The New

CENTURY CYCLOPEDIA

OF

Names

EDITED BY

Clarence L. Barnhart

with the assistance of

William D. Halsey

and a staff of more than 350
consulting scholars, special editors, and
other contributors

VOLUME ONE

A—Emin Pasha

APPLETON-CENTURY-CROFTS, INC.
NEW YORK

Library of Congress Card Number: 52–13879

PRINTED IN U.S.A.

CONTENTS OF VOLUME I

CONTENTS OF VOLUME II

CONTENTS OF VOLUME III

PREFACE

The *New Century Cyclopedia of Names* is a unique reference work consisting solely of information about proper names having importance in the English-speaking world. We give the most frequently used English and native spellings and pronunciations, as well as the essential facts, about more than 100,000 proper names of every description—persons, places, historical events, plays and operas, works of fiction, literary characters, works of art, mythological and legendary persons and places, and any other class of proper names of interest or importance today. The only condition of insertion has been that the name should be one about which information would be likely to be sought.

The original *Century Cyclopedia of Names* was for over fifty years the chief English-language source of information about all kinds of proper names. Benjamin E. Smith, the editor of the original work, wrote on September 1, 1894, that "it is entirely independent in subject and use, . . . primarily a dictionary of proper names, giving their orthography and pronunciation and such explanation of them as is necessary for their identification; and, secondarily, a condensed encyclopedia in its . . . treatment of several thousands of the more important articles." So well were the high editorial standards of the original book maintained that the original cyclopedia was still used fifty-eight years after its original publication, to obtain information about proper names entered in no other generally available reference work. For many years there has been a persistent demand by librarians and scholars that the original *Century Cyclopedia of Names* be brought up to date. In 1947 the publisher acceded to this demand, and work was begun on the modernization and revision of the *Century Cyclopedia of Names*.

Because of the wide extent of modern knowledge the editor formed an Editorial Advisory Committee (see page xv) of eminent scholars in various fields of knowledge or in the making and use of reference books to assist in the framing of basic policies. The scope of the original cyclopedia was unchanged but its size was greatly enlarged so that all useful names might be included. Two world wars and the closer linking together of distant parts of the world have greatly expanded the range of human interests and knowledge, and hence the number of names with which everyone comes in contact. In order to include the proper names important to the modern reader, we made the present work over twice as large as the original one. Even so the selection of names to be included was one of the first and most important problems before the Committee. In order to evaluate properly names for inclusion we decided, on the advice of this Editorial Advisory Committee, to enlist the help of additional scholars in a wide range of special fields. Before we could know where our chief problems lay, and in which fields we would be likely to encounter the greatest amount of difficulty, we analyzed the names in the original *Century Cyclopedia of Names* against a variety of special and general sources, and undertook a classification of all the names being considered for entry in the new work. We divided our master list of over 500,000 proper names into 1,248 categories, and the terms contained within each of these categories were subjected to further analysis against standard textbooks in each field, and other special works. On the recommendation of members of the Committee or of the Consulting Editors immediately responsible, systematic checks were made against a wide range of authoritative sources to ensure completeness and accuracy of the facts included. As a result, many important facts which have not hitherto been available in any general reference work have been added.

At the same time we turned to scholars recommended by members of the Editorial Advisory Committee for help in writing articles on the names in all the most difficult categories (see list of Consulting Editors beginning on page xvi). In still other cases, there were single names which were in themselves of such great importance as virtually to comprise separate categories; for these we obtained the help of nearly 200 Special Consultants (see list beginning on page xix).

In the *New Century Cyclopedia of Names* the reader will, so to speak, "find each name where it belongs"—which is simply to say that he will find it where experience has taught him to expect it. We use a system of entry based on those found in the two reference books which are probably most familiar to the greatest possible number of people, the telephone book and the dictionary. By combining the conventions of entry used in these two reference works we believe we have been able to produce an order-of-entry system with which most readers will already be completely familiar.

We have given precise and detailed facts instead of general information as a matter of policy. All dates have been carefully checked. In addition, exact places and dates of birth and death are given wherever they could be ascertained. Population, area, height and other comparable statistics are cited and dated from official sources; where no adequate official source could be obtained, the reader is clearly informed that the information given is an approximation, even though many of these approximations have been derived from documents of considerable authority. Readers interested in a fuller discussion of this highly technical matter are referred to the section "How to Use the New Century Cyclopedia of Names," beginning on page xi.

The bulk of the names in this work are entered as we believe they are most likely to be spelled by the greatest number of American readers. Such items as "Washington, D.C.," or "John Adams" present no problems. The more obscure American place names or those that have been changed (as "Governors Island," now written without an apostrophe) are entered according to the decisions of the U.S. Board on Geographic Names or the spellings used by the Bureau of the Census; personal names now in some doubt follow the spellings in the *Dictionary of American Biography* or the *Dictionary of National Biography*.

Entries on people or places of foreign countries using Roman alphabets are given in native spellings except where American usage is overwhelmingly against this practice, and the accents or diacritics of these alphabets are used. Thus we give as a main entry "Brașov," a city in Rumania, not "Brashov" as it was formerly often spelled to approximate the pronunciation, nor yet "Stalin," now its official designation but not well known. However, we prefer "Bucharest" to "Bucuresti," "Prague" to "Praha," and "Rome" to "Roma," all these first-named being manifestly the more familiar forms in the United States.

Names transliterated from non-Roman alphabets are presented as simply as possible, with almost no use of accented letters or diacritical marks, since most such marks (largely used to indicate pronunciation, which we give following the entry word) are puzzling in ordinary texts. So far as we could ascertain it, we have thus endeavored to follow the mandate of usage by literate Americans.

The letters of the alphabet are directions to say sounds, but the directions are often confusing since one letter or a combination of letters may represent more than one sound. Therefore, we use a system of diacritics to make the directions more precise. We use the pronunciation key of the *New Century Dictionary*, which is known to the hundreds of thousands of the users of that book. Such a pronunciation key, based upon the usual English sound-values of the letters, is one to which most of us are most accustomed and is therefore one which enables English-speaking consulters of a reference work to reproduce with a fair degree of accuracy the sounds indicated.

We provide the educated speaker of American English with standard pronunciations of names drawn from nearly every known language and every period of history. English names, of course, present no special difficulty. Moreover, many familiar American names are of non-English origin. Names of this latter type are "foreign" in origin only; they are anything but foreign in their application to present-day American people or places. Furthermore, many unquestionably "foreign" names (for instance, *Caesar*, *Nineveh*, *Balboa*, *Tokyo*, *Pravda*) are established words in our speech and have an established pronunciation among us. This established pronunciation may fall entirely within patterns of speech that are normal for English words, thus: (sē′za̤r, nin′ẹ.vẹ, bal.bō′a̤, tō′ki.ō, präv′da̤). In some details, however, we often imitate the native pronunciation of a foreign name; thus, educated speakers usually pronounce *Bach*, the name of the German composer, as (bäċh), employing a sound which does not occur in English. It is possible, too, for the English pronunciation of a foreign name to vary from rather complete imitation, as in *Versailles* (ver.säy′, approximating the French pronunciation), through Anglicization partially imitating the foreign pronunciation (in our example, vėr.sī′), to a complete Anglicization suggested by the written form (here, vėr.sālz′, which is, of course, the regular pronunciation of this name when applied to places in America).

There remain many foreign names for which there is no established English pronunciation, but which nevertheless occur frequently in atlases, histories, translated literature, current news dispatches, and the like. In the absence of a traditional English pronunciation of these names, a work such as this must supply pronunciations according to some general principle, either respelling them with sounds suggested to Americans by the written forms, or imitating, so far as the resources of the English sound-system permit, the pronunciation of the original. The former practice was very commonly followed until recent times and unfamiliar names were freely Anglicized according to the spelling. At the present time, however, the tendency to approximate the native pronunciation is very strong, particularly in the United States, and the respellings in this volume reflect that fact. The closeness of the approximation naturally depends to some extent on the certainty (for Americans) of the pronunciation represented by the written form; this is quite exact in case of languages such as French and German, written in our Latin alphabet, rather less so for names transliterated from less familiar languages employing other alphabets or other forms of writing, and still less so for names recorded by European observers from native speech in remote parts of the world; in the less certain instances, the indicated pronunciation is what may be considered a reasonable spoken equivalent of the written form in which the name reaches us. The closeness of approximation varies, of course, with the degree of difference between American English speech patterns and those of the language imitated; thus, it is relatively easier for us to imitate most German names than it is to imitate most French names.

This work has been, in the truest possible sense, a coöperative effort by scholars, editors, and publisher. Without the invaluable policy-making advice of the nine members of the Editorial Advisory Committee many of the most valuable features of the work would never have come into being. Equally important, but with reference to particular fields of knowledge or particular individuals in history, was the work of the many consulting editors and consultants who gave so generously of their time for a period of several years in order to be sure that the information we gave would be the very best we could possibly obtain. Two persons on the staff deserve special mention: Mr. W. D. Halsey, the managing editor, who has devoted many long hours to detailed editing and has also participated in planning the cyclopedia, and Mr. R. A. Goodwin, who has spent much time on problems of transliteration and pronunciation. Invaluable assistance was also obtained from Mr. George Sarton, who generously made available to us all of the authoritative materials contained in his monumental *Introduction to the History of Science*. Finally, great thanks are due to Mr. W. Morgan Shuster and Mr. Dana Ferrin, of Appleton-Century-Crofts, without whose patience and understanding this work would certainly never have been possible. Much credit is due also to Mr. Joseph Giebel, of Appleton-Century-Crofts, and to the many people at the H. Wolff Book Manufacturing Company who were involved in work on the book, for solutions to a vast number of very difficult problems of composition and manufacture.

Clarence L. Barnhart

HOW TO USE THE NEW CENTURY CYCLOPEDIA OF NAMES

It is the belief of the editors of this work that the mechanics of its use—where and how to find particular entries, and the like—will be, for all practical purposes, self-explanatory. However, to those users who may be interested in knowing the technical details of its organization, the following sections may be of some interest.

Order of Entries

Perhaps the first thing to bear in mind in a discussion of this matter is that the term "strict alphabetical order," in the sense in which it is understood by most people, cannot be applied in any work as complex as this one. By their nature, dictionaries have been able to come somewhat closer to applying it than encyclopedias, and the result is that dictionaries are somewhat easier for many people to use than most encyclopedias. Realizing the great difficulties involved, we have nevertheless done our utmost in this work to achieve a blending of dictionary techniques with others desirable in such a work as this. A few examples may make it easier for the user of the book to understand what is meant by this. The sequence

Albert
Alberta
Albertville

is simple, and there are no two ways of alphabetizing it; if this work were a simple glossary there would be no problem. But where in that sequence would one look for the entry "Albert the Bear"? In a telephone book it would be second in the sequence, in a dictionary third; in an encyclopedia or the index to a historical text it might be either place according to the convention adopted by the editors of the book. This question of arrangement can become complex indeed where the editor is faced with such a long list, for example, as that under *Charles* in this work: first, how to arrange the many kings, princes, and literary characters known only as "Charles"; second, how to arrange the many names containing the element "Charles," whether they are single words (*Charleston*) or phrases (*Charles the Bold*). In a biographical dictionary or a gazetteer the kinds of names are relatively few. Yet even in biographical works the ways of distinguishing among the persons known as Charles may be various and intricate (as for example emperors before kings, kings before dukes, dukes before earls, and so on—helpful provided the reader remembers that dukes rank higher than earls). And even in the indexes to two different atlases one may find *Charles Town* and *Charlestown* next to each other or separated by a column or two.

We have kept the system of placement simple and easy to use by combining the conventions of those reference books which are probably most familiar to most readers, the telephone book and the dictionary. The primary principle of arrangement in the telephone book is what is called "directory style," i.e., that people's names are entered in reverse, surname followed by prename. The comma between these two elements, though not printed in many directories, is strictly taken into account, and the user will not find *Alberts, Andrew* before *Albert, William*. It might be said that the primary system of ordering is based on what precedes the comma (assumed or actual): the *Albert* group comes before the *Alberts* group; and secondary ordering goes by what follows the comma: within the *Albert* group *Albert, Charles* precedes *Albert, Daniel*. This is also our principle. The comma between the elements of a reversed or "directory-style" name is rigidly observed, and primary and secondary ordering go according to what precedes and what follows the comma:

Andersen, Hans Christian
Andersen, Karl
Andersen Nexø, Martin
Anderson
Anderson, Adam

Finally, for the user of this work, which contains many multiple-word entries, it is important to have a convention that enables him easily to find an item (as *Charles Town* or *Charlestown*) even if he does not know whether it is written with or without a space. In this we follow dictionary style, which is familiar to most readers and easily used by them, though they may not be aware that the spaces between words are ignored. In a dictionary

alphabet
alphabetize
alphabet noodles

would be found in that order. To return to the simple "glossary" sequence cited above and add to it the troublesome phrase, we have

Albert
Alberta
"Albert the Bear" (placed the same as if it were written "*Albertthebear*")
Albertville

These three simple principles of the glossary, the directory, and the dictionary cover the ordering of the great majority of entries in this work, and the treatment of any sequence of items involving the same name may be summarized as follows:

I. the name alone: Albert

before

II. the name as a surname: Albert, Heinrich
or as other main element of a reversed or directory-style name: Albert, Lake

before

III. the name as part of a longer name, whether several words: Albert Avogadro
"Albert the Bear"
or one word: Albertville

Under these classes of entry there are sometimes enough cases otherwise identical as to need ways of distinguishing. Given several items the names of which are all simply "Albert," the arrangement is:

(1) people (biographical entries):

Albert (ȧl.ber). [Called **"l'ouvrier Albert,"** meaning "Albert the Worker"; original name, **Alexandre Martin.**] b. at Bury, Oise, France, April 27, 1815; d. at Mello, Oise, France, May 28, 1895. French politician. . . .

Albert (al'bėrt), Prince. [Full name, **Albert Francis Charles Augustus Emmanuel of Saxe-Coburg-Gotha.**] b. at the Rosenau, near Coburg, Germany, 1819; d. at Windsor Castle, 1861. Husband of Queen Victoria and prince consort of England. . . .

before

(2) places (geographical entries):

Albert (ȧl.ber). [Former name, **Ancre.**] Town in N France. . . .

before

(3) things (entries neither biographical nor geographical):

Albert (al′bėrt). In Goethe's *Sorrows of Werther*, a young farmer. . . .

Albert. [Title, **Count of Geierstein.**] Character in Sir Walter Scott's novel *Anne of Geierstein*. . . .

(*It will be noted that neither the lightface title, in this case "Prince," nor the boldface variant names given in brackets have any bearing on order of main entry.*)

Within categories 1 and 3 (people and things) the order is chronological: Albert born in 1815 precedes Albert born in 1819; because of earlier publication date the character from Goethe's work precedes the one from Scott's.

Within category 2 (places) the order is:

(a) alphabetical by place of location, which is the largest meaningful and well-known unit. (By "meaningful" is meant that we do not locate by the units United States, Canada, or Europe, since these are too large to make any distinction, in many cases, among places of the same name.) We use states of the United States, provinces of Canada, and countries elsewhere (further distinguishing, where there are two or more places of the same name in one country, by the name of the next unit in size thereunder, such as a county or department). The name of the locating unit appears close to the beginning of the entry, where it may be easily spotted:

Paris. City in W Arkansas.
Paris. City in N France.
Paris. City in E Illinois.
Paris. City in N Kentucky.
Paris. Town in SW Maine.
Paris. Town in Ontario, Canada.

(b) by size, when the difference is specifically known and the reader may be expected to use this as a guide:

Quebec. . . . Largest province of the Dominion of Canada.
Quebec. . . . City in SE Quebec.

(c) chronological:

Israel. Kingdom of the northern tribes of the Israelites who seceded during the 10th century B.C. from the southern tribes. . . .
Israel. Independent Jewish state in W Asia, formed from the N, W, and S parts of the former mandated territory of Palestine on May 14, 1948. . . .

In a small proportion of entries there are enough identical names to need still further means of distinction and thus of ordering. Probably most numerous is the list of Charleses, many of them kings, who cannot be spotted quickly even by the numerals that accompany many of the names. To arrange these simply in order of date would be to make a hopeless jumble as to numbers and to lead the reader interested in a dynasty, for instance, through many pages in his effort to trace the monarchs of one country. Therefore we have introduced, where it is needed, a phrase in parentheses designating the country or empire (in italic type) most familiarly associated with the ruler in question:

Charles I (of *England*).

This name, used as a secondary element in alphabetical order just as the prename is in common directory style, keeps the rulers of one country together and makes possible chronological order within each such group:

Charles I (of *England*).
Charles II (of *England*).
Charles I (of *France*).
. . .
Charles X (of *France*).
Charles I (of the *Holy Roman Empire*).

The numeral is regarded only as a plus element, in that name-plus-numeral (in the absence of country-designation) follows name alone:

Charles.
Charles (of *Anjou*).
Charles (of *England*), Prince.
Charles I.
Charles I (of *England*).

(Since the order of numerals parallels chronological order, they need not be considered as affecting sequence in themselves.)

Variant Names

All variant forms are given that have considerable usage, either in current reading matter or in historical sources. These are divisible generally into other spellings and other names. Where another spelling is virtually interchangeable with the one preferred it is presented in this style:

Manicheans or Manichaeans.

Most other spellings and other names now (or until recently) current are entered, however, in brackets after the main entry, preceded by the word "also":

Mahanadi. [Also, **Mahanuddy.**]
Magyars. [Also, **Hungarians.**]

There are other names of various special kinds, chief of which are the following (note that all are labeled as to kind):

1. Former names, whether:

(a) recent:

Malaya, Federation of. [Former name, **Union of Malaya.**]

(b) or ancient:

Málaga. [Ancient name, **Malaca.**]

(c) original names of persons or places whose names have been changed:

Mackenzie, Alexander Slidell. [Original name, **Alexander Slidell.**]
Mansfield, Katherine. [Maiden name, **Beauchamp.** . . .]

(d) or of persons better known by their titles:

Marlborough, 1st Duke of. [Title of **John Churchill.**]

(e) or of persons or places whose names are now commonly shortened:

Malraux, André. [Full name, **Georges André Malraux.**]

(Full names are also indicated by parentheses in the main entry where alphabetical order is not affected, thus: **Markham, Edwin (Charles).**)

2. Names current in modern languages other than that of the entry, including:

(a) Native forms where the English or Anglicized form has been used as main entry:

Magellan, Strait of. [Spanish, **Estrecho de Magallanes.**]

(b) Names in the languages of adjoining countries or countries of which a place has been part or with which a person was associated:

Mariánské Lázně. [German, **Marienbad.**]

(c) Names in other languages official or widely used in the same country, as are French, German, Italian, and Romansh in Switzerland, French and Flemish in Belgium, English and Irish in Ireland, and English and French in parts of Canada:

Matterhorn. [French, **Mont Cervin;** Italian, **Monte Cervino.**]

(d) Titles in other languages, if they have current or contemporary usage, of operas, books, and the like:

Nozze di Figaro, Le. [English title, **The Marriage of Figaro.**]

3. Additional names, assumed or conferred, as:
   (a) Pseudonyms:
   Marston, John. [Pseudonym, **W. Kinsayder.**]
   (b) Nicknames or epithets:
   Magnus I (of *Denmark* and *Norway*). [Called **Magnus the Good.**]
   (c) Titles:
   Mancini, Hortense. [Title, Duchesse **de Mazarin.**]

Cross References

The user of this work will find that a great deal of space has been given to cross references. This has been done in recognition of the number of names by which a person or place may be known (or have been known), and of the great variety of forms or spellings under which a name may be encountered by a reader whose range includes old works as well as new or the publications of regions and countries other than his own.

A suggestion of the kinds of variants included has been given in the section on Form of Entry. All of these are cross-referred if there is a reasonable possibility of their being looked up. Exceptions are: (1) spellings so close to that of the main entry that there is no likelihood of the desired article being overlooked (as *Bilolj* for *Bitola*), and (2) names or forms given as useful or interesting information but unlikely to be found in most reading (as *Bermingham*, the Middle English form of *Birmingham*).

Cross references are pronounced, like main entries, unless they are proper names derived from common words (such as *White Mountain*). Noncross-referred forms under category (1) of the preceding paragraph are pronounced unless pronunciation is identical with that of the preferred spelling or easily ascertainable from it. Most "information" variants are not pronounced.

In addition to cross references for variant forms the reader will find placement cross references, especially for:

(1) Middle names which may be confused with surnames:
Acuña de Figueroa, Francisco. See **Figueroa, Francisco Acuña de.**

(2) Multiple surnames:
Alexis, Pierre Nord. See **Nord Alexis, Pierre.**

(3) Surnames unconventionally used:
Brooke-Popham, Sir **Henry Robert Moore.** See **Popham,** Sir **Henry Robert Moore Brooke-.**

(4) "Switches," i.e., entries which might reasonably be looked for under more than one element:
East Africa, British. See **British East Africa.**

(5) Unfamiliar geographical generic words (such names being usually entered straight, not reversed as the more familiar "Lake" or "Mount" names are):
More, Ben. See **Ben More.**

Generic terms, particles, and other subordinate elements in foreign languages, which may appear only in variants or be treated as secondary parts of entries, are in many cases covered by general cross references explaining their uses and how to find names containing them. Among these are the particles *Abd* and *Al*, the geographical terms *Cabo*, *Laguna*, *Wadi*, and many others.

Entry of Pronunciations

1. Ordinarily, only the part of a name preceding the comma is pronounced. Thus:
   Smith (smith), **Adam.**

   Prenames are pronounced in a separate list in the back of the book. However, such elements as *l'*, *d'*, and *dell'*, pronounced as part of the name, are included in the pronunciation. Thus:
   Abbadie (dȧ.bȧ.dē), **Antoine Thomson d'.**
   Abbate (del.läb.bä'tā), **Niccolò dell'.**

2. Generic geographical terms (in English) and other unequivocally generic words used in a literal sense are not pronounced. Thus:
   Andaman Islands (an'dạ.mạn).
   Brother Jonathan (jon'ạ.thạn).
   Good Hope, Cape of.

   Otherwise, all names are pronounced. Thus:
   Roan Mountain (rōn).
   White (hwīt), **Alma.**

3. When a name occurs with identical pronunciation in two or more successive entries, it is pronounced only at the point of first entry. Thus:
   Cumberland (kum'bėr.lạnd).
   Cumberland, Richard.
   Cumberland Gap.

   When successive entries have the same spelling but different pronunciations, as in **Adam** (English, ad'ạm; as a German surname, ä'däm; as a French surname, ȧ.däṅ), the pronunciation is given at every point of change from one pronunciation to another, and omission of any pronunciation indicates that the name is pronounced the same as the closest preceding entry where pronunciation was given.

4. When a name which has been pronounced is repeated (without change of pronunciation) as part of a successive entry, unhyphenated, only the new part of the compound entry is pronounced. Thus:
   López (lō'pes), **Carlos Antonio.**
   López Contreras (kōn.trā'räs), **Eleázar.**

   For hyphenated names the full pronunciation is given, except that if each part of the compound has a primary accent, the repetition of the first element may be indicated by a hyphen. Thus:
   Åbenrå (ô'bẹn.rô).
   Åbenrå-Sönderborg (-sėn'nėr.bôrg).

Handling of Statistics

Figures for populations, areas, elevations above sea level, and the like, have been obtained from official sources wherever possible, and elsewhere from the most reliable unofficial ones available to us. Populations are dated in all cases where official sources have been used. A general prefatory statement, to the effect that latest census figures are cited, has not been considered sufficient; if no census has been held since 1930 on a certain South Pacific island, the reader should be so informed as he reads the entry. Therefore, the great majority of our population statistics are dated, even though they must occasionally bear old dates.

Every plain date, such as "(1951)" or "(1948)," means that an official census figure for that year is given. An official estimate is indicated by the abbreviation "est." preceding the date. For example:

Aerschot. Town in C Belgium. . . . 10,589 (1947).
Afghanistan . . . . Pop. ab. 12,000,000 (est. 1946).

In cases where the unit may be expected to have a focal point (or capital) and area, as well as population, all of this information is ordinarily supplied:

Ağri. *Il* (province or vilayet) in E Turkey. . . . Capital, Doğubayazit; area, 5,142 sq. mi.; pop. 155,545 (1950).

In cases where the name applies to two legally different units, one of which may entirely encompass the other, an effort has been made to provide exact statistics for each:

East Hampton. Town (in New York the equivalent of township in many other states) and village in SE New York. . . . Pop. of town, 6,325 (1950); of village, 1,737 (1950).

In certain other cases, where a significant population change may have taken place in recent years, two dated figures are often given in order that this important fact may be made adequately clear to the reader:

Mexico City. City in S central Mexico. . . . 1,448,422 (1940), 2,113,451 (1950).

How to Use the New Century Cyclopedia of Names

Consistent use is made of the abbreviation "ab." (for "about") with all statistics not confirmable in detail (for example, round numbers for populations, areas computed from the metric or some other system of measurement, or elevations of mountain peaks where two or more equally reliable surveys have produced different figures or where no exact measurement is known to have been made).

Distances between places are given only as rough guides, chiefly for the location of points on the map. There are too many variables (such as changes in the routes of connecting roads or railroads and relocation of city lines or even of the "center of town") for accurate reporting of these mileages. Therefore such figures are frankly labeled "ab." and exactness is not implied where it cannot be established.

The lengths of rivers are among the most debatable of statistics, since all change their courses more or less, many are unnavigable and not yet reached by aerial surveys, and some even have never been accurately mapped. Here also the qualification "ab." is freely used wherever the reader should be informed that figures are open to any doubt.

In the case of biographical entries, a comparable effort has been made to provide the reader with vital statistics which are both detailed and precise:

> **Ahlwardt, Christian Wilhelm.** b. at Greifswald, Prussia, Nov. 23, 1760; d. there, April 12, 1830.

Exceptions occur in all cases where such precise information could not be adequately confirmed or was not available in the sources at our disposal:

> **Ahumada y Villalon, Agustín de.** b. c1700; d. at Mexico City, Feb. 6, 1760.

EDITORIAL ADVISORY COMMITTEE

CONSULTING EDITORS, WITH THEIR SPECIAL FIELDS

Burt W. Aginsky
Chairman of the Department of Sociology and Anthropology
City College of New York
WESTERN AND CENTRAL EUROPEAN ETHNOLOGY

Edward D. Andrews
Dean of Students and Head of the Department of History
Scarborough School
Author: *The Community Industries of the Shakers*
SHAKER HISTORY AND BIOGRAPHY

Martin S. Allwood
Director of the Institute of Social Research
Mullsjo, Sweden
MODERN SWEDISH LITERATURE

Ralph C. Altman
INDONESIAN ARCHAEOLOGY

John C. Archer
Hoober Professor of Comparative Religion (1932–50)
Yale University
POLITICAL BIOGRAPHY AND HISTORY OF MODERN INDIA, PAKISTAN, AND AFGHANISTAN

C. Rankin Barnes
Secretary of the General Convention and of the National Council of the Protestant Episcopal Church
Author: *The General Convention: Offices and Officers, 1785–1950*
EPISCOPAL HISTORY AND BIOGRAPHY

William R. Bascom
Associate Professor, Department of Anthropology
Northwestern University
Author: *The Sociological Role of the Yoruba Cult Group*
AFRICAN ETHNOLOGY

Robert H. Bass
Instructor in History (1949–51)
Mount Holyoke College
MODERN CZECHOSLOVAKIAN POLITICAL BIOGRAPHY AND HISTORY

Cyril E. Black
Associate Professor, Department of History
Princeton University
Author: *Establishment of Constitutional Government in Bulgaria*
POLITICAL BIOGRAPHY AND HISTORY OF THE BALKANS IN MODERN TIMES

H. Boeschenstein
Professor of German
University of Toronto
MODERN SWISS LITERATURE

Carl B. Boyer
Professor of Mathematics
Brooklyn College
Author: *The Concepts of the Calculus*
MODERN MATHEMATICS AND MATHEMATICIANS

Edwin G. Burrows
Professor of Anthropology
University of Connecticut
Author: *Western Polynesia; Hawaiian Americans*
ETHNOLOGY OF OCEANIA

Werner J. Cahnman
EUROPEAN GEOGRAPHY

Shepard B. Clough
Professor of European History
Columbia University
Author: *France, 1789–1939, A Study in National Economics; The Rise and Fall of Civilization*
MODERN FRENCH POLITICAL BIOGRAPHY AND HISTORY

A. P. Coleman
President of Alliance College
POLISH LITERATURE

Carleton S. Coon
Professor of Ethnology and Curator of the University Ethnology Museum
University of Pennsylvania
Author: *Tribes of the Rif; The Riffian; Measuring Ethiopia; Southern Arabia: A Problem for the Future; Cave Explorations in Northern Iran*
NORTH AFRICAN AND NEAR EASTERN ETHNOLOGY

George B. Cressey (See Editorial Advisory Committee)
Maxwell Professor of Geography
Syracuse University
Author: *China's Geographic Foundations; Asia's Lands and Peoples; The Basis of Soviet Strength*
RUSSIAN AND ASIATIC GEOGRAPHY

Taraknath Das
Lecturer in the Department of History
Columbia University;
Adjunct Professor of Public Affairs
New York University
Author: *India in World Politics; Sovereign Rights of Indian Princes; The War Comes to India; Status of Hyderabad Before and After the British Rule in India*
MODERN INDIAN POLITICAL BIOGRAPHY AND HISTORY

John DeFrancis
Assistant Professor of International Relations
Walter Hines Page School
The Johns Hopkins University
Author: *Nationalism and Language Reform in China*
MODERN CHINESE POLITICAL BIOGRAPHY AND HISTORY

Robert E. Dickinson
Professor of Geography
Syracuse University
Author: *Germany: A General and Regional Geography; The West European City*
EUROPEAN GEOGRAPHY

John F. Embree (deceased)
Associate Professor of Sociology and Anthropology, and Director of Southeast Asia Studies
Yale University
Author: *The Japanese Nation; Bibliography of the Peoples and Cultures of Mainland Southeast Asia* (in collaboration)
JAPANESE AND INDONESIAN ETHNOLOGY

José Famadas
MODERN BRAZILIAN AND PORTUGUESE LITERATURE

Pedro Villa Fernandez
Professor of Spanish
University of Florida
MODERN SPANISH LITERATURE

Josef Frejlich
MODERN POLISH POLITICAL BIOGRAPHY AND HISTORY

Wilbur M. Frohock
Professor of French
Wesleyan University
Author: *André Malraux and the Tragic Imagination*
MODERN FRENCH LITERATURE

Iago Galdston
Executive Secretary of the Medical Information Bureau of The New York Academy of Medicine and Lecturer at the New York Medical College, Flower and Fifth Avenue Hospitals
MEDICAL HISTORY AND BIOGRAPHY

John W. Gassner
Associate Professor of English
Queens College

Consulting Editors, with Their Special Fields

Author: *Masters of the Drama; Producing the Play; A Treasury of the Theatre; Our Heritage of World Literature*
Senior Contributing Editor, *Theatre Arts Magazine*
MODERN EUROPEAN THEATER

William J. Gibbons
Associate Editor of *America* (1945–48)
ROMAN CATHOLIC HISTORY AND BIOGRAPHY

Alexander Gode-von Aesch
Lecturer in Germanics and Linguistics
Barnard College, Columbia University
Author: *National Science in German Romanticism*
GERMAN LITERATURE

Eugene Golomshtok
RUSSIAN AND SIBERIAN ARCHAEOLOGY

C. Hartley Grattan
Carnegie Corporation Fellow in Australia (1937–38)
Author: *Introducing Australia*
POLITICAL BIOGRAPHY AND HISTORY OF AUSTRALIA AND NEW ZEALAND IN MODERN TIMES

André von Gronicka
Associate Professor of Germanic Languages and Literatures
Columbia University
MODERN AUSTRIAN LITERATURE

Robert W. Habenstein
MODERN SOCIOLOGY

Robert S. Harper
Assistant Professor of Psychology
Knox College
PSYCHOLOGY

Einar Haugen
Thompson Professor of Scandinavian Languages
University of Wisconsin
Author: *The Norwegian Language in America*
MODERN DANISH, NORWEGIAN, AND ICELANDIC LITERATURE

Rufus S. Hendon
Director of the Indonesia Project
Center for International Studies
Massachusetts Institute of Technology
JAPANESE AND INDONESIAN ETHNOLOGY

E. H. Hespelt
Professor Emeritus of Spanish
New York University
Chief Editor: *An Outline History of Spanish American Literature; An Anthology of Spanish American Literature*
LATIN AMERICAN LITERATURE

Hajo Holborn
Randolph W. Townsend Professor of History
Yale University
Author: *The Political Collapse of Europe*
MODERN INTERNATIONAL HISTORY

Fred W. Householder, Jr.
Associate Professor of Classics
Indiana University
MODERN GREEK POLITICAL BIOGRAPHY AND HISTORY

Arthur W. Hummel
Chief of the Division of Orientalia
Library of Congress
Editor: *Eminent Chinese of the Ch'ing Period*
CHINESE ETHNOLOGY

Benjamin Hunningher
Queen Wilhelmina Professor of the History, Literature, and Language of The Netherlands
Columbia University
MODERN DUTCH, FLEMISH, AND SOUTH AFRICAN LITERATURE

Bernard Jaffe
Chairman of the Physical Science Department
James Madison High School, Brooklyn, New York
Author: *Crucibles, the Story of Chemistry; New World of Chemistry; Chemical Calculations; New World of Science*
CHEMISTRY

Preston E. James
Professor of Geography (Chairman of Department)
Syracuse University;
United States Member, Commission on Geography of the Pan American Institute of Geography and History
Author: *An Outline of Geography; Latin America; A Geography of Man*
LATIN AMERICAN GEOGRAPHY

Henry M. Kendall
Professor of Geography (Chairman of Department)
Miami University
NORTH AMERICAN GEOGRAPHY

Hibberd V. B. Kline, Jr.
Associate Professor of Geography
Syracuse University;
Consultant to the Dependent Areas Branch of the Mutual Security Agency
AFRICAN GEOGRAPHY

Bertram S. Kraus
Professor, Department of Anthropology
University of Arizona
Editor: *The Prehistory of Japan,* by G. Groot
JAPANESE ARCHAEOLOGY

Ursula Lamb
Barnard College, Columbia University
MODERN SPANISH POLITICAL BIOGRAPHY AND HISTORY

Bruno Lasker
Consultant on Southeast Asia, Social Affairs Department, United Nations
Author: *Standards and Planes of Living in the Far East; New Forces in Asia; Asia on the Move; Peoples of Southeast Asia*
POLITICAL BIOGRAPHY AND HISTORY OF INDONESIA AND SOUTHEAST ASIA

John Lotz
Associate Professor of General and Comparative Linguistics
Columbia University
MODERN HUNGARIAN LITERATURE

D. G. Mandelbaum
Professor of Anthropology
University of California
INDIAN ETHNOLOGY

M. F. Ashley Montagu
Professor of Anthropology (Chairman of Department)
Rutgers University
Editor: *Atlas of Human Anatomy*
ANATOMY

Dana Gardner Munro
Professor of Latin American History and Affairs;
Director of the Woodrow Wilson School of Public and International Affairs
Princeton University
Author: *Five Republics of Central America; The U. S. and the Caribbean Area; Latin American Republics: A History*
MODERN LATIN AMERICAN POLITICAL BIOGRAPHY AND HISTORY

Ants Oras
Former Professor of English Language and Literature
University of Tartu (Estonia);
Professor of English
University of Florida
MODERN LATVIAN, LITHUANIAN, AND ESTONIAN LITERATURE

John A. Pope
Assistant Director of the Freer Gallery of Art, Washington, D.C.
CHINESE ARCHAEOLOGY

Hugh W. Puckett
Professor of German Literature
Barnard College, Columbia University
GERMAN LITERATURE

Irving Rouse
Associate Professor of Anthropology and Associate Curator of the Peabody Museum of Natural History
Yale University
NORTH AMERICAN ARCHAEOLOGY

Thomas A. Sebeok
Assistant Professor of Linguistics
Indiana University
LINGUISTICS

Consulting Editors, with Their Special Fields

Demitri Shimkin
Research Associate, Russian Research Center;
Assistant Curator of Siberian Ethnology of the Peabody Museum
Harvard University

RUSSIAN AND SIBERIAN ETHNOLOGY

George N. Shuster
President of Hunter College
Author: *The Germans; Strong Man Rules; Like a Mighty Army; Germany: A Short History*

MODERN GERMAN POLITICAL BIOGRAPHY AND HISTORY

David B. Stout
Associate Professor of Anthropology
University of Iowa

NORTH AMERICAN AND LATIN AMERICAN ETHNOLOGY

John W. Streeter
Assistant Director of the Fels Planetarium
The Franklin Institute, Philadelphia
Author: *Understanding the Stars*

ASTRONOMY

Theo Suranyi-Unger
Professor of Economics
Syracuse University

MODERN HUNGARIAN POLITICAL BIOGRAPHY AND HISTORY

R. Stanley Thomson
Head of the Department of History and Government
Russell Sage College

POLITICAL BIOGRAPHY AND HISTORY OF BELGIUM, LUXEMBOURG, AND THE NETHERLANDS SINCE 1900

John H. Wuorinen
Professor of History
Columbia University

Author: *Nationalism in Modern Finland; Finland and World War II*

MODERN SCANDINAVIAN POLITICAL BIOGRAPHY AND HISTORY

Avrahm Yarmolinsky
Chief of the Slavonic Division
New York Public Library

MODERN RUSSIAN LITERATURE

J. H. Young

Assistant Professor, Department of Classics
The Johns Hopkins University

MODERN GREEK LITERATURE

SPECIAL CONSULTANTS, WITH THE SUBJECTS OF THEIR ASSISTANCE

Nabia Abbott
Professor of Islamic Studies
University of Chicago
Author: *Aishah, The Beloved of Mohammed*
MOHAMMED

Martin Ray Adams
Professor of English (Chairman of Department)
Franklin and Marshall College
Author: *Political Radicalism in England, 1789–1799; Studies in the Literary Backgrounds of Political Radicalism in England*
WILLIAM GODWIN

Frederick Lewis Allen
Editor in Chief of *Harper's Magazine*
Author: *The Great Pierpont Morgan*
JOHN PIERPONT MORGAN

Gay Wilson Allen
Professor of English
New York University
Author: *Walt Whitman Handbook; American Prosody; Masters of American Literature* (in collaboration)
WALT WHITMAN

Fulton H. Anderson
Professor of Philosophy (Head of Department)
University of Toronto
Author: *The Philosophy of Francis Bacon*
FRANCIS BACON

A. Joseph Armstrong
Professor of English (Head of Department)
Baylor University
Editor: *Letters of Robert Browning to Isa Blagdon; Browning the World Over; Browning's Testament of Hope*
ROBERT BROWNING

Newton Arvin
Professor of English
Smith College
Author: *Herman Melville*
HERMAN MELVILLE

Brooks Atkinson
Drama Critic of the New York *Times*
Author: *Henry Thoreau, the Cosmic Yankee*
Editor: *Walden and Other Writings of Henry David Thoreau*
HENRY DAVID THOREAU

John Bakeless
Author: *Daniel Boone, Master of the Wilderness; Fighting Frontiersman; Eyes of Discovery*
DANIEL BOONE

Robert Cecil Bald
Professor of English
University of Chicago
Author: *Donne's Influence in English Literature*
JOHN DONNE

William Thomas Bandy
Professor of French
University of Wisconsin
Author: *Baudelaire Judged by His Contemporaries; A Word Index of Baudelaire's Poems*
CHARLES PIERRE BAUDELAIRE

Theodore Howard Banks
Professor of English
Wesleyan University
Author: *Milton's Imagery*
JOHN MILTON

Eugene Campbell Barker
Professor of American History
University of Texas
Author: *Life of Stephen F. Austin; Mexico and Texas, 1821–1835*
Editor: *The Austin Papers, 1765–1836*
STEPHEN F. AUSTIN

Jacques Barzun
Professor of History
Columbia University
Author: *Berlioz and the Romantic Century*
HECTER BERLIOZ

Paull Franklin Baum
Professor of English
Duke University
Editor: *Rossetti's The House of Life: Dante Gabriel Rossetti—An Analytical List of Manuscripts in the Duke University Library, with Hitherto Unpublished Verse and Prose; Rossetti's Letters to Fanny Cornforth*
DANTE GABRIEL ROSSETTI

Adelaide Brooke Baylis
JOAN OF ARC

John Yokum Beaty
Author: *Luther Burbank, Plant Magician*
Editor: *Luther Burbank's Autobiography*
LUTHER BURBANK

Arthur Eugene Bestor, Jr.
Professor of History
University of Illinois
Author: *Backwoods Utopias: A History of Communitarian Socialism in America; Education and Reform at New Harmony: Correspondence of William Maclure and Marie Duclos Fretageot, 1820–1833*
ROBERT OWEN

Bernard Bloch
Professor of Linguistics and Chairman of the Department of Indic and Far Eastern Languages and Literatures
Yale University
LEONARD BLOOMFIELD

Marguerite Beck Block
Associate in Religion, Department of Philosophy and Curator of the Bush Collection in Religion and Culture
Columbia University
Author: *The New Church in the New World: A Study of Swedenborgianism in America*
Managing Editor: *Review of Religion*, Columbia University
EMANUEL SWEDENBORG

Special Consultants, with the Subjects of Their Assistance

Richmond Pugh Bond
Professor of English
University of North Carolina
JOSEPH ADDISON

Catherine Drinker Bowen
Author: *John Adams and the American Revolution*
JOHN ADAMS (in collaboration with John H. Powell)

Frederick Edward Brasch
Consultant in Bibliography
Stanford University;
Consultant in History of Science (1944–48)
Library of Congress
Editor: *Sir Isaac Newton 1727–1927* (memorial volume); *Portfolio of Newton's Portraits and Statues*
SIR ISAAC NEWTON

Crane Brinton
Professor of History (Chairman of Department)
Harvard University
Author: *The Lives of Talleyrand*
TALLEYRAND

S. H. Brockunier
Professor of History
Wesleyan University
Author: *The Irrepressible Democrat: Roger Williams*
ROGER WILLIAMS

Robert B. Brown
BENJAMIN FRANKLIN

Geoffrey Bruun
Visiting Professor of History
Cornell University
Author: *Clemenceau; Saint-Just, Apostle of the Terror*
CLEMENCEAU,
SAINT-JUST

Storm Bull
Professor of Music and Head of the Division of Piano of the College of Music
University of Colorado
JOHANN SEBASTIAN BACH

Kenneth Walter Cameron
Assistant Professor of English
Trinity College
Author: *Emerson the Essayist; Ralph Waldo Emerson's Reading*
RALPH WALDO EMERSON

Carl Carmer
LATTER-DAY SAINTS

Edward Hallett Carr
MICHAEL BAKUNIN

Thomas Caldecot Chubb
Author: *Aretino: Scourge of Princes*
PIETRO ARETINO

Paul S. Clarkson
Author: *A Bibliography of William Sydney Porter (O. Henry)*
RUFUS CHOATE,
THOMAS DE QUINCEY,
LUTHER MARTIN,
WILLIAM SYDNEY PORTER (O. HENRY)

Cyril Clemens
Editor: *Mark Twain Quarterly*
SAMUEL LANGHORNE CLEMENS

Reginald L. Cook
Professor of American Literature and Director of the Bread Loaf School of English
Middlebury College
ROBERT FROST

Edward Samuel Corwin
McCormick Professor (Emeritus) of Jurisprudence
Princeton University;
Lecturer on Constitutional Law and History
The New School
Author: *The Doctrine of Judicial Review; John Marshall and the Constitution; Court over Constitution*
JOHN MARSHALL

Richard N. Current
Associate Professor of History
Mills College
Author: *Old Thad Stevens*
PHILETUS SAWYER,
CHRISTOPHER LATHAM SHOLES,
THADDEUS STEVENS

David Daiches
Formerly Professor of English
Cornell University;
University Lecturer in English
Cambridge University, England
Author: *The Place of Meaning in Poetry; New Literary Values: Studies in Modern Literature; Poems in English 1930–1940; Poetry and the Modern World*
T. S. ELIOT

Dominic de la Salandra
VASCO NUÑEZ DE BALBOA

René Jules Dubos
Author: *Louis Pasteur—Free Lance of Science*
Editor: *Journal of Experimental Medicine*
LOUIS PASTEUR

Clement Eaton
Professor of History
University of Kentucky
Author: *Freedom of Thought in the Old South; A History of the Old South*
ALEXANDER HAMILTON STEPHENS

Alfred Einstein (deceased)
Professor of Music
Smith College
Author: *Mozart, His Character, His Work*
WOLFGANG AMADEUS MOZART

David Ewen
Author: *Haydn: A Good Life*
JOSEPH HAYDN

DeLancey Ferguson
Chairman of the English Department
Brooklyn College
RUDYARD KIPLING

Louis Filler
Associate Professor of American Civilization and Literature
Antioch College
Author: *Crusaders for American Liberalism*
WILLIAM LLOYD GARRISON

Paul Abraham Freund
Charles Stebbins Fairchild Professor of Law
Harvard Law School
LOUIS DEMBITZ BRANDEIS

Claude Moore Fuess
Headmaster (1933–47)
Phillips Andover Academy
Author: *Calvin Coolidge, The Man from Vermont*
CALVIN COOLIDGE

Leo Gershoy
Professor of History
New York University
NAPOLEON I

Special Consultants, with the Subjects of Their Assistance

Lawrence Henry Gipson
Research Professor of History
Lehigh University
Author: *The Great War for the Empire; The American Revolution as an Aftermath of the Great War for the Empire and Other Essays in American Colonial History; The British Empire in the Eighteenth Century*
THE FRENCH AND INDIAN WARS

Louis Gottschalk
Professor of History
University of Chicago
Author: *Lafayette Comes to America; Lafayette Joins the American Army; Lady-in-Waiting—The Romance of Lafayette and Aglaé de Hunolstein; Lafayette and the Close of the American Revolution; The Letters of Lafayette to Washington; Lafayette between the American and the French Revolution (1783–1789)*
MARQUIS DE LAFAYETTE

Garland Greever
Professor Emeritus of English
University of Southern California;
Visiting Professor of English
George Pepperdine College
Author: *Facts and Backgrounds of Literature, English and American* (in collaboration)
Editor: *Tiger-Lilies and Southern Prose*
SIDNEY LANIER

Elizabeth Hazelton Haight
Professor Emeritus of Latin
Vassar College
Author: *Horace and His Art of Enjoyment*
HORACE

Lewis Francis Haines
Professor of Humanities and Director of the University Press
University of Florida
CHARLES READE

Abram L. Harris
Professor of Economics and Professor of the Social Sciences in the Division of the Social Sciences
University of Chicago
KARL MARX

Seale Harris
Author: *Banting's Miracle*
SIR FREDERICK BANTING

Lodwick Hartley
Professor of English (Head of Department)
North Carolina State College
Author: *This Is Lorence: A Narrative of the Reverend Laurence Sterne*
LAURENCE STERNE

Paul Harold Heisey
Professor of Bible and Religious Education
Newberry College
Author: *Three Essays on Luther*
MARTIN LUTHER

Robert Selph Henry
Author: *The Story of the Confederacy; "First With the Most" Forrest*
NATHAN BEDFORD FORREST,
ROBERT E. LEE

William Best Hesseltine
Professor of History
University of Wisconsin
Author: *Ulysses S. Grant*
ULYSSES S. GRANT

Eldon Cleon Hill
Associate Professor of English
Miami University
Author: *A Biographical Study of Hamlin Garland 1860–1895*
HAMLIN GARLAND

David Hinshaw
Author: *Herbert Hoover, American Quaker*
HERBERT HOOVER

Fletcher Hodges, Jr.
Curator of the Foster Hall Collection
University of Pittsburgh
STEPHEN COLLINS FOSTER

Stanley F. Horn
Author: *The Army of Tennessee*
THOMAS JONATHAN JACKSON

Mark DeWolfe Howe
Professor of Law
Harvard University
Editor: *Holmes Pollock Letters (Correspondence of Mr. Justice Holmes and Sir Frederick Pollock, 1874–1932); Touched with Fire (Civil War Letters of O. W. Holmes Jr.); Holmes Laski Letters (Correspondence of Mr. Justice Holmes and Harold J. Laski, 1916–1935)*
OLIVER WENDELL HOLMES

Allan F. Hubbell
Assistant Professor of English
University of Denver
Editor: *American Speech*
ENGLISH

William Thomas Hutchinson
Professor of American History and Chairman of the Department of History
University of Chicago
Author: *Cyrus Hall McCormick: Seed-Time (1809–1856); Cyrus Hall McCormick: Harvest (1856–1884)*
CYRUS HALL MC CORMICK

Clyde Kenneth Hyder
Professor of English
University of Kansas
Author: *Swinburne's Literary Career and Fame*
ALGERNON CHARLES SWINBURNE

Marquis James
Author: *Andrew Jackson, The Border Captain; Andrew Jackson: Portrait of a President*
ANDREW JACKSON

Frederick Lafayette Jones
Professor of English
University of Pennsylvania
Author: *An Examination of the Shelley Legend* (in collaboration)
PERCY BYSSHE SHELLEY

Henry Donaldson Jordan
Professor of English History
Clark University
RICHARD COBDEN

Harnett Thomas Kane
Author: *Louisiana Hayride: The American Rehearsal for Dictatorship*
HUEY LONG

Sheila Kaye-Smith
Author: *Speaking of Jane Austen* (in collaboration with G. B. Stern); *More about Jane Austen* (in collaboration with G. B. Stern)
JANE AUSTEN

Special Consultants, with the Subjects of Their Assistance

Abraham C. Keller
Associate Professor of French
University of Washington
FRANÇOIS RABELAIS

Eric Philbrook Kelly
Professor of Journalism
Dartmouth College
Author: *Helena Modjeska*
HELENA MODJESKA

Fred C. Kelly
Author: *George Ade—Warmhearted Satirist*
Editor: *The Permanent Ade*
GEORGE ADE

Geoffrey Keynes
Consulting Surgeon
St. Bartholomew's Hospital, London
Author: *Bibliography of William Harvey*
WILLIAM HARVEY

Pearl Kibre
Associate Professor of History
Hunter College
ALBERTUS MAGNUS

Willard Leroy King
Author: *Melville Weston Fuller*
MELVILLE WESTON FULLER

Lewis Mansfield Knapp
Professor of English (Chairman of Department)
Colorado College
Author: *Tobias Smollett, Doctor of Men and Manners*
TOBIAS SMOLLETT

Bernhard Knollenberg
Associate Fellow
Saybrook College
Yale University
Author: *Washington and the Revolution: A Re-Appraisal*
GEORGE WASHINGTON

Edwin B. Knowles
Professor of English
Pratt Institute
MIGUEL DE CERVANTES

Dayton Kohler
Associate Professor of English
Virginia Polytechnic Institute
WILLA CATHER

Louis Knott Koontz
ROBERT DINWIDDIE

Laurence J. Lafleur
Head of the Department of Philosophy
University of Akron
Author: *Bentham's Principles of Morals and Legislation*
JEREMY BENTHAM

Wheaton Joshua Lane
Former Instructor in History
Princeton University
Author: *Commodore Vanderbilt*
CORNELIUS VANDERBILT

Lewis Leary
Professor of English
Columbia University
Author: *That Rascal Freneau: A Study in Literary Failure; The Last Poems of Philip Freneau*
PHILIP FRENEAU

Paul F. Leedy
Professor of English
Bowling Green State University
ALEXANDER POPE

Wilmarth Sheldon Lewis
Editor: *A Selection of the Letters of Horace Walpole; Horace Walpole's Fugitive Verses;* Yale Edition of *Horace Walpole's Correspondence*, 16 Volumes, to be completed 1965 in 50 Volumes
HORACE WALPOLE

David Alexander Lockmiller
President of the University of Chattanooga
Author: *Sir William Blackstone*
SIR WILLIAM BLACKSTONE

Rupert Clendon Lodge
Visiting Professor
Long Island University
Author: *Plato's Theory of Ethics; Plato's Theory of Education; Plato's Theory of Art*
PLATO

Louis Eleazer Lord
Professor Emeritus of Classics
Oberlin College
Author: *Aristophanes*
ARISTOPHANES

Robert Phillips Ludlum
President of Blackburn College
JOSHUA REED GIDDINGS

Gerstle Mack
Author: *Paul Cézanne; La Vie de Paul Cézanne* (translation by Nancy Bouwens)
PAUL CÉZANNE

Malcolm Lorimer MacLeod
Associate Professor of English
University of Florida
Author: *A Concordance to the Poems of Robert Herrick; An Analysis of Herrick's Vocabulary*
ROBERT HERRICK

Kemp Malone
Donovan Professor of English Literature
The Johns Hopkins University
Author: *The Thorkelin Transcripts of Beowulf*
ALFRED (THE GREAT),
BEOWULF

Watt Pearson Marchman
Director of the Hayes Memorial Library
RUTHERFORD B. HAYES

Helen Edith Marshall
Professor of Social Science
Illinois State Normal University
Author: *Dorothea Dix: Forgotten Samaritan*
DOROTHEA LYNDE DIX

Special Consultants, with the Subjects of Their Assistance

John Sedberry Marshall
Professor of Philosophy
University of the South
ARISTOTLE

Bernard Mayo
Professor of American History
University of Virginia
Author: *Henry Clay, Spokesman of the New West*
HENRY CLAY

Walter Flavius McCaleb
Fellow in History
University of Chicago
Author: *The Aaron Burr Conspiracy*
AARON BURR

George Leslie McKay
Author: *A Bibliography of Robert Bridges*
ROBERT BRIDGES

Silas Bent McKinley
Author: *Old Rough and Ready*
ZACHARY TAYLOR

James G. McManaway
Consultant in Literature and Bibliography
The Folger Shakespeare Library
Editor: *Shakespeare Quarterly*
WILLIAM SHAKESPEARE

John Robert Moore
Professor of English and Library Consultant in Augustan Literature
Indiana University
Author: *Daniel Defoe and Modern Economic Theory; Defoe in the Pillory and Other Studies; Defoe's Sources for "Robert Drury's Journal"*
Editor: *Defoe's Essay on the Regulation of the Press*
DANIEL DEFOE

Glenn R. Morrow
Adam Seybert Professor of Moral and Intellectual Philosophy and Dean of the College
University of Pennsylvania
Author: *The Ethical and Economic Theories of Adam Smith*
ADAM SMITH

George Henry Nettleton
Lampson Professor (Emeritus) of English
Yale University
Author: *English Drama of the Restoration and Eighteenth Century; The Major Dramas of Richard Brinsley Sheridan; British Dramatists from Dryden to Sheridan*
RICHARD BRINSLEY SHERIDAN

Roy Franklin Nichols
Professor of History and Dean of the Graduate School of Arts and Sciences
University of Pennsylvania
Author: *Franklin Pierce*
FRANKLIN PIERCE

Russell Blaine Nye
Professor of English (Head of Department) and Director of Language and Literature
Michigan State College
Author: *George Bancroft: Brahmin Rebel; Fettered Freedom: Civil Liberties and Slavery*
GEORGE BANCROFT

Whitney J. Oates
Andrew Fleming West Professor of Classics (Chairman of Department) and Chairman of the Special Program in the Humanities
Princeton University
Author: *The Stoic and Epicurean Philosophers*
EPICURUS

Charles W. Olsen
Author: *John Brown*
JOHN BROWN

Howard Rollin Patch
Professor of English
Smith College
Author: *The Tradition of Boethius*
ANICIUS BOETHIUS

Rembert W. Patrick
Professor of American History and Social Sciences and Chairman of the Department of History
University of Florida
Author: *Jefferson Davis and His Cabinet*
JEFFERSON DAVIS

Donald Culross Peattie
Author: *Singing in the Wilderness: A Salute to John James Audubon; Forward the Nation*
JOHN JAMES AUDUBON,
SACAJAWEA

Kenneth Wiggins Porter
Author: *John Jacob Astor, Businessman*
ABRAHAM,
JOHN JACOB ASTOR,
COACOOCHEE,
SAMUEL GORTON,
OSCEOLA

Levi Arnold Post
Professor of Greek
Haverford College
Editor of the Loeb Classical Library
Translator: *Menander—Three Plays*
MENANDER

Frederick A. Pottle
Sterling Professor of English
Yale University
Author: *The Literary Career of James Boswell*
Editor: *Boswell's London Journal, 1762–1763; Boswell in Holland, 1763–1764*
JAMES BOSWELL

John H. Powell
Research Librarian
Free Library of Philadelphia
JOHN ADAMS (in collaboration with Catherine Drinker Bowen)

Lawrence Clark Powell
Director of the William Andrews Clark Memorial Library
University of California
Author: *An Introduction to Robinson Jeffers; Robinson Jeffers, the Man and His Work*
ROBINSON JEFFERS

Julius William Pratt
Professor of American History and Dean of the Graduate School of Arts and Sciences
University of Buffalo
JAMES MONROE

Special Consultants, with the Subjects of Their Assistance

Robert A. Pratt

Professor of English
University of North Carolina

Author: *Sources and Analogues of Chaucer's Canterbury Tales* (in collaboration)

GEOFFREY CHAUCER

Benjamin Quarles

Dean of Instruction
Dillard University

Author: *Frederick Douglass*
Assistant Editor: *The Journal of Negro History*

FREDERICK DOUGLASS

J. G. Randall (deceased)

Professor of History
University of Illinois

Author: *The Civil War and Reconstruction; Lincoln the President; Lincoln and the South; Lincoln the Liberal Statesman*

ABRAHAM LINCOLN

Fannie Elizabeth Ratchford

Director of Rare Book Collections
University of Texas

Author: *The Brontës' Web of Childhood; The Legends of Angria*

BRONTË FAMILY

Gordon Norton Ray

Professor of English (Head of Department)
University of Illinois

Author: *The Letters and Private Papers of William Makepeace Thackeray; The Buried Life: a study of the relation between Thackeray's fiction and his personal history*

WILLIAM MAKEPEACE THACKERAY

Thomas Middleton Raysor

Professor of English
University of Nebraska

Editor: *Coleridge's Shakespearean Criticism; Coleridge's Miscellaneous Criticism*

SAMUEL TAYLOR COLERIDGE

Richard Ashley Rice

Professor of English Literature
Smith College

Author: *Studies of Wordsworth and Byron; The Best of Byron*

GEORGE GORDON NOEL BYRON

Lawrence Melville Riddle

Professor Emeritus of French
University of Southern California

Author: *Sources of Pierre Corneille's Tragedies from Médée to Pertharite*

Editor: *Corneille's Cinna*

PIERRE CORNEILLE,
JEAN ROTROU

Frank Humphrey Ristine

Professor Emeritus of English Literature
Hamilton College

JOHN GREENLEAF WHITTIER

William J. Roach

Professor of Romance Languages
University of Pennsylvania

Author: *The Continuations of the Perceval of Chrétien de Troyes*

CHRÉTIEN DE TROYES

Roy Marvin Robbins

Professor of History and Political Science (Head of Department)
Butler University

Author: *Our Landed Heritage: A History of the Public Domain, 1776–1936*

HORACE GREELEY

Charles Alexander Robinson, Jr.

Professor of Classics
Brown University

Author: *The Ephemerides of Alexander's Expedition; Alexander the Great*

ALEXANDER THE GREAT

George Washington Robinson

Author: *Errata in Cotton Mather's Magnalia*

COTTON MATHER

Charles Alfred Rochedieu

Associate Professor of French
Vanderbilt University

JEAN JACQUES ROUSSEAU

Frederick William Roe

Professor Emeritus of English
University of Wisconsin

Author: *Carlyle as a Critic of Literature; Social Philosophy of Carlyle and Ruskin*

Editor: *Ruskin—Selections and Essays; Carlyle—Sartor Resartus*

THOMAS CARLYLE,
JOHN RUSKIN

Woodburn O. Ross

Professor of English
Wayne University

W. SOMERSET MAUGHAM

Kenneth R. Rossman

Professor of History (Chairman of Department)
Doane College

Author: *Chester A. Arthur and the Civil Service Reform; Thomas Mifflin and the Politics of the American Revolution*

CHESTER A. ARTHUR,
THOMAS MIFFLIN

William Hobart Royce

Founder and President of The Balzac Society of America

Author: *A Balzac Bibliography*

HONORÉ DE BALZAC (in collaboration with N. E. Saxe)

Una Bernard Sait

Former Professor of Philosophy
Scripps College

Author: *Implications of Bergson's Philosophy*

HENRI LOUIS BERGSON

N. E. Saxe

Chairman of the Division of Humanities and Head of the Department of Modern Languages
Washburn University

HONORÉ DE BALZAC (in collaboration with William Hobart Royce)

J. Salwyn Schapiro

Professor Emeritus of History
The City College of New York

Author: *Condorcet and the Rise of Liberalism*

CONDORCET

Special Consultants, with the Subjects of Their Assistance

Ferdinand Schevill
Former Professor of Modern History
University of Chicago
Author: *History of Florence*
MACHIAVELLI

Paul Arthur Schilpp
Professor of Philosophy
Northwestern University
ALBERT EINSTEIN

Martha Hale Shackford
Professor Emeritus of English Literature
Wellesley College
Author: *E. B. Browning, R. H. Horne—Two Studies; The Brownings and Leighton*
Editor: *Letters from Elizabeth Barrett to B. R. Haydon*
ELIZABETH BARRETT BROWNING

Robert Shafer
Professor of Literature
University of Cincinnati
GEORGE GISSING

Samuel Shellabarger
CHEVALIER DE BAYARD

Clifford Kenyon Shipton
Custodian of Archives
Harvard University
Author: *Isaiah Thomas*
ISAIAH THOMAS

Roger Vernon Shumate
Professor of Political Science
University of Nebraska
HENRY ADAMS

Charles Southward Singleton
Professor of Romance Languages
Harvard University
BOCCACCIO

St. George L. Sioussat
Professor of American History
University of Pennsylvania (1920–38);
Honorary Consultant in American Historiography
Library of Congress
ANDREW JOHNSON

Emily Ellsworth Ford Skeel
Author: *Mason Locke Weems, His Work and Ways* (in collaboration)
MASON LOCKE WEEMS

Donald Smalley
Professor of English
Indiana University
Editor: *Domestic Manners of the Americans ... with a History of Mrs. Trollope's Adventures in America*
FRANCES TROLLOPE

Charles G. Smith
Professor of English
Baylor University
Author: *Spenser's Theory of Friendship*
EDMUND SPENSER

Herman Dunlap Smith
President of the Chicago Historical Society
Author: *War Journals of Henry Dearborn, 1773–1783, with Biographical Essay*
HENRY DEARBORN

Theodore Clarke Smith
Professor Emeritus of American History
Williams College
Author: *Life and Letters of James Abram Garfield*
JAMES ABRAM GARFIELD

Harold Edwin Blame Speight
Former Professor of Biography
Dartmouth College
Author: *Life and Writings of John Bunyan*
Editor: *Creative Lives*
JOHN BUNYAN

Benjamin Townley Spencer
Professor of English
Ohio Wesleyan University;
Visiting Professor of English (1952–53)
Universities of Uppsala and Stockholm
Author: *Seventeenth Century Studies* (in collaboration)
Editor: *The Bondman*
PHILIP MASSINGER

Robert E. Spiller
Professor of English
University of Pennsylvania
Author: *Fenimore Cooper, Critic of His Times*
Editor: *A Descriptive Bibliography of James Fenimore Cooper* (in collaboration); *James Fenimore Cooper, Representative Selections*
JAMES FENIMORE COOPER

Matthew Spinka
Waldo Professor of Church History
Hartford Theological Seminary
Author: *John Hus and the Czech Reform*
JOHN AMOS COMENIUS, JOHN HUS

William Edward Bloomfield Starkweather
Assistant Professor of Art and Lecturer on Spanish Art
Hunter College
Author: *Drawings and Paintings of Francisco Goya in the Collection of the Hispanic Society of America*
GOYA

Herbert Willmarth Starr
Assistant Professor of English
Temple University
Author: *Gray as a Literary Critic*
THOMAS GRAY

Vincent Starrett
Book Columnist of the Chicago *Tribune*
Author: *Ambrose Bierce*
AMBROSE GWINETT BIERCE

Lawrence D. Steefel
Professor of History
University of Minnesota
OTTO VON BISMARCK

Jack M. Stein
Assistant Professor of German
Columbia University
RICHARD WAGNER

Kate Steinitz
Librarian of the Elmer Belt Library of Vinciana
Author: *Leonardo da Vinci's Manuscripts* (in collaboration)
LEONARDO DA VINCI

Special Consultants, with the Subjects of Their Assistance

Randall Stewart
Professor of English
Brown University
Author: *Nathaniel Hawthorne: A Biography*
NATHANIEL HAWTHORNE

George Winchester Stone, Jr.
Professor of English Literature
The George Washington University
Author: *The Journal of David Garrick, 1763*
DAVID GARRICK

Dirk J. Struik
Professor of Mathematics
Massachusetts Institute of Technology
Author: *Yankee Science in the Making*
ASA GRAY

Frank Sullivan
Professor of English
Loyola University
SIR THOMAS MORE

Carl Brent Swisher
Thomas P. Stran Professor of Political Science
The Johns Hopkins University
Author: *Roger B. Taney*
ROGER B. TANEY

Robert Emmett Taylor
Professor of Business Law and Accounting
University of Cincinnati
Author: *The Story of Robert Emmet*
ROBERT EMMET

Charles Dewey Tenney
Vice-President and Provost, and Professor of Philosophy
Southern Illinois University
GEORGE MEREDITH

Adelaide Eve Thein
Former Chairman of the English Department
Doane College
WILLIAM COWPER

Helen Lewis Thomas
JOHANN KEPLER

Samuel M. Thompson
Professor of Philosophy (Head of Department)
Monmouth College
IMMANUEL KANT

Clarence DeWitt Thorpe
Professor of English
University of Michigan
Author: *The Mind of John Keats*
Editor: *The Complete Poems and Selected Letters of John Keats*
JOHN KEATS

Lewis Paul Todd
HORACE MANN

William Troy
Lecturer in Comparative Literature
The New School
HENRY JAMES

Berthold Louis Ullman
Kenan Professor of Classics (Head of Department)
University of North Carolina
Author: *The Identification of the MSS. of Catullus*
CATULLUS

Carl Van Doren (deceased)
JONATHAN SWIFT

Mark Van Doren (See Editorial Advisory Committee)
JOHN DRYDEN

Albert Tangeman Volwiler
Professor of History (Chairman of Department)
Ohio University
Editor: *Correspondence between Benjamin Harrison and James G. Blaine*
BENJAMIN HARRISON

Ira Owen Wade
Professor of Modern Languages (Chairman of Department)
Princeton University
Author: *The Clandestine Organization and Diffusion of Philosophic Ideas in France from 1700 to 1750; Voltaire and Mme. du Châtelet; Studies in Voltaire*
VOLTAIRE

Edward Wagenknecht
Professor of English
Boston University
Author: *The Man Charles Dickens: A Victorian Portrait; An Introduction to Dickens*
CHARLES DICKENS

Eva Ingersoll Wakefield
Editor: *The Letters of Robert G. Ingersoll*
ROBERT G. INGERSOLL

Gerald Groveland Walsh (deceased)
Professor of Medieval Cultural History
Fordham University
DANTE

Harry R. Warfel (See Editorial Advisory Committee)
Author: *Noah Webster: Schoolmaster to America; Charles Brockden Brown: American Gothic Novelist*
CHARLES BROCKDEN BROWN, NOAH WEBSTER

Carl J. Weber
Roberts Professor of English Literature and Curator of Rare Books
Colby College
Author: *Hardy's Lost Novel; Hardy of Wessex; Hardy in America; New Light on Hardy's "Woodlanders"; Hardy and the Lady from Madison Square*
THOMAS HARDY

Stanley T. Williams
Sterling Professor (Emeritus) of English
Yale University
Author: *Washington Irving*
WASHINGTON IRVING

Special Consultants, with the Subjects of Their Assistance

Wayne Cullen Williams
Author: *The Life of William Jennings Bryan*
WILLIAM JENNINGS BRYAN

Barnie F. Winkelman
Author: *John D. Rockefeller*
JOHN D. ROCKEFELLER

Ione Stuessy Wright
Associate Professor of Hispanic American History
University of Miami
JOSÉ DE SAN MARTÍN

Morton Dauwen Zabel
Professor of English
University of Chicago
Editor: *The Portable Joseph Conrad*
JOSEPH CONRAD

Casimir Douglass Zdanowicz (deceased)
Professor of Romance Languages
University of Wisconsin
MOLIÈRE

Donald Joseph Zinn
Assistant Professor of Zoölogy
University of Rhode Island
ALEXANDER AGASSIZ, LOUIS AGASSIZ

PRONUNCIATION EDITORS AND CONSULTANTS

W. Cabell Greet
(See Editorial Advisory Committee)

R. A. Goodwin
(Editor in Charge)

Special Assistants:

Harriet Cassell

R. A. Hall, Jr.
Professor of Linguistics
Cornell University

Special Consultants:

Fang-Kuei Li
Professor of Far Eastern and Slavic Languages and Literatures
University of Washington

Joseph K. Yamagiwa
University of Michigan

SPECIAL WRITERS, WITH THEIR FIELDS

George T. Beck
MODERN POLITICAL BIOGRAPHY AND HISTORY OF INDIA

Bruno Blau
EUROPEAN GEOGRAPHY

Imre Cholnoky
MODERN HUNGARIAN LITERATURE

Henry W. Dearborn
BRITISH PHYSICAL AND SOCIAL GEOGRAPHY

Dora Edinger
MODERN GERMAN BIOGRAPHY AND HISTORY

Richard N. Fried
MODERN FINE ARTS OF EUROPE AND THE UNITED STATES

Helen Hause
Lecturer in Anthropology
Northwestern University
NORTH AFRICAN AND NEAR EASTERN ETHNOLOGY

Robert E. Huke
RUSSIAN AND ASIATIC GEOGRAPHY

Lionel F. Jaffe
MODERN CHEMISTRY

Edward J. Miles
Instructor in Geography and Economics
University of Maryland
GEOGRAPHY OF THE ARCTIC AND ANTARCTIC, CANADA, AFRICA, AUSTRALIA, NEW ZEALAND, AND THE ISLANDS OF THE PACIFIC

Walter M. Mosse
Instructor in Theological German
Princeton Theological Seminary
MODERN EUROPEAN BIOGRAPHY

Hoh-Cheung Mui
Social Science Analyst of the United States Department of State
MODERN JAPANESE POLITICAL BIOGRAPHY AND HISTORY

Jerome P. Pickard
Instructor in Geography
University of Maryland
SPECIAL PROBLEMS IN GEOGRAPHY

Curt Proskauer
Consultant to the Library of the New York Academy of Medicine; Consulting Editor of the *Journal of the History of Medicine and the Allied Sciences*
MEDICAL BIOGRAPHY AND HISTORY

Herbert H. Rowen
Assistant Professor of History
State University of Iowa
MODERN FRENCH AND SCANDINAVIAN BIOGRAPHY AND HISTORY

OFFICE STAFF

Editors: Harriet Cassell, Jerome Fried, W. M. Frohock, R. A. Goodwin, William Greenleaf, Maria Leach, Frances Murlin, Herbert Spencer Robinson, Grace G. Shaw

Associate Editors: Caroline Brady, Harry Freeman, Natalie Frohock, Charles Goodrich, Leo Hamalian, Anne Heffner, Ruth Hein, Winifred M. Irwin, Celia Koron, Margaret Madden, Shaemas O'Sheel, Ethel M. Ryan, Elizabeth St. Vincent, Pamela Taggard, Katherine Theda, Frederick Tozer, Irving Weiss, Carolyn D. Werley, Phyllis Ruckgaber Winant

Editorial Assistants: W. T. Atwood, Martha H. Decrouez, Barbara Fairberg, Ramona Grayson, Herbert J. Landar, Ellen L. Nelson, N. Bryce Nelson, Mary Guion Randel, John Wasley, Roger Williams

Office Assistants: Vincenta P. Adams, Helen Areinoff, Elizabeth Ballard, Helen Barlow, Anna-Luise Bartling, Marshall Brigham, Leroy Brightman, Joan Carvon, Dannydelle W. Dandridge, Filomene Della Donne, Dorothy Alma Druschen, Pat Ferrara, Thomas Gelardi, Esther Golden, Angelina Guido, William S. Hemingway, Jane E. Herrick, Emma Jean Huff, Jean G. Leftwich, Nancy Mastro, Mary F. Noble, Catherine T. Piacentino, James W. Porter, Cynthia A. Rogers, Harriette Roseth, Agnes Seaman, Sophie Shupín, Jaime Burnet Spencer, Janet Stone, Ruth C. Vickery, Marjorie C. Waldo

ABBREVIATIONS USED GENERALLY IN THESE VOLUMES

ab.	about
A.D.	year of our Lord (*anno domini*)
A.M.	before noon (*ante meridiem*)
b.	born
B.A.	Bachelor of Arts
B.C.	before Christ
B.S.	Bachelor of Science
C	central
c	about (*circa, circiter*, or *circum*)
ch.	chapter
d.	died
E	east, eastern
E.	east longitude
ed.	edition
Eng. trans.	English translation
est.	estimated
etc.	and so forth (*et cetera*)
et seq.	and afterward (*et sequens*)
F.	French
fl.	flourished (*floruit*)
ft.	feet
i.e.	that is (*id est*)
kw.	kilowatt
M.A.	Master of Arts
M.D.	Doctor of Medicine
mi.	miles
M.S.	Master of Science
N	north, northern
N.	north latitude
NE	northeast, northeastern
NW	northwest, northwestern
Ph.D.	Doctor of Philosophy
P.M.	after noon (*post meridiem*)
pop.	population
S	south, southern
S.	south latitude
Sc.	Scottish
SE	southeast, southeastern
sq.	square
SW	southwest, southwestern
UN	United Nations
U.S.	United States
U.S.S.R.	Union of Soviet Socialist Republics
v.	verse
vol.	volume
vols.	volumes
W	west, western
W.	west longitude

ABBREVIATIONS FOR STATES

Ala.	Alabama
Ariz.	Arizona
Ark.	Arkansas
Calif.	California
Colo.	Colorado
Conn.	Connecticut
D.C.	District of Columbia
Del.	Delaware
Fla.	Florida
Ga.	Georgia
Ill.	Illinois
Ind.	Indiana
Kan.	Kansas
Ky.	Kentucky
La.	Louisiana
Mass.	Massachusetts
Md.	Maryland
Me.	Maine
Mich.	Michigan
Minn.	Minnesota
Miss.	Mississippi
Mo.	Missouri
Mont.	Montana
N.C.	North Carolina
N.D.	North Dakota
Neb.	Nebraska
Nev.	Nevada
N.H.	New Hampshire
N.J.	New Jersey
N.M.	New Mexico
N.Y.	New York
Okla.	Oklahoma
Ore.	Oregon
Pa.	Pennsylvania
R.I.	Rhode Island
S.C.	South Carolina
S.D.	South Dakota
Tenn.	Tennessee
Tex.	Texas
Va.	Virginia
Vt.	Vermont
Wash.	Washington
Wis.	Wisconsin
W.Va.	West Virginia
Wyo.	Wyoming

ABBREVIATIONS FOR BOOKS OF THE BIBLE

Gen.	Genesis
Ex.	Exodus
Lev.	Leviticus
Num.	Numbers
Deut.	Deuteronomy
Josh.	Joshua
1 Sam.	I. Samuel
2 Sam.	II. Samuel
1 Chron.	I. Chronicles
2 Chron.	II. Chronicles
Neh.	Nehemiah
Ps.	Psalms
Prov.	Proverbs
Eccl.	Ecclesiastes
Cant.	Canticles (Song of Solomon)
Isa.	Isaiah
Jer.	Jeremiah
Lam.	Lamentations
Ezek.	Ezekiel
Dan.	Daniel
Hos.	Hosea
Obad.	Obadiah
Hab.	Habakkuk
Zeph.	Zephaniah
Hag.	Haggai
Zech.	Zechariah
Mal.	Malachi
Mat.	Matthew
Rom.	Romans
1 Cor.	I. Corinthians
2 Cor.	II. Corinthians
Gal.	Galatians
Eph.	Ephesians
Phil.	Philippians
Col.	Colossians
1 Thes.	I. Thessalonians
2 Thes.	II. Thessalonians
1 Tim.	I. Timothy
2 Tim.	II. Timothy
Phile.	Philemon
Heb.	Hebrews
Jas.	James
1 Pet.	I. Peter
2 Pet.	II. Peter
Rev.	Revelation

Ecclus.	Ecclesiasticus
Bar.	Baruch
1 Mac.	I. Maccabees
2 Mac.	II. Maccabees

The New

CENTURY CYCLOPEDIA

OF

Names

KEY TO PRONUNCIATION

a as in fat, man, pang, parrot.

ā as in fate, mane, dale.

ä as in far, father, palm, guard.

ȧ as in ask, fast, ant.

ã as in fare, hair, bear.

e as in net, pen, bless.

ē as in me, meet, meat.

ė as in her, fern, herd, hurt.

i as in pin, it, biscuit.

ī as in pine, fight, file.

o as in not, on, gloss, forest, dog, god (a variable sound: in the speech of some, or in some words, approaching ä; in other cases, approaching ô).

ō as in note, poke, floor.

ö as in move, spoon, room.

ô as in nor, song, off.

u as in up, son, blood.

ū as in mute, few, lute, tube (in many words, after l, t, etc., replaced in common speech by ö).

u̇ as in pull, book, could.

oi as in oil, joint, boy.

ou as in out, proud, now.

A single dot under a vowel in an unaccented syllable indicates shortening and lightening, without absolute loss of the distinctive quality. Thus:

ạ̄ as in aviary, prelate, captain.

ẹ̄ as in elect, ablegate, episcopal.

ọ̄ as in agony, abrogate, democrat.

ọ̈ as in into, injury.

ụ̄ as in unite, singular, educate.

Two dots under a vowel in an unaccented syllable indicate that its sound is obscured. Thus:

a̤ as in errant, publican, rural.

e̤ as in ardent, prudence, towel.

o̤ as in actor, valor, idiot.

ṳ̄ as in nature, feature, natural.

ch as in chip, much.

g as in go, bag.

s as in say, yes, vice.

th as in thin.

ᴛʜ as in then.

y as in you, yet.

A mark (˯) under the consonants d, s, t, z, indicates that they are variable to j, sh, ch, zh. Thus:

d̮ as in arduous, educate.

s̮ as in nausea, appreciation.

t̮ as in nature, adventure.

z̮ as in aphasia, usury.

o as in French cloche, German schloss (a short or medium open o-sound, intermediate in character between ō and ô: not an English sound).

ü as in French menu, German kümmel, Müller.

ċh as in Scotch loch, German ach.

ṅ nasal n, as in French bonbon.

ʙ as in Spanish Habana, Córdoba (sounded almost like v).

ʜ as in Spanish jacal, gitana (a strongly aspirated, guttural h-sound).

as in French faille, Swedish Strindberg (to indicate an obscure vowel-sound following a consonantal y-sound).

′ denotes a primary accent, ″ a secondary accent. (A secondary accent is not ordinarily marked if it occurs at its regular interval of two syllables from the primary, or from another secondary.)

In the pronunciation of French words (except such as are regarded as at least partially Anglicized) no accents are indicated. This is the usage of French dictionaries, and is better suited to the light, nearly uniform accentuation of French words than the use of marks customarily denoting the heavier tonic accent of English words.

The New CENTURY CYCLOPEDIA OF Names

A. In colonial New England, as an abbreviation for "adulterer" or "adulteress," the letter "A" was branded on individuals found guilty of thus violating the marriage oath. In Nathaniel Hawthorne's *Scarlet Letter,* a piece of scarlet cloth worn by Hester Prynne is made to assume the shape of this letter; in another, earlier story, *Endicott and the Red Cross,* Hawthorne employed the device in somewhat similar fashion.

Aa (ä). River in N France, flowing from Pas-de-Calais department to Gravelines on the North Sea between Calais and Dunkerque. The term "Aa" is applied as a proper name not only to this particular stream, but also to many others in N and W Europe, and from this usage the term has come to be an element of hundreds of European names of villages, towns, and cities near to or on the banks of rivers named "Aa." It has as its root the same Indo-European form as the Latin word "aqua."

Aa. River in NE Netherlands, in the province of Groningen, consisting of two branches, the Mussel Aa and Ruiten Aa, which join near Ohstwedde and flow NE into the Dollart.

Aa. River in S Netherlands, in the province of North Brabant, which flows NW to unite with the Dommel near 's Hertogenbosch.

Aa. River in N central Switzerland, in the cantons of Lucerne and Aargau, which flows N through Baldegg and Hallwil lakes into the river Aare.

Aa. [Also, **Sarner-Aa.**] River in C Switzerland, in the canton of Unterwalden, which flows NE through Lake Sarnen into the Lake of Lucerne near Alpnachstadt.

Aa. River in C Switzerland, in the canton of Unterwalden, which flows generally N into the Lake of Lucerne near Buochs. It should not be confused with the slightly larger river of the same name covered by the entry immediately preceding, and flowing also into the Lake of Lucerne.

Aa. Former name of the **Gauja,** a river in Latvia.

Aa. Former name of the **Lielupe,** a river in Latvia.

Aa, Pieter van der. fl. last half 17th century. Dutch publisher and engraver who, with his brothers, formed (c1682) a publishing house at Leiden. They edited and published several collections of travels in French and Dutch.

AA. See **Alcoholics Anonymous.**

AAA. See **Agricultural Adjustment Administration.**

Aabenraa (ô'bẹn.rô). [Also: **Åbenrå;** German, **Apenrade.**] Town in S Denmark, in the *amt* (county) of Aabenraa-Sønderborg, in SE Jutland, situated at the head of a fjord that opens on the Little Belt, ab. 15 mi. S of Haderslev. It has a port, fisheries, and some importance as a shipping point in the lumber trade. The town's chief point of tourist interest is Castle Bruunlund, a structure dating from the 15th century. The community received town privileges in 1335; as part of Schleswig-Holstein, it belonged (1864–1920) to Prussia. After a plebiscite following World War I it was returned (1920) to Denmark. The population includes a German-speaking minority. 12,189 (1945).

Aabenraa-Sønderborg (sėn'nėr.bôrg). [Also, **Åbenrå-Sönderborg.**] *Amt* (county) of Denmark, in S Jutland, consisting of the island of Als and a strip of the nearby mainland. Capital, Sønderborg; area, 475 sq. mi; pop. 46,260 (1945).

Aach (äċh). Small village in SW Germany, in the *Land* (state) of South Baden, French Zone, ab. 20 mi. NW of Konstanz, Switzerland. It was the scene of a battle between the French and the Austrians on March 25, 1799.

Aachen (ä'ċhẹn). [French, **Aix-La-Chapelle;** Dutch, **Aken;** Latin, **Aquae Grani, Aquisgranum.**] City in W Germany, in the *Land* (state) of North Rhine-Westphalia, British Zone, formerly in the Rhine Province, Prussia, situated on the border of Belgium, ab. 40 mi. SW of Cologne. It is a center of German textile manufacturing, and also has important glass (mirror) and needle industries; other manufactures include automobile parts and electrical equipment, brushes, and rubber and paper goods. The city has canneries and breweries of some importance. Its hot alkaline and sulfurous springs have been known for some 2,000 years, and there are numerous bathing establishments still used by people suffering from rheumatism, paralysis, and various intestinal and skin diseases. It is the seat of a Roman Catholic bishopric, and of an institute of technology and other educational institutions. In World War II, it was the first German city taken by the Allies (Oct. 20, 1944), having first been reduced virtually to ruins by artillery fire and aerial bombardment. 129,811 (1950).

Architecture. Of the once numerous historical buildings, only the *Münster* (cathedral) remains standing, although badly damaged. It is largely in the Romanesque style, but smaller parts of it were built at various times, the earliest dating back to the period of Charlemagne. This oldest section is the Emperors' Chapel, a domed octagonal building (796–804) designed for Charlemagne by Udo of Metz, largely after the Byzantine style of the Church of San Vitale at Ravenna, and consecrated by Pope Leo III. A later section of some importance is the Gothic choir, dating from 1414. Six chapels surround the central building, which contains the tombs of Charlemagne and Emperor Otto III. It was this building, or its sections, that served as the place of coronation of the German kings as Holy Roman emperors in the period of the 9th–16th centuries, the first being Louis the Pious (813), and the last Ferdinand I (1531). The 14th-century *Rathaus* (town hall) built on the site of Charlemagne's palace was formerly a structure of considerable historical and architectural interest, but it is now largely ruined.

History. Founded by the Romans as a watering place, Aachen became Charlemagne's northern (and favorite) capital; it was because they were technically his successors as Holy Roman emperors that the German kings of the Middle Ages were crowned here. Seventeen diets and eleven synods were convoked at Aachen during this period. Like most major European cities, Aachen suffered from several serious fires during the Middle Ages and later, the most serious of which took place in 1656 (but of course even this did relatively little damage compared to the wholesale destruction wrought during World War II). Aachen belonged to France in the period 1801–15; at the Congress of Vienna it was ceded to Prussia. Among the international agreements concluded at Aachen (under its French name) were the first Treaty of Aix-la-Chapelle (1668), which ended the war of Louis XIV against Spain, and the second Treaty of Aix-la-Chapelle (1748), which ended the War of the Austrian Succession. The Congress of Aix-la-Chapelle, which took place here in 1818 after the final downfall of Napoleon, was the first meeting of the Holy Alliance. Economically, Aachen developed greatly during the 19th and 20th centuries, but it was dealt a tremendous blow in World War II and the resultant decrease of population (1939–46) amounted to 31.9 percent. The majority of the population is Catholic.

Aagesen (ô'gẹ.sẹn), **Svend.** [Also, **Aageson.**] fl. 1185. Danish historian. His *Compendiosa historia regum Daniae*, from the reign of King Skjold (c300) to that of Canute VI (1170–1202), is considered by some authorities to be the first connected history of Denmark. He also probably edited, and may have translated, a Latin version of the military laws of Canute the Great (c995–1035).

Aahhotep (ä.hō'tep). [Also, **Ahhotpe.**] Egyptian queen; wife of Kamose, last king of the XVIIth dynasty, and mother of Ahmose I, first king of the XVIIIth dynasty. Her coffin was found (1860) at Thebes in the ancient necropolis of No, placed in the museum at Bulaq, removed to Giza, and thence (1902) to Cairo.

Aakjaer (ôk'yer), **Jeppe.** [Called **"the Danish Burns."**] b. in Jutland, Denmark, Sept. 10, 1866; d. April 23, 1930. Danish lyric poet and novelist. A farm worker and herder who worked his way through the University of Copenhagen and was at one time imprisoned for socialistic writing, he made his Jutland farm a peasants' center for festivals and lectures on social theory. His novels include *Bondens Søn* (The Peasant's Son, 1899) and *Vredens Børn; et Tyendes Saga* (Children of Wrath; the Saga of a Servant, 1904). He wrote also *Rugens Sange* (Songs of the Rye, 1906), and other works of poetry.

Aakon (ä'kọn), Saint. See Saint **Aaron** (d. c305).

Aaland Islands (ä'lạnd, ô̊'-). See **Ahvenanmaa.**

Aalborg (ôl'bôrg). [Also, **Ålborg.**] *Amt* (county) of Denmark, in N Jutland, bounded by the amts of Randers, Viborg, and Hjørring, and by the Kattegat. It is traversed from E to W by the Lim Fjord. Capital, Aalborg; area, 1,129 sq. mi.; pop. 218,335 (1945).

Aalborg. [Also, **Ålborg.**] City in N Denmark, the capital of the *amt* (county) of Aalborg, ab. 130 mi. NW of Copenhagen, located on the S shore of the Lim Fjord, which joins the Kattegat and the North Sea. The name is Danish for "eel-town." A seaport and railroad center, it is important for its fisheries, for its exports of dairy products and livestock, and for its distilleries (it produces a major portion of Denmark's annual output of aquavit). It is the seat of a Lutheran bishopric, and has a museum, naval school, and other educational institutions. The community is noted for its medieval houses, for Budolphi Cathedral (erected in the 14th century, rebuilt in the 18th century), and for a castle built in the 17th and 18th centuries. Town privileges received in the 14th century; occupied by Prussian troops in 1864; airfield used as a base for the German attack on Norway during World War II. 60,880 (1945).

Aalen (ä'lẹn). City in S Germany, in the *Land* (state) of Württemberg-Baden, American Zone, formerly in the Jagst *Kreis* (district) of Württemberg, situated on the Kocher River, ab. 42 mi. E of Stuttgart. Primarily a manufacturing town, it has metalworking, lumber, leather, and pharmaceutical industries, and manufactures costume jewelry, linen, and lace, but it also has livestock markets of considerable local importance. The town (which has preserved in its streets and buildings much of its medieval character) was a free imperial city in the period 1360–1802, and came under Württemberg in 1803. The population increase (1939–46) amounted to 39.6 percent. 21,941 (1946), 25,375 (1950).

Aalesund (ô'lẹ.sùn). See **Ålesund.**

Aali Pasha (ä'lē pȧ.shä'; pȧsh'ä), **Mehemet.** [Also, **Mehemet Ali Pasha.**] b. at Constantinople, 1815; d. at Erenkoi, in Asia Minor, Sept. 6, 1871. Turkish diplomat and political leader. He served as ambassador to Great Britain (1842–45), was five times grand vizier (1852 *et seq.*), and was a delegate to the London conference (1871) on Black Sea sovereignty. He was a vigorous proponent of Turkish Westernization.

Aalsmeer (äls'mār). Town in the W Netherlands, in the province of North Holland, ab. 8 mi. SW of Amsterdam. It is located near the center of one of the most fertile districts in the country, and is important as a distribution point for bulbs, plants, and various other horticultural products. The community also has some local importance as a shipbuilding center. 10,420 (1939).

Aalst (älst). [Also: **Aelst;** French, **Alost.**] Town in NW Belgium, in the province of East Flanders, situated on the Dender River, ab. 16 mi. NW of Brussels: lace, cotton, and linen textile manufactures; breweries; sugar refineries; grain and hops trade; railroad junction. Of particular historical and architectural interest are its 13th-century bell-tower, the beautiful but unfinished Church of Saint Martin, in late Gothic style, containing a painting by Rubens, the Church of Saint Rochus, and the medieval town walls. A former capital of the counts of Flanders (1056 *et seq.*), the town was conquered by a French army under Marshal Turenne in 1667 and was occupied by the French from 1667 to 1706. It was occupied by the Germans in World Wars I and II. 41,960 (1947).

Aalten (äl'tẹn). Town in the E Netherlands, in the province of Gelderland, situated near the German border, ab. 29 mi. E of Arnhem: manufactures combs, buttons, and brushes. 11,966 (1939).

Aalto (äl'tō), **Aino.** [Maiden name, **Marsio.**] d. at Helsinki, Finland, cJan. 13, 1949. Finnish architect and furniture designer. She was the wife of Alvar Aalto, with whom she collaborated professionally.

Aalto, Alvar. [Full name, **Hugo Alvar Henrik Aalto.**] b. at Kuortane, near Helsinki, Finland, Feb. 3, 1898—. Finnish architect and industrial designer. He was a member of a small group which adopted and tried to introduce into Finland the advanced architectural ideas of Gropius, Le Corbusier, and Oud. He won the competition (1927) for the design of the municipal library at Viipuri, Finland (although actual construction was delayed until 1934 by opposition of the local clergy to its modern design) and won an international first prize for the Finnish pavilion at the Paris Exposition (1937). He first came to the U.S. in 1938; as research professor in architecture at the Massachusetts Institute of Technology, he was later (1947) commissioned to plan a new dormitory. As a designer of furniture, he exhibited his first chair in 1932; made of plywood, it was based on studies of sitting postures. He founded (1935) the firm of Artek, Ltd., at Helsinki for the manufacture and distribution of Aalto furniture. He was awarded (1947) an honorary degree by Princeton University as a doctor of fine arts.

Aanrud (ôn'röd), **Hans.** b. in the Gudbransdal valley, Norway, 1863—. Norwegian writer of peasant stories, satiric comedies, and poems. His novelette, *Lisbeth Longfrock*, was translated (1907) into English. His books for children, *Sidsel Sidsaerk* (1903) and *Sølve Solfeng* (1910), were published (1935) as one volume in English.

Aar (är). See **Aare.**

Aaraaf (ar'af), **Al.** See **Al Aaraaf.**

Aarau (ä'rou). Town in N central Switzerland, the capital of the canton of Aargau, on the Aare River, ab. 180 mi. SE of Paris. It is the site of an ancient fortress, and ab. 8 mi. away is the castle (now in ruins) that was the first seat of the Hapsburg family. The modern town has foundries and manufactures of textiles, cutlery, and scientific instruments. 12,900 (1941).

Aarburg (är'bůrk). Small manufacturing town in NW Switzerland, in the canton of Aargau, on the Aare River, near Aarau, ab. 180 mi. SE of Paris. 2,932 (1941).

Aare (ä′rẹ). [Also, **Aar.**] River in Switzerland, rising in the Aare glaciers of the Bernese Oberland (Bernese Alps) near the Grimsel Pass. It crosses the Hasli valley and forms the Handegg Falls (ab. 200 ft. high), traverses the lakes of Brienz and Thun, flows through Bern, Solothurn, and Aargau cantons, and joins the Rhine opposite Waldshut. On it are the cities and towns of Bern, Solothurn, Aarau, Aarburg, and Brugg. The largest river totally within Switzerland, it is ab. 180 mi. long and navigable below Unterseen.

Aarestrup (ô′rẹ.ströp), **Carl Ludvig Emil.** b. at Copenhagen, Dec. 4, 1800; d. 1856. Danish lyric poet and physician, author of *Digte* (1838) and *Elfterladte Digte* (1863).

Aargau (är′gou). [French, **Argovie.**] Canton in N Switzerland, bounded on the N by the Rhine: a fertile, hilly region on the plateau between the Alps and the Jura Mountains, traversed by the Aare River. It has vineyards, tobacco and dairy farms, and some manufactures, particularly of ribbon. Baden, in the E part, is a tourist center. Seat of the Hapsburgs in the 13th century, Aargau was annexed in part to the Swiss Confederation in 1415, comprised the cantons of Aargau and Baden in 1798, and took its present form in 1803. Capital, Aarau; area, 548 sq. mi.; pop. 270,463 (1941).

Aarhus (ôr′hös). [Also: **Århus, Aarhuus.**] *Amt* (county) of Denmark, in E Jutland, bounded by the amts of Vejle, Ringkøbing, Viborg, and Randers, and by the Great Belt. Capital, Aarhus; area, 971 sq. mi.; pop. 183,808 (1945).

Aarhus. [Also: **Århus, Aarhuus.**] City in E Jutland, Denmark, the capital of the *amt* (county) of Aarhus, situated on the Bay of Aarhus, ab. 100 mi. NW of Copenhagen. The second largest city in Denmark, it has a large harbor, important shipping activities, and much trade. Its industrial facilities include oil mills, and factories for the manufacture of machinery and railroad equipment. It is the seat of a Lutheran bishopric. The *Domkirke* (cathedral), in the brick-Gothic style, dates from the 14th and 15th centuries, and the Church of Our Lady from the 13th century. The university dates officially from 1933, but many of its facilities were available to students several years earlier. It was here that the Prussians defeated the Danes on May 31, 1864, in one of the decisive battles of the war by which Denmark lost to Germany until the end of World War I a great part of its S territory. It was occupied by Germany again in World War II and an explosion of German ammunition-ships destroyed part of the harbor facilities in 1944. Pop. 107,393 (1945).

Aarlen (är′lẹn). Flemish name of **Arlon.**

Aarö (ôr′ė″). See **Ærø.**

Aaron (ãr′ọn). [Hebrew, **'Aharon.**] fl. c15th–16th centuries B.C. In the Old Testament, the first high priest of the Israelites and companion of Moses on the Exodus from Egypt; eldest son of Amram and Jochebed of the tribe of Levi, and brother of Moses and Miriam. He is often represented as the traditional religious representative of Yahweh (Jehovah), while Moses was the secular; in the opinion of some authorities, he was a rival of, if not actually hostile to, Moses, as in the making of the golden calf and in his subsequent revolt, with Miriam, against Moses. Consecrated as high priest after the revelation on Mount Sinai, he subsequently obtained confirmation of his position against a challenge by his opponents. From Aaron and his tribe, by tradition, are descended the priests of Israel. The period of his life has been variously given as ranging from the 16th to the 13th centuries B.C. Conflict exists within the Old Testament as to the place of his death, but he is usually said to have died at the age of 123 on Mount Hor. The most important Old Testament references to him are found in Exodus, Numbers, and Deuteronomy.

Aaron, Saint. [Also, **Aakon.**] d. c305. British martyr who, according to tradition, was put to death with Saint Julius and others at Caerleon-upon-Usk (near what is now Newport, Monmouthshire, England), in the reign of Diocletian.

Aaron, Saint. fl. 6th century. British hermit and abbot, superior of a monastery of hermits which he founded on the island in the Atlantic Ocean off the coast of Brittany which is now called (after one of Aaron's disciples) St. Malo.

Aaron. Moorish lover of the Gothic queen, Tamora, in *Titus Andronicus*, a play attributed to Shakespeare. His remarkable villainy has caused some scholars to suspect a definite link in authorship between this character and Barabas in Marlowe's *Jew of Malta*, and to attribute the tragedy for this reason to Marlowe. In the play, Aaron is ruthlessly punished by Titus for his treachery and cruelty on behalf of Tamora against Titus's family.

Aaron ben Moses ben Asher (ãr′ọn ben mō′zis ben ash′ėr). b. 900 A.D.; d. at Jerusalem, 960 A.D. Jewish scholar who contributed to the Masorah, i.e., the vowels and accents which make up the text of the Hebrew Masoretic Bible now used. His contemporary and opponent was Moses ben David ben Naphtali; when these authorities differ, both readings are given in the rabbinical Bibles.

Aaron of Alexandria. [Hebrew, **'Aharon;** Arabic, **Harun.**] fl. c610 to c641. Author, possibly Jewish, of a Greek medical encylopedia (*Pandectae medicinae*), divided into 30 sections. It contained a description of smallpox and was translated into Syriac and Arabic. The writer, about whom little else is known, was almost certainly a contemporary of the Byzantine emperor Heraclius, father of Constantine III.

Aaron's Rod. In the Old Testament, a rod which turned into a serpent and by which Aaron thus surpassed the performance of the Egyptian magicians before Pharaoh (Ex. vii. 10). Later Aaron's Rod was one of the 12 rods of the 12 tribes of Israel. Representing the tribe of Levi, it was the only one that sprouted, budded, flowered, and bore ripe almonds, as a sign of the endowment of the priesthood upon Aaron and his descendants (Num. xvii. 8).

Aaron's Rod. Novel (1922) by D. H. Lawrence, written in Italy, partly Italian in setting.

Aarschot (är′sċhōt). See **Aerschot.**

Aarssens (är′sẹns), **Frans van.** [Also, **Francis Van Aarssen.**] b. 1572; d. 1641. Dutch diplomat and writer of memoirs, now chiefly remembered as a member of the "packed" court which condemned Jan van Olden Barneveldt in 1619. He was at various times ambassador to England, France, and Venice, and his memoirs have been considered valuable by historians concerned with his period.

Aartsen (ärt′sẹn), **Pieter.** See **Aertszen** or **Aertsen, Pieter.**

Aasen (ô′sẹn), **Ivar Andreas.** b. at Ørsta, Norway, Aug. 5, 1813; d. at Christiania (now Oslo), Sept. 23, 1896. Norwegian lexicographer, philologist, and poet. Convinced by a study of Norwegian dialects that they, rather than the Dano-Norwegian which was at that time standard in most Norwegian literature, comprised (with some modification) the proper vehicle for writers in his country, he produced (1853) a new national language (*Landsmaal*) by standardizing the various dialects. He himself used this "country language" in his own work, and lived to see it widely established among Norwegian writers, teachers, and government officials. Author of *Det norske Folkesprogs Grammatik* (Grammar of the Norwegian Dialects, 1848), *Ordbog over det norske Folkesprog* (Dictionary of the Norwegian Dialects, 1850), later enlarged and issued under the title *Norsk Ordbog* (Norwegian Dictionary, 1873), and others.

Aat or **Aath** (ät). Flemish names of **Ath.**

Aavik (ä′vik), **Johannes.** b. on the Estonian island of Saare, in the Baltic Sea, Dec. 8, 1880—. Estonian linguist and language reformer. He studied linguistics and literature at Tartu, Nezhin, and Helsinki, and was for a time thereafter a high-school teacher, but subsequently became an instructor and professor at the University of Tartu. He influenced the development of the Estonian language by numerous bold suggestions for reform, extending to certain morphological features, and through the invention of new words, many of which entered the common language. A voluminous writer on linguistic and literary subjects, he has translated into Estonian various works by Edgar Allan Poe, Gabriele d'Annunzio, and others. In 1951 he was living in exile in Sweden.

Ab (ab, äb). Fifth month of the Jewish ecclesiastical calendar and eleventh month of the Jewish civil calendar (except in leap years, when the insertion of a new seventh month makes it twelfth). It falls variously in the period

July-August. The word is of Babylonian origin and is said to have been adopted, with the names of the other months, after the Babylonian exile.

Ab, Ninth of. [Also, **Fast of Ab.**] Jewish fast day commemorating the destruction of the second Temple. It is strictly observed only by Orthodox Jews; the day falls variously in July or August.

Ababda (ä.bäb′dä) or **Ababdeh** (ä.bäb′de). See **Abadba.**

Ababua (ä.bä.bö′ä). See **Bwa.**

Abaco Islands (ab′ą.kō). Two islands (called Great Abaco and Little Abaco) in the British West Indies, at the extreme N end of the Bahamas group ab. 180 mi. E of Florida. With them, as an administrative district, are included a number of small surrounding islets (or cays). Although they are now, of course, all British subjects, many inhabitants of the district are descendants of Southern families that emigrated here after the collapse of the Confederacy. Area, 776 sq. mi.; pop. 3,461 (1943).

Abad (ä.bäd′). See **Abbad.**

Abadan (ä.bä.dän′, ab.ą.dan′). Island in a delta near the coast of SW Iran, in Khuzistan province, with access to the Persian Gulf. It has been the site of human settlements since the 5th century B.C. or earlier, but gained great international importance only in the 20th century through its position as the terminus of the oil pipe line from the interior of Iran and as the site of the chief refineries in Iran. Chief city, Abadan.

Abadan. City on the island of Abadan, in a delta near the coast of SW Iran, in Khuzistan province. It is a focal point for one of the world's greatest oil-refining centers, the terminus of the pipe line from the Iranian oil fields, and a major port for oil tankers. Pop. ab. 110,000 (est. 1948).

Abadba (ä.bäd′bä). [Also: **Ababda, Ababdeh.**] One of the predominantly Caucasoid Beja peoples of NE Africa, inhabiting NE Anglo-Egyptian Sudan and SE Egypt. They speak Arabic.

Abaddon (ą.bad′ǫn). Place of destruction; the depth of hell. It is mentioned in the Talmud and Milton's *Paradise Regained*, iv. 624. The term is also sometimes applied to the destroyer personified, or angel of the bottomless pit, more usually known by his Greek name Apollyon. Rev. ix. 11.

Abadeh (ä.bä.dā′). Town in C Iran, ab. 110 mi. N of Shiraz. A comparatively cool climate and ample moisture make it an important agricultural center, notably in the cultivation of fruit. It is known also for wood handicrafts of various kinds. Pop. ab. 7,000.

Abadites (ab′ą.dīts). See **Abbadides.**

Abad y Queypeo (ä.bäth′ ē kä.pā′ō), **Manuel.** [Also, **Abad y Queipo** (kāy′pō).] b. in Asturias, Spain, c1770; d. in prison, in Spain, 1824. Spanish ecclesiastic in Mexico, bishop (1809–20) of Michoacán. A close friend of Hidalgo y Costilla, with whom he had come (1800) to the attention of the Inquisition for admiring the works of Rousseau, Montesquieu, and other French writers, he was nevertheless one of the bishops who excommunicated him in 1810. Driven out of Mexico by the revolutionists, he returned in 1813. In 1820 he was deposed and imprisoned in Spain for opposition to the Inquisition; on his release he became a member of the government junta and bishop of Tortosa, Spain. Again imprisoned (1823) by the Inquisition, he died in confinement.

Abae (ā′bē). [Also, **Abai** (ā′bī).] In ancient geography, a city in Phocis, Greece, noted for its temple and oracle of Apollo. Looted and largely destroyed during one of the Persian invasions of Greece, it was later partly rebuilt under the Roman emperor Hadrian. Ruins of parts of the town still exist.

Abaelard or **Abailard** (ab′ę.lärd), **Peter.** See **Abelard, Peter.**

Abafi (ô′bô.fi), **Michael.** See **Apafi, Michael.**

Abakan (ä.bä.kän′). [Also: **Abakansk** (ä.bä.känsk′); former name, **Ust-Abakanskoye.**] City and river port in the U.S.S.R., in Asia, in the Khakass autonomous *oblast* (region) of the Russian Soviet Federated Socialist Republic, ab. 2,000 mi. E of Moscow, on the Yenisei River near Minusinsk. It is an agricultural trading center and is connected by a branch of the Trans-Siberian Railroad through Minusinsk to the main line at Achinsk. An 18th-century prison fort was located here. Bronze Age tumuli and statues covered with hieroglyphs have been discovered in the vicinity. Pop. ab. 37,000.

Abaliget (ô′bô.lē.get). Village in SW Hungary, situated NW of Pécs. It is noted for a large stalactite cave ab. 3,000 ft. in length.

Aballum (ą.bal′um). Latin name of **Avallon.**

"Abalone Song" (ab.ą.lō′nę). Humorous poem composed in honor of a large, edible mollusk found in the coastal waters of California. Authorship of the work has been attributed to the poet George Sterling, although as many as 20 other writers, including Sinclair Lewis, are said to have written verses at various times during the second and third decades of the 20th century. The poem was conceived of originally primarily as a joke (Sterling used to sing its verses intentionally off-key to the tune of the hymn "Old Sarum"), but it has become during the past 20 years a true folksong of western America. Among the best-known of its many stanzas is the one that goes

Oh! Some folks boast of quail on toast,
Because they think it's tony;
But I'm content to owe my rent
And live on abalone.

Abalus (ab′ą.lus). In ancient geography, an island reputedly abounding in amber, located by the Greek explorer Pytheas in the "Northern Ocean." Variously identified, it may have been near what is now the SW Baltic coast, between Danzig and Memel.

Abamonti (ä.bä.mōn′tē) or **Albamonte** (äl.bä.mōn′tā), **Giuseppe.** b. c1759; d. Aug. 8, 1818. Italian political leader. He was secretary-general (1798) under the Cisalpine Republic and a member of the executive committee at Naples. Arrested and condemned to death on the restoration (1799) of the monarchy, he was amnestied and again made secretary-general at Milan, serving in that post until 1805.

Abana (ab′ą.ną, ą.bā′ną). Biblical name of the **Barada** River. 2 Kings, v. 12.

Abancay (ä.BÄng.kī′). Town in S Peru, capital of Apurímac department, on the Abancay River ab. 300 mi. SE of Lima: mining and sugar-refining center. It was the site of several battles during the Spanish conquest. 5,789 (1940).

Abancay River. Small river in S Peru, a tributary stream of the Apurímac, W of Cusco, and crossed by the road to Lima. The site of this crossing was a military point of some importance in the local wars of the 16th century. It was here that Alonso de Alvarado was defeated by the elder Diego de Almagro, and captured with his whole army, on July 12, 1537. On another occasion (May 21, 1554), at a point close by, Alvarado again suffered defeat, this time at the hands of the rebel Francisco Hernández Girón.

Abancourt (då.bäṅ.kör), **Charles Xavier Joseph de Franqueville d'.** b. 1758; killed at Versailles, Sept. 8, 1792. French minister of war (July, 1792), last to hold office under Louis XVI. He was killed by officials of the revolutionary government, who were escorting him and other prisoners from Orléans to Paris, when word reached them of the massacres then taking place in the capital.

Abano (ä′bä.nō). [Also: **Abano Bagni, Abano Terme.**] Town and commune in NE Italy, in the *compartimento* (region) of Veneto, in the province of Padova, SW of Padua. It has been known from ancient times for its hot springs (Aponi Fons or Aquae Patavinae), which are visited by people suffering from arthritis, rheumatism, and various other diseases. It is reputed to be the birthplace of Livy. Buildings of interest to tourists were undamaged in World War II. Pop. of commune, 7,062 (1936); of town, 1,232 (1936).

Abano (dä′bä.nō), **Pietro d'.** [Also: **Pietro di Apono**; Anglicized, **Peter of Abano**; Latinized: **Petrus Aponensis, Petrus Aponus.**] b. at Abano, Italy, c1250; d. at Padua, c1316. Italian philosopher, physician, and translator from Greek and from French into Latin. He is said to have traveled considerably, and it is certain that he spent some time in Constantinople, probably before 1293, when he was established in Paris for the continuation of his studies. His residence in Paris may have lasted ten years or more. He then returned to Padua, where he taught in the university and spent the remainder of his life. He talked with Marco Polo (c1295–1310) and spoke of him in his *Conciliator*, this being the only reference to

Marco Polo in a contemporary scientific work. Pietro was primarily an astrologer, but he had a good knowledge of astronomical theory, was genuinely interested in science and medicine, anxious on the one hand to understand nature and man, and on the other hand to apply his knowledge to medical or other needs. His most famous work, *Conciliator differentiarum philosophorum et praecipue medicorum,* was well advanced c1303, but was not completed until 1310. Its main purpose was to settle as far as possible the moot questions of human knowledge. Pietro aims at reconciling conflicting opinions (Greek, Arabic, Jewish, Latin) on more than two hundred questions (*differentiae*). For each of them the authorities are reviewed, a solution is offered, and objections are discussed. These questions concern science in general, medical philosophy, medical art, astrology, and similar subjects. The central interests are medical and astrological. His *Lucidator astronomiae,* dating from the same year, 1310, is the most important astronomical treatise written during the first part of the 14th century in Italy. In it the author incidentally reveals his scientific philosophy: the purpose of science is to account for the facts as faithfully and as simply as possible. During his stay at Constantinople Pietro found a copy of the Problems of Aristotle and made the first Latin translation of the work. He began a commentary on these problems while in Paris, and completed it in Padua in 1310. It is clear that Pietro had an unusually extensive knowledge of Greek literature. He did not hesitate to defend the fundamental doctrine of astrology (that man's fate is controlled by planetary and stellar events), and its applications to medicine and to practical life in general. Pietro may have fallen into trouble with the Inquisition because of his astrology. He may have been suspected of practicing black magic, and he is said to have denied the miracles of Christ. It is said that the Inquisition instituted proceedings against him twice, first in 1306 (or before 1303), when he was acquitted, and then in 1315, when he died during trial. Thomas of Strasbourg, general of the Augustinian order from 1345 to his death in 1357, stated that he witnessed the burning of Pietro's bones in Padua as a posthumous punishment for heresy.

Abarbanel (ä.bär.bä.nel'), **Isaac.** See **Abravanel, Isaac.**

Abarim (ab'ą.rim). In the Old Testament, a general term for the region E of the Dead Sea and Jordan River (now included in the kingdom of Hashemite Jordan) and, more specifically, the high tableland in this region, often called Pisgah. It was from the highest point of this tableland, known as Mount Nebo, that Moses is said to have looked into Palestine.

Abaris (ab'ą.ris). [Called **"the Hyperborean."**] Mythical Greek sage, assigned by Pindar to the 6th century B.C., by Eusebius to the 7th. According to these writers and to Herodotus, Apollo gave him a magic arrow on which he traveled and which he gave to Pythagoras in exchange for instruction in the latter's philosophy. He was believed to have worked miraculous cures, and was widely invoked by the ancient Greeks in oracles and charms.

Abasalo (ä.Bä.sä'lō), **Mariano.** b. at Dolores (now Dolores Hidalgo), Mexico, 1783; d. at Cádiz, Spain, 1819. Spanish soldier in Mexico who joined the revolutionary movement (1810) of Hidalgo y Costilla and became lieutenant-general of the insurgents. Captured and sent to Spain, he died in prison.

Abascal y Sousa (ä.Bäs.käl' ē sō'sä), **José Fernando.** [Created in 1812 Marqués **de la Concordia Española del Peru.**] b. at Oviedo, Spain, June 3, 1743: d. at Madrid, June 30, 1821. Spanish general and politician. Governor of Cuba (1796) and viceroy of Peru (until 1816), he reconciled Spanish-Creole friction in those areas. He reorganized the Peruvian army, suppressed local rebellions, and led campaigns against the Argentinian and Chilean rebels.

Abasgi (ą.baz'jī) or **Abasci** (ą.bas'ī). See **Abkhazians.**

Abasgia (ą.baz'ji.ą). [Also, **Abasia** (ą.bas'i.ą).] In ancient geography, the region occupied by the Abkhazians (or Abasgi), approximately coextensive with what is now the Abkhaz Autonomous Soviet Socialist Republic of the U.S.S.R.

A Basso Porto (ä bäs'sō pôr'tō). [Eng. trans., *"At the Lower Harbor."*] Opera by Nicola Spinelli, with libretto by Eugene Checchi, based on a work by Goffredo Cognetti. It was produced in German (1894) at Cologne and in English (1900) at New York. It tells the story of a mother who, in order to save her son from committing the crime, kills her daughter's lover, betrayer of the Camorra, an Italian secret society to which her son belongs.

Abate (del.lä.bä'tā) or **Abati** (del.lä.bä'tē), **Niccolò dell'.** See **Abbate, Niccolò dell'.**

Abauzit (ȧ.bō.zēt), **Firmin.** b. at Uzès, France, Nov. 11, 1679; d. at Geneva, Switzerland, March 20, 1767. French Protestant philosopher, theologian, and mathematician. He included among his friends such figures as Newton, Rousseau, and Voltaire, by each of whom he was at various times warmly and publicly praised. Educated from the age of six in Switzerland (his family had been compelled to take refuge at Geneva after the revocation (1685) of the Edict of Nantes), he was later offered patronage by William III of England and a professorship of philosophy at Geneva, but preferred a librarianship which permitted leisure for his extensive scholarly pursuits. His name was taken by Voltaire as a pseudonym.

Abaye (ą.bä'yę). [Also: **Abayi;** original name, **Nachmani** or **Nahmani.**] b. c280; d. 338. Babylonian *amora* (Rabbinic teacher and scholar). He was the director (333–338) of the Hebrew academy at Pumbeditha, in Babylonia.

Abazgi (ą.baz'jī). See **Abkhazians.**

Abba (äb'bä), **Marta.** b. at Milan, 1907—. Italian actress. She studied for three years while still under age at the Academy of the Theatre in Milan, and at 17 joined the Paollodini company. In 1925, Pirandello engaged her for his company at the Odescalchi Theatre, having remembered her from a performance in Chekhov's *The Sea Gull.* The same year she played at London in Pirandello's *Six Characters in Search of an Author* and *Each In His Own Way,* and repeated her success under Sacha Guitry's management at Paris. The next year she toured Europe, and in 1927, South America. In 1928 she formed her own company, playing in Molnar's *The Good Fairy,* Pirandello's *As You Desire Me,* and a dramatization of Tolstoy's *Anna Karenina.* In 1934 she played Portia at Venice under Reinhardt's direction and the next season at London. Pirandello, who regarded her highly as an artist and friend, dedicated many of his plays to her. She made her New York debut in Robert Sherwood's adaptation of *Tovarich* (1937). In January, 1938, she married and retired from the stage.

Abba Arika (ab'ą ą.rē'ką). [Also: **Abba Aricha** (or **Arecha**); called **Rab.**] b. c175 A.D.; d. 247 A.D. Jewish teacher and leader, one of the Babylonian *amora* (Rabbinic teachers and scholars). Born of a Babylonian family, he was educated in Palestine; he returned to Babylonia in 219, settling first at Nehardea, then at Sura on the Euphrates. He founded here the Academy of Sura, a school for the systematic study of scriptural materials, and was himself reckoned to be one of the outstanding Haggadists of Jewish religious history. This Academy flourished for nearly eight centuries and became one of the greatest intellectual centers of Israel. It soon made Babylonia independent from Palestine and gave it a predominant position in the Jewish world. A large part of the Babylonian Talmud is constituted by the opinions of Abba Arika and of his immediate disciples.

Abbad I (äb.bäd'). [Also, **Abad.**] d. 1042. Cadi and first Abbadide king of Seville; reigned 1023–42. He took advantage (1023) of political chaos at Córdoba to throw off the rule of that city, and to establish his independence as ruler of Seville. During the next 19 years he attained a position of unquestioned leadership in the Spanish Moslem world, and made Seville the strongest of Spain's city-states.

Abbad II. [Also: **Abad;** called **Abbad al-Mutadid.**] d. 1069. Second Abbadide king of Seville; reigned 1042–69. Poet, poisoner, filicide, and patron of the arts, he sought to expand his realm at the expense of his fellow Moslems, but in the attempt, weakened his own power to the point of having to send tribute to Ferdinand I of León and Castile.

Abbad III. [Also: **Abad;** called **Abbad al-Mutamid.**] d. at Morocco, 1095. Third and last Abbadide king of Seville; reigned 1069–91. He made Seville a center of the arts, particularly poetry, but had little success with his military and political ventures. When his war against

Alfonso VI of León and Castile met with reverses, he obtained aid from the Almoravides, a sect of African Moslems, and was thus able finally (1086) to defeat Alfonso. However, he was thereupon himself attacked and deposed by the Almoravides, and is said to have bought his own life by compelling his sons to surrender (1091). He spent his last four years an exile in Morocco.

Abbadides (ab'ą.dīdz). [Also: **Abbadids** (ab'ą.didz), **Abadites** (ab'ą.dīts).] Moslem dynasty (1023–91) at Seville, in Spain, of whom the reigning members were Abbad I, Abbad II, and Abbad III. The dynasty lasted until the capture of Seville by the Almoravides in 1091.

Abbadie (dȧ.bȧ.dē), **Antoine Thomson d'.** b. at Dublin, Jan. 3, 1810; d. at Paris, 1897. French explorer of Ethiopia (1838–48). With his brother and fellow explorer, Arnaud Michel d'Abbadie, he published *Géodésie d'une partie de la Haute-Éthiopie* (1860–73). Although both he and his brother were born at Dublin, they were taken (1818) by their family to live in France, with which country they were identified for the rest of their lives.

Abbadie, Arnaud Michel d'. b. at Dublin, July 24, 1815; d. 1893. French explorer; brother and companion of Antoine Thomson d'Abbadie. Author of *Douze ans dans la Haute-Éthiopie* (1868), which contains an account of the two brothers' joint explorations in the period 1838–48 and of Arnaud Michel d'Abbadie's subsequent expedition in 1853.

Abbadie (ȧ.bȧ.dē), **Jacques.** [German, **Jakob Abbadie** (ä.bä.dē'); English, **James Abbadie** (ab'ą.di).] b. at Nay, France, c1654; d. at London, Sept. 25, 1727. French Protestant theologian and preacher at Berlin, in England, the Savoy, and Ireland. His zealous preaching to French Protestant refugees at Berlin (c1680–88) and his treatises in refutation of atheism, deism, Socinianism, and other disputed religious positions of the time won him the patronage of William III and George I of England, the former of whom appointed him (1699) dean of Killaloe, Ireland. Among his works, which were widely translated, were *Traité de la vérité de la religion chrétienne* (1684; Eng. trans., 1719, 1777), essays in support of the English revolution of 1688, *The Art of Knowing One-Self* (1694), *Le Triomphe de la providence et de la religion* (1723), and others.

Abba Jared (äb'bä yä'red). [Also, **Abba Yared.**] Mountain in E Africa, in N Ethiopia, NE of Gondar. Elevation ab. 15,000 ft.

Abbas (ab'ąs, äb.bäs'). b. c566; d. 652. Arab merchant and proselytizer of Islam; paternal uncle of Mohammed. He was the progenitor of the family that produced the Abbasside dynasty of caliphs.

Abbas I (of *Egypt*). b. at Jidda, Arabia, 1813; assassinated in Egypt, July 13, 1854. Turkish viceroy and pasha of Egypt (1849–54); nephew and successor of Ibrahim. He abolished the commercial monopolies established by his grandfather, Mehemet Ali, but his government otherwise did little that could be expected to help Egypt or win the affection of the people. His reign saw the beginning by the British government (but with his permission) of the Alexandria-Cairo railroad.

Abbas II (of *Egypt*). [Also, **Abbas Hilmi Pasha.**] b. at Cairo, July 16, 1874; d. at Geneva, Switzerland, Dec. 21, 1944. Egyptian khedive (1892–1914); eldest son of Mohammed Tewfik Pasha. He held the khedivate until the outbreak of World War I, when Great Britain established a protectorate over Egypt and replaced him with his uncle, Hussein Kamil. Nominally subject to Turkey throughout his reign and sympathetic to the Turkish Central Power alignment in 1914, he sought to retain some degree of autonomy, but actually at every point he was compelled to accept the authority of Great Britain's representative at Cairo, who was at first the Earl of Cromer and subsequently Lord Kitchener.

Abbas I (of *Persia*). [Called **Abbas the Great.**] b. 1557; d. at Kazvin, Persia, Jan. 27, 1628. Shah of Persia (1586–1628), notable for a reign which was both prosperous and, for its time, extremely enlightened. When he ascended the throne Persia was threatened by enemies within and beyond her borders, and the administration of the country was in a state of chaos. The most immediate threat was presented by the Uzbek tribe of Tartars, who had succeeded in occupying a part of Persia, and it was against them that he made his first major military effort. Following their defeat (1597) near Herat, he diverted his chief force to war against the Turks, whom he defeated (1605) at Basra and from whom he wrested a considerable amount of territory. In 1622, with help from soldiers in the employ of the British East India Company, he took the island of Hormuz, off the S coast of Persia, from the Portuguese, and in the following year, after a lengthy siege in his intermittent war with Turkey, became master of Baghdad. Two years later (1625), with the capture of Kandahar, he expanded his realm in the east to include a considerable portion of what is now Afghanistan and N India. He encouraged commerce within all the vast territories thus included under his rule, and saw to it that builders of roads and bridges should follow closely behind the armies that enabled him so greatly to expand the boundaries of Persia.

Abbas, Ferhat. b. at Tahar, Constantine department, Algeria, Oct. 24, 1899—. Algerian political leader, an advocate of Algerian autonomy and opponent of French colonization. By profession a pharmacist, he entered politics (1931) as a supporter of assimilation policies. After the liberation of North Africa in World War II, he published a *Manifesto to the Algerian People* (December, 1942) supporting a federalist, autonomist position. He was arrested (May 8, 1945) as a result of a conflict between French troops and native Algerians, but was amnestied in March, 1946. He was elected to the French constituent assembly in June, 1946.

Abbas Effendi (e.fen'di). See **Abdul Baha.**

Abbas Hilmi Pasha (hil'mi pą.shä', pash'ą). See **Abbas II** (of *Egypt*).

Abbas Mirza (äb.bäs' mēr'zä). b. c1783; d. at Meshed, Persia, in December, 1833. Persian soldier and prince; younger son of the shah Fath Ali. He commanded (1811–13, 1826–28) in two unsuccessful wars against Russia. By the first war Persia lost its remaining possessions in the Caucasus and was compelled to acknowledge Russian control of the Caspian Sea; by the second it lost Armenia.

Abbassides (ą.bas'īdz, ab'ą.sīdz). [Also: **Abbasids** (ab'ą.sidz), **Abbasides.**] Dynasty (750–1258) of 37 caliphs at Baghdad, succeeding the Ommiad dynasty after a victory (750) over Marwan II, the last Ommiad caliph, by Abu-al-Abbas, who was thereafter (750–754) first caliph of the new dynasty. Abu-al-Abbas, who claimed descent from Abbas, the uncle of Mohammed, was succeeded by al-Mansur, who made (762) Baghdad the seat of the caliphate. The line was overthrown, so far as the caliphate was involved, in 1258 by Mongols under command of a grandson of Genghis Khan. The most famous of the Abbassides was Harun al-Rashid; the last of the line genealogically (but not one of the 37 caliphs included in the dynasty) was Mutawakkal III, who died (1538) at Cairo.

Abbas the Great (ab'ąs, äb.bäs'). See **Abbas I** (of *Persia*).

Abbate (del.läb.bä'tā), **Niccolò dell'.** [Also: **Abate, Abati;** called **Messer Niccolino.**] b. at Modena, Italy, c1512; d. in France, 1571. Italian painter of the Lombard school, known for his frescoes. He assisted in decorating the palace at Fontainebleau.

Abbatis Villa (ą.bā'tis vil'ą). Ancient name of **Abbeville,** France.

Abbatucci (ȧ.bȧ.tö'chē; Italian, ä.bä.töt'chē), **Charles.** b. 1771; killed in battle, Dec. 2, 1796. French general; son of Jacques Pierre Abbatucci. He served under Napoleon in the Army of the Rhine.

Abbatucci, Jacques Pierre. b. 1726; d. 1812. Corsican partisan commander. He was an antagonist of the Corsican patriot, Pasquale Paoli, and later a divisional general in the French service under Napoleon in Italy.

Abbatucci, Jacques Pierre Charles. b. 1791; d. 1857. French jurist and politician; grandson of Jacques Pierre Abbatucci. He was for a time minister of justice in the French government under Napoleon III.

Abbaye (lȧ.be.ē), **L'.** French military prison once connected with the monastery of St.-Germain-des-Prés, at Paris. It was the scene of the murder (1792) of 164 prisoners by revolutionists during the massacres that took place at Paris in September of that year. Originally built in 1522, it was finally destroyed in 1854.

Abbazia (äb.bä.tsē'ä). Italian name of **Opatija.**

Abbe (ab'ẹ), **Cleveland.** [Called the **"Father of the Weather Bureau."**] b. at New York, Dec. 3, 1838; d. Oct. 28, 1916. American astronomer and meteorologist; brother of Robert Abbe. A pioneer (1869 *et seq.*) in demonstrating the feasibility of weather forecasts based on telegraphic reports, he was instrumental in the founding (1870) of a government weather service. He also took a leading part in establishing the use of standard time throughout the U.S. He was director (1868–73) of Cincinnati Observatory, meteorologist (1871–1916) of the U.S. Weather Bureau, and for many years editor of *The Monthly Weather Review*. Author of *Report on Standard Time* (1879), *Mechanics of the Earth's Atmosphere* (1892–1910), *Relation between Climate and Crops* (1901), *Physical Basis of Long-range Forecasting* (1902), and other works.

Abbe (äb'ẹ), **Ernst.** b. at Eisenach, Germany, Jan. 23, 1840; d. at Jena, Germany, Jan. 14, 1905. German physicist, industrialist, and specialist in optics. Professor at Jena (1870–91), he was associated with Carl Zeiss as research director (1866 *et seq.*) and as a partner (1875 *et seq.*) in the Zeiss firm. He became head of the firm after the death (1888) of Zeiss and reorganized it (1896) as a foundation that would share its profits between its employees and the university. He invented Jena glass and the Abbe refractometer, and conducted experiments which largely made possible the high quality of the initial Zeiss instruments.

Abbe (ab'ẹ), **Robert.** b. at New York, April 13, 1851; d. March 7, 1928. American surgeon; brother of Cleveland Abbe. He received his M.D. from Columbia University (College of Physicians and Surgeons) in 1874. Notable as both teacher and practicing surgeon, he took great interest in the radiological work of the Curies (of whom he was a personal friend) and did pioneer work in the use of radium to treat cancer.

Abbé Constantin (là.bā kôṅ.stäṅ.taṅ), **L'.** Novel by the French dramatist and satirist Ludovic Halévy, published in 1882. It was enthusiastically received for its benevolent treatment of characters, in contrast to the types then being depicted by Zola.

Abbeokuta (ab"ẹ.ō.kö'tạ). See **Abeokuta.**

Abberville (ab'ėr.vil), **Lord.** Principal character in the sentimental comedy *The Fashionable Lover* (1772), by the English dramatist Richard Cumberland.

Abbeville (àb.vēl; Anglicized, ab'ẹ.vil). [Ancient name, **Abbatis Villa.**] City in N France, in the department of Somme, ab. 90 mi. NW of Paris, on the canal of the Somme River, ab. 12 mi. from the English Channel. It belonged in the 9th century to the abbey at St.-Riquier, and was a gathering point in the first and second Crusades. Among its several medieval churches is that of Saint Wulfram, begun in the 15th century and now partly demolished, a rich example of the flamboyant Gothic style. A major Allied base in World War I, the city was severely damaged in World War II, and many of its ancient and modern buildings have been destroyed. It is important as a trading center for various agricultural products, chiefly grain, and has carpet and woolen industries. The nearby area is notable for the fossil remains and prehistoric implements which have been found there. 16,780 (1946).

Abbeville (ab'ẹ.vil). Town in S Louisiana, parish seat of Vermilion Parish, ab. 125 mi. W of New Orleans: center of a rice-producing district. 9,318 (1950).

Abbeville. City in NW South Carolina, county seat of Abbeville County, ab. 70 mi. W of Columbia: textile mills. It was named for Abbeville, France, by Huguenot settlers, and is known in American history as the site of the last meeting in 1865 of the Confederate cabinet under Jefferson Davis. This fact, plus its earlier importance as a focal point of secessionist sentiment, has caused it to be referred to occasionally as "the cradle and the grave of the Confederacy." 5,395 (1950).

Abbeville (dàb.vēl), **Claude d'.** See **Claude d'Abbeville.**

Abbeville (àb.vēl; Anglicized, ab'ẹ.vil), **Treaty of.** Treaty concluded (1259) between Henry III of England and Louis IX of France, formalizing the end of England's claims to Anjou, Poitou, Normandy, Touraine, and Maine, and acceptance of Guienne as a fief of the French throne.

Abbey (ab'i), **Edwin Austin.** b. at Philadelphia, April 1, 1852; d. at London, Aug. 1, 1911. American painter and illustrator. On the staff of *Harper's Weekly* (1871 *et seq.*), he was sent (1878) to London by Harper and Brothers on an assignment to provide illustrations for an edition of the poems of Robert Herrick. He subsequently also illustrated editions of Shakespeare and Goldsmith. Elected to the Royal Academy (1898), the National Academy (1902), and others; exhibited at London, Paris, Berlin, Vienna, Philadelphia, and elsewhere. He did mural paintings for the Boston Public Library (*Quest of the Holy Grail*, 1890–1902), the British Houses of Parliament (1910), and the state capitol at Harrisburg, Pa. (1911). He was, by royal request, official painter at the coronation of Edward VII of England.

Abbey, Henry Eugene. b. at Akron, Ohio, June 27, 1846; d. Oct. 17, 1896. American opera and theater impresario. He acquired Buffalo's Academy of Music with J. B. Schoeffel (1876); became leading New York producer with Schoeffel and Maurice Grau (1880 *et seq.*); and brought together the team of William H. Crane and Stuart Robson. He also managed the elder Sothern, Barrett, Henry Irving, and Edwin Booth; brought U.S. audiences Sarah Bernhardt, the de Reszkes, Emma Eames, Calvé, Adelina Patti, and the London Gaiety company; managed the Metropolitan Opera House and opened Abbey's Theater (1893).

Abbey Theatre. Irish company of actors and the theater at Dublin which is used by them. The company was founded in 1904 as a development of an earlier group, the Irish Literary Theatre (1899 *et seq.*), on a subsidy from Mrs. A. E. F. Horniman, who also enabled the group at that time to use the Dublin theater-building from which the name of the modern company is derived. Prominent among the members of the original group were Lady Gregory, J. M. Synge, and W. B. Yeats, all of whom wrote plays first produced by the Abbey Theatre; other playwrights whose works have been brought to the public through the Abbey Theatre include Padraic Colum, Sean O'Casey, Lord Dunsany, James Stephens, and Paul Vincent Carroll. In addition to giving plays at Dublin, the company has on several occasions toured the U.S. and other countries.

Abbiategrasso (äb.byä.tā.gräs'sō). Town and commune in NW Italy, in the *compartimento* (region) of Lombardy, in the province of Milano, situated on the Naviglio Grande Canal, ab. 15 mi. SW of Milan. Economically important as the center of a rich agricultural region, it is also of some historical and architectural interest for its Church of Santa Maria Maggiore, erected in the 14th century, and altered in the 15th century according to plans by Bramante. Pop. of commune, 16,759 (1936); of town, 13,704 (1936).

Abbitibbe or **Abbitibbi** (ăb.i.tib'ẹ). See **Abitibi.**

Abbon of Fleury (à.bôṅ; flė.rē). [Also, **Abbo of Fleury;** Latinized, **Abbo Floriacensis.**] b. near Orléans, France, c945; d. at La Réole, France, Nov. 13, 1004. French theologian and diplomat under Robert II of France, for whose period his letters (collected by Aimoin) are a valuable historical source. He was educated in France and England, and was abbot of Fleury (now St.-Benoît-sur-Loire) from 985. He wrote before 987 a commentary on Victorius's Calculus (second half of fifth century): *De numero mensura et pondere super calculum Victorii.* He wrote also *Quaestiones grammaticales* dealing with prosody and pronunciation.

Abbon of Paris. [Latinized, **Abbo Parisiensis;** called **Cernuus,** meaning "the Crooked."] d. c923. French Benedictine monk of St.-Germain-des-Prés, at Paris. He was the author of a Latin poem, *De bellis Parisiacae urbis,* on the siege of Paris (885–86) by the Normans.

Abbot (ab'ọt). See also **Abbott.**

Abbot, Benjamin. b. at Andover, Mass., Sept. 17, 1762; d. Oct. 25, 1849. American educator. He was principal (1788–1838) of Phillips Exeter Academy, where he taught Edward Everett, Jared Sparks, Daniel Webster, and others. He was notable among educators of his time for maintaining discipline without resort to corporal punishment.

Abbot, Charles. [Title, 1st Baron **Colchester.**] b. at Abingdon, Berkshire, Oct. 14, 1757; d. May 7, 1829. English politician. As speaker (1802–16) of the House of Commons, he was highly respected for his impartiality and the quality of his speeches. He initiated the practice of publishing annual tables of temporary laws, advocated (unsuccessfully) improving the language of laws, and introduced (1800) the first British census act. As chief secretary (1801–02) for Ireland under Addington, he compiled diaries now valuable to historians. An anti-Canning Tory, his published speeches (1828, 1829) include some opposing admission of Roman Catholics to Parliament.

Abbot, Charles Greeley. b. at Wilton, N. H., May 31, 1872—. American astrophysicist, notable as a specialist in research on solar radiation. Director of Smithsonian Astrophysical Observatory (1907 *et seq.*); secretary of Smithsonian Institution (1928 *et seq.*); home secretary of the National Academy of Sciences (1918–23). He has published papers on solar eclipses, the infra-red spectrum, solar variability, and on instruments for solar measurement. Author of *The Sun* (1911), *The Earth and the Stars* (1925), *The Sun and the Welfare of Man* (1929), *Fundamentals of Astronomy* (1927, with S. A. Mitchell), and other works.

Abbot, Ezra. b. at Jackson, Me., April 28, 1819; d. at Cambridge, Mass., March 21, 1884. American Biblical scholar. He was professor of New Testament criticism and interpretation at Harvard (1872–84) and a member (1871 *et seq.*) of the American committee for New Testament revision. His written works include *Literature of the Doctrine of a Future Life* (1864), *The Authorship of the Fourth Gospel* (1880), and some 400 articles in the American edition of Smith's *Dictionary of the Bible* (1867–70).

Abbot, Francis Ellingwood. b. at Boston, Nov. 6, 1836; d. Oct. 23, 1903. American philosophical writer. He was editor (1870–80) of *The Index*, a journal of free thought, and founder (1867) of the Free Religious Association. Author of *Scientific Theism* (1885), *The Way out of Agnosticism* (1890), and other works, several of which (and particularly the first) were subjected to strong criticism by Josiah Royce and his followers.

Abbot, George. b. at Guildford, Surrey, Oct. 29, 1562; d. at Croydon, Surrey, Aug. 4, 1633. English prelate, archbishop of Canterbury (1611–33), and one of the translators of the New Testament in the Authorized (or King James) Version of the Bible. A militant Protestant, he was influential in state affairs during the reign of James I, but was largely deprived of his power under Charles I.

Abbot, George. [Called **"the Puritan."**] b. at Easington, Yorkshire, 1603; d. 1649. English scholar, lay writer on religious subjects, and member of the Long Parliament. Author of the *Whole Book of Job Paraphrased* (1640), which had a simplicity of style in striking contrast to that of other commentators then living, of *Vindiciae Sabbathi* (1641), which was influential in the Sabbatarian controversy, and others.

Abbot, Gorham Dummer. b. at Brunswick, Me., Sept. 3, 1807; d. at South Natick, Mass., Aug. 3, 1874. American educator and clergyman. For five years (1837–41) a Presbyterian pastor at New Rochelle, N. Y., he was later (1843) associated with his brothers, Jacob Abbott and John S. C. Abbott, in establishing a girls' school at New York. He subsequently founded and headed (until 1870) the institution that was to become known as the Spingler Institute, a school for girls. His enthusiasm for the education of women was imparted during his later life to Matthew Vassar. The spelling of his name with a single "t" was retained throughout his life, except for a brief period at Bowdoin, when he emulated his brothers' double-t spelling.

Abbot, Henry Larcom. b. at Beverly, Mass., Aug. 13, 1831; d. Oct. 1, 1927. American military engineer. Early in his career he assisted Captain A. A. Humphreys in a survey (1857) of the Mississippi flood problem and possible means of control. He served with the Union army in the Civil War, acting as commander of siege artillery at Petersburg and Richmond (1864–65). He later developed the Engineer School of Application at Willett's Point, N. Y. (1865 *et seq.*), and assisted with plans for the Panama Canal, both with the French Comité Technique and with the U.S. board which succeeded it in 1904.

Abbot, Joel. b. at Westford, Mass., Jan. 18, 1793; d. at Hong Kong, Dec. 14, 1855. American naval officer. He served as a midshipman in the War of 1812, notably under Macdonough on Lake Champlain. He is best remembered, however, as commander (1852 *et seq.*) of the frigate *Macedonian* in Matthew Calbraith Perry's expedition to Japan, and as successor to Perry as fleet commander when the latter returned (1854) to the U.S.

Abbot, Sir **Maurice** (or **Morris**). b. at Guildford, Surrey, 1565; d. at London, Jan. 10, 1642. English merchant, deputy-governor (1615–24) and governor (1624–c1635) of the British East India Company, and lord mayor (1638–39) of London; brother of George Abbot (1562–1633), archbishop of Canterbury. One of the original directors and earliest investors in the East India Company, he was its representative in the long disputes over trading and fishing rights with its Dutch counterpart. He was able during a great part of his career virtually to control the English merchant service, and took a major part in sending expeditions to look for the Northwest Passage. Elected (1621) to Parliament, he was a member (1624) of the council for establishing the colony of Virginia.

Abbot, Robert. b. at Guildford, Surrey, c1560; d. March 2, 1617. English prelate, bishop of Salisbury (1615–17); brother of George Abbot (1562–1633), archbishop of Canterbury, and of Sir Maurice Abbot (1565–1642). A vigorous opponent of Roman Catholicism and supporter of Calvinism as against Arminianism in the Anglican church, he was in great favor with James I for such works as the *Mirror of Popish Subtleties* (1594), *Antichristi Demonstratio* (1603), *Defence of the Reformed Catholike of Mr. William Perkins* (1606–09), and others.

Abbot, Robert. b. c1588; d. c1662. English Puritan divine. He was vicar (1616–43) of Cranbrook, and later pastor of St. Austin's, at London. Author of *Triall of our Church Forsakers* (1639), and other works.

Abbot, Samuel. b. at Andover, Mass., Feb. 25, 1732; d. April 12, 1812. Boston merchant and philanthropist. He was one of the founders (1807) of the Andover Theological Seminary, which has been since 1908 a part of Harvard University.

Abbot, The. Novel by Sir Walter Scott, published in 1820. A sequel to *The Monastery*, it is based on incidents from the life of Mary Queen of Scots, covering the period from her imprisonment in Lochlevel to her flight into England after the battle of Langside.

Abbot, Willis John. [Also, **Abbott.**] b. at New Haven, Conn., March 16, 1863; d. at Brookline, Mass., May 19, 1934. American journalist, author, and worker for world peace, especially as editor (1921–27) and contributing editor (1927–34) of the *Christian Science Monitor*. At one time a reporter for the New Orleans *Times-Democrat* and New York *World* (1885–86), he became part-owner (1887–88) of the Kansas City *Evening News* and was associated with papers at Chicago, New York, and Washington, participating in the highly nationalistic journalism of the Spanish-American war period and in several political campaigns before he joined (1921) the staff of the *Christian Science Monitor* and became interested in its peace plan.

Abbotsford (ab'ọts.fọrd). Residence (1812 *et seq.*) of Sir Walter Scott, on the Tweed ab. 3 mi. from Melrose, Scotland. A 100-acre farm nicknamed Clarty ("muddy") Hole when he bought it in 1811, it was enlarged and renamed by Scott, who built on it in 1817 a mansion in baronial style. The Abbotsford Club, which published (1835–64) historical books connected with Scott's works, was named by its founder, Turnbull, for Scott's home.

Abbotsford and Newstead Abbey (nū'sted). Second volume of *The Crayon Miscellany* (3 vols., 1835), by Washington Irving containing recollections of his visit to Scotland and a visit to Sir Walter Scott's home.

Abbott (ab'ọt). See also **Abbot.**

Abbott, Alexander Crever. b. at Baltimore, Feb. 26, 1860; d. near Woods Hole, Mass., Sept. 11, 1935. American bacteriologist who, after graduate studies at Johns Hopkins, Munich, and Berlin, became (1897) professor of hygiene and bacteriology at the University of Pennsylvania. Author of *Principles of Bacteriology* (1892, 1921), *Hygiene of Transmissible Diseases* (1899, 1902), and others.

Abbott, Austin. b. at Boston, Dec. 18, 1831; d. at New York, April 19, 1896. American lawyer and legal writer; son of Jacob Abbott (1803–79). He collaborated with his brother, Benjamin Vaughan Abbott (1830–90), on numerous legal works (1855 *et seq.*). The most useful of the many works of which he was sole author is generally considered to be *Trial Evidence, The Rules of Evidence Applicable on the Trials of Civil Actions* (1880).

Abbott, Benjamin Vaughan. b. at Boston, June 4, 1830; d. at Brooklyn, Feb. 17, 1890. American lawyer and legal writer; son of Jacob Abbott (1803–79). He collaborated with his brother, Austin Abbott (1831–96), on a *Digest of New York Statutes and Reports* (1860) and many other works. As a member of the New York Code Commission (1864), he drafted a plan which provided a basis for the present penal code of that state. He was later (1870–72) one of the commissioners selected to revise the Statutes of the U.S. Author of *Judge and Jury* (1880), *The Travelling Law School* (1884), *Addison on Contracts* (1888), and others.

Abbott, Charles. [Title, 1st Baron **Tenterden of Hendon.**] b. at Canterbury, England, Oct. 7, 1762; d. Nov. 4, 1832. British jurist, notable as chief justice (1818–32) of the King's Bench. He began practice at the Inner Temple (1796), and was subsequently appointed recorder of Oxford (1801) and a judge in the court of common pleas (1818). As chief justice, he presided over the trials of the Cato Street conspirators and of Arthur Thistlewood, and became known for his strong opposition to the Catholic Relief and Reform Bills and Romilly's reform of criminal law. He is now perhaps best remembered for the soundness and clarity of his decisions, and for his *Law Relative to Merchant Ships and Seamen* (1802), long a standard work in its field.

Abbott, Charles Conrad. b. at Trenton, N. J., June 4, 1843; d. July 27, 1919. American naturalist and archaeologist. Author of *Days Out of Doors, Recent Rambles, Upland and Meadow, Travels in a Treetop;* his autobiography, *Ten Years Digging in Lenape Land* (1912), is still of some importance to archaeologists. He wrote, in addition to his books, more than 100 articles for popular scientific journals.

Abbott, Claude Colleer. b. 1889—. English scholar and poet. He has been a professor (1932 *et seq.*) at Durham University and editor (1939 *et seq.*) of the Durham University *Journal.* His discovery (1930–31, although formal announcement was not made until 1936) in Scotland of some 1,600 previously unknown letters and other papers written by, or to, Samuel Johnson, James Boswell, and other figures of note in 18th-century English letters, has been of great value to specialists in the field of literary history. Author of *Poems* (1921), *Early Medieval French Lyrics* (1932), and *The Sand Castle and other Poems* (1946).

Abbott, Edith. b. at Grand Island, Neb., Sept. 26, 1876—. American social worker and dean of the University of Chicago School of Social Service Administration (1924 *et seq.*); sister of Grace Abbott (1878–1939). Author of *Women in Industry* (1910), *The Tenements of Chicago* (1936), and *Public Assistance* (1939), as well as numerous articles and books on immigration problems; editor of *Social Service Review* and *Social Service Monographs.*

Abbott, Edward. b. at Farmington, Me., July 15, 1841; d. April 5, 1908. American Congregational and Episcopal clergyman; youngest son of Jacob Abbott (1803–79). Congregational minister (1863–69) in and near Boston; assistant editor (1869–78) of the *Congregationalist.* Disturbed by what he considered to be an undesirable development of liberalism in Congregational thought, he transferred his religious affiliation to the Episcopal church in 1878.

Abbott, Edwin Abbott. b. at London, 1838; d. 1926. English clergyman, educator, and Shakespearean scholar, notable as headmaster (1865–89) of the City of London School; brother of Evelyn Abbott (1843–1901). Author of *A Shakespearian Grammar* (1870), *Bacon and Essex* (1877), *Francis Bacon* (1885), *The Kernel and the Husk* (1887), *The Anglican Career of Newman* (1892), and works of New Testament criticism (1900–17).

Abbott, Eleanor Hallowell. [Married name, **Coburn.**] b. at Cambridge, Mass., Sept. 22, 1872—. American short-story writer and novelist; granddaughter of Jacob Abbott (1803–79) and niece of Lyman Abbott (1835–1922). Her works include *Molly Make-Believe* (1910), *Sick-Abed Lady and Other Stories* (1911), *Peace on Earth* (1920), *Rainy Week* (1921), *Fairy Prince and Other Stories* (1922), *Silver Moon* (1923), *Love and the Ladies* (1928), *But Once a Year* (1929), *The Minister Who Kicked the Cat and Other Stories* (1932), and the autobiographical *Being Little in Cambridge When Everybody Else Was Big* (1936).

Abbott, Emma. b. at Chicago, Dec. 9, 1850; d. at Salt Lake City, Utah, Jan. 5, 1891. American soprano, successful both in Europe and America as an operatic singer.

Abbott, Evelyn. b. 1843; d. 1901. English classical scholar and librarian; younger brother of Edwin Abbott Abbott (1838–1926). Author of *History of Greece* (3 vols., 1888–1900), and various works on classical philology.

Abbott, Francis Lemuel. See **Abbott, Lemuel.**

Abbott, Frank. b. at Shapleigh, Me., Sept. 5, 1836; d. April 20, 1897. American dentist, known for the development of various dental instruments, notably an automatic mallet patented in 1887. He was on the faculty of the New York College of Dentistry (1866–97), serving as dean after 1869. Elected head of the American Dental Association (1888) and National Association of Dental Faculties (1895); author of *Dental Pathology and Practice* (1896), and numerous articles.

Abbott, Frank Frost. b. at Redding, Conn., March 27, 1860; d. at Montreux, Switzerland, July 23, 1924. American classical scholar. After serving for seven years (1884–91) as a Latin tutor at Yale, he received the first appointment to the faculty of the newly established University of Chicago, for which he drew up a curriculum and which he thereafter served as associate professor (1891–94) and professor (1894–1908) of Latin. He was subsequently (1908–24) Kennedy Professor of Latin at Princeton. Author of numerous scholarly works and articles on Roman history, language, and society.

Abbott, George. b. at Forestville, N. Y., June 25, 1889—. American playwright, producer, film director (1927–30), and former actor (1913–18). Adaptor of themes from Shakespeare's *Comedy of Errors* and classic Greek comedy in *The Boys from Syracuse;* coauthor, with J. C. Holm, and director of *Three Men on a Horse;* coauthor, with Philip Dunning, of *Broadway* (1926); collaborator with J. V. A. Weaver on *Love 'em and Leave 'em* (1928) and with Ann P. Bridgers on *Coquette.*

Abbott, Grace. b. at Grand Island, Neb., Nov. 17, 1878; d. June 19, 1939. American social worker and writer on social problems; younger sister of Edith Abbott (1876—). After serving as chief of the U.S. Department of Labor's Child Labor Division (1917–20) and Children's Bureau (1921–34), she became (1934) public welfare professor at the University of Chicago. Author of *The Immigrant and the Community* (1917), *Federal Aid for the Protection of Maternity and Infancy* (1923), and *The Child and the State* (2 vols., 1938).

Abbott, Horace. b. at Sudbury, Mass., July 29, 1806; d. near Baltimore, Md., Aug. 8, 1887. American iron manufacturer. With his brother, he secured (1836) control of Peter Cooper's Canton Iron Works in Maryland and began manufacture of wrought-iron machinery components, notably the power shaft of the Russian frigate, *Kamchatka,* which was the first large steamship shaft to be manufactured in the U.S. His ownership of four rolling mills (including one which was believed capable of handling the largest wrought-iron plate in the U.S.) proved invaluable to the U.S. government during the Civil War, as Abbott was thus enabled to produce armor for the original *Monitor* and for virtually all subsequent vessels of its type built on the Atlantic coast.

Abbott, Jacob. [Original surname, **Abbot.**] b. at Hallowell, Me., Nov. 14, 1803; d. at Farmington, Me., Oct. 31, 1879. American Congregational clergyman, educator, and prolific author of children's books; father of Austin Abbott (1831–96), Benjamin Vaughan Abbott (1830–90), and Lyman Abbott (1835–1922). He was the founder (1829) and first principal of Boston's Mt. Vernon School, one of the first women's academies in the U.S., but after the huge success of *The Young Christian* (1832) he devoted himself primarily to writing. A bibliography of his works lists 180 by him alone, including the 28-volume *Rollo* series, and 31 more on which he collaborated.

Abbott, Sir **John Joseph Caldwell.** b. at St. Andrew's, Quebec, March 12, 1821; d. at Montreal, Oct. 30, 1893. Canadian politician and jurist, premier of Canada (1891–92). A graduate (1847) and later dean of the law faculty at McGill University, he became queen's counsel in 1862 and was a member (1859–74) of the Canadian parliament.

Abbott, John Stevens Cabot. b. at Brunswick, Me., Sept. 18, 1805; d. at Fair Haven, Conn., June 17, 1877. American Congregational clergyman and historian; brother of Jacob Abbott (1803–79). Active for several years in the administration of a pioneer school for girls established by his brothers at New York in 1843, he returned (1853) to Brunswick, Me., where he completed his *History of Napoleon Bonaparte* (1855). His eulogies of Napoleon in this work, which appeared serially in *Harper's Magazine* (1851–55) before publication in book form, detracted greatly from its worth as a historical source, and led to hints by Horace Greeley and Charles Dana that interested parties in France might have given financial aid to the author. Abbott returned to the pulpit in 1861, and was thereafter engaged until his death in preaching and writing. His literary work eventually totalled 54 titles, in the fields of history, ethics, popular science, and juvenile stories.

Abbott, Joseph Carter. b. at Concord, N. H., July 15, 1825; d. at Wilmington, N. C., Oct. 8, 1881. American politician, journalist, and officer with the Union army during the Civil War. Editor (1859–61) of Boston's Whig *Atlas and Bee*, he was also adjutant-general of New Hampshire, in which latter capacity he offered his services to Lincoln in April, 1861, and served thereafter with the 7th New Hampshire Volunteers, being promoted to colonel in 1863. He established himself as leader of North Carolina's Republicans after the war, drawing his chief support from newly enfranchised Negroes, but became involved (1868 *et seq.*) in political and financial irregularities, and was eventually ousted from North Carolina politics.

Abbott, Josiah Gardner. b. at Chelmsford, Mass., Nov. 1, 1815; d. at Wellesley Hills, Mass., June 2, 1891. American jurist and politician. He was judge of the Superior Court of Massachusetts for Suffolk County (1855–59), a Democratic member of Congress (1876–77), and a member of the electoral commission (1877). He was twice (1875, 1877) an unsuccessful Democratic candidate for U.S. senator, and once (1878) for governor.

Abbott, Lemuel. [Sometimes signed his work **Francis Lemuel Abbott.**] b. 1760; d. 1803. English portrait painter, chiefly at London, where he did likenesses of various notable figures, including Lord Nelson and other naval heroes of the period, and the poet Cowper. He is said to have died of insanity brought on by an unhappy marriage.

Abbott, Lyman. b. at Roxbury, Mass., Dec. 18, 1835; d. at New York, Oct. 22, 1922. American Congregational clergyman, author, and editor; son of Jacob Abbott (1803–79). Appointed by the American Tract Society to be editor of the *Illustrated Christian Weekly* (1870), he later became co-editor with Henry Ward Beecher of the *Christian Union* (1876) and editor-in-chief upon Beecher's withdrawal (1881), continuing in that position when the name of the paper was changed (1893) to the *Outlook.* He succeeded Beecher also as minister (1890 *et seq.*) of the Plymouth Congregational Church at Brooklyn, but in 1899 withdrew from the pulpit to devote himself to editorial work and lecturing. Author of *Theology of an Evolutionist* (1897), *The Other Room* and *Henry Ward Beecher* (1903), *The Great Companion* (1904), *The Spirit of Democracy* (1910), *What Christianity Means to Me* (1921), and others.

Abbott, Mount. Culminating peak of the southward-projecting mountain mass that forms the W side of the N half of Terra Nova Bay, in Antarctica, in Victoria Land, at ab. 74°50′ S., 163°46′ E. It was probably first located by Captain Robert F. Scott's *Discovery* expedition (1901–04). Elevation, ab. 3,000 ft.

Abbott, Samuel Warren. b. at Woburn, Mass., June 12, 1837; d. Oct. 22, 1904. American physician and pioneer public health statistician. After service as a surgeon with the Union army during the Civil War he established a private practice in Massachusetts, and became, for his day, unusually concerned with problems of community health. He formulated what were probably the first Massachusetts standards for manufacture of a reliable smallpox vaccine, and was appointed (1886) secretary of the Massachusetts Board of Health (the first state body of its kind in the U.S.), in which capacity he served until 1904. In addition to summaries which were for many years models of U.S. public health statistics, he produced *Past and Present Condition of Public Hygiene and State Medicine in the United States* (1900), which was possibly the first adequate study of public health developments to be published in the U.S.

Abbott, Thomas Kingsmill. b. at Dublin, March 26, 1829; d. 1913. Irish clergyman and scholar. He was a graduate and fellow of Trinity College, Dublin, in which he occupied the chairs of moral philosophy (1867–72), of Biblical Greek (1875–88), and of Hebrew (1879–1900).

Abbott, Wilbur Cortez. b. at Kokomo, Ind., Dec. 28, 1869—. American historian. He was professor of history at Kansas (1902–08), Yale (1908–20), and Harvard (1920–37). Author of *The Expansion of Europe* (1917), *Conflicts with Oblivion* (1924), and others.

Abbott, William Hawkins. b. at Middlebury, Conn., Oct. 27, 1819; d. Jan. 8, 1901. American pioneer in petroleum production and refining. His ownership of an Ohio mercantile business led to a trip (1859) into the Pennsylvania oil fields shortly after the first Titusville well was completed. Interested by the business possibilities of this achievement, he made a small investment in adjoining oil land, which was followed in the next year by the sale of 200 barrels of Pennsylvania petroleum to the New York drug firm of Schieffelin Brothers, an achievement which is considered by many to have marked the actual opening of the U.S. oil trade. This, in turn, was followed in 1861 by the opening of the first Titusville refinery, and in 1862 by Abbott's removal to Pennsylvania, where he engaged in extensive coal-mining operations and was a cofounder (1867) of the first oil pipe-line consolidation, under the name of the Pennsylvania Transportation Co.

Abbott, Willis John. See **Abbot, Willis John.**

Abbt (äpt), **Thomas.** b. at Ulm, Germany, Nov. 25, 1738; d. at Bückeburg, Germany, Nov. 3, 1766. German professor of mathematics and philosophy. A friend of Moses Mendelssohn and C. F. Nicolai, he contributed to the latter's famous *Litteraturbriefe* (1759–65) after Lessing had withdrawn. He wrote *Vom Tode fürs Vaterland* (1761) and *Vom Verdienste* (1765).

ABC (ä'bā'thā'). Spanish newspaper, considered by many to be the leading news publication of modern Spain. Published (with occasional interruptions) since 1904, it reflects a conservative and monarchist point of view. Its circulation in 1949 was approximately 120,000.

A.B.C., An. Poem by Chaucer, designed as a prayer to the Virgin Mary. It contains 26 stanzas beginning in each case with a different letter of the alphabet. It is a loose translation from a work of Guillaume de Deguileville, a Cistercian monk who died c1360.

A.B.C. Conference. [Also, **A.B.C. Mediation.**] International conference (May-July, 1914) at Niagara Falls, N. Y., at which representatives from Argentina, Brazil, and Chile attempted mediation between the U.S. and the Huerta government of Mexico following the U.S. bombardment of Veracruz. The conference proposed that a provisional government of Mexico be chosen by agreement between the warring Huerta and Carranza factions, but the proposal was rejected by Carranza following his military victories over his opponents. Huerta, whom the Wilson administration considered a usurper, resigned, and Carranza became president on Aug. 22, 1914.

A.B.C. Powers. Term sometimes applied to Argentina, Brazil, and Chile, particularly in those cases where the three powers have acted jointly (1910 *et seq.*) to arrive at a treaty or agreement involving the U.S. or a major European power.

Abd (äbd, abd). Initial element of many Arabic and other Semitic proper names. Compound names containing "Abd" (which means "servant") are usually formed by the combination, through a linking element, of "Abd" with the name of a place, person, quality, etc., as in "Abd-al-Aziz," below. The spelling, in English, of names containing "Abd" has been subject, over a period of centuries, to widely differing systems of transliteration and transcription, with the result that the single name given above might also be found in some sources with such spellings as "Abdul Aziz," "Abdool Aziz," "Abdul-Aziz," "Abd-el-Aziz," "Abdel Aziz," and many more. The user of a general reference book will find it helpful to bear in mind that no one of these forms is necessarily more or less "correct" than another; methods of transcription have differed from country to country and from century to century. In this work, if usage does not clearly indicate preference for another form, we have written such names in the manner here first cited: "Abd-al-Aziz," "Abd-al-Malik," "Abd-al-Muttalib," and so forth. However, we have deferred first of all to the needs of the reader, which require that a name should be entered where it is most likely to be looked for by the greatest number of people, and this is a matter finally determined not by any one system but by actual usage in newspapers, magazines, works of history, textbooks, and novels. Where usage appears to be divided between two or more forms we have made liberal use of cross references in order to guide the reader to the main entry.

Abd-al-Aziz IV (äbd″äl.ä.zēz′). [Also: **Abd-el-Aziz, Abdul-Aziz.**] b. 1878; d. 1943. Sultan of Morocco (1894–1908); member of the Filali dynasty. His attempts to Westernize his country and his inability to control the state budget finally led to a popular revolt and the loss of his throne. He was instrumental in calling the Algeciras conference (1906), but his apparent submission to France and the chaos in his own country made his fall inevitable. He was deposed in 1908 by a junta under the leadership of his brother and successor, Abd-al-Hafid.

Abd-al-Aziz ibn-Saraya al-Hilli (äbd″äl.ä.zēz′ ib″n.sä-rä′yạ äl.hil′li). b. in August, 1278; d. at Baghdad, in March, 1349. Iranian poet and musician. He was a court poet at various royal establishments (perhaps most notably in 1326 at that of the Mamelukes, in Cairo) and remains even today a favorite of many young Arab intellectuals. He was the author of a treatise on musical composition that urged the desirability of putting melodies together according to the zodiac (a kind of musical astrology that had a considerable tradition in the Arab world).

Abd-al-Hakam (äb″däl.hä.käm′). b. in Egypt; d. at Cairo (in what is now called locally al-Fustat, the older part of the city), 870 or 871. Egyptian historian. His account of the conquest of Egypt, North Africa, and Spain is the earliest Moslem history of its kind. It is a critical work and was used extensively by later historians.

Abdaldar (abd.al′där). One of the three great magicians (Lobaba and Mohareb are the other two) in *Thalaba the Destroyer*, by Robert Southey.

Abd-al-Hafid (äbd″äl.hä.fēd′). [Also: **Abd-el-Hafid, Abd-al-Hafiz, Abdul-Hafiz.**] b. c1875—. Sultan of Morocco (1908–12); member of the Filali dynasty. He overthrew his brother and predecessor, Abd-al-Aziz IV, but was himself deposed by the French when he interfered with the expansion of their domain in N Africa.

Abd-al-Kaaba (äbd.äl.kä′ä.bä). Original name of **Abu-Bakr.**

Abd-al-Kadir (äbd.äl.kä′dir). [Also, **Abd-el-Kader.**] b. near Mascara, Algeria, c1807; d. at Damascus, May 26, 1883. Arab chief and scholar, notable as leader of the tribes of Oran in a Moslem holy war (1832–47) against the French. With Abd-er-Rahman, sultan of Morocco, he was defeated by a French force under Marshal Bugeaud near the river Isly on Aug. 14, 1844. Imprisoned (1847 *et seq.*) in France, he was freed (1852) by Napoleon III. He was given the Grand Cross of the Legion of Honor (1860) for pro-French action in Moslem anti-Christian riots at Damascus, and later (1871) urged Algerian submission to France. During his last years he lived as a pensioner of the French Government.

Abdalla (ab.dal′ạ). The Mufti, a character in John Dryden's tragedy *Don Sebastian.*

Abdalla (äb.däl′lä), **Baba.** See **Baba Abdalla.**

Abdallah (ab.dal′ạ, äb.däl.lä′). See also **Abdullah.**

Abdallah. [Also, **Abdullah.**] b. at Mecca, Arabia, c545; d. at Medina, Arabia, 570. Father of Mohammed, son of Abd-al-Muttalib (d. 578).

Abdallah-ibn-Yasin. (ib″n.yä.sēn′). [Also: **Abdallah ben Yasim, Abdullah ibn-Yasin.**] d. c1058. Arab scholar. He was the founder, chief lawmaker, and spiritual leader of the Almoravides, a Berber people of the African mountains whom he converted to Islam. Under his leadership they conquered much of the country between the Sahara and ancient Gaetulia. Under his successor, Yussuf ibn-Tashfyn, Almoravide power spread over much of N Africa, establishing (1062) Marrakech as a capital and eventually reaching (1086) Spain, at the behest of Abbad III of Seville, who sought their aid against Alfonso VI of León and Castile. In 1091 they turned on Abbad, ousted him, and were themselves for a brief period in control of Seville.

Abdallatif (äb″däl.lä.tēf′). [Also, **Abd-al-Latif.**] b. at Baghdad, 1162; d. there, Nov. 8, 1231. Arab physician, philosopher, scientist, and traveler. He was one of a group of scholars at the court of Saladin, and at various times a teacher at Cairo, Damascus, and Aleppo.

Abd-al-Malik (äbd″äl.mä.lik′). b. c646; d. 705. Fifth caliph (685–705) of the Ommiad dynasty. He defeated various rivals for the caliphate and united Islam, but his war against the Byzantine emperors was protracted and indecisive. He is perhaps most noteworthy as the first caliph to use Arabic coins, although he also improved postal facilities, reorganized the government, and made the Arabic language official in the area under his control.

Abd-al-Malik. b. at Basra (in what is now Iraq), c740. Arab doctor. An instructor of Harun al-Rashid, he was noted for his extraordinary memory. He is reputed to have written part, if not all, of one version of the Arabic romance of Antar.

Abd-al-Malik. b. at Córdoba, Spain, 801; d. 853. Spanish Moslem historian and theologian.

Abd-al-Mumin (äbd″äl.mö′min). See **Abdul-Mumin.**

Abd-al-Muttalib (äbd.äl.möt′tạ.lib). d. 578. Grandfather of Mohammed and his guardian for two years; father of Abdallah (c545–570).

Abd-al-Rahman (äbd″äl.rä.män′). See **Abd-er-Rahman.**

Abdara (ab.dãr′ạ). Ancient name of **Adra.**

Abdas (or **Abda**) **of Susa** (äb′däs; äb′dä; sö′zạ, -sạ). d. c420. Persian bishop killed in a persecution of Christians brought about by his destruction of a Zoroastrian fire temple. He is said to have aided in driving a demon out of Yezdigerd, a king of Persia.

Abd-el- (äbd″el-). See under **Abd.**

Abdelazar (äb.del.ä′zạr). Tragedy derived by Aphra Behn from the play *Lust's Dominion*, first acted in 1676, and published the next year. It is notable for inclusion of the song *Love in fantastic triumph sat.*

Abd-el-Aziz IV (äbd″el.ä.zēz′). See **Abd-al-Aziz IV.**

Abd-el-Hafid (äbd″el.hä.fēd′). See **Abd-al-Hafid.**

Abd-el-Kader (äbd.el.kä′dėr). See **Abd-al-Kadir.**

Abd-el-Kadir (äbd.el.kä′dir). fl. 14th century. Arab musicologist. He was the author of several treatises on musical theory.

Abd-el-Krim (äbd.el.krim′). [Also: **Abdel Krim**; full name, **Mohammed ibn Abd al-Karim al-Khattabi.**] b. c1880—. Moroccan chieftain, notable as the leader of the Berber tribes of the Er Rif region of North Africa in their war (1920 *et seq.*) against Spain and, later, France. His education and intelligence enabled him while still a young man to attract (1908) the attention of the Spanish authorities in Morocco, and he became a member of the Spanish civil service at Ceuta. In 1920 he turned against the Spanish and led a rebellion of the tribesmen of the Er Rif, winning (1921) an important victory at Annual. In 1924 he forced Primo de Rivera, the Spanish dictator, again to withdraw his troops from their frontier positions, but Abd-el-Krim then made the mistake of attacking also his French neighbors. As a result, by 1925, Spain and France had agreed to coöperate against the tribesmen, and in 1926 Abd-el-Krim was defeated by a two-front offensive under Marshal Pétain. Within the next few weeks all remaining resistance was suppressed and the entire Er Rif region was once again securely under European control. Abd-el-Krim himself was captured and sent into exile on the French island of Réunion, in the Indian Ocean. In 1947, while on his way to France, he escaped on an Australian ship to take refuge in Cairo. He announced (1948) a decision to renew his struggle against European control of North Africa.

Abdemon (ab′dẹ.mọn). [Also, **Abdesmun.**] By ancient tradition, a Tyrian, the subject of King Hiram of Tyre. He allegedly vindicated his country's honor and won a wager for his ruler by answering a series of riddles put to Hiram by King Solomon, and by posing riddles which Solomon was unable to answer. Despite Solomon's earlier success with riddles set by Hiram, and Hiram's inability to solve the problems set by Solomon, Abdemon's success was considered to have won the contest for the Tyrian monarch and the forfeit was paid by Solomon.

Abdenago (ab.den'ą.gō). See **Abed-nego.**

Abdera (ab.dir'ą). [Greek, **Avdera.**] In ancient geography, a maritime city in Thrace, on Cape Balastra, opposite the island of Thasos in NE Greece. Although there is an ancient legend that it was founded by Hercules, it is now known actually to have been colonized (c650 B.C.) by people from Clazomenae. Destroyed sometime before 550 B.C. by Thrace, it was resettled (c540) by refugees from the Persian occupation of Teos, and became during the next 200 years one of the most prosperous of Greek cities. It thereafter declined in importance, and the ancient city is now entirely in ruins, although a small agricultural community still occupies part of the original site. It was thought in ancient times that the air of the region caused people to become dull, and from this came a folk belief among the ancient Greeks that all Abderites were stupid. This conviction persisted despite the fact that a number of famous men, including Protagoras and Democritus, were either born at or residents of Abdera.

Abdera. Ancient name of **Adra.**

Abderhalden (äb'dėr.häl.dẹn), **Emil.** b. in Switzerland, 1877—. Swiss biochemist and physiologist. His extensive work in the field of nutrition, especially with proteins and amino acids, includes discovery of norleucine and of protective enzymes (proteinasas). He is the editor of *Handbuch der Biologischen Arbeitsmethoden*, a handbook of biochemical techniques in nine volumes (1910 *et seq.*), and director (1911 *et seq.*) of the Halle Physiological Institute.

"Abderite (ab'dẹ.rīt), **The."** An epithet of **Democritus.**

Abd-er-Rahman (äbd.ėr.rä'män). [Also: **Abd-al-Rahman, Abd-ar-Rahman, Abdurrahman.**] d. 732. Moslem emir (731–732) of Spain and governor (721 *et seq.*) of southern Gaul. He invaded France with a large army, but was defeated and slain (732) by Charles Martel near Tours.

Abd-er-Rahman. b. Nov. 28, 1778; d. in August, 1859. Sultan of Fez and Morocco (1822–59). The piracy practiced in the Mediterranean trade routes by his subjects involved him at intervals throughout his reign in conflicts with Austria, England, and Spain. He supported Abd-al-Kadir (c1807–83) against France, but made peace after a decisive defeat (1844).

Abd-er-Rahman I. [Also: **Abd-al-Rahman, Abd-ar-Rahman, Abdurrahman.**] b. at Damascus, 731; d. 788. Founder (756) of the Ommiad dynasty of emirs of Córdoba, Spain. He survived the overthrow by the Abbassides of the Ommiad dynasty of caliphs, and took refuge in Syria. Invited by a faction of Arabs in Spain to be their sovereign, he quickly established his power in that country by overcoming (756) the rival emir Yusuf in a battle near the Guadalquivir River. He was thereafter successful in several encounters with the Franks, but never actually met Charlemagne in battle. (In the one instance when a meeting seemed inevitable, Charlemagne withdrew before battle was joined. According to legend, however, this was the occasion of the gallant stand of the Frankish rearguard that gave rise to the *Song of Roland.*) Abd-er-Rahman I is also generally credited with having begun construction of the great mosque which still stands at Córdoba.

Abd-er-Rahman II. [Also: **Abd-al-Rahman, Abd-ar-Rahman, Abdurrahman.**] b. 788; d. 852. One of the emirs of the Ommiad dynasty at Córdoba, Spain. He encouraged writing, painting, and architecture, but his rule (822–852) was marked, politically, by weakness and vacillation.

Abd-er-Rahman III. [Also: **Abd-al-Rahman, Abd-ar-Rahman, Abdurrahman.**] b. 891; d. in Spain, 961. Ommiad ruler of Córdoba (912–961), the first to assume (929) the title of caliph, which had previously been used only by the rulers of the holy cities of Islam. He strengthened and centralized the government; a great patron of the arts and sciences, he made Córdoba a center of European learning and brought Moslem Spain to the height of its power.

Abd-er-Rahman Khan (kän). [Also, **Abdurrahman Khan.**] b. c1844; d. Oct. 1, 1901. Amir of Afghanistan (1880–1901); grandson of Dost Mohammed Khan (1793–1863). He came to the throne partly as a result of the Second Afghan War (1878–81) with Great Britain, during which the British coöperated in his installation as amir at Kabul. He later consolidated his control, ruling independently except for the British Indian government's voice in foreign affairs. He established a strong national army, set up efficient tax collection, and brought about a considerable reduction of crime. It was in his reign also that border clashes with Russia (1885) and India (1893) resulted in the fixing by Great Britain of the boundaries of Afghanistan.

Abdias (ab.dī'ąs). See **Obadiah.**

Abdiel (ab'di.el). Seraph in Milton's *Paradise Lost* (v. 896), the only seraph who remained loyal when Satan stirred up the angels to revolt. He is mentioned also by the Jewish cabalists.

Abdi-Milkut (äb'dẹ.mil.köt'). fl. 7th century B.C. King of Sidon, a contemporary and dependent ruler of Esar-Haddon, king of Assyria (c681–668 B.C.). He attempted to repudiate his allegiance to Assyria, was attacked, and, after a prolonged resistance, fled, probably to the island of Cyprus. He was caught and decapitated in 676.

Abdool (äb'döl). See under **Abd.**

Abduction from the Seraglio (se.ral'yō, -räl'-), **The.** [German title, **Die Entführung aus dem Serail.**] Opera (1782) by Mozart, with libretto based on a play by Bretzner. It is a romance, set in the 16th century, of Belmonte's rescue of his sweetheart, Constanze, who has been captured by Selim Pasha.

Abdul-, Abdu-l- (äb'dụl). See under **Abd.**

Abdul-Aziz (äb'dụl.ä.zēz'). b. Feb. 9, 1830; d. June 4, 1876. Sultan of Turkey (1861–76). He was the brother and successor of Abdul-Medjid (1823–61). He is sometimes credited with attempts to Westernize Turkey, and he displayed an interest in some aspects of European culture on his tour (1867) of France, England, Austria, and Germany. Nevertheless, few reforms were actually made, and the financial position of the country reached in 1875 a point so hopeless that Turkey was unable to pay the interest on its bonds. Partly as a result of this, and partly because of widespread unrest in Turkey's Balkan possessions, he was deposed on May 29, 1876. He died (probably murdered, but possibly a suicide) a few days thereafter.

Abdul-Aziz IV. See **Abd-al-Aziz IV.**

Abdul Baha (äb'dụl bä.hä'). [Also: **Abbas Effendi;** as an English knight, Sir **Abdul Baha Bahai.**] b. 1844; d. 1921. International Bahai leader and son of Baha Ulla, originator of the Bahai sect. He was exiled and imprisoned (1868–1908) by the Turks at Acre, in Palestine, but meanwhile became (1892) leader of Bahaism on his father's death. He was liberated during the "Young Turk" regime and won international acceptance for Bahaism through world-wide preaching (1911–13). He was knighted (1920) by Great Britain for various services to that country during World War I.

Abdul-Hafiz (äb'dụl.hä.fēz'). See **Abd-al-Hafid.**

Abdul-Hamid I (äb'dụl.hä.mēd'). b. May 30, 1725; d. April 7, 1789. Sultan of Turkey (1774–89). He inherited from his brother and predecessor, Mustafa III, a disastrous war with Russia which, by the treaty of Kuchuk Kainarji (1774), resulted in the loss by Turkey of the Crimea and adjacent regions.

Abdul-Hamid II. [Called the **"Great Assassin"** and the **"Red Sultan."**] b. Sept. 22, 1842; d. 1918. Sultan of Turkey (1876–1909); second son of Abdul-Medjid (1823–61), brother and successor of the insane Murad V (1840–1904), and nephew of Abdul-Aziz (1830–76), whom he accompanied (1867) on a European tour. Possessed of considerable astuteness and a notable capacity for international intrigue, he was determined to share the reins of government with no one, for which reason his early promise of reforms was soon abandoned. Nevertheless, his bloody suppression of uprisings in Bulgaria and elsewhere led to protests by the great European powers, and finally to the temporary restoration of the constitution of 1876. In the meantime, war with Russia (1877–78) had ended with the Treaty of San Stefano by which, as later modified by the Berlin Treaty, Turkey lost considerable territory in Europe and Asia. Called the "Great Assassin" and the "Red Sultan" by many western European newspapers for his part in the Armenian atrocities of 1894–96, he nonetheless escaped punishment for the treaty violation implicit in these atrocities by his shrewd intrigues among the great powers. He exchanged favors to German business, especially in connection with the proposed Berlin-to-Baghdad railway, for aid in reorganization of the Turkish army and navy. A true despot, with an army of spies, he was finally forced by the reformist political faction known as the "Young Turks" to abdicate (1909), was exiled, and later imprisoned.

Abdul Illah (äb'dụl il.lä'). [Also, **Abdul Ilah.**] b. Nov. 24, 1913—. Regent of Iraq (1939 *et seq.*) during the minority of King Feisal II (b. 1935), his nephew.

Abdul-Kerim Pasha (äb'dụl.ke.rēm' pä.shä'). b. 1811; d. 1885. Turkish general. He was honored for his services in the Crimean War (1853–56) and against the Serbians (1876), but was banished for his failure as Turkish commander in the Russian war of 1877–78.

Abdulla (ab.dul'ạ). Malay trader in *Outcast of the Islands* and *Almayer's Folly*, by Joseph Conrad.

Abdullah (ab.dul'ạ, äb.döl.lä'). See also **Abdallah.**

Abdullah. [Full name, **Abdullah ibn-Husein** (äb.döl-lä' ib"n.hö.sīn').] b. at Mecca, Arabia, 1882; assassinated at Jerusalem, July 20, 1951. King of Hashemite Jordan (in popular usage, often called the king of Transjordan, or Trans-Jordan, but since 1949, at his request and in accord with the constitution of his country, "Hashemite Jordan" or, simply, "Jordan" have been more often used). The son of Husein, a Hashemite leader who was crowned king of Hejaz after World War I, Abdullah was one of the Arab leaders who revolted against Turkey during World War I and who supported the British during that war in the Near East. As emir of Transjordan (1921–46) he maintained close relations with the British, receiving from them an annual subsidy and aid in maintaining the so-called "Arab Legion," the small, efficient army which has made Transjordan one of the most powerful states in its part of the world. He became king of Jordan in 1946. For some 30 years a bitter rival of ibn-Saud of Saudi Arabia for leadership and territory in the Arab world, Abdullah after World War II, and particularly in connection with opposition to the state of Israel, took a leading part in the loose federation of Arab states known as the Arab League. His assassination in the summer of 1951 was alleged to have taken place at the instigation of the Grand Mufti, a prominent Arab leader resident at Cairo, notable for both his anti-British convictions (which would by themselves have tended to alienate him from the pro-British Abdullah) and for his opposition to the Hashemite dynasty of Arab rulers.

Abdullah (ab.dul'ạ), **Achmed.** b. (probably) at Yalta, in the Crimea, May 12, 1881; d. at New York, May 12, 1945. Novelist and short-story writer. Educated at Eton, Oxford, the University of Paris, and elsewhere, he served with the British army in the Near East, India, China, and France before becoming a writer. He produced a vast amount of superficial but quick-moving and colorful fiction, and also contributed works to the stage and, during his later years, to the films.

Abdullah (ab.dul'ạ, äb.döl.lä'), Sheik **Mohammed.** [Called **"Sher-i-Kashmir."**] b. at Srinagar, in Kashmir, 1905—. Indian Moslem leader, prominent as head of the movement in Kashmir to accede to the Union of India.

Abdullah ibn-Yasin (äb.döl.lä' ib"n.yä.sēn'). See **Abdallah ibn-Yasin.**

Abdul-Medjid I (äb'dụl.me.jēd'). [Also, **Abdul-Mejid.**] b. April 23, 1823; d. June 25, 1861. Sultan of Turkey (1839–61); brother of Abdul-Aziz (1830–76), his successor, and father of Murad V (1840–1904) and Abdul-Hamid II (1842–1914). Defeated in war (1839) by Mehemet Ali, viceroy of Egypt, at what is now the town of Nizip, in S Turkey, he was protected from the consequences of his defeat by the intervention (1840) of England, Austria, and Russia. He promulgated the documents of Turkish constitutional reform known as the *Hatti-sherif* of Gülhanè (the imperial palace whence it was formally announced) in 1839, and the *Hatti-y-humayun* (1856), which avowedly guaranteed security of life and property, impartial justice, and civil and religious liberty to his subjects. He also introduced certain fiscal, educational, and military reforms, which were, however, imperfectly enforced, because of strong opposition by the privileged classes. He sheltered Kossuth after the Hungarian uprising of 1849. Influenced to some extent throughout his reign by the British foreign office and its representatives in Turkey, he was the ruler of Turkey during the Crimean War (1853–56). Thereafter, by increasing extravagance, he helped to bring on the financial disintegration of Turkey that took place during the latter part of the 19th century.

Abdul-Medjid (II) Effendi (e.fen'di). b. 1868—. Last Turkish caliph at Constantinople. He served (1922–24) as caliph after the national assembly at Ankara abolished the office of sultan and provided that the caliphate should be filled by election from among the princes of the Osmanli (or Ottoman) dynasty. When the assembly dissolved (March 2, 1924) the Turkish caliphate and deprived him of his Turkish citizenship, he took up residence in Switzerland.

Abdul-Mumin (äb'dụl.mö'min). [Also, **Abd-al-Mumin.**] b. in Africa, c1101; d. 1163. Arab chief, political founder of the Almohade dynasty, and claimant (1130–63) to the title of caliph. A disciple of and successor to Mohammed ibn-Tumart (the spiritual founder of the Almohades), he extended his power into Morocco and Algeria (1139–47), and, by defeating the Almoravides, into Spain (1148 *et seq.*).

Abdul the Bulbul Ameer (ab'dul ᴛʜẹ böl'böl ä.mir'). [Also: **Abdul the Bul Bul Ameer, Abul Abulbul Ameer,** and many others.] Humorous song popular for several generations in American schools and colleges. Some authorities have considered that it may have had its original inspiration in the Crimean War. It recounts the tale of a fabulous contest between the Moslem Abdul and the Cossack Ivan Skivinsky Skivar (whose name also exists in innumerable variant forms, some of which are covered by Carl Sandburg in his *American Songbag*). It begins

The sons of the Prophet are hardy and bold,
And quite unaccustomed to fear;
But of all the most reckless of life and of limb
Was Abdul the Bulbul Ameer. . . .

Abdurrahman (äb.dụr.rä'män). See **Abd-er-Rahman.**

Abdurrahman, Abu Zeid. See **ibn-Khaldun.**

Abdurrahman Khan (kän). See **Abd-er-Rahman Khan.**

Abe (ä.be), **Isoo.** b. in Fukuoka prefecture, Japan, Feb. 4, 1865; d. at Tokyo, Feb. 10, 1949. Japanese politician, known as the "father of baseball" in Japan. Educated in Japan and the U.S., he served as professor of political economy at Waseda University until 1926, and also as head of the baseball department at that institution.

Abe, Nobuyuki. b. in Ishikawa prefecture, Japan, 1875—. Japanese general and government official. Twice prime minister (August-September, 1939, and September, 1939-January, 1940), he is sometimes held to have been a member of Japan's peace-seeking group because of his statement (August, 1939) that Japan would have no part in Europe's war. Later (1944–45) governor general of Korea, he was removed from office and arrested by U.S. troops under Lieutenant General John R. Hodge.

Abecedarians (ā"bē.sē.dãr'i.ạnz). German Anabaptist sect of the 16th century, led by Nicholas Stork, a Zwickau weaver. Members of the sect rejected all learning, even down to the alphabet, as a hindrance to religion, and claimed possession of mystically revealed truth superseding the Bible. Their tendency to back up with actual deeds their predicted overthrow of existing governments did not increase their popularity with the civil authorities of the time.

Abéché (ȧ.bā.shā). [Also, **Abeshr.**] Caravan center and principal town in Wadai, in the C Sudan, situated in the E central part of the Chad territory (formerly a colony), French Equatorial Africa, near the border of Darfur, Anglo-Egyptian Sudan. It became a portion of the colony of Chad under French rule in 1920, although it had already been under French control for 17 years in an unaffiliated status.

à Becket (ạ bek'ẹt), **Thomas.** See **Thomas à Becket.**

à Beckett (ạ bek'ẹt), **Arthur William.** b. 1844; d. 1909. British playwright, journalist, and lawyer; son of Gilbert Abbott à Beckett. Author of *The À Becketts of Punch,* (1903).

à Beckett, Gilbert Abbott. b. at London, Jan. 9, 1811; d. at Boulogne, France, Aug. 30, 1856. British lawyer and journalist, chiefly noted for his contributions to *Punch,* although he also wrote for the London *Times.* Author of

Comic History of England (1848), *Comic History of Rome* (1852), and others.

à Beckett, Gilbert Arthur. b. 1837; d. 1891. British playwright and journalist, a member (1879 *et seq.*) of the staff of *Punch;* son of Gilbert Abbott à Beckett. In addition to his contributions to *Punch*, he wrote works for the stage, most notably *The Happy Land* (1873), in collaboration with W. S. Gilbert.

Abed-nego (a̤.bed'nē̤.gō). [Also: **Abednego;** in Douay Version, **Abdenago.**] In the Old Testament, one of the three Hebrews (Shadrach and Meshach were the others) cast by Nebuchadnezzar into the fiery furnace. By intervention of an angel, all three were miraculously delivered unharmed from the flames. Abed-nego's Hebrew name was Azariah, Abed-nego being substituted for it by the prince of the eunuchs of the king of Babylon. Dan. i. 7.

Abegg (ä'bek), **Julius Friedrich Heinrich.** b. at Erlangen, Bavaria, March 27, 1796; d. at Breslau, May 29, 1868. German jurist, author of *Versuch einer Geschichte der preussischen Civilprozessgesetzgebung* (1848), and others.

Abegg, Richard Wilhelm Heinrich. b. at Danzig, 1869; d. in Pomerania, 1910. German physical and inorganic chemist. He outlined a valency theory (with Bodländer, 1899), and carried out experiments on the freezing points of various solutions, ice's dielectric constant, and potentials in nonaqueous solutions (with Neustadt). He was a professor (1909–10) at Breslau.

Abeilard (ab'e̤.lärd), **Peter.** See **Abelard, Peter.**

Abel (ā'be̤l). In the Old Testament, the second son of Adam, slain by his brother Cain. Gen. iv. 1–8.

Abel (ä'be̤l), **Carl.** b. at Berlin, Nov. 25, 1837; d. 1906. German comparative philologist. He was Ilchester lecturer on comparative lexicography at Oxford, and served as Berlin correspondent of the London *Times* and *Standard*. Author of *Linguistic Essays* (1880) and others.

Abel (ā'be̤l), Sir **Frederick Augustus.** b. at Woolwich (now part of London), 1827; d. at London, 1902. English chemist, notable as a specialist in explosives. He was the inventor (with Sir James Dewar) of cordite and of the Abel test for the flash point of petroleum. He also developed improved techniques for the manufacture of guncotton. Professor at the Royal Military Academy (1851–55); war department chemist (1854–88); president of the Institute of Chemistry and other learned societies.

Abel (ä'be̤l), **Heinrich Friedrich Otto.** b. at Reichenbach, Württemberg, Jan. 22, 1824; d. at Leonberg, Württemberg, Oct. 28, 1854. German historian. He was a collaborator on the *Monumenta Germaniae historica,* and author of *König Philipp der Hohenstaufe* (1852) and others.

Abel (ā'be̤l), **John Jacob.** b. at Cleveland, Ohio, May 19, 1857; d. May 26, 1938. American pioneer in endocrinology and modern physiological chemistry. He is credited with having first produced insulin in its crystalline form, and with having isolated (1926) the pituitary hormone. His finding of amino acids in the blood stream, as well as his work with adrenal glands (which facilitated Takamine's development of adrenalin and in connection with which he himself isolated epinephrine), made him a leader in international science. He was professor of pharmacology at Johns Hopkins (1893–1932), and thereafter professor emeritus and director of that university's Laboratory for Endocrine Research.

Abel (ä'be̤l), **Joseph.** b. at Aschach, Austria, 1768; d. at Vienna, Oct. 4, 1818. Austrian historical and portrait painter.

Abel, Karl Friedrich. b. at Köthen, Germany, 1725; d. at London, June 20, 1787. German composer, notable as a performer on the viola da gamba. He studied under Johann Sebastian Bach at Leipzig, and was later court musician to the elector of Saxony (1748–58) and to Queen Charlotte of England (1758 *et seq.*). He conducted (c1764 *et seq.*) Bach and Abel concerts at London.

Abel (ā'be̤l), **Mr.** The narrator and chief male character of *Green Mansions*, by William Henry Hudson.

Abel (ä'be̤l), **Niels Henrik.** b. at Findø, Norway, Aug. 5, 1802; d. near Arendal, Norway, April 6, 1829. Norwegian mathematician, a leader in improving methods of analysis, and noted especially for his researches on elliptic functions. His complete works, edited by Holmbø, were published in 1839.

Abel (ā'be̤l), **Thomas.** See **Abell, Thomas.**

Abela (ab'e̤.la̤). An ancient name of **Ávila,** city.

Abelard (ab'e̤.lärd), **Peter.** [French, **Pierre Abélard** (á.bā.lår); Latinized, **Petrus Abelardus;** older spellings, **Abaelard, Abailard, Abeilard.**] b. of a noble family at Pallet (Palais) near Nantes, France, 1079; d. at the abbey of St. Marcel near Châlons-sur-Saône, April 21, 1142. French logician, philosopher, theologian, and teacher.

Life. Abelard was the eldest son of a minor vassal in Brittany. His father had some education and wanted his children to have more, so he gave his son the best instruction available in the district. Abelard became inflamed with the desire for knowledge and abandoned his birthright, preferring to spend the rest of his life in study rather than to take over the government of the family estates. After he left home, he wandered about France, studying under various masters, especially William of Champeaux, a leader of the realist school of philosophy; he may also have studied under Roscellin of Compiègne. He soon attacked the views of William of Champeaux and forced him to modify his position. At the age of twenty-two he opened a school of his own at Melun. Finally, he reached Paris where he finished his work in logic and taught there with considerable success. Employed by Fulbert, a canon of Paris, to supervise the education of his niece Héloïse, Abelard fell in love with his pupil and seduced her. Her uncle eventually learned of the affair and forced Abelard to marry her. Abelard tried to keep the marriage secret and persuaded Héloïse to hide herself in a convent. Fearing that Abelard planned to repudiate Héloïse, Fulbert hired some ruffians who broke into Abelard's house at night and castrated him. Abelard then took refuge in monastic life at St. Denis. Cited (1121) before the Synod of Soissons on a charge of disseminating Sabellianism (explanation of the doctrine of the Trinity on philosophical principles) and compelled to burn his *Introductio ad Theologiam,* he retired to Nogent-sur-Seine, where he was sought out by devoted students who built for him the Oratory of the Paraclete. Abbot of St. Gildas, Brittany, from 1125 to c1134, he was accused (1140) of heresy at the Council of Sens by Bernard of Clairvaux (who believed that faith must be mystical and intuitive rather than rationalistic) and was condemned by the Council in 1141, and, finally, in Rome by the Pope in 1142. Abelard was buried at the Paraclete and in 1164 Héloïse was buried there also at the side of her lover. They are now supposed to be buried in the Père Lachaise, Paris, where their tomb is shown to visitors.

Philosophy and Writings. Abelard defended a sort of compromise between Roscellin's nominalism and Champeaux's extreme realism; this middle doctrine, called conceptualism, was a sort of mitigated and disguised nominalism (universals exist, but only as concepts in the minds of men, and previous to that, in the mind of God). Partly because of Abelard's eloquence and dialectical power, partly because of its intermediate nature, this doctrine became very popular; it remained for three centuries (the twelfth to the fourteenth) the favorite solution of the problem of universals. Though Abelard's views were less objectionable to the Church than pure nominalism, they were repeatedly condemned. Abelard's philosophy is best expressed in his *Glossulae super Porphyrium.* His dialectical attitude is illustrated by the *Sic et Non* (Yes and No), a collection of scriptural and patristic extracts showing the pro and con of a number of theological and casuistic questions. Abelard exposed these contradictions without trying to solve them. He was essentially a dialectician and may be considered one of the founders of the scholastic method; his teaching prepared for the reception of Aristotle and the Aristotelian supremacy. His own work was done before the arrival of Arabic philosophy—either in Latin or in Hebrew; it is interesting to note that he deplored the fact that the latter language was generally unknown.

Summary. Abelard was the completely questioning mind for whom reason was superior to faith. He was a rationalist but not a freethinker; he relied on orthodox authorities and not on his own observation. He never denied the doctrines of the Church, though he loved to reason about them. His methods and many of his results were adopted by later theologians who were never accused of heresy. Abelard's method of collecting arguments on both sides of a question was followed by all theologians of the twelfth and thirteenth centuries. For example, Peter Lombard, who wrote the first of the great theological encyclopedias, the *Book of Sentences*, cited authorities, pro and con, for every statement, but he did one thing more—he indicated a preferred solution to the problem. This was safer than Abelard's system of leaving the question open for discussion, for it affirmed the orthodoxy of the writer.

Abel de Pujol (à.bel dẹ pü.zhol), **Alexandre Denis.** b. at Valenciennes, France, c1785; d. at Paris, Sept. 28, 1861. French historical painter, a pupil of Jacques Louis David.

Abelin (ä'bẹ.lin), **Johann Philipp.** [Pseudonyms: **Philipp Arlanibäus, Johann Ludwig Gottfried,** or **Gothofredus.**] b. at Strasbourg; d. c1635. German historian, founder of *Theatrum Europaeum*, a 21-volume serial work on contemporary history, later carried forward by Schieder, Oräus, and others into the 18th century, and illustrated by Matthäus Merian (1593–1650). He was the author also of a history of the West Indies, *Historia Antipodum*, and other works.

Abe Lincoln in Illinois. Play by Robert Sherwood, produced in 1938 and published in 1939, when it was awarded a Pulitzer prize. A simple chronicle play, in many scenes, covering the years between 1830 and Lincoln's election to the presidency, there is no extraneous comment in the text, simply the implication that in the figure of Lincoln there is an imperishable example of faith and courage.

Abelites (ā'bẹl.īts). [Also: **Abelonites, Abelonians, Abelians** (ab'ẹ.lọn.īts, ā.bẹl.ō'ni.ạnz, ạ.bē'li.ạnz).] Christian sect in Africa which spurned procreation in order not to perpetuate inherited sin, following the traditional example of Abel, son of Adam. Abelite couples, in order to continue their sect, would adopt the children of others. The sect is mentioned (c400) by Augustine as having within recent years utterly disappeared.

Abell (ā'bẹl), **Arunah Shepherdson.** b. at East Providence, R. I., Aug. 10, 1806; d. at Baltimore, Md., April 19, 1888. American printer and newspaper publisher. After an apprenticeship (1822 *et seq.*) on the Providence *Patriot* and a period as a journeyman printer at Boston and New York, he formed an association with William M. Swain and Azariah H. Simmons to found a paper patterned on the highly successful New York *Sun*, first of the American "penny papers." The Philadelphia *Public Ledger* (March 24, 1836) and Baltimore *Sun* (May 17, 1837) were the result, the latter entirely managed by Abell although owned jointly with Swain and Simmons.

Abell (ä'bẹl), **Kjeld.** b. at Ribe, Denmark, Aug. 28, 1901—. Danish dramatist, notable in his own country and elsewhere as an innovator of new and popular stage techniques. His *Melodien der blev væk* (1935; Eng. trans., *The Melody That Got Lost*, 1939) is a tuneful revue-drama suggesting the evanescence of youth, while his *Anna Sophie Hedvig* (1939) is a serious study of the spirit of resistance to all forms of tyranny.

Abell (ā'bẹl), **Thomas.** [Also, **Abel.**] Executed at Smithfield, London, July 30, 1540. Roman Catholic clergyman, a rector at Bradwell, Essex, and chaplain to Catherine of Aragon, wife of Henry VIII. He actively supported the queen in her endeavor to prevent the divorce sought by Henry, and was thereupon condemned and executed on a charge of concealing the alleged treason of Elizabeth Barton, called the "Nun of Kent." Author of *Invicta veritas* (c1532).

Abellinum (ab.ẹ.lī'num). Latin name of **Avellino,** city.

Abe Martin (āb' mär'tin). Character in the newspaper columns and humorous books by Frank McKinney Hubbard.

Abenak (ab.ẹ.näk') or **Abenaki** (ab.ẹ.nä'kẹ). See **Abnaki.**

Abencérages (à.bän.sā.ràzh). Opera by Cherubini, with a libretto by Jouy. First performed (1813) for Napoleon I, at the Paris Opéra, it is now infrequently played, except for the overture. Its basis is the tragic story of the famous family of Spanish Moors called, in English, the Abencerrages.

Abencerrages (ạ.ben'sẹ.rāj.iz). [Spanish, **Abencerrajes** (ä.ben.thä.rä'hās).] Moorish family in Granada, famous in Spanish romance. The tale of the struggle of the Abencerrages with the family of the Zegris, and of their final destruction in the Alhambra near the end of the period of Moslem rule in Granada, is recounted by Pérez de Hita (as a story based on history, but not as actual fact) in his *Historia de las guerras civiles de Granada* (1595). The accounts of this family later served as the groundwork of a romance by Chateaubriand (1826) and of an opera by Cherubini (1813).

Åbenrå (ô'bẹn.rô). See **Aabenraa.**

Åbenrå-Sönderborg (-sėn'nėr.bôrg). See **Aabenraa-Sønderborg.**

Abensberg (ä'bẹns.berk). [Latin, **Castra Abusina.**] City in S Germany, in the *Land* (state) of Bavaria, American Zone, in the *Kreis* (district) of Lower Bavaria-Upper Palatinate, situated on the Abens River, ab. 18 mi. SW of Regensburg. A center of the Lower Bavarian hops trade, it has ferruginous thermal springs and a brewery. Its Gothic town hall has attracted some tourist interest. It was the scene of a victory (April 20, 1809) by Napoleon I over the Austrians under the archduke Louis. 4,010 (1946).

Abeokuta (ab″ẹ.ọ.kö'tạ). [Also: **Abbeokuta.**] City in W Africa, in Nigeria, capital, chief trading center, and principal town of Abeokuta province, Western Provinces. Under British control, it is situated approximately 64 mi. N of Lagos. Founded (c1830) by members of the Egba tribe of Yorubas seeking refuge from slave hunters, its government was semi-autonomous for much of the 19th century. 54,000 (est. 1950).

Aber (ab'ėr). Element in many place names of ancient British origin, signifying "a confluence of waters," either of two rivers or of a river with the sea, as in Aberdeen, Aberdour, Abergavenny, Aberystwyth, and others.

Aberavon (ab.ėr.ā'vọn). Former municipal borough, now officially comprising two wards of Port Talbot, in S Wales, in Glamorganshire, situated near the mouth of the river Avon, on Swansea Bay (an inlet of Bristol Channel), ab. 7 mi. E of Swansea. It has no direct rail connections for passengers, except through Port Talbot, ab. 178 mi. W of London. Situated in the South Wales coal field, the community has large manufacturing works, and easy access to iron ore from mines in the vicinity. 16,848 (1931).

Aberbrothock (ab″ėr.brọ.thok') or **Aberbrothwick** (ab-ėr.broth'ik). Former names of **Arbroath.**

Abercarn (ab.ėr.kärn'). Urban district in W England, in Monmouthshire, ab. 10 mi. NW of Newport, ab. 144 mi. W of London by rail: tin-plating factories; coal mining. 18,757 (1951).

Aberconway (ab'ėr.kon.wā). See **Conway,** Wales.

Abercorn (ab'ėr.kôrn). Civil parish in S Scotland, in West Lothian, situated on the Firth of Forth, ab. 10 mi. W of Edinburgh. It was the seat of a bishopric from 681 to 685. Pop. 775 (1931).

Abercrombie (ab'ėr.krom.bi, -krum.bi), **James.** See **Abercromby, James** (1706–81).

Abercrombie, John. b. at Aberdeen, Scotland, Oct. 10, 1780; d. at Edinburgh, Nov. 14, 1844. Scottish physician, pathologist, and philosophical writer. He was the author of *Pathological and Practical Researches on Diseases of the Brain and Spinal Cord* (1828), *Pathological and Practical Researches on Diseases of the Stomach, the Intestinal Canal, etc.* (1828), *Enquiries Concerning the Intellectual Powers and the Investigation of Truth* (1830), *Philosophy of the Moral Feelings* (1883), and others.

Abercrombie, Lascelles. b. at Ashton-on-Mersey, Cheshire, England, Jan. 9, 1881; d. at London, Oct. 27, 1938. British poet, critic, playwright, and professor. He taught English literature at the universities of Leeds (1922–29) and London (1929–35). Abercrombie did not attempt to sever himself completely from the Victorian tradition; there are, in fact, many signs of Browning's influence on him. He made frequent use of the dialogue form in his verse, which included *Interludes and Poems* (1908), *Emblems of Love* (1912), and *Twelve Idylls* (1928). Of his six plays from *The Adder* (1913) to *Phoenix* (1923), the best-known and the best-liked was *Deborah* (1913). Perhaps *The Sale of Saint Thomas* (published in part in 1911 but not entire till 1930) is the most memorable. His reputation was academic rather than popular, and his hold upon the intellectuals was strengthened by his work in criticism and aesthetics: *An Essay towards a Theory of*

Art (1922), *Principles of English Prosody* (1923), *The Idea of Great Poetry* (1925), *Romanticism* (1926), and *Principles of Literary Criticism* (1932).

Abercrombie, Sir **Leslie Patrick.** b. 1879—. British architect and town planner, a member of the comimttee appointed to supervise post-World War II reconstruction of London and Plymouth.

Abercromby (ab′ėr.krom.bi, -krum.bi), **David.** d. c1702. Scottish physician and philosophical writer. Author of *A Discourse of Wit* (1685), and a medical treatise (1684) which was translated into French, Dutch, and German.

Abercromby, James. [Also, **Abercrombie.**] b. at Glassaugh, Banffshire, Scotland, 1706; d. at Stirling, Scotland, April 28, 1781. British army officer. He served (1756 *et seq.*) against the French in Canada, as second in command (1756–58) and as commander of all British troops in America (1758). In this same year, however, a costly defeat in the assault on Fort Ticonderoga led to his replacement by Jeffrey Amherst and recall to England.

Abercromby, James. [Title, 1st Baron **Dunfermline.**] b. Nov. 7, 1776; d. in Midlothian, Scotland, April 17, 1858. British lawyer and politician; third son of Sir Ralph Abercromby (1734–1801). He entered Parliament in 1807, and was subsequently appointed judge-advocate-general (1827), chief baron of exchequer of Scotland (1830), master of the mint (1834), and speaker of House of Commons (1835). Author of a memoir (1861) on his father.

Abercromby, Sir **John.** b. 1772; d. at Marseilles, Feb. 14, 1817. English soldier; second son of Sir Ralph Abercromby (1734–1801). He served in Flanders (1793–94), was arrested by Napoleon and imprisoned at Verdun in 1803, was exchanged in 1808, and was appointed commander in chief at Bombay in 1809. He captured Mauritius in 1810.

Abercromby, Patrick. b. at Forfar, Scotland, 1656; d. c1716. Scottish physician, antiquarian, and historian. He was the author of *Martial Achievements of the Scots Nation* (1711–16), pamphlets in favor of the union with England, and others.

Abercromby, Sir **Ralph.** b. at Menstry, Clackmannan, Scotland, Oct. 7, 1734; d. near Alexandria, Egypt, March 28, 1801. British general, generally considered to have been an expert on military discipline and efficiency. He was commander in chief in the West Indies (1795–97).

Abercromby, Sir **Robert.** b. at Tullibody, Clackmannan, Scotland, 1740; d. at Airthrey, near Stirling, Scotland, in November, 1827. British general; brother of Sir Ralph Abercromby (1734–1801). He served in the French and Indian War, and in the Revolutionary War (at the battles of Brooklyn, Brandywine, and Germantown, and later at Charleston and Yorktown). He subsequently (1792 *et seq.*) commanded in India.

Aberdare (ab.ėr.dãr′). Urban district, market town, and coal-mining center in S Wales, in Glamorganshire, situated at the confluence of the rivers Dar and Cynon, ab. 4 mi. SW of Merthyr Tydfyl, ab. 163 mi. W of London by rail. It was a center of the British iron industry in the 19th century, until rail transportation made it more economical to smelt iron elsewhere. Since that time (c1875) coal mining has been the major industry of the community. 40,916 (1951).

Aberdare, 1st Baron. Title of **Bruce, Henry Austin.**

Aberdeen (ab.ėr.dēn′). See also **Aberdeenshire.**

Aberdeen (ab′ėr.dēn). [Former name, **Dundee.**] City in NE Mississippi, county seat of Monroe County, on the Tombigbee River, ab. 125 mi. SE of Memphis, in a cotton-growing area. It was a thriving plantation town before the Civil War, and the community still retains several excellent examples of the architecture of that period. 5,282 (1950).

Aberdeen (ab.ėr.dēn′). [Called the **"Granite City,"** and **"Silver City by the Sea."**] City, royal burgh, seaport, holiday resort, and manufacturing and shipbuilding center in C Scotland, in Aberdeenshire, situated on the North Sea between the mouths of the rivers Dee and Don, ab. 131 mi. NE of Edinburgh, and ab. 524 mi. N of London by rail. It comprises Old Aberdeen (in the N portion of the city) and New Aberdeen (in the S portion). It is the county seat of Aberdeenshire, and the third-ranking town in Scotland in population. Aberdeen is the principal seaport in Scotland N of Edinburgh and Glasgow, and has had a long history of commerce with Europe, beginning at least as early as the 13th century. It is an important port in herring fishery and has large exports of the cured fish. Granite working is an important activity in the vicinity, both for local use (many houses in the city are built of granite) and for export. At the beginning of the 19th century Aberdeen was Scotland's principal shipbuilding center, specializing in clipper ships. It now builds smaller craft for the fisheries trade. Aberdeen has been an important Scottish cultural center since the Middle Ages and has a university over 400 years old (King's College, in Old Aberdeen, and Marischal College, in New Aberdeen). In more recent years the town has become one of the principal holiday resorts of Scotland. 188,853 (est. 1948).

Aberdeen (ab′ėr.dēn). City in NE South Dakota, county seat of Brown County, ab. 120 mi. NE of Pierre: second largest city in South Dakota; rail and truck distributing center for agricultural products. It is the seat of Northern State Teachers College. Hamlin Garland resided here at one time. 21,051 (1950).

Aberdeen. City in SW Washington, in Grays Harbor County, on the N shore of Grays Harbor, ab. 43 mi. W of Olympia: manufactures of paper, lumber products, and canned seafood. It was platted in 1884, but a settlement had been established on the site of the present city some 20 years earlier. 19,475 (1950).

Aberdeen (ab.ėr.dēn′), **Old.** Former registration district (abolished 1931) and historic community in C Scotland, in Aberdeenshire, situated on the S bank of the river Don at its mouth, ab. 1 mi. N of New Aberdeen. Together with New Aberdeen it forms the city and royal burgh of Aberdeen. It contains the Cathedral of Saint Machar, and King's College in the University of Aberdeen. The old cathedral (begun c1366) is now a parish church, with only the spacious nave remaining of the original building.

Aberdeen Proving Grounds (ab′ėr.dēn). Installation of the U.S. Army in N Maryland, NE of Baltimore. It is used for the testing and development of guns, tanks, and other heavy weapons.

Aberdeenshire (ab.ėr.dēn′shir) or **Aberdeen** (ab.ėr.dēn′). Maritime county in NE Scotland, bounded on the N and E by the North Sea, on the S by Kincardineshire, Angus, and Perthshire, on the W by Inverness-shire, and on the NW by Banffshire. The coastline is generally bold and rocky with few inlets or bays. The surface is hilly, becoming mountainous in the SW portion where it reaches an altitude of 4,296 ft. in Ben Macdhui. Much of the county is wooded, the most densely wooded portion of Scotland being on the Buchan Plateau in the E part of the county. In this county beef cattle are raised in some quantity, the meat being shipped largely to London. About one half of the total area of the county is under cultivation or in pasture. The most important commercial crop is oats, which are of fine quality; except for a little barley, the county produces no other grains in quantities sufficient to have commercial importance. However, some root crops are produced, such as potatoes, turnips, and rutabagas. The chief industries are agriculture and fisheries, notably of herring, whitefish, and salmon. Granite-working (especially in the vicinity of the city of Aberdeen) is also important. County seat, Aberdeen; area, ab. 1,971 sq. mi.; pop. 334,400 (est. 1949).

Aberdeen University (ab.ėr.dēn′). Incorporated under this name in 1860 as a union of King's College, which was founded in 1494 by Bishop Elphinstone at what is now called Old Aberdeen, and Marischal College, which was founded in 1593 by Earl Marischal in the newer part of the city. It included, by 1943, three readerships, 34 chairs, and 68 lectureships. Conjointly with the universities of St. Andrews, Edinburgh, and Glasgow, it sent, until after World War II, the three "Scottish Universities" members to Parliament.

Aberdour (ab.ėr.dör′). Civil parish and summer resort in C Scotland, in Fifeshire, situated on the N bank of the Firth of Forth, ab. 8 mi. N of Edinburgh, ab. 411 mi. N of London by rail. It has the ruins of Aberdour Castle nearby. 2,055 (1931).

Aberfoyle (ab.ėr.foil′). Civil parish in C Scotland, in Perthshire, situated on the river Forth, ab. 8 mi. SW of

Callander, ab. 462 mi. N of London by rail. It figures in Scott's novel *Rob Roy*. 1,014 (1931).

Abergavenny (ab″ėr.gạ.ven′i). [Latin, **Gobannium.**] Municipal borough and market town in W England, in Monmouthshire, situated at the confluence of the rivers Gavenny and Usk, ab. 20 mi. N of Newport, ab. 153 mi. W of London by rail. During the 19th century it was important for its coal mines and ironworks, and as a market center, but has now lost much of its commercial importance. It was involved constantly in the border struggles of the Middle Ages and was burned (1404) by Owen Glendower. It has the ruins of a Norman castle, and also an ancient priory church containing the tombs and effigies of the lords of Bergavenny, once owners of the castle. 8,844 (1951).

Abergele (ab.ėr.gāl′). Urban district and market town in N Wales, in Denbighshire, ab. 5 mi. W of Rhyl, ab. 214 mi. NW of London by rail. It is a seaside resort, situated on the S shore of Liverpool Bay. 7,539 (1951).

Aberhart (ā′bėr.härt), **William.** b. near Seaforth, Ontario, 1878; d. at Vancouver, British Columbia, April 23, 1943. Canadian politician who served (1935–43) as premier of Alberta and there introduced a program of social credit based on the theories of C. H. Douglas. During his early career, he taught school at Brantford (1905–10) and Calgary (1910 *et seq.*).

Abernethy (ab.ėr.nē′thi, -neth′i). Police burgh in C Scotland, in Perthshire, ab. 7 mi. SE of Perth, ab. 442 mi. N of London by rail. It was in ancient times a seat of Culdee worship and a Pictish royal residence. The community has a round tower, said to date from the 10th century. 676 (est. 1948).

Abernethy, George. b. at New York, Oct. 7, 1807; d. May 2, 1877. American merchant, administrator, and first provisional governor (1845 *et seq.*) of what is now the state of Oregon. Chosen financial director of a Methodist mission in Oregon, he arrived there (1840) on the *Lausanne* with the earliest American colonizers. He established the first newspaper in the area, and embarked upon such commercial enterprises as fisheries and lumbering in successful rivalry with the Hudson's Bay Company. Twice (1845, 1847) elected governor of the provisional administrative machinery that preceded the territorial government, his administrations were marked by the Whitman massacre, retaliatory war against the Indians, and efforts to secure aid of Congress.

Abernethy, John. b. at Coleraine, Ireland, Oct. 19, 1680; d. in December, 1740. Irish Presbyterian clergyman, appointed (1717) by the synod to leave his parish at Antrim for one at Dublin. His refusal to obey caused a schism in Irish Presbyterianism which resulted (1726) in the separation of the "non-subscribers" (as those who refused to accept the authority of the ecclesiastical courts were called) from the main body of Presbyterians. Abernethy was, as might be expected from his position in this conflict, the author of several controversial writings on freedom of worship.

Abernethy, John. b. at London, April 3, 1764; d. at Enfield, England, April 28, 1831. English surgeon. He was a lecturer on anatomy and physiology at London's College of Surgeons (1814–17) and surgeon at St. Bartholomew's Hospital (1815–27). His medical works were collected (c1830) in five volumes. He is now perhaps best remembered for developing (1797) a technique for ligation of the external iliac artery.

Abershaw (ab′ėr.shô), **Louis Jeremiah.** [Also: **Avershawe;** called **"Jerry."**] b. c1773; d. 1795. English highwayman. He was for several years able to exact tribute from travelers by coach and horseback on the roads from London to Kingston and Wimbledon, which were then some ten miles SW of the city proper.

Abersychan (ab.ėr.suk′ạn). Former urban district, now in Pontypool, in W England, in Monmouthshire, ab. 147 mi. W of London by rail. It is a coal-mining town, and has ironworks. 25,748 (1931).

Abert (ä′bėrt), **Hermann.** b. at Stuttgart, Germany, March 25, 1871; d. there, 1927. German musicologist and teacher; son of Johann Joseph Abert (1832–1915). He was successor (1920) to the professorship held earlier and made famous by Hugo Riemann at Leipzig.

Abert (ā′bėrt), **John James.** b. probably at Shepherdstown, Va., Sept. 17, 1788; d. at Washington, D. C., Jan. 27, 1863. American topographical engineer. He assisted F. R. Hassler in topographical and geodetic surveys (to 1829) of rivers, harbors, and canals in the eastern U.S., and afterward (1831) became chief of the Topographical Bureau of the War Department. As commissioner (1832–34) for Indian affairs, he was instrumental in establishing western reservations. He was a cofounder and director of the National Institute of Science.

Aberteifi (ab.ėr.tī′vi). Welsh name of **Cardigan.**

Abertillery (ab.ėr.til′ėr.i). Urban district in W England, in Monmouthshire, ab. 15 mi. NW of Newport, ab. 151 mi. W of London by rail, in a coal and iron producing region. 27,617 (1951).

Aberystwyth (ab.ėr.ist′with). [Also, **Aberystwith.**] Municipal borough, seaport, seaside resort, and national cultural center in W Wales, in Cardiganshire, situated at the mouths of the rivers Ystwyth and Rheidol on Cardigan Bay, ab. 38 mi. NE of Cardigan, ab. 234 mi. W of London by rail. It is notable as the seat of the University College of Wales and of the Welsh National Library, which contains nearly a million books in addition to valuable manuscripts in Welsh. The Welsh National Library is one of six libraries entitled to receive a free copy of every book printed in the United Kingdom. 9,323 (1951).

Abeshr (a.besh′ėr). See **Abéché.**

Abessa (ạ.bes′ạ). Character in Spenser's *Faerie Queene* who personifies superstition and ecclesiastical corruption, particularly with reference to abbeys and convents.

Abetti (ä.bāt′tē), **Giorgio.** b. at Padua, Italy, Oct. 5, 1882—. Italian astronomer. Director (1922 *et seq.*) of the observatory at Arcetri, near Florence, he is noted for solar studies with a tower telescope. Author of *Il Sole.*

Abetz (ä′bets), **Otto.** b. 1903—. German government official and propaganda agent of the Nazi party. He was for several years (1932 *et seq.*) before the outbreak of World War II active as a German propagandist in France. At one time a student and teacher of drawing, he purported to be interested chiefly in cultural matters and in a better understanding by both France and Germany of each other's problems. He was expelled from France in 1935 but returned almost immediately as a member of the German diplomatic staff at Paris. After the fall of France in 1940 he was appointed German ambassador to the Pétain-Laval government at Vichy and also served as German commissioner for occupied France. After the liberation of France he was held by the French for trial as a war criminal. Convicted (July 22, 1949) at Paris of having taken part in the arrest and deportation of French army officers during the period 1940–45, he was sentenced to prison for 20 years.

Abgar (ab′gär). [Latinized, **Abgarus** (ab′gạ.rus).] An appellation of the kings of Edessa, used as was "Caesar" among the Romans, "Pharaoh" and "Ptolemy" in Egypt, and "Antiochus" in Syria. It is said that there were 29 Abgars and that the dynasty lasted from 99 B.C. to 217 A.D. According to Eusebius, Abgar V (who was called Ukkāmā or Ucomo, meaning "the Black") wrote to Christ asking him to take up his abode with him and to cure him of leprosy. Tradition has it that Christ promised to send him one of his disciples after his ascension, and accordingly, through Thomas, sent Thaddeus. By another account, the man who bore the message to Christ was a painter, and desired to make a portrait of Jesus, but was so dazzled by the splendor of his countenance that he was unable to carry out his plan. Thereupon Christ washed his face and dried it with a linen cloth, upon which his features were miraculously impressed. This cloth, according to the legend, was then taken back to Edessa by the messenger. These tales, and others, as well as the supposed correspondence of Abgar V, have been the cause of much discussion within Christian churches, but the letters are now considered by virtually all Christian sects to be spurious.

Abhiras (ab.hē′rạz). [Also, **Abhira.**] Term sometimes used as a generic name for the peoples inhabiting the NW coast of India, on the Arabian Sea E of the mouth of the Indus River. This region has been identified by some scholars with the Ophir of the Old Testament.

Abhorson (ab.hôr′sọn). An executioner in Shakespeare's *Measure for Measure.*

Abiad (äb′yäd), **Bahr el.** See **White Nile.**

Abiah or **Abia** (a̤.bī'a̤). See also **Abijah** (second king of Judah).

Abiah. [Also, **Abijah.**] The second son of Samuel, one of the judges whose injustice led to the establishment of the kingdom. 1 Sam. viii. 2, 1 Chron. vi. 28.

Abiathar (a̤.bī'a̤.thär). fl. probably c1000–980 B.C. In the Old Testament, a high priest of Israel, a supporter and companion of David during his exile, appointed for his services high priest conjointly with Zadok, the appointee of Saul. 1 Sam. xxii. 20, etc.

Abibe (ä.bē'be). See **Dabaiba.**

Abich (ä'bich), **(Otto) Wilhelm Hermann von.** b. at Berlin, Dec. 11, 1806; d. at Gratz, Austria, July 1, 1886. German mineralogist, geologist, and traveler in Russia, Armenia, Persia, and elsewhere. Professor at Dorpat (1842 *et seq.*), he was a specialist in volcanic structure and deposits. Author of *Geologische Forschungen in den Kaukasischen Ländern* (1878–87) and other works.

Abidjan (ab.i.jän'). Town in W Africa, the capital of the French territory of the Ivory Coast, French West Africa, situated on a lagoon near the coast. It is important as an administrative center and as the terminus of the railway to Bobo-Dioulasso in the interior. It is also an educational center. Its seaport is Port Bouet, ab. 7 mi. away, with which it is connected by rail. 33,000 (1945).

Abie's Irish Rose. Comedy by Anne Nichols, which after a success in California was produced at the Fulton Theatre, New York, May 23, 1922, and ran for over 2,500 performances. The plot concerns itself with practically every form of love known to human beings. There is, first, the love a boy, Abraham Levy, and a girl, Rose-Mary Murphy, who have been married secretly, knowing the religious prejudice of their respective fathers. Next is the love of Solomon Levy and Patrick Murphy for their children; third, the love, sanctified by memory, of the dead mothers of the young couple; and finally the love of the grandfathers for their twin grandchildren, through whom the reconciliation is brought about. There is thus secured an appeal to all ages and conditions, sharpened by shrewdly conceived dialogue, which is based on the century-old principle of antithesis, and borrowed from the variety show.

Abiezer (ā.bi.ē'zėr). [Also, **Abiezar.**] In the Old Testament, a grandson of Manasseh and nephew of Gilead, founder of an important family to which also, collectively, the name was applied.

Abiezer. In the Old Testament, one of David's chief warriors, an inhabitant of Anathoth, of the tribe of Benjamin.

Abigail (ab'i.gāl). In the Old Testament, mother of Amasa and stepsister of David.

Abigail. In the Old Testament, wife of Nabal and, after his death, of David. By hastening to meet David with a supply of provisions when he was marching to take vengeance upon Nabal she succeeded in arresting his anger. 1 Sam. xxv.

Abigail. Lady's maid in Beaumont and Fletcher's *Scornful Lady*, and in other plays, presumably after the Abigail of the Bible, who called herself (1 Sam. xxv. 24) the handmaid of David. This Elizabethan usage later caused the name to become a literary synonym for lady's maid.

Abigail. Daughter of Barabas in Christopher Marlowe's *The Jew of Malta.* The dialogue between father and daughter is in some ways very close to that between Shylock and Jessica in Shakespeare's *The Merchant of Venice.*

Abigor (ab'i.gôr). In medieval demonology, a demon of high degree, grand duke in the infernal realms, with 60 legions at his command; an authority on war. He was represented as a knight carrying a lance, standard, or scepter.

Abihu (a̤.bī'hū). In the Old Testament, the second of the sons of Aaron by Elisheba. For neglecting to burn incense with fire taken from the great altar and using "strange" or common fire, he was slain with his elder brother Nadab by fire from heaven. Lev. x.

Abijah (a̤.bī'ja̤). See also **Abiah.**

Abijah. [Also: **Abijam, Abiah, Abia.**] In the Old Testament, the second king of Judah; son of Rehoboam and grandson of Solomon. He reigned for approximately three years in the late 10th century B.C. A victory over Jeroboam in which 400,000 men are said to have fought for Abijah and 800,000 for Jeroboam, leaving 500,000 dead (obviously somewhat exaggerated numbers), was a notable event of his reign. 2 Chron. xii.

Abijah. [Also, **Abijam.**] Name of various minor persons mentioned in the Old Testament: **1.** a son of Becher, one of the sons of Benjamin (1 Chron. vii. 8). **2.** the wife of Hezron and mother of Ashur (1 Chron. ii. 24). **3.** a priest, a descendant of Eleazar, the chief of the eighth of the 24 courses into which the priesthood was divided by David (1 Chron. xxiv. 10). **4.** a son of Jeroboam the son of Nebat (1 Kings, xiv. 1). **5.** the mother of Hezekiah (2 Chron. xxix. 1). **6.** a priest mentioned in Nehemiah (x. 7).

Abildgaard (ä'bil.gôr), **Nikolaj Abraham.** b. at Copenhagen, 1743; d. at Fredericksdal, Denmark, June 4, 1809. Danish historical painter. He was (1786 *et seq.*) professor at, and later (1789 *et seq.*) director of, the Copenhagen Academy.

Abilene (ab'i.lēn). City in E central Kansas, county seat of Dickinson County, on the Smoky Hill River ab. 115 mi. W of Kansas City. Settled in 1856 and given (1867) a Syrian name meaning "grassy plain," it was an important cattle town, being at various times (1867 *et seq.*) the terminus of both the Abilene and Chisholm trails over which Texas cattle were brought for eastern shipment. "Wild Bill" Hickok was town marshal in 1871. Still a cattle-shipping point, it is now more important as a grain and flour-milling center. 5,775 (1950).

Abilene (ab.i.lē'nḛ). In ancient geography, a district of Syria, lying E of the Antilibanus (Anti-Lebanon) mountains. A kingdom of Ituraea, which came under Roman domination with Pompey's conquest (c62 B.C.) of Syria, it became (c37 A.D.) a tetrarchy.

Abilene (ab'i.lēn). City in N central Texas, county seat of Taylor County, ab. 200 mi. NW of Austin: marketing and shipping center for the cattle, cotton, and dairy products of the southern high plains. Settled c1881, it was named for Abilene, Kansas. It is the seat of Hardin-Simmons University, Abilene Christian College, and McMurry College. Abilene State Park is nearby. 47,102 (1950).

Abilene Trail. Cattle trail from Texas to Abilene, Kan., over which the first cattle from the Texas ranges were driven northwards in 1866 (although it was not known by this name until 1867, when Abilene was formally named). Differences exist as to its precise route because of the trail's many branches. Although it had the same terminus in Kansas, it was not identical with the Chisholm Trail.

Abimelech (a̤.bim'ḛ.lek). In the Old Testament, a name believed by some scholars to have been used as a general title (like the Egyptian "Pharaoh") for the Philistine kings. In Gen. xx. allusion is made by this name to a king of Gerar who, supposing Sarah to be Abraham's sister, as Abraham asserted, took her into his harem, but dismissed her when he found she was Abraham's wife. In Gen. xxvi. another allusion by the same name is made to a king of Gerar in the time of Isaac, with whom Isaac found refuge during a famine. According to some authorities, these two were actually a single ruler; in other sources, however, they are cited as having been separate individuals.

Abimelech. In the Old Testament, a son of Gideon by a concubine, a native of Shechem, made "king" of Israel (for about three years) by the Shechemites. Judges, ix.

Abimelech. See **Ahimelech.**

Abimelech Jackwood (jak'wůd). See **Jackwood, Abimelech.**

Abingdon (ab'ing.dọn), 4th Earl of. Title of **Bertie, Willoughby.**

Abingdon. [Latin, **Abindonia** (ab.in.dō'ni.a̤).] Municipal borough and grain-marketing town in S England, in Berkshire, ab. 7 mi. S of Oxford on the Thames. It was an important river port for coal shipped up from London during the 16th and 17th centuries, and contains the remains of a 7th-century Benedictine abbey, at one time one of the wealthiest and most beautiful in England. 10,176 (1951).

Abingdon. City in NW Illinois, in Knox County, in a farming region. 3,289 (1950).

Abingdon. [Former name, **Wolf Hills.**] Town in SW Virginia, county seat of Washington County: manufactures of chemicals, wagons, lumber, condensed milk, and cigars; shipping point for burley tobacco. It was established in 1778. The Barter Theater, one of the first and best known of U.S. summer theaters, was founded here in 1933. Pop. 4,709 (1950).

Abington (ab'ing.tọn). Town in SE Massachusetts, in Plymouth County, ab. 20 mi. S of Boston: shoes, textiles, garments, and ice cream. Settled in 1668 and incorporated c1712, it produced many of the boots worn by Union soldiers in the Civil War. During the 1850's, nearby Island Grove Park was the site of antislavery meetings led by William Lloyd Garrison and others. 7,152 (1950).

Abington, Frances. [Maiden name, **Barton.**] b. at London, 1737; d. there, March 4, 1815. English actress. From flower girl and street singer, she rose to a position of eminence on the stage which she held for 43 years. Garrick's leading lady at the Drury Lane for 18 years, she was the first to play the role of Lady Teazle in Sheridan's *School for Scandal.*

Ab-Initio Movement (ab.i.nish'i.ō). Political and legal position that came into being in Texas in 1866 during the state constitutional convention that followed the Civil War. It involved the question of whether or not secession had been invalid from the outset (i.e., *ab initio*) or whether it had been invalidated as a result of the war. If the Ab-Initio position were to be held sound, it meant that the laws (and hence most public and private contracts of the period 1860–65) operative under secession could be disregarded. Controversy over this point caused a considerable rift among Texas politicians of the day, but the Ab-Initio position was finally, with some compromises, set aside in the formulation of the new state constitution.

Abipon (ab.i.pōn'). [Also, **Abipones** (ab.i.pō'nās).] Name given to a tribe of South American Indians, now extinct, which during the 16th century occupied both banks of the river Paraguay ab. 600 mi. above the Paraná. They later moved to the Chaco region, whence they were driven southward by the Spaniards. According to the accounts of that day and later, they were savage and intractable, wandering in their habits, and lived by hunting and fishing. After the introduction by the Spaniards of horses to South America, the tribe acquired considerable numbers of them and attained great skill in horsemanship. For many years the Abipon were a serious hindrance to colonial settlement. Their language was of the Guaycuruan family.

Abisa (ä.bē'sä). See **Bisa.**

Abishag (ab'i.shag). In the Old Testament, a Shunammite woman taken by David to comfort him in his old age. 1 Kings, i. 1–4.

Abishai (ạ.bish'ā.ī). In the Old Testament, a stalwart soldier of David, and son of his sister, Zeruiah. 2 Sam. ii. 18.

Abitibi Lake (ab.i.tib'i). [Also: **Abbitibbe, Abbitibbi.**] Lake in E central Canada, in Ontario, S of James Bay, on the boundary between the provinces of Ontario and Quebec. Elevation, 868 ft.; length, ab. 60 mi.; area, ab. 350 sq. mi.

Abitibi River. [Also: **Abbitibbe, Abbitibbi.**] River in E central Canada, the outlet of Abitibi Lake, Ontario, flowing generally N to join the Moose River, which flows into James Bay, an arm of Hudson Bay. Length, ab. 220 mi.

Abkhaz Autonomous Soviet Socialist Republic (ab.kaz'; Russian, äp.ʜäs'). [Also: **Abkhazia** (ab.kā'zhạ), **Abkhazian Autonomous Soviet Socialist Republic.**] Autonomous republic of the U.S.S.R., the westernmost of those comprising the Georgian Soviet Socialist Republic, on the E coast of the Black Sea and the S slope of the Caucasus Mountains. The chief occupations of the people are stock raising and lumbering. There are several health resorts here, including Sukhumi, on the Black Sea. The republic includes much of the ancient region of Colchis, which was conquered by the Abasgi in the 7th century; they called their kingdom Abasgia and united (978 A.D.) with Iberia to the E to form an empire powerful until the Mongol invasion (1234 A.D.). Capital, Sukhumi; area, 3,155 sq. mi.; pop. 198,854 (1939).

Abkhazians (ab.kā'zhạnz). [Also: **Abazgi;** earlier spellings, **Abasgi, Abasci, Abasges.**] A Circassian people of the Black Sea coast of the Transcaucasus, numbering about 59,000 (1939).

Ableman v. Booth, 21 Howard 506 (1859) (ā'bl.mạn; böth). U.S. Supreme Court decision, handed down by Chief Justice Roger B. Taney for a unanimous court, upholding the validity of the federal Fugitive Slave Act of 1850 and prohibiting state interference with federal prisoners. The case arose over the freeing of Sherman Booth, who had violated the Fugitive Slave Law, by the supreme court of Wisconsin, which discharged him from custody on a writ of habeas corpus. After U.S. District Marshal Ableman had secured a writ of error, Booth was tried again before the U.S. district court, and sentenced to imprisonment and fine. The supreme court of Wisconsin again ordered his release on the ground that the Fugitive Slave Law was unconstitutional. Chief Justice Taney's opinion in this case is considered notable by historians of American jurisprudence for its masterly analysis of the nature of federal and state powers.

Able McLaughlins (mạk.lôf'linz), **The.** Novel by Margaret Wilson, published in 1923. It was awarded a Pulitzer Prize in 1924.

Ablesimov (äb.lyi.sē'mọf), **Aleksandr Anisimovich.** b. 1742; d. c1783. Russian satirical playwright and composer of comic operas, notable as the first to utilize peasant songs and legends on the Russian stage. His opus *The Miller*, which ran for nearly two months at Moscow, is considered by some music historians to have been the first successful Russian opera.

Abnaki (ab.nä'kē). [Also, **Abenak;** often, in American history, **Abenaki.**] Confederacy of Indian tribes in NE North America, speaking languages of the Algonquian linguistic stock of the Central-Eastern New England type. They withdrew from territory in Maine after the French, to whom they were allied, were defeated by the British in the French and Indian War. Their name became almost a synonym for savagery among the New England colonists of the 18th century (who called them also Tarrateens), by reason of the repeated forays made by them, under the influence of the French, against the British settlers. Their descendants now live chiefly in Quebec, New Brunswick, and Maine.

Abner (ab'nėr). In the Old Testament, a blood relative of Saul and the commander in chief of his army. After Saul's death he maintained the interests of the royal house, supporting Ishbosheth against David. In his flight, after his defeat by David, he slew Joab's brother, Asahel, who was pursuing him. Later, when he was about to effect a compromise with David prejudicial to Joab's interest, Joab treacherously slew him. 1 Sam. xxvi.

Abney (ab'ni), Sir **Thomas.** b. at Willesley, Derbyshire, England, in January, 1640; d. at Theobalds, Hertfordshire, England, Feb. 6, 1722. English merchant (originally a fishmonger), sheriff of London and Middlesex (1693–94), one of the original directors of the Bank of England, and lord mayor of London (1700–01). He was a friend and patron of the noncomformist theologian, Isaac Watts, who for the last 36 years (1712–48) of his life made his home at the Abney residence.

Abney, Sir **William de Wiveleslie.** b. at Derby, England, 1843; d. at Folkestone, England, 1920. English physicist and chemist, known for his work in photographic chemistry, color photography, and spectroscopy. President of the Royal Astronomical Society (1893–95) and of the Physical Society (1895–97), he was knighted in 1900.

Åbo (ō'bö). Swedish name of **Turku.**

Aboan (ạ.bō'ạn). Slave in the play *Oroonoko*, adapted by Thomas Southerne from the novel by Aphra Behn. Though of secondary importance in the play, the part was for many years esteemed by critics.

Aboccis (ạ.bok'is). An ancient name of **Abu Simbel.**

Abolitionist. In U.S. history before and during the Civil War, a term applied to one sympathetic to extreme antislavery doctrines, but more characteristically to one engaged in militant agitation against Negro slavery, employing such means as political action, moral condemnation, or force. Sentiment against the institution of slavery existed in the American colonies as early as 1688, when the Society of Friends at Germantown, Pa., registered its disapproval in a formal vote on the question. Until c1830 antislavery societies were active in the South, where they were actually more numerous than their Northern counterparts, but mounting fears of slave uprisings and the emerging Southern defense against Northern abolitionism discouraged further effort in the South and led to the effective end of the movement there. Northern abolitionism after c1830 was associated with the general development of humanitarian movements, particularly in New England and the older Middle West. Far from being unified, the abolitionist movement was beset by many differences, as witness the history of the extremists best represented by William Lloyd Garrison. Political developments after the Mexican War saw the progressive rise of abolitionism in national affairs, and the Compromise of 1850 ushered in an era that witnessed the amalgamation of the abolitionist moral crusade with political interests in the North. Among the prominent abolitionist leaders, in addition to Garrison, were William Ellery Channing, Theodore Weld, Theodore Parker, and Wendell Phillips. The outstanding literary work of the movement was *Uncle Tom's Cabin* (1852), by Harriet Beecher Stowe.

Abomey (ạ.bō′mi, ä.bō.mā′). Town in W Africa, in Dahomey, ab. 70 mi. from the S coast of French West Africa, ab. 1,900 mi. S of Algiers. Before its capture by the French in 1892, it was capital of the native kingdom of Dahomey. It is connected by rail with the port of Cotonou and with Porto-Novo, the capital of Dahomey. Pop. ab. 15,000.

Abominations, Tariff of. Name given to the U.S. tariff law of 1828, by which congressional supporters of Andrew Jackson for the presidency sought through very high duties on raw materials to create an issue which could be identified with the administration of John Quincy Adams, and which would be equally offensive to the South (already considered safe for Jackson) and New England (believed to be firmly behind Adams). The plan of Jackson's supporters was simple: to weaken Adams in his own stronghold of New England so seriously as to enable his defeat It was expected that the tariff would be defeated and that Jackson could then turn to the protectionist Middle Atlantic states for sufficient additional votes to make his election a certainty. The measure had little or no regard for the actual needs of the country; as John Randolph pointed out, it was concerned with "manufactures of no sort or kind but the manufacture of a president." Much to the surprise of its sponsors, it secured enough New England support actually to be passed as law, and was immediately and bitterly attacked by the South. It was nullified by a South Carolina ordinance in 1832.

Abongo (ạ.bong′gō). See **Bongo.**

Abony (ô′bōny′). [Also, **Nagy Abony.**] Town in C Hungary, in the county of Pest, ab. 50 mi. SE of Budapest, between Cegléd and Szolnok. 15,585 (1948).

Aborn (ā′bôrn), **Milton.** b. at Marysville, Calif., May 18, 1864; d. at New York, Nov. 12, 1933. American opera producer who did much to popularize with American audiences the works of Gilbert and Sullivan and Victor Herbert, and other operas in English. Starting with his own opera company, he was subsequently an actor and stage director (1887–95) for the Keith-Albee chain, and later managed companies with his brother, Sargent Aborn, under the sponsorship (1913–15) of Otto H. Kahn.

Ab'-o'th'-Yate (ab′ọ.ᴛʜẹ.yāt′). Pseudonym of **Brierley, Benjamin.**

Abou ben Adhem (ä′bö ben ä′dem). Short poem by Leigh Hunt in which Abou ben Adhem discovers, from an angel who appears to him at night, that his name is not listed in the golden book of those who love the Lord. He thereupon prays that he may at least be listed as one who loves his fellow men, and discovers on the following night that he is therefore entered with those who love the Lord.

Aboukir (ä.bö.kēr′). See also **Abukir.**

Aboukir. British heavy cruiser which, together with the cruisers *Hague* and *Cressy*, was sunk (Sept. 22, 1914) while on patrol in the North Sea by the German submarine U–9. The sinking of the three ships was the first major British naval disaster of World War I, and indicated clearly the need for special tactics in combating German submarines. One immediate result was that British heavy vessels were forbidden to stand by to pick up survivors in a submarine attack (the *Hague* and *Cressy* presented easy targets to the U–9 when they halted to pick up crew members of the *Aboukir*). The loss of life reached approximately 1,400 men from the total crews of the three ships.

Aboukir, Bay of. See **Abukir, Bay of.**

Abou-Klea (ä′bö klā′ạ). See **Abu Klea.**

About (à.bö), **Edmond François Valentin.** b. at Dieuze, France, Feb. 14, 1828; d. at Paris, Jan. 16, 1885. French satirical novelist, journalist, and dramatist. He studied archaeology at the French school, at Athens, and after his return (1853) to France, wrote for *Le Moniteur* and *Le Soir;* his political articles supported Napoleon III.

A. B. Plot. Term applied to the so-called plot (1823–24) stemming from the political differences between U.S. Secretary of the Treasury William H. Crawford and Senator Ninian Edwards of Illinois, a supporter of Calhoun. It takes its name from a number of articles signed "A.B." which appeared (1823) in the Washington (D. C.) *Republican.* The articles, which came from the pen of Edwards, charged Crawford with official misconduct in the use of western banks for collecting public-land revenues, and it was believed by some that they were written primarily, if not solely, in order to damage Crawford's chances in the presidential campaign of 1824. In 1824 Edwards' charges against Crawford were formally presented to the House of Representatives, and the committee report which cleared Crawford also served to cast doubts on Edwards' character and probity.

Abra (ä′brä). See also **Abra River.**

Abra. Province of the Philippine Islands, in NW Luzon, bounded by Ilocos Norte on the N, Ilocos Sur on the W and S, and Mountain Province on the E. Capital, Bangued; area, 1,475 sq. mi.; pop. 86,600 (1948).

Abra (ab′rạ). Favorite concubine of Solomon, notable in Matthew Prior's *Solomon on the Vanity of the World* for her docility:

"Abra was ready ere I called her name;
And, though I called another, Abra came."

Abrabanel (ä.brä.bä.nel′), **Isaac.** See **Abravanel, Isaac.**

Abradatas (ab.rạ.dā′tạs). fl. 6th century B.C. King of Susa. He was at first an enemy, then an ally, of the Persians under Cyrus the Great. In the *Cyropaedia* of Xenophon is told as an episode (the earliest example of a sentimental romance) the story of the loves of Abradatas and his wife Pantheia, which ends with the death of Abradatas in battle and the suicide of Pantheia and her eunuchs.

Abraham (ā′brạ.ham). [Also, **Abram.**] First of the patriarchs, traditional progenitor of the Hebrew people, and also, through his son Ishmael, a traditional ancestor of the Arabs. Many critical scholars do not consider Abraham a historical figure, and it is unquestionably true that particular stories about him in the scriptures comprise something which is closer to saga than to any other easily classifiable type of religious writing. In the case of Abraham, however, what might be called strict historical fact is secondary to his position as the bearer of the promise of God to his people. For this reason, such stories as that of his son Isaac (whom he was willing to sacrifice, if need be, to God) must be taken as indicating the quality of his devotion to God, rather than as strictly factual accounts of a historical episode in the usual sense. The question of the date of his life is a difficult one, but the 14th chapter of Genesis contains enough specific references to identifiable contemporary historical figures to suggest a tentative dating between 1550 and 1450 B.C. Abraham is equally revered by Jews, Christians, and Mohammedans. We are told that he was buried in the cave of Machpelah (the double cave) at Hebron, now said to be enclosed by the Great Mosque (Haram) of that place.

Abraham. b. c1787–1791; d. on the Little River, Seminole Nation, Indian Territory, sometime after 1870. Seminole interpreter and counselor. Originally a slave at Pensacola, Fla., he escaped to the Seminoles, with whose principal chief he became closely associated and whom he served as an interpreter when the tribe sent a delegation to Washington, D. C., in 1825. He was prominent in the Seminole War of 1835–37, and a principal negotiator of the treaty of Fort Dade (March 6, 1837). Shipped to Indian Territory in 1839, he later visited Florida, Washington, and New York with a delegation to Billy Bowlegs, a recalcitrant Florida Seminole chief, in 1852.

Abraham, John. See **Braham, John.**

Abraham, Plains of. Elevated plain SW of the city of Quebec, above the St. Lawrence River, on which was fought (Sept. 13, 1759) the deciding battle of the French and Indian War in its last phase. The British were led by General James Wolfe and the French by the Marquis de Montcalm; both commanders were killed in the battle. The British victory in this battle was one of the chief factors in determining that the further development of North America would rest primarily with the English rather than the French. A portion of the area is now preserved by the Canadian government as a national park.

Abraham, William. [Called **Mabon.**] b. in Afon Valley, Wales, 1842; d. 1922. British labor leader and politician, for many years (1885–1920) member of Parliament from Glamorganshire (Rhondda division), in Wales. He was influential with the Welsh miners throughout his political life, and served as first president of the South Wales Miners' Federation.

Abraham Adams (ad′ąmz). See **Adams, Abraham.**

Abraham a Sancta Clara (ä′brä.häm ä zängk′tä klä′rä). [Original name, **Hans Ulrich Megerle.**] b. at Kreenheinstetten, near Messkirch, Baden, July 2, 1644; d. at Vienna, Dec. 1, 1709. Austrian theologian and satirical writer. An Augustinian monk (1662 *et seq.*), he was court preacher (1667 *et seq.*) at Vienna. Author of a satirico-religious romance entitled *Judas the Arch-rascal* (*Judas der Erzschelm*) (1686–95), of *Gack, Gack, Gack a Ga of a Marvellous Hen in the Duchy of Bavaria, or a Detailed Account of the Famous Pilgrimage of Maria Stern in Taxa* (1687), and others. His collected works were published after his death in 21 volumes.

Abraham ben Meïr ibn-Ezra (ā′brą.ham ben mār′ ib″n.ez′rä). See **ibn-Ezra, Abraham ben Meïr.**

Abraham Cresques (kres′kęs). [Called **Cresques lo Juheu,** meaning "Cresques the Jew"; **Lo Jueu buscolor,** meaning "the map Jew"; **El Judio de las brujulas,** meaning "the compass Jew."] fl. at Palma de Mallorca, on Majorca island; d. 1387. Cartographer, believed to have been a member of a Jewish family from Catalonia. One of the greatest cartographers of his age and generally recognized to have been founder of the Jewish cartographical school at Palma de Mallorca, he was for most of his life in the service of the rulers of Aragon. He was probably (although there is no archival proof) the author of *Atlas Catalan*, originally made in 1375 for Charles V of France (Charles the Wise) and now considered by geographers to have been one of the outstanding cartographical achievements of the Middle Ages.

Abrahamites (ā′brą.ham.īts). Christian sect in Syria during the 9th century, linked by some scholars with the Paulicians. Their name derived from Abraham, or Ibrahim, of Antioch, whose denial of Christ's divinity became a distinguishing characteristic of their theology and caused them to be branded as heretics by the established Church.

Abrahamites. Bohemian deists of the 18th century who professed to follow the religion of Abraham before his circumcision. Their refusal to accept identification with either Christians or Jews led to their exclusion from the edict of tolerance laid down by Joseph II in 1781 and to their banishment in 1783. They had disappeared as a sect by the end of the century.

Abraham Lincoln. Critical estimate of Abraham Lincoln by James Russell Lowell, originally published (1864) in the *North American Review* as "The President's Policy." It now appears in the *Political Essays* as "Abraham Lincoln," with a short addition written after Lincoln's death. It treats of Lincoln's difficult task in preserving the Union and is, on the whole, a tribute to him.

Abraham Lincoln. Eulogistic poem (1865) by William Cullen Bryant, written at the request of the committee of arrangements when Lincoln's body was carried in funeral procession through the city of New York.

Abraham Lincoln. A biographical writing (1865) by Ralph Waldo Emerson. It prophesied that Lincoln would "serve his country even more by his death than by his life."

Abraham Lincoln. Historical play (1918) in six episodes by John Drinkwater. It was first produced at the Birmingham Repertory Theatre and was staged at London in 1919.

Abraham Lincoln. Biography by Carl Sandburg, in two parts: *Abraham Lincoln: The Prairie Years* (2 vols., 1926) and *Abraham Lincoln: The War Years* (4 vols., 1939). Unquestionably his major prose work, its research and writing occupied a major part of Sandburg's effort for some 20 years.

Abraham Lincoln: A History. Ten-volume biography of Abraham Lincoln, written by John Hay, with the help of John G. Nicolay. It was published in 1890.

Abraham Lincoln Walks at Midnight. Poem by Vachel Lindsay, published in *The Congo and Other Poems* (1914), in which Lincoln is seen pacing the dark streets of Springfield in an agony of distress over the war in Europe.

Abraham-man (ā′brą.hąm.man″). [Also, **Abram-man.**] Name originally applied to a mendicant lunatic from London's Bethlehem (Bedlam) Hospital, notably one from the ward named after the patriarch Abraham. On certain days of the year, patients from this ward were permitted to beg on the London streets, wearing a distinctive badge and becoming known in time as "Abraham-men." Their success as beggars led others to wear the badge, and to feign lunacy, until the term came to mean any imposter who sought alms under pretense of madness. The once common term "to sham Abraham," in the sense of pretending sickness, derives from this usage.

Abraham of Antioch (an′ti.ok). [Also, **Ibrahim.**] fl. 9th century A.D. Founder of the Christian sect known, after him, as Abrahamites.

Abraham's Oak. Ancient oak or terebinth which stood for many years on the plain of Mamre, near Hebron in Palestine, and was said to be that under which the patriarch Abraham pitched his tent.

Abrahamsohn (ä′brä.häm.zōn), **Otto.** See **Brahm, Otto.**

Abraham the Jew and the Merchant Theodore. Medieval story devised to support iconolatry, in which the friendless and penniless Theodore pledges himself before the statue of Christ, set up by Constantine at Byzantium, to repay a loan by Abraham. When, after a period of prosperous travel, he finds himself with the money but without a messenger to return it, he places it in a box and "commits it, in the name of Christ, to the waves," by which it is thereupon washed to the feet of Abraham at Byzantium. But when Theodore returns, Abraham, to test him, feigns not to have received repayment, upon which Theodore demands that Abraham should make an oath to this effect before the statue of Christ. The oath is never made, however, for as Theodore himself prays before the image, Abraham's heart is filled with faith in the trustworthiness of men who, like Theodore, have been at one time friendless, and he acknowledges receipt of the money.

Abrahen (ab′rą.hen). Second son of the caliph in George Chapman's tragedy, *Revenge for Honor.*

Abram (ā′brąm). See also **Abraham.**

Abram (ab′rąm). Urban district in NW England, in Lancashire, ab. 2 mi. SE of Wigan, ab. 208 mi. NW of London by rail. It is a coal-mining center, located on the south Lancashire coal field. 6,286 (1951).

Abram (ā′brąm). Montague's servant in Shakespeare's *Romeo and Juliet.*

Abrams (ā′brąmz), **Albert.** b. at San Francisco, Dec. 8, 1863; d. Jan. 13, 1924. American physician, author of a controversial theory of diagnosis based on changes in electronic vibration measurable at the skin, known as "Electronic Reactions of Abrams," or "ERA." Practicing in San Francisco, he acquired an international reputation for his extensive researches and publications, particularly his discovery of the visceral reflexes named for him. His attempt to combine the latter with the claims of chiropractors, and his development on a commercial basis of expensive apparatus for diagnosis and treatment by means of ERA, prompted ridicule among his colleagues and finally an investigation (1923) by the *Scientific American* (although, at the same time, others were inclined to credit him with the beginnings of revolutionary discoveries). Author of *The Blues* (*Splanchnic Neurasthenia*) (1904–14), *Spondylotherapy; Spinal Concussion* (1910), *New Concepts in Diagnosis and Treatment* (1916), and others.

Abrams v. United States, 250 U.S. 616 (1919). Majority opinion of the U.S. Supreme Court, in its first decision involving the Sedition Act of 1918, upholding that statute and the conviction of the appellants. The latter had been charged with the publication of two leaflets denouncing the U.S. government and calling for a general strike to frustrate Allied intervention in Russia. The case is memorable for the dissenting opinion of Justice Oliver Wendell Holmes, who made it a vehicle for a characteristic expression of his philosophical views. With the concurrence of Justice Louis D. Brandeis, he declared that "when men have realized that time has upset many fighting faiths, they may come to believe . . . that the ultimate good desired is better reached by free trade in ideas—that the best test of truth is the power of the thought to get itself accepted in the competition of the market, and that truth is the only ground upon which their wishes safely can be carried out. That at any rate is the theory of our Constitution. It is an experiment, as all life is an experiment."

Abrantes (ạ.brun'tę̄sh). [Latin, **Aurantes.**] Town and *concelho* (commune) in C Portugal, in the province of Ribatejo, in the district of Santarém, situated on the Tejo River at the head of navigation, ab. 75 mi. NE of Lisbon. In a hilly location of some strategic importance, the town has a large medieval castle, and contains the Church of São Vicente, considered by some to be one of the most remarkable churches in Portugal. Conquered by the Arabs in 1116, the town was reconquered by the Portuguese in 1148. It was taken by the French under Junot in 1807, but returned to Portugal in 1808. Pop. of concelho, 43,733 (1940); of town, 8,881 (1940).

Abrantes, Marquis and Viscount of. Titles of **Calmón du Pin e Almeida, Miguel.**

Abrantès (då.bräṅ.tes), Duc **d'.** Title of **Junot, Andoche.**

Abra River (ä'brä). River in Luzon, Philippine Islands, rising in Mountain Province and taking a circuitous course through Abra and Ilocos Sur provinces to the South China Sea. Length, ab. 100 mi.

Abravanel (ä.brä.vä.nel'), **Isaac.** [Also: **Abrabanel, Abarbanel.**] b. at Lisbon, 1437; d. at Venice, 1508. Jewish scholar, theologian, and statesman. The most notable member of a Sephardic family which claimed descent from the royal house of David and which produced a number of scholars and scientists during the 15th and 16th centuries, Abravanel is now perhaps best known for his commentaries on the Old Testament, particularly those on the books of Kings and Samuel. Convinced that such scholarship was most productive if it dealt with the meaning of a book in its entirety, rather than with the mere interpretation of isolated words and sentences, he sought also to have his commentaries reflect an understanding of the social, political, and economic conditions of the period within which a particular book of the Old Testament was actually prepared. The result was a body of theological writing widely used by both Christian and Jewish religious scholars for centuries after his death. In his own lifetime, Abravanel was treasurer to Alfonso V of Portugal until that ruler died in 1481, and was thereafter for eight years in the service of King Ferdinand and Queen Isabella at Madrid. Forced to quit Spain after the expulsion of the Jews in 1492, he lived successively at Naples, Sicily, Corfu, and Venice, being employed by the Venetian republic as a member of its diplomatic corps.

Abreu (ạ.brā'ọ̄), **Casimiro José Marques de.** b. on a farm near Barra de São João, Brazil, Jan. 4, 1839; d. there, Oct. 18, 1860. One of Brazil's most popular romantic poets. He lived for some time (1853–57) in Portugal, where he wrote part of his work. Author of *Camões e o Jau* (1856), and of *Primaveras* (1859), a book of poems which has had many editions in Brazil and Portugal.

Abreu, João Capistrano de. b. at Maranguape, Ceará, Brazil, Oct. 23, 1853; d. at Rio de Janeiro, Aug. 13, 1927. Brazilian historian, scholar, and essayist, notable as the author of several important works dealing with the colonial period in Brazil. He was assistant at the National Library at Rio de Janeiro, and professor (1883–99) at Pedro Segundo College. Among his best known writings are *O Brasil no Século XVI* (1880), *O descobrimento do Brasil* (1883), *Materiais e achegas para a história e geografia do Brasil* (1886), and *Capítulos da história colonial* (1907).

Abreu, José de. [Created in 1826 Baron of **Serro Largo.**] b. in Rio Grande do Sul, Brazil, c1775; killed at the battle of Ituzaingó, Feb. 20, 1827. Brazilian general. He was of obscure parentage and enlisted in the army as a common soldier, but rapidly rose in rank and is considered to have been one of the most distinguished Brazilian leaders in the campaigns (1816–20) against Artigas. In 1820 he became field marshal, and in 1826 took part in the Uruguayan campaign under the marquis of Barbacena.

Abricatae (ab.ri.kā'tē) or **Abrincatae** (ab.rin.kā'tē). Ancient name of **Avranches.**

Abricium (ạ.brish'i.um). [Also, **Abrutum.**] In ancient geography, a place in Moesia, a Roman province in SE Europe. In the vicinity Decius was defeated and killed by the Goths in 251 A.D.

Abrikosov (äb.rē.kô'sọf), **Aleksey Ivanovich.** b. in Russia, 1875—. Russian pathologist. He was surgeon (1911) at the Botkin Hospital, Moscow, and became (1920) director of the Institute of Pathologic Anatomy of the Moscow Medical Institute. He discovered a muscle tumor with which his name is associated.

Abrocomes and Atheia (ạ.brok'ọ.mēz; ạ.thē'ạ). [Called **Ephesian Stories;** also, **Abrocomas and Anthia, Habrocomas and Anthia.**] Romance in five books by a Hellenistic writer named Xenophon of Ephesus, in which he describes the premarital and domestic adventures of a young Greek couple of the period. The later writers Chariton and Heliodorus are believed to have used this work as a pattern for some of their writing.

Abrolhos (ạ.brō'lyös). [Full name, **Parcel dos Abrolhos.**] Group of islets and reefs off the coast of Brazil.

Abron (ä.brōn'). [Also: **Abrono, Brong.**] One of the Sudanic-speaking Guang peoples of W Africa, inhabiting the C part of the Gold Coast.

Abrutum (ạ.brö'tum). See **Abricium.**

Abruzzi (ä.bröt'tsē). Former division of Italy, comprising the provinces of Chieti, Teramo, and L'Aquila; a part of the former kingdom of Naples. Within it were the highest and wildest portions of the Apennines. Although, strictly speaking, the term is without significance in the political geography of Italy today, it is still used as a general regional designation by many people.

Abruzzi, Duke of the. [Additional title, Prince **Luigi Amedeo of Savoy-Aosta.**] b. at Madrid, 1873; d. 1933. Italian explorer, mountaineer, and naval officer; third son of Prince Amedeo of Aosta, one-time king of Spain. He was the first to climb Mount St. Elias, Alaska (1897) and Mount Ruwenzori, East Africa (1906), and leader of the polar expedition (1899–1900) on the *Stella Polare*, which reached the farthest northern latitude (86°33′ N.) gained up to that time. He also climbed Mount Godwin-Austen (or K2), in the Himalayas, to a height of 20,000 ft., and Bride Peak, to 24,600 ft. (1909). He was commander (until 1917) of the Italian Adriatic fleet in World War I.

Abruzzi e Molise (ā mō.lē'zā). *Compartimento* (region) in E central Italy, containing the modern provinces of Campobasso, Chieti, L'Aquila, Pescara, and Teramo. It is comprised for the most part of mountainous territory, and situated between the Adriatic Sea and the Apennines, which here attain their greatest height. Livestock raising and forestry are the most important activities of the region, but some olives, wine, and grain are produced. Part of the duchy of Spoleto under the Lombards and of Apulia under the Normans, the region was unified under Emperor Frederick II in 1240. Later a part of the kingdom of Naples, it was incorporated into Italy in 1860. Most of the inhabitants have long been, and remain, the victims of extreme poverty, which has led to frequent uprisings, much banditry, and (in the 20th century) large-scale emigration. Area, 5,883 sq. mi.; pop. 1,600,631 (1936), 1,663,000 (est. 1949).

Abruzzo Citeriore (ä.bröt'tsō chē.tā.ri.ō'rā). Former name of **Chieti,** province.

Abruzzo Ulteriore I (öl.tā.ri.ō'rā ö'nō). Former name of **Teramo,** province.

Absalom (ab'sạ.lọm). In the Old Testament, the third son of David, king of Israel. He slew his brother Amnon for the rape of his sister Tamar, and thereupon fled the wrath of David. He subsequently returned and was accepted by his father, but later rebelled (with David's counselor Ahithophel) against him, and was defeated and slain in the forest of Ephraim. 2 Sam. xiii–xix.

Absalom. An undutiful son, intended to represent the Duke of Monmouth, in John Dryden's satirical *Absalom and Achitophel.*

Absalom, Absalom! Novel by William Faulkner, published in 1936, describing the maniacal design of Colonel Sutpen to build a big house and establish a landed family.

Absalom and Achitophel (ą.kit'ǫ.fel). Political satire in heroic couplets by John Dryden, published in 1681. After the excitement of the Popish Plot (1678) there had been repeated attempts to force a bill through Parliament excluding Catholics (and thus the legitimate heir, the duke of York) from the throne of England. The villain in these attempts was the Whig leader, the earl of Shaftesbury, who in the summer of 1681 was under arrest charged with high treason. At the suggestion of the King, *Absalom and Achitophel* was written and its publication timed to fall just a week before Shaftesbury's fruitless arraignment. The poem makes use of biblical story to suggest how Achitophel (Shaftesbury) is tempting to rebellion Absalom (the duke of Monmouth, illegitimate son of Charles II and the Whig candidate to succeed his father). Since Monmouth had not yet rebelled, the poem lacks action, but not tenseness. It consists largely of satirical portraits and of eloquent argumentative speeches in Dryden's epical style. A second part, chiefly written by Nahum Tate, but revised by Dryden and containing 200 lines written by him, was published in 1682 against the lesser figures in the conspiracy. The name "Achitophel" was taken from the Vulgate Bible, and corresponds to the "Ahithophel" of the King James version. The poem, which still ranks as one of the leading political satires in English verse, had an immediate success, and was to a large extent responsible for the quick waning of the Shaftesbury cabal.

Absalon (äp'sä.lôn). [Also, **Axel.**] b. 1128; d. at Sorø, Zealand, Denmark, 1201. Danish prelate, statesman, and warrior; archbishop of Lund (1178–1201). Under his counselorship to Valdemar I and Canute VI, there occurred a considerable expansion of the territory controlled by Denmark, particularly in the general region of what is now Estonia. He also repudiated the claim of the German emperor Frederick Barbarossa to fealty from the Danish crown. A naval commander of considerable skill, he defeated the Wendish pirates (1168) and the Pomeranian fleet (1184). He is remembered also as the founder of schools and of religious orders, and as the patron of Saxo Grammaticus and Svend Aagesen.

Absaroka (ab.sä'rǫ.ką). Name which has been applied to the entire tribe of Crow Indians, of the Siouan linguistic family, and too, by some historians of the American West, to a subdivision or remnant of the Crows in S Montana. Etymologically speaking, all Crows may be called Absaroka, in view of the fact that "Crow" stems ultimately to the word "Absaroke," meaning crow or sparrow-hawk, which was the Indians' own name for themselves.

Absaroka Mountains. Range of the Rocky Mountains, in NW Wyoming and S Montana. The range is named after the Crow Indians who were once numerous in this area. Touching at one point on Yellowstone National Park, the range is variously estimated to be 150–180 mi. in length.

Absecon (ab.sē'kǫn). [Also, **Absecum.**] Name of a bay and an inlet on the coast of New Jersey, NE of Atlantic City.

ABSIE (ab'si). [Full name, **American Broadcasting Station in Europe.**] Agency of the U.S. government, under the State Department, established (April 30, 1944) at London to convey news, coded instructions to the various underground groups on the Continent, and communications from the various Allied commanders to the peoples of Europe. As the reader will note, its most usual name is an acronym from its full name. It continued to exist for several months after the close of World War II (broadcasting in English, Norwegian, Danish, French, Dutch, and German) and anticipated to some extent the type of work which was later taken over by the Voice of America.

Absolon (ab'sǫ.lon). In Chaucer's *Miller's Tale,* an amorous parish clerk who comes to grief in his wooing of the carpenter's wife.

Absolon, John. b. at London, May 6, 1815; d. there, June 26, 1895. English painter, best known for his water colors.

Absolute (ab'sǫ.löt), **Captain Jack.** In Richard Brinsley Sheridan's *The Rivals,* the son of Sir Anthony Absolute. He is a spirited soldier and persistent lover who appears as the impecunious Ensign Beverley (and is thus his own rival) to win the affections of the romantic Lydia Languish. She, in turn, scorns a match with one so suitable as the son of Sir Anthony Absolute, but falls in love with him, unknowingly, as Ensign Beverley, and is thereby persuaded to accept him when his real identity becomes known.

Absolute, Sir Anthony. Character in Richard Brinsley Sheridan's comedy *The Rivals,* an obstinate, passionate, self-willed, but generous old man.

Absyrtus (ab.sėr'tus). In Greek legend, the brother of Medea, killed by her on her flight from Colchis with Jason, to delay the pursuit of her father, Aeëtes. She cast the pieces of Absyrtus's body into the sea and Aeëtes, stopping to recover them, was left behind.

Abt (äpt), **Franz.** b. at Eilenburg, Saxony, Dec. 22, 1819; d. at Wiesbaden, Hesse, March 31, 1885. German conductor and composer. One of the best known of his songs is *When the Swallows Homeward Fly.*

Abt Vogler (fō'glėr). Poetic work by Robert Browning, published (1864) in *Dramatis Personae.* The work is written in the form of a dramatic monologue from the mouth of a certain "Abbe (or Abt) Vogler," in real life (1749–1814) court chaplain at Mannheim, Germany, notable for devising various improvements in the organ. In the poem, Vogler at first expresses his sorrow that the beautiful musical structure which he has just extemporized on the organ should disappear with the sound that brought it into being, but is then heartened to recall that nothing beautiful or true can ever really be lost: God hears or knows it, and it thus acquires an existence transcending human understanding.

Abu (ä'bö). Initial element of many Arabic proper names. It means "father." For a discussion of the relative "correctness" of the various methods of transcribing such Arabic forms as this, see the note under **Abd.**

Abu, Mount. Plateaulike area in NW India, in Bombay state: notable for its Jain temples. Parts of the area have long been popular as resorts. Highest point, 5,650 ft.

Abu Abdallah Mohammed (äb.däl'lä mō.häm'med). See **ibn-Batuta.**

Abu Abdullah (äb.döl.lä'). Arabic name of **Boabdil.**

Abu-al-Abbas (ä'böl.äb.bäs'). [Also: **Abul Abbas;** called **as-Saffah,** meaning "the Bloodspiller."] b. c721; d. 754. First Abbasside caliph. He established the Abbasside dynasty after defeating (750) Marwan II, the last Ommiad caliph, near the river in Mesopotamia now called the Great Zab. He based his claim to the caliphate on his descent from Mohammed's uncle, Abbas, and was named caliph at Kufa, in Mesopotamia, which was later superseded by Baghdad as the capital. He is noted in history for his ruthless treatment of his opponents.

Abu-al-Ala al-Maarri (ä'böl.ä.lä' äl.mä.är'rē). b. at Maarrah, near Aleppo, Syria, 973; d. 1057. Arab poet and skeptic, blind from infancy. His rationalist iconoclasm was important for several generations in the philosophy and literature of the Arabic world.

Abu-al-Atahiya (ä'böl.ä.tä'hē.yä). b. at Anbar, in Mesopotamia, 748; d. 828. Arab philosophic poet and moralist. Befriended and aided by Caliphs al-Mamun and Harun al-Rashid, he lived at Kufa and Baghdad. He developed a simple verse form to replace the archaic *qasīda,* or elegy, and established a technique of Arabic sacred poetry which held for generations. Despite the fact that he has been called the "father of Arabic sacred poetry," he was accused by some of his contemporaries of being a heretic.

Abu-al-Faraj al-Isfahani (ä'böl.fä.räj' äl.ēs.fä.hä'nē). [Also, **Abulfaraj.**] b. at Isfahan, Persia, 897; d. 967. Arab historian and anthologist. Born of a Qurashite family, he was a descendant of the last Ommiad caliph, and some of his many books were dedicated to his relatives in Spain. He lived at Baghdad, Aleppo, and elsewhere. His *Book of Songs* is a treasury of Arab poetry, music, and archaeology; it embodies the researches of earlier humanists, is by far the most important work of its kind, and is an invaluable source for the study of Arab antiquity.

Abu 'Arish (ä'bö ä.rēsh'). Town in SW Arabia, ab. 24 mi. from the Red Sea and ab. 40 mi. N of the border of Yemen: trading center. The irrigated area around the town produces various crops. Pop. ab. 8,000.

Abu-Bakr (ä'bö.bäk'ėr). [Also: **Abu-Bekr;** original name, **Abd-al-Kaaba;** called **al-Siddik,** meaning "the Faithful."] b. at Mecca, Arabia, 573; d. at Medina, Arabia, 634. First Moslem caliph (632–634); father-in-law and one of chief supporters of Mohammed, whom he accompanied on the Hegira. He was the immediate successor (632) to Mohammed as leader of Islam, which gained its first great strength in Arabia under his rule. He completed the first written record of Mohammed's sayings, the basis of the Koran. His dispute with Ali (who was Mohammed's nephew and son-in-law) over the succession began the schism between Sunnites and Shiites, the two chief Moslem sects. His daughter Ayesha was Mohammed's wife, and the source of the name by which he is now usually known (it means, in Arabic, "father of the virgin"). He was succeeded by Omar I.

Abu Beker ibn-el-Tufeil (ä'bö bek'ėr ib"n.el.tö.fīl'). See **ibn-Tufail.**

Abu-Bekr (ä'bö.bek'ėr). See **Abu-Bakr.**

Abu-Hanifah (ä'bö.hä.nē'fä). [Also: **Abu-Hanifa;** full name, **Abu-Hanifah al-Numan ibn-Thabit** (äl.nö'män ibn.thä'bit).] b. at Kufa, in Mesopotamia, c699 or c680; d. at Medina, c768. Moslem jurist, notable as the founder of the Hanifite school of Moslem law, based on free interpretation of the Koran by judges.

Abu Hassan (ä'bö häs.sän'). Opera by Carl Maria von Weber, first performed in 1811.

Abu-Hassan (ä'bö.has'ạn). In the story of "The Sleeper Awakened" in *The Arabian Nights' Entertainments,* a citizen of Baghdad who while entertaining the disguised caliph expresses a wish to "be caliph for one day." The wish is granted in such a way that Abu-Hassan is entirely deceived as to the caliph's real identity, to the great amusement of the caliph, who in the end makes him his companion and favorite. Shakespeare has adopted this idea, from an older play, in the deception practiced on Sly, the tinker, in the induction to the *Taming of the Shrew.*

Abukir (ä.bö.kēr'). [Also, **Aboukir.**] Small village in N Egypt, on the Bay of Abukir, ab. 13 mi. NE of Alexandria, near the site of the ancient Canopus, probably a little to the west. Here, July 25, 1799, Napoleon with 5,000 French defeated 15,000 Turks. On March 8, 1801, the English under Sir Ralph Abercromby captured the town from the French.

Abukir, Bay of. [Also, **Bay of Aboukir.**] Bay N of Egypt, between Abukir and the Rosetta mouth of the Nile, the scene of the Battle of the Nile (Aug. 1–2, 1798), in which an English fleet under Nelson defeated the French fleet under Brueys, who lost 13 out of 17 vessels and some 9,000 men.

Abu Klea (ä'bö klā'ạ). [Also, **Abou-Klea.**] Wells in the Nubian desert in the bend of the Nile on the route between Korti and Shendi, where, on Jan. 17, 1885, the Mahdists attacked the British, and were repulsed with severe losses on both sides.

Abul-Abbas (ä'böl.äb.bäs'). See **Abu-al-Abbas.**

Abulfaragius (ab"ul.fạ.rā'ji.us). See **Bar-Hebraeus.**

Abulfaraj (ä'böl.fä.räj'). See **Abu-al-Faraj al-Isfahani;** see also **Bar-Hebraeus.**

Abulfazl (ä'böl.fä'zl). [Also, **Abul Fazl.**] b. 1551; d. 1602. Minister of state and historiographer of the Mogul emperor Akbar. He was the author of *Akbar Namah* (Book of Akbar), comprising a history of Akbar's reign and an account of the religious and political constitution and administration of the empire.

Abulfeda (ä'böl.fe.dä'). [Also, **Abulfida.**] b. at Damascus, 1273; d. in Syria, Oct. 26, 1331. Arab geographer and historian; a collateral descendant of Saladin. He warred against the Crusaders (1285 *et seq.*); served at the court of Malik al-Nasir (1298); and was governor (1310), prince (1312), and sultan (1320–31) of Hama, in Syria. A patron of letters, he was himself the author of a geographical work of some importance and *An Abridgement of the History of the Human Race,* a valuable source of Arab history to 1329 (published in modern times in 1869 at Constantinople).

Abulghazi Bahadur (ä.böl.gä'zē bä.hä.dör'). [Also, **Abul Ghazi Bahadur Khan.**] b. 1605; d. c1665. Khan of Khiva (1643–64). He is now best known as the author of a history of the Mongols and Tatars, which has been translated into French and various other European languages. By some accounts, this work was completed after he had abdicated as khan.

Abul Kasim (ä'böl kä'sim). [Also: **Abu-l-Qasim;** Latinized, **Abulcasis, Albucasis, Alsaharavius.**] b. near Córdoba, Spain; d. near Córdoba, Spain, c1013. Arab surgeon, considered the greatest in the Spanish-Moslem culture. His great medical encyclopaedia in 30 sections, *al-Tasrif* (*Vade mecum*), contains interesting methods of preparing drugs by sublimation and distillation, but its most important part is the surgical, in three books. Great importance is attached to cauterization and styptics. Parts of the surgery are devoted to obstetrics and to the surgical treatment of eyes, ears, and teeth. This work was illustrated with views of the surgical instruments. It was early translated into Latin, Provençal, and Hebrew. Moslem prejudices against surgery stifled his fame in Islam, but in the Christian world his prestige was soon immense.

Abul Kasim (or **Qasim**) **Mansur** (or **Hasan**) (män.sör'; hä'sạn). See **Firdausi.**

Abuncis (ạ.bun'sis). An ancient name of **Abu Simbel.**

Abu-Nuwas (ä'bö.nö.wäs'). b. in Persia, c756; d. at Baghdad, 810. Arab lyric poet at the courts of Harun al-Rashid and al-Amin, caliphs of Baghdad. He is notable among Arab poets for his songs of love and wine, and his satires of Baghdad society and of traditional poetic forms, especially the *qasīda* (elegy).

Aburi (ä.bö'rē). Town in W Africa, in Gold Coast colony, ab. 15 mi. inland from Accra. Owing to its altitude, it is used as a health resort by British residents and officials.

Abury (ā'bėr.i). See **Avebury.**

Abus (ā'bus). Latin name of the **Humber.**

Abuses Stript and Whipt. Long moralistic poem (1613) by George Wither, divided into two books.

Abu Shahrein (ä'bö shä.rān'). Modern name of **Eridu.**

Abushehr (ä.bö.sher'). See **Bushire.**

Abu Simbel (ä'bö sim'bel). [Also: **Ipsambul;** ancient names, **Abuncis, Aboccis.**] Place in Upper Egypt situated on the Nile, famous for its two rock temples, one large and the other smaller, built (c1250 B.C.) in the steep face of a cliff by Rameses II. For the great temple the rock has been cut away to form a smooth façade ab. 100 ft. wide and high, with a cornice of seated cynocephali.

Abusina (ab.ụ.sī'nạ), **Castra.** Latin name of **Abensberg.**

Abusir (ä.bö.sēr'). [Ancient name, **Busiris.**] Small town in Egypt, in the Nile valley S of Cairo, containing pyramids said to have been erected by kings of the Vth dynasty.

Abu-Tammam (ä'bö.täm.mäm'). [Also, **Abu-Teman;** full name, **Abu-Tammam Habib ibn-Aus.**] b. in Syria, 807; d. at Mosul, in Mesopotamia, c845. Arab poet and anthologist. Author of the *Diwan,* a collection of his own poems, and more notably of the *Hamasa,* an anthology of early Arabic poetry. He served as court poet at Baghdad.

Abu-Ubaida (ä'bö.ö.bī'dä). [Also, **Abu-Ubayda.**] b. at Basra, 728; d. there, c825. Arab scholar and writer. Employed (803 *et seq.*) by Harun al-Rashid at Baghdad as an antiquarian and philologist, he wrote a vast number of essays and verses, of which 105 are mentioned in the *Fihrist* (a catalogue of early Arabic writing), but of them all only one now survives. Affiliated with the Kharijite sect in politics and religion, and of Jewish-Persian parentage, he was a champion of the non-Arab Moslems.

Abyad (äb'yäd), **Bahr el.** See **White Nile.**

Abydos (ạ.bī'dọs). In ancient geography, a town in Upper Egypt on the W bank of the Nile, near what is now the village of Arabat-el-Madfuneh, famous for a temple of Osiris built by Seti I, and also for a temple built by Rameses II. The former is described by Strabo as the "Memnonion." The plan is a square facing the NE, with a large rectangular projection from the back of the SE side. From the outer court is entered the long first hall, with two ranges of columns, and from it the second hall, with three ranges. Both these great halls are ornamented with reliefs. From the second hall there is access to an extensive series of chambers, corridors, and smaller halls, all decorated with colored reliefs. In one of the corridors is the important Tablet of Abydos, from which much of our present knowledge of Egyptian chronology was deduced.

Abydos. [Also, **Abydus.**] In ancient geography, a town in Mysia, Asia Minor, on the Hellespont, noted in the legend of Hero and Leander, in Byron's *Bride of Abydos*, and as the location of the famous bridge of boats by which the Persians, under Xerxes, crossed from Asia into Europe in their assault on Greece.

Abydos, Tablet of. A block of stone in a corridor of the temple built at Abydos, in Egypt, by the Pharaoh Seti I. The inscriptions on it enabled archaeologists to establish a tentative chronology for 65 Egyptian rulers over a period of some 2,200 years.

Abydos, The Bride of. See **Bride of Abydos, The.**

Abyla (ab'i.lą). [Also: **Abyla Columna, Abyla Mons.**] In ancient geography, a promontory in Africa, the modern Jebel Musa, opposite the ancient Calpe (the modern Gibraltar). The two together constitute the famous "Pillars of Hercules" of the ancient geographers.

Abyla. An ancient name of **Ávila,** city.

Abyssinia (ab.i.sin'i.ą). See **Ethiopia.**

Acacians (ą.kā'shąnz). An early Christian sect, in some respects close to the Arians, but not actually an Arian group. The sect was named after Acacius, a bishop of Caesarea.

Acacius (ą.kā'shus). [Surnamed **Monophthalmus,** meaning "the One-eyed."] d. after 365 A.D. Bishop of Caesarea and founder of the Acacian sect, an early Christian group that favored the Arian heresy. Condemned by the semi-Arian Synod of Lampsacus in 365, he was deposed.

Academic Festival Overture. Name given to an overture (opus 80) by Johannes Brahms, written for the University of Breslau in appreciation of the conferring of an honorary degree upon the composer, and embodying a number of German student songs.

Academic Legion. Name once generally applied to armed student corps in the European insurrections of 1848, and particularly to one at Vienna which was prominent in the revolt of that year.

Académie de Musique et de Danse (à.kà.dā.mē dę mü.zēk ā dę däṅs). A state-supported institution at Paris for the performance of opera and ballet. Established (1669) by a grant from Louis XIV and opened (1671) as the Académie des Opéras with Cambert's pastoral *Pomone*, its official title has been changed several times since 1672; popularly, it is now known as the "Opéra."

Academy. See also under other elements of the full name for important academies not listed immediately below. Where usage has indicated the desirability of doing so (as with "French Academy" and "Royal Academy") entry has been made under the initial element of the name rather than under the word "Academy."

Academy. [Greek, **Akademeia, Akademia.**] Name applied to what was originally a public pleasure-ground on the Cephissus, about one mile NW of ancient Athens, on land said to have belonged, in the time of the Trojan war, to the hero Academus. It was surrounded with a wall by Hipparchus and further adorned by Cimon, the son of Miltiades, who bequeathed it to the citizens of Athens. It was the resort of Plato, who taught in its groves for nearly 50 years.

Academy. Term applied to the Platonic school of philosophy down to the time of Cicero; so called from the pleasure-ground of the same name. It is commonly divided into the Old, the Middle, and the New Academy. The chief representatives of the first were, in addition to Plato himself, Speusippus, Xenocrates of Chalcedon, Polemo, Crates, and Crantor. The Middle Academy was founded by Arcesilaus ab. 244 B.C., and the New Academy by Carneades ab. 160 B.C. Sometimes the academies of Philo and Antiochus are spoken of as the Fourth Academy and the Fifth Academy, respectively.

Academy, Royal Spanish. [Spanish, **Real Academia Española.**] Organization founded at Madrid in 1713 by the Duke of Escalona, and established by royal confirmation in 1714, with the object of cultivating and improving the national language.

Academy, Swedish. [Earlier names: **Royal Swedish Academy, Academy of Sciences at Stockholm.**] Society, originally private, founded June 2, 1739, and originally incorporated March 31, 1741, as the Royal Swedish Academy. Its quarterly publications, *Svenska Akademiens Handlingar*, are issued in annual volumes, of which the first 40 (1779) form a series known in English as the *Old Transactions*.

Academy of Ancient Music. Organization established (c1710) at London by a group of instrumental performers for the purpose of learning and performing group works. It was active until 1792.

Academy of Arcadians (är.kā'di.ąnz). [Also, **Society of Arcadians.**] Society founded in 1690 in Italy by Giovan Mario Crescimbeni and Gian Vincenzo Gravina. Its chief aim was to establish in literature the simplicity of the shepherds of the fabled golden age of Arcadia.

Academy of Fine Arts. [French, **Académie des Beaux-Arts** (à.kà.dā.mē dā bō.zàr).] Institution at Paris, originating in a private association of painters in the 14th century, recognized by royal French authority in 1648 as the Academy of Painting and Sculpture, and definitively constructed in 1655 by Cardinal Mazarin. At the creation of the National Institute in 1795 it was united with the Academy of Architecture, founded by Colbert in 1671, to form the fourth class of the institute; and since 1819 this class has borne the name of Academy of Fine Arts. It consists of 40 members and a secretary, ten honorary academicians, ten foreign associates, and 50 correspondents. It publishes its memoirs and transactions and the *Dictionnaire géneral des beaux-arts*.

Academy of Fine Arts. Institution at Florence, Italy, occupying the building formerly known as the Ospedale di San Matteo. The pictures in the collection represent especially the Italian painters of the 15th century. In the "domed room" is Michelangelo's statue of David and a collection of casts of the sculptor's work.

Academy of Fine Arts. Institution at Venice which occupies the old Scuola di Santa Maria della Carità on the Grand Canal. The gallery, which was founded in 1798, is devoted to paintings by Venetian masters.

Academy of France at Rome. [French, **Académie de France à Rome** (à.kà.dā.mē dę fräṅs à rom).] School of fine arts founded at Rome by Louis XIV, where those artists are sent, at the public expense, who obtain the annual prizes of the Academy of Fine Arts at Paris.

Academy of Inscriptions and Belles-Lettres. [French, **Académie des Inscriptions et Belles-Lettres** (à.kà-dā.mē dā.zaṅ.skrēp.syôṅ ā bel.letr).] Association composed originally of four members, chosen by Colbert from among the members of the French Academy to draw up inscriptions for the monuments erected by Louis XIV and the medals struck in his honor. It received a separate organization in 1701, which was confirmed by the letters patent of Louis XIV in 1712. It was suppressed by the Convention in 1793, but at the creation of the National Institute in 1795 its members were incorporated in that body. In 1816 the title was restored by Louis XVIII for the second class of the Institute. It has 40 members, 15 free members, 12 foreign associates, and 30 French and 40 foreign correspondents.

Academy of Medicine. [French, **Académie de Médecine** (à.kà.dā.mē dę māt.sēn).] Organization founded in France in 1820 to preserve vaccine matter and act as a bureau of information to the government on sanitation and the public health. It publishes memoirs and carries on an extensive correspondence.

Academy of Moral and Political Sciences. [French, **Académie des Sciences Morales et Politiques** (à.kà-dā.mē dā syäṅs mo.ràl ā po.lē.tēk).] Organization founded as the fifth class of the French National Institute. It was originally established in 1795, suppressed by Napoleon in 1803, and reëstablished by Louis Philippe in 1832. It has 40 members, 10 honorary academicians, 12 foreign associates, and 60 corresponding members.

Academy of Motion Picture Arts and Sciences. Organization founded in the U.S. in 1927 for the purpose of advancing the arts and sciences of motion pictures. It maintains headquarters at Los Angeles, Calif., has a library of some 3,000 volumes on the history and development of motion pictures, and makes "Annual Awards of Merit" (usually called "Oscars") for outstanding achievement in various phases of motion-picture acting, writing, and production.

Academy of Natural Sciences of Philadelphia. A scientific institution organized at Philadelphia in 1812, and incorporated in 1817, possessing a valuable library relating chiefly to natural history, and an extensive collection of specimens in natural history. Its publications consist of *Proceedings* from 1841, *Frontiers* (1936 *et seq.*), and *Notulae Naturae* (1939 *et seq.*).

Academy of Political Science. Organization established in the U.S. in 1880 for the purpose of contributing toward an informed public opinion. It maintains headquarters at Columbia University and publishes the *Political Science Quarterly* and *Proceedings*.

Academy of Science of St. Louis. Organization founded at St. Louis in 1856 for the purpose of promoting science and establishing a museum and library of scientific works. The latter contains more than 70,000 volumes. The academy issues *Transactions* (irregularly).

Academy of Sciences. [French, **Académie des Sciences** (à.kà.dā.mē dā syàṅs).] Institution founded at Paris in 1666 by Colbert, approved by Louis XIV in 1699, suppressed by the Convention in 1793, and reconstituted in 1795 as a class of the National Institute. It numbers 66 members, 10 honorary academicians, 12 foreign associates, and 110 corresponding members.

Academy of Sciences and Letters, Royal Danish. [Danish, **Det Kongelige Danske Videnskabernes Selskab.**] An academy established as a private society in 1742, and received under royal Danish protection in 1743.

Academy of Sciences at Berlin, German. [German, **Deutsche Akademie der Wissenschaften zu Berlin** (doi′chẹ ä.kä.dā.mē′ dėr vis′ẹn.shäf.tẹn tsö ber.lēn′).] Institution founded in 1700 by Frederick I, according to plans submitted by Leibniz, and opened in 1711. It was formerly known as the Royal Academy of Sciences at Berlin. It has 55 members, more than 100 correspondents, a library containing some 55,000 volumes, and has sections on natural science, mathematics, history, and philosophy.

Acadia (ạ.kā′di.ạ). [French, **Acadie** (à.kà.dē).] Former French colony in North America, approximating the modern Nova Scotia in geographical extent, bounded by the Atlantic Ocean, the Gulf of St. Lawrence, the St. Lawrence River, and westward by a line running N from the mouth of the Penobscot River. It was colonized by France in 1604, on the Bay of Fundy, and ceded (except for Cape Breton Island, which remained French until 1763) to Great Britain by the Treaty of Utrecht, in 1713. The French settlers in Nova Scotia were deported by the British in 1755, from which event Longfellow derived the basis for his poem *Evangeline*.

Acahaí (ä.kä.ī′). City in SW Paraguay, in Paraguarí department. 13,000 (est.).

Acajutla (ä.kä.ʜöt′lä). Town in SW El Salvador, in Sonsonate department, ab. 40 mi. W of San Salvador: seaport and railroad terminus; exports coffee. Pop. under 5,000 (est. 1942).

Acámbaro (ä.käm′bä.rō). City in C Mexico, in Guanajuato state, ab. 90 mi. NW of Mexico City. 17,643 (1940).

Acampichtli or **Acampixtli** (ä.käm.pēsh′tlē). [Eng. trans., "*Handful of Reeds.*"] d. 1403. Chief of the Aztecs of Mexico, who, according to one chronology, was elected in 1375. He led the Indians of Tenochtitlan in their wars with Tecpan, and canals and stone houses were first made in his time. Although sometimes called a "king," his power was very limited.

Acapulco (ä.kä.pöl′kō). [Full name, **Acapulco de Juárez.**] City in SW Mexico, in Guerrero state, on the Pacific Ocean. It has been developed during the 20th century as a major Mexican resort, and today attracts many tourists from the U.S. Possessed of one of the best harbors in the country, it had a large commerce during the 17th and 18th centuries, particularly during the Spanish colonization of the Philippines. It suffered a severe earthquake in July, 1909. Pop. 9,993 (1940).

Acarahy Mountains (ä″kạ.rạ.ē′). [Portuguese, **Serra Acaraí.**] Mountain range in NE South America, forming part of the border between Brazil and British Guiana.

Acarnania (ak.ạr.nā′ni.ạ). [Also, **Akarnania.**] In ancient geography, a division of Greece, bounded by the Ambracian Gulf on the N, by Amphilochia on the NE, by Aetolia on the E (partly separated by the Achelous River), and by the Ionian Sea on the W. Its ancient inhabitants were the Leleges and Curetes. They were considered rude mountaineers by the people of the Greek city-states, but were nevertheless regarded as Hellenes, and as such were allowed to participate in the Panhellenic games.

Acaste (à.kàst). Character in Molière's play *Le Misanthrope*, a gay and brilliant marquis, a lover of Célimène.

Acasto (ạ.kas′tō). Character in Thomas Otway's play *The Orphan*, a nobleman, the father of Polydore and Castalio, retired from the court and living on his estates.

Acastus (ạ.kas′tus) or **Akastos** (-tos). In Greek legend, a son of King Pelias of Iolcos, an Argonaut, and one of the hunters of the Calydonian boar; father of Laodamia. He was killed by Peleus, king of the Myrmidons, whom his wife had falsely accused and whose magic sword he had stolen.

Acawa (ak′ạ.wạ). See **Chewa.**

Acawai (ä.kä.wä.ē′). [Also: **Akawai, Wakawai.**] Indian tribe of British Guiana, whose settlements were once located on the Cuyuni, Barama, Barima, and Pomeroon rivers. The Acawai language belongs to the Cariban linguistic stock.

Acaxee (ä.käsh′ē). Indian tribe, now extinct, which once inhabited part of the state of Durango, Mexico. Its language was a member of the Uto-Aztecan stock.

Acca (ak′ạ). Arabic name of **Acre,** Palestine.

Accad (ak′ad, äk′äd). See **Akkad.**

Accademia della Crusca (äk.kä.dā′myä del.lä krös′kä). Academy founded at Florence in 1582 by the poet Grazzini, with the object of purifying the Italian language and literature. It published in 1612 the first edition of the *Vocabolario degli Accademici della Crusca*, long the standard dictionary of the Italian language.

Acca Larentia (or **Laurentia**) (ak′ạ lạ.ren′shi.ạ; lô.ren′shi.ạ). Variously identified in Roman legend: **1.** as the wife of Faustulus and nurse of Romulus and Remus, her nickname Lupa (she-wolf, or courtesan) being perhaps the source of the story that they were raised by a wolf. **2.** as a beautiful woman won in gambling by Hercules, wife of an Etruscan whose wealth she bequeathed to the Romans, honored by their festival called Larentalia.

Accau or **Accault** (à.kō), **Michel.** See **Aco, Michel.**

Accho (ak′ō). Old Testament name of **Acre,** Palestine.

Acciajuoli (ät.chä.ywô′lē) or **Acciajoli** (ät.chä.yô′lē), **Donato.** b. at Florence, 1428; d. at Milan, Aug. 28, 1478. Italian scholar and government official. He was gonfalonier, or chancellor, of Florence in 1473. Author of lives of Hannibal, Scipio, and Charlemagne, of a translation of some of Plutarch's *Lives*, and of commentaries on Aristotle's *Ethics* and *Politics*.

Acciajuoli or **Acciajoli, Nerio.** Italian nobleman, a member of the Florentine family of that name, created Duke of Athens in 1394. The title and the Athenian seat were retained by his successors till 1456, when the Turks put an end to the domination of parts of Greece by various of the Italian city-states.

Acciajuoli or **Acciajoli, Niccolò.** d. 1365. Florentine banker and statesman. He served for many years as the chief adviser of Joanna, Queen of Naples, and was invested in 1358 with the barony and hereditary governorship of the fortress of Corinth, in Greece.

Accioli de Cerqueira e Silva (äk.syō′lē dẹ ser.kā′rạ ẹ sēl′vạ), **Ignacio.** b. at Coimbra, Portugal, 1808; d. at Rio de Janeiro, Aug. 1, 1865. Brazilian geographer. When very young he emigrated with his father to Brazil, and in 1833 began the publication of a series of geographical works on the Brazilian empire, of which he was made official chronicler.

Accius (ak′shi.us), **Lucius.** [Also, **Attius.**] b. c170 B.C.; d. c90 B.C. Roman tragic poet and prose writer notable for his Greek adaptations, though he dealt also with Roman subjects.

Acco (ak′ō). Old Testament name of **Acre,** Palestine.

Accolon (ak′ọ.lon). Character in the *Morte d'Arthur*, a knight of Gaul, celebrated for his combat with King Arthur. In this combat the latter sought to regain his enchanted sword and scabbard, of which Accolon had gained possession through the aid of Morgan le Fay.

Accolti (äk.kôl'tē), **Benedetto.** b. at Arezzo, Italy, 1415; d. at Florence, 1466. Italian jurist and writer, gonfalonier, or chancellor, of the Florentine republic (1459–66). He was a brother of Leonardo Accolti.

Accolti, Benedetto. b. at Florence, 1497; d. 1549. Italian cardinal and poet; nephew of Pietro Accolti (1455–1532). He was the author of Latin poems collected in *Carmina illustrium poetarum Italorum.*

Accolti, Bernardo. [Called **"l'Unico Aretino."**] b. c1465; d. c1535. Italian poet; son of Benedetto Accolti (1415–66). He was famous in his day, particularly as an extemporaneous poet, and is known (partly through Castiglione's *The Courtier*) to many modern readers of Italian literature.

Accolti, Francesco. b. at Arezzo, Italy, 1418; d. at Siena, Italy, 1483. Italian jurist, professor of law at Bologna and Ferrara, and secretary to the duke of Milan; brother of Benedetto Accolti (1415–66).

Accolti, Leonardo. fl. 15th century. Italian historian and writer. He shared the authorship, with his brother, Benedetto Accolti (1415–66), of a history of the First Crusade used by Tasso as a source for *Jerusalem Delivered.*

Accolti, Pietro. [Called **"Cardinal of Ancona."**] b. at Florence, 1455; d. there, 1532. Italian cardinal and legate in Ancona; brother of Bernardo Accolti (c1465–c1535). As abbreviator under Pope Leo X, he drew up the bull against Luther in 1520. He was made archbishop of Ravenna in 1524 by Pope Clement VII.

Accoramboni (äk"kō.räm.bô'nē), **Vittoria.** [Title, Duchess of **Bracciano.**] b. at Rome, c1557; d. at Padua, Dec. 22, 1585. Italian beauty, whose tragic story has been used by numerous writers in the centuries since her death. Her first husband, Francesco Peretti, was murdered (1581) at the instigation of Paolo Giordano Orsini, Duke of Bracciano, whom she subsequently married. On his death (1585) she became involved in litigation with Lodovic Orsini concerning the inheritance, and was murdered by him. These events were adapted in Webster's tragedy *The White Devil, or Vittoria Corombona* (1612), recounted by the biographer Gnoli (1870), and made the subject of a novel by Ludwig Tieck, *Vittoria Accoramboni* (1840).

Accorso (äk.kōr'sō), **Buono.** [Also: **Buonaccorso;** Latinized, **Accursius.**] b. at Pisa, Italy, c1450. Italian classical scholar and rhetorician, a commentator on Caesar and other Latin authors.

Accorso, Francesco. [Latinized, **Franciscus Accursius.**] b. at Bagnolo, Tuscany, or in Florence, c1182; d. at Bologna, c1260. Italian jurist, for a time teacher of law at Bologna. His most celebrated work was a methodical compilation of all the commentaries on Roman law, called, in English, *The Great Gloss.* This work remained the final authority until the time of Bartolo (late 14th century).

Accorso, Francesco. [Latinized, **Franciscus Accursius.**] b. at Bologna, 1225; d. there, 1293. Italian jurist; son of Francesco Accorso (c1182–c1260). He was professor of law at Bologna, entered the service of Edward I of England, and lectured on law at Oxford (c1275).

Accorso, Mariangelo. [Latinized, **Accursius.**] b. at Aquila, Italy, c1490; d. 1544. Italian literary critic at the court of Charles V. He was the author of *Diatribae in Ausonium, Jul. Solin Polyhistora, et in Ovidii Metamorphoses* (1524), and editor of *Ammianus Marcellinus* (1553), and others.

Account of Corsica. Narrative (1768) by James Boswell, written as a result of a visit to Corsica in 1765. In it Boswell clearly reveals his sympathy for the Corsicans in their lengthy period of rebellion (1729–68) against control by Genoa. The book was published in the year that Corsica was sold by Genoa to France.

Accra (ak'ra̤, a̤.krä'). [Also: **Akkra, Akra.**] City in W Africa, the capital and largest city of the Gold Coast, situated on the Gulf of Guinea ab. 60 mi. W of the mouth of the Volta River. An important port, it is connected by rail with the cocoa-growing districts and the major towns of the interior. It is the educational center of the area, with several schools and a college. The chief exports of the port are cocoa, kola, lumber, and palm oil. 135,926 (1948).

Accrington (ak'ring.to̤n). Municipal borough and market town in NW England, in Lancashire, situated on the river Hinburn, ab. 20 mi. NW of Manchester, ab. 205 mi. NW of London by rail. Its industries include the manufacture of cheap cotton cloth, calico printing, dyeing, iron founding, and the manufacture of textile machinery, 40,671 (1951).

Accum (äk'ům), **Friedrich Christian.** b. at Bückeburg, Germany, 1769; d. at Berlin, June 28, 1838. German chemist, long resident in London. He is known chiefly for his *Practical Treatise on Gas-light* (1815), and his efforts to promote the use of gas for purposes of illumination.

Accursius (a̤.kėr'shi.us; -shus). Latinized form of **Accorso.**

Aceldama (a.sel'da̤.ma̤). Field said to have been situated S of Jerusalem, the Potter's Field, purchased with the bribe which Judas took for betraying Jesus (whence the name, meaning "field of blood" in Aramaic). It was later appropriated to the interment of strangers, and it was from this use that the term "potter's field" came to mean a burying ground for paupers. Mat. xxvii. 8; Acts, i. 19.

Acelum (as'e̤.lum). Ancient name of **Asolo.**

Acephali (a̤.sef'a̤.lī). Name given to various 5th and 6th century Christian groups who repudiated the authority of all bishops and other church heads (the name derives from a Greek word meaning "without a head"). Most notable among them were the Monophysites, who in 482 rejected the authority of Peter Mongus, bishop of Alexandria, on doctrinal grounds.

Acerbas (a̤.sėr'ba̤s) or **Akerbas** (-kėr'-). [Also, **Sicharbas.**] In classical legend, uncle and husband of Elissa, a wealthy and powerful Tyrian noble, high priest of the Tyrian god Melkarth. In Vergil's *Aeneid* Acerbas was Sichaeus, husband of Dido (Elissa), murdered for his riches by her brother Pygmalion. Dido was able, however, when she fled from Tyre and founded Carthage, to take the treasure with her.

Acerbi (ä.cher'bē), **Giuseppe.** b. at Castel-Goffredo, near Mantua, Italy, May 3, 1773; d. Aug. 26, 1846. Italian scholar, traveler, and naturalist. One of the founders (1816) of *Biblioteca Italiana,* a literary magazine, he is remembered also as the author of *Travels through Sweden, Finland, and Lapland to the North Cape in the Years 1798 and 1799* (Eng. trans., 1802).

Acernus (a̤.sėr'nus), **Sebastian.** See **Klonowicz, Sebastjan Fabjan.**

Acerra (ä.cher'rä). [Latin, **Acerrae.**] Town and commune in S Italy, in the *compartimento* (region) of Campania, in the province of Napoli, situated on the Carmignano Canal, ab. 10 mi. NE of Naples. It is an agricultural community. Pop. of commune, 21,973 (1936); of town, 19,177 (1936).

Acesines (a̤.ses'i.nēz). Ancient name of the **Chenab.**

Acestes (a̤.ses'tēz). In Greek legend, a son of the Sicilian river-god Crimisus and Egesta (Segesta), a Trojan woman. He figured in the Trojan War, and was introduced by Vergil in the *Aeneid.*

Acevedo Díaz (ä.sā.ʙā'ᴛʜō dē'äs), **Eduardo.** b. 1851; d. in exile, 1924. Uruguayan historical novelist whose work, written entirely in his several periods of exile, stimulated and was a model for much modern *gaucho* prose in Uruguay and Argentina. Author of *Ismael* (1888), *Nativa* (1890), *Grito de gloria* (1894), and *Soledad* (1894), the first three of which have been said to constitute a nationalistic "hymn to blood."

Ach (äċh), **Narziss.** b. Oct. 29, 1871—. German psychologist, a member of Külpe's "Würzburg School." In his *Über die Willenstätigkeit und das Denken* (1905) he presented three notable contributions to psychology: (1) the concept of determining tendency, (2) the concept of awareness (*bewusstseinlage*), and (3) the technique of systematic experimental introspection. He accepted a professorial chair at Göttingen upon the retirement of G. E. Müller in 1921.

Achá (ä.chä'), **José María de.** b. c1805; d. at Cochabamba, Bolivia, 1868. Bolivian revolutionist. He served under Santa Cruz (1829–39), and under José Ballivián in the war against Peru (1841). Appointed (1858) minister of war by President Linares, he revolted, and in May, 1861, was proclaimed president of Bolivia. During the four years of his administration Bolivia was the victim of much civil strife, and he was himself deposed (1865) through the successful revolt of a rival politician.

Achaea (ą.kē′ą). [Also: **Achaia** (ą.kā′ą); called **Achaea Phthiotis** (thī.ō′tis).] In ancient geography, a small region in S Thessaly, containing Phthia. It was probably the original home of the Achaean people, and it retained its name as late as the time of Herodotus.

Achaea. [Also: **Achaia;** original name, **Aegialus** or **Aegialeia,** meaning "The Coast."] In ancient geography, a mountainous district in the Peloponnesus, bordering on the Gulf of Corinth, N of Elis and Arcadia.

Achaea. [Also, **Achaia.**] In ancient geography, a collective term applied to the states forming the Achaean League (c280–146 B.C.).

Achaea. [Also, **Achaia.**] In ancient geography, a Roman province, of uncertain limits, but corresponding approximately to modern Greece, formed probably in the first century B.C. Its northern boundary was probably drawn south of Thessaly and Epirus. The province was abolished by Nero, but was reëstablished by Vespasian.

Achaea. [Also, **Achaia.**] In medieval geography, a Frankish principality in Greece, corresponding generally to the Peloponnesus.

Achaea. [Also: **Akhaia, Achaia.**] In modern geography, a *nomos* (department) in S Greece, situated on the N coast of the Peloponnesus. It includes the provinces of Aegialia, Kalavryta, and Patras. Capital, Patras; area, 2,065 sq. mi. pop. 221,633 (1940).

Achaean League (ą.kē′ąn). A religious confederation in Achaea, consisting at the time of Herodotus of 12 cities: Pellene, Aegeira, Aegae, Bura, Helike, Aegion, Rhypes, Patrae, Pharae, Olenos, Dyme, and Tritaea. Somewhat later, Rhypes and Aegae fell into decay, and their places in the confederacy were taken by Leontion and Keryneia.

Achaean League. A political confederation of Achaean and other Greek cities extending over the period of 281 B.C. to 146 B.C. After the death of Lysimachus in 280 B.C., the Achaean cities Dyme, Patrae, Tritaea, and Pharae formed a confederation to resist the Macedonian domination, and were afterward joined by the other Achaean cities, except Olenos and Helike. In 251 B.C. the confederation acquired new strength by the accession of Sikyon, under the leadership of Aratus. In 245 B.C. Aratus was elected strategus of the league, which under his guidance rapidly rose to national importance. In a short time it embraced Athens, Aegina, Salamis, and the whole of Peloponnesus, with the exception of Sparta, Tegea, Orchomenos, Mantineia, and Elis. It was destroyed by the Romans in 146 B.C., and with it fell the last stronghold of freedom in Greece. The Achaean League is remarkable as one of the most perfect types of federal government which has been handed down from antiquity. The confederation was inseparable, every city having equal rights with the others; in foreign affairs the federal government was supreme. Common affairs were regulated at general meetings held twice a year by the citizens of all the towns.

Achaeans (ą.kē′ąnz). [Also: **Achaei** (ą.kē′ī), **Achaians** (ą.kā′ąnz), **Achivi** (ą.kī′vī).] One of the four principal peoples of ancient Greece (the Aeolians, Dorians, and Ionians were the other three). Their chief places of abode were S Thessaly and the E part of the Peloponnesus. The name is applied generally to all Greeks in Homeric poetry, and to some extent by poets in later times. The Achaeans formed the ethnic basis of the Achaean League which lasted until 146 B.C., when the Romans finally subjugated the Greeks.

Achaemenes (ą.kē′mę.nēz). [Old Persian, **Hakhāmaniš,** meaning "the Friendly."] fl. c7th cent. B.C. Eponymous founder (possibly mythical) of the ancient Persian royal family of the Achaemenidae. He was, initially, ruler of Anshan, in SW Persia. His name was later used as a family name, beginning (550 B.C.) with Cyrus.

Achaemenidae (ak.ę.men′i.dē). [Also: **Achaemenides** (-dēz), **Achemenides, Achemenids.**] Ancient royal family of Persia, founded c600 B.C. Its leading members were Achaemenes, Cyrus the Great, Cambyses (Gomates, the Magian usurper), Darius Hystaspis, Xerxes I, Artaxerxes I, Xerxes II, Sogdianos, Darius Ochus, Artaxerxes Mnemon, Ochus, Arses, and Darius Codomannus.

Achaeus (ą.kē′us) or **Achaios** (ą.kā′os). fl. c484–448 B.C. Greek poet of Eretria in Euboea. He was the author of 44 dramas, only fragments of which remain, and of which the titles of only 17 are now known. He contended with Sophocles and Euripides in the great Hellenic drama contests of his day.

Achalm (äċh′älm). Mountain peak in S Germany, in Württemberg, near Reutlingen. 2,313 ft.

Achamoth (ak′ą.moth). Name given by the Gnostic philosopher Valentinus to a lower or imperfect Wisdom, the weakest aeon, the form under which spirit surrenders itself completely to matter and becomes the foundation of the real world.

Achan (ā′kan). [Also, **Achar** (ā′kär).] In the Old Testament, an Israelite of the tribe of Judah, stoned to death, with his family, for plundering during the sack of Jericho. Josh. vii; 1 Chron. ii. 7.

Achard (äċh′ärt), **Franz Karl.** b. at Berlin, April 28, 1753; d. in Silesia, April 20, 1821. German chemist, notable as a pioneer in beet-sugar manufacture and as the discoverer of a method for working platinum. Following Marggraf's discovery of sugar in beets, he conducted experiments and a school in beet-sugar manufacture on a government-granted Silesian estate.

Achard (å.shȧr), **Louis Amédée Eugène.** b. at Marseilles, in April, 1814; d. at Paris, March 25, 1875. French novelist and dramatist. He was the author of *La Belle Rose* (1847), *La Chasse Royale* (1849–50), and others.

Achard, Marcel. b. at Sainte-Foy-lès-Lyon, France, July 5, 1899—. French dramatist, particularly successful with whimsical comedy. His plays include *Voulez-vous jouer avec moâ* (1923), *La Vie est belle* (1928), *La Belle Marinière* (1929), and *Jean de la Lune* (1929). The last is his best-known work, because of the international success of the motion picture based upon it.

Acharius (ä.kä′ri.ùs), **Erik.** b. at Gefle, Sweden, Oct. 10, 1757; d. at Wadstena, Sweden, Aug. 14, 1819. Swedish physician and botanist. A specialist in lichens, he was a pupil of Linnaeus. Author of *Lichenographia universalis* (1804) and *Synopsis methodica Lichenum* (1814).

Acharnians (ą.kär′ni.ąnz), **The.** Comedy of Aristophanes, first brought out, under the name of Callistratus, at the Lenaea, or country Dionysia, at Athens, in 425 B.C. It was an attempt to support the aristocratic peace-party against the intrigues and intimidations of the democratic war-party represented by the chorus of Acharnians. In form it is an extravagant farce rather than a comedy.

Achates (ą.kā′tēz). Faithful companion (called *fidus Achates*) of Aeneas, and hence in literary usage sometimes used to mean any follower, adherent, or companion of great loyalty.

Ache (dȧsh), **Caran d'.** See **Caran d'Ache.**

Acheen (ä.chēn′). See **Atjeh.**

Achehnese (ach.ę.nēs′, -nēz′). [Also: **Achenese, Achinese, Atjehnese, Atjenese.**] A Malayo-Polynesian-speaking, rice-growing coastal people of N Sumatra.

Achelous (ak.e.lō′us). [Modern Greek, **Akheloos, Aspropotamos.**] River in NW Greece which rises in Epirus, in the Pindus Mountains, forms part of the boundary between what was ancient Aetolia and Acarnania, and flows into the Ionian Sea. It is not commercially navigable, but it is important in modern Greece as a source of hydroelectric power. Length, ab. 130 mi.

Achelous. In Greek mythology, a river god, defeated by Hercules in a struggle over Deianira.

Achemenides (ak.ę.men′i.dēz) or **Achemenids** (ak.ę-men′idz). See **Achaemenidae.**

Achenbach (ä′ċhęn.bäċh), **Andreas.** b. at Cassel, Germany, Sept. 29, 1815; d. 1910. German landscape and marine painter; brother of Oswald Achenbach (1815–1910). He was a pioneer in 19th-century German realism.

Achenbach, Max. [Stage name, **Max Alvary.**] b. at Düsseldorf, Germany, c1858; d. 1898. German operatic tenor; son of Andreas Achenbach (1815–1910). He made his debut at Weimar, and later (1884–89) performed at New York.

Achenbach, Oswald. b. at Düsseldorf, Germany, Feb. 2, 1827; d. there, 1905. German landscape painter, chiefly of Italian subjects; brother of Andreas Achenbach (1815–1910). His paintings are notable for their richness of color.

Acheng (ä′cheng′). [Also: **Ajeho, Alchoku, Ashehoh.**] Town in NE China, in the province of Sunkiang, Manchuria, ab. 20 mi. SE of Harbin, in a wheat and millet growing area. Pop. ab. 5,000.

Achen Lake (äċh'ẹn). [German, **Achensee** (äċh'ẹn.zā).] Small lake in W Austria, in the Tirol, lying N of the valley of the lower Inn. It empties into the Isar. Length, ab. 5½ mi.

Achenwall (äċh'ẹn.väl), **Gottfried.** b. at Elbing, Prussia, Oct. 20, 1719; d. at Göttingen, Germany, May 1, 1772. German scholar, professor of philosophy (1748 *et seq.*) and of law (1761 *et seq.*) at the University of Göttingen. He is considered by some authorities to have been the founder of the science of statistics.

Achern (äċh'ėrn). Town in S Germany, in the *Land* (state) of Baden, French Zone, ab. 31 mi. SW of Karlsruhe: wine trade; metallurgical and paper manufactures. The insane asylum of Illenau is in the vicinity. 4,391 (1947).

Achernar (a.kėr'när). Name given to the blue first-magnitude star α Eridani, at the southern extremity of the constellation Eridanus, 32½ degrees from the South Pole.

Acheron (ak'ẹ.ron). In ancient geography, the name of several small rivers in Greece, of which the chief (the modern Gurla) was in Thesprotia in Epirus. It flowed through the lake Acherusia, received the waters of the Cocytus (the modern Vuvos), and emptied into the Ionian Sea.

Acheron. In Greek mythology, one of the five rivers surrounding Hades, the river of woe. The souls of the dead had to bathe in it or cross it. Later it became synonymous with the lower world in general.

Acheron. An ancient name of **Fusaro Lake.**

Acherusia Palus (ak.ẹ.rö'si.ạ pā'lus). [Eng. trans., "*Acherusian Bog.*"] In ancient geography, the name of several small lakes supposed to be connected with the lower world. The most important were the lake through which the Acheron flowed, and one ab. 11 mi. W of Naples, the modern Fusaro Lake. Like Acheron, the name came to be applied, in ancient literary usage, to the lower world itself.

Acheson (ach'ẹ.sọn), **Dean Gooderham.** b. at Middletown, Conn., April 11, 1893—. American lawyer and statesman. He was graduated (1915) from Yale, and in 1918 received his law degree from Harvard. He then served (1919–21) as private secretary to Supreme Court Justice Louis D. Brandeis, and in 1921 joined the law firm of Covington, Burling, and Rublee (Washington, D. C.), of which he became a partner in 1934. During the early New Deal period he was undersecretary of the treasury (May 19–Nov. 15, 1933). In 1941 he was named assistant secretary of state, and in 1945 was appointed undersecretary of state, holding that post until 1947. On Jan. 7, 1949, he was named U.S. secretary of state, succeeding George C. Marshall. During the first year of his service he took a leading role in the discussions which culminated in the signing of the Atlantic Pact by the U.S., France, Great Britain, Norway, Italy, and other nations. He presided in 1951 over the meeting of the Allies at San Francisco that saw the signing of a peace treaty with Japan, and was succeeded as secretary of state in January, 1953, by John Foster Dulles.

Acheson, Edward Goodrich. b. at Washington, Pa., March 9, 1856; d. at New York, July 6, 1931. American inventor and technician, notable for his development of carborundum. With Edison, he installed the first electric lights in Belgium, the Netherlands, and Italy (c1885). He later organized the Acheson Graphite Company (1899), and patented processes for Egyptianizing clay and for producing synthetic graphite.

Acheulean Period (ạ.shė'lẹ.ạn). Stage of early Paleolithic development during which the techniques of Chellean hand-axe manufacture were further developed. In time it apparently coincides with the gradual onset of the last glaciation in Europe; the woolly rhinoceros and the mammoth are associated with the period. It seems to have been succeeded by the Mousterian Period.

Achewa (ach'ẹ.wạ). See **Chewa.**

Ach Gott vom Himmel (äċh got fom him'ẹl). Hymn by Martin Luther published in 1524, the melody of which is used in Mozart's *Magic Flute.*

Achikunda (ach.i.kůn'dạ). See **Chikunda.**

Achill (ak'il). [Also: **Achil, Eagle Island.**] Island in W Ireland, in Connacht province of the Irish Republic, County Mayo. It lies off the W coast of that county, and is the largest island off the coast of Ireland, with which it is connected by a bridge. Its highest elevation is Slievemore (2,204 ft.). Area, 80 sq. mi.

Achilleis (ak.i.lē'is). [Also, **Achilleid** (-id).] Unfinished epic poem by the Roman poet Publius Papinius Statius.

Achilleis. [Also, **Achilleid.**] Name given to the part of the *Iliad* comprised by Books I, VIII, and XI–XXII, regarded by some critics as constituting a poem of which the theme is the "wrath of Achilles," and which is distinct from, and older than, the rest of the *Iliad.* The name *Achilleis* was first applied to these books by George Grote.

Achilles (ạ.kil'ēz). In Greek legend, a great warrior, one of the chief heroes of the Trojan War. He is said to have been the son of Peleus and Thetis, the grandson of Aeacus, and chief of the Myrmidons, a Thessalian tribe. According to the legend of his life, he was educated by the centaur Chiron. He is the central hero of Homer's *Iliad,* which is largely occupied with his quarrel with Agamemnon, leader of the Greek host, and with his martial exploits. He was the slayer of Hector, and was himself slain by Paris, who pierced his heel, Achilles' only vulnerable spot (all other portions of his body had been rendered invulnerable when his mother, holding him by the heel, had immersed him as a child in the river Styx).

Achilles Tatius (tā'shus). fl. in the late 2nd century (or during the 3rd century) A.D. Greek astronomer who was one of the many commentators on the astronomical work, in verse, now usually spelled *Phenomena* (or *Phainomena*), written by Aratos of Soli. His commentary, entitled *On the Sphere* is preserved only in a fragmentary condition.

Achilles Tatius. fl. probably in 4th century A.D. Greek rhetorician at Alexandria, in Egypt. He was the author of the Greek romance *Adventures of Leucippe and Cleitophon.*

Achilleum (ak.i.lē'um). In ancient geography, a place on the promontory of Sigeum, in NW Asia Minor, in the Troad, containing, according to tradition, the tomb of Achilles.

Achill Head (ak'il). Promontory in W Ireland, at the W extremity of the island of Achill, in Connacht province of the Irish Republic, County Mayo. Elevation, 2,192 ft.

Achillini (ä.kēl.lē'nē), **Alessandro.** [Called **"the Second Aristotle."**] b. at Bologna, Italy, Oct. 29, 1463; d. Aug. 2, 1512. Italian anatomist and philosopher. One of the first European medical scholars to dissect cadavers; he served as professor of both philosophy and medicine at the universities of Bologna and Padua. He was the author of works in both fields, but is best known for his contributions as an anatomist.

Achin (ä.chēn'). See **Atjeh.**

Achinese (ach.ẹ.nēs', -nēz'). See **Achehnese.**

Achinsk (ä'chinsk). [Also, **Atchinsk.**] Town in the U.S.S.R., in the Krasnoyarsk *oblast* (region) of the Russian Soviet Federated Socialist Republic, on the Trans-Siberian Railroad, situated on the Chulym River ab. 100 mi. W of Krasnoyarsk: important rail and highway junction, and trading center. Manganese is mined in the vicinity. Pop. ab. 17,000.

Achipeta (ach.i.pē'tạ). See **Chipeta.**

Achish (ā'kish). In the Old Testament, a Philistine king of Gath with whom David sought refuge when fleeing from Saul. 1 Sam. xxi. 10–15; 1 Sam. xxix.

Achish. In the Old Testament, a king of Gath who reigned in the time of Solomon. 1 Kings, ii. 39–40.

Achithophel (ạ.kit'ọ.fel). A character in Dryden's poem *Absalom and Achitophel,* intended to represent the Earl of Shaftesbury, who was called by this name by his contemporaries, implying a treacherous friend and adviser. The name is intended, of course, to suggest the counselor of David, in the Old Testament, who joined Absalom in his revolt against his father. Dryden took his spelling from the Vulgate Bible; the King James Bible shows "Ahithophel," which is now the spelling most commonly used for the Old Testament character, but Dryden's character retains the Vulgate spelling.

Achitophel. Variant spelling of **Ahithophel** found in the Vulgate and Douay Bibles. It was from the former of these that John Dryden derived the spelling used in his satiric poem *Absalom and Achitophel.*

Achivi (a̤.kī′vī). See **Achaeans.**

Achmet (äch′met). See also under **Ahmed.**

Achmet Pasha (pä.shä′, påsh′ä). See **Bonneval, Claude Alexandre,** Comte **de.**

Acholi (ä.chō′lē). [Also: **Atscholi, Gang, Schuli, Shuoli.**] Nilotic-speaking people of E Africa, inhabiting Acholi district of N Uganda and a small portion of S Anglo-Egyptian Sudan. Their population is estimated at ab. 180,000 (by M. A. Bryan, *Distribution of the Nilotic and Nilo-Hamitic Languages of Africa*, 1948).

Achray (a̤.krā′), **Loch.** Lake in C Scotland, in Perthshire, situated in the Trossachs, between Loch Katrine and Loch Vennachar, ab. 19 mi. NW of Stirling. Length, ab. 2 mi.

Achúcharro (ä.chö′chär.rō), **Nicolás.** b. at Bilbao, Spain, 1881; d. at Madrid, 1918. Spanish histologist. A pupil of Ramón y Cajal, he took postgraduate work with Pierre Marie at Paris (1901–02), with E. Kraepelin and A. Alzheimer at Munich, and with G. Lugaro at Florence, and became (1908) director of the laboratory of St. Elizabeth's Hospital, Washington, D. C. His investigations (1909) of the changes in the nervous systems of animals suffering from rabies led him to the study of neuroglial reactions in this disease and thence to an understanding of the need for a better neuroglial staining method. He developed (1911) the tannic acid and silver technique which bears his name. With the help of Ramón y Cajal he set up a neuropathology laboratory in the museum of natural history at Madrid which was later united with Ramón y Cajal's Laboratorio de Investigaciones Biológicas. Among his more important neuropathologic works were those on general paresis (1911, 1912, 1914), functions of the neuroglia (1909, 1913, 1915), brain tumors (1912, 1913), and Alzheimer's disease (1914).

Acidalius (as.i.dā′li.us; German, ä.tsē.dä′li.u̇s), **Valens.** b. at Wittstock, Prussia, May 25, 1567; d. at Neisse, Prussia, May 25, 1595. German philologist and critic, author of several commentaries on the Latin classics.

Acilia gens (a̤.sil′i.a̤ jenz). In ancient Roman history, a clan or house whose family names were Aviola, Balbus, and Glabrio. Members of the last two families were frequently tribunes of the plebs.

Acilium (a̤.sil′i.um). Latin name of **Aiguillon.**

Acireale (ä″chē.rā.ä′lā). City and commune in S Italy, on the island of Sicily, in the province of Catania, situated on the E coast of Sicily and on the E slope of Mount Etna, ab. 9 mi. N of Catania. It is the center of a fertile citrus and wine producing district, and contains numerous churches and houses in the Sicilian baroque style. World War II damage included the Chiesa del Suffragio, the roof and windows of the *Duomo* (cathedral), and the dome and windows of San Sebastiano, but repairs are now completed or being carried out. Nearby are the hot springs of Santa Venera, which are visited by people suffering from neuritis, gout, and respiratory diseases. Pop. of commune, 36,871 (1936); of city, 19,440 (1936).

Acis (ā′sis). In classical mythology, a beautiful Sicilian, son of Faunus and Symaethis, beloved by Galatea, and slain by Polyphemus the Cyclops, his unsuccessful rival.

Acis and Galatea (gal.a̤.tē′a̤). Pastoral opera by Handel, composed c1721. The words by John Gay, with additions by Alexander Pope and John Dryden, spiritedly burlesque one of Ovid's *Metamorphoses*.

Acis et Galatée (å.sēs ā gå.lå.tā). Opera by Jean Baptiste Lully, with words by Jean Galbert de Campistron, first produced in 1686.

Acken (äk′e̤n). See **Aken.**

Acker (ak′ėr), **Charles Ernest.** b. at Bourbon, Ind., March 19, 1868; d. at Ossining, N. Y., Oct. 18, 1920. American electrical engineer and manufacturer, inventor of numerous processes in electrochemistry and electrometallurgy. Beginning with his electrolytic process for caustic soda and chlorine production (1896), on which was founded the Acker Process Company, Niagara Falls, N. Y., he obtained over 40 patents for inventions including methods of producing caustic alkalis, gases, nitrides, carbon and tin tetrachlorides, detinning processes, and others. He was director of the American Electro-chemical Society (1905–10) and of the Westchester County Bureau of Municipal Research.

Ackermann (äk′ėr.män), **Alexander.** Original name of **Agricola, Alexander.**

Ackermann, Johann Christian Gottlieb. b. Feb. 17, 1756; d. at Altdorf, Bavaria, March 9, 1801. German medical writer. He was the author of *Institutiones historiae medicinae* (1792), and lives of Hippocrates, Theophrastus, Dioscorides, Aretaeus, Rufus Ephesius, and Galen.

Ackermann, Konrad Ernst. b. in Schwerin, Germany, Feb. 1, 1712; d. at Hamburg, Nov. 13, 1771. German actor, usually credited with establishing the basic standards of the German theater in his day. He appeared on the stage first at Lüneburg (1740), traveled with various companies, and built and operated (1764–67) a theater at Hamburg. He was the stepfather of Friedrich Ludwig Schröder.

Ackermann (å.ker.mån), **Louise Victorine.** [Maiden name, **Choquet.**] b. at Paris, Nov. 30, 1813; d. at Nice, France, Aug. 2, 1890. French poet. Author of *Contes* (1855), *Contes et poésies* (1863), *Poésies philosophiques* (1874), and a volume of prose, *Pensées d'une solitaire* (1883).

Ackermann (ak′ėr.ma̤n), **Rudolph.** b. at Schneeberg, Saxony, April 20, 1764; d. at Finchley, Middlesex, England, March 30, 1834. German art publisher and bookseller at London (1795 *et seq.*). A one-time coach-builder and harness-maker, he patented (1801) a method of making cloth and paper waterproof, which had considerable value to publishers of books. He himself published (1817–28) the monthly *Repository of Arts, Literature, Fashions, etc.* and travel books, illustrated with lithographs by Rowlandson and others. The establishment of lithography as a fine art in England is often credited to him.

Ackermann aus Böhmen (äk′ėr.män ous bė′me̤n), **Der.** German dialogue written in 1400 by Johannes von Saaz. In this most human document of the period a man who has just lost his wife argues with death only to be shown by God in the end that death must be.

Ackland (ak′la̤nd), **Rodney.** b. 1908—. English playwright. His *Strange Orchestra* (1932) was much admired at London, but failed after a single performance at New York. Other plays include *The Old Ladies* (1935), an adaptation of Sir Hugh Walpole's novel about three aged gentlefolk, and the Chekhovian *After October* (1936) and *Remembrance of Things Past* (1938). He also adapted (1949) *Crime and Punishment* for the stage.

Acklins Island (ak′linz). Island in the Atlantic Ocean, a British possession in the Bahamas, ab. 120 mi. NE of Cuba. Area, 120 sq. mi.; pop. 1,744 (1943).

Ackté-Jalander (äk.tā′yä′län.dėr), **Aino.** [Maiden name, **Stoemer-Ackté.**] b. at Helsinki, Finland, April 23, 1876; d. there, 1944. Finnish operatic soprano. She won fame at the Grand Opéra (1897–1904), the Metropolitan (1904–06), and Covent Garden (1907, 1910).

Acla (ä′klä). In early Spanish-American history, a Spanish colonial town in N Panama, in Colón province, on the Caribbean side of the Isthmus of Panama, probably near San Blas Bay. It was founded by Pedrarias in 1515, and was the place where Balboa built his ships to be transported across the isthmus in 1517, and where he was executed. The settlement, for a time important, was abandoned before 1580.

Acland (ak′la̤nd), Lady **Christian Henrietta Caroline.** [Called Lady **Harriet.**] b. Jan. 3, 1750; d. at Tetton, near Taunton, England, July 21, 1815. Wife of John Dyke Acland, whom she accompanied in North America during the Revolutionary War on Burgoyne's Saratoga campaign in 1777.

Acland, Sir **Henry Wentworth Dyke.** b. at Exeter, England, Aug. 23, 1815; d. at Oxford, England, 1900. English physician. As regius professor of medicine at Oxford (1858–94), he took a leading part in the revival of the medical school at Oxford, and made himself known as an advocate of public-health legislation. He was also for many years a friend of Ruskin, and attended the Prince of Wales on a voyage to America in 1860.

Acland, John Dyke. d. near Dulverton, England, Oct. 31, 1778. English soldier and politician. As a member of Parliament, he was a vigorous opponent of the demands of the American colonies, and joined Burgoyne's Saratoga campaign (1777) during the Revolutionary War as a major. During the decisive battle of this campaign, near

Saratoga in the autumn of 1777, he was wounded and taken prisoner.

Aco (à.kō), **Michel.** [Also: **Accau, Accault, Ako.**] b. at Poitiers, France; fl. 1680–1702. French explorer and trader in colonial America. Sent (1680) by La Salle, with Auguel and Hennepin, to explore the upper Mississippi, he was captured with them by the Sioux. After rescue by Duluth, the three made their way through the Great Lakes and arrived (1681) at Montreal. Later (1693) appearing in Illinois as a trader at the fort erected by Tonty, Aco married the daughter of a Kaskaskia chief.

Acoemetae (as.ẹ.mē′tē). [Called **Studites.**] Monastic order founded (c430) by Alexander, a Syrian monk. Their religious zeal led the members of the order to divide the 24-hour day into three equal parts, during each of which one third of the monks would engage in prayer, so that the religious devotion of the order might be uninterrupted.

Acolastus (ak.ọ.las′tus). Latin comedy composed by Gulielmus Fullonius (Willem de Volder), a schoolmaster at The Hague. It was translated into English prose and published (1540) by John Palsgrave, in a volume which also contained the Latin version. It was first acted, in Latin, in 1529. It was designed for use in schools, and there were 40 different issues of it during the lifetime of the author.

Acolhuas (ä.kọ.lö′ạz). [Also, **Acolhuans** (ä.kọ.lö′ạnz).] Name which has been applied to a Nahuatl-speaking tribe of Indians which, according to tradition, preceded the Aztecs in the valley of Mexico.

Acoma (ä′kọ.mạ). Pueblo Indian village in W central New Mexico; the language is of the Keresan family. Pop. ab. 600.

Acomat (à.ko.mà). In Jean Baptiste Racine's tragedy *Bajazet*, an ambitious vizier.

Aconcagua (ä.kông.kä′gwä). Province in C Chile, bounded by Coquimbo on the N, and by Santiago and Valparaíso on the S. Capital, San Felipe; area, 3,940 sq. mi.; pop. 121,206 (est. 1943).

Aconcagua. Mountain in W Argentina, on the border of Chile. An inactive volcano, it is the tallest mountain in South America and the Western Hemisphere. 22,835 ft.

Aconcagua River. River in C Chile, N of Valparaíso. It empties into the Pacific Ocean.

Aconcio (ä.kōn′chō) or **Aconzio** (ä.kōn′tsyō), **Giacomo** (or **Jacopo**). [Also: **Concio**; Latinized, **Jacobus Acontius.**] b. at Trent, in the Tirol, c1500; d. at London, c1566. Italian theologian and engineer. A refugee (1559 *et seq.*) in Elizabethan England because of his repudiation of Catholic doctrine, he there wrote *Stratagemata Satanae* (Stratagems of Satan, 1565), in which he sought to articulate a basis for belief which might be shared by all Christians (the "stratagems of Satan" were, in his eyes, the conflicting dogmas that lay behind the conflicts between various Christian groups).

Aconquija (ä.kōng.kē′hä), **Sierra de.** See **Sierra de Aconquija** or **Anconquija.**

Acontius (ạ.kon′shi.us, -shus). Principal character in the tale of Acontius and Cydippe, told by Aristaenetus and by Ovid. "Acontius gathered an orange in the garden of Venus, and having written on the rind the words, 'By Artemis, I will marry Acontius,' threw it in Cydippe's way. She took it in her hand, read out the inscription, and threw it from her. But Artemis heard the vow, and brought about the marriage." William Morris took the legend for the subject of one of his poems in *The Earthly Paradise.*

Açores (ạ.sō′rẹsh). Portuguese name of the **Azores.**

Acosta (ạ.kôsh′tạ), **Christovão de.** d. 1580. Portuguese traveler and naturalist, author of *Tratado de las drogas y medecinas de la Indias orientales* (1578).

Acosta, Gabriel. [Also: **Gabriel da Costa, Gabriel d'Acosta;** after conversion, **Uriel da Costa, Uriel Acosta, Uriel d'Acosta, Uriel de Acosta.**] b. at Oporto, Portugal, 1591; d. a suicide, 1647. Portuguese philosopher and religious skeptic. He moved to Amsterdam as a young man and was converted to Judaism from Catholicism, but was thereafter twice excommunicated by the synagogue for his outspoken skepticism. His autobiography, *Exemplar humanae vitae* (1687), was reprinted in 1847 and used as a source by K. F. Gutzkow for his tragedy, *Uriel Acosta* (1847).

Acosta (ä.kôs′tä), **Joaquín.** b. in Colombia, c1795; d. 1852. Colombian patriot, soldier, and historian, notable for his service (1819) with Bolívar. His subsequent activity as a member of the Colombian legislature was followed by diplomatic appointments, and by historical research in the Spanish archives at Madrid (1845), and later at Paris. He was the author of *Compendio histórico del descubrimiento y colonización de la Nueva Granada* (1848).

Acosta, José de. b. at Medina del Campo, Spain, 1540; d. at Salamanca, Spain, Feb. 15, 1600. Spanish Jesuit historian, archaeologist, and missionary. The first two books of his *Natural and Moral History of the Indies,* in Latin, appeared at Salamanca in 1588 and 1589. The entire work was published in Spanish at Seville in 1590.

Acosta, Julio. [Full name, **Julio Acosta Garcia.**] b. May 23, 1872—. Costa Rican politician and diplomat who was during World War II the foreign secretary of his country. Earlier served as president (1920–24) and member of congress (1906–10, 1932–36, 1938–42); chairman (1945) of the Costa Rican delegation to the San Francisco United Nations conference.

Acqs (àks). See **Ax.**

Acquaviva delle Fonti (äk.kwä.vē′vä del.lā fôn′tē). Town and commune in S Italy, in the *compartimento* (region) of Apulia, in the province of Bari, ab. 18 mi. S of Bari. It is the center of a wine, olive, almond, and fruit producing district, and contains several distilleries. Pop. of commune, 12,809 (1936); of town, 11,934 (1936).

Acqui (äk′kwē). [Ancient name, **Aquae Statiellae.**] Town and commune in NW Italy, in the *compartimento* (region) of Piedmont, in the province of Alessandria, situated on the Bormida River, ab. 29 mi. NW of Genoa. The town is renowned for its hot springs, which are visited by people suffering from respiratory, skin, and certain other diseases. The cathedral and castle, dating from the 11th and 13th centuries, were undamaged in World War II. Remains of a Roman aqueduct may still be seen in the vicinity. Originally a Roman provincial town, and later under Lombard rule, Acqui was subsequently part of the county of Monferrato; it fell to the house of Savoy in 1708. Pop. of commune, 18,336 (1936); of town, 9,643 (1936).

Acragas (ak′rạ.gạs). Greek name of **Agrigento.**

Acrasia (ạ.krā′zi.ạ). In Spenser's *Faerie Queene* a beautiful woman, the personification of intemperance in all things, living in the "Bower of Bliss," which contains everything to delight the senses. She was suggested originally by Circe and, more directly, by the Alcina of Ariosto.

Acrates (a.krā′tēz). Male character in Spenser's *Faerie Queene,* personifying the intemperate love of pleasure.

Acre (ä′krẹ). See also **Acre River.**

Acre. [Former name, **Aquiry.**] Territory in W Brazil, N of the Acre River, bordering on Bolivia and Peru. The boundary dispute between Bolivia and Brazil with regard to this territory was adjusted by a treaty in November, 1903, and an agreement to adjudicate a similar dispute between Brazil and Peru was reached in July, 1904. Capital, Rio Branco; area, 59,139 sq. mi.; pop. 116,124 (1950).

Acre (ā′kėr, ä′kėr). Former subdistrict of the Galilee district, in N Palestine, now part of Israel.

Acre. [Arabic, **Acca** or **Akka**; French, **St.-Jean-d'Acre;** in the Old Testament, **Accho, Acco,** or **Akko;** in the New Testament, **Ptolemaïs.**] City and seaport in Palestine, in NW Israel, ab. 9 mi. NE of Haifa. Once a leading port and trading center of the E Mediterranean, Acre has in modern times lost much of its economic importance through the development of feeder rail-lines to other cities and ports. Its population fluctuated from approximately 8,000 to 11,000 over the period from 1900 to the end of World War II, but dipped sharply in 1948 when an estimated two thirds of the city's predominantly Arab population fled Israel to live in adjoining Arab states. From a 1948 low point of 4,000 (est.), the population had risen to 12,200 (1950), including 8,200 Jews.

History. Although it was in the territory assigned to the tribe of Asher (Judges, i. 31.), Acre was never conquered in Biblical times by the Israelites. Its kings were reckoned next in importance to those of Tyre and Sidon. It was conquered by the Assyrian king Sennacherib, and again by his grandson, Assurbanipal, who sacked it. Subsequently it was captured by the Arabs (638), by the Crusaders (1104), by Saladin (1187), and again by the Crusaders (1191). It was thereafter held by the Knights of St. John until 1291, being the last Palestinian stronghold to be held by the Christians of western Europe. It was taken by Turkey in 1517, who held it against various attacks (including one by Napoleon in 1799), until it was absorbed (1832) as part of Syria into Egypt, falling again (with British help) to the Turks in 1840. In World War I the British captured it from the Turks in 1918, and administered it thereafter until 1948.

Acre, Bay of. Bay of the E Mediterranean, on the W coast of Palestine, in NW Israel. It serves as a harbor for vessels calling at the major port of Haifa and the lesser port of Acre. Width, ab. 8 mi.

Acrelius (a̤.krē′li.us; Swedish, ä.krā′li.us), **Israel.** b. at Öster-Åker, Sweden, Dec. 4, 1714; d. at Fellingsbro, Sweden, April 25, 1800. Swedish Lutheran pastor (1749–56) of Christina (now Wilmington), Delaware. Besides organizing Swedish ecclesiastical affairs in that region, he contributed to the work of the Pennsylvania German Lutherans and wrote a *History of New Sweden* (1759; English trans., 1874), a scholarly history of the colony under the Swedes, Dutch, and English.

Acre River (ä′krē). [Former name, **Aquiry.**] River in C South America, in Brazil. For part of its length it forms the boundary between Brazil and Bolivia. Length, ab. 330 mi.

Acres (ā′kėrz), **Bob.** A character in Richard Brinsley Sheridan's comedy *The Rivals*, an awkward and simple country gentleman changed into a boasting coward by the sudden excitement of high society at fashionable 18th-century Bath, England. His brag, his ludicrous vanity, and his assurance are combined with a comic trepidation and an uneasy gaiety.

Acri (ä′krē). Town and commune in S Italy, in the *compartimento* (region) of Lucania, in the province of Cosenza, situated on the Mucone River, ab. 13 mi. NE of Cosenza. It has wine, oil, cattle, and hog markets, and produces various sausage products. The palace of the princes of Bisignano dates from the 17th century. Pop. of commune, 16,213 (1936); of town, 5,387 (1936).

Acrisius (a̤.kris′i.us). In Greek mythology, a king of Argos, father of Danaë.

Acroceraunia (ak″rō̤.sē̤.rô′ni.a̤). [Also: **Akrokeraunia;** modern Greek, **Glossa;** Italian, **Linguetta.**] In ancient geography, a promontory projecting from what was then the NW part of Epirus (and is now SW Albania) into the Ionian Sea. The name has sometimes been incorrectly extended to the whole range of the Ceraunian Mountains.

Acroceraunian Mountains (ak″rō̤.sē̤.rô′ni.a̤n). Occasional name of the **Ceraunian Mountains.**

Acrocorinthus (ak″rō̤.kō̤.rin′thus). [Also: **Akrokorinthos, Acro-Corinth** (ak.rō̤.kor′inth).] Height (ab. 1,885 ft.) covered with ruins, under the N slope of which lies the city of Corinth, Greece. It is celebrated for its extensive view. The medieval fortifications form a triple line, 1½ mi. in circuit, below the summit. Of the ancient fortifications, and the celebrated temple of Aphrodite and other religious structures, the remains are very scanty.

Acropolis (a.krop′ō̤.lis). General name for the citadel of an ancient Greek city, but especially appropriated to that of Athens, famous for the placing on its summit in the 5th century B.C. of the highest achievements of Greek art, the Parthenon and the Erechtheum, with the sculptures which adorned them without and within, and the Propylaea, or monumental gate, inside of the walls at the W end. The Acropolis is a precipitous rock which rises about 260 ft. above the city, and extends 1,000 ft. from E to W, and 400 in its greatest width. It was the site of the earliest Athens known to history, was strongly fortified, and contained the palace of the king until the expulsion of the Pisistratids.

Sacred Ground and Fortress. From this time it ceased to be inhabited, and was reserved as sacred ground and as a last refuge in time of danger. It was taken and sacked by the Persians in 480 B.C.; shortly afterward its fortifications were strengthened and completed and its area increased by retaining-walls and filling, especially by Cimon, who had much to do with devising the plans for monumental embellishment which were carried out under Pericles. The ancient entrance to the Acropolis was on the southwest, by a narrow, winding path commanded by the battlements above. Among the other monuments of the Acropolis are the pre-Persian temple of Athena, correctly identified and studied by Dorpfeld in 1885, the colossal bronze statue, by Phidias, of Athena Promachos, and the temple of the Wingless Victory. The slopes of the Acropolis were occupied by important foundations, particularly on the south, where lie the Odeum of Herodes, the sanctuary of Aesculapius, and the Dionysiac theater.

Fate in Medieval and Modern Times. Under the medieval Franks and Turks the Acropolis was the citadel and abode of the dukes and pashas. The Parthenon was in turn cathedral and mosque; the Propylaea became the palace and government offices; and the Erechtheum, after being a church, was fitted as the pasha's harem. These great monuments remained comparatively unharmed until a late date in the Turkish domination. The Propylaea were shattered by an explosion of gunpowder induced by lightning, the Erechtheum was destroyed by the overweighting of the roofs in the effort to make them bombproof, and the Parthenon was cut in two in 1687, during the Venetian siege of Athens under Königsmark, by a bomb purposely shot into the powder stored in it.

Acropolita (ak″rō̤.pō̤.lī′ta̤), **George.** [Greek, **Georgios Akropolites.**] b. at Constantinople, 1217; d. in December, 1282. Byzantine historian. In 1233 he went to the Nicaean court, where he was trained for the diplomatic service; in 1257 he was entrusted the command of an army by his former pupil Theodoros II Lascaris, but failed and was made prisoner; Michael VIII Palaeologos freed him in 1260 and used him as a diplomat. After 1261 he lived chiefly at Constantinople. In 1273 he was sent to Pope Gregory X to negotiate the reconciliation of the Latin and Greek churches, and in the following year, at the council of Lyon, he acknowledged in the emperor's name the supremacy of the Roman pontiff. In 1282 he was sent to John II, emperor of Trebizond. He died soon after his return to Constantinople in the same year, a few months before Michael VIII. His main work is a chronicle dealing with the period extending from the conquest of Constantinople by the Latins to the Byzantine restoration (1204–61).

Across Spoon River. Autobiographical work (1936) by the poet Edgar Lee Masters.

Across the Plains. Autobiographical narrative by Robert Louis Stevenson, originally published (1883) in *Longman's Magazine* and expanded into book form in 1892.

Acta Diurna (ak′ta̤ dī.ėr′na̤). [Eng. trans., *"Daily Events."*] Roman official daily chronicle, which, in addition to official reports of events in the imperial family, and state and city affairs, contained regulations by the magistrates, transactions and decrees of the senate, accounts of accidents, and family news communicated to the editors. The *Acta* were publicly exhibited on a whitened board (*album*), which any one might read and copy, and there were men who made a business of multiplying and transmitting such news to the provinces. After a time the originals were placed among the state archives for the benefit of those who wished to consult them. The publication of such news was made official by Caesar; it ceased, apparently, on the transfer of the capital to Constantinople. The 11 fragments of *Acta* (*diurna*) *populi* first published in 1615 (called *"fragmenta Dodwelliana,"* from Henry Dodwell, the chief defender of their genuineness) are now regarded as spurious.

Actaeon (ak.tē′o̤n). In Greek mythology, a hunter, who, having seen Artemis (Diana) bathing, was changed by her into a stag and (according to the most usual account of his death) torn to pieces by his own dogs.

Acta Eruditorum (ak′ta̤ e.rö.di.tō′rum). Latin journal, the first literary periodical in Germany, founded by Otto Mencke at Leipzig, 1682, and discontinued in 1782. After his death (1707) his son Burkhard Mencke became editor. In 1732 the title was changed to *Nova Acta Eruditorum*, a new series edited by F. O. Mencke, son of Burkhard Mencke. A total of 117 volumes appeared. Leibniz was one of the contributors.

Acta Pilati (pi.lā'tī). Report formerly believed to have been sent by Pontius Pilate to the emperor Tiberius on the trial and death of Christ. The *Acta Pilati* written in the 4th century is a part of the apocryphal Latin *Gospel of Nicodemus.*

Acta Sanctorum (sangk.tō'rum). [Eng. trans., *"Acts of the Saints."*] Title that may be applied to all collections of accounts of saints and martyrs, both of the Roman and Greek churches; specifically, the great Roman Catholic work begun (1643) by the Bollandists, a society of Jesuits. It now consists of more than 60 folio volumes, including an index published in 1875.

Acte (ak'tę). See **Athos.**

Action Française (àk.syôṅ fräṅ.sez). [Eng. trans., *"French Action."*] French royalist organization known for its extreme political and social conservatism and for its advocacy of the violent overthrow of the French Third Republic. Established (1898) during the period of the Dreyfus Affair as the *Comité d'Action Française* (Committee of French Action), with Henri Vaugeois and Maurice Pujo as principal initiators, it became (1905) the *Ligue de l'Action Française* (League of French Action). The principal leaders were Charles Maurras, Léon Daudet, Pujo, and (until 1925) Georges Valois. An auxiliary group of supporters who engaged in demonstrations, street riots, and other forms of violence was formed (1908) under the name of *Camelots du Roi* (The King's Pedlars). The organization sponsored the publication *L'Action Française.* The French Catholic hierarchy and the Vatican rejected (1926) the support of the group, and placed its newspaper on the Index. During World War II, the group supported the Pétain regime. Many of its leaders were convicted (1945) of collaboration with the Germans during World War II.

Actium (ak'shi.um, -ti.um). [Greek, **Aktion.**] In ancient geography, a promontory on the NW coast of Acarnania, in Greece. The ancient *peribolos* or sacred enclosure, rectangular in plan and built in *opus reticulatum,* the seat of the famous Actian games of Augustus, still remains. Modern excavations have laid bare extensive ruins of several successive temples, one of the latest of which is that dedicated by Augustus after the victory of 31 B.C. A famous naval battle was fought (Sept. 2, 31 B.C.) near Actium between Octavius and Mark Antony and Cleopatra. It was decided by the flight of Cleopatra, Mark Antony's land forces thereupon surrendering to Octavius. The victory secured for Octavius supreme rule over the Roman dominion.

Act of Chapultepec (chä.pöl'te.pek). Doctrine proclaimed (1945) by the Inter-American Conference on Problems of War and Peace at Chapultepec Castle, Mexico City. The act, in effect, made the guardianship of the Monroe Doctrine the responsibility of all nations of the Western Hemisphere, even in the event of aggression originating among them. Argentina was the only Latin American nation absent from the conference but subscribed to it upon declaration (March 27, 1945) of war against the Axis.

Act of Havana (hą.van'ą). Pact approved (July 30, 1940) by the second meeting of Foreign Ministers of the American Republics at Havana. It provided that European-owned territory in the Western Hemisphere in danger of enemy attack might be taken into the "collective trusteeship" of the American republics for the duration of the emergency.

Acton (ak'tǫn). Municipal borough in SE England, in Middlesex, ab. 4 mi. W of Paddington station, London. Acton is a western suburb of London. 67,424 (1951).

Acton, Lord. [Full name, **John Emerich Edward Dalberg-Acton;** title, 1st Baron **Acton of Aldenham.**] b. at Naples, Italy, Jan. 10, 1834; d. at Tegernsee, in Bavaria, June 19, 1902. English historian. He succeeded his father as eighth baronet in 1837, and was successively member of Parliament for Carlow (1859–65) and for Bridgenorth (1865–66). He was a Liberal and a close friend of Gladstone, who obtained his elevation to the peerage in 1869. He was appointed regius professor of modern history at Cambridge University in 1895. His famous historical library of about 60,000 volumes was purchased by Andrew Carnegie, who, after Acton's death, gave it to John Morley, who presented it to the University of Cambridge. He was a leader of liberal British Roman Catholics in opposing the doctrine of papal infallibility, but accepted it when it was promulgated officially. He published *Lecture on the Study of History* (1895), and outlined the plan of the *Cambridge Modern History* (which was completed, however, by others after his death, except for the first volume). His famous *Lectures on the French Revolution,* edited by J. Neville Figgis and Reginald Vere Laurence, were published in 1910.

Acton. [Former name, **Concord Village.**] Town in E Massachusetts, in Middlesex County: wool textiles, radio cabinets, and metal products. 3,510 (1950).

Acton, Charles Januarius Edward. b. at Naples, Italy, March 6, 1803; d. there, June 23, 1847. English ecclesiastic; the second son of Sir John Francis Edward Acton (1736–1811). He entered the service of the Pope, was made cardinal in 1842, and played an important part in papal politics, especially in matters relating to England.

Acton, Eliza. b. at Battle, England, April 17, 1799; d. at Hampstead, England, Feb. 13, 1859. English poet and prose writer, now best known, however, as the author of *Modern Cookery* (1845).

Acton, Sir **John Francis Edward.** b. at Besançon, France, 1736; d. at Palermo, Italy, Aug. 12, 1811. English soldier of fortune and political adventurer. He was an officer in the Tuscan navy during the campaign against Algiers (1775), and later army and navy commander, minister of finance, and prime minister at Naples (1779 *et seq.*), where he instituted a regime of ruthless oppression but was forced to flee by French entry (1806) into the city.

Acton, Thomas Coxon. b. at New York, Feb. 23, 1823; d. there, May 1, 1898. American banker and public official, president of the board of New York police during the Civil War draft riots in 1863.

Acts of the Apostles. Book of the New Testament, a continuation of the third gospel (Luke), and, according to tradition, written by the same author. It is a history of the early progress of Christianity after (and including) the ascension of Christ.

Acuña (ä.kö'nyä), **Cristóbal de.** b. at Burgos, Spain, 1597; d. at Lima, Peru, c1676. Spanish Jesuit missionary and author. He accompanied Pedro Teixeira on an exploration of the Amazon (1639), and published (1641) at Madrid his *Nuevo descubrimiento del gran río de las Amazonas,* the first known eyewitness account of that river.

Acuña, Hernando de. b. c1500; d. 1580. Spanish poet and soldier. He served in the expedition of Charles V against Tunis, and translated Olivier de la Marche's *Le Chevalier délibéré.* His own poems were published after his death, under the title *Varias Poesías* (1591).

Acuña de Figueroa (dā fē.gä.rō'ä), **Francisco.** See **Figueroa, Francisco Acuña de.**

Acuña y Bejarano (ä.kö'nyä ē bā.Hä.rä'nō), **Juan de.** [Title, Marquis of **Casa Fuerte.**] b. at Lima, Peru, 1657; d. in Mexico, 1734. Spanish soldier and colonial administrator in America. He was governor of Messina, viceroy of Aragón and Mallorca, member of the supreme council of war, and viceroy of New Spain from 1722 until his death.

Acushnet (ą.kush'nęt). Town in SE Massachusetts, in Bristol County: site of a battle (September, 1776) between the Minute Men and British troops. 4,401 (1950).

Acusilaus (ą.kū.si.lā'us). b. at Argos, probably mid-6th century B.C. Greek commentator on, or prose paraphrast of, the *Theogony* of Hesiod. He was by some regarded as one of the seven wise men.

Ada (ā'dą). City in S central Oklahoma, in Pontotoc County, in an oil-producing, cattle-ranching, and agricultural region: cotton, corn, sorghum, wheat, oats, hay, and sugar cane; manufactures of flour and cement. It is the seat of East Central State College. The city was established in 1889. Pop. 15,995 (1950).

Ada (ä'dä). Village and *varos* (township) in NE Yugoslavia, in the region of Bačka, in the autonomous province of Vojvodina, federative unit of Serbia, former *banovina* (province) of Dunavska, situated on the right bank of the Tisa River, between Stari-Bečej and Senta. The town belonged to Hungary prior to 1919. Pop. 10,414 (1948).

Ada (ā'dạ). Greek form of **Adah.**

Ada. Former name of **Brookings,** S. D.

Adabazar (ä"dä.bä.zär'). See **Adapazari.**

Adachi (ä.dä.chē), **Kenzo.** b. in Kumamoto prefecture, Japan, Oct. 23, 1864–. Japanese politician. Founder of several newspapers in Korea and long a member of the Japanese house of representatives, to which he was elected 14 times (1902–40), he was also founder and president of the Kokumin Domei (1932–40), a political party of the extreme right.

Adachi, Mineichiro. b. in Yamagata prefecture, Japan, 1869; d. at Amsterdam, The Netherlands, Dec. 28, 1943. Japanese diplomat and jurist, remembered chiefly as president (1931–33) of the Permanent Court of International Justice. A graduate of Imperial University at Tokyo, he served in various Japanese embassies, and was chief interpreter (1905) for the peace conference at Portsmouth, N. H., after the Russo-Japanese War (1904–05). He was subsequently minister to Mexico (1916–17), ambassador to Belgium (1917–27), and ambassador to France and principal Japanese delegate to the League (1928–30).

Ada Clare (ā'dạ klãr). See **Clare, Ada.**

Adad (ā'dad). See **Hadad;** see also **Ramman.**

Adad-Nirari (ā'dad.ni.rä'ri). See **Ramman-Nirari.**

Adah (ā'dạ). [Greek, **Ada.**] In the Old Testament: 1. The first of the two wives of Lamech. Gen. iv. 19–23. 2. One of the wives of Esau and the mother of Eliphaz. Gen. xxxvi.

Adah. Wife of Cain, a character in *Cain*, by Byron.

Adaiel (ä.dī'el). See **Adal.**

Adai Kokh (ä.dī' kôʜ'). [Also, **Adai Khokh.**] Mountain peak in the U.S.S.R., in the Caucasus. 15,240 ft.

Adair (ạ.dãr'), **James.** b. c1709; d. c1783. English trader and American pioneer who lived (1735–70) with the Chickasaw and Cherokee Indians. He wrote a *History of the American Indians* (1775), which maintains that the Indians are descendants of the Jews.

Adair, John. b. in Chester County, S. C., Jan. 9, 1757; d. at Harrodsburg, Ky., May 19, 1840. American politician and soldier. He served in the Revolutionary War, in the Indian wars, and commanded the Kentucky troops at the battle of New Orleans; U.S. senator from Kentucky (1805–06), governor of Kentucky (1820–24), and a member of Congress from Kentucky (1831–33).

Adair, Sir **Robert.** b. at London, May 24, 1763; d. there, Oct. 3, 1855. English diplomat and writer of historical memoirs. He was sent on diplomatic missions to Vienna (1806–07), to Constantinople (1808–09), where he concluded the treaty of the Dardanelles, and to the Low Countries (1831–35).

Adair, Robin. See **Robin Adair.**

Adair v. United States, 208 U.S. 161 (1908). Decision of the U.S. Supreme Court which held unconstitutional Section 10 of the Erdman Act of 1908 prohibiting "yellow dog" labor contracts. The majority opinion held that the provision impaired liberty of contract in violation of the due process clause of the Fifth Amendment and also declared that the federal government had exceeded its powers under the commerce clause of the Constitution.

Adajel (ä.dä'yel). See **Adal.**

Adak (ā'dak). One of the Aleutian Islands, in the Andreanof group, off the SW coast of Alaska. Its surface is barren and rocky, but it has good harbors and was important in World War II as the site of a U.S. air base (1942 *et seq.*) which supported the campaign against the islands then still held by the Japanese further to the west.

Adal (ä.däl'). [Also: **Adaiel, Adajel, Adel.**] Region in E Africa, bordering on the Red Sea, mainly included in the former Italian colony of Eritrea and now part of Ethiopia. Its S end lies in French Somaliland. Its inhabitants are the Danakil.

Adalberon (a.dal'bẹ.ron) or **Adalbero** (a.dal'bẹ.rō). d. 988. Bishop of Reims and chancellor of France under Lothaire and Louis V. In 963 he was made archbishop, and in 987 he officiated at the coronation of Hugh Capet.

Adalbert (ad'ạl.bėrt). See also **Adelbert.**

Adalbert, Saint. d. c740. English saint, perhaps a grandson of Oswald, king of Deira. He devoted himself to missionary work among the Friesians, and is said to have been the first archdeacon of Utrecht.

Adalbert. [Called **"Apostle of the Slavs."**] d. 981. German missionary to Russia (961) and archbishop of Magdeburg.

Adalbert, Saint. [Also: **Adelbert;** Czech, **Vojtěch;** called **"Apostle of the Prussians."**] b. near Prague, c955; killed in Pomerania, 997. Bohemian prelate and nobleman. Bishop of Prague (983 *et seq.*), he incurred the dislike of various powerful nobles and withdrew (988) to Rome, but returned (993) to Bohemia at the behest of Pope John XV. He found the situation in that country still difficult and obtained permission to undertake missionary work first in Hungary, then in Poland and northern Germany. He is said to have been assassinated by an agent of the non-Christian Poles.

Adalbert (of *Prussia*). [Full name, **Heinrich Wilhelm Adalbert.**] b. at Berlin, Oct. 20, 1811; d. at Karlsbad, June 6, 1873. Prince of Prussia; son of Prince Wilhelm, youngest brother of King Frederick William III. He entered the army as an artillery officer (1832). In 1842 he visited southern Brazil, traveling over parts of the Amazon and Xingú rivers. A description of this voyage was published for private circulation, and republished in English (2 vols., 1849). After the revolution of 1848 he was employed in the organization of the German fleet, and was for much of the rest of his life a leading figure in the development of German naval strength.

Adalia (ä.dä'lē.ä). Former name of **Antalya,** city.

Adalia, Gulf of. See **Antalya, Gulf of.**

Adam (ad'ạm; French, à.däṅ). See also **Adenet.**

Adam (ad'ạm). The first man; the father of all humanity, according to the account of the creation in Genesis. In its etymology, the word "Adam" derives from a Babylonian term meaning "man" in the general sense, and is found used in this sense in both Hebrew and Assyrian. Adam may therefore be taken to refer to both "mankind" and to the specific and particular individual of the male sex from one of whose ribs was derived Eve, and from whom mankind is said to have descended. Some scholars have pointed particularly to the fact that there is in the Bible no attempt to link Adam to God as having been himself a semi-divinity, or as having derived from a linking genealogy of demi-gods or heroes; in other words, original man is not of the substance of God, but a creation of God. The fact that man is nevertheless capable of moral judgment, of reason, and of communion with God (all of which are qualities possessed by no other living beings) is taken by many to be one of the noblest conceptions of the three great monotheistic religions (Christianity, Islam, and Judaism) which share the account of man's beginning as told in Genesis.

Adam. City in Palestine mentioned in the third chapter of Joshua.

Adam. Character in Shakespeare's *As You Like It*, an old and faithful servant of Oliver, but following the fortunes of the exiled Orlando. There is a tradition that Shakespeare himself acted this part.

Adam (à.däṅ), **Adolphe Charles.** b. at Paris, July 24, 1803; d. there, May 3, 1856. French composer of comic operas. His best-known works are *Cantique de Noël*, the opera *Le Postillon de Longjumeau* (1836), and the ballet *Giselle*, but he composed in all more than 50 musical works for the stage.

Adam (ä'däm), **Albrecht.** b. at Nördlingen, Germany, April 16, 1786; d. at Munich, Aug. 28, 1862. German painter, engraver, and lithographer, chiefly known for his battle-pieces and paintings of horses.

Adam (ad'ạm), **Alexander.** b. near Forres, Scotland, June 24, 1741; d. at Edinburgh, Dec. 18, 1809. Scottish educator, rector of the High School of Edinburgh (1768–1809), and antiquarian. He published *Roman Antiquities* (1791), and other works.

Adam (à.däṅ), **Antoine Edmond.** b. 1816; d. 1877. French politician and police official; second husband of Juliette Adam. He was prefect of the Paris police (1870 *et seq.*) and a life-member of the French senate.

Adam, François Balthasar Gaspard. b. 1710; d. 1761. French sculptor, much of whose work was done for Frederick the Great at Sans Souci. He is generally considered, however, to have been less talented than his brothers, Nicolas Sébastien Adam (1705–78) and Lambert Sigisbert Adam (1700–59).

Adam (ä′däm), **Franz.** b. at Milan, Italy, May 4, 1815; d. 1886. German painter, once well known for his battle scenes; son of Albrecht Adam (1786–1862).

Adam (ad′ąm), **James.** b. 1730; d. 1794. British architect; brother of Robert Adam (1728–92), with whom he collaborated in the design of London's Adelphi terrace (1768–71).

Adam, Jean. b. near Greenock, Scotland, 1710; d. at Glasgow, 1765. Scottish poetess and schoolmistress, now remembered chiefly as the author of *Poems* (1734), a collection of religious verse. She died in a poorhouse after a life of extreme hardship.

Adam (à.däṅ), **Jean Louis.** b. at Miettershelz, in Alsace, Dec. 3, 1758; d. at Paris, April 8, 1848. French pianist and composer.

Adam, Juliette. [Also: **J. La Messine;** pseudonym, **Comte Paul Vasili;** maiden name, **Lamber.**] b. at Verberie, France, Oct. 4, 1836; d. 1936. French writer, a founder and editor of the *Nouvelle Revue* (1879–99).

Adam (ä′däm), **Karl.** b. Oct. 22, 1876—. German theologian and professor (1919 *et seq.*) of Catholic dogma at the University of Tübingen. His publications include *Der Kirchenbegriff Tertullians* (1907), *Die Geistige Entwicklung d. hl. Augustinus* (1931), and *Una Sancta, Zur Wiedervereinigung im Glauben* (1947).

Adam (à.däṅ), **Lambert Sigisbert.** [Called **Adam l'aîné,** meaning "Adam the elder."] b. 1700; d. 1759. French sculptor and antiquarian; brother of Nicolas Sébastien Adam (1705–78) and François Balthasar Gaspard Adam (1710–61).

Adam (ä′däm), **Melchior.** b. at Grottkau, in Silesia, 1551; d. 1622. German Protestant divine and biographer; author of *Vitae Germanorum philosophorum* (1615–20), and other works.

Adam (à.däṅ), **Nicolas Sébastien.** [Called **Adam le jeune,** meaning "Adam the younger."] b. 1705; d. 1778. French sculptor. He created the tomb of Catherine Opalinska, queen of Poland, and is generally considered to have been more talented than either of his brothers, Lambert Sigisbert Adam (1700–59) and François Balthasar Gaspard Adam (1710–61).

Adam, Paul Auguste Marie. b. at Paris, Dec. 7, 1862; d. there, Jan. 2, 1920. French novelist and essayist, cofounder of several important French literary periodicals.

Adam, Quirin François Lucien. b. at Nancy, France, May 31, 1833; d. 1900. French magistrate and philologist, noted for his researches on American Indian and other languages.

Adam (ad′ąm), **Robert.** b. at Kirkcaldy, Scotland, 1728; d. at London, March 3, 1792. British architect, furniture designer, and landscape painter. Impressed during travels (c1754) in Italy and Dalmatia by the architecture of the ancient Romans, he patterned much of his work, as architect (1762–68) to King George III, upon it. He was assisted in virtually all his work (perhaps most notably in connection with London's famous Adelphi terrace) by his brother, James (1730–94). Adam's architecture, with its delicate and graceful interior designs, probably influenced him in the selection of the wreaths, paterae, honeysuckle, and fan ornaments which are the characteristic marks of his furniture style.

Adam, William. b. at Maryburgh, Kinross, Scotland, Aug. 2, 1751; d. at Edinburgh, Feb. 17, 1839. British lawyer and politician. He was a manager in Parliament of the impeachment proceedings against Warren Hastings (1788) and chancellor of the Duchy of Cornwall (1806).

Adam, William Patrick. b. Sept. 14, 1823; d. at Ootacamund, India, May 24, 1881. British politician. He was parliamentary whip of the Liberal party from 1874 to 1880, and governor of Madras from 1880 till his death.

Adam Anglicus (or **Anglo-Scotus**) (ang′gli.kus; ang′glō.skō′tus). See **Adam Scotus.**

Adamastor (ad.ąm.as′tǫr). Phantom of the Cape of Good Hope in the *Lusiad*, a terrible spirit described by Camões as appearing to Vasco da Gama and prophesying the misfortunes which should fall upon other expeditions to India.

Adamawa (à.dä.mä′wä). [Ancient name, **Fumbina.**] Region in W Africa, in E Nigeria and W Cameroun, having an area of ab. 70,000 sq. mi., approximately coextensive with a former native kingdom. The region is dominated by the Fulah class but the population consists of several Negro tribes with Bantu admixtures. Germany, France, and England divided the region among them until c1900. Later it was divided between the French and English, the French section being included in French Equatorial Africa and the British part becoming a province in Nigeria.

Adamawa. One of the Northern Provinces of Nigeria, in W Africa, paralleling the E boundary of the protectorate and straddling the Benue River. The administrative center is Yola; area, ab. 35,000 sq. mi.; pop. ab. 650,000.

Adam Bede (ad′ąm bēd). See also **Bede, Adam.**

Adam Bede. Novel by George Eliot, published in 1859. It was her first full-length novel.

Adam Bell (bel). See **Bell, Adam.**

Adam Bell, Clym of the Cloughe, and Wyllyam of Cloudeslee. Old ballad of outlaw life printed (c1550) by William Copland, and in the collections of both Thomas Percy and Joseph Ritson. The 19th-century American scholar Francis James Child repeated it from Ritson, with some variations from an edition older than Copland's recovered by Payne Collier.

Adamberger (ä′däm.ber.gėr), **Valentin.** [Stage name in Italy, **Adamonti.**] b. at Munich, July 6, 1743; d. at Vienna, Aug. 24, 1804. Operatic tenor and friend of Mozart, who wrote for Adamberger several songs and the opera part of Belmonte in *The Abduction from the Seraglio.*

Adam Cupid (ad′ąm kū′pid). Nickname of Cupid in Shakespeare's *Romeo and Juliet.*

Adam de La Halle (à.däṅ dẹ là àl). [Called **"Le Bossu d'Arras** (lẹ bo.sü dà.räs), meaning "the Hunchback of Arras."]. b. at Arras, France, c1230; d. in Italy, c1287. French poet and dramatist. He was educated as a monk, but forsook his religious seclusion and married; later he abandoned his native town and his family, and went first to Douai, and then with Robert of Artois to Italy. His *Le Jeu de la feuillée* has been regarded as the earliest comedy in the French tongue, while his pastoral drama, *Robin et Marion,* ranks as the earliest specimen of French comic opera.

Adam de Marisco (ad′ąm dẹ mą.ris′kō). [Also, **Adam Marsh.**] b. in Somerset, England; d. 1257 or 1258. English Franciscan monk. He entered the Franciscan order, at Worcester, c1237. He is not mentioned because of his writings, which are lost, but rather because he was the real founder of the great Franciscan school at Oxford, the friend and counselor of such men as Robert Grosseteste, with whom he attended the Council of Lyon in 1245. He exerted a moderating influence on Simon de Montfort, Earl of Leicester, the main leader of the crusade against the Albigenses, and upon various other statesmen and churchmen.

Adamello Alps (ä.dä.mel′lō). Mountain range in S central Europe, a group of the Alps near the border between Italy and the Tirol, S of the Ortler group. The highest point is ab. 11,693 ft.

Adamic (ad′ą.mik), **Louis.** b. at Blato, in Slovenia (then under Austria-Hungary, now part of Yugoslavia), March 23, 1899; d. Sept. 4, 1951. American writer. He entered the U.S. in 1913 and served in the U.S. army during World War I, becoming a citizen in 1918. Author of *The Native's Return* (1934), *What's Your Name* (1942), *My Native Land* (1943), *A Nation of Nations* (1945), *Dinner at the White House* (1946), *The Eagle and the Roots* (1952), and others.

Adamites (ad′ąm.īts). Sect which originated in N Africa during the 2nd century A.D. and claimed to have attained the primitive innocence of Adam. They spurned marriage and, in their assemblies or "paradises," made a rite of nudity. Their beliefs derived to a great extent from a gnostic espousal of sensualism as a path to mystic revelation. The sect reappeared in Savoy during the 14th century and among the Brethren and Sisters of the Free Spirit in Germany, Bohemia, and Moravia during the 15th century, being suppressed in the latter instance for immorality. The edict of toleration proclaimed (1781) by Joseph II brought them again into existence for a brief period, but they were proscribed almost at once and did not again reappear until the period of European political unrest in 1848–49, after which they appear to have vanished utterly as a religious group.

Adam Kadmon (ad′ąm kad′mǫn). Name of the first man, in cabalistic doctrine, where he is presented as the second divine principle and the personification of the ten Sephiroth, which are the direct emanations of God.

Adamnan (ad′ạm.nạn) or **Adomnan**, Saint. b. in Ulster, Ireland, c625; d. at Iona, Scotland, 704. Irish ecclesiastic, abbot of Iona (679–704). He was the author of *Vita Columbae* and of *De Locis Sanctis*, an account of Palestine and other countries.

Adam of Bremen. [Latinized, **Adamus Bremensis.**] b. in Upper Saxony, probably at Meissen, before 1045; d. c1076. German geographer, considered to have been the first German in his field. His history of the diocese of Hamburg down to 1072 is the fundamental source for the early history, geography, and ethnography of N Europe and of the Scandinavian colonies. It contains the earliest known record of Wineland (Vineland) and a very valuable account of North European trade. It was largely based on oral information collected in Bremen and in Denmark.

Adam of Murimuth (mur′i.muth). [Latinized, **Adamus Murimuthensis.**] b. in Oxfordshire, c1274; d. 1347. English chronicler. He was educated at Oxford, where he became a doctor of civil law in 1312 or soon before. From c1312–18 and even later he spent much time at Avignon, representing the archbishop of Canterbury or the king, and defending English ecclesiastical interests before the curia. By 1323, he was canon at Hereford, and he held other ecclesiastical offices at Exeter and London. Having observed that the chronicles of Exeter did not extend beyond 1302 and those of Westminster beyond 1305, he decided to write a "continuatio ex visu et auditu mei temporis." This work, entitled *Continuatio chronicorum*, covers the period from 1303 to 1347. He began to write it c1325 and worked at it until the last year of his life. The information for the years 1303–37 is quite meager; for the last ten years the material is more abundant, although he never wrote in great detail. This part of the chronicle is of particular value for the account of the English campaigns in France and of the negotiations between the two countries. The chronicle is of special interest from the ecclesiastical point of view. There is an anonymous continuation down to 1380.

Adam of Orlton (ôrl′tọn). b. at Hereford, England; d. at Farnham, England, July 18, 1345. English prelate, made bishop of Hereford in 1317, of Worcester in 1327, and of Winchester in 1333. He took the part of the barons against Edward II, was tried by Parliament for treason as an adherent of Mortimer (the first English bishop, it is said, ever tried before a lay court), and was influential in political affairs during the reign of Edward III.

Adamonti (ä.dä.mōn′tē). Italian stage name of **Adamberger, Valentin.**

Adamov (ä′dä.môf). [German, **Adamsthal.**] Village in Czechoslovakia, in C Moravia, on the Svratka River, N of Brno: ironworks. The stalactite caves of the Moravian Karst are in the vicinity. 1,432 (1947)

Adamowski (ä.dä.môf′skē), **Joseph.** b. at Warsaw, July 4, 1862; d. 1930. American concert cellist and music teacher; married (1896) Antoinette Szumowska. Debut (1883) as soloist at Warsaw; joined (1889) Boston Symphony after concert tours (1883 *et seq.*) and teaching (1885–87) in Russia and Germany; member of Adamowski Trio and Quartet; professor (1903 *et seq.*) at New England Conservatory; trustee of Paderewski Fund; a founder and director of the Boston Symphony Orchestra pension fund.

Adamowski, Timothée. b. at Warsaw, March 24, 1858; d. at Boston, 1943. American concert violinist and conductor; brother of Joseph Adamowski (1862–1930). Arrived (1879) in the U.S. and made tours with Clara Louise Kellogg and others; member of the Adamowski Trio and Quartet; member (1884–1908) of the Boston Symphony Orchestra; taught (1885 *et seq.*) at the New England Conservatory at Boston.

Adams (ad′ạmz). Town in NW Massachusetts, in Berkshire County, ab. 47 mi. NW of Springfield: manufactures of textiles and paper; stone quarries. It was incorporated in 1778. Pop. 12,034 (1950).

Adams, Abigail. [Maiden name, **Smith.**] b. at Weymouth, Mass., Nov. 11, 1744; d. at Quincy, Mass., Oct. 28, 1818. Wife of John Adams (second president of the U.S.) and mother of John Quincy Adams (sixth president). She supported her husband in his political views and work, joined him in France (1784), and accompanied him to London, where he was U.S. minister (1785–88). Her letters are not only important to historians but possess literary quality as well. The general impression from the letters is that of a woman of extraordinary character, a fit mate for a president and the mother of a president, who had strong prejudices but had a mind far above the usual man or woman of the time and who wrote in a style that is direct and often brilliant. *The Letters of Mrs. Adams, The Wife of John Adams: With an Introductory Memoir, by Her Grandson, Charles Francis Adams* (Boston, 1840) contains some of the best of Abigail Adams's correspondence, altered unfortunately at times by the editor. Additional collections of her letters are preserved at the American Antiquarian Society in Worcester, Mass. One hundred and forty-two of these were published in the *Proceedings* of the Society. These were reprinted with a revised introduction as *New Letters of Abigail Adams, 1788–1801* (Boston, 1947).

Adams, Abraham. [Called **"Parson Adams."**] In Henry Fielding's novel *Joseph Andrews*, a poor curate whose amusing adventures in the company of Joseph Andrews and his betrothed, Fanny, constitute a large part of the book. Usually considered to be a portrait of Fielding's friend William Young (a classical scholar with whom Fielding had collaborated on a translation of Aristophanes' *Plutus*), he is a good-natured but naïve scholar. As a character in fiction, he is ranked by many authorities with Oliver Goldsmith's "Vicar" and Laurence Sterne's "Uncle Toby."

Adams, Alva. b. in Iowa County, Wis., May 14, 1850; d. Nov. 1, 1922. American businessman and banker, twice (1886, 1896) elected and seated as governor of Colorado. He contributed to the development of state educational and penal institutions and advocated strong reforms in state taxation. Elected in his second campaign as a candidate of the fusion of the Democrats with the Free Silver Republicans, he was defeated in a challenge of a third election (1904) instituted by the retiring governor. He later served on the Democratic National Committee (1908) and as a commissioner for the Panama-Pacific exposition (1915).

Adams, Alvin. b. at Andover, Vt., June 16, 1804; d. Sept. 1, 1877. Pioneer in the U.S. express business. He established what later became the Adams Express Company with Ephraim Farnsworth (1840) by purchasing two season round-trip railroad tickets between Boston and New York and making daily journeys between the two cities for his customers. He expanded (1841) with Farnsworth's successor, William B. Dinsmore, and incorporated (1854) the ten-million-dollar Adams Express Company, which carried on a tremendous business during the Civil War in both parcels and mail.

Adams, Andrew. b. at Stratford, Conn., Dec. 11, 1736; d. Nov. 27, 1797. American jurist. He was a prominent member (1776 *et seq.*) of the Connecticut General Assembly, a delegate (1777–80) to the Continental Congress, and chief justice (1793–97) of the Connecticut superior court.

Adams, Andy. b. in Whitley County, Ind., May 3, 1859; d. Sept. 26, 1935. American writer of cowboy stories based on his experiences in the 1880's as a Texas cowhand.

Adams, Brooks. b. at Quincy, Mass., June 24, 1848; d. Feb. 13, 1927. American lawyer and historian; son of Charles Francis Adams (1807–86) and brother of Henry Adams (1838–1918). He was secretary to his father when the latter was U.S. arbitrator at the Geneva tribunal (1871–72) that met to settle the U.S. claims against Great Britain for damages suffered by U.S. shipping from the *Alabama* and other Confederate raiders outfitted in British yards. Author of *The Emancipation of Massachusetts* (1887), *The Law of Civilization and Decay* (1895), *America's Economic Supremacy* (1900), *The New Empire* (1902), *The Degradation of Democratic Dogma* (1920), and others.

Adams, Charles. [Original name, **Karl Adam Schwanbeck.**] b. in Pomerania, Dec. 19, 1845; d. at Denver, Colo., Aug. 19, 1895. American soldier, Indian fighter, and diplomat. He joined a Massachusetts regiment soon after his arrival in the U.S. and served throughout the Civil War; subsequently he enlisted with the 3rd Cavalry and fought Indians in New Mexico and Texas. Appointed (1870) brigadier general of Colorado militia, he later served as Ute Indian agent, with which tribe he attained sufficient influence to arbitrate the Ute uprising of Sept.

29, 1879. Sent (1880) by President Hayes as U.S. ambassador to Bolivia, he successfully reconciled differences that existed between that country and Chile. A term (1882–85) as post-office inspector was terminated by President Cleveland for "offensive partisanship," and he spent the rest of his life in private business.

Adams, Charles Baker. b. at Dorchester, Mass., Jan. 11, 1814; d. Jan. 18, 1853. American naturalist. Employment (1836) with New York geological survey followed by teaching at Amherst; appointed (1838) chemistry and natural history professor at Middlebury and later (1845) Vermont state geologist; recalled (1847) to Amherst, where he served as professor of astronomy and natural history until his death. He is notable for his work in tropical zoology, which resulted in *Contributions to Conchology* (1849–52) and *Catalogue of Shells Collected at Panama* (1852).

Adams, Charles Christopher. b. at Clinton, Ill., July 23, 1873—. American zoologist. Director of N.Y. State Museum (1926 *et seq.*); author of *Guide to the Study of Animal Ecology* (1913) and numerous magazine articles.

Adams, Charles Follen. b. at Dorchester, Mass., April 21, 1842; d. March 8, 1918. American writer of German-dialect verse. His work was collected in the volume *Yawcob Strauss and Other Poems* (1910).

Adams, Charles Francis. b. at Boston, Aug. 18, 1807; d. there, Nov. 21, 1886. American diplomat, lawyer, and biographer; son of John Quincy Adams (1767–1848). He was Free Soil vice-presidential candidate (1848), a member of Congress (1858–61), minister to England (1861–68), and U.S. arbitrator at the Geneva tribunal that met (1871–72) to settle the *Alabama* claims. He published *Life and Works of John Adams* (10 vols., 1850–56) and *Diary of John Quincy Adams* (12 vols., 1874–77).

Adams, Charles Francis. b. at Boston, May 27, 1835; d. at Washington, D.C., March 20, 1915. American lawyer, historian, and railroad authority; son of Charles Francis Adams (1807–86). Served in Civil War, attaining brevet rank as brigadier general; member Massachusetts Board of Railroad Commissioners (1869–79), and chairman after 1872; through influence of Carl Schurz, appointed (1878) chairman of government board for the Union Pacific Railroad and later (1884) its president; lost post (1890) through pressure by Jay Gould, but not until Adams had put railroad on a solid footing. Three lectures made by him at Oxford (1913) were published under the title *Trans-Atlantic Historical Solidarity;* author also of *A College Fetich* (1883), *Chapters of Erie and Other Essays* (1871), *Railroads: Their Origin and Problems* (1878), *Richard Henry Dana, A Biography* (2 vols., 1890), *Life of Charles Francis Adams* (1900), *Studies Military and Diplomatic* (1911), and others.

Adams, Charles Francis. b. at Quincy, Mass., Aug. 2, 1866—. American financier and lawyer; grandson of Charles Francis Adams (1807–86). Secretary of the navy (1929–33) under Herbert Hoover; board chairman of State Street Trust Company, Boston.

Adams, Charles Kendall. b. at Derby, Vt., Jan. 24, 1835; d. at Redlands, Calif., July 26, 1902. American educator and historian. Professor of history at Michigan (1867–85), he was later president of Cornell (1885–92) and Wisconsin (1892–1901). Author of *Democracy and Monarchy in France* (1874), *Manual of Historical Literature* (1882), and others.

Adams, Clement. b. at Buckington, Warwickshire, c1519; d. Jan. 9, 1587. English writer and teacher, schoolmaster to the royal "henchmen" (pages) at Greenwich. His transcription of Richard Chancellor's narrative of the journey to Moscow (1553) is the first written account of the earliest Anglo-Russian contact. It was published by Richard Hakluyt in his *Collections* (1589).

Adams, Comfort Avery. b. at Cleveland, Ohio, Nov. 1, 1868—. American electrical engineer and professor. At one time an associate of Albert Abraham Michelson, he has been Lawrence professor of engineering at Harvard (1914–35) and Gordon McKay professor of electrical engineering at Harvard (1935–36). Author of *Dynamo Design Schedules* and numerous technical articles.

Adams, Cyrus Cornelius. b. at Naperville, Ill., Jan. 7, 1849; d. at New York, May 4, 1928. American geographer, president (1889–93) of the department of geography at the Brooklyn Institute. He wrote a biography of David Livingstone, and was the editor (1908 *et seq.*) of the *Bulletin* of the American Geographical Society.

Adams, Daniel. b. at Townsend, Mass., Sept. 29, 1773; d. at Keene, N.H., June 8, 1864. American physician, educator, and civic benefactor. He was during his early career (1799 *et seq.*) a practicing physician at Leominster, Mass., but largely abandoned active practice when he undertook publication of a weekly newspaper, the *Telescope,* and preparation (1801 *et seq.*) of improved elementary textbooks, notably *The Scholar's Arithmetic* (1801), *Geography or a Description of the World* (1814), and works on the nature and use of language. He moved (1813) to New Hampshire, to become again a practicing physician, after teaching school (1805 *et seq.*) and editing a monthly agricultural journal at Boston.

Adams, Daniel Weissiger. b. at Lynchburg, Va., 1820; d. at New Orleans, La., June 13, 1872. American lawyer and soldier, with Confederate army in Civil War. Appointed (1861) member of a three-man military committee responsible for organizing Louisiana for war, he entered one of two regiments thus prepared, and fought at Shiloh, Stone's River, Chickamauga, and elsewhere, being three times wounded and rising to the rank of brigadier general. He resumed (1865) practice of law at New Orleans.

Adams, Ebenezer. b. in New Hampshire, Oct. 22, 1765; d. Aug. 15, 1841. American educator. He was prevented by poverty from entering college until the age of 22, but graduated (1791) with honors from Dartmouth, and served (1792–1806) as preceptor of an academy at Leicester, Mass., becoming also local justice of the peace and first postmaster of the town. Appointed (1808) first professor of mathematics and natural science at Phillips Academy, Exeter, N.H., after two years of teaching at Portland, Me., he returned (1809) to Dartmouth as professor of languages, and succeeded (1810) to the chair of mathematics and philosophy on the death of John Hubbard, which post he held until 1833. During the period of the "Dartmouth University" controversy with the state of New Hampshire, he remained a stalwart champion of Dartmouth College, and was active in raising funds to carry the issue to the Supreme Court of the U.S.

Adams, Edwin. b. at Medford, Mass., Feb. 3, 1834; d. at Philadelphia, Oct. 28, 1877. American actor, notable for his performances in light comedy. His debut (1853) at Boston's National Theatre was followed a few years later by his first great popular success at Baltimore; subsequently he played Shakespearian roles with Kate Bateman, Edwin Booth, and others. He is, however, probably chiefly remembered for his characterization of Enoch Arden, in the dramatization of Tennyson's poem of the same name, in which role he toured the U.S.

Adams, Eliphalet. b. at Dedham, Mass., March 26, 1677; d. at New London, Conn., Oct. 4, 1753. American clergyman, notable as a missionary to the Indians and leader of the New England Puritans. Successor to Gurdon Saltonstall as pastor at New London, he held his pulpit for 43 years (c1709 *et seq.*) against the attacks of Baptists, Episcopalians, and New Light adherents within his own congregation.

Adams, Ephraim Douglass. b. at Decorah, Ia., Dec. 18, 1865; d. Sept. 1, 1930. American historian. Professor at Stanford University (1906 *et seq.*); author of *Great Britain and the American Civil War* (1925) and others.

Adams, Frank Dawson. b. at Montreal, 1859; d. 1942. Canadian geologist. As Logan professor of geology at McGill University (until 1931), he was an outstanding teacher of his science in North America; received honors from scientific societies in Canada, Great Britain, and elsewhere. Author of *Birth and Development of the Geological Sciences* (1938).

Adams, Franklin Pierce. [Pseudonym, **F.P.A.**] b. at Chicago, Ill., Nov. 15, 1881—. American humorous author, journalist, and radio performer. He began his newspaper career at Chicago, but moved to New York where his column, "The Conning Tower," was successively carried by three papers (1922–41). He was a charter performer on the radio program, "Information Please" (1938 *et seq.*). Author of *The Diary of Our Own Samuel Pepys* (1935), *The Melancholy Lute* (1936), and others.

Adams, Frank Ramsay. b. at Morrison, Ill., July 7, 1883—. American novelist, musical-comedy writer, and motion-picture scenarist. Author of 15 novels, including *Men on Foot* (1937) and *Fathers of Madelon* (1939), he also did the books for seven musical comedies and scripts for the films *Trade Winds* and *The Cowboy and the Lady*.

Adams, Frederick Upham. b. at Boston, Dec. 10, 1859; d. at Larchmont, N.Y., Aug. 28, 1921. American engineer, inventor of electrical devices, and author. Developed electric lamp post (1886) and signal tower (1887); built record-breaking experimental train for Baltimore and Ohio Railroad (1900); founder and editor (1896–98) of reformist *New Time;* author of several novels as well as works on engineering and social problems.

Adams, George Burton. b. at Fairfield, Vt., June 3, 1851; d. at New Haven, Conn., May 26, 1925. American historian. Professor of history at Yale (1888–1925); author of *Civilization during the Middle Ages* (1894), *Origin of the English Constitution* (1912), and others.

Adams, Hannah. b. at Medfield, Mass., Oct. 2, 1755; d. at Brookline, Mass., Dec. 15, 1831. American writer, author of *View of Religious Opinions* (1784, later entitled *Dictionary of Religions*), and others. She is credited by some authorities with having been the first woman in the U.S. to make even a meager commercial success of writing.

Adams, Harry William. b. at Worcester, England, Nov. 3, 1868—. English landscape-painter, noted particularly for his winter scenes. In 1896 he became a member of the Royal Academy, and in 1900 his painting *Winter's Sleep* was purchased under the terms of the Chantrey Bequest.

Adams, Henry. b. at Boston, Feb. 16, 1838; d. March 28, 1918. American historian, author, and philosopher; son of Charles Francis Adams (1807–86), grandson of John Quincy Adams (1767–1848), and great-grandson of John Adams (1735–1826). He graduated from Harvard in 1858 and studied briefly in Germany, after which he spent two years traveling in Europe, mostly in Germany and Italy. He then served as secretary to his father, who was U.S. minister (1861–68) to England, returning thereafter to the U.S., avowedly to seek a career in journalism. From 1870 to 1877 he served as assistant professor of history at Harvard, and as editor of the *North American Review*. While at Harvard he introduced the seminar method of instruction in history. After leaving Harvard he devoted the remainder of his life to writing, traveling, and reflecting upon the relationship between man and the universe. His best-known works are *Mont-Saint Michel and Chartres* (privately printed, 1904; published, 1913) and *The Education of Henry Adams* (privately printed, 1907; published, 1918). His most scholarly work, however, is his nine-volume *History of the United States During the Administrations of Jefferson and Madison* (1885–91). Other works include *The Life of Albert Gallatin* (1879), *Democracy* (1880), *John Randolph* (1882), *Esther* (1884), *A Letter to American Teachers of History* (1910), and *The Degradation of the Democratic Dogma* (1919). He also collaborated with his brother, Charles Francis Adams, in writing *Chapters of Erie and Other Essays* (1871) and with three of his students at Harvard in writing *Essays on Anglo-Saxon Law* (1876). In his search for a philosophy of history he extended his studies to politics, economics, astronomy, physics, chemistry, mathematics, geology, anthropology, and psychology. As a result of his study and reflection, he concluded that the second law of thermodynamics is as applicable to human society as it is to mechanical energy, i.e., that institutions, like individuals, must follow the law of senescence and decay, and that both man and the "celestial universe" are doomed. Despite his vast learning and the recognition which he received, he professed to believe that his education was wholly inadequate and his life a failure.

Adams, Henry Carter. b. at Davenport, Ia., Dec. 31, 1851; d. Aug. 11, 1921. American economist, writer, and educator. For many years (1887 *et seq.*) professor of political economy and finance at Michigan, he is now perhaps best known as the author of *The State in Relation to Industrial Action* (1887). He was the author also of *Public Debts* (1887), *The Science of Finance* (1898), *American Railway Accounting* (1918), and others.

Adams, Henry Cullen. b. in Oneida County, N.Y., Nov. 28, 1850; d. en route from Washington, D.C., to Wisconsin, July 9, 1906. American politician, congressman (1902–06) from Wisconsin. After serving (1895–1902) as Wisconsin dairy and food commissioner, he was elected (1902) to Congress, where he became known for his support of the National Food and Drugs Act, and of a law providing for federal inspection of meat. He also espoused the act admitting Arizona and New Mexico into the U.S. as separate states, and was responsible for the Adams Act, which provided for an annual appropriation of one million dollars for agricultural research.

Adams, Herbert. b. at West Concord, Vt., Jan. 28, 1858; d. May 21, 1945. American sculptor. Although he was best known for his busts of women, many of them done in polychrome, he also did statues and busts of many men important in American history, including William Cullen Bryant and William Ellery Channing. In addition to this, he executed the figures for the McMillan fountain at Washington, D.C., as well as the Vanderbilt memorial bronze doors of New York's Saint Bartholomew's Church.

Adams, Herbert Baxter. b. at Shutesbury, Mass., April 16, 1850; d. at Amherst, Mass., July 30, 1901. American historian and political scientist. Awarded degrees with highest honors by Amherst (1872) and Heidelberg (1876), he was a faculty member (1876 *et seq.*) at Johns Hopkins, serving (1891 *et seq.*) as professor of American and institutional history. He was a founder (1884) and first secretary (1884–1900) of the American Historical Association, and author of the *Life and Writings of Jared Sparks* (1893) and many others.

Adams, Isaac. b. at Adams Corner, Rochester, N.H., Aug. 16, 1802; d. July 19, 1883. American inventor and manufacturer of printing machinery. His invention (1827) of the "Adams Power Press" and establishment (1836) of the manufacturing firm of I. and S. Adams was of enormous importance in the history of printing in 19th-century America. For more than 50 years, until it was replaced with the cylinder press, Adams's press, which handled 30- by 40-inch sheets, was standard equipment for much of the American book-printing industry.

Adams, James Hopkins. b. in South Carolina, March 15, 1812; d. there, July 13, 1861. American politician and cotton planter, governor (1854 *et seq.*) of South Carolina. Terms at various times (1834 *et seq.*) in both houses of the state legislature were followed by a successful campaign for the governorship, but his administration was marred by espousal of a bill to reopen the African slave trade. Probably because of this, and his fiery advocacy of secession at a time when most South Carolinians still disapproved it, he was defeated (1858) in a campaign for a seat in the U.S. Senate. His secessionist views, however, made him a prominent member of the convention which voted for withdrawal from the Union in 1860 and he was elected one of three commissioners to negotiate transfer of federal property to state ownership.

Adams, James Truslow. b. at Brooklyn, N.Y., Oct. 18, 1878; d. at Westport, Conn., May 18, 1949. American historian and former stockbroker (1900–12). Won Pulitzer Prize with *Founding of New England* (1921); wrote *The Epic of America* (1931), now published in nine languages; recent works are *The American* (1943) and *Frontiers of American Culture* (1944); editor-in-chief of the *Dictionary of American History*.

Adams, Jasper. b. at East Medway, Mass., Aug. 27, 1793; d. Oct. 25, 1841. American college administrator and Episcopal clergyman. As president (1824–36) of Charleston College, in South Carolina, he raised that institution from poverty and ill repute to respectable rank among southern colleges, although indifference on the part of the trustees led him at one point (1826) to accept a post as first president of Hobart College, Geneva, N.Y. (but his absence awakened Charlestonians to his value and he was recalled in 1828). He later served (1838–40) as chaplain and professor of geography, history, and ethics at West Point. Author of *Elements of Moral Philosophy* (1837).

Adams, John. b. at what is now Quincy (then part of Braintree), Mass., Oct. 19, 1735; d. there, July 4, 1826. American political philosopher, revolutionist, diplomat, second president of the U.S. (1797–1801); father of John Quincy Adams (1767–1848). He was graduated from Harvard College in 1755, studied law at Worcester with James Putnam and by 1770 had attained the position of leading barrister in Massachusetts. From the year 1765, he was a principal figure of the Revolutionary movement in Massachusetts, opposing the governors Bernard and Hutchinson in their enforcement of the Stamp Act, the Townsend Acts, and other measures of the British government. Adams's numerous pamphlets on political issues were influential and he acted as constitutional adviser to the Massachusetts Assembly, the committees of correspondence, and to a number of Massachusetts town meetings. In 1770 he defied public opinion by defending the constitutional rights of the British soldiers involved in the Boston Massacre. From 1774 to 1778, Adams represented Massachusetts in the Continental Congress, where he tutored the several states in their constitution-making and drafted the Plan of Treaties establishing the new nation's conduct of its foreign relations. His diary of these years and his letters are the source of most of our knowledge of the personal history of the Congress. The years from 1778 to 1788 Adams spent abroad as our diplomatic representative in France and Holland; at the close of the War for Independence he was one of the peace makers and first minister of the U.S. to Great Britain. While abroad he wrote his three-volume *Defence of the Constitutions of the United States of America against the Attacks of Mr. Turgot* (London, 1787–88), which was influential in the reform of the American government. When the new Constitution went into effect, Adams was chosen vice-president (1789–97), and after Washington's retirement was elected president and served during four years of political strife at home and our quasi-war with France abroad. John Adams is responsible for the early growth of the navy and for our policy of naval defense. As a Federalist, he mistrusted the French Revolution, believing in the Anglo-Saxon heritage of reform by "gradual abolition." He ran for a second term, was defeated by Jefferson, and in 1801 returned to Quincy where he lived in retirement until his death on July 4, 1826, the 50th anniversary of American independence. He married Abigail Smith of Weymouth. His eldest son, John Quincy Adams, was sixth president of the U.S.

Adams, John. [Also, **Alexander Smith.**] b. in England, c1760; d. on Pitcairn Island, in the Pacific Ocean, 1829. English seaman and leading mutineer of the *Bounty* (1789). The only mutineer not massacred (1794) by the Tahitians, he eventually became governor of Pitcairn Island.

Adams, John. b. at Canterbury, Conn., Sept. 18, 1772; d. April 24, 1863. American educator, principal (1810–32) of Phillips Academy, Andover, Mass. His administration of Phillips Academy was notable for successful efforts to reimpose discipline and to restore the original high standing of the institution, but a slackening of his control led trustees to request his resignation in 1832, despite his earlier success. The last 31 years of his life were spent variously as principal of an academy at Elbridge, N.Y., as seminary president at Jacksonville, Ill., and as an agent for the American Sunday School Union.

Adams, John. b. at Nashville, Tenn., July 1, 1825; killed in battle at Franklin, Tenn., Nov. 30, 1864. American army officer, with Confederate forces in Civil War.

Adams, John Coleman. [Called **"the Dean of the Hartford Ministry."**] b. at Malden, Mass., Oct. 25, 1849; d. at Hartford, Conn., June 22, 1922. American Universalist clergyman and author. Pastorates at Newton, Mass., Lynn, Mass., Chicago, and Brooklyn were followed (1901) by a call to All Souls' Church, Hartford, Conn., where he soon became known for his liberal, but firm, theological views, and his feeling for nature.

Adams, John Couch. b. at Lidcot, Cornwall, England, June 5, 1819, d. at Cambridge, England, Jan. 21, 1892. English astronomer, notable as professor of astronomy and director of the observatory at Cambridge University. He shares with Leverrier the honor for discovery of the planet Neptune in 1845–46. In addition to this, he brought out a tabulation of moon's parallax (1852), published findings (1853) on secular acceleration of the moon's mean motion which partly superseded the theories of Laplace, and conducted research into Leonids of the meteor shower in 1866.

Adams, John Quincy. b. at what is now Quincy (then part of Braintree), Mass., July 11, 1767; d. at Washington, D.C., Feb. 23, 1848. Sixth president of the United States (1825–29); son of President John Adams (1735–1826). Minister to the Netherlands (1794–97) and to Prussia (1797–1801); senator from Massachusetts (1803–08); minister to Russia (1809–14); a negotiator of the Treaty of Ghent (1814) which ended the War of 1812; minister to England (1815–17); secretary of state (1817–25). A candidate for president in 1824 (with his support coming chiefly from New England and New York), he ran second to Andrew Jackson (99 vs. 84 votes) in the Electoral College, but was elected by the House of Representatives, largely through the instrumentality of Henry Clay (Jackson, although the leader of the four candidates in the Electoral College, lacked a majority). In his campaign (1828) for a second term, Adams was defeated by Jackson. He was a Whig member of Congress thereafter (1831–48). His *Memoirs* were posthumously edited and published (1874–77) by his son, Charles Francis Adams (1807–86).

Adams, John Quincy (2nd). b. at Boston, Sept. 22, 1833; d. Aug. 14, 1894. American politician; eldest son of Charles Francis Adams (1807–86). He was the unsuccessful Democratic candidate for governor of Massachusetts in 1867 and 1871.

Adams, Joseph Alexander. b. at New Germantown, N.J., 1803; d. 1880. American wood-engraver, believed by some to have been the first electrotyper in America. Aided during his apprenticeship as a printer by Dr. Alexander Anderson, a pioneer American wood-engraver, he is now perhaps chiefly remembered for his 1,600 illustrations in Harper's *Illuminated Bible* (1843). His work has been commended for firmness and clarity of line by such authorities as W. J. Linton in *History of Wood Engraving in America* (1882).

Adams, Joseph Quincy. b. at Greenville, S.C., March 23, 1881; d. Nov. 10, 1946. American Shakespearean scholar. He was professor of English at Cornell University (1919-31), and director of the Folger Shakespeare Library, at Washington, D.C. (1931 *et seq.*). Author of *Shakespearean Playhouses* (1917); editor of *Chief Pre-Shakespearean Dramas* (1924), *The Adams Shakespeare* (1929), *The Passionate Pilgrim* (1939); general editor of *The New Variorum Shakespeare.*

Adams, Léonie Fuller. b. at Brooklyn, N.Y., 1899—. American poet. She has taught at New York University and Bennington College. She was an early advocate of breaking with the established tradition in American poetry. Her works include *Those Not Elect* (1925), *High Falcon* (1929), and *This Measure* (1933).

Adams, Maude. [Original name, **Maude Kiskadden.**] b. at Salt Lake City, Utah, Nov. 11, 1872; d. near Tannersville, N.Y., July 17, 1953. American actress. She made her first professional appearance in 1888 with E. H. Sothern's company. She first became well known for her role in *Men and Women* while with the Charles Frohman Stock Company, and later supported John Drew for five years in *The Masked Ball, The Butterflies,* and others (1892–97). Her principal successes include *The Little Minister, Quality Street, Peter Pan,* and *What Every Woman Knows* (all by J. M. Barrie) and also *L'Aiglon, Romeo and Juliet, Joan of Arc,* and *Chantecler.*

Adams, Moses. A pseudonym of **Bagby, George William.**

Adams, Mount. Mountain in N New Hampshire, in the Presidential Range, second highest summit of the White Mountains, near Mount Washington. 5,798 ft.

Adams, Mount. Peak of the Cascade Mountains in the state of Washington. 12,307 ft.

Adams, Nehemiah. b. at Salem, Mass., Feb. 19, 1806; d. Oct. 6, 1878. American Congregational clergyman, notable for his defense of orthodox trinitarian Congregationalism against Unitarianism and for his arguments on behalf of a solution by the South of the problem of slavery. The latter view is covered in *A South-side View of Slavery* (1854), which brought Adams violent criticism from many of his own Boston parishioners. His sermons and other writings, in a style based on Addison and Jeremy Taylor, brought him international renown.

Adams, Oscar Fay. b. at Worcester, Mass., 1855; d. at North Truro, Mass., April 30, 1919. American editor and author, chiefly known for his *Through the Years with the Poets* (12 vols., 1886) and *Dictionary of American Authors* (1897). Author also of *The Archbishop's Unguarded Moment and Other Stories* (1899). He was U.S. editor of *The Henry Irving Shakespeare.*

Adams, Point. Northwesternmost headland of Oregon, at the mouth of the Columbia River.

Adams, Samuel. b. at Boston, Sept. 27, 1722; d. there, Oct. 2, 1803. American patriot and political agitator, one of the leaders of the American Revolution. Opposed Sugar Act (1764) and Stamp Act (1765); as member of Massachusetts legislature (1765–74) thrust James Otis aside as leader of popular party; organized committee of correspondence (1772) to acquaint colonial leaders with latest political developments; delegate to first Continental Congress (1774), and an influential member thereafter until 1781; a signer of the Declaration of Independence; member of Massachusetts ratifying convention (1788); lieutenant governor of Massachusetts (1789–94); governor of Massachusetts (1794–97).

Adams, Samuel Hopkins. b. at Dunkirk, N.Y., Jan. 26, 1871—. American novelist and magazine writer. During his early career he was, successively, a New York *Sun* reporter (1891–1900), an editor of *McClure's Magazine* (1903–05), and author of a famous exposé (1905) of quack medicine for *Collier's Magazine*. He has written numerous novels, several of which have received film adaptation, including *It Happened One Night* (1934), *Gorgeous Hussy* (1934), and *The Harvey Girls* (1942).

Adams, Sarah Flower. b. at Great Harlow, Essex, Feb. 22, 1805; d. in August, 1848. English poet, now remembered chiefly as the author of the hymn *Nearer, My God, to Thee* (1840).

Adams, Sherman. b. at East Dover, Vt., Jan. 8, 1899—. American politician. He was elected to the New Hampshire legislature in 1940, serving as speaker (1943–44). He became a member of Congress in 1945, and in 1949 was sworn in as governor of New Hampshire. After playing a leading role in Dwight D. Eisenhower's presidential campaign, he was appointed (1953) the new president's chief administrative assistant.

Adams, Thomas. d. c1655. English Puritan divine and writer. He published *The Happiness of the Church* (1618, a collection of sermons), a collection of occasional sermons (1629), and a commentary on the second epistle of Saint Peter (1633).

Adams, Walter Sydney. b. at Antioch, Turkey, Dec. 20, 1876—. American astronomer. He was a staff member (1904 *et seq.*) of the Mt. Wilson Observatory, Pomona, Calif., and Observatory director (1923–46). Author of numerous articles on stellar and solar spectroscopy, and other subjects.

Adams, William. [Called **Will Adams**; Japanese title, **Anjin Sama**, meaning "Mr. Pilot."] b. at Gillingham, near Chatham, England, sometime between 1564 and 1575; d. in Japan, 1620. English navigator, notable as the first Englishman to reach Japan. He joined (1598) as pilot major a Dutch fleet of five ships fitted out by Rotterdam merchants for the India trade, and after an unfortunate voyage in which all the ships except the *Charity*, in which he sailed, returned to Holland or were lost, arrived (1600) at Kyushu. Although he remained in Japan at first under compulsion, he rose into favor at the Japanese court, and received from the reigning shogun an estate near Yokosuka. In 1613 he obtained for the English a trading-station at Hirado. He later married a Japanese woman and made voyages to Siam (1616) and Cochin-China (1617–18).

Adams, William. b. at Colchester, Conn., Jan. 25, 1807; d. Aug. 31, 1880. American Presbyterian clergyman. Ordained (1831) after graduation (1827) from Yale at the head of his class in classical scholarship, he was one of the founders of the Union Theological Seminary in 1836, and later (1874 *et seq.*) its president (in which post he had much to do with increasing its endowment). He was regarded by many as the leading Presbyterian divine of his day, and was after 1837 a leading member of the "New School" group within the Presbyterian church.

Adams, William. b. 1814; d. 1848. English clergyman and writer, vicar of Saint Peter's at Oxford (1840). Author of *The Shadow of the Cross* (1842), *Distant Hills* (1844), and other sacred allegories.

Adams, William Henry Davenport. b. at London, May 5, 1828; d. at Wimbledon, near London, Dec. 30, 1891. English author, editor, compiler, private tutor, and French translator. He founded (1870) and edited (1870–78) the *Scottish Guardian*, later editing several volumes in the *Whitefriars Library of Wit and Humor*. Author of *Memorable Battles in English History* (1862), *The Bird World* (1877), *Good Queen Anne* (1886), and a *Concordance to the Works of Shakespeare* (1886).

Adams, William Lysander. b. at Painesville, Ohio, Feb. 5, 1821; d. April 26, 1906. American editor, physician, Campbellite preacher, and a founder of the Republican Party in Oregon. He emigrated (1848) to Oregon, after studying under William Campbell, and spent the period until 1855 as farmer, schoolteacher, preacher, and occasional contributor to newspapers; owner, publisher, and editor of the Oregon City *Argus* (1855–61) and federal collector of customs at Astoria (1861 *et seq.*); student of medicine (1873) at Philadelphia, and subsequently a practicing physician and founder of the Hood River sanitarium in Oregon. He is probably chiefly remembered for his ruthless campaign against the "Salem Clique," which he apparently suspected of secessionist plots on behalf of Brigham Young and the Mormons.

Adams, William Taylor. [Pseudonym, **Oliver Optic.**] b. at Bellingham, Mass., July 30, 1822; d. at Boston, March 27, 1897. American teacher and fiction writer, chiefly of works for young boys, including the series entitled the *Boat Club*, *Young America Abroad*, *Starry Flag*, *Riverdale Series*, and *Onward and Upward*. Founded and edited *Oliver Optic's Magazine;* teacher for 20 years in Boston public schools.

Adam's Bridge. [Also, **Rama's Bridge.**] Series of shoals between NW Ceylon and SE India, a considerable hindrance to shipping in the area. By tradition, the shoals are the remains of a causeway built by Rama, the hero of the *Ramayana*, in order that he might cross from India to Ceylon to rescue his wife Sita; geologically, it seems probable that the gap between India and Ceylon was actually once bridged by an isthmus, and that Adam's Bridge may be what is left of it. Length, ab. 30 mi.

Adam Scotus (ad'ąm skō'tus). [Also: **Adam Anglicus, Adam Anglo-Scotus.**] fl. c1180. Scottish theologian and religious writer. He was a Christian mystic and advocate of asceticism whose works (first published in 1518) gained him international repute.

Adams Express Company (ad'ąmz). American shipping concern whose origin as a corporation may be said to date from the small carrying trade instituted (1840) by Alvin Adams and Ephraim Farnsworth between Boston and New York. The enterprise enjoyed a rapid expansion, reaching into the Middle States, the South, and the Pacific Coast. The company's considerable stock holdings gave it an important financial position and considerable influence in the years after the Civil War. Its shipping activity was eventually absorbed by the American Railway Express Company.

Adamson (ad'ąm.sǫn), **John.** b. at Gateshead, England, Sept. 13, 1787; d. at Newcastle, England, Sept. 27, 1855. English archaeologist and scholar of Portuguese.

Adamson, Patrick. [Original surname, **Conston, Constant, Consteane,** or **Constantine.**] b. at Perth, Scotland, March 15, 1537; d. at St. Andrew's, Scotland, Feb. 19, 1592. Scottish prelate. Archbishop at St. Andrew's (1576 *et seq.*), he was excommunicated on various charges in 1588, but the sentence was later nullified.

Adamson, Robert. b. 1852; d. 1902. Scottish philosophical writer, professor of philosophy at Owens College, Manchester, and of logic and rhetoric at Glasgow (1895–1902). Author of *Roger Bacon: the Philosophy of Science in the Middle Ages* (1876), *On the Philosophy of Kant* (1879), *Fichte* (1881), and others.

Adamson, William Charles. b. at Bowdon, Ga., Aug. 13, 1854; d. Jan. 6, 1929. American lawyer and politician, notable for the introduction in Congress of the Adamson Act specifying the eight-hour day as normal for railroad laborers. After admission (1876) to the bar, he was judge (1885–89) of the city court at Carrollton, Ga.; representative (1897–1917) in Congress until his resignation (1917) to accept a post on the Board of U.S. General Appraisers of the Customs Court.

Adamson Act. Act passed (Sept. 2, 1916) by the U.S. Congress during the first Wilson administration. Part of the "New Freedom" program, it regulated the working hours of railroad employees engaged in interstate commerce by reducing the work day from ten to eight hours.

Adams-Onís Treaty (ad'ąmz.ō.nēs'). Treaty between the U.S. and Spain signed (Feb. 22, 1819) at Washington, D.C., by the U.S. secretary of state, John Quincy Adams, and the Spanish minister, Luis de Onís. The treaty provided for the termination of the West Florida controversy, the cession to the U.S. of East Florida, the U.S. assumption of claims of its own nationals against Spain, the fixing of a boundary line from the Gulf of Mexico to the Pacific Ocean, and the reaffirmation of certain provisions of Pinckney's Treaty (1795). The Adams-Onís Treaty is considered by most authorities to have been a landmark in the history of American expansionism.

Adam's Peak (ad'ąmz). Conical mountain near the W shore of Ceylon. There is a Buddhist temple on the summit, but it is a holy place also for Hindus and Moslems (according to Moslem legend, a small indentation in one of its topmost rocks was formed by Adam, the first man, who was compelled to stand there, on one foot, for 1,000 years as a penance for eating the apple in the Garden of Eden). 7,420 ft.

Adamsthal (ä'däms.täl). German name of **Adamov.**

Adams v. Tanner, 244 U.S. 590 (1917) (ad'ąmz; tan'ėr). Decision of the U.S. Supreme Court which voided a Washington law prohibiting the acceptance of fees as payment for assistance in obtaining employment. The majority opinion held that this statute affecting employment agencies violated the constitutional guarantee of due process of law.

Adana (ä.dä'ną). [Also: **Seyhan, Seihan.**] City in S Turkey, on the Seyhan River and capital of the *il* (province or vilayet) of Seyhan: fourth largest city in Turkey. Founded in the 1st century B.C. by the Romans, it was for several centuries thereafter an important point on one of the great military highways built by them to link the various portions of their eastern empire, but subsequently waned in importance until the 8th century A.D., when it was restored by Harun al-Rashid. It is now an important commercial and agricultural center, with rail and air connections to other major Turkish cities. 117,799 (1950).

Adana (ad'ą.ną). An ancient name of **Aden.**

Adangme (ä.däng'mā). [Also, **Adangbe** (-bā).] Sudanic-speaking people of W Africa, inhabiting the coastal towns of the SE Gold Coast. They are considered a subgroup or an eastern extension of the Ga, to whom they are closely related in language and culture.

Adans (å.däṅs). See **Adenet.**

Adanse (ä.dän'sā). One of the Sudanic-speaking Akan peoples of W Africa, inhabiting the S part of the Gold Coast, to the S of Kumasi.

Adanson (å.däṅ.sôṅ), **Michel.** b. at Aix, France, April 7, 1727; d. at Paris, Aug. 8, 1806. French naturalist and traveler in Senegambia. He was the author of *Histoire naturelle du Sénégal* (1757), *Familles des plantes* (1763), and others.

Adapazari (ä.dä.pä.zä.ri'). [Also: **Adabazar**; Turkish, **Adapazarı**).] Town in NW Turkey, on the Sakarya River in the *il* (province or vilayet) of Kocaeli; commercial and textile center. 29,386 (1945).

Adar (ą.där'). [Also, **Adar Sheni.**] Name of the 12th month (falling variously in February-March) of the Babylonian calendar, from which it was adopted by the Jews, along with the rest of the names of the months, after the Exile. It stands as 12th month in the Jewish ecclesiastical calendar, sixth in the civil calendar. On leap years, a new seventh month is added to the calendar, and in such years the variant "Adar Sheni" becomes the name of the seventh month.

Adara (a.dä'rą). Name of the second-magnitude star ε Canis Majoris, second brightest in the constellation Canis Major ("Great Dog"), situated in the animal's thigh.

Adare (ą.dãr'), **Cape.** Cape in Antarctica, the E entrance point of Robertson Bay and the NE extremity of Victoria Land, in 71°17′ S., 170°15′ E. It was named (1841) by Sir James Clark Ross after a friend, Viscount Adare. Here the first landing on the Antarctic mainland was made (1895) by a party from the Norwegian ship *Antarctic.*

Adar Sheni (ą.där' she.nē'). See **Adar.**

Adbeel (ad'bē.el). Name of the third son of Ishmael. Gen. xxv. 13, 1 Chron. i. 29. An Arabian tribe, *Idiba'il,* is mentioned in the cuneiform inscriptions. It was probably located on the Egyptian border. The name has also been found in a Minaean inscription.

Adda (äd'dä). [Latin, **Addua.**] River in N Italy, in the *compartimento* (region) of Lombardy. It rises in the Alps W of the Ortler Spitze (highest mountain in the Ortler range), traverses the Valtellina and Lake Como, and joins the Po River ab. 8 mi. W of Cremona. Length, ab. 180 mi.; navigable ab. 75 mi.

Addams (ad'ąmz), **Jane.** b. at Cedarville, Ill., Sept. 6, 1860; d. May 21, 1935. American social worker, author, and advocate of international peace. She graduated from Rockford College (1881) and, with Ellen Gates Starr, opened (1889) Chicago's Hull House, of which she was head resident until her death. President of Women's International League for Peace, she presided at conventions at The Hague (1915–22), Zurich (1919), Vienna (1921), Washington (1924), Dublin (1926), and Prague (1929). She shared the Nobel Peace Prize with Nicholas Murray Butler in 1931. Author of *Democracy and Social Ethics* (1902), *Newer Ideals of Peace* (1907), *Twenty Years at Hull House* (1910), *A New Conscience and an Ancient Evil* (1911), *The Second Twenty Years at Hull House* (1930), *The Excellent Becomes the Permanent* (1932), and others.

Addar (ad.där'), **Ras.** Arabic name of **Bon, Cape.**

Adding Machine, The. Play by Elmer Rice, produced and published in 1923, satirizing the commercial spirit and social and economic regimentation. Its chief character, Mr. Zero, loses his job as an accountant when he is replaced by an adding machine, and thereupon murders his employer, is executed, and goes to heaven, where he derives pleasure from the operation of a giant adding machine. Ordered to return to earth, he at first defies the command, but is informed that it is his cosmic destiny to be an eternal slave to the machine age.

Addington (ad'ing.tǫn), **Henry.** [Title, 1st Viscount **Sidmouth.**] b. at Reading, England, May 30, 1757; d. Feb. 15, 1844. English politician, at one time the leader of the parliamentary faction known as the "king's friends." He entered Parliament in 1783, and was subsequently speaker (1789–1801) and prime minister (1801–04). During his office as home secretary under Liverpool (1812–22), his suspension (1817) of the Habeas Corpus Act and alleged encouragement of police repression infuriated a large section of the English public. He withdrew from the government entirely in 1824.

Addis Ababa (ad'is ab'ą.bą). [Also: **Adis Ababa, Adis Abeba.**] City in E Africa, the capital of Ethiopia, in the province of Shoa, ab. 487 mi. inland from the Gulf of Aden, at the end of the railway from Djibouti, in French Somaliland. A treaty of peace with Italy was concluded here on Oct. 26, 1896, after Italy's first attempt to conquer Ethiopia had ended in disaster. The second Italian invasion, during the 1930's, ended with the occupation (1936) of Addis Ababa. The city was freed during the collapse of the Italian empire in Africa during World War II. It is the only large urban area in Ethiopia, and because of its altitude (over 8,000 ft.) it enjoys a fine, healthful climate. Pop. ab. 300,000.

Addiscombe (ad'is.kum). Ward of Croydon, county borough, in SE England, in Surrey, ab. 13 mi. S of Charing Cross station, London. It was formerly the seat of a college for the cadets of the East India Company. 14,048 (1931).

Addison (ad'i.sǫn), **Christopher.** [Title, 1st Viscount **Addison of Stallingborough.**] b. in Lincolnshire, 1869; d. Dec. 11, 1951. English politician and professor of anatomy. Active in the government during and after World War I, he was later minister of agriculture in MacDonald's second Labour cabinet (1930–31), Labour leader in the House of Lords (1940), and secretary for the dominions (1945).

Addison, John. b. at London, c1766; d. there, Jan. 30, 1844. English composer and performer on the double-bass. His work includes several operettas which were very popular in his day, as well as a number of songs.

Addison, Joseph. b. at Milston, Wiltshire, England, 1672; d. at Holland House, London, 1719. English essayist, poet, and statesman; son of Lancelot Addison (1632–1703). He was a graduate of Charterhouse School (where he first met Richard Steele) and Oxford (where he won high praise for his Latin verse). Partly because of a poem in Latin on the Peace of Ryswick, he was appointed to receive a subsidy to enable him to prepare for diplomatic service by travel (1699–1703) on the Continent. In 1705, he wrote *Campaign* in couplets to celebrate the victory at Blenheim, and won political preferment among Whigs; the same year also saw publication of his long *Remarks on Italy*, in prose. He was under-secretary of state (1706–08), chief secretary to the lord lieutenant of Ireland (1709–10), and a member of Parliament (1708 *et seq.*). During this period he wrote the opera *Rosamond* (1707) and the classical tragedy *Cato* (1713), the latter an immediate success partly because of its political implications. He contributed also to the *Tatler*, writing (1709–11) approximately 80 papers alone or with Steele; he also wrote about 250 *Spectators* (1711–12) and about 50 *Guardians* (1713). He edited and was the main contributing author of the revived *Spectator* (1714), as well as the *Free-Holder* (1715–16). He married (1716) the Countess of Warwick, and served (1717–18) in the cabinet as secretary of state.

Addison, Julia de Wolf. b. at Boston, Mass., 1866—. American muralist, author, composer, and designer.

Addison, Lancelot. b. at Crosby Ravensworth, Westmorland, England, 1632; d. at Lichfield, Staffordshire, England, 1703. English clergyman and writer; father of Joseph Addison (1672–1719). A zealous royalist and Episcopalian, he was appointed after the Restoration to a post as English chaplain at Dunkerque, on the Channel coast of France.

Addison, Thomas. b. 1793; d. 1860. British physician. He discovered "Addison's disease," an illness involving adrenal gland destruction, ordinarily caused by tuberculosis.

Addison of Stallingborough (stôl'ing.bėr.ǫ), 1st Viscount. Title of **Addison, Christopher.**

Addison's Walk. A walk in the grounds of Magdalen College, Oxford, said to have been a favorite promenade of the English essayist, Joseph Addison (1672–1719), who in 1689 held a demyship (foundation scholarship) in that college.

Addled Parliament. Nickname of the second Parliament of James I (April-June, 1614), which was dissolved without having passed any acts, on its refusal to grant supplies until the king's imposition of customs and the restoration of the nonconforming clergy ejected from the Anglican Church in 1604 had been considered.

Addua (ad'ö̤.ạ). Latin name of the **Adda.**

Addums (ad'umz), **Mozis.** A pseudonym of **Bagby, George William.**

Addyston Pipe and Steel Co. v. United States, 175 U.S. 211(1899) (ad'is.tọn). Unanimous decision of the U.S. Supreme Court holding illegal under the terms of the Sherman Antitrust Act an association of cast-iron pipe manufacturers established for the purpose of fixing prices and eliminating competition.

Ade (ād), **George.** b. at Kentland, Newton County, Ind., Feb. 9, 1866; d. at Brook, Newton County, Ind., May 16, 1944. American journalist, columnist, humorist, and playwright. On the staff of the Chicago *Record* (1890–1900), he conducted a column, "Stories of the Streets and of the Town," and became nationally famous with his widely syndicated "Fables in Slang," beginning in 1900. His fables were a reflection of the common sense of the plain people. The form of the fable, with capital letters plentifully bestowed on important words and an aphoristic moral in italics at the end, served to garnish what was often a crisp short story dealing with familiar human types in well-worn situations. Ade in his fables was Ring Lardner in the germ, except that he was the inventor of novel turns of speech rather than a reporter mimicking the idiom actually spoken. The first book of his collected "fables" (entitled *Fables in Slang*, like his column) was a national best-seller from the day of its publication in 1900. His other books of fables, about a dozen, included *The Girl Proposition* (1902), *People You Know* (1903), and *Knocking the Neighbors* (1912). He also wrote *Single Blessedness*, a volume of humorous essays (1922), and *The Old Time Saloon* (1931). *In Babel*, made up of short stories that originally appeared in his newspaper column, includes stories acclaimed by the critic H. L. Mencken as among the best ever written by an American. He became one of the most successful playwrights of his time and wrote at least 17 plays, including the musical comedies *The Sultan of Sulu* (1902) and *The Sho-gun* (1904), and continued his dramatic work until 1914. *The County Chairman* (1903) is a study of the human politician in a small town in Indiana. In *The College Widow* (1904) Ade presented a picture of Atwater College, evidently in the Middle West. *Just Out of College* (1905) is a satire on the college man who has available from his education nothing that he can sell in the business world.

Adee (ā'dē), **Alvey Augustus.** b. at Astoria, N.Y., Nov. 27, 1842; d. July 5, 1924. American career diplomat, sometimes called "the anchor of the State Department" because of his 37-year tenure as second assistant secretary of state (1886 *et seq.*). He was also chief of the diplomatic bureau (1878–82) and third assistant secretary of state (1882–86).

Adel (ä.dāl'). See also **Adal.**

Adel (ā.del'). City in S Georgia, county seat of Cook County. 2,776 (1950).

Adela (ad'ę.lạ). b. c1062; d. 1137. Fourth daughter of William the Conqueror. She was the wife of Stephen, earl of Blois and Chartres, and mother of Stephen, king of England, whose claim to the throne derived through her.

Adelaer (ä'dę.ler), **Cort Sivertsen.** [Also, **Cort Sivertsen Adeler,** meaning "Cort Sivertsen the Eagle"; original name, **Cort Sivertsen.**] b. at Brevig, Norway, Dec. 16, 1622; d. at Copenhagen, Nov. 5, 1675. Scandinavian naval commander. He was successively in the service of the Netherlands (1637 *et seq.*), of Venice against Turkey (1642 *et seq.*), and of Denmark (1663 *et seq.*). Adelaer or Adeler was added to his original name as a tribute to his boldness.

Adelaide (ad'ę.lād), Saint. [German, **Adelheid.**] b. c931; d. at Seltz, in Alsace, 999. German noblewoman and religious figure; wife of Otto I of Germany (951–973) and founder of the Benedictine cloister at Seltz, in Alsace. Daughter of Rudolph II of Burgundy, she was first married to Lothair of Italy (947–950). Imprisoned by his successor, Berengar II, she escaped and married Otto I (951), being crowned empress in 962 by Pope John XII. She had great influence during the first part of the reign (973–983) of her son, Otto II, but in 978, possibly because her generosity to religious groups was depleting the exchequer, her power waned. With Otto's widow, the Empress Theophano, she defended the right of the infant Otto III to the throne and was sole regent (991–996).

Adélaïde (ȧ.dā.lȧ.ēd). b. at Paris, Aug. 25, 1777; d. Dec. 31, 1847. Princess of Orléans; sister of Louis Philippe, King of France. She is said to have persuaded her brother to accept the crown in 1830.

Adelaide (ad'ę.lād). [Full name, **Amelia Adelaide Louise Theresa Caroline.**] b. Aug. 13, 1792; d. Dec. 2, 1849. Princess of Saxe-Coburg-Meiningen and queen of England; wife of the Duke of Clarence (later William IV), whom she married on July 18, 1818.

Adelaide. City in SE Australia, the capital of the state of South Australia, on the Torrens River, ab. 7 mi. SE of Port Adelaide. Named for Adelaide, queen of England and wife of William IV, the city was founded in 1836. It contains the University of Adelaide, founded in 1874. Today the city is the industrial and commercial center of the state. Pop. including suburbs, ab. 422,000 (1950).

Adelaide Island. Island in Antarctica, lying N of Marguerite Bay on the W side of the Palmer Peninsula, in 67°15′ S., 68°40′ W. It was discovered on Feb. 14, 1832, by John Biscoe and named by him for Adelaide, then queen of England. Length, ab. 68 mi.; width, ab. 20 mi.

Adelard of Bath (ad'ę.lärd). [Also: **Æthelhard;** Latinized, **Adelardus Bathoniensis.**] b. at Bath, England; fl. c1116 to c1142. English mathematician, scientist, philosophical writer, and traveler, known for his knowledge of Arabic learning, and considered to have been the greatest in his field before Grosseteste and Bacon. He studied at Tours and Laon, and then traveled in Italy, Sicily, Greece, Asia Minor, and Africa, returning to England in the reign of Henry I. Before 1116 he wrote a philosophical treatise on identity and difference (*De eodem et diverso*), and before 1137 (probably much earlier) a dialogue (*Questiones naturales*) divided into 76 chapters, each of which treats of a scientific question, the whole purporting to expound Arabic knowledge on these questions. In chapter 51, apropos of an experiment carefully described by him, he explains the impossibility of a vacuum by a theory of universal continuity (developed later by Roger Bacon). The *De eodem et diverso* is a dialogue explaining Platonic views similar to those of the School of Chartres and opposing exaggerated Realism: genera and species are nothing but individuals considered from different points of view. This attitude has been regarded as preparing Abelard's conceptualism. Adelard's most important contributions, however, were in the field of mathematics. Early in life (before his Arabic contacts) he wrote a treatise on the abacus (*Regule abaci*). Later, in 1126, he translated from Arabic into Latin a revised edition of the astronomical tables of al-Khowarizmi; they included tables of sines. Thus was Moslem trigonometry, and more specifically the sine and tangent functions, introduced into the Latin world. He was also in all probability the "Magister A" who translated al-Khowarizmi's mathematical treatise (*Liber ysagogarum Alchorismi*). Thus Adelard was an abacist at the beginning of his career, and later became an algorist, the earliest (or one of the earliest) of them. Finally, he translated Euclid's works from the Arabic, this being the earliest Latin translation known to us, though he would seem to have made use of an earlier version from the Greek. There are many manuscripts of this, yet they are very divergent, and the exact nature of Adelard's original work, whether it was an abridgment, a close translation, or a commentary, is not clear. His translation of Euclid included the determination of the sum of the angles of stellated polygons. One of his latest writings was a treatise on the astrolabe (*De opere astrolapsus;* c1142–46). To complete this brief account of Adelard's mathematical activity, he was probably instrumental in introducing some knowledge of Moslem music into the West, for he had studied music in France, and al-Khowarizmi's mathematical treatise, covering the whole quadrivium, contains a section on music.

Adelbert (ad'ẹl.bėrt). See also **Adalbert.**

Adelbert or **Adalbert.** b. c1000; d. at Goslar, Prussia, March 16, 1072. German prelate, archbishop of Bremen and Hamburg (c1045). He attempted the formation of a northern European patriarchate with 12 suffragan bishoprics.

Adelboden (ä'dẹl.bō.dẹn). [Also, **Engstligenthal.**] Alpine valley in S central Switzerland, in the canton of Bern, connecting with the Kander valley, ab. 15 mi. SW of Interlaken.

Adeler (ä'dẹ.lėr), **Cort Sivertsen.** See **Adelaer, Cort Sivertsen.**

Adeler, Max. See under **Clark, Charles Heber.**

Adelheid (ä'dẹl.hīt). German form of **Adelaide.**

Adelheid. Character in Goethe's *Götz von Berlichingen.*

Adélie Coast (ad'ẹl.ẹ̄, à.dā.lē'). [Also, **Adélie Land.**] Region in Antarctica, a part of the coast of Wilkes Land, lying between 136°20′ E. and 142°20′ E. It was discovered and named in 1840 by the French naval commander Dumont d'Urville for his wife. It was later explored by Sir Douglas Mawson, and has been since 1938 within the area placed under French administration. According to some authorities, this part of Antarctica has the strongest winds in the world.

Adeliza (ad.ẹ.lī'zạ). d. in March, 1151. Second queen of Henry I of England; daughter of Godfrey (Barbatus) of Louvain, duke of Brabant or Lower Lotharingia, and a descendant, in the male line, of Charlemagne. She was married to Henry I on Jan. 24, 1120 (or 1121), and after his death married William de Albini.

Adelon (àd.lôṅ), **Nicolas Philibert.** b. at Dijon, France, Aug. 20, 1782; d. July 19, 1862. French medical writer.

Adelphi (ạ.del'fī; -fẹ̄). Section in W central London, in Westminster metropolitan borough, comprising several streets on the S side of the Strand, on the approximate site (now occupied by office buildings) of the Adelphi terrace, facing the river. The name was given from the Greek *adelphoi* ("brothers") from the fact that the terrace which formerly occupied it was designed (c1768) by the Adam brothers.

Adelphi Theatre. Theater on the Strand, London, first built in 1806, and rebuilt and enlarged in 1858.

Adelphoe (ạ.del'fē). [Also, **Adelphi.**] Comedy by Terence, adapted from Menander's work of the same name in Greek, with the addition of a scene from a play of Diphilos. It suggested Molière's *École des maris* and Baron's *L'École des pères.*

Adelung (ä'dẹ.lụng), **Friedrich von.** b. at Stettin, Prussia, Feb. 25, 1768; d. at St. Petersburg, Russia, Jan. 30, 1843. German philologist; nephew of Johann Christoph Adelung (1732–1806). He wrote *Rapport entre la langue sanscrite et la langue russe* (1811), *Übersicht der Reisenden in Russland bis 1700,* and others.

Adelung, Johann Christoph. b. at Spantekow, Prussia, Aug. 8, 1732; d. at Dresden, Sept. 10, 1806. German philologist, librarian at Dresden (1787–1806). He wrote *Grammatischkritisches Wörterbuch der hochdeutschen Mundart* (1774–86), and others. His *Mithridates* contained the Lord's Prayer in nearly five hundred languages and attempted a vast survey of languages throughout the world. Publication was begun in the year of Adelung's death (1806); the work was completed by Johann Severin Vater, the last volume appearing in 1817. *Mithridates* reflects the state of linguistic knowledge in the latter part of the 18th century immediately before the dawn of the scientific study of language in the 19th century.

Aden (ä'dẹn, ā'-). [Ancient names: **Adana, Attanae.**] City in the SW Arabian peninsula, seaport and capital of the British colony and protectorate of Aden, on the Gulf of Aden, situated on a rocky peninsula connected with the mainland by a narrow isthmus. It is an important coaling station, and a port of call of ships to and from the Orient via the Suez Canal. The production of salt and cigarettes are among its chief industries. It was captured and annexed by the British in 1839. Aden and the settlements adjoining (Aden Settlement), with the island of Perim at the S entrance to the Red Sea, and the Kuria Muria Islands S of Muscat and Oman, constitute a crown colony. Area of the colony, ab. 110 sq. mi.; of Aden Settlement, 75 sq. mi.; pop. of Aden city, 80,516 (1946).

Aden, Gulf of. Arm of the Indian Ocean, S of the Arabian Peninsula and N of the "horn" of Africa, connected with the Red Sea by the strait of Bab el Mandeb. British Somaliland occupies most of the S shore of the Gulf.

Adena (ạ.dē'nạ). Collective name for a North American Indian culture revealed archaeologically at sites in Ohio, Kentucky, Indiana, West Virginia, and W Pennsylvania. It is dated at about 500–900 A.D., during the Burial Mound I period, and consists of large earthen burial mounds and village sites which contain pottery of particular styles, a variety of stone and bone tools, and ornaments of shell, copper, mica, and stone.

Adenauer (ä'dẹn.ou.ėr), **Konrad.** b. at Cologne, Germany, Jan. 5, 1876—. German politician, first chancellor of the West German federal republic after World War II. Mayor of Cologne (1917–33), he was banished from Cologne by the Nazis and twice arrested. He was appointed to his former post by the British after the overthrow of the Hitler regime. He was thereafter zonal chairman of the CDU (Christian Democratic Union), president of the parliamentary council at Bonn in 1948, and chancellor in 1949, taking the additional post of foreign minister in 1951.

Aden Colony (ä'dẹn, ā'-). See under **Aden.**

Adenet (àd.ne). [Also: **Adam, Adans, Adenès, Adenez;** called **le Roi,** meaning "the King."] French trouvère of the 13th century. He is known for his refashioning of three chansons de gestes, *Les enfances Ogier, Berte aus grans Piés,* and *Bueves de Commarchis;* author of *Cléomadès,* a roman d'aventure of 20,000 verses.

Adenis (àd.nē), **Jules.** [Full name, **Jules Adenis-Colombeau.**] b. at Paris, 1821; d. there, 1900. French journalist and dramatist. He was on the editorial staff of the *Corsaire* (1847–49), and wrote many comedies, vaudevilles, and librettos. Among his independent works are *Philanthropie et repentir* (1855), *Une Crise de ménage* (1857), *Les Chasseurs et la laitière* (1865; music by Gavaert), *La Fiancée d'Abydos* (1865; music by Barthe), *Le Nouveau Sorcier* (1867), and *Les Trois Souhaits* (1873; music by Poise).

Aden Protectorate (ä'dẹn, ā'-). British protectorate in S Arabia, E, W, and N of the colony of Aden, consisting of the territories of a number of sultans and Arab chiefs in protectorate treaty relations with the British crown. It is divided for administrative purposes into Western Aden

Protectorate, which includes some 19 sultanates in the vicinity of the city of Aden, and Eastern Aden Protectorate, which includes the Hadhramaut region, the island of Socotra in the Arabian Sea, and several smaller divisions W of the sultanate of Muscat and Oman. Government is by the individual sultans, subject to the governor of Aden colony. Fishing is important along the coast; in the interior the main occupation is herding. Capital, Aden; length of coastline, 750 mi.; area, 112,000 sq. mi.; pop. 600,000 (est. 1946).

Aden Settlement. See under **Aden.**

Adeodatus I (ā.dẹ.od′ą.tus). See **Deusdedit,** Saint.

Adeodatus II, Saint. Pope from 672 to 676. He was an upholder of monastic discipline and opponent of the Monothelite heresy.

Aderar (ä.de.rär′) or **Aderer** (-rār′). See **Adrar.**

Adernò (ä.der.nô′). See **Adrano.**

Adeste fideles (ä.des′tā fē.dā′lās). [English, **O Come, All Ye Faithful.**] Hymn, originally in Latin, beginning with these words. It has been ascribed to Bonaventura (1221–74), but is more probably of the 17th or 18th century and of French or German authorship. The familiar arrangement, commencing "O come, all ye faithful, joyfully triumphant," first appeared in Murray's *Hymnal* in 1852 and is an adaptation of the translation made by the Reverend Frederick Oakeley in 1841. It has also been published in many other translations. The tune is ascribed to John Reading (1677–1764), organist, and was at first called the "Portuguese Hymn" in England because it was sung at the chapel of the Portuguese embassy in 1797.

Adhemar (ȧ.de.mär). See under **Bourbon.**

Adhémar de Chabannes (ȧ.dā.mȧr dẹ shȧ.bȧn). [Latinized, **Ademarus Cabannensis** (or **Engolismensis,** meaning "of Angoulême").] b. at Chabannes, near Châteauponsac, Haute-Vienne, France, 988; d. at Jerusalem, 1034. French monk and chronicler, active for most of his life at Limoges and Angoulême. His main work is a chronicle of French history with special reference to Aquitania (*Chronicon aquitanicum*), from mythical ages down to 1028, in three books. The first two books are largely copied from older chronicles, but Book 3, dealing with the period 814 to 1028, is the most important source for the history of Aquitania in the 10th and 11th centuries.

Adherbal (ad.hėr′bąl). d. c112 B.C. Son of Micipsa and king of Numidia (118 B.C.), sharing the rule with his brother Hiempsal and cousin Jugurtha. Hiempsal was slain by Jugurtha, and Adherbal sought protection of the Romans, who restored him to the throne (117 B.C.), but he was ousted and slain (c112 B.C.) by Jugurtha.

Adiabene (ad″i.ą.bē′nē). In ancient geography, a small Assyrian district on the Tigris not far from Nisibis. It was a vassal of Parthia, and succumbed to Rome under Trajan. Its queen, Helen, and her sons Izates and Monabaz, embraced Judaism c18 A.D.

Adi-Buddha (ä′dẹ.bůd′ą). Deity appearing (c10th century A.D.) in northern Buddhism, probably under the influence of Christianity. He was believed to be infinite, self-existent, and omniscient and by the exercise of the five meditations to have evolved out of himself the five Buddhas of contemplation, each of whom created a Bodhisattva, who in turn created out of his immaterial essence a material world.

Adicia (ą.dish′i.ą). In Spenser's *Faerie Queene*, the wife of the Soldan, an unrighteous woman, transformed into a raging tiger.

Adige (ä′dē.jā). [German, **Etsch;** Latin, **Athesis.**] River in N Italy. It rises near the frontier of Switzerland, flows S through the Alps to the plain of the Po, sends arms to the Po, and flows into the Adriatic N of the mouths of the Po. Its length is ab. 255 mi., and it is navigable for ab. 180 mi. On it are Trent and Verona.

Adigetto (ä.dē.jāt′tō). Canal or arm of the Adige, in N Italy, which separates from it near Badia, and flows past Rovigo into the Adriatic N of the Po.

Adighe (ä.di.gā′). See **Adyge.**

Adi-Granth (ä′dẹ.grănth′). Bible of the Sikhs, compiled by the fifth successor of Nanak, Guru Arjun (1584–1606).

Adin (ā′din). Head of a Hebrew family which returned from Babylon with Zerubbabel. Ezra, ii. 15, Neh. vii. 20.

Adipurana (ä″dẹ.pö.rä′ną). See **Brahmapurana.**

Adirondack Mountains (ad.i.ron′dak). Range of mountains in NE New York, the highest in the state. The main group is in Hamilton, Essex, Franklin, and Clinton counties, but the name is extended to the whole NE region of New York. The highest peak is Mount Marcy (5,344 ft.). Other notable summits are Mount Dix, Mount McIntyre, Mount Seward, Mount Whiteface, and Haystack.

Adirondack State Forest. [Also, **Adirondack Park.**] Park established by act of the New York State legislature in 1892 within the counties of Hamilton, Essex, Franklin, Warren, St. Lawrence, and Herkimer, for the use of the public. Further provision for the park was made by act of 1893. Area, 2,171,690 acres.

Adis Ababa (ad′is ab′ą.bą) or **Adis Abeba** (ä.bā.bä′). See **Addis Ababa.**

Adites (ad′īts). Early Arabian (Cushite) rulers.

Aditi (ä′di.ti). Term used in the Vedas as an adjective to mean "unbound," "free," "limitless," "infinite," "exhaustless," and, as a noun, to mean "freedom," "security," and then "infinity," in particular that of heaven in contrast with the finitude of earth and its spaces. The last conception personified is the goddess Aditi, the mother of the Adityas.

Adityas (ä′dit.yąz). [Eng. trans., "*Sons of Aditi.*"] In the Vedic literature, the seven gods of the heavenly light, at whose head stands Varuna, who is the Aditya *par excellence.* They are Varuna, Mitra ("the friend"), Aryaman ("the bosom friend"), Bhaga ("the liberal"), Daksha ("the capable"), Ansa ("the apportioner"), and an uncertain seventh. Mitra and the rest are only a splitting up and reflection of Varuna, the god of the vast luminous heavens, viewed as embracing all things and as the primary source of all life and every blessing. In the Brahmanas and later, the Adityas are 12 in number, with manifest reference to the number of the months. The term Aditya is also used from the earliest times as a designation for the sun.

Adjunta (ą.jun′tą). See **Ajanta.**

Adjusted Compensation Act of 1924. Measure passed by the U.S. Congress over presidential veto in 1924 providing a bonus for honorably discharged servicemen who had been members of the U.S. armed forces during World War I. The bonus credits were based upon length of service, domestic service bringing one dollar a day, while foreign service brought one dollar and twenty-five cents a day. The act stipulated deferral of payment until 1945 for all eligible veterans except those receiving a bonus of less than 50 dollars. More than 3,500,000 veterans received Adjusted Compensation Certificates which became redeemable in 1936 after long agitation by ex-servicemen's groups brought congressional sanction of payments in a move overriding President Franklin D. Roosevelt's veto.

Adkins v. Children's Hospital, 261 U.S. 525 (1923) (ad′kinz). Minimum-wage case in which the U.S. Supreme Court, by a vote of five to three, declared void an act of the U.S. Congress fixing minimum wages for women and children in the District of Columbia. The statute was held unconstitutional on the grounds that it impaired freedom of contract and violated the due process clause.

Adler (äd′lėr), **Alfred.** b. at Penzing-Vienna, Austria, Feb. 7, 1870; d. at Aberdeen, Scotland, May 28, 1937. Austrian psychiatrist, a chief proponent of the "inferiority complex" as a key to problems in psychopathology. At one time professionally close to Sigmund Freud, he later asserted that Freud overemphasized the sexual motive in behavior. He studied medicine, psychology, and philosophy at Vienna, where he served (1895–97) at the General Hospital and Polyclinic, and was later (1897–1927) a general practitioner and nerve specialist. He became privatdocent (1924) at the Pedagogical Institute of the city of Vienna, and was a lecturer (1928) at Columbia University medical center, being also appointed in the same year clinical director of the Mariahilfer Ambulatorium, at Vienna. He became in 1932 visiting professor of medical psychology at the Long Island College of Medicine, at New York. At the time of his death he was connected with the faculty of Aberdeen University, at Aberdeen, Scotland, where he had been lecturing on psychopathology. He established the School of Individual Psychology at Vienna, and founded (1914) the *Journal of Individual Psychology.* Convinced that his techniques could help to prevent neurosis and delinquency in childhood, he organized child guidance centers in 30 schools at Vienna, and began educating teachers to apply his methods in them. Author of *Studie über Minderwertigkeit von Organen und ihre seelische Kompensation* (1907; Eng. trans., *Study of Organ Inferiority and its Psychical Compensation*, 1917), *Über den nervösen Charakter* (1912), *Heilen und Bilden* (1914), *Praxis und Theorie der Individualpsychologie* (1918), *Problem der Homosexualität* (1919), *Menschenkenntnis* (1921), *Technik der Individualpsychologie* (1928), *The Science of Living* (1929), *Problems of Neurosis* (1929), *Education of Children* (1930), *The Pattern of Life* (1930), *Der Sinn des Lebens* (1932), and *Social Interest: A Challenge to Mankind* (1936).

Adler (ad'lėr), **Cyrus.** b. at Van Buren, Ark., Sept. 13, 1863; d. April 7, 1940. American archaeologist, educator, and Jewish historian. He was a librarian (1892–1905) and assistant secretary (1905–08) of the Smithsonian Institution. Subsequently president (1908 *et seq.*) of Dropsie College, at Philadelphia, he was during the latter part of his life acting president (1916–24) and president (1924 *et seq.*) of the Jewish Theological Seminary of America, at New York. He was also an editor of the *Jewish Encyclopedia*, editor of the *American Jewish Year Book* (1899–1906), and a council member of the Jewish Agency for Palestine.

Adler (ad'lėr, äd'-), **Felix.** b. at Alzey, Germany, Aug. 13, 1851; d. April 24, 1933. American lecturer, writer, and reformer, notable as the founder (1876) of the New York Society for Ethical Culture. He was professor of political and social ethics at Columbia (1902 *et seq.*) and Hibbert lecturer at Oxford (1923). Author of *Creed and Deed* (1877), *Life and Destiny* (1903), *Marriage and Divorce* (1905), *Religion of Duty* (1905), *The World Crisis and Its Meaning* (1915), *An Ethical Philosophy of Life* (1918), and others.

Adler (äd'lėr), **Friedrich.** b. at Berlin, Oct. 15, 1827; d. there, Sept. 15, 1908. German architect and archaeologist. He is now best known as a writer on the medieval and Renaissance architecture of Germany, but he was also a chief associate of Ernst Curtius in the excavations on the plain of Olympia, in Greece, the results of which were published between 1890 and 1897.

Adler, Friedrich. b. at Vienna, July 9, 1879—. Austrian socialist; son of Viktor Adler (1852–1918). He joined the pacifist left wing of the Social Democratic Party during World War I and killed (1916) the Austrian prime minister, Count Carl Stürgkh, as a protest against the government's militarism. For this he was condemned to death, but the sentence was commuted, and he was amnestied in 1918 at the time of the collapse of the Hapsburg regime.

Adler (ad'lėr, äd'-), **George J.** b. at Leipzig, 1821; d. in Bloomingdale Asylum, New York, Aug. 24, 1868. American philologist. He arrived in the U.S. in 1833, and graduated (1844) as class valedictorian from New York University, where he became (1846) professor of modern languages. The publication (1849) of his *Dictionary of the German and English Languages*, which added nearly 30,000 new terms and numerous articles on synonyms to an earlier dictionary by the German scholar Johann Gottfried Flügel, marked him as one of the great philologians of his period, but the staggering labor of preparation entailed by this work permanently damaged Adler's mental health. After a trip (1849) to Europe, during which he met and became intimate with Herman Melville, he undertook once again his university work, but fell subject (1853) to delusions of persecution which necessitated confinement in Bloomingdale Asylum, where he nevertheless completed several philological works before his death.

Adler (äd'lėr), **Ludwig.** b. at Vienna, Austria, Nov. 7, 1878—. Austrian gynecologist and obstetrician. He served at the general hospital and at the institute of pathological anatomy of the University of Vienna, where he became privatdocent (1912) and professor (1919) of gynecology and obstetrics. He was also for many years director of the gynecological department of the Wilhelminespital at Vienna. He is known for his work (with F. Hitschmann) on the endometrium (1908), his studies on the pathology of the uterus, function of the ovaries, and X-ray treatment of uterus carcinoma.

Adler (ad'lėr), **Mortimer Jerome.** b. at New York, Dec. 28, 1902—. American educator and author. He was an instructor in psychology at Columbia (1923–29) and associate professor (1930–42) and professor (1942–52) of the philosophy of law at Chicago. Author of *Dialectic* (1927), *How To Read a Book* (1940), *The Problems of Species* (1940), and *How To Think about War and Peace* (1944), and associate editor of *Great Books of the Western World* (1945 *et seq.*).

Adler (ad'lėr, äd'-), **Nathan Marcus.** b. at Hanover, Germany, Jan. 15, 1803; d. at Brighton, England, Jan. 21, 1890. Chief rabbi of the United Congregations of Jews of the British Empire. Elected (1844) chief rabbi of London, he founded (1855) and was first president of the college for Jewish teachers at London. He proposed (1860) the plan which in 1870 was passed by Parliament as the United Synagogue Act.

Adler, Samuel. b. at Worms, Germany, Dec. 3, 1809; d. June 9, 1891. American rabbi and proponent of Reform Judaism. His appointment (1857) as head of Congregation Emanu-El at New York brought him to the U.S., where he subsequently completed a revision of the prayer book started by Dr. L. Merzbacher and aided in the establishment of New York's Hebrew Orphan Asylum. Prior to this, in Europe, a deep interest in bringing new vigor to the practice of Judaism had led him to the Rabbinical Reform Conferences at Brunswick (1844), Frankfort on the Main (1845), and Breslau (1846) which prepared the way for Reform Judaism, and he continued throughout his life to urge every change which he felt would open the way to a fuller religious life by his congregation.

Adler (äd'lėr), **Viktor.** b. at Prague, June 24, 1852; d. Nov. 12, 1918. Austrian journalist and Socialist leader. Founder (1886) of the newspaper, *Gleichheit*, which later became *Die Arbeiterzeitung*, the chief organ of the Austrian Social Democrats, he was a member of the Austrian Diet (1902) and of the Reichsrat (1905 *et seq.*), and played a leading role in securing (1907) universal suffrage for Austria. He was for a few days before his death foreign minister of the provisional government that immediately preceded the Austrian republic established at the close of World War I.

Adlerberg (äd'lėr.berk), Count **Vladimir.** b. at St. Petersburg, Russia, Nov. 10, 1790; d. there, March 20, 1884. Russian general and minister in the service of the Russian czars Nicholas I and Alexander II.

Adlerbeth (äd'lėr.bet), **Gudmund Göran.** b. 1751; d. 1818. Swedish poet, dramatist, translator (of old Norse poetry, Vergil, Horace, Ovid, and others), and historical writer.

Adlercreutz (äd'lėr.kroits), Count **Karl Johan.** b. near Borgå (now Porvoo, Finland), April 27, 1757; d. Aug. 21, 1815. Swedish general, defeated (1808) in Finland by the Russians. He took part in deposing (1809) Gustavus IV of Sweden, and later served in Germany (1813) and in Norway (1814).

Adlersparre (äd'lėr.spär.rẹ), Count **Georg.** b. in Jemtland, Sweden, March 28, 1760; d. in Wermland, Sweden, Sept. 23, 1835. Swedish author, editor, government official, and general. He contributed (1809) to the overthrow of Gustavus IV of Sweden, and was later appointed major general in the Swedish army and made a member of the nobility.

Adlersparre, Karl August. b. June 7, 1810; d. May 5, 1862. Swedish poet and historian; son of Count Georg Adlersparre (1760–1835).

Adlum (ad'lum), **John.** b. at York, Pa., April 29, 1759; d. March 1, 1836. American horticulturist and viticulturist. He is remembered for his development of the Catawba grape and, among botanists, as the source of the plant name *Adlumia*. Author of *Adlum on Making Wine* (1826) and *A Memoir on the Cultivation of the Vine in America and the Best Mode of Making Wine* (1823, 1828).

Admah (ad'mạ). In the Old Testament, one of the cities destroyed with Sodom. Gen. xiv. 2.

Ad Mediam (ad mē'di.ạm). Ancient name of **Mehadia.**

Admetus (ad.mē'tus). [Also, **Admetos** (-tos).] In Greek mythology, a Thessalian king, son of Pheres, king of Pherae, delivered from death by the voluntary sacrifice of his wife Alcestis (who was thereupon rescued from Hades by Hercules). He took part in the expedition of the Argonauts and in the chase of the Calydonian boar.

Administration of Justice Act. See under **Coercive Acts.**

Admirable Bashville (bash'vil), **The.** Drama (1901) by George Bernard Shaw. It is based on *Cashel Byron's Profession,* written by Shaw in 1882 and generally considered to be the best of his five novels.

Admirable Crichton (krī'tọn), **The.** Dramatic work (1902) by J. M. Barrie. Crichton is the butler in a wealthy household whose head, Lord Loam, likes to pretend that class distinctions are actually meaningless, and who accordingly once a year entertains his servants at tea. Believing firmly that such an arrangement violates the laws of nature, Crichton resists, but without avail until during a yachting trip the family is wrecked on a desert island and left there for two years. Now the situation is different, and the laws of nature clearly dictate that the most competent member of the party (obviously Crichton) shall be the leader. He cheerfully assumes the responsibility, and accepts all the prerogatives of an absolute master: the others are reduced to the status of slaves, and he proposes to marry his former master's daughter. However, when rescue comes and the party returns to England, Crichton punctiliously returns to his original menial rank, and life goes on as it had before the shipwreck except for one important difference: Crichton's point about the relative positions of master and servant has now been clearly driven home to Lord Loam. In real life, there was a man actually called "the Admirable Crichton" (a Scottish scholar and adventurer of the late 16th century, named James Crichton) whose accomplishments were comparable in their variety (although not in kind) to those of Barrie's character.

Admirable Doctor. See **Bacon, Roger.**

Admiralty Inlet (ad'mi.rạl.ti). Arm of Puget Sound, on the W coast of the state of Washington, E of Juan de Fuca Strait.

Admiralty Island. Island W of the SE part of Alaska, SW of Juneau, belonging to the U.S.

Admiralty Islands. Archipelago in the Pacific, NE of the island of New Guinea, discovered by the Dutch in 1616, and annexed by Germany in 1885. In 1920 the League of Nations included the islands in the New Guinea mandate to Australia, and they remained, as a trust territory of the United Nations, still under Australian control after World War II. The islands are important chiefly for their coconut plantations and pearl fisheries. They were occupied by the Japanese early in World War II, and Allied forces of liberation landed on the small subgroup of Los Negros in 1944. There are ab. 18 islands in the group, of which the chief is Manus (the name Manus is also used in reference to the entire group). Area, ab. 800 sq. mi.; pop. 13,172 (1941).

Admiralty Islands, Battle of the. Name usually given to a series of amphibious attacks carried out by U.S forces against the Japanese in the early part of 1944 as a part of the overall campaign in the SW Pacific area. Action centered on Los Negros, invaded on Feb. 29, and Manus, which fell into U.S. hands on March 18 (although organized resistance did not end until April 17). As a result of the operation the Allies obtained several air strips from which to harass the Japanese garrisons stranded at Rabaul and in New Britain. Another and possibly more important result of the victory was that it gave the Allies air bases within easy reach of the Japanese sea lanes to all territory S of the Admiralty Islands, and thus made possible the launching of a sustained attack against the vessels carrying supplies to the Japanese forces (estimated at 100,000 men) throughout the Bismarck archipelago. In General MacArthur's words, the battle enabled the Allies to "put the cork in the bottle," so far as any important strategic use of the Japanese forces S of the Admiralty Islands was concerned.

Admiralty Range. Name given to the N part of the great mountain system W of the Ross Sea, in Victoria Land, in Antarctica. The largest mountains in the range reach a height of ab. 10,000 ft.

Admiralty Sound. Arm of the Strait of Magellan, in SE Chile, on the W coast of King Charles's South Land. Tierra del Fuego.

Admonitionists (ad.mō.nish'ọn.ists). Sect of 16th-century English Puritans who followed Thomas Cartwright in urging church government by presbyters rather than bishops and demanding recognition of church authority as superior to that of the state. The name derives from *An Admonition to Parliament,* published in 1572 by two members of the sect, which was followed by a second work of the same nature under Cartwright's own name.

Admont (äd'mont). Town in E Austria, in Styria, situated on the Enns River ab. 50 mi. S of Linz. It is noted for its scenery and a Benedictine abbey, founded 1074, of which the main buildings, particularly the library, are considered to be excellent examples of the Austrian baroque style of the 18th century. The library contains 100,000 volumes and manuscripts. 2,221 (1946).

Ado (ä'dō), Saint. b. c800; d. 875. Archbishop of Vienne, in France (859 *et seq.*). He was notable among the church leaders of his day for his zeal in reforming the morals of the people and in enforcing church discipline.

Adolf of Nassau (ad'olf, ā'dolf; German, ä'dolf). [Latinized, **Adolphus.**] b. c1255; d. in battle at Göllheim, in the Rhine Palatinate, 1298. King of Germany, elected in 1292 and deposed in 1298; son of Walram, count of Nassau. He was chosen to succeed Rudolph I. His position in relation to the nominally subordinate princes who elected him was always unsure, and was made even more precarious by his seizure (1294–96) of Meissen and Thuringia.

Adolf of Nassau. [Full German name, **Wilhelm August Karl Friedrich Adolf.**] b. July 24, 1817; d. Nov. 17, 1905. Last duke of Nassau. He succeeded to the duchy in 1839. In 1866 he allied himself with Austria (thereby sharing in the Hapsburg defeat in the Austro-Prussian War) and Nassau was annexed to Prussia in the same year. He became grand duke of Luxembourg in November, 1890.

Adolph (ä'dolf), **Karl.** b. at Vienna, May 19, 1869; d. there, Nov. 22, 1931. Austrian writer of novels on social themes. He is considered noteworthy by some critics of modern Austrian fiction for his naturalistic style.

Adolphe (à.dolf). [Full title, **Adolphe: anecdote trouvée dans les papiers d'un inconnu.**] Romance by Benjamin Constant, first published in 1816, which ranks as one of the major novels of the French Romantic period.

Adolphus (ạ.dol'fus). Latinized form of **Adolf.**

Adolphus, John. b. at London, Aug. 7, 1768; d. there, July 16, 1845. English barrister and historian. He was the author of *History of England from the Accession of George III, to the Conclusion of Peace in 1783* (1802), and others.

Adolphus, John Leycester. b. May 11, 1795; d. Dec. 24, 1862. English barrister and man of letters, now remembered as the author of *Letters to Richard Heber containing Critical Remarks on the Series of Novels beginning with Waverley* (1822), in which he asserted Sir Walter Scott's authorship of the Waverley novels. His argument was based on resemblances between Scott's poems (which were acknowledged by their author) and the novels (which had been published anonymously because Scott considered it beneath his dignity as an official of the law to attach his name to a novel). Adolphus's work made clear beyond all reasonable doubt a fact that had been known or suspected from the first by such good judges of literary style as Jane Austen, and in 1825, in the introduction to one of his later series of novels, Scott himself affirmed what everyone by that time knew: that he was "the sole and unaided author of these Novels of Waverley."

Adolphus Frederick (of *England*). [Title, Duke of **Cambridge.**] b. at London, Feb. 24, 1774; d. July 8, 1850. English general and prince of the royal house; youngest son of George III. He was viceroy of Hanover in the period 1816–37.

Adolphus Frederick (of *Sweden*). [German, **Adolf Friedrich**; Swedish, **Adolf Fredrik.**] b. May 14, 1710; d. Feb. 12, 1771. King of Sweden (1751–71) and duke of Holstein-Eutin. He was chosen as heir to the Swedish throne in 1743.

Adomnan (ad'ọm.nạn, ạ.dom'nạn), Saint. See **Adamnan,** Saint.

Adonai (ad.ọ̄.nā'ī, ạ.dō'nī). Name substituted by the Hebrews in place of the ineffable name YHWH (the tetragrammaton from which, with greater or lesser error, Yahweh and Jehovah were derived) wherever it occurs in the Scriptures. The term "Adonai" means "my lord" in Hebrew.

Adonais (ad.ọ.nā′is). Elegiac poem by Percy Bysshe Shelley, commemorating the death of John Keats, published in 1821, and generally considered to rank second only to *Lycidas* among English elegies.

Adonijah (ad.ọ.nī′ją). In the Old Testament, the fourth son of David. He plotted near the close of David's reign to obtain the succession to the throne in place of Solomon. 1 Kings, i.

Adonijah. In the Old Testament, a Levite, a teacher of the law, mentioned in 2 Chron. xvii.

Adonis (ą.don′is, ą.dō′nis). [Modern, **Nahr-Ibrahim.**] In ancient geography, a small river in Syria, rising in Lebanon, and flowing into the Mediterranean ab. 13 mi. N of what is now Beirut.

Adonis. In ancient Greek mythology, a young man of extraordinary beauty who was loved by Aphrodite. He died, according to the usual account, from the wound of a boar's tusk, received while hunting. Acceding partly to the entreaties of Aphrodite that he be restored to life, Zeus thereupon decreed that he should pass half the year in the upper and half in the lower world. Adonis has been considered by some scholars to have been originally an oriental deity of nature, typifying the withering of nature in winter, and its revival in summer. By way of Asia Minor his cult came first to Greece, then passed to Egypt, and thence finally was brought to Rome. The yearly festival of Adonis in the spring was a special favorite with women. In the Old Testament reference is made to the weeping of the women over Tammuz, the Babylonian equivalent of Adonis (Ezek. viii. 14).

Adoptive Emperors. Collective term for the Roman emperors Nerva, Trajan, Hadrian, Antoninus Pius, and Marcus Aurelius; so called because after Nerva, who was elected by the senate on the death of Domitian, each was the adopted son of his predecessor. They are usually considered to have been, as a group, the greatest of the Roman emperors, and the period of their reigns the most beneficent in Roman history (indeed, according to Gibbon, the happiest in the history of the world).

Ador (à.dôr), **Gustav.** b. at Geneva, Switzerland, Dec. 23, 1845; d. there, March 31, 1928. Swiss diplomat, Red Cross official (1910 *et seq.*), and League of Nations delegate (1920 *et seq.*). He was president of Switzerland (properly termed, in strict political usage, the Swiss Confederation) in the period 1918–19.

Adoration of the Lamb. [Also: **Agnus Dei, Ghent Altarpiece, Mystic Lamb,** and **Worship of the Lamb.**] Large altarpiece in oil on wood begun (1420) by Hubert van Eyck and finished (1432) by his brother Jan for the church of Saint Bavon, at Ghent. Many authorities consider it to be the van Eycks' greatest single work. The central painting depicts the worship of the lamb of God by a company consisting of groups of angels, martyrs, hermits, prophets, apostles, and knights; the rest of the 24 panels show Christ in judgment, Adam and Eve, the Annunciation, and the prophets of the birth of Christ.

Adoration of the Magi. A subject much used by medieval and Renaissance painters, characteristically showing the Virgin and Child in a stable, ruin, or similar setting, with wise men and often kings and other personages, accompanied by their retinues, worshiping and presenting gifts. Noteworthy examples include: **1.** A number of paintings (at Berlin, New York, and elsewhere) by the Flemish artist Hieronymus Bosch, with whom it was a favorite subject. **2.** Several paintings by the Florentine painter Sandro Botticelli, notably one in tempera (at the Uffizi, in Florence) done originally for the church of Santa Maria Novella, Florence, in which the three kings are portraits of Cosimo, Giuliano, and Giovanni de' Medici and which, according to Vasari, got the artist a commission from Pope Sixtus IV to decorate the Sistine Chapel. **3.** A painting (at the Uffizi, in Florence) by the German artist Albrecht Dürer, one of his first important works, showing the influence of both German and Italian masters. **4.** A monochrome painting (at the Uffizi, in Florence), one of several unfinished studies by the Florentine artist Leonardo da Vinci for an altarpiece intended for the church of San Donato at Florence. In this work the story is subordinated to an elaborate and masterful exercise in design and perspective. **5.** A large triptych, called the *Dombild*, done for the Cologne Cathedral by the German artist Stephan Lochner. Painted against an interwoven gold background, the Virgin and kings in this work are flanked by Ursula and Gereon, patron saints of Cologne, and their followers. An outstanding example of the work of the early Renaissance in Germany, this altarpiece combines certain medieval features of decorative treatment with a new feeling of plasticity and realism. **6.** One of the later paintings (at Buckingham Palace, London) of the Dutch artist Rembrandt. In it the Virgin and Child sit at the right, the Magi kneel before them, kings and old men stand in the background, and a camel caravan is seen in the distance. **7.** Several paintings (at New York, Madrid, and elsewhere) by the Flemish artist Peter Paul Rubens, including a large one (at Antwerp) in oil on a wooden panel in which the life-size figures are disposed with a spirit of magnificence and movement typical of Rubens' most admired work. **8.** A copper engraving by the German artist Martin Schongauer, containing a rich composition of many figures skilfully treated in its small area. **9.** An altarpiece (at Siena) by the Italian painter Sodoma, done for the church of San Agostino at Siena. **10.** One of a series by the Venetian painter Tintoretto, done for the Scuola di San Rocco at Venice. In this the problem of making the Child's radiance the only source of light is typical of the experiments this artist set for himself. **11.** An early painting (at Madrid) by the Spanish artist Velasquez. **12.** A large painting (at Dresden) by the Venetian artist Paolo Veronese, done as a companion-piece for his *Marriage at Cana.* In this the numerous attendants, camels, and horses of the kings provide occasion for the pageantry and lively composition characteristic of Tintoretto's work.

Adour (à.dör). [Ancient name, **Aturus.**] River in SW France which rises in the Pyrenees and flows into the Bay of Biscay ab. 5 mi. W of Bayonne. Length, ab. 200 mi.; navigable for ab. 70 mi.

Adowa (ä′dọ.wä). See **Aduwa.**

Ad Pirum (ad pī′rum). In historical geography, a Roman military station in what is now NW Yugoslavia, NE of Trieste, on the road across the Alps into Italy, noted in connection with Theodosius' victory at the Frigidus, 394 A.D.

Adra (ä′drä). [Ancient name, **Abdera** or **Abdara.**] Commune in Spain, in the province of Almería, situated on the Mediterranean coast at the mouth of the Almería River, ab. 30 mi. W of the town of Almería. It is a seaport, exporting lead and iron ore. The climate is subtropical, and sugar cane is grown in the vicinity. Originally a Phoenician colony, taken over by the Carthaginians, it was later occupied and settled by the Romans, probably under Tiberius. It was the last Moslem possession in medieval Spain, under Boabdil. 12,443 (1940).

Adrain (ad′rān), **Robert.** b. at Carrickfergus, Ireland, Sept. 30, 1775; d. at New Brunswick, N.J., Aug. 10, 1843. American mathematician and one-time Irish patriot, notable for his hypothecation of the curve *catenaria volvens* and two proofs of the exponential law of error which anticipated the demonstration of the same law by the German mathematician Karl Friedrich Gauss (for whom the law is now generally named) by one year. Largely self-educated, Adrain began teaching in Ireland, but emigrated to the U.S. after joining the Irish separatists and being nearly killed in battle with British authorities. He taught at Queen's College (now Rutgers), Columbia, and the University of Pennsylvania, where he became (1828) vice-provost.

Adrammelech or **Adramelech** (ą.dram′ẹ.lek). In the Old Testament: **1.** An idol worshiped, with the sacrifice of children, by the inhabitants of Sepharvaim with whom Sargon, king of Assyria, colonized Samaria. 2 Kings, xvii. 31. **2.** A son of Sennacherib, king of Assyria. With the help of his brother Sharezer he slew his father in the so-called temple of Nisroch, on his return from his expedition against Hezekiah. 2 Kings, xix. 37; Isa. xxxvii. 38. This event is mentioned also in the Babylonian chronicles (cuneiform).

Adrammelech or **Adramelech.** In angelology, one of the fallen angels.

Adramyti (ad.rą.mit′i). See **Edremit.**

Adramyttium (ad.rą.mit′i.um). Biblical name of **Edremit.**

Adramyttium, Gulf of. See **Edremit, Gulf of.**

Adrano (ä.drä′nō). [Also: **Adernò**; Latin, **Adranum, Hadranum.**] Town and commune in SW Italy, on the island of Sicily, in the province of Catania, situated near the Simeto River on the W slope of Mount Etna, ab. 17 mi. NW of Catania. It is the market center of a wine and citrus growing district. The town, which was founded by the Greeks, has Siculian, Greek, and Roman remains. Considerable damage was suffered during World War II by some buildings of tourist interest, but repairs have now been completed or are being carried out. Pop. of commune, 24,515 (1936); of town, 24,307 (1936).

Adrar (ä.drär′). [Also: **Dhar Adrar, Aderar, Aderer.**] Mountainous region in the western Sahara desert, within the territory of Mauritania, French West Africa, near the protectorate of Spanish Sahara. The chief place is Atar, which is connected by road with St.-Louis, Senegal.

Adraste (à.dràst). Principal character of Molière's play *Le Sicilien*, a young French gentleman who succeeds in carrying off Isidore, the beautiful Greek slave of Don Pèdre, by disguising himself as a portrait painter (and hence the second title of the play, *L'Amour peintre*).

Adrasteia (ad.ras.tī′ạ). In Greek mythology: **1.** A name of Nemesis and of Rhea-Cybele. **2.** A Cretan nymph, daughter of Melisseus, to whom Rhea entrusted the infant Zeus to be reared in the Dictaean grotto.

Adrastos of Aphrodisias (ạ.dras′tos). fl. at Aphrodisias, in Caria, about the beginning of the 2nd century B.C. Greek philosopher who wrote commentaries on Aristotle (ethics, logic, physics), on Theophrastos (ethics), and on Plato's *Timaeos.* His commentary on the *Timaeos* dealt with mathematical and astronomical questions. He also wrote a treatise upon the order of the Aristotelian writings.

Adrastus (ạ.dras′tus). [Also, **Adrastos** (-tos).] In Greek legend, a king of Argos, leader and only survivor of the original expedition of the "Seven against Thebes." Some ten years later he led the sons of the Seven in a successful campaign to avenge their fathers, and on this occasion was able to capture Thebes. He was worshiped as a hero in several places, among them Megara.

Adrea (ā′drē.ạ). Tragedy by David Belasco and John Luther Long, produced in 1904.

Adria (ā′dri.ạ). In ancient geography, the sea now called the Adriatic, and also (about the first century A.D.) that part of the Mediterranean which lies between Crete and Sicily.

Adria (ä′drē.ä). [Also: **Adria Veneta** (ve.nā′tä); ancient names, **Atria, Hadria, Hatria.**] Town and commune in NE Italy, in the province of Rovigo, situated on an island in the delta of the Po River, on the Bianco Canal between the Adige and the Po Grande rivers, ab. 16 mi. SW of Venice. The town, now far inland, was in ancient times situated much nearer the Adriatic Sea, which derived its name from the name of the town. It was successively an Etruscan, Greek, and Roman town, the remains of which have been excavated, and some of which are in the civic museum. The *Duomo* (cathedral) and the Church of Santa Maria della Tomba were undamaged in World War II. Pop. of commune, 32,762 (1936); of town, 9,435 (1936).

Adrian (ā′dri.ạn). City in S Lower Michigan, on the Raisin River, ab. 55 mi. SW of Detroit, county seat of Lenawee County: center of a manufacturing and agricultural area. It is the seat of Siena Heights College and Adrian College. 18,393 (1950).

Adrian. A lord in Shakespeare's *The Tempest.*

Adrian I. [Also, **Hadrian.**] d. 795. Pope from 772 to 795. He summoned (773) Charlemagne to quell the Lombard king, Desiderius, who was threatening Rome, and presided over and accepted the decree of the second Nicaean Council (787) upholding the veneration of images and anathematizing iconoclasts. His firm and constructive rule included restoration of the ancient Roman aqueducts and maintenance of close ties with Charlemagne.

Adrian II. [Also, **Hadrian.**] Pope from 867 to 872. He passed a sentence of deposition on Photius, patriarch of Constantinople, which was confirmed at the fourth Council of Constantinople (869–870).

Adrian III, Saint. [Also, **Hadrian.**] Pope from 884 to 885.

Adrian IV. [Also: **Hadrian**; original name, **Nichola Breakspear.**] b. at Langley, near St. Albans, in Hertfordshire, England, before 1100; d. at Anagni, Italy, 1159. Pope from 1154 to 1159, the only Englishman ever to occupy the papal chair. Created cardinal-bishop of Albano (1146) by Pope Eugenius III, he was legate to Denmark and Norway (1152–54). As pope, he is said to have bestowed (c1156) Irish sovereignty on Henry II of England (this point has long been a center of controversy among historians, but it is now generally agreed that it is true and that the documents supporting it are genuine). He also opened the great conflict between the papacy and the Hohenstaufens by his firm assertion of papal prerogatives against the emperor Frederick I (Frederick Barbarossa).

Adrian V. [Also: **Hadrian**; original name, **Ottoboni Fiesco.**] Pope in 1276. A native of Genoa, he lived only five weeks after his accession.

Adrian VI. [Also, **Hadrian.**] b. at Utrecht, 1459; d. 1523. Pope from 1522 to 1523. He studied at the University of Louvain, of which he later became vice-chancellor, and was chosen by the emperor Maximilian to tutor his grandson, the archduke Charles (who was later to be the emperor Charles V). Bishop of Tortosa and grand inquisitor of Aragon (1516), he was created a cardinal by Leo X (1517), and was for a short time regent of Spain (1520). He attempted as Pope to check the Reformation and the Turkish attack on Rhodes, but failed in both.

Adrian, Edgar Douglas. b. Nov. 30, 1889—. British physiologist, winner of the Nobel Prize in medicine (1932) for his work with Sir Charles Scott Sherrington in the field of nerve impulses. He is the author of *The Basis of Sensation* (1928), *The Mechanism of Nervous Action* (1932), and numerous technical articles.

Adriana (ā.dri.ā′nạ). Character in Shakespeare's *Comedy of Errors;* the wife of Antipholus of Ephesus.

Adriana Lecouvreur (ä.drē.ä′nä lẹ.kö.vrėr′). [French, **Adrienne Lecouvreur.**] Opera by Francesco Cilea, with words based on a play by Augustin Eugène Scribe and Gabriel Jean Baptiste Ernest Wilfrid Legouvé. It was first produced at Milan in 1902.

Adrian de Castello (ā′dri.ạn dẹ kas.tel′ō). [Also, **Adrian de Corneto** (dē kôr.net′ō).] b. at Corneto, Tuscany, Italy, c1460; d. c1521. Italian ecclesiastic and scholar, nuncio of Pope Innocent VIII in Scotland in 1488, agent at Rome of Henry VII of England, collector of Peter's pence in England, and papal prothonotary. He obtained in 1492 the prebend of Ealdland in Saint Paul's Cathedral, and the rectory of Saint Dunstan-in-the-East, but returned to Rome on the death of Innocent VIII. He was made bishop of Hereford in 1502, bishop of Bath and Wells in 1504, and cardinal in 1503. In 1517 he was implicated in the conspiracy of Cardinals Petrucci, De Sauli, and Riario to poison Pope Leo X, and was deprived of his cardinalate (1518) and of his dignities in England. He was probably assassinated. He wrote *Venatio*, a poem (1505), *De Vera Philosophia* (1507), *De Sermone Latino et modo Latine Loquendi* (1513), and others.

Adriani (ä.drē.ä′nē), **Giovanni Battista.** b. at Florence, 1513; d. 1579. Florentine statesman and historian. With the patronage of Cosimo de' Medici, he wrote a useful history of the period 1536–74 (published 1583; modern edition, 1872).

Adrianople (ā″dri.ạn.ō′pl). Former name of **Edirne.**

Adrianople, Battle of. Name given to: **1.** The victory of the Visigoths over the emperor Valens in 378 A.D. **2.** The victory of the Bulgarians over the Byzantines in 551 A.D.

Adrianople, Peace or **Treaty of.** Treaty between Russia and Turkey, signed at Adrianople (now Edirne), on Sept. 14, 1829. By its terms, Turkey ceded to Russia important fortresses and districts on the NE coast of the Black Sea; granted to Russian subjects freedom of trade in Turkey, and freedom of navigation in the Black Sea, on the Danube, and through the Dardanelles; confirmed and extended the protectorate exercised by the czar over the Danubian principalities; gave Russia control of a part of the left bank of the lower Danube, and of one of the mouths of that river; and recognized the independence of Greece.

Adrianopolis (ā″dri.ạn.op′ọ.lis). A Latin name of **Edirne,** city.

Adriatic Sea (ā.dri.at′ik, ad.ri.at′ik). [Italian, **Mare Adriatico** (mä′rā ä.drē.ä′tē.kō); Latin, **Adria, Mare Adriaticum.**] That part of the Mediterranean Sea which lies between Italy on the W and NW, and Yugoslavia and Albania on the E, and is connected with the Ionian Sea by the Strait of Otranto. Its chief arms are the Gulfs of Manfredonia, Venice, Trieste, and Quarnero (Velik· Kvarner), and its largest tributaries are the rivers Po and Adige. Length, ab. 500 mi.; area, ab. 51,000 sq. mi.; average depth, ab. 795 ft.; greatest known depth, 4,590 ft.

Adrienne Lecouvreur (à.drē.en lę.kö.vrėr). French prose drama in five acts, by Augustin Eugène Scribe and Gabriel Jean Baptiste Ernest Wilfrid Legouvé, first presented on April 14, 1849.

Adrienne Lecouvreur. French title of the opera **Adriana Lecouvreur.**

Adrienne Toner (ā′dri.en tō′nėr). Novel by Anne Douglas Sedgwick, published in 1922.

Adua (ä′dö.ä). Italian name of **Aduwa.**

Aduatici (ad.ū.at′i.sī) or **Aduatuci** (-ū.sī). Tribe in Belgic Gaul, living W of what is now the Meuse River. They are considered by some authorities to have been descendants of the Cimbri and Teutones, and may therefore have been either Celtic or Germanic in their ethnic origin. In 57 B.C. they were suspected (with the other Belgic tribes) of planning a general attack on the Romans, and were compelled by Julius Caesar to lay down their arms. To avoid possible further difficulties with them, Caesar thereupon sold the entire tribe into slavery.

Adula (ä′dö.lä). [German, **Rheinwaldgebirge.**] Group of Alps in the W part of the canton of Graubünden, Switzerland, the source of the Hinter Rhein, a tributary of the river Rhine. The highest point is the Rheinwaldhorn (ab. 11,174 ft.).

Adulateur (ad′ū.lā.tėr), **The.** Satirical play by Mercy Otis Warren, published at Boston in 1773. It attacks Thomas Hutchinson, the Boston merchant who was until 1774 royal governor of Massachusetts. Hutchinson's acceptance of the Stamp Act in 1765, and continuing support thereafter of British policy, had infuriated the population of Boston. However, as is implied by the title of the play, many people were doubly offended by the fact that official support for this policy had come from a fellow Bostonian, who therefore seemed to them clearly to be acting as a toady of the British crown.

Adulis (ad′ū.lis). See under **Zula.**

Adullam (ą.dul′ąm). City and "cave" (scribal error for "stronghold") in the territory of Judah in the low country; originally a Canaanite city. It was used by David as a hiding place. It has been identified with various places in modern geography, the most usual one being Aid-el-ma, ab. 10 mi. NE of Hebron. A traditional, and highly conjectural, identification with Khareitun, near Bethlehem, is now generally discounted by scholars.

Adullam, Cave of. In the Old Testament, the stronghold to which David withdrew from Gath (see immediately above). 1 Sam. xxii.

Adullamites (ą.dul′ąm.īts). Group of English Liberals who in 1866 withdrew from their party and supported the Conservatives after the introduction by Lord John Russell and Gladstone of a bill to broaden the elective franchise. Their action, which was bitterly attacked by their former colleagues in the Liberal Party, brought them their name when they were likened by John Bright to the malcontents who took refuge with David in the Cave of Adullam, for which reason they were often thereafter referred to collectively as "The Cave of Adullam" or simply "The Cave." The term is said to have been used earlier (1864) by President Lincoln to characterize a somewhat similar situation in U.S. politics.

Aduwa (ä′du.wä). [Also: **Adowa;** Italian, **Adua.**] Town in NE Ethiopia, in Tigré province, just inside the old Eritrean frontier. It was here that Ethiopian forces under Menelik II defeated the Italians in 1896 and brought world attention to their country for the first time in modern history. Pop. ab. 5,000.

Advaita (ą.dvī′tą). See under **Chaitanya.**

Advance. Vessel used in the 1850's by the American, Elisha Kane, in his search through the Arctic regions for the lost expedition of Sir John Franklin.

Advent. Christian religious season commemorating the coming of Christ. It encompasses the four Sundays before Christmas and begins on the Sunday closest to Saint Andrew's Day (Nov. 30). In the Roman Catholic Church the season is observed by fasting; most Protestant groups observe it as a liturgical season only.

Adventure. Sloop constructed (1791–92) on Nootka Sound, on the coast of Vancouver Island, by two Boston captains, John Kendrick and Asa Gray, who were members of a trading and exploring party in the Northwest region. The vessel was the first American sailing craft built on the Pacific coast.

Adventure. Ship used by the pirate captain, William Kidd.

Adventure. Ship in which Captain Philip Parker King (associated with Robert Fitzroy, commander of the *Beagle*) explored the coasts of South America in the period 1826–30.

Adventures of Alonso (ą.lon′zō). Romance (1775) attributed to Thomas Atwood Digges.

Adventures of an Atom, The. Political satire by Tobias Smollett, published in 1769. It pretended to be about Japan, but was recognized by all its readers as being actually a coarse and virulent satire on important political issues and persons in the early part of the reign of George III.

Adventures of a Young Man. Novel by John Dos Passos, published in 1939, portraying the disillusionment of a too hasty adherent of Communism.

Adventures of Brown, Jones, and Robinson, The. See **Brown, Jones, and Robinson, The Adventures of.**

Adventures of Captain Bonneville, The. Account by Washington Irving, published in 1837, of the adventures in the West of a U.S. army officer of this name. It was this officer (whose full name was Benjamin Louis Eulalie de Bonneville) after whom the Bonneville Dam was later named.

Adventures of Cléomadès (klā.o.mà.des′). See **Cléomadès, Adventures of.**

Adventures of Huckleberry Finn, The. See **Huckleberry Finn, The Adventures of.**

Adventures of Philip (fil′ip). Novel by W. M. Thackeray, published in 1862. It was the last of Thackeray's novels to be published in his lifetime, and is considered by most critics to reflect a waning of the novelist's creative power.

Adventures of Robin Day (rob′in dā), **The.** Picaresque novel (1839) by Robert Montgomery Bird.

Adventures of Sherlock Holmes, The. See under **Sherlock Holmes.**

Adventures of Tom Sawyer, The. See **Tom Sawyer, The Adventures of.**

Advertisements for the Unexperienced Planters of New England, or Anywhere. Work by Captain John Smith (1580–1631) dealing with colonial settlement, and based on his own experiences (1606 *et seq.*) in the Virginia colony. It was published in 1631.

Advice to a Raven in Russia. Last poem written by Joel Barlow, published posthumously in 1843. It was a bitter attack upon Napoleon's allegedly tyrannical tactics in Russia.

Advice to the Privileged Orders. Tract by Joel Barlow, published in 1792. Most historians consider that it reflects Barlow's political beliefs more clearly than any of his other works, and see in it clear evidence of an influence by Thomas Paine, who had become Barlow's friend during the 1780's. Written in France, within the atmosphere of equalitarianism produced by the early phases of the French Revolution, it urges that the state should be representative of all the people, rather than of a particular class or group, and that it should also be finally responsible for the welfare of each individual it represents.

Adwick-le-Street (ad′ik.lę.strēt′). Urban district in C England, in the West Riding of Yorkshire, ab. 5 mi. NW of Doncaster, ab. 160 mi. NW of London by rail. 18,808 (1951).

Ady (ô′dē), **Endre.** [English, **Andrew Ady.**] b. at Érdmindszent, Hungary, Nov. 22, 1877; d. at Budapest, Jan. 27, 1919. Hungarian poet, leader in his country of the modernist symbolist movement. He is generally regarded as the greatest Hungarian poet of the 20th century. His career began with the publication of a volume *Uj versek* (New Poems, 1906), which caused a split in the entire modern Hungarian literary world. Although he spent a great part of his life at Paris, his verse reflects a deep love for his native country. He was the author also of seven volumes in prose.

Adye (ā′di), Sir **John Miller.** b. at Sevenoaks, Kent, Nov. 1, 1819; d. Aug. 26, 1900. English general and military writer. He was the author of *Recollections of a Military Life* (1895), and others.

Adyge (ä.di.gā′). [Also: **Adighe, Adygei, Adyghe.**] A people of the NW slopes of the Caucasus Mountains, near Krasnodar.

Adyge. [Also: **Adighe, Adygei.**] Autonomous *oblast* (region) of Krasnodar Territory, Russian Soviet Federated Socialist Republic, U.S.S.R., in the foothills of the Caucasus Mountains. The occupations of the people have been agriculture, herding, and (in modest quantities) lumbering. However, the discovery in comparatively recent years of oil has given the region a position of vital importance in the industrial economy of Russia, and has made Maikop, the chief city of the oblast, an important oil center. Of the inhabitants today, less than half belong to the Circassian tribe known as the Adyge; the remainder of the population is divided between people of Russian stock and a slightly smaller number of Ukrainians. Capital, Maikop; area, ab. 1,700 sq. mi.; pop. ab. 250,000 (est. 1941), but some recent estimates have ranged upwards of 300,000.

Adzhar Autonomous Soviet Socialist Republic (ạ.jär′, ä′jär). [Also: **Adjar;** often called **Adzharia.**] Autonomous republic in the SW Georgian Soviet Socialist Republic, in the U.S.S.R. A great part of the republic is in the coastal area of the Black Sea, and in its S part it touches on the border of Turkey. In the level areas along the coast the climate is subtropical, which has permitted the republic to become the largest Russian tea-producing area; considerable quantities of rice, cotton, and Indian corn are also grown. Tobacco is grown in the central portion of the republic, and livestock breeding is important in the mountains. However, the most significant occupation of the people is not agriculture, but oil production, refining, and distribution; Batum, the chief city of the republic, has been for many years one of the world's great oil centers. Because of this, the republic as a whole, and Batum in particular, comprised a chief objective of the Germans in World War II. In August, 1942, the Germans occupied a great part of the area, but it was liberated by the Russians approximately six months later in the great offensive of early 1943. Capital, Batum; area, ab. 1,080 sq. mi.; pop. ab. 170,000 (est. 1941), but more recent estimates have ranged as high as 200,000.

Æ. See **Russell, George William.**

Aeacus (ē′ạ.kus). In Greek mythology, the son of Zeus and Aegina, renowned for his justice, and made a judge in the lower world. He was a reputed grandfather of Achilles.

Aedhan (ad′han), Saint. See **Aidan,** Saint.

Aëdon (ā.ē′dọn). In Greek legend, a daughter of Pandareus of Ephesus. According to Homer she was the wife of Zethus, king of Thebes, and the mother of Itylus. Inspired by envy of Niobe, the wife of her brother Amphion, who had six sons and six daughters, she formed the design of killing Niobe's eldest son, but by mistake destroyed her own son Itylus. To relieve her grief she was changed by Zeus into a nightingale.

Aedua (ed′ū.ạ, ē′dū.ạ). A Latin name of **Autun.**

Aedui (ed′ū.ī). [Also: **Haedui, Hedui.**] Celtic people in C Gaul, W of the Sequani between what are now the Saône and the Loire rivers. Their capital was Bibracte (the Roman Augustodunum, and the modern French Autun). They were allies of the Romans, but joined in the revolt of 52 B.C.

AEF. See **American Expeditionary Forces.**

Aegadian Isles (ē.gā′di.ạn) or **Aegates** (ē.gā′tēz). Ancient names of the **Egadi Islands.**

Aegae (ē′jē). An ancient name of **Edessa.**

Aegaeon (ē.jē′ọn). See **Briareus.**

Aegaleos (ē.gā′lẹ.os), **Mount.** In ancient geography, a mountain in W Attica, W of Athens. It ended in a promontory (Amphiale), opposite the island of Salamis, from which Xerxes is said to have witnessed (480 B.C.) the defeat of his forces by the Greeks in the Battle of Salamis. Elevation, ab. 1,534 ft.

Aegean Islands (ẹ.jē′ạn). [Modern Greek, **Nēsoi Aigaiou.**] In modern political geography, a district of E Greece. It includes the *nomoi* (departments) of Chios, Lesbos, Lemnos, and Samos. Area, 1,506 sq. mi.; pop. 311,751 (1940).

Aegean Sea. [Greek, **Aigaion Pelagos;** Latin, **Mare Aegaeum.**] Name given to that part of the Mediterranean Sea which lies between Greece on the W and N, and Turkey on the E. It communicates with the Sea of Marmara, and thence with the Black Sea, by the strait of the Dardanelles. It contains many islands, as Aegina, Euboea, the Cyclades, the Sporades, Samos, Chios, Lesbos, Samothrace, Thasos, and others. Its chief arms are the Gulf of Nauplia, the Gulf of Aegina (Saronic Gulf), the Channels of Evripos and Talanta, and the Gulfs of Lamia, Volos, Salonika, Cassandra, Monte Santo, Contessa, Saros, Edremit, İzmir, Kuşadasi (Scala Nuova), Mendelia, and Kos. Its chief tributaries are the Salembria, Vardar, Strymon, Maritsa, Gediz, and Menderes rivers. Length, ab. 400 mi.; greatest width, over 200 mi.; area, ab. 69,000 sq. mi.; average depth, 1,910 ft.

Aegeon (ē.jē′on). Character in Shakespeare's *Comedy of Errors;* a merchant of Syracuse and the father of the Antipholus twins.

Aegeri (ā′gẹ.rē). See **Ägeri.**

Aegeus (ē′jẹ.us, -jös). In Greek legend, the father of Theseus, and king of Athens. He is said to have drowned himself in what is now called the Aegean Sea (whence, according to one tradition, its name) out of grief at the supposed killing of his son by the Minotaur.

Aegialus (ẹ.jī′ạ.lus) or **Aegialeia** (ē″ji.ạ.lē′ạ). Original name of the ancient district of **Achaea,** in the Peloponnesus.

Aegidi (ā.gē′dē), **Ludwig Karl.** b. at Tilsit, in East Prussia, April 10, 1825; d. at Berlin, Nov. 19, 1901. German jurist, publicist, and politician. He was professor of jurisprudence at Bonn (1868 *et seq.*) and at Berlin (1877 *et seq.*).

Aegidia (ẹ.jid′i.ạ). An ancient name of **Capodistria.**

Aegidius (ẹ.jid′i.us). fl. second half of the 5th century. Roman commander in Gaul under the emperor Majorian (457–461). After the death of the emperor he is said to have maintained an independent sovereignty, possibly with the title of king, at what is now Soissons. He was voluntarily chosen king of the Franks during the temporary exile of the unpopular Childeric I, father of Clovis.

Aegidius a Columnis (ā kọ.lum′nis). b. probably at Rome c1247; d. 1316. Scholastic philosopher and general of the Augustine order, surnamed "Doctor Fundatissimus."

Aegidius of Assisi (ạ.sē′zẹ). [Also, Blessed **Giles.**] d. 1262. Friar, philosopher, and companion of Saint Francis of Assisi, by whom he was called "the Knight of our Round Table." His aphorisms were collected and printed as the *Dicta* after his death; an English translation of this was made by Paschal Robinson under the title *The Golden Words of the Blessed Brother Giles* (1906).

Aegina (ẹ.jī′nạ). [Modern Greek: **Aigina, Aiyina.**] Island in SE Greece, in the Aegean Sea, in the Gulf of Aegina, in the *nomos* (department) of Attica and Boeotia, ab. 22 mi. SW of Athens. It was conquered and colonized in very ancient times by the Dorians, and was an important Greek commercial state and center of art in the 6th and 5th centuries B.C. In 459 B.C. it was defeated for the first time by Athens, and some three decades later (431 B.C.) relegated to a position of comparative insignificance when the Athenians carried out a mass deportation of its population. In the 12th century A.D. it achieved brief notoriety as a nest of pirates, and partly as a result of their suppression it later came under the control of Venice. It was invaded and sacked in 1537 by the Algerian pirate Khair ad-Din Barbarossa. It was under Turkish rule for several centuries before the Greek war for independence in the early 19th century. Length, 9 mi.; pop. 10,762 (1940).

Aegina. [Also: **Aiyina, Aigina.**] Town in SE Greece, in the *nomos* (department) of Attica and Boeotia, the capital of the island of Aegina, situated on the W coast: center of the island's sponge-fishing industry. Aegina was the seat of the Greek government after its defeat by the Turks in 1826. Pop. 5,814 (1940).

Aegina. [Also, **Aigina.**] In Greek mythology, a river nymph, the daughter of Asopus, the river-god, and mother of Aeacus, a reputed grandfather of Achilles. She was beloved by Zeus, and carried by him to the island of Aegina (whence, according to one tradition, its name).

Aegina, Gulf of. [Also: **Saronic Gulf**; Greek, **Saronikós Kólpos**; Latin, **Saronicus Sinus.**] Arm of the Aegean Sea, lying SW of Attica and NE of Argolis, Greece. It contains the islands of Salamis and Aegina. Length, ab. 50 mi.

Aeginetan Marbles (ej.i.nē'tạn). Name given to an important collection of ancient Greek sculptures from the temple of Athena at Aegina, now the property of a museum at Munich. Discovered in 1811, these sculptures consist for the most part of the remains of the series of statues from both pediments of the temple. Five figures survive from the eastern pediment, and 10 from the western, which is probably complete. Both groups represent the exploits of Greek heroes in the Trojan War, with Athena as the central figure.

Aegion (ē'ji.on). See **Aigion.**

Aegipan (ē'ji.pan). In Greek mythology, a name sometimes used for the goat Pan. In some forms of the myth he is identical with Pan, and in others different from him. He is called the son of Zeus and Aega, Pan's wife, and also the father of Pan.

Aegir (ā'gir, ē'jir). [Also: **Gymir**; Old Norse, **Hlér.**] In Old Norse mythology, the god of the ocean. He was the principal water-demon and by race a giant, but personifies the more propitious characteristics of the sea. His wife is Ran.

Aegisthus (ẹ.jis'thus). In Greek legend, a son of Thyestes and cousin of Agamemnon. According to the older accounts, he seduced Clytemnestra, and procured the murder of Agamemnon, although in the *Agamemnon* of Aeschylus it is Clytemnestra, incited to the act by Aegisthus, who commits the murder.

Aegium (ē'ji.um). See **Aigion.**

Aeglamour (ē'glạ.mör). The "Sad Shepherd" in Ben Jonson's play of that name. He grieves at the reported drowning of the shepherdess Earine.

Aegle (eg'lē). In Greek mythology: **1.** A naiad, mother of the Graces. **2.** One of the Hesperides.

Aegospotami (ē.gọs.pot'ạ.mī). [Also, **Aegospotamos** (-mos).] In ancient geography, a small river and a town in that part of ancient Thrace known as the Chersonesus Thracica (geographically identical with what is now called the Gallipoli Peninsula of Turkey in Europe). The area of the river's mouth is noted as the scene of the decisive naval victory of the Spartans under Lysander over the Athenians, in 405 B.C., which led to the close of the Peloponnesian War.

Aegusa (ẹ.gū'sạ). A Latin name of **Favignana.**

Aegydius (ẹ.jid'i.us), Saint. See Saint **Giles.**

Aegyptus (ẹ.jip'tus). In Greek mythology, a son of Belus and twin brother of Danaüs. He received from Belus the sovereignty of Arabia and conquered Egypt. It is from his name, by one tradition, that the name "Egypt" is derived.

Aegyptus. Latin name of **Egypt.**

Aehrenthal (ā'rẹn.täl), **Alois Lexa,** Count **von.** b. in Bohemia, 1854; d. Feb. 17, 1912. Austro-Hungarian diplomat, notable as the foreign minister (1906–12) of his country during most of the international crises that set the stage for World War I. During his earlier career he was ambassador to Rumania (1895) and to Russia (1899). As foreign mi ister, he maneuvered the annexation of Bosnia-Hercegovina (1908) after the Buchlau conference with Russia, guided Austria through the Moroccan crisis, the Algeciras conference, and the First Balkan War, and tightened the Triple Alliance of Austria-Hungary, Germany, and Italy.

Aeken (ä'kẹn), **van.** See **Bosch, Hieronymus.**

Aelana (ẹ.lā'nạ). An ancient name of **Aqaba.**

Aelen (ā'lẹn). German name of **Aigle.**

Ælfheah (alf'he"ạċh), Saint. [Also: **Alphege, Elphege.**] b. 954; d. 1012. Anglo-Saxon bishop of Winchester (984) and archbishop of Canterbury (1006). He obtained a peace promise from the Danes in 994, but was later (1011) captured by them and slain (1012).

Ælfred (al'frẹd). See **Alfred,** king of England.

Ælfric (al'frik). [Called **Grammaticus.**] b. c955; d. c1020. Anglo-Saxon abbot, author of homilies (edited by Benjamin Thorpe and published 1844–46), a Latin grammar and glossary, a treatise on the Old and New Testaments, a volume of lives of the saints, and others. He was abbot of Cernel (now Cerne Abbas, in Dorsetshire), and later of Eynsham (in what is now Oxfordshire). The clarity and fluency of his prose has led some authorities to class it as the best in Anglo-Saxon literature.

Ælfthryth (alf'thrith). See **Elfrida.**

Aelia (ē'li.ạ) or **Aelia Capitolina** (kap"i.tọ.lī'nạ). See under **Jerusalem,** city.

Aelia gens (ē'li.ạ jenz). In ancient Rome, a plebeian clan or house whose family names and surnames were Bala, Catus, Gallus, Gracilis, Lamia, Ligur, Paetus, Sejanus, Staienus, Stilo, and Tubero. To this gens belonged the emperor Hadrian and through him, by adoption, several (Antonius Pius, Marcus Aurelius, and Lucius Aurelius Verus) of the so-called Antonine emperors.

Aelianus (ē.li.ā'nus), **Claudius.** [Called **Aelian** (ē'li.ạn).] b. at Praeneste, in Latium; d. probably after 222. Roman rhetorician. He was the author of *Variae historiae*, *De natura animalium*, and others. His works, most of which were written originally in Greek, cover a wide range of animal curiosa and human anecdote.

Aelianus Tacticus (tak'ti.kus). [Sometimes called **Aelian** (ē'li.ạn).] fl. c100 A.D. Greek military historian and writer, residing at Rome. He was the author of a work in Greek on the military tactics of the Greeks and the constitution of a Roman army.

Aelius Donatus (ē'li.us dọ.nā'tus). See **Donatus, Aelius.**

Aelius Herodianus (hẹ.rō.di.ā'nus). See **Herodianus, Aelius.**

Aelius Paetus (pē'tus), **Sextus.** fl. in the 2nd century B.C. Roman jurist, consul in 198, censor in 193. Author of the *Tripartita* (or *Jus Aelianum*) containing a recension of the Twelve Tables (450 B.C.) with commentary.

Ælla (al'ạ). d. 588. King of the Deirans from 559 to 588, the son of Iffa, ealdorman of the Deirans. He cast off the supremacy of the Bernicians at the death of Ida.

Aello (ā.el'ō). In Greek mythology, one of the Harpies.

Aelst (älst). See **Aalst.**

Aelst, Willem van. b. at Delft, in the Netherlands, 1620; d. at Amsterdam, 1679. Dutch painter, known particularly for his pictures of flowers and fruit.

Aemilia (ẹ.mil'i.ạ). In the fourth book of Spenser's *Faerie Queene*, a lovely lady "rapt by greedie lust," into the power of a cannibal giant who held Amoret also captive. She was saved by Belphoebe.

Aemilia. In Shakespeare's *Comedy of Errors*, the wife of Aegeon, acting as the abbess of Ephesus.

Aemilia. Ancient name of **Emilia-Romagna.**

Aemilia gens (ẹ.mil'i.ạ jenz). One of the most ancient patrician houses at Rome, probably of Sabine origin, which regarded as its ancestor Mamercus, called Aemilius on account of his persuasive language, who was variously represented as the son of Pythagoras, or of Numa, or as the descendant of Ascanius. The first member of the gens who obtained the consulship was L. Aemilius Mamercus (in 484 B.C.). Its family names are Barbula, Buca, Lepidus, Mamercus or Mamercinus, Papus, Paulus, Regillus, and Scaurus.

Aemilian Way (ẹ.mil'i.ạn). See **Via Aemilia.**

Aemilius (ẹ.mil'i.us). In *Titus Andronicus*, attributed to Shakespeare, a noble Roman.

Aenaria (ẹ.nãr'i.ạ). An ancient name of **Ischia.**

Aeneas (ẹ.nē'ạs). In classical legend, a Trojan prince, son of Anchises, king of Dardanus, and Aphrodite. The accounts of his life and achievements vary considerably, depending on the period of their writing. According to Homer, having been robbed of his cattle by Achilles, he took sides, with his Dardanians, against the Greeks, played an important part in the Trojan War, and after the sack of Troy, and the extinction of the house of Priam, reigned (as did also his descendants) in Troas (or the Troad, as the territory in the vicinity of Troy was known). In post-Homeric accounts he is sometimes represented as absent from the sack of Troy, sometimes as seeking refuge, on the admonition of Aphrodite, on Mount Ida, and carrying his father thither on his shoulders (with other variations), and as settling in the peninsula of Pallene, or in the Arcadian Orchomenos. Most of the accounts, however (including that in Vergil's *Aeneid*), represent him as landing in Italy, and becoming the ancestral hero of the Romans.

Aeneas, Dido and. See **Dido and Aeneas.**

Aeneas Tacticus (tak'ti.kus). fl. c360 B.C. Greek writer on tactics. He was an Arcadian or, at any rate, Peloponnesian, who had seen service in the Aegean and in Asia Minor. In the fragment that has come down to us he explains how to conduct defensive warfare and how to resist a siege (*Commentarius poliorceticus*). This book was very probably composed in 357–356 B.C. The hydraulic telegraph invented by Aeneas was described by Polybios. Aeneas also explains a system of cryptography.

Aeneid (ẹ.nē'id). [Also, **Aeneis.**] Epic poem, in 12 books, by Vergil, recounting one version of the adventures of Aeneas after the fall of Troy, founded on the Roman tradition that Aeneas settled in Latium and became the ancestral hero of the Roman people. The hero, driven by a storm onto the coast of Africa, is hospitably received by Dido, queen of Carthage, to whom he relates the fall of Troy and his wanderings. An attachment between them is broken by the departure of Aeneas in obedience to the will of the gods, and the suicide of Dido follows. After a visit to Sicily, Aeneas lands at Cumae in Italy. In a descent to the infernal regions he sees his father, Anchises, and has a prophetic vision of the glorious destiny of his race as well as of the future heroes of Rome. He marries Lavinia, daughter of Latinus, king of the Latini, and a contest with Turnus, king of the Rutuli, the rejected suitor, follows, in which Turnus is slain. The poem is a glorification of Rome and of the emperor Augustus, who, as a member of the Julian gens, traced his descent from Julus (sometimes identified with Ascanius), the grandson of Aeneas. The poem was completed, but not finally corrected, at the death of the author in 19 B.C. Among the more noteworthy English translations of the poem into English are those by Gavin Douglas (in rhyme, 1512–13), by Henry Howard, called by courtesy "the earl of Surrey" (whose translation in the middle of the 16th century is believed to mark the first appearance of blank verse in English poetry), by John Dryden (1697), and by William Morris (a translation notable more for the fact that it was done (1876) by Morris than for its quality).

Aenesidemus (ẹ.nes.i.dē'mus). b. at Cnossus, on the island of Crete; fl. 1st century B.C. Greek skeptical philosopher, notable for his teaching at Alexandria, in Egypt. He was the author of *Pyrrhonian Principles* and others.

Aenos (ē'nos). An ancient name of **Enez.**

Aenus (ē'nus). An ancient name of **Enez.**

Aenus. A Latin name of the **Inn.**

Aeoliae Insulae (ẹ.ō'li.ē in'sū̦.lē). A Latin name of the **Lipari Islands.**

Aeolian Hall (ẹ.ō'li.ạn). London concert hall opened in 1904: the remodeled Grosvenor Gallery.

Aeolian Islands. Ancient name of the **Lipari Islands.**

Aeolians (ẹ.ō'li.ạnz). [Also: **Aeoles** (ē.ō'lēz), **Aeoli** (-lī).] One of the four great divisions of the ancient Greeks (the Achaeans, Dorians, and Ionians were the other three).

Aeolis (ē'ọ.lis). [Also, **Aeolia** (ẹ.ō'li.ạ).] In ancient geography, originally the W coast of Asia Minor between the river Hermus and Lectum, settled by Aeolians. Later it extended along Troas (the Aegean coastal territory in the vicinity of the ancient city of Troy).

Aeolus (ē'ọ.lus, ẹ.ō'lus). In Greek mythology: **1.** The god of the winds, which he confined in a cavern. **2.** The son of Hellen, and the eponymic founder of the division of the ancient Greek people known as the Aeolians.

Aepinus (ā.pē'nus), **Franz Maria Ulrich Theodor.** [Original surname, **Hoch.**] b. at Rostock, on the Baltic Sea, 1724; d. at Dorpat (now Tartu, Estonia), 1802. German physicist, author of *Tentamen theoriae electricitatis et magnetismi* (1759), and others. He derived his name of "Aepinus" (as did Johann Aepinus, immediately following) by translating his original surname (which means "high" in German) into its Greek equivalent, which he then Latinized.

Aepinus, Johann. [Original surname, **Hoch.**] b. at Ziesar, Prussia, 1499; d. at Hamburg, May 13, 1553. German Protestant theologian, an opponent of Melanchthon, and author of a work entitled *De Purgatorio*.

Aequi (ē'kwī). Tribe in Latium, E of Rome and N of the Hernici, often allied with the Volscians and at war with the Romans. They were subdued at the end of the second Samnite war in 304 B.C.

Aërians (ā.ē'ri.ạnz). Reformist Arian sect which developed in Pontus, Asia Minor, during the 4th century under Aërius. Held by some scholars to have been a forerunner of modern Presbyterianism, the sect maintained that a presbyter or elder has equal authority with a bishop, repudiated prayers for the dead, and rejected church fasts.

Aërius (ā.ē'ri.us). fl. middle of the 4th century A.D. Early Christian leader, notable as a presbyter at Sebastia, in Pontus, Asia Minor. He was the founder of the sect known, from him, as Aërians.

Ærø (er'ė"). [Also: **Aarö, Arröe.**] Island of Denmark in the Little Belt, S of Fyn island, in the *amt* (county) of Svendborg. Length, 15 mi.; area, 33 sq. mi.; pop. 10,723 (1945).

Aerschot (är'sċhôt). [Also: **Aarschot, Arschot.**] Town in C Belgium, in the province of Brabant, situated on the Demer River, ab. 23 mi. NE of Brussels. At the center of an agricultural district, it has a considerable grain trade. During World War I it was the scene of severe fighting between the Belgians and Germans in August-September, 1914. In World War II the convent building of the lay order known as the Beguines was gutted and partly destroyed. 10,589 (1947).

Aertszen or **Aertsen** (ärt'sẹn), **Pieter.** [Also, **Aartsen.**] b. at Amsterdam, c1507; d. 1573. Dutch painter, noted for his realistic portrayal of furniture, kitchen utensils, and other simple furnishings of the peasant cottages which he used as background material in his work. An excellent example of his style is provided by a small *Crucifixion* in the Antwerp Museum.

Aescanes (es'kạ.nēz). Character in Shakespeare's *Pericles;* a lord of Tyre.

Aeschines (es'ki.nēs). fl. latter half of 5th century B.C. Athenian philosopher, a contemporary and disciple of Socrates. The three extant dialogues ascribed to him are now considered to be spurious.

Aeschines. b. 389 B.C.; d. on the island of Samos, in the Aegean Sea, 314 B.C. Athenian orator and political antagonist of Demosthenes, twice (347–346 B.C.) an envoy to Philip of Macedon. At one time anti-Macedonian, he later advocated a pro-Macedonian policy for Athens and was accused (343) by Demosthenes of accepting bribes from Philip. He was defeated (330) in a suit brought by him against Demosthenes' friend, Ctesiphon, and fled to Rhodes.

Aeschines the Orator. Greek statue from Herculaneum, in the National Museum at Naples, of high rank among works of its class. The orator stands quietly, his arm wrapped in his mantle; the expression is preoccupied, but full of dignity.

Aeschylus (es'ki.lus). b. at Eleusis, Greece, 525 B.C.; d. at Gela, Sicily, 456 B.C. Athenian tragic dramatist. He was a soldier of Athens in the war against the Persians, and is believed by many to have been at the battles of Marathon, Artemisium, Salamis, and Plataea (490–479). In his career as a playwright, he entered the annual Athenian competition of tragic drama more than 20 times (499–458), and won first prize 13 times (484–468), being finally defeated by Sophocles. Of his approximately 90 plays, seven survive: *The Suppliants, The Persians, The Seven against Thebes, Prometheus Bound* (sole surviving drama of his Promethean trilogy), and the Orestean trilogy, consisting of *Agamemnon, Choëphoroe,* and *Eumenides.*

Aesculapius (es.kū̦.lā'pi.us). [Also: **Asclepius, Asklepios.**] In Greek mythology, the god of medicine; son of Apollo and Coronis. He was killed with a thunderbolt by Zeus, because Pluto complained that, through his efforts, Hades was being depopulated. At the request of Apollo, he was, after death, placed among the stars. He is commonly represented as an old man with a beard, his usual attribute being a staff with a serpent coiled around it. The common offering to him was a cock.

Aesernia (ẹ.sėr'ni.ạ). Ancient name of **Isernia.**

Aeshma Daeva (ä.esh′mą dä′ā.vą). In Zoroastrian mythology, the demon of anger, identified with the Asmodeus of the Book of Tobit.

Aesir (ē′sėr, ā′sir). Collective name for the gods of the Scandinavian mythology. There were 12 gods and 26 goddesses, dwellers in Asgard.

Aesis (ē′sis). Ancient name of **Iesi.**

Aeson (ē′sǫn). In Greek legend, the father of Jason, and stepbrother of Pelias, who excluded him from his share of the kingdom of Thessaly. One account has it that when Pelias, on the reported return of the Argonauts, attempted to kill him, he committed suicide. According to Ovid, he was rejuvenated by Medea after the return of the Argonauts.

Aesop (ē′sǫp). [Also, **Esop.**] According to tradition, a Greek fabulist of the 6th century B.C., represented as a dwarf and originally a slave. Samos and other places claimed the honor of being his birthplace. After obtaining his freedom he visited Lydia and Greece. Of the so-called fables of Aesop there have been several editions, but they are all considered to be spurious. Indeed, Aesop was probably not an actual historical personage. Several of the fables which he is popularly supposed to have written have been traced to sources which considerably antedate his own alleged period of life; some, in fact, may be found in Egyptian materials dating from approximately the 14th century B.C. He was represented in later art as deformed, "perhaps to indicate his nearer approach to the lower animals and his peculiar sympathy for their habits."

Aesopus (ę.sō′pus), **Clodius.** [Also, **Aesop.**] fl. 1st century B.C. Roman tragic actor, a contemporary and intimate friend of Cicero, regarded by Horace as the equal of the great actor Roscius.

Aestii (es′ti.ī). People of the Baltic coast mentioned (1st century A.D.) by Tacitus. Some authorities believe they may have been the progenitors of the modern Estonians, who are ethnically close to the Finns; other sources classify them, tentatively, as a Balto-Slavic tribe.

Aeta (ä.ā′tä). [Also, **Eta.**] Negrito peoples of the Philippines, found chiefly in the mountains of Luzon, Palawan, and Mindanao. The group is believed to be aboriginal in the Philippines, and is known certainly to have been in the archipelago before the tribes which now predominate. They depend for their sustenance primarily upon game, wild fruits, and plants. Most of them now speak one of the Philippine dialects of the Indonesian group of the Malayo-Polynesian languages. This, and much else of their present culture, they have borrowed from their more advanced neighbors.

Aeth (ät). Flemish name of **Ath.**

Aethalia (ę.thā′li.ą). An ancient name of **Elba.**

Æthelhard of Bath (ath′ęl.härd). See **Adelard of Bath.**

Ætheling (a′thę.ling), **Edgar** (or **Eadgar**). See **Edgar** (or **Eadgar**) **Ætheling.**

Aethiopia (ē.thi.ō′pi.ą). See ancient **Ethiopia.**

Aethiopis (ę.thī′ǫ.pis). [Also, **Lay of Aethiopia.**] Greek epic poem of the Trojan cycle (by Arctinus of Miletus, the oldest (c776 B.C.) certainly known epic poet), so named from one of its heroes, Memnon the Aethiopian. It was a continuation of the *Iliad*, reaching "from the death of Hector to that of Achilles, and telling of the arrival of the Amazons and the Aethiopians to aid Troy."

Aethusa (ę.thū′zą). A Latin name of **Favignana.**

Aëtion (ā.ē′shi.ǫn). fl. c350 B.C. Greek painter, probably a contemporary of Apelles. He is noted for his painting *The Marriage of Alexander and Roxana.*

Aëtius (ā.ē′shi.us). [Greek, **Aëtios** (-os).] b. at Amida, Mesopotamia; fl. c500. Greek writer and physician. He was the compiler of a medical work, in Greek, of 16 books (Latin translation, 1542).

Aëtius, Flavius. b. at Durostorum (now Silistra, Rumania), c396; murdered at Rome, 454. Roman general and commander in chief under Valentinian III. He maintained the crumbling northern borders of the empire against the Visigoths (West Goths), Franks, and Burgundians (433 *et seq.*). He is remembered particularly for his decisive defeat (451) of Attila and the Huns near what is now Châlons-sur-Marne (this battle, which was the last major triumph of Roman arms, is often said to have saved Europe from the barbarians). He was killed in 454 by Valentinian, who suspected that he might covet the throne.

Aëtius of Antioch. [Greek, **Aëtios** (ā.ē′shi.os); called **"the Atheist."**] b. at Antioch; d. at Constantinople, 367. Syrian theologian. He was the founder of a sect of extreme Arians, called Aetians from him, Eunomians from his disciple Eunomius, and Anomoeans from their espousal of the doctrine that the Son was unlike (Greek, *anomoios*) the Father. Exiled (359) by Constantius, he was recalled (c361) by Julian, who retained him at the court in Constantinople.

Aetna (et′ną). Latin didactic poem, which has been erroneously attributed to Vergil. It combats the mythical theory (still popular at the time the poem was written) as to the causes of volcanic action.

Aetna. Latin name of **Etna,** Italy.

Aetolia (ę.tō′li.ą). [Also, **Aitolia.**] In ancient geography, a district of Greece, bounded by Epirus and Thessaly on the N, Doris on the NE, Locris on the E and SE, the Corinthian Gulf on the S, and Acarnania on the W. In modern Greece, it forms part of the *nomos* (department) of Aetolia and Acarnania.

Aetolia and Acarnania (ak.ąr.nā′ni.ą). [Also spelled **Aitolia and Acarnania.**] *Nomos* (department) in N Greece. Capital, Missolonghi; area, 3,004 sq. mi.; pop. 220,208 (1951).

Aetolian League (ę.tō′li.ąn). Confederation of Greek cities whose organization was copied from that of the Achaean League. It waged war against Macedon in 323 B.C., against the Gauls in 279, and against the Achaean League in 220. In the period 211–192 B.C., it was allied with Rome. It was dissolved in 167 B.C.

Afanas'evo (ä.fä.nä′syi.vǫ). Early Neolithic culture in the area of what is now the central U.S.S.R., widely distributed throughout the Minusinsk area and in W Siberia. It apparently flourished c2000–1500 B.C.

Afanasyev (ä.fä.nä′syif), **Aleksandr Nikolayevich.** b. 1826; d. 1871. Russian folklorist and archaeologist. He published numerous collections of tales and poems from the folklore of various groups in W and C Russia, and is to some extent responsible for their becoming known to non-Russian readers during the latter part of the 19th century. The most recent English translation of fairy tales from his various collections was published in 1945.

Afar Country (ą.fär′). See **Danakil.**

Afema (ä.fā′mä). [Also, **Sanwi Agni.**] One of the Sudanic-speaking Anyi peoples of W Africa, inhabiting the SE part of the Ivory Coast, to the E of Bingerville.

Afer (ā′fėr), **Domitius.** b. at Nemausus (now Nîmes, France); d. 60 A.D. Roman orator, a teacher of Quintilian. In 26 A.D. he conducted the accusation for the government against Claudia Pulchra, the cousin of Agrippina, and in 27 A.D. appeared against Varus Quintilius, her son.

Affair of Dishonor, An. Historical romance by William De Morgan, published in 1910.

Affleck (af′lek), **Thomas.** b. at Dumfries, Scotland, July 13, 1812; d. Dec. 30, 1868. American agricultural writer, notable as an advocate of improved methods of farming in the southern U.S. He became a junior editor (1840) of *Western Farmer and Gardener* at Cincinnati eight years after arriving in the U.S. Subsequently he moved to Mississippi and Texas, where he acquired extensive properties, including the only gristmill in Texas.

Affonso (ą.fon′sō; Portuguese, ą.fōn′sö). See **Alfonso.**

Affre (âfr), **Denis Auguste.** b. at St.-Rome, Tarn, France, Sept. 27, 1793; d. at Paris, June 27, 1848. French ecclesiastic, appointed (1840) archbishop of Paris. He was mortally wounded in the insurrection of 1848 while attempting to admonish the insurgents.

Afghanistan (af.gan′i.stan). [Also: **Pukhtun-Khtun;** ancient name, **Aryana.**] Country in W central Asia, bounded by the U.S.S.R. on the N, Pakistan on the E and S, and Iran on the W. It is ab. 700 mi. long and ab. 600 mi. wide. The prevailing religion is Mohammedanism (predominantly of the Sunnite sect).

Government, Population, and Area. Since 1926, the government has been a constitutional monarchy, consisting of the king (the title of amir was abolished in 1926), a supreme council of state (or cabinet), a senate of 45 members (appointed for life by the king), and a national assembly of approximately 138 members elected by popular vote. There are seven major provinces (Kabul,

Mazar, Kandahar, Herat, Kataghan, Simat-i-Mashriqi, Simat-i-Junubi) and three minor provinces (Badakhshan, Farah, Maimana), each of which is administered by a governor responsible to the monarchy. Capital, Kabul; area, ab. 250,000 sq. mi.; pop. ab. 12,000,000 (est. 1946).

Topography and Climate. The Hindu Kush range of mountains, and its various extensions, is the chief topographical feature of Afghanistan, although in the N and S parts of the country there are arid plains of considerable extent. The principle rivers are four: the Kabul, the Kunduz, the Herat, and the Helmand. For obvious reasons, a major part of the country's agricultural activity is found in the valleys of these rivers, but the plateau region in C Afghanistan provides valuable grazing areas for the camels, goats, and sheep vital to the existence of many of the country's inhabitants. The average annual rainfall of the country is not great (10 to 11 inches), and occurs chiefly in the period from October through May. The range in temperature, even within a 24-hour span, is often considerable; the seasonal range is, of course, very much greater, running from a low of ab. 0° F. in the winter to a high of ab. 100° in the summer.

Industry, Agriculture, and Trade. Afghanistan has little industry in the usual Western sense of the word (the total electric-power output of the country is only slightly over 6,000 kilowatts), but there are cotton and woolen mills of some size. However, the bulk of the material produced by these mills, and by the other, smaller manufacturing enterprises of the country, is consumed domestically. Some evidence exists that worthwhile mineral resources may exist, but thus far lack of capital and the extraordinary difficulties of transportation (Afghanistan has no railroad facilities, and uncertain highways) have prevented their exploitation. In agriculture, and in the raising of livestock, the Afghan economy finds its chief basis, perhaps most notably with the famous karakul sheep, which produce the fur usually spelled "caracul" in the U.S. There are an estimated 4,000,000 of these sheep now on the Afghan ranges. Other products exported by the country include wheat, nuts, and many fruits. Some cotton is grown, but not in sufficient quantity to be significant except for domestic use.

History. Afghanistan was included in the Persian empire of Darius I, in the empire of Alexander the Great, in the Mogul empire of India, and others. The country became an autonomous unit in 1747, when it achieved independence of Persia under the Durani dynasty (which was itself derived from a governor responsible to Persia). Under the last member of the Durani dynasty, Dost Mohammed Khan, the First Afghan War broke out with the British in 1838. The latter captured Kandahar, Ghazni, and Kabul in 1839, and succeeded briefly in establishing a new amir at Kabul, but in 1841 the British agent was killed, and the British army was largely annihilated in 1842 as it withdrew from Kabul through the Kurd-Kabul Pass. Later in the same year, a British force under Sir George Pollock forced its way back into Kabul, but the victory was only temporary, and sporadic outbreaks of British-Afghan hostility occurred throughout the next several decades. In 1878, under the amir Shere Ali, the Second Afghan War broke out, and the British captured Jalalabad and Kandahar. Shere Ali fled, and Yakub Khan was proclaimed amir in 1879. A massacre of the British at Kabul followed, and brought another British invading force, under Frederick Sleigh Roberts (the "Bobs Bahadur" of Kipling's stories), and Yakub Khan abdicated. The latter's brother Ayub Khan in 1880 at first defeated the British forces, but again under Roberts the British relieved Kandahar in 1880, defeated Ayub Khan, and recognized Abd-er-Rahman Khan as amir. Although Abd-er-Rahman Khan was nominally an independent ruler (except in foreign affairs), the British interest in Afghanistan was now evident at Kabul and generally recognized by the European powers. Various disputes arose during the next decade regarding the boundary between Afghanistan and the Russian possessions, and when the Russians seized Panjdeh in 1885, war between Great Britain and Russia was narrowly averted. An Anglo-Russian commission arranged the delimitation of the N frontier in 1886–87, and the so-called Pamir Commission of 1895 defined the NE border. The government and domestic affairs of Afghanistan were thereafter relatively stable until just after World War I, when resentment of British interference in combination with sympathy for their Moslem co-religionists, the Turks, led the Afghans into a brief war against Great Britain in 1919. Thereafter, during the 1920's and 1930's, a considerable effort was made by various rulers to modernize the country, but with comparatively little success. (One of the chief reasons for this was, and continues to be, that the majority of Afghans is suspicious of any change which appears to threaten the cultural conservatism that has been produced by the intense devotion to orthodox Mohammedanism characteristic of the country.) Some U.S. financial aid was extended to Afghanistan during and after World War II, but the country still remains, by Western standards, comparatively undeveloped. In 1948 a new boundary agreement was negotiated and signed with Russia.

Afghan Turkistan (af'gan tėr'ki.stan). [Also, **Afghan Turkestan.**] Name sometimes applied to a region in N Afghanistan, a low plain between the Amu Darya (Oxus) River and the Hindu Kush mountains to the S.

Afghan Wars. Two wars between Great Britain and Afghanistan during the years 1838–42 and 1878–80.

Afinger (ä'fing.ėr), **Bernhard.** b. at Nuremberg, Bavaria, May 6, 1813; d. at Berlin, Dec. 25, 1882. German sculptor.

Afinogenov (ä.fē.no.gye'nof), **Aleksandr Nikolayevich.** b. 1904; killed by a bomb during a German air raid on Moscow, Nov. 4, 1941. Russian playwright. Some half a dozen of his plays, all dealing with Soviet life, are available in English.

Afium (or **Afiun**) **Karahissar** (ä.fyöm'; ä.fyön'; kä.rä.hi-sär'). See **Afyon,** town.

AFL or **A. F. of L.** See **American Federation of Labor.**

Afloat and Ashore. Romance by James Fenimore Cooper, published in 1844.

Afontova Mountain (ä.fôn'to.va). [Russian, **Afontova Gora** (go.rä').] Upper Paleolithic site situated near Krasnoyarsk, Siberia, and first excavated (1886) by I. T. Savenko. Another series of excavations, under N. K. Auerbach, was started in 1923.

Afragola (ä.frä.gô'lä). Town and commune in S Italy, in the *compartimento* (region) of Campania, in the province of Napoli, ab. 10 mi. NE of Naples. The center of a rich agricultural district, it belongs to the metropolitan region of Naples; it has hat manufactures and a considerable agricultural trade. Pop. of commune, 29,281 (1936); of town, 29,156 (1936).

Afranius (a.frā'ni.us), **Lucius.** fl. c100 B.C. Roman comic poet, an imitator of the Greek Menander. Extant fragments of his work indicate that he dealt, like Menander, chiefly with middle-class life.

Afranius, Lucius. d. in Africa, 46 B.C. Roman general. An adherent of Pompey, who assisted him to become consul (60 B.C.), he was defeated by Caesar at Ilerda, Spain in 49 B.C. Despite a promise not to serve thereafter against Caesar, he joined Pompey's forces and was present at the defeats of Pompey at Pharsalus (48 B.C.) and Thapsus (46 B.C.). He was captured in the last-named battle and taken to Caesar, by whose soldiers he was thereupon put to death.

Africa (af'ri.ka). [Called the **"Dark Continent."**] Continent in the Eastern Hemisphere, next to Asia the largest grand division of the world. It is bounded on the N by the Mediterranean Sea (which separates it from Europe), on the E by the Isthmus of Suez (which connects it with Asia), the Red Sea (which separates it from Asia), and the Indian Ocean, by the Southern Ocean (or the Indian and South Atlantic oceans) on the S, and the Atlantic Ocean on the W. The length of the continent is 4,970 mi., its breadth 4,700 mi.; area, 11,698,830 sq. mi.; pop. ab. 198 million (est. 1950).

Political Divisions. The principal political divisions are: Egypt; the Anglo-Egyptian Sudan (an Anglo-Egyptian condominium); Ethiopia, including Eritrea; United Nations trust territories of Italian, British, and French Somaliland; the British territories of East Africa (Kenya colony and protectorate, Uganda protectorate, and the trust territory of Tanganyika); Mozambique (Portuguese); the British colonies of Northern and Southern Rhodesia, Nyasaland protectorate, and Bechuanaland protectorate; the French colony of Madagascar;

the Union of South Africa (Cape of Good Hope Province, Natal, Orange Free State, Transvaal, and the trust territory of South-West Africa); the British native protectorates of Basutoland and Swaziland; the Belgian Congo; Angola (Portuguese); French Equatorial Africa; British Cameroons; Cameroun (French); the British West-African territories (Nigeria, the Gold Coast, Sierra Leone, and Gambia); Liberia; Portuguese Guinea; the French West African federation consisting of Mauritania, Senegal, the Ivory Coast, French Guinea, French Togo, Dahomey, French Sudan, and Niger; Spanish Sahara; French Morocco; Algeria; Tunisia; Spanish Morocco; and the former Italian colony of Libya (which after World War II was divided between France, Great Britain, and Italy as trust territories under the United Nations, and in 1951 became an independent kingdom).

Physical Geography. The more distinctive physiographic features of the continent are the Atlas Mountains, the Sahara desert, the great equatorial forests, the lake region (Albert, Victoria, Tanganyika, and others), and the S central plateau. Principal rivers: Nile, Congo, Niger, and Zambezi (with Victoria Falls, the "African Niagara"). Africa has few high mountains; the highest are the glacier-covered Kilimanjaro (19,565 ft.) in Tanganyika, and Kenya (17,040 ft.) in Kenya colony.

History. Even to this day the least-known of the earth's grand divisions, Africa has been called the "Dark Continent." Its northern portions were early seats of civilization, and part of the Roman Empire; but some of its interior remains even today still unexplored. It was circumnavigated by the Phoenicians as early as the 7th century B.C. Coastline exploration was undertaken by the Portuguese in the middle of the 15th century, and the Portuguese navigator, Vasco da Gama, rounded the Cape of Good Hope, from the Atlantic Ocean into the Indian Ocean, in 1497. Explorations of the interior have been made since the last part of the 18th century by Bruce, Mungo Park, Hornemann, Burckhardt, Denham, Clapperton, Lander, Oudney, Rebmann, Barth, Richardson, Overweg, Vogel, Livingstone, Burton, Speke, Grant, Baker, Stanley, Schweinfurth, Mauch, Nachtigal, De Brazza, Holub, Wissmann, Serpa Pinto, Cameron, Rohlfs, Lenz, Du Chaillu, Emin Pasha, and others. During the last decade of the 19th century and in the early years of the 20th century the great European powers engaged in a scramble for colonial possessions in Africa. The main participants were France, Great Britain, Portugal, and Spain, but Belgium also obtained a share as did Italy, which was late in entering the race for territory. After World War I, Germany lost her colonies, which became mandated territories under France, Great Britain, and the Union of South Africa. A similar disposition was made of portions of the Italian Empire as a result of World War II.

Africa. Diocese of the later Roman prefecture of Italy. It comprised the Roman provinces of Africa, Numidia, and a part of Mauritania, and corresponds to modern Algeria, Tunisia, and Tripoli. To the Arabs, Africa meant the province of Carthage or Tunis and its capital, which was not at first Tunis but successively Kairouan and Mahdiya. Throughout the later Middle Ages the name "Africa" was applied by Christian writers to the latter city.

Africaine (là.frē.ken), **L'.** Opera by Meyerbeer, with a libretto by Augustin Eugène Scribe, produced at the Académie at Paris, on April 28, 1865, in the year following the composer's death.

Africanus (af.ri.kā'nus), **Scipio.** See **Scipio.**

Africanus, Sextus Julius. fl. at Rome, c200–250. Christian historian, traveler, and author. He wrote an account of the world from its creation (which he calculated at 5499 B.C.) to 221 A.D. His chronology, which moved back the birth of Christ three years, was thereafter for many years accepted by virtually all Eastern churches. Fragments of his writing are extant in Eusebius's *Chronicon* and elsewhere.

African War. Name sometimes applied to the war between Julius Caesar and the followers of Pompey, who had collected in the Roman province of Africa after the defeat at Pharsalus, in Greece, in 48 B.C., and were overthrown at Thapsus in 46 B.C.

Africa Orientale Italiana (ä'frē.kä ō.ryān.tä'lā ē.tä.lyä'nä). Italian name of **Italian East Africa.**

Afrikaans (af.ri.känz'). A creolized Germanic language, modified Dutch, spoken among the Boers in South Africa.

Afrikander Bond (af.ri.kan'dėr bond) or **Afrikander Bund** (äf.rē.kän'dėr bunt). South African association originally established in 1879, and which assumed the name here cited in 1880. It aimed not only at the furtherance of Afrikander influence, but at the ultimate complete independence of South Africa. In 1910 the group merged with others of a similar point of view into the South African Party.

Afrique Équatoriale Française (à.frēk ā.kwà.to.ryàl frän.sez). French name of **French Equatorial Africa.**

Afrique Occidentale Française (ok.sē.dän.tàl). French name of **French West Africa.**

Aftalion (àf.tà.lyôn), **Albert.** b. at Nancy, France, Oct. 21, 1874—. French economist, noted for his studies in the field of monetary theory. He was a professor at the University of Paris. Author of *Les Crises périodiques de surproductions* (2 vols., 1913), *Monnaie, prix et change* (1927), and *L'Équilibre dans les relations économiques internationales* (1937).

Afyon (äf.yōn'). [Also, **Afyonkarahisar** (äf.yōn"kä.rä-hi.sär').] *Il* (province or vilayet) in W central Turkey, long known for its hand-loomed rugs and for its opium trade. Several caravan routes cross the mountainous terrain included within its boundaries. The chief crops are wheat, cotton, and tobacco. Capital, Afyon; area, 4,880 sq. mi.; pop. 372,566 (1950).

Afyon. [Also: **Afium** (or **Afiun**) **Karahissar, Afyonkarahisar** ("Black Castle of Opium"), **Karahissar.**] Town in W central Turkey, capital of the *il* (province or vilayet) of Afyon, ab. 175 mi. SE of Istanbul: an important rail junction with large railroad shops; center of a large opium-growing area; wheat and tobacco are other important crops. It was the birthplace of Othman, founder of the Turkish empire. Near it is the site of the ancient Synnada (Eskikarahisar). Pop. ab. 27,000 (1945).

Afzelius (äf.sā'lē.ůs), **Adam.** b. at Larf, Sweden, Oct. 7, 1750; d. Jan. 30, 1837. Swedish naturalist and founder (1802) of the Linnaean Institute at Uppsala. He was variously an explorer (1792) in Sierra Leone, secretary (1796) of the Swedish legation at London, and professor of materia medica (1812) at Uppsala. He published (1823) the autobiography of Linnaeus.

Afzelius, Arvid August. b. Oct. 8, 1785; d. at Enköping, Sweden, Sept. 25, 1871. Swedish clergyman, writer, and collector of folksongs. He was pastor (1828 *et seq.*) at Enköping.

Aga (ä'gä). Modern name of the **Allia.**

Agabus (ag'ą.bus). Prophet and martyr of the early Christian church, supposed to have been one of the 70 disciples of Christ. In 43 A.D., while Paul and Barnabas were in Antioch, he came from Judea to Antioch, where he predicted the approach of a famine. (Acts, xi. 27, 28.)

Agada (ag'ą.dą). [Also: **Agadta, Haggadah.**] Name given in Aramaic to one of the two great divisions of post-Biblical Hebrew literature. The spelling of the name here shown is the one preferred by most authorities in the field, but the spelling "Haggadah" is also common and the term "Haggadist" is generally used to describe a Talmudic scholar who concerns himself chiefly with this division of Hebrew literature. It denotes that portion of the Talmudic literature not devoted to religious law; thus the exegetical and homiletical portions, fables, proverbs, the ethics, as well as everything relating to natural science and history, are included under the Agada, which is thus complementary to the Halacha, the legal portions.

Agade (ą.gā'dē). See under **Akkad.**

Agadès (à.gà.des, ag'ą.dēz). City in W Africa, former capital of the old sultanate of Air, in Niger territory, French West Africa, between Nigeria and Algeria. It is connected by caravan route with Nigeria and Dahomey in the S and with Ghardaïa and Laghouat in Algeria. It is also the name of a district, of which Agadès is the administrative center. Pop. of district, 32,448 (1946).

Agadir (à.gà.dēr, ag.ą.dir'). Seaport in NW Africa, in French Morocco, on the Atlantic coast near the mouth of the Sous River, in the SW part of the country. It is connected by road with Mogador and Marrakech. 5,730.

Agadir Crisis. European crisis which precipitated (1911) the second Moroccan Crisis. It arose when the German gunboat *Panther* arrived (July 1) at Agadir harbor on the Moroccan coast, avowedly to protect German interests. In effect, the visit was designed to bring action by the French on a settlement which would give to Germany concessions in the French Congo. Eventually, on Nov. 4, a settlement was reached by which Germany gained a slice of French Congo and recognized Morocco as a French protectorate.

Agag (ā′gag). In the Old Testament, an Amalekite king, defeated but spared by Saul, killed by Samuel. 1 Sam. xv.

Agag. Character in John Dryden's *Absalom and Achitophel*, generally believed to be a satirical portrait of Sir Edmund Berry Godfrey, a magistrate who received the declaration of Titus Oates. His mutilated body was found in a country ditch shortly thereafter, which led Dryden to the allusion:

"And Corah might for Agag's murder call
In terms as coarse as Samuel used to Saul."

The name "Corah" applies, of course, to Titus Oates.

Aga Khan I (ä′gä ċhän). [Title of **Hasan Ali Shah.**] b. 1800; d. 1881. First of the Ismaili Moslem leaders of this name to settle in India, under British protection. At one time he held temporal authority under the Persian shah, but fled after a quarrel. He traced his descent and spiritual authority from Mohammed's daughter, Fatima. He aided the British in restraining the Moslems on India's N border.

Aga Khan II. d. 1885. Ismaili Moslem leader in India; eldest son of Aga Khan I. He continued the policy of coöperation with the British which had been established by his father and was, like him, given by the British a degree of support. He was for part of his life a member of the Bombay legislative council.

Aga Khan III. b. at Karachi (now in Pakistan), 1875—. Indian statesman, spiritual leader since 1885 of the Ismaili Moslem sect, numbering followers in E Africa, C Asia, and India; son of Aga Khan II. Member (1902–04) of the viceroy's council; obtained Moslem support in India and elsewhere for the British in World War I; aided Turkey in peace negotiations with Allies; a founder and benefactor of Moslem Aligarh University; proposed (1924) for Nobel peace prize by Indian council of state.

Agamemnon (ag.a̤.mem′non). In Greek legendary history, the son of Atreus, king of Mycenae, and the most powerful ruler in Greece. He led the Greek expedition against Troy and on his return was slain, according to Homer, by Aegisthus, and according to Aeschylus, by his wife Clytemnestra, who was incited to the deed partly by jealousy of Cassandra, and partly through fear on account of her adultery with Aegisthus.

Agamemnon. Tragic drama by Aeschylus, considered by some to have been his greatest. The scene is laid in Argos, in the palace of Agamemnon, at the time of the king's return from the capture of Troy. The catastrophe is the murder (behind the scenes) of Agamemnon and Cassandra (whom he has brought captive with him) by the queen Clytemnestra urged on by her paramour Aegisthus.

Agamemnon of Aeschylus. Translation (1877) by Robert Browning of the Greek play by Aeschylus. Many critics consider that Browning attempted deliberately to reproduce in this work the harshness and obscurity of the original Greek in order to increase, by comparison, the stature of Euripides (whom Browning greatly admired) at the expense of Aeschylus (who was receiving at that time a degree of acclaim which seemed to Browning a reflection on Euripides).

Agaña (ä.gä′nyä). Seat of the U.S. government, and formerly the largest settlement, on the island of Guam, Pacific Ocean. It was largely destroyed when Guam was recaptured (1944) from the Japanese during World War II; reconstruction was begun in 1946. 10,004 (1940), 1,330 (1950).

Aganippe (ag.a̤.nip′ę̄). In ancient geography, a fountain near Mount Helicon, in Boeotia, Greece, sacred to the Muses. It was believed to inspire those who drank of it, and it gave the name "Aganippides" to the Muses.

Agape (ag′a̤.pē). In Spenser's *Faerie Queene*, a fay (or fairy), the mother of three knights, Diamond, Priamond, and Triamond, for whom she obtained the gift that if one were killed his strength should pass into the remaining brothers or brother.

Agapetus I (ag.a̤.pē′tus), Saint. [Also, **Agapitus.**] Pope from May, 535, to April, 536; son of Gordianus, a Roman priest. He went to Constantinople in 536 and deposed Anthimus the Eutychian, patriarch of Constantinople, but died before returning to Rome.

Agapetus II. Pope from 946 to 955, a Roman by birth. He strove to restore church discipline and to uphold temporal power, but was frustrated by Alberic, ruler of the independent Roman state.

Agar (ā′gär), **Herbert Sebastian.** b. at New Rochelle, N.Y., Sept. 29, 1897—. American editor and writer. London correspondent for the Louisville *Courier-Journal* and Louisville *Times* (1929–34); editor, Louisville *Courier-Journal* (1940 *et seq.*); collaborated with his second wife, Eleanor Carroll Chilton, on volumes of verse; author of *The People's Choice* (1933), which won him a Pulitzer prize. He has also written *Bread and Circuses* (1930), *Land of the Free* (1935), *Pursuit of Happiness* (1938), *A Time for Greatness* (1942), *A Declaration of Faith* (1952), and others.

Agard or **Agarde** (a̤.gärd′), **Arthur.** b. at Foston, Derbyshire, 1540; d. at London, Aug. 22, 1615. English antiquary, clerk in the British Exchequer, and (1603) deputy chamberlain. He prepared catalogues of state papers, compiled a list of all the leagues, treaties of peace, "intercourses," and marriages arranged between England and other countries down to the end of the 16th century, and wrote a Latin treatise on the Doomsday Book. He bequeathed his numerous manuscripts partly to the Exchequer and partly to his friend Robert Cotton. Most of them are now in the British Museum.

Agardh (ä′gärd), **Jakob Georg.** b. at Lund, Sweden, 1813; d. there, 1901. Swedish naturalist; son of K. A. Agardh. He served as professor of botany at Lund. Author of *Species, Genera, et Ordines Algarum*, of *Theoria Systematis Naturalis Plantarum* (1858), and other works.

Agardh, Karl Adolf. b. at Bastad, Sweden, Jan. 23, 1785; d. at Karlstad, Sweden, Jan. 28, 1859. Swedish naturalist and political economist, professor of botany and economics at the University of Lund (1812), and bishop of Karlstad (1834). His most important scientific works are *Systema Algarum* (1824), *Icones Algarum Europaearum* (1828–35), and *Lärobok i Botanik* (1830–32).

Agarrib (ag′a̤.rib), **Gebel** (or **Jebel**). See **Gharib, Gebel.**

Agasias (a̤.gā′shi.a̤s). Name of two Greek sculptors of the Ephesian school who lived sometime during the 1st century B.C.: **1.** Son of Dositheus. His name is inscribed on the base of the *Borghese Gladiator* in the Louvre, at Paris. **2.** Son of Menophilus. A military statue done by him is in the Athens national museum.

Agassiz (ag′a̤.si; French, à.gà.sē), **Alexander.** b. at Neuchâtel, Switzerland, Dec. 17, 1835; d. in mid-Atlantic, on the steamship *Adriatic*, March 27, 1910. American morphologist, geologist, zoölogist, oceanographer, museum director, and mining engineer; son of Louis Agassiz. His early schooling at Neuchâtel and Baden was under the guidance of Braun and von Siebold; he arrived in the U.S. in 1849 and took further education at Cambridge High School, Harvard (1855), and Lawrence Scientific School (1857, 1862). He went with the U.S. Coast Survey to California (1859) and to Panama (1860). In the latter year he married Anna Russell; their children were George, Maximilian, and Rodolphe. Business manager, a curator, and finally director of the Museum of Comparative Zoology (1860–98), he became a naturalized U.S. citizen in 1861. He published *Embryology of the Starfish* in 1864, and *A Catalogue of North American Acalephae* in 1865. Superintendent (1867–68) and president (1871–1910) of the Calumet and Hecla copper mines; traveled in Europe (1869–70). His authoritative *Revision of the Echini* was published in 1873. Conducted collecting expedition to Lake Titicaca (1874–75); established marine laboratory at Newport, R.I. (1877–98); in charge of the three important oceanographic cruises of the steamer *Blake* (1877–80), results published (1888). Investigated and collected in Mexico (1881–82), India (1883–84), Sandwich (now Hawaiian) Islands (1885), Egypt (1885–86), northern Africa (1889–90), Japan (1891–92), the Bahamas and Bermudas (1893–94), the Great Barrier Reef (1896), the

Fijis (1897–98), South Africa (1898–99), tropical Pacific (1899–1900), and the Maldives (1900–02). In charge of the first three Albatross Expeditions (1891, 1899, 1904). Published a great many papers on coral reefs and the Echinoderms, especially *Hawaiian and Other Pacific Echini* (1897). He was primarily a great investigator with many interests, who contributed more to the advancement of pure science than his more famous father.

Agassiz, Elizabeth Cabot. [Maiden name, **Cary.**] b. at Boston, Dec. 5, 1822; d. at Arlington Heights, Mass., June 27, 1907. American teacher and author; second wife (1850 *et seq.*) of Louis Agassiz. She was a founder (1879) of Radcliffe College and its president (1894–1902). Author and editor of *Louis Agassiz: His Life and Correspondence* (1885) and others.

Agassiz, Lake. Extensive post-glacial lake which once occupied the valley of the Red River in North Dakota, Minnesota, and Manitoba. The retreating ice sheet ponded waters in front of it, and in these were laid down sediments, now the fertile wheat fields of this region.

Agassiz, Louis. [Full name, **Jean Louis Rodolphe Agassiz.**] b. at Motier-en-Vuly, Switzerland, May 28, 1807; d. at Cambridge, Mass., Dec. 14, 1873. American teacher, naturalist, biologist, geologist, paleontologist, and ichthyologist. After early schooling at Bienne, Switzerland, he attended college at Lausanne, Zurich, Heidelberg, Erlangen (Ph.D., 1829), Munich (M.D., 1830); taught by Leuckart, Tiedmann, Braun, Oken, Döllinger, Fuchs, and others. Published Martius's and Spix's collection in Latin, *Brazilian Fishes* (1829); studied prevention and treatment of cholera (1831). Cuvier directed his work on fossil fishes at the Jardin des Plantes at Paris (1831–32). Humboldt's generosity and guidance led to a professorship of natural history in the lyceum at Neuchâtel (1832–46), where he included among his pupils Desor, Guyot, and Vogt. He married Cecile Braun in 1833; their children were Alexander, Pauline, and Ida. Published his monumental *Recherches sur les poissons fossiles* (1833–43) and an important monograph *The Fossil Fish of the Old Red Sandstone* (1844). His ice-age hypothesis was presented in *Études sur les glaciers* (1840). followed by *Système glaciare* (1847). Investigations (mostly paleontological) resulted in *Monographie d'echinodermes vivans et fossiles* (1838) and *Études critiques sur les mollusques fossiles* (1840–44). The comprehensive *Nomenclator Zoölogicus* (1842–46, 1848) preceded the *Bibliographia Zoölogiae et Geologiae* (1854). Arrived (1846) in America; gave eight series of Lowell Institute Lectures (1846–70); professor of zoölogy and geology at Harvard (1848–73); conducted (and published on) exploration of Lake Superior (1848). He married Elizabeth Cabot Cary in 1850. Executed Coastal Survey of Florida (1850–51); served as professor of comparative anatomy at the Medical College of Charleston, S.C. (1852–53); founded (1855) Agassiz School for girls, predecessor of Radcliffe College; established (1859) Museum of Comparative Zoölogy at Harvard, the parent stem of all American natural history museums. He became a naturalized U.S. citizen in 1861. Issued four volumes of a prospective ten on *Contributions to the Natural History of the United States* including his famous *Essay on Classification* (1857–62); wrote *Geological Sketches* in two series (1853–54; 1864–65); published *Methods of Study in Natural History* (1863); gave lecture series at Cornell (1868); conducted (and published on) zoölogical expeditions to Brazil (1865), and to San Francisco by way of the West Indies and Cape Horn (1871–72). He established (1873) the Anderson School of Natural History on Penikese Island, Buzzards Bay, Mass., the forerunner of all modern marine and lacustral biological stations. His bibliography consists of more than 425 published books and papers.

Agassiz (ä.gä.sēs'), **Mount.** Peak in SE Chile, in the territory of Magallenes. Elevation, ab. 10,000 ft.

Agassiz (ag'ą.si), **Mount.** A peak of the Uinta Mountains in Utah. Elevation, ab. 13,000 ft.

Agate (ā'gąt), **Alfred T.** b. at Sparta, in Westchester County, N.Y., Feb. 14, 1812; d. at Washington, D.C., Jan. 5, 1846. American illustrator and painter of miniatures; brother of Frederick Styles Agate (1803–44). He was artist for the Wilkes Exploring Expedition (1838–42), and a member of the National Academy. One of the best-known of his works is *Cocoanut Grove*.

Agate, Frederick Styles. b. at Sparta, in Westchester County, N.Y., Jan. 29, 1803; d. there, May 1, 1844. American religious and historical painter; brother of Alfred T. Agate (1812–46). He was a student of S. F. B. Morse, and a founder (1826) of the National Academy of Design. His paintings include *Ugolino*, *Pietá*, *The Assumption*, *Columbus and the Egg*, and *The Old Oaken Bucket*.

Agate, James Evershed. b. at Manchester, England, 1877—. British critic and author. He served as dramatic critic of the London *Sunday Times*, film critic of *The Tatler*, and literary critic of the London *Daily Express*. He was also the author of the *Ego* autobiographical volumes, most lately *Ego 7* (1945).

Agatha (ag'ą.thą), Saint. b. at Catania or Palermo, Sicily; d. 251. Sicilian virgin martyr, tortured and killed by Quintianus, governor of Sicily, whose advances she had spurned. She is a patron saint of Catania and is also invoked against storms.

Agatha. Latin name of **Agde.**

Agatharchides of Cnidos (ag.ą.thär'ki.dēz; nī'dǫs). [Also: **Agatharcus, Agatharchus.**] b. at Cnidos; fl. 2nd quarter 2nd century B.C., at Alexandria. Greek geographer and historian. His *On the Erythraean Sea*, which has been preserved through Photius, contains valuable geographic and ethnographic information on Arabia and Ethiopia. He also wrote a geography and history of Asia (in 10 books) and a geography and history of Europe (in 49 books).

Agatharchus (ag.ą.thär'kus). b. on the island of Samos, in the Aegean Sea; fl. c460–417 B.C. Athenian painter, said by Vitruvius to have painted a scene for a tragedy by Aeschylus, and thus sometimes credited with having been the inventor of scene painting for the theater.

Agathias (ą.gā'thi.ąs). b. at Myrina, in Asia Minor, c536; d. c582. Byzantine poet and historian.

Agathinos (ag.ą.thī'nos). [Full name, **Claudios Agathinos.**] b. in Sparta; fl. second half of the 1st century A.D. Greek physician. He wrote a treatise on the pulse, another on the action of hellebore (partly based on experiments), and recommended the use of cold (as opposed to warm) baths.

Agatho (ag'ą.thō), Saint. b. at Palermo, Sicily; d. 681. [Surnamed **Thaumaturgus.**] Pope from 678 to 681.

Agathocles or **Agathokles** (ą.gath'ǫ.klēz). b. at Thermae, Sicily, 361 B.C.; d. 289 B.C. Sicilian despot, tyrant of Syracuse (317–289 B.C.). He seized power with an army of exiles and Campanian hirelings, and shortly became involved in war with Carthage, traditional enemy of the Sicilian Greeks. He made his way through the Carthaginian forces around Syracuse and crossed the Mediterranean to attack Carthage in 310 B.C., but returned to find Syracuse rumbling with incipient revolt. He thereupon made peace with the Carthaginians, and put down his opposition, but died before he could renew attack on Carthage.

Agathon (ag'ą.thon). b. c450 B.C.; d. c400 B.C. Athenian tragic poet; friend of Euripides and Plato. His house on the occasion of his winning his first dramatic victory (416 B.C.) at Lenaea is the scene of Plato's *Symposium*. He is considered to have been the first Athenian dramatist to devise an original plot and to sever the link between plot and choral odes.

Agathon. Unknown author referred to by Chaucer in the prologue to the *Legend of Good Women*.

Agathon. Philosophical novel by Christoph Martin Wieland, published in 1766: so named from its chief character in whom the author depicted himself.

Agave (ą.gā'vē). In Greek legend, the daughter of Cadmus, wife of the Spartan Echion, and mother of Pentheus, king of Thebes, whom she destroyed in a fit of frenzy.

Agawam (ag'ą.wom, -wôm). Town in S Massachusetts, in Hampden County, on the Connecticut River: a suburb of Springfield. 10,166 (1950).

Agawam. Original name of **Ipswich,** Mass.

Agbatana (ag.bat'ą.ną). Ancient name of **Hamadan.**

Agde (ägd). [Latin, **Agatha.**] Town in S France, in the department of Hérault, situated on the Hérault River and the Canal du Midi, near the Mediterranean, ab. 29 mi.

SW of Montpellier. Founded by the Phoenicians, it was occupied by the Goths in the 6th century. Alaric II called a council here in 506. It was frequently sacked during the Middle Ages, and was held for some years by the Huguenots. The cathedral of Saint Étienne dates from the 12th century. 7,594 (1946).

Ageladas (aj.ẹ.lā'dạs). [Also: **Hageladas, Hagelaidas.**] fl. c520–c460 B.C. Greek sculptor, a native of Argos, thought by some to have been instructor to Myron, Phidias, and Polycleitus. None of his work is now known to exist.

Agelaus (aj.ẹ.lā'us). In Greek mythology, a servant of Priam, who exposed Paris on Mount Ida.

Agelaus. In Greek mythology, the bravest of the suitors of Penelope. He was one of the last to be slain by Ulysses.

Agen (à.zhaṅ). [Latin, **Aginnum.**] City in SW France, the capital of the department of Lot-et-Garonne, situated on the Garonne River between Bordeaux and Toulouse. It is a center of trade for the fruit growers of the vicinity. The cathedral of Saint Caprais dates from the 11th to the 16th centuries, with Romanesque and Gothic architectural elements. There are a number of buildings, including a library and a museum, from the medieval and the Renaissance periods. The town was the capital of the ancient Nitiobriges, and came under French control in 1439. It suffered considerable damage during the Albigensian and Huguenot religious wars. 33,397 (1946).

Agen (dà.zhaṅ), **Augustin Boyer d'.** See **Boyer d'Agen, Augustin.**

Agendicum (ạ.jen'di.kum). A Latin name of **Sens.**

Agenois (àzh.nwà) or **Agenais** (àzh.ne). Former district of France, comprised in the modern department of Lot-et-Garonne.

Agenor (ạ.jē'nôr, -nọr). In Greek legend, a king of Phoenicia; son of Poseidon and Libya, and father of Cadmus and Europa.

Agenor. In Greek legend, a brave Trojan warrior, son of Antenor, who appears in the Iliad as a leader in the attack on the fortifications of the Greeks. He fought with and wounded Achilles, and Apollo assumed his form in order to lead Achilles away from his pursuit of the retreating Trojans.

Age of Innocence. An oil painting (in the National Gallery, London) by the English artist Sir Joshua Reynolds (1723–92). The subject is a little girl seated on the ground in a wooded landscape.

Age of Innocence, The. Novel by Edith Wharton, published in 1920, and awarded a Pulitzer prize the following year. It was dramatized (1928) by Margaret Ayer Barnes.

Age of Reason, The. Deistic work by Thomas Paine published at Paris, in two parts (Part I, 1794; Part II, 1796). Shortly after the publication of the first part, the author was arrested. Part I asserts the existence of God, suggests that the Word of God is contained in His creation, and deprecates the machinery of national churches. Part II endeavors to point out the fallibility of the Bible by presenting examples of its inconsistency. The work was in its time regarded as revolutionary and has been called "the atheist's bible."

Ager (ā'gėr), **Captain.** Character in Middleton and Rowley's play *A Fair Quarrel*, a soldier of delicate and noble nature who makes, in his consideration of a point of family honor, a fine distinction between moral and physical courage.

Ägeri (ā'gẹ.rē). [Also: **Aegeri, Egeri.**] Small valley in the E part of the canton of Zug, Switzerland.

Ägeri, Lake of. [Also: **Lake of Aegeri, Lake of Egeri.**] Lake in the canton of Zug, Switzerland. It drains by way of the Lorze River into the Lake of Zug. Length, ab. 3½ mi.

Ages, The. Poem by William Cullen Bryant, published in 1821.

Agesander (aj.ẹ.san'dėr) or **Agesandros** (-dros). fl. 42–21 B.C. Greek sculptor, a native of Rhodes. With Athenodorus and Polydorus of Rhodes he carved the famous sculptured group known as the Laocoön, which is now in the Vatican, and which shows Laocoön and his two sons struggling with the serpents sent by the gods to kill them.

Agésilan de Colchos (à.zhā.zē.läṅ dẹ kol.kos). [English, **Agesilan of Colchos.**] Principal character in the romance of that name in the eleventh and twelfth books of the *Amadis de Gaule*.

Agésilan de Colchos. A tragicomedy by Rotrou, produced in 1635 or 1636. It is based on the *Amadis*.

Agésilas (à.zhā.zē.làs). Tragedy by Pierre Corneille, produced in 1666.

Agesilaus (ạ.jes.i.lā'us) or **Agesilaos** (-os). b. c444 B.C.; d. in Egypt, c360 B.C. King of Sparta (c399–c360); son of Archidamus II of the Eurypontid line of Spartan rulers. He aided the Asiatic Greeks against Persia (396–395 B.C.). Called home to subdue the Corinthian league of Greek states allied against Sparta, he defeated them at the battle of Coronea in Boeotia (394 B.C.) and withstood a series of attacks on Sparta, culminating in a campaign by four armies against the unwalled city (369). He died in Egypt, where he had led a force of Spartan mercenaries.

Agger of Servius Tullius (ag'ėr; sėr'vi.us tul'i.us). Name given to a stretch of the Servian Wall of Rome, extending from the Colline Gate across the low ground to the Esquiline Gate, adjoining the existing Arch of Gallienus, at the foot of the Esquiline. In the middle of the Agger there was a third gate, the Porta Viminalis. The Agger consisted of a great mound of earth, in front of which there was a ditch 30 ft. deep and 100 ft. wide. The mound had a very massive retaining-wall in front, rising 30 ft. above the top of the ditch, and a lighter wall at the back.

Aggershus (äg'ėrs.hös). See **Akershus.**

Aggtelek (ôg'te.lek). [Also, **Agtelek.**] Village in NE Hungary, situated on the Czechoslovakian border N of the city of Miskolc. It is noted for its cavern (Hungarian, *Baradla*), which is, after the one at Postonje, in Yugoslavia, the largest stalactite grotto in Europe.

Agha Jari (ä'gä jä'rē). Region in W Iran, ab. 75 mi. SE of Ahwaz, at the foot of the W slopes of the Zagros Mountains: an important oil-field area and the terminus of a pipe line to Khorramshahr.

Aghlabites (ag'lạ.bīts). See **Aglabites.**

Aghrim (ôg'rim, ôċh'-). See **Aughrim.**

Agiadae (ạ.jī'ạ.dē). See under **Agis I.**

Agias (ā'ji.ạs). fl. c740 B.C. Greek cyclic poet of Troezen, in the Peloponnesus; author of the *Nostoi* (*Homeward Voyages*) of the Achaean heroes after the siege of Troy.

Agias (ä.yäs'). [Also: **Agyia, Ayiá.**] Town in Thessaly, N Greece, in the *nomos* (department) of Larissa, situated at the foot of Mount Ossa. 3,001 (1940).

Agilolfinger (ä.gi.lol'fing.ėr). The family of the earliest dukes of Bavaria. The line began in the 6th century and ended in 788.

Agilulf (ä'gi.lu̇lf). d. 616. Duke of Turin and king of Lombardy.

Agincourt (aj'in.kōrt; French, à.zhaṅ.kör). [Modern French, **Azincourt.**] Village in the department of Pas-de-Calais, France, ab. 29 mi. SE of Boulogne, noted for the victory gained there on Oct. 25, 1415, by English bowmen under Henry V over a very much larger force of heavily armed French knights under the Constable d'Albret.

Aginnum (ạ.jin'um). Latin name of **Agen.**

Agion Oros (ä'yôn ô'rôs). [Also: **Hagion Oros, Ayion Oros**; English, **Mount Athos.**] *Nomos* (department) in N Greece, situated in Macedonia. On the mountain of the same name are 20 monasteries, mostly of the Greek Orthodox Church, forming an autonomous community, first established in the 10th century, which promulgated its own constitution in 1783, and renewed it in 1926. Capital, Karyai; pop. 3,100 (1951).

Agira (ä.jē'rä). [Also: **San Filippo d'Argirò**; ancient name, **Agyrium.**] Town and commune in SW Italy, on the island of Sicily, in the province of Enna, situated on the Salso River, ab. 30 mi. W of Catania. It is the center of a rich agricultural and sulfur-mining district. The church of San Filippo dates from the 17th century. One of the oldest cities in the interior of Sicily, it flourished under the Greeks and retained its importance under the Romans and later the Moslems and the Normans. Pop. of commune, 15,350 (1936); of town, 14,411 (1936).

Agis I (ā'jis). King of Sparta (c1032 B.C.). He was the reputed founder of the royal line known as the Agiadae.

Agis II. King of Sparta (c427–399 B.C.); victorious at Mantinea in 418 B.C.

Agis III. King of Sparta (338–331 B.C.). He was allied with Persia against Macedon, and was defeated and killed in 331.

Agis IV. King of Sparta (244–240 B.C.); son of Eudamidas II of the Eurypontid line of Spartan rulers. He proposed to recruit additions to the ranks of the Spartans from among the Perioeci, and advocated a redistribution of the landed property. In these measures of reform he was opposed by his colleague, Leonidas II, of the royal line known as the Agiadae, and was, after some transient successes, captured and sentenced to death by the Spartan ephors. Alfieri produced a tragedy which used his story as its basis.

Aglabites (ag'la̤.bīts). [Also: **Aghlabites, Aglabides** (-bīdz).] Arab dynasty which reigned in N Africa (capital at Kairouan) for approximately 100 years, from the beginning of the 9th century to 909. It was succeeded by the Fatimites.

Aglaia (a̤.glā'a̤). In Greek mythology, one of the three Graces.

Aglaia. Asteroid (No. 47) discovered by R. Luther at Düsseldorf, Germany, on Sept. 15, 1857.

Aglaura (a̤.glô'ra̤). Tragedy by Sir John Suckling, acted in 1637–38 and printed in 1646.

Aglauros (a̤.glô'ros), **Agraulos** (-grô'los), or **Agraule** (-lē). In Greek mythology, the wife of Cecrops; also, the daughter of Cecrops, noted in legends of Attica.

Agnano (ä.nyä'nō), **Lake.** [Italian, **Lago d'Agnano.**] Formerly a small lake, now an open crater, in S Italy, ab. 5 mi. W of Naples, noted for the Grotta del Cane. It was drained in 1870.

Agnes (ag'ne̤s), Saint. fl. probably in middle of 3rd century. Virgin and child martyr, said to have been beheaded at the age of 12 or 13 after being cast into a brothel. She is the patron saint of young maidens, and the source of the legend that on Saint Agnes's Eve (Jan. 20) a girl might perform a certain ritual and discover the visage of her future husband, a superstition important in Keats's *Eve of Saint Agnes.* The date of her martyrdom is very uncertain. The *Acts* of Agnes are regarded as spurious, and the latest studies suggest that she did not suffer under Diocletian (304), but during a persecution just after or before the reign of Decius (251).

Agnès (à.nyes). Character in Molière's *L'École des Femmes,* an ingénue. She contrives to make extremely suggestive allusions while speaking with the utmost simplicity of mind. Wycherley took his *Country Wife* from this character. The name has become proverbial for a person of this kind.

Agnes (ag'ne̤s), **Black.** See **Dunbar, Agnes.**

Agnès (à.nyes), **Mère.** See **Arnauld, Jeanne Catherine Agnès.**

Agnes (ag'ne̤s), **The Eve of Saint.** Poem by John Keats, written in 1818.

Agnes' Eve, Saint. Poem by Alfred Tennyson, published in 1842.

Agnes Grey (grā). Novel by Anne Brontë, published (1847) under the pseudonym Acton Bell.

Agnesi (ä.nyā'zē), **Maria Gaetana.** b. at Milan, 1718; d. there, 1799. Italian mathematician; sister of Maria Teresa Agnesi. Professor at Bologna (1752 *et seq.*); author of *Instituzioni Analitiche* (1748; Eng. trans., 1801), and others.

Agnesi, Maria Teresa. b. at Milan, 1724; d. c1780. Italian composer and pianist; sister of Maria Gaetana Agnesi. She composed five operas (including *Sofonisbe, Ciro in Armenia, Nitocri,* and *Insubria Consolato*), two piano concertos, and several cantatas.

Agnes of Austria. b. 1281; d. 1364. Daughter of the German king Albert I, and wife (1296 *et seq.*) of Andrew III of Hungary. She is remembered in history for her unceasing efforts to wreak vengeance against John the Parricide (her first cousin) and all others connected with the murder of her father.

Agnes of Meran (mā.rän'). d. at Poissy, France, 1201. Wife of Philip II of France; daughter of Duke Berthold of Meran. Philip's divorce of his previous wife, Ingeborg of Denmark, was held to be invalid by the Pope, and Philip was thereupon forced by an interdict to give up Agnes.

Agnes of Poitou (pwà.tö'). d. Dec. 14, 1077. Second consort of the emperor Henry III, and daughter of William V, duke of Aquitaine. At the death of Henry III, on Oct. 5, 1056, she became guardian of her son, Henry IV.

Agnes's Eve (ag'ne̤s.e̤z), **Saint.** Christian feast, celebrated on the night of Jan. 20. It is especially a holiday for young maidens. It was supposed possible by various forms of divination for a girl on this night to see the form of her future husband. A narrative poem by John Keats, *The Eve of Saint Agnes,* is based on this tradition.

Agnew (ag'nū), **David H.** b. in Lancaster County, Pa., Nov. 24, 1818; d. at Philadelphia, March 22, 1892. American surgeon, professor of clinical surgery (1870) and professor of surgery (1871–89) at University of Pennsylvania. He was chief surgical consultant when President Garfield was shot (1881) by Guiteau.

Agnew, Eliza. b. at New York, Feb. 2, 1807; d. in Ceylon, June 14, 1883. American missionary and teacher.

Agnew, Patrick. b. 1822; d. at Multan, India, April 21, 1848. English civil servant in India, murdered with his companion, Lieutenant W. A. Anderson, by the retainers of Mulráj, *dewan* (governor) of Multan. It was this incident that precipitated the second Sikh war.

Agni (ä'nyē). See also **Anyi.**

Agni (ag'ni). In Hindu mythology, the god of fire.

Agni Purana (ag'ni pọ.rä'na̤). Epic poem (grouped by some scholars with 18 others in the Sanskrit work known collectively as the *Puranas* and so named because it is supposed to have been communicated by Agni to Vasishtha) devoted ostensibly to the glorification of Siva.

Agno (äg'nō). River in C Luzon, Philippines. It rises in the northern mountains of Mountain Province, and flows S into Pangasinan, where it divides and turns W, entering Lingayen Gulf by channels at Dagupan, Lingayen, San Isidro, and San Fabian. The produce of the N part of the C valley of Luzon is carried by branches of the Agno to Lingayen Gulf. Length, ab. 128 mi.

Agnoëtae (ag.nọ.ē'tē). [Also: **Agnoïtoe** (-ī'tē), **Agnoïtes** (ag'nọ.īts).] Christian sect of the 4th century A.D., which denied the omniscience of God, maintaining that He knows the past only by memory and the future only by inference from the present.

Agnoëtae. [Also: **Agnoïtoe, Agnoïtes;** Greek, **Agnoetai.**] Christian sect of the 6th century A.D., followers of Themistius, deacon of Alexandria. The group was notable for its contention that Christ, as man, was ignorant of many things, including the time of the day of judgment.

Agnolo (dä'nyō.lō), **Baccio d'.** b. at Florence, c1461; d. 1543. Florentine architect.

Agnolo da Siena (ä'nyō.lō dä sye'nä). fl. 1310–c1350. Italian architect and sculptor, with **Agostino da Siena.**

Agnone (ä.nyō'nä). Town and commune in C Italy, in the province of Campobasso. Buildings of interest to tourists were undamaged in World War II. Pop. ab. 10,000.

Agnus Dei (ag'nus dē'ī). See **Adoration of the Lamb.**

Agnyi (ä'nyē). See **Anyi.**

Agobard (à.go.bàr). b. c799; d. 840. Frankish theologian, archbishop of Lyons (816 *et seq.*). He was important in the renaissance of scholarship that came into existence for a brief period in western Europe under the aegis of Charlemagne. Said to have had "the clearest head of his time," he was a champion of reason against superstition, denouncing the fallacies involved in persecution for witchcraft, trial by ordeal, judicial duel, image worship, and the magical explanation of storms.

Agora (ag'ọ.ra̤). Large irregular area at Athens, Greece, which may be entered beneath the NE angle of the Colonus Agoraeus hill (on which stands the so-called Theseum) by the broad portico-bordered Dromos Street running to the Dipylon Gate, thence passing along the base of the "Theseum" hill, and extending one branch north of the Areopagus, and another around the W end of the Areopagus, and between the Pnyx and the Acropolis. This last portion was especially the political agora, or place of assembly, while the portion north of the Areopagus was more particularly the original commercial agora or market place.

Agoracritus (ag.ǫ.rak′ri.tus) or **Agorakritos** (-tos). b. on the island of Paros, in the Aegean Sea; fl. 5th century B.C. Greek sculptor, favorite pupil of Phidias and rival of Alcamenes. He is now remembered chiefly for his *Nemesis at Rhamnus,* fragments of which are in the British Museum and Athens Museum.

Agosta (ä.gōs′tä). See **Augusta,** Italy.

Agostini (ä.gō.stē′nē), **Leonardo.** b. at Siena, Italy; fl. in the 17th century. Italian scholar, appointed inspector of antiquities by Pope Alexander VII. He was editor of a new edition of Paruta's *Sicilian Medals* and of other works.

Agostini, Paolo. b. at Vallerano, Italy, 1593; d. at Rome in September, 1629. Italian composer, chiefly of sacred music. He was successor (1627) to Ugolini as maestro of the Vatican chapel.

Agostino (ä.gō.stē′nō) and **Agnolo da Siena** (ä′nyō.lō dä sye′nä). fl. 1310–c1350. Italian architects and sculptors who together designed the Sienese church and convent of Saint Francis and who are often mistakenly treated as brothers. Their best sculptural work is usually considered to have been Bishop Tarlati's tomb at Arezzo, which was destroyed by the French during the Napoleonic period.

Agostino di Duccio (dē döt′chō). b. at Florence, Italy, c1418; d. at Perugia, Italy, c1498. Florentine sculptor, noted for his glazed terra-cotta reliefs. His façade for the church of San Bernardino at Perugia is considered to be an outstanding example of Italian polychrome architectural adornment.

Agotes (à.got). See **Colliberts.**

Agotime (ä.gō.tē′mā). Sudanic-speaking people of W Africa, inhabiting S French Togo. They form a small group and are surrounded by Ewe peoples, but are related culturally and linguistically to the Ga.

Agoult (dà.gö), **Marie Catherine Sophie de Flavigny,** Comtesse **d'.** [Pseudonym, **Daniel Stern.**] b. at Frankfort on the Main, 1805; d. at Paris, 1876. French authoress; mistress of Franz Liszt, by whom she had three children. One of them, Cosima, married Hans von Bülow and later Richard Wagner; another, Blandine, married Emile Olliver. Her novel *Nélida* contains a thinly veiled account of her breach with Liszt. She was mentioned as "Arabella" in *Lettres d'un voyageur,* by George Sand; contributed to *Revue des deux Mondes;* wrote *Esquisses morales et politiques* (1849), *Histoire de la Révolution de 1848* (1851), and others.

Agoust (dà.göst), **Bertrand d'.** Original name of Pope **Clement V.**

Agra (ä′grą). Division of Uttar Pradesh state, in N Union of India, ab. 120 mi. S of Delhi: rice, wheat, sugar, and cotton. Capital, Agra; area, ab. 9,000 sq. mi.; pop. 5,326,768 (1941).

Agra. District of the division of Agra, Union of India. Capital, Agra; area, ab. 1,800 sq. mi.; pop. ab. 1,000,000.

Agra. City in N India, the capital of the division and district of Agra, Union of India, on the Jumna River, ab. 120 mi. S of Delhi. Agra is chiefly famous for its architectural monuments, though its manufactures of carpets, embroideries, and stone work are considerable. It was the capital of the Mogul empire during the last part of the 16th and the first part of the 17th century, and was captured by the British in 1803. The English in Agra were besieged in the fort by the Sepoy mutineers, during July–October, 1857. Pop. 284,149 (1941).

Agrae (ā′grē). Suburb of ancient Athens extending E from opposite the temple of Olympian Zeus over the hills on the S bank of the Ilissus. In it lies the Panathenaic Stadium.

Agramante (ä.grä.män′tā). In Boiardo's *Orlando Innamorato* and Ariosto's *Orlando Furioso,* the young king of Africa.

Agramonte (ä.grä.mōn′tā), **Arístides.** b. at Puerto Príncipe (now Camagüey), Cuba, June 3, 1869; d. at New Orleans, in August, 1931. Cuban bacteriologist, pathologist, and physician, notable as a member of the four-man commission which demonstrated (1901) the transmission of yellow fever by the mosquito *Aëdes calopus.*

Agramonte y Loinaz (ē loi.näs′), **Ignacio.** b. at Puerto Príncipe (now Camagüey), Cuba, 1841; killed at Jimaguayú, Cuba, July 1, 1873. Cuban revolutionist and patriot. Leader in the revolts of 1867 and 1868 against Spain, he was commissioned a major general by Céspedes.

Agrarian Party. Group of several Czechoslovak parliamentary parties, among which the republican party was the largest, that came into being with the 20th-century development of Czech and Slovak national sentiment.

Agraulos (ą.grô′los) or **Agraule** (-lē). See **Aglauros.**

Agraviados (ä.grä.ʙyä′ᴛʜōs). In Spanish history, the adherents of the Hapsburgs in Spain in the 18th century, who opposed recognition of the Bourbons; also, the partisans of an unsuccessful absolutist revolt in 1826–28.

Agreda (ä.grā′ᴛʜä), **María de.** [Original name, **María Fernández Coronel.**] b. at Agreda, Spain, 1602; d. there, 1665. Spanish mystic. She was abbess (1627 *et seq.*) of the convent of the Immaculate Conception at Agreda, and a correspondent of Philip IV, who seems to have given considerable weight to her advice; author of a life of the Virgin Mary, which was later termed indecent by Bossuet and censured by the Sorbonne, despite her assertions of divine revelation. Her *Mystic City of God* (1668) was for a time under ecclesiastic ban, but this was later lifted.

Agreeable Surprise, The. Farce by John O'Keeffe, produced in 1781.

Agreeb (ag′rēb), **Gebel** (or **Jebel**). See **Gharib, Gebel.**

Agreement of St.-Jean-de-Maurienne. Secret treaty, one of several defining spheres of interest in the Near East, signed in April, 1917, by Great Britain, France, and Italy. In it France and Great Britain promised to Italy a sphere N of Smyrna and possession of the southern third of Anatolia.

Ağri (äg.ri′). [Also, **Karaköse.**] *Il* (province or vilayet) in E Turkey, in mountainous country where subsistence crops, wool, and opium are raised. Capital, Doğubayazit; area, 5,142 sq. mi.; pop. 155,545 (1950).

Ağri. A former name of **Doğubayazit.**

Agrib (ag′rib), **Gebel** (or **Jebel**). See **Gharib, Gebel.**

Agricane (ä.grē.kä′nā). In Boiardo's *Orlando Innamorato,* a king of Tatary who is in command of an enormous army, but is killed by Orlando in single combat.

Agricola (ą.grik′ǫ.lą), **Alexander.** [Original surname, **Ackermann.**] b. probably in the Netherlands, c1446; d. at Valladolid, Spain, c1506. Composer of religious music. He was employed at the court of France, by Lorenzo de' Medici, and elsewhere. His works include motets, songs, and several masses.

Agricola, Christoph Ludwig. b. at Ratisbon (now better known as Regensburg), Bavaria, 1667; d. there, 1719. German landscape and portrait painter.

Agricola, Georg. [Original surname, **Bauer.**] b. at Glauchau, Saxony, March 24, 1494 (or possibly 1490); d. at Chemnitz, Saxony, Nov. 15 (or 21), 1555. German mineralogist, author of numerous scientific books. His most important work was *De re metallica,* published posthumously in 1556. An English translation by Herbert C. Hoover, later president of the U.S., and Lou H. Hoover, appeared in 1912.

Agricola, Gnaeus Julius. b. at Forum Julii (now Fréjus, France), 37 A.D.; d. at Rome, 93 A.D. Roman soldier and politician; father-in-law of Tacitus. Quaestor in Asia (63) under Salvius Titianus; made commander (70) of the XXth Legion in Britain by Vespasian; governor of Aquitania (74–78); elected consul (78) and assigned to southern Britain, where in seven campaigns (78–84) he extended Roman law to the northern boundary of Perth and Argyll. He may have been poisoned by agents of the emperor. Tacitus' *Agricola,* an account of his life and accomplishments, is generally considered to be an outstanding example of good classical biography.

Agricola, Johann. [Called **"Magister Islebius";** original surname, **Schneider,** later **Schnitter.**] b. at Eisleben, Saxony, 1492; d. at Berlin, 1566. German Protestant theologian. He was at one time a follower of Luther, but separated from him in 1536 on the issue of the Antinomian heresy, which Agricola espoused. Author of various theological works and a collection of German proverbs (1529–48).

Agricola, Johann Friedrich. b. at Dobitschen, Saxe-Altenburg, Jan. 4, 1720; d. at Berlin, Nov. 12, 1774. German organist and composer, director (1759–74) of the Royal Chapel at Berlin. He was at one time a pupil of J. S. Bach.

Agricola, Martin. [Original surname, **Sohr** or **Sore.**] b. at Sorau, Brandenburg, c1486; d. at Magdeburg, Saxony, June 10, 1556. German writer on music and musical director at Magdeburg, notable for his attempt to improve musical notation. Author of *Ein kurtz deutsche Musica* (1528), *Musica instrumentalis deudsch* (1529), and others.

Agricola, Rodolphus. [Original name, **Roelof Huysmann** (or **Huysman**).] b. at Baflo, near Groningen, the Netherlands, 1443; d. at Heidelberg, Germany, 1485. Dutch scholar, painter, and musician. He was a lecturer (1482 *et seq.*) on Greek and Roman literature at Worms and Heidelberg.

Agricultural Adjustment Act. Act passed by the U.S. Congress in 1933 to meet national economic distress by cutting down farm surpluses and increasing agricultural income. Its provisions, including soil-conservation measures, were carried out by the Agricultural Adjustment Administration. An important part of the early New Deal legislative program, it was declared unconstitutional in 1936 on the ground that its taxing provisions exceeded the powers allotted to the federal government.

Agricultural Adjustment Act. [Full title, **Agricultural Adjustment Administration Act of 1938.**] Act passed by the U.S. Congress in 1938 which placed upon a permanent basis the farm-relief and soil-conservation measures of the Soil Conservation and Domestic Allotment Act (1936). This act introduced the policy of the "ever normal granary" through commodity loans and storage against less productive years of the surplus thus obtained. It continued also the earlier provision of benefit payments to farmers and restored the 1909–14 "parity" ratio of agricultural prices.

Agricultural Adjustment Administration. [Called **"the AAA."**] National agency established by the Agricultural Adjustment Acts (1933, 1938) to administer the farm-relief and soil-conservation measures provided for by these acts. Its activities were altered early in World War II toward the end of increasing food production.

Agricultural Marketing Act of 1929. Measure designed to aid U.S. agricultural production and marketing by means of voluntary coöperation under official agencies. It stressed the development of farm coöperatives, set up a Federal Farm Board of eight members, and established a revolving fund of five hundred million dollars for loans to coöperatives.

Agricultural Wheel. U.S. farm movement initiated (1882) by W. W. Tedford for the purpose of improving agricultural conditions. In 1886 it changed its name to the National Agricultural Wheel; three years later it was amalgamated with the National Farmers' Alliance and Co-operative Union of America.

Agriculture, U.S. Department of. Department of the national government established by an act of the U.S. Congress, May 5, 1862. It is the eighth of the national departments, and was elevated to cabinet status on Feb. 9, 1889. Between 1862 and 1889 it was headed by a commissioner, and confined the scope of its functions to experimentation, research, seed distribution, and the collection and dissemination of information. During this period it established new divisions, including those of botany, chemistry, forestry, and pomology. After attaining cabinet status it expanded rapidly and penetrated numerous special phases of agricultural activity. It carries out service functions (including the activities of the Weather Bureau); administers more than 50 regulatory laws relating to the inspection of foodstuffs in interstate commerce, the supervision of stockyards and packers, and the like; undertakes information and extension activities; pursues important research and planning programs, ranging from studies in animal and plant pathology to erosion control; participates in the control or eradication of animal and plant diseases and pests; supervises crop-credit, insurance, and subsidy plans; and takes part in road-construction programs.

Agrigento (ä.grē.jen′tō). [Former name, **Girgenti.**] Province in SW Italy, on the island of Sicily. Capital, Agrigento; area, 1,172 sq. mi.; pop. 418,265 (1936), 458,000 (est. 1946).

Agrigento. [Former name, **Girgenti**; Latin, **Agrigentum**; Greek, **Acragas, Akragas.**] City and commune in SW Italy, on the island of Sicily, the capital of the province of Agrigento, situated on the Girgenti River, near the S coast of Sicily. Some war damage was suffered by buildings of tourist interest, but repairs have now been completed or are being carried out. Pop. of commune, 32,951 (1936); of city, 27,785 (1936).

Agrigentum (ag.ri.jen′tum). [Modern name, **Agrigento**; Greek, **Acragas, Akragas.**] City founded (c582 B.C.) by Greek colonists from Gela. In the middle of the 6th century B.C. it was ruled by the tyrant Phalaris; afterward its government was in turn oligarchic and republican. It was most flourishing in the 5th century B.C., when it was a great commercial center, with (according to some estimates) nearly one million inhabitants.

Agrinion (ä.grē′nyôn). [Former name, **Vrakhori.**] Town in C Greece, in the *nomos* (department) of Aetolia and Acarnania, Trikhonis province, situated ab. 24 mi. inland from the W coast of Greece, in a tobacco-growing region. 20,981 (1940).

Agrippa (ạ.grip′ạ), **Marcus Vipsanius.** b. at Rome, 63 B.C.; d. in Campania, 12 B.C. Roman soldier and politician, who rose from a humble birth to become son-in-law, friend, and counsellor to Augustus. He put down the Aquitanian revolt (38 B.C.) in Gaul, was elected consul (37) and defeated (36) Sextus Pompeius Magnus (often called Pompey the Younger) at Mylae and Naulochus. He became an aedile in 33, and defeated (31) Antony's fleet at Actium. Recalled from the governorship of Syria to become (23) Augustus's chief counsellor, he shared the tribuneship with Augustus (18 *et seq.*). He is also known for his geographical writings.

Agrippa, Menenius. Character in Shakespeare's *Coriolanus.*

Agrippa Postumus (pos′tū̦.mus). b. 12 B.C.; d. 14 A.D. Posthumous son of Marcus Vipsanius Agrippa by Julia, the daughter of Augustus; adopted by Augustus in 4 B.C. He was exiled and murdered on the accession of Tiberius, probably by the order of Livia.

Agrippa von Nettesheim (ä.grip′ä fon net′ẹs.hīm), **Heinrich Cornelius.** b. at Cologne, Germany, Sept. 14, 1486; d. at Grenoble, France, Feb. 18, 1535. German physician, philosopher, and student of alchemy. Author of *De incertitudine et vanitate scientiarum* (1527), *De occulta philosophia* (1510), and others.

Agrippina (ag.ri.pī′nạ), **Julia.** [Called **Agrippina the Younger.**] b. at Oppidum Ubiorum (later named, for her, Colonia Agrippina, now Cologne), c15 A.D.; killed near Baiae (now Baia), on the Bay of Naples, 59. Daughter of Germanicus and Vipsania Agrippina, and wife of Domitius Ahenobarbus, by whom she was mother of Nero. She later married Crispus Passienus, and in 49 her uncle, Claudius, whom she poisoned (54) after excluding his son, Britannicus, from the throne in favor of Nero. She was influential during the early part of Nero's reign, but was eventually killed by him after she threatened to support the claims of Britannicus.

Agrippina, Vipsania. [Called **Agrippina the Elder.**] b. c13 B.C.; d. at Pandataria, near what is now Naples, 33 A.D. Roman matron, known for the loftiness of her character; youngest daughter of Marcus Vipsanius Agrippa and Julia, daughter of Augustus; wife of Germanicus and mother of Caligula. She accompanied her husband on his military campaigns and was with him at Antioch when he was poisoned (19 A.D.); returned to Rome and publicly denounced the governor of Syria, Calpurnius Piso, as the poisoner; incurred the jealous hatred of Tiberius and Sejanus, and was banished by them to Pandataria; believed by some to have starved herself to death, and by others to have been starved by order of Tiberius.

Agtelek (ôg′te.lek). See **Aggtelek.**

Agua (ä′gwä). [Spanish, **Volcán de Agua.**] Volcanic mountain ab. 25 mi. SW of Guatemala City, Guatemala. In 1541 it apparently discharged water, and destroyed by floods the old city of Antigua Guatemala. Elevation, ab. 12,300 ft.

Aguadilla (ä.gwä.ᴛʜē′yä). Department in NW Puerto Rico. It is bounded by the Atlantic Ocean on the N, Arecibo and Ponce on the E, Mayaguez (separated by mountains) on the S, and the Atlantic Ocean on the W. Capital, Aguadilla; area, 240 sq. mi.; pop. ab. 100,000.

Aguadilla. City at the NW extremity of Puerto Rico, on the Caribbean Sea, capital of Aguadilla department. It is a seaport from which fruit, cotton, sugar, and other produce is exported. 13,468 (1940).

Aguado (ä.gwä′ᴛʜō), **Juan de.** Spaniard who accompanied Columbus on his second voyage to America (1493), returned to Spain the next year, and was made royal commissioner to investigate the affairs of Hispaniola.

Agua Fria (ä′gwä frē′ä). River in C Arizona, a northern tributary of the Gila River.

Aguán (ä.gwän′). River in N Honduras, that flows NE and empties into the Caribbean Sea, at Santa Rosa de Aguan.

Aguanaval (ä″gwä.nä.ʙäl′). River in N Mexico, forming part of the border between the states of Durango and Coahuila. It flows NE to Lake Viesca.

Aguascalientes (ä″gwäs.kä.lyen′tās). State in C Mexico, NE of Mexico City. Capital, Aguascalientes; area, 2,499 sq. mi.; pop. 188,104 (1950).

Aguascalientes. City in C Mexico, capital of Aguascalientes state, on the Aguascalientes River: textile mills, tobacco factories, and breweries. There are hot springs in the vicinity (whence the name). 117,409 (1950).

Aguecheek (ā′gū̦.chēk), **Sir Andrew.** Character in Shakespeare's comedy, *Twelfth Night*, a timid, silly, but amusing country squire. He is the friend of Sir Toby Belch.

Agüero (ä.gwā′rō), **Cristóbal.** b. at San Luis de la Paz, Michoacán, Mexico, 1600; date of death not known. Dominican missionary, who spent the greater part of his life working among the Zapotecan Indians. He left several works on their language.

Agüero, Joaquín de. b. at Puerto Principe (now Camagüey), Cuba, Nov. 15, 1816; executed there, Aug. 12, 1851. Cuban revolutionist. He was a planter of moderate fortune and lofty ideals. In 1843 he freed his slaves and took measures to have them educated. Later he endeavored to bring white immigrants to Cuba. He engaged in the insurrection of 1851, and was captured and shot.

Aguesseau (dȧ.ge.sō), **Henri François d'.** [Original surname, **Daguesseau.**] b. at Limoges, France, 1668; d. at Paris, 1751. French jurist and three times chancellor of France (1717–18, 1720–22, 1737–50). A selection of his works was published in two volumes (Paris, 1865) under the title *Oeuvres choisies*.

Aguilar (ä.gē.lär′). [Also, **Aguilar de la Frontera.**] Commune in Spain, in the province of Córdoba, ab. 35 mi. S of Córdoba: the center of a rich agricultural district; olives, fruits, and excellent wines are produced in the vicinity. The upper town has a Moorish castle. 16,091 (1940).

Aguilar (ą.gwil′ąr, ä.gē.lär′), **Grace.** b. at London, 1816; d. at Frankfort on the Main, 1847. English writer on Jewish history, best known for *The Spirit of Judaism* (1842). She also wrote several novels, including *Home Influence* (1847) and *The Vale of Cedars* (1850).

Aguilar (ä.gē.lär′), **Manuel.** b. c1800; d. in Guatemala, June 6, 1846. Central American statesman, president (1837–38) of Costa Rica. He occupied various public posts in Costa Rica, represented that state in the assembly of 1828, and was elected president on April 7, 1837. He was deposed by Carillo in May, 1838.

Águilas (ä′gē.läs). [Also, **San Juan de las Águilas.**] Commune in Spain, in the province of Murcia, situated on a peninsula on the Mediterranean coast, ab. 40 mi. SW of Cartagena: seaport, important for the export of the lead and copper ores of the Sierra Almagrera; trade in esparto grass; medieval castle. 15,166 (1940).

Aguilera (ä.gē.lā′rä), **Francisco Javier** (or **Xavier**). b. at Santa Cruz, Bolivia, c1775; killed at Valle Grande, Bolivia, Nov. 23, 1828. Royalist guerrilla chief of Charcas (approximately coextensive with what is now Bolivia), notorious for his cruelty. He received a commission as brigadier general, and for a time was military commandant of Santa Cruz. In 1828, with a small force, he captured a Spanish post, and proclaimed Ferdinand VII as king. He was soon captured and shot.

Aguinaldo (ä.gē.näl′dō), **Emilio.** b. near Cavite, Luzon, Philippine Islands, c1869—. Philippine patriot and insurrectionary leader. He headed Philippine forces in revolt against Spain (1896–98) and in resistance to the U.S. (1899–1901). Captured by General Frederick Funston at Palawan, he took an oath of allegiance to U.S.

Aguirre (ä.gēr′rä), **José Antonio.** b. at Bilbao, Spain, 1904—. Basque nationalist and statesman. Trained in law, he became leader of the Basque Catholic youth in 1929, mayor of Biscay in 1931, and (having served as deputy for Navarre and Biscay in the Spanish Cortes), was elected president of the newly established Basque republic in 1936. His book *De Guernica a Nueva York Pasando por Berlin* describes his experiences during and after the Spanish Civil War (1936–39). In 1942–43 he was visiting professor at Columbia University.

Aguirre, Josef Sáenz de. b. at Logroño, in Castile, March 24, 1630; d. at Rome, Aug. 19, 1699. Spanish cardinal and theologian, author of *Defensio cathedrae S. Petri* (1682), *Collectio maxima Conciliorum* (1693), *Theologia S. Anselmi*, and others.

Aguirre, Lope de. [Called **"Aguirre the Madman."**] b. at Oñate, Spain, c1508; killed Oct. 27, 1561. Spanish adventurer who early in life drifted to America, engaged in several rebellions, was outlawed, and joined the expedition of Pedro de Ursua in search of El Dorado and the kingdom of the Omaguas on the upper Amazon (1559). Ursua was murdered by Aguirre at Machiparo (1561), and Fernando de Guzman (whom Aguirre afterward murdered) was made general with Aguirre as his lieutenant. The band declared themselves rebels, proceeded down the Amazon, plundering Indian villages, and finally reaching the island of Margarita (July 20, 1561), where Aguirre murdered the governor, and robbed the royal treasury. He was captured at Barquisimeto, and shot by his own followers.

Aguirre Cerda (ser′ᴛʜä), **Pedro.** b. 1879; d. Nov. 25, 1941. Chilean politician, landowner, and student of viticulture, elected (1938) president of Chile as candidate of the so-called Popular Front coalition. His presidency was marked by strict neutrality with reference to the war in Europe. A millionaire and political "moderate," he received last-minute electoral support from the *Nacistas* (Chilean Nazis), who later (1939) re-formed as the "Popular Socialist Vanguard" and opposed his government. Dissension among Communist, Socialist, and Radical party members of the Popular Front was bitter throughout Aguirre Cerda's administration and he withdrew (1941) in favor of the minister of the interior.

Agujari (ä.gö.yä′rē), **Lucrezia.** [Called **"La Bastardella"** or **"La Bastardina."**] b. at Ferrara, Italy, 1743; d. at Parma, Italy, May 18, 1783. Italian soprano. Mozart observed after hearing her at Parma (1770) that her voice ranged a full octave higher than that of the average professional; her illegitimate birth, which brought her the sobriquet "La Bastardella," was openly admitted and used freely to increase public interest in her career.

Agulhas (ą.gul′ąs; Portuguese, ą.gö′lyąsh), **Cape.** Southernmost point in Africa, ab. 100 mi. SE of the Cape of Good Hope.

Agusan (ä.gö′sän). Province of the Philippine Islands, occupying most of the NE corner of Mindanao island. It is bounded on the NE by Surigao, on the N by the Mindanao Sea, on the W by Misamis Oriental and Bukidnon, and on the S by Davao. The Diuata Mountains form the E boundary of the province, and most of the C part is occupied by the Agusan River and its drainage basin. Capital, Butuan; area, 4,120 sq. mi.; pop. 126,448 (1948).

Agustina (ä.gös.tē′nä). [Called the **"Maid of Saragossa."**] d. at Cueta, Spain, June, 1857. Spanish patriot, noted for her bravery in the defense of Saragossa (1808–09).

Agustini (ä.gö.stē′nē), **Delmira.** b. 1886; killed by her husband, 1914. Uruguayan modernist poet, considered by some critics the greatest of Spanish-American poetesses. Author of *El Libro blanco* (1907) and others.

Agyia (ä.yä′). See **Agias.**

Agylla (ą.jil′ą). See **Caere.**

Agyrium (ą.jir′i.um). Ancient name of **Agira.**

Ahab (ā′hab). d. c853 B.C. Israel's seventh ruler (c875–853 B.C.); son of King Omri. He was the husband of Jezebel, daughter of the king of Tyre, and the father-in-law of the heir to Judah. His astute diplomacy brought

Israel to its peak of power and united adjoining realms by war (854) against Assyria's Shalmaneser II; he was killed at Ramoth Gilead in battle against Benhadad of Damascus. His acquiescence in the worship of Baal and Astarte by his wife and others provoked the anger of Elijah.

Ahab, Captain. Whaler in *Moby Dick* (1851), a novel by Herman Melville. His unceasing quest for the white whale exemplifies the theme of the book.

Ahaggar (ą.hag'ąr). Large plateau and mountainous region in N central Africa, in the Sahara, in the SE part of Algeria ab. 700 mi. NW of Lake Chad. It rises in some places to more than 9,000 ft. The chief place in the region is Ideles.

Ahala (ą.hā'lą), **Gnaeus Servilius Structus.** Roman patrician, master of the horse in 439 B.C. (according to the common chronology), and slayer of the popular leader Spurius Maelius.

Ahanta (ä.hän'tą). District of Gold Coast colony, W Africa, in the W part. The chief town in the district is Axim.

Ahanta. [Also, **Akanta.**] One of the Sudanic-speaking Akan peoples of W Africa, inhabiting the SW part of the Gold Coast, to the E of Axim.

Aharon (ä.hä.rōn'). Hebrew name of **Aaron.**

Ahasuerus (ą.has.ụ̄.ē'rus). In the Old Testament, a Persian shah, mentioned as the father of Darius the Mede (Dan. ix. 1). He has been variously identified as Astyages and Cyaxeres.

Ahasuerus. In the Old Testament, a great ruler of Persia, and husband of Esther, probably identical with Xerxes I. He is mentioned in Ezra, iv. 6., and throughout the Book of Esther.

Ahasuerus. Name sometimes given to the legendary Wandering Jew.

Ahava (ą.hā'vą). In the Old Testament, the name of a place and river, or canal, in Babylon at which the Jews assembled who formed the second expedition which returned to Jerusalem with Ezra. Its exact location is unknown. Ezra, viii. 15.

Ahaz (ā'haz). d. c727 B.C. King of Judah, now believed to have reigned from c731 B.C. to c727 B.C. He was a contemporary of the prophet Isaiah. On his accession to the throne, which took place in his youth, Rezin, king of Syria, and Pekah, king of Israel, formed a conspiracy against him. Contrary to the advice of Isaiah he sought (and obtained) the assistance of the Assyrian king, to whom he paid homage and tribute. (This latter fact is mentioned both in the Bible and in cuneiform inscriptions. In the latter he is called *Iauhazi*, which would indicate that his name is shortened from *Joahaz*.) The price of Assyrian aid was paid for partly in gold (which Ahaz obtained from the Temple at Jerusalem) and partly by a loss of independence. Ahaz was bitterly criticized by Isaiah and others, both for his sacrilegious use of the Temple treasure and for his political dalliance with the Assyrians. He was succeeded by his son Hezekiah. 2 Kings, xvi.

Ahaziah (ā.hą.zī'ą). In the Old Testament, son of Ahab and king of Israel, c853–851 B.C. 1 Kings, xxii. 40.

Ahaziah. In the Old Testament, son of Jehoram and Athaliah, and king of Judah, c844–c843 B.C. After his accidental death at Jezreel he was succeeded by his mother. 2 Kings, viii. 25.

Ahenobarbus (ą.hē.nọ.bär'bus, ą.hen.ọ-). A plebeian family of Rome, of the gens Domitia, to which the emperor Nero belonged.

Ahenobarbus, Gnaeus Domitius. fl. 104–92 B.C. Roman official; father of Lucius Domitius Ahenobarbus. A tribune (104 B.C.), pontifex maximus (103 B.C.), consul (96 B.C.), and censor (92 B.C.), he framed the law, later repealed by Sulla, that certain types of priests should be selected by the lay citizenry rather than by each other.

Ahenobarbus, Lucius Domitius. fl. 34–48 B.C. Roman official and political opportunist; son of Gnaeus Domitius Ahenobarbus. He was a consul in 54 B.C. and Caesar's successor as governor of Gaul in 49 B.C. He opposed both Caesar and Pompey, but later attached himself to the latter and was slain after the defeat at Pharsalus.

Ahhotpe (ä.hōt'pe). See **Aahhotep.**

Ahi (u'hē). See **Vritra.**

Ahijah (ą.hī'ją) or **Ahiah** (ą.hī'ą). In the Old Testament, the name of several persons, of whom the most notable was a son of Ahitub and high priest in the reign of Saul (1 Sam. xiv. 3, 18). He is probably the same as Ahimelech, high priest at Nob, who was killed by Saul for assisting David.

Ahimaaz (ą.him'ą.az). In the Old Testament, the father of Ahinoam, wife of Saul. 1 Sam. xiv. 50.

Ahimaaz. In the Old Testament, a high priest, the son and successor of Zadok. He distinguished himself by his services to King David during the revolt of Absalom. 2 Sam. xv, xviii.

Ahimelech (ą.him'ẹ.lek). In the Old Testament, a high priest at Nob; father of Abiathar, the friend of David. He gave to David, who was fleeing from Saul, the sacred bread and the sword of Goliath from the tabernacle. For this Saul slew him. 1 Sam. xxi. 1–9. See also **Ahijah.**

Ahimelech. [Also, **Abimelech.**] In the Old Testament, a priest in David's time; son of Abiathar and grandson of Ahimelech, the priest at Nob. 1 Chron. xviii. 16.

Ahir (ä.ēr'). See **Air.**

Ahithophel (ą.hith'ọ.fel). In the Old Testament, a counselor of King David and, later, of Absalom in his revolt against his father. He was famous for his political wisdom, and his defection caused David great apprehension. His advice, however, was rejected by Absalom, and he thereupon retired to his home, set his affairs in order, and hanged himself. He is thought to have been the grandfather of Bathsheba.

Ahl (äl), **Henry Hammond.** b. at Hartford, Conn., 1869; d. at Newburyport, Mass., May 21, 1953. American painter and sculptor. He studied with Gérôme, at the École des Beaux-Arts, Paris. His works include church murals and many portraits.

Ahlat (ä.lät'). [Also, **Akhlat.**] Town in E Turkey, in the *il* (province or vilayet) of Erzurum, on the NW shore of Lake Van over a mile above sea level: a minor trading center. Near it are the ruins of the ancient Khelat. Pop. ab. 2,000.

Ahle (ä'lẹ), **Johann Georg.** b. at Mühlhausen, in Thuringia, Germany, 1651; d. there, Dec. 2, 1706. German composer and organist; son of Johann Rudolph Ahle.

Ahle, Johann Rudolph. b. at Mühlhausen, in Thuringia, Germany, Dec. 24, 1625; d. there, in July, 1673. German composer and organist. His hymn, *Liebster Jesu, wir sind hier*, is still occasionally sung in Germany.

Ahlen (ä'lẹn). City in W Germany, in the *Land* (state) of North Rhine-Westphalia, British Zone, formerly in the province of Westphalia, Prussia, situated on the Werse River, ab. 19 mi. SE of Münster: shoe factories; zinc industry; manufactures tools, machines, vehicles, and other metallurgical articles; cannery; coal mines are in the vicinity. The population is predominantly Catholic. Buildings of interest to tourists were undamaged in World War II. 33,141 (1950).

Ahlheide (äl'hī.dẹ). A barren plain in the C part of Jutland, Denmark.

Ahlquist (äl'kvist), **August Engelbert.** b. at Kuopio, Finland, Aug. 7, 1826; d. Nov. 29, 1889. Finnish philologist, poet, and traveler in Russia and Siberia. He was appointed (1862) professor of Finnish language and literature at the University of Helsingfors (now Helsinki).

Ahlwardt (äl'värt), **Christian Wilhelm.** b. at Greifswald, Prussia, Nov. 23, 1760; d. there, April 12, 1830. German philologist, rector successively of several public schools, and later professor of ancient literature at the University of Greifswald. His work was chiefly upon the Greek poets (edited Pindar, 1820).

Ahlwardt, Theodor Wilhelm. b. July 4, 1828; d. Nov. 1, 1909. German orientalist; son of Christian Wilhelm Ahlwardt. He was professor of oriental languages at the University of Greifswald.

Ahmadabad (ä"mạd.ą.bäd'). See **Ahmedabad.**

Ahmadnagar (ä.mạd.nug'ėr). [Also: **Ahmednagar, Ahmednuggur.**] District of Bombay, Union of India, ab. 100 mi. E of the city of Bombay: teakwood, wheat, and millet. Capital, Ahmadnagar; area, 6,646 sq. mi.; pop. 1,142,229 (1941).

Ahmadnagar. [Also: **Ahmednagar, Ahmednuggur.**] City in W India, the capital of the district of Ahmadnagar, Union of India, ab. 120 mi. E of the city of Bombay: important road junction and trading center. In the

15th and 16th centuries it was the capital of a Mohammedan kingdom. It surrendered to the British under Wellington in 1803. Pop. 54,193 (1941).

Ahmad Shah (ä'mäd shä). [Also, **Ahmad Shah Durrani** (or **Durani**).] b. 1724; d. 1773. Ruler of Afghanistan (1747 *et seq.*).

Ahmed (ä'med). [Full name, **Sidi Ahmed-esh-Sherif es-Senusi** (or **Senussi**).] b. 1872; d. at Medina, Arabia, 1933. Chieftain (1902–18) of the Senusi, a Moslem sect in Africa; successor to his uncle, Senusi al-Mahdi. He resisted (1904–11) the French, who succeeded in conquering Oudai from the Senusi; as a supporter of the pan-Islamic movement, he aided (1911) the Turks in their struggle against the Italian invasion of Tripolitania and Cyrenaica; after the conclusion (1912) of the Treaty of Lausanne, he independently pursued a military campaign against the Italians. During World War I he sided with the Central Powers and carried out attacks against British positions in Egypt and the Sudan; his forces were defeated at Agaya (Feb. 26, 1916) and at Siwa (February, 1917). He left (1918) Cyrenaica and settled in Turkey, where he was active in the pan-Islamic movement.

Ahmed I. [Also, **Achmet I.**] b. 1589; d. Nov. 22, 1617. Sultan of Turkey; son of Mohammed III, whom he succeeded (1603). He began his reign with promise, but later became dissolute. He concluded (1606) the peace of Sitvatorok with Austria, abolishing, for a large settlement, Austrian payment of tribute and observing for the first time certain principles of modern international law in diplomatic relations. He fought (1603–12) an unsuccessful war with Persia under Abbas I.

Ahmed II. [Also, **Achmet II.**] b. 1642; d. Feb. 6, 1695. Sultan of Turkey; son of Ibrahim, brother of Suleiman II, whom he succeeded in 1691. He lost control of Hungary at the battle of Slankamen (1691) in which the grand vizier Mustafa Kuprili was defeated and slain by the Austrians under Louis William I (of Baden).

Ahmed III. [Also, **Achmet III.**] b. 1673; d. 1736. Sultan of Turkey (1703–30); son of Mohammed IV, brother of Mustafa II, whom he succeeded. He became involved through Charles XII of Sweden in a war with Russia under Peter the Great, which ended in the Peace of the Pruth (1711). He took Morea and the Ionian islands from Venice (1715), but was defeated at Peterwardein (1716) and Belgrade (1717) by the Austrians under Prince Eugene, and signed the Treaty of Passarowitz in 1718. Compelled by the Janizaries to resign, he died of poison in prison. He was succeeded by his nephew, Mahmud I.

Ahmedabad (ä"med.ä.bäd'). [Also, **Ahmadabad.**] District of Bombay state, Union of India, ab. 280 mi. N of the city of Bombay, at the head of the Bay of Cambay: cotton and wheat. Capital, Ahmedabad; area, ab. 3,800 sq. mi.; pop. 1,372,171 (1941).

Ahmedabad. [Also, **Ahmadabad.**] City in W India, capital of the district of Ahmedabad, on the Sabarmati River, ab. 50 mi. N of the head of the Bay of Cambay. One of the most important manufacturing cities of India, it is now the second in India in the production of cotton and has become highly industrialized. It is the former home of Mohandas K. Gandhi. It was captured by the British in 1780, and was ceded to them in 1818. The Jumma Musjid of Ahmedabad, built by Ahmed Shah in the early 15th century, is one of the most beautiful of mosques. The gross dimensions are 382 by 258 ft., three sides of the court being surrounded by a colonnaded gallery, and the sanctuary, 95 ft. deep, occupying one end. The sanctuary contains 260 columns, which support three rows each of five domes, the central one of which is the largest and highest, flanked by two which are higher than the other 12. The front facing the court is formed by a fine screen, with three pointed arches, flanked on each side by a lower arcade. 591,267 (1941).

Ahmed Bey (ä'med bā). [Also, **Achmet Bey.**] d. July 16, 1822. Turkish commander in the Greek war of independence. He was repulsed (May 27, 1821) by the Greeks in an attack on the fortified post at Valtetzi.

Ahmed Fuad II (fö.äd'). b. at Cairo, Egypt, Jan. 16, 1952—. King of Egypt (1952 *et seq.*); son of King Farouk. After the forced abdication of his father in July, 1952, the six-month-old crown prince was named king and a council of regents was established to rule in his name.

Ahmednagar or **Ahmednuggur** (ä"med.nug'ėr). See **Ahmadnagar.**

Ahmedpur (ä.med.pör'). [Also, **East Ahmedpur.**] Town in the state of Bahawalpur, Pakistan, S of the Sutlej River. Cotton and wheat are raised intensively in the area around the city as a result of the irrigation from the dams on the Sutlej. Located on a railroad, the town is a large trading and shipping center. Pop. ab. 10,000.

Ahmed Riza Bey (ä'med rē.zä' bā). b. c1870; d. 1930. Turkish politician. Active in the Young Turk party, he served (1908) as president of the Turkish parliament and was a member of the Turkish peace commission after World War I.

Ahmed Shah (shä). [Also, **Ahmed Mirza.**] b. 1898; d. 1930. Last shah of Persia in the Kajar dynasty. He ruled under a regency (1909–14) following the deposition of his father, Mohammed Ali. He lived in Paris (1923 *et seq.*) and was deposed (1925) in favor of Riza Shah Pahlavi by the National Assembly when he declined to return.

Ahmes Papyrus (ä'mēz). [Also, **Rhind Papyrus.**] The most important surviving work of ancient Egyptian mathematics, containing tables of unit fractions and numerous questions involving linear equations arising from problems in mensuration. It was copied c1650 B.C. by a scribe named Ahmes from an older treatise.

Ahn (än), **Johann Franz.** b. at Aix-la-Chapelle (now Aachen, Germany), Dec. 15, 1796; d. at Neuss, Germany, Aug. 21, 1865. German teacher and grammarian, noted for his methods of teaching modern languages. He published *The Poetry of Germany* (1859), and numerous grammars.

Ahnen (ä'nẹn), **Die.** Series of historical romances by Gustav Freytag, illustrating German history (published 1870–80). It comprises *Ingo und Ingraban, Das Nest der Zaunkönige, Die Brüder vom deutschen Hause, Markus König, Die Geschwister*, and *Aus einer kleinen Stadt.*

Ahnfeld (än'felt), **Arvid Wolfgang Nathanael.** b. Aug. 16, 1845; d. Feb. 17, 1890. Swedish journalist, author of a *History of the Literature of the World* (1874–76), and other encyclopedic works.

Aholibamah (ạ.hol.i.bā'mạ). One of the wives of Esau. Gen. xxxvi. 2.

Aholibamah. Name of an Edomite tribe.

Aholibamah. Character in Byron's *Heaven and Earth*, the proud, ambitious granddaughter of Cain.

Ahom (ä'hôm). Originally, a Thai-speaking people who in 1229 founded a kingdom which by the 18th century ruled much of Assam (which owes its name to them).

Ahoskie (ạ.hos'ki). Town in NE North Carolina, ab. 40 mi. W of the Atlantic coast. It is a local trading center for tobacco, some cotton, and light lumber products manufactured in the area. 3,579 (1950).

Ah Puch (ä pöch'). In Maya religion, the lord of death and, in one of his aspects, the deity who presided over the ninth layer of the underworld.

Ahr (är). River in W Germany, in the former Rhine Province of Prussia, which flows generally NE and joins the Rhine at Sinzig (above Bonn). On its banks are produced the noted Ahr wines. Length, ab. 55 mi.

Ahrens (ä'rẹns), **Franz Heinrich Ludolf.** b. at Helmstedt, Germany, June 6, 1809; d. at Hanover, Germany, Sept. 24, 1881. German philologist, noted as a student of the Greek dialects. Author of *De Graecae linguae dialectis* (1839–43).

Ahrens, Heinrich. b. at Kniestedt, Prussia, 1808; d. at Salzgitter, Prussia, Aug. 2, 1874. German philosophical writer and jurist, professor at Brussels (1834–50), at Gratz (1850–59), and at Leipzig (1859).

Ahrensbök (ä'rẹns.bėk). [Also, **Ahrensböck.**] Town in NW Germany, in the *Land* (state) of Schleswig-Holstein, British Zone, formerly the province of Schleswig-Holstein, Prussia, NW of Lübeck: manufactures rubber, asbestos, cotton and woolen textiles, and furniture. The *Marienkirche* (Church of Mary), in the Gothic style, dates from 1328. Prussia ceded the place to Oldenburg (Enclave of Eutin) in 1867. It has a predominantly Protestant population. 10,169 (1950).

Ahrensburg (ä'rẹns.bůrk). Town in NW Germany, in the *Land* (state) of Schleswig-Holstein, British Zone, formerly the province of Schleswig-Holstein, Prussia, NE of Hamburg, of which it is a residential suburb:

electrical, metallurgical, cement, and foodstuff industries. The population is predominantly Protestant. 17,586 (1950).

Ahrweiler (är'vī.lėr). Town in W Germany, in the *Land* (state) of Rhineland-Palatinate, French Zone, formerly in the Rhine Province, Prussia, situated on the Ahr River ab. 20 mi. S of Cologne, in a wine-growing community. 6,688 (1947).

Ahtena (ä'te.nä). North American Indian tribe inhabiting the Copper River area, Alaska. The language is of the Athabaskan family.

Ahuachapán (ä.wä.chä.pän'). Department in W El Salvador, bordering on Guatemala and the Pacific Ocean. It is the chief commercial and industrial department of the country, and has a widely varied agriculture and some mining. Capital, Ahuachapán; area, 804 sq. mi.; pop. 103,198 (est. 1942).

Ahuachapán. City in W El Salvador, capital of Ahuachapán department: distribution center for cereals, coffee, sugar, and tobacco. 10,290 (1950).

Ahuizotl or **Ahuitzotl** (ä.wē'tsō.tl). d. 1502. Aztec chief of Tenochtitlan (in what is now Mexico) from 1486.

Ahumada (ä.ö.mä'ᴛʜä), Duke of. [Title of **Pedro Girón;** additional title, Marqués **de las Amarillas.**] b. at San Sebastián, Spain, 1788; d. at Madrid, May 17, 1842. Spanish politician and general, chief of the general staff of the Spanish army in the war of independence, minister of war for a short time in 1820, member of the regency during the minority of Isabella, and again minister of war in 1835.

Ahumada y Villalon (ē ʙē.lyä.lōn'), **Agustín de.** [Title, Marqués **de las Amarillas.**] b. c1700; d. at Mexico City, Feb. 6, 1760. Spanish general and administrator. He distinguished himself in the Italian and Peninsular wars, and served (Nov. 10, 1755 *et seq.*) as viceroy of Mexico.

Ahura Mazda (ä'hö.rä mäz'dä). [Also: **Ormazd, Ormuzd;** Eng. trans., "*The Wise Lord.*"] Good Spirit in the dual system of Zoroaster. He is the modern Persian Ormazd or Ormuzd.

Ahuréi (ä.ö.rā'). [Also, **Aurai.**] Seaport on the island of Rapa, Austral Islands, South Pacific: a coaling station on the steamship route from Panama to New Zealand and Sydney. It is a French possession.

Ahvenanmaa (ä've.nän.mä'). [Also: **Aaland** (or **Aland**) **Islands;** Swedish, **Åland** or **Ålandsöerna.**] Group of about 300 small islands at the entrance of the Gulf of Bothnia, belonging to Finland. They were ceded to Russia by Sweden in 1809 and remained Russian until 1917 when Finland and the islands became independent. In 1921 they were awarded to Finland as an autonomous department by the League of Nations. Capital, Maarianhamina; area, ab. 581 sq. mi.; pop. 22,569 (1951).

Ahwaz (ä.wäz', -hwäz'). City in W Iran, in Khuzistan, on the Karun River ab. 70 mi. NE of the city of Abadan. At this point several oil pipe lines join and run into Abadan and the refineries there. Near here was a bridge of boats which made it possible for Nearchus to join the land forces of Alexander in 325 B.C. The town was an ancient residence of Persian kings, and a flourishing center under the Arabs in the early Middle Ages. 30,000 (1942).

Ah, Wilderness! Comedy by Eugene O'Neill, produced in 1932.

Ai (ī). See also **Ai River.**

Ai (ā'ī). In the Old Testament, a city of the Canaanites, in the territory of Benjamin, ab. 10 mi. N of Jerusalem. It was conquered by Joshua. Josh. vii. 1–5.

Aiblinger (ī'bling.ėr), **Johann Kaspar.** b. at Wasserburg, Bavaria, Feb. 23, 1779; d. at Munich, May 6, 1867. German composer of religious music.

Aicard (ā.kȧr), **Jean.** b. at Toulon, France, 1848; d. 1921. French poet, author, and playwright. Among his works are *Les Jeunes croyances* (1867), *Poèmes de Provence* (1874), *La Chanson de l'enfant* (1876), *Le Père Lebonnard* (1889), *Le Manteau du roi* (1907), and others.

A.I.C.C. See **All-India Congress Committee.**

Aichi (ī.chē). Prefecture of Japan, in C Honshu. The area, which is of considerable industrial importance, was heavily bombed by the U.S. Air Force in World War II. Capital, Nagoya; area, 1,950 sq. mi.; pop. 3,390,585 (1950).

Aïda (ä.ē'dą). Opera in four acts composed by Giuseppe Verdi, with libretto by Ghislanzoni, first performed at the Cairo Opera House at Cairo, Egypt, on Dec. 24, 1871.

Aidan (ā'dąn). d. 606. King of Scottish Dalriada. In 575, at the council of Drumceat, he declared the independence of his kingdom, which had been formed in the 5th century by emigrants from Irish Dalriada, and which had hitherto been treated as an Irish dependency.

Aidan, Saint. [Also, **Aedhan.**] d. 651. Irish monk, first bishop of Lindisfarne, and founder of the church in Northumbria, to which he was sent by the monks of Hii or Iona in answer to a request by King Oswald that someone be dispatched to his realm in order to convert his heathen subjects. After the defeat (642) of Oswald by Penda, Aidan joined Oswin, king of the Deirans.

Aïdé (å.ē.dā', ī.dā'), **Hamilton.** b. at Paris, c1829; d. 1906. English novelist and poet. Son of an Armenian father and English mother, he was for a time (1845–52) an officer in the British army. His poetic works include *Eleanore and Other Poems* (1856), *The Romance of the Scarlet Leaf* (1865), and *Songs Without Music* (1882); his novels include *Rita* (1859), *The Marstons* (1868), *Passages in the Life of a Lady* (1887), and others.

Aid-el-ma (īd.el.mä'). See under **Adullam.**

Aidenn (ā'dẹn). Paradise: an Anglicized form of the Arabic for *Eden*, used, for the rhyme's sake, by Edgar Allan Poe in *The Raven.*

Aïdin (ī.din'). See **Aydin.**

Aiea (ä.ē.ā'ä). Town in Hawaii, in the S part of the island of Oahu, NW of Honolulu, touching on the E side of Pearl Harbor. 3,714 (1950).

Aigai (ī'gī). [Modern name, **Nimrud-Kalessi.**] In ancient geography, a town in Aeolia, Asia Minor. On its site are the ruins of various ancient structures.

Aigaion Pelagos (e.ye'ôn pe'lä.gôs). Greek name of the **Aegean Sea.**

Aigaiou (e.ye'ö), **Nesoi.** Modern Greek name of the **Aegean Islands.**

Aigina (e'yē.nä). See **Aegina.**

Aigion (e'yôn). [Also: **Aiyion, Aegion, Aegium.**] Town in S Greece, in the *nomos* (department) of Achaea, Aiyalia province, situated on the NW coast of the Peloponnesus on the Gulf of Corinth, ab. 22 mi. E of Patras: railroad station; exports currants. 16,047 (1940).

Aigle (egl). See also **Laigle.**

Aigle. [German, **Aelen.**] Small town in S Switzerland, in the canton of Vaud, on the Grande Eau River, near the Rhône, S of Villeneuve. 3,918 (1941).

Aiglon (le.glôn), **L'.** See **Napoleon II.**

Aiguebelle (eg.bel). Small town in SE France, in the department of Savoie, ab. 17 mi. E of Chambéry. Here, in 1742, the French and Spaniards defeated the Sardinians.

Aiguebelle (deg.bel), **Paul Alexandre Neveue d'.** b. Jan. 7, 1831; d. Feb. 21, 1875. French naval officer, in the Chinese service during the Taiping rebellion (1862–64).

Aigueperse (eg.pers). Town in S central France, in the department of Puy-de-Dôme, ab. 19 mi. NE of Clermont-Ferrand. Pop. ab. 2,000.

Aiguesmortes or **Aigues-Mortes** (eg.môrt). [Latin, **Aquae Mortuae.**] Town in S France, in the department of Gard, near the Mediterranean, ab. 22 mi. SW of Nîmes, founded by Saint Louis in 1246. From here he embarked on his Crusades (1248 and 1270) to Egypt and Tunis. The modern town has salt works and fisheries. Its fortifications, constructed (1270–85) by Philip III, are among the most remarkable in France. The town has a theater, *hôtel de ville* (town hall), and the Church of Notre-Dame-de-Sablons. 3,616 (1946).

Aiguille d'Argentière (e.gwēy' dȧr.zhäṅ.tyer). Alpine peak in E France, NE of Mont Blanc. 12,832 ft.

Aiguille de la Grande-Sassière (dẹ lȧ gräṅd.sȧ.syer). One of the chief peaks of the Tarentaise Alps, France, on the Italian border. 12,325 ft.

Aiguille du Midi (dü mē.dē). Alpine peak NE of Mont Blanc. 12,605 ft.

Aiguille du Midi. Peak in the Alps of Oisans, Isère, France. Elevation, ab. 11,025 ft.

Aiguille Verte (vert). Alpine peak NE of Mont Blanc. 13,540 ft.

Aiguillon (e.gwē.yôṅ). [Latin, **Acilium.**] Town in SW France, in the department of Lot-et-Garonne, on the

Lot River near its junction with the Garonne, ab. 16 mi. NW of Agen. It has Roman ruins and an 18th-century castle of the dukes of Aiguillon. 2,778 (1946).

Aiguillon (de.gwē.yôn), **Armand de Vignerot du Plessis de Richelieu,** Duc **d'.** b. 1750; d. at Hamburg, 1800. French aristocrat, republican sympathizer during the first days of the French Revolution; son of Emmanuel Armand Vignerot du Plessis de Richelieu, Duc d'Aiguillon. Despite his renunciation of aristocratic privilege, he fell under suspicion (1792) and was compelled to flee France.

Aiguillon, Emmanuel Armand Vignerot du Plessis de Richelieu, Duc **d'.** b. 1720; d. 1782. French politician, minister of foreign affairs (1771–74) under Louis XV. He was related to Cardinal Richelieu, and linked himself to the group at court which opposed Madame de Pompadour and the Jansenists.

Aigun (ī.gön'). [Also: **Aihun** (-hön'); Chinese, **Heilungkiang-cheng** or **Heilungkiang-chieng.**] City in NE China, in the province of Heilungkiang, Manchuria, on the Amur River. It was opened to international trade in 1905. Important placer gold mines are located nearby. 38,112 (est. 1931).

Aijalon (ā'ja̤.lon, ī'ja̤-). [Also, **Ajalon.**] In Biblical geography, a town in Palestine, the later Yâlo, ab. 14 mi. NW of Jerusalem.

Aikawa (ä.ē.kä.wä). City in Japan, situated on the W coast of the island of Sado, ab. 165 mi. NW of Tokyo. There are rich gold and silver mines in the area. 8,621 (1945).

Aikawa, Yoshisuke. b. in Yamaguchi prefecture, Japan, 1880—. Japanese industrialist, active in the industrial development of Manchuria when it was under Japanese domination.

Aiken (ā'ke̤n). [Called the **"Polo Capital of the South."**] City in W South Carolina, county seat of Aiken County: notable as a winter resort. It has textile mills, kaolin refineries, granite quarries, and lumber mills. It was platted in 1834 and incorporated in 1835. Since 1951 Aiken has had a great increase in population due to the construction ab. 15 mi. S of the city, on the Savannah River, of a major plant of the Atomic Energy Commission. 7,083 (1950).

Aiken, Charles Avery. b. at Georgia, Vt., 1872—. American muralist and print-maker. He originated and first exhibited prints produced from plaster blocks. Examples of his work may be seen at the National Collection of Fine Arts, Washington, D.C., and elsewhere.

Aiken, Conrad Potter. b. at Savannah, Ga., Aug. 5, 1889—. American poet, anthologist, critic, and fiction writer. A leader among the "new poets" immediately after World War I, he was one of the editors (1916 *et seq.*) of *The Dial;* awarded (1929) Pulitzer prize for *Selected Poems.* Author also of *Earth Triumphant* (1914), *The Jig of Forslin* (1916), *The Charnel Rose* (1918), *Priapus and the Pool* (1922), *John Deth* (1930), *Time in the Rock* (1936), and *And in the Human Heart* (1940); novels, including *Blue Voyage* (1927), *Great Circle* (1933), *King Coffin* (1935), and *The Conversation* (1940); anthologies, including *Twentieth Century American Poetry* (1945), and *A Comprehensive Anthology of American Poetry;* and the autobiographical *Ushant* (1952).

Aiken, George L. b. at Boston, Dec. 19, 1830; d. April 27, 1876. American playwright and actor. He adapted numerous 19th-century prose works for the stage, but is now remembered for only one of them: *Uncle Tom's Cabin.* His version of this work was first performed in 1852, at Troy, N.Y., and ran for 200 performances during the next year in the city of New York. It was the first successful dramatization of Harriet Beecher Stowe's enormously successful novel, and the prototype of virtually all subsequent stage versions.

Aikens (ā'ke̤nz), **Andrew Jackson.** b. at Barnard, Vt., Oct. 31, 1830; d. Jan. 22, 1909. American newspaper editor and owner, and pioneer of "boiler-plate" in journalism. As a proprietor of Milwaukee's *Evening Wisconsin* he headed a syndicate which offered mats of complete pages, including advertisements, to country papers (1864).

Aikin (ā'kin), **Anna Letitia.** See **Barbauld, Anna Letitia.**

Aikin, Arthur. b. at Warrington, Lancashire, England, May 19, 1773; d. at London, April 15, 1854. English chemist and mineralogist; son of John Aikin (1747–1822).

Aikin, John. b. at Kibworth, England, Jan. 15, 1747; d. at Stoke Newington, England, Dec. 7, 1822. English physician and writer. Author of *General Biography* (1799–1815), *Evenings at Home* (1792–95, written in conjunction with his sister, Anna Letitia Barbauld), and others.

Aikin, Lucy. b. at Warrington, Lancashire, Nov. 6, 1781; d. at Hampstead, England, Jan. 29, 1864. English writer; daughter of John Aikin (1747–1822). Author of *Memoirs of the Court of Queen Elizabeth* (1818), *Memoirs of the Court of James I* (1822), *Memoirs of the Court of Charles I* (1833), *Life of Addison* (1843), and others.

Aikipyak (ī.kēp'yäk). [Also: **Ilaikipyak, Laikipia.**] Former subgroup of the Nilo-Hamitic-speaking Masai of S Kenya and N Tanganyika in E Africa.

Aikman (āk'ma̤n), **William.** b. at Caerney, Scotland, Oct. 24, 1682; d. at London June 7 1731. Scottish portrait-painter.

Aikwe (ī'kwā). [Also, **Naron.**] Central Bushman group of S Africa, inhabiting W Bechuanaland.

Ailly or **Ailli** (dȧ.yē), **Pierre d'.** [Latinized name, **Petrus d'Alliaco**; called the **"Hammer of Heretics"** and **"Eagle of the Doctors."**] b. 1350; d. at Avignon, France, c1420. French cardinal and theologian. An advocate of nominalism, he endeavored to end the schism in the Roman Catholic Church. His proposal that a clerical council should have authority even over the Pope was in later years condemned by the Roman Catholic Church as heretical, but d'Ailly urged it after the Council of Pisa (1409), which produced a third Pope, as the only solution; at the Council of Constance (1414–18) he continued his efforts toward reform, but accepted the condemnation of Huss.

Ailsa Craig (āl'sa̤ krāg). Rocky island in S Scotland, in Ayrshire, situated near the entrance of the Firth of Clyde, ab. 25 mi. SW of Ayr. It is conical in shape, and rises to a height of 1,114 ft.

Aimar (e.mȧr). See under **Bourbon.**

Aimard (e.mȧr), **Gustave.** [Pseudonym of **Olivier Cloux**; sometimes called the **"French Fenimore Cooper."**] b. at Paris, 1818; d. there, 1883. French novelist and traveler in the U.S., Mexico, Spain, Turkey, and the Caucasus. His works include *Les Trappeurs de l'Arkansas* (1858), *La Grande Flibuste* (1860), *Nuits mexicaines* (1863), and others.

Aimeo (ī.mā'ō). See **Moorea.**

Aimoin of Fleury (e.mwaṅ; flė.rē). [Latinized, **Aimoinus Floriacensis.**] b. at Périgord, France, c960; d. some time after 1010. French chronicler. His main work (begun before 1004) is a history of the Franks (*Historia Francorum*) from their origins (which he believed to have been in ancient Troy) to 654. It is actually merely a compilation, but it enjoyed much popularity. He also wrote a life of Abbo, one of his predecessors as abbot of Fleury, and an account of the miracles wrought by Saint Benedict's relics at Fleury from 887 to 1003. The history of the Franks is preceded by a topographical introduction in eight chapters. Various continuations of it were successively compiled, the latest between 1169 and 1174.

Aimon (ā'mo̤n). See **Aymon.**

Aimoré (ī.mō.rā'). See **Botocudo.**

Aimorés (ī.mö.res'), **Serra dos.** Mountain range in E South America, near the Brazilian coast, extending from the Parahyba do Sul River N nearly to the mouth of the São Francisco River. They are properly a northern prolongation of the Serra da Mantiqueira, which here becomes the Coast Range, the Serra do Mar dying out.

Aimwell (ām'wel"). In George Farquhar's comedy *The Beaux' Stratagem,* a young gentleman of a romantic temperament, who has dissipated his fortune and who, with his cooler-headed friend Archer disguised as his servant, impersonates a rich lord, with a view to retrieving their losses by a rich marriage for either or both, making a journey from one town to another, and taking turns in being master and man. The stratagem is successful at the end of the play.

Aimwell. In James Shirley's play *The Witty Fair One,* the lover of Violetta.

Ain (aṅ). See also **Ain River.**

Ain. Department in E France, formerly belonging to Burgundy, bounded by the departments of Saône-et-Loire and Jura on the N, Haute-Savoie and Savoie (from both of which it is separated by the Rhone) and Switzerland on the E, the department of Isère (from which it is separated by the Rhone) on the S, and the departments of Rhône and Saône-et-Loire (from both of which it is separated by the Saône) on the W. The city of Lyons is situated near the SE corner of the department. Ain is essentially an agricultural department, producing corn, wine, hemp, and flax, and raising fowl and hogs. Among the industries, the plastics industry of Oyonnax, the optical industry of Gex, and the manufacture of silks and other textiles are outstanding. There are important asphalt and stone quarries. Winter sports enthusiasts are attracted to the Jura Mountains on the E border of the department. It is on the main line of the railway between Paris and Geneva. Capital, Bourg; area, 2,248 sq. mi.; pop. 306,778 (1946).

Ainad (ī.näd'). Trading town in Hadhramaut, S Arabia, in Aden Protectorate, ab. 175 mi. NE of Aden.

Ainger (ān'jėr), **Alfred.** b. at London, Feb. 9, 1837; d. at Darley Abbey, Derbyshire, Feb. 8, 1904. English clergyman, author, and editor. He wrote biographies of Lamb (1882) and of Crabbe (1903), and published annotated editions of Lamb's *Essays of Elia* (1883), of Lamb's *Letters* (1888), and of Hood's *Poems*, with a biographical memoir (1897).

Ain Hersha (īn her'shä). [Also, **Ain Herché** (her.shā').] Village in E Lebanon, ab. 30 mi. W of Damascus. It contains a Roman temple *in antis*, practically complete except the roof.

Ain Jidy or **'Ain Jidi** (ān ji'dē). Modern name of **En-gedi.**

Ain Kadish (kä.dēsh'). Modern name of **Kadesh,** in Edom.

Ainmiller (īn'mil.ėr), **Max Emanuel.** [Also, **Maximilian Emmanuel Ainmüller** (-mül.ėr).] b. at Munich, Feb. 14, 1807; d. there, Dec. 8, 1870. German painter of architectural subjects and on glass. He developed a modern variant of the Renaissance enamel process of producing colored glass windows.

Aino (ī'nō). See **Ainu.**

Ain Qadis (ān kä.dēs'). Modern name of **Kadesh,** in Edom.

Ain River (aṅ). River in E France, which joins the Rhone ab. 17 mi. E of Lyons. It is narrow in its lower course. Length, ab. 100 mi.

Aïn-Sefra (īn se.frä'). [Official name, **Territoire d'Aïn-Sefra.**] One of the Territoires du Sud of Algeria, in NW Africa. It is bounded on the N by French Morocco and the Oran department of Algeria, on the W by the Spanish Sahara and French Mauritania, on the S by French West Africa, and on the E by the territories of Ghardaïa and Oasis Sahariennes. The administrative center is the town of Aïn-Sefra. Area, ab. 251,000 sq. mi.; pop. 250,894 (1948).

Ainslie (ānz'li), **Douglas.** [Original full name, **Douglas Ainslie Grant Duff.**] b. at Paris, 1865—. English poet, critic, and diplomat. Translated works of Benedetto Croce into English; author of *Chosen Poems* (1928), *The Conquest of Pleasure* (1942), and others.

Ainsworth (ānz'wėrth), **Frederick Crayton.** b. at Woodstock, Vt., Sept. 11, 1852; d. June 5, 1934. American army officer. Entered medical corps (1874); remembered for efficient reorganization of Record and Pension Office, of which he was chief (1892–1907); adjutant general (1907–12); reached rank of major general (1904).

Ainsworth, Henry. b. at Pleasington, Lancashire, England, 1571; d. at Amsterdam, c1622. English separatist clergyman and rabbinical scholar. Driven (1593) from England by persecution of the Brownists, a Nonconformist sect with which he was affiliated, he became porter to an Amsterdam bookseller and later (1596) teacher to the refugee members of Francis Johnson's London congregation; pastor of his own congregation (1610–22); author of several Brownist tracts and a body of rabbinical studies.

Ainsworth, Robert. b. near Manchester, England, 1660; d. at London, 1743. English lexicographer and teacher; author of a Latin-English dictionary, *Thesaurus linguae Latinae compendiarius* (1736).

Ainsworth, William Francis. b. at Exeter, England, Nov. 9, 1807; d. at Hammersmith, in London, Nov. 27, 1896. English geologist and traveler. He published *Researches in Assyria, Babylonia, etc.* (1838), *Travels* and *Researches in Asia Minor, Mesopotamia, etc.* (1842), *Travels in the Track of the 10,000 Greeks* (1844), *A Personal Narrative of the Euphrates Expedition* (1888), and others.

Ainsworth, William Harrison. b. at Manchester, England, 1805; d. at Reigate, England, 1882. English editor, publisher, and writer. He was editor (1840 *et seq.*) of *Bentley's Miscellany*, *Ainsworth's Magazine*, and the *New Monthly.* His novel *Rookwood* (1834) established him as a successful writer, and by 1881 he had published 39 novels, including *Crichton* (1837), *Jack Sheppard* (1839), *Tower of London* (1840), *Old St. Paul's* and *Guy Fawkes* (both 1841), *Windsor Castle* (1843), *The Flitch of Bacon,* and others. Seven of his novels were illustrated by Cruikshank.

Ainsworth, William Newman. b. at Camilla, Ga., Feb. 10, 1872; d. 1942. American Methodist Episcopal bishop. President of Wesleyan College, Macon, Ga. (1909–12); elected bishop (1918); president of American Anti-Saloon League (1935–36).

Aintab (īn.täb'). Former name of **Gaziantep,** city.

Aintree (ān'trē). Small area in W England, in Lancashire, ab. 5 mi. N of Liverpool, comprising a racecourse over which the steeplechase known as the Grand National is run in March of each year. The racecourse, which was founded over 100 years ago, is ab. 4½ mi. long and notable as one of the most difficult for riders in the world.

Ainu (ī'nö). [Also, **Aino.**] The aboriginal inhabitants of Japan, now found only on Hokkaido and Sakhalin islands; they number ab. 17,000. They live along the coasts and river banks, subsisting chiefly upon sea food.

Aiposha (ī.pō.shä'). [Also, **Naivasha.**] Former subgroup of the Nilo-Hamitic-speaking Masai of S Kenya and N Tanganyika in E Africa.

Air (ä.ēr'). [Also: **Ahir, Asben, Azbine.**] Mountainous oasis and former sultanate in the Sahara desert, in Niger territory, French West Africa, between Nigeria and the Territoires du Sud of Algeria. Chief town, Agadès; area, ab. 20,000 sq. mi.; pop. 60,000 (est.)

Airay (ãr'ā), **Henry.** b. at Kentmere, England, c1560; d. Oct. 6, 1616. English Puritan divine, vice-chancellor of Oxford (1606), and author of a *Commentary on Philippians* (1618).

Aircastle (ãr'kàs"l). Character in Samuel Foote's comedy *The Cozeners*, originally played in an amusingly prolix and digressive manner by Foote himself, burlesquing Gahagan, a highly educated young Irish gentleman who was hanged (1749) for "filing or diminishing the current coin of the realm."

Air Corps Ferrying Command, U.S. See **Air Transport Command.**

Airdrie (ãr'dri). Parliamentary burgh and market town in S Scotland, in Lanarkshire, ab. 10 mi. E of Glasgow, ab. 426 mi. N of London by rail. The town is situated on the Lanarkshire coal field. It has an iron and steel industry, which now uses mostly imported iron ores. 30,645 (est. 1948).

Aire (ãr). [Also: **Aire-sur-l'Adour;** Latin, **Vicus Julii, Atura.**] Town in SW France, in the department of Landes, situated on the Adour River, between Bayonne and Tarbes. An old town, it has been a bishopric since the 6th century. The episcopal palace dates from the 12th, 14th, and 18th centuries. The cathedral is partly in the Romanesque style and partly in the Gothic. 4,298 (1946).

Aireborough (ãr'bėr.ō). Urban district in C England, in the West Riding of Yorkshire, ab. 208 mi. NW of London by rail. It has been formed from parts of the former urban districts of Guiseley, Otley, Rawdon, and Yeadon. 27,533 (1951).

Aire River (ãr). River in C England, in the West Riding of Yorkshire. It rises in Malham Tarn, a small lake ab. 11 mi. NW of Skipton, and flows SE past Skipton, Bingley, Leeds, Rothwell, Castleford, and Knottingley to a confluence with the river Ouse ab. 18 mi. SE of York. Length, ab. 70 mi.; navigable above Leeds.

Aire River. Small river in E France, which joins the Aisne in the department of Ardennes.

Aires (ī'rēs), **Matias.** [Full name, **Matias Aires Ramos da Silva de Eça.**] b. at São Paulo, Brazil, March 27, 1705; d. at Lisbon, Portugal, Dec. 10, 1763. Brazilian moralist, regarded as one of the classical writers in the Portuguese language and best known for his *Reflexões* *sôbre a vaidade dos homens* (1752), which has appeared in several editions. He studied at the University of Coimbra, Portugal, and at Bayonne, France.

Aire-sur-l'Adour (ãr.sür.lȧ.dör). See **Aire.**

Aire-sur-la-Lys (ãr.sür.lȧ.lēs). Town in N France, in the department of Pas-de-Calais, situated at the junction of the Lys and Melde rivers and various canals, ab. 30 mi. SE of Calais. It was formerly a fortified place, and has preser ed the aspect of the 17th and 18th centuries. The *hôtel du ville* (town hall) dates from the 18th century. The Church of Saint Pierre was reconstructed in the 16th century. 8,213 (1946).

Air Force, U.S. Department of the. Executive agency established under the military unification act passed by the U.S. Congress on July 25, 1947. The department is part of the National Military Establishment embracing all the armed forces of the U.S. The air force secretary, equal in rank to the secretaries of the army and the navy, does not have cabinet rank. The first secretary of the air force was W. Stuart Symington. Unification established the air force as an independent arm, but it did not affect the status of naval aviation, which still remains a part of the U.S. navy. The commander in chief of the air force is the president of the U.S.; its executive head is the chief of staff of the U.S. Air Force. The air force had its inception (Aug. 1, 1907) in the Aeronautical Division of the Signal Corps, U.S. Army. It saw service in World War I as the Army Air Service, and later became the Army Air Corps. During World War II, as one of the three major components of the U.S. Army, it functioned under the designation of the Army Air Forces. The chief functions of the U.S. Air Force, which includes air combat and service forces, is to assure ability to carry out prompt and sustained combat operations in the air, to be responsible (in line with policies established by the Joint Chiefs of Staff) for the defense of the U.S. against air attack, to be responsible for strategic air warfare, and to gain and maintain general air supremacy. Its combat operations are divided into three categories: air reconnaissance and observation, air attack, and air fighting. Its basic combat unit is the squadron, consisting of two or more flights (a flight may number as few as three planes). A group is made up of two or more squadrons; a wing consists of two or more groups; and a command is made up of two or more wings. The various commands comprise the U.S. Air Force. Commissioned officers of the U.S. Air Force (except administrative and other ground officers) are the pilots, bombardiers, navigators, aerial photographers, and flight surgeons. At the close of World War II the Army Air Forces had in service more than 43,000 combat aircraft and a total enrollment of approximately 2,500,000 officers and men. Shortly before it was placed under the National Military Establishment, its personnel numbered 388,000.

Ai River (ī). River in NE China, in the province of Liaoning, Manchuria, which flows into the Yalu River opposite Gishu, Korea. It played an important part in the attack of the right wing of the Japanese forces upon the Russians in the battle of the Yalu River, May 1, 1904. Length, ab. 100 mi.

Airlanga (er.läng'gä). [Also: **Erlanga, Erlangga.**] b. in Bali, 1001; d. in Java, 1049. King of an East Javanese empire. His memorial statue from his tomb, now in the Modjokerto museum, is one of the most famous stone sculptures of Java.

Airolo (ī.rô'lō). [German, **Eriels.**] Small town in S Switzerland, in the canton of Ticino (German, Tessin), at the S entrance to the St. Gotthard railway tunnel, on the Ticino River. It is the first Italian-speaking community reached when traveling south by this route. 1,719 (1941).

Air Raid. Radio play by Archibald MacLeish, produced in 1938.

Air Service Command. [Abbreviation, **ASC.**] American air-supply arm in World War II, formed in October, 1941, with its own depots, warehouses, and over 300,000 employees. It maintained a world-wide supply network. Meeting day-to-day as well as emergency needs, it became one of the largest supply lines the Allies had in the war, carrying everything from cigarettes to munitions.

Air Transport Command. [Original name, **U.S. Air Corps Ferrying Command.**] Branch of the U.S. Air Force established in World War II to ferry planes from the U.S. to various theaters of operations, and to perform for the U.S. land and air forces generally the duty of flying urgently needed freight and passengers to or between operational areas. It was established formally in July, 1942, on a basis of the U.S. Air Corps Ferrying Command, which had been established primarily to ferry planes to Great Britain and the Middle East. Using to a great extent the planes and personnel of private air companies and carriers on a contract basis, it carried out important supply deliveries to all parts of the world in World War II. Its best-known single achievement was perhaps the operation (called "flying the hump") by which supplies were flown over the Himalaya Mountains from India to China. It became important again with the outbreak in June, 1950, of war in Korea, serving in this case not only to transport supplies to the combat area, but also as a primary means of evacuating casualties to hospitals in Japan and the U.S.

Airways, Inc. Play by John Dos Passos, published in 1928 and produced in 1929.

Airy (ãr'i), Sir **George.** The successful lover of Miranda in Susannah Centlivre's comedy *The Busybody.*

Airy, Sir **George Biddell.** b. at Alnwick, Northumberland, 1801; d. at Greenwich, London, 1892. English astronomer. As director of the Greenwich observatory and astronomer royal (1835–1881), he made 8,000 lunar observations of earlier dates available to astronomers (1846), and calculated mean density of earth (1854). His discovery of new inequality in the motions of Venus and the earth is considered to have been one of the outstanding achievements of 19th-century astronomy.

Aisén (ī.sān'). [Also, **Aysen.**] Province in S Chile. It is wooded, mountainous, rainy, cool, and largely unexplored. Lumbering is the principal source of livelihood. Capital, Aisén; area, 34,348 sq. mi.; pop. 23,430 (est. 1950).

Aisne (ān; French, en). Department in NE France, bounded by Belgium and the department of Nord on the N, by the departments of Ardennes and Marne on the E, by Seine-et-Marne department on the S, and the departments of Oise and Somme on the W; formed from parts of the former provinces of Picardy, Brie, and Île-de-France. Ravaged in the civil and religious wars of former centuries, it was overrun by German armies in World Wars I and II; its rivers (Aisne, Marne, Oise) and chief towns (Château-Thierry, Laon, Soissons, St. Quentin) have seen much bitter fighting and widespread destruction. Important for sugar-beet, potato, and flax production, cattle-raising, dairying, and various other agricultural activities; it also has metallurgical, textile, glass, and other industries. It contains many fine (and still essentially undamaged) examples of medieval architecture. Capital, Laon; area, 2,866 sq. mi.; pop. 453,411 (1946).

Aisne, Battles of the. Three separate engagements of World War I, which occurred in the vicinity of the Aisne River, France. The first battle (Sept. 15–18, 1914) was an Allied effort to follow up the successful counter-thrusts on the Marne, but was blocked by German resistance. A second Allied offensive (April, 1917) on the Aisne River failed in conjunction with the third battle of Champagne. The final battle of the Aisne (May 27–June 6, 1918) was part of Ludendorff's final plunge toward Paris, in which the Germans again reached the Marne River.

Aisne-Marne Offensive (ān'märn'). World War I operation in France, involving U.S. troops and allied French forces, which took place from July 18 to Aug. 6, 1918. The Allied strategy called for a counterattack against the German right flank NW of Soissons. The operation compelled a German retreat from the Marne, eliminated their salient, and marked the end of major German offensive action in World War I. The engagement was notable for its demonstration of the battle vigor and fitness of the American Expeditionary Forces. Among the U.S. divisions participating in the operation were the 1st, 2nd, 3rd, 4th, 26th, 28th, 32nd, 42nd, and 77th.

Aisne River (ān; French, en). [Ancient name, **Axona.**] River in N France, which rises in the department of Meuse, flows through Marne, Ardennes, Aisne, and Oise, and joins the Oise River near Compiègne. On it are Rethel and Soissons. Its chief affluents are the Aire and Vesle, and it communicates by canals with the Meuse and Marne. Its valley was the scene of several important battles in World War I. Length, ab. 175 mi.; navigable for ab. 75 mi.

Aïssé (à.ē.sā), Mlle. **Haidée.** b. c1694; d. at Paris, 1733. Daughter of a Circassian chief, who gained fame as a writer of letters at Paris. Sold by the Turks at the age of four to the French ambassador at Constantinople, she was educated at Paris, where she became renowned for her beauty and wit. Her *Letters*, which were first edited (1787) by Voltaire, are an excellent source of certain kinds of historical material for the early 18th century.

Aist (īst), **Dietmar von.** See **Dietmar von Aist.**

Aistulf (īs'tůlf) or **Astolf** (as'tolf). d. 756. King of the Lombards (749–756). His conquest (752) of the exarchate of Ravenna aroused the Pope's fears for the safety of Rome, and Pepin, king of the Franks, was called by Pope Stephen II to repel the Lombard threat. In the campaign that followed (755-756), Aistulf was defeated and driven out of Ravenna (755–756).

Aitken (āt'kẹn), **Robert.** b. at Dalkeith, Scotland, 1734; d. July 15, 1802. American printer, publisher, engraver, and bookseller. He opened his original bookstore in Philadelphia in 1769; in 1771 he reopened the store and added bookbinding. He published the *Pennsylvania Magazine* (1775–76), with contributions from Hopkinson, Witherspoon, and Thomas Paine, and produced America's first complete English Bible (1782.)

Aitken, Robert. b. at Crailing, Scotland, Jan. 22, 1800; d. in Paddington Station, London, July 11, 1873. Clergyman of the Church of England, from which he temporarily withdrew (1824–40).

Aitken, Robert Grant. b. at Jackson, Calif., Dec. 31, 1864; d. at Berkeley, Calif., Oct. 29, 1951. American astronomer at Lick Observatory, Calif. (1895 *et seq.*); observatory director (1930–35); awarded (1932) gold medal of Royal Astronomical Society for his discovery of more than 3,000 double-stars.

Aitken, Robert Ingersoll. b. 1878; d. Jan. 3, 1949. American sculptor and designer.

Aitken, William Maxwell. See **Beaverbrook,** 1st Baron

Aitkenites (āt'kẹn.īts). Party in the Church of England led by Robert Aitken, a minister originally ordained (1823 by the Church of England, but for some 16 years (1824–40' a preacher in Methodist and various other Nonconformist churches. In 1840 he rejoined the Church of England, as a High Churchman, and was vicar of Pendeen, in Cornwall, from 1849 to 1873. The object of the Aitkenites was to engraft certain Methodist practices and views upon the Anglican Church.

Aitolia (e.tô.lē'ä). See **Aetolia.**

Aiton (ā'tọn), **William.** b. near Hamilton, Scotland, 1731; d. at Kew, near London, Feb. 2, 1793. Scottish botanist. He was for many years (1759–93) director of the Royal Botanical Gardens at Kew, near London. He published *Hortus Kewensis* in 1789.

Aiton, William Townsend. b. 1766; d. 1849. British botanist; eldest son of William Aiton (1731–93). He was successor to his father as director of the Royal Botanical Gardens at Kew and brought out an expanded edition of his father's work, *Hortus Kewensis,* in the period 1810–13.

Aitos (ī'tôs). See **Aytos.**

Aitutaki (ī.tö.tä'kē). [Also, **Aitutake.**] One of the chief islands of the Cook Islands, in the Pacific Ocean: a possession, since 1901, of New Zealand. Area, 3,900 acres; pop. 2,590 (est. 1949).

Aiud (ä'yöd). [Hungarian, **Nagyenyed;** German, **Strassburg.**] Town in NW Rumania, in Transylvania province, situated on the Mureş River, ab. 45 mi. S of Cluj: theological seminary and teachers college; winegrowing in the environs. The people are mostly Hungarians. 9,535 (1948).

Aivalik (ī.vä.lik') or **Aivali** (-li'). See **Ayvalik.**

Aivazovski (ī.vä.zôf'ski), **Ivan Konstantinovich.** b. at Feodosia, in the Crimea, July 7, 1817; d. there, May 2, 1900. Armenian painter. He was for many years professor at the Imperial Academy of Fine Arts, St. Petersburg.

Aix (eks). See also **Aix-les-Bains.**

Aix (āks; French, eks). [Also: **Aix-en-Provence;** Latin, **Aquae Sextiae.**] City in S France, in the department of Bouches-du-Rhône, ab. 15 mi. N of Marseilles: seat of an archbishopric; has various old churches, among them the cathedral of Saint Sauveur with Romanesque nave and Roman columns, an art museum, a museum of ancient furniture, an art academy, and a public library with about 200,000 volumes. It is the seat of the University of Aix-Marseilles. It is a center for trade in olive oil and fruit, and has textile, ceramics, and food industries. Aix is the site of the oldest Roman establishment in Gaul; founded in 124 B.C. by the proconsul Gaius Sextius Calvinus (for whom it was named Aquae Sextiae), it soon became renowned for its baths. Here took place the great victory of Marius over the Teutones, Ambrones, and some other Germanic tribes in 102 B.C. Aix flourished as the capital of Provence until the 6th century. It was sacked by the Saracens in 731. It was the temporary residence of Charles V (1536). After the reunion of Provence with France (1481), it again became the capital of Provence and the seat of the provincial parliament (1501–1790). The historian Mignet and the painter Cézanne were born here. 46,053 (1946).

Aix (deks), **Île d'.** Island off W France, in the department of Charente-Maritime, situated between the mouth of the Charente River and the island of Oléron. The island was the last refuge of the Emperor Napoleon I, before his deportation (1815) to St. Helena. There are a Napoleonic museum and an African museum. 161 (1946).

Aix-en-Provence (eks.äṅ.pro.väṅs). See **Aix.**

Aix-la-Chapelle (eks.là.shà.pel; Anglicized, āks''lä.shä-pel'). French name of **Aachen.**

Aix-la-Chapelle, Congress of. Meeting of the powers of the Quadruple Alliance which resulted (Oct. 9, 1818) in a convention providing for withdrawal of occupation forces from France. Although the sovereigns of Russia, Austria, and Prussia were present, actual negotiations were largely in the hands of Wellington and Castlereagh (England), Metternich (Austria), Nesselrode (Russia), and Hardenberg and Bernstorff (Prussia). The congress reaffirmed the reactionary design of the Holy Alliance and, through the duc de Richelieu, invited French participation.

Aix-la-Chapelle, Treaty of. [Sometimes called **"Peace of Aix-la-Chapelle."**] **1.** Treaty (May 2, 1668) which ended the War of Devolution between France and Spain, and which was guaranteed (May 7, 1669) by the Triple Alliance (England, Sweden, and the Netherlands). It permitted France to retain the Flemish acquisitions of 1667, but compelled French return to Spain of Cambrai, Aire, and St.-Omer, and the province of Franche-Comté. **2.** Treaty (Oct. 18, 1748) which ended the War of the Austrian Succession. Based on mutual restitution of conquests, except that Austria was compelled to cede Parma, Piacenza, and Guastalla to Spain's *infante,* Philip, and to confirm Prussian possession of Silesia and Gratz, it confirmed the pragmatic sanction (i.e., the right of female succession to the Hapsburg throne) and reaffirmed recognition of Protestant succession to the English throne.

Aix-les-Bains (eks. lā. baṅ). [Also: **Aix;** Latin, **Aquae Gratianae, Aquae Domitianae.**] Town in E France, in the department of Savoie, situated near Lake Bourget, ab. 8 mi. N of Chambéry. It is a famous summer and winter resort and has been known since Roman times for its hot sulfur springs, in which many have bathed in an attempt to cure such ailments as rheumatism and gout. The poet Lamartine was born here. Nearby is the abbey of Hautecombe founded (1125) by Saint Bernard and Count Amédée III and later reconstructed (1824–43); it is occupied by the Cistercians and is the ancient funeral place of the princes of the house of Savoy. 14,556 (1946).

Aiyina (e'yē.nä). See **Aegina.**

Aiyion (e'yôn). See **Aigion.**

Aizani (ī.zä'nē). See **Azani.**

Aizu (ī.zö). Former name of **Wakamatsu,** Honshu, Japan.

Ajaccio (ä.yät'chō). Town on the island of Corsica, the capital of the French department of Corse, situated on the Gulf of Ajaccio, on the W coast of the island. It is a winter resort and a center for the trade in fruit, olive oil, and other products. Napoleon Bonaparte was born here; the 16th-century cathedral contains the font where he was baptized. The town has a statue of Napoleon and a museum. 31,434 (1946).

Ajalbert (à.zhàl.ber), **Jean.** b. at Clichy-la-Garenne, France, 1862; d. 1947. French lawyer, novelist, and author of various discussions of public questions.

Ajalon (aj'ạ.lon). See **Aijalon.**

Ajan (ä'jan). [Also, **Ajam** (-jam).] Region in E Africa, on the Somaliland coast, S of Cape Guardafui.

Ajanta (ạ.jun'tạ). [Also: **Adjunta, Ajunta.**] Small place in Hyderabad, Union of India, celebrated for its cave-temples.

Ajax (ā'jaks). In Greek legend, one of the leading Greek heroes in the Trojan War, famous for his size and physical strength and beauty; son of Telamon and half-brother of Teucer. According to Homer he was, next to Achilles, the bravest of the Greek warriors. He engaged several times in victorious single combat with Hector, and was always a source of terror to the Trojans. There are various accounts of his exploits after the war and of his death. According to the common poetical tradition, he died by his own hand. The decision of Agamemnon (on the advice of Athena) to award the arms of Achilles to Odysseus drove Ajax mad, and, according to Sophocles, in his insanity he furiously attacked and slew the sheep of the Greeks, imagining them to be his enemies. Shame for this conduct drove him to suicide. According to other accounts he was murdered. From his blood was said to have sprung up a purple flower bearing on its leaves the letters *ai*, which were the first letters of his name in Greek and also an exclamation of woe. His story was dramatized by Sophocles.

Ajax. Locrian legendary king, son of Oïleus, and one of the heroes in the Trojan War. Having incurred the displeasure of Athena, he was shipwrecked and drowned on his return from the war. He is often called the "Lesser Ajax."

Ajeho (ä.je'hō). See **Acheng.**

Ajiba (aj'i.bạ). See **Beir.**

Ajmer (aj.mēr'). [Also: **Ajmeer, Ajmere, Ajmir;** former name, **Ajmer-Merwara** (mėr.wä'rạ)]. State of the Union of India, in the NW part, a former chief-commissionership of Rajputana. It consists of two former districts, Ajmer and Merwara, united in 1871. Ajmer district was ceded to the British in 1818. Forest products and cattle raising are important here. Capital, Ajmer; area, 2,425 sq. mi.; pop. 692,506 (1951).

Ajmer. [Also: **Ajmeer, Ajmere, Ajmir.**] City in NW India, the capital of the state of Ajmer, Union of India, ab. 275 mi. NE of the city of Ahmedabad: important junction and trading center, particularly for salt and cotton textiles. The Mosque of Ajmer was founded in the early 13th century, and is one of the first established in India. It occupies the spacious square court of a 12th-century Jain temple, whose old colonnades of graceful and well-carved columns remain in place around the walls and support a series of low domes. The great beauty of the monument lies in the screen of seven keel-shaped Mohammedan arches carried across the W side of the court in front of the colonnade. This screen is covered with bands of Cufic and Togra inscriptions separated by diaper-work, admirable in decorative motive, and cut with great delicacy. 147,258 (1941).

Ajo (ä'hō, ā'jō). Unincorporated community in S Arizona, in Pima County: copper mining and smelting. 5,817 (1950).

Ajodhya (ạ.jōd'yạ). [Also: **Ayodhya, Oudh.**] Town in N India, in Fyzabad district, United Provinces, Union of India, across the Gogra River from Fyzabad, with which it is united for administrative and census purposes. It is a trading center, on the site of an important ancient city.

Ajtos (ī'tôs). See **Aytos.**

Ajunta (ạ.jun'tạ). See **Ajanta.**

Ajuti (ä.jö'tē). [Also: **Atyuti, Adjati.**] One of the Sudanic-speaking Guang peoples of W Africa, inhabiting N British Togo.

Aka (ä'kä). [Also: **Aca, Akowa, Baca, Wochua.**] One of the eastern pygmy groups discovered by Miani and Schweinfurth in C Africa, inhabiting the Ituri forests of NE Belgian Congo. They speak a Sudanic language.

Akaba or **Akabah** (ä'kạ.bạ). See **Aqaba.**

Akademeia or **Akademia** (ạ.kad.ẹ.mī'ạ). Greek name of the **Academy.**

Akakia (à.kà.kē.à). [Original name, **Martin Sans-Malice.**] b. at Châlons-sur-Marne, France; d. 1551. French physician, lecturer at the Collège de France founded by Francis I. He published several medical works. The name "Akakia," by which he is known, is a translation into Greek of the French words "sans malice," which made up his own original surname.

Akalkot (ä'kạl.kōt). Former state of the Union of India, in the Deccan States, ab. 230 mi. SE of Bombay, now part of Bombay state, in a tobacco and millet growing area. Capital, Akalkot; area, 498 sq. mi.; pop. 103,903 (1941).

Akan (ä'kän). Group of Sudanic-speaking peoples of W Africa, inhabiting the S part of the Gold Coast, all of whom speak dialects of Tshi (or Twi). The Akan include the Adanse, Ahanta, Akim, Akwapim, Aowin, Ashanti, Asini, Denkyira, Efutu, Etsi, Fanti, Kyefo, Nzima, Sefwi, and Wasa. They are closely related to the Anyi of SE Ivory Coast; the Guang peoples of C Gold Coast, who were formerly classed as Akan, are also related. The Akan peoples established a number of kingdoms of varying size, which controlled the Guinea Coast in this area, the most important being that of the Ashanti.

Akanta (ä.kän'tä). See **Ahanta,** a Sudanic-speaking people.

Akarnania (ak.ạr.nā'ni.ạ). See **Acarnania.**

Akarnania (ä.kär.nä'nē.ä). See **Acarnania.**

Akashi (ä.kä.shē). City in Japan, situated on the shore of the Inland Sea ab. 12 mi. W of Kobe: an industrial suburb of Kobe, with some heavy industry and much general light industry. It has a good deep-water harbor. The city is administered as a part of Kobe. 65,642 (1950).

Akassa (ä.käs'ạ). Seaport in W Africa, in Nigeria, situated on the W side of the Nun mouth of the Niger River.

Akastos (ạ.kas'tos). See **Acastus.**

Akawai (ä.kä.wä.ē'). See **Acawai.**

Akbar (ak'bär). [Also: **Akber** (äk'bėr), **Akhbar;** full Arabic name, **Jelal-ed-Din-Mohammed;** called **Akbar the Great.**] b. at Amarkote, India, 1542; d. at Agra, India, 1605. Greatest of India's Mogul emperors; reigned 1556–1605. He was born during the exile of his father, Humayun, who 12 years later recovered his throne at Delhi but died within the year; ruled (1556–60) under the regency of Bairam Khan, a tyrannical Turkoman noble whom he displaced upon reaching 18 years of age. Akbar engaged (1560–67) in constant warfare to consolidate his realm, conducting campaigns in the Punjab, and against Chitor and Ajmer (1567). Later campaigns (1572 *et seq.*) brought conquest of Gujarat, Bengal, Orissa, Kabul, Kashmir, and Kandahar, including, finally, Berar in the Deccan; his empire at time of his death included all India N of the 20th parallel. His achievements as a civil administrator rivaled his military feats; he instituted laws against extortion, a uniform system of weights and measures, banned child marriage below a certain age, and compelled toleration of religious diversity. His chief minister, Abulfazl, recorded the emperor's achievements in the biography *Akbar-nameh.*

Ak-Denghiz (äk.deng.gēz'). See **Balkhash.**

Aké (ä.kā'). One of the principal ruined cities of Yucatán, Mexico, situated ab. 30 mi. E of Mérida, noted for its pyramid.

Akeley (āk'li), **Carl Ethan.** b. at Clarendon, N.Y., May 19, 1864; d. in the Belgian Congo, Africa, Nov. 17, 1926. American naturalist, taxidermist, sculptor, and author. He developed a technique, now used by many museums, of mounting animals in habitat groups; headed expeditions to Africa for Chicago's Field Museum (1896, 1905) and for the American Museum of Natural History (1909, 1920–22, 1926). His bronze sculptures include *The Wounded Comrade, Lion and Cape Buffalo* and *The Nandi Spearmen and Lions.* He invented the cement gun used in mounting many of his subjects and the "Akeley camera" used by naturalists.

Akeley, Mary. [Maiden name, **Jobe.**] b. at Tappan, Ohio. American explorer, teacher, author; second wife (1924 *et seq.*) of Carl Akeley. Explored Canadian Rockies (1914–18); accompanied her husband on African expedition (1926–27) and headed it after his death; author of *Carl Akeley and the Great Adventure* (1940), *Rumble of a Distant Drum* (1946), and others.

Akeman Street (āk'mạn). Ancient Roman road in England connecting what is now Bath, through Speen and

Wallingford, with London. Parts of it are still discernible near Oxford.

Aken (ä'kẹn). [Also, **Acken.**] Town in C Germany, in the *Land* (state) of Saxony-Anhalt, Russian Zone, formerly in the province of Saxony, Prussia, situated on the Elbe River, near the influx of the Mulde and Saale rivers, ab. 25 mi. SE of Magdeburg. It is an important river port, and before World War II had manufactures of oils and essences, textile factories, and sugar refineries. The population is chiefly Protestant. 14,624 (1946).

Aken. Dutch name of **Aachen.**

Akenside (ā'kẹn.sīd), **Mark.** b. at Newcastle, England, 1721; d. at London, 1770. English poet and physician.

Akerbas (ạ.kėr'bạs). See **Acerbas.**

Akerblad (ä'kėr.bläd), **Johan David.** b. in Sweden, 1760; d. at Rome, Feb. 8, 1819. Swedish orientalist and diplomat, author of works on oriental inscriptions.

Akerman (ä'kėr.män; Russian, ä.kir.män'). Former name of **Belgorod-Dnestrovski.**

Akerman (ā'kėr.mạn), **Amos Tappan.** b. at Portsmouth, N.H., Feb. 23, 1821; d. at Cartersville, Ga., Dec. 21, 1880. American lawyer and politician. He settled at Elberton, Ga., in 1850 and followed his adopted state in secession from the Union in 1861, but became a Republican and reconstructionist after the war. He was attorney general (1870–71) under Grant.

Akerman (ä'kėr.män), **Convention of.** Treaty concluded between Russia and Turkey, Oct. 6, 1826, by which Russia secured the navigation of the Black Sea, and various agreements were entered into concerning Moldavia, Wallachia, and Serbia. The nonfulfillment of the treaty by Turkey led to the war of 1828–29 between Russia and Turkey.

Akerman (ā'kėr.mạn), **John Yonge.** b. at London, June 12, 1806; d. at Abingdon, England, Nov. 18, 1873. English numismatist.

Akers (ā'kėrz), **Benjamin Paul.** [Called **"St. Paul Akers."**] b. at Saccarappa, Me., 1825; d. at Philadelphia, 1861. American sculptor. Among his works are *Una and the Lion, Saint Elizabeth of Hungary, The Dead Pearl-Diver*, and others.

Akers, Elizabeth Chase. [Also: **Elizabeth Allen**; maiden name, **Chase**; pseudonym, **Florence Percy.**] b. at Strong, Me., Oct. 9, 1832; d. at Tuckahoe, N.Y., Aug. 7, 1911. American poetess; wife of Benjamin Paul Akers.

Akers, Floyd. A pseudonym of **Baum, Lyman Frank.**

Akershus (ä'kėrs.hös). [Also, **Aggershus.**] *Fylke* (county) in SE Norway, bordering on Sweden in the E and bounded by the *fylker* (counties) of Østfold, Hedmark, Opland, and Buskerud. Capital, Oslo; area, 1,894.7 sq. mi.; pop. 170,133 (1946).

Akeyem (ä.kā.yem'). See **Akim.**

Akha (ä'kä). [*Chinese*, **Wo-ni.**] A Tibeto-Burman-speaking hill people of S Yunnan in China, N Laos in Indo-china, N Thailand (Siam), and the E Shan States of Burma.

Akhaia (ä.ċhä'yä). See **Achaea,** a department of modern Greece.

Akhal Tekke (ä.ċhäl' tek'ke). Oasis in the U.S.S.R., in the Turkmen Soviet Socialist Republic, in C Asia, N of Iran.

Akhaltsikhe (ä.ċhäl'tsē.ċhe). [Also, **Akhalzikh** (-tsēċh).] Town in the U.S.S.R., in the Georgian Soviet Socialist Republic, famous for silver filigree work. It is the ancient capital of Turkish Georgia, and was captured by the Russians under Paskevich on Aug. 27, 1828. A Turkish attack upon it was repulsed in March, 1829, and near it a Russian victory was gained on Nov. 26, 1853. Pop. ab. 15,000.

Akhbar (ak'bär). See **Akbar.**

Akheloos (ä.ċhe.lô'ôs). See **Achelous.**

Akhinos (ä.ċhē.nôs') or **Akhinou** (-nö'). Modern Greek names of **Cercinitis.**

Akhisar (äk.hi.sär'). [Also: **Akhissar**; ancient name, **Thyatira.**] Town in W Turkey, in the *il* (province or vilayet) of Manisa, ab. 58 mi. NE of Izmir (formerly Smyrna): a trading center served by a railway. It exports grapes, figs, olives, and opium. Pop. ab. 21,000.

Akhissar (äk.hi.sär'). Turkish name of **Krujë.**

Akhlat (äċh.lät'). See **Ahlat.**

Akhmatova (äн.mä'tọ.vạ), **Anna.** [Pseudonym of **Anna Andreyevna Gorenko.**] b. at Odessa, Russia, 1888—. Russian poet. Between 1912 and 1923 she published half a dozen slim volumes of delicately wrought personal lyrics, but it was not thereafter until World War II that her name reappeared in the press under a few poems. In the summer of 1946 her work was scathingly denounced by the secretary of the Communist party as harmful to Soviet youth, and was proscribed. A group of her poems is to be found in Avrahm Yarmolinsky's *A Treasury of Russian Verse.*

Akhmim (äċh.mēm'). [Also: **Ekhmim**; ancient names, **Khemmis, Panopolis.**] Town in Egypt, on the E bank of the Nile between Asyut and Thebes. It was the seat of the cult of Ammon Khem, and its ancient necropolis was discovered by Maspero in 1884. Pop. ab. 25,000.

Akhmim Papyrus. Greek papyrus which is interesting because it gives what might be called a last glimpse of Egyptian mathematics. Strangely enough, it is also the earliest document on Greek practical arithmetic. The author was a Christian. The papyrus is Byzantine and anterior to the Arab invasion of 640–641. It dates probably from the sixth or seventh century.

Akhtal (äċh'täl), **al-.** [Original name, **Ghiyath ibn-Harith.**] b. in Iraq, c640; d. c710. Arab poet.

Akhtiar (uċh.tyàr'). See **Sevastopol.**

Akhtuba (äн'tö.bạ). River in the U.S.S.R., an arm of the Volga River which branches from the main stream near Stalingrad, and flows parallel with it to the Caspian Sea. Length, ab. 300 mi.

Akhtyrka (äн.tir'kạ). Town in the U.S.S.R., in the Ukrainian Soviet Socialist Republic, ab. 75 mi. NW of Kharkov: industrial center. Pop. ab. 28,000.

Akim (ä.kim'). [Also, **Akeyem.**] One of the Sudanic-speaking Akan peoples of W Africa, inhabiting the SE part of the Gold Coast.

Akins (ā'kinz), **Zoë.** [Married name, Mrs. **Hugo Cecil Levinge Rumbold.**] b. at Humansville, Mo., Oct. 30, 1886—. American poet, playwright, and film writer. Her poetry includes *Interpretations* (1911), *The Hills Grow Smaller* (1937); her plays include *Déclassée* (1919), *Daddy's Gone a-Hunting* (1921), *A Royal Fandango* (1924), *The Greeks Had a Word for It* (1929), and *The Little Miracle* (1936). She won a Pulitzer prize in drama for her adaptation of *The Old Maid* (1935), and is the author of the novel *Forever Young* (1941).

Akir (ä.kēr'). Modern name of **Ekron.**

Akita (ä.kē.tä). Prefecture in Japan, in N Honshu. It is important for its resources of oil and copper, which (although modest by U.S. standards) are among the largest in Japan. Capital, Akita; area, 4,484 sq. mi., pop. 1,309,091 (1950).

Akita. City and port in Japan, in NW Honshu. It has considerable industrial importance for its oil refineries, and is politically significant as the capital of the prefecture of Akita. Its population, which increased throughout World War II, was 126,074 in 1950.

Akka (äk'kạ). Arabic name of **Acre,** Palestine.

Akkad (ak'ad, äk'käd). [Also, **Accad.**] One of the four cities of Nimrod's empire (Gen. x. 10.) in Shinar or Babylonia; in the cuneiform inscriptions it is usually the name of a region. The kings of Babylonia and those of Assyria who conquered Babylonia called themselves kings "of Sumer and Akkad," whence it is usually assumed that Sumer denominated S Babylonia and Akkad N Babylonia. The boundaries of this district are not certain, but it seems to have lain between the Tigris River and the Elamitic and Median mountains, its northern limit being the upper Zab. The name of a city, Agade, discovered in an inscription of Nebuchadnezzar, is held by some to be identical with the city of Akkad. Agade was the residence of the earliest known Babylonian king, Sargon I (c3800 B.C.). Cyrus mentioned this city as still existing in his time. Friedrich Delitzsch considered it part of the city of Sepharvaim; other scholars, however, have doubted this identification. Akkadian is the name given to the people and dialect of Akkad.

Akkerman (ä.kir.män'). Former name of **Belgorod-Dnestrovski.**

Akko (ak'ō). Old Testament name of **Acre,** Palestine.

Akkra (ak'rạ, ạ.krä'). See **Accra.**

Aklavik (ą.klav′ik, ä.klä′vik). Largest settlement in the far northern area of Canada, situated in the Northwest Territories, on the delta near the mouth of the Mackenzie River. It is the most northerly town not only on the continent of North America but also in the entire British Commonwealth. It is the headquarters for Anglican and Roman Catholic missions in the area; each denomination maintains its own cathedral, school, and hospital here. Pop. ab. 760 (including 170 whites, 213 Indians, and 377 Eskimos).

Akmolinsk (äk.mo.lēnsk′). [Also, **Akmollinsk.**] *Oblast* (region) of the Kazakh Soviet Socialist Republic, in the U.S.S.R., ab. 600 mi. NW of Alma-Ata. It is level in the N, hilly in the center, and a desert steppe in the S.

Akmolinsk. City in the U.S.S.R., the capital of the Akmolinsk *oblast* (region) of the Russian Soviet Federated Socialist Republic, situated on the Ishim River. A rail junction with lines to Magnitogorsk and Karaganda, it is also a caravan center. 44,700 (1935).

Ako (ȧ.kō), **Michel.** See **Aco, Michel.**

Akola (ą.kō′lą). District of Madhya Pradesh, Union of India, NE of Bombay. Cotton and millet are the chief crops. Capital, Akola; area, 4,093 sq. mi.; pop. 907,742 (1941).

Akola. Capital of Akola district, Madhya Pradesh, Union of India, ab. 300 mi. NE of Bombay: important trading center, especially for cotton. 62,564 (1941).

Akowa (ä′kō.wä). See **Aka.**

Akra (ak′rä, ą.krä′). See **Accra.**

Akrabbim (ą.krab′im). [Also, **Maaleh-acrabbim.**] In Biblical geography, a group of hills S of the Dead Sea, variously identified.

Akragas (ak′rą.gąs). Greek name of **Agrigento.**

Akrokeraunia (ak″rō.kę.rô′ni.ą). See **Acroceraunia.**

Akrokorinthos (ak″rō.kǫ.rin′thos). See **Acrocorinthus.**

Akron (ak′rǫn). City in NE Ohio, county seat of Summit County, ab. 36 mi. S of Cleveland, on the divide between the Lake Erie and Ohio River watersheds. It is known as the rubber capital of the world and is the chief supplier of automobile tires to nearby Detroit. Other manufactures include dirigibles, clay products, breakfast foods, and matches. It is the seat of the University of Akron and the Goodyear Industrial University. It was platted in 1825 and was an important shipping point on the Ohio and Erie Canal. Pop. of city, 244,791 (1940), 274,605 (1950); of urbanized area, 366,765 (1950).

Akropolites (ak″rō.pǫ.lī′tēz), **Georgios.** See **Acropolita, George.**

Ak-sai (äk.sī′). See **Ak Su Darya.**

Aksakov (äk.sä′kǫf), **Ivan Sergeyevich.** b. at Ufa, Russia, 1823; d. at Moscow, 1886. Russian Slavophile author, journalist, and politician; son of Sergey Timofeyevich Aksakov (1791–1859). He edited or founded several papers, including the *Sbornik* (1852), the *Den* (1861–65), the *Moskva* (1867), and the Slavophile organ, *Rus* (1880 *et seq.*). All of his journalistic ventures were at one time or another banned by the government.

Aksakov, Konstantin Sergeyevich. b. at Moscow, 1817; d. on the Greek island of Zante, in the Ionian Sea, 1860. Russian poet and prose writer; son of Sergey Timofeyevich Aksakov (1791-1859). Author of several Slavophile works, including *The Prince Lupuvitski* and *Moscow Delivered in 1812.*

Aksakov, Sergey Timofeyevich. b. at Ufa, Russia, 1791; d. at Moscow, 1859. Russian novelist and friend of Gogol, influential in the development of realism in Russian literature. Author of *A Family Chronicle* (1856) and other books, most of which are now remembered for their accurate portrayal of life on the estates of the Russian rural aristocracy, in the region of the Ural frontier.

Aksaray (äk.sä.rī′). [Also: **Akserai**; ancient name **Archelais.**] Town in C Turkey, in the *il* (province or vilayet) of Kirşehir, ab. 110 mi. NW of Adana. It is a trading center for various nomads of the region, who sell Angora wool here, and has a rug industry. Pop. ab. 9,000

Akşehir (äk.she.hēr′). [Also: **Akshehr, Ak-Sheher**; ancient name, **Philomelion.**] Town in W central Turkey, in the *il* (province or vilayet) of Konya, ab. 120 mi. N of Antalya: scene of the victory of Frederick Barbarossa over the Seljuks, on May 18, 1190. Bajazet I died here in 1403. Pop. ab. 10,000.

Akserai (äk.se.rī′). See **Aksaray.**

Akshehr (äk.sher′) or **Ak-Sheher** (-she.her′). See **Akşehir.**

Ak Su Darya (äk sö där′yą). [Also: **Aksu, Ak-sai.**] River in China, in the province of Sinkiang, a northern tributary of the Tarim. It rises in the Tien Shan. Length, ab. 300 mi.

Aksum (äk.söm′). [Also, **Axum.**] Ancient town in Tigré, Ethiopia, noted for its antiquities including, according to tradition, the Ark of the Covenant. It was the capital of the Axumite Kingdom, and a coptic religious center.

Akte (äk′tē). See **Athos.**

Aktion (ak′ti.on, -shi.on). Greek name of **Actium.**

Aktyubinsk (äk.työ′binsk). City in Asia, in the U.S.S.R., in the Kazakh Soviet Socialist Republic. Its location on a major rail line from the Caspian Sea plus considerable mineral resources in the area resulted in its development even before World War I as an industrial center of some importance. It is now believed to contain sizeable machine shops, plants for the working of chrome and nickel, and a chemical factory. The oil pipe line N from the Caspian Sea passes through the city. 41,500 (1935).

Akuapen (ä.kwä.pen′). See **Akwapim.**

Akunakuna (a.kö.nä.kö′nä). [Also, **Akurakura.**] Semi-Bantu-speaking people of W Africa, inhabiting an area SE of Afikpo on the E bank of the Cross River in S Nigeria. Their number has been estimated at 9,000 (by P. A. Talbot, *The Peoples of Southern Nigeria,* 1926).

Akupara (äk.ö.pä′rą). In Hindu mythology, the tortoise which upholds the world.

Akureyri (ä′kür.ā.ri). Seaport in N Iceland, situated on the Eyja Fjord, on the N coast of the island. It is a tourist center, and the second largest community in Iceland. 7,439 (1950).

Akwapim (ä.kwä.pēm′). [Also, **Akuapen.**] One of the Sudanic-speaking Akan peoples of W Africa, inhabiting the SE part of the Gold Coast in the neighborhood of Koforidua. Their dialect was reduced to writing in 1838, and since then has become the literary form of Tshi used by the Akan peoples of the Gold Coast.

Akyab (ak.yab′, äk.yäb′). District in the division of Arakan, on the W coast of Burma, ab. 350 mi. SE of Calcutta, isolated from the rest of the country by mountains and dense jungles. Rice paddies occupy 90 percent of the cultivated land; fishing is the chief nonagricultural occupation. Area, ab. 5,000 sq. mi.

Akyab. Seaport in NW Burma, capital of the district of Akyab, and capital and chief port of the Arakan division of Burma, ab. 325 mi. NW of Rangoon. The major exports are fish and rice. 38,094 (1931).

Akyerman (ä.kir.män′). Former name of **Belgorod-Dnestrovski.**

Al- or **al-** (äl, al). Particle in many Arabic names, similar in use to *de* and *von.* Most such names are entered in this book under the element following the *al-* (as "Gazali, Abu Hamid Mohammed al-"); in some cases names have become better known in a westernized form such as "Alcazarquivir" and are thus entered. For such Arabic or Arabic-derived names not found under A, look under the second element.

Ala (ä′lä). Town and commune in NE Italy, in the *compartimento* (region) of Trentino-Alto Adige, in the province of Trento, situated on the Adige River, ab. 23 mi. SW of Trent. It was formerly a border community of the Austrian Tirol; incorporated into Italy in 1919. Pop. of commune, 6,171 (1936); of town, 2,301 (1936).

Ala-ad-Din (ä.lä′äd.dēn′). See **Ala-ed-Din.**

Al Aaraaf (al ar′af). Allegorical poem by Edgar Allan Poe published (1829) as the title-piece of a volume. It is written in octosyllabic divisions, heroic couplets, and songs. Deriving in some measure from the "Al Araf" of Mohammedan theology (a partition between heaven and hell wherein reside the souls of those who have been neither virtuous enough for heaven nor wicked enough for hell) the Al Aaraaf of Poe is conceived of as a star from which the Idea of Beauty originates. The youth Angelo is transported from the Earth to Al Aaraaf, where his love for the maiden Ianthe takes him out of the ideal realm. The couple are punished for their defection by being sentenced to hell.

Alabama (al.ạ.bam′ạ). [Called the **"Cotton State"** and the **"Yellowhammer State."**] State in the S United States, bounded by Tennessee on the N, Georgia (partly separated by the Chattahoochee) and Florida (separated by the Perdido) on the E, Florida and the Gulf of Mexico on the S, and Mississippi on the W: one of the Gulf States.

Population, Area, and Political Divisions. Alabama is divided for administrative purposes into 67 counties. It sends 9 representatives to Congress and has 11 electoral votes. Capital, Montgomery; area, 51,279 sq. mi. (51,998 sq. mi. including water); pop. 3,061,743 (1950). The state ranks 28th in area, and 17th (on the basis of the 1950 census) in population. The chief cities are Birmingham, Mobile, Montgomery, Gadsden, Tuscaloosa, and Anniston.

Terrain and Climate. The Raccoon and Lookout ranges of the S Appalachians lie in the NE part of the state. The Cumberland Plateau, a low hilly range in the NE, is traversed by the Tennessee River, which flows across the N part of the state. Muscle Shoals, formerly ab. 37 mi. of rapids on the Tennessee in the NW, has been submerged by Lake Wilson, formed by Wilson Dam, a part of the Tennessee Valley Authority. At the head of Lake Wilson, and forming Wheeler Lake, is Wheeler Dam, on the Tennessee River and also a part of the Tennessee Valley Authority. The S part of the state consists of a fertile coastal plain with a general elevation of no more than 600 ft. The Tallapoosa and Coosa rivers, joining above Montgomery, form the Alabama River. The Alabama unites with the Tombigbee River, ab. 35 mi. above Mobile. From their confluence to Mobile Bay, an inlet of the Gulf of Mexico, the combined streams are known as the Mobile River. Another river formed by the confluence of the Alabama and Tombigbee rivers is the Tensaw, or Tensas, which branches off ab. 5 mi. N of the Mobile and also flows into Mobile Bay. Other rivers in the state include the Chattahoochee, forming the SE boundary, the Conecuh and the Pea in the SE and S, the Choctawhatchee in the S, and the Black Warrior (a tributary of the Tombigbee) in the N.

Industry, Agriculture, and Trade. With agriculture as the state's chief industry, Alabama produces approximately one tenth of the nation's cotton. Peanuts, corn, potatoes (including sweet potatoes), sugar cane, tobacco, oats, fruits, and hay are other important crops, and the raising of livestock is a major occupation. Valuable deposits of coal and iron, particularly in the Birmingham region, make mining the second most important industry of the state. Limestone, clay, bauxite, marble, and sandstone are also abundant. The state's many forests supply material for a lumber industry of some scope. Annual income in the state from agriculture ranges as high as $315,000,000 and from mineral output as high as $112,000,000. The extensive system of waterways provides excellent facilities for transportation of goods, and Mobile is a busy port with considerable foreign trade.

History. Alabama was explored in the 16th century by the Spanish, chiefly De Soto, in c1540. The French established a temporary settlement on the Mobile River in 1702, making the first permanent settlement in 1711 on the site of the modern city of Mobile. The territory N of lat. 31° N. was ceded to Great Britain in 1763, and to the U.S. in 1783. The S portion became part of West Florida, falling (1783) to Spain; claimed (1803) by the U.S. under the Louisiana Purchase. Alabama was created a territory in 1817. The first constitutional convention was held in 1819 and Alabama became a state of the Union (the 22nd) on Dec. 14, 1819; seceded (Jan. 11, 1861) from the Union at a state convention. The government of the Confederate States of America was formed (Feb. 4, 1861) at Montgomery. Secession was declared null and void and slavery was abolished by a constitutional convention in 1865. The state rejoined the Union in June, 1868, after the constitutional convention of 1867. The present constitution was adopted in 1901.

Culture. A large rural segment is contained in the population. Negroes comprise approximately a third of the total. Institutions of higher learning include the Univeristy of Alabama, with branches at Birmingham, Mobile, and Montgomery, and the Alabama Polytechnic Institute at Auburn, both state-supported, as is Alabama College for Women, Montevallo; five state teachers colleges, including one for Negroes; and Tuskegee Institute. State motto: *Audemus Jura Nostra Defendere* ("We Dare Defend Our Rights"); state flower, goldenrod; state bird, yellowhammer; state song, "Alabama."

Alabama. One of the several North American Indian communities, now extinct, that formed the Creek Confederacy, and after which the state of Alabama is named.

Alabama. Wooden steam-sloop of 1,040 tons built during the Civil War for the Confederacy, at Birkenhead, England. Her commander was Captain Raphael Semmes of the Confederate navy. Her crew and equipment were English. She cruised (1862–64), destroying American shipping, and was sunk by the *Kearsarge,* off Cherbourg, France, on June 19, 1864.

Alabama Claims. Claims for damages preferred by the U.S. against Great Britain for losses caused during the Civil War by Confederate raiders on the high seas, the chief of which was the *Alabama,* fitted out or supplied in British ports under the direction of the Confederate government. The adjustment of these claims was provided for by the treaty of Washington, concluded May 8, 1871, which referred them to a tribunal of arbitration to be composed of five members, named respectively by the governments of the U.S., Great Britain, Italy, Switzerland, and Brazil. The tribunal assembled at Geneva, Switzerland, on Dec. 15, 1871, and was composed of the following arbitrators: Count Federigo Sclopis, of Italy; Baron Itajuba, of Brazil; Jacques Staempfli, of Switzerland; Charles Francis Adams, of the U.S.; and Lord Chief Justice Sir Alexander Cockburn, of Great Britain. The agent for Great Britain was Lord Tenterden, the counsel Sir Roundell Palmer; the agent for the U.S., J. C. Bancroft Davis, the counsel William M. Evarts, Caleb Cushing, and Morrison R. Waite. Count Sclopis was elected president, and Alexandre Favrot, of Switzerland, secretary. After having received the cases of the contending parties, the tribunal adjourned till June 15, 1872. The U.S. claimed, in addition to direct damages, consequential or indirect damages; Great Britain contended against any liability whatever, and especially against any liability for indirect damages. The decision of the tribunal was announced on Sept. 14, 1872, a gross sum of 15,500,000 dollars in gold being awarded the U.S. in satisfaction for all claims. The Geneva tribunal is of importance in the history of international law on account of the rules relating to neutrals which it adopted to guide its action.

Alabama Platform. Political formula adopted (1848) by the state convention of Democrats in Alabama which enlisted the support of other elements in the South. Designed as a reply to the doctrine of squatter sovereignty and the Wilmot Proviso, the platform called for congressional safeguards for slavery in the territory ceded by Mexico to the U.S.

Alabama River. River in Alabama, which is formed by the Coosa and Tallapoosa above Montgomery, flows SW and unites with the Tombigbee to form the Mobile, ab. 32 mi. N of Mobile. Its chief tributary is the Cahawba. Length, ab. 315 miles; navigable to Montgomery.

Alabanda (al.ạ.ban′dạ). Ancient city of Caria, Asia Minor, on the site of the modern Hissar.

Alabaster (al′ạ.bas.tėr), **William.** [Also, **Arblastier.**] b. at Hadleigh, Suffolk, 1567; d. in April, 1640. English poet and clergyman. Author of a Latin tragedy *Roxana* (acted at Cambridge c1592, printed 1632), and of various learned works.

Alabat (ä.lä.bät′). Elongated island in Lamon Bay on the N coast of the SE peninsula of Luzon, Philippine Islands: part of Tayabas province. Chief town, Alabat; area, 73.8 sq. mi.; pop. 11,723 (1939).

Alacaluf (ä.lä.kä.löf′). [Also: **Alakaluf, Halakwulup.**] South American Indian tribe inhabiting the archipelago on the S Chilean coast from ab. latitude 48° S. to W of the island of Tierra del Fuego. Greatly reduced in population today, they possessed an extremely simple material culture, much like the Yahgan, gaining their food principally from the sea and therefore spending much of the time in their bark canoes. The Alacaluf language forms an independent stock unrelated to any others.

Alacranes (ä.lä.krä'nes). See **Arrecife Alacrán.**

Aladağ (ä.lä.däg'). [Also, **Ala-Dagh.**] Range of the Taurus Mountains in the SE part of Turkey, N of Adana, a continuation of the Bulgar-Dagh. The range runs E and W for a distance of 200 mi. and reaches a height of 12,250 ft. Through these mountains engineers built a road in 1,000 B.C.

Aladağ. [Also: **Ala-Dagh, Allah Dagh.**] Mountain range in N part of Turkey. It runs NE to SW for a distance of ab. 220 mi. and reaches a height of 8,451 ft.

Aladağ. [Also, **Ala-Dagh.**] Mountain range in E Turkey, N of Lake Van, the source of the Eastern Euphrates. Elevation, ab. 11,545 ft.

Aladağ. [Also: **Ala Dagh, Aladja-Dagh.**] Mountain near Kars, in Turkish Armenia, the scene of a victory (Oct. 13–15, 1877) of the Russians under the Grand Duke Michael over the Turks under Mukhtar Pasha.

Aladdin (a.lad'in). See also **Ala-ed-Din.**

Aladdin. In the story of "Aladdin or the Wonderful Lamp," in *The Arabian Nights' Entertainments*, the son of a poor widow in China, who becomes possessed of a magic lamp and ring, which command the services of two powerful jinns. Learning the magic power of the lamp by accidentally rubbing it, Aladdin becomes rich and marries the Princess of Cathay through the agency of the "slave of the lamp," who also builds in a night a palace for her reception. One window of this palace is left unfinished, and no one can complete it to match the others. Aladdin therefore directs the jinns to finish it, which is done in the twinkling of an eye (hence the phrase "to finish Aladdin's window"; that is, to attempt to finish something begun by a greater man). After many years the original owner of the lamp, a magician, in order to recover it, goes through the city offering new lamps for old. The wife of Aladdin, tempted by this idea, exchanges the old and rusty magic lamp for a new and shining useless one (hence the phrase "to exchange old lamps for new"), and the magician transports both palace and princess to Africa, but the ring helps Aladdin to find them. He kills the magician, and, possessing himself of the lamp, transports the palace to Cathay, and at the sultan's death succeeds to the throne.

Ala-Denghiz (ä'lä.deng.gēz'). See **Balkhash.**

Ala-ed-Din (ä.lä'ed.dēn'). [Also: **Aladdin, Ala-ad-Din.**] fl. 14th century. Ottoman statesman; son of Othman, the founder of the Ottoman Empire. Orchan, Ala-ed-Din's elder brother, offered to share the empire with him, but he would accept only revenues from a single village and the post of vizier. With Orchan, he organized the corps of Janizaries (the élite military force that consisted of non-Turks captured as children and carefully schooled for their military career), with which he gained (1330) a victory over the emperor Andronicus and took Nicaea, chief defense of the Greek empire in Asia.

Alagez (al.a.gez'; Russian, ä.lä.gyôs'). [Also: **Alaghez, Alagöz, Ali-Ghez, Aragats.**] Extinct volcano in the U.S.S.R., in the Armenian Soviet Socialist Republic, ab. 30 mi. NW of Erivan. 13,436 ft.

Alagôas (ä.la.gō'as). State in E Brazil, bounded by Pernambuco on the N and NW, the Atlantic on the SE, and Sergipe on the SW. Its chief products are cotton, sugar, and tobacco. Capital, Maceió; area, 11,016 sq. mi.; pop. 1,106,454 (1950).

Alai (ä.lī'). Mountain range in Asia, in the Kirghiz Soviet Socialist Republic, in the U.S.S.R. Its highest peaks reach an altitude of between 19,000 and 20,000 ft.

Alain (å.laṅ). Pseudonym of **Chartier, Émile.**

Alain de Lille (de lēl). [Latinized name, **Alanus ab** (or **de**) **Insulis;** called **"Doctor Universalis."**] b. c1128; d. 1202. French monk, theologian, and scholastic philosopher. Author of the satirical poem *De planctu naturae*, and the encyclopedic poem *Anticlaudianus* (1536), which attempts to encompass morality, science, and the arts.

Alain le Gros (le grō). See **Aleyn.**

Alais (å.le, -les). Former name of **Alès.**

Alaiye (ä.lī'ye). See **Alanya.**

Alajuela (ä.lä.hwā'lä). Province in W Costa Rica: agriculture. Capital, Alajuela; area, 3,652 sq. mi.; pop. 148,850 (1950).

Alajuela. Capital of Alajuela province, in C Costa Rica: center of the sugar industry, and a summer resort. 13,903 (1950).

Alakaluf (ä.lä.kä.löf'). See **Alacaluf.**

Ala Kul (ä'lä köl). [Also, **Ala Kol.**] Lake in the U.S.S.R., in the Kazakh Soviet Socialist Republic, Asiatic Russia, near the Chinese frontier. It has no outlet. Area, ab. 900 sq. mi.

Alamán (ä.lä.män'), **Lucas.** b. at Guanajuato, Mexico, Oct. 18, 1792; d. in Mexico, June 2, 1853. Mexican historian and politician. He was secretary of the interior for the provisional government (1823–25), foreign minister under Bustamante, and again under Santa Anna.

Alamanni or **Alemanni** (al.a.man'ī). Confederation of Suevic-speaking Germanic tribes which occupied the region from the Main to the Danube in the first part of the 3rd century A.D. Their territory extended later across the Rhine, including Alsace and part of E Switzerland.

Alamanni (ä.lä.män'nē) or **Alemanni** (-lā-), **Luigi.** b. at Florence, 1495; d. at Amboise, France, 1556. Italian poet, author of eclogues, hymns, satires, elegies, a didactic poem *La Coltivazione* (1546), an epic poem *Girone il cortese* (1548), and others. He conspired against Guilio de' Medici and escaped to Venice, from which place he went to Genoa, and in 1523 to the court of France, where, after returning to Florence for a short time (1527–30), he spent most of his later life. Through Wyatt, who imitated him, he exerted considerable influence upon English poetry.

Alamannia or **Alemannia** (al.a.man'i.a). Division of ancient Germany, which first appears about the end of the 3rd century. It lay in the SW part of Germany and adjoining parts of Switzerland and the Tirol, the region settled largely by the Alamanni (ancestors of the Swabians, German Swiss, and others).

Alamannic Federation (al.a.man'ik). [Also, **Alemannic Federation.**] A federation of several German tribes, chiefly Suevi, which appeared in the area of the Main River in the third century after Christ. Caracalla engaged in war with them in 214. Under Aurelian they invaded the empire, but were defeated in three battles in 271. In 356 and 357 they were defeated by Julian; in 366 by Jovinus; and in 496 they were completely subjugated by Clovis.

Alambagh (a.lum'bäg). [Also, **Alumbagh.**] An enclosure near Lucknow, India. It was held by Sir James Outram against the Sepoys from November, 1857, until March, 1858.

Alameda (al.a.mē'da). City in C California, in Alameda County, ab. 9 mi. E of San Francisco, on San Francisco Bay: naval air station; shipbuilding and fishing. 64,430 (1950).

Alameda. Village in SE Idaho, in Bannock County, near Pocatello. 4,694 (1950).

Alameda. Unincorporated community in C New Mexico, in Bernalillo County, ab. 9 mi. N of Albuquerque, on the Rio Grande River, in an agricultural region producing chiefly sorghum, chili peppers, and alfalfa. Nearby are the Alameda Pueblo ruins, a pre-Columbian Tigua Indian village. The Indian Pueblo was burned (1681) during Indian uprisings against the Spanish. 1,792 (1950).

Alaminos (ä.lä.mē'nōs), **Antón** or **Antonio.** fl. 1499–1520. Spanish navigator. He accompanied Columbus in 1499 and 1502, and was chief pilot of successive expeditions (1517–20) made by Cordova, Grijalva, and Cortés to Mexico. He discovered the Bahama channel in 1520.

Alamo (al'a.mō). City in S Texas, NW of Brownsville: trading center for an agricultural area. 3,017 (1950).

Alamo. Mission building at San Antonio, Texas, begun in 1744. It was used as a parish church until 1793, when the mission was secularized. In February, 1836, it was occupied by William B. Travis with about 150 Texans in revolt against the government of Mexico. After withstanding a lengthy siege by Mexican forces under Santa Anna, it was taken by assault on March 6, and the surviving members of the garrison (including David Crockett and James Bowie) were killed. The American casualties, which included reinforcements, were 187 dead. The Mexicans, who employed between 6,000 and 7,000 men in the operation, lost about 1,500 killed. Although the affair involved, as defenders of the mission, Texas settlers who had emigrated from the U.S. to live in what was at the time of their emigration still Mexican territory, and the U.S. itself was therefore not directly involved, the "Battle of the Alamo" has come to be regarded as one of the most heroic of U.S. military achievements.

Alamogordo (al"ạ.mọ.gôr'dō). Town in S New Mexico, county seat of Otero County: railroad repair shops and a marble works. Near here, at the Alamogordo Air Base, the first successful test of the atomic bomb was made on July 16, 1945. Pop. 6,783 (1950).

Alamo Heights. City in C Texas, in Bexar County, N of San Antonio, of which it is a suburb. 8,000 (1950).

Alamos (ä'lä.mōs). Town in NW Mexico, in Sonora state. Pop. under 5,000 (1940).

Alamosa (al.ạ.mō'sạ). City in S Colorado, county seat of Alamosa County, on the Rio Grande: shipping point for potatoes and meat. 5,354 (1950).

Álamos de Barrientos (ä'lä.mōz ᴛʜā bär.ryen'tōs). b. at Medina del Campo, Spain, 1550; d. c1635. Spanish philologist.

Alamut (ä.lä.möt'), **Rock of.** Place in N Iran, in the Elburz Mountains, ab. 70 mi. NW of the city of Tehran. In medieval times it was a stronghold of the Assassins.

Åland (ō'länd) or **Ålandsöerna** (ō'länds.ė'ėr.nä). Swedish names of **Ahvenanmaa.**

Alanda (ạ.lan'dạ). Celtic name of **Lodi,** Italy.

Aland Islands (ä'lạnd, ô'-). See **Ahvenanmaa.**

Alane (al'ạn), **Alexander.** See **Alesius, Alexander.**

Alani (ạ.lā'nī) or **Alans** (ā'lạnz). A people of Scythian origin, dwelling originally in the Caucasus. With the Huns they defeated the Ostrogoths (or East Goths) in 375 A.D., and invaded Gaul with the Suevi and Vandals in 406, and Spain in 409. They were defeated (c418) by the Visigoths (or West Goths) and disappeared as a nation in the 5th century.

Alantika (ä.län'ti.kä). Mountain range in W central Africa, in Adamawa, on the border between Nigeria and Cameroun. Average elevation, ab. 5,000 ft.

Alanus ab (or **de**) **Insulis** (ạ.lā'nus ab, dē, in'sụ.lis). Latinized name of **Alain de Lille.**

Alanya (ä.län'yä). [Also: **Alaiye, Alaya.**] Town in S Turkey, ab. 75 mi. SE of Antalya, on the coast of the Mediterranean Sea, in a rich lowland area producing cotton, tobacco, wheat, grapes, and barley. It has a small flour mill and a macaroni factory. Pop. ab. 6,000.

Alaotra (ä.lä.ō'trä), **Lake.** Largest lake in Madagascar, NW of Tamatave. Length, ab. 30 mi.; width, ab. 5 mi.

Alapaevsk (ä.lä.pä'yifsk). [Also, **Alapayevsk.**] Town in the U.S.S.R., in the Sverdlovsk *oblast* (region) of the Russian Soviet Federated Socialist Republic; situated on the Neiva River ab. 80 mi. NE of the city of Sverdlovsk. High-grade iron and aluminum ores are found near it, and it is an iron-smelting center. Pop. ab. 12,000.

Alapaha (ạ.lap'ạ.hä). [Also, **Allapaha.**] River in S Georgia, which flows S into N Florida, a tributary of the Suwannee.

Alapalli (ạ.lap'ạ.li). See **Alleppey.**

Al Araf (äl ä'räf). In Mohammedan theology, a partition between heaven and hell (described in the Koran, *Surah,* vii. 44) in which may be found the souls of those who have not yet entered into heaven but desire to do so. It is regarded by some as a limbo for the patriarchs and prophets, or for other holy persons, and by others as a place of abode for those whose good and evil works are about equally balanced.

Alarbus (ạ.lär'bus). In *Titus Andronicus,* attributed to Shakespeare, a son of Tamora, queen of the Goths.

Alarcón (ä.lär.kōn'), **Hernando de.** b. (possibly) at Trujillo, Spain, 1500; date of death not known. Spanish navigator and sea captain. He was sent (c1540) to support by sea Francisco Vasquez de Coronado's expedition into what is now the southwestern U.S., and proved by penetration of the Gulf of California that California was not an island. The first to explore the Colorado River, he made two attempts to ascend it, planting a cross (subsequently found by Melchior Diaz) at the highest point he reached. His report is contained in Hakluyt's *Voyages.*

Alarcón, Pedro Antonio de. b. at Guadix, in Granada, Spain, March 10, 1833; d. at Madrid, July 20, 1891. Spanish poet, novelist, journalist, and politician. He accompanied the Spanish army to Morocco as a newspaper correspondent in 1859, and in 1864 was elected a member of the Cortes from Cádiz.

Alarcone (ä.lär.kō'nā). In Torquato Tasso's *Jerusalem Delivered,* the king of Barca who fought against the Crusaders with the Egyptians.

Alarcón y Mendoza (ä.lär.kōn' ē men.dō'thä), **Juan Ruiz de.** b. at Taxco, Mexico, c1580; d. at Córdoba, Spain, Aug. 4, 1639. Spanish dramatic poet. He went to Spain after 1606, obtained a position under the Council of the Indies, and began to publish his comedies in 1628. They are regarded by some judges as the finest in the Spanish language. Perhaps the best known is *La Verdad sospechosa,* which was imitated by Corneille in *Le Menteur.*

Alard (ȧ.lȧr), **Jean Delphin.** b. at Bayonne, France, March 8, 1815; d. Feb. 22, 1888. French violinist, music teacher, and composer. Taught (1843–75) at the Paris conservatory, where he included Sarasate among his pupils.

Alardo (ä.lär'dō). Younger brother of Bradamant in Ariosto's *Orlando Furioso.*

À la recherche du temps perdu (ȧ lȧr.shersh dü täṅ per.dü). French novel (1913–27: in 13 to 16 vols., depending on the edition; Eng. trans., *Remembrance of Things Past,* 1922–32) by the French writer Marcel Proust (1871–1922). The individual parts of the novel are *Du côté de chez Swann* (1913; Eng. trans., *Swann's Way*), *A l'ombre des jeunes filles en fleurs* (1918; Eng. trans., *Within a Budding Grove*), *Du côté de Guermantes* (1920; Eng. trans., *Guermantes Way*), *Sodome et Gomorrhe* (4 vols. 1921–1922; Eng. trans., *Cities of the Plain*), *La Prisonnière* (2 vols., 1923; Eng. trans., *The Captive*), *Albertine disparue* (2 vols., 1925; Eng. trans., *The Sweet Cheat Gone*), and *Le Temps retrouvé* (2 vols., 1927; Eng. trans., *Time Regained*). Essentially a reconstruction of memories projected into fiction, the series records the disintegration of the French aristocracy and the rise to social primacy of the rich middle class.

Alaric (al'ạ.rik). b. on the island of Peucè, in the Danube, c370; d. at Cosentia, Italy, 410. King of the West Goths (or Visigoths) and conqueror of Rome. He commanded the Gothic auxiliaries under the emperor Theodosius in the war against Eugenius and Arbogastes (394), but left the Roman service upon the death of Theodosius and was elected (395) king of the West Goths. In the same year he invaded Greece but was compelled by Stilicho to retire (396) to Epirus; appointed prefect of eastern Illyricum by Arcadius; invaded Italy (400) but halted by Stilicho at Polentia (402); appointed prefect of western Illyricum by Honorius; invaded Italy (408) and after twice besieging Rome, captured and sacked it on Aug. 24, 410. He died while making preparations for an invasion of Sicily and Africa.

Alaric II. Killed in battle near what is now Poitiers, France, 507. King (484 *et seq.*) of the West Goths (or Visigoths); defeated and slain by Clovis, king of the Franks. He established a commission to draw up *Breviarium Alaricianum* (Breviary of Alaric), which was based on Roman law and formed a legal code for his subjects in Spain.

Alascans (ạ.las'kạnz). Name given to the foreign Protestants in London during the reign of Edward VI, taken from the name of the superintendent of the foreign (German, French, and other) churches in London, John Laski, a Polish refugee and follower of Zwingli.

Alasco (ạ.las'kō). [Also called **Dr. Demetrius Doboobie.**] Old astrologer in Sir Walter Scott's novel *Kenilworth,* secretly in the employ of Richard Varney.

Alaşehir (ä.lä.she.hėr'). [Also: **Alashehr** (-sher'); ancient name, **Philadelphia.**] Town in W Turkey, situated on the slope of Tmolus ab. 80 mi. E of Izmir (formerly, Smyrna): a small trading center, on two railways, of some local importance in the export of wool. It is the seat of a Greek archbishopric. Pop. ab. 8,000.

Alaska (ạ.las'kạ). Territory of the U.S., in NW North America, the largest territorial unit under U.S. control (in square miles, including areas of inland water, it is slightly more than twice the size of Texas). It is bounded on the N by the Arctic Ocean, on the E by Canada, on the S by the Pacific Ocean, and on the W by Bering Strait and the Bering Sea. At its westernmost point, at the tip of the Seward Peninsula, it is only ab. 50 mi. by air from the easternmost point of Siberia, in the U.S.S.R. During and since World War II it has received considerable attention as a strategic military outpost by the tacticians of the U.S. Department of Defense. Capital, Juneau; area, 571,065 sq. mi. (land only), 586,378 sq. mi. (including areas of water); pop. 72,524 (1940), 128,643 (1950).

Terrain and Climate. The chief mountain ranges are the Alaska range in the S and C part of the territory, the Aleutian range, extending SW from the main body of the territory over a considerable part of the Aleutian peninsula (and often included under the Alaska range), the Brooks range, in the N part of the territory, N of the Arctic Circle, and the Coast range in the S part of the territory. The highest mountain is Mount McKinley, which is at its peak (20,300 ft.) not only the highest point in Alaska, but also the highest in North America. About 125 mi. SE of Mount McKinley is Matanuska Valley, notable for its fertility and relatively mild climate. The longest river in Alaska is the Yukon, which is navigable during the summer all the way from the Bering Sea to the territory of Yukon, under Canadian jurisdiction; its overall length of ab. 2,000 mi. makes it one of the longest rivers in North America. The seasonal temperature range in some parts of Alaska is considerable (at Fort Yukon, which lies almost exactly on the Arctic Circle, there are recorded instances of —78° Fahrenheit in the winter and of 100° Fahrenheit in the summer), but the greater part of the territory lies in the North Temperate Zone, S of the Arctic Circle, and considerable portions of the S coastal area are comparable in their climate to the NW coast of the U.S.

Industry, Agriculture, and Trade. Alaska's major exports derive chiefly from the territory's gold mines and fisheries: gold production in recent years has reached a peak of more than $25,000,000 per annum in value; exported fish, 90 percent of which are salmon, bring an annual revenue of millions of dollars. Agricultural products still play a comparatively modest part in Alaska's economy, but the development of such areas as the Matanuska Valley is expected vastly to increase their quantity and value. Other products of some importance include furs, lumber, and a growing volume of processed (either by canning or quick-freezing) fish.

History. The first white men known to have reached the area of what is now Alaska were members of the expedition headed by Vitus Bering, who touched on the islands off the coast in 1741 and claimed the area for Russia. It was not until 1784, more than 40 years later, that the Russians established their first permanent settlement (on Kodiak island), but Russian interest in the furs which could be obtained from Alaska was considerable almost from the time of Bering's voyage. In 1799, after many years of collection and marketing by individuals, the fur trade was consolidated officially in the hands of the Russian American Fur Company, under the direct management of Aleksandr Baranov, who proceeded forcefully and effectively to exploit the native inhabitants of Alaska, both fur-bearing and human. Baranov's tactics in dealing with the Aleuts, Tlingits, and other native tribes were ruthless to the point of inhumanity, but he made the territory a profitable one for his employers in Moscow and their agents in Alaska. After his death, in 1819, the value of Alaskan fur-exports declined, and when (as a result of the cost of the Crimean War and possible further difficulties with England) the Russian government was willing to consider selling the territory, an interested listener was found in U.S. Secretary of State William H. Seward. Largely through Seward's efforts, Alaska was purchased by the U.S. from Russia in 1867 for $7,200,000, but there were few in the U.S. at the time who could appreciate the value of the territory; Seward was ridiculed and abused for what was generally considered to be a piece of wanton extravagance involving the taxpayers' money. In 1897, however, the discovery of gold in the Yukon brought a complete reversal of this attitude, and by 1898 there had developed a rush of prospectors from the U.S. to Alaska that rivaled the California gold rush of 1849. It was at this time largely because of the now obvious value of the region that a boundary dispute between the U.S. and Canada concerning the extreme southern portion of Alaska reached a point of climax; it was solved, in favor of the U.S., by the Alaska Boundary Tribunal in 1903. During the first decade of the 20th century, as the quantity of easily accessible gold became steadily less, a considerable portion of the population of the territory returned to the U.S., and Alaska was for a short time seemingly destined to become once again a neglected appendage of one of the world's great powers. In the 1920's, however, completion of the Alaska railroad, an increasing amount of tourist interest, and the development of modest farming communities all combined to hasten a new development of the territory. A full understanding of the strategic importance of the region was brought home to most Americans by the events of World War II, and the status of the territory by the beginning of the sixth decade of the century was that of both a key military bastion and of a steadily developing economic asset to the U.S. as a whole.

Alaska Boundary Tribunal. Convention called (1903) between the U.S. and Great Britain to determine the boundary between SE Alaska and Canada. The Canadians had made claims to land which would give them access to the sea through inlets and thus facilitate transportation into the Klondike gold fields. The tribunal, composed of three Americans, two Canadians, and the Lord Chief Justice of England, met at London, and rejected the principal Canadian claims. The two Canadians dissented, but Lord Alverstone voted with the American delegation, thus arousing the charge that President Theodore Roosevelt had influenced his decision.

Alaska Highway. [Called the **"Alcan Highway"**; former names, **Alaska Military Highway, Alaskan International Highway.**] An all-weather highway for motor vehicles between Dawson Creek, in British Columbia, and Fairbanks, Alaska. Based on the distance between these two points, its length is generally given as 1,523 mi., but if certain branches and short feeder-roads are included it may be said to be some 150 mi. longer. It came into being as the result of an agreement between Canada and the U.S. in World War II, and was built (largely in the period March-November, 1942, although some work continued into 1943) by a force of some 10,000 men of the U.S. Army Corps of Engineers, aided by civilian contractors. Its primary purpose was to provide a wartime road-link between Alaska and supply bases in Canada and the U.S.; some authorities have questioned whether its military use in World War II ever justified its cost of approximately 139 million dollars, but the continuing strategic importance of Alaska makes it more than likely that the road will be a worthwhile long-term investment. The highway was maintained as a military road until April, 1946, when the 1,221-mile section of it that lies in Canada was turned over by the U.S. military authorities to administration by the Canadian government. However, it was not opened for ordinary tourist traffic until 1948, since which time a considerable number of people have driven over all or part of its length (overnight accommodations and gasoline stations are maintained at intervals along its route). Its width is at no point less than 24 ft., and it has no grades of more than four percent. The name "Alcan Highway," which is still used by many people, has had no official status since 1945.

Alaska Peninsula. Peninsula in SW Alaska, extending toward the Aleutians from Iliamna Lake, and partly enclosing the Bering Sea.

Alaska Range. Mountain range in S Alaska. Its highest peak, Mount McKinley (20,300 ft.), is also the highest in North America.

Alaska-Yukon-Pacific Exposition (ạ.las'kạ.ū'kon.pạ.sif'ik). Exposition held at Seattle, Wash., from June to October, 1909, for the purpose of exhibiting the resources and demonstrating the progress of northwestern America and the Pacific coast generally. It occupied 250 acres of the campus of the University of Washington.

Alassio (ä.läs'syō). Town and commune in N Italy, in the *compartimento* (region) of Liguria, in the province of Savona, situated on the Gulf of Genoa, ab. 48 mi. SW of Genoa: a fashionable winter health resort and bathing place on the Italian Riviera, favored by English tourists. It is also a fishing port. Buildings of interest to tourists suffered little damage during World War II; the church of San Ambrogio is intact. Pop. of commune, 8,090 (1936); of town, 5,609 (1936).

Alastor (a̦.las′to̦r). In Greek mythology, a surname of Zeus as the avenger; also applied to any avenging deity or demon.

Alastor. In medieval demonology, a spirit of evil who carries out the sentences of the king of hell.

Alastor. Poem by Shelley, published in 1816, named from its chief character, "Alastor or the Spirit of Solitude."

Alatau or **Ala Tau** (ä.lä.tou′). Series of mountain ranges located around and near the lake Issyk Kul in C Asia.

Alatheus (a̦.lā′thē̦.us) or **Odotheus** (o̦.dō′thē̦.us). d. 386 A.D. Military leader of the East Goths (Ostrogoths).

Alatri (ä.lä′trē). [Ancient name, **Alatrium.**] Town and commune in C Italy, in the *compartimento* (region) of Latium, in the province of Frosinone, situated on a hillside above the Cosa River, ab. 45 mi. SE of Rome. It has stone quarries and garment factories. There are many important architectural remains from Roman antiquity. The Church of Santa Maria Maggiore is in the Romanesque style of the early Middle Ages. The town was active on the side of the Papacy in the struggle against Emperor Frederick II. Considerable damage was suffered during World War II by some buildings of tourist interest; the Church of San Francesco, however, is intact. Pop. of commune, 18,616 (1936); of town, 4,702 (1936).

Alatyr (ä.lä.tir′). Town in the U.S.S.R., in the Chuvash Autonomous Soviet Socialist Republic of the Russian Soviet Federated Socialist Republic, on the Sura River ab. 125 mi. SW of Kazan: agricultural trade; machinery and lumber industries. Pop. ab. 22,000.

Alausí (ä.lou.sē′). Town in C Ecuador, in Chimborazo province. 12,238 (est. 1944).

Álava (ä′lä.ʙä). Province in N Spain, bounded on the N by Vizcaya and Guipúzcoa, on the E by Navarra, on the S by Logroño, and on the W by Burgos. It is one of the Basque provinces, preserving Basque language and customs. The terrain is generally mountainous, the climate more humid than in other parts of Spain. Capital, Vitoria; area, 1,175 sq. mi.; pop. 122,334 (1950).

Álava, Miguel Ricardo de. b. at Vitoria, Spain, 1771; d. at Barèges, France, 1843. Spanish politician and general. He fought under Wellington in the Peninsular campaign, attaining the rank of brigadier general; president of the Cortes (1822); fought in the same year under Ballasteros and Murillo in support of the Cortes against the rebels; went into exile (1823) on the restoration of Ferdinand by French intervention; espoused the cause of Maria Christina against Don Carlos on the death of Ferdinand; was ambassador to London (1834) and to Paris (1835); retired to France after the insurrection of La Granja.

Álava y Navarete (ē nä.ʙä.rā′tā), **Ignacio Maria de.** b. at Vitoria, Álava, Spain, c1750; d. at Chiclana, near Cádiz, Spain, May 26, 1817. Spanish admiral and explorer. He is best known for his voyage of circumnavigation of the globe, begun in 1794, in which he explored the coasts of South America and the East Indies, and added considerably to the geographical knowledge of his day. He commanded a squadron at Trafalgar, and in 1816 was made grand admiral and chief of marine.

Alaya (ä.lä′yä). See **Alanya.**

Alayrac (då.lā.råk), **Nicolas d'.** See **Dalayrac** or **d'Alayrac, Nicolas.**

Alazan (ä.lä.zän′). River in the U.S.S.R., in the Azerbaijan Soviet Socialist Republic, a northern tributary of the Kura. Length, ab. 150 mi.

Alba (äl′bä). [Ancient name, **Alba Pompeia.**] Town and commune in NW Italy, in the *compartimento* (region) of Piedmont, in the province of Cuneo, situated on the Tanaro River, ab. 31 mi. SE of Turin. It is a commercial town, with brickyards, machine factories, distilleries, and a large trade in wine, grain, and cattle; it is one of the wine centers of Piedmont. There are Roman remains and the Cathedral of San Lorenzo in Gothic-Lombard style. A member of the Lombard League in the Middle Ages, Alba became later part of the territory of Monferrato; it was incorporated into Sardinia at the end of the 18th century. Some damage was suffered during World War II by buildings of tourist interest, but repairs have now been completed or are being carried out. Pop. of commune 17,308 (1936); of town, 11,072 (1936).

Alba (al′ba̦), Duke of. See **Berwick and Alba,** Duke of.

Albacete (äl.bä.thā′tā). Province in E Spain, bounded by Cuenca on the N, Valencia and Alicante on the E, Murcia on the SE, Granada on the S, and Jaén and Ciudad Real on the W. The province is partly mountainous, arid, and thinly settled. Livestock raising is more important than agriculture; iron and copper are mined. Capital, Albacete; area, 5,739 sq. mi.; pop. 400,821 (1950).

Albacete. [Arabic, **Al-basit.**] City in E Spain, the capital of the province of Albacete, situated on the Canal de Albacete (or Canal de María Cristina) and the junction of the Júcar and Segura rivers, ab. 138 mi. SE of Madrid. One of the larger towns of Castile, it is a center of the grain trade, manufactures fine cutlery and matches, and is known for its fairs. The irrigation system dates from the period of Charles IV. 71,822 (1950).

Alba de Liste (äl′ʙä dā lē′stā), Count of. See **Henríquez de Guzmán, Luis.**

Alba Fucense (äl′bä fö.chen′zā). [Also: **Albe;** Latin, **Alba Fucentia.**] Village near Avezzano, in C Italy, in the province of Aquila. It contains an ancient amphitheater of the usual Roman elliptical plan, 114 by 305 ft., estimated to have seated 20,000 people. The arena measures 68 by 159 ft. The Church of San Pietro, damaged in the earthquake of 1915, was not further harmed in World War II, although repairs of the original damage had still not been completed.

Alba Iulia (äl′bä yö′lyä). [Also: **Alba Julia;** German, **Karlsburg,** formerly **Weissenburg;** Hungarian, **Gyulafehérvár;** Latin, **Apulum.**] Town in NW Rumania, in the province of Transylvania, situated on the Mureş River, ab. 30 mi. NW of Sibiu. It is a railroad junction, in a wine-growing region. Since the 11th century seat of a bishopric, it is now that of a Roman Catholic bishopric; it was the seat also of the Transylvanian princes from the 16th century. Once a Roman colony, it now has a museum of Roman discoveries. There is a beautiful Romanesque cathedral with the tomb of the Hungarian national hero János Hunyadi, and a college for priests. The citadel, known as the Karlsburg, was built by the emperor Charles VI in 1716–35. The town was long a center of the Rumanian nationalist movement; here, in 1918, the National Committee of Transylvania proclaimed union with Rumania. On Oct. 15, 1922, the coronation of King Ferdinand I and Queen Marie took place here. 14,420 (1948).

Alba Longa (al′ba̦ long′ga̦). In ancient geography, a town in Latium, Italy, ab. 15 mi. SE of Rome, the ancient center of the Latin League. Its foundation is traditionally ascribed to Ascanius, son of Aeneas, and its destruction (665 B.C.) to Tullus Hostilius.

Alba Marla or **Albamarla** (al.ba̦.mär′la̦). Medieval Latin name of **Aumale.**

Albamonte (äl.bä.mōn′tā), **Giuseppe.** See **Abamonti** or **Albamonte, Giuseppe.**

Alban (ôl′ba̦n, al′-), Saint. Killed at Verulamium (now St. Albans, Hertfordshire, England), c304. Roman soldier and first martyr of Britain, executed for sheltering a Christian priest. He is said to have been a native of the town where he was killed. The famous monastery of Saint Alban was founded in his honor by King Offa c795. His festival is celebrated in the Roman Catholic Church on June 22, and in the Anglican Church on June 17.

Albanenses (al.ba̦.nen′sēz). Small medieval sect, named from the city of Alba in Piedmont, Italy, which professed Manichaean doctrines. They were closely allied to the Albigenses.

Alban Hills (al′ba̦n). [Italian, **Monti Laziali, Monti Albani.**] Mountain group SE of Rome, near Albano Laziale. Its highest point is Monte Cavo.

Albani (äl.bä′nē), Mme. **Emma.** [Stage name of **Marie Louise Cécile Emma Lajeunesse.**] b. at Chambly, near Montreal, Nov. 1, 1852; d. at London, 1930. Canadian operatic soprano. She derived her stage name from Albany, N.Y., where she moved with her family in 1864.

Albani or **Albano** (äl.bä′nō), **Francesco.** b. at Bologna, Italy, 1578; d. there, 1660. Italian painter. A student with Guido Reni under Calvaert and the Carracci, he produced over 40 altarpieces and a number of frescoes.

Albani, Giovanni Francesco. Original name of Pope **Clement XI.**

Albani, Giovanni Girolamo. b. at Bergamo, Italy, 1504; d. 1591. Italian soldier, diplomat, and cardinal.

Albani, Mathias. b. 1621; d. at Botzen, 1673. Violinmaker, a pupil of Stainer.

Albani, Villa. Palace in the N part of Rome, celebrated for its art collections.

Albania (al.bā'ni.ą). In ancient geography, a country of W Asia, lying W of the Caspian Sea, N of Armenia, and E of Iberia, and corresponding nearly to the modern Azerbaijan and S Daghestan in the U.S.S.R. It was part of the Assyrian empire, and the theater of some of the wars of Sargon and Sennacherib.

Albania. [Albanian, **Shqipni**; French **Albanie**; German, **Albanien**; Serbo-Croatian, **Albanija**; Turkish, **Arnautlik.**] Country in SE Europe, bounded by Yugoslavia on the N and E, Greece and the Ionian Sea on the S, and the Ionian Sea, the Strait of Otranto, and the Adriatric Sea on the W. It corresponds largely to the ancient Illyria and part of Epirus. Occupied by the Turks in the first part of the 15th century, it revolted (1443–67) under Scanderbeg, and was subdued by the Turks in 1478. Several rebellions against the Turks occurred about the beginning of the 19th century. Albania resisted the treaty of Berlin (1878) and the cession of territory to Montenegro in 1880. It was annexed (1939) by Italy, but regained its independence in 1946. The country is largely mountainous or hilly. The inhabitants are almost entirely engaged in agricultural and pastoral activities. Corn and wheat are the chief subsistence crops. The only railroad line in the country runs between the port of Durrës and Tirana. The Moslem religion is predominant, but there is a large Christian minority. Capital, Tirana; area, 10,629 sq. mi.; pop. 1,150,000 (est. 1947).

Albania. Ancient name of **Aubagne.**

Albaniae Pylae (al.bā'ni.ē pī'lē). See **Caspian Gates.**

Albanian (al.bā'ni.ąn). Language of the Albanians, a member of the Indo-European family. It shows heavy borrowings from Latin and also from Greek, Turkish, and Slavic. It is supposed to be the descendant of the ancient Illyrian, of which only scanty records are extant. The two chief dialects are Tosk and Geg. Albanian is also called Skipetar, from the native name of the people (Shgipetár, meaning "highlanders").

Albanian Gates. See **Caspian Gates.**

Albano (äl.bä'nō), **Lake.** [Italian, **Lago di Albano, Lago di Castello;** Latin, **Albanus Lacus.**] Small lake in C Italy, near Albano Laziale, noted for its picturesque scenery, occupying the crater of an extinct volcano and drained by an underground channel constructed in the 4th century B.C.

Albano, Monte (or **Mount**). See **Cavo, Monte.**

Albano Laziale (lä.tsyä'lā). [Ancient name, **Albanum.**] Town and commune in C Italy, in the *compartimento* (region) of Latium, in the province of Roma, situated in the Alban Hills, ab. 13½ mi. SE of Rome. The town, in a beautiful location near Lake Albano, is the center of a wine and olive growing district. It contains a number of churches dating from the Middle Ages and the 18th century, and the palatial country homes of the Roman nobility. There are some architectural remains from ancient times, particularly of the villa of Pompey and a pretorian camp built by Domitian. The papal summer residence at Castel Gandolfo is nearby. The town was incorporated into the Papal States in 1697. Damage was suffered during World War II by some buildings of tourist interest, but repairs have now been completed or are being carried out. Pop. of commune, 11,469 (1936); of town, 9,414 (1936).

Albanova (äl.bä.nô'vä). Town and commune in S Italy, in the *compartimento* (region) of Campania, in the province of Napoli, N of Naples. It belongs to the metropolitan region of Naples and has a considerable agricultural trade with that city. Pop. of commune, 17,875 (1936); of town, 9,351 (1936).

Albany (ôl'bą.ni). See also **Breadalbane.**

Albany, Countess of. [Title of **Louise Maria Caroline Stuart.**] b. 1753; d. at Florence, Italy, Jan. 29, 1824. German princess; daughter of Gustavus Adolphus, prince of Stolberg-Gedern, and wife (married March 28, 1772) of the "Young Pretender," Charles Edward Stuart, Duke of Albany. She was later (1784–1803) the mistress of Vittorio Alfieri.

Albany. Small seaport in SW Australia, in the state of Western Australia, situated on King George Sound, ab. 250 mi. SE of Perth. 4,761 (1947).

Albany. Residential city in C California, in Alameda County, NE of San Francisco. 17,590 (1950).

Albany. City in SW Georgia, capital of Dougherty County, on the Flint River at the head of navigation, ab. 90 mi. SW of Macon: packing center for the pecan orchards of the surrounding region. 31,155 (1950).

Albany. City in E New York, capital of the state and county seat of Albany County: inland seaport and port of entry. It is an important shipping center on the Mohawk route for petroleum, soda ash, and wheat, and has manufactures of automobile accessories, sheet metal, paper, clay products, chemicals, and iron products. It is the seat of the New York State College for Teachers, the College of Saint Rose, the Albany College of Pharmacy, the Albany Law School, and the Dudley Observatory of Union College. Among its notable old houses is the Schuyler Mansion. Albany was settled by the Dutch in 1614, was granted a city charter in 1686, and was the meeting place of the Albany Congress (1754), which approved Benjamin Franklin's plan to form a colonial union; it became the permanent state capital in 1797. Pop. of city, 130,577 (1940), 134,995 (1950); of urbanized area (including Troy), 291,897 (1950).

Albany. City in W Oregon, county seat of Linn County, at the confluence of the Calapooya and Willamette rivers ab. 63 mi. SW of Portland: trading and shipping center for an agricultural region producing chiefly wool, grain, rye-grass, vetch seed, and cascara bark. Manufactures include leather, chairs, boxes, iron, dairy and meat products, and flour. It was founded in 1848. Pop. 10,115 (1950).

Albany, Duke of. Character in Shakespeare's *King Lear*, the husband of Goneril, Lear's eldest daughter.

Albany Congress. Congress at Albany, N.Y., called in 1754 at the behest of the British government with the aim of winning the confidence of the Iroquois and obtaining their aid in the conflict with France. The chiefs of the Iroquois met with commissioners from Pennsylvania, Maryland, New York, Connecticut, Massachusetts, New Hampshire, and Rhode Island, but the negotiations with the Indians were inconclusive. The outstanding accomplishment of the congress was its adoption of the so-called Albany Plan of colonial union set forth by Benjamin Franklin. It provided for an improved scheme of colonial defense and a more effective supervision and control of Indian affairs. The plan called for a general government in which each colony would retain its separate identity; the executive would be appointed by the crown, while the delegates would be named by the various colonial legislative bodies. The British crown rejected the plan as an invasion of royal powers; the colonies frowned upon the scheme because it seemed to them a threat to their independence. The Albany Plan, even though never placed in operation, had a genuine value, for it served as a guide to the basis of union in the critical years between 1765 and the beginning of the Revolutionary War.

Albany Convention. Meeting of military and civil officers of Albany which gathered on Aug. 1, 1689, and established an interim regime awaiting the instructions of the British crown. The threat of armed attack by the French led the convention to request support from Jacob Leisler, then in power in lower New York; when Leisler refused, and the French attack materialized, the convention finally agreed to make Leisler commander in chief.

Albany Regency. Name given to a clique of New York politicians who controlled (c1820–54) the machinery of the Democratic Party in the state of New York. It is generally recognized as the first fully developed political machine in the U.S. Among its members were Martin Van Buren, William L. Marcy, Azariah C. Flagg, Silas Wright, John A. Dix, and Benjamin F. Butler.

Albany River. River in N Ontario, Canada, flowing into James Bay. Length, ab. 610 mi.

Alba Pompeia (al'bą pom.pē'ą). Ancient name of **Alba.**

Albareto di Borgotaro (äl.bä.rā'tō dē bôr.gō.tä'rō). A former name of **Borgo Val di Taro.**

Albatross (al'bą.tros). New England sailing vessel used by W. P. Hunt of the Pacific Fur Company in withdrawing from the Astoria fur post upon learning of the commencement of hostilities (1812) between the U.S. and Great Britain. It was Hunt's object to prevent seizure by the British of the American-owned furs at Astoria.

Albay (äl.bī'). Province in SE Luzon, Philippine Islands. It is bounded by Camarines Sur on the N, the Pacific Ocean and Sorsogon on the E, Sorsogon on the S, and the Burias Pass on the SW and W. Besides its area in Luzon it includes several islands, among them Catanduanes and Batan. Albay, including Catanduanes, is the largest abacá-producing province of the Philippines. A good quality of coal is mined in Batan. Gold and mercury are reported in other parts of the province. The NE coast is indented by Albay Gulf. Mountains extend from E to W, the eastern extremity being Mayon volcano. The inhabitants are chiefly Bicols. Capital, Legaspi; area, 1,554 sq. mi.; pop., including Catanduanes, 506,815 (1948).

Albay. Former capital of Albay province, SE Luzon, Philippine Islands: now incuded in Legaspi, on the W side of Albay Gulf.

Albay Gulf. Gulf on the NE coast of Albay province, SE Luzon, in the Philippine Islands.

Albazin (äl.bä.zēn'). [Also: **Albasin, Yaksa.**] Former fortified town in the U.S.S.R., in what is now the Chita *oblast* (region) of the Russian Soviet Federated Socialist Republic, on the northern bend and along the gorges of the Amur River: a center of Russian colonization in the 17th century.

Albe (äl'bā). See **Alba Fucense.**

Albe (dȧlb), Baron **Bacler d'.** See **Bacler d'Albe, Louis Albert Ghislam,** Baron.

Albee (ôl'bē̜), **Edward Franklin.** b. at Machias, Me., Oct. 8, 1857; d. at Palm Beach, Fla., March 11, 1930. American theater-chain manager and owner. Organize the Keith-Albee vaudeville circuit of approximately 70 theaters with B. F. Keith; president of the Keith-Albee vaudeville exchange, which at one time handled bookings for vaudeville players in 317 theaters in the U.S. an Canada.

Albee, Ernest. b. at Langdon, N.H., Aug. 8, 1865 d. May 25, 1927. American philosopher and author. He was on the faculty of Cornell's Sage School of Philosophy as an instructor (1892–1902), an assistant professor (1902–07), and professor (1907–27). Author of *The History of English Utilitarianism* (1902), which was the best and most comprehensive work in that field in its time.

Albee, Fred Houdlett. b. at Alna, Me., April 13, 1876; d. at New York, Feb. 15, 1945. American orthopedic surgeon and specialist in bone grafting. Author of *Bone Graft Surgery* (1915), *Orthopedic and Reconstructional Surgery* (1919), *Injuries and Diseases of the Hip* (1937), and numerous technical pamphlets.

Albeladory (al.bel.ä.dōr'i). See **Beladori, Abul Hassan Ahmed al-.**

Albemarle (al'bē̜.märl). Town in S central North Carolina, county seat of Stanly County: agricultural marketing center; lumber and brickyards; manufactures of textiles, cottonseed oil, and flour. It was incorporated as a town in 1842. Pop. 11,798 (1950).

Albemarle. Confederate ironclad ram, built on the Roanoke River ab. 30 mi. below Weldon, N.C., in 1863. She did much damage to Union shipping during the spring of 1864, but was destroyed by Lieutenant W. B. Cushing during the night of Oct. 27, 1864. He attacked her in a small launch carrying a torpedo. Forcing his way within the chain of logs which formed part of her defense, he exploded the torpedo under the ram's overhang. (Cushing's daring exploit made him a national hero for the rest of his life. Although the feat can hardly be said to have materially hastened the Union victory, it is nevertheless, and quite understandably, one of the most often told stories of individual bravery in the U.S. Navy.) The *Albemarle* was afterward raised, towed to Norfolk, and in 1867 stripped and sold.

Albemarle, 1st Duke of. See **Monck** or **Monk, George.**

Albemarle, 1st Earl of. See **Keppel, Arnold Joost van.**

Albemarle. English name of **Aumale,** medieval countship.

Albemarle and Chesapeake Canal. Inland waterway in NE North Carolina, constructed (1856–60) as a link between Albemarle Sound and Chesapeake Bay. It consists of two canals, set 30 mi. from each other; one joins Currituck Sound with the North River, while the other links North Landing River with the Elizabeth River.

Albemarle Point. See under **Charleston,** S.C.

Albemarle Sound. Shallow body of water in the NE part of North Carolina, separated from the Atlantic by sand beaches, and communicating with Pamlico Sound on the S through Croatan and Roanoke Sounds. It receives the Roanoke, Chowan, and Alligator rivers, and is connected with Chesapeake Bay by the Albemarle and Chesapeake Canal and the Dismal Swamp Canal. Length, ab. 55 mi.

Albenga (äl.beng'gä). [Latin: **Albium Ingaunum, Albingaunum.**] Town and commune in NW Italy, in the *compartimento* (region) of Liguria, in the province of Savona, situated near the Cento River on the Riviera di Ponente, between Genoa and San Remo. It contains a Roman bridge and the Gothic Cathedral of San Michele. Some damage was suffered during World War II by buildings of tourist interest; however, the Baptistery, the *Duomo* (cathedral), the Chapel of Santa Maria in Fontibus, and the Ponte Lungo are intact. Pop. of commune, 10,698 (1936); of town, 5,848 (1936).

Albéniz (äl.bā'nēth), **Isaac.** b. at Camprodón, Spain, May 29, 1860; d. in the Pyrenees, 1909. Spanish composer and pianist. He studied under Franz Liszt, and was appointed official pianist to the queen of Spain. During his lifetime he made a number of international concert tours, and wrote several operas and zarzuelas (a kind of operetta), but he is now best known for piano works such as *Iberia* and *Catalonia,* which are based on Spanish folk melodies.

Albéniz, Pedro. b. at Logroño, Spain, April 14, 1795; d. at Madrid, April 12, 1855. Spanish organist, pianist, and composer. Choirmaster at San Sebastián and subsequently first organist at the Capilla Real, he is noted for his compositions for the pianoforte.

Alberdi (äl.ber'dē), **Juan Bautista.** b. in Argentina, 1810; d. at Paris, 1884. Argentine political scientist, jurist, and sociologist. Exiled (1839–52) for opposition to the dictator, J. M. de Rosas, he was important as a political adviser and diplomat in the administration of Urquiza that followed the overthrow of Rosas. He published (1852) at Valparaíso, his *Base for the Organization of the Argentine Republic* (which he wrote in five days), and contributed in great part to the framing of the Argentine constitution.

Alberdingk Thijm (äl'bėr.dingk tīm'), **Karel J. L.** See **Deyssel, Lodewijk van.**

Albères Mountains (ȧl.ber). [French, **Monts Albères.**] The eastern ramification of the Pyrenees, between Spain and the department of Pyrénées-Orientales, France.

Alberic I (al'bėr.ik). Killed by the Romans at Orta, Italy, c925. Lombard nobleman, patrician (also called senator, consul, and prince) of the Romans and duke of Spoleto; expelled from Rome by Pope John X. He married Marozia, daughter of Theodora.

Alberic II. d. 954. Patrician and senator of the Romans; son of Alberic I and Marozia.

Alberoni (äl.bā.rō'nē), **Giulio.** b. near Piacenza, Italy, 1664; d. 1752. Statesman and cardinal. Representative of the Duke of Parma at the Spanish court; negotiator of the marriage of Philip V and Elizabeth Farnese; prime minister of Spain (1715–19). His foreign policy led to the Quadruple Alliance and a war disastrous to Spain; exiled from Spain, he spent his last years in Italy.

Albers (äl'bėrs), **Johann Friedrich Hermann.** b. at Dorsten, Westphalia, Nov. 14, 1805; d. at Bonn, May 12, 1867. German physician and professor at Bonn, author of *Atlas der pathologischen Anatomie* (1832–62), and others.

Albers, Josef. b. in Westphalia, Germany, 1888—. Abstract painter, glass designer, photographer, and typographer, who has been in recent years a teacher at Black Mountain College, North Carolina, and guest lecturer at Harvard University. He obtained his schooling at Berlin in the Royal Art School. He has painted much of his work on glass and has sandblasted designs on glass surfaces with an original process devised by him.

Albers-Schönberg (äl'bėrs.shėn'berk), **Heinrich Ernst.** b. at Hamburg, Germany, Jan. 21, 1865; d. there, June 4, 1921. German roentgenologist. He founded (1897) an institute of roentgenology at Hamburg and became the first specialist in this field. He was appointed (1919) professor of roentgenology at the University of Hamburg.

He described (1903–04) a bone-marrow disease (osteopetrosis) causing marmorization of the long bones, called also marble bones or ivory bones, and named after him.

Albert (al′bėrt). Antipope in 1102. He claimed the papacy in opposition to Pascal II.

Albert (ål.ber). [Called **"l'ouvrier Albert,"** meaning "Albert the Worker"; original name, **Alexandre Martin.**] b. at Bury, Oise, France, April 27, 1815; d. at Mello, Oise, France, May 28, 1895. French politician and workingman, known chiefly as a member of the provisional government of the Second French Republic (February–May, 1848). He served as vice-president of the so-called "Luxembourg commission." He was sentenced to deportation for complicity in the riot of May 15, 1848, and recovered his liberty by the amnesty of 1859. In 1870 he took a prominent part in the defense of Paris against the Germans.

Albert (al′bėrt), Prince. [Full name, **Albert Francis Charles Augustus Emmanuel of Saxe-Coburg-Gotha.**] b. at the Rosenau, near Coburg, Germany, 1819; d. at Windsor Castle, 1861. Husband of Queen Victoria and prince consort of England; second son of the Duke of Saxe-Coburg-Gotha. He first met Queen Victoria in 1836; after their marriage (1840) he managed to overcome the initial distrust of the English people by his tact and diligent interest in the arts and scientific development; the great Exhibition of 1851 was successful largely through his efforts. He was given the formal title of Prince Consort in 1857; his death (1861) through typhoid fever plunged Victoria into the deepest grief and left a nation of friends to mourn him.

Albert (ål.ber). [Former name, **Ancre.**] Town in N France, in the department of Somme, situated on the Ancre River, ab. 28 mi. NE of Amiens. It is a center of the French metallurgical industry. Nearby, in Meaulte, are important airplane factories. The town, including the Church of Notre-Dame-de-Brebières, was almost completely destroyed in World War I and suffered damage again in World War II. The population declined from 7,343 in 1914 to 3,040 in 1924, but has since risen to a point slightly above the level before World War I. 8,900 (1946).

Albert (al′bėrt). In Goethe's *Sorrows of Werther*, a young farmer who marries Charlotte, with whom Werther is in love. He represents Kestner, one of Goethe's friends.

Albert. [Title, **Count of Geierstein** (gī′ėr.stīn).] Character in Sir Walter Scott's novel *Anne of Geierstein*, a restless intriguer and head of the Vehmgericht. Pursued by Charles of Burgundy, he takes refuge in a monastery and is known as the "Black Priest of St. Paul's." By order of the Vehmgericht he kills Charles of Burgundy in battle.

Albert, Blessed. See **Albert Avogadro.**

Albert (of *Austria*). [German, **Albrecht;** called **"Albert the Pious."**] b. 1559; d. 1621. Archduke of Austria, sixth son of Emperor Maximilian II; cardinal and diplomat. He was educated for the Church at the Spanish court, and became cardinal (1577) and archbishop (1584) of Toledo. After serving as viceroy of Portugal (1584–96) and governor of the Spanish Netherlands (1596), he forsook the Church in 1598 and married the Infanta Isabella of Spain. In his campaign against the Dutch he was defeated (1600) at Nieuport, in Flanders, by Maurice of Nassau. He subsequently concluded (1609) a 12-year armistice with the Netherlands.

Albert (of *Austria*). [Full German prename, **Friedrich Rudolph Albrecht.**] b. at Vienna, 1817; d. at Arco, in the Tirol, 1895. Archduke of Austria; eldest son of Archduke Charles of Austria. He was noted as a soldier, military writer, and proponent of the tactical theories of Radetsky. After serving (1848–49) in Italy, he was an Austrian commander (1860–63) there, and was there promoted to field marshal (1863) and commanded at the victory of Custozza (1866). He was made Austrian commander in chief in the same year, but assumed command too late to alter the outcome of the war with Prussia. He served (1866 *et seq.*) as inspector general in the reorganization of the Austrian army.

Albert I (of *Austria*). See **Albert I** (of *Germany*).

Albert II (of *Austria*). [German, **Albrecht.**] b. 1298 d. 1358. Duke of Austria and son of Albert I of Germany.

Albert III (of *Austria*). [German, **Albrecht.**] d. 1395. Son of Albert II of Austria. He ruled alone as duke of Austria (1379 *et seq.*).

Albert V (of *Austria*). See **Albert II** (of *Germany*).

Albert IV (of *Bavaria*). [German, **Albrecht;** called **"Albert the Wise."**] b. Dec. 15, 1447; d. March 18, 1508. Duke of Bavaria. In 1465, after the death of his oldest brother John, he became co-regent with his second brother Sigismund, and later (1467) sole ruler of Bavaria.

Albert I (of *Belgium*). b. at Brussels, April 8, 1875; d. Feb. 17, 1934. King of the Belgians; younger son of Philip, Count of Flanders, and nephew of Leopold II. As a ruler, he was popular and admired for his interest in social reforms in his country. He became heir presumptive to the throne after the death of the king's only son and the death of his own elder brother, Prince Baudouin. He married (Oct. 2, 1900) Elizabeth, daughter of Duke Charles Théodore of Bavaria. They had three children: Leopold, b. Nov. 3, 1901, later King Leopold III; Charles, b. Oct. 10, 1903, later prince regent; and Marie José, b. Aug. 4, 1906 (who married Prince Umberto of Italy, later (1946) for a short time king of Italy after his father's abdication). Albert became king of Belgium on Dec. 23, 1909. Taking command of the Belgian army at the outbreak of World War I, he remained at its head throughout the war, with headquarters at La Panne. He commanded the northern army group of French and Belgian troops in the final offensive of October, 1918, and entered Brussels amid popular enthusiasm on Nov. 22, 1918. Later he visited and worked to rehabilitate devastated areas. Albert traveled widely, visiting the U.S., England, South Africa, and the Belgian Congo. He was killed in an accidental fall while mountain climbing near Namur.

Albert (of *Brandenburg*). [German, **Albrecht;** called **"Albert Alcibiades."**] b. at Ansbach, Germany, March 28, 1522; d. at Pforzheim, Germany, Jan. 8, 1577. Margrave of Brandenburg, partisan and later opponent of the emperor Charles V. He was defeated by Maurice of Saxony at Sievershausen, near Lüneburg, in Hanover, on July 9, 1553.

Albert I (of *Brandenburg*). [German, **Albrecht;** called **"Albert the Bear."**] b. at Ballenstädt, Germany, c1100; d. there, 1170. Margrave of Brandenburg (1150 *et seq.*); son of Otto the Rich. He accompanied Emperor Frederick I (Frederick Barbarossa) on the Italian campaign (1162). His territories were divided (1169) among six sons, who carried on the line in his name.

Albert III (of *Brandenburg*). [German, **Albrecht;** called **"Albert Achilles," "Albert Ulysses."**] b. at Tangermünde, Prussia, 1414; d. at Frankfort on the Main, Germany, 1486. Elector of Brandenburg, third son of Frederick I, on whose death (1440) he acquired Ansbach. He inherited Bayreuth (1464) from his brother John, and Brandenburg (1470) from his brother Frederick II. He engaged in successful campaigns against Mecklenburg and Pomerania, and resisted the attempt of the Teutonic Knights to repossess Neumark. He was the author of *Dispositio Achillea* (1473), which some authorities believe to be the original instance in written German law of the custom of primogeniture.

Albert (of *Brandenburg-Ansbach*). [German, **Albrecht.**] b. at Ansbach, Germany, 1490; d. 1568. Margrave of Brandenburg-Ansbach, last grand master (1511 *et seq.*) of the Teutonic Knights, and first duke of Prussia; younger son of Frederick of Ansbach, who was the second son of Albert III of Brandenburg. He carried on war (1519–25) with the king of Poland in a futile attempt to regain the independence of Prussia, but secured, by the Treaty of Cracow (1525), the conversion of Prussia into a secular duchy, hereditary to his family. He championed the policies of Luther and introduced them (1525) to his realm. He was the founder (1544) of the University of Königsberg, Europe's third Protestant university.

Albert (of *Brunswick-Lüneburg*). [German, **Albrecht;** called **"Albert the Tall."**] b. 1236; d. Aug. 15, 1279. Duke of Brunswick-Lüneburg; son of the first duke, Otto the Child. He was captured (Oct. 27, 1263) by the sons of the margrave Henry, in the war of the Thuringian succession, and was released in 1264, on the payment of 8,000 marks in silver and the cession of the Guelph cities and castles on the Werra.

Albert I (of *Germany*). [German, **Albrecht.**] b. c1250; killed at Windisch, Switzerland, 1308. Duke of Austria (1282 *et seq.*) and king of Germany (1298 *et seq.*), who was murdered by his nephew John, thereafter called "the Parricide." At Göllheim, near Worms, he deposed Adolf of Nassau, his predecessor as king of Germany. Albert obtained Bohemia (1306) for his son, but failed in his campaign (1307) against Thuringia. His abolition of tolls on the Rhine, in existence since 1250, united the archbishops and the leading nobility of the Rhine against him.

Albert II (of *Germany*). [Also, **Albert V** (of *Austria*).] b. 1397; d. 1439. First Hapsburg Holy Roman Emperor; son-in-law of the Emperor Sigismund. His rule of Hungary, Austria, and Bohemia was marked by revolts. He died of dysentery during an unsuccessful war against the Turks.

Albert I (of *Mecklenburg* and *Schwerin*). [German, **Albrecht.**] b. c1317; d. 1379. Founder of the former reigning house of Mecklenburg, created duke of Mecklenburg in 1348 by Emperor Charles IV. He came into possession of the duchy of Schwerin in 1358, and secured the establishment of Albert, his second son by his first wife Euphemia of Sweden, as king of Sweden in 1365.

Albert (of *Meissen*). [German, **Albrecht**; called **"Albert the Proud."**] b. 1158; d. June 25, 1195. Margrave of Meissen from 1190 to 1195. In attempting to oppress his younger brother Dietrich, who had inherited Weissenfels, he incurred the enmity of Emperor Henry VI of Germany, and died by poison administered, it is said, by an agent of the emperor.

Albert I (of *Monaco*). [Full name, **Honoré Charles Grimaldi,** Prince **Albert I of Monaco.**] b. at Paris, Nov. 13, 1848; d. there, June 26, 1922. Prince of Monaco (1889–1922), notable as an oceanographer.

Albert (of *Prussia*). [Full German prename, **Albrecht Friedrich Heinrich.**] b. Oct. 4, 1809; d. Oct. 14, 1872 Prince of Prussia; fourth son of Frederick William III

Albert (of *Saxe-Teschen*). [German, **Kasimir Albrecht** title, Duke of **Saxe-Teschen.**] b. near Dresden, Germany, 1738; d. at Vienna, 1822. Austrian general; son o Augustus III of Poland. He was defeated (1792) by a French army under Dumouriez.

Albert (of *Saxony*). [Full German prename, **Albrecht Friedrich August.**] b. at Dresden, Germany, 1828; d. a the Castle of Sibyllenort, in Silesia, 1902. King o Saxony; son of King John of Saxony, whom he succeede on Oct. 29, 1873. He commanded an army corps in th Franco-Prussian War and later the army of the Meuse.

Albert III (of *Saxony*). [German, **Albrecht**; calle **"Albert the Bold."**] b. 1443; d. at Emden, Prussia 1500. Duke of Saxony; younger son of Frederick th Gentle, and founder of the Albertine Saxon line. He rule (1464–85) with his brother Ernest; in the division of th Saxon dominions under the treaty of Leipzig (1485) he received Meissen.

Albert II (of *Sweden*). [German, **Albrecht.**] d. 141 Son of Albert I of Mecklenburg and Schwerin; establishe as king of Sweden in 1365. He was defeated (Sept. 2 1389) by Queen Margaret of Denmark and Norwa (widow of Haakon) at the battle of Falköping, and take prisoner. On his release in 1395 he renounced the thron of Sweden.

Albert (of *Thuringia* and *Meissen*). [German, **Albrecht** called **"Albert the Bad."**] d. 1314. Landgrave o Thuringia after 1265, and margrave of Meissen fron 1288 to 1293. His second wife, Cunegonde of Eisenberg persuaded him to exclude his sons by his first marriag from the succession in Thuringia in favor of Apitz, his so by Cunegonde. A war followed, in which Albert was take captive by his son Frederick, and forced to sign a dis advantageous treaty at Rochlitz, on Jan. 1, 1289.

Albert (dal′bėrt; German, däl′bert), **Eugène Franci Charles d'.** b. at Glasgow, April 10, 1864; d. at Riga Latvia, 1932. Pianist and composer, at one time a pupi of Franz Lizt. After a début (1881) at London, he wa court conductor (1885) at Weimar and director (190 *et seq.*) of the Hochschule at Berlin. He made severa concert tours (1889–90, 1892, 1904–04) in the U.S., an was the composer of 16 operas, three concertos, a symphony, and other works.

Albert (äl′bėrt), **Heinrich.** b. at Lobenstein, Saxony 1604; d. at Königsberg, Oct. 6, 1651. German composer, organist, and poet; nephew and student of Heinrich Schütz, with whom he helped to create the form of later German opera and *lieder*.

Albert, Joseph. b. at Munich, 1825; d. there, 1886. German photographer; inventor of Albertype, a gelatine process of photomechanical printing which permits great numbers of copies from a single plate.

Albert (al′bėrt), **Lake.** [Also, **Albert Nyanza.**] Lake in E central Africa, on the border between Uganda and the Belgian Congo: one of the main sources of the Nile River. It was discovered by Sir Samuel Baker, on March 14, 1864. Length, ab. 97 mi.; area, ab. 2,064 sq. mi.

Albert (ål.ber), **Paul.** b. at Thionville, France, Dec. 14, 1827; d. at Paris, June 21, 1880. French literary historian.

Alberta (al.bėr′tạ). Westernmost of the prairie provinces of Canada, bounded on the N by the Mackenzie district of the Northwest Territories; on the W by British Columbia, from which it is separated by the Rocky Mountains; on the S by Montana; and on the E by the province of Manitoba. The province was created on Sept. 1, 1905 from the provisional districts of the Northwest Territories, which had been set up in 1882 and included the former district of Alberta, the W half of Athabaska, and a strip of Assiniboia and Saskatchewan. It is represented in the Dominion Parliament by 6 senators and 57 representatives, and has a legislative assembly of 17 members. Besides extensive areas suitable for grain-growing and ranching, Alberta has valuable reserves of coal and oil, first exploited on a large scale in the 1940's. Capital, Edmonton; area, 255,285 sq. mi. (including 6,485 sq. mi. of fresh water); pop. 939,501 (1951).

"Albert Achilles" (al′bėrt ạ.kil′ēz). See **Albert III** (of *Brandenburg*).

"Albert Alcibiades" (al.si.bī′ạ.dēz). See **Albert** (of *Brandenburg*).

Albert Avogadro (ä.vō.gä′drō). [Also, Blessed **Albert.**] b. at Gualteri, near Parma, Italy, 1149; d. 1215. Italian prelate and diplomat, canon regular of St. Augustine and patriarch of Jerusalem. He founded Carmelite houses at Ptolemais, Tyrus, Sarepta, Sidon, and Tripolis, and drew up a rule for this order which was of such extraordinary asceticism that it was later (1246) mitigated by Innocent IV. He took a prominent part in the attempt to mediate disputes which arose during his lifetime between the Holy See and the emperor Frederick Barbarossa.

Albert Edward Nyanza (ed′wạrd ni.an′zạ, nī-). Former name of **Edward, Lake.**

Albert Hall. A covered amphitheater in London, finished in 1871 and named in honor of Prince Albert, Queen Victoria's husband. Its axes are 270 and 240 ft., those of the arena 100 and 70 ft., and it can seat 8,000 persons.

Alberti (äl.ber′tē), **Conrad.** [Original surname, **Sittenfeld.**] b. at Breslau, July 9, 1862; d. at Berlin, June 24, 1918. German writer and editor. He was in business, turned actor, then settled at Berlin, where he joined the young revolutionaries of naturalism. Later he became editor of the Berlin *Abendpost.* Among his critical works are *Herr L'Arronge und das deutsche Theater* (1884), *Bettina von Arnim* (1885), and *Der moderne Realismus in der deutschen Literatur* (1889). Of his plays, *Brot* (1888) treats the historical Thomas Münzer, and *Im Suff!* (1890) is a satire on naturalism. He was tried and fined for his novel *Die Alten und die Jungen* (1889). This is one of six novels in a series called *Der Kampf ums Dasein.*

Alberti, Domenico. b. at Venice, c1710; d. at Formio, Italy, 1740. Venetian singer and composer known for sonatas utilizing a broken-chord bass accompaniment, since termed the "Alberti bass."

Alberti, Leon Battista. b. at Florence, 1404; d. at Rome, 1472. Italian poet, musician, painter, sculptor, and architect. His churches of Sant' Andrea at Mantua, San Francesco at Rimini, as well as the Palazzo Strozzi and façade for Santa Maria Novella at Florence, are early Renaissance landmarks; author of *De re aedificatoria* (1485), and others.

Albertina (äl.ber.tē′nä). Library and gallery at Vienna, built for the Austrian archduke Albert in 1804.

Albertine (ål.ber.tēn). Character in *À la recherche du temps perdu* (1913–27; Eng. trans., *Remembrance of Things Past*, 1922–32), by Marcel Proust; object of the pathologically jealous love of Marcel, the narrator.

Albertine Line (al′bėr.tin, -tēn). [Also, **Wittenberg Line.**] Younger and royal branch of the Saxon house which descended from Albert, duke of Saxony (1443–1500). He ruled jointly with his brother Ernest from 1464 to 1485, when they came into possession of Thuringia by inheritance, and agreed upon a division, Albert taking an eastern and a western portion, with the Ernestine lands intervening.

Albertinelli (äl.ber.tē.nel′lē), **Mariotto.** b. at Florence, 1474; d. there, 1515. Florentine painter. An admirer and fellow student of Fra Bartolommeo under Piero di Cosimo, he completed Bartolommeo's *Last Judgment.*

Albertini (äl.ber.tē′nē), **Luigi.** b. at Ancona, Italy, Oct. 19, 1871; d. at Rome, Dec. 29, 1941. Italian statesman and journalist. After studying at London, where he observed the operation of the *Times,* he joined (1896) the staff of the *Corriere della Sera,* becoming its administrator in 1898 and managing editor in 1900. A conservative liberal, he advocated (1914) Italy's entry into World War I; he was appointed (1914) to the senate, where he favored the Italo-Yugoslav accord (1918–20) and opposed the annexation of Dalmatia. Although under his management the *Corriere* had become a leading European newspaper, his consistently anti-Fascist policy (1922 *et seq.*) caused him to be relieved (Nov. 29, 1925) of the editorship by the Crespi brothers, owners of the publication. He devoted his later years to historical studies and land conservation.

Albertis (däl.ber′tēs), **Luigi Maria d'.** b. at Voltri, Italy, Nov. 21, 1841; d. at Sassari, Italy, Sept. 2, 1901. Italian explorer and discoverer of the Fly River. After following (1860) Garibaldi to Sicily, he joined (1871) Odoardo Beccari on a geographical and naturalistic expedition to New Guinea, then still almost unexplored. After its arrival there in 1872, the expedition was cut short by disease; Albertis returned (1874) on a second trip. On a third visit he discovered (1875) and was the first to navigate (1876) the Fly River. He recorded his experiences in *Alla Nuova Guinea* (1881).

Albert Lea (al″bėrt lē′). City in S Minnesota, county seat of Freeborn County, ab. 92 mi. S of St. Paul: railroad center; oil and dairy coöperatives. It has meat-packing plants and gas-stove factories, and a fish hatchery. 13,545 (1950).

Albert Memorial. Monument in London, erected to the memory of Prince Albert, Queen Victoria's husband, on the S side of Kensington Gardens, built from the designs of Sir Gilbert Scott. It consists of a colossal bronze statue of the prince, seated, beneath an ornate spired canopy which rises to a height of 175 ft. Statue and canopy rest on a basement bearing reliefs of artists of all countries and times. At the angles four pedestals project with groups of statuary representing Agriculture, Commerce, Engineering, and Manufacture. Steps descend on all sides in pyramidal form, and at the lower angles are placed sculptures personifying Europe, America, Asia, and Africa.

Albert Nyanza (ni.an′zạ, nī-). See **Albert, Lake.**

Albert of Brandenburg. [German, **Albrecht.**] b. June 28, 1490; d. at Aschaffenburg, Sept. 24, 1545. German prelate; youngest son of the elector Johannes Cicero of Brandenburg. He became archbishop of Magdeburg (1513), archbishop and elector of Mainz (1514), and cardinal (1518). To him was entrusted the sale of indulgences in one district of Germany, with Johann Tetzel acting as his commissioner.

"Albert of Westphalia." See **Aldegrever, Heinrich.**

Albertrandy (äl.ber.trän′di), **John Baptist.** [Polish, **Jan Chrzciciel.**] b. at Warsaw, Dec. 7, 1731; d. there, Aug. 10, 1808. Polish Jesuit and historian, of Italian parentage, librarian to Bishop Zaluski at Warsaw, and later to Stanislaus Augustus, and a notable collector of manuscripts relating to Polish history. He was appointed bishop of Zenopolis and decorated with the Order of Saint Stanislaus.

Alberts (al′bėrts). A former name of **Ashley.**

Albert Savarus (ȧl.ber sȧ.vȧ.rüs). Tale by Honoré de Balzac, published in 1844, one of the *Scenes from Private Life.* Savarus is said to be a portrait of the author. The book contains many details of his life and work.

"Albert the Bad" (al′bėrt). See **Albert** (of *Thuringia* and *Meissen*).

"Albert the Bear." See **Albert I** (of *Brandenburg*).

"Albert the Bold." See **Albert III** (of *Saxony*).

"Albert the Pious." See **Albert** (of *Austria*), 1559–1621.

"Albert the Proud." See **Albert** (of *Meissen*).

"Albert the Tall." See **Albert** (of *Brunswick-Lüneburg*).

"Albert the Wise." See **Albert IV** (of *Bavaria*).

"Albert Ulysses" (ū.lis′ēz). See **Albert III** (of *Brandenburg*).

Albertus Magnus (al.bėr′tus mag′nus), Saint. [Called **"Albert the Great," "Doctor Universalis"**; hereditary title, Count **von Bollstädt.**] b. at Lauingen, Swabia, c1193 (or 1205); d. at Cologne, Prussia, 1280. German scholastic philosopher, member (1223 *et seq.*) of the Dominican order, and teacher at Paris, Cologne, Strasbourg, and elsewhere. He was noted as one of the foremost scholars of his time by Roger Bacon, his contemporary, and was named by later writers the most powerful expositor of the intellectual efforts of the 13th century. Chiefly known for his interest in Aristotle, whose works he endeavored to free from Arabic interpolations, he was excelled in his pioneering efforts to reconcile the study of Aristotelian logic and philosophy with Catholic theology by his favorite pupil, Thomas Aquinas. He was, however, without a rival in his day, preëminently successful as a teacher in interpreting and making comprehensible to his contemporaries the Aristotelian works in natural philosophy. Raised (1260) to the bishopric of Ratisbon, he retired two years later in order to continue his teaching at Cologne. His scientific studies based on the Aristotelian method and plan were supplemented by his own observations of the animal and plant life around him, and by his visits to the mines, mineral deposits, and the laboratories of alchemists in the vicinity of his residence at Cologne. He was canonized (1932) by Pope Pius XI.

Albert Victor Christian Edward (al′bėrt vik′tọr kris′chạn ed′wạrd). [Title, Duke of **Clarence and Avondale.**] b. Jan. 8, 1864; d. Jan. 14, 1892. Eldest son of Edward VII. He was created Duke of Clarence and Avondale in 1890.

Albertville (al′bėrt.vil). City in N Alabama, in Marshall County, ab. 63 mi. NE of Birmingham: cotton mill, cotton gins, and a cottonseed-oil mill. 5,397 (1950).

Albertville. Town in C Africa, in the Belgian Congo, in Elisabethville province, on the W shore of Lake Tanganyika, ab. 130 mi. from Kigoma, Tanganyika. It is connected by rail with Kabalo, ab. 170 mi. W on the upper Congo (Lualaba River); from Kabalo goods can reach Léopoldville and the sea via rail and river. However, because of the long, roundabout trip necessitated by this route, much trade and commerce are carried on by shipment to Kigoma and from there by rail to Dar es Salaam on the Indian Ocean. The town has railroad offices and a cotton mill; ground nuts are exported. Pop. ab. 10,000.

Albertville (ȧl.ber.vēl). Town in SE France, in the department of Savoie, situated on the Arly River, near its junction with the Isère River, ab. 23 mi. NE of Chambéry. It consists of the picturesque old quarter of Conflans on the left bank and the new commercial quarter of Hôpital on the right bank. 7,147 (1946).

Alberus (äl′be.rus), **Erasmus.** b. at Sprendlingen, Germany, 1500; d. at Neubrandenburg, Germany, 1553. German poet and scholar, staunch supporter of the Reformation and a close associate of Luther. The latter wrote the preface to his satire *Barfüssermönche Eulenspiegel und Alkoran* (1542). His poems and fables are contained in *Das Buch von der Tugend und Weisheit* (1550). He is best remembered for his hymns, which are still found in hymnals today.

Albery (al′bėr.i), **James.** b. at London, 1838; d. there, 1889. English dramatist. His play *Two Roses* was used (1870) as a vehicle by Henry Irving; his other dramas, none of which achieved success to match that of *Two Roses,* include *Pink Dominoes* and *Oriana.*

Albi (ȧl.bē). [Also: **Alby;** Latin, **Albiga.**] Capital of the department of Tarn, S France, situated on the Tarn River, NE of Toulouse. It is one of the most picturesque cities in France. The Cathedral of Sainte Cécile is a unique Gothic monument, massively built of brick, with openings high above the ground and generally constructed in such a way as to serve military as well as ecclesiastical purposes. There is an archiepiscopal palace. The town was the capital of the Celtic tribe of the Albigenses, and in the 12th and 13th centuries gave its name to the Albigensian heretical movement, which was suppressed by the Roman Catholic Church. The modern city has chemical, textile, and food industries; coal mines are in the vicinity. 34,342 (1946).

Albia (al′bi.ạ). [Former name, **Princeton.**] City in S Iowa, county seat of Monroe County. Coal mining is the principal industry. 4,838 (1950).

Albigenses (al.bi.jen′sēz). [Also, **Cathari.**] Collective name for the members of several anti-sacerdotal sects in the S part of France in the 12th and 13th centuries; so called after Albi, in Languedoc, where they were dominant. They revolted against the established church, were charged with Manichaean errors, and were so vigorously persecuted that, as sects, they had in great part disappeared by the end of the 13th century. A crusade against them was preached by Pope Innocent III in 1208, and was led by Arnold of Citeaux and Simon de Montfort. The war of extermination, which lasted for several years, was one of the bloodiest in history. Their doctrines are now known chiefly from the writings of their orthodox enemies.

Albigeois (ȧl.bē.zhwȧ). Former district of Languedoc, S France, comprised in the modern department of Tarn.

Albina (al.bī′nạ). Former city in Multnomah County, Oregon, on the Willamette River; now a part of Portland.

Albingaunum (al.bin.gô′num). A Latin name of **Albenga.**

Albingians (al.bin′ji.ạnz). Saxon tribe living N of the Elbe (whence the name) in what was later to be Holstein.

Albini (äl.bē′nē), **Franz Joseph,** Baron **von.** b. May 14, 1748; d. Jan. 8, 1816. German statesman, head of the government of the electorate of Mainz during the French revolutionary period.

Albino (äl.bē′nō). Town and commune in N Italy, in the *compartimento* (region) of Lombardy, in the province of Bergamo, situated on the Serio River, in the foothills of the Alps NE of Milan. It has cotton mills and cement factories. Pop. of commune, 11,048 (1936); of town, 4,256 (1936).

Albinovanus Pedo (al.bin.ọ.vā′nus pē′dō). fl. 1st century A.D. Roman poet of the Augustan period. A friend of Ovid and praised by Martial, he is known today only through a fragment of his work preserved by Seneca.

Albinus (al.bī′nus; German, äl.bē′nůs). [Original name, **Bernhard Siegfried Weiss.**] b. at Frankfort on the Oder, Germany, 1697; d. at Leiden, the Netherlands, 1770. German anatomist, professor of medicine and anatomy at Leiden; author of *Tabulae sceleti et musculorum corporis humani* (1747), and others.

Albinus. See **Alcuin.**

Albinus. See **Brutus, Decimus Junius.**

Albinus, Decimus Clodius Ceionius Septimius. Killed after the battle of Lyons, 197 A.D. Roman commander, proclaimed emperor by the armies in Gaul and Britain in 193 A.D., and probably recognized as Caesar by Severus in 194. He was defeated and killed by Severus in 197.

Albinus, Spurius Postumius. fl. late 4th century B.C. Roman consul (334 and 321 B.C.) and commander at the defeat of the Caudine Forks.

Albion (al′bi.ọn). City in S Lower Michigan, in Calhoun County, on the Kalamazoo River, ab. 38 mi. SW of Lansing: industrial center. It is the seat of Albion College. 10,406 (1950).

Albion. Village in W New York, county seat of Orleans County, ab. 43 mi. NE of Buffalo: canning center for tomatoes and peas. 4,850 (1950).

Albion. Ancient name of Britain, specifically, England. The Romans associated the term with *albus,* "white," and identified it with the Dover chalk cliffs.

Albion and Albanius (al.bā′ni.us). An operatic entertainment by Dryden, produced in 1685, allegorically representing the chief events of King Charles II's reign

Albireo (al.bir′ẹ.ō). Usual name for the third-magnitude double star β Cygni. It is in the beak of the figure of the swan in the northern constellation Cygnus, and consists of a yellow star with a fainter blue companion.

Albis (äl′bis). Low mountain range in the canton of Zurich, Switzerland, W of Lake Zurich. Its best-known summit is the Ütliberg.

Albis (al′bis). Latin name of the **Elbe.**

Albistan (äl.bi.stän′). See **Elbistan.**

Albitte (ȧl.bēt), **Antoine Louis.** d. 1812. French revolutionist, member (1791) of the Legislative Assembly. He was condemned to death for participation in the revolt of May 20, 1795, against the Convention, but succeeded in avoiding capture. Under the Directory he was appointed mayor of Dieppe. After the 18th Brumaire he was engaged in military affairs, and finally perished in the retreat from Moscow.

Albium Ingaunum (al′bi.um in.gô′num). A Latin name of **Albenga.**

Albizzi (äl.bēt′tsē). Noted Italian family, originally from Arezzo, which played a conspicuous part in Florentine affairs during the 14th and 15th centuries. They belonged to the democratic Guelph party.

Albizzi, Bartolommeo. [Latinized, **Bartholomaeus Albicius Pisanus.**] b. at Rivano, in Tuscany; d. at Pisa, Dec. 10, 1401. Franciscan monk and religious writer; author of *Liber conformitatum sancti Francisci cum Christo* (first ed. folio, Venice, undated).

Albona (äl.bō′nä). Italian name of **Labin.**

Alboni (äl.bō′nē), **Marietta.** [Title, by marriage, Contessa **Pepoli.**] b. at Cittá di Castello, Italy, 1826; d. at Ville d'Avray, France, June 23, 1894. Italian operatic contralto. Student of Rossini at Bologna; made début (1843) at La Scala; sang with great success in Europe, England (1847 *et seq.*), and the U.S. (1852).

Al Borak (äl bō′räk). [Arabic, **al-Boraq.**] Legendary animal, white in color, between a mule and an ass in size, with two wings and of great swiftness, on which Mohammed is said to have made a nocturnal journey to the seven heavens, conducted by the angel Gabriel.

Ålborg (ôl′bôrg). See **Aalborg.**

Albornoz (äl.bôr′nōth), **Gil Álvarez Carilio de.** b. at Cuenca, Spain, c1300; d. at Viterbo, Italy, Aug. 24, 1367. Spanish prelate (archbishop of Toledo) and soldier.

Albrecht (äl′brecht). fl. c1270. German poet, author of the later *Titurel,* a continuation of the *Titurel* of Wolfram von Eschenbach: generally, but probably wrongly, named Albrecht von Scharfenberg.

Albrecht. German form of **Albert.**

Albrecht, Wilhelm Eduard. b. at Elbing, Prussia, March 4, 1800; d. at Leipzig, Germany, May 22, 1876. German jurist, one of the seven Göttingen professors removed on account of liberalism in 1837.

Albrechtsberger (äl′brechts.ber.gėr), **Johann Georg.** b. at Klosterneuburg, Austria, Feb. 3, 1736; d. at Vienna, March 7, 1809. Austrian musician, theorist, and contrapuntist; teacher of Beethoven, Hummel, and others.

Albrecht von Eyb (or **Eybe**) (äl′brecht fon īp′; ī′bẹ). b. in Franconia, Germany, 1420; d. at Eichstätt, Germany, 1475. German cleric and author. His witty *Ehestandsbuch* (1472) debates whether a man should marry or tarry and contains among other things the translations of two Italian stories. Likewise his posthumous *Spiegel der Sitten* (1511) was accompanied by translations of Ugolini's *Philogenia* and Plautus's *Menaechmi* and *Bachides.* He published an anthology of Latin classics in the original called *Margarita poetica* (1472).

Albrecht von Halberstadt (fon häl′bėr.shtät). fl. c1210. Middle High German poet. At the suggestion of Landgrave Hermann of Thuringia, he translated Ovid's *Metamorphoses* directly from the Latin. His version is extant in fragments only, but in the 16th century a complete text was available to Jörg Wickram, who produced from it a popular prose adaptation.

Albret (ȧl.bre), **House of.** Gascon family which arose in the 11th century, and derived its name from the Château d'Albret. Its best-known members are Charles d'Albret, count of Dreux, who was killed in the battle of Agincourt in 1415; Louis d'Albret (d. 1465), cardinal bishop of Cahors; Jean d'Albret, who became king of Navarre by his marriage with Catherine of Foix in 1484; Jeanne d' Albret; and César-Phébus d'Albret, marshal of France and the last descendant of the house in the male line.

Albret (dàl.bre), **Jeanne d'**. b. at Pau, Jan. 7, 1528; d. at Paris, June 9, 1572. Queen of Navarre; daughter of Henry, king of Navarre, and Margaret of Valois, wife of Antony of Bourbon, and mother of Henry IV of France.

Albright (ôl'brīt), **Jacob.** b. near Pottstown, Pa., May 1, 1759; d. May 18, 1808. American clergyman, founder of a movement known as the Evangelical Association, now the Evangelical Church.

Albright, Malvin Marr. [Pseudonym (as painter), **Zsissly.**] b. at Chicago, 1897—. American sculptor. He has exhibited at the Chicago World's Fair (1933–34), Golden Gate Exposition (1939), and New York World's Fair (1939), as well as in numerous museums and private collections.

Albrizzi (äl.brēt'tsē), **Isabella Teotochi,** Contessa **d'.** b. on the island of Corfu, in the Ionian Sea, c1763; d. at Venice, 1836. Italian author and patroness, particularly of Canova and Foscolo; called by Byron "The Madame de Staël of Venice." Author of *Descrizione delle opere di Canova* (1809–25), a biography of Vittoria Colonna (1836), and others.

Albuféira (äl.bö.fā'rạ). Town and *concelho* (commune) on the S coast of Portugal, in the province of Algarve, in the district of Faro, ab. 21 mi. W of Faro: a picturesque seaport with tuna and sardine fisheries. Pop. of concelho, 13,892 (1940); of town, 6,452 (1940).

Albufera (äl.bö.fā'rä). [Full name, **Albufera de Valencia.**] Lagoon in E Spain, ab. 7 mi. S of Valencia. The rights to it belonged at one time to the Duke of Wellington. Length, ab. 10 mi.

Albufera (àl.bü.fä.rà), Duc **d'.** Title of **Suchet, Louis Gabriel.**

Albula (äl'bö.lä). Pass in the canton of Graubünden, Switzerland, ab. 25 mi. SE of Coire, connecting the valleys of the Albula and Hinter Rhein rivers with that of the Inn. Elevation, 7,595 ft.

Albula. Town in E Switzerland in the canton of Graubünden. 7,533 (1941).

Albumazar (äl.bö.mä'zär). b. at Balkh, Turkestan, 805; d. at Wasid, in central Asia, 885. Arab astronomer and astrologer at Baghdad, who made important contributions to the study of tides. A prolific writer, he compiled astronomical tabulations based on the Persian system, differentiating it from the Jewish. He predicted the end of the world in his *De magnis conjunctionibus.* He was used as a prototype of a knavish astrologer in Gian Battista del Porta's play *L'Astrologo* (1606), on which were based John Tomkis's *Albumazar,* played (1614) before James I, revived by Dryden (1748) and Garrick, and Ralph's *The Astrologer* (1734). He was the author of some 50 works including *Flores astrologici* (Augsburg, 1488), *De Magnis conjunctionibus* (Augsburg, 1489), and *Introductorium in astronomiam* (Venice, 1506).

Albuquerque (äl.bö.kėr'kā). See also **Alburquerque.**

Albuquerque (al'bu.kėr.ki, -bū-). City in C New Mexico, county seat of Bernalillo County, on the Rio Grande, ab. 58 mi. SW of Santa Fe: health resort; manufactures of bricks and sheet metal; railway shops and petroleum refineries; trading center for a livestock-raising and irrigated farming area. It is the seat of the University of New Mexico. The modern city comprises two settlements, the old town (founded 1706), and the new town (founded 1880). Pop. of city, 96,815 (1950); of urbanized area, 124,901 (1950).

Albuquerque (äl.bö.ker'kā), Duke of. Title of **Fernández de la Cueva, Francisco,** and **Fernández de la Cueva Henríquez, Francisco.**

Albuquerque (äl.bö.ker'kẹ), **Affonso de.** b. at Alhandra, Portugal, 1453; d. at sea near Goa, India, 1515. Portuguese navigator and colonial administrator, founder of the Portuguese empire in the East. He was educated at the court of Alfonso V. His first expedition to India was made in 1503–04; on the second, with Tristão da Cunha, he carried secret orders from King Emmanuel to replace Almeida, Portuguese viceroy in India, by whom he was imprisoned (1508) until the grand marshal's fleet came (1509) to his support. He conquered Goa (1510), Malacca, the Malabar coast (1512), Ceylon, the Sunda Islands, and Ormuz (1515), the last of which gave Portugal a foothold in the Red Sea. An able and beneficent colonial administrator, he gained the respect of both Hindus and Moslems

Albuquerque, Duarte Coelho de. See **Coelho de Albuquerque, Duarte.**

Albuquerque, Jeronymo de. b. c1514; d. at Olinda, near Pernambuco, Brazil, c1594. Portuguese soldier, leader in various wars against the Indians in Brazil, whither he went in 1535. In 1548 he was captured by the Cahetes tribe, but gained their good will and married the daughter of a chief.

Albuquerque, José Joaquim de Campos da Costa de Medeiros e. b. at Recife, Brazil, Sept. 4, 1867; d. at Rio de Janeiro, June 9, 1934. Brazilian polygraph, journalist, poet, essayist, novelist, short-story writer, educator, and critic. He was a professor at the National School of Fine Arts and director of the Department of Education of Rio de Janeiro. Among his books are *Canções da decadência,* poems (1887); *Um homem prático* (1898) and *Contos escolhidos* (1907), short stories; *Pontos de vista* (1913) and *Graves e fúteis* (1922), essays; *Literatura alheia* (1914) and *Páginas de crítica* (1920), criticism; *Marta* (1920), novel; *Homens e coisas da Academia* (1933) and *Minha vida* (1934), memoirs.

Albuquerque, Mathias de. b. probably in Brazil; d. at Lisbon, 1647. Portuguese general. Governor of Pernambuco (1624); after the Dutch capture of Bahia (1624), he was acting governor-general of northern Brazil. Recovered Bahia (1625), and after a visit to Madrid returned to Pernambuco (1629) as governor; abandoned Olinda and Recife (1630) to the Dutch; ordered back to Madrid (1635) and sent to Portugal in disgrace. In the war which followed the Portuguese revolt (1640) against Spain, Albuquerque's victory of Montijo or Campo Mayor (1644) won him the titles of Count of Allegrete and grandee of Portugal.

Albuquerque (däl.bö.ker'kẹ), **Pedro d'.** b. at Pernambuco, Brazil, c1575; d. at Belém (Pará), Brazil, Feb. 6, 1644. Brazilian colonial administrator; son of Jeronymo de Albuquerque Maranhão. He was appointed governor of Maranhão and Pará in 1642.

Albuquerque Coelho (äl.bö.ker'kẹ kwā'lyö), **Duarte de.** See **Coelho, Duarte de Albuquerque.**

Albuquerque Coelho, Jorge de. See **Coelho, Jorge de Albuquerque.**

Albuquerque Maranhão (mạ.rạ.nyouṅ'), **Jeronymo de.** b. at Pernambuco, Brazil, 1548; d. in Maranhão, Brazil, Feb. 11, 1618. Brazilian soldier; son of Jeronymo de Albuquerque and an Indian mother. He conquered Rio Grande do Norte from the Indians (1598–99) and Ceará in 1613. In November, 1615, he took Maranhão from the French, and was made captain-general of that colony.

Alburquerque (äl.bör.ker'kā). [Also, **Albuquerque.**] Town in W Spain, in the province of Badajoz, situated near the Portuguese border, ab. 24 mi. N of Badajoz: old frontier fortifications. 10,015 (1940).

Albury (al'bėr.i). Town in SE Australia, in the state of New South Wales, situated on the border of Victoria ab. 200 mi. NE of Melbourne: shipping and trading center at the head of steam navigation on the Murray River. 14,419 (1947).

Albus (al'bus), **Mons.** Latin name of **Blanc, Mont.**

Albuzdschani (äl.böz.jä'nē). [Also: **Abul Wafa** (or **Wefa**).] b. 940; d. 998. Arab astronomer and mathematician. A student of Greek mathematics, he devised the Arabic table of tangents and cotangents. His *Almagest* suggests that he may have noted those movements of the moon later to be recognized as "variation."

Alby (àl.bē). See **Albi.**

Alcácer do Sal (äl.kä'sėr dö säl'). [Latin, **Salacia.**] Town and *concelho* (commune) in S Portugal, in the province of Estremadura, in the district of Setubal, situated at the mouth of the Sado River, ab. 50 mi. SE of Lisbon: manufactures of straw and esparto products, and of salt from sea water. The town, which was the scene of much fighting in the Moslem wars, has the ruins of a Moorish castle. Pop. of concelho, 23,000 (1940); of town, 14,109 (1940).

Alcaeus (al.sē'us) or **Alkaios** (-kī'os). fl. in Mytilene, c611–580 B.C. Greek poet whose lyrics in Aeolic dialect, known through fragments, are thought to have been a prototype of Sappho's. He was the probable inventor of Alcaics, a meter much used by later classical poets.

Alcaforado (äl''kạ.fö.rä'dö), **Francisco.** Portuguese navigator who took part in the expedition (of which he wrote an account) of João Gonzales Zarco to Madeira in 1420.

Alcalá de Guadaira (äl.kä.lä′ dā gwä.ᴛʜī′rä). [Also: **Alcala, Alcala de los Panaderes** (pä.nä.ᴛʜā′res).] Town in S Spain, in the province of Sevilla, situated on the Guadaira River, ab. 9 mi. E of Seville: flour mills. There is a Moorish castle of the 12th century, and other Moorish remains. The town was taken (1244) from the Moslems by Ferdinand III of Castile. 20,477 (1940).

Alcalá de Henares (ā.nä′res). [Latin name, **Complutum.**] Town in C Spain, in the province of Madrid, situated on the Henares River, ab. 20 mi. NE of Madrid: terra cotta, leather, chocolate, and soap factories. There is a 12th-century Magistral Church, rebuilt in the 15th century. The town was formerly a royal Castilian residence, and was the birthplace of Catherine of Aragon and of Cervantes. The university, once second only to that of Salamanca, was founded by Cardinal Francis Ximénes Cisneros in 1508 and moved to Madrid in 1836; here was produced (1513–17) the Complutensian Polyglot Bible. The Church of San Ildefonso contains a collection of more than 60,000 documents. 18,419 (1940).

Alcalá la Real (lä rā.äl′). Commune in Spain, in the province of Jaén, ab. 25 mi. NW of Granada: the center of a wine, vegetable, and wool producing district; thermal springs. The town was taken from the Moslems in 1213, retaken by them in 1219, and again occupied by Ferdinand III in 1249. The French won (1810) a victory here in the Peninsular War. 25,558 (1940).

Alcalá Zamora y Torres (thä.mō′rä ē tôr′res), **Niceto.** b. in Spain, 1877; d. Feb. 18, 1949. Spanish statesman and politician. Upon completion of the study of law he became an officer of the Spanish council of state in 1899, professor of law at the University of Madrid in 1903, and deputy in the Cortes of 1906. He held various ministerial posts until 1923 when dictator Primo de Rivera took over the government. He subsequently transferred his sympathies to the republican cause and became titular head of the provisional government which was formed upon the fall of the monarchy, and first president of the Spanish republic founded in 1931. He represented Catholic conservative middle-class interests, and was deposed in 1936, before expiration of his legal term, due to the widening gulf between the left and right and the impossibility of further compromise. In *Los defectos de la Constitución de 1931* (Madrid, 1936) he gives his political views.

Alcamenes or **Alkamenes** (al.kam′ẹ.nēz). b. at Lemnos or Athens; fl. c448–c404 B.C. Greek sculptor, according to Pausanius the most skillful pupil of Phidias, whom he probably assisted in the decoration of the Parthenon. He is known to have done *Aphrodite of the Gardens* (now at Athens), which is considered a masterpiece of his period.

Alcamo (äl′kä.mō). [Arabic, **Alqamah.**] Town and commune in SW Italy, on the island of Sicily, in the province of Trapani, situated S of the Gulf of Castellammare, between Palermo and Trapani. The town is the center of a wine and grain producing district; the population is largely of Arabic descent. The site of the town was moved by Emperor Frederick II in 1233; later it belonged to the domain of the Peralta family. There are a number of churches, mainly from the 17th and 18th centuries; the ruins of the ancient town of Segesta are nearby. Damage was suffered during World War II by some buildings of tourist interest. Pop. of commune, 38,396 (1936); of town, 38,129 (1936).

Alcandre (ål.kändr). Character in Mademoiselle de Scudéry's romance *Clélie;* a flattering portrait of Louis XIV, then only about 18 years of age.

"Alcan Highway" (al′kan). See **Alaska Highway.**

Alcântara (äl.kun′tạ.rạ). Seaport in N Brazil, in the state of Maranhão. Pop. under 5,000 (1940).

Alcântara. Western suburb of Lisbon, Portugal, noted for the victory gained there in 1580 by the Duke of Alva over the Portuguese army.

Alcántara (äl.kän′tä.rä), **Francisco Martín.** b. in what was then the province of Estremadura, Spain probably c1480; killed at Lima, Peru, June 26, 1541 Spanish soldier; half-brother of Francisco Pizarro on the maternal side. He left Spain with Pizarro in 1529, and was with him during part of the conquest of Peru. He received a large inheritance which was unjustly taken from the younger Almagro. Alcántara was killed with Pizarro.

Alcantarilla (äl.kän.tä.rē′lyä). Town in E Spain, in the province of Murcia, situated in a well-watered plain, ab. 4 mi. W of Murcia: agricultural trade center. 10,744 (1940).

Alcatraz (al′kạ.traz). [Also, **Pelican Island.**] Small rocky island N of San Francisco, the seat of a federal penitentiary (until 1933, a military prison only), a torpedo station, and a lighthouse.

Alcaudete (äl.kou.ᴛʜā′tā). Town in S Spain, in the province of Jaén, situated on a tributary of the Guadalquivir River, ab. 23 mi. SW of Jaén: agricultural trade center. 18,442 (1940).

Alcázar (äl.kä′thär), **Baltasar de.** b. 1530; d. 1606. Spanish poet and wit. An edition of his collected poems published in 1910 displays the acid but charming phraseology which brought him his reputation.

Alcázar de San Juan (dā säng hwän). [Also: **Alcázar;** Arabic, **Al-Qaṣr,** meaning "the castle"; Latin, **Alces.**] Town in C Spain, in the province of Ciudad-Real, situated on a dry steppe, ab. 80 mi. SE of Madrid: a center of the local cattle and sheep trade, with small industries; zinc and iron ore are mined in the vicinity. The town was destroyed in the struggle between the Moslems and the Christians, and later rebuilt. 26,141 (1940).

Alcazarquivir (äl.kä″thär.kē.ʙēr′). [Also: **Alcázar, Lxor;** Arabic, **Al-Qaṣr al-Kabir, El Ksar el Kebir.**] City in Spanish Morocco, ab. 60 mi. S of Tangier and 48 mi. from Larache, on the Atlantic coast, connected by rail with both places. The town is almost on the border between Spanish and French Morocco. Here, on Aug. 4, 1578, King Sebastian of Portugal was defeated and slain by the Moslems. The Spanish occupied the town in 1912 and built a European quarter. 33,196 (1940).

Alcazava Sotomayor (äl.kạ.zä′vạ sō″tö.mạ.yōr′), **Simão de.** [Also: **Alcazaba, Alcazova, Alcaçoba.**] b. c1490; d. on the coast of Patagonia early in 1536. Portuguese explorer, from 1522 in the service of Spain as a naval officer. In 1534 he fitted out, at his own expense, two vessels and 240 men, with the object of reaching Peru by the Straits of Magellan. Leaving San Lucar on Sept. 21, he touched at the Abrolhos islands, Brazil, and arrived at the Straits in January, 1535; attempting to pass, he was driven back by a storm, and wintered at Puerto de los Lobos (probably St. Joseph's or St. Matthew's Bay). From there he led a land expedition which crossed the country to the Andes and was the first to explore the Patagonian plateau. Alcazava himself was obliged by sickness to return to the ship, where he was shortly after murdered in a mutiny.

Alcedo (äl.thā′ᴛʜō), **Antonio de.** b. at Quito, in what is now Ecuador, 1735; date of death not recorded. Spanish soldier and geographer. Best known for his *Diccionario geográfico-histórico de las Indias occidentales ó América* (5 vols., 1786–89), of which an English translation was later (1812–15) published at London.

Alcedo y Herrera (ē er.rā′rä), **Dionisio de.** b. at Madrid, 1690; d. there, 1777. Spanish administrator. From 1706 to 1752 he was almost constantly in Spanish America in various civil capacities. As president and captain-general of Quito (1728–37), he received the French commission sent to measure an arc of the meridian. He published some works of considerable importance on the geography and history of South America.

Alces (al′sēz). Latin name of **Alcázar de San Juan.**

Alceste (al.sest′). Tragic opera in three acts, by Gluck, with a libretto by Calzabigi, first presented at Vienna, Dec. 16, 1767.

Alceste (ål.sest). Principal character in Molière's comedy *The Misanthrope;* an upright but tactless man who scorns the excessive civilities of courtly life and the shams of society. Wycherley took him as the model for his rude and brutal Manly in *The Plain Dealer.*

Alcester (ôl′stėr, ôs′tėr). Rural district and market town in C England, in Warwickshire, situated at the confluence of the rivers Alne and Arrow, ab. 19 mi. S of Birmingham, ab. 136 mi. NW of London by rail. It is the site of an ancient Roman encampment. 13,264 (1951).

Alcester, 1st Baron. Title of **Seymour, Frederick Beauchamp Paget.**

Alcestis (al.ses′tis) or **Alceste** (-tē). In Greek legend, the daughter of Pelias and wife of Admetus, king of Pherae in Thessaly. When her husband was stricken with a mortal sickness she sacrificed her life for him, in accordance with the promise of Apollo that by this means he should be saved. According to one form of the legend she was allowed to return to the upper world by Persephone; according to another she was rescued by Hercules. She is the subject of a play by Euripides.

Alchemb (al.kemb′). A rarely used name for the second-magnitude star α Persei, in the northern constellation Perseus; usually called Mirfak, and sometimes Algenib.

Alchemist, The. Comedy by Ben Jonson, first acted in 1610. It is a satire on the reigning folly of the time, the search for the philosopher's stone. It observes strictly the unities of time and place, and, in point of intellectual power, is regarded by some as the best of Jonson's plays.

Alchevsk (a̧l.chefsk′). Former name of **Voroshilovsk.**

Alchfrith (älch′frith). Son of Oswui, king of the Northumbrians, and Eanflæd, daughter of Eadwine. He married Cyneburh, daughter of Penda, king of the Mercians. He was created under-king of the Deirans by his father, whom he joined in the defeat (655) of Penda, near the river Winwæd. Later he waged an unsuccessful war against his father, and probably fled to Mercia.

Alchoku (äl.chō′kö). See **Acheng.**

Alchuine (al′kwin). See **Alcuin.**

Alchymist (äl.chē.mest′), **Der.** Opera by Louis Spohr, composed about the end of 1829, and first performed at Kassel, Germany, on July 28, 1830. The libretto is based on a story by Washington Irving.

Alciati (äl.chä′tē), **Andrea.** b. at Alzano, Italy, 1492; d. 1550. Italian legal scholar. He made a pioneer study of civil law which was based on original classical sources and was not merely a reworking of contemporary glosses; author of *Emblems*, a collection of aphorisms in Latin which was later published (Padua, 1661) with commentaries.

Alcibiades (al.si.bī′a̧.dēz). b. at Athens, c450 B.C.; killed at Melissa, Phrygia, 404 B.C. Athenian politician and general; member of the Alcmaeonidae; pupil and friend of Socrates. After his father's death, he was brought up by Pericles, a relative. He was leader of the radical party against Nicias (421), commanded the Athenian League (420–418), and was appointed a commander of the expedition against Sicily (415), which he had actively promoted. Accused of profanation in Athens, he fled (415) to Sparta, becoming an open enemy of Athens. Suspected of intrigue in Sparta, with death sentence awaiting him in Athens, he then went over (412) to the Persians. Recalled by the Athenian army, he was commander in the victory over the Spartan fleet at Abydos (411) and Cyzicus (410), which restored Chalcedon, Byzantium, and rule of the sea to Athens. Failure at Andros and defeat of his general at Notium (407) lost him command; after Athenian defeat at Aegospotami, sought refuge with Pharnabazus in Phrygia, where he was murdered on order of Lysander of Sparta. He was celebrated for great charm and military talent, but never fully trusted because of his capricious self-will.

Alcibiades. Tragedy by Thomas Otway, produced in 1675.

Alcida: Greene's Metamorphoses (al′si.da̧). Pamphlet by Robert Greene, licensed in 1588, probably published in 1589. It consists of stories exposing the evils of women's pride and vanity.

Alcidamas (al.sid′a̧.ma̧s). b. at Elaea, Asia Minor; fl. 4th century B.C.; Greek rhetorician; pupil of Gorgias. He was instructor in eloquence at Athens, last of the purely sophistical school of rhetoricians. Two extant declamations and fragments of other works are ascribed to him.

Alcimona (al.si.mō′na̧). A Latin name of the **Altmühl.**

Alcimus (al′si.mus). fl. 2nd century B.C. Jewish high priest, whose efforts to Hellenize the Hebrew community and religious customs won him favor at court but infuriated the Maccabees.

Alcina (äl.chē′nä). Fairy, the embodiment of carnal delights, in Boiardo's *Orlando Innamorato* and Ariosto's *Orlando Furioso*. She is described as the sister of Logistilla (Reason) and Morgana (Lasciviousness). When tired of her lovers she changed them into trees, beasts, and other objects. She was finally, by means of a magic ring, displayed in her real senility and ugliness.

Alcinous (al.sin′ǫ.us). In Greek legend, a king of the Phaeacians, in the island of Scheria, mentioned in the *Odyssey*. A considerable part of the poem (Books VI–XIII) is devoted to the events of Odysseus's stay in his dominions.

Alcionius (al.si.ō′ni.us), **Petrus.** See **Alcyonius, Petrus.**

Alciphron (al′si.fron). fl. 2nd century A.D. Greek writer, particularly of imaginary letters which, though models of Attic style, purported to be the work of contemporary lower-class Athenians. The approximately 124 which are extant constitute a valuable description of social conditions and manners of the period; those supposedly written by famous hetaerae reflect the work of New Comedy writers, especially Menander.

Alciphron. Character in Thomas Moore's romance *The Epicurean*, published in 1827. Moore also wrote a poem with this title, published in 1839.

Alciphron, or the Minute Philosopher. Philosophical dialogue by Bishop Berkeley, written to expose the weakness of infidelity. It was composed while Berkeley was at Newport, R.I., and was published in 1732.

Alcira (äl.thē′rä). Town in E Spain, in the province of Valencia, situated on an island in the Júcar River, ab. 23 mi. S of Valencia: center of a fertile agricultural district; rice, sugar cane, citrus fruit, and silkworms. A Roman bridge across the Júcar River is preserved; there are a number of old churches and monasteries. 24,518 (1940).

Alcmaeon (alk.mē′ǫn). In Greek legend, the son of Amphiaraus and Eriphyle and the leader of the Epigoni in the expedition against Thebes. In accordance with the command of his father, given when he joined the first expedition against Thebes, and the advice of the oracle, he slew his mother, and was driven mad and pursued by the Furies in consequence. Having, under false pretenses, obtained from Phegeus the Arcadian the necklace and robe of Harmonia for his wife Callirrhoe, he was waylaid and slain by Phegeus's order.

Alcmaeonidae (alk.mę.on′i.dē). Noble family of Athens, a branch of the family of the Neleidae which came from Pylos in Messenia to Athens about 1100 B.C. Among the more notable members of the family are Alcmaeon, an Athenian general in the Cirrhaean war; Megacles, a son of Alcmaeon, and a rival of Pisistratus; Clisthenes, the legislator, son of Megacles; Pericles, the celebrated Athenian statesman, great-grandson of Megacles; and the scarcely less famous Alcibiades, cousin of Pericles. The family was banished for sacrilege about 596 B.C. on account of the action of the Alcmaeonid archon Megacles who in 612 B.C. put to death the participants in the insurrection of Cylon while they clung for protection to the altars. They returned through an alliance with Lycurgus, carried on with varying fortunes a struggle with Pisistratus and the Pisistratidae, and were finally restored in 510 B.C.

Alcmaeon of Crotona (alk.mē′ǫn; krō.tō′na̧). b. at Crotona, Italy; fl. c500 B.C. Greek physician and philosopher; younger contemporary of Pythagoras and perhaps his disciple. He was the most famous of the Greek physicians preceding Hippocrates, and has been called "the father of Greek medicine." His book is lost and only a few fragments of his writings have remained, but it is known that he was the first to make sections, by means of which he discovered the optic nerve, distinguished in the cadaver empty veins and veins carrying blood, and knew the trachea. He gave explanations of sleep, of the origin of sperm, of sense impressions, and made physiological experiments. He was the first to recognize that the brain is the central organ of intellectual activity, and held that health and disease are respectively an equilibrium and a rupture of equilibrium of the organism.

Alcman or **Alkman** (alk′ma̧n) or **Alcmaeon** (alk.mē′ǫn). b. at Sardis, Lydia; fl. middle of the 7th century B.C. Greek poet, founder of the Doric school. Formerly a slave, he was freed and made a citizen of Sparta. He is often considered the inventor of lyric poetry; he wrote, especially for choral performance, hymns, paeans, processionals, and *parthenia* (maidens' songs); one of the latter was discovered (1855) on an Egyptian papyrus.

Alcmene or **Alkmene** (alk.mē'nē). In Greek mythology, the wife of Amphitryon and mother, by Zeus, of Hercules.

Alcmona (alk.mō'na). A Latin name of the **Altmühl.**

Alcoa (al.kō'a). City in E Tennessee, in Blount County, in the Tennessee Valley near the foothills of the Great Smoky Mountains: one of the principal centers in the U.S. for the production of aluminum ingots. It was founded in 1913. Pop. 6,355 (1950).

Alcobaça (äl.kö.bä'sa). Small town in W Portugal, in the province of Estremadura, ab. 50 mi. N of Lisbon. It contains a Cistercian monastery, founded in 1148, and believed to have been at one time the largest of the order. Pop. of *concelho* (commune), 42,890 (1940); of town, 3,823 (1940).

Alcock or **Alcocke** (ôl'kok), **John.** b. at Beverly, Yorkshire, England, 1430; d. at Wisbeach, England, 1500. English prelate, scholar, and architect. Successively bishop of Rochester, Worcester, and Ely, he restored churches and colleges; founded (1496) and built Jesus College, Cambridge.

Alcock, Sir John William. b. at Manchester, England, 1892; killed in crash at Côte d'Evrard, Normandy, 1919. English aviator. During World War I, as a military aviator, he was captured by the Turks on his return flight from the bombing (1917) of Constantinople. With Lt. A. W. Brown as navigator, he crossed the Atlantic from St. John's, Newfoundland, to Clifden, Ireland, in 16 hours and 12 minutes (June 14, 1919).

Alcock, Sir Rutherford. b. at London, 1809; d. there, 1897. English diplomat and physician. He forsook medicine to become (1844) consul at Foochow, China, which had just (1842) been opened to British trade; consul general (1858) and minister plenipotentiary (1859 *et seq.*) to Japan; emissary of Great Britain at Peking (1865–71); author of *The Capital of the Tycoon* (1863), *Art in Japan* (1878), and others.

Alcoforado (äl"kö.fö.rä'dö), **Marianna.** b. 1640; d. 1723. Portuguese nun. She entered (c1656) the Franciscan convent at Béja. Her five letters to her lover, Noël Bouton (later the Marquis de Chamilly and a marshal of France), vividly portray the phases of her grief after their separation. The letters were later translated into French and published (Paris, 1669) anonymously.

Alcofribas Nasier (ål.ko.frē.bås nå.zyā). Pseudonym of **Rabelais, François.**

Alcoholics Anonymous. [Also: **Alcoholic Foundation, Inc.**; abbreviation, **A. A.**] Organization incorporated in 1938 to assist alcoholics desiring to break the drinking habit. A nonprofit organization without national officers and supported entirely by voluntary contributions, the Foundation grew out of a group formed in 1935. It holds that the moral support of others is desirable, if not a necessity, for the habitual drunkard who desires to end his addiction to liquor; Alcoholics Anonymous undertakes to strengthen the will, through company and prayer, of the drinker who desires to reform, maintaining that the cure from within is more efficacious than physical cures, such as isolation or "tapering off." Its 4,000 groups had a membership of ab. 120,000 in 1951.

Alcolea (äl.kō.lā'ä). Locality in the province of Córdoba, Spain, on the Guadalquivir River ab. 8 mi. NE of Córdoba, where, on Sept. 28, 1868, the Spanish revolutionists under Serrano defeated the royalists. The battle resulted in the overthrow of Queen Isabella.

Alcools (ål.ko.ol). Collection of French modernist poems (1913) by Guillaume Apollinaire (1880–1918). They were taken as models by the surrealists and members of similar schools after World War I.

Alcor (al'kôr). Fifth-magnitude star very near to Mizar (ζ Ursae Majoris). It is easily seen with the naked eye if the eye is normal, but not otherwise: hence sometimes used as a test of vision. It is called Aliore in the Latin version of the *Almagest.*

Alcott (ôl'kot), **Amos Bronson.** b. at Wolcott, Conn., Nov. 29, 1799; d. at Boston, March 4, 1888. American educator and transcendentalist philosopher; father of Louisa May Alcott. A book-peddler (1808–23) in Virginia and Carolinas, he was inspired chiefly by his reading of and association with Quakers to take up teaching (Connecticut 1823–27; Boston 1828–30; Germantown, Pa., 1831–33) in which he advanced ideas on religion and education shocking to most of his contemporaries, based on learning through pleasure and imagination rather than discipline. On these principles, fortified by Neo-Platonism, he founded (1834) in Boston an "infant-school" where he attempted to develop mind and moral sense through a question-and-answer method. His *Record of a School* (1835) and *Conversations with Children on the Gospels* (1836–37), together with his refusal to dismiss a Negro pupil, brought the disapproval of parents and failure (1839) of his school. Founder of Fruitlands (1844–45) and member of Brook Farm Association, coöperative communities; made lecture tours (1853 *et seq.*); superintendent of Concord schools (1859); conducted Concord Summer School of Philosophy and Literature (1879–88); friend of Emerson, Thoreau, Hawthorne, Channing. Author of *Observations on the Principles and Methods of Infant Instruction* (1830), *The Doctrine and Discipline of Human Culture* (1836), *Concord Days* (1872), *New Connecticut* (1881–87), *Ralph Waldo Emerson* (1865–82), and others.

Alcott, Louisa May. b. at Germantown, Pa., Nov. 29, 1832; d. at Boston, March 6, 1888. American novelist and writer of children's books; daughter of Amos Bronson Alcott, whose financial failures left much of the family support to Louisa. Teaching, dressmaking, and domestic service preceded the publication (1854) of *Flower Fables,* a book of stories written for Emerson's daughter, and the appearance (1860) of stories in *Atlantic Monthly.* Letters written while she was a Civil War nurse at Georgetown (*Hospital Sketches,* 1863) aroused wide interest; her first novel, *Moods,* appeared in 1864. She was editor (1867) of *Merry's Museum,* a children's magazine. *Little Women* (1868–69), enormously successful, was translated into several languages and assured financial independence of family. She championed woman suffrage, abolition, and temperance. Her books for children, largely autobiographical, had wide appeal for their cheerful and sympathetic quality, particularly *An Old Fashioned Girl* (1870), *Little Men* (1871), *Eight Cousins* (1875), *Under the Lilacs* (1878), *Aunt Jo's Scrap-Bag* (1872–82), and *Jo's Boys* (1886).

Alcott, William Andrus. b. at Wolcott, Conn., Aug. 6, 1798; d. at Newton, Mass., March 29, 1859. American educator and writer; cousin and co-worker of Amos Bronson Alcott. Worked for better schools and better teaching in 19th-century America; author of *Confessions of a Schoolmaster* (1839), *Forty Years in the Wilderness of Pills and Powders* (1859), and many others.

Alcoy (äl.koi'). City in E Spain, in the province of Alicante, situated above the Molinar River near its junction with the Alcoy River, ab. 22 mi. N of Alicante: important factories for cigarette paper; manufactures of leather, cotton and woolen textiles, garments, and soap; distilleries; agricultural markets. There are a number of old churches and some educational institutions, including an industrial high school. There are health resorts in the vicinity. The city was founded by the Carthaginians in 236 B.C. 45,792 (1940).

Alcudia (äl.kö'THyä). Town on the N coast of the island of Majorca, Balearic Islands, in the Spanish province of Baleares, situated on the Bay of Alcudia: formerly the chief fortress of the island; fisheries. Pop. ab. 5,000.

Alcuin (al'kwin). [Also: **Albinus, Albinus Flaccus, Alchuine**; Anglo-Saxon, **Ealhwine.**] b. at York (then Eboracum), England, 735; d. at Tours, France, 804. English prelate and scholar, a leader in the medieval revival of learning in Europe. At Charlemagne's invitation, he settled at Aachen (Aix-la-Chapelle); he served as abbot of Ferrières and Troyes, as head of the palace school, and as mentor for the Frankish educational and ecclesiastical reform that took place in his day. At the Council of Frankfort (794), he led the opposition to the adoptionist heresy, causing its leader, Felix of Urgel, to recant. As abbot of Tours (796–804), he conducted the foremost school of Carolingian Europe. The value of Alcuin's services can hardly be exaggerated; he was the main instrument in the transmission to the ignorant Franks of the relatively high culture which had been attained in English monasteries under Bede's guidance.

Alcuin: A Dialogue. Tract (1798) by Charles Brockden Brown.

Alcyone (al.sī'ǫ.nē). In classical mythology, the daughter of Aeolus and wife of Ceÿx. After the loss of her husband she cast herself into the sea and was changed into a kingfisher.

Alcyone. In classical mythology, a Pleiad, daughter of Atlas and Pleione.

Alcyone. Third-magnitude star, the brightest of the Pleiades; η Tauri.

Alcyonius or **Alcionius** (al.si.ō'ni.us), **Petrus.** b. at Venice, 1487; d. at Rome, 1527. Italian scholar, corrector of the press of Aldus Manutius, and professor of Greek at Florence; author of *Medicis legatus, sive de Exilio* (1522), and other works.

Alda (äl'dạ), **Frances.** [Original name, **Frances Davis.**] b. in New Zealand, 1883; d. Sept. 18, 1952. Operatic soprano. After studying under Marchesi in Paris, she made her début (1904) at the Opéra Comique. Her first appearance (1908) in New York was at the Metropolitan in the part of Gilda; she continued at the Metropolitan until 1930. She married Giulio Gatti-Casazza in 1910, and divorced him in 1929.

Aldabella (äl.dä.bel'lä). Wife of Orlando in Ariosto's poems, the sister of Oliviero and Brandimarte and daughter of Monodantes; in the old French and Spanish poems she is called "Alda" and "Auda."

Aldabella. Character in Henry Hart Milman's play *Fazio*, a handsome, shameless woman who beguiles Fazio when he becomes rich, and after his execution is condemned to imprisonment in a nunnery for life through the interposition of Bianca, the wife of Fazio.

Aldabra Islands (al.dab'rạ). Group of small coral islands in the W part of the Indian Ocean, ab. 200 mi. NW of the island of Madagascar: part of the British crown colony of Seychelles.

Aldan (ôl'dạn). Borough in SE Pennsylvania, in Delaware County, near Philadelphia. 3,430 (1950).

Aldana (äl.dä'nä), **Lorenzo de.** b. in Estremadura, Spain, c1500; d. at Arequipa, Peru, probably in 1556. Spanish soldier who served with Alvarado in Guatemala and Peru, and in 1536 went with Juan de Rada to reinforce Almagro in Chile. In 1554 he was with Alonzo de Alvarado in the campaign against Giron, and shared in the defeat at the Abancay River (May 21, 1554). Authorities are not in accord as to the date of his death, Calancha placing it in 1571.

Aldanov (äl.dä'nǫf), **M. A.** [Pseudonym of **Mark Aleksandrovich Landau.**] b. at Kiev, Russia, Nov. 7, 1886—. Russian novelist, biographer, and political writer, an émigré since 1919 in France, and more recently in the U.S. His sequence of novels entitled *The Thinker* has to do with the French revolution and its aftermath. It includes *The Ninth Thermidor, The Devil's Bridge, The Conspiracy,* and *St. Helena.* All of them except *The Conspiracy* were published in English between 1924 and 1929. His anti-communist novel *The Fifth Seal* was chosen (1943) as a selection in America by the Book of the Month Club. A later work, published in English as *Before the Deluge* (1947), is an historical novel through the pages of which move Alexander II and many leading Russians and Europeans who flourished in the last years of Alexander's reign. His "philosophical novelette" *The Tenth Symphony* was published in English in 1948. He is the author of a biography of Lenin, published in English in 1922, and of a fictional life of Byron translated into English as *For Thee the Best* (1945). *To Live as We Wish* (1952) is concerned with totalitarianism.

Aldan Plateau (äl.dän'). [Also, **Aldan Mountains.**] Spur of the Stanovoi Mountains, in E Siberia, U.S.S.R., near the river Aldan, running NE-SW. Gold is mined in these mountains.

Aldan River. River in the U.S.S.R., in the Yakutsk *oblast* (region) of the Russian Soviet Federated Socialist Republic, Siberia; it rises in the Aldan Plateau, E of the Yablonoi Mountains, and joins the Lena. Much gold has been found in this river. Length, ab. 1,393 mi.

Aldborough (ôld'bėr.ǫ). See also **Aldeburgh.**

Aldborough (ôld'bėr.ǫ; locally ô'brǫ). [Latin, **Isurium.**] Civil parish and hamlet in C England, in the West Riding of Yorkshire, ab. 16 mi. NW of York. It is noted for its Roman antiquities, including the pavements, foundations, and other remains of an ancient Roman city. 543 (1931).

Aldebaran (al.deb'ạ.rạn). Name of the standard first-magnitude orange star α Tauri, in the northern constellation Taurus ("the Bull"), in the eye of the animal; most conspicuous member of the group known as the Hyades. Its diameter is 50 times that of the sun. One of the stars with which Halley discovered the proper motion of stars (1718); known to Hesiod and Homer. It is also often called Palilicium.

Aldeburgh (ôld'bėr.ǫ). [Also, **Aldborough.**] Municipal borough and seaport in E England, in East Suffolk, ab. 100 mi. NE of London and ab. 21 mi. NE of Ipswich. 2,684 (1951).

Aldegrever (äl'dẹ.grā.vėr), **Heinrich.** [Also: **Aldegraf** (-gräf); original name, **Heinrich Trippenmeker;** sometimes called **"Albert of Westphalia."**] b. at Paderborn, Prussia, 1502; d. at Soest, Prussia, c1562. German engraver and painter; one of a group known as the Little Masters. He is noted particularly for his expert and delicate engravings, influenced by the Italian Renaissance masters and by Albrecht Dürer.

Alden (ôl'dẹn). Town in W New York, in Erie County ab. 20 mi. E of Buffalo: resort. 4,899 (1950).

Alden, Ebenezer, b. at Randolph, Mass., March 17, 1788; d. Jan. 26, 1881. American physician, medical historian, bibliophile, and genealogist. He is notable for his research in the history of medicine in Massachusetts, as evidenced by his *Historical Sketch of the Origin and Progress of the Massachusetts Medical Society* (1838), and others. His library, particularly in connection with medicine, the Civil War, and the ecclesiastical history of New England, was one of the most complete in the U.S. during the 19th century.

Alden, Henry Mills. b. at Mt. Tabor, Vt., Nov. 11, 1836; d. at New York, Oct. 7, 1919. American editor, author, and scholar of the classics. An early intention to enter the ministry was forsaken after graduation (1860) from Andover Theological Seminary; he gained some literary success during next three years with articles in the *Atlantic Monthly.* He collaborated (1863 *et seq.*) with Alfred H. Guernsey on *Harper's Pictorial History of the Great Rebellion*, serving also as managing editor (1863–69) of *Harper's Weekly*, and from 1869 until his death as editor of *Harper's Magazine.* Under his guidance *Harper's Magazine* attained the largest magazine circulation in the U.S., never surrendering its policy of printing only those portions of good literature which "could . . . be read aloud in the home."

Alden, Ichabod. b. at Duxbury, Mass., Aug. 11, 1739; killed in massacre at Cherry Valley, N.Y., Nov. 11, 1778. American Revolutionary officer. Appointed (1778) to defend the settlement at Cherry Valley, N.Y., he was led by inexperience in Indian warfare to underestimate the tactical cunning of the Indian force under British and Loyalist leadership and was massacred, with most of his troops and many of the settlers, in a surprise attack on Nov. 11, 1778.

Alden, Isabella Macdonald. [Pseudonym: **Pansy.**] b. at Rochester, N.Y., Nov. 3, 1841; d. at Palo Alto, Calif., Aug. 5, 1930. American writer of books and stories for children. Editor (1873–96) of the juvenile publication known as *Pansy;* wrote over 70 "Pansy Books," a life of Christ, and some fiction for adults.

Alden, James. b. at Portland, Me., 1810; d. at San Francisco, Calif., Feb. 6, 1877. American naval officer, appointed rear admiral (1871). He served in the Mexican War; in the Civil War, he commanded the *Richmond* in the New Orleans campaign of 1862, and the *Brooklyn* in Mobile Bay (1864).

Alden, John. b. in England, c1599; d. at Duxbury, Mass., 1687. One of the "Pilgrim Fathers," a cooper of Southampton, who was engaged in repairing the *Mayflower* and became one of the party which sailed in her. He is said to have been the first to step on Plymouth Rock after the arrival (1620) in America, though this honor is also assigned to Mary Chilton. He settled at Duxbury and married (c1623) Priscilla Mullens. The incidents (probably apocryphal) of their courtship form the theme of Longfellow's *Courtship of Miles Standish.* He was an official in the colony for more than 50 years, serving (1633–41, 1650–86) as governor's assistant. He is said to have outlived all the other signers of the Mayflower Compact.

Alden, Raymond Macdonald. b. at New Hartford, N.Y., March 30, 1873; d. at Philadelphia, Sept. 27, 1924. American philologist and Shakespearian scholar, known for his variorum edition of *The Sonnets of Shakespeare* (1916); author of numerous textbooks and some short fiction.

Alden, Timothy. b. at Yarmouth, Mass., Aug. 28, 1771; d. July 5, 1839. American Congregational minister, founder and first president of Allegheny College. He served (1817–31) as president, and professor of Oriental language and ecclesiastical history, of the college at Meadville, Pa., which was forced to close by poverty, but was reopened under Methodist auspices in 1833.

Aldenham (ôl'dẹn.ạm), 1st Baron. [Title of **Henry Hucks Gibbs.**] b. at London, 1819; d. at Aldenham, Hertfordshire, 1907. English scholar, merchant, and banker. Director (1853–1901) and governor (1875–77) of the Bank of England; aided Sir James Murray with *Oxford English Dictionary* (1880 *et seq.*) and wrote many of its banking and commercial definitions; edited (1868) *Romance of the Chevelere Assigne* for Early English Text Society; author of numerous pamphlets on banking, including several which argued for bimetallism.

Aldenhoven (äl'dẹn.hō.fẹn). Town in W Germany, in the former Rhine Province, Prussia, ab. 12 mi. NE of Aachen. Here on March 1, 1793, the Austrians under the Prince of Coburg and Archduke Charles defeated the French, and on Oct. 2, 1794, a French army under Jourdan defeated the Austrian forces under Clairfayt. Pop. ab. 2,000.

Alderamin (al.dėr.am'in). Usual name of the 2½-magnitude star α Cephei, in the northern constellation Cepheus.

Alderman (ôl'dėr.mạn), **Edwin Anderson.** b. at Wilmington, N.C., May 15, 1861; d. April 29, 1931. American educator and historian. Professor of education (1893–96) and president (1896–1900), University of North Carolina; president of Tulane (1900–04) and University of Virginia (1904–31); editor-in-chief of the Library of Southern Literature.

Alderney (ôl'dėr.ni). [French, **Aurigny**; ancient names, **Aurinia, Riduna.**] One of the Channel Islands, situated ab. 23 mi. NE of Guernsey and ab. 7 mi. W of the Cap de la Hague, France: noted for its breed of cattle The island, a British possession, is politically a dependency of the bailiwick of Guernsey, but has its own government, vested in a judge, 6 jurats, and 12 representatives. Both English and Norman-French are spoken, the latter being the official language. Capital, St. Anne; length, ab. 4 mi.; greatest width, ab. 1 mi.; area, ab. 3 sq. mi.; pop. 1,469 (1950).

Alderney, Race of. [French, **Ras d'Aurigny.**] That part of the English Channel which lies between the island of Alderney and the Cap de la Hague, France. It is a dangerous tidal race. The French fleet escaped here after a defeat (1692) at the battle of La Hogue. Width, ab. 9 mi.

Aldersgate (ôl'dėrz.gāt). Gate in old London wall which stood in the reëntering angle of the old city between Newgate and Cripplegate and at the junction of Aldersgate Street and St. Martin's Lane. It is called Ealdred's gate in the laws of Ethelred.

Aldershot (ôl'dėr.shot). Municipal borough in S England, in Hampshire, near the Hampshire-Surrey border, ab. 34 mi. SW of London: site of the largest military post in Great Britain (est. 1854–55). The Basingstoke Canal divides the camp. 36,184 (1951).

Aldfrith (äld'frith). [Also: **Eahfrith, Ealdfrith.**] d. 705. King of the Northumbrians, an illegitimate son of Oswiu, and brother of Ecgfrith, whom he succeeded in 685.

Aldgate (ôld'gāt). Eastern gate of old London wall, situated near the junction of Leadenhall Street, Houndsditch, Whitehall, and the Minories. It must have been one of the seven double gates mentioned by Fitz Stephens (who died 1191), not one of the Roman gates. The great road to Essex by which provisions were brought to the Roman city crossed the Lea at Old-ford and entered the city by way of Eormine (Ermine) Street, not at Aldgate but at Bishopsgate. Aldgate may have been opened in the reign of King Eadgar, or that of Edward the Confessor, but probably dates from the first years of Henry I, at which time Bow Bridge across the Lea at Stratford is supposed to have been built by his queen, Matilda.

Aldhelm (ôld'helm). b. c640; d. at Doulting, England, 709. English scholar and cleric; abbot of Malmesbury (675–709) and first bishop of Sherborne (705–709). He settled the controversy between Britons and Rome on the date of Easter. He founded schools and built several churches. A student of the classics, he is believed to have been the first Englishman to write Latin verse. He was also the author of *Epistola ad Acircium*, a treatise on Latin prosody which included 101 riddles in Latin hexameters; *De laude virginitatis sive virginitate sanctorum* (c705), a commemorative treatise on the saints; and of Anglo-Saxon poems and songs. Aldhelm was later canonized, his feast falling on May 25.

Aldiborontephoscophornio (al"di.bọ.ron"tẹ.fos"kọ.fôr'ni.ō). Character in Henry Carey's burlesque *Chrononhotonthologos*. It was given as a nickname to James Ballantyne the printer, on account of the solemn pomposity of his manner, by Sir Walter Scott.

Aldiger (al'di.gėr). In Ariosto's *Orlando Furioso*, a Christian knight and the brother of the enchanter Malagigi.

Aldine (ôl'dēn, al'dīn), **The.** Journal of art and typography (1868–79), known for the high quality of its technical craftsmanship. Originally a house organ of a New York printing establishment, it became (1871) a magazine aimed at a wider audience.

Aldine Press. The press established at Venice by Aldus Manutius.

Aldingar (al'ding.gär). Prior of St. Cuthbert's Abbey in Sir Walter Scott's poem *Harold the Dauntless*.

Aldingar, Sir. Ballad concerning a false steward who sought to take away the honor of his queen. In the ballad with this title from the Percy Manuscript the queen's name is Elinore, the wife of Henry II, but the story occurs repeatedly in connection with historical personages of nearly all the European nations.

Aldington (ôl'ding.tọn), **Richard.** b. in Hampshire, England, 1892—. English poet and novelist; leader of the Imagist school of English verse writing. He was for a short time in 1919 a staff-member of the London *Times* literary supplement after service (1916–18) in World War I; lived until outbreak of World War II in Switzerland, Italy, France, and elsewhere, becoming in 1939 a resident of the U.S.; married (1913–37) to American poet, Hilda Doolittle ("H.D."), and since 1937 to Netta McCulloch. Author of *Images Old and New* (1915), *War and Love* (1918), *Images of Desire* (1919), *A Fool i' the Forest* (1925), *Collected Poems* (1928), and many other volumes of verse; his novels include *Death of a Hero* (1929), *The Colonel's Daughter* (1931), *All Men Are Enemies* (1933), *Very Heaven* (1937), *Rejected Guest* (1939), and others; has also written the autobiographical *Life for Life's Sake* (1941), as well as a play, several short stories, and a number of translations from Greek, Latin, Italian, and French.

Aldini (äl.dē'nē), Count **Antonio.** b. at Bologna, Italy, 1756; d. at Pavia, Italy, Oct. 5, 1826. Italian statesman, minister of the Italian republic and kingdom under the Napoleonic regime.

Aldini, Giovanni. b. at Bologna, Italy, 1762; d. at Milan, Italy, 1834. Italian physicist, professor of physics at Bologna; brother of Antonio Aldini and nephew of Galvani.

Al-Djesirat-al-hadra (äl.je.sē'rạt.äl.hä'drä). An Arabic name of **Algeciras.**

Aldo (al'dō), **Father.** In John Dryden's play *Limberham, or the Kind Keeper*, an abandoned but kind-hearted old debauchee.

Aldobrandini (äl"dō.brän.dē'nē). Celebrated Florentine family, originally from the village of Lasciano, near Pistoia, established in Florence since the 12th century.

Aldobrandini, Giovanni. b. 1525; d. at Rome, 1573. Italian cardinal; son of Silvestro Aldobrandini.

Aldobrandini, Giovanni Francesco. b. 1546; d. 1601. Papal general; nephew of Pope Clement VIII.

Aldobrandini, Ippolito. Original name of Pope **Clement VIII.**

Aldobrandini, Pietro. b. 1571; d. 1621. Italian cardinal; grandson of Silvestro Aldobrandini.

Aldobrandini, Silvestro. b. at Florence, Nov. 23, 1499; d. at Rome, Jan. 6, 1558. Italian jurist and opponent of the Medici family.

Aldobrandini, Tommaso. b. c1530; d. 1572. Italian man of letters; son of Silvestro Aldobrandini. He is the author of a Latin translation of Diogenes Laërtius.

Aldred (al'drẹd). [Also: **Alred, Ealdred.**] d. at York, England, 1069. English ecclesiastic; bishop of Worcester (1044) and archbishop of York (1060). He was commissioned by Edward the Confessor to negotiate the return to the throne of Edward the Aetheling. Failing in this, he submitted to William I (the Conqueror), whom he crowned in 1066; he later (1068) also crowned Matilda.

Aldrich (ôl'drich), **Bess Streeter.** b. at Cedar Falls, Iowa, Feb. 17, 1881—. American novelist and short-story writer. Author of *A White Bird Flying* (1931), *Miss Bishop* (1933), *Spring Came on Forever* (1935), *Song of Years* (1939), *The Drum Goes Dead* (1941), as well as short-story collections including *The Man Who Caught the Weather* (1936), and others. Before 1918 she used the pseudonym Margaret Dean Stevens.

Aldrich, Edgar. b. at Pittsburg, N.H., Feb. 5, 1848; d. Sept. 15, 1921. American jurist. His outstanding ability as a lawyer led to an appointment (1891) as U.S. district judge for New Hampshire and to selection (1907) as legal head of the inquiry into the ability of Mrs. Mary Baker Eddy to manage her considerable financial interest.

Aldrich, Henry. b. at Westminster, England, 1647; d. at Oxford, 1710. English theologian, musician, and architect; dean of Christ Church, Oxford, from 1689.

Aldrich, Louis. [Original name **Louis Lyon;** called the **"Ohio Roscius."**] b. in Ohio, Oct. 1, 1843; d. at Kennebunkport, Me., June 17, 1901. American actor. He began his stage career as a boy, notably in Richard III, and first starred in 1858, when he also adopted the surname Aldrich. He later played with Kate Bateman, Charles Kean, Edwin Forrest, Charlotte Cushman, and others. He was elected president of the American Actors' Fund in 1897; he suggested the establishment of a home for destitute actors, which subsequently came into being as the Staten Island Actors' Home.

Aldrich, Nelson Wilmarth. b. at Foster, R.I., Nov. 6, 1841; d. at New York, April 16, 1915. American politician and financier. As a Republican senator (1881–1911) from Rhode Island, he was a brilliant parliamentarian and political strategist. Senate leader during the McKinley, Roosevelt, and Taft administrations, he influenced the passage of the McKinley Tariff Act (1890), the Silver Purchase Act (1890), the Anti-Trust Act (1890), the Gold Standard Act (1900), and the Payne-Aldrich Tariff Act (1909) against strong opposition and in spite of party splits. As chairman of the National Monetary Commission, created by the Aldrich-Vreeland Act (1908), he made the study of banking reform (1908–11) later largely embodied in the Federal Reserve Act (1913).

Aldrich, Richard. b. at Providence, R.I., July 31, 1863; d. at Rome, June 2, 1937. American music critic. On staff of Providence *Journal* (1885–89) and New York *Tribune* (1891–1902); New York *Times* music critic (1902–24); contributor to *International Cyclopedia of Music and Musicians* (1938); author of *Guide to Parsifal* (1904), *Guide to Nibelungen Ring* (1905), *Musical Discourse* (1928), and others.

Aldrich, Thomas Bailey. b. at Portsmouth, N.H., Nov. 11, 1836; d. at Boston, March 19, 1907. American story writer, editor, and poet. Editor of *Every Saturday* (1865–74) and of the *Atlantic Monthly* (1881–90) during one of its chief periods as a standard of excellent literary craftsmanship, he is perhaps best known for *The Story of a Bad Boy* (1870). Author also of volumes of verse, of novels, including *Prudence Palfrey* (1874), *The Queen of Sheba* (1877), and *Stillwater Tragedy* (1880), sketches such as *Ponkapog Papers* (1903), and of short stories, especially those collected in *Marjorie Daw and Other People* (1873).

Aldrich, Winthrop Williams. b. at Providence, R.I., Nov. 2, 1885—. American banker and diplomat; son of Nelson W. Aldrich. Chairman of the board of the Chase National Bank of New York, he has served also as director of a number of business and industrial firms and as a trustee of several institutions. He was appointed (1953) U.S. ambassador to Great Britain.

Aldrich Deep. Very deep portion of the Pacific Ocean, lying NE of New Zealand and E of the Kermadec Islands. It is part of the Kermadec Trench. Depth, 30,930 ft.

Aldrich-Vreeland Act (ôl'drich.vrē'lạnd). Act passed by the U.S. Congress in 1908 as an emergency measure following the brief financial panic of 1907. Its chief aims were the encouragement of an elastic currency and the creation of a reform banking policy and structure to serve until more permanent legislation could be devised. It established the National Monetary Commission to study fiscal and banking systems and to report to Congress on the advisability of making changes in the U.S. banking system. This law expired on June 30, 1915, but its chief goals had already been secured by the Federal Reserve Act (1913).

Aldridge (ôl'drij). Urban district in C England, in Staffordshire, ab. 10 mi. E of Wolverhampton, ab. 129 mi. NW of London by rail. 29,167 (1951).

Aldridge, Ira Frederick. [Called the **"African Roscius."**] b. probably at New York, c1805; d. at Łódź, Poland, Aug. 10, 1867. American Negro tragedian. A protégé of Edmund Kean, whose valet he probably was for a time, he made his début (1826) as Othello at the Royalty Theatre, London. He was poorly received at Baltimore (c1830) but played successfully at London (1833 *et seq.*) and met with considerable acclaim in Europe (1853–56; 1858–67), particularly for Shakespearian roles such as Othello, Lear, Aaron, and Macbeth. He was honored by the governments of Prussia, Austria, Russia, and others.

Aldringen (äl'dring.ẹn) or **Aldringer** (-ėr), Count **Johann.** [Also, **Altringer.**] b. at Thionville (Diedenhofen), in Lorraine, Dec. 10, 1588; killed at Landshut, in Bavaria, 1634. Austrian imperial general in the Thirty Years' War. He succeeded Tilly as commander of the army of the League in 1632, and served under Wallenstein at Nuremberg (1632). He was in command of the campaign against the Swedes on the Danube (1634).

Aldrovand (al'drọ.vand), **Father.** A Dominican friar, the warlike chaplain of Lady Eveline Berenger in Sir Walter Scott's novel *The Betrothed.*

Aldrovandi (äl.drō.vän'dē), **Ulisse.** [Latin, **Ulysses Aldrovandus.**] b. at Bologna, Italy, 1522; d. there, 1605. Italian naturalist; professor of natural history at Bologna (1560); founder (1568) and director of the Bologna botanical gardens. As inspector of drugs, he published *Antidotarii Bononiensis Epitome* (1574); his chief work, a monumental *Natural History* (1599–1642) on birds, insects, and mollusks, is profusely illustrated with his own drawings.

Aldstone or **Aldstone Moor** (ôl'stọn). See **Alston.**

Aldwych (ôld'wich). Street in W London, in Westminster metropolitan borough. It is a crescent (100 ft. wide) extending ab. ¼ mi. from its intersection with the Strand at St. Clement's to intersect again with the Strand at the S end of Catherine Street. The Gaiety Theatre, Bush House, and Australia House are on Aldwych.

Aleandro (ä.lā.än'drō), **Girolamo.** [Latinized, **Hieronymus Aleander.**] b. at Motta, near Venice, Italy, Feb. 13, 1480; d. at Rome, Jan. 31, 1542. Italian cardinal and scholar. He was at various times Vatican librarian, rector of the University of Paris, and papal nuncio to Germany, the Netherlands, and France. He was a determined opponent of the Reformation, and particularly of Luther. He was the author of a *Lexicon Graeco-Latinum* (1512) and other works.

Aleardi (ä.lā.är'dē), Count **Aleardo.** [Original surname, **Gaetano.**] b at Verona, Italy, 1812; d. there, 1878. Italian poet and patriot, an active partisan of the insurrection in Venetia (1848–49); imprisoned by the Austrians in 1852 and 1859. The best edition of his poems is usually considered to have been that published at Florence in 1862 (5th ed., 1878).

Alecsandri (ä.lek.sän'drē), **Vasili.** [Also, **Basile Alexandri.**] b. in Moldavia, 1821; d. at Mircesti, Moldavia, 1890. Rumanian poet, politician, and journalist, notable as a collector of Rumanian songs. Active in politics after 1848, he served as foreign minister (1859–60) and minister to France (1885 *et seq.*). He published lyric and dramatic poems, *Despot Voda* (1880), *Ovidiu* (1885), collections of native songs (1844, 1852–53), and others.

Alecto (ạ.lek'tō). In Greek mythology, one of the three Erinyes.

Aledo (a.lē'dō). City in NW Illinois, county seat of Mercer County, SW of Rock Island: center of an agricultural area. 2,919 (1950).

Alegrete (ä.le.grā'te). City in S Brazil, in the state of Rio Grande do Sul. 20,160 (1950).

Alegría (ä.lā.grē'ä), **Ciro.** b. at Sartimbamba, Peru, 1909—. Peruvian novelist and political journalist. He joined (1930) the Aprista party and was twice jailed (1931, 1933) for political activity; exiled (1934) and for a time resident in Chile; came to the U.S. (1941) and served with the Coördinator of Inter-American Affairs and Office of War Information. Author of the prize-winning *La Serpiente de oro* (1935), the first great work to depict life in the Peruvian jungle, of *Los Perros hambrientos* (1938), *El Mundo es ancho y ajeno* (1941), winner of the first Latin American Prize Novel contest in the U.S., and others.

Alekhine (ä.lye'hin), **Aleksandr Aleksandrovich.** [Also, **Aljechin.**] b. at Moscow, Nov. 1, 1892; d. at Lisbon, Portugal, March 24, 1946. Russian chess master and world chess champion (1927–35; 1937–46). He was an eminently successful match and tournament player, chess theoretician, and author, whose principal works were *My Best Games of Chess, 1908–1923, New York 1924 Tournament Book*, and *My Best Games of Chess, 1924–1937.* His chief international tournament victories were first prize at Stockholm 1912, Scheveningen 1913, Moscow 1914 (equal first), Budapest 1921, The Hague 1921, Carlsbad 1923 (equal first), Baden-Baden 1925, Kecskemet 1927, San Remo 1930, Berne 1932, and Zurich 1934.

Aleksandr Aleksandrovich (ä.lik.sän'dėr ä.lik.sän'dro.vich). Russian name of **Alexander III** (of *Russia*).

Aleksandr Nikolayevich (nē.ko.lä'yi.vich). Russian name of **Alexander II** (of *Russia*).

Aleksandropol (al.ig.zan'drō.pôl; Russian, ä.lik.sän.drô'-pol). Former name of **Leninakan.**

Aleksandrov (ä.lik.sän'drof). [Also: **Alexandrov, Alexandroff.**] City in the U.S.S.R., in the Vladimir *oblast* (region) of the Russian Soviet Federated Socialist Republic, ab. 65 mi. NE of Moscow. Pop. ab. 12,000.

Aleksandrovsk (ä.lik.sän'drofsk). [Full name, **Aleksandrovsk-Sakhalinski.**] City and port in Asia, in the Russian Soviet Federated Socialist Republic, in the U.S.S.R. Situated on the W coast of Sakhalin, N of Japan, it was until after World War II of little importance in the Russian economy (before the Russian Revolution it was considered so remote and of such small value as to be used as a place of exile), but the discovery in recent years of extensive oil and coal reserves in the vicinity, and the acquisition by Russia from Japan of the S portion of Sakhalin, have given it immense importance since World War II. The last official census estimate gives it a population of only ab. 10,000, but recent unofficial estimates of its size run as high as 100,000.

Aleksandrovsk-Grushevski (ä.lik.sän'drofsk.grů.shef'-ski). Former name of **Shakhty.**

Aleksandr Pavlovich (ä.lik.sän'dėr päv'lo.vich). Russian name of **Alexander I** (of *Russia*).

Alekseyev (ä.lik.sā'yif), **Mikhail Vasilyevich.** b. 1857; d. at Ekaterinodar (now Krasnodar), Russia, 1918. Russian army officer. He entered the army in 1876 and became a general in 1904, during the early part of the Russo-Japanese War. In World War I, he was a commander in the sector of the Galician victory over Austria-Hungary (1914) and later (1915) rescued the Russian armies from defeats on the northwestern front. During the early period of the Russian Revolution, he attempted mediation between Kerensky and Kornilov; later he joined the counter-revolutionary forces, becoming their political head after Kornilov's death, and leaving the military leadership to Denikin.

Alekseyev, Yevgeni Ivanovich. [Also, **Eugenii Ivanovitch Alexeief.**] b. 1843; d. 1918. Russian admiral, appointed imperial lieutenant with control of both diplomatic and military affairs in the Far East on July 30, 1903, shortly before the outbreak of the Russo-Japanese War. From 1883 to 1893 he was naval attaché of the Russian embassy in Paris. He commanded the Russian squadron during the Chinese-Japanese war of 1894–97, and took possession of Port Arthur. In 1898 he was promoted to vice-admiral, took part in the work of the allies in China during 1900–01, and became chief of the Russian Pacific squadron. His conduct of affairs after his appointment to the imperial lieutenancy did not prevent war, and after the early Japanese successes he was deprived (April, 1904) of most of his power. He retired in November and returned to Russia. Reinstated (1914) as chief of staff, he headed (1915–16) the general staff and actively resisted (1917–18) the new revolutionary regime.

Aleksey Mikhailovich (ä.lik.sā' mē.hī'lo.vich). [Also, **Alexis Mikhailovich.**] b. March 19, 1629; d. Feb. 8, 1676. Czar of Russia, son of Michael Féodorovitch, the son of Czar Michael Romanoff, whom he succeeded in 1645. He waged a war (1654–67) with Poland, acquiring possession of Smolensk and the eastern Ukraine. In a war (1655–58) with Sweden he conquered a part of Livonia and Ingermanland, but was forced by domestic troubles to relinquish this territory at the treaty of Cardis (June 21, 1661). He suppressed with difficulty the revolt (1669–71) led by Stenka Razin. He extended his conquests to eastern Siberia, codified the laws of the various provinces of Russia, and, by beginning to introduce European civilization, prepared the way for the later rule of his younger son Peter the Great.

Aleksey Petrovich (pi.trô'vich). [Also, **Alexis Petrovich.**] b. at Moscow, Feb. 18, 1690; d. in prison at St. Petersburg, July 7, 1718. The eldest son of Peter the Great and father of Peter II. He fled (1717) to Vienna after voicing his disapproval of his father's policies. He returned, however, at Peter's request, and was then condemned for high treason and imprisoned.

Aleksin (ä.lyôk'sin). [Also, **Alexin.**] Town in the U.S.S.R., in the Tula *oblast* (region) of the Russian Soviet Federated Socialist Republic, situated on the Oka River ab. 85 mi. SW of Moscow.

Aleksinac (ä'lek.sē.näts). [German, **Alexinatz.**] Town in E Yugoslavia, in the federative unit of Serbia, in the former *banovina* (province) of Moravska, situated near the Morava River, N of Niš: scene of several armed contests between the Serbians and the Turks in 1876. Pop., predominantly Greek-Orthodox, 7,383 (1948).

Alem (ä.lem'), **Leandro N.** b. at Buenos Aires, c1845; d. 1896. Argentine political reformer, notable as chief organizer (1889) of the Unión Cívica and later (1891) of the Unión Cívica Radical. Both groups aimed at political reform within the country, but failed when Alem's attempt (1892) at a coup d'état was crushed. The Unión Cívica had earlier, however, compelled the resignation of President Juárez Celmán in 1890.

Alemán (ä.lā.män'), **Mateo.** b. near Seville, Spain, 1547; d. in Mexico, c1610. Spanish novelist and physician, first writer known to have produced a picaresque novel. Controller of finance (1571–88) under Philip II, he emigrated (1608) to Mexico and is thought to have been a printer at Mexico City. Author of *La vida y hechos del pícaro Guzmán de Alfarache* (1599–1604/5), which went into more than 16 editions in five years and was translated into French (1600), English (*The Rouge*, 1623), and Latin (1623).

Alemán, Miguel. b. at Sayula, Veracruz, Mexico, Sept. 29, 1903—. Mexican statesman, president of Mexico (1946–52). A noted labor attorney and a justice of the federal court, he was elected (1936) governor of Veracruz, serving until 1940, when he resigned to manage the successful presidential campaign of Manuel Ávila Camacho. He was minister of the interior (1940–45) under Camacho and was elected president to succeed him in 1946. Alemán's presidency was marked by a campaign to industrialize the country and to modernize its agricultural methods, of expanding the educational system, and of attracting foreign capital to Mexico to help build the country's prosperity.

Alemanni (al.e.man'ī). See **Alamanni** or **Alemanni.**

Alemannia (al.e.man'i.a). See **Alamannia.**

Alemannic Federation (al.e.man'ik). See **Alamannic Federation.**

Alembert (då.läṅ.ber), **Jean le Rond d'.** [Original name, **Jean le Rond.**] b. at Paris, 1717; d. there, 1783. French mathematician, physicist, and philosopher; cofounder and an editor of Diderot's *Encyclopédie;* son of Mme. Claudine Alexandrine de Tencin. As secretary (1772–83) of the French Academy, he was the spokesman and, after Voltaire's death (1778), the leader of the *parti des philosophes.* Author of numerous scientific works, chiefly the *Traité de dynamique* (1743) in which he proposed what is now called "d'Alembert's principle," *Recherches sur différents points importants du système du monde* (1754–56), and *Histoire des membres de l'Académie française.*

Alemquer (ä.lãng.ker'). See **Alenquer.**

Alencar (ä.lãng.kär'), **José (Martiniano) de.** b. at Mecejana, Ceará, Brazil, May 1, 1829; d. at Rio de Janeiro, Dec. 12, 1877. Brazilian novelist, playwright, essayist, poet, and political writer. The most famous novelist of the romantic period in Brazil, he is best known for his stories of Indian and colonial life, particularly *O guarani* (1857) and *Iracema* (1865). An English translation of the latter was published at London (1886). Among his other well-known novels are *As minas de prata* (1862–65), *Diva* (1864), *O gaucho* (1870), *A pata da gazela* (1870), *O tronco do ipê* (1871), *Ubirajara* (1875), *O sertanejo* (1876), and *Guerra dos Mascates* (1877).

Alençon (à.läṅ.sôṅ). Former countship and duchy of France, whose counts and dukes were prominent in the 14th, 15th, and 16th centuries. The duchy was an appanage of the house of Valois.

Alençon. Town in NW France, the capital of the department of Orne, situated at the junction of the Briante and Sarthe rivers, between Le Mans and Caen. It is an important trade center and has manufactures of lace (renowned as *point d'Alençon*), linen and woolen goods, and pottery. There is a museum, and a castle of the dukes of Alençon. The Church of Notre Dame dates from the 15th century. The town changed hands frequently in the English and Holy League wars. It was occupied by the Germans in 1871 and in 1940. Pop. 19,715 (1946).

Alençon (dà.läṅ.sôṅ), **Charles IV,** Duc **d'.** b. 1489; d. April 11, 1525. Prince of the blood and constable of France; husband of Margaret of Valois, sister of Francis I. His cowardice is said to have caused the loss of the battle of Pavia in 1525 and the capture of Francis I.

Alençon, Charles de Valois, Duc **d'.** d. 1346. French nobleman; brother of Philip VI of France. He was killed in the battle of Crécy.

Alençon, Emmanuel, Duc **de Vendôme et d'.** [Title of **Philippe Emmanuel Maximilien Marie Eudes d'Orléans.**] b. at Obermais, near Merano, Italy, Jan. 18, 1872; d. at Cannes, France, Feb. 1, 1931. Member of the house of Bourbon-Orléans; son of Ferdinand Philippe Marie d'Orléans, Duc d'Alençon (1844–1910).

Alençon, Ferdinand Philippe Marie d'Orléans, Duc **d'.** b. at Château Neuilly, Seine department, France, July 12, 1844; d. at Belmont Castle, England, June 29, 1910. Member of the house of Bourbon-Orléans. He refused (1870) to accept his nomination by the dictator Serrano as king of Spain, and also declined a later proposal (1886) concerning the Bulgarian throne. He campaigned (1865) with the Spanish army in the Philippines and served (1871–83) in the French army.

Alençon, Jean II, Duc **d'.** d. 1476. He supported the Dauphin against his father Charles VII, and was condemned to death in 1456, the sentence being, however, commuted to life imprisonment, followed by a pardon.

Alenio (ä.lā'nyō), **Giulio.** b. at Brescia, Italy, 1582; d. in China, c1644. Italian Jesuit, a missionary in China after 1610. He published several theological works in Chinese.

Alenquer (ä.lãng.ker'). [Also, **Alemquer.**] Town in N Brazil, in the state of Paraná, on the Amazon River opposite the mouth of the Tapajós River. 2,801 (1940).

Alenquer. [Also, **Alemquer.**] Small town and *concelho* (commune) in W Portugal, in the province of Estremadura, in Lisboa district, ab. 29 mi. NE of Lisbon. Pop. of concelho, 32,415 (1940); of town 7,553 (1940).

Alentejo (ä.lān.tā'zhö). [Also, **Alemtejo.**] Former province of Portugal, in the SE part of the country, now included in the provinces of Alto Alentejo and Baixo Alentejo.

Alentejo, Alto. See **Alto Alentejo.**

Alentejo, Baixo. See **Baixo Alentejo.**

Alenuihaha Channel (ä.le.nö.ē.hä'hä). Sea passage of the Pacific Ocean separating the islands of Maui and Hawaii, in the Hawaiian Islands. Width, 26 sea mi.

Aleppo (ạ.lep'ō). [French, **Alep** (à.lep).] Former *il* (province or vilayet) of the Turkish empire, now mostly in Syria.

Aleppo. [Arabic, **Haleb, Haleb-es-Shahba;** French, **Alep;** Greek, **Khalepion;** ancient name, **Beroea.**] City in NW Syria, on the Kuweik. The most important trading center of N Syria, it is a major road junction and rail center near the Turkish border. In 638 it was conquered by the Saracens; it was the seat of a Seljuk sultanate in the 11th and 12th centuries. Captured by the Crusaders under Baldwin in 1170, and plundered by the Mongols and by Tamerlane, it was conquered and annexed by the Turks in 1517. The city suffered severely from plagues, and in 1170 and 1822 from earthquakes; it was the scene of an outbreak against the Christians in 1850. Pop. 362,541 (1950).

Aler (ä'lèr), **Paul.** b. at St.-Guy, Luxembourg, 1656; d. at Düren, Germany, 1727. German Jesuit, author of the school treatise *Gradus ad Parnassum* (1702), and others.

Alert (ạ.lėrt'). One of the steam vessels of the British polar expedition (1875–76) under Sir George Strong Nares; the other was the *Discovery.* The *Alert* passed through Kennedy Channel and wintered at Floeberg Beach, the most northerly point reached by ship up to that date.

Alès (à.les). [Former name, **Alais.**] Town in S France, in the department of Gard, situated on the Gardon River, ab. 25 mi. NW of Nîmes. It is an industrial town, with silk, leather, chemical, and iron industries. Nearby are coal, iron, silver, zinc, antimony, and asphalt mines. It is also a lumber trade center. A fortification was erected here by Vauban on the site of a medieval castle. 34,731 (1946).

Alesia (ạ.lē'zhạ). In ancient geography, the capital of the Mandubii in C Gaul, usually identified with modern Alise, a small town in the French department of Côte-d'Or.

Alesius (ạ.lē'zhi.us), **Alexander.** [Also surnamed: **ab Ales** (**äb** ä'les), **Alane** (al'ạn), **Ales, Aless, Alesse** (ä'les).] b. at Edinburgh, 1500; d. at Leipzig, 1565. Scottish Lutheran controversialist and exegete; canon of Saint Andrew's, Edinburgh. Imprisoned as a result of his reformism, he escaped (1532) to Wittenberg, Germany; there he became the friend of Luther and Melanchthon and signed the Augsburg Confession. He returned to England (1535), and was an intimate associate of Thomas Cranmer, Thomas Cromwell, and other English reformers.

Alessandra (ä.les.sän'drä). Queen of the Amazons in Ariosto's *Orlando Furioso.*

Alessandri (ä.les.sän'drē), **Alessandro.** b. at Naples, Italy, c1461; d. 1523. Italian jurist and antiquarian, author of *Dies geniales* (1522), and others.

Alessandria (ä.les.sän'drē.ä). Province in the *compartimento* (region) of Piedmont in NW Italy. Capital, Alessandria; area, ab. 1,376 sq. mi.; pop. 493,698 (1936).

Alessandria. City and commune in NW Italy, in the *compartimento* (region) of Piedmont, the capital of the province of Alessandria, situated at the junction of the Bormida and Tanaro rivers, E of Turin. It is an important railroad junction, has railroad repair shops, metallurgical, cotton textile, and hat manufactures (Borsalino), and trade in agricultural products. In a strategic location, it was a center of liberal movements, aiming at the liberation and unification of Italy, in the 19th century. The churches of San Rocco, Santa Maria di Castello, and San Francesco date from the 13th and 14th centuries; there are a number of palatial houses from the Renaissance period, including the episcopal palace and the town hall, and an art gallery. Little damage was suffered by buildings of tourist interest during World War II. Pop. of commune, 79,327 (1936); of city, 59,372 (1936).

Alessandria, Armistice of. Armistice agreed upon between Napoleon and the Austrian general Melas, on June 16, 1800, after the battle of Marengo. The Austrians retired behind the Mincio, abandoning to the French every fortress in N Italy to the west of that river.

Alessandri Palma (ä.lā.sän'drē päl'mä), **Arturo.** b. Dec. 20, 1868; d. Aug. 24, 1950. Chilean lawyer and politician, president of Chile (1920–25; 1932–37); father of Arturo Alessandri Rodríguez (1895—). Minister of industry and public works (1908 *et seq.*); minister of finance (1913 *et seq.*); minister of interior (1918 *et seq.*); successful presidential candidate (1920) of the Liberal Alliance, an anti-Conservative coalition party. His efforts to reform the government and to enact socialist legislation brought a reaction, and his government was overthrown (1924) by an army revolt. He was elected president the second time (1932) on a moderate socialist ticket.

Alessandri Rodríguez (rō.ᴛʜrē'ges), **Arturo.** b. at Santiago, Chile, May 8, 1895—. Chilean lawyer and legal scholar; son of Arturo Alessandri Palma (1868—).

Alessandro Stradella (ä.les.sän'drō strä.del'lä). [Original title, **Stradella.**] Opera by Flotow, first produced as a short lyrical piece at Paris in 1837, and afterward rewritten and produced in its present form at Hamburg, Dec. 30, 1844.

Alessi (ä.les'sē), **Galeazzo.** b. at Perugia, Italy, c1512; d. 1572. Italian architect, builder of the Church of Santa Maria di Carignano, at Genoa, and of palaces and churches at Genoa, Milan, and elsewhere.

Ålesund (ô'lẹ.sůn). [Also, **Aalesund.**] City in W Norway, in the *fylke* (county) of Møre og Romsdal, situated on two islands at the mouth of the Stor Fjord, between Bergen and Trondheim: a seaport and headquarters for cod, herring, and seal fishing fleets. Formerly only a landing station by the name of Borgundsund, it was established in 1848; rebuilt after a fire in 1904. Pop. 18,143 (1946).

Alet (à.lā). Town in the department of Aude, S France, on the Aude River ab. 15 mi. SW of Carcassonne. It contains a ruined cathedral.

Aletsch Glacier (ä'lech). Largest glacier in Switzerland, situated in the canton of Valais, N of Brigue and S of the Jungfrau. Length, ab. 13 mi.

Aletschhorn (ä'lech.hôrn). Peak of the Bernese Alps, in Valais canton, S Switzerland, near the Aletsch Glacier. Elevation, ab. 13,763 ft.

Aleut (al'i.öt). Division of the Eskimo, inhabiting the Alaskan peninsula and the Aleutian Islands. The languages of the various Aleut groups comprise a family related to the Eskimo linguistic family.

Aleutian Islands (ạ.lö'shạn). [Also, **Catharine Archipelago.**] Chain of ab. 150 islands belonging principally to Alaska. It extends W from the peninsula of Alaska, and separates Bering Sea from the Pacific Ocean. The islands were discovered by the Russians in the middle of the 18th century.

Aleutian Range. Mountain range in SW Alaska, extending W into the Aleutian peninsula. It includes a number of large volcanoes.

Aleutians Campaign. American campaign in World War II. Extending over a whole year from August, 1942, to August, 1943, this campaign wrested from Japanese control the islands in the Aleutian chain which Japan had taken almost without resistance earlier in the war, and on which it had sought to construct airfields. The action centered first on Attu, which was invaded in May, and was made more difficult by snowstorms and dense fogs. The ultimate point of attack, however, was Kiska, to the E of Attu. After heavy American bombardment of this island, Japanese troops made a skillful evacuation, aided by the fogs of the Bering Sea, and U.S. troops moved in.

Alexander (al.eg.zan'dėr). [Called **Alexander Lyncestes.**] fl. 4th century B.C. A native of Lyncestis in Macedonia (whence his surname "Lyncestes"), implicated with his brothers in the murder of Philip II of Macedonia in 336 B.C. Because he was the first to do homage to Alexander the Great, the latter pardoned him and raised him to a high position in the army, but afterward put him to death for a treasonable correspondence with Darius.

Alexander. [Called **Alexander Jannaeus.**] b. 128 or 129 B.C.; d. 78 B.C. King of the Jews from 104 till 78 B.C. He was a younger son of John Hyrcanus.

Alexander, Saint. d. at Alexandria, 326 A.D. Patriarch of Alexandria (312 *et seq.*) and opponent of Arius, whom he excluded from the patriarchate. He took a leading part in the General Council at Nicaea, which he attended with his deacon, Saint Athanasius.

Alexander I, Saint. Pope from 105 to 115, successor of Saint Evaristus. He has been identified by some scholars with an Alexander martyred on the Via Nomentana, at Rome.

Alexander II. [Original name, **Anselmo Baggio**; Latinized, **Anselmus Badajus.**] d. 1073. Pope from 1061 to 1073. Endeavored to enforce celibacy of clergy; occupancy of papal chair at first threatened by election of an antipope, Honorius II, at Basle, but threat removed when rapprochement reached with German bishops and court, who were Honorius's chief supporters; Alexander formally recognized (1064) as Pope by all parties.

Alexander III. [Original name, **Orlando** (or **Rolando Ranuci**) **Bandinelli.**] b. at Siena, Italy; d. 1181. Pope from 1159 to 1181, successor of Adrian IV. A champion of ecclesiastical independence, he carried out the policy of Hildebrand in opposition to Frederick Barbarossa (whom he excommunicated) and Henry II of England. Three antipopes, Victor IV, Pascal III, and Calixtus III (elected 1159, 1164, and 1168, respectively) were confirmed by Frederick, and disputed the authority of Alexander, who was compelled to take refuge (1162–65) in France and again (1167) at Venice and elsewhere. His struggle with Henry II, who had murdered (1173) Thomas à Becket, most outspoken English supporter of papal claims of supremacy, ended in the penance (1174) of the king and the canonization of Thomas. His contest with the emperor ended in decisive defeat of the latter at the battle of Legnano (1176), reconciliation (1177) at Venice, and the abdication (1178) of antipope Calixtus III. At the third Lateran Council (1179), he established the law of papal succession.

Alexander IV. [Original name, **Rinaldo,** Conti **di Segni.**] b. at Anagni, Italy; d. at Viterbo, Italy, 1261. Pope from 1254 to 1261, successor of Innocent IV; nephew of Gregory IX. He established the Inquisition in France and encouraged mendicant friars, especially the Franciscans. He engaged in a long struggle with the Hohenstaufen family, especially Manfred, Ghibelline leader and king (1258) of Naples and Sicily, whose influence in Rome gave rise to factional struggles which drove Alexander to Viterbo, where he spent the last years of his pontificate.

Alexander V. [Earlier name, **Pietro Philarghi**; original name, **Petros Philargos**; called **Pietro di Candia.**] b. at Candia, Crete, c1339; d. at Bologna, Italy, 1410. Antipope. He claimed the papal chair from 1409 to 1410, as a successor to rival popes Benedict XIII and Gregory XII after their deposition by the Council of Pisa. He was elected by this council on a basis of his efforts, as cardinal (1405–10) under Innocent VII, to reconcile the Great Schism (1378–1417). He was prevented from reaching Rome and died at the castle of Balthasar Cossa, who succeeded him as John XXIII and who was accused, though without proof, of having poisoned him. Alexander V has been carried by some sources as a Pope, but is now definitely listed among the antipopes by the Roman Catholic Church. Gregory XII is regarded as having been the rightful Pope, and his deposition unlawful.

Alexander VI. [Original name, **Rodrigo Lanzol y Borgia.**] b. at Xativa, near Valencia, Spain; d. at Rome, 1503. Pope from 1492 to 1503, successor (probably through bribery) of Innocent VIII. He may be taken as typical of wealthy and corrupt Renaissance popes. He was a nephew of Calixtus III (Alfonso Borgia), who made him a cardinal and vice-chancellor of the church (1456), and whom he succeeded as archbishop of Valencia. Although he was a patron of artists, including Bramante, Michelangelo, Raphael, and others, his complex career, directed toward temporal aggrandizement of the papacy and of his own family, contributed otherwise to an unprecedented degradation of the church and the downfall of powerful families such as Sforza, Orsini, and Colonna which opposed him. Prominent as conspirators in his schemes and profiters by them were his four natural children by Rosa Vanozza, especially Cesare and Lucrezia Borgia. These children he begot between 1474 and 1482, while still a cardinal. He issued a bull (1493) dividing the New World between Spain and Portugal. Unsuccessfully opposed the entrance (1494) of Charles VIII of France into Naples; joined (1495) the league between Maximilian I, Milan, Venice, and Spain which drove Charles from Italy. In 1498 he ordered the execution of Savonarola, outspoken critic of his corruption, intrigues, and secular display; and in 1501 he instituted a censorship of books. His death, popularly attributed to poison, was probably caused by malaria.

Alexander VII. [Original name, **Fabio Chigi.**] b. at Siena, Italy, 1599; d. at Rome, 1667. Pope from 1655 to 1667, successor of Innocent X. He promulgated the bull against the Jansenists (1665). In a conflict (1662) with Louis XIV of France, he lost Avignon. Though he practiced the nepotism customary at the time, he preferred the arts and philosophy to affairs of state; enlarged the Sapienza and Vatican libraries, improved the plan of Rome, and built Saint Peter's colonnade, designed by Bernini.

Alexander VIII. [Original name, **Pietro Ottoboni.**] b. at Venice, 1610; d. at Rome, 1691. Pope from 1689 to 1691, successor of Innocent XI. He condemned doctrine of "philosophical sin"; assisted Venice against Turks; enriched Vatican library by purchase of Queen Christina of Sweden's collection of books and manuscripts.

Alexander I (of *Bulgaria*). [Also, Prince **Alexander of Battenberg.**] b. April 5, 1857; d. Nov. 17, 1893. A ruler of Bulgaria and titular prince of Battenberg; the second son of Prince Alexander of Hesse-Darmstadt. He served in the Hessian army, and, during the Russo-Turkish war of 1877–78, in the Russian army. Elected (April 29, 1879) prince of Bulgaria, he suspended constitutional government there for the period 1881–83. By the revolution (September, 1885) at Philippopolis he became prince of Eastern Rumelia also; he commanded in the repulse of the consequent Serbian invasion (November, 1885).

Alexander I (of *Epirus*). d. 326 B.C. King of Epirus, son of Neoptolemus and brother of Olympias, the mother of Alexander the Great. His youth was spent at the court of Philip II of Macedon, who made him king of Epirus.

Alexander II (of *Epirus*). King of Epirus, son of Pyrrhus and Lanassa, the daughter of Agathocles, tyrant of Syracuse. He succeeded his father in 272 B.C. He was dispossessed of Epirus and Macedonia by Demetrius, whose father, Antigonus Gonatas, he had deprived of Macedonia; but Epirus was recovered by the aid chiefly of the Acarnanians.

Alexander I (of *Greece*). [**Alexander of the Hellenes.**] b. at Athens, 1893; d. Oct. 25, 1920. King of Greece (1917–20). He became ruler after the deposition of his father, King Constantine, because the Allies distrusted the sympathies of his elder brother, George (later, King George II). The reins of government were actually in the hands of Venizelos during the greater part of his reign.

Alexander III (of *Macedonia*). See **Alexander the Great.**

Alexander I (of *Russia*). [Russian, **Aleksandr Pavlovich.**] b. at St. Petersburg, Dec. 23, 1777; d. at Taganrog, Russia, Dec. 1, 1825. Emperor of Russia; son of Paul I of Russia, on whose deposition he succeeded to the throne in 1801. He was influenced by his Swiss tutor to promote liberal ideas and reforms in education and science, and encouraged the introduction to Russia of Western civilization. He carried out many reforms, including the abolition of serfdom in the Baltic provinces, and promoted trade and manufactures. During the last years of his reign, however, he became increasingly reactionary and unpopular. In 1805 he joined the coalition against Napoleon. He was present at the battle of Austerlitz and joined Prussia against Napoleon in 1806. He signed the Treaty of Tilsit in 1807. He conquered Finland in 1808. Under his aegis, a successful war was waged with Turkey in 1806–12. In 1812 Napoleon invaded Russia, and Alexander was thenceforth a leader in the coalition (1813–14) against France. He took part in the battles of Dresden and Leipzig in 1813, entered Paris in 1814, and was present at the Congress of Vienna. He became king of Poland in 1815, again entered Paris in 1815, formed the Holy Alliance in 1815, and took part in the conferences of Aix-la-Chapelle (1818), Troppau (1820), Laibach (1821), and Verona (1822). He married Princess Elizabeth of Baden.

Alexander II (of *Russia*). [Russian, **Aleksandr Nikolayevich.**] b. April 29, 1818; d. at St. Petersburg, March 13, 1881. Emperor of Russia; son of Nicholas I, whom he succeeded in 1855. His greatest achievement was the emancipation (1861) of the serfs. He reorganized the army and the departments of administration and justice, and developed commerce and manufactures. In 1856 he concluded the Treaty of Paris which ended the Crimean War. He suppressed the Polish insurrection (1863–64), and carried on war (1877–78) with Turkey. During the latter part of his reign he was closely allied with Germany and Austria. The attacks of the Nihilists led him to enter upon a reactionary policy in 1879, and he was finally assassinated by them. He married Princess Maria of Hesse-Darmstadt.

Alexander III (of *Russia*). [Russian, **Aleksandr Aleksandrovich.**] b. March 10, 1845; d. at Livadia, in the Crimea, Nov. 1, 1894. Emperor of Russia; son of Alexander II whom he succeeded on March 13, 1881. He continued the reactionary policy inaugurated late in his father's reign. A meeting of the emperors of Russia, Germany, and Austria, at Skierniewice in Poland, in September, 1884, cemented the personal union of these rulers for the time, but after the formation of the Triple Alliance in 1883, Russia became a virtual ally of France.

Alexander I (of *Scotland*). b. c1078; d. at Stirling, Scotland, April 27, 1124. King of Scotland; the fourth son of Malcolm Canmore and Margaret of Scotland, and brother of Edgar, whom he succeeded in 1107. He married Sibylla, a natural daughter of Henry I of England. During the early years of his reign he quelled an insurrection in the north of Scotland. He upheld throughout his reign the supremacy of the Scottish church in his country.

Alexander II (of *Scotland*). [Called **"Alexander the Peaceful."**] b. at Haddington, Scotland, Aug. 24, 1198; d. in Kerrera, Scotland, July 8, 1249. King of Scotland; son of William the Lion, whom he succeeded in 1214.

Alexander III (of *Scotland*). b. at Roxburgh, Scotland, Sept. 4, 1241; d. near Kinghorn, Fifeshire, Scotland, March 16, 1285. King of Scotland; son of Alexander II, whom he succeeded in 1249. He aided Henry III of England, his father-in-law, in 1264, but opposed him on the question of the overlordship of Scotland. His army defeated the Norwegians in 1263, finally consolidating the islands near Scotland, including the Isle of Man, with Scotland. He maintained friendly relations with Norway, proposing his granddaughter Margaret, daughter of Eric of Norway, as Scottish heiress-presumptive.

Alexander I (of *Serbia*). [Also, **Alexander Obrenović.**] b. at Belgrade, Serbia, Aug. 14, 1876; assassinated there, June 11, 1903. King of Serbia (1889–1903), noted for his attempt to strengthen the position of the Obrenović dynasty at the expense of the national assembly; son of Milan I and Queen Natalie. On March 6, 1889, he was proclaimed ruler, under a regency, upon the abdication of his father. On April 13, 1893, he assumed personal control of affairs; he suspended (April 7, 1903) the liberal constitution and annuled a series of laws passed by the radical government. His marriage to a commoner added to his general unpopularity and on the night of June 10, 1903, he was assassinated, with Queen Draga, in the palace. He was the last ruler of the Obrenović dynasty and was succeeded by Peter Karageorgević, the choice of the military party.

Alexander I (of *Yugoslavia*). [Also, **Alexander Karageorgevich.**] b. at Cetinje, Montenegro, 1888; assassinated at Marseilles, France, Oct. 9, 1934. King of Yugoslavia (1921–34), who contributed greatly to the unification of the rival peoples of Serbia, Croatia and Slovenia; son of Peter I, and grandson of Alexander Karageorgević. He was educated at the Russian court at St. Petersburg, and at Geneva; he served (1914–19) as commander in chief of the Serbian army. When party feuds threatened national security, he established a personal dictatorship (1931) under an authoritarian constitution.

Alexander, Albert V. b. at Weston-super-Mare, England, 1885—. British politician, active in the coöperative movement. He was parliamentary secretary to the board of trade (1924); first lord of the Admiralty (1929–31, 1940–45, 1945–46); member of special cabinet delegation to India (1946); and minister of defense (1946 *et seq.*).

Alexander, Archibald. b. at Lexington, Va., April 17, 1772; d. at Princeton, N.J., Oct. 22, 1851. American Presbyterian minister. He was president (1796–1807) of Hampden Sydney College, Va. He was also the first professor (1812–51) at Princeton Theological Seminary.

Alexander, Barton Stone. b. in Kentucky, Sept. 4, 1819; d. at San Francisco, Dec. 15, 1878. American military engineer and officer in the Civil War. With General Barnard he shared the chief credit for the chain of forts which eventually protected Washington, D. C.

Alexander, Cecil Frances. [Maiden name, **Humphreys.**] b. in Ireland, 1818; d. at Londonderry, Ireland, 1895. Irish poet and writer of hymns. In 1850 she married

Bishop William Alexander. She is the author of hymns including *All Things Bright and Beautiful*, *Once in Royal David's City*, and *Jesus Calls Us o'er the Tumult*, as well as a number of poems.

Alexander, Edmund B. b. at Haymarket, Va., Oct. 6, 1802; d. at Washington, D.C., Jan. 3, 1888. American officer. He served in the Mexican War, commanded the Utah expedition (1857–58), and was brevetted brigadier general on Oct. 18, 1865.

Alexander, Edward Porter. b. at Washington, Ga., May 26, 1835; d. at Savannah, Ga., April 28, 1910. American engineer, author, teacher, and Confederate soldier. He served as artillery commander under Longstreet at Gettysburg and elsewhere. He was president (1887–93) of the Georgia Railroad and Banking Company after serving (1885–87) as a government director of the Union Pacific. His writings include volumes on railroading, a book of verse, and numerous works on the Civil War, including the highly regarded critical work known as *Military Memoirs of a Confederate* (1907).

Alexander, Francis. b. at Killingly, Conn., 1800; d. (probably) at Florence, Italy, 1881. American painter and lithographer. After studying (1820 *et seq.*) under Alexander Robertson at New York, he painted portraits at Providence and Boston until 1831, when he left for Italy. His style after his return (1832) to the U.S. was less colorful, but brought him great popularity. His paintings include portraits of Daniel Webster, Benjamin R. Curtis, and Dickens. During his last years, which he spent at Florence, he did virtually no painting.

Alexander, Sir **George.** [Original name, **George Samson.**] b. at Reading, England, 1858; d. 1918. English actor. In 1881 he appeared with Sir Henry Irving. From 1891 to his death he was actor-manager at St. James's Theatre at London.

Alexander, Grover Cleveland. [Called **"Old Pete."**] b. Feb. 26, 1887; d. Nov. 4, 1950. American baseball player, pitcher (1911–30) successively for Philadelphia, Chicago, and St. Louis in the National League. He is famed for 16 shutout games in 1916, and 90 in his entire career. In 1938 he was elected to baseball's Hall of Fame at Cooperstown, N.Y.

Alexander, Harold Rupert Leofric George. [Title, 1st Viscount **Alexander of Tunis.**] b. in Tyrone, Ireland, Dec. 10, 1891—. British field marshal; son of the 4th earl of Caledon; governor-general of Canada (1946–52). During World War I he was several times decorated for service in France; he later saw action on India's northwest frontier (1935). After commanding the first division (1938–40), he supervised the evacuation from Dunkerque (1940) and had charge of the Burma retreat (1942). As Middle East commander in chief (1942) he was in charge of the successful African campaign. He served as deputy commander in chief (1943) of Allied forces in the Mediterranean, with responsibility for the invasions of Sicily and Italy. In 1944 he was created field marshal and given the supreme Allied command in the Mediterranean. He later served (1944–46) as aide-de-camp general to King George VI. He became minister of defense in 1952.

Alexander, Hartley Burr. b. at Lincoln, Neb., April 9, 1873; d. July 27, 1939. American philosopher and university professor. Staff member of *New International Encyclopedia* (1903); philosophy professor at Nebraska (1908–27) and at Scripps College (1927 *et seq.*); president (1919) of the American Philosophical Association; author of *God's Drum* (1927), *Pueblo Indian Painting* (1931), *God and Man's Destiny* (1936), and others.

Alexander, James. b. in Scotland, 1691; d. at Albany, N.Y., April 2, 1756. American lawyer and politician, notable for his efforts on behalf of Peter Zenger. Descendant and heir of the Earls of Stirling (and father of William Alexander, the Revolutionary general), he came to America following the collapse of the Scottish uprising in 1715. His career as lawyer and public official in New York and New Jersey was marked by attacks on misuse of power, culminating in aid to Peter Zenger in the establishment (1733) of his New York *Weekly Journal* and his subsequent defense (1735) against a suit for criminal libel. The efforts of Alexander, Zenger, and others in this case represented the first great victory for freedom of the press in the American colonies, and set a precedent which tremendously influenced the course of subsequent U.S. law in such matters.

Alexander, Sir **James Edward.** b. in Scotland, 1803; d. 1885. British general and explorer. Conducted (1836–37) expedition into Namaqualand and Damaraland, Africa; instrumental in transfer to England (1877) of Cleopatra's Needle. Author of *Travels through Russia and the Crimea* (1830), *Expedition of Discovery into the Interior of Africa* (1838), and others.

Alexander, James Waddel. b. in Louisa County, Va., March 13, 1804; d. at Red Sweet Springs, Va., July 31, 1859. American Presbyterian clergyman; son of Archibald Alexander. He was professor of rhetoric and belles-lettres (1833–44) at Princeton College, and of ecclesiastical history and church government (1844–51) in Princeton Theological Seminary, and pastor (1851–59) of the Fifth Avenue Presbyterian Church, New York.

Alexander, Jerome. b. at New York, Dec. 21, 1876—. American chemist, specialist in the chemistry of colloids. Author of *Colloid Chemistry* (1919), and numerous technical articles, as well as the chapter on colloid chemistry in Liddell's *Handbook for Chemical Engineers* (1920); translated (1909) Zsigmondy's *Colloids and the Ultramicroscope.*

Alexander, John Henry. b. at Annapolis, Md., June 26, 1812; d. March 2, 1867. American scientist, advocate of a standardized system of weights and measures. He was sent (1857) to Europe by the U.S. government on a mission dealing with unification of coinage. His *Universal Dictionary of Weights and Measures, Ancient and Modern* (1850) has been termed "one of the most complete . . . ever published."

Alexander, John White. b. at Allegheny, Pa., 1856; d. 1915. American painter, for many years connected with *Harper's Magazine.*

Alexander, Joshua Willis. b. at Cincinnati, Jan. 22, 1852; d. Feb. 27, 1936. American lawyer and government official. He was secretary of commerce (1919–21).

Alexander (al.eg.zan′dėr), **Romance of.** One of the most famous romances of the Middle Ages. Callisthenes, a companion of Alexander the Great, wrote an account of the Asiatic expedition of Alexander, but it is lost. His name, however, is attached to a fabulous account which is supposed to have been written in Alexandria in the early part of the 3rd century. There are three Latin translations of this pseudo-Callisthenes: one by Julius Valerius, before 340; the *Itinerarium Alexandri;* and the *Historia de preliis*, by Archpresbyter Leo. The later ones are based on these. It was translated into Syriac and Armenian in the 5th century. The Persians and Arabs made use of the myth, and in the 11th century Simeon Seth, keeper of the imperial wardrobe at the Byzantine court, translated it back from the Persian into the Greek. In the 11th century it entered into French literature as a troubadour poem; the earliest extant form of this is in fragments by Aubry or Alberic. Lamprecht, a priest, translated the French of Aubry, or Alberic, of Besançon, into German, and called it the *Alexanderlied*, in the 12th century. The *Alexandreis* of the Austrian Siegfried was written c1350. In the 15th century Alexander again appeared as the hero of prose romances in Germany. Alexander myths are to be found in many other of the old French poems, and he becomes a knightly conqueror surrounded by 12 paladins. The poems do not properly form a cycle, as they are quite independent of one another.

Alexander, Stephen. b. at Schenectady, N.Y., Sept. 1, 1806; d. June 25, 1883. American astronomer, professor (1840–77) in astronomy, mechanics, and mathematics at Princeton. The scientific findings of the Labrador party, headed by him to observe the solar eclipse of 1860, were published in the *U.S. Coast and Geodetic Survey Report* of that year. In 1862 he was chosen one of the 50 original members of the National Academy of Sciences.

Alexander, Sir **William.** [Title, Earl of **Stirling.**] b. c1567; d. at London, Sept. 12, 1640. Scottish poet and statesman, tutor to Prince Henry and adherent of King James I of England. He is the author of *Monarchicke Tragedies* (1603–07), *Paraenesis to the Prince* (1604), *Doomesday, etc.* (first part, 1614), and others. He received on Sept. 21, 1621, the grant of New Scotland (Nova Scotia and New Brunswick), which was transferred to

De la Tour in 1630. In 1626 he was appointed secretary of state for Scotland.

Alexander, William. [Called Lord **Stirling.**] b. at New York, 1726; d. at Albany, N.Y., Jan. 15, 1783. American Revolutionary general. Although his claim of descent from the earls of Stirling was rejected (1762) by the House of Lords, he nevertheless assumed the title. An astronomer, he held political offices in New Jersey and was one of the governors of Kings College (now Columbia University). He was made brigadier general after the capture (1776) of a British transport at Sandy Hook: directed the building of Forts Lee and Washington; was captured after the battle of Long Island; and promoted to major general (1777) after the battle of Trenton. He fought at Brandywine, Germantown, and Monmouth, and took part in the exposure of the Conway Cabal and in the court of inquiry (1780) on John André.

Alexander, William. b. in Derry, Ireland, 1824; d. at Torquay, England, 1911. Irish Anglican prelate and poet. He was bishop of Derry (1867–93) and archbishop of Armagh (1893–1911). In 1892 he lectured in the U.S.

Alexander, William Dewitt. b. at Honolulu, April 2 1833; d. there, Feb. 22, 1913. American historian, natural scientist, and Hawaiian public official. He graduated (1855) from Yale and returned (1858) to Hawaii after teaching in the U.S. He served as professor of Greek and as president (1864–70) of Punahou School. In 1872 he was appointed surveyor general of the kingdom of Hawaii. He was a founder of the Hawaiian Historical Society, and a member of many other scientific and scholarly groups. The most important of his written works is probably his *Brief History of the Hawaiian People* (1891).

Alexander and Campaspe (kam.pas′pē). See **Campaspe, Alexander and.**

Alexander Archipelago. Group of islands off the W coast of SE Alaska, which includes Sitka, Prince of Wales, Admiralty, and other islands.

Alexanderbad (ä.lek.sän′dėr.bät). [Also, **Alexandersbad** (-dėrs.bät).] Village in S Germany, in the *Land* (state) of Bavaria, American Zone, district of Upper and Middle Franconia, situated in the Fichtelgebirge, ab. 21 mi. NE of Bayreuth: health resort. It has ferruginous thermal springs which are visited by people suffering from nervous and circulatory diseases. 873 (1946).

Alexander Balas (al.eg.zan′dėr bā′lạs). b. at Smyrna; killed in Arabia, 145 B.C. Usurper of the Syrian throne (150–145 B.C.). Of humble origin, he was the self-alleged son of Antiochus Epiphanes. He was the protégé of a coalition including Ptolemy Philometor of Egypt which seized the throne from the Selencid king Demetrius Soter.

Alexander Balus (bā′lus). Oratorio by George Frederick Handel, with words by Thomas Morell, written in 1747 and first performed at Covent Garden, London, on March 9, 1748.

Alexander City. [Former name, **Youngville.**] City in E Alabama, in Tallapoosa County, ab. 42 mi. NE of Montgomery: textile and knitting mills, and cotton gins. 6,430 (1950).

Alexander Column. Column erected at St. Petersburg in 1832 in honor of Alexander I of Russia. The polished shaft of red granite, 84 ft. high and 14 in diameter, was remarkable for years as the greatest modern monolith.

Alexander Cornelius (kôr.nē′li.us, -nēl′yus). [Called **Alexander Polyhistor.**] fl. 1st cent. B.C. Greek writer, a native either of Ephesus or Cotiaeum in Lesser Phrygia. He wrote a geographico-historical account in 42 books of nearly all the countries of the ancient world, and many other works, of which only the titles and fragments have been preserved.

Alexander I Island. [Former name, **Alexander I Land.**] Large island at the SW base of the Palmer Peninsula in Antarctica. Discovered in 1821 by Admiral Thaddeus von Bellingshausen, it was proven to be an island in 1940. Length, ab. 235 mi.; greatest width, 150 mi.

Alexander Jagellon (jạ.gel′ọn, yä.gel′ôn). b. in 1461; d. in 1506. King of Poland and grand duke of Lithuania; second son of Casimir IV of Poland. He succeeded (1492) to the grand duchy at the death of his father, and was elected (1501) king of Poland at the death of his brother.

Alexander John I (of *Rumania*). [Original name, **Alexander John Cuza** (or **Cusa**).] b. at Hush, Moldavia, March 20, 1820; d. at Heidelberg, Baden, May 15, 1873. Prince of Moldavia and Wallachia, 1859. After being arrested as a member of the unsuccessful revolution of Jassy (1848), he was made (1850) prefect of Galati. The Turks recognized him in 1861 as ruler of the united principalities, but he was dethroned in 1866.

Alexander Karageorgevich (kä.rạ.jôr′jẹ.vich). b. at Topola, Serbia, Oct. 11, 1806; d. at Temesvar, Hungary, May 2, 1885. Prince of Serbia (1842–58); son of the Serbian patriot Karageorge. He succeeded Prince Michael Obrenovich of Serbia, but lost the throne in 1858 to Prince Milosh Obrenovich (Michael's father). Alexander vacillated in his policies and allegiances; his allegiance to Austria caused his deposition. He made repeated attempts to regain the throne, and was accused of complicity in the murder (1868) of Prince Michael (who had succeeded his father in 1860) and imprisoned, but was soon pardoned.

Alexander Manette (ma.net′), **Doctor.** See **Manette, Doctor Alexander.**

Alexander Nevski (nef′ski, nyef′ski). b. at Vladimir, Russia, c1220; d. 1263. Russian national hero; patron of St. Petersburg. Prince of Novgorod (1238), he fought in defense of Novgorod and Pskov against Germans, Lithuanians, and Swedes, defeating the latter (1240) on the Neva River (whence his surname) and the Teutonic Knights (1242) on the ice of Lake Peipus. As grand duke of Kiev, Novgorod, and Vladimir (1252–63), he was a vassal of the Tartars, whose friendship toward Russia he fostered, securing a reduction in the tribute and abolishment of the military service formerly required by them of Russia. The Order of Alexander Nevski was established (1725) by Peter the Great.

Alexander of Aphrodisias (af.rọ.diz′i.ạs). [Also: **Alexander Aphrodisiensis;** called **"the Exegete"** or **"the Expositor."**] b. at Aphrodisias, in Caria; fl. at Athens 200 A.D. Greek philosopher, notable as the foremost commentator on Aristotle. His commentaries are extensive and very valuable; many are still extant, and others are partly known through later commentaries or Arabic translations. Alexander tried to free the Aristotelian doctrine from Neoplatonic syncretism and Stoic tendencies.

Alexander of Hales (hālz). [Also: **Alexander Halensis;** called **Doctor Irrefragabilis.**] b. at Hales, Gloucestershire, c1175; d. 1245. English scholastic philosopher and theologian. He lectured (c1220) at Paris, and in 1222 joined the Franciscan order. He wrote *Summae Universae Theologiae* (printed, 1475), the first amalgamation of Augustinian Christian doctrine with the Aristotelian system and Arabian thought; this work was much used by Thomas Aquinas and others.

Alexander of the Hellenes. See **Alexander I** (of *Greece*).

Alexander of Tralles (tral′ēz). [Also, **Alexander Trallianus** (tral.i.ā′nus).] b. at Tralles, Lydia; fl. mid-6th century A.D. Greek medical writer. He is the author of *De Lumbricis* (printed at Venice, 1570), and others.

Alexander Severus (sẹ.vir′us), **Marcus Aurelius.** [Original name, **Alexianus Bassianus.**] b. at Arca Caesarea, Phoenicia, c208; d. near Mainz, Germany, 235. Roman emperor (222–235); son of Gessius Marcianus and Julia Mammaea, and cousin of the emperor Heliogabalus, who adopted him in 221 and whom he succeeded as emperor.

Alexander's Feast. Ode by John Dryden, written in 1697, in honor of Saint Cecilia's day.

Alexander's Feast. Musical setting by George Frederick Handel to the poem by John Dryden, completed in 1736 and first performed at Covent Garden, London, on Feb. 19, 1736.

Alexanderson (al.eg.zan′dėr.sọn), **Ernst Frederik Werner.** b. at Uppsala, Sweden, Jan. 25, 1878—. American electrical engineer, notable for his inventions in radio and television. He arrived in the U.S. in 1901 and entered (1902) the employ of the General Electric Company at Schenectady, N.Y., as a draftsman. He became a member (1904) of the engineering staff and has since been responsible for more than 200 patents. His high-frequency alternator, plus a magnetic amplifier and multiple tuned antenna, were important in the development of transoceanic radio communication. He developed the use of a high-power vacuum tube which was employed in all radio transmission, and also aided in the development of a selective receiver. He has also done important pioneering work in television, as well as developmental research in electric ship propulsion and railroad electrification.

Alexander's Wall (al.eg.zan'dėrz). See under **Derbent.**

Alexander the Great. [Also, **Alexander III** (of Macedonia).] b. at Pella, Macedonia, 356 B.C.; d. at Babylon, June 13, 323 B.C. Macedonian ruler, conqueror of the civilized world. Legend has it that he inherited his military ability from his father, Philip II of Macedonia, a rough mountain king of genius, while from Olympias, the Epirote princess who was his mother, came his mysticism and impetuousness. He was educated by Aristotle. He was a handsome man, whose temper was his greatest enemy; contrary to legend, he rarely drank. With Philip, he defeated (338) the armies of Greek city-states at Chaeronea. In 336 Philip was murdered, and Alexander became king of Macedonia and leader of the Greeks in war against the predatory Persian empire. Two years were spent pacifying tribes to his rear; rebellious Thebes was destroyed. His highly professional army, which was devoted to him, consisted of 30,000 heavy- and light-armed infantry and 5,000 cavalry, with a superior siege train, commissary, and intelligence service. In 334 he crossed to Asia, defeated the Persians at the Granicus River and the following year at Issus. Taking Tyre en route, he continued (332) to Egypt, where he built Alexandria, the first of 70 communities founded by him which became powerful forces for the Hellenization of the non-Greek world. With the eastern Mediterranean coasts now in his possession, he turned inland and at Gaugamela (at the battle sometimes called the Battle of Arbela) overwhelmed (331) the armies of Darius III. Alexander's march next carried him across Iran to India (326). When his men refused to follow him farther, he returned by way of the Indus Valley and Baluchistan to Babylon. Here, not yet 33 years of age, he died from fatigue and disease. Napoleon called him the greatest general in history. Alexander strongly believed in the fusion of races; both of his wives, Roxane and Barsine, were eastern princesses. His life altered the course of history, for he created a new world society based on a common Greek culture. He became after his death a legendary figure to medieval Europe and to the Orient of all periods.

Alexander the Paphlagonian (paf.lą.gō'ni.ạn). b. at Abonuteichos (Ionopolis), Paphlagonia, Asia Minor; fl. c100 A.D. Roman charlatan who set up a false oracle of Aesculapius and pretended Eleusinian mysteries with large financial success. He was exposed by Lucian, whose account of the incident has been preserved.

"Alexander the Peaceful." See **Alexander II** (of *Scotland*).

Alexandra (al.eg.zan'drą). See also **Cassandra.**

Alexandra. [Full prename, **Alexandra Caroline Maria Charlotte Louisa Julia.**] b. at Copenhagen, Dec. 1, 1844; d. 1925. Queen of England; daughter of Christian IX of Denmark and wife of Edward VII, king of England, whom she married on March 10, 1863. Her second son subsequently became King George V of England. "Alexandra Day" was instituted (1913) in her honor.

Alexandra. The 54th asteroid, discovered by H. Goldschmidt at Paris, Sept. 10, 1858.

Alexandra Fyodorovna (fyō'dọ.rọv.nạ). [Original prename, **Victoria Alice** (or **Alix**) **Helena Louise Beatrice.**] b. at Darmstadt, Germany, 1872; d. 1918. Empress of Russia; fourth daughter of Ludwig IV, Grand Duke of Hesse-Darmstadt, and Princess Alice, daughter of Queen Victoria. She married Nicholas II of Russia in 1894.

Alexandra Land. Name at one time given to a vast region of Australia, under the administration of South Australia, regarded as the same as the Northern Territory, or as that part of it which is included between lat. 16°–26° S. and long. 129°–138° E. The name is obsolete.

Alexandrapol (al.eg.zan'drą.pôl) or **Alexandropol** (-drǭ-). Former name of **Leninakan.**

Alexandre (ä.lek.sän'dėr), **Aaron.** b. at Hohenfeld, Bavaria, c1766; d. at London, Nov. 16, 1850. German chessplayer, author of *Encyclopédie des échecs* (1837).

Alexandre le Grand (å.lek.sändr lẹ grän). Tragedy by Jean Baptiste Racine, produced in 1665. It was the cause of a serious quarrel between Molière and Racine, who both loved the same woman, an actress who played the part of Axiane.

Alexandretta (al"ig.zan.dret'ą). Former name of **Hatay**, also of **Iskenderun.**

Alexandretta, Gulf of. See **Iskenderun, Gulf of.**

Alexandrette (å.lek.säṅ.dret). Former French name of **Iskenderun.**

Alexandri (ä.lek.sän'drē), **Basile.** See **Alecsandri, Vasili.**

Alexandria (al.eg.zan'dri.ą). [Arabic, **Al-Iskandariyah, Iskanderiyeh.**] Seaport in NE Africa, in Egypt, founded (332 B.C.) by Alexander the Great, from whom the city took its name: chief port and second city of Egypt; summer residence of the Egyptian court. It is situated at the NW extremity of the Nile delta on the strip of land which lies between the Mediterranean Sea and Lake Mareotis, ab. 133 mi. NW of Cairo. The modern city occupies what was anciently the island of Pharos, together with the isthmus now connecting it with the mainland where the ancient city stood. Ancient Alexandria was the capital of Egypt during the Ptolemaic period, and became an important seat of Greek culture and learning. In 30 B.C. it was annexed by Rome. It long ranked as the second city of the Roman empire, and continued as the chief commercial city under the Byzantine empire. It was an important center of Christianity, and the seat of a patriarchate. In 641 it was taken by the Moslems, and was entered by the French in 1798, who were defeated near here by the British in 1801. The present city was largely rebuilt under Mehemet Ali. It was bombarded by a British fleet of eight ironclad vessels under Sir Frederick Seymour, July 11, 1882, and was taken by the British on July 12. It is the chief seaport in N Africa and until February, 1947, was the main British naval base in the Middle East. 928,237 (1947).

Alexandria. City in C Indiana, in Madison County, on Pipe Creek, ab. 11 mi. N of Anderson: manufactures rock-wool insulation. 5,147 (1950).

Alexandria. City in C Louisiana, parish seat of Rapides Parish, on the Red River ab. 100 mi. NW of Baton Rouge, in the geographic center of the state: trading center for cotton, sugar cane, and fish. It was invaded (1864) by Union forces under General Nathaniel P. Banks, when the Red River was dammed up at this point to permit passage of a Union squadron. 34,913 (1950).

Alexandria. City in W Minnesota, county seat of Douglas County, ab. 125 mi. NW of St. Paul: rail center for a rich agricultural area; fishing and golf resort. The noted "Kensington Runestone" was found (1898) in the vicinity. 6,319 (1950).

Alexandria. Town in S Rumania, province of Muntenia, ab. 50 mi. SW of Bucharest, on the railroad to Zimnicea: wheat and mill center. It contains six Orthodox churches. 17,840 (1948).

Alexandria. Small manufacturing town comprising three electoral districts of the Vale of Leven District, in C Scotland, in Dunbartonshire, situated on the river Leven, ab. 3 mi. N of Dumbarton, ab. 419 mi. N of London by rail. Pop. of electoral districts, 5,818 (1931).

Alexandria. City in N Virginia, in Arlington (formerly Alexandria) County, on the Potomac River, ab. 7 mi. S of Washington, D.C. It has manufactures of fertilizer, refrigerator cars, chemicals, iron, shirts, bricks, pottery, and automobile assembly plants, but is now best known as a residential suburb of Washington. It was entered by Federal troops during the Civil War on May 24, 1861. It was incorporated in 1779; from 1789 to 1846, it was part of the District of Columbia. 61,787 (1950).

Alexandria Arachosiae (ar.ą.kō'si.ē). Ancient name of **Kandahar,** city.

Alexandria Arion (ãr'i.ọn, ą.rī'ọn). See **Herat,** city.

Alexandria Bay. Village in N New York, in Jefferson County, on the St. Lawrence River, ab. 32 mi. SW of Ogdensburg: summer resort community for the Thousand Islands region. 1,688 (1950).

Alexandria Conference. In U.S. history, a meeting (March 28, 1785) between Virginia and Maryland for the purpose of dealing with commerce and navigation on the Pocomoke and Potomac rivers and Chesapeake Bay. Although Alexandria, Va., had been designated as the meeting place, the conference actually conducted its business at Mount Vernon, where George Washington acted as its host. The conference proposed a convention of all the states for the purpose of formulating a body of uniform rules governing commercial relations among the states. The resulting Annapolis Convention was the genesis of the Federal Convention.

Alexandria Eschata (es.kā'tạ). Ancient name of **Leninabad.**

Alexandrian Codex (al.eg.zan'dri.ạn). [Latin, **Codex Alexandrinus.**] Important manuscript of the Scriptures now in the British Museum, sent to Charles I of England by the Patriarch of Constantinople. It is written in Greek uncials on parchment, and contains the Septuagint version of the Old Testament complete, except parts of the Psalms, and almost all the New Testament. It has been assigned to the 5th century.

Alexandria Troas (al.eg.zan'dri.ạ trō'as). [Also, **Troas.**] Ancient seaport on the NW coast of Turkey, near the island of Tenedos (Bozcaada), ab. 10 mi. S of Troy. It contains archaeologically important ruins of a building that contained a Roman bath.

Alexandrina (al.eg.zan.drē'nạ), **Lake.** [Also, **Lake Victoria.**] Expansion of the Murray River, Australia, at its mouth, in South Australia state.

Alexandrine War (al.eg.zan'drin, -drēn). A war (48–47 B.C.) between Julius Caesar and the guardians of Ptolemy (elder brother of Cleopatra), in Egypt. It resulted in favor of Caesar, who placed Cleopatra and her younger brother (the elder having died) on the Egyptian throne as joint rulers.

Alexandroúpolis (ä"le.ksän.drö'pô.lēs). [Turkish, **Dede Agach.**] Town in NE Greece, the capital of the *nomos* (department) of Evros, situated on the NE coast of the Aegean Sea, 19 mi. W of the Turkish border: seaport. 17,081 (1940).

Alexandrov or **Alexandroff** (ä.lik.sän'drọf). See **Aleksandrov.**

Alexas (ạ.lek'sạs). Minor character in Shakespeare's *Antony and Cleopatra*, an attendant of Cleopatra.

Alexeief (ä.lik.sā'yif), **Eugenii Ivanovitch.** See **Alekseyev, Yevgeni Ivanovich.**

Alexianus Bassianus (ạ.lek.si.ā'nus bas.i.ā'nus). Original name of **Alexander Severus, Marcus Aurelius.**

Alexin (ä.lyôk'sin). See **Aleksin.**

Alexinatz (ä.lek'si.näts). German name of **Aleksinac.**

Alexis (ạ.lek'sis). b. at Thurii, Magna Graecia, Italy, fl. 4th and 3rd centuries B.C. Greek dramatist at Athens, a master of the Middle Comedy. A prolific writer, he was the author of about 245 plays, fragments of which are extant.

Alexis (á.lek.sē), **Paul.** b. at Aix-en-Provence, France, June 10, 1847; d. at Triel, France, July 29, 1901. French playwright, novelist, essayist, and faithful collaborator of his lifelong friend, Émile Zola, in the development of French naturalism. Although his novels about the demimonde of Paris, including *Le Collage* (1883), *Madame Meuriot* (1891), and *Vallotra* (1901) are still read, he is best remembered for his famous telegram to Zola (when the latter's novel, *La Terre*, was attacked by the Paris press): "Naturalism not dead, letter follows."

Alexis, Pierre Nord. See **Nord Alexis, Pierre.**

Alexis (ä.lek'sis), **Wilibald.** [Pseudonym of **Georg Wilhelm Heinrich Häring.**] b. at Breslau, in Silesia, June 29, 1798; d. at Arnstadt, in Thuringia, Dec. 16, 1871. German novelist. He introduced to Germany historical fiction in the style of Sir Walter Scott. After establishing his reputation with *Walladmor* (1823) and *Schloss Avalon* (1827), which purported to be actually translations of Scott, he wrote several novels dealing with various periods of Brandenburg's history, running from the 14th to the 19th century.

Alexis Mikhailovich (ạ.lek'sis mē.ʜī'lọ.vich). See **Aleksey Mikhailovich.**

Alexis Petrovich (pi.trô'vich). See **Aleksey Petrovich.**

Alexius (ạ.lek'si.us), Saint. fl. early 5th century. Holy man of the Byzantine empire, believed by some to have been a Roman nobleman who fled to Edessa on the night before his marriage, there to devote his life to asceticism.

Alexius V. [Also, **Alexios V**; called **Dukas Murtzuphlos.**] d. 1204. Byzantine emperor. He usurped the throne of Alexius IV Angelus in 1204, but was driven from Constantinople by members of the Fourth Crusade who had resolved on the partition of the empire.

Alexius III Angelus (an'jẹ.lus). [Also, **Alexios III Angelos.**] d. 1210. Byzantine emperor from 1195 to 1203. He usurped the throne of his brother Isaac II, but was deposed by an army of Crusaders who besieged Constantinople and reinstated Isaac II with his son Alexius IV Angelus as colleague. Alexius III died in exile.

Alexius IV Angelus. [Also, **Alexios IV Angelos.**] d. 1204. Byzantine emperor in 1203 and 1204; son of Isaac II Angelus. He was put to death by Alexius V after a reign of six months.

Alexius I Comnenus (kom.nē'nus). [Also, **Alexios I Komnenos.**] b. at Constantinople, 1048; d. 1118. Byzantine emperor from 1081 to 1118; nephew of Isaac Comnenus. With the aid of the militia he supplanted the emperor Nicephorus III. He defended the empire against the Turks, the Normans, and others. In his reign occurred the First Crusade. His life, the *Alexiad*, was written by his daughter Anna Comnena.

Alexius II Comnenus. [Also, **Alexios II Komnenos.**] b. c1168; d. 1183. Byzantine emperor from 1180 to 1183; son of Manuel I, whom he succeeded. He was very unpopular with his subjects, and was deposed and strangled by Andronicus I.

Alexius I Comnenus (of *Trebizond*). [Also, **Alexios Komnenos; called the "Grand Comnenus."**] d. 1222. Emperor of Trebizond from 1204 to 1222; grandson of the Byzantine emperor Andronicus I. At the capture of Constantinople by the Crusaders in 1204 he made himself master of Trebizond, later raising it from the position of a province of the Byzantine Empire to that of an independent empire. He also attempted, but failed in, an attack on Theodore I of Nicea.

Alexius II Comnenus (of *Trebizond*). [Also, **Alexios II Komnenos.**] d. 1330. Emperor of Trebizond from 1297 to 1330; son of Joannes II, whom he succeeded.

Alexius III Comnenus (of *Trebizond*). [Also, **Alexios III Komnenos.**] d. 1390. Emperor of Trebizond from 1349 to 1390; son of Basilius by Irene of Trebizond.

Alexius IV Comnenus (of *Trebizond*). [Also, **Alexios IV Komnenos.**] b. ?; d. 1446. Emperor of Trebizond from 1417 to 1446; son of Manuel III and Eudocia of Georgia.

Aleyn (ạ.lān'). One of the Cambridge students (clerks of Cantebregge) in Chaucer's *Reeve's Tale.*

Aleyn. [Also: **Alain, Alain le Gros.**] In the legendry of the Grail, the twelfth son of Bron who was the brother-in-law of Joseph of Arimathea. Aleyn was selected by Joseph as the keeper of the Holy Grail.

Aleyn (al'in), **Charles.** d. 1640. Minor English poet, author of *The Battailes of Crescey and Poictiers* (1631).

Alfadir (äl'fä"dir). [Icelandic, **Alfadhir** (-ᴛʜēr).] In Old Norse mythology, one of the many appellations of Odin as the supreme god of all mankind.

Al Falluja (äl fäl.lö'jạ). Town in C Iraq, on the Euphrates River, ab. 35 mi. W of Baghdad: an important crossing, since ancient times, on the road between Syria and Persia.

Alfana (äl.fä'nä). Horse of Gradasso in Ariosto's *Orlando Furioso.*

Alfano (äl.fä'nō), **Franco.** b. near Naples, Italy, March 8, 1877—. Italian composer. His opera, *Madonna Imperia*, was performed (1928) at the Metropolitan, but received an indifferent reception. He completed Puccini's *Turandot* after that composer's death (1924). He composed numerous other operas, piano pieces, and one symphony.

Alfaro (äl.fä'rō), **Eloy.** b. at Montecristi, Ecuador, 1864; killed by a Quito mob, in January, 1912. Ecuadorian revolutionist and political leader, president of Ecuador (1895–1901; 1907–11). He led the revolution against President Luis Cordero, declaring himself (1895) president. Though an avowed anti-clerical, he was moderate in his handling of church and state separation, although the law of patronage (enacted 1899) gave the civil authority some control over the church. Having left office in 1901, he returned to power after deposing (1906) Lisardo García. During his second administration a new constitution (lasting 22 years) was put into effect, the authority of the Church was abridged, and the Quito-Guayaquil railway was completed (1908).

Alfaro, Francisco de. b. at Seville, Spain, c1565; d. at Madrid, c1650. Spanish lawyer. He was successively fiscal of the Audience of Panama (1594), member of the

Audience of Lima (c1601), president of the Audience of Charcas (1632), and member of the Council of the Indies.

Alfaro, Ricardo Joaquín. b. at Panama City, Panama, Aug. 20, 1882—. Panamanian lawyer, politician, and diplomat. Foreign minister and head of the cabinet (1918–22); minister to the U.S. (1922–30; 1933–36); vice-president (1928–30) and president (1931–32) of Panama; member of the Hague Permanent Court of Arbitration (1929–41); delegate to the San Francisco Conference (1945); foreign minister (1945 *et seq.*).

Alfeld (äl'felt). Town in NW Germany, in the *Land* (state) of Lower Saxony, British Zone, formerly in the province of Hanover, Prussia, situated on the Leine River, ab. 28 mi. S of Hanover: metallurgical, wooden-ware, paper, shoe, and ceramics industries. The Nikolai Church is in the Gothic style; the town hall (*Rathaus*), built in 1585, is in the early Renaissance style. Both buildings were undamaged in World War II. The population is predominantly Protestant. 13,323 (1950).

Alfen aan den Rijn (äl'fen än den rīn). [Also, **Alphen aan den Rijn.**] Town in the W Netherlands, in the province of South Holland, ab. 19 mi. NE of Rotterdam: agricultural trade center; metallurgical and construction industries; large printing establishment. 18,941 (1939).

Alfeta (al'fe.tä). The name given in the *Almagest* and Alphonsine tables to the second-magnitude star α Coronae Borealis. The star is also widely known as Alphecca or Gemma.

Alfheim (älf'hīm). [Old Norse, **Alfheimr** (-hām.ėr).] In Old Norse mythology, the abode of the light elves. It was conceived to be near the sacred well of the Norns, at the foot of the ash Yggdrasil.

Alfieri (äl.fyā'rē), **Cesare.** [Title, Marchese **di Sostegno.**] b. at Turin, Italy, Aug. 13, 1796; d. at Florence, Italy, April 17, 1869. Piedmontese politician and Italian nationalist, premier for a short time in 1848.

Alfieri, Conte **Vittorio.** b. at Asti, Piedmont, Italy, Jan. 16, 1749; d. at Florence, Italy, Oct. 10, 1803. Italian tragic dramatist and satirist, whose works had a strong influence on Italian nationalism. Heir to a large fortune, he wandered (1767–74) over Europe, passing through various adventures and amours before settling for a time at Turin. The success of his first play, *Cleopatra* (1775), began his career, which he pursued at Florence; there he fell in love (1777) with the Countess of Albany, with whom he lived (1784–1803) in Alsace, Paris, and Florence. His initial enthusiasm for the French Revolution was turned to disgust by its excesses, and in 1799 he published one of his best-known works, the *Misogallo*, a bitter diatribe against France. He was the author also of some 19 tragedies, including *Saul* (1782), *Antigone* (1783), *Sophonisba* (1788), *Maria Stuart* (1804), *Merope*, and *Myrrha;* six comedies; five odes (1776–83) on American independence; prose works including an autobiography (1804) and *Del principe e delle lettere* (1801); and others.

Alfinger (äl'fing.ėr), **Ambrosio de.** d. 1532. German soldier, appointed (1528) agent of the mercantile house of the Welsers (of Augsburg), which held Venezuela as a grant from the Spanish throne on condition of completing the conquest of the country for Castile and colonizing it.

Alföld (ôl'fėld). Name given to the great central plain of Hungary.

Alfonsine (äl.fôn'sē.nā). Town and commune in N Italy, in the *compartimento* (region) of Emilia-Romagna, in the province of Ravenna, situated in the midst of a system of canals near the Po di Primaro River, between Ravenna and Ferrara. It is the center of an agricultural district producing grain, vegetables, hemp, and sugar beets, and has small industries. Pop. of commune, 11,889 (1936); of town, 4,138 (1936).

Alfonso I (of *Aragon*) (al.fon'sō). See **Alfonso I** (of *Aragon and Navarre*).

Alfonso II (of *Aragon*). [Also: **Alphonso, Alonzo.**] b. 1152; d. 1196. King of Aragon (1162–96); son of Raymondo, count of Barcelona, and Petronilla, daughter of Ramiro II of Aragon. He is especially noted as a patron of Provençal poetry.

Alfonso III (of *Aragon*). [Also: **Alphonso, Alonzo;** called **"Alfonso the Magnificent."**] b. 1265; d. June 18, 1291. King of Aragon (1285–91); son of Pedro III.

Alfonso IV (of *Aragon*). [Also: **Alphonso, Alonzo;** called **"Alfonso the Good."**] b. 1299; d. 1336. King of Aragon (1327–36); son of James II of Aragon. His entire reign was occupied by a war with the Genoese over the possession of Corsica and Sardinia.

Alfonso V (of *Aragon*). [Also: **Alphonso, Alonzo;** called **"Alfonso the Magnanimous;"** additional title, **Alfonso I** (of *Sicily and Sardinia* and of *Naples*).] b. c1385; d. at Naples, Italy, June 27, 1458. King of Aragon and, as Alfonso I, king of Sicily and Sardinia and of Naples. He was the son of Ferdinand I of Aragon (Ferdinand the Just), whom he succeeded in 1416 as king of Aragon and of Sicily and Sardinia. In 1420 he was adopted as heir and prospective successor by Joanna I of Naples, but was disinherited in 1423 in favor of Louis of Anjou. He captured Naples in 1442, seven years after the death of Joanna, and enforced his claim to the succession. He was a patron of learning and was considered to be a model of chivalric virtues.

Alfonso I (of *Aragon and Navarre*). [Also: **Alphonso, Alonzo;** called **"Alfonso the Battler."**] d. 1134. King of Aragon and Navarre (1104–34); father of Alfonso VII of León and Castile. In 1109 he married Urraca, daughter and heiress of Alfonso VI of León and Castile. He conquered Saragossa (1118) and Calatayud (1120) from the Moors.

Alfonso I (of *Asturias*). [Also: **Alphonso, Alonzo;** called **"Alfonso the Great."**] b. c693; d. at Cangas, Spain, 757. King of Asturias (739–757), famous for his zeal in erecting and endowing monasteries and churches.

Alfonso II (of *Asturias*). [Also: **Alphonso, Alonzo;** called **"Alfonso the Chaste."**] d. at Oviedo, Spain, 842. King of Asturias (791–842). He defeated Mohammed, the Moorish governor of Merida, in 830.

Alfonso III (of *Asturias*). [Also: **Alphonso, Alonzo;** called **"Alfonso the Great."**] b. 848; d. 912. King of Asturias and (by conquest) León (866–910); eldest son of Ordoño I of Asturias and León. His reign was filled with internal struggles and external conflicts, especially with the Moors, over whom he was almost uniformly victorious. His successes extended his dominions from the Duero (Douro) River to the Guadiana River. In 910 he abdicated in favor of his son Garcia on account of civil wars raised by his sons.

Alfonso I (of *Castile*). See **Alfonso VI** (of *León and Castile*).

Alfonso II (of *Castile*). See **Alfonso VII** (of *León and Castile*).

Alfonso III (of *Castile*). See **Alfonso VIII** (of *León and Castile*).

Alfonso I (of *Este*). [Also, **Alphonso.**] b. 1476; d. Oct. 31, 1534. Duke of Ferrara (1505–34). He commanded papal troops in the war of the League of Cambrai in 1509, and fought against Pope Julius II at Ravenna in 1512. In 1501 he married Lucretia Borgia.

Alfonso I (of *León and Castile*). See **Alfonso I** (of *Asturias*).

Alfonso II (of *León and Castile*). See **Alfonso II** (of *Asturias*).

Alfonso III (of *León and Castile*). See **Alfonso III** (of *Asturias*).

Alfonso IV (of *León and Castile*). [Also: **Alphonso, Alonzo;** called **"Alfonso the Monk."**] d. c933. King of León (c924–927); eldest son of Ordoño II of Asturias and León. He abdicated, on the death of his wife, in favor of his brother Ramiro, and retired to a cloister. He was taken prisoner at León in an attempt to regain the throne, was blinded, and was thereafter confined until his death in the monastery of Saint Julian.

Alfonso V (of *León and Castile*). [Also: **Alphonso, Alonzo;** called **"Alfonso the Noble."**] b. c994; d. 1027. King of León and Castile (999–1027); son of Bermudo II, whom he succeeded. He recaptured León, which had been lost during his minority, and was killed at the siege of what is now Viseu, Portugal.

Alfonso VI (of *León and Castile*). [Also: **Alphonso, Alonzo;** called **"Alfonso the Valiant"**; additional title, **Alfonso I** (of *Castile*).] b. 1030; d. 1109. King of León and Castile; son of Ferdinand the Great, whom he succeeded in León in 1065. He succeeded his brother Sancho in Castile in 1072. From 1068 until 1072, when Sancho died, the brothers were at war, and in 1071 Alfonso was defeated and taken prisoner. In 1085 he captured Toledo from the Moors but was himself defeated near Zallaka by the Almoravid leader, ibn-Tashfin, in 1086. His reign witnessed the exploits of the Cid.

Alfonso VII (of *León and Castile*). [Also: **Alphonso, Alonzo**; additional title, **Alfonso II** (of *Castile*).] b. c1106; d. in August, 1157. King of León and, as Alfonso II, king of Castile (1126–57). He extended the frontiers of Castile from the Tagus (Tajo) River to the Sierra Morena Mountains, and proclaimed himself emperor of Spain in 1135.

Alfonso VIII (of *León and Castile*). [Also: **Alphonso, Alonzo**; called **"Alfonso the Noble"** and **"Alfonso the Good"**; additional title, **Alfonso III** (of *Castile*).] b. 1155; d. 1214. King of Castile (1158–1214); son of Sancho III. He was defeated by the Moors at Alarcos in 1195, and in alliance with Aragón and Navarre defeated the Moors at Las Navas de Tolosa in 1212. He established, at Palencia, the first Spanish university.

Alfonso IX (of *León and Castile*). [Also: **Alphonso, Alonzo.**] d. 1230. King of León (1188–1230); son of Ferdinand II of León and Castile. He gained a brilliant victory over Mohammed ibn-Hud at Mérida in 1230. He was married first to Theresa, daughter of Sancho I of Portugal, and later to Berengaria, daughter of the king of Castile. Both marriages were dissolved by the Pope as being within the degree of affinity proscribed by the canon law.

Alfonso X (of *León and Castile*). [Also: **Alphonso, Alonzo**; called **"Alfonso the Wise"** and **"Alfonso the Astronomer."**] b. in Burgos, Spain, Nov. 23, 1221; d. at Seville, Spain, April 4, 1284. King of León and Castile (1252–82); son of Ferdinand III of León and Castile. He laid claim to the duchy of Swabia, and twice was a candidate for the imperial crown; the first time he was defeated by Richard of Cornwall, and the second by Rudolf I of Hapsburg. From 1261 to 1266 he waged war with the Moors. He was dethroned by his son Sancho in 1282. Alfonso is celebrated as the author of the code *Las Siete Partidas*, the basis of Spanish jurisprudence, and for the Alphonsine tables, a set of astronomical observations compiled at his command.

Alfonso XI (of *León and Castile*). [Also: **Alphonso, Alonzo**; called **"Alfonso the Avenger."**] d. March 26, 1350. King of León and Castile (1312–50), son of Ferdinand IV. He defeated the Moors of Morocco and Granada at the Salado River (Rio Salado) (Oct. 29, 1340); in 1342 he laid successful siege to Algeciras. He was noted for his severity in quelling civil disorder.

Alfonso XII (of *León and Castile*). See **Alfonso XII** (of *Spain*).

Alfonso XIII (of *León and Castile*). See **Alfonso XIII** (of *Spain*).

Alfonso II (of *Naples*). [Also, **Alphonso.**] b. 1448; d. Nov. 19, 1495. King of Naples (1494–95); eldest son of Ferdinand I of Naples and Isabella. He defeated the Florentines at Poggio (1479) and the Turks at Otranto (1481); disliked by his subjects, he abdicated (Jan. 23, 1495) in favor of his son, Ferdinand II, when Charles VIII of France threatened Naples.

Alfonso (of *Poitou*). [French, **Alphonse.**] d. 1271. Count of Poitou; brother of Louis IX of France, and ruler of Poitou and Toulouse.

Alfonso I (of *Portugal*). [Also: **Affonso, Alphonso.**] b. c1110; d. Dec. 6, 1185. First king of Portugal; son of Henry of Burgundy, count of Portugal, and Teresa of Castile. On his father's death in 1112 he became, under his mother's tutelage, count of Portugal, and was declared sole ruler in 1128. In that year he made successful war upon his mother, who refused to yield up the government, and also warred against her ally, Alfonso VIII of León and Castile, from whom he wrested the independence of Portugal. He was proclaimed king by his soldiers, probably after the victory over the Moors at Ourique, on July 26, 1139; took Santarem from the Moors in 1146; captured Lisbon in 1147; and was taken captive near Badajoz in 1167 by the Leonese and made to pay a heavy ransom (the surrender of all his conquests in Galicia).

Alfonso II (of *Portugal*). [Also: **Affonso, Alphonso**; called **"Alfonso the Fat."**] b. April 23, 1185; d. March 25, 1223. King of Portugal (1211–23). He defeated the Moors at Alcácer do Sal, Portugal, in 1217. Pope Honorius III excommunicated him as a result of Alfonso's rulings against the Church.

Alfonso III (of *Portugal*). [Also: **Affonso, Alphonso.**] b. May 5, 1210; d. Feb. 16, 1279. King of Portugal (1248–79) and Count of Boulogne. Early in his reign Algarve was incorporated in Portugal. Alfonso encouraged financial reforms and commercial progress, and promoted French culture in his domain.

Alfonso IV (of *Portugal*). [Also: **Affonso, Alphonso**; called: **"Alfonso the Brave," "Alfonso the Fierce."**] b. at Coimbra, Portugal, Feb. 8, 1290; d. May 28, 1357. King of Portugal (1325–57). He consented to the murder of Inés de Castro, secretly married to his son Pedro, who, in consequence, headed a revolt against his father.

Alfonso V (of *Portugal*). [Also: **Affonso, Alphonso**; called **"Alfonso the African."**] b. at Cintra (now Sintra), Portugal, Jan. 15, 1432; d. there, Aug. 28, 1481. King of Portugal (1438–81); son of King Duarte (Edward) of Portugal. He defeated the Moors in Africa in 1458 and 1471, and was defeated at Toto in 1476 by Ferdinand the Catholic. A civil war resulted from the conflict between Alfonso and his uncle, Dom Pedro; the latter assumed the regency while Alfonso was still under age, and was made to relinquish it only by force. His marriage to Juana la Beltraneja of Castile led Alfonso to attempt without success the annexation of Castile to his throne.

Alfonso VI (of *Portugal*). [Also: **Affonso, Alphonso.**] b. 1643; d. Sept. 12, 1683. King of Portugal; second son of John IV. He succeeded to the throne in 1656 and was deposed, in 1667, by his younger brother, Pedro II of Portugal. Alfonso was driven into exile.

Alfonso I (of *Sicily and Sardinia* and of *Naples*). See **Alfonso V** (of *Aragon*).

Alfonso XII (of *Spain*). [Also: **Alphonso, Alonzo.**] b. at Madrid, Nov. 28, 1857: d. at Madrid, Nov. 26, 1885. King of Spain (1874–85). The son of Isabella II, he was proclaimed king of Spain in December, 1874. He landed in Spain (January, 1875), and suppressed the Carlist rebellion in 1876. He was respected and liked for the benevolence and justice of his reign.

Alfonso XIII (of *Spain*). [Also: **Alphonso, Alonso**; full prename, **León Fernando María Isídro Pascual António.**] b. at Madrid, 1886; d. at Rome, 1941. King of Spain (1886–1931). Posthumous son of Alfonso XII by his second wife, Maria Christina of Austria, he was proclaimed king under the regency of his mother on the day of his birth. On May 17, 1902, he took over the government and in 1906 married Eugenia Victoria of Battenberg. During the regency of his mother Spain had lost the Philippines and Cuba, and Spanish policy in Morocco had remained unsuccessful and costly, leading to riots in Madrid and Barcelona in 1909 and 1911. Beset by problems in the wake of World War I (in which Spain stayed neutral) and suffering repeated setbacks in Morocco through the activities of Abd-el-Krim, the king sanctioned the establishment of a dictatorship under Primo de Rivera in 1923. At the fall of the dictatorship in 1930 the king was forced to abdicate and went into exile with his family. In 1941, just before his death, General Franco restored Alfonso's civil rights, and he was buried in Spain.

"Alfonso the African." See **Alfonso V** (of *Portugal*).

"Alfonso the Astronomer." See **Alfonso X** (of *León and Castile*).

"Alfonso the Avenger." See **Alfonso XI** (of *León and Castile*).

"Alfonso the Battler." See **Alfonso I** (of *Aragon and Navarre*).

"Alfonso the Brave." See **Alfonso IV** (of *Portugal*).

"Alfonso the Chaste." See **Alfonso II** (of *Asturias*).

"Alfonso the Fat." See **Alfonso II** (of *Portugal*).

"Alfonso the Fierce." See **Alfonso IV** (of *Portugal*).

"Alfonso the Good." See **Alfonso IV** (or *Aragon*); also **Alfonso VIII** (of *León and Castile*).

"Alfonso the Great." See **Alfonso I** (of *Asturias*) and **Alfonso III** (of *Asturias*).

"Alfonso the Magnanimous." See **Alfonso V** (of *Aragon*).

"Alfonso the Magnificent." See **Alfonso III** (of *Aragon*).

"Alfonso the Monk." See **Alfonso IV** (of *León and Castile*).

"Alfonso the Noble." See **Alfonso V** (of *León and Castile*); also **Alfonso VIII** (of *León and Castile*).

"Alfonso the Valiant." See **Alfonso VI** (of *León and Castile*).

"Alfonso the Wise." See **Alfonso X** (of *León and Castile*).

Alfonso und Estrella (äl.fōn'sō ůnt es.trel'ä). Opera in three acts by Franz Schubert, with a libretto by F. von Schober, first performed at Weimar, Germany, on June 24, 1854.

Alfonso y Castro (äl.fôn'sō ē käs'trō). See **Castro, Alfonso y.**

Alford (ôl'fo̤rd), **Henry.** b. at London, 1810; d. at Canterbury, England, 1871. English Biblical scholar. Graduate (1832) and fellow (1834) of Trinity College, Cambridge; dean of Canterbury (1857–71). He was the first editor (1866–70) of the *Contemporary Review.* His publications include an important critical edition of the Greek Testament (1849–61), *A Plea for the Queen's English* (1866), *New Testament for English Readers* (1867), poems, hymns, and others.

Alford, Michael. [Original surname, **Griffith.**] b. at London, 1587; d. at St. Omer, 1652. English Jesuit, active in Great Britain during the period of 17th-century anti-Catholic persecution. He is the author of various works on ecclesiastical history.

Alfortville (àl.fôr.vēl). Town in N France, in the department of Seine, situated at the confluence of the Seine and Marne rivers, SE of Paris, of which it is a suburb. It is the seat of a national veterinary school established in 1766. Pop. 27,940 (1946).

Alfred (al'fre̤d). [Also: **Ælfred**; called **Alfred the Great.**] b. at Wantage, in Berkshire, England, 849; d. Oct. 28, 899. King of England (871–899); youngest son of Ethelwulf, king of the West Saxons, and his wife Osburh (daughter of Oslac, Ethelwulf's cup-bearer), and brother of Ethelbald, Ethelbert, and Ethelred, the last of whom he succeeded. He fought against the Danes in the defensive campaign of 871, serving under his brother Ethelred at Ashdown, Basing, and Merton, and commanded as king at Wilton. In 878 he withdrew before the Danes to Athelney, but later obtained a decisive victory over them at Ethandun. By the treaty of Wedmore, which followed, the Danish Guthrum consented to receive baptism and to retire north of Watling Street. Alfred fortified London in 886, and carried on a defensive war (892–896) with the Danes, which ended in the withdrawal of the invaders, and in which, by the aid of ships of improved model, the English for the first time gained a decisive naval advantage over the Vikings. His success against the Danes was due largely to his reform of the national *fyrd* or militia, by which half the force of each shire was always ready for military service. His administration was also marked by judicial and educational reforms. He compiled a code of laws, rebuilt the schools and monasteries, and invited scholars to his court. Himself a man of learning, he translated into English the *Epitome of Universal History* of Paulus Orosius, the *Consolations of Philosophy* of Boethius, and the *Pastoral Rule* of Gregory the Great; and had translations made of the *Dialogues* of Gregory the Great and the *Ecclesiastical History* of Bede. The popular accounts of his life abound in legends which are devoid of historical foundation.

Alfred, Prince. [Full prename, **Alfred Ernest Albert;** titles: Duke of **Edinburgh,** Duke of **Saxe-Coburg and Gotha.**] b. Aug. 6, 1844; d. July 30, 1900. Duke of Saxe-Coburg and Gotha (1893 *et seq.*); second son of Queen Victoria. He was elected king of Greece in 1862, but declined the offer. He married the Grand Duchess Maria of Russia.

Alfred Club. Club organized at London in 1808.

Alfred Jingle (jing'gl). See **Jingle, Alfred.**

Alfred of Beverley (bev'ėr.li). [Also: **Alured of Beverley**; Latin, **Alredus** (or **Aluredus**) **Beverlacensis.**] fl. in the middle of the 12th century. English chronicler.

Alfred the Great. See also **Alfred.**

Alfred the Great. Historical play by J. Sheridan Knowles, produced in 1831.

Alfreton (ôl'fre̤.to̤n). Urban district and market town in C England, in Derbyshire, ab. 13 mi. NE of Derby, ab. 136 mi. NW of London by rail. There are five townships contained within the civil parish. 23,388 (1951).

Alfvén (äl.vān'), **Hugo.** b. at Stockholm, Sweden, May 1, 1872—. Swedish composer and violinist. Music director (1910 *et seq.*) at Upsala University; composer of three symphonies, two symphonic poems, as well as numerous choral and short orchestral pieces.

Algardi (äl.gär'dē), **Alessandro.** b. at Bologna, Italy, 1602; d. at Rome, June 10, 1654. Italian sculptor and architect. A student of Lodovico Carracci, he collaborated with Borromini on the decoration of St. Peter's Church.

Algarotti (äl.gä.rôt'tē), Conte **Francesco.** b. at Venice, Italy, Dec. 11, 1712; d. at Pisa, May 3, 1764. Italian littérateur and art connoisseur, a friend of Voltaire and Frederick the Great.

Algarve (äl.gär've̤). [Arabic, **Al-Gharb.**] Southernmost province of Portugal, bounded by the province of Baixo Alentejo on the N, by Spain, from which it is separated by the Guadiana River, on the E, and by the Atlantic Ocean on the S and W. It forms the district of Faro, with the town of Faro as capital. The province is divided into a mountainous northern belt, a densely populated and fertile southern belt growing wine, figs, olives, bananas, and oranges, and a partly sandy and swampy, partly rocky, coastal area. Shipping and fishing are the chief occupations on the coast. Algarve originally also comprised that part of the Moroccan coast immediately to the southeast, and the neighboring Spanish districts, and was a stronghold of the Islamic Moors in the early Middle Ages; its name is derived from the Arabic *al-gharb.* It was conquered (1212–51) by the Christians. Portuguese voyages of discovery started from here, chiefly from the ports of Lagos and Sagres. Capital, Faro; area, 1,958 sq. mi.; pop. 317,628 (1940).

Algäu (äl'goi). [Also, **Allgäu.**] Region in the SW part of Bavaria and the neighboring portions of Württemberg-Hohenzollern, Germany, and the Austrian land of Vorarlberg; the larger part of it is in the Bavarian government district of Swabia. It is rich in pasture land, and is the chief center of the German dairy industry.

Algäu Alps. [Also: **Allgäu Alps**; German, **Algäuer Alpen** (äl'goi.ėr äl'pe̤n).] Mountain group in Algäu (N Tirol, Austria, and SW Bavaria, Germany). Its highest point is the Parseyer Spitz (ab. 9,960 ft.).

Algazel (äl.gä.zel'). See **Gazali, Abu Hamid Mohammed al-.**

Algebar (al'je.bär). **1.** An Arabic and poetical name of the constellation Orion. **2.** Name occasionally used to designate Rigel (β Orionis), the brightest star in that constellation.

Algeciras (al.je̤.sir'a̤s; Spanish, äl.hä.thē'räs). [Arabic, **Al-Djesirat-al-hadra, Al-Jazira** or **Al-Jezira,** meaning "the island" or "peninsula"; Latin, **Portus Albus.**] Commune in S Spain, in the province of Cádiz, on the W shore of the Bay of Algeciras, ab. 6 mi. W of Gibraltar: seaport and railroad terminal; fisheries; exports of wine, liquor, cork, leather, and stone. There is a castle and an aqueduct built by the Moors; the Church of Santa María della Palma dates from the 18th century. The city was founded by the Carthaginians, and later occupied by the Romans. The Moslem invaders of Spain landed on the Bay of Algeciras in 710; Algeciras was the first Spanish town conquered by them, and they held it until 1344. The town was devastated by the Normans in 845 and 859; and besieged by Alfonso X of León and Castile in 1278; the final siege, by Alfonso XI of León and Castile, lasted from 1342 to 1344. A French-Spanish fleet defeated the British near here on July 6, 1801, but was defeated in a second engagement on July 12, 1801. The international conference of Algeciras, dealing with the international problems involved in the administration of Morocco, was held here in 1906. Pop. 25,671 (1940).

Algeciras, Bay of. Inlet of the Strait of Gibraltar, S Spain, situated W of the town of Gibraltar.

Algeciras Conference. Meeting (Jan. 16–April 7, 1906) of the European powers, called largely at the insistence of Germany, to discuss the international status of Morocco, upon whose sultan the French were making further demands for concessions. The results of the conference redounded to Germany's disadvantage, although during the conference she had only the support of Austria-Hungary. Moroccan independence was nominally preserved, its eight ports were put under French and Spanish guard, and France was given general direction over its new international bank, but the completely free hand which France desired in the Moroccan area was for the moment denied. By decision of the delegates, various reforms were urged upon the sultan of Morocco, such as the removal of disabilities placed upon citizens of the U.S. (by the U.S. delegate), the abolition of slavery (Great Britain), the establishment of lighthouses (Germany), the publication of commercial statistics (Austria), and the immediate construction of railways (Spain). The U.S. was represented by Henry White, at that time ambassador to Italy.

Algeiba or **Algieba** (al.jē′bạ). The second-magnitude double star γ Leonis. By Ulugh Beigh the name Algeiba was applied to three stars, η, γ, and ζ Leonis.

Algemesí (äl″ʜä.mā.sē′). Commune in Spain, in the province of Valencia, situated on the Júcar River, ab. 6 mi. N of Alcira: paper factories; trade in rice, wine, oranges, and olive oil. 17,373 (1940).

Algenib (al′je.nib). The third-magnitude star γ Pegasi, at the extremity of the wing. The same name is also given to α Persei, better known as Mirfak. It is also called Alchemb.

Algenubi (al.je.nö′bi). A name of the third-magnitude star ϵ Leonis.

Alger (ȧl.zhā). French name of **Algiers.**

Alger (al′jėr), **Cyrus.** b. at Bridgewater, Mass., Nov. 11, 1781; d. Feb. 4, 1856. American inventor and iron manufacturer. He established (1809) an iron foundry at South Boston, and was thereafter responsible for production in the U.S. of the first cylinder stoves (1822), the first rifle (1834), a malleable cast-iron plow, and the casting of the first "Columbiad" mortar, the largest weapon of its kind to be produced in the U.S. before 1850.

Alger, Horatio. b. at Revere, Mass., Jan. 13, 1834; d. July 18, 1899. American author of boy's books and Unitarian clergyman. He terminated a brief career as minister (1864–66) to devote himself to writing, which eventually produced 119 works and brought Alger juvenile readers throughout the English-speaking world. *Ragged Dick* (1867) was the first story in what was to be Alger's typical and most popular series; his later books (one of which was written in two weeks) produced through their similarity of theme a pattern of writing which has indissolubly linked Alger's name to a certain type of "rags to riches" fiction.

Alger, Russell Alexander. b. at Lafayette, Ohio, Feb. 27, 1836; d. at Washington, Jan. 24, 1907. American politician; Secretary of War (1897–99) during the Spanish-American War. During his secretaryship, the War Department was severely criticized for unpreparedness and maladministration; the Dodge report on the conduct of the war, plus that of the "embalmed beef" commission, resulted in Alger's resignation at McKinley's request. He served as a colonel (1864) under Sheridan in the Civil War, and was brevetted a major-general of volunteers (1865). He was governor of Michigan (1885–87) and a senator from Michigan (1902–07).

Alger, William Rounseville. b. at Freetown, Mass., Dec. 28, 1822; d. Feb. 7, 1905. American Unitarian clergyman and author, an outspoken opponent of slavery. He wrote *The Poetry of the East* (1856), *Critical History of the Doctrine of a Future Life* (1864), *Life of Edwin Forrest, The American Tragedian* (1877), and others.

Algeria (al.jir′i.ạ). [French, **Algérie** (ȧl.zhā.rē).] Country in NW Africa (consisting of the ancient Numidia and E Mauritania), organized as a colonial possession of France in 1834 (conquest begun in 1830). In 1870 the northern part of the country was divided into three departments and became part of metropolitan France. Algeria is bounded by the Mediterranean Sea on the N, by Tunisia on the E, by the Sahara on the S, and by French Morocco on the W; it is traversed by the Atlas range. Capital, Algiers; area (including Algiers and the Algerian part of the Sahara), 847,500 sq. mi.; pop., 8,676,016 (1948).

Physical and Economic Geography. It comprises three distinct regions: the Tell, or mountainous and cultivated region, in the north; the steppe region, with various brackish lakes, in the center; and the Sahara, which extends indefinitely southward. Agriculture is the leading occupation, but the country contains considerable mineral wealth (especially iron, lime phosphate, and copper), and exports wheat, barley, oats, wine, olive oil, esparto grass, wool, fruits, and livestock.

Political Divisions. Algeria is organized in two divisions, Territoire du Nord (including the departments of Algiers, Oran, and Constantine) and Territoires du Sud (including Aïn-Sefra, Ghardaïa, Touggourt, and Oasis Sahariennes). Its chief cities include Algiers, Constantine, and Oran. The government is vested in a governor general appointed from France, in the French *Corps Législatif*, and in a superior council. Each of the three departments sends a senator and three deputies to the French assembly, with the exception of Algiers, which sends four deputies.

Culture and History. The prevailing religion is Mohammedanism, and the inhabitants are chiefly Berbers, Arabs, Europeans (largely French and Spanish), Moors, and the descendants of Turks. The country was annexed by Rome in the first century B.C., was conquered by the Vandals in the 5th century and by the Moslems in the 7th century, passed into the possession of the Turks in 1519, and was a piratical power from the 16th to the 19th century, becoming independent of Turkey in 1710. The office of dey was established in 1600. Defeated by the U.S. in 1815. Conquest by France, begun in 1830 with the taking of Algiers, was continued by the taking of Constantine in 1837, the subduing of the Kabyles, and the capture of Abd-al-Kadir in 1847. In 1871 there was another revolt, but after this was suppressed the French had little trouble in later years. A campaign for control of the Sahara was begun in 1891, and was finally completed in 1919 as far as actual warfare was concerned. Since then the penetration and extension of French control has been carried on with little opposition. Under the Vichy government in World War II, the country was invaded by the Allies in 1942.

Alger of Liége (lẹ.āzh′, lyezh). b. at Liége, in what is now Belgium, c1055; d. at Cluny, France, 1132. French ecclesiastic. He was for 20 years canon of the Cathedral of St. Lambert, and then (1121 *et seq.*) monk of Cluny. A well-known ecclesiastical writer, he opposed the error of the Berengarians.

Alghero (äl.ge′rō). [Also, **Algheri** (-rē).] Town and commune in Italy, on the island of Sardinia, in the province of Sassari, situated on the Rada d'Alghero, on the W coast of the island, SW of Sassari. The fortified town was at various times contested between Venice, Genoa, and Aragon; in 1353 the rebellious inhabitants were expelled by King Pietro IV of Aragon and replaced by settlers from Spain; after preserving Spanish habits for a long time, they fused with the Sardic inhabitants of the surrounding countryside. The population is engaged in seafaring activities and fishing; excellent wines and other agricultural products are grown in the vicinity. Pop. of commune, 15,998 (1936); of town, 14,519 (1936).

Al Ghiraybah (äl gē.rī′bạ). City on the island of Bahrein, in the Persian Gulf, E of Arabia. It is in the center of the rich Bahrein oil fields, and near it is located a large refinery with a capacity of over 10 million barrels a year.

Algieba (al.jē′bạ). See **Algeiba.**

Algiers (al.jirz′). [French, **Alger**; Arabic, **Al-Jezair.**] Middle department of Algeria, in NW Africa, consisting of five *arrondissements* (administrative divisions). It is headed by a prefect (appointed by the president of France), who is aided by several minor officials. Capital, Algiers; area, 21,052 sq. mi.; pop. 2,765,898 (1948).

Algiers. [French, **Alger**; Arabic, **Al-Jezair**; Latin, **Icosium.**] Seaport, the capital of Algeria and of Algiers department, on the Bay of Algiers, on the NW coast of Africa midway on the Algerian coast; founded by the Arabs c935 on the site of the ancient Roman city of Icosium. It was held by Spain 1509–17, and unsuccessfully attacked by Charles V in 1541. It was a focal point for piracy on American shipping, which ended with the appearance there of Decatur's fleet (1815). It was bombarded by the British in 1816, and occupied by the French in 1830. In World War II, Algiers served as a headquarters for the Allied forces in Africa after the city was taken by the Allies on Nov. 8, 1942. The city, with its suburbs, is the largest urban area in French northern Africa. It is the leading industrial and commercial center of the country, a chief port, and principal coaling station. 266,165 (1948).

Algiers. District of New Orleans, Louisiana, in Orleans Parish: at one time frequented by the pirate, Lafitte.

Algoa Bay (al.gō′ạ). Bay on the S coast of Cape of Good Hope province, Union of South Africa. The important harbor of Port Elizabeth is situated on the W side of the bay.

Algol (al′gol). The remarkable second-magnitude variable star β Persei, in the head of Medusa, who is the monster referred to in the name. This is the most celebrated of eclipsing binaries, its faint companion passing in front every two days, 20 hours, 49 minutes, and reducing the brightness to one-third normal. Its variability was noted in 1670 by Montanari, and its periodicity discovered in 1782 by Goodricke, who suggested the eclipse cause.

Algoma (al.gō′mạ). City in E Wisconsin, in Kewaunee County: resort community on Lake Michigan. 3,384 (1950).

Algona (al.gō′nạ). [Former name, **Call's Grove.**] City in N Iowa, county seat of Kossuth county, on the Last Fork of the Des Moines River. It was settled in 1854. Pop. 5,415 (1950).

Algonac (al′gọ.nak). Village in S Michigan, in St. Clair County, NE of Detroit: resort center. 2,639 (1950).

Algonquian (al.gon′ki.ạn). [Also, **Algonkin** (-kin).] One of the major North American Indian linguistic families. It covers an area greater than any of the others. It was distributed over large portions of the NE U.S., and C and E Canada, though its continuity of distribution in the E Great Lakes area and the St. Lawrence valley was interrupted by the Iroquoian family of languages.

Algorab (al.gọ.räb′) or **Algores** (al′gọ.rēz). The third-magnitude star δ Corvi.

Algrange (ȧl.gräṅzh). [German, **Algringen** (äl′gring.ẹn).] Town in E France, in the department of Moselle, W of Thionville, near the Luxembourg border. It is an industrial town. Iron ore is mined in the vicinity. 7,953 (1946).

Algrind (al′grind). An anagram of Edmund Grindal, archbishop of Canterbury, used in Spenser's *Shepherd's Calendar.*

Al Habbaniya (äl häb.bä.nē′yạ). Town in C Iraq, on the Euphrates River N of Lake Habbaniya, ab. 50 mi. W of Bagdad: called by some scholars the traditional site of the Garden of Eden; now a small trading center.

Alhama de Murcia (ä.lä′mä dā mör′thyä). [Also, **Alhama.**] Town in SE Spain, in the province of Murcia, situated at the foot of the Sierra de Espuña, ab. 17 mi. SW of Murcia: center of a fertile, irrigated agricultural district. It is a health resort, with hot sulfur springs. There is a Moorish castle. 10,740 (1940).

Alhamarides (ä.lä.mär′idz). The last Moorish dynasty in Spain. It ruled in Granada from the middle of the 13th century until 1492.

Alhambra (al.ham′brạ). City in S California, in Los Angeles County, ab. 7 mi. NE of Los Angeles: residential and manufacturing center, in a fruit-growing region. 51,359 (1950).

Alhambra (al.ham′brạ; Spanish, ä.läm′brä). Moslem fortress and palace, with additional buildings, at Granada, Spain, built chiefly (1248–1354) by the king Mohammed Ibn Al Ahmar and his successors; the outstanding example of Moslem architecture and decoration in Spain. Damaged after the expulsion (1492) of the Moslems from Spain and by the emperor Charles V (Charles I of Spain), who replaced part of the old structure with a Renaissance palace in the 16th century, it was extensively restored in the 19th century. Standing on a plateau about 35 acres in area and surrounded by heavy brick walls, the buildings are composed mainly of small rooms laid out around open courtyards which contain the fountains and rich gardens characteristic of Moslem landscape architecture. Most noted of these is the Court of Lions, in which a covered passage, or arcade, of tall arches on 124 paired or grouped white marble columns surrounds a paved patio with the Fountain of Lions in the center. The interior and exterior decoration, in the style known as Arabesque, consists of infinitely varied interwoven patterns of foliage-like forms, Arabic script in gold on blue background, and geometric tracery, done in majolica tiles, carved wood, pressed plaster and stucco, and pierced stone heightened with brilliant colors; ceilings and doorways present the intricate repetition of geometrical forms resulting in what is known as "honeycomb" and "stalactite" vaulting.

Alhambra, The. Series of 41 sketches published in 1832 by Washington Irving. The material for the book was gathered during Irving's residence in the old royal palace of the Moors at Granada. The author's avowed purpose was to describe the half-Spanish, half-Oriental character of the place against the background of its legends, history, and traditions.

Alhaurín el Grande (ä.lou.rēn′ el grän′dā). [Also, **Alhaurín.**] Town in S Spain, in the province of Málaga, ab. 20 mi. SW of Málaga. The town trades in olive oil; marble quarries are in the vicinity. 10,681 (1940).

Alhazen (äl.hä.zen′). b. at Basra, Iraq, c965; d. at Cairo, c1038. Arabian mathematician and astronomer; important contributor to the science of optics. Called to Egypt by Hakim to control Nile floods, he pretended insanity to avoid carrying out an impracticable plan. Author of works on geometry, philosophy and medicine, particularly his *Opticae thesaurus* (Latin translation, 1270) and studies of twilight and clouds, the latter three of which were published together in 1572.

Alhena (al.hen′ạ). The third-magnitude star γ Geminorum, in the foot or ankle of Pollux. It is sometimes called Almeisam.

Ali (ä′lē). [Called (by members of the Shiite sect) **Sher-i-Khuda,** meaning "the Lion of God."] b. at Mecca, in Arabia, c600; killed at Kufa, in what is now Iraq, 661. Fourth Moslem caliph (656–661); cousin, adopted son, and son-in-law of Mohammed, one of his earliest converts. His descendants were the Alids who founded the Shiite sect and also, through Fatima (his wife and Mohammed's daughter), the Fatimites. Ali's struggle for succession, first against Abu-Bakr, Mohammed's immediate successor, and Ayesha, Mohammed's widow, and later against Muawiyah, founder of the Ommiads, was the cause of his death and the original source of the great Shiite-Sunnite schism in the Moslem world. Assuming the caliphate on the death (656) of Othman, he defended it against the armies of Ayesha (Battle of the Camel, 656) and Muawiyah (657), with whom he attempted peaceful settlement. He was betrayed (658) by arbitrators and assassinated (661) by Kharijite fanatics. He is venerated as a martyr by the Shiite Moslems of Afghanistan, Iran, and India.

Ali, Asaf. b. 1888—. Indian statesman and nationalist Moslem leader, first ambassador (1947–48) of the Union of India to the U.S. He has served also as governor of Orissa (1948 *et seq.*). An active participant in the independence movement, he was a member of the Congress Working Committee in 1942 and later deputy leader of the Congress Party in the central assembly.

Ali, Fath (or **Feth**). See **Fath Ali.**

Ali, Mohammed. b. in Rampur State, United Provinces, India, 1878; d. at London, Jan. 4, 1931. Indian Moslem leader, an advocate of Indian independence. The son of a small landowner, he was graduated from Allahabad University (1898) and from Oxford (B.A., 1902), but failed (1902) the India Civil Service examination. He took part in the formation (1906) of the All-India Moslem League. Pro-Turkish in World War I and a pan-Islamist until Turkey's abolition (1924) of the caliphate, he was imprisoned (1914 *et seq.*, 1919, 1921) by the British. Long associated with Mohandas K. Gandhi and the non-coöperation movement, he was president (1923) of the India National Congress, but as president (1931) of the All-India Moslem Conference he attacked the policy of Gandhi, fearing loss of freedom for India's Moslems.

Alia (ā′li.ạ). See **Allia.**

Ali Baba (ä′lē bä′bä). Character in *The Arabian Nights' Entertainments*, in the story "Ali Baba and the Forty Thieves." He is a poor woodcutter who, concealed in a tree, sees a band of robbers enter a secret cavern, and overhears the magic words "open sesame," which open its door. After the departure of the thieves he repeats the spell and the door opens, disclosing a room full of treasures with which he loads his donkeys and returns home. His brother Cassim, who discovers his secret, enters the cave alone, forgets the word "sesame," and is found, killed, and dismembered by the robbers. The thieves, discovering that Ali Baba knows their secret, resolve to kill him, but are outwitted by Morgiana, Ali Baba's slave.

Ali Baba. Opera by Cherubini, founded on his *Koukourgi*, produced at Paris, July 22, 1833.

Alibaud (ä.lē.bō), **Louis.** b. at Nîmes, France, May 2, 1810; guillotined at Paris, July 11, 1836. Frenchman who attempted to assassinate Louis Philippe, the king of France, on June 25, 1836.

Alibert (à.lē.ber), **Jean Louis,** Baron. b. at Villefranche, Aveyron, France, May 12, 1766; d. at Paris, Nov. 6, 1837. French medical writer; author of *Traité complet des maladies de la peau* (1806–27), and other works.

Alibert, Paul. b. at Carcassonne, France, March 15, 1873—. French poet. His reputation as a master of the elegy is based upon his *Odes* (1922), *Églogues* (1923), and *Élégies romaines* (1923).

Ali Bey (ä'lę bā). See also **Badía y Leblich, Domingo.**

Ali Bey. b. in Abkhazia (in what is now part of the U.S.S.R.), c1728; d. 1773. Mameluke *bey* (ruler) of Egypt. Originally a slave, he became leader of the Mamelukes (the slave-soldiers who for centuries made up one of the most effective fighting forces in the region of the E Mediterranean) in 1763 and declared himself independent of the Porte (Turkey) in 1768. He made many conquests in Arabia, Syria, and elsewhere; taken prisoner in battle in 1773.

Alibunar Marsh (ä.lē.bö'när). Large morass in NE Yugoslavia, in Vojvodina, NE of Belgrade.

Alicante (ä.lē.kän'tā). Province in SE Spain, bounded by Valencia on the N, the Mediterranean Sea on the E and SE, and Murcia and Albacete on the SW and W. Large parts of the hilly country along the Mediterranean coast are fertile, producing grain, wine, olive oil, almonds, and citrus fruits. The climate is mild, and date palms grow in the subdistrict of Elche. Capital, Alicante; area, 2,267 sq. mi.; pop. 648,435 (1950).

Alicante. [Latin, **Lucentum.**] Town in SE Spain, capital of the province of Alicante, situated on the Mediterranean Sea, ab. 77 mi. S of Valencia. It has a good harbor, and exports grain, almonds, castor and olive oil, red Alicante wines, and other agricultural products. There are tobacco, textile, ceramics, and food industries in the area, and it has some importance also as a seaside resort. Among the noteworthy buildings of the town are a castle, the town hall, various churches in baroque style, and the Gothic church of Santa María (which takes the place of a former mosque). A Roman town in ancient times, Alicante retained some degree of independence under the Moors, but was subject to Moslem overlordship; it was later much contested between Christians and Moslems. Finally taken from the Moors by James I of Aragon in 1296, it was thereafter alternately in the hands of Aragon and Castile. It was besieged by the French in 1709 and was the scene of revolutionary fighting in 1873 and 1936. Pop. 107,596 (1950).

Alice (al'is). City in S Texas, county seat of Jim Wells County, W of Corpus Christi in a petroleum and cotton producing area. 16,449 (1950).

Alice. Wife of Bath in Chaucer's tale of that name. Her "gossib," to whom she alludes, has the same name.

Alice. Lady in attendance on Princess Katherine in Shakespeare's *Henry V*.

Alice. Principal female character in *The Tragedy of Mr. Arden of Feversham*, a play of unknown authorship which was first published in 1592. Some scholars have thought that the author might have been Shakespeare.

Alice. Little girl in *Alice's Adventures in Wonderland* and *Through the Looking-Glass* by Charles Lutwidge Dodgson (Lewis Carroll). In real life, "Alice" was Alice Liddell, daughter of the classical scholar Henry George Liddell.

Alice Adams. Novel by Booth Tarkington, published in 1921 and awarded a Pulitzer prize in 1922.

Alice Bridgenorth (brij'nôrth"). See **Bridgenorth, Alice.**

Alice-for-Short. Novel by William De Morgan, published in 1907.

Alice of Old Vincennes (vin.senz'). Novel by Maurice Thompson, published in 1900.

Alice, or The Mysteries. Novel by Edward Bulwer-Lytton, published in 1838 as a sequel to *Ernest Maltravers*.

Alice's Adventures in Wonderland. Novel by Charles Lutwidge Dodgson (writing under the pseudonym of Lewis Carroll), published in 1865. Alice, the child heroine, falls asleep and dreams that she falls down a rabbit hole. In the world she finds there she has bizarre encounters with such strange characters as the Mad Hatter, the Cheshire Cat, the King and Queen of Hearts and their court, the March Hare, and many others. Although Dodgson wrote the book for children, it has been variously interpreted by 20th-century critics as a satire on Victorian England and as a Freudian allegory.

Alice Springs. [Original name, **Stuart.**] Town in C Australia, in the Northern Territory, approximately midway between Adelaide and Darwin. In a section of the Macdonnell Ranges, at an elevation of ab. 2,000 ft., it has a very low annual rainfall (ab. 11 inches) and a temperature range that is sometimes as great as 40° within a single 24-hour span. The chief occupation of the inhabitants of the area is the grazing of livestock, although there is some opal mining and the town itself is an administrative center and a major station on the telegraph line across Australia. Railways and highways pass through it to Adelaide and Darwin, and it has become in recent years a focal point for air service throughout the C part of Australia. In World War II (largely because of the completion of the highway to Darwin in 1941), the town became a point of considerable strategic importance for the shipment of both munitions and troops from the S part of Australia to Darwin on the N coast. The first white man known to have reached the site of the present town was John McDouall Stuart, in 1860, and the settlement was named for him until 1931. Pop. 2,078 (1947).

Aliceville (al'is.vil). Town in W Alabama, in Pickens County, ab. 35 mi. SW of Tuscaloosa. 3,170 (1950).

Alicia (a.lish'ą). One of the principal female characters in Nicholas Rowe's tragedy *Jane Shore*, a woman of strong passions who by her jealousy ruins her former friend Jane Shore. The name was given by Lillo in his *Arden of Feversham* to the Alice of the earlier (and anonymous) *The Tragedy of Mr. Arden of Feversham.*

Alidor (à.lē.dôr). Character in Pierre Corneille's comedy *La Place Royale*. He is the first of a long line of headstrong (usually referred to as "willful") characters in the dramatist's plays.

Alids or **Alides** (al'idz). Name applied to the descendants of Ali, the fourth Moslem caliph. It was the Alids in Persia who founded the Shiite sect which, in opposition to the Sunnites, has since split the Moslem world. Even today, in modern Afghanistan and Iran most Moslems are members of the Shiite sect and venerate Ali as second only to Mohammed, whereas in Turkey the Sunnite sect is dominant and Ali's name is held in contempt. A revolt of the Alids in the 8th century, some 100 years after Ali's death, was suppressed by the Abbasside caliphs.

Aliena (ā.li.ē'ną). Name assumed by Celia in Shakespeare's *As You Like It*, when, disguised as a shepherdess, she follows Rosalind.

Alien and Sedition Acts. Collective expression now applied to four acts passed (1798) by the U.S. Congress in the administration of President John Adams. The acts came as the climax of almost a decade of political strife between the Federalists and their opponents, who had emerged as the Jeffersonian Republicans; the difficulties with France, which aroused a spirit of nationalism, also played their part, for the publication (April, 1798) of the XYZ correspondence almost obliterated for the moment old party antagonisms. The Federalists, irritated by the assaults of journalists and pamphleteers, and fearing the effects of abuse and misrepresentation when war with France appeared inevitable, passed the legislation despite serious and able opposition. The animus of the acts was directed particularly against a group of anti-Federalist journalists of French and English extraction. The Naturalization Act of June 18, 1798, provided for 14 years' residence before the granting of full U.S. citizenship and required registration of resident aliens as well as new arrivals. The Alien Act of June 25, 1798, authorized the president to order such aliens as he might deem dangerous or to be engaged in "treasonable or secret machinations" against the government to depart from the country. If anyone so ordered should be "found at large" and without a license to remain, he should upon conviction thereof be imprisoned for not more than three years and become ineligible for citizenship. The Alien Enemies Act of July 6,

1798, provided that whenever a proclamation by the president announcing war or predatory invasion was issued, alien enemies should be liable to apprehension and removal. The Sedition Act of July 14, 1798, was directed against unlawful combination or conspiracy with intent to oppose governmental measures or impede their operation. In sweeping terms, it further provided for punishing anyone publishing or causing to be published scandalous and malicious writings against the government, or either house of Congress, or the president, with intent to defame them or to bring them "into contempt or disrepute," or to stir up sedition, or excite unlawful combinations for resisting any law of the U.S. or any act of the president done in pursuance of such laws. The act provided for punishment by a fine of not more than two thousand dollars and by imprisonment not exceeding two years. The Naturalization Act was repealed in 1802, under the administration of Jefferson. The Alien Enemies Act was not repealed. The Alien Act was limited by its terms to two years and was not renewed. Though the Alien Acts were never enforced, a number of French refugees fled the country or went into hiding. The Sedition Act expired in 1801 and was not renewed. Under it some 25 persons were arrested, and ten convicted. The most prominent of these was Dr. Thomas Cooper. The Alien and Sedition Laws excited protests among the several states of the Union, and brought forth the Virginia and Kentucky Resolution in protest.

Alien Contract Labor Laws. Series of national acts (1885–1910) aimed at excluding the entry into the U.S. of dependent immigrant laborers under contract. Their general purpose was the prevention of depressed wage levels for U.S. workers. The initial act of Feb. 26, 1885, was supplemented by legislation enacted in 1891, 1903, 1907, and 1910.

Alien Corn. Play (1933) by Sidney Howard.

Alien Property Custodian, Office of. U.S. government agency set up in 1942 for maintaining control over enemy-alien property in the U.S. during World War II. It was dissolved in October, 1946, and its duties were absorbed by the U.S. Department of Justice.

Alien Registration Act. Act passed by the U.S. Congress on June 29, 1940, requiring all aliens resident in the U.S., except government officials and their families, to be fingerprinted and to submit a statement setting forth their political beliefs and personal and occupational history. The act also requires aliens to notify the U.S. Immigration and Naturalization Service upon making a change of address. The enforcement of the act applied to approximately five million aliens.

Alifánfaron (ä.lē.fän′fä.rōn). Emperor of the Island of Trapoban, mentioned by Cervantes' *Don Quixote.* When he sees two flocks of sheep coming toward him Don Quixote says of one of them: "Know, friend Sancho, that yonder army before us is commanded by the Emperor Alifánfaron, sovereign of the Island of Trapoban. . . ."

Aligarh (u.lē.gur′, al′i.gär). District of the Agra division, Uttar Pradesh, Union of India, ab. 80 mi. SE of Delhi: barley and rice. Capital, Aligarh; area, 1,946 sq. mi.; pop. 1,372,641 (1941).

Aligarh. [Also, **Koil.**] City in N central India, capital of the Aligarh district, Agra division, Uttar Pradesh, in the Union of India. It is a trading center for the wheat, corn, millet, and cotton produced in the vicinity, and is assuming steadily greater importance as a processing center for these agricultural products. It is still best known, however, for its Moslem university, which was opened in 1875 and which has become one of the leading educational institutions of the East. 112,655 (1941).

Aligarh, Fort. Fort in the district of Aligarh, India, defended by the Mahrattas and stormed by the British in 1803. It is one of the historic monuments of the city of Aligarh, within the limits of which it is now included.

Ali-Ghez (ä′li.gez′). See **Alagez.**

Alighieri (ä.lē.gyā′rē), **Dante.** Full name of **Dante.**

Ali Gur-Ber (ä′lẹ gur′ber′). Pseudonym of **Cloots** or **Clootz, Baron de.**

Ali ibn-Husein (ä′lē ib″n.hö.sīn′). b. 1878; d. 1935. King of Hejaz; elder brother of Abdullah ibn-Husein (1882–1951), king of Jordan. During World War I he commanded Arab troops against the Turks. In 1924 he became king of Hejaz, succeeding to the throne upon the abdication of his father, Husein ibn-Ali. He resigned (1925) under pressure from ibn-Saud (now king of Saudi Arabia, but at that time sultan of Nejd), and until his death lived at Baghdad. He was the last ruler of the independent kingdom of Hejaz.

Alijos Islands (ä.lē′hōs). Group of small islands in the Pacific, W of Lower California.

Ali Khan (ä′lē kän), **Liaqat.** See **Liaqat Ali Khan.**

Alima (ä.lē′mạ). River in W central Africa, a right (or western) affluent of the Congo River, having its headwaters near those of the Ogooué River, in Middle Congo, French Equatorial Africa. It was discovered by Brazza in 1878, and is navigable for a short distance from its mouth.

Alin (ä.lēn′), **Oscar Josef.** b. at Falun, Sweden, 1846; d. 1900. Swedish politician and historian; rector of Uppsala University. He was the author of *Den svensk-norsk Unionen* (1889–91), an outstanding presentation of the Swedish viewpoint on the question of Norwegian-Swedish union, as well as of numerous other books and articles.

Alinda (ạ.lin′dạ). Daughter of Alphonso in John Fletcher's *Pilgrim.*

Alinda. Name assumed by young Archas when disguised as a woman, in John Fletcher's *Loyal Subject.*

Alinda. Character in Thomas Lodge's romance *Rosalynde.*

Alingsås (ä′lings.ōs). Town in S Sweden, in the *län* (county) of Älvsborg, situated near the mouth of the Säfvea River into Mjörn Lake, ab. 25 mi. NE of Göteborg. It has textile industries. 12,327 (1949).

Aliore (al′i.ōr). See under **Alcor.**

Alioth (al′i.oth). Name in the Alphonsine tables, and still in ordinary use, of the bright second-magnitude star ϵ Ursae Majoris. The name is also sometimes (rarely) given to α Serpentis, and even to θ Serpentis.

Ali Pasha (ä′lē pä.shä′). [Called the **"Lion of Janina."**] b. at Tepeleni, Albania, 1741; assassinated at Janina (now Ioannina, Greece), Feb. 5, 1822. Turkish governor (1788–1820) of Albania. On the death (1755) of his father, governor of S Albania, he joined the mountain brigands. He soon became a leader among them and depended on them for most of his power as pasha. Sent by the Turkish government to put down a rebellion in Albania at Scutari (now Shkodër), he was made governor of Janina (1788) and Rumelia (1803); extended power into Greece and, contemplating further expansion, made a series of alliances with France, Russia, and England. He was deposed (1820) and assassinated (1822) on the order of the Turkish sultan Mahmud II. Accounts of his brigand court at Janina were written by various travelers, including Lord Byron (*Childe Harold's Pilgrimage*). He is a legendary hero among the Albanian and Greek mountaineers.

Ali Pasha, Mehemet. See **Aali Pasha, Mehemet.**

Aliquippa (al.i.kwip′ạ). Borough in W Pennsylvania, in Beaver County, important for the great amount of steel manufactured in its mills. It was named for "Queen" Aliquippa, an Iroquois Indian. 26,132 (1950).

Alisal (al′i.sal). Unincorporated community in S California. 16,714 (1950).

Aliscans (ȧ.lēs.kän̄). [Also, **Aleschans.**] Chanson of the 12th century, dealing with the contest between "William of Orange," a great Christian hero of the south of France, and the Saracens. It forms, according to custom, the center of a whole group of chansons dealing with the earlier and later adventures of the hero, his ancestors and descendants. Some of these are *Le Couronnement Loys, La Prise d'Orange, Le Charroi de Nîmes, Le Moniage Guillaume.* The series formed by these and others has been considered to be among the most interesting of these groups.

Alise (ȧ.lēz). See under **Alesia.**

Aliso (al′i.sō). Fortress near the river Lippe, in what is now NW Germany, built by the Romans under Drusus, in 11 B.C., as a military center to be used by the Roman legions against the Germanic tribes. It has been variously identified with Elsen (near Paderborn), and localities near Hamm, Dortmund, and elsewhere.

Alison (al′i.sọn), **Archibald.** b. at Edinburgh, Nov. 13, 1757; d. at Colinton, near Edinburgh, May 17, 1839. Scottish Anglican clergyman in Shropshire (1790–1800) and Edinburgh (1800–31). He was the author of *Essays on the Nature and Principles of Taste* (1790), which formed the basis of Francis Jeffrey's association theory of esthetics, of collected sermons (1814–15), and others.

Alison, Sir **Archibald.** b. at Kenley, Shropshire, England, Dec. 29, 1792; d. at Glasgow, May 23, 1867. British historian; son of Archibald Alison (1757–1839).

Alison, Sir **Archibald.** b. at Edinburgh, Jan. 21, 1826; d. at London, 1907. British general (1887–93); son of Sir Archibald Alison (1792–1867).

Alison, Francis. b. at Leck, Ireland, 1705; d. Nov. 28, 1779. American Presbyterian clergyman and educator. He established (1743) a school at Philadelphia which he later moved to Newark, Del. (where it became a precursor of the modern University of Delaware). Recalled (1752) to serve as rector of the Philadelphia Latin Academy, he remained to the end of his life with this institution, seeing it grow into a college from which later came the University of Pennsylvania.

Alison, William Pulteney. b. near Edinburgh, 1790; d. 1859. Scottish physician. Professor of medical jurisprudence (1820–22) and of physiology (1822 *et seq.*) at Edinburgh, he sought to reform the archaic Scottish poor-laws, on the grounds that poverty was a prime source of disease. He was the author of numerous medico-sociological pamphlets and technical works in physiology and pathology.

Alison's House (al'i.sǫnz). Play by Susan Glaspell, produced in 1930 and awarded a Pulitzer prize in the following year.

Alithea (al.i.thē'ạ). One of the principal characters in William Wycherley's comedy *The Country Wife*, a woman of the world, brilliant and cool. She also appears in David Garrick's *The Country Girl*.

Aliwal (u.lē.wäl'). Village in Punjab state, Union of India, ab. 70 mi. SE of Lahore, near the Sutlej River. It was the scene of a British defeat (Jan. 28, 1846) of the Sikhs.

Aljechin (ä.lye'ᴛʜin), **Aleksandr Aleksandrovich.** See **Alekhine, Aleksandr Aleksandrovich.**

Aljubarrota (äl.zhö.bạr.rô'tạ). Village in W Portugal, ab. 63 mi. N of Lisbon. Here, on Aug. 14, 1385, John I of Castile was defeated by John I of Portugal. The battle established the independence of Portugal.

Aljustrel (äl.zhö.strel'). Town and *concelho* (commune) in S Portugal, in the province of Baixo Alentejo, in the district of Beja, SW of Beja: agricultural trade center. Pop. of concelho, 17,239 (1940); of town, 9,397 (1940).

Al Kadhimain (äl kä.ᴛʜi.mīn'). [Also: **Kadhimain, Kazemain.**] City in C Iraq, near the capital city of Baghdad: a Moslem holy place visited each year by many pilgrims. The domes of its minarets are covered with gold leaf; many of the buildings show signs of cracking from earthquakes.

Alkaid (al.kād'). Second-magnitude star η Ursae Majoris, at the extremity of the bear's tail, or "dipper-handle." It is by many often called Benetnasch.

Alkaios (al.kī'os). See **Alcaeus.**

Alkalurops (al.kạ.lū'rops). A name, now seldom used, for the fourth-magnitude star μ Boötis, situated in the staff which Boötes carries in his right hand.

Alkamenes (al.kam'ẹ.nēz). See **Alcamenes.**

Alkan (àl.käṅ). [Original full name, **Charles Henri Valentin Morhange.**] b. at Paris, Nov. 30, 1813; d. there, March 20, 1888. French pianist, composer, and teacher. He entered the Paris Conservatory in 1819; later visited (1833) London, and settled as a teacher at Paris. His compositions include études, concertos, sonatas, and numerous other works for the piano.

Alkes (al'kẹs). The fourth-magnitude star α Crateris.

al-Khowarizmi (äl.ċhö.wä.rēz'mē), **Mohammed ibn-Musa.** [Sometimes called the **"Father of Algebra."**] b. in Khwarizm (now Khiva, in the U.S.S.R.), c780; d. between 835 and 845. Arab mathematician. His most famous work was *Al-jabr wa'l muqabalah*, from the title of which the word "algebra" arose. English translations of this treatise were published in 1831 and 1915. He wrote also *De numero indorum*, and it was his authorship of this work that led to the corruptions *algorism* and *algorithm*, which at first meant only calculation by the use of the Hindu-Arabic numerals. He is, with the Greek Diophantus, sometimes referred to as the "Father of Algebra."

Alkmaar (älk.mär'). Town in the W Netherlands, in the province of North Holland, situated on the North Holland Canal ab. 20 mi. N of Amsterdam: center of a fertile agricultural district. It has renowned grain, cattle, butter, and cheese markets, particularly for the Edam type of cheese, as well as foodstuff and paper-ware manufactures. The name of the town (meaning "All Sea") occurs first in the 10th century and recalls its original location in the midst of marshes and lakes. The town's charter dates from 1254; the Middle Ages saw many contests between Hollanders, Gelderlanders, and Frisians here; in 1573 it was unsuccessfully besieged by the Spaniards. The prosperity of Alkmaar started after the reclamation of the surrounding swamps at the end of the 17th century. 39,240 (1949).

Alkmaar, Convention of. Convention concluded (October, 1799) at Alkmaar, in the Netherlands, by which the Anglo-Russian army under the Duke of York evacuated the Netherlands.

Alkmaar, Heinrik von. fl. second half 15th century. German translator of the poem *Reineke de Vos* (Reynard the Fox), published in Low German at Bremen in 1498.

Alkman (alk'mạn). See **Alcman.**

Alkmene (alk.mē'nē). See **Alcmene.**

Al Kufa (äl kö'fä). [Also: **Cufa, Kufa.**] In medieval history, a city on the Euphrates, near Ctesiphon; a leading city of the caliphate in the 7th and 8th centuries.

Alla (al'ạ) or **Ella** (el'ạ). King in *The Man of Law's Tale*, one of Chaucer's *Canterbury Tales*. He marries Constance, the heroine of the tale.

Allacci (äl.lät'chē), **Leone.** [Latinized, **Leo Allatius** (ạ.lā'shus).] b. on the island of Chios, in the Aegean Sea, 1586; d. 1669. Greek theologian, scholar, author, and librarian. He was librarian at the Vatican (1661 *et seq.*).

Allagash (al'ạ.gash). [Also: **Allegash, Alleguash.**] River in N Maine, in Aroostook and Piscataquis counties, a branch of the St. John River.

Allah (al'ạ; Arabic, äl.lä'). The Mohammedan name of God.

Allahabad (al''ạ.hạ.bad'). Division of Uttar Pradesh, N central Union of India, in the C and upper Ganges valley: wheat, rice, sugar, barley, cotton, and tobacco. Capital, Allahabad; area, 17,270 sq. mi.; pop. 6,014,813 (1941).

Allahabad. District of the Allahabad division, Uttar Pradesh, Union of India. Capital, Allahabad; area, ab. 2,800 sq. mi.; pop. 1,812,981 (1941).

Allahabad. [Eng. trans., "*City of God.*"] City in N central India, the capital of Allahabad division and district and formerly of the United Provinces, Union of India, situated at the junction of the Jumna River with the Ganges: important railway center with large railway shops. It is the emporium for C India, a celebrated place of Hindu pilgrimage, and the seat of an annual fair. Among its major buildings are the citadel built by Akbar (which was during the period of English rule one of the chief British strongholds in India), the Juma Masjid (mosque), and the serai of Khosru. Allahabad was taken by the British in 1765 and by them granted to the emperor of Delhi and later to the nawab of Oudh; it was ceded to the British in 1801. Pop. 260,630 (1941).

Allah Dagh (ä'lä däg). See **Aladağ.**

Allain-Targé (à.laṅ.tàr.zhā), **François Henri René.** b. at Angers, Maine-et-Loire, France, May 7, 1832; d. at Targé château, Maine-et-Loire, France, July 16, 1902. French political leader and jurist. He resigned (1864) his judgeship under Napoleon III and became a prefect after the Third Republic was formed. As a deputy (1876–89), he held the posts of finance minister (1881) and interior minister (1885). He was a friend of Léon Gambetta.

Allaire (ạ.lãr'), **James Peter.** b. 1785; d. May 20, 1858. American master-mechanic and builder of steam engines, particularly for use in ships. The lease (1815) and transfer to New York of Robert Fulton's Jersey City engine-shop made Allaire a key figure in the founding of New York's first steam-engine manufacturing facility. Later he established works in Monmouth County, N.J., near a source of iron ore, but was placed at an economic disadvantage by the discovery of adjoining soft coal and iron-ore fields in Pennsylvania, and the plant was ultimately abandoned.

Prior to this, however, Allaire constructed the first marine compound steam-engine in the world.

Allamand (å.lå.mäṅ), **Jean Nicolas Sébastien.** b. at Lausanne, Switzerland, 1713; d. at Leiden, March 2, 1787. Swiss physicist, professor of philosophy (1749) and later of natural history at Leiden. He was the first to explain the phenomena of the Leyden jar.

All-American Canal. Main trunk of the system of irrigation canals carrying water from the Colorado River to the Imperial Valley, in California. The canal, which was completed in 1940, feeds its waters into three subordinate canals, which in turn irrigate the Imperial Valley. Length, ab. 80 mi.

Allan (al'ạn), **Barbara.** See under **Barbara Allen's Cruelty.**

Allan, David. b. at Alloa, Scotland, Feb. 13, 1744; d. at Edinburgh, Aug. 6, 1796. Scottish painter and etcher. He studied (1764 *et seq.*) at Rome and maintained a portrait studio at London from 1777 to 1780. In 1786 he was named director of the Edinburgh Academy of Arts. His works include illustrations for Ramsay's *Gentle Shepherd* (1788); humorous genre pictures such as *Scotch Wedding, Repentance Stool,* and *Highland Dance;* historical paintings; and others. He has been called the "Scottish Hogarth" for his caricatures and early genre works.

Allan, George. A pseudonym of **Kremnitz, Marie.**

Allan, Sir **Hugh.** b. at Saltcoats, Ayrshire, Scotland, Sept. 29, 1810; d. at Edinburgh, Dec. 9, 1882. Scottish merchant, identified (1826 *et seq.*) with Canadian mercantile interests, and founder (1853) of the Allan Line of steamships. He was one of the original group that planned what is now the Canadian Pacific Railway, but became involved in the "Pacific Scandal" (1873) and was forced to withdraw from the enterprise.

Allan, John. b. at Edinburgh, Scotland, in January, 1746 or 1747; d. Feb. 7, 1805. American Revolutionary soldier and emissary to the Indians. He fled (1776) into Maine from his home in Nova Scotia when his anti-British activity led to a charge of treason; later efforts on behalf of the revolting colonists brought his appointment (1777) as colonel of the garrison at Machias, Me. Despite inadequate supplies and lack of reinforcements, he was able to secure Indian support and to maintain his post throughout the Revolutionary War.

Allan, Sir **William.** b. at Edinburgh, 1782; d. there, Feb. 23, 1850. Scottish historical and genre painter. After a long tour (1805–14) of Russia, on which were based his many pictures of Russian life, he was launched on a successful career by the patronage of Sir Walter Scott. He was later president (1838) of the Royal Scottish Academy and limner (1841) to Queen Victoria in Scotland.

Allan-a-Dale (al"ạn.ạ.dāl'). See **Allen-a-Dale.**

Allapaha (ạ.lap'ạ.hä). See **Alapaha.**

Allapalli (ạ.lap'ạ.li). See **Alleppey.**

Allardice (al'ạr.dīs), **Robert Barclay.** [Called **"Captain Barclay."**] b. 1779; d. 1854. British army officer and pedestrian, known for his feat of walking one mile in each hour for 1,000 hours in succession, at Newmarket, June 1 to July 12, 1809.

Allatoona (al.ạ.tö'nạ). Place in N Georgia, ab. 35 mi. NW of Atlanta. Here, on Oct. 5, 1864, Union forces under John Murray Corse defeated a section of the Confederate forces.

Allauch (å.lōsh). Town in SE France, in the department of Bouches-du-Rhône, NE of Marseilles, of which it is a suburb.

Allbutt (ôl'but), Sir **Thomas Clifford.** b. at Dewsbury, England, 1836; d. at Cambridge, 1925. English physician; inventor of the short clinical thermometer, and an important contributor to the knowledge of heart disease, ophthalmoscopy, history of medicine, and various diseases affecting the nervous system, especially syphilis. Graduate (1860) and regius professor of physics (1892–1925) at Cambridge, he was also commissioner in lunacy (1889–92). He made studies of tetanus and hydrophobia, described (1868) the effect of syphilis on the arteries of the brain, and wrote *The Use of the Ophthalmoscope in Diseases* (1871), *Diseases of the Heart* (1896), *Historical Relations of Medicine and Surgery* (1905), and others. He was an editor of *A System of Medicine* (1896), and others.

Alle (äl'ẹ). River in N Poland and W U.S.S.R., which joins the Pregel at Wehlau. Length, ab. 130 mi.

Allectus (ạ.lek'tus). b. c250; d. c296. Prime minister to Marcus Aurelius Valerius Carausius, a soldier with the Roman legions in Britain who seized control of the province, proclaimed himself emperor, and was actually for a short time (290–292) able to command a degree of acceptance from Rome. Allectus murdered him in 293, and claimed the title for himself, but was himself slain three years later near London by Roman soldiers.

Allée Blanche (å.lā bläṅsh). Alpine valley in N Italy, S of Mont Blanc.

Allefonsce (ål.fôṅs), **Jean.** b. at Saintonge, France, c1482; d. c1557. French explorer and navigator; chief pilot to Roberval in the French exploration of Canada (1542 *et seq.*). His sketch maps pertaining to the search for a northwestern water route to China were published in *Cosmographie* (1545).

Allegan (al'ẹ.gan). City in S Lower Michigan, on the Kalamazoo River, county seat of Allegan County: hydroelectric power plant; manufactures of drugs and machine parts. 4,801 (1950).

Allegany (al.ẹ.gā'ni). Town in S New York, in Cattaraugus county: seat of St. Bonaventure College and Seminary. Allegany State Park and Allegany Indian Reservation are nearby. 1,738 (1950).

Allegash or **Alleguash** (al'ẹ.gash). See **Allagash.**

Allegheny (al.ẹ.gā'ni). Former city in SW Pennsylvania, in Allegheny County, on the Allegheny River, now a part of the city of Pittsburgh, with which it was incorporated in 1907.

Allegheny Mountains. [Also: **Allegany** (or **Alleghany**) **Mountains, Alleghenies, Alleghanies.**] Name given sometimes to the Appalachian Mountains, and sometimes to that part of this system which lies W and S of the Hudson River, but usually applied, in a restricted sense, to the chain which in Pennsylvania lies E of the Laurel Hill range. This chain crosses the W extremity of Maryland, traverses West Virginia, and forms part of the boundary between Virginia and West Virginia. Elevation, ab. 2,000–4,000 ft.

Allegheny Portage Railway. Railway connecting the eastern and western canals of the Pennsylvania system of canals, built in 1831–35 and covering the 36 mi. between Hollidaysburg and Johnstown, Pa. It was notable for its ten inclined planes, five on each side of Blair's Gap in the Allegheny Mountains. The planes, powered by stationary engines, made possible the ascent of the steep gradient. They were replaced by a continuous roadbed in 1856, and in the following year the Pennsylvania Railroad purchased the portage railway; soon thereafter it fell into disuse.

Allegheny River. Chief headstream of the Ohio River. It rises in Potter County, Pennsylvania, flows NW into Cattaraugus County, New York, reënters Pennsylvania, flows SW, and unites with the Monongahela at Pittsburgh to form the Ohio. Its chief tributaries are French Creek, the Clarion, and the Kiskiminetas. Length, ab. 325 mi.; navigable ab. 200 mi.

Allegri (äl.lā'grē), **Gregorio.** b. at Rome, 1582; d. there, Feb. 18, 1652. Italian composer of church music, especially of a *Miserere* for nine voices in two choirs still sung annually in the Sistine Chapel during Holy Week. The composition was at one time so treasured that its transcription was punishable by excommunication; it was copied, nevertheless, by Mozart and others. Allegri also wrote concertos, motets, and other works.

Alleine (al'in), **Joseph.** b. at Devizes, England, 1634; d. Nov. 17, 1668. English Puritan clergyman, scholar, and popular evangelist; associated with the founders of the Royal Society of London. He was assistant minister (1655–62) at Taunton until his ejection from the Church of England for nonconformity; thereafter he continued evangelical preaching in various parts of England in spite of frequent fines and imprisonment. He was the author of the enormously successful *Alarm to the Unconverted* (1672, republished as *A Sure Guide to Heaven,* 1675). He also wrote *Remains* (1674), and others.

Allemagne (ål.mány'). French name of **Germany.**

Allemaine (al.ẹ.mān'). An early English name of **Germany.**

Allemand (ål.mäṅ), Comte **Zacharie Jacques Théodore.** b. at Port Louis, Mauritius, 1762; d. at Toulon, France, March 2, 1826. French naval commander.

Allemane (ál.mán), **Jean.** b. at Sauveterre, Haute-Garonne, France, 1843; d. at Herblay, Seine-et-Oise, France, 1917. French political leader and journalist, known for his advocacy of the general strike as a weapon of the labor and socialist movements. He took part (1871) in the Paris Commune; was deported (1871) to New Caledonia, where he remained until 1880; and formed (1890) his own socialist party, called the *Parti ouvrier socialiste-révolutionnaire*, which found its principal strength among manual workers.

Allen (al'ęn), **Alexander Viets Griswold.** b. at Otis, Mass., May 4, 1841; d. July 1, 1908. American clergyman, educator, and author. Ordained in the Episcopal Church (1866), he was instructor (1867–69) and professor (1869–1908) of church history at Cambridge Theological Seminary. He was the author of *Continuity of Christian Thought* (1884), and others.

Allen, Andrew. b. at Philadelphia, in June, 1740; d. at London, March 7, 1825. American lawyer and Loyalist during the Revolutionary War. Although elected to the Committee of Safety (1775) and present at the First Continental Congress, he opposed, probably from principle rather than self-gain, the decision to establish a government separate from Great Britain. His subsequent resignation from Congress and flight to Lord Howe at Trenton caused him in 1778 to be declared a traitor. Cooling of tempers after the war brought a pardon in 1792, but when he was unable to recover confiscated property he left for England, where he lived for the rest of his life on a pension of 400 pounds per year from the British government.

Allen, Anthony Benezet. b. in Hampshire County, Mass., June 24, 1802; d. Jan. 12, 1892. American stockbreeder, agricultural writer, and manufacturer of farming equipment. He was cofounder and editor (1842–56) of the *American Agriculturist* and a dealer in and manufacturer of farm machinery, much of it based on patented improvements developed by him, from 1847 to the end of his life.

Allen, Arabella. In Charles Dickens's *Pickwick Papers*, a young lady, afterward Mrs. Nathaniel Winkle.

Allen, Arthur Augustus. b. at Buffalo, N.Y., Dec. 28, 1885—. American ornithologist, a lecturer and explorer in bird lore since 1912. He was an assistant professor (1915–25) and in 1925 became a professor of ornithology at Cornell. His publications include *The Book of Bird Life* (1930), *The Golden Plover and Other Birds* (1939), and others.

Allen, Barbara. See under **Barbara Allen's Cruelty.**

Allen, Benjamin. In Charles Dickens's *Pickwick Papers*, "a coarse, stout, thick-set" young surgeon, "with black hair cut rather short and a white face cut rather long."

Allen, Bennet Mills. b. at Greencastle, Ind., July 4, 1877—. American zoölogist and endocrinologist. A professor of zoölogy (1924 *et seq.*) at the University of California at Los Angeles, he is the author of papers on germ-cell origin, influence of endocrine glands upon growth, and others.

Allen, Bog of. Group of peat bogs of great extent, in Leinster province, in the Irish Republic, Counties Kildare, Westmeath, Offaly, and Laoighis. Specifically, the name applies to the bogs in the E portion of County Offaly and the NW portion of County Kildare. It occupies over 375 sq. mi.

Allen, Charles. b. at Greenfield, Mass., April 17, 1827; d. at Boston, Jan. 13, 1913. American jurist and occasional student of the Shakespeare-Bacon controversy. He served (1867–72) as Massachusetts attorney general, after six years as reporter to the Massachusetts supreme court. Selected (1880) to head the commission which revised the Massachusetts general statutes, he was elevated (1882) to the post of associate justice of the state supreme court, which he held until 1898. He published in 1900 *Notes on the Bacon-Shakespeare Question*, in which he examined, through a lawyer's eyes, the evidence on both sides and concluded that the Baconians were without a case.

Allen, Charles Herbert. b. at Lowell, Mass., April 15, 1848; d. April 20, 1934. American banker and politician. He was a member of Congress (1885–89), assistant secretary of the navy (1898–1900), following Theodore Roosevelt in that post, and governor (1900–02) of Puerto Rico.

Allen, David Oliver. b. at Barre, Mass., Sept. 14, 1799; d. at Lowell, Mass., July 19, 1863. American Congregational missionary in India, notable for his work as translator and chief editor of the Marathi-dialect Bible published in 1855. He was the author also of *India, Ancient and Modern* (1856), and others.

Allen, Edgar. b. at Canon City, Colo., 1892; d. 1943. American endocrinologist and professor of anatomy. In 1919 he was an investigator for the U.S. Bureau of Fisheries at Woods Hole, Mass. After serving as professor of anatomy (1923–33) and dean of the medical school (1929–33) at Missouri, he became, in 1933, a professor of anatomy at Yale. Contributor of numerous technical papers to endocrinological, anatomical, and physiological journals.

Allen, Elisha Hunt. b. at New Salem, Mass., Jan. 28, 1804; d. at Washington, D.C., Jan. 1, 1883. American lawyer, politician, and diplomat. He was a member of the Maine House of Representatives (1835–40) and a Whig member of Congress (1841–43). In 1850 he was named consul to Hawaii and served later as Hawaiian minister of finance, chancellor, and chief justice until 1876; later he was the Hawaiian minister to the U.S. (1876–83).

Allen, Elizabeth. See **Akers, Elizabeth Chase.**

Allen, Ethan. b. at Litchfield, Conn., Jan. 10, 1738; d. at Burlington, Vt., Feb. 12, 1789. American Revolutionary commander. After serving (1757) in the French and Indian War, he took up residence (c1769) in the New Hampshire Grants (now Vermont), where, to resist New York's efforts at control, he organized (1770) and was colonel of the militia known as the "Green Mountain Boys"; this unit he used in the capture (1775), with Benedict Arnold, of Fort Ticonderoga from the British. A captive (1775–77) of the British after an unsuccessful attempt to take Montreal, he was, on his return, made a major general of the Vermont militia. In 1778 he presented Vermont's claim for statehood to the Continental Congress, but without success; thereafter, with his brothers Ira and Levi Allen, he negotiated with British forces, but whether to make Vermont a British province or simply to force recognition by Congress has never finally been established. Author of *A Narrative of Col. Ethan Allen's Captivity* (1779) and of *Reason the Only Oracle of Man* (1784), a work on deism.

Allen, Florence Ellinwood. b. at Salt Lake City, Utah, March 23, 1884—. American lawyer, the first American woman to be elevated to a state supreme court bench. She was an assistant county prosecutor (1919–20) and common pleas judge (1921 *et seq.*) in Ohio. After two terms as an Ohio supreme court judge (1922–34), she was in 1934 made a judge of the sixth U.S. circuit court of appeals.

Allen, Francis Richmond. b. at Boston, Mass., 1843; d. 1931. American architect. A student (1877–78) at the École des Beaux-Arts, Paris, he was later a member (1904–26) of the architectural firm of Allen and Collens. He designed twelve buildings at Vassar College and eight at Williams College, as well as many hospitals, churches, and residences, chiefly in the modern Gothic style.

Allen, Frederic De Forest. b. at Oberlin, Ohio, May 25, 1844; d. Aug. 4, 1897. American classical scholar. His teaching at Knoxville's University of East Tennessee (1868–73) was interrupted by two years at Leipzig under Georg Curtius, and followed by posts at the University of Cincinnati (1874–79) and Yale (1879). In 1880 he was appointed professor of classical philology at Harvard, and remained there for the rest of his life. Notable among his works is a revision (1884) of Hadley's *Greek Grammar.*

Allen, Frederick Lewis. b. at Boston, Mass., July 5, 1890—. American magazine-editor and historian. He served as assistant editor (1914–16) of the *Atlantic Monthly*, managing editor (1916–17) of the *Century*, and has been on the staff of *Harper's Magazine* since 1923, as associate editor (1931–41) and as editor (1941 *et seq.*). Author of *Only Yesterday* (1931), *The Lords of Creation* (1935), *Since Yesterday* (1940), *I Remember Distinctly* (1947), *The Great Pierpont Morgan* (1949), and *The Big Change* (1952).

Allen, Frederick Madison. b. at Des Moines, Ia., March 16, 1879—. American physician, notable as a specialist in diabetes. Author of *Studies Concerning Glycosuria and Diabetes* (1913).

Allen, Frederic Sturges. b. at Norwalk, Conn., Oct. 1, 1861; d. Aug. 8, 1920. American lexicographer. He was chief editor of the supplement (1900) to *Webster's International Dictionary*, a contributor of law material to the supplement of Appleton's *Universal Encyclopedia*, and general editor of *Webster's New International Dictionary* (1909). Author of *Synonyms and Antonyms* (1920), and others.

Allen, Fred Hovey. b. at Lyme, N.H., Oct. 1, 1845; d. Dec. 24, 1926. American Congregational clergyman and writer on fine arts. After ordination (1874) he served (1875–1902) various New England churches, and was also a director of an art gallery. He inaugurated the photogravure reproduction process in the U.S. by using it to produce plates for his *Masterpieces of Modern German Art* (1884). Author also of *Glimpses of Parisian Art* (1882), *Modern German Masters* (1885), *Recent German Art* (1885), *Great Cathedrals of the World* (1886), *Famous Paintings* (1887), and *Grand Modern Paintings* (1888). In addition to these works on art he wrote *Popular History of the Reformation* (1887).

Allen, George. b. at Milton, Vt., Dec. 17, 1808; d. May 28, 1876. American educator, author, and one-time Episcopal clergyman. Ordained (1834) and for three years minister at St. Albans, Vt., he returned to teaching (1837) at Delaware College, Newark, Del., from which he was appointed (1845) to the chair of Latin and Greek at the University of Pennsylvania. Two years later, in accord with his convictions as a member of the Oxford group, he joined the Roman Catholic church. His publications in the field of classical literature are negligible, and fail utterly to indicate the remarkable ability which contemporary accounts indicate he must have had as a teacher.

Allen, Glover Morrill. b. at Walpole, N.H., Feb. 8, 1879; d. Feb. 14, 1942. American naturalist and professor of zoölogy. He was a member of expeditions to the Bahamas (1904), to Liberia (1926), to Brazil (1929), and elsewhere. Author of *Birds and Their Attributes* (1925), *Bats* (1939), and others.

Allen, Grant. [Full name, **Charles Grant Blairfindie Allen**; pseudonyms: **Cecil Power** and **J. Arbuthnot Wilson.**] b. at Kingston, Ontario, Canada, Feb. 24, 1848; d. at Hindhead, Surrey, England, Oct. 25, 1899. English novelist, poet, essayist, scientist, and philosopher. Author of *Strange Stories* and *Philistia* (both 1884), *The Devil's Die* (1888), *The Woman Who Did* (1895), his best-known work and a sensation in its day because of its then startlingly frank discussion of freedom in sex, *The British Barbarians* (1896), *An African Millionaire* (1897), and other novels; of *The Lower Slopes* (1894), poetry; *Falling in Love* (1889) and *Postprandial Philosophy* (1894), collected essays; and of scientific and philosophical works including *Physiological Aesthetics* (1877; dedicated to Herbert Spencer), *Color Sense* (1879), *Vignettes from Nature*, *An Evolutionist at Large*, and *Anglo-Saxon Britain* (all 1881), *Colors of Flowers* (1882), *Colin Clout's Calendar: The Record of a Summer* and *Flowers and Their Pedigrees* (both 1883; the former highly praised by Huxley and Darwin), *Force and Energy* (1888), and *Evolution of the Idea of God* (1897).

Allen, Harrison. b. at Philadelphia, April 17, 1841; d. there, Nov. 14, 1897. American anatomist and naturalist. He served as assistant surgeon in the U.S. army (1862–65) and was professor of comparative anatomy and later of physiology at the University of Pennsylvania (1865 *et seq.*).

Allen, Henry. See **Alline, Henry.**

Allen, Henry Tureman. b. at Sharpsburg, Ky., April 13, 1859; d. at Buena Vista Spring, Pa., Aug. 30, 1930. American army officer who was commander (1919–23) of the American army of occupation in Germany after World War I. A graduate (1882) and instructor (1888–90) at West Point, he was a military attaché in Russia (1890–95) and Germany (1897–98). After the Spanish-American War, he was governor (1901) of Leyte, and organizer and head (1903) of the Philippine constabulary. He also served with the Mexican punitive expedition (1916). He held the rank of brigadier general in World War I. Author of *The Rhineland Occupation* (1926) and others.

Allen, Henry Watkins. b. in Prince Edward County, Va., April 29, 1820; d. at Mexico City, April 22, 1866. American soldier and public administrator, with the Confederate army in the Civil War. The early period of his life was marked by idealistic fervor, which led him into the Texan army (1842) and later (1854) into sailing to Europe for service under Garibaldi. He joined the Confederate army at the outset of the Civil War, and rose to brigadier general after displaying great personal courage at Shiloh, the defense of Vicksburg, and elsewhere. Elected (1864) governor of Louisiana, he showed extraordinary ability in organizing the resources of the state. Largely through his efforts, the Trans-Mississippi Department of the Confederacy was actually stronger at the end of the war than during it. Allen wisely counseled against attempting further resistance, however, and fled to Mexico to escape Union imprisonment.

Allen, Hervey. [Full name, **William Hervey Allen.**] b. at Pittsburgh, Pa., Dec. 8, 1889; d. at Miami, Fla., Dec. 28, 1949. American novelist, biographer, and poet, author of the tremendously successful *Anthony Adverse* (1933), a long historical novel. His two-volume *Israfel* (1926), although never so widely read, is considered to be among the best biographies of Poe. He collaborated with Du Bose Heyward on *Carolina Chansons* (1922), a volume of verse; among his other novels are *Action at Aquila* (1937) and *It Was Like This* (1940), as well as a series of three related novels, *The Forest and the Fort* (1943), *Bedford Village* (1944), and *Toward the Morning* (1948).

Allen, Horace Newton. b. at Delaware, Ohio, April 23, 1858; d. Dec. 11, 1932. American Presbyterian clergyman, medical missionary, and diplomat. Sent to Korea (1884), he became medical consultant to the Korean royal family, and aided the Koreans in setting up a diplomatic service at Washington. He was secretary of the U.S. legation at Seoul (1890 *et seq.*), and was appointed (1897) U.S. minister to Korea.

Allen, Horatio. b. at Schenectady, N.Y., May 10, 1802, d. near South Orange, N.J., Jan. 1, 1890. American civil engineer and pioneer railroad authority. He was employed (1825–29) by the Delaware and Hudson Company, for whom he purchased (1828) four locomotives in England; his trial operation (Aug. 9, 1829) of the first of these at Honesdale, Pa., made him the first man to operate a steam locomotive in the U.S. As chief engineer (1829–35) for the South Carolina Railroad, he directed the construction of the locomotive "Best Friend of Charleston." For many years consulting engineer to the Erie Railroad, he was at one time (1843) its president; he was retained after his retirement (1870) as consulting engineer for the construction of the Brooklyn Bridge and Panama Railroad.

Allen, Sir **Hugh Percy.** b. at Reading, England, Dec. 23, 1869; d. at Oxford, England, 1946. English organist; conductor (1907 *et seq.*) of the London Bach Choir; professor (1918 *et seq.*) of music at Oxford, and successor (1918) to Sir Hubert Parry as director of the Royal College of Music. He retired from the latter post in 1938.

Allen, Ira. b. at Cornwall, Conn., May 1, 1751; d. at Philadelphia, Jan. 15, 1814. American Revolutionary soldier and politician; brother of Ethan Allen (1738–89). He was a leader in the Windsor Convention (1777) which declared the independence of Vermont and drew up its constitution; thereafter he was, with his brothers, instrumental in maintaining Vermont's independence and working for recognition of its statehood. He served as a member of the governor's council (1777), first state treasurer (1778), and representative of the state in negotiations (1781–91) with other states and with British forces. He was a sponsor and donor of land (1789) in the founding of the University of Vermont. Author of *Natural and Political History of the State of Vermont* (1798), and others.

Allen, Sir **James.** b. in South Australia, 1855; d. 1942. New Zealand politician and dominion official. Taken to New Zealand from Australia by his parents in infancy, he was educated in England. After election (1887) to the New Zealand legislature, he became minister of defense (1915–20) and high commissioner from New Zealand at London (1920–26). Author of several pamphlets and articles pertaining to the development and defense of New Zealand.

Allen, James Lane. b. near Lexington, Ky., Dec. 21, 1849; d. at New York, Feb. 18, 1925. American novelist. A schoolmaster (1872 *et seq.*) and professor of Latin and English (1880–83) at Bethany College, in West Virginia, he published critical essays and poetry in *Harper's*, *Atlantic Monthly*, and other journals. Author of such stories and novels on the Old South as *Flute and Violin* (1891), *A Kentucky Cardinal* (1894), *Aftermath* (1895), *A*

Summer in Arcady (1896), *The Choir Invisible* (1897), *The Reign of Law* (1900), *The Mettle of the Pasture* (1903), *The Bride of the Mistletoe* (1909), *The Doctor's Christmas Eve* (1910), and *The Sword of Youth* (1914).

Allen, Jeremiah Mervin. b. at Enfield, Conn., May 18, 1833; d. Dec. 29, 1903. American engineer and businessman, notable as a pioneer in steam-boiler insurance. In 1867 he was selected to head a newly established company at Hartford, Conn., for the inspection and insurance of steam boilers. He remained in this post to the end of his life, serving also at various times as president of Hartford's board of trade, of the Y.M.C.A., and of the board of trustees for what is now the Hartford Theological Seminary.

Allen, Joel Asaph. b. at Springfield, Mass., July 19, 1838; d. at Cornwall-on-Hudson, N.Y., Aug. 29, 1921. American zoölogist, a specialist in mammalogy; student of J. L. R. Agassiz, whom he accompanied (1865) on the expedition to Brazil. He was curator of birds at the Harvard Museum of Comparative Zoölogy (1867–85), and of the department of birds and mammals at the American Museum of Natural History, New York (1885–1921). Author of *Mammals and Winter Birds of Eastern Florida* (1871), *The American Bisons, Living and Extinct* (1876), *History of North American Pinnipeds* (1880), and others.

Allen, John. b. at Colinton, near Edinburgh, Feb. 3, 1771; d. at Dulwich, England, April 10, 1843. British political and historical writer, secretary to Lord Holland; author of *Growth of the Royal Prerogative in England* (1830), and others.

Allen, John. b. in Broome County, N.Y., Nov. 4, 1810; d. March 8, 1892. American dentist. His invention of a denture employing platinum plate and gum-colored porcelain (patented 1851) involved him in eventually unsuccessful litigation for patent infringement with Dr. W. M. Hunter, but Allen is still regarded as a pioneer in denture development in the U.S. He aided in the establishment (1845) of Ohio College of Dental Surgery, the second dental college to be established in the U.S., and of the New York College of Dentistry (1865).

Allen, John F. b. in England, 1829; d. Oct. 2, 1900. American engineer and inventor. He devised a valve motion which made possible a pioneer high-speed steam engine, developed an inclined-tube vertical water-tube boiler, and originated two kinds of pneumatic riveting, for which he manufactured air compressors and pneumatic hammers.

Allen, John James. b. at Woodstock, Va., Sept. 25, 1797; d. at Botecourt, Va., Sept. 18, 1871. American jurist, an ardent partisan of the Confederacy. Service in the state legislature and one term (1833–35) in Congress were followed by judicial appointments culminating in that of president (1851–65) of the court of appeals. His cogency of thinking was displayed in a striking manner by a statement of Virginia's attitude toward secession which was adopted as the preamble to a resolution (Dec. 10, 1860) urging withdrawal from the Union.

Allen, Joseph Henry. b. at Northboro, Mass., Aug. 21, 1820; d. at Cambridge, Mass., March 20, 1898. American author, editor, Latin scholar, and Unitarian clergyman. He was associate editor (1863–65) of the *Christian Examiner* and editor (1887–91) of the *Unitarian Review;* he also prepared a *Latin Primer* (1870), as well as numerous other once widely used Latin textbooks, in association with his brother, W. F. Allen (1830–89), and with J. B. Greenough.

Allen, Lewis Falley. b. at Westfield, Mass., Jan. 1, 1800; d. May 2, 1890. American stock-breeder and agricultural writer; brother of A. B. Allen (1802–92) and R. L. Allen (1803–69). He was the founder and first editor of the *American Shorthorn Herdbook*, a contributor to A. B. Allen's *American Agriculturist,* and author of *Rural Architecture* (1852), *American Cattle* (1868), and *History of the Shorthorn Cattle* (1872).

Allen, Lough. Lake in Connacht province, Irish Republic, in Counties Leitrim and Roscommon. An expansion of the river Shannon, ab. 7 mi. below its headwaters, it is the highest of the numerous lakes on that river. Elevation, 161 ft.; length, ab. 8 mi.; greatest width, ab. 4 mi.

Allen, Nathan. b. at Princeton, Mass., April 25, 1813; d. Jan. 1, 1889. American physician and medical writer, notable for his studies of insanity and birth-rate phenomena. Early service (1839–41) as editor of the *American Phrenological Journal and Miscellany* (which at that time still attracted reputable scientific attention) was followed by the practice of medicine at Lowell, Mass. His *Physiological Laws of Human Increase* (1868, 1870) and *Changes in the New England Population* (1877) dealt, respectively, with the possible adverse effect on fertility of hyperactivity in a single organ, and the theory that the falling birthrate of native New Englanders as opposed to immigrants might be explained by relatively poorer health.

Allen, Nathan Hale. b. at Marion, Mass., April 14, 1848; d. 1925. American organist and composer. Study (1867–70) in Germany was followed by service as organist at New Bedford and Worcester, Mass., and at Hartford, Conn. Composer of *The Apotheosis of Saint Dorothy* (1891), *The New-Born King* (1904), and others.

Allen, Paul. b. at Providence, R.I., Feb. 15, 1775; d. at Baltimore, Md., Aug. 18, 1826. American poet, historical writer, and editor. Graduation (1793) from what is now Brown University was followed by the publication of *Original Poems, Serious and Entertaining* (1801) and subsequent editorial posts at Philadelphia and Baltimore.

Allen, Philip. b. at Providence, R.I., Sept. 1, 1785; d. Dec. 16, 1865. American politician and textile manufacturer. He was governor of Rhode Island (1851–53) and a U.S. senator (1853–59).

Allen, Ralph. b. 1694; d. at Bath, England, June 20, 1764. English philanthropist, known chiefly as a friend of Fielding, Pope, and the elder Pitt. He acquired a fortune by devising (1720) a postal system for England and Wales. He is said to have been the original of Squire Allworthy in Fielding's *Tom Jones.*

Allen, Richard. b. at Philadelphia, Feb. 14, 1760; d. March 26, 1831. American clergyman. Born a Negro slave, he obtained his freedom when Methodist religious convictions won over his master; he was accepted as a Methodist preacher and held pulpit as an itinerant minister (1784 *et seq.*) in numerous churches. Following a display of race prejudice at Philadelphia's Saint George Methodist Church (c1786), he aided in the establishment of the African Methodist Episcopal Church and became its first bishop in 1816.

Allen, Richard Lamb. b. at Westfield, Mass., Oct. 20, 1803; d. at Stockholm, Sweden, Sept. 22, 1869. American stock-breeder, agricultural editor, and manufacturer of farm machinery; cofounder with his brother, A. B. Allen (1802–92), of the *American Agriculturist.* He was a member (1847 *et seq.*) of the firm of A. B. Allen and Company, which sold and manufactured various kinds of farm machinery. His *Brief Compend of American Agriculture* (1846), which was reissued (1869) as the *New American Farm Book,* was for decades widely used by farmers.

Allen, Robert. b. in Ohio, in July, 1812; d. at Geneva, Switzerland, Aug. 5, 1886. American soldier, member of the Union army during the Civil War. He served in the Mexican War and in California. During most of the Civil War he was chief quartermaster for armies based on St. Louis and, later, Louisville, in support of campaigns against Vicksburg, Atlanta, and elsewhere.

Allen, Samuel. b. in England, c1636; d. at Newcastle, N.H., May 5, 1705. English merchant, proprietor and colonial governor of what is now the state of New Hampshire.

Allen, Thomas. b. at Uttoxeter, England, Dec. 21, 1542; d. at Oxford, England, Sept. 30, 1632. English mathematician, astrologer, and antiquary; collector of manuscripts on history, astronomy, mathematics, and philosophy, some of which are still preserved in the Bodleian Library at Oxford. Patronized by the earls of Northumberland and Leicester, he was popularly considered a magician.

Allen, Thomas. b. at Pittsfield, Mass., Aug. 29, 1813; d. at Washington, D.C., April 8, 1882. American railroad financier, politician, and one-time newspaper editor. He established (1837) the *Madisonian* at Washington, D.C., to support William Henry Harrison against the Van Buren wing of the Democratic Party, but withdrew on Harrison's death and moved (1842) to St. Louis, where he became a key figure in the 19th-century financing of western railroads, particularly with the founding (1858) of the banking firm of Allen, Copp and Nisbet. He served (1880–82) in Congress.

Allen, Thomas M. b. in Virginia, Oct. 21, 1797; d. Oct. 10, 1871. American minister of the Disciples of Christ, farmer, and philanthropist. Baptized (1823) by B. W. Stone and ordained two years later, he was for many years an influential member of his sect, establishing churches and preaching widely in Kentucky and Missouri. Although himself a slave-owner, he opposed secession. He was active in raising funds for the University of Missouri and was a founder of Missouri's Christian Female College.

Allen, Timothy Field. b. at Westminster, Vt., April 24, 1837; d. Dec. 5, 1902. American homeopathic physician, ophthalmic surgeon, and botanist. Professor (1867 *et seq.*) of materia medica and therapeutics at New York Homeopathic Medical College; surgeon (1884 *et seq.*) at New York Ophthalmic Hospital; a founder (1871) of the Torrey Botanical Club, and owner of an outstanding collection of stoneworts. Author of a ten-volume *Encyclopedia of Materia Medica* (1874 *et seq.*), *Ophthalmic Therapeutics* (1876), and others.

Allen, Viola. b. at Huntsville, Ala., Oct. 27, 1869; d. at New York, May 9, 1948. American actress. She made her stage debut at the age of 15 in *Esmeralda.*

Allen, William. b. at Rossall, Lancashire, England, 1532; d. at Rome, Oct. 16, 1594. English cardinal and controversialist. He was principal of St. Mary's Hall, Oxford (1556); opposed to the accession of Elizabeth, he fled (1561) to Louvain, returning to England to live in hiding (1562–65). He founded the English Catholic seminary at Douai (1568), under Spanish patronage, but was forced by a Flemish uprising to move to Reims (1578), where he began what is now known as the Douay version of the Bible (1582–1609). Created a cardinal (1587) by Pope Sixtus V and commissioned to reorganize English ecclesiastical affairs after Philip II's proposed Spanish conquest of England, he wrote *An Admonition to the Nobility and People of England* (1588) to stir up sentiment against Elizabeth. After the failure of the Armada, he was made Vatican librarian under Pope Gregory XIV, and a member of the commission to revise the Vulgate.

Allen, William. b. Aug. 5, 1704; d. Sept. 6, 1780. American jurist and merchant, prominent in the pre-Revolutionary development of Pennsylvania. He served (1750–51) on the Pennsylvania-Maryland boundary commission; laid out (1765) the community later to be known as Allentown; urged compromise with England in 1774; and retired to the mother country when these recommendations were refused.

Allen, William. b. at Pittsfield, Mass., Jan. 2, 1784; d. at Northampton, Mass., July 16, 1868. American Congregational clergyman, educator, and author. He sided with New Hampshire in its attempt to reorganize Dartmouth College as Dartmouth University, and headed the latter institution from 1817 until the Supreme Court decision of 1819 put it out of existence. As president of Bowdoin (1819 *et seq.*), he was once nearly forced out of office by the Maine legislature, and finally resigned (1838) because of unpopularity with both students and trustees.

Allen, William. [Called **"Earthquake Allen," "Petticoat Allen,"** and **"the Ohio Gong."**] b. at Edenton, N.C., Dec. 18, 1803; d. near Chillicothe, Ohio, July 11, 1879. American politician; Democratic congressman from Ohio (1833–35), U.S. senator (1837–49), and governor of Ohio (1874–76). He was a leading expounder of the "Ohio Idea," a scheme (1868–76) for the payment in greenbacks of U.S. bonds issued during the Civil War and later, and for the general use of greenbacks in place of national-bank notes.

Allen, William Frederick. b. at Bordentown, N.J., Oct. 9, 1846; d. Nov. 9, 1915. American railroad engineer and editor, notable for his efforts on behalf of standard time. His early career (1862–72) on the technical staff of the Camden and Amboy Railroad was followed by work with the *Official Guide of the Railways and Steam Navigation Lines*, an omnibus volume of travel data. His experience with this publication enabled him to argue effectively for standard time when it was urged by the railroads in the late 19th century, and brought him the post of secretary and treasurer to the American Railway Association.

Allen, William Harvey. b. at Leroy, Minn., Feb. 9, 1874—. American social worker. He studied at Leipzig and Berlin; became the first editor of the *New Jersey Review of Charities;* acted as general agent of the New York Association for Improving the Condition of the Poor (1903–07) and as director of the Bureau of Municipal Research (1908). A member of the American Academy of Political and Social Science and of the American Sociological Society, he has written *Civics and Health, Efficient Democracy*, and *Modern Philanthropy.*

Allen, William Henry. b. at Providence, R.I., Oct. 21, 1784; d. in Mill Prison, Plymouth, England, Aug. 18, 1813. American naval officer, commander of the 20-gun sloop-of-war *Argus.* He was wounded during an engagement in the War of 1812 with the English brig *Pelican* in the Irish Channel, and died of his wounds in a British prison. He had seen earlier service aboard the frigate *Chesapeake*, on which he was the man who snatched a hot coal from the galley to fire the only shot of that vessel's ill-fated encounter (1807) with the *Leopard.*

Allen, William Henry. b. at Manchester, Me., March 27, 1808; d. at Philadelphia, Aug. 29, 1882. American educator. He was professor of natural philosophy and afterward of philosophy and English literature at Dickinson College (1836–49); president (1865–66) of Pennsylvania Agricultural College at Gettysburg; and president (1850–62 and 1867–82) of Girard College.

Allen, William Vincent. b. at Midway, Ohio, Jan. 28, 1847; d. Jan. 12, 1924. American Populist politician, senator from Nebraska (1894–1901). Elected by a coalition of Populists and Democrats, Allen was a vigorous spokesman for free coinage of silver and for other planks in the Populist platform. His 15-hour filibuster against the repeal of the Sherman Silver Purchase Act failed in its purpose, but marked him as a third-party force to be reckoned with. Hailed by some as "the intellectual giant of Populism," he supported a Populist-Democratic merger in 1896, and subsequently joined the Democratic Party.

Allen, Young John. b. in Burke County, Ga., Jan. 3, 1836; d. at Shanghai, May 30, 1907. American Methodist missionary, educator, and Far Eastern journalist. He arrived (1860) in China as Georgia's first "missionary ambassador" to that nation and was forced by the American Civil War to sustain the entire mission establishment for the next 15 years virtually without aid from his American sponsors. He translated upwards of 90 volumes from English into Chinese and, particularly with his *Review of the Times* (1867 *et seq.*), advanced the cause of Western journalism in China; founder (1882) of Shanghai's Anglo-Chinese College, which later became part of Soochow University.

Allen, Zachariah. b. at Providence, R.I., Sept. 15, 1795; d. there, March 17, 1882. American scientist and inventor. He was the first to construct (1821) a hot-air furnace for heating dwelling-houses; he also invented the automatic cut-off valve for steam-engines (patented 1834). Author of *The Science of Mechanics* (1829), *Philosophy of the Mechanics of Nature* (1852), *The Rhode Island System of Treatment of the Indians and of Establishing Civil and Religious Liberty* (1876), *Solar Light and Heat, the Source and Supply* (1881), and others.

Allen-a-Dale (al″ẹn.ạ.dāl′). [Also, **Allan-a-Dale.**] In the Robin Hood tales, a brave, gaily dressed, and musical youth whom Robin Hood assisted to elope with his bride who was to be married against her will to an old knight. He is usually introduced as "chaunting a round-de-lay." He appears as Robin Hood's minstrel in Scott's *Ivanhoe.*

Allenburg (äl′ẹn.bůrk). Small town in what was formerly the province of East Prussia, situated on the Alle River ab. 30 mi. SE of Königsberg. This area is now under control of the U.S.S.R.

Allenby (al′ẹn.bi), **Edmund Henry Hynman.** [Title, 1st Viscount **Allenby of Megiddo and Felixstowe.**] b. in Suffolk, England, April 23, 1861; d. at London, May 14, 1936. British field marshal. He served in Bechuanaland (1884–85) and against the Zulus (1888), and fought with cavalry forces in the relief of Kimberley and elsewhere in the Boer War (1899–1902). After entering World War I as commander of a cavalry division, he was cited for the record at Mons, on the Aisne, and at Ypres, and was given command of a cavalry corps, finally becoming (1916) III Army commander. His transfer (1917) to the command of the Egyptian Expeditionary Force led to the invasion of Palestine and capture (Dec. 9, 1917) of Jerusalem; his victory at Megiddo (1918) led to the fall of Damascus and Aleppo, and final Turkish capitulation.

He was subsequently British high commissioner for Egypt (1919–25).

Allendale (al′en.dāl). Civil parish in NE England, in Northumberland, situated on the East Allen River, ab. 27 mi. W of Newcastle-upon-Tyne. In a region where formerly extensive lead mining was carried on, it is now of little importance. 2,218 (1931).

Allendale. Town in S South Carolina, county seat of Allendale County, ab. 67 mi. SW of Columbia, in an agricultural area. 2,474 (1950).

Allende (ä.yen′dā). [Former name, **San Bartolomé.**] Hamlet and hacienda in N Mexico, in S Chihuahua, the first Spanish establishment in Chihuahua (1570). Pop. ab. 2,000.

Allende, Ignacio José. b. at San Miguel el Grande (now San Miguel de Allende, in his honor), in what is now the state of Guanajuato, Mexico, Jan. 27, 1779; executed at Chihuahua, Mexico, June 26, 1811. Mexican revolutionary patriot, and a captain in the Spanish army; son of a Spaniard, Narciso Allende. With his regiment, he declared for Mexican independence (1810) and joined (with Juan Aldama) the insurrection of Miguel Hidalgo y Costilla, whom he succeeded (1811) as actual commander.

Allen Park. Village in S Lower Michigan, in Wayne County: a suburb of Detroit. 12,329 (1950).

Allentown (al′ẹn.toun). Borough in C New Jersey, in Monmouth County, ab. 11 mi. SE of Trenton. 931 (1950).

Allentown. [Former names, **Northampton, Northamptontown.**] City in E Pennsylvania, county seat of Lehigh County, on the Lehigh River, ab. 50 mi. NW of Philadelphia: the chief trading center of the Lehigh valley. Manufactures include cotton and silk textiles, clothing, steel, barbed wire, and cement. It is the seat of Muhlenberg College and Cedar Crest College. Platted in 1762, it was incorporated in 1811 and renamed (1838) for William Allen. Pop. of city, 96,904 (1940), 106,756 (1950); of urbanized area (including Bethlehem), 225,962 (1950).

Alleppey (ạ.lep′i). [Also: **Alapalli, Allapalli, Alleppi.**] Seaport in Travancore state, Union of India, ab. 130 mi. below Calicut. Coconuts are shipped from here. 56,333 (1941).

Aller (ä.lyer′). Town in NW Spain, in the province of Oviedo, ab. 20 mi. SE of Oviedo: an agricultural trade center, with small industries. There are coal, iron, and lead mines in the vicinity. 23,600 (1940).

Allerheim on the Ries (äl′ėr.hīm; rēs). [Also, **Allersheim** (äl′ėrs.hīm).] Village ab. 6 mi. SE of Nördlingen, Bavaria. Here, on Aug. 3, 1645, during the Thirty Years' War, the French under Condé defeated the forces of the Holy Roman Empire under Franz von Mercy (who fell). This encounter is sometimes called the second battle of Nördlingen.

Aller River (äl′ėr). River in N Germany which joins the Weser ab. 18 mi. SE of Bremen. Length, ab. 100 mi.; navigable from Celle.

Allerton (al′ėr.tọn), **Isaac.** b. probably in England, c1586; d. at New Haven, Conn., 1659. One of the "Pilgrim Fathers" who arrived (1620) in America on the *Mayflower.* He served as assistant (1621–24) to Governor Bradford; as agent in Europe (1625–31), he secured enough supplies to end the colony's poverty, transportation for the remaining "Leyden Pilgrims" (1629), and the Patent of 1630 giving the colony title to its lands. Deprived of his position (1631) for unauthorized trading, he settled (c1644) at New Haven.

Allerton, Samuel Waters. b. at Amenia Union, N.Y., May 26, 1828; d. at South Pasadena, Calif., Feb. 22, 1914. American meat-packer, banker, and leader in the development of modern Chicago. His early farming and trading ventures were followed (1860) by a coup that cornered the Chicago pork market; later interests in the First National Bank of Chicago (1863 *et seq.*) and various stockyards increased his wealth. He advocated (1865) the union stockyards which came into being the next year, and which contributed considerably to Chicago's preëminence as a meat-packing center.

Allestree (al′ẹs.trē), **Richard.** b. at Uppington, Shropshire, England, in March, 1619; d. at London, Jan. 28, 1681. English royalist clergyman and scholar. He was a soldier and emissary for Prince Charles (later to be Charles II) in the English Civil War. After the Restoration, he was made chaplain to Charles II, canon of Christ Church College, and regius professor of divinity at Oxford (1663); in 1665 he became provost of Eton. Author of many tracts, including *Privileges of the University of Oxford* (1647), sermons, and, at least in part, of *The Whole Duty of Man.*

Allevard (àl.vàr). Town in SE France, in the department of Isère, situated on the Breda River ab. 23 mi. NE of Grenoble. Pop. ab. 2,000.

Alley (al′i), **Rewi.** b. at Springfield, New Zealand, Dec. 2, 1899—. New Zealand industrial organizer in China. Of Anglo-Irish parentage, he was named by his father after a Maori chieftain. A sheep farmer (1920–26) in New Zealand, he served as factory inspector (1927–32) and chief factory inspector (1932–37) for the Shanghai Municipal Council. After the fall (1937) of Shanghai to the Japanese, he organized (1937–42), with the sanction of Chiang Kai-shek, a chain of industrial coöperatives for the Chinese National Government throughout China.

Alleyn (al′in), **Edward.** [Also: **Alleyne;** called **Ned Allen.**] b. at London, Sept. 1, 1566; d. Nov. 25, 1626. English actor; son-in-law of John Donne. He was the founder (1613) and director (1619–26) of Dulwich College (the College of God's Gift), at London. Rated by Jonson, Nash, and others as the foremost actor, especially of tragedy, of his time, he was a member of the Earl of Worcester's players (1586 *et seq.*), head of the Lord Admiral's (Earl of Nottingham's) company (c1592), and owner-manager, with Henslowe, of various London theaters including the Rose and the Fortune (built in 1600), and of a bearbaiting house at Paris Garden (1594–1626). He played leads in Marlowe's *Jew of Malta, Tamburlaine,* and *Doctor Faustus;* his last known appearance was at a reception address to James I (c1604).

All Fools' Day. See **April Fools' Day.**

All Fools, or All Fools but the Fool. Tragi-comedy by George Chapman, printed in 1605. It was first called *The World on Wheels,* and registered in 1599. It is considered by some to be the best of his comedies.

All for Love, or the World Well Lost. Tragedy by John Dryden, produced in 1678. It is based on Shakespeare's *Antony and Cleopatra.* In this play Dryden abandoned rhyme.

Allgäu (äl′goi). See **Algäu.**

Allgeyer v. Louisiana, 165 U.S. 578 (1897) (ôl′gī″ėr). U.S. Supreme Court decision remembered for Justice Rufus W. Peckham's comprehensive definition of the right to contract as an essential part of liberty guaranteed by due process of law. His interpretaton was repeatedly cited in later decisions holding illegal various types of social and economic legislation.

All God's Chillun Got Wings. Drama by Eugene O'Neill, produced and published in 1924. The plot involves the difficulties arising from the marriage of Jim Harris, a Negro, and Ella Downey, a white girl whose confusions finally manifest themselves in insanity.

All-Hallows Day (ôl″hal′ọz). See **All Saints Day.**

Allia (al′i.ạ). [Also, **Alia;** modern name, **Aga.**] In ancient geography, a small river in Latium, Italy, joining the Tiber ab. 10 mi. N of Rome. On its banks in c390 B.C., the Gauls under Brennus defeated the Romans. The battle was followed by the capture and sack of Rome.

Alliaco (dal.yā′kō), **Petrus d'.** Latinized name of **Ailly, Pierre d'.**

Alliance (ạ.lī′ạns). City in NW Nebraska, county seat of Box Butte County: trading center in an agricultural region, one of the chief crops being potatoes. 7,891 (1950).

Alliance. City in NE Ohio, in Stark County, on the Mahoning River, ab. 48 mi. SE of Cleveland: important for the manufacture of steel cranes and heavy mill machinery. Car wheels and twist drills are shipped from here. Manufactures also include pipe organs, safes, cash registers, ceramics, and paints. It is the seat of Mount Union College. The city was formed (1854) by the union of an early 19th-century Quaker settlement with Freedom, Williamsport, and Mount Union, and incorporated in 1889. Pop. 26,161 (1950).

Alliance. Frigate in the American service built in 1778 which saw action until the last naval engagement (March 10, 1783) of the Revolutionary War. It carried 36 guns.

Allibone (al′i.bōn), **Samuel Austin.** b. at Philadelphia, April 17, 1816; d. at Lucerne, Switzerland, Sept. 2, 1889. American bibliographer; librarian (1879–88) of the

Lenox Library, New York. Author of *A Critical Dictionary of English Literature and British and American Authors* 1858–71), *Poetical Quotations from Chaucer to Tennyson* (1873), *Prose Quotations from Socrates to Macauley* (1876), and others.

Allied Advisory Council for Italy. Advisory body established in accord with agreements reached during World War II by the Allies at the 1943 Moscow Conference. With a membership that included the U.S., the U.S.S.R., Great Britain, France, Greece, and Yugoslavia, it sought to advise the Allied commander in chief in Italy on general political matters. Meeting first at Algiers, it was moved in April, 1944, to Italy.

Allied Airborne Army, First. Anglo-American military force that took part in several major operations during World War II. Its existence under the command of U.S. General Lewis Hyde Brereton was officially revealed on Aug. 10, 1944, although three of its five major fighting units (the British 6th Airborne Division, the U.S. 82nd Airborne Division, and the U.S. 101st Airborne Division) had already participated in the invasion (June 6, 1944) of Normandy. At its peak strength, the First Allied Airborne Army consisted of the U.S. XVIIIth Corps (17th, 82nd, and 101st Airborne divisions), the British Airborne Troops Command (1st and 6th Airborne divisions), three major troop-carrier groups (one from the U.S. Army Air Force and two from the Royal Air Force), and several smaller units of various kinds. Sizable elements of the army took part in the unsuccessful effort (Sept. 17, 1944) to win a bridgehead across the Rhine at Arnhem, in the Netherlands, and in the later (March 24, 1945) successful landing across the Rhine and behind the enemy line, in Germany.

Allied Commission on Reparations. International body established at the Yalta Conference in February, 1945. The commission (which had its seat at Moscow) was charged with the formulation of a common reparations policy for Germany after World War II. It was never truly successful in defining such a policy, partly because of Russia's looting of territory under its control in Germany and partly because of the entanglement of reparations problems with that of German demilitarization. It did, however, advance a general plan calling for (1) the payment of reparations in goods rather than money, and on a basis of loss suffered by the claimant nations; (2) removal of German industrial equipment not required for the minimum economy deemed essential for that country, in order that no surplus might be available for rearmament; and (3) the maintenance of a German economic structure which would enable German self-support. The plan was completed during the first two weeks of July, 1945, and submitted for approval at the Potsdam Conference (July 17–Aug. 2, 1945). With certain qualifications (the chief one being that reparations should be obtained largely on a zonal rather than interzonal basis) it was accepted. However, this qualification, plus the increasing dissension between the U.S.S.R. and the other occupying powers, effectively defeated the avowed purpose of both the Commission and its plan.

Allied Control Commission for Austria. International body formally set up after World War II by Allied agreement on June 28, 1946, with representation from the U.S., Great Britain, the U.S.S.R., and France. Through zonal commands, it was entrusted with maintaining the integrity of the Austrian state, with helping the Austrian government establish a democratic national life, and with eradication of traces of Nazi life. Its avowed chief purpose was to bring into being as soon as possible a full-fledged popular government in Austria. By the terms of its establishment, and until the signing of a peace treaty acceptable to the four occupying powers, the U.S. zone includes the province of Salzburg and most of Upper Austria; the French, the province of Vorarlberg-Tirol other than East Tirol; the British, East Tirol, Carinthia, and Styria; and the Russian, Lower Austria, part of Upper Austria, and Burgenland. The Commission meets in Vienna, which in turn is divided into four zones.

Allied Control Commission for Finland. International body established during World War II by the terms of the armistice agreement signed at Moscow on Sept. 19, 1944, by Finland, Great Britain, and the U.S.S.R. Its purpose was to supervise and ensure the carrying out by Finland of the terms of the armistice. Although the commission included representatives of Great Britain, it was for all practical purposes dominated by its Russian members, whose chief aim was to secure the existence of a Finnish government which could be counted on to coöperate with Moscow.

Allied Control Commission for Germany. Term sometimes applied to the group of deputy Allied commanders in Germany charged with the preparation of drafts of plans and decisions for the Allied Control Council for Germany. The term is also sometimes applied to the Allied Control Council itself.

Allied Control Commission for Italy. Joint commission of Great Britain and the U.S. created on Nov. 10, 1943, by General Eisenhower to regulate and execute the terms of armistice for Italy. It was assimilated in January, 1944, with the formal agency for Allied military government. As time went on, its functions became less and less administrative, taking on a general supervisory character. The word "Control" in its title was dropped in the fall of 1944. It formally ceased to exist after the Italian peace treaty was signed in 1947.

Allied Control Council for Germany. International body which was, at the time of its establishment after World War II, the highest organ of the Allied Military Government organization for Germany. Its plan and scope were worked out by the European Advisory Commission and finally approved by the Potsdam Conference. The Allied Control Council which began to function officially at the beginning of August, 1945, consisted of the four Allied military commanders in Germany (General Eisenhower, for the U.S.; Field Marshal Montgomery, for Great Britain; Marshal Zhukov, for the U.S.S.R.; General Koenig, for France). It was supposed, through its meetings at Berlin, to implement the Potsdam Agreement, but soon proved incapable of reaching agreement on common policies for Germany. It finally broke up in April, 1948.

Allied Council for Japan. International body established (December, 1945) by joint decision at Moscow of the foreign ministers of Great Britain, the U.S., and the U.S.S.R. It was conceived of as an advisory and consultative organization subordinate, for all practical purposes, to the occupying military authorities. Its original membership consisted of a representative of the U.S., a representative of the U.S.S.R., a representative of China, and a joint representative of Great Britain, India, Australia, and New Zealand. Its permanent chairman was General MacArthur, who held that office by virtue of his position as supreme commander of the Allied forces in the Far East. Its permanent seat was at Tokyo.

Allied Military Government. [Abbreviation, **AMG**; original abbreviation, **AMGOT.**] Term applied to the various interim governmental structures, usually under military control, established during and immediately following World War II in Japan and various parts of Europe and N Africa. In this sense all the governmental machinery of the occupying powers in Germany, Austria, and Japan may be called Allied Military Government (although in certain cases a particular power may be so dominant as to make the term "Allied" somewhat of a misnomer). In a specific sense, the term is often applied to the military government set up (July, 1943) in Sicily under the overall direction of General Eisenhower, who was at that time supreme commander of Allied forces in the Mediterranean. The functions of this organization, as well as a considerable portion of its Anglo-American staff, were transferred in November, 1943, to the Allied Control Commission for Italy.

Allier (ȧ.lyā). Department in C France, bounded by the department of Cher on the NW, Nièvre department on the N, Saône-et-Loire department on the E, Loire department on the SE, Puy-de-Dôme department on the S, and Creuse department on the W. It was formed chiefly from part of the old province of Bourbonnais. Vichy, its mineral-water spa, has long been known as a resort, and in World War II became even better known as the seat of the Pétain government. Important for its agricultural products, particularly lumber, cattle, and grain, it also has coal mines, stone quarries, and metallurgical and rubber industries. It contains several notable examples of 11th–15th century medieval architecture. Capital, Moulins; area, 2,848 sq. mi.; pop. 373,381 (1946).

Allier River. [Ancient name, **Elaver.**] River in C France which rises in the mountains of Lozère, flows N, and joins the Loire ab. 5 mi. W of Nevers. Length, ab. 220 mi.; navigable from Fontanes.

Allies. Term used in World Wars I and II to describe the coalition of nations aligned against various powers, of which Germany was in both wars the most important. In World War I the primary Allies were Great Britain, France, Russia (until 1917), Italy (after 1915), Japan, and the U.S. (after 1917). In World War II the Allies were those nations led by the U.S., the U.S.S.R., and Great Britain in alignment against the three Axis powers (Germany, Italy, and Japan). The term came in this war to be synonymous with the 26 United Nations tentatively formed on Jan. 1, 1942. With the outbreak (June, 1950) of hostilities in Korea the word came to be used more or less interchangeably with the term "UN forces" to describe the various nations contributing to the army there fighting against the forces of North Korea and Communist China.

Allies (al'is), **Thomas William.** b. near Bristol, England, 1813; d. 1903. English religious writer and classical scholar. In 1850 he left the Anglican church for the Roman Catholic after the publication (1849) of his *Journal in France*, which urged a reunion of the Anglican and Roman Catholic churches. Author of *The See of St. Peter* (1850), the eight-volume *Formation of Christendom* (1861–95), and others.

Alligator Swamp. Large swamp in E North Carolina, between Pamlico and Albemarle Sounds.

Allin (al'in), **Norman.** b. at Ashton-under-Lyne, Lancashire, England, 1884—. English operatic and concert basso. A founder of the British National Opera Company, he was for many years a professor at the Royal Academy of Music. In 1918 he became principal basso at Covent Garden opera house.

Allin, Sir **Thomas.** b. at Lowestoft, England, 1612; d. at Somerleyton, England, 1685. English naval officer. Knighted and appointed admiral (1665) after the victory over the Dutch in the North Sea off Lowestoft, he commanded a squadron in the defeat (1666) of De Ruyter, and led punitive expeditions (1668–70) against the Barbary pirates.

All-India Congress Committee. [Often called the **A.I.C.C.**] Legislative body of the Congress Party of India, which is charged with the execution of the Congress Party's program, formulated in annual sessions, and which exercises certain rule-making powers. The assemblage varies from three to four hundred members and consists of approximately one eighth of the number of provincial delegates who are elected to attend the annual sessions of Congress.

Alline (al'īn), **Henry.** [Also, **Allen.**] b. at Newport, R.I., June 14, 1748; d. at North Hampton, N. H., Feb. 2, 1784. American religious leader, notable for the establishment in Nova Scotia of a religious movement not unlike that of the New Light group. The often-made statement that he was founder of a "short-lived religious sect . . . named . . . 'Allenites' " is not untrue, but obscures the more important fact that he started a revivalist spirit which is discernible even to this day in Nova Scotia.

Allingham (al'ing.am), **William.** b. at Ballyshannon, Ireland, 1824; d. at London, 1889. Irish poet. Editor (1874–79) of *Fraser's Magazine*, he was a friend of Dante Gabriel Rossetti (who illustrated some of his books), Tennyson, Thomas Carlyle, and Leigh Hunt.

All in the Day's Work. Autobiography (1939) by Ida M. Tarbell.

Allis (al'is), **Edward Phelps.** b. at Cazenovia, N.Y., May 12, 1824; d. April 1, 1889. American manufacturer of industrial machinery. His early career as owner of leather tanneries in Wisconsin terminated in 1854 and was followed in 1861 by his purchase of a small ironworks, which was developed during the next 28 years into one of the largest industrial establishments in the U.S. Such diverse products as the Corliss engines, flour-milling machinery, and heavy pumps were built at Allis's Milwaukee plant and shipped throughout the world. He was said to be worth three million dollars at the time of his death. Allis became a Greenbacker in the 1870's and was nominated by that party for governor of Wisconsin in 1877.

Allison (al'i.son), **Fred.** b. at Glade Spring, Va., 1882—. American physicist. He devised the magneto-optic analytical method which enabled his discovery (in collaboration with others) of Element 87 (francium), in 1930, and Element 85 (astatine), in 1931. He received the Ph.D. (1922) from the University of Virginia and in the same year became professor of physics at the Alabama Polytechnic Institute. He received (1933) the Herty research medal.

Allison, William Boyd. b. at Perry, Ohio, March 2, 1829; d. at Dubuque, Ia., Aug. 4, 1908. American politician. He was a Republican congressman from Iowa (1862–71), U.S. senator (1872–1908), and senate chairman of appropriations (1881–1908). A moderationist on tariff questions and Western railroad demands, he worked with N. W. Aldrich against the Silverites, especially in the Bland-Allison Act (1878), limiting silver coinage, and the Gold Standard Act (1900), and against the currency expansion advocated by Theodore Roosevelt.

Allix (à.lēks), **Jacques Alexandre François.** b. Sept. 21, 1776; d. Jan. 26, 1836. French general and military writer. He served as a colonel at Marengo in 1800; later he was in the service of Jérôme Bonaparte, king of Westphalia. He was exiled from France on July 24, 1815, but was recalled in 1819. Author of *Système d'artillerie de campagne* (1827).

Allix, Pierre. b. at Alençon, France, 1641; d. at London, March 3, 1717. French Protestant divine and controversialist, an exile at London after 1685.

Allman (ôl'man), **George James.** b. at Cork, Ireland, 1812; d. at Parkstone, England, Nov. 24, 1898. British biologist, a pioneer in marine zoölogy. In 1844 he was appointed professor of botany at Dublin; later he served (1855–70) as regius professor of natural history and curator of natural history at Edinburgh (1855–70). He published a monograph (1871–72) on hydrozoa, and numerous other studies in coelenterate and polyzoan morphology.

All Men Are Brothers. Translation (1933) by Pearl S. Buck of a 13th-century Chinese novel about bandits.

All Men Are Enemies. Satirical novel, a product of his experiences in World War I, by Richard Aldington, published in 1933.

Allmers (äl'mėrs), **Hermann.** b. at Rechtenfleth, Germany, Feb. 11, 1821; d. there, March 9, 1902. German poet and dramatist. He was the author of *Marschenbuch* (1858), *Dichtungen* (1860), *Römische Schlendertage* (1869), the drama *Elektra* (1872), and others.

Alloa (al'ō.a). Police burgh and seaport in C Scotland, in Clackmannanshire, situated on the N bank of the Firth of Forth, ab. 2 mi. W of Clackmannan, ab. 424 mi. N of London by rail. The largest town in Clackmannanshire, it manufactures tweeds and other items. 14,438 (est. 1948).

Allobriges (a.lob'ri.jēz). Germanic tribe situated, at the time of Caesar, between the Menapi and the Batavii.

Allobroges (a.lob'rō.jēz) or **Allobrogi** (-jī). In ancient history, a Celtic people of SE Gaul, dwelling between the Rhone and the Isère rivers, northward to Lake Geneva. They occupied also a tract on the W bank of the Rhone. The chief town of the tribe was Vienne. They were made subject to Rome in 121 B.C.

Allori (äl.lō'rē), **Agnolo di Cosimo.** See **Bronzino, Il.**

Allori, Alessandro. [Called **Alessandro Bronzino.**] b. 1535; d. 1607. Florentine painter; student of Il Bronzino, and father of Cristofano Allori. His work is marked by elements of Michelangelo's grand manner; his best-known painting, a portrait of Giuliano de' Medici, is in the collection of the Uffizi, Florence, as are many of his other paintings.

Allori, Cristofano. b. 1577; d. 1621. Florentine painter; son of Alessandro Allori. His best work, *Judith and Holofernes*, as well as his *Saint Julian* and *Sacrifice of Isaac*, are in the collection of the Pitti Palace, Florence.

Allott (al'ot), **Robert.** [Also, **Allot.**] fl. 1600. English anthologist and editor. He is the probable compiler of *England's Parnassus* (1600), which contains extracts from the works of Spenser, Shakespeare, Michael Drayton, George Chapman, and numerous other writers.

Allouez (al'ō.wā). Unincorporated community in E Wisconsin, in Brown County, S of Green Bay. 4,094 (1950).

Allouez (à.lö.ā), **Claude Jean.** b. in St.-Didier, France, 1622; d. in what is now Indiana or Michigan, 1689. French Jesuit missionary in North America, one of the first in the Great Lakes region. He came in 1658 to Canada, and explored (1665 *et seq.*) the country surrounding Lake Superior and parts of the Mississippi valley.

All Our Yesterdays. Novel by H. M. Tomlinson, published in 1930, dealing with World War I.

Alloway (al'ǫ.wā). See under **Ayr.**

Alloway Kirk. Ruined church in the parish of Ayr, Scotland, near the Doon, rendered famous by Robert Burns in *Tam o'Shanter.*

All Passion Spent. Novel by V. (Victoria Mary) Sackville-West, published in 1931.

Allport (ôl'pōrt), **Gordon Willard.** b. at Montezuma, Ind., Nov. 11, 1897—. American psychologist. He was appointed (1942) professor of psychology at Harvard.

All Quiet on the Western Front. [German, **Im Westen nichts Neues** (im ves'tẹn nic̄hts noi'ẹs).] Novel by Erich Maria Remarque, published in 1929 (both the original German and the first English editions came out in this year). It tells the story of a small group of young German soldiers, with their occasional memories of days before the war, their constant awareness of the perilous and necessarily brutal day-to-day existence thrust upon them by the life of the trenches, and their growing sense of closeness to and dependence upon one another. It imparts to the reader with great clarity Remarque's conviction that war is one of the most horrible and most futile activities of which man is capable, and it had an immediate and overwhelming success in a world which was for the most part as opposed to war as Remarque himself. The novel was translated into virtually every European language, made into a film, and remains even today, in the opinion of most literary historians, one of the outstanding war novels of all time.

All Religions Are One. Critical work (c1789) by William Blake. It was printed in booklet form as an experiment in "illuminated printing" (which means that the text as well as the illustrations were engraved, and that each copy was then colored by hand).

All Saints Bay. [Portuguese, **Baía de Todos os Santos.**] Arm of the Atlantic Ocean, off the coast of Bahia state, E Brazil. The city of Salvador is located on it. Circumference, ab. 100 mi.

All Saints Day. [Former name, **All-Hallows Day.**] Christian feast day, falling on November 1. It is marked by church services in memory of all the saints on the various religious calendars. The feast has been celebrated in the Western world since the 9th century.

Allschwil (älsh'vēl). Village in NW Switzerland, in the half-canton of Basel-Land, near the border of Alsace, France. 7,315 (1941).

All's Lost by Lust. Play by William Rowley, a leading English comic actor of his day. Resembling in many ways what is now called melodrama, it was first performed in 1633.

Allsop (ôl'sọp), **Thomas.** b. near Wirksworth, England, April 10, 1795; d. at Exmouth, England, 1880. English stockbroker and author. He was an intimate friend of Samuel Taylor Coleridge and also shared the theories and was a friend of William Cobbett and Giuseppe Mazzini.

All Souls College. College of Oxford University, England, founded in 1437 by Archbishop Henry Chichele, to provide masses for the souls of the departed, especially those killed in the Hundred Years' War. The first quadrangle, with its fine gate, remains substantially as when first built; the chapel possesses beautiful fan tracery and reredos. The second quadrangle, with its two towers, was built in 1720. The statutes of the college were formally issued on April 2, 1443.

All Souls' Day. Roman Catholic holy day for the liturgical commemoration of the souls of the faithful dead still in Purgatory. It falls on November 2. The observance is believed to date from the 9th century, when it was introduced at the monasteries of Cluny.

Allstedt (äl'shtet). Town in S central Germany, in the *Land* (state) of Thuringia, Russian Zone, situated in the Goldene Aue valley ab. 32 mi. N of Weimar. It was at one time, with its territory, an enclave surrounded by Prussia. Pop. ab. 3,000.

Allston (ôl'stọn), **Robert Francis Withers.** b. in All Saints' Parish, S.C., April 21, 1801; d. April 7, 1864. American civil engineer, plantation owner, and politician.

Allston, Washington. b. at Waccamaw, S.C., 1779; d. at Cambridge, Mass., 1843. American painter, notably of religious subjects. He was a student of Benjamin West, teacher of S. F. B. Morse, and friend of Washington Irving, Bertel Thorvaldsen, and Samuel Taylor Coleridge. Influenced by Raphael, Michelangelo, and particularly the Venetian school, he is known for a portrait of Coleridge and for such Biblical paintings as *Dead Man Revived by Touching the Bones of the Prophet Elisha* (Pennsylvania Academy), *The Agony of Judas* (which he destroyed), *Jeremiah* (Yale University), *Witch of Endor* (Gardner Collection, Boston), *The Deluge* (Metropolitan Museum, N.Y.), and the unfinished *Belshazzar's Feast* (Boston Athenaeum). Author of *The Sylphs of the Seasons with other Poems* (1813), *Monaldi* (1841), *and Lectures on Art* (1850).

All's Well that Ends Well. Comedy by Shakespeare, played as early as c1596. Portions of this play were written not later than 1593, but the play as we have it was probably written in large part after 1600. It was first printed in the folio of 1623. The plot is from "Giletta of Narbonne" in Painter's *Palace of Pleasure* who took it in 1566 from the *Decameron* of Boccaccio. The story is followed closely, but the countess, the clown, Lafeu, and Parolles are Shakespeare's own.

All the Sad Young Men. Collection of short stories (1926) by F. Scott Fitzgerald. It is grouped by most critics of Fitzgerald's writing with the work of his second phase, in which his own personal crack-up paralleled the collapse of the supposedly flamboyant, extravagantly gay life of the 1920's with which he was first identified.

All-the-Talents Administration. Name given ironically to the English ministry of 1806–07. Among the leading members were William Wyndham Grenville (prime minister), Charles James Fox (foreign secretary), Thomas Erskine (1st Baron Erskine of Restormel), William Wentworth Fitzwilliam (2nd Earl Fitzwilliam), Henry Addington (1st Viscount Sidmouth), and Edmund Law (1st Baron Ellenborough).

All the Year Round. Periodical established and conducted by Charles Dickens. Its first issue appeared in 1859. It was a successor to Dickens's earlier family-magazine, *Household Words.*

Allward (ôl'wạrd), **Walter Seymour.** b. at Toronto, Canada, 1875—. Canadian sculptor. His works include the Vimy Ridge memorial to Canada's dead in World War I and the symbolic *Peace* of Toronto's Northwest Rebellion monument.

Allwit (ôl'wit"). Character in Thomas Middleton's *Chaste Maid in Cheapside*: a dupe.

Allworth (ôl'wėrth), **Lady.** Rich widow in Philip Massinger's play *A New Way to Pay Old Debts.*

Allworth, Tom. In Philip Massinger's play *A New Way to Pay Old Debts*, a young gentleman, page to Lord Lovell.

Allworthy (ôl'wėr"ᴛʜi), **Thomas.** [Called **"Squire Allworthy."**] In Henry Fielding's novel *Tom Jones*, a squire of large fortune, the foster father of the foundling Tom Jones. He is depicted as a man of the most upright and attractive character, a sharp contrast to Squire Western. He is generally considered to have been a portrait of Fielding's friend Ralph Allen.

Allyn (al'in), **Robert.** b. at Ledyard, Conn., Jan. 25, 1817; d. Jan. 7, 1894. American educator. As Rhode Island commissioner of schools (1854–57) he established the *Rhode Island Schoolmaster*, which was later (1875) combined with the *New England Journal of Education.* He was president of Wesleyan Female Academy at Cincinnati (1859 *et seq.*) and of McKendree College (1863 *et seq.*), as well as a founder and the first president (1874–92) of Southern Illinois State Normal University.

Alm (älm). See **Alp.**

Alma (al'mạ). City in SE Georgia, county seat of Bacon County. 2,588 (1950).

Alma. City in C Lower Michigan, on the Pine River, in Gratiot County: beet-sugar processing and oil refining. It is the seat of Alma College. 8,341 (1950).

Alma. In Edmund Spenser's *Faerie Queene*, the Queen of Body Castle, the personification of the soul.

Almaach or **Almak** (al′mak). The second-magnitude triple star γ Andromedae, in the foot of the constellation.

Alma-Ata (äl′mä.ä′tä). [Former name, **Verny** or **Vernyy.**] City in the U.S.S.R., capital of the Kazakh Soviet Socialist Republic. Important for the manufacture of silk and woolen textiles, it is also a junction on the Turkistan-Siberia railroad and for roads to China. 230,528 (1939).

Almack (ôl′mak), **William.** d. 1781. English valet and gamester; founder of the club (now Brook's) and owner (1764 *et seq.*) of the assembly rooms both known as Almack's. It has been established that he arrived in London as valet to the Duke of Hamilton, but whether from Yorkshire, Galway, or Atholl is not known; his establishment was for many years a center of London social life, holding its reputation even to the middle of the 19th century.

Almack's (ôl′maks). Gaming club established by William Almack in Pall Mall, London, before 1763, afterward the Whig club known as "Brook's." Among the 27 original members were William Henry Cavendish Bentinck (3rd Duke of Portland) and Charles James Fox; it was later joined by Edward Gibbon and William Pitt, among others.

Almack's. Famous assembly rooms built by William Almack in 1764, and opened on Feb. 20, 1765, in King Street, St. James, London. It remained a popular gathering place until the middle of the 19th century. These rooms were later also called "Willis's," after the next proprietor.

Almada (äl.mä′dą). Town and *concelho* (commune) in C Portugal, in the province of Estremadura, in the district of Setubal, at the mouth of the Tejo River opposite Lisbon. It has a wine trade, fisheries, and a small port. A medieval castle is situated above the town. Scene of a battle (July 23, 1833) in the Portuguese civil war. Pop. of concelho, 28,976 (1940); of town, 8,578 (1940).

Alma Dagh (or **Dağ**) (äl′mä däg). Modern name of **Amanus.**

Almaden (al′mą.dęn). [Former name, **New Almaden.**] Unincorporated community in C California, ab. 57 mi. SE of San Francisco: resort community. Cinnabar, the mercury ore, was mined here in some quantity from c1853 to the early 1900's. Pop. 250 (1949).

Almadén (äl.mä.ᴛʜān′). [Also: **Almadén del Azogue** (del ä.thō′gā); ancient name, **Sisapon** or **Sisapo.**] Mining town in C Spain, in the province of Ciudad-Real, situated above the Alcudia River, ab. 50 mi. SW of Ciudad-Real. Some of the richest quicksilver mines of the world are in the vicinity, producing about one third of the world supply of mercury; prior to the opening (1853–57) of new sources of mercury near New Almaden, Calif., they held a near monopoly. There are also lead and sulfur mines, and schools of mining. The mines were exploited by the Romans and later by the Moslems; in the 16th and 17th centuries they were leased to the banking house of Fugger, and in the 19th century to the banking house of Rothschild. The town was of strategic importance in the Spanish Civil War of 1936–39 and remained in Loyalist hands until the end of the conflict. 12,988 (1940).

Almagest (al′mą.jest). Scientific treatise, in 13 books, by Ptolemy. The title, from the Arabic translation of Ptolemy's Greek *Syntaxis,* means "the greatest synthesis"; the work embodies Ptolemy's astronomic theories, establishing a geocentric universe, and, by his own system of eccentrics and epicycles, fixing the length of the year at 365¼ days. The work also gives a modified list of Hipparchus's catalogue of stars. The translation of this work into Latin was unquestionably one of the most important events in European astronomy before the Renaissance. Actually, there were two translations, both made in the 12th century. The first was made by anonymous scholars in Sicily about 1160 from a Greek manuscript brought to Sicily from the library of one of the Byzantine rulers. The second was made at Toledo, in Spain, from an Arabic manuscript some 15 years after the first. However, the first translation (from the Greek), remained practically unknown (despite the fact that most scholars consider that it was probably the superior of the two), and the Almagest became known in Europe chiefly through the translation from Arabic. In this translation, it remained the standard astronomic authority of Europe until the time of Copernicus.

Almagro (äl.mä′grō), **Diego de.** b. probably at Aldea del Rey, Spain, c1475 (but according to some accounts a foundling in Almagro, Spain, in 1464); executed on July 10 (or 12), 1538. Spanish soldier, one of the conquerors of Peru; father of Diego de Almagro (1520–42). He went to Panama with Pedrarias in 1514, and in 1525 joined Francisco Pizarro in an enterprise for conquest toward the south. He went down the coast with Pizarro as early as 1526; and when, after his return from Spain, Pizarro sailed for Peru in January, 1531, Almagro followed, late in the same year, with three vessels and 150 men, and joined him at Cajamarca, on the Peruvian slope of the Andes, about the middle of February, 1533, before the death of Atahualpa. Here a violent quarrel (the second) took place between them, but a reconciliation was effected and Almagro took an active part in the march on Cusco. In 1535 he was sent to conquer Chile, of which he was made governor. He went as far south as Coquimbo, but, finding nothing of the coveted riches, turned back, laid claim to Cusco as the territory assigned to him, and seized the city by surprise (April 8, 1537), capturing Hernando and Gonzalo Pizarro. He was attacked by Alonzo Alvarado, who was captured (July 12, 1537) with his whole army. Almagro was finally defeated by Hernando Pizarro at Las Salinas, near Cusco, April 26, 1538, and he was soon after captured, tried, and beheaded.

Almagro, Diego de. b. in Panama, 1520; executed at Cusco, Peru, 1542. Political adventurer; son of Diego de Almagro and an Indian woman. He was with his father in Chile in the period 1535–36 and was proclaimed (1541) governor of Peru on Pizarro's death, although he probably was not an active member of the group which killed him. Defeated (Sept. 16, 1542) at Chupas by royalists under Vaca de Castro, he was beheaded.

Almahide (äl.mȧ.ēd). Romance by Madeleine de Scudéry, based on the 15th-century feud in Spain between the Moorish family of the Abencerrages and the Zegris. An English translation was made in 1677 by John Phillips.

Almahide (äl.mä.ē′dā). Anonymously composed opera first performed at London in 1710. It is presumed to have been the first work wholly in Italian to be sung in England.

Almahyde (al′mą.hīd). Queen of Granada in John Dryden's *Almanzor and Almahyde, or The Conquest of Granada by the Spaniards.* The name was taken from Madeleine de Scudéry's novel *Almahide.*

Almain (al.mān′). An early English name of **Germany.**

Alma Island (al′mą). Island in the Saguenay River, Quebec, Canada, at the outlet of Lake St. John.

Almali (äl.mä.li′). See **Elmali.**

Almansa (äl.män′sä). [Also, **Almanza.**] Town in E Spain, in the province of Albacete, situated on the Rio Grande river, ab. 43 mi. E of Albacete: textile, leather, and soap manufactures; distilleries; railroad junction. On a rock above the town is a picturesque Moorish castle. 16,025 (1940).

Almansa or **Almanza, Battle of.** Victory gained at Almansa, in E Spain, by the French and Spanish under James Fitzjames, Duke of Berwick, over the allied British, Dutch, and Portuguese under Henri de Massue, 1st Earl of Galway, on April 25, 1707. It established Philip V on the Spanish throne.

Almansa, Martín Henríquez de. See **Henríquez de Almansa, Martín.**

Almansor (äl.män′sōr). See **Mansur, al-.**

Almanzor (al.man′zǫr). Caliph of Arabia in George Chapman's *Revenge for Honour.*

Almanzor and Almahyde, or The Conquest of Granada by the Spaniards. Heroic tragedy in two parts, by John Dryden, produced in 1670. It was partly taken from Madeleine de Scudéry's *Almahide,* and is usually known as *The Conquest of Granada.* The character of Almanzor, a knight errant of extravagant egotism, is caricatured as Drawcansir in *The Rehearsal.*

Alma River (äl′mą). River in the U.S.S.R., in the Crimean *oblast* (region) of the Russian Soviet Federated Socialist Republic, which flows into the Black Sea ab. 20 mi. N of Sevastopol. Near its mouth, on Sept. 20, 1854, the Allies (British, French, and Turks) defeated the Russians under Menshikov.

Alma-Tadema (al′mą.tad′ę.mą), Sir **Laurence** (or **Lawrence**). b. at Dronrijp, Netherlands, Jan. 8, 1836; d. at Wiesbaden, Germany, June 25, 1912. British painter noted especially for representations of Egyptian, Greek, and Roman life; knighted in 1899. He settled at London in 1870 and became a British citizen in 1873. Among his works are *The Vintage*, *Catullus*, *The Siesta*, *Entrance to a Roman Theatre*, *Tarquinius Superbus*, *Phidias*, and *An Audience at Agrippa's*.

Almaviva (äl.mä.vē'vä), **Count.** Brilliant, attractive, and philandering nobleman in Pierre Augustin Caron de Beaumarchais's comedy *Le Barbier de Séville*. He is the lover of Rosine, and succeeds, with the aid of Figaro the barber, his former valet, in rescuing her from old Bartholo and marrying her himself. He appears in *Le Mariage de Figaro*, already tired of Rosine his wife, and in *La Mère Coupable*, as an old and faded beau. He also appears in the operas by Giovanni Paisiello and Gioacchino Antonio Rossini founded on *Le Barbier de Séville*, as well as in Mozart's *Le Nozze di Figaro*, based on *Le Mariage de Figaro*.

Almayer's Folly (ôl'mī.ėrz). Novel (1895) by Joseph Conrad.

Almazán (äl.mä.sän'), **Juan Andreu.** b. in Guerrero, Mexico, 1891—. Mexican army officer and politician.

Almeida (äl.mā'dạ). Town and *concelho* (commune) in E Portugal, in the province of Beira Alta, in Guarda district. It was captured by the French in 1810, and retaken by the Duke of Wellington in 1811. Pop. of concelho, 16,390 (1940); of town, 1,654 (1940).

Almeida, Antônio José de. b. 1866; d. 1929. Portuguese politician and physician. He was elected a republican member of parliament (1906) and became successively minister of the interior and prime minister. From 1919 to 1923 he was president of Portugal.

Almeida, Francisco de. b. at Lisbon, c1450; killed near the Cape of Good Hope, South Africa, March 1, 1510. Portuguese naval commander, notable as the first viceroy (1505–09) of the Portuguese possessions in India. He established forts and trading posts in Africa (at Kilwa and elsewhere) and in the East (at Calicut, India, and elsewhere). His activities so greatly threatened the trade of Egypt with Africa and the East that a fleet was built by Egypt (with the help of Venice) in order to attack him; an initial Egyptian success (1508) was followed (1509) by complete defeat off the coast of India at the hands of a fleet under Almeida.

Almeida, Guilherme de. b. at Campinas, Brazil, July 24, 1890—. Brazilian poet, journalist, and lawyer. Among his books of poetry are *Nós* (1917), *A dança das horas* (1919), *Messidor* (1919), *Simplicidade* (1929), *Você* (1931), *Cartas a minha noiva* (1931), and *Cartas que eu não mandei* (1932). His prose works include *Gente de cinema* (1929) and *O meu Portugal* (1934). He translated into Portuguese the *Gitanjali* of Rabindranath Tagore.

Almeida, José Américo de. b. at Areia, Paraíba, Brazil, 1887—. Brazilian novelist and lawyer, who has held several important posts in his country. His best known work, *A bagaceira* (1928), is regarded as a landmark in the history of the regional novel in Brazil. His other two well-known novels are *Coiteiros* and *O boqueirão* (1935), which also deal with social problems of the northeast of Brazil.

Almeida, Manuel Antônio de. b. at Rio de Janeiro, Nov. 17, 1831; d. in the shipwreck of the *Hermes* near Macaé, Brazil, Nov. 28, 1861. Brazilian novelist, journalist, and physician. His well-known novel, *Memórias de um sargento de milícias*, which first appeared in a newspaper supplement (1852–53) and later (1854–55) in book form, is generally regarded as a forerunner of realism in the literature of Brazil. He also wrote *Dois amores* (1861), a lyric drama.

Almeida, Miguel Calmón du Pin e. See **Calmón du Pin e Almeida, Miguel.**

Almeida, Nicolau Tolentino de. See **Tolentino de Almeida, Nicolau.**

Almeida-Garrett (äl.mā'dạ.gạ.ret'), **João Batista da Silva Leitão de.** See **Garrett, João Batista da Silva Leitão de Almeida.**

Almeirim (äl.mā.rēn'). Town and *concelho* (commune) in C Portugal, in the province of Ribatejo, in the district of Santarém, situated near the left bank of the Tejo River, opposite Santarém: wine trade. Once a royal residence, it was largely destroyed in the earthquake of 1755. Pop. of concelho, 15,916 (1940); of town, 9,175 (1940).

Almeisam (al.mī'sạm). A name for the star γ Geminorum. It is also often called Alhena.

Almelo (äl'mẹ.lō). [Also, **Almeloo.**] Town in E Netherlands, in the province of Overijssel, situated at the junction of the Almelo and Overijssel canals, ab. 22 mi. NE of Deventer. It is connected with the Ems River through the Almelo-Nordhorn Canal. Linen and cotton textiles are important manufactures. Among the notable buildings is a castle of the counts of Rechteren and Limpurg; the town developed, beginning in the Middle Ages, under the overlordship of these two families. 41,308 (1949).

Almendralejo (äl''men.drä.le'ʜō). Town in W Spain, in the province of Badajoz, ab. 27 mi. SE of Badajoz: agricultural trade center; sheep fair; distilleries. The palace of the Marquis of Monsalad contains a collection of Roman antiquities. 21,276 (1940).

Almería (äl.mä.rē'ä). Province in SE Spain, bounded by Murcia on the NE, the Mediterranean Sea on the E and S, and Granada on the W and NW: a part of the region of Andalusia. The province is mountainous, comprising the E section of the Sierra Nevada. Wine, citrus fruit, and sugar cane are produced; there are iron and lead mines. Capital, Almería; area, 3,388 sq. mi.; pop. 370,635 (1950).

Almería. [Arabic, **Al-Merya;** ancient names, **Urci, Portus Magnus.**] City in SE Spain, capital of the province of Almería, situated on the Gulf of Almería, near the mouth of the Almería River, ab. 60 mi. SE of Granada: exports iron, lead, and zinc ores, silver, and agricultural products, particularly esparto grass, citrus fruit, and white grapes. 84,719 (1950).

Almeria (al.mir'i.ạ). In Congreve's play *The Mourning Bride*, the supposedly widowed bride of Alphonso, prince of Valentia. It is she who utters (Act 1, Scene 1) the familiar words: "Music hath charms to soothe a savage breast, To soften rocks, or bend a knotted oak."

Almirante (äl.mē.rän'tā). Town and port on the coast of NW Panama. It is important chiefly as a point of export for the bananas produced further inland. Pop. ab. 1,600.

Almodóvar (äl.mō.ᴛʜō'ʙär), Count of. [Title of **Ildefonso Díaz de Ribera.**] b. at Granada, Spain, 1777; d. at Valencia, Spain, 1846. Spanish statesman. He was imprisoned and exiled in the reign of Ferdinand VII, was afterward minister of war and president of the Cortes, and was minister of foreign affairs (1842–43).

Almodóvar. [Also, **Almodóvar del Campo** (del käm'pō).] Town in C Spain, in the province of Ciudad-Real, situated above the Alcudia River, ab. 21 mi. SW of Ciudad-Real. The Puertollano coal field and also mines of argentiferous lead are in the vicinity. The Alcudia valley contains pasture land for large flocks of sheep. The town was a Moslem stronghold in the Middle Ages; the castle still stands. 14,633 (1940).

Almogaver (äl''mō.gä.ʙer'), **Juan Boscán.** See **Boscán Almogaver, Juan.**

Almohades (al'mọ.hādz). Moslem dynasty in N Africa and Spain, which superseded the Almoravides about the middle of the 12th century.

Almolonga (äl.mō.lōn'gä). See under **Ciudad Vieja.**

Almon (al'mọn), **John.** b. at Liverpool, England, Dec. 17, 1737; d. at Boxmoor, England, Dec. 12, 1805. English publisher and Whig political pamphleteer; friend of John Wilkes. His sale (1763 *et seq.*) of pamphlets against the government then ruling England brought him continual harassment by the attorney general and others.

Almond (ôl'mọnd), **Edward Mallory.** b. at Luray, Va., Dec. 12, 1892—. American soldier. A graduate of Virginia Military Institute, he was commissioned (1916) and fought with the American Expeditionary Forces in France during World War I. He served with the army of occupation in Germany and subsequently became a military instructor. In World War II he commanded (1942–45) the 92nd infantry division; he served as deputy chief of staff at Tokyo (1946–49) and chief of staff of the Far East Command (1949–50). With the outbreak of the Korean War, he assumed command (1950) of the U.S. 10th Corps, leading it until 1951, when he became commandant of the Army War College at Carlisle Barracks, Pa.

Almondbury (ä'mọnd.ber.i; locally, äm'bri). Civil parish and ward of Huddersfield, in C England, in the West Riding of Yorkshire, situated on the river Calder. It is a part of Huddersfield. 8,435 (1931).

Almonde (äl.môn'dẹ), **Philippus van.** b. at Briel, the Netherlands, 1646; d. near Leiden, Jan. 6, 1711. Dutch naval officer, made commander of the fleet on the death of Michel Adriaanszoon de Ruyter (1676). He accompanied William of Orange to England in 1688. After commanding the Dutch fleet at La Hogue in 1692, he commanded, with Sir George Rooke, the allies at the destruction of the Spanish fleet in the Bay of Vigo (1702).

Almond for a Parrot. Essay (1590) probably by Robert Greene in reply to the Martin Marprelate pamphlets. Some literary historians believe that Thomas Nash may have been its actual author.

Almonte (al'mont). Town in E Ontario, Canada, situated on the Mississippi River (a branch of the Ottawa River), ab. 43 mi. SW of Ottawa: important rail junction on the main line of the Canadian Pacific Railway. 2,672 (1951).

Almonte (äl.mōn'tā), **Juan Nepomuceno.** b. in Guerrero, Mexico, c1804; d. at Mexico City, 1869. Mexican general and political opportunist; government official under Antonio López de Santa Anna, Paredes, and Maximilian. Part Indian, perhaps a son of Morelos, he was U.S.-educated. He served with Santa Anna in Texas, and was taken prisoner (1836) by Sam Houston at the battle of San Jacinto. As secretary of state and minister to Washington (1841 *et seq.*) under Santa Anna, he entered a formal protest (1845) against the annexation of Texas and demanded his passport. He was a candidate (1845) for the Mexican presidency, and claimed to have been elected; he then aided in the deposition (1845) of Herrera by Paredes and was the latter's minister of war. In the war against the U.S., he fought at Buenavista, Cerro Gordo, and Churubusco. In Santa Anna's second administration (1854–55), he was again made minister to Washington, retaining that post until 1860 and negotiating the Gadsden Purchase; later, as minister to France, he was involved in the diplomacy which precipitated the French expedition (1862) to Mexico. He was regent and, later, grand marshal under Maximilian who, becoming suspicious of him, sent him (1866) as minister to France.

Almora (äl.mō'rạ). District of Kumaun division, Uttar Pradesh (United Provinces), Union of India, near the NW border of Nepal: important silk-producing area. Capital, Almora; pop. 687,281 (1941).

Almora. Capital of Almora district, Kumaun division, Union of India, ab. 160 mi. NE of the city of Delhi: trading center, particularly for silk. 9,688 (1941).

Almoradi (äl.mō.rä'ᴛʜē). Town in E Spain, in the province of Alicante, situated near the Segura River, between Alicante and Murcia: agricultural trade. 10,459 (1940).

Almoravides (al.mō'rạ.vīdz). Moslem sect and dynasty in NW Africa and Spain, founded by Abdallah ibn-Yasin, who was killed in battle c1058. His successor, ibn-Tashfin (who is usually thought of also as a founder of the dynasty), established his capital at Marrakech, in what is now French Morocco, in 1062. The Almoravides under ibn-Tashfin defeated Alfonso VI of León and Castile at Zalaca in 1086, having been invited into Spain by Abbad III. In 1091 they ousted Abbad and their dynasty was established in Spain. It was overthrown (1146–47) by the Almohades. In the course of their domination of NW Africa, the religious leaders of the Almoravides succeeded in converting the Tukulor, Sarakole, Songhai, and other Sudanese peoples to Mohammedanism.

Almqvist (älm'kvist), **Karl Jonas Ludwig.** [Assumed name, **Professor Westermann.**] b. at Stockholm, Nov. 28, 1793; d. at Bremen, Sept. 26, 1866. Swedish writer and proponent of socialism. He is best known for his novel collection, *The Book of the Thorn-Rose* (1832–35); his later activities and writing are linked to the cause of socialism.

Almuñécar (äl.mö.nyā'kär). Town in S Spain, in the province of Granada, situated on the Mediterranean Sea, ab. 35 mi. S of Granada: seaport, chiefly for coastwise shipping. It was the landing place in 755 of Abd-er-Rahman I, Ommiad caliph who became emir with his capital at Córdoba. 11,110 (1940).

Almus Pickerbaugh (al'mus pik'ėr.bô), **Dr.** See **Pickerbaugh, Dr. Almus.**

Almy (al'mi), **John Jay.** b. at Newport, R.I., April 24, 1815; d. at Washington, D.C., May 16, 1895. American naval officer, active in the Union blockade of Southern ports during the Civil War. He was appointed commodore (1869) and rear admiral (1873).

Alnaschar (al.nash'ạr, -nas'kär). The "Barber's Fifth Brother" in *The Arabian Nights' Entertainments.* He invests his inheritance in glassware. While awaiting customers he fancies himself already a millionaire, and an incautious movement upsets his basket, breaking its contents and destroying all his prospects (hence the phrase "visions of Alnaschar," that is, counting one's chickens before they are hatched; daydreams).

Alnilam (al.ni.läm'). The second-magnitude star ε Orionis, in the middle of the giant's belt.

Alnitak (al.ni.tak'). The triple second-magnitude star ζ Orionis, at the SE end of the belt.

Alnwick (an'ik). Urban district and market town in NE England, in Northumberland, situated on the river Alne, ab. 38 mi. N of Newcastle-upon-Tyne, ab. 306 mi. N of London by rail. It is famous for Alnwick Castle (held by the Percy family since 1309), the residence of the dukes of Northumberland. Here, in 1174, an English force defeated the Scots. Near Alnwick are the ruins of Hulne Abbey (1240). Pop. 7,366 (1951).

Alnwick, William of. d. 1449. English ecclesiastic; bishop of Norwich (1426–36) and Lincoln (1436–49). He was a friend of Henry V and confessor to Henry VI, and an opponent of the Lollards. He produced the *Novum Registrum* (1440), which codified the statutes of Lincoln Cathedral.

Alnwick Castle. Poem by Fitz-Greene Halleck, published in his *Alnwick Castle, with Other Poems* (1827).

Aloadae (a.lō'ạ.dē). See **Aloidae.**

Alofi (ä.lō'fẹ). Seaport and main center on the Pacific island of Niue, owned by New Zealand. It is the site of a wireless and meteorological station.

Alofi. See also under **Futuna Islands.**

Aloidae (al.ọ.ī'dē). [Also: **Aloiadae** (-ī'ạ.dē), **Aloadae.**] In Greek mythology, two giants, Otus and Ephialtes, sons of Poseidon. See under **Ephialtes.**

Aloisi (ä.lō.ē'zē), Baron **Pompeo.** b. 1875; d. Jan. 15, 1949. Italian diplomat. He was minister to Denmark (1920–22), Rumania (1923–25), and Albania (1926–27); ambassador to Japan (1928–29) and Turkey (1930–32); cabinet chief in the foreign ministry (1932–36); League of Nations delegate (1932–37); and senator (1939 *et seq.*).

Alompra (ạ.lom'prạ). [Also, **Aloung P'Houra.**] b. 1711; d. 1760. Founder of the last dynasty of Burma (named from him). He reigned c1754–60.

Alonesos (ä.lô'nē.sôs). [Also: **Alón** (ä.lôn'), **Iliodhromia, Khiliodhromia, Khiliodromia, Khilidromi;** ancient name, **Halonnesus.**] Island in the Sporades, Aegean Sea, belonging to Greece, E of Skopelos and N of Euboea. Length, ab. 13 mi.

Alonso (ạ.lon'sō), **Adventures of.** See **Adventures of Alonso.**

Alonzo (ạ.lon'zō). See also under **Alfonso.**

Alonzo. In Beaumont and Fletcher's *The Custom of the Country*, a young Portuguese gentleman, the enemy of Duarte.

Alonzo. King of Naples in Shakespeare's *The Tempest.*

Alonzo. In Richard Brinsley Sheridan's translation of August Friedrich Ferdinand Kotzebue's *Pizarro*, the commander of the army of Ataliba, king of Quito.

Alonzo of Aguilar (ä.gē.lär'). In Spanish literature, a brave knight who lost his life in trying to plant King Ferdinand's banner on the heights of Granada, in 1501. There are several Spanish ballads on the subject.

Alopeus (ạ.lō'pẹ.us), **Maximilian.** b. at Viborg, Finland, Jan. 21, 1748; d. at Frankfort on the Main, Germany, May 16, 1822. Russian diplomat. He was accredited as minister plenipotentiary to the court of Prussia in 1790 by Catherine II.

Alor (ä'lôr). [Also: **Ombai, Ombay.**] One of the Lesser Sunda Islands, situated N of Timor, from which it is separated by Ombai Passage.

Álora (ä'lō.rä). [Ancient name, **Iluro.**] Town in S Spain, in the province of Málaga, situated on the Guadalhorce River, ab. 17 mi. NW of Málaga: health resort, with hot sulfur springs; distilleries. The irrigated *vega* (meadow area) is important for oranges, lemons, dates, and other fruits. 13,968 (1940).

Aloros (ą.lō'ros). In ancient mythology, the first of the ten kings who reigned over Babylonia before the Deluge.

Alorton (al'ǫr.tǫn). Town in SW Illinois, in St. Clair County. 2,547 (1950).

Alost (ȧ.lost). French name of **Aalst.**

Aloung P'Houra (ä.lông' pę.hö'rä). See **Alompra.**

Aloysius (al.ǭ.ish'us), Saint. [Original name, **Luigi Gonzaga.**] b. at the castle of Castiglione, near Mantua, Italy, 1568; d. 1591. Italian nobleman and Jesuit. He spent much of his childhood in one of the Medici courts, and in that of the duke of Mantua. Resigning his titles to his brother, he entered the Society of Jesus, despite opposition from his father. He died while still a student in 1591, having caught a fever from hospital patients whom he attended. Known from childhood for the purity of his life, he was declared patron of youth by Pope Benedict XIII three years after his canonization in 1726.

Alp (älp). [Also, **Alm.**] Local name of the elevated and sparsely inhabited meadow and pasture tracts of Switzerland and the Tirol.

Alp (alp). Principal character in Byron's poem *The Siege of Corinth*, a renegade shot in the siege.

ALP. See also **Anna Livia Plurabelle.**

ALP. Abbreviation of **American Labor Party.**

Alp Arslan (älp ärs.län'). [Earlier name, **Mohammed ibn-Daud.**] b. 1029; d. 1072. Sultan of the Seljuk Turks, who reigned, as successor to his father, Daud, in Khurasan, in what is now Iran, from 1059 to 1072. He also succeeded (1063) his uncle Toghrul Beg as chief ruler of the Seljuk empire in Persia; subdued (c1064) Georgia and Armenia; conquered Aleppo and defeated and took prisoner the Byzantine emperor Romanus Diogenes near the Araxes (now the Araks) River in 1071, a victory which led to the establishment in Asia Minor of the Seljuk empire of Rum.

Alpen (äl'pęn). German name of the **Alps.**

Alpena (al.pē'ną). City in N Lower Michigan, on Thunder Bay, Lake Huron, county seat of Alpena County: center for lumber products. 13,135 (1950).

Alpensinfonie (älp'ęn.zin.fo.nē''), **Eine.** [Eng. trans., "*An Alpine Symphony.*"] Tone poem by Richard Strauss depicting a day of mountain climbing; it was first performed at Berlin on Oct. 28, 1915.

Alpes (al'pēz). Latin name of the **Alps.**

Alpes (ȧlp). French name of the **Alps.**

Alpes, Basses-. See **Basses-Alpes.**

Alpes-Maritimes (ȧlp.mȧ.rē.tēm). Department in SE France, bounded by Italy on the N and E, by the Mediterranean Sea on the S, and by the departments of Var and Basses-Alpes on the W. It was formed from the territory of Nice (ceded by Italy in 1860), and from part of Var. The department had previously been French from 1793 to 1815. Although severe weather prevails in the mountainous N part, the climate is exceptionally mild along the coast, which forms part of the French Riviera and where world-famous resorts, such as Cannes, Antibes, Cagnes, Nice, and Menton, are situated. The tourist industry is highly developed. Agriculture is hampered by the nature of the terrain, and more than 40 percent of the surface is uncultivated. The commune of Grasse and other places along the coast are centers of intensive cultivation of flowers, both for export and for the production of essential oils which are used in the French perfume industry. It is the largest area in the world devoted to this specialty. Capital, Nice; area, 1,443 sq. mi.; pop. 448,973 (1946). (The territories of Brigue and Tende, ceded to France by Italy in 1947, are not included in these figures.)

Alpes Maritimes (ȧlp mȧ.rē.tēm). French name of the **Maritime Alps.**

Alph (alf). Sacred underground river in Xanadu, in Coleridge's poem *Kubla Khan.*

Alphand (ȧl.fäṅ), **Hervé.** b. May 31, 1907—. French government official, active (1941–44) in the Free French movement. He served (1940–41) as French commercial attaché at Washington and was a delegate (1945) to the United Nations conference at San Francisco.

Alphard (al.färd'). The second-magnitude star α Hydrae, or Cor Hydrae.

Alphecca (al.fek'ą). See **Alfeta.**

Alphege (al'fej), Saint. See **Ælfheah,** Saint.

Alphen (äl'fęn), **Hieronymus van.** b. at Gouda, the Netherlands, Aug. 8, 1746; d. at The Hague, April 2, 1803. Dutch poet and jurist.

Alphen aan den Rijn (än dęn rīn). See **Alfen aan den Rijn.**

Alpheratz (al.fę.rats'). The usual name of the second-magnitude star α Andromedae, in the head of the constellation. It is also often called Sirrah.

Alpheus (al.fē'us, al'fę.us) or **Alpheius** (äl.fyôs'). In Greek mythology, a river god, son of Oceanus and Tethys.

Alpheus River. [Also (for parts of its course): **Rouphia, Rufia, Ruphia**; Greek, **Alpheios** (al'fā.ǫs).] River in Greece, in the Peloponnesus, flowing generally NW from S Greece into the Ionian Sea. The plain of Olympia touches its N bank, and its name is mentioned repeatedly in the legend and history of Greece. In more modern times, it occurs in English literature as the original of Coleridge's river Alph, mentioned in *Kubla Khan.* In Greek mythology, it was the river diverted by Hercules in order to clean the Augean stables. It flows at one point under the ground, and was for this reason believed by the ancient Greeks actually to flow under the sea to Sicily.

Alphirk (al.fėrk'). The third-magnitude double star β Cephei.

Alphonsa (al.fon'są), Mother. [Original name, **Rose Hawthorne.**] b. at Lenox, Mass., May 20, 1851; d. July 9, 1926. American philanthropist and religious superior; youngest child of Nathaniel Hawthorne. She was married (1871) in England to George Parsons Lathrop, with whom she was converted (1891) to Roman Catholicism; after her husband's death (1896) she founded a sisterhood named Servants of Relief for Incurable Cancer. Subsequently she established homes at Hawthorne, N.Y. (1901) and New York City (1912) for destitute victims of incurable cancer.

Alphonse (ȧl.fôṅs) or **Alphonso** (al.fon'sō). See also under **Alfonso.**

Alphonsus a Sancta Maria (al.fon'sus ä sangk'tą mą.rē'ą). [Also, **Alfonso de Cartagena.**] b. at Cartagena, Spain, 1396; d. July 12, 1456. Spanish prelate and historian. He succeeded his father, Paulus, as bishop of Burgos. Deputed in 1431 by John II of Castile to attend the Council of Basle, he succeeded in effecting a reconciliation between Albert V of Austria and Ladislaus, king of Poland. His principal work is a history of Spain to 1496 (printed 1545).

Alphonsus Liguori (lē.gwô'rē), Saint. See **Liguori,** Saint **Alfonso Maria de'.**

Alpi (äl'pē). Italian name of the **Alps.**

Alpiew (al'pū). In Susannah Centlivre's comedy *The Basset-Table*, Lady Reveller's waiting-woman, a pert, adroit soubrette. The name is taken from "alpieu," a term in the once popular game of basset implying the continuance of the bet on a card that has already won.

Alpi Lepontine (äl'pē lā.pōn.tē'nā). Italian name of the **Lepontine Alps.**

Alpi Marittime (mä.rēt'tē.mā). Italian name of the **Maritime Alps.**

Alpine (al'pīn). Town in W Texas, county seat of Brewster County, SE of El Paso, in a region producing copper, lead, gold, silver, marble, zinc, potash, and cinnabar. The area is also important for the raising of Highland Herefords, and is sometimes called "Cow Heaven." It is the seat of Sul Ross State Teachers College. Kokernot State Park is nearby. 5,261 (1950).

Alpini (äl.pē'nē), **Prospero.** [Latinized, **Prosper Alpinus.**] b. at Marostica, near Venice, Nov. 23, 1553; d. at Padua, Feb. 6, 1617. Italian botanist and physician. His study of Egyptian palms led him to a theory of sexual reproduction of plants similar to that later established by Linnaeus. He was also notable as the first European scientist to mention the prevalence of trachoma in Egypt, and as the author of *De plantis Aegypti liber* (1592) and *De medicina Aegyptiorum* (1591), the latter containing what many believe to be the first European account of the coffee plant.

Alpi Retiche (äl'pē rā'tē.kā). Italian name of the **Rhaetian Alps.**

Alps (alps). [French, **Alpes**; German, **Alpen**; Italian, **Alpi**; Latin, **Alpes.**] The most extensive mountain system in Europe, comprising a part of SE France, most of Switzerland, a part of N Italy, a part of S Germany, and parts of Austria and Yugoslavia. It was anciently divided into the Maritime, Cottian, Graian, Pennine, Rhaetian, Noric, Carnic, Venetian, and Julian Alps. The modern division is into the Western, Central, and Eastern Alps. The Western Alps include the Ligurian, Maritime, Cottian, and Graian Alps, Montagnes des Maures and Esterel Mountains, Mountains of Provence (or of Vaucluse, Ventoux group), Alps of Dauphiné, Limestone Alps of Savoie, and the Mountains of Chablais and Faucigny. The Central Alps include the Pennine, Lepontine, Rhaetian, Otzthaler, Bernese, Fribourg, Emmenthal, and Urner and Engelberg Alps, the Tödi range, Schwyzer Alps, St. Gall and Appenzell Alps, Vorarlberg and Allgäu Alps, North Tirolese and Bavarian Alps, and the Luganer, Bergamasker, Ortler, Nonsberg, Adamello, and Tridentine Alps. The Eastern Alps include the Zillerthal Alps, Hohe Tauern, Niedere Tauern, Carinthian and Styrian Alps, Styrian Nieder Alps, and Kitzbühler, Salzburg, Upper Austrian, North Styrian, Lower Austrian, Lessinian, Cadoric (Dolomite), Venetian, Carnic, Karawanken, Bacher, and Santhaler Alps, and Julian Alps. There are also various outliers of the system in Hungary and Yugoslavia, etc. The length of the range from the Pass of Giovi (N of Genoa) to Semmering Pass is over 600 mi., and its width is from 90 to 180 mi. Its highest peak is Mont Blanc (15,781 ft.), on the borders of France and Italy; highest in Switzerland, the Monte Rosa; average height of the range ab. 7,700 ft. Its largest glacier is the Aletsch, ab. 13 mi. long.

Alps, Bernese. See **Bernese Oberland.**

Alps, Eastern. Division of the Alps which extends from the Brenner Pass eastward to the Semmering Pass, often made to include all the Alps lying E of a line connecting Lake Constance with Lago Maggiore.

Alps, Western. Division of the Alps which is separated from the Apennines by the Pass of Giovi (N of Genoa) and extends to the Pass of Great St. Bernard; often made to include all the Alps lying W of a line connecting Lake Constance with Lago Maggiore.

Alpujarras (äl.pö.ʜär′räs), **Las.** Mountainous region in S Spain, in the provinces of Granada and Almería. It contains many picturesque and fertile valleys. After the fall of the Moorish (Moslem) kingdom of Granada in 1492 it was a refuge of the Moriscos in Spain.

Alqamah (äl.kä′mạ). Arabic name of **Alcamo.**

Alred (al′rẹd). See **Aldred.**

Alredus Beverlacensis (al.rē′dus bev″ėr.lạ.sen′sis). See **Alfred of Beverley.**

Alright Island (ôl′rīt″). One of the Magdalen Islands, in the Gulf of St. Lawrence. It is part of the province of Quebec.

Als (äls). [German, **Alsen.**] Island belonging to Denmark, in the Little Belt SE of Jutland. The chief town is Sønderborg, capital of the *amt* (county) of Aabenraa-Sønderborg. Area, ab. 120 sq. mi.; pop. 34,294 (1945).

Alsace (al.sās′, al′sas; French, ȧl.zȧs). [German, **Elsass;** Latin, **Alsatia.**] Region in NE France, comprising the departments of Haut-Rhin and Bas-Rhin. One of the most bitterly contested regions in Europe, it was long (1871–1919) part (see Alsace-Lorraine) of the German Empire, comprising the *Bezirke* (districts) of Upper Alsace and Lower Alsace. The Vosges mountains form its W frontier. Its soil is fertile, and it has important iron and coal mines, and considerable manufactures. The chief city is Strasbourg. Both German and French are spoken by most of the inhabitants. Alsace was a part of ancient Gaul and afterward of the Frankish kingdom. In the 9th and 10th centuries it was a part of Lotharingia, and later of the duchy of Swabia, and gradually came to be divided between imperial cities, bishops, and other rulers. Part of it was conquered by France in the Thirty Years' War, and ceded to her in 1648. Strasbourg was seized by Louis XIV in 1681, and the remainder of Alsace was annexed to France in 1791. It was ceded to Germany in 1871 as a result of the Franco-Prussian War. Returned to France (1919) by the treaty of Versailles, it was occupied by German forces in 1940 and held until 1945.

Alsace, Lower. [German, **Unter-Elsass.**] District of the former German province of Alsace-Lorraine, occupying the N portion of Alsace. The chief city is Strasbourg (German, Strassburg).

Alsace, Upper. [German, **Ober-Elsass.**] District of the former German province of Alsace-Lorraine, occupying the S portion of Alsace. Its chief city is Mulhouse (German, Mülhausen).

Alsace-Lorraine (al′sās.lọ.rān′, al′sas-; French, ȧl.zȧs-lo.ren). [German, **Elsass-Lothringen.**] Region in E France, from 1871 to 1918 a *Reichsland* (imperial territory) of the German Empire, capital Strasbourg, bounded by Luxemburg, Prussia, and the Rhine Palatinate on the N, by Baden (from which it is separated by the Rhine) on the E, by Switzerland and France on the S, and by France on the W. It is traversed by the Vosges mountains; the soil is generally fertile, producing grain, wine, tobacco, and other agricultural products, and it has important iron and coal mines, and large manufactures of iron, cotton, and other items. It was divided under German rule into three districts: Upper Alsace, Lower Alsace, and Lorraine. By the constitution granted in May, 1911, it was ruled by a governor and a Diet of two chambers, and sent 3 members to the Bundesrath and 15 deputies to the Reichstag. The prevailing religion (about 78 percent of the population) is Roman Catholic. Both German and French are spoken. It was ceded by France to Germany in 1871, as a result of the Franco-Prussian War. Restored to France (1919) by the Treaty of Versailles, it was occupied (1940–45) by Germany in World War II. Area, 5,604 sq. mi.

Alsager (al′sạ.jėr). Urban district in W England, in Cheshire, ab. 6 mi. E of Crewe, ab. 154 mi. NW of London by rail. 5,574 (1951).

Alsatia (al.sā′shạ). Formerly a cant name (Alsace being a debatable ground or scene of frequent contests) for Whitefriars, a district in London between the Thames and Fleet Street, and adjoining the Temple, which possessed certain privileges of sanctuary derived from the convent of the Carmelites, or White Friars, founded there in 1241. The locality became the resort of libertines and rascals of every description, whose abuses and outrages, and especially the riot in the reign of Charles II, led in 1697 to the abolition of the privilege and the dispersion of the Alsatians. The term "Alsatia" was later applied offensively to the English stock-exchange, because of the supposedly questionable character of some of its proceedings. The name first occurs in Shadwell's plays *The Woman Captain* (1680) and *The Squire of Alsatia* (1688).

Alsatia. Latin name of **Alsace.**

Alsberg (als′bėrg), **Carl Lucas.** b. at New York, April 2, 1877; d. at Berkeley, Calif., Nov. 1, 1940. American biochemist, a specialist in the chemistry of foods. He headed (1921–37) the Stanford Food Research Institute, and was director (1937 *et seq.*) of the Giannini Agricultural Economics Foundation at the University of California.

Alsdorf (äls′dôrf). Town in W Germany, in the *Land* (state) of North Rhine-Westphalia, British Zone, formerly in the Rhine Province, Prussia, situated near the Dutch border, ab. 10 mi. N of Aachen. It has chemical and paper manufactures; coal mines are in the vicinity. The town suffered considerable damage during World War II. The population is predominantly Roman Catholic. 22,205 (1950).

Alsen (äl′zẹn). German name of **Als.**

Alsfeld (äls′felt). Town in W Germany, in the *Land* (state) of Hessen, American Zone, formerly in the province of Upper Hesse, grand duchy of Hesse, situated on the Schwalm River, ab. 41 mi. SW of Kassel. It has cotton and linen textile industries, considerable lumber trade, and furniture factories. Architectural points of interest include the remains of medieval fortifications and numerous old buildings, among them the *Rathaus* (town hall; 1512–16), the Wine House (1533), and the Wedding-Hall (1565–71); the Walpurgis Church and Holy Trinity Church are in the Gothic style. There is also a local museum and a library. The population is predominantly Protestant. 8,191 (1946).

Alshain (al.shān′). A seldom-used name for the fourth-magnitude star β Aquilae.

Alshemali (al.shẹ.mä′li). The fourth-magnitude star μ Leonis, in the head of the animal.

Al Sirat (äl si.rät′). Bridge over which must pass all who enter the Mohammedan paradise. It is of inconceivable narrowness, finer than the edge of a razor; hence those burdened by sins are sure to fall off and are dashed into hell, which lies below the bridge. A somewhat similar conception has occurred at various times in other theologies, most notably the Jewish and that of the Zoroastrians.

Alsleben (äls'lā"bẹn). Town in C Germany, in the *Land* (state) of Saxony-Anhalt, Russian Zone, formerly in the province of Saxony, Prussia, situated on the Saale River, ab. 30 mi. S of Magdeburg. Before World War II it had important flour mills, sugar refineries, and manufactures of building materials. The population is predominantly Protestant. 5,066 (1946).

Alsop (ôl'sọp), **George.** b. 1638; date of death not known. English colonist in America, remembered chiefly as the author of an early work about the Maryland colony.

Alsop, Richard. b. at Middletown, Conn., Jan. 23, 1761; d. at Flatbush (now part of Brooklyn), N.Y., Aug. 20, 1815. American writer, particularly of antidemocratic satire; one of the "Hartford Wits," also called "Connecticut Wits," a literary group interested in the growth of indigenous American writing. The author of adaptations from European writers and of eclectic poetry, he is best remembered for *The Echo*, on which he collaborated with Theodore Dwight (in *American Mercury*, 1791–1805; published 1807), a satire in verse on John Hancock, Samuel Adams, and others, and *The Political Greenhouse* (1798), a similar work.

Alsop, Vincent. d. May 8, 1703. English nonconformist divine and controversialist. Author of *Antisozzo* (1675), *Melius Inquirendum* (1679), *Mischief of Impositions* (1680), and others.

Alstaetten (äl'shtet.ẹn). See **Altstätten.**

Alsted (äl'shtet), **Johann Heinrich.** b. at Ballersbach, near Herborn, Prussia, 1588; d. at Weissenburg, in Transylvania, Nov. 8, 1638. German Protestant theologian and writer. Professor of philosophy (1615) and theology (1619) at Herborn, and later at Weissenburg. His *Encyclopaedia* (1630) was highly esteemed for several generations after his death.

Alster (äl'stėr). River in NW Germany, a small tributary of the Elbe, which traverses Hamburg, forming two basins, one (the larger) outside the town (Aussen Alster), and one within it (Binnen Alster). Before World War II the latter was surrounded with fine buildings and was a favorite pleasure resort.

Alston (ôl'stọn). [Also: **Aldstone, Alston** (or **Aldstone**) **Moor, Alston with Garrigill** (gar'i.gil).] Rural district and market town in NW England, in Cumberland, ab. 20 mi. SE of Carlisle, ab. 319 mi. NW of London by rail. It was formerly a lead-mining center. 2,327 (1951).

Alston, Joseph. b. in South Carolina, c1779; d. Sept. 10, 1816. American politician and rice-planter; son-in-law of Aaron Burr. He was governor (1812–14) of South Carolina, and a strong supporter of the War of 1812.

Alströmer (äl'strė"mėr), **Jonas.** [Also, **Alstroemer.**] b. at Alingsås, Sweden, Jan. 7, 1685; d. June 2, 1761. Swedish merchant, philanthropist, and pioneer industrialist. He went (1707) to London as clerk to a Swedish merchant, and later amassed (1710–24) a fortune through independent activity as a London ship-broker. He returned to Alingsås and established successively a woolen factory, a sugar refinery, and a business in sheep importation to improve the breeds in Sweden. He developed improved techniques of potato cultivation, textile dyeing, shipbuilding, tanning, and cutlery manufacture.

Alt (ält). See **Olt.**

Alta Fjord (äl'tä). See **Alten Fjord.**

Alta Gracia (grä'syä). City in C Argentina, in Córdoba province: principal resort in the Sierras. 11,570 (1947).

Altai (äl.tī'). Mountain system in E central Asia, which lies partly in the S central Russian Soviet Federated Socialist Republic, and continues SE into Outer Mongolia and the province of Sinkiang, China. The main range is also known as the Ektag Altai. Length, ab. 1,000 mi. The highest known elevation, the Belukha (White Mountain), reaches 14,783 ft.

Altaic (al.tā'ik). Linguistic group inconclusively set up to include Turkic, Mongol, Tungus-Manchu, and, recently, Korean.

Altair (al.tār') or **Atair** (a-). The first-magnitude star α Aquilae.

Altai Territory (äl.tī'). [Also, **Altai Mining District.**] Territory of the U.S.S.R., a *krai* (subdivision) of the Russian Soviet Federated Socialist Republic, C Asia, ab. 1,000 mi. W of Lake Baikal. It is noted for its mineral wealth. Area, ab. 101,000 sq. mi.; pop. 2,358,653 (1939).

Altamaha (ôl"tạ.mạ.hô'). River in Georgia which is formed by the junction of the Oconee and Ocmulgee rivers, and flows into the Atlantic ab. 55 mi. SW of Savannah. Length, ab. 137 mi.

Altamira (äl.tä.mē'rä). Caverns in N Spain, SW of Santander, in which were discovered (1879) a number of prehistoric drawings of animals (most of which are recognizable as bulls). This was the first discovery of an example of prehistoric art of the cave-dweller period and still ranks as one of the major archaeological findings of all time.

Altamirano (äl"tä.mē.rä'nō), **Ignacio Manuel.** b. in Guerrero, Mexico, c1834; d. at San Remo, Italy, Feb. 14, 1893. Mexican poet, orator, and journalist, said to have been a descendant of the Aztec monarchs. He was a member of the constituent congress of 1861; joined the army under Juárez during the French invasion, attaining the rank of colonel. Author of *Clemencia* (1869), *Rimas* (1871), *La Navidad en las montañas* (1871), and others. His *El Zarco*: *Episodios de la vida mexicana en 1861–63* was republished (1935) at New York.

Altamira y Crevea (äl.tä.mē'rä ē krā.ᴃā'ä), **Rafael.** b. 1866—. Spanish jurist and historian. He taught the history of Spanish law at Oviedo (1897–1910) and the history of American political and civil institutions at Madrid (1914–36). He was also on the bench (1922–45) of the Permanent Court of International Justice. Author of numerous works in the fields of Spanish and Spanish-American law and political history.

Altamont (al'tạ.mont). Unincorporated community in S Oregon, in Klamath County. 9,419 (1950).

Altamont. In Nicholas Rowe's play *The Fair Penitent*, the husband of Calista.

Altamont. In W. M. Thackeray's novel *Pendennis*, the name assumed by the returned convict Amory. He is the first husband of Lady Clavering and father of the emotional Blanche Amory.

Altamont. In Thomas Wolfe's *Look Homeward, Angel*, the name of the town in which the chief events of the novel take place. It is used, but less frequently, in Wolfe's later novels as the hero's point of return from the great cities of the world. It is now generally conceded to be, in real life, the city of Asheville, N.C., which was Wolfe's birthplace.

Altamura (äl.tä.mö'rä). [Ancient name, **Lupatia.**] City and commune in SW Italy, in the *compartimento* (region) of Apulia, in the province of Bari, ab. 28 mi. SW of Bari. It is the center of a rich agricultural district, producing grain, wine, fruit, and livestock. The cathedral, begun by Emperor Frederick II in 1232 and built in Romanesque style, has a beautiful Gothic portal dating from the 16th century. Pop. of commune, 31,431 (1936); of city, 31,099 (1936).

Altan Bulak (äl.tän' bö.läk'). [Also: **Altan-Bulag, Kiachta, Kyakhta;** former name, **Maimachin, Maimaichin, Maimatchin.**] Town in the Mongolian People's Republic, ab. 100 mi. S of Lake Baikal, on the Siberian frontier opposite Kyakhta, U.S.S.R. It is one of the most active commercial centers of the nation, being on a main trade route to the U.S.S.R. The chief exports are wool and meat products. Pop. ab. 20,000.

Altar (äl.tär'). [Also: **Altar de Collanes** (dā kō.yä'näs), **Capac-Urcu.**] Extinct volcano in the Andes of Ecuador, E of Riobamba. 17,725 ft.

Altaroche (äl.tȧ.rosh), **Marie Michel.** b. at Issoire, France, April 18, 1811; d. at Vaux, France, May 14, 1884. French journalist, poet, and dramatist. He edited *Charivari.*

Altar of Righteousness, The. Poem by Algernon Charles Swinburne. The burden of this poem is Swinburne's belief in his later years that there is no star to guide a man "save his own soul." It is probably now notable not so much for its subject matter as for being Swinburne's last poem before his death in 1909.

Altar of the Dead, The. Short story (1909) by Henry James, one of his stories of the occult.

Altar-Piece, The. Novel by Naomi Royde-Smith, published in 1939.

Altar Steps, The. Novel by Compton Mackenzie, published in 1922. The first of a trilogy, it deals with the spiritual development of Mark Lidderdale, an Anglican minister. His story is continued in *The Parson's Progress* (1923) and *The Heavenly Ladder* (1924).

Alt-Aussee (ält'ous'zā). Town in C Austria, in the northernmost part of Styria, in the Salzkammergut region, situated on the lake of Alt-Aussee. It is a summer resort. The author Jakob Wassermann lived here. 2,707 (1946).

Alta Verapaz (äl'tä BĀ.rä.päs'). Department in C Guatemala. Capital, Cobán; area, 4,472 sq. mi.; pop. 194,321 (1950).

Altavilla (al.tą.vil'ą). Roman name of **Eltville.**

Altavista (al.tą.vis'tą). Town in S Virginia, in Campbell County, on the Roanoke River. Manufactures include rayon and cedar chests. 3,332 (1950).

Alt-Breisach (ält"brī'zäch). See **Breisach.**

Altdorf (ält'dôrf). [Also, **Altorf.**] Town in S Germany, in the *Land* (state) of Bavaria, American Zone, in the *Regierungsbezirk* (government district) of Middle and Upper Franconia, situated on the Schwarzach River, ab. 13 mi. SE of Nuremberg: seat of an agricultural school. A university located here from 1623 to 1814 was united in the latter year with the University of Erlangen. Wallenstein was among its students. Altdorf belonged to the city of Nuremberg from 1505 to 1806. The population is predominantly Protestant. 5,306 (1946).

Altdorf. [Also, **Altorf.**] Capital of the canton of Uri, in C Switzerland, situated near the Reuss River and near the SE extremity of the Lake of Lucerne, on the St. Gotthard route, ab. 20 mi. SE of Lucerne, in the center of a fruit-growing district. It is the locale of the legends of William Tell, to whom a statue was erected here in 1861. Friedrich Schiller's dramatic play *Wilhelm Tell* is performed annually by residents of Altdorf at the William Tell Theater. 5,692 (1941).

Altdorfer (ält'dôr"fėr), **Albrecht.** b. probably at Regensburg, Bavaria, c1480; d. there, 1538. German engraver, landscape painter, and architect for the city of Regensburg; one of the "Little Masters" (a name given to a group of 16th-century German artists, all of them followers of Dürer). One of his most important paintings is *The Battle of Arbela* (1529), which is in the collection of the Pinakothek at Munich; a collection of his etchings and engravings is at Regensburg. His style was close to that of Dürer, with whom many scholars believe he may have studied.

Alte Fritz (ält'ę frits), **Der.** See **Frederick II** (of *Prussia*).

Alten (äl'tęn), Count **Karl August von.** b. at Burgwedel, near Hanover, Germany, Oct. 20, 1764; d. at Bozen, in the Tirol, April 20, 1840. Hanoverian soldier whose service in the British army won him the rank of major general. He served with the "German Legion" against Napoleon Bonaparte; campaigned under Sir John Moore and the Duke of Wellington in the Peninsular campaign; and was wounded at Waterloo. He later returned (1818) to Hanover, where he attained the rank of field marshal, and held posts as minister of war and foreign affairs.

Altena (äl'tę.nä). Town in W Germany, in the *Land* (state) of North Rhine-Westphalia, British Zone, formerly in the province of Westphalia, Prussia, situated on the Lenne River, ab. 40 mi. NE of Cologne: important iron and steel manufactures, particularly of wire, needles, nails, and screws; also instruments, cotton textiles, shoes, and leather goods. The castle above the town, built in 1122, belonged formerly to the counts of Mark; it contains the local museum of the Sauerland. The important Thomée Collection of medieval paintings and sculptures remained intact during World War II. The population is predominantly Protestant. 22,162 (1950).

Altenahr (äl'tęn.är). Village in W Germany, in the *Land* (state) of Rhineland-Palatinate, French Zone, formerly in the Rhine Province, Prussia, situated on the Ahr River, ab. 30 mi. S of Cologne: wine culture; summer resort. The castle, built in the 10th century, was destroyed by the archbishop of Cologne in 1714. The population is predominantly Roman Catholic. 1,402 (1946).

Altenberg (äl'tęn.berk). Town in C Germany, in the *Land* (state) of Saxony, Russian Zone, situated in the Erzgebirge, ab. 21 mi. S of Dresden: noted for its bismuth mines; in former centuries also a tin-mining center. The population is predominantly Protestant. 1,796 (1946).

Altenberg, Peter. [Pseudonym of **Richard Engländer.**] b. at Vienna, March 9, 1859; d. there, Jan. 8, 1919. Austrian author and publisher.

Altenburg (äl'tęn.bu̇rk). City in C Germany, in the *Land* (state) of Thuringia, Russian Zone, situated near the Pleisse River, ab. 25 mi. S of Leipzig. Before World War II it had important grain and livestock trade, specialized in the manufacture of playing cards, and also manufactured gloves, hats, brushes, chemicals, and cotton textiles. The *Rathaus* (town hall) is a Renaissance building built in 1562–64. High above the city is the castle, built in the 15th century, which was until 1919 the residence of the ruling dukes of Saxe-Altenburg; now it is a local and archaeological museum. There is also a museum of natural history and an art museum, a library, and various educational institutions. One of the oldest towns in the region, it was first mentioned in 976, became an imperial city in the 12th century, and came under the house of Wettin in 1329. It was burnt down by the Hussites in 1430; scene of the "robbery of the princes" in 1455, and of the religious disputation of Altenburg between Philippists and Lutherans in 1568–69; twice capital (1603–72 and 1826–1918) of the duchy of Saxe-Altenburg; incorporated into the newly formed state of Thuringia in 1918. Pop. 51,805 (1946).

Alten Fjord (äl'tęn). [Also, **Alta Fjord.**] Fjord on the N coast of Norway.

Altenkirchen (äl'tęn.kir.chęn). [Also, **Altenkirchen im Westerwald** (im ves'tėr.vält).] Town in W Germany, in the *Land* (state) of Rhineland-Palatinate, French Zone, formerly in the Rhine Province, Prussia, situated on the Wied River, ab. 34 mi. SE of Cologne: manufactures wooden and rubber articles; agricultural trade. The French and Austrians twice fought near here in 1796. Pop. 3,567 (1946).

Alten-Ötting (äl'tęn.ėt'ing). See **Altötting.**

Altenstein (äl'tęn.shtīn). Summer castle of the dukes of Saxe-Meiningen, in the Thuringian forest ab. 10 mi. S of Eisenach, connected with the histories of the English Benedictine missionary, Saint Boniface, and of Luther (1521).

Altenstein, Karl. [Title, Baron **von Stein zum Altenstein.**] b. at Anspach, Bavaria, Oct. 7, 1770; d. at Berlin, May 14, 1840. Prussian minister of finance (1808–10) and of public worship (1817–38).

Altenzelle (äl'tęn.tsel.ę). Former Cistercian monastery near Nossen, in Saxony, secularized in 1544.

Alter (ôl'tėr), **David.** b. in Westmoreland County, Pa., Dec. 3, 1807; d. Sept. 18, 1881. American physicist and physician, noted for his work in the field of spectrum analysis. His discovery that elemental gases have dissimilar spectra permitted the spectroscopic determination of their chemical nature. This discovery, now incorporated in the second of Kirchhoff's Laws, has led some biographers to make undeserved charges of theft against Kirchhoff, despite the fact that Alter himself never suggested such a possibility and seems to have been at first incompletely aware of the true import of his work.

Alterf (al.tėrf'). The seldom-used name of the fourth-magnitude star λ Leonis, in the mouth of the animal.

Altgeld (ält'gelt, ôlt'geld), **John Peter.** b. at Nieder Selters, Germany, Dec. 30, 1847; d. at Joliet, Ill., March 12, 1902. American politician. He was a judge (1886–91) of the Superior Court of Cook County, Ill. As Democratic governor (1892–96) of Illinois he attracted wide attention by his pardon in 1893 of Neebe, Schwab, and Fielden, anarchists concerned in the Haymarket riot (1886) at Chicago. He protested Cleveland's use of the army in the Pullman strike (1894); was a prominent advocate of free coinage of silver and a supporter of William Jennings Bryan for the Presidency in 1896 and 1900. Author of *Our Penal Machinery and its Victims* (1884), *Live Questions* (1890), and others.

Althaea or **Althea** (al.thē'ą). In Greek legend, a daughter of Thestius, wife of Oneus, king of Calydon, and mother of Tydeus, Meleager, and Deïaneira.

Altham (ôlt′ham), **John.** [Original name possibly **Gravenor** or **Grosvenor.**] b. 1589; d. in Maryland, 1640. English Jesuit missionary, active in the establishment of the Maryland colony. He sailed (1633) from England with 220 people in Leonard Calvert's Maryland expedition and later served as missionary to the Indians, among whom he achieved great influence.

Althea (al.thē′a). Name by which Richard Lovelace poetically addressed a woman, supposed to have been Lucy Sacheverell, whom he also celebrated by the name of Lucasta.

Althen (French, ȧl.täṅ), **Jehan** or **Jean.** b. in Persia; d. in France, 1774. Persian aristocrat, son of the governor of a Persian province, who introduced the cultivation of madder into France. Captured by the Turks and sold as a slave at Smyrna, he made his escape to France with some seeds of madder, the exportation of which was at that time forbidden under penalty of death.

Althing (äl′thing). Name of the parliament of Iceland. It is notable as the oldest European parliamentary body in existence, dating (although not as a continuously active body) from 930 A.D. Its most important act in recent years, from an international point of view, was to vote the independence of Iceland from Denmark in 1944. Its name (which means "general assembly" in Icelandic) is derived from the same original root as the word "Thing," which still has generic usage as the name of parliaments, assemblies, or diets in Scandinavian-speaking countries.

Althouse (ôlt′hous″), **Paul Shearer.** b. at Reading, Pa., 1889—. American operatic and concert tenor. He was the first singer trained entirely in the U.S. to obtain leading roles at the Metropolitan Opera, where he made his debut in 1913.

Altichiero da Zevio (äl.tē.kye′rō dä dze′vyō). [Also, **Aldighero da Zevio.**] b. at Zevio, near Verona, Italy, c1320; d. c1385. Italian painter of the Veronese school.

Altieri (äl.tye′rē), **Emilio.** Original name of Pope **Clement X.**

Altilia (äl.tē′lyä). [Ancient name, **Saepinum.**] Small place in C Italy ab. 20 mi. N of Benevento. The Roman walls of the ancient town (the Samnite Saepinum), ab. 2 mi. from the modern site, remain practically perfect.

Alting (äl′ting), **Johann Heinrich.** b. at Emden, Prussia, Feb. 17, 1583; d. at Groningen, Aug. 25, 1644. German Protestant theologian, professor of dogmatics (1613) at Heidelberg and later of theology (1627) at Groningen. He opposed the Remonstrants in the synod of Dordrecht.

Altin Tagh (äl′tin täg). See **Altyn Tagh.**

Altiplano de México (äl.tē.plä′nō dā me′hē.kō). Spanish name of the **Mexican Plateau.**

Altisidora (äl″tē.sē.dō′rä). Character in the "Curious Impertinent," an episode in Cervantes' *Don Quixote.* An attendant of the duchess, she torments Don Quixote by pretending to be in love with him.

Altkirch (ält′kirċh). Town in E France, in the department of Haut-Rhin (formerly Upper Alsace), situated on the Ill River ab. 18 mi. NW of Basel, Switzerland. The chief place in the old Sundgau district, it has remnants of medieval fortifications. Cotton textiles are the principal manufactures. 3,807 (1946).

Altman (ôlt′man), **Benjamin.** b. at New York, July 12, 1840; d. there, Oct. 7, 1913. American merchant, philanthropist, and art patron. Following small independent ventures and partnerships, he opened (1906) a store at the NE corner of Fifth Ave. and 34th St., which is the site of the present-day department store bearing his name. He was characterized by John Wanamaker as the first among New York's retail merchants. He established also the Altman Foundation to aid the welfare of employees, and amassed a collection of works of art which was appraised at 20 million dollars when it was given to the Metropolitan Museum at New York.

Altmark (ält′märk). See under **Nordmark.**

Altmark Incident. Famous international incident in World War II involving the *Altmark*, a German auxiliary cruiser, which was discovered by the British in February, 1940, in Norwegian territorial waters. Believed to be carrying British prisoners, the *Altmark* was boarded on Feb. 19, 1940, by sailors from the British destroyer *Cossack* despite protests by the Norwegians. The British prisoners found aboard were freed and returned to England on the *Cossack.*

Altmeyer (ôlt′mī″ėr), **Arthur Joseph.** b. at De Pere, Wis., May 8, 1891—. American public servant and teacher. A high-school teacher (1914–16) and principal (1916–18), Wisconsin state official (1918–33), and federal government official (1933 *et seq.*), he became, in 1937, chairman of the Social Security Board.

Altmeyer (ält′mī″ėr), **Jean Jacques.** b. at Luxembourg, Jan. 24, 1804; d. at Brussels, Sept. 15, 1877. Belgian historian. Among his works are *Histoire des relations commerciales et politiques des Pays-Bas*, *Résumé de l'histoire moderne* (1842), and various works on Dutch and Belgian history.

Altmühl (ält′mül). [Latin, **Alcimona, Alcmona.**] River in SE Germany, in Bavaria, which joins the Danube at Kelheim ab. 14 mi. SW of Regensburg. It crosses the Franconian Jura and is connected with the Main River system by the Ludwigs-Canal at Dietfurt. Length, ab. 125 mi.

Altmünster (ält′mün″stėr). [Also, **Altmuenster.**] Village in C Austria, in the province of Upper Austria, situated on the W side of the Traunsee, SW of Gmunden. It is a summer resort. 7,566 (1946).

Alto Alentejo (äl′tö ä.lān.tā′zhö). Province of Portugal, bounded by Beira Baixa, Ribatejo, and Estremadura on the NW, W, and SW, by Baixo Alentejo on the S, and by Spain on the E. It comprises the districts of Portalegre and Évora. Wine, grain, and cork are among the chief agricultural products; minerals including copper, iron ore, and manganese are also important. Capital, Évora; area, 5,219 sq. mi.; pop. 375,511 (1940).

Alton (ôl′ton). Urban district and market town in S England, in Southampton (an administrative county of the geographical county of Hampshire), ab. 47 mi. SW of London by rail. 8,636 (1951).

Alton. City in SW Illinois, in Madison County, on the Mississippi River, ab. 21 mi. N of St. Louis. Important manufactures include glass, lead, steel, and chemicals. It is the seat of Shurtleff College. The seventh and final Lincoln-Douglas debate took place at Alton on Oct. 15, 1858. Pop. 32,550 (1950).

Alton (däl′ton), **Johann Wilhelm Eduard d'.** b. at Aquileia, Austria-Hungary (now in Italy), Aug. 11, 1772; d. at Bonn, Prussia, May 11, 1840. German naturalist and engraver, author of *Naturgeschichte des Pferdes* (1810) and *Vergleichende Osteologie* (1821–31).

Altona (äl′tō.nä). Former city in NW Germany, in the *Land* (state) of Hamburg, British Zone, formerly in Schleswig-Holstein province, Prussia, situated on the right bank of the Elbe River below Hamburg: a part of Hamburg since 1937. It has extensive trade and numerous manufactures, particularly of foodstuffs and textiles, as well as fish and livestock markets. Altona received town privileges through King Frederick III of Denmark (1664), was burned down by the Swedes in 1713, and came under Prussian rule in 1866. Extensive damage was done to the community in World War II.

Altoona (al.tö′na). City in S Pennsylvania, in Blair County, at the base of the Allegheny Mountains: important for its railroad shops; manufactures silk and rayon textiles. Horseshoe Curve, where the Pennsylvania Railroad ascends the Allegheny plateau, is nearby. The curve, a noted engineering feat, has a central angle of 220° and is graded 91 ft. to the mile. It was constructed in 1852 and is 2,375 ft. long. Pop. of city, 77,177 (1950); of urbanized area, 86,614 (1950).

Alto Perú (äl′tō pā.rö′). Spanish name of Upper Peru; see **Charcas.**

Altorf (äl′tôrf). See **Altdorf.**

Altos (äl′tōs). City in S Paraguay, in Cordillera department. 11,000 (est.).

Altötting (ält′ėt″ing). [Also, **Alten-Ötting.**] Town in S Germany, in the *Land* (state) of Bavaria, American Zone, in the *Kreis* (district) of Upper Bavaria, situated near the Inn River and the Austrian border, ab. 50 mi. NE of Munich: machine industry and agricultural trade. It is a famous place of pilgrimage. The black, wood-carved statue of the Holy Virgin, contained in a silver tabernaculum in the Romanesque Holy Chapel, is considered to have miraculous properties; the hearts of the rulers of Bavaria, since the elector Maximilian I, are preserved in silver vessels. The parish church contains a treasury and the tomb of the field marshal Johann Tserclaes Tilly; the Jesuit Church of Mary Magdalene, built in 1593, is in the baroque style. 8,529 (1946).

Altranstädt (ält'rän''shtet). Village in C Germany, in the *Land* (state) of Saxony-Anhalt, Russian Zone, formerly in Prussian Saxony, ab. 9 mi. SE of Merseburg. Here a treaty was concluded (1706) between Charles XII of Sweden and Augustus II of Saxony, by which the latter lost Poland. A treaty was also made here in 1707, between Charles XII of Sweden and Emperor Joseph I of Austria, by which religious toleration was secured for the Protestants in Silesia. 1,817 (1946).

Altrincham (ôl'tring.ạm). [Also, **Altringham.**] Municipal borough in W England, in Cheshire, ab. 8 mi. SW of Manchester, ab. 185 mi. NW of London by rail. 39,787 (1951).

Altringer (ält'ring.ėr), Count **Johann.** See **Aldringen,** Count **Johann.**

Altruria (al.trö'ri.ạ). Imaginary commonwealth, the government and institutions of which are founded upon the principles of altruism. William Dean Howells described such a community in his book *A Traveler from Altruria* (1894). The practical application of the principles resulted in the abolition of monopoly and competition and the establishing of social and economic equality.

Altschuler (ält'shö''lėr), **Modest.** b. at Mogilev, Russia, 1873—. Russian cellist and symphony conductor. After studying (1884–86) at the Warsaw Conservatory, he came to the U.S. and organized (1903) the Russian Symphony Orchestra, which gave (1904–20) concerts under his baton at New York and elsewhere.

Altsheler (ôlt'shel'ėr), **Joseph Alexander.** b. at Three Springs, Ky., April 29, 1862; d. June 5, 1919. American editor and author of six series of historical novels for boys. He was on the staff of the New York *World* from 1892 on, for which publication he wrote his first adventure story when no other suitable tale could be obtained.

Altstätten (ält'shtet''ẹn). [Also: **Alstaetten, Altstädten, Altstetten.**] Town in NE Switzerland, in the canton of St. Gallen, near the Rhine River, S of Rorschach. It has cotton manufactures. 8,213 (1941).

Altstrelitz (ält'shtrā''lits). [Also, **Strelitz.**] Town in N Germany, once capital of the duchy of Mecklenburg-Strelitz, situated S of Neustrelitz, which replaced it as capital in the 18th century.

Alturas (al.tůr'ạs). City in NE California, on the Pit River, county seat of Modoc County. It is a trading center for the lumber and agricultural products of the area. 2,819 (1950).

Altus (al'tus). City in SW Oklahoma, in Jackson County: marketing center for a petroleum and cotton producing region. 9,735 (1950).

Altvater Mountains (ält'fä''tėr). [Also, **Moravian Snow Mountains.**] Group of mountains in the Sudetic system, situated in N Moravia, Czechoslovakia. Highest point, Gross Altvater, ab. 4,850 ft.

Altyn Tagh (äl'tin täg). [Also: **Altin Tagh, Astin Tagh.**] Mountain system in W China, between Sinkiang and Tibet, running generally E to W and arching N. It forms the S boundary of the Takla Makan desert, extending for 700 mi. and reaching a height of 19,728 ft.

Aludra (al.ö'drạ). The third-magnitude star η Canis Majoris.

Alula Borealis and Alula Australis (al'ū̦.lạ bō.rẹ.al'is; ôs.trā'lis). The two fourth-magnitude stars ν and ξ Ursae Majoris, which mark the S hind foot of the beast. Xi, which is a fine binary star with a period of only 59.8 years, is also known as El Acola.

Alumbagh (ạ.lum'bäg). See **Alambagh.**

Alungu (ä.löng'gö). [Also: **Ulungu, Urungu.**] District of Northern Rhodesia, C Africa, S and SE of Lake Tanganyika.

Alunno (ä.lön'nō), **Niccolò.** [Original name, **Niccolò di Liberatore.**] b. at Foligno, Italy, c1430; d. 1502. Umbrian painter, believed by some scholars to have been the teacher of Perugino and Pinturicchio. His work consisted largely of banners for religious processions, and altarpieces.

Alur (ä.lör'). [Also: **Aluri** (-lö'rē), **Jo Alur, Lur.**] Nilotic-speaking people of E Africa, in NW Uganda and NE Belgian Congo, inhabiting an area N of Lake Albert and W of the branch of the Nile deriving from Lake Albert. Their population is estimated at 140,000 (by M. A. Bryan, *Distribution of the Nilotic and Nilo-Hamitic Languages of Africa*, 1948). Culturally and linguistically they resemble the Lango and Shilluk.

Alured of Beverley (al'ū̦.red). See **Alfred of Beverley.**

Aluredus Beverlacensis (al.ū̦.rē'dus bev''ėr.lạ.sen'sis). See **Alfred of Beverley.**

Aluta (o.lů'to). See **Olt.**

Alva (äl'ʙä; Anglicized, al'vạ), Duke of. [Also: Duke of **Alba;** birth name, **Fernando Alvarez de Toledo.**] b. 1508; d. c1582. Spanish general and governor of the Netherlands (1567–73). He served as an officer under Charles V from the siege of Tunis (1535) through the victory at Mühlberg (1547) over Elector John of Saxony, and as commander in chief (1553 *et seq.*) in Italy. He was appointed by Philip II of Spain after the abdication of Charles V to suppress the revolt in the Netherlands, which he put down with ruthlessness until checked (1572 *et seq.*) by the prince of Orange, William I of Nassau ("William the Silent"). His Council of Troubles (known popularly as the Council of Blood) imposed death sentences on leading patriots of the Netherlands, including Counts Egmont, Hoorn, and others, and reaching a total of approximately 18,000 persons by the end of his regime. He fell from favor on his return to Spain, but was recalled (1580) to head the attack on Portugal which resulted in the collapse of the Portuguese government and a massacre of the Lisbon populace.

Alva (al'vạ). City in NW Oklahoma, county seat of Woods County. It was designated a land-office town when the Cherokee Strip was opened (1893) for settlement; named for Alva Adams, a governor of Colorado. 6,505 (1950).

Alvan (al'vạn), **Sigismund.** In George Meredith's novel, *The Tragic Comedians* (1880), the fictional name of Ferdinand Lassalle.

Alvarado (äl.ʙä.rä'ᴛʜō), **Alonso de.** b. at Burgos, Spain, c1490; d. in Peru, c1556. Spanish cavalier who joined (1518) Hernando Cortés in the conquest (1519–21) of Mexico. With Pedro de Alvarado he went (1534) to Peru, where he remained with Francisco Pizarro. Defeated (July 12, 1537) by Pizarro's enemy, Diego de Almagro, at Abancay, he revenged himself (April 26, 1538) when Almagro was in turn defeated by him at Las Salinas.

Alvarado, Diego de. d. in Spain, 1540. Spanish soldier. He is believed to have been either a brother or an uncle of Pedro de Alvarado, who went with him to Peru in 1534.

Alvarado, Juan Bautista. b. at Monterey, California, 1809; d. 1882. Mexican politician. He was governor (1836–42) of California, at a time when that area, although technically still Mexican, was in fact virtually independent of the mother country. His period of authority saw the decay of political power which facilitated acquisition of California by the U.S. a few years later.

Alvarado, Pedro de. [Called by the Indians **"Tonatiuh,"** a Nahuatl word meaning "sun," in allusion to his ruddy complexion and blond hair and beard.] b. in Badajoz, Spain, 1485; d. at Guadalajara, Mexico, June 4, 1541. Spanish cavalier, famous as a companion of Hernando Cortés in the conquest of Mexico. He went to the West Indies in 1510, and in 1511 joined the expedition of Diego Velasquez (c1465–1522) to Cuba, where he received a grant of land. In 1518 he commanded a vessel in the expedition of Grijalva to Yucatán, and in the following year followed Cortés in the Mexican conquest. He was present at the seizure of Montezuma, and when Cortés went to the coast to meet Pánfilo de Narvaez, Alvarado was left in command of the force at what is now Mexico City. During Cortés's absence the Mexicans rose and besieged the Spaniards. In the disastrous nocturnal retreat (the *noche triste,* of July 1, 1520), Alvarado commanded the rear guard and escaped with difficulty, saving his life, according to the tradition, by leaping across a great gap in the causeway, at the spot later called "Alvarado's Leap." In the subsequent operations and the siege of Mexico he took a prominent part. In December, 1523, he was sent with 420 Spaniards and a large force of Indians to conquer Guatemala; after a desperate battle with the Quiché Indians near Quezaltenango, he marched to Utitlán and burned that town, after conquering the inhabitants, in April, 1524. He defeated another army near Lake Atitlán, and founded the old city of Guatemala, on July 25, 1524. He returned (1527) to Spain to meet charges of defrauding the royal treasury, but was acquitted, and went back to Guatemala in 1530 as governor, with a large number of colonists. In 1534 he headed an expedition of 400 men against Quito, claiming that the region was not included in the grant made to Pizarro, and was thus open to conquest. Landing on the coast, he led his men over the mountains in a terrible march, during which large numbers of them perished. Near Riobamba he met the forces of Almagro and Sebastián de Benalcazar, and was induced to retire, receiving, it is said, a large sum of gold from Pizarro. Returning to Guatemala, he took part in the conquest of Honduras, which was added to the territory under his control as governor. In 1540 he went to Mexico, was engaged in subduing a revolt in Jalisco, and died there from a fall with his horse.

Alvarenga (äl.vą.rāng′gą), **Manuel Inácio da Silva.** b. at Vila Rica (now Ouro Preto) or at São Joao del-Rei, Brazil, 1749; d. at Rio de Janeiro, Nov. 1, 1814. Brazilian poet, best remembered for his *Glaura: poemas eróticos* (1799), and considered by some critics to have been a forerunner of romanticism in Brazil. He studied law (1771–76) at the University of Coimbra, Portugal, and taught rhetoric and poetics at Rio de Janeiro.

Alvarenga Peixoto (pā.shō′tö), **Ignácio José de.** See **Peixoto, Ignácio José de Alvarenga.**

Alvares (äl′vą.rēsh), **Diogo.** [Full surname, **Alvares Corrêa**; Indian name, **Caramurú.**] d. near Bahia, Brazil, Oct. 5, 1557. Portuguese adventurer who in 1510 was shipwrecked on the coast of Brazil near what was later to be known as Bahia. He succeeded in gaining the friendship of the Tupinambá Indians, and subsequently brought about friendly relations between them and the first Portuguese colonists.

Álvares de Azevedo (äl′vą.rēz dē ä.zę.vā′dö), **Manuel Antônio.** See **Azevedo, Manuel Antônio Álvares de.**

Álvarez (äl′ʙä.reth), **Gonzales Melquíades.** See **Melquíades Álvarez, Gonzales.**

Alvarez, José. [Full name, **José Álvarez de Pereira y Cubero.**] b. 1768; d. 1827. Spanish sculptor, an outstanding member of the classicist school. He aided in the decoration of the Quirinal palace at Rome, and was later made sculptor to Ferdinand VII of Spain, of whom he made a bust. His other works include statues of Charles IV, Maria Louisa, Isabella de Braganza, and other notable Spanish figures.

Álvarez (äl′ʙä.res), **Juan.** b. at Concepción de Atoyac (now Ciudad Álvarez), Mexico, c1790; d. Aug. 21, 1867. Mexican Indian revolutionary general and political leader.

Álvarez (äl′ʙä.reth), **Luis.** b. at Madrid, 1836; d. there, 1901. Spanish historical painter, also known for his genre and portrait work.

Alvarez (al′vą.rez), **Walter Clement.** b. at San Francisco, July 22, 1884—. American physician. After serving on the staffs of the medical schools at Stanford (1911–12) and the University of California (1915–26), he joined the staff of the Mayo Clinic in 1926. In 1934 he became professor of medicine at Minnesota's Mayo Foundation.

Álvarez de Arenales (äl′ʙä.res dā ä.rā.nä′les), **Juan Antonio.** b. 1774; d. 1831. Argentine general in the war for independence. He served under José de San Martín in the invasion of Chile and Peru, and in the latter country led two expeditions to the interior, in December, 1820, and in May, 1821. In the first of these he defeated and captured (Dec. 6, 1820) the Spanish general, O'Reilly. In 1822 he commanded the garrison of Lima.

Álvarez de Cienfuegos (äl′ʙä.reth dā thyen.fwā′gōs), **Nicasio.** See **Cienfuegos, Nicasio Álvarez de.**

Álvarez de Toledo (dā tō.lā′ᴛʜō), **Fernando.** See **Alva,** Duke of.

Alvarez Quintero (kēn.tā′rō), **Joaquín.** b. at Utrera, Spain, 1873; d. 1944. Spanish dramatist who wrote in collaboration with his brother, Serafín Alvarez Quintero.

Álvarez Quintero, Serafín. b. at Utrera, Spain, 1871; d. 1938. Spanish dramatist. He collaborated with his brother Joaquín in writing more than 100 comedies, one-act plays, and satires, almost all of which have an Andalusian setting. Among the most popular are *El genio alegre*, *La buena sombra*, *El patio*, *La reja*, *Puebla de las mujeres*, *Doña Clarines o Las de Caín*, and *Los galeotes*.

Alvary (äl.vä′rē), **Max.** Stage name of **Achenbach, Max.**

Alvear (äl.ʙā.är′), **Carlos María.** b. in Misiones, Argentina, 1789; d. at Montevideo, Uruguay, c1853. Argentine politician and soldier, prominent in the war for independence. Having joined the party of Posadas, he commanded the besieging army to which Montevideo capitulated in June, 1814, but was worsted in a struggle with the Uruguayan, José Gervasio Artigas. In January, 1815, he succeeded Posadas as dictator, but was soon deposed by the army. He commanded the Argentine forces against the Brazilians in Uruguay in 1826 and won the indecisive victory of Ituzaingó (Feb. 20, 1827). He was minister to the U.S. in 1823. During the dictatorship of Juan Manuel de Rosas he was banished.

Alvear, Marcelo Torcuato de. b. at Buenos Aires, 1868; d. 1942. Argentine politician and diplomat whose administration (1922–28) as president was marked by moderate reforms, chiefly in the field of aid to farmers. Active in the revolutions of 1890, 1893, and 1905, he is believed also to have been a leading figure in the unsuccessful revolt of December, 1932, in company with his successor as president (and erstwhile) political opponent, Hipólito Irigoyen.

Alvensleben (äl′vęns.lā.bęn), Count **Albrecht von.** b. at Halberstadt, Prussian Saxony, March 23, 1794; d. at Berlin, May 2, 1858. Prussian politician and diplomat. As minister of finance (1836–42), he furthered the development of the Zollverein, the customs union among the German states that preceded political union later in the century.

Alvensleben, Gustav Hermann von. b. at Rathenow, Germany, Jan. 17, 1827; d. at Möckmühl, Germany, Feb. 1, 1905. Prussian lieutenant general. He participated in the Prussian wars against Denmark and Austria in the 1860's, and commanded an Uhlan regiment in the Franco-Prussian War (1870–71).

Alvensleben, Gustav von. b. at Eichenbarleben, Germany, Sept. 30, 1803; d. at Gernrode, Germany, June 30, 1881. Prussian general, chief of staff in the military department of the Rhine provinces and Westphalia. He commanded an army corps in the Franco-Prussian War (1870–71), distinguishing himself at Sedan and elsewhere.

Alvensleben, Konstantin von. b. at Eichenbarleben, Germany, Aug. 26, 1809; d. at Berlin, March 28, 1892. Prussian general; brother of Gustav von Alvensleben.

Alver (äl′ver), **Betti.** b. in Tartumaa, Estonia, 1906—. Estonian poet and novelist. She is regarded by some critics as the subtlest master of form in Estonian poetry.

Alverdes (äl.ver′des), **Paul.** b. at Strasbourg, May 6, 1897—. German poet, story writer, and novelist. He deals with young people and their crises, more particularly with their war experiences. *Die Pfeiferstube* (1929; Eng. trans., *The Whistlers' Room*, 1930), a story of soldiers wounded in the throat, is considered to be the most effective of these. *Reinhold oder die Verwandelten* (1931; Eng. trans., *Changed Men*, 1933) treats a similar theme on a broader canvas. A drama, *Die feindlichen Brüder* (1923), was less successful. Together with Karl Benno von Mechow he founded (1934) the journal *Das Innere Reich*.

Alves (äl′vęs), **(Antônio de) Castro.** [Called the **"Poet of the Slaves."**] b. on a farm near Curralinho (now Castro Alves), Bahia, Brazil, March 14, 1847; d. at Cidade do Salvador, Brazil, July 6, 1871. Brazilian romantic poet (both lyric and epic) of extraordinary power, regarded by many critics as the greatest poetic genius of Brazil. An apostle of social justice, he used to recite his own poems at rallies and became known as "the poet of the slaves." He studied law at Recife and São Paulo.

Alves Branco (brung′kö), **Manoel.** [Created in 1854, Visconde **de Caravellas.**] b. at Bahia, Brazil, June 7, 1797; d. at Nictheroy, Brazil, July 13, 1855. Brazilian lawyer and politician. He entered political life as a deputy in 1830, and soon became a leader of the liberal party.

Alvey (al′vi), **Richard Henry.** b. in St. Mary's County, Md., March 6, 1826; d. at Hagerstown, Md., Sept. 14, 1906. American jurist and Confederate sympathizer during the Civil War. His advocacy of states' rights was incorporated (January, 1861) in the "Alvey Resolution," produced at a county meeting held to discuss the question of secession; his attitude led to a period of probably unjustified imprisonment (February, 1861–February, 1862) as a Confederate agent.

Alvin (al′vin). City in E Texas, in Brazoria County, S of Houston, in a petroleum-producing region. 3,701 (1950).

Alvinczy (ôl′vin.tsē) or **Alvinzi** (äl′-), **Josef.** [Title, Baron **von Barberek.**] b. at Alvincz, in Transylvania, Feb. 1, 1735; d. at Budapest, Nov. 25, 1810. Austrian field marshal. He served in the Seven Years' War, attaining the rank of colonel; after an unsuccessful attempt to storm Belgrade in 1789, he distinguished himself at Neerwinden in 1793, but later in the same year he was defeated at Hondschooten. As an Austrian commander in Italy (1796–97), he was defeated by Napoleon at Arcole (1796) and at Rivoli (1797).

Alvord (ôl′vord, al′-), **Benjamin.** b. at Rutland, Vt., Aug. 18, 1813; d. Oct. 16, 1884. American general and military writer, member of the Union forces during the Civil War, serving as commander of volunteers and paymaster in Oregon. He was the author also of numerous articles on mathematics and geography.

Alvord, Clarence Walworth. b. at Greenfield, Mass. May 21, 1868; d. Jan. 24, 1928. American historian.

Alvord, Corydon Alexis. b. at Winchester, Conn., May 12, 1813; d. Nov. 28, 1874. American printer. A printing firm which he established (1845) at New York acquired one of the largest stocks of seldom-used type faces in America, and became for that reason one of the chief 19th-century U.S. printers of special works of all kinds.

Alvord, Henry Elijah. b. at Greenfield, Mass., March 11, 1844; d. Oct. 1, 1904. American educator, specialist in dairy husbandry, and Union soldier in the Civil War. He studied agriculture at Massachusetts Agricultural College, after having been the first U.S. army officer detailed to serve (1869–71) as a military instructor at a land-grant college. A pioneer (1876 *et seq.*) in the establishment of coöperative creameries in New England, he was head of the Dairy Division of the U.S. Department of Agriculture's Bureau of Animal Husbandry from the time it was set up in 1895 until his death.

Älvsborg (elfs′bôry′). *Län* (county) of Sweden, in the SW part. Capital, Vänersborg; area, 4,919 sq. mi.; pop. 358,700 (1950).

Alwaid (al.wīd′). The second-magnitude star β Draconis, in the monster's eye. It is called Rastaban on some star-maps.

Alwand (äl.vänd′). [Also: **Arwand, Elwend, Elwund;** ancient name, **Orontes.**] Mountain in NW Iran, a few miles S of Hamadan (formerly called Ecbatana). 11,719 ft.

Alwar (ul′wur). [Also, **Ulwar.**] Former state of Rajputana, now merged with Rajasthan, Union of India, ab. 50 mi. S of Delhi: wheat, barley, and cotton. Capital, Alwar; area, 3,127 sq. mi.; pop. 823,055 (1941).

Alwar. Capital of the former state of Alwar, Union of India, ab. 80 mi. SW of Delhi. 54,143 (1941).

Alyattes (al.i.at′ēz). Reigned c617–560 B.C. King of Lydia; father of Croesus. He made conquests in Asia Minor, carried on war against Cyaxares of Media, and laid the foundation of the Lydian empire. His tomb N of Sardis was an outstanding monument of antiquity.

Alypius (a̤.lip′i.us) or **Alypios** (-os). fl. c360 A.D. Greek theorist whose *Introduction to Music*, consisting of vocal and instrumental symbols, is a chief source for the study of the Greek system of musical notation.

Alz (älts). River in SE Germany, a tributary of the Inn, in Upper Bavaria: the outlet of Chiem Lake.

Alzey (äl′tsī). [Also, **Alzei.**] Town in W Germany, in the *Land* (state) of Rhineland-Palatinate, French Zone, formerly in the department of Rhine Hesse, Hesse, situated on the Selz River, ab. 19 mi. SW of Mainz. A center of the local wine and livestock trade, it also contains machine, shoe, and leather factories. The *Nikolaikirche* (Church of Saint Nicholas) dates from the 15th century, and the *Rathaus* (town hall) from the 16th century; there is a museum of antiquities. Founded by the Romans, it is mentioned in the medieval *Nibelungenlied.* Throughout the Middle Ages it belonged to the Rhenish Palatinate, and was at various times the residence of the electors of the Palatinate. Sacked by the Spaniards in 1620, burned down by the French in 1689, it was ceded to France in 1797, and to Hesse in 1816. Considerable damage was done in World War II. Approximately two thirds of the population are Protestants, one third Roman Catholics. 10,555 (1950).

Alzheimer (älts′hī.mėr), **Alois.** b. at Marktbreit, Bavaria, Germany, June 14, 1864; d. at Breslau, in Silesia, Dec. 19, 1915. German psychiatrist.

Alzire (al.zēr). Tragedy, and its titular heroine, by Voltaire, produced on Jan. 27, 1736, in which are contrasted the virtues of the noble natural man with those of Christianized and civilized man. The heroine, Alzire, is a noble Peruvian captive.

Alzog (äl′tsōk), **Johann Baptist.** b. at Ohlau, in Silesia, June 29, 1808; d. at Freiburg, Baden, Feb. 28, 1878. German Roman Catholic historian, professor at Posen, Hildesheim, and Freiburg. Author of *Lehrbuch der Universalkirchengeschichte* (1840), and others.

Alzubra (al′zu̇.bra̤). The rarely used name of a star of the fifth magnitude, 72 Leonis, in the animal's hind quarters.

Amabaca (ä.ma̤.bä′ka̤). See **Bhaca.**

Amabomvana (ä″ma̤.bôm.vä′na̤). See **Bomvana.**

Amacuro (ä.mä.kö′rō). [Also, **Amacura** (-rä).] Small river in E Venezuela which enters the delta of the Orinoco ab. 15 mi. W of the mouth of the Barima.

Amadah (ä.mä′dä). Place in NE Africa, in the old region of Nubia, on the bend of the Nile near Derr: noted for the temple of the Egyptian pharaoh Thutmose III.

Amadas (am′a̤.da̤s), **Philip.** [Also, **Amidas.**] b. at Hull, England, 1550; d. c1618. English navigator. He was sent (1584) by Raleigh, with Arthur Barlowe, to explore the coast of America from Florida northward. He landed on islands off what is now North Carolina and, with Sir Richard Grenville (c1541–91) and Sir Ralph Lane (c1530–1603), established a colony there in 1585.

Amadeo (ä.mä.dā′ō). [Title, Duke of **Aosta;** Latinized, **Amadeus.**] b. May 30, 1845; d. at Turin, Italy, Jan. 18, 1890. King of Spain; the second son of Victor Emmanuel II of Italy. He was elected king of Spain in November, 1870; he entered Madrid on Jan. 2, 1871, and abdicated Feb. 11, 1873.

Amadeo, Giovanni Antonio. [Also: **Omodeo;** Latinized, **Amadeus.**] b. near Pavia, in Lombardy, c1447; d. Aug. 27, 1522. Lombard sculptor. He was associated during his early career with the work on the façade of the Certosa at Pavia. With his brother Protasius he also made the tomb of San Lanfranco in the church of that saint near Pavia. He made the monument to Medea Colleoni (or Coleoni) at Basella near Bergamo, and the chapel and tomb of Bartolommeo Colleoni himself at Bergamo, the latter in 1509. In 1490 he was appointed chief architect of the Certosa at Pavia, and made a new design for the façade which was subsequently carried out by his successors. He constructed the cupola of the cathedral at Milan, and two important monuments for the chapel of the Borromeo family at Isola Bella.

Amadeus V (am.a̤.dē′us). [French, **Amédée;** called **"the Great."**] b. at Bourge, Savoy, 1249; d. 1323. Count of Savoy, who reigned from 1285 to 1323. He was the ancestor of the house of Savoy (from which came, until the establishment of the republic in 1946, the kings of modern Italy). He increased the possessions of Savoy by marriage and conquest, and was made a prince of the Holy Roman Empire in 1313.

Amadeus VI. [Called the **"Green Count."**] b. 1334; d. 1383. Count of Savoy; a grandson of Amadeus V. He reigned 1343–83, and acquired various territories in Piedmont and elsewhere.

Amadeus VII. [Called **"Amadeus the Red."**] Count of Savoy; a son of Amadeus VI. He reigned 1383–91, and acquired Nice.

Amadeus VIII. b. at Chambéry, Savoy, Sept. 4, 1383; d. at Geneva, Switzerland, Jan. 7, 1451. Count (later duke) of Savoy; son of Amadeus VII. He succeeded to the title of count in 1391, was created duke in 1416, and abdicated in 1434. He was elected Pope in 1439, and ruled (1440–49) as Felix V.

Amadeus, Lake. Salt Lake in W central Australia, in the SW corner of the Northern Territory. Length, ab. 150 mi.

"Amadeus the Red." See **Amadeus VII.**

Amadis of Gaul (am′a̤.dis). [French, **Amadis de Gaule** (à.mà.dēs de̤ gōl); Spanish **Amadís de Gaula** (ä.mä-ᴛʜēs' dā gou'lä).] Legendary and titular hero of a famous medieval romance of chivalry, the center of a cycle of romances. He is the oldest of the heroes of chivalry. He is represented as the illegitimate son of Perion, king of Gaul, and Elisena, princess of Brittany. His mother abandoned him soon after his birth, putting him, in his cradle, in the sea. Rescued by a Scottish knight, he was educated at the court of the king of Scotland, and fell in love with, and eventually married, Oriana, daughter of Lisuarte, king of England. After being knighted he returned to Gaul, and during the rest of his life performed there and elsewhere a number of impressive exploits. It is believed that the *Amadis* was originally translated by the Spaniard Montalvo from a lost Portuguese original of the 14th century. There is no trace of a French original, the existence of which has been assumed by French critics. The first known edition was prepared by Garci Rodríguez de Montalvo in Spanish and published at Saragossa, Spain, in 1508. It contained four books and stated that the first three had not been originally written by him. The authorship of the romance is a controversial matter. It has been ascribed to the Portuguese Vasco de Lobeira (d. c1403) by some scholars; to João de Lobeira (13th century, also a Portuguese, by others; still others have ascribed one part (the third book) to the former and another part (the first two books) to the latter. References to the first three books of the romance are often found in the literature of the 14th century. In 1540, Nicolas d' Herberay des Essarts undertook to give a French version of it. His version, in turn, had sequels, but none which equaled the popularity or power of his work. The book became immensely popular in France. It had, moreover, a great influence on the heroic romances of the early 17th century.

Amadis of Greece. Continuation of the seventh book of *Amadis of Gaul.* It was in Spanish, and said to be by Feliciano de Silva. It relates the exploits of the son of Lisuarte of Greece who was the son of Esplandian, the son of Amadis of Gaul.

Amado (ą.mä'dö), **Jorge.** b. at Ilhéus, Brazil, August 12, 1912—. Brazilian novelist, journalist, and lawyer.

Amador de los Ríos (ä.mä.ᴛʜōr' dā lōz rē'ōs), **José.** b. at Baena, Spain, May 1, 1818; d. at Seville, Spain Feb. 17, 1878. Spanish critic and literary historian.

Amador Guerrero (ger.rā'rō), **Manuel.** b. at Cartagena, Colombia, 1833; d. 1909. First president (1904–08) of the republic of Panama. Having been a leader of the movement by which Panama declared its independence (1903) of Colombia, he was unanimously chosen by the constitutional convention despite a clause in the constitution stipulating that the president must be a native of the area now comprising the republic.

Amagasaki (ä.mä.gä.sä.kē). City in Japan, in Hyogo prefecture, in the W part of the island of Honshu, within the metropolitan area of Osaka. It is an important industrial center, most notably in the production of iron, steel, and chemicals, and was heavily bombed by U.S. planes during the latter part of World War II. 279,264 (1950).

Amager (ä'mä.gẹr). [Also, **Amak.**] Island of Denmark, in the Øresund, opposite the main part of Copenhagen and partly within the limits of that city. Area, 25 sq. mi.; pop. 150,775 (1945).

Amaimon (ą.mā'mon). [Also: **Amaymon, Amoymon.**] In medieval demonology, one of the four kings of hell, of which he governed the eastern portion. Asmodeus was his lieutenant and first prince of his realm. Shakespeare alludes to Amaimon in the *Merry Wives of Windsor* and in *Henry IV.*

Amak (ä'mäk). See **Amager.**

Amakusa Islands (ä.mä.kö.sä). Group of islands off the W coast of the island of Kyushu, Japan. There are two large islands in the group, and some 68 smaller ones.

Amakusa Sea. [Japanese, **Amakusa Nada** (nä.dä).] Arm of the East China Sea, on the W coast of the island of Kyushu, Japan.

Amalarius (am.ą.lā'ri.us). b. at Metz, France, before 800; d. c850. French ecclesiastic. A disciple of Alcuin, he was a liturgical writer during the period when a fusion of Gallican and Roman rites took place. He was head of the church at Lyons during the deposition of Agobard, in 833–837. His work *De ecclesiasticis officiis* describes the order of service observed in the Roman Church in the 9th century.

Amalasontha (am''ą.lą.son'thą), **Amalasuentha** (-sū-en'thą), **Amalasuntha** (-sun'thą), or **Amalaswintha** (-swin'thą). b. 498; killed 535. Daughter of Theodoric, king of the East Goths. After her father's death (526) she became regent for her son Athalaric. In 534, when Athalaric also died, she became co-ruler for a year.

Amalek (am'ą.lek). [In the Douay Version, **Amalech.**] A grandson of Esau, eponymic of a tribe in the early history of the Hebrews. In Biblical history the Amalekites are represented as nomads, doomed to extermination after the attack on the Israelites under Joshua.

Amalfi (ä.mäl'fē). Town and commune in S Italy, in the *compartimento* (region) of Campania, in the province of Salerno, situated on the Gulf of Salerno, ab. 22 mi. SE of Naples. It has a port, fisheries, and paper and macaroni factories. It is the seat of an archbishopric. The ancient town, picturesquely situated on a hilly slope in the midst of orchards and vineyards, is a major attraction for tourists. The former convent of San Francesco is now used as a hotel. The cathedral was built in the Norman-Saracenic style in the 10th–13th centuries. In the early Middle Ages a leading commercial center, carrying on large-scale trade with the Near East, Amalfi preserved its republican autonomy against Byzantines, Lombards, and Moslems, but succumbed temporarily to the Normans. Its sea power was destroyed by the Pisans who, rivals in commerce, plundered the town in 1135. The maritime law of Amalfi (*Tabula Amalfitana*) was widely accepted throughout the eastern Mediterranean area in the 10th–16th centuries (see Amalfitan Code). The castle, the Church of Atrani (10th century), and the small town of Ravello are in the vicinity. The town suffered severe damage during World War II prior to the Allied invasion in the summer of 1944. Pop. of commune, 7,654 (1936); of town, 4,259 (1936).

Amalfitan Code or **Tables** (ą.mal'fi.tąn). Oldest existing code of maritime law, compiled about the time of the first Crusade by the authorities of Amalfi, which then possessed considerable commerce and maritime power.

Amalia (ä.mä'lẹ.ä), **Anna.** [Full title, Duchess of **Saxe-Weimar-Eisenach.**] b. at Wolfenbüttel, Germany, Oct. 24, 1739; d. at Weimar, Germany, April 10, 1807. Wife of Duke Ernest, and mother of Duke Karl August, of Saxe-Weimar. She was regent (1759–75), and is known as a patroness of literature and art, especially as the friend of Christoph Martin Wieland, Johann Gottfried von Herder, and Johann Wolfgang von Goethe.

Amalias (ä.mä.lyäs'). Town in S Greece, in the Peleponnesus, in the *nomos* (department) of Elis, near the W coast, ab. 18 mi. NW of Pyrgos on the Patras-Pyrgos railroad line: wine and currants. 16,031 (1940).

Amalie (ä.mä'lẹ.ẹ), **Marie Friederike.** b. Dec. 21, 1818; d. May 20, 1875. Princess of Oldenburg; eldest daughter of the grand duke Augustus, and wife of Otto I, king of Greece (whom she married on Nov. 22, 1836). Her husband's reign was never popular with the Greeks, and his deposition (1862) is attributable at least partly to his wife's interference in affairs of state.

Amalie Marie Friederike Auguste (mą.rē' frē.dẹ.rē'kẹ ou.gùs'tẹ). [Pseudonym, **Amalie Heiter.**] b. Aug. 10, 1794; d. Sept. 18, 1870. German dramatist and a duchess of Saxony; sister of King John of Saxony. Author of *Der Oheim, Die Fürstenbraut, Vetter Heinrich,* and other works.

Amalings (am'ą.lingz) or **Amals** (-alz). English name of the **Amelungen.**

Amalric I (ą.mal'rik, am'ąl-). See **Amaury I** (of *Jerusalem*).

Amalricians (am.ą.lrish'ąnz). Followers of Amalric (Amaury) of Bena (in the diocese of Chartres), a pantheist who was condemned by the University of Paris (in which he was a professor of logic and exegesis), by the Pope, and by a synod of Paris. Ten of the Amalricians were burned (1209) as heretics.

Amalric of Bena (ą.mal'rik, am'ąl-; bē'ną). [French, **Amalric de Bène** (à.màl.rēk dẹ ben), **Amauri** (or **Amaury**) **de Chartres**; Latin, **Amalricus** (ą.mal'ri.kus), **Amauricus** (ą.mô'ri.kus), **Almaricus** (al.mar'i.kus).] b. at Bène, near Chartres, France; d. c1206. French theologian and mystic philosopher, teacher at the University of Paris. He was the founder of the Amalricians, a pantheistic sect claiming to derive from Aristotle and Erigena. Their belief that sin was impossible, since God was in all men, led to much license and brought down upon it the wrath of university and Church. Amalric was ordered (1204) by Pope Innocent III to recant, ten of his followers were burned (1209) at Paris for heresy, and his doctrines were condemned (1215) by the fourth Lateran Council. Aristotle's works were banned for a time, and Erigena's *De divisione naturae* was condemned (1225) as Amalric's source.

Amalric of Lusignan (lü.zē.nyäṅ). See **Amaury II** (of *Jerusalem*).

Amalthaea or **Amalthea** (am.al.thē′a). In Greek mythology, the nurse of Zeus, in most versions a goat.

Amalthaea or **Amalthea.** In Roman legend, the Sibyl who sold the Sibylline books to Tarquin.

Amambara (ä.mäm.bä′rä). River in W Africa, a tributary of the Niger River, S of the Benue River.

Amana (a.man′a). See also **Barada.**

Amana. Community in E Iowa, in Iowa County, ab. 20 mi. SW of Cedar Rapids: the oldest of seven villages owned by the Amana Society, the "Community of True Inspiration." The society was founded c1715, in Württemberg, as a revolt against the dogmatism of the Lutheran church. Under the leadership of Christian Metz, its members came to the U.S. in 1843 and settled in the W part of New York. In 1855 the community moved to Amana, since noted for its furniture craftsmanship and wool textile products. The people work for the common good of the community, and the profits are distributed on an equal basis. In 1932, the organization was modified to allow for secular control of economic activities. Pop. ab. 200.

Amanda (a.man′da). In Colley Cibber's comedy *Love's Last Shift*, and in its continuation by Sir John Vanbrugh, *The Relapse*, a virtuous and charming woman, wife of Loveless. In the Cibber play, she wins Loveless. *The Relapse* shows her, recently married, already deserted but successful, in the end, in recapturing her husband's affection.

Amandola (ä.män′dō.lä). Town and commune in C Italy, in the *compartimento* (region) of Marche, in the province of Ascoli Piceno, ab. 45 mi. S of Ancona. It is a market for the agricultural products of the district and has an ancient castle and the Gothic Church of San Francesco. Pop. of commune, 6,348 (1936); of town, 1,235 (1936).

Aman-Jean (å.mäṅ.zhäṅ), **Edmond.** b. at Chevry-Cossigny, France, c1856; d. 1936. French painter. He won recognition at first by historical and allegorical paintings, but later devoted himself especially to portraiture.

Amann (ä′män), **Max.** b. at Munich, Germany, Nov. 24, 1891—. German politician. He served in the German army, in the same company as Hitler, during World War I. He became business manager of the Nazi party, and was sentenced with Hitler after the abortive "Beer Hall Putsch" in 1923. Later he became the editor of the Nazi paper *Völkischer Beobachter;* after 1933 he was *Reichsleiter* (chief) of the German press and president of the *Reichspressekammer* (national chamber of the press).

Amants magnifiques (lā zå.mäṅ må.nyē.fēk), **Les.** Dramatic work by Molière, written in 1670 at the order of the king.

Amanullah Khan (ä.ma.nül′lä kän). b. June 1, 1892—. Amir and king of Afghanistan (1919–29). He was ruler of Afghanistan when, in the early 1920's, that country formally repudiated any British influence over its foreign affairs. In 1924 he announced a new constitution, under which he would serve as a constitutional monarch along Western lines (he actually took the title of king at this time), but certain aspects of the constitution (most notably those relating to education and other advantages for women) aroused great opposition, and he was thereafter, until 1929, when he abdicated, faced with constantly recurring revolts. After 1929 he lived in Europe, and during World War II attempted to enlist German aid in regaining his throne.

Amanus (a.mā′nus). [Modern name, **Alma Dagh** (or **Dağ**).] In ancient geography, a mountain group, a branch of the Taurus range, on the borders of Cilicia and Syria.

Amapá (ä.ma.pä′). Territory in NE Brazil. Capital, Macapá; area, 51,659 sq. mi.; pop. 38,374 (1950).

Amapá. [Also, **Montenegro.**] Town in Amapá territory, in NE Brazil: former capital. 444 (1940).

Amapala (ä.mä.pä′lä). Town in SW Honduras, on the island of Tigre, in the Gulf of Fonseca, near the Pacific Ocean: Honduras' best Pacific port. Pop. under 5,000 (1940).

Amapala, Gulf of. See **Fonseca, Gulf of.**

Amara (ä.mä′rä). *Liwa* (province) in SE Iraq, lying across the Tigris River, ab. 100 mi. NW of the city of Basra. It is a low-lying area of rich farmland and unused swamps; many shallow lakes are formed here by the waters of the Tigris. Capital, Amara; pop. 308,108 (1947).

Amarakantaka (am″a.ra.kan′ta.ka). [Eng. trans., "*Peak of the Immortals.*"] Place of pilgrimage in N central India, in the tableland E of the Vindhya Mountains, SW of Allahabad.

Amarakosha (am″a.ra.kō′sha). See under **Amara Sinha.**

Amarant (am′a.rant). In English legend, a giant killed in the Holy Land by Guy of Warwick.

Amaranta (am.a.ran′ta). In Beaumont and Fletcher's *Spanish Curate*, the wife of Bartolus, "as cunning as she's sweet."

Amarante (ä.ma.run′te). Small town and *concelho* (commune) in N Portugal, in Douro Litoral province, N of Oporto. Pop. of concelho, 40,884; of town, 4,427 (1940).

Amarante, Count of. See **Chaves, Manoel de Silveira Pinto de Fonseca,** Marquis **de.**

Amaranth (am′a.ranth). Verse narrative by Edwin Arlington Robinson, published in 1934.

Amaranth, Lady. Character in John O'Keeffe's farce *Wild Oats.*

Amarapura (am′a.ra.pö′ra). Town in N central Burma, near the Irrawaddy River, ab. 25 mi. S of Mandalay. It contains the former royal palace. It was built in 1783, and was for many years a capital of Burma. 8,254 (1931).

Amarar (ä.mä′rär). One of the Cushitic-speaking Beja peoples of NE Africa, inhabiting NE Anglo-Egyptian Sudan E of Port Sudan. Their population is estimated at ab. 50,000 (by G. E. R. Sandars, *The Amarar, Sudan Notes*, vol. 17, 1935). They are predominantly Caucasoid in physical type.

Amara Sinha (am′a.ra sin′ha). [Also, **Amarasinha.**] fl. c550 A.D. Sanskrit lexicographer, poet, and grammarian. He was the author of *Amarakosha* or *Amarakosa* (Treasury of Amara), also called *Trikanda* (Tripartite), a three-volume vocabulary (in 1,500 verses) of Sanskrit roots arranged in meter to facilitate memorizing. It is essentially a dictionary of synonyms, the words being entered according to subject matter.

Amaravati (am.a.rä′va.tē). Former important city, now in ruins, in the E part of the Union of India, in the state of Madras. It was the capital (c100 B.C. *et seq.*) of an ancient Buddhist kingdom, and is found, with the same spelling, in Hindu mythology, as the capital of Indra's heaven.

Amargosa (am.är.gō′sa). [Also, **Amargoza.**] Small river in E California, which flows into Death Valley.

Amargosa Desert. See **Death Valley.**

Amari (ä.mä′rē), **Emerico.** b. at Palermo, Sicily, May 9, 1810; d. there, Sept. 20, 1870. Italian publicist. He was appointed (1841) professor of criminal law at the University of Palermo. Author of *Critica di una scienza delle legislazioni comparate* (1857).

Amari, Michele. b. at Palermo, Sicily, July 7, 1806; d. at Florence, July 16, 1889. Italian historian, Arabic scholar, and statesman. Opposed to Bourbon rule in Naples, he joined the Carbonari and wrote a book (1842) for which he was forced to leave Italy; returning for the revolution of 1848, he was again forced into exile by the Bourbon restoration. He was professor of Arabic at Pisa (1859 *et seq.*) and Florence (1864), and minister of education in the Farini and Minghetti cabinets until 1864. Author of important bibliographies on Moslem rule in Sicily, *Biblioteca Arabo-Sicula* (Rome, 1880) and *I diplomi arabi del archivio fiorentino* (1863–67), and of the histories *La guerra del Vespro Siciliano* (1841) and *Storia dei Musulmani in Sicilia* (1853–72).

Amarillas (ä.mä.rē′lyäs), Marqués **de las.** Additional title of **Ahumada,** Duke of.

Amarillas, Marqués **de las.** Title of **Ahumada y Villalon, Agustín de.**

Amarillo (am.a.ril'ō). [Former name, **Ragtown.**] City in NW Texas, in the Panhandle, county seat of Potter County, in Randall and Potter counties; produces helium; center for a cattle and wheat district. Its industries include oil refining, flour milling, zinc smelting, meat packing, and the manufacture of boots, saddles, and ceramic products. 74,246 (1950).

Amarinna (ä.mä.rin'nä). See **Amharic.**

Amaro (ä.mä'rō), **Monte.** Highest summit of the Maiella group of the Apennines, C Italy. 9,170 ft.

Amar-Sin (ä.mär'sin'). Babylonian king of the oldest Babylonian period, residing in Ur. His name is found on several archaic cuneiform inscriptions which, however, do not give much information concerning him or his reign.

Amaryllis (am.a.ril'is). Shepherdess or country maiden in the *Idyls* of Theocritus and the *Eclogues* of Vergil.

Amaryllis. In Edmund Spenser's *Colin Clout's Come Home Again*, a personage described with adulation, intended to represent Alice Spenser, countess of Derby, with whose family Spenser claimed an alliance. It was for Alice Spenser that Milton wrote his *Arcades.*

Amaryllis. In John Fletcher's pastoral *The Faithful Shepherdess*, a shepherdess who is in love with Perigot, and uses foul means to part him from Amoret.

Amaryllis. In *The Rehearsal*, attributed to George Villiers, duke of Buckingham, a female character intended to cast ridicule on John Dryden. The part was taken by Ann Reeve, whose intrigue with John Dryden was mentioned in the play.

Amasa (am'a.sa, a.mā'sa). In the Old Testament, a son of Abigail, sister of David, and Jether, an Ishmaelite. He joined Absalom in his rebellion and was made commander of his forces. After Absalom's defeat Amasa was pardoned by David and offered the command of the army in place of Joab, who later slew him. 2 Sam. xvii. 25.

Amasis (a.mā'sis). [Also: **Amosis, Aahmes, Ahmes.**] Egyptian captain who fought against the Hyksos in c1700 B.C. and whose tomb was found in the 19th century near ancient Thebes.

Amasis I. [Also: **Amosis, Aahmes, Ahmes.**] d. c1557 B.C. Egyptian king, conqueror of the Hyksos and founder of the XVIIIth dynasty. The building of the New Empire was begun by his campaigns in the northeastern Delta, Palestine, and Nubia; these gains were consolidated by his son and successor, Amenhotep I, second Diospolite ruler.

Amasis II. [Also: **Amosis, Aahmes, Ahmes.**] fl. c569–525 B.C. Egyptian king, the fifth of the XXVIth dynasty. Of lowly origin, according to Herodotus, he was made king by the revolting soldiers of his predecessor Apries, whom they suspected of betrayal at Cyrene. He maintained friendly relations with the Greek states, sending gifts in 548 B.C. for rebuilding the burnt temple at Delphi; he also confirmed the Greek commercial settlement at Naucratis, and brought unprecedented prosperity to Egypt. Remains of his monuments in Lower Egypt still exist.

Amasya (ä.mä.syä'). [Also, **Amasia.**] *Il* (province or vilayet) in N Turkey, at the W end of the Pontus Mountains: subsistence agriculture and herding. Capital, Amasya; area, 2,142 sq. mi.; pop. 163,494 (1950).

Amasya. [Also, **Amasia.**] City in N central Turkey, capital of the *il* (province or vilayet) of Amasya, on the Yeşil Irmak, ab. 350 mi. E of Istanbul: the later residence of the kings of Pontus, and the birthplace of Strabo, the Greek geographer. It is known for its forest products, used for construction and shipbuilding. There are several sawmills in the city. Pop. ab. 12,000.

Amat (ä.mät'), **Felix.** b. at Sabadell, near Barcelona, Spain, Aug. 10, 1750; d. Sept. 28, 1824. Spanish ecclesiastic and writer, archbishop of Palmyra *in partibus infidelium* (which means "in infidel parts," and applies to an ecclesiastic whose see, although it has geographical existence, is beyond the immediate physical reach of its bishop. Many such sees formerly existed in Moslem countries.) He became confessor to Charles IV in 1806, and is the author of an ecclesiastical history, *Tratado de la Iglesia de Jesu Cristo* (1793–1803).

Amat, Manuel de. b. in Catalonia, Spain, c1705; d. at Barcelona, Spain, c1780. Spanish general and administrator. After serving with distinction in Africa, Italy, and on the Peninsula, he was captain-general (1755–61) of Chile, and viceroy (1761–76) of Peru. He carried out (1767) the decree for the expulsion of the Jesuits.

Amateis (ä.mä.tā'ēs), **Louis.** b. at Turin, Italy, 1855; d. 1913. American sculptor, notable for his work in the architectural field. He came to the U.S. in the early 1880's and was employed on several projects by the architectural firm of McKim, Mead and White. Examples of his work may be found at Washington and in Connecticut, and very widely in Texas, a state for which he did a tremendous amount of work.

Amaterasu (ä.mä.tā.rä.sö). [Full name, **Amaterasu-o-mikami.**] The Japanese sun goddess and supposed divine ancestress of the Emperor. Born from the left eye of the creator-god Izanagi, she is the most important deity of the Shinto pantheon. There is a great national shrine in her honor at Ise.

Amateur Emigrant, The. Autobiographical narrative by Robert Louis Stevenson, published in 1894.

Amathus (am'a.thus). In ancient geography, a city of Phoenician origin on the S coast of Cyprus, near the site of the modern Limassol. It contained a sanctuary of Aphrodite.

Amati (ä.mä'tē), **Andrea.** b. at Cremona, Italy, c1520; d. there, 1611. Italian violinmaker and first of his family to become internationally known for the quality of his instruments. Few of his instruments are now known to exist, but those that do support the claim that he was the first craftsman to produce a modern violin.

Amati, Antonio. b. at Cremona, Italy, 1550; d. there, 1638. Italian musical-instrument maker, notable for his violins, bass viols, and cellos; son and successor to Andrea Amati (c1520–1611). With his brother, Geronimo Amati, he developed the style toward the peak reached by the house in its next generation.

Amati, Geronimo or **Girolamo.** b. at Cremona, Italy, 1551; d. there, 1635. Italian musical-instrument maker; son and successor to Andrea Amati (c1520–1611). He is usually considered to have been more talented than his brother and coworker, Antonio Amati (1550–1638); he prepared the way for the brilliant achievements of his son, the second Nicolo Amati.

Amati, Geronimo or **Girolamo.** b. at Cremona, Italy, 1649; d. there, 1740. Italian violinmaker and son of the second Nicolo Amati (1596–1684). He was the last of the house to achieve distinction in the craft.

Amati, Nicolo or **Nicola.** fl. 1568–86. Italian maker of violins and bass viols; younger brother of Andrea Amati (c1520–1611).

Amati, Nicolo or **Nicola.** b. at Cremona, Italy, 1596; d. there, 1684. Italian maker of violins, bass viols, and cellos; son of Geronimo Amati (1551–1635). A teacher of Andrea Guarnieri and Antonio Stradivari, he brought the work of his house to its highest point of quality, in beauty as well as in tone.

Amatitlán (ä.mä.tē.tlän'). Town in S Guatemala in Guatemala department, S of Guatemala City. It is in a cochineal-producing area. 6,683 (1950).

Amatitlán Lake. [Spanish, **Lago de Amatitlán.**] Lake in S Guatemala, in Guatemala department, near Amatitlán. Length, ab. 9 mi.

Amato (dä.mä'tō), **Giovanni Antonio d'.** [Called **"Il Vecchio,"** meaning "the Old One."] b. 1475; d. 1555. Neapolitan painter, known chiefly for religious work in the style of Pietro Perugino. His painting of the *Holy Family* was hung in a chapel of the San Dominico Maggiore church at Naples.

Amato (ä.mä'tō), **Pasquale.** b. at Naples, 1878; d. 1942. Italian operatic baritone. He studied and made his debut (1900) at Naples, and later sang in leading opera houses on the Continent, at London, and at Buenos Aires. He was introduced to New York audiences by Gatti-Casazza at the Metropolitan Opera House in *Traviata* (November, 1908). In 1921 he retired from the Metropolitan and spent the rest of his life chiefly as a teacher of operatic singing.

Amatongaland (am.a.tong'ga.land). [Also, **Tongaland.**] Region in SE Africa, in the Union of South Africa, a former native state, under British rule, on the E coast N of Zululand. In 1897 it was incorporated with the colony (later province) of Natal, along with the Ingwavuma district. It is often included in the larger area of Zululand. Area, ab. 600 sq. mi.; pop. ab. 13,500.

Amatus Lusitanus (ạ.mā′tus lö.si.tā′nus). b. 1511; d. 1568. Portuguese physician. He is said to have been the second author to describe the valves in the veins.

Amauri or **Amaury de Chartres** (à.mō.rē dẹ shȧrtr). See **Amalric of Bena.**

Amaury I (of *Jerusalem*) (ạ.mô′ri; French, à.mō.rē). [Also, **Amalric I.**] b. 1135; d. 1174. King of Jerusalem (Count of Joppa); a younger son of Fulc of Jerusalem, and brother of Baldwin III, whom he succeeded in 1162.

Amaury II (of *Jerusalem*). [Title of **Amaury** (or **Amalric**) **of Lusignan.**] d. 1205. King of Cyprus from 1194, and titular king of Jerusalem from 1197 (through his marriage with Isabella, widow of Henry, count of Champagne). He was unable to maintain himself against the Moslems, and died at Ptolemais.

Amaury, Giles. Grand master of the Knights Templars in Sir Walter Scott's tale *The Talisman.* He conspired against King Richard and was killed by Saladin.

Amaymon (ạ.mā′mon). See **Amaimon.**

Amaziah (am.ạ.zī′ạ). King of Judah (c797 B.C. *et seq.*); son of King Joash of Judah. He conquered Edom and attacked King Joash of Israel, but was defeated and captured. Assassinated at Lachish, he was succeeded by his son, Uzziah.

Amazon (am′ạ.zon). [Former name, **Orellana.** Portuguese, **Rio Amazonas;** Spanish, **Río de las Amazonas;** French, **Fleuve des Amazones;** German, **Amazonenstrom;** earlier English, **Amazone.**] The principal river of South America, and the largest in the world, in N Brazil. It has two chief headstreams: one is the Marañón (or Tunguragua) which rises in N Peru; the other is the Ucayali, which has for its southernmost headstream the Apurímac. The Ucayali is formed in C Peru by the junction of the Apurímac and Urubamba rivers. The Marañón (for most of its course taken as the Amazon) flows NW between ranges of the Andes, turns E, enters Brazil, and after discharging water through several narrow channels into the lower Tocantins or Pará River, thus cutting off the island of Marajó, flows into the Atlantic near the equator. It is connected on the N with the Orinoco by the Negro and Casiquiare. The basin of the Amazon comprises ab. 2,700,000 sq. mi. Its leading tributaries are, on the N, the Napo, Içá, Japurá, and Negro; on the S the Huallaga, Javarí, Jutaí, Juruá, Purús, Madeira, Tapajóz, Tocantins, and Xingú. Length: with the Marañón, over 3,000 mi.; with the Ucayali and Apurímac, ab. 3,900 mi. It is navigable ab. 2,300, for steamships ab. 2,200 mi. The width of the main mouth is 50 mi.; and at the Peruvian frontier the river is 1 mi. wide. The mouth was discovered by Pinzón in 1500, and Orellana descended it in 1541. Steamers first plied on it in 1853. In 1867 it was made a free highway to all nations.

Amazonas (ä.mạ.zō′nạs). State in NW Brazil, bordering Venezuela, Colombia, Ecuador, Peru, and Bolivia: largest state of Brazil. Capital, Manaus; area, 616,148 sq. mi.; pop. 530,920 (1950).

Amazonas (ä.mä.sō′näs). Intendancy in SE Colombia. Capital, Leticia; area, 48,008 sq. mi.; pop. 6,500 (est. 1950).

Amazonas. Department in N Peru, W of Loreto. Capital, Chachapoyas; area, 13,947 sq. mi.; pop. 103,559 (est. 1950).

Amazonas. [Official name, **Territorio Federal** (or **T.F.**) **Amazonas;** also, **Territorio Amazonas** (ter.rē-tō′ryō).] Federal territory in S Venezuela, on the Brazilian border: densely forested. Capital, Puerto Ayacucho; area, 67,857 sq. mi.; pop. 6,945 (1950).

Amazone (am.ạ.zōn′). An earlier English form of the Portuguese name of the **Amazon** River.

Amazonia (am.ạ.zō′ni.ạ). Name sometimes given to the valley of the Amazon.

Amazons (am′ạ.zonz). In Greek legend, a race of women supposed to have dwelt on the coast of the Black Sea and in the Caucasus Mountains. The Amazons and their contests were a favorite theme in Grecian art and story. They were represented as forming a state from which men were excluded, as devoting themselves to war and hunting, and as being often in conflict with the Greeks in the heroic age.

Amazons. Fabled tribe of female warriors said to have existed in South America. The report originated in an Indian myth which was found from the West Indies to Paraguay, and still exists among the Caribs and others; it is interesting for its similarity to the Old World myth.

Ambacia (am.bā′shi.ạ). Latin name of **Amboise.**

Ambala (um.bä′lạ). [Also, **Umballa.**] Name of a former division of the Punjab, India. Area, ab. 4,014 sq. mi.

Ambala. District of Punjab state, Union of India, ab. 120 mi. N of Delhi: sugar and wheat. Capital, Ambala; area, 1,851 sq. mi.; pop. ab. 800,000.

Ambala. City in NW India, the capital of the district of Ambala, Punjab state, Union of India, ab. 120 mi. N of Delhi: important station on the North-Western Railway. 62,419 (1941).

Ambalema (äm.bä.lā′mä). Town in W Colombia, on the Magdalena River ab. 55 mi. W of Bogotá: center of an extensive tobacco-producing district. Pop. under 5,000 (1938).

Ambassadors, The. Novel by Henry James, published in 1903. Lambert Strether, a middle-aged American editor, is sent by Mrs. Newsome to reclaim her son Chad from his attachment to Paris. Strether finds that Chad has not only succumbed to the fascination of Continental life but is also presumably the lover of the Countess de Vionnet. Strether himself begins to surrender to the color and tone of Europe, and all but abandons his original mission. A second set of emissaries is sent to secure the return of Strether, who is engaged to Mrs. Newsome. Strether responds to convention as typified in Mrs. Pocock, and returns; Chad, however, remains abroad.

Ambato (äm.bä′tō). Town in C Ecuador, capital of Tungurahua province, ab. 65 mi. S of Quito, on the Ambato River: fruit, textile and flour mills, and tanneries. 21,692 (est. 1944).

Ambatondrazaka (äm″bä.tōn.drä′zä.kä). Town on the island of Madagascar, off SE Africa, in the E central part, near Lake Alaotra. It is connected by rail with Tananarive and Tamatave, via Moramanga. 16,152 (1946).

Ambedkar (äm.bed′kär), **Bhimrao Ramji.** b. 1892—. Indian politician, lawyer, and educator, best known for his advocacy of the cause of the untouchables of India. He was educated in part at American universities. Minister of law in the government of India (1947 *et seq.*), he is also one of the principal framers of the Indian constitution. He presided over various provincial and district conferences of the depressed classes, and was a delegate to the Round Table Conferences (1930–32).

Ambelakia (äm.vē.lä′kyä). Small town in E Greece, in the vale of Tempe, Thessaly, ab. 18 mi. NE of Larissa.

Amber (am′bėr). Ancient town near Jaipur, Union of India, the former capital of the state of Jaipur.

Amber, Cape. [French, **Cap d'Ambre.**] Cape on the Indian Ocean, the northernmost point of the island of Madagascar. The Bay of Diégo-Suarez is on the E side of the headland forming the cape.

Amberg (äm′berk). Town in S Germany, in the *Land* (state) of Bavaria, American Zone, in the *Kreis* (district) of Lower Bavaria-Upper Palatinate, situated on the Vils River, ab. 32 mi. NW of Regensburg. It is the former capital of the Upper Palatinate; has enamel and ironware, ceramics, garment, shoe, leather, and furniture factories. The population, predominantly Catholic, increased 26.4 percent between 1937 and 1946 largely because of the influx of Sudeten Germans. 37,920 (1950).

Amberger (äm′ber″gėr), **Christoph.** b. c1500; d. 1562. German portrait painter. He employed a style so close to that of Hans Holbein the Younger that some of his work has been attributed to that painter.

Ambérieu-en-Bugey (äṅ.bā.ryė.äṅ.bü.zhe). [Also, **Ambérieu.**] Town in E France, in the department of Ain, situated at the confluence of the Valsérine and Ain rivers, between Bourg-en-Bresse and Chambéry. It is the site of a ruined castle which belonged to the dukes of Savoy. 7,142 (1946).

Amber Islands (am′bėr). [Also, **Electrides.**] In ancient geography, a name given by the Greeks in later times to the islands in the North Sea off what is now Denmark, Germany, and the Netherlands. See also **Glessariae.**

Ambert (äṅ.ber). Town in C France, in the department of Puy-de-Dôme, situated near the Dore River, ab. 37 mi. SE of Clermont-Ferrand: manufactures cheese, paper, furniture, wooden shoes, and religious articles. The Gothic Church of Saint Jean dates from the 15th and 16th centuries. 7,004 (1946).

Amber Witch, The. Opera in four acts by W. V. Wallace, words by Henry Fothergill Chorley, first produced at London, on Feb. 28, 1861. It was founded on a popular German romance by Johann Wilhelm Meinhold, published in 1843.

Ambianum (am.bi.ā′num). An ancient name of **Amiens.**

Ambiorix (am.bī′ǫ.riks). fl. 1st century B.C. Gallic chief, leader of the Eburones. He is famous for his campaigns against the Romans (54–53 B.C.) in which, with Catuvolcus, he twice defeated the Romans in what is now Belgium, but fled across the Rhine at the approach of Julius Caesar.

Ambitious Statesman, or The Loyal Favorite, The. Tragedy by John Crowne, acted in 1679.

Ambitious Stepmother, The. Tragedy by Nicholas Rowe, printed in 1700. It is a drama of palace intrigue, with echoes of the type of heroic play popular during the Restoration a few decades earlier.

Ambler (am′blėr). Borough in SE Pennsylvania, in Montgomery County, near Philadelphia: manufactures include asbestos, chemicals, hosiery, and boilers. It was settled c1728. Pop. 4,565 (1950).

Ambler, James Markham Marshall. b. at Markham, Va., Dec. 30, 1848; d. on *Jeannette* expedition to the Arctic, Oct. 30, 1881. American explorer, naval surgeon, and Confederate soldier in the Civil War. He enlisted at the age of 16 in the 12th Virginia Cavalry, entered college, and acquired (1865) a medical degree, being appointed (1874) assistant surgeon in the U.S. Navy. He sailed (July 8, 1879) as surgeon of the *Jeannette* expedition to the Arctic and was subsequently lost with most of his fellow explorers in their effort to regain civilization after the *Jeannette* sank in the ice fields north of the Arctic Circle.

Ambleside (am′bl.sīd). Town and former urban district in NW England, in Westmorland, situated ab. 1 mi. N of Lake Windermere, ab. 12 mi. NW of Kendal. It has no direct rail connections for passengers, being reached via Windermere, ab. 260 mi. NW of London. Ambleside is in the Lake District, and is noted for its picturesque scenery. Near it are Rydal Mount, Fox How, and Grasmere. It contains Roman antiquities. 2,343 (1931).

Ambleteuse (äṅ.blę.tėz). Beach resort and former seaport in N France, in the department of Pas-de-Calais, ab. 7 mi. N of Boulogne. Pop. ab. 900.

Amboina (am.boi′nạ). [Also: **Amboyna**; Malay, **Ambon, Ambun.**] One of the chief islands of the Moluccas, situated between Celebes and New Guinea, in Indonesia. The island consists of two parts connected by a narrow isthmus. Its chief product is cloves. It was settled by the Portuguese in the 16th century, and was taken by the Dutch in 1605. Length, 32 mi.; area, ab. 314 sq. mi.; pop. 66,821.

Amboina. [Also: **Amboyna**; Malay, **Ambon, Ambun.**] Seaport in Indonesia, capital of the island of Amboina: Allied naval base, lost to the Japanese in 1942, during World War II. 17,334.

Amboina, Massacre of. Name applied to the execution (1623) of eight Englishmen for an alleged attempt with the aid of Japanese mercenaries to seize this outpost of the Netherlands Indian empire for British rule.

Amboina, Revolt of. One of several uprisings (c1660) in the Moluccas against the oppressive rule of the Netherlands East India Company which, through pressure on local princes, attempted to enforce its monopoly over the trade in cloves and nutmeg and greatly to increase the supply of these spices. This revolt opened a rift between the Moslem majority of the population and a Christianized minority which coöperated with the European colonists. The special position of the Amboinese Christians has continued until recent times, and Amboinese soldiers have remained a strong and reliable nucleus of Netherlands Indian military forces.

Amboise (äṅ.bwȧz). [Latin, **Ambacia.**] Town in W France, in the department of Indre-et-Loire, situated on the Loire River, ab. 14 mi. E of Tours: wine-trade center; manufactures of woolens, shoes, and agricultural machinery; steel and iron foundries. The castle, once a favorite residence of the Valois kings and the scene of the conspiracy of Amboise in 1560, later became the property of the Orléans family. The Algerian rebel leader Abd-al-Kadir was confined here in 1848–52. A large part of the town was destroyed in World War II. 4,443 (1946).

Amboise, Conspiracy of. Unsuccessful conspiracy of the Huguenots to seize the French king (Francis II), first at Blois and afterward at Amboise in 1560, and to remove him from the influence of the Guises. Louis I of Bourbon, the 1st prince of Condé, was the chief of the conspirators.

Amboise, Edict of. Edict of pacification between the French Catholics and Huguenots, authorizing (1563) worship by Huguenots in the houses of the nobility, throughout all the domains of the justiciary nobles, and in one city of each bailiwick. It ended the first war between the two parties.

Amboise (däṅ.bwȧz), **Georges d'.** b. at Chaumont-sur-Loire, France, 1460; d. at Lyons, France, 1510. French cardinal; chief minister (1498–1515) under Louis XII of France, and director of his foreign policy. He was the archbishop of Narbonne and of Rouen (1493–98), and a member of Louis' party before his accession. Directing his efforts toward the increase of French power in Italy and toward a papacy for himself, he organized the campaign of 1500 for the conquest of Milan but, preferring diplomacy, let slip the opportunity to force himself on the papal conclave as the successor of Pope Alexander VI.

Ambon (äm′bôn). Malay name of **Amboina.**

Ambonese (am.bǫ.nēz′), **Amboinese,** or **Amboynese** (-boi-). The Christian and Moslem (as distinguished from the pagan) inhabitants of Amboina (Ambon) and neighboring islands in Indonesia; they number 232,000 (1930), 60 percent being Christian (chiefly Protestant).

Ambos Camarines (äm′bōs kä.mä.rē′nās). Former province of the Philippine Islands, now divided between Camarines Norte and Camarines Sur.

Amboyna, or The Cruelties of the Dutch to the English Merchants (am.boi′nạ). Tragedy by John Dryden, produced in 1673. Part of the plot was taken from one of the Italian novels in the *Hecatommithi* of Giovanni Battista Giraldi (known as Cinthio), and part has reference to occurrences of the time.

Ambracia (am.brā′shi.ạ). An ancient name of **Arta,** city.

Ambracian Gulf (am.brā′shi.ạn). [Also, **Gulf of Amvrakía** (or **of Arta**).] Inlet of the Ionian Sea, in W Greece. Length, ab. 25 mi.; greatest breadth, ab. 10 mi.

Ambre (däṅbr), **Cap d'.** French name of **Amber, Cape.**

Ambree (am′brē), **Mary.** Woman who is said to have fought against the Spanish at the siege of Ghent in 1584 to revenge her lover's death. She is frequently mentioned in old ballads, and is the subject of one preserved by Thomas Percy. Ben Jonson refers to her in the *Epicoene*, *The Tale of a Tub*, and in *The Fortunate Isles*, where he quotes the words of this ballad. John Fletcher also mentions her in *The Scornful Lady*. The ballad in Percy's *Reliques* is often quoted by the writers of Jonson's time, and, like him, they frequently gave the name of Mary Ambree to any remarkable woman who adopted man's attire.

Ambridge (am′brij). Borough in W Pennsylvania, in Beaver County, on the Ohio River: manufactures bridge and structural steel, and electrical machinery. It occupies the site of Economy, a communal settlement founded here by the Harmony Society in 1825. It was incorporated from part of Harmony township in 1905. Pop. 16,429 (1950).

Ambriz (äm.brēz′). Coast town in Angola, in SW Africa, capital of the *concelho* (commune) of the same name. Its chief export is coffee, which is brought down from the mountains. It was occupied by the Portuguese in 1855. Pop. ab. 2,200.

Ambrones (am.brō′nēz). Germanic tribe mentioned by Livy and Strabo in connection with the Teutones, whose near neighbors they seem to have been on the North Sea, and with whom they were allied in the Cimbrian wars. They suffered a crushing defeat by Marius at Aquae Sextiae in 102 B.C. There is no certain record of their subsequent fate.

Ambros (äm′brōs), **August Wilhelm.** b. at Mauth, in Bohemia, Nov. 17, 1816; d. at Vienna, June 28, 1876. Composer and musicologist. He was a professor at the Prague Conservatory (1869) and the Vienna Conservatory (1872 *et seq.*). Author of a history of music (1862 *et seq.*), books of essays on music, and others; composer of *Bretislav a Jitka* (a Czech opera), orchestral and church music, songs, and others.

Ambrose (am′brōz), Saint. [Latinized, **Ambrosius.**] b. at what is now Trier, Germany, c340; d. at Milan, Italy, 397. One of the fathers of the Roman Church; bishop of Milan (374–397). As consular prefect (c369) in upper Italy, he demonstrated his interest in public welfare; he was elected (374), though a layman and unbaptized, bishop of Milan. A champion of Catholics against paganism and heresy, he resisted the Arianism of the empress Justina and accomplished the deposition of the Arian prelates Palladius and Secundianus by persuading the emperor Gratian to limit the synod of Aquileia (381) to western bishops. Sent twice under Valentinian II to dissuade Maximus from invading Italy, he succeeded on the first occasion but failed on the second. Remaining in Milan under Gallic occupation, he melted down church vessels for the relief of the poor; after the reconquest by Theodosius, Emperor of the East, Ambrose forced penance on him for the massacre in Thessalonica. Forced to flee at the time of the assassination of Valentinian II, he returned to intercede with Theodosius (who again reconquered the West in 394) for the Arian supporters of the usurper Eugenius. Following the doctrine of Saint Basil of Caesarea and other Greeks, but with a characteristically western emphasis on divine grace and individual faith, he was, with Paul, a main precursor of Augustine. Author of commentaries on early Old Testament narratives of Hexaëmeron, Abraham, and others, of hymns such as *Deus Creator Omnium* and *Veni redemptor gentium,* and of treatises including *De Spiritu Sanctu, De mysteriis, De officiis ministrorum.*

Ambrose, Isaac. b. at Ormskirk, Lancashire, England, 1604; d. at Preston, England, 1664. English Puritan clergyman and devotional writer. He was one of the approximately 2,000 nonconformists deprived of their religious posts by the Uniformity Act of 1662. Author of *Looking unto Jesus* (1658).

Ambrose and the Emperor Theodosius. Painting by Peter Paul Rubens. The archbishop, in full canonicals, stands with his attendants before the door of the cathedral, and forbids the emperor to enter.

Ambrose Channel. [Former name, **East Harbor.**] One of the chief points at which vessels entering New York harbor cross Sandy Hook bar. The time of a voyage is reckoned to (or from) Ambrose Channel lightship. Width of channel, ab. 1,800 ft.; depth, ab. 40 ft.

Ambrose of Alexandria. [Latin, **Ambrosius** (am.brō′zi.us).] d. c250. Roman nobleman, a friend of Origen.

Ambrose of Camaldoli (kä.mäl.dō′lē), Saint. [Original name, **Ambrose Traversari.**] b. at Portico, near Florence, 1386; d. at Florence, 1439. Italian theologian and writer. He entered the order of Camaldoli, and became its general in 1431; sent by Eugene IV to the Council of Basel, he upheld there the primacy of Rome.

Ambrose's Tavern. Old tavern in Edinburgh, now destroyed, the scene of John Wilson's *Noctes Ambrosianae.*

Ambrosian Library (am.brō′zhan). Library at Milan, founded by Cardinal Federigo Borromeo in 1609, and named for Saint Ambrose. It contains over 500,000 printed volumes and more than 30,000 manuscripts. Its early Greek texts and the collection of incunabula are outstanding; it also contains a painting collection.

Ambrosiaster (am.brō′zi.as.tėr) or **Pseudo-Ambrosius** (sö″dō.am.brō′zhus). Name usually given to the unknown author of "Commentaria in XIII. Epistolas B. Pauli," which has found its way into the Benedictine edition of the works of Ambrose. The author is sometimes identified with Saint Hilary of Poitiers or Saint Hilary of Pavia.

Ambrosius (am.brō′zhus) or **Ambrose** (am′brōz), **Father.** Last abbot of St. Mary's, Edward Glendinning, in Sir Walter Scott's novel *The Abbot.*

Ambrosius (äm.brō′zē.ůs), **Hermann.** b. at Hamburg, Germany, 1897—. German composer. He was a coach (1924) at the Leipzig opera, and a teacher (1926 *et seq.*) of musical theory at the Leipzig conservatory. His works include symphonies, piano and violin concertos, and a choral opus on the theme of Goethe's *Faust,* as well as chamber music and songs.

Ambrosius Aurelianus (am.brō′zhus ô.rē.li.ā′nus). [Welsh, **Emrys.**] fl. c440 A.D. Roman emperor of Britain, Gaul, and Spain under Honorius; leader of the Britons against the Saxon invasion; said by some chroniclers to have been a son of Constantine. He drove back the Saxons, and, as king of Britain, defeated the opposition of Hengist. He was poisoned at Winchester by a Saxon.

Ambrus (ôm′brůsh), **Zoltán.** b. at Debrecen, Hungary, 1861; d. at Budapest, 1932. Hungarian novelist, representative of the French influence in Hungarian literature.

Ambun (äm′bön). Malay name of **Amboina.**

Amchitka (am.chit′ka). Island off the coast of SW Alaska, one of the Aleutian Islands. It was garrisoned by U.S. forces in World War II, and was the site of a military air base important in the campaign to recapture Attu and Kiska.

Ameca (ä.mā′kä). Town in SW Mexico, in Jalisco state. 13,003 (1940).

Amecameca (ä.mā.kä.mā′kä). [Full name, **Amecameca de Juárez.**] Town in C Mexico, in México state, SE of Mexico City. The community dates back to the pre-Spanish civilization of Mexico, as a part of which it was an important and highly developed urban center. It is today the site of Sacro Monte, a hillock built over a cave in which lived an early Christian missionary, which has been for generations a shrine visited by thousands of people on Ash Wednesday. The town is also of some importance as a starting point for tourists making ascents of Mexico's two famous mountain peaks, Popocatepetl and Ixtacihuatl. 7,573 (1940).

Amédée V (å.mā.dā). French name of **Amadeus V.**

Ameer Ali (ä.mēr′ ä′lē), **Syed.** [Also, **Seyyid Amir Ali.**] b. at Cuttack, Orissa, India, April 6, 1849; d. in England, Aug. 3, 1928. Indian Shiite Moslem, jurist, author, and political leader. Educated at Hoogli College, the University of Calcutta, and at the Inner Temple, London, he was called (1873) to the bar, returning at once to India, where he became a lecturer (1873–77) on Mohammedan law at Presidency College, Calcutta. He was a magistrate (1878) and chief magistrate (1879–81) at Calcutta, a member (1878–83) of the Bengal legislative assembly, a professor of law (1884–85) and president (1891–92) of the faculty of law at Calcutta University, and a judge (1890–1904) of the high court of judicature at Fort William, in Bengal. Resident (1904–28) in England, where he had married (1884) into an English family, he was appointed (1909) a privy councillor, the first Indian to be thus honored; he was also at one time chairman of the Woking Mosque committee. A constant friend of Great Britain and of British rule in India, he was an advocate of India's use of English as a common language and a friend of the Caliphate movement, although not himself a pan-Islamist.

Ameghino (ä.mā.gē′nō), **Fiorino** (or **Florentino**). b. in Italy, 1854; d. 1911. Argentine paleontologist and anthropologist, prominent in the late 19th century for his theory that South America was the area where man originated.

Ameland (ä′me.länt). Island in the N part of the Netherlands, belonging to the province of Friesland, situated ab. 4 mi. off the N coast of Friesland, from which it is separated by the Wadden Sea, the fourth island from the W of five large islands fringing the NW coast of the Netherlands. It contains four villages. Length, ab. 13 mi.; width ab. 2 mi.; pop. 2,000 (1939).

Amelia (ä.me′lyä). [Ancient name, **Ameria.**] Town and commune in C Italy, in the *compartimento* (region) of Umbria, in the province of Terni, ab. 45 mi. N of Rome. It is a walled city with a medieval cathedral reconstructed in the 17th century. It suffered from an earthquake in 1832. Pop. of commune, 11,055 (1936); of town, 2,583 (1936).

Amelia (a.mēl′ya, -mē′li.a). Opera (1732) in the Italian manner, but written in English. It is presumed to have been written by Henry Carey.

Amelia. Heroine of Henry Fielding's novel of that name (published 1751), a virtuous and devoted wife, said to be a portrait of Fielding's own wife. She is represented as having suffered an injury to her nose (like Mrs. Fielding), which impaired her popularity among Fielding's readers. Thackeray considered her "the most charming character in English fiction."

Amelia Island. Small island off the NE coast of Florida.

Amelia Island Affair. Attempt made by Luis Aury, a former pirate, to establish (1817) a so-called republic on Amelia Island, off the coast of Spanish Florida. Aury appealed to Florida to oust the Spanish tyrants; U.S.

naval forces, in December, 1817, put an end to this flouting of American laws, and the island was handed back to the Spanish.

Amélie-les-Bains (à.mā.lē.lā.baṅ). [Former name, **Arles-les-Bains.**] Town in SW France, in the department of Pyrénées-Orientales, situated on the Tech River, N of the Spanish border and ab. 20 mi. SW of Perpignan. It assumed its present name in 1840 in honor of the wife of King Louis Philippe. It is a health resort and a tourist center; its thermal springs are considered useful in the treatment of rheumatism and respiratory ailments; excursions into the surrounding mountainous area are made from the town. It was severely damaged toward the end of World War II. Pop. 3,210 (1946).

Amelot de la Houssaye (àm.lō de là ö.sā), **Abraham Nicolas.** b. at Orléans, 1634; d. at Paris, 1706. French historian; author of *Histoire du gouvernement de Venise* (1676), which caused him to be imprisoned, and was widely read in France and England.

Amelotte (àm.lot), **Denis.** [Also: **Amelote, Amlote.**] b. at Saintes, France, 1609; d. at Paris, Oct. 7, 1678. French theologian, author of a translation of the New Testament (1666–68), and an opponent of Jansenism.

Amelungen (ä'mẹ.lung.ẹn). [English, **Amalings** or **Amals.**] Ruling family of the Ostrogoths (and possibly at an earlier date, before the division of the Goths, of the Visigoths as well) which first came to prominence in the 4th century under their king Ermanric and attained their greatest fame under Theodoric the Great (c454–526).

Amen (ā'mẹn). [Also: **Ammon, Amon, Amun, Hammon.**] In Egyptian mythology, a deity variously represented as a ram with large curving horns, as a being with a ram's head and a human body, and as a man enthroned or standing erect. In art his figure is colored blue. On his head he wears the royal symbol and two long feathers, and in one hand he carries a scepter and in the other the sign of life. His chief temple and oracle were on an oasis in the Libyan desert near Memphis. Later he became identified with the sun god Ra and was worshiped as Amen-Ra, the chief deity of Egypt.

Amenemhet (ä.mẹn.em'het). [Also, **Amenemhat.**] Egyptian official under Sesostris I. An inscription recording the events of his life was found in a rock-tomb at Beni-Hassan. It contains a reference to a famine which has, by some, been supposed to be that which occurred during Joseph's sojourn in Egypt.

Amenemhet I. [Also: **Amenemhat, Ammenemez** (am.ẹ.nē'mēz).] d. 1970 B.C. Egyptian king, the founder of the XIIth dynasty, who reigned 2000–1970 B.C. He was a successful ruler and general, and founded the temple of Amun in Thebes. There is considerable documentary evidence concerning his reign. In 1980 B.C., his son Sesostris I became his co-regent, after Amenemhet had considerably strengthened the royal authority.

Amenemhet II. [Also: **Amenemhat, Ammenemes.**] d. 1903 B.C. Egyptian king, the third of the XIIth dynasty, who reigned 1938–1903 B.C.; son of Sesostris I with whom he was co-ruler 1938-1935 B.C. He was succeeded by his son, Sesostris II, with whom he reigned from 1906 B.C. until his death. During his reign expeditions were undertaken to Sinai and the Nubian mines.

Amenemhet III. [Also: **Amenemhat, Ammenemes.**] d. 1801 B.C. Egyptian king, the sixth of the XIIth dynasty, who reigned 1849–1801 B.C.; son of Sesostris III. He constructed Lake Moeris and the Labyrinth. Inscriptions of his time have been found on the rocks in the peninsula of Sinai. There is also a mark (with an inscription) on the rocks of Semneh showing the height of the inundation of the Nile in the 14th year of his reign.

Amenemhet IV. [Also: **Amenemhat, Ammenemes.**] d. 1792 B.C. Egyptian king, the seventh of the XIIth dynasty, who reigned 1801–1792 B.C.

Amenhotep I (ä.mẹn.hō'tep). [Also: **Amenhotpe** (-hōt'pe), **Amenophis** (am.ẹ.nō'fis).] Egyptian king, the second of the XVIIIth dynasty, who reigned 1557–1501 B.C. He was successful in campaigns in Cush (in what is now Ethiopia), and Libya.

Amenhotep II. [Also: **Amenhotpe, Amenophis.**] d. 1420 B.C. Egyptian king, the seventh of the XVIIIth dynasty, who reigned 1448–1420 B.C. He made a successful campaign in Asia, which is commemorated in an inscription in a temple at Amadah in Nubia. There are also inscriptions bearing his name in the temple of Amen at Karnak.

Amenhotep III. [Also: **Amenhotpe, Amenophis.**] Egyptian king, the ninth of the XVIIIth dynasty, who reigned 1411–1375 B.C. He was a successful warrior and a great builder. The two colossal statues of Memnon, near Thebes, are portrait-statues of him. Amenhotep III was as great in peace as in war. In his reign Egypt lost none of her military prestige, and from some large scarabaei—one of which is in the Giza Palace—we learn that under his rule Egypt stretched from Mesopotamia to the country of Karoy in Ethiopia. At the same time that he consolidated the empire left him by preceding monarchs, Amenhotep raised, along the banks of the Nile, monuments which for their grandeur and the perfection of their workmanship are unsurpassed. The temple at Gebel Barkal, in the Sudan, was erected by this king; so also was that at Soleb, near the third cataract; and further evidence of his reign may be found at Aswan, Elephantine, Gebel Silsileh, El Kab, Turah, the Serapeum at Memphis, and Serabit el Khadim. He added considerably to Karnak, and built that portion of the temple at Luxor that bears his name. He also erected on the left bank of the Nile—opposite to Luxor—a sacred edifice which once must have been one of the most important in Egypt. Destroyed completely by causes unknown to us, all that is now left of it are the two enormous colossi which originally stood at the entrance.

Amenhotep IV. See **Ikhnaton.**

Amenophis IV (am.ẹ.nō'fis). See **Ikhnaton.**

Ament (ā'ment), **William Scott.** b. at Owosso, Mich., Sept. 14, 1851; d. in China, Jan. 6, 1909. American Congregational clergyman and missionary to China. A preacher of remarkable vigor, Ament carried out hazardous refugee missions during the Boxer Rebellion, and showed great personal courage in aiding the Chinese Christians during and after hostilities. Inaccurate reporting of an interview led to attacks by several papers in the U.S., and accusations by Mark Twain in the *North American Review* (in February and April, 1901) of extortion and looting, but the charges were later shown to be without foundation.

Amenti (ạ.men'tē). In Egyptian mythology, the underworld; the world of the dead.

Amer (ä'mėr). See **Amr ibn-al-As.**

Amerbach (äm'ėr.bäċh), **Johannes.** b. c1445; d. at Basel, Switzerland, Dec. 25, 1514. Swiss printer who published, for the most part, religious books, with the coöperation of Erasmus, Johann Reuchlin, Albrecht Dürer, and other leading figures in the early development of humanism.

Ameria (ạ.mir'i.ạ). Ancient name of **Amelia.**

America (ạ.mer'i.kạ). [Portuguese and Spanish, **América** (ä.mā'rē.kä).] Name often applied specifically to the United States of America, particularly in the U.S. and in parts of the world outside of the Western Hemisphere. The designation is also often (and in the eyes of many, more properly) applied to either of the continents of the Western Hemisphere, i.e., North America or South America. The Americas (a plural form of the name meaning the entire Western Hemisphere, including the West Indies) were probably visited first by the Northmen, who are believed to have reached North America in about 1000 A.D. Christopher Columbus discovered the island of San Salvador, in the Bahamas, on Oct. 12, 1492; in subsequent voyages he visited Central America and South America. The North American mainland was reached by John Cabot in 1497. The name America was proposed by Martin Waldseemüller (a German teacher of geography) who suggested (1507), in a treatise called *Cosmographia,* that the New World be named after Amerigo Vespucci (Latinized as Americus Vespucius, thus America), the Florentine navigator who is believed by some to have reached North America 18 days before Cabot, and who wrote the earliest extensive account of the New World.

America. Name given in the U.S. to the tune which is used in Great Britain for *God Save the King* after its adaptation for use in connection with the American hymn *My Country 'Tis of Thee,* written by Samuel F. Smith in 1832. The author of the hymn stated, "I found the tune in a German music-book, put into my hands by Lowell Mason."

America. American yacht which was awarded a trophy cup in 1851, was placed in service as a Confederate dispatch vessel during the Civil War, and after being seized was converted into a practice craft at the U.S. Naval Academy. After the war she defended (1870) the cup, became the property of Benjamin F. Butler in 1873, was sold (1917) to Charles H. W. Foster, and in 1921 was docked permanently at the Naval Academy. The vessel was broken up during the 1940's.

America Comes of Age. Critical work by André Siegfried, published in 1927. It is an interpretation of American institutions and social life.

America First Committee. Organization established in 1940 with the general object of opposing U.S. involvement in foreign wars. During its existence the committee took a leading part in urging the "Isolationist" viewpoint upon the U.S. It was dissolved shortly after the U.S. entry into World War II.

American (ạ.mer'i.kạn), **The.** Novel by Henry James, published in 1877. Christopher Newman, a wealthy American, falls in love with a Parisian lady, Claire de Cintré. Newman, a fairly direct and sincere individual, is appalled by the subtleties of European life and particularly by the contrivings of Claire's family, who succeed in breaking the couple's engagement. Newman learns that Claire's mother and brother were instrumental in the death of her father, but instead of revealing this information he destroys the evidence and surrenders the opportunity for revenge.

American Academy in Rome. Organization founded in 1894 as the American School of Architecture in Rome which received its present designation in 1897. Since 1913 it has included also the American School of Classical Studies at Rome. It is devoted to the advancement of arts and letters in America, awards annual fellowships in fine arts and classical studies, and maintains a school of fine arts and a school of classical studies. The academy's library contains some 50,000 volumes on art, classics, and archaeology. The organization has headquarters at New York and issues *Papers and Monographs* and *Memoirs of the American Academy in Rome.*

American Academy of Arts and Sciences. Society for the encouragement of art and science, founded at Boston in 1780. It has published *Memoirs* from 1785, and *Proceedings* from 1848. Its headquarters are at Boston.

American Academy of Political and Social Science. Organization founded in 1889 for the purpose of providing a forum for the discussion of the political, social, and industrial problems affecting the U.S. and other nations. It maintains headquarters at Philadelphia and in addition to its *Annals* (bimonthly) issues a series of monographs and pamphlets.

American Anthropological Association. Organization incorporated in 1902 at Washington, D.C., for the purpose of advancing the science of anthropology and promoting the professional interests of American anthropologists. It issues the *American Anthropologist* (quarterly), a quarterly *News Bulletin*, and a series of *Memoirs*.

American Antiquarian Society. Organization at Worcester, Mass., founded in 1812 by Isaiah Thomas, which maintains a comprehensive library of Americana (comprising some 700,000 titles) and is devoted to the promotion of research in American history. It possesses the world's best and largest single collection of American colonial newspapers. The society publishes its *Proceedings* semi-annually.

American Association for the Advancement of Science. Organization founded in 1848 (incorporated in 1874) for the purpose of promoting science and its application to human welfare and the fostering of coöperation among scientists. It maintains headquarters at Washington, D.C. In 1947 the association had 201 officially associated or affiliated organizations. It publishes *Science* (weekly) and *Scientific Monthly*.

American Association of University Professors. Organization founded in 1915 for the purpose of advancing professional standards and ideals and the fostering of more effective coöperation among teachers and scholars in universities, colleges, and professional schools. It maintains headquarters at Washington, D.C., and publishes a *Bulletin* (quarterly).

American Astronomical Society. Organization founded in 1897 as a conference of astronomers, and which received its present designation in 1914. It is devoted to the advancement of astronomy, astrophysics, and related branches of physics. Its headquarters are at the Dearborn Observatory, Evanston, Ill. The society formerly issued (1899–1946) the *Publications of the American Astronomical Society* and is associated with the publication of the *Astrophysical Journal* and the *Astronomical Journal*.

American Automobile Association. Body founded (March 4, 1902) at Chicago by delegates from nine automobile clubs for the purpose of encouraging and advancing the use of the automobile. It conducts racing and endurance contests, seeks the improvement of public roads, and promotes the passage of sound motor-vehicle laws. Its federated membership consists of some 750 motor clubs and branches and state associations; in 1948 the association listed its membership at 2,350,000. National headquarters are maintained at Washington, D.C.

American Bar Association. Nation-wide professional body established (1878) for the purpose of improving legal education and promoting sound judicial and legal standards in the U.S. The creation (1891) of the U.S. circuit court of appeals, and the consolidation (1911) of the U.S. circuit and district courts, was in large measure owing to the proposals of the association. It maintains its headquarters at Chicago; in 1948 its membership was listed at 42,000.

American Bible Society. Organization established (1816) at New York for the purpose of publishing and distributing the Bible in all lands and languages. Up to shortly before World War II it had distributed more than 7,700,000 Bibles, Testaments, or portions thereof, publishing the Bible in 176 separate tongues and the New Testament in 214. It also conducts a service for the blind. The society maintains its headquarters at New York; in 1948 it listed its membership at 150,000.

American Broadcasting Station in Europe. See **ABSIE.**

American Chemical Society. Organization originally founded in 1876 and incorporated under a federal charter in 1937. It is devoted to the advancement of chemistry in all its branches, to the promotion of research in chemical science and industry, and to the improvement of professional standards. It maintains headquarters at Washington, D.C., and has 125 geographic sections. It awards numerous medals and awards for outstanding services in the field, among them the Willard Gibbs Medal and the Eli Lilly and Company Award in biological chemistry. Among its publications are the *Journal* (monthly), *Chemical Abstracts* (semi-monthly), *Chemical and Engineering News* (weekly), and *Analytical Chemistry*.

American Civil Liberties Union. Organization established in 1920 for the purpose of maintaining and protecting civil liberties endangered by various forms of social and political prejudice. It provides legal counsel and engages in informational activities.

American Claimant, The. Story by Samuel Langhorne Clemens, written under his pseudonym of Mark Twain and published in 1892. It is noted for its matchless description of a typical American boarding-house of the early 1890's.

American Council of Learned Societies. Council established in 1919 and incorporated in 1924 for the purpose of promoting the interests of the humanistic sciences in America and stimulating and carrying out major research projects. It also acts as a clearing house for information relating to scholarly activities. The council comprises 24 constituent societies and maintains headquarters at Washington, D.C.

American Council on Education. Organization founded in 1918 for the advancement of American education through voluntary coöperative action. It maintains headquarters at Washington, D.C., and issues the *Educational Record* (quarterly).

American-Danish Treaty of 1916. Agreement (Aug. 4, 1916) by which Denmark ceded to the U.S. the Virgin Islands for a payment of 25 million dollars. Totaling almost 100 islands, covering 132 sq. mi., with a population of 26,000, the group covered by the treaty was formally taken into U.S. possession on March 31, 1917, with Danish laws temporarily remaining in effect.

American Defense Society. Organization active c1915–17 in disseminating preparedness propaganda shortly before the U.S. entry into World War I.

American Dental Association. Organization founded in 1859 for the purpose of improving professional standards and knowledge in the interests of public health and welfare. It maintains headquarters at Chicago, has a library of more than 6,000 volumes on dental science and practice, and publishes a monthly *Journal* and the *Journal of Oral Surgery* (quarterly).

American Ethnology, Bureau of. Bureau established in 1879 for collecting and disseminating information pertaining to American aborigines. It is supported by U.S. Congressional appropriation and is under the direction of the Smithsonian Institution. It maintains a library of more than 34,000 volumes on anthropology and issues an *Annual Report* and *Bulletin*.

American Expeditionary Forces. [Abbreviation, **AEF.**] Official name applied to the entire body of U.S. troops serving in the European theater during World War I. The AEF was under the command (1917–19) of John J. Pershing. From it, the first American troops (of the 1st Division) entered the battle line on the night of Oct. 20, 1917, and took their first ground when the 1st Division captured Cantigny, France, on May 28, 1918. The AEF participated in major engagements including the Aisne defensive, the Montdidier-Noyon defensive, the Champagne-Marne defensive, the Aisne-Marne offensive, the reduction of the St.-Mihiel salient, and the Meuse-Argonne offensive. Overall command of the combat elements of the AEF was initially relinquished to the Allied commander in chief, Marshal Foch, and it was not until Aug. 10, 1918, when 24 U.S. combat divisions were in France, that the First (American) Army was formed with headquarters at Ligny-en-Barrois. By the time the armistice was declared (Nov. 11, 1918) more than 2,000,000 troops, including 29 combat divisions, had been transported to France, of which 1,390,000 saw action against the enemy. The last division of the AEF departed from France in August, 1919.

American Express Company. Shipping concern established in 1850 by the merger of Livingston, Fargo and Company with Wells, Butterfield and Company, and which is now chiefly important for its banking and tourist-service activities. The guiding spirits of the enterprise were Henry Wells, who served as its first president, and William G. Fargo. Its rapid development and penetration into the American West brought about the organization (1852) of Wells, Fargo and Company as an associated body. In 1854 the American Express Company established the United States Express Company, but this subsidiary later emerged as a chief competitor. In 1918 the American Railway Express Company consolidated the shipping activities of the various concerns, and the American Express Company thereafter confined itself to banking and tourist services. In 1929 the American Railway Express Company was taken over by the Railway Express Agency.

American Farm Bureau Federation. National organization formed in 1919 of state and local farm bureaus which were originally established for educational purposes on an extension basis. It soon thereafter became a powerful guardian of farmers' interests in Congress, establishing permanent offices at Washington, D.C.

American Federation of Labor. [Abbreviations: **AFL** and **A. F. of L.**] Organization composed of self-governing craft unions which was formed at Columbus, Ohio, in 1886. Its forerunner was the Federation of Organized Trades and Labor Unions of the United States of America, founded at Terre Haute, Ind., in 1881. The traditional policy of the AFL has been oriented towards a firm support of the craft-union principle. Organizationally, the AFL is a loose federation of more than 100 national and international unions with a total of some 39,000 locals. Its first president, Samuel Gompers, who headed the AFL from 1886 to 1924 (with the exception of 1895), was succeeded by William Green. The contest within the AFL between advocates of craft unionism and supporters of industrial unionism was climaxed by the expulsion of several unions and the formation (1938) of the Congress of Industrial Organizations. In 1947 the AFL claimed a membership of some 7,400,000 workers.

American Fur Company. Commercial enterprise incorporated in 1808 under the laws of the state of New York, with John Jacob Astor (1763–1848) as its sole stockholder. Astor's aim in establishing the concern was to compete with British interests in Canada for control of the rich fur-trade of the American West. By 1820 Astor was well on his way toward securing a monopoly of the U.S. fur trade, and in 1827 his company merged with its chief rival, the Columbia Fur Company. Astor's peak years came between 1828 and 1834, when he enjoyed an effective monopoly of the U.S. fur trade. In 1834 Astor sold his interests and withdrew from the company, and a portion of the enterprise continued active under the old title. It suffered a financial failure in 1842 and thereafter had little if anything to do with the fur trade.

American Geographical Society. Organization founded in 1851 (incorporated in 1852) for the purpose of collecting and disseminating geographical information and encouraging exploring expeditions likely to yield valuable discoveries in geography and allied fields. Its headquarters at New York maintain a library containing some 118,000 volumes, 145,000 maps, 2,400 atlases, and 29,600 photographs. It awards the David Livingstone Centenary Medal and the S. F. B. Morse Medal. The society's publications include the *Geographical Review* (quarterly) and *Current Geographical Publications* (monthly).

American Geographical Society Bay. See **Gardner Bay.**

American Historical Association. Organization founded on Sept. 9, 1884 (incorporated on Jan. 4, 1889) for the purpose of promoting professional and public interest in history in the U.S. It awards the Albert J. Beveridge Memorial Fellowship and the George Louis Beer Prize. The chief cultural agency of its kind in the U.S., its activities extend to the organization and promotion of research and the classification of manuscript and archival materials. It maintains committees on various aspects of scholarly endeavor in historical studies. The association maintains headquarters at Washington, D.C., and publishes the *American Historical Review* (quarterly), *Social Education* (issued nine times a year), and an *Annual Report.* In 1948 it listed its membership at approximately 5,000. The Pacific Coast branch of the association, established in 1902, publishes the *Pacific Historical Review.*

American Independence, War of. See **Revolutionary War.**

American Insurance Co. v. Canter, 1 Peters 511 (1828) (kan'tėr). [Also called **American Insurance Co. v. 356 Bales of Cotton.**] U.S. Supreme Court decision upholding the right of the U.S. government to acquire and govern territory. The case arose over a suit by the American Insurance Company to recover a cargo of cotton which had been sold by order of the territorial legislature of Florida. The plaintiffs alleged that the territorial court which ordered the sale was not a legally constituted court because the acquisition of Florida by the U.S. was unconstitutional. Chief Justice John Marshall declared that "the Constitution conferred absolutely on the government of the Union the powers of making war and of making treaties; consequently, that government possesses the power of acquiring territory, either by conquest or treaty," and also has the constitutional right of making all needful rules and regulations respecting such territory. This is the leading U.S. case on the constitutionality of acquired territory: it gave a constitutional basis to the incorporation of the Louisiana Purchase.

American Iron and Steel Institute. Organization incorporated in 1908 for the purpose of promoting the interests of the iron and steel industry. Its membership is composed of company and personal members. The institute maintains headquarters at New York and issues *Steel Facts* (six times a year) and *Iron and Steel Works Directory of the United States and Canada* (irregularly).

Americanization of Edward Bok (bok), **The.** Autobiographical narrative by Edward W. Bok, published in 1920 and awarded the Pulitzer Prize. The book recounts the author's arrival in America and the progress of his career.

American Labor Party. [Abbreviation, **ALP.**] Third-party organization set up at New York in 1936 with independent and labor support. It was instrumental in carrying New York state for Franklin D. Roosevelt in the presidential election of 1936. A split in the party in 1944 led to the secession of right-wing elements which subsequently emerged as the Liberal Party. During the latter part of the decade 1940–50 it lost much of the power and support which it had enjoyed during the late 1930's and early 1940's.

American Language, The. Study (1919; revised, 1921; 3rd edition, 1923; 4th edition, 1936; First Supplement, 1946; Second Supplement, 1948) of the English language in the U.S., by Henry Louis Mencken. It is considered by most critics and scholars to be his most lasting monument.

American Legion. National organization composed of honorably discharged veterans who served in the U.S. armed forces during World Wars I and II. It was initially organized at Paris (February–March, 1919) and was chartered by the U.S. Congress on Sept. 16, 1919. The largest single veterans' society in the U.S., it has thousands of local posts at home and abroad and maintains national headquarters at Indianapolis, Ind. The organization has been active in securing veterans' benefits, and in the promotion of patriotic sentiment and community endeavor. In 1949 it claimed 3,272,060 members.

American Liberty League. Organization established in 1934 by conservative Democrats and others with the declared aim of supporting constitutional government and combating radical tendencies in the U.S. A great part of its activity was devoted to attacking the policies of the New Deal. It was dissolved in 1940.

American Library Association. Organization founded in 1876 for the purpose of extending library facilities throughout the U.S. and Canada, elevating standards and ideals of library service, and promoting the interests and welfare of the profession. It is affiliated with more than 50 other library associations. It maintains headquarters at Chicago and publishes a monthly *Bulletin*, the *Booklist* (semimonthly), *College and Research Libraries* (quarterly), *Hospital Book Guide* (quarterly), and *Subscription Books Bulletin* (quarterly).

American Medical Association. Organization founded in 1847 for the purpose of promoting professional knowledge and efficiency and improving public health. Its membership is composed of the members of 53 constituent state and territorial medical associations. The association maintains headquarters at Chicago. Among its publications are the *Journal* (weekly), *American Journal of Diseases of Children* (monthly), *Archives of Dermatology and Syphilology* (monthly), *Archives of Neurology and Psychiatry* (monthly), *Occupational Medicine*, and *Hygeia* (monthly).

American Mercury, The. Monthly publication founded by H. L. Mencken and George Jean Nathan, with help from Alfred Knopf, in 1924. Under their editorship the magazine burlesqued national institutions and presented a sharply critical view of contemporary American mores and customs. Contributors included Theodore Dreiser, Eugene O'Neill, Sinclair Lewis, and Edgar Lee Masters. The character of the publication was modified after Mencken resigned in 1934.

American Museum of Natural History. Institution at New York, incorporated in 1869 for the purpose of establishing and maintaining a museum and library of natural history, and of encouraging and developing the study of natural science. Its buildings, including the memorial to Theodore Roosevelt (1858–1919) and the Hayden Planetarium, occupy an area lying W of Central Park and extending from 77th Street to 81st Street. The museum is supported in part by an annual appropriation from the city, and in part by the income from a permanent endowment, from membership fees, and from gifts for special purposes. The affairs of the museum are administered by a board of trustees who serve without compensation. The exhibits include extensive collections in anthropology, paleontology, geology, mineralogy, conchology, entomology, mammalogy, ornithology, the lower animals, and forestry. The library contains about 130,000 volumes on natural history. The museum conducts scientific investigations at home and in the field, publishes memoirs, a bulletin, a journal, and anthropological papers, and is a center for the meetings of local scientific societies. It also offers free lectures to the public and to school children, and lends small collections to the public schools.

American National Red Cross. See **American Red Cross.**

American Party. [Also called **Know-nothing Party.**] In U.S. politics, a party which advocated the control of the government by native citizens, and fostered anti-Catholic sentiment. Because it was at the outset a secret fraternity and its members refused to give information concerning it, they received the name of "Know-nothings." In 1855 it discarded its secret machinery. The party nominated Millard Fillmore for president in 1856, and soon after its defeat in the election of that year began a rapid decline.

American Philosophical Society. Learned society, the oldest of its kind in America, founded at Philadelphia by Benjamin Franklin in 1743, and united in 1769 with his Junto of 1727, or Society for Promoting Useful Knowledge. Franklin was the first president after the union of the two societies. Incorporated in 1780, it has a library of more than 102,000 volumes, and issues *Memoirs*, *Proceedings*, and *Transactions*. Its headquarters are at Philadelphia. Its membership is limited to 500, and is not restricted to U.S. nationals.

American Political Science Association. Organization founded in 1903 for the purpose of encouraging the study of political science, including political theory, government and politics, public law and administration, and international politics. It maintains headquarters at Ohio State University, Columbus, Ohio, and issues the *American Political Science Review* (bimonthly).

American Practical Navigator. [Full title, **The New American Practical Navigator**; commonly called **Bowditch's Navigator.**] Work by Nathaniel Bowditch (1773–1838), published under his name in 1802. A revision of *Moore's Practical Navigator*, it became a standard work on navigation for American seamen. More than 60 editions have been issued since 1802. In 1866 the responsibility for publication and revision was taken over by the U.S. Navy Hydrographic Office.

American Protective Association. [Abbreviation, **APA.**] Secret nativist organization established (March 13, 1887) by Henry F. Bowers, a lawyer of Clinton, Iowa. The APA fostered prejudice against immigrants and Catholics and circulated propaganda designed to expose the alleged designs of the Papacy for dominating the U.S. It agitated for greater restrictions on immigration and naturalization, the prevention of state aid to parochial schools, and the exclusion of Roman Catholics from political and, as far as possible, from industrial affairs. Its members took secret oaths binding them not to employ or vote for Catholics. The APA's following, which stood at 70,000 in 1893 and rose to 1,000,000 by 1896, was drawn largely from rural areas in the Midwest. Its membership dwindled rapidly after 1896.

American Psychiatric Association. Organization originally founded in 1844 as the Association of Medical Superintendents of American Institutions for the Insane which received its present title in 1921. It is devoted to the advancement of psychiatric knowledge, education, and research, the application of such knowledge to other branches of medicine, and the elevation of standards of institutions for the care of the mentally ill. It maintains headquarters at New York and issues the *American Journal of Psychiatry* (monthly).

American Psychological Association. Organization founded in 1892 (incorporated 1925) for the purpose of advancing psychology as a science and profession. It maintains headquarters at Washington, D.C., and issues publications including *Psychological Abstracts* (monthly), *Psychological Bulletin* (bimonthly), *Psychological Review* (bimonthly), *Journal of Abnormal and Social Psychology* (quarterly), *Journal of Applied Psychology* (bimonthly), and *Journal of Experimental Psychology* (bimonthly).

American Public Health Association. Organization founded in 1872 for the purpose of promoting and protecting personal and public health. It maintains headquarters at New York and issues the *American Journal of Public Health and The Nation's Health* (monthly).

American Railway Association. Body of U.S. railway managers and executive operating officials which had its genesis in the so-called Time Table Conventions held as early as 1872 (and out of which came, among other things, the railroads' decision to establish and apply the four zones of standard time in the U.S.). It was known by the name above after 1891, and was included (1934) in the Association of American Railroads.

American Railway Union. Labor organization in the U.S., adhering to the principles of industrial unionism, established under the leadership of Eugene V. Debs on June 20, 1893. It grew rapidly under Debs's guidance and within a year after its founding had 465 lodges and a membership of 150,000. The union called the Pullman strike of 1894, which became the occasion for a noted antilabor injunction and led to Debs's imprisonment on the charge of contempt of court. The organization is now defunct.

American Red Cross. [Also, **American National Red Cross.**] Organization organized in 1881 by Clara Barton and others for the purpose of furnishing volunteer aid to the sick and wounded of armies in time of war, and to carry on a system of national and international relief in time of peace to mitigate the sufferings caused by pestilence, famine, and natural disasters. It was chartered by the U.S. Congress in 1905. It maintains headquarters at Washington, D.C., and issues the *Red Cross Courier* (monthly), *Junior Red Cross News* (monthly), and *Junior Red Cross Journal* (monthly).

American Republican Party. [Later name, **Native American Party.**] Nativist political body in the U.S., with an animus against Catholics and immigrants, organized in 1843 at New York. It rose to prominence by winning (1844) the municipal contests at New York and Philadelphia, and held its first national convention in 1845. The party then changed its name to the Native American Party and adopted a program demanding radical reforms in the naturalization laws. The party declined rapidly after the outbreak of the Mexican War.

American Revolution, War of the. See **Revolutionary War.**

American River. River in N central California, flowing generally SW into the Sacramento River at Sacramento. It rises near Lake Tahoe, in the Sierra Nevada mountains. Several of the gold strikes made in 1848 occurred on its banks, and it was thereafter of considerable importance in the development of California. Length, ab. 30 mi.

American Samoa (sa.mō′a). [Also, **Eastern Samoa.**] Term applied to the E half of the Samoan islands, owned by the U.S. In 1872 the harbor of Pago Pago was ceded to the U.S. as a coaling and naval station. In 1899, when Great Britain gave up all her claims to the Samoan islands, the group was divided between Germany and the U.S.; Western Samoa became a League of Nations mandate after World War I and later a trust territory of the United Nations, administered by New Zealand. The American islands comprise Tutuila, Aunuu, Rose Island, and the Manua Islands (Tau, Ofu, and Olosega). In 1925 Swains Island was added to the territory. The commandant of the naval station at Pago Pago is also the governor of American Samoa. There is a native legislature of two houses (one elected), and a high court presided over by an American chief justice. The islands produce copra, coconuts, taro, yams, and fruit. Capital, Pago Pago; area, 76 sq. mi.; pop. 18,937 (1950).

American Scholar, The. Address delivered by Ralph Waldo Emerson before the Phi Beta Kappa Society of Harvard on Aug. 31, 1837. It has been described as "our intellectual Declaration of Independence." The author asserts that the scholar's function is to understand and interpret the society of which he is a part, to assume an active as well as a contemplative role, to escape the tyranny of popular opinion, and to consecrate his talents to the highest good of the community. From it was derived the name of the magazine (quarterly) of the Phi Beta Kappa Society.

American School of Classical Studies at Athens. School founded at Athens, Greece, by the Archaeological Institute of America, opened in 1882, and supported by individuals and by leading American colleges and universities. Its main purpose is the study of Greek archaeology.

American School of Classical Studies at Rome. School founded at Rome in 1895 by the Archaeological Institute of America, and supported by individuals and by leading American colleges and universities. In 1913 it was consolidated with the American Academy in Rome.

American's Creed, The. Expression of American political faith written in 1917 by William Tyler Page, at that time clerk of the U.S. House of Representatives. It was chosen to receive an award of one thousand dollars offered in a national contest by the city of Baltimore. On behalf of the American people it was accepted (April 3, 1918) by the House of Representatives. The text is as follows: "I believe in the United States of America as a Government of the people, by the people, for the people; whose just powers are derived from the consent of the governed; a democracy in a republic; a sovereign Nation of many sovereign States; a perfect union, one and inseparable; established upon those principles of freedom, equality, justice and humanity for which American patriots sacrificed their lives and fortunes. I therefore believe it is my duty to my country to love it; to support its Constitution; to obey its laws; to respect its flag, and to defend it against all enemies."

American Society of Composers, Authors and Publishers. [Abbreviation, **ASCAP.**] Non-profit group organized (1914) by Victor Herbert whose voluntary membership includes composers, authors, and music publishers. It represents its members in dealing with entertainment and public-communications establishments, and in matters connected with copyright protection.

American Society of Tropical Medicine. Organization founded in 1903 for the purpose of promoting the knowledge of tropical diseases by means of research and publication. It awards the Walter Reed Medal for meritorious achievement in tropical medicine and publishes the *American Journal of Tropical Medicine* (bimonthly).

American Sociological Society. Organization established in 1905 for the purpose of encouraging research, discussion, teaching, and publication in the field of sociology. It publishes the *American Sociological Review* (bimonthly).

American Songbag, The. Collection of folk songs and ballads compiled by Carl Sandburg and published in 1927.

American Speech. Quarterly magazine founded (1925) by Louise Pound, who served as its editor until 1933. It is a scholarly publication devoted to research and discussion in such fields as pronunciation, vocabulary, regional and local dialects, technical definitions, and slang.

American System. Name applied by Henry Clay to the system of protective tariffs and internal improvements advocated by him in a famous speech (March 30–31, 1824) before the U.S. Congress. It looked to the encouragement of agrarian and industrial interests for the development of a domestic market freed from dependence on foreign sources. Clay also advocated as part of his program the distribution by the national government among the states of the revenues from the sale of public lands. In the broader sense, the term "American System" was used by Clay to raise the standard of a hemispherical unity of republican belief against the monarchical rule of Europe.

American Tract Society. Body established (1825) at New York for the purpose of producing and distributing Christian tracts. It was incorporated in 1841. An interdenominational body, it has published well over eight hundred million copies of leaflets and tracts, many of which have been distributed by its colporteurs.

American Tragedy, An. Novel by Theodore Dreiser, published in 1925. Clyde Griffiths, in a desperate attempt to escape the stultifying effects of a poverty-stricken life in a midwest town, seeks a life of wealth and ease. Almost coincident with his love affair with Roberta Alden is his attraction to Sondra Finchley, who exemplifies affluence and social prestige. When Roberta tells Clyde that she is pregnant, he takes her to a lake resort, planning to murder her. Clyde lacks the courage to perform the crime, but when a rowboat carrying them overturns, Clyde swims away, leaving Roberta to drown. He stands trial and is sentenced to death. The novel was dramatized by Patrick Kearney in 1926 and was subsequently filmed.

American Veterans Committee. [Abbreviation, **AVC.**] National organization of honorably discharged veterans who served in the U.S. armed forces during World War II. Formally organized in 1944 under the leadership of Charles G. Bolté, it declared its general objectives under the slogan, "Citizens First, Veterans Second." It has been active in promoting legislation for veterans' benefits, government housing, and full employment.

American Veterans of World War II. [Abbreviation, **Amvets.**] National organization of honorably discharged veterans who served in the U.S. armed forces during World War II. The group obtained a national charter in 1947.

American Zone. See under **German Federal Republic.**

Americus (ạ.mer′i.kus). City in W Georgia, county seat of Sumter County, in a kaolin and bauxite mining region. It is the seat of Georgia Southwestern College. 11,389 (1950).

Amerighi (ä.me.rē′gē), **Michelangelo.** See **Caravaggio, Michelangelo Amerighi** (or **Merighi**) **da.**

Amerling (ä′mėr.ling), **Friedrich von.** b. 1803; d. 1887. Austrian portrait painter.

Amersfoort (ä′mėrs.fōrt). Town in the C part of the Netherlands, in the province of Utrecht, situated on the Eem River, ab. 12 mi. NE of Utrecht: manufacturing and commercial community, with textile mills producing damask, cotton, and woolen goods, the Erdal chemical works, cigar factories, and breweries. The town has preserved its medieval character; the 13th-century Church of Saint Joris contains the tomb of Jacob van Kampen, a famous Dutch architect. There is a Jansenist church and college. The town was occupied by the Germans in May, 1945. Pop. 57,653 (1949).

Amery (ā′mėr.i), **Leopold Charles Maurice Stennett.** b. at Gorakhpur, India, 1873—. English politician and journalist. After serving on the staff of the London *Times* (1899–1909), he was elected (1911) to Parliament on the Unionist ticket from a Birmingham constituency. He served in the army (1914–16) and as War Cabinet secretary (1917–18); thereafter he held numerous cabinet posts, becoming in 1940 secretary of state for India and Burma, which post he surrendered in 1945 after the victory of the Labour party at the polls. Author of the seven-volume *Times History of the South African War* (1909), as well as of numerous works pertaining to empire and international affairs.

Ames (āmz). [Former name, **College Farm.**] City in C Iowa, in Story County. Manufactures include canned foods, pottery, and garden tools. It is the seat of Iowa State College of Agriculture and Mechanic Arts. It was platted in 1864 and incorporated in 1870. Pop. 22,898 (1950).

Ames, Adelbert. b. at Rockland, Me., Oct. 31, 1835; d. April 13, 1933. American general in the Civil and Spanish-American Wars, Reconstruction governor of Mississippi. He was awarded the Congressional Medal of Honor for gallantry at the first battle of Manassas (Bull Run). He fought also at Malvern Hill, Antietam, Gettysburg, and other battles, and was brevetted major general of volunteers in 1865 and of the regular army in 1866. Appointed by Grant provisional governor (1868–70) of Mississippi, he served as a Republican U.S. senator (1870–74) from that state, and as its governor (1874–76). His governorship was troubled by the Vicksburg riot (1874) and other disorders. As brigadier general of volunteers, he served in the Santiago campaign (1898) in the Spanish-American War.

Ames, Charles Gordon. b. at Dorchester, Mass., Oct. 3, 1828; d. April 15, 1912. American Baptist and Unitarian clergyman, newspaper editor, and vigorous supporter of the Union in the Civil War. The period (1851–56) he spent as a Baptist pastor at Minneapolis was marked by his editorship (1855–57) of the Minnesota *Republican* (forerunner of the Minneapolis *Tribune*) and his activity on behalf of the Minnesota Republican Party, which in 1854 he helped to found. Disillusionment with parishioners led to his withdrawal from the ministry, but he returned in 1859 as a Unitarian. Although rejected for military service for physical reasons, he paid for a substitute and argued for the Union cause and Abraham Lincoln (whom he had met earlier at Bloomington, Ill.).

Ames, Edward Raymond. b. at Amesville, Ohio, May 20, 1806; d. at Baltimore, April 25, 1879. American Methodist bishop and itinerant minister. He traveled upwards of 25,000 miles between Minnesota and Texas as a corresponding secretary for the Methodist Missionary Society in the West. A vigorous supporter of the North during the Civil War, he was the sole Methodist bishop to be appointed chaplain with the army. His selection (1862) as a commissioner to enter Richmond, Va., with comforts for the Union soldiers there imprisoned, led to violent outbursts in the South, where it was felt his mission of mercy would play a secondary role to his Unionist political sympathies, and he was refused a pass into the Confederacy.

Ames, Ezra. b. at Framingham, Mass., 1768; d. 1836. American portrait painter. His early career as a carriage painter was followed by commissions to paint miniature, bust, and full-length portraits of Governor George Clinton of New York, Alexander Hamilton, Charles Genet, and others.

Ames, Fisher. [Pseudonyms, **Lucius Junius Brutus,** and **Camillus.**] b. at Dedham, Mass., April 9, 1758; d. there, July 4, 1808. American Federalist leader and political writer; supporter of Hamilton in Congress. He began a law practice at Dedham in 1781, and was a member (1787) of the Massachusetts ratifying committee. As a Federalist member (1788–97) of Congress from Massachusetts, having defeated Samuel Adams, he made memorable speeches opposing (1794) Madison's proposal of commercial war against Britain and in support (1796) of Jay's Treaty. In 1805 he declined the presidency of Harvard College. Author of essays advancing the Hamiltonian theory of selective democracy and opposing Jeffersonian libertarianism, such as *The Dangers of American Liberty* (written 1805); his works were collected in *Works of Fisher Ames* (1809, 1854) and *Speeches of Fisher Ames in Congress* (1871).

Ames, Frederick Lothrop. b. at North Easton, Mass., June 8, 1835; d. Sept. 13, 1893. American banker, railroad official, and Boston real-estate owner, son of Oliver Ames (1807–77). He was nominated and elected (1872) to the Massachusetts senate.

Ames, James Barr. b. at Boston, June 22, 1846; d. at Wilton, N.H., Jan. 8, 1910. American educator and writer on law. A graduate of Harvard (1868) and the Harvard Law School (1872), he replaced Henry Adams at Harvard as teacher of medieval history (1872–73); subsequently he was also professor of law (1877) and dean of the law school (1895–1910). Through his teaching methods and case books, he furthered Christopher Columbus Langdell's system of teaching law by case study; he was also instrumental in founding (1897) the *Harvard Law Review*. Authority on legal history; author of *Lectures on Legal History and Miscellaneous Legal Essays* (1913).

Ames, James Tyler. b. at Lowell, Mass., May 13, 1810; d. Feb. 16, 1883. American manufacturer; brother of N. P. Ames (1803–47). As head of the Ames tool-manufacturing concern after the death of his brother, he expanded his works to include textile machinery, water turbines, sewing machines, and bicycles. During the Civil War, the Ames shops turned out sabers, rifles, and cannon for the North, and later executed large munitions contracts for France and Turkey.

Ames, Joseph. b. at Yarmouth, England, Jan. 23, 1689; d. at London, Oct. 7, 1759. English antiquary and bibliographer, publisher of *Typographical Antiquities* (1749, ed. by Herbert 1785–90), an account of English printing to 1600, called by some the foundation of English bibliography. He was the author also of descriptive catalogs of coins (1746) and old prints (1747), a memoir of Christopher Wren (1750), and others.

Ames, Joseph Alexander. b. at Roxbury, Mass., 1816; d. at New York, 1872. American painter, notable for his portraits of Pope Pius IX, Rufus Choate, William H. Seward, and Emerson. A painting done by him of Daniel Webster in 1852 is believed to have been the last painted of Webster from life.

Ames, Joseph Sweetman. b. at Manchester, Vt., July 3, 1864; d. at Baltimore, Md., June 24, 1943. American physicist and college administrator. He conducted research in aerodynamics and was chairman (1927–39) of the National Advisory Committee for Aeronautics. He served also on the staff of Johns Hopkins' physics department (1888 *et seq.*), becoming professor in 1899 and director of the physical laboratories in 1901; from 1929–35 he was president of Johns Hopkins.

Ames, Mary Clemmer. See **Clemmer, Mary.**

Ames, Nathaniel. b. at Bridgewater, Mass., 1708; d. at Dedham, Mass., 1764. American almanac-maker, physician, and one-time tavern-keeper. In 1725 he published the first edition of his *Almanac*, which preceded Benjamin Franklin's *Poor Richard's Almanac* by eight years and was destined to be for two generations the best known of New England's almanacs.

Ames, Nathan Peabody. b. at Chelmsford, Mass., Sept. 1, 1803; d. Apr. 3, 1847. American manufacturer, notable for his establishment (1834) of the Ames Manufacturing Company. Ames first specialized in the production of edged tools, which led to the operation of the first U.S. sword-company, and expansion into various industrial fields peculiar to New England. He was sent (1840) with a commission from the U.S. army ordnance department to study arms manufacture in Europe.

Ames, Oakes. b. at Easton, Mass., Jan. 10, 1804; d. at North Easton, Mass., May 8, 1873. American manufacturer, financier, and politician; father of Oliver Ames (1831–95). With his brother, Oliver (1807–77), he managed the Ames shovel-factory, which prospered from gold rushes, development of the Northwest, and the Civil War. As a Republican congressman from Massachusetts (1863–73), he became interested in the building of the Union Pacific Railroad, of which Oliver became president while he obtained control of the Crédit Mobilier. Exposure of its manipulations began in the election year of 1872 with the publication in the New York *Sun* of his letters to a congressman who claimed Ames had withheld stock from him. He was found guilty by the Poland Committee of bribery, and by the Wilson Committee of defrauding the government, and was publicly condemned by a House resolution for his conduct, which many colleagues and constituents maintained was not intentionally corrupt.

Ames, Oakes. b. at North Easton, Mass., Sept. 26, 1874; d. in Florida, April 28, 1950. American botanist, a specialist in orchidology.

Ames, Oliver. b. at West Bridgewater, Mass., April 11, 1779; d. Sept. 11, 1863. American shovel-manufacturer, notable for his belief (unusual in his day) that the tool was easier to replace than its user, and that shovels should therefore be lighter and easier to use than was the standard of his time. He established shops at North Easton, Mass. (1803), Braintree, Mass. (1823), and Canton, Mass. (1844), which were taken over by his sons Oakes Ames (1804–73) and Oliver Ames (1807–77) during the 1840's.

Ames, Oliver. b. at Plymouth, Mass., Nov. 5, 1807; d. Mar. 9, 1877. American industrialist, railroad official, and banker; son of Oliver Ames (1779–1863) and brother of Oakes Ames (1804–73). His business success was originally based on the shovel factory founded by his father. He was associated (1855 *et seq.*) with his brother in the construction of the Easton Branch Railroad; subsequently he was acting president (1866–68) and president (1868–71) of the Union Pacific. Though connected with the Crédit Mobilier (which financed the Union Pacific), he was not involved in the scandals that followed the exposure of its manipulations, because he was not connected with the wholesale legislative corruption upon which the scandals were based.

Ames, Oliver. b. at North Easton, Mass., Feb. 4, 1831; d. Oct. 22, 1895. American industrialist, railroad official, and politician; son of Oakes Ames (1804–1873). He was three times (1886, 1887, 1888) elected governor of Massachusetts, despite bitter personal attacks based on his failure to serve in the armed forces during the Civil War.

Ames, Samuel. b. at Providence, R.I., Sept. 6, 1806; d. there, Dec. 20, 1865. American jurist, chief justice of the Rhode Island supreme court (1856 *et seq.*). His service (1841–51) as a member for Providence in the Rhode Island general assembly was marked by his support of state authority in the "Dorr Rebellion" (1842); later (1861) he represented Rhode Island in unsuccessful peace negotiations between the North and the South in the Civil War.

Ames, William. [Latinized, **Amesius.**] b. at Ipswich, England, 1576; d. at Rotterdam, 1633. English Puritan theologian who was forced by his controversial preaching to live (c1610–33) in the Netherlands, where he was professor (1622–26) and rector (1626–33) of the university at Franeker. A Calvinist, he was opposed to the strong Arminian doctrines in the English church. Author of *Medulla theologiae, De conscientia eius iure et casibus* (1632), and others.

Ames, Winthrop. b. at North Easton, Mass., Nov. 25, 1871; d. at Boston, Nov. 3, 1937. American theatrical producer and theater manager at Boston (1905–08) and New York (1909 *et seq.*). He built the Little Theatre (1912) and the Booth Theatre (1913), both at New York; his production of *Snow White* was the first New York play designed specially for children. He was active also in the revival of Gilbert and Sullivan and in a variety of other productions, many of which set a high standard of dramatic excellence.

Amesbury (āmz'ber"i, -bėr.i). Town in S England, in Wiltshire, ab. 8 mi. N of Salisbury. It is probably now chiefly known outside of England as being the community closest to Stonehenge, but it is important also as the site of a portion of one of England's largest military training centers.

Amesbury (āmz'ber"i). Name of a town and village in NE Massachusetts, in Essex County, on the Merrimack River, ab. 34 mi. N of Boston: manufactures hats. Pop. of town, 10,851 (1950); of village, 9,711 (1950).

Amestratus (ą.mes'trą.tus). Ancient name of **Mistretta.**

Amestris (ą.mes'tris). Daughter of Otanes according to Herodotus, of Onophas according to Ctesias, and the favorite wife of Xerxes, whom she bore at least five children. Her crimes and cruelties are related by Ctesias at some length, and are mentioned by Herodotus. She is believed by some to be the Vashti of the Book of Esther.

Ameto (ä.mā'tō). Prose idyl by Boccaccio, with poetical interludes. Seven nymphs over whom Ameto, a young hunter, presides recount the story of their loves. Each story concludes with eclogues, which were among the first in Italian literature.

Amfissa (am.fis'ą). See **Amphissa.**

Amfiteatrov (äm.fi.tyi.ä'trọf), **Aleksandr Valentinovich.** b. Dec. 26, 1862; d. 1923. Russian man of letters, prolific as a novelist, playwright, and liberal journalist.

AMG. Abbreviation of **Allied Military Government.**

Amga (äm'gą). River in the U.S.S.R., in the Yakutsk *oblast* (region) of the Russian Soviet Federated Socialist Republic, E Siberia, which joins the Aldan. Length, ab. 500 mi.

AMGOT. Original abbreviation of **Allied Military Government.**

Amhara (äm'hä.rä, am.har'ą). Former province in N Ethiopia, in E Africa, situated in the vicinity of Lake Tana. This high region, which possesses good soil and climate, was to be the nucleus of the empire of Italian East Africa; because of its altitude it was considered fit for European colonization. It is inhabited by Amharans, who have long been the ruling group in Ethiopia. Capital, Gondar; area, 76,235 sq. mi.; pop. ab. 2,000,000.

Amharic (am.har'ik). [Also, **Amarinna.**] Semitic language of NE Africa, derived from Geez or Ethiopic. Since the 14th century it has been the official and literary language throughout the Ethiopian state. It is spoken by some 3,000,000 to 5,000,000 people (estimated by E. Ullendorf, *Exploration and Study of Abyssinia*, 1945).

Amherst (am'ėrst). District in Tenasserim division, SE Burma, with its center ab. 150 mi. SE of Rangoon. Tungsten is mined in the area. The most important crop is rice. Area, ab. 7,000 sq. mi.

Amherst. Name of a town and village in C Massachusetts, in Hampshire County, ab. 20 mi. N of Springfield: seat of Amherst College and of the University of Massachusetts. Pop. of town, 10,856 (1950); of village, 7,900 (1950).

Amherst. Seaport in Nova Scotia, Canada, the capital of Cumberland County, situated on Cumberland Basin, an arm of Chignecto Bay, near the New Brunswick boundary. It has manufactures and a considerable trade in lumber and shipbuilding, and is a junction point on the main railway line into the province. 9,870 (1951).

Amherst. Village in N Ohio, in Lorain County: sandstone quarries. 3,542 (1950).

Amherst, Jeffrey. [Title, Baron **Amherst.**] b. at Sevenoaks, Kent, England, Jan. 29, 1717; d. there, Aug. 4,

1797. British field marshal, commander against the French in North America. He served under Ligonier and Cumberland in Europe in the War of the Austrian Succession. Sent (1758) by William Pitt to take Louisburg from the French, he was victorious there, at Crown Point and Ticonderoga (1759), and at Montreal (1760), securing British control of Canada. He was appointed (1761) governor-general of British North America, but returned (1763) to England after an unsuccessful campaign against the Indians. He later acted as an adviser to the British government during the American Revolution. For his services, he was made a baron (1787), commander in chief of the army (1793), and a field marshal (1796).

Amherst, Nicholas. See **Amhurst, Nicholas.**

Amherst, William Pitt. [Title, Earl **Amherst of Arakan.**] b. in January, 1773; d. 1857. English government official and diplomat; nephew of Jeffrey Amherst (1717–97). He was ambassador to China (1816–17).

Amherstburg (am′ėrst.bėrg). Town in Essex County, Ontario, Canada, situated at the entrance of the Detroit River into Lake Erie, ab. 20 mi. S of Detroit: agricultural and resort region; several industries. 3,638 (1951).

Amhurst (am′ėrst), **Nicholas.** [Also: **Amherst**; pseudonym, **Caleb D'Anvers of Gray's Inn.**] b. at Marden, Kent, England, Oct. 16, 1697; d. at Twickenham, England, April 12, 1742. English poet and pamphleteer. As editor (1726 *et seq.*) of the political journal *The Craftsman*, he published many papers by Henry St. John, 1st viscount Bolingbroke, and William Pulteney, earl of Bath, who apparently abandoned him when their campaign against the Walpole government succeeded. Expelled (1719) from Oxford for irregular conduct or, according to his account, for his liberal opinions, he retaliated by satirizing the university in *Terrae filius* (1721–26), a prose work, and *Oculus Britanniae* (1724), a poem.

Ami (ä′mē). Largest of the Malayo-Polynesian-speaking tribes of Formosa, on the E coast of the island.

Amici (ä.mē′chē), **Giovanni Battista.** b. at Modena, Italy, March 25, 1786; d. at Florence, April 10, 1863. Italian optician and astronomer who developed, besides the dioptric or achromatic microscope which bears his name, important improvements in the mirrors of reflecting telescopes.

Amicis (ä.mē′chēs), **Edmondo De.** See **De Amicis, Edmondo.**

Amico Fritz (lä.mē′kō frēts′), **L'.** Opera in three acts by Pietro Mascagni, with a libretto by P. Suardon, first performed in the Teatro Costanzi at Rome on Oct. 31, 1891.

Amida (ä.mē.dä). Central figure in the most popular Buddhist sect in Japan. Friendly to man, Amida is regarded as a savior; sincere faith in him assures his worshipers a place in paradise.

Amida (am′i.dạ). Ancient name of **Diyarbakir,** city.

Amidas (am′i.dạs), **Philip.** See **Amadas, Philip.**

Amidas and Bracidas (bras′i.dạs). Twin brothers whom Artegall reconciles in Book V of Edmund Spenser's *Faerie Queene*.

Amie (ā′mi). In Ben Jonson's *Sad Shepherd*, a gentle shepherdess.

Amiel (ā′mi.ẹl). In John Dryden's *Absalom and Achitophel*, a character supposed to have been intended for Edward Seymour, speaker of the House of Commons, who was an adherent of William of Orange and the head of the house of Seymour.

Amiel (å.myel), **Denys.** b. at Villegailhenc, near Carcassonne, France, Oct. 5, 1884—. French dramatist, specializing in a form of subtle comedy in which the most important lines are left unsaid, to be inferred by the audience. His plays include *La Souriante Madame Obey* (1921, in collaboration with André Obey), *La Carcasse* (1926), *Décalage* (1931), and *L'Age du fer* (1932).

Amiel, Henri Frédéric. b. at Geneva, Switzerland, Sept. 27, 1821; d. there, May 11, 1881. Swiss philosopher and poet. After studying philosophy at Berlin 1844–48, he served as professor of aesthetics and French literature (1849 *et seq.*) and of moral philosophy (1854) at the academy at Geneva. Author of *Fragments d'un journal intime*, published after his death (2 volumes, 1883), translated (1885) by Mrs. Humphry Ward and praised by Matthew Arnold.

Amiens (am′i.ẹnz; French, å.myaṅ). [Ancient names, **Samarobriva, Ambianum.**] City in N France, the capital of the department of Somme, situated at the junction of the Selle and the Somme rivers. It was the capital of the old province of Picardy and is now one of the leading manufacturing and commercial centers of France. Among its various industries are metallurgical, leather-goods, and garment factories, cotton and jute processing plants, and flour mills. The Cathedral of Notre Dame, begun in 1220 and renovated in 1902–03, is considered one of the largest and finest examples of Gothic church architecture in France. The façade is richly sculptured and the choir stalls, dating from 1508–19, are of great beauty. The slender central spire is ab. 370 ft. high. The city suffered severely in World Wars I and II and as a result of the latter, most of the city's ancient buildings, with the exception of the cathedral, and many of its industries were partially or totally destroyed. Among the buildings wholly destroyed were the Church of Saint Germain, the courthouse of the royal bailiff, and the Sagittaire mansion. 84,787 (1946).

Amiens (ä′mi.ẹnz). In Shakespeare's *As You Like It*, a gentleman in attendance on the duke.

Amiens (am′i.ẹnz; French, å.myaṅ), **Battle of.** Victory gained on Nov. 27, 1870, in the Franco-Prussian War by the Germans under Edwin Hans Karl Manteuffel over the French. It was followed by the taking of Amiens on Nov. 28, and the surrender of its citadel on Nov. 30.

Amiens, Mise of. Award pronounced on Jan. 23, 1264, by Louis IX of France, to whom the question as to the obligation of Henry III to observe the Provisions of Oxford had been referred on Dec. 16, 1263. By this award the King of France entirely annulled the Provisions of Oxford, and all obligations made under them.

Amiens, Treaty of. Peace concluded at Amiens, March 27, 1802, between Great Britain on one side, and France, Spain, and the Batavian republic on the other. England restored all conquests except Ceylon and Trinidad, the Ionian republic was acknowledged, the French were to abandon Rome and Naples, and Malta was to be restored to the Knights of St. John.

Amiet (å.mye), **Cuno.** b. at Solothurn, Switzerland, March 28, 1868—. Swiss genre painter and landscape and portrait artist who decorated the City Hall at Basel, Switzerland. He studied in Switzerland (1885–91), and at Paris with Adolphe William Bouguereau. Given a one-man show (1928) at Bern, Switzerland, he has also exhibited his work at Berlin, Munich, and Zurich. *Winter Landscape, Mother and Child*, and *Beauty of the Evening* are among his principal paintings.

Amigoni (ä.mē.gō′nē), **Jacopo.** b. at Venice, 1675; d. at Madrid, 1752. Venetian painter and etcher. He spent a large part of his life in England, where his work was at one time extremely popular. His paintings include numerous portraits and historico-mythological scenes.

Amin (ä.mēn′). Eldest son of Harun al-Rashid in "The Three Ladies of Baghdad" in *The Arabian Nights' Entertainments*. He marries Amine.

Amina (ä.mē′nä). The principal character, a soprano, in Vincenzo Bellini's opera *La Sonnambula*.

Aminadab (ạ.min′ạ.dab). Name often used by the English dramatists of the 18th century to designate a Quaker.

Amine (ä.mēn′). In the story of "Sidi Nouman" in *The Arabian Nights' Entertainments*, the wife of Sidi Nouman. Her habit of eating only a few grains of rice, at meal-times, arouses his suspicions, and he discovers her feasting at night with a ghoul.

Amine. In the story of "The Three Ladies of Baghdad" in *The Arabian Nights' Entertainments*, Zobeide's sister. Without knowing his rank, she marries Amin, eldest son of Harun al-Rashid.

Aminta (ä.mēn′tä). Pastoral drama by Torquato Tasso, produced in 1573. The drama is allegorical, presenting Arcadia as a reflection of the Ferrara court, where the work was acted in 1573.

Aminte (å.maṅt). Neighbor of Sganarelle in Molière's *L'Amour Médecin*.

Amintor (ạ.min′tôr). One of the principal male characters in Beaumont and Fletcher's play *The Maid's Tragedy*. Loyalty to his king is his outstanding trait.

Amiot (å.myō), **Jean Joseph Marie.** [Also, **Amyot.**] b. at Toulon, France, Feb. 8, 1718; d. at Peking, China,

Oct. 8, 1794. French Jesuit missionary, after 1740, in China, whose *Mémoires concernant l'histoire, les sciences, et les arts des Chinois* (1776–91), and *Dictionaire tatar-mantchou-francais* (1789, a Manchu dictionary) were notable contributions to the European knowledge of Chinese culture.

Amirabad (ą.mir'ą.bad, ä.mēr''ä.bäd'), **Camp.** U.S. Army camp in World War II, in N Iran, ab. 15 mi. N of the city of Tehran. Built by the U.S. Army, it was the headquarters of the Persian Gulf Command.

Amir Ali (ä.mēr' ä'lē), **Seyyid.** See **Ameer Ali, Syed.**

Amirante Islands (am'i.rant). Group of small islands in the Indian Ocean, SW of the Seychelles Islands and included in the British crown colony of Seychelles.

Amis et Amiles (ä.mēs ā ä.mē.lęs). [Also, **Amys and Amyloun.**] Middle English metrical romance, dating probably from the 12th century, and probably of French origin. It tells the story of two perfect friends, born the same day and alike in beauty, courage, and devotion. Amiles saves the honor of Amis in a trial by combat, and is punished with leprosy. Amis in true devotion cures Amiles with the blood of his own children. As reward for such perfect friendship the children are restored to life.

Amish (am'ish, ä'mish). Christian sect, formerly Mennonites, in the U.S. whose practices are based upon the teachings of Jacob Amman. They broke off from the main body of Mennonites in Europe toward the close of the 17th century and appeared in Pennsylvania as early as c1714. Among their distinguishing outward characteristics are their simple, old-fashioned attire, their use of hooks and eyes (buttons are forbidden), and the wearing of beards, but not moustaches, by the men. Their code of personal conduct is extremely conservative; in the affairs of daily life, they are highly industrious and frugal. Their individualism is almost proverbial; during the era of the New Deal they scorned, in more than one community, unsolicited aid in the form of public projects.

Amisia (ą.mis'i.ą). Latin name of the **Ems River.**

Amistad Case (ä.mēs.täᴛʜ'). Case of the U.S. against the Spanish vessel *Amistad.* This vessel, while coming from Africa in 1839 with a cargo of kidnaped Negroes, was seized by the Negroes near Cuba and taken to the coast of Connecticut, and there captured by a U.S. vessel. On a libel for salvage the U.S. Supreme Court held on appeal that the Negroes were free and not pirates.

Amis the Parson (ä'mis). [German, **Der Pfaffe Amis.**] Comic poem in Middle High German, composed by the German poet Der Stricker, probably c1230.

Amite City (ą.mēt'). Town in SE Louisiana, parish seat of Tangipahoa Parish: trading center for cotton, dairy products, and corn yielded by the farms in the vicinity. 2,804 (1950).

Amitu (am'i.tö). See **Amytis.**

Amityville (am'i.ti.vil). Village in SE New York, in Suffolk County, on Long Island: residential community. 6,164 (1950).

Amlet (am'lęt), **Dick** (or **Richard**). In Vanbrugh's comedy *The Confederacy,* a gamester, the son of a garrulous old woman who sells paint, powder, and toilet luxuries to ladies. He attempts with her assistance to pass himself off as a fine gentleman, but fails.

Amlote (åm.lot), **Denis.** See **Amelotte, Denis.**

Amlwch (äm'löċh). Urban district and seaport in N Wales, in Anglesey, ab. 24 mi. NW of Bangor, ab. 263 mi. NW of London by rail. During the 19th century, it was noted for its copper mines, once the largest in Europe, and the town was a copper-smelting center. 2,700 (1951).

Amman (äm'män, am'ąn). [Ancient names, **Rabboth** (or **Rabbah** or **Rabbath**) **Ammon, Philadelphia.**] Capital of Jordan (formerly Transjordan), located ab. 40 mi. NE of Jerusalem. It is linked by a main highway with Jerusalem and Jaffa, and served by the railroad line which runs N to Damascus. It is a trading center for the area, and exports wool. According to Biblical history it was the chief city of the Ammonites. Later it was built up by Ptolemy II Philadelphus, whence it received the name Philadelphia. It contains a number of Roman ruins, including a theater ab. 360 ft. in diameter, in part excavated from a hillside. 170,000 (est. 1950).

Amman (äm'än), **Johann Konrad.** b. at Schaffhausen, Switzerland, 1669; d. at Warmond, near Leiden, Holland, c1730. Swiss physician, one of the earliest to write on instruction for deaf-mutes, particularly in *Surdus loquens* (1692) and *Dissertatio de loquela* (1700).

Amman, Jost. b. at Zurich, Switzerland, June 13, 1539; d. at Nuremberg, Germany, May 17, 1591. Swiss engraver and painter who worked in Nuremberg after 1560; one of the "Little Masters." He was a prolific producer of paintings, drawings, and stained glass as well as of prints (for which he is best remembered). Chief among the latter are a series of copper engravings of kings of France (Frankfort, 1576), woodcuts for Sigmund Feierabend's Bible (1564–71), and 115 woodcuts in a series on the arts and trades (Frankfort, 1586).

Amman or **Ammann** (äm'än), **Paul.** b. at Breslau, Aug. 30, 1634; d. Feb. 4, 1691. German physician and botanist. He was appointed professor of botany at Leipzig in 1674, and of physiology in 1682, and was the author of *Praxis Vulnerum lethalium* (1690), *Character naturalis Plantarum* (1676), and others.

Ammanati (äm.mä.nä'tē), **Bartolommeo.** b. at Settignano, near Florence, Italy, June 18, 1511; d. there, April 22, 1592. Italian architect and sculptor who worked with Jacopo Sansovino, Giacomo da Vignola, and Giorgio Vasari; in 1557 he became an architect to Cosimo de' Medici. He designed the Ponte della Trinità at Florence and the court façade of the Pitti Palace at Florence.

Ammanford (am'ąn.fǫrd). Urban district and market town in S Wales, in Carmarthenshire, ab. 7 mi. S of Llandilo, ab. 213 mi. W of London. 6,578 (1951).

Ammen (am'ęn), **Daniel.** b. in Ohio, May 16, 1819; d. July 11, 1898. American naval officer in the Civil War; friend of Ulysses S. Grant. In 1836 he became a midshipman; he was subsequently in command of the gunboat *Seneca* at Port Royal in 1861, of the monitor *Patapsco* at Fort McAllister in 1863, and of the steam sloop *Mohican* at Fort Fisher in 1864–65. He was made captain (1866) and rear admiral (1878). Author of *The Atlantic Coast* (1883), *The Old Navy and the New* (1891), and others.

Ammen, Jacob. b. at Fincastle, Va., Jan. 7, 1807; d. at Lockland, Ohio, Feb. 6, 1894. American soldier and engineer, a general with the Union Army in the Civil War; brother of Daniel Ammen. He was graduated from West Point in 1831, resigned from the army in 1837, and became captain of volunteers on April 18, 1861. He took part in the West Virginia campaign under McClellan, was promoted to brigadier general of volunteers on July 16, 1862, and was in command of the district of east Tennessee from April 10, 1864, to Jan. 14, 1865, when he resigned. He was subsequently (1874) a member of a commission to study possible routes for the Panama Canal.

Ammendorf (äm'ęn.dôrf). Town in C Germany, in the *Land* (state) of Saxony, Russian Zone, formerly in the province of Saxony, Prussia, situated on the White Elster River, ab. 3 mi. S of Halle: manufacturing community; chemical and dye works, and paper mills. The population is predominantly Protestant. 18,723 (1946).

Ammenemez (am.ę.nē'mēz). See under **Amenemhet.**

Ammer Lake (äm'ėr). [German, **Ammersee** (äm'ėr.zā).] Lake in Upper Bavaria, Germany, traversed by the Ammer River. It lies W of Würm Lake (or Starnbergersee). Length, ab. 10 mi.

Ammer River. [Also, **Amper.**] River in Upper Bavaria, Germany, which rises in the Alps, traverses Ammer Lake (Ammersee), and joins the Isar River ab. 30 mi. NE of Munich. It receives the outlet of Würm Lake (or Starnbergersee). Length, ab. 125 mi.

Ammers-Küller (äm'ėrs.kül'ėr), Mrs. **Jo (Johanna) van.** b. at Delft, the Netherlands, 1884—. Dutch novelist, playwright, and short-story writer, internationally active in the feminist movement. She first achieved international standing as an author with *The Rebel Generation* (1925; Eng. trans., 1928), which was widely translated and later dramatized in Dutch. Author also of *Tantalus* (1930, based on a visit to the U.S.), *Jenny Heysten's Career* (1930), a suffragette novel, *No Surrender* (1931), *The House of Tavelinck* (1938), and others.

Ammianus Marcellinus (am.i.ā'nus mär.sę.lī'nus). b. at Antioch, c330; d. c395. Greek soldier in the Roman army, and a historian of the Roman empire. His work, continuing that of Tacitus, is an account in Latin covering the period from the accession of Nerva (96) to the death of Valens (378), originally in 31 books of which 13 (for the period 96–352) have been lost. Though the language is often faulty and the background of the writer that of a professional soldier rather than a scholar, the observation is impartial and provides a valuable source on the dissolution of the Roman empire.

Ammirato (äm.mē.rä′tō), **Scipione.** b. at Lecce, Italy, 1531; d. 1601. Italian historian. Aided in his work by the de' Medici duke of Florence, Cosimo I; best known for *Istorie Fiorentine* (1600), a history of Florence and neighboring areas up to his time.

Ammon (am′on, ä′mon). See also **Amen.**

Ammon (am′on). Eponymic ancestor of a people, the children of Ammon, or Ammonites, frequently mentioned in the Old Testament: according to the account in Genesis, the son of Lot by Ammon's younger daughter was Ben-Ami (Gen. xix. 38).

Ammon, Saint. [Also: **Amon, Amun.**] b. in Egypt, c285; d. 348. Christian saint. A friend of Saint Anthony, he was bishop of an Egyptian see and founder of a settlement of hermits in Nitria.

Ammon (äm′ōn), **Christoph Friedrich von.** b. at Bayreuth, Bavaria, Jan. 16, 1766; d. at Dresden, Saxony, May 21, 1850. German Protestant preacher and rationalist theologian, professor at Erlangen (1789–1804) and at Göttingen (1794).

Ammon, Friedrich August von. b. at Göttingen, Hanover, Sept. 10, 1799; d. May 18, 1861. German ophthalmologist; son of Christoph Friedrich von Ammon.

Ammonias (a.mō′ni.as). fl. late 5th century A.D. Architect who, according to an epigram in the Anthology, restored the Pharos of Alexandria in the time of the emperor Anastasius, about the end of the 5th century A.D. He is also credited with the construction of an aqueduct.

Ammonius (a.mō′ni.us). [Called **Saccas** or **Saccophorus,** meaning "Sack-bearer."] b. c175; d. 242. Alexandrian philosopher, a former porter. Possibly a Christian, he was a founder of Neoplatonism; according to some accounts, he attempted to reconcile the teachings of Plato and Aristotle. Plotinus, Longinus, and Origen were among his pupils.

Ammonius Hermiae (hėr′mi.ē). fl. 5th century A.D. Greek philosopher at Alexandria, author of commentaries on Plato and Ptolemy, now lost, and on Aristotle. He was the reputed author of a life of Aristotle, which was, in fact, probably the work of his pupil, John Philoponus.

Ammonoosuc (am.ō.nö′suk). [Also, **Lower Ammonoosuc.**] River in New Hampshire, which rises near Mount Washington and joins the Connecticut River ab. 7 mi. N of Haverhill, N.H. Length, ab. 100 mi.

Ammons (am′onz), **Elias Milton.** b. in Macon County, N.C., July 28, 1860; d. May 29, 1925. American cattleman and governor (1913–14) of Colorado.

Amol (ä.môl′). See **Amul.**

Amometus (am.ō.mē′tus). Greek writer of uncertain date, author of a poetical description of a nation of "Attacori," supposedly dwelling beyond the Himalayan range, resembling the ancient account of the Hyperboreans.

Amon (ä′mon, ā′-). See also **Amen.**

Amon (ā′mon). In the Old Testament, a governor of Samaria under Ahab. Amos, vii.

Amon. fl. in the middle of the 7th century B.C. Son of Manasseh and king of Judah. He was assassinated through a court conspiracy, and was succeeded by his son Josiah.

Amon, Saint. See Saint **Ammon.**

Amöneburg (ä.mė′ne.bůrk). Small town in W central Germany, in the former province of Hesse-Nassau, Prussia, situated on the Ohm River, ab. 7 mi. E of Marburg. It was formerly a strong fortress.

Amontons (à.môṅ.tôṅ), **Guillaume.** b. at Paris, Aug. 31, 1663; d. Oct. 11, 1705. French physicist. He was the inventor of a system of telegraphy which operated by means of manual signals between stations, set up in such a fashion that each one was within eyesight of the one immediately preceding and following it.

Amoor (ä.mör′). See **Amur River.**

Amore dei tre re (lä.mō′rā dā trā′rā′), **L'.** Opera in three acts, composed by Italo Montemezzi, with a libretto by Sem Benelli, first performed at La Scala, Milan, on April 10, 1913. The symbolic story centers around Fiora, captive princess of Archibaldo, king of Altura, and his son Manfredo. Fiora rejects Manfredo in favor of Avito, her own countryman.

Amoret (am′ō.ret). Twin sister of Belphoebe in Edmund Spenser's *Faerie Queene.* Her mother is the nymph Chrysogone.

Amoret. In John Fletcher's *Faithful Shepherdess,* a shepherdess in love with, and loved by, Perigot, and enduring many trials with sweetness and constancy.

Amoretti (am.o.ret′i). Group of sonnets (1595) by Edmund Spenser. They are largely autobiographical, and give an account of his wooing of Elizabeth Boyle, who had come to Ireland with her brother and settled in County Cork, near Youghal, on the coast.

Amorgos (a.môr′gos; Greek, ä.môr.gôs′). Island in the Aegean Sea, one of the Cyclades, ab. 16 mi. SE of Naxos. It belongs to Greece, in the *nomos* (department) of Cyclades. Olives are an important crop. It was the birthplace of the Greek poet Simonides. Area, ab. 50 sq. mi.

Amorites (am′ō.rīts). Name used in the Old Testament in general for the Canaanites as well as for a subdivision of the Canaanites. Biblical critics assert that in the set of documents known as J (Jahvist) all the pre-Israelitish inhabitants of Palestine are called Canaanites, while in the documents known as E (Elohist) (by others R = Redactor) they are called Amorites. This general use of the term "Amorite" finds further confirmation in a suggested reading of a geographical term in the cuneiform inscriptions, *mat Amurri,* country of the Amorites, which denominates in the inscriptions Phoenicia and Syria in general, particularly Palestine; it was previously read *mat Aharri.* Even in the restricted sense it is obvious that they were one of the chief races of Canaan. As early as the 13th century B.C., they seem to have been antagonists of the Hittites. They appear on the Egyptian monuments as *Amaru;* they lived E of the Jordan where Sihon and Og, their kings, were defeated by Moses. The land thus conquered became the territory of the tribes of Reuben, Gad, and half of Manasseh. Those W of the Jordan were conquered by Joshua, and their territory was given to the tribe of Judah.

Amorous Bigotte (big′ot), **The.** Comedy (1690) by Thomas Shadwell. Many of the incidents and characters of the play were conceived with the deliberate intent of pleasing the Whigs (in his political sympathies, Shadwell was a "true-blue" Whig), and this fact won the work considerable partisan popularity.

Amorous Complaint Made at Windsor, An. Poem attributed to Geoffrey Chaucer.

Amory (ā′mō.ri). City in NE Mississippi, in Monroe County: shipping point for dairy products, cotton, grain, and timber. 4,990 (1950).

Amory, Blanche. In W. M. Thackeray's novel *Pendennis,* a pretty, worldly, frivolous, and selfish girl, whose real name is Betsy. She is the daughter of Lady Clavering.

Amory, Thomas. b. at Limerick, Ireland, in May, 1682; d. at Boston, June 20, 1728. American merchant. A successful trader (1706–19) between the Azores and Portugal, Holland, England, and America, he came to South Carolina to settle his father's estate. Having lost his promised wife, and been forced to engage in a lawsuit to acquire his property, he settled (1720) at Boston, where he developed extensive trading enterprises, a shipbuilding business, and a rum and turpentine distillery.

Amory, Thomas. b. c1691; d. Nov. 25, 1788. English writer, author of *Memoirs Containing the Lives of Several Ladies of Great Britain* (1755), *Life of John Buncle, Esq.* (1756–66), and others. Likened to Rabelais and Dickens, he included in his books an extraordinary combination of theology, amorous adventure, scenic description, and autobiography.

Amoryus and Cleopes (a.môr′yus; klē′ō.pēz). Verse work (1448–49) by John Metham. A poem of 2,200 lines in rime royal, it deals with a variant of the Pyramus and Thisbe theme loosely associated with the story of Alexander the Great.

Amos (ā′mos). fl. c750 B.C. Hebrew prophet, contemporary of Isaiah and Hosea, and native of Tekoa, near Bethlehem. Author of the Book of Amos, the third of the Minor Prophets in the Bible, exhorting people to righteousness and warning of the doom that would inevitably follow wickedness.

Amos. Town in W central Quebec, on the main line of the Canadian National Railway, ab. 55 mi. N of Val d'Or. 4,265 (1951).

Amos, Sheldon. b. c1835; d. near Alexandria, Egypt, Jan. 3, 1886. English jurist and publicist, professor of jurisprudence at University College, London (1869–79). He was author of *Capital Punishment in England* (1864), *Codification in England and the State of New York* (1867), *Difference of Sex as a Topic of Jurisdiction and Legislation* (1870), *Policy of the Contagious Diseases Acts Tested* (1870), *A Systematic View of the Science of Jurisprudence* (1872), *Science of Politics* (1883), and others.

Amos Barton (bär'tọn). Short story (1857) by George Eliot. Originally published in *Blackwood's* it was one of her first works of fiction.

Amosis (ạ.mō'sis). See **Amasis.**

Amos Judd (ā'mọs jud). Novel by John Ames Mitchell, published in 1895.

Amour Médecin (là.mör māt.saṅ), **L'.** Comedy by Molière, produced (1665) at Versailles. In this play the author ridicules pedantry and charlatanism in the medical profession, which he mistrusted.

Amoy (ạ.moi'). [Also, **Szeming.**] Seaport in SE China, in the province of Fukien, situated on the island of Amoy opposite Formosa. It is a former treaty port, and has one of the best harbors in the country; tea is exported. It was captured by the British in 1841, and was opened to British commerce in 1842. One of its largest sources of wealth is money received from Chinese overseas, amounting to about 40 million Chinese dollars a year. 124,075 (est. 1947).

Amoymon (ạ.moi'mon). See **Amaimon.**

Ampato (äm.pä'tō). Mountain in the Cordillera Blanca of Peru. 21,681 ft.

Ampelius (am.pē'li.us), **Lucius.** fl. probably sometime before 100 B.C. Roman author. He is best known for a concise history entitled *Liber Memorialis*, which contains also a number of geographical and mythological entries. Although much of the material is not trustworthy, it includes the only known classical reference to the sculptures at Pergamum.

Amper (äm'pėr). See **Ammer River.**

Ampère (äṅ.per), **André Marie.** b. at Polémieux, near Lyons, France, Jan. 22, 1775; d. at Marseilles, June 10, 1836. French physicist and mathematician, discoverer of the relationship between magnetism and electricity (Ampère's law), which is the basis of the science of electrodynamics; inventor of the astatic needle. The ampere, unit of electric-current flow, is named for him. He was a professor of mathematics at the École Polytechnique (1809) and the Collège de France (1824), at Paris. Author of *Recueil d'observations électrodynamiques* (1822), *Théorie des phénomènes électrodynamiques* (1830), *Essai sur la philosophie des sciences*, and others.

Ampère, Jean Jacques Antoine. b. at Lyons, France, Aug. 12, 1800; d. at Pau, France, March 27, 1864. French literary historian; son of André Marie Ampère. A professor at Marseilles and at the Collège de France at Paris, his lectures on Scandinavian and German epics were among the first of their kind in Europe. One of these was published (1830) as *De l'histoire de la poésie;* author also of *La Grèce, Rome, et Dante* (1848), *Histoire romaine à Rome* (1861–64), and others.

Ampersand Mountain (am'pėr.sand). Peak of the Adirondacks, in N New York, situated S of the Saranac Lakes. Elevation, ab. 3,365 ft.

Ampezzaner Alps (äm.pe.tsä'nėr). Group of the Dolomite Alps on the borders of the S Austrian Tirol and Italy.

Ampezzo (äm.pet'tsō). See also **Cortina d'Ampezzo.**

Ampezzo. Valley in NE Italy, near the Austrian Tirol, ab. 26 mi. SE of Bressanone. Its chief town is Cortina d'Ampezzo.

Ampfing (ämp'fing). Village in SE Germany, in Upper Bavaria, ab. 5 mi. W of Mühldorf.

Ampfing, Battle of. Victory gained at Ampfing by the Austrians over the French, on Dec. 1, 1800.

Amphiale (am.fī'ạ.lē). See under **Aegaleos.**

Amphialus (am.fī'ạ.lus). In Sir Philip Sidney's *Arcadia*, the valiant and virtuous son of the wicked Cecropea, and the lover of his cousin Philoclea.

Amphiaraus (am"fi.ạ.rā'us). In Greek mythology, a seer and hero of Argos, who took part in the Argonautic expedition, the hunt of the Calydonian boar, and the expedition of the Seven against Thebes. He was saved from his enemies by Zeus, who ordered the earth to swallow him, and a sanctuary called the Amphiareion was erected on the supposed spot.

Amphiareion (am"fi.ạ.rī'ọn). Sanctuary and oracle of Amphiaraus, near Oropus, in Boeotia, Greece. In Greek legend, Amphiaraus was one of the Seven who marched against Thebes, and was here swallowed up by the earth at the will of Zeus, to save him in his flight. The sanctuary occupies a narrow area on the bank of a torrent; it includes a temple and altar, a large portico, a long range of bases for votive statues, and a theater. All the existing ruins are of Hellenistic date. The oracle enjoyed great renown, and the deified seer had a high reputation for healing sickness. Excavations were made (1884 *et seq.*) here by the Archaeological Society of Athens.

Amphictyony (am.fik'ti.ọ.ni) or **Amphictyonic League** (am.fik.ti.on'ik). In Greek history, a league of peoples inhabiting neighboring territories or drawn together by a community of origin or interests, for mutual protection and the guardianship in common of a central sanctuary and its rites. There were several such confederations, but the name is specially appropriated to the most famous of them, that of Delphi. This was composed of 12 tribes, and its deputies met twice each year, alternately at Delphi and at Thermopylae. Its origin dates back to the beginnings of Greek history. It exercised paramount authority over the famous oracular sanctuary of the Pythian Apollo and over the surrounding region, and conducted the Pythian games; and it constituted, though in an imperfect way, a national congress of the many comparatively small and often opposed states into which Greece was divided. The 12 members of the Delphic Amphictyonic League were the Thessalians, the Boeotians, the Dorians, the Ionians, the Perrhabeans, the Magnetes, the Locrians, the Oeteans, the Phtyiots, the Malians, the Phocians, and the Dolopians.

Amphilochus (am.fil'ọ̄.kus). In Greek legend, a seer, son of Amphiaraus and brother of Alcmaeon; one of the Epigoni.

Amphion (am.fī'on, am'fi.ọn). In Greek mythology, a skillful musician; son of Zeus and Antiope, twin brother of Zethus, and husband of Niobe. The brothers slew Dirce, who had ill-treated their mother, by causing her to be dragged to death by a bull. They took possession of Thebes, and when the walls were building, the stones moved of their own accord to their places under the influence of Amphion's lyre.

Amphipolis (am.fip'ọ̄.lis). In ancient geography, a city in Macedonia, on the Strymon River, ab. 3 mi. from the Aegean Sea. Originally a Thracian town, it was colonized by Athens in c436 B.C., and was captured (424 B.C.) by Sparta. Near it the Spartans under Brasidas defeated (422 B.C.) the Athenians under Cleon. It later became a Macedonian and then a Roman possession.

Amphissa (am.fis'ạ; Greek, äm'fē.sä). [Also: **Salona, Amfissa.**] Town in C Greece, capital of the *nomos* (department) of Phocis, N of the Gulf of Corinth, situated at the foot of the W slope of Mount Parnassus ab. 51 mi. NW of Corinth: large olive plantations. It is the seat of a bishopric. In ancient times it was a Locrian city. 5,546 (1951).

Amphitheater. Unincorporated community in S Arizona, in Pima County, N of Tucson. 12,664 (1950).

Amphitrite (am.fi.trī'tē). In Greek mythology, the goddess of the sea; daughter of Nereus and wife of Poseidon.

Amphitrite. Asteroid (No. 29) discovered by A. Marth, at London, on March 1, 1854.

Amphitryon (am.fit'ri.ọn) or **Amphitruo** (-rö.ō). In Greek legend, husband of Alcmene and father of Iphicles. To secure Alcmene (who would not wed him until the death of her brothers had been avenged) he undertook, for his uncle Creon, to catch a ravaging fox, which by a decree of fate could not be captured, with the help of an Athenian dog which fate had decreed should catch every animal it might pursue. This conflict was resolved when both animals were turned into stone. He attacked the Taphians, but could not overcome them so long as the chief, Pterelaus, who was rendered immortal by one golden hair, continued to live. Comaetho, daughter of Pterelaus, cut off this hair for love of Amphitryon, and Pterelaus perished. The application, in later literature, of the name Amphitryon to a host is from that part of the story where Jupiter assumes the former's shape in order to visit Alcmene. He gives a feast and is interrupted by the real Amphitryon. This gives rise (in Molière's comedy) to a dispute which is settled by the phrase "Le véritable Amphitryon est l'Amphitryon où l'on dine" (translatable as, "he who gives the feast is the host").

Amphitryon. [Also, **Amphitruo.**] Play by Plautus. A comedy founded on the fable of Jupiter and Alcmene, it has been adapted or imitated by Molière, John Dryden, and many others. Its source is uncertain, but it is possibly from Archippus, a writer of the old comedy (415 B.C.).

Amphitryon (äṅ.fē.trē.ôṅ). Comedy by Molière, produced in 1668; a version of Plautus's play.

Amphitryon. Opera by Michel Jean Sedaine, produced in 1781.

Amphitryon. Comedy by François Guillaume Jean Stanislas Andrieux, produced in 1782.

Amphitryon 38 (French, äṅ.fē.trē.ôṅ tränt.wet). Philosophical comedy (1929; Eng. trans., 1938) on the ancient theme, in French, by the French writer Jean Giraudoux (1889–1944). The figure in the title indicates the author's surmise that there have been 37 previous treatments.

Amphitryon, or The Two Socias (am.fit'ri.ǫn; sō'shạz). Comedy by John Dryden, performed in 1690. It is an altered version of Molière's play.

Ampin (äm'pēn). [Also: **Anpei, Anping.**] Town in SE China, on the SW coast of the island of Formosa, ab. 20 mi. N of Kaohsiung (Takao).

Amplepuis (äṅ.plę.pwē). Town in E France, in the department of Rhône, situated on the railroad line from Paris to Lyons, ab. 29 mi. NW of Lyons: manufactures silk, cotton, and linen. 5,290 (1946).

Ampsancti (amp.sangk'tī), **Vallis.** See **Amsancti.**

Ampsivarii (amp.si.vā'ri.ī). [Also: **Amsivarii, Ansibarii.**] German tribe described by Tacitus as originally neighbors, in the region of the Ems River, of the Chauci who had driven them out. In the year 58 A.D. they appeared on the Rhine, whence they were dislodged by the Romans, and were thought to have been annihilated. They reappeared, however, in the 4th century in incursions into Roman territory. They were ultimately merged with the Franks.

Ampthill (amt'il). Urban district and market town in SE England, in Bedfordshire, ab. 42 mi. NW of London by rail. 2,873 (1951).

Ampthill, 2nd Baron. Title of **Russell, Arthur Oliver Villiers.**

Ampudia (äm.pö'ᴛʜyä), **Pedro de.** fl. in the middle of the 19th century. Mexican general, in command of the Mexican army on the Rio Grande at the beginning of the Mexican War (1846). As commander at Monterey he surrendered to General Taylor on Sept. 24, 1846.

Ampurdán (äm.pör.ᴛʜän'). Valley-plain in the province of Gerona, Spain, in the vicinity of Figueras.

Amraoti (um.rou'tē). [Also, **Amrawati.**] District of Madhya Pradesh, Union of India, ab. 80 mi. W of Nagpur: wheat and tobacco. 988,524 (1941).

Amraoti. City in Amraoti district, Union of India, ab. 85 mi. W of Nagpur: important trading center. 61,971 (1941).

Amraphel (am'rạ.fel, am.rā'fęl). In the Old Testament, a king of Shinar (southern Babylonia) who, allied with Chedorlaomer of Elam and two other kings, marched, in the time of Abraham, against the five kings of the Vale of Siddim. He is tentatively identified by some with Hammurabi. Gen. xiv.

Amr ibn-al-As (äm'ėr ib''ęn.äl.äs'). [Also: **Amru ben-el-Ass**; sometimes called **Amer** or **Amru.**] d. 664 A.D. Arab general, conqueror and first Moslem governor of Egypt. A Koreish tribesman, he was early an opponent of Mohammed, but later (629) became his follower at Mecca. Sent by the caliph Abu-Bakr, Mohammed's successor, he participated (633) in the conquest of Syria; he also headed an expedition (639–42) to Egypt, sent by the caliph Omar I, taking Pelusium, Heliopolis, Babylon, and (by treaty with Cyrus) Alexandria. Replaced, under Omar and Othman, by another commander, he was recalled (645) to put down a revolt in Alexandria. He extended Moslem influence into Tripoli, and sided with Muawiyah in the war which followed Ali's seizure of the caliphate on the death of Othman. He served as Muawiyah's representative during the arbitration with Ali, and as his governor (658–64) after the reconquest of Egypt.

Amrit Kaur (äm'rēt kour'), **Rajkumar.** b. 1887— Indian social worker and feminist leader, member of the Indian cabinet (1947 *et seq.*). Secretary (1930) of the All-India Women's Conference, she served as its chairman (1931–33) and president (1938). She had the distinction of being the first woman to be a member (1942) of the advisory board of education to the Indian government. She was head (1950–51) of the World Health Organization.

Amritsar (um.rit'sạr). [Also, **Umritsir.**] District of the division of Lahore, Punjab state, Union of India, NE of the city of Lahore: important wheat and sugar area. It is divided into the three subdistricts Amritsar, Ajnala, and Tarn Taran. Capital, Amritsar; area, ab. 1,600 sq. mi.; pop. 1,413,876 (1941).

Amritsar. [Also, **Umritsir.**] City in NW India, the capital of the Amritsar district, Punjab state, Union of India, ab. 30 mi. E of Lahore: one of the most important commercial and manufacturing cities in N India. Its carpets are famous all over the world, it has a large hide industry, and is a collecting and distributing center for much of the grain of the area. Founded by Ram Das in the 16th century, it is the religious center for the Sikhs, and contains the Golden Temple, a Sikh temple attended by 500 to 600 priests. 391,010 (1941).

Amritsar Massacre. See under **Dyer, Reginald Edward Harry.**

Amru-al-Kais (äm'rö.äl.kīs'). [Also, **Imru-al-Qays.**] fl. early 6th century A.D. Arab poet, one of the greatest included in the anthology known as the Muallaqat. According to legend, he devoted his life to avenging his murdered father, wandering in search of aid and spending a long period at the Byzantine court. He was given troops by the emperor but poisoned on his way back to Arabia for having seduced a Byzantine princess. Technical excellence and beauty of feeling made his work a model for later Arab poets, particularly in the field of erotic verse.

Amru ben-el-Ass (äm'rö ben.el.äs'). See **Amr ibn-al-As.**

Amrum (äm'rum). Island in NW Germany, in the *Land* (state) of Schleswig-Holstein, British Zone, formerly in the province of Schleswig-Holstein, Prussia, situated in the North Sea, W of the island of Föhr. It has several seaside resorts. Area, 8 sq. mi.; pop. ab. 3,000.

Amsancti (äm.sängk'tē). [Also, **Vallis Amsancti** (or **Ampsancti**).] Valley in the province of Avellino, SW Italy, E of Naples, noted for its sulfurous lake and cave.

Amsdorf (äms'dôrf), **Nikolaus von.** b. at Torgau, Germany, Dec. 3, 1483; d. at Eisenach, Germany, May 14, 1565. German Protestant reformer; friend of Luther, whom he accompanied to Leipzig (1519) and Worms (1521), and whom he aided in the translation of the Bible. He was instrumental in introducing the Reformation into Magdeburg (1524), Goslar (1528), and elsewhere; consecrated (1542) Bishop of Naumburg by Luther, he was driven (1546) from his see in the Schmalkaldic war. In the adiaphoristic controversy, he opposed Melanchthon.

Amshewitz (am'shę.wits), **John Henry.** b. at Ramsgate, England, Dec. 19, 1882; d. 1942. English painter and illustrator, noted for his portraits, mural decorations, etchings, and cartoons. He studied at the Royal Academy school, where he won the prize for mural decoration. He exhibited repeatedly at London, and also at Paris, Florence, New York, and Philadelphia, and in South Africa and the Straits Settlements. His paintings are in several royal collections and in museums at London, Cape Town, and other cities in South Africa. Among the books he illustrated are *Everyman* and *Myths and Legends of Ancient Greece*. His other works include historical panels in the Liverpool town hall and in the Royal Exchange at London.

Amsivarii (am.si.vā'ri.ī). See **Ampsivarii.**

Amsler (äms'lėr), **Jakob.** [Also, **Amsler-Laffon** (-läf'ōn).] b. at Stalden, near Brugg, Switzerland, Nov. 16, 1823; d. at Schaffhausen, Switzerland, in January, 1912. Swiss mathematician and scientist who wrote on mechanical integration, magnetism, and thermodynamics. He took his doctorate at Schaffhausen in 1856 and taught there. From 1892 he served as corresponding member of the Paris Académie des Sciences. His works include *Ueber die mechanische Bestimmung des Flächeninhaltes* and *Zur Theorie der Vertheilung des Magnetismus im weichen Eisen.*

Amsler, Samuel. b. at Schniznach, Switzerland, Dec. 17, 1791; d. at Munich, May 18, 1849. Swiss engraver at Rome (1816 *et seq.*) and Munich (from 1829). An admirer of Raphael, he is best known for reproductions of such works of Raphael's as the *Entombment of Christ.*

Amsteg (äm′shtek). [Also, **Amstäg.**] Village in C Switzerland, in the canton of Uri, amid magnificent scenery, on the Reuss River: has a power station for the St. Gotthard railway.

Amstel (äm′stel). Small river in the NW part of the Netherlands, which flows through Amsterdam and empties into the Ij. Amsterdam was named for it (formerly Amsteldam).

Amstelland (äm′stel.länt). Formerly, the name given to the region, in the NW Netherlands, which lies near the Amstel River.

Amsterdam (am′stėr.dam). Small uninhabited island in the S Indian Ocean, halfway between Australia and Africa, below the N limit of drift ice. A volcanic island, almost 3,000 ft. high, named by Anton Van Diemen in 1633, it belongs to France.

Amsterdam. [Former name, **Amsteldam** (äm.stel-däm′).] City in the W part of the Netherlands, in the province of North Holland, built on marshy ground at the junction of the Amstel River, the Ij (or Y), and the North Sea Canal, and traversed by numerous small waterways: the largest city and the commercial metropolis of the country. 832,935 (1949).

Commerce and Industry. It has a port serving seagoing as well as river navigation, with extensive quays, warehouse facilities, docks, and shipyards; it is connected with the Rhine River system through the Merwede Canal. The mainstay of Amsterdam's shipping activities is the trade with the East Indies and with the Americas, particularly in tobacco, coffee, tea, cocoa, rice, drugs, spices, and sugar, but also in grain, coal, timber, and petroleum. Among the industries, diamond cutting was predominant until the 20th century, when Antwerp and then Israel began to outrank Amsterdam; other industries include tobacco manufacture, sugar refineries, oil, soap, margarine, glass, and chemical factories, tanneries, distilleries, breweries, and shipyards. Amsterdam is of considerable importance as a banking place; the stock exchange is among the leading institutions of its kind in Europe; it is the seat of the Bank of the Netherlands and of numerous other banking and insurance institutions.

Cultural Institutions. Amsterdam is the cultural center of the Netherlands. It has a municipal university, a Calvinist university, and a People's University, a colonial institute, a zoölogical and a botanical garden, numerous vocational schools, literary societies, newspaper and periodical offices; it is the seat of the Royal Academy of the Sciences. There is a renowned conservatory of music; the performances of the Concertgebouw Orchestra are famous. Amsterdam is an international market for paintings and art objects, and has an academy of arts. It is a city of museums. The Rijks Museum contains the best existing collection of paintings and etchings of Netherlands masters (Rembrandt, Frans Hals, Jan Vermeer, Jan Steen, Jan van Goyen, Pieter de Hooch, Adriaen van Ostade, the Ruysdaals, and others) besides a collection of arts, crafts, and folklore objects. The municipal museum contains a collection of furniture and one of paintings, including works by Vincent van Gogh. The Joseph Fodor Museum contains French and Dutch pictures; the Willet Holthuysen Museum has exhibits of furniture and porcelain. There is an ethnological and a natural history museum. The university library, with more than 100,000 volumes and manuscripts, includes the Rosenthal collection of Jewish literature.

Architecture. The nucleus of the old city of Amsterdam, marking the city limits in the 14th century, lies between the innermost crescent canal (*Gracht*) and the harbor area on the Ij; the city limits of the 17th century are marked by the outermost crescent canal (*Single*); toward the outskirts are the newer quarters including model settlements and garden suburbs. The canals divide the old city into numerous islands; the houses are erected on piles because of the swampy ground. Many tree-bordered quays and old-fashioned houses, mostly of the 16th, 17th, and 18th centuries, are preserved. The royal palace, built in the classical style by Jacob van Kampen in 1648–55, served originally as the town hall; the Nieuwe Kerk ("New Church," or Saint Catherine's Church), a Gothic building dating from 1408, contains the monument to Admiral Michel Adrianszoon de Ruyter. The Oude Kerk ("Old Church," or Saint Nicholas) has beautiful stained-glass windows. The North Church was built (1565–1621) by Hendryk de Keyser. The Great Synagogue of the Portuguese Jews dates from 1670. Various important buildings were added in the 19th and 20th centuries.

History. In the 13th century a small sea-fishing settlement, Amsterdam came under the rule of the counts of Holland in 1327; extensive privileges, including freedom from tolls, were granted by Count William IV in 1342. Walls were added in 1482. The city attained commercial importance first as a member of the Hanseatic League and then, during the period of the religious troubles, through the admission of refugees, such as Protestants from Antwerp and Brabant, and Jews from Portugal. Influenced, however, by its trading interests, Amsterdam did not join the other towns of the Netherlands in their revolt against Spain until 1578. The closing of the Schelde River estuary through the treaty of Westphalia in 1648 eliminated Antwerp as a rival; in 1602 the East India Company, in 1621 the West India Company, in 1609 the Bank of Amsterdam were founded; the Edict of Nantes (1681) brought French Huguenots to the city. In this period Amsterdam, thanks to the achievements of Dutch seapower and overseas enterprise, was the leading commercial city of Europe, a center of the arts and sciences, and a citadel of religious freedom. The painter Rembrandt lived here and the philosopher Spinoza was a native of Amsterdam. The city defended itself against William II of Nassau in 1650 and against Louis XIV in 1672 by opening the dikes. A decline set in during the 18th century; Amsterdam was occupied by the Prussians in 1787 and by the French in 1794. In 1810 it was incorporated into the French empire. The new prosperity started with the building of the North Sea Canal, connecting Amsterdam with Ijmuiden, in 1876 and the modernization of the harbor. The city suffered only slight damage during the five-day German attack in May, 1940. However, the harbor area was heavily damaged later in World War II; the Fokker aircraft works near Amsterdam were stripped of their machinery and equipment.

Amsterdam. City in E New York, in Montgomery County, on the Mohawk River, ab. 30 mi. NW of Albany: center for the manufacture of carpets, rugs, knitted goods, and brooms; also produces underwear, gloves, linseed oil, and pearl buttons. 32,240 (1950).

Amstetten (äm′shtet″en). Town in E Austria, in the province of Lower Austria, situated on the Ybbs River ab. 28 mi. SE of Linz: a station on the railroad from Linz to Vienna. Nearby is the Benedictine abbey of Seitenstetten, founded in 1112 and rebuilt (1718–47) in the baroque style. The library contains some 80,000 volumes, manuscripts, and incunabula. 11,341 (1951).

Amstutz (am′stuts), **Noah Steiner.** b. at Milton, in Wayne County, Ohio, Nov. 5, 1864—. American research engineer and patent attorney who originated the first phototelegraphy system (1891) and the first automatic half-tone engraving machine. He was manager (1903–05) of the British Automatic Photographic Company at London, and was admitted (1903) to the bar of the Supreme Court. Author of *Handbook of Photo Engraving* (1907), technical serials, *Physical Characteristics of Relief Engravings* (1906–07), and other works.

Amucú (ä.mö.kö′), **Lake.** See **Amuku, Lake.**

Amu Darya (ä.mö′ där′ya). [Arabic, **Jihun, Jaihun,** or **Gihon**; ancient name (still sometimes used), **Oxus.**] Principal river in Central Asia, in the U.S.S.R. It rises in the plateau of the E Pamirs, in the Tadzhik Soviet Socialist Republic; flows generally W, separating, in part of its course, Bukhara, in the U.S.S.R., from Afghanistan, flows then NW, and empties by a delta into the S part of the Aral Sea. It is generally thought to have emptied into the Caspian Sea in ancient times. At Chardzhou it is crossed by the Transcaspian Railway. Length, ab. 1,578 mi.; navigable by vessels for ab. 300 mi.

Amuku (ä.mö.kö'), **Lake.** [Also, **Lake Amucú.**] Small lake in S central British Guiana, connected with the Essequibo River and, through the Branco River, with the Amazon.

Amul (ä.möl'). [Also, **Amol.**] City in N Iran, in Mazanderan, situated on the Heraz River, ab. 70 mi. NE of Tehran: an important trading center. It was a flourishing city in the Middle Ages. Pop. ab. 10,000.

Amulree (ā'mul.rē), 1st Baron. [Title of **William Warrender Mackenzie.**] b. 1860; d. at Winterbourne, Wiltshire, England, May 5, 1942. British jurist and expert on industrial arbitration. He was chairman (1917–18) of a committee on production, a member (1918–19) of a committee of inquiry on women in industry, and joined (1930) the cabinet of Ramsay MacDonald as secretary of state for air. Coauthor of works on highway laws, licensing and education acts, and industrial arbitration.

Amun (am'un), Saint. See Saint **Ammon.**

Amun (ä'mön). See **Amen.**

Amunátegui (ä.mö.nä'tā.gē), **Miguel Luis.** b. Jan. 11, 1828; d. Jan. 22, 1888. Chilean historian. Coauthor of *Memoria sobre la reconquista española* (1850), *Compendio de la historia politica y eclesiástica de Chile* (1856), *Descubrimiento y conquista de Chile* (1862), and *Los precursores de la independencia de Chile* (1872–73).

Amundsen (am'und.sen; Norwegian, ä'mün.sen), **Roald.** b. in Borge, Norway, July 16, 1872; d. 1928. Norwegian polar explorer. As commander of the *Gjöa* (1903–06), he navigated the Northwest Passage, and located the exact geographic position of the north magnetic pole. Having bought Fridtjof Nansen's *Fram*, he altered his plans for further Arctic exploration, and sailed (1910) from Norway for the Antarctic, reaching the South Pole on Dec. 14, 1911. He was ahead of Robert Falcon Scott by 34 days and is thus known as the discoverer of the South Pole. He negotiated (1918–20) the Northeast Passage in the *Maud*. With Lincoln Ellsworth and others, he undertook a polar exploration by air, using both planes and airships, and flew across the North Pole (1926) in the semi-rigid dirigible *Norge*, built by Umberto Nobile. On June 17, 1928, he set out from Bergen to rescue Nobile, who had crashed after crossing the pole in the *Italia*, and was never heard from again. Author of the two-volume *North West Passage* (1908), the two-volume *South Pole* (1912), of *Our Polar Flight* (1925) and *First Crossing of the Polar Sea* (1927), both with Lincoln Ellsworth, and others.

Amundsen Gulf. Arm of Beaufort Sea, in the Arctic Ocean, separating Victoria and Banks islands of the Canadian Arctic Archipelago from the NW North American mainland. It was named for Roald Amundsen, the Norwegian polar explorer, who traversed it in 1903.

Amur (ä.mör'). Former province in E Siberia, situated N of the Amur River, ceded by China to Russia in 1858: now incorporated in the Khabarovsk *Krai* (subdivision) of the Russian Soviet Federated Socialist Republic.

Amurath (ä.mö.rät'). See **Murad.**

Amur River. [Also: **Amoor**; Chinese, **Heilungkiang.**] River in NE Asia, formed by the junction of the Shilka and Argun rivers. It flows generally SE then NE, and then E, and enters the Gulf of Tartary. In part of its course it forms the boundary between the Russian Soviet Federated Socialist Republic and Manchuria. Its chief tributaries are, on the right, the Sungari and Ussuri; on the left, the Zeya, Bureya, Urmi, Gorin, and Amgun. Length, including the Argun, ab. 2,713 mi.; navigable for ab. 2,400 mi.

Amussat (å.mü.så), **Jean Zuléma.** b. at St. Maixent, Deux-Sèvres, France, Nov. 21, 1796; d. May 14, 1856. French surgeon and surgical writer; author of *Torsion des artères* (1829) and other works. He invented a probe used in lithotrity.

Amuyao (ä.mö.yä'ō). [Also, **Anuyao.**] Mountain in C Mountain province, Luzon, Philippine Islands. 8,865 ft.

Amvets (am'vets''). See **American Veterans of World War II.**

Amvrakia (äm.vrä.kē'ä), **Gulf of.** See **Ambracian Gulf.**

'Amwas (äm.wäs'). See under **Emmaus,** Palestine.

Amy (ā'mi), **Ernest Valentine.** b. at New York, 1892—. American radio engineer. He invented (independently and in collaboration with others) many devices used in the noise-reduction systems of radio networks. He was graduated as an electrical engineer (1917) from Columbia University, served in France with the American army during World War I, was associated (1922–28) with the Radio Corporation of America, and in 1928 became a consulting engineer at New York. He supervised (1922–23) the installation of the first two-way radio telephone, on the transatlantic liner *America.*

Amyas (am'i.as). In Edmund Spenser's *Faerie Queene*, the captive lover of Aemilia, a squire of low degree.

Amyclae (a.mī'klē). In ancient geography, a town in Laconia, Greece, ab. 3 mi. S of Sparta, the legendary seat of Tyndareus. It long retained its Achaean population. According to a legend, the inhabitants of Amyclae had been so often alarmed by false reports of the hostile approach of the Spartans that all mention of the subject was forbidden; hence, when they did come, no one dared announce the fact, and the town was captured. "Amyclaen silence" thus became a proverb.

Amynta (a.min'ta). Character in Thomas D'Urfé's romance *Astrea.*

Amyntas I (a.min'tas). d. c498 B.C. King of Macedonia; son of Alcetas, and fifth in descent from Perdiccas, the founder of the dynasty. He presented earth and water, as a token of his submission, to the Persian commander Megabazus, whom Darius, on returning to Persia, had left at the head of 80,000 men in Europe.

Amyntas II. King of Macedonia (394–370 B.C.); nephew of Perdiccas II. He obtained the crown of Macedonia proper in 394 by the murder of Pausanias, son of the usurper Aëropus. He was driven from Macedonia by Argaeus, the son of Pausanias, supported by Bardylis, an Illyrian chief. He was subsequently restored by the Thessalians, with whom he had taken refuge.

Amyntas III. d. 336 B.C. King of Macedonia (360–359 B.C.); grandson of Amyntas II. He was an infant at the death of his father in 360 B.C., and was excluded (359 B.C.) from the throne by the regent, his uncle Philip of Macedon, at whose court he was brought up, and whose daughter he married. He was executed by Alexander the Great for a conspiracy against the king's life.

Amyntas, or The Impossible Dowry. Pastoral drama of the Italian type by Thomas Randolph, first printed in 1638, and performed before Charles I and Queen Henrietta at Whitehall, in London.

Amyot (å.myō), **Jacques.** b. at Melun, France, Oct. 30, 1513; d. at Auxerre, France, Feb. 6, 1593. French prelate and classical scholar whose translations of ancient writers, especially Plutarch, had a great influence on later writers. Tutor to Charles IX and Henry III of France, he was also bishop of Auxerre (1570–93). His version of Plutarch's *Lives*, entitled *Vies des hommes illustres de Plutarque* (1559–65), as translated (1579) into English by Sir Thomas North, was the source on which Shakespeare drew for his Roman plays. He also produced *Théagène et Chariclée* (1547 *et seq.*, after Heliodorus), *Daphnis et Chloé* (1559, after Longus), *Oeuvres morales de Plutarque* (1572, from *Opera Moralia*), and others.

Amyot, Jean Joseph Marie. See **Amiot, Jean Joseph Marie.**

Amyraut (å.mē.rō), **Moïse.** [Also: **Moïse Amyrault**; Latinized, **Moses Amyraldus.**] b. in September, 1596; d. 1664. French Protestant theologian, professor (1633–64) at Saumur. He was charged with Arminianism, and although he was acquitted at the synods of Alençon (1637) and Charenton (1644), the *Formula Consensus Helvetica* (1657) was directed chiefly against him.

Amytis (am'i.tis). [Also, **Amitu.**] Median wife of Nebuchadnezzar, king of Babylon. It was for her that he is said to have built the famous "hanging gardens."

Anabaptists (an.a.bap'tists). Christian sect that holds baptism in infancy to be invalid, and requires adults who have received it to be baptized on joining their communion. The name is best known historically as applied to the followers of Thomas Münzer (a leader of the Peasants' War in Germany, who was killed in battle in 1525), and to those of John Matthias and John Bockold, or John of Leiden, who attempted to establish a socialistic kingdom of New Zion or Mount Zion at Münster in Westphalia, and were defeated in 1535, their leaders being killed and hung up in iron cages. The name has also been applied to bodies of very different character in other respects, usually in an approbrious sense, since believers in the sole validity of adult baptism refuse to regard it as rebaptism in the case of persons who have received the rite only in infancy. The Mennonite sect in the U.S. derives originally from an Anabaptist group.

Anabar (ä.nä.bär'). [Also, **Anabara** (-bä'rą).] River in the N part of the U.S.S.R., in the Yakutsk Autonomous Soviet Socialist Republic of the Russian Soviet Federated Socialist Republic, in Siberia; it flows into the Arctic Ocean ab. 250 mi. W of the Lena River. Length, ab. 561 mi.

Anabasis (ą.nab'ą.sis). Account by Xenophon, in seven books, of the campaign of the Persian prince Cyrus (the Younger) against his brother Artaxerxes II of Persia, and of the retreat (401–399) of the 10,000 Greeks who had fought under Cyrus, after his death at Cunaxa. Xenophon himself, a volunteer soldier, was one of those who led the 10,000 and, after a long and arduous march through Armenia and Georgia, brought them to the sea at Trebizond (now Trabzon).

Anabasis of Alexander. Important historical work by Arrian, in seven books, all of which, with the exception of a few pages, has survived. It begins with the accession of Alexander the Great, and describes his campaigns and victories.

Anacáona (ä.nä.kä'ō.nä). [Eng. trans., "*Golden Flower.*"] d. at Santo Domingo (now Ciudad Trujillo, in the Dominican Republic), c1503. Indian woman; sister of Behechio and wife of Caonabo, caciques (tribal chiefs) of Haiti when it was discovered by Columbus (1492). After the capture and death of Caonabo, she counseled submission to the Spaniards, and herself received Bartholomew, brother of Christopher Columbus, with great hospitality in 1498. She succeeded her brother Behechio as ruler of his tribe, and friendly relations with the Spanish continued until 1503; in that year she entertained Ovando and his forces, but in the midst of a festival in their honor they attacked her village, massacred a great number of Indians, and carried her to the settlement of Santo Domingo, where she was hanged.

Anacapri (ä.nä.kä'prē). The W part of the island of Capri, in the *compartimento* (region) of Campania, S Italy.

Anacharsis (an.ą.kär'sis). fl. c600 B.C. Scythian prince brother of Saulius, king of Thrace, a contemporary of Solon. He visited Athens, where he obtained a great reputation for wisdom. On returning to Thrace he was slain by his brother. By some he was reckoned among the legendary seven great sages of ancient times.

Anacker (ä'näk.ėr), **Heinrich.** [Called the **"Lyricist of the Brown Front."**] b. at Aarau, Switzerland, 1901—. German poet, many of whose poems enjoyed the popularity of true folk songs with the German youth of the Nazi period. His numerous lyrical collections include *Die Trommel* (The Drum, 1931), *Die Fanfare* (The Fanfare, 1933), *Der Aufbau* (The Reconstruction, 1935), and *Kämpfen und Singen* (Fighting and Singing, 1937).

Anacletus (an.ą.klē'tus), Saint. [Also: **Cletus** and (probably) **Anencletus.**] fl. 1st century A.D. Third Pope (76–88 A.D.), said to have been director, with Linus, of the Church during Saint Peter's lifetime. He is believed by some scholars not to have been identical with Anencletus or Cletus, although he is listed under these names in some sources.

Anacletus II. [Also: **Anaclete** (an'ą.klēt); original name, **Pietro Pierleone** or **Pierleoni.**] d. 1138. Antipope from 1130 to 1138, in opposition to Innocent II. His popularity in Rome caused Innocent's flight to France and Pisa, but the influence of Saint Bernard healed the schism after Anacletus's death.

Anaconda (an.ą.kon'dą). City in W Montana, county seat of Deer Lodge County, ab. 23 mi. W of Butte. It is a major copper-smelting center. 11,254 (1950).

Anacortes (an.ą.kôr'tęz). City in NW Washington, in Skagit County, on Fidalgo Island: fishing and lumbering center. 6,919 (1950).

Anacostia (an.ą.kos'ti.ą). Small river rising in C Maryland and flowing generally S into the Potomac River at Washington, D.C. It has given its name to a section of Washington that lies on its banks, and also to a large U.S. naval air base situated near the point of its junction with the Potomac.

Anacreon (ą.nak'rē.ǫn). b. at Teos, in Asia Minor, c563 B.C.; d. there, c478 B.C. Greek lyric poet, whose work concerns itself chiefly with love and wine. He was widely imitated in the Alexandrian period, and later, in a form of verse called, from him, Anacreontics. He is supposed to have been driven from Teos by the invasion (545) of Cyrus the Great, to have fought briefly in the resisting army, and to have been tutor to Polycrates of Samos, at whose court he became a favorite. He was called to Athens on Polycrates' death by Hipparchus, the patron of Simonides and other literary figures; he probably returned to Teos after Hipparchus was assassinated (514). Pliny's account, probably mythical, of his death by choking on a grapeseed, gives the key to his reputation as a celebrator of the gay and leisurely life, though various writers attest to his sobriety. Although only fragments of his work are now extant, imitations, from the pseudocollection by Stephens (1554) to Thomas Moore (1800), demonstrate the popularity of his short, facile lyrics.

Anacreon (å.nå.krā.ôṅ). Ballet-opera in two acts, by Cherubini, produced at Paris on Oct. 4, 1803.

Anadarko (an.ą.där'kō). See also **Nadaaku.**

Anadarko. City in W Oklahoma, W of Chickasha, county seat of Caddo County, in a petroleum-producing area. Cotton, wheat, alfalfa, corn, and watermelons are produced nearby and marketed here; there are facilities for processing cotton and cottonseed. It was established in 1901, and named for an Indian tribe. 6,184 (1950).

Anadolu (ä.nä.dō.lö') or **Anadoli** (-li'). Turkish names of **Anatolia.**

Anadyomene (an"ą.dī.om'ę.nē). A surname of Aphrodite, in allusion to her origin from the sea.

Anadyr or **Anadir** (ä.nä.dir'). River in the NE part of the U.S.S.R., in the Khabarovsk *Krai* (subdivision) of the Russian Soviet Federated Socialist Republic, Siberia; it flows into the Gulf of Anadyr. Length, ab. 694 mi.

Anadyr or **Anadir, Gulf of.** Arm of the Bering Sea, E of Siberia, in the NE corner of the U.S.S.R.

Anafi (ä.nä'fē). See **Anaphi.**

Anagni (ä.nä'nyē). [Ancient name, **Anagnia** (ą.nag'ni.ą).] Town and commune in C Italy, in the *compartimento* (region) of Latium, in the province of Frosinone, ab. 36 mi. SE of Rome. In ancient times the capital of the Hernicians, it owes its continued historical importance to its location high above the Sacco River, dominating the line of communication between Rome and Naples. In spite of frequent devastations by occupying armies, it flourished during the Middle Ages as the residence of a number of popes. It has grandiose architectural works, such as the 11th-century cathedral, the *palazzo communale* (town hall), built in the 13th century, and the palace of Pope Boniface VIII. Only minor damage was suffered by buildings of tourist interest in World War II. Pop. of commune, 12,396 (1936); of town, 6,590 (1936).

Anagnos (ą.nag'nos), **Michael.** [Original name, **Michael Anagnostópoulos.**] b. at Papingo, Greece, Nov. 7, 1837; d. June 29, 1906. American educator and Greek patriot. He arrived in the U.S. as a protégé of Dr. Samuel G. Howe, whose daughter he later married; he succeeded Howe as head of the Perkins Institution in 1876. His outstanding ability as a fund raiser manifested itself at once, culminating in a one-million-dollar endowment brought together to support a kindergarten for the blind. He retained throughout his life a burning desire for Greek independence and social betterment, and left a will providing that his entire estate should be used for the establishment of schools in Greece.

Anaheim (an'ą.hīm). City in S California, in Orange County, SE of Los Angeles, in a citrus-growing region: canneries and other industries. It was founded as an experiment in communal living by German settlers in 1857. Pop. 14,556 (1950).

Anaides (ą.nā'dēz). In Ben Jonson's *Cynthia's Revels*, an impudent ruffian. Thomas Dekker imagined that in this character he was caricatured. Others, however, think John Marston was intended.

Anaitis (ą.nī'tis). [Also: **Anait** (ä.nīt'), **'Anat**; Egyptian, **Anta.**] Syrian goddess whose worship was introduced into Egypt in the 15th century B.C. She was a war goddess, and is usually depicted with helmet, shield, and battle-ax. The Greeks identified her with Athena.

Anak (ā'nak). In the Old Testament, the progenitor of a tribe or race of giants, the Anakim, or a collective name for this tribe itself. Num. xiii. 33.

Anakim (an'a.kim). In the Old Testament, the sons of Anak, a race of giants dwelling in S Palestine. See **Anak.**

Anak Krakatoa (an'ak krak.ạ.tō'ạ). See under **Krakatoa.**

Analysis of the Human Mind. Prose work (1829) by James Mill. It was one of the earliest works in English to concern itself explicitly with something approaching what is now called psychology (the word, in its modern sense, was virtually never used in Mill's day, but his theory of "associationism" was nevertheless a pioneering effort in an area of science then still almost unknown).

Anam (ạ.nam'). See **Annam.**

Anamabo (ä.nä.mä'bō). See **Anomabu.**

Anambas Islands (ä.näm'bäs). [Dutch, **Anambas Eilanden.**] Group of small islands E of the Malay Peninsula and W of Borneo, in the Republic of Indonesia.

Anammelech (ạ.nam'ẹ.lek). Divinity of the Babylonian Sepharvites, whose worship they continued to practice in Samaria. 2 Kings, xvii. 31.

Anamosa (an.ạ.mō'sạ). [Former names: **Dartmouth, Lexington.**] City in E Iowa, county seat of Jones County. It is the seat of a state reformatory. 3,910 (1950).

Anand (ä'nạnd), **Mulk Raj.** b. 1905—. Indian novelist and critic, one of the outstanding novelists of India writing in English. Author of *The Barbers Trade Union and Other Stories*, *Untouchable*, *Coolie*, and *The Sword and the Sickle.*

Ananda (ä'nạn.dạ). fl. 5th century B.C. Cousin and favorite disciple of Buddha. He is believed to have persuaded Buddha to accept women as nuns, and is important in Buddhist religious literature of the early period, some of which he is thought to have written himself.

Ananev (ä.nä'nyif). [Also: **Ananiev, Ananieff.**] Town in the W part of the U.S.S.R., in the Ukrainian Soviet Socialist Republic: center for a grain-producing region. Pop. ab. 6,000.

Anang (ä.näng'). Subgroup of the Semi-Bantu-speaking Ibibio peoples of W Africa, inhabiting SE Nigeria E of Obete. Their population is estimated at more than 250,000 (by P. A. Talbot, *The Peoples of Southern Nigeria*, 1926). With the Anang proper, who number ab. 150,000, are included eight related subgroups, the Abak, Afaha, Ibechitt, Ika, Inen, Okana, Okun, and Ukpum.

Ananias (an.ạ.nī'ạs). In the New Testament: **1.** An early Christian of Jerusalem who with his wife Sapphira was struck dead for lying. (Acts v.) His name has since become a generally used term for one who lies. **2.** Early Damascene Christian and friend of Paul. **3.** Jewish high priest (48–59 A.D.) and friend of the Romans before whom Paul was tried.

Ananias. In Ben Jonson's comedy *The Alchemist*, a hypocritical Puritan deacon of Amsterdam.

Ananias Club. Term in U.S. history applied to a group which had no formal organization or membership save as President Theodore Roosevelt exercised his personal prerogative of "electing" to its ranks those newspaper reporters whom he accused of having diverged from the truth in dispatches covering political developments. The "club" was in existence before the fairly recent regulation which prohibits White House newspapermen from quoting directly informal remarks made by the president. Thus, Roosevelt used nominations to the body as a convenient instrument for repudiating such published quotations of presidential observations as had become politically embarrassing. The record demonstrates that Roosevelt's motives in naming journalists as members of the Ananias Club (a term whose Biblical associations with Ananias, struck dead for lying, made its meaning clear) often were flexible enough to indicate a not entirely unbiased interest on his part.

Ananino (ä.nä'nyi.nọ). Burial ground situated on the left bank of the Toima River, in the Viatka district of C Russia. First excavated in the middle of the 19th century, it gave its name to the culture of the people inhabiting this region in the period 800–400 B.C. No iron objects were found in the Kotlov burial ground, which is the oldest remains of this culture; at the Ananino itself, which belongs to a later date, some iron objects were found, together with copper and bronze. The dead were buried in pits or on a level ground, with mounds built over them; full and partial burials were practiced, with an occasional cremation. A close tie with the Altai cultures of Siberia may be seen in the implements found, especially in hammers, knives, and metal mirrors. It is therefore possible that the Scythian daggers, arrows, and animal-style of some ornaments was influenced not only by the Scythians, but by the Altai cultures as well. Flame-shaped spears, with an oblong core and side slashes, indicate contact with C Asia, and some objects at Ananino resemble the later, local, definitely Finnish cultures. There is a possibility that the people of Ananino were of Finnish origin. The presence of stone arrows in some graves shows that the stone industry had not, as yet, been completely abandoned. Pottery was fairly primitive, consisting mostly of small round-bottom pots, with the horizontal "rope" ornament along the upper edge. Forged iron and cast copper and bronze were also found, sometimes in cases made of birch bark.

Anansi (ạ.nan'si). See under **Tar Baby.**

Anantnag (ä.nänt.näg'). [Former name, **Islamabad.**] Town in S central Asia, in Kashmir, situated on the Jhelum River, ab. 35 mi. SE of Srinagar: trading center.

Ananus (an'ạ.nus). See also **Annas.**

Ananus. High priest of the Jews; son of Seth. He was appointed by Cyrenius and removed by Valerian, and is apparently the Annas mentioned in the gospels.

Ananus. High priest of the Jews; grandson of Seth. He held office for three months in 62 A.D., was removed by King Agrippa at the demand of the Pharisees because of his attempt to revive Sadduceeism, and was put to death in 67 A.D. by the Zealots.

Anapa (ä.nä'pạ). Seaport and naval station in the U.S.S.R., on the Black Sea, in the Krasnodar Territory of the Russian Soviet Federated Socialist Republic, ab. 60 mi. SE of Kerch. It is also a bathing resort. Pop. ab. 13,000.

Anaphi (ä.nä'fē). [Also: **Anafi, Anaphe.**] Island in the SE Cyclades, in the *nomos* (department) of Cyclades, Greece, situated ab. 40 mi. SE of Naxos. Length, ab. 7 mi.

Anaquito (ä.nä.kē'tō). Plain about a mile from Quito, Ecuador, where the army of Gonzálo Pizarro defeated that of the viceroy Vasco Nuñez Vela, on Jan. 18, 1546.

Anarchiad (an.är'ki.ad), **The.** Twelve satirical papers written in mock-heroic verse by the "Connecticut Wits" (David Humphreys, Lemuel Hopkins, Joel Barlow, Timothy Dwight, and John Trumbull) and published (1786–87) in *The Connecticut Magazine* and the New Haven *Gazette.* The writings opposed democratic and agrarian tendencies, advocated the establishment of a monetary system on Hamiltonian lines, and supported national allegiance as against state loyalties.

Anarkali (ä.när'kạ.li). Suburb of Lahore, in the West Punjab, Pakistan.

Anarutha the Great (ä.nä.rö'thä). fl. 11th century. King of Pagan, in C Burma. He extended his realm from the Irrawaddy River to the Menam valley of what is modern Thailand and, by defeating the remnant of Khmer power, made possible the infiltration of Thai warrior tribes from the north, and the creation of a powerful Thai state.

Anasazi (ä.nä.sä'zē). One of the major patterns of culture in the American Southwest, including the Basket Maker and Pueblo cultures, which was spread over the plateau area from about the time of Christ on, in what is now NE Arizona, NW New Mexico, SE Utah, and SW Colorado. The name is taken from the Navaho word meaning "ancient ones." In contrast to Hohokam, Mogollon, and Patayan, the other major patterns, the Anasazi is characterized by pit dwellings and masonry pueblos, kivas, inhumation, black-on-white painted pottery, and dry farming.

Añasco (ä.nyäs'kō), **Pedro de.** b. at Lima, Peru, 1550; d. at Tucumán, in what is now Argentina, April 12, 1605. Peruvian Jesuit. He left several works on the language of the Indians among whom he had worked.

Anastasia (an.ạs.tā'zhạ), Saint. Titular saint of the ancient church below the Palatine Hill at Rome. She is commemorated in the canon of the Roman mass. The

"Acts" of her martyrdom are spurious. Her cult first appeared in Sirmium, in Pannonia, where she was martyred.

Anastasia. [Called **"the Elder."**] Figure in the early church. She is supposed to have been a noble Roman virgin, martyred during the middle of the 3rd century A.D. under Valerian. However, aside from legend, little is known about her, and modern scholars tend to consider even her existence doubtful.

Anastasian Law (an.as.tā'zhan). Law of the emperor Anastasius I (506), directed against usurers.

Anastasius (an.as.tā'zhus). [Surnamed **Bibliothecarius.**] d. 886. Librarian of the Vatican and abbot of Santa Maria Trans-Tiberim at Rome. He was sent to Constantinople to arrange a marriage between the daughter of Louis II and a son of Basil of Macedonia in 869, and while there assisted, by his knowledge of Greek, the papal ambassador in attendance at the eighth ecumenical council. His fame rests upon his numerous translations from the Greek and his supposed connection with the *Liber Pontificalis.*

Anastasius. Antipope from August to September, 855, in opposition to Benedict III, while the latter was awaiting confirmation by the emperors Lothaire and Louis II.

Anastasius I, Saint. Pope from 399 to 401, successor to Saint Siricius; friend of Augustine, Jerome, and Paulinus. He is remembered for his condemnation of the Donatist heresy and of the errors of Origen.

Anastasius II. Pope from 496 to 498. He sought to end the schism between the sees of Constantinople and Rome, but his manner of doing so met with disapproval among Romans, and he is among those listed as having been consigned to Hell in the works of Dante. He has been supposed, probably erroneously, to have been the author of a letter congratulating Clovis, king of the Franks, on his conversion to Christianity.

Anastasius III. Pope from 911 to 913, successor to Sergius III. He was active in establishing the ecclesiastical division of Germany.

Anastasius IV. [Original name, **Conrad.**] b. at Rome; d. there, 1154. Pope from 1153 to 1154, successor to Eugenius III. His occupancy of the papal chair was disturbed by the activities of the reformer Arnold of Brescia. He achieved a settlement of long disputes over appointments to the sees of York and Magdeburg, making terms on the latter with Emperor Frederick I (Frederick Barbarossa) of the Holy Roman Empire.

Anastasius I. [Called **Anastasius I Dicorus.**] b. at Dyrrachium (now Durrës, Albania), c430; d. 518. Byzantine emperor (491–518). He was raised to the throne by an intrigue with the empress Ariadne whom he married after the death of the emperor Zeno. As a Eutychian he opposed the orthodox who rose in arms under Vitalianus but were bought off by the faithless promise of a general council.

Anastasius II. [Original name, **Artemius.**] Byzantine emperor (713–716). He was deposed by the fleet which he had sent to the coast of Syria to destroy the naval stores of the Arabs, but which was repulsed, mutinied under its commander, John, and proclaimed Theodosius III emperor. He was put to death in 721 (or 719) by Leo III for conspiring against the throne.

'Anat (ä.nät'). See **Anaitis.**

'Anata (ä.nä'tä). See under **Anathoth.**

Anathoth (an'a.thoth). In Biblical geography, a city of Benjamin in Palestine, the birthplace of Jeremiah. The traditional site is Kenyet-el-'Enat, ab. 10 mi. NW of Jerusalem, but the true site is probably 'Anata, ab. 3 mi. NE of that city.

Anatolia (an.a.tō'li.a). [Turkish, **Anadolu,** formerly also **Anadoli**; Eng. trans., *"Eastern Land."*] Large region in Asiatic Turkey, nearly identical with Asia Minor. There was a *theme* (province) of Anatolia in the Byzantine empire situated in the interior of Asia Minor. An area of little rainfall and poor soil, its chief means of livelihood is stock raising, with sheep and goats most important. The chief exports are mohair and Angora wool; others are opium, wheat, and mastic and tragacanth gums. The making of rugs is an important occupation.

Anatomy Lesson, The. See **Lesson in Anatomy, The.**

Anatomy of Melancholy, The. Famous work by Robert Burton (1577–1640), published in 1621 under the pseudonym "Democritus Junior," and frequently republished and abridged. The sixth edition is the last which contains changes by the author; it was published, shortly after his death, from an annotated copy. The work is the result of many years of humorous study of men and of books, and abounds in quotations from authors of all ages and countries. It is divided into three parts which treat (1) of the causes and symptoms of melancholy, (2) of its cure, and (3) of erotic and religious melancholy.

Anau (ä.nou'). Archaeological site in what is now the Turkmen Soviet Socialist Republic of the U.S.S.R. It shows a transition from late Stone Age culture with the beginnings of agriculture to an early Bronze Age civilization. Its date is uncertain, possibly 5500 to 2500 B.C.

Anaxagoras (an.aks.ag'ō.ras). b. at Clazomenae, in Ionia, c500 B.C.; d. at Lampsacus, in Mysia, c428 B.C. Greek philosopher, teacher at Athens (c464–c434) of Pericles, Thucydides, Euripides, and perhaps Socrates. His theory of the universe, based on astronomical observation and the teachings of Anaximander, led to a charge of impiety that forced him, in spite of Pericles' defense, into exile. He introduced a dualistic explanation of the universe as deriving from a chaotic and inextricable mass in which infinitely small particles (or "seeds"), existing in larger or smaller numbers, constitute the distinction between different kinds of matter; on these the controlling function of mind (*nous*) is exercised to bring order via motion. The first half of this concept (which is fundamental to the atomic theory) and his description of the sun as a mass of molten metal, of heavenly bodies as rocks torn from earth, and of men and animals as being born from moist clay, were abhorrent to the pantheism of his time; the second half, through Aristotle and Averroës, became an absorbing topic of medieval speculation.

Anaxarchus (an.aks.är'kus). fl. c350 B.C. Greek philosopher of Abdera, a disciple of Democritus. He attended Alexander in his Asiatic campaigns, and is said to have consoled the king after the murder of Cleitus by maintaining that a king can do no wrong.

Anaxilaus (a.nak.si.lā'us) or **Anaxilas** (-nak'si.las). d. 476 B.C. Tyrant of Rhegium (c494 B.C. *et seq.*).

Anaxilaus. fl. 1st century B.C. Pythagorean philosopher and physician, banished as a magician from Italy by Augustus in 28 B.C.

Anaximander (a.nak.si.man'dėr). b. at Miletus, c611 B.C.; d. c547 B.C. Greek philosopher (the second of the Ionian or Milesian school) and mathematician; friend and pupil of Thales. He taught that the principle of all things is a substance of indeterminate quality and limitless quantity, "immortal and imperishable," out of which all things arise and to which all return; eternal motion creates opposites, conflict between which brings about order and destroys it, in a continuing cycle. This substance, according to some accounts, he regarded as having a nature intermediate between that of water and air. He was probably the author of the first philosophical treatise in Greek prose. He is said to have discovered obliquity of the ecliptic, to have introduced the sundial and gnomon to Greece, and to have made the first map. His teachings had, after his death, some considerable influence on the theories of Anaxagoras.

Anaximenes of Lampsacus (an.ak.sim'ē.nēz; lamp'sa.kus). b. at Lampsacus in Mysia; fl. 4th century B.C. Greek rhetorician, historian, and a companion of Alexander the Great on his Persian campaigns. Author of histories of Greece, and biographies of Philip of Macedon and of Alexander, the latter in epic form, he is also the probable author of a treatise on rhetoric, *Rhetorica ad Alexandrum,* the only existing work on the subject prior to Aristotle (and formerly attributed to him).

Anaximenes of Miletus (mī.lē'tus, mi-). b. at Miletus, in Asia Minor; fl. 6th century B.C. Greek philosopher, the third of the Ionian or Milesian school, a contemporary and friend of Thales and Anaximander, usually reckoned a disciple of the latter. He regarded air as the principle of all things, various kinds of matter being created by its expansion with heat and contraction with cold.

Anaya (ä.nä'yä), **Pedro Maria.** b. at Huichapan, Mexico, 1795; d. at Mexico City, March 21, 1854. Mexican general in the war with the U.S. He entered the Spanish army as a cadet in 1811, joined Augustín de Iturbide's independence movement in 1821, and was a captain in Nicaragua in 1823. In 1833 he became brigadier general. Adhering to the federalist party in Mexico, he was forced to leave the country. He invaded Tabasco in November, 1840, with federalist forces from Texas and Yucatán, but was defeated at Cometán, on May 15, 1841, and fled to Yucatán. Under José Joaquín Herrera in 1845 he was minister of war. He adhered to Antonio Lopéz de Santa Anna, and while the latter was resisting the advance of Winfield Scott, was acting president (April 2–May 20, 1847) of Mexico. He commanded the Mexican force of 800 men which defended the convent of Churubusco, and surrendered (Aug. 20, 1847) only after his ammunition was exhausted. In 1852 he was secretary of war under Mariano Arista, and on Santa Anna's restoration (1853) was made postmaster general, a position which he held until his death.

An Cabhán (ą koun'). Irish name of County **Cavan.**

Ancaeus (an.sē'us). In Greek classical legend, a son of Poseidon. He was told by a seer that he would not live to enjoy the wine from a vineyard which he had planted. He lived, however, to have wine from his own grapes, and, in scorn of the prophet, raised a cup of it to his mouth. The seer replied, "There is many a slip between the cup and the lip," and at the same instant a tumult arose over a wild boar in the vineyard. Ancaeus put down the cup, and was killed in an attempt to destroy the animal.

Ancaeus. In Greek classical legend, son of the Arcadian Lycurgus, and one of the Argonauts. He was killed in the Calydonian boar hunt.

Ancash (äng.käsh'). [Former spelling, **Ancachs.**] Department in W Peru, N of Lima, corresponding to the colonial *intendencia* of Huailas, or Huaylas. Capital, Huarás; area, 14,705 sq. mi.; pop. 540,845 (est. 1950).

Ancelot (äṅs.lō), **Jacques Arsène François Polycarpe.** b. at Le Havre, France, Feb. 9, 1794; d. at Paris, Sept. 7, 1854. French dramatist. His works include *Louis IX* (1819), *Fieque* (1824), *Le maire du palais* (1825), *Marie de Brabant* (1825), *Olga* (1828), *Elizabeth d'Angleterre* (1829), *Epîtres familières*, and others.

Ancelot, Marguerite Louise Virginie. [Maiden name, **Chardon.**] b. at Dijon, France, March 15, 1792; d. at Paris, March 21, 1875. French dramatist and novelist; wife of Jacques Arsène F. P. Ancelot (1794–1854). Her *Théâtre complet* (1848) contains 20 plays.

Ancenis (äṅ.sę.nē). Town in W France, in the department of Loire-Inférieure, situated on the Loire River, ab. 17 mi. NE of Nantes. It is a river port. A suspension bridge spans the Loire at this point. The town has cattle markets. 4,851 (1946).

Anchieta (uṅ.shyā'tą), **José de.** [Called the **"Apostle of Brazil."**] b. at Tenerife, in the Canary Islands, 1533 or 1534; d. at Reritigbá (now Anchieta), Brazil, June 9, 1597. Jesuit missionary educated in Portugal at the University of Coimbra and sent (1553) to Brazil, where he dedicated his life to the conversion and education of the natives. Besides the first grammar of one of the native languages (1595), he wrote plays, letters, and poems which are generally counted among the beginnings of Brazilian literature.

Anchises (an.kī'sēz, ang-). In Greek legend, a prince of the royal house of Troy, father (by Aphrodite) of Aeneas.

Anchorage (ang'kǫr.ąj). City in S Alaska, in the Third Judicial Division, at the head of Cook Inlet: supply center for the Willow Creek gold district, and for a coal-mining, fishing, canning, and fur-farming area, the Matanuska Valley, and surrounding military bases. It was founded in 1914, and has grown in recent years to become the largest city in Alaska. 3,495 (1939), 11,254 (1950).

Ancient Mariner, The Rime of the. Poem by Samuel Taylor Coleridge, published in the *Lyrical Ballads* in 1798 as his principal contribution to the book. The narrative of the poem is told for the most part by the Ancient Mariner himself, as he stops a man bound for a wedding. The mariner is doomed by a curse to go through the world teaching universal love through the recounting of his own awful deed, which consisted in the heartless killing of a storm-tossed albatross.

Ancient Music, Academy of. See **Academy of Ancient Music.**

Ancillon (äṅ.sē.yôṅ), **Charles.** b. at Metz, France, July 28, 1659; d. at Berlin, July 5, 1715. French historian and judge. He was a historian for the Protestant colony at Brandenburg, where he settled after being driven from France by the revocation (1685) of the Edict of Nantes. A historian to the elector of Brandenburg, he was associated with Gottfried Wilhelm von Leibnitz in the founding of the Berlin Academy. Author of a history (1690) of the Brandenburg refugees.

Ancillon, David. b. at Metz, France, March 17, 1617; d. at Berlin, Sept. 3, 1692. French Protestant divine, a refugee in Germany after the revocation of the Edict of Nantes (1685). He was the father of Charles Ancillon.

Ancillon, Jean Pierre Frédéric. [German, **Johann Peter Friedrich Ancillon.**] b. at Berlin, April 30, 1767; d. April 19, 1837. Prussian minister of foreign affairs (1832 *et seq.*) to Frederick William IV, whose tutor he had been, and over whom he exerted a strong influence. Great-grandson of Charles Ancillon, French Protestant refugee, he was pastor to the French colony at Berlin and author of a psychological study of European history; he was also a member (1814) of the ministry of state. He used his influence to support Metternich's policy, embodied in the Vienna Final Act (1834), of solidifying Prussian class-distinctions as the basis of the state.

Anckarström (äng'kär.strėm), **Johan Jakob.** [Also, **Ankarström.**] b. May 11, 1762; executed at Stockholm, April 27, 1792. Swedish assassin of Gustavus III. A former army officer, who had been tried for sedition, he joined the conspiracy to murder the king in 1792.

Anckarswärd (äng'kärs.verd), Count **Karl Henrik.** b. April 22, 1782; d. at Stockholm, Jan. 25, 1865. Swedish soldier and statesman. He joined (1809) the revolutionary party, but being opposed to the policy of Jean Baptiste Jules Bernadotte, was retired (1813) from the army, in which he held the post of colonel. In 1817 he became a member of the *Riksdag* (Swedish parliament), where as leader of the opposition he distinguished himself by the bitterness of his attacks on the government.

Anclam (äng'kläm). See **Anklam.**

An Clár (ą klôr). Irish name of County **Clare.**

An Cób (ą kōv) or **An Cóf** (ą kōf). See **Cóbh.**

Ancohuma (äng.kō.ö'mä). [Full Spanish name, **Nevado de Ancohuma.**] Mountain in Bolivia NNW of La Paz. It is one of the peaks of the Nevado de Sorata. 21,490 ft.

Ancon (ang'kon). [Spanish, **Ancón** (äng.kōn').] Town in the Canal Zone, adjoining Panama City but legally separate from it. It is the site of a U.S. hospital. 1,695 (1950).

Ancon (äng.kōn'). Archaeological site midway of the coast of Peru, representative of an early period in Peruvian Indian archaeology. It is believed to be between 1,950 and 2,450 years old.

Ancona (äng.kō'nä). Medieval march (or mark) of Italy, extending from Tronto on the Adriatic NW to San Marino, and W to the Apennines. It was afterward part of the Papal States, and passed with them to the kingdom of Italy.

Ancona. Province in C Italy, in the *compartimento* (region) of Marches. Capital, Ancona; area, 748 sq. mi.; pop. 372,229 (1936).

Ancona. City and commune in C Italy, in the *compartimento* (region) of Marches, the capital of the province of Ancona, situated on the Adriatic Sea SE of Ravenna. Along with Venice the chief Adriatic seaport of Italy and the port of call of various steamship lines, it exports grain, hemp, silk, skins, and similar products and imports coal. It has Roman antiquities, including the Arch of Trajan, a cathedral dating from the 12th century, and a number of early medieval churches, such as San Ciriaco, Santa Maria della Piazza, and Santa Maria Maggiore; other churches, such as Santa Maria della Misericordia, date from the Renaissance period. The Church of San Francesco della Scala contains a museum of antiquities. Colonized by the Greeks, it became a naval station under the Romans, and was later ravaged by the Goths and the Moslems. Much contested during the Middle Ages, it was annexed to the Papal States in 1532 and remained with them, except during the Napoleonic era, until the papal army surrendered the town to the Sardinians in 1860. It was bombarded by the Austrian navy in the beginning of World War I. Considerable damage was suffered during World War II by many buildings of tourist interest, but repairs have now been completed or are being carried out. The Church of San Agostino, the Palazzi Benincasa and Ferretti, and the Arch of Trajan, however, were undamaged. Pop. of commune, 89,198 (1936); of city, 57,068 (1936).

Ancona (däng.kō'nä), **Alessandro d'.** b. at Pisa, Italy, Feb. 20, 1835; d. at Florence, Italy, Nov. 9, 1914. Italian literary historian; he served as professor (1860 *et seq.*) at the universities of Pisa and Florence. Author of *Origini del teatro in Italia* (Origins of the Theater in Italy, 1877).

Anconquija (än.kōng.kē'hä), **Sierra de.** See **Sierra de Aconquija** or **Anconquija.**

Ancre (äṅkr). Former name of **Albert,** France.

Ancre (däṅkr), Marquis **d'.** [Also, Baron **de Lussigny**; original name, **Concino Concini.**] Assassinated at Paris, April 14, 1617. Florentine adventurer, marshal and chief minister of France at the beginning of the reign of Louis XIII. Though a great favorite of Marie de' Medici, who made him marshal of France in 1613, after her marriage to Henry IV, he was much hated. His wife, Leonora Galigai, was his partner in his intrigues.

Ancren Riwle (angk'ren röl; Middle English, ängk'ren rü'lẹ). Term meaning the "rule of anchoresses," used as the name of a specific work on the rules and duties of monastic life. It was written, first in English and afterward in Latin, for a society of anchoresses (three in number) at Tarente, or Tarrant-Kaines (Kaineston or Kingston), near Crayford Bridge in Dorsetshire. It is ascribed to Simon of Ghent (died 1315), bishop of Salisbury in 1297. Five manuscripts are extant. It was edited for the Camden Society by James Morton in 1853.

Ancud (äng.köᴛʜ'). [Also: **San Carlos;** original name, **San Carlos de Ancud.**] Seaport in SW Chile, capital of Chiloé province, on the island of Chiloé: trade center for agricultural and lumber products; seat of a bishopric. Pop. under 5,000 (1940).

Ancus Marcius (ang'kus mär'shi.us, -shus). Fourth king of Rome (c640–616 B.C.); grandson of Numa Pompilius and the reputed founder of Ostia, fortifier of the Janiculum, and builder of a bridge over the Tiber.

Ancy-le-Franc (äṅ.sē.lẹ.fräṅ). Town in N central France, in the department of Yonne, ab. 29 mi. E of Auxerre. It has a noted château.

Ancyra (an.sī'rạ). A Latin name of **Ankara.**

Andagoya (än.dä.gō'yä), **Pascual de.** b. in the province of Alava, Spain, c1495; d. at Manta, Peru, June 18, 1548. Spanish soldier. He went (1514) with Pedrarias to Darien and was engaged in many explorations. In 1522 he was appointed inspector-general of the Indians, and about the same time made an expedition southward into a province called Birú, between the river Atrato and the Pacific. Here he had the first tidings of the Inca empire.

Åndalsnes (ôn'däls.nās''). See under **Romsdal.**

Andalucía (än.dä.lö.thē'ä), **Fuentes de.** See **Fuentes de Andalucía.**

Andalusia (an.dạ.lö'zhạ, -shạ). [Former name, **New Site.**] City in S Alabama, county seat of Covington County, ab. 75 mi. S of Montgomery. 9,162 (1950).

Andalusia. [Spanish, **Andalucía** (än.dä.lö.thē'ạ).] Region in S Spain, comprising the provinces of Almería, Jaén, Granada, Córdoba, Málaga, Sevilla, Cádiz, and Huelva. It is traversed by the Sierra Nevada and other mountain ranges, and belongs in large part to the basin of the Guadalquivir River. From the fertility of its soil it has been called the "garden" and "granary" of Spain; it is also rich in minerals. It was a part of the Roman Baetica, was overrun by the Vandals and Visigoths in the 5th century, and became the nucleus of the Moslems' power and their last stronghold in Spain.

Andamanese (an''dạ.mạn.ēz', -ēs') or **Andaman Islanders** (an'dạ.mạn). [Also, **Mincopies.**] The Negrito inhabitants of the Andaman Islands, numbering 460 (est. 1931). They speak a language without known affinities.

Andaman Islands (an'dạ.mạn). [Also, **Andamans.**] Group of islands belonging to the Union of India, a penal colony from 1858 to 1942, situated in the E part of the Bay of Bengal, ab. 780 mi. SE of Calcutta. It comprises the Great Andaman group and the Little Andaman group. The chief islands are North, Middle, and South Andaman, and Rutland. Together with the Nicobar Islands, to the S, they comprise the province of Andaman and Nicobar Islands. Capital of the province, Port Blair; area, of the Andamans, 2,508 sq. mi.; of the province, 3,143 sq. mi.; total pop. 30,963 (1951).

Andaman Sea. Arm of the Bay of Bengal, enclosed by the Andaman Islands on the W and Burma on the N and E. Its major arm is the Gulf of Martaban; receives the Irrawaddy River. Length, ab. 800 mi.; width, ab. 350 mi.

Andean Cultures (an.dē'ạn, an'dẹ-). Native Indian cultures of the highland areas of Colombia, Ecuador, Peru, Bolivia, NW Argentina, and Chile, and the W coastal plains of Ecuador, Peru, and Chile. They have now disappeared, or merged with European culture patterns. They were similar in having primary dependence on intensive agriculture for subsistence, with maize, squash, beans, sweet potatoes, peppers, peanuts, manioc, and coca being grown, as well as many varieties of fruits. Irrigation, terracing, crop rotation, and food preservation were practiced. The llama and alpaca were important domesticated animals because of their value for wool, meat, transportation, hides, fertilizer, sinew, and bone. Hunting was secondary to agriculture and herding, as was gathering. Large-scale building, with adobe on the coast and stone in the highlands, was characteristic of the Andes. High standards of skill were attained in such crafts as ceramics, weaving, and metallurgy. A distinctive costume of woven material was worn by both men and women in the Andes, in contrast to the scanty costume usual among most of the South American tribes. The intensity of these diagnostic traits diminished N, S, and E of the central area.

Andecavi (an.dẹ.kā'vī) or **Andegavi** (-gā'vī). See under **Anjou.**

Andechs (än'deks). Village in S Germany, in the *Land* (state) of Bavaria, American Zone, in the *Kreis* (district) of Upper Bavaria, situated above Ammer Lake, SW of Munich: has a Benedictine abbey, with baroque church and brewery. The counts of Andechs were mentioned in the 9th century. The abbey was secularized in 1803, but restored in 1846 by King Ludwig I. 1,664 (1946).

Andeer (än'dār). Village in SE Switzerland, in the canton of Graubünden, near the S end of the Via Mala. 614 (1941).

Andegavia (an.dẹ.gā'vi.ạ) or **Andegavum** (-gā'vum). Latin names of **Angers.**

Andenne (äṅ.den). Town in S central Belgium, in the province of Namur, situated on the Meuse River ab. 10 mi. E of Namur: manufacturing center, particularly of ceramic products. Pop. ab. 8,000.

Anderab (än.dėr.äb'). [Also, **Inderab.**] Town in Afghanistan, situated on the river Anderab on the N slope of the Hindu Kush, ab. 85 mi. NE of Kabul. Pop. ab. 6,000.

Anderida (an.der'i.dạ). Roman encampment in England, generally identified with Pevensey. It was destroyed (491) by the South Saxons.

Anderlecht (än'dėr.leċht). Town in C Belgium, in the province of Brabant, situated on the Senne River, SW of Brussels, of which it is a suburb: has textile spinning, weaving, printing, and dyeing mills. The Church of Saint Peter, built in the 15th century, is in the Gothic style; the town hall is in the Renaissance style. 86,412 (1947).

Anderledy (än.dėr.lā'dē), **Anton Maria.** b. at Berisal, Switzerland, 1819; d. at Fiesole, Italy, 1892. General of the Society of Jesus (1887–92). He completed his studies for the priesthood in the U.S. after the Jesuits were expelled (1848) from Switzerland; later (1850–70) served as a missionary and teacher in Germany.

Anderlues (äṅ.der.lü). Town in S Belgium, in the province of Hainaut, ab. 60 mi. S of Brussels: coal mining; metal products; breweries. 12,383 (1947).

Andermatt (än'dėr.mät). [Also: **Ursern;** Italian, **Orsera.**] Village in S Switzerland, in the canton of Uri, S of Altdorf, at the junction of the St. Gotthard railway, the Furka pass railway, and the Oberalp railway, near the N entrance to the St. Gotthard tunnel. It is a center for summer and winter sports, and the last German-speaking community on this route from N to S. 1,496 (1941).

Andernach (än'dėr.näċh). [Latin, **Antunnacum, Castellum Ante Nacum.**] Town in W Germany, in the *Land* (state) of Rhineland-Palatinate, French Zone, formerly in the Rhine Province, Prussia, situated on the left bank of the Rhine River, ab. 12 mi. NW of Koblenz. Manufactures include millstones, wooden floors, cigars, foodstuffs, chemicals, and paper goods. The town, which was badly damaged in World War II, has walls and fortifications dating from the 12th century, a 12th-century parish church in the Romanesque style, and a Gothic *Rathaus* (town hall) built in the 16th century. The population is predominantly Catholic. Andernach was founded by Drusus in 12 B.C. as a Roman frontier fortification. Charles the Bald was defeated here by Ludwig III in 876; the dukes of Lorraine and Franconia, by Otto I in 939. Donated by Emperor Frederick I to the archbishop of Cologne in 1167, it was conquered by the Swedes in 1622; in 1688 it was burned down by the French. It was incorporated into France in 1801, into Prussia in 1815. Pop. 15,879 (1950).

Anders (än′ders), **Wladyslaw.** b. 1892—. Polish general. Imprisoned by the Russians in the early part of World War II when they occupied the eastern half of Poland, he was, after the Sikorski-Maisky pact (1941), nominated commander of a Polish army recruited in the same year from prisoners of war and deportees in Russia. He brought this army through Iran to the Near East and led it in the battles in North Africa and Italy. His name became famous at Monte Cassino, which he helped take from the Germans after a bloody battle. He wrote *Bez ostatniego rozdzialu* (An Army in Exile, 1949).

Andersen (an′dėr.sn̦; Danish, än′nėr.sn̦), **Hans Christian.** b. at Odense, Denmark, April 2, 1805; d. at Copenhagen, Aug. 4, 1875. Danish poet and novelist, best known for fairy tales. Son of a poverty-stricken shoemaker, he went (1819) to Copenhagen to become an actor; a failure in the theater, he nevertheless won friends in the musical and dramatic world, and attracted the attention of King Frederick VI, who sent him to school. He achieved his first success with a curious work entitled *A Journey on Foot from Holmen's Canal to the East Point of Amager* (1829), which was followed by a volume of verse. Critical approval began to come his way with his first novel, *Improvisatoren* (The Improvisator, 1835), and was further stimulated by the first volume of fairy tales, under the title *Eventyr*, published the same year. Thereafter, until 1872, he averaged a volume of these tales a year, establishing himself not only as Denmark's best-known author, but as one of the leading story-tellers of history. Included among his best-known fairy tales are *The Fir Tree, The Tinder Box, The Ugly Duckling, The Red Shoes,* and *The Emperor's New Clothes.*

Andersen, Karl. b. at Copenhagen, Oct. 26, 1828; d. there, Sept. 1, 1883. Danish lyric and epic poet. He lived (1837–48) in Iceland, returning in the latter year to Denmark, where he became inspector and intendant of Castle Rosenborg at Copenhagen. His works include *Strit og Fred* (1858), *Genrebilleder* (1867–81), *Romanser og Sanger* (1880), and others.

Andersen Nexø (nek′sė), **Martin.** b. at Christianshavn, near Copenhagen, Denmark, June 26, 1869—. Danish novelist. Son of a fisherman, descended from peasant stock, he worked at manual labor until at the age of 20 he entered a folk high-school. After travels in the U.S.S.R. during the 1920's he produced several works based on the experiment being undertaken there. He was seized (1940) and placed in a concentration camp by the Germans. His early experiences gave him the materials and impulses for his masterpieces of proletarian description, *Pelle Erobreren* (3 vols., 1906–10; Eng. trans., *Pelle The Conqueror,* 3 vols., 1914–17) and *Ditte Menneskebarn* (4 vols., 1917–21; Eng. trans., *Ditte, Girl Alive!,* 1920–22).

Anderson (an′dėr.sn̦). City in C Indiana, county seat of Madison County, on the W fork of White River, ab. 34 mi. NE of Indianapolis: manufactures automotive parts, machinery, glass, wire fencing, and corrugated containers. It was the site of a natural-gas boom during the 1860's. 46,820 (1950).

Anderson. City in NW South Carolina, county seat of Anderson County, ab. 97 mi. NW of Columbia, in the Blue Ridge Mountains, in a grain, cotton, and truck-gardening area. Manufactures include cotton textiles, brooms, mattresses, bricks, tiles, cottonseed products, fertilizer, meal, flour, metal shingles, eyeglasses, monuments, and lumber products. It is the seat of Anderson Junior College. 19,770 (1950).

Anderson, Adam. b. in Scotland, 1692; d. at London, 1765. Scottish economist and commercial historian. He served as clerk for 40 years at South Sea House, London, and is believed to have been a trustee in the establishment of the Georgia colony. His *Historical and Chronological Deduction of the Origin of Commerce* (1764) was consulted by Adam Smith and, despite possible errors in its earlier chapters, cited by Macpherson for periods after 1492.

Anderson, Alexander. b. at New York, 1775; d. at Jersey City, 1870. American engraver, self-taught. Inspired by Hogarth's work to make copper engravings and by that of Bewick to try wood, he produced (1794) the first American wood-engravings. Also a physician, he illustrated many books, chiefly Bell's *Anatomy,* Webster's *Spelling Book, Emblems of Mortality* (1800, after Holbein's *Dance of Death*), and the first American edition of Bewick's *General History of Quadrupeds* (1804).

Anderson, Alexander. [Pseudonym, **"Surfaceman."**] b. at Kirkconnel, Upper Nithsdale, Scotland, April 30, 1845; d. at Edinburgh, July 11, 1909. Scottish railway worker, dialect poet, and librarian. He received a meagre education at the village school of Crocketford, and worked on the Glasgow and Southwestern Railway system as a track-layer (surfaceman) from the age of 17 to 35, writing dialect verse on labor and child themes in his free time.

Anderson, Benjamin McAlester. b. at Columbia, Mo., May 1, 1886; d. Jan. 19, 1949. American economist.

Anderson, Carl David. b. at New York, Sept. 3, 1905—. American physicist. He shared, with Victor Hess, the 1936 Nobel prize in physics for the discovery of positron. In 1937 he discovered, at the same time as J. C. Street and Edward Stevenson, the presence of heavy electrons in cosmic rays, and photographed (1938) their path with a Wilson cloud chamber. Professor of physics (1939 *et seq.*) at California Institute of Technology.

Anderson, Carl Thomas. b. at Madison, Wis., Feb. 14, 1865—. American cartoonist and illustrator, noted especially for his cartoon strip *Henry.* He attended the School of Industrial Art of Philadelphia, and then worked on the staffs of several newspapers in Pennsylvania and New York, drawing cartoons and illustrations. In 1906, he became a free-lance cartoonist, contributing to many widely distributed magazines. His character *Henry* was created in 1932, and became a syndicated feature in 1934. Other works include *Dusty—the Story of a Dog and His Adopted Boy* and *How to Draw Cartoons Successfully.*

Anderson, Chandler Parsons. b. at Lakeville, Conn., Sept. 5, 1866; d. Aug. 2, 1936. American lawyer. He graduated (1887) from Yale, and attended (1888–89) the Harvard Law School; in 1891 he was admitted to the New York bar. Specializing in international arbitration, he served as special counsel (1905–10) to the U.S. Department of State in negotiations with Britain over British North American treaties. Subsequently he was a counselor (1910–13) to the U.S. Department of State, arbitrator (1913–23) for the U.S. in the British-American pecuniary claims arbitration, a counsel (1917–18) to the U.S. War Industries Board, a commissioner (1923 *et seq.*) for the U.S. on the mixed claims commission (U.S. and Germany), and a commissioner (1933) on the body representing the U.S., Austria, and Hungary. He served also on the editorial staff of the *American Journal of International Law.*

Anderson, Clinton Presba. b. at Centerville, S.D., Oct. 23, 1895—. American politician and farmer, U.S. secretary of agriculture (1945–48), a Democratic congressman (1941–45) and senator (1948 *et seq.*) from New Mexico.

Anderson, David. b. July 6, 1880—. English civil engineer, specializing in bridge and tunnel construction. His principal works include the design and execution of Southwark Bridge, Tyne Bridge, Wearmouth Bridge, Tees Bridge, Londonderry Bridge, and the Mersey Tunnel.

Anderson, David Lawrence. b. at Summerhill, S.C., Feb. 4, 1850; d. in China, Feb. 16, 1911. American Methodist missionary in China who founded and was the first president (1901–11) of Soochow University. Sent to Shanghai (1883) and then to Soochow (1884), he was given charge (1886) of the latter district by the Methodist China Mission Conference. Here he found a strong interest in liberal education, established (1894) an Anglo-Chinese school, and planned for the new university despite the anti-Western feeling during the Boxer Rebellion. Under his guidance, Soochow University developed departments of literature, medicine, and theology, and an enrollment by 1909 of 350.

Anderson, Sir **David Murray.** b. April 11, 1874; d. at Sydney, Australia, Oct. 29, 1936. British admiral and government administrator. He served with the Grand Fleet during World War I, was temporary commander in chief of the China station (1925) and commander in chief of the Africa station (1927–29), and was the first governor of and commander in chief (1933–36) at Newfoundland.

Anderson, Sir **Edmund.** b. at Flixborough or Broughton, England, 1530; d. at Eywroth, England, Aug. 1, 1605. English jurist, lord chief justice of Common Pleas (1582–1605). A bitter opponent of the Puritans and Catholics, he was notorious for his severity in the trials of Sir Walter Raleigh in 1603, of John Udall, and of others, and was one of the commissioners who tried Mary Queen of Scots in 1586.

Anderson, Edwin Hatfield. b. at Zionsville, Ind., Sept. 27, 1861; d. at Evanston, Ill., April 29, 1947. American librarian and director (1913–34) of the New York Public Library. He organized (1895) and directed (1895–1904) the Carnegie Free Library of Pittsburgh, was appointed (1906) director of the New York State Library and Library School, and was made (1908) assistant director of the New York Public Library. He received (1927) the Order of the White Lion from Czechoslovakia for public service.

Anderson, Elizabeth. [Maiden name, **Garrett.**] b. at Aldeburgh, England, 1836; d. there, 1917. English physician, a pioneer in opening the medical professions in Britain to women, and the first woman mayor in England. She secured her medical training from qualified physicians after surmounting numerous obstacles, and was licensed to practice in 1865; a dispensary, opened in 1866, later became a small hospital staffed by women physicians, and has been known since 1918 as the Elizabeth Garrett Anderson Hospital. She was elected (1908) England's first woman mayor by Aldeburgh.

Anderson, Elizabeth. [Maiden name, **Milbank.**] b. at New York, Dec. 20, 1850; d. Feb. 22, 1921. American philanthropist. A trustee (1894 *et seq.*) of the board of Barnard College (to which she gave extensive properties), she was the founder (1905) of what became the Milbank Memorial Fund, which after her death reached an endowment of ten million dollars, to be used by the directors as a source of income for humanitarian projects of the widest possible scope.

Anderson, Galusha. b. at Clarendon, N.Y., March 7, 1832; d. July 20, 1918. American Baptist clergyman, president of the University of Chicago (1878–85) and of Denison University (1887–90). Having attracted attention by his able pastorship (1856–58) at Janesville, Wis., he was called (1858) to St. Louis, where he devoted himself to the Union cause in Missouri. He was a pastor at Brooklyn (1873–76), Chicago (1876–78), and Salem, Mass. (1885–87), and a teacher at Newton (1866–73) and Baptist Union (1890–92) seminaries, and at the new University of Chicago (1892–1904). Author of *A Border City During the Civil War* (1908), *Science and Prayer* (1915), and others.

Anderson, George Thomas. b. in Georgia, March 3, 1824; d. at Anniston, Ala., April 4, 1901. American soldier, brigadier general (1862) in the Confederate army; often confused with other Civil War generals of the same surname. He was, as of 1863, in Hood's division, Longstreet's corps, Army of Northern Virginia. Serving throughout the war, he was prominent at Antietam, Gettysburg, and Knoxville.

Anderson, Henry Tompkins. b. in Caroline County, Va., Jan. 27, 1812; d. at Washington, Sept. 19, 1872. American clergyman and student of the classics who devoted most of his life to a translation of the New Testament from the Greek into contemporary English. Averse to teaching and administrative work, in both of which fields various positions were offered him, he would have liked to combine farming and study; failing this, he was often dependent on the help of friends to support his family. Besides his *New Testament* (1864), he made a translation (published in 1918) of the then newly discovered *Codex Sinaiticus*.

Anderson, Isabel. [Maiden name, **Perkins.**] b. at Boston, 1876; d. there, Nov. 3, 1948. American author of books and plays for juveniles; wife of Larz Anderson. She served as a Red Cross worker in Europe during World War I and in 1923 was chosen as librarian general of the Daughters of the American Revolution. Author of *The Great Sea Horse* (1909), *Topsy Turvy and the Gold Star* (1920), *Polly the Pagan* (1922), and *A Yacht in the Mediterranean Seas* (1930). Among her plays are *Everyboy* (1920), *The Witch in the Woods* (1925), *The Gee Whiz* (1933), and *Sir Frog Goes A-Traveling* (1935).

Anderson, James. b. at Edinburgh, 1662; d. at London, 1728. Scottish genealogist and antiquarian. In 1705 he published *An Historical Essay Showing That The Crown, and Kingdom of Scotland Is Imperial and Independent* to demonstrate that a pamphlet by William Atwood, chief justice of York, on the supremacy of the English crown over the Scottish, was a forgery. After receiving a reward for the exposé, he devoted himself to his great work, collecting facsimiles of Scottish charters and other muniments, which he published (1729) under the title of *Diplomata;* he also published *Collections Relating to Mary Queen of Scots* (1727–28). He served (1715–17) as postmaster general for Scotland.

Anderson, James. b. at Hermiston, near Edinburgh, 1739; d. Oct. 15, 1808. Scottish economist and writer on agriculture. Publisher of *The Bee* (1790–94), a weekly journal of economics and politics; author of essays, tracts, and pamphlets, particularly *An Inquiry into the Nature of the Corn Laws, with a View to the Corn Bill Proposed for Scotland* (1777), which contains a statement of the theory of rent generally attributed to David Ricardo. He was the inventor of the "Scotch plow."

Anderson, James Patton. b. in Franklin County, Tenn., Feb. 12, 1822; d. Sept. 1, 1872. American soldier, major general in the Confederate army under Braxton Bragg, who cited him for heroism at the battles of Shiloh and Murfreesboro and sent him to the assistance of John Bell Hood in 1864 after the latter's failure to take Atlanta from W. T. Sherman. Severely wounded at Jonesboro, he returned to duty in North Carolina against medical advice, an act characteristic of the courage which made him a successful commander.

Anderson, John. b. at Roseneath, Scotland, 1726; d. at Glasgow, Jan. 13, 1796. Scottish physicist, professor of Oriental languages (1756) and natural philosophy (1760) at Glasgow, interested particularly in the application of science to industry. He founded, by bequest, Anderson's College at Glasgow, now part of the Glasgow and West of Scotland Technical College. A sympathizer with the French Revolution, he wrote essays on military science, and invented a cannon and a method of smuggling newspapers by means of small balloons. Author of *Institutes of Physics* (1786).

Anderson, John. b. Oct. 4, 1833; d. Aug. 16, 1900. Scottish zoölogist. He was appointed superintendent of the Indian Museum at Calcutta in 1865, and was scientific officer on expeditions to western China in 1868 and 1874.

Anderson, Sir **John.** b. 1882—. British politician and civil servant. In 1905 he entered the Colonial Office and held various positions in it prior to World War I; subsequently he was permanent under-secretary of state in the Home Office (1922–32), governor of Bengal (1932–37), and lord privy seal (1938–39). As home secretary and minister of home security (1939–40), he supervised the design and installation of bomb-shelters (one of the best-known types of which was named for him), and was in charge of the interning of enemy aliens. He was also lord president of the council (1940–43) and chancellor of the exchequer (1943–45).

Anderson, John Alexander. b. in Washington County, Pa., June 26, 1834; d. at Liverpool, England, May 18, 1892. American Presbyterian clergyman, president (1873–88) of Kansas State Agricultural College, and congressman (1878–91) from Kansas. An associate of Thomas Starr King in the reform of state institutions in California, Anderson obtained with the former's help a post on the U.S. Sanitary Commission in the Civil War. He reorganized Kansas State from a small liberal arts school into an industrial and agricultural institution according to the intent of the land grant of 1862. As a Kansas representative in Congress, he was responsible for increasing the taxation of railroad land-grants and for giving cabinet status to the Department of Agriculture.

Anderson, John August. b. at Rollag, Minn., 1876—. American astronomer. He was graduated (Ph.D., 1907) from Johns Hopkins, where he served (1908–16) as associate professor of astronomy. In 1916 he was named physicist at the Mount Wilson Observatory in California. Author of *Absorption Spectra of Solutions* (in collaboration with H. C. Jones, 1908).

Anderson, John Henry. [Called **"Professor Anderson, the Wizard of the North."**] b. 1815; d. 1874. English conjurer and actor, memorable for his connection with the burning (March 5, 1856) of Covent Garden Theatre, London. He acted in *Black-Eyed Susan* and *Rob Roy.* The *bal masqué* with which he ended his 1855–56 season was the occasion of the fire which destroyed the entire building.

Anderson, Joseph. b. at White Marsh, near Philadelphia, Nov. 5, 1757; d. at Washington, D.C., April 17, 1837. American lawyer, politician, and officer in the Revolutionary War. He was the leader in the Tennessee constitutional convention of 1796, a U.S. senator from Tennessee (1797–1815), and the first comptroller (1815–36), appointed by Madison, of the U.S. Treasury.

Anderson, Joseph Reid. b. near Fincastle, Va., Feb. 6, 1813; d. at Isles of Shoals, N.H., Sept. 7, 1892. American iron manufacturer whose Tredegar Iron Works were a chief source of Confederate munitions and thus a focal point of Confederate strategy during most of the Civil War. Graduated (1836) from West Point, he served (1837) in the Corps of Engineers, but resigned to become an engineer in civilian life, and build (1838–41) the Staunton-Winchester turnpike in Virginia. Acquiring (1848) the Tredegar company, he developed it into a leading supplier to railroads and the government. Brigadier general (1861) in command of the Cape Fear district and later (1862) commander of a brigade in the Peninsular Campaign, he returned (1862) to the management of the ironworks and became its president in 1867.

Anderson, Judith. b. at Adelaide, Australia, 1898—. American actress, noted for her performance of tragic roles, particularly those based on the Greek, as in Eugene O'Neill's *Mourning Becomes Electra* (1931) and Robinson Jeffers' *Medea* (1947–48). She has become well known also as a Shakespearian actress, most notably with her performances as Hamlet's mother (1936) and as Lady Macbeth (1937, 1941). She has also played in *Strange Interlude* (1930), *The Old Maid* (1935), and others.

Anderson, Karl. b. at Oxford, Ohio, 1874—. American painter; brother of Sherwood Anderson. His work is represented in the permanent collections of the Art Institute of Chicago, the Pennsylvania Academy of the Fine Arts, the Boston Museum of Fine Arts, and elsewhere. He has done illustrations for *Collier's, The Saturday Evening Post,* and numerous books.

Anderson, Kenneth Arthur Noel. b. at Dharwar, India, Dec. 25, 1891—. English army officer. He served in World War I (1914–18), on the northwest frontier of India (1930–31), and in World War II (1939–45), where he took part (1940) in the Dunkerque evacuation operation. After heading (1942–43) the First Army in the African campaign, and holding the Eastern command (1944–45) and the East Africa command (1945–46), he became governor of Gibraltar in 1947. In 1943 he was named lieutenant general.

Anderson, Larz. b. at Paris, France, Aug. 15, 1866; d. April 13, 1937. American diplomat.

Anderson, Marian. b. at Philadelphia, 1902—. American concert contralto. After winning (1925) the first place in a contest with 300 other singers for an appearance with the New York Philharmonic Orchestra, she was awarded a scholarship by the National Association of Negro Musicians and sent (1933) to Europe for an extensive and outstandingly successful concert tour. She returned for a concert on Dec. 30, 1935 at New York, and has since made several tours of the U.S. In 1936 she sang at the White House. Her honors include the degree of Mus.D. from Howard University (1938), and the Spingarn medal (1939).

Anderson, Martin Brewer. b. at Brunswick, Me., Feb. 12, 1815; d. at Lake Helen, Fla., Feb. 22, 1890. American Baptist clergyman and scholar, first president (1853–88) of the University of Rochester. Working in a shipyard and then at the college, Anderson made his own way through Waterville (now Colby) College, returning there, after a year of theological study, as instructor of mathematics and the classics, and later (1843–50) professor of rhetoric. The influential position in Baptist affairs which he attained through his editorship (1850–53) of the *New York Recorder* he maintained during his presidency of Rochester. In the latter capacity he raised funds enabling the establishment of a separate theological department, obtained an enrollment that necessitated a new building within ten years, and fostered the scientific method and historical research. He was a coeditor of *Johnson's Cyclopaedia.*

Anderson, Mary. b. at Lidköping, Sweden, 1872—. American labor-union leader. She arrived in the U.S. in 1888, and was employed in a garment factory near Chicago; later she worked for 18 years in a shoe factory. She headed Local 94, National Boot and Shoe Workers' Union, before being named, in 1919, the director of the Women's Bureau of the U.S. Department of Labor.

Anderson, Mary Antoinette. b. at Sacramento, Calif., July 28, 1859; d. in England, May 29, 1940. American actress. She made her debut in 1875 as Juliet at Louisville, Ky., and played Rosalind in *As You Like It* for the opening performance (1877) of the Shakespeare Memorial theater at Stratford-on-Avon. The role of Clarice in W. S. Gilbert's *Comedy and Tragedy* was written for her. She was also associated with Robert Hichens in the dramatization of his novel, *The Garden of Allah.* She retired (1889) from the stage and soon after married Antonio de Navarro, a British subject, with whom she settled in England.

Anderson, Mary Reid. [Maiden name, **Macarthur.**] b. at Glasgow, Scotland, Aug. 13, 1880; d. at Golder's Green, London, Jan. 1, 1921. British organizer of the National Federation of Woman Workers, founded in 1906. She was responsible for the establishment of a minimum wage for women workers, and was one of the authors of the Wages (Temporary Regulation) Act of 1918.

Anderson, Maxwell. b. at Atlantic, Pa., Dec. 15, 1888—. American playwright. He taught school (1911 *et seq.*) in North Dakota and California, and was on the staff of the San Francisco *Chronicle* and others prior to 1918, when he became an editorial writer for the *New Republic*, the New York *Evening Globe*, and the New York *World.* He first made his name in the theater when he collaborated with Laurence Stallings on the tremendously successful *What Price Glory* (1924) and others. His later plays include *Saturday's Children* (1927), *Elizabeth the Queen* (1930), *Night over Taos* (1932), *Mary of Scotland* (1933), *Valley Forge* (1934), *Star-Wagon* (1937), *Key Largo* (1939), *Eve of St. Mark* (1942), *Anne of The Thousand Days* (1948), and *Barefoot in Athens* (1951). His *Both Your Houses* (1933) won a Pulitzer prize, while *Winterset* (1935) and *High Tor* (1936) both received the Critics' award. He wrote the text for *Lost in the Stars* (1949), a musical adaptation by Kurt Weill of Alan Paton's *Cry, the Beloved Country.*

Anderson, Rasmus Björn. b. at Albion, Wis., Jan. 12, 1846; d. March 2, 1936. American scholar and translator of Scandinavian. He was a professor at Wisconsin (1875–83), minister to Denmark (1885–89), and publisher and editor of *Amerika* (1897–1922). Author of *America not Discovered by Columbus* (1874), *Norse Mythology* (1875), and *Viking Tales of the North* (1877), as well as an autobiography (1915) and numerous translations from the Scandinavian dialects.

Anderson, Richard Clough. b. in Hanover County, Va., Jan. 12, 1750; d. Oct. 16, 1826. American soldier in the Revolutionary War; father of Richard Clough Anderson (1788–1826) and Robert Anderson (1805–71). As a captain, he had, on the eve of the battle of Trenton, an encounter with Hessian sentries which may have led the latter to mistake George Washington's army for a band of scouts. In the attack (1779) on Savannah he cared for the dying Casimir Pulaski, who gave him his sword.

Anderson, Richard Clough. b. at Louisville, Ky., Aug. 4, 1788; d. at Turbaco, Colombia, July 24, 1826. American politician and diplomat; son of Richard Clough Anderson (1750–1826) and half-brother of Robert Anderson (1805–71). After graduating (1804) from William and Mary College, he studied and practiced law, entering politics in 1812 as a member of the Kentucky house of representatives. Elected (1817, 1819) Kentucky representative to Congress, he proved a distinguished speaker and negotiator with a lively interest in South American independence. Selected (1823) by Monroe as minister to Colombia, he was instrumental in the first American treaty with a republic of South America, and was a delegate to the Panama Congress at the time of his death.

Anderson, Richard Heron. b. at Statesburg, S.C., Oct. 7, 1821; d. at Beaufort, S.C., June 26, 1879. American Confederate general under Braxton Bragg and James Longstreet. A graduate (1842) of West Point, he participated in the siege of Veracruz and the capture of Mexico City, under Winfield Scott. A brigadier general (1861) and lieutenant general (1864) in the Confederate army, he fought at Antietam, Gettysburg, Spottsylvania, Richmond, and elsewhere.

Anderson, Robert. b. near Louisville, Ky., June 14, 1805; d. at Nice, France, Oct. 26, 1871. American army officer who was in command of Fort Sumter during the Confederate attack (1861) at the beginning of the Civil War. A graduate (1825) of West Point, he served in the Black Hawk, Seminole, and Mexican wars. Given command (1860) of troops in Charleston Harbor, he garrisoned Fort Sumter with the intention of keeping peace by establishing an impregnable position. Still hoping to avoid bloodshed and in the absence of definite orders from Washington, he failed to support the *Star of the West* when it brought reinforcements; faced with the Confederate demand for surrender, he defended the fort until it was untenable. He served as brigadier general (1861) in Kentucky.

Anderson, Robert Bernerd. b. at Burleson, Tex., June 4, 1910—. American administrator. He served (1932–37) in Texas as a legislator, assistant attorney general, tax commissioner, racing commissioner, and director of the state unemployment commission, before returning to the private practice of law. He was named (1953) U.S. secretary of the navy by President Eisenhower.

Anderson, Rudolph Martin. b. near Decorah, Iowa, June 30, 1876—. Canadian zoölogist. He has been assistant (1902–06) in zoölogy at the Museum of Natural History of the University of Iowa, explorer and field agent (1908–13) for the American Museum of Natural History, New York, zoölogist (1913–20) for the Geological Survey of Canada, and head (1920–46) of the division of biology at the National Museum of Canada, as well as a consulting zoölogist for the Ottawa Department of Mines and Resources. Author of *Birds of Iowa* (1907), *Recent Explorations on the Canadian Arctic Coast* (1917), and *Mammals of Quebec* (1940).

Anderson, Rufus. b. at North Yarmouth, Me., Aug. 17, 1796; d. at Boston, May 30, 1880. American Congregational clergyman, secretary (1832–66) of the American Board of Commissioners for Foreign Missions, and the author of several works on missions.

Anderson, Sherwood. b. at Camden, Ohio, Sept. 13, 1876; d. at Colón, Panama, March 8, 1941. American novelist, short-story writer, poet, and journalist. His managership of an Elyria, Ohio, paint factory was followed by service in the Spanish-American War, and was terminated by Anderson's characteristically abrupt decision to seek more meaningful employment. He spent a period with his brother Karl Anderson as an advertising copy writer at Chicago, where he became a protegé of the "Chicago Group," then emerging in American letters, and published *Windy McPherson's Son* (1916), based on the character of his father. He first received general recognition with *Winesburg, Ohio* (1919). He settled at Marion, Va., where he became editor of two weekly newspapers, one Republican and one Democratic. He is the author also of the verse volume *Mid-American Chants* (1918). Other works by him include *Marching Men* (1917), *Poor White* (1920), *The Triumph of the Egg* (1921), *Horses and Men* (1923), *Many Marriages* (1923), *A Story Teller's Story* (1924), *Tar, a Midwest Childhood* (1926), *Dark Laughter* (1925), *Home Town* (1940), and *Memoirs* (1942).

Anderson, Thomas Victor. b. at Ottawa, July 4, 1881—. Canadian soldier. He was graduated (1900) from the Royal Military College at Kingston and granted (1901) the B.Sc. degree from McGill before serving as an instructor (1902–06) of civil engineering at the Royal Military College. In 1905 he joined the Canadian regular army. Wounded while serving (1915–17) in World War I, he was awarded the Distinguished Service Order. Subsequently he was director (1925–29) of military training at the National Defense Headquarters in Canada, quartermaster general (1935–38) and chief (1938–40) of the general staff in Canada, and inspector-general (1940–42) for central Canada.

Anderson, Walter. b. at Minsk, Russia, 1885—. Estonian folklorist. He was a professor (1920–40) at the University of Tartu, and subsequently a political refugee.

Anderson, William. b. probably in Accomack County, Va., in December 1762; d. at Chester, Pa., in December, 1829. American Revolutionary soldier, lawyer, congressman (1808–17) from Pennsylvania, and leader in the affairs of that state. He served on the Marquis de Lafayette's staff in the Revolutionary War, and as a colonel of the Pennsylvania militia. Thereafter he was a resident and prominent figure of Chester and Delaware counties; in the latter, he led the agitation for the election of voting delegates from unrepresented districts to the legislative caucus.

Anderson, William. b. at Edinburgh, Dec. 10, 1805; d. Aug. 2, 1866. Scottish writer, compiler, and editor; his chief works are *Poetical Aspirations* (1830), *Landscape Lyrics* (1839), *Popular Scottish Biography, being Lives of Eminent Natives of Scotland* (1842), *The Scottish Nation, or the Surnames, Families, Literature, Honors, and Biographical History of the People of Scotland* (3 vols., 1853, 1859–63, and many editions), *Treasury of the Animal World* (c1859), and *Genealogy and Surnames, with some Heraldic and Biographical Notices* (1865). He was described (1882) by James Grant, in *Old and New Edinburgh*, as a "hard-working and industrious literary man who died poor, unpensioned, and neglected."

Andersonville (an'dėr.sǫn.vil). Village in W Georgia, in Sumter County, ab. 62 mi. SW of Macon. During the Civil War it contained a Confederate military prison, opened in 1864. Pop. ab. 200.

Andersonville Prison. Confederate military prison in Georgia which was used (February, 1864–April, 1865) during the closing phases of the Civil War for the confinement of enlisted men of the Union forces. Of hasty construction, it was a log stockade occupying 16½ and later 26 acres. The slim resources of the Confederacy prevented adequate food and medical care from being furnished to the prisoners, and the suffering and heavy casualties among the Union troops there inflamed Northern feeling against the South. In the summer of 1864 there were as many as 31,678 prisoners inside the stockade. The National Cemetery at Andersonville contains 12,912 graves; some estimates have placed the mortality figures even higher. After the war a military commission tried (August, 1865) Captain Henry Wirz, who had been responsible for the internal management of the prison. He was found guilty and hanged. During the Reconstruction period and shortly thereafter the name of Andersonville was brought up by Republican politicians who desired to reawaken and exploit popular sentiment against the South and the Democratic Party.

Anderssen (än'dėr.sẹn), **Adolf.** b. at Breslau, July 6, 1818; d. there, March 13, 1879. German chess master, noted for his brilliant attacking style of play. The winner of the first International Master tournament at London, 1851, he took first prize in tournaments at London in 1862, and at Baden-Baden in 1870.

Andersson (än'dėrs.sôn), **Karl Johan.** b. in Sweden, 1827; d. in South Africa, July 5, 1867. Swedish explorer in Africa. He made three successful expeditions: to Damaraland (1850, with Francis Galton), to Lake Ngami (alone, 1853–54), and to the Okavango River (1859). He died in an attempt to reach the upper Kunene River. Author of *Lake Ngami* (1855), *The Okavango River* (1861), and others.

Andersson, Lars. Original name of **Andreä, Laurentius.**

Andersson, Nils Johan. b. Feb. 20, 1821; d. at Stockholm, March 27, 1880. Swedish botanist, author of works on the plants of Scandinavia and Lapland.

Andes (an′dēz). [Spanish, **Los Andes, Cordillera de los Andes.**] Principal mountain system of South America. It extends from Cape Horn to the vicinity of the Isthmus of Panama, and comprises the Patagonian Andes, the Chilean Andes (which lie partly in the Argentine Republic), the Bolivian and Peruvian Andes (each with two ranges nearly parallel), the Ecuadorian Andes, and the Colombian Andes (with three main ranges) branching E into the Venezuelan Andes. The range rises abruptly from the Pacific coast and contains many celebrated volcanoes. Among the chief summits are Aconcagua, Sorata, Illimani, Chimborazo, Cotopaxi, Antisana, and Tolima. On its E slope rise the headwaters of the Amazon. It is rich in gold, silver, and other metals. Length, ab. 4,500 mi.; average width, ab. 100 mi.; average elevation, ab. 12,500 ft.

Andes. In ancient geography, a village near Mantua, Italy, famous as the birthplace of Vergil.

Andesians (an.dē′zhạnz) or **Antesians** (-tē′-). General name for a number of native tribes in the Andes region. Its significance is geographical rather than ethnographical.

And Even Now. Volume of essays (1920) by Max Beerbohm.

Andhaka (än′dạ.kạ). In Hindu mythology, a demon having a thousand arms and heads, two thousand eyes and feet, and called Andhaka because he walked like a blind man, though he saw well. Shiva slew him when he tried to carry off the tree of paradise from heaven.

Andilly (däṅ.dē.yē), **Angélique Arnauld d′.** See **Arnauld d′Andilly, Angélique.**

Andilly, Robert Arnauld d′. See **Arnauld d′Andilly, Robert.**

Andino (än.dē′nō), **Tiburcio Carías.** See **Carías Andino, Tiburcio.**

Andizhan (än.dē.zhän′). [Also, **Andijan.**] City in the U.S.S.R., in the Uzbek Soviet Socialist Republic, situated near the Syr Darya ab. 75 mi. NE of Kokand, in a cotton-producing region. 83,691 (1939).

Andkhui (änd.kö′ē). [Also, **Andkho** (änd.kō′).] Town in Afghanistan, ab. 300 mi. NW of Kabul: former capital of a khanate. It is a trading center near the Russian border. Pop. ab. 15,000.

Andlaw-Birseck (änt′läf.bir′zek), **Franz Xaver von.** b. at Freiburg, Baden, Oct. 6, 1799; d. Sept. 4, 1876. German diplomat. He was the author of *Erinnerungsblätter aus den Papieren eines Diplomaten* (1857), *Mein Tagebuch 1811–61* (1862), and others.

Andler (äṅd.ler), **Charles.** b. at Strasbourg, March 11, 1866; d. at Malesherbes, France, April 1, 1933. French educator and philosopher, active in behalf of Franco-German amity.

Andocides (an.dos′i.dēz). b. at Athens, c440 B.C.; d. c391 B.C. Athenian politician and orator, banished for implication in the mutilation (415) of Hermae, of which Alcibiades was also accused. Readmitted to Athens under the democracy (403), he was later an ambassador to Sparta.

Andoni (än.dō′nē). Small subgroup of the Sudanic-speaking Ibibio peoples of W Africa, inhabiting SE Nigeria to the S of Opobo. Their population is estimated at ab. 10,000 (by P. A. Talbot, *The Peoples of Southern Nigeria*, 1926).

Andorra (an.dôr′ạ). [French, **Andorre** (äṅ.dôr).] Independent republic in the Pyrenees Mountains, bounded on the N by France (Pyrénées Orientales and Ariège departments), and on the S and W by Spain (province of Lérida). The republic of Andorra has existed uninterruptedly since 1278, and its continued independence is guaranteed jointly by the president of the republic of France and the bishop of Urgel in Spain against a yearly payment of 960 francs and 460 pesetas respectively. The official language of the republic is Catalan. The terrain is mountainous. There are iron-ore and lead mines, thermal springs, pine forests, and pasture lands. There is some agriculture. Capital, Andorra; area, 191 sq. mi.; pop. 5,000 (est. 1946).

Andover (an′dō.vėr). Municipal borough in S England, in Southampton (an administrative county of the geographical county of Hampshire), situated on the Anton River, ab. 67 mi. SW of London by rail. 14,661 (1951).

Andover. Town in NE Massachusetts, in Essex County, ab. 22 mi. NW of Boston: seat of Phillips Academy and the Abbot Academy, and formerly of Andover Theological Seminary (Congregational; founded in 1807). Its factories produce woolen and rubber goods. It was the home of Harriet Beecher Stowe. 12,437 (1950).

Andøy (än′ė′′i). [Also: **Andö, Andöy.**] Northernmost of the Vesterålen islands, NW Norway: cod fisheries. Length, ab. 35 mi.; area, ab. 189 sq. mi.

Andrada (un.drä′dạ), **Antônio de.** b. at Oleiros, Portugal, c1580; d. at Goa, in India, March 19, 1634. Portuguese Jesuit missionary in the East Indies and Tibet, author of *Novo descobrimento do Grão Catayo, ou dos Reynos de Tibet* (1626).

Andrada, Diego Payva de. b. at Coimbra, Portugal, 1528; d. at Lisbon, 1575. Portuguese theologian, sent as a delegate by Dom Sebastian to the Council of Trent (1561). He wrote *Orthodoxarum Quaestionum libri X. . . contra Kemnitii petulantem audaciam* (1564) and others.

Andrada, Gomes Freire de. [Also, **Andrade** (un.drä′dẹ).] b. in Portugal, 1684; d. at Rio de Janeiro, Jan. 1, 1763. Portuguese administrator. From 1733 until his death he was governor of Rio de Janeiro, then comprising most of southern Brazil, and the period of his administration was the most prosperous in the colonial history of that country. In 1758 he was made count of Bobadella.

Andrada e Silva (ẹ sēl′vạ), **Antonio de.** [Called the **"Mirabeau of Brazil"**; full name, **Antonio Carlos Ribiero de Andrada Machado e Silva.**] b. at Santos, Brazil, Nov. 1, 1773; d. at Rio de Janeiro, Dec. 5, 1845. Brazilian politician; brother of José Bonifácio and Martim Francisco de Andrada e Silva. He was involved in the rebellion of 1817 at Pernambuco and imprisoned until 1821. In the Brazilian constituent assembly of 1823 he led the radicals and was banished with his two brothers to France. He returned in 1828, was elected deputy (1835), and was one of the liberal leaders. He was one of the first ministers of Pedro II, and in 1845 entered the senate.

Andrada e Silva, José Bonifácio de. See **Bonifácio, José.**

Andrada e Silva, Martim Francisco de. b. 1776; d. 1844. Brazilian statesman; brother of José Bonifácio and Antonio de Andrada e Silva. He was exiled (1823) to France with his brothers for his advocacy of democratic government under Pedro I.

Andrade (an′drād), **Edward Neville da Costa.** b. at London, Dec. 27, 1887—. English physicist. He studied at University College, London, the universities of Heidelberg, Cambridge, and Manchester, and was a professor (1920–28) of physics at the Military College of Science at Woolwich, before becoming, in 1928, Quain professor of physics at the University of London. Author of *Structure of the Atom* (1923), *Airs* (1924), *Engines* (1928), *Mechanism of Nature* (1930), *The New Chemistry*, and in collaboration with Julian Huxley, *Simple Science* (1934).

Andrade (un.drä′dẹ), **Manuel de Carvalho Paes de.** See **Carvalho Paes de Andrade, Manuel de.**

Andrade, Mário de. b. at São Paulo, Brazil, Oct. 9, 1893; d. at Rio de Janeiro, Feb. 15, 1945. Brazilian poet, novelist, critic, essayist, folklorist, one of the central figures of the Brazilian modernist movement of the 1920's, and an authority on Brazilian music. Among his books of poems are *Há uma gota de sangue em cada poema* (1917), *Paulicéia desvairada* (1922), *Losango cáqui* (1926), *Clã de jabotí* (1927), and *Remate de males* (1930). He also wrote *Macunaíma* (1928), *Ensaio sôbre a música brasileira* (1928), and *Belazarte*, short stories (1933). One of his novels, *Amar, verbo intransitivo* (1927), was translated into English as *Fräulein* (1933).

Andrade (än.drä′ᴛʜā), **Olegario Victor.** b. in Entre Ríos province, Argentina, 1841; d. 1882. Argentine poet and editor-in-chief (1880–82) of the government newspaper, *La tribuna nacional*. He has been compared by some critics to Walt Whitman in the manner and effect of his art as well as his patriotism. Author of *El nido de cóndores* (c1877), *Prometeo* (1877), *San Martín* (1878), *Victor Hugo* (1881), and *Atlántida* (1881).

Andrade Neves (un.drä′dẹ nā′vẹs), **José Joaquim de.** [Created in 1867, Baron of **Triumpho.**] b. at Rio Pardo, Rio Grande do Sul, Brazil, Jan. 22, 1807; d. at Asunción,

Paraguay, Jan. 6, 1869. Brazilian general. He distinguished himself in the war in Rio Grande do Sul (1835–45), and especially as a cavalry commander in the Paraguayan war (1867–69).

Andrade y Portugal (ē pōr.tö.gäl′), **Pedro Fernández de Castro.** See **Fernández de Castro Andrade y Portugal, Pedro.**

Andrae (än′drā), **Walter.** b. at Anger, near Leipzig, Germany, Feb. 18, 1875—. German archaeologist, on the faculty (1927 *et seq.*) of the Technische Hochschule at Charlottenburg. He directed (1894 *et seq.*) the excavations at Babylon and elsewhere in Mesopotamia. Author of *Hatra* (1908–12), *Die Festungswerke von Assur* (The Fortifications of Assur, 1913), and *Die Archäischen Ischtar-Tempel in Assur* (The Archaic Ishtar-Temples at Assur, 1922).

Andral (äṅ.dràl), **Gabriel.** b. at Paris, Nov. 6, 1797; d. at Châteauvieux, Loir-et-Cher, France, Feb. 13, 1876. French physician, professor (1828–66) at the University of Paris. Among his works are *Clinique médicale* (1823 *et seq.*), *Précis d'anatomie pathologique* (1829), and *Cours de pathologie interne* (1836–37).

Andrássy (ôn′drä.shē; Anglicized, an.dras′i), Count **Gyula.** b. at what is now Košice, Czechoslovakia, March 8, 1823; d. at Volosca, on the Istrian peninsula, Feb. 18, 1890. Hungarian statesman and diplomat; father of Gyula Andrássy (1860–1929). He was a member of the Hungarian diet (1847) and governor of Zemplin (1848). Leader, with Kossuth and Deák, of the Hungarian insurrection (1848–49), he was in exile until 1857. Again in the diet (1861), he engineered with Deák a compromise (1867) creating the Austro-Hungarian dual monarchy, and became the first constitutional premier of Hungary (1867–71). As foreign minister for Austria-Hungary (1871–79) he consolidated a cordial relationship with Bismarck and framed the Andrássy Note (1876) which helped bring on the Russo-Turkish War; as a representative at the Congress of Berlin (1878), he obtained a mandate over Bosnia and Hercegovina, a move which proved unpopular at home and led finally to his resignation. He negotiated a treaty with Bismarck in 1879 which formed the basis of the Triple Alliance.

Andrássy, Count **Gyula.** b. 1860; d. 1929. Austro-Hungarian politician and government official; son of Gyula Andrássy (1823–90). He was minister of the interior (1906–10) in the coalition cabinet, and an advocate (1915) of a separate peace with the Allies; he succeeded Burian as foreign minister in 1918 and once more sought separate peace, but failed. Imprisoned (1921) for his part in the plot to restore Charles to the throne, he was amnestied and headed the royalist opposition to Horthy and Bethlen. In 1922 he was elected to the national assembly of Hungary.

Andrássy Note. Declaration relating to the disturbed state of Bosnia and Hercegovina, drawn up by the governments of Austria, Russia, and Germany with the approval of England and France, and presented to the government of Turkey on Jan. 31, 1876. It demanded the establishment of religious liberty, the abolition of the farming of taxes, the application of the revenue derived from direct taxation in Bosnia and Hercegovina to the needs of these provinces, the institution of a commission composed equally of Christians and Moslems to control the execution of these reforms, and the improvement of the agrarian population by the sale of surplus lands belonging to the state.

André (äṅ.drā), **Albert.** b. at Lyons, May 24, 1869—. French painter, designer of tapestries, and illustrator, who followed the impressionist school. Although he studied with Adolphe William Bouguereau, he was strongly influenced by Renoir and Cezanne; he has been exhibiting in France, the U.S., and Argentina since 1894. As director of the Museum of Bagnols-sur-Cèze, he has encouraged many modern artists of schools more extreme than his own. His work consists mainly of still lifes, interior scenes, and landscapes, many of which have won prizes. *Café Interior, Bagatelle, Fruits, Flower Merchant, Portrait of Renoir, Girl Reading,* and *The Beige Hat* are among his more popular works. He illustrated Charles Maurras' *L'Étang de Berre,* and other books.

André, Bernard. [Also, **Andreas** (an.drē′as).] French poet and historian, poet laureate of England in the reign of Henry VII (the first laureate appointed by an English king), tutor of Arthur, prince of Wales, and royal historiographer. In spite of blindness he attained a high degree of scholarship. He wrote a life of Henry VII.

André (än.drā′), **Johann.** b. at Offenbach, Germany, March 28, 1741; d. there, June 18, 1799. German composer and music publisher; founder of the publishing firm expanded by his son, Johann Anton André (1775–1842).

André, Johann Anton. b. at Offenbach, Germany, Oct. 6, 1775; d. 1842. German composer, teacher, and publisher, who, with his four sons, developed the publishing firm founded by his father, Johann André. He was a collector of musical memorabilia, especially those connected with Mozart.

André (än′drā, an′dri), **John.** b. at London, 1751; executed at Tappan, N.Y., Oct. 2, 1780. English officer hanged as a spy by Washington in the Revolutionary War. A lieutenant (1774 *et seq.*) in the Royal Fusileers, he was aide-de-camp to Grey and Clinton, made by the latter adjutant general with rank of major. As Clinton's representative, he arranged (1780) with Benedict Arnold, near Stony Point, for the surrender of West Point; returning in civilian disguise, he mistook some intercepting soldiers for British and revealed his identity; captured near Tarrytown, he was tried and condemned at Tappan. His charm, talent, and avowed lack of sympathy for his mission aroused strong American sentiment and some censure of George Washington for the execution.

André (äṅ.drā), **Louis.** b. at St.-Rémy, France, May 28, 1631 (or 1623); d. at Quebec, Sept. 19, 1715. French Jesuit missionary and student of American Indian languages, particularly (1672–82) in what is now Wisconsin.

Andrea (un.drā′a), **Francisco José Soares de.** [Title, Baron of **Caçapava.**] b. at Lisbon, Portugal, Jan. 29, 1781; d. at Rio de Janeiro, Oct. 2, 1858. Portuguese-Brazilian general, a supporter of Brazilian independence. He went to Brazil in 1808; was adjutant-general in the Cisplatine campaign of 1827; commandant of Pará (1831); president and commandant of Pará (1835); and president of Santa Catherina (1839), of Rio Grande do Sul (1841), of Minas Gerais (1843), of Bahia (1845), and again of Rio Grande do Sul (1848). He attained the rank of marshal in the Brazilian army.

Andrea (än.drā′ä), **Girolamo.** b. at Naples, Italy, April 12, 1812; d. at Rome, May 14, 1868. Italian cardinal and diplomat. His liberalism in religion and politics (especially his leaning toward Italian national unity) led to his suspension (1866) from his dignities by the papal Curia, but he was reinstated after a humble submission in 1867.

Andreä (än.drā′e), **Jakob.** b. at Waiblingen, Württemberg, March 25, 1528; d. at Tübingen, Württemberg, Jan. 7, 1590. One of the chief Protestant theologians of the 16th century, appointed professor of theology and chancellor of the University of Tübingen in 1562. He was the principal author of the *Formula Concordiae,* and wrote over 150 works, chiefly polemical.

Andreä, Johann Valentin. b. at Herrenberg, Germany, Aug. 17, 1586; d. at Stuttgart, Germany, June 24, 1654. German Protestant theologian and satirical writer; grandson of Jakob Andreä. Author of *Menippus* (1648) a satire, and possibly of *Chymische Hochaeit Christiani Rosenkreuz* (1616), and other works on the Rosicrucians.

Andreä, Laurentius. [Original name, **Lars Andersson.**] b. 1480; d. 1552. Swedish reformer, chancellor under Gustavus Vasa. Together with Olaus Petri he translated (1536) the Bible into Swedish, and was the principal agent in introducing (1527) the Lutheran Reformation at the diet of Westeras. In 1540 he was charged with having failed to disclose a conspiracy against the king, and was sentence to death, but bought a pardon.

Andrea Chénier (än.drā′ä shā.nyā′). Opera in four acts, by Umberto Giordano, libretto by Luigi Illica, first produced at La Scala, Milan, March 28, 1896.

Andrea del Sarto (än.drā′ä del sär′tō). See **Sarto, Andrea del.**

Andreae (än.drā′e), **Wilhelm Friedrich.** b. at Magdeburg, Germany, April 8, 1888—. German political economist, on the faculties (1926 *et seq.*) of the universities of Graz and Giessen. Author of *Bausteine zu einer universalistischen Steuerlehre* (Bricks for a Universalistic Science of Taxes, 1927), and *Kapitalismus, Bolschevismus, Faschismus* (Capitalism, Bolshevism, and Fascism, 1933).

Andreani (än.drā.ä'nē), **Andrea.** b. at Mantua, Italy, c1540; d. at Rome, 1623. Italian chiaroscuro engraver on wood. His prints (now rare) are valued for their excellent technique, particularly in the handling of light and shade. He is best known for *The Deluge* and *Destruction of Pharaoh's Host* (after Titian), *The Miraculous Draught of Fishes* (after Raphael), and the series entitled *Triumph of Julius Caesar* (after Mantegna).

Andreanof Islands (än.dri.ä'nof, an.drē.an'of). Group of islands SW of Alaska, midway of the Aleutian archipelago. U.S. bases were established on two of the islands (Adak and Atka) during World War II.

Andreas (än.drā'äs), **Willy.** b. at Karlsruhe, Germany, Oct. 30, 1884—. German historian. He served as professor (1914 *et seq.*) at Karlsruhe, Rostock and Heidelberg. His main work is *Deutschland vor der Reformation* . . . (Germany before the Reformation, 1932). He edited *Bismarck's Gespräche* (Bismarck's Conversations, 1924–26).

Andreasberg (än.drā'äs.berk). [Also, **St. Andreasberg.**] Town in NW Germany, in the *Land* (state) of Lower Saxony, British Zone, formerly in the province of Hanover, Prussia, situated in the Harz Mountains, ab. 28 mi. NE of Göttingen. Formerly noted for its silver mines, it now produces toys and metallurgical, wooden and paper goods. 4,799 (1946).

Andreas-Salomé (än.drā'äs.zä'lō.mā), **Lou.** b. at St. Petersburg, Russia, Feb. 13, 1861; d. At Göttingen, Germany, Feb. 11, 1937. German novelist, biographer, and psychoanalyst; intimate friend of Friedrich Wilhelm Nietzsche and Rainer Maria Rilke. Her international connections (her father, General Salomé, was a Russian of French descent; her German husband, Professor Andreas, was an Orientalist at Göttingen) may account for her liberal and wide interests. She wrote *Über Ibsens Frauengestalten* (1892) with considerable psychological insight, and her numerous novels (*Im Kampf um Gott*, 1885; *Aus fremder Seele*, 1896; *Ma*, 1901) tend to the psychological. Eventually she came to know Freud, and took up psychoanalysis. She exercised a marked influence on Nietzsche, and her lifelong friendship with Rilke was the most constant factor in his existence. She wrote *Nietzsche in seinen Werken* (1894) and *Rainer Maria Rilke* (1928).

Andree (än'drā), **Karl Theodor.** b. at Brunswick, Germany, Oct. 20, 1808; d. at Wildungen, Germany, Aug. 10, 1875. German geographer and journalist, founder (1862) of *Globus*, a geographical journal carried on by his son, Richard. Author of geographies of North America (1854) and Argentina (1856), *Geographische Wanderungen* (1859), *Geographie des Welthandels* (1859), and others.

Andree, Richard. b. at Brunswick, Germany, Feb. 26, 1835; d. at Munich, 1912. German ethnographer and geographer; son of Karl Theodor Andree, of whose *Globus* he was editor (1891–1903). Author of a German atlas (1877), *Algemeiner Handatlas* (1881), and others.

Andrée (än.drā'), **Salomon August.** b. at Grenna, Sweden, 1854; d. on White Island, near Greenland, 1897. Swedish aeronaut and engineer. He attempted (1897) with two companions to reach the North Pole from Spitzbergen in a balloon equipped with sails and ropes designed to guide a course. His fate was unknown until 1930, when sailors discovered his remains on White Island; his diaries and other material pertaining to the disaster were printed in *Andrée's Story* (1930).

Andreini (än.drā.ē'nē), **Francesco.** b. at Pistoia, Italy, 1548; d. 1624. Italian comedian, popular actor, and scenarist in the Gelosi, a troupe of strolling players in Italy and France who improvised their lines from scenarios, summoned to Paris by Henry IV to entertain Marie de' Medici. He was the husband of Isabella Andreini and father of Giovanni Battista Andreini. Author of *Le Bravure del Capitano Spavento* (1607) and other plays translated into French.

Andreini, Giovanni Battista. [Stage name in Paris, **Leylio.**] b. at Florence, c1578; d. at Paris, c1650. Italian comedian and poet; son of Francesco and Isabella Andreini. Member of the Gelosi, founder of the Fidele, companies of players; author of *L'Adamo* (1613), from which Milton was said to have borrowed several scenes for *Paradise Lost*.

Andreini, Isabella. b. at Padua, Italy, 1562; d. at Lyons, France, 1604. Italian actress and poet, prima donna of the Gelosi, a group of improvising comedians who traveled in Italy and France, of which her husband, Francesco Andreini, and son, Giovanni Battista Andreini, were also members. Playing parts in scenarios by Flaminio Scala, she became one of the most popular actresses in Europe. Author of *Mirtilla*, a pastoral fable (1588), poems and songs, and letters published (1607, 1647) after her death.

Andreis (än.drās'), **Andrew James Felix Bartholomew de.** [Called **Felix de Andreis.**] b. in Italy, Dec. 12, 1778; d. Oct. 15, 1820. Italian priest, rector (c1818–20) of the cathedral at St. Louis, Mo. A teacher of theology (1806 *et seq.*) at Monte Citorio, Rome, who conducted missions in nearby towns, he attracted by his scholarship and preaching the notice of Pope Pius VII, who made it possible for him to accompany Louis Du Bourg to Louisiana in 1816. He was preparing to extend his missionary work among the Indians in Missouri when he died, probably of typhoid fever.

Andréossy or **Andréossi** (dän.drā.*o*.sē), **Antoine François**, Comte **d'**. b. at Castelnaudary, France, March 6, 1761; d. at Montauban, France, Sept. 10, 1828. French general and diplomat under Napoleon. He served in the wars of the Revolution, took part in the coup d'état of the 18th Brumaire, and was ambassador at London, Vienna (1808–12), and Constantinople (1812–14). Recalled by Louis XVIII, he wrote on military history and science.

Andrés (än.drās'), **Juan.** b. at Planes, Spain, Feb. 15, 1740; d. at Rome, Jan. 17, 1817. Spanish Jesuit and scholar. Author of *Dell' origine, dei progressi e dello stato attuale d'ogni Letteratura* (On the Origin, Progress, and Present Condition of all Literature, 1782–99), and others.

Andreu (än.drā'ö), **Mariano.** b. at Barcelona, Spain, 1888—. Spanish portraitist, illustrator, and genre painter who has exhibited in France and Spain since 1920. *The Artist and His Wife*, *Portrait of Jean Giraudoux*, *Bathers*, and *Woman with Guitar*, are among his outstanding works.

Andrew (an'drö), Saint. fl. first half of 1st century A.D. One of the twelve disciples of Jesus, a brother of (Simon) Peter and an apostle to the Gentiles. He is honored by the Scotch as their patron saint, and by the Russian church as its founder. He suffered death by crucifixion. The X-shaped cross of Saint Andrew is named for him.

Andrew I. d. 1060. King of Hungary (1046–60). He carried on wars with the Germans (1046–52) and with his brother Béla. He was killed in the struggle against the latter.

Andrew II. b. 1175; d. 1235. King of Hungary (1205–35); son of Béla III, and father of Béla IV and of Elizabeth of Hungary. He took part in the fifth Crusade in 1217, and in his Golden Bull (1222), urged on him by his nobles and known as the "Hungarian Magna Charta," decreed that royal violation of the privileges of the nobility should be considered as a just cause for resistance by force against the king. Later provisions (1231) established other limits on the royal power, chiefly by strengthening the position of the nobles. He also granted (1224) self-government to Transylvania.

Andrew III. d. 1301. King of Hungary (1290–1301); grandson of Andrew II, and the last of the Árpád dynasty. On the murder of Ladislaus IV the Pope claimed Hungary as a fief of the church, and invested Charles Martel, son of the King of Naples, with its throne. In 1291 however, Andrew defeated him at Agram (now Zagreb).

Andrew, James Osgood. b. in Wilkes County, Ga., May 3, 1794; d. at Mobile, Ala., March 2, 1871. American bishop of the Methodist Episcopal Church, a source of the controversy (1844) which led to the split into northern and southern branches of the church. His ownership, through marriage, of slaves, though he renounced property rights over them, aroused the Northern delegates to a Methodist conference (1844), resulting in the resolution that he desist from office. Southern members, maintaining that the church should wait for national antislavery sentiment, refused to accept this decision and formed (1845) the Methodist Episcopal Church, South. Andrew was one of its first bishops (1846).

Andrew, John Albion. b. at Windham, Me., May 31, 1818; d. at Boston, Oct. 30, 1867. American antislavery leader; governor of Massachusetts during the Civil War. He was one of the founders of the Free Soil Party, and a defender of John Brown. As governor (1860–66) he organized the first wartime regiment to reach Washington (6th Massachusetts) and the first Negro regiment (54th Massachusetts).

Andrew, Samuel. b. at Cambridge, Mass., Jan. 29, 1656; d. Jan. 24, 1738. American Congregational clergyman and educator. A founder (1701) of Yale and its rector (1707–19), he taught a class at Milford, Conn., and supervised others at Saybrook, Conn., during the period when the final site of the institution was still undetermined.

Andrew Aguecheek (ā′gū.chēk), **Sir.** See **Aguecheek, Sir Andrew.**

Andrewes (an′dröz), **Christopher Howard.** b. at London, June 7, 1896—. English pathologist, an expert on virus infections. He served as house physician (1921–23, 1925–26) at St. Bartholomew's Hospital, and assistant resident physician (1923–25) at the Hospital of the Rockefeller Institution at New York. He became in 1927 a member of the staff of the National Institute for Medical Research at London.

Andrewes, Lancelot. b. at Barking, England, 1555; d. at London, Sept. 25, 1626. English prelate, leader and spokesman of the High Church (Anglican) party against Roman Catholics and Puritans, respected even by his opponents for his scholarship, high principles, and brilliant preaching. He was chaplain to Elizabeth, James I, and Charles I; dean of Westminster (1601); bishop of Chichester (1605), Ely (1609), and Winchester (1619); privy councillor for England (1609) and Scotland (1617); and one of the translators (1607–11) of the Bible into the King James Version. Author of *Tortura Torti* (1609), an anti-Catholic defense of James I, manuals of devotions and prayers (1648), and others.

Andrew of Crete (an′drö). [Latinized, **Andreas Cretensis.**] b. at Damascus, in Syria, 660; d. 720 or 740. Archbishop of Crete and writer of religious poetry. He took part in the Monothelite synod of 712, but later returned to orthodoxy. He is regarded by most authorities as the inventor of the musical canon.

Andrews (an′dröz). Town in E South Carolina, in Williamsburg and Georgetown counties NE of Charleston. It contains pulp and lumber mills, and is a trading center for the agricultural products of the vicinity. 2,702 (1950).

Andrews. Town in NW Texas, county seat of Andrews County. 3,294 (1950).

Andrews, Alexander Boyd. b. near Franklinton, N.C., July 23, 1841; d. April 17, 1915. American railroad builder and operator whose part in the expansion of railroads in North Carolina contributed to the building up of the South after the Civil War. Severely wounded and financially ruined in the war, he opened a passenger and freight ferry-service on the Roanoke River; he then became superintendent of the Raleigh and Gaston (1867), the Chatham (1868), and later the North Carolina Railroad, building numerous lines, particularly one through the mountains in the western part of the state. On the formation (1894) of the Southern Railway he became its first vice-president.

Andrews, Avery DeLano. b. at Massena, N.Y., April 4, 1864—. American lawyer and soldier, brigadier general (1918) in World War I. A graduate (1886) of the U.S. Military Academy, he practiced law (1891 *et seq.*) at New York, where he also served as police commissioner (1895–98). He was assistant chief of staff (1918 *et seq.*) to General Pershing, about whom he wrote in *My Friend and Classmate, John J. Pershing* (1939).

Andrews, Charles. b. at Whitestown, N.Y., May 27, 1827; d. Oct. 22, 1918. American lawyer. He was district attorney (1853–56) of Onondaga County, N.Y., mayor (1861, 1862, 1868) of Syracuse, and chief justice (1881, 1892–97) of the New York court of appeals, which he had been instrumental in reëstablishing (1867).

Andrews, Charles Bartlett. b. Nov. 4, 1836; d. Sept. 12, 1902. American lawyer, governor (1879–81) of Connecticut, and judge (1881 *et seq.*) of the superior court of Connecticut.

Andrews, Charles Freer. [Called (by Gandhi) **Dinahandbu,** meaning "Friend of the People."] b. at Newcastle-on-Tyne, England, 1871; d. at Calcutta, India, April 4, 1940. English writer, resident in India for 35 years; a close friend of Mohandas Gandhi and Rabindranath Tagore, and one of the few Englishmen generally trusted by Indian natives. An outstanding authority on India, Indian labor, and the drink and opium problems, he was the author of *Indian Independence* (1922), *The ½ndian Problem* (1922), *The Drink and Opium Evil* (1923), *Mahatma Gandhi's Ideas* (1929), *The Indian Earthquake* (1935), *India and Britain* (1935), *India and the Pacific* (1937), and *The True India* (1939).

Andrews, Charles McLean. b. at Wethersfield, Conn., Feb. 22, 1863; d. at New Haven, Conn., Sept. 9, 1943. American historian. He was professor at Bryn Mawr (1889–1907), Johns Hopkins (1907–10), and Yale (1910–31). Author of the four-volume *Colonial Period of American History* (1934–38), the first volume of which won a Pulitzer prize in 1935, he also wrote the two-volume *Historical Development of Modern Europe* (1896–98), *The Colonial Background of the American Revolution* (1924, 1931), and others.

Andrews, Chauncey Hummason. b. at Vienna, Ohio, Dec. 2, 1823; d. Dec. 25, 1893. American mine and railroat promoter. Having developed coal mines in the Mahoning valley of Ohio and Mercer County, Pa., and needing transportation facilities, he was instrumental in the building of railroads including the Pittsburgh and Lake Erie (1876), the Pittsburgh, Youngstown and Chicago, and the Pittsburgh, Chicago and Toledo; he was the owner also of a farm-machinery factory at Youngstown.

Andrews, Christopher Columbus. b. at Hillsboro, N.H., Oct. 27, 1829; d. at St. Paul, Minn., Sept. 21, 1922. American diplomat, lawyer, author, and Union soldier during the Civil War. He practiced law (1857 *et seq.*) at St. Cloud, Minn., and in 1859 entered state politics. Having enlisted in the Union army as a private, he was captured, exchanged, and finally reached the brevet rank of major general. Subsequently he served as minister (1869–77) to Sweden and Norway and consul general (1882–85) to Brazil. Author of numerous works pertaining to his military, diplomatic, and legal careers.

Andrews, Edward Gayer. b. Aug. 7, 1825; d. Dec. 31, 1907. American Methodist Episcopal bishop and educator. In 1848 he entered the Methodist ministry and was elected bishop in 1872. He was appointed (1876) by Methodist officials to undertake the coördination of congregations in Sweden, Norway, and India with the church in the U.S.

Andrews, Elisha Benjamin. b. at Hinsdale, N.H., Jan. 10, 1844; d. at Interlachen, Fla., Oct. 30, 1917. American educator and Baptist clergyman. He was a soldier in the Civil War, president of Denison (1875–79) and Brown (1889–98) universities, and a professor at Newton Theological Institution (1879–82), Brown (1882–88), and Cornell (1888–89). He resigned in 1897 from the presidency of Brown (where he had established in 1891 a Women's College) over the issue of freedom of expression, his views on the silver question having differed from those of university officers; on protests from the faculties of other universities, he was asked to remain. He was also superintendent of the Chicago schools (1898–1900), and chancellor of the University of Nebraska (1900–08). Author of *An Honest Dollar* (1889), *Wealth and Moral Law* (1894), *The United States in Our Own Time* (1903), *The Call of the Land* (1913), and others.

Andrews, Ethan Allen. b. at New Britain, Conn., April 7, 1787; d. there, March 24, 1858. American educator, teacher of classics, and head of female seminaries; editor of Latin textbooks and of *A Copious and Critical Latin-English Lexicon* (1850).

Andrews, Frank Maxwell. b. at Nashville. Tenn., Feb. 3, 1884; d. in airplane crash in Iceland, in May, 1943. American air-force officer. A graduate (1906) of the U.S. Military Academy, he served in the Philippines and in Hawaii, and later (1917–20) in the aviation section of the signal corps. He was assigned in 1920 to the U.S. army of occupation in Germany. In 1935 he was appointed colonel, after serving as executive officer (1923–25) at Kelly Field, Texas. He was the organizer and first head (1936–39) of General Headquarters Air Force, with the rank of major general; appointed lieutenant general (1941), he headed the U.S. Caribbean defense command (1942) and the Middle East command (November, 1942–February, 1943). He succeeded General Dwight Eisenhower as commander (February, 1943) of U.S. forces in the European theater.

Andrews, Garnett. b. May 15, 1837; d. May 6, 1903. American soldier and lawyer. After graduating (1861) from the University of Georgia law school, he served in the Confederate army, where he was the organizer (1864) and commander of the regiment of foreigners known as the "Galvanized Yankees." He practiced law with distinction at Yazoo City, Miss., and Chattanooga, Tenn., serving one term (1891–93) as mayor of the latter. Author of *Andrews' Digest of the Decisions of the Supreme Court of Mississippi* (1884).

Andrews, George Leonard. b. at Bridgewater, Mass., Aug. 31, 1828; d. April 4, 1899. American soldier, engineer, law officer, and teacher. Graduated (1851) from West Point, he became an army engineer (1851–55) and a civil engineer (1855–61). Having been commissioned in the Union army, he trained and led the 2nd Massachusetts infantry; he also commanded the Baton Rouge district and trained Negro troops for service with the Union army. He was appointed (1867) U.S. marshal for Massachusetts. Later he served as professor of French (1871–82) and head of the modern language department (1882–92) at West Point.

Andrews, George Pierce. b. at Bridgton, Me., Sept. 29, 1835; d. May 24, 1902. American lawyer, corporation counsel (1882) to the City of New York, and associate justice (1883–97, 1898–1902) of the New York supreme court. After graduating (1858) from Yale, he began the practice of law in the office of the U.S. district attorney for southern New York and gained his reputation as prosecutor of the first slave-trader to be hanged (1862) for piracy under a law of 1820. Retained by Cornelius K. Garrison, he obtained a knowledge of corporation law, in which he was later regarded as a leading authority.

Andrews, Israel Ward. b. at Danbury, Conn., Jan. 3, 1815; d. at Hartford, Conn., April 18, 1888. American educator, teacher (1838–88) at and president (1855–85) of Marietta College, Ohio, during its formative period. After his graduation (1837) from Williams College, he became an instructor in mathematics in 1838 at Marietta on the recommendation of Mark Hopkins, and was professor of mathematics and natural philosophy (1839–55), and professor of political science (1855–88) there. Active in a number of educational associations and in the field of political science, he attracted wide attention with a paper (1863) on allegiance during the Civil War. Author of the college textbook *Manual of the Constitution* (1874), and others.

Andrews, James Pettit. b. near Newbury, England, c1737; d. at London, Aug. 6, 1797. English antiquary and historian. He was the author of translations, satires, and two histories of Great Britain (1794–95 and 1796).

Andrews, John. b. in Cecil County, Md., April 4, 1746; d. March 29, 1813. American Episcopal clergyman, classical scholar, and provost (1810–12) of the University of Pennsylvania. A graduate (1764) of the College of Philadelphia, he headed classical schools at Lancaster (1765–67) and York (c1776–82), Pa., and the Protestant Episcopal Academy (1785–91), Philadelphia, which became part in 1791 of the University of Pennsylvania. He was active (1784) in the separation of the Maryland Protestant Episcopal Church from the British church, and was an advocate of the merging of the Episcopal with the Methodist church. Author of *A Compend of Logick* (1801), *Elements of Rhetorick and Belles Lettres* (1813), and others.

Andrews, John Miller. b. July 17, 1871—. British statesman. He headed the ministry of Labour (1921–37) and that of Finance (1937–40), and was Prime Minister (1940–43) of Northern Ireland, as well as a member (1921–29) from County Down of the Northern Irish Parliament.

Andrews, Joseph. b. at Hingham, Mass., c1805; d. there, or at Boston, May 7, 1873. American engraver, particularly of portraits and other paintings. Besides *Plymouth Rock, 1620*, on which he worked 14 years, he did portraits of Benjamin Franklin, George Washington, John Quincy Adams, and many others.

Andrews, Launcelot Winchester. b. at London, Canada, June 13, 1856; d. 1938. American chemist. He was a professor of chemistry at the Iowa State College of Agriculture (1884–85) and at the State University of Iowa (1885–1904), a consulting chemist (1904–10) to the Mallinckrodt Chemical Works at St. Louis, and a research chemist (1915–21) at the Victor Chemical Works at Chicago. Author of *An Introduction to the Study of Qualitative Analysis* (1891).

Andrews, Lorrin. b. at East Windsor (now part of Vernon), Conn., April 29, 1795; d. at Honolulu, Hawaii, Sept. 29, 1868. American missionary, teacher, and official of the Hawaiian government. A missionary (1828 *et seq.*) to Hawaii, he headed (1831) the teachers college at Lahainaluna and published (1834) the first Hawaiian newspaper; he resigned (1841) as a missionary when the American Board of Missions accepted contributions from slaveholders. Thereafter he was a member (1846 *et seq.*) of the Hawaiian privy council, and the first associate justice (1852–55) of the Hawaiian supreme court. He was also active in the translation of the Bible into Hawaiian, and published (1865) a Hawaiian-English dictionary of approximately 17,000 words.

Andrews, Mary Raymond. [Maiden name, **Shipman.**] b. at Mobile, Ala., c1865; d. Aug. 2, 1936. American novelist; wife (1884 *et seq.*) of William Shankland Andrews. Author of *Bob and the Guides* (1906), *A Good Samaritan* (1906), *The Perfect Tribute* (1906), *Enchanted Forest* (1909), *The Eternal Masculine* (1913), *Three Things* (1915), *The Eternal Feminine* (1916), *His Soul Goes Marching* (1922), *Yellow Butterflies* (1922), and *Lost Commander* (1929).

Andrews, Roy Chapman. b. at Beloit, Wis., Jan. 26, 1884—. American natural scientist, explorer, and author. He became in 1906 a staff member of the American Museum of Natural History and was its director from 1935 to 1941. He accompanied expeditions to Alaska (1908), Netherlands East Indies (1909–10), and northern Korea (1911–12), and went (1913) again to Alaska with the Borden expedition. After 1914 he specialized in explorations of central Asia to test the validity of H. F. Osborn's theory that this area was the dispersal point of northern mammalian life; his earlier specialization in water mammals, chiefly whales, produced *Whale Hunting with Gun and Camera* (1916) and others. He also participated in expeditions (1917–30) to SW and N China, Tibet, Burma, and particularly Mongolia, on which he unearthed great fossil-fields, new geological formations, dinosaur eggs, and remains of the *Baluchitherium*, largest land mammal yet known to have existed. Author of *Across Mongolian Plains* (1921), *On the Trail of Ancient Man* (1926), *The New Conquest of Central Asia* (1932), and others.

Andrews, Stephen Pearl. b. at Templeton, Mass., March 22, 1812; d. at New York, May 21, 1886. American abolitionist and writer on language, law, phonography, and philosophy; uncle of Elisha Benjamin Andrews (1844–1917). Author of *Discoveries in Chinese* (1854), *The Basic Outline Of Universology* (1877), and others.

Andrews, Thomas. b. at Belfast, Dec. 19, 1813; d. there, Nov. 26, 1885. Irish physicist and chemist. He was a professor of chemistry (1845–79) at Queen's College, Belfast. His research led to the discovery and naming of the "critical temperature" in gases, i.e., that point beyond which a given gas cannot be liquefied at any pressure.

Andrews, William Loring. b. at New York, Sept. 9, 1837; d. March 19, 1920. American bibliophile and businessman. He was an active member of the Grolier Society, which was so named (1884) at his home, as well as the founder (1895) of the New York Society of Iconophiles. He published (1865–1908) 26 volumes of his own work and ten by others which are outstanding as examples of printing and binding craftsmanship.

Andrews' Raid. Attempt (April 12, 1862) by 22 Union secret agents to demolish the railroad between Chattanooga, Tenn., and Atlanta, Ga. They seized the engine *General*, but were captured by a party from the locomotive *Texas* after a breath-taking race. Eight of the Union agents were subsequently hanged as spies.

Andreyev (än.drā′if), **Leonid Nikolayevich.** b. in Orel, Russia, 1871; d. at Kuokkala, Finland, 1919. Russian playwright and short-story writer. His writings for the stage combine symbolism with melodrama, while his short stories dwell on themes of death and horror, and are marked by an emotionalism verging on hysteria. His early career as a reporter was followed by the publication of the short story *They Lived* in 1899; his obvious talent brought him to the attention and won him the friendship of Gorki. He is notable for the anti-war story *The Red Laugh* (1904), and for *The Seven Who Were Hanged* (1909), which argued against capital punishment; his other works include the plays *Life of Man* (1906) and *He Who Gets Slapped* (1916; Eng. trans., 1921). His last work, *S.O.S.* (1919), was a scathing denunciation of terrorism under the Communists; to escape them he fled to Finland.

Andrézel (äṅ.drā.zel), **Pierre.** See under **Dinesen, Isak.**

Andria (än′drē.ä). City and commune in SE Italy, in the *compartimento* (region) of Apulia, in the province of Bari, W of Bari. It was a residence and one of the strongholds of the emperor Frederick II (Frederick I of Sicily) in his struggle against the Papacy. The cathedral dates in part from the 11th, in part from the 14th century. The surrounding district is fertile; there are a number of agricultural industries. Buildings of interest to tourists were undamaged in World War II. Pop. of commune, 56,152 (1936); of city, 51,597 (1936).

Andrian-Werburg (än′drē.än.ver′bürk), **Leopold von.** b. at Vienna, May 9, 1875—. Austrian writer, one of the founders of the *Jung-Wien* (Young-Vienna) group of writers; member of the so-called *George-Kreis* (or "George Circle," referring to the group of writers influenced by the German poet Stefan George). He is best known for his lyric poetry and prose.

Andrieux (äṅ.drē.ė), **François Guillaume Jean Stanislas.** b. at Strasbourg, May 6, 1759; d. at Paris, May 9, 1833. French lawyer and dramatist. As professor of literature at the Collège de France, he championed classicism. He wrote *Les Étourdis* (1788), *Le Meunier sans-souci* (1797), *Molière avec ses amis* (1804), *La Comédienne* (1816), *Lucius Junius Brutus* (1830), and others.

Andrieux, Louis. b. at Trévoux, France, July 23, 1840; d. at Paris, Aug. 27, 1931. French politician and government official, whose *Souvenirs d'un préfet de police* (1885) attracted wide attention. First elected a deputy in 1876, he was Paris police chief (1879–81) and ambassador to Madrid (1882); returned in 1885 to the Chamber of Deputies, he became an "elder statesman" of the Third Republic.

Andriscus (an.dris′kus). Pretended son of Perseus, king of Macedon, and a claimant to the throne. He was defeated and sent captive to Rome in 148 B.C.

Androcles and the Lion (an′drǫ.klēz). Comedy (1912) by George Bernard Shaw. It is a satirical treatment of early Christianity, mingling buffoonery with the serious presentation of different types of Christian faith.

Androclus (an′drǫ.klus) or **Androcles** (-klēz). fl. 1st century A.D. Roman slave noted for his friendship with a lion, subject of Shaw's play *Androcles and the Lion.* According to Aelian and Aulus Gellius, Androclus, escaping from his master in Africa, hid in a cave and there removed a thorn from a lion's foot; years later the animal, remembering him, refused to harm him in the arena.

Andromache (an.drom′ą.kē). In Greek legend, the wife of Hector, and, after his death, of Neoptolemus, son of Achilles; later the wife of Helenus, brother of Hector. She was the daughter of the king of Thebae in Cilicia, who, with his seven sons, was slain by Achilles when he captured Thebae.

Andromache. Tragedy by Euripides. It was probably composed during or shortly after the Peloponnesian war, as it shows a considerable bitterness of feeling against Sparta, plausible enough in view of Euripides' probable sentiments as a citizen of Athens.

Andromachus (an.drom′ą.kus). fl. middle of the 1st century A.D. Physician to the emperor Nero, the first to bear the title of "Archiater," or chief physician. He was the inventor of a celebrated medicine and antidote (called from him "theriaca Andromachi").

Andromaque (äṅ.dro.mȧk). Tragedy by Jean Baptiste Racine, produced in 1667.

Andromaque. Opera by André Ernest Modeste Grétry, produced at Paris in 1780.

Andromeda (an.drom′ę.dą). In Greek legend, the daughter of Cepheus and Cassiopeia. Poseidon, angered by boasts that there were women more beautiful than the Nereids, sent against the country a sea monster which could only be appeased by the sacrifice of the king's daughter. Andromeda was consequently offered to the monster, but was rescued by Perseus. The legend states that Andromeda, Perseus, and the monster were all three changed into constellations upon their deaths.

Andromeda. A northern constellation surrounded by Pegasus, Cassiopeia, Perseus, Pisces, Aries, and others, supposed to represent the figure of a woman chained. The constellation contains three stars of the second magnitude, of which the brightest is Alpheratz.

Andromeda. Poem (1858) by Charles Kingsley. This work, in hexameters, is Kingsley's most ambitious undertaking in verse, although not so well known as his *The Sands of Dee.*

Andromède (äṅ.dro.med). Tragedy by Pierre Corneille, produced in 1650.

Andronica (än.drô′nē.kä). One of the handmaids of Logistilla (Reason) in Ariosto's *Orlando Furioso.* She represents Fortitude.

Andronicus IV (an.dron′i.kus, an.drǫ.nī′kus). Name sometimes given to the son of John V Palaeologus who usurped the Byzantine throne and held it from 1376 to 1379.

Andronicus, Livius. See **Livius Andronicus, Lucius.**

Andronicus, Marcus. In *Titus Andronicus,* attributed to Shakespeare, the brother of Titus and tribune of the people.

Andronicus I Comnenus (kom.nē′nus). b. c1110; d. at Constantinople, Sept. 12, 1185. Byzantine emperor (1183–85); grandson of Alexius I Comnenus. Having contrived to get himself appointed regent during the minority of Alexius II, he put the prince and his mother, the empress Maria, to death, and ascended the throne in 1183. However, his cruelty and debauchery brought about insurrection under Isaac Angelus, who put him to death after subjecting him to torture.

Andronicus of Cyrrhus (sir′us). [Called **Cyrrhestes.**] b. at Cyrrhus; fl. 1st century B.C. Greek astronomer, builder, at Athens, of the "tower of the winds," still partly standing, an octagonal tower decorated with sculptured figures of the winds, and surmounted by a bronze Triton which turned with the wind. It was perhaps the first weather-vane in history.

Andronicus of Rhodes (rōdz). fl. in the middle of the 1st century B.C. Greek philosopher, head of the peripatetic school at Rome. He was the author of commentaries on, and paraphrases of, Aristotle, and of editions of Aristotle and Theophrastus.

Andronicus II Palaeologus (pā.lę.ol′ǫ.gus). b. c1259; d. 1332. Byzantine emperor (1282–1328); son of Michael Palaeologus. During his reign the empire was ravaged by the revolt (1306–08) of the so-called Catalan Grand Company, a body of Spanish mercenaries employed against the Ottoman Turks, and by a civil war (1321–28) with his grandson Andronicus III, by whom he was finally dethroned and compelled to retire to a cloister.

Andronicus III Palaeologus. b. c1296; d. June 15, 1341. Byzantine emperor (1328–41); grandson of Andronicus II, whose throne he usurped. He carried on war with the Ottoman Turks, who detached (1326–38) nearly the whole of Asia Minor from the Empire.

Andronovo (än.drô′nǫ.vǫ). Culture named after the village of Andronovo, in the Achinsk region of Siberia, and found in W Siberia from the Yenisei River to the Urals, and from Tomsk to Semipalatinsk. It is dated as occurring from 1500 B.C. onward. The graves of the Andronovo culture are situated haphazardly, covered with a low, flat hill, and often surrounded by circular enclosures of stone slabs. The burial chambers, in ground pits, are made of stone or wood slabs. Skeletons were placed on their side, with flexed arms and legs, and oriented to the east. Some additional graves were found, where bodies were cremated. The graves contained mostly flat-bottom pots, some of them crude, with straight sides, often completely covered with deep, pitted or incised ornamentation. The second type of vessels were well made, with concave-convex sides covered with geometrical ornamentation. The latter type is characteristic of the Andronovo culture. Stone scrapers and points were still present, but metal objects were found in greater profusion than in the Afanas'evo culture, and consisted of copper daggers and copper ornaments, sometimes covered with thin gold leaf. The bones of sheep, horses, and bulls show developed animal domestication.

Andros (an′dros). Island in the Atlantic Ocean, largest of the Bahamas, SE of Miami, Fla.: a British possession. It is the only island in the Bahamas traversed by streams. Length, ab. 95 mi.; pop. 6,718 (1943).

Andros. Northernmost island of the Cyclades, E Greece, in the *nomos* (department) of Cyclades, situated in the Aegean Sea, ab. 6 mi. SE of Euboea, anciently a possession successively of Athens, Macedon, Pergamum, and Rome. It has a silk industry and oil refinery, and produces lemons and wine. The surface is mountainous. The Venetians founded a principality here under Marino Dandolo. In 1566 it became Turkish and in 1829 Greek. It is the seat of a Catholic bishopric. The population on the E coast is in the majority Albanian. Length, 25 mi.; greatest width, 10 mi.; pop. ab. 18,000.

Andros, Sir **Edmund.** b. at London, Dec. 6, 1637; d. there in February, 1714. English colonial governor of New York (1674 *et seq.*), the dominion of New England (1686–89), and Virginia (1692–97). He succeeded his father as bailiff of Guernsey in 1674. Chosen for his military background to settle border disputes and maintain defense, first of New York and then of the newly formed dominion of New England, which later (1688) also included New York and the Jerseys, he antagonized the people by his severity. Fired by resentment over the loss of their charters and by the Puritan fanaticism of Cotton Mather and others, the colonists revolted (1689), imprisoning Andros with other officials, and returned to charter government. Acquitted in England of the colonists' charges and considered an able administrator, Andros was made governor of Virginia (1692–97) and lieutenant-governor of Guernsey (1704–06).

Androscoggin (an.dro̤s.kog′in). [Early name, **Pejebscot,** corrupted to **Bishopscote** or **Bishopscott.**] River in the NE part of the U.S., whose headstreams rise in N New Hampshire and N Maine, and which drains Lake Umbagog and the Rangeley Lakes, and joins the Kennebec River ab. 5 mi. N of Bath, Me. Length, 171 mi.

Androtion (an.drō′shi.on). fl. c350 B.C. Athenian orator, a contemporary of Demosthenes and pupil of Isocrates, possibly the chronicler of Attica mentioned by Pausanius. He is known chiefly as a subject of attack by Demosthenes in one of his early orations.

Androuet du Cerceau (äṅ.drö.e dü ser.sō), **Baptiste.** b. c1544; d. 1602. French architect; son of Jacques Androuet du Cerceau (c1510–84). Designer of the Pont Neuf across the Seine, and successor to Pierre Lescot as superviser of building under the crown in Paris. He collaborated with his brother, Jacques Androuet du Cerceau, on work on the Louvre.

Androuet du Cerceau, Jacques. [Original surname, **Androuet.**] b. c1510; d. 1584. French architect and founder of the line, better known from his writings and etched drawings than from actual buildings. He was a pioneer of the Italian Renaissance in France. The family name of Androuet du Cerceau derived from the trademark of a circle which marked his place of work.

Androuet du Cerceau, Jacques. d. 1614. French architect; son of Jacques Androuet du Cerceau (c1510–84). He worked on the design and construction of the Tuileries, and was associated with his brother, Baptiste Androuet du Cerceau, in work on the Louvre.

Androuet du Cerceau, Jean. d. sometime after 1649. French architect; son of Baptiste Androuet du Cerceau. Designer of Paris mansions including the Sully, the Bellegarde, and others.

Andrugio (än.drö′jō). In John Marston's *Antonio and Mellida*, the noble but turbulent Duke of Genoa. He utters the speech beginning, "Why, man, I never was a prince till now."

Andrusovo (än.drö′so̤.vo̤). [Also: **Andrussof, Andrusov** (än.drö′so̤f), **Andrussovo.**] Small village in the U.S.S.R., in the Smolensk *oblast* (region) of the Russian Soviet Federated Socialist Republic, noted for the treaty (1667) between Russia and Poland, by which the latter ceded Kiev, Smolensk, and the E Ukraine.

Andújar (än.dö′ʜär). [Celtiberian, **Illiturgis.**] Commune in Spain, in the province of Jaén, situated on the Guadalquivir River, ab. 44 mi. NE of Córdoba. It has hot mineral springs; produces pottery and porous jars (*alcarrazas*). There is a Moorish castle. Located at a strategic river crossing, the town has been frequently contested. 24,765 (1940).

Anecdotes of Painting in England. Prose work (4 vols., 1762–71) by Horace Walpole. It was based on the notebooks of the engraver George Vertue, which Walpole had purchased from Vertue's widow, and has led many scholars to consider Walpole an authentic pioneer in the history of English painting.

Anécho (ä.nā′kō). [Also, **Little Popo.**] Seaport and district in the French trust territory of Togo, W Africa, situated on the Bight of Benin, and connected with Lomé, ab. 27 mi. to the W, by rail. Pop. of district 181,936 (1946).

Anegada (an.e̤.gä′da̤). One of the British Virgin Islands, in the Caribbean Sea, NE of Puerto Rico. The chief occupation is vegetable gardening. During the 17th century, it was used by the Dutch and British as a base for buccaneering expeditions. Length, ab. 10 mi.

Aneho (ä.nā′hō). Sudanic-speaking people of W Africa, inhabiting S French Togo. They form a small group, surrounded by Ewe peoples, but are related culturally and linguistically to the Ga.

Aneirin (ä′nī.re̤n). See **Aneurin.**

Anel (à.nel), **Dominique.** b. 1679; d. 1730. French surgeon. He introduced improvements in the operation for aneurysm, and invented a syringe still used in the treatment of fistula lacrymalis.

Anelida and Arcite (a̤.nel′i.da̤; är′sīt). Unfinished poem by Goeffrey Chaucer. It was among those printed by Caxton, and is mentioned in both Lydgate's and Thynne's lists of Chaucer's works. In the latter it is mentioned as "Of Queen Anelida and False Arcite." There are passages in it from Boccaccio's *Teseide*, and the *Thebaid* of Statius was also drawn upon. Chaucer himself tells us that he took it from the Latin. Elizabeth Barrett Browning modernized the poem about the middle of the 19th century. Anelida was the Queen of Armenia. In the poem is included "The Complaint of Fair Anelida upon False Arcite," occasioned by the fact that the Theban knight (who is not the true Arcite of the *Knight's Tale*) deserted her for another. The poem breaks off at the end of her complaint (which is considered to be, by itself, one of the most polished and charming examples of perfect balance of strophe and antistrophe in medieval literature).

Anencletus (an.e̤n.klē′tus). See Saint **Anacletus.**

Anerio (ä.nā′ryō), **Felice.** b. at Rome, c1560; d. there, c1614. Italian composer of sacred music who succeeded Giovanni Palestrina, on the latter's death, as composer (1594–1602) to the papal chapel.

Anerio, Giovanni Francesco. b. at Rome, c1567; d. c1620. Italian composer of sacred music, the adapter of Giovanni Palestrina's *Papae Marcelli*, he became (c1609) maestro di cappella to Sigismund III, king of Poland.

Anesus (a̤.nē′sus). A Latin name of the **Enns River.**

Anethan (dàn.täṅ), **Jules Joseph,** Baron **d'.** b. at Brussels, 1803; d. there, 1888. Belgian politician. He was premier from 1870 to 1871.

Aneto (ä.nā′tō), **Pico de.** [French, **Pic de Néthou.**] Peak in NE Spain, in the Maladetta group close to the French border: the highest peak in the Pyrenees. Elevation, ab. 11,170 ft.

Aneurin (an′ū.rin, a̤′nī.re̤n). [Also: **Aneirin, Neurin.**] fl. c600 A.D. Welsh bard, author of *Gododin*, an epic of the struggle between Britons and Saxons, one of the oldest works in Welsh literature. Son of a chief (Caw ab Geraint or Gildas) of the Otadini or Gododin, a sea-coast tribe living south of the Firth of Forth, he is variously thought to have been Gildas the historian or his son.

Aney (ä.nā′), **Madhao Shrihari.** b. 1880—. Indian statesman and lawyer, representative (1943) of India in Ceylon and governor (1948) of Bihar, Union of India. Vice-president of the Indian Home Rule League (1916–18), he later became a prominent figure in the civil disobedience campaign. He served as a member (1924–30, 1935) of the legislative assembly of Berar, member (1924–25, 1931–34) of the Congress Working Committee, and acting president (1933) of the Indian National Congress. He was the member (1942–43) for Indians overseas in the viceroy's executive cabinet.

Anfossi (än.fôs′sē), **Pasquale.** b. at Naples, April 25, 1727; d. at Rome, in February, 1797. Italian operatic composer who served as Lateran maestro (1792 *et seq.*); studied under Piccinni. He composed *L'Incognita perseguitata* (1773), and other operas, on two of which Mozart collaborated; he also wrote church music.

Anfu Clique (än'fö'). Organization founded (1918) by the Chinese warlord Tuan Ch'i-jui to aid his pro-Japanese group in monopolizing public office. During its control (1918–20) of the capital, the clique made valuable concessions to the Japanese in return for extensive loans.

Angara (än.gä.rä'). [Also, in part of its course, **Upper Tunguska.**] Chief tributary of the Yenisei River, in the U.S.S.R., in S Siberia. It rises (as the Upper Angara) NE of Lake Baikal, traverses Lake Baikal, flows NW and W, and joins the Yenisei above Krasnoyarsk. Length, ab. 1,152 mi.; navigable for almost its entire course.

Angas (äng'gäs). [Also, **Angassawa** (äng.gäs.sä'wä).] Sudanic-speaking people of W Africa, inhabiting C Nigeria to the SE of Joa. Their population is estimated at ab. 50,000 (by C. K. Meek, *The Northern Tribes of Nigeria*, 1925). They practice hoe agriculture, and their principal crop is sorghum.

Angas (ang'gas), **George Fife.** b. at Newcastle, England, 1789; d. at Adelaide, South Australia, 1879. English merchant and shipowner; a founder of South Australia.

Angel (ang'gel). Extensive Middle Mississippi site in Vanderburgh County near Evansville, Ind., which dates from the Temple Mound II period (about 1300–1700 A.D.). This site, covering an area of about 100 acres, consisted of a central plaza, houses, and mounds surrounded by a palisade.

Angel (ān'jel). Novel (1926) by DuBose Heyward. It is a story of life in the mountains of the SE part of the U.S.

Angel, Benjamin Franklin. b. at Burlington, N.Y., Nov. 28, 1815; d. at Geneseo, N.Y., Sept. 11, 1894. American lawyer and diplomat. He was commissioner to China (1855) under President Pierce, and minister to Sweden and Norway (1857–61) under President Buchanan.

Angel, John. b. at Newton Abbot, Devonshire, England, Nov. 1, 1881—. English sculptor who came to the U.S. in 1925 and became especially noted for his religious works and his war memorials. He studied in England, at the Albert Memorial, Lambeth, and Royal Academy art schools, and exhibited (1912–27) at the Royal Academy. He has also lectured at several universities, and illustrated (for *The Cathedral Age*) an article on cathedral sculpture. His other works include a bronze door and a life-size figure of Saint Patrick, for Saint Patrick's Cathedral, New York; figures on the Cathedral of Saint John the Divine, New York; *Statue of William M. Rice*, for Rice Institute, Houston, Tex.; *War Memorial*, Milton Academy, Milton, Mass.; and *Madonna and Child.*

Angela Merici (än'jä.lä mā.rē'chē), Saint. b. at Desenzano, Italy, 1474; d. at Brescia, Italy, 1540. Italian nun and founder of the Ursuline Order. She became a tertiary of Saint Francis at an early age, and established the Ursuline Order (1535) at Brescia with a group of 12 virgins, serving as their superior until her death.

Angeli (än'jä.lē), **Heinrich von.** b. in Hungary, July 8, 1840; d. 1925. Genre and portrait painter at Vienna; an Austro-Hungarian historical and portrait painter who was engaged by many of the courts in Europe (Germany, Austria, England, and Russia). He studied at Vienna; from 1859 to 1862 he painted historical subjects there and at Munich. Later he did portraits of Queen Victoria, the Empress Marie of Russia, Emperor William II of Germany, and many persons of lesser rank. His paintings were acquired by galleries at Berlin, Vienna, and London.

Angelica (an.jel'i.ka). In Matteo Maria Boiardo's *Orlando Innamorato* and Ludovico Ariosto's *Orlando Furioso*, a beautiful but coquettish and faithless princess, daughter of Galaphron, king of Cathay. His unrequited love for her was the cause of Orlando's madness.

Angelica. Principal female character in William Congreve's play *Love for Love*, a witty and piquant woman, and the author's favorite character.

Angelica. Character in George Farquhar's comedy *The Constant Couple* and also in its sequel *Sir Harry Wildair.*

"Angelical Salutation." See **Ave Maria.**

Angelic Brothers (an.jel'ik). Sixteenth-century community of Dutch Pietists, who believed that they had attained that state of angelic purity in which there is "neither marrying nor giving in marriage."

Angelicus (an.jel'i.kus), **Doctor.** Epithet of **Aquinas, Saint Thomas.**

Angelina (an.je.lī'na). Heroine of Oliver Goldsmith's ballad *The Hermit, or Edwin and Angelina.*

Angelina. In John Dryden's tragi-comedy *The Rival Ladies*, a sister of Don Rhodorigo, in love with Gonsalvo. She disguises herself as a man and goes by the name of Amideo.

Angel in the House, The. Poem (1854) by Coventry Patmore. Its theme of wedded love may be traced, for its inspiration, to Patmore's own relationship with his wife (whose beauty was so great as to attract the comment also of many of Patmore's fellow Pre-Raphaelites). It was published in four parts: *The Betrothal* (published anonymously in 1854), *The Espousals* (1856), *Faithful Forever*, a poem of disappointed love (1860), and *The Victories of Love*, a poem of bereavement (1862).

Angélique (äṅ.zhā.lēk). One of the principal characters in Molière's *Le Malade Imaginaire.* She is the daughter of Argan, the imaginary invalid, who wishes to marry her to the son of his physician, Diafoirus, but is finally induced to give her to Cléante, the man she loves.

Angélique. Wife of George Dandin, in Molière's comedy *George Dandin.*

Angélique, Mère. See **Arnauld, Jacqueline Marie** and **Arnauld d'Andilly, Angélique.**

Angel Island (ān'jel). Island in San Francisco Bay, N of San Francisco. It was until 1946 the site of a U.S. Army base.

Angell (ān'jel), **George Thorndike.** b. at Southbridge, Mass., June 5, 1823; d. March 16, 1909. American reformer and lawyer; a founder (with Mrs. William Appleton) of the Massachusetts Society for the Prevention of Cruelty to Animals. He established the periodical *Our Dumb Animals* (1868 *et seq.*), and aided (1869) the British S.P.C.A. to set up its publication, *The Animal World.* He denounced Theodore Roosevelt for advocating both militarism and hunting.

Angell, James Burrill. b. near Scituate, R.I., Jan. 7, 1829; d. at Ann Arbor, Mich., April 1, 1916. American educator, journalist, and diplomat. A graduate (1849) and professor of modern languages (1853–60) at Brown, he was successor to H. B. Anthony as editor (1860–66) of the Providence *Journal.* He served also as president of the universities of Vermont (1866–71) and Michigan (1871–1909), at the latter of which he established the first professorships of education (1879) and forestry (1882), and advocated a separate graduate school, which was organized in 1910. As minister to China (1880–81), he negotiated the treaty of 1880 on Chinese immigration; he later (1897–98) was minister to Turkey. Cofounder (1884) and president (1893–94) of the American Historical Association.

Angell, James Rowland. b. at Burlington, Vt., May 8, 1869; d. at Hamden, Conn., March 4, 1949. American psychologist and educator; son of James Burrill Angell. A graduate of Michigan (1890) and Harvard (1892), he studied at Berlin, Halle (1893), Leipzig, and elsewhere abroad. He served in the psychology department at Chicago (1894–1919), and as a professor and head of the department from 1905; later he was dean of the university faculties (1911–19) and acting president (1918–19). Appointed president of Yale in 1921, he left that post in 1937 to become an educational counselor to the National Broadcasting Company. President of the American Psychological Association (1906); chairman of the National Research Council (1919–20); president of the English Speaking Union (1939 *et seq.*). Author of *Chapters from Modern Psychology* (1911), *American Education* (1937), and others; editor of *Psychological Monographs* (1912–22).

Angell, Joseph Kinnicutt. b. at Providence, R.I., April 30, 1794; d. at Boston, May 1, 1857. American legal writer. He was editor (1829–31) of the *United States Law Intelligencer and Review*, and author of *Common Law in Relation to Watercourses* (1824), *The Right of Property in Tide Waters* (1826), *The Law of Private Corporations Aggregate* (1832), and other books.

Angell, Sir **Norman.** [Original name, **Ralph Norman Angell Lane.**] b. at Holbeach, England, Dec. 26, 1874—.

Anglo-American economist, pacifist, journalist, and author. He received his early education at St.-Omer, France, and Geneva, Switzerland, and lived in the western U.S. as a rancher, prospector, and newspaperman, becoming a citizen before his return (1898) to Europe as a newspaper correspondent. He was general manager of the Paris edition of the London *Daily Mail* (1905–14) and editor of *Foreign Affairs* (1928–31). A Labour member of Parliament (1929–31), he was awarded (1934) the Nobel peace prize for 1933. He is also the inventor of "The Money Game" which utilizes cards to teach economic principles of currency and banking. Author of *The Great Illusion* (1910), *The Great Illusion, 1933* (1933), *America's Dilemma* (1940), *Let the People Know* (1943), *After All* (1952, autobiography), and others.

Angellier (äṅ.zhe.lyā), **Auguste Jean.** b. at Dunkerque, France, 1848; d. at Boulogne-sur-Mer, France, 1911. French poet and critic, expert on English literature. Author of *Étude sur la vie et les oeuvres de Robert Burns* (1892) and similar studies, as well as of *À l'amie perdue* (1896), *Le Chemin des saisons* (1903), and other volumes of verse.

Angeln (äng'e̜ln). Small district in N Germany, in the former province of Schleswig-Holstein, Prussia, lying between the Flensburg Fjord on the N, the Baltic Sea on the E, and the Schlei River on the S. It is noted for its fertility, and is supposed to have been the original home of the Angles.

Angelo (an'je̜.lō). Character in Shakespeare's *Measure for Measure*. He is the duke's deputy, who unjustly condemns Claudio to death.

Angelo. Character in Shakespeare's *Comedy of Errors;* a goldsmith.

Angelo (än'jā.lō), **Castle of Sant'.** [Also, **Hadrian's Mole.**] Remodeled mausoleum of Hadrian in Rome. It is a huge circular tower about 230 ft. in diameter on a basement about 300 ft. square, with medieval chambers and casements excavated in its solid concrete.

Angelus (an'je̜.lus). Prayer in the Roman Catholic Church, in honor of the Incarnation, repeated three times daily (by tradition, at six a.m., at noon, and at six p.m.). The devotion consists on each occasion of a Hail Mary, with certain introductory and concluding versicles, and is announced by a distinctive tolling of the church bell, usually three units of three strokes each (the units are traditionally separated by "the space of one Pater and one Ave") or two units of three strokes followed by nine strokes.

Angelus, Isaac. See **Isaac II.**

Angelus Silesius (sī.lē'zhus). [Original name, **Johann** (or **Johannes**) **Scheffler.**] b. at Breslau, 1624; d. there, July 9, 1677. German religious poet. At first a Lutheran and a physician, he became (1661) a Catholic priest. Author of hymns and of *Geistreiche Sinn- und Schlussreime* (1657), published later as *Cherubinischer Wandersmann* (1674), a rhymed work on mysticism based on Jakob Böhme, and others.

Angely (äṅ.zhe̜.lē'), **Louis.** b. at Berlin, c1788; d. there, 1835. German actor and dramatist. Author of *Sieben Mädchen in Uniform*, *Das Fest der Handwerker*, and others, mainly adaptations of French plays (collected in 4 vols., Berlin, 1842).

Angerapp (äng'e̜.räp). River in N Poland and the W part of the U.S.S.R., a headstream of the Pregel River, which drains Mamry Lake.

Ångerman (ōng'ėr.män). River in Sweden, in the *län* (counties) of Västernorrland and Västerbotten, which flows into the Gulf of Bothnia near Härnösand. It drains several lakes and forms many waterfalls. Length, ab. 280 mi.; navigable in its lower course.

Ångermanland (ōng'ėr.män.länd). District in N Sweden, mainly included in the modern *län* (counties) of Västerbotten and Västernorrland.

Angermünde (äng.ėr.mün'de̜). City in NE Germany, in the *Land* (state) of Brandenburg, Russian Zone, formerly in the province of Brandenburg, Prussia, situated on the Mündesee (lake), ab. 42 mi. NE of Berlin: railroad junction; agricultural trade. The Church of Mary, in the Gothic style, dates from the 13th century. 10,813 (1946).

Angerona (an.je̜.rō'na̜) or **Angeronia** (-ni.a̜). In Roman mythology, a goddess whose attributes and powers are not definitely known. She was, perhaps, the goddess connected with anguish and secret grief. Her statue stood in the temple of Volupia (sensual pleasure), and she was represented with her finger upon her bound and sealed lips.

Angers (äṅ.zhā). [Latin, **Andegavia, Andegavum, Juliomagus.**] Capital of the department of Maine-et-Loire, W central France, situated on both banks of the Maine River, ab. 5 mi. from its influx into the Loire River, between Nantes and Le Mans. The Gothic cathedral of Saint Maurice, dating mainly from the 12th century but with later additions, is an example of the Angevin pointed style. It contains stained-glass windows from the 13th century and tapestries from the 14th century. The town has collections of tapestries, ceramics, engravings, and paintings. The castle dates from the period of Saint Louis. There is a medical school and a school for arts and crafts. The town has metallurgical and chemical industries; among its manufactures are stained glass for church windows, wines, liqueurs, shoes, rope, and thread. Angers was formerly the capital of the old province of Anjou and suffered severely in the Huguenot and Vendean wars. 94,408 (1946).

Angers (däṅ.zhā), **David d'.** See **David, Pierre Jean.**

Angerstein (ang'gėr.stīn), **John Julius.** b. at St. Petersburg, Russia, 1735; d. at Blackheath, England, Jan. 22, 1823. English merchant, philanthropist, and art amateur. As an underwriter (1756 *et seq.*) at Lloyd's, he became an influential commercial figure and helped transform the business from the original, more or less unorganized character which had marked it in its coffee-house days to the present highly coördinated system of insurance underwriting represented by Lloyd's. Guided by Benjamin West and Sir Thomas Lawrence, he collected paintings which were acquired (1824) by the British government and formed the nucleus of the National Gallery.

Angevin (an'je̜.vin). Dynastic name sometimes applied to the Plantagenet rulers of England. The term, taken from French, is a derivative of "Anjou," from which French house the Plantagenets were descended; the first three Plantagenets (Henry II, Richard I, and John) were actually counts of Anjou as well as kings of England, and the Plantagenets (or Angevins) are ordinarily listed as a separate and rightful house under the counts of Anjou.

Angilbert (ang'gil.bėrt), Saint. [Called **"Homer"** at Charlemagne's court.] b. c740; d. 814. Frankish poet. He was a minister under Charlemagne, and abbot of Centula (now St.-Riquier) from 790; pupil and friend of Alcuin; said to be the father, by Charlemagne's daughter, Bertha, of Nithard, Frankish chronicler. He is the probable author of an epic describing the meeting between Charlemagne and Pope Leo III, of which a part is extant.

Angirases (an'ji.ra̜s.e̜z). In Hindu mythology, a class of beings standing between gods and men. They are called the sons of heaven, sons of the gods. They appear in company with the gods, with the Asvins, Yama, the gods of the sun and light. Angi is called the first and highest Angiras. At the same time the Angirases are called the fathers of men, and many families trace their descent from them. The hymns of the *Atharvaveda* are called *Angirasas*, and the Angirases were especially charged with the protection of sacrifices performed in accordance with the *Atharvaveda*.

Angkor (ang'kôr). [Also, **Angkor Thom** (tôm').] Ancient city in Indochina, in NW Cambodia, near Siemréap, ab. 150 mi. NW of Pnompenh. It was the capital of Cambodia from 802 until its capture by the Siamese in 1432, when the court removed to the vicinity of Pnompenh. Discovered by French archaeologists in 1860, it is now one of the greatest tourist attractions in Cambodia. It is believed to have been a city of a million people, with a wall which had five gates. Extensive ruins, including many buildings and several high towers, have been cleared of jungle growth and partly restored. These and the nearby temple, Angkor Wat, all elaborately decorated with bas-reliefs, constitute one of the world's richest finds for students of archaeology and art history.

Angkor Wat (wät). [Also: **Angkor Vat** (vät), **Nakhon Wat** (or **Vat**).] Temple situated ab. 5 mi. S of Angkor, the ancient capital of Cambodia. It is generally considered to be the finest architectural creation of Cambodia, dating from the 12th century. The plan presents three concentric rectangular enclosures, the exterior one measuring 570 by 650 ft. and each rising above that surrounding it, so that the general form is pyramidal, an effect which is enhanced by the flanking of the great pointed tooth-battlemented central tower by similar smaller side towers. The exterior is colonnaded with coupled square pillars on a raised basement. Above the pillars there is an elaborate entablature with a frieze of projecting serpent-heads and very rich moldings. In the middle of each face there is a large triple portal. The back walls of the porticos which extend from these bear remarkable friezes in low relief, most of the subjects being battle scenes from the *Ramayana* or *Mahabharata*, about 6½ ft. high and 2,000 ft. in aggregate length. The entrance-hall contains over 100 square columns. The temple proper, 200 by 213 ft., stands in the central court; it surrounds four large water tanks so disposed that the middle portion of the structure is cruciform. The plan is closely similar to Indian types, but the constructive and decorative details are purely local. The capitals are almost classical in form, and there are no bracket-capitals.

Anglante's Knight (äng.glän'tāz). Name given to Orlando, lord of Anglante, in Lodovico Ariosto's *Orlando Furioso*.

Angles (ang'glz). [Latin, **Angli.**] A Germanic-speaking people which in the earliest period of its recorded history dwelt in the neighborhood of the district now called Angeln, in the region of Schleswig, and which in the 5th century and later, accompanied by kindred tribes, the Saxons, Jutes, and Friesians, crossed over to Britain, and colonized the greater part of it. The Angles were originally the most numerous of these settlers, and founded the three kingdoms of East Anglia, Mercia, and Northumbria. From them the entire country derived its modern name of England.

Anglesey or **Anglesea** (ang'gl.si). [Latin, **Mona.**] Island and county in N Wales, lying NW of the mainland, from which it is separated by Menai Strait; the strait is crossed by a famous suspension bridge, reconstructed in 1940. The surface of Anglesey is generally flat, the highest elevation being Holyhead Hill (703 ft.). The county has much land in permanent pasture, and beef-cattle raising and sheep raising are important. Oats are the principal crop. Copper ore was discovered at Amlwch in 1768 and the mine was once the largest in Europe. By the end of the 19th century, however, the ore was largely exhausted, and the mines are now of negligible value. Anglesey was an ancient seat of the Druids, was conquered by the Romans under Suetonius Paulinus in 61 A.D., and by Agricola in 78, and later became a Welsh stronghold. Length, ab. 28 mi.; width, ab. 20 mi.; area of county, ab. 276 sq. mi.; pop. 50,637 (1951).

Anglesey, 1st Earl of. Title of **Annesley, Arthur.**

Anglet (äṅ.gle). Town in SW France, in the department of Basses-Pyrénées, situated near the Atlantic coast, between Bayonne and Biarritz. A summer and winter resort, it has an airport. 11,320 (1946).

Angleterre (äṅ.glẹ.ter). French name of **England.**

Angleton (ang'gl.tọn). City in SE Texas, county seat of Brazoria County, ab. 40 mi. S of Houston: railroad and marketing center in a region producing oil and farm products. 3,399 (1950).

Angli (ang'glī). See **Angles.**

Anglia (ang'gli.ạ). Latin name of England; specifically, that part of England which was settled by the Angles.

Anglian (ang'gli.ạn). Name most often used for the dialect spoken by the Angles. It is used also, but less often, as an ethnic term for one of the people who spoke this dialect.

Anglicus (ang'gli.kus), **Bartholomaeus.** See **Bartholomaeus Anglicus.**

Anglin (ang'glin), **Francis Alexander.** b. at St. John, New Brunswick, Canada, April 2, 1865; d. at Ottawa, Canada, March 2, 1933. Canadian supreme court justice. He was a member (1906) of the commission to revise the Ontario statutes, and an associate justice (1909–24) and chief justice (1924–33) of the supreme court of Canada. Author of *Trustees' Limitations and Other Relief*.

Anglin, Margaret Mary. b. at Ottawa, Canada, April 3, 1876—. American actress. In 1894 she made her debut as Madeline West in Charles Frohman's New York production of *Shenandoah;* later she played Roxane in *Cyrano de Bergerac* (1898), appeared with Henry Miller in *Camille*, and had a part in *The Devil's Disciple*. In 1906–07, she starred with Miller in *The Great Divide*. She also played in several Greek tragedies, notably Sophocles' *Antigone* and *Electra*, between 1910 and 1927, and headed a cast of 1,200 in *As You Like It* during the Shakespeare tercentenary (1916) at St. Louis. She was awarded the Laetare medal by Notre Dame University in 1927 and last starred in *Fresh Fields* (1935–36).

Anglo-American Caribbean Commission (ang'glō.ạ-mer'i.kạn kar.i.bē'ạn, kạ.rib'ē.ạn). See **Caribbean Commission.**

Anglo-American Committee of Inquiry. Joint committee established by the governments of Great Britain and the U.S. in 1946 to investigate conditions in Palestine. It was set up after the British Labour Party had affirmed its adherence to the British White Paper of 1939 and President Truman had urged the immediate immigration of 100,000 Jews into Palestine. The chief recommendation of the report it rendered was that the 100,000 immigration should be permitted. This and other recommendations were not accepted by the British government, and later in 1946 the problem of Palestine was submitted to the United Nations.

Anglo-American Oil Agreement. Agreement concluded (Sept. 24, 1945) at London to supersede earlier tentative arrangements which had failed for various reasons to obtain final approval. It was signed by Harold Ickes, for the U.S., and by Emanuel Shinwell, for Great Britain; it was intentionally drafted in such a way as to permit the signatures of other nations which would be affected by its provisions. It called for the establishment of an Anglo-American Petroleum Commission which was to promote the orderly development of the international petroleum trade with the eventual aim of negotiating an oil agreement among all oil-producing and consuming nations. The effect of the agreement was circumscribed by American unwillingness to accept any regulation of its domestic oil industry and British insistence that its control over overseas oil sources not be restricted.

Anglo-Boer War (ang'glō.bör'). See **Boer War** (*1899–1902*).

Anglo-Egyptian Sudan (ang'glō.ẹ.jip'shạn sö.dan'). Anglo-Egyptian condominium occupying a large portion of NE Africa. It is bounded on the N by Egypt, on the W by Libya and French Equatorial Africa, and on the S by the Belgian Congo, Uganda, and Kenya, and on the E by Ethiopia, Eritrea, and the Red Sea. Capital, Khartoum; area, 967,500 sq. mi.; pop., 8,350,000 (est. 1950; a census has never been held).

History. The country was ruled by Egypt until 1882 when a revolt under the Mahdi wrested it from Egyptian control. In 1896 an Anglo-Egyptian army began a campaign to regain control of the area and finally succeeded (1899) in doing so with the defeat of the rebels at the Battle of Omdurman. Great Britain and Egypt signed a convention in the same year, constituting the condominium and providing for its government and administration. This agreement was reaffirmed by the Anglo-Egyptian Treaty of 1936. Self-government was granted in 1953, with a guarantee that self-determination would occur in 1956.

Government. There is an appointed governor-general agreed upon by both nations; since 1910 he has been assisted by a governor-general's council, and since 1943 by an advisory council for the northern Sudan. The members of both these bodies are either ex-officio or appointed persons. The country is divided into 8 provinces, each having a governor responsible to the governor-general; and into 46 districts, each in charge of a district commissioner who is responsible to the governor concerned.

Cultural and Economic Geography. The population of the northern provinces is Arabic-speaking, Mohammedan in religion, and accounts for about two-thirds of the total; the population of the southern provinces is largely composed of Negro African tribes. Except for the area on the banks of the Nile River and its main tributaries (Sobat and Atbara rivers) and headstreams (White and Blue Niles), the country is desert and of little value for agriculture or development. The S part is covered by dense tropical forests and swamps. Cotton, cottonseed, gum arabic (in which it leads the world), sesame, ground nuts, and numerous other tropical products are exported. Gold is mined in the Red Sea hills and some is exported.

Anglo-French Entente (ang′glō.french′). Relationship established on April 8, 1904, when Great Britain and France signed a treaty by which they settled their colonial conflicts in Africa, SE Asia, the Pacific, and Newfoundland. Most important was the French recognition of British control in Egypt and the British promise of a free hand for France in Morocco. France agreed in the open treaty not to change the political status of Morocco. In secret clauses, however, the two powers envisaged great modifications of the existing French and British control methods in Egypt and Morocco, with consequent diminution of native autonomy. The opposition of Germany to one-sided changes in Morocco (which was a chief reason for the Algeciras Conference) forced Britain and France into ever closer diplomatic coöperation and the treaty thus became the cornerstone of the Anglo-French alliance of 1914.

Anglo-German Naval Agreement of 1935 (ang′glō.jėr′-mạn). Agreement that developed from conversations held between Germany and Great Britain after Hitler's declaration in May, 1935, that the German navy would be in a 35:100 ratio to that of the United Kingdom. The accord recognized a 35:100 ratio between the two navies, though Germany was allowed to build submarines on parity within the overall ratio. At the time, the British were condemned for a unilateral violation of the Versailles Treaty. In April, 1939, Hitler canceled the agreement with the assertion that Great Britain had accepted the inevitability of war and was already "encircling" Germany.

Anglo-German Yangtze Agreement (yang′tsi). Agreement signed on Oct. 16, 1900. stating that the two signatory powers would use all their influence to keep the Yangtze River and the Chinese coastal ports open to international trade. It also gave assurance of no interest in territorial aggrandizement at the expense of China as a result of the Boxer Rebellion and promised joint consultation if another power should attempt territorial acquisitions. Great Britain viewed this agreement as a defense against Russia, Germany as a way of smoothing relations with Russia. The applicability of this agreement to Manchuria later aroused controversy.

Anglo-Italian Mediterranean Agreement (ang′glō.i-tal′yạn med″i.tẹ.rā′nẹ.ạn). Joint statement of Jan. 2, 1937, made by British Ambassador Sir Eric Drummond and Italian Foreign Minister Galeazzo Ciano disclaiming any desire to change the status quo in the Mediterranean area. It was made in an effort to dispel the Anglo-Italian friction which existed at that time in that area. Both countries gave assurances of mutual transit rights in the Mediterranean. During the same negotiations Italy and Great Britain settled disputes involving grazing and watering rights of tribes in their adjoining East African colonies and Italian transit rights in British Somaliland.

Anglo-Japanese Alliance (ang′glō.jap.ạ.nēz′). Agreement reached on Jan. 30, 1902, between Japan and Great Britain. Japan had earlier, but without success, sought an understanding with Russia concerning the fluid Far Eastern situation at that time. The Anglo-Japanese Alliance recognized the independence of China and Korea and stipulated that, in the event of a threat to the commercial or industrial interests of either Japan or Great Britain, each could take action with the assurance of the other's neutrality or active support in the case of hostilities. The agreement also disavowed separate arrangements in the Far East without prior consultation.

Anglo-Latin (ang′glō.lat′in). Name applied to medieval Latin as written in England in the Middle Ages, the ordinary language of the church and the courts until the modern period. It is characterized by the liberal inclusion and free Latinizing of technical and vernacular English and Norman or Anglo-French terms.

Anglo-Normandes (äṅ.glo.nôr.mäṅd), **Îles.** A French name of the **Channel Islands.**

Anglo-Portuguese Alliance (ang′glō.pôr′ṭū.gēz). Treaty of friendship and alliance between Portugal and Great Britain, notable as the oldest diplomatic instrument still in existence. It was concluded in 1688 when England assisted Portugal in liberating herself from a century of Spanish domination. In World War II it was partly because of this centuries-old relationship that Portugal approved in October, 1943, a British request that the Royal Air Force and Royal Navy be permitted to establish bases in the Azores.

Anglo-Russian Entente (ang′glō.rush′ạn). Relationship established on Aug. 31, 1907, when Great Britain and Russia signed an agreement at St. Petersburg. The immediate motivation for the agreement was provided by certain conflicts between the two powers in the Near and Middle East, especially in Persia and Afghanistan. Complementing the Anglo-French Entente of 1904, it became the basis of Allied coöperation in World War I. By setting up spheres of influence in Persia, it gave protection to the British frontier in India, but gave Russia an almost free hand in the north. The clauses on Afghanistan were never put into effect.

Anglo-Saxon (ang′glō.sak′sọn). Name sometimes applied to one of the Angles or original "English" Saxons. The term is sometimes, however, restricted to the Saxons who dwelt chiefly in the southern districts (Wessex, Essex, Sussex, Middlesex—names which contain the form of Saxon—and Kent) of the country which came to be known as the land of the Angles, now England; more usually, since the 16th century, the term is extended to include the whole people or nation formed by the aggregation of the Angles, Saxons, and other early Germanic settlers in Britain, or the whole people of England before the Norman Conquest.

Anglo-Saxon. A term referring to stereotypic individuals of English nationality and extended to certain sections of the population of the U.S. The term has no validity as a racial classification, despite its widespread use, being essentially a linguistic term; thus a Negro whose native language is English is in fact an Anglo-Saxon.

Anglo-Saxon. The language of the Anglo-Saxons; Saxon; the earliest form of the English language, constituting with Old Saxon, Old Friesic, and other dialects, a group belonging to the West Germanic division of the Teutonic speech.

Anglo-Saxon Chronicle. Name applied to a group of manuscripts that serve as chief source for the history and literature of England during the 10th, 11th, and part of the 12th centuries. The "chronicle" is actually clearly divisible into several distinct units, which are nevertheless ordinarily treated as parts of the same overall series of annals. Work on the earliest portion now known to exist was probably commenced (c892) by monks at Winchester, almost certainly at the behest of (and possibly with the actual editorial aid of) Alfred the Great. Certain parts of the work contain material from Bede's *Ecclesiastical History* and other earlier records, but the greater portion of the chronicle consists of entries about events that took place at approximately the time of writing. The annals come to a close some years after the Norman conquest, at about the middle of the 12th century.

Anglo-Soviet Treaty (ang′lō.sō.vi.et′, -sō.vyet′). Twenty-year treaty signed on May 26, 1942, by Great Britain and the U.S.S.R. It was designed to affirm the unity of the two powers in their opposition to Germany during and after hostilities in World War II, and to express a common desire to work with the United Nations. Stipulating joint military effort against Germany and her European allies, and a promise to forsake separate peace treaties with the Axis, it also provided for common support in the event of aggression by another power in the post-war period. A clause was also inserted assuring economic support and assistance after the war.

Angmagssalik (äng.mäg′sä.lik). [Also, **Angmagsalik.**] Trading post and meteorological station in E Greenland, just S of the Arctic Circle, established by the Danes. Its weather reports are transmitted by a radio station built in 1925. The settlement is of considerable importance also in the military air strategy of the nations linked by the North Atlantic Treaty Organization. During World War II it was the site of a U.S. air base. Pop. ab. 700.

Angol (äng.gōl′). Capital of Malleco province, in C Chile. It was the capital of the former territory of Angol. 12,398 (1940).

Angola (ang.gō′lạ). [Full Portuguese name, **Reino e Conquistas de Angola.**] Former Portuguese colony in SW Africa, founded within the boundaries of the ancient native kingdom of Angola.

Angola. [Also, **Portuguese West Africa.**] Modern Portuguese colony in SW Africa which comprises the old kingdoms of Congo, Angola, and Benguela, the district of Mossâmedes, and the later accessions between the Cuangu and Kasai rivers. This colony extends along the W coast of Africa between the mouths of the Congo and Cunene rivers, and inland as far as the Cuango, Kasai, and Zambezi rivers. It is bounded by the Belgian Congo on the N, by the Belgian Congo and Northern Rhodesia on the E, by Bechuanaland and South-West Africa on the S, and by the Atlantic Ocean on the W. Capital, Luanda; area, 481,350 sq. mi.; pop. 4,111,796 (1950).

Government. It is divided into five provinces (since 1946): Luanda, Malange, Benguela, Bie, and Huila. The administration is in the hands of a governor-general, residing at Luanda; in the late 1940's plans were under way to make Nova Lisboa the capital.

Economic Geography. Angola is the only central African possession which has a large white population (ab. 51,363 in 1946) and in which agriculture flourishes on a large scale. There are valuable deposits of diamonds, and some large deposits of copper and lignite, which are as yet not extensively worked. The highlands of the interior are believed to be one of the most favorable regions in C Africa for European settlement. The railway from Benguela to the Katanga region of the Belgian Congo provides the shortest and best route for transporting products of the Katanga to the sea. It has been of great importance in the development of the country and is one of the main revenue-producers.

Angola. City in NE Indiana, county seat of Steuben County: seat of Tri-State College. 5,081 (1950).

Angolalla (äng.gō.läl'ą). One of the chief towns in Shoa province of Ethiopia, in E Africa, N of the capital, Addis Ababa.

Angora (ang.gō'rą). See **Ankara.**

Angostura (äng.gōs.tö'rä). Former name of **Ciudad Bolívar.**

Angoulême (äṅ.gö.lem). [Latin, **Inculisma.**] City in W France, the capital of the department of Charente, situated on the Charente River, W of Rochefort and NE of Bordeaux. It is the seat of highly specialized paper and printing industries, and a great variety of paper articles are produced. The liquor and brandy industry of the region has a world-wide reputation; there are also several smaller industries. The cathedral dates from the 12th century. Other points of interest include an art museum, a statue of the poetess Marguerite of Valois (a sister of the French king Francis I), who was born in Angoulême in 1492, and medieval ramparts. Angoulême became the seat of a bishopric in the 3rd century. The city was ceded to the British in 1360, but they were driven out in 1373. It later suffered greatly during the religious wars. At various times, the houses of Savoy, Valois, and Berry held title to the duchy of Angoulême. 44,244 (1946).

Angoulême (däṅ.gö.lem), Duc **d'.** [Family name, **Charles de Valois.**] b. April 28, 1573; d. Sept. 24, 1650. French politician and general; illegitimate son of Charles IX and Marie Touchet. He was made Duc d'Angoulême in 1619. He was imprisoned (1605–16) in the Bastille for his intrigues with Henriette de Balzac d'Entragues, Marquise de Verneuil. As a soldier he served with distinction at Arques and Ivry, and directed the sieges of Soissons and La Rochelle. He is the reputed author of *Mémoires* (1662).

Angoulême, Duc **d'.** [Family name, **Louis Antoine de Bourbon.**] b. at Versailles, Aug. 6, 1775; d. in what was then Austria, June 3, 1844. Last dauphin of France; the eldest son of Charles X of France (Comte d'Artois) and Maria Theresa of Savoy, princess of Sardinia. He opposed Napoleon in the south of France on his return from Elba, and was a commander in the French invasion of Spain (1823); he went into exile in 1830.

Angoulême, Duchesse **d'.** See also **Diane de France.**

Angoulême, Duchesse **d'.** [Family name, **Marie Thérèse Charlotte de Bourbon.**] b. at Versailles, Dec. 19, 1778; d. at Frohsdorf, Austria, Oct. 19, 1851. French noble woman; daughter of Louis XVI, and wife of the Duc d'Angoulême (1775–1844). An active adherent of the ultra-royalists, she was a prisoner (1792–95) during the French Revolution.

Angoumois (äṅ.gö.mwȧ). Former division of W France, which, with Saintonge, formed a subordinate political unit previous to the French Revolution. As a region, it corresponds nearly to the modern department of Charente. It contains numerous vineyards, and is probably best known outside of France for the fact that it produces much of the world's best cognac (the town of Cognac, from which the brandy derives its name, is in Angoumois).

Angra do Heroísmo (ung'grą dö ę.rö.ēzh'mö). District of Portugal, in the Azores islands. Capital, Angra do Heroísmo; area, 268 sq. mi.; pop. 86,979 (1950).

Angra do Heroísmo. Town and *concelho* (commune) in the Azores islands, capital of the Portuguese district of Angra do Heroísmo, situated on the S coast of the island of Terceira. It has a protected harbor and exports wine, grain, and pineapples. It is the seat of a bishopric. Founded in 1534, it was the capital of the Azores islands until 1832. Some of the old fortifications remain. The words "do heroísmo" were added to the name of the town for its patriotic opposition (1830–32) to the pretender Dom Miguel. Pop. of concelho, 36,225 (1940); of town, 10,642 (1940).

Angra Pequena (ang'grą pę.kwē'ną). Region in the former German protectorate of South West Africa, from the Orange River N to Angola, N of Cape Frio, but excluding Walvis Bay. It passed under German protection in 1884, and was lost by the Germans as a result of World War I.

Angri (äng'grē). Town and commune in S Italy, in the *compartimento* (region) of Campania, in the province of Salerno, situated S of Mount Vesuvius, between Salerno and Torre Annunziata, ab. 19 mi. SE of Naples. It has cotton mills and is a center of the local lumber trade. Pop. of commune, 19,468 (1936); of town, 11,851 (1936).

Ångström (ông'strėm; Anglicized, ang'strǫm), **Anders Jöns.** b. at Lödgö, Sweden, Aug. 13, 1814; d. at Uppsala, Sweden, June 21, 1874. Swedish physicist, a specialist in spectrum analysis and pioneer in spectroscopy. A graduate, privatdocent (1839 *et seq.*), and professor of physics (1858 *et seq.*) at Uppsala, he was also on the staff (1843 *et seq.*) of the Uppsala Observatory. His *Optiska Undersökningar* (1853), describing the spectra of the electric spark and of incandescent gases, is one of the fundamental works in spectroscopy. He published a demonstration of the presence of hydrogen in the sun's atmosphere (1862), a map of the solar spectrum (1869), and a description of the spectrum of the aurora borealis (1867), and was the discoverer of the line in the latter now often called the "Ångström line." The Ångström unit, a measure equal to one hundred-millionth of a centimeter, is used in the scientific handling of wave-lengths of light.

Ångström, Knut Johan. b. at Uppsala, Sweden, Dec. 1, 1857; d. March 4, 1910. Swedish physicist; son of Anders Jonas Ångström. A professor of physics (1896–1910) at Uppsala, he invented (1893) the Angström pyrheliometer for measuring solar radiation, and devised (1895) a means of photographing the infrared spectrum.

Anguier (äṅ.gyā), **François.** b. in Normandy, 1604; d. 1669. French sculptor; brother of Michel Anguier. He created the mausoleum of Henry II, the duke of Montmorency, at Moulins.

Anguier, Michel. b. in Normandy, 1614; d. 1686. French sculptor; brother of François Anguier. His *Nativity* at the church of Val de Grâce has, with his other work, brought him high rank among French sculptors of the Baroque period.

Anguilla (ang.gwil'ą). [Also: **Anguila, Snake Island.**] Island in the Caribbean Sea, E of Puerto Rico: part of the British colony of the Leeward Islands, governed under St. Christopher-Nevis (or St. Kitts-Nevis) presidency. The major occupations are fishing, cotton culture, and cattle raising; salt is also produced. Area, 50 sq. mi.; pop. 5,036 (1946).

Anguille (ang.gwil'), **Cape.** Point of land projecting W from the SW coast of Newfoundland toward the Gulf of St. Lawrence. At its tip it is the westernmost point in Newfoundland.

Anguisciola (än.gwē'shō.lä) or **Angussola** (-gös'sō-), **Sofonisba.** [Also, **Angussciola.**] b. at Cremona, Italy, c1535; d. at Genoa, 1626. Italian portrait-painter; a pupil of Bernardino Campi. At the invitation of Philip II (1560), she painted portraits of members of the royal family of Spain; she is known also for several self-portraits.

Angus (ang′gus). [Former name, **Forfarshire.**] Maritime county, in E central Scotland. It is bounded on the N by Aberdeenshire, on the NE by Kincardineshire, on the E by the North Sea, and on the S and SW by the Firth of Tay and Perthshire. The coastline is sandy S of Arbroath, and rises to cliffs N of it. The county is mountainous in the NW, where the Braes of Angus reach an altitude of 3,077 ft. in Mount Keen. The Sidlaw Hills are in the SW portion. Strathmore (or the Howe of Angus), a lowland running generally SW–NE, separates these two ranges. E and S of the Sidlaw Hills to the coast the land is level and well-cultivated. The NW region is sheep pasture, deer forests, or moorland. Principal crops of the county are oats, potatoes, wheat, turnips, barley, and hay. Angus is the chief seat of Scottish linen manufacture, and the city of Dundee is the most important center of jute manufacture in the British Isles. There are shipyards and fisheries. County seat, Forfar; area, ab. 874 sq. mi.; pop. 247,870 (1951).

Angus, Earl of. Title held by various members of the Douglas family of Scotland, within the branch of the family sometimes called the "Red Douglases." The title came into being in 1389, when it was granted to George Douglas, and passed out of existence in 1660, with the death of William Douglas, 11th Earl of Angus and 1st Marquis of Douglas. For information about particular holders of the title, see under **Douglas.**

Angus. In Shakespeare's *Macbeth*, a thane of Scotland.

Angussola (än.gös′sō.lä) or **Angussciola** (-shō-), **Sofonisba.** See **Anguisciola, Sofonisba.**

Anhalt (än′hält). Former duchy in N Germany, later a *Land* (state) of the German Empire, now part of Saxony-Anhalt, in that part of Germany under Russian occupation. It was surrounded by Prussia and consisted of two chief portions, an eastern (Dessau-Köthen-Bernburg), which is level, and a western (Ballenstedt), which is hilly and mountainous. It had also several enclaves. Its capital was Dessau, and its government a hereditary constitutional monarchy under a duke and *Landtag* (parliament). It sent one member to the Bundesrat and two members to the Reichstag. It became an independent principality in the first part of the 13th century and was often divided and reunited. The last duchy was formed in 1863 by the union of the duchies of Anhalt-Dessau-Köthen and Anhalt-Bernburg. Area, 888 sq. mi.; pop. (of the region), less than 450,000 (1939).

Anhanguera (u.nyung.gā′ra̤). See **Bueno de Silva, Bartholomeu.**

Anholt (än′hôlt). Island belonging to Denmark, part of the *amt* (county) of Randers, situated in the Kattegat ab. 47 mi. N of Zealand. Length, ab. 7 mi.

Anholt (än′holt). Small town in W Germany, in the former province of Westphalia, Prussia, situated on the Ijssel River, on the Dutch frontier, ab. 16 mi. NW of Wesel. The town suffered considerable damage during World War II; however, the *Schloss* (castle) still stands and repairs are under way, and the Salm-Salm Archives are reasonably well preserved.

Anhwei (än′hwā′). [Also: **Anhui** (-hwā′), **Nganhui, Nganhwei.**] Province in E China, bounded by Kiangsu on the NE, by Kiangsu and Chekiang on the E, by Kiangsi on the S, by Hupeh and Honan on the W, and by Honan on the NW. It contains part of the green-tea district, and also grows much rice and has considerable trade on the Yangtze-Kiang. Capitals, Hofei and Wuhu; area, ab. 56,500 sq. mi.; pop. 24,473,693 (1950).

Ani (ä′nē). See **Anni.**

Aniakchak (an.i.ak′chak). Volcano in SW Alaska, in the Aleutian Range, with a crater ab. 6 mi. across at its widest point (and thus the largest known crater of its kind in the world). Its last eruption took place in 1931.

Anian (ā′ni.a̤n), **Straits of.** Early name of **Bering Strait.**

Anicet-Bourgeois (ȧ.nē.se.bör.zhwȧ), **Auguste.** b. at Paris, Dec. 25, 1806; d. at Pau, France, Jan. 12, 1871. French dramatist and author of vaudevilles, melodramas, and other works for the stage.

Anicetus (an.i.sē′tus). fl. c60 A.D. Roman freedman. He was a tutor of Nero.

Anicetus, Saint. Pope from 155 to 166, successor to Pius I He was visited by Saint Polycarp for an indecisive conference on the Paschal controversy.

Aniche or **Aniches** (ȧ.nēsh). Town in N France, in the department of Nord, between Douai and Valenciennes. It has coal mines, glass manufactures, and other industries. 9,037 (1946).

Aniene (ä.nyā′nā). [Also (in its lower course), **Teverone;** Latin, **Anio.**] River in C Italy that flows into the Tiber just above Rome. It is the source of a famous waterfall, ab. 330 ft. high, at a point just below Tivoli. It has been since ancient times a source of water for the city of Rome, and is now used also to produce hydroelectric power. Length, ab. 70 mi.

Animal Kingdom, The. Play by Philip Barry, produced in 1932.

Animuccia (ä.nē.möt′chä), **Giovanni.** [Called **"Father of the Oratorio."**] b. at Florence, c1500; d. at Rome, 1571. Italian composer of sacred music; predecessor (1555 *et seq.*) of Palestrina as maestro di cappela at Saint Peter's and source of some of the latter's ideas. He has been called "Father of the Oratorio" for his dramatic laudi, which were sung at the Oratorio of San Filippo, and which have been considered predecessors of the later form.

Animuccia, Paolo. d. 1563. Italian composer, who was for three years (1550–52) maestro di cappella at the Lateran. He composed chiefly religious music, most of which survives only in manuscript.

Animula (a̤.nim′ṳ̄.la̤). Poem by T. S. Eliot, usually grouped with the six-poem sequence *Ash-Wednesday* (1930), and dealing, like it, primarily with the difficulty and cost of attaining the religious life, and also with its paradoxical nature. The poem *Animula* specifically expresses the perplexities of the soul projected into an existence from which it shrinks.

Anio (an′yō). Latin name of the **Aniene.**

Anisfeld (ä′nis.felt), **Boris Israelevich.** b. at Bieltsy, in Bessarabia, Oct. 2, 1879—. Painter and stage decorator, resident since 1917 in the U.S. He is noted for his mystical, decorative paintings, and for his sets and décor for the ballet and opera. He studied at the Odessa Art School, and then at the Petrograd Imperial Academy of Art. Later, he went to Paris, and thence to the U.S. His work has been influenced by the impressionists, and has been exhibited in Russia, France, and the U.S. Among his better known works are *Flowers and Woman, The Garden of Eden, The Blue Statue, September, Self-Portrait with Sunflower and Cat, The Dream,* and décor for *Boris Godounov, Les Sylphides, Le Coq d'Or,* and many other ballets and operas.

Anisius (a̤.nis′i.us). A Latin name of the **Enns River.**

Anjala (än.yä′lä). In Swedish history, a name sometimes given to an unsuccessful league of noblemen against Gustavus III, in 1788.

Anjar (än.jär′). Small town in Kutch, Union of India, ab. 180 mi. W of Ahmedabad: trading center and rail junction. Pop. ab. 18,000.

Anjengo (än.jeng′gō). [Also, **Anjutenga.**] Village in Travancore, Union of India, ab. 70 mi. NW of Cape Comorin. Once an important seaport, it is now a local trading center, with a small export of coconuts.

Anjer Lor (an′jėr lôr′). [Also, **Anjer.**] Small seaport in Indonesia, at the NW corner of Java, on the Sunda Strait. It was overwhelmed by a tidal wave following the eruption of Krakatoa in 1883.

Anjin Sama (än.jēn sä.mä). Japanese title of **Adams, William** (d. 1620).

Anjos (uṅ′zhōs), **Augusto (de Carvalho Rodrigues) dos.** b. in the state of Paraíba, Brazil, April 20, 1884; d. at Leopoldina, Minas Gerais, Brazil, Nov. 12, 1914. Brazilian poet, author of the book *Eu* (1912), whose poems are characterized by a scientific terminology and sad tone. He was a bachelor of law and taught social sciences at several schools in Brazil.

Anjou (an′jö; French, äṅ.zhö). Medieval countship and duchy of France. It was bounded by Maine in the N, by Touraine on the E, by Poitou on the S, and by Brittany on the W. It comprised a territory approximating what is now the department of Maine-et-Loire and small portions of adjoining departments. The name is derived from the Andecavi, or Andegavi, a Gallic tribe in that region. Anjou was united with Touraine in 1044, and with Maine in 1110. By the marriage of Geoffrey IV (Geoffrey Plantagenet) with Matilda, heiress of Henry I of England, the way was opened for the eventual joining of Anjou, England, and Normandy under an English ruler. This step took place in 1154 when Geoffrey's son, Henry, already in possession of the French territories, ascended the English throne as Henry II, and founded the Plantagenet (or Angevin) house of English rulers. Anjou was conquered (c1204) by Philip Augustus of France and was subsequently united with Naples and Provence. It was annexed finally and formally to the French crown in 1480 by Louis XI. Capital, Angers.

Anjou, Counts and Dukes of. The origin of the countship has been referred to Ingelger, seneschal of Gâtinais, who in 870 received from Charles the Bald that portion of what was later to be the province of Anjou which lies between the Maine and the Mayenne rivers. Among his descendants were Fulke, count of Anjou, a Crusader, who became king of Jerusalem in 1131, and Fulke's son, Geoffrey IV (Geoffrey Plantagenet), who married Matilda, the daughter and heiress of Henry I of England, and is usually considered for this reason to have been not only the progenitor of the English royal house of Plantagenet, but also of the second house of Anjou, which was thus a branch of the royal family of France. However, King John of England lost (1204) his French fiefs to Philip II of France, and in 1246 Anjou passed into the hands of Charles, the brother of Louis IX. Charles established the house of Anjou on the throne of Naples in 1266. His son, Charles II of Naples, gave Anjou and Maine to his son-in-law, Charles de Valois, and from 1290 the counts of Valois took the title of duke of Anjou and count of Maine. The son of Charles de Valois became (1328) king of France as Philip VI, thus putting Anjou for the moment under the French crown. John II of France bestowed it, as a duchy, on his son Louis in 1356. This third house of Anjou became extinct in the direct line on the death (1480) of Charles, nephew of René. The title of duke of Anjou has also been borne, without implying territorial sovereignty, by Charles VIII of France, by the four sons of Henry II, by the second son of Henry IV, by the two sons of Louis XIV, by Louis XV, and by Philip V of Spain.

Anjouan (äṅ.zhwäṅ). [Also: **Anzuan, Johanna.**] One of the Comoro Islands, in Mozambique Channel, E of Africa and W of Madagascar, to which it is attached as an autonomous territory. Until 1912 it was governed by a sultan residing at Johanna, the main town; in that year the entire archipelago was made a French colony with Anjouan included. Area, 89 sq. mi.; pop. ab. 20,000.

Anju (än.jö'). [Japanese, **Anshu.**] Town in NW Korea, situated near the coast at the head of Korea Bay, in the province of Pyongan-namdo, ab. 45 mi. N of Pyongyang. Pop. ab. 25,000.

Anjutenga (an.ju.teng'gạ). See **Anjengo.**

Ankara (äng'kä.rä; Anglicized, ang'kạ.rạ). [Also: **Angora, Engüri;** Greek, **Ankyra;** Latin, **Ancyra, Sebaste Tectosagum.**] Capital of Turkey, situated on a headstream of the Sakarya River, in the geographic center of Turkey and on what have been in history the main overland trade routes from Europe to the East. The city has a commanding position on top of a hill of volcanic origin. A cosmopolitan city, it is the seat of a university (founded 1934) and of a British institute of archaeology (opened 1948). It was an ancient Galatian town, the capital of the Roman province of Galatia, and an important commercial center on the route between Byzantium and Syria, and it is still one of the chief commercial places in Asia Minor. The district is celebrated for its breed of goats, commonly called Angora goats. The ancient town was founded, according to the legends, by Midas, son of Gordius. It became the chief town of the Tectosages, a Gallic tribe which settled (c277 B.C.) in Galatia, and passed (25 B.C.) into the possession of Rome, when it received the name of Sebaste Tectosagum, and under which it had an important trade. The temple of Augustus, built by the Romans in the town, contained a famous inscription in Latin and Greek (*Monumentum,* or *Marmor, Ancyranum;* discovered in 1554), a transcript of the record of his deeds which Augustus ordered in his will to be cut on bronze tablets for his mausoleum. An ecclesiastical council held (c314) here passed 25 canons relating chiefly to the treatment of those who had betrayed their faith or delivered up the sacred books during the Diocletian persecution. A battle was fought here, on June 16, 1402, between Bajazet and Tamerlane, in which Bajazet was defeated. As a result, Asia Minor fell into the hands of Tamerlane and the Mongols. (An interesting historical sidelight of this conquest is that Bajazet, as a prisoner, was carried in a barred litter in Tamerlane's victory processions, and it was thus that the legend arose that he had been kept in an iron cage). Since 1923, when the seat of government was transferred from Istanbul, it has been the political center of Turkey. 286,781 (1950).

Ankarström (äng'kär.strėm), **Johan Jakob.** See **Anckarström, Johan Jakob.**

Anker Larsen (äng'kėr lär'sẹn), **Johannes.** b. on the island of Langeland, Denmark, 1874—. Danish novelist. He is the author of *The Philosopher's Stone* (Eng. trans., 1924) which won the Danish Gyldendal prize in 1923.

Anklam (äng'kläm). [Also, **Anclam.**] City in NE Germany, in the *Land* (state) of Mecklenburg, Russian Zone, formerly in the province of Pomerania, Prussia, situated on the Peene River, ab. 45 mi. NW of Stettin. Before World War II it had an important sugar refinery, machine factory, iron foundries, and woolen and cotton spinning mills. Its Gothic churches of Saint Mary and Saint Nicholas, of the 13th and 14th centuries, are impressive monuments, as are the city's medieval walls. Anklam was founded in the 11th century, joined the Hanseatic League in 1244, suffered gravely in the Thirty Years' War, was sacked by the Russians in 1713, and came under Prussian rule in 1720. The population is predominantly Protestant. 19,449 (1946).

Ankober (än.kō'bėr). [Also, **Ankobar** (-bär).] Former capital of Shoa province, Ethiopia, in E Africa, situated in the highlands ab. 70 mi. NE of Addis Ababa. Pop. ab. 2,000.

Ankogel (än'kō.gẹl). Mountain peak in the Hohe Tauern in Austria, on the borders of Salzburg and Carinthia, SE of Gastein. Elevation, ab. 10,700 ft.

Ankole (äng.kō'lā). [Also, **Ankori** (-rē).] Highland region in E Africa, in Uganda, W of Lake Victoria. The area is, for this part of Africa, densely populated; the bulk of the native inhabitants are of Galla stock. Elevation, ab. 6,000–7,000 ft.

Ankyra (äng'gē.rä). Greek name of **Ankara.**

Ann (an), **Cape.** Peninsula in E Massachusetts, projecting E into the Atlantic Ocean, N of Massachusetts Bay. It contains Gloucester and several other communities long important for their fishing fleets, and now important also as resort centers.

Anna (an'ạ). In the New Testament, a prophetess of Jerusalem noted for her piety. Luke, ii. 36.

Anna. City in S Illinois, in Union County: center for fruit shipments; seat of a state hospital for the insane. 4,380 (1950).

Anna. One of the principal female characters in John Home's play *Douglas.*

Anna, Saint. See **Anne** or **Anna, Saint.**

Anna (än'nä), **Donna.** One of the principal characters, a soprano, in Mozart's opera *Don Giovanni.*

Anna Amalia (än'ä ä.mä'lẹ.ä). See **Amalia, Anna.**

Annabel (an'ạ.bel). Character in John Dryden's *Absalom and Achitophel,* intended as a satirical portrait of the Duchess of Monmouth.

Annabella (an.ạ.bel'ạ), **Queen.** In Sir Walter Scott's novel *The Fair Maid of Perth,* the wife of King Robert III and mother of Rothsay.

Annabel Lee (an''ạ.bel lē'). Lyrical ballad in six stanzas by Edgar Allan Poe, posthumously published (Oct. 9, 1849) in the New York *Tribune.* The work has the theme, frequently employed by Poe, of separation by death from a loved one.

Annaberg (än'ä.berk). Town in C Germany, in the *Land* (state) of Saxony, Russian Zone, situated in the Erzgebirge mountains near the border of Czechoslovakia, ab. 18 mi. SE of Chemnitz. Before World War II it was one of the foremost centers in Germany for the manufacture of lace and ribbons, largely in the form of home industries: the lace-making industry was introduced by Barbara Uttmann in 1550, in order to provide employment for the poor population; the making of ribbon was introduced by Protestant refugees from Belgium in 1590. Originally a mining town, Annaberg was famed for its cobalt, bismuth, tin, and silver mines in the 16th century; the last mines were exhausted in 1892. The exact character of the town's present industrial activities cannot be determined, but it is in a region from which the Russians are known to derive considerable quantities of low-grade radioactive ores, and it is believed that this may considerably have altered the industrial pattern of the community. 19,584 (1946).

Anna Christie (an″ą kris′ti). Play by Eugene O'Neill, produced in 1921 and published in 1922, rewritten from his play *Chris Christopherson* (1920). It was awarded a Pulitzer prize in 1922. In it, Chris Christopherson, a Swedish-American captain, is reunited with his daughter, Anna, ignorant of the fact that she has turned to prostitution. Chris and Mat Burke, a sailor who loves Anna, leave her when she discloses her past. The three are eventually reunited, however, and Anna promises to provide a home for them. The sea is used throughout the play as a symbol of undefined longing. Pauline Lord created the title part on the stage; it was played in the motion-picture version by Greta Garbo.

Anna Comnena (kom.nē′ną). b. at Constantinople, Dec. 1, 1083; d. c1150. Byzantine princess and historian; daughter of Alexius I Comnenus. Having unsuccessfully conspired against her brother, John II, she retired to a convent where she wrote the *Alexiad*.

Anna Ivanovna (än′ną ē.vä′nǫv.ną). b. Jan. 25, 1693; d. Oct. 28, 1740. Empress of Russia (1730–40); daughter of Ivan V and niece of Peter the Great. She was elected by the secret high council, consisting of eight of the chief nobles, in preference to other claimants, after having promised important concessions to the nobility. However, she frustrated the attempt of the council to limit her power, exiled or executed its members, and surrounded herself with German favorites, of whom Biron was the leader. Allying herself with Austria, she waged (1736–39) successful war against the Turks, gaining Azov for Russia; earlier (1735) she had gained ascendancy over Poland as a result of the War of the Polish Succession.

An Najaf (än nä′jäf). [Also: **Meshhed-Ali, Nedjef, Nejef.**] City in S central Iraq, near the Euphrates River, ab. 90 mi. S of Baghdad, on several major highways. It is a holy city of the Shiite Moslems, by great numbers of whom pilgrimages are made each year to the tomb of Ali, son-in-law of Mohammed. Pop. ab. 25,000.

Anna Karenina (än′ną kä.rā′nyi.ną). Novel by Leo Tolstoy, published in 1855–57. The book, which has as its theme the nature of marriage, is set in the Russian society of the middle 19th century. The titular heroine, unhappy in her marriage to the much older Alexis Karenin, finds an affinity in Count Vronski; the rules of society, however, so far prevent the two from enjoying any happiness together that Anna, driven to desperation, commits suicide by throwing herself under a train after Vronski has rejoined his regiment.

Anna Leopoldovna (li.o.pôl′dǫv.ną) or **Anna Karlovna** (kär′lǫv.ną). [Original full prename, **Elizabeth Catherine Christine.**] b. Dec. 18, 1718; d. March 18, 1746. Grand duchess and regent (1740–41) of Russia; daughter of Charles Leopold, duke of Mecklenburg-Schwerin, and wife of Anton Ulric, duke of Brunswick. On the death (Oct. 28, 1740) of her aunt, the czarina Anna Ivanovna, she became regent for her son, Ivan VI, who had been appointed her successor by Anna, but was deprived of this post on Dec. 6, 1741, by a conspiracy which deposed Ivan and placed Elizabeth, daughter of Peter the Great, on the throne.

Anna Livia Plurabelle (an′ą liv′i.ą plö′rą.bel). Heroine of James Joyce's *Finnegan's Wake*. She exemplifies, on a local scale, the River Liffey, and, on a broader scale, the whole female principle; concretely, she appears as Maggie Earwicker, the publican's wife. Her initials, ALP, are woven through the narrative, juxtaposed against those of the hero (HCE, for Humphrey Chimpden Earwicker).

Annals of Cuauhtitlan (kwou.tē.tlän′). Name given to an early post-conquest Indian manuscript, written in the Nahuatl language, with the Spanish alphabet, in which is recorded in incomplete and confusing form the history of the Toltecs. The work appears to be made up of interpretations of the pre-conquest native pictographic writings.

Annals of the Cakchiquel (käk.chē.kel′). Name given to several manuscript books, written in the Cakchiquel dialect of the Quiche Indian language, but with a modified Spanish alphabet. They contain records of Cakchiquel history during the Spanish conquest and early post-conquest times.

Annam (ą.nam′, an′am). [Also: **Anam**; official name since 1949, **Central Viet-Nam.**] Former French protectorate in SE Asia, in the E part of the Indochinese peninsula: now largely included in the state of Viet-Nam as part of the federation of French Indochina. It lies between Tonkin (North Viet-Nam) on the N, the China Sea on the E, Cochin-China (South Viet-Nam) on the S, and Laos and Cambodia on the W. It is rich in agricultural and natural resources, having oil wells, and gold, copper, iron, coal, and zinc mines. The chief product of the region is rice, but sugar, cinnamon, paper, and tea are also exported. The government was until 1949 a monarchy, with a French resident; it is now administered by a governor under the Viet-Namese chief of state. The inhabitants are Annamites (in the towns and along the coasts) and Moïs (in the hill districts), and the prevailing religions are Buddhism, Confucianism, spirit-worship, and Christianity. It was formerly a Chinese possession, and gained its independence in 1428. It became a French protectorate by a treaty signed in 1884. Capital, Hué; area, 56,973 sq. mi.; pop. 7,183,827 (1943).

Annamaboe (än.nä.mä.bö′). See **Anomabu.**

Anna Matilda (an′ą mą.til′dą). Name adopted by Mrs. Hannah Cowley, dramatist and poet, in a poetical correspondence with Robert Merry (who called himself "Della Crusca"). With two others of her school (the "Della Cruscans") she was held up to scorn by the critic William Gifford in his *Baviad and Maeviad*, and the name "Anna Matilda" acquired considerable usage as a synonym for namby-pamby verse and sentimental fiction.

Annamese (an.ą.mēz′, -mēs′) or **Annamites** (an′ą.mīts). Name sometimes applied to the Vietnamese people of Indochina. Vietnamese is the name which they themselves prefer.

Annamese. [Also: **Annamite, Vietnamese, Viet-Namese.**] Language spoken by ab. 16 million people in Indochina.

Annan (an′ąn). Royal burgh, seaport, and market town in S Scotland, in Dumfriesshire, situated near the entrance of the river Annan into Solway Firth, ab. 15 mi. SE of Dumfries, ab. 317 mi. N of London by rail. The town possesses salmon-fishing rights to a considerable portion of Solway Firth. Annan was the birthplace (1792) of Edward Irving. 4,562 (est. 1948).

Annandale (an′ąn.dāl). Valley of the river Annan, in S Scotland, in Dumfriesshire. It forms the middle one of the three divisions of Dumfriesshire. Length, ab. 30 mi.; width, ab. 15 mi.

Annan River (an′ąn). River in S Scotland, in Dumfriesshire. It rises on the Dumfriesshire-Peeblesshire boundary, ab. 5 mi. N of Moffat and flows southward into the Solway Firth ab. 2 mi. S of Annan. Length, ab. 49 mi.

Anna of the Five Towns (an′ą). Novel by Arnold Bennett, published in 1902. A study of a young middle-class woman, it is the first volume in the first "Five Towns" trilogy, which also contains *Leonora* (1903) and *Sacred and Profane Love* (1905; revised, 1911, as *The Book of Carlotta*). The "Five Towns" comprised a district in Staffordshire known as "the Potteries," a grimy and unlovely locality. Bennett himself came from one of the towns and his affectionate knowledge of it made him one of the foremost of the regionalists.

Anna Petrovna (än′ną pi.trôv′ną). b. 1708; d. 1728. Russian grand duchess; eldest daughter of Peter the Great and Catherine I, wife of Charles Frederick, duke of Holstein-Gottorp, and mother of Peter III of Russia.

Annapolis (ą.nap′ǫ.lis). [Former names, **Providence, Anne Arundel Town.**] City in C Maryland, capital of the state and county seat of Anne Arundel County, on the Severn River, ab. 2 mi. from Chesapeake Bay: the seat of the U.S. Naval Academy and St. John's College. The town was founded in 1649 and became a city in 1696; it was one of the meeting places (November, 1783 to June, 1784) of the Continental Congress, and Washington here resigned his commission as commander in chief, in December, 1783. It was the seat of the Annapolis Convention (1786), predecessor of the Federal Convention of 1787. Pop. 10,047 (1950).

Annapolis Basin. Arm of the Bay of Fundy, on the W coast of Nova Scotia, in Canada. The Annapolis River flows into it, and it reaches the bay through an opening (ab. ½ mi. wide) known as Digby Gut. Both the basin as a whole, and Digby Gut in particular, are known for their extremely high tides.

Annapolis Convention. Convention of 12 delegates from the states of New York, New Jersey, Pennsylvania, Delaware, and Virginia, which met at Annapolis, on Sept. 11, 1786, to promote commercial interests. It recommended calling another convention at Philadelphia in 1787, which became the Federal Convention.

Annapolis River. River in W Nova Scotia, in Canada, flowing generally W into Annapolis Basin at the town of Annapolis Royal. Its valley is famous for fruit farms. Length, ab. 75 mi.

Annapolis Royal. [Former name, **Port Royal.**] Seaport in Nova Scotia, Canada, near the Bay of Fundy, on the W side of the peninsula that forms the major portion of the province. It was founded by the French in 1604, and was ceded to the British in 1713. It is one of the main commercial centers for the famous Annapolis valley apple-growing region. Pop. ab. 800.

Ann Arbor (an' är'bo̤r). City in S Lower Michigan, on the Huron River, ab. 38 mi. W of Detroit, county seat of Washtenaw County: seat of the University of Michigan. Its factories produce radios, cameras, and steel articles; trading center for an agricultural and fruit-growing region. 48,251 (1950).

Annas (an'a̤s). [Also, **Ananus.**] A high priest of the Jews, called Ananus by Josephus, according to whom he was appointed high priest by Quirinus, proconsul of Syria, in c7 A.D., and deposed by Valerius Gratus, procurator of Judea, in 14 A.D. He was followed by Ishmael, the son of Phabaeus; Eleazar, the son of Annas; and Simon, the son of Camithus, when Joseph, surnamed Caiaphas, the son-in-law of Annas, was elevated to the office c27 A.D. In the New Testament (Luke, iii. 2, John, xviii. 13, Acts, iv. 6) Annas is mentioned as high priest conjointly with Caiaphas. The first hearing of Jesus was before Annas, who sent him bound to Caiaphas.

An Nasiriya (än nä.sē.rē'ya̤). See **Nasiriya.**

Anna St. Ives (an'a̤ sānt īvz'). Novel (1792) by Thomas Holcroft. In it the revolutionary program of "perfectibility" is put into the form of fiction. The idealistic hero confounds the machinations of the aristocratic villain and in the end converts him to a better view of life.

Anne (an) or **Anna** (an'a̤), Saint. According to tradition, the mother of the Virgin Mary. Her life and the birth of the Virgin are recorded in several of the apocryphal gospels. In art she is often represented wearing a veil.

Anne (of *England*). b. at London, Feb. 6, 1665; d. at Kensington, England, Aug. 1, 1714. Queen of Great Britain and Ireland (1702–14); daughter of James II of England and Anne Hyde, and wife of Prince George of Denmark (married 1683). She was for much of her reign under the influence of the Duke and Duchess of Marlborough, and later of Mrs Abigail Masham. She sided with William of Orange (who, as William III, was king of England from 1689 to 1702) in the English revolution that unseated her father, James II. Among the notable events of her reign were the War of the Spanish Succession and the union of England and Scotland. Her name is given to the graceful style of interior decoration associated with the early 18th century.

Anne (of *England*), Princess. [Full name, **Anne Elizabeth Alice Louise.**] b. at London, Aug. 15, 1950—. English princess; second child of Elizabeth II and Philip, Duke of Edinburgh, and younger sister of Prince Charles.

Anne, Fort. See under **Fort Anne National Park.**

Anne, Mount. Mountain in Antarctica, in the Queen Alexandra Range, rising on the S side of the Socks Glacier and W of the Beardmore Glacier, at the head of the Ross Shelf Ice, in ab. 83°56′ S., 169°20′ E. It was discovered and named by the British Antarctic Expedition (1908–09) under the leadership of Sir Ernest Shackleton. Elevation, ab. 10,270 ft.

Anne, Sister. Sister of Bluebeard's last wife, Fatima. She watched for the cloud of dust which was to indicate the arrival of their brothers to rescue Fatima and herself.

Anne Arundel Town (a̤.run'de̤l). A former name of **Annapolis.**

Anne Boleyn (bůl'in, bů.lēn'). Tragedy by Henry Hart Milman, produced in 1821.

Annecy (ån.sē). [Latin, **Anneciacum** (an.ẹ.sī'a̤.kum).] Capital of the department of Haute-Savoie, E France, beautifully situated on the Lake of Annecy, between Geneva and Grenoble. It has an old castle, a cathedral dating from the 16th century, and a bishop's palace. Industries include textile, metal, chemical, and shoe manufactures. A fair is held annually at which the agricultural and industrial products of the region are exhibited; the town is a summer resort and tourist center. It was formerly the seat of the counts of Geneva but fell later to the dukes of Savoy. In 1535 it became, and was for many years thereafter, the seat of the diocese of Geneva. It was taken by Henry IV in 1600, by Louis XIII in 1630, and by the troops of Louis XIV in 1703. Annecy was annexed to France during the French Revolution, was returned to Sardinia, but was ceded to France in 1860. Pop. 26,122 (1946).

Annecy, Lake. Lake in the department of Haute-Savoie, E France, near Annecy. Its outlet is through the Fier River to the Rhône River. Length, ab. 9 mi.

Anne de France (ån dẹ fräṅs). [Also, **Anne de Beaujeu.**] b. c1460; d. 1522. Regent of France (1483–90); daughter of Louis XI. She served as regent for her brother, Charles VIII.

Annemasse (ån.mås). Town in E France, in the department of Haute-Savoie, E of Geneva. It is an important railroad junction, and a tourist center in the French Alps. 8,831 (1946).

Annen (än'ẹn). Manufacturing town in W Germany, in the *Land* (state) of North Rhine-Westphalia, British Zone, formerly in the province of Westphalia, Prussia, situated ab. 6 mi. SW of Dortmund. It has coal mines, chemical and glass factories and steelworks. It is incorporated into the community of Witten-Annen. Pop. ab. 18,000.

Annenkov (än'nyin.ko̤f), **Mikhail.** b. April 30, 1835; d. 1899. Russian general and engineer who projected and superintended the construction of the Russian Transcaspian Railway.

Annensky (än'nyin.ski), **Innokenty Fyodorovich.** b. 1856; d. 1909. Russian classical scholar and symbolist poet. He wrote poems and plays, after having made a name for himself with a translation into Russian of the works of Euripides.

Anne of Austria (an). b. at Madrid, Sept. 22, 1601; d. Jan. 20, 1666. Queen of France; daughter of Philip III of Spain, and wife of Louis XIII of France. She was regent (1643–61) for her son Louis XIV, with Jules Mazarin as her principal adviser.

Anne of Bohemia. b. at Prague, Bohemia (in what is now Czechoslovakia), May 11, 1366; d. June 7, 1394. Queen of England; daughter of the emperor Charles IV and wife of Richard II of England. It was while she was queen that Richard, infuriated because its bankers refused his request for a loan, revoked the rights of the City of London, and it was largely through the persuasive efforts of Anne that Richard was prevailed upon to restore them.

Anne of Brittany. [French, **Anne de Bretagne** (brẹ-tȧny').] b. at Nantes, France, 1476; d. at Blois, France, 1514. Queen of France; the daughter and heiress of Francis II, duke of Brittany. She married (1491) Charles VIII of France and, after his death, became (1499) the wife of his successor, Louis XII. Through her, Brittany, the last of the great fiefs of France, was permanently united to the French crown.

Anne of Cleves (klēvz). b. at Cleves, Germany, 1515; d. in England, 1557. Queen of England; daughter of the Duke of Cleves and fourth wife of Henry VIII. She was selected for Henry by Thomas Cromwell, for political reasons. She was married in January, 1540, and divorced in July of the same year. Having agreed to live in England for the rest of her life, she died there, and is buried in Westminster Abbey.

Anne of Denmark. b. at Skanderborg, Denmark, Dec. 12, 1574; d. March 2, 1619. Queen of England and Scotland; daughter of Frederick II of Denmark and wife of James VI of Scotland (James I of England). She was interested in elaborate entertainments, personally taking part in masques by Ben Jonson and Thomas Dekker.

Anne of Geierstein (gī′ėr.shtīn, -stīn). Romance by Sir Walter Scott, published in 1829. The scene is laid mainly in the Switzerland of the 15th century. This is one of the works that Scott wrote during the last seven years of his life, when he was burdened by debt and forced himself to unremitting toil to satisfy his creditors.

Anne of Savoy (sa̤.voi′). b. 1320; d. 1359. Empress-regent of the Byzantine empire; daughter of Amadeus V, duke of Savoy. She was married (1337) to the emperor Andronicus III, and, after his death (1341), served as regent during the minority of her son John V Palaeologus.

Anne of the Thousand Days. Historical play (1948) by Maxwell Anderson. Considered by many critics to be among Anderson's best plays, it centers upon the brief passion of Henry VIII and Anne Boleyn.

Anne Severn and the Fieldings (sev′ėrn; fēl′dingz). Novel by May Sinclair, published in 1922.

Annesley (anz′li), **Arthur.** [Title, 1st Earl of **Anglesey** (or **Anglesea**).] b. at Dublin, July 10, 1614; d. at Bletchingdon, England, April 26, 1686. British politician and government official under Charles II. He was member for Dublin in Richard Cromwell's parliament (1658); as president of the council of state (1660), he aided in the restoration of Charles II. He also served as vice-treasurer and receiver-general for Ireland (1660–67), and as lord privy seal (1673–82). He was dismissed (1682) from office for criticism of the government in a paper (1681) on Irish affairs and another addressed to Charles II, entitled *The Account of Arthur, Earl of Anglesea, to your Most Excellent Majesty on the true state of your Majesty's government and kingdom* (1682).

Annesley, James. b. 1715; d. Jan. 5, 1760. English claimant to nobility, the subject of Charles Reade's *Wandering Heir*. His legitimacy as son of Lord Altham (d. 1727) being disputed, he was sent into slavery (1728–40) in America by his uncle who also claimed the title. His subsequent lawsuit to establish his claim was used in part in Smollett's *Peregrine Pickle* and Scott's *Guy Mannering*.

Annesley Bay. See **Zula, Gulf of.**

Annett (an′e̤t), **Henry Edward.** b. June 5, 1871—. English pathologist. Educated at University College at Liverpool and Victoria University at Manchester, he was professor (1906–11) of comparative pathology, lecturer (1922–28) in animal pathology, and cancer researcher (1923–30) at the University of Liverpool. He served as Turner Research Fellow (1930–38) in cancer, after having been superintendent (1911–22) of the research laboratories at Higher Runcorn. He took part in the first (1891) and led the second (1900) expedition to West Africa of the Liverpool School of Tropical Medicine, and headed subsequent expeditions to Uruguay (1905) and the West Indies (1906–07).

Anni (än′nē). [Also, **Ani.**] Ruined medieval city in the S part of the U.S.S.R., in the Armenian Soviet Socialist Republic, situated on the Arpachai River ab. 28 mi. SE of Kars, Turkey: the ancient capital of Armenia.

Annie Kilburn (an′i kil′bėrn). Novel by William Dean Howells, published in 1888. After an 11-year residence in Italy, Annie returns to New England receptive to liberal ideas and interested in philanthropic activities. With the help of a local Unitarian minister, Mr. Peck, she performs beneficent deeds. Rejecting the conventional and, in their eyes, ineffectual type of New England charity, Annie and Mr. Peck organize a progressive "Social Union." Upon the death of the clergyman, Annie adopts his daughter, Idella, and marries Dr. Morrell, who has been her adviser.

Annie Laurie (lô′ri). Song written by William Douglas of Kirkcudbright and widely popular in Great Britain, the U.S., and other English-speaking countries.

Anning (an′ing), **Mary.** b. at Lyme Regis, England, 1799; d. 1847. English collector of fossils. While still a child of 12, she found the first fossil specimen of *Icthyosaurus* known to scientists; later she found the remains of *Plesiosaurus* (1821) and of a pterodactyl, which was identified (1828) as *Dimorphodon*.

Anniston (an′is.to̤n). City in NE Alabama, county seat of Calhoun County, ab. 60 mi. E of Birmingham: center of a great iron-mining region. Iron and steel products, textiles, and chemicals are manufactured in this city. Fort McClellan is nearby. 31,066 (1950).

Annius of Viterbo (an′i.us; vē.ter′bō). [Original name, **Giovanni Nanni.**] b. at Viterbo, Italy, 1432; d. Nov. 13, 1502. Italian Dominican monk and scholar. He published a collection of spurious lost classics.

Anno (an′ō) or **Hanno** (han′ō), Saint. b. 1010; d. 1075. Archbishop of Cologne (1056 *et seq.*); son of the Swabian count, Walter of Pfullingen. He is said to have headed a group of princes in revolt (1062) against the regent, Agnes of Poitou, kidnaping the youthful King Henry IV and usurping the regency. He obtained recognition of Alexander II as Pope at the Council of Mantua (1064). He was canonized in 1183.

Annobón (än.o̤.bōn′). Small island off the W coast of Africa, belonging to Spain and forming part of the colony of Spanish Guinea. It is S of the Portuguese island São Tomé and ab. 200 mi. W of Cape Lopez, French Equatorial Africa. The island was uninhabited when given to Spain by Portugal in 1778. Length, 4 mi.; width, 2 mi.; area, 7 sq. mi.; pop. ab. 1,200.

Annœullin (á.nė.laṅ). Town in N France, in the department of Nord, ab. 11 mi. S of Lille. It has a number of industries. 6,283 (1946).

Annolied (än′ō.lēt). Early Middle High German narrative poem (c1090), a chronicle of creation culminating in the life and works of Saint Anno (or Hanno), archbishop of Cologne. It is known to us through Martin Opitz' edition (1639).

Annonay (á.no.ne). [Ancient name, **Annoniacum** (an-o̤.nī′a̤.kum).] Town in S France, in the department of Ardèche, situated near the N border of the department, ab. 37 mi. SW of Lyons. It is located between two ravines. Manufactures include paper, paperware, silk goods, and glove leather; it is a skin and hide trade center. The town has a monument to the Montgolfier brothers, who were born nearby, and who are remembered for their pioneer efforts as balloonists. 15,462 (1946).

Annonce faite à Marie (lá.nôṅs fet à má.rē), **L'.** Poetic drama (1910) by Paul Claudel, French poet, dramatist, and diplomat, on the theme of human weakness and divine compassion. It is called by some critics one of the few masterpieces of drama since Shakespeare and Racine. An earlier version was entitled *La Jeune Fille Violaine*.

Annual, Battle of. Battle in Morocco between the Spanish and the Rif leader, Abd-el-Krim, on June 23, 1921, one of the greatest disasters ever suffered by a Spanish army. As a result of it, control of Spanish Morocco was for several years in doubt. The fatal offensive move made by Spanish forces under General Silvestre was unknown to his superior, General Berenguer, but was probably encouraged by King Alfonso XIII. The terrible loss of life and prestige for Spain (10,000 killed, 4,000 prisoners), brought down the Maura government and very much enhanced the stature of Abd-el-Krim.

Annual Register, The. Periodical founded in 1758 and published by Robert Dodsley, a fashionable bookseller of the time and the leading publisher of English poetry. Edmund Burke was the first contributor. Each annual volume contained a retrospective account of the year, even including reviews of a few chosen books. Somewhat imitative in concept of early registers, such as John Meres's *Historical Register* for the years 1714–38, it surpassed its predecessors by being more inclusive and more literary. Burke remained the principal conductor of this undertaking, of which he made an enormous success, for over 31 years.

Annunciation, Feast of the. [Also, **Lady Day.**] Roman Catholic holy day observed on March 25. It commemorates the Annunciation (the announcement to the Virgin Mary by the angel Gabriel that she was to be the mother of Christ).

Annunciation, The. Subject of many paintings important in the history of art, particularly by artists of the Italian Renaissance and those influenced by the work of that period. Some of the best known are: **1.** Fresco painting by Fra Angelico, in the Convent of San Marco at Florence. **2.** Painting by Andrea del Sarto, belonging to the collection of the Galleria Pitti at Florence. **3.** Painting by Lucca Signorelli, painted in the San Carlo Chapel of the *Duomo* (cathedral) at Volterra, Italy; one of this master's best works. **4.** Painting by Titian, in the collection of the Scuola di San Rocco at Venice. **5.** Characteristic Pre-Raphaelite painting by Dante Gabriel Rossetti, in the National Gallery at London. The model for the Virgin was Christina Rossetti.

Annunzio (dän.nön'tsyō), **Gabriele D'.** See **D'Annunzio, Gabriele.**

Annus Mirabilis (an'us mi.rab'i.lis). [Eng. trans., *"The Year of Wonders."*] Poem (published 1667) by John Dryden, descriptive of the Dutch war and the London fire of 1666. Dryden regards his material as historical rather than epic, but insists on the lofty heroic quality of the events, and he makes them majestic both by the sound of the verse and by the use of grandiose imagery. Many critics feel that the poem is on the whole less interesting than its preface, in which Dryden sets forth his notion of poetic imagination.

Ann Veronica: A Modern Love Story (an' vę.ron'i.ką). Novel by H. G. Wells, published in 1909. It is a realistic story of a middle-class heroine and of her struggle to be free and independent.

Annville (an'vil). [Former name, **Millerstown.**] Unincorporated community in SE Pennsylvania, in Lebanon County, on Quitapahilla Creek, in a dairying and quarrying region: manufactures shoes and hosiery. It is the seat of Lebanon Valley College. The town was platted in 1762. 3,564 (1950).

Ano (ä'nō). [Also, **Mango.**] One of the Sudanic-speaking Anyi peoples of W Africa, inhabiting the SE part of the Ivory Coast.

Anoka (ą.nō'ką). City in SE Minnesota, county seat of Anoka County, at the confluence of the Rum and Mississippi rivers: flour milling. 7,396 (1950).

Anomabu (ä.nǫ.mä'bö). [Also: **Anamabo, Annamaboe.**] Town in the Gold Coast colony, W Africa, ab. 10 mi. E of Cape Coast: formerly of some importance as a seaport.

Anomoeans (an.ǫ.mē'ąnz). [Also: **Aëtians, Eudoxians, Eunomians.**] Sect of extreme Arians in the 4th century A.D. They held that the Son is of an essence not even similar to that of the Father (whence their name), while the more moderate Arians held that the essence of the Son is similar to that of the Father, though not identical with it. The sect was founded at Antioch, and was first led by Aëtius, and after him by Eunomius and by Eudoxius, whence its members were also called Aëtians, Eunomians, and Eudoxians. Its beliefs were finally condemned at the Council of Constantinople (381).

Anpei (än'pā') or **Anping** (-ping'). See **Ampin.**

Anpu and Bata (än'pö; bä'tą). See **Tale of the Two Brothers.**

Anquetil (äṅk.tēl), **Louis Pierre.** b. at Paris, Jan. 21, 1723; d. there, Sept. 6, 1808. French historian. He collaborated on *Histoire de France* (1805), and was the author of *Esprit de la ligue* (1767), *Précis de l'histoire universelle* (1797), and others.

Anquetil-Duperron (äṅk.tēl.dü.pe.rôṅ), **Abraham Hyacinthe.** b. at Paris, Dec. 7, 1731; d. there, Jan. 17, 1805. French Orientalist; brother of Louis Pierre Anquetil. He is best known for his three-volume *Zend-Avesta* (1771), which was the first translation in Europe of Zoroastrian scripture. He was the author also of *Législation orientale* (1778) and others, including a Latin translation of the Upanishads.

Ans (äṅs). Town in E Belgium, in the province of Liége, situated on a branch of the Meuse River NW of Liége, of which it is a suburb: coal mines; railroad-equipment works; manufactures mine cables and bricks. 15,476 (1947).

Ansarii (an.sär'i.ī). [Also, **Nossarii.**] Members of an Arabic-speaking religious sect in Syria, dwelling in the mountains between the Orontes River to the N and Tripoli, in Lebanon, to the S.

Ansbach (äns'bäċh). [Also: **Anspach, Onolzbach.**] City in S Germany, in the *Land* (state) of Bavaria, American Zone, the capital of the *Kreis* (district) of Middle and Upper Franconia, situated on the Franconian Rezat River, ab. 25 mi. SW of Nuremberg. Manufactures include shoes, gloves, combs, paper, motors, and stoves; the city is an agricultural trade center, with important livestock markets. There is a library, historical museum, and various educational institutions. Formerly the residence of the margraves of Ansbach-Bayreuth, it took on the delightful character of the rococo style of the period; the castle (1713–32) is one of the finest examples of 18th-century architecture in S Germany. 33,170 (1950).

Anschar (ans'kär), Saint. [Also: **Ansgar, Anskar;** Latinized, **Anscharius, Ansgarius;** called the **"Apostle of the North."**] b. near Amiens, France, 801; d. at Bremen, Germany, 865. Frankish Benedictine missionary to Denmark, Sweden, and northern Germany. He was appointed (831) bishop of Hamburg and later (857) first archbishop of the newly formed see of Hamburg and Bremen.

Anschluss (än'shlůs''). German word, meaning union (literally, connection), and especially the union (1938) of Germany and Austria. Historically, the desire for union between Austria and Germany has long existed in the German-speaking world, but it became especially acute immediately after the collapse and partition of the Hapsburg empire of Austria-Hungary in 1918. The Austrian constituent assembly declared the country a part of Germany, and the Weimar republic responded with similar declarations. However, the Allied powers prevented the union by imposing upon Austria, through Article 88 of the peace treaty of St.-Germain, the obligation to maintain her full sovereignty. The propaganda in favor of union flared up again in 1921 when plebiscites aiming at the union with Germany were held in some Austrian provinces. Austria, nevertheless, reaffirmed Article 88 by the Geneva Convention of November, 1922, through which she received economic and financial assistance from the League of Nations. The European powers saw in the German-Austrian customs union treaty of March, 1931, another attempt at the achievement of union. Their strong opposition induced Germany and Austria to renounce the project before the League of Nations a day before the International Court at The Hague declared the treaty to be in violation of Article 88 and the Geneva Convention. Hitler tried to bring about an Anschluss in July, 1934, by an abortive coup which culminated in the assassination of the Austrian chancellor Dollfuss. With Italian support the Austrians thereafter maintained their independence until March, 1938, when Hitler marched troops into an Austria prepared by propaganda, a resurgence of pan-German feeling, and native fascist elements to accept him without resistance.

Anschütz-Kämpfe (än'shüts.kemp'fę), **Hermann.** b. at Zweibrücken, Germany, Oct. 3, 1872; d. at Munich, Germany, May 6, 1931. He invented (1908) a gyrocompass employing the flotation method.

Ansdell (anz'del), **Richard.** b. at Liverpool, England, 1815; d. at Farnborough, England, April 20, 1885. English painter, chiefly of animal life. He first exhibited at the Royal Academy in 1840 and became a member of that body in 1870. His works include *Stag at Bay*, *Combat of Red Stags*, and *Hunting the Boar.*

Anse (äṅs). Small community in E central France, in the department of Rhône, situated on the Azergue River near the Saône River, ab. 14 mi. NW of Lyons. It was an important place in the Middle Ages.

Ansedonia (än.sä.dō'nyä). [Ancient name, **Cosa.**] Small town in C Italy, in the *compartimento* (region) of Tuscany, on the coast near Orbetello. Its remains of Etruscan fortifications, the most perfect in Italy, are in plan an approximate square of about a mile in circuit. The lower part of the walls is of huge polygonal blocks so exactly fitted that a knifeblade cannot be inserted in the joints.

Anseel (än'säl), **Edward.** b. at Ghent, 1856—. Belgian publicist and politician. He was minister of railroads in the period 1925–27.

Ansegis (an'sę.jis) or **Ansegisus** (an.sę.jī'sus), Saint. b. c770; d. July 20, 833. Abbot of Fontanelle (823 *et seq.*). He enlarged the library at Fontanelle until it was among the greatest of its time in Europe. He also compiled the laws and decrees of Charlemagne and his son, Louis le Debonnaire, in a four-volume work (826) entitled *Quatuor Libri Capitularium Regum Francorum*, sometimes known as *Capitularies* from the general name applied to the collective laws of the Carolingian and Merovingian kings.

Anselm (an'selm), Saint. b. at Aosta, Italy, 1033; d. at Canterbury, England, 1109. Burgundian prelate who became archbishop of Canterbury; forerunner of the great medieval scholastic philosophers. In 1060 he became a monk at Bec, in Normandy; he studied under Lanfranc and succeeded him as prior (1063–78) of Bec, in the latter year becoming abbot. Made archbishop of Canterbury in 1093 by William II of England (William Rufus), he accepted reluctantly, with the stipulation that church rule of prelates, rather than royal sanction (inaugurated by Gregory VII), be observed, thus beginning a long struggle with William (1087–1100) and with Henry I (1100–35) over the right of investiture, ending in compromise (1107) with Henry. An expositor of Augustinian doctrine and of the priority of faith over reason, he anticipated the thought of later scholastics, though he was not accepted by them because he wrote tracts and dialogues (as distinguished from treatises) on separate questions. He is now most noted for his ontological proof of the existence of God, which states that the concept of perfection encompasses all desirable traits, including real existence. Immanuel Kant, among others, attempted a refutation of this reasoning, but it remains nevertheless one of the most often cited of arguments in support of the existence of God. He was the author of *Monologion* and *Proslogion* (on God) and *Cur Deus Homo* (on atonement). He was canonized (1494) by Pope Alexander VI.

Anselme (äṅ.selm). Character in the drama *L'Avare*, by Molière.

Anselme (däṅ.selm), **Jacques Bernard Modeste d'.** b. at Apt, France, July 22, 1740; d. 1812. French general, commander of the army of the Var in 1792.

Anselm of Laon (an'selm; läṅ). [French, **Anselme de Laon** (äṅ.selm dẹ läṅ); Latinized, **Anselmus Laudinensis.**] b. at Laon, France, c1030; d. July 15, 1117. French theologian, author of *Glossa interlinearis* (Antwerp, 1634), an interlinear gloss of the Vulgate Bible.

Anselm of Lucca (lök'kä), Saint. b. at Mantua, Italy, c1036; d. 1086. Italian Benedictine ecclesiastic and reformer; nephew of Pope Alexander II.

Ansermet (äṅ.ser.me), **Ernest.** b. at Vevey, Switzerland, Nov. 11, 1883—. Swiss conductor of music. A former professor of mathematics, he is the composer of the symphonic poem *Feuilles de Printemps.* He was the conductor (1915 *et seq.*) for the Ballet Russe under Diaghilev, and came to be highly regarded as an interpreter of Stravinsky and other moderns. He was the founder (1918) and permanent conductor of the Orchestre de la Suisse Romande.

Ansgar (ans'gär), Saint. See **Anschar,** Saint.

Anshan (än'shän'). City in NE China, in the province of Liaotung, Manchuria, on the railroad halfway between Mukden and Yingkow. There is coal and some low-grade iron ore in the vicinity; the principal iron and steel works of Manchuria are located here. Area of municipality, ab. 140 sq. mi.; pop. 185,159 (1950).

Anshu (än.shö). Japanese name of **Anju.**

Ansibarii (an.si.bãr'i.ī). See **Ampsivarii.**

Anskar (ans'kär), Saint. See **Anschar,** Saint.

Ansley (ānz'li), **Clarke Fisher.** b. at Swedona, Ill., Dec. 29, 1869; d. Feb. 14, 1939. American editor and teacher. He was on the staff (1894–99) of the University of Nebraska, head (1899–1917) of the English department at the State University of Iowa, and director (1922–23) of the New School for Social Research at New York. After serving as editor (1921–22) of *The New State* at Lincoln, Neb., he was editor-in-chief (1927 *et seq.*) of the Columbia University Press and the *Columbia Encyclopedia.*

Anslo (äns'lō), **Reinier.** b. at Amsterdam, 1626; d. at Perugia, Italy, May 10, 1669. Dutch poet. He wrote *The Martyr Crown of Saint Stephen, The Plague at Naples,* and *The Paris Wedding* (on the subject of the massacre of Saint Bartholomew's Eve).

Anson (an'sọn). City in W central Texas, county seat of Jones County, ab. 24 mi. N of Abilene: cotton processing and shipping. Once a cattle town, it still holds an annual Cowboys' Christmas Ball. 2,708 (1950).

Anson, Adrian Constantine. [Called **"Cap" Anson.**] b. at Marshalltown, Iowa, April 17, 1852; d. April 14, 1922. American baseball player. He was employed by the Philadelphia Athletics (1872–76) and the Chicago National League team (1876–97); as captain and manager, he led the latter to pennants in 1880, 1881, 1882, 1885, and 1886. Best known for his hitting prowess, he attained an overall average of .331 in his 22 years with Chicago.

Anson, George. [Title, Baron **Anson.**] b. at Shugborough, England, April 23, 1697; d. at Moor Park, England, June 6, 1762. English admiral, notable for his successes against the Spanish and the French. He circumnavigated the globe, and made important reforms in the British navy. As a captain, he was assigned (1724) to protect South Carolina from pirates and Spaniards. He was the commodore of a squadron of six ships sent (1740) to attack Spanish holdings on the Pacific coast of South America; although his fleet was finally reduced by storms to one ship, the *Centurion,* he harassed the enemy's commerce and captured (1743) the Spanish treasure-ship, *Nuestra Señora de Covadonga,* on its way from Manila to Acapulco, taking booty valued at 500,000 pounds, and returned (1744) to England via the Cape of Good Hope. Made rear admiral (1745) and vice-admiral (1746) with command of the Channel fleet, he defeated (1747) a French convoy off Cape Finisterre. As first lord of the admiralty (1751–56 and 1757–62), he reorganized naval administration, supply, and discipline, creating (1755) the corps of marines. He was in office during the conquest of Canada; in 1761 he was named admiral of the fleet.

Anson, Sir **William Reynell.** b. at Walberton, Sussex, England, 1843; d. 1914. English jurist, university official, and member of Parliament. He was vice-chancellor of Oxford (1898–99) and Liberal Unionist member of Parliament (1899 *et seq.*). Author of *Principles of the English Law of Contract* (1879), the two-volume *Law and Custom of the Constitution* (1886, 1892), and others.

Ansonia (an.sō'ni.ạ). City in SW Connecticut, in New Haven County, on the Naugatuck River, ab. 10 mi. NW of New Haven: manufactures include copper, brass, and electrical goods. 18,706 (1950).

Anspach (äns'päċh). See **Ansbach.**

Anspach, Caroline of. See **Caroline of Anspach.**

Anspacher (äns'pä.kėr), **Louis Kaufman.** b. at Cincinnati, Ohio, March 1, 1878; d. at Nashville, Tenn., May 10, 1947. American writer. Author of *Tristan and Isolde* (1904), *Embarrassment of Riches* (1906), *Anne and the Archduke John* (1907), *All the King's Horses* (1920), *A Way of Life* (1937), *They Saw the Light* (1941), *The Story of Liberty* (1944), *Study of the Master Race Mentality* (1945), and others.

Ansted (an'sted), **David Thomas.** b. at London, Feb. 5, 1814; d. May 20, 1880. English geologist, professor of geology (1840–53) at King's College, London. He was a consultant (1850 *et seq.*) in mining and other fields. Author of *Geology* (1844), *Great Stone Book of Nature* (1863), and others.

Anster (an'stėr). Local name of **Anstruther, Easter** and **Wester.**

Anster, John. b. at Charleville, County Cork, Ireland, 1793; d. at Dublin, June 9, 1867. Irish scholar and poet, regius professor of civil law at Dublin (1850–67). He translated Goethe's *Faust* (1835, 1864), works by Schiller, La Motte-Fouqué, and others. Author of biographies (in the *North British Review,* 1847 *et seq.*) of Shelley, Swift, and others.

Anster Fair. Poem (1812) by William Tennant. It is notable chiefly for the fact that it served to introduce the Italian mock-heroic style into English literature.

Anstett (än'shtet), **Johann Protasius von.** b. at Strasbourg, 1766; d. at Frankfort on the Main, May 14, 1835. Russian diplomat. He represented Russia with plenary powers at the congress of Prague (1813). From 1815 to his death he was ambassador extraordinary and minister plenipotentiary to the German Confederation.

Anstey (an'sti), **Christopher.** b. at Brinkley, England, Oct. 31, 1724; d. at Chippenham, England, Aug. 3, 1805. English satirical poet. He was a fellow (1745) of King's College, Cambridge, where he wrote Latin verses and was refused the degree of master of arts because of his opposition to regulations. Author of *New Bath Guide* (1766) and *The Election Ball* (1776), letters in varied verse poking fun at Bath society, the first of which was in its day enormously popular.

Anstey, F. Pseudonym of **Guthrie, Thomas Anstey.**

Anstruther (an'struтн''ėr), **Easter** and **Wester.** [Locally called **Anster.**] Two civil parishes in Kilrenny and Anstruther, royal burgh, in C Scotland, in Fifeshire, situated on the Firth of Forth, ab. 9 mi. SE of St. Andrews, ab. 443 mi. N of London by rail. Anstruther is a seaport and market town. Pop. of Kilrenny and Anstruther, 3,184 (est. 1948).

Anta (än'tä). An Egyptian name of **Anaitis.**

Antaeus (an.tē'us). In Greek mythology, a Libyan giant and wrestler, son of Poseidon, god of the sea, and Gaea, the earth. He was invincible so long as he remained in contact with his mother. He compelled strangers in his country to wrestle with him, and built a house to Poseidon of their skulls. Hercules discovered the source of his strength, and, lifting him into the air, crushed him.

Antakia (än.tä.kē'ą), **Antakiya** (-yą), or **Antakya** (-kyä'). See **Antioch,** Turkey.

Antalcidas (an.tal'si.dąs). fl. in the first half of the 4th century B.C. Spartan diplomat, politician, and warrior. Dispatched (c393 B.C.) to undermine Athenian relations with the Persian satrap in Asia Minor, he proceeded (388 B.C.) to the Persian court, where aid against Athens was finally obtained, and shortly thereafter he defeated the Athenian fleet near the Hellespont. He exacted the "Peace of Antalcidas" (or "King's Peace") in 386, which provided that all of Asia Minor, as well as Cyprus and Clazomenae, would become Persian, while all remaining Greek city-states would be independent, except for Imbros, Lemnos, and Skyros, which remained Athenian.

Antalya (än.täl.yä'). *Il* (province or vilayet) in SW Turkey, bordering on the Gulf of Antalya (or Adalia). It consists of a flat plain where dates, figs, grapes, and other fruit are grown and a very hilly hinterland where subsistence agriculture is the main occupation. Capital, Antalya; area, 7,519 sq. mi.; pop. 312,102 (1950).

Antalya. [Also: **Antaliyeh;** former name, **Adalia;** in the Crusades, **Satali, Satalia, Sataliah, Satalieh;** in the Bible, **Attalia;** ancient name, **Attaleia.**] City in S Turkey, situated on the Gulf of Antalya, capital of the *il* (province or vilayet) of Antalya: flour mills, and macaroni, canning, and spirit factories. The city was built by Attalus II of Pergamum, and was a leading city of ancient Pamphylia. Louis VII of France launched the second Crusade from here. Pop. ab. 25,000.

Antalya, Gulf of. [Former name, **Gulf of Adalia;** ancient name, **Pamphylian Gulf;** Latin, **Pamphylicus Sinus.**] Arm of the Mediterranean Sea, on the S coast of Turkey, on which the city of Antalya is located. Length, ab. 100 mi.; width, ab. 40 mi.

Antara (än.tä'rą). [Also, **Antar** (-tär').] fl. 6th century. Arab poet and warrior. His part in a war between two related Arab tribes has become the basis of a folk romance in which he is the hero and ideal of Arab chivalry. The only poem now extant known to have come from his pen is in the *Muallaqat.* He is supposed by some scholars to have been, by birth, a Christian slave.

Antarctica (ant.ärk'ti.ką). [Also: **Antarctic Continent, the Antarctic** (ant.ärk'tik, -är'tik, ant'är"tik).] All that portion of land in the Southern Hemisphere which lies close to the Antarctic Circle and the South Pole. Explorations on the continent started as early as 1800 and have continued to the present day. Various countries have sponsored expeditions but Great Britain, the U.S., and Norway have been the most active. Voyages were made by James Cook (1772–75), James Weddell (1822–24, penetrating to 74°15′ S.), Dumont D'Urville (1837–40), Charles Wilkes (1838–42), James C. Ross (1839–43), the *Challenger* expedition (1874), the *Belgica* expedition (1897–99), C. E. Borchgrevink (1898–1900), and the *Discovery* expedition under Captain R. F. Scott (1901–04, to lat. 82°17′ S., the farthest point reached up to that date). Sir Ernest Shackleton penetrated (1908–09), to 88°23′ S. A notable scientific result of this last expedition was the location of the S magnetic pole at lat. 72°25′ S., long. 155°16′ E. Antarctic expeditions were led by Jean B. Charcot in 1903–05 and 1908–10, and by R. F. Scott and Roald Amundsen between 1910 and 1913, Amundsen attaining the South Pole on Dec. 17, 1911, and Scott reaching it Jan. 17, 1912. Valuable work was done by the Argentine government in establishing a number of meteorological stations. Since 1912 there have been numerous expeditions to Antarctic waters. Sir Ernest Shackleton and Sir Hubert Wilkins both made two trips to the continent. Rear Admiral Richard E. Byrd and Lincoln Ellsworth, both Americans, have made numerous expeditions and have brought back valuable information. Various countries that sent expeditions have laid claim to sections of Antarctica. Great Britain (Falkland Islands) and New Zealand (Ross Dependency) have actually annexed areas, while Australia, Norway, France, and the U.S. have merely laid claims. In late years, some South American nations have challenged certain of these claims and even some actual territorial holdings (perhaps most notably the British rights to the Falkland Islands, which have never been recognized by Argentina) and the situation is in a state of flux and indecision. No trace of animal life belonging to the land surface has yet been discovered in the Antarctic tract. Nearly all of the land is covered with ice and snow, but there are occasional bare mountain peaks. The climate is severely cold and windy. Peaks include Mount Erebus, an active volcano (13,200 ft.), and Mount Melbourne (ab. 8,500 ft.). Area, ab. 5,450,000 sq. mi.

Antarctic Circle (ant.ärk'tik, -är'tik, ant'är"tik). Line (shown as broken on most globes) hypothesized by geographers as the N extreme of Antarctica. It circles the globe (and parallels the equator) ab. 23½ degrees N of the South Pole.

Antarctic Ocean. That part of the ocean which is included between the South Pole and the Antarctic Circle.

Antares (an.tãr'ēz). A red star of the first magnitude, the middle one of three in the body of the Scorpion; α Scorpii.

Antelope Island (an'tę.lōp). [Also, **Church Island.**] Largest island in Great Salt Lake, Utah. Length, ab. 18 mi.

Antenor (an.tē'nǫr). fl. 6th century B.C. Athenian sculptor who executed the first bronze statues of Harmodius and Aristogiton which the Athenians set up in the Agora and which were carried off to Susa by Xerxes. After his conquest of Persia, Alexander the Great sent the statues back to Athens. He is also believed to be the creator of a statue of a woman in marble, which is still extant.

Antenor. In Greek legend, a Trojan, according to Homer the wisest of the elders. He was the host of Menelaus and Odysseus when they visited Troy, and strongly advised the Trojans to surrender Helen. His friendliness toward the Greeks in the end amounted, from the Trojan point of view, to treason.

Antequera (än.tā.kā'rä). [Latin, **Antiquaria.**] City in S Spain, in the province of Málaga, situated on the Guadalhorce River, ab. 20 mi. N of Málaga: center of a rich agricultural district; trades in olive oil, sugar, and grain; woolen, silk, and leather manufactures; marble quarries. Numerous caves and prehistoric monuments are in the vicinity. The town was captured from the Moslems in 1410. Pop. 37,531 (1940).

Anteros (an'tėr.os), Saint. [Also, **Anterus** (-us).] b. in Greece. Pope from 235 to 236, successor to Saint Pontianus. His tomb was discovered in the catacombs at Rome by De Rossi in 1854.

Anteros. In Greek mythology, a son of Aphrodite and Ares, and brother of Eros. He was the god of unhappy love, the avenger of unrequited affection: the opposite of Eros.

Antesians (an.tē'zhąnz). Name sometimes applied to several Andean Indian tribes. See **Andesians.**

Antevs (an'tevz; Swedish, än.tefs'), **Ernst Valdemar.** b. at Vartofta, Sweden, Nov. 20, 1888—. American geologist notable for research on glacial history, tree growth in relation to climate, and early American anthropology. A graduate (1917) of the University of Stockholm, he has been associated at Washington, D.C., with the Carnegie Institution (1922–23, 1928–29, 1934–40).

Antheil (an'tīl), **George.** b. at Trenton, N.J., 1900—. American pianist and composer. He studied at the Sternberg Conservatory, Philadelphia, and with Ernest Bloch, and received (1931) a Guggenheim award. He first attracted attention in the U.S. with his *Ballet Mécanique* (1925), which shocked conservative music listeners by its use of mechanical pianos and various electrical devices. His other compositions include *Zingareska* (first performed 1922), *American Symphony* (1937), *Symphony No. 4* (1943), and *Symphony No. 5* (1945); the operas *Transatlantic* (1929), and, with John Erskine, *Helen Retires* (1932); and musical scores for the films *Once in a Blue Moon, The Scoundrel,* and others. Composer also of much chamber music, a piano work, and several violin sonatas. He is the author of *Bad Boy of Music* (1945).

Anthemius (an.thē′mi.us). d. 472. Emperor of the West (467–472); son of Procopius and son-in-law of the eastern emperor Marcian. He was nominated emperor of the West by the eastern emperor Leo, on the application of Ricimer for a successor to Majorian, and was confirmed at Rome.

Anthemius. b. at Tralles, in Lydia; fl. 6th century. Greek mathematician and architect. He was one of the architects employed by the emperor Justinian in building (532–37) the church of Saint Sophia (or Hagia Sophia) at Constantinople. Author of a treatise on burning-glasses which contains the first recorded instance of the practical use of the directrix.

Anthology, The. Collection of several thousand short Greek poems by many authors, written for the most part in the elegiac meter. In it every period of Greek literature is represented, from the Persian war to the decadence of Byzantium. The first *Anthology* was compiled by Meleager of Gadara in the 1st century B.C., and to this additions were made by Philippus of Thessalonica about 40 A.D. In the collection by Agathias of Myrina (6th century) the poems are (for the first time) arranged by subjects. The so-called Palatinate Anthology, a version compiled probably in the 10th century by Constantius Cephalas, is the oldest one still extant.

Anthon (an′thǫn), **Charles.** b. at New York, Nov. 19, 1797; d. there, July 29, 1867. American classical scholar, leader in his time of Greek and Latin study based on German scholarship. He was a professor (1820–67) at Columbia College, and an editor of classical dictionaries including Lemprière's (2nd ed., 1833), and Smith's. Author of textbooks, including *A System of Latin Prosody and Metre* (1838) and *A System of Ancient and Medieval Geography* (1850), and of *Horatii Poemata* (1830), the first critical and interpretative edition of a classical author to appear in America.

Anthony (an′thǫ.ni, -tǫ-), Saint. [Also: **Antony;** called **"the Great."**] b. at Coma, Egypt, c251; d. c350. Egyptian hermit and early monastic founder. He withdrew (285) completely from society, after having already passed 15 years as a hermit; his solitary life on a mountain near the Nile River was, by his own statements, tormented by constant pressure from the Devil in a variety of forms. His sanctity attracted numerous disciples, whom he gathered (c300) into an ascetic community near Fayum, thus establishing the first monastery in Christian history. He emerged into society only twice, once to encourage martyrs (311), and again a few years before his death in order to attack Arianism. Saint Anthony and his temptations have been a favorite theme in literature and art since the Renaissance.

Anthony (an′thǫ.ni). City in S Kansas, county seat of Harper County. 2,792 (1950).

Anthony, Henry Bowen. b. at Coventry, R.I., April 1, 1815; d. at Providence, Sept. 2, 1884. American journalist and politician. He was editor (1838–60) of the Providence *Journal*, and served as a U.S. senator (1858–84).

Anthony, Katherine Susan. b. at Roseville, Ark., Nov. 27, 1877—. American biographical writer. She is the author of *Margaret Fuller* (1920), *Catherine the Great* (1925), *Queen Elizabeth* (1929), *Marie Antoinette* (1932), *Louisa May Alcott* (1938), *The Lambs* (1945), and *Dolly Madison, Her Life and Times* (1949). She attended Peabody College of Teachers, graduated (1905) from the University of Chicago, and studied at the universities of Heidelberg and Freiburg. Author also of *Feminism in Germany and Scandinavia* (1915), *Labor Laws of New York* (1917), and *Mothers Who Must Earn.*

Anthony, Susan Brownell. b. at Adams, Mass., Feb. 15, 1820; d. at Rochester, N.Y., March 13, 1906. American abolitionist and militant agitator for female and Negro suffrage, temperance, and women's civil rights. Her father's house was a gathering place for reformers such as William Ellery Channing, William Lloyd Garrison, and Frederick Douglass; she was associated with Amelia Bloomer, Lucy Stone, and others, especially with Elizabeth Cady Stanton, with whom she lectured and wrote. She was an organizer of the Woman's State Temperance Society of New York (c1852) and of the National Woman Suffrage Association (1869); after the latter merged (1890) with the American Woman Suffrage Association, she served (1892–1900) as president of the larger group. Arrested (1872) and tried for voting at Rochester, she refused to pay the fine. Coauthor of *History of Woman Suffrage* (1881–1900).

Anthony Absolute (ab′sǫ.löt), **Sir.** See **Absolute, Sir Anthony.**

Anthony Adverse (ad′vėrs). Historical novel by Hervey Allen, published in 1933, which had a sale of some 500,000 copies within two years after its appearance. Written in a romantic vein, it is set against a background of the Napoleonic era.

Anthony Branville (bran′vil), **Sir.** See **Branville, Sir Anthony.**

Anthony Chuzzlewit (chuz′l.wit). See **Chuzzlewit, Anthony.**

Anthony of Bourbon (bör′bǫn). English name of **Antoine de Bourbon.**

Anthony of Padua (pad̦′ū.a̦), Saint. [Also, **Antony.**] b. at Lisbon, Portugal, Aug. 15, 1195; d. near Padua, Italy, June 13, 1231. Franciscan friar, theologian, and preacher in France and Italy. He taught at Montpellier, Toulouse, and Padua. According to the legend, he one day preached to a school of fish and was heard with attention. There is a noted painting of him by Bartolomé Esteban Murillo in the cathedral at Seville. The figure of the saint was cut from the painting in 1874, but was recovered at New York and replaced. There is another painting of Anthony, also by Murillo, in the museum at Seville. In this painting, the saint is shown as kneeling, with one arm about the infant Christ, who is seated before him on an open book. Anthony was canonized by Pope Gregory IX in 1232.

Anthonys Nose (an′thǫ.niz). Promontory near the S entrance of the Highlands, in Westchester County, New York, projecting into the Hudson River from its E shore, near Peekskill.

Anti (än′tē). Province of the Inca empire of Peru, at the base of the eastern mountains, bordering the Ucayale valley: so called from the Indians who inhabited it. By some it has been supposed that the Andes took their name from this province.

Anti. [Also, **Chuncho.**] Collective term applied by the Inca to several Indian tribes in the lowlands of E Peru who spoke languages of the Arawakan stock. Principal tribes included in the Anti were the Campa, Piro, and Machiguenga.

Antibes (äṅ.tēb). [Ancient name, **Antipolis.**] Town in SE France, in the department of Alpes-Maritimes, situated on the Mediterranean Sea between the Gulf of Juan and the Gulf of Nice, ab. 13 mi. SW of Nice. It is a seaport and winter resort on the French Riviera, and one of the foremost horticultural centers in the region, shipping flowers to Paris and to foreign markets. It also has trade in such items as wine, fish, olives, and oil. In the vicinity is the beautiful Cap d'Antibes, an internationally popular resort. The town was founded by the Greeks. 23,574 (1946).

Antic Hay. Novel (1923) by Aldous Huxley.

Anti-Comintern Pact (an.ti.kom′in.tėrn, -tī-). Treaty signed on Nov. 25, 1936, by Germany and Japan. It denounced the Communist International and bound the signatory powers to take certain joint steps against its subversive activities. By design, the Pact left room for further signatures, and among the nations that later added their names were Italy in 1937, Spain and Hungary in 1939, and the Japanese-sponsored Nanking government of China in 1941.

Anti-Corn Law League. Association formed in 1839, with headquarters at Manchester, England, to further the repeal of the British corn laws. Among its leaders were Richard Cobden, John Bright, George William Frederick Villiers, Joseph Hume, and John Arthur Roebuck.

Anticosti (an.ti.kos′ti). Thinly inhabited island in the province of Quebec, Canada, situated in the Gulf of St. Lawrence, NE of the Gaspé Peninsula. It is swampy, rocky, and unfruitful. The chief settlement is Port Menier. Length, ab. 135 mi.; greatest width, ab. 35 mi.; area, ab. 3,043 sq. mi.

Anticyra (an.tis′i.ra̦). In ancient geography, a city in Locris, Greece, situated near Naupactus.

Anticyra. In ancient geography, a city in Phocis, Greece, situated on the Corinthian Gulf. It was noted for the hellebore (the ancient remedy for madness) obtained in its neighborhood.

Anticyra. In ancient geography, a city in Thessaly, Greece, situated on the Sperchius. Like Anticyra in Phocis, it was noted for hellebore, the ancient remedy for madness.

Antietam (an.tē′tạm). Creek in S Pennsylvania and W Maryland, which joins the Potomac River ab. 6 mi. N of Harpers Ferry. On its banks near Sharpsburg, Sept. 17, 1862, a battle (called by the Confederates the battle of Sharpsburg) was fought between Union forces (87,164, of whom about 60,000 bore the brunt of the battle) under George Brinton McClellan, and Confederates (40,000 according to Robert E. Lee, 45,000 to 70,000 according to Edward Alfred Pollard, 97,000 according to McClellan) under Lee. The total loss of the Union army was 12,410 (2,108 killed); of the Confederates, 11,172. Other estimates of the Confederate loss are 8,000 to 26,000. Lee retreated across the Potomac on the 18th. The battle has been variously described as a Union victory and as too indecisive to be considered either a victory or a defeat for either side.

Anti-Federalist Party. [Also, **Anti-Federal Party.**] In U.S. history, the name given to those elements which opposed the adoption and ratification of the Constitution of the U.S., and which, failing in this, strongly favored the strict construction of the Constitution. Its fundamental principle was opposition to the strengthening of the national government at the expense of the states. Soon after the close of Washington's first administration (1793) the name Anti-Federalist went out of use, Republican and afterward Democratic-Republican taking its place.

Antigo (an′ti.gō). City in C Wisconsin, county seat of Langlade County: manufactures of wood products and processed cheese; marketing center for potatoes. 9,902 (1950).

Antigone (an.tig′ọ.nē). In Greek legend, a daughter of Oedipus by his mother Jocasta. She accompanied Oedipus, as a faithful daughter, in his wanderings until his death at Colonus; she then returned to Thebes. According to Sophocles, Haemon, the son of Creon (who in other accounts was then dead), fell in love with her. Contrary to the edict of Creon, she buried the body of her brother Polynices, who had been slain in single combat with his brother Eteocles, and (according to Sophocles) was shut up in a cave where she perished by her own hand. Haemon also slew himself. Various other accounts of her life and death are given.

Antigone. Tragedy by Sophocles, of uncertain date.

Antigone (äṅ.tē.gon). Tragedy by Robert Garnier, published in 1580.

Antigone. Tragedy by Jean de Rotrou, produced in 1637.

Antigone (än.tē′gō.nā). Tragedy by Count Vittorio Alfieri, a sequel to *Polynices*, published in 1783.

Antigonidae (an.ti.gon′i.dē). The descendants of Antigonus I of Macedonia, one of the generals of Alexander the Great. The principal members of the family were Demetrius I (Poliorcetes), king of Macedonia (d. 283 B.C.), son of Antigonus I; Antigonus II (Gonatas), king of Macedonia (d. 239 B.C.), son of Demetrius I; Demetrius of Cyrene (d. 250 B.C.), son of Demetrius I; Demetrius II, king of Macedonia (d. 229 B.C.), son of Antigonus II; Antigonus III (Doson), king of Macedonia (d. 220 B.C.), son of Demetrius of Cyrene; Philip V, king of Macedonia (d. 179 B.C.), son of Demetrius II; and Perseus, king of Macedonia, conquered by the Romans in 168 B.C.

Antigonish (an″ti.gọ.nish′). Seaport, capital of Antigonish County, Nova Scotia, Canada, situated on George Bay ab. 38 mi. E of Pictou, on the E end of the peninsula. It is the seat of St. Francis Xavier University. 3,196 (1951).

Antigonus (an.tig′ọ.nus). b. c80 B.C.; executed at Antioch, 37 B.C. King of Judea who reigned in the period 40–37 B.C.; the last Maccabean king. He was defeated by Herod, the son of Antipater, and put to death by Mark Antony as a common criminal.

Antigonus. Character in Shakespeare's *The Winter's Tale;* a lord of Sicilia.

Antigonus. In John Fletcher's *Humorous Lieutenant*, an old and licentious king.

Antigonus I (of *Macedonia*). [Surnamed **Cyclops** or **Monophthalmos**, meaning the "One-Eyed."] b. c382 B.C.; killed at the battle of Ipsus, 301 B.C. King of Macedonia (306–301); one of the generals of Alexander the Great. After the death of Alexander he received the provinces of Greater Phrygia, Lycia, and Pamphylia. He carried on war against Perdiccas and Eumenes, made extensive conquests in Asia, assumed the title of king in 306, and was overthrown at Ipsus by a coalition of his enemies.

Antigonus II (of *Macedonia*). [Called **Antigonus Gonatas.**] b. c320 B.C.; d. 239 B.C. King of Macedonia (283–239); son of Demetrius Poliorcetes. He assumed the title in 283, after the death of his father, but did not actually reign until 276. He suppressed the Celtic invasion and was temporarily driven from his land by Pyrrhus in 273.

Antigonus III (of *Macedonia*). [Called **Antigonus Doson.**] d. 220 B.C. King of Macedonia (229–220); nephew of Antigonus II and a great-grandson of Antigonus I, Alexander's general. He was appointed guardian of Philip, son of Demetrius II, and on the death of Demetrius (229 B.C.) he married his widow, and ascended the throne. He successfully supported Aratus and the Achaean League against Cleomenes, king of Sparta, and the Aetolians, and defeated the former at Sellasia in 221. He is said to have been dubbed "Doson" because "he was always about to give, and never did."

Antigonus of Carystus (kạ.ris′tus) or **Antigonus Carystius** (-ti.us). b. at Carystus, Euboea; fl. c250 B.C. Greek writer, chiefly at Pergamum. Author of biographical works on the philosophers and of a natural-history work entitled *Collection of Wonderful Tales*, portions of which are still extant.

Antigua (an.tē′gạ). One of the Leeward Islands in the Caribbean Sea, SE of Puerto Rico: a British possession. The chief products are sugar, molasses, and rum. It is also the site of U.S. military and naval bases, and a major stop for Caribbean air flights. It was discovered in 1493 by Columbus and settled in 1632. Capital, St. Johns; area, 108 sq. mi.; pop. 40,777 (1946), 43,504 (est. 1948).

Antigua (än.tē′gwä). [Also: **Antigua** (or **Old**) **Guatemala, Guatemala Antigua.**] Town in S Guatemala, capital of Sacatepéquez department, ab. 24 mi. SW of Guatemala City. The original city of Guatemala, founded 1527, was destroyed (1541) by a flood, apparently from the Volcán de Agua; refounded (1542) on a new site, it was almost completely destroyed by the great earthquake of July 29, 1773; the capital was then removed to its present site, but the town of Antigua grew up about the ruins of the second city. 10,691 (1950).

Antihuenó (än.tē.wā.nō′) or **Antigüenú** (-gwā.nö′). d. 1564. Araucanian Indian of Chile who, in 1559, was made *toqui* (war-chief) of his tribe. In 1563 he defeated and killed a son of the Spanish governor Villagra at Mariguenu, attempted to take Concepción but failed, and drove the Spaniards from Cañete and Arauco, but was defeated and killed in an attack on Angol the following year.

Anti-Lebanon (an.ti.leb′ạ.nọn). [French, **Anti-Liban** (äṅ.tē.lē.bäṅ); ancient name, **Anti-Libanus** (an.ti.lib′ạ-nus).] Mountain range in E Lebanon and SW Syria, E of the Lebanon range, and separated from it by the valleys of the Orontes and Litani rivers. Its highest peak is Mount Hermon (9,232 ft.).

Antilles (an.til′ēz; French, äṅ.tēy′). [Spanish, **Antillas** (än.tē′yäs).] General name for the West Indies, in the Caribbean Sea SE of the U.S., excluding the Bahamas. The Greater Antilles comprise Cuba, Jamaica, Hispaniola, and Puerto Rico; the Lesser Antilles (sometimes also called the Caribbees) comprise four chief groups: the Virgin Islands (U.S. and Great Britain), the Leeward Islands (Great Britain and France), the Windward Islands (Great Britain and France), and the islands off the N coast of Venezuela (Netherlands and Venezuela).

Antilochus (an.til′ọ.kus). In Greek legend, a son of Nestor conspicuous in the Trojan War. He was a close friend of Achilles and was chosen to break to him the news of Patroclus's death. Memnon (or, in another account, Hector) slew him and Achilles avenged his death, as he did that of Patroclus. The three friends were buried in the same mound, and were seen by Odysseus walking together over the asphodel meadows of the lower world.

Antimachus (an.tim′ạ.kus). [Called **"the Colophonian."**] fl. c410 B.C. Greek epic and elegiac poet of Claros, a part of the dominion of Colophon. His chief work was the *Thebais*, a voluminous epic poem. His elegy on Lyde, his wife (or mistress), was highly praised in antiquity. He also published a critical edition of Homer.

Anti-Masonic Party (an″ti.mạ.son′ik). In U.S. politics, a political party which opposed the alleged influence of freemasonry in civil affairs. It originated in W New York after the kidnaping, in 1826, of William Morgan, who had threatened, it was said, to disclose the secrets of the order. A national convention nominated William Wirt for the presidency in 1831, thus making it the first "third party" in U.S. political history. The organization was soon after absorbed by the Whigs.

Anti-Matrimony. Comedy (1910) by the American dramatist Percy MacKaye. It satirizes the effect of Ibsen and other Continental dramatists on American would-be intellectuals.

Anti-Monopoly parties. [Also called **Independent** or **Reform parties.**] In U.S. history, political organizations (1873–76) which drew their following from agrarian elements in the Midwest and parts of the Far West and called for government reforms similar to those advocated by the Granger movement. These organizations vanished after the national elections of 1876.

Antin (däṅ.taṅ), Duc **d'.** [Original name, **Louis-Antoine de Pardaillan de Gondrin.**] b. 1665; d. at Paris, Dec. 2, 1736. French courtier; son of Madame de Montespan. He gained the favor of Louis XIV and the dauphin, and was a member of the regency under the duke of Orleans.

Antin (an′tin), **Mary.** b. at Polotsk (or Polotzk), Russia, 1881; d. 1949. American author and authority on the immigrant. She came to the U.S. in 1894, and studied at Columbia University. She is best known for *The Promised Land* (1912). Author also of *From Polotzk to Boston* (1899), and *They Who Knock at Our Gates* (1914).

Antinomian Controversy (an.ti.nō′mi.ạn). In American colonial history, a celebrated theological controversy in the Massachusetts Bay colony which involved Mistress Anne Hutchinson and her interpretation of the doctrine of the Covenant of Grace. It had its inception (1636) at Boston, where her lectures created alarm among the New England clergy; perhaps the central point of her theological differences with the established clergy was her insistence that they stressed too much the doctrine of salvation by works and neglected the basic Protestant principle of salvation by faith. Her teachings threatened a revolution in the prevailing concept of moral law, and finally became an issue of high policy in Massachusetts. Mrs. Hutchinson's movement was suppressed; she was examined by a synod, which found her guilty of 80 theological errors, and was brought before the General Court, where she asserted that she had been in communication with the Holy Ghost. In punishment, she was excommunicated (March, 1638) and banished from the Massachusetts Bay colony.

Antinori (än.tē.nō′rē), Marchese **Orazio.** b. at Perugia, Italy, Oct. 28, 1811; d. at Marefia, Africa, Aug. 26, 1882. Italian explorer and scientist; a founder of the Italian Geographical Society. He explored the Upper Nile (1860–61) and later (1869) the territory N of Abyssinia. In 1876 he led a scientific expedition into the Shoa region and established the station Marefia, where he died.

Antinoüs (an.tin′ọ.us). b. in Bithynia, Asia Minor; fl. c110–130 A.D. Page, attendant, and favorite of the emperor Hadrian. After he was drowned in the Nile during a trip to Egypt, Hadrian established a cult to deify him, named cities in his honor, and commissioned statues which portray him as an ideal of youthful beauty.

Antioch (an′ti.ok). Town in C California, in Contra Costa County, NE of San Francisco: shipping point for industrial and agricultural products; canneries. 11,051 (1950).

Antioch. [Turkish and Arabic, **Antakya**; Arabic, also, **Antakia, Antakiya**; Greek, **Antiokheia** (an″ti.ọ.kē′ạ); Latin, **Caesarea,** or **Antiochia** (-kī′ạ).] City in S Turkey, in the *il* (province or vilayet) of Hatay (formerly Alexandretta), on the Orontes River ab. 15 mi. from the Mediterranean Sea: site of Saint Paul's first ministry. It was founded by Seleucus c300 B.C., at that time at a point on the borders of Pisidia and Pamphylia, was the capital of Syria until 65 B.C., and rose to great splendor. It was called "the Crown of the East," and "Antioch the Beautiful." Under the early Roman Empire it was a famous market town, the most important after Rome and Alexandria, and one of the earliest and most influential seats of Christianity, the center of a patriarchate. It was the scene of a serious riot in 387 A.D., suppressed by Theodosius. It was often ravaged by earthquakes (especially in 115, 341, 458, 507–508, and 525–526), was destroyed by Chosroes in 538 and by the Moslems in 635, and was besieged and taken by the Crusaders in 1098. From 1099 until its capture by the Egyptian sultan in 1268 it was the seat of a Christian principality. It passed to the Turks in 1516. It is now an unimportant town with few relics of antiquity. In 1872 it was devastated by an earthquake. Pop. ab. 28,000.

Antioche (äṅ.tyosh). *Chanson de geste* of the group entitled *Le Chevalier au Cygne*. It narrates the exploits of the Christian host during the Crusades in attacking and then defending Antioch.

Antiochus (an.tī′ọ.kus). In the drama *Pericles, Prince of Tyre*, attributed to Shakespeare, the king of Antioch.

Antiochus. In Philip Massinger's *Believe as You List*, the king of Lower Asia, a fugitive; the son of a daughter of Charles V of Portugal.

Antiochus I (of *Commagene*). d. c30 B.C. King of Commagene, a petty principality between the Euphrates and Mount Taurus, capital Samosata, at one time a part of the Syrian kingdom of the Seleucidae. He concluded (64 B.C.) a peace with Pompey, and later (49 B.C.) supported him in the civil war with Caesar.

Antiochus II (of *Commagene*). fl. late 1st century B.C. King of Commagene, successor to Mithridates I. He was summoned to Rome and executed (29 B.C.) for having caused the murder of an ambassador sent to Rome by his brother.

Antiochus III (of *Commagene*). fl. early 1st century A.D.; d. 17 A.D. King of Commagene; probably the father of Antiochus IV of Commagene. Very little is known about either his accomplishments or dates of rule.

Antiochus IV (of *Commagene*). [Called **Antiochus IV Epiphanes.**] fl. middle of 1st century A.D. King of Commagene; probably a son of Antiochus III of Commagene. He was a friend of Caligula, who restored (38 A.D.) to him the kingdom of Commagene, which had been made a Roman province at the death of his father in 17 A.D. Subsequently, however, he was deposed by Caligula, but was restored (41 A.D.) on the accession of Claudius. He was finally deprived (72 A.D.) of his kingdom.

Antiochus I (of *Syria*). [Called **Antiochus I Soter.**] b. 324 B.C.; killed c261 B.C. King of Syria (280–261); son of Seleucus I Nicator. It is said that when he fell sick, from love of Stratonice, the young wife of his father, the latter, on the advice of the physician Erasistratus, allowed Stratonice to marry his son, and invested him with the government of Upper Asia, allowing him the title of king. On the death of his father, Antiochus succeeded to the whole of his dominions, but relinquished his claims to Macedonia on the marriage of Antigonus II of Macedonia to Phila, the daughter of Seleucus and Stratonice.

Antiochus II (of *Syria*). [Called **Antiochus II Theos.**] killed 247 B.C. King of Syria; son of Antiochus I, whom he succeeded in 261 B.C. He became involved in a ruinous war with Ptolemy Philadelphus, king of Egypt, during which Syria was further weakened by the revolt of the provinces of Parthia and Bactria, Arsaces establishing the Parthian empire in c250 B.C., and Theodotus the independent kingdom of Bactria about the same time. Peace was concluded with Egypt in 250 B.C., Antiochus being obliged to reject his wife Laodice, and to marry Berenice, the daughter of Ptolemy. On the death of Ptolemy (247 B.C.), he recalled Laodice (who, it is thought, caused his murder) and also Berenice and her son. The connection between Syria and Egypt is referred to in Daniel, xi. 6.

Antiochus III (of *Syria*). [Called **Antiochus the Great.**] b. c241 B.C.; d. 187 B.C. King of Syria (223–187 B.C.), the most famous of the Seleucidae. He was the son of Seleucus II, and grandson of Antiochus II, and succeeded his brother Seleucus Ceraunus at the age of 15. His epithet "the Great" was earned by the magnitude of his enterprises rather than by what he accomplished. He subdued (220 B.C.) his rebellious brothers Molo and Alexander, satraps of Media and Persia, and was forced (after having undertaken an aggressive war against Ptolemy Philopator) by the battle of Raphia, near Gaza, to relinquish (217 B.C.) his claims to Coele-Syria and Palestine. He defeated and killed (214 B.C.) Achaeus, the rebellious governor of Asia Minor; attempted (212–205 B.C.) to regain the former provinces Parthia and Bactria; and was compelled to recognize (205 B.C.) the independence of Parthia. The victory of Paneas (198 B.C.) gave him back the Egyptian provinces of Coele-Syria and Palestine. He made peace, however, with Ptolemy Epiphanes, to whom he betrothed his daughter Cleopatra, promising Coele-Syria and Palestine as a dowry. He conquered (196 B.C.) the Thracian Chersonese from Macedonia; received (195 B.C.) Hannibal at his court; carried on (192–189 B.C.) a war with the Romans who demanded the restoration of the Egyptian provinces and the Thracian Chersonese; was defeated at Thermopylae in 191, and at Magnesia in 190; and sustained naval losses at Chios (191) and at Myonnesus (190). He purchased peace by consenting to the surrender of all his European possessions, and his Asiatic possessions as far as the Taurus, the payment of 15,000 Euboean talents within 12 years, and the surrender of Hannibal, who escaped, and by giving up his elephants and ships of war. Antiochus was killed by his subjects in an attempt to plunder the rich temple of Elymais to pay the Romans, an event which, like his defeat by the Romans, is supposed by some to be referred to in Daniel, xi. 18, 19.

Antiochus IV (of *Syria*). [Called **Antiochus IV Epiphanes.**] d. 163 B.C. King of Syria (175–c163 B.C.); son of Antiochus III. He reconquered Armenia, which had been lost by his father, and made war on Egypt in the period 171–168 B.C., recovering Coele-Syria and Palestine. His policy of destroying the Jewish religion, in pursuance of which he took Jerusalem by storm in 170 B.C. (when he desecrated the temple), and again in 168 B.C., led to the successful revolt under Mattathias, the father of the Maccabees (167 B.C.).

Antiochus V (of *Syria*). [Called **Antiochus V Eupator.**] b. c173 B.C.; d. 162 B.C. King of Syria (163–162 B.C.); son of Antiochus IV, whom he succeeded at the age of nine years, under the guardianship of Lysias. He concluded a peace with the Jews, who had revolted under his father, and was defeated and killed by Demetrius Soter (the son of Seleucus Philopator) who laid claim to the throne.

Antiochus VII (of *Syria*). [Called **Antiochus VII Sidetes.**] b. c159 B.C.; d. c129 B.C. King of Syria (c139–c129 B.C.); second son of Demetrius Soter. He carried on war with the Jews, taking Jerusalem in 133 B.C., after which he concluded peace with them on favorable terms. He was killed in a war with the Parthians.

Antiochus VIII (of *Syria*). [Called **Antiochus VIII Grypus,** meaning "the Hook-nosed."] d. 96 B.C. King of Syria (125–96 B.C.); second son of Demetrius Nicator.

Antiochus XIII (of *Syria*). [Called **Antiochus XIII Asiaticus.**] King of Syria, the last of the Seleucidae. He took refuge in Rome during the mastery of Tigranes in Syria, in the period 83–69 B.C. Given (69 B.C.) possession of the kingdom by Lucullus, he was deprived (64 B.C.) of it by Pompey.

Antiochus of Ascalon (as'ka̜.lon). b. in Palestine; fl. early in the 1st century B.C. Greek eclectic philosopher, founder of the so-called Fifth Academy. He sought to reconcile the philosophies of the stoic Mnesarchus and the skeptic Philo, each of whom had been his teacher.

Antiochus of Syracuse (sir'a̜.kūs). fl. 5th century B.C. Greek historian. His *History of Syracuse* provided a record to 424 B.C. and was used as source by Thucydides. He also wrote an account of the Greek colonization of Italy which is referred to by Strabo and Dionysius of Halicarnassus.

Antiope (an.tī'o̜.pē). In Greek legend, daughter of the Boeotian river-god Asopus, and mother, by Zeus, of Amphio and Zethus.

Antiope. In Greek legend, sister or daughter of Hippolyte, queen of the Amazons, and wife of Theseus.

Antioquia (än.tyō'kyä). Department in NW Colombia: chiefly a mining region. Capital, Medellín; area, 25,402 sq. mi.; pop. 1,486,300 (est. 1950).

Antioquia. Town in NW Colombia, in Antioquia department, on the Cauca River, at an altitude of ab. 2,000 ft. Pop. under 5,000 (1938).

Antiparos (an.tip'a̜.ros). [Ancient name, **Oliaros.**] Island in the Cyclades, SW of Paros, celebrated for a stalactite grotto. Length, ab. 8 mi.

Antipater (an.tip'a̜.tėr). b. c398 B.C.; d. 319 B.C. Macedonian general and diplomat. He was appointed (334) regent of Macedonia by Alexander during the expedition to the east. Earlier service, partly under Philip, included a mission (346) to Athens as ambassador, and negotiations for peace after the battle at Chaeroneia (338). As regent, he suppressed Spartan revolt through a victory at Megalopolis (331). On Alexander's death (323) the partition of the empire left Macedonia under his control as joint ruler with Craterus; he defeated a Greek attempt (322) to throw off Macedonian rule in the Lamian war. He is believed by some scholars to have died of illness and by others to have been killed in battle.

Antipater. [Surnamed **"the Idumean."**] d. 43 B.C. Procurator of Judea, governor of Idumea, and the father of Herod the Great. He secured, by his participation in the Alexandrine war (48 B.C.), the confirmation by Caesar of his political tool Hyrcanus as high priest in 47 B.C., and was himself appointed procurator of Judea in c46 B.C.

Antipater. d. 4 B.C. Son of Herod the Great by his first wife, Doris. He is described by Josephus as a "mystery of wickedness," and was put to death for conspiring against the life of his father, after having previously succeeded, by arousing his father's suspicions, in bringing about the death of Alexander and Aristobulos, Herod's sons by Mariamne, his second wife.

Antipater, Lucius Coelius. fl. 123 B.C. Roman jurist and historian. He wrote a history of the second Punic war, fragments of which are extant.

Antipatrea or **Antipatria** (an.ti.pat'ri.a̜, -pā'tri.a̜). Ancient name of **Berat.**

Antiphanes (an.tif'a̜.nēz). b. c408 B.C.; d. c334 B.C. Greek comic poet, outstanding writer of the so-called Middle Comedy. He is believed not to have been a native Athenian, but he settled there and began writing in c387 B.C. Titles of more than 200 of his plays are known, as well as fragments of text from a smaller number.

Antiphellos (an.ti.fel'os). In ancient geography, a town on the SW coast of Lycia, Asia Minor. Its site contains a Lycian necropolis of rock-cut tombs, which are architecturally important because the façades are in exact reproduction of a framed construction of square wooden beams, with doors and windows of paneled work, and ceilings of round poles laid closely together. These tombs evidently represent ancient dwellings, and the imitation is carried out in some of the interiors. There is also an ancient theater, the *cavea* of which is well preserved, with 26 tiers of seats.

Antiphilus (an.tif'i.lus). fl. 2nd half of 4th century B.C. Greek painter. His work included portraits of Philip of Macedonia, Alexander the Great, and others.

Antipholus of Ephesus (an.tif'o̜.lus; ef'e̜.sus) and **Antipholus of Syracuse** (sir'a̜.kūs). In Shakespeare's *Comedy of Errors*, twin brothers, the first of a violent and the latter of a mild nature. They are the sons of Aegeon, a merchant of Syracuse.

Antiphon (an'ti.fon). b. at Rhamnus, Attica, c480 B.C.; executed at Athens, 411 B.C. Athenian orator and politician, the oldest of the "ten Attic orators." A member of the aristocratic party, he was condemned to death (411 B.C.) for his share in establishing government by the Four Hundred. A professional writer of speeches, his work was sold to litigants; his own trial is the only instance of public delivery by him of one of his own speeches.

Antipodes (an.tip'o̜.dēz). Cluster of small uninhabited islands in the South Pacific, ab. 450 mi. SE of New Zealand, to which they belong. They are so called from their nearly antipodal position to Greenwich (near London), from which longitude is counted. Area, ab. 24 sq. mi.

Antipolis (an.tip'o̜.lis). Ancient name of **Antibes.**

Antipsara (an.tip'sa̜.ra̜). Small island in the E Aegean Sea, just W of Psara.

Antiquaria (an.ti.kwãr'i.a̜). Latin name of **Antequera.**

Antiquary, The. Novel by Sir Walter Scott, published in 1816. It is so named after its principal character, Jonathan Oldbuck the Antiquary, and repeats the missing-heir plot which Scott had already used in *Guy Mannering*.

Antique (än.tē'kā). Province of the Philippine Republic, occupying most of the W coast of Panay island and several offshore islands. It is bordered on the W by Sulu Sea, on the S by the Gulf of Panay, on the E by Cápiz and Iloilo provinces, and on the N by Cápiz and the Sibuyan Sea. It is separated from the E portion of the island by a mountain range with peaks as high as 6,000 ft. Capital, San José de Buenavista; area, 1,034 sq. mi.; pop. 233,506 (1948).

Antiquity of Freedom, The. Poem by William Cullen Bryant, inspired by his fight against oligarchy at home and by his outspoken sympathy with struggles for freedom abroad. It is included in a volume of poems published in 1842. Its theme may be most clearly expressed in Bryant's own words:

O Freedom! thou are not, as poets dream,
A fair young girl, with light and delicate limbs. . .
A bearded man,
Armed to the teeth, art thou; one mailed hand
Grasps the broad shield, and one the sword; thy brow,
Glorious in beauty though it be, is scarred
With tokens of old wars. . . .

Anti-Rent Party. In U.S. politics, a party in the state of New York which had its origin in dissatisfaction among the tenants under the patroon system which then prevailed in the E part of the state. The tenants refused to pay rent in 1839, resisted force, and a few years later carried their opposition into politics. The matter was settled by compromise in 1850.

Anti-Saloon League. Organization established at Oberlin, Ohio, in 1893, for the purpose of preventing the liquor traffic by legislative means. This original unit, progenitor of the "Ohio plan," served as the model for similar local units. The Anti-Saloon League of America, founded at Washington, D.C., in 1895, was one of the major forces in securing the passage of the Eighteenth Amendment establishing national prohibition in 1919. However, the social evils prevailing during the following decade, which saw the rise of bootlegging and gangsterism, contributed toward lowering the League's prestige in the eyes of many voters. After the repeal of the Eighteenth Amendment in 1933, the League reverted to operations on a local basis.

Antisana (än.tē.sä'nä). Village in N Ecuador, on the slope of Mount Antisana; one of the highest inhabited spots in the world (ab. 13,350 ft.). Pop. under 5,000 (est. 1944).

Antisana, Mount. [Spanish, **Cerro Antisana.**] Volcano of the Ecuadorian Andes, ab. 35 mi. SE of Quito. It was formerly believed to be the only great mountain in the world almost immediately upon the equator. 19,335 ft.

Antistates (an.tis'tạ.tēz). fl. middle of 6th century B.C. Greek architect, associated with Callaeschrus and Porinus in planning and beginning the great temple of Zeus at Athens in the time of Pisistratus (c560 B.C.). This work was interrupted by the downfall of Pisistratus, resumed by the Roman architect Cossutius in the time of Antiochus IV of Syria (Antiochus Epiphanes; 175–163 B.C.), and finished by the emperor Hadrian. The unfinished building was compared by Aristotle with the pyramids of Egypt.

Antisthenes (an.tis'thẹ.nēz). b. at Athens, c444 B.C.; d. there after 371 B.C. Athenian philosopher, founder of the school of the Cynics. He was a pupil of Socrates and taught in a gymnasium at Athens.

Anti-Taurus (an.ti.tô'rus). Range of mountains in C Turkey, lying NE of and parallel to the Taurus, regarded as a continuation of the Ala-Dagh range. They run roughly E and W for a distance of ab. 150 mi. and reach a height of 12,481 ft.

Antium (an'shum, -shi.um). Ancient name of **Anzio.**

Antivari (än.tē'vä.rē). Italian name of **Bar,** Yugoslavia.

Antlers (ant'lėrz). Town in SE Oklahoma, county seat of Pushmataha County, in a lumbering region: processing center for lumber. It was the site of the "Locke War" (1892–93). Pop. 2,506 (1950).

Antofagasta (än"tō.fä.gäs'tä). Province in N Chile, acquired from Bolivia by treaty (1884). Capital, Antofagasta; area, 47,502 sq. mi.; pop. 196,585 (est. 1950).

Antofagasta. Seaport in NW Chile, the capital of Antofagasta province and principal commercial center of N Chile; chief port for Bolivian commerce: minerals; rail and air service. Ceded to Chile by Bolivia in 1884. Pop. 49,106 (est. 1950).

Antofalla (än.tō.fä'yä). [Spanish, **Volcán Antofalla.**] Volcanic mountain in NW Argentina. Elevation, ab. 20,900 ft.

Antogast (än'tō.gäst). Small town in SW Germany, in the *Land* (state) of Baden, French Zone, on the slope of the Kniebis near Oberkirch: tourist resort.

Antoine (äṅ.twȧn), Père. [Original name, **Antonio de Sedilla.**] b. in Granada, Spain, 1748; d. at New Orleans, La., 1829. Spanish Capuchin priest at New Orleans. He arrived (1780) in Louisiana, where he became curé (1785) and auxiliary vicar (1787) of St. Louis parish. The governor, fearing that he intended to establish an Inquisition in the colony, had Antoine sent back to Spain in 1790, ostensibly for "canonical reasons" but nonetheless bound in irons. Antoine returned (1795) to his parish at the order of the Spanish king, who supported him (1805) in his dispute with superior ecclesiastics in Louisiana. The transfer of the colony to France and later to the U.S. found him loyal to Spain and acting (1813–16) as Spanish secret agent. In relations with parishioners, he invariably showed remarkable devotion, and his death was mourned by the entire city.

Antoine, André Léonard. b. at Limoges, France, 1858; d. at Camaret, in Brittany, France, in October, 1943. French actor, stage director, manager, and dramatic critic, who founded (1887) the Théâtre Libre, France's first naturalistic theater. For eight years Antoine managed to maintain his theater with meager means, producing 124 plays, among them many naturalistic dramas by Eugène Brieux, François de Curel, Tolstoy, Ibsen, and Hauptman. In 1894, worn out by his duties, he withdrew from the Théâtre Libre, which was a small subscription theater and always suffered financial difficulties. Three years later, after a season (1896) with the Odéon, he opened his own popular theater, the Théâtre Antoine (1897–1906), where he gave a memorable production of Henri François Becque's *La Parisienne* (1897), playing the main male role to Mme. Réjane's Clotilde. After the first World War, he became a drama critic, and was honored as the dean of the French theater.

Antoine de Bourbon (äṅ.twȧn dẹ bör.bôṅ). [English, **Anthony of Bourbon.**] b. in Picardy, April 22, 1518; d. Nov. 17, 1562. French nobleman; son of Charles de Bourbon, duke of Vendôme; husband (1548 *et seq.*) of Jeanne d'Albret. He became king of Navarre in 1555.

Antommarchi (än.tōm.mär'kē), **Francesco.** b. in Corsica, c1780; d. April 3, 1838. Italian surgeon, physician (1818 *et seq.*) to Napoleon at St. Helena. He wrote *Les Derniers moments de Napoléon* (1823).

Antonelli (än.tō.nel'lē), **Giacomo.** b. at Sonnino, Italy, April 2, 1806; d. at Rome, Nov. 6, 1876. Italian prelate and diplomat. He became a cardinal in 1847 and was selected by Pope Pius IX to be premier of the papal states' first constitutional ministry (1848).

Antonello da Messina (än.tō.nel'lō dä mes.sē'nä). [Original name, **Antonello di Giovanni degli Antonj.**] b. at Messina, Sicily, c1430; d. there, in February, 1479. Italian painter, said to have introduced oil painting from Flanders into Italy. Having studied with the followers of Jan van Eyck, he certainly brought, on his return to Italy, a Flemish sense of design expressed through detail. He worked a good deal at Venice. His works include *Saint Jerome in his Study* and *Christ on the Cross* (National Gallery, London), *Saint Sebastian* (Dresden), *Calvary* (Antwerp), *Madonna del Rosario* (Messina), and others.

Antonescu (än.tō.nes'kö), **Ion.** b. in Rumania, 1882; executed there, 1946. Rumanian military and political leader. A member of the fascist Iron Guard organization, he was prime minister (1940–44) until arrested (1944) and sentenced to death for treason.

Antongil Bay (äṅ.tôṅ.zhēl). [French, **Baie d'Antongil.**] Bay in Madagascar, on the E coast of the N part of the island.

Antoniadi (äṅ.to.nyȧ.dē), **Eugen.** b. at Constantinople, March 10, 1870—. French astronomer, of Greek parentage. He has devoted his life to planetary studies at Mendon Observatory. Author of *La Planète Mars* (1930) and *La Planète Mercure* (1934).

Ántonia Shimerda (än'tō.nyä shē'mer.dä). Pioneer heroine of *My Ántonia* (1918), novel by Willa Cather.

Antonina (an.tọ.nī'nạ). The wife of Belisarius.

Antonine Column (an'tọ.nīn). See **Column of Marcus Aurelius.**

Antonines (an'tọ.nīnz), **Age of the.** In Roman history, the period of the reigns of Antoninus Pius and Marcus Aurelius (who was surnamed Antoninus). It was generally characterized by domestic tranquility.

Antoninus (an.tọ.nī'nus), Saint. [Original name, **Antonio Pierozzi;** called **Antonio de' Forciglioni.**] b. at Florence, 1389; d. 1459. Italian Dominican friar (1405 *et seq.*) and archbishop of Florence (1446 *et seq.*). He took part as theologian in the Council of Florence (1439). Author of *Summa Theologica Moralis* (Venice, 1477), which was printed in 15 editions during the succeeding 50 years. He was canonized by Pope Adrian VI in 1523.

Antoninus, Marcus Aurelius. See **Caracalla.**

Antoninus Liberalis (lib.ẹ.rā'lis). fl. c150 A.D. Greek grammarian, author of a collection of mythical metamorphoses.

Antoninus Pius (pī'us). [Full name, **Titus Aurelius Fulvus Boionius Arrius.**] b. near Lanuvium, Italy, Sept. 19, 86 A.D.; d. at Lorium, Italy, March 7, 161 A.D. Emperor of Rome (138–161 A.D.). He was consul and proconsul in Asia under Hadrian, and was adopted by Hadrian in 138. His reign was marked by general internal peace and prosperity.

Antonio (an.tō'ni.ō). In Shakespeare's *The Merchant of Venice*, the princely merchant who gives the play its name. He is of a sensitive, susceptible, melancholy nature, with a presentiment of evil and danger. Being obliged to borrow money from Shylock to meet the needs of Bassanio, his friend, he is induced to sign a bond agreeing to forfeit a pound of flesh if he does not repay the money within a specified time. Not being able to pay, he nearly loses his life to satisfy the demands of Shylock, but is saved by Portia who, disguised as a lawyer, points out to Shylock the impossibility of taking the flesh—his legal right—without spilling a drop of blood—a criminal act.

Antonio. Brother of Leonato, governor of Messina, in Shakespeare's *Much Ado About Nothing.*

Antonio. In Shakespeare's *The Tempest*, the usurping duke of Milan.

Antonio. Sea captain devoted to Sebastian, in Shakespeare's *Twelfth Night.*

Antonio. In Shakespeare's *Two Gentlemen of Verona*, the father of Proteus.

Antonio. One of the principal characters in John Marston's *Antonio and Mellida* and *Antonio's Revenge;* the son of Andrugio, in love with Mellida.

Antonio. In John Webster's tragedy *The Duchess of Malfi*, the steward of the household of the duchess, and, secretly, her husband. He is killed by Bosola, henchman of the Duchess' two vengeful brothers.

Antonio. In Thomas Tomkis's comedy *Albumazar*, an old gentleman, supposedly drowned, who returns in time to frustrate the schemes of the thievish Albumazar.

Antonio. In Thomas Middleton's play *The Changeling*, a secondary character who pretends for his own purposes to be an idiot or a changeling; it is from this that the play takes its name.

Antonio. In Thomas Otway's play *Venice Preserved*, a foolish speechmaker and senator whose buffooneries were intended to ridicule the first earl of Shaftesbury. The part is usually omitted from the acting version on account of its indecency.

Antonio. In John Dryden's tragedy *Don Sebastian*, a young Portuguese nobleman, a slave at the time the play begins. Dorax, another character in the same play, calls him "The amorous airy spark, Antonio."

Antonio (sänt.än.tô'nyō), **Church of Sant'.** Remarkable church in Padua, Italy, built by Niccola Pisano in the 13th century, and combining pointed forms with Byzantine domes modeled after those of the church of San Marco (St. Mark) at Venice. The aisles and chapels have groined vaults, and pointed and round arches are used together. The church contains fine paintings and tombs, and several magnificent chapels, among them the Cappella del Santo, whose marble reliefs are among the most notable of the Renaissance, and the Cappella San Felice.

Antonio (än.tō'nyō), **Nicolás.** [Latinized, **Nicolaus Antonius.**] b. at Seville, 1617; d. 1684. Spanish bibliographer and critic. He was the author of the *Bibliotheca Hispanica*, an index of Spanish authors from the time of Augustus. It is in two parts, each of two folio volumes.

Antonio and Mellida (an.tō'ni.ō; mel'i.dạ). Tragedy in two parts by John Marston, printed in 1602. It uses the conventional Italian setting which Marston liked and had been played in 1601 prior to its printing. This play was ridiculed by Ben Jonson in *The Poetaster* and in *Cynthia's Revels*. The second part is also known as *Antonio's Revenge.*

Antonio Balladino (än.tô'nyō bäl.lä.dē'nō). See **Balladino, Antonio.**

Antonio's Revenge (an.tō'ni.ōz). See under **Antonio and Mellida.**

Antonius (an.tō'ni.us), **Marcus.** b. 143 B.C.; killed at Rome, 87 B.C. Roman orator, consul (99 B.C.), and censor (97). He was put to death by the Marian party.

Antonj (än.tô'nē), **Antonello di Giovanni degli.** Original name of **Antonello da Messina.**

Anton Ulrich (än'tōn ůl'rich). [Title, Duke of **Brunswick-Wolfenbüttel.**] b. at Hitzacker, in Lüneburg, Germany, Oct. 4, 1633; d. March 27, 1714. German novelist and poet. He was the author of the romances *Die durchlauchtige Syrerinn Aramena* (1699–73) and *Römische Octavia* (1677).

Antony (äṅ.to.nē). Town in N France, a suburb of Paris, in the department of Seine, situated on the Bièvre River, S of Sceaux. 21,233 (1946).

Antony. Tragedy by the elder Alexandre Dumas, produced in 1831.

Antony (an'tọ.ni), Saint. See **Anthony,** Saint (c251–c350).

Antony, Mark. [Also: **Marc Antony;** Latin, **Marcus Antonius.**] b. c83 B.C.; d. at Alexandria, in August, 30 B.C. Roman triumvir and general; grandson of Marcus Antonius the orator. He served in Palestine and Egypt, and was quaestor in 52 and tribune in 50 B.C. He became a prominent adherent of Caesar, and when he was expelled from Rome he fled to Caesar, who thereupon commenced the civil war. He commanded the left wing at the battle of Pharsalus, was master of the horse in 47, and became consul in 44. He engaged in intrigues after Caesar's death, and was denounced by Cicero; after having fled from Rome, he formed with Octavian and Lepidus the 2nd triumvirate in 43. He defeated Brutus and Cassius at Philippi in 42, summoned Cleopatra to Asia, and later followed her to Alexandria, and renewed the triumvirate in 40 and 37. From c40 he lived chiefly at Alexandria with Cleopatra. He conducted an unsuccessful expedition against Parthia, during which he was defeated by Octavian at Actium in 31. Returned to Egypt, he committed suicide.

Antony and Cleopatra (klē.ọ.pā'trạ, -pat'rạ, -pä'trạ). Tragedy by Shakespeare, written and produced c1607, entered on the Stationers' Register in 1608 and printed in 1623. It was founded on North's translation of Plutarch's *Lives* and in it Shakespeare followed history more closely than in any other of his plays. The subject was used by John Dryden in *All for Love* (1678), and by John Fletcher and Philip Massinger in *The False One*. The character of Mark Antony is incomparably stronger in Shakespeare's play than in the others. Dryden makes him a weak voluptuary entirely given up to his passion for Cleopatra, whereas Shakespeare shows him as brave and noble.

Antony of Padua (pad'ū.ạ), Saint. See **Anthony of Padua,** Saint.

Antraigues (däṅ.treg), **Emmanuel Louis Henri de Launay,** Comte **d'.** b. at Ville-Neuve, France, 1755; assassinated near London, July 22, 1812. French politician, author of *Mémoires sur les États-Généraux* (1788).

Antrim (an'trim). Maritime county of Ulster province, in Northern Ireland. It is bounded on the N by the Atlantic Ocean, on the E by the North Channel, on the SE by Belfast Lough, on the S by County Down, on the SW by Lough Neagh, and on the W by County Londonderry. The county includes Rathlin Island and the Skerries off the N coast. The coastline is largely hilly, especially along the North Channel. The greatest elevation is

Trostan (1,817 ft.), in the Mountains of Antrim, in the NE portion of the county. Antrim is notable for its unusual basaltic formations, among them the Giant's Causeway on the N coast. Farming, including sheep raising, dairying, and extensive potato growing, is the chief occupation; there are important fisheries along the coast. Minerals found include rock salt, limestone, and bauxite, the bauxite being mainly exported to Scotland. Belfast is the chief city. Various industries, including shipbuilding, are carried on there. County Antrim was largely colonized from Scotland. County seat, Belfast; area, ab. 1,098 sq. mi.; pop. 213,761 (est. 1947).

Antrim. Town in Ulster province, Northern Ireland, in County Antrim, situated on Six-Mile-Water, near its influx to Lough Neagh, ab. 14 mi. NW of Belfast. Antrim is a market town. Near it are Antrim Castle, founded in 1662, Shane's Castle, and an ancient round tower, an unusually fine example of this characteristic type of medieval Irish structure. It is ab. 95 ft. high and 18 ft. in diameter at the base, and tapers to the top, which is covered with a conical block replacing the original one, which was destroyed by lightning. The small, low door is raised ab. 10 ft. above the ground, and has monolithic jambs and lintel. Antrim was the scene of a royalist victory over the Irish insurgents, on June 7, 1798. Pop. 1,628 (1937).

Antsirabé (änt.sē.rä'bā). Town on the island of Madagascar, off SE Africa, situated at the terminus of the railway from Tananarive, ab. 99 mi. to the N: noted for its thermal springs. 14,222 (1946).

Antsirane (ant.si.rän'). See **Diégo-Suarez.**

Antuco (än.tö'kō). Volcano in Chile, SE of Concepción. Elevation, ab. 9,000 ft.

Antung (än'tu̇ng'). Former province of Manchuria, created from the SE portion of Liaoning province in 1934. It was abolished in 1949. The capital was Tunghwa; area, 22,468 sq. mi.; pop. 3,214,000 (est. 1947).

Antung. City in NE China, in the province of Liaotung, Manchuria, situated near the mouth of the Yalu River: a seaport, rail terminal, and lumber center. It was opened to foreign trade, by agreement between China and the U.S., in January, 1904, and after the Russo-Japanese War was reopened by Japan in 1906. The Japanese left approached it on the N on May 1, 1904, during the Battle of the Yalu River. The city is on the border of Korea, with which it is linked by a railroad bridge. Most of the overland traffic between China and Korea passes through Antung. 315,242 (est. 1947).

Antunnacum (an.tun'a̤.kum). A Latin name of **Andernach.**

Antura (an.tū'ra̤). An ancient name of the **Eure River.**

Antwerp (ant'wėrp). [Flemish and German, **Antwerpen** (änt'ver''pe̤n); French, **Anvers.**] Province of Belgium, bounded by the Netherlands on the N, by Limbourg on the E, by Brabant on the S, and by East Flanders on the W. The border toward East Flanders is marked by the Schelde River, Belgium's chief outlet to the sea. The capital city, situated on the Schelde River, is the principal commercial city of Belgium and one of the largest seaports of the European continent. Almost the entire province is a fertile plain; both agriculture and manufacturing are important occupations. Apart from the Schelde, the principal rivers are the Rupel, Nèthe, and Dyle, all tributaries of the Schelde; it is traversed by the Albert, Schelde-Meuse, and Antwerpen-Turnhout canals. The population is Flemish. Capital, Antwerp; area, 1,104 sq. mi.; pop. 1,281,333 (1947).

Antwerp. [Flemish and German, **Antwerpen**; French, **Anvers.**] City in N Belgium, the capital of the province of Antwerp, situated on the Schelde River, ab. 60 mi. from the North Sea and ab. 23 mi. N of Brussels: the chief commercial city of Belgium and one of the principal seaports of the European continent. 263,233 (1947).

Commerce and Industry. It is the terminus of the Belgian canal system, and has extensive docks and quays lined with cranes and warehouses; ship-repairing is done, and river boats are constructed for export to Africa. The commercial activities of the harbor of Antwerp come largely under the heading of transport; it exports the iron and steel, metallurgical, chemical, and other products not only of Belgium and Luxembourg but also of Germany, Switzerland, Alsace, and Lorraine, and imports grain, raw materials, and colonial products destined for these countries; grain has long been the predominant commodity in the import trade. There is a stock exchange, established in the 15th century. Antwerp is one of the principal seats of the world diamond industry; it also has sugar refineries and distilleries, and other industries which are only of local importance.

Art and Architecture. The inner city of Antwerp, in the area between the former town walls, contains a number of historical monuments, such as the cathedral (with one unfinished tower), a notable example of the late Gothic style of Flanders; the town hall, built (1561–65) in the Renaissance style by Cornelius de Vriendt; the *Vleeschhuis* (meat market), dating back to the Middle Ages; numerous guild houses; and the 16th-century Church of Saint Paul (with paintings by Peter Paul Rubens, Jacob Jordaens, and David Teniers), the 15th-century Church of Saint Jacob (with Rubens's tomb), the 17th-century Church of the Augustines, now the academy of arts, and others.

Cultural and Educational Institutions. Masterworks of old Dutch and Flemish and of modern Belgian painters are exhibited in the museum of fine arts. There is also a museum of antiquities and the Museum Platin-Moretus, the latter containing a unique collection pertaining to the early history of printing. Antwerp is a center of Flemish culture in Belgium; it has a Flemish opera house as well as a French theater, a museum of Flemish folklore, and similar institutions. There are a famous academy of art, an academy of commerce, a music conservatory, a nautical college, and other vocational schools.

History. Antwerp, of little importance in the early Middle Ages, was incorporated into Brabant in the 11th century; it became a member of the Hanseatic League in 1315. In the 14th century, the city began to attract the English cloth and woolen trade; in the 15th century the foreign trades guilds were transferred from Bruges to Antwerp; the stock exchange was founded in 1460. High prosperity was reached in the 16th century, particularly in the reign of Emperor Charles V, who was himself a native of Flanders; at this time it was the center of the transit trade for the Spanish and Portuguese colonies in the New World and harbored business firms of all European nationalities. In the same period, Antwerp was the seat of a famous school of painting (Quentin Massys, Rubens, Jordaens, and others). The decline of the city began with the religious wars; it was plundered by the Spanish soldiery in 1576; conquered, after a long siege, by Alexander Farnese in 1585; all Protestant citizens were then exiled. The heaviest blow came when Holland stipulated in the peace of Münster (1648) that the Schelde River should be closed to shipping. Freedom of navigation was restored only after 1794, when the city was under French sovereignty. Napoleon I, using Antwerp against England, had the first modern docks and quays built. In 1863 the Dutch rights to levy a toll on the Schelde were redeemed and the port from then on grew rapidly in shipping tonnage, ushering in the second period of prosperity in the history of the city. It became the second largest port on the European continent. At the same time it was heavily fortified, yet unable to resist for long the German onslaught at the start of World War I; it fell on Oct. 9, 1914. During World War II, Antwerp was again occupied (May 18, 1940) by the Germans in the course of their drive against the Channel ports. Subsequently, it was for months under the destructive fire of the V-bombs; about one third of all buildings suffered damage. After its liberation (August, 1944) by the Allies, Antwerp served as an important supply base during the remainder of World War II.

Anu (ä'nö). In Assyro-Babylonian mythology, the supreme god of the pantheon. He was especially the god of heaven, and his consort, earth, was the "mother of the gods." His ancient seat of worship was in Uruk and later in Ur. In the time of the Assyrian ascendancy his cult fell into the background, though theoretically he maintained the first place in the hierarchy of the Assyro-Babylonian divinities.

Anuak (an'ū.ak). [Also: **Anywa, Anywak.**] Nilotic-speaking people of W Ethiopia and SE Anglo-Egyptian Sudan, living SE of Malakal in NE Africa. Their population is estimated at ab. 45,000 (by Cranzzolara, *Uganda*

Journal, vol. 5, 1937). Political authority is divided among hereditary village headmen. Although among the southeastern Anuak a circulating hereditary king is recognized, he has no political authority beyond the particular village in which he resides. The Anuak have patrilineal clans composed of exogamous lineages, and age grades, but circumcision is not performed. The Anuak practice agriculture, and their principal food is millet.

Anubis (ạ.nū'bis). In Egyptian mythology, the son of Osiris, often identified by the Greeks with Hermes. He is represented with a jackal's head, and was the ruler of graves and supervisor of the burial of the dead.

Anunaki (ä.nö.nä'kē). In Assyro-Babylonian mythology, the spirits of the earth. With the Igigi, spirits of heaven, they constituted the "host of heaven and earth," subordinate to the higher gods, especially to Anu, the supreme god of heaven.

Anuradhapura (ạ.nö″rä.dạ.pö'rạ). [Also, **Anuradhpura** (-räd″pö'rạ).] Sacred city in N Ceylon, ab. 60 mi. SW of Trincomalee: noted for extensive ruins dating from its period as capital of Ceylon (4th century B.C. to about the 8th century A.D.). 8,975 (1931).

Anuyao (ä.nö.yä'ō). See **Amuyao.**

Anvers (äṅ.ver). French name of **Antwerp.**

Anville (däṅ.vēl), **Jean Baptiste Bourguignon d'.** b. at Paris, July 11, 1697; d. there, Jan. 28, 1782. French geographer and cartographer. He revolutionized mapmaking by insisting on adequate sources and refusing to accept without proof positions indicated on earlier maps.

Anxanum (anks'ạ.num). Ancient name of **Lanciano.**

Anyang (än'yäng'). Town in Honan province, China, some 150 mi. NE of Loyang; it was the site of the last capital of the Shang dynasty from ab. the 14th century B.C. down to the Chou conquest. Excavations conducted there intermittently since 1929 have yielded rich materials for the study of Shang culture and history.

Anyi (än'yē). [Also: **Agni, Agnyi.**] Group of Sudanic-speaking peoples of W Africa, inhabiting the SE part of the Ivory Coast. The Anyi include the Afema, Ano, Baule, Betie, Bonda, Bini, Diabe, Moronu, and Ndenie. Culturally and linguistically they are related to the Akan peoples of the S Gold Coast, but they are divided into smaller kingdoms. Like the Akan, they have exogamous matrilineal clans, and do not perform circumcision. They practice hoe agriculture, and their principal crops are yams and maize.

Anything for a Quiet Life. Play by Thomas Middleton, printed in 1662.

Anywa (an'i.wä) or **Anywak** (-wäk). See **Anuak.**

Anza (än'sä), **Juan Bautista de.** b. at Fronteras, Mexico, 1735; d. 1788 or later. Spanish explorer in SW North America and founder (1776) of San Francisco. He was leader (1775–76) of the Anza Expedition to Alta California. Appointed (1777) governor of New Mexico, he lost favor after the colonies established (1780) by him on the Colorado River were wiped out (1781) by Yuma Indians; he was relieved (1788) of the governorship and disappears thereafter from written records of the time.

Anzac (an'zak). Australian-New Zealand term formed from the initial letters of the Australian and New Zealand Army Corps in World War I. Originally, it was applied only to men who fought at Gallipoli; it was gradually extended to all Australian and New Zealand soldiers, no matter where they had served, and applied also to such soldiers in World War II.

Anzac Pact. Agreement between Australia and New Zealand, signed at Canberra, Australia, on Jan. 21, 1944, whereby the two dominions agreed to collaborate in promoting and advancing certain regional and international policies; it provides for a permanent consultation machinery.

Anza Expedition (än'sä). Expedition dispatched (1775) to Alta California by Antonio Bucareli, viceroy of New Spain, for the purpose of preserving Spanish interests in that region against Russian and English designs. Consisting of 244 persons, it was led by Juan Bautista de Anza, and extended from Oct. 23, 1775, to Jan. 4, 1776.

Anzasca Valley (än.tsäs'kä). [Italian, **Val d' Anzasca** (dän-).] Alpine valley in the province of Novara, N Italy, near the Swiss border.

Anzengruber (än'tsẹn.grö.bėr), **Ludwig.** b. at Vienna, Nov. 29, 1839; d. there, Dec. 10, 1889. Austrian playwright and novelist, best known for his dramas of peasant life. He eked out a living as a journalist and police clerk until the success of *Der Pfarrer von Kirchfeld* (1870), after which he wrote a novel, several short stories, and a number of other plays, including *Der Meineidbauer* (1872; English trans., *The Farmer Forsworn*, 1913–15).

Anzhero-Sudzhensk (än.zhe'rọ.sö.jensk'). City in the U.S.S.R., in the Novosibirsk *oblast* (region) of the Russian Soviet Federated Socialist Republic, ab. 85 mi. W of Marinsk on the Trans-Siberian railroad: coal-mining center. 71,079 (1939).

Anzin (äṅ.zaṅ). Town in N France, in the department of Nord, ab. 1 mi. W of Valenciennes. It is the center of a rich coal-mining region; the Compagnie d'Anzin, founded in 1717, still holds large mining concessions here. The town was destroyed in World War I, rebuilt after 1919, and in World War II again severely damaged. 14,235 (1946).

Anzio (än'tsyō; Anglicized, an'zi.ō). [Former name, **Porto d'Anzio;** ancient name, **Antium.**] Town in C Italy, in the *compartimento* (region) of Latium, in the province of Latina (formerly Littoria), situated on the Tyrrhenian Sea, ab. 32 mi. S of Rome, at one time part of the nearby community of Nettuno: a seaside resort, already known to the Romans, now also a seaport and fishing town. In ancient times a Volscian stronghold, it was incorporated into Rome in 338 B.C., and colonized by the emperor Nero, who also improved the harbor. It was sacked by the Moslems in the 9th and 10th centuries. The harbor was restored by Pope Innocent XII in 1698 and a new settlement created at the same time; excavations of ancient remains were made near here, including the so-called Maiden of Anzio. The statue known as the Apollo Belvedere was discovered here in 1485. Anzio was the birthplace of Nero and possibly of Caligula. In World War II an amphibious landing was made here by American forces on Jan. 22, 1944; severe fighting took place, with large-scale destruction, before the drive on Rome could be started (May 25, 1944). Pop. 7,025 (1936).

Anzoátegui (än.sō.ä'tā.gē). State in NE Venezuela, on the Caribbean coast: oil, and agricultural and forest products. It was the site of some of the earliest Spanish settlements in South America. Capital, Barcelona; area, 16,718 sq. mi.; pop. 238,082 (1950).

Anzuan (än.zö.än'). See **Anjouan.**

Aoki (ä.ō.kē), Viscount **Shuzo.** b. in Choshu, Japan, in January, 1844; d. at Tokyo, Feb. 16, 1914. Japanese statesman and diplomat. He studied in Germany and was appointed secretary of the Japanese legation at Berlin in 1873 and minister in 1875, was vice-minister of foreign affairs in 1886–89, and was minister of foreign affairs in 1889–91 and 1898–1900. In 1906 he was appointed first Japanese ambassador to the U.S., retiring in 1907. He was a member of the privy council of the empire.

Aomori (ä.ō.mō.rē). Prefecture of Japan, in N Honshu. It produces some timber and a quantity of foodstuffs. Capital, Aomori; area, 3,716 sq. mi.; pop. 1,282,867 (1950).

Aomori. City and seaport in Japan, in N Honshu, capital of Aomori prefecture. 106,417 (1950).

Aonia (ā.ō'ni.ạ). In ancient geography, a district in Boeotia, Greece. The name is often used as synonymous with Boeotia.

Aorangi (ä.ō.räng'gē). See **Cook, Mount.**

Aornus (ā.ôr'nus). [Also, **Aornos** (-nos).] In ancient geography, a rock stronghold, situated near the Indus (or possibly near the Kabul) river, taken (c327 B.C.) by Alexander the Great from native defenders.

Aosta (ä.ôs'tä). Province in the *compartimento* (region) of Valle d'Aosta, NW Italy, bordering on France and Switzerland and including the S slopes of Mont Blanc, Monte Rosa, and the Matterhorn. Capital, Aosta; pop. 227,500 (1936).

Aosta. [French, **Aoste** (å.ost); ancient name, **Augusta Praetoria.**] Town and commune in NW Italy, the capital of the autonomous region of Valle d'Aosta, and of the province of Aosta, situated on the Dora Baltea River at the terminus of the Great St. Bernard and Little St. Bernard passes: tourist center; has an important hydroelectric plant. The ancient capital of the Gallic tribe of the Salassi, it became a Roman colony under Augustus; Roman walls, towers, gates, arches, and theaters are preserved. The cathedral dates from the 11th century with later additions; the Church of SS. Pietro and Orso is chiefly in the Gothic style. Except for short intervals, the town was under the house of Savoy from the 11th century on. Buildings of interest to tourists were undamaged in World War II. Pop. of commune, 23,641 (1936); of town, 13,466 (1936).

Aosta, Duke of. Title of **Amadeo** (1845–90).

Aowin (ä'ō.wēn). [Also: **Awowin, Brissa, Brussa.**] One of the Sudanic-speaking Akan peoples of W Africa, inhabiting the SW part of the Gold Coast.

A.P. or **AP.** Abbreviation of **Associated Press.**

Apa (ä'pä). River in South America that constitutes for most of its course part of the boundary between Paraguay (to the W) and Brazil (to the E). Length, ab. 125 mi.

Apaches (a̤.pach'ēz). Collective term for a number of North American Indian tribes, speaking closely related languages of the Athabaskan family, who ranged during historic times over large areas of N Mexico, SW Texas, nearly all of New Mexico (where they surrounded the settled Pueblo tribes), and E Arizona. All were mainly hunting peoples and after the introduction of the horse, which was eagerly adopted by them, they became aggressive raiders and a threat to the white settlement of the area.

Apafi (ô'bô.fi), **Michael.** [Also: **Apaffy, Abafi.**] b. Sept. 25, 1632; d. April 15, 1690. Prince of Transylvania, under protection of Turkey until 1686, when he made a treaty with Leopold I, the reigning Hapsburg emperor. He was succeeded by his son, Michael II, who died in 1713.

Apalachee (ap.a̤.lach'ē). [Also, **Apalachi.**] North American Indian tribe, now extinct, which formerly inhabited the Gulf coast area of N central Florida. The language was of the Muskogean language family.

Apalachee Bay. [Also, **Appalachee Bay.**] Arm of the Gulf of Mexico, on the W coast of Florida.

Apalachicola (ap"a̤.lach.i.kō'la̤). [Also, **Appalachicola.**] City in NW Florida, county seat of Franklin County, at the mouth of the Apalachicola River, W of Jacksonville: important for oyster beds. It was a leading cotton-shipping port before the Civil War. 3,222 (1950).

Apalachicola Bay. [Also, **Appalachicola Bay.**] Arm of St. George's Sound, NW Florida, in Franklin County, at the mouth of the Apalachicola River.

Apalachicola River. [Also, **Appalachicola River.**] River in W Florida, formed by the union of the Flint and Chattahoochee rivers, which flows into St. George's Sound, Gulf of Mexico. Length, ab. 90 mi.; navigable.

Apamea (ap.a̤.mē'a̤). [Also, **Apamea Cibotus** (si.bō'tus).] In ancient geography, a city in Phrygia, Asia Minor, near the modern Dinar, Turkey.

Apamea. [Also, **Apamea ad Orontem** (ad ō.ron'tem).] In ancient geography, a city in Syria, situated on the Orontes River ab. 50 mi. SE of Antioch; the medieval Famieh, and the modern Qal'at el Mudiq, originally called Pharnake.

Apappus (a̤.pap'us). In Egyptian mythology, a giant, traditionally described as being nine cubits high (approximately 15 feet). His name has been found on many ancient inscriptions.

Aparri (ä.pär'rē). Town and seaport in Cagayan province, in the N part of Luzon, Philippine Islands, at the mouth of the Rio Grande de Cagayan. 10,125 (1948).

Apatin (ä'pä.tēn). Town in N Yugoslavia, in the region of Bačka, autonomous province of Vojvodina, federative unit of Serbia, former *banovina* (province) of Dunavska, situated near the Danube River NE of Osijek. It is an important marketing town in the center of one of the richest agricultural regions of Yugoslavia. 13,537 (1948).

Apaturia (ap.a̤.tū'ri.a̤). In Greek antiquity, the solemn annual meeting of the *phratries* (family brotherhoods) for the purpose of registering the children of the preceding year whose birth entitled them to citizenship. It took place in the month Pyanopsion (falling variously in October or November), and lasted three days. The registration took place on the third day.

Apel (ä'pe̤l), **Johann August.** b. at Leipzig, Germany, 1771; d. 1816. German writer. Author of *Gespensterbuch* (1810–14), a collection of ghost stories, including one upon which Weber based his opera *Der Freischütz.*

Apeldoorn (ä'pe̤l.dōrn). City in the E part of the Netherlands, in the province of Gelderland, situated on the Grift and Dieren canals, ab. 17 mi. N of Arnhem: a garden city; has paper mills, chemical, pharmaceutical, and metallurgical industries, and cigar factories; it is a railroad junction. In the vicinity is Loo (Dutch, Het Loo), the summer palace of the royal family. 85,841 (1949).

Apellas (a̤.pel'a̤s). fl. c400 B.C. Greek sculptor.

Apelles (a̤.pel'ēz). b. in Ionia; fl. 4th century B.C. Greek painter, considered one of the great ancient artists. He is said to have been a pupil first of an otherwise unknown Ephoros of Ephesus, later of Pamphilos of Sicyon, and his style is described as a blend of Ionian and Dorian elements. He was celebrated particularly for his portraits, including one of Alexander with the thunderbolts of Zeus, and those of such other Macedonian notables as Archelaus, Clitus, and Antigonus. He also painted a procession of the high priest of Artemis, Artemis and her nymphs, and the *Aphrodite Anadyomene* (Aphrodite wringing out her hair as she rises from the sea), painted for the temple of Aesculapius at Cos. This last was probably his most noted work. None of his pictures are preserved. The nearest to a copy remaining is Raphael's drawing (now in the collection of the Louvre), from Lucian's description, of the allegory *Calumny.*

Ap Ellis (ap el'is), **Augustine.** b. 1886—. British military aviator. Having entered (1915) the Royal Flying Corps from the Royal Engineers, he served with the air ministry and the Royal Air Force after World War I, and headed (1931–44) air training centers.

Apelt (ä'pe̤lt), **Ernst Friedrich.** b. at Reichenau, Saxony, March 3, 1812; d. Oct. 27, 1859. German philosophical writer, professor of philosophy at Jena. He was the author of *Epochen der Geschichte der Menschheit* (1845; 2nd ed. 1852), *Theorie der Induktion* (1854), *Religionsphilosophie* (1860), and others.

Apemantus (ap.ē.man'tus). In Shakespeare's *Timon of Athens*, a cynical and churlish philosopher.

Apennines (ap'e̤.nīnz). [Italian, **Appennino**; French, **Apennins** (à.pe.naṅ); German, **Apenninen** (ä'pe̤-nē'ne̤n); Latin, **Appenninus.**] Central mountain system of Italy. It forms the backbone of the peninsula and extends from the Ligurian Alps in the neighborhood of Savona SE to the extremity of the peninsula. The highest point is Monte Corno (9,585 ft.), in the Gran Sasso d'Italia. Length, ab. 800 mi.; average elevation, ab. 4,000 ft.

Apenrade (ä'pe̤n.rä.de̤). German name of **Aabenraa.**

Apepi (ä'pe.pē). See also **Apophis.**

Apepi. In ancient Egyptian mythology, the great serpent, the embodiment of evil.

Aper (ä'per) or **Aperiu** (ä.per'yö). See **Apiru.**

Apfelstedt (äp'fe̤l.shtet). Small river in C Germany, in Thuringia, which joins the Gera River S of Erfurt.

Aphraates (af.rä'tēz), **Jacob.** [Called the **"Persian Sage."**] fl. 4th century A.D. Christian convert and a bishop of the Syrian Church. He was an opponent of Arianism, and was the author of a collection of homilies.

Aphrodisias (af.rō̤.diz'i.a̤s). In ancient geography, a town in Caria, Asia Minor, situated on the Maeander River (modern, Menderes) in what is now SW Turkey. The site contains the remains of an ancient hippodrome which coincide on one side with the city walls. Both ends are semicircular. The length is 919 ft., the breadth 270; the arena is 747 by 98 ft. There are 26 tiers of seats, divided into sections by flights of steps and bordered above by an arcaded gallery. There is also a comparatively well preserved Roman temple of Venus. It is Ionic, octastyle, pseudodipteral, with 15 columns on the flanks, in plan 60 by 119 ft. The peristyle columns are 35¾ ft. high.

Aphrodisias, Chariton of. See **Chariton of Aphrodisias.**

Aphrodite (af.rō̤.dī'tē). In Greek mythology, the goddess of love and wedlock, according to one legend daughter of Zeus and Dione (a female Titan), according to another risen from the foam of the sea at Cyprus, whence she is called Kypris. Many scholars give her an Asiatic origin and connect her with the Phoenician Astarte (the Assyro-Babylonian Ishtar) who corresponds to her. She was originally conceived of as a power of nature, and later specifically as the deity of reproduction and love. She sometimes appears as the wife of Hephaestus, and in her train are her son Eros and the Graces. The chief seats of her worship were Paphos, Amathus, and Idalion on the island of Cyprus, Cnidus in Asia Minor, Corinth, and Eryx in Sicily. Among plants the myrtle, rose, and apple were specially sacred to her; among animals the ram, he-goat, dove, and swan. Of her representations in classical art the most famous are the replica of her statue of Cnidus by Praxiteles, the original statues of Melos in the Louvre, of Capua at Naples, the Medicean at Florence, and the Capitoline at Rome. The Romans identified Aphrodite with Venus, who was originally a Latin goddess of spring.

Aphrodite against Artemis (är'tẹ.mis). Play (1901) by Thomas Sturge Moore.

Aphroditopolis (af''rọ.di.top'ọ.lis). Name of several cities in ancient Egypt.

Aphthartodocetae (af.thär''tọ.dọ.sē'tē). [Sometimes called **Phantasiasts.**] Monophysite sect which existed from the 6th to the 9th century A.D. or later. They held that the body of Christ was incorruptible even before the resurrection, and that he suffered death only in a phantasmal appearance. From this they are sometimes called Phantasiasts, a name more properly belonging to the Docetae, who denied even the reality of Christ's body.

Aphthonius (af.thō'ni.us), **Aelius Festus.** fl. at Antioch, c4th century A.D. Greek rhetorician, author of a textbook on rhetoric and a collection of fables.

Apia (ä.pē'ä). Seaport and chief town of Upolu island, Samoa: capital of Western Samoa territory; site of a high-power wireless station. It was the center of German commerce in the W Pacific, under German rule from 1899 to 1920, when it became part of the mandated territory of Western Samoa, assigned by the League of Nations to New Zealand. On March 15, 1889, a hurricane struck the harbor of Apia, destroying the American men-of-war *Vandalia* and *Trenton*, and the German men-of-war *Adler* and *Eber*, with several merchant vessels. The American *Nipsic* and the German *Olga* were beached, and many lives were lost. Pop. ab. 2,000.

Apiacá (ä''pi.ą.kä'). South American Indian tribe, now extinct, once centered in the area between the Arinos and Juruena rivers, S and C Brazil. Their language belonged to the Tupí-Guaraní stock.

Apianus (ap.i.ā'nus, ā.pi-; German, ä.pē.ä'nủs), **Petrus.** [Also: **Peter Apian** (ā'pi.ạn); original name, **Peter Bienewitz** or **Bennewitz.**] b. at Leisnig, Saxony, 1501; d. April 21, 1552. German mathematician and cosmographer. A professor of mathematics at Ingolstadt, he was knighted by Charles V. Author of an astronomical work and *Cosmographicus liber* (1524; published later as *Cosmographia*), a mathematical geography containing some of the earliest known maps of America.

Apicata (ap.i.kā'tạ). In Ben Jonson's play *The Fall of Sejanus*, the wife of Sejanus.

Apicius (ạ.pish'i.us, ạ.pish'us), **Marcus Gabius** or **Gavius.** fl. 1st century A.D. Roman epicure during the reigns of Augustus and Tiberius. He is said to have committed suicide rather than economize, after having spent most of his fortune inventing and procuring rare foods.

Apion (ā'pi.on, ap'i-). b. in Libya; fl. at Alexandria and Rome, 1st century A.D. Greek grammarian and commentator on Homer, whose complaints against Jews, as head of a deputation (38) of Alexandrians to Caligula, and books on the same theme were dealt with in Josephus's *Contra Apioneum.* Aulus Gellius's story of Androclus was taken from Apion.

Apiru (ä.pē'rö). [Also: **Aper, Aperiu, Apuirai.**] Egyptian variant of the Akkadian word *habiru*, a word which probably meant "wanderer." For the most part the Apiru were soldiers of fortune, mercenaries, and wandering craftsmen.

Apis (ä'pēs). See also **Dimitrijević, Dragutin.**

Apis (ā'pis). In Egyptian mythology, the sacred bull of Memphis, worshiped by the ancient Egyptians. He was believed to be the incarnation of Osiris, and was the sacred emblem of that god. Sometimes he is portrayed as a man with a bull's head.

Apo (ä'pō), **Mount.** Volcano in the S part of Mindanao, Philippines: an active volcano, and highest mountain in the Philippines. 9,690 ft.

Apocalypse. Autobiographical work (1932) by D. H. Lawrence. It was published posthumously.

Apocrypha (ạ.pok'ri.fạ). Collection of 14 books subjoined to the canonical books of the Old Testament in the authorized version of the Bible, as originally issued, but now generally omitted. They do not exist in the Hebrew Bible, but are found with others of the same character scattered through the Septuagint and Vulgate versions of the Old Testament. They are: First and Second Esdras (otherwise Third and Fourth Esdras, reckoning Nehemiah as Second Ezra or Esdras), Tobit or Tobias, Judith, the Rest of Esther, Wisdom of Solomon, Ecclesiasticus, Baruch (as joined to Jeremiah), parts of Daniel (namely, Song of the Three Children, the History of Susanna, the Destruction of Bel and the Dragon), the Prayer of Manasses, and First and Second Maccabees. Most of these are recognized by the Roman Catholic Church as canonical, though theologians of that church often distinguish them as deutero-canonical, on the ground that their place in the canon was decided later than that of the other books, limiting the name Apocrypha to the two books of the Esdras and the Prayer of Manasses, and other books not in the above collection, namely, Third and Fourth Maccabees, a book of Enoch, an additional or 151st Psalm of David, and 18 Psalms of Solomon. With these sometimes are included certain pseudepigraphic books, such as the Apocalypse of Baruch and the Assumption of Moses. The name Apocrypha is also occasionally made to embrace the Antilegomena of the New Testament. The Greek Church makes no distinction among the books contained in the Septuagint.

Apodaca (ä.pō.ᴛʜä'kä), **Juan Ruiz de.** [Title, Count of **Venadito;** called **"the Unfortunate."**] b. at Cádiz, Spain, Feb. 3, 1754; d. at Madrid, Jan. 11, 1835. Spanish naval officer and administrator. He fought against England, and in the Napoleonic and French Revolutionary wars. In 1808 he was sent as ambassador to England. He was captain-general (1812–16) of Cuba, and viceroy (1816–22) of New Spain (Mexico). He repressed the revolutionists, defeating Mina, who was captured and executed (1817), and drove Vicente Guerrero to the mountains. When Iturbide rebelled (1821), Apodaca was obliged to temporize, and was replaced by Novella, leader of the Masonic insurgents.

Apolda (ä.pol'dä). City in C Germany, in the *Land* (state) of Thuringia, Russian Zone, ab. 9 mi. NE of Weimar: before World War II a manufacturing center for hosiery, woolen goods, and knitwear; there were various metallurgical industries. It has a library and vocational schools. The population is predominantly Protestant. 33,439 (1946).

Apollinaire (ȧ.po.lē.ner), **Guillaume.** [Original name, **Guillaume de Kostrowitski.**] b. at either Monaco or Rome, Aug. 26, 1880; d. at Paris, Nov. 9, 1918. French poet. Son of a Polish mother and an unidentified father, he came to Paris in 1898 and emerged shortly after 1900 as a modernist poet, art theorist, editor of *Curiosa*, and friend and apologist of the cubists and similar schools. Among his works are the manifestoes *Les Peintres cubistes* (1913) and "L'Esprit nouveau" (in the *Mercure de France*, December, 1918); novels, *Le Poète assassiné* (1916) and *La Femme assise* (1920); plays, *Les Mamelles de Tirésias* (1917) and *Couleur du temps* (1920); and two important collections of poems, *Alcools* (1913) and *Calligrammes* (1918).

Apollinare in Classe (sänt.ä.pōl.lē.nä'rā ēn kläs'sā), **Sant'.** Church at Ravenna, Italy, begun in 534, the most important existing early-Christian basilica in Italy. In plan it is 93 by 173 ft., measuring inside, with nave and aisles separated by 24 gray marble columns with round arches, and a raised semicircular tribune. There is a clerestory of double round-arched windows, and the wooden roofs are open. The narthex, now walled up, originally had open arcades. Nave and aisles have painted medallion-friezes of busts of the bishops and archbishops of Ravenna. The vault and walls of the tribune are covered with splendid mosaics of the 6th and 7th centuries. The picturesque circular campanile is of brick, 120 ft. high, with many round-arched windows.

Apollinare Nuovo (nwô′vō), **Sant'.** Church at Ravenna, Italy, built by Theodoric in the 6th century. In plan it is 115 by 315 ft., with a single raised apse (*bema*), and a handsome narthex with a portico. The nave, 51 ft. wide, with fine coffered ceiling, has 24 columns brought from Constantinople; the Corinthian capitals are surmounted by heavy Byzantine abaci. Above the arcades of the nave the walls are covered with very beautiful 6th-century mosaics.

Apollinarians (a̤.pol.i.nãr′i.a̤nz). Religious sect deriving their name from Apollinaris the Younger, bishop of Laodicea in the 4th century. Apollinaris denied the proper humanity of Christ, attributing to him a human body and a human soul, or vital principle, but teaching that the Divine Reason (or *Logos*) took in him the place which in man is occupied by the rational principle.

Apollinaris (a̤.pol.i.nãr′is), Saint. Early Antiochian, presumed in tradition to be the founder and bishop of the Church of Ravenna whither he had been sent by Saint Peter, who had ordained him at Rome. He is venerated as a martyr.

Apollinaris Fountain. Mineral spring near Neuenahr, ab. 25 mi. NW of Koblenz, Germany, discovered in 1853. Its waters are largely exported.

Apollinaris Sidonius (sī.dō′ni.us, si-), **Gaius Sollius.** b. at Lyons, France, c430; d. c487. Christian writer, bishop, and politician. Appointed (472) bishop of Clermont after a period as prefect of Rome, he was active in resistance to and mediation with the Huns and Goths. Author of *Panegyrics* on various emperors of Rome, as well as nine books of letters and poems which are important to historians of the 5th century.

Apollinaris the Younger. [Also, **Apollinaris of Laodicea** (lā.od.i.sē′a̤).] d. c390 A.D. Bishop of Laodicea who with his father, Apollinaris the Elder, rewrote and taught parts of the Bible after the manner of Euripides, Menander, Pindar, and Plato in order to preserve Greek literature, after the edict (362) by Emperor Julian (the Apostate) against teaching of the classics by Christians. He was the founder of Appollinarianism, a theory advanced to combat Arianism but condemned as heresy by the Council of Constantinople (381) and others. In writings formerly ascribed to Gregory Thaumaturgus, whose name he probably used, he gained wide circulation for his beliefs (chiefly, that Christ possessed the *Logos*, or holy principle, in place of a rational human mind), later espoused by the Vitalians and Polemeans, and a probable source of Monophysitism.

Apollino (ä.pōl.lē′nō). Statue in the collection of the Uffizi, Florence. It is an antique copy from a Greek original, probably of the 4th century B.C., representing a delicately built type of the youthful Apollo, standing easily and gracefully.

Apollinopolis Magna (a̤.pol.i.nop′ǫ.lis mag′na̤). See **Edfu.**

Apollo (a̤.pol′ō). [Former name, **Warren.**] Borough in W Pennsylvania, in Armstrong County: manufactures of sheet steel. It was renamed in 1848. Pop. 3,015 (1950).

Apollo. In Greek and later in Roman mythology, one of the great Olympian gods, the son of Zeus and Leto, representing the light- and life-giving influence, as well as the deadly power, of the sun, and often identified with the sun-god Helios. He was the leader of the Muses, god of music, poetry, and healing, and patron of these arts; a mighty protector from evil, all-seeing, and hence the master of prophecy; also the destroyer of the unjust and insolent, and ruler of pestilence. In art he was represented in the full majesty of youthful manhood, usually unclothed or only lightly draped, and usually characterized by the bow and arrows, the laurel, the lyre, the oracular tripod, the serpent, or the dolphin. He was the father of Aesculapius, to whom he granted his art of healing. Apollo was honored, both locally and generally, under many special titles, of which each had its particular type in art and literature: as, *Apollo Citharoedus* (Apollo who sings to the accompaniment of the lyre), equivalent to *Apollo Musagetes*, the conductor of the Muses; *Apollo Chresterios* (the Apollo of oracles), *Apollo Sauroktonos* (the lizard-killer), and others. In Roman mythology he was primarily a god of healing.

Apollo Belvedere (bel.vẹ.dir′; Italian, ä.pôl′lō bel.vā.dā′rā). Most famous extant statue of Apollo, a marble figure carved during the early Roman empire, now in the collection of the Belvedere, Vatican, Rome, discovered (1485) at Antium (now Anzio, Italy). It was copied from a Greek original in bronze. Just over life size, it depicts a vigorous, youthful god wearing a chlamys around the neck and over the extended left arm. The left hand, one of the parts restored by Montorsoli, a pupil of Michelangelo, holds part of an object variously thought to have been an aegis, a bow from which he has shot an arrow, or another weapon. The original may have been a commemorative figure erected at Delphi to celebrate the expulsion of the Gauls (279 B.C.) from the temple of Apollo.

Apollodorus (a̤.pol.ǫ.dō′rus). [Surnamed **Skiagraphas,** meaning "Shadow Painter" or "Shadower."] b. at Athens; fl. late 5th century B.C. Greek painter, contemporary of Zeuxis and Parrhasius. He seems to have been the first important painter to abandon the old schematic arrangements for chiaroscuro and foreshortening observed from nature.

Apollodorus. fl. 2nd century B.C. Athenian grammarian and historian, author of an extant *Bibliotheca*, an important work on Greek mythology; probably an abridgment.

Apollodorus of Carystus (ka̤.ris′tus). b. at Carystus, in Euboea; fl. at Athens 300–260 B.C. Greek comic poet of the new Attic comedy, author of 47 plays, and five times a prize-winner. He supplied Terence with models for his *Hecyra* and *Phormio.*

Apollodorus of Damascus. b. at Damascus; fl. 2nd cent. A.D. Greek architect in Rome under Trajan; designer of the Forum and Column of Trajan at Rome, a stone bridge over the Danube (c105), triumphal arches at Ancona and Beneventum, and public buildings. He was banished and put to death by Hadrian, presumably for criticizing a design by Hadrian for a temple.

Apollonia (ap.ǫ.lō′ni.a̤). [Modern name, **Marsa Susa.**] In ancient geography, the port of Cyrene, a Greek city in N Africa, in what is now E Libya.

Apollonia. In ancient geography, a city in Illyria, in what is now W Yugoslavia.

Apollonia. [Modern name, **Arsuf.**] In ancient geography, a town in Palestine, situated on the Mediterranean between Joppa (modern Jaffa) and Caesarea.

Apollonia. [Modern name, **Sozopol.**] In ancient geography, a city in Thrace, situated on the Black Sea. It is now only a small village, in Bulgaria.

Apollonia. Former station on the Gold Coast, West Africa.

Apollonia, Diogenes of. See **Diogenes of Apollonia.**

Apollonius (ap.ǫ.lō′ni.us). [Called **"the Sophist."**] fl. late 1st century A.D. Alexandrian grammarian, author of a Homeric lexicon (still extant) based on Aristarchus and Apion.

Apollonius Dyscolus (dis′kǫ.lus). b. at Alexandria. fl. 2nd century A.D. Alexandrian grammarian, first critical student of Greek syntax. His only extant works are *On Syntax* and three treatises on adverbs, pronouns, and conjunctions.

Apollonius Molon (mō′lon). b. at Alabanda, Caria; fl. 1st century B.C. Greek rhetorician at Rhodes; instructor of Cicero and Caesar. He advocated "Atticizing," or moderating, the florid Asiatic style.

Apollonius of Perga (pėr′ga̤). [Also, **Apollonius Pergaeus** (pėr′jẹ̄.us).] b. at Perga, Asia Minor; fl. 247–205 B.C. Greek geometrician educated at Alexandria, author of a treatise on *Conic Sections* in eight books, of which four are extant in Greek and three others in Arabic; it includes the theories of Euclid and others, as well as new deductions.

Apollonius of Tralles (tral′ēz). b. at Tralles, in Caria: fl. probably in the 1st century B.C. Greek sculptor who, with his brother, Tauriscus, carved the so-called *Farnese Bull.*

Apollonius of Tyana (tī′a̤.na̤). [Also, **Apollonius Tyanaeus** (tī.ā′ni.us, tī.a̤.nē′us.] b. at Tyana, Asia Minor; fl. 1st century A.D. Greek Neo-Pythagorean philosopher and reputed magician and wonder-worker. He studied in Greek schools at Tarsus, traveled in Babylonia, Persia, and India, where he absorbed Eastern mysticism, and set up a school at Ephesus. A life of him by Philostratus, largely fabulous and no doubt written for a controversial purpose, presents similarities with that of Jesus. He was considered divine by some for his supposed miracles, and his bust was placed by Alexander Severus in his lararium with those of Abraham, Orpheus, and Christ.

Apollonius of Tyre (tīr). Stoic philosopher living in the reign of Ptolemy Auletes, mentioned by Diogenes Laërtius as the author of a work on Zeno, and by Strabo as the author of another work which seems to have been a résumé of the philosophers and their writings from the time of Zeno.

Apollonius Rhodius (ap.o̤.lō'ni.us rō'di.us). [Also, **Apollonius of Rhodes** (rōdz).] fl. at Alexandria and Rhodes 3rd century B.C. Greek epic poet, author of *Argonautica*, on the legend of the Golden Fleece, an imitation of Homer which was in turn used by Vergil, Marianus, and others. He is known to have been, for a time, librarian at Alexandria.

Apollos (a̤.pol'o̤s). fl. middle of 1st century A.D. Alexandrian Jew and early Christian missionary, converted (c49 A.D.) by Aquila and Priscilla at Ephesus (Acts, xviii). He was renowned for his preaching at Corinth, which later led a group in the Corinthian church to claim him as their founder (1 Cor. i. 10–12). He is thought by some scholars to have been the author of the *Epistle to Hebrews*, although evidence for this is at best questionable.

Apollo Sauroktonos (a̤.pol'ō sô.rok'to̤.nos). [Also, **Sauroctonus** (-nus); Eng. trans., "*the Lizard-slayer.*"] Name of two copies, one in bronze (Vatican, Rome) and one in marble (Paris), of a lost bronze statue by the Greek sculptor Praxiteles. The god leans against a tree and is apparently about to strike with an arrow, possibly as a method of divination, the lizard which climbs up the trunk. The relaxed, curving figure is typical of Praxiteles' choice of youthful subjects and his graceful, humanizing treatment of the gods.

Apollyon (a̤.pol'yo̤n). Angel of destruction. The name is a Greek rendering of Abaddon, the Hebrew term which originally meant the bottomless pit of which Apollyon is the keeper (Rev. ix. 11); introduced by Bunyan as antagonist of Christian in *Pilgrim's Progress*.

Apology for Actors, An. Work in three books by Thomas Heywood, published in 1612, and reprinted in 1658 by William Cartwright, with some alterations, under the title of *The Actors' Vindication*. It is one of the most successful apologias in English, and, though it opens with a sharp rebuke of "the sundry exclamations of many seditious sectists in this age, who in the fatness and rankness of a peaceable commonwealth grow up like unsavory tufts of grass," it proceeds with modesty and common sense.

Apology of Socrates (sok'ra̤.tēz). Plato's version of the defense of Socrates before his judges. A similar work attributed to Xenophon is spurious.

Aponensis (ap.o̤.nen'sis) or **Aponus** (ap'o̤.nus), **Petrus.** Latinized name of **Abano, Pietro d'.**

Aponi Fons (ap'o̤.nī fonz). See under **Abano,** Italy.

Apono (ä'pō.nō), **Pietro di.** See **Abano, Pietro d'.**

Apophis (ap'ō̤.fis). [Also: **Apopi, Apopy** (ä.pô'pē), **Apepi.**] Hyksos king of Egypt who ruled at Avaris (Zoan) c1600 B.C.: probably the Aphobis of Manetho, and perhaps a contemporary of Joseph.

Apopka, Lake (a̤.pop'ka̤). Lake in C Florida, much frequented by tourists for the fish in its waters.

Apostle Islands. Group of islands in the SW part of Lake Superior, belonging to Ashland and Bayfield counties, Wisconsin.

"Apostle of Andalusia." See **Ávila, Juan de.**

"Apostle of Brazil." See **Anchieta, José de.**

"Apostle of Caledonia." See Saint **Columba.**

"Apostle of Germany." See Saint **Boniface.**

"Apostle of Livonia." See **Berthold of Lokkum** (or **Loccum**).

"Apostle of the English." See **Augustine of Canterbury,** Saint.

"Apostle of the Franks." See Saint **Remi** or **Remy.**

"Apostle of the Frisians." See Saint **Willibrod.**

"Apostle of the North." See Saint **Anschar**; also Saint **Hyacinth**; also **Macdonald, John** (1779–1849).

"Apostle of the Prussians." See Saint **Adalbert**; also Saint **Methodius.**

"Apostle of the Slavs." See Saint **Adalbert** (d. 981).

Apostles' Creed, The. Primitive creed of the Christian Church, not of apostolic origin, but a product of the Western Church during the first four centuries, not now assignable to any individual author. It was originally a baptismal confession, and was intended to be a popular summary of apostolic teaching.

"Apostle to the Prussians." See Saint **Bruno.**

"Apostle to the Sioux." See **Hare, William Hobart.**

Apostolic Canons. Certain ordinances and regulations, usually reckoned as 85 in number, belonging to the first centuries of the Christian Church, and incorrectly ascribed to the apostles.

Apostolic Constitutions. Collection of diffuse instructions, relating to the duties of the clergy and laity, to ecclesiastical discipline, and to ceremonies. It is divided into eight books. They profess to be the words of the apostles, written down by Clement of Rome, but are considerably later than apostolic times. It is believed that the major portion of the first six books was composed in Syria or Asia Minor at the end of the 3rd century, and that the seventh and eighth books were later additions, dating possibly from the 4th century.

Apostolic Council, The. First conference or synod of the Christian Church. It was held (c50 A.D.) at Jerusalem by the churches of Jerusalem and Antioch to settle the personal relation between the Jewish and gentile apostles, to divide the field of labor between them, to decide the question of circumcision, and to define the relation between the Jewish and gentile Christians. Acts, xv.

Apostolic Delegation, The. Papal representation established (Jan. 24, 1893) at Washington, D.C., by Pope Leo XIII, and accredited to the Catholic Church of the U.S. The first apostolic delegate was Archbishop Satolli.

Apostolic Fathers, The. Those fathers of the church who were during any part of their lives contemporary with the apostles. They are six: Barnabas (lived c70–100 A.D.), Clement of Rome (d. c100), Hermas (lived probably about the beginning of the 2nd century), Ignatius (d. probably 107), Papias (lived probably c130), and Polycarp (d. 155).

Apostolius (ap.o̤s.tō'li.us), **Michael.** d. in Crete, c1480. Greek scholar of Constantinople, who fled (1453) to Italy at the time of the Turkish invasion.

Apostool (ä.pôs.tōl'), **Samuel.** b. 1638; d. c1700. Dutch Mennonite preacher at Amsterdam. He became involved in a dispute in 1662 with his colleague Hans Galenus, who maintained that Christianity is not so much a body of dogma as a practical way of life. The formation of two parties, Galenists and Apostoolians or Apostoolists, resulted. The two groups were reunited in 1801.

Appalachee Bay (ap.a̤.lach'ē̤). See **Apalachee Bay.**

Appalachia (ap.a̤.lach'i.a̤, -lā'chi.a̤, -lach'a̤, -lā'cha̤). Region in the W part of Virginia, lying W of the valley of Virginia. Area, ab. 4,500 sq. mi.

Appalachia (ap.a̤.lach'i.a̤). Town in SW Virginia, in Wise County. Coal mining is the principal industry. 2,915 (1950).

Appalachian Mountain Club (ap.a̤.lach'i.a̤n, -lā'chi.a̤n, -lach'a̤n, -lā'cha̤n). Organization founded in 1876 (incorporated 1878) for the purpose of exploring the mountains of New England and adjacent regions. It maintains headquarters at Boston and issues *Appalachia* (semiannual).

Appalachian Mountains. Great mountain system, named from the Apalachee (or Apalachi) Indians, in the E part of North America, which extends (according to the definition of the U.S. Geographic Board) from N Maine to Alabama; often, but less properly, called the Allegheny Mountains, from its chief division. The system is sometimes considered as including also the mountains of Gaspé Peninsula (St. Anne Mountains, Shickshock Mountains). In the U.S., the principal ranges are: the White Mountains, the Green Mountains, the Hoosac Range, the Taconic Range, The Helderberg Mountains, the Shawangunk Mountains, the Blue Ridge, the Alleghenies proper, the Blue Mountains (Pa.), the Laurel Hill and Chestnut Ridge ranges, the Black Mountains, the Stone Mountains, the Bald Mountains, the Cumberland Mountains, the Great Smoky Mountains, the Unaka Mountains, and some lesser groups. It contains large deposits of coal and iron. It is cut by the Connecticut, Hudson, Delaware, Susquehanna, Potomac, Kanawha, Tennessee, and other rivers. Length, ab. 1,500 mi.;

greatest width (in Pennsylvania), ab. 130 mi.; highest point, Mount Mitchell (6,684 ft.), in North Carolina.

Appalachian Plateau. Name defined (1907) by the U.S. Geographic Board as including the entire plateau forming the western member of the Appalachian system, known in the north as the Allegheny plateau and in the south as the Cumberland plateau.

Appalachian Trail. Hikers' trail extending from Mount Katahdin, in C Maine, to Mount Oglethorpe, in N Georgia. It passes over or near every major peak in the Appalachian system (the highest peak it actually traverses is Clingman's Dome (6,642 ft.) in the Great Smoky Mountains, in E Tennessee, but from this point easy access is had to Mount Mitchell (6,684 ft.) in W North Carolina, the highest point in the Appalachians). Length, ab. 2,050 mi.

Appalachicola (ap″a̤.lach.i.kō′la̤). See **Apalachicola.**

Appassionata (äp.päs.syō.nä′tä). [Also, **Sonata Appassionata.**] Name commonly applied to Beethoven's piano sonata opus 57, although the composer himself did not use it.

Appeasement, Period of. Phrase applied to the era in the 1930's which culminated in Neville Chamberlain's efforts to achieve a settlement with Germany in 1938. In a political sense, the term "appeasement" has from this gained meaning as a general expression for callous submission to naked or aggressive power. Many English leaders, some of whom believed that Hitler was merely seeking the redress of rightful grievances, followed a course of successive concessions culminating in the Munich Conference.

Appel (ap′e̤l), **Benjamin.** b. at New York, Sept. 13, 1907—. American novelist. He was graduated (1929) from Lafayette College and during World War II served with the Office of Civilian Defense and the War Manpower Commission at Washington, D.C. His novels include *Brain Guy* (1934), *Four Roads to Death* (1935), *Runaround* (1937), *The Powerhouse* (1939), *The Dark Stain* (1943), and *Fortress in the Rice* (1951). He is the author of a documentary report, *The People Talk* (1940).

Appendini (äp.pen.dē′nē), **Francesco Maria.** b. near Turin, Italy, Nov. 4, 1768; d. in January, 1837. Italian historian and critic.

Appennino (äp.pen.nē′nō). Italian name of the **Apennines.**

Appenninus (ap.e̤.nī′nus). Latin name of the **Apennines.**

Appenzell (äp′e̤n.tsel). Canton of Switzerland, surrounded by the canton of St. Gallen and divided into two half-cantons, Appenzell Inner Rhoden and Appenzell Ausser (outer) Rhoden. It has manufactures of muslin, silk, and embroidery. The prevailing language is German. At one time under the control of the abbots of St. Gallen, Appenzell won its independence in the beginning of the 15th century; it was allied with the confederated cantons in 1452, was admitted into the Swiss Confederation in 1513, and was divided into the half-cantons in 1597. Appenzell sends three representatives to the Swiss national council. Capital of Appenzell Inner Rhoden, Appenzell; of Appenzell Ausser Rhoden, Herisau; total area, 161 sq. mi.; pop. 61,474 (1950).

Appenzell. City in NE Switzerland, the capital of the half-canton of Appenzell Inner Rhoden: manufactures of hand and machine embroideries. All burghers entitled to vote meet on the "Landsgemeinde Platz" on the last Sunday in April to elect officers and to enact laws. 4,756 (1941).

Appenzell Ausser Rhoden (ous′ėr rō′de̤n). [English, **Appenzell Outer Rhodes.**] Half-canton of Switzerland, which occupies the N and W parts of the canton of Appenzell. The religion is predominantly Protestant, and the language German. It sends two representatives to the Swiss national council. Capital, Herisau; area, 94 sq. mi.; pop. 48,026 (1950).

Appenzeller (ap′e̤n.zel.ėr), **Henry Gerhard.** b. at Suderton, Pa., Feb. 6, 1858; drowned in shipwreck off Korean coast, June 11, 1902. American Methodist missionary to Korea. He translated a portion of the New Testament into Korean, and established (1886) the Pai Chai school for boys. His daughter, Alice Appenzeller, was the first white child ever born (1885) in Korea.

Appenzell Inner Rhoden (äp′e̤n.tsel in′ėr rō′de̤n). [English, **Appenzell Inner Rhodes.**] Half-canton of Switzerland, occupying the SE portion of the canton of Appenzell. The religion is predominantly Roman Catholic and the language German. It sends one representative to the Swiss national council. Capital, Appenzell; area, 67 sq. mi.; pop. 13,448 (1950).

Apperley (ap′ėr.li), **Charles James.** [Pseudonym, **Nimrod.**] b. at Plasgronow, Wales, 1777; d. at London, May 19, 1843. English writer on sporting matters, author of *The Life of a Sportsman* (1842), and others, popular with collectors, as well as sportsmen, for their illustrations by Henry Alken and others.

Appert (à.per), **François.** [Original prename, **Nicolas.**] b. 1750; d. c1840. French scientist and chef. He devised a method of food preservation without chemicals by heating and sealing in a container; the technique, which is basically similar to that still used in home canning, is explained in his *Art of Preserving Animal and Vegetable Substances* (1811).

Appia (à.pyà), **Adolphe.** b. at Geneva, Switzerland, Sept. 1, 1862; d. at Nyon, Switzerland, Feb. 29, 1928. Swiss stage designer and producer. He made notable contributions to the art of the theater, chiefly through his concepts of stage lighting and scenery construction. He was associated with the festivals of the Dalcroze school at Hellerau. Author of *Mise en scène du drame wagnérien* (1895) and *Musik und Inszenierung* (1899).

Appian (ap′i.a̤n). [Latin, **Appianus** (ap.i.ā′nus); Greek, **Appianos** (-nos).] b. at Alexandria; fl. at Rome 2nd century A.D. Roman historian, author of a history of Rome (in Greek) in 24 books, of which 11 are extant, together with a few fragments. Chiefly a compilation from earlier writers, it is nevertheless a valuable source, especially on the civil wars.

Appiani (äp.pyä′nē), **Andrea.** [Surnamed, **"the Elder"**; called **"Painter of the Graces."**] b. at Milan, May 23, 1754; d. there, Nov. 18, 1817. Italian painter, pupil and imitator of Correggio, pensioned by Napoleon (until 1814) as artist for the kingdom of Italy. His frescoes include those in the royal palace and church of Santa Maria presso San Celso, Milan; among his oils are *Venus and Cupid* and *Rinaldo in the Garden of Armida.*

Appiano (äp.pyä′nō). Italian family, rulers of Piombino from the 14th to the 17th century. Its founder was Jacopo I, lord of Pisa (1392–98).

Appian Way. [Latin, **Via Appia** (vī′a̤ ap′i.a̤).] Most famous of the ancient Roman highways. It ran from Rome to Brundisium (now called Brindisi), and is probably the first great Roman road which was formally undertaken as a public work. It was begun in 312 B.C. by Appius Claudius Caecus, the censor, who carried it as far as Capua. The next stage of the work extended it to Beneventum (Benevento), and it probably did not reach Brundisium until 244 B.C., when a Roman colony was inaugurated there. At present the Appian Way, for a long distance after it leaves Rome, forms one of the most notable memorials of antiquity in or near Rome, bordered as it is by tombs and the ruins of monumental buildings. Long stretches of the pavement remain perfect, and show that the width of the roadway proper was only 15 ft. Length, ab. 350 mi

Appii Forum (ap′i.ī fō′rum). In ancient geography, a station on the Appian Way, ab. 40 mi. SE of Rome.

Appin (ap′in). Registration district, village, and seaport in Lismore and Appin civil parish, in C Scotland, in Argyllshire, extending ab. 18 mi. along the E coast of Loch Linnhe, ab. 12 mi. NE of Oban, ab. 512 mi. N of London by rail. 529 (1931).

Appius and Virginia (ap′i.us; vėr.jin′ya̤). Tragedy attributed to John Webster and Thomas Heywood, printed in 1654 as by Webster alone. The story, originally told by Livy, forms the first novel of the 19th day in the *Pecorone di Giovanni Fiorentino* (1378), and was reproduced in Painter's *Palace of Pleasure* (1st ed., 1566) two centuries later. There is a version of it in the *Roman de la Rose.* Chaucer tells it in *The Doctor's Tale,* and Gower embodied it in his *Confessio Amantis.* There was an earlier play, *The Tragical Comedy of Apius and Virginia,* by an unknown author whose initials were R.B. It was probably acted as early as 1563, though not printed till

1575. John Dennis also wrote a tragedy with this name in 1709.

Appleby (ap'l.bi). Municipal borough in NW England, county seat of Westmorland, situated on the river Eden, ab. 28 mi. SE of Carlisle, ab. 280 mi. NW of London by rail: noted for Saint Michael's Church, which has a Norman doorway, the lintel of which is a Saxon tombstone. Appleby Castle occupies the site of an old Roman encampment. 1,704 (1951).

Appleby, John Francis. b. at Westmoreland, N.Y., May 23, 1840; d. Nov. 8, 1917. American inventor. He constructed (1859) the first model of what was later (1878 *et seq.*) to be the Appleby knotter, a basic component of most of the world's grain binders; he also worked out a rifle-cartridge magazine and automatic feeder while in the trenches before Vicksburg during the Civil War as a member of the 23rd Wisconsin Infantry.

Apple Cart, The. Play (1930) by George Bernard Shaw.

Applegarth (ap'l.gärth), **Robert.** b. in England, 1834; d. there, 1924. English trade-union leader. As general secretary (1862 *et seq.*) of the Amalgamated Society of Carpenters and Joiners, he became the leader of the aggressive cadre within the British labor movement which secured the legislative acceptance of unions and their right to amass funds for benefit payments and other purposes. In 1872 he retired from active participation in union activities to enter private business.

Applegate (ap'l.gāt), **Jesse.** b. in Kentucky, July 5, 1811; d. April 2, 1888. American surveyor, legislator, and pioneer to Oregon. In 1843 he emigrated to Oregon, where he became at once influential in public affairs, becoming (1845) a member of the provisional government which lasted until the territory was attached (1849) to the U.S. A member (1857) of the state constitutional convention, he withdrew when his leadership was challenged. First a Whig and then a Republican, he had much to do with upholding Lincoln and the cause of the North in Oregon. He is thought to have been refused a seat in the U.S. Senate because acceptance would have required a degree of subservience to the railroads which he had himself helped to develop. He is important as the author of documents and newspaper articles pertaining to the settlement of Oregon.

Appleton (ap'l.tọn). City in E Wisconsin, county seat of Outagamie County, at the falls of the Fox River: center of a livestock-raising and dairying region; manufactures pulp and paper. It is the seat of Lawrence College. The magician Harry Houdini was born here. 34,010 (1950).

Appleton, Charles Edward Cutts Birch. b. at Reading, England, March 16, 1841; d. at Luxor, Egypt, Feb. 1, 1879. English journalist and man of letters; founder (1869) of the *Academy* and its editor until 1879.

Appleton, Daniel. b. at Haverhill, Mass., Dec. 10, 1785; d. at New York, March 27, 1849. American bookseller and publisher, at first a merchant of "English goods," including books. With his son, W. H. Appleton, he founded (1831) the publishing house which became (1838) D. Appleton and Company, New York.

Appleton, Sir **Edward Victor.** b. 1892—. English physicist, notable for discovery in the upper atmosphere of a conducting layer since known as the "Appleton layer," and important in the development of radar. He was awarded a Nobel prize in physics in 1947.

Appleton, Jesse. b. at New Ipswich, N.H., Nov. 17, 1772; d. at Brunswick, Me., Nov. 12, 1819. American clergyman and educator, president of Bowdoin College (1807–19); father-in-law of President Franklin Pierce.

Appleton, John. b. at Beverly, Mass., Feb. 11, 1815; d. at Portland, Me., Aug. 22, 1864. American politician, and diplomat. He practiced law at Portland (1837 *et seq.*), and was a Democratic member of Congress (1851–53). Appointed minister to Russia by President Buchanan in 1860, he resigned upon the election of Lincoln.

Appleton, John Howard. b. at Portland, Me., Feb. 3, 1844; d. Feb. 18, 1930. American chemist. He was an instructor (1863–68) and professor of chemistry applied to the arts (1868–72), and professor of chemistry (1872–1914) at Brown University, as well as a member (1891) of the U.S. Mint Commission. Author of numerous textbooks and technical articles.

Appleton, Nathan. b. at New Ipswich, N.H., Oct. 6, 1779; d. at Boston, July 14, 1861. American cotton-manufacturer and politician. With his brother Samuel and other pioneers in the textile industry, he developed cotton-producing centers at Waltham and Lawrence, Mass., and Manchester, N.H. He was also one of the founders of Lowell, Mass. As a congressman from Massachusetts (1830–33 and 1842), he supported Adams and Jackson on the protective tariff, and wrote *Currency and Banking* (1841) on the Bank of the United States controversy. He was one of the organizers of the Boston Athenaeum.

Appleton, Samuel. b. at New Ipswich, N.H., June 22, 1766; d. at Boston, July 12, 1853. American merchant and philanthropist. Established (1794) an importing business at Boston with his brother Nathan; later he was profitably engaged in cotton manufacture at Waltham and Lowell, Mass., and in real estate and railroads. He gave generously to various institutions, including Harvard, which built the Appleton Chapel with his bequest.

Appleton, William Henry. b. at Haverhill, Mass., Jan. 27, 1814; d. Oct. 19, 1899. American publisher; son of Daniel Appleton. He formed a partnership (1838) with his father under the name of D. Appleton and Company; the enterprise expanded prodigiously after the retirement (1848) of his father, publishing the scientific volumes which first acquainted the American public with the theories of Charles Darwin, Thomas Huxley, and Herbert Spencer. The sale of the *Webster Spelling Book* is said to have reached 1,596,000 in a single year (1866), while scientific interest brought in 1872 the first issue of what is now the *Popular Science Monthly.* He also published the *Appleton Cyclopedia of Biography* (1856). He urged international copyright laws and served as president (1887) of the American Publishers' Copyright League.

Apple-Tree Table and Other Sketches, The. Ten prose sketches by Herman Melville, first published in 1922.

Appold (ap'ọld), **John George.** b. at London, April 14, 1800; d. at Clifton, England, Aug. 31, 1865. English inventor who devised a form of centrifugal pump and a break used in laying the first Atlantic cable.

Appomattox (ap.ọ.mat'ọks). [Also, **Appomattox Courthouse.**] Town in C Virginia, county seat of Appomattox County, situated ab. 25 mi. E of Lynchburg. Here, on April 9, 1865, General Robert E. Lee surrendered the Confederate army of Northern Virginia to General Ulysses S. Grant, virtually ending the Civil War. 1,094 (1950).

Appomattox River. River in Virginia, joining the James River ab. 20 mi. SE of Richmond. Length, ab. 150 mi.; navigable for ab. 15 mi.

Apponyi (ô'pō.nyē), Count **Albert György.** b. at Vienna, May 29, 1846; d. at Geneva, Switzerland, Feb. 7, 1933. Hungarian political leader; son of Count György Apponyi (1808–99). He was a member of the Hungarian parliament (1872–1933) first, with Gyula Andrássy, as a Deák follower, and later as a conservative leader and successor to Kossuth as president of the party for Hungarian independence. A delegate to the World Peace Conference at St. Louis (1904), and minister of education (1906–10) in Sándor Wekerle's cabinet, he was appointed (1919) head of the Hungarian peace delegation to Paris, and served as Hungarian representative (1926 *et seq.*) in the League of Nations. Author of *Aesthetics and Politics* (1905), *A Brief Sketch of the Hungarian Constitution and of the Relation Between Austria and Hungary* (1908), and others.

Apponyi, Count **Antal.** b. Sept. 7, 1782; d. Oct. 17, 1852. Hungarian diplomat; son of Antal György, Count Apponyi (1751–1817).

Apponyi, Count **Antal György.** b. 1751; d. 1817. Hungarian founder of the Apponyi Library at Bratislava.

Apponyi, Count **György.** b. 1808; d. 1899. Hungarian statesman; grandson of Count Antal György Apponyi (1751–1817). Court chancellor (1847) and conservative leader before the insurrection of 1848–49, he was later (1859 *et seq.*) a nationalist leader instrumental in securing the Austro-Hungarian compromise (*Ausgleich*) with Ferenc Deák and Gyula Andrássy, and in the restoration of the Hungarian constitution.

Apponyi, Count **Rudolph.** b. Aug. 1, 1812; d. at Venice, May 31, 1876. Hungarian diplomat; son of Count Antal Apponyi (1782–1852). He was appointed Austrian minister (1856) and ambassador (1860) at the court of St. James, was relieved in 1871, and was transferred to Paris, in 1872.

Apprentice, The. Play (1756) by Arthur Murphy. His own brief career as an actor contributed to this farce, his first play.

Apprenti sorcier (là.prañ.tē sôr.syā), **L'.** French title of **Sorcerer's Apprentice, The.**

Appuleia gens (ap.ū̦.lē'a̦ jenz). In ancient Rome, a plebeian clan or house whose family names are Decianus, Pansa, and Saturninus.

Appuleius (ap.ū̦.lē'us), **Lucius.** See **Apuleius, Lucius.**

Apraksin (ä.präk'sin), Count **Fyodor Matveyevich.** [Also, **Apraxin.**] b. 1671; d. Nov. 10, 1728. Russian admiral, chief collaborator of Peter the Great in the founding of the Russian navy. A page at the court under Czar Fyodor III and his half-brother Peter, he became a lifelong friend of the latter. He began his career of building ships as governor of Arkhangelsk (1692), served at the siege of Azov (1696), and was chief of the admiralty (1700–06). In the war between Peter the Great and Charles XII of Sweden, he built fleets, fortifications, and harbors, defended St. Petersburg (1708), and followed up the Russian victory at Poltava (1709) by capturing Viborg (1710), Helsingfors, and Borgo (1713), securing Finland and the Baltic States (by the Treaty of Nystad, 1721) for Russia.

Apraksin, Stefan. [Also, **Apraxin.**] d. in prison, Aug. 31, 1758. Russian general; nephew of F. M. Apraksin. He defeated (1757) the Prussian army of Frederick the Great at Gross-Jägerndorf. He was arrested for a court conspiracy and died in prison.

Après-midi d'un faune (là.pre.mē.dē dėñ fōn), **L'.** [Full title, **Prélude à l'après-midi d'un faune;** English title, **The Afternoon of a Faun.**] Eclogue, or tone-poem, for orchestra by Claude Debussy, composed (1892–94) after a poem of the same title by Stéphane Mallarmé. It is one of the pieces which established Debussy's reputation as an innovator in impressionist technique and composition. It was performed (1912) at Paris as a ballet with Nijinsky.

Apries (ap'ri.ēz). [Called in the Bible, **Hophra.**] Egyptian ruler, fourth king of the XXVIth dynasty; reigned c588–c569 B.C. as successor to his father, Psamtik II. Rivalry with Babylon's Nebuchadnezzar led him to attack Tyre and Sidon, as well as to attempt the relief of Jerusalem, which was besieged by the Babylonians. He failed (586 B.C.) to save Jerusalem or to overthrow Babylonian rule in Syria, despite a series of military and naval victories, and was finally himself overthrown and killed by his erstwhile ally, Amasis II.

April (ā'pril). The fourth month of the year, containing 30 days. Among poets April has traditionally symbolized inconstancy, because of the changeableness of its weather.

April Fools' Day. [Also, **All Fools' Day.**] April 1, the day for playing practical jokes on unsuspecting victims.

Apsheron (äp.shi.rôn'). Peninsula in the S part of the U.S.S.R., in the Azerbaijan Soviet Socialist Republic, which projects into the Caspian Sea and terminates in Cape Apsheron. It is noted for its petroleum wells (in the vicinity of Baku) and its mud volcanoes.

Apsley (aps'li), Baron. See **Bathurst, Henry** (1714–94).

Apsley House. Name of what was at one time the residence of the Duke of Wellington, at Hyde Park Corner in London. It was built for Lord Bathurst (whose family name was Apsley) in 1785, purchased by the government in 1820, and presented to the Duke of Wellington as part of the national reward for his services.

Apsyrtos (ap.sėr'to̦s). b. at Prusa (now Bursa) or Nicomedia (now Izmit), in Bithynia; fl. at Constantinople, c332–334. Greek veterinary surgeon. He wrote a treatise (in two books) on the veterinary art, which was used considerably by later authors.

Apt (àpt). [Ancient name, **Apta Julia** (ap'ta̦ jöl'ya̦, jö'li.a̦).] Town in SE France, in the department of Vaucluse, situated on the Calavon River, ab. 30 mi. E of Avignon. It has an annual fair, marble quarries, sulfur and ocher mines, and small industries. The Church of Saint Anne is in the Romanesque style. 6,259 (1946).

Apuan Alps (ap'ū.a̦n). Chain of the N Apennines, situated near Carrara, Italy.

Apuania (ä.pwä'nyä). Former commune in N Italy, in the *compartimento* (region) of Tuscany, formed (1938) from the communities of Massa, Carrara, and Montignoso. It was abolished after World War II. 106,378 (1936).

Apuania. Former name of **Massa e Carrara.**

Apuirai (a̦.pwē'rā). See **Apiru.**

Apuleius (ap.ū.lē'us), **Lucius.** [Also, **Lucius Appuleius.**] b. in Numidia (or, according to some authorities, at what is now Bône, Algeria), c125 A.D.; fl. chiefly at Carthage. Roman rhetorician and Platonic sophist, notable as a clever and versatile writer with an encyclopedic range of interests. He is probably now best known for his *Metamorphoses*, or *The Golden Ass*, one of the few Latin romances still extant. The extraordinary adventures (including metamorphosis into the shape of an ass) attributed by Apuleius to the hero of this fictional work were later freely adapted and used by Fielding, Smollett, Boccaccio, and Cervantes. However, Apuleius is also of some considerable importance, although less well known, for his scientific writings. His most important work in this field (particularly for the historian of medicine) was his book on magic (*De magia* or *Apologia*), which dealt with various matters not unrelated to those which were the concern of the first alchemists, and thus historically linked to what was later to emerge as modern science. All of his other scientific writings, including a translation of an early text on arithmetic, have now been lost, except for *De mundo* (*On the World*), and some scholars have even questioned the authenticity of extant copies of this.

Apulia (a̦.pū'li.a̦). [Italian, **Puglia, Puglie.**] *Compartimento* (region) in SE Italy, containing the provinces of Bari, Brindisi, Foggia, Lecce, and Ionio. It is the heel of the Italian boot, lying between the Adriatic Sea on the N and E and the E slope of the Apennines and the Gulf of Taranto on the S and W. The coastal plain produces rich harvests of olives, wine, grain, fruits, almonds, and tobacco. There are fisheries, livestock farms, salt works, and flourishing agricultural industries. Ancient Apulia lay S of the Frentani and E of Samnium; it was conquered by Rome in the 4th century B.C. Later it included the Messapian Peninsula. The ancient inhabitants were the Dauni, Peucetii, and Salentini or Messapians. After the dissolution of the Roman Empire, the district was under Lombard, Byzantine, Norman, and Hohenstaufen rule until it was incorporated into the Kingdom of Naples and the Two Sicilies. The region saw bitter fighting in the Punic Wars and in the struggle between Emperor Frederick II and Pope Gregory IX; many architectural works from this time still stand. Throughout the centuries, Apulia was a place of entrance for Greek and Oriental influences. It was joined to Italy in 1860. Area, 7,470 sq. mi.; pop. 2,642,076 (1936), 3,210,411 (1951).

Apulum (ap'ū̦.lum). Latin name of **Alba Iulia.**

Apure (ä.pö'rā). State in W Venezuela, at the Colombian border. Capital, San Fernando de Apure; area, 29,537 sq. mi.; pop. 84,806 (1950).

Apure River. River in W Venezuela, one of the principal tributaries of the Orinoco. Length, ab. 600 mi.; navigable in its lower part.

Apurímac (ä.pö.rē'mäk). Department in S Peru. Capital, Abancay; area 8,189 sq. mi.; pop. 280,213 (1940), 336,379 (est. 1950).

Apurímac River. River in W South America, the S headstream of the Ucayali River, and hence of the Amazon, rising in S Peru and flowing N. From the confluence of the Montaro River it is called the Ené to its junction with the Perené River; thence to the Urubamba River, which it joins to form the Ucayali, it is known as the Tambó. Length to the Ucayali, ab. 600 mi.

Apus (ā'pus). One of the southern constellations formed in the 16th century, probably first classified by Petrus Theodori; the Bird of Paradise. It is situated S of the Triangulum Australe, and its brightest star is of the fourth magnitude.

Aqaba (ä'kä.bä). [Also: **Akaba, Akabah, 'Aqaba;** ancient names, **Aelana, Elath, Eloth.**] Village in SW Jordan, at the head of the Gulf of Aqaba. It is a minor seaport. Near it was the ancient Ezion Geber.

Aqaba, Gulf of. [Also: **Akaba, Akabah**; Arabic, **Bahr el 'Aqaba.**] One of the northward extensions of the Red Sea, separating the Sinai Peninsula from the Arabian Peninsula, and Africa from Asia. Israel and Jordan meet at its N end.

Aquae (ak'wē). Latin name of **Ax.**

Aquae Augustae (ô.gus'tē). A Latin name of **Dax.**

Aquae Bigerrionum Balneariae (bi.ger.i.ō'num bal.nē-âr'i.ē). Latin name of **Bagnères-de-Bigorre.**

Aquae Bormonis (bôr.mō'nis). Latin name of **Bourbon-l'Archambault.**

Aquae Borvonis (bôr.vō'nis). Latin name of **Bourbonne-les-Bains.**

Aquae Calidae (kal'i.dē). [Eng. trans., "*Hot Springs.*"] In ancient geography, a place in Mauretania Caesariensis, S of Caesarea.

Aquae Calidae. Latin name of **Vichy**; see also **Bath,** England.

Aquae Domitianae (dọ.mish.i.ā'nē). A Latin name of **Aix-les-Bains.**

Aquae Flaviae (flā'vi.ē). Latin name of **Chaves.**

Aquae Grani (grā'nī). A Latin name of **Aachen.**

Aquae Gratianae (grā.shi.ā'nē). A Latin name of **Aix-les-Bains.**

Aquae Helveticae (hel.vē'ti.sē). Latin name of **Baden,** Switzerland.

Aquae Mattiacae (mạ.tī'ạ.sē). Latin name of **Wiesbaden.**

Aquae Mortuae (môr'tụ.ē). Latin name of **Aigues-mortes.**

Aquae Nisinei (ni.sī'nẹ.ī). Latin name of **Bourbon-Lancy.**

Aquae Pannonicae (pạ.non'i.sē). Latin name of **Baden,** Austria.

Aquae Patavinae (pat.ạ.vī'nē). See under **Abano,** Italy.

Aquae Sextiae (seks'ti.ē). Latin name of **Aix.**

Aquae Statiellae (stā.shi.el'ē). Latin name of **Acqui.**

Aquae Solis (sō'lis) or **Sulis** (sö'lis). A Latin name of **Bath,** England.

Aquae Tarbellicae (tär.bel'i.sē). A Latin name of **Dax.**

Aquambo (ä.kwäm'bō). Name applied at one time to a region on the Gold Coast, W Africa.

Aquapim (ä.kwä.pēm'). District of the Eastern province, Gold Coast, W Africa; at one time the name applied to a whole region.

Aquarium (ạ.kwãr'i.um). See **Castle Garden.**

Aquarius (ạ.kwãr'i.us). A zodiacal constellation supposed to represent a man standing with his left hand extended upward, and with his right pouring out of a vase a stream of water which flows into the mouth of the Southern Fish. Its symbol is designed to represent a stream of water.

Aquaviva (ä.kwä.vē'vä), **Claudio** or **Claudius.** [Also, **Acquaviva.**] b. at Naples, Italy, 1543; d. at Rome, 1615. Italian ecclesiastic, fifth general (1581–1615) of the Society of Jesus. He was substantially the author of *Ratio Studiorum,* a basic Jesuit educational work.

Aqueduct of Valens (vā'lẹns). Aqueduct in Istanbul (Constantinople), finished 378 A.D., and still in use. The main bridge is 2,000 ft. long and 75 high, and consists of two tiers of arches of about 30 ft. span.

Aquila (ak'wi.lạ). See also **Arno.**

Aquila. fl. 1st century A.D. Early Christian who shares with his wife Priscilla (or Prisca) fame for their devoted companionship with Paul and for the conversion of Apollos at Ephesus. Probably originally from Pontus, the couple settled at Rome, were driven out by edict of Claudius, and took up the trade of tent-making at Corinth, where they met and sheltered Paul (Acts, xviii. 2–3), with whom they later journeyed to Ephesus.

Aquila. [Full name, **Aquila et Antinoüs.**] Northern constellation situated in the Milky Way nearly south of Lyra, and containing the bright star Altair. It has for its outline the figure of a flying eagle carrying in its talons the boy Antinoüs, the page of the emperor Hadrian.

Aquila (ak'wi.lạ; German, ä'kvē.lä), **Kaspar.** [Original name, **Kaspar Adler.**] b. at Augsburg, Bavaria, Aug. 7, 1488; d. at Saalfeld, Thuringia, Nov. 12, 1560. German Protestant theologian, an assistant of Luther in the translation of the Old Testament. He became (1527) pastor at Saalfeld, and was outlawed (1548) by Charles V for his violent opposition to the Interim; he saved himself by flight, returning after the treaty of Passau (1552) to his pastorate at Saalfeld.

Aquilante (ä.kwē.län'tā). Brother of Gryphon, descended from Olivero, a character in works by Matteo Maria Boiardo and Lodovico Ariosto. The brothers were brought up by two fairies.

Aquileia (ä.kwē.lā'yä). Town and commune in NE Italy, in the *compartimento* (region) of Friuli-Venezia Giulia, in the province of Udine, situated near the head of the Adriatic Sea, S of Udine. Founded by the Romans in 181 B.C., it was one of the chief cities of the Empire, the key to Italy on the NE. Destroyed by the Huns under Attila in 452 A.D., it was rebuilt and became the seat of one of the most important patriarchates of the early Christian church and the scene of a number of church councils. The cathedral, in basilica style, dates from the 11th century, with Gothic additions from the 14th century. The town became less important as the Adriatic Sea retreated, but excavations on the site of the Roman town have yielded a great variety of antiquities. Pop. of commune, 9,495 (1936); of town, 1,116 (1936).

Aquilino (ä.kwē.lē'nō). Horse of Raymond, in *Jerusalem Delivered,* by Torquato Tasso. His sire was the wind.

Aquillia gens (ạ.kwil'i.ạ jenz). In ancient Rome, a patrician and plebeian clan or house of great antiquity, whose family names under the Republic were Corvus, Crassus, Flourus, Gallus, and Tuscus.

Aquin (dȧ.kaṅ), **Louis Claude d'.** See **Daquin** or **d'Aquin, Louis Claude.**

Aquinas (ạ.kwī'nạs), Saint **Thomas.** [Called **Doctor Angelicus, "Father of Moral Philosophy,"** and (in fun by his schoolmates) the **"Dumb Ox."**] b. at Rocca Secca, near Aquino, Italy, c1225; d. at Fossanuova, Italy, 1274. Italian theologian, leading scholastic philosopher, ranked with the fathers of the Latin Church. He was educated at Monte Cassino and Naples, and joined (c1243) the Dominican order. A student at Paris (1245–48) under Albertus Magnus, he followed him to Cologne (1248), where he began teaching. His great fame was attained at Paris (1252–56 and 1268–72) and Rome (1259–68). At Paris he engaged in a great controversy with Siger de Brabant and the Averroists over the interpretation of Aristotle, which ended in a triumph for scholasticism. Founder of the philosophical system now called Thomism, and synthesizer of the theology which was pronounced (1879) as official for the Roman Catholic Church, he was a great medieval scholar in breadth of scope and brilliance of logic. He was the author of a *Mass for Corpus Christi* (1264), containing hymns considered among the finest in the Christian church and examples of masterful Latin prosody; also of a body of writing leading up to his *Summa Theologica,* chiefly a commentary (1254–56) on the *Sentences* of Peter Lombard, a work following Albertus Magnus and Augustinianism; commentaries (1265–73) on the *Physics, Metaphysics, De anima, Ethics,* and other works of Aristotle; and the *Summa de Veritate Catholicae Fidei contra Gentiles* (1258–60), an attempt to persuade non-Christians by distinguishing and reconciling reason and faith. The *Summa Theologica* (1267–73) a three-part work dealing with God, Man, and Christ, and intended to summarize all learning and to demonstrate his fundamental belief in the compatibility of faith and intellect, is still studied as one of the greatest philosophical works of all time. It was not, however, completed by him.

Aquincum (ạ.kwing'kum). Latin name of **Budapest.**

Aquino (ä.kwē'nō). [Ancient name, **Aquinum** (ạ.kwī'num).] Town and commune in C Italy, in the *compartimento* (region) of Latium, in the province of Frosinone, ab. 55 mi. NW of Naples. It has Roman antiquities and the ruins of the early medieval Church of Santa Maria della Libera. It was the birthplace of Saint Thomas Aquinas, the leading philosopher of the medieval church. Pop. of commune, 3,359 (1936); of town, 1,697 (1936).

Aquiry River (ä.kē.rē'). Former name of the **Acre River.**

Aquisgranum (ak.wis.grā'num). A Latin name of **Aachen.**

Aquitaine (ak.wi.tān', ak'wi.tān; French, ȧ.kē.ten). Medieval division of SW France, lying between the Garonne and Loire rivers. A Visigothic kingdom was founded there in the first part of the 5th century. It was conquered (507) by Clovis, became (c700) a duchy, and was conquered by Charlemagne and made a kingdom (including all S Gaul and the Spanish March) for his son Louis. In 838 Neustria was united to it, and it became soon after a duchy and one of the great fiefs of the French crown. Gascony was united to it in 1052. In 1137 it passed temporarily to France, by the marriage of Eleanor of Aquitaine with Louis VII of France, but in 1152 was united (by the marriage of Eleanor with Henry II of England) to Normandy and Anjou, and in 1154 to England, which retained it under John. It became (c1258) nominally a French fief, but was freed from French vassalage and granted to Edward III of England in 1360. Part of it was recovered from the English in the reign of Charles V of France, but was won back for England by Henry V. It was finally conquered by the French in 1451–53. It included (as Guienne) properly Bordelais, Rouergue, Périgord, Quercy, Agénois, and Bazadois, and comprised nearly the modern departments of Gironde, Dordogne, Lot, Lot-et-Garonne, and Aveyron.

Aquitaine, Prince of. A title of **Edward,** the Black Prince.

Aquitania (ak.wi.tā′ni.ạ). In ancient geography, the SW division of Gaul, as described by Julius Caesar, comprising the region between the Pyrenees and the Garonne River. It was extended by Augustus northward to the Loire River, and made a Roman province.

Aquitanian Sea (ak.wi.tā′ni.ạn). Occasional name of **Biscay, Bay of.**

Aquitania Tertia (ak.wi.tā′ni.ạ tėr′shi.ạ). See under **Gascony.**

Aquitanicus Sinus (ak.wi.tan′i.kus sī′nus). A Latin name of **Biscay, Bay of.**

Ara (ā′rạ). One of the 15 ancient southern constellations; the Altar. It is situated S of the Scorpion. Its two brightest stars are of the third magnitude.

'Arab (ä′rạb), **Bahr al.** Arabic name of the **Arabian Sea.**

Araba (ä′rạ.bạ). [Also: **Arabah;** Arabic, **Wadi el 'Araba.**] Valley, or wadi, between Israel and Jordan, running from the Dead Sea S to the Gulf of Aqaba. Length, ab. 100 mi.

Arabah (ä′rạ.bạ), **Sea of the.** See under **Dead Sea.**

Arabat (ä.rä.bät′). Small place in the S part of the U.S.S.R., in the Crimea, at the head of the Tongue of Arabat.

Arabat, Tongue of. [Also: **Arabat;** Russian, **Arabatskaya Strelka** (ä.rä.bät′skạ.yạ strel′kạ).] Long and narrow, sandy peninsula in the S U.S.S.R., in the Crimean *oblast* (region) of the Russian Soviet Federated Socialist Republic, separating the Sea of Azov from the Sivash.

Arabat Bay. Arm of the Sea of Azov, in the S part of the U.S.S.R., in the Crimean *oblast* (region) of the Russian Soviet Federated Socialist Republic.

Arabat-el-Madfuneh (ä.rä′bät.el.mäd.fö′ne). See under **Abydos, Egypt.**

Arabella (ar.ạ.bel′ạ). Character in David Garrick's play *The Male Coquette.*

Arabella. Romantic heroine of Charlotte Lennox's novel *The Female Quixote; or, the Adventures of Arabella* (2 vols., 1752).

Arabella Allen (al′ẹn). See **Allen, Arabella.**

Arabġir (ä.räb.gėr′) or **Arabkir** (-kėr′). See **Arapkir.**

Arabia (ạ.rā′bi.ạ). Turkish and Persian, **Arabistan** (ä.rä.bē.stän′).] Peninsula in SW Asia, with the shape of an irregular triangle, between Iran and Egypt, bounded on the W by the Red Sea and the Gulf of Aqaba, on the S by the Gulf of Aden and the Arabian Sea, on the E by the Gulf of Oman and the Persian Gulf, and on the N by Iraq and Jordan. Area, 1,200,000 sq. mi.; pop. 12,000,000 (est. 1950).

Main Divisions. The Greeks and Romans divided Arabia into Arabia Petraea (the "stony"), Arabia Deserta (the "desert"), and Arabia Felix (the "flourishing" or "happy"). Modern geographers recognize from 8 to 12 districts: the Hejaz, along the coast of the Red Sea, including the Haram (i.e., the sacred territory of Mecca and Medina); Yemen (the Sheba of Biblical geography), on the S coast of the Red Sea; Aden, a British protectorate including Hadhramaut, situated toward the Indian Ocean; Muscat and Oman on the SE coast; Nejd, or Central Arabia; the Trucial Oman, Qatar, and Kuwait on the Persian Gulf; and the Syrian desert. The Hejaz, Nejd, and the N desert region are included in the kingdom of Saudi Arabia.

Physical and Economic Geography. The peninsula averages 700 mi. in width and 1,200 mi. in length. Countless *wadis* (river valleys), which carry rain water, take the place of ordinary rivers, which Arabia lacks. One third of Arabia is a sandy desert. Intense heat during the day is followed by cool nights. The deserts of the interior hold wide oases which support large numbers of men and animals, which move to other locations only after a succession of adverse seasons. Dates and coffee are major products, followed by gums, hides, and wool. Nomads raise the famous Arab horses near the Syrian desert. Nomadic pastoral tribes also raise small cattle, fat-tailed sheep, and black goats. The principal seaports are Jedda, in Hejaz, Muscat, the key to the Persian Gulf, and Aden, the key to the Red Sea. Other important cities are Mecca, Medina, and Riyadh. The chief commercial product is petroleum, obtained from oil fields in the E part of the peninsula.

Early History; Mohammed. The period preceding the era of Mohammed was characterized by the formation of local monarchies and federal governments of a rude form. The religion of that period had elements of fetishism, and animal and ancestor worship. The Koran enumerates ten idols of pre-Islamitic times. But in the midst of the old idolatry there had arisen some perception of a supreme god, Allah, the other gods being termed his children. Mecca with its Kaaba was the center of Arab worship under the guardianship of the noble tribe of Koreish. Out of Mecca and the Koreishites came Mohammed (570–632), who by his new religion consolidated the Arabs into a theocracy, so that on his death the Arab peninsula was, with a few exceptions, under one scepter and one creed. He was succeeded (632) by Abu-Bakr, the father of his favorite wife, Ayesha, his title being caliph, or successor. Abu-Bakr was followed by Omar (634–644), who conquered Syria, Persia, and Egypt. He was followed by Othman (644–656), who in turn was succeeded by Ali, the prophet's nephew and son-in-law. All of these except Abu-Bakr died at the hands of assassins.

Ommiad Dynasty. Next came the dynasty of the Ommiads (661–750), with 14 princes, having their capital at Damascus. During the reign of Yezid I, the second prince (679–683), a rebellion took place which split the Mohammedan world into two great sects, the Sunnites and Shiites. The Ommiads conquered other portions of Asia and Africa, and even invaded (732) France. Their most important military achievement was the conquest of Spain in 711. Spain soon became independent of the main Arab realm (but a part remained for centuries under the Moors). In the Orient the Ommiads succumbed to Ibrahim and his brother, Abu al-Abbas, who founded the dynasty of the Abbassides (q.v.).

Modern History. Before World War I, Arab Asia was part of the Ottoman Empire; parts of this were divided between Syria, Palestine, and Iraq, leaving the present Arab kingdom. Hejaz in the W and Yemen in the S were for a time Turkish provinces. Nejd and other districts came under the influence of the Wahhabees, a politico-religious faction named after Mohammed ibn-Abdul Wahhab, who arose (c1740) as a reformer. In a revival of this nationalistic movement ibn-Saud began (1913) the unification of the country by driving the Turks out of Hasa, on the Persian Gulf. The end of World War I saw the Turks completely ejected from the peninsula. Unification was practically completed by 1926, when ibn-Saud, then sultan of Nejd, was proclaimed king of Hejaz; he became king of Nejd also, in 1927, and the name of his domain was changed to Saudi Arabia in 1932. Only comparatively small units remain outside the kingdom, chief among them Yemen and Oman, which are independent, and Aden and Kuwait, which are British protectorates.

Arabia Deserta (dẹ.zėr′tạ). [Eng. trans., "*desert,*" or "*uninhabited,*" *Arabia.*] In ancient geography, the N and C portions of Arabia.

Arabia Felix (fē′liks). [Eng. trans., "*flourishing,*" or "*happy,*" *Arabia.*] In ancient geography, the region in the SE and S parts of Arabia, or perhaps the peninsula proper.

Arabia Felix. Prose work (1932) by Bertram Thomas.

Arabian Nights' Entertainments, The. [Also, **A Thousand and One Nights.**] Collection of tales, originally in Arabic, of which the plan and name are very ancient. The source of some of the stories has been traced, others are traditional. In 943 al-Masudi speaks of a Persian work *A Thousand Nights and a Night.* In the course of centuries it was added to and taken from to a great extent, and in 1450 it was reduced to its present form in Egypt, probably at Cairo. The tales show their Persian, Indian, and Arabian origin. The stories are separate from each other in plot and the work as a whole is held together by the device of Scheherazade, the supposed teller of the tales. She is supposedly under sentence of death from her husband, but postpones her execution night after night by telling him a story almost to the end, but withholding the climax until the following night. The modern editions are Antoine Galland's, from the oldest known manuscript (1548), published in French, at Paris, in 1704–17, in 12 volumes, an inaccurate translation; E. W. Lane's English scholarly translation, published in 1840; Payne's English translation, 1882–84; and Sir Richard Burton's English translation, printed (1885 *et seq.*) by the Kamashastra Society, for subscribers only, at Benares. Lady Burton issued an expurgated edition for popular reading, at London, 1886–88, in six volumes. One of the most recent editions is that by Pourys Mathers, from the French (4 vols., 1937).

Arabian Sea. [Arabic, **Bahr al 'Arab.**] Part of the Indian Ocean, nearly corresponding to the ancient Mare Erythraeum, which is bounded by Africa on the W, Arabia on the NW, Iran and Pakistan on the N, and India on the E, and is connected with the Red Sea by the strait of Bab el Mandeb, and with the Persian Gulf by the Strait of Oman. Its chief arms are the Gulfs of Aden, Oman, Kutch, and Cambay; its islands, Socotra, and the Laccadive Islands. Length, ab. 1,000 mi.; width, ab. 600 mi.

Arabia Petraea (ạ.rā'bi.ạ pẹ.trē'ạ). [Eng. trans., "*stony*" *Arabia.*] In ancient geography, the NW part of Arabia.

Arabic (ar'ạ.bik). A language of the Semitic family. It is the language of the Koran, and with Arab conquests and the spreading of Islam from the 7th and 8th centuries it came to be spoken in many countries outside of Arabia. In Iraq, Syria, Palestine, Egypt, Malta, North Africa, the Sudan, Nigeria, the western Sahara, and Zanzibar and even in Arabia itself, various Arabic dialects are spoken. The written language, however, has almost everywhere conformed to the type known as classical Arabic.

Arabicus (ạ.rab'i.kus), **Sinus.** Latin name of the **Red Sea.**

Arabi Pasha (ä.rä'bē pä.shä'), **Ahmed.** b. in Egypt, c1839; d. at Cairo, Sept. 21, 1911. Egyptian officer and revolutionary leader. A conscript in the army, he was commissioned in 1862; having been charged (1875) with peculation, he was reduced to half pay. He joined a movement against the government, serving as its spokesman against Anglo-French control of the Tewfik Pasha government and as a participant in military demonstrations which forced Tewfik to reorganize his cabinet and finally to make Arabi minister of war (1882). His influence was alarming to the British (who feared for the Suez Canal) and incited anti-European feeling, leading to bloody riots in Alexandria and a British punitive expedition. Defeated by Garnet Joseph Wolseley at Tell el-Kebir on Sept. 11, 1882, he surrendered and was tried at Cairo, receiving a death sentence which was commuted to banishment to Ceylon. Pardoned by Abbas II, he returned (1901) to Egypt.

Arabistan (ä.rä.bē.stän'). See **Arabia;** see also **Khuzistan.**

Arab League. Name applied to a loosely organized federation that formally came into existence between the states within the general area of the old Turkish empire during the latter part of World War II. Though movements for Arab unity were strong after the dissolution of the Turkish (or Ottoman) empire in 1923, this drive did not take concrete shape until March 22, 1945, when the Arab League was formed at Cairo. Signatories to the pact were Egypt, Iraq, Saudi Arabia, Lebanon, Syria and Transjordan (now Jordan), with Yemen becoming an associate state. A League Council representing all members was set up with the primary purpose of seeking measures to deter aggressors in disputes affecting two member states, or a member state and a third power, and to develop common military and economic policies. In the sense that it is used by the League members, the term "Arab" is applied to the entire body of people in W Asia and N Africa who share a common religious tradition of Islam, but it is an avowed principle of the Arab League that its members shall permit complete religious freedom within their boundaries.

Aracajú (ä"rạ.kạ.zhö'). Capital of the state of Sergipe, in E Brazil: a river port for cotton, hides, oils, and sugar. 68 686 (1950).

Aracan (ä.rä.kän'). See **Arakan.**

Aracatí (ä"rạ.kạ.tē'). [Also, **Aracaty.**] Seaport in the state of Ceará, in NE Brazil, on the Juaguaribe River near its mouth on the Atlantic. 6,803 (1940).

Araçatuba (ä"rạ sạ.tö'bạ). City in S Brazil, in the state of São Paulo. 27,692 (1950).

Arachne (ạ.rak'nē). In Greek legend, a Lydian maiden who challenged Athena to a contest in weaving, and was changed by her into a spider.

Arachosia (ar.ạ.kō'zhạ, -zhi.ạ). In ancient geography, a region in ancient Persia corresponding to part of the modern Afghanistan.

Aracthus (ạ.rak'thus). Latin name of the **Arakhthos.**

Aracthus. Latin name of **Arta,** city.

Arad (ä.räd'). [Also, **Old Arad.**] City in NW Rumania, in the region of Crişana, situated on the Mureş River, ab. 30 mi. E of the Hungarian border: one of the most beautiful cities in Rumania, and a cultural center. It has a large trade in grain, wine, tobacco, spirits, and cattle; manufactures textiles, soap, shoes, furniture, automobiles, and railway carriages; railroad junction. It was a fortress in the 17th century and belonged after 1699 to Hungary; previously it had belonged to Turkey (1551 *et seq.*) and Austria (1685 *et seq.*). In the revolution of 1849 it played an important part; it was taken from the Austrians after a long siege, was surrendered by the Hungarians in August, 1849, and was the scene of the military executions by Julius von Haynau, in October, 1849. It became Rumanian in 1920 by the Peace of Trianon. 87,291 (1948).

Aradus (ar'ạ.dus). [Old Testament name, **Arvad;** modern names, **Arwad, Rouad, Ruad.**] In ancient geography, a Phoenician city, situated on a rocky island, ab. 3 mi. from the coast of what is now Syria, N of Sidon; founded by fugitives from that place, according to Strabo. It is mentioned in Ezek. xxvii. 11 and 1 Mac. xv. 23. After Tyre and Sidon it was the most important city in Phoenicia. Remains of its walls still exist.

Araf (ä'räf), **Al.** See **Al Araf.**

Arafat (ä.rä.fät'). Sacred mountain of the Mohammedans in W Arabia, situated ab. 15 mi. SE of Mecca. 1,980 ft.

Arafura Sea (ä.rä.fö'rä). That part of the Pacific Ocean which lies N of Australia, E of Timor, Indonesia, and SE of the island of New Guinea.

Aragats (ä.rä.gäts'). See **Alagez.**

Arago (à.rà.gō), **Étienne Vincent.** b. at Perpignan, France, Feb. 9, 1802; d. at Paris, March 6, 1892. French dramatist, journalist, politician, and poet; brother of François Arago. Author of *Les Aristocrates* (1847), and others.

Arago, François. [Full name, **Dominique François Jean Arago.**] b. at Estagel, near Perpignan, France, Feb. 26, 1786; d. at Paris, Oct. 2, 1853. French astronomer and physicist who made important contributions to modern optics and electromagnetism. He was engaged (1806–08), with Biot, in geodetic surveys in the Pyrenees and Balearic Islands when the French invaded Spain, and was imprisoned by the Spanish. On his release (1809) he was elected to the Academy of Sciences and appointed professor of analytical geometry at the École Polytechnique, Paris, at the age of 23. He was also director of the Royal Observatory. In 1830 he became a member of the Chamber of Deputies. As minister of war and marine under the provisional government (after 1848), he improved conditions for sailors and abolished Negro slavery in the French colonies; he withheld his allegiance to Louis Napoleon in 1852. He made discoveries in the magnetic properties of nonferruginous substances and the magnetism of rotation, and traced the connection between the aurora borealis and magnetic elements. With Alexander von Humboldt, he supported Augustin

Jean Fresnel's undulatory theory of light against the emission theory of Pierre Simonde Laplace and others; his experiments with Fresnel led to the formulation of the laws of polarization. His final experiment (1832–50) on the velocity of light in media of varying density was completed by A. H. L. Fizeau and J. B. L. Foucault, and established the undulatory theory. Founder (1816), with Joseph Louis Gay-Lussac, of *Annales de chimie et de physique;* author of *Astronomie populaire* (published in his collected works, 1854–62), and others.

Arago, Jacques Étienne Victor. b. at Estagel, near Perpignan, France, March 10, 1799; d. in Brazil, in January, 1855. French traveler, journalist, and playwright; brother of François Arago. Author of *Voyage autour du monde* (1843), and others.

Aragon (ar'ą.gon). [Spanish, **Aragón** (ä.rä.gōn').] Medieval kingdom, subsequently a province of Spain, bounded by France on the N, by Catalonia on the E, by Valencia on the S, and by New Castile, Old Castile, and Navarre on the W, comprising the modern provinces of Huesca. Zaragoza, and Teruel. It is traversed by mountains and intersected by the Ebro River. During the Middle Ages it was one of the two chief Christian powers in the peninsula. In 1035 it became a kingdom; it was united to Catalonia in 1137, rose to great influence through its acquisitions, in the 13th and 14th centuries, of Valencia, the Balearic Islands, Sardinia, and the Sicilies, and was united with Castile in 1469 through the marriage of Ferdinand of Aragon with Isabella of Castile. Capital, Saragossa; area, 18,294 sq. mi.

Aragon (à.rà.gôn), **Louis.** b. Oct. 3, 1897—. French poet, novelist, journalist, and essayist. He was in turn a member of the cubist and dadaist movements, and subsequently (1924) a surrealist. He joined the Communist Party in 1930 and was several times an editor or staff member of *Commune, L'Humanité,* and *Ce Soir.* Sentenced to five years imprisonment for his poem *Front rouge* (1931; Eng. trans., *The Red Front,* 1933), he emerged during World War II as a great poet of patriotism and love, as well as a leader (1940–44) in the French Resistance movement. His work includes the novels *Les Cloches de Bâle* (1934; Eng. trans., *The Bells of Basel,* 1936), *Les Beaux Quartiers* (1936; Eng. trans., *Residential Quarter,* 1938), *Les Voyageurs de l'impériale* (1941; Eng. trans., *The Century Was Young,* 1941), and *Aurélien* (1944); representative of his early poetry is *Feu de joie* (1920), of his more recent mood, *Le Crève-coeur* (1941) and *Les Yeux d'Elsa* (1942); *Louis Aragon, Poet of the French Resistance* (1945) is an anthology of work written during World War II.

Aragona (ä.rä gō'nä). Town and commune in SW Italy, on the island of Sicily, in the province of Agrigento, situated on the Platani River, ab. 8 mi. N of Agrigento Most of the buildings date from the 17th century. The surrounding district has rich almond orchards; sulfur is mined in the vicinity. Pop. of commune, 14,839 (1936); of town, 10,840 (1936).

Aragon River (ar'ą.gon). [Spanish, **Río Aragón** (rē'ō ä.rä.gōn').] River in N Spain, which rises in the Pyrenees, flows W and SW through Huesca, Zaragoza, and Navarra, and joins the Ebro River near Milagro. Length, ab. 100 mi.

Aragua (ä.rä'gwä). State in N Venezuela, bounded on the NW by the Caribbean Sea. Agriculture is the principal occupation. Capital, Maracay; area, 2,162 sq. mi.; pop. 192,555 (1950).

Aragua. Valley in N Venezuela, E of Lake Valencia. It gave its name to the state of Aragua.

Araguaia (ä.rą.gwī'ą). [Also, **Araguaya.**] River in C Brazil which flows N, is separated in its middle course for a long distance into two arms, and joins the Tocantins River. The upper part of the Araguaia is sometimes called Rio Grande. Length, ab. 1,100 mi.; navigable for ab. 750 mi.

Araguarí (ä"rą.gwą.rē'). [Also, **Araguary.**] City in C Brazil, in the state of Minas Gerais. 25,789 (1950).

Araguarí River. [Also, **Araguary.**] River in NE Brazil, which flows into the Atlantic N of the Amazon.

Aragua River (ä.rä'gwä). Short river in N Venezuela, emptying into the Lake of Valencia.

Arahal (ä.rä.äl'), **El.** See **El Arahal.**

Araja (ä.rä'yä), **Francesco.** b. at Naples, c1700; d. there, c1770. Italian composer; maestro di cappella (c1734–59) at St. Petersburg. Composer of several operas, including *Cephalus and Procris,* which some scholars believe to have been the first ever sung in Russian.

Ara Jovis (ãr'ą jō'vis). Ancient name of **Aranjuez.**

Arakan (ä.rä.kän'). [Also, **Aracan.**] Division in the W part of Burma, ab. 200 mi. NW of Rangoon. Rice is the most important crop; teakwood is of secondary importance. Capital, Akyab; area, 16,001 sq. mi.; pop. 1,008,535 (1931).

Arakan Hill District (or **Tracts**). Northernmost district of the division of Arakan, W Burma, ab. 230 mi. NW of Rangoon.

Arakcheyev (ä.räk.chā'yif), Count **Aleksey Andreyevich.** b. Oct. 4, 1769; d. at Gruzina, Russia, May 3, 1834. Russian army officer and minister of war under Paul I and Alexander I. His organization of Paul's Gatchina corps and imperial forces, though so severe as to arouse strong opposition and to lead twice (1798, 1799) to his dismissal, contributed to reforms in hygiene and discipline. As inspector-general of artillery (1803) and war minister (1808) under Alexander, he played important roles in the Napoleonic wars and the war with Sweden. He later became chief counsellor to Alexander, and organized (1822–25) military colonies in Russia.

Arakhthos (ä'räch.thôs). [Also: **Arta;** Latin, **Aracthus.**] River in NW Greece, in Epirus, which flows into the Ambracian Gulf, ab. 8 mi. below Arta.

Arakhthos. An ancient name of **Arta, city.**

Araki (ä.rä.kē), **Sadao.** b. at Tokyo, 1877—. Japanese general. He was war minister (1931–33) and education minister (1937–39), and author of *Japan's Mission in Showa.* Indicted as a war criminal after World War II, he was found guilty of conspiracy and of aggressive-war charges, and sentenced to life imprisonment. He was a chief exponent of the Japanese ambition to dominate the world.

Araks (ä.räks'). See **Aras.**

Aral Sea (ar'ąl). [Also: **Lake** (or **Lake of**) **Aral;** Russian, **Aralskoe More** (ä.räl'skǫ.yę mô'ryę).] Brackish inland sea in the U.S.S.R., between the Kazakh Soviet Socialist Republic and the Uzbek Soviet Socialist Republic. in C Asia. It receives the waters of the Amu Darya and Syr Darya (rivers), but has no outlet and is thought to have been formerly dry, the Amu Darya and Syr Darya then emptying into the Caspian Sea. The Aral is generally shallow (maximum depth, ab. 222 ft.), and is subject to storms. It is now important for the water it provides for cotton irrigation in the Uzbek and Kazakh Republics. Length, ab. 225 mi.; greatest width, ab. 185 mi.; area, 24,650 sq. mi.; elevation, ab. 174 ft.

Aram (ā'ram; ãr'ąm). [Also: **Aramaea, Aramea** (ar.ą-mē'ą).] Biblical name of the country extending from the W frontiers of Babylonia to the highlands of W Asia. The inhabitants of this country were called Arameans. The Septuagint and Vulgate refer to it as Syria. The Old Testament mentions six divisions of the country, among them being Aram Naharaïm (Gen. xxiv. 10), i.e., of the two rivers; Mesopotamia, probably the territory between the Euphrates and the Chabor where the Judean exiles were settled (2 Kings, xvii. 6); Paddanaram, probably the designation for the flat country in N Mesopotamia; and Damascus. In the Assyrian cuneiform inscriptions the names Aramu, Arimu, and Arumu are used, but only of Mesopotamia and the peoples on the W bank of the Euphrates. The principal river of Aram was the Orontes. The Arameans were Semitic in race, language (Aramaic), and religion. As early as the period of the Judges an Aramean king extended his conquests to Palestine (Judges, iii. 8, 10). David took Damascus from them, but Solomon was obliged to restore it. The last king of Damascus, Rezin, allied himself with Pekah, king of Israel, against Judah, but succumbed to Tiglath-pileser of Assyria (745–727 B.C.). Aram Naharaïm appears on Egyptian monuments and in the Tel-el-Amarna tablets under the form Naharina. Thothmes I, Thothmes III, and Amenhotep III conquered it several times but after repeated attacks it finally fell to the Assyrians. The Arameans became an important component of the Assyrian state; their language seems to have become the common speech of trade and diplomacy, and gradually to have supplanted Assyrian in Assyria and Hebrew in Palestine.

Aram (ãr′ąm), **Eugene.** b. at Ramsgill, Yorkshire, England, 1704; executed Aug. 6, 1759. English scholar, executed for murder. A schoolmaster at Knaresborough, which he left (1745) under suspicion of fraud in company with a certain Daniel Clark (who subsequently disappeared), he taught at various places until arrested (1758) at Lynn Regis. He was convicted of Clark's murder on testimony by an admitted accomplice, in spite of a brilliant defense in which he accused Clark of seducing his wife; he was executed and his body hanged in chains at Knaresborough. A self-taught authority on French, Arabic, and other languages, he was among the first to point out the affinity of Celtic to Indo-European, and disputed the derivation of Latin from Greek. His life is the subject of a novel (1832) by Bulwer-Lytton, a poem, *The Dream of Eugene Aram*, by Thomas Hood, and a play, *Eugene Aram*, by W. G. Wills produced (1873) by Henry Irving.

Aramaic (ar.ą.mā′ik). Name applied as a general term to a group of Semitic languages, and also sometimes specifically to certain dialects within the group, spoken (c300 B.C. *et seq.*) in Mesopotamia, Palestine, and Syria. It includes Syriac as one of its important subdivisions, and was for many centuries the language of trade and commerce throughout that portion of the world which now comprises Lebanon, Syria, Israel, Saudi Arabia, Iraq, and Jordan. It is notable also as having been the language spoken by Jesus Christ.

Aramanik (ä.rä.mä′nēk). [Also, **Laramanik.**] Subgroup of the Nilo-Hamitic-speaking Dorobo people of E Africa, living among the Masai in N Tanganyika.

Araminta (ar.ą.min′tą). The principal female character in William Congreve's comedy *The Old Bachelor*.

Araminta. In John Vanbrugh's comedy *The Confederacy*, the wife of Moneytrap, an extravagant, luxurious woman with a marked leaning toward "the quality."

Aramis (à.rà.mēs). One of the "Three Musketeers," in the novel *The Three Musketeers*, by the elder Alexandre Dumas.

Aram Naharaïm (ā′ram nā.hā.rā′im). See **Mesopotamia**; see also under **Aram.**

Arana (ä.rä′nä), **Diego Barros.** See **Barros Arana, Diego.**

Aranda (ä.rän′dä), Conde **de.** [Title of **Pedro Pablo Abarca y Bolea.**] b. at Saragossa, in Aragon, 1719; d. at Epila, in Aragon, 1798. Spanish officer and diplomat. He introduced Prussian drill in the Spanish army, resigned under Ferdinand VI, and was recalled by Charles III to put down riots at Madrid in 1766; as president of the Council of Castile (to 1773), he effected the expulsion (1767) of the Jesuits from Spain and South America. An erratic and outspoken minister, he was generally held responsible for a diplomatic error involving the Falkland Islands; he was thereupon immediately sent (1773) to Paris, where he served as ambassador until 1787. As prime minister (1792) under Charles IV, he was involved in the intrigues of Maria Louisa and Godoy, and was dismissed and imprisoned by the king.

Aranda Memorial. Document said to have been sent (c1783) to Charles III of Spain by the Spanish statesman Pedro Pablo Abarca y Bolea, Conde de Aranda, expressing regret that Spain and France were aiding the American colonies against Great Britain and predicting that the American republic would emerge as an "irresistible colossus" threatening Spanish possessions in the New World.

Arango y Parreno (ä.räng′gō ē pär.rā′nō), **Francisco de.** b. at Havana, Cuba, May 22, 1765; d. at Güines, Cuba, March 21, 1837. Cuban lawyer, best known for his numerous works on economic questions connected with Cuba. He was twice the representative of Cuba in the Spanish Cortes, was councilor of state, and held other public offices.

Aranha (ą.ru′nyą), **José Pereira da Graça.** See **Graça Aranha, José Pereira da.**

Aranha (ą.ru′nyą), **Oswaldo.** b. at Alegrete, Rio Grande do Sul, Brazil, Feb. 15, 1894—. Brazilian lawyer and diplomat. A leader during the Vargas revolution (1930), he served as minister of justice (1930–31), finance (1931–34), and foreign affairs (1938–44). After a term as ambassador (1934–38) to the U.S., he was the Brazilian representative (1946–47) to the United Nations, and served as president (1947) of the United Nations Assembly.

Aran Islands (ar′ąn). [Also: **Arran Islands, South Aran.**] Three islands at the entrance of Galway Bay, in Connacht province, in the Irish Republic, included in County Galway. The islands form a chain ab. 15 mi. long, stretching from NW to SE. The largest, Inishmore (also called Aran-na-naomh), is ab. 9 mi. long; the others are Inishmaan and Inisheer.

Aran Islands, The. Prose work (1907) by John Millington Synge.

Aranjuez (ä.räng.ʜweth′). [Ancient name, **Ara Jovis.**] Commune in Spain, in the province of Madrid, situated ab. 25 mi. S of Madrid: center of a fertile plain, providing vegetables and fruit (particularly asparagus and strawberries) for the Madrid markets. The hippodrome attracts visitors from the capital. The fame of Aranjuez rests on its castle, long a favorite summer residence of the Spanish court. A number of wings were erected under Philip II and Charles III, in the 16th and 18th centuries. There is a park and gardens. The town was built (1746–59) according to a plan drawn up by Ferdinand VI. 23,646 (1940).

Aranjuez, Convention of. Agreement (April 12, 1779) providing for Spain's entry as an ally of France into the war against Great Britain undertaken by the American colonies. Spain was to participate in the war in the event that Great Britain should turn down the Spanish offer of mediation. Upon British rejection of the offer, Spain joined the conflict. One of the provisions of the convention called for the cession of Gibraltar to Spain in any future peace negotiations.

Aran Mawddwy (ä′rän mouᴛʜ′wi). Mountain in N Wales, in Merionethshire, situated ab. 8 mi. NE of Dolgelley. 2,970 ft.

Aransas Bay (ą.ran′sąs). Arm of the Gulf of Mexico, in Texas, NE of Corpus Christi Bay.

Aransas Pass. City in S Texas, in Aransas and San Patricio counties, NE of Corpus Christi: processing and shipping point for petroleum; shrimp and oyster fisheries. 5,396 (1950).

Aransas Pass. Strait of the Gulf of Mexico, off the coast of S Texas, the entrance to Aransas Bay.

Aranta (ą.ran′tą). A language of central Australia.

Arán Valley (ä.rän′). [Spanish, **Valle de Arán** (bä′lyā ᴛʜā).] Valley in the Pyrenees, in the province of Lérida, Spain, NE of the Maladetta range: the source of the Garonne River.

Arany (ô′rôny′), **János.** b. at Nagyszalonta (now Salonta, Rumania), March 2, 1817; d. at Budapest, Oct. 22, 1882. Hungarian epic poet and writer of ballads.

Arany, László. b. at Nagyszalontá (now Salonta, Rumania), March 24, 1844; d. at Budapest, Aug. 1, 1898. Hungarian poet; son of János Arany, whose correspondence and later works he published (1887–89).

Aranyos (ô′rô.nyōsh). River in Hungary which flows generally E to join the Mureş (Hungarian, Maros) River. Length, ab. 80–90 mi.

Arapaho (ą.rap′ą.hō). North American Indian tribe formerly centered in the headwaters area of the Platte and Arkansas rivers, but which also ranged widely from the Yellowstone River to the Rio Grande. Remnants of the tribe are now on the Wind River reservation, Wyoming. The language was of the Algonquian family.

Arapahoe Peak (ą.rap′ą.hō). Mountain in N central Colorado, in the Front Range of the Rocky Mountains. 13,506 ft.

Arapkir (ä.räp.kēr′). [Also: **Arabgir, Arabkir.**] Town in E central Turkey, ab. 40 mi. N of Malátya: a trading center in the Anatolian plateau; exports wool, rugs, and opium. Pop. ab. 7,000.

Araraquara (ą.rä.rą.kwä′rą). City in S Brazil, in the state of São Paulo. 34,671 (1950).

Ararat (ar′ą.rat). [Also: **Van**; Assyrian, **Urartu.**] Ancient name of a district in E Armenia between the river Araxes (modern Aras) and lakes Van and Urmia; also used for all of Armenia, and for the mountain ridge in the S part of that region. The usual statement that Noah's ark rested on Mount Ararat has no foundation in the Hebrew text, which reads "on the mountains of Ararat." In the Assyrian cuneiform inscriptions the country is mentioned under the name Urartu, and many expeditions of the Assyrian kings against it are enumerated.

Ararat. Town in SE Australia, in the state of Victoria, on the Hopkins River, ab. 120 mi. NW of Melbourne, in a gold-mining region. 5,960 (1947).

Araripe Junior (ą.rą.rē'pę zhö'nyōr), **Tristão de Alencar.** b. at Fortaleza, Brazil, June 27, 1848; d. at Rio de Janeiro, Oct. 29, 1911. Brazilian critic, novelist, journalist, and jurist, author of many articles and books about some of the leading Brazilian writers. Among his novels and stories are *Contos brasileiros* (1868), *O ninho do beija-flor* (1874), *Jacina, a marabá* (1875), *Um motim na aldeia* (1877), *O reino encantado* (1878), *Luizinha* (1878), and *Miss Kate* (1909).

Araros (ar'ą.ros). fl. early 4th century B.C. Athenian comic poet; son of Aristophanes. He brought out his father's *Plutus* in 388 B.C. and appeared as an original poet in 375 B.C.

Aras (ä.räs'). [Also: **Araks;** ancient name, **Araxes.**] River which rises in Turkey, NW of Lake Van, flows E to the border of the U.S.S.R., turns SE and forms part of the boundary between Turkey and the U.S.S.R., and of Iran and the U.S.S.R., and empties into the Kura River. Length, 666 mi.

Aras, Tevfik Rüştü or **Tewfik Rushdi.** b. at Çanakkale, Turkey, 1883—. Turkish statesman and diplomat. A physician (1908–09) at Smyrna, he served (1909–10) as inspector general of public health at Salonika and became inspector general of public health of the Ottoman empire. He was a medical officer in the Turkish army during World War I. He took an active role in the Turkish revolution of 1908 and in the Turkish war of independence (1918–22), served as minister of public health and minister for foreign affairs (1925–38) in the republic of Turkey, and was delegate and president in the League of Nations council and assembly. He was Turkish ambassador (1939–42) to Great Britain.

Arason (ä'rä.sôn), **Jón.** [Also: **Areson, Aresson.**] b. 1484; d. 1550. Icelandic poet and last Roman Catholic bishop of Iceland before the Reformation. Consecrated bishop of Holar in 1524, he was a man of great sagacity and courage, but openly in disagreement with the rule concerning the celibacy of the clergy. Outlawed by the king, chiefly because of his forthright opposition to the Reformation, he was executed by Danish soldiers. He is said to have established the first printing press in Iceland.

Arator of Liguria (ą.rā'tǫr, -tôr; li.gū'ri.ą). fl. 6th century A.D. Christian poet and historian. Author of *De actibus apostolorum,* which was widely used during the Middle Ages as an apostolic history.

Aratus of Sicyon (ą.rā'tus; sish'i.on, sis'i-). b. at Sicyon, near Corinth, Greece, 271 B.C.; d. 213 B.C. Greek general, leader of the second Achaean League. He liberated (251) Sicyon from the usurper Nicocles, and set up a democracy; elected (245) strategus (military leader) of the Achaean League, he took the citadel of Corinth in 243, and brought Athens and Argos into the League. Defeated in a succession of campaigns by the Spartans under Cleomenes III, he formed an alliance with Antigonus III of Macedonia (Antigonus Doson), who defeated Cleomenes at the battle of Sellasia, near the city of Sparta, in 221, but thus brought the League under Macedonian domination. He carried on an unsuccessful defensive war (221–219) against the Aetolians.

Aratus of Soli (sō'lī). b. at Soli, in Cilicia, c315 B.C.; d. in Macedonia, c240 B.C. Greek didactic poet at the court of Antigonus II of Macedonia (Antigonus Gonatas) and Antiochus I of Syria. He was the author of *Phenomena* (or *Phaenomena* or *Phainomena*), a work in 1,154 verses on astronomy, later very popular with Roman writers. It contained a section on weather signs (*Prognostica* or *Diosemeia*) used by Cicero, Vergil, and others, and an invocation to Zeus quoted by Saint Paul in his address to the Athenians on the Areopagus (Mars' Hill). Acts, xvii. 28.

Arauca (ä.rou'kä). Commissary in NE Colombia. Capital, Arauca; area, 9,970 sq. mi.; pop. 11,300 (est. 1950).

Arauca. Town in E Colombia, capital of Arauca commissary, on the Arauca River at the Venezuelan border. Pop. under 5,000 (1938).

Araucana (ä.rou.kä'nä), **La.** Heroic poem, in 37 cantos, by the Spanish poet Alonso de Ercilla y Zúñiga. It is partly a geographical and statistical account of the region of Araucania and partly the story of the expedition for the Spanish conquest of the territory of the Araucanian Indian tribes in South America in which the author took part.

Araucania (ä.rou.kä'nyä). Region in S Chile which included the territory S of the Bío-Bío River to the Gulf of Ancud, i.e., approximately the modern provinces of Bío-Bío, Arauco, Malleco, Cautín, and Valdivia.

Araucanian (ar.ô.kā'ni.ąn). [Also: **Araucanos** (-nōz), **Aucas, Oucas, Aucanos, Proaucas, Pampeans.**] Term applied to a number of more or less indeoendent tribes who formed an independent linguistic family in the main valley of C Chile. They are now to be found mainly in S middle Chile, S of the Maule River and, since c1700, in the Andean foothills and W pampas of Argentina. They resisted fiercely both the Incas in the 15th century, forcing the Inca boundary to be fixed at the Maule River, and the Spaniards, who first began invasion under Pedro de Valdivia in 1541. He was killed by them in 1553, as was one of his successors, Martin Garcia Oñez de Loyola, in 1598, when the Spanish settlements in Araucanian territory were almost totally destroyed. The last uprising of the Araucanians was put down in 1883 and reservation privileges were given by Chile in 1887. The name of one of the chief Araucanian tribal groups, the Mapuche, is sometimes used for the linguistic family as a whole. Maize and potatoes were important in their economy. Many, especially in the Argentine pampas, became nomadic hunters and raiders after the introduction of the horse by the Spaniards. It is estimated that there are about 300,000 Araucanians in Chile today. For Argentina the estimates run from a few hundred to 4,000. The main tribal divisions are the Picunche, Mapuche, and Huilliche in Chile, Pehuenche in the highland region on the boundary between Chile and Argentina, and Ranquel in the Argentine pampas. The Spanish conquest of the Araucanians is the chief subject of the epic poem *La Araucana* by Ercilla y Zúñiga.

Arauca River (ä.rou'kä). River in NE Colombia, flowing E through Venezuela to join the Orinoco River.

Arauco (ä.rou'kō). Province in S central Chile. Capital, Lebú; area, 2,222 sq. mi.; pop. 65 504 (est. 1950).

Arauco. Fort and city in C Chile, S of Concepción, and originally ab. 6 mi. from the sea: founded by Pedro de Valdivia in 1552. During the early Araucanian wars it was a post of great importance. Besieged by the Indians, it was abandoned and destroyed in 1553, rebuilt (1559) by Mendoza, again abandoned (1563) when attacked by Antihueno, rebuilt in 1566, and withstood what might be called a continuous siege from 1559 to 1590, when it was removed to the present site on the coast. Pop. under 5,000 (1940).

Araújo (ä.rą.ö'zhö), **Joaquim Aurélio Barreto Nabuco de.** See **Nabuco, Joaquim.**

Araujo de Azevedo (ä.rą.ö'zhö dę ä.zę.vā'dö), **Antônio de.** [Title, Conde de **Barca.**] b. at Sa, near Ponte de Lima, Portugal, 1754; d. at Rio de Janeiro, 1817. Portuguese politician and diplomat. He was made minister of war and foreign affairs (1804), and prime minister (1807). It was by his advice that the Portuguese court fled to Brazil in 1807. Arrived at Rio de Janeiro (1808), he resigned (but remained a member of the council of state), and in 1815 was created Conde de Barca. In 1814 he was minister of marine, and in 1817 was again called to be prime minister, holding the position until his death.

Araujo Jorge (zhôr'zhę), **Arthur Guimarães de.** b. at Paulo Affonso, Alagôas, Brazil, Sept. 29, 1884—. Brazilian writer, editor, and diplomat. He entered the diplomatic service in 1905, and held posts in Bolivia, Panama, Cuba (1927–29), Uruguay (1931–33), Germany (1933–35), and other countries, and was ambassador to Chile (1935–36) and Portugal (1936–43). Editor (1909–20) of *Revista americana.* Author of *Problemas de philosophia biológica* (1905), *História diplomática do Brasil colonial* (1915), and other books.

Araujo Lima (lē'mą), **Pedro de.** [Titles: Viscount (1841) and Marquis (1854) of **Olinda.**] b. at Antas, Pernambuco, Brazil, Dec. 22, 1793; d. at Rio de Janeiro, June 7, 1870. Brazilian statesman, regent of Brazil during the minority of the emperor Pedro II, from April 22, 1838, to July 23, 1840. He was a senator, and several times prime minister (1848–49, 1857–59, 1862–64, 1865–66).

Araújo Pôrto-Alegre (ä.rạ.ö'zhö pōr'tö.ạ.le'grẹ), **Manuel de.** See **Pôrto-Alegre, Manuel de Araújo.**

Aravalli Range (ar.a.vä'lē). [Also, **Aravali** or **Aravulli Range** (or **Hills**).] Range of mountains in Rajputana, W central Union of India, ab. 300 mi. in length, extending from NE to SW. Its highest point is Mount Abu (ab. 5,650 ft.).

Ara Vos Prec (ar'ạ vōs prek). Volume of poems (1919) by T. S. Eliot.

Arawak (ä'rä.wäk). Term sometimes incorrectly applied to the extinct **Arhuaco** Indian tribes of N Colombia.

Arawak. [Also: **Arrawac, Arrua.**] Collective term for a large number of Indian tribes distributed widely, but discontinuously, in the tropical forested portion of South America and the Antilles, and speaking languages of the Arawakan linguistic stock. Culturally the Arawak tribes are quite diverse, sharing details of custom with other tribes of various language groups in the several regions of lowland South America, rather than possessing a body of practices setting them apart from all others. Among characteristic traits possessed by the Arawak tribes in one or another degree, depending upon circumstances, have been cultivating manioc, corn, sweet potatoes, beans, and cotton; hunting with traps, bows and arrows, and blowguns; fishing with poisons, bows and arrows, and weirs; use of dugout and bark canoes; and manufacture of a great variety of basketry objects, pottery, and cloth woven on vertical looms. Socially and politically the Arawak tribes were limited to small villages or towns, headed by a chief of restricted power, and never banded together. Religion was for the most part animistic, with the principal power of rapport with the supernatural being vested in medicine men. Among the main ceremonial activities were harvest festivals, puberty ordeals, and mourning rites. Some of the Arawak tribes also practiced forms of cannibalism. The broken distribution of the Arawak tribes suggests an early establishment in the tropical forests of South America and subsequent widespread movement along the various rivers, often after displacement by the more aggressive Carib.

Arawakan (ä.rä.wä'kạn). One of the major South American linguistic stocks, widely but discontinuously distributed throughout the tropical-forest areas of W Brazil lowland Colombia, Venezuela, the Guianas, Ecuador Bolivia, and Paraguay, as well as at one time through the Antilles. A small representation probably once existed in S Florida, and thus Arawakan may be said to be the only American Indian language stock to have representation on both of the American continents.

Araxá (ä.rạ.shä'). City in SE Brazil, in the state of Minas Gerais. 14,997 (1950).

Araxes (ạ.rak'sēz). Ancient name of the **Aras.**

Arayat (ä.rä'yät), **Mount.** See under **Pampanga.**

Arbaces (är'bạ.sēz, är.bā'-). Founder of the Median empire. He reigned from c876 to 848 B.C.

Arbaces. In Beaumont and Fletcher's *King and No King*, the king of Iberia, whose nature is a compound of vainglory and violence.

Arbaces. In Byron's *Sardanapalus*, the governor of Media, who became, in place of Sardanapalus, the king of Nineveh and Assyria.

Arbaïlu (är.bī'lö). See **Arbela.**

Arbasto, the Anatomie of Fortune (är.bas'tō). Prose narrative (1584) by Robert Greene. It is a romantic tale about Arbasto, king of Denmark, who, while warring against the French king, fell in love with his daughter, Doralicia. She scorned him, but her sister Myrania loved him, released him from prison, fled with him to Denmark, and there died of a broken heart because of his indifference. Doralicia then repented and offered love, but was rebuffed and she too died. Arbasto's subjects revolted and banished him, and he found content as a hermit.

Arbate (ȧr.bȧt). Character in Jean Baptiste Racine's play *Mithridate.*

Arbate. Character in Molière's comedy *La Princesse d'Élide.*

Arbaud (dȧr.bō), **Louis d'.** b. at Meyrargues, in Provence, France, 1874—. French poet, novelist, and editor, writing in French and modern Provençal. His poems, collected in *Lou Lausié d'Arle* (The Laurel of Arles, 1913) and others published only in pamphlet form, with his novel *La Bèstio dóu Vacarés* (The Beast of the Vacares, 1924), are frequently cited as samples of modern French regional literature. He has, at recurrent intervals, edited the regionalist review *Le Feu* and has been instrumental in prolonging the Provençal local-culture movement.

Arbedo Castione (är.bā'dō käs.tyō'nā). Village in S Switzerland, in the canton of Ticino, situated at the junction of the Arbedo and Ticino valleys, NE of Bellinzona. It was the scene of a Swiss victory (1422) over the much larger army of the Milanese. 1,302 (1941).

Arbela (är.bē'lạ). [Also: **Arbaïlu**; modern name, **Erbil.**] In ancient geography, a town in Assyria. It was an early seat of the worship of Ishtar, and a place of considerable importance. Near here, at Gaugamela, a Macedonian force (said to have numbered 47,000) under Alexander the Great defeated a much larger Persian army (some estimates have run as high as one million) under Darius, in 331 B.C. This battle led to the final overthrow of the Persian empire.

Arbella (är.bel'ạ). Flagship of the fleet which, between April 8 and June 12, 1630, transported John Winthrop and other members of the Massachusetts Bay Company from England to Salem, thus inaugurating the so-called "Great Migration" which provided the basis for the settlement of Massachusetts.

Arbenz Guzmán (är'bāns gös.män'), **Jacobo.** b. at Quezaltenango, Guatemala, Sept. 14, 1913—. Guatemalan politician, president of Guatemala (1951 *et seq.*). An army officer, he became minister of national defense in 1945 after acting as one of the leaders of the revolt of 1944.

Arber (är'bėr). Mountain group in E Germany, the highest group of the Böhmerwald (Bohemian Forest), situated in Bavaria ab. 50 mi. E of Regensburg. Elevation of the Grosser Arber, ab 4,780 ft.

Arber, Edward. b. at London, Dec. 4, 1836; killed by a London taxicab, Nov. 23, 1912. English admiralty clerk, professor, and research scholar. He edited a series of works of tremendous value to students and scholars, including *Arber's English Reprints* (14 vols., 1868–71), *An English Garner: Ingatherings from Our History and Literature* (10 vols., 1877–96, usually called *Arber's English Garner*), *English Scholar's Library* (16 vols., 1878–84), *Transcript of the Registers of the Company of Stationers of London, 1554–1640* (5 vols., 1875–94), *Term Catalogues 1668–1709* (3 vols., 1903–06).

Arbères (dȧr.ber), **Bernard de Bluet d'.** See **Bluet d'Arbères, Bernard de.**

Arbil (är'bil). See **Erbil.**

Arblastier (är.blas'tyėr), **William.** See **Alabaster, William.**

Arblay (där'blā), Madame **d'.** See **Burney, Fanny.**

Arboga (är.bö'gä). Town in the *län* (county) of Västmanland, Sweden, ab. 76 mi. NW of Stockholm. It was formerly of great importance, the seat of many councils and diets. 9,262 (1950).

Arbogast (är'bọ.gast). [Also, **Arbogastes** (är.bọ.gas'tēz).] d. 394 A.D. Frankish general in Roman service under Theodosius I (the Great). He fought the Goths in Thrace, and defeated (388) Maximus, usurper of the western empire. He was made minister to Theodosius' brother-in-law, Valentinian II, who died (392) suddenly, probably murdered by Arbogast in order to install Eugenius as western emperor. Defeated (394) by Theodosius at the battle of Frigidus, he committed suicide.

Arbois (ȧr.bwȧ). Town in E France, in the department of Jura, situated on the Cuisance River, between Lons-le-Saunier and Besançon. It is famous for its wines. The chemist Louis Pasteur spent his youth here; the town has a Pasteur museum. 3,457 (1946).

Arbois de Jubainville (dȧr.bwȧ dẹ zhü.baṅ.vēl), **Marie Henri d'.** b. at Nancy, France, Dec. 5, 1827; d. in February, 1910. French archaeologist and Celtic scholar. He was archivist (until 1880) for the Aube department, and a professor of Celtic at the Collège de France (1882 *et seq.*). Founder of *Revue Celtique;* author of *Cours de littérature celtique,* and other important works on ancient Celtic literature and law.

Arboleda (är.bō.lā'ᴛʜä), **Julio.** b. at Barbacoas, Colombia, 1817; assassinated Nov. 12, 1862. Colombian poet and revolutionist. He early took his place among the first poets of Spanish America, but the manuscript of his greatest work, *Gonzalo de Oyón*, was destroyed by a personal enemy, and only portions which had been copied were published. In 1856 he joined the conservative revolt in Antioquia, became its leader, and in alliance with the president of Ecuador, carried on a war against Tomás Cipriano de Mosquera and the federalists. The states of western Colombia adhered to him, and he was elected president, but only a few months later he was assassinated.

Arbon (är'bōn). Town in NE Switzerland, in the canton of Thurgau, situated on Lake Constance between Rorschach and Egnach. 7,897 (1941).

Arbor Day. American holiday dedicated to the planting of new trees. Although observed in almost every state and territory, its dates vary from one locality to another. It is a legal holiday in a few states.

Arbor of Amorous Devices, The. Anthology of poetry (1597) issued by Richard Jones under Nicholas Breton's name. Breton is not the sole author of these poems, although a good many are his. There was an edition of the *Arbor* in 1594, but no copy is known still to exist.

Arbós (är.bōs'), **Enrique Fernández.** b. at Madrid, Spain, Dec. 25, 1863; d. at San Sebastián, Spain, June 3, 1939. Spanish violinist, conductor, and composer. He taught at the Hamburg Conservatory, the Madrid Conservatory, and at the Royal College of Music, London (1894 to 1916); he also served as concert master of the Berlin Philharmonic Orchestra, the Boston Symphony Orchestra, and the Madrid Symphony Orchestra. His compositions include *El Centro de la Tierra* (1895), a comic opera.

Arbroath (är.brōTH'). [Former names, **Aberbrothock, Aberbrothwick.**] Royal burgh and seaport, in E Scotland, in Angus, situated on the North Sea, at the mouth of the river Brothock, ab. 17 mi. NE of Dundee, ab. 469 mi. N of London by rail. The town is scenically situated near some cliffs, and has a fine sandy beach. The ruins of Arbroath Abbey, founded in 1178, are nearby. 19,584 (est. 1948).

Arbuckle (är'buk"l), **John.** b. at Pittsburgh, 1839; d. March 27, 1912. American coffee merchant, sugar refiner, and inventor. He was a leader in the development (1871 *et seq.*) of machinery to weigh, pack, and seal ground coffee, which was adapted to use with sugar; his success led to the termination (1896) by the Havemeyers' American Sugar Company of an agreement whereby Arbuckle shared in the profits derived from packaging their sugar. A five-year fight took Arbuckle into sugar refining and the Havemeyers into the coffee trade; the end result saw Arbuckle in the sugar business and eliminated the Havemeyers as competitors in coffee. He subsequently expanded his merchant-vessel holdings until it was believed that he was the largest individual American owner of seagoing vessels.

Arbuckle Mountains. Range of low mountains, of very great geological age, in S Oklahoma. The range has now, by process of erosion, been so leveled off as to have an overall average height of less than 800 ft., but it remains, because of its age and unusual rock formations, an area of great interest to geologists.

Arbuthnot (är.buth'nọt, är'buth.not), **Alexander.** b. in Kincardineshire, Scotland, 1538; d. 1583. Scottish Protestant poet, divine, and lawyer. Author of three short poems (*The Praises of Women*, *The Miseries of a Pure Scholar*, and *On Love*), a Latin work on the origin and dignity of the law, and a manuscript history, also in Latin, of his family.

Arbuthnot, John. b. at Arbuthnot, Scotland, 1667; d. at London, 1735. British physician, wit, and man of letters. He was physician extraordinary (1705), and later (1709) in ordinary to Queen Anne. The Tory ministry employed him as a political writer. He joined Jonathan Swift, Alexander Pope, John Gay, and Thomas Parnell to form (c1713) the Scriblerus Club, and was a friend of Philip Dormer Stanhope, 4th Earl of Chesterfield, William Congreve, Swift, who mentions him frequently in *Journal to Stella*, and Pope, who dedicated to him the *Epistle to Dr. Arbuthnot* (1735). Author of satirical pamphlets, chiefly *Law is a Bottomless Pit, exemplified in the case of Lord Strutt, John Bull, Nicholas Frog, and Lewis Baboon, who spent all they had in a lawsuit* (1712), later known as *The History of John Bull*, a lively attack on Whig war policy which established (though it did not invent) the popular character of John Bull as the symbol personified of Great Britain; *Memoirs of Martinus Scriblerus*, published (1741) in Pope's works but mainly written by Arbuthnot, is a satire of contemporary pedantry and antiquarianism.

Arc (ärk). River in E France, in the department of Savoie, which joins the Isère River at Chamousset. Length, ab. 90 mi.

Arcachon (ȧr.kȧ.shôṅ). Town in SW France, in the department of Gironde, situated on the Bassin d'Arcachon, a vast inlet on the Atlantic coast, ab. 35 mi. SW of Bordeaux. It is surrounded by sand dunes and pine forests; has fisheries and is a noted summer and winter resort. It has a port which is connected with the open ocean. 14,603 (1946).

Arcadelt (är'kä.delt), **Jacob.** [Also: **Archadelt, Archadet, Arcadet** (är'kä.det), **Harcadelt.**] b. in the Netherlands, c1514; d. at Paris, c1570. Dutch composer, active (c1539–49) at Rome in the papal choir, and in the service (after 1557) of the duke of Guise at Paris. He composed masses and other church music, but is best known for secular contrapuntal pieces, especially madrigals.

Arcades (är'ka.dēz). Masque by John Milton, acted shortly after *Comus* in 1634, and printed in 1645.

Arcadia (är.kā'di.ạ). City in S California, in Los Angeles County, NE of Los Angeles, of which it is a suburb. In the decade between the last two U.S. censuses its population more than doubled. 9,122 (1940); 23,066 (1950).

Arcadia. City in C Florida, county seat of De Soto County, SE of Tampa. 4,764 (1950).

Arcadia. In ancient geography, a region in Greece, in the heart of the Peloponnesus, bounded by Achaea on the N, by Argolis on the E, by Laconia and Messenia on the S, and by Elis on the W. All but isolated by mountains and intersected by them, it was proverbial for its rural simplicity. Its cities Tegea, Mantinea, and others formed a confederation c370–360 B.C.

Arcadia. [Also, **Arkadia.**] *Nomos* (department) in S Greece, situated on the Peloponnesus. It includes the provinces of Gortynia, Cynouria, Mantinea, and Megalopolis. Capital, Tripolis; area, ab. 1,600 sq. mi.; pop. 154,318 (1951).

Arcadia. Unincorporated community in NW South Carolina, in Spartanburg County: a suburb of Spartanburg. 2,554 (1950).

Arcadia. Description of shepherd life, in prose and verse, by Jacopo Sannazaro, written toward the end of the 15th century, but not published until 1504. Although it is not a pastoral romance, it appears to have first opened the field to that species of composition.

Arcadia. [Full title, **The Countess of Pembroke's Arcadia.**] Pastoral romance by Sir Philip Sidney, published in 1590, but written in 1580–81.

Arcadia. Romance by Robert Greene, published in 1589. It is modeled on Sir Philip Sidney's celebrated pastoral of the same name, which, although not printed until after the publication of Greene's *Arcadia*, had actually been written several years before it.

Arcadia. Pastoral romance by Lope de Vega, modeled on the *Arcadia* by Jacopo Sannazaro. It was not printed until 1598, although written many years before that date.

Arcadia. Pastoral play by James Shirley, printed in 1640, although presented on the stage some time previously. This is a dramatization of Sir Philip Sidney's romance of the same name.

Arcadians (är.kā'di.ạnz), **Academy** (or **Society**) **of.** See **Academy of Arcadians.**

Arcadius (är.kā'di.us). b. in Spain, c377 A.D.; d. May 1, 408. Byzantine emperor (395–408); the elder of the two sons of Theodosius I and Flaccilla. He succeeded, under the guardianship of Rufinus, to the eastern half of the empire on the death of his father and the permanent division of the Roman Empire. Rufinus claimed the civil government also of the western Roman empire, and was murdered (395) by Gainas, commander of the Gothic mercenaries at Constantinople, who acted under the instructions of Stilicho, the guardian of Arcadius's brother Honorius, emperor in the west. Arcadius then fell under the influence of the eunuch Eutropius, supported by

Gainas. After the death of Eutropius (399) and of Gainas (401) he was governed entirely by his wife Eudoxia. In this reign Alaric settled with his Visigoths (West Goths) in Illyria, and was appointed governor there.

Arcae Remorum (är'sē rē.mō'rum). A medieval name of **Charleville**.

Arcagnolo (är.kä.nyô'lō). See **Orcagna, Andrea.**

Arcata (är.kā'ta). [Former name, **Union Town.**] City in NW California, in Humboldt County, on Humboldt Bay, ab. 6 mi. N of Eureka, in a lumbering and dairy-farming region: seat of a state teachers college. Bret Harte worked here as a newspaper man and Wells Fargo agent. 3,729 (1950).

Arc de Triomphe (ärk de trē.ônf). [English, **Arch of Triumph;** full name, **Arc de Triomphe de l'Étoile.**] Triumphal arch at the head of the Champs Élysées, Paris. It was begun in 1806 by Napoleon I, but not finished until 1836. The structure is 146 ft. wide, 160 high, and 72 deep. Its chief fronts are pierced with a single archway 67 ft. high and 46 wide, and the ends have smaller archways. The spandrels of the large archway are adorned with Victories by James Pradier, and flanked by large rectangular panels representing military episodes, as do the reliefs of the frieze. Above the heavy cornice there is an attic with shields bearing titles of French victories. Against the four piers of the fronts are placed pedestals, upon which are colossal high reliefs representing (east front) triumph of Napoleon and Peace of Vienna (1810), by Jean Pierre Cortot, departure of troops for the frontier in 1792, by François Rude; (west front) blessings of peace (1815), and resistance of France to invasion (1814), both by Antoine Etex. The vaults are inscribed with the names of battles won by France, and of officers of the French army during the Napoleonic and first republican periods. The tomb of the unknown soldier of World War I was placed under the arch. The arch has long been a symbol of French military achievement, and has been so recognized by non-Frenchmen; significantly (to emphasize the completeness of German victory), Hitler marched his troops under the arch in 1940, while on a happier occasion, after the liberation of France in 1944, French and other Allied troops also marched under it.

Arc de Triomphe du Carrousel (dü kà.rö.zel). Triumphal arch built by Napoleon I at Paris, in commemoration of his victories of 1805–06, in the square enclosed by the Tuileries and the Louvre. It imitates, on a smaller scale, the Arch of Constantine at Rome. It has a large archway between two small ones, flanked by Corinthian columns, an entablature, and a high attic. Reliefs over the small archways represent incidents of the campaigns; over the columns are placed statues of soldiers of the empire, and in the spandrels of the large archway are sculptured Victories. On the summit is a group in bronze representing a four-horse chariot. The height is 48 ft., the width 63½.

Arce (är'sā), **Manuel José.** b. at San Salvador, in what is now El Salvador, c1783; d. 1847. Central American politician. He was elected (1825) first president of the Central American confederation after the break with Spain because of his known opposition to absorption by Mexico. Having repudiated his liberal following, he was replaced (1829) by Francisco Morazán. His later attempts at coups d'état were uniformly unsuccessful.

Arcesilaus (är.ses.i.lā'us) or **Arcesilas** (är.ses'i las). b. at Pitane, in Aeolis, c315 B.C.; d. c241 B.C. Greek skeptic philosopher, founder of the so-called second Academy, an opponent of Stoicism and exponent of the Socratic method. Holding that both senses and reason are untrustworthy, he based his system of ethics on assumption of probability.

Arcesilaus (of *Cyrene*). See under **Battiadae.**

Arcevia (är.chā'vyä). Town and commune in C Italy, in the *compartimento* (region) of Marches, in the province of Ancona, situated on the slopes of the Apennines, W of Ancona. Its religious buildings, which were undamaged in World War II, contain art treasures by Giovanni della Robbia, Luca Signorelli, and others. Pop. of commune, 12,478 (1936); of town, 1,145 (1936).

Arch (ärch), **Joseph.** b. at Barford, England, Nov. 10, 1826; d. there, 1919. English politician and reformer: founder (1872) and president of the National Agricultural Labourers' Union, which was broken up by farmers 18 months later. He studied labor problems in the U.S. and Canada. As a member of Parliament from northwest Norfolk (1885–86, 1892–1900), he was one of the first workingmen to hold a seat in the House of Commons.

Archadelt (är'ċhà.delt) or **Archadet** (-det), **Jacob.** See **Arcadelt, Jacob.**

Archaeological Institute of America. Society for the promotion of archaeological research, founded at Boston in 1879, and incorporated in 1906. It has since established affiliated societies in different cities. The Institute founded the American School of Classical Studies at Athens (opened 1882), the American School of Classical Studies at Rome (1895), the American Schools of Oriental Research in Palestine (1900), School of American Research (1907), and American School of Prehistoric Research (1921). Its official organ is the *American Journal of Archaeology.* It also issues reports and special publications relating to archaeology. Its headquarters are at Cambridge, Mass.

Archaic. Term applied to the preagricultural peoples and cultures of the eastern U.S., particularly to those late groups which are transitional between the Paleo- and Neo-Indians. These are often assumed to constitute a single pattern, contrasting with the Woodland and Mississippi patterns which made their appearance with the introduction of agriculture. Shell middens without accompanying mounds and earthworks are characteristic.

Archambault (är.shäm'bō), **Anna Margaretta.** b. at Philadelphia—. American portrait painter, director of the Philadelphia School of Miniature Painting, lecturer and writer, noted for her miniature portraits of such dignitaries as Presidents Warren G. Harding and Calvin Coolidge.

Archangel (ärk'ān"jel). English name of **Arkhangelsk.**

Archangel Bay or **Gulf of Archangel.** Former names of **Dvina Gulf.**

Archas (är'kas). Person in John Fletcher's *The Loyal Subject* whose character gives the play its name. He is a general of the Muscovites whose loyalty is pictured as being of the kind that bears all kinds of outrage from an unworthy king. Young Archas, the son of the general, disguises himself as a woman, and takes the name of Alinda.

Archbald (ärch'bôld). [Former name, **White Oak Run.**] Borough in NE Pennsylvania, in Lackawanna County, ab. 6 mi. NE of Scranton: coal mining; manufactures of textiles. 6,304 (1950).

Archbold (ärch'bōld), **John Dustin.** b. at Leesburg, Ohio, July 26, 1848; d. Dec. 5, 1916. American oil-company executive. He led the resistance of Titusville, Pa., oil men to the restrictive schemes of John D. Rockefeller's South Improvement Company, and was thereupon taken into the growing Standard Oil empire; prominent (1882 *et seq.*) in Standard Oil policy-making, he was a company spokesman in numerous Congressional and state investigations. He became president of the Standard Oil Company of New Jersey when the parent company was dissolved (1911) by a Supreme Court decision.

Archdale (ärch'dāl), **John.** b. in England, 1642; d. 1717. English governor of Carolina (1694–98). He was the emissary of Charles II in the dispute (1664) with Massachusetts over the Maine colony.

Archean Era (är.kē'an). The Pre-Cambrian Era. See table at end of Vol. III.

Archelais (är.ke.lā'is). Ancient name of **Aksaray.**

Archelaus (är.ke.lā'us). In ancient Greek history, one of the Heraclidae, the traditional founder of the Macedonian royal house.

Archelaus. fl. c1st century A.D. Greek sculptor. A bas-relief, the *Apotheosis of Homer,* carved by him, is in the British Museum.

Archelaus (of *Athens*). [Surnamed **Physicus,** meaning "the Physicist."] fl. c450 B.C. Greek philosopher of the Ionian (or Milesian) school, a pupil of Anaxagoras, and said to have been an instructor of Socrates and Euripides. He regarded heat and cold, derived by condensation and rarefaction of "primitive matter" or "original substance" (which he took to be air) mixed with mind, as the basic principles of generation.

Archelaus (of *Cappadocia*). fl. 1st century B.C. Cappadocian general under Mithridates II in Parthian campaigns against Rome. Sent to Greece (87) with a large force, he occupied Piraeus; defeated by Sulla at Chaeronea (86) and at Orchomenus (85), and incurring Mithridates' distrust, he deserted to the Romans in 81.

Archelaus (of *Cappadocia*). King of Cappadocia from c34 B.C. to 17 A.D.; a grandson of Archelaus (of Egypt). He owed his elevation to Mark Antony, who was captivated by the charms of Archelaus's mother, Glaphyra. He sided with Antony in the war with Octavian, but was permitted, after the defeat of Antony, to retain his kingdom, to which was subsequently added part of Cilicia and Lesser Armenia. He was, finally, summoned to Rome by Tiberius, where he was held prisoner until his death. Cappadocia became, after his death, a Roman province.

Archelaus (of *Egypt*). King of Egypt in 56 B.C.; a son of the general Archelaus (of Cappadocia). He became high priest at Comana in 63 B.C., and secured the hand of Berenice, queen of Egypt, by representing himself to be the son of Mithridates VI Eupator. He was defeated and slain by the Romans after a reign of six months.

Archelaus (of *Macedonia*). d. 399 B.C. King of Macedonia (c413–399 B.C.); son of Perdiccas II. He was a patron of Hellenic art and literature, and attracted to his court Zeuxis, Euripides, and Agathon, and invited Socrates, who declined.

Archenholz (är'ċhen.holts), Baron **Johann Wilhelm von.** b. near Danzig, Sept. 3, 1743; d. near Hamburg, Germany, Feb. 28, 1812. German historian. He served in the Seven Years' War, and lived (1769–79) in England. Author of *England und Italien* (1785) and *Geschichte des siebenjährigen Krieges* (1793); editor (1792–1812) of *Minerva*, a literary and historical journal.

Archeozoic Period (är"kē.ō.zō'ik). That part of the Pre-Cambrian Era in which life arose. See table at end of Vol. III.

Archer (är'chėr). River in NE Australia, in Cape York Peninsula, Queensland, which flows generally W into the Gulf of Carpentaria.

Archer. In George Farquhar's comedy *The Beaux' Stratagem*, a friend of Aimwell who pretends to be his servant in order to further the success of the stratagem. He carries on various lively adventures on his own account.

Archer, Branch Tanner. b. in Virginia, 1790; d. Sept. 22, 1856. American leader in the Texas revolution. After moving to Texas in 1831, he presided over the conference (1835) on Santa Anna's changes in the constitution which adopted a resolution to fight for republican principles; as a commissioner to New Orleans (1836) to obtain a loan, he helped arouse sympathy for the Texas declaration of independence. He was a supporter of Stephen Fuller Austin for the presidency of Texas, a member of its first congress, and President Lamar's secretary of war.

Archer, Frederic. b. at Oxford, England, June 16, 1838; d. at Pittsburgh, Oct. 22, 1901. Organist and conductor. After studying at Oxford, London, and Leipzig, he gave organ recitals at Alexandra Palace, London, and elsewhere. He came (1881) to the U.S., becoming church organist at Brooklyn, New York, and Chicago, conductor (1887–88) of the Boston Oratorio Society, organist and music director (1895 *et seq.*) at the Carnegie Institute, Pittsburgh, and conductor (1896–98) of the Pittsburgh Orchestra. He was a leader in removing the organ recital from its narrow field and popularizing it in the U.S.

Archer, Frederick J. b. at Cheltenham, England, 1857; shot himself at Newmarket, England, 1886. English jockey. He competed in 2,746 races, and was five times winner of the Derby and several times winner of virtually every other important English stake race of his day.

Archer, Frederick Scott. b. at Bishop's Stortford, England, 1813; d. 1857. English photographer and one-time sculptor who invented (1850) the collodion process of making photographic plates. He also developed a version of the liquid-filled lens and was the first in England to use the so-called triplet lens.

Archer, Isabel. Heroine of *The Portrait of a Lady* (1881), a novel by Henry James.

Archer, James. b. at Edinburgh, 1823; d. 1904. British portrait painter. His early work includes a number of Biblical and classical studies, as well as several scenes from the Arthurian legend, but his reputation is based on his later portraits of children, and on costume pictures, most of which were exhibited at the Royal Academy.

Archer, James J. b. at Stafford, Md., Dec. 19, 1817; d. Oct. 24, 1864. American soldier, Confederate general in the Civil War. Educated at Princeton and at Bacon College in Kentucky, he achieved the brevet rank of brigadier general for service at Chapultepec in the Mexican War, but left the army in 1848. He returned (1855) with the rank of captain, and aligned himself with the Confederacy (1861). He commanded a brigade in the Army of Northern Virginia in every notable battle of 1862–63; captured at Gettysburg, he died soon after his exchange (1864).

Archer, John. b. near Churchville, Md., May 5, 1741; d. Sept. 28, 1810. American physician, teacher, Revolutionary soldier, and one-time theologian. He gave up theology for medicine after preaching a trial sermon, began to practice medicine while still a student at the Philadelphia College of Medicine, and received (1868) the first medical degree involving attendance at lectures to be awarded in America. He became a major in January, 1776, in the Revolutionary army and was later a member of the Maryland state constitutional convention. He was also a member of Congress (1801–07), and an examiner and founder (1799) of the Medical and Chirurgical Faculty of Maryland.

Archer, Newland. Hero of *The Age of Innocence* (1920), novel by Edith Wharton.

Archer, William. b. at Perth, Scotland, 1856; d. 1924. British drama critic and playwright; translator and popularizer of Ibsen in England. Newspaper work in Scotland, Australia, and London was followed by the translation of Ibsen's *Pillars of Society*, the production of which (1880) at the Gaiety Theatre gave the London public its first taste of Ibsen. He edited *Ibsen's Prose Dramas* (5 vols., 1890–91). His own works included the prose volume *God and Mr. Wells* (1917), as well as several plays, including *The Green Goddess* (1921), a melodrama successful on both sides of the Atlantic.

Archers, The. [Full title, **The Archers: or, The Mountaineers of Switzerland.**] Opera by Benjamin Carr, with libretto by William Dunlap, first performed at New York on April 18, 1796. One of the earliest American operas, the work is based on the William Tell legend.

Archibald (är'chi.bôld), Sir **Adams George.** b. at Truro, Nova Scotia, May 18, 1814; d. there, Dec. 14, 1892. Canadian politician and jurist, active in conferences (1857, 1864, 1866) on the union of the Canadian provinces, and secretary of state (1867–68) for the new Dominion of Canada. He was also the first lieutenant governor (1870–72) of Manitoba under dominion status.

Archibald, Jules François. [Original name, **John Feltman.**] b. at Kildare, Victoria, Australia, Jan. 14, 1856; d. at Sydney, Australia, Sept. 10, 1919. Australian journalist and editor, founder (1880) with John Haynes of the *Bulletin* of Sydney, one of the most influential political, financial, and literary weeklies in Australia's history.

Archibald, Raymond Clare. b. at South Branch, Nova Scotia, Oct. 7, 1875—. American mathematician and historian, author of works on the history of mathematics. He held numerous offices in mathematical and scientific organizations, and served on the editorial boards of many periodicals. He was educated at Harvard, Berlin, and Strasbourg, at the last of which he received his doctorate in 1900. From 1908 on he taught at Brown University. Besides bio-bibliographical studies, especially of Simon Newcomb (1905, 1924), Benjamin Peirce (1925), J. J. Sylvester (1936), and mathematical table-makers (c1948), his books include *The Cardioid and Some of Its Related Curves* (1900) and an *Outline of the History of Mathematics* which has gone through many editions since its original publication in 1932.

Archidamus (är.ki.dā'mus). Bohemian lord in Shakespeare's *A Winter's Tale.*

Archidamus II. King of Sparta from c469 to c427 B.C. He led the army under Sparta against Athens in the beginning of the Peloponnesian War.

Archidamus III. King of Sparta from c361 to 338 B.C. He defeated the Arcadians and Argives in the "Tearless Battle" (367), and was killed in battle in 338.

Archigenes (är.kij'ē.nēz). b. at Apamea, in Syria; fl. at Rome, 98–117 A.D. Greek physician, who practiced at Rome in the time of Trajan. A celebrated eclectic, he was the author of a treatise on the pulse (the most elaborate of ancient times) to which Galen added a commentary. He distinguished four stages in the development of disease, and established a classification system for fevers. In addition to this, he made considerable refinement in diagnostic technique, and also produced descriptions of leprosy (then little understood) and Hindu therapeutics (then almost completely unknown in Europe).

Archilochus (är.kil'ǫ.kus). b. at Paros, in the Cyclades; fl. c700–650 B.C. Greek lyric poet, probable inventor of iambic and trochaic meters. Embittered by poverty and by the refusal of a fellow townsman to give him his daughter in marriage, he became a wanderer and soldier, being eventually killed in battle. He used iambics in satires praised by Horace and Hadrian, among others. Author also of hymns (one of which was sung in the Olympics), elegies, and lampoons; he used the trochee in his serious works, and was the first to alternate long and short verses in the form called epode.

Archimage (är'ki.māj). [Also, **Archimago** (är.ki.mā'gō).] Personification of Hypocrisy in Edmund Spenser's *Faerie Queene*, a magician and a compound of deceit and credulity. He deceives Una by assuming the appearance of the Red Cross Knight, but his falsehood is exposed. The whole story is taken from Ariosto's *Orlando Furioso.*

Archimage. [Also, **Archimago.**] Personification of Indolence in James Thomson's *Castle of Indolence.*

Archimedes (är.ki.mē'dēz). b. at Syracuse, Sicily, c287 B.C.; killed there, 212 B.C. Greek mathematician, engineer, and physicist, now usually considered to have been in each of these fields the outstanding figure of the ancient world. He was the discoverer of principles and the author of treatises basic to the subsequent study of geometry and calculus, particularly on the dimensions of the circle, sphere, cylinder, and parabola; in physics, developer of the displacement theory known as Archimedes' principle, and supposedly also of that of the lever (of which, according to tradition, he said, "Give me the place to stand, and I will move the world"); in mechanics he was the inventor of the Archimedean screw and various machines of war. The son of an astronomer, he was a student at Alexandria, and was probably associated with Conon of Samos. He spent much of his life at the court of Hiero II of Syracuse (who is said to have been his relative). Given the problem of analyzing the gold content of Hiero's crown, he is supposed to have cried "Eureka!" ("I have found [it]"), as, stepping into his bath, he discovered the relationship between weight and displacement of water, the principle now applied to determining the displacement of ships and specific gravity. His engines of war, which struck terror among the Romans and held them off for three years in their siege of Syracuse (214–212 B.C.), were considered unimportant by him. According to one tradition he was killed at the fall of Syracuse while drawing geometrical figures in the sand, though the Roman commander had ordered him spared for his great learning.

Archipelago (är.ki.pel'ą.gō). [Also: **Greek Archipelago;** Turkish, **Jezairi-Bahri-Sefid.**] In ancient geography, a name for the various islands in the Aegean Sea, or for the sea itself; in recent times, a former vilayet of Turkey including some of the Aegean islands.

Archipel des Comores (ȧr.shē.pel dā ko.mor). A French name of **Comoro Islands.**

Archipenko (Anglicized, är.ki.peng'kō; Russian, är-ʜē'pin.kǫ), **Aleksandr.** b. at Kiev, Ukraine, May 30, 1887—. Russian sculptor and painter, resident (since 1924) in the U.S. A leader of modernists in the field of sculpture, he is best known for his abstractions based on the female nude figure; the use of unusual materials characterizes much of his work.

Archipiélago (är.chē.pyā'lä.gō). Spanish word for "archipelago": for entries not listed here, see the specific element of the name.

Archipiélago de Colón (är.chē.pyā'lä.gō ᴛʜā kō.lōn'). [Also called **Galápagos Islands.**] Civil division of Ecuador, comprising the Galápagos Islands. Capital, San Cristóbal; area, 3,029 sq. mi.; pop. 661 (est. 1944).

Archipropheta (är.ki.prof'ę.tą). Tragedy (1547) written in Latin by Nicholas Grimald.

Archive War. Incident (1842) involving a struggle between Houston and Austin, Tex., over the possession of the state archives. In 1839 Austin was named as the capital of Texas. A raid conducted by the Mexicans against San Antonio in 1842 created fears that the archives might be destroyed, and President Houston, of the Texan republic, ordered the records moved to Houston. However, the residents of Austin pursued the wagons bearing the archives and compelled them to turn back to Austin.

Arch of Augustus. [Also, **Porta Romana.**] Roman triumphal arch at Rimini, Italy, built in 27 B.C., in honor of the restoration of the Flaminian Way. It is of white travertine, 45.9 ft. high and 28.8 thick, with a single arch 29.5 ft. high and 26.9 wide. A Corinthian fluted column on each side of the archway supports an entablature, above which there is a low pediment.

Arch of Constantine. Roman arch built in 312 A.D. in honor of Constantine's triumph over Maxentius. It has a large central archway between two smaller ones, and four Corinthian columns on each front. The attic bears a long inscription.

Arch of Drusus. Roman arch (wrongly named) built by Caracalla to carry an aqueduct for the supply of his thermae over the Appian Way near the gate of San Sebastiano. It is built of travertine, faced with white marble, and decorated with composite columns, and originally had on each side an entablature and a pediment. The style is usually considered to be very poor.

Arch of Hadrian. Triumphal gateway at Athens, probably built by Hadrian, between the old city and his new quarter. It is 59 ft. high, with a single arch 20 ft. high. Above the arch there is an attic with three large openings, originally closed. Above the central opening there is a pediment. The arch was decorated on each side with Corinthian columns.

Arch of Janus Quadrifrons. Roman arch at the NE extremity of the Forum Boarium. It is a four-way arch of marble, largely built of older architectural fragments. The interior is covered with a simple groined vault. The four fronts bear 32 niches for statues of divinities, and on the massive piers there are 16 blind niches flanking the archways. The structure was used in antiquity as a kind of financial exchange.

Arch of Septimius Severus. Roman arch in the Forum, dedicated 203 A.D., in commemoration of victories over the Parthians. It is of Pentelic marble, with a central arch and two side arches, flanked by four Corinthian columns on each face. There are panels over the side arches and a frieze above all with reliefs of Roman triumphs. The attic bears inscriptions.

Arch of Titus. Roman arch in the Forum, built in commemoration of the taking of Jerusalem. It has a single archway, the opening flanked on each face by four composite columns. The spandrels bear Victories in relief, and on the high attic is the dedicatory inscription. The vault is richly coffered and sculptured, and the interior faces of the piers display reliefs of Titus in triumph, with the plunder of the temple at Jerusalem, in which the seven-branched candlesticks are conspicuous.

Arch of Trajan. Arch over the Appian Way at Benevento, Italy, dedicated in 114 A.D., and one of the finest of ancient arches. It is of white marble, 48 ft. high and 30½ wide, with a single arch measuring 27 by 16½ ft. On each face there are four engaged Corinthian columns, with an entablature, above which is a paneled attic. The arch is profusely sculptured with reliefs illustrating Trajan's life and his Dacian triumphs. There are Victories in the spandrels and dedicatory inscriptions on the central panels of the attic.

Arch of Trajan. Arch erected at Ancona, Italy, in 115 A.D. It is of white marble, and stands at the end of the breakwater built by Trajan, and is perhaps the best-proportioned of all Roman triumphal arches. It has a single opening 46 by 29½ ft., two engaged Corinthian columns on the face of each pier, and a high attic above the entablature.

Arch of Triumph. See **Arc de Triomphe.**

Archon (är'kon). In John Dryden's poem *Albion and Albanius*, a character intended to represent George Monck.

archy and mehitabel (är'chi; mę.hit'ą.bel). Collection of verse by Don Marquis, published in 1927. A cockroach in whom resides the soul of a poet, archy uses a typewriter to compose free verse, all of which is unencumbered with capital letters because of his inability to operate the shift key; mehitabel is a cat, archy's occasional companion and conversational foil, with a soul which belonged in an earlier incarnation, by her own claim, to Cleopatra.

Archytas of Tarentum (är.kī'tas; ta.ren'tum). fl. c400–350 B.C. Greek Pythagorean philosopher, mathematician, statesman, and general; a friend of Plato. Believed by some to have furnished certain ideas used by Plato and Aristotle, he is known to have been the first to set up a system of analytical geometry and to distinguish harmonic progression. He was a notable contributor to the theory of proportion and the study of acoustics and music. Finally, he was the inventor of a method of doubling the cube, supposedly also of the pulley, and even, according to Aulus Gellius, of a flying machine.

Arcignano (är.chē.nyä'nō). [Also, **Arzignano.**] Town and commune in NE Italy, in the *compartimento* (region) of Veneto, in the province of Vicenza, situated in the foothills of the Alps, W of Vicenza. Pop. of commune, 13,382 (1936); of town, 4,597 (1936).

Arciniegas (är.sē.nyā'gäs), **Germán.** b. at Bogotá, Colombia, Dec. 6, 1900—. Colombian historian and diplomat. He has served as vice-consul (1930 *et seq.*) at London, counsellor (1940) at Buenos Aires, minister of education (1941, 1946), and a visiting professor at Columbia (1942, 1948 *et seq.*), the University of Chicago (1943), and the University of California (1944). Editor of *Revista de America*, and author of *The Knight of El Dorado* (1943), *Germans in the Conquest of America* (1943), *The Green Continent* (1944), and *The Caribbean* (1946).

Arcis-sur-Aube (år.sēs.sür.ōb). Town in the department of Aube, France, situated on the Aube River ab. 17 mi. N of Troyes. It was the birthplace of Georges Jacques Danton. Here a battle was fought, on March 20 and 21, 1814, between the French under Napoleon I and the Allies under Karl Phillip Schwarzenberg. Napoleon was unsuccessful in his attempt to prevent the junction of Schwarzenberg and Blücher, and retreated, leaving the route to Paris open, with the intention of attacking the Allies in the rear. Pop. ab. 3,000.

Arciszewski (är.chē.shef'skē), **Crestofle d'Artischau.** See **Artichofsky, Crestofle d'Artischau.**

Arciszewski, Tomasz. b. Sept. 14, 1877—. Polish socialist. Active in secret political organizations under the Czarist regime, he was later a member (1919–35) of the Polish parliament. During the German occupation (1939 *et seq.*) he belonged to the underground council of national unity, and was flown (1944) to London, where he served (1944–45) as premier of the Polish government-in-exile.

Arcite (är'sīt). Theban knight. An account of him is given in Geoffrey Chaucer's *Knight's Tale*, and John Dryden's *Palamon and Arcite*. The name was also given by Chaucer to a false knight in his *Anelida and Arcite.*

Arco (är'kō). Town and commune in NW Italy, in the *compartimento* (region) of Trentino-Alto Adige, in the province of Trento, situated on the Sarca River, near Lake Garda, ab. 16 mi. SW of Trent. It is a health resort, with a generally mild climate. There is a castle of the counts of Arco; seat of the Arco family, of Bavarian origin, from the 12th century. Pop. of commune, 9,215 (1936); of town, 3,448 (1936).

Arcole (är'kō.lā). [Also, **Arcola** (-lä).] Village and commune in NE Italy, in the *compartimento* (region) of Veneto, in the province of Verona, situated on the Alpone River, ab. 15 mi. SE of Verona. Here a victory was gained by the French under Napoleon I over the Austrians under Josef Alvinczy, on Nov. 15, 16, and 17, 1796. It was fought largely in the swamps near Arcole, laying the foundation of Napoleon's reputation as a strategist and military leader. Pop. of village, 1,945 (1936); of commune, 4,480 (1936).

Arçon (dår.sôṅ), **Jean Claude Eléonore Le Michaud d'.** b. at Pontarlier, France, 1733; d. July 1, 1800. French military engineer and writer. He was the inventor of floating batteries used at the siege of Gibraltar (1782), and the author of *Considérations militaires et politiques sur les fortifications* (1795).

Arcos (år.kos), **René.** b. at Clichy-la-Garenne, near Paris, Nov. 16, 1880—. French poet, author of *L'Âme essentielle* (1903), *L'Île perdue* (1913), and others. He is known as a member, with Georges Duhamel, Jules Romains, and others, of the "Abbaye de **Créteil**," a unanimist group.

Arcos de la Frontera (är'kōs dā lä frōn.tā'rä). City in S Spain, in the province of Cádiz, situated on the Guadalete River, ab. 30 mi. NE of Cádiz: agricultural trade center. The city is located on a high rock, which is surmounted by a Gothic church. A Roman town in ancient times, it preserves remains of the ancient fortifications. Under Moslem rule in the early Middle Ages, the town was captured by Ferdinand III of Castile and León in 1250, and served subsequently as a fortified frontier stronghold in the wars between Castile and Granada. 18,146 (1940).

Arcot (är.kot'). [Tamil, **Arkat** or **Arucati,** meaning "Six Forests."] Town in the district of North Arcot, Madras state, Union of India, situated on the Palar River ab. 67 mi. W of the city of Madras: once the capital of the Carnatic. It was taken by Robert Clive in August, 1751, and defended by him from September to November of that year against the French and natives. Later it was successively held by the French, British, and Hyder Ali, and was ceded to the British in 1801. Pop. ab. 15,000.

Arctedius (ärk.tē'di.us), **Petrus.** Latinized name of **Artedi, Peter.**

Arctic (ärk'tik). Passenger steamship belonging to the Collins Line (the first American line of steamships), which was sunk by collision in the Atlantic Ocean in 1854.

Arctic Archipelago. [Also, **Canadian Arctic Islands.**] Island group in the Arctic Ocean, N of Canada and included within the political jurisdiction of the Northwest Territories of Canada. The chief islands of the group are Baffin Island, Banks Island, Ellesmere Island, Melville Island, and Victoria Island. The archipelago has been formally under Canadian control since 1880. Area, ab. 550,000 sq. mi.

Arctic Circle. Hypothetical line shown on most globes to separate the Arctic region from the rest of the world to the S. It is at every point in its circumference ab. 23½° S of the North Pole, and represents the latitude at which the sun is tangent to the horizon at midnight on June 22. Everywhere N of the Arctic Circle there is continuous sunshine (during clear weather) for a period in midsummer, and during the same period continuous daylight or twilight prevails in a zone several degrees S of the Arctic Circle.

Arctic Ocean. Part of the ocean which lies about the North Pole. Partially enclosed by Europe, Asia, North America, and Greenland, it communicates with the Pacific Ocean by Bering Strait, and is open to the Atlantic. It is generally regarded as extending S to the Norwegian Sea. Among the lands in it are Greenland, Novaya Zemlya, Severnaya Zemlya, Svalbard, Franz Josef Land, Jan Mayen, New Siberia, Wrangel Island, Banks Island, Prince Patrick Island, Melville Island, Victoria Island, King William Island, Prince of Wales Island, Bathurst Island, Somerset Island, Devon Island, Baffin Island, and Ellesmere Island. Among its arms or divisions are Kotzebue Sound, Beaufort Sea, Viscount Melville Sound, McClintock Channel, Gulf of Boothia, Lancaster Sound, Baffin Bay, Smith Sound, Lincoln Sea, Kara Sea, Barents Sea, Gulf of Ob, Yenisei Gulf, White Sea, Laptev Sea, East Siberian Sea, and Chuckchee Sea. Area, ab. 5,440,000 sq. mi.

Arctic Red River. River in NW Canada, in the Northwest Territories, flowing generally NW to the Mackenzie River. There is a Hudson's Bay Company post, and also a station of the Royal Canadian Mounted Police, at the point of its junction with the Mackenzie. Length, ab. 230 mi.

Arctinus (ärk.tī'nus). fl. c776 B.C. Greek poet of Miletus, believed to have been a pupil of Homer. Author of *Aethiopis*, an epic poem which picks up the narrative at the point where it is dropped by the *Iliad.*

Arcturus (ärk.tū'rus). An orange star, α Boötis, sixth brightest in the sky. It is situated between the thighs of Boötes, behind the Great Bear, and is easily found by following out the curve of the bear's tail. It may be recognized by its forming a nearly equilateral triangle with Spica and Denebola.

Arcueil (år.kėy'). [Latin, **Arculi** (är'kū.lī), **Arcus Julianus** (är'kus jö.li.ā'nus).] Town in N France, in the department of Seine: southern suburb of Paris. Nearby are the ruins of a Roman aqueduct on the site of which another was built (1613–24) to convey water to the gardens of the Luxembourg. A new aqueduct was built in 1868–72. Arcueil has been known for its quarries, and has had some popularity as a resort. 16,340 (1946).

Ardabil (är.dą.bēl'). See **Ardebil.**

Ardahan (är.dä.hän'). [Also, **Ardagan** (-gän').] Fortress in NE Turkey, situated on the Kura River ab. 41 mi. NW of Kars: stormed by the Russians in May, 1877, and ceded to Russia by Turkey in 1878, but later returned. Pop. ab. 3,000.

Ardashir (är.dä.shēr'). [Called **"Ardashir i Papakau,"** meaning "Ardashir the son of Papak"; Old Persian, **Artaxerxes.**] Founder of the Sassanid dynasty. He reigned c226–c241 A.D. From Papak's capital at Istakhr, near Persepolis, he subdued Kerman and Susiana. In 224 he defeated and killed Ardavan, the last Parthian emperor, and from that time he called himself "king of kings." Alexander Severus led a large force against him. While Istakhr was in theory the capital, his real capital consisted of Ctesiphon and Veh-Ardashir (Seleucia), on the opposite bank of the Tigris. He established the Zoroastrian religion as the official religion of the state.

Ardea (är'dę.ą). In ancient geography, a town in Latium, Italy, ab. 24 mi. S of Rome. It was the chief town of the Rutulians, and later a Roman colony.

Ardebil (är.dę.bēl'). [Also, **Ardabil.**] City in NW Iran, in Azerbaijan region, ab. 30 mi. W of the Caspian Sea. It is situated on the chief trade route between Iran and the U.S.S.R. (the S boundary of the latter is only a few miles to the N of Ardebil), and has been at various times under Russian political control. It is the historical capital of the Azerbaijan nation, and remains a chief cultural center of the Azerbaijan people in both Iran and the U.S.S.R. It was at one time also a residence of the court of Persia. Pop. ab. 63,500.

Ardèche (ȧr.desh). Department in S France, bounded by the department of Loire on the N, the department of Drôme (separated by the Rhone River) on the E, the department of Gard on the S, and the departments of Lozère and Haute-Loire on the W; formed chiefly from the ancient district of Vivarais. The territory slopes down from the Cévennes mountains to the valley of the Rhone; agricultural products are consequently of great variety. Grain and pasture lands prevail in the W, and vineyards, orchards, and mulberry groves in the Rhone valley and the valleys leading to it. There are various industries, the silk and paper manufactures of Aubenas, Tournon, and Annonay being the most important. Capital, Privas; area, 2,144 sq. mi.; pop. 254,958 (1946).

Ardèche River. Small river in S France, in the department of Ardèche, which joins the Rhone River ab. 26 mi. NW of Avignon.

Ardelan (är.de.län'). District in W Iran, ab. 150 mi. NE of the city of Baghdad, Iraq: oil wells and herds of sheep are the principal sources of revenue.

Arden (är'dęn), **Forest of.** English forest which in former times extended through Warwickshire and other midland counties of England. Many scholars of Shakespeare have held that the Forest of Arden of *As You Like It* was the Forest of Ardennes in French Flanders. Wherever the scene of the play was laid, it is likely from the allusions to Robin Hood and the bits of description that it is the English forest that Shakespeare meant, though some of the characters have French names. A comparatively small wooded area in N Warwickshire is all that remains today of the original forest.

Ardennes (är.den'; French, ȧr.den). Department in NE France, bounded by Belgium on the N and NE, the department of Meuse on the E, the department of Marne on the S, and the department of Aisne on the W. It is formed largely from part of the old provinces of Champagne and Sédannais, and smaller territories. It lies in a heavily forested region sometimes called "the Forest of Ardennes," which falls within France, Belgium, and Luxembourg. It was the scene of decisive battles in the wars following the French Revolution, in the Franco-Prussian War of 1870–71, and in the two World Wars. In 1870, the French army under Marshal Marie Edme Patrice Maurice de MacMahon capitulated to the Germans near Sedan, and it was likewise near Sedan that the German Panzer divisions made their major break through the French lines in 1940. Later in World War II the Ardennes region saw severe fighting in the "Battle of the Bulge" (December, 1944–January, 1945). Many of its cities, industries, and architectural masterpieces were destroyed in the course of these disasters, and the population has dropped. The soil is generally poor. Among the industries, the metallurgical and textile industries are outstanding. Capital, Mézières; area, 2,027 sq. mi.; pop. 245,335 (1946).

Ardennes (dā.zȧr.den), **Charles Baudin des.** See **Baudin des Ardennes, Charles.**

Ardennes (är.den'; French, ȧr.den), **Forest of.** [French, **Forêt des Ardennes**; Latin, **Arduenna Silva.**] In ancient geography, a large forest in Gaul which extended from the Rhine River at Koblenz to the Sambre River; now restricted to S Belgium and a part of NE France, the present department of Ardennes (*q.v.*), a plateau rich in minerals and timber.

Ardennes Offensive. See **Battle of the Bulge.**

Arden of Feversham (är'dęn; fev'ėr.shąm). Tragedy, published by George Lillo in 1736, founded on the earlier *Tragedy of Mr. Arden of Feversham,* and played first in 1759. It was unfinished when Lillo died in 1739, and was thereafter completed by other hands. It was considerably altered and revised by Dr. John Hoadley in 1762, and was produced in this form in 1790.

Arden of Feversham, The Tragedy of Mr. Tragedy first printed (anonymously) in 1592, sometimes attributed to Shakespeare, and dramatized from Raphael Holinshed's account of the murder of a leading citizen of Faversham in Kent in 1551. According to Frederick Gard Fleay, who dates it 1585, there is some ground for attributing it to Thomas Kyd. Ludwig Tieck translated it into German as Shakespeare's work.

Arderne (är'dėrn), **John.** fl. c1370. English surgeon who performed an operation for fistula believed by most medieval European surgeons to be impossible, although not unknown to Arab medical men. His patients probably included Edward the Black Prince and other leading men of the time. He derived his surgical precepts largely from actual practice rather than from written sources, although his *Liber de fistulis* and *De arte medicinae* indicate an awareness of Galen's works.

Ardigò (är.dē.gô'), **Roberto.** b. at Casteldidone, Italy, Jan. 28, 1828; d. at Mantua, Italy, Sept. 15, 1920. Italian philosopher, outstanding in the Italian positivistic philosophical movement. He served (1881 *et seq.*) as professor at the University of Padua.

Arditi (är.dē'tē), **Luigi.** b. in Piedmont, Italy, in July, 1822; d. in England, May 1, 1903. Italian violinist and conductor of opera at Vercelli (1843), New York (1852–56, c1880), London (1857–78), St. Petersburg, Vienna, and elsewhere. He was a composer of songs, particularly *Il Bacio,* overtures, and operas such as *I Briganti* (1841), *Il Corsaro* (1846), and *La Spia* (1856, based on Cooper's *The Spy*).

Ardmeanach (ärd.men'ąċh). See **Black Isle.**

Ardmore (ärd'mōr). City in S Oklahoma, county seat of Carter County, ab. 120 mi. SE of Guthrie, in a petroleum-producing area. Manufactures include automobile tires, refined petroleum, guns, cigars, stoves; processing center for cotton and pecans. It was settled in 1887 and named after a suburb of Philadelphia. 17,890 (1950).

Ardnamurchan (ärd.ną.mėr'ċhąn). Peninsula in W Scotland, in Argyllshire, ab. 25 mi. NW of Oban. It forms a parish of Argyllshire. Length, ab. 17 mi.; greatest width, ab. 8 mi.; area, ab. 171 sq. mi.

Ardnamurchan Point. Promontory in W Scotland, in Argyllshire, situated at the W extremity of the Ardnamurchan peninsula. It is the most westerly point of the mainland of Scotland.

Ardoch (är'doċh). Parish in S Perthshire, Scotland, ab. 12 mi. N of Stirling. It has noted Roman military antiquities (the best-preserved Roman camp in Great Britain), and is the probable site of the victory of Agricola over the North Britons in 84 A.D.

Ardoin (är'doin, -dǫ.in) or **Ardoino** (är.dō.ē'nō). See **Arduin.**

Ardres (är'dėr; French, ȧrdr). Town in N France, in the department of Pas-de-Calais, situated ab. 9 mi. SE of Calais. Near here was the meeting on the "Field of the

Cloth of Gold" between Francis I of France and Henry VIII of England in 1520.

Ardrossan (är.dros'ạn). Police burgh, seaport, and holiday resort in S Scotland, in Ayrshire, situated on the Firth of Clyde, ab. 26 mi. SW of Glasgow, ab. 407 mi. N of London by rail. The town is situated on the Ayrshire coal field; it imports iron ore and exports coal and iron. Ardrossan formerly had a shipbuilding industry, but the shipyards have now been closed. 8,783 (est. 1948).

Arduenna Silva (är.dū.en'ạ sil'vạ). Latin name of **Ardennes, Forest of.**

Arduin (är'dụ̄.in), **Ardoin** (är'doin, -dọ.in), or **Ardoino** (är.dō.ē'nō). d. c1015. King of Italy or Lombardy (1002–13), and marquis of Ivrea. He was proclaimed king of Italy in Pavia on the death of Otto III, but was overthrown by the emperor Henry II.

Ardven (ärd'ven). In the poems of Ossian, a name given to a region on the W coast of Scotland.

Ardys (är'dis). Son of Gyges, king of Lydia. Assurbanipal, king of Assyria (668–626 B.C.), relates in his annals that Gyges rebelled against him, but that his son Ardys, as a result of the invasion of Lydia by the Cimmerians, submitted to him and invoked his help.

Are (ä'rẹ). Ruined castle near Altenahr, W Germany, in the former Rhine Province of Prussia.

Arecibo (ä.rā.sē'ʙō). [Full name, **San Felipe de Arecibo.**] City on the N coast of Puerto Rico, on the Grande de Arecibo River. 22,134 (1940).

Areius (ạ.rī'us) or **Areios** (-os). See also **Arius.**

Areius. fl. c30 B.C. Stoic or Pythagorean philosopher of Alexandria, the friend and preceptor of Augustus Caesar. He is said to have overcome the latter's hesitation to put to death Caesarion, the reputed son of Julius Caesar and Cleopatra, by the following parody of Homer's famous praise of monarchy: "'Tis no good thing, a multitude of Caesars."

Arel (ä'rẹl). German name of **Arlon.**

Arelate (ar.ẹ.lā'tẹ̄). A Latin name of **Arles.**

Aremberg (ä'rẹm.berk), Prince **August Marie Raymond von.** See **Arenberg,** Prince **August Marie Raymond von.**

Aremorica (ar.ẹ.môr'i.kạ). See **Armorica.**

Arena Chapel. [Italian, **Cappella degli Scrovegni** (käp.pel'lä de'lyē skrō.vā'nyē), **Cappella Annunziata dell' Arena** (än.nön.tsyä'tä del.lä.rā'nä).] Chapel at Padua, Italy. It is a plain vaulted building without aisles, stands in the precincts of the ancient amphitheater. and is famous for its series of frescoes by Giotto, which were begun in 1303, and cover all the interior walls except those of the choir.

Arenacum (ar.ẹ.nā'kum). See **Arnhem.**

Arenales (ä.rā.nä'lās), **Juan Antonio Álvarez de.** See **Álvarez de Arenales, Juan Antonio.**

Arenberg (ä'rẹn.berk; French, å.raṅ.ber) or **Aremberg** (ä'rẹm.berk; French, å.raṅ.ber), Prince **August Marie Raymond von.** [Also, Comte **de La Marck.**] b. at Brussels, Aug. 30, 1753; d. there, Sept. 26, 1833. Austrian general and French political figure. He was elected to the French States-General (1789), and was a friend of Mirabeau, upon whose death he emigrated to Austria. He obtained the rank of major general in the Austrian army, and was employed by the Austrian government in negotiations with the French.

Arenberg, Duke **Engelbert Ludwig von.** b. July 3, 1750; d. at Brussels, March 7, 1820. Austrian landholder. He lost his possessions west of the Rhine by the Peace of Lunéville (1801), receiving Meppen and Recklinghausen in compensation (1803).

Arenberg, Duke **Karl Leopold von.** b. 1721; d. 1775. Commander in the Austrian service; son of Leopold Philipp Karl Arenberg (1690–1754). During the Seven Years' War he led the right wing of the Austrians at Hochkirch, in Saxony, where, on Oct. 14, 1758, a Prussian army under Frederick the Great was defeated by the Austrians. He was himself defeated by the Prussians in 1759.

Arenberg, Duke **Leopold Philipp Karl von.** b. 1690; d. 1754. Commander in the Austrian service. He fought under Prince Eugene at Belgrade in 1717, and obtained the rank of field marshal in 1737, with command of the army in Flanders.

Arenberg-Meppen (ä'rẹn.berk.mep'ẹn). Former German duchy, later forming the *Kreis* (district) of Meppen. province of Hanover, Prussia; now in the *Land* (state) of Lower Saxony, British Zone.

Arenberg-Meppen, Duke **Prosper Ludwig von.** b. April 28, 1785; d. Feb. 27, 1861. Austrian landholder: son of Engelbert Ludwig von Arenberg (1750–1820). He became duke von Arenberg in 1803, was deprived of his sovereignty by Napoleon in 1810 (receiving in 1813, as an indemnification, a rental of 240,800 francs), and was reinstated in 1815.

Arendal (ä'rẹn.däl). City in S Norway, capital of the *fylke* (county) of Aust-Agder, situated on the Skagerrak near the mouth of the Nid River, SW of Oslo. It is connected with Oslo by rail. It is a seaport, and has important shipyards, lumber trade, and fisheries. 11,570 (1946).

Arène (å.ren), **Paul Auguste.** b. at Sisteron, France, June 26, 1843; d. at Antibes, France, Dec. 18, 1896. French journalist, dramatist, novelist, and Provençal poet, a member of the group known as "Les Félibres."

Arensky or **Arenski** (ä.ren'ski), **Anton Stepanovich.** b. at Novgorod, Russia, Aug. 11, 1861; d. at Terijoki, Finland, Feb. 25, 1906. Russian composer and conductor. A student of Rimsky-Korsakov, he was professor (1882 *et seq.*) of harmony and counterpoint at the Moscow Conservatory. He is chiefly remembered for his piano pieces, including a trio in D minor and three suites for two pianos, and his songs. Composer also of church music, two symphonies, and the operas *A Dream on the Volga* (1892), *Raphael* (1894), and *Nal and Damayanti* (1899).

Arensville (ar'ẹnz.vil). A former name of **Tottenville.**

Arents (ä'rents), **Albert.** b. at Clausthal, Germany, March 14, 1840; d. May 15, 1914. American metallurgist and inventor. Arrived in the U.S. in 1865, he soon after entered the employ of a lead-mining company at Eureka, Nevada. He was the designer of a "siphon lead-well" (sometimes called "Arent's lead-well") which permitted the continuous withdrawal of molten lead from the furnace in place of the periodic tapping previously required; he also contributed to the improvement of silver smelting and cement manufacturing.

Areopagite (ar.ẹ̄.op'ạ.jīt), **Dionysius the.** See **Dionysius the Areopagite.**

Areopagitica (ar"ẹ̄.ọ.pạ.jit'i.kạ). [Full title, **Areopagitica, or Speech for the Liberty of Unlicensed Printing.**] Pamphlet by John Milton, published in 1644. It is an argument in behalf of liberty of conscience and freedom of the press. It is one of the first and most famous of English works on this subject.

Areopagus (ar.ẹ̄.op'ạ.gus). [Eng. trans., *"Hill of Mars"* (Ares).] Low rocky hill at Athens, Greece, continuing westward the line of the Acropolis, from which it is separated by a depression of ground. On the S side near the top there is a flight of 15 rock-cut steps, and portions of the summit are hewn smooth to form platforms, doubtless for altars. Upon this hill sat the famous court of the same name, which originally exercised supreme authority in all matters, and under the developed Athenian constitution retained jurisdiction in cases of life and death and in religious concerns, and exercised a general censorship. From the slopes of the Areopagus Saint Paul delivered his address to the Athenians (Acts, xvii.), who were probably assembled on the border of the Agora below.

Arequipa (ä.rā.kē'pä). Department in S Peru. Capital, Arequipa; area, 21,952 sq. mi.; pop. 319,896 (est. 1950).

Arequipa. City in SW Peru, capital of Arequipa department, on a plain near the foot of the Misti volcano 7,611 ft. above the sea. It is connected by rail with the port of Mollendo, ab. 107 mi. distant, with Lake Titicaca, ab. 218 mi., and with Cusco. The plain, watered by irrigation, is very fertile, and the city has a large trade. The major industrial products are textiles and soap. It is an episcopal town, and the seat of a university and three *collegios* (schools). It was founded by Francisco Pizarro in 1540. It has frequently suffered from earthquakes, and was almost entirely destroyed by that of Aug. 13, 1868. In 1856 and 1857 the city was in rebellion against the government of President Castilla. 97,110 (est. 1950).

Ares (är'ēz). In Greek mythology, the god of war (son of Zeus and Hera), typical particularly of the violence, brutality, confusion, and destruction it calls forth. The corresponding Roman deity was Mars.

Areson or **Aresson** (ä′rę.sôn), **Jón.** See **Arason, Jón.**

Aretaeus of Cappadocia (ar.ę.tē′us). b. in Cappadocia; fl. sometime between 120–200 A.D. Greek physician and medical writer of the eclectic school.

Arete (ą.rē′tē). In the *Odyssey*, the wife of Alcinous, king of the Phaeacians, "a noble and active superintendent of the household of her husband."

Arete. Companion of Cynthia, in Ben Jonson's *Cynthia's Revels*, a dignified, grave lady, personifying Virtue or Reasonableness.

Arethusa (ar.ę.thū′są). Name of various springs in ancient Greece, especially of one on the island of Ortygia in the harbor of Syracuse. With it was connected the legend that Arethusa, a nymph of Elis, while bathing in the Alpheus, was surprised by a lover, the river god, and fled from him to Ortygia; he followed under the sea and overtook her.

Arethusa. In Beaumont and Fletcher's play *Philaster*, a princess, a woman of the greatest self-abnegation and womanly devotion.

Aretin (ä.re.tēn′), Baron **Christoph von.** b. at Ingolstadt, Germany, Dec. 2, 1773; d. at Munich, Dec. 24, 1824. Bavarian political and legal writer. He was appointed (1806) librarian of the Centralbibliothek at Munich, but was forced to resign on account of the sensation caused by his treatise *Die Pläne Napoleons und seiner Gegner in Deutschland* (The Plans of Napoleon and his Opponents in Germany, 1809).

Aretin, Baron **Karl Maria von.** b. at Wetzlar, Germany, July 4, 1796; d. at Berlin, April 29, 1868. Bavarian historical writer; son of Christoph von Aretin.

Aretino (ä.rā.tē′nō), **Guido.** See **Guido d'Arezzo.**

Aretino, Leonardo. See **Bruni, Leonardo.**

Aretino, Pietro. [Called the **"Scourge of Princes"**; original surname, **Bacci.**] b. at Arezzo, Italy, April 20, 1492; d. at Venice, Oct. 21, 1556. Italian writer of poems, satires, comedies, letters, and dialogues. Born of plebeian parents, he left home at 14 to become an art student and then a vagabond. In 1516, he took a menial position with the Roman banker, Agostino Chigi, whence he attracted the attention of Pope Leo X with a mordant satire. Thereafter, as a hired wit and literary bravo, he served Leo, the marquis of Mantua, Pope Clement VII, and the Medici warrior, Giovanni delle Bande Nere, until a threat against his life caused him, in 1527, to take refuge at Venice, where he remained until his death. There, living like a magnifico in a palace filled with great art and rowdy hangers-on, he discovered that by having many employers, he could dispense with subservience to one patron. By 1537, his pen had earned him 10,000 crowns, and he had become friend and adviser to Titian (whose portrait of Aretino is now in the Metropolitan Museum at New York). The Emperor Charles V was but one of many who paid him tribute money. Most of his voluminous writings were published during his Venetian stay, including his lively comedy *La Cortegiana*, his vivid, but pornographic *Ragionamenti*, and the six volumes of his "Letters." Once neglected, the latter are now widely regarded as his most important work. With their variety of subject matter and their colorful, informal style, they have established his present-day reputation as the father of journalism.

Aretinus (ar.ę.tī′nus), **Guido.** See **Guido d'Arezzo.**

Arévalo Bermejo (ä.rā′ʙä.lō ʙer.mä′ʜō), **Juan José.** b. at Taxisco, Guatemala, Sept. 10, 1904—. Guatemalan statesman and professor, president (1945 *et seq.*) of Guatemala. He received the Ph.D. (1934) from the University of La Plata, and was a member (1924, 1934) of the ministry of education. An exile in Argentina during the Ubico regime, he served on university staffs at Tucumán (1936), La Plata (1937), Buenos Aires (1939), and Mendoza (1943), and founded and directed (1941–42) the Institute of Pedagogy at San Luis, Argentina. A member of the Partido Acción Revolucionaria, he was elected (1944) president of Guatemala after the downfall of Ubico.

Arévalo Martínez (ä.rā′ʙä.lō mär.tē′nes), **Rafael.** b. at Guatemala City, Guatemala, July 25, 1884—. Guatemalan poet and novelist, whose poetry is akin to the classical Spanish, while his prose is considered by some to be in the forefront of contemporary American fiction. He was director (1926–44) of the Guatemalan national library. His verse works include *Maya* (1911) and *Los Atormentados* (1914). His outstanding work is the novelette *El Hombre que parecía un caballo* (1915).

Arezzo (ä.rāt′tsō). Province in C Italy, in the *compartimento* (region) of Tuscany. Capital, Arezzo; area, ab. 1,250 sq. mi.; pop. 316,380 (1936).

Arezzo. [Ancient name, **Arretium.**] City and commune in C Italy, in the *compartimento* (region) of Tuscany, the capital of the province of Arezzo, situated in the Chiana Valley, near the junction of the Arno and Chiana rivers, ab. 38 mi. SE of Florence. It is the center of the local trade in grain, wine, olive oil, and silk; has railroad shops, and metallurgical and textile industries. It was the birthplace of Maecenas, Petrarch, Guido and Pietro Aretino, and Vasari. The city contains many art treasures, from the Etruscan, Roman, medieval, and Renaissance periods, and has interesting churches, palaces, and art collections. The Gothic cathedral dates from the 13th, Santa Maria delle Pieve from the 11th and 13th centuries, San Francesco, containing frescoes by Piero della Francesca, from the 15th century. An ancient Etruscan city called Arretium, it was colonized by the Romans and became the terminus of the Via Flaminia. Arretium refused to take part in an Italian coalition against Rome (285–282 B.C.) and was besieged by the whole force of the confederacy, including paid hordes of Gallic Semones. Lucius Caecilius Metellus went to the relief of the city, but was defeated and slain, with seven military tribunes and 13,000 men, the rest of the army being made prisoners. Adhering to the Ghibelline party in the Middle Ages, Arezzo contested the power of Florence among the cities of Tuscany. Considerable damage was suffered during World War II by some buildings of tourist interest, but repairs have now been completed or are being carried out. Pop. of commune, 60,284 (1936); of city, 24,411 (1936).

Arfak (är′fäk). Mountain group in the NW part of the island of New Guinea.

Arfe y Villafañe (är′fā ē ʙē.lyä.fä′nyā), **Juan de.** b. 1535; d. c1603. Spanish silversmith and sculptor.

Arga (är′gä). Small river in Navarra, N Spain, a tributary of the Aragon River.

Argaeus (är.jē′us). Ancient name of **Erciyas Daği.**

Argalia (är.gä.lē′ä). Brother of Angelica in Matteo Maria Boiardo's *Orlando Innamorato.* He was killed by the Spanish knight Ferraù, and his ghost reappears in Ariosto's *Orlando Furioso.* He had an enchanted lance which overthrew everyone whom it touched, and which finally came into the possession of Astolfo.

Argall (är′gôl, -gąl), Sir **Samuel.** b. at Bristol, England, c1572; d. 1626. English adventurer, deputy governor (1617–19) of the Virginia colony.

Argalus (är′gą.lus). In Sir Philip Sidney's romance *Arcadia*, the husband of Parthenia. He was killed by Amphialus in single combat.

Argalus and Parthenia (pär.thē′ni.ą). Tragedy (1629) by Francis Quarles. It was based on Sir Philip Sidney's *Arcadia* and attained equal popularity in its day.

Argan (år.gäṅ). Principal character in Molière's *Le Malade Imaginaire*, a hypochondriac whose mind is divided between his diseases, his remedies, and his desire to reduce his apothecary's bill.

Argand (år.gäṅ), **Aimé.** b. at Geneva, Switzerland, 1755; d. Oct. 24, 1803. Swiss physician and chemist, inventor of the "Argand lamp," introducing the circular wick which, by admitting a current of air in the center, made for faster combustion and thus a brighter light. A modification of such a wick is used in many modern gas and oil burners.

Argandab (är.gän.däb′). River in Afghanistan, which flows from NE to SW and joins the Helmand River W of Kandahar. Length, ab. 200 mi.

Argante (är.gan′tę). Giantess in Spenser's *Faerie Queene*, the personification of Licentiousness.

Argante (är.gän′tā). In Torquato Tasso's *Jerusalem Delivered*, the bravest of the infidel knights.

Argante (år.gäṅt). Father of Octavia and Zerbinetta, in Molière's *Les Fourberies de Scapin.* He is fooled by Scapin into giving up his plans and falling in with those of his son and daughter.

Arganthonius (är.gan.thō′ni.us). In ancient geography, a mountain ridge in Bithynia, Asia Minor, near the Propontis.

Argao (är.gä′ō). City in the E part of Cebu province, Cebu island, Philippine Islands. 3,706 (1948).

Argelander (är′ge.län.dėr), **Friedrich Wilhelm August.** b. at Memel, on the Baltic Sea, March 22, 1799; d. at Bonn, Germany, Feb. 17, 1875. German astronomer, noted for his research on the motion of the solar system in space (1837) and on changes of light in variable stars. He was a student and assistant (1820) to Friedrich Wilhelm Bessel at Königsberg; director of the Åbo Observatory (1823) and of that at Helsingfors (1832); and professor (1837) of astronomy at Bonn. He wrote various astronomical works, including *Über die eigene Bewegung des Sonnensystems* (1837) and *Untersuchungen über die Eigenbewegung von 250 Sternen* (1869); with Schönfeld, he published *Durchmusterung* (1859–63), a work which included a celestial atlas and charted the positions and magnitudes of over 324,000 stars in the northern hemisphere.

Argenlieu (dȧr.zhäṅ.lyė), **Georges Thierry d'.** b. at Brest, France, Aug. 8, 1889—. French naval officer and ecclesiastical figure, commander of the Free French naval forces during World War II. After a period (1912–20) of naval service, he joined the Carmelite order, becoming a provincial in 1939. He returned (1939) to military service, escaped (1940) from German captivity, joined the Free French régime at London, and was high commissioner (1941–42) for French Pacific territories. He was commander in chief (1943–45) of Free French naval forces in England, and vice-president of the supreme naval council and naval inspector-general (1945 *et seq.*). He campaigned (1946 *et seq.*) against a revolt in Annam.

Argensola (är.ʜen.sō′lä), **Bartolomé** (or **Bartolomeo**) **Leonardo de.** [Called, with his brother Lupercio, one of the **"Spanish Horaces."**] b. at Barbastro, in Aragon, Aug. 26, 1562; d. at Saragossa, Feb. 4, 1631. Spanish poet and historian, closely associated with his brother, Lupercio Leonardo de Argensola (1559–1613), whom he succeeded (1613) as historiographer for Aragon. He served as rector of Villahermosa (1588), chaplain to the empress Maria of Austria, and at the court of the viceroy of Naples (1610). Author of *Conquista de las Islas Molucas* (1609), a supplement to Zurita's *Anales de Aragón* (1630), and poems published with those of his brother in *Rimas* (1634).

Argensola, Lupercio Leonardo de. [Called, with his brother Bartolomé, one of the **"Spanish Horaces."**] b. at Barbastro, in Aragon, Dec. 14, 1559; d. at Naples, Italy, in March, 1613. Spanish poet and historian: brother of Bartolomé Leonardo de Argensola (1562–1631), with whom he was a protégé of Maria of Austria. Both were at the court of the viceroy of Naples, Lupercio as state secretary (1610–13). Lupercio preceded (1599–1613) his brother as historiographer of Aragon. Besides satires and translations of Latin poems, published with Bartolomé's works in *Rimas* (1634), the elder brother was author of tragedies in the classical manner, notably *Filis* (now lost), and *Isabela* and *Alejandra* (printed in 1772).

Argenson (dȧr.zhäṅ.sôṅ), **Marc Antoine René de Voyer,** Marquis **de Paulmy d'.** b. 1722; d. 1787. French diplomat and man of letters; son of René Louis de Voyer d'Argenson (1694–1757). He was minister of war (1757–58), and ambassador to Poland (1762–64) and Venice (1766–70). The Bibliothèque de l'Arsenal was formed from his collection of 150,000 volumes, which he sold (1785) to the Comte d'Artois. Author of *Mélanges tirés d'une grande bibliothèque* (1779–88), and others.

Argenson, Marc Pierre de Voyer de Paulmy, Comte **d'.** b. at Paris, 1696; d. there, 1764. French government official; brother of René Louis de Voyer d'Argenson (1694–1757). In 1740 he was intendant of Paris. As secretary of state for war (1743–57) he shared with René virtual control of the government during the War of the Austrian Succession; thereafter he instituted army reforms and founded (1751) the École Militaire. He was a friend of Voltaire, to whom he furnished material for *Siècle de Louis XIV*, and of Denis Diderot and Jean le Rond d'Alembert, who dedicated their encyclopedia to him.

Argenson, Marc René de Voyer, Marquis **de Paulmy** et Marquis **d'.** b. at Venice, 1652; d. at Paris, 1721. French lawyer and politician. As lieutenant-general of police (1697–1718) under Louis XIV he became an intimate of the king. It was he who ordered the destruction (1709) of the Jansenist monastery, Port Royal. Keeper of seals and president of the council of finance (1718–20), he was involved in the confused schemes of John Law to reorganize the treasury. He was an academician (1718), and patron of letters.

Argenson, René Louis de Voyer de Paulmy, Marquis **d'.** [Called **"d'Argenson la Bête."**] b. Oct. 18, 1694; d. Jan. 26, 1757. French lawyer and government official; son of Marc René de Voyer d'Argenson (1652–1721); friend of Voltaire. As secretary of state for foreign affairs (1744–47) under Louis XV, he attempted to bring about international arbitration in the War of the Austrian Succession, but was thwarted by military opposition, intrigue, and the influence of the Spanish Court. President of the Académie des Inscriptions (1747); author of *Considérations sur le gouvernement ancien et présent de la France* (1764), memoirs, and others.

Argenta (är.jen′tä). Town and commune in N Italy, in the *compartimento* (region) of Emilia-Romagna, in the province of Ferrara, between Ferrara and Ravenna. It is the center of a rich agricultural district, producing grain, hemp, and tobacco; it has many canals. Severe damage was suffered during World War II by buildings of tourist interest, some of which are beyond repair. Pop. of commune, 28,032 (1936); of town, 3,684 (1936).

Argentan (ȧr.zhäṅ.täṅ). Town in NW France, in the department of Orne, situated on the Orne River, ab. 21 mi. N of Alençon. It is an agricultural trade center for the surrounding region; has stained-glass, linen, leather goods, lace, and glove manufactures. There is a castle dating from the 15th and 16th centuries. Most of the town, including the Church of Saint Germain, built (1421–1641) in flamboyant Gothic style, is in ruins as a result of the heavy fighting that occurred here in the wake of the Normandy invasion. In August, 1944, the gap between Argentan and Falaise was closed by the Allied armies, but part of the German forces escaped eastward toward the valley of the Seine. 6,711 (1946).

Argentario (är.jen.tä′ryō), **Monte.** [Also, **Monte Argentaro** (-tä′rō).] Promontory on the coast of Tuscany, Italy, near Orbetello. Elevation, ab. 2,090 ft.

Argenteuil (ȧr.zhäṅ.tėy′). City in N France, in the department of Seine-et-Oise, situated on the Seine River, ab. 6 mi. NW of Paris: a river port belonging to the suburban region of Paris. It has various industries, particularly chemical, metallurgical, and construction works; other manufactures include automobiles, bicycles, hosiery, and paper. Fruits and vegetables are grown in the area, which is famous for its asparagus. The ruined priory, founded in 656, was at one time a nunnery of which Héloïse was an abbess. The city suffered large-scale destruction in World War II. 53,543 (1946).

Argentière (dȧr.zhäṅ.tyer), **Aiguille d'.** See **Aiguille d'Argentière.**

Argentina (är.jen.tē′na; Spanish, är.ʜen.tē′nä) or **Argentine Republic** (är′jen.tēn, -tīn). [Sometimes called **"the Argentine"**; official Spanish name, **Republica Argentina**; former name, **Argentine Confederation.**] Nation in SE and C South America, the continent's second largest in population and area, bounded on the W by Chile, on the E by Uruguay, Brazil, and the Atlantic Ocean, on the S by the arc of the Chilean boundary and the Atlantic Ocean, on the N by Bolivia and Paraguay.

Population, Area, and Political Divisions. Argentina is divided for administrative purposes into 16 provinces, 8 territories, and a Federal District. Capital, Buenos Aires; area, 1,084,360 sq. mi. (exclusive of the disputed Falkland Islands); pop. 15,893,827 (1947).

Terrain and Climate. The Andes range in the west includes some of the highest peaks in the world, notably Mount Aconcagua (22,834 ft.); the Pampa region in C Argentina is a virtually treeless plain of enormous fertility; the Gran Chaco is a heavily forested, lowland area in the north; Patagonia in the south is for much of its area mountainous, cold, and without rainfall comparable to the rest of the country. The chief river system is that of the Río de la Plata, which is itself actually a bay into which such true rivers as the Uruguay and the Paraná empty. Because of its position below the equator, Argentina has its warm season in the winter and its cold season in the summer. The climate ranges from the extreme heat of the subtropical north to the cold of S Patagonia.

Industry, Agriculture, and Trade. One of the world's first three wheat-exporting nations and the top corn exporter, Argentina's chief industry is meat-packing, which makes it a leading producer also of hides, tallow, wool, and other animal products. Its agricultural industries also produce flax, linseed, sugar, *maté* (Paraguay tea), and hardwood lumber. Oil, copper, lead, and some precious metals are produced, but manufacturing and mining are secondary to agriculture in the national economy, despite vigorous government efforts to stimulate them.

History. The country was colonized by Spain in the middle of the 16th century and remained under Spanish rule until 1810, when Buenos Aires established an autonomous governmental junta. National independence of the territory adjoining Buenos Aires was declared in 1816 under the name United Provinces of La Plata, which subsequently became (1825) the Argentine Confederation. Recurrent political chaos and an extended dictatorship (1835–52) under Juan Manuel de Rosas were followed by the adoption (1853) of a national constitution and the presidency of Justo José de Urquiza. Unwilling to accept Urquiza, the people of Buenos Aires established a separate government under Bartolomé Mitre, and Argentina had two governments until 1862, when Mitre defeated Urquiza and became president. The next 25 years were the great period of Argentine expansion and development; a depression in 1890 halted economic growth momentarily, but gave birth to the Radical Party, which provided leadership against the hitherto absolute control of Argentine government by the great landowners and ultimately (1912) compelled passage of a law ensuring free elections. Argentina maintained neutrality throughout World War I and during World War II until March, 1945, when war was declared against the Axis Powers. The present government, which purports to seek the support of all groups except the Left, is conservative and intensely nationalistic. It is headed by President Juan Domingo Perón.

Culture. The Argentine people are still predominantly Spanish, despite heavy immigration from Italy, Great Britain, and Germany during the latter part of the 19th century and the early 20th century. A considerable Indian population exists in the areas outside of the great cities. The dominant religious group is Roman Catholic. Under President Perón and his immediate predecessors close cultural relationships with the Spanish regime of General Franco have been encouraged.

Argentina, La. [Stage name of **Antonia Mercé.**] b. at Buenos Aires, c1890; d. 1936. Argentine dancer who headed a company of dancers that toured (1927 *et seq.*) the U.S. and Europe. She specialized in modern Spanish dances, for many of which she used music composed by Manuel de Falla.

Argentine (är′jẹn.tēn). Former city in NE Kansas, in Wyandotte County, on the Kansas River: noted for silver and lead smelting. It was annexed to Kansas City by petition in 1909.

Argentine Confederation (är′jẹn.tēn, -tīn). Name formerly used (1825 *et seq.*) for Argentina. Except for the period from 1852 to 1859, when Buenos Aires withdrew, the Confederation included all the important subdivisions of modern Argentina.

Argentine Mesopotamia (mes″ǫ.pǫ.tā′mi.ạ). See **Mesopotamia, Argentine.**

Argentino (är.HEn.tē′nō), **Lake.** [Spanish, **Lago Argentino.**] Lake in SW Argentina, in Santa Cruz territory, near the border of Chile. It is the southernmost of the marginal lakes. Area ab. 570 sq. mi.

Argentoratum (är.jen.tǫ.rā′tum). Latin name of **Strasbourg.**

Arginusae (är.ji.nū′sē). In ancient geography, a group of small islands off the coast of Asia Minor, SE of Lesbos. Near here the Athenian fleet under Conon defeated (406 B.C.) the Spartans under Callicratidas.

Argives (är′jīvz). Name often used for the Greeks of Argolis. As a result of the important part they played under their king Agamemnon in the Trojan War, their name is extended by Homer in the *Iliad* to all the Greeks.

Argo (är′gō). Island in the Nile River, between Dongola and the third cataract, in the Anglo-Egyptian Sudan.

Argo. In Greek legend, the ship which bore the Argonauts.

Argolis (är′gǫ.lis). In ancient geography, a division of the Peloponnesus, Greece, surrounded by Sicyonia, Corinthia, the Aegean (with the Saronic and Argolic gulfs), Laconia, and Arcadia, and containing the plain of Argos and the cities of Argos and Mycenae.

Argolis. *Nomos* (department) in SE Greece, situated on the Peloponnesus, including Spetsai and other islands. Argolis and Corinthia, formerly combined, were separated after World War II. Capital, Nauplia; pop. 85,264 (1951).

Argonautica (är.gǫ.nô′ti.kạ). Epic poem by Apollonius of Rhodes. It deals with Jason's legendary voyage in search of the Golden Fleece.

Argonauts (är′gǫ.nôts). In Greek legend, the heroes who sailed to Colchis in the ship *Argo* to carry off the Golden Fleece. The expedition took place not long after the Trojan War. Jason was its leader, and it included demigods and heroes from all parts of Greece.

Argo Navis (är′gō nā′vis). Ancient southern constellation, the largest in the heavens. It contains Canopus, after Sirius the brightest of the fixed stars. By modern astronomers it is commonly divided into parts: *Carina, Puppis, Pyxis,* and *Vela,* meaning keel, stern, compass, and sail.

Argonne Forest (är.gon′, är′gon; French, år.gon). [Also: **Argonne, Forest of Argonne.**] Rocky plateau in NE France, on the borders of Lorraine and Champagne, containing several difficult defiles which lead from the basin of the Meuse River to that of the Seine River, famous in the "Argonne Campaign" of Charles François Dumouriez in 1792. During World War I the section was the scene of heavy fighting.

Argos (är′gos, -gǫs). Town in S Greece, on the Peloponnesus, in the *nomos* (department) of Argolis and Corinthia, situated ab. 9 mi. NW of Nauplia and the coast: the leading Dorian city prior to the middle of the 8th century B.C. It remained an important town in later times, was often in conflict with Sparta, and flourished under the Romans. It was ruled by the legendary dynasties of Inachus, Danaus, and Pelops. It produced many noted sculptors. The modern town is a railroad junction. 13,440 (1940).

Ancient Architecture. Argos contains the remains of an ancient theater. The upper tiers of seats of the cavea are rock-hewn; below these are tiers of masonry. Twenty tiers in all survive, the lowest consisting of thrones of honor. There are remains of a Roman stage, and of several modifications of the Greek stage structure. An underground passage ran from behind the proscenium to the middle of the orchestra, as at Eretria and others. There are important remnants of the Heraion, or sanctuary of Hera, the national shrine of Argolis, which lay at some distance from the city. The temple was rebuilt after a fire in the 5th century B.C., a little below the old site, as a Doric hexastyle peripteros about 65½ by 130 ft. The cult statue was an admirable chryselephantine work by Polycleitus. The Heraion was excavated (1892 *et seq.*) by the American School at Athens, to which is due nearly all our knowledge of the architectural and sculptural remains of both temples and their peribolos, as well as a very valuable collection of archaic terra cottas.

History. Argos was a city-state under King Phaedon in 680 B.C. Under Rome it was the headquarters of the Achaean powers. From 1261 to 1460 it was under Byzantine rule and from 1460 to 1830 under the Ottoman Empire. In 1822 it was the seat of the national assembly in the movement for Greek independence. It was destroyed by Ibrahim Pasha in 1825 and later rebuilt.

Argostolion (är.gô.stô′lyôn). [Also, **Argostoli** (är.gôs-tô′lē).] Town in W Greece, the capital of the *nomos* (department) of Cephalonia, one of the Ionian Islands, situated on the SW coast. It is a flourishing trade center and mill town, and the seat of a bishopric. 8,711 (1951).

Argout (dår.gö), **Antoine Maurice Apollinaire,** Comte **d'.** b. at Isère, France, Aug. 27, 1782; d. Jan. 15, 1858. French politician and financier. In 1830 he was mediator between Charles X and the popular leaders. Appointed (1834) governor of the Bank of France, he became minister of finance in 1836. Reappointed governor of the Bank of France in 1836, he continued in that post under the republic of 1848.

Argovie (ȧr.go.vē). French name of **Aargau.**

Argüedas (är.gwā′ᴛʜäs), **Alcides.** b. at La Paz, Bolivia, July 15, 1879—. Bolivian novelist, sociologist, and historian, considered by many to be Bolivia's foremost contemporary writer. His *Wuatu-Wuaru* (1904), *Pueblo enfermo* (1900), and *Raza de bronce* (1919) are outstanding for their understanding of the problems of the Indian. Besides serving in several government positions at home, he has represented his country in England, France, Spain, Colombia, and Venezuela.

Argüelles (är.gwā′lyās), **Agustín** (or **Augustín**). [Called **"the Spanish Cicero."**] b. at Ribadesella, Spain, Aug. 28, 1776; d. at Madrid, March 23, 1844. Spanish revolutionist and liberal politician. He was a member of the patriotic party in the war for independence (1808 *et seq.*) and was prominent in the Cortes (1812–14), where he gained a reputation as an orator. Upon the restoration of Ferdinand VII, he was imprisoned (1814–20). He served as minister of the interior after the revolution of 1820, resigned (1821) in protest against the narrowness of the court, and on the fall of the constitution (1823) was exiled to England. He returned under the amnesty of deputies; as president and vice-president of the Cortes, he was a consistent reformer; he was guardian of Isabella during Espartero's regency.

Argüelles, José Canga. See **Canga Argüelles, José.**

Argüello (är.gwā′lyō), **Luis Antonio.** b. at San Francisco, 1784; d. there, 1830. Spanish *commandante* (1806–22) and governor (1822–25), under the short-lived Mexican empire, of California; first native-born Californian to hold either post. In 1821 he conducted an exploratory expedition to the Columbia River.

Argüello (är.gwā′yō), **Octavio Béeche.** See **Béeche Argüello, Octavio.**

Arguin (är.gwēn′). [Also, **Banc d'Arguin.**] Small island in the Atlantic Ocean W of Africa, S of Cape Blanc. It is sometimes shown on maps as a reef or bank.

Argun (är.gön′). River in N China, one of the two chief headstreams of the Amur River. It rises as the Kerulen River in Outer Mongolia, traverses Dalai Nor (or Hulun Nor) lake, flows along the boundary between Manchuria and the Russian Soviet Federated Socialist Republic, and unites with the Shilka River to form the Amur on the N border of China, in the province of Heilungkiang. Length, ab. 945 mi.

Arguri (är.gö′rē). Former village in what was known as Russian Armenia, on the N slope of Ararat, buried by an earthquake and landslide from Ararat in 1840.

Argurion (är.gū′ri.ǫn). Semiallegorical personification of Money, in Ben Jonson's *Cynthia's Revels.* The character is afterward expanded in *The Staple of News* as Lady Pecunia.

Argus (är′gus). In Greek legend, the guardian of Io. Slain by Hermes, he is said to have had one hundred eyes, which were rendered useless when Hermes, through a charm, caused him to fall asleep.

Argyll (är.gīl′), Dukes, Earls, and Marquises of. Titles held by various members of the Campbell family of Scotland. The first Campbell to hold title as Argyll was Colin Campbell, who was created 1st Earl of Argyll in 1457. For entries on the particular holders of the title, see **Campbell.**

Argyllshire (är.gīl′shir) or **Argyll** (är.gīl′). Maritime county, partly mainland and partly insular, in W Scotland. It is bounded on the N by Inverness-shire, on the E by Perthshire, Dunbartonshire, and the Firth of Clyde, on the S by Buteshire and the North Channel, and on the W by the North Channel and the Atlantic Ocean. The mainland is deeply indented by sea lochs and firths, which form Kintyre and other peninsulas. Argyllshire includes the islands Mull, Iona, Colonsay, Staffa, Ulva, Rum, Coll, Tiree, Jura, Islay, Gigha, and others (virtually the entire Inner Hebrides group). The surface is generally mountainous. Within the county are Lochs Awe, Eil, Etive, Fyne, Goil, Leven, Linnhe, Long, Shiel, and Striven. Ben Cruachan (3,611 ft.) is in the NW portion of the county on the mainland. The leading industries are the rearing of cattle and sheep, the quarrying of building stone (especially slate for export), lead mining, and fishing (herring, salmon, and trout). Loch Fyne is fished for herring. There are distilleries at Campbeltown and on the island of Islay. Argyllshire is the second largest county in Scotland. County seat, Inveraray; area, ab. 3,110 sq. mi.; pop. 63,270 (1951).

Argyrippa (är.ji.rip′ą). See **Arpi.**

Argyrocastro (är″gē.rō.käs′trō) or **Argyrokastron** (är.yę̄-rô′käs.trôn). See **Gjinokastër.**

Argyropoulos (är″ji.rǫ.pö′lǫs), **Johannes.** [Also: **Argyropulus** (-pū′lus) or **Argyropulo** (-pö′lō).] b. at Constantinople, c1416; d. at Rome, c1486. Greek scholar, one of the earliest humanist teachers in the West. He was a teacher at Constantinople, Padua (1434 *et seq.*), the University of Florence (c1456–71) (to which he was invited by Cosimo de' Medici and where he taught Piero and Lorenzo de' Medici), and at Rome (1471 *et seq.*). Among his pupils were Angelus Politianus and Johann Reuchlin. Author of a work on Aristotle's *Ethics* and Latin translations of various works of Aristotle.

Argyropoulos, Perikles. [Also, **Argyropulos.**] b. at Constantinople, Sept. 17, 1809; d. at Athens, Dec. 22, 1860. Greek politician and publicist. He was professor of law at Athens in 1837, and foreign minister in 1854–55.

Arhuaco (är.wä′kō). Collective name for Indian tribes that spoke a Chibchan language in the mountains of Santa Marta in N Colombia. The most important of these tribes were the Cagaba and, very likely, the Tairona. They are sometimes incorrectly termed Arawak.

Århus (ôr′hös). See **Aarhus.**

Aria (ãr′i.ą, ą.rī′ą). In ancient geography, a region in Asia corresponding nearly to W Afghanistan and E Khurasan, Iran; often confused with Ariana.

Aria. Ancient name of **Herat.**

Ariadne (ar.i.ad′nē). d. 515 A.D. Byzantine empress; daughter of Leo I. She was married to Zeno, who became emperor in 474, and after his death (491) she became the wife of Anastasius I.

Ariadne. In Greek mythology, the daughter of Minos, king of Crete. She gave Theseus the unwinding strand by means of which he retraced his steps out of the Labyrinth after killing the Minotaur. She then went with Theseus to the island of Naxos, where, according to the common account, she was abandoned by him, and became the wife of Dionysus.

Ariadne. An asteroid (No. 43) discovered by Pogson at Oxford, April 15, 1857.

Ariadne auf Naxos (ä.rę̄.äd′nę ouf näk′sōs). Opera in one act composed by Richard Strauss as an interlude to Molière's *Le Bourgeois Gentilhomme,* with a libretto by Hugo von Hofmannsthal; first performed at Stuttgart in 1912. Revised (1916) to full length, the new version was first presented at London in 1924. The opera, based on the old Greek legend, is presented as a play-within-a-play, the prologue taking place in the 18th-century setting appropriate to the Molière comedy. The prologue itself has been arranged as an orchestral suite under the title of *Le Bourgeois Gentilhomme.*

Ariana (ar.i.ā′ną, ar.i.an′ą). In ancient geography, a region in Asia, of vague boundaries, extending from Media on the W to the Indus River on the E, and from Hyrcania and Bactriana on the N to the Persian Gulf and Arabian Sea on the S.

Ariane (ȧ.ryȧn). Tragedy by Thomas Corneille, composed in 1672.

Ariano Irpino (ä.ryä′nō ēr.pē′nō). [Also, **Ariano di Puglia** (dē pö′lyä).] Town and commune in SE Italy, in the *compartimento* (region) of Campania, in the province of Avellino, situated in the Apennines, ab. 50 mi. NE of Naples: textile and pasta factories. In a dominating position near the Appian Way, the town changed hands at various times during the Middle Ages. Its rulers were Byzantines, Normans, Frederick of Swabia, Charles of Anjou, and a number of feudal lords. The Castello, a medieval castle, was undamaged during World War II. Pop. of commune, 24,357 (1936); of town, 9,473 (1936).

Ariano nel Polesine (nel pō.lā′zē.nā). Town and commune in NE Italy, in the *compartimento* (region) of Veneto, in the province of Rovigo, situated in the Polesine region of the Po Delta, on the Po di Goro River, S of Venice. It is the center of a rich agricultural district in the formerly swampy delta area, producing grain, rice, tobacco, and vegetables. Pop. of commune, 12,372 (1936); of town, 2,552 (1936).

Arians (ãr′i.ąnz). Followers of Arius, a deacon of Alexandria, who in the 4th century A.D. maintained, in opposition to both Sabellianism and Tritheism, that the Son is of a nature similar to (not the same as) the Father, and is subordinate to him. The tendency of these doctrines, in the eyes of orthodox theologians, was toward the denial of the divinity of Christ. The Arian discussion raged fiercely in the 4th century, and though Arianism was condemned by the Council of Nicaea (325), the heresy long retained great importance, both theological and political. The strongholds of the Arians were in the East and among the Goths and other barbarians who were converted by Arian missionaries.

Arias (ä′ryäs), **Arnulfo.** b. 1897—. Panamanian politician, president (1940–41, 1949–51) of Panama. Educated in Panama and at the University of Chicago, he received an M.D. degree from Harvard. He retired from medical practice to enter the diplomatic service, holding posts as minister to Italy, France, and Great Britain, and serving as Panamanian delegate to the League of Nations. As president of Panama (October, 1940–October, 1941), he was the author of a new constitution (adopted 1941) providing for government regulation of monopolies, exempting church property from taxation, and terminating the U.S. protectorate. Exiled as a Fascist sympathizer, he returned in October, 1945. Claiming to have won the 1948 election to the presidency, he was placed in that office by a military coup in 1949; in 1951 he was overthrown and barred from public office for life.

Arias, Harmodio. b. at Penonomé, Panama, July 3, 1886—. Panamanian politician, lawyer, and diplomat, president of Panama (1932–36). Educated in England as a lawyer, he thereafter held various government posts, including those of minister to the U.S. and Argentina, and delegate to the first League of Nations assembly. During his presidency a treaty was signed (March 2, 1936) with the U.S. providing joint responsibility for the security of the republic and the canal. Author of *The Non-Responsibility of States for Damages Suffered by Foreigners* (1912), and other legal works.

Arias de Ávila (ä′ryäs dā ä′ʙē.lä), **Pedro.** See **Pedrarias.**

Arias de Saavedra (sä.ä.ʙä′ᴛʜrä), **Hernando.** [Also, **Hernandarias.**] b. at Asunción, Paraguay, c1561; d. c1634. Spanish governor (1597–99, 1602–09, 1615–18) of Río de la Plata province, which was at first part of, then (1617) separated from, Paraguay (at that time Guairá). He encouraged settlement by the Jesuits, made expeditions to Chaco, the Straits of Magellan, and elsewhere, and built up cities such as Buenos Aires and Santa Fé.

Arias Montanus (ā′ri.ạs mọn.tā′nus), **Benedictus.** [Spanish, **Benito Arias Montano** (bä.nē′tō ä′ryäs mōn-tä′nō).] b. at Frejenal de la Sierra, Spain, 1527; d. at Seville, May 22, 1598. Spanish Benedictine Orientalist and linguist. He was the author of *Jewish Antiquities* and other works, and editor (appointed by Philip II) of the Antwerp Polyglot Bible (1568–73).

Arica (ä.rē′kä). Northernmost seaport in Chile, in Tarapacá province. It is also a rail center, important principally for trade with Bolivia in minerals and agricultural produce. The harbor is a roadstead protected by a point of land and a small island. The town was nearly destroyed by earthquakes in 1868, 1877, and 1906. Possession of the port became a matter of armed dispute between Chile and Peru in 1879–80. In the latter year it became a part of Chile, having previously belonged to Peru. The city has, in recorded history, never been known to have a rainfall. 14,064 (1940).

Ariccia (ä.rēt′chä). [Latin, **Aricia** (ạ.rish′ạ).] Town and commune in C Italy, in the *compartimento* (region) of Latium, in the province of Roma, situated in the Alban Hills, SE of Rome. An ancient Latin town, the site of which has been excavated, it belonged in later centuries to the States of the Church. It has buildings from this period, among others the Church of Santa Maria dell'Assunta, built by Giovanni Lorenzo Bernini in 1664. Damage was suffered during World War II by some buildings of tourist interest, but repairs have now been completed or are being carried out. Pop. of commune, 5,596; of town, 4,854 (1936).

Arichat (ar′i.shat). Small seaport on Madame Island, off the S coast of Cape Breton Island, Nova Scotia, Canada. Pop. ab. 800.

Arici (ä.rē′chē), **Cesare.** b. at Brescia, Italy, July 2, 1782; d. there, July 2, 1836. Italian didactic poet. He was appointed (1810) professor of history and literature at the Brescia lyceum, and became professor of Latin in 1824.

Arided (ar′i.ded). The first-magnitude star α Cygni, often called Deneb Cygni.

Ariège (à.ryezh). [Also, **La Riège.**] Department in S France, bounded by the department of Haute-Garonne on the W and N, the department of Aude on the E, and the department of Pyrénées-Orientales, Andorra, and Spain on the S. It generally corresponds to the medieval countship of Foix, which went to the French crown under Henry IV. The climate is mild and warm in the north but characterized by strong contrasts in the mountainous south. The N region is fertile and produces grains, vegetables, and fruits, while the inhabitants of the S part depend mainly on forest culture and pastures. There is an active trade in sheep and goats with places across the Pyrenees. There are stone quarries and iron deposits, iron and steel mills, and construction, textile, and other industries. Capital, Foix; area, 1,892 sq. mi.; pop. 145,956 (1946).

Ariège River. [Latin, **Aurigera.**] River in S France which rises in the Pyrenees, flows past Tarascon and Foix, and joins the Garonne River near Toulouse. Length, ab. 100 mi.

Ariel (ãr′i.ẹl, ā′ri.el). In the Old Testament: **1.** One of the chief men sent by Ezra to procure ministers for the sanctuary. Ezra, viii. 16. **2.** A Moabite whose sons were killed by Benaiah. 2 Sam. xxiii; 1 Chron. xi. 22. **3.** Name used symbolically to mean Jerusalem. Isa. xxix.

Ariel. In cabalistic demonology, one of the seven princes of angels, or spirits who preside over the waters, under the archangel Michael. In medieval European folklore, a spirit of the air.

Ariel. "An ayrie spirit" in Shakespeare's *The Tempest*, employed by Prospero.

Ariel. Sylph, guardian of Belinda, in Alexander Pope's *Rape of the Lock.* This particular spirit was the chief of those whose

"Humbler province is to tend the fair . . .
To save the powder from too rude a gale,
Nor let the imprison'd essences exhale . . .
. . . to curl their waving hairs,
Assist their blushes and inspire their airs."

Ariel. One of the rebel angels in John Milton's *Paradise Lost.*

Arienzo San Felice (ä.ryen′tsō sän fä.lē′chä). Town and commune in S Italy, in the *compartimento* (region) of Campania, in the province of Caserta, situated between Caserta and Avellino, NE of Naples. It is the center of an agricultural district. Pop. of commune, 13,682 (1936); of town, 3,126 (1936).

Aries (ãr′ēz, -i.ēz). One of the zodiacal constellations.

Aries. The first sign of the zodiac, which the sun enters at the vernal equinox, March 21, and leaves April 20. Owing to the precession of the equinoxes, the constellation Aries has moved completely out of the sign of the same name, which is now occupied by the constellation Pisces.

Ari Frodi Thorgilsson (ä′rē frō′ᴛʜē thôr′gils.sōn). [Also, **Ari Froði Thorgilsson.**] b. c1067; d. 1148. Icelandic historian whose works, compiled from oral report, poetry, and tradition, are by some called the foundation of Icelandic prose style and of Icelandic history, later developed by Snorri Sturluson and others. Author of *Konungabók* (Book of Kings), a history of the kings of Norway comparable to the English *Domesday Book;* also of *Landnámabók* (Land-taking Book, or book of settlements), describing the discovery of Iceland and the genealogy and history of each settler and his descendants, and of *Islendingabók* (Book of Icelanders, c1127), a history from c870 to 1120, containing an epitome of the other two plus the constitutional history of Iceland.

Arika (ạ.rē′kạ), **Abba.** See **Abba Arika.**

Arikara (ạ.rē′kạ.rạ). North American Indian tribe formerly inhabiting NW South Dakota and SW North Dakota. The language was of the Caddoan family.

Arimaspians (ar.i.mas′pi.ạnz). In classical mythology, a one-eyed people of Scythia. They were at war with the Griffins, whose gold they sought.

Arimathea (ar″i.mạ.thē′ạ). In the New Testament, a town in Judea, Palestine, of undetermined location;

probably the Ramah of 1 Sam. i. 1, 19. It was the home of Joseph of Arimathea, the Israelite who placed the body of Jesus in his own tomb. Mat. xxvii. 57–60.

Arimu (ar'i.mö). See under **Aram.**

Arinos (a.rē'nös). River in C Brazil, which flows NW to join the Juruena River, forming the Tapajós. Length, ab. 400 mi.

Arinos, Afonso. [Full name, **Afonso Arinos de Melo Franco.**] b. at Paracatú, Minas Gerais, Brazil, May 1, 1868; d. at Barcelona, Spain, Feb. 19, 1916. Brazilian short-story writer, novelist, and journalist, one of the creators of regional literature in the south of Brazil, chiefly remembered for his *Pelo sertão* (1898), a book of short stories. Among his other works are *Jagunços* (1898), *Lendas e tradições brasileiras* (1917), *Histórias e paisagens* (1921), and his historical drama, *O contratador de diamantes* (1917).

Ariobarzanes (ar"i.ọ.bär.zā'nēz). Soldier and satrap of the Persian empire in Persis (now Fars) who, after the battle of Gaugamela (331 B.C.), secured the pass through the so-called "Persian Gates." Alexander was able to force the pass and continue to the east only by stratagem.

Ariobarzanes I (of *Cappadocia*). [Also, **Ariobarzanes I Philoromaeus** (fil"ọ.rō.mē'ụs).] fl. about the beginning of the 1st century B.C. King of Cappadocia. He was several times expelled by Mithridates II of Parthia and restored by the Romans.

Ariobarzanes II (of *Cappadocia*). [Also, **Ariobarzanes II Philopator** (fi.lop'ạ.tôr).] King of Cappadocia; son of Ariobarzanes I, whom he succeeded c63 B.C.

Ariobarzanes III (of *Cappadocia*). [Also: **Ariobarzanes III Eusebes** (ū.sē'bēz), **Ariobarzanes III Philoromaeus** (fil"ọ.rọ.mē'us).] d. 42 B.C. King of Cappadocia; son of Ariobarzanes II, whom he succeeded c51 B.C. He aided Pompey against Julius Caesar in the civil war, but was pardoned by Caesar. He was put to death by Cassius.

Ariobarzanes I (of *Pontus*). fl. 5th century B.C. Satrap of Pontus; father of Mithridates I of Pontus.

Ariobarzanes II (of *Pontus*). King of Pontus (363–337 B.C.); son and successor of Mithridates I of Pontus. He revolted (362 B.C.) against Artaxerxes II of Persia, and founded the independent kingdom of Pontus.

Ariobarzanes III (of *Pontus*). King of Pontus (266–c240 B.C.); son of Mithridates III of Pontus.

Arioch (ar'i.ok). In the Old Testament: **1.** A king of Ellasar, one of four kings who at the time of Abraham made an attack on the cities in the valley of Siddim. Gen. xiv. **2.** Captain of the guard of Nebuchadnezzar. Dan. ii. 14 *et seq.*

Arioch. In Milton's *Paradise Lost*, one of the rebellious angels overthrown by Abdiel.

Ariodante (ä.ryō.dän'tā). In Ariosto's *Orlando Furioso*, the lover of Ginevra, princess of Scotland.

Arioi (ä'rē.ō.ē). Society of strolling players that flourished in the Society Islands in pre-missionary times. The members traveled in flotillas of canoes from island to island, enacting mythical and legendary stories in song and dance. They were regarded as sacred, were feasted and honored, and their performances, voyages, and initiation or promotion ceremonies were attended with elaborate ritual. Special buildings were maintained for them. Membership was divided into a series of ranks or grades, each distinguished by special tattooing. Members were forbidden to have children and were required to kill any born to them. Apparently, their performances, which were dedicated to the god Oro, were thought to stimulate the fertility of man and nature; these performances ended in sexual orgies. The Arioi was the peak development of an institution found in simpler form elsewhere in Polynesia: the Karioi of New Zealand, the Kaioi of the Marquesas, perhaps also the hula dancing of Hawaii and the merrymaking in the young men's houses of W Polynesia.

Arion (a.rī'on). b. on the island of Lesbos, in the Aegean Sea; fl. c700–625 B.C. Greek musician and poet at the court of Periander of Corinth, subject of a legend made famous by Herodotus. He is represented among constellations by his lyre and the dolphin which, according to tradition, saved him from robbers at sea. He has been credited with the first literary use of the dithyramb.

Arion. In Greek legend, a fabulous horse. It was said to be the offspring of Poseidon by Demeter (or, in other accounts, Gaea or a harpy) who to escape him had metamorphosed herself into a mare. It was successively owned by Copreus, Oncus, Hercules, and Adrastus. It possessed marvelous powers of speech, and its right feet were those of a man.

Ariosti (ä.rē.ôs'tē), **Attilio.** b. at Bologna, Italy, c1660; d. c1740. Italian operatic composer. After serving as maestro di cappella (1698 *et seq.*) at Berlin, he was one of the first directors (1720), with George Frederick Handel and Giovanni Battista Bononcini, of the London Academy of Music. Composer of *Dafne* (1686), *Atys* (1700), *La Festa d'Imeneo* (1700), *Nabucodonosor* (1706), *Amor tra Nemici* (1708), *Ciro* (1721), *Coriolanus* (1723), and *Teuzone* (1727).

Ariosto (ä.rē.ôs'tō), **Lodovico** or **Ludovico.** [Called **"Divino Lodovico."**] b. at Reggio, Italy, Sept. 8, 1474; d. at Ferrara, Italy, June 6, 1533. Italian poet, author of *Orlando Furioso*, an epic of Roland considered one of the masterpieces of Renaissance literature. A student of law, then of the classics, he was early connected with the court at Ferrara. He began (c1495) to write comedies, among which *La Cassaria* and *I Suppositi* (performed c1512) found him a patron in Cardinal Ippolito d'Este. He was poorly paid for missions to Pope Julius II and other diplomatic services, and for his epic, which he had begun (1503) with the aim of completing Matteo Maria Boiardo's *Orlando Innamorato*. He dedicated the first version (1516) to Cardinal Ippolito. Ariosto left (c1517) the cardinal's service for that of his brother Alfonso d'Este, duke of Ferrara. Rewarded only with the governorship (1522–25) of the bandit-ridden Italian district of Garfagnana, he retired (1525) to write comedies and revise *Orlando* (final version, 1532). Besides those mentioned, his works include comedies such as *Il Negromante*, satires in the manner of Horace, Latin poems, and sonnets; only his Italian lyrics and his epic receive unmixed acclaim; *Orlando Furioso* has been widely translated, and was used by Cervantes, Spenser, Scott, Byron, and others.

Ariovistus (ar"i.ō.vis'tus). fl. c71–58 B.C. Germanic leader, chief of the Suevi, who crossed the Rhine and invaded Gaul c71 B.C. to aid the Sequani, conquering the Aedui in 61. He was made an ally of Rome by Julius Caesar, but on an appeal by the Gauls Caesar engaged him in battle at Vesontio (now Besançon, France) and finally defeated him near what is now Mulhouse, France, in 58.

'Arish (ä.rēsh'), **El.** See **El 'Arish.**

Arispe (ä.rēs'pā). See **Arizpe.**

Arista (ä.rēs'tä), **Mariano.** b. in San Luis Potosí, Mexico, July 26, 1802; d. at sea near Lisbon, Portugal, Aug. 7, 1855. Mexican general and politician, president (1851–53) of Mexico. He was an officer in the Mexican army which was defeated (1836) in the Texan revolution, and commanded the Mexican Army of the North which was defeated (1846) by General Zachary Taylor at Palo Alto and Resaca de la Palma. After serving (1848–50) as minister of war under Herrera, he was elected (Jan. 8, 1851) president of Mexico, but resigned (1853) to avoid civil war.

Aristabulus Bragg (ar'is.tab'ū.lus brag). See **Bragg, Aristabulus.**

Aristaeus (ar.is.tē'us). In Greek mythology, a beneficent deity, protector of husbandmen and shepherds. He is especially considered the patron of beekeeping. According to Vergil, his swarms of bees were destroyed by the nymphs after he had unintentionally brought death on Euridyce, but on his offering a penitential sacrifice, his bees were restored to him.

Aristagoras (ar.is.tag'ọ.rạs). d. 497 B.C. Persian governor of Miletus, and leader in the Ionian revolt (500 B.C. *et seq.*) against Persia.

Aristander (ar.is.tan'dėr). Lycian soothsayer, a favorite of Alexander the Great.

Aristarchus (ar.is.tär'kus) or **Aristarchos** (-kos). fl. 51–57 A.D. Macedonian associate of the apostle Paul, whom he accompanied on several of his missionary journeys, and with whom he was imprisoned at Rome. Acts, xix, xx, xxvii. He is represented by the Greek Church as a bishop of Apamea in Phrygia, and by the Roman as a bishop of Thessalonica.

Aristarchus of Samos (sā'mos). [Also, **Aristarchos.**] fl. c280–264 B.C. Greek astronomer and mathematician of the Alexandrian school. According to Archimedes and Copernicus, he was the first to maintain the heliocentric theory of the universe and the rotation of the earth on its axis. In order to reconcile the apparent immobility of the fixed stars with the revolution of the earth around the sun, he assumed that the sphere of the fixed stars was incomparably greater than that containing the earth's orbit. That is, the universe conceived by him was incomparably greater than that conceived by his predecessors. In his only extant treatise, "on the sizes and distances of the sun and moon," he gave a scientific method to make these measurements. His results were grossly inaccurate, but the method was sound. This treatise is also of great mathematical interest because of its containing the calculation of ratios which are in fact trigonometrical ratios. Aristarchos added $\frac{1}{1623}$ of a day to the existing estimate of 365¼ days for the solar year; he estimated the length of the "great year" (luni-solar cycle) to be 2.484 years (he probably meant 2.434 years). The discovery of an improved sun dial (a concave hemispherical surface with a gnomon in the center) was ascribed to him. He also wrote on vision, light, and colors.

Aristarchus of Samothrace (sam'ō.thrās). [Also: **Aristarchos**; called **"Coryphaeus of Grammarians."**] fl. at Alexandria, c217–c145 B.C.; d. on Cyprus. Greek grammarian and critic, a leading Homeric scholar of antiquity, now considered to have been one of the greatest philologists of the ancient world. A student of Aristophanes of Byzantium, and his successor (c180) as librarian at Alexandria, he was the founder of a school of philology known as Aristarcheans. A prolific commentator on and editor of Hesiod, Pindar, Aeschylus, Sophocles, and other Greeks, his version of the Homeric language and the arrangement into 24 books of the *Iliad* and *Odyssey* is a basis of many modern texts.

Ariste (à.rēst). Brother of Chrysale, in *Les Femmes Savantes* by Molière.

Aristeas (a.ris'tē.as). [Sometimes called the **"Wandering Jew."**] Greek poet, assigned to various periods, from the 6th century B.C. to the time of Homer; reputed author of an epic poem, *Arimaspea*, in three books. The accounts of his life are legendary; he is represented as a magician who rose after death, and whose soul could occupy or abandon his body at will.

Aristeas or **Aristaeos.** [Surnamed **"the Elder."**] fl. about the end of the 4th century B.C. Greek mathematician who collaborated with Euclid in the composition of the "treasury of analysis," a geometrical method for advanced students. He wrote on the "comparison of the five figures" (i.e., the five regular solids) and proved that "the same circle circumscribes both the pentagon of the dodecahedron and the triangle of the icosahedron when both solids are inscribed in the same sphere." He also wrote five books of solid loci connected with the conics (that is, a treatise on conics regarded as loci). This treatise is now usually considered by historians of science to be more important and more original than the one written later by Euclid on the same subject, although its object and point of view were different. Aristeas called the conics, respectively, sections of right-angled, acute-angled, and obtuse-angled cones, and he discussed the three-line and four-line locus.

Aristeus, Aristaeus (ar.is.tē'us), or **Aristeas** (a.ris'tē.as). fl. 3rd century B.C. Official at the court of Ptolemy II (of Egypt) who was formerly believed to have obtained from Eleazar, Jewish high priest at Jerusalem, a copy of the Pentateuch for translation into Greek. The *Letter of Aristeus* which bears this out is now known to be false in this respect, but is nonetheless of use to scholars as a historical source for the period.

Aristides (ar is.tī'dēz). [Also: **Aristeides**; surnamed **"the Just."**] b. c530 B.C.; d. probably at Athens, c468 B.C. Athenian statesman and general. One of the ten Greek generals at Marathon (490), he is said to have ensured victory over the Persians by persuading his colleagues to give full command to Miltiades. He served (489-488) as chief archon of Athens. A conservative, he advocated land power for Athens in opposition to the naval policy of Themistocles; he was ostracized in c483 as a result of this conflict. Returning under the amnesty of 480 to help the defense of Athens against the Persians under Xerxes, he served (480–479 and 479–478) as strategus, took part in the victory of Salamis (480) by capturing Psyttaleia from the Persians, was a commander at Plataea (479) and Byzantium (c478), and succeeded Pausanius as admiral after the Ionian revolt. He was in charge of taxation for the Delian League (c477) and thereafter influential in Athenian affairs. An administrator of ability and integrity, he was probably not the great democrat he has been called.

Aristides. [Also, **Aristeides.**] fl. 2nd century A.D. Greek Christian and theologian, author of what is believed by most scholars to be Christianity's earliest apology. Written on the occasion of Christian persecution after Hadrian's initiation into the Eleusinian mysteries, the *Apology of Aristides* was long known to exist but no complete manuscript of it was available until J. R. Harris discovered a Syriac copy of it on Mount Sinai in 1889.

Aristides, Publius Aelius. [Also: **Aristeides**; surnamed **Theodorus.**] b. in Mysia, Asia Minor, c120 A.D.; d. at Smyrna, c180 A.D. Greek rhetorician, author of treatises on speech, declamations, sacred discourses, and others, used as models of Attic style. His account to Marcus Aurelius of the destruction (178) of Smyrna by earthquake is said to have induced that emperor to rebuild the city.

Aristides, Quintilianus. [Also, **Aristeides.**] fl. between 1st and 4th centuries A.D. Greek author of a treatise on music (printed in a collection in 1652), considered by some as the most important ancient book on the subject.

Aristides of Miletus. [Also, **Aristeides.**] fl. c150–100 B.C. Greek author of the *Milesiaca* or *Milesian Tales*, considered to have been the first Greek prose romance.

Aristides of Thebes. [Also, **Aristeides.**] fl. 4th century B.C. Greek painter. He did battle scenes, hunting scenes, and other works, prized by Alexander and others for their expression of the mind and passions of man.

Aristippus (ar.is.tip'us). b. at Cyrene, Africa; fl. c435–386 B.C. Greek philosopher; pupil of Socrates, and founder of the Cyrenaic school. Starting with the Socratic principles of virtue and happiness, he based his ethics on the pursuit of pleasure, tempered with prudence in order to avoid pain. Little is known of his life, and it is uncertain how much of his theory actually originated with him, and how much was developed by his followers.

Aristo (à.rēs.tō). Brother of Sganarelle, in Molière's *École des Maris.*

Aristobulus (a.ris.tō.bū'lus, ar"is.tō-). fl. 4th century B.C. Greek historian from Cassandreia who was a companion of Alexander the Great on the Asiatic expedition. His account of Alexander's campaigns was later used by Plutarch, Arrian, and others.

Aristobulus. b. at Paneas (now Baniyas), in ancient Palestine; fl. at Alexandria c180–160 B.C. Greek Peripatetic philosopher and Jewish scholar who attempted to reconcile the Jewish and Greek philosophies. Author of a commentary on Moses which sought to trace certain Greek writings to scriptural origin; the authenticity of his quotations is a subject of controversy among scholars.

Aristobulus I (of *Judea*). [Called **Judah.**] b. c140 B.C.; d. 103 B.C. King and high priest of Judea (c104–103 B.C.); son of John Hyrcanus. He is said to have been the first of the Maccabees (or Hasmoneans) to assume the title of king. During his brief reign he extended Judea in the regions of Iturea and Trachonitis.

Aristobulus II (of *Judea*). d. c48 B.C. King and high priest of Judea; son of Alexander Jannaeus. He was designated high priest by his mother, the queen-regent Alexandra, while the throne was bequeathed to his elder brother Hyrcanus II. After her death a contest took place between the two brothers which brought Pompey for the first time to Jerusalem (63 B.C.); he defeated Aristobulus and led him captive to Rome. Like Aristobulus I, he was a member of the priestly family of the Maccabees (or Hasmoneans).

Aristobulus III (of *Judea*). Prince and high priest of Judea; grandson of Aristobulus II, brother of Mariamne, and thus brother-in-law of Herod I. In 36 B.C. he was made high priest with the approval of Herod, but, fearing his great popularity, Herod had him assassinated (c35

B.C.). He was the last representative of the Maccabees (or Hasmoneans) to be high priest.

Aristodemus (a̤.ris.tō̤.dē'mus). fl. 8th century B.C. King of Messenia (c731–724 B.C.). A hero in the first war (c727) against the Spartans, he committed suicide because he feared eventual defeat. His life has been the subject of various legends.

Aristomenes (ar.is.tom'ē̤.nēz). fl. 7th century B.C. Messenian national hero in the second war against Sparta (c650–630 B.C.). According to the account of Pausanius, based on the epic *Messeniaea* (c230 B.C.), he was the instigator and leader of the revolt against Sparta (which ended in disaster for the Messenians, but has been remembered as a valiant struggle against tyranny).

Ariston (a.ris'ton) or **Aristo** (-tō). b. on the island of Chios, in the Aegean Sea; d. c250 B.C. Greek Stoic philosopher, a disciple of Zeno and later, according to Diogenes Laertius, of the Platonist Polemo. Of the various branches of philosophy he recognized only ethics as a legitimate study.

Aristonicus (a̤.ris.tō̤.nī'kus). d. c130 B.C. Natural son of Eumenes II (of Pergamum). When Attalus II, the brother and successor of Eumenes, died, he was succeeded by Attalus III, his nephew, who bequeathed the kingdom on his death (133 B.C.) to the Romans. Aristonicus disputed the inheritance with the latter, defeating (131 B.C.) and taking prisoner the Roman commander sent to oppose him. He was himself defeated and taken prisoner in 130 B.C., carried to Rome, and beheaded.

Aristophanes (ar.is.tof'a̤.nēz). b. between c450 and 446 B.C.; d. c380 B.C. Athenian writer of Greek comedies. Out of the buffoonery of Greek comic plays Aristophanes created an artistic comedy. A conservative and passionate believer in the good old days of Marathon, he attacked with triumphant vigor "progressive" education (Socrates), new ideas in philosophy (the Sophists), melodrama, rhetorical claptrap, and bizarre musical innovations in contemporary tragedy (Euripides), and above all demagoguery and corruption in politics (Cleon and Hyperbolus). His criticism of the tragedies of Aeschylus and Euripides in *The Frogs* is the earliest and one of the best pieces of literary criticism in existence. His comedies are characterized by a wealth of imagination, a freshness of wit, a pungency of satire, and bursts of pure lyric poetry that can be found in no other comedies except perhaps those of Shakespeare. He took the role of public critic seriously and his political satire was so effective that he was awarded by the Athenian state a crown of wild olive for the good advice he had given the city. Of his many comedies these eleven survive: *The Acharnians* (425), *The Knights* (424), *The Clouds* (423), *The Wasps* (422), *The Peace* (421), *The Birds* (414), *Lysistrata* (411), *The Thesmophoriazusae* (411), *The Frogs* (405), *The Ecclesiazusae* (c393), and *The Plutus* (388).

Aristophanes' Apology. Poem by Robert Browning, published in 1875. It is the sequel to *Balaustion's Adventure* and sets forth a defense of Euripides against the detraction current at the time, as well as a statement of Browning's own poetic faith and practice.

Aristophanes of Byzantium. b. c257 B.C.; d. c180 B.C. Greek grammarian, critic, and lexicographer, now considered to have been perhaps the greatest philologist of the ancient world. He was for many years librarian at the Alexandria museum. A pupil of Zenodotus and Callimachus, he was an instructor of Aristarchus of Samothrace, who succeeded him both as librarian at Alexandria and as the leading Homeric scholar of the day. Besides Homer, he edited Hesiod, Alcaeus, Anacreon, Pindar, Plato, and the Greek dramatists, wrote commentaries on Aristophanes (the playwright) and on Callimachus's literary history (*Pinakes*), compiled word lists, and introduced diacritical marks in an effort to systematize the pronunciation and accentuation of Greek. The invention of punctuation is sometimes ascribed to Aristophanes, but systematization is perhaps a more exact description of his contribution.

Aristotle (ar'is.tot.l). [Sometimes called the **"Stagirite."**] b. at Stagira (whence the name above), on the NW Aegean coast, 384 B.C.; d. at Chalcis, in Euboea, 322 B.C. Greek philosopher, one of the greatest thinkers of antiquity, and a continuing influence on philosophic speculation. He was the son of Nicomachus, the personal physician of Amyntas II of Macedonia, and probably spent part of his childhood at the Macedonian court. When he was 17 he went to Athens and attended the academy of Plato, where he remained until Plato's death. He then went to Assos as the guest (348–347) of Hermias, the ruler of Atarneus and Assos, and married Hermias's niece, Pythias. After the death of Hermias in 345, he went to Mytilene, and there carried on zoölogical studies. In 343–42 Philip of Macedonia invited him to Pella to act as the tutor of his son, Alexander. In 335, after Philip's death, he returned to Athens and founded outside the city a school which took its name (the Peripatetic School) from a covered court, or *peripatos*, in the garden of the school. The school had a communal life and an extensive library, and was a center of research in every field of contemporary knowledge. When Alexander died there was an outbreak of feeling against the Macedonians, and Aristotle was charged with impiety. He left Athens and went to Chalcis, and there died in 322 of a digestive disease.

Written Works. His works were of three kinds: (1) early writings in the form of Platonic dialogues, and Platonic in spirit, which survive only in fragments, e.g. the *Protrepticus;* (2) later didactic works in which he moved away from Platonism towards his more mature views, and which also survive only in fragments, e.g. the *Theodectea;* and (3) the works of his maturity, many of which still survive. The body of his surviving works does contain some which are spurious, but for the most part the works are genuine. The extant writings may be conveniently divided into the classes used by the ancient editors: (1) the *Organon*, or group of logical writings, which includes the *Prior* and *Posterior Analytics;* (2) the works on natural science which include the *Physics, On the Soul,* and the *History of Animals;* (3) miscellaneous writings, which include the *Problems;* (4) the work on primary philosophy, called the *Metaphysics;* (5) the works on moral philosophy, which include the *Nicomachean Ethics* and the *Politics;* and (6) the works on art, the *Rhetoric,* and the *Poetics.* To these must be added one historical work, the *Constitution of Athens*, written on papyrus and discovered in Egypt in the latter part of the 19th century.

Influence as Philosopher. Aristotle has been the philosopher *par excellence* of the western world, and his influence is still significant. He was primarily a philosopher of moderation and common sense. In metaphysics he believed in both matter and mind, in both the natural and the supernatural. In ethics he believed in both physical well-being and spiritual contemplation. In political theory he believed in both constitutional government and a leadership of merit. Aristotle's philosophy is an inspired common sense governed by a critical insight into the meaning of human experience.

Aristotle and the History of Science. Aristotle was one of the founders of the inductive method. He was the first to conceive the idea of organized research, and himself contributed considerably to the organization of science by his systematic survey and classification of the knowledge of his time. He took pains to make as clear as possible the fundamental principles of each science in particular, and of science in general. He may be called the founder of logic, and his systematization of it in the *Organon* was so masterful that it still dominates much of the teaching of today. He prepared the systematization of geometry by his investigations of its more fundamental and philosophical aspect, in particular by his introduction of new or better definitions and his discussion of the concepts of continuity and infinity. He completed the system of homocentric spheres of Eudoxus and Callippus, using a total of 55 spheres to account for all the celestial motions. His is the oldest attempt to estimate the size of the earth. To the four elements he added the quintessence called aether, the natural movement of which was circular. The celestial bodies are made of aether and are perfect and incorruptible (this theory stood until 1610). If the mechanical writings be genuine, Aristotle had done much profound thinking on the subject, but whether he was fundamentally right or fundamentally wrong depends entirely upon one's interpretation of his thought. He is said to have discovered the law of the lever, and that sound is transmitted by vibrations of the air. He made the first systematic study (and wrote the first textbook) of meteorology, as well as the first treatise on chemistry.

Contributions to the Natural Sciences. Aristotle carried on immense botanical, zoölogical, and anatomical investigations. He clearly recognized the fundamental problems of biology: sex, heredity, nutrition, growth, adaptation. He outlined both a theory of evolution (*scala naturae*) and a scientific classification of animals. He proposed theories of generation and heredity. He may be called the founder of comparative anatomy (e.g., comparative study of the womb). Many of his anatomical descriptions are admirable (e.g., reproduction of selachians, especially placental development of the dog-fish, embryonic development of the chick, stomach of ruminants, and others). Some of Aristotle's errors are extremely important, however, because of their far-reaching influence. Thus his denial of the sexuality of plants (he assimilated their reproduction to nutrition and growth) was the main cause of the enormous delay in its discovery (Camerarius, 1694). In spite of earlier Hippocratic views, he considered the heart as the seat of intelligence, the function of the brain being then simply to cool the heart by the secretion of phlegm and to prevent its overheating. He realized that the arterial system duplicates the venous system, but failed to understand the real difference between arteries and veins; he believed that arteries contain air as well as blood. Here again Aristotle's views were the main cause of the extraordinary tardiness of the discovery of the circulation of the blood (Harvey, 1628).

Other Contributions and Summary. He attempted an inductive study of politics, and wrote a history and critical account of Greek constitutional law. One of the modern definitions of psychology as "the positive science of the behavior of living things" is a return to the standpoint of Aristotle. His theory of dreams was far more rational than that of Democritus (he tried to explain them by the persistence of sense impressions, having observed the exaggerated excitement caused by slight stimuli if they interrupt a dream). Aristotle's influence, for good or evil, in every department of knowledge, was so tremendous that a good history of Aristotelianism would include a large part of the history of science and of thought down to the 18th century. The prodigious activity of Aristotle marks the climax of the golden age of Greece. The very existence of his works proves not simply that he had an encyclopedic mind of the highest order, but also that a large amount of scientific research had already been accomplished by his time. Unlike his teacher Plato, Aristotle was not essentially a mathematician. He had a deep mathematical knowledge, but that knowledge was happily balanced by a very extensive acquaintance with every branch of natural history.

Aristoxenus (ar.is.tok'sē.nus). b. at Tarentum (now Taranto), Italy; fl. 4th century B.C. Greek music theorist and philosopher of the Peripatetic School; student of Aristotle. Now usually considered to have been the greatest music theoretician of ancient times, he was the founder of the school of musicians known as Aristoxeneans; his *Elements of Harmony* (which exists in its entirety) is of value to music historians. Author also of *Elements of Rhythm* (which exists in fragments), and of more than 430 other works, which have been lost.

Arita (ä.rē.tä), **Hachiro.** b. in Japan, in September, 1884—. Japanese diplomat, foreign minister from 1936 to 1939.

Arius (a.rī'u̧s, ãr'i.us). [Also: **Areius, Areios, Arios.**] b. in Libya or at Alexandria, c256 (or, according to some authorities, c280) A.D.; d. at Constantinople, 336. Presbyter of Alexandria, a pupil of Lucian of Antioch, from whom he derived the beginnings of the doctrine known as Arianism or the Arian heresy. This, which maintained that Christ, a combination of divine *Logos* and created body, was neither perfect God nor perfect man, i.e., less divine than God, was the subject of a controversy in the Christian church for three centuries. Excommunicated by the provincial synod at Alexandria (321), he defended his views, which were nevertheless condemned, before the Council of Nicaea (325); he was banished, but was possibly about to be reinstated by Constantine when he (Arius) died. The Arians, especially in the Eastern empire, then split into several groups, and disputes raged between these groups and others in the church, chiefly between adherents of Athanasius (who supported the essential Nicene doctrine of consubstantiality, i.e., that God and Christ are of one substance) and the heretic emperor Valens. Indeed, after the death (337) of Constantine, the new emperor reversed the decision of the council of Nicaea and a kind of Arianism became for a time (until 378) the orthodox doctrine. A point of interest here is that Ulfilas, apostle of the Goths, was consecrated bishop by Eusebius in 341, during this Arian supremacy, and because of this initial accident, the Goths were, and remained, Arians, as did other Teutonic tribes—Suevi, Vandals, Burgundians, Lombards—which were either Arian from the beginning or became so because of the Gothic example. Thus, for a time, Teutonic Christianity was Arian, while Latin Christianity was Catholic. Both religions were essentially the same, but there was enough theological difference to add some religious rancor to racial enmities. No international hatred is truly perfect unless the selfrighteousness of both parties is enhanced by a feeling of religious superiority. In this case, the theologians of Nicaea had provided the necessary touch of perfection; a single iota (identical essence vs. similar essence) made the whole difference between good people and others. This state of affairs lasted until the 6th century. The Franks were the first Germanic tribe to become Catholic, in 496, and by the middle of the sixth century, the greatest part of Gaul was Catholic.

Arius. Ancient name of the **Hari Rud.**

Arizona (ar.i.zō'na̧). [Called the **"Grand Canyon State."**] State of the SW United States, bounded by Utah on the N, New Mexico on the E, Mexico on the S, and California and Nevada (partly separated by the Colorado River) on the W.

Population, Area, and Political Divisions. Arizona is divided for administrative purposes into 14 counties. It sends two representatives to Congress and has 18 electoral votes. Capital, Phoenix; area, 113,580 sq. mi. (113,909 sq. mi., including water); pop. 499,261 (1940), 749,587 (1950). The state ranks fifth in area, and 38th (on the basis of the 1950 census) in population. The chief cities are Phoenix and Tucson.

Terrain and Climate. Arizona's surface consists of a high plateau traversed by mountain ranges and cut by deep canyons, which occupies the N, C, and E parts, and a dry desertlike lowland, traversed by jagged mountain ranges, which occupies the SW and S central parts. The highest mountain is Mount Humphreys (12,665 ft.), in the San Francisco range, in the N part of the state. Other principal ranges are the Bradshaws, in the C part, the White Mountains and the Grahams, in the E part, and the Santa Catalina Mountains, the Chiricahua Mountains, and the Santa Rita Mountains, in the S part of the state. The chief river system is that of the Colorado, which flows into the state from the N and along its W boundary, draining into the Gulf of California. Where the river turns S, in the NW part of the state, and partly in SE Nevada, is Lake Mead, the largest artificial lake in the world, a reservoir formed by Hoover Dam (formerly Boulder Dam) and utilized for power, irrigation, and control of flood waters. In the NW is the Grand Canyon, formed by the Colorado's course; more than 200 mi. in length, it lies within a plateau ranging in height from 5,000 to 7,000 ft. above sea level. Grand Canyon National Park (established 1919), including part of the canyon and the surrounding area, comprises ab. 1,009 sq. mi. West of the park is the Grand Canyon National Monument (established 1932) consisting of 196,051 acres. Principal tributaries of the Colorado are the Little Colorado, flowing NW into it, and the Gila, flowing SW into it. The Salt River, flowing W into the Gila, has been made a valuable source of power and irrigation by means of Roosevelt Dam, Mormon Flat Dam, Horse Mesa Dam, Stewart Mountain Dam, and the lakes formed by these dams. The Verde River flows S into the Salt at a point somewhat E of Phoenix. The Petrified Forest National Monument in NE Arizona consists of 85,304 acres of cedar and pine forests turned into stone by the action of mineral-laden waters flowing toward the Colorado. Also in the NE part of the state is the Painted Desert, a stretch of ab. 200 mi. of colored rock surfaces. Arizona's clear air attracts many invalids as winter visitors or year-round residents. The climate of the S lowland is dry, with hot summers and mild winters. The plateau has warm summers and cold winters, with snow common above ab. 5,000 ft. elevation.

There is enough rainfall in the high regions of the plateau to permit a fine forest growth of pine, juniper, and cedar.

Industry, Agriculture, and Trade. Although Arizona ranks as the nation's leading copper-producing state, agriculture (including stock raising) is its chief industry. Extensive irrigation has redeemed great stretches of arid land for general farming. Alfalfa, cotton, truck vegetables, fruits (including semitropical fruits), dairy products, and hay are important crops. Mining since 1858 has produced more than three billion dollars in metals, of which 87 percent was in copper. Minerals found in addition to copper are gold, silver, lead, zinc, mercury, and tungsten. Manufacturing centers primarily on the smelting and refining of copper and on meat products. Annual income in the state from agriculture ranges as high as $176,000,000; from mining, as high as $115,000,000; from manufacturing, as high as $127,000,000. The tourist industry is also important.

History. Vast ruins testify to the existence of a prehistoric culture in Arizona; they include canals, cities, and fortifications. The first Europeans to explore the state were the Spaniards, the Franciscan friar Marcos de Niza reaching it in 1539 and leading a second expedition into the region the following year. The region was governed by Spain as a part of Mexico; the N part was acquired (1848) by the U.S., with New Mexico, as the result of the Mexican War; that part S of the Gila was retained by Mexico as part of the Mexican state of Sonora until the Gadsden Purchase in 1853. Arizona was not separated from New Mexico until 1863 when it became a separate territory. It refused (1906) statehood when Congress proposed that it join with New Mexico as one state, and was admitted to the Union (as the 48th state) on Feb. 14, 1912.

Culture. Indian arts, crafts, and architecture, as well as Spanish architecture, still maintain a dominant influence in Arizona. The state has proven a rich field for the investigation of anthropologists and archaeologists. Indian reservations make up ab. 27,000 sq. mi. The inhabitants of the state are about equally divided between rural and urban areas (on the basis of the 1950 census urban population constituted 55.5 percent of the total). Arizona's institutions of higher learning include the state-supported University of Arizona, at Tucson, and state colleges at Flagstaff and Tempe. The state motto is *Ditat Deus*, meaning "God Enriches." The state flower is the blossom of the *Cereus Giganteus* (giant cactus) or saguaro.

Arizpe (ä.rēs′pā). [Also, **Arispe.**] Town in NW Mexico, in Sonora state, on the Sonora River: formerly the state capital. It was probably the site of an Opata village as early as 1540. The Mission of Arizpe dates from about 1640, and is one of the oldest in the Sonora River valley. Pop. under 5,000 (1940).

Arjish Dagh (är.jēsh′ däg′). See **Erciyas Daği.**

Arjish Lake. See **Ercis Lake.**

Arjona (är.hō′nä). City in NW Colombia, in Bolívar department. 10,416 (1938).

Arjona. Town in S Spain, in the province of Jaén, ab. 20 mi. NW of Jaén: center of an agricultural district. 11,111 (1940).

Arjuna (är′jö.na). In Hindu mythology, one of the chief heroes of the *Mahabharata.*

Arkab (är′kab). Name occasionally used for the third-magnitude star β Sagittarii.

Arkadelphia (är.ka.del′fi.a). City in SW Arkansas, on the Ouachita River, county seat of Clark County, ab. 63 mi. SW of Little Rock: seat of Ouachita College and Henderson State Teachers College. 6,819 (1950).

Arkadia (är.kä.ᴛʜē′ä). See **Arcadia,** department, Greece.

Ark and the Dove. Sailing vessels which transported (Nov. 22, 1633–March 27, 1634) the first permanent English settlers to Maryland. The vessels left from Cowes on the Isle of Wight, and anchored off the site of what is now St. Mary's (and which was so named by the settlers), near the mouth of the Potomac River.

Arkansas (är′kan.sô). [Official nickname, the **"Wonder State."**] State of the S and C United States, bounded by Missouri on the N, Tennessee and Mississippi (separated by the Mississippi River) on the E, Louisiana on the S, and Oklahoma and Texas on the W.

Population, Area, and Political Divisions. Arkansas is divided for administrative purposes into 75 counties. The state sends 7 representatives to Congress and has 18 electoral votes. Capital, Little Rock; area, 52,725 sq. mi. (53,102 sq. mi., including water); pop. 1,909,511 (1950). The state ranks 26th in area, and 30th (on the basis of the 1950 census) in population. Leading cities are Little Rock, Fort Smith, Hot Springs, Helena, North Little Rock, Pine Bluff, and El Dorado.

Terrain and Climate. Arkansas' surface is about equally divided between lowlands and highlands, with the Ozark Mountains (including the Boston Mountains) in the NW and the Ouachita Mountains slightly S of them. Highest spots in the state are Magazine Mountain (2,800 ft.) in the Boston Mountains and Rich Mountain (formerly Blue Mountain, 2,750 ft.) in the Ouachita Mountains. At Hot Springs National Park in the Ouachitas are 47 thermal springs, ranging from 95° to 147° in temperature, which have made the surrounding area a popular tourist and health resort. Traversing the state, the Arkansas River flows from W to E, joining the Mississippi ab. 30 mi. N of Greenville, Miss. The Mississippi forms the state's E boundary and provides an important commercial passage. Flowing SE from Missouri is the White River, which is joined by the Black and Cache Rivers before it discharges into the Arkansas near the point where that river joins the Mississippi. The Red River in the SW corner of the state flows E and S. The Ouachita rises in the W and flows SE into Louisiana. The state is extensively forested. It has hot summers and cool winters, with occasional cold waves in winter.

Industry, Agriculture, and Trade. One of the top cotton and rice producing states, Arkansas is heavily agricultural. Corn, hay, fruits, and soybeans are other major crops, and livestock raising is important. The state is rich in minerals, supplying about 95 percent of the country's bauxite, and having abundant deposits of bituminous coal, petroleum, and natural gas. Titanium (containing uranium and thorium), clay, limestone, and manganese are also found. In 1906 the first and only deposit of diamonds in North America was found near Murfreesboro. The manufacture of lumber products, cotton products, machinery, and pottery are leading occupations. Annual income in the state from agriculture ranges as high as $539,818,000; from industrial output, as high as $719,000,000.

History. Spanish explorers led by De Soto were the first Europeans to visit (1641) Arkansas. Later explorations were undertaken by Joliet and Marquette, La Salle, de Tonti, and the missionary Hennepin. The first permanent settlement was made (1686) by the French under de Tonti at Arkansas Post. The territory went (1762) from France to Spain, was returned (1780) to France, and was included (1803) in the Louisiana Purchase. Arkansas was part of the territory of Louisiana and later of the territory of Missouri before becoming (1819) a state (the 25th) of the Union on June 15, 1836. The state seceded (1861) to join the Confederate States; adopted (1863) a constitution prohibiting slavery and was readmitted to the Union in the same year.

Culture. Arkansas has a preponderantly rural population (urban population, on the basis of the 1950 census, constituted 33 percent of the total). Among its institutions of higher learning are the state-supported University of Arkansas, at Fayetteville, and teachers' colleges at Conway and Arkadelphia. State motto: *Regnat Populus* ("The People Rule"); state flower, apple blossom; state bird, mocking bird; state song, *The Arkansas Traveler.*

Arkansas City (är.kan′zas). City in SE Kansas, in Cowley County, on the Arkansas River: important for petroleum refining. During the 1870's, when horse thieves made the community their headquarters, "Buffalo Bill" Cody was U.S. marshal here. 12,903 (1950).

Arkansas Post (är′kan.sô). Village in SE Arkansas, on the Arkansas River, in Arkansas County, ab. 73 mi. SE of Little Rock. Established in 1686, it was the first permanent white settlement in the lower Mississippi valley. It was captured by Union forces on Jan. 11, 1863. Pop. under 100.

Arkansas Post, Battle of. Engagement (January, 1863) in SE Arkansas, between besieged Confederate forces at Arkansas Post (Fort Hindman) under General Thomas J.

Churchill and attacking Union forces (30,000 troops) under General John A. McClernand. The Union assault was aided by a fleet of ironclads on the Arkansas River under Admiral David D. Porter. The Confederates surrendered on Jan. 11, 1863.

Arkansas River (är.kan′zạs, är′kạn.sô). River in the W central U.S., a major tributary of the Mississippi River. It rises in Lake County, Colo., in the Rocky Mountains, flows E through Colorado and Kansas, and SE through Kansas, Oklahoma, and Arkansas, and joins the Mississippi ab. 30 mi. N of Greenville, Miss. Length, ab. 1,450 mi.; greatest width, ab. 1 mi.; navigable for ab. 800 mi.

Arkansas Traveler (är′kan.sô). American folk dialogue and fiddle tune. It is a dialogue between a lost traveler and an Arkansas squatter whom he finds fiddling in front of his cabin. The tune was first published in 1847 as *The Arkansas Traveler and Rackinsac Waltz.*

Arkat (är′kät). A Tamil name of **Arcot.**

Arkell (är′kẹl, är.kel′), **Reginald.** b. at Lechlade, Gloucestershire, England, 1882—. English journalist, librettist, and playwright. His musical comedies include an adaptation (1935) of *1066 and All That;* among his other works are *Colombine and Other Verses* (1912), *Tragedy of Mr. Punch* (1920), *Green Fingers* (1934), *War Rumours* (1939), *Green Fingers Again* (1942), and *Old Herbaceous* (1951). Editor (1946 *et seq.*) of *Men Only* and *London Opinion.*

Arkhangelsk (är.hän′gilsk). [English, **Archangel** (ärk′ān″jẹl).] *Oblast* (region) in the NE part of the U.S.S.R. in Europe, in the Russian Soviet Federated Socialist Republic, S of the White Sea and the Arctic Ocean, centered ab. 500 mi. NE of Leningrad. The greater portion of its area is a plain, but it is traversed SE to NW by a narrow range of low hills. The land is sparsely settled, and is covered in the N by frozen tundra and in the S by coniferous forests. There is little farming and the production of minerals is negligible. Prior to the Russian Revolution it was the largest of the governments of Russia, but its area was considerably reduced in 1919. Capital, Arkhangelsk; area, 252,397 sq. mi.; pop. 1,199,178 (1939).

Arkhangelsk. [English, **Archangel.**] Seaport in the N part of the U.S.S.R., in the Arkhangelsk *oblast* (region) of the Russian Soviet Federated Socialist Republic, situated on the Dvina River near the White Sea: the chief commercial town in the N region of Russia, and long the only Russian seaport. It was an important receiving point for materials from the U.S. during World War II. The harbor is open from May to September. Exports from Arkhangelsk include grain, flax, linseed, pitch, skins, and tar. It has sawmills, woodworking plants, fish canneries, and shipyards. A Russian fort was built there in 1584. Pop. 281,000 (1939).

Arkhangelsky (är.hän′gil.ski), **Aleksandr Andreyevich.** b. in Pensa, Russia, 1846; d. at Prague, 1924. Russian composer and choral conductor. He was the first to replace boy choristers with women in Russian churches. Composer of several masses and other religious works.

Arklow (ärk′lō). [Irish, **Inbhear Mor.**] Market town and seaport in Leinster province, Irish Republic, in County Wicklow, situated at the mouth of the river Avoca, ab. 39 mi. S of Dublin. It is the largest fishing port in the country, fishing being virtually the only industry of the town. Coal and general cargo are also landed here. A force of Irish insurgents, numbering about 30,000, was defeated by the royal troops near here on June 10, 1798. Pop. 5,193 (1951).

Arkona (är.kō′nạ), **Cape.** [German, **Kap Arkon.**] Northernmost point of the island of Rügen, Germany, projecting into the Baltic Sea. It contained a Wendish sanctuary.

Ark Royal. British aircraft carrier. The vessel played a decisive part in the successful hunt for and sinking of the German battleship *Bismarck* on May 26–27, 1941, some 400 mi. off the French coast. The 22,000-ton carrier was herself torpedoed by a German submarine during the early evening of Nov. 12, 1941, at a point ab. 25 mi. E of Gibraltar, and sank early the next morning.

Arkwright (ärk′rīt), Sir **Richard.** b. at Preston, England, Dec. 23, 1732; d. at Cromford, England, Aug. 3, 1792. English inventor of a cotton-spinning frame (patented 1769), and manufacturer of cotton cloth. His frame, using rollers for the first time and producing hard thread particularly suitable for warp (which Hargreaves's jenny (1770) could not do) was nevertheless not used at first by manufacturers. He established his first mill, horse-driven, at Nottingham in 1768, established water-powered stocking factories at Cromford and elsewhere, used (1790 *et seq.*) a steam engine at Nottingham, was among the first to employ machinery on a large scale as a substitute for hand labor in textile manufacture, and was thus a contributor to the industrial revolution. His calico made with cotton warp (1773) was the first all-cotton textile produced in England. He added improvements in carding, roving, and spinning (patented 1775), and defended his patent against other claims in a long lawsuit (1781 *et seq.*).

Arland (år.läṅ), **Marcel.** b. at Varennes, France, July 5, 1899—. French novelist and essayist; awarded (1929) the Goncourt prize for *L'Ordre.* Other works by him include *Terres étrangères* (1924), *Antarès* (1932), *La Vigie* (1935), and *Zélie dans le désert* (1944). Among his essays are *La Route obscure* (1925), *Essais critiques* (1931), *Le Promeneur* (1944), and *Les Échanges* (1945).

Arlanibäus (är″lä.nē.bā′ůs), **Philipp.** A pseudonym of **Abelin, Johann Philipp.**

Arlanza (är.län′thä). Small river in N Spain, a tributary of the Arlanzón River.

Arlanzón (är.län.thôn′). Small river in N Spain, a tributary of the Pisuerga River and subtributary of the Douro River.

Arlberg (ärl′berk; Anglicized, ärl′bėrg). Pass on the border of Tirol and Vorarlberg, Austria, 5,895 ft. high. A railroad tunnel ab. 6½ mi. long passes under it ab. 1,600 ft. below its highest point.

Arlberg Tunnel. Tunnel under the Arlberg, in W Austria, forming part of the railway which runs from Bludenz in Vorarlberg via Landeck to Innsbruck. It is ab. 6½ mi. long, and was opened in 1884.

Arlen (är′lẹn), **Michael.** [Original name, **Dikran Kouyoumdjian.**] b. at Roustchouk, Bulgaria, 1895—. British novelist recently resident in the U.S. He became a British citizen in 1922 and served (1940 *et seq.*) as a public relations officer for the west Midlands area during World War II. His novel *The Green Hat* (1924), with its boyish, unconventional heroine, was a huge success, and was subsequently dramatized and filmed. Among Arlen's other works are *Man's Mortality* (1933), *The Crooked Coronet* (1937), and *The Flying Dutchman* (1939).

Arles (ȧrl; Anglicized, ärlz). [Latin, **Arelate,** (under Constantine) **Constantia.**] City in SE France, in the department of Bouches-du-Rhône, situated on the left bank of the E arm of the Rhone River, near its mouth, S of Avignon. It is a river port accessible to seagoing vessels through the canal from Arles to Bouc. There are various industries, particularly stone quarrying, and manufactures of paper and of sausage. Arles is of considerable importance to archaeologists and art historians. It has the largest Roman amphitheater in France, another Roman theater where the Venus of Arles was found, a Roman obelisk, the Roman cemetery of Aliscamps, two museums (Musée Lapidaire and Musée Arlatin), and the cathedral of Saint Trophime, one of the most beautiful Romanesque churches in Provence. The city was colonized by the Phoenicians and prospered under Roman rule to such an extent that it was called "the little Gallic Rome." The emperors Constantine and Honorius favored the city. In 480 it fell victim to the Visigothic invasion. From 1150 to 1251 it was a republic, but then submitted to Charles of Anjou, count of Provence. It was united with France in 1481. The city was in the invasion path of the Seventh U.S. Army and a French army in the fall of 1944 and suffered severe damage. 35,017 (1946).

Arles, Kingdom of. In medieval history, a kingdom which was formed by the union of the kingdoms of Transjurane Burgundy and Cisjurane Burgundy in 933. In 1032 its territories were annexed to the Holy Roman Empire. Cisjurane Burgundy, formed in 879, is sometimes called the kingdom of Arles.

Arlésienne (lȧr.lā.zyen), **L'.** Two orchestral suites by Georges Bizet arranged from his incidental music to Alphonse Daudet's play of the same name.

Arles-les-Bains (ȧrl.lā.baṅ). Former name of **Amélie-les-Bains.**

Arlincourt (dȧr.laṅ.kör), **Charles Victor Prévot,** Vicomte **d'.** b. at the Château de Mérantris, near Versailles, Sept. 28, 1789; d. at Paris, Jan. 23, 1856. French poet and novelist. Author of *Le Solitaire* (1821), and others.

Arline (är.lēn′). The "Bohemian Girl," in Michael William Balfe's opera of that name.

Arlington (är′ling.tọn), 1st Earl of. [Title of **Henry Bennet.**] b. at Arlington, Middlesex, England, 1618; d. July 28, 1685. English politician and diplomat, created earl of Arlington by Charles II in 1672. A member of the Royalist army during the English Civil War, he was, after the Restoration, made (1661) keeper of the privy purse, and served (1662–74) as secretary of state, with charge of foreign affairs during the "Cabal ministry" after the fall (1667) of Edward Hyde, 1st earl of Clarendon. He opposed Sir William Temple's triple alliance with Holland and Sweden, and was confidential adviser to Charles II in the negotiation of the secret Treaty of Dover (1670). Impeachment proceedings were initiated (1674) against him in the House of Commons on charges of his being linked to the papacy, of being the king's chief instrument in corruption, and for breach of trust; even though the charges were not sustained, Arlington's power waned and his only further office was that of lord chamberlain (1674–85).

Arlington. Town in E Massachusetts, in Middlesex County, ab. 6 mi. NW of Boston: residential suburb. 44,353 (1950).

Arlington. Unincorporated community in SE New York, in Dutchess County. 5,374 (1950).

Arlington. Unincorporated community in SW North Carolina, in Gaston County. 5,085 (1950).

Arlington. City in C Texas, in Tarrant County, W of Dallas: marketing and shipping center for roses; processing of medicinal crystals. It is the seat of the North Texas Agricultural College. 7,692 (1950).

Arlington. Village in N Virginia, in Arlington County, opposite Washington, D.C. It contains a national cemetery in which many famous Americans are buried, and which is the site of the Tomb of the Unknown Soldier.

Arlington Heights. Village in NE Illinois, in Cook County: horse races. 8,768 (1950).

Arlington House. Mansion on the heights opposite Washington, D.C., in the midst of the Arlington National Cemetery (which is often popularly called Arlington Cemetery). It was once the property of George Washington, and descended through George Washington Parke Custis to Robert E. Lee. It was occupied as a headquarters in the Civil War by the Union army, the estate being a camp of the troops. It is now the property of the U.S. government.

Arlington National Cemetery. Cemetery at Arlington, Va., ab. 3 mi. from Washington, D.C. It is the site of the Tomb of the Unknown Soldier. In it are also buried the bodies of American soldiers from every war since the Civil War, as well as many American citizens whose contributions to the national welfare were of a less explicitly military nature.

Arliss (är′lis), **George.** b. at London, 1868; d. there, 1946. English actor. He made his stage debut (1887) as an extra at the Elephant and Castle, London, after a short career in his father's printing and publishing office; in 1901 he arrived in the U.S. with Mrs. Patrick Campbell for an appearance in Sir Arthur Wing Pinero's *The Second Mrs. Tanqueray.* Thereafter he appeared in a series of plays including *Disraeli* (1911), which was written particularly for him, and in which he toured the U.S. from 1912 to 1915. He began his film career in 1920, and after 1929 completely forsook the legitimate stage. His films include many of his earlier stage successes as well as such biographical productions as *Voltaire, Cardinal Richelieu,* and others. His autobiography, *Up the Years from Bloomsbury,* was published in 1927.

Arlon (år.lôṅ). [Flemish, **Aarlen**; German, **Arel**; Latin, **Orolaunum.**] Town in SE Belgium, the capital of the province of Luxembourg, situated near the border of the Grand Duchy of Luxembourg, SE of Namur. There are iron mines in the vicinity; the town has iron foundries, woolen and pottery manufactures, and grain and livestock markets. There is a German-speaking minority. Arlon was fortified in 1671, and occupied by the French in 1684–97. The French under Jean Baptiste Jourdan defeated the Austrian imperial forces here in 1794. In World War II it was reached by the German offensive in the Battle of the Bulge (December, 1944, to January, 1945). 11,180 (1947).

Armada (är.mä′dạ, -mā′-), **Spanish.** [Also, **Invincible Armada.**] A great fleet sent by Philip II of Spain against England in 1588. It consisted of 129 (or more) vessels, with an estimated 19,295 soldiers and 8,460 sailors, and was commanded by the Duke of Medina Sidonia. It was met and defeated by an English fleet of about 80 vessels, under Charles Howard, in the English Channel and Strait of Dover, in August, 1588. The best-known English captains serving under Howard were Sir Francis Drake, Sir Martin Frobisher, and Sir John Hawkins.

Armadale (är′mạ.dāl). Police burgh in S Scotland, in West Lothian, ab. 7 mi. SW of Linlithgow, ab. 414 mi. N of London by rail. The town has a paraffin factory. 5,831 (est. 1948).

Armadale. Novel by Wilkie Collins, published in 1866.

Armado (är.mä′dō), **Don Adriano de.** In Shakespeare's *Love's Labour's Lost,* a bragging Spanish soldier. His prototype is found in old Italian comedy.

Armageddon (är.mạ.ged′ọn). [Also, **Har-Magedon.**] Name used in Rev. xvi. 16, and signifying "the mountain of Megiddo." The reference in the passage in Revelation is probably to Megiddo, but some refer it to the plain of Esdraelon in Galilee and Samaria, famous as a battlefield.

Armagh (är.mä′). [Called the **"Orchard of Ireland."**] Inland county of Ulster province, in Northern Ireland. It is bounded on the N by Lough Neagh, on the E by County Down, on the S by County Louth (Irish Republic), on the SW by County Monaghan (Irish Republic), and on the NW by County Tyrone. The surface is low and undulating in the north and south, becoming hilly in the southeast, where Slieve Gullion rises to 1,893 ft. Beef cattle are raised on the lowlands, and sheep on the uplands. The county is noted for its pleasant farming country and orchards. There are linen and cotton mills. County seat, Armagh; area, ab. 489 sq. mi.; pop. 112,457 (1947).

Armagh. Urban district of Ulster province, Northern Ireland, county seat of County Armagh, situated near the river Callan, ab. 33 mi. SW of Belfast: customs station. It is the seat of an Anglican archbishop (primate of Ireland) and a Roman Catholic archbishop. Armagh was the ancient metropolis of Ireland and a center of learning. Saint Patrick founded his church here in 432 A.D. The cathedral (Protestant) of Armagh, the metropolitan church of the primate of Ireland, is a late Gothic structure which was well restored some years ago. The town was sacked by Shane O'Neill in 1564. Pop. 8,540 (est. 1947).

Armagh. Township in C Pennsylvania, in Mifflin County. It was settled in 1792. Pop. 2,953 (1950).

Armagnac (år.må.nyåk). In medieval history, a district in S France corresponding in general to the modern department of Gers. It was made a countship in the 10th century, and was united to the crown in the 16th century.

Armagnac (dår.må.nyåk), **Bernard VII,** Comte **d'.** d. 1418. French politician and soldier, leader of the Orléanist faction (known, from him, as Armagnacs) in the war against the Burgundians. Military victories made the Armagnacs virtual rulers of France, and Bernard held office (1415–18) as constable of France. When oppressive measures aroused the ire of the Parisian populace, he was murdered in the massacres which followed the capture of that city by the Burgundians under John the Fearless.

Armagnac, Jean V, Comte **d'.** b. c1420; d. 1473. French political agitator; grandson of Bernard VII d'Armagnac. He formed an incestuous union with his sister, Jeanne Isabelle, which brought upon him the censure of the church and deprivation of his possessions by Charles VII. He was reinstated after the death of Charles, joined the League of the Public Weal against Louis XI in 1465, and was put to death by the royalists at the capture of the castle of Lectoure.

Armagnacs (Anglicized, är′mạn.yaks). The party of the house of Orléans, opponents of the house of Burgundy during the reign of Charles VI: so named from Bernard VII d'Armagnac, their leader.

Armagnacs. Bands of lawless mercenaries, consisting chiefly of natives of Armagnac, in France, trained in the civil wars between the Armagnac and Burgundian parties. To rid France of them they were sent by Charles VII to aid the emperor Frederick III in enforcing his claims against the Swiss (by whom they were roundly, and for Charles VII conveniently, defeated on Aug. 26, 1444).

Armagnac War. [German, **Armegeckenkrieg** (är.mẹ-gek'ẹn.krēk).] Contest between the Armagnac mercenaries of the emperor Frederick III and the Swiss in 1444, which ended in the total defeat of the Armagnacs on Aug. 26, 1444.

Armançon (ȧr.mäṅ.sôṅ). River in E France, which joins the Yonne River E of Joigny. Length, ab. 100 mi.

Armand (ȧr.mäṅ), **Charles.** See **Rouarie** or **Rouërie, Marquis de la.**

Armande (ȧr.mäṅd). One of the learned ladies in Molière's comedy *Les Femmes Savantes*. She loves Clitandre, but he loves her sister Henriette, who is not a *femme savante*.

Armansperg (är'mäns.perk), Count **Joseph Ludwig von.** b. at Kötzting, in Lower Bavaria, Feb. 28, 1787; d. at Munich, April 3, 1853. Bavarian minister of foreign affairs (1826), and later of the interior. Dismissed for anticlerical views, he went to Greece with King Otto (1830), where he was president (1833–35) of the Greek regency, and Greek chancellor of state (1835–37).

Armatoles (är'mạ.tōlz) or **Armatoli** (är.mạ.tō'lī). Body of irregular Greek local militia, in the employ of the sultans of Turkey (although themselves Christians) from the 15th century to the Greek revolution in 1821. The Armatoles had existed in the Byzantine empire, and had served, in a measure, to protect the Greek population from the Franks, Albanians, and Serbians. The institution was accepted by the sultans and incorporated in their administration. After the peace of Belgrade (1739) the power of the Armatoles was undermined by the Turkish government, and it steadily declined. Large numbers of them joined the Greeks in the war of independence.

Armavir (är.mä.vēr'). City in the S part of the U.S.S.R., in the Russian Soviet Federated Socialist Republic, on the Kuban River. It is a rail junction (the line from Rostov to Baku passes through it) and an agricultural trading center of some importance. It was founded in 1848. In World War II, during the latter part of 1942, it was held by the Germans for approximately four months. 83,677 (1939).

Armbruster (ärm'brös"tėr), **Charles Hubert.** b. at London, 1874—. English colonial official in Africa, a student of Amharic. He accompanied Sir Francis Reginald Wingate on a mission to Somaliland (1909). Author of *Amharic Grammar* (1908), *Amharic-English Vocabulary* (1920), and others.

Ärmelkanal (er'mẹl.kä.näl"). A German name of the **English Channel.**

Armellina (är.mẹ.lī'nạ). Shrewd maidservant of Antonio, in Thomas Tomkis's comedy *Albumazar*. She is loved and finally won by Trincalo.

Armendaris (är.men.dä'rēs), **Lope Díaz de.** See **Díaz de Armendaris, Lope.**

Armendariz (är.men.dä.rēth'), **José de.** [Title, Marqués **de Castelfuerte.**] b. at Rivagorza, in Navarre, c1670; d. c1740. Spanish general. He served in the War of the Spanish Succession (1701–14), commanding troops in Spain and Sicily. Later was governor (1724–36) of Peru.

Armendariz de Toledo (dā tō.lā'ᴛʜō), **Alonso Henriquez de.** b. in Navarre, 1543; d. in Mexico, Nov. 5, 1628. Spanish Franciscan friar. He was successively vicar-general of Peru, bishop of Sidonia in 1603, bishop of Cuba from 1610 to 1623, and bishop of Michoacán in Mexico from 1624 until his death.

Armenia (ar.mē'ni.ạ, -mēn'yạ). Country and region in W Asia. It has not been in modern times an autonomous political unit, but remains an ethnic and political entity, the inhabitants of which have a strong sense of their own distinct nationality. It is now usually considered to include the territory SE of the Black Sea and SW of the Caspian Sea, comprising geographical territory under the control of the U.S.S.R., Turkey, and Iran. Within it may be found the headwaters of the Euphrates and Araks rivers, and also Mount Ararat, of Biblical fame.

Armenia (är.mä'nyä). City in W Colombia, in Caldas department: center of a coffee district; railway terminus. 29,673 (1938).

Armenian (är.mē'ni.ạn, -mēn'yạn). The Indo-European language of Armenia.

Armenians (är.mē'ni.ạnz, -mēn'yạnz). Inhabitants of the Armenian Soviet Socialist Republic of the U.S.S.R., found also in Turkey and elsewhere in the Near East, numbering about 2,500,000. The Armenian language is one of the primary branches of Indo-European. Several sharply differing dialects exist. The first historical record of the Armenians (Khayi) comes in the chronicles of Darius, in the 5th century B.C. By the 1st century B.C., the Armenian kingdom under Tigran II dominated the Transcaucasus; it was soon eclipsed by Roman conquest. The oldest documents in Armenian date to the 5th century A.D., when the Armenians had already been converted to Christianity. Since that time, Armenia has been largely a pawn of the surrounding powers (Iran, Turkey, and later Russia). Although the Armenians are noted traders and craftsmen, the bulk of the population is agricultural, and formerly lived in extended, patriarchal families under one roof.

Armenian Soviet Socialist Republic. Southernmost republic of the European division of the U.S.S.R. It borders on Turkey and Iran between the Black Sea and the Caspian Sea, S of the Caucasus Mountains. Capital, Erivan; area, 11,500 sq. mi.; pop. 1,281,599 (1939), 1,400,000 (est. 1951).

Armentières (ȧr.mäṅ.tyer). Town in N France, in the department of Nord, situated on the Lys River, near the Belgian frontier, ab. 9 mi. NW of Lille. It has textile manufactures, particularly of table linen and cotton cloth, and machine industries. The town was largely destroyed during the German World War I offensive of April, 1918, but was rebuilt after the end of the war. The population was 28,625 in 1914, dropped to 14,758 in 1925, and later rose to 22,667 (1946).

Armfelt (ärm'felt), Count **Gustaf Mauritz.** b. at Åbo, Finland, April 1, 1757; d. at Tsarskoe Selo, Russia, Aug. 19, 1814. Swedish general and diplomat. He was a trusted adviser of Gustavus III in the war with Russia (1788-90), and leader of the Dalecarlian levies in the defense of Gothenburg (1788) against the Danes. A member of the council of regency on the death (1792) of the king, he was forced by an anti-Gustavian intrigue to flee to Russia. He was restored on the majority of Gustavus IV, and served as ambassador (1802–04) to Vienna, and commander in chief (1805–07) in Pomerania. Driven from Sweden again for support of Gustavus, he entered (1811) the service of Alexander I of Russia; as governor general of Finland, he was the organizer of the Russian defense there.

Armfelt, Baron **Karl Gustaf.** b. in Ingermanland, Sweden, Nov. 9, 1666; d. in Finland, Oct. 24, 1736. Swedish general. He entered the French service in 1685, and returned to Sweden in 1700. Entrusted by Charles XII with the defense of Finland in 1713, he was overpowered by Dmitri Mikhailovich Gallitzin at Storkyro in 1714; later he was sent on an unsuccessful expedition to the north of Norway in 1718. He was commander in chief in Finland at his death.

Armida (är.mē'dä). [French, **Armide** (ȧr.mēd).] Enchantress in Torquato Tasso's *Gerusalemme Liberata* (*Jerusalem Delivered*). She used her charms to seduce the Crusaders from their vows and duty. Her palace, surrounded by magnificent pleasure grounds, was so luxurious and splendid that "the gardens of Armida" have become a synonym for gorgeous luxury. She also possessed a magic girdle which surpassed even the cestus of Venus in its power. Her voluptuous witchery was finally destroyed by a talisman brought from the Christian army, and Rinaldo, who had been enslaved by her, escaped. She followed him, and he finally defeated her in battle, persuaded her to become a Christian, and became her knight.

Armida. [French, **Armide.**] Title of operas by (among others) Lully (produced in 1686), Jommelli (Naples, 1771), Cherubini (1782), and Rossini (Naples, 1817).

Armide (ȧr.mēd). Opera in five acts, by Christoph Willibald Gluck, with a libretto by Philippe Quinault, first performed at the Académie Royale at Paris in 1777. The plot is based on an episode in Torquato Tasso's *Gerusalemme Liberata* (*Jerusalem Delivered*).

Armijo (är.mē'hō). Unincorporated community in W central New Mexico, in Bernalillo County, near Albuquerque. 4,516 (1950).

Armin (är′min), **Robert.** [Nicknamed **Robin.**] fl. c1610. English actor and playwright, probable successor to Richard Tarlton as actor, in the Lord Chamberlain's company of players, of Shakespearean clowns and fools; he also played in Ben Jonson's *The Alchemist* (1610). Author of *Nest of Ninnies* (1608) and others.

Arminians (är.min′i.ạnz). The followers of Arminius (1560–1609), also known as Remonstrants.

Arminius (är.min′i.us). [Latinized name of **Armin** (är′min); German, **Hermann.**] b. c17 B.C.; assassinated 21 A.D. German chieftain of the Cherusci (near modern Hanover), a liberator of the Germans from Roman rule. He entered the Roman military service in 1 A.D., and became a Roman citizen of the equestrian order, but on his return to Germany he organized a revolt of the Cherusci and destroyed (9 A.D.) three legions of the Roman governor Quintilius Varus in the Teutoburger Wald forcing withdrawal of the Roman frontier from the Elbe to the Rhine. Defeated (16) by Germanicus Caesar, he still maintained the independence of the right bank of the Rhine. He overthrew Marbo, head of the Marcomanni, but was killed in a feud among rival chiefs. He became a hero of 19th-century German nationalism, a monument having been erected to him at Detmold.

Arminius (är.mē′nē.ụs), **Jacobus.** [Original name, **Jacob Harmensen, Hermanns,** or **Hermansz.**] b. at Oudewater, in South Holland, Oct. 10, 1560; d. at Leiden, Oct. 19, 1609. Dutch theologian and founder of the anti-Calvinist Dutch reformed movement in Protestant theology known as Arminianism. His doctrines became the basis of the Arminian, or Remonstrant, sect in Holland, and are evident today in Methodist and certain other Protestant theologies. He studied at Geneva (1582 *et seq.*), served as a minister (1588–1603) at Amsterdam, and was a professor of theology (1603–09) at Leiden. His early acceptance of the Calvinist doctrine of predestination was modified as a result of studies undertaken when he was selected to defend the belief against its opponents; the reversal in his point of view brought on bitter controversy (1604 *et seq.*) with Franciscus Gomarus, a leading Calvinist also on the faculty at Leiden. The Arminian doctrine of ultimate redemption and predestination mitigated by divine prescience was carried even further by his followers in the five articles called *The Remonstrance* (1610), which precipitated internecine strife between the Calvinist House of Orange and the allegedly republican Arminian Remonstrants.

Armistead (är′mi.sted, -stẹd), **George.** b. at New Market, Va., April 10, 1780; d. at Baltimore, April 25, 1818. American army officer. He was prominent in the capture (1813) of Fort George from the British, and commander (1814) of Fort McHenry, his successful defense of which prevented a British assault on Baltimore and was the occasion of Francis Scott Key's writing the *Star Spangled Banner*.

Armistead, Lewis Addison. b. at Newbern, N.C., Feb. 18, 1817; killed in battle at Gettysburg, Pa., July 3, 1863. American soldier, a Confederate general in the Civil War; nephew of George Armistead. He served (1846–47) in the Mexican War, became (1862) a brigadier general in the Confederate army, and was killed in the charge of Pickett's division at Gettysburg.

Armistice Day. Holiday (November 11) celebrated in most states of the U.S. and in several other countries. It commemorates the anniversary of the signing (1918) of the World War I armistice.

Armistice of World War I. See **Compiègne Armistice (1918).**

Armisticio (är.mēs.tē′syō). Former territory of Venezuela, now forming the W part of the state of Bolívar.

Armitage (är′mi.tạj), **Edward.** b. at London, 1817; d. at Tunbridge Wells, England, 1896. English historical painter. His scenes from British and Biblical history, in fresco and on canvas, adorn many English public buildings.

Armitage, Merle. b. at Mason City, Iowa, Feb. 12, 1893—. American impresario. After a brief career as a civil engineer and stage designer (until 1911) he became a booking agent for Alice Nielsen, John McCormack, Alma Gluck, Ernestine Schumann-Heink, Amelita Galli-Curci, Mary Garden, and others; he was also director of publicity for the Diaghilev ballet (1915 *et seq.*) and later for Pavlova. A founder and general manager (1924–30) of the Los Angeles Grand Opera Association, he served also as manager of the Philharmonic Auditorium (1933 *et seq.*). He is the author of *Biography of Rockwell Kent* (1932), *Igor Stravinsky* (1936), *George Gershwin* (1938), *So-called Abstract Art* (1939), and others.

Armitage-Smith (är′mi.tạj.smith′), Sir **Sydney Armitage.** b. Sept. 3, 1876; d. at London, Oct. 31, 1932. English financial expert. He was a member (1911–12) of the West African currency committee, a representative (1919) at the Paris Peace Conference, a financial adviser (1920–21) to the Persian government, and secretary general (1924–30) of the Reparations Commission. He investigated (1931) the revenue of the Leeward and Windward Islands.

Armorica (är.môr′i.kạ). [Also, **Aremorica.**] In ancient geography, the NW part of France, comprising, in general, the region which lies between the mouths of the Seine and Loire rivers. It was restricted in the Middle Ages to Brittany.

Armorican (är.môr′i.kạn). See **Breton.**

Armour (är′mọr), **Herman Ossian.** b. 1837; d. 1901. American grain merchant and meat packer; brother of Philip Danforth Armour. He established the Chicago grain-commission house known as H. O. Armour and Company in which Philip Danforth Armour became interested and which was to become (after 1870) the meat-packing firm of Armour and Company.

Armour, John Douglas. b. 1830; d. 1903. Canadian jurist. He served (1887–90) as chief justice of the Queen's Bench, Ontario, and was a Canadian supreme court justice (1902–03).

Armour, Jonathan Ogden. b. at Milwaukee, Wis., Nov. 11, 1863; d. at London, Aug. 16, 1927. American meat packer; son of Philip Danforth Armour. He joined (1883) Armour and Company and became a partner in 1884. After the death of his father in 1901, he headed the firm.

Armour, Norman. b. at Brighton, England, Oct. 14, 1887—. American career diplomat, minister to Hait, (1932–35) and to Canada (1935–38), ambassador to Chile (1938), Argentina (1939–44), and Spain (1944–45), assistant secretary of state (1947–48). His major diplomatic feat was the negotiation of an agreement under which U.S. marines withdrew from Haiti. He served (1950–51) as U.S. ambassador to Venezuela.

Armour, Philip Danforth. b. at Stockbridge, N.Y., May 16, 1832; d. at Chicago, Jan. 6, 1901. American industrial promoter who headed (1875–99) Armour and Company, meat packers. Starting (1863) in the commission business (grain and meat) at Cincinnati, he made some two million dollars speculating in pork futures at the close of the Civil War; invested in the Chicago grain business of his brother, Herman Ossian Armour, adding (1868) a pork-packing plant and becoming (1875) head of the company. An innovator in the use of slaughtering by-products, he took advantage of the introduction of refrigeration to expand, shipping in his own refrigerated cars. He established distributing plants and an export business, and inaugurated the large-scale canning of meat. He founded (1893) the Armour Institute of Technology.

Armour Wherein He Trusted. Unfinished novel by Mary Webb, published in 1929. The time of the story is the First Crusade (1096).

Arms (ärmz), **John Taylor.** b. at Washington, D.C., 1887—. American etcher. He was elected (1933) to the National Academy. Examples of his work are owned by galleries throughout the U.S., and also in France and Great Britain.

Arms and the Man. Play by George Bernard Shaw, included in his *Plays: Pleasant and Unpleasant* (1898). It is a satirical treatment of the traditonal regard for martial prowess. The scene is set in Bulgaria, and the leading character is the Swiss Bluntschli, an unwilling soldier. Oskar Straus's operetta *The Chocolate Soldier* uses this same plot and character.

Armsby (ärmz′bi), **Henry Prentiss.** b. at Northbridge, Mass., Sept. 21, 1853; d. Oct. 19, 1921. American agricultural chemist. He organized and directed (1887–1907) the Pennsylvania Agricultural Station, and was director (1907–21) of the Pennsylvania Institute of Animal Nutrition. Aided by grants from the U.S. Bureau of Animal

Industry, he headed the Pennsylvania staff which devised a respiration calorimeter with which he demonstrated the conservation of energy in cattle; his research showed that an economic loss is entailed in feeding to livestock agricultural products which are capable of direct use by humans. Author of *The Conservation of Food Energy* (1918), and others.

Armstead (ärm′sted, -sted), **Henry Hugh.** b. at London, 1828; d. there, 1905. English sculptor and silversmith, known for work in silver, gold, and bronze, particularly his *St. George's Vase* and *Outram Shield*. Taking up sculpture in 1863, he was employed by Sir Gilbert Scott, architect of the Albert Memorial, for which he did reliefs and figures; his other works include decorations at Whitehall and a fountain at King's College, Cambridge.

Armstrong (ärm′strông), **Andrew Campbell.** b. at New York, Aug. 22, 1860; d. Feb. 22, 1935. American psychologist and educator, professor of philosophy at Wesleyan University (1888–1930). He was the author of *Transitional Eras in Thought* (1904) and a translation, *History of Modern Philosophy* (1893).

Armstrong, Archibald. [Called **Archie** or **Archy.**] b. in Cumberland, England, or in S Scotland; d. 1672. Jester to James I and Charles I (of England), discharged, after attaining considerable power, for ridiculing William Laud. He is the original of a charcater in Sir Walter Scott's novel *The Fortunes of Nigel*.

Armstrong, David Maitland. b. at Newburgh, N.Y., 1836; d. 1918. American muralist and maker of stained glass. He studied at Paris and at Rome, and was U.S. consul general (1869–72) to the Papal States, Italy. He was made a Chevalier of the Legion of Honor for his directorship of the American department at the Paris Exposition (1878); he also executed frescoes for Machinery Hall at the Chicago World's Fair (1893). His works in glass include windows in All Souls' Chapel, Biltmore, N.C., and Columbia University Chapel, at New York.

Armstrong, Edwin Howard. b. at New York, Dec. 18, 1890—. American electrical engineer and inventor of radio improvements. A graduate of Columbia University in 1913, he remained there as associate in research with Michael I. Pupin and as professor (1934 *et seq.*). His inventions include a regenerative circuit (1912), a superheterodyne receiving set (1918), a superregenerative circuit (1920), and the development of wide-band frequency modulation (1939).

Armstrong, George Buchanan. b. at Armagh, Ireland, Oct. 27, 1822; d. at Chicago, May 5, 1871. American post-office employee, a pioneer of postal sorting facilities in mail cars; distant relative of President Buchanan. Appointed (1852) to the Post Office Department, Washington, D.C., and transferred two years later to Chicago, he resigned (1856) to enter private business, but reëntered the postal service when his business failed (1858). He held the title of colonel of Illinois volunteers during the Civil War, but seems to have spent the period with the Post Office. In 1864 he proposed reforms of the postal system which would eliminate distributing stations in favor of sorting facilities on mail cars; experiments on the Chicago and Northwestern Railroad during the same year brought further trials and the adoption of the innovation by Congress in 1865. Later controversy over the possibility that others (including William A. Davis) may have conceived and even tried the scheme at an earlier date arose (1881) with the dedication of a statue of Armstrong near Chicago's Federal Building.

Armstrong, George Ellis. b. in Lawrence County, Ind., Aug. 4, 1900—. American army officer and surgeon, surgeon general of the U.S. army (1951 *et seq.*).

Armstrong, Hamilton Fish. b. at New York, April 7, 1893—. American writer and editor; son of David Maitland Armstrong. He served as managing editor (1922–28) and editor (1928 *et seq.*) of *Foreign Affairs*. He was also a special adviser (1945) to the U.S. secretary of state, and an adviser (1945) to the U.S. delegation at the San Francisco Conference. Author of *The New Balkans* (1926), *Where the East Begins* (1929), *Hitler's Reich—the First Phase* (1933), *Europe Between Wars?* (1934), *When There Is No Peace* (1939), *Chronology of Failure* (1940), *Tito and Goliath* (1951), and other works.

Armstrong, Helen Maitland. b. at Florence, Italy, Oct. 14, 1869; d. at New York, Nov. 26, 1948. American artist; daughter of David Maitland Armstrong. She studied at the Art Students League and with W. M. Chase. Her work, consisting chiefly of stained-glass windows, is owned by a number of churches in the U.S.

Armstrong, Henry W. b. at Somerville, Mass., July 22, 1879; d. at New York, Feb. 28, 1951. American popular composer. Among the songs to which he wrote the music were *Eyes of Blue, I Love My Wife But Oh You Kid,* and *Sweet Adeline.*

Armstrong, John. [Called **Johnie** (or **Johnnie**) **Armstrong of Gilnockie.**] Killed c1528. Scottish freebooter, subject of many Scottish and English ballads. Chief of a band of over 150 men, he is supposed to have levied tribute from the English almost as far south as Newcastle, though tradition has it that he never harmed a Scot. When James V (of Scotland) undertook (c1528) to suppress the turbulent border marauders, Armstrong, one of the most notorious, appeared before him with 36 of his band and offered his services; the king had them all hanged on trees near Hawick (or, according to other accounts, killed them in a bloody battle, or had them ambushed). This, and the rest of the legend, became the material for *Armstrong's Good-Night*, *Johnie Armstrong*, and other popular ballads.

Armstrong, John. b. in Roxburghshire, Scotland, 1709; d. at London, 1779. British physician, poet, and essayist. He was the author of the blank verse *Art of Preserving Health* (1744). At one time a close friend of John Wilkes (who is believed by some to have obtained for him a post as physician to the army in Germany), he severed the relationship as the result of disputes arising from the publication (c1761) by Wilkes of his verse *Day*.

Armstrong, John. [Called the **"Hero of Kittanning."**] b. in Brookborough Parish, Ireland, Oct. 13, 1717; d. at Carlisle, Pa., March 9, 1795. American soldier in the French and Indian Wars, a general in the Revolutionary War. A surveyor, he laid out the town of Carlisle; commissioned to defend the colony from Indians after Edward Braddock's defeat (1755), he led a successful night attack (1756) on the Delawares at Kittanning.

Armstrong, John. b. at Carlisle, Pa., Nov. 25, 1758; d. April 1, 1843. American general, politician, and diplomat; son of John Armstrong (1717–95). He served under John Francis Mercer and Horatio Gates in the Revolutionary War; later he admitted to the authorship of the "Newburgh Letters" (1783) which threatened army action if Congress failed to make good arrears in pay. He obtained a U.S. senatorship (1800–02, 1803–04) from New York through an alliance between the Clintons and the Livingstons (his wife's family) which made George Clinton governor of the state and De Witt Clinton mayor of the city of New York. As minister to France (1804–10) he has been held partly responsible, through the failure to investigate Napoleon's policy, for the outbreak of the War of 1812 with Great Britain. He served as secretary of war (1813–14) under Madison, but was hampered by insufficient Congressional appropriations, the enmity of Monroe, and his own unwise decisions. He has been considered responsible for the failure of the Montreal and Plattsburg campaigns and, in part, for the British capture (1814) of Washington.

Armstrong, Margaret Neilson. b. at New York, Sept. 24, 1867; d. there, July 18, 1944. American writer; daughter of David Maitland Armstrong (1836–1918). Author of *Fanny Kemble: a Passionate Victorian* (1938), *Murder in Stained Glass* (1939), *Trelawny: a Man's Life* (1940), *The Man with No Face* (1941), and others.

Armstrong, Martin Donisthorpe. b. at Newcastle, England, 1882—. English poet and short-story writer. Educated at Cambridge as a mechanical engineer, he forsook science for a literary career two years after his graduation. Author of *Exodus, and Other Poems* (1912), *The Puppet Show* (1922), *Sir Pompey and Madame Juno* (1927), *Lover's Leap* (1932), *General Buntop's Miracle* (1934), *The Butterfly* (1941), *Chichester Concert* (1944), *Said the Cat to the Dog* (1945), and others.

Armstrong, Paul. [Pseudonym (on New York newspapers) **"Right Cross."**] b. at Kidder, Mo., April 25, 1869; d. at New York, Aug. 30, 1915. American playwright. He was a reporter for newspapers at Buffalo (until 1896) and Chicago (1896–98), and a specialist on prize fights for New York newspapers (1898–1904). His play *Heir to the Hoorah* (1905) opened an eight-year period of tremendous success with such works as *Salomy Jane* (1907), based on a story by Bret Harte; *Going Some* (1908), written in collaboration with Rex Beach; *Via Wireless* (1908), with Winchell Smith; and *The Greyhound* (1912), with Wilson Mizner. He is probably best known for *Alias Jimmy Valentine* (1909), which was written in one week and set a pattern in crime melodrama that lasted for years.

Armstrong, Robert. b. at Abingdon, Va., Sept. 28, 1792; d. at Washington, Feb. 23, 1854. American soldier, diplomat, and newspaper owner. He served on the staff of Andrew Jackson at the battle of New Orleans and was later appointed brigadier of volunteers in the second Seminole war (1836) by Jackson, who was then in the White House. Appointed consul at Liverpool by President Polk (1845), he returned (1849) to the U.S. to become the owner (1851 *et seq.*) of the Washington *Union*, and a staunch supporter of Democratic policies.

Armstrong, Samuel Chapman. b. in the Hawaiian Islands, Jan. 30, 1839; d. at Hampton, Va., May 11, 1893. American educator, founder (1868) and principal of Hampton Normal and Industrial Institute, in Virginia, for Negroes. Colonel of colored troops in the Civil War and, as an agent of the Freedmen's Bureau, head of a Negro camp (1866), he secured the support of the American Missionary Association in 1867, and patterned the school on the Hilo Manual Labor School in Hawaii. The name of the school was subsequently officially shortened to Hampton Institute, and Indians were also admitted.

Armstrong, Thomas Henry Wait. b. at Peterborough, England, June 15, 1898—. English organist, music teacher, and composer. After serving as organist (1928–33) at Exeter Cathedral, he was appointed (1933) to an equivalent post at Christ Church Cathedral, Oxford. Composer of choral works, as well as compositions for piano, violin, and chorus and orchestra.

Armstrong, Sir **Walter.** b. in Roxburghshire, Scotland, 1850; d. at London, 1918. British art critic; director (1892–1914) of the National Gallery at Dublin.

Armstrong, William. [Called **"Kinmont Willie."**] fl. c1587. Scottish marauder on the border between Scotland and England. Captured in 1587, he escaped and continued his depredations until again imprisoned (1596) by the English; his subsequent rescue by the Scotch led almost to a break in relations between England and Scotland. He should not be confused with the more famous Scottish freebooter and border raider, John Armstrong.

Armstrong, William George. [Title, Baron **Armstrong of Cragside.**] b. at Newcastle, England, Nov. 26, 1810; d. at Rothbury, England, Dec. 27, 1900. English inventor, in particular of the Armstrong gun, which was much used by the British army during the latter half of the 19th century. At first a lawyer, his study of hydraulics and hydroelectric power produced the invention of an improved rotary water-motor (1839), a hydraulic crane (patented 1846), and a hydroelectric machine (c1843) to produce frictional electricity. Crimean War ordnance orders to a factory set up (1847) at Elswick to manufacture hydraulic machinery led to the development (1855) of his field gun, on the principle of a steel cylinder kept in a state of tension by shrunk-on iron rings of smaller diameter, also including new designs for breech-loading, rifling, and elongated projectile. He formed (1859) the Elswick Ordnance Company and developed (1880) a 6-inch breech-loading gun substituting wire wound at high tension for metal rings. He also made important experiments (1855 *et seq.*) with smoke prevention. Having expanded (1868) his factory to include shipbuilding, he produced (1882) what some have considered the first modern armored cruiser. Author of *Electric Movement in Air and Water* (1897), and others.

Armstrong Legislative Committee. Joint committee of the New York Legislature, appointed July 20, 1905, to investigate the condition and the methods of the various life insurance companies of the state and to recommend suitable legislation in the interests of policy holders. Of its eight members, three, including the chairman, W. W. Armstrong, were appointed from the Senate and five from the Assembly. Charles Evans Hughes was chosen by the committee as its chief counsel. The sessions for receiving testimony opened on Sept. 6, 1905, and closed on Dec. 30, 1905. Many facts in regard to the mismanagement of the insurance companies of New York were brought to light, and important legislation resulted (1906) from the investigation.

Army, U. S. Department of the. Government department, one of three under the National Military Establishment created in 1947 (the other two are the Department of the Navy and the Department of the Air Force). It is headed by the secretary of the army, who does not have cabinet status and is responsible to the secretary of defense. Before unification of the armed forces was achieved, the War Department (as it was then called) had separate status as an executive department, and its head enjoyed cabinet rank. The commander in chief of the army is the president of the U.S.; the executive head of the army is the chief of staff. The Regular Army of the U.S. is a peacetime unit consisting of volunteers and of recruits raised through selective service. The chief function of the U.S. Army is to assure the ability to carry out prompt and sustained combat operations on land. The army general staff, with headquarters at Washington, D.C., has six divisions in charge of the entire administration of the army: personnel and administration; organization and training; service, supply, and procurement; plans and operations; research and development; and special. Six general administrative units (called army areas) are in charge of this number of field armies assigned to regional areas of the continental U.S. The combat units of the U.S. Army include the infantry, field artillery, coast artillery, mechanized cavalry, armored divisions, tank destroyer command, and the amphibian training command. Technical services include the Chemical Corps, Transportation Corps, Ordnance Department, Medical Department, Quartermaster Corps, Corps of Engineers, and Signal Corps. Administrative services include the Special Services Division, Provost Marshal General's Office, Corps of Chaplains, Finance Department, and Adjutant General's Department. The Women's Army Corps, originally an auxiliary service, became an integral part of the army in 1943. Under legislation approved in 1948, women enjoy equal military status with men. The smallest unit in the army is the squad (consisting of not more than nine men); the largest is the field army (consisting in full combat strength of 500,000 to 800,000 men). Intermediate units include the company (80 to 200 men), the regiment (800 to 3,700 men), the division (15,500 to 18,500 men), and the corps (65,000 to 90,000 men). Individual grades among enlisted men range from private to master sergeant; corporals and sergeants are known as noncommissioned officers. Warrant officers (of two grades) rank above enlisted men but below commissioned officers; the latter range in rank from second lieutenant to general (of which there are several ranks, the highest being general of the army). Among the peacetime reserves of the army are the National Guard, the Organized Reserves, the Enlisted Reserve Corps, and the Reserve Officers' Training Corps. Technically, the U.S. Army had its inception in 1789, with the birth of the national government, and in its present form dates from the National Defense Act of 1916, but American armies fought on a large scale in the French and Indian Wars and in the Revolutionary War. The U.S. Army has participated in the War of 1812, the Mexican War, the Civil War, the Spanish-American War, World Wars I and II, and the Korean War, in addition to taking part in such actions as campaigns against the Indians, the China expedition, and the Mexican border campaign.

Army War College. Military educational institution founded in 1901 by U.S. Secretary of War Elihu Root for the purpose of training specifically chosen officers for general staff and other high post commands. It is the top-ranking body of its kind in the U.S. Army.

Arn (ärn). See **Arno,** German ecclesiastic.

Arnaboldi (är.nä.bôl′dē), **Alessandro.** b. at Milan, Nov. 19, 1827; d. 1898. Italian lyric poet. He resigned (1873) from municipal office at Milan to devote himself to literature. Author of *Versi* (1872), *Nuovi versi* (1888), and others.

Arnaldo da Brescia (är.näl′dō dä brā′shä). Italian name of **Arnold of Brescia.**

Arnall (är′nạl, -nôl), **Ellis Gibbs.** b. at Newnan, Ga., March 20, 1907—. American lawyer and politician. After serving as attorney general (1939–43), he was elected (1943) governor of Georgia, defeating Eugene Talmadge. In 1947, when his term ended, Talmadge had been voted his successor. Upon Talmadge's death (in December, 1946) only a few weeks before he was to assume office, the question arose of who was to become governor instead, the state having no provision for such an eventuality. Arnall, backed by the attorney general of the state, protested the popular nomination of Talmadge's son Herman, and refused to relinquish his post. He was ousted, however, by the adherents of Herman Talmadge. In 1948 he became president of the Society of Independent Motion Picture Producers. In 1952 he served briefly as director of the Office of Price Stabilization. Author of *The Shore Dimly Seen* (1946) and *What the People Want* (1948).

Arnason (är′nä.sôn), **Jón.** [Called, **"the Grimm of Iceland."**] b. at Reykjavík, Iceland, Nov. 13, 1819; d. Aug. 17, 1888. Icelandic writer and librarian. He published, as coauthor, *Popular Legends of Iceland* (1862–64).

Arnaud (ȧr.nō), **Henri.** b. at Embrun, France, 1641; d. at Schönenberg, Germany, 1721. Waldensian clergyman and Swiss patriot. He was pastor (1685) at La Tour, in Piedmont, and leader of the Waldenses (or Vaudois) after their expulsion (1686) from that district by Victor Amadeus, duke of Savoy, under the terms of an alliance with Louis XIV of France. He conducted 3,000 exiles to Switzerland and there, with the aid of William of Orange, organized a band of 1,000 men who crossed the Alps, withstood the siege (1689–90) of 4,000 French and Savoyard troops at Balsille, and reached La Tour. During Victor Amadeus's temporary shift of allegiance from France to England and Holland, Arnaud led the Waldenses in Victor's service; forced into exile again (1698) by the peace between France and Savoy, he settled in Württemberg, where he became (1699) pastor of refugees. Author of *Histoire de la glorieuse rentrée des Vaudois dans leurs vallées* (1710).

Arnauld (ȧr.nō). [Also: **Arnault, Arnaut.**] French family prominent in the Jansenist movement, chiefly through the connection of most of them with the Cistercian Abbey at Port-Royal (near Versailles; later also at Paris). It included Antoine Arnauld (1560–1619) and his 20 children, notably Robert Arnault d'Andilly (c1588–1674), Jacqueline Marie (1591–1661), Jeanne Catherine Agnes (1593–1671), Henri (1597–1692), and Antoine (1612–94) Arnauld, and Robert's daughter, Angélique Arnauld d'Andilly (1624–84).

Arnauld, Antoine. b. at Paris, Feb. 6, 1560; d. there, Dec. 29, 1619. French supporter of Henry IV, celebrated for his speech (1594) against the Jesuits in defense of the University of Paris; father of a large family important in the Jansenist movement.

Arnauld, Antoine. [Called **"the Great Arnauld."**] b. at Paris, Feb. 16, 1612; d. at Brussels, 1694. French philosopher and Jansenist theologian; youngest son of Antoine Arnauld (1560–1619). His exposition of the Jansenist movement, *De la fréquente communion* (1643), directed against the Jesuits, resulted in his expulsion from the Sorbonne; this event was the occasion of *Provincial Letters* by his friend Blaise Pascal. He retired (1656) to Port-Royal, where he collaborated on *Logique de Port-Royal* (also called *Art de penser*). Author, with Pierre Nicole, of the anti-Calvinist *La Perpétuité de la foi* (1669–72) and, after his flight (1679) to the Netherlands under new persecution, of numerous works in opposition to the Jesuits and Calvinists. A follower of René Descartes, he engaged also in later years (1683–85) in a long controversy with Nicolas de Malebranche.

Arnauld, Henri. b. at Paris, 1597; d. at Angers, France, June 8, 1692. French Jansenist ecclesiastic; brother of Antoine Arnauld (1612–94). He became bishop of Angers in 1649 and was one of the four bishops who refused to sign the acceptance of the papal bull condemning the *Augustinus* of Jansen.

Arnauld, Jacqueline Marie. [Called (as abbess) **Mère Angélique**; religious name, **Marie Angélique de Sainte-Madeleine.**] b. Sept. 8, 1591; d. Aug. 6, 1661. French nun; second daughter of Antoine Arnauld (1560–1619). According to some accounts she became abbess of Port-Royal at the age of eight or eleven. In 1608 she began the reforms under the guidance of Saint Francis of Sales which made Port-Royal nuns widely noted for piety. In 1626 she removed her charges to Paris for more healthful surroundings; the old buildings were thereafter, in strict parlance, known as Port-Royal-des-Champs and the new as Port-Royal-de-Paris, the former becoming the seat of a group of ascetics led by men of the Arnauld family and of the Port-Royal schools. In ordinary usage, the term "Port-Royal" continued to apply to the original establishment near Versailles. Under the influence of Jean Du Vergier de Hauranne, abbé of Saint-Cyran, she followed Jansenism, establishing Port-Royal as a stronghold of this movement. Author of writings and letters collected in *Mémoires pour servir à l'histoire de Port-Royal* (1742–44) by her niece, Angélique Arnauld d'Andilly.

Arnauld, Jeanne Catherine Agnès. [Called (as abbess) **Mère Agnès.**] b. 1593; d. 1671. French Jansenist nun; daughter of Antoine Arnauld (1560–1619). Author of *L'Image d'une religieuse parfaite et d'une imparfaite* (1660) and of *Le Chapelet secret du Saint Sacrement* (1663). The latter, a small treatise on the sacrament of love, was condemned by the Sorbonne and was the subject of an apology by Jean Du Vergier de Hauranne, abbé of Saint-Cyran, which precipitated a scandal and began his Jansenist influence over her sister, Jacqueline Marie Arnauld.

Arnauld d'Andilly (ȧr.nō dän.dē.yē), **Angélique.** [Called (as abbess) **Mère Angélique**; religious name, **Angélique de Saint-Jean.**] b. at Paris, Nov. 28, 1624; d. Jan. 29, 1684. French Jansenist nun; daughter of Robert Arnauld d'Andilly. As abbess of Port-Royal (1678 *et seq.*), she bravely resisted persecutions which ended with the expulsion (1710) of the nuns. Author of *Mémoires pour servir à l'histoire de Port-Royal* (1742–44), containing writings of her aunt, Jacqueline Marie Arnauld.

Arnauld d'Andilly, Robert. b. at Paris, c1588; d. at Port-Royal, Sept. 27, 1674. French lawyer and theological writer; eldest son of Antoine Arnauld (1560–1619). An official of and favorite at the court of Anne of Austria, he became in 1646 a Jansenist ascetic at Port-Royal. He translated Augustine's *Confessions* and other works into French.

Arnault (ȧr.nō), **Antoine Vincent.** b. at Paris, Jan. 1, 1766; d. near Le Havre, France, Sept. 16, 1834. French dramatist and poet, who was exiled (1815–19) for his support of Napoleon. Author of *Marius à Minturnes* (1791), *Fables et poésies* (1812), *Souvenirs d'un sexagénaire* (1833), and others.

Arnautlik (är.nä.öt″lik′). Turkish name of **Albania.**

Arnauts (är′nôts) or **Arnaout** (är.nä.öt′). [Modern Turkish, **Arnavut** (är.nä.vöt′).] Turkish name for the Albanians.

Arndt (ärnt), **Ernst Moritz.** b. at Schoritz, on the island of Rügen (then under Sweden), in the Baltic Sea, Dec. 26, 1769; d. at Bonn, Germany, Jan. 29, 1860. German poet and historian; writer of nationalistic pamphlets and songs against Napoleon. He became privatdocent (1800) and professor (1806) of history at Greifswald, and in 1818 at Bonn. He was the author of *Versuch einer Geschichte der Leibeigenschaft in Pommern und Rügen* (1803), a history of serfdom in Pomerania and Rügen which led to the abolishment (1806) of the system by the Swedish king Gustavus IV. He also wrote *Der Geist der Zeit* (1806–18), containing a bitter attack on Napoleon which forced Arndt's flight to Sweden (1806), and criticism of reactionary tendencies in the Prussian government which led to his arrest (1819) and suspension of his professorship (1820–40). He is known also for his songs, such as *Was ist des Deutschen Vaterland?* and *Was blasen die Trompeten?*

Arndt or **Arnd** (ärnt), **Johann.** b. at Ballenstädt, in Anhalt, Germany, Dec. 27, 1555; d. at Celle, Germany, May 11, 1621. German Lutheran theologian, semimystic, and religious writer. He supported Melanchthon in the crypto-Calvinist dispute (1577 *et seq.*); also engaged in various iconological disputes as well as a controversy over the baptismal ritual. He is best known for *Vom Wahren Christentumb* (1609), since translated into English as *True Christianity.*

Arne (ärn), **Michael.** b. at London, 1741; d. there, Jan. 14, 1786. English harpsichordist and composer; son of Thomas Augustine Arne (1710–78). He wrote music for David Garrick's *Cymon* (1767), Hannah Cowley's *The Belle's Stratagem* (1780), and other plays, and popular songs such as *The Highland Laddie.*

Arne, Susannah Maria. Maiden name of **Cibber, Susannah Maria.**

Arne, Thomas Augustine. b. at London, March 12 1710; d. there, March 5, 1778. English composer of songs, especially for Shakespearean plays, and of oratorios and operas. In his first production, a setting of Addison's *Rosamund* (1733), the lead was played by his sister, Susannah Maria Cibber; in *Opera of Operas* (1733), based on Fielding's *Tragedy of Tragedies,* his brother played Tom Thumb. His most noteworthy works include music for John Milton's *Comus* (1738) and for James Thomson and David Mallet's masque *Alfred* (1740), the finale of which is now known as *Rule Britannia;* music for *Under the Greenwood Tree* and other songs in Shakespeare's *As You Like It* (1740), and for *Where the Bee Sucks,* among others, in *The Tempest* (1746); and the oratorios *Abel* (1744) and *Judith* (1764), a performance (1773) of the latter using female voices in an oratorio chorus for the first time. He also composed the operas *Artaxerxes* (1762) and *Love in a Village* (1762), and others.

Arneb (är'neb). The third-magnitude star α Leporis. It is sometimes called Arsh.

Arneiro (ar.nā'rö), Visconde **de.** [Title of **José Augusto Ferreira Veiga.**] b. at Macao, China, 1838; d. at San Remo, Italy, in July, 1903. Portuguese composer. He is now known chiefly for his operas *L'Elisire di Giovinezza* (1876) and *La Derelitta* (1885), and a *Te Deum* (1871).

Arnér (är.nār'), **Sivar.** [Full name, **Ernst Nils Sivar Erik Arnér.**] b. at Arbyar, Småland, Sweden, 1909—. Swedish novelist and short-story writer, professor at Skara and at Norrköping. Arnér first acquired literary fame as the result of short stories in *Skon som krigaren bar* (The Warrior's Shoe, 1943).

Arneth (är'net), **Alfred von.** b. at Vienna, July 10, 1819; d. there, July 30, 1897. Austrian historian; son of Joseph Calasanza von Arneth. Author of works on Eugene of Savoy, Maria Theresa, Marie Antoinette, and numerous others; of them all the *Geschichte Maria Theresas* (10 vols., 1863–79) is best known.

Arneth, Joseph Calasanza von. b. Aug. 12, 1791; d. Oct. 31, 1863. Austrian archaeologist and numismatist. Appointed director of the cabinet of numismatics and antiquities at Vienna in 1840; author of *Synopsis numorum antiquorum* (1837–42), and others.

Arnheim (ärn'hīm), Baron **Johann** (or **Hans**) **Georg von.** See **Arnim,** Baron **Johann** (or **Hans**) **Georg von.**

Arnhem (ärn'hem). [German, **Arnheim** (-hīm); Latin, probably, **Arenacum.**] City in NE Netherlands, the capital of the province of Gelderland, situated on the right bank of the Rhine River, near its confluence with the Ijssel River, ab. 33 mi. E of Utrecht. It is surrounded by garden suburbs, has beautiful parks, and is a favorite residence of retired merchants and government officials. It is a river port, and has many commercial and banking enterprises; the factories produce nylon, hosiery, furniture, ceramics, cigars, and foodstuffs; there are metallurgical and chemical establishments. There is a museum of antiquities, a concert hall, and a theater. The 15th-century Groote Kerk had a famous chime of bells; the town hall dates from the 16th century. Arnhem received town privileges in 1233, was a residence of the dukes of Gelder in the 13th–16th centuries, and a member of the Hanseatic League in 1343. Conquered by Charles the Bold of Burgundy in 1473, it was contested between the Spaniards and the dukes of Gelder until the death of the last duke of Gelder in 1538; joined the Union of Utrecht in 1579 and the States General in 1585. It was taken by the French in 1795, and by the Prussians in 1813. A large part of the center of the town was destroyed in World War II, when Arnhem was the site of a large Allied airborne invasion (1944); the Groote Kerk is beyond repair. 102,434 (1949).

Arnhem (är'nem), **Cape.** Headland at the entrance of the Gulf of Carpentaria, in the Northern Territory of Australia: the easternmost point of Arnhem Land.

Arnhem Bay. Indentation on the N coast of the Northern Territory, Australia, in NE Arnhem Land.

Arnhem Land. [Also, **Arnhemland.**] District in N Australia, in the Northern Territory. It occupies most of the large peninsula between the Gulf of Carpenteria and the Timor Sea. A large part of it has been set aside as an aboriginal reserve.

Arnim (är'nim), Count **Adolf Heinrich von.** b. April 10, 1803; d. Jan. 8, 1868. Prussian politician and historical writer. He was the leading cabinet minister during the tense days of March 19–29, 1848, when the Prussian government was a chief target of the reformist insurrections of that year in Europe.

Arnim, Elisabeth (or **Bettina**) **von.** [Maiden name, **Brentano.**] b. at Frankfort on the Main, Germany, April 4, 1785; d. at Berlin, Jan. 20, 1859. German writer; wife of Ludwig Achim von Arnim and sister of Clemens Brentano. She was a member of a circle including Karl Wilhelm von Humboldt, Leopold von Ranke, the brothers Grimm, and the poet Karoline von Günderode, whose biography (*Die Günderode,* 1840) she wrote. Author also of *Goethe's Briefwechsel mit einem Kinde* (1835), a partly fictitious correspondence with Johann Wolfgang von Goethe, and *Dies Buch gehört dem König* (1843), an account of poverty and bad government in Berlin. It was addressed to Frederick William IV.

Arnim, Count **Harry Karl Kurt Eduard von.** b. at Moitzelfitz, in Pomerania, Oct. 3, 1824; d. at Nice, May 19, 1881. German diplomat under Bismarck. He was Prussian envoy at the papal court (1864–70) and ambassador at Paris (1872–74), and leader in the negotiation of the treaty of Frankfort (1871). He protested the doctrine of papal infallibility and proposed (1869) sending government representatives to the Vatican council, in the first of his series of struggles against Bismarck; he was recalled (1874) from his post at Paris for differences over policy and assigned to Constantinople. Dismissed for permitting the publication of diplomatic papers and charged with theft of state documents, he remained in exile (1875–81), publishing anti-Bismarck pamphlets including *Pro nihilo* (1876) and *Der Nunzius kommt!* (1878).

Arnim, Baron **Heinrich Alexander von.** b. at Berlin, Feb. 13, 1798; d. at Düsseldorf, Jan. 5, 1861. Prussian diplomat and politician. He was ambassador at Brussels (1840–46) and Paris (1846–48), and was minister of foreign affairs from March 21 to June 8, 1848.

Arnim, Baron **Johann** (or **Hans**) **Georg von.** [Also, **Arnheim.**] b. at Boitzenburg, Brandenburg, Prussia, 1581; d. at Dresden, April 18, 1641. German general and diplomat. He served with the Swedes under Gustavus Adolphus (Gustavus II) against Russia and later with the Poles against Turkey. He was persuaded (1626) by the Austrian general, Wallenstein, to join the newly formed imperial army and quickly rose to the rank of field marshal despite his known Protestant religious convictions; he quit the imperial service after the dismissal of Wallenstein and later fought on the side of the Swedes at Breitenfeld (1631) as commander of an army raised by the elector of Saxony. His later life found him less and less trusted by the Swedes, who imprisoned him in 1638 for alleged plots against them. At the time of his death he was striving to raise an army which would free German soil of foreign military forces.

Arnim, Karl Otto Ludwig von. b. at Berlin, Aug. 1, 1779; d. there, Feb. 9, 1861. German writer of travel works.

Arnim, Ludwig Achim (or **Joachim**) **von.** b. at Berlin, Jan. 26, 1781; d. at Wiepersdorf, Germany, Jan. 21, 1831. German romantic novelist and poet; husband of Elisabeth von Arnim. With his wife's brother, Clemens Brentano, he published the collection of folk songs entitled *Des Knaben Wunderhorn* (1806–08). He was the author of novels and tales, notably *Die Kronenwächter* (1817), laid in the 16th century and considered to have been the best historical novel of the day; among his other works are *Der Wintergarten* (1809), *Gräfin Dolores* (1810), and *Halle und Jerusalem* (1811).

Arniston the elder (är'nis.ton), Lord. See **Dundas, Robert** (1685–1753).

Arniston the younger, Lord. See **Dundas, Robert** (1713–87).

Arno (är′nō). [Also: **Arn, Aquila.**] b. c750; d. 821. German ecclesiastic and diplomat; friend of Alcuin; appointed (798) archbishop of Salzburg. He is said to have converted many Avars and Wends to Christianity, to have presided at several synods, and to have enjoyed the esteem of Charlemagne and Pope Leo III. He was active in both church and government, and established a library at Salzburg.

Arno. [Latin, **Arnus.**] River in Tuscany, N central Italy, which rises in the Apennines, flows S, W, NW, and then W, and empties into the Mediterranean ab. 6 mi. SW of Pisa. Florence and Pisa are situated on it. Length, ab. 154 mi.

Arno, Peter. [Original name, **Curtis Arnoux Peters, Jr.**] b. at New York, Jan. 8, 1904—. American cartoonist, designer, and author, best known for his cartoons, which have appeared both in periodicals and book form. He was educated at Yale University, and became associated with *The New Yorker* magazine in 1925. Since then he has written and produced musical revues, served as a writer and designer for films, and designed automobiles. Exhibitions of his work have been held at Paris, London, and in the U.S. Among his better known works are the books *Peter Arno's Parade, Peter Arno's Circus, For Members Only, Man in the Shower, Peter Arno's Sizzling Platter*, and cartoons, illustrations, and articles for the *New Yorker, Saturday Evening Post, Harper's Bazaar*, and other periodicals.

Arnobius (är.nō′bi.us). [Surnamed **Afer.**] fl. in Numidia, c300 A.D. Rhetorician and Christian apologist. He was the author of *Adversus Gentes*, a treatise on Christianity written shortly after his conversion (and based more on Plato and Lucretius than on the Scriptures) which sought to refute contemporary charges that Christian impiety was a cause of the world's troubles, and attacked heathenism and polytheism.

Arnold (är′nọld). Urban district in C England, in Nottinghamshire, ab. 3 mi. NE of Nottingham, of which it is a suburb. It has no direct rail connections for passengers, being reached by rail to Nottingham, ab. 124 mi. N of London. 21,474 (1951).

Arnold. Borough in W Pennsylvania, in Westmoreland County, on the Allegheny River NE of Pittsburgh: manufactures glass. 10,263 (1950).

Arnold, Sir **Arthur.** b. at Gravesend, Kent, England, May 28, 1833; d. at London, May 20, 1902. English editor, reformer, and novelist; brother of Sir Edwin Arnold.

Arnold, Benedict. b. in England, Dec. 21, 1615; d. June 20, 1678. English colonial governor of Rhode Island (1663 *et seq.*).

Arnold, Benedict. b. at Norwich, Conn., Jan. 14, 1741; d. at London, June 14, 1801. American general in the Revolutionary War, chiefly remembered for his attempt to betray West Point to the British in 1780. Commissioned as a colonel in 1775, he took part in Ethan Allen's capture of Fort Ticonderoga, commanded the winter expedition through the Maine wilderness to Quebec, and was wounded, but maintained the blockade of Quebec, and in 1776 was promoted to brigadier general. He twice defeated the British in their attempted expedition down Lake Champlain in 1776, and defeated them again in 1777 at Norwalk, Conn., for which Congress gave him a delayed promotion to major general, though permitting certain junior officers to outrank him until after Saratoga, where his initiative and reputation for audacity were important factors leading to Burgoyne's surrender. Appointed (1778) commander at Philadelphia, he there met and married (1779) Margaret ("Peggy") Shippen, member of a wealthy Philadelphia family. He attempted to maintain a social position and household establishment not unlike that to which his wife was accustomed, and soon found himself seriously in debt. A court-martial for private use of the militia under his control, plus continuing indignation at slights by Congress and opposition to the French alliance, led in 1779 to the opening of the correspondence with Sir Henry Clinton, the British commander in chief in North America, that culminated (1780) in the arrangement with Major John André, of Clinton's staff, to betray West Point (which Arnold then commanded) to the British. Fleeing to the British lines after André's capture, he was appointed a brigadier general in the British army and subsequently led raids on Virginia (1780) and Connecticut (1781). He settled in England during the latter year, but was never able to collect the full amount of the reward he had expected from the British and spent the last years of his life in comparative poverty.

Arnold, Bion Joseph. b. at Casnovia, Mich., Aug. 14, 1861; d. Jan. 29, 1942. American electrical engineer. As a consulting engineer (1893 *et seq.*) he contributed to the development of street railway systems in many American cities; he was also a consultant in the building of New York subways and in the third-rail electrification of the Grand Central terminal at New York. He was the inventor of a magnetic clutch and innovator of alternating-current and single-phase traction systems.

Arnold (är′nolt), **Christoph.** b. at Sommerfeld, near Leipzig, Dec. 17, 1650; d. April 15, 1695. German astronomer, noted for his observations of the comets of 1682 and 1686, and of the transit of the planet Mercury in 1690.

Arnold (är′nọld), Sir **Edwin.** b. at Gravesend, Kent, England, June 10, 1832, d. at London, March 24, 1904. English poet, journalist, educator, Oriental student and translator, and author of *The Light of Asia;* brother of Sir Arthur Arnold. He was educated at King's College, Rochester, King's College, London, and University College, Oxford, winning the Newdigate prize (1852) with his poem, *Belshazzar's Feast.* Thereafter he taught at Birmingham at the King Edward's School, and was principal (1856–61) of the Deccan Government College at Poona, Bombay. Returning to England in 1861, he joined the staff of the London *Daily Telegraph,* serving as editorial writer (until 1873) and as chief editor from 1873 until his death. He traveled in Japan (marrying a Japanese woman as his third wife) and along the U.S. Pacific coast (1889), and traveled and lectured elsewhere in the U.S. (1891). Author of *Poems Narrative and Lyrical* (1853), *Griselda* (1856), *The Wreck of the Northern Belle* (1857), *The Light of Asia* (1879), an epic poem on the life of Buddha, once his best-known and most popular work, but now little read; *Pearls of the Faith* (1883), *Secret of Death* (1885), *Lotus and Jewel* (1887), *The Light of the World* (1891), the last of which dealt with Christ in somewhat the same fashion as *The Light of Asia* did with Buddha. His other poetry includes *Potiphar's Wife* (1892), *The Tenth Muse* (1895), and *The Voyage of Ithobal* (1901). History, travel books, and comment include *History of the Marquis of Dalhousie's Administration* (2 vols., 1862–65), *India Revisited* (1886), *Seas and Lands* (1891), *Japonica* (1892), *Wandering Words* (1894), and *East and West* (1896). He also translated poetry by Victor Hugo and Giuseppe Garibaldi, *Poets of Greece* (1869), the *Hero and Leander* (1873) of Musaeus, several volumes of Indian poetry, and wrote (1877) a Turkish grammar.

Arnold, Elliott. b. at New York, Sept. 13, 1912—. American journalist and novelist. He was a reporter (1933–42) for the New York *World-Telegram* and served (1942 *et seq.*) in the U.S. army during World War II. Among his novels are *Two Lovers* (1934), *Personal Combat* (1936), *Only the Young* (1939), *The Commandos* (1942), *Tomorrow Will Sing* (1945), *Blood Brother* (1947), and *Everybody Slept Here* (1948).

Arnold, George. [Pseudonyms: **McArone, George Garrulous,** and others.] b. at New York, June 24, 1834; d. at Strawberry Farms, N.J., Nov. 9, 1865. American poet and essayist. He was a member of a 19th-century American literary group known as the "Bohemians."

Arnold (är′nolt), **Gottfried.** b. at Annaberg, in Saxony, Sept. 5, 1666; d. at Perleberg, in Prussia, May 30, 1714. German Pietist theologian and church historian, author of *Die erste Liebe zu Christo* (1696). His work was rediscovered and brought again to public attention during the 19th century by Leo Tolstoy.

Arnold (är′nọld), **Henry Harley.** [Nicknamed **"Hap" Arnold.**] b. at Gladwyne, Pa., June 25, 1886; d. Jan. 15, 1950. American air-force officer. He served (1916–17) with the signal corps aviation division and was thereafter a member of the army air force; he was awarded the Mackay trophy (1912, 1935), the Collier trophy (1943), the Distinguished Flying Cross (1934), and others. He served as flight commander on the army air force flight to Alaska in 1934, assistant chief (1936–38) and chief (1938 *et seq.*) of the army air corps, and commanding general of U.S. army air forces (1942–46). Appointed (1944) general of the army, highest regular U.S. military rank, he retired from active service in January, 1946. Author of *Air Men and Aircraft* (1929), and others; collaborator with General Ira C. Eaker on *Winged Warfare* (1941), *Army Flyer* (1942), and others.

Arnold, Isaac Newton. b. at Hartwick, N.Y., Nov. 30, 1815; d. at Chicago, April 24, 1884. American politician and biographical writer, a member of Congress from Illinois (1861–65). Author of *Life of Abraham Lincoln* (1885), his best-known work, *Life of Benedict Arnold* (1880), and others.

Arnold, John. b. at Bodmin, Cornwall, England, 1736; d. 1799. English watchmaker who improved and named the chronometer. He was assisted in establishing a watchmaking shop by George III, to whom he gave a watch set into a ring; later he developed improvements in the instrument now known, from the name he gave it, as the chronometer.

Arnold (är′nolt), **Karl.** b. at Württemberg, March 21, 1901—. German politician. Originally a leather worker, he became a trade-union official; he was arrested after the attempt to assassinate Hitler in July, 1944. Mayor of Düsseldorf in 1945, he was elected Minister President of the *Land* (state) of North Rhine-Westphalia in 1947.

Arnold (är′nọld), **Matthew.** b. at Laleham, England, Dec. 24, 1822; d. at Liverpool, England, April 15, 1888. English critic, poet, and essayist; son of Thomas Arnold (1795–1842), headmaster of Rugby. Educated at Winchester, Rugby, and Balliol College, Oxford, Matthew became a fellow of Oriel College, Oxford, in 1845, and secretary to the marquis of Lansdowne in 1847; he was lay inspector of schools (1851–83) and professor of poetry at Oxford (1857–67). His teaching at Oxford prompted him to devote the greater part of his interest, over a period of years, to criticism in the widest sense and the formulation of his own standards in the evaluation of literature and literary techniques. This was first evident in his own poem on Wordsworth, Byron, and Goethe in *Empedocles on Etna and Other Poems* (1852) and in his preface to *Poems by Matthew Arnold* (1853). In the latter work he included his *Requiescat*, *The Scholar-Gipsy*, and *Sohrab and Rustum* (which last was taken from the works of the Persian epic poet, Firdausi, and which embodied Arnold's own standard of unity). This interest in critical writing was again apparent in *Merope* (1858), which was intended as a poetical manifesto and was, at least partly for this reason, not successful as a tragedy. Most modern critics consider that his poetry from this date on lacked the power of his earlier work, with certain notable exceptions such as the elegies *Rugby Chapel* (1857) on his father, *A Southern Night* (1859) on his brother, *Thyrsis* (1861) on Arthur Hugh Clough, and *Westminster Abbey* (1881) on Arthur Penrhyn Stanley, the dean of Westminster Abbey. His critical works, on which his fame as a master of clear and felicitous English may be said chiefly to rest, include published lectures *On Translating Homer* (1861–62) and *On the Study of Celtic Literature* (1867); two volumes of *Essays in Criticism* (1865, 1888), the first of which contains the essay depicting Heine as a great intellectual liberator, such as Arnold himself wanted very intensely to be; and *Culture and Anarchy* (1869), reprinted from the *Cornhill Magazine*, in which Arnold put forth his so-called "sweetness and light" theory. His other works include theological studies such as *Literature and Dogma* (1873), and such works of essays as *Discourses in America* (1885) and *Civilization in the United States* (Boston, 1888), both based on his American lecture tours (1883–84 and 1886).

Arnold, Ralph. b. at Marshalltown, Ia., April 14, 1875—. American geologist and petroleum consultant. He served (1900–09) on the staff of the U.S. Geological Survey, and has made oil surveys in Texas, Wyoming, Mexico, Trinidad, Venezuela, and elsewhere. Author of numerous technical articles, including *Tertiary and Quaternary Pectens of California*, *Two Decades of Petroleum Geology*, and *Petroleum in the United States and Possessions*.

Arnold, Richard. b. at Providence, R.I., April 12, 1828; d. on Governor's Island, N.Y., Nov. 8, 1882. American soldier, Union general in the Civil War. He served in the Peninsular Campaign in 1802, and commanded a cavalry division in 1864. He received promotions for gallantry at Savage Station, Port Hudson, and Fort Morgan.

Arnold, Richard. b. at Eilenburg, near Leipzig, Germany, 1845; d. at New York, 1918. American violinist and music teacher, concert master (1880–1909) of the New York Philharmonic Orchestra. He came to the U.S. as a child, already proficient as a violinist, and was an orchestra conductor and violin performer at the age of 12.

Arnold, Samuel. b. at London, Aug. 10, 1740; d. there, Oct. 22, 1802. English composer and musicologist, organist (1793–1802) at Westminster Abbey. He composed operas such as *The Maid of the Mill* (1765), oratorios including *The Cure of Saul* (1767), overtures, pantomimes, harpsichord pieces, and others; he also published 40 volumes of an edition of George Frederick Handel's works.

Arnold, Samuel Greene. b. at Providence, R.I., April 12, 1821; d. there, Feb. 13, 1880. American historian. He was several times (1852, 1861, 1862) lieutenant governor of Rhode Island, and was a U.S. senator in 1862–63. Author of *History of Rhode Island and Providence Plantation* (1859), *Historical Sketch of Middletown* (1880), and others.

Arnold, Thomas. [Called **"Arnold of Rugby."**] b. at West Cowes, on the Isle of Wight, June 13, 1795; d. at Rugby, England, June 12, 1842. English educator and historian, headmaster of Rugby (1828–42); father of Matthew Arnold. Educated at Winchester and at Corpus Christi College, Oxford, he was a fellow (1815–19) at Oriel College, Oxford. Ordained deacon in 1818, he settled (1819) at Laleham, where he tutored young men for universities. At Rugby, he set the modern pattern for the English public-school system. His leadership was widely recognized, in spite of outspoken criticism by certain elements of the clergy, and he was given an appointment (1841) as regius professor of modern history at Oxford. His works include a collection of sermons (1829–34), an edition of Thucydides (1830–35), *History of Rome* (3 vols., 1838–43), and *Lectures on Modern History* (1842).

Arnold, Thomas. b. at Laleham, England, 1823; d. at Dublin, 1900. English scholar; son of Thomas Arnold (1795–1842) and brother of Matthew Arnold. Inspector of schools in Tasmania (1850–56), he joined (1856) the Roman Catholic Church. He was professor of English literature at Dublin, appointed by Newman to New Catholic University there, and later at St. Stephen's Green. Author of *Manual of English Literature, Historical and Critical* (1862), of editions of Wycliffe (1869–71), *Beowulf* (1876), and others; also of *Passages in a Wandering Life* (1900), containing much material on Newman and the Tractarian (now better known as the Oxford) Movement.

Arnold, Thomas Kerchever. b. at Stamford, England, 1800; d. at Lyndon, England, March 9, 1853. English clergyman and writer of classical textbooks, including an English-Latin lexicon (with J. E. Riddle, 1847), based on an earlier work by a German scholar. He also produced Hebrew and various modern-language grammars (also based on German scholarship), pamphlets on the Oxford Movement, and others.

Arnold, Thurman Wesley. b. at Laramie, Wyo., June 2, 1891—. American jurist and author. Holding degrees from Princeton (1911), Harvard (1914), and Yale (1931), he was professor of law (1931–38) at Yale. Thereafter he served as assistant U.S. attorney general (1938–43) in charge of the antitrust division in the U.S. Department of Justice, and as associate justice (1943–45) of the federal court of appeals for the District of Columbia. Author of *The Symbols of Government* (1935), *Cases on Trials, Judgments and Appeals* (1936), *The Folklore of Capitalism* (1937), *The Bottlenecks of Business* (1940), and *Democracy and Free Enterprise* (1942).

Arnold, William Delafield. [Pseudonym, **Purjabee.**] b. at Laleham, near Staines, England, April 7, 1828; d. at Gibraltar, April 9, 1859. English educator and novelist; son of Thomas Arnold (1795–1842) and brother of Matthew Arnold. He was educated at Rugby, and was a student at Christ Church, Oxford, in 1847. In 1848 he went to India, as an ensign, and became an assistant commissioner in the Punjab, and, in 1856, director of public instruction. He wrote the novel *Oakfield* (1853).

Arnold, William Rosenzweig. b. at Beirut, Lebanon, Nov. 14, 1872; d. Dec. 11, 1929. American Orientalist, philologist, and teacher. After serving as curator of antiquities (1896–98) at the Metropolitan Museum of Art at New York, he was professor of Hebrew language and literature at Andover Theological Seminary (1903–22) and at Harvard (1922–29). Author of *The Rhythms of the Ancient Hebrews* (1908), *The Passover Papyrus from Elephantine* (1912), and others.

Arnold, William Thomas. b. at Hobart, Tasmania, Sept. 18, 1852; d. at London, May 29, 1904. English historian, journalist, and editor; grandson of Thomas Arnold (1795–1842) and son of Thomas Arnold (1823–1900). He was author of a *Manual of English Literature*, and an inspector of schools in Tasmania. Educated at Rugby and at University College, Oxford, he was on the staff of the *Manchester Guardian* for many years. Author of *The Roman System of Provincial Administration to the Accession of Constantine the Great* (1879), a standard work in its field, and *Studies in Roman Imperialism* (1906). In 1886, he edited his grandfather's *History of Rome: The Second Punic War.* Matthew Arnold was his uncle, and Mary Arnold, better known as Mrs. Humphry Ward (1851–1920), the novelist, was his sister.

Arnold (är.nôlt'), **Yurij** (or **Yuri**) **von.** b. at St. Petersburg, Nov. 13, 1811; d. in the Crimea, July 20, 1898. Russian composer and writer on music. He served in the cavalry (1831 *et seq.*), and later taught music (1870) and history of music (1888) at Moscow.

Arnold-Forster (är'nold.fôr'stėr), **Hugh Oakeley.** b. at Dawlish, England, 1855; d. at London, March 12, 1909. British politician and writer on imperial and military affairs; grandson of Thomas Arnold (1795–1842). He was called to the bar in 1879, and served as member of Parliament for Belfast (West) (1892–1905) and for Croydon (1906–09). He was also parliamentary secretary to the admiralty (1900–03) and secretary of state for war (1903–05). Author of *In a Conning Tower* (1891), *Our Home Army* (1891–92), *Our Great City* (1900), *War Office, Army, and Empire* (1900), and *English Socialism of Today* (1908).

Arnold of Brescia (är'nold; brā'shä). [Also: **Arnaldus, Arnoldus, Ernaldus;** Italian, **Arnaldo da Brescia.**] b. at Brescia, Italy, c1100; executed at Rome, 1155. Italian religious reformer and political agitator. Possibly a student of Abelard at Paris, he excoriated the corruption of the clergy and the power they exercised through ownership of the land. He was banished (1139) by Pope Innocent II for arousing the people against the bishop of Brescia; in France, he probably reprimanded Saint Bernard of Clairvaux, whose measures against him, including condemnation (with Abelard) by the Council of Sens (1140), drove him to Zurich and thence (1143 or 1145) to Italy, where he did penance to Pope Eugene III (but soon afterward took leadership of the republican faction at Rome which drove Eugene into exile). Though excommunicated (1148) by Eugene, Arnold remained powerful until the accession (1154) of Pope Adrian IV who, supported by the emperor Frederick I (Barbarossa), laid an interdict (1155) on Rome, driving out the republicans and reëstablishing papal power.

Arnold of Villanova. [French, **Arnauld** (or **Arnaud**) **de Villeneuve;** Latinized, **Arnaldus Villanovanus.**] b. c1240; d. 1313. Physician, alchemist, and astrologer, possibly originally from the region of Catalonia, in Spain. He taught at Paris, Barcelona, and Montpellier, and is said to have discovered the poisonous quality of what is now called carbon monoxide gas. He has been incorrectly credited with the discovery of sulfuric, nitric, and hydrochloric acids, which, according to some authorities, were known before his time.

Arnoldson (ȧr'nůld.sôn), **Klas Pontus.** b. at Göteborg, Sweden, Oct. 27, 1844; d. at Stockholm, Feb. 20, 1916. Swedish writer, politician, and worker for international peace. He was a winner of the Nobel peace prize in 1908, with Fredrik Bajer. He introduced a motion for permanent neutrality while a member (1882–87) of the Swedish *Riksdag* (parliament), and opposed war with Norway in the Swedish-Norwegian union crisis of 1906. He is best known for his *Hope of the Centuries, a Book on World Peace* (1900).

Arnoldson, Sigrid. b. at Stockholm, March 20, c1862; d. 1943. Swedish operatic soprano. She distinguished herself in the opera houses of Paris, Amsterdam, Budapest, Stockholm, St. Petersburg, Moscow, and London.

Arnoldstein (är'nolt.shtīn). Market village in S Austria, in Carinthia, SW of Villach. It is situated immediately N of the Italian and Yugoslav borders and is a station on the railroad from Villach to Venice. The population is partly German, partly Slovenian. 5,418 (1946).

Arnolfo di Cambio (är.nôl'fō dē käm'byō). [Also, **Arnolfo di Lapo** (lä'pō).] b. at Colle, in Tuscany, c1232; d. at Florence, c1300. Tuscan architect and sculptor, a pupil of Niccola Pisano. His work includes the churches of Santa Croce (1294–95) and Santa Maria del Fiore (1298 *et seq.*) at Florence.

Arnolphe (ȧr.nolf). Cynical and morose man in Molière's *École des Femmes.* He is imbued with the idea that a woman can only be good and virtuous in proportion as she is ignorant. He brings up a young girl, Agnes, on these principles with the view of marrying her, but this system results in making her so ignorant that she says and does without a blush many things which normal society considers shocking. His warnings teach her exactly how to deceive him, and she marries her younger lover, Horace.

Arnon (är'non). [Arabic, **Wadi Mojib.**] In the Old Testament, a small river flowing into the Dead Sea. It formed the boundary between the Moabites on the S and the Amorites (and later the Israelites) on the N.

Arnon (ȧr.nôṅ). River in N central France, a tributary of the Cher River, lying chiefly in the department of Cher.

Arnot (är'not), **William.** b. at Scone, Scotland, Nov. 6, 1808; d. at Edinburgh, June 3, 1875. Scottish minister and theological writer. He was ordained minister of Saint Peter's Church, Glasgow, in 1838, joined Chalmer's Free Church movement in 1843, and became minister of a Free Church congregation at Edinburgh in 1863. He visited America (1845, 1870, 1873), and was well received in the N part of the U.S. for his antislavery stand. Author of *Laws from Heaven for Life on Earth,* and others.

Arnott (är'not), **Neil.** b. at Arbroath, Scotland, May 15, 1788; d. at London, March 2, 1874. Scottish physician, physicist, and inventor. As ship's surgeon (1807–11) on China voyages for the East India Company, he made a study of meteorology, which served as foundation for his *Elements of Physics* (1827–29). In the same period he began the study of sanitation which led to his invention of a smokeless grate ("Arnott's Stove") and other devices, described in his *Warming and Ventilation* (1833), and for further development of which he gave up his London practice in 1855.

Arnould (ȧr.nö), **Madeleine Sophie.** [Called **Sophie Arnould.**] b. at Paris, in February, 1744; d. there, in October, 1802. French actress and opera singer; leading soprano (1757–78) at the Paris Opéra. A friend of Claude Adrien Helvétius, Jean le Rond d'Alembert, Denis Diderot, Jean Jacques Rousseau, and others, she was known in her time as a wit. Her epigrams were collected in *Arnouldiana* (1813).

Arnouville-les-Gonesse (ȧr.nö.vēl.lā.go.nes). Town in N France, in the department of Seine-et-Oise, situated NE of St.-Denis, between Paris and Senlis. It belongs to the metropolitan region of Paris. 6,879 (1946).

Arno Valley (är'nō). [Italian, **Val d'Arno** (val där'nō).] The fruitful valley of the upper Arno River, in N central Italy.

Arnprior (ärn"prī'or). Small industrial town on the S bank of the Ottawa River, E Ontario, Canada, ab. 42 mi. W of Ottawa. 4,381 (1951).

Arnsberg (ärns'berk). Town in W Germany, in the *Land* (state) of North Rhine-Westphalia, British Zone, formerly in the province of Westphalia, Prussia, situated on the upper Ruhr River. Industries include metallurgical, electrical, chemical, and shoe factories, and breweries. There is a ruined castle. Arnsberg was formerly the seat of the dreaded Vehmgericht of Westphalia. Originally an independent countship, it passed to Cologne in 1368, to Hesse in 1802, and to Prussia in 1815. Pop. 18,884 (1950).

Arnstadt (ärn'shtät). City in C Germany, in the *Land* (state) of Thuringia, Russian Zone, situated on the Gera River, ab. 11 mi. SW of Erfurt: a manufacturing center, which before World War II produced shoes, gloves, rayon, and machinery. It is one of the oldest cities in Thuringia, references to it having been found from as early as 704; it came into the possession of the counts of

Schwarzburg in the 13th century, and was capital of the independent principality of Schwarzburg-Sondershausen until 1919, when it was incorporated into the free state of Thuringia. The population is predominantly Protestant; the increase between 1939 and 1946 amounted to 23.1 percent, largely due to the influx of East-German refugees. 27,846 (1946).

Arnstein (ärn′stīn), **Karl.** b. at Prague, March 24, 1887—. American designer and builder of dirigibles and other airships. He arrived in the U.S. in 1924 after employment (1914–24) as a designer and engineer by the Zeppelin works at Friedrichshafen, Germany; he became a U.S. citizen in 1930. Technical director in aircraft construction for the Goodyear Tire and Rubber Company (1924) and chief engineer of the Goodyear-Zeppelin Corporation (1925 *et seq.*), he was in charge of designing and building the airships *Akron* and *Macon.*

Arnulf (är′nůlf). b. c850; d. at what is now Regensburg, Bavaria, Dec. 8, 899. Emperor of the Holy Roman Empire; illegitimate son of Carloman, king of Bavaria. He was elected king of the East Franks in 887, and was crowned emperor in 896. He defeated the Normans near Louvain in 891, fought with the Moravians, and invaded Italy and stormed Rome in 895.

Arnulf. Roman Catholic ecclesiastic, archbishop of Reims during the period 989–991.

Arnus (är′nus). Latin name of the **Arno.**

Arod (ā′rod) or **Arodi** (ar′ǫ.dī). Son of Gad. Num. xxvi. 17. In Gen. xlvi. 16 the same person is called Arodi.

Arod. In the second part of *Absalom and Achitophel* (which was written in the main by Nahum Tate and revised by John Dryden), a character intended for Sir William Waller.

Aroe Islands (ä′rö). [Also: **Aru** (or **Arru** or **Arroe**) **Islands;** Dutch, **Aroe Eilanden.**] Group of more than 90 islands, SE of New Guinea, in E Indonesia. Chief town, Dobo; area, 3,300 sq. mi.; pop. ab. 18,000.

Arolas (ä.rō′läs), **Juan.** b. at Barcelona, Spain, June 20, 1805; d. at Valencia, Spain, Nov. 25, 1849. Spanish poet, author of *Poesias caballerescas y orientales* (1840–50) and others.

Arolsen (ä′rol.zẹn). Town in W Germany, in the *Land* (state) of Hessen, American Zone, formerly in Waldeck, ab. 22 mi. N of Kassel: a summer resort; also has livestock markets and small industries. The castle of the princes of Waldeck-Pyrmont (erected 1710–25) is in the baroque style; it contains art collections and a valuable library. Arolsen was the birthplace of the sculptor Christian Rauch and the painter Friedrich Kaulbach. It was formerly the capital of the independent principality of Waldeck. 4,726 (1946).

Arona (ä.rō′nä). Town and commune in NW Italy, in the *compartimento* (region) of Piedmont, in the province of Novara, situated on Lago Maggiore, ab. 38 mi. NW of Milan. It is a railroad junction, has cotton textile mills, and is a resort town. A monument to Cardinal Carlo Borromeo is outside the town. Arona, fortified from Roman times, was at various later periods in the hands of the Lombards, of Milan, and of Austria until it was ceded to Sardinia in 1743. Buildings of interest to tourists were undamaged in World War II. Pop. of commune, 8,632 (1936); of town, 5,667 (1936).

Arondight (ar′ǫn.dīt). In later versions of the Arthurian legend, the sword of Lancelot.

Aronhold (ä′ron.holt), **Siegfried Heinrich.** b. at Angerburg, in East Prussia, July 16, 1819; d. at Berlin, March 13, 1884. German mathematician, one of the most important contributors to the theory of invariants of algebraic forms. He wrote on kinematics and was largely responsible, through "Aronhold's notation," for the modern symbolic methods in algebraic geometry. He took his doctorate at Königsberg in 1851 and taught at Giessen, Zurich, Heidelberg, and Berlin. Besides numerous papers, especially in Crelle's *Journal*, he wrote *Ueber eine fundamentale Begründung der Invariantentheorie* (1863).

Aroostook (ą.rös′tůk). River in N and NE Maine, which joins the St. John River in W New Brunswick. Length, ab. 140 mi.

Aroostook War. So-called war (February–May, 1839) along the Maine-New Brunswick boundary involving Maine troops who were dispatched to the area to contest Canadian claims in the region. The dispute had no formal status and did not occasion any shedding of blood on either side; it had its roots in the absence of a definite boundary line (later established by the Webster-Ashburton Treaty of 1842 between the U.S. and Great Britain). Although the U.S. government made provisions for funds and troops should war break out, the dispute ended in the negotiation of a truce by General Winfield Scott and the lieutenant governor of New Brunswick.

Arosa (ä.rō′zä). Summer and winter resort in E Switzerland, in the canton of Graubünden at the head of the Plessur Valley, E of Chur, at an elevation of 6,000 ft. It is one of the leading winter-sport centers in Switzerland. 1,980 (1941).

Arosemena (ä.rō.sā.mā′nä), **Florencio Harmodio.** b. 1873; d. 1945. Panamanian politician, president (1928–31) of Panama. His administration was overthrown (Jan. 2, 1931) by the Acción Comunal, a nationalist Panamanian patriotic society.

Arp (ärp), **Hans.** b. at Strasbourg, Sept. 16, 1887—. Swiss painter of the dadaist school. He is best known for his compositions superimposing free forms on a flat background, several of which are in the Museum of Modern Art at New York.

Arpachshad (är.pak′shad). [Also: **Arphaxad, Arphaxhad.**] Third son of Shem, and a remote ancestor of Abraham, according to Genesis and 1 Chronicles. However, Arpachshad is not necessarily a single person. From the structure of the genealogical tables the name may be that of a tribe or land of which the people were descendants from that son of Shem. The name long referred to the mountainous country on the Upper Zab N and NE of Nineveh, called by the Greek geographers Arrapachitis. Gen. x. 22, 24; xi. 10.

Árpád (är′päd). d. 907. A Magyar national hero, founder (c890) of the Árpád dynasty in Hungary. It is said that he led the Magyars into Hungary c895.

Arpad (är′pad). [Also: **Arphad;** in Assyrian inscriptions, **Ar-pad-da;** modern name, **Tel-Erfad.**] Ancient city in N Syria, ab. 15 mi. N of Aleppo. In the Old Testament it is always mentioned in conjunction with Hamath (the modern Hama), on the Orontes River (Isa. x. 9, Jer. xlix. 23). It was taken by Tiglath-pileser II in 740 B.C., after a siege of three years.

Árpád Dynasty. Dynasty of Hungarian sovereigns, ruling as kings from 997 to 1301. The first actual sovereign of this dynasty (as distinct from Árpád, a national hero who was its progenitor) was Stephen I (called Saint Stephen); the last was Andrew III, who reigned from 1290 to 1301.

Arpasia (är.pā′zhą). Greek princess, in Nicholas Rowe's tragedy *Tamerlane.*

Arphad (är′fad). See **Arpad.**

Arphaxad or **Arphaxhad** (är.fak′sad). See **Arpachshad.**

Arpi (är′pī). [Also, **Argyrippa.**] In ancient geography, a city in Apulia, Italy.

Arpino (är.pē′nō). [Ancient name, **Arpinum** (är.pī′num).] Town and commune in C Italy, in the *compartimento* (region) of Latium, in the province of Frosinone, situated near the Garigliano River, SE of Rome: marble quarries; woolen mills. In ancient times a Roman town, the birthplace of Marius and Cicero, it was later sacked by Lombards, Hungarians, and Moslems, and became a stronghold of the Papal States. It preserves walls and fortifications from both Roman and medieval times. World War II damage to buildings of tourist interest consisted chiefly of broken windows in the churches of Sant' Andrea, Santa Maria Assunta in Cività, and San Michele Arcangelo. Pop. of commune, 10,564 (1936); of town, 2,613 (1936).

Arpino (där.pē′nō), **Cavaliere d'.** See **Cesari, Giuseppe.**

Arquà Petrarca (är.kwä′ pā.trär′kä). Village in NE Italy, in the province of Padova, ab. 13 mi. SW of Padua: the place where Petrarch died (1374).

Arquebusiers of Saint Andrew. Oil painting (1633) by Frans Hals in the town hall at Haarlem, Holland. It comprises 14 figures, colonel, captains, lieutenants, ensigns, and sergeants of the company, and is characteristic in color and expression of the artist's middle period.

Arques (ȧrk). [Full name, **Arques-la-Bataille** (lȧ.bȧ.täy′).] Town in N France, in the department of Seine-Inférieure, on the Arques River near its junction with the Eaulne and Béthune rivers, ab. 3 mi. E of Dieppe. It contains a ruined castle, built in the 11th century by William the Conqueror. Nearby is the battlefield of Archelles, where Henry IV defeated Charles de Lorraine Duc de Mayenne, on Sept. 21, 1589. The church, built in flamboyant Gothic style, was damaged during World War II. 2,462 (1946).

Arquipélago (är.kē.pe′lạ.gö). Portuguese word for "archipelago": see the specific element of the name.

Arrah (är′rạ). City in E Union of India, in Bihar, ab. 35 mi. W of Patna: rail junction and trading center. In 1857 it was successfully defended against the Sepoy rebels. 53,122 (1941).

Arraignment of Paris (par′is), **The.** Play, combining the elements of a pageant and a masque, which was published anonymously in 1584, but is thought to have been written by George Peele. It is written mainly in varied lyrical measures, with about 200 lines of blank verse, considered by critics to be the loveliest written before those of Marlowe.

Arrakis (ar′ạ.kis). The fourth-magnitude double-star μ Draconis, in the Dragon's tongue.

Arran (ar′ạn). Island in C Scotland, in Buteshire, lying between the Firth of Clyde and Kilbrennan Sound. The surface is hilly and mountainous, rising to 2,866 ft. in Goatfell, the highest summit. Length, ab. 20 mi.; width, ab. 12 mi.; area, ab. 166 sq. mi.; pop. 4,506 (1931).

Arran Islands. See **Aran Islands.**

Arras (ar′ạs; French, à.räs). [Gallic, **Atrabate, Atrebates;** Latin, **Nemetacum, Nemetocenna.**] City in N France, the capital of the department of Pas-de-Calais, situated at the influx of the Crinchon River into the Scarpe River, at the point where the latter becomes navigable. It is a trade center for the agricultural products of the region, having been one of the major French grain markets, and has manufactures of lace and of beet sugar. In medieval times it was noted for its tapestry. Arras was the capital of the Atrebates and later of the county of Artois; it later belonged to Burgundy, and passed with the Netherlands to Spain. It was taken by the French in 1640, besieged by the Spaniards in 1654, and ceded to France in 1659. Robespierre was born at Arras. During World War I, Arras was in the front line and was uninterruptedly bombarded. Almost the entire inner city, including the architecturally interesting Petite-Place and Grande-Place, the cathedral, the theater, the museum, and the railroad station, was completely destroyed. The city was again the scene of fighting in World War II and was largely destroyed for the second time. Reconstruction was initiated along modern lines 33,346 (1946).

Arras, Battle of. British assault (April 9, 1917) on the Western Front in World War I. It was carried out by General Allenby's Third Army and a Canadian corps Preceded by long and heavy artillery bombardment, it managed to take Vimy Ridge. The British lost 84,000 troops, but inflicted a loss of 75,000 men on the Germans, took 13,000 prisoners, and managed to retain Vimy Ridge, which was to prove an invaluable defensive position against the German offensive of March, 1918.

Arras, Lines of. Fortifications extending from Arras to Bouchain on the Scheldt River, crossed by John Churchill, 1st Duke of Marlborough, in 1711.

Arras, Treaty of. In French history: **1.** Treaty concluded between the Armagnacs and the Burgundians in 1414. **2.** Treaty between Charles VII of France and Philip the Good of Burgundy, concluded in 1435. **3.** Treaty between Louis XI of France and Maximilian I of Germany, concluded in 1482. By its terms, France was to receive Artois, Franche-Comté, and other territories.

Arrate y Acosta (är.rä′tä ē ä.kôs′tä), **José Martin Félix.** b. at Havana, Cuba, 1697; d. there, 1766. Cuban historian. Author of *Llave del nuevo mundo y antemural de las Indias occidentales* (begun 1761, published 1830), a history of Cuba.

Arrawac (ar′ạ.wak). See **Arawak.**

Arrebo (ä′rẹ.bō), **Anders Christensen.** [Also, **Arreboe.**] b. on the island of Ærø, Denmark, Jan. 2, 1587; d. at Vordingborg, Denmark, March 12, 1637. Danish poet, a leader of the Italian Renaissance influence in Danish literature. Author of *Hexaëmeron* (1641 and 1661), translations of Psalms, and others.

Arrecife Alacrán (är.rā.sē′fā ä.lä.krän′). [Also, **Alacranes.**] Group of coral islets in the Gulf of Mexico, N of Yucatán, Mexico.

Arrée (dà.rā), **Monts d'.** Mountain group in the department of Finistère, France, culminating in Mont St.-Michel (ab. 1,275 ft.).

Arrest (dä.rest′, dä re′), **Heinrich Ludwig d'.** b. at Berlin, July 13, 1822; d. at Copenhagen, June 14, 1875. German astronomer. He was appointed professor at Leipzig in 1852 and at Copenhagen in 1857; noted for discoveries of comets and observations of nebulae.

Arretium (ạ.rē′shum, -shi.um). Ancient name of **Arezzo.**

Arrhenius (är.rā′nẹ.ůs), **Svante August.** b. at Wijk, near Uppsala, Sweden, Feb. 19, 1859; d. at Stockholm, Oct. 2, 1927. Swedish physical chemist. He was winner of the Nobel prize in chemistry (1903) for his theory of electrolytic dissociation (or ionization) in conductivity of solutions, first presented (1884) as his doctoral thesis at Uppsala, later revised and extended (1887), and the basis of his work thereafter. He was professor of physics (1895–1904) at Stockholm, and director (1905–27) of the Nobel Institute for Physical Chemistry, near Stockholm. Author of *Immunochemistry* (1907), based on lectures given at the University of California in 1904, *Worlds in the Making* (Eng. trans., 1908, a refutation of Clausius's theory of exhaustion of energy), *Quantitative Laws in Biological Chemistry* (1915), *Destinies of the Stars* (1918), and others.

Arrhidaeus (ar.i.dē′us). Killed 317 B.C. Macedonian soldier; half brother of Alexander the Great. He was one of the military leaders who disputed the empire after Alexander's death in 323 B.C., being elected by the soldiers under his command in Babylonia. He was put to death by order of Olympias, mother of Alexander.

Arria (ar′i ạ). d. 42 A.D. Roman woman whose husband, Caecina Paetus, was condemned to death for conspiracy against the emperor Claudius. As he hesitated to destroy himself, she stabbed herself and handed him the dagger with the words *"Paete, non dolet"* ("Paetus, it does not pain me").

Arriaga (dạr.ryä′gạ), **Manoel José d'.** [Full name, **Manoel José d'Arriaga Brun da Silveira e Peyrelongue.**] b. at Horta, in the Azores, c1842; d. 1917. Portuguese educator and politician, first constitutional president (1911–15) of the Portuguese republic. He was rector of the University of Coimbra, and professor at Lisbon, as well as a republican deputy for Funchal (1882) and for Lisbon (1890–92). He was a leader in the revolution of 1910. His administration was disturbed by royalist rebellions (1911, 1912) and a coup d'état (1915), following which he resigned.

Arriaga (är.ryä′gä), **Pablo José.** b. at Vergara, Spain, c1564; perished in shipwreck near Havana, 1622. Spanish Jesuit and author. He spent most of his life in Peru, where he was the first rector of the College of San Martin at Lima. Author of *Estirpación de la idolatría de los Indios del Perú.*

Arrian (ar′i.ạn). Fl. first half of the 2nd century B.C. Greek meteorologist. He wrote a book on meteorology and a short monograph on comets, but his work was largely absorbed in later writings and only three fragments of it now remain extant.

Arrian (ar′i.ạn). [Latin, **Flavius Arrianus.**] b. at Nicomedia, Bithynia; fl. 2nd century A.D. Greek historian and philosopher. Made a Roman citizen and governor of Cappadocia (c131) by Hadrian, he served as consul (c146) under Antoninus Pius. He was a friend and follower of Epictetus, whose lectures he published and on whose philosophy he wrote a manual. Author also of valuable historical works in the style of Xenophon, notably his *Anabasis* of Alexander, based on first-hand accounts by Aristobulus and others, the *Indica* on Nearchus's expedition to India, the *Periplus of the Euxine* (Black Sea), and the *Cynegeticus*, on hunting.

Arriaza y Superviela (är.ryä′thä ē sö.per.ʙyā′lä), **Juan Bautista de.** b. at Madrid, 1770; d. there, 1837. Spanish poet, author of *Emilia* (1803), *Poesías patrióticas* (3rd ed., 1815), and *Poesías líricas* (6th ed., 1829–32). A supporter of an absolute monarchy, he was made a royal councilor and chamberlain by Ferdinand VII (of Spain).

Arriba (är.rē′bȧ). Spanish Falangist newspaper founded in 1939. It reflects the point of view and policies of one faction of the Franco government.

¡Arriba España! (es.pä′nyä). Slogan of the Falange and of the nationalist forces during the Spanish Civil War (1936–39). The forces of the republican government used the slogan ¡Viva España!

Arrieta (är.ryā′tä), **Rafael Alberto.** b. at Rauch, Argentina, Oct. 28, 1889—. Argentine poet and critic, on the faculties of both La Plata and Buenos Aires universities. His verse, marked by simplicity of expression and form, is based on humble themes. Author of *Alma y momento* (1910), *Estío serrano* (1926), *Etudias en tres literaturas* (1940), *Don Gregório Beeche y los bibliografos americanistas de Chile y del Plata* (1941), *Antología poética* (1942), and *Centuria portena* (1944).

Arrigal (ar.i.gôl′), **Mount.** See **Errigal, Mount.**

Arrivabene (är.rē.vä.bā′nā), **Ferdinando.** b. at Mantua, Italy, 1770; d. there, June 29, 1834. Italian jurist and miscellaneous author.

Arrivabene, Count **Giovanni.** b. at Mantua, Italy, June 24, 1787; d. there, Jan. 11, 1881. Italian patriot and political economist. He was arrested by the Austrian government in 1820 for political activity and fled the country; he returned (1860) to Italy, where he was created a senator. He was for many years president of the Italian association of political economy.

Arröe (ar.ō′). See **Ærø.**

Arroe Islands (är′ö). See **Aroe Islands.**

Arrol (ar′ol), Sir **William.** b. in Scotland, 1839; d. at Ayr, Scotland, 1913. Scottish construction engineer and bridge builder. He established (1872) the Dalmarnock iron works, specializing in bridge building. After building the Caledonian railway bridge at Glasgow, he successfully undertook (1882–87) the reconstruction of the Tay bridge after its disastrous collapse. He also built the Forth Bridge (1882–89), as well as part of London's Tower Bridge and all of Cairo's Nile bridge.

Arrom (är.rōn′), **Cecilia Francisca Josefa de.** See **Caballero, Fernán.**

Arroux (ȧ.rö). River in E central France, a tributary of the Loire River, lying chiefly in the department of Saône-et-Loire. It flows past Autun. Length, ab. 75 mi.

Arrow (ar′ō), **Lough.** Small lake in Connacht province, Irish Republic, situated on the County Roscommon-County Sligo boundary, ab. 14 mi. SE of Sligo. Length, ab. 5 mi.; greatest width, ab. 3 mi.

Arrow and the Song, The. Poem by Henry Wadsworth Longfellow, published in *The Belfry of Bruges and Other Poems* (1845).

Arrow Lake, Upper and **Lower.** Expansions of the Columbia River in the SE part of British Columbia. Elevations: Upper Arrow, 1,395 ft., Lower Arrow, 1,379 ft.; areas: Upper Arrow, 88 sq. mi., Lower Arrow, 59 sq. mi.

Arrow of Gold. Novel (1919) by Joseph Conrad. It is a reworking of his earlier *The Mirror of the Sea.* Both books draw upon his own experiences when (1874) he made his way to Marseilles, where he was involved in gun-running adventures for the Spanish Carlists.

Arrowpoint (ar′ō.point), **Catharine.** In George Eliot's novel *Daniel Deronda*, a girl accomplished to a point of exasperating thoroughness, but possessing much good sense.

Arrowsmith (ar′ō.smith). Novel by Sinclair Lewis, published in 1925. Awarded a Pulitzer prize for this work, the author refused to accept it. The obstacles that confront a man of science in a society devoted to the pursuit of material success supply the theme of this novel.

Arrowsmith, Aaron. b. at Winston, England, July 14, 1750; d. at London, April 23, 1823. English geographer and cartographer. His publication of *A Chart of the World as on Mercator's projection, showing all the New Discoveries, etc.* (1790), *Map of Scotland* (1807), *Atlas of Southern India* (1822), and others, began a distinguished family enterprise, carried on by his sons and particularly by his nephew John Arrowsmith.

Arrowsmith, John. b. 1790; d. at London, May 1, 1873. English geographer and cartographer; nephew of Aaron Arrowsmith. He was one of the founders (1830) of the Royal Geographical Society. His *London Atlas* (1834) was the first of a long series of meticulous and authoritative cartographic works produced under his direction.

Arrowsmith's Map. Map published (Jan. 1, 1795) at London by Aaron Arrowsmith which bore the designation, *A Map Exhibiting All The New Discoveries In The Interior Part of North America.* It was a large-scale map printed on six sheets; at least 17 editions were brought out between 1795 and 1850.

Arroyo (är.rō′yō). Town and port of entry in SE Puerto Rico. 4,930 (1950).

Arroyo de China (dā chē′nä). Former name of **Concepción del Uruguay.**

Arroyo de la Luz (dā lä löth). [Also called **Arroyo, Arroyo del Puerco** (del pwer′kō).] Town in W Spain, in the province of Cáceres, W of Cáceres: center of an agricultural district. 10,265 (1940).

Arroyo del Río (del rē′ō), **Carlos Alberto.** b. 1893—. Ecuadorian statesman, president (1940–44) of Ecuador. He served as a national deputy (1922–23), and was later president of the chamber of deputies. He was also a professor, later dean of jurisprudence, at Guayaquil University. Elected president in January, 1940, he resigned following a coup d'état on May 28, 1944.

Arroyo Hondo (hon′dō). [Eng. trans., "*Deep Gorge.*"] Name of two deep sluices or gorges in New Mexico, one running W of Taos a distance of ab. 12 mi., the other running ab. 5 mi. S of Santa Fé toward the Santa Fé Creek. On the sides of the latter there are the ruins of two ancient villages of the Tehuas called Kukuä.

Arroyos y Esteros (är.rō′yōs ē es.tā′rōs). City in C Paraguay, in Cordillera department. Pop. ab. 20,000.

Arrua (ar′ö.ạ). See **Arawak.**

Arruda da Câmara (ạ.rö′dạ dạ ku′mạ.rạ), **Manoel.** b. in Alagôas, Brazil, 1752; d. at Pernambuco (now Recife), Brazil, 1810. Brazilian botanist and physician, author of various works on the economic botany of Brazil. He studied medicine in France and during the latter part of his life was a practicing physician at Pernambuco.

Arru Islands (är′ö). See **Aroe Islands.**

Arsaces I (är′sạ.sēz, är.sā′sēz). Founder of the Parthian kingdom. He is variously represented as the chief of a nomad tribe of Scythians, Bactrians, or Parthians who headed (c250 B.C.) a revolt of the Parthians against Syria, and established the independent kingdom of Parthia (250 B.C.–226 A.D.).

Arsacidae (är.sas′i.dē). Dynasty of Parthian kings, established by Arsaces I in c250 B.C. and overthrown by the Persians in 226 A.D. The most noteworthy of the Arsacidae are Phraates III (d. c60 B.C.), Orodes I (d. c37 B.C.), Phraates IV (d. c4 A.D.), Artabanus II (d. 44 A.D.), Vologeses I (d. c90 A.D.), and Chosroes (d. c122 A.D.).

Arsames (är′sạ.mēz). [Persian, **Arsama** (är.shä′mä).] The father of Hystaspes and grandfather of Darius I.

Arsames. Son of Darius I and a commander in the army of Xerxes I.

Arsames. Illegitimate son of Artaxerxes Mnemon.

Ars an der Mosel (ärs′ än dėr mō′zel). German name of **Ars-sur-Moselle.**

Arschot (är′sċhôt). See **Aerschot.**

Arsenal at Springfield, The. Poem by Henry Wadsworth Longfellow, published in *The Belfry of Bruges and Other Poems* (1845).

Arsenaria (är.sẹ.nãr′i.ạ). Latin name of **Arzeu.**

Arsenius (är.sē′ni.us), Saint. [Surnamed **"the Great."**] b. at Rome, c354; d. at Troë, near Memphis, Egypt, c450. Roman scholar who became famous as a monk in Egypt. He was for a time (c383–394) tutor to Arcadius and Honorius, sons of Theodosius the Great, and subsequently (394–434) a hermit under Saint John the Dwarf in the monastic wilderness of Scetis in Egypt. Driven from that refuge by an uprising of barbarians, he established himself at Troë until 444, going then to the island of Canopus for three years and finally returning to Troë.

Arsenius Autorianus (ar.sē′ni.us ô.tō.ri.ā′nus). fl. 13th century A.D. Patriarch of Constantinople, appointed, with Georgios Mouzalon, guardian of John IV Lascaris, son of the emperor Theodore II Lascaris. He was deposed and banished by the usurper Michael VIII Palaeologus, whom he had excommunicated for blinding John IV.

Arsh (ärsh). See **Arneb.**

Arsinoë (är.sin′ọ.ē). See also under **Fayum,** city.

Arsinoë. In ancient geography, a town in NE Egypt near the head of the Gulf of Suez.

Arsinoë. [Also, **Crocodilopolis.**] In ancient geography, a town in Lower Egypt, situated near Lake Moeris ab. 34 mi. SW of Memphis.

Arsinoé (är.sē.no.ā). In Molière's comedy *Le Misanthrope*, a woman whose advancing age and ugliness have forced her to give up being admired by men; she assumes a hypocritical and prudish kind of piety.

Arsinoë (är.sin'ǫ.ē). Opera by Thomas Clayton, produced in 1705. It was composed of a number of Italian songs which he brought with him from Italy and adapted to the words of an English play by Peter Motteux called *Arsinoë, Queen of Cyprus*. He called it his own composition. According to some critics, it was the first attempt to establish, in England, opera as it was produced in Italy.

Arsinoë. Ancient name of **Famagusta.**

Arsinoë I. fl. in Egypt, c280 B.C. The daughter of Lysimachus of Thrace, and first wife of Ptolemy II. Suspected of plotting against her husband's life, she was for a time banished to Coptos.

Arsinoë II. b. 316 B.C.; d. c270 B.C. Daughter of Ptolemy I of Egypt, wife of Lysimachus and, afterward, of Ptolemy II.

Arsinoë III. fl. c220 B.C. The wife of Ptolemy IV Philopator, by whose order she was put to death.

Arsinoë IV. Killed at Miletus, 41 B.C. Queen of Egypt in 47 B.C., put to death by Mark Antony at the instigation of her sister Cleopatra.

Arsonval (dȧr.sôṅ.vȧl), **Arsene d'.** b. 1851; d. 1940 French physicist and physician, notable as a pioneer in electrotherapy (he was the originator of the term "diathermy"). On the faculty of the Collège de France from 1882 until the early 1930's, he is remembered also for his development of the "D'Arsonval galvanometer."

Arsuf (är.söf'). Modern name of **Apollonia,** Palestine.

Arsuk Fjord (äċh'sůk). See under **Frederikshaab.**

Arta (är'tä). See also **Arakhthos.**

Artá (är.tä'). Town in the Balearic Islands, in the Spanish province of Baleares, situated near the E coast of the island of Majorca. Pop. ab. 8,000.

Arta (är'tä). *Nomos* (department) in NW Greece, in Epirus. Capital, Arta; pop. 72,738 (1951).

Arta. [Also: **Narda;** ancient names, **Ambracia, Arakhthos;** Latin, **Aracthus.**] City in NW Greece, the capital of the *nomos* (department) of Arta, situated on the Arakhthos River, N of the Ambracian Gulf. It was founded by the Corinthians in the 7th century B.C., and became the capital of Epirus under Pyrrhus in 295 B.C. In the 13th and 14th centuries it was the seat of the despots of Epirus; it was taken by the Turks in 1449, and by Ali Pasha in 1789. Here, in 1822, Reshid Pasha defeated the Greeks; it became a Greek city in 1881. It is the seat of a bishopric. 9,054 (1940).

Arta, Gulf of. See **Ambracian Gulf.**

Artabasdes (är.tą.baz'dēz). [Also, **Artabazes** (-bā'zēz).] Son of Tigranes the Great (king of Armenia), coruler with his father, and his successor c55–34 B.C.

Artabazus (är.tą.bā'zus). Persian general of the Parthians and Chorasmians in the campaigns of 480 and 479 B.C. He retreated to Asia after the defeat of Plataea.

Artabazus. fl. c362–328 B.C. Persian general under Artaxerxes II. He rebelled (c356) against Artaxerxes III, was pardoned (c349) through the intercession of Mentor, fought at Arbela (331) under Darius, and was made satrap of Bactria by Alexander.

Artabazus. In Xenophon's *Cyropedeia*, a Median, a friend and adviser of Cyrus.

Artachaees (är.tak.a'ēz). d. c481. Persian engineer who directed the construction of a canal across the Athos peninsula, near Acanthos, in Greece, to allow the passage of Xerxes's fleet in 480.

Artachshast (är.tak.shast') or **Artachshasta** (-shas'tą). In passages of the Old Testament (Ezra, iv. 7, 8; vi. 14; vii. 1, 11, 21; Neh. ii. 1, v. 14, xiii. 6), a name referring to Artaxerxes I.

Artagnan (dȧr.tȧ.nyäṅ; Anglicized, där.tan'yąn), **D'.** One of the principal characters in *The Three Musketeers* by the elder Alexandre Dumas, and also in its sequels.

Artagnon (dȧr.tȧ.nyôṅ), **Charles de Baatz d'.** [Also, **Artagnan.**] b. c1611; d. in the siege of Maastricht, 1673. French soldier, originally from Gascony. He was captain of musketeers for Louis XIV and is the prototype for the elder Dumas' character D'Artagnan, who appears in several novels, including *The Three Musketeers*.

Artamène, or The Grand Cyrus (ȧr.tȧ.men). Romance by Magdeleine de Scudéry, published in 1650 in ten volumes. Artamène is intended to represent the second Louis Condé, marshal of France and friend of Molière, Jean Baptiste Racine, and others.

Artaphernes (är.tą.fėr'nēz). fl. c500 B.C. Persian general; brother of Darius Hystaspis (of Persia), by whom he was appointed satrap of Sardis. He interfered ineffectually in behalf of Hippias, the expelled tyrant of Athens, and took part in suppressing the revolt (499–498 B.C.) of the Ionians against Persian rule.

Artaphernes. Persian general; son of the foregoing Persian general of the same name. He commanded, with Datis, the Persian army which invaded (490 B.C.) Greece and was defeated at Marathon, and led the Lydians in the expedition of Xerxes I against Greece some ten years later which ended in the naval defeat of the Persians at Salamis.

Artaxata (är.tak'są.tą). [Armenian, **Artashat** (är.tä-shät').] In ancient geography, the capital of Armenia in the 2nd and 1st centuries B.C., situated in the plain of the Araxes (modern Aras) River, probably NE of Ararat. It is said to have been built (180 B.C.) in accordance with a plan of Hannibal, destroyed (58 A.D.) by Nero's general Corbulo, and restored by Tiridates I.

Artaxerxes (är.tą.zėrk'sēz). See also **Ardashir.**

Artaxerxes I. [Surnamed **Longimanus,** meaning "the Long-handed"; name in the Old Testament, **Artachshast.**] King of Persia (c465–c425 B.C.); son of Xerxes I. His reign, which followed upon the assassination of his father, was marked by an Athenian uprising (c460 B.C.); he is presumed to have instigated the mission of Ezra and Nehemiah to Jerusalem, thus furthering Judaism. His forces were defeated (449 B.C.) on sea and land in the double action of Salamis in Cyprus. He won the epithet "Longimanus" because of the excessive length of his right hand.

Artaxerxes II. [Surnamed **Mnemon.**] King of Persia (c405–c361 B.C.); son of Darius II. He defeated (401) his younger brother Cyrus (who was killed in the battle) at Cunaxa, and concluded the Peace of Antalcidas with Sparta.

Artaxerxes III. [Surnamed **Ochus.**] King of Persia (c361–338 B.C.); son of Artaxerxes II. He reconquered Egypt and reduced Phoenicia, and was poisoned by the eunuch Bagoas, his chief minister. His reign was marked by violence and terror.

Artedi (är.tā'dē), **Peter.** [Latinized, **Petrus Arctedius.**] b. at Anund, Sweden, Feb. 22, 1705; drowned at Leiden or Amsterdam, Sept. 27, 1735. Swedish naturalist; friend of Carolus Linnaeus at Uppsala (1728–32), where Artedi was distinguished for his reclassification of ichthyology and where the two scientists willed their manuscripts to each other. Linnaeus published (1738) Artedi's *Bibliotheca Ichthyologia* and *Philosophia Ichthyologica,* with a biography.

Artegall (är'tę.gąl), **Sir.** [Also: **Arthegall, Artegal, Arthegal.**] In Edmund Spenser's *Faerie Queene,* a knight errant, the personification of Justice, supposed to have been intended to represent Arthur Grey, 14th Baron Grey de Wilton, Spenser's patron.

Arteijo (är.tā'hō). Commune in N Spain, in the province of La Coruña, situated on the Atlantic coast, ab. 6 mi. SW of the city of La Coruña: seaport; sardine fisheries. 10,528 (1940).

Artemas (är'tę.mąs). fl. 1st century A.D. Companion of Saint Paul and, according to tradition, bishop of Lystra.

Artemidorus Daldianus (är"tę.mi.dō'rus dal.di.ā'nus). fl. c170 A.D. Greek soothsayer of Daldis, in Lydia, author of a four-book treatise on the interpretation of dreams, valuable to modern scholars as a source of information on ancient rites and superstitions. He also wrote treatises on auspices (divination based upon the observation of birds) and on chirognomy (palmistry), but these have been lost.

Artemidorus of Cnidos (nī'dǫs). In Shakespeare's tragedy *Julius Caesar*, a teacher of rhetoric.

Artemidorus of Ephesus (ef'ę.sus). fl. c104–100 B.C. Greek geographer. He was at one time the Ephesian ambassador at Rome. He is better known, however, as the author of an 11-volume geographical work, now lost, largely based on earlier writers and in turn used by Strabo and others. It purported to deal with the whole "inhabited world," and attached much importance to physical geography and distances between places cited.

Artémire (år.tā.mēr). Tragedy by Voltaire, produced in 1720. It was not successful, and the author preserved the best of it in *Mariamne*, which was produced in 1724.

Artemis (är'tę.mis). [Latin, **Diana.**] In Greek mythology, one of the Olympian deities; daughter of Zeus and Leto, and twin sister of Apollo. She may be regarded as a feminine counterpart of Apollo. She chastised evil with her keen shafts and with deadly sickness, and also protected mortals from danger and pestilence. Unlike Apollo, she was not connected with poetry or divination, but, like him, she was a deity of light, and to her was attributed authority over the moon, which belonged more particularly to her kinswomen Hecate and Selene. In art Artemis is represented as a young woman of noble and severe beauty, tall and majestic, and generally bearing bow and quiver as the huntress or mountain goddess. She was identified by the Romans with their Diana, an original Italian divinity.

Artemis. A court lady in John Dryden's comedy *Marriage-à-la-Mode.*

Artemis, Temple of. See under **Ephesus.**

Artemisa (är.tā.mē'sä). City in W Cuba, in Pinar del Río Province. 13,084 (1943).

Artemisia (of *Caria*) (är.tę.miz'i.ą, -mish'i.ą). fl. middle of 4th century B.C. Queen of Caria, in Asia Minor, 352–c350 B.C. In memory of her husband Mausolus, she built at Halicarnassus the mausoleum which was reckoned by the ancients one of the seven wonders of the world. To give further proof of her affection she is said to have mixed her husband's ashes with a precious liquid and to have drunk the potion so prepared.

Artemisia (of *Halicarnassus*). fl. early 5th century B.C. Queen of Halicarnassus and vassal of Persia. She was an ally of Xerxes I and added her ships to his in the fleet which met defeat (480 B.C.) at the hands of the Greeks at Salamis. By tradition, she is said to have showed great valor at the battle.

Artemisium (är.tę.mish'i.um). In ancient geography, a promontory in N Euboea, Greece, near which occurred (480 B.C.) an indecisive naval battle between the Greeks under Eurybiades and the Persians under Achaemenes.

Artemovsk (är.tyô'mǫfsk). [Former name, **Bakhmut.**] City in the U.S.S.R. in the Ukrainian Soviet Socialist Republic, ab. 52 mi. N of Stalino by railroad. Salt is mined here, and the city is an important chemical center. 55,165 (1939).

Artemus Ward: His Book (är'tę.mus wôrd). Humorous prose work (1862) by Charles Farrar Browne. "Artemus Ward" was first introduced in 1858 in the pages of the Cleveland *Plain Dealer* as a traveling showman writing letters to the press and anxious to exhibit his wax works and a zoo. The name and character became so well known within a few years as completely to overshadow the actual name of Browne, their creator. Browne published only this and one other book, *Artemus Ward: His Travels* (1865). Both were widely read and frequently imitated, not only at the time of their first appearance but for many years thereafter.

Artenay (årt.ne). Village in N central France, in the department of Loiret, ab. 13 mi. N of Orléans. It was the scene of German victories in 1870. The buildings were largely destroyed during the Allied advance in 1944. Pop. 1,177 (1946).

Artesia (är.tē'zhą). Unincorporated community in S California, in Los Angeles County. 5,837 (1940), 14,446 (1950).

Artesia. City in SE New Mexico, in Eddy County: refining and shipping center for a petroleum-producing region. Angora goats are raised in the area. In the decade between the last two U.S. censuses the city's population doubled. 4,071 (1940), 8,244 (1950).

Artevelde (är'tę.vel.dę), **Jacob van.** [Also: **Arteveld**; called the **"Brewer of Ghent."**] b. at Ghent, c1290; killed there, 1345. Flemish popular leader, supposedly a brewer, chosen (1337) to represent Ghent during hostilities between England and France (at the beginning of the Hundred Years' War) which threatened Flemish trade. He made a treaty (1338) with England establishing Flemish neutrality and assuring Flemish weavers of their supply of English wool; by bringing Bruges and Ypres to the support of Ghent, he began the federation of Netherlands towns of which he became head. In 1339 he recognized Edward III's claim to France (thus also to the Netherlands); he also built up commerce, reviving communal institutions. Suspected of supporting Edward the Black Prince to replace Louis as count of Flanders, he was killed by a mob.

Artevelde, Philip van. [Also, **Arteveld.**] b. c1340; killed at Roosebeke, in what is now Belgium, 1382. Flemish popular leader; son of Jacob van Artevelde. He led the people of Ghent in a revolution (1381) against Count Louis of Flanders (son of his father's enemy) and defeated him at Bruges. He was thereafter for a short time in control of all Flanders, but was conquered and slain by an army of Charles VI of France, who came to Louis' support. His life is the subject of Sir Henry Taylor's tragedy, *Philip van Artevelde* (1834).

Artevelde, Philip van. Play by Sir Henry Taylor published in 1834. It was an attempt to revive the traditions of the tragic school of Marlowe and Shakespeare.

Arth (ärt). Town in C Switzerland, in the canton of Schwyz, at the S tip of the Lake of Zug: the starting point of a railway up the Rigi Mountain. 5,146 (1941).

Arthénice (år.tā.nēs). Anagram of "Catherine" (the marquise de Rambouillet), invented by the poets François de Malherbe and Jean Baptiste Racine.

Arthur (är'thėr). fl. c6th century. British chieftain who led armies against the invading Saxons. He was first celebrated as an actual person by the Welsh chronicler Nennius (c796), according to whom Arthur defended the Christian cause against the pagan Saxons in many battles, including the great victory at the Mount of Badon (c516). Later historians add his death (537) at the battle of Camlan (*Annales Cambriae*, c956) and burial at Glastonbury (Giraldus Cambrensis, c1195). Tales added to history, which originated in Brythonic mythology, spread through Europe by Welsh, Cornish, and Breton troubadours, built up the Arthurian Cycle (*q.v.*) of legend, so that he appears in Geoffrey of Monmouth's *Historia Regum Britanniae* (1147) as king of all western Europe and becomes part of French, German, and Italian lore. According to tradition he was the illegitimate son of Uther Pendragon, and demonstrated his royalty by drawing a sword from a stone when a boy; he fought with the miraculous sword Excalibur given him by the Lady of the Lake, and was the leader of the Knights of the Round Table at Camelot (variously identified, possibly Caerleon, in Monmouthshire). He is the subject of European and British literary tradition, chiefly through the writings of Sir Thomas Malory, down to Alfred Lord Tennyson and William Morris.

Arthur (of *Brittany*). b. at Nantes, France, March 29, 1187; killed at Rouen, France, April 3, 1203. Count (or duke) of Brittany; posthumous son of Geoffrey Plantagenet. He was murdered probably by order of his uncle, King John, who feared him as a claimant to the English throne. He is a leading character in Shakespeare's *King John.*

Arthur, Chester Alan. b. at Fairfield, Vt., Oct. 5, 1830; d. at New York, Nov. 18, 1886. American statesman, 21st President of the United States (1881–85). He graduated from Union College, New York, in 1848, and married in 1859 Ellen Lewis Herndon (1837–80), daughter of an officer in the U.S. navy. He served as a lawyer at New York, was on the staff of the governor of New York during the Civil War, and was inspector general and quartermaster general of New York state. An active Republican, he was appointed (1871) collector of the port of New York by President Grant, but removed (1878) from that office by President Hayes because of undue political activity. Elected (1880) Republican vice-president, he became president on Garfield's death (1881), serving to 1885. He gave earnest support to the Pendleton Civil Service Reform Bill passed (1883) in his administration, prosecuted with some vigor but without effective convictions the Star Route frauds in the Post Office Department, courageously vetoed an extravagant Rivers and Harbors appropriation bill passed (1882) by Congress, and approved laws modernizing the U.S. navy.

Arthur, Joseph Charles. b. at Lowville, N.Y., Jan. 11, 1850; d. April 30, 1942. American botanist, professor at Purdue and staff member of the Indiana Agricultural Experiment Station (1887–1915). He is best known for his work in the physiology and pathology of vegetables, particularly in reference to fungous diseases and rusts.

Arthur, Julia. [Pseudonym of **Ida Lewis.**] b. at Hamilton, Ont., May 3, 1869; d. at Boston, Mass., March 28, 1950. Actress. She first appeared at London with Henry Irving at the Lyceum in 1895. Her New York performances included *A Lady of Quality*, *As You Like It*, and *More than Queen*.

Arthur, King. In Henry Fielding's burlesque *Tom Thumb the Great*, a "passionate sort of king," husband to Dollallolla (of whom he is afraid) and in love with Glumdalca.

Arthur, Mount. See under **Grinnell Land.**

Arthur, Timothy Shay. b. near Newburgh, N.Y., June 6, 1809; d. at Philadelphia, March 6, 1885. American journalist, of whose many editing ventures only *Arthur's Home Magazine* (1850–85) was successful. He was also a prolific writer of moral tales and tracts, particularly on temperance, the best known of which is *Ten Nights in a Barroom and What I Saw There* (1854).

Arthur Clarington (klar'ing.tọn), **Sir.** See **Clarington, Sir Arthur.**

Arthur Clennam (klen'ạm). See **Clennam, Arthur.**

Arthurian Cycle of Romances (är.thū'ri.ạn), **The.** Series of romances relating to the exploits of Arthur and his knights. They were Breton romances amplified in Wales and adopted at the court of the Plantagenets as the foundation of the epic of chivalry.

Arthur Kill (är'thur kil). [Former name, **Staten Island Sound.**] Arm of the Atlantic which separates Staten Island from New Jersey, and connects Newark Bay on the N with Raritan Bay on the S.

Arthur's (är'thėrz). London club established in 1765. It was named from the former keeper of White's Chocolate House, who died in 1761.

Arthur's Seat. Hill in S Scotland, in Midlothian, in the SE quarter of the city of Edinburgh. It has an extensive view of the city. 822 ft.

Arthur's Show. A representation, principally an exhibition of archery, by 58 city worthies who called themselves by the names of the Knights of the Round Table, referred to in Shakespeare's *Henry IV, Part II*.

Arthus (är.tü), **Nicolas Maurice.** b. at Angers, Maine-et-Loire, France, Jan. 9, 1862; d. 1945. French experimental physiologist. He became (1890) *chef de conférence physiologiques* at the Sorbonne, was appointed (1896) professor of physiology at the University of Fribourg, Switzerland, was named (1900) *chef de laboratoire* at the Pasteur Institute at Lille, and was called (1907) to the chair of physiology at the University of Lausanne, Switzerland. He is known for his discovery (1903) of a form of allergy, the so-called Arthus phenomenon, and is credited with the first mention (1890) of the essential role of calcium in the mechanics of blood coagulation. Author of *Coagulation des liquides de l'organisme* (1894), *Précis de chimie physiologique* (1895), *Nature des enzymes* (1896), *Injections répétées de sérum du cheval chez le lapin* (1903), *De l'anaphylaxie à l'immunité* (1921), and *Précis de physiologie microbienne* (1921).

Artibonite (är.tē.bo.nēt). [French, **Rivière Artibonite**; Spanish, **Río Artibonito** (är"tē.bō.nē'tō).] River in the W Dominican Republic and C Haiti.

Artichofsky (är.tē.shôf'skē), **Crestofle d' Artischau.** [Also, **Arciszewski.**] b. in Poland, c1585; date of death unknown. Polish soldier who entered (1623) the service of the Dutch West India Company, and distinguished himself in the wars (1631–39) with the Portuguese in Brazil. He returned (1637) to Holland, and was sent back (December, 1638) in command of a reinforcement, with a rank so high that it conflicted with the powers of the Dutch governor. A quarrel ensued, and in 1639 Artichofsky was ordered back to Holland.

Article 10. Article of the Covenant of the League of Nations stating that League members would undertake to "respect and preserve as against external aggression the territorial integrity and existing political independence of all members." In case of aggression or its threat the Council was to "advise upon means" to fulfill the obligation. Its precise meaning and obligation was subject to much dispute, particularly in the U.S. Senate during debates on the League. Though cited in several instances, the article was never invoked. It is, nevertheless, the best known and most often mentioned of the articles that made up the Covenant of the League.

Articles of Confederation. See **Confederation, Articles of.**

Articles of Prague (präg). See under **Calixtines.**

Artifice, The. Comedy by Susannah Centlivre.

Artigas (är.tē'gäs). Department in N Uruguay, bounded by Argentina and Brazil. Gem stones are mined here. Capital, Artigas; area, 4,393 sq. mi.; pop. 57,854 (est. 1947).

Artigas. [Also, **San Eugenio.**] City in N Uruguay, capital of Artigas department, near the Brazilian border: agricultural center. Pop. ab. 16,500.

Artigas, José Gervasio. b. near Montevideo, Uruguay, c1774; d. in Paraguay, Sept. 23, 1850. Uruguayan revolutionary general, national hero, and dictator (1811–20). He entered the general South American revolution against Spain in 1811, but repudiated the revolutionary junta at Buenos Aires, and compelled the cession of Uruguay to his group by the defeat of Buenos Aires forces in 1814. His power waned after he sustained military defeat in 1817, and he was finally (1820) forced into exile in Paraguay. Uruguay later honored him by naming a town and a province after him.

Artist of the Beautiful, The. Allegorical story by Nathaniel Hawthorne, originally published (1844) in the *Democratic Review* and collected in *Mosses from an Old Manse* (1846).

Art of Fugue, The. [German, **Die Kunst der Fuge.**] Set of contrapuntal compositions (1749) by Johann Sebastian Bach furnishing practical examples of technique. Long considered merely study material, the fugues were subsequently arranged for two pianos, for orchestra, and for string quartet.

Artois (är.twä). Region and former province in N France, corresponding nearly to the modern department of Pas-de-Calais. The capital was Arras. The name may be derived from Latin *Atrebates*, name of a Celtic tribe inhabiting the district in the time of Caesar. It was a county under Flemish rule in the Middle Ages, was annexed to France under Philip Augustus in 1180, made a countship by Saint Louis in 1237 for his brother Robert, and passed to Philip the Bold of Burgundy in 1384; on the death of Charles the Bold it was temporarily taken (1477) by Louis XI of France. It passed, by the marriage (1477) of Mary of Burgundy with Maximilian of Austria, to the Hapsburgs, and was ceded in part to France in 1659, the cession being completed in the treaties of Nijmegen (1678–79).

Artois, Battles of. Two battles of World War I, the major French attempt to capitalize fully on the German retreat from the Marne in September, 1914. The first battle (Sept. 27–Oct. 10, 1914) brought no real gains for the French. The later battle of Artois (May 9–June 18, 1915) gave General Henri Philippe Pétain's forces slender advances on a narrow front, with heavy casualties and no significant improvement in position.

Artois (där.twä), **Comte d'.** See **Charles X** (of *France*).

Artois, Henri Charles Ferdinand Marie Dieudonné d'. See **Chambord,** Comte de.

Artôt (är.tō), **Alexandre Joseph.** b. at Brussels, Jan. 25, 1815; d. at Ville d'Avray, France, July 20, 1845. Belgian composer and concert violinist; son of Maurice Montagney Artôt (1772–1829).

Artôt, Jean Désiré. b. at Paris, 1803; d. in Belgium, 1887. Belgian horn player and music teacher; son of Maurice Montagney Artôt (1772–1829).

Artôt, Marguerite Joséphine Désirée. b. at Paris, July 21, 1835; d. at Berlin, April 3, 1907. Belgian operatic soprano; daughter of Jean Désiré Artôt (1803–87).

Artôt, Maurice Montagney. [Original surname, **Montagney.**] b. at Gray, France, 1772; d. at Brussels, 1829. Belgian band conductor and horn player. The name Artôt, which he adopted for professional use, was later used by his entire family.

Artotyrites (är.tọ.tī'rīts). Sect in the primitive Christian church which used bread and cheese in the Eucharist, alleging that the first oblations of man were the fruits of the earth and the produce of their flocks. They admitted women to the priesthood and to the episcopate.

Art Poëtique (år po ā.tĕk). Critical work (1674) by Nicolas Boileau-Despréaux, translated (1683) into English, shortly after its publication, by Sir William Soames and John Dryden.

Artsybashev (är.tsi.bä'shif), **Mikhail Petrovich.** See **Artzybashev, Mikhail Petrovich.**

Artusi (är.tö'sē), **Giovanni Maria.** b. at Bologna, Italy, c1550; d. Aug. 18, 1613. Italian composer and musical theorist. He opposed Claudio Monteverdi and others who urged changes in musical theory. Author of *Delle imperfezioni della musica moderna* (1600, 1603), which upholds his views. He was a composer chiefly of religious music. Among his writings are *Arte del contrapunto ridotta in tavole* (1586, 1589) and *Considerazioni musicali* (1607).

Artvin (ärt.vēn'). See **Çoruh.**

Artzybasheff (är.tsi.bä'shif), **Boris Mikhailovich.** b. at Kharkov, Russia, 1899—. American illustrator and author; son of Mikhail Petrovich Artzybashev. After serving (1918–19) in the Ukrainian army, he arrived in the U.S. in 1919 and became a citizen in 1926. Known for magazine illustrations, perhaps most notably for his covers for *Time,* he is the author of *Poor Shaydullah* (1931), *Seven Simeons* (1937), and others.

Artzybashev (är.tsi.bä'shif), **Mikhail Petrovich.** [Also, **Artsybashev.**] b. at Kharkov, Russia, 1878; d. at Warsaw, 1927. Russian novelist and playwright; a great-grandson of Thaddeus Kosciusko and father of Boris Artzybasheff. He began his career as a caricaturist. He made a sensation with the novel *Sanine* (1907; Eng. trans., 1915), which, with others of his works, was forbidden by the imperial government and the Bolsheviks alike for its protest against restraints of all kinds (although the work is perhaps best known for its opposition to sexual restraint). He founded the anarchist journal *Svoboda,* several times suppressed, which he later revived in Poland, attacking the Soviet regime. Author also of *The Breaking Point* (Eng. trans., 1915), *Ivan Lande* (Eng. trans., 1915), *Tales of the Revolution* (Eng. trans., 1917); the plays *War* (Eng. trans., 1916), *Jealousy* (Eng. trans., 1917), *The Law of the Savage* (Eng. trans., 1923), *Lovers and Enemies* (produced 1927), and others.

Aruba (ä.rö'bä). [Also, **Oruba.**] Island in the Caribbean Sea, N of Venezuela: a possession of the Netherlands, part of Curaçao. It is the site of one of the largest petroleum refineries in the world, and the refining of Venezuelan oil is the principal industry. There have been many experiments in hydroponics (soilless gardening), and gold mining was formerly important. Chief town, Oranjestad; area, ab. 70 sq. mi.; pop. 51,110 (1949).

Arucas (ä.rö'käs). Town in the Canary Islands, in the Spanish province of Santa Cruz de Tenerífe, situated on the W shore of the island of Gomera: sugar and bananas are produced. 21,804 (1940).

Arucati (ä.rö.kä'tē). A Tamil name of **Arcot.**

Aru Islands (ä'rö). See **Aroe Islands.**

Arumu (ar'u.mö). See under **Aram.**

Arundel (ar'un.dẹl). Municipal borough in SE England, in West Sussex, situated at the water-gap of the river Arun through the Downs, ab. 19 mi. W of Brighton, ab. 59 mi. SW of London by rail. It is known for Arundel Castle, the seat of the dukes of Norfolk. 2,680 (1951).

Arundel. Horse of Sir Bevis of Hampton in some versions of the Arthurian legend and in Michael Drayton's *Polyolbion.*

Arundel, Earl of. Title held by various members of the **Howard** family.

Arundel, Thomas. [Family surname, **Fitzalan.**] b. 1353; d. 1414. English prelate. He was archbishop of Canterbury (1396–97, 1399–1412), and was involved, with his brother Richard Fitzalan, the 4th Earl of Arundel, in the struggle between Richard II and Parliament. As bishop of Ely (1374–88), he was instrumental in inducing the king to submit to Parliament, which set up a council of regency (that included his brother), made Thomas chancellor in 1386, and imposed sentences of treason on the king's advisers. He became archbishop of York in 1388. Declaring himself of age, the king deprived Thomas of the chancellorship in 1389, and later (1397) secured his impeachment and banishment for complicity in the regency of 1386. A year before this happened, Thomas had been made archbishop of Canterbury, but his occupancy of this office was now interrupted. Returning with Henry of Lancaster in 1399, Thomas conspired with him to prevent Richard's escape, crowned him Henry IV, was restored by him to Canterbury and the chancellorship (1399, 1407, 1412). He played a chief role in the execution of Sir John Oldcastle and other Lollards.

Arundel Club. [Original name, **Arundel Society.**] An English society for the promotion of art, founded at London in 1849. It was known as the Arundel Society until 1897, when for a period of some seven years it became inactive, and reappeared in the first decade of the 20th century as the Arundel Club.

Arundel House. House belonging to the earls of Arundel (in the Howard line), which formerly stood near Highgate, London. Francis Bacon died there in 1626.

Arundel House. Mansion belonging to the earls of Arundel (in the Howard line) which formerly stood on the Strand, London, where Arundel, Norfolk, Surrey, and Howard streets now are. In its gardens were originally placed the Arundel Marbles.

Arundell (ar'un.dẹl), Lady **Blanche.** b. 1583; d. at Winchester, England, 1649. English royalist; daughter of Edward Somerset, 4th Earl of Worcester (1553–1638). She is remembered for her stout nine-day defense (1643) of Wardour Castle in Wiltshire with 25 men against some 1,300 Parliamentarians during the English Civil War. The castle was recovered for Charles I the following year by her son, Henry Arundell.

Arundell, Henry. [Title, 3rd Baron **Arundell of Wardour.**] b. c1606; d. at Breamore, England, 1694. English statesman and son of Lady Blanche Arundell. In 1644 he dislodged the Parliamentarians who had captured (1643) the Arundell family estate of Wardour Castle and made it once again a stronghold for the forces of Charles I. Imprisoned (1678) for allegedly plotting against Charles II, he became after his release in 1678 privy councillor (1686) and keeper of the privy seal (1687).

Arundell, Isabel. Maiden name of **Burton,** Lady **Isabel.**

Arundell, Thomas. [Title, 1st Baron **Arundell of Wardour.**] b. 1562; d. at Oxford, England, 1639. English soldier of fortune and father-in-law of Lady Blanche Arundell. He was made a count of the Holy Roman Empire by the emperor Rudolph II for his service (1595) against the Turks in Hungary. He was said to have been a great favorite of Queen Elizabeth, and was created baron Arundell of Wardour by James I in 1605.

Arundel (or **Oxford**) **Marbles.** Part of a group of ancient sculptures and antiquities collected by Thomas Howard, 14th Earl of Arundel, presented to the University of Oxford in 1667. It includes the Parian Chronicle, a marble slab detailing events in Greek history.

Arunta Desert (ạ.run'tạ). [Also, **Simpson Desert.**] Name given to the C desert area of Australia E of the telegraph line that links the S coast of the continent to Darwin on the N coast. Elongated in shape, it is an uninhabited region of dunes and dry salt lakes. The name "Arunta" was first applied (c1930) to the area by Griffith Taylor, an Australian geographer. Area, ab. 43,500 sq. mi.

Arusha (ạ.rö'shạ). Town and district in E Africa, in Tanganyika Territory, situated on the slopes of Mount Meru in the center of the coffee-growing district. The town is the terminus of the railway to Tanga on the coast (ab. 272 mi.). The district is a rich agricultural one and has had extensive European settlement. Pop. of district, 840 Europeans (1946).

Aruwimi (ä.rö.wē'mẹ). River in C Africa, a western affluent of the Congo River, which eventually joins the Congo in N central Belgian Congo. It runs through a thick forest region. On its banks was Sir Henry Morton Stanley's Yambuya camp. Length, ab. 800 mi.

Arvad (är'vad). Old Testament name of **Aradus.**

Arval Brothers (är'vạl). In ancient Rome, a priesthood of 12 members, including the emperor, who offered public sacrifices for the fertility of the fields.

Arve (årv). River in the department of Haute-Savoie, E France, which rises in the Col de Balme, traverses the valley of Chamonix, and joins the Rhone River ab. 1 mi. S of Geneva. Length, ab. 50 mi.

Arverni (är.vėr'nī). Gallic name of **Auvergne.**

Arveyron (är.vä.rôn̄). River in E France, a tributary of the Arve River, the outlet of the Mer de Glace. It joins the Arve in the valley of Chamonix.

Arvida (är.vī′dạ). Industrial city in Quebec, Canada, situated on the Saguenay River ab. 25 mi. E of Lake St. John. One of the great centers of Canadian aluminum production, it derives its power from the Shipshaw Dam and power-development project. The bulk of the ore processed at Arvida is imported from British Guiana. 11,078 (1951).

Arvika (är.vē′kä). Town in S Sweden, in the *län* (county) of Värmland, W of Stockholm. It has lumber industries. 14,938 (1949).

Arvin (är′vin). Unincorporated community in S California, in Kern County near Bakersfield. 5,007 (1950).

Arviragus (är.vir′ạ.gus). Knight, the husband of Dorigen, in the *Franklin's Tale*, by Geoffrey Chaucer.

Arviragus. In British mythology, a mythical son of Cymbeline. In Shakespeare's *Cymbeline* he is the real son of Cymbeline, but is brought up as Cadwal, the son of Belarius, who is disguised as Morgan.

Arwad (är.wäd′). A modern name of **Aradus.**

Arwand (är.vänd′). See **Alwand.**

Arwidsson (är′vits.sôn), **Adolf Ivar.** b. at Padasjoki, Finland, Aug. 7, 1791; d. at Viborg (now Vyborg, in the U.S.S.R.), June 21, 1858. Swedish poet and historian. A docent in history (1817–22) at Åbo, he was dismissed for his criticism of the university and later banished for his pamphlet against the Russian government; he served as director of the royal library, Stockholm (1843 *et seq.*). Author of *Svenska fornsånger* (1834–42), a collection of Swedish folk songs, also of collected poems (1832), and others.

Arx (ärks), **Cäsar von.** b. at Basel, Switzerland, May 23, 1895; d. at Nieder-Erlinsbach, Switzerland, 1949. Swiss dramatist writing in German. He attained wide European recognition with his highly effective and at the same time often deeply philosophical plays, notably *Der Verrat von Novara* (1933), *Der heilige Held* (1936), and *Brüder in Christo* (1947).

Aryana (ăr.i.an′ạ). Ancient name of **Afghanistan.**

Arzamas (är.zä.mäs′). City in the U.S.S.R., in the Russian Soviet Federated Socialist Republic, ab. 60 mi. S of Gorki. On the rail line between Moscow and Kazan, it is a shipping point for the agricultural produce of the vicinity. Pop. ab. 19,000.

Arzano (är.dzä′nō). Town and commune in S Italy, in the *compartimento* (region) of Campania, in the province of Napoli, N of Naples. It belongs to the metropolitan district of Naples, and produces vegetables and fruit for the Neapolitan markets. Pop. of commune, 10,819 (1936); of town, 10,710 (1936).

Arzeu (är.zē.ö′). [Also: **Arzew;** Latin, **Arsenaria.**] Port in Oran department, Algeria. Extensive improvements in the port facilities have been made in recent years. Arzeu is one of the main North African centers for the export of esparto grass. 8,805 (1936).

Arzignano (är.dzē.nyä′nō). See **Arcignano.**

Arz von Straussenburg (ärts ′fon shtrou′sẹn.bu̇rk), **Artur von.** b. at Hermannstadt, in the Transylvanian Alps, June 16, 1857; d. 1935. Austro-Hungarian general. As a commander on the Eastern front in World War I, he opposed (1915) Russian attacks at Brest-Litovsk, and later served in Rumania. In 1917 he replaced Conrad von Hötzendorf as chief of the Austrian general staff.

Aš (äsh). [German, **Asch.**] Town in Czechoslovakia, in the extreme NW corner of Bohemia, ab. 15 mi. NW of Cheb in the immediate vicinity of the German border (Bavaria and Saxony), situated in a narrow strip of Czech territory protruding into German territory. Aš was the home town of the Sudeten-German leader Konrad Henlein, who supported the separation of Sudetenland from Czechoslovakia. Until 1945 a number of industries were located in the town itself as well as in the surrounding region, especially various textile industries including hosiery mills and dyeing establishments; also tanneries, shoe factories, breweries, sawmills, and others. Most of them, however, have now been transferred either to Germany or to the interior of Czechoslovakia. The German population, predominantly Lutheran in religion, has departed. From 1930 to 1947 the population declined from 22,930 to 11,378.

As (äs). In Old Norse mythology, a member of one of the principal races of gods, the inhabitants of Asgard. There were two groups, the high gods, the Aesir, and the Vanir, who dwelt in Vanaheim (Old Norse, *Vanaheimr*). They were originally at war with each other, but were subsequently reconciled, and several of the Vanir (Njord, Frey, and Freya) were received into Asgard.

Asa (ā′sạ). d. c875 B.C. King of Judah (c917–c875 B.C.); son of Abijam or Abijah. A vigorous opponent of idolatry (2 Chron. xiv–xvi), he recaptured Ramah from the Israelite king Baasha with the help of Benhadad of Damascus; he was succeeded by his son Jehoshaphat (1 Kings, xv).

Asaheim (ä′sä.hīm). See **Asgard.**

Asahikawa (ä.sä.hẹ.kä.wä) or **Asahigawa** (-gä-). City in Japan, in W central Hokkaido. It is a trading and distribution point for the agricultural products (particularly rice) of the area surrounding it. 123,238 (1950).

Asakasa Pagoda (ä.sä.kä.sä). Buddhist tower in Tokyo, Japan. It consists of five square red-lacquered stages with widely projecting roofs upturned at the corners, from which bells are suspended, and is surmounted by a tall hooped finial.

Asamayama (ä.sä.mä.yä.mä). [Also, **Mount Asama.**] Volcano on the island of Honshu, Japan, ab. 75 mi. NW of Tokyo. 8,341 ft.

Asángaro (ä.säng′gä.rō). [Also, **Azángaro.**] Village in SE Peru, in Puno department, in the basin of Lake Titicaca. Pop. under 5,000 (1940).

Asaph (ā′sạf). In Biblical history, a musician (or family of musicians) in the time of David. From him the choristers of the temple at Jerusalem were called the "sons of Asaph."

Asaph. The name under which Nahum Tate wrote of John Dryden in the second part of *Absalom and Achitophel* (the part which was written originally almost entirely by Tate and edited by Dryden).

Asben (az.ben′). See **Air.**

Asberg (äs′berk). See **Asperg.**

Asbestos (az.bes′tọs). Town in S Quebec, Canada, ab. 35 mi. N of Sherbrooke. It derives its name from the large asbestos mines located nearby. 8,190 (1951).

Asbjørnsen (äs′byėrn.sẹn), **Peter Christen.** b. at Christiania (now Oslo), Norway, Jan. 15, 1812; d. there, Jan. 6, 1885. Norwegian folklorist and zoölogist. He was so closely associated with the poet Jörgen Engebretsen Moe in such works as *Norske Folkeeventyr* (1842–44) that their names are virtually never mentioned separately, although Asbjörnsen did publish by himself *Norske Huldreeventyr og Folksagn* (1845). His zoölogical work was all but forsaken at an early date in favor of folklorism.

Asboth (as′both; Hungarian, ôsh′bōt), **Sándor.** b. at Keszthely, Hungary, Dec. 18, 1811; d. at Buenos Aires, Jan. 21, 1868. American general, active with the Union army in the Civil War. He arrived in the U.S. (1851) with Kossuth, under whom he had previously fought in the Hungarian rebellion of 1848–49; having volunteered for the Union army at the outbreak of Civil War, he commanded divisions under John Charles Frémont and Newton Martin Curtis; when he resigned (1865) he held the brevet rank of major general. He also served as U.S. minister (1866–68) to the Argentine republic. He was generally referred to in the U.S. as "Alexander Asboth," "Alexander" being the English form of "Sándor."

Asbru (äs′brö). See **Bifrost.**

Asbury (az′ber″i, -bẹ.ri), **Francis.** b. near Birmingham, England, Aug. 20 (or 21), 1745; d. at Spottsylvania, Va., March 31, 1816. American Methodist Episcopal clergyman, the first to hold the rank of bishop in the colonies. He landed (1771) at Philadelphia and was appointed (1772) John Wesley's superintendent in America, but was superseded (1773) by Thomas Rankin; his fierce religious convictions led to friction with Rankin, resulting in Asbury's recall (1775) to England by Wesley. Asbury disobeyed the order and remained, aligning himself with the growing movement for political separation from England, becoming a Delaware citizen (1778), and anticipating the split with English Methodism which appeared inevitable. Ordained a Methodist superintendent in 1784, he shortly thereafter took the title of bishop, which he retained until his death.

Asbury, Herbert. b. at Farmington, Mo., Sept. 1, 1891—. American journalist and author. Educated at Baptist College and Carleton College, he served in World War I, worked on the staff of the New York *Sun* (1916–20), New York *Herald* (1920–24), and New York *Herald Tribune* (1924–28) before becoming an associate editor of *Collier's* magazine. He is the author of a life of Francis Asbury, *A Methodist Saint* (1927), *The Gangs of New York* (1928), *Life of Carry Nation* (1929), *The Barbary Coast* (1933), *The French Quarter* (1936), *Sucker's Progress* (1938), *Gem of the Prairie* (1940), *The Golden Flood* (1942), and *The Great Illusion* (1950).

Asbury Park. City in C New Jersey, in Monmouth County, on the Atlantic Ocean, ab. 6 mi. S of Long Branch and ab. 35 mi. S of New York: summer resort. 17,094 (1950).

ASC. See **Air Service Command.**

Ascagne (ȧs.kȧny'). Name given to the daughter of Albert, in Molière's comedy *Le Dépit Amoureux*. She is substituted for her brother Ascagne, who is dead, and appears in his dress. However, she reveals herself as actually a woman by falling in love with Valère, whom she contrives to marry secretly.

Ascalon (as'ka.lon). See also **Ashkelon.**

Ascalon. Sword of Saint George, in the collection of medieval tales known as the *Seven Champions of Christendom.*

Ascania (as.kā'ni.a), **Lake.** [Modern Turkish, **İsnik** or **Iznik.**] In ancient geography, a lake in Bithynia, Asia Minor, draining finally into the Sea of Marmara. Nicaea was situated at its E extremity. Length, ab. 11 mi.

Ascanio (as.kä'ni.ō). Page in Philip Massinger's play *The Bashful Lover.*

Ascanio. Son of Don Henriques, in John Fletcher and Philip Massinger's play *The Spanish Curate.* He is a modest, affectionate boy of great tenderness.

Ascanio. Page in John Dryden's play *The Assignation.*

Ascanius (as.kā'ni.us). [Also, **Iulus.**] In classical legend, the son of Aeneas and (in the Roman version) the ancestor of the Roman Julii.

ASCAP. Abbreviation of **American Society of Composers, Authors, and Publishers.**

Ascapart (as'ka.pärt) or **Ascabart** (-bärt). Giant in the romance of *Sir Bevis of Hampton.* Bevis conquered him. He is said to have been 30 feet high. There are frequent allusions to him by the Elizabethan writers.

Ascásubi (äs.kä'sö.ʙē), **Hilario.** b. in Argentina, 1807; d. 1875. Argentine poet of the gaucho, who was variously a runaway schoolboy, sailor, soldier, prisoner, and exile. Both his major works were published outside his own country; *Paulino Lucero* (1839–51) is a collection of anti-Rosas ballads written during the siege of Montevideo, while *Santos Vega, el payador* is a gaucho epic completed (1872) at Paris. Between 1852 and 1860 he wrote political commentary in prose and verse for *Aniceto el gallo*, a Buenos Aires periodical.

Ascension (a.sen'shon). Island of volcanic origin in the South Atlantic Ocean, ab. 900 mi. NW of St. Helena. For administrative purposes, it is classed as a part of the British colony of St. Helena. Until 1922 the island was administered by officials of the British navy. It was important as a base of operations in World War II. Area, 38 sq. mi.; pop. 169 (1940).

Ascensión (ä.sen.syōn'). Town in NW Mexico, in Chihuahua state, ab. 12 mi. S of the boundary line of New Mexico. Ruins of considerable archaeological interest exist in the vicinity, along the Casas Grandes River. Pop. under 5,000 (1940).

Ascension Bay (a.sen'shon). [Spanish, **Bahía de la Ascensión** (ä.sen.syōn').] Arm of the Caribbean Sea, off the coast of Quintana Roo territory, SE Mexico.

Ascension Day. [Also, **Feast of the Ascension.**] Christian feast day falling on the last Thursday before Pentecost, commemorating the ascent of Christ into Heaven.

Ascensius (a.sen'shus, -shi.us), **Jodocus Badius.** See **Badius, Jodocus.**

Ascent of F. 6, The. Play (1936) by Wystan Hugh Auden and Christopher Isherwood.

Asch (äsh). German name of **Aš.**

Asch, Sholem. [Prename also written: **Shalom** or **Sholom.**] b. at Kutno, near Warsaw, Poland, Nov. 1, 1880—. American novelist and playwright, notable for works in both Yiddish and English. He was educated in rabbinical theology in his native village, and moved (1899) to Warsaw, where he began his career as an author, writing at first in Hebrew and then in Yiddish. He settled (1914) in the U.S., of which he became (1920) a naturalized citizen. His novels and short stories include *The Mother* (1930), *Three Cities* (1933), *Salvation* (1934), *The War Goes On* (1936), *The Nazarene* (1939), *Children of Abraham* (1942), *The Apostle* (1943), *East River* (1946), *Mary* (1949), and *Moses* (1951). Among his plays are *Mottke the Thief* (1917; new trans., 1935) and *The God of Vengeance* (1918). He is also the author of *What I Believe* (1941).

Aschaffenburg (ä.shäf'en.bůrk). City in S Germany, in the *Land* (state) of Bavaria, American Zone, in the *Kreis* (district) of Lower Franconia, situated on the Main River, ab. 23 mi. SE of Frankfort on the Main: cement and béton works; shoe, leather, felt, hosiery, garment, and paper factories; brewery. It is a river port, with trade in lumber, coal, and stone. The castle, erected in 1605–14, one of the finest examples of the German Renaissance style, with a valuable library and collections of paintings and etchings, along with other monuments and a large part of the town, was destroyed during the latter part of World War II. The decrease of population in the period 1939–46 was 19.8 percent. 36,383 (1946), 45,499 (1950).

Ascham (as'kam), **Roger.** b. at Kirby Wiske, Yorkshire, England, 1515; d. at London, 1568. English classical scholar and author. At St. John's College, Cambridge (B.A., 1534), then a center of humanism, he became an accomplished Greek scholar. As tutor (1548–50) to Elizabeth Tudor (later to be Queen Elizabeth of England), he can probably be held responsible for her great interest in the classics. He was subsequently secretary (1550–53) to Sir Richard Morysin, ambassador to the emperor Charles V, and Latin secretary (1553–68) to both Mary and Elizabeth. His chief works are *Toxophilus* (1545), a treatise in dialogue form on archery, an early masterpiece of modern English prose, and *The Scholemaster* (1570), highly valued for its method of teaching Latin.

Aschbach (äsh'bäch), **Joseph von.** b. at Höchst, Prussia, April 29, 1801; d. at Vienna, April 25, 1882. German historian. He was a professor of history at Bonn (1842), and at Vienna (1853–72). Author of *Geschichte der Westgoten* (1827), *Geschichte der Omajjaden in Spanien* (1829), *Geschichte Kaiser Sigismunds* (1834–38–45), a work (1833–37) on the Almoravide and Almohade invasions of Spain, and others.

Aschenbrödel (äsh'en.brė.del). See **Cenerentola.**

Aschersleben (äsh'ėrs.lā.ben). City in C Germany, in the *Land* (state) of Saxony-Anhalt, Russian Zone, formerly in the province of Saxony, Prussia, situated on the Eine River near the Wipper River, ab. 28 mi. SW of Magdeburg: center of an important manufacturing district. It produces woolen articles (especially blankets), paper, chemicals, and machinery, and has large sugar refineries. Potash, salt, and lignite mines are in the vicinity. It belonged in the early Middle Ages to the Abbey of Fulda; it came under Anhalt in 1315, the *Hochstift* (ecclesiastical territory) of Halberstadt in 1332, and Brandenburg-Prussia in 1648. The population is predominantly Protestant; the increase in population from 1939 to 1946 amounted to 34.1 percent. 42,196 (1946).

Aschheim (äsh'hīm), **Selmar.** b. at Berlin, Oct. 4, 1878—. German gynecologist and biochemist. He became (1930) a privatdocent of biological research in gynecology at the University of Berlin, where he was named (1931) a professor. While working on gynecological histology and hormones he detected (1927) hormone contents in the urine of pregnant women and showed (in collaboration with B. Zondek) that the anterior-lobe implants in immature rodents produced premature sexual development. This has been further broken down to a "follicle-stimulating" and a "luteinizing hormone." With his collaborator Zondek, he introduced the well-known Aschheim-Zondek test for pregnancy.

Aschoff (äsh'of), **Ludwig.** b. at Berlin, Jan. 10, 1866; d. at Freiburg im Breisgau, Germany, June 24, 1942. German pathologist. Aschoff was appointed (1903) to the chair of pathological anatomy at Marburg and served

(1906–36) in a similar post at Freiburg. He made studies of appendicitis, classifying its several varieties, and elucidated the various ways that it might be caused; also worked on cholecystitis, on the concept of the reticulo-endothelial system (1913), and on the problems of icterus, thrombosis, and tuberculosis. In 1904 he described a special kind of inflammatory nodule in the heart muscle characteristic of the rheumatic process ("Aschoff's bodies").

Asclepiades of Bithynia (as.klē.pī'ạ.dēz; bi.thin'i.ạ). fl. c100 B.C. Greek physician, notable as the first eminent one of his country to practice at Rome. He opposed the theories of Hippocrates, asserting that disease springs from a disordered movement of the corpuscles and that a cure is achieved by soothing remedies, such as diet, moderate exercise, bathing, wine, and (for the insane) music. He achieved considerable success in Rome by his methods. Portions of his written works are preserved in C. G. Gumpert's *Asclepiadis Bithyni Fragmenta* (1798).

Asclepiades of Samos (sā'mos). fl. early 3rd century B.C. Greek lyric poet and epigrammatist. He is the earliest, and considered by some the most important, of his school; some scholars believe that the type of verse known as Asclepiadean is so named from him.

Asclepius (as.klē'pi.us). See **Aesculapius.**

Ascoli (däs'kō.lē), **Cecco d'.** See **Cecco d'Ascoli.**

Ascoli (äs'kō.lē), **Graziadio Isaia.** b. at Gorizia, Italy, July 16, 1829; d. at Milan, Italy, Jan. 21, 1907. Italian comparative philologist and professor at Milan. He was the originator and chief representative in Italy of the Ario-Semitic theory, which supposes a close connection between the Aryan and Semitic families of languages. In the treatise *Studi orientali e linguistici* he endeavored to prove the presence of Semitic elements in the Etruscan dialect. He was founder and editor (1873 *et seq.*) of *Archivio glottologico italiano*, in which he printed (1873) his *Saggi ladini*.

Ascoli Piceno (pē.chā'nō). Province in the *compartimento* (region) of Marches, in C Italy. Capital, Ascoli Piceno; area, ab. 807 sq. mi.; pop. 303,869 (1936).

Ascoli Piceno. [Also: **Ascoli**; ancient name, **Asculum Picenum.**] City and commune in C Italy, in the *compartimento* (region) of Marches, the capital of the province of Ascoli Piceno, situated at the confluence of the Tronto and Castellano rivers in a strongly fortified location, S of Ancona. It is the seat of a bishopric. There are renowned silk and ceramics manufactures and other, particularly agricultural, industries based on the development of waterpower in the vicinity. It is rich in monuments from many ages, including a Romanesque *battistero* (baptistery), which dates from the 12th century, the Church of SS. Vincenzo and Anastasio from the 13th, the Church of San Francesco from the 15th, and the cathedral from the 16th century; the *palazzo communale* (town hall) was rebuilt in the 17th and 18th centuries. Buildings of interest to tourists were undamaged in World War II. Pop. of commune, 38,111 (1936); of city, 20,665 (1936).

Ascoli Satriano (sä.tryä'nō). [Ancient name, **Asculum Apulum.**] Town and commune in SW Italy, in the region of Apulia, in the province of Foggia, 2 mi. S of Foggia. It is the seat of a bishopric. The Church of San Potito dates from the 12th century, with Renaissance additions. Founded by the Romans (scene of the costly victory (279 B.C.) of Pyrrhus over the Romans), the town was burned to the ground in the early Middle Ages by the Moslems; it was subsequently under Byzantine and Norman rule. Pop. of commune, 8,421 (1936); of town, 7,989 (1936).

Asconius Pedianus (as.kō'ni.us pē.di.ā'nus), **Quintus.** b. probably at Padua, c2 B.C.; d. c83 A.D. Roman historian and grammarian, notable for his commentaries on Cicero's speeches.

Ascot (as'kọt). Name of a famous English horse-race meeting, held annually in June at Ascot Heath. The distance of the course is slightly over 2½ mi. The first race was run in 1711, and the meeting has since been regarded (with the Derby in England, and the Kentucky Derby in the U.S.) as one of the world's most important horse-racing events.

Ascot Heath. Site of a famous race track in S England, in Berkshire, ab. 6 mi. SW of Windsor.

Ascrivium (as.kriv'i.um). See under **Kotor.**

Ascue (as'kū), **Anne.** See **Askew, Anne.**

Asculum Apulum (as'kụ.lum ap'ụ.lum). Ancient name of **Ascoli Satriano.**

Asculum Picenum (pī.sē'num). Ancient name of **Ascoli Piceno.**

Ascutney Mountain (as.kut'ni). [Also, **Mount Ascutney.**] Mountain in Windsor County, Vermont, ab. 30 mi. SE of Rutland. 3,320 ft.

Asdudu (äs'dö.dö). Assyrian name of **Ashdod.**

Aselli (ạ.sel'ī). The two fifth-magnitude stars γ and δ Cancri, γ being the northern one.

Aselli (ä.sel'lē) or **Asellio** (-lyō), **Gasparo.** [Latinized, **Gaspar Asellius.**] b. at Cremona, Italy, 1581; d. at Pavia, Italy, 1626. Italian anatomist and physician. His account of the lacteal vessels, which he discovered but seems not to have completely understood, is contained in his *De Lactibus* (1627).

Asem the Man Hater (ā'sẹm). Tale (1759) by Oliver Goldsmith. It appeared in *The Bee*, a periodical of the day, which was issued on eight Saturdays in October and November, 1759. The figure of Asem is a center for a fantasy of Goldsmith's favorite ideas. Asem is taught the necessity of having the life of pure reason stimulated by emotion and he is cured of his misanthropy by means of regenerated social emotions.

Asenappar (as.ẹ.nap'ạr). [Also, **Asnappar.**] In the Bible, a ruler mentioned in Ezra, iv. 10, who had transplanted certain tribes to the cities of Samaria. He was, in actual history, Assurbanipal, king of Assyria.

Aser (ā'sėr). See **Asher.**

Aseyev (ä.sā'yif), **Nikolay Nikolayevich.** b. 1889—. Russian futurist poet, a disciple and collaborator of V. V. Mayakovsky (1893–1930).

Asfandiyar (as.fan.di.yär'). [Also: **Aspandiyar, Isfendiyar.**] Hero of the *Shahnamah;* son of King Gushtasp, the Constantine of the Zoroastrians. After many exploits he was called to conquer Arjasp, a demon king, who had taken captive two daughters of Gushtasp, and to restore his sisters. For this he undertook his "seven labors." Choosing, like Rustam, the shortest and most perilous way to the enemy's stronghold, he first slew two monstrous wolves; secondly, conquered a fierce lion and his mate; thirdly, slew a fierce dragon; fourthly, withstood the wiles of a beautiful woman who, caught in Asfandiyar's noose, became first a cat, then a wolf, and finally a black, flame-vomiting demon, and was then slain by him; fifthly, he slew a Simurgh, a gigantic bird, which tried to bear him away; sixthly, brought his troops through a furious storm of wind and snow; and seventhly, traversed a deadly desert. Reaching the brazen fortress, Asfandiyar collected 100 camels and entered it with his warriors disguised as a merchant caravan, while his brother Bishutan attacked it from without. After this success Gushtasp wished Asfandiyar to go against Rustam, to whom Kaikhusrau had given Zabul, Kabul, and Nimruz. Asfandiyar pleaded the nobility and services of Rustam, but the king was obdurate. Rustam came out to welcome Asfandiyar, but when told the errand of the latter refused to yield. The heroes fought on two successive days. Rustam was wounded but recovered and, guided by the Simurgh which had cared for his infancy, on the second day lodged an arrow, made by the Simurgh's direction from the Kazu tree, in the eye of his antagonist, who fell. Zal and Rustam both came to offer sympathy, but Asfandiyar died, entrusting his son Bahman to the care of Rustam.

Asgalan (äs.gä.län'). Modern name of **Ashkelon.**

Asgard (as'gärd). [Also, **Asaheim**; Old Norse, **Asaheimr, Asgardhr.**] Realm of the gods and goddesses in Old Norse mythology. It was apparently located in the heavens above the earth. Asgard contained different regions as well as separate abodes. The principal of these was Valhalla, the assembling-place of the gods and heroes.

Asgeirsson (äs'gār.sōn), **Asgeir.** b. 1894—. Icelandic statesman, president of Iceland (1952 *et seq.*). A member of the legislature (1924 *et seq.*), he was Iceland's minister of finance (1931) and prime minister (1932–34).

Asgill (az'gil), **John.** [Called **"Translated Asgill."**] b. at Hanley Castle, in England, 1659; d. 1738. English lawyer and pamphleteer, expelled on a charge of blasphemy from the Irish House of Commons (1703) and from the English House of Commons (1707), chiefly for a book

(1700) which sought to prove that, the penalty for original sin having been paid by Christ, death was no longer legal, and Christians would therefore pass to eternity by "translation."

Ash (ash), **John.** b. in Dorsetshire, England, c1724; d. 1779. English lexicographer and author. His works include a grammar and a two-volume *New and Complete Dictionary of the English Language* (1775), based on both those of Samuel Johnson and Nathan Bailey, and including the latter's vocabulary of cant, plus provincial words.

Ashangi Lake (ä.shäng'gē). Small lake in E Africa, in E Ethiopia.

Ashango Land (ä.shäng'gō). Country in W Africa, in the S part of French Equatorial Africa, in the territory of Gabon.

Ashanti (ä.shän'tē). [Also: **Ashantee, Sianti.**] Former kingdom in W Africa, which lay N of the Gold Coast, now replaced by the British protectorate and reconstituted kingdom of Ashanti, with different boundaries. Capital, Kumasi.

Ashanti. African kingdom and British protectorate, N of the Gold Coast colony, W Africa, attached to Gold Coast for administrative purposes. Its chief city, Kumasi, is linked to Accra and the port of Takoradi by rail and road. There are valuable forests in the W part of the area, and lumber, cocoa, and ground nuts make up the chief exports. Capital, Kumasi; area, 24,560 sq. mi.; pop. 737,000 (est. 1940).

Ashanti. [Also: **Ashantee, Asante.**] One of the Sudanic-speaking Akan peoples of W Africa, inhabiting an area N of the Gold Coast colony. Their population is estimated at ab. 600,000 (based on 1931 census). At the beginning of the 18th century, under the leadership of a chief named Osai Tutu, they threw off the rule of the Denkyira and established a powerful kingdom with its capital at what is now the city of Kumasi. The Ashanti were conquered in the course of a series of military encounters with the British throughout much of the 19th century, culminating in the Ashanti War (1873–74). The Golden Stool, which is believed to contain the soul of the Ashanti nation, was indirectly a cause of some of these. The Ashanti War ended when Kumasi was burned to the ground (it has since been rebuilt), and King Prempeh was exiled.

Ashanti War. War (1873–74) between Great Britain and the Ashanti, in W Africa. Ashanti was invaded by a British army under Garnet Joseph Wolseley, who conquered and burned Kumasi in February, 1874, and exacted from the Ashanti a treaty that prepared the way for a British protectorate some 22 years later.

Ashbel (ash'bel). In the Old Testament, a son of Benjamin. Gen. xlvi. 21.

Ashbourne (ash'bo̤rn), 1st Baron. [Title of **Edward Gibson.**] b. at Dublin, 1837; d. at London, 1913. British politician and jurist, raised to the peerage in 1885. He was a member of Parliament in 1875–85, holding the post of attorney general for Ireland under Disraeli, and lord chancellor of Ireland in 1885–92 and 1895–1905.

Ashbourne or **Ashbourn.** Urban district and market town in C England, in Derbyshire, situated on the river Henmore, ab. 14 mi. NW of Derby, ab. 159 mi. NW of London by rail. 5,440 (1951).

Ashburn (ash'bėrn). City in SW Georgia, county seat of Turner County, NE of Albany: marketing center for a farming and livestock-raising region. 2,918 (1950).

Ashburner (ash'bėrn"ėr), **Charles Albert.** b. at Philadelphia, Feb. 9, 1854; d. at Pittsburgh, Dec. 24, 1889. American geologist. He was commissioned (1876) to survey four counties in the oil-producing section of W Pennsylvania, and produced (1878) a topographical map and other materials which permitted an accurate appraisal of the area's oil-bearing possibilities. He conducted (1880–86) a survey of Pennsylvania's anthracite field, resigning to accept (1886) a position as consultant to the Westinghouse Company at Pittsburgh.

Ashburnham (ash'bėr.na̤m), **John.** b. 1603; d. 1671. English politician under Charles I and Charles II. A member (1640 *et seq.*) of the Long Parliament, he was treasurer of the Royalist army during the English Civil War and a commissioner in the Uxbridge negotiations (1644). He accompanied Charles I in flight, joined him at Hampton Court when he was captured (1647), and inadvertently brought about his recapture on the Isle of Wight after his escape later in the same year. Restored to favor during the Restoration, he served as a member of Parliament from 1661 to 1667, when he was expelled for accepting bribes from French vintners.

Ashburton (ash'bėr"to̤n, -bėr.to̤n), 1st Baron. [Title of **John Dunning.**] b. at Ashburton, England, Oct. 18, 1731; d. at Exmouth, England, Aug. 18, 1783. English lawyer who, as a member of Parliament, opposed a restrictive policy toward the American colonies. He first became known as a lawyer for his defense (1762) of the British East India Company against the Dutch; he was solicitor general in 1768–70. As a member of Parliament (1768–83) he spoke against the harsh treatment of the colonies and for the relief of Roman Catholics. He moved a resolution (1780) that "the influence of the crown has increased, is increasing, and ought to be diminished."

Ashburton. Urban district, market town, and holiday resort in SW England, in Devonshire, ab. 18 mi. SW of Exeter, ab. 212 mi. SW of London by rail. It has a small woolen-serge weaving industry. Ashburton was one of the four coinage towns in Devonshire during the Middle Ages. 2,704 (1951).

Ashburton, 1st Baron (second creation). Title of **Baring, Alexander.**

Ashburton, 2nd Baron. Title of **Baring, William Bingham.**

Ashburton River. River in W Australia which flows into the Indian Ocean N of Exmouth Gulf.

Ashby (ash'bi), **Turner.** b. in Fauquier County, Va., Oct. 23, 1828; d. June 6, 1862. American soldier, a Confederate general in the Civil War. He raised a company of cavalry at the outbreak of hostilities, became a brigadier general in 1862, and was killed in a skirmish preliminary to the battle of Cross Keys, Va.

Ashby-de-la-Zouch (ash'bi.del.a̤.zöch'). Urban district in C England, in Leicestershire, situated on the river Mease, ab. 16 mi. NW of Leicester, ab. 120 mi. N of London by rail. It is an important coal-mining center located on the Leicestershire coal field. It contains a ruined castle in which Mary Stuart was confined (1569). Pop. 6,406 (1951).

Ashby-Sterry (ash'bi.ster'i), **Joseph.** b. at London; d. June 1, 1917. English journalist and author. He studied painting and actually began a career as an illustrator illustrating for *Punch*, but soon gave this up for writing. He was the author of *Nutshell Novels* (1890), *Lazy Minstrel* (1892), *Naughty Girl* (1893), *A Tale of the Thames in Verse* (1896), *Sketches in Song* (1903), and *River Poems* (1909). He also created and wrote (1890–1909) the popular "Bystander" column in the London *Graphic*, and was art critic (1891–1907) for the London *Daily Graphic*.

Ashcroft (ash'kroft), **Peggy.** [Full name, **Edith Margaret Emily Ashcroft.**] b. 1907—. English actress. She made her debut (1926) as Margaret in James Barrie's *Dear Brutus* with the Birmingham Repertory Theatre; later she played Desdemona to Paul Robeson's *Othello* (1930), and appeared in a revival of *The Importance of Being Ernest* (1942), and in *The Duchess of Malfi* (1944). In 1950 she appeared at Stratford-on-Avon opposite John Gielgud. Her film appearances include *The Wandering Jew, The 39 Steps*, and others.

Ashdod (ash'dod). [Greek, **Azotos**; Assyrian, **Asdudu**; modern name, **Esdud.**] In Biblical geography, one of the five cities of the Philistine confederacy, and a seat of the worship of Dagon the fish god (1 Sam. v. 5), in Palestine between Gaza and Jaffa. It was strategically important because of its location on the highway to Egypt. It was assigned to the tribe of Judah (Josh. xv. 47), but was never subdued by the Israelites. It was conquered (722–705 B.C.), by the Assyrians under Sargon, and in the annals of Esarhaddon (680–668 B.C.) is mentioned (under the form Asdudu) as paying homage to the Assyrian king. Psammetichus, king of Egypt from 666 to 610 B.C., took it from the Assyrians (Herod. II. 157). It is, however, mentioned as an independent power in alliance with others against Jerusalem at the time of Nehemiah (iv. 7). It was destroyed by the Maccabees (1 Mac. v. 68; x. 84), and afterward restored (55 B.C.) by Gabinius.

Ashdown (ash'doun). City in SW Arkansas, county seat of Little River County, ab. 125 mi. SW of Little Rock:

rail and marketing center in a cotton and vegetable producing region. 2,738 (1950).

Ashdown. Locality in S England where Ethelred and Alfred the Great defeated (871) the Danes.

Ashe (ash), **John.** b. probably at Grovely, N.C., c1720; d. in Sampson County, N.C., in October, 1781. American patriot and officer in the Revolutionary War. His lack of military skill led to a defeat (1778) at Briar Creek, in North Carolina, which permitted British military control of Georgia, opened communications between Georgia and the Carolinas, and considerably lengthened the war.

Ashe, Samuel. b. near Beaufort, N.C., 1725; d. at Rocky Point, N.C., Feb. 3, 1813. American jurist and politician; brother of John Ashe. Despite his connections as a member of the bar with the British government, he became a forthright supporter of the republican movement in the colony, serving successively as president (1776) of the North Carolina Council of Safety and captain (1779) of a cavalry troop. He was governor of North Carolina (1795–97) after serving as state supreme court chief justice for a period of years.

Ashe, Thomas. b. at Stockport, Cheshire, England, 1836; d. at London, 1889. English schoolmaster, minor poet, and one-time clergyman. He forsook the clergy to become a teacher in 1865. His verse was collected in the volume *Poems* (1885).

Asheboro (ash'bur.ọ). Town in C North Carolina, county seat of Randolph County: manufactures furniture, chemicals, hosiery, boxes, mattresses, garters, and brooms. Fox hunting is popular in the surrounding region. It was founded c1740, and was named for Samuel Ashe, later (1795–97) a governor of the state. 7,701 (1950).

Ashehoh (ash'ẹ.hō). See **Acheng.**

Ashenden, or the British Agent (ash'ẹn.dẹn). Novel by W. Somerset Maugham, published in 1928.

Asher (ash'ėr). [Also, **Aser.**] In the Old Testament, the eighth son of Jacob. The name was also applied to the tribe of which Asher was the progenitor. Their territory on the north extended to the Palestine border, and in the south to the S boundary of Carmel; on the east its boundaries were the territories of Zebulun and Naphtali, and on the west along the Mediterranean. However, the tribe's failure to capture and occupy the Phoenician plain along the sea left them with only inland hill country except near Carmel. Gen. xxx. 12–13.

Asher, Aaron ben Moses ben. See **Aaron ben Moses ben Asher.**

Asheville (ash'vil). [Former name, **Morristown.**] City in W North Carolina, county seat of Buncombe County, near the Great Smoky Mountains National Park, at an elevation of 2,216 ft.: noted as a tourist and health resort. It is the commercial and financial center for the 18 mountain counties of the W part of the state and produces textiles, forest and mica products, and foodstuffs. Formerly part of the Cherokee Indian hunting grounds, it was settled in 1794 and incorporated and named in 1797. It is a tobacco-marketing point. It is the burial place of William Sydney Porter (O. Henry) and Thomas Wolfe (who was also born in Asheville). It is the "Altamont" of Wolfe's novels. Pop. of city, 53,000 (1950); of urbanized area, 58,437 (1950).

Ashfield (ash'fēld), 1st Baron. [Title of **Albert Henry Stanley.**] b. at Derby, England, Nov. 8, 1874; d. at London, Nov. 4, 1948. British industrialist and transport specialist who headed (1933-47) the unified transport system of London. He emigrated with his family to the U.S., where he was associated with the Detroit Tramway Company, served in the Spanish-American War, and reorganized the New Jersey transport system. Called to England to help reorganize London's electric transportation system, he was president (1916–19) of the Board of Trade and chairman (1933–47) of the London Passenger Transport Board.

Ashford (ash'fọrd). Urban district, market town, and industrial center in SE England, in Kent, situated on the Stour River, ab. 13 mi. SW of Canterbury, ab. 56 mi. SE of London by rail: manufactures railroad locomotives. 24,777 (1951).

Ashford, Bailey Kelly. b. at Washington, D.C., Sept. 18, 1873; d. at San Juan, Puerto Rico, Nov. 1, 1934. American army physician and officer, notable as an authority on tropical diseases. He graduated from the Georgetown University Medical School (1896) and the Army Medical School (1898), before serving (1898) in Puerto Rico during the Spanish-American War. As a colonel, he headed (1917–18) battle training for medical officers of the U.S. forces in France. He was a professor of tropical medicine and mycology for Columbia University at the School of Tropical Medicine in Puerto Rico, a member (1916) of the Rockefeller Foundation's medical commission to Brazil, and U.S. delegate (1928) to the International Congress of Tropical Medicine and Hygiene at Cairo. Author of *Anemia in Porto Rico* (1904), *Uncinariasis in Porto Rico* (with Gutierrez, 1911), and *A Soldier in Science* (1934).

Ashford, Margaret Mary. [Pen name, **Daisy Ashford.**] English child-author known for works written at the age of eight and earlier; she was introduced to English readers by Sir James M. Barrie, and to the American public by Irvin S. Cobb. She was the author of *The Young Visiters, or Mr. Salteena's Plan* (published 1919, written when she was nine), *Daisy Ashford: Her Book* (published in the U.S. in 1920), containing *A Short History of Love and Marriage* (written when she was eight and dictated by her to her father), *The True History of Leslie Woodcock* (when she was eleven), *Where Love Lies Deepest* (when she was twelve), and *The Hangman's Daughter* (when "about thirteen"). An earlier manuscript, *Mr. Chapmer's Bride,* was lost. The stories, published as originally written, owed their popularity and appeal to a combination of childish wisdom, ignorance, imagination, sentence structure, spelling, and punctuation. Barrie's preface to the 1919 volume, as Daisy Ashford gladly admitted, played a large part in securing favorable attention to her work. One English reviewer expressed the opinion that *The Young Visiters* was a literary hoax, having been written by Barrie himself; though entirely without foundation, this theory gained a certain credence, and made the book something of a literary curiosity.

Ashhurst (ash'hėrst), **John.** b. at Philadelphia, Aug. 23. 1839; d. July 7, 1900. American surgeon. He served as medical officer in U.S. army hospitals at Chester, Pa., and Germantown, Pa., during the Civil War before being chosen (1877) professor of clinical surgery at the University of Pennsylvania, later (1888) becoming professor of surgery. A prolific writer, he was the author of nearly all the surgical reviews carried by the *American Journal of the Medical Sciences* from 1867 to 1877; his work as editor of the *International Encyclopedia of Surgery* (1881–86) brought him renown on both sides of the Atlantic as a historian of surgery and surgeons.

Ashikaga (ä.shē.kä.gä). City in Japan, in C Honshu, situated ab. 65 mi. NW of Tokyo. It is an old cultural center and an important modern trading center, and has some small industries, especially the making of silk cloth. 52,810 (1950).

Ashingdon (ash'ing.dọn). Civil parish and village in SE England, in Essex, ab. 2 mi. N of Rochford, ab. 33 mi. NE of London. 504 (1931). See **Assandun.**

Ashington (ash'ing.tọn). Urban district in NE England, in Northumberland, ab. 4 mi. E of Morpeth, ab. 288 mi. N of London by rail. It is an important coal-mining center (and claims to be the site of the largest colliery in the world). 28,723 (1951).

Ashkelon (ash'kẹ.lon). [Also: **Ascalon, Askelon, Eshkalon**; Assyrian, **Isqaluna**; modern name, **Asgalan.**] In ancient geography, one of the five chief cities of Philistia, situated on the Mediterranean ab. 39 mi. SW of Jerusalem. Near it were the temple and sacred lake of Derceto. It is mentioned in Phoenician and Assyrian inscriptions; the names of four of its kings (Sidka, Sarludari, Rukibti, and Mitenti) appear in the annals of Sennacherib (705–681 B.C.) and Esarhaddon (680–668 B.C.). Herod I, whose birthplace it was, adorned the city with many edifices. On August 12, 1099, it was the scene of a victory of the Crusaders under Godfrey of Bouillon over a superior army sent by the sultan of Egypt to recapture Jerusalem; the city was taken by the Crusaders in 1153, recaptured for Islam by Saladin in 1187, and was destroyed in 1270.

Ashkenaz (ash'kẹ.naz). The eldest son of Gomer, as referred to in Genesis and 1 Chronicles. Whether or not the name originally referred to a person, a tribe, or a country, it did designate a people who in the time of

Jeremiah dwelt in the neighborhood of Ararat and Minni (near what is now eastern Armenia).

Ashkenaz (ash.kẹ.naz'). Name sometimes applied in rabbinical literature to Germany, giving rise to the appellation "Ashkenazim" used both in rabbinical literature and in modern Jewish terminology to mean those Jews who were resident, in the Middle Ages, in Germany and France, and to their descendants. They are distinguished from the "Sephardim," the Jews of Spain and Portugal.

Ashkhabad (äsh ɦä.bät'). [Also: **Askabad, Askhabad;** former name, **Poltoratsk.**] City in the U.S.S.R., capital of the Turkmen Soviet Socialist Republic. It is an important cotton-shipping center, and has cotton-textile, silk-reeling, glass, and food-processing industries. 126,580 (1939).

Ashland (ash'lạnd). [Former name, **Poage Settlement.**] City in NE Kentucky, in Boyd County, on the Ohio River, in an area rich in natural gas and petroleum. It manufactures steel products, bricks, tile, and coke, and is the principal city in E Kentucky. It was settled in 1815, platted in 1850, and incorporated in 1858. Pop. 31,131 (1950).

Ashland. [Former name, **Uniontown.**] City in N Ohio, county seat of Ashland County, ab. 52 mi. SW of Cleveland: manufactures windmills, men's clothing, pumps, boxes, hardware, rubber goods, and medicines. It was founded (1815) as Uniontown and assumed its present name in 1822. It is the seat of Ashland College. 14,287 (1950).

Ashland. City in SW Oregon, in Jackson County, on Bear Creek, in a mining, lumbering, quarrying, and apple and pear producing area: shipping center for fruit, granite, and marble. It holds an annual Shakespeare festival. 7,739 (1950).

Ashland. Borough in E Pennsylvania, in Schuylkill and Columbia counties, ab. 40 mi. NW of Reading: coal mining; manufactures of shirts, knitted goods, and metal products. It was platted in 1847. Pop. 6,192 (1950).

Ashland. Town in E central Virginia, in Hanover County, ab. 16 mi. N of Richmond: seat of Randolph-Macon College for men. The town was named for the country estate of Henry Clay, who was born nearby. 2,610 (1950).

Ashland. City in N Wisconsin, county seat of Ashland County, on a bay of Lake Superior, ab. 62 mi. SE of Duluth: manufactures of paper and gabbro (black granite) products; shipping point for Canadian pulp and for the iron ore of the vicinity. It was settled in 1854. It is the seat of Northland College. 10,640 (1950).

Ashley (ash'li). [Former names: **Scrabbletown, Coalville, Skunktown, Peestone, Hightown, Newton, Hendricksburg, Nanticoke Junction,** and **Alberts.**] Borough in E Pennsylvania, in Luzerne County, S of Wilkes Barre, in an anthracite coal region; coal mining; railroad shops; manufactures lace. It was settled c1810; the present name was adopted in 1871. Pop. 5,243 (1950).

Ashley, Chester. b. at Westfield, Mass., June 1, 1790; d. at Washington, D.C., April 27, 1848. American politician, a senator from Arkansas in the period 1844–48.

Ashley, James Mitchell. b. in Alleghany County, Pa., Nov. 14, 1824; d. Sept. 16, 1896. American abolitionist, politician, journalist, lawyer, and businessman. His fervent antislavery convictions drove him (1848) from the Democratic into the Free Soil Party and thence (1854) into the newly formed Republican Party (1854), as a member of which he served as a congressman from 1858 to 1868. On Dec. 14, 1863, he introduced the first proposition for a Constitutional amendment to abolish slavery. He initiated (Jan. 7, 1867) the impeachment proceedings against President Andrew Johnson, and withdrew as a force in national politics when these were not sustained.

Ashley, William Henry. b. in Powhatan County, Va., c1778; d. March 26, 1838. American fur trader and politician. He forsook the manufacture of gunpowder and lead mining for fur trading in 1822, sending parties up the Missouri River to the Yellowstone (1822–23) and into Wyoming (1823–24). He replaced (1824) the fixed trading post with an annual rendezvous method of collecting furs, and led two parties from St. Louis in a great swing through the west, crossing the eastern Rockies and nearly reaching Great Salt Lake in the period 1824–26. After unsuccessful campaigns for the governorship of Missouri (1824) and a seat in the U.S. Senate (1829), he was elected congressman (1831) on an anti-Jackson ticket and became known at Washington for his consistent support of aggressive western measures and his opposition to temporizing with the Indians.

Ashley, Sir **William James.** b. at London, 1860; d. 1927. English economist. Professor of political economy and constitutional history at Toronto (1888–92), of economic history at Harvard (1892–1901), and of commerce and public finance at Birmingham, England (1901–25), he was the author of the two-part *Introduction to English Economic History* (1888, 1893), a leading reference work in its field. He also wrote *Tariff Problem* (1903, 1920), *Gold and Prices* (1912), *Commercial Education* (1926), and others.

Ashley River. Small river in South Carolina, at the mouth of which Charleston is situated. Length, ab. 40 mi.

Ashmead (ash'mēd), **Isaac.** b. at Germantown, Pa., Dec. 22, 1790; d. March 1, 1870. American printer. He was the founder (1819) of the Sunday and Adult School Union, now known as the American Sunday School Union. He introduced to the American printing industry the composition roller and hydraulic press for smooth-pressing wet sheets of paper.

Ashmead-Bartlett (ash'mēd.bärt'lẹt), Sir **Ellis.** b. at Brooklyn, N.Y., 1849; d. at London, 1902. English politician. Educated at Torquay and Christ Church, Oxford (1872, 1874), he was called to the bar of the Inner Temple in 1877. He served as member of Parliament for Eye, Suffolk (1880–84), and for Ecclesall, Sheffield (1885–1902); as civil lord of the admiralty (1885–92); and as an observer in the war between Turkey and Greece (1897) and the Boer War (1899). A strong imperialist and opponent of Gladstone, he was much in demand as a speaker at meetings of the Conservative Party. Founder and editor (1880–98) of *England*, a conservative weekly paper; author of *Shall England Keep India?* (1886), *The Battlefields of Thessaly* (1897), and others.

Ashmole (ash'mōl), **Elias.** b. at Lichfield, England, May 23, 1617; d. at London, May 18, 1692. English antiquary, founder of the Ashmolean Museum at Oxford. He was a Royalist (1642 *et seq.*) and subsequently an official under Charles II. He took up mathematics, alchemy, botany, and other studies. Author of *Institutions, Laws, and Ceremonies of the Order of the Garter* (1672).

Ashmolean Museum (ash.mō'lẹ.ạn). Museum at Oxford University, founded (c1679) by Elias Ashmole. The original building was designed and built by Sir Christopher Wren in the period 1682–83. The museum collections have been removed from the Old Ashmolean Museum (Broad Street), which is now occupied in part by the Bodleian Library, to the New Ashmolean Museum, on Beaumont Street. The museum contains some of the Arundel marbles, the Cretan antiquities discovered by Sir Arthur Evans, and others.

Ashmun (äsh'mön). See **Eshmun.**

Ashmun (ash'mun), **George.** b. at Blandford, Mass., Dec. 25, 1804; d. at Springfield, Mass., July 17, 1870. American politician. As a Whig member of Congress (1845–51) he opposed the Mexican War and supported Daniel Webster, whose growing unpopularity ultimately led to Ashmun's withdrawal from Congress. He was chairman (1860) of the Republican national convention at Chicago.

Ashmun, Jehudi. b. at Champlain, N.Y., April 21, 1794; d. at New Haven, Conn., Aug. 25, 1828. American colonial agent, notable for his efforts on behalf of Liberia. He forsook the Congregational ministry in 1818 to become an editor of the Episcopalian *Theological Repertory*, which was then supporting the establishment of Liberia as a haven for returned slaves. His interest in this undertaking led to his appointment as supervisor of 37 people who were being thus returned (1822) to Africa. His discovery, on arrival in Liberia, that the settlement was fever-ridden, deserted by its white agents, and threatened with attack by native chiefs compelled him to remain and head a reorganization which led to his official appointment (1824) as chief agent, a position he retained until 1828.

Ashokan Reservoir (ạ.shō'kạn, ash'ọ-). Reservoir in the system supplying water to the city of New York, in SE New York, near Kingston. Peak capacity, ab. 130 billion gallons; area, ab. 13 sq. mi.

Ashraf (äsh.räf'). [Also, **Eshref.**] Town in N Iran, in Mazanderan, situated near the Caspian Sea ab. 120 mi. NE of Tehran. It was a favorite residence of Abbas I of Persia (Abbas the Great). Pop. ab. 5,000.

Ashraf, Gulf of. See **Asterabad Bay.**

Ashtabula (ash.tą.bū'lą). City in NE Ohio, in Ashtabula County, on the Ashtabula River, near Lake Erie, ab. 50 mi. NE of Cleveland: shipping center for iron ore and coal; manufactures include agricultural implements, leather goods, and boats. 23,696 (1950).

Ashtaroth (ash'tą.roth). In Biblical geography, a city in Bashan, Syria, E of the Sea of Galilee.

Ashton (ash'tǫn), **Algernon Bennet Langton.** b. at Durham, England, Dec. 9, 1859; d. at London, 1937. English composer and pianist. He was a professor of piano at the Royal College of Music (1885–1910) and at the London College of Music (1913–37). Composer of symphonies, overtures, a variety of chamber music, concertos, sonatas, and others.

Ashton, Ernest Charles. b. at Brantford, Ontario, Oct. 28, 1873—. Canadian army officer and physician. After serving as a staff surgeon (1901–15) at the Brantford General Hospital, he was chief surgeon (1935–38) of the Canadian general staff, and was appointed (1939) inspector general of the Canadian military forces, a post which he relinquished in 1941.

Ashton, Helen Rosaline. b. at London, 1891—. English novelist. She is perhaps best known for *Doctor Serocold* (1930), which was a choice of the Book of the Month Club, and also wrote *A Lot of Talk* (1927), *Bricks and Mortar* (1932), *Family Cruise* (1934), *People in Cages* (1937), *The Swan of Usk* (1939), *Tadpole Hall* (1941), *Parson Austen's Daughter* (1949), and others. Her *William and Dorothy* (1938) is a fictionalized biography of the Wordsworths.

Ashton, John William. [Called **"Will" Ashton.**] b. at York, England, Sept. 20, 1881—. English landscape and seascape painter, who has been in recent years a member of the art advisory board of the government of Australia. In 1914 he was awarded an honorable mention at the Carnegie International art show at Pittsburgh; he received the Wynne art prize at Sydney in 1908 and 1930. Many of his paintings are owned by the Australian national galleries at Adelaide, Melbourne, Perth, Sydney, and New South Wales. Among his principal works are *The Cornish Coast*, *Barge on the River Seine*, and *Building Sydney Harbor Beach.*

Ashton, Lady. Wife of Sir William and mother of Lucy, the "bride of Lammermoor," in Sir Walter Scott's novel of that name.

Ashton, Lucy. Bride of Lammermoor in Sir Walter Scott's novel of that name, the daughter of Sir William and Lady Ashton. Betrothed to Edgar Ravenswood, she is forced by her mother to marry Frank Hayston. Grief makes her insane and she dies on her wedding night. The leading characters of this novel also appear, with slightly altered names, in Gaetano Donizetti's opera *Lucia di Lammermoor*, and in several dramas founded upon the incidents of the story.

Ashton, Sir William. In Sir Walter Scott's *Bride of Lammermoor*, the Lord Keeper of Scotland, father of Lucy Ashton.

Ashton, Winifred. See **Dane, Clemence.**

Ashton-in-Makerfield (ash'tǫn.in.mā'kėr.fēld). Urban district, coal-mining town, and small manufacturing center in NW England, in Lancashire, ab. 15 mi. NE of Liverpool, ab. 226 mi. NW of London by rail. It has manufactures of cotton. 19,053 (1951).

Ashton-under-Lyne (ash'tǫn.un'dėr.līn'). [Also, **Ashton.**] Municipal borough in NW England, in Lancashire, situated on the E edge of the South Lancashire coal field, ab. 7 mi. E of Manchester, ab. 185 mi. NW of London by rail. It is connected by canal with Manchester. Industries include coal mining, cotton finishing, and the spinning of coarse cotton yarns. 46,490 (1951).

Ashtoreth (ash'tǫ.reth). See **Astarte.**

Ashuanipi Lake (ash.wą.nip'i). Lake near the source of the Ashuanipi River in the SW corner of Labrador, near the Quebec boundary.

Ashuanipi River. [Also, **Grand River.**] River in Labrador flowing into Hamilton Inlet.

Ashuapmuchuan (ąsh.wäp.mö.chwän'). [Also: **Ashuapmouchouan, Chamouchouane.**] Middle course of the Saguenay River, in Quebec, Canada, flowing into Lake St. John. Length, 165 mi.

Ashuelot (ash.wil'ǫt). River in SW New Hampshire, a tributary of the Connecticut River.

Ashur (ash'ėr). A variant spelling of **Assur,** the national deity of ancient Assyria. It is an element in the names of many Assyrian rulers (**Assurbanipal,** etc.) and in the name of the country itself.

Ashurst (ash'ėrst), **Henry Fountain.** b. in a covered wagon near Winnemucca, Nev., Sept. 13, 1874—. American politician whose five terms (1912–40) as senior senator from Arizona were marked by some of the most colorful oratory in modern American political history. Elected for his first term one month after Arizona achieved statehood, he subsequently supported Woodrow Wilson on the Versailles Treaty, fought tax-exempt securities, and rose to the chairmanship of the Senate Judiciary Committee. Generally a supporter of New Deal measures, he introduced (1937) the bill by which F. D. Roosevelt hoped to add six justices to the Supreme Court, although he had only a few weeks before denounced the plan as "ridiculous, absurd, and unfair." He was defeated (1940) in the Democratic primary elections and withdrew from active political life.

Ashwander v. Tennessee Valley Authority, 297 U.S. 288 (1936) (ash'wąn.dėr). Decision of the U.S. Supreme Court upholding the authority of the U.S. government to dispose of surplus electrical power generated at Wilson Dam, a plant of the Tennessee Valley Authority. The majority opinion delivered by Chief Justice Charles Evans Hughes stressed the commerce and war powers and invoked the federal government's power, under the Fourth Article of the Constitution, "to dispose of and make all needful rules and regulations respecting the territory or other property belonging to the United States."

Ash Wednesday. Christian holy day marking the beginning of Lent and occurring seven weeks before Easter. In some churches, notably the Roman Catholic, the day, which is one of repentance and of sorrowing for human sinfulness, is marked by the symbolic application of ash to the forehead.

Ash Wednesday. Six-poem sequence by T. S. Eliot, published in 1930.

Asia (ā'zhą). [French, **Asie;** German, **Asien.**] Continent of the Eastern Hemisphere, the largest grand division of the world. It is bounded by the Arctic Ocean on the N, Bering Strait (which separates it from North America) on the NE, the Pacific Ocean on the E, and the Indian Ocean on the S. The Red Sea and Suez Canal (in the Isthmus of Suez) separate it from Africa, and the Mediterranean, Black, and Caspian seas separate it in part from Europe. The European boundary is vague, but is roughly represented by the Urals and the Caucasus. Asia extends from lat. 1°16′ N. to 77°40′ N., and long. 26°3′ E. to 169°40′ W. The chief divisions of the mainland are Korea, the U.S.S.R., China, Indochina, Burma, India, Turkey, and Arabia. Area, with islands, 16,495,345 sq. mi. (est.); pop. 1,317,500,000 (est. 1950).

History and Cultures. With the ancients the name also embraced the few parts of Africa known to them, and it was only after the Nile began to be considered as a dividing river that the countries W of it were separated from Asia, while Egypt was still included in it. Moreover, the knowledge of the ancients with regard to Asia did not reach far beyond the boundaries of the Perso-Macedonian empire. The parts S of the Himalaya range were called India, those to the N Scythia. The west was termed Upper and Lower Asia, the Tigris being the dividing line between both. In the books of the Maccabees "Asia" designates the parts of the kingdom of the Seleucides excepting Syria, i.e., the greatest part of Asia Minor; in the New Testament it is taken to be the Roman province, namely, the W part of the peninsula of Asia Minor, with Ephesus as capital, which was bequeathed to the republic by Attalus, king of Pergamum (133 B.C.). In Asia, it is assumed, stood the "cradle of mankind": according to legends of the oldest Asiatic nations, in the region of the Hindu Kush. Western Asia was, and is still, occupied by Semites.

Physical Geography. The principal physiographic

divisions of Asia are the Siberian and Turanian lowlands (steppes, in part), the desert regions of Arabia, Iran, and Mongolia, the plateau of the Deccan, in India, and the vast mountain complex which centers about the Pamirs and in various branches traverses the greater part of the continent S and SE of Turkistan and Siberia. Mount Everest, in the Himalayas (29,002 ft.), is the highest point on the globe. Rivers of the first magnitude are numerous, the longest being the Yangtze, Yenisei, and Ob.

Asia. Roman province, in Asia Minor, formed c130 B.C., comprising Mysia, Lydia, Caria, and Phrygia.

Asiago (ä'zyä.gō). Town and commune in NE Italy, in the *compartimento* (region) of Veneto, in the province of Vicenza, the chief place in the Sette Communi, ab. 38 mi NW of Padua. (The Sette Communi was an exclave of German speech within the territory of the Venetian Republic until the early 19th century.) Asiago was destroyed during the Austrian offensive in World War I, but was afterward reconstructed. Pop. of commune, 6,318 (1936); of town, 3,051 (1936).

Asia Minor (mī'nọr). Peninsula of W Asia which lies between the Black Sea and the Sea of Marmara on the N, the Aegean Sea on the W, and the Mediterranean Sea on the S; the E boundary is vague. The chief divisions in ancient times were Mysia, Lydia, Caria, Lycia, Pamphylia, Pisidia, Phrygia, Bithynia, Paphlagonia, Galatia, Lycaonia, Cilicia, Cappadocia, and Pontus. It is now roughly coextensive with Asiatic Turkey, or Anatolia. The surface is in the main a plateau, traversed by the Taurus and other ranges. The chief rivers are the Sakarya, Kizil Irmak, Menderes, Seyhan, and Gediz. It was the seat of Troy, Lydia, and other ancient powers, and of the Ionian Greek civilization; its possession has been disputed by Persia, Macedonia, Syria, Rome, the Byzantine empire, Parthia, the Saracens, the Seljuks, and the modern Turks. According to Herodotus, there were 15 races or nations in Asia Minor: in the S part the Cilicians, Pamphylians, Lycians, and Caunians; W of the great central plateau, close to the coast, the Carians, Lydians, Mysians, and Greeks; on the shores of the Euxine or Black Sea, Thracians, Marlandynians, Paphlagonians, and Cappadocians; in the interior, the Phrygians, Chalybes, and Matieni.

Asiatic Russia (ā.zhi.at'ik rush'ạ). Name often applied to those regions of Asia which are under Russian rule. The term Asia has various meanings but the most popular division between Europe and Asia is along a line following the crest of the Ural Mountains to a point ab. 55° N. latitude, then following the Ural River to the Caspian Sea. Thus Asiatic Russia includes all of the Turkmen, Uzbek, Tadzhik, and Kirgiz Soviet Socialist Republics as well as most of the Kazakh, and a large part of the Russian Soviet Federated Socialist Republic.

Asie (à.zē). French name of **Asia.**

Asien (ä'zyẹn). German name of **Asia.**

Asiento (ä.syen'tō). License conferring (1713) upon the English South Sea Company the monopoly of selling over a 30-year period 144,000 Negro slaves in the Spanish colonies. The license was granted by the royal government of Spain, which was paid the equivalent of 200,000 dollars for the privilege.

As I Lay Dying. Stream-of-consciousness novel by William Faulkner, published in 1930.

Asinara (ä.sē.nä'rä). [Ancient name, **Insula Herculis.**] Island off the NW coast of Sardinia, belonging to the Italian province of Sassari. Length, ab. 11 mi.

Asinara, Gulf of. Arm of the Mediterranean, off the NW coast of Sardinia.

Asinarus (as.i.nā'rus). [Italian names, **Falconare, Fiume di Noto.**] In ancient geography, a small river in the province of Syracuse, Sicily. Near here the Syracusans defeated (413 B.C.) the Athenians.

Asini (ä.sē'nē). [Also, **Assini.**] One of the Sudanic-speaking Akan peoples of W Africa, inhabiting the S Gold Coast.

Asinia gens (ạ.sin'i.ạ jenz). In ancient Rome, a plebeian clan or house, originally from Teate, the principal town of the Marrucini, whose family names were Agrippa, Celer, Dento, Gallus, Pollio, and Saloninus.

Asioli (ä.zyô'lē), **Bonifacio.** b. at Correggio, Italy, Aug. 30, 1769; d. May 18, 1832. Italian composer. A child prodigy, he had written three masses by the age of eight. Author of *Principi elementari di musica* (1809).

Asir (ä.sēr'). [Also, **Asyr.**] Mountainous region in W Arabia, along the coast of the Red Sea, between Hejaz on the N and Yemen on the S.

Asís Cambó (ä.sēs' käm.bō'), **Francisco de.** See **Cambó, Francisco de Asís.**

Asisi (ä.sē'zē). See **Assisi.**

Ask (äsk) and **Embla** (em'blä). [Old Norse, **Askr** and **Embla.**] In Old Norse mythology, the first man and woman, created in Midgard by the three gods Odin, Hoenir, and Lodur (Old Norse, Lodhurr), out of trees found on the seashore. Odin gave them life; Hoenir, sense; and Lodur, blood and color.

Askabad (as'kạ.bad). See **Ashkhabad.**

Askanazy (äs.kä.nä'tsē), **Max.** b. at Stallupönen, in East Prussia, Feb. 24, 1865; d. at Geneva, Switzerland, Oct. 23, 1940. Swiss pathologist. He was graduated (1890) from Königsberg, was professor of pathological anatomy (1905–39) at the University of Geneva, and became (1935) an honorary citizen of the city of Geneva. He made original studies of the blood, malignant tumors, animal parasites, and the pathology of bones, and called attention (1904) to a relationship between the parathyroid glands and decalcification of the bones. He reorganized the department of pathology at Geneva and was instrumental in the creation of a special building for the Pathological Institute. He was the founder of the International Society for Geographical Pathology. Author of *Zur Regeneration der quergestreiften Muskelfasern* (1890), *Die Dermoidcysten des Eierstockes* (1905), *Knochenmark* (1927), *Erreichte und erstrebte Ziele der Geschwulstforschung* (1928), *Äussere Krankheitsursachen* (1928), and *Die Entzündung* (1929).

Askanien (äs.kä'ni.ẹn). Ancient countship of Germany, named from a castle near Aschersleben.

Aske (ask), **Robert.** Executed at York, England, 1537. English lawyer, leader of the Yorkshire Catholic insurrection called the "Pilgrimage of Grace."

Askelon (as'kẹ.lon). See **Ashkelon.**

Askenazy (äs.ke.nä'zi), **Szymon.** b. 1866; d. 1935. Polish historian and diplomat. A professor of modern history at the University of Lemberg (now Lvov) and a member of the Polish academy of sciences, he founded a school of history famous for its researches in the field of diplomatic history during the period of the Polish partitions. He was a delegate (1920–23) to the League of Nations. Author of many historical works, among them *Die letzte polnische Königswahl* (1894), *Przymierze polsko-pruskie* (1900), *Ksiaże Józef Poniatowski* (1904; German edition, 1912; French edition, 1921), *Rosja a Polska, 1815–1830* (1907), *Łukasiński* (2 vols., 1908), *Napoleon a Polska* (3 vols., 1918–19), and *Gdańsk a Polska* (1919; English edition, 1920).

Askew (as'kū), **Anne.** [Also: **Ascue, Ayscough.**] b. at Stallingborough, England, c1521; burned at Smithfield, in London, July 16, 1546. English Protestant who, accused of heresy in regard to the sacraments, was imprisoned and tortured, but refused to recant. Her self-possession and skill in argument drew much sympathy, and her account of the events leading up to her martyrdom, published by John Bale, strengthened the Protestant cause.

Askew, Sir **George.** See **Ayscue,** Sir **George.**

Askhabad (as'kạ.bad). See **Ashkhabad.**

Askia Mohammed (äs'kẹ.ä mọ.ham'ẹd). Founder of the Askia dynasty which ruled the Songhai of W Africa from 1493 until 1591, when it was defeated and overthrown by Moorish troops from Morocco. Mohammed was a Sarakole general who overthrew the ruling Sonni dynasty and took the title of Askia, ruling from 1493 to 1529. By recruiting a professional army from slaves and prisoners of war, he avoided the economic disruptions formerly caused by the practice of conscripting farmers, traders, and merchants, and his troops established an empire which stretched thousands of miles from W of Djenné in what is now French Sudan to the conquered Hausa states of N Nigeria. He showed great respect for scholars and religious leaders, and under his patronage the cities of Gao, Walata, Djenné, and especially Timbuktu became intellectual centers whose scholarship was famed throughout the Mohammedan world.

Askja (äsk'yä). Volcano in the interior of Iceland. It was in eruption in 1875. Elevation, ab. 3,200 ft.

Asklepios (as.klē'pi.os). See **Aesculapius.**

Askwith (as'kwith), **George Ranken.** [Title, 1st **Baron Askwith.**] b. 1861; d. at London, June 3, 1942. English expert on industrial arbitration, who served (1911–19) as chief English industrial commissioner. He settled the cotton dispute of 1911 and the great strike at Belfast, was umpire (1913–15) of the Scottish Coal Conciliation Board, and served as chairman (1915–17) of the government arbitration committee. Author of *Industrial Problems and Disputes* (1920), and other books.

Aslaugas Ritter (äs.lou'gäs rit'ėr). [Eng. trans., "*Aslauga's Knight.*"] German story (1814) by Baron de La Motte-Fouqué, translated into English in Carlyle's *German Romance*. Aslauga is a spirit chosen by the Knight in preference to any earthly ladylove. She appears to him at important moments in his career, and he dies fancying himself clasped in her arms and shrouded in her wonderful golden hair.

Asmai (äs'mä.ē), **al-.** [Full name, **abu-Said Abd al-Malik ibn-Koraib al-Asmai.**] b. at Basra, c739; d. at Baghdad, 831. Arab writer and scholar, believed by some authorities to have written the romance known as *Antar*. He sought to keep Arabian literature and language free of foreign influence, thus directly opposing abu-Ubayda, who espoused the cause of imported elements in Arabic culture; he was employed by Harun al-Rashid as tutor to his son. Author of *Book of Wild Animals, Book of Distinction, Book of the Horse,* and others, most of which are no longer extant.

Asmara (äs.mä'rä). City in E Africa, the capital of the former Italian colony of Eritrea. It is situated ab. 75 mi. from the coast port of Massawa on a plateau ab. 8,000 ft. above sea level; the altitude gives it a pleasant climate. It is connected by rail with Massawa and other towns on the plateau. It is included in the area voted (1949) to Ethiopia by the United Nations, and along with Massawa it is given special status in order to provide for the protection of the large Italian population. Pop. 85,000, including 50,000 Europeans (1939).

Asmodeus (as.mǭ.dē'us, az-). [Hebrew, **Ashmodai.**] In later Jewish demonology, a destructive demon. In the *Book of Tobit* he is said to have loved Sara and to have destroyed in succession her seven husbands, appearing as a succubus on their bridal nights. He is hence jocularly spoken of as the destroyer of domestic happiness. When, however, Sara was married to the son of Tobit, Asmodeus was driven away by the fumes from the burning heart and liver of a fish (hence the allusion in *Paradise Lost*, iv. 168). King Solomon, in his search for the mysterious and miraculous Shamir, ordered Asmodeus, who knew the secret, to be brought to him. He resisted the summons violently, upsetting trees and houses. A poor widow begging him not to injure her little hut, he turned aside so sharply that he broke his leg and has been a "lame devil" ever since. Probably drawing from a Spanish source, Alain René Le Sage made him the hero of his romance *Le Diable Boiteux,* from which Samuel Foote took his play *The Devil on Two Sticks*. He appears in Le Sage's work as the companion of Don Cleofas, whom he takes with him in his wonderful flight over the roofs of Madrid, showing him by his diabolical power the insides of houses as they fly over them. In the novel he is a witty, playful, malicious creature. He is also introduced in Christoph Martin Wieland's *Oberon*.

Asmun (äs'mön). See **Eshmun.**

Asnappar (as.nap'ạr). See **Asenappar.**

Åsnen (ōs'nẹn), **Lake.** Lake in S Sweden, in the S central part of Kronoberg, S of Växjö.

Asnières (å.nyer). Town and river port in N France, in the department of Seine; it is a suburb of Paris, situated on the Seine River, ab. 1 mi. NW of the former fortifications of that city, on the route from Paris to Argenteuil. It has manufactures of dyes and perfume, and is known for its yacht races. The town suffered considerable damage in World War II. 2,273 (1946).

Asnyk (äs'nik), **Adam.** b. at Kalisz, in Russian Poland, Sept. 11, 1838; d. at Cracow (now Kraków), Aug. 2, 1897. Polish poet, a leading representative of the "Cracow School" of poets in the positivist era following the anti-Russian uprising of 1863. He was one of the "discoverers" of the Tatra mountain folk and scene as literary material. Much of his work was published in *Poezye* (1872–80). He was a friend of the actress Helena Modjeska.

Aso (ä.sō), **Mount.** See **Asosan.**

Asoka (ạ.sō'kạ). [Also: **Açoka, Piyadasi.**] d. 232 B.C. A king of the Maurya dynasty of Magadha, ruler of an empire that embraced most of N and C India; son of Bindusara, and grandson of Chandragupta. He reigned c272–232 B.C. In consequence of a quarrel with his father, he fled to Rajputana and the Punjab. Returning at the moment of his father's death, he massacred his brothers and obtained the throne. In time (261 B.C. *et seq.*) he extended his sway over Hindustan, the Punjab, and Afghanistan, while he claimed to rule also over South India and Ceylon. Converted by a miracle, he openly adopted Buddhism and became what might be called the Buddhist Constantine. Especially noted are his edicts enjoining the practical morality of Buddhism, which are engraved in different Prakrit dialects on pillars or rocks in various parts of India.

Asola (ä'zō.lä). Town and commune in N Italy, in the *compartimento* (region) of Lombardy, in the province of Mantova, situated on the Chiese River, ab. 19 mi. NW of Mantua. The town has ancient Venetian walls. Chestnuts are among the chief products of the surrounding district. Pop. of commune, 10,809 (1936); of town, 3,908 (1936).

Asolando: Facts and Fancies (as.ǭ.lan'dō). Volume of poems by Robert Browning, published in London on Dec. 12, 1889, the day on which the poet died at Venice. It is a collection of love lyrics, versified anecdotes, and philosophical pronouncements. It closes with the *Epilogue* in which Browning describes himself as

"One who never turned his back but marched breast
forward,
Never doubted clouds would break,
Never dreamed, though right were worsted, wrong
would triumph,
Held we fall to rise, are baffled to fight better,
Sleep to wake."

Asolo (ä'zō.lō). [Ancient name, **Acelum.**] Town and commune in NE Italy, in the *compartimento* (region) of Veneto, in the province of Treviso, situated in the foothills of the Alps, NW of Treviso. It is a resort and tourist center, frequented especially by Venetians. It is the site of important paleolithic excavations, and has Roman remains and a medieval castle. In the 19th century it was a favorite sojourning place of Robert Browning and of Eleonora Duse. Buildings of interest to tourists were undamaged in World War II. Pop. of commune, 10,042 (1936); of town, 760 (1936).

Asopus (ạ.sō'pus). [Modern name, **Oropo.**] In ancient geography, a small river in Boeotia, Greece, flowing into the Euripus in N Attica.

Asopus. [Modern name, **Hagios Georgios.**] In ancient geography, a small river in Sicyonia, Greece, flowing into the Corinthian Gulf ab. 4 mi. NE of Sicyon.

Asopus. In Greek mythology, the god of the Sicyonian river Asopus. He was struck by a thunderbolt from Zeus.

Asosan (ä.sō.sän). [Also, **Mount Aso.**] Active volcano on the island of Kyushu, Japan, whose crater is one of the largest in the world. 5,225 ft.

Asotus (ạ.sō'tụs). In Ben Jonson's *Cynthia's Revels,* a foolish and prodigal coxcomb, the hanger-on of Amorphus, whom he imitates in every way.

Aspadana (as.pạ.dā'nạ). Ancient name of **Isfahan.**

Aspandiyar (as.pan.di.yär'). See **Asfandiyar.**

Asparagus Gardens. In 16th and 17th century England, a place of public entertainment, not far from Pimlico (which is now a district of London near Westminster). It is to this that Richard Brome refers in his *Sparagus Garden*.

Aspasia (as.pā'zhạ). b. at Miletus, in Ionia; fl. c440 B.C. Greek courtesan, renowned for her wisdom, beauty, and wit. She was for many years the mistress of Pericles, who was so attracted to her that he left his wife and would have married her except for his own law of 451 B.C., which forbade Athenians to take foreign wives. Her brilliance made her house a center of Athenian literary and philosophical life. Accused of impiety, she was saved from death by Pericles' eloquence; her son, by Pericles, was legitimized under his father's name by a special Athenian decree.

Aspasia or **Aspatia** (as.pā'sha). The heroine of Beaumont and Fletcher's *The Maid's Tragedy.* She is betrothed to Amintor and is deserted by him. Heartbroken, she seeks her death by disguising herself as a man and challenging Amintor to a duel in which he kills her.

Aspasia the Younger. [Original name (according to Plutarch), **Milto.**] b. at Phocaea, in Asia Minor; fl. late 5th century B.C. Greek beauty, mistress of Cyrus the Younger and of his brother Artaxerxes. She was named after Aspasia, consort of Pericles, by Cyrus in tribute to her beauty and wit. She became the mistress of Artaxerxes on the death of Cyrus and was made by him a priestess when Darius sought to claim her as part of his perquisites in succeeding to the throne.

Aspasius (as.pā'zhus). b. at Ravenna, Italy; fl. c225–238 A.D. Roman rhetorician and Sophist philosopher who served as secretary to the first emperor Maximinus (173–238).

Aspects of Modern Poetry. Critical work by Edith Sitwell, published in 1934.

Aspects of the Novel. Critical work (1927) by Edward Morgan Forster.

Aspen (as'pen). City in C Colorado, the county seat of Pitkin County, W of Leadville: formerly important for silver mining, now a winter sports resort. In the summer of 1949, an international festival commemorating the 200th birthday of Goethe was held here. 916 (1950).

Aspendos (as.pen'dos). [Also, **Aspendus** (-dus).] In ancient geography, a city in Pamphylia, Asia Minor, on the Eurymedon. It contains a Roman theater, which is one of the best-preserved of all ancient structures of the kind. The cavea is quite intact. There is also a Roman aqueduct which crosses the valley by a long range of arches.

Asper (as'pėr). In Ben Jonson's *Every Man out of his Humour,* a character which he designed as a portrait of himself.

Asper. Pseudonym of Samuel Johnson in the *Rambler.* It was under this name that he launched his attacks on David Garrick.

Asperg (äs'perk). [Also, **Asberg.**] Town in S Germany, in the *Land* (state) of Württemberg-Baden, American Zone, formerly in the *Neckar-Kreis* (Neckar district) of Württemberg, ab. 9 mi. N of Stuttgart: chemical, metallurgical, ceramics manufactures. North of it, situated on a steep elevation, is the fortress of Hohenasperg, until 1883 the state prison of Württemberg, from which the place gained much ill fame in the 18th and 19th centuries: Joseph Süss Oppenheimer, Christian Friedrich Daniel Schubart, and Friedrich List the economist, were all prisoners here. 5,329 (1946).

Aspern (äs'pėrn). Former village in E Austria, in the province of Lower Austria, since 1905 incorporated into the city of Vienna, situated on the N bank of the Danube River, ab. 5 mi. NE of downtown Vienna. Here, on May 21–22, 1809, the Austrians under the archduke Charles gave battle to the French army under Napoleon I and succeeded in forcing Napoleon's retreat. 5,661 (1946).

Aspern, Battle of. [Also, **Battle of Essling.**] Victory gained at Aspern and Essling, near Vienna, on May 21 and 22, 1809, by the Austrians (80,000) under the archduke Charles over the French (40,000 and later 80,000) under Napoleon. The loss of the Austrians was about 24,000; that of the French considerably more, including Jean Lannes, one of Napoleon's marshals.

Aspern Papers (as'pėrn). Novelette by Henry James, published in 1888.

Aspe Valley (åsp). [French, **Vallée d'Aspe** (vå.lā dåsp).] Valley in the department of Basses-Pyrénées, France, near the Spanish frontier, traversed by one of the main routes across the Pyrenees. It formed a medieval republic under the protection of Béarn.

Asphaltites (as.fal.tī'tēz), **Lacus.** A Latin name of the **Dead Sea.**

Aspidiske (as.pi.dis'kē) or **Asmidiske** (-mi-). The fourth-magnitude star ι Argus, situated in the shield which ornaments the vessel's poop. There is some confusion in the lettering of the stars of this constellation, and some star-maps assign this name to ξ instead of ι.

Aspinall (as'pi.nal), Sir **Algernon Edward.** b. 1871—. English author of books on the West Indies, and president and secretary (1898–1938) of the West India Committee. Educated at Eton and at Magdalen College, Oxford (B.A. 1894), he was called to the bar of the Inner Temple, London, in 1897. Author of *Pocket Guide to the West Indies* (1910), *West Indian Tales of Old* (1912), and *A Wayfarer in the West Indies* (1928).

Aspinwall (as'pin.wôl). Borough in SW Pennsylvania, in Allegheny County: residential suburb of Pittsburgh. 4,084 (1950).

Aspinwall. A former name of **Colón**, Panama.

Aspinwall, William Henry. b. at New York, Dec. 16, 1807; d. there, Jan. 18, 1875. American merchant, banker, and railroad promoter. He was the head of the group which financed the building (1850–55) of the Panama Railroad, the eastern terminus of which (now Colón) was originally named for him. He was also active in the establishment (1848) of the Pacific Mail Steamship Company which, with the railroad, put a through water-rail route to California in the hands of a single group and made Aspinwall in less than a decade one of New York's wealthiest men. A founder of New York's Union League Club and a firm supporter of Abraham Lincoln, he served as a secret emissary of the Union to persuade Great Britain to halt the building of iron-clads for the Confederacy.

Aspiroz (äs.pē.rōs'), **Manuel de.** b. at Puebla, Mexico, June 9, 1836; d. at Washington, D.C., March 24, 1905. Mexican soldier and diplomat. He was graduated (1855) from the University of Mexico. He was active in the Juárez insurrection (1863) against Maximilian, and was judge advocate of the court which sentenced the emperor to death. Assistant secretary of state for foreign affairs (1867 *et seq.*), he participated (1872) in the amicable settlement of U.S.-Mexican claims. In 1899 he became the first Mexican ambassador to the U.S., a post he held until his death.

Aspramonte (äs.prä.mōn'tā). Italian epic poem, by an unknown author, which appeared at Milan in 1516, in the same year as the first version of Lodovico Ariosto's *Orlando Furioso.* The subject is the defeat of the Saracens by the French when the former came over in large numbers under Garnier, king of Carthage, to sack Rome. This accomplished, they went across to France where Charlemagne and the great paladins under him defeated them near Aspramonte (Aspremont), a small place in France (not to be confused with the mountain named Aspromonte in S Italy, in Calabria).

Aspre (däs'pre), Baron **Konstantin d'.** b. 1789; d. 1850. Austrian general. He distinguished himself in the Italian campaigns of 1848–49.

Aspromonte (äs.prō.mōn'tā). Mountain in Calabria, Italy, ab. 10–20 mi. NE of Reggio. Near it Giuseppe Garibaldi was defeated and captured by Italian troops on Aug. 29, 1862. Elevation, nearly 7,000 ft.

Aspropotamos (äs.prô.pô'tä.môs). See **Achelous.**

Aspull (as'pul). Urban district in NW England, in Lancashire, ab. 3 mi. NE of Wigan. It has no direct rail connections, being reached by rail to Wigan, ab. 194 mi. NW of London. 6,522 (1951).

Asquith (as'kwith), **Elizabeth.** [Married name, Princess **Bibesco.**] b. 1897; d. at Bucharest, Rumania, April 8, 1945. English novelist, dramatist, and poet; daughter of Herbert Henry and Margot Asquith. She was the author of *I Have Only Myself to Blame* (1921), *Balloons* (1923), *The Fir and the Palm* (1924), *There Is No Return* (1927), *Portrait of Caroline* (1931), and *The Romantic* (1940), all fiction; *The Painted Swan* and *Points of View* (both 1926), three-act plays; and *Poems* (1927).

Asquith, Herbert. b. March 11, 1881—. English novelist, poet, soldier, and lawyer; son of Herbert Henry Asquith, 1st Earl of Oxford and Asquith, and brother of Elizabeth Asquith. He saw service (1915–18) in France and Flanders in World War I. Author of poetry including *The Volunteer* (1915), *A Village Sermon* (1920), *Pillicock Hill, Poems 1912–1933* (1934), and *Youth in the Skies* (1940); of the novels *Wind's End, Young Orland* (1927), *Roon* (1929), and *Mary Dallon;* and of *Moments of Memory: Recollections and Impressions* (1937).

Asquith, Herbert Henry. [Title, 1st Earl of **Oxford and Asquith.**] b. at Morley, Yorkshire, England, Sept.

12, 1852; d. at Sutton Courtney, Berkshire, England, Feb. 15, 1928. English statesman. He was educated at Balliol College, Oxford, and was called to the bar in 1876. In 1886 he became a Liberal member of Parliament for East Fife. He was secretary of state for the home department (1892–95), ecclesiastical commissioner (1892–95), chancellor of the exchequer (December, 1905, to 1908), and prime minister (1908–16). During his term as prime minister, the Liberal Party had some of its most successful years. Asquith managed, against heavy opposition, to restrict somewhat the veto power of the House of Lords, but did not succeed in passing the Home Rule Bill, of which he had been for many years a strong advocate. In 1926, a year after he had been raised to the peerage, he resigned his leadership of the Liberal Party.

Asquith, Margot. [Maiden name, **Emma Alice Margaret Tennant;** title, Countess of **Oxford and Asquith.**] b. near the Scottish border, 1864; d. at London, July 28, 1945. British author, known for her controversial writings on public problems; daughter of Sir Charles Tennant, a Glasgow industrialist and art patron, and second wife of Herbert Henry Asquith (1852–1928), whom she married in 1894. She was the author of a lively *Autobiography* (1922), *Octavia* (1928), *More Memories* (1933), and *Off the Record* (1944), a series of frank character sketches of eleven prime ministers.

Ass, Feast of the. See **Feast of the Ass.**

Assab (ä'säb). Port in NE Africa, in the former Italian colony of Eritrea, situated on the W Red Sea coast near the Bab el Mandeb strait, just above French Somaliland. It is the terminus of a road leading into the interior. Assab was the first Italian settlement in the colony of Eritrea. It is included in the part of Eritrea voted (1949) by the United Nations to Ethiopia.

Assab, Bay of. Bay on the E coast of Africa, in the Red Sea, near the S end of Eritrea. From 1881 to 1941 it belonged, with adjacent villages, to Italy as part of the colony of Eritrea, which Italy surrendered to the Allies in World War II.

Assad (as'sad). In the story of "Prince Amgiad and Prince Assad," in *The Arabian Nights' Entertainments*, the son of Camaralzaman and Haiatalnefous.

Assal (äs.säl'). Salt lake in E Africa, inland from the Gulf of Tadjoura, an arm of the Gulf of Aden. 571 ft. below sea level.

Assam (as.sam'). State in the NE part of the Union of India, bordering on East Bengal, in Pakistan, and extending up the valley of the Brahmaputra River to the borders of China. Rice, rubber, tea, and tobacco are the important crops of the area. In the SW end of the state much jute is raised, and in the NE oil has been discovered. Capital, Shillong; area, 54,951 sq. mi.; pop. 9,129,442 (1951).

Assamese (as.ạ.mēz'). An Indo-European language spoken by about two million people in Assam, the easternmost state of the Union of India. It is closely related to Bengali, and its script resembles that of Bengali, but there has been a distinctive Assamese literature since the 14th century A.D. This modern Indian language is not to be confused with the entirely unrelated Assamese groups of dialects belonging to the Tibeto-Burman family.

Assandun (ạ.san'dun). Locality, identified with Ashingdon, Essex, England, where Edmund Ironsides was defeated (1016) by Canute.

Assanovgrad (äs.sä'nùv.grät). [Also, **Stanimakai.**] Town in S Bulgaria, in the department of Plovdiv, situated on the Karajska River, ab. 13 mi. SW of Plovdiv, at the foot of the Rhodope Mountains, in a wine and silkworm producing region. 20,920 (1946).

Assassin, The. Novel by Liam O'Flaherty, published in 1928.

Assassination Plot. Name given to a conspiracy against the life of William III of England, by Sir George Barclay and Robert Charnock, detected in 1696.

Assassins. Military and religious order in Syria, founded (c1090) in Persia by Hasan ibn-al-Sabbah. A colony migrated from Persia to Syria, settled in various places, with their chief seat on the mountains of Lebanon, and became notorious for their secret murders in blind obedience to the will of their chief. Their religion was a compound of Magianism, Judaism, Christianity, and Mohammedanism. One article of their creed was that the Holy Spirit resided in their chief and that his orders proceeded from God himself. The chief of the sect was best known by the denomination "old man of the mountain" (in Arabic, *sheik al-jebal*, meaning "chief of the mountains"). These chieftains and their followers spread terror among nations far and near for almost two centuries. In the time of the Crusades they totaled some 50,000, and presented a formidable obstacle to the arms of the Christians. They were eventually subdued by the Mongols about 1256. Their name is derived from the Arabic word for the drug hashish, which they are generally believed to have used to prepare themselves for their terroristic assignments. From the standpoint of strict etymology, the name does not stem from the fact that assassinations were carried out under influence of the drug, but from a play on the word itself, which is "hashishiyun" in Arabic. Although they are best known in the western world for the fanaticism and ferocity which was unquestionably a characteristic of part of the sect at one time, they carried out a certain amount of scientific research at their fortress in Syria, and also amassed a considerable library (which was destroyed by the Mongols). Some remnants of the sect may be found scattered through the Moslem world even today, but they have long since ceased to have any international significance.

Assaye (äs.sī'). [Also, **Assye.**] Village in Hyderabad, C Union of India, ab. 210 mi. NE of the city of Bombay. Here 9,500 men under Wellesley (Duke of Wellington) defeated more than 40,000 Mahrattas on Sept. 23, 1803. The loss of the British was ab. 1,800.

Asse (äs'ẹ). [Also, **Assche-lez-Bruxelles** (åsh.lā.brü-sel).] Town in C Belgium, in the province of Brabant, ab. 7 mi. NW of Brussels: tanneries; breweries; Gothic church. 11,111 (1947).

Assebroek (äs'ẹ.brök). Town in NW Belgium, in the province of West Flanders, ab. 1 mi. SE of Bruges, of which it is a suburb. 11,337 (1947).

Asselbergs (äs'ẹl.berks), **W. J. M. A.** See **Duinkerken, Anton Van.**

Asselyn (äs'ẹ.līn), **Jan.** [Surnamed **Krabbetje.**] b. c1610; d. at Amsterdam, c1660. Dutch painter of landscapes, animals, and battles.

Assemani (äs.sä.mä'nē), **Giuseppe Aloysio.** b. at Tripoli, in Syria, c1710; d. at Rome, Feb. 9, 1782. Syrian Orientalist; nephew of Giuseppe Simone Assemani. He served as professor of Oriental languages at Rome.

Assemani, Giuseppe Simone. b. at Tripoli, in Syria, 1687; d. at Rome, Jan. 14, 1768. Syrian Orientalist. Sent (1717, 1735) by the Vatican library to the Near East, he obtained several hundred extremely valuable manuscripts, and was thereafter appointed Vatican librarian and titular archbishop of Tyre. Author of the incomplete but valuable *Bibliotheca Orientalis Clementino-Vaticana* (1719–28).

Assemani, Simone. b. at Tripoli, in Syria, 1752; d. at Padua, Italy, 1821. Syrian scholar; a relative of Giuseppe Aloysio Assemani. He was professor of Oriental languages at Padua, and author of several works on Oriental numismatics.

Assemani, Stefano Evodio. b. at Tripoli, in Syria, c1707; d. 1782. Syrian Orientalist; nephew of Giuseppe Simone Assemani, whom he assisted at the Vatican library. His works include *Bibliothecae Mediceo-Laurentianae et Palatinae cod.* (1742), *Acta Sanctorum Martyrum* (1748), and others.

Assembly of Ladies, The. Poem attributed to Geoffrey Chaucer, but now considered spurious. It is an imitation of Chaucer's *Parliament of Fowles.*

Assen (äs'ẹn). Town in NE Netherlands, the capital of the province of Drenthe, ab. 16 mi. S of Groningen. It is connected by canal with Groningen, Meppel, and the Wadden Zee. It has canneries, cement works, and other industries. Peat bogs are in the vicinity; also the "Giant's Caves" and other prehistoric monuments, and there is an archaeological museum. The town, built around an old nunnery, attained importance only in the 19th century. 20,235 (1939).

Asser (as'ėr). d. at Sherborne, England, c909 A.D. Welsh monk, bishop of Sherborne (c900 *et seq.*); tutor and companion of Alfred the Great. Author of a life of Alfred (c893), containing also a history of England (849–87), which was used by later chroniclers.

Asser (äs'ėr), **Tobias Michael Carel.** b. at Amsterdam, 1838; d. at The Hague, 1913. Dutch statesman and student of international law. An authority on international law, he was professor of law at the Athenaeum of Amsterdam and held (1876 *et seq.*) the same post at the University of Amsterdam. He was appointed counsellor (1875) to the Dutch foreign office and a member (1893) of the council of state, and served as delegate to numerous international conferences, notably the Hague Conference (1899). He shared the Nobel peace prize (1911) with A. H Fried. Author of *La Codification du droit international privé* (1901) and *Arbitrage international entre les États-Unis d'Amérique et la Russie* (1902).

Assideans (as.i.dē'ạnz). See **Hasidim.**

Assignation, The. Story by Edgar Allan Poe, originally published (1834) in *Godey's Lady's Book* under the title "The Visionary." It was included in his collection, *Tales of the Grotesque and Arabesque* (1840).

Assing (äs'ing), **Ludmilla.** b. at Hamburg, Feb. 22, 1821; d. at Florence, March 25, 1880. German author, editor of various works by Varnhagen von Ense (her uncle) and of his correspondence with Alexander von Humboldt. Charged with libel by the Prussian government for political references in von Ense's diary (published 1861–71), she fled to Florence.

Assini (äs.sē'nē). See also **Asini.**

Assini. Former small French protectorate on the W coast of Africa, W of the British Gold Coast, on a river of the same name. It is now part of the French territory of Ivory Coast, French West Africa.

Assiniboia (ạ.sin.i.boi'ạ). Formerly a provisional district in the NW part of Canada, formed in 1882. It extended to the N nearly to lat. 52° N., and to the W to a little beyond long. 111°. It was bounded on the S by the U.S. and on the E by Manitoba. On the establishment in 1905 of the provinces of Alberta and Saskatchewan, by far the larger part of it was incorporated in the latter province. Today it is the name of a small town in S Saskatchewan ab. 77 mi. S of Moose Jaw and ab 67 mi. N of the U.S. border. 1,349 (1941).

Assiniboin (ạ.sin'i.boin). North American Indian tribe whose language was a member of the Siouan family, formerly inhabiting what is now NE Montana, NW North Dakota, and SW Saskatchewan.

Assiniboine (ạ.sin'i.boin). River in the S part of Manitoba, Canada, which joins the Red River at Winnipeg Manitoba. Length, ab. 590 mi.

Assiniboine, Mount. Mountain in W Canada, in the Rocky Mountains, ab. 25 mi. SW of Banff. It is one of the peaks on the Continental Divide. 11,870 ft.

Assiout or **Assiut** (äs.yöt'). See **Asyut.**

Assís (ạ.sēs'), **Joaquim Maria Machado de.** b. at Rio de Janeiro, Brazil, June 21, 1839; d. there, Sept. 29, 1908. Brazilian novelist, short story writer, poet, critic, journalist, and playwright, an outstanding figure of Brazilian literature and considered one of the best writers in the Portuguese language. His most notable novels are *Memórias póstumas de Braz Cubas* (1881), *Quincas Borba* (1891), and *Dom Casmurro* (1900). Among his books of poetry are *Crisálidas* (1864), *Falenas* (1870), and *Americanas* (1875). His complete works have been published in 31 volumes.

Assís Figueiredo (fē.gā.rā'dö), **Afonso Celso de.** See **Celso, Afonso.**

Assisi (äs.sē'zē). [Also: **Asisi**; ancient name, **Assisium** (ạ.sizh'i.um).] Town and commune in C Italy, in the *compartimento* (region) of Umbria, in the province of Perugia, situated on the slope of Mount Subasio, ab. 12 mi. SE of Perugia. There are remains of Etruscan walls, and a Roman temple of Minerva. Assisi became famous as the birthplace and home of Saint Francis of Assisi (1182–1226), who also died here. The Gothic Franciscan monastery and the upper and lower church contain (in the crypt) his tomb and also paintings by Cimabue, Giotto, and other masters, portraying events in the life of the saint. The town, which has preserved its medieval character, has many other churches, including Santa Chiara, San Damiano, San Ruffino, and Santa Maria degli Angeli, the latter dating from 1569; there is a medieval castle. It was at various times part of the States of the Church until it was definitely attached to Rome in the pontificate of Pope Paul III. The town escaped serious damage in World War II. Pop. of commune, 22,514 (1936); of town, 4,686 (1936).

Assize of Clarendon (klar'ẹn.dọn). English ordinance, issued in 1166, which introduced important changes in the administration of English justice.

Assize of Northampton (nôrth.amp'tọn). English ordinance, a reissue and expansion of the Assize of Clarendon, issued at Northampton in 1176, drawn up in the form of instructions to the judges. The new articles relate to tenure, reliefs, dower, and other matters.

Assizes of Jerusalem (jẹ.rö'sạ.lẹm). Two codes of laws, drawn up under the authority of Godfrey of Bouillon, the first Crusader to serve as ruler of Jerusalem, and in force under the Christian sovereignty at Jerusalem and Cyprus. One code had jurisdiction over the nobility, the second over the common people. Both were conceived with a wisdom and enlightenment beyond their age, and were based on contemporary French law and customs.

Assmannshausen (äs'mäns.hou.zẹn). [Also, **Bad Assmannshausen.**] Village in W Germany, in the *Land* (state) of Hessen, American Zone, formerly in the province of Hesse-Nassau, Prussia, situated on the Rhine River, ab. 16 mi. W of Mainz. It is celebrated for its red wines. It is a health resort, with thermal springs, which are visited by people suffering from gout and rheumatism. 1,504 (1946).

Associated Counties. In English history, a name given to the counties of Norfolk, Suffolk, Essex, Hertford, Cambridge, Huntingdon, and Lincoln, because they combined (1642–46) to join the Parliamentary side in the English Civil War, and to keep their territory free from invasion.

Associated Loyalists (of *New England*). [Also, **Loyal Associated Refugees.**] Groups organized in Rhode Island during the British occupation (December, 1776–October, 1779) in the Revolutionary War. They were established under the leadership of Colonel Edward Winslow, Jr, and carried out raids against the coast of Long Island Sound in revenge for actions taken by colonial supporters of the Revolutionary cause.

Associated Press. [Abbreviation, **A.P.** or **AP**] American news-gathering agency, with headquarters at New York, originally organized in 1848. In its present form it dates from the organization of a coöperative association by Victor F. Lawson in 1892. Its services of news and picture collection and distribution cover the world. The unit has approximately 7,200 staff newsmen in the U.S. and foreign countries, and provides service to some 1,500 member newspapers. The association is under the ownership and control of the member publishers.

Associated Press v. National Labor Relations Board, 301 U.S. 103 (1937). Decision of the U.S. Supreme Court upholding the enforcement of the Wagner Labor Relations Act of 1935 as applicable to the labor-management relations of newspapers and press associations. The case involved a challenge by the Associated Press of an order issued by the National Labor Relations Board prohibiting the discharge of employees for membership in the American Newspaper Guild and for activities associated with the union.

Associated Press v. United States, 326 U.S. 1 (1946). Decision of the U.S. Supreme Court holding illegal under the Sherman Antitrust Act the bylaws of the Associated Press forbidding members to sell news to nonmembers and empowering each member to exclude rival newspapers from membership in the press association. In delivering the majority opinion, Justice Hugo Black declared: "Freedom to publish means freedom for all and not for some. Freedom to publish is guaranteed by the Constitution, but freedom to combine to keep others from publishing is not."

Association of American Colleges. Organization founded in 1915 for the purpose of promoting higher education in American colleges and the furthering of greater efficiency among its member institutions. It maintains headquarters at Washington, D.C., and publishes a *Bulletin* (quarterly).

Association of American Railroads. Organization established in 1934 by merger of various railway units including the American Railway Association. It furthers the interests of U.S. railroads by public relations programs and similar activities. The greater part of its membership is composed of major railroads classified by the Interstate Commerce Commission as Class I roads. It maintains headquarters at Washington, D.C., and has a library of some 30,000 volumes covering the railroad field.

Association of American Universities. Organization founded in 1900 for the purpose of considering matters of common interest related to graduate study and research. Its membership is composed of universities with well-developed graduate schools. The association issues an annual *Journal of Proceedings and Addresses.*

Associators. Military body organized (1747) by Benjamin Franklin for the purpose of defending the Philadelphia port. The action was taken in face of the refusal of the Quaker-dominated city and provincial governments to adopt defensive measures.

Assollant or **Assolant** (ä.so.läṅ), **Jean Baptiste Alfred.** b. at Aubusson, France, March 20, 1827; d. at Paris, Feb. 4, 1886. French novelist and journalist. He brought a charge of plagiarism against Victorien Sardou, alleging that the latter's play *Oncle Sam* was taken from Assollant's *Scènes de la vie des États-Unis.* The charge was referred to a commission of authors who gave a verdict in favor of Sardou.

Assos (as′os). [Also: **Assus;** modern Turkish, **Behram** or **Behramköy.**] In ancient geography, a city situated on the Gulf of Adramyttium, Mysia. The site, in what is now W Turkey, was thoroughly explored and excavated (1881–82) by the Archaeological Institute of America, with the important result of illustrating the architectural and topographical development of a minor Greek city with a completeness comparable to the body of information supplied by Pompeii concerning Roman towns under somewhat similar conditions. The remains studied include very extensive fortifications of successive periods, and temples ranging from the archaic Doric to foundations from within the Christian era, a theater, baths, porticos, a gymnasium, private dwellings in great variety, a remarkable and highly adorned street of tombs, and a Greek bridge.

Assouan or **Assuan** (äs.wän′). See **Aswan.**

Assuay (ä.swī′). See **Azuay.**

Assumption, Feast of the. Christian feast day, notably of the Roman Catholic Church, celebrated on August 15, commemorating the miraculous ascent into heaven of the Virgin Mary.

Assumption of the Virgin. Subject much used by religious painters in the Renaissance and later. Some of the best known are: **1.** Painting by Perugino in the collection of the Academy of Fine Arts at Florence. The Virgin is one of Perugino's most beautiful figures; the four saints in the foreground are also considered admirable. **2.** Fresco by Gaudenzio Ferrari in the Church of San Cristoforo at Vercelli, Italy. The figures include the Father, the Virgin, angels, and apostles, in a dramatic composition. **3.** Painting by Titian in the collection of the Academy of Fine Arts at Venice, one of the best known of this artist's works. The Virgin ascends on glowing clouds, surrounded by ranks of rejoicing angels which recede behind the hovering figure of the Father. The apostles, looking up in amazement from the earth below, are dramatic in pose and foreshortening. **4.** Painting by Titian in the cathedral at Verona, Italy, splendid and characteristic in coloring. **5.** Series of frescoes by Correggio and his pupils in the dome of the cathedral at Parma, Italy. These paintings, which have been much admired for their color and light, were damaged by moisture, but escaped further injury in World War II. **6.** Large painting by Guido Reni, at London. **7.** Painting by Rubens, possibly largely executed by students, although designed by him, in Antwerp Cathedral, Belgium. The Virgin, surrounded by angels, is borne up to heaven in glory; the apostles and women are gathered about the empty tomb below. The coloring is less brilliant than is usual with Rubens.

Assur (as′ėr). [Also: **Asur, Ashur.**] The ancient national god of Assyria. The names of both the country and the people are derived from his name.

Assur. See also under **Assyria.**

Assurbanipal (ä.sör.bä′nę.päl). [Also: **Ashurbanipal;** Greek, **Sardanapalus;** name in the Old Testament, **Asenappar.**] King of Assyria (668–c626 B.C.); son of Esarhaddon and grandson of Sennacherib. He was the last of the great kings of the vigorous Sargonide dynasty. The Greeks called him Sardanapalus: in the Old Testament (Ezra, iv. 10) he is mentioned under the name Asenappar, meaning "the great and majestic." His reign was marked by great external prosperity and splendor, and the flourishing of art and literature, but also by frequent revolts and disturbances, which shook the huge empire to its foundations, and foreboded its near fall, which took place (608 B.C.) a score of years after his death. At the beginning of his reign he had to suppress a revolt in Egypt instigated by the dethroned Ethiopian king Taharka or Tarqu (the Tirhakah mentioned in the Old Testament, 2 Kings, xix. 9, Isa. xxxvii. 9). The most significant uprising, however, was that of the coalition of Babylonia, Arabia, Ethiopia, Phoenicia, and Palestine, brought about by his own brother Shamash-shum-ukin (the Greek Saosduchinos), the viceroy of Babylonia, which was also quelled by Assurbanipal. Among the most important of his victories and conquests was the capture and destruction of Susa, after many expeditions, between 646 and 640 B.C. Assurbanipal held together the Assyrian empire under his iron scepter with great rigor, not shrinking from the most atrocious cruelties, inflicting punishment on so-called "rebels." Under his protection and promotion Assyrian art, especially architecture, attained the height of its development, and literature celebrated its golden age. Being of a literary turn of mind, or, as he expresses himself, "endowed with attentive ears" and inclined to the study of "all inscribed tablets," he ordered the collecting and reëditing of the whole cuneiform literature then in existence, and the tablets, well arranged and marked, were deposited in the royal library of his palace. A great part of this library was discovered in the ruins of that palace on the mound of Kuyunjik, and transferred to the British Museum, and to it is due the larger part of our present knowledge of Assyrian history and civilization.

Assurbelnisesu (ä″sör.bel.nē.sā′sö). King of Assyria (c1480 B.C.). He is the first Assyrian king about whom some definite and certain knowledge is preserved. He is mentioned in the cuneiform inscriptions as having entered into a treaty with the king of Babylonia.

Assurdan I (ä.sör.dän′). King of Assyria (c1208–1150 B.C.). He conducted a victorious campaign against Babylonia, and conquered many cities. He had the temple of Anu and Ramman in the city of Assur, which was threatening to fall, torn down, without, however, rebuilding it. This was done by Tiglath-pileser I (1120–1100 B.C.).

Assurdan II. King of Assyria (c930–911 B.C.); son and successor of Tiglath-pileser II.

Assurdan III. King of Assyria (772–743 B.C.). The most interesting event recorded of his reign is the mention of an eclipse of the sun at Nineveh in 763. As this is confirmed by the calculations of astronomers, who fix the date of this event on the 15th of June, 763, it has served as a basis for the establishment of the whole chronology of W Asia.

Assuretililaniukinni (ä′sör.ā′tēl.ē.lä′nē.ö.kēn′nē). King of Assyria (626 B.C. *et seq.*); son and successor of Assurbanipal. Under him began the downfall of the Assyrian empire, inaugurated by an invasion of the Scythians. The length of his reign is not known.

Assurnadinsum (ä.sör.nä′dēn.söm). Eldest son of Sennacherib; king of Assyria (705–681 B.C.). He was established by his father as king of Babylonia, but was made captive by the king of Elam.

Assurnazirpal (ä.sör.nä′zēr.päl). King of Assyria (c884–c859 B.C.). He was one of the greatest and most warlike of the Assyrian kings, and inaugurated a period of prosperity and power of the Assyrian empire. He made numerous and successful campaigns especially to "the countries of Nairi" and Syria, and extended the boundaries of Assyrian dominion westward. His victorious expeditions were marked, according to his own annals, by atrocious cruelties and barbarous devastations. He also distinguished himself by works of peace. He rebuilt Calah, which he made his capital, adorning it with a temple of Adar (the god of war), his favorite divinity, and a palace for himself, and constructed a canal. The ruins of his buildings excavated show a great advance in architecture and sculpture over the preceding period.

Assurnirari (ä″sör.nē.rä′rē). King of Assyria, in 754–745 B.C.

Assus (as′us). See **Assos.**

Asswan (äs.wän′). See **Aswan.**

Assye (äs.sī′). See **Assaye.**

Assynt (as′int), **Loch.** Lake in N Scotland, in Sutherland, ab. 41 mi. NW of Dornoch. It is noted for its picturesque scenery. Length, ab. 6 mi.; width, ab. 1 mi.

Assyria (a̤.sir′i.a̤). [Greek, **Syria**; ancient name, **Assur, Asur,** or **Ashur**; Persian, **Athura.**] Ancient Asiatic state, which at the period of its greatest power covered a territory of ab. 75,000 sq. mi., bounded by Armenia on the N, the Lower Zab River on the S, the Zagros Mountains on the E, and the Euphrates River on the W. In Gen. x. 2 the name is given to a small district ab. 24 by 17 mi. on the left bank of the Tigris River. The name was derived from that of the national deity, Assur, and was first applied to the city situated ab. 50 mi. S of the modern Mosul. This city of Assur is not mentioned in the Old Testament, but it survived Nineveh, being still in existence in the time of Cyrus of Persia (Cyrus the Great), the conqueror of Babylon. The name Assur, besides being given to the city (and thence to the country), was also an element in the names of many Assyrian rulers. The Persians called the city Athura. The Greeks included under the name Assyria, or its shortened form Syria, the entire territory between Babylonia and the Mediterranean, sometimes applying it even to Babylonia. The N and E portions of the country were mountainous, but the greater part was flat, being an extension of the Babylonian plain. Its principal rivers were the Tigris, the Upper and Lower Zab, the Kurnib, the Khoser, and the W Khabur. It was a fertile country, and abounded in all sorts of animals, among others the stag, roebuck, wild bull, and lion. The hunting of the lion was the favorite sport of the Assyrian kings. According to Genesis (x. 8–12, 22) the Assyrians were descendants of Shem and emigrants from Babylon. Their Semitic-Babylonian origin is fully attested by their sculptures and inscriptions. Their language is, apart from a few dialectical and orthographical variations, identical with Babylonian, and closely akin to Hebrew. Assyria derived its civilization from Babylonia. Its religion was the same as that of the mother-country, with the exception of the national god Assur, who was placed by them at the head of the pantheon. Assyrian architecture was a slavish copy of that of Babylonia. Although stone abounded in Assyria, bricks continued to be used in imitation of the practice in Babylonia, where no stone existed. The Babylonian emigrants who founded Assyria have been dated by some scholars as leaving Babylonia c2000 B.C., although some recent archaeological research indicates the probability of a settlement at an even earlier date. In the 15th century B.C., Assyria was involved in a war with Babylonia. War continued between the two countries for a long time with varying success. Finally, however, Assyria became supreme and Babylonia the vassal state. The chief maker of Assyria's glory was Tiglath-pileser I (c1120–1100 B.C.), who conquered the city of Babylon, other cities of Babylonia, and penetrated as far as the Mediterranean. His more important successors were Assurdan II (930–911 B.C.), Assurnazirpal (884–860 B.C.), Shalmaneser III (860–824 B.C.), who came in contact with Damascus and Israel, Tiglath-pileser III (Phul in the Old Testament), 745–727 B.C., whose power extended to the confines of Egypt and who put the crown of Babylon on his head; Sargon (722–705 B.C.), the conqueror of Samaria, who defeated the Egyptians of Raphia, Sennacherib (705–681 B.C.), and Esarhaddon (680–668 B.C.). These last two kings mark the height of Assyrian power, and Esarhaddon was enabled by his conquests to add to his name the title king of Upper and Lower Egypt and Ethiopia. Under Assurbanipal (the Sardanapalus of Greek writers), 668–626 B.C., the decline of the empire began. In some respects this reign was most prosperous and brilliant; it was the golden age of art and literature. Under this reign too, Susa was conquered and destroyed. But signs of the approaching disintegration were seen in the constant uprisings of the oppressed nations. The downward course was rapid. Once, c625, Assyria succeeded in repelling an attack of the Medes and Persians, but later, Cyaxares in union with Nabopolassar of Babylon repeated the attack (606 B.C.), Nineveh fell, and the Assyrian power entirely disappeared.

Assyrian Question (a̤.sir′i.a̤n). Name given in modern international history to the problem of an Assyrian minority in Iraq, brought to the attention of the League of Nations Council in 1932. A special investigating committee examined relocation possibilities such as Brazil, Guinea, Nigeria, and elsewhere, but all were deemed impractical. In 1937 the upper Khabur valley in Syria was approved. Both Great Britain and Iraq contributed to the expenses involved. The situation was further alleviated by Iraq's recognition of the Assyrians as an equal minority.

Ast (äst), **Georg Anton Friedrich.** b. at Gotha, Germany, Dec. 29, 1778; d. at Munich, Oct. 31, 1841. German philologist and scholar of philosophy, notable for his work in Platonic philosophy. Author of *Platos Leben und Schriften* (1816) and compiler of a Latin edition of Plato's works (last volume published 1832) with commentary.

Astacus (as′ta̤.kus). [Modern Turkish name, **İzmit.**] In ancient geography, a Greek colony in Bithynia, Asia Minor, near Nicomedia.

Astaire (a̤.stãr′), **Fred.** [Original surname, **Austerlitz.**] b. at Omaha, Neb., May 10, 1899—. American actor and dancer. He made his theatrical debut (1904) with his sister, Adele Astaire, with whom he played as a team (1916–32) in *Over the Top* and *Apple Blossoms.* He starred on the stage in *Gay Divorcee* (1932), and then was teamed with Ginger Rogers in films such as *Gay Divorcee, Roberta* (1935), *Follow the Fleet* (1936), and *Carefree* (1938). Other appearances on the screen include *Yolanda and the Thief* (1945), *Blue Skies* (1947), *Barkleys of Broadway* (1949), and *Royal Wedding* (1951).

Asta Pompeia (as′ta̤ pom.pē′a̤). An ancient name of **Asti,** city.

Astarabad (äs″tä.rä.bäd′). See **Asterabad.**

Astarte (as.tär′tē). [Also, **Ashtoreth.**] Semitic goddess of fecundity and love, among the Phoenicians equivalent to the Ishtar of the Assyro-Babylonians; often considered to be an equivalent of the Greek Aphrodite. She is the female counterpart of Baal, with whom she held the first place in the Phoenician pantheon. Baal was identified with the sun, and Astarte with the moon, and she is often represented under the symbol of the crescent. The chief seat of her worship was at Sidon. The pomegranate and the dove were sacred to her. The favorite places of her worship were sacred groves, and she herself was often adored under the symbol of a tree, the *asherah* (translated "grove") often denounced in the Old Testament. Her cult in later times was combined with orgiastic celebration.

Astarte. Woman guiltily beloved by Manfred (in Byron's *Manfred*), and because of whom he suffers an undying remorse.

Astell (as′te̤l), **Mary.** b. at Newcastle, England, 1668; d. 1731. English writer. She was the author of *A Serious Proposal to Ladies,* published anonymously (1694–97) suggesting the construction of a home for religious and academic retirement, to be conducted under the rules of the Church of England, a scheme which was attacked as "popish," particularly in the *Tatler* (Nos. 32, 59, and 63), where she was called Madonella and Platonne. Among her other works, also controversial and also published anonymously, were *The Christian Religion* (1705) and *Occasional Communion* (1705).

Aster (äs′tėr), **Ernst Ludwig von.** b. at Dresden, 1778; d. at Berlin, 1855. German military engineer who planned the fortresses of Torgau (for Napoleon), Koblenz, and Ehrenbreitstein.

Asterabad (äs.te.rä.bäd′). See also **Gurgan.**

Asterabad. [Also: **Astarabad, Astrabad, Gurgan.**] Mountainous region and former province in N Iran, adjoining Mazanderan on the W. The chief occupation of the people is herding. Capital, Gurgan; area, 5,737 sq. mi.; pop. ab. 80,000.

Asterabad Bay. [Also: **Astrabad Bay, Gulf of Ashraf.**] Southeasternmost bay of the Caspian Sea, ab. 160 mi. NE of Tehran. Length, ab. 25 mi.; width, ab. 6 mi.

Asteria (as.tir′i.a̤). An ancient name of **Delos.**

Asterope (as.ter′o̤.pē). One of the Pleiades, composed of two stars, each of the seventh magnitude, and just too faint to be seen by most eyes without telescopic assistance.

It is sometimes regarded as the "lost Pleiad," though more usually Pleione is so considered.

Asti (äs′tē). Province in the *compartimento* (region) of Piedmont, NW Italy. Capital, Asti; pop. 245,764 (1936).

Asti. [Ancient name, **Hasta** (or **Asta**) **Pompeia.**] City and commune in NW Italy, in the *compartimento* (region) of Piedmont, the capital of the province of Asti, situated at the junction of the Borbore and Tanaro rivers, in the Monferrato hills, ab. 28 mi. SE of Turin. Formerly famous for its potteries, it now has agricultural markets, cotton and silk mills, and is noted for the production of a sparkling wine called *Asti spumante.* It is the seat of a bishopric, and has a medieval castle, baptisteries dating from the 8th and 11th centuries, a cathedral from the 14th century, the Romanesque-Gothic Church of San Secondo, and a number of old houses and palaces. One of the most powerful Lombard republics in the early Middle Ages, the town was destroyed by Frederick I (Barbarossa) in 1155; fell (1348) to the rulers of Milan and later (1387) to France; in the Peace of Cambrai (1529) it was given to Spain, but ceded to the house of Savoy in the same year Buildings of interest to tourists were undamaged in World War II. Pop. of commune, 48,898 (1936); of city, 26,476 (1936).

Astié (às.tyā), **Jean Frédéric.** b. at Nérac, France, Sept. 21, 1822; d. at Lausanne, Switzerland, May 20, 1894. French Protestant clergyman and writer on philosophy and history. He was pastor of a French-Swiss church at New York (1848–53), and professor of theology and philosophy (1856 *et seq.*) at Lausanne. Author of *Histoire de la république des États-Unis* (1865), and others.

Astier, François Pierre Raoul, Baron. b. at Le Mans, France, March 7, 1886—. French aviator and air force commander; head (1942–45) of Free French military aviation in Great Britain during World War II.

Astier, Paul. In Alphonse Daudet's *Struggle for Life,* an unscrupulous egoist.

Astigi (as′ti.jī) or **Astigis** (-jis). An ancient name of **Écija.**

Astin Tagh (äs′tin täg′). See **Altyn Tagh.**

Astle (as′l), **Thomas.** b. at Yoxall, England, Dec. 22, 1735; d. at Battersea Rise (now part of London), Dec. 1, 1803. English paleographer and antiquary. He was keeper of records in the Tower of London (1783 *et seq.*), and a notable collector in his own right of books and manuscripts. He was the author of *The Origin and Progress of Writing* (1784), containing a valuable study of medieval handwriting, and others.

Astley (ast′li), Sir **Jacob.** [Title, Baron **Astley.**] b. in Norfolk, England, 1579; d. at Maidstone, England, in February, 1652. English soldier, a leading Royalist general in the English Civil War. He served in the Netherlands in the Thirty Years' War, and later, under Charles I, commanded troops at Edgehill, Gloucester, Naseby, and elsewhere. He was defeated and taken prisoner by the Parliamentarians at Stow-on-the-Wold, in Gloucestershire, in 1646.

Astley, Sir **John Dugdale.** [Called **"the Mate."**] b. at Rome, Feb. 19, 1828; d. at London, Oct. 10, 1894. English patron of sport. He served with British forces in the Crimean War (1854–55), and was a member of Parliament for North Lincolnshire in the period 1874–80. For many years a devotee of the turf and of prize fighting, he was the author of a breezy memoir, *Fifty Years of My Life in the World of Sport at Home and Abroad* (1894).

Astley, Philip. b. at Newcastle-under-Lyme, England, 1742; d. at Paris, 1814. English horse-trainer, equestrian, and theater manager. A cabinet-maker during his youth, he joined a regiment of light horse in Holland as a rough-rider (1759), and opened an exhibition of horsemanship at Lambeth, in London. He subsequently developed a prosperous business as proprietor of circuses there and elsewhere. His first circus and hippodrome (opened in 1770), known as "Astley's," became Astley's Royal Amphitheatre in 1798, under the patronage of the Prince of Wales and the Duke of York.

Astolat (as′tǫ.lat). In the later Arthurian romances, a name applied to what is now Guildford, Surrey, England.

Astolf (äs′tolf). See **Aistulf.**

Astolfo or **Astolpho** (as.tol′fō). Important character in the Charlemagne romances and in the *Orlando Innamorato* and *Orlando Furioso:* a noble, kindhearted, and eccentric English knight. The most notable of his knightly feats and adventures is his journey to the moon, where he enters the Valley of Lost Things, and among a mass of broken resolutions, lovers' tears, days lost by idlers, and similar items, finds Orlando's lost wits in a vessel larger than all the others (he also finds his own wits in another vase). He is permitted to take Orlando's back to their original owner (and also to have back his own). Alexander Pope, in the *Rape of the Lock,* speaking of the same place, says:

"Where the heroes' wits are kept in ponderous vases,
And beaux' in snuff boxes and tweezer cases."

Astolfo was also the possessor of a wonderful horn which spread universal terror when it was sounded.

Astolfo or **Astolpho.** King of Lombardy in an episode in Lodovico Ariosto's *Orlando Furioso.* He is introduced from the tale of Astolfo and Jocunde, two men who, finding their wives false, set about to procure true ones.

Aston (as′tǫn) or **Aston Manor.** Ward of Birmingham, in C England, in Warwickshire. It is situated in the NE portion of the city. 35,612 (1931).

Aston, Antony. [Called **"Tony Aston."**] fl. c1700–35. English actor and dramatic writer. He is the first English actor definitely known to have appeared on the stage in the American colonies.

Aston, Francis William. b. at Birmingham, England, 1877; d. 1945. English physicist and chemist. He proved that a number of elements contain atoms different in mass but chemically identical; work with these materials, known as isotopes, produced mass spectra, by which each isotope shows a line proportionate to its weight. He was awarded the Nobel prize in chemistry (1922), the Paterno Medal (1923), and others. Author of *Isotopes* (1922), *Mass Spectra and Isotopes* (1933), and numerous technical articles.

Aston, Hugh. fl. early 16th century. English composer. He was one of the first composers of instrumental music, and his *Hornpipe for Virginals* is believed by some scholars to be the earliest extant composition for a keyboard instrument.

Aston, William George. b. near Londonderry, Ireland, 1841; d. at Beer, England, 1911. English diplomat and scholar of Japanese. Appointed (1864) to the staff of the British legation at Tokyo, he shares with Sir Ernest Satow the credit for advising Great Britain that the revolutionary efforts of 1868 would produce a stable government; he served as assistant secretary of the Tokyo legation (1875–80), as consul at Hiogo (1880–83), as consul general in Korea (1884–86), and as secretary at Tokyo (1886–89). Author of two early Japanese-English grammars, as well as *Japanese Literature* (1899) and *Shinto* (1905); translator of *Ancient Chronicles of Japan* (1896).

Aston Hall. Old hall in the Elizabethan style, near Birmingham, England, repaired and converted into a museum, having been sold by the owner, Charles Holt Bracebridge, to the town of Birmingham. It is said to have been the original of Irving's *Bracebridge Hall.*

Astor (as′tǫr), Viscountess. [Maiden name, **Nancy Witcher Langhorne.**] b. at Greenwood, Va., 1879—. British politician; wife of Waldorf Astor, 2nd Viscount Astor of Hever Castle, whom she succeeded (1919) in Parliament upon his succession to the peerage. She was the first woman to sit in the House of Commons. In 1903 she divorced Robert Shaw, and 1906 she married Astor. A member of the Conservative Party, she has been active during most of her political career in such reforms as temperance, betterment of conditions pertaining to widows, illegitimate children, and others. At her country home, Cliveden (presented by her to the government in 1942), she entertained many of the leading statesmen of the 1920's and 1930's, and from this came the term "Cliveden Set" which came to be applied to those politicians of the 1930's who were convinced that appeasement would ensure peace with Germany.

Astor, John Jacob. b. at Waldorf, in Baden, Germany, July 17, 1763; d. at New York, March 29, 1848. American merchant, fur trader, real-estate owner, and financier. Son of a Waldorf butcher, he joined his brother George, a musical-instrument manufacturer, at London in 1779, and in 1784 joined his brother Henry, a butcher, at New York, where he worked as a baker's boy, furrier's clerk, and peddler. He married Sarah Todd on Sept. 19, 1785, and opened (1786) a music shop in his mother-in-law's house at 81 Queen St. He entered the fur trade in c1787, making fur-buying expeditions up the Hudson Valley, into W New York, and to Montreal. In 1797 he began importing general merchandise from Europe; when he entered the China trade in 1800, he is said to have been worth $250,000. In the same year he began investing in Manhattan Island real estate, which was to be chiefly responsible for the great fortune of his family. He bought the Park Theatre in 1806 and rebuilt it in 1822. He incorporated the American Fur Company on April 6, 1808, as the first step in gaining control of the U.S. fur trade as far west as the Pacific coast; organized the Pacific Fur Company on June 23, 1810, for trade with the Pacific Northwest and Alaska; established the fur-trading post of Astoria near the mouth of the Columbia River in 1811, but the outbreak of war with Great Britain forced its sale (1814) to the North West Company (Canadian); and organized on Jan. 28, 1811, with two Montreal firms, the South West Fur Company for trade on the Great Lakes and the upper Mississippi River, but this was interrupted by the War of 1812, as was his trade with Europe and China. He subscribed (1813) for over two million dollars of the 6-percent government loan at 88 percent of par, and subscribed for $200,000 of the 1814 loan at 80 percent, payable in depreciated bank notes. He entered (1815) the complex interrelated trade in furs and China goods involving New York, the Mediterranean, Canton, the Hawaiian Islands, and the Russian and Spanish settlements of the Pacific. In the same year he resumed the drive for supremacy in the U.S. fur trade and in 1817 bought out his partners in the South West Fur Company. He established the Western Department in partnership with St. Louis traders in 1822, and the Upper Missouri Outfit in partnership with Scottish traders in 1827. He withdrew from foreign trade in his own vessels in 1825, and retired from the American Fur Company and from the fur trade in general in 1834, at which time he controlled the fur trade of the Great Lakes, the Mississippi, and the Missouri, but not the Rocky Mountains. Thereafter he devoted himself primarily to Manhattan Island real estate, money lending, and investment in bonds and stocks. He bought the City Hotel in 1828 and built the Park Hotel (later the Astor House) in 1834–36. He also sponsored the writing of Washington Irving's *Astoria*, published in 1836. His estate was estimated at twenty million dollars, $507,000 of which was left to public objects, principally the Astor Library.

Astor, John Jacob. b. at New York, June 10, 1822; d. there, Feb. 22, 1890. American capitalist and real-estate owner; grandson of John Jacob Astor (1763–1848) and son of William Backhouse Astor (1792–1875). He served on the staff of General George B. McClellan as a colonel during the Civil War. He was involved (1871) with five other prominent New York businessmen in the report commending books kept by City Controller Connolly, a member of the so-called "Tweed Ring:" He administered (1875–90) the Astor estate.

Astor, John Jacob. b. at Rhinebeck, N.Y., July 13, 1864; d. in sinking of *Titanic*, April 15, 1912. American capitalist, inventor, and real-estate owner; great-grandson of John Jacob Astor (1763–1848). He built (1897) the Astoria section of the original Waldorf-Astoria Hotel. He placed his yacht, *Nourmahal*, at the disposal of the U.S. government and equipped a battery of artillery in the Spanish-American War, in which he served as a lieutenant colonel. Author of a semi-scientific novel entitled *A Journey in Other Worlds* (1894), and inventor of several mechanical devices, including a bicycle brake and an improved turbine engine.

Astor, John Jacob. b. 1886—. British publisher and politician; son of William Waldorf Astor, 1st Viscount Astor of Hever Castle (1848–1919). A member (1906 *et seq.*) of a Guards regiment, he was aide-de-camp (1911–14) to the viceroy of India, and served (1914–18) in World War I. In 1922 he purchased control of the (London) Times Publishing Company, which he thenceforth served as chairman. He is notable for having established a non-political body of trustees to secure the future control of the *Times* from owners who might abuse it.

Astor, Vincent. [Full name, **William Vincent Astor.**] b. at New York, 1891—. Son of the fourth John Jacob Astor, whom he succeeded as head of the Astor family in America.

Astor, Waldorf. [Title, 2nd Viscount **Astor of Hever Castle.**] b. at New York, 1879; d. Sept. 30, 1952. British politician; son of William Waldorf Astor, 1st Viscount Astor of Hever Castle, and husband of Viscountess (Nancy) Astor. He was a member of Parliament (1910–19), serving as parliamentary secretary to the prime minister, who was then Lloyd George. For many years he has been owner of the London *Sunday Observer*, which is considered by many to be one of the outstanding news journals of Great Britain.

Astor, William Backhouse. [Called the **"Landlord of New York."**] b. at New York, Sept. 19, 1792; d. there, Nov. 24, 1875. American capitalist and real-estate owner; son of John Jacob Astor (1763–1848). He administered the family fortune after the death of his father, increasing it by over 25 million dollars in less than three decades. He gave about 550,000 dollars to the library founded by his father.

Astor, William Waldorf. [Title, **1st Viscount Astor of Hever Castle.**] b. at New York, March 31, 1848; d. at Brighton, England, Oct. 18, 1919. Anglo-American capitalist, real-estate owner, and one-time diplomat, who settled (1890) in England and became, in 1899, a British subject; great-grandson of John Jacob Astor (1763–1848) and son of John Jacob Astor (1822–90). He was U.S. minister (1882–85) to Italy, after a period (1877 *et seq.*) in the New York legislature. He entered British journalism in 1893 with the purchase of the *Pall Mall Gazette* and the establishment of the *Pall Mall Magazine*, later followed (1911) by his acquisition of the London *Sunday Observer*. His last years were marked by bitter prejudice against his former countrymen in America. Author of the novels *Valentino* (1885) and *Sforza* (1889).

Astor, William Waldorf. [Title, 3rd Viscount **Astor of Hever Castle.**] b. in England, Aug. 13, 1907—. British politician; eldest son of Waldorf Astor, 2nd Viscount Astor of Hever Castle. He was parliamentary secretary to Sir Samuel Hoare when the latter was first lord of the admiralty (1936–37) and home secretary (1937–39).

Astorga (äs.tôr′gä). [Ancient name, **Asturica Augusta.**] City in NW Spain, in the province of León, situated on the Tuerto River, ab. 29 mi. SW of León: linen textile and chocolate factories; seat of a bishopric. The Gothic cathedral dates from the 15th century. The city's ancient Roman walls have been preserved, and present a curious spectacle with their long series of projecting semicircular towers which do not rise above the flat portions of the wall. In ancient times, it was the Roman capital of Asturias, and in the 8th and 9th centuries a Spanish stronghold in the struggle against the Moslems. 14,523 (1940).

Astorga (dä.stôr′gä), Baron **Emanuele Gioacchino Cesare Rincón d'.** b. at Augusta, Sicily, March 20, 1680; d. c1755. Spanish composer, best known for his *Stabat Mater* (c1707). He also composed the pastoral opera *Dafni* (1709), a volume of chamber cantatas (1726), and others.

Astoria (as.tō′ri.ą). [Original name, **Hallett's Cove.**] Section of SE New York, situated on Long Island, in the NW part of the borough of Queens, New York City. Formerly a village (incorporated in 1839), it was at one time important for the manufacture of pianos. Today it is a residential and manufacturing community of Long Island City and a terminal point of the Triborough Bridge.

Astoria. [Former name, **Fort George.**] City in NW Oregon, county seat of Clatsop County, at the mouth of the Columbia River, ab. 75 mi. NW of Portland, in a lumbering, fishing, dairying, and agricultural region: flour mills, sawmills, salmon canneries, and grain elevators. The site of the first permanent settlement in the Oregon country, it was chosen by and named for John Jacob Astor in 1811. It was held (c1813–18) by the British as Fort George. 12,331 (1950).

Astoria. Prose work (1836) by Washington Irving. Edgar Allan Poe based his unfinished *The Journal of Julius Rodman* partially upon *Astoria*.

Astor Library (as′tọr). Library in the city of New York, founded by John Jacob Astor, and opened in 1854. It was a reference library only, and contained about 260,000 volumes. It was combined with the Lenox and the Tilden libraries as the New York Public Library, founded in 1895 and opened in 1911.

Astor Place Riot. Riot at New York, on May 10, 1849, involving the partisans of the American actor Edwin Forrest and the English actor William Charles Macready. The latter was acting at the time in the Astor Place Opera House. It was suppressed by the militia. Twenty-two people were killed and 36 wounded.

Astrabad (äs.trä.bäd'). See **Asterabad.**

Astraea or **Astrea** (as.trē'ạ). In classical mythology, the goddess of justice.

Astraea or **Astrea.** An asteroid (the fifth) discovered by Henke at Driesen, on Dec. 8, 1845.

Astraea Redux (rē'duks). A poem by John Dryden celebrating the restoration of Charles II, first published in 1660.

Astrakhan (äs'trạ.ʜạn; Anglicized, as'trạ.kạn). Former district of SE Russia.

Astrakhan. City in the U.S.S.R., in the Russian Soviet Federated Socialist Republic: major port in the delta of the Volga River. It has extensive commerce by the Volga and the Caspian Sea, and is the chief port for the latter; it has also a large transit trade with Iran and Transcaucasia, various manufactures, valuable fisheries, and other industries. It was formerly the capital of a Tartar state, and was conquered by Russia in 1554. Pop. 254,000 (1939).

Astrée (ȧs.trā), **L'.** Pastoral romance by Honoré d'Urfé, published in five volumes in the period 1607–10. It is a work in which, under the disguise of pastoral incidents and characters, the author depicts the history of his own family, and the amours at the court of Henry IV of France It had a considerable influence on much of the French literature which came after it and John Fletcher based his tragicomedy *Monsieur Thomas* on Part Two of this novel.

Astrolabe (as'trǫ.lāb), **The Treatise on the.** [Also, **The Conclusions of the Astrolabe.**] Unfinished prose work by Geoffrey Chaucer, written by him for the instruction of his son Lewis, then ten years old. It is inferred that it was written in 1391. This is not proved, however; and of the child nothing more is known than that in the introduction to this treatise Chaucer mentions him by name and gives his reasons for the "enditing" of the work for him. It contains some very slight autobiographical allusions, but is essentially a translation of the work of an Arab astronomer, Messahala (8th century), from a Latin version.

Astrolabe Bay. Arm of the Pacific Ocean, on the NE coast of the island of New Guinea, in the Australian trusteeship of North-East New Guinea.

Astroni (äs.trō'nē). Crater of an extinct volcano in W Italy, ab. 5 mi. W of Naples.

Astropalia (as.trǫ.pā'li.ạ). See **Astypalaia.**

Astrophel (as'trǫ.fel). Name assumed by Sir Philip Sidney in the series of sonnets entitled *Astrophel and Stella,* often considered to have been his greatest literary work. These sonnets, 110 in number, chronicle the growth of Sidney's love for Stella (the name by which he alluded to Penelope Devereaux, sister of the Earl of Essex, afterward Lady Rich). It contains about one-third of Sidney's extant poetry.

Astrophel. Elegy written by Edmund Spenser in 1586, lamenting the death of Sir Philip Sidney. It was printed in the same volume as *Colin Clout's Come Home Again* and was the first of a group of poems by various authors on Sidney's death.

Astrophel. Collection of poems (1894) by Algernon Charles Swinburne.

Astruc (ȧs.trük), **Jean.** b. at Sauve, France, March 19, 1684; d. at Paris, May 5, 1766. French physician. Distinguished in his day as an anatomist and as the author of a treatise on venereal diseases (1736), he is now remembered chiefly for his *Conjectures sur les mémoires originaux, dont il paroit que Moyse s'est servi pour composer le livre de la Genèse* (1753), in which he points out that use of the names Elohim and Yahveh for the Deity indicates two parallel narratives drawn upon for Genesis; his work is considered by many to have been the starting point of modern criticism of the Pentateuch.

Astrup (äs'tröp), **Eivind.** b. at Christiania (now Oslo), Norway, Sept. 17, 1871; d. on expedition in Dovrefjeld, Norway, December, 1895. Norwegian arctic explorer; companion of Robert Edwin Peary in the explorations of Greenland during the periods 1891–92 and 1893–95. He was the first to survey the N coast of Melville Bay.

Astura (äs.tö'rä). Small river in C Italy, S of Rome, which rises near Velletri and flows into the Mediterranean.

Asturias (as.tū'ri.ạs; Spanish, äs.tö'ryäs). Ancient province of NW Spain, officially called Oviedo since 1833. It was a nucleus of the Spanish kingdom. The Christian kingdom of Asturias was founded c718 by Pelayo, and was merged with the kingdom of León in the 10th century. From the year 1388 the title "Prince of the Asturias" was borne by the heir apparent to the Spanish throne.

Asturias. Region in N Spain, comprising the modern province of Oviedo. Iron, zinc, and a chief portion of Spain's coal are mined in this region, which is also (particularly in its largest city, Oviedo) a major Spanish industrial area. For centuries the Asturians have cherished a sense of almost national identity, although they have never (unlike the Basques) sought national autonomy; nevertheless, they are keenly conscious of their own regional traditions, and have been ever since the period of Napoleon, among the most courageous of Spanish soldiers.

Asturica Augusta (as.tū'ri.kạ ô.gus'tạ). Ancient name of **Astorga.**

Astyages (as.tī'ạ.jēz). Son and successor of Cyaxares; king of the Medes in the period 584–c549 B.C. In the latter year Cyrus the Great dethroned him and united Media with Persia. According to Herodotus, Astyages was the grandfather of Cyrus.

Astyanax (as.tī'ạ.naks). [Also, **Scamandrius.**] In Greek legend, the son of Hector and Andromache, killed in the capture of Troy.

Astypalaia (äs.tē.pä'le.ä). [Also: **Astropalia, Astypalaea;** Italian, **Stampalia.**] Greek island in the Aegean Sea, ab. 77 mi. NW of Rhodes: one of the Dodecanese Islands. Length, ab. 13 mi.; pop. ab. 2,000.

Asunción (ä.sön.syōn'). [Original name, **Nuestra Señora de la Asunción.**] City in C Paraguay, in the territory of the Capital, on the Paraguay River: the capital of Paraguay, and its principal commercial center and river port. Founded in 1536; taken by the Brazilians on Jan. 5, 1869. Pop. 100,000 (est. 1944).

Asur (as'ėr). A variant spelling of **Assur,** the national deity of ancient Assyria. It is an element in the names of many Assyrian rulers (**Assurbanipal,** etc.) and in the name of the country itself.

Aswan (äs.wän', as.won'). [Also: **Assouan, Assuan.**] Province of Egypt, in NE Africa, occupying land on both sides of the river Nile in the vicinity of the city of Aswan, its capital. It is bordered by the Anglo-Egyptian Sudan on the S and the province of Qena on the N, with the desert on the E and W. Settled area, 363 sq. mi.; pop. 285,155 (1947).

Aswan. [Also: **Assouan, Assuan, Asswan;** ancient name, **Syene.**] Town in NE Africa, in Upper Egypt, capital of the province of Aswan, on the Nile River near the first cataract, ab. 552 mi. S of Cairo; formerly supposed to be on the tropic of Cancer. It is noted for its granite, but its chief importance to modern Egypt results from the Aswan Dam (*q.v.*), built there in 1902. This was the place to which Juvenal was banished. 25,397 (1947).

Aswan Dam. [Also: **Assouan** (or **Assuan** or **Asswan**) **Dam.**] Dam in NE Africa, in Upper Egypt, constructed across the Nile River at Aswan for purposes of irrigation; it was completed in 1902. Between 1902 and 1912 the height of the dam was raised 23 ft., and in 1929 work was started on another addition of 28 ft. to bring the dam to 394 ft. This work was completed in 1934, and the capacity of the dam is now ab. 5,300,000,000 cubic meters. It is 1¼ mi. long and is pierced by some 180 sluice gates.

Asyoot (äs.ūt'). See **Asyut.**

As You Find It. Comedy by Charles Boyle, 4th Earl of Orrery, printed in 1703.

As You Like It. Comedy by Shakespeare. Some scholars believe it was produced in 1599, but no copy of it is known to exist earlier than the folio of 1623. It was founded on Thomas Lodge's romance *Rosalynde.* In the comedy the characters of Touchstone, Audrey, and Jaques are Shakespeare's; otherwise he has followed Lodge quite closely. The main setting is the Forest of Arden. Rosalind, daughter of a banished duke, falls in love with Orlando, and he with her, after only one meeting. When Rosalind, disguised as a boy, goes into the forest to join her father, she again meets Orlando, who is now also an outcast, and encourages him in his admiration for Rosalind. Just when Rosalind reveals herself to Orlando, word comes that the Duke is again ruler of his lands. Touchstone, the clown, and Jaques, the cynical, melancholy philosopher, furnish moments of comedy considered by many to be among the best in Shakespeare.

Asyr (ä.sēr'). See **Asir.**

Asyut (äs.yöt'). [Also: **Assiout, Assiut, Asyoot, Siut.**] Province of Upper Egypt, NE Africa, on both sides of the Nile River in the vicinity of the city of Asyut, its capital, and between the provinces of Minya and Girga. Settled area, 812 sq. mi.; pop. 1,379,875 (1947).

Asyut. [Also: **Assiout, Assiut, Asyoot, Siut**; ancient name, **Lycopolis.**] Capital of Asyut province, Upper Egypt, in NE Africa, near the left bank of the Nile River, ab. 234 mi. S of Cairo: one of the oldest towns in Egypt, noted for its pottery. It is a railroad terminus, a Coptic center, and the site of one of the judicial tribunals. An important irrigation barrage on the Nile is nearby. 88,730 (1947).

Ata (ä'tä). Ancient Egyptian king, usually considered to have been the fourth of the Ist dynasty. His dates, and even his existence, are still, at best, only conjectural.

Atabalipa (ä tä.bä'lē pä). See **Atahualpa.**

Atacama (ä.tä.kä'mä). Province in N Chile. It is rich in copper and nitrates, but its surface is largely a desert. Formerly a maritime department of Bolivia, it was occupied by the Chileans in 1879. Capital, Copiapó; area, 30,843 sq. mi.; pop. 80,858 (est. 1950).

Atacama Desert. [Spanish, **Desierto** (or **Salar**) **de Atacama.**] Desert in N Chile extending from Antofagasta to the Peruvian border: one of the most arid regions in the world, receiving an average annual rainfall of one-tenth of an inch. The scarcity of rainfall has caused this to be the only region in the world with extensive natural nitrate deposits, first mined in 1831 and a chief basis for the War of the Pacific (1879–83), won by Chile against Peru and Bolivia. The revenue of the Chilean government was for many years dependent upon the tax placed on Chilean exports. With the onset of World War I, the Germans dispatched the submarine *Graf Spee* to prevent nitrate export through the Panama Canal to the U.S. for use in the manufacture of explosives. This resulted in the synthetic production of nitrate outside of Chile, causing at the time and during the early 1920's a severe crisis in the Chilean economy. The major cities are Antofagasta, Iquique, Arica, Chile; and Tacna, Peru. Area, ab. 30,835 sq. mi.

Atacameño (ä.tä.kä.mā'nyō). [Also: **Atacama, Atacamana** (ä.tä.kä.mä'nä).] Kunza-speaking people who once occupied the desert and highland regions of N Chile and contiguous Chaco areas of NW Argentina. Their culture may have reached a peak c1000 A.D., but absolute dating is uncertain since their culture and language have been replaced by those of the Aymara and the Spanish. Archaeology reveals that the Atacameño practiced agriculture with irrigation and herding of llama and alpaca. Trade played a very important role in their economy. Stone architecture and metallurgy are other traits. Kunza, the name of their language, is sometimes also used as the name of the Atacameño.

Atahualpa (ä.tä.wäl'pä). [Also: **Atahuallpa, Atabalipa.**] b. c1502; strangled at Cajamarca, Peru, Aug. 29, 1533. Last Inca chief of Peru, notable for his offer (1532) to Francisco Pizarro of a room filled with gold in exchange for freedom. He succeeded to the throne on the death (1525) of his father, Huaina Capac, but lost the rest of the Inca empire to his half-brother, Huáscar, whom he later (1532) attacked and displaced. His rule as emperor was interrupted in the same year by the arrival of Pizarro, whose attempts at conversion to Christianity he rebuffed and by whom he was thereupon treacherously made prisoner. He was put to death in the spring of the following year on a charge of ordering the assassination of Huáscar and of plotting against the Spaniards.

Atair (a.tär'). See **Altair** or **Atair.**

Atak (ä.täk'). See **Attock.**

Atakapa (ä.tä'kä.pä). North American Indian tribe, now extinct, which inhabited the coastal areas of E Texas and W Louisiana. The language formed an independent linguistic family.

Atala (à.tà.là). Romance by François René Auguste de Chateaubriand which first appeared (1801) in the newspaper *Le Mercure de France.*

Atalanta (at.a̤.lan'ta̤) or **Atalante** (-tē). In Greek legend, a maiden whose story appears in two versions: In the Arcadian version, she is a daughter of Zeus by Clymene, exposed by her father in infancy, suckled by a bear, and brought up by a party of hunters, under whose care she develops into a beautiful and swift huntress. She takes part in the Calydonian boar hunt, is the first to strike the boar, and receives from Meleager the head and skin as prize of victory. She is also connected with the expedition of the Argonauts, and marries Milanion. In the Boeotian version, she is a daughter of Schoeneus, son of Athamas, of great beauty and very swift of foot. She is warned by an oracle not to marry, and rids herself of her suitors by challenging them to a race, and smiting them with a spear in the back on overtaking them. Hippomenes, however, overcomes her by throwing before her in the race three golden apples given to him by Aphrodite, which she stoops to pick up; she is thus tricked into pausing long enough to lose the race to Hippomenes. (However, because Hippomenes fails to give thanks to Aphrodite, the goddess subsequently changes the pair into lions.)

Atalanta or **Atalante.** An asteroid (No. 36) discovered by H. Goldschmidt at Paris, Oct. 5, 1855.

Atalanta in Calydon (kal'i.don). Tragedy based on the classical theme of Atalanta and the Calydonian boar hunt, by Algernon Charles Swinburne, published in 1864.

Atalanti (at.a̤.lan'ti; Greek, ä.tä.län'dē), **Channel** (or **Gulf**) **of.** [Also, **Channel** (or **Gulf**) **of Atalante** (or **Talanti**).] The NW portion of the sea passage which separates Euboea from the mainland of Greece.

Ataliba (at.a̤.lē'ba̤). In Richard Brinsley Sheridan's translation of August Friedrich Ferdinand von Kotzebue's *Pizarro*, the king of Quito (the Inca of Peru). He is the equivalent, of course, of the actual historical figure usually now called Atahualpa.

Atalide (àt.à.lēd). In Jean Baptiste Racine's tragedy *Bajazet*, a princess in love with Bajazet. She kills herself on hearing of his assassination (instigated by her rival Roxana), reproaching herself with being in some way the cause.

Atall (at'ôl). In Colley Cibber's comedy *The Double Gallant*, the son of Sir Harry Atall. He courts Clarinda under the disguise of Colonel Standfast, falls in love with Silvia and makes love to her as Mr. Freeman, and finally discovers that she is the woman to whom he had been betrothed by his father years before.

Atall, Sir Positive. In Thomas Shadwell's comedy, *The Sullen Lovers or The Impertinents* (1668), a foolish knight who pretends to understand everything, and will not permit any one in his company to understand anything. He is supposed to have been intended as a caricature of Sir Robert Howard, who was also a dramatist (he collaborated with John Dryden on the *Indian Queen*).

Atami (ä.tä.mē). City in Japan, in C Honshu. Its chief importance is as a resort. Pop. ab. 35,000.

Atanua (ä.tä.nö'a̤). See under **Papa.**

Atarés Massacre (ä.tä.rās'). Name sometimes given to the death by shooting (Aug. 16, 1851) of 50 members (most of them Americans) of the López filibustering party. The execution was carried out by the Spaniards at Havana, and was justified by them on the ground that the filibusterers were pirates. By modern standards of international law this was a judgment which few would now care to dispute; the 19th-century filibustering expeditions of North American adventurers in countries S of the Rio Grande River and in the Caribbean Sea were for the most part comprised of looters and scoundrels who would hesitate at nothing to achieve their ends.

Atargatis (a̤.tär'ga̤.tis). Syrian goddess, worshiped in Carchemish, corresponding approximately to Astarte and the Assyro-Babylonian Ishtar. At Ashkelon she was worshiped by the Philistines under the name of Derceto in the form of a woman terminating in a fish. She also had a temple at Ephesus, and her numerous retinue of priestesses, which the Greeks found there, is supposed by some to have given rise to the legend of the Amazons.

Atascadero (ạ.tas.kạ.der'ō). Unincorporated community in SW California, in San Luis Obispo County, on the Salinas River ab. 200 mi. SE of San Francisco. 3,443 (1950).

Ataulphus (at.ạ̄.ul'fus). [Also: **Atawulf** (at'ạ.wůlf), **Ataulf** (-ạ̄.ulf), **Athaulf, Adaulf.**] d. 415. King of the Visigoths (West Goths); brother-in-law of Alaric I, whom he succeeded in 410. He evacuated Italy in 412; conquered Aquitaine, in Gaul; formed a treaty with the emperor Honorius, whose sister Galla Placidia he married in 414; crossed into Spain to subdue a revolt of the Vandals and Suevi against the empire; and was assassinated at Barcelona.

Atax (ā'taks). Ancient name of the **Aude River.**

Atbara (ät'bä.rä). Town in NW Africa, in NE Anglo-Egyptian Sudan, situated at the point where the Atbara River meets the Nile. In this vicinity, Anglo-Egyptian forces under Kitchener defeated (1898) a Mahdist army. 34,700 (est. 1949).

Atbara River. River in NE Africa, the largest tributary of the Nile River with the exception of the Blue Nile. It rises near Lake Tana in Ethiopia, flows generally NW, and joins the Nile S of Berber, at Atbara in the Anglo-Egyptian Sudan. Its chief affluent is the Takazze River. Length, ab. 500 mi.

Atbo (ät'bō). Coptic name of **Edfu.**

Atchafalaya Bayou (ạ.chaf.ạ.lī'ạ). [Also, **Atchafalaya Bay.**] Outlet of the Red and Mississippi rivers, in S Louisiana. Length, ab. 150 mi.

Atchafalaya River. River in S Louisiana, flowing generally S into Atchafalaya Bay. It is navigable for most of its course. Length, ab. 200 mi.

Atchin or **Atcheen** (ä.chēn'). See **Atjeh.**

Atchinsk (ä.chēnsk'). See **Achinsk.**

Atchison (ach'i.sọn). City in NE Kansas, county seat of Atchison County, on the Missouri River ab. 21 mi. NW of Leavenworth: former terminus of the Atchison, Topeka and Santa Fe Railway. It is a wholesale and jobbing center, and also manufactures flour, locomotive parts, industrial alcohol, and leather goods. 12,792 (1950).

Atchison, David Rice. b. at Frogtown, Ky., Aug. 11, 1807; d. in Clinton County, Mo., Jan. 26, 1886. American politician. As a senator from Missouri (1843–55), he was notable for his pro-slavery activity, particularly in connection with border raids (1855–56) into Kansas.

Ate (ā'tē). In Greek mythology, a daughter of Zeus (according to Homer) or of Eris, strife (according to Hesiod); the goddess of mischief and discord.

Ate. In Edmund Spenser's *Faerie Queene,* a hag, a liar and slanderer; friend of Duessa.

Atea (ä.tā'ä). Polynesian god who personifies space or sky He plays a varying role in creation myths, usually as father of the gods. The name is taken from the Polynesian word meaning space; in other dialects it is Vatea or Wakea.

Atella (ạ.tel'ạ). In ancient geography, a town in Campania, Italy, ab. 10 mi. N of Naples.

Atellan Plays (ạ.tel'ạn). Early Roman comedies so named from Atella, where they were first produced. Originally simple and coarse farces, they were gradually raised to burlesque comedy. They had a stock set of characters, somewhat in the manner of "Punch and Judy" shows.

Aten (ä'ten). In Egyptian mythology, the sun's disk. The worship of Aten was introduced by Ikhnaton (or Amenhotep IV).

Aterno (ä.ter'nō). [Latin, **Aternus** (ạ.tėr'nus).] Upper course of the river Pescara, in C Italy.

Aternum (ạ.tėr'num). An ancient name of **Pescara,** town.

Atessa (ä.tes'sä). Town and commune in C Italy, in the *compartimento* (region) of Abruzzi e Molise, in the province of Chieti, situated in the Apennines, ab. 24 mi. SE of Chieti. It has cattle and fruit markets of some local importance. Slight damage was suffered during World War II by buildings of tourist interest. Pop. of commune, 10,596 (1936); of town, 3,515 (1936).

Ateste (ä.tes'tā). Ancient name of **Este.**

Ath (ät). [Flemish, **Aat, Aath, Aeth.**] Town in S Belgium, in the province of Hainaut, situated on the Dender River, ab. 30 mi. SW of Brussels. An industrial town, it has woolen, linen, cotton, lace, glove, and dye manufactures, ironworks, and nail and cutlery factories. Little now remains of the medieval town; the place was conquered by the French under Vauban in 1697. The discoverer of the Mississippi River, Louis Hennepin, was born here in 1701. Pop. 10,296 (1947).

Athabaska (ath.ạ.bas'kạ). [Also, **Athabasca.**] Formerly a provisional district in the Northwest Territories, Canada, lying N of Alberta and E of British Columbia. It occupied the area around and mainly to the S of Lake Athabaska. In 1905 it was divided between the new provinces of Alberta and Saskatchewan.

Athabaska, Lake. [Also, **Lake Athabasca.**] Lake in the NE corner of Alberta, and the NW corner of Saskatchewan, Canada. It receives the Athabaska River, and drains by way of the Slave River through Great Slave Lake and the Mackenzie River into the Arctic Ocean. Length, 230 mi.; breadth, 20–30 mi.; elevation, 699 ft.; area, 3,058 sq. mi.

Athabaskan (ath.ạ.bas'kạn). [Also: **Athapascan, Dene, Tineh.**] A major North American Indian linguistic family. It contains over a score of languages widely distributed in the interior of Alaska, the NW interior of Canada, and scattered areas of the coasts of Oregon and N California, with an outlying distribution also in New Mexico, E Arizona, SW Texas, and N Mexico.

Athabaska Pass. [Also, **Athabasca Pass.**] Pass over the Rocky Mountains, between Mounts Brown and Hooker on the border between British Columbia and Alberta, Canada. It is little used because the railroad uses Yellowhead Pass a little further N.

Athabaska River. [Also, **Athabasca River.**] River in the province of Alberta, Canada, which rises in the Rocky Mountains, flows generally NE, crosses the W end of Athabaska Lake, and unites with the Peace River to form Slave River. It is properly the upper course of the Mackenzie. Length, 765 mi.

Athalaric (ạ.thal'ạ.rik) or **Athalric** (ạ.thal'rik). b. 516; d. 534. Gothic prince; son of Euthelric or Eutharic and Amalasuintha, daughter of Theodoric I. On Theodoric's death in 526 he became king of the Ostrogoths (East Goths) in Italy under Amalasuintha's regency.

Athalia (ath.ạ.lī'ạ). Oratorio by George Frederick Handel, produced in 1733.

Athaliah (ath.ạ.lī'ạ). d. c837 B.C. The daughter of Ahab, king of Israel, and Jezebel. She was the wife of Jehoram, king of Judah. On the death of Jehoram and that of his son and successor, Ahaziah, she usurped (c843 B.C.) the throne of the kingdom of Judah. In order to remove all rivals she put to death all the male members of the royal house, Joash alone escaping. She was put to death by command of Jehoida.

Athalie (ȧ.tȧ.lē). Tragedy composed by Jean Baptiste Racine for the scholars of St.-Cyr, but not performed there. The subject was from sacred history, and it was his last dramatic work. It was written at the instigation of Madame de Maintenon, was first performed in 1690 (printed in 1691) at Versailles with choruses, and has since been produced from time to time with music by various composers.

Atha Melik (ä'thä mā'lik). [Also, **Ala-ed-Din.**] b. in Khurasan, Persia, c1227; d. at Baghdad, 1282. Persian historian, author of *Conquest of the World.*

Athanagild (ạ.than'ạ.gild). [Latin, **Athanagildus** (ạ.than.ạ.gil'dus).] d. 567. King of the Visigoths (West Goths). He became king in 554 by the aid of a Byzantine fleet, and in return for this service ceded to the emperor Justinian all the seaboard towns from Valencia to Gibraltar. Of his two daughters, Brunhilda and Galswintha, the former was married to Sigebert I, king of Austrasia, and the latter to Chilperic, king of Neustria.

Athanaric (ạ.than'ạ.rik). d. at Constantinople, 381. Chief (c366–380) of a Visigoth (West Goth) tribe, in Dacia. He negotiated a peace after a defeat in 369 by the emperor Valens but was crushed utterly in 376 by Huns and forced to flee eastward; he died while seeking aid from the emperor Theodosius.

Athanasian Creed (ath.ạ.nā'zhạn). [Also, **Quicunque vult.**] One of the three great creeds of the Christian church, supposed at one time to have been composed by Athanasius. The name was probably given to it during the

Arian controversy in the 6th century, Athanasius having been the chief upholder of the system of doctrine opposed to the Arian system. It is included in the Greek, Roman, and English services, but is not retained in the Book of Common Prayer most commonly used in the U.S. It is also called *Quicunque vult*, after its first words.

Athanasius (ath.ą.nā'shus), Saint. [Called the **"Father of Orthodoxy"** and **"Athanasius contra mundum"**; surnamed **"the Great."**] b. at Alexandria, c298; d. there, 373. Greek bishop and father of the church, notable as a defender of orthodoxy against Arianism. His stubborn advocacy of his own beliefs throughout his life brought him the epithet *"contra mundum"* and led to his exile on five occasions. His theological brilliance attracted the attention of Alexandria's bishop, Alexander, at an early date and he was appointed (319) deacon; he was present at the Council of Nicaea (325) as Alexander's secretary. He was consecrated bishop of Alexandria on Alexander's death (328) despite the opposition of the Arians, against whom both Athanasius and Alexander had fought, at Nicaea and elsewhere. His refusal to reinstate Arius led to his trial by the Council of Tyre (335), against whose unjust verdict of deposition Athanasius appealed to Emperor Constantine with proof of his innocence, but when his enemies brought additional (and equally false) charges, Constantine exiled him to Trier, Germany, without a hearing. Returned to Alexandria on the death of Constantine, he was again (339 or 340) forced into exile by the Arian intrigue; he took refuge with Pope Julius I, was sustained (c343) by a council of the western Church at Sardica, and was permitted (346) to return again to Alexandria. During the peaceful decade that followed he wrote *Defense against the Arians;* his next exile (356–62) permitted the continuation of this work under the title of *History of the Arians*, as well as the magnificent doctrinal work *Discourses against the Arians*. It was during this period that Athanasius fully formulated his concept of the Homoousian reply to the various shades of Arianism. He returned (362) to Alexandria, but was exiled again in same year by Julian; returned again (363) under Jovian, but was banished (365) by Valens, who permitted his return during the next year; he spent his last years in comparative peace at Alexandria.

Athapascan (ath.ą.pas'kąn). See **Athabaskan.**

Athar (ä.thär'). See **Attar.**

Atharva-Veda (ą.tär'vą.vā'dą). [Eng. trans., *"Veda of the Atharvans."*] Fourth of the Vedas. It is also called *Brahma-Veda*, where *brahma* means "sacred utterance" in the sense of "charm, incantation." It comprises nearly six thousand verses in about 730 hymns, which are divided into 20 books. The first 18 books are arranged upon a like system, of which the length of the hymn is the principle.

Athaulf (ath'ā.ulf). See **Ataulphus.**

Atheist, or The Second Part of The Soldier's Fortune, The. Comedy by Thomas Otway, first acted in 1684.

Atheist's Tragedy, or The Honest Man's Revenge, The. Play by Cyril Tourneur. It is said to have been acted between 1601 and 1604, and printed in 1611. It was founded on a tale in Boccaccio's *Decameron*.

Athelney (ath'ę̣l.ni), **Isle of.** [Anglo-Saxon, **Æthelmga Ig.**] Place, once surrounded by marsh, near Taunton, Somersetshire, England, the refuge of Alfred the Great in 878. He founded (888) a Benedictine abbey here.

Athelstan (ath'ę̣l.stan). [Also, **Æthelstan;** surnamed **"the Glorious."**] b. 895; d. 940. King of the West Saxons and Mercia (924–940); a son of Edward the Elder. He defeated the Danes and Celts at Brunanburh in 937, thus making himself ruler over all of England. Through the marriage of his sisters, he was brother-in-law to Charles III (Charles the Simple), king of the West Franks; Louis, king of Lower Burgundy; Hugh, the "Great Duke" of the French; and the emperor Otto the Great.

Athelstane (ath'ę̣l.stān). In Sir Walter Scott's novel *Ivanhoe*, the Thane of Coningsburgh, suitor of Rowena. called "The Unready," from the slowness of his mind.

Athelston (ath'ę̣l.stǫn). Poem (c1350) of unknown authorship. In its approximately 800 lines a purely fictitious story is told about a king who was famous in English history. It uses scraps of history, legend, folklore, and commonplaces of romance.

Athena (ą.thē'ną) or **Athene** (-nē). [Also, **Pallas Athena.**] In Greek mythology, the goddess of knowledge, arts, sciences, and righteous war. She was particularly the tutelary deity of Athens, and was identified by the Romans with Minerva. She personified the clear upper air as well as mental clearness and acuteness, embodying the spirit of truth and divine wisdom, and was clothed with the aegis, symbolizing the dark storm-cloud, and armed with the resistless spear (the shaft of lightning). According to myth, she sprang full-grown from the forehead of Zeus.

Athenaeum (ath.ę̣.nē'um). A famous school or university at Rome, founded by the emperor Hadrian. It was named for Athens, and was situated on the Capitoline Hill.

Athenaeum, The. London club established in 1824. It was designed for the "association of individuals known for their scientific or literary attainments, artists of eminence in any class of the Fine Arts, and noblemen and gentlemen distinguished as liberal patrons of Science, Literature, or the Arts."

Athenaeus (ath.ę̣.nē'us). fl. possibly about the end of the 2nd century B.C. Greek mechanician. He wrote a book on siege engines which contains historical information on these engines.

Athenaeus. b. at Naucratis, Egypt; fl. c200 A.D. Greek grammarian, rhetorician, and philosopher. His only extant work, *Deipnosophistae* (in 15 books, ten of which exist in their entirety), contains quantities of detailed information about the food, music, and pleasures of the period. The work also contains what is believed to be the first account in history of a rain of fishes.

Athenaeus of Attalia. fl. at Rome, c41–68 A.D. Greek physician, founder of the Pneumatic school of medicine, a development of Stoic physics. He wrote a comprehensive treatise on medicine in at least 30 books, containing many definitions and highly praised by Galen. Fragments of it are extant, and deal with the study of food and drink, the influence of air (in different places and at different times), and the education of children and women.

Athenagoras (ath.ę̣.nag'ǫ.rąs). b. at Athens; fl. c177 A.D. Greek Platonist philosopher and early Christian, author of an apology addressed to the emperors Marcus Aurelius and Commodus which states and refutes the accusations of atheism, cannibalism, and incest made against the Christians.

Athena Parthenos (ą.thē'ną pär'thę̣.nos). Ivory and gold statue by Phidias, once in the Parthenon. It was one of the most admired works of antiquity. Only copies of the work survive, the most important of which, for its careful reproduction of details, is the Roman copy belonging to the collection of the National Museum at Athens.

Athenäum (ä.tā.nā'ům). German journal edited (1798–1800) at Berlin by August Wilhelm Schlegel and his brother Friedrich. The latter, who has been called the founder of the romantic school in his country, laid down in this publication the theories that formed the basis of early romanticism in Germany.

Athenia (ą.thē'ni.ą). British passenger ship sunk on the very evening (Sept. 3–4, 1939) of the beginning of hostilities in World War II. The vessel was torpedoed by a German U-boat at a point some 250 mi. NW of Ireland, while en route from England to Canada, and sank with a loss of some 125 people (of whom 30 were Americans).

Athenian Gazette: or Casuistical Mercury, The. Periodical published from 1691 to 1697. It was a project of the eccentric bookseller John Dunton, whose staff included Richard Sault, John Norris, Samuel Wesley, and others. These men composed an "Athenian Society" and undertook to answer questions on all topics in the *Mercury*.

Athenion (ą.thē'ni.on). Leader in the second slave insurrection in Sicily, 103–99 B.C. He is said to have been the commander of banditti in Cilicia, where he was captured and sold as a slave into Sicily. He was chosen leader of the insurgents in the western part of the island, made an unsuccessful attack on Lilybaeum, joined Tryphon (Salvius), king of the rebels, by whom he was for a time thrown into prison, fought under Tryphon in the battle with Lucius Licinius Lucullus, and on the death of Tryphon became king. He was slain in battle by the hand of Marcus Aquillius who put down the revolt.

Athenodorus (a̤.thē.nō̤.dō′rus). b. at Rhodes; fl. 1st century B.C. Greek sculptor. He collaborated, according to Pliny the Elder, with Agesander (believed by some to have been his father) and Polydorus on the group of the *Laocoön*.

Athenodorus Cananites (kā.na̤.nī′tēz). b. at Tarsus, Asia Minor; fl. 1st century B.C. Stoic philosopher and tutor of Augustus. His influence over his one-time pupil is alleged to have been great even in later years; he was a friend also of Strabo and Cicero.

Athenodorus Cordylion (kôr.dil′i.o̤n). fl. early 1st century B.C. Stoic philosopher and librarian at Pergamum. He lived at Rome during most of his later life.

Athens (ath′e̤nz, -inz). City in N Alabama, county seat of Limestone County, ab. 88 mi. N of Birmingham: seat of Athens College. 6,309 (1950).

Athens. City in N Georgia, county seat of Clarke County, on the Oconee River, ab. 62 mi. NE of Atlanta. It is the seat of the University of Georgia (founded 1801). 28,180 (1950).

Athens. [Greek, **Athenai, Athinai** (ä.thē′ne); Latin, **Athenae** (a̤.thē′nē).] Capital of Greece and of the *nomos* (department) of Attica and Boeotia, situated ab. 5 mi. from its seaport Piraeus (on the Saronic Gulf) in E central Greece and Euboea at the SW end of the Attic peninsula, on the Attic plain: the leading commercial, financial, administrative, and manufacturing city of Greece, though not a great center when compared with many other modern cities of Europe. Its chief industry is the production of carpets. Piraeus is the center of its industrial activity. Athens is the center of the railroad traffic of the country and has an airport. Pop. 1,315,571 (1951); with the 8 surrounding towns including Piraeus, 1,368,142 (1951).

City and Surroundings. Athens has developed into a modern large city in only 100 years; it grew from 14,900 inhabitants in 1836 to 487,045 in 1940, an increase of more than 3,000 percent. The Greeks like to call their capital the "Paris of the East." The city is 350 ft. above sea level; summers are hot and dry; winters are mild. The chief surrounding mountains are Aegaleos, Parnes, Pentelikon, and Hymettus on the W and E, and, within the city limits, the steep, rocky hill of Lycabettus; on Lycabettus stands the monastery of Saint George. The Acropolis, around which the ancient city grew up, rises in the center of the city; it is the site of the earliest settlement and a place of many historical remains. To the W is the Areopagus, or Hill of Mars, where Saint Paul preached; farther W are the Hill of the Muses, the Pnyx, and the Hill of the Nymphs. Long walls once joined the city to its port. The modern city has extended NE around Lycabettus; it has well laid out streets and fine buildings, while the older section near the Acropolis has poor houses and narrow streets. The chief public buildings of the modern city are palaces with fine gardens; a university (1837); national library (1833); national museum (1866), one of the richest of the world; polytechnic institute (1837); Byzantine Museum (1914); Greek, French, and British archaeological schools; American School of Classical Studies (1882).

Architecture. The ancient architectural masterpieces are mostly on the Acropolis, the chief ancient landmark. The most important structures are: the Dionysiac Theater, on the S slope of the Acropolis, where all the famous Greek dramas were produced. It was originally of wood, and was not completed in stone until about 340 B.C. The existing remains of orchestra and stage-structure are modifications of Roman date. The Gate of the Oil-Market, or New Agora, a gate built with gifts from Julius Caesar and Augustus, is also noteworthy. The "Long Walls," now mostly in ruins, two massive fortification walls extending from the ramparts of the city to those of the Piraeus, at a distance apart, except near their diverging extremities, of about 550 ft. They made the port and the metropolis practically one huge fortress, and assured Athenian supplies by sea while rendering possible Athenian naval triumphs at times when the Spartans held their land without the walls. They were destroyed when Athens fell before Sparta toward the end of the 5th century B.C., but were restored in 393 B.C. by Conon The Long Walls followed the crests of the group of hills SW of the Acropolis. The foundations of the old Temple of Athena, between the Erechtheum and the Parthenon, were recognized and studied by Dörpfeld in 1885. It was Doric, peripteral, hexastyle, with 12 columns on the flanks, and measured 70 by 137 ft. A number of the column drums, capitals, and other architectural elements are built into the N wall of the Acropolis. The temple had a large cult-cella toward the E, behind which there was a treasury with two chambers opening on a vestibule. One authority has disputed Dörpfeld's restoration, and suggests that the temple may have been Ionic, of 8 by 16 columns. This temple remained standing certainly until 406 B.C., and probably until the reign of Hadrian and later. It is of unusual historical and archaeological importance. The arena of the Panathenaic stadium, a stadium still practically complete except for its sheathing of marble, measures 109 by 670 ft., and is bordered on its long sides and its semicircular E end by the slopes which supported the seats (about 60 tiers) for the spectators. There were at intervals 29 flights of steps to give access to the seats. Notable also are the Academy of Sciences, a beautiful building in Pentelic marble, completed in modern times in the classical Greek style for the accommodation of a learned body modeled after the French Institute, and the Convent of Daphni, a convent founded by the French dukes of Athens in the 13th century.

History. Athens was founded, according to the old account, by an Egyptian colony led by Cecrops. It became the chief place in Attica, with Pallas Athena as its especial divinity, and was ruled by kings, among whom Erechtheus, Theseus, and Codrus are famous. It was then (from the legendary date 1132 B.C.) ruled by the nobles (*Eupatrids*), and had archons as magistrates, who were successively perpetual, decennial, and (after 683 B.C.) annual. The laws of Draco were enacted in 621 B.C., and those of Solon in 594 B.C. Pisistratus became tyrant in 560, and his sons were expelled in 510. The reforms of Cleisthenes (508) made Athens (for its day) a pure democracy; popular assemblies of all its citizens (but not all, or even most, of its adult inhabitants were citizens) made the laws. The glorious period began with the Persian wars, in which Athens took a leading part, as at Marathon (490) and Salamis (480). The city was temporarily held by the Persians in 480. Under Themistocles, immediately thereafter, the Long Walls were built. Athens became the head of the confederacy of Delos in c477, and for a short period had an extensive empire and was the first power in Greece. The "Age of Pericles" (c461–429) was noted for the adornment of the city. The Peloponnesian war (431–404) resulted in the displacement of Athens by Sparta in the hegemony of Greece. Athens was taken by Sparta in 404 and an aristocratic faction was put in power, but moderate democracy was restored by Thrasybulus in 403. Athens under Demosthenes resisted Macedonia, but was overthrown at the battle of Chaeronea (338), and was generally after this under Macedonian influence. It was subjugated by Rome in 146 B.C., and pillaged by Sulla in 86 B.C. It continued to form part of the Roman and later of the Byzantine empire. Conquered by the Crusaders in 1205, it became a lordship and soon a duchy under French, Spanish, and Italian rulers successively till its conquest by the Turks in 1456. It was devastated by a Venetian bombardment in 1687, and also in the war for Greek independence in 1821–27. It became the capital of the new kingdom of Greece in 1834. In World War II it was occupied (1941–44) by German forces.

Athens. City in SE Ohio, county seat of Athens County, on the Hocking River, ab. 35 mi. W of Marietta. It is the seat of Ohio University. It was established in the early 1800's and was incorporated as a city in 1912. Pop. 11,660 (1950).

Athens. Borough in NE Pennsylvania, in Bradford County, at the confluence of the Chemung and Susquehanna rivers, near the New York border: manufactures of silk textiles, machine tools, and iron; railroad shops. Settled in 1778, it occupies the site of the former Indian town of Tioga. 4,430 (1950).

Athens. City in SE Tennessee, county seat of McMinn County, ab. 50 mi. NE of Chattanooga: seat of Tennessee Wesleyan College. 8,618 (1950).

Athens. City in E Texas, county seat of Henderson County, SE of Dallas: distributing point for fruit, peanuts, vegetables, pigs, and poultry; pottery manufactures. 5,194 (1950).

Athens, Duke of. See under **Acciajuoli** or **Acciajoli, Nerio.**

Athens: an Ode. Poem by Algernon Charles Swinburne. It is a patriotic poem in which Swinburne draws a parallel between Greece and England.

"Athens of America." See under **Boston,** Mass.

"Athens of the North." See under **Edinburgh.**

Atherstone (ath'ėr.stōn). Rural district and market town in C England, in Warwickshire, ab. 17 mi. NE of Birmingham, ab. 102 mi. NW of London by rail. It has a famous milestone which is 100 mi. equidistant from London, Liverpool, and Lincoln. 23,662 (1951).

Atherstone, Edwin. b. at Nottingham, England, April 17, 1788; d. at Bath, England, Jan. 29, 1872. English author of romances and of epic poems such as *The Last Days of Herculaneum* (1821), *The Fall of Nineveh* (30 books, 1828–68), and others.

Atherton (ath'ėr.tọn). Residential town in W California, in San Mateo County, ab. 25 mi. SE of San Francisco. Incorporated in 1923, it was formerly the site of palatial mansions financed by mining speculations, including that of the father-in-law of Gertrude Atherton. 3,630 (1950).

Atherton. [Also, **Chowbent.**] Urban district and coal-mining center in NW England, in Lancashire, situated on the South Lancashire coal field, ab. 10 mi. NW of Manchester, ab. 194 mi. NW of London by rail. 20,591 (1951).

Atherton, Charles Gordon. b. at Amherst, N.H., July 4, 1804; d. at Manchester, N.H., Nov. 15, 1853. American politician and lawyer. Elected to the House of Representatives in 1836 and to the Senate in 1842 and 1852 as a Democrat, he was a tariff opponent and a champion of an independent treasury system. He fiercely defended states' rights, proposing the tabling of all memorials in Congress relating to slavery on grounds that the federal government could not legally intervene.

Atherton, Gertrude. [Full name, **Gertrude Franklin Atherton;** maiden name, **Horn.**] b. at San Francisco, Oct. 30, 1857; d. there, June 14, 1948. American novelist. Author of *The Doomswoman* (1892), *The Californian* (1898), *The Conqueror* (1902), *Tower of Ivory* (1910), *Julia France and Her Times* (1912), *Black Oxen* (1923), *The Sophisticates* (1931), *Golden Peacock* (1936), *The House of Lee* (1940), *The Horn of Life* (1942), and many others.

Atherton Company. In American colonial history, a company of land speculators taking its name from a certain Major Humphrey Atherton. Between 1659 and 1662 the company, by negotiations with the Indians, secured claims to virtually the entire Narragansett country. The ensuing jurisdictional dispute between Rhode Island and Connecticut brought violent differences, including armed clashes, which were settled only when the English Board of Trade assigned (1727) jurisdiction to Rhode Island.

Atherton Moor, Battle of. Victory gained in the English Civil War near Bradford, England, in 1643, by the Royalists under the Earl of Newcastle over the Parliamentarians under Ferdinando Fairfax.

Athesis (ath'ẹ.sis). Latin name of the **Adige.**

Áth Í (ô'ē'). Irish name of **Athy.**

Athinai (ä.thē'ne). Greek name of **Athens,** Greece.

Athlete, The. Greek statue, held to be a copy of the famous Doryphorus (spear-bearer), the canon or type of Polyclitus, found at Pompeii, and added to the collection of the Museo Nazionale, Naples. The undraped figure is well proportioned and holds a simple, naturalistic pose.

Athlone (ath.lōn'), 1st Earl of (2nd creation). [Title of **Alexander Augustus Frederick William Alfred George Cambridge,** Prince **Alexander of Teck.**] b. at London, April 14, 1874—. English soldier and politician. He married (1904) Princess Alice, a granddaughter of Queen Victoria. He served in the Matabele War (1896), the Boer War (1899–1900), and World War I. After serving as governor general of the Union of South Africa (1923–30), he was appointed (1940) to the same post for Canada.

Athlone. [Irish, **Áth Luain** (ô lö'in).] Urban district, market town, railway junction, and road center, in Leinster province, Irish Republic, in County Westmeath, situated on the river Shannon, ab. 26 mi. SW of Mullingar. It was taken from the Irish by General Ginkel in June, 1691. Pop. 9,015 (1951).

Athmallik (ät.mul'ik). Former state of the Union of India, one of the Eastern States, merged (1948) with Orissa, ab. 130 mi. W of Cuttack. Timber and coal mining are carried on, and the main crops are rice and maize. Area, 711 sq. mi.; pop. 72,755 (1941).

Athol (ath'ol). Name of a town and village in N Massachusetts, in Worcester County, on Miller's River, ab. 23 mi. W of Fitchburg: manufactures include precision tools, thread, cigars, toys, and furnaces. Pop. of town, 11,554 (1950); of village, 9,708 (1950).

Atholl (ath'ọl), 8th Duke of. [Title of **John George Stewart-Murray.**] b. 1871; d. in Perthshire, Scotland, March 16, 1942. Scottish cavalry officer; son of John James Hugh Henry Stewart-Murray (1840–1917). He was in charge of a unit of Scottish cavalry during the Boer War and in World War I. After attending Eton, he took part 1896–98 in the Nile expedition, serving in the battles at Atbara and Khartum. In World War I he saw action at Gallipoli and in Egypt. He was a member of Parliament from 1910 to 1917; in 1922 he was made lord chamberlain.

Atholl or **Athole** (ath'ọl). [Also, **Athol.**] Hilly district in C Scotland, in Perthshire, situated at the base of the Grampian Mountains, which lie immediately north. The region is largely barren. It contains the "Forest of Atholl" (area over 150 sq. mi.). Area, ab. 450 sq. mi.

Atholstan (ath'ọl.stan), 1st Baron. [Title of **Hugh Graham.**] b. at Atholstan, Quebec, 1848; d. at Montreal, Jan. 28, 1938. Canadian publisher who founded (1869) and published (1869–1938) the Montreal *Star.* He was a staff member of the Montreal *Telegraph* and Montreal *Gazette.* Knighted (1907) and raised to the peerage (1917), he served (1920 *et seq.*) in the British House of Lords.

Athos (ath'os). [Also: **Acte, Akte.**] Easternmost peninsula of Chalcidice in Macedonia, NE Greece. It projects into the Aegean Sea and is connected with the mainland by a narrow isthmus (pierced by a canal during the invasion of Xerxes). Length, ab. 30 mi.

Athos (ā'thos; French, å.tos). One of the "three Musketeers" in the novel *The Three Musketeers,* by the elder Alexandre Dumas.

Athos (ath'os), **Mount.** See also **Agion Oros.**

Athos, Mount. [Called the **"Holy Mountain."**] Mountain at the extremity of the peninsula of Athos, famous since the early Middle Ages for its communities of monks, which form what is in many respects an autonomous republic. Elevation, ab. 6,350 ft.

Athribis (ä.thrē'bēs). See under **Benha.**

Athura (ä.thö'rạ). Persian name of **Assyria.**

Athy (ạ.thī'). [Irish, **Áth Í.**] Urban district and market town in Leinster province, Irish Republic, in County Kildare, situated on the river Barrow and on a branch of the Grand Canal, ab. 39 mi. SW of Dublin. 3,753 (1951).

Atia or **Attia gens** (at'i.ạ jenz). In ancient Rome, a plebeian clan or house whose family names were Balbus, Labienus, Rufus, and Varus.

Atilia or **Atillia gens** (ạ.til'i.ạ jenz). In ancient Rome, a patrician and plebeian clan or house whose family names were Bulbus, Calatinus, Longus, Regulus, and Serranus. The first member of this gens who became consul was Marcus Atilius Regulus, 335 B.C.

Atin (ā'tin). The personification of Strife in Edmund Spenser's *Faerie Queene.*

Atitlán (ä.tē.tlän'). [Also, **Santiago Atitlán.**] Volcano in Guatemala, W of Guatemala City, near Lake Atitlán. Elevation, ab. 12,000 ft.

Atitlán, Lake. Lake in W Guatemala, ab. 50 mi. W of Guatemala City, noted for its great depth (ab. 1,000 ft.). Length, ab. 24 mi.; width, ab. 10 mi.

Atiu (ä.tē.ö'). See under **Cook Islands.**

Atjeh (ä'che). [Former spellings: **Achin, Atchîn;** also, **Acheen, Atcheen.**] Region in Indonesia, in N Sumatra. A war with the Dutch, which began in 1873, resulted in the virtual subjugation of the country. In January, 1942, it was occupied by the Japanese; at the end of World War II it was returned to the Dutch: now part of the new Republic of Indonesia. Oil and rubber are found in the region. Area, 21,386.9 sq. mi.; pop. 1,003,062 (1930).

Atjenese or **Atjehnese** (ach.ẹ.nēz'). See **Achehnese.**

Atka (at'ka). Largest of the Andreanof Islands, Aleutian Archipelago, W of Alaska: U.S. military base in World War II.

Atkins (at'kinz), Sir **Ivor Algernon.** b. near Cardiff, Wales, Nov. 29, 1869—. English organist and composer. He served as choirmaster (1897 *et seq.*) at Worcester Cathedral, and was president (1935–36) of the Royal College of Organists. Composer of *Hymn of Faith* (1905), for which Sir Edward Elgar arranged the libretto, and others.

Atkinson (at'kin.son), **Brooks.** [Original full name, **Justin Brooks Atkinson.**] b. at Melrose, Mass., Nov. 28, 1894—. American journalist and drama critic. A graduate (1917) of Harvard, he joined the staff of the New York *Times* as book review editor (1922–25) and drama critic (1925–42, 1946 *et seq.*). During World War II he was a news correspondent at Chungking, China (1942–44), and Moscow (1944–46). Author of *Skyline Promenades* (1925), *Henry Thoreau, The Cosmic Yankee* (1927), *East of the Hudson* (1931), *The Cingalese Prince* (1934), and *Once Around the Sun* (1951).

Atkinson, Edward. b. at Brookline, Mass., Feb. 10, 1827; d. at Boston, Dec. 11, 1905. American economist, industrialist, and statistician. He was a pioneer in the field of mutual insurance for factories by aiding the establishment in the 1880's of the Boston Manufacturers Mutual Insurance Company, one of the first organizations to reduce insurance risk by urging improvements in the construction and use of industrial establishments. Author of *Our National Domain* (1879), *Railroads of the United States* (1880), and others.

Atkinson, Eleanor. [Maiden name, **Stackhouse;** pseudonym, **Nora Marks.**] b. at Rensselaer, Ind., 1863; d. 1942. American writer. She was on the staff of the Chicago *Tribune* until her marriage (1891), writing under the name of Nora Marks; subsequently (1900–07) she served as an editor of the *Little Chronicle*, a journal for children. Among her best-known works are *Greyfriars Bobby* (1912) and *Johnny Appleseed* (1915); she was also the author of *Mamzelle Fifine* (1903), *Poilu, a Dog of Roubaix* (1918), and others.

Atkinson, George Francis. b. at Raisinville, Mich., Jan. 26, 1854; d. at Tacoma, Wash., Nov. 15, 1918. American naturalist, professor of botany at Cornell from 1896. He was an associate editor of the *Botanical Gazette* in the period 1896–98. Author of *Studies of American Fungi* (1900), *Mushrooms* (1903), and others.

Atkinson, George Wesley. b. in Kanawha County, Va. (now W. Va.), June 29, 1845; d. at Charleston, W. Va., April 14, 1925. American writer, lecturer, lawyer, and politician. He was elected (1896) governor of West Virginia, being the first Republican to win that office in some 25 years. He served as editor (1877–78) of the Wheeling *Evening Standard* and joint editor for nine years of the West Virginia *Journal*. Author of *History of Kanawha County* (1876), *West Virginia Pulpit* (1878), *Bench and Bar of West Virginia* (1919), and many others.

Atkinson, Sir **Harry Albert.** b. at Broxton, Cheshire, England, November 1, 1831; d. at Wellington, New Zealand, June 28, 1892. New Zealand political leader, four times premier. He arrived in New Zealand in 1853, and distinguished himself as a leader in the wars against the Maori tribesmen. He served in the New Zealand Parliament from 1861; became a cabinet minister in 1874, and put through Parliament bills abolishing provinces and setting up a centralized system of government. He served as treasurer for a total of ten years in several ministries. He was three times premier (1876–77, 1883–84, 1887–91).

Atkinson, Henry. b. in North Carolina, 1782; d. at Jefferson Barracks, Mo., June 14, 1842. American general, leader of two expeditions to the mouth of the Yellowstone River. The first of these (1819) accomplished little, largely because of War Department interference; the later expedition (1825) was an outstanding success, achieving treaties with Indian tribes and returning to St. Louis without loss of any kind. A commander in the Black Hawk War (1832), he was credited with the decisive victory over the Sacs at Bad Axe.

Atkinson, John. b. at Deerfield, N.Y., Dec. 6, 1835; Dec. 8, 1897. American Methodist clergyman and historian. He is best known for his *Memorials of Methodism in New Jersey* (1860), *Centennial History of American Methodism, 1784–1816* (1884), and *Beginnings of the Wesleyan Movement in America, 1766–73* (1896). He was the author also of the widely known hymn *Shall We Meet Beyond the River?*

Atkinson, John Christopher. b. at Eddhangor, England, 1814; d. 1900. English clergyman and antiquary, remembered chiefly for *Forty Years in Moorland Parish* (1891), a collection of local legends and traditions. He received his bachelor's degree from Cambridge University in 1838, served as vicar (1847–1900) of Danby, Yorkshire, and became prebendary of York in 1891. He published minor antiquarian works, and books for children.

Atkinson, Sergeant. Character in Henry Fielding's *Amelia*. With his devotion to Booth and Amelia, and his self-sacrificing generosity, he is an embodiment of goodness of heart.

Atkinson, Thomas. b. in Dinwiddie County, Va., Aug. 6, 1807; d. at Wilmington, N.C., Jan. 4, 1881. American Episcopal bishop and one-time lawyer. He forsook the legal profession for the ministry in 1836, was consecrated bishop of North Carolina in 1853, and aided in the preliminary efforts to establish what was later to be the University of the South at Sewanee, Tenn. He was instrumental in reëstablishing the link between the northern and southern branches of the Episcopal Church severed during the Civil War. In 1867 he was a delegate to the first Lambeth conference, at London.

Atkinson, Thomas Dinham. b. 1864—. English architect and writer. His chief works include the Cambridge observatory and library, and various buildings adjoining Ely Cathedral. Author of *English Architecture* (1904; 12th edition, 1946), *Key to English Architecture* (1936), *Local Style in English Architecture* (1946), and others.

Atkinson, Wilmer. b. in Bucks County, Pa., June 13, 1840; d. May 10, 1920. American journalist and publisher. A cofounder (1866) of the Wilmington *Daily Commercial*, the first daily newspaper in Delaware, he was also the founder (1877) at Philadelphia of the *Farm Journal*, which later attained a circulation of over a million and was the first periodical in the U.S. to bar patent-medicine advertising. President (1915) of the Pennsylvania Men's League for Woman Suffrage.

Atkyns (at'kinz), **Richard.** b. 1615; d. at London, 1677. English writer on the history of printing. He was the author of *The Origin and Growth of Printing, etc.* (1664).

Atkyns, Sir **Robert.** b. in Gloucestershire, England, 1621; d. Feb. 18, 1709. English jurist, chief lord of the exchequer. His defense of the Whig leader, William Russell (1639–83), against a charge of treason, and other similar cases, earned him a wide reputation for honesty and brilliance in a time of corrupt courts. Author of *Parliamentary and Political Tracts* (1734), and others.

Atlanta (at.lan'ta). [Sometimes called the **"Gate City."**] City in NW Georgia, capital of Georgia and of Fulton County, on the Chattahoochee River. It is an important railway center, and has manufactures of textiles, chemicals, confectionery, fertilizers, and paper products. It is the seat of Emory University, the Georgia Institute of Technology, Oglethorpe University, Atlanta University, Clark College, Gammon Theological Seminary, Morris Brown College, and other educational institutions, and of a federal penitentiary. Atlanta was taken by William Tecumseh Sherman on Sept. 2, 1864, and was partly burned (Nov. 15, 1864) previous to his departure on his "March to the Sea." It became the state capital in 1868. Pop. of city, 302,288 (1940), 331,314 (1950); of urbanized area, 507,887 (1950).

Atlanta. City in NE Texas, in Cass County near the borders of Arkansas and Louisiana, ab. 150 mi. NE of Dallas. Oil and lumber are produced in the surrounding area. 3,782 (1950).

Atlanta, Battle of. Military operation in the Civil War, E of Atlanta, Ga., on July 22, 1864, involving Union forces under William Tecumseh Sherman and Confederate forces under John Bell Hood, who had made a sortie from the city. Sherman lost about 3,600 men. The Confederates were compelled to fall back upon Atlanta on Sept. 1, 1864.

Atlante (ät.län'tā). Magician, in Matteo Maria Boiardo's *Orlando Innamorato* and Lodovico Ariosto's *Orlando Furi-*

oso. He lived on Mount Carena in a castle, surrounded with a wall of glass, where he educated the young Rogero.

Atlantic (at.lan′tik). City in SW Iowa, county seat of Cass County, on the East Nishnabotna River, ab. 47 mi. E of Omaha: canning center for agricultural produce, particularly corn and pumpkins. 6,480 (1950).

Atlantic, Battle of the. Term often applied to the extended series of separate naval and air actions in World War II that arose from the German effort to cut British sea-routes of supply and from the countermeasures instituted by the naval and air forces of Great Britain and, later, the U.S. The German attack depended chiefly upon submarines (although a few aircraft were used), and the Allied defense was organized around the convoy system, and the use of aircraft and light surface vessels ranging widely over the areas of known submarine activity. During the period 1939–42 the German submarine campaign achieved considerable success (in the first ten months of 1942 alone, the Allies lost a total of over four and a half million tons of shipping). At the beginning of the war the bulk of the German submarine effort was aimed at the destruction of vessels in waters immediately adjoining the British Isles (the northwest approaches to which, for several hundred miles off the coasts of N Scotland and Ireland, were a favorite hunting ground for many U-boat commanders); at a later date, immediately after the U.S. entered the war, the weight of submarine attack shifted to the coastal waters of North America. However, by the beginning of 1942, Allied countermeasures had reached a level of effectiveness which caused German submarine losses to rise prohibitively, and even with the development of the so-called Schnorkel (or "breather-tube") and other devices, the German submarines were never again in World War II able to offer a serious threat to the Allied lines of supply. Many authorities therefore consider the Battle of the Atlantic to have ended in 1942; other historians, however, consider that it paralleled the entire course of World War II, on the grounds that even after the invasion of Germany, some local submarine activity continued in the North Sea and off the W coast of Scotland.

Atlantic Charter. Eight-point joint declaration of principles drafted by U.S. President Franklin D. Roosevelt and British Prime Minister Winston S. Churchill in August, 1941, when the U.S. was still a nonbelligerent in World War II. It was drawn up during conferences aboard British and U.S. war vessels off Newfoundland and released for publication on Aug. 14. Incorporated later in the United Nations Declaration, the Charter was intended to publicize common principles on which the signatories "base their hopes for a better future for the world." The Charter was actually signed on Aug. 14 1941, on the British battleship *Prince of Wales.* Its chief points were: (1) no territorial aggrandizement; (2) no territorial changes contrary to the wishes of the people involved; (3) right of people to choose their own forms of government; (4) equal access of all nations to trade and raw materials; (5) world-wide collaboration for economic and social progress; (6) freedom from fear and want; (7) freedom of the seas; (8) abandonment of force, disarming of aggressor nations, and reduction in armaments.

Atlantic City. City in SE New Jersey, in Atlantic County, ab. 60 mi. SE of Philadelphia: summer and winter resort. It is the site of annual bathing beauty contests and business conventions, and has a famous boardwalk, many hotels, and a number of large amusement piers. Pop. of city, 61,657 (1950); of urbanized area, 105,083 (1950).

Atlantic Coast Line Railroad. One of the chief railroad systems of the Southern region of the U.S. It was chartered (1836) as the Richmond and Petersburg Railroad and took its present designation in 1900. Its main line operates between Richmond, Va., and Tampa, Fla.

Atlantic Conference. Meeting from Aug. 9 to Aug. 14 1941, on warships in Placentia Bay, off Newfoundland, between Prime Minister Churchill and President Franklin D. Roosevelt. It was the first face-to-face meeting of these two national leaders. The discussions ranged over the whole military position of the Allies and gave general consideration to postwar organization. At its conclusion the Atlantic Charter was issued.

Atlantic Highlands. Borough in E New Jersey, in Monmouth County, on Sandy Hook Bay ab. 40 mi. NE of Trenton: seaside resort and residential community. 3,083 (1950).

Atlantic Monthly. Magazine of literature, art, and current events, published (1857 *et seq.*) at Boston.

Atlántico (ät.län′tē.kō). Department in N Colombia: the smallest in the country. Capital, Barranquilla; area, 1,340 sq. mi.; pop. 406,500 (est. 1950).

Atlantic Ocean (at.lan′tik). [French, **Mer Atlantique** (mer at.läṅ.tēk); German, **Atlantisches Meer** (ät.län′tish.ęs mär); Latin, **Atlanticum Mare** (at.lan′ti.kum mā′rē).] That part of the ocean which is bounded by the Arctic Ocean on the N, Europe and Africa on the E, the Antarctic Ocean on the S, and America on the W. It is sometimes regarded as terminating at lat. 40° S., the part southward being reckoned as belonging to the so-called Southern Ocean. Its chief currents are the Gulf Stream, Greenland Current, North Atlantic Drift Current, Labrador Current, Equatorial Currents, South Connecting Current, Guinea Current, and Brazil Current. Length, 10,000 mi.; average breadth, 3,000 mi.; average depth, ab. 13,000 ft.; area, excluding fringing seas (Caribbean, Mediterranean, etc.), ab. 31,837,000 sq. mi.

Atlántida (ät.län′tē.ᴛʜä). Department in NW Honduras. Rubber is the principal product. Capital, La Ceiba; area, 1,656 sq. mi.; pop. 63,582 (1950).

Atlantis (at.lan′tis). Legendary island in the Atlantic Ocean, NW of Africa, referred to by Plato and other ancient writers, which with its inhabitants (who had achieved, according to most accounts, a high degree of civilization) was said to have disappeared in a convulsion of nature. The belief in the possibility of such a place has continued to exist even into modern times, and many writers (including Francis Bacon in his work *The New Atlantis*) have taken the name as an equivalent for a utopian state.

Atlas (at′lạs). Unincorporated community in E central Pennsylvania, in Northumberland County, ab. 45 mi. NE of Harrisburg. 3,090 (1950).

Atlas. In Greek mythology, a Titan, brother of Prometheus and Epimetheus; son of Iapetus and Clymene (or Asia), and father (by Pleione) of the Pleiades and (by Aethra) of the Hyades, and also (in Homer) of Calypso. According to Hesiod he was condemned by Zeus, for his part in the battle of the Titans, to stand at the western extremity of the earth, near the habitation of the Hesperides, upholding the heavens with his shoulders and hands. His station was later said to be in the Atlas Mountains in Africa. According to some accounts he was the father of the Hesperides; also a king to whom the garden of the Hesperides belonged. The details of the myth vary greatly.

Atlas. The fourth-magnitude star 27 Tauri at the E extremity of the "handle" of the Pleiades.

Atlas Mountains. Mountain system in NW Africa, in Morocco, Algeria, and Tunisia, sometimes regarded as limited to Morocco. The mountains are often divided into the Tell, Riff, High (or Great), Saharan, and Anti-Atlas. The highest summit of this system, Jebel Ajashi, in Morocco, is 14,600 ft. high. Length, of the system, ab. 1,500 mi.

Atlee (at′lē), **Washington Lemuel.** b. at Lancaster, Pa., Feb. 22, 1808; d. Sept. 6, 1878. American surgeon. A specialist in ovariotomies (of which he had performed 378 by 1878), he encountered the censure (1843 *et seq.*) of other surgeons, who in some cases termed the operation a form of murder; but endorsements of leading Philadelphia surgeons and continued success brought him the eventual approval of his colleagues.

Atli (ät′lē). In the *Volsunga Saga*, the name of Attila, king of the Huns, who married Gudrun.

Atlin Lake (at′lin). Lake in NW Canada, in NW British Columbia, extending N for a very short distance into Yukon Territory; ab. 375 mi. NW of Victoria, B.C., and 27 mi. NE of Juneau, Alaska. On its E shore there is some gold mining. Length, ab. 58 mi.; greatest width, ab. 18 mi.; area, ab. 308 sq. mi.

Atlixco (ä.tlēs′kō). City in S Mexico, in Puebla state. 17,034 (1940).

Atm (ä'tẹm). [Also: **Atmu, Tmu.**] In Egyptian mythology, the setting sun, a double of Ra, represented in human form, worshiped at Heliopolis.

Atmore (at'mōr). City in SE Alabama, in Escambia County, ab. 40 mi. NE of Mobile: shipping point for agricultural produce, including potatoes, cabbage, and beans. 5,720 (1950).

Atmu (ät'mö). See **Atm.**

Atna (at'nạ). See **Copper.**

Atoka (ạ.tō'kạ). City in SE Oklahoma, county seat of Atoka County. It was named for a subchief of the Choctaws. 2,653 (1950).

Atom, The Adventures of an. See **Adventures of an Atom, The.**

Atomic Energy Commission. U.S. government five-man board, composed of civilian members appointed by the president, which was created by the Atomic Energy Act of 1946. It is empowered with the control of raw fissionable materials and lands producing them, atomic weapons, and all U.S. patents and inventions relating to atomic energy. It also controls pertinent information in the interests of national security and assists research and development in the theory and production of atomic energy.

Atomic Energy Commission. Commission set up within the United Nations which studies and advises upon the problems related to atomic energy.

Atonement, Day of. [Hebrew, **Yom Kippur.**] Jewish fast day, among Orthodox Jews the most solemn occasion of the year. It falls on the tenth day of Tishri (variously in September or early October) as the culmination of ten penitential days following Rosh Hashanah. On this day, according to tradition, individual fates for the ensuing year are decreed by God. The commemoration is marked by a synagogue service which includes the blowing of a ram's horn and prayers for the dead.

Atossa (ạ.tos'ạ). fl. 6th century B.C. Queen of Persia; daughter of Cyrus ("the Great") and mother of Xerxes I. She was the wife, successively, of Cambyses II (who was her brother), of the "false Smerdis" (a Magian priest who successfully passed himself off as the true Smerdis, also a brother of Atossa, but murdered by Cambyses. The pose enabled the "false Smerdis" briefly to usurp the throne.), and of Darius I, by whom she was the mother of Xerxes I.

Atossa. Poetical name given to Sarah (Jennings) Churchill, the first duchess of Marlborough, by Alexander Pope in his *Moral Essays.*

Atoyac (ä.tō.yäk'). [Spanish, **Río Atoyac.**] River in SE Mexico. It flows SW to join the Mexcala River.

Atrabate (ạ.tra'bạ.tē). A Gallic name of **Arras.**

Atrai (ä'trī). [Also, **Atri.**] River in East Bengal, Pakistan, which joins the Jamuna (right branch of the Brahamaputra River) near Pabna. Length, ab. 300 mi.

Atrato (ä.trä'tō). [Spanish, **Río Atrato.**] River in NW Colombia which flows N into the Gulf of Darien. Length, ab. 400 mi.; navigable for over half its course.

Atrebates (ạ.treb'ạ.tēz, at.rẹ.bā'tēz) or **Atrebati** (-tī). In ancient history, a tribe of Belgic Gaul, dwelling chiefly in what later was Artois. It joined the confederation against Julius Caesar. One branch dwelt in Britain near the Thames.

Atrek (ä'trek). [Also, **Attruck.**] River in N Iran which flows E into the Caspian Sea and for part of its length forms the boundary between Iran and the U.S.S.R. Length, ab. 280 mi.

Atreus (ā'trẹ.us, -trös). In Greek legend, a king of Mycenae; son of Pelops and father of Agamemnon. He brought upon himself the curse of his brother Thyestes when, to revenge himself for the seduction, by Thyestes, of his wife, Atreus killed three of Thyestes' sons, and served them at a meal as meat to their father. Aegisthus, the only surviving son of Thyestes, subsequently slew Atreus.

Atri (ä'trī). See also **Atrai.**

Atri (ä'trē). [Ancient names, **Hadria, Hatria.**] Town and commune in C Italy, in the *compartimento* (region) of Abruzzi e Molise, in the province of Teramo, situated near the Adriatic Sea, ab. 14 mi. SE of Teramo: manufactures ceramics, silk articles, and pasta. It is the seat of a bishopric; the Romanesque-Gothic cathedral dates from the 13th century. Buildings of interest to tourists were undamaged in World War II. Pop. of commune, 12,735 (1936); of town, 3,837 (1936).

Atria (ā'tri.ạ). See **Adria.**

Atropatene (at"rọ.pạ.tē'nē). See under **Azerbaijan.**

Atropos (at'rọ.pos). In Greek mythology, that one of the three Fates who severs the thread of human life.

Atscholi (ä.chō'lē). See **Acholi.**

Attaché; or Sam Slick in England, The. Humorous sketches by Thomas Chandler Haliburton, published (1843, 1844) under the pseudonym Sam Slick, in two series.

Attakapas (ạ.tak'ạ.pô). Popular name for a district in S Louisiana comprising the parishes of St. Mary's, St. Martin's, Vermilion, Iberia, and Lafayette.

Attaleia (at.ạ.lē'ạ). Ancient name of **Antalya,** city.

Attalia (at.ạ.lī'ạ). Biblical name of **Antalya,** city.

Attalla (ạ.tal'ạ). City in NE Alabama, in Etowah County, ab. 53 mi. NE of Birmingham: shipping point for cotton. 7,537 (1950).

Attalus (at'ạ.lus). [Also, **Attalos** (-los).] d. c336 B.C. Macedonian general under Philip II. He was assassinated for his opposition to Alexander the Great.

Attalus. [Also, **Attalos.**] fl. c325 B.C. Macedonian officer in the service of Alexander the Great.

Attalus I. [Also: **Attalos;** surnamed, **Soter.**] b. c269 B.C.; d. 197 B.C. King of Pergamum (c242–197). He carried on war with the Galatians, with Syria, and with Macedonia, and was allied with Rome against Macedonia in the latter part of his reign. Votive groups were set up by him on the Acropolis at Athens, in honor of his victory over the Gauls. These groups, of figures of about half life-size, depicted a battle of the gods and giants, combat between Athenians and Amazons, the victory of Marathon, and destruction of the Gauls by Attalus. Four figures from these groups were acquired by the National Museum at Naples: a fallen giant, a dead Amazon, a fallen Persian, and a dying bearded Gaul.

Attalus II. [Also: **Attalos;** surnamed **Philadelphus.**] b. 220 B.C.; d. 138 B.C. King of Pergamum (c159–138); son of Attalus I and successor to his brother Eumenes II. He was an ally of Rome.

Attalus III. [Also: **Attalos;** surnamed **Philometor.**] b. 171 B.C.; d. 133 B.C. King of Pergamum (138–133); nephew of Attalus II. By his will he left his kingdom to the Romans. He is of some interest to historians of science for his studies in botany and, more narrowly, in agriculture (a treatise by him in this latter field was used by Pliny). However, his interests in these fields seem to have had a very practical motive, and one not unrelated to the political hazards of his day: his chief interest was in poisonous plants, and he prepared and experimented with a number of poisons.

Attalus, Flavius Priscus. fl. early 5th century B.C. Emperor of the Roman Empire in the west. He was probably an Ionian by birth, was prefect of Rome when the city was taken (Aug. 24, 410) by Alaric, and was proclaimed emperor by Alaric in opposition to Honorius. He was deposed by Alaric in the same year, and was banished to Lipari by Honorius in 416.

Attanae (at'ạ.nē). An ancient name of **Aden.**

Attaque du moulin (là.tàk dü mö.laṅ), **L'.** [Eng. trans., "*The Attack on the Mill.*"] Opera in three acts by Alfred Bruneau, based on a tale by Émile Zola, first performed at the Opéra Comique at Paris on Nov. 23, 1893.

Attar (ät.tär'). [Also: **Athar;** full name, **Mohammed ibn-Ibrahim Ferid Eddin Attar.**] b. near Nishapur, in Persia, 1119; d. c1229. Persian poet and mystic. By profession originally a maker of medicines and perfumes (from which comes his name Attar, meaning "perfume"), he wrote 40 poetical works, admired for their elegance of style and insight into the Sufi doctrines, of which *Mantig-ut-Tair* (The Language of Birds) is the best known. It was translated into English by Edward FitzGerald. He is said to have been killed when some 90 years of age by a Mongol soldier.

Attawapiskat (at"ạ.wạ.pis'kat). River in C Canada, in N Ontario, flowing generally E into James Bay, the southernmost arm of Hudson Bay. Length, ab. 465 mi.

Atterberg (ät'tėr.bery'), **Kurt.** b. at Göteborg, Sweden, Dec. 12, 1887—. Swedish composer and orchestra conductor. Educated as an electrical engineer, he early forsook science for music, serving as a conductor of orchestras throughout Scandinavia and Germany. He is best known for his seven symphonies, but also wrote operas, ballets, concertos, and others.

Atterbom (ät'tėr.bům), **Per Daniel Amadeus.** b. at Åsbo, Östergötland, Sweden, Jan. 19, 1790; d. July 21, 1855. Swedish poet, professor of philosophy, and a leader in the Swedish romantic movement. He taught (1828 *et seq.*) at Uppsala, after having founded (1807) the Aurora league, which served as the vanguard of the Swedish romantic literary movement. His most celebrated work is *The Fortunate Island* (1824), a romantic drama: he also wrote *The Blue Bird*, a fairy tale in play form of which, unfortunately, only fragments still exist, and *Swedish Seers and Bards* (1841–55), and others.

Atterbury (at'ėr.ber.i, -bėr.i), **Francis.** b. at Milton, Buckinghamshire, England, March 6, 1662; d. at Paris, Feb. 15, 1732. English prelate, politician, and controversialist. He was appointed bishop of Rochester and dean of Westminster in 1713. From his tutorship at Christ Church a pamphleteer (1687 *et seq.*) against the Reformation, he was celebrated in Swift's *Battle of the Books* as leader of the attack on Richard Bentley. Involved in the plot (1721) to restore the Stuart pretender to the throne, he was imprisoned (1722) and banished (1723) as a Jacobite.

Atterbury, Grosvenor. b. at Detroit, July 7, 1869—. American architect. He was graduated from Yale University (1891) and from the École des Beaux-Arts, Paris (1895), and studied also at the Columbia School of Architecture. His special interest in town-planning and home-building led to his appointment as architect of Forest Hills Gardens, the model town built by the Russell Sage Foundation at Forest Hills, L.I.

Atterbury, William Wallace. b. at New Albany, Ind., Jan. 31, 1866; d. Sept. 20, 1935. American railway executive. He became an apprentice in the Altoona, Pa., shops of the Pennsylvania Railroad immediately after his graduation (1886) from the Sheffield Scientific School, at Yale. Selected (1902) by A. J. Cassatt, then president of the railroad, for his grasp of traffic problems, he served (1912 *et seq.*) as vice-president in charge of operations and later (1925–35) as president. He served also (1918–19) as a brigadier general on the staff of General John J. Pershing during World War I, as coördinator of American army transport on French railways.

Atteridge (at'ėr.ij), **Andrew Hilliard.** b. at Liverpool—. English author, journalist, correspondent, and specialist on military and naval subjects. Educated at London and Louvain universities, he later served as an assistant editor of the London *Month*, correspondent for the London *Daily Chronicle*, and war correspondent (1896) in Kitchener's Anglo-Egyptian Dongola campaign. He wrote *Popular History of the Boer War* (1901), *Napoleon's Brothers* (1909), *Modern Battles from Alma to Mukden* (1910), *The First Phase* and *The Second Phase of the Great War* (1914, 1915), and *The World-Wide War* (1915). Author also of articles on "Sir Henry Hawkins," "The Irish in South Africa," and "English Catholic Periodical Literature" in the *Catholic Encyclopedia* (vols. 7, 8, 11).

Atter Lake (ät'ėr). [Also: **Kammer Lake**; German, **Attersee** (ät'ėr.zā), **Kammersee.**] Lake in N Austria, the largest lake in the province of Upper Austria, situated in the Salzkammergut ab. 20 mi. E of Salzburg. Its outlet is by the Ager River into the Traun River. Length, ab. 13 mi.

Attia gens (at'i.ą jenz). See **Atia or Attia gens.**

Attic (at'ik). One of the dialects of ancient Greek, spoken in Athens and the surrounding district (Attica). Three periods can be distinguished in the history of the Attic dialect: (a) Ancient Attic, till the end of the 5th century B.C.; (b) Middle Attic, from the end of the 5th century B.C. to the middle of the 4th century B.C.; and (c) New Attic, from the middle of the 4th century B.C. to the death of Alexander the Great. Attic was considered the most highly cultivated of the Hellenic dialects.

Attica (at'i.ką). In ancient geography, a division of C Greece, bounded by Boeotia (partly separated by Cithaeron) on the NW, the Gulf of Evripos (separating it from Euboea) on the NE, the Aegean Sea on the E, the Saronic Gulf on the SW, and Megaris on the W. It contained several mountains (Cithaeron, Parnes, Pentelicus, and Hymettus) and the plain of Attica, watered by the Cephissus and Ilissus rivers. Its chief city was Athens, with whose history it is in general identified.

Attica. [Also, **Attike** (ä.tē.kē').] *Nomos* (department) in C Greece. Capital, Athens; area, 1,310 sq. mi.; pop. 1,546,234 (1951).

Attica. City in W Indiana, in Fountain County, on the Wabash River, ab. 70 mi. NW of Indianapolis: manufacturing center. Its products include overalls, steel casings, and bricks. 3,862 (1950).

Attica. Village in W New York, in Wyoming County, ab. 25 mi. E of Buffalo: railroad junction; seat of a state prison. 2,676 (1950).

Atticus (at'i.kus), **Titus Pomponius.** b. at Rome, 109 B.C.; d. 32 B.C. Roman scholar and bibliophile. He is best known for a collection of letters from Cicero, his intimate friend, which he edited and published. A man of great political discretion, he was also simultaneously the friend of Pompey and Caesar, both of whom Cicero opposed. His surname derives from a 20-year residence at Athens during the Roman civil war.

Atticus Herodes (hẹ.rō'dēz). See **Herodes Atticus, Tiberius Claudius.**

Attigny (à.tē.nyē). Town in N France, in the department of Ardennes, situated on the Aisne River ab. 22 mi. SW of Mezières. It is an ancient town, of importance in the Merovingian and Carolingian periods. There are remains from this time, and from the later Middle Ages. 1,210 (1946).

Attila (at'i.lą, ą.til'ą). [Old High German, **Azzilo, Ezzilo**; Middle High German, **Etzel**; Icelandic, **Atli**; Hungarian, **Ethele.**] d. 453 A.D. Famous king of the Huns; son of Mundzuk and brother of Bleda, together with whom he ascended the throne in c433; surnamed the "Scourge of God" by medieval writers, on account of the ruthless and widespread destruction wrought by his arms. On the death (which may have been by assassination) of his brother in 445 he became sole ruler and extended his sway over German as well as Slavonic nations, including the East Goths, Gepidae, Alani, Heruli, Longobards, Thuringians, and Burgundians. He laid waste the provinces of the Eastern Empire south of the Danube in the period 442–447, exacting from Theodosius II a tribute of six thousand pounds of gold, and establishing the annual subsidy at two thousand pounds. He laid claim to one half of the Western Empire as the betrothed husband of Honoria, the sister of Valentinian, who years previously had secretly sent him her ring and the offer of her hand in marriage; having been refused his demands, he invaded Gaul in 451, in alliance with Genseric, king of the Vandals, and was defeated in the same year by the Roman general Aëtius with the aid of the Visigothic king Theodoric at Châlons-sur-Marne. He led (452) an army into Italy, destroying Aquileia, but retired without attacking Rome, having been, according to legend, dissuaded from sacking that city by Pope Leo I; and died, probably from the rupture of a blood vessel, on the night of his marriage with the Gothic Ildico or Hilda. He appears in German legend, notably in the *Nibelungenlied*, as Etzel, who, in his turn, is the Atli of the heroic lays of the older *Edda*. Between Etzel and Atli there are differences as well as correspondences. According to the *Edda*, Atli, who married Gudrun, the widow of Sigurd (the Siegfried of the *Nibelungenlied*), possessed a kingdom in the south. He is, however, nowhere called a king of the Huns. "Hûnaland," located in the south of Germany, is here a possession of Sigurd's ancestors, the Volsungs, and he himself is frequently called the "Hunnish." In the *Nibelungenlied* the land of the Huns is located in the east, and belongs to Etzel as king. In the later legend, as in this case, the whole external circumstances of Attila have been transferred to Etzel, and the historical and legendary person are regarded as one. Atli, in the Icelandic *Volsunga Saga*, was the husband of Gudrun and brother of Brynhild.

Attila (à.tē.là). Tragedy by Pierre Corneille, produced in 1667.

Attila (ät'tē.lä). Opera by Giuseppe Verdi, produced at Venice in 1846.

Attila, or The Triumph of Christianity (at'i.lą, ą.til'ą). Epic poem in 12 books, by William Herbert (London, 1838), with a historical preface, on the career of Attila from his defeat (451) on the Catalaunian plains, at what is now Châlons-sur-Marne, France, till his death (453).

Attinghausen (ät'ing.hou.zen). Village in C Switzerland, in the canton of Uri, situated on the Reuss River, SE of Lucerne. 890 (1941).

Attiret (à.tē.rā), **Jean Denis.** b. at Dôle, France, July 31 1702; d. at Peking, in December, 1768. French painter and Jesuit missionary in China. He was employed as a painter by the emperor of China, who later also made him a mandarin. His painting style became finally that of the Chinese artists, abandoning the use of oils for water color and distemper.

Attis (at'is). See **Atys** or **Attis.**

Attius (at'i.us), **Lucius.** See **Accius, Lucius.**

Attius (at'i.us) or **Attus** (at'us), **Navius.** Augur under Tarquinius Priscus.

Attleboro (at'l.bur.ọ). City in SE Massachusetts, in Bristol County, ab. 31 mi. SW of Boston: a center for jewelry and emblem manufacture; also produces optical goods, machinery, and dyes. 23,809 (1950).

Attleborough (at'l.bėr.ọ). Civil parish and small market town in E England, in Norfolk, ab. 14 mi. SW of Norwich, ab. 108 mi. NE of London by rail. It formerly had manufactures of high-grade worsteds, but this industry has now declined. 2,608 (1931).

Attlee (at'lẹ), **Clement Richard.** b. at London, Jan. 3, 1883—. English politician, Labour Party leader, and prime minister (1945–51). After his admission to the bar (1905), he was employed as a social worker, and as lecturer at the London School of Economics, until 1914; he then served in World War I, attaining the rank of major. He was elected (1922) member of Parliament from Stepney. He served in the Ramsay MacDonald cabinets of 1924 and 1929, but remained outside the coalition cabinet of 1931. He followed George Lansbury as Labour Party head, and was taken into the Winston Churchill cabinet as lord privy seal (1940–42), deputy prime minister (1942–45), dominions secretary (1942–43), and lord president of the council (1943–45). He was succeeded as prime minister by Churchill when the Labour government was defeated in the 1951 general election. Despite the bitter opposition of Aneurin Bevan and his followers in the Labour Party to Attlee's generally "moderate" and pro-American policies, Attlee has been able successfully to retain his post as party leader.

Attnang-Puchheim (ät'näng pöċh'hīm). [Also, **Attnang.**] Town in Austria, in the province of Upper Austria, situated on the Ager River between Salzburg and Linz. It is a station on the Salzburg-Linz railroad and the starting point for the local railroad line leading to Gmunden and Ischl. 5,894 (1946).

Attock (ạ.tok'). [Also, **Atak.**] Fort and strategic point in the West Punjab, Pakistan, ab. 185 mi. NW of the city of Lahore, situated on the Indus River, at the head of navigation: built by Akbar in 1581. The Indus is crossed here by a railway bridge. Pop. ab. 2,000.

Attruck (at'ruk). See **Atrek.**

Attu (at'tö, at.tö'). Island in the N Pacific Oecan, the westernmost of the Aleutian Islands, S of the Bering Sea, ab. 460 mi. E of the coast of Siberia. Attu is in the Eastern Hemisphere, but the international date line is altered to go just west of it. Rocky, volcanic, subject to heavy fog and rain all year, it is sparsely inhabited (chiefly by Aleuts who live by fishing, trading in furs and baskets, and cultivation of subsistence vegetables). It contains one village, Attu, with a population of 44 (1942). Attu was invaded by the Japanese in 1942, and recaptured May 11, 1943, by U.S. and Canadian forces.

Attu, Battle of. Military operation in World War II in which a division of U.S. ground troops, with sea and air support, was able to recapture from a Japanese garrison (estimated at 2,200 men) the strategically important Aleutian island of Attu. It had been seized by the Japanese in June, 1942; the battle for its recapture lasted from May 11 to May 30, 1943, with the major fighting taking place in the key area of Chichagof harbor. Because of its position at the extreme west of the Aleutian chain, Attu was vital to the Japanese hold on certain of the other islands, most notably Kiska, and its recapture by the U.S. enabled these other islands to be retaken with comparatively little difficulty (Kiska itself was liberated in August).

Attucks (at'uks), **Crispus.** b. c1723; killed at Boston, March 5, 1770. American anti-British agitator who led the group which precipitated the so-called Boston Massacre. Variously believed to have been a runaway mulatto slave, a Natick Indian, or half Indian-half Negro, Attucks was a man of tremendous physical stature and boldness who, on March 5, 1770, headed the group of 50 or 60 men, chiefly sailors, which was fired on at Boston by British soldiers. Attucks and two others died instantly, and thus was created a dramatic situation which further exacerbated the already tense relations between the Boston populace and the British troops in the area.

Attu Deep (at'tö). Deepest part of the ocean trench paralleling, and S of, the Aleutian Islands. Depth, 24,219 ft.

Attus (at'us), **Navius.** See **Attius** or **Attus, Navius.**

Attwood (at'wu̇d), **Thomas.** b. at London, Nov. 23, 1765; d. at Chelsea (now part of London), March 24, 1838. English musician; pupil (1785–87) of Wolfgang Amadeus Mozart. He was organist of Saint Paul's Cathedral, and composer (1796 *et seq.*) to the Chapel Royal. A founder (1813) of the Philharmonic Society, he composed anthems for the coronations of George IV and William IV, as well as a number of glees, stage compositions, and other works.

Attwood, Thomas. b. at Halesowen, Worcestershire, England, 1783; d. at Great Malvern, Worcestershire, England, 1856. English politician and reformer. A founder (1830) of the Political Union (an organization under whose guidance mass meetings were held at Birmingham to urge reform of the franchise), he was elected (1832) to Parliament from a new Birmingham constituency after the passage of the Reform Act in the same year. He supported currency reforms which proposed to replace the then existing coinage with paper money intended to reflect fluctuating prices.

Atuana (ä.tö.ä'nä). See **Atuona.**

Atuel (ä.twel'). [Spanish, **Río Atuel.**] River in W Argentina, flowing SE to join the Salado River.

Atuona (ä.tö.ō'nä) or **Atuana** (-ä'-). Village in the Marquesas Islands, in the S Pacific Ocean, on the S coast of Hiva Oa island, ab. 2,000 mi. SE of Honolulu. It is the center of French political administration for the Marquesas group. Pop. ab. 600.

Atura (ạ.tū'rạ). A Latin name of **Aire.**

Aturus (ạ.tū'rus). Ancient name of the **Adour.**

Atwater (at'wô"tėr, -wot"ėr). City in C California, in Merced County ab. 100 mi. SE of San Francisco, in a farming and dairying region. 1,235 (1940), 2,856 (1950).

Atwater, Lyman Hotchkiss. b. at New Haven, Conn., Feb. 3, 1813; d. at Princeton, N.J., Feb. 17, 1883. American clergyman, educator, and editor of the *Princeton Review.* He was appointed professor of mental and moral philosophy at Princeton in 1854, and later (1869) of logic and moral and political science. Author of *Manual of Elementary Logic* (1867) and over 100 polemics against unorthodoxy in theology and philosophy.

Atwater, Wilbur Olin. b. at Johnsburg, N.Y., May 3, 1844; d. at Middletown, Conn., Sept. 22, 1907. American physiologist and agricultural chemist. He was a professor (1873 *et seq.*) at Wesleyan University, Middletown, Conn., the first director (1875–77) of the Connecticut Agricultural Experiment Station, itself the first in the U.S., and organizer (1888) and first director (1888 *et seq.*) of the U.S. Department of Agriculture's Office of Experiment Stations. With E. B. Rosa, then professor of physics at Wesleyan, he constructed (1892–97) a calorimeter which demonstrated that the law of conservation of energy holds true for human functions. In 1896 he published calorific tables which are still widely used.

Atwill (at'wil), **Edward Robert.** b. at Red Hook, N.Y., Feb. 18, 1840; d. 1911. American Protestant Episcopal clergyman, consecrated (1890) first bishop of western Missouri. He served previously as a rector at Burlington, Vt. (1867–82), and at Toledo, Ohio (1882–90).

Atwood (at'wu̇d), **Charles B.** b. at Charlestown, Mass., May 18, 1849; d. at Chicago, Dec. 19, 1895. American architect. He was designer in chief (1891–93) of the Chicago World's Fair (1893), where he created the Fine Arts Building, the Peristyle, and approximately 60 other structures.

Atwood, George. b. 1746; d. at London, July 11, 1807. English mathematician. He was a graduate (1769), fellow, and tutor at Trinity College, Cambridge (to 1784), where his lectures and experiments were influential. He wrote *A Treatise on the Rectilinear Motion and Rotation of Bodies* (1784), containing a description of "Atwood's machine" for measuring the accelerative action of gravity. Author also of two works on natural philosophy (1776, 1784), and others.

Atwood, Isaac Morgan. b. at Pembroke, N.Y., March 24, 1838; d. at Washington, D.C., Oct. 26, 1917. American Universalist clergyman, editor, and teacher. After his ordination (1861), he was general superintendent (1898–1906) of the Universalist Church in the U.S. and Canada, and secretary (1905–12) of the Universalist General Conventions. After a term as president (1879–99) of the Canton Theological Seminary, he was a professor (1911 *et seq.*) of theology and philosophy at St. Lawrence University. Editor (1867–72) of the Boston *Universalist*; author of *Have We Outgrown Christianity?* (1870), *Revelation* (1893), and *A System of Christian Doctrines* (1900).

Atwood, Julius Walter. b. at Salisbury, Vt., June 27, 1857; d. at Washington, D.C., April 10, 1945. American Episcopal clergyman; a friend of Franklin D. Roosevelt. Ordained a deacon in 1882, he was rector of Trinity Church, Columbus, Ohio (1894–1906), and Trinity Church, Phoenix, Arizona (1906–11). Subsequently he was archdeacon (1907–11) of an Arizona diocese and bishop of Arizona (1911–25).

Atwood, Wallace Walter. b. at Chicago, Oct. 1, 1872; d. July 24, 1949. American geologist and geographer. He was on the faculties at Chicago (1903–13) and Harvard (1913–20), and served as president of Clark University (1920 *et seq.*). Founder (1925) and first editor of *Economic Geology;* author of several technical volumes and articles.

Atyoulo (ä.työ'lō). See **Awuna.**

Atyrá (ä.tē.rä'). City in S central Paraguay, in Cordillera department. Pop. ab. 10,000.

Atys (ā'tis) or **Attis** (at'is). Mythical personage in the worship of the Phrygian goddess Cybele, son of the Lydian supreme god Manes, or of Nana, daughter of the river-god Sangarius, and beloved of Cybele. He met his death in early youth at a pine tree, which received his spirit while from his blood sprang violets. A tomb was raised to him on Mount Dindymum, in the sanctuary of Cybele the priests of which had to be eunuchs. A festival of orgiastic character, lasting three days, was celebrated in his honor in the spring. A pine tree covered with violets was carried to the shrine of Cybele as a symbol of the departed Atys. Then, amidst tumultuous music and the wildest exhibition of grief, the mourners sought for Atys on the mountains. On the third day he was found, and the rejoicing which followed was as extravagant as the mourning which preceded. The myth may be considered as the counterpart of the Greek legend of Aphrodite and Adonis, which itself is borrowed from the Semitic legend of Tammuz and Ishtar.

Atyuti (ä.työ'tē). See **Ajuti.**

Atzapozalco (ät"sä.pō.säl'kō). See **Azcapotzalco.**

Atzgersdorf (äts'gėrs.dorf). Town in E Austria, in the municipal district of Vienna, a station on the Südbahn railroad line. It has factories producing chemicals, shoes, furniture, pianos, and electric bulbs, and lumber mills. 7,144 (1946).

Aubagne (ō.bány'). [Ancient name, **Albania.**] Town in SE France, in the department of Bouches-du-Rhône situated on a high elevation near the Huveaune River ab. 11 mi. E of Marseilles. It is an old town; has brick and ceramics manufactures. 16,061 (1946).

Aubanel (ō.bà.nel), **Théodore.** [Full name, **Joseph Marie Jean-Baptiste Théodore Aubanel.**] b. at Avignon, France, March 26, 1829; d. there, Oct. 31, 1886 French Provençal poet. A printer by trade, he was one of seven, including Frédéric Mistral and Joseph Roumanille, who founded (1854) a group known as Félibrige (or Les Félibres) near Avignon, to foster and purify the Provençal language as a literary medium. Affected by the loss of his sweetheart, "Zani," who entered a convent, he wrote poignant poems collected in *Lou miougrano entre duberto* (1860) and *Li Fiho d'Avignoun* (1883). Author of a successful play, *Lou pan dóu pecat* (performed in 1878).

Aube (ōb). Department in N France, bounded by the departments of Marne and Meuse on the N, the department of Haute-Marne on the E, the department of Côte-d'Or on the S, the department of Yonne on the SW, and the department of Seine-et-Marne on the W. It consists of parts of the old provinces of Champagne and Burgundy. Aube has frequently been a theater of war. The Huns under Attila were defeated here; it was ravaged in the civil and religious wars and was also affected by the battles of the French Revolution. In World War II the Allied armies passed through this region in pursuit of the Germans. The climate is mild and the surface consists generally of level land and rolling hills. Agriculture is highly developed, with grain, wine, potatoes, and livestock the chief products. Milk, butter, and cheese are shipped from here to Paris. There are textile mills and other industries. The capital, Troyes, was an important cultural center in the Middle Ages. Area, 2,326 sq. mi.; pop. 235,237 (1946).

Aubé (ō.bā), **Jean Paul.** b. at Longwy, Meurthe-et-Moselle, France, July 3, 1837; d. at Capbreton, Landes, France, 1916. French sculptor of portrait statues, allegorical groups, and monuments in the 19th-century European academic tradition. He is best known for his monument (1888) of Léon Gambetta at Paris, for which Louis Charles Boileau did the architectural features, and for his bust of Prosper Mérimée, also at Paris. His schooling at the École des Beaux-Arts at Paris was followed by studies in Italy. He exhibited at Paris, where he was awarded the grand prize at the World's Fair (1900); his work was also shown at Copenhagen, Antwerp, Chicago, and St. Louis.

Aubenas (ōb.näs). Town in SE France, in the department of Ardèche, situated on the Ardèche River, between Avignon and St.-Étienne. It is noted for its silk manufactures, and has small food industries. It has a castle dating from the 13th–16th centuries. 8,195 (1946).

Auber (ō.ber), **Daniel François Esprit.** b. at Caen, in Normandy, Jan. 29, 1782; d. at Paris, May 13, 1871. French operatic composer; pupil of Cherubini, friend and collaborator of Augustin Eugène Scribe. His *La Muette de Portici* (1828), often called *Masaniello* after its hero, partook to a great extent of the revolutionary sentiments of the time and actually helped to set off the Brussels uprising (1830) which drove the Dutch out of Belgium. Other works include *La Bergère Châtelaine* (1820), his first popular success, *Le Dieu et la Bayadère* (1830), and *Les Diamants de la Couronne* (1841), most of which reveal the influence of François Adrien Boieldieu.

Auber (ô'bėr), **Harriet.** b. at London, Oct. 4, 1773; d. at Hoddesdon, Hertfordshire, Jan. 20, 1862. English poetess. She was the author of several hymns published (1829) in *The Spirit of the Psalms. Hasten Lord, the glorious time* and *Our blest Redeemer ere he breathed* are two of her best-known hymns.

Auberge Rouge (lō.berzh rōzh), **L'.** [Eng. trans., *"The Red Inn."*] Tale by Honoré de Balzac, written in 1831.

Aube River (ōb). River in N France which rises in the plateau of Langres, and joins the Seine River ab. 25 mi. NW of Troyes. Length, ab. 150 mi.

Auberlen (ou'bėr.lẹn), **Karl August.** b. at Fellbach, Germany, Nov. 19, 1824; d. at Basel, Switzerland, May 2, 1864. German Protestant theologian, professor of theology at Basel (1851–64). At first a proponent of Ferdinand Christian Baur's point of view, as set forth at the University of Tübingen, he became more conservative in later years.

Aubert (ô'bėrt), **Alexander.** b. at London, May 11, 1730; d. at Wygfair, St. Asaph, Wales, Oct. 19, 1805. English astronomer.

Aubert (ō.ber), **Jacques.** b. c1680; d. at Belleville, France, 1753. French violinist and composer. He was a member (1727 *et seq.*) of the royal orchestra, first violin (1728–52) at the Paris Opéra, and composer of the opera *La Reine des Péris* (1725), and others.

Aubert, Jean-Louis, Abbé. b. at Paris, 1731; d. there, 1814. French poet and journalist, best known for fables patterned on those of Jean de La Fontaine. His work, eclectic as to style, was praised by Voltaire.

Aubert, Louis François Marie. b. at Paramé, France, Feb. 19, 1877—. French composer. He enrolled at the Paris Conservatory at the age of nine. Composer of the opera *La Forêt Bleue* (produced at Boston in 1913), the orchestral work *La Habanera*, and others.

Aubertin (ō.ber.taṅ), **Charles.** b. at St.-Dizier, France, Dec. 24, 1825; d. 1908. French scholar, appointed rector of the academy of Poitiers in 1874. He published *Étude critique sur les rapports supposés entre Sénèque et Saint-Paul* (1857), *L'Esprit public au XVIII*[e] *siècle* (1872), *Les Origines de la langue et de la poésie française* (1875), and *Histoire de la langue et de la littérature française au moyen-âge* (1867–78).

Aubervilliers (ō.ber.vē.yā). [Former name, **Notre Dame des Vertus.**] Town in N France, in the department of Seine. It is a suburb of Paris, ab. 1 mi. N of the fortifications of that city, on the Canal of St.-Denis. Among its manufactures are chemicals, glass, rubber, and perfumes. 53,010 (1946).

Aubignac (dō.bē.nyȧk), **François Hédelin,** Abbé **d'.** b. at Paris, Aug. 4, 1604; d. there, July 27, 1676. French dramatic critic and playwright. He was the author of four tragedies which, perhaps most notably in the case of *Zénobie* (1647), are considered by most scholars to have suffered from his effort to make them vehicles of dramatic theory rather than emotion. He engaged in literary controversies through most of his life, writing *Conjectures académiques sur l'Illiade d'Homère* (published posthumously in 1715), which questioned the authorship of the Homeric epics, and *Pratique du théâtre* (1657), which formulated his own rigid conception of permissible dramatic technique.

Aubigné (dō.bē.nyā), **Françoise d'.** See **Maintenon,** Madame **de.**

Aubigné (dō.bē.nyā), **Théodore Agrippa d'.** b. in Saintonge, France, Feb. 8, 1552; d. at Geneva, Switzerland, April 29, 1630. Huguenot historian, satirist, and soldier. He served under the Prince de Condé and Henry IV (of France), breaking with the latter as a result of his out-spoken Protestant convictions. He spent the last ten years of his life in exile at Geneva for the expression of these beliefs in his *Histoire universelle depuis 1550 jusqu'à l'an 1601* (1620), one volume of which was subsequently ordered burned by the Paris authorities.

Aubigny (ō.bē.nyē), Duchess of. See **Kéroualle, Louise Renée de.**

Aubin (ō.baṅ). Town in S France, in the department of Aveyron, S of Décazeville. It has alum, sulfur, and coal mines, and various industries. The church dates from the 12th–15th centuries. 7,982 (1946).

Aublet (ō.ble), **Jean Baptiste Christophe Fusée.** b. in Provence, France, Nov. 4, 1720; d. at Paris, May 6, 1778. French botanist. In 1752 he went to Mauritius, where he spent several years. From 1762 to 1764 he traveled in French Guiana, and in the latter year was on the island of Hispaniola. The results of his voyages were published in 1775, in his *Histoire des plantes de la Guyane françoise* (4 vols.), containing also descriptions of species from Mauritius, and many notes of general interest.

Auboin (ō.bwaṅ), **Roger.** [Full name, **Camille Henri Roger Auboin.**] b. at Paris, May 15, 1891—. French banker, director-general (1938 *et seq.*) of the Bank for International Settlements at Basel, Switzerland.

Aubrac Mountains (ō.brȧk). [French, **Montagnes d'Aubrac** (môṅ.tȧny' dō.brȧk).] Mountain group in S France, in the departments of Aveyron and Lozère, connected with the system of the Cévennes. Its highest point is nearly 4,800 ft.

Aubray (dō.bre), **Marie Madeleine d'.** See **Brinvilliers, Marie Madeleine d'Aubray,** Marquise **de.**

Aubrey (ô'bri). In Richard Cumberland's play *The Fashionable Lover*, the father of Augusta Aubrey. He rewards those who have befriended her.

Aubrey, Augusta. Principal female character in Richard Cumberland's *Fashionable Lover*, persecuted by Lord Abberville, but finally married to Francis Tyrrel.

Aubrey, John. b. in Wiltshire, England, 1626; d. at Oxford, in June, 1697. English antiquary. Reduced to poverty by various lawsuits and amorous adventures, he was commissioned (1671) to make surveys of antiquities, which he described in *Perambulation of Surrey* and other manuscripts published after his death. Supported mainly by wealthy friends, he collected anecdotes of such notables as Francis Bacon, John Milton, Thomas Hobbes, and Sir Walter Raleigh, which he contributed to the historian Anthony à Wood, as *Minutes of Lives* (first published separately in 1813; called *Brief Lives* in 20th-century editions), for his *Athenae Oxonienses* (1690). Author also of *Miscellanies* (1696), a collection of ghost stories and dreams.

Aubrey, Mr. Principal character in Samuel Warren's novel *Ten Thousand a Year*.

Aubriot (ō.brē.ō), **Hugh.** fl. late 14th century. French municipal official. As provost of Paris, he improved the streets and constructed numerous public buildings, including the original section of the Bastille. His wealth, together with his outspoken defense of the Jews and attacks on the clergy, brought him enemies who, after the death of Charles V in 1381, obtained his imprisonment for heresy.

Aubry (dō.brē), **Claude Charles,** Comte **d'.** b. at Bourg-en-Bresse, France, Oct. 25, 1773; d. Oct. 19, 1813. French general under Napoleon. He fought in the campaigns of 1812–13, was rewarded with a title and promoted to general for his services in restoring a bridge over the Beresina, and was fatally wounded at the battle of Leipzig.

Aubry de Montdidier (ō.brē dẹ môṅ.dē.dyā). d. c1371. French courtier, a favorite of Charles V. He was murdered in the forest of Montargis by another courtier, named Richard de Macaire. It is said that Macaire would have escaped unpunished but for Aubry's dog, which followed him until, suspicion being aroused, the king ordered Macaire to fight the dog, as his accuser. Though armed with a club, Macaire was knocked down, confessed, and was hanged. The story is the subject of many ballads and plays, including the French-Italian chanson *Macaire.*

Aubry's Ride (ô'briz). Incident in the history of the American West, involving a certain Francis Xavier Aubry, who won a wager by riding a horse (1848) from Santa Fe to Independence, Mo., in less than eight full days.

Auburn (ô'bėrn). City in E Alabama, in Lee County, ab. 50 mi. NE of Montgomery: seat of Alabama Polytechnic Institute. 12,939 (1950).

Auburn. City in N California, county seat of Placer County, NE of San Francisco: originally settled (1848) by prospectors as a mining camp. 4,653 (1950).

Auburn. City in NE Indiana, county seat of De Kalb County, on Cedar Creek, ab. 22 mi. N of Fort Wayne: manufacturing center for automotive parts. 5,879 (1950).

Auburn. City in SW Maine, county seat of Androscoggin County, on the Androscoggin River, ab. 34 mi. N of Portland, opposite Lewiston: manufactures of shoes. 23,134 (1950).

Auburn. Town in S Massachusetts, in Worcester County: residential suburb of Worcester. 8,840 (1950).

Auburn. City in SE Nebraska, county seat of Nemaha County, in a fruit-producing area. 3,422 (1950).

Auburn. City in W New York, county seat of Cayuga County, on Owasco Lake. Manufactures include rope, carpets, Diesel engines, farm machinery, and shoes. Auburn was the home of William H. Seward. It is the seat of the Auburn State Prison. 36,722 (1950).

Auburn. [Former name, **Slaughter.**] City in W Washington, in King County: railroad repair shops; manufactures of pottery and toys. 6,497 (1950).

Auburn. Hamlet described by Oliver Goldsmith in his *The Deserted Village,* commonly identified with Lissoy, County Westmeath, Irish Republic.

Auburndale (ô'bėrn.dāl). City in C Florida, in Polk County, E of Tampa, in a fruit-growing region. 3,763 (1950).

Aubusson (ō.bü.sôṅ). Town in C France, in the department of Creuse, situated on the Creuse River, SW of Guéret: noted for its production of carpets and tapestry. It has a tapestry museum. 5,512 (1946).

Aubusson (dō.bü.sôṅ), **Pierre d'.** [Called the **"Shield of the Church."**] b. in France, 1423; d. at Rhodes, July 13, 1503. Grand master (1476–1503) of the Knights of Saint John of Jerusalem, at Rhodes, and cardinal (1489–1503) under Pope Innocent VIII. He defended Rhodes against the Turks (1480), and gave refuge to Jem, brother of Bajazet II of Turkey, after the quarrel (1481 *et seq.*) over the succession to the throne. Six years later he accepted a bribe from Bajazet in return for which he violated his pledge and placed Jem in the hands of

Pope Innocent VIII, who gave Jem, as a Turk and an infidel, short shrift, and thus coincidentally removed the threat to Bajazet. Aubusson was later elevated (1489) to a cardinal's rank and awarded a number of valuable privileges not previously available to his order. He organized an expedition against the Turks which failed (1501). His zeal for Christianity led to the expulsion of all adult Jews from Rhodes and the forcible baptism of children.

Auby (ō.bē). Town in N France, in the department of Nord, situated on the Deule River, ab. 4 mi. N of Douai. It has coal mines, important zinc works, and chemical factories. 7,165 (1946).

Aucas (ou'käs) or **Aucanos** (ou.kä'nōs). Term sometimes applied to the South American Indian language group known usually as Araucanians.

Aucassin et Nicolette (ō.kȧ.saṅ ā nē.ko.let). French romance of the 13th century, named after its hero and heroine. Aucassin, the son of the count of Beaucaire, falls in love with Nicolette, a captive Saracen maiden, who is in reality a king's daughter. After overcoming many obstacles the two are finally united.

Aucassin et Nicolette. Opera by André Ernest Modeste Grétry, first produced in 1780.

Auch (ōsh). [Gallic, **Elimberrum**; Latin, **Augusta Auscorum.**] City in SW France, the capital of the department of Gers, situated on the Gers River, between Toulouse and Bayonne. It is a railroad junction and a flourishing trade center for agricultural products, particularly wine, brandy (Armagnac), and poultry. There are flour mills, furniture factories, and other industries. The Cathedral of Sainte-Marie, dating from 1489–1662, is a beautiful Gothic monument, with Renaissance additions. The choir stalls, with sculptures, and the stained-glass windows are notable. Auch was the capital of the Ausci, and later one of the chief towns in Gascony and Armagnac. 15,253 (1946).

Auchel (ō.shel). Town in N France, in the department of Pas-de-Calais, situated near the Belgian border, between Béthune and Lillers. It is a coal-mining town and has various industries. 14,168 (1946).

Auchinleck (ô.ċhin.lek'). Civil parish and village in S Scotland, in Ayrshire, situated on Lugar Water, ab. 13 mi. E of Ayr, ab. 376 mi. N of London by rail. Here was the country estate of Alexander Boswell, Lord Auchinleck, the father of James Boswell. 6,626 (1931).

Auchinleck, Lord. Title of **Boswell, Alexander.**

Auchinleck, Sir **Claude John Eyre.** b. at Aldershot, England, June 21, 1884—. English army officer. He studied at Wellington College and Sandhurst, served in Egypt (1914–15), at Aden (1915), and in Mesopotamia (1916–19), where he was awarded (1917) the Distinguished Service Order. Later he took part (1933, 1935) in operations on the northwestern Indian frontier, commanded (1933–36) the Peshawar brigade in India, and was deputy chief (1936–38) of staff in India. He was transferred (1939) to England where he was in charge (May, 1940) of the attempted occupation of Narvik, in Norway. Subsequently he was commander in chief in India (December, 1940–July, 1941, and June, 1943, *et seq.*) and the Middle East (January, 1942, *et seq.*), until his replacement in the latter theater in August, 1942, by General Harold Alexander. An aide-de-camp (1941–46) to King George VI, he was appointed (1946) field marshal.

Auchmuty (ôk.mū'ti), **Richard Tylden.** b. at New York, July 15, 1831; d. at Lenox, Mass., July 18, 1893. American philanthropist, architect, and Union soldier in the Civil War. He studied architecture in the office of James Renwick, and was later admitted to partnership there. For his service at Gettysburg during the Civil War, he was brevetted colonel. In 1881 he established the New York Trade School to aid young men of slender means in obtaining skills which, in Auchmuty's opinion, were being restricted by the conditions of apprenticeship imposed by trade unions.

Auchmuty (ôk.mū'ti), **Samuel.** b. at Boston, Jan. 26, 1722; d. at New York, March 4, 1777. Clergyman, a Loyalist in the Revolutionary War. Rector of New York's Trinity Church (1764–77), he supported the British cause from the pulpit, referring to the Revolutionary leaders as a "rascally Whig mob."

Auchmuty, Sir **Samuel.** b. at New York, 1756; d. at Dublin, 1822. British general; son of Samuel Auchmuty (1722–77). He served with the British forces against the Continental army in the Revolutionary War, and later (1783–97) in India, where he earned the patronage of Charles Cornwallis and Ralph Abercromby; he was knighted (1803) for his service in Egypt (1800–03). Sent to reinforce British forces at Buenos Aires (1806), he captured (1807) Montevideo. He was also commander in chief (1810) at Madras, and in the victory (1811) which determined the British conquest of Java.

Auchterarder (ôċh'tėr.är.dėr). Police burgh and market town in C Scotland, in Perthshire, ab. 12 mi. SW of Perth, ab. 436 mi. N of London by rail. The town has a famous golf course, and there are the remains of a castle in the vicinity. 2,387 (est. 1948).

Auchterhouse Hill (ôċh'tėr.hous). See under **Sidlaw Hills.**

Auckland (ôk'lạnd), 1st Baron. [Title of **William Eden.**] b. in England, April 3, 1744; d. near Beckenham, Kent, England, May 28, 1814. English diplomat and statesman. After gaining a considerable reputation as a barrister, he was appointed undersecretary of state in 1772. He was sent (1778) to America as one of five commissioners to attempt a settlement of disturbances. As chief secretary (1780 *et seq.*) to the viceroy of Ireland, and a member of the Irish privy council and of its parliament, he took a leading part in the establishment of the Bank of Ireland. He was appointed vice-treasurer of Ireland in 1783, was chosen (1786) by Pitt to negotiate a commercial treaty with France, served as ambassador extraordinary to Spain (1788), and to Holland (1790–93), and was president of the board of trade (1806) under Grenville. Author of *Principles of Penal Law* (1772) and *History of New Holland* (1788).

Auckland, 1st Earl of. [Title of **George Eden.**] b. near Beckenham, Kent, England, Aug. 25, 1784; d. Jan. 1, 1849. English statesman; son of William Eden, 1st Baron Auckland. He was president of the board of trade and master of the mint in Charles Grey's cabinet (1830–34), first lord of the admiralty in 1834 and 1835, and governor general of India (1835–42). He favored removal of Dost Mohammed Khan from the throne of Afghanistan in 1838, and his activity on behalf of a rival claimant contributed greatly to the outbreak of the first war between Afghanistan and the forces of Great Britain. He was created earl of Auckland in 1839.

Auckland. Provincial district in the N part of North Island, New Zealand. Chief town, Auckland; area, 25,420 sq. mi.; pop. 745,099 (1951).

Auckland. Largest city and second largest port of New Zealand, situated on Hauraki Gulf in the NE part of the North Island. The former capital of New Zealand, it is the chief town of Auckland district. It has one of the best harbors in New Zealand, and is the seat of Auckland University College (a branch of the University of New Zealand), a school for the deaf, an institute for the blind, and a cathedral. Pop., with suburbs, 329,123 (1951).

Auckland Islands. Group of uninhabited islands in the South Pacific Ocean, ab. 290 mi. S of New Zealand, to which they belong. They were discovered by the British in 1806. Area, 234 sq. mi.

Auctioneer, The. Play (1901) by Charles Klein.

Auda (ou'dạ). See under **Aldabella.**

Audaeans (ô.dē'ạnz). Monastic Christian sect founded by Audaeus, in Scythia, in the 4th century A.D.

Audaeus (ô.dē'us), **Audius** (ô'di.us), or **Udo** (ū'dō). b. in Mesopotamia; d. in Scythia, c370 A.D. Founder (c330) of a monastic Christian sect in Scythia. The group, known as Audaeans, shared his anthropomorphism and remained in existence for only a few years after his death.

Aude (ōd). See also **Aude River.**

Aude. Department in S France, bounded by the departments of Tarn and Hérault on the N, the Mediterranean on the E, the department of Pyrénées-Orientales on the S, department of Ariège on the W, and the department of Haute-Garonne on the NW. It formed part of the old province of Languedoc. In the early Middle Ages it suffered frequent Moslem invasions and was later one of the main theaters of the destructive Albigensian wars. Agriculture is well developed; products are wine, olives, fruits, grains, and dairy products. There are stone quarries and chemical, textile, construction, and food industries; among the latter, the manufacture of candied fruits and the distilleries are most important. The spas of Alet and Rennes are well known. The cities of Carcassonne and Narbonne contain outstanding architectural remnants of the high culture of the region during the Middle Ages. Capital, Carcassonne; area, 2,448 sq. mi.; pop. 268,889 (1946).

Audebert (ōd.ber), **Jean Baptiste.** b. at Rochefort, France, 1759; d. at Paris, 1800. French naturalist and artist, noted for his engravings of birds and animals.

Audefroy le Bâtard (ōd.frwȧ lę bä.tȧr). fl. early 13th century. French minstrel, some of whose romances have been preserved.

Audeley (ôd'li), Sir **James.** See **Audley, Sir James.**

Auden (ô'dęn), **Wystan Hugh.** b. at York, England, Feb. 21, 1907—. English poet, resident in the U.S. since 1939 and an American citizen since 1946. He was an early member of the group including Stephen Spender, Christopher Isherwood, and C. Day Lewis which oriented itself at that time to the left politically and against established conventions in writing technique. He collaborated with Isherwood on the plays *The Dog beneath the Skin* (1935), *The Ascent of F. 6* (1936), and *On the Frontier* (1938), as well as on *Journey to a War* (1939), a prose record of experiences in China; in collaboration with Louis MacNeice he wrote *Letters from Iceland* (1937). Editor of *The Oxford Book of Light Verse* (1938), and others. His recent volumes include *The Double Man* (1941), *For the Time Being* (1944), *The Age of Anxiety* (1947), and *Nones* (1951). A collection of his poems was published in 1945. Auden's use of common words and metaphors in preference to the poetic language of 19th-century romanticism is characteristic of his style both in his lyrics and in his longer, didactic poems. He has also written the libretto to the *The Rake's Progress* (1951), an opera by Igor Stravinsky.

Audenaarde or **Audenarde** (ōd.nȧrd). See **Oudenarde.**

Audenshaw (ô'dęn.shô). Urban district in NW England, in Lancashire, ab. 6 mi. E of Manchester, ab. 183 mi. NW of London by rail. 12,656 (1951).

Auderghem (ou'dėr.ċhęm). [Also, **Oudergem.**] Town in C Belgium, in the province of Brabant, SE of Brussels, of which it is a suburb. 18,640 (1947).

Aude River (ōd). [Ancient name, **Atax.**] River in S France which rises in the Pyrenees and flows into the Mediterranean Sea ab. 11 mi. E of Narbonne. Carcassonne is situated on it. Length, ab. 139 mi.

Audhumla (ou.ᴛʜum'lä). Cow, in the Old Norse cosmogony, from whose udders flowed the milk which nourished the first created being, the giant Ymir, and his race. She licked out of the salty ice a being whose son was the father of Odin.

Audiberti (ō.dē.ber.tē), **Jacques.** b. 1900—. French poet, novelist, and journalist. Audiberti's richly eloquent poetry, collected in *Race des hommes* (1937), reminded critics of Victor Hugo and Arthur Rimbaud, and was a momentary sensation in France just before World War II. He has also written novels including *Abraxas* (1938) and *Septième* (1939), and plays, *Quoat-Quoat* (1946), and *Le Mal Court* (1947).

Audience. [Spanish, **Audiencia** (ou.ᴛʜyen'syä).] Originally, a superior court of Spain. The Audience as established in the Spanish colonies of America had very extensive powers, frequently in legislative and administrative matters as well as in judicial ones. In the latter respect it was the superior of crown governors, but inferior to the viceroys. In criminal suits its decisions admitted of no appeal; in civil cases an appeal lay open to the Council of the Indies only where a large amount was involved. Audiences could appoint temporary governors and remove them; in the case of crown governors and captains-general, their powers were often so nearly balanced by those of the Audience as to give rise to constant disputes. The first Audience established in America was that of Santo Domingo; later there were Audiences of Panama, Los Reyes (Lima), Confines (Central America), New Spain, Charcas, Chile, Bogotá, and others.

Audiencia de los Confines (ou.ᴛʜyen'thyä dā lōs kōn.fē'nās). See **Confines, Audience of the.**

Audierne (ō.dyern). Town in NW France, in the department of Finistère, situated on the Bay of Audierne at the mouth of the Goyen River, ab. 22 mi. W of Quimper. It is a picturesque fishing port, particularly for sardine fisheries, and a seaside resort. 3,777 (1946).

Audiffredi (ou.dēf.frā'dē), **Giovanni Battista.** b. at Saorgio, near Nice, 1714; d. July 3, 1794. Italian astronomer and bibliographer.

Audiffret (dō.dē fre), **Charles Louis Gaston,** Marquis, **d'.** b. at Paris, Oct. 10, 1787; d. there, April 28, 1878. French financier and government official. He was the author of *Système financier de la France* (1840).

Audiffret-Pasquier (dō.dē.fre.pä.kyā), **Edmé Armand Gaston,** Duc **d'.** b. at Paris, Oct. 20, 1823; d. June 4, 1905. French politician. He was president (1875) of the national assembly during the formulation of the constitution of the Third Republic, and president of the senate from 1876 to 1879, when his party lost power.

Audincourt (ō.dań.kör). Town in E France, in the department of Doubs, situated near the Swiss border, SE of Montbéliard. It is a center of the metallurgical industry of the region; has ironworks and the Peugot machine factory. 9,040 (1946).

Audius (ô'di.us). See **Audaeus.**

Audley (ôd'li), Sir **James.** [Also, **Audeley.**] b. c1316; d. at Fontenay-le-Comte, France, 1386. English commander under Edward III and Edward, the Black Prince. He fought with great bravery at Poitiers (1356), was governor of Aquitaine (1362), and grand seneschal of Poitou (1369). He was one of the original 25 knights of the Order of the Garter, founded (c1344) by Edward III.

Audley, Thomas. [Title, Baron **Audley of Walden.**] b. in Essex, England, 1488; d. at London, 1544. English politician and lord chancellor of England (1533–44) under Henry VIII. As speaker of the House of Commons (1529), he presided over the Black Parliament which abolished papal authority in England. Backed by Henry in his attack on the clergy, he began his support of the king which continued throughout his career: in Henry's divorce from Catherine of Aragon, the trials of Bishop Fisher and Sir Thomas More (1535), the imprisonment of Anne Boleyn (1536), the trials (1537) of Robert Aske and other Catholic rebels in the "Pilgrimage of Grace," the Act of Six Articles (1539), the attainder of Cromwell, and the annulment (1540) of Henry's marriage with Anne of Cleves. Said to have been a large, impressive man, he was actually weak physically and based his ethics on expediency; his opportunism was rewarded by Henry with gifts of many monastic estates.

Audouin (ō.dwań), **Jean Victor.** b. at Paris, April 27, 1797; d. there, Nov. 9, 1841. French entomologist. Founder of an entomological society and professor at the Paris natural history museum; author of *Histoire des insectes nuisibles à la vigne* (1842); contributor to Cuvier's *Règne Animal.*

Audoux (ō.dö), **Marguerite.** b. at Sancoins, France, 1863; d. at Hyères, France, in February, 1937. French seamstress and writer. Author of *Marie-Claire* (1910), *L'Atelier de Marie-Claire* (1920), and others.

Audran (ō.dräń), **Charles.** b. at Paris, 1594; d. there, 1674. French engraver. His prints, which are numerous, are marked "C." and (later) "K."

Audran, Claude. b. at Paris, 1597; d. at Lyons, 1677. French engraver; brother of Charles Audran (1594–1674).

Audran, Edmond. b. at Lyons, 1842; d. at Tierceville, France, 1901. French composer; son of Marius Audran (1816–87). He is best known as a composer of light operas, of which he produced nearly 40. He won his first success at Paris with *Les Noces d'Olivette* (1879), and was soon also popular at London for such works as *The Grand Mogul* (1884).

Audran, Gérard. b. at Lyons, 1640; d. at Paris, 1703. French engraver; third son of the engraver Claude Audran (1597–1677) and generally considered to have been the most talented of the family. He is notable for his engravings of Charles Le Brun's historical paintings. Author of *Proportions du corps humain* (1693).

Audran, Marius. b. at Aix, France, 1816; d. at Marseilles, 1887. French tenor singer. He was a performer (c1840 *et seq.*) at the Opéra Comique, and director (1863 *et seq.*) of the Marseilles Conservatory.

Audrey or **Awdrey** (ô'dri). Bride, in Ben Jonson's *Tale of a Tub*, a bright and perverse little person.

Audrey. In Shakespeare's comedy *As You Like It*, an awkward country girl.

Audubon (ô'du.bon, -bọn). City in W Iowa, county seat of Audubon County, ab. 65 mi. W of Des Moines in a farming region: canneries. It was platted in 1878 by the Chicago, Rock Island and Peoria Railroad. 2,808 (1950).

Audubon. Borough in S New Jersey, in Camden County, S of Camden. 9,531 (1950).

Audubon, John James. b. at Cayes, Santo Domingo (now Haiti), April 26, 1785; d. at New York, Jan. 27, 1851. American ornithologist and artist; son of Captain Jean Audubon of the French navy, and of a woman known only as Mlle. Rabin. He was legitimatized by adoption (1794) by Captain Audubon and his French wife, by whom he was reared from the age of four in and near Nantes, France. From childhood he exhibited a passion for drawing birds. Sent (1803) to his father's estate near Philadelphia to enter business, he married in 1808 Lucy Bakewell and with her migrated to Kentucky where he failed in various businesses, owing partly to his long absences for collecting and studying birds. He was sent to jail (1819) for debt; declared bankrupt; saving only his gun and his drawings (regarded as worthless by the sheriff), he took to drawing sidewalk portraits. He traveled (1820) down the Mississippi in a flatboat to fulfill his cherished dream of drawing all the birds of America, life-size, in crayon and water color. In New Orleans and the countryside he supported himself as a portraitist and a teacher of dancing, fencing, and the violin. Failing to find an American publisher for his monumental work, he sailed (1826) with his drawings for Britain. Acclaimed in Edinburgh and London as a genius, he secured many subscribers and arranged with a London engraver for publication. For the next 11 years he was engaged in exploring eastern North America for further bird subjects. His *Birds of America* (issued 1827–38) in elephant folio, consisting of 435 hand-colored copper-plate engravings (the edition numbered probably less than 200 copies), are still recognized, despite some flaws, as the finest of all ornithological illustration, marked by the innovation of showing birds in action, with a wealth of native vegetation and wilderness scenery. He published (1831–39) his *Ornithological Biography* (5 vols.), containing original life-histories of birds and rich in personal experiences with frontier human types. Always a man of much personal beauty and magnetism, he was recognized in the closing years of his life as the greatest American naturalist of his age, and he still stands highest in popularity. In 1843, with the collaboration of his two sons in painting, and of John Bachman in the text, he began *Quadrupeds of North America*, completed by his sons after death found him at his home (now known as Audubon Park). The claim of some of his descendants that he was the "lost Dauphin" is contradicted by documents surrounding his birth.

Audubon Societies, National Association of. Organization in the U.S. devoted primarily to carrying out educational activities in the field of wild-life conservation Incorporated on Jan. 5, 1905, it consists of federated state and local Audubon clubs. Its chief phase of activity concerns the protection of bird life. The organization maintains the Junior Audubon Clubs and issues the periodical *Bird-Lore*.

Aue (ou'ẹ). Name of various small rivers in Germany, and elsewhere in C Europe.

Aue. City in E Germany, in the *Land* (state) of Saxony, Russian Zone, situated on the Zwickauer Mulde River, near the border of Czechoslovakia, ab. 14 mi. SE of Zwickau: before World War II had cotton mills, lingerie manufactures, and metallurgical industries. It is most important as the center of a uranium and bismuth mining district. The territory belongs to the Wismut Company which, in turn, is dependent upon the Russian Metal Trust. It is among the few territories in the Eastern Zone definitely known, shortly after World War II, to be guarded by a large force of Russian troops. Aue is a railroad junction; it has vocational schools for the textile and metal trades, and a library. 25,567 (1946).

Auen (ou'ẹn). [Also, **Kauen.**] Northern Bushman group of S Africa, inhabiting E South-West Africa and numbering ab. 500.

Auenbrugger von Auenbrug (ou'ẹn.brüg.ėr fon ou'ẹn-brůk), **Leopold.** b. at Graz, Austria, Nov. 19, 1722; d. at Vienna, May 17, 1809. Austrian physician. He devised a method of ascertaining the presence of thoracic disease by percussion; the technique is explained in his *Inventum novum ex percussione* (1761), but was not taken up generally in the medical profession until after his death.

Auer (ou'ėr), **Leopold.** b. at Veszprém, Hungary, June 7, 1845; d. 1930. Hungarian violinist and teacher. He was appointed concertmaster at Düsseldorf in 1863, and at Hamburg in 1866. He served as a violin professor (1868–1917) at the St. Petersburg conservatory before coming to the U.S. in 1918. His pupils included Mischa Elman, Efrem Zimbalist, and Jascha Heifetz.

Auerbach (ou'ėr.bäch). Small town in SE Germany, in the Franconian Jura mountains, Bavaria, ab. 31 mi. NE of Nuremberg.

Auerbach. City in E Germany, in the *Land* (state) of Saxony, Russian Zone, formerly in the *Kreis* (district) of Zwickau, Saxony, situated on the Göltzsch River, in the Vogtland region, ab. 15 mi. SW of Zwickau: before 1945 manufactured cotton and woolen textiles (shirts, curtains, carpets, and other articles), and embroideries. 18708 (1946).

Auerbach, Berthold. b. at Nordstetten, Württemberg, Feb. 28, 1812; d. at Cannes, France, Feb. 8, 1882. German novelist, poet, and student of Spinoza. Originally destined by his family for a rabbinical career, he was diverted, partly by his reading of Spinoza, into other fields. He was imprisoned (1836) for his participation in the students' uprising of that year. He is notable for his portrayal of Black Forest peasant life in such works as *Schwarzwälder Dorfgeschichten* (1843), *Barfüssele* (1856), *Edelweiss* (1861), *Auf der Höhe* (1871; Eng. trans., *On the Heights*), and others. The impact of Spinoza on his life is shown by a novel based on the life of the philosopher, and a five-volume translation of his works published in 1841.

Auerbach's Keller (ou'ėr.bächs kel'ėr). Wine cellar in Auerbach's Hof at Leipzig, famous from its connection with the Faust legends, with Goethe's *Faust*, and with the academic years of the youthful Goethe.

Auernheimer (ou'ėrn.hīm.ėr), **Raoul.** [Pseudonyms: **Raoul Heimern, Raoul Othmar.**] b. at Vienna, April 15, 1876; d. at Oakland, Calif., Jan. 7, 1948. Austrian writer, exponent of Viennese comedy, in the Bauernfeld tradition, and novelist.

Auersperg (ou'ėrs.perk), Prince **Adolf Wilhelm Daniel.** b. July 21, 1821; d. at his castle Goldegg, in Austria, Jan. 5, 1885. Austrian statesman; brother of Prince Karlos Auersperg (1814–90). He was premier of the Cisleithan ministry (1871–79).

Auersperg, Count **Anton Alexander von.** [Pseudonym, **Anastasius Grün.**] b. at Laibach (now Ljubljana, in Yugoslavia), April 11, 1806; d. at Graz, Austria, Sept. 12, 1876. Austrian poet and politician. His criticism of the government at Vienna, voiced as a member of the Laibach diet, was followed (1848) by membership in the Frankfort parliament which sought a liberalized pan-Germany. Known as a writer of epic, lyric, and political verse, including such works as *Spaziergänge eines Wiener Poeten* (1831), *Schutt* (1835), *Gedichte* (1837), and others.

Auersperg, Prince **Karlos.** b. May 1, 1814; d. Jan. 4, 1890. Austrian army officer and several times president (1861 *et seq.*) of the upper chamber of the Reichsrat.

Auerstädt (dȧ.wer.stät), Duc **d'.** A title of **Davout, Louis Nicolas.**

Auerstedt (ou'ėr.shtet). [Also, **Auerstädt.**] Village in E central Germany, in the former province of Saxony, Prussia, ab. 14 mi. NE of Weimar. A famous victory was gained here, on Oct. 14, 1806, by the French (ab. 35,000) under Louis Nicolas Davout over the Prussians (ab. 50,000) under Karl Wilhelm Ferdinand, Duke of Brunswick (with Frederick William III also present). The loss of the French was ab. 7,500; of the Prussians, over 10,000 (including the Duke of Brunswick). On the same day Napoleon defeated another Prussian army at Jena.

Auerswald (ou'ėrs.vält), **Alfred von.** b. at Marienwerder, Prussia, Dec. 16, 1797; d. at Berlin, July 3, 1870. Prussian official and politician, minister of the interior in Ludolf Camphausen's cabinet (March 29–June 14, 1848).

Auerswald, Hans Adolf Erdmann von. b. Oct. 19, 1792; d. Sept. 18, 1848. Prussian general; brother of Alfred von Auerswald (1797–1870). He was killed by rioters during the uprising of 1848 against the Prussian government.

Auerswald, Rudolf von. b. Sept. 1, 1795; d. at Berlin, Jan. 15, 1866. Prussian official and politician. He was entrusted with the formation of a cabinet on June 10, 1848, on the resignation of Ludolf Camphausen, remaining in office till Sept. 10 of the same year.

Auffenberg (ouf'ẹn.berk), Baron **Joseph von.** b. at Freiburg im Breisgau, Baden, Germany, Aug. 25, 1798 d. there, Dec. 25, 1857. German soldier (in the service of Austria and then of Baden) and dramatic poet. On a journey to Spain, in 1832, he was severely wounded by robbers near Valencia, was nursed through a long convalescence in the Convent del Cid at Valencia, and in his will made the convent his heir. He became seneschal of Baden in 1839. His chief works are *Pizarro* (1823), *Alhambra* (1829–30), and *Das Nordlicht von Kasan.*

Auffenberg-Komarów (ouf'ẹn.berk.kô.mä'röf), Baron **Moritz von.** b. at Troppau, Austria, May 22, 1852; d. 1928. Austro-Hungarian general. He was close to the archduke Franz Ferdinand, and served (1911–12) as minister of war. In World War I, he won the battle of Komarów (Aug. 26–Sept. 3, 1914) against the Russians, but was defeated at the second battle of Lemberg (1915). In April, 1915, he was arrested for alleged irregularities while minister of war, but was acquitted by a court martial and withdrew from public life.

Aufidia gens (ô.fid'i.ạ jenz). In ancient Rome, a plebeian clan or house whose family names were Lurco and Orestes. The first member of this gens who rose to the consulship was Gnaeus Aufidius Orestes in 71 B.C.

Aufidius (ô.fid'i.us), **Tullius.** In Shakespeare's *Coriolanus,* the general of the Volscians.

Aufrecht (ouf'recht), **Theodor.** b. at Leischnitz, Upper Silesia, Germany, 1822; d. at Bonn, Germany, 1907. German philologist, notable as a specialist in Sanskrit. He was professor of Sanskrit and comparative philology at Edinburgh (1862–75) and at Bonn (1875–89). He worked with Johann Wilhelm Adolf Kirchhoff on his *Die umbrischen Sprachdenkmäler* (1851), and with Max Müller on his edition of the *Rig-Veda;* he was cofounder, with F. F. A. Kuhn, of *Zeitschrift für vergleichende Sprachforschung* (1852). Author of a treatise on Sanskrit (1847), an edition of the *Rig-Veda* (2nd ed., 1877), a catalogue of Sanskrit literature (1896–1903), and others.

Augarten (ou'gär.tẹn). Public garden at Vienna, situated in the Leopoldstadt suburb between the Danube River and the Donau canal. It is noted as the place where many musical masterpieces were first performed. It was opened in 1775, at first only as a garden; then a concert room was built, and in 1782, with the help of Mozart, morning concerts were started. From that time until 1830 the place was a resort for music lovers, but interest dwindled and the place became again simply a garden or park.

Auge (ōzh). [Also, **Vallée d'Auge.**] District in NW France, in the E part of the department of Calvados, Normandy.

Auge (ô'jē) or **Augeia** (ô.jī'ạ). In Greek mythology, a priestess of Athena, mother by Hercules of Telephus.

Augeas (ô'jē.ạs, ô.jē'ạs) or **Augeias** (ô.jē'ạs). In Greek mythology, a son of Helios (or of Phorbas) and Hermione, king of the Epeians in Elis, and one of the Argonauts. He was the owner of a herd of 3,000 oxen, including 12 white bulls sacred to the sun, which he kept in a stable that had not been cleaned for 30 years. The task of cleaning this stable was deemed impracticable, but Hercules accomplished it in a single day by channeling the waters of two rivers through it. Augeas was slain by Hercules.

Auger (ō.zhā), **Athanase.** b. at Paris, Dec. 12, 1734; d. there, Feb. 7, 1792. French classical scholar and ecclesiastic. He translated, among other classics, works by Demosthenes, Aeschines, and Isocrates. His principal work is a treatise, *De la constitution romaine.*

Augereau (ōzh.rō), **Pierre François Charles.** [Title, Duc **de Castiglione.**] b. at Paris, Nov. 11, 1757; d. near Melun, France, June 12, 1816. French marshal (1804 *et seq.*) and politician. He served with distinction in the Italian campaigns of 1796–97, particularly at Lodi, Castiglione, and Arcole. A leader in the coup d'état of 18 Fructidor (Sept. 4, 1797), he served later under Napoleon at Jena (1809), Eylau (1807), Leipzig (1813), and elsewhere. He was elevated to the French peerage by Louis XVIII after the fall of Napoleon.

Aughrim (ôg'rim). [Also, **Aghrim.**] Town in Connacht province, Irish Republic, in County Galway, ab. 4 mi. SW of Ballinasloe. Here, on July 12, 1691, the English forces of William III under Ginkel defeated the Irish and French forces of James II under Saint-Ruth. 112 (1936).

Augier (ō.zhyā), **Guillaume Victor Émile.** b. at Valence, France, Sept. 17, 1820; d. at Croissy, France, Oct. 25, 1889. French dramatist. He became a member of the Academy in 1857. Opposition to romanticism and criticism of the customs of the Second Empire characterize much of his work, which includes *L'Aventurière* (1848), *Gabrielle* (1849), *Le Gendre de M. Poirier* (1854; in collaboration with Jules Sandeau), *Mariage d'Olympe* (1855), *Les Effrontés* (1861), *Maître Guérin* (1864), *Lions et renards* (1869), *Madame Caverlet* (1876), *Les Fourchambault* (1878), and others.

Augila (ou.jē'lạ). [Also, **Aujila.**] Oasis in the Libyan desert, Africa, SE of Sidra Gulf, on the route between Egypt and Murzuk: noted for its dates.

Auglaize (ô.glāz'). River in W Ohio, a tributary of the Maumee River.

Augsburg (ôgz'bėrg; German, ouks'bůrk). [Latin, **Augusta Vindelicorum.**] City in S Germany, in the *Land* (state) of Bavaria, American Zone, the capital of the *Kreis* (district) of Swabia, situated at the junction of the Wertach River with the Lech River, ab. 30 mi. NW of Munich: important center of the cotton textile industry, with a number of spinning and weaving mills, dye works, shirt, lace, and upholstery manufactures, and an equally important metallurgical center, producing motors, agricultural machinery, freezing machinery, and the like; markets. The I.G. Farbenindustrie has a chemical factory in the suburb of Gersthofen. During World War II, Augsburg was a center of aircraft production (Messerschmitt works). It was from here that Rudolf Hess took off for his flight to Scotland. 185,183 (1950).

Architecture. Before World War II, Augsburg was one of the outstanding examples of a German Renaissance town, particularly through the architectural genius of Elias Holl. The *Rathaus* (town hall), erected 1615–20 and of monumental size, contained the superbly decorated Golden Hall, running through three stories, which was burned out in World War II. Next to it is the Perlach Tower, also by Holl; the latter was damaged, but still standing after the war. The arsenal dates from 1602–07. The cathedral has both Romanesque and Gothic features; it was begun in 994, and numerous additions made at later periods. The Church of Saint Maurice, founded in the 11th century, was rebuilt in 1300 and 1440; the Church of Saint Ann, founded in the 14th century, was rebuilt 1847–97; the Church of Saint Ulrich dates from the 15th century. Augsburg has many beautiful 16th-century fountains, such as the Augustus, Mercurius, and Hercules fountains, the latter by Adriaan de Vries; it had a number of patrician houses, the most remarkable one being the Fugger House, built in 1512–15 for Jakob Fugger, member of a family of merchant princes and sponsors of the arts and sciences; it was later used as a museum. The so-called Fuggerei, consisting of 53 small houses for working men, erected in 1519, is one of the earliest housing projects for low-income families. Most of these buildings are now badly damaged or completely ruined; the Fugger House was almost completely destroyed by fire.

History. Augsburg was founded by Augustus in 15 B.C. as a Roman military colony; it was chief town of the province called Vindelicia or Rhaetia Secunda, became a bishopric in the 6th century, and was besieged by the Hungarians in 955. In the early Middle Ages the town was held in fief by the church until it was confirmed as a free imperial city in 1276. In the 15th and 16th centuries it was one of the leading commercial centers of the North, and had important trade also with Italy and the Near East; it owed its economic dominance largely to its location at the northern exit of the Alpine routes leading up from Venice. In the 16th century, it was one of the seats of early capitalistic enterprise in Europe; the Fugger and Welser families financed textile, metallurgical, and mining enterprises in many parts of the continent, engaged in a colonization project in Venezuela, and functioned as bankers to the German emperors of the house of Hapsburg and to the crown of Spain. In the same period Augsburg was a center of German art and humanistic studies; the painters Albrecht Altdorfer, Christoph Amberger, Hans Burgkmair, and Hans Holbein lived here. The city accepted Protestantism in 1534–38, but the surrounding countryside remained Roman Catholic. Augsburg was the seat of many diets; Luther defied the papal legate here in 1518, the Confessio Augustana (known as the Augsburg Confession) was declared in 1530, and the religious peace of Augsburg was concluded in 1555. The city suffered severely in the Thirty Years' War; it was conquered by the Swedes in 1632, and by the Imperialists in 1635; the population declined from 45,000 to 16,000. During the War of the Spanish Succession Augsburg was occupied (1703) by the Franco-Bavarian army. It was annexed to Bavaria in 1806. The industrial development of the 19th century was based on water power. The city was frequently bombed and badly damaged in World War II; it was occupied by American forces on April 28, 1945.

Augsburg, Diet of. Convened April 8, 1530, opened June 20, and closed in November. It was summoned by the emperor Charles V, in an invitation dated at Bologna, Jan. 21, 1530, for the purpose of settling the religious dispute in Germany, and to prepare for war against the Turks.

Augsburg, League of. Treaty (July 9, 1686) between Holland, the Holy Roman emperor, the kings of Sweden and Spain, and the electors of Bavaria, Saxony, and the Palatinate, for the purpose of maintaining, against France, the treaties of Münster and Nijmegen.

Augsburg, Religious Peace of. Treaty between the Lutheran and Catholic groups in Germany, concluded Sept. 25, 1555, at a diet held at Augsburg in conformity with the Convention of Passau. It secured the triumph of the Reformation by providing that the individual states of the Holy Roman Empire should be permitted to prescribe the form of worship within their limits. The benefits of this peace, however, were not extended to the Calvinists.

Augsburg Confession. The chief Lutheran creed, prepared by Melanchthon and read before the Diet of Augsburg in 1530.

Augsburg Interim. Provisional arrangement for the settlement of religious differences between Protestants and Roman Catholics in Germany during the Reformation epoch, pending a definite settlement by a church council. It was proclaimed by the emperor Charles V, May 15, 1548, but ignored by many Protestants.

Augur (ô'gėr), **Hezekiah.** b. at New Haven, Conn., Feb. 21, 1791; d. there, Jan. 10, 1858. American sculptor and inventor. His sculpture reveals wood-carving techniques picked up in his youth, and includes a bust of Oliver Ellsworth at Washington, D.C. He also worked in marble; in the latter medium *Jephthah and his Daughter* is well known. His inventions include a wood-carving machine, the bracket-saw, and others, none of which ever brought him financial success.

Augurs, The Mask of. Masque by Ben Jonson, acted in 1622.

August (ô'gust). The eighth month of the year, containing 31 days, reckoned the first month of autumn in Great Britain, but the last of summer in the U.S. It was so named by the emperor Augustus Caesar in his own honor. The earlier Roman name of the month was Sextilis.

August (ou'gůst), **Ernst Ferdinand.** b. at Prenzlau, Prussia, Feb. 18, 1795; d. at Berlin, March 25, 1870. German scientist, the inventor of the psychrometer.

August, Friedrich Eberhard. b. at Stuttgart, Württemberg, Jan. 24, 1813; d. Jan. 12, 1885. Prince of Württemberg; uncle of Charles I of Württemberg. A general in the Prussian service, he served with distinction at the battles of Königgrätz, Gravelotte, and Sedan.

August, Friedrich Wilhelm Heinrich. b. Sept. 19, 1779; d. July 19, 1843. Prince of Prussia; nephew of Frederick the Great, and an officer distinguished in the Napoleonic wars.

August, Paul Friedrich. b. July 13, 1783; d. Feb. 27, 1853. Grand duke of Oldenburg (1829–53).

Augusta (ô.gus'tạ). City in E Georgia, county seat of Richmond County, on the Savannah River at the head of navigation. It has a large cotton trade, and important manufactures, especially of cotton goods and cottonseed products. It is the seat of the University of Georgia School of Medicine and of Paine College. Captured by the British in the Revolutionary War, it was besieged and taken by American troops in 1781. Pop. of city, 71,508 (1950); of urbanized area, 87,733 (1950).

Augusta (ou.gös'tä). [Also, **Agosta.**] Town and commune in SW Italy, in the *compartimento* (region) of Sicily, in the province of Siracusa, situated on a small island in the Gulf of Augusta, ab. 13 mi. N of Syracuse. The town, connected by a bridge with the mainland of Sicily, has an excellent harbor; it has sardine fisheries, and exports olive oil, wine, fruit, and cheese; imports petroleum. Augusta was named after the Roman Emperor Augustus; it was sacked and destroyed by the Moslems, and rebuilt by the emperor Frederick II in 1232; later under French and Spanish rule but repeatedly threatened by Turkish pirates from the Barbary states; it was destroyed by earthquake in 1693. There was large emigration from here in the 19th century. In World War II it was occupied by the British in July, 1943. The castle sustained considerable war damage, but other buildings of tourist interest escaped. Pop. of commune, 19,690 (1936); of town, 17,716 (1936).

Augusta (ô.gus'tạ). City in SE Kansas, in Butler County, in an oil-producing region. It has a refinery. 4,483 (1950).

Augusta. City in SW Maine, capital of the state and county seat of Kennebec County, on the Kennebec River at the head of navigation: manufactures pulp, paper, lumber, and shoes. 20,913 (1950).

Augusta. In ancient Rome, a title conferred as a supreme honor upon women of the imperial house. It was first borne by Livia, then by Antonia, grandmother of Caligula, and first as consort of the emperor by Agrippina, wife of Claudius. Later it was bestowed, with the consent of the emperor, upon others beside the consort of the reigning Caesar.

Augusta. British warcraft which led the assault (1777) on the American fleet protecting Fort Mercer, on the Delaware River. The *Augusta* went aground and exploded (Oct. 23, 1777) following an attack by an American force.

Augusta. American cruiser noted in connection with a number of international conferences during World War II. During the Atlantic Charter meeting off Newfoundland in August, 1941, the *Augusta* together with the British battleship *Prince of Wales* afforded the meeting ground for President F. D. Roosevelt, Prime Minister Winston Churchill, and their staffs. In early 1945 the *Augusta* took President Roosevelt to and from the Mediterranean on his way to the Yalta Conference.

Augusta, Congress of. In American colonial history, a meeting (Nov. 5–10, 1763) at Augusta, Ga., of the governors of Georgia and North and South Carolina and the lieutenant governor of Virginia, for the purpose of effecting a settlement of trade and boundary differences with the Indians of the Southern regions. The colonial representatives, together with John Stuart, superintendent of Indian affairs in the Southern district, convened with 700 Indians and signed a treaty of friendship which obtained for the Americans land in Georgia ceded by the Creeks. The Congress of Augusta was called at the behest of the British government at the close of the French and Indian War.

Augusta (ou.gůs'tä), **Marie Luise Katharina.** b. at Weimar, Germany, Sept. 30, 1811; d. at Berlin, Jan. 7, 1890. The second daughter of Karl Friedrich, grand duke of Saxe-Weimar, and Princess Maria Paulovna. She was the wife (1829 *et seq.*) of William I (of Prussia), afterward emperor of Germany.

Augusta (ô.gus'tạ), **Treaty of.** In American colonial history, a treaty negotiated (1773) by John Stuart, superintendent of Indian affairs in the Southern district, and the governor of Georgia, James Wright, with the chiefs of the Cherokee and Creek nations. The initiative for the treaty came from the Indians, who were motivated by a desire to clear themselves of a huge debt burden. By the terms of the treaty, Georgia received two tracts of land embracing over 2,100,000 acres, and the proceeds from the sale of these holdings were to be paid in settlement of the debts owed by the Indians to white traders. Although many of the participants were the same, this treaty was not connected with the earlier Congress of Augusta and should not be confused with it.

Augusta Aubrey (ô'bri). See **Aubrey, Augusta.**

Augusta Auscorum (ôs.kō'rum). Latin name of **Auch.**

Augusta Felix (fē'liks). See under **Beirut.**

Augusta Firma (fėr'mạ). An ancient name of **Écija.**

Augustan History (ô.gus'tạn), **The.** Collection (date and authorship unknown) of lives of the Roman emperors from Hadrian to Numerianus.

Augusta Praetoria (ô.gus'tạ prē.tō'ri.ạ). Ancient name of **Aosta,** town.

Augusta Taurinorum (tô.ri.nō'rum). A Latin name of **Turin.**

Augusta Trevirorum (trev.i.rō'rum). Latin name of **Trier.**

Augusta Ubiorum (ū.bi.ō'rum). A Latin name of **Cologne.**

Augusta Veromanduorum (ver.ọ.man.dụ.ō'rum). Latin name of **St.-Quentin,** France.

Augusta Victoria (vik.tō'ri.ạ). [German, **Auguste Viktoria** (ou.gůs'tẹ vik.tō'rē.ä).] b. Oct. 22, 1858; d. 1921. Daughter of Duke Friedrich of Schleswig-Holstein-Sonderburg-Augustenburg, and (as the wife of William II) empress of Germany.

Augusta Vindelicorum (vin.del.i.kō'rum). Latin name of **Augsburg.**

Augustenburg (ou.gůs'tẹn.bůrk). Castle on the island of Als, E of Jutland, Denmark, and formerly in Schleswig-Holstein, whence the noble house of Augustenburg was named.

Augustenburg Line. Branch of the royal house of Denmark and Oldenburg founded by Ernst Günther (1609–89), son of Duke Alexander (d. 1627). To this line belonged Caroline Amalie, queen of Christian VIII of Denmark, and the German empress Augusta Victoria.

Augustine (ô'gus.tēn, ô.gus'tin), Saint. [Latin, **Aurelius Augustinus.**] b. at Tagaste (now Souk-Ahras), in Numidia, 354; d. at Hippo (now Bône, Algeria), in Numidia, 430. Early Christian philosopher and father of the church. He was bishop of Hippo (396 *et seq.*), and defender of orthodoxy against the Pelagians, Donatists, and Manichaeans, of which last group he was himself for nine years a member. Despite his Christian parents, his early years were marked by skepticism, which continued during the period (384 *et seq.*) he spent as lecturer at Milan, but was ended by a mystic experience which was followed by baptism (387) at the hands of Ambrose, bishop of Milan, with whom Augustine had already conversed. Returned to the family property at Tagaste, he was thrust forward in 391 by the congregation at the nearby town of Hippo for ordination as a priest. His growing fame led to his consecration (395) as bishop, with the provision that he would succeed to the see of Hippo when it became vacant. His occupancy of the bishopric was marked by brilliant and voluminous correspondence defending orthodoxy against the heresies of his day. He was the author of the great *De Civitate Dei* (completed in 22 books by 426; Eng. trans., *City of God*), the *Confessiones,* and others.

Augustine (ô.güs.tēn). Stage name of **Brohan, Joséphine Félicité Augustine.**

Augustine of Canterbury (kan'tėr.ber.i, -bėr.i), Saint. [Also: **Austin**; called **"Apostle of the English."**] d. at Canterbury, England, c604 or 613. Roman Benedictine monk chosen (595 or 596) by Pope Gregory I to head a group of 40 missionaries to the English. He was received (597) by the powerful and tolerant King Ethelbert of Kent, whose wife Bertha was a Christian, and installed at his capital, Canterbury. Probably with Bertha's aid, he converted the king. Made archbishop of the English at Arles, he baptized ten thousand converts in 597. Created first archbishop of Canterbury (601), he set up the dioceses of London, Rochester, York, and others, but failed to reconcile differences of practice, such as the date of Easter, with the Celtic bishops. He consecrated Christ Church, Canterbury, in 603, which was replaced by the present cathedral (begun by Lanfranc in 1070).

Augustine of Trent (trent). [Also, **Augustinus de Tridento** (ô.gus.tī'nus dē trī.den'tō).] b. at Brescia, Italy; fl. in the middle of the 14th century. Italian friar and medical astrologer. He is of considerable interest in the history of science for a treatise which he dedicated on July 12, 1340, to the bishop of Trent on the pestilence of 1340 (which destroyed approximately one sixth of the population of Florence). This treatise, which was anterior to the Black Death and its abundant literature, was nevertheless not essentially different from much of that literature.

Augustinians (ô.gus.tin'i.ạnz). Name applied to various religious orders in the Roman Catholic Church which follow the "Rule of Saint Augustine." The most venerable Augustinian group in the Church today comprises the "Canons and Canonesses Regular," who are, indeed, often called simply "Augustinians," and whose organization may be said to date from the 11th century. Historically, the Augustinians must also be taken to include the fourth of the mendicant orders (the first three being the Franciscans, Dominicans, and Carmelites), which was founded about the middle of the 13th century, and which spread rapidly throughout Europe (Luther was a member of a separatist Augustinian congregation in Germany). These Augustinian (or Austin) Friars (both names are used, and the latter has been retained also as the name of one of the most interesting historic sites in London) exist today in at least three different active orders within the Church.

Augustodorus (ô.gus.tọ.dō'rus). Latin name of **Bayeux.**

Augustodunum (ô.gus.tọ.dū'num). A Latin name of **Autun.**

Augustonemetum (ô.gus.tọ.nem'ẹ.tum). Latin name of **Clermont-Ferrand.**

Augustów (ou.gö'stöf). [Also: **Augustowo** (ou.gö.stô'vô); Russian, **Avgustov.**] Town in E Poland, in the *województwo* (province) of Białystok, situated on the Netta River, ab. 50 mi. N of Białystok, in the vicinity of the former German (East Prussian) border. It is connected by a canal with the Niemen River N of Grodno. Before World War II it had lumber trade, lake fisheries, and a brewery. The town was founded by King Sigismund II Augustus of Poland in 1650. In World War I, a battle took place here between Germans and Russians on Oct. 4, 1914. In World War II, it was occupied by the Germans, and was retaken by the Russians on Oct. 24, 1944. It was returned to Poland in 1946. Pop. 8,338 (1946).

Augustulus (ô.gus'tū.lus), **Romulus.** Last Roman emperor of the West (475–476 A.D.); son of Orestes who deposed the emperor Julius Nepos, and seized the government of empire, while he had the title of emperor conferred on his son. Augustulus was compelled by Odoacer to abdicate after the defeat and death of his father at Pavia. His original name of Augustus was popularly changed to the diminutive Augustulus in derision of the emperor's youth.

Augustus (ô.gus'tus). [Original name, **Gaius Octavius;** called later **Caius Julius Caesar Octavianus.**] b. at Velitrae, in Latium, or at Rome, Sept. 23, 63 B.C.; d. at Nola, Campania (now in Italy), Aug. 19, 14 A.D. The first Roman emperor, son of Caius Octavius by Attia, daughter of Julia, the sister of Julius Caesar whose chief heir he became. After Caesar's death he went from Epirus to Rome in the spring of 44 B.C. There he gained the influence of Cicero, the senate, and the people against Mark Antony. He was reconciled with Antony, and formed with him and Lepidus the second triumvirate in 43. He took part in the proscription of 43, and in the victory over Brutus and Cassius at Philippi in 42. He carried on the Persian war in the period 41–40. He became more closely allied with Antony in 40, and was ruler over the West. In 37 he renewed the triumvirate. In 36 he subdued Sextus Pompey. His defeat of Antony and Cleopatra at Actium in 31 left him sole ruler of the Roman dominion. In 28 he was made princeps senatus, and received the title of "Augustus" in 27. Augustus preserved the republican forms, but united in his own person the consular, tribunician, proconsular, and other powers. His generals carried on various wars in Spain, Africa, Germany, and elsewhere, but the Roman advance in the last-named country received a definite setback through the defeat of Varus by Arminius in 9 A.D. Under Augustus Roman literature reached its highest point, and the temple of Janus was closed, indicating world peace. The birth of Jesus Christ occurred during his reign.

Augustus. [German, **August** (ou'gůst).] b. July 31, 1526; d. Feb. 12, 1586. Elector of Saxony (1553–86); brother of Maurice, whom he succeeded. Originally a

Calvinist, he was induced by his wife Anna of Denmark to embrace Lutheranism, and was one of the major influences in securing the adoption of the *Formula Concordiae* (1580).

Augustus II (of *Poland*). [As Saxon elector, **Frederick Augustus I**; German, **Friedrich August**; called **"Augustus the Strong."**] b. at Dresden, May 12, 1670; d. at Warsaw, Feb. 1, 1733. Elector of Saxony (1694–1733). He was elected king of Poland in 1697. Having joined Peter the Great and Denmark against Charles XII of Sweden in 1699, he invaded Livonia in the same year, but was defeated by the Swedes at Riga (1701) and at Klissow (1702). He was deposed from the Polish throne through the influence of Charles XII in 1704, but was reinstated (1709) after the defeat of Charles at Poltava.

Augustus III (of *Poland*). [As Saxon elector, **Frederick Augustus II**; German, **Friedrich August.**] b. at Dresden, Oct. 17, 1696; d. there, Oct. 5, 1763. Elector of Saxony; son of Augustus II, whom he succeeded as elector in 1733; he was elected king of Poland in the same year. He supported Prussia in the first Silesian War. In the second Silesian War he sided with Austria, being compelled at its close (settled by the Peace of Dresden, on Dec. 25, 1745) to pay to Prussia a war indemnity of one million rix-dollars. He became involved in the third Silesian, or Seven Years', War (1756–63) through a secret treaty with Austria. The electorate was occupied by the Prussians during the whole of the war.

Augustus, Titus Flavius Domitianus. See **Domitian.**

Augustus Frederick, Prince. [Additional title, Duke of **Sussex.**] b. at London, Jan. 27, 1773; d. at Kensington, London, England, April 21, 1843. Prince of Great Britain and Ireland and Duke of Sussex; the sixth son of George III. He was a patron of literature and art, and president of the Royal Society in the period 1830–39.

August Wilhelm (ou'gůst vil'helm). b. Aug. 9, 1722; d. June 12, 1758. Prussian prince and general; brother of Frederick the Great.

Aujila (ou.jē'lạ). See **Augila.**

Aulard (ō.lår), **François Victor Alphonse.** b. at Montbron, France, 1849; d. 1928. French historian, notable for works dealing with the French Revolution. He founded the Société de l'Histoire de la Révolution and its monthly journal *La Révolution française.* Author of *Les Orateurs de la constituante* (1882), *La Société des Jacobins* (1889–97), *Histoire politique de la Révolution française* (1901), and others.

Auld Lang Syne (ôld' lang' zīn'). Song by Robert Burns, written c1789. Burns stated that the tune was not original with him, but was the first written version of an old folk melody which he had heard.

Auld Licht Idylls (licht). Play (1888) by Sir James M. Barrie. It is a Scottish regional play.

"Auld Reekie" (rē'ki). Nickname of **Edinburgh.**

Auld Robin Gray (rob'in grā'). Ballad by Lady Anne Barnard, published in 1772. It was written to an old Scottish tune, "The Bridegroom grat," which was later superseded by an English air.

Aulia gens (ô'li.ạ jenz). In ancient Rome, a clan, probably plebeian, whose only family name was Cerretanus. Quintus Aulius Cerretanus held the consulship twice (323 and 319 B.C.) in the Samnite war.

Aulic Council (ô'lik). In the old German Empire, the personal council of the emperor, and one of the two supreme courts of the empire which decided without appeal. It was instituted c1501, and organized under a definite constitution in 1559, modified in 1654. In its final form it consisted of a president, a vice-president, and 18 councilors, six of whom were Protestants; the unanimous vote of the latter could not be set aside by the others. The Aulic Council ceased to exist on the extinction of the German Empire in 1806. The title was later given to the council of state of the emperor of Austria.

Aulich (ou'lich), **Ludwig.** b. at Pressburg (now Bratislava, in Czechoslovakia), 1795; hanged at Arad (now in Rumania), Oct. 6, 1849. Hungarian general and minister of war during the revolution of 1848. He was one of 13 generals executed by the Austrians after the Hungarian surrender at Világos.

Aulick (ô'lik), **John H.** b. at Winchester, Va., 1789; d. at Washington, D.C., April 27, 1873. American naval officer. Having entered the navy as a midshipman in 1809, he commanded the *Vincennes* in 1847. He was for a time commander of the East India squadron. He was retired on April 4, 1867, with the rank of commodore.

Aulie-Ata (ou'li.e.ä'tä) or **Auliye-Ata** (ou'li.ye-). Former name of **Dzhambul.**

Aulin (ou.lēn'), **Tor.** b. at Stockholm, 1866; d. there, 1914. Swedish violinist, composer, and conductor. He was founder (1887) of the Aulin String Quartet, and at various times leader of the Royal Opera and conductor of the Stockholm Kunstverein. As a composer he is best known for his shorter violin and piano pieces, some of which have been played by Leopold Auer and Mischa Elman.

Aulis (ô'lis). In ancient geography, a town on the E coast of Boeotia, Greece. It was the rendezvous of the Greek fleet in the expedition against Troy.

Aulnay-sous-Bois (ō.ne.sö.bwä). Town in N France, in the department of Seine-et-Oise, NE of Paris, situated on the railroad line from Paris to Soissons. It is an industrial town belonging to the suburban region of Paris. 32,356 (1946).

Aulne (ōn). See **Aune.**

Aulnoy or **Aunoy** (dō.nwå), **Marie Catherine Jumel de Berneville,** Comtesse **d'.** b. c1650; d. 1705. French writer of romances and memoirs, best known for her fairy stories. Her short tales include *L'Oiseau Bleu, La Belle aux Cheveux d'Or,* and others. Her novels, often imitations of Comtesse de La Fayette's work, include *Histoire d'Hippolyte, Comte de Duglas* (1690), and others.

Aulps (dōlps), **Blacas d'.** See **Blacas d'Aulps.**

Aumale (ō.mål). Town and commune in Algiers department, Algeria, ab. 78 mi. SE of Algiers. Pop. (of the commune), ab. 7,000.

Aumale. [Medieval Latin, **Alba Marla, Albamarla;** English, **Albemarle.**] Medieval countship of France, formed by William the Conqueror in 1070. It passed to various families, finally to that of Lorraine, and was created a duchy in 1547. By marriage it passed to the house of Savoy, from whom it was purchased by Louis XIV in 1675 for his illegitimate son the Duc du Maine.

Aumale. [Latin, **Alba Marla, Albamarla, Aumalcum.**] Town in N France, in the department of Seine-Inférieure, between Rouen and Amiens. It has a church dating from the 16th century. The town was almost entirely destroyed in World War II. 2,152 (1946).

Aumale (dō.mål), Duc **d'.** [Original name, **Claude de Lorraine.**] b. 1526; d. 1573. French Roman Catholic partisan leader in the civil wars.

Aumale, Duc **d'.** [Original name, **Charles de Lorraine.**] b. c1556; d. 1631. One of the French Leaguers, commander at the battles of Arques and Ivry; son of Claude de Lorraine.

Aumale, Henri Eugène Philippe Louis d'Orléans, Duc **d'.** b. at Paris, Jan. 16, 1822; d. at Zucco, Sicily, May 7, 1897. French soldier; fifth son of Louis Philippe (of France). He served (1840–47) with distinction in the army in Algeria, was governor general of Algeria (1847–48), and became (1871) a member of the Assembly. He was named a member of the French Academy, and was appointed general of a division in 1872. In 1873 he was president of the Bazaine tribunal. In 1886 he was expelled from France. He published *Histoires des Princes de Condé* (1869) and *Institutions militaires de la France* (1867).

Aumonier (ô.mon'yā), **Stacy.** b. 1887; d. in Switzerland, Dec. 21, 1928. English novelist, short-story writer, landscape painter, and society entertainer. He began his career as entertainer in 1908, and began writing in 1913. Author of *Three Bars' Interval* (1917), *The Querrils* (1919), *One After Another* (1920), and *Heartbeat* (1922), all novels, and *Fifteen Tales* (1924), a collection of short stories.

Aune or **Aulne** (ōn). River in NW France, in Brittany, which flows into the Roads of Brest. Length, ab. 90 mi.

Aungerville (än'jėr.vil), **Richard.** [Also: **Aungervyle;** called **Richard de Bury.**] b. at Bury St. Edmunds, Suffolk, 1281; d. 1345. English cleric, bibliophile, and writer. He was appointed tutor to young Edward of Windsor and was involved in the plotting that brought about the deposition of Edward II, and the accession of Richard's pupil to the throne as Edward III; he was favored thereafter with rapid promotion. Twice (1330, 1333) ambassador to the papal court, he was appointed in the latter year to the bishopric of Durham, and was also made (1334) lord treasurer and lord chancellor. Known throughout Europe as a bibliophile, Aungerville left an account of his book-collecting in his *Philobiblon* (trans. 1888).

Aunis (ō.nēs). Region in W France, the smallest of the former provinces of France, lying between Poitou on the N and Saintonge on the S, and principally comprised in the modern department of Charente-Maritime. It was conquered (1223–26) by Louis VIII. In general it shared the fortunes of Aquitaine.

Aunoy (dō.nwȧ), **Marie Catherine Jumel de Berneville,** Comtesse **d'.** See **Aulnoy** or **Aunoy, Marie Catherine Jumel de Berneville,** Comtesse **d'.**

Aunt Fanny (fan'i). Pseudonym of **Barrow, Frances Elizabeth.**

Aurai (ä.ö.rā'). See **Ahuréi.**

Aurangabad (ou.rung.gạ.bäd'). [Also: **Aurengabad, Aurungabad.**] District of Hyderabad, Union of India, ab. 170 mi. NE of Bombay. Cotton, millet, oranges, tobacco, and wheat are the crops here. Capital, Aurangabad; area, ab. 6,212 sq. mi.; pop. 945,000 (est. 1941).

Aurangabad. [Also: **Aurengabad, Aurungabad.**] City in C India, headquarters of the district of Aurangabad, in Hyderabad, Union of India, ab. 165 mi. NE of Bombay: the former Mogul capital and the favorite residence of Aurangzeb, now partly in ruins. It is a trading center. 29,000 (est. 1941).

Aurangzeb (ô'rung.zeb). [Also: **Aurungzeb, Aurangzib** (-zib), **Aurungzebe, Aureng-Zebe;** surnamed **Alum-Geer** or **Alamgir,** meaning "Conqueror of the World."] b. Nov. 3, 1618; d. at Ahmadnagar, March 3, 1707. Emperor of Hindustan (1658–1707); third son of Shah Jehan. He became governor of the Deccan in 1638, and usurped the throne in 1658, after having murdered his two elder brothers Dara and Shuja and imprisoned his father and younger brother. He incorporated the vassal states of Bijapur and Golconda in the empire in the period 1683–87, and is regarded by the Moslems of India as one of their greatest monarchs, although his religious intolerance impaired the resources of the country.

Auranitis (ô.rạ.nī'tis). See under **Bashan.**

Aurantes (ô.ran'tēz). Latin name of **Abrantes.**

Auray (ō.rā). Town in NW France, in the department of Morbihan, situated on the Loc River, which connects the town with the Bay of Quiberon, ab. 10 mi. W of Vannes. It is a seaport and one of the foremost centers of oyster culture in France; manufactures furniture. Nearby is the church of Sainte-Anne-d'Auray, a place of pilgrimage. 8,642 (1946).

Auray, Battle of. Victory gained (1364) by John IV (of Brittany), and the English commander Sir John Chandos over the French under Charles de Blois and Bertrand Du Guesclin.

Aurea (ô'rē.ạ), **Chersonesus.** Ancient name of the **Malay Peninsula.**

Aurelia (ô.rē'li.ạ, -rē'lyạ). In John Marston's *The Malcontent,* the duchess, a dissolute, proud woman.

Aurelia. Pretty but impertinent and affected coquette in John Dryden's comedy *An Evening's Love, or The Mock Astrologer.*

Aurelia gens (jenz). In ancient Rome, a plebeian clan or house whose family names were Cotta, Orestes, and Scaurus. The first member of this gens who obtained the consulship was Aurelius Cotta, in 252 B.C.

Aurelian (ô.rē'li.ạn, -rēl'yạn). [Full name, **Claudius Lucius Valerius Domitius Aurelianus.**] b. probably at Sirmium, in Pannonia, c212 A.D.; killed near Byzantium, 275. Emperor of Rome (270–275). He was of obscure birth, and rose from the rank of a private to the highest post in the army, was designated by Claudius as his successor, and defeated the Alemanni (271) and Zenobia, queen of Palmyra (272–273). He was called by the senate the "Restorer of the Roman Empire."

Aurelianus (ô.rē.li.ā'nus), **Ambrosius.** See **Ambrosius Aurelianus.**

Aurelianus, Caelius. b. in Numidia; fl. probably in the 5th century A.D., although placed by some scholars in the 2nd century A.D. Roman physician and medical writer. He was the author of works on acute diseases (three books), chronic diseases (five books), and a compendium on medical science. The former two works were largely a translation of material from Soranus, a 2nd-century Greek physician.

Aurelian Way (ô.rē'li.ạn, -rēl'yạn). See **Via Aurelia.**

Aurelius (ô.rē'li.us, -rēl'yus). Amorous squire in Geoffrey Chaucer's *Franklin's Tale.*

Aurelius Antoninus (an.tọ.nī'nus), **Marcus.** See **Caracalla.**

Aurelius Augustinus (ô.gus.tī'nus). Latin name of **Augustine,** Saint.

Aurelius Victor (vik'tọr), **Sextus.** b. in Africa; fl. c360–389. Roman historian. He was the reputed author of a brief history of the Roman rulers and emperors (*De Caesaribus*) from Julius Caesar to Constantine I, probably an extract, as is the *Epitome,* in which history is brought down to the death of Theodosius I. *Origo gentis Romanae* and *De viris illustribus Urbis Romae,* which have been ascribed to him, were written later.

Aurelle de Paladines (dō.rel dẹ pȧ.lȧ.dēn), **Louis Jean Baptiste d'.** b. at Malzieu, Lozère, France, Jan. 9, 1804; d. at Versailles, France, Dec. 17, 1877. French general in the Crimean and Franco-Prussian wars. Chosen (1870) by Léon Gambetta to replace La Motte-Rouge after the latter's defeat at Orléans, he reorganized the troops ("Army of the Loire"), and defeated the Prussians near Coulmiers, but was beaten by them at Beaune-la-Rolande and again at Orléans. He served (1875–77) in the French senate.

Aurengabad (ou.rung.gạ.bäd'). See **Aurangabad.**

Aureng-Zebe (ô'rung.zeb'). See also **Aurangzeb.**

Aureng-Zebe, or The Great Mogul. A rhymed tragedy by John Dryden, produced in 1675; it was read by Charles II in manuscript, and partly revised by him.

Aurevilly (dōr.vē.yē), **Jules Amédée Barbey d'.** See **Barbey d'Aurevilly, Jules Amédée.**

Auric (ō.rēk), **Georges.** b. at Lodève, France, Feb. 15, 1899—. French composer, youngest member of a modernist group known as "les Six." He was the composer of incidental music to Molière's *Les Fâcheux,* which was later converted into a ballet. His early work reveals an interest in jazz which produced compositions such as *Adieu New York.*

Aurich (ou'rich). Town in NW Germany, in the *Land* (state) of Lower Saxony, British Zone, formerly in the province of Hanover, Prussia, situated on the Ems-Jade Canal, E of Emden. It is the chief town of East Friesland and a center of the livestock trade, formerly famous for its horse markets. The castle dates from the 19th century. Outside the town is the Upstallsbom, a hill where the Friesian assemblies met until the 14th century. The town passed to the counts of East Friesland in 1438, to Prussia in 1744, was French in the period 1807–14, again under Hanover in the period 1814–66, and once more part of Prussia from 1866 to 1945. Pop. 11,284 (1950).

Aurifaber (ou.rẹ.fä'bėr), **Johann.** [Latinized name of **Johann Goldschmied.**] b. at Breslau, Jan. 30, 1517; d. there, Oct. 19, 1568. German Lutheran clergyman appointed (1550) to the professorship of theology at Rostock, on the recommendation of Melanchthon.

Aurifaber, Johann. [Latinized name of **Johann Goldschmied.**] b. 1519; d. at Erfurt, Prussia, Nov. 18, 1575. German Lutheran pastor, friend and assistant of Luther, and an editor of his works. In his theology, he opposed Melanchthon. His name is identical in both its original and Latinized forms with that of the Johann Aurifaber born two years earlier at Breslau, but there is no other connection between the two.

Auriga (ô.rī'gạ). A northern constellation, the Charioteer or Wagoner, containing the first-magnitude star Capella. It is supposed to represent a charioteer kneeling in his vehicle. He is often represented with a kid on his left shoulder.

Aurigera (ô.rij'ẹ.rạ). Latin name of the **Ariège River.**

Aurignac (ō.rē.nyȧk). Village in S France, in the department of Haute-Garonne, ab. 37 mi. SW of Toulouse: site of tanneries. In nearby caves were found some of the most important known paleolithic remains. 716 (1940).

Aurignacian Period (ô.rig.nā'shạn, -ri.nyā'-). Earliest stage of upper Paleolithic development, succeeding the Mousterian and giving way to the Solutrean. It appears to have occurred at the close of the last glaciation. The people associated with this culture are closer to modern man than the Neanderthal Man, and *Homo sapiens* is generally considered to have made his appearance here; Cro-Magnon Man and Grimaldi Man are two of the several types who apparently made the artifacts left from this age. The Aurignacians were hunters and bone tools and ornaments are found; sea-shell ornaments, often found far inland, indicate some trade. Tools became more wieldy and smaller, and the blade made its appearance.

Aurigny (ō.rē.nyē). French name of **Alderney.**

Aurillac (ō.rē.yȧk). Town in S France, capital of the department of Cantal, situated on the Jordanne River, between Clermont-Ferrand and Montauban. The former capital of the Auvergne, it has a number of churches and secular buildings dating from the 16th and 17th centuries. It is a trade center for cattle, cheese, and horses; has manufactures of umbrellas and shoes, especially wooden shoes. The first French Pope, Sylvester II, formerly Bishop Gerbert, was born near here. 22,174 (1946).

Auringer (ôr'in.jėr), **Obadiah Cyrus.** b. at Glens Falls, N.Y., June 4, 1849; d. Oct. 2, 1937. American writer and Presbyterian clergyman. Ordained in 1890, he preached until 1916 at various churches in New York state. Author of *Scythe and Sword* (1887), *Friendship's Crown of Verse* (1908), *The Eagle's Bride* (1911), and *Quest of the Lamp* (1922), all poems; also of *Aboriginal Stone Implements of Queensbury* (1909), *In Praise of Books* (1930), and *The Eye of the Plain* (1931).

Aurinia (ô.rin'i.ạ). An ancient name of **Alderney.**

Auriol (ō.ryol), **Vincent.** [Pseudonyms (as a member of the French Resistance movement), **Dr. André Viaud** and **Jules Morel.**] b. at Revel, Haute-Garonne, France, Aug. 27, 1884—. French statesman and lawyer, first president of the French Fourth Republic. A Socialist deputy (1914–40), he was secretary (1919–39) of the Socialist group in parliament. The Popular Front election victory (1936) resulted in his appointment (1936) as minister of finance in the first Blum cabinet. He was minister of justice (1937–38) and minister of coördination of ministerial services (1938) in the second Blum cabinet. He was a French Socialist Party delegate (1924–39, 1944–45) to the Second (Socialist) International. A specialist in financial law, he took part (1924, 1925) in international economic conferences as a French delegate; as finance minister, he devalued the franc and reorganized (1936) the Bank of France. After Germany's defeat of France, he voted (July 10, 1940) against the grant of dictatorial powers to Henri Pétain, was imprisoned (1940–41), was active (1942–43) in the Resistance movement in France using the names Dr. André Viaud and Jules Morel, and escaped (1943) to London by airplane. Following the liberation of France, he was a deputy (1945–47), minister of state (1945–46), and delegate (1946) to the first assembly of the United Nations and to the U.N. security council. He was president (1946–47) of the two Constituent Assemblies and of the National Assembly, was one of the principal authors of the Constitution of the Fourth Republic, and was elected (Jan. 16, 1947) president of the republic.

Aurispa (ou.rē'spä), **Giovanni.** b. at Noto, Sicily, c1369; d. at Ferrara, Italy, c1459. Italian scholar, notable for his efforts to awaken contemporary interest in Greek classics. He voyaged (1418) to Constantinople, where he obtained approximately 250 manuscripts, including works by Pindar, Sophocles, Plato, and others. After his return to Italy he aroused the interest of Cosimo de' Medici and was aided by him. He served also for several years as a papal secretary.

Aurivillius (ô.ri.vil'i.us; Swedish, ou.rē.vēl'lē.ủs), **Karl.** b. at Stockholm, 1717; d. 1786. Swedish Orientalist.

Aurora (ô.rō'rạ). City in C Colorado, in Adams and Arapahoe counties: a suburb of Denver. In the decade between the last two U.S. censuses its population more than tripled. 3,437 (1940), 11,421 (1950).

Aurora. City in NE Illinois, in Kane County, on the Fox River, ab. 39 mi. W of Chicago: railroad shops; manufactures of machinery and flour. It is the seat of Aurora College. 50,576 (1950).

Aurora. City in SE Indiana, in Dearborn County, on the Ohio River, ab. 22 mi. SW of Cincinnati: furniture, coffins, and other manufactures. 4,780 (1950).

Aurora. City in SW Missouri, in Lawrence County: trade and processing center for an agricultural community formerly important for zinc and lead mining. 4,153 (1950).

Aurora. Small residential town in Ontario, Canada, on the main highway, ab. 24 mi. N of Toronto: seat of a private boarding school for boys. 3,358 (1951).

Aurora. [Greek, **Eos.**] In Roman mythology, the goddess of the dawn. The poets represented her as rising out of the ocean in a chariot, her rosy fingers dropping gentle dew.

Aurora. Anti-Federalist newspaper published (1794–1835) at Philadelphia.

Aurora. Former name of **Makatea.**

Aurora Leigh (lē). Narrative poem by Elizabeth Barrett Browning, published in 1857, named from its heroine.

Aurungabad (ou.rung.gạ.bäd'). See **Aurangabad.**

Aurungzebe (ô'rung.zeb). See **Aurangzeb.**

Au Sable (ô sā'bl). River in Michigan, in Iosco County, which flows into Lake Huron N of Saginaw Bay.

Ausable (ô.sā'bl). Small river in NE New York, in Essex and Clinton counties, which flows from the Adirondacks and empties into Lake Champlain.

Ausable Chasm. Deep, narrow, and picturesque chasm formed by the Ausable River near Keeseville, N.Y.

Ausci (ô'sī) or **Auscii** (-si.ī). [Also, **Auscenses** (ô.sen'sēz).] Aquitanian tribe conquered by the Romans in 56 B.C. From them was derived the name of the Roman city Augusta Auscorum, the modern Auch, France.

Aus der Ohe (ous dėr ō'ẹ), **Adèle.** b. at Hanover, Germany, 1864; d. at Berlin, 1937. German pianist and composer. A pupil of Franz Liszt and Franz Kullak, she gave concerts (1886–1903) in the U.S. Composer of several pieces for the piano and a sonata for piano and violin.

Auslander (ôs'lan"dėr), **Joseph.** b. at Philadelphia, Oct. 11, 1897—. American poet and anthologist. He served as an instructor at Harvard (1919–23), and poetry consultant at Columbia (1929–37), before taking (1937) a post as a consultant in English poetry to the Library of Congress. Author of *Sunrise Trumpets* (1924), *Cyclops' Eye* (1926), *Hell in Harness* (1930), *No Traveler Returns* (1933), *More than Bread* (1936), *Riders at the Gate* (1939); co-editor (with F. E. Hill) of *The Winged Horse* (1927) and *The Winged Horse Anthology* (1928); translator of *Fables of La Fontaine* (1930), *Sonnets of Petrarch* (1931), and others.

Ausona (ô.sō'nạ). A Latin name of **Vich.**

Ausonius (ô.sō'ni.us), **Decimus Magnus.** b. at Burdigala (now Bordeaux, France), c310 A.D.; d. c394 A.D. Roman Christian poet and teacher. He was employed by the emperor Gratian as tutor for his son, Valentinian; when Valentinian became emperor he was appointed (379) consul. He was converted, possibly by expediency as much as faith, to Christianity during the period of his tutorship. His works include summaries of the *Iliad* and *Odyssey;* also *Caesares,* memorials in verse to Roman rulers after Julius Caesar, *Mosella,* a travel narrative, and others.

Auspicius (ô.spish'i.us), Saint. d. c130. Bishop of Trier (or, according to some scholars, of Toul). He should not, however, be confused with the Saint Auspicius who is known to have been bishop of Toul more than 300 years later.

Auspicius, Saint. d. c475. Bishop of Toul, said to have been one of most learned prelates of his time. An epistle in Latin verse addressed by him to a contemporary nobleman, Count Arbogastes, is extant.

Aussa (ou'sä). Region in Adal, E Africa, in E central Ethiopia, near the border of French Somaliland.

Aussee (ous'zā"), **Alt-.** See **Alt-Aussee.**

Aussee, Bad. See **Bad Aussee.**

Aussen Alster (ous'ẹn äl'stėr). See under **Alster.**

Aust-Agder (oust"äg'dėr). *Fylke* (county) in S Norway, bordering on the Skagerrak in the E, and bounded by the *fylker* (counties) of Vest-Agder, Telemark, and Rogaland. Capital, Arendal; area, 3,606.8 sq. mi.; pop. 74,861 (1946).

Austen (ôs'tẹn), **Jane.** b. at Steventon, Hampshire, England, 1775; d. at Winchester, England, 1817. English novelist; seventh and youngest child of George Austen, rector of Deane and Steventon. Unmarried, she lived with her family, writing apparently chiefly for their amusement, at Steventon, Bath (1801), Southampton (1805), Chawton (1809), and Winchester (1817), making a humorous, ironical study of middle-class society for which she is unrivaled. Her first novel to be sent to a publisher, *Susan* (afterwards *Abbey*), did not appear till after her death. But *Sense and Sensibility*, published in 1811, brought her immediate recognition. It was followed by *Pride and Prejudice* (1813), *Mansfield Park* (1814), and *Emma* (1816). Her last, and as many think her best, novel, *Persuasion*, did not appear till a year after her death, when it was published with *Northanger Abbey*. In her lifetime she was conceded rank possibly equal to that of Fanny Burney or Maria Edgeworth; later appreciation of her peculiar gifts of proportion and composition (which she called those of a miniaturist), began probably with Richard Whately and Sir Walter Scott, and was seconded enthusiastically by George Henry Lewes, Samuel Taylor Coleridge, Thomas Babington Macaulay, and others. Published writing by her, in addition to the novels already cited, includes various shorter and unfinished works, recently reissued as curiosities, and two volumes of her letters.

Austen, Peter Townsend. b. on Staten Island, N.Y., Sept. 10, 1852; d. Dec. 30, 1907. American chemist. He taught successively at Dartmouth, Rutgers, and Brooklyn Polytechnic Institute (1876–96); thereafter he headed his own laboratory and served as an industrial consultant (1896 *et seq.*). He translated and revised Pinner's *Introduction to the Study of Organic Chemistry* (1883), and wrote numerous technical articles.

Auster (ôs'tėr). In Latin, the south wind.

Austerlitz (ôs'tėr.lits; German, ou'stėr-). [Czech, **Slavkov.**] Town in Czechoslovakia, in E central Moravia, where, on Dec. 3, 1805, the French under Napoleon I defeated the Russo-Austrian army under Mikhail Ilarionovich Kutuzov in what was perhaps the most brilliant victory in Napoleon's career. Another name for the battle was "Battle of the Three Emperors" because Alexander I of Russia, Francis of Austria, and Napoleon all participated. The battle was followed by the peace of Pressburg (now Bratislava) between France and Austria.

Austerlitz, Sun of. The bright sun which dispersed the clouds and mist on the morning of the battle of Austerlitz, proverbial as a symbol of good fortune.

Austin (ôs'tin). Unincorporated community in S Indiana, in Scott County, ab. 75 mi. S of Indianapolis. 2,906 (1950).

Austin. City in SE Minnesota, county seat of Mower County, on the Cedar River, ab. 97 mi. S of St. Paul: a food-packing center. 23,100 (1950).

Austin. Township in C Nevada, county seat of Lander County, ab. 146 mi. NE of Carson City: formerly important for gold and silver mining. 419 (1950).

Austin. [Former name, **Waterloo.**] City in C Texas, capital of Texas and county seat of Travis County, on the Colorado River, near the Texas cotton-belt region: marketing and processing center for agricultural products. It is the seat of the University of Texas, Samuel Houston College, Tillotson College, St. Edward's University, the O. Henry Museum, and the Elizabeth Ney Museum. It was established as capital in 1839, renamed for Stephen F. Austin, and was incorporated (1840) as a town. Pop. of city, 87,930 (1940), 132,459 (1950); of urbanized area, 135,971 (1950).

Austin, Alfred. b. at Headingley, Leeds, England, May 30, 1835; d. at Ashford, Kent, England, June 2, 1913. English poet, essayist, and novelist. He was named poet laureate in 1896, although most critics consider his abundant verse of little worth. His critical views are indicated by the fact that he attacked Tennyson, Robert Browning, Matthew Arnold, Algernon Charles Swinburne, William Morris, Arthur Hugh Clough, and Victor Hugo as inferior poets in his *Poetry of the Period* (1870), and Wordsworth in his *The Bridling of Pegasus* (1910), a volume of collected essays.

Austin, Ernest. b. at London, Dec. 31, 1874—. English composer. He forsook business for music at the age of 33 and thereafter produced compositions ranging from symphonic works to schoolroom piano pieces. He is best known for works based on old English folk tunes, such as *The Vicar of Bray* and *Phantasy on Old Tunes*.

Austin, Frederic. b. at London, March 30, 1872—. English baritone and composer. A leading bass-baritone (1915 *et seq.*) with the Beecham Opera Company, he also arranged the scores for Hammersmith productions of *The Beggar's Opera* (1920) and *Polly* (1922). In 1924 he was named artistic director of the British National Opera Company. Composer of a symphony, a symphonic poem, and others.

Austin, Frederick Britten. b. May 8, 1885; d. at Weston-super-Mare, Somerset, England, March 12, 1941. English novelist, short-story writer, dramatist, and scenarist. Author of *The Shaping of Lavinia* (1911), *A Saga of the Sea* (1928), *The Road to Glory* (1935), novels; *The Thing That Matters* (1921), a drama; *On the Borderland* (1923), a collection of stories; *When Mankind Was Young* (1927), a fictional picture of prehistoric man; and *The Red Flag* (1934), an account of revolutions from Spartacus to Lenin (published 1933 in Spanish as *La Bandera Roja*).

Austin, Herbert. [Title, 1st Baron **Austin.**] b. at Little Missenden, England, 1866; d. near Bromsgrove, England, May 23, 1941. English motorcar manufacturer, especially of light automobiles. After serving as an apprentice engineer and manager of engineering companies (1883–90) at Melbourne, Australia, he headed (1890 *et seq.*) the Wolseley Sheep-Shearing Machine Company in England, before settling (1905) at Birmingham to manufacture motorcars.

Austin, Jane Goodwin. b. at Worcester, Mass., Feb. 25, 1831; d. March 30, 1894. American novelist and short-story writer. Creator of the "Pilgrim Books" series, including *Standish of Standish* (1889), *Betty Alden* (1891), *A Nameless Nobleman* (1881), and *Dr. Le Baron and His Daughters* (1890), in order of historical sequence; her other works consisted of novels and collected short pieces.

Austin, John. b. at Creeling Mill, Suffolk, England, March 3, 1790; d. at Weybridge, Surrey, England, December, 1859. English lawyer and writer on jurisprudence. He has been praised for his work in establishing definitions of legal ideas and terms, and credited with laying a scientific foundation for legal analysis and a modern philosophy of law. He was a professor of jurisprudence (1826–32) at University College, London, where John Stuart Mill was his student; in 1834 he was royal commissioner on criminal law. Author of *Province of Jurisprudence Determined* (1832), *A Plea for the Constitution* (1859, a pamphlet against Charles Grey's proposal of parliamentary reform), *Lectures on Jurisprudence* (1869), and others.

Austin, Jonathan Loring. b. at Boston, Jan. 2, 1748; d. there, May 10, 1826. American Revolutionary soldier and government official. He was sent (1777) to Paris with dispatches to Benjamin Franklin announcing the surrender of General John Burgoyne, and remained two years with Franklin as his private secretary, engaging (1778) in a secret mission to English political leaders.

Austin, Louis Winslow. b. at Orwell, Vt., Oct. 30, 1867; d. June 27, 1932. American physicist. He was on the staff of the Bureau of Standards, Washington, D.C. (1904 *et seq.*) and chief of the Special Radio Transmission Research Laboratory, also at Washington, D.C. (1923 *et seq.*). Author (with C. B. Thwing) of *Physical Measurement* (1896).

Austin, Mary. [Maiden name, **Hunter.**] b. at Carlinville, Ill., Sept. 9, 1868; d. at Santa Fe, N.M., Aug. 13, 1934. American novelist, playwright, feminist, and devotee of the American Southwest. Known chiefly for her literary interest in the peoples and cultures in the area of the Mojave Desert, she was also influenced by a sympathy for Fabian socialism and by her passionate belief in (and espousal of) women's rights. Her best novel is thought by many to be *A Woman of Genius* (1912). Author also of *The Land of Little Rain* (1903), *Isidro* (1905), *Lost Borders* (1909), *The Man Jesus* (1915), which was revised as *A Small Town* (1925), *The Ford* (1917), and many others; her plays include the New Theater project entitled *The Arrow Maker* (1911), and others; she also wrote the semi-autobiographical *Experiences Facing Death* (1931) and an autobiography, *Earth Horizon* (1932).

Austin, Moses. b. at Durham, Conn., Oct. 4, 1761; d. June 10, 1821. American mine owner, merchant, and pioneer. His fortune, based on lead mines and other properties in Missouri, was wiped out during the financial panic of 1819. He thereupon became interested in the possibility of settlement in Texas and negotiated (1820) with the Spanish governor at San Antonio to this end, but died before carrying out his scheme (which was actually approved by the Spanish officials on Jan. 17, 1821). The plan was then carried on by his son, Stephen Fuller Austin.

Austin, Oscar Phelps. b. at Newark, Ill.; d. at New York, Jan. 6, 1933. American statistician. He was chief (1898 *et seq.*) of the Bureau of Statistics in the U.S. Treasury Department, and a statistician (1914–25) for the National City Bank of New York; he also taught (1903–14) commerce and statistics at George Washington University, at Washington, D.C. He was, in addition, the author of a series of juvenile novels.

Austin, Samuel. b. at New Haven, Conn., Oct. 7, 1760; d. at Glastonbury, Conn., Dec. 4, 1830. American Congregational clergyman, president of the University of Vermont (1815–21). As pastor (1790–1815) of the First Congregational Church, Worcester, Mass., he became known as an effective supporter of theological orthodoxy in the school of Jonathan Edwards and Samuel Hopkins.

Austin, Sarah. [Maiden name, **Taylor.**] b. at Norwich, Norfolk, England, 1793; d. at Weybridge, Surrey, England, Aug. 8, 1867. English writer; wife of John Austin (1790–1859). Besides editions of her husband's lectures (1861–63), she was the author of painstaking translations from German and French, of which the best known are *Characteristics of Goethe from the German of Falk, Von Müller, and Others* (1833), Friedrich Wilhelm Carové's *Story Without an End* (1834), Leopold von Ranke's *History of the Popes* (1840), *History of the Reformation in Germany* (1845), and Guizot's *Causes of the Success of the English Revolution* (1850).

Austin, Stephen Fuller. b. in Wythe County, Va., Nov. 3, 1793; d. Dec. 27, 1836. American pioneer and Texas colonizer. He continued (1821 *et seq.*) the colonization scheme envisioned by his father, Moses Austin, successfully negotiating, after the establishment (1821) of Mexican control, the continuance of an arrangement originally made with the Spanish to settle 300 families in Texas (by 1833, however, almost 1,000 families had arrived). He held office under the Mexican government and directed the government of his colony in Texas until 1827, when local government, as a part of Mexico, was established under a modified state constitution. In 1833 he undertook a mission to persuade the Mexican national government to permit the full separation of Texas from Coahuila and its admission to the Mexican republic as a full-fledged state. However, a misunderstanding with Gomez Farias, the Mexican vice-president, led to Austin's imprisonment and subsequent detention (January, 1834–July, 1835) under bond. Appointed a commissioner to the U.S. by the provisional government of Texas before the declaration of independence of the republic of Texas (1835–36), he also served (1836) for two months as secretary of state of the short-lived republic of Texas under President Sam Houston.

Austin, Warren Robinson. b. at Highgate, Vt., Nov. 12, 1877—. American statesman, a senator from Vermont (1931–46) and head of the U.S. delegation to the United Nations (1946–53). His longstanding internationalist outlook, along with Yankee shrewdness and integrity, led President Harry Truman to cross party lines (Austin is and was a Republican) to appoint him leader of the U.S. delegation in the then new international organization. In the Senate he advocated lend-lease and collaborated in drafting the first peacetime compulsory military training bill (1940) in U.S. history. At Mexico City (1945) he was a leader in framing the formula for inter-American defense known as the Act of Chapultepec.

Austin, William. b. 1587; d. Jan. 16, 1634. English lawyer and writer. His works include *Devotionis Augustinianae Flamma, or Certayne Devout, Godly, and Lerned Meditations* (1635), *Haec Homo, wherein the Excellency of the Creation of Woman is described by way of an Essay* (1637), and a translation of Cicero's *Cato Major*.

Austin, William. b. at Lunenburg, Mass., March 2, 1778; d. at Charlestown, Mass., June 27, 1841. American lawyer and writer. His *Peter Rugg, the Missing Man* (1824) is still read, and is considered, with *Rip Van Winkle*, an outstanding example of American story-telling up to that time; his other works, although once popular, are now little read.

Austin, William Lane. b. in Scott County, Miss., Jan. 25, 1871—. American statistician and government official. He joined the staff of the U.S. Bureau of the Census in 1900, and became its director in 1933.

Austin Colony. Settlement in Texas carried out by Stephen F. Austin under a grant originally made (Jan. 17, 1821) to Moses Austin by Spanish officials in Mexico. The eventual settlement of over 1,000 families, most of whom had arrived by 1833, created an important stepping-stone for the separation of Texas from Mexico.

Austin Friars. [Also, **Augustinian Friars.**] Former monastery of the Friars Eremite of the order of Saint Augustine, on the N side of Broad Street, in the City of London, founded by Humphrey Bohun, Earl of Hereford and Essex, in 1253. The ground was considered especially sacred, and the tombs were deemed by many to be equal in beauty to those of Westminster Abbey. Here were buried Hubert de Burgh; Edmund Plantagenet, half-brother of Richard II; many of those who fell in the battle of Barnet; Richard Fitzalan, Earl of Arundel, who was beheaded in 1397; the Earl of Oxford, beheaded in 1463; and Edward Stafford, Duke of Buckingham, beheaded in 1521. At the dissolution of the monastery under Henry VIII the spire was destroyed and the monuments sold by the Marquis of Winchester. The nave was walled up, and was used as a church by the Dutch residents of London.

Austin of Canterbury, Saint. See **Augustine of Canterbury,** Saint.

Austral (ôs'trạl), **Florence.** [Stage name of **Florence Wilson.**] b. near Melbourne, 1894—. Australian concert and opera soprano. She made her debut (1922) with the British National Opera Company at Covent Garden as Brünnehilde, and subsequently toured England and Scotland. Her American debut (1925) in the mid-West was followed by a tour (1926). In 1930 she appeared with the Berlin State Opera.

Australasia (ôs.trạ.lā'zhạ). Name given to a division of Oceania, comprising Australia, New Guinea, Tasmania, New Zealand, New Caledonia, the Bismarck Archipelago, and some lesser islands. It is often regarded as comprising only the Australian possessions of Great Britain, including New Zealand, Tasmania, and Fiji, but is sometimes taken as an equivalent to Oceania in its entirety.

Australia (ôs.trāl'yạ). [Official name, the **Commonwealth of Australia**; former name, **New Holland.**] Island continent and dominion of the British Commonwealth of Nations, S of Asia, bordered by the Pacific Ocean on the E, by the Indian Ocean on the NW, W, and SW, and separated from New Guinea by Torres Strait on the N, and from Tasmania by Bass Strait on the S. Capital, Canberra; area, 2,974,581 sq. mi.; pop. 8,649,000 (est. 1952).

Physical Geography. Its principal natural features are mountains along the E and S coasts (Australian Alps, Blue Mountains, Liverpool Range), the Murray River system in the SE, the lake district in the S, and extensive desert regions in the interior. The chief products are wheat, maize, and other cereals, wool, hay, cotton, sugar, and wine. It is also rich in gold, silver, copper, and coal.

Political Divisions. Its political divisions are the states forming the Commonwealth of Australia (consisting of New South Wales, Victoria, Queensland, South Australia, Western Australia, Tasmania: all former British colonies and known as the "original states"), and the Northern Territory, Australian Capital Territory, and the Territory of Papua. Australia also administers the trust territory of New Guinea, which includes the NE part of the island of New Guinea and several of the neighboring islands. Australia's chief cities are Melbourne and Sydney.

History and Government. In 1606 the continent was visited by Spanish and Dutch explorers; it was explored by Cook in 1770–77. The first settlement was at Port Jackson in 1788. Gold was discovered in 1851. Among the explorers of Australia have been George Bass (for whom was named Bass Strait, separating Australia and Tasmania), Matthew Flinders (an associate of Bass in the late 18th century, who first surveyed much of the W coast of Australia), Charles Sturt (who discovered the Darling River in SE Australia in 1828), Edward John Eyre (who explored much of the interior during the middle of the 19th century), Friedrich Wilhelm Ludwig Leichardt (a German explorer and geologist who crossed the continent in 1844–45), Robert O'Hara Burke (who, during the early

1860's, made the first north-south crossing of the continent), William John Wills (an associate of Burke), John McDouall Stuart (an associate of Sturt, for whom the town now called Alice Springs was originally named), and John Forrest (who in 1890 became the first prime minister of Western Australia). The federal government was inaugurated Jan. 1, 1901, a new site for a national capital was acquired at the city of Canberra in 1911, and the first Australian Parliament opened there in 1927. Legislative power is vested in a federal Parliament, consisting of a governor general (representing the king), a Senate, and a House of Representatives. There is an executive council of ministers of state. Australia has participated actively in both world wars as a member of the British Commonwealth of Nations.

Australia Felix (fē'liks). Novel by Henry Handel Richardson (pseudonym of Mrs. Henrietta Robertson), published in 1917. It is the first volume of the trilogy *The Fortunes of Richard Mahony* (1930), and deals with goldminers in Australia.

Australian (ôs.trāl'yạn). Name sometimes given to the native languages (taken collectively) of Australia, forming a geographic rather than a linguistic group. All are often assumed to be of common origin, but this is not established and Wilhelm Schmidt, who has done the most careful work on the subject, finds no connection between his northern and southern groups, nor even among the southern languages themselves. Relationships outside Australia have been suggested, but never proved.

Australian Alps. Mountain range in SE Australia, in the E part of Victoria and New South Wales, nearly parallel with the coast: the S part of the Great Dividing Range, containing the highest point in Australia, Mount Kosciusko (7,324 ft.).

Australian Capital Territory. [Former names, **Federal Capital Territory, Yass-Canberra.**] Federal territory in Australia composed of two segments of land, one (911 sq. mi.) within the S part of the state of New South Wales near the national capital at Canberra, and the other (28 sq. mi.), ab. 100 mi. E of the capital, on the coast of New South Wales at Jervis Bay. The former contains the government buildings and the latter a naval college. Both these areas were obtained by the Commonwealth of Australia by agreement with the state of New South Wales. General control over the area is exercised by the Australian minister for the interior. 25,366 (est. 1951).

Austrasia (ôs.trā'zhạ). [Also, **Ostrasia.**] Eastern kingdom of the Merovingian Franks from the 6th to the 8th century A.D. It embodied an extensive region on both sides of the Rhine, with Metz as its capital. In some older works the variant form "Austria" is also (and not illogically) hypothesized for this kingdom; in fact, however, there is no historical or geographical connection between this early realm and any political unit resembling what was later to be Austria.

Austrasia, Duke of. See **Charles Martel.**

Austria (ôs'tri.ạ). See also **Austria-Hungary.**

Austria. Historical region in C Europe between the rivers Inn and Leitha, on both banks of the Danube River and bounded on the N by the Bohemian-Moravian hill country, on the S by the northernmost ranges of the eastern Alps. It comprises the present Austrian *Länder* (provinces) of Upper Austria (German, Oberösterreich) and Lower Austria (German, Niederösterreich) and the city of Vienna, and forms the historical nucleus from which the Austro-Hungarian monarchy of the Hapsburgs grew. It came into being in the 7th to 10th centuries as the Austrian (meaning the "eastern") *Mark* (realm) of the duchy of Bavaria and as a protective frontier against the Huns, Avars, and Magyars. It was colonized by German knights, clerics, burghers, and peasants who mingled with the originally Slavic population. The Hapsburg family attained sovereignty in the 13th century. The region now forms an integral part of the republic of Austria.

Austria. The Cisleithan part (that portion W of the Leitha River) of the former Austro-Hungarian monarchy as it emerged after the compromise with Hungary in 1867. It comprised, apart from the territory of the present republic of Austria, and exclusive of the Burgenland, what is now the Italian part of the Tyrol, the territories, now Yugoslav, of S Styria, Krain, Istria, and Dalmatia, and Bohemia, Moravia, Silesia, Galicia, and Bucovina. It was united with the Transleithan part of the monarchy, namely Hungary, in personal union, the emperor of Austria at the same time being designated as the king of Hungary. The internal history of the country (even excluding Hungary) was marked by strife between its diverse national groups and numerous attempts were made to achieve compromise solutions to the problem. The Germans comprised close to 40 percent of the total, followed by the Czechs, Poles, Ruthenians, Slovenians, and Italians. Austria had thus become a term equivalent to the western half of the Hapsburg domain. The Austria of the Hapsburgs collapsed at the end of World War I.

Austria. [German, **Österreich, Oesterreich**; official German name, **Republik Österreich**; during German occupation, **Ostmark**; French, **Autriche,** formerly also **Austrie.**] Republic in E central Europe, bounded on the W by Switzerland, on the N by Germany (specifically, Bavaria), on the NE by Czechoslovakia (specifically, Bohemia and Moravia), on the E by Czechoslovakia (specifically, Slovakia) and Hungary, and on the S by Yugoslavia and Italy. Capital, Vienna; area, 32,374 sq. mi.; pop. 6,918,959 (1951).

Terrain and Climate. The country has a roughly oblong shape, with its base on the Danube River between the Bavarian and Hungarian borders but with a narrow section pointing westward toward the valley of the upper Rhine River and the Lake of Constance. Most of the area, particularly toward the S and W, is mountainous. There are four principal areas: the hill country N of the Danube, a continuation of the Bohemian-Moravian uplands; the valley of the Danube, including the Viennese basin and the N part of Burgenland; the Alpine mountain ranges, reaching high peaks in the W and C parts of the country (Vorarlberg, Tirol, Salzburg) and gradually sloping off toward the E; finally the southern slopes and valleys of the Alps in Styria, Carinthia, and S Burgenland (the corresponding southern valleys in the Tyrol now belong to Italy); there are also many subregions, such as the Inn, Salzach, and Mur valleys. Accordingly, there are variations in the generally central-European character of the climate, ranging from high precipitation and long winters in the Alpine valleys to a mild climate permitting extensive vine cultivation in Lower Austria (German, Niederösterreich), the Burgenland, and lower Styria.

Agriculture, Industry, and Trade. Owing to its largely mountainous character, Austria is not self-supporting in regard to foodstuffs. Grains, potatoes, and sugar are grown mainly in the N, E, and SE parts of the country, while the raising of livestock, particularly of cattle and pigs, is of importance in the other sections. Forests, which used to be one of the most valuable assets of Austria, were ruthlessly cut down during and after World War II. The tourist trade has not yet fully recovered from the war. Oil is produced in Lower Austria, iron ore in Styria, lignite, salt, and some other minerals in various parts of the country. Industries, apart from lumbering, paper manufacture, and the production of foodstuffs, are largely concentrated in the Viennese basin, in Styria, and in Vorarlberg. By a government bill passed on July 26, 1946, some 70 industrial concerns were nationalized. These include all or most of the firms in the following fields: banking, oil producing and refining, river navigation, coal extraction, nonferrous and ferrous mining and refining, pig-iron and steel production, and the manufacture of iron and steel products (including structural materials, machinery, railroad equipment, and shipbuilding) and of electrical machinery and appliances.

History. The independent existence of Austria came about with the breakdown of the old Austro-Hungarian monarchy of the Hapsburgs at the end of World War I. The republic was declared to be in existence on Nov. 12, 1918. The idea was at first to have Austria become a part of the German republic and to include in it all linguistically German regions of the former monarchy. However, the S Tyrol was occupied by Italy, S Styria by Yugoslavia, and the German parts of Bohemia and Moravia by Czechoslovakia. Only the Burgenland, formerly a part of W Hungary, was added to pre-Hapsburg Austria to form the new republic. In the fall of 1919, the peace of St.-Germain granted further territorial inroads in favor of

Czechoslovakia and specifically barred incorporation (*Anschluss*) with the German Reich. A plebiscite returned Ödenburg (Hungarian, Sopron) to Hungary, but prevented S Carinthia from falling to Yugoslavia. The new country was hardly viable. In regard to foodstuffs it was far from being self-sufficient, while the industrial, commercial, and financial apparatus, designed to serve large parts of the monarchy, was now outgrown. The financial aid coming from the League of Nations was insufficient and a destructive inflation was the result. The collapse in 1931 of the Österreichische Boden-Credit Anstalt, the leading banking enterprise of Austria, made the crisis of the Austrian economy obvious and was at the same time indicative of a larger crisis in C Europe. Internal unrest had been growing during the same period, with the Christian-Social (clerical) and the Social-Democratic (socialist) parties contending for supremacy while militantly nationalistic groups, first the *Heimwehren* and later the National Socialists (Nazis), attempted to supersede them both. In 1931, the Schober-Curtius attempt at a customs union between Germany and Austria failed, mainly because of the opposition of France and Czechoslovakia. Austria's foreign policy thereupon became oriented toward Italy. After Hitler's accession to power in Germany and the Hitler-Mussolini alliance, Austria's independence was doomed. Chancellor Dollfuss was murdered by Nazis on July 25, 1934. On March 12, 1938, Hitler marched into Austria without encountering resistance. Between 1938 and 1945 Austria was administered (as *Ostmark*) by a *Gauleiter* of the Nazi party. By May, 1945, the whole of Austria was occupied by the troops of the four Allied powers and a provisional government was set up within the frontiers of 1937.

Government. Austria is a democratic, parliamentary republic consisting of nine provinces (*Länder*), one of which is the city of Vienna. There is in every *Land* an elected provincial assembly. The *Länder* are: Vienna (German, Wien), Lower Austria (German, Niederösterreich), Upper Austria (German, Oberösterreich), Salzburg, Styria (German, Steiermark), Carinthia (German, Kärnten), Tirol, Vorarlberg, and Burgenland. Pending the peace treaty, the country is divided into four zones of occupation. Lower Austria, Burgenland, and Upper Austria N of the Danube are in the Russian zone, Salzburg and Upper Austria S of the Danube in the American zone, Styria and Carinthia including East Tirol in the British zone, and Tirol and Vorarlberg in the French zone. The city of Vienna is jointly occupied by the four powers.

Culture. The Austrian population is almost entirely German as to language and Roman Catholic as to religion. Yugoslavia claims those parts of S Carinthia where part of the population is Slovenian in origin. Only small Protestant communities survived the Counter Reformation. The formerly considerable Jewish population of Vienna has almost entirely disappeared. There is a marked difference in cultural backgrounds between the Alpine regions of Austria and the city of Vienna. In the former many survivals of the medieval peasant culture are still to be found, while Vienna has a cosmopolitan character owing to the fusion over many centuries of German, Latin, Slavic, Jewish, and Hungarian elements. However, the German dialect spoken is a variant of the Bavarian throughout the country, with the exception of Vorarlberg where an Alemannic dialect is still spoken. The literacy rate is high, elementary education compulsory. There are three universities, at Vienna, Graz, and Innsbruck, two institutes of technology, at Vienna and Graz, an agricultural college at Vienna, and a mining college at Leoben.

Austria, Archduke of. See **John** (of *Austria*).

Austria, Allied Control Commission for. See **Allied Control Commission for Austria.**

Austria, Lower. See **Lower Austria.**

Austria, Upper. See **Upper Austria.**

Austria-Hungary (ôs'tri.ạ.hung'gạ.ri). [Also: **Austro-Hungarian Monarchy**; sometimes shortened to **Austria**; German, **Österreich-Ungarn, Österreichisch-Ungarische Monarchie.**] Former empire of Europe, capital Vienna, one of the "Great Powers" of the globe until the close of World War I, bounded by Germany (partly separated from it by the Erzgebirge and Sudetic Mountains) and Russia (partly separated from it by the Vistula River) on the N, Russia and Rumania on the E, Rumania (separated from it by the Carpathians), Serbia (partly separated from it by the Danube River), and Montenegro on the S, the Adriatic Sea and Italy (mainly separated from it by the Alps) on the SW, and Switzerland and Germany (partly separated from it by the Inn and Bohemian Forest) on the W. The area was 261,035 sq. mi. Politically the monarchy was divided into the Cisleithan division, comprising Upper Austria, Lower Austria, Tirol and Vorarlberg, Salzburg, Styria, Carinthia, Carniola, Küstenland, Dalmatia, Bohemia, Moravia, Silesia, Galicia, and Bucovina (these were represented in the Reichsrath, which met at Vienna, and was composed of an upper house, and a lower house of 516 members); and the Transleithan division, comprising Hungary (including Transylvania), Croatia-Slavonia, and Fiume, which were represented at Budapest by the Diet, composed of a "House of Magnates," and a house of 453 representatives. Legislation for the monarchy as a whole was vested in the "Delegations" (60 members from each of the two parliaments). Bosnia and Hercegovina were annexed by Austria-Hungary in 1908. The government was a constitutional hereditary monarchy. The inhabitants belonged to various races whose relations were exceedingly complicated. The Slavs (Czechs, Poles, Ruthenians, Slovaks, Slovenes, Serbs, and Croats) led, numerically forming about one half of the whole; the Germans constituted one fourth, the Magyars less than one sixth, and the Rumanians about one fifteenth. There were also Jews, Bulgarians, Armenians, Italians, Gypsies, and Ladins. The religion of the majority was Roman Catholic; there were several millions of Protestants, and about an equal number belonged to the Greek Church. The S and W regions belonged at one time to the Roman Empire. The country was thereafter at various times overrun by the Goths, Huns, Lombards, Avars, and other invaders. The nucleus was the *Mark* (realm) of Austria, which was constituted a duchy in 1156. To this Styria was united in 1192. The Babenberg dynasty was extinguished in 1246, and was followed after some years by the Hapsburg line. Rudolf of Hapsburg (the ruler of various districts in Switzerland, Alsace, Swabia, and Breisgau) was elected emperor of Germany in 1273. In 1282 he conferred Austria, Styria, and Carniola (having wrested them from Ottocar II of Bohemia in 1276) upon his sons. Carinthia was acquired in 1335, Tirol in 1363, and Trieste in 1382. The continuous line of Hapsburg emperors of Germany began in 1438. Austria itself was made an archduchy in 1453. Bohemia, with Moravia, Silesia, and Lusatia, was added to the Hapsburg dominions in 1526. In the same year began the rule of the Hapsburgs in Hungary, at that time mainly in the possession of the Turks, who were not completely dispossessed until 1718. Austria took the leading part in the Thirty Years' War, and at its close (1648) had to cede her possessions in Alsace to France; she also took part in the War of the Spanish Succession, and acquired in 1714 the Spanish Netherlands, Milan, Mantua, Naples, and Sardinia (the latter was exchanged for Sicily in 1720). By the treaties of 1735 and 1738 Naples and Sicily were ceded to the Bourbons, part of NW Italy was ceded to Sardinia, and Austria received Parma and Piacenza. The accession of Maria Theresa in 1740 raised the question of accession to the throne through the female line, and thus provided a technical basis for the War of the Austrian Succession. The greater part of Silesia was ceded to Prussia in 1742; and by the treaty of 1748 Parma, Piacenza, and Guastalla were ceded to Spain. Austria also took a leading part in the Seven Years' War. By the first partition of Poland (1772) she acquired Galicia and Lodomeria. Bucovina was acquired in 1777, and Bavaria ceded the Innviertel in 1779. War was waged with France in the period 1792–97, and by the treaty of Campo-Formio (1797) Austria lost her Netherlands territory and Lombardy, but received Venice, Venetia, Istria, and Dalmatia. Much of Galicia (afterward lost) was obtained in the third partition of Poland (1795). War with France was again carried on in the period 1799–1801, resulting in the treaty of Lunéville (1801), by which the previous treaty was confirmed. Members of the Hapsburg family received cessions in the arrangements of 1803. The emperor Francis took the title of "Emperor of Austria" in 1804. A disastrous war with France broke out in 1805, and Austria was forced to cede (1805) Tirol, Vorarlberg, Breisgau, various territories in Swabia, Venetia, Dalmatia, and others to France and French allies, and received Salzburg and Berchtesgaden. The dissolution of the German Empire took place in 1806. War with France again occurred in 1809, and Austria ceded in the same year Carniola, Trieste, Croatia, part of Carinthia, Salzburg, the Innviertel, and part of Galicia, to Napoleon. Austria formally joined the Allies for the last time against Napoleon in 1813. By the Congress of Vienna (1815) she regained many of her former dominions, including Tirol, the Illyrian territories, Venetia, and Lombardy. She became the head of the German Confederation (1815–66), a member of the Holy Alliance, and a leader in the European political reaction that followed the Napoleonic era. Revolutionary movements in Austrian and Italian dominions (1848–49) were repressed, and a rebellion in Hungary which took place at the same time was subdued with the aid of Russia. The republic of Kraków was annexed in 1846. By the war of 1859 against France and Sardinia, Austria lost Lombardy and her influence in Italy. She joined with Prussia in a war against Denmark in 1864. In 1866 Prussia, in alliance with Italy, made war (the Austro-Prussian War) upon Austria, and completely defeated her at Königgrätz. Austria was thereupon forced to retire from the German Confederation and to cede Venetia to Italy. The formation of the dual monarchy took place in 1867. In 1878 the administration of Bosnia and Hercegovina was given to Austria-Hungary, and they were formally annexed in 1908. In 1883 Austria entered into the Triple Alliance with Germany and Italy. The empire was dissolved (1918) at the close of World War I.

Austrian People's Party (ôs'tri.an). Political party, active in Austria since World War II, drawing its strength from the middle class and farmers, and following a strongly Roman Catholic program.

Austrian Succession, War of the. Designation of the war, or series of wars, between Austria and England on the one side, and France, Bavaria, Prussia, Spain, Sardinia, and various lesser allies on the other, which broke out on the succession of Maria Theresa (daughter of the emperor Charles VI) to the Austrian lands in 1740. The states whose adhesion to the pragmatic sanction Charles VI had secured took up arms to despoil Maria Theresa of her dominions. In its early phase, in the conflict with Prussia which was terminated in 1742, it is known also as the First Silesian War. England became allied with Austria in 1741, and King George II defeated the French at Dettingen, in Bavaria, in 1743. The Second Silesian War, in which Saxony, originally the ally of Prussia, joined Austria, followed in 1744–45. French victories were gained at Fontenoy (1745), Raucoux (1746), and Laafelt (1747). The chief American phase of the war between England and France is known as King George's War. The expedition of Charles Edward Stuart (the "Young Pretender") in Scotland and England (1745–46) was a diversion in the French favor. Russia joined Austria in 1747. The war was ended by the Treaty of Aix-la-Chapelle (1748) and a mutual restitution of conquests, except in regard to Austria, which came out of the struggle with the loss of Silesia, as well as of Parma and Piacenza.

Austric (ôs'trik). A proposed linguistic stock in which some authorities group the Austroasiatic (i.e., Mon-Khmer and Munda) and the Malayo-Polynesian languages. Others use the term to cover only the Mon-Khmer and Malayo-Polynesian families, excluding the Munda languages as unrelated.

Austrie (ōs.trē). Former French name of **Austria.**

Austroasiatic (ôs'trō.ā.zhi.at'ik). A proposed linguistic stock including the Mon-Khmer languages of SE Asia and the Munda languages of India. Most authorities, however, do not accept a genetic relationship between these two families.

Austro-German Agreement of 1936. Agreement concluded on July 11, 1936, between Austria and Germany, with the knowledge and assent of the Italian government under Mussolini. Although it affirmed the mutual sovereignty of Germany and Austria, it stipulated that Austrian foreign policy be based on principles acknowledging Austria as a German state. An effect of the agreement was to bring both Austria and Italy more closely into the German orbit.

Austro-Prussian War. [Also, **Seven Weeks' War.**] War between Austria (allied with Bavaria, Hanover, Hesse-Kassel, Nassau, and Saxony) and Prussia (allied with Italy). It is now generally agreed that Bismarck, the Prussian chancellor, deliberately brought about a situation in which Austria had either to renounce hegemony among the German states, or fight. Hostilities opened on June 15, 1899; on July 3 Austria sustained one of the most crushing military defeats experienced by any nation up to that time in the battle variously known by the names of Sadowa and Königgrätz, two villages near the battlefield. In the Treaty of Prague signed on Aug. 23, 1866, Prussia granted Austria moderate terms, but Austria acknowledged its exclusion from German affairs and conceded the right of Prussia to form a union of German states N of the Main River. Prussia annexed Austria's allies excepting Saxony, adding to her domain some 25,000 sq. mi. and 5,000,000 subjects, and constrained Austria to cede Venetia to Italy. By this war Austria's predominance in Germany was broken, and she was unable to intervene in the Franco-Prussian War (1870–71) or to prevent the formation of the German Empire at the close of that conflict. This defeat also ended Austrian power in Italy, and made Austria amenable to proposals for reform of relations with Hungary, which led to the establishment of the dual monarchy of Austria-Hungary.

Ausugum (ô.sö'gum). Ancient name of **Borgo.**

Auténtico Party (ou.tän'tē.kō). Cuban political party, having a membership of diverse political opinion, and containing such opposing leaders as Ramón Grau San Martín and Carlos Prío Socarrás.

Auteroche (dōt.rosh), **Jean Chappe d'.** See **Chappe d'Auteroche, Jean.**

Autesiodorum (ô.tē"si.ō.dō'rum). Latin name of **Auxerre.**

Auteuil (ō.tėy'). Former village in N France, in the department of Seine, now part of Paris; situated on the right bank of the Seine River E of Boulogne-Bilancourt. It is noted as the place of residence of Nicolas Boileau-Despréaux, Molière, Claude Adrien Helvétius, Charles Maurice de Talleyrand, Adolphe Thiers, and other distinguished literary and political figures. It is the site of a well-known racecourse.

Authari (ô.thär'ī). d. 590. Third king of the Lombards after they entered Italy. Elected in 584 A.D., he reigned until his death in 590. He ended ten years of anarchy caused by the ambitions of the Lombard dukes, consolidated Lombard power, and repelled three invasions by the Frankish king Childebert II.

Author, The. A comedy by Samuel Foote, produced and printed in 1757.

Authoress of the Odyssey, The. Prose work (1897) by Samuel Butler. Butler's reputation as an ironist led many to take this for a hoax, but he was convinced that the *Odyssey* had been written at Trapani in Sicily and by a woman.

Author's Farce, The. Play by Henry Fielding, originally produced in 1730 and revived in 1734. It contains humorous portraits of Colley Cibber and his son Theophilus, and burlesques the amusements of the town.

Autlán de Navarro (ou.tlän' dā nä.bär'rō). [Also, **Autlán.**] City in SW Mexico, in Jalisco state. 10,915 (1940).

Autobiography of Alice B. Toklas (tok'las). Narrative by Gertrude Stein, published in 1933. Ostensibly dealing with the life of the author's secretary, the book is actually an account of Miss Stein's own life and literary development. It was this book which brought Miss Stein to the attention of a wide popular audience.

Autobiography of an Ex-Colored Man, The. Novel (1912) by James Weldon Johnson.

Autocracy of Mr. Parham (pär'am), **The.** Novel (1930) by H. G. Wells. It is one in a series of his Utopian novels.

Autocrat of the Breakfast-table, The. A series of papers by Oliver Wendell Holmes, published serially (1857–58) in the first 12 numbers of the *Atlantic Monthly*, and collectively in 1858. The autocrat (Holmes himself) discourses on matters in general from his position at the head of a boarding-house breakfast-table. The collection of 1858 includes also such poems as *The Chambered Nautilus*, *The Living Temple*, *Contentment*, and *The*

Deacon's Masterpiece; or, The Wonderful "One-Hoss Shay."

Autolycus (ô.tol'i.kus). b. at Pitane, in Aeolis; fl. late 4th century B.C. Greek mathematician and astronomer. He was the author of two treatises still extant: one a work on the motion of points on a sphere (the oldest Greek mathematical work preserved as a whole) and the other a study of the apparent rising and setting of fixed stars. Autolycus was the first to try to explain certain difficulties involved in the theory of homocentric spheres in astronomy, notably the fact that the apparent differences in the relative sizes of the sun and moon, and in the brightness of the planets, suggest variations in their distances from the earth.

Autolycus. In Greek legend, a son of Hermes (or Daedalion) and Chione, and father of Anticleia, the mother of Odysseus. He was a famous thief, and possessed the power of making himself and the things that he stole invisible, or of giving them new forms.

Autolycus. In Shakespeare's *The Winter's Tale*, a witty thieving peddler, a "snapper up of unconsidered trifles." He indulges in grotesque self-raillery and droll soliloquizing on his own sins.

Automedon (ô.tom'ẹ.don). In Greek legend, the son of Diores, and, according to Homer, the comrade and charioteer of Achilles. In another account, he had an independent command of ten ships in the Trojan War. Vergil makes him the companion in arms of Pyrrhus, son of Achilles.

Autorianus (ô.tō.ri.ā'nus), **Arsenius.** See **Arsenius Autorianus.**

Autran (ō.trän), **Joseph Antonine.** b. at Marseilles, in June, 1813; d. there, March 6, 1877. French poet. He was the author of *La Fille d'Eschyle*, a tragic drama which gained him a seat in the French Academy; he also wrote *Poèmes de la mer* (1852), and others.

Autriche (ō.trēsh). French name of **Austria.**

Autricum (ô'tri.kum). An ancient name of **Chartres.**

Autronia gens (ô.trō'ni.ạ jenz). In ancient Rome, a clan or house whose only known family name is Paetus. The first member of this gens who obtained the consulate was P. Autronius Paetus, in 65 B.C.

Autry (ô'tri), **(Orvon) Gene.** b. at Tioga, Tex., Sept. 29, 1907—. American actor, noted as a singing cowboy in western films. He began his motion-picture career in 1934 after having been a singer on radio at Chicago from 1930 to 1934. Autry is also known as a composer of popular songs.

Autumn. Selections (1892) from Henry David Thoreau's notebooks. This collection was the last in a series of such selections published after Thoreau's death in 1862.

Autun (ō.tėn). [Latin, **Aedua, Augustodunum.**] City in the department of Saône-et-Loire, C France, situated on the Arroux River, NW of Le Creusot. Near the site of Bibracte, the capital of the ancient Aedui, it was among the most important Gallo-Roman cities and contains many Roman remains. The Porte d'Arroux and the Porte Saint-André are Roman gateways. The so-called Temple of Janus is a defensive outwork of the ancient fortifications. The Roman town was destroyed by Tetricus, but was rebuilt by Constantius Chlorus and Constantine. It was sacked by Germanic and Moslem invaders. The Cathedral of Saint-Lazare was started in the 12th century in early Romanesque style but shows mainly the characteristics of the Gothic style of the 15th century. Autun has chemical, metallurgical, and leather industries, among others, and is situated within the coal-mining region of d'Épinac-Autun. 14,438 (1946).

Autunois (ō.tü.nwȧ). Former division of Burgundy, France, corresponding in general to the modern department of Saône-et-Loire and part of Côte-d'Or.

Auvergne (ō.verny'). [Gallic, **Arverni.**] Region and medieval government of France. It was bounded by Bourbonnais on the N, Lyonnais on the E, Languedoc on the SE, Guienne on the SW, and Limousin and Marche on the W. It corresponded approximately to the modern departments of Puy-de-Dôme and Cantal, and part of Haute-Loire. It was a countship and then a duchy, and was finally united to the French crown in the 16th and 17th centuries. Capital, Clermont.

Auvergne, Countess of. Minor character in Shakespeare's *Henry VI, Part I.*

Auvergne (dō.verny'), **Henri de La Tour d'.** See **Turenne,** Vicomte de.

Auvergne Mountains (ō.verny'). Branch of the Cévennes, situated chiefly in the departments of Cantal and Puy-de-Dôme, France. They are volcanic in structure. The chief peaks are Puy-de-Sancy (6,185 ft.), Plomb du Cantal, and Puy-de-Dôme.

Auwers (ou'vėrs), **Arthur von.** b. at Göttingen, Germany, 1838; d. 1915. German astronomer. He served (1866 *et seq.*) as astronomer at the Imperial Academy of Sciences, Potsdam. Notable for his observations of the transits of Venus (1874, 1882), he also completed the nebular observations initiated by Sir J. F. W. Herschel and carried out research on the proper motion of fixed stars.

Aux Cayes (ō ke). See **Cayes.**

Auxentius (ôk.sen'shi.us). d. 374. Arian bishop of Milan (355–374). He was condemned by a synod held at Rome in 370 (or 369) for his continued opposition to Nicaean doctrine, but maintained his hold on the bishopric until his death.

Auxerre (ō.ser). [Latin, **Autesiodorum.**] Capital of the department of Yonne, C France, situated on the Yonne River, SW of Paris. It is noted for its wines and has various industries, particularly food manufactures. The Cathedral of Saint-Étienne (begun in 386, rebuilt in 1030 and again from 1215 to 1235, and completed in 1543) was erected in the Gothic style. The museum and other buildings were either damaged or destroyed during World War II. There are a number of educational institutions. 24,052 (1946).

Auxerrois (ō.se.rwȧ). Medieval countship of France, formerly part of the duchy of Burgundy. It was incorporated in France under Louis XI. Capital, Auxerre.

Auxois (ō.swȧ). Medieval countship in Burgundy, France, corresponding to the modern arrondissement of Avallon in the department of Yonne and the modern arrondissement of Sémur in the department of Côte-d'Or.

Auxonne (ō.son). Town in E France, in the department of Côte-d'Or, situated on the Saône River, ab. 20 mi. SE of Dijon: river port; manufactures plaster of Paris and textiles. The town was fortified by Vauban; it resisted the army of the Holy Roman Empire in 1526, surrendered to Austria in 1815 only two months after the abdication of Napoleon I, and resisted the Germans in 1870. There is a collegiate church dating from the 14th century. 5,164 (1946).

Auxonnois (ō.so.nwȧ). Former small district of France, whose capital was Auxonne.

Aux Plaines River (ō plānz). See **Des Plaines River.**

Aux Sources (ō sörs), **Mont.** See under **Drakensberg.**

Auzout (ō.zö), **Adrien.** d. 1691. French mathematician, astronomer, and maker of telescopes. He was the inventor of the filar micrometer.

Auzoux (ō.zö), **Théodore Louis.** b. at St.-Aubin-d'Escroville, France, 1797; d. at Paris, May 7, 1880. French physician, inventor of a method of making paste models for anatomical study.

Ava (ä'fä). [Called **Frau Ava.**] d. Feb. 7, 1127. Austrian hermit. She lived for part of her life as wife and mother, but withdrew to a life of seclusion and devoted her later years to the composition of three early poems in the German language on the life of Jesus, the Antichrist, and Judgment Day. She seems to have been the first woman author writing in German.

Ava (ä'vạ). Former capital of Burma, situated on the Irrawaddy River, ab. 12 mi. SW of the present city of Mandalay: now largely in ruins.

Avacha (ä.vä'chạ). [Also: **Avatcha, Gorelaya**; Russian, **Avachinskaya Sopka** (ä.vä'chin.skạ.yạ sôp'kạ).] Volcano in the NE U.S.S.R., in the Khabarovsk *krai* (subdivision) of the Russian Soviet Federated Socialist Republic, in the Kamchatka Mountains. Elevation, ab. 8,983 ft.

Avacha Bay. [Also, **Avatcha Bay**; Russian, **Avachinskaya Guba** (ä.vä'chin.skạ.yạ gö.bä').] Bay in the NE U.S.S.R., in the Khabarovsk *krai* (subdivision) of the Russian Soviet Federated Socialist Republic, on the E coast of Kamchatka. Petropavlovsk is situated on it.

Aval Islands (av'ạl). See **Bahrein.**

Avallenau (ä.väl'ẹ.nou), **The.** Welsh poem ascribed to the ancient Merlin. It is thought to have been written in the latter part of the reign of Owain Gwynedd, and to contain distinct historical allusion to affairs of the years 1165–70. The title means "of the apple trees."

Avallon (å.vå.lôn). [Latin, **Aballum.**] Town in C France, in the department of Yonne, picturesquely situated on the Cousin River, ab. 27 mi. SE of Auxerre: chemical and leather industries. It is the center of a wine-growing district, giving its name to a Burgundy wine. The Church of Saint-Lazare dates from the 12th century. 5,637 (1946).

Avalokiteshvara (äv″ä.lō.ki.tesh′vą.rą). One of the two Bodhisattvas, the other being Manjushri, who had become objects of worship among the followers of the Great Vehicle, the northern school of Buddhism, at least as early as 400 A.D. Avalokiteshvara is the personification of power, the merciful protector of the world and of men.

Avalon (av′ą.lon). Main settlement and resort center on Santa Catalina Island, off the coast of S California near Los Angeles, located on the SE tip of the island. 1,506 (1950).

Avalon. [Former name, **West Bellvue.**] Residential borough in SW Pennsylvania, in Allegheny County, near Pittsburgh. Settled in 1802, it was renamed in 1894. Pop. 6,463 (1950).

Avalon or **Avallon** (av′ą.lon). [Also: **Avelion, Avilion, Vale of Avalon.**] In Arthurian legend, the Land of the Blessed, or Isle of Souls, an earthly paradise in the western seas. The great heroes, such as Arthur and Ogier the Dane, are supposed to have been carried there at death, and the fairy Morgana or Morgan le Fay holds her court there.

Avalon Peninsula. Peninsula at the SE extremity of Newfoundland, on which St. John's is situated, connected with the rest of the island by a narrow isthmus. The U.S. was granted bases here during World War II.

Avalos (dä′vä.lōs), **Fernando Francesco d'.** See **Pescara,** Marquis of.

Avaré (ä.vą.re′). City in SE Brazil, in the state of São Paulo. 12,245 (1950).

Avare (lå.vår), **L'.** [Eng. trans., "*The Miser.*"] Comedy by Molière, produced in 1668. The plot was borrowed from the *Aulularia* of Plautus. Henry Fielding founded his *Miser* upon it. In this version, Cléante is in rivalry with his father, Harpagon, the miser of the title, for the hand of Marianne. Cléante wins her by stealing his father's money, and then giving Harpagon the choice between his wealth and the girl. Most critics consider Fielding's translation to be the best English version.

Avaricum (ą.var′i.kum). Latin name of **Bourges.**

Avars (ä′värz). [Latin, **Avari** (ą.vā′rī).] People allied to the Huns. They settled (c555 A.D.) in Dacia. They aided Justinian, and later assisted the Lombards against the Gepidae; occupied Pannonia and, later, Dalmatia, and invaded Germany, Italy, and the Balkan Peninsula. Their power was broken (c796) by Charlemagne, and they disappeared with the establishment of the Moravians and Magyars.

Avars. A people, probably allied to the Lesghians, who dwell in Dagestan, in the Caucasus, and speak a North Caucasian language.

Avarua (ä.vä.rö′ä). Administrative center of the Cook Islands, owned by New Zealand. It is situated on Rarotonga Island and is the chief port for the islands.

Avatcha (ä.vä′chą). See **Avacha.**

AVC. Abbreviation of **American Veterans Committee.**

Avdeyenko (äv.dyā′yin.kǫ), **Aleksandr Yevstigneyevich.** b. 1908—. Russian novelist. His reputation rests on a novel translated into English under the title *I Love* (1935), the story of a Magnitogorsk workman, who overflows with enthusiasm for the Soviet way of life.

Ave atque Vale (ā′vę at′kwę vā′lę). Poem (1867) by Algernon Charles Swinburne. It is a tribute to Baudelaire.

Avebury (āv′bėr.i, ā′bėr.i). [Also, **Abury.**] Civil parish and small village in S England, in Wiltshire, ab. 6 mi. W of Marlborough. It is noted for its megalithic antiquities. Nearby is the ancient burial mound called Silbury Hill. 561 (1931).

Ave Imperatrix (ā′vę im.pę.rā′triks). Poem by Rudyard Kipling included among his *Schoolboy Lyrics* (1881). It is significant in that it strikes for the first time the authentic Kipling note of service to the British Empire.

Aveiro (ą.vā′rö), Duke of. [Title of **José Mascarenhas.**] b. 1708; executed Jan. 13, 1759. Portuguese nobleman, condemned to death for his alleged participation in an attempted murder of the king of Portugal in 1758.

Aveiro. District in C Portugal, in the province of Beira Litoral. Capital, Aveiro; area, 1,070 sq. mi.; pop. 481,804 (1950).

Aveiro. Town and *concelho* (commune) in W Portugal, in the province of Beira Litoral, the capital of the district of Aveiro, situated at the mouth of the Vouga River on the lagoon of Aveiro, ab. 35 mi. S of Oporto. A canal connects the town with the ocean. Aveiro trades in agricultural products, produces sea salt, and exports sardines. It is the seat of a bishopric, and is known also for its Church of the Carmelites and the Monastery of Jesus, which includes the tomb of Santa Joana. Pop. of concelho, 35,303 (1940); of town, 11,247 (1940).

Avé-Lallemant (ä.vā′läl.män′), **Robert Christian Berthold.** [Also, **Avé-Lallement.**] b. at Lübeck, Germany, July 25, 1812; d. there, Oct. 10, 1884. German traveler in South America. He was a physician at Rio de Janeiro, and the author of books on his travels in Brazil.

Aveling (āv′ling), **Edward Bibbins.** b. at Stoke Newington, England, 1851; d. 1898. English socialist and scientist; son-in-law of Karl Marx.

Aveling, Francis Arthur Powell. b. at St. Catherine's, Ontario, Canada, 1875; d. at London, 1941. British psychologist. A professor of psychology at King's College, London, he was converted (1896) to Roman Catholicism and ordained (1899) as a priest. He was the author of numerous volumes pertaining to psychology and faith.

Avelion (ą.vēl′yǫn). See **Avalon.**

Avellaneda (ä.bā.yä.nā′ᴛʜä). City in E Argentina, in Buenos Aires province, within the industrial part of metropolitan Buenos Aires, but politically independent: meat-packing plants, stockyards, and textile mills. 278,621 (1947).

Avellaneda (ä.bā.lyä.nā′ᴛʜä), **Alonso Fernández de.** Name assumed by the writer of a spurious continuation (1614) of Miguel de Cervantes' *Don Quixote.* The work may have served as a stimulus for Cervantes' completion of his own promised second volume (1615). Its authorship, never decided, has been variously attributed to Blanco de Paz (an enemy of Cervantes), to Bartolomé Leonardo de Argensola (a friend), to the dramatists Lope de Vega, Ruiz de Alarcón, and Tirso de Molina, and various others. Ridicule of Cervantes' appearance, conduct, and writing in the preface called forth a reply in the last chapters of Cervantes' own work.

Avellaneda (ä.bā.yä.nā′ᴛʜä), **Nicolás.** b. at Tucumán, Argentina, c1837; d. Dec. 26, 1885. Argentine journalist and educator, president of Argentina (1874–80). He was a professor of political economy at Buenos Aires, and minister of education (1868–74) under Domingo F. Sarmiento, whom he succeeded as president. Under his administration Julio A. Roca, then minister of war, completed the conquest of the Argentine Araucanian Indians.

Avellaneda y Arteaga (ä.bā.lyä.nā′ᴛʜä ē är.tā.ä′gä), **Gertrudis Gómez de.** [Pseudonym, **La Peregrina.**] b. at Puerto Príncipe (now Camagüey), Cuba, March 23, 1814; d. at Madrid, Feb. 2, 1873. Spanish author. She arrived (1836) in Spain from Cuba. She is best known for her lyric verse and for such dramas as *Saúl* (1849) and *Baltasar* (1858). Her novels, which include *El Mulato Sab* (1839), *Dos Mujeres* (1842), and *Espatolino* (1844), are now largely unread, despite the possible sociological interest of the first one mentioned, which was a sort of Cuban *Uncle Tom's Cabin.*

Avellino (ä.vel.lē′nō). [Former name, **Principato Ulteriore.**] Province in the *compartimento* (region) of Campania, S Italy. Capital, Avellino; area, ab. 1,082 sq. mi.; pop. 451,466 (1936).

Avellino. [Latin, **Abellinum, Avellinum** (av.ę.lī′num).] City and commune in S Italy, in the *compartimento* (region) of Campania, the capital of the province of Avellino, ab. 29 mi. NE of Naples, near the site of an ancient town of the Hirpini. It is the seat of a bishopric, with a cathedral that dates from the 10th century. Its convent of Monte Vergine, founded in 1193, is a place of pilgrimage. Excellent wines are produced in the vicinity. A Samnite and Roman town in ancient times, Abellinum was destroyed in the wars of the Greeks and Lombards. There was a large emigration from here to the U.S. and South America in the 19th century. Some damage was suffered during World War II by some buildings of tourist interest, but repairs have now been completed or are being carried out. Pop. of commune, 29,955 (1936); of city, 20,578 (1936).

Avellino, Antonio di Pietro. See **Filarete.**

Ave Maria (ä'vā mä.rē'ä). [Also: the **"Angelical Salutation"**; English, **Hail Mary.**] Among Roman Catholics, the prayer most frequently addressed to the Virgin Mary. It is often known as the Hail Mary, from the meaning of the first two words in English. The words of the prayer as used today are, in English: "Hail, Mary, full of grace, the Lord is with Thee; blessed art thou among women, and blessed is the fruit of thy womb, Jesus. Holy Mary, Mother of God, pray for us sinners, now and at the hour of our death. Amen." The words up to and including "women" are the salutation of the angel Gabriel to Mary at the Annunciation, as given in Luke, i. 28 (Douay Version), with the name of Mary inserted; the next phrase is that spoken to Mary by Saint Elizabeth, according to Luke, i. 42, with the addition of the name Jesus. Beginning in the 6th century or earlier the prayer evolved through popular usage and the approval of various popes until its inclusion in its present form in the Roman Breviary, in 1568.

Avempace (ä.vem.pä'thā, ā'vẹm.pās). [Also: **Avenpace, Aben Pace.**] b. at Saragossa during late 11th century; d. at Fez, Morocco, 1138. Spanish-Arab philosopher, important for his influence on Averroës. His work, virtually none of which survives, developed a philosophy which rejected sectarianism in favor of intellectual union with a universal, all-embracing Mind. This thinking, in some ways close to Neoplatonism, led orthodox Moslems of his own day to term him a heretic, although it is not clear that he ever explicitly forsook Islam.

Avenal (av'ẹ.nạl). Unincorporated community in C California, in Kings County, NW of Los Angeles. 3,982 (1950).

Avenare (ä.ve.nä'rạ). See **ibn-Ezra, Abraham ben Meïr.**

Avenarius (ä.vā.nä'ri.ůs; Anglicized, av.ẹ̄.nãr'i.us), **Ferdinand.** b. at Berlin, Dec. 20, 1856; d. at Kampen, on the island of Sylt, in the North Sea, Sept. 22, 1923. German literary and art critic, and anthologist. After extensive travels he founded in 1887 *Der Kunstwart*, a critical journal of high standing. His own verse (*Wandern und Werden*, 1881; *Stimmen und Bilder*, 1898) now attracts little attention, but his anthologies, particularly *Hausbuch deutscher Lyrik* (1903), have become German classics. He founded (1903) the *Dürerbund* and did much to bring good reproductions of the best in art before the public. His *Faust* (1919) is an ethically interesting if somewhat unpoetical continuation of Goethe's *Faust, Part I.*

Avenarius, Richard. b. at Paris, Nov. 19, 1843; d. at Zurich, Aug. 18, 1896. German philosopher; brother of Ferdinand Avenarius and a nephew of Richard Wagner. He was professor (1877–96) at Zurich and a founder of the Akademischphilosophische Verein at Leipzig. Employing the principle of economy of thinking as a basis, he sought to relate pure experience with intellect and environment, producing the philosophy known as "Empiriocriticism." He was the author of *Philosophie als Denken der Welt gemäss dem Princip des Kleinsten Kraftmasses* (1876), *Kritik der reinen Erfahrung* (1888–90), and others.

Avenches (à.väṅsh). [German, **Wifflisburg**; Latin, **Aventicum** (ạ.ven'ti.kum).] Town in W Switzerland, in the canton of Vaud (German, Waadt), near the S end of the Lake of Morat, NW of Fribourg: a Roman town and the ancient capital of the Helvetii. There are remains of a Roman theater and other relics of antiquity, some of them in the museum of the archaeological society. 1,565 (1941).

Avenel (dȧv.nel), Vicomte **Georges d'.** b. at Neuilly, France, c1850; d. c1922. French writer, an expert on the ecclesiastical history of Paris. He was the author of *Les Évêques et Archevêques de Paris depuis Saint Denys jusqu'à nos jours* (1878).

Avenel (āv'nẹl), **Julian.** Usurper of Avenel Castle and the uncle of Mary Avenel in Sir Walter Scott's novel *The Monastery.*

Avenel, Mary. One of the principal characters in Sir Walter Scott's novel *The Monastery*, the wife of Halbert Glendinning. She reappears in *The Abbot.*

Avenio (ạ.vē'ni.ō). Latin name of **Avignon.**

Avenol (ȧv.nol), **Joseph Louis Anne.** b. Sept. 7, 1879; d. Sept. 2, 1952. French statesman; second secretary-general of the League of Nations. He held various financial posts in the French government from 1905 to 1919. He then served (1920–23) on the finance committee of the League, as deputy secretary-general (1923–32), and as secretary-general (1933–40).

Avenpace (ä.vem.pä'thā, ā'vẹn.pās). See **Avempace.**

Aventine Hill (av'ẹn.tīn). [Latin, **Mons Aventinus** (mons av.ẹn.tī'nus); Italian, **Monte Aventino** (môn'tā ä.ven.tē'nō).] Name of the southernmost of the seven hills of ancient Rome, rising on the left bank of the Tiber, S of the Palatine. Below it to the N lay the Circus Maximus, and to the E the thermae of Caracalla.

Aventinus (av.ẹn.tī'nus; German, ä.ven.tē'nůs). [Called the **"Bavarian Herodotus"**; original name, **Johannes Turmair** or **Thurmayr.**] b. at Abensberg, Bavaria, July 4, 1477; d. at Regensburg, Bavaria, Jan. 9, 1534. Bavarian historian. He is now best known for his *Annales Boiorum* (written 1517–21; published 1524), a history of Bavaria to 1460, which the author later translated into German. The work, which was prepared with painstaking care, is notable for the way in which it seemingly anticipates the modern scientific concept of writing history.

Avenzoar (av.ẹn.zō'ạr) or **Abumeron** (ạ.bö.mẹ.ron'). [Also: **ibn-Zohr** or **ibn-Zuhr.**] b. at Seville, c1090; d. 1162. Spanish-Arab physician and medical writer, thought to have been a teacher of Averroës. He was an admirer of Galen and an opponent of quackery in medicine, particularly of remedies based on astrology; his best known medical work, *Teisir*, was translated (1280) into Hebrew and later (1490) into Latin.

Averell (ā'vẹr.ẹl), **William Woods.** b. at Cameron, in Steuben County, N.Y., Nov. 5, 1832; d. at Bath, N.Y., Feb. 3, 1900. American inventor, a general with the Union army in the Civil War. His inventions include a process of making cast steel directly from ore, a variety of asphalt pavement, and a conduit insulation system for electric wiring.

Averescu (ä.ve.res'kö), **Alexandru.** b. in Bessarabia, 1859; d. at Bucharest, 1938. Rumanian politician and army officer. After serving (1877–78) against Turkey in the war for Rumanian independence, he commanded an army corps in the Balkan Wars (1912–13) and against the Central Powers in World War I. He was selected (1918) to conduct Rumania's peace negotiations. He was twice (1920–21, 1926–27) premier of Rumania. A member of the industrial clique which actually ruled Rumania during this period, Averescu led the diplomatic effort to achieve a rapprochement with Italy.

Averlino (ä.ver.lē'nō), **Antonio di Pietro.** See **Filarete.**

Averno (ä.ver'nō), **Lake.** [Italian, **Lago d'Averno** (lä'gō dä-); Latin, **Lacus Avernus** (lā'kus ạ.vėr'nus).] Small lake in Campania, Italy, ab. 9 mi. W of Naples, anciently believed to be the entrance to the infernal regions. Circumference, ab. 2 mi.; depth, ab. 200 ft.

Averreest (ä.vẹ.rāst'). [Also, **Avereest.**] Town in E Netherlands, in the province of Overijssel, ab. 13 mi. NE of Zwolle: hosiery and furniture manufactures; cement works. 10,229 (1939).

Averroës or **Averrhoës** (ạ.ver'ọ̄.ēz). [Arabic, **ibn-Roshd** or **ibn-Rushd.**] b. at Córdoba, Spain, 1126; d. at what is now Marrakech, Morocco, Dec. 10, 1198. Spanish-Arab philosopher and physician, most celebrated of the scholars produced by Spain's remarkable Moslem culture, notable particularly for his commentaries on Aristotle. He served as cadi (1169 *et seq.*), first of Seville and then of Córdoba; he was favored, for a time, by the Almohade caliph, al-Mansur, but fell victim to a growing distrust of speculative philosophy and was briefly confined (1195) near Córdoba for his allegedly dangerous lack of orthodoxy. In addition to treatises on astronomy, grammar, jurisprudence, and medicine, he produced the extensive commentaries on Aristotle upon which a great part of medieval Christian scholastic thought depended. In fact, Averroës's fame in history largely developed through use of his work by Christian (rather than Moslem) theologians, one group of whom became known as Averroists through their virtually complete acceptance of his metaphysics. Despite his studies of Aristotle, however, there is in his own epistemology an element of Neoplatonism, which makes some portions of his thought strikingly similar to certain aspects of Christianity. Although his fame as a philosopher has completely eclipsed his fame as a physician, we know (from his medical encyclopedia) that he had a knowledge of medicine which would have been, by itself, enough to assure any ordinary person of a secure place in the history of science. For example, he recognized that a person who has smallpox and recovers may be assured thereafter of immunity to the disease, and he also understood the function of the retina in the eye.

His Philosophy and Its Impact. His philosophical work, despite its almost incalculable value, was not at all as original as various distortions of it have led us to believe. It continued the tradition of Moslem scholasticism, and in a sense might be said to have represented the culmination of Moslem effort in one essential direction: the understanding of Aristotle's thought. For generations every Moslem philosopher had done his best to understand that thought, but most of them had failed because they mistook various Neoplatonic works for ones actually produced by the Peripatetic school. However, the latter had gradually reached the world of Moslem scholarship, and by the time of Averroës the genuine Aristotelian works were entirely available in Arabic. It was from these that he worked, and from within this framework that he sought a return to what one might call Aristotelian positivism, as much as this could be reconciled with Moslem theology. For example, he tried to reconcile the Aristotelian notion of the eternity of the world, which seems to imply a denial of creation, with Moslem creationism: God is eternal, and His creative effort is perpetual; He creates time (or duration) as well as the world, and He may have created it from all eternity, inasmuch as He is Himself without cause (note that it is easy to reconcile this notion with that of evolution, though in this case it is not so much the creature as the creating power that evolves, but the final result remains the same). Under the circumstances it is paradoxical indeed that he should have gained a reputation in the Moslem world for heterodoxy: he sought not to disturb the basis of Moslem theology but rather to give it added strength. Nevertheless, in the worlds of Christian and Jewish as well as Moslem theological thought, his works soon became a rallying point for what was considered by the orthodox in each of these groups to be dangerously heterodox thinking.

Aversa (ä.ver′sä). City and commune in S Italy, in the *compartimento* (region) of Campania, in the province of Napoli, ab. 9 mi. N of Naples, near the site of the ancient Atella. It is famous for its fruits and its sparkling white wine, known as Asprino. It was rebuilt by the Normans in 1038 as one of their first settlements in S Italy. The Church of San Paolo was founded in the 11th century. Damage was suffered during World War II by some buildings of tourist interest, but repairs have now been completed. Pop. of commune, 36,960 (1936); of city, 26,538 (1936).

Avershawe (av′ėr.shô), **Louis Jeremiah.** See **Abershaw, Louis Jeremiah.**

Averulino (ä″vä.rö.lē′nō), **Antonio di Pietro.** See **Filarete.**

Avery (ā′vėr.i), **Elroy McKendree.** b. at Erie, Mich., July 14, 1844; d. Dec. 1, 1935. American educator and historical writer. He served with the Union army during the Civil War. Author of numerous textbooks in chemistry and physics, as well as a 12-volume *History of the United States and Its People* (1913).

Aves (ä′vās). [Also, **Bird Islands.**] Group of small islands in the Caribbean Sea, belonging to Venezuela, E of Bonaire.

Avesnes (å.ven). [Also, **Avesnes-sur-Helpe** (-sür.elp).] Town in N France, in the department of Nord, situated on the Helpe River, ab. 26 mi. SE of Valenciennes: local trading center of a cheese-producing region. Its Church of Saint Nicholas dates from the 13th and 16th centuries. Avesnes grew up around a castle built in the 11th century. It changed hands several times during the 15th and 16th centuries, and was fortified by Vauban. From 1914 to 1918 it was occupied by the Germans. Hindenburg established his headquarters here on March 18, 1918. Pop. 5,247 (1946).

Avesta (ą.ves′tą). Bible of Zoroastrianism and the Parsis. The name comes from the Pahlavi *avistak*, which possibly means "knowledge." The name *Zendavesta* arose by mistake from inverting the Pahlavi phrase *Avistak va Zand*, "Avesta and Zend," or "the Law and Commentary," *Zend*, "knowledge, explanation," referring to the later version and commentary in Pahlavi.

Aveyron (å.vā.rôṅ). Department in S France, bounded by the department of Cantal on the N, the departments of Gard and Lozère on the E, the departments of Hérault and Tarn on the S, and the departments of Lot, Tarn-et-Garonne, and Tarn on the W. It was formed from the ancient Rouergue, which was a part of Aquitania in the early Middle Ages and of Guienne before 1789. The climate is mild in the SE but severe in the more mountainous NW. Thus the production of wine, fruits, and aromatic essences prevails in the SE, while the C and N parts of the department are given over to raising livestock, particularly cattle and sheep, to dairying, and to woolen and leather manufactures. Aveyron is also a center for the manufacture of gloves and of cheeses (the cheeses of Roquefort are world renowned, and it is an interesting fact that the huge caves in which cheeses of this type are matured were known as early as 1070). There are also stone quarries, coal mines, and a number of minor industries. Capital, Rodez; area, 3,385 sq. mi.; pop. 307,717 (1946).

Aveyron River. River in S France which joins the Tarn River ab. 9 mi. NW of Montauban. On it are Rodez and Villefranche. Length, ab. 150 mi.

Avezzano (ä.vāt.tsä′nō). Town and commune in C Italy, in the *compartimento* (region) of Abruzzi e Molise, in the province of L'Aquila, situated on the border of the Lago di Fucino (which is now nearly drained), ab. 53 mi. E of Rome. The town is the seat of a bishopric and has various old churches, but most of its buildings were badly damaged by an earthquake in 1915 and suffered more damage during World War II. Pop. of commune, 18,463 (1936); of town, 15,003 (1936).

Avgustov (äv.gös′tǫf). See **Augustów.**

Avianus (ā.vi.ā′nus) or **Avianius** (-ni.us), **Flavius.** fl. c4th century A.D. Roman writer of fables. He wrote 42 fables in elegiac meter, which were, as a collection, once much used as a schoolbook.

Avicenna (av.i.sen′ą). [Also: **ibn-Sina;** called the **"Prince of Physicians."**] b. near Bukhara, 980; d. at Hamadan, Persia, 1037. Arab philosopher and physician, considered by some scholars to have been the greatest produced by the culture of the eastern Arab world. He displayed (c997) his medical proficiency while still a youth, by curing a Persian ruler of a critical illness, and was thereafter variously physician and adviser to rulers at Khiva (c1004) and Hamadan (until 1037). He was the author of more than 100 works, of which his *Canon of Medicine* is unquestionably the most important. Still valued in some sections of the Orient as a medical reference, this work was widely translated in Europe during the Middle Ages (initially by Gerard of Cremona in the 12th century). His philosophy, which is largely covered by a modern translation into Latin under the title *Avicennae Metaphysices Compendium*, is rooted in Aristotelian thought, with a distinct element of Neoplatonism in its cosmology.

Avienus (ā.vi.ē′nus), **Rufus Festus.** fl. second half of the 4th century A.D. Roman poet and geographer. He was the author of *Descriptio orbis terrae* (based on the *Periegesis* of Dionysios Periegetes), *Ora maritima* (a description of the W and S coasts of Europe), *Aratea phenomena* (a translation of the *Phenomena* of Aratus of Soli), and others. In the fragment of *Ora maritima* that is still extant there may be found the only known account of a Carthaginian expedition along the W coast of Europe under Himilco in the 5th century B.C.

Avigliana (ä.vē.lyä′nä). Small town in the province of Torino, Italy, ab. 14 mi. W of Turin. Its elaborate 15th-century houses, and other buildings of interest to tourists, were undamaged in World War II.

Avigliano (ä.vē.lyä′nō). Town and commune in S Italy, in the *compartimento* (region) of Basilicata, in the province of Potenza, situated on the Bianco River NW of Potenza. Trading center of a cattle, goat, and sheep raising district, it also has woolen manufactures and stone quarries. Pop. of commune, 13,006 (1936); of town, 4,485 (1936).

Avignon (à.vē.nyôṅ). [Latin, **Avenio;** Italian, **Avignone** (ä.vē.nyō'nā).] City in SE France, the capital of the department of Vaucluse, situated on the E bank of the Rhone River, at the influx of the Durance River, NW of Marseilles. The old city is located on a steep rock above the river and entirely surrounded by ramparts. The papal palace, dating mainly from the 14th century and built like a fortress, with battlemented towers and walls, is now a museum. The Cathedral of Notre-Dame-des-Doms was built in the early Christian era and was reconstructed in the 12th century. There are other historical monuments, churches and palaces, an art museum, and a natural history museum. Avignon is the seat of an archbishopric. The new city is a commercial center and has various food industries, producing flour, sugar, olive oil, canned olives and fruits, and candies; silk and leather are also manufactured. The ancient Avenio was a town of the Cavares, in Gallia Narbonensis. In the early Middle Ages Avignon was of Albigensian sympathies; it attained world distinction in the 13th and 14th centuries, when the Roman popes, insecure in the Vatican, fled to France and made Avignon and the Comtat Venaissin a papal territory. Pope John XXII, a former bishop of Avignon, took permanent residence there in 1316. Later popes returned to Rome but the city remained under papal administration until 1791. It was the scene of bloody encounters during the French Revolution. Parts of the new city were damaged in World War II. 60,053 (1946).

Avignon (dà.vē.nyôṅ), **Comtat d'.** See **Comtat Venaissin.**

Ávila (ä'ʙē.lä). Province in C Spain, bounded by Valladolid on the N, Segovia and Madrid on the E, Toledo on the S, Cáceres on the SW, and Salamanca on the W. It is a part of old Castile. The surface is hilly or mountainous and the climate continental. Merino sheep are raised. Capital, Ávila; area, 3,107 sq. mi.; pop. 254,505 (1950).

Ávila. [Also: **Ávila de los Caballeros** (dā lōs kä.ʙä.lyā'rōs); ancient names, **Abela, Abyla, Ovila.**] City in C Spain, the capital of the province of Ávila, situated on the Adaja River, ab. 58 mi. NW of Madrid: center of a sheep-raising and wheat-growing district; seat of a bishopric. The city is medieval in appearance, and its walls, gates, and battlemented towers are in an excellent state of repair. The cathedral is in the Gothic style. Other old churches are San Vicente, Santo Tomas, San Pedro, and San Segundo. The Convent and Church of Santa Teresa, which date from the 16th century, are said to occupy the site of the house where the saint was born. In the Spanish Civil War, Ávila was occupied early in 1936 by the nationalist forces. 20,261 (1940).

Ávila, Alonzo de. [Often written **Alonzo Dávila.**] b. c1485; d. after 1537. Spanish soldier and adventurer in America. He went to America, where his name first appears as commander of a vessel in the Spanish expedition of 1518 to the Mexican coast. In 1519 he joined Cortés, was one of his most trusted captains, marched with him to Mexico and against **Pánfilo de Narváez,** and in 1521 was his agent to the Audience of Santo Domingo, on the island of Hispaniola, where he obtained important concessions. In June, 1522, he was sent to Spain with treasure and dispatches; near the Azores his ships were captured by French corsairs, and the treasure was lost. Ávila managed to have his dispatches sent to Spain, but was himself kept a prisoner for several years. Finally ransomed, he returned to Spain, was appointed *contador* of Yucatán, and set out for that region as second in command of the Spanish expedition of 1527. Arrived there, he was appointed to lead an expedition to a region on the west coast, in search of gold. He provoked conflicts with the Indians, was unable to return, and, after terrible sufferings, made his way to Trujillo in Honduras. In 1537 he was engaged in another unsuccessful expedition to Yucatán.

Ávila, Juan de. [Called the **"Apostle of Andalusia."**] b. at Almodóvar del Campo, Spain, c1500; d. May 10, 1569. Spanish preacher who won a tremendous following during a 40-year mission in Andalusia, in Spain. He was the author of *Epistolario espiritual* (1578), and others.

Ávila, Pedro Arias de. See **Pedrarias.**

Ávila Camacho (kä.mä'chō), **Manuel.** b. at Tezuitlán, Puebla, Mexico, 1897—. Mexican politician, army officer, and president (1940–46). He served in the revolution (1914 *et seq.*) and attained the rank of general. He later held a series of government offices during the 1930's, becoming finally minister of national defense under Lázaro Cárdenas. Nominated for president by Cárdenas in opposition to General J. A. Almazán, he was seated after an election (July 7, 1940) which was protested by his opponents. His administration was conservative and pro-U.S.

Ávila y Zúñiga (ē thö'nyē.gä), **Luis de.** b. at Placencia, Spain, c1500; d. c1564. Spanish historian. He wrote *Comentarios de la guerra de Alemaña, hecha por Carlos V, 1546–47* (1547).

Avilés (ä.ʙē.läs'). City in NW Spain, in the province of Oviedo, situated on the Bay of Avilés, an inlet of the Bay of Biscay, ab. 14 mi. N of Oviedo. It has a port from which coal from the Oviedo mines is exported, and is also the home port of a large fishing fleet. Iron, copper, and coal mines are in the vicinity. 18,037 (1940).

Avilés, Pedro Menéndez de. See **Menéndez de Avilés, Pedro.**

Avilés y del Fierro (ē del fyer'rō), **Gabriel.** [Title, Marquis of **Avilés.**] b. c1745; d. at Valparaíso, Chile, 1810. Spanish soldier and administrator. He was a colonel and later a general in the Spanish army in Peru, and took part in suppressing the Indian rebellion (1780–81) of Tupac Amaru (who was known in Spanish, after 1771, as José Gabriel Condorcanqui, and was the last known direct descendant of the pre-Spanish Inca rulers of Peru). He was one of the judges who condemned the rebels after their defeat to torture and death. He was successively president of Chile (1795–99), viceroy of Buenos Aires (1799–1801), and viceroy of Peru (1801–06), attaining the military grade of lieutenant general. He died while on his way from Peru to Spain.

Avilion (ạ.vil'yọn). See **Avalon.**

Avion (à.vyôṅ). Town in N France, in the department of Pas-de-Calais, ab. 9 mi. NE of Arras: coal mining. It was the scene (1917) of bitter fighting in World War I. 16,080 (1946).

Avis (ạ.vēsh'). See **Aviz.**

Avisa (ạ.vī'sạ), **Willobies.** Volume of short poems by an English writer named Henry Willobie (or Willoughby). It was first printed in 1594, and prefixed to the second edition in 1596 are some verses which allude to Shakespeare's *Rape of Lucrece.* The poems exemplify the character of a chaste woman resisting all the temptations to which her life exposes her. This is the earliest known work to make printed mention of Shakespeare's name.

Avison (av'i.sọn), **Charles.** b. at Newcastle, England, c1710; d. there, May 9, 1770. English musical theorist, composer, critic, and organist. He is best known for his *Essay on Musical Expression* (1752), which clashed with the general opinion of his time by placing some German music, particularly that of Handel, below certain French and Italian compositions which were later considered by critics to be, in some respects, superior to much of Handel's work.

Avitus (ạ.vī'tus), Saint. [Full name, **Sextus Alcimus Ecdicius** (or **Ecdidius**) **Avitus.**] d. c518–523. Bishop (490 *et seq.*) of Vienne in Gaul, of the Roman family of the emperor Avitus, possibly his grandson or nephew, notable as a contender for orthodoxy against Arianism, from which he converted King Sigismund of Burgundy (516–523). He was the author of a long poem (five books) on the Bible, of letters, homilies, and other works.

Avitus, Marcus Maecilius. d. at what is now Auvergne, France, 456 A.D. Emperor of the Roman Empire in the West, 455–456. As master of the armies in Gaul he distinguished himself against the Huns and Vandals. He obtained the throne on Aug. 15, 455, by the aid of Theodoric II, king of the Visigoths (or West Goths), but was deposed after a reign of only 14 months by the Suevic-born Roman general Ricimer.

Aviz (ạ.vēsh'). [Also, **Avis.**] Small town and *concelho* (commune) in E central Portugal, in the province of Alto Alentejo, in Portalegre district, situated on a tributary of the Zatas River, ab. 75 mi. NE of Lisbon. Pop. of concelho, 8,799 (1940); of town, 1,424 (1940).

Avoca (ạ.vō'kạ) or **Ovoca** (ọ-). River and valley in the E part of the Irish Republic, in County Wicklow, ab. 43 mi. S of Dublin, formed by the union of the small rivers Avonmore and Avonbeg. The Avoca flows SW to the Irish Sea at Arklow. Thomas Moore celebrated the "Sweet Vale of Avoca" in his song *The Meeting of the Waters.*

Avoca. [Former name, **Pleasant Valley.**] Borough in E Pennsylvania, in Luzerne County, in an anthracite coal mining area. 4,040 (1950).

Avogadro (ä.vō.gä′drō), **Albert.** See **Albert Avogadro.**

Avogadro, Amedeo. [Title, Conte **di Quaregna.**] b. at Turin, Italy, Aug. 9, 1776; d. there, July 9, 1856. Italian chemist and physicist, professor (1820 *et seq.*) at Turin. He was the first to hypothesize (1811) what has since become known as "Avogadro's law": that equal volumes of gas at equal temperature contain equal numbers of molecules.

Avola (ä′vō.lä). Town and commune in SW Italy, in the *compartimento* (region) of Sicily, in the province of Siracusa, situated near the Gulf of Noto on the E coast of Sicily, ab. 12 mi. SW of Syracuse. It is a seaport for local produce, including citrus fruits, wine, almonds, and sugar cane; it also has a sugar refinery. Pop. of commune, 21,883 (1936); of town, 21,462 (1936).

Avon (av′ǫn). Village and town (in New York the equivalent of township in many other states) in W New York, in Livingston County, in a horse-breeding region. It is a dairying and canning center and was formerly noted as a health resort. Pop of village, 2,412 (1950); of town, 3,725 (1950).

Avon (ā′von). Village in N Ohio, in Lorain County, near the S shore of Lake Erie, ab. 15 mi. W of Cleveland. 2,773 (1950).

Avondale (av′ǫn.dāl). Town in S central Arizona, in Maricopa County, on the Agua Fria River ab. 15 mi. W of Phoenix. 2,505 (1950).

Avondale, Earl of. A title of **Douglas, James** (c1371–1443).

Avon Lake (ā′von). Village in N Ohio, in Lorain County, on the S shore of Lake Erie ab. 17 mi. W of Cleveland: resort and residential community. 4,342 (1950).

Avonmouth (ā′vǫn.mouth). Ecclesiastical district, seaport, and manufacturing town in W England, in Gloucestershire, situated at the mouth of the river Avon, ab. 6 mi. NW of Bristol, ab. 121 mi. W of London by rail. It is part of the port of Bristol and handles imports from the West Indies and Central America, especially bananas and other tropical fruits. The tidal change is exceptionally large, being ab. 45 ft.; large vessels are compelled to wait for high tide before leaving the dock. Avonmouth also has a zinc-refining industry and large oil refineries.

Avon Park (ā′von). City in C Florida, in Highlands County, SE of Tampa: important for the production of oranges and avocados. 4,612 (1950).

Avon River (ā′vǫn, av′ǫn). [Also, **Upper Avon.**] River in C and W England, rising near Naseby, Northamptonshire, forming part of the boundary between Northamptonshire and Leicestershire, and flowing through Warwickshire, Worcestershire, and Gloucestershire to a confluence with the Severn River at Tewkesbury. It passes Rugby, Warwick, Stratford, and Evesham. Its chief tributaries are the Alne, Leame, Stour, Sow, and Swift. Length, ab. 100 mi.

Avon River. [Also, **East Avon.**] River in S and W England, in Wiltshire and Hampshire. It rises near Devizes, and flows past Salisbury into the English Channel at Christchurch. Length, ab. 65 mi.; navigable to Salisbury.

Avon River. [Also: **Lower Avon, Bristol Avon.**] River in W and SW England, in Wiltshire and Somersetshire, and on the boundary between Somersetshire and Gloucestershire, flowing into Bristol Channel ab. 7 mi. NW of Bristol, at Avonmouth. On it are Bath and Bristol. Length, ab. 80 mi.; navigable for large vessels to Bristol, for small vessels to Bath.

Avowals and Denials. Prose work by G. K. Chesterton published during the decade 1925–35.

Avranches (ȧ.vräṅsh). [Ancient names, **Ingena, Abricatae, Abrincatae.**] Town in NW France, in the department of Manche, situated near the English Channel, ab. 30 mi. E of St.-Malo in a location dominating the Bay of St.-Michel. It has fisheries and small industries, and is a commercial center for the surrounding district. In the Middle Ages it was repeatedly occupied by the British. The revolt of the Nu-Pieds broke out here in 1639. The town was largely destroyed (1944) in the course of the Normandy invasion by the Allies during World War II. 7,554 (1946).

Avranchin (ȧ.vräṅ.shaṅ). Medieval division of Normandy, France, forming part of the modern department of Manche.

Awaji (ä.wä.jē). [Also, **Awadsi.**] Island of Japan, lying between Honshu and Shikoku islands. Length, ab. 30 mi.; width, ab. 5 mi.; area, 229 sq. mi.; pop. ab. 186,000.

Awake and Sing. Play by Clifford Odets, produced and published in 1935.

Awata (ä.wä.tä). Village in Japan, near Kyoto. It is noted for its pottery, a yellow faïence, first made in the 7th century.

Awdelay or **Awdeley** (ôd′lā), **John.** [Also called **Sampson Awdelay** and **John Sampson.**] fl. 1559–77. English printer and writer. He is best known for his *Fraternitye of Vacabondes* (1565), a detailed account of beggars and their organizations in the 16th century.

Awdrey (ô′dri). See **Audrey** or **Awdrey.**

Awe (ô), **Loch.** Lake in C Scotland, in Argyllshire, ab. 8 mi. W of Inveraray. Ben Cruachan is at its N end. The lake drains into Loch Etive by the river Awe, which flows through the Pass of Brander. Length, ab. 24 mi.; width, ab. 1 mi.

Awemba (ä.wem′bä). See **Bemba.**

Awkward Age, The. Novel by Henry James, published in 1899.

Awori (ä.wô′rē). [Also, **Aworri.**] Subgroup of the Sudanic-speaking Yoruba of W Africa, inhabiting SW Nigeria, NW of Lagos. Their population is estimated at ab. 90,000 (by P. A. Talbot, *The Peoples of Southern Nigeria*, 1926).

Awo-Sima (ä.wō.shē.mä). See **O Shima.**

Awowin (ä.wō′win). See **Aowin.**

Awuna (ä.wö′nä). [Also, **Atyoulo.**] One of the Sudanic-speaking Gurunsi peoples of W Africa, inhabiting the Northern Territories of the Gold Coast. They practice hoe agriculture, and their principal food is millet. They are non-Mohammedan.

Ax (äks). See also **Dax.**

Ax. [Also: **Acqs, Ax-les-Thermes;** Latin, **Aquae.**] Town in SW France, in the department of Ariège, situated on the Ariège River, at the foot of the Pyrenees, ab. 21 mi. SE of Foix and near the border of Spain and Andorra. It is a tourist center and a health resort; the baths of Ax were known in antiquity and in the Middle Ages, and are still considered useful in the treatment of arthritis, skin ailments, and other diseases. In 1260, Louis IX of France (Saint Louis) had a hospital constructed here for his soldiers. 1,501 (1946).

Axar Fjord (äċh′sär). [Also, **Aksar.**] Bay in NE Iceland, an inlet of the Arctic Ocean, ab. 200 mi. NE of Reykjavík.

Axayacatl (ä.shä.yä′kä.tl) or **Axayacatzin** (ä″shä.yä.kä′tsin). [Eng. trans., *"Face-in-the-Water."*] d. 1477. Aztec war-chief and emperor (1464–77) in Mexico; according to some accounts, the father of Montezuma II, whom Hernán Cortés conquered. His military expeditions considerably expanded the Aztec empire (or confederation), which lasted until the Spanish conquest.

Axel (äk′sel). See **Absalon.**

Axel Heiberg Island (ak′sel hī′bėrg). Island in the Arctic Ocean W of Ellesmere Island, under Canadian control, part of the Arctic Archipelago. Area, 13,248 sq. mi.

Axenfeld (äk′sen.felt), **Karl Theodor Paul Polykarpos.** b. at Smyrna, Turkey, June 24, 1867; d. at Freiburg, Germany, July 29, 1930. German ophthalmologist. He served (1901–30) as a professor at the University of Freiburg. He isolated (simultaneously with V. Morax) the hemophilus duplex, the so-called Morax-Axenfeld bacillus, which causes chronic conjunctivitis (known as Morax-Axenfeld conjunctivitis), and gave a classic account of metastatic ophthalmia.

Axhausen (äks′hou.zen), **Georg.** b. at Landsberg an der Warthe (now Gorzów, Poland), March 24, 1877—. German surgeon. He served as a military surgeon, worked (1904–24) at the surgical clinic at Kiel, and at the anatomical institute of Friedrichshain Hospital and the surgical clinic of the Charité Hospital, both at Berlin. He became (1908) privatdocent of surgery at the University of Berlin, was named professor in 1912, and became (1924) director of the surgical department of the dental school of the University of Berlin. He is known for his methods of transposition of the nipple, of bone transplantations, and the theory that carcinoma cells secrete a substance which stimulates osteogenesis.

Axholme (aks'ōlm), **Isle of.** [Also: **Isle of Axholm, Axholme** (or **Axholm**) **Isle.**] Lowland area, formerly marshy but now drained, in C England, in NW Lincolnshire, in the Parts of Lindsey. The "island" is formed by the rivers Trent, Don, Torne, and Idle. Its marshes were reclaimed by Flemish settlers in the 17th century. Length, ab. 18 mi.; width, ab. 5 mi.

Axim (äk'sim). Port in Gold Coast colony, W Africa, situated at the mouth of the Ankobra River, ab. 15 mi. W of Cape Three Points. Pop. ab. 5,000.

Axis. [Full name, **Rome-Berlin-Tokyo Axis.**] Term used to describe the coalition of Germany and Italy, and later Japan, which was opposed by the Allies in World War II. The term was first given formal status by the German-Italian pact of Oct. 25, 1936, which was nominally a simple treaty of coöperation, but which provided over a period of time a basis for the close "community of interests and policies" which was to mark the foreign policies of the two countries until 1943. The Anti-Comintern Pact between Germany and Japan, signed in November, 1936, was in many respects the second step toward the full three-way form finally assumed by the Axis, although Japan remained technically outside of the Axis until the outbreak of war with the U.S. In the meantime, however, the Rome-Berlin relationship was further strengthened by the "pact of steel" signed in May, 1939, and the three powers together concluded a treaty (Sept. 27, 1940) that asserted a joint interest in achieving a "new world order."

Axius (ak'si.us). Latin name of the **Vardar.**

Ax-les-Thermes (åks.lā.term). See **Ax.**

Axminster (aks'min.stėr). Urban district and market town in SW England, in Devonshire, situated on the river Axe, ab. 24 mi. E of Exeter, ab. 145 mi. SW of London by rail: famous formerly for its carpet manufactures. 2,673 (1951).

Axona (ak'sō.na). Ancient name of the **Aisne River.**

Axum (äk.söm'). See **Aksum.**

Axumite Kingdom (aks'ū.mīt). See ancient **Ethiopia.**

Ay (å.ē). Town in NE France, in the department of Marne, situated on the Marne River, ab. 18 mi. NW of Châlons-sur-Marne. It is noted for its wines of the champagne type. The town was damaged during World War II. 6,272 (1946).

Ayacucho (ä.yä.kö'chō). Small plain in the valley of the Venda-Mayu streamlet, near the village of Quinua, about midway between Lima and Cusco, S Peru. It was the scene of an important battle in the history of South America, in which a veteran force of 9,000 Spaniards, under the viceroy José de la Serna, was defeated by 5,780 patriots under General Antonio José de Sucre, on Dec. 9, 1824. The battle lasted about an hour; the viceroy himself was taken prisoner, his army was completely routed and forced to capitulate, and the independence of Spanish South America was finally secured.

Ayacucho. Department in SW Peru. Capital, Ayacucho; area, 18,190 sq. mi.; pop. 485,897 (est. 1950).

Ayacucho. [Former name, **Guamanga, Huamanga.**] City in S Peru, capital of Ayacucho department, in a valley 7,900 ft. above the sea. The city is the seat of a bishopric and has a university. It was founded by Francisco Pizarro in 1539; the name was changed in honor of the battle on the plain of Ayacucho. 22,389 (est. 1950).

Ayala (ä.yä'lä), **Juan Manuel de.** fl. 1775. Spanish naval commander. Sent by the viceroy of New Spain, Antonio Maria Bucareli, he was the first to explore (August–September, 1775) San Francisco Bay and its environs, reporting it to be the best port seen by him north of Cape Horn.

Ayala, Ramón Pérez de. See **Pérez de Ayala, Ramón.**

Ayala y Herrera (ē er.rā'rä), **Adelardo López de.** b. at Guadalcanal, Spain, 1828; d. 1879. Spanish dramatist and politician. His first play, *Un hombre de estado* (performed in 1851), was followed by *Castigo y perdon, Lo Dos Guzmanes,* and *Rioja* (1854). At first a political conservative, he later joined the progressives, for the expression of which sympathies his play *El Conde de Castralla* was suppressed (1856) by the government; in 1857 he was elected a liberal deputy. He later (1871) reverted to conservatism and was appointed a cabinet minister under Alfonso XII, under whom he also served as president of the Cortes. He was the author also of *El Tanto por ciento* (1861), *El Tejado de vidrio, El Nuevo Don Juan* (1863), *Consuelo* (performed in 1878), and others.

Ayamonte (ä.yä.mōn'tā). Town in S Spain, in the province of Huelva, situated on the left bank of the Guadiana River near its mouth, ab. 25 mi. W of Huelva: seaport, with shipyards and fisheries; exports olive oil and canned fish. Across the river is the Portuguese town of Vila Real de Santo António. The nearby Isla Cristina was settled by Catalan fishermen. 12,136 (1940).

Ayasaluk or **Ayasalouk** (ä"yä.sä.lök'). [Also, **Aya Soluk.**] Village in SW Turkey, in the valley of the Caÿster River, on what is approximately the site of the ancient Ephesus, Asia Minor.

Aycock (ā'kok), **Charles Brantley.** b. in Wayne County, N.C., Nov. 1, 1859; d. April 4, 1912. American politician and advocate of public-school reform. He was elected (1900) governor of North Carolina by the largest majority received up to that time by any candidate for that office. He is best known, however, for his educational reforms, which culminated in the establishment (1907) of a system of rural high schools. His campaign platform included a policy of white supremacy, Aycock urging that Negro members of the community should be prepared by education for proper use of the ballot.

Aydelotte (ā'de.lot), **Frank.** b. at Sullivan, Ind., Oct. 16, 1880—. American educator and author. Holding degrees from Indiana University (1900) and Harvard (1903), and with a background as a Rhodes scholar (1905–07) at Oxford, he was a professor of English (1915–21) at the Massachusetts Institute of Technology, American secretary (1918 *et seq.*) to the Rhodes Trustees, president (1921–40) of Swarthmore College, and director (1939–47) of the Institute of Advanced Study at Princeton, N.J. Author of *Elizabethan Rogues and Vagabonds* (1913), *The Oxford Stamp* (1917), *English and Engineering* (1917), *Breaking the Academic Lock-Step* (1944), *The Vision of Cecil Rhodes* (1946), and other works.

Aydin (ī.din'). [Also, **Aïdin.**] *Il* (province or vilayet) in SW Turkey, lying on both sides of the Menderes River. It consists of rolling plain close to the sea and a hilly hinterland. The farming population raises olives, grapes, figs, cotton, cattle, and sheep. Capital, Aydin; area, 2,926 sq. mi.; pop. 337,977 (1950).

Aydin. [Also: **Aïdin**; ancient name, **Tralles.**] Town in SW Turkey, capital of the *il* (province or vilayet) of Aydin, situated near the Menderes River, ab. 55 mi. SE of Smyrna (Izmir), near the ruins of ancient Tralles: trade in figs, cotton, olives, olive oil, emery, and grapes. Pop. ab. 15,000.

Ayenbite of Inwyt (ä.yen'bīt; in'wit"), **The.** Translation into the Kentish dialect in 1340, by Dan Michel of Northgate, Kent, a brother of the Cloister of Saint Austin at Canterbury, from the French of Frère Lorens (called in Latin *Laurentius Gallus*), of a treatise composed by the latter in 1279 for the use of Philip III of France, called *Le Somme des Vices et des Vertus.* Geoffrey Chaucer's *Parson's Tale* is considered to have been partly taken from the French treatise; it is also believed that he was familiar with Dan Michel's version. The title means "the againbiting of the inner wit," or "the remorse of conscience."

Ayer (ãr). Town (in Massachusetts the equivalent of township in many other states) and unincorporated village in NE Massachusetts, in Middlesex County. Near it is Fort Devens, a major training center of the U.S. army. Pop. of town, 5,740 (1950); of village, 3,107 (1950).

Ayer, Edward Everett. b. at Kenosha, Wis., Nov. 16, 1841; d. at Pasadena, Calif., May 3, 1927. American lumberman, bibliophile, and Union soldier in the Civil War. After service (1861–64) with the 1st California Cavalry, he returned to Illinois where he became chief supplier of ties, telegraph poles, and other lumber to western railroads. He became interested in history (particularly of the western U.S. and Pacific) after reading William Hickling Prescott's *Conquest of Mexico,* and subsequently built up a 17,000-volume collection on the subject which is now in Chicago's Newberry Library. He was also a founder and the first president (1893–98) of the Field Museum of Natural History at Chicago.

Ayer, Francis Wayland. b. at Lee, Mass., Feb. 4, 1848; d. March 5, 1923. American advertising executive and one-time schoolteacher. He entered the advertising business in 1869 under the firm name of N. W. Ayer and Son, and was one of the chief contributors to the growth of the American advertising business during the next 54 years.

Ayesha (ä'yẹ.shä). [Also: **Aisha, Ayeshah;** called (by Mohammedans) **Ummu al-Muminin,** meaning "Mother of the Believers."] b. at Medina, Arabia, c611; d. c678. Daughter of Abu-Bakr, first Moslem caliph; child-wife and favorite of Mohammed. She opposed Ali, Mohammed's cousin and the husband of his daughter Fatima, in his dispute with Abu-Bakr over the caliphate. When Ali took office after the death of Othman (656), she raised an army against him, but was defeated and taken prisoner by him at the "Battle of the Camel."

Ayia (ä.yä'). See **Agias.**

Ayion Oros (ä'yôn ô'rôs). See **Agion Oros.**

Aylesbury (ālz'ber"i, -bėr.i). Municipal borough and market town in S England, the county seat of Buckinghamshire, ab. 38 mi. NW of London by rail. Many people who work in London live here. Aylesbury has one of the most important markets (held twice weekly) in the Home Counties. It is noted for its poultry (particularly its ducks) and dairy products. 21,054 (1951).

Aylesford (ālz'fọrd). Civil parish and village in SE England, in Kent, situated on the river Medway, ab. 4 mi. NW of Maidstone, ab. 39 mi. SE of London by rail. Sands for glass making are quarried here. It is the birthplace of Charles Sedley. There are British antiquities in the neighborhood. Here the Jutes under Horsa defeated the Britons in 455 A.D. 3,644 (1931).

Aylesford, 1st Earl of. A title of **Finch, Heneage** (c1647–1719).

Aylesworth (ālz'wėrth), Sir **Allen Bristol.** b. at Newburgh, Ontario, Nov. 27, 1854; d. at Toronto, Feb. 13, 1952. Canadian lawyer. A graduate (1874) of Toronto University, he was called to the bar in 1878. He was a member of the Alaska Boundary Tribunal of 1903, and an agent (1910) for Great Britain at The Hague in the international litigation over the North Atlantic fisheries. A member (1905–11) of the Canadian House of Commons, he served as postmaster general and minister of labor (1905), and as minister of justice (1906–11).

Ayllón or **Aillón** (ī.lyōn'), **Lucas Vásquez de.** b. c1475 d. probably in what is now South Carolina, 1526. Spanish adventurer and explorer. After arrival (1502) in Santo Domingo from Spain, he became interested (c1520) in the possibilities of colonizing the area between what is now Virginia and Florida. He sailed (1526) with approximately 500 colonists to settle land on this coast, establishing a colony which was probably in what is now South Carolina, although thought by some to have been near Jamestown, Va. The effort collapsed with the onset of an epidemic fever, of which Ayllón himself was a victim. The expedition was notable for including what some authorities believe to have been the first instance of shipbuilding in North America (which Ayllón undertook when one of his vessels was wrecked) and also for the first importation into North America of African slaves.

Aylmer (āl'mėr), **John.** b. at Tivetshall St. Mary, Norfolk, England, 1521; d. at Fulham (now part of London), June 3, 1594. English prelate, bishop of London (1576–94) under Queen Elizabeth. He served as chaplain to Henry Grey, the duke of Suffolk, and tutor (1541) to his daughter Lady Jane Grey. Deprived of an archdeaconship for his opposition to Mary's restoration of the Roman Catholic Mass, he fled to Switzerland, where he remained during her reign (1553–58) and where he collaborated on John Foxe's translation of the *Acts of the Martyrs.* A relentless opponent of Roman Catholicism and Puritanism alike, he was bitterly attacked in the Martin Marprelate tracts (1588) and is supposed to be "Morrell' ("the proude and ambitious pastour") of Edmund Spenser's *Shepheard's Calendar.*

Aylmer, Lake. Lake in the Mackenzie District of the Northwest Territories, Canada, NE of Great Slave Lake. Elevation, 1,230 ft.; area, 340 sq. mi.

Aylmer, Matthew. [Title, Baron **Aylmer of Balrath.**] d. 1720. British naval officer.

Aylwin (āl'win). Romance (1898) by Walter Theodore Watts-Dutton. It caused a momentary sensation because of the recognizable portraits of Rossetti and other celebrities it contained.

Aymará (ī.mä.rä'). Group of linguistically allied but politically independent Indian tribes of the Titicaca basin and the regions around Lake Poopo in the highlands of Peru and Bolivia. The Aymará language comprises an independent linguistic family. The most powerful of these tribes were the Colla and the Lupaca, the latter of which allied itself with the Incas when the Aymará were conquered in the 15th century. The coming of the Spanish in force into Aymará territory in 1535 was followed by a renewal of the rivalry between the Colla and the Lupaca, the former this time aiding the invaders. Spanish rule was established by 1542. The Titicaca basin is still predominantly populated by Aymará-speaking peoples who, it is estimated, number 600,000 (1935). They practice agriculture with the potato as the main crop and keep the llama, alpaca, sheep, pig, guinea-pig (which is eaten), and chicken. Fishing and trade in community specialties are important.

Aymará. Name sometimes given to a small tribe of Indians once found in the highlands near Cusco, Peru, and conquered by the Incas.

Aymar-Vernay (e.mär.ver.ne), **Jacques.** b. 1662; d. after 1692. French peasant, once famous as a successful impostor in divination.

Aymé (e.mā), **Marcel.** b. at Joigny, in Burgundy, France, 1902—. French novelist and short-story writer. After ventures in bricklaying, insurance, selling, and journalism, and a period of very serious illness, he turned (1926) to writing fiction. Following three failures *Brûlebois* (1926), *Aller et retour* (1927), and *Les Jumeaux du diable* (1928), he discovered his formula for popularity with *La Table aux crevés* (1929) and has since found an ever-widening public. His best-known work is *La Jument verte* (1933). Since World War II his work has appeared regularly in American mass-circulation periodicals.

Aymer (ā'mėr), **Prior.** In Sir Walter Scott's *Ivanhoe,* the prior of Jorvaulx Abbey, a fat and cautious voluptuary who is captured by Locksley.

Aymer de Valence (or **de Lusignan**) (dẹ val'ẹns; lü.zē.nyäṅ). [Also: **Æthelmær** or **Ethelmar de Valence.**] d. at Paris, 1260. Anglo-French ecclesiastic; younger son of Isabella, widow of King John of England, and Hugh X, the count of La Marche, her second husband. He was elected bishop of Winchester in November, 1250, but not consecrated by the pope until the year of his death. He was half brother to Henry III of England.

Aymer de Valence. [Title, Earl of **Pembroke.**] b. c1265; d. 1324. English soldier and statesman; third son of William de Valence, and nephew of Aymer de Valence (d. 1260), also a half brother of Henry III of England. He succeeded to the earldom of Pembroke in 1296; led (as "Guardian of Scotland") the van of the English forces in the attack on Robert VIII ("the Bruce") in 1306, in the defeat of the Scots at Methven; and was himself defeated (1307) by Robert at Loudon Hill. Under Edward II he was one of the chief opponents of Gaveston, favorite and foster brother of Edward.

Aymestrey or **Aymestry** (ām'stri). Parish and village in W England, in Herefordshire, situated on the river Lugg, ab. 6 mi. NW of Leominster. It is noted for its limestone. 484 (1931).

Aymon (ā'mọn). [Also: **Aimon, Haimon, Haymon;** title, **Count of Dordogne.**] fl. early 8th century. French nobleman, much of whose story is based on legend rather than verifiable fact. He appears in the old French romances, a prince of Ardennes, possibly of Saxon origin, who took the title of Duke of Dordogne. He was the father of Renaud (Rinaldo), Guiscard (Guicciardo), Alard (Alardo), and Richard (Richardetto), the "four sons of Aymon" whose adventures were written in a *chanson de gestè* of the 13th century (first printed in 1493), supposed to be by Huon de Villeneuve, under the title of *Les Quatre Fils d'Aymon.* The brothers appear in Torquato Tasso's *Gerusalemme Liberata* (*Jerusalem Delivered*), Luigi Pulci's *Morgante Maggiore,* Matteo Maria Boiardo's *Orlando*

Innamorato, Lodovico Ariosto's *Orlando Furioso*, and other French and Italian romances.

Ayodhya (a̤.yōd'ya̤). See **Ajodhya.**

Ayolas (ä.yō'läs), **Juan de.** [Also, **Ayola** (-lä).] d. c1537. Spanish soldier and explorer of the Río de la Plata and the Paraguay River. He was a lieutenant of Pedro de Mendoza, who led a Spanish expedition to what is now Argentina in 1535, and assumed command when, discouraged as famine and sickness decimated his forces, Mendoza returned to Spain. Ayola continued up the Río de la Plata to the point where the Paraguay and Paraná Rivers enter it, and then up the Paraguay toward Peru; en route he built a fort where Asunción now stands. His party reached the Peruvian mines, but while returning to its base, was ambushed and its members killed by natives.

Ayotla (ä.yō'tlä), **Plan of.** See **Ayutla, Plan of.**

Ayoub Khan (ä.yöb' kän'). See **Ayub Khan.**

Ayr (ãr). Royal burgh and seaport in S Scotland, county seat of Ayrshire, situated on the Firth of Clyde, at the mouth of the river Ayr, ab. 18 mi. NE of Girvan, ab. 406 mi. N of London by rail. The town has manufactures of woolens and other items, and exports coal. It is famous as the center of the Robert Burns country, Burns's birthplace being at Alloway, on the outskirts of the town. The "Auld Brig" mentioned by Burns (for 500 years the only bridge in town) still stands in the center of the town. 43,011 (1951).

Ayrer (ī'rėr), **Jakob.** b. c1540; d. at Nuremberg, Germany, March 26, 1605. German dramatic poet, author of a large number of plays, 66 of which are preserved in his *Opus Theatricum* (1618). He was influenced by his fellow townsman, Hans Sachs, and also by the English comedians. He is known as the initiator of the German "Singspiel" or operetta.

Ayres (ãrz), **Anne.** b. at London, Jan. 3, 1816; d. at New York, Feb. 9, 1896. American religious author and first woman in U.S. to become a member of a Protestant Episcopal sisterhood. Arrived in the U.S. (1836), she was consecrated (1845) as a Sister of the Holy Communion, although the group was not formally organized until 1852. Author of *Evangelical Sisterhoods* (1867), and others.

Ayres, Brown. b. at Memphis, Tenn., May 25, 1856; d. Jan. 28, 1919. American educator. A professor of physics and electrical engineering (1880–1900) and of physics and astronomy (1900–04) at Tulane, he served as president of the University of Tennessee (1904–19). He is chiefly known for his efforts at the latter institution to arouse the legislature to support it in a suitable manner, with the result that in 1917 special taxes and a million-dollar bond issue provided Tennessee with what many consider to have been the first properly financed state educational institution in the South.

Ayres, Leonard Porter. b. at Niantic, Conn., Sept. 15, 1879; d. at Cleveland, Ohio, Oct. 29, 1946. American statistician and one-time educator. He served (1908–20) as director of education and statistics for the Russell Sage Foundation, after teaching for several years in Puerto Rico; was chief statistician to the army and several other U.S. government agencies during World War I, and later to the American commission to negotiate peace; and acted as economic adviser (1924) to the Dawes Plan Commission. Author of *Price Changes and Business Prospects* (1921), *Business Recovery Following Depression* (1922), *Economics of Recovery* (1933), *Inflation* (1936), *Turning Points in Business Cycles* (1939), and others.

Ayres, Romeyn Beck. b. at East Creek, N.Y., Dec. 20, 1825; d. at Fort Hamilton, N.Y., Dec. 4, 1888. American army officer, with the Union forces in the Civil War. Garrison duty during the Mexican War was followed by combat service at Gettysburg, the Wilderness, Spottsylvania Court House, Chancellorsville, and elsewhere, during the Civil War.

Ayres, Ruby Mildred. b. 1883—. English novelist. Her novels, published serially in the London *Daily Chronicle, Daily Mirror*, and elsewhere, brought her an enormous audience. Among her numerous works are *Richard Chatterton, V.C., The Remembered Kiss, The Scar, The Bachelor Husband, The Big Fellah, Compromise, Sunrise for Georgie*, and *The Lady from London*. Her play *Silver Wedding* was produced in 1932.

Ayres de Cazal (ī'rez dē ka̤.zäl'), **Manuel.** b. 1754; d. at Lisbon, c1823. Portuguese historian and priest. He went (1780) to Brazil and lived at Rio de Janeiro, returning to Portugal in 1821. He wrote the *Corografia Brasilica* (Rio de Janeiro, 1817 and 1845), a work on the geography and history of Brazil.

Ayr River (ãr). River in S Scotland, in Ayrshire. It rises ab. 24 mi. E of Ayr and flows generally W across the county to the Firth of Clyde at Ayr. Length, ab. 38 mi.

Ayrshire (ãr'shir) or **Ayr.** Maritime county in S Scotland. It is bounded on the N by Renfrewshire, on the NE by Lanarkshire, on the E by Dumfriesshire, on the SE by Kirkcudbrightshire, on the S by Wigtownshire, and on the W by the Firth of Clyde. The surface is hilly and mountainous in the S and E, sloping toward the coast in a series of gentle undulations. The highest point in the county is Blackcraig Hill (2,298 ft.). About 45 percent of the total area of the county is under cultivation or in pasture. Dairy cattle are raised in the N portion, about 30 percent of the milk being made into cheese. Early potatoes are raised, especially in the vicinity of Girvan. The Ayrshire coal field is worked mainly in the N in the vicinity of Kilmarnock and Ardrossan. The iron and steel industry is concentrated around Irvine and Kilbirnie; most of the iron ore is now imported. Limestone and sandstone are quarried. Other industries include woolen and carpet manufactures (especially at Kilmarnock and Ayr), cotton manufactures (at Catrine), and lace-making (at Newmilns and Darvel). Ayr is the county seat; area, ab. 1,132 sq. mi.; pop. 321,184 (1951).

Ayrshire Legatee, The. Satirical sketch (1820) by John Galt.

Ayrton (ãr'to̤n), **Hertha.** [Maiden name, **Marks.**] b. at Portsea, England, 1854; d. 1923. English scientist; wife (1885 *et seq.*) of William Edward Ayrton. Daughter of a Polish refugee, she entered Girton College as a protegée of George Eliot. Having invented (1884) a draftsman's line-divider, she entered Finsbury Technical College, where she studied under her future husband; she was elected (1899) the first woman member of the Royal Society of Electrical Engineers and awarded (1906) a medal for work on both sand ripples and the electric arc. She collaborated (1904–08) with her husband on problems pertaining to an electric searchlight, and developed (1915) an anti-gas fan for use by the British army. She was active (1906 *et seq.*) in the suffragette Women's Social and Political Union.

Ayrton, William Edward. b. at London, 1847; d. there, Nov. 8, 1908. English physicist and electrical engineer. He was a student (1867–68) of Lord Kelvin (then Sir William Thomson) in preparation for work (1868–72) in the Indian telegraph service, in which he made outstanding technical improvements. He served as a professor of physics and telegraphy (1873–78) at the Imperial Engineering College, Tokyo; there, and at London (1879–81), Finsbury (1881–84), and South Kensington technical colleges, he worked with John Perry on instruments for electrical measurement and other devices. Their inventions included the surface-contact system and block system for electric railways and (with Fleeming Jenkin) the telpherage system of transport. Author of *Practical Electricity* (1887), and others.

Ayscough (as'kū), **Anne.** See **Askew, Anne.**

Ayscough (ās'kō), **Florence.** [Maiden name, **Wheelock.**] b. at Shanghai, 1878; d. 1942. American poet, also known as a specialist in Chinese literature. She lectured on that subject at the University of Chicago (1938 *et seq.*). Author of *Fir-Flower Tablets* (in collaboration with Amy Lowell, 1922), *A Chinese Mirror* (1925), *The Autobiography of a Chinese Dog* (1926), *Pictures of the Chinese World* (1931), and *Firecracker Land* (1932).

Ayscough (as'kū), **John.** Pseudonym of **Bickerstaffe-Drew,** Monsignor Count **Francis Browning Drew.**

Ayscough, Samuel. b. at Nottingham, England, 1745; d. at London, 1804. English librarian, index-maker, and clergyman. He prepared (1780–82) a two-volume index of undescribed manuscripts in the British Museum; later he indexed the *Monthly Review* (1786, 1796), the *Gentleman's Magazine* (1789), and was responsible for one third of the British Museum book catalogue printed in 1787. His *Index* to Shakespeare, which was published in 1790, was the first Shakespeare concordance in history.

Ayscue (ās'kū, as'-), Sir **George.** [Also: **Askew, Ayscough.**] d. c1672. English admiral in wars against the

Dutch. A captain (1646) in the English fleet, he was one of those who adhered to Parliament, and was sent by Cromwell to America in 1651, in command of a squadron of ships. He reduced Barbados and other islands which had remained faithful to the royalists, and visited the coast of Virginia. He encountered De Ruyter's Dutch fleet off Plymouth in 1652, both sides claiming victory. He was deprived of his command and made naval advisor to Sweden in 1658. Returning under the Restoration, he was made a commissioner of the navy. He again served against the Dutch, notably at Lowestoft (1665); an admiral under Monk (1666), he was captured and imprisoned (1666–67) in Holland.

Aysen (ī.sän'). See **Aisén.**

Ayton or **Aytoun** (ā'tọn), Sir **Robert.** b. near St. Andrew's, Scotland, 1570; d. at London, in February, 1638. Scottish poet at the court of James I of England. One of the first Scots to use English as a literary language, he was also a friend of Ben Jonson. Besides Latin poems including a panegyric on the accession (1603) of James I and an elegy on the death of Buckingham (1628), he wrote lyrics such as *Inconstancy Upbraided* and, probably, *I Do Confess Thou'rt Smooth and Fair.*

Aytos (ī'tôs). [Also: **Aitos, Ajtos.**] Town in SE Bulgaria, department of Burgas, situated on the Ajtos River, ab. 22 mi. NW of Burgas, at the foot of the Ajtosbalcan Mountains: it has warm springs. 9,972 (1946).

Aytoun (ā'tọn), **William Edmonstoune.** b. at Edinburgh, June 21, 1813; d. near Elgin, Scotland, Aug. 4, 1865. Scottish poet and humorist. Though called to the Scottish bar in 1840, he had been more interested in writing than in law since the publication of his first book, *Poland, Homer, and Other Poems* (1832), and did virtually nothing to further his career as a barrister. He became a contributor to *Blackwood's Magazine* (in 1836, and later served on the staff), especially of satirical articles on politics and contemporary affairs. He was also a popular lecturer as professor (1845–65) of rhetoric and belles-lettres at Edinburgh. Author of *Lays of the Scottish Cavaliers* (1848), *Firmilian, a Spasmodic Tragedy* (1852, a satire on contemporary writers); with Sir Theodore Martin, of *The Bon Gaultier Ballads* (1855, reprinted from *Blackwood's*), a series of parodies imitated by W. S. Gilbert (*Bab Ballads*) and others; translated, with Martin, *Poems and Ballads of Goethe* (1858); and collected and annotated *Ballads of Scotland* (1858).

Ayubite (ä.yö'bīt). See **Ayyubid.**

Ayub Khan (ä.yöb' kän'). [Also, **Ayoub Khan.**] b. c1855; d. at Lahore, India, April 6, 1914. A younger son of Shere Ali, claimant (1879) to the Afghan throne after the death of his father. As governor of Herat, he opposed the British (by whom he was defeated in 1880) and Abd-er-Rahman Khan (by whom he was overthrown in 1881).

Ayudhya (ä.yöd'yä). See **Ayutthaya.**

Ayut'ia (ä.yö'tē.ä). [Also: **Ayuthia, Ayutthaya.**] Siamese kingdom founded in 1350 by Rama Tibodi. The kingdom achieved its greatest power in the 15th century, when it extended also over part of the Malay Peninsula. After several previous invasions, it was conquered by Burma in 1569 and again in 1766–67. Soon after, through a series of internal wars, the Chakri dynasty secured supreme rule of Siam and Ayut'ia lost its independent statehood. Its name remains (usually in a variant spelling) as that of a city ab. 45 mi. N of Bangkok.

Ayutla (ä.yö'tlä), **Plan of.** [Also, **Plan of Ayotla.**] The announcement of principles made by Mexican revolutionists at Ayutla in S Mexico, March 1, 1854. It led to the revolution overthrowing Santa Anna in 1855.

Ayutthaya (ä.yö'tä.yä) or **Ayudhya** (ä.yöd'yä). [Also: **Ayuthia, Ayut'ia, Juthia, Yuthia.**] Former capital of Thailand, situated on the Chao Phraya River, ab. 45 mi. N of Bangkok. It was sacked and destroyed by the Burmese in 1555 and in 1767, and also saw later fighting. Now a trading center, it has rice mills and is served by one rail line and one major highway. Pop. ab. 20,000.

Ayvalik (ī.vä.lik'). [Also: **Aivalik, Aivali;** Turkish, **Ayvalık;** ancient name, **Heraclea.**] Seaport in W Turkey, in the *il* (vilayet) of Balikesir, situated on the Gulf of Edremit ab. 66 mi. NW of Smyrna (Izmir). Pop. ab. 13,000.

Ayyubid (ī.yö'bid). [Also, **Ayubite.**] Moslem dynasty (1169–1250), established in Egypt (1173) by Saladin.

Azad (ä.zäd'), **Abul Kalam (Maulana).** b. at Mecca, Arabia, 1889—. Indian Nationalist Moslem leader, president (1939–46) of the Indian National Congress, and spokesman for the Congress in the negotiations (1945) for independence. Equally well-known as a Moslem divine and an Oriental scholar, he was one of the earliest prominent Moslem leaders to urge Indian Moslems to join with the Hindus in the nationalist struggle under Gandhi. Minister of education in the Indian government since 1947, he is the author of commentaries on the *Koran* and other books on theology.

Azaïs (à.zà.ēs), **Pierre Hyacinthe.** b. at Sorèze, France, March 1, 1766; d. at Paris, Jan. 22, 1845. French philosopher. His chief work, *Des Compensations dans les destinées humaines* (1809), propounds the thesis that happiness and misery always balance themselves in life and that it is thus foolish to attempt by revolution to alter a government which already offers as much as man may logically hope for. This reasoning so gratified Napoleon that he rewarded its author with a professorship at St. Cyr.

Azamgarh (ä.zạm.gur'). [Also, **Azimgarh.**] District of Gorakhpur division, Uttar Pradesh (United Provinces), Union of India, ab. 45 mi. N of Benares: rice, sugar, and wheat. Capital, Azamgarh; area, ab. 2,217 sq. mi.; pop. 1,822,893 (1941).

Azamgarh. [Also, **Azimgarh.**] Capital of the district of Azamgarh, Union of India, on the Tons River, ab. 55 mi. NE of Benares: trading center; rail and road junction. Pop. ab. 25,000.

Azaña y Díez (ä.thä'nyä ē dē'eth), **Manuel.** [Often shortened to **Manuel Azaña.**] b. at Alcalá de Henares, Spain, 1880; d. at Montauban, France, 1940. President of the Spanish republic (May, 1936–March, 1939). He was educated at the College of the Escorial and made a reputation as an author and critic, being elected to the presidency of the Madrid Ateneo in 1930. As founder (1930) of the political group, Acción Republicana, he established himself as a liberal and was active in the overthrow of the monarchy in 1931. He was chosen to be minister of war in the cabinet of the provisional government and was prime minister of the republic (1931–33). He attempted many reforms which were unpopular with the army and the clerical party, and some of which led to strife, as in the matter of Catalonian autonomy. In 1934, during the Catalonian revolt, he was briefly imprisoned and upon his release defended himself in *Mí rebellión en Barcelona* (1935). In 1936 he succeeded Alcalá Zamora as president of the republic, appointing as prime minister the moderate Diego Martínez Barrio. But the cleavage between right and left could no longer be bridged and Azaña led the government into the northeast of Spain during the latter part of the Spanish Civil War. He resigned his post and went into exile in March, 1939.

Azanchevsky (ä.zän.chef'ski), **Mikhail Pavlovich.** b. at Moscow, 1838; d. there, 1881. Russian composer and teacher of music. He was director (1870–76) of the St. Petersburg Conservatory, a composer of chamber music, and collector of a library of musical texts.

Azángaro (ä.säng'gä.rō). See **Asángaro.**

Azani (ạ.zā'nī). [Also: **Azanion** (-ni.on), **Aizani.**] In ancient geography, a city in Phrygia, Asia Minor, situated in lat. 39°16′ N.

Azanza (ä.thän'thä), **Miguel José de.** [Called by Mexicans the **"Bonapartist Viceroy."**] b. at Aviz, Spain, 1746; d. at Bordeaux, France, June 20, 1826. Spanish politician and soldier. He was minister of war (1793 *et seq.*), and as viceroy (1798–1800) of New Spain (Mexico), put down the rebellion known as the "Conspiracy of the Machetes." Minister of finance during the short first reign (1808) of Ferdinand VII, he was later a member of the junta which negotiated (1808) with Napoleon at Bayonne over the appointment of his brother, Joseph Bonaparte, as king of Spain; he became the latter's minister of justice, of the Indies, and of ecclesiastical affairs. After Joseph's abdication (1813), Azanza retired to Bordeaux.

Azara (ä.thä'rä), **Félix de.** b. at Barbunales, Aragon, May 18, 1746; d. in Aragon, 1811. Spanish naturalist and traveler; brother of José Nicolás de Azara. From 1781 to 1801 he was in Paraguay as one of the commissioners to settle the boundaries between Spanish and Portuguese possessions, and he devoted much of his time there to studying local geography, history, and zoölogy. The results were published in *Voyage dans l'Amérique méridionale* (Paris, 1809, 4 vols., with atlas).

Azara, José Nicolás de. b. at Barbunales, Aragon, 1731; d. at Paris, 1804. Spanish diplomat, a collector of Italian paintings and antiquities; brother of Félix de Azara. He served as an agent (1765–85) and ambassador (1785–98) of Spain at the Vatican, and ambassador (1798 *et seq.*) to France. He was active in the suppression (1773) of the Jesuits.

Azarian: An Episode (ạ.zãr'i.ạn). Tale by Harriet Prescott Spofford, published in 1864.

Azarias (az.ạ.rī'ạs), Brother. [Original name, **Patrick Francis Mullany.**] b. in Ireland, June 29, 1847; d. at Plattsburg, N.Y., Aug. 20, 1893. American Catholic educator and author. He arrived in the U.S. (c1853) and became a member of the congregation of Brothers of the Christian Schools; he taught at Rock Hill College, Ellicott City, Md., and later (1879) became its president. He was notable as a lecturer and writer for his ability to present the Roman Catholic arguments in a manner attractive to non-Catholics as well as to Catholics. Author of *The Development of Old English Thought* (1879), *Aristotle and the Christian Church* (1888), and others.

Azay-le-Rideau (à.ze.lẹ rē.dō). Small town in W central France, in the department of Indre-et-Loire, near Tours. It contains a château, a very fine example of the Renaissance manor house of the 16th century, with cylindrical flanking towers, high roofs, and dormer windows. Pop. ab. 1,400.

Azazel (ạ.zā'zel, az.ạ.zel'). [Arabic, **Azazil** (ä.zä'zil).] Name which occurs in the ritual of the Day of Atonement, Lev. xvi. 8, 10–26. The high priest had among other ceremonies to cast lots upon two goats. One lot was inscribed "for Yahveh" (Jehovah), the other "for Azazel." The goat upon which the lot "for Yahveh" fell was offered as a sacrifice, while on the goat upon which the lot "for Azazel" had fallen the high priest laid his hands and confessed all the sins of the people. The goat was then led by a man into the desert, "unto a land not inhabited," and was there let loose. The authorized version of the Old Testament renders Azazel on the margin by "scape-goat"; the revised version has Azazel in the text and "or dismissal" on the margin. Arabic writers describe Azazel as one of the jinn who for transgression were taken prisoners by the angels. Azazel was their chief, until he refused to prostrate himself before Adam, when he became father of the Shaitans (evil spirits). This is reëchoed in Milton's *Paradise Lost,* where Azazel is represented as the standard-bearer of the infernal hosts, cast out from heaven and becoming the embodiment of despair. The identification of Azazel with Satan is also met in some of the church fathers.

Azaziel (ạ.zā'zi.el). Seraph in Byron's *Heaven and Earth.*

Azbine (az.bēn'). See **Air.**

Azcapotzalco (äs"kä.pōt.säl'kō). [Also: **Atzapozalco, Azcapozalco, Azcaputzalco.**] City in S Mexico, in the Distrito Federal, ab. 5 mi. NW of Mexico City. It was an old Aztec town, founded by the Tecpanecs on the W side of the lake of Tezcuco in 1168. At the time of the Spanish conquest it was the great market of Mexico, where there was a regular sale of produce and slaves. Hernán Cortés and his army took refuge there after the flight of the *Noche Triste.* It was the scene of a battle between the Spanish forces and those of Iturbide, Aug. 19, 1821: both sides claimed the victory. 31,496 (1940).

Azcárate (äth.kä'rä.tā), **Gumersindo de.** b. at León, Spain, 1840; d. at Madrid, 1917. Spanish politician, social reformer, and jurist. He was interested in the thought and scholarship of England, translating Mackenzie's *Roman Law* and Fawcett's *Free Trade and Protection* into Spanish. Appointed lecturer in political economy at the University of Madrid and subsequently professor of comparative law, he joined the staff of *La Voz del Siglo* and was dismissed from his university post upon the collapse (1874) of the Spanish republic. Upon his return to Spain after some years in exile he became a member of the Cortes for León and coöperated with the reformist movement of 1898. He founded and headed the *Institución de Reformas Sociales* (1903–17). Representative of the intellectual and social reform movements of his day and of the pragmatic approach to problems of government, he became the *gran anciano* ("grand old man") of the intelligentsia and commercial middle class in Spain.

Azeglio (dä.dze'lyō), **Massimo Taparelli,** Marchese **d'.** b. at Turin, Italy, Oct. 24, 1798; d. there, Jan. 15, 1866. Italian patriot, politician, and author; son-in-law of A. F. T. A. Manzoni. He was active in the Risorgimento, particularly with such writings (1846) as the anti-papal *Gli ultimi casi di Romagna;* served (1848) in the war against Austria; headed (1849–52) the government under Victor Emmanuel II, withdrawing in favor of Cavour when the cabinet initiated a rapprochement with the Left which his aristocratic background made it impossible for him to accept; and served thereafter on various diplomatic missions, notably to France and England. Besides polemical works such as the one mentioned above, he wrote two novels, *Ettore Fieramosca* (1833) and *Nicolò de' Lapi* (1841), both of which reflect his preoccupation with Italian history; his autobiography, *I Miei Ricordi,* was published posthumously.

Azerbaidzhani (ä"zer.bī.jä'nē). People (predominantly Moslem in religion) of the SW shores of the Caspian Sea, now divided about equally between the U.S.S.R. and Iran, and totaling some 3,000,000. The Azerbaidzhani, who are most closely related to the Osmanli Turks of Turkey, and the Turkmen of Central Asia, entered their present home beginning in the 13th century A.D., at the time of the Mongol invasions.

Azerbaijan (ä"zer.bī.jän'). Region and former province in NW Iran, separated from the Azerbaijan Soviet Socialist Republic of the U.S.S.R. by the Aras River. Since 1938 it has consisted officially of the *Ustan Yakum* (First Province) and *Ustan Duwum* (Second Province). It corresponds in general to the region anciently known as Atropatene or Media Atropatene, which was the N part of Media. After the death of Alexander the Great it was for a time an independent kingdom, but in the 11th century was colonized by Seljuk Turks and two centuries later was occupied by Mongols. Still later Azerbaijan was invaded by the Arabs, and became a Moslem country. The inhabitants of Azerbaijan are predominantly of Mongol and Turkic strains. From the mid-16th century to the mid-18th Azerbaijan was ruled by Persia, but thereafter Russia took over much of it, and in 1827 the boundary line was fixed which still separates Iranian Azerbaijan from Soviet Azerbaijan. In November, 1945, the Azerbaijan Democratic Party, supposedly at the instigation of the U.S.S.R., attempted to set up an autonomous government; Iranian troops were stopped by Soviet forces, and an election was held. On Jan. 19, 1946, the Iranian representative in the United Nations called the attention of the Security Council to alleged interference by the U.S.S.R. in Iranian internal affairs; this was denied by the Russians. On Jan. 30, the Security Council noted that both parties were willing to negotiate and resolved that the Council should be kept informed of developments. Iran and the U.S.S.R. had negotiated an agreement by which Soviet forces were to withdraw from Azerbaijan by March 2, 1946; on March 18, Iran complained in the Security Council that this agreement had not been kept. After further debate and maneuvers within the United Nations, it was stated by Iran on May 21 that the Soviet forces had evacuated Azerbaijan on May 6, and discussion of Iranian matters was suspended. The Iranian government had on April 6, 1946, signed an agreement with the U.S.S.R. for joint exploitation of Azerbaijan oil resources, but on Oct. 22, 1947, Iran repudiated this commitment, and on Nov. 24 rejected a Russian protest. No oil areas are now being exploited in Azerbaijan, but it is thought that there are vast fields of high-grade oil in the region. Other resources of this mountainous but fertile area are fruit, minerals, and marble. Capital, Tabriz; area, 41,150 sq. mi.; pop. ab. 1,500,000.

Azerbaijan (or **Azerbaidzhan**) **Soviet Socialist Republic** (ä"zer.bī.jän'). One of the southern Soviet Socialist Republics, located E of the Armenian Soviet Socialist Republic, S of the Caucasus Mountains, and W of the Caspian Sea. Capital, Baku; area, 33,100 sq. mi.; pop. 3,209,727 (1939), 3,100,000 (est. 1951).

Azevedo (ä.zę.vä′dö), **Aluízio** (**Belo Gonçalves de**). b. at São Luís, Brazil, April 14, 1857; d. at Buenos Aires, Argentina, Jan. 21, 1913. Brazilian novelist, playwright, and author of short stories, the best-known writer of the naturalist school in Brazil. *O mulato* (1881), *Casa de pensão* (1883), and *O cortiço* (1890) are his most famous novels.

Azevedo, Antônio de Araujo de. See **Araujo de Azevedo, Antônio de.**

Azevedo, Artur (**Nabantino Gonçalves de**). b. at São Luís, Brazil, July 7, 1855; d. at Rio de Janeiro, Brazil, Oct. 22, 1908. Brazilian playwright, drama critic, journalist, short story writer, and poet; brother of Aluízio Azevedo, with whom he wrote some of his plays. The most prolific playwright of Brazil, his works include scores of plays, among which are *A princesa dos cajueiros* (1880), *A filha de Maria Angú* (1894), *Amor por anexins*, and *A Capital Federal*.

Azevedo, Manuel Antônio Álvares de. b. at São Paulo, Brazil, Sept. 12, 1831; d. at Rio de Janeiro, Brazil, April 25, 1852. One of the outstanding romantic poets of Brazil. A note of sadness, fear, and doubt marks his writings. His collections of poems (*Poesias diversas, Lira dos vinte anos, Poema do frade, O conde Lopo*) and his book of short stories (*A noite na taverna*) were published after his death.

Azevedo Coutinho (kō.tē′nyö), **José Joaquim da Cunha.** b. at Campos, Brazil, Sept. 8, 1742; d. Sept. 12, in Portugal, 1821. Portuguese prelate. In 1794 he was made bishop of Pernambuco, and in 1818 became inquisitor-general of Portugal and Brazil, the last to hold this office.

Azilia (ą.zil′i.ą), **Margravate of.** Name applied to Sir Robert Montgomery's proposed new colony S of Carolina in the region between the Altamaha and Savannah rivers. He received the grant (1717) from the Carolina proprietors, but failed to carry out the process of settlement within the three years specified in the grant.

Azim (ä′zim). Lover of Zelica in "The Veiled Prophet of Khorassan," one of the tales in Thomas Moore's *Lalla Rookh* (1817). He kills her by mistake for the latter.

Azimech (az′i.mek). A name applied both to α Virginis (Spica) and to Arcturus, but rarely to the latter.

Azimgarh (ä.zim.gur′). See **Azamgarh.**

Azincourt (ȧ.zaṅ.kör). Modern French name of **Agincourt.**

Azo (ä′dzō) or **Azzo** (äd′-). [Latinized, **Azolinus Porcius.**] b. at Bologna, c1150; d. c1230. Bolognese jurist. He is now best known for *Summa codicis et institutionem*, a summary of Roman law. He was the author also of *Apparatus ad codicem*.

Azof or **Azoff** (ā′zof, ä.zôf′). See **Azov.**

Azogues (ä.sō′gās). City in S central Ecuador, capital of Cañar province. 15,068 (est. 1944).

Azoic Period (ą.zō′ik). The early part of the Pre-Cambrian Era. See volume 3.

Azolinus Porcius (az.ǫ.lī′nus pōr′shus). Latinized name of **Azo.**

Azor (ā′zôr). Name of the Beast in Jean François Marmontel's *Beauty and the Beast*.

Azores (ą.zōrz′). [Portuguese, **Açores,** in full, **Arquipélago dos Açores.**] Group of islands, belonging to Portugal, situated in the Atlantic Ocean ab. 800 mi. W of Portugal. They form the districts of Angra do Heroísmo, Horta, and Ponta Delgada. The nine main islands are São Miguel, São Jorge, Santa Maria, Terceira, Pico, Fayal, Graciosa, Flores, and Corvo. They form three widely separated groups; the E and W groups are ab. 100 mi. and ab. 150 mi., respectively, from the central one. The islands of São Miguel, Terceira, and Pico contain over half of the total population of the archipelago. Capital, Angra do Heroísmo; area, 890 sq. mi.; pop. 318,686 (1950).

Azorín (ä.thō.rēn′). [Pseudonym of **José Martínez Ruiz.**] b. at Monóvar, Alicante, Spain, 1874—. Spanish novelist, essayist, critic, and playwright. He was the first to designate the Spanish intellectuals who were his contemporaries as the "generation of 1898," and was a leading figure among them. His novels have little plot but are notable for their descriptions. His writings show great skill in evoking a nostalgic sense of the past. He is the author of two plays, *Old Spain* and *Brandy, mucho brandy,* but it is in the field of the essay and in literary criticism that the greater part of his work has been done. *Los Hidalgos, El Alma castellana, Los Pueblos, La Ruta de Don Quijote, Las Nubes, Las Confesiones de un pequeño filósofo, La Voluntad, Antonio Azorín,* and *Don Juan y Doña Inés* are among his most popular books.

Azotos (ą.zō′tos). Greek name of **Ashdod.**

Azov (ā′zof; ä.zôf′). [Also: **Azof, Azoff.**] Town in the U.S.S.R., in the Rostov *oblast* (region) of the Russian Soviet Federated Socialist Republic, situated on the Don River near its mouth: food industries; fisheries. It was taken from the Turks by Peter the Great in 1696, and annexed to Russia in 1774. Pop. ab. 18,000.

Azov, Sea of. [Also: **Sea of Azof** (or **Azoff**); Russian, **Azovskoe More** (ä.zôf′skǫ.yę mô′ryę); ancient name, **Palus Maeotis.**] Sea S of the U.S.S.R., communicating with the Black Sea by Kerch Strait. Its largest arm is the Gulf of Taganrog, and its chief tributary the Don River. It is very shallow. Length, ab. 220 mi.; width, ab. 80 mi.; area, ab. 14,000 sq. mi.

Azpeitia (äth.pā′tyä). Town in N Spain, in Guipúzcoa province, ab. 17 mi. SW of San Sebastián and ab. 180 mi. NE of Madrid, on the Urcola River: noted for its mineral springs. A monastery situated W of Azpeitia is said to stand on the site of the birthplace of Saint Ignatius of Loyola.

Azrael (az′rą.el). In certain writings of Judaism and Islam, the angel who separates the soul from the body at the moment of death, for which he watches.

Azraq or **Azrak** (äz′räk), **Bahr el.** See **Blue Nile.**

Aztalan (az′tą.lą̇n). North American Indian archaeological site on the Crawfish River, in S Wisconsin, dated about 1300–1600 A.D., consisting of a palisaded town containing houses made of poles, grass, and clay, and truncated pyramids of earth on which wooden temples were once placed. The site contains a variety of pottery forms and implements which indicate it was at one time inhabited by an invading outpost of the settled agricultural tribes once centered about the Cahokia area near what is now East St. Louis, Illinois.

Aztec (az′tek). Dominant Nahua Indian nation in the C plateau of Mexico at the time of the Spanish conquest, with its capital at Tenochtitlán, now the site of Mexico City. The language of its people was a Nahuatl dialect, a member of the great Uto-Aztecan linguistic stock to which the Maya language of Yucatán also belongs. The correlation of the results of extensive archaeological researches, legendary history, and the extension backward of the 52-year calendrical cycles which the Aztec employed to reckon elapsed time, and which are reflected in successive additions to the temple pyramids, reveals that the Aztec became clearly distinguished as a tribal state during the 13th century. They were still, however, only one of a number of competing groups in the central Mexican plateau, and did not become firmly established at Tenochtitlán, on an island in Lake Texcoco, until early in the 14th century, after several centuries of aggressive wanderings throughout the region. During the 14th and 15th centuries the Aztecs, through a sustained series of conquests and alliances, gradually extended their political control until they dominated a large region of Mexico and influenced, through warfare, trade, and colonial effort, a great many of the various tribes and nations in Middle America.

Aztec. Large ruin of the Great Pueblo period, built between 1100 and 1125 A.D. in NW New Mexico, near what is now a small community of the same name. This ruin is in the architectural style of the Chaco branch of Anasazi culture. It has been restored as a national monument, and there is a small museum alongside.

Aztlan (äs.tlän′). Mythical point of origin of the Aztec Indians, whence they are said to have begun their southward movement to the plateau of C Mexico.

Azua (ä′swä). Province in S Dominican Republic. Capital, Azua; area, 936 sq. mi.; pop. 50,166 (1950).

Azua. [Full name, **Azua de Compostela.**] Town in S Dominican Republic, capital of Azua province. 7,419 (1950).

Azuaga (ä.thwä′gä). Town in W Spain, in the province of Badajoz, ab. 57 mi. NE of Seville: livestock market for the upland pastures of the district. 16,453 (1940).

Azuay (ä.swī'). [Also, **Assuay.**] Province S Ecuador. Capital, Cuenca; area, 3,011 sq. mi.; pop. 263,873 (est. 1944).

Azucena (ä.dzö.chā'nä). Contralto character in Giuseppe Verdi's opera *Il Trovatore*, the old gypsy who stole Manrico.

Azuela (ä.swā'lä), **Mariano.** [Pseudonym, **Beleño.**] b. at Lagos de Moreno, Mexico, Jan. 1, 1873; d. in March, 1952. Mexican novelist. Besides his "modern classic" *Los de abajo* (1915), which has been widely translated, *Los Caciques* (1917) and *Las Moscas* (1918) also depict the events of the revolution. He is also the author of *Mala yerba* (1909), *La Luciérnaga* (1932), *La Nueva Burguesía* (1941), and others. He filled the double role of physician and writer throughout his life.

Azufre (ä.sö'frā). See **Copiapó.**

Azul (ä.söl'). City in E Argentina, in Buenos Aires province, ab. 160 mi. SSW of the city of Buenos Aires: agricultural products and marble quarries. 28,609 (1947).

Azulai (ä.zö'lī), **Hayim Joseph David.** b. at Jerusalem, 1724; d. at Leghorn, Italy, 1806. Jewish bibliographer, of whose numerous works the best known are *Shem-ha-Gedolim* (The Names of the Great) and *Wa'ad ha-Hakamim* (Assembly of the Wise). The first of these works lists more than 1,300 Jewish writers and more than 2,200 of their works. Azulai was one of the first to write of the history of rabbinical literature, and he dealt with almost every field of rabbinical lore, thus preserving much that might otherwise have been lost. A systematic arrangement of his work was published in 1852. His life was spent mostly at Leghorn.

Azul River (ä.söl'). [Spanish, **Río Azul.**] River in NE Guatemala, flowing N to join the Hondo River, forming part of the border between Mexico and British Honduras.

Azuni (ä.dzö'nē), **Domenico Alberto.** b. at Sassari, Sardinia, Aug. 3, 1749; d. at Cagliari, Sardinia, Jan. 23, 1827. Italian jurist and legal historian. Author of *Sistema universale dei principii del diritto maritimo dell Europa* (1795), *Dizionario universale raggionato della giurisprudenza mercantile* (1786–88), and others.

Azusa (ą.zö'są). City in S California, in Los Angeles County, NE of Los Angeles, in an orange-growing area: citrus-shipping center. In the decade between the last two U.S. censuses its population more than doubled. 5,209 (1940), 11,042 (1950).

Azzo (äd'dzō). See **Azo.**

B

"B.A." Short for **Buenos Aires,** city.

Baader (bä'dėr), **Franz Xaver von.** b. at Munich, March 27, 1765; d. there, May 23, 1841. German scholar, appointed (1826) honorary professor of philosophy and speculative theology at the University of Munich. He is chiefly known for his philosophical writings. He devoted himself at first to the study of medicine and the natural sciences, held the position of superintendent of mines at Munich in 1797, and published various scientific and technical works. His philosophy was conceived under Roman Catholic influences, and was theosophical in character.

Baal (bā'ąl). Name specifically of the supreme god of the Phoenicians and the Canaanites. The word derives from Assyro-Babylonian (Akkadian), the oldest of the Semitic languages, and had originally a common-language meaning of "owner" or "lord." It is cognate with the Babylonian "Bel." In those theologies of which he was the chief male god, Baal was conceived of as the productive power of generation and fertility, his female counterpart Astarte (Ashtoreth or Ishtar) being the receptive. His statue was placed on a bull, the symbol of generative power, and he was usually represented with bunches of grapes and pomegranates in his hands. He was also worshiped as the sun god, and was in this conception represented with a crown of rays. His cult was attended by wild and licentious orgies. Baal-worship came to Israel under Ahab and his wife, who was a Phoenician princess. For reasons of nation and politics, as well as theology, the Jews opposed not only the worship of Baal (or the plural "Baalim," taking cognizance of the various related gods already cited), but also, as the "Baalim" became increasingly identified with the polytheism of the Canaanites and other opponents of the Jews, even found it advisable to give the name a connotation almost equivalent to that of the Antichrist in Christian theology; it is ultimately from this, of course, that we may trace the development of Beelzebub as a name of the Devil.

Baalah (bā'ą.lä). See **Kirjath-jearim.**

Baalath (bā'ąl.ath). In Biblical geography, a town in Dan, situated probably on the site of the later Bel'ain, ab. 2 mi. N of Beth-horon.

Baalbek (bäl'bek). [Also: **Baalbec, Ba'albek;** called by the ancient Greeks **Heliopolis.**] Ancient city of Syria, situated on the slope of the Anti-Libanus (now Anti-Lebanon) mountains, ab. 34 mi. NW of Damascus; now a small town in E Lebanon. Famous in modern times chiefly for its ruins, it was a center of the worship of Baal as sun god, whence both the original and the Greek names. The city was a Roman colony (Colonia Julia Augusta Felix) under Augustus, and was adorned, especially with the great temple of Jupiter, by Antoninus Pius. There are also remains of temples to Bacchus and Venus. Its decline began with its capture by the Arabs, and it was totally destroyed by an earthquake in 1759. The site is famous for the ruins of the great temples on its acropolis. The older portions of the acropolis wall, made of huge stones, are of Phoenician or kindred origin, and date from the time when the worship of Baal was still supreme. Aside from these sections of the wall, all the structures now remaining are Roman or later in time, and are interesting for their grouping, their great size, and the beauty of the materials. Baalbek has been known to Europeans since the 16th century, and its monuments have been studied and sketched by many explorers.

Baal-Hermon (bā'ąl.hėr'mǫn). See under **Hasbeya.**

Baal Shem-Tob (bäl shem'tōv). [Also, **Baal Schem-Tov;** known also by the initialism, **BeSHT** or **BeShT;** original name **Israel ben Eliezer.**] b. in the Ukraine, c1700; d. in Podolia, in the Ukraine, 1760. Jewish teacher and religious leader, known also in his lifetime as a healer. He was the founder of the Hasidim (or Chassidim), as a modern sect; his beliefs (which constitute the basis of modern Hasidism) had as their basis the conviction that God is omnipresent, existent in all things. From this pantheistic foundation he developed the doctrine that God might best be reached by ecstatic prayer, that asceticism was in direct opposition to the will of God, and that the truly religious man was characterized by a capacity for inward prayer rather than highly sophisticated and intellectualized study of the forms of religion. Finally, he preached the imminent approach of the Messiah. The doctrine brought him thousands of devoted followers throughout Europe, and attracted the bitter enmity of most orthodox Jewish theologians and scholars of the time. His own life was a simple one: he was at various times a teacher, a *shohet* (a rabbinically ordained slaughterer of meat), and tavern keeper. He lived part of his life as a hermit, studying among other things the herbs and other plants he found about him in the forests (and with this knowledge enabled himself to perform acts of healing which seemed miraculous to the people of his day). The two first elements of his name (Baal Shem) have the meaning "master of the Name" (the "Name" being, of course, the Deity).

Baan (bän), **Jacob van der.** b. at The Hague, in March, 1672; d. at Vienna, in April, 1700. Dutch portrait painter; son of Jan van der Baan (1633–1702).

Baan, Jan van der. [Also, **Jan de Baen.**] b. at Haarlem, Feb. 20, 1633; d. at Amsterdam, 1702. Dutch portrait painter.

Baanes (bā'ą.nēz). d. 801. Founder of a Paulician sect in the early Church known, after him, as Baanites.

Baanites (bā′a̤n.īts). Paulician sect, in the early Church, comprised of the followers of Baanes. They repudiated the hierarchy and rituals of the established Church, and were themselves by that Church branded as heretics. This particular sect appears to have disappeared in the 9th century a few years after the death of its founder.

Baar (bär). Town in N Switzerland, in the canton of Zug, situated between the lakes of Zug and Zurich. It has cotton manufactures and other industries. 6,193 (1941).

Baar, The. Elevated and broken region in S Germany, in SW Württemberg and SE Baden, lying about the headwaters of the Neckar and Danube rivers.

Baarn (bärn). Town in the C Netherlands, in the province of Utrecht, situated near the Eem River, ab. 11 mi. NE of Utrecht: a garden city. The settlement of Soestdijk, site of the Dutch royal summer residence, is in the vicinity. 13,248 (1939).

Baasha (bā′a̤.sha̤). d. probably c888 or 886 B.C. King of Israel (c910 *et seq.*). The third ruler of the kingdom of Israel, he is considered also to have been the founder of the second dynasty of Israelite kings (dating from the time Israel was separated, under Jeroboam I, from Judah). He usurped the throne after killing Nadab, son of Jeroboam I (and forthwith slew also a number of others whose kinship with Jeroboam might conceivably have jeopardized his position). He made his capital the city of Tirzah, and reigned for approximately 24 years (a great number of which were spent in war with Asa, king of Judah). Like Jeroboam, he was accused (by the prophet Jehu) of encouraging idolatry. 1 Kings, xv. 27–34; xvi. 1–7.

Bab (bab). [Full form, **Bab ed-Din,** meaning "Gate of Faith"; original name, **Ali Mohammed.**] b. at Shiraz, in what is now Iran, 1819; executed at Tabriz, in what is now Iran, July 9, 1850. Religious leader who founded (May 23, 1844) at Shiraz the sect known as Babism. Although his beliefs were in many respects basically those of the Shiite Moslems who were (and are) the dominant religious group in Iran, and although one of his aims was simply to achieve a degree of moral reform within the traditional framework of Islam, he also assumed the role of a prophet, equal in stature to Mohammed himself, and proclaimed the imminence of a Messiah. His success in persuading his followers to accept him in this role was so great as to threaten the established religious framework of the country, and to become a source of rebellion even against the civil authority of the state itself. As a result, after sentence by leading figures of the Shiite Moslem faction, he was shot by soldiers of the government and his sect was repressed with a degree of ruthlessness considered by some authorities to have been as great as any in the history of religious persecution (some estimates of the number of his followers who were killed have run as high as 20,000). Belief remained alive, however, in the 19-year interval (1844–63) which he had forecast before arrival of the Messiah, and in 1863 Baha Ullah was accepted by surviving Babists as the "Manifestation" prophesied by the Bab. Thereafter Babism, as such, disappeared, being replaced by Bahaism (although modern Bahaists reckon both Baha Ullah and the Bab as founders of their sect).

Bab, Lady. Character in James Townley's farce *High Life Below Stairs.*

Baba (bä′bä). Ethnic and linguistic group in Malaya (particularly in Singapore, Malacca, and Penang) who are the descendants of Chinese immigrants and speak a Chinese-influenced Malay dialect (called Baba Malay) as their mother tongue.

Baba, Cape. [Turkish, **Baba Burnu.**] Promontory at the W extremity of Turkey, at the entrance of the Gulf of Edremit, ab. 180 mi. SW of the city of Istanbul.

Baba, Hajji. Principal character in a novel by James Justinian Morier, *The Adventures of Hajji Baba of Ispahan,* published in 1824.

Baba Abdalla (äb.däl′a̤). Blind man, in a story in *The Arabian Nights' Entertainments,* who becomes rich through the kindness of a dervish. His covetousness makes him demand also a box of magic ointment which, when applied to the left eye, reveals all hidden treasures, but when used on the right produces total blindness. Doubting this, he applies it to both, and loses both sight and riches.

Baba Gurgur (bä′bä gör.gör′). Oil field in NE Iraq, in the foothills of the mountains of W Kurdistan, ab. 150 mi. N of Baghdad, at the head of a pipe line. ab. 550 mi. long to Tripoli, in Lebanon.

Babahoyo (bä.ʙä.ō′yō). City in W Ecuador, capital of Los Ríos province. 13,429 (est. 1944).

Babbage (bab′a̤j), **Charles.** b. near Teignmouth, Devonshire, England, Dec. 26, 1792; d. at London, Oct. 20, 1871. English mathematician, a founder, secretary, and vice-president of the Royal Astronomical Society, and professor of mathematics (1829–39) at Cambridge. He is now possibly best known as the inventor of a calculating machine which, after many years of toil and a large expenditure of money, he failed to perfect. He published a treatise *On the Economy of Machinery and Manufactures* (1832), a table of logarithms, and many minor works.

Bab Ballads (bab), **The.** Volume of humorous verse by W. S. Gilbert, published at London in 1868. The poems in the collection appeared originally in the magazine *Fun.*

Babbie (bab′i). Heroine of J. M. Barrie's novel *The Little Minister.*

Babbitt (bab′it). Novel by Sinclair Lewis, published in 1922. George F. Babbitt, who exemplifies the American business man of the 1920's, tires of the provincialism in the city of Zenith and makes tentative gestures of escape from the accepted values of those around him. In the end, however, he returns to Zenith's formalized code of behavior. The novel was variously, and vociferously, received by the American public; many found it a vigorous and welcome satire, others considered it a gratuitous attack on solid, middle-class virtue. Its most lasting effect was perhaps that it introduced the term "Babbitt" into the language as a noun describing a type of cautious, middle-class American.

Babbitt, Benjamin Talbot. b. at Westmoreland, N.Y., 1809; d. Oct. 20, 1889. American inventor and soap manufacturer who developed and improved soap-making processes, inventing much of the machinery used in his plant. His widely used "Babbitt's Best Soap" brought him a fortune. He also devoted his mechanical ingenuity to steam boilers, pumps, gas engines, and ordnance, taking out 108 patents between 1842 and 1889.

Babbitt, George Folansbee. The full name of the chief character of Sinclair Lewis's novel *Babbitt* (*q.v.*). He is better known, and usually referred to, as "George F. Babbitt."

Babbitt, Irving. b. at Dayton, Ohio, Aug. 2, 1865; d. at Cambridge, Mass., July 15, 1933. American teacher and author. After graduating (1889) from Harvard, he there served as an instructor (1894–1902), assistant professor (1902–12), and professor (1912 *et seq.*) of French. He was an originator (with Paul Elmer More) of the 20th-century humanistic development called the "New Humanism." Editor of Taine's *Introduction à l'histoire de la littérature anglaise* (1898), Voltaire's *Zadig* (1905), and Racine's *Phèdre* (1910). Author of *Literature and the American College* (1908), *The New Laokoön* (1910), *The Masters of Modern French Criticism* (1912), *Rousseau and Romanticism* (1919), and *Democracy and Leadership* (1924).

Babbitt, Isaac. b. at Taunton, Mass., July 26, 1799; d. at Somerville, Mass., May 26, 1862. American inventor, metal manufacturer, and one-time goldsmith, notable as the discoverer of the antifriction bearing-metal (an alloy of tin, copper, lead, and antimony) which bears his name. Originally only an incidental part of a journal box patented by him in 1839, the alloy was of tremendous importance in the development of high-speed machinery. As superintendent (1834 *et seq.*) of the South Boston Iron Works (also known as Alger's Foundry and Ordnance Works), Babbitt contributed to the first U.S. casting of a brass cannon.

Babcock (bab′kok), **George Herman.** b. at Unadilla Forks, N.Y., June 17, 1832; d. Dec. 16, 1893. American inventor and manufacturer, notable as one of the inventors of the Babcock and Wilcox steam engine and high-pressure boiler, and (with his father, Asher M. Babcock) of the first polychromatic printing press. Originally a job printer in Westerly, R.I., he joined his partner, Stephen Wilcox, at Providence, R.I., where they invented and manufactured the automatic cut-off engine bearing their names.

Babcock, Harold Delos. b. at Edgerton, Wis., Jan. 24, 1882—. American physicist and spectroscopy specialist. After receiving (1907) his B.S. from the University of California, he served as a staff member (1909–48) of Mount Wilson Observatory, Pasadena, Calif.

Babcock, James Francis. b. at Boston, Feb. 23, 1844; d. July 19, 1897. American chemist, notable for his work in the assaying of milk and liquors. After having attended the Lawrence Scientific School at Harvard, he acted as professor of medical chemistry (1869–74) at the Massachusetts College of Pharmacy, later holding a similar post at Boston University; he was also Massachusetts assayer of liquors (1875–85). His skill, as Boston inspector of milk, at revealing milk adulteration brought adoption of his methods by other cities. He was the inventor of a fire extinguisher bearing his name.

Babcock, James Woods. b. at Chester, S.C., Aug. 11, 1856; d. March 3, 1922. American physician and psychiatrist, responsible for early surveys of tuberculosis and pellagra.

Babcock, Joseph Weeks. b. at Swanton, Vt., March 6, 1850; d. at Washington, D.C., April 27, 1909. American politician. After a term as a member (1890 *et seq.*) of the Wisconsin legislature, he was a member of Congress (1892–1906), serving (1894 *et seq.*) as chairman of the Committee on the District of Columbia. He was also chairman (1894 *et seq.*) of the Republican Congressional Campaign Committee.

Babcock, Maltbie Davenport. b. at Syracuse, N.Y., Aug. 3, 1858; d. at Naples, Italy, May 18, 1901. American Presbyterian clergyman and author. A graduate of Syracuse University in 1879 and of Auburn Theological Seminary in 1882, he was ordained in the latter year, after taking the pastorate of the First Presbyterian Church, Lockport, N.Y. He later served as pastor of the Brown Memorial Church, Baltimore (1887–99), and of the Brick Presbyterian Church, at New York (1899 *et seq.*). His works, all published posthumously, include *Three Whys and Their Answer* (1901) and *The Success of Defeat* (1905).

Babcock, Orville E. b. at Franklin, Vt., Dec. 25, 1835; d. at Mosquito Inlet, Fla., June 2, 1884. American general, with the Union army in the Civil War. After graduation (1861) from West Point, he served with the Army of the Potomac and as aide-de-camp (1864 *et seq.*) to General Ulysses S. Grant. As private secretary to Grant, when he became president, and superintendent of buildings and grounds at Washington, D.C., he was associated with the notorious "Whisky Ring" and was indicted (1875) by a grand jury at St. Louis for complicity in revenue frauds, but was acquitted with the aid of a deposition on his good character by Grant.

Babcock, Rufus. b. at North Colebrook, Conn., Sept. 18, 1798; d. at Salem, Mass., May 4, 1875. American Baptist clergyman. He was graduated (1821) from Brown University, was president (1833–37) of Waterville College (now Colby College), Maine, served as pastor of several Baptist congregations, and was the founder and editor of the *Baptist Memorial.*

Babcock, Stephen Moulton. b. at Bridgewater, N.Y., Oct. 22, 1843; d. July 2, 1931. American agricultural chemist, noted for devising (1890) the Babcock test for the percentage of butterfat in milk. He served as professor (1887–1903) of agricultural chemistry at the University of Wisconsin, and as chief chemist (1887–1913) and assistant director (1901–13) at the Wisconsin Agricultural Experiment Station.

Babcock, Washington Irving. b. at Stonington, Conn., Sept. 26, 1858; d. at New York, Aug. 7, 1917. American naval architect, notable for introducing the mold system of ship construction into American shipbuilding and for improvements in the design of lake carriers. Graduated (1876) from Brooklyn Polytechnic Institute and in 1878 from Rensselaer Polytechnic Institute, he served (1880–85) on the staff of the Delaware Iron Shipbuilding and Engine Works, Chester, Pa. He was thereafter assistant superintendent (1885–87) of the Providence and Stonington Steamship Company and superintendent (1887 *et seq.*) of the Union Drydock Company, Buffalo, N.Y. He was manager (1889–1900), and later president, of the Chicago Shipbuilding Company.

Babek (bä′bek). [Surnamed **Khoremi,** meaning the "sensualist."] d. 837. Persian rebel and religious leader. He acquired his surname from the allegedly libertine principles which he taught. He was taken prisoner and put to death, after having defied, for a time, the entire forces of the caliph al-Mutasim, the eighth Abbaside caliph and son of Harun al-Rashid.

Babel (bā′bel, bab′el). See **Babylon,** Mesopotamia.

Babel (bä′bil), **Isaak Emanuilovich.** b. at Odessa, Russia, 1894—. Russian author. His book of sketches and short stories about the Russo-Polish conflict of 1920 had an extensive popular success when published in Russia (1926). It was translated into English as *Red Cavalry* (1929). His *Benya Krik, the Gangster and Other Stories* (1948) contains an English rendering of most of his autobiographical sketches and Jewish "gangster stories." In the U.S.S.R., he appeared in print for the last time in 1938. It is believed that he may have died in a Soviet concentration camp.

Babel (bā′bel, bab′el), **Tower of.** In the Old Testament, a tower built in the valley of Shinar by the descendants of Noah, who sought by this means to reach the heavenly realm above the earth. Displeased at their temerity, God thereupon threw their language into a multitude of languages, which made it impossible for the builders of the tower to understand each other or work together, and thus halted construction of the tower. Many scholars have interpreted this Biblical account (Gen. xi. 1–9) as a primitive explanation of the diversity of the world's languages.

Bab el Mandeb (bäb el män′deb, bab el man′deb). [Eng. trans., *"Gate of Tears."*] Sea passage separating the E "horn" of Africa from the Arabian Peninsula. It connects the Gulf of Aden with the Red Sea and separates French Somaliland from Aden protectorate. In it is the island of Perim, part of the British colony of Aden: a strategic point on one of the most important of the British-controlled trade routes.

Bab el Mandeb, Cape. [Arabic, **Ras Bab el Mandeb.**] Headland at the SW point of the Arabian peninsula, which projects into the strait of Bab el Mandeb near the Aden-Yemen boundary.

Babelon (bab.lôn), **Ernest Charles François.** b. at Sarrey, France, Nov. 7, 1854; d. at Paris, Jan. 3, 1924. French numismatist and archaeologist. He served as curator of the Paris department of numismatics. His main work is *Traité des monnaies grecques et romaines* (Treatise on Greek and Roman Coins, 1901–32).

Babemba (bä.bem′bä). See **Bemba.**

Babenberg (bä′ben.berk). Princely family of Franconia, prominent in the 9th and 10th centuries, whose castle stood on the site of the modern German city of Bamberg, in Bavaria. The Austrian dynasty of Babenberg, which ruled from 976 to 1246, held (1156–1246) the duchy of Austria before the establishment of the house of Hapsburg. The last of the Babenberg line was Frederick II ("The Quarrelsome"), who died in battle in 1246.

Babenhausen (bä′ben.hou.zen). Town in S Germany, in the *Land* (state) of Bavaria, American Zone, situated on the Günz River, ab. 22 mi. SE of Ulm: small industries; agricultural trade; school of agriculture and of home economics. It was formerly (1538–1806) the seat of an independent knightship. 3,493 (1946).

Babenhausen. Town in W Germany, in the *Land* (state) of Hessen, American Zone, formerly in the province of Starkenburg, Hesse, situated on the Gersprenz River, ab. 15 mi. SE of Frankfort on the Main: pharmaceutical and other industries. From the 15th to the 18th century it was the residence of the counts of Hanau-Lichtenberg. 3,343 (1946).

Baber, Babar, or **Babur** (bä′bėr). [Mongol surname (meaning the "Tiger") of **Zahir ud-Din Mohammed.**] b. Feb. 4, 1483; d. Dec. 28, 1530. Indian ruler, notable as the founder of the Mogul empire in India; great-grandson of Tamerlane. He succeeded his father in Fergana in 1495, conquered Kashgar, Kunduz, Kandahar, and Kabul (thus establishing himself as the ruler of Afghanistan), and, in 1525 and 1526, proceeded to the conquest of most of India. He wrote in the Tatar language memoirs afterward translated into Persian and from that into various Western languages.

Babeş (bä'besh), **Victor.** b. at Vienna, July 28, 1854; d. at Bucharest, Rumania, Oct. 19, 1926. Rumanian physician and bacteriologist. Active (1886) at the Pasteur Institute at Paris in the investigation of rabies, he demonstrated the protective value of the serum from an immunized animal. He described (1888) the metachromatic granules (called Babeş-Ernst bodies) found in the protoplasm of bacteria; recommended (1891) the mallein reaction for use in the early diagnosis of glanders; and discovered a group of small protozoon parasites, called Babesia, which invade the red cells of various animals (except humans).

Babes in the Wood. See **Children in the Wood.**

Babeuf (bå.bėf), **François Noël.** [Also: **Baboeuf**; pseudonym, **(Caius) Gracchus Babeuf.**] b. at St.-Quentin, France, Nov. 23, 1760; d. at Vendôme, France, May 27, 1797. French agitator and communist. He founded (1794) a journal called (eventually, but not at first) *Tribun du Peuple*, in which he advocated absolute equality and community of property. His beliefs anticipated those of Karl Marx; it was his conviction that the French Revolution would fail if it was able to achieve only political equality, and he asserted as equally important the common ownership of property and the right of each individual to share equally in the fruits of an economy which would be owned and served by all. In 1796 he took part in organizing a conspiracy against the Directory for the purpose of putting his theories into practice, but was betrayed, and executed, together with his principal accomplice, Darthé. His system of communism, known as Babouvism (in French, *Babouvisme*), is set forth in his two principal works, *Cadastre perpétuel* (1789) and *Du système de population* (1794).

Babia Góra (bä'byä gö'rä). [Also, **Babia-Gura.**] Peak in the Carpathian Mountains, near the borders of Czechoslovakia and Poland, SW of Kråkow. 5,659 ft.

Babieça (bä.ʙyā'thä). See **Bavieça.**

Babil (bā'bil, bab'il). See under **Babylon,** Mesopotamia.

Babine Mountains (ba.bēn', bab'ēn). Minor mountain chain in the coastal range of W Canada, in the W central part of British Columbia. The highest peak has an elevation of ab. 8,000 ft.

Babinet (bå.bē.ne), **Jacques.** b. at Lusignan, France, March 5, 1794; d. at Paris, Oct. 21, 1872. French physicist, meteorologist, and astronomer. He invented (or made improvements in) several devices, including a polariscope and an air pump, used in physics.

Babington (bab'ing.ton), **Anthony.** b. at Dethick, Derbyshire, England, in October, 1561; executed Sept. 20, 1586. English Roman Catholic conspirator. He was page for a time to Mary Queen of Scots during her imprisonment at Sheffield, and became chief (under the guidance of various Catholic priests, particularly of John Ballard) of a conspiracy for the murder of Elizabeth, the release of Mary, and a general rising of the Catholics. The plot was discovered, and he was sentenced to death for high treason.

Babington, Benjamin Guy. b. at Guy's Hospital, Southwark (now part of London), 1794; d. 1866. English physician and linguist. After serving in the navy, with the rank of midshipman, at Walcheren and Copenhagen, he joined the Indian civil service; poor health, however, forced him to retire from this career after service in the Madras presidency. Turning to medicine, he received his M.D. degree at Cambridge in 1830, and served as a physician (1840–58) at Guy's Hospital, London, where his father had been the resident apothecary; in 1861 he was president of the Royal Medical and Chirurgical Society. He was the author of *A Grammar of the High Dialect of the Tamil Language* (1822), *The Adventures of the Gooroo Paramartan* (1822) from the Tamil, *The Vedala Cadai* (1831), a Tamil version of certain Vedic tales, and Hecker's *Epidemics of the Middle Ages* (1844), from the German.

Babington, Churchill. b. in Leicestershire, England, 1821; d. 1889. English classical scholar and archaeologist.

Babisa (bä.bē'sä). See **Bisa.**

Babism (bäb'iz.em). [Also, **Babi.**] Persian sect from which developed modern Bahaism. It was called "Babism" from its founder, Bab, who took his name from *bab*, meaning "gate." He claimed that no one could come to know God except through him, and hence called himself, in full, "Bab ed-Din," which means "Gate of Faith." The sect of Babism was, essentially, a pantheistic offshoot of Mohammedanism, tinctured with Gnostic, Buddhistic, and Jewish ideas. It inculcated a high morality, discountenanced polygamy, forbade concubinage, asceticism, and mendicancy, recognized the equality of the sexes, and encouraged the practice of charity, hospitality, and abstinence from intoxicants of all kinds.

Babits (bô'bich), **Mihály.** b. at Szekszárd, Hungary, Nov. 26, 1883; d. at Budapest, 1941. Hungarian poet and novelist, one of the outstanding representatives of the modernist *Nyugat* (West) group. His lyrical poetry is marked by many experiments in formal expression. His *Elza Pilota, vagy a tökéletes társadalom* (Elza Pilota, or the Perfect Society, 1933), a utopian novel, describes a future stage of mankind in which permanent war will prevail between two superstates. He was the author also of *Halál fia* (Son of the Death, 1927).

Babócsa (bô'bō.chô). Town in SW Hungary, W of Pécs, situated near the Drawa River and the Yugoslav border.

Babol (bä.bōl'). See **Babul.**

Baboon (ba.bön'), **Lewis** and **Philip.** Characters in John Arbuthnot's *History of John Bull*, representing, respectively, Louis XIV of France and Philip of Bourbon, Duc d'Anjou.

Babrius (bā'bri.us). [Also: **Babrias, Gabrias.**] fl. possibly in Syria, 1st century A.D., or later. Greek writer who put into choliambic verse the fables attributed to Aesop.

Babson (bab'son), **Roger Ward.** b. at Gloucester, Mass., July 6, 1875—. American financial statistician and author. A graduate (1898) of the Massachusetts Institute of Technology, he founded Babson's Statistical Organization and the Babson Institute. He is the author of *Business Barometers* (1909), *The Future of South America* (1915), *Business Fundamentals* (1923), *Looking Ahead Fifty Years* (1942), *Better Living for Less Money* (1943), and other works.

Babudja (bä.bö'jä). See **Buja.**

Babul (bä.böl'). [Also: **Babol**; former name, **Balfrush, Barfrush,** or **Barfurush.**] Town in N Iran, former capital of the province of Mazanderan, on the Bawal River near the Caspian Sea, ab. 89 mi. NE of Tehran: an important center for commerce between the U.S.S.R. and Iran. 30,000 (1942).

Babushkin (bä'bush.kin). [Former name, **Losinoostrovsk.**] City in the U.S.S.R., in the Moscow *oblast* (region) of the Russian Soviet Federated Socialist Republic, a northern suburb of Moscow: light industries. 70,480 (1939).

Babuyan Islands (bä.bö.yän'). Group of small islands in the Philippines, N of Luzon, separated from that island by the Babuyan Channel. Among the most important of the islands are Calayan and Camiguin.

Babwa (bä'bwä). See **Bwa.**

Babylon (bab'i.lon). In ancient geography, a name sometimes given to a town in Egypt, on the Nile River opposite the Pyramids.

Babylon. [Possibly the Biblical **Babel**; ancient Persian, **Babirus.**] In ancient geography, a city in Mesopotamia, the capital of Babylonia, situated on both sides of the Euphrates River, above the modern city of Hilla, S central Iraq, ab. 50 mi. S of Baghdad. The etymology of the name is, as ascertained by many passages in the cuneiform inscriptions, Bab-Ili (meaning "Gate of God"), from "bab" (meaning "gate") and "ilu" (meaning "god"). Babylon was one of the oldest cities of Mesopotamia (compare Gen. x. 10), and was the undisputed capital of Babylonia at the time of the Elamite conquest, in the third millennium B.C. As capital of the country it shared in all its vicissitudes, and was the principal aim of the Assyrian invasions. It was first conquered (c1270 B.C.) by the Assyrian king Tukulti-Adar, then (c1110 B.C.) by Tiglath-Pileser I. Of Shalmaneser II (860–824 B.C.) and his son and grandson it is recorded that they victoriously entered Babylon and sacrificed there to the gods. It was customary with the Assyrian kings, in order to be recognized as fully legitimate kings, to go to Babylon and there perform the mysterious ceremony termed by them "seizing the hands of Bel." Sennacherib sacked it (690 B.C.), and completely razed it to the ground. His son and successor Esarhaddon undertook, 11 years later, the restoration of the city. But it was under Nabopolassar (625–604 B.C.), the founder of the new Babylonian empire, and especially under his successor Nebuchadnezzar (605–562 B.C.) that it became "Babylon the Great." The ruins, now covering both banks of the Euphrates, are those of the Babylon of these kings and their successors, and convey some idea of its former magnitude and splendor. Nebuchadnezzar, who took more pride in the buildings constructed under his auspices than in his victorious campaigns, concentrated all his care upon the adorning and beautifying of his residence. To this end he completed the fortification of the city begun by his father Nabopolassar. The city itself was adorned with numerous temples, chief among them Esagila ("the high-towering house"), temple of the city and of the national god Merodach (Babylonian, Marduk) with his spouse Zirpanit. In the neighborhood of it was the royal palace, the site of which was identified with the ruins of Al-Kasr. Sloping toward the river were the Hanging Gardens, one of the seven wonders of the world, the location of which is in the N mound of ruins, Babil. The temple described by Herodotus is that of Nebo in Borsippa, not far from Babylon, which Herodotus included under Babylon, and which also in the cuneiform inscriptions is called "Babylon the second." This temple, which in the mound of Birs Nimrud represents the most imposing ruin of Babylonia, is termed in the inscriptions Ezida ("the eternal house"), an ancient sanctuary of Nebo (Assyrian, Nabu), and was restored with great splendor by Nebuchadnezzar. It represents in its construction a sort of pyramid built in seven stages, whence it is sometimes called "temple of the seven spheres of heaven and earth," and it has been assumed that the narrative of the Tower of Babel in Gen. xi. may have been connected with this temple. Concerning Babylon proper Herodotus mentions that it had wide streets lined with houses of three and four stories. In the conquest (538 B.C.) of Cyrus of Persia, the city of Babylon was spared. Darius Hystaspes razed its walls and towers. Xerxes (486–465 B.C.) despoiled the temples of their golden statues and treasures. Alexander the Great wished to restore the city, but was prevented by his early death. The decay of Babylon was hastened by the foundation (300 B.C.) in its neighborhood of Seleucia, which was built from the ruins of Babylon. The last who calls himself in an inscription "king of Babylon, restorer of Esagila and Ezida," was Antiochus the Great (223–187 B.C.). In the time of Pliny (23–79 A.D.) Babylon was a deserted and dismal place. In the Apocalypse, Babylon is used for the city of the Antichrist.

Babylon. Village in SE New York, in Suffolk County, Long Island, on Great South Bay: residential and yachting center. 6,015 (1950).

Babylon. Middle English ballad. It tells how a young outlaw kills two of three sisters before he learns from the third that he is their brother.

Babylonia (bab.i.lō'ni.ạ, -lōn'yạ). In ancient geography, a region and country of SW Asia. Its extent and boundaries are matters of divergence of opinion, some scholars considering it to have been coextensive with the whole, but others with the S part only, of Mesopotamia. Before the rise of Babylon to power, S Mesopotamia was known as Chaldea and as Sumer. A line running from the Euphrates near Hit to a little below Samarra on the Tigris has been suggested as an approximate boundary between Sumer to the south and Akkad to the north. Some, however, apply the name Sumer to the whole region; some also identify it with the Biblical Shinar (also spelled Shanhar, Shenar), which others differentiate from Sumer and apply only to N Mesopotamia.

Culture. The N part of the area between the Tigris and the Euphrates is an upland; the S part is an alluvial plain resulting from deposits of silt by the two rivers. This alluvial land advances into the Persian Gulf at the rate of ab. 115 ft. a year. From this it is known that Eridu, anciently a seaport and now 130 mi. inland, existed 6,000 years ago. It is widely believed that man first attained civilization in this alluvial plain. The ruins of many cities and towns have been discovered, with artifacts of Stone Age and Bronze Age cultures. There is evidence that from an early age this was a region where many peoples met. The Sumerians drained swamps, built canals, practiced flood control, developed agriculture and trade, and developed skill in metal working, pottery, and textiles. They had an advanced understanding of astronomy and also practiced astrology, and acquired such a reputation for magic that their other name, Chaldeans, was for ages a synonym for magicians. Their religion was polytheistic; different Semitic and non-Semitic deities were popular in different periods, and each city had its particular god or goddess. At Nippur, Bel was especially worshiped, but within the precincts of his temple there were shrines to 24 other deities. One of the great Sumerian achievements was the cuneiform alphabet, perhaps the first ever to take form. Systems of weights, measures, and accounting were also invented in Sumer and later highly developed in Babylon.

History. The Sumerians, a non-Semitic people, were conquered by the Akkadians, generally supposed to have been Semites, under Sargon I; the Akkad dynasty may be dated c2400–2200 B.C. At this time the city of Babylon began to dominate the entire region from the mountains E of the Tigris to the Arabian or Syrian Desert and from the Persian Gulf to the borders of what is now Armenia. Thus the ancient Babylonian empire occupied approximately the area now comprised in the kingdom of Iraq. From about 2200 B.C. it was ruled for some centuries by the Guti, a highland people; about 1850 B.C. it was conquered by the Amorites, who were probably Semites. The capture of Mari, chief city of the Amorites, by the Sumerian Hammurabi is now generally dated about 1700 B.C. Under Hammurabi the village of Babylon became a great city, and the laws were written down in the famous Hammurabian Code. Babylonia, however, was far from through with invasions, being conquered thereafter by Horites and Hittites and, about 1270 B.C. by the Assyrians. For centuries Assyria had been a vassal state of Babylonia, but now for more than 600 years the Assyrians were supreme. Under Nebuchadnezzar (605–562 B.C.) Babylonia enjoyed its greatest power and Babylon its peak of wealth and glory; but in 538 B.C. Cyrus of Persia put an end to Babylonian power. After the Persians, Babylonia was ruled by Alexander the Great, by the Seleucids, the Parthians, the Arabs, and the Turks. Throughout the later centuries the ancient system of drainage and irrigation was neglected, and the land became almost a wilderness, while ancient cities and towns were leveled by war or abandoned by their inhabitants.

Babylonian Captivity (bab.i.lō'ni.ạn). [Also: **Exile**; sometimes shortened to **Captivity.**] Term applied to the period of the exile of the Jews in Babylon; usually reckoned as 70 years, although the actual period from the destruction of the temple and capture of Jerusalem to the return was not more than 50 years. In 605 B.C. Nebuchadnezzar attacked Jerusalem and carried off many prisoners. In 597 the city was again attacked and the king Jehoiachin, his household, and some 10,000 others are said to have been carried away. In 586 the city was captured after a siege, and the city and temple were burned. This was the date of the beginning of the Babylonian captivity proper. A considerable part of the remaining population, including the city's most prosperous and influential citizens, were carried off to Babylonia. The mass deportation had obvious advantages so far as the conquering power was concerned, if only because of the hostages it provided; indeed, such measures appear to have been usual in the policy of both Babylonia and Assyria in their conquests, although it is this particular one that has become best known. Nearly 50 years later (c538), the Persian king Cyrus, after capturing Babylon, granted the exiles permission to return, and a group of more than 42,000 persons is said to have availed itself of the opportunity. Jerusalem at this time once more became for the Jews both a national and religious center, and rebuilding of the temple was at once undertaken. With its completion (c516) the 70 years of the scriptural prophecy were completed.

Babylonian Captivity. Term often applied to that period in Roman Catholic history when the popes lived at Avignon, France. During this period of some 70 years the popes (all of whom were French) were subject, in greater or lesser degree, to direct political control by the French throne. The term derives from the original Babylonian Captivity, of the Jews in the 6th century B.C., which is traditionally reckoned also as having lasted for 70 years.

Babylonica (bab.i.lon'i.ką). Ancient romance in 39 books, by Iamblichus, a Syrian rhetorician of the time of the Roman emperor Trajan. It existed in manuscript until near the end of the 17th century, when it was destroyed by fire. An epitome of it is given by Photius. It narrates the adventures of two lovers, Rhodanes and Sinonis, in their flight from King Garmus of Babylon, and their attempt to evade his two eunuchs, Damas and Saca, sent in pursuit of them.

Baca (bā'ką), **Valley of.** Valley referred to in the Old Testament (Ps. lxxxiv. 6), probably the later El-Bakei'a, between Jerusalem and Bethlehem. The Biblical reference ("valley of weeping" in the King James Version) is clearly allegorical, and has been suggested as the probable source of the phrase "vale of tears."

Bacarra (bä.kär'rä). Town in Ilocos Norte province, in NW Luzon, Philippine Islands. 6,566 (1948).

Bacău (bä.ku'ö). [Also: **Bakau, Bakeu.**] Town in NE Rumania, in the region of Moldavia, situated on the Bistrița River, ab. 55 mi. SW of Iași, on the railroad from Chernovtsy to Bucharest: railroad junction; textile mills; factories for leather, shoes, and paper; vegetable, fruit, and meat canneries. 34,461 (1948).

Bacbuc (bak.bük). Priestess of the temple in François Rabelais' *Pantagruel.*

Baccarat (bå.kå.rå). Town in E France, in the department of Meurthe-et-Moselle, situated on the Meurthe River, ab. 15 mi. SE of Lunéville. It has large glass and crystal works. The town was severely damaged in World War II. 5,034 (1946).

Baccelli (bät.chel'lē), **Guido.** b. at Rome, Nov. 25, 1830; d. Jan. 10, 1916. Italian statesman and professor (1856 *et seq.*) of clinical medicine at the University of Rome. After being named (1874) to the chamber of deputies, he served as minister of instruction under Agostino Depretis (1880–84), Francesco Crispi (1893–96), and Luigi Pelloux (1898–1900) and as minister of agriculture, industry, and commerce (1901–03) under Giuseppe Zanardelli.

Bacchae (bak'ē) or **Bacchantes** (bą.kan'tēz). [Also, **Maenads.**] In ancient Greece and Italy, female worshipers of the god of wine, generally called by the Greeks Dionysus, and by the Romans Bacchus.

Bacchae, The. Tragedy by Euripides, usually assigned to a late period in the life of the dramatist.

Bacchanalia (bak.ą.nā'li.ą, -nāl'yą). Festival in honor of Bacchus (Dionysus). Introduced into Rome from the Greek communities in S Italy, the Bacchanalia (the name is a Latin translation of the Greek *Dionysia*) originally consisted of secret rites practiced by women only (the Bacchae or Bacchantes) on three days of the year. Later the rites were opened to men and were celebrated five days each month; they became drunken orgies, at which it was supposed that crimes were plotted and conspiracies were hatched, and the Roman Senate by decree in 186 B.C. prohibited them throughout Italy, under penalty of severe punishments.

Bacchiadae (ba.kī'ą.dē) Ruling family of Corinth, a branch of the Heraclidae; reputedly so named from Bacchis, said to have been king of Corinth in the period 926–891 B.C. Members of the family ruled Corinth, first under a monarchical form of government, then as a close oligarchy, from 926 B.C. till their deposition (c657 B.C.) by Cypselus.

Bacchides (bak'i.dēz). fl. 160 B.C. Governor of Mesopotamia who was sent by Demetrius I (Demetrius Soter), king of Syria, into Judea to investigate the rebellion of the Maccabees and to install the renegade, Alcimus, as high priest. He treacherously slew Jewish priests and leaders who submitted to him, and thereafter conducted several campaigns aiming at the subjugation of Judea, but being defeated by Jonathan and Simon he made peace and returned to his own country.

Bacchiglione (bäk.kē.lyō'nā). [Latin, **Medoacus Minor.**] River in NE Italy which flows past Vicenza and Padua and empties into the Gulf of Venice. Length, ab. 65 mi.

Bacchus (bak'us). In classical mythology, a name of Dionysus, the son of Jupiter (Zeus) and Semele. He was the god of wine, personifying both its good and its bad qualities. Bacchus was the current name of the god among the Romans. The orgiastic worship of Bacchus was especially characteristic of Boeotia, where his festivals were celebrated on the slopes of Mount Cithaeron, and extended to those of the neighboring Parnassus. In Attica the rural and somewhat savage cult of Bacchus underwent a metamorphosis, and reached its highest expression in the choragic literary contests, in which originated both tragedy and comedy, and for which were written most of the masterpieces of Greek literature. Bacchus was held to have taught the cultivation of the grape and the preparation of wine.

Bacchus and Ariadne (ar.i.ad'nē). Oil painting (1523) by Titian in the National Gallery, London. In it, Bacchus descends from his leopard-chariot, attended by satyrs and maenads, while Ariadne turns away startled. The background is of woodland, meadow, and sea, glowing with color and light, harmonious, and beautiful in form.

Bacchylides (bą.kil'i.dēz). b. on the island of Ceos (now Keos), in the Aegean Sea; fl. 5th century B.C. Greek lyric poet; nephew and pupil of Simonides and a contemporary and rival of Pindar. He lived for a time at the court of Hiero I of Syracuse.

Bacci (bät'chē). Original surname of **Aretino, Pietro.**

Bacci, Baccio Maria. b. Jan. 8, 1888—. Florentine painter. He studied at Florence, at Paris, and in Germany; his first important work was *The Café des Artistes.* Other works include *La Mère*, *Le Fils Prodigue*, and *Paysage de Fiesole.* His works have been exhibited in Italy and France, and he received (1931) the silver medal from the Éducation Nationale at Rome.

Bacciocchi (bät.chôk'kē), **Felice Pasquale.** b. at Ajaccio, Corsica, May 18, 1762; d. at Bologna, Italy, April 27, 1841. French army officer; husband of Maria Anna Elisa Bonaparte and brother-in-law of Napoleon I. Through his wife (with whom he was raised to the nobility by Napoleon I) he became the prince of Lucca and Piombino, and the duke of Tuscany.

Baccio della Porta (bät'chō del'lä pôr'tä). See **Bartolommeo,** Fra.

Bach (bäċh), **Aleksey Nikolayevich.** b. 1857—. Russian biochemist and revolutionary. He wrote a famous political work, *Czar Hunger* (1883), and did important scientific work on peroxides in slow autoxidations (1897), metabolism (1901–10), and on redox enzymes (1911–26). In 1881 he joined the "People's Will Party," a terrorist group, on returning from exile in N Russia. He lived in France and Switzerland in the period 1885–1917; returned to Russia in 1917, and organized (1920) the Biochemical Institute of the People's Commissariat of Health.

Bach, Baron **Alexander von.** b. at Loosdorf, Austria, Jan. 4, 1813; d. Nov. 13, 1893. Austrian Ultramontane statesman, minister of justice (July 19, Oct. 8, and Nov. 21, 1848) and of the interior (1849–59), and later (1859–67) ambassador at Rome, where he negotiated a concordat with the Vatican.

Bach, Carl Philipp Emanuel. [Called **"the Berlin"** or **"the Hamburg" Bach.**] b. at Weimar, Germany, March 8, 1714; d. at Hamburg, Germany, Dec. 14, 1788. German composer; third son of Johann Sebastian Bach (1685–1750). He went to Berlin in 1737, and in 1740 entered the service of Frederick the Great as court musician, remaining in this position until 1767; he then went to Hamburg. He was a voluminous composer of concertos, sonatas, chamber music, and oratorios. Author of *Versuch über die wahre Art Klavier zu spielen* (Essay on The True Art of Clavier Playing, 1753), the first methodical work of its kind.

Bach, Christoph. b. April 19, 1613; d. at Arnstadt, Germany, in September, 1661. German organist and composer; son of Hans Bach (d. 1626) and grandfather of Johann Sebastian Bach (1685–1750). He was musician for the town and court at Eisenach, Germany.

Bach, Hans. [Called **Der Spielmann,** meaning "the Player."] d. Dec. 26, 1626. German musician, active in Thuringia, Germany; great-grandfather of Johann Sebastian Bach (1685–1750).

Bach, Heinrich. b. Sept. 16, 1615; d. at Arnstadt, Germany, in July, 1692. German musician; son of Hans Bach (d. 1626). He was organist (1641 *et seq.*) at Arnstadt.

Bach, Johann (or **Johannes**). b. Nov. 26, 1604; d. May 13, 1673. German organist at Schweinfurt and Erfurt, Germany; son of Hans Bach (d. 1626).

Bach, Johann Ambrosius. b. at Erfurt, Germany, Feb. 22, 1645; d. at Eisenach, Germany, 1695. German organist; son of Christoph Bach (1613–61) and father of Johann Sebastian Bach (1685–1750). He was town musician at Eisenach.

Bach, Johann Bernhard. b. Nov. 23, 1676; d. June 11, 1749. German organist and composer, known as "the most distinguished of the Erfurt line" of the great family of Bach; cousin of Johann Christoph Bach (1642–1703). He served as organist at the Kauffmannskirche at Erfurt, and also at Magdeburg and at Eisenach. At the time of his death he was *Kammer-Musikus* (chapel musician) in the court orchestra of Duke Johann Wilhelm of Saxe-Eisenach.

Bach, Johann Christian. b. at Erfurt, Germany, 1640; d. there, 1682. Member of the Bach family of musicians; son of Johann Bach (1604–73) of Schweinfurt and Erfurt.

Bach, Johann Christian. [Called **"the Milanese"** or **"the English" Bach.**] b. at Leipzig, Germany, Sept. 5, 1735; d. at London, Jan. 1, 1782. German musician; son of Johann Sebastian Bach (1685–1750). He was for much of his life resident at Milan (where he was organist of the cathedral, 1754–59) and at London (where he taught music to the royal family, 1759–82). He composed operas, masses, and Te Deums.

Bach, Johann Christoph. b. in December, 1642; d. March 31, 1703. German organist; son of Heinrich Bach (1615–92). He was court organist at Eisenach, Germany.

Bach, Johann Christoph. b. at Erfurt, Germany, Feb. 22, 1645; d. at Arnstadt, Germany, 1693. German musician at the court of the count of Schwarzburg; son of Johann Bach of Schweinfurt and Erfurt (1604–73).

Bach, Johann Christoph. b. at Erfurt, Germany, June 16, 1671; d. Feb. 22, 1721. German organist; son of Johann Ambrosius Bach (1645–95) and older brother of Johann Sebastian Bach (1685–1750). He was organist to the court at Ohrdruff.

Bach, Johann Christoph Friedrich. [Called **"the Buckeburg" Bach.**] b. at Leipzig, Germany, June 21, 1732; d. at Bückeburg, Germany, Jan. 26, 1795. German composer; ninth son of Johann Sebastian Bach (1685–1750). He was *Kapellmeister* (choirmaster) to Count Schaumburg at Bückeburg.

Bach, Johann Michael. b. Aug. 9, 1648; d. 1694. German composer and instrument maker; son of Heinrich Bach (1615–92).

Bach, Johann Nikolaus. b. at Eisenach, Germany, Oct. 10, 1669; d. 1753. German organist at Jena; son of Johann Christoph Bach (1642–1703). He was director of university music at Jena. Also composer of orchestral music, none of it preserved, and of vocal works, he was perhaps best known as an instrument maker.

Bach, Johann Sebastian. b. at Eisenach, Germany, March 21, 1685; d. at Leipzig, Germany, July 28, 1750. German composer and instrumentalist, noted as one of the foremost musicians of all time; son of Johann Ambrosius Bach (1645–95). Orphaned at an early age, he went in 1695 to Ohrdruff to live with his organist brother Johann Christoph. In 1700 he entered the Michaelisschule at Lüneburg. Although he was 15 years of age his unusually beautiful soprano voice won him free schooling in return for choir participation. He became a violinist in the chamber orchestra of Prince Johann Ernst at Weimar in 1703 and, later that same year, organist at Arnstadt. He was organist at Mülhausen in 1707, court organist and violinist at Weimar in 1708, and *Kapellmeister* (choirmaster) to the prince of Anhalt Köthen in 1717. He was cantor at the Thomasschule (1723–50), a position which entailed the additional work of director of music in several Leipzig churches as well as musical duties in connection with the university; he was also honorary *Kapellmeister* (choirmaster) to the duke of Weisenfels in 1729, and in 1736 honorary court composer to the elector of Saxony. He became totally blind in 1749 after an unsuccessful operation to restore his failing sight. He composed both secular and religious music for solo performance and for diverse vocal and instrumental combinations. His 48 preludes and fugues for *"Das wohltemperierte Klavier"* ("The Well-tempered Clavier") represented the first wholehearted use of the equally tempered scale throughout all keys. He was master of counterpoint, and his many organ preludes and fugues are still often played, both in their original form and in orchestral transcriptions. Of his secular instrumental works the best-known are the six Brandenburg Concertos (so called because they were composed at the request of the elector of Brandenburg) for chamber orchestra. Of his vocal works, the sacred cantatas and oratorios are the most important; outstanding among them are the *St. John's Passion* and the *St. Matthew Passion.* He also composed over 30 secular cantatas, and set over 300 of Luther's hymns to music.

Bach, Paul. Pseudonym of **Baumbach, Rudolf.**

Bach, Wilhelm Friedemann. [Called **"the Halle" Bach.**] b. at Weimar, Germany, 1710; d. at Berlin, July 1, 1784. German composer and organist; eldest son of Johann Sebastian Bach (1685–1750). He was organist of the Church of St. Sophia at Dresden (1733) and of St. Mary's at Halle (1747–67).

Bach, Wilhelm Friedrich Ernst. b. 1759; d. at Berlin, Dec. 25, 1845. Organist and composer; son of Johann Christoph Friedrich Bach (1732–95). *Kapellmeister* (choirmaster) at Berlin, he taught music to Frederick William III of Prussia. He also wrote songs, cantatas, and works for piano.

Bachan or **Bachian** (bä.chän′). See **Batjan.**

Bacharach (bäċh′ä.räċh). Town in W Germany, in the *Land* (state) of the Rhineland Palatinate, French Zone, formerly in the Rhine Province, Prussia, situated on the Rhine River, ab. 24 mi. above Koblenz: wine trade. It is picturesquely situated, and has fortifications dating from the 14th century, the 13th-century Peters Church, and the ruined Werner's Chapel. Above the town is the ruin of the castle Stahleck, once the residence of the *Pfalzgrafen* (counts of the Palatinate), destroyed by the French in 1689 under Mélac. Bacharach was the center of the Rhenish wine trade until the 16th century. It suffered severe damage in World War II. 1,962 (1946).

Bach Choir. English choral society, founded (1875) at London by amateur singers under the direction of Otto Goldschmidt. Subsequent directors have been C. V. Stanford (1885–1902), H. Walford Davies (1902–07), H. P. Allen (1907–20), R. Vaughan Williams, Adrian Boult, and Reginald Jacques. The group specializes in performances of Bach chorales, giving an annual performance of the complete St. Matthew Passion.

Bache (bāch), **Alexander Dallas.** b. at Philadelphia, July 19, 1806; d. at Newport, R.I., Feb. 17, 1867. American physicist and educator; great-grandson of Benjamin Franklin, grandson of Richard Bache, and cousin of Benjamin Franklin Bache. After graduation (1825) from West Point, he served as professor of natural philosophy and chemistry (1828 *et seq.*) at the University of Pennsylvania, and later as superintendent (1843–67) of the U.S. Coast Survey. First president (1836 *et seq.*) of Girard College, at Philadelphia, he also reorganized the Philadelphia public schools. Most of his work as a physicist was done in the field of terrestrial magnetism.

Bache, Benjamin Franklin. b. at Philadelphia, Aug. 12, 1769; d. there, Sept. 10, 1798. American journalist; grandson of Benjamin Franklin, son of Richard Bache, and cousin of Alexander Dallas Bache. After studying abroad, he founded (1790) the Philadelphia *General Advertiser* (later known as the *Aurora*), an organ which supported the Democratic-Republican cause against the Federalists with such vigor that Bache was arrested (1798) for libel. It was Thomas Jefferson's opinion that the Sedition Act was framed by the Federalists with suppression of the *Aurora* particularly in mind.

Bache, Francis Edward. b. at Birmingham, England, Sept. 14, 1833; d. there, Aug. 24, 1858. English composer; brother of Walter Bache (1842–88). He was the author of music for the piano, as well as operas, songs, and others.

Bache, Franklin. b. at Philadelphia, Oct. 25, 1792; d. March 19, 1864. American physician, chemist, and teacher; first son of Benjamin Franklin Bache. After receiving (1814) his M.D. from the University of Pennsylvania, he served as a military surgeon in the War of 1812. He was a professor of chemistry (1826–32) at the Franklin Institute, holding similar posts at the Philadelphia College of Pharmacy and Science from 1831 to 1841, and at Jefferson Medical College (1841 *et seq.*). As early as 1813, in three papers appearing in the *Memoirs of the*

Columbian Chemical Society, he made notable contributions to the progress of chemical theory in the U.S.; he edited (1826–31) the *North American Medical and Surgical Journal;* revised (1830) the *Pharmacopoeia of the United States;* and produced the *Dispensatory of the United States of America*, which passed through numerous editions during his lifetime.

Bache, Jules Semon. b. at New York, Nov. 9, 1861; d. March 24, 1944. American financier and collector of works of art. He began his business career as cashier of Leopold Cahn and Company, New York bankers, and became head of this firm in 1892, when it became J. S. Bache and Company. The Bache firm played an important financial role in an era of expanding American industry, and Bache himself was a director of many companies. Deeply interested in art, Bache acquired one of the world's outstanding collections of paintings and sculptures, which was given in the year of his death (1944) to the Metropolitan Museum, at New York.

Bache, Richard. b. at Settle, in the West Riding, Yorkshire, England, 1737; d. July 29, 1811. American merchant and Revolutionary patriot; son-in-law of Benjamin Franklin. When he emigrated (1765) to New York, he joined his brother Theophylact in business. In 1767, after moving to Philadelphia, he married Franklin's only daughter, Sarah. He served on the Committee on Non-Importation Agreements, on the Committee of Correspondence, and on the Board of War. He was postmaster general (until 1782), succeeding Franklin in that office.

Bache, Sarah. b. at Philadelphia, Sept. 11, 1744; d. Oct. 5, 1808. Daughter of Benjamin Franklin and wife of Richard Bache.

Bache, Theophylact. b. at Settle, in the West Riding, Yorkshire, England, Jan. 17, 1734/35; d. at New York, Oct. 30, 1807. American merchant; brother of Richard Bache. Having arrived (1751) at New York, he entered the mercantile and shipping business, and on the eve of the Revolutionary War was prominent in the city's merchant community. His reputation as a Loyalist brought the dissolution of a business partnership with his brother Richard Bache.

Bache, Walter. b. at Birmingham, June 19, 1842; d. at London, March 26, 1888. English pianist; brother of Francis Edward Bache. He is noted for his advocacy of Franz Liszt.

Bachelder (bak'ẹl.dėr), **John.** b. at Weare, N.H., March 7, 1817; d. at Houghton, Mich., July 1, 1906. American inventor and machinist. He improved the sewing machine invented by Elias Howe by adding the horizontal table, the continuous feed, and the vertical needle.

Bacheller (bach'ẹ.lėr), **Irving (Addison).** b. at Pierpont, N.Y., Sept. 26, 1859; d. at White Plains, N.Y., Feb. 24, 1950. American journalist and author. For a number of years he was on the staff of the Brooklyn *Times* and on that of the New York *World*. He was the author of 28 novels, including *The Master of Silence* (1890), *The Still House of O'Darrow* (1894), *Eben Holden, a Tale of the North Country* (1900), *D'ri and I* (1901), *Darrel of the Blessed Isles* (1903), *Vergilius* (1904), *Silas Strong, Emperor of the Woods* (1906), *The Hand-made Gentleman* (1909), *Keeping up with Lizzie* (1911), *A Man for the Ages* (1919), *Opinions of a Cheerful Yankee* (1926), *Coming Up the Road* (1928), *A Candle in the Wilderness* (1930), and *The Winds of God* (1941).

Bachelor of Salamanca, The. [French title, **Le Bachelier de Salamanque, ou les mémoires de Don Chérubin de la Ronda.**] Romance by Alain René Le Sage.

Bacher (bä'kėr), **Otto Henry.** b. at Cleveland, Ohio, March 31, 1856; d. at Bronxville, N.Y., Aug. 16, 1909. American painter, etcher, and illustrator. He was a student at Paris of Jules Joseph Lefebvre and Carolus Duran, later going to Venice, where he was a pupil of Frank Duveneck and a friend of Whistler. The special kind of monotype called "Bachertype" was first printed on Bacher's press by members of Duveneck's group. He is remembered chiefly for his etchings and pen-and-ink drawings, and for illustrations in *Harper's* and the *Century* magazines.

Bachergebirge (bä'ċhėr.gẹ.bir"gẹ). German name of a mountain group in what is now NW Yugoslavia, formerly S Styria, S of the Drava River, an eastern continuation of the Karawanken mountains.

Bachewa (bä.che'wä). See **Chewa.**

Bach Gesellschaft (bäċh gẹ.zel'shäft). Organization founded (1850) in Germany by leading musicians for the publication of a critical edition of the entire works of Johann Sebastian Bach; the society issued (1850–1900) 46 annual publications. Among the editors were Wilhelm Rust, A. Dörffel, Ernst Naumann, and Count Paul Waldersee. After its reincorporation (1900) as the Neue Bach Gesellschaft, the society issued a yearbook, founded a Bach museum at the composer's birthplace, and sponsored Bach festivals.

Bachka (bäch'kä). See **Bačka.**

Bachman (bak'mạn), **John.** b. at Rhinebeck, N.Y., Feb. 4, 1790; d. at Charleston, S.C., Feb. 24, 1874. American naturalist and Lutheran clergyman, chiefly remembered for his collaboration with J. J. Audubon upon *The Viviparous Quadrupeds of North America* (3 vols., 1845–49, with numerous editions and revisions). Schoolteacher at Ellwood, Pa., and Philadelphia, he was licensed (1813) as a Lutheran preacher, and ordained in 1814. He took (1815) a pulpit at St. Johns, Charlestown, S.C., where he organized the Lutheran Synod of South Carolina and founded the state's Lutheran theological seminary. Bachman's connection with Audubon, which began in 1831, developed into a working partnership after 1835; some scholars believe Bachman actually wrote much of and edited all of the classic work on the North American viviparous quadrupeds. He was a leader in founding the South Carolina Horticultural Society (1833), and author of *The Unity of the Human Race* (1850), which attempted to tread a middle way between theology and science.

Bacho (bā'kō), **John.** See **Baconthorpe, John.**

Bachokwe (bä.chôk'we). See **Chokwe.**

Bächtold (beċh'tolt), **Jakob.** b. at Schleitheim, Switzerland, Jan. 27, 1848; d. at Zurich, Switzerland, Aug. 8, 1897. Swiss critic and historian of literature, writing in German. He was professor of German at the University of Zurich. He wrote *Geschichte der deutschen Literatur in der Schweiz* (1892) and published the first extensive biography of Gottfried Keller, whose personal friendship he enjoyed: *Gottfried Kellers Leben, seine Briefe und Tagebücher* (1893–96). This basic study has since been revised and gone through many editions.

Bacis (bā'sis) or **Bakis** (-kis). In Greek legend, a name given to several seers or prophets, the most celebrated of whom was the Boeotian Bacis, whose oracles were delivered at Heleon in Boeotia. Specimens of these (spurious) oracles, in hexameter verse, have been preserved.

Back (bak), Sir **George.** b. at Stockport, Cheshire, England, Nov. 6, 1796; d. at London, June 23, 1878. English admiral and Arctic explorer. He accompanied Sir John Franklin to the Spitzbergen region (1818) in the *Trent*, to the Coppermine River (by land) and the Arctic coasts of America (1819–22), and to the Mackenzie River (1825–27). He conducted (1833–35) an expedition overland, and discovered the Great Fish, or Back, River. He commanded the *Terror* in an Arctic expedition (1836–37). He was made admiral in 1857. His chief works are *Narrative of the Arctic Land Expedition to the Mouth of the Great Fish River* and *Narrative of an Expedition in H.M.S. Terror*.

Bačka (bäch'kä). [Also: **Bachka;** Hungarian, **Bácska;** German, **Batschka.**] Region in N Yugoslavia, formerly in S Hungary, in the autonomous province of Vojvodina, federative unit of Serbia, situated between the Tisa and the Danube rivers. Its chief city is Novi Sad. The region is very fertile, and until recently had a strong German minority. However, the Germans were expelled as Nazi sympathizers after World War II and have been replaced by Serbian colonists.

Bačka Topola (tô'pô.lä). Town and township in N Yugoslavia, in the region of Bačka, autonomous province of Vojvodina, federative unit of Serbia, former *banovina* (province) of Dunavska, situated S of Subotica. It is a market town in the center of a rich agricultural region. 14,177 (1948).

Back Bay. Name applied to what was originally an expansion of the Charles River, in Boston, Mass. In the 19th century it was largely filled in and the area is now the site of a residential quarter in which are situated the residences of many of Boston's oldest and wealthiest families.

Backbite (bak'bīt), **Sir Benjamin.** A slanderer in Richard Brinsley Sheridan's comedy *The School for Scandal.*

Backbone Mountain. Mountain ridge in NW Maryland, in Garrett County, extending SW into West Virginia along the North Branch of the Potomac River. Its peak is the highest point in Maryland. Elevation, ab. 3,360 ft.

Backergunge (bak.ėr.gunj'). See **Bakarganj.**

Backhaus (bäk'hous), **Wilhelm.** b. at Leipzig, Germany, March 26, 1884—. German pianist. He studied at the Leipzig conservatory and became (1899) a pupil of Eugen d'Albert. He taught (1905) at the Royal College of Music, Manchester, England, and toured (1906 *et seq.*) as a virtuoso.

Backhouse (bak'us), Sir **Roger Roland Charles.** b. Nov. 24, 1878; d. at London, July 15, 1939. British naval officer. He was appointed admiral (1934), admiral of the fleet (1939), and was named commander in chief of the home fleet (1935) and first sea lord and chief of the naval staff (1938); he retired in 1939.

Backhuysen (bäk'hoi.zẹn), **Ludolf.** [Also, **Bakhuyzen.**] b. at Emden, in East Friesland, Germany, Dec. 18, 1631; d. at Amsterdam, Nov. 17, c1708. Dutch marine painter.

Backlog Studies. Prose work (1873) by Charles Dudley Warner.

Backlund (bäk'lünd), **Johann Oskar.** b. in Sweden, April 28, 1846; d. at Pulkovo, Russia, Aug. 30, 1916. Swedish astronomer. He was appointed (1876) observer at the observatory at Dorpat (now Tartu, in Estonia), adjunct astronomer at Pulkovo (1878), astronomer of the Academy of Sciences at St. Petersburg (1887), and director of the observatory at Pulkovo (1895).

Backnang (bäk'näng). Town in S Germany, in the *Land* (state) of Württemberg-Baden, American Zone, formerly in the Neckar *Kreis* (district) of Württemberg, situated on the Murr River, ab. 15 mi. NE of Stuttgart. It manufactures machinery and vehicles; has metallurgical, chemical, shoe, leather, and textile industries, and livestock markets. The *Stiftskirche* (collegiate church) dates from the 15th century, the *Rathaus* (town hall) from the 17th century. Backnang has a number of educational institutions, a library, and a local museum. The population is predominantly Protestant. 18,189 (1950).

Back River. [Former name, **Great Fish River.**] River in the district of Mackenzie, Northwest Territories, Canada, which flows generally NE from the neighborhood of Great Slave Lake into the Arctic Ocean. It is named for the English explorer, Sir George Back, who discovered it during an expedition in the period 1833–35. Length, 605 mi.

Bäckström (bek'strėm), **Per Johan Edvard.** b. at Stockholm, Oct. 27, 1841; d. there, Feb. 12, 1886. Swedish poet and dramatist. He was editor of *Teater och Musik* (1876), of *Nu* (1877), and of *Post och Inrikes Tidningar* (from 1878 to his death). Author of the tragedy *Dagvard Frey* (1877) and others.

Back to Methuselah (mẹ.thö'zẹ.lạ). Cycle of five plays by George Bernard Shaw, published in 1921. The work is a satirical treatment of the theme of purposive evolution and the perfectibility of man. The separate parts, set in the Garden of Eden, England, and in the future, are entitled *In the Beginning*, *Gospel of the Brothers Barnabas*, *The Thing Happens*, *Tragedy of an Elderly Gentleman*, and *As Far As Thought Can Reach.*

Backus (bak'us), **Azel.** b. near Norwich (at what is now Franklin), Conn., Oct. 13, 1765; d. Dec. 9, 1817. American Congregational clergyman and educator, first president (1812 *et seq.*) of Hamilton College. A Federalist, he attacked Thomas Jefferson in a sermon, published (1798) as *Absalom's Conspiracy*, and in 1806 was formally charged with (but never tried for) libeling President Jefferson.

Backus, Isaac. b. at Norwich, Conn., Jan. 9, 1724; d. Nov. 20, 1806. American Separatist, Baptist clergyman, religious historian, and fighter for religious freedom. His interest in religion was aroused during the "Great Awakening" inspired by George Whitefield; he joined (1746) with his family in forming a Separatist church and set out on a preaching tour which took him to the precinct of Titicut (near Middleborough), Mass., where he was ordained in 1748. As a Separatist, he became noted for his preaching tours; his doctrinal controversies over baptism finally led him to organize (1756) a Baptist church at Middleborough, where, except for his far-ranging tours, he lived for the rest of his life. He was one of the most capable church leaders of his time and as a vigorous supporter of religious freedom in America stands squarely in the tradition of Roger Williams. His outstanding contribution to colonial and subsequent religious history was made in *A History of New England, with Particular Reference to the Denomination of Christians Called Baptists* (3 vols., 1777–96; revised edition, 2 vols., 1871).

Backus, Truman Jay. b. at Milan, N.Y., Feb. 11, 1842; d. March 25, 1908. American educator. After graduation (1864) from the University of Rochester (where he later received his M.A.) he taught (1867–83) rhetoric and English at Vassar College. He served as president (1883–1908) of the Packer Collegiate Institute of Brooklyn.

Backward Glance O'er Travel'd Roads, A. Prose epilogue to *Leaves of Grass* by Walt Whitman, published in the edition of 1889. It was earlier used as the preface to Whitman's *November Boughs* (1888).

Backward Sun, The. Novel by Stephen Spender, published in 1940.

Backwater. Novel by Dorothy M. Richardson, published in 1916. It is the second section of *Pilgrimage*, a novel sequence in 12 parts (published collectively in 1938), employing the stream-of-consciousness technique.

Backwell (bak'wel), **Edward.** d. 1683. London goldsmith and alderman who played an important part in state financial affairs under Oliver Cromwell and Charles II of England. He is regarded as a chief founder of the modern English system of banking.

Bacler d'Albe (bå.kler dålb), **Louis Albert Ghislam,** Baron. b. at St.-Pol, France, Oct. 21, 1762; d. at Sèvres, France, Sept. 12, 1824. French painter, cartographer, and soldier. He served (1796–1814) with distinction under Napoleon, especially as director of the topographical bureau, and attained (1813) the rank of brigadier general. His best-known work is a picture of the battle of Arcole, Italy, in which he took part.

Bacninh (bäk.nin'). Town in Indochina, SE Asia, in the E part of Tonkin (North Viet-Nam) on the Red River, ab. 20 mi. NE of Hanoi. Near it several engagements in the French war in Tonkin took place in 1884. In the period after World War II it was again the site of military activity by French troops, this time against the forces of the Viet Minh faction in Indochina. Pop. ab. 10,000.

Bacoli (bä'kō.lē). Town and commune in S Italy, in the *compartimento* (region) of Campania, in the province of Napoli, situated on the Bay of Pozzuoli, near Cape Miseno, W of Naples. Pop. of commune, 10,438 (1936); of town, 5,506 (1936).

Bacolod (bä.kō'lōd). City in the Philippine Islands, the capital of Negros Occidental province, in NW Negros island, on Guimaras Strait. 42,820 (1948).

Bacon (bā'kọn), **Alice Mabel.** b. at New Haven, Conn., Feb. 6, 1858; d. May 1, 1918. American writer, teacher, and lecturer. She taught (1883–88, 1889–99) at the Hampton Institute and for one year at the Peeress' School of the imperial Japanese household, describing her experiences at the latter institution in *Japanese Girls and Women* (1891) and in *A Japanese Interior* (1893). She revisited Japan in 1899, teaching for two years at the Tokyo Higher Normal School. In 1890 she founded the Dixie Hospital, an institution for the training of Negro nurses.

Bacon, Anthony. b. 1558; d. May, 1601. English diplomat; son of Sir Nicholas Bacon by his second wife, and brother of Francis Bacon. In 1593 he attached himself to Robert Devereux, the 2nd earl of Essex, and followed his fortunes until his death, acting for seven years as his private foreign secretary.

Bacon, Augustus Octavius. b. in Bryan County, Ga., Oct. 20, 1839; d. at Washington, D.C., Feb. 14, 1914. American legislator and lawyer, a soldier in the Confederate Army during the Civil War. He received his law degree (1860) at the University of Georgia, after which he practiced law (c1865 *et seq.*) at Macon, Ga.

After serving as a member (1870 *et seq.*) of the Georgia House of Representatives, he was elected (1894), a senator from Georgia. In 1912 he was one of the first U.S. senators to be elected under the Constitutional amendment providing for the popular election of senators. At the time of his death he was chairman of the Senate Committee on Foreign Relations.

Bacon, David. b. at Woodstock, Conn., Sept. 4, 1771; d. at Hartford, Conn., Aug. 27, 1817. American Congregational clergyman, missionary, and pioneer; father of Delia Bacon (1811–59) and Leonard Bacon (1802–81). Sent (1800) by the Connecticut Missionary Society to work among the Indians W of Lake Erie, he continued his missionary activities on Mackinac Island in the following year; later he bought a 12,000-acre tract in the Western Reserve and laid out (1807) the town of Tallmadge, Ohio.

Bacon, Delia Salter. b. at Tallmadge, Ohio, Feb. 2, 1811; d. Sept. 2, 1859. American writer and lecturer; sister of Leonard Bacon (1802–81). Her best-known work, *Philosophy of the Plays of Shakespeare Unfolded* (1857), in which she attempted to prove that the plays attributed to Shakespeare are the work of Francis Bacon and others, touched off the Shakespeare-Bacon controversy which continues to this day. She wrote the book in England, after abandoning a successful career as a lecturer in the U.S., conducting her researches at London and elsewhere for three years before making her literary contribution.

Bacon, Edward Payson. b. at Reading, N.Y., May 16, 1834; d. at Daytona, Fla., Feb. 16, 1916. American grain trader. As a freight and ticket clerk (1856–65) for the Milwaukee and Mississippi Railroad, he developed equipment for handling passenger coupon tickets which was still in use decades after his death. He was one of the founders (1865) of the Milwaukee grain-trading firm of Bacon and Everingham, and later, as an independent operator, the foremost grain trader in the Middle West. He was one of the leading spirits behind the law of 1906 which enlarged the powers of the Interstate Commerce Commission, and was the founder of the Bacon Fellowships at Beloit College.

Bacon, Edwin Munroe. b. at Providence, R.I., Oct. 20, 1844; d. at Cambridge, Mass., Feb. 24, 1916. American journalist and author. An early career (1863 *et seq.*) as a reporter on the Boston *Daily Advertiser* was followed by employment (1868–72) with the New York *Times*. He served as editor (1873–78) of the Boston *Globe*, resigning to rejoin the *Daily Advertiser* as chief editor (1883–86). After holding the editorship (1886–91) of the Boston *Post*, he retired from newspaper activity, and wrote a number of regional and local travel books, including *Boston Illustrated* (1893), *Historic Pilgrimages in New England* (1902), and *Rambles Around Old Boston* (1914).

Bacon, Ezekiel. b. at Boston, Mass., Sept. 1, 1776; d. at Utica, N.Y., Oct. 18, 1870. American jurist and politician. He served (1807–13) as a member of Congress from Massachusetts, and later (1813–15) as first comptroller of the U.S. Treasury.

Bacon, Francis. [Titles: 1st Baron **Verulam of Verulam,** Viscount **St. Albans.**] b. Jan. 22, 1561; d. April 9, 1626. English essayist, philosopher, jurist, and statesman; son of Sir Nicolas Bacon, Lord Keeper of the Great Seal, and related through his mother to the Cecils, a family politically powerful in the reigns of Elizabeth and James I. Bacon studied at Cambridge (1573–75) and at Gray's Inn (1576 *et seq.*). He was admitted to the bar in 1582, and entered Parliament in 1584. As a learned counsel under Elizabeth he was commissioned to prosecute his erstwhile friend and benefactor Robert Devereux, 2nd Earl of Essex, for treason. Under James I he was knighted in 1603. In 1607 he became solicitor-general, in 1608 secretary to the Council of the Star Chamber (this office he had formerly held by reversion), in 1612 a judge of the Court of the Verge, in 1613 attorney general, in 1617 Lord Keeper, and in 1618 Lord Chancellor. He was created Baron Verulam of Verulam in 1618, and Viscount St. Albans in 1621. From his boyhood he lived close to the court. He was an "adviser" of James in a continuous battle waged between king, court, and lords on the one side and the House of Commons and courts of common law on the other. At the instigation of his political enemies, he was tried in 1621 for bribery, condemned, fined, and deprived of office. He had accepted, after a fashion of the time, presents from litigants in the courts over which he presided. He called the verdict just, and contended, probably in all sincerity, that no gift had ever influenced him in his reaching judicial decisions.

Quest for Knowledge. Bacon pursued high place and power largely to obtain control of foundations, such as colleges, and of collectors of scientific data for the inauguration and perpetuation of a "new learning." He sought to encompass all scientific information and set out to be a "second Aristotle." He hoped that his new method of investigation (*novum organum*) would supplant the organon of that influential Greek thinker. He called his purported reform of learning the Great Instauration. This included a "refutation" of all previous opinions and theories, especially those of Aristotle; a freeing of the human mind from its predispositions to error, which he called Idols (false images); a new method of investigation; and a naturalistic philosophy to be based on conclusions reached through an inductive collecting and observing of the data of natural history. His logic he designed as a "machine" which was to keep the intellect from soaring in "speculation" and would at the same time enlighten the senses. His philosophy was materialistic. He gave over to revealed theology questions concerning God's nature, the rational soul and its processes, and the basic rules of morality.

Influence on Later Thought. Bacon's influence became considerable about the middle of the 17th century when many members of the Royal Society professed to be his followers. By the end of the century speculative opponents regarded him as a "dictator" in English philosophy. His followers were in the main naturalistic thinkers who refused to accept any opinion, those of revealed theology excepted, which could not be "proven" by "observation and experiment." Few of them were materialists. Bacon himself made no appreciable discoveries, but he did much to implement an inductive investigation of nature. He was instrumental in founding a philosophical tradition in which systematic thought became identified with generalized and organized conclusions obtained in the empirical sciences. He construed the purpose of human knowledge as the control of nature for the relief of human misery, and he gave prominence to a doctrine of education which rejected textual study as "useless" and identified "sound" and "solid" learning with technical information and skill gained in the practice of the pure and applied sciences.

Written Works. His most important works are *Essays* (1597, 1612, 1625), *Advancement of Learning* (1605), *De Sapientia veterum* (1609), *Novum Organum* (1620), *Phenomena universi* (1622), *De dignitate et augmentis scientiarum* (1623), and the following pieces published posthumously: *Cogitationes de rerum natura, Valerius Terminus, Delineatio et argumentum, Cogitata et visa, Redargutio philosophiarum, New Atlantis, De principiis atque originibus,* and *Sylva Sylvarum.* Most of his Latin writings are translated in his *Works*, edited by Robert Leslie Ellis, James Spedding, and Douglas Denon Heath. His *Life* has been written with painstaking care by Spedding.

Bacon, Frank. b. at Marysville, Calif., Jan. 16, 1864; d. at Chicago, Nov. 19, 1922. American actor and playwright, notable for his homespun role of Lightnin' Bill Jones in the once (1918–21) tremendously popular *Lightnin'* (of which he was coauthor with Winchell Smith). He first appeared on the stage in 1890, in *Ten Nights in a Barroom* at the Garden Theater at San José, Calif.; arrived at New York after the San Francisco earthquake, he scored successes in *Stop Thief, The Cinderella Man, The Miracle Man,* and *The Fortune Hunter.* He was coauthor of *Me and Grant* and *Five o'Clock.*

Bacon, Henry. b. at Watseka, Ill., Nov. 28, 1866; d. Feb. 16, 1924. American architect, notable as the designer of the Lincoln Memorial at Washington, D.C. While on the staff of the New York architectural firm of McKim, Mead, and White, he won (1889) the Rotch Traveling Fellowship and spent two years studying architecture in Europe. He established (1897) a partnership with James Brite, and in 1902 founded his own firm. His work is characterized by Greek influence, as in his great Lincoln Memorial (for which he received the gold medal of the American Institute of Architects), and he designed many monuments in collaboration with sculptors, among them Augustus Saint-Gaudens and Daniel Chester French. The numerous buildings, memorials, and monuments he designed include the Union Square Savings Bank, New York, the Longfellow Monument, Cambridge Mass., the Parkman Monument, Jamaica Plain, Mass., the Lafayette Monument, Brooklyn, N.Y., and the war memorial for the State of Massachusetts, St. Mihiel, France.

Bacon (bȧ.kôṅ), **Jean Paul.** b. at Paris, Nov. 1, 1907—. French political leader, a leading participant in the founding of the *Mouvement républicain populaire* (MRP). A Catholic youth leader before World War II, he was a Resistance leader (1941–44), and served (1944 *et seq.*) as a member of the Chamber of Deputies. He was minister of labor (1950 *et seq.*) in several cabinets.

Bacon (bā'kọn), **John.** b. at Canterbury, Conn., April 9, 1738; d. Oct. 25, 1820. American Congregational clergyman, jurist, and legislator. He graduated (1765) from the College of New Jersey (now Princeton University), and in 1771 became pastor of Old South Church at Boston. His theological views drew the criticism of his parishioners, and in 1775, after his dismissal from the Boston pastorate, he took up farming at Stockbridge, Mass. A champion of civil liberty, he was instrumental in removing discriminatory provisions in the state constitution adopted in 1780. He served as associate judge (1779–1807) and presiding judge (1807–11) of the court of common pleas of Berkshire County, and was a member of Congress (1801–03).

Bacon, John. b. at London, Nov. 24, 1740; d. there, Aug. 4, 1799. English sculptor. Among his works are monuments to William Pitt, 1st earl of Chatham (Guildhall and Westminster Abbey), Dr. Samuel Johnson (St Paul's Cathedral), and Sir William Blackstone (All Souls, Oxford).

Bacon, John Mosby. b. in Kentucky, April 17, 1844; d. at Portland, Ore., March 19, 1913. American soldier, in the Union army in the Civil War. He was brevetted colonel for Indian warfare (1867) on the Rio Pecos, Texas, and for action (1869) near the headwaters of the Brazos River in Texas. He served as aide-de-camp (1871–84) to General William Tecumseh Sherman.

Bacon, Josephine Dodge. [Maiden name, **Daskam.**] b. at Stamford, Conn., Feb. 17, 1876—. American author. She was graduated from Smith College in 1898. Among her works are *Smith College Stories* (1900), *The Imp and the Angel* (1901), *The Madness of Philip* (1902), *Whom the Gods Destroyed* (1902), *Her Fiancé* (1904), *An Idyll of All Fools' Day* (1908), *The Strange Cases of Dr. Stanchon* (1913), *Square Peggy* (1919), *Kathy* (1933), *The House by the Road* (1937), and *The Root and the Flower* (1939).

Bacon, Leonard. b. at Detroit, Mich., Feb. 19, 1802; d. Dec. 24, 1881. American Congregational clergyman, editor, teacher; brother of Delia Salter Bacon (1811–59). He was graduated (1820) from Yale, and later from Andover Theological Seminary; ordained as an evangelist (1824), he became (1825) minister of the First Church of New Haven, Conn., whose parishioners included Noah Webster and Eli Whitney. He was its only pastor until 1866 and thereafter pastor emeritus until he died; he was also acting professor of revealed theology (1866–71) in the Yale Divinity School and lecturer on church polity and American church history (1871 *et seq.*) at the same institution. He was editor (1826–38) of the *Christian Spectator*, a founder and editor of the *New Englander*, and a founder and senior editor (1848 *et seq.*) of the *Independent*, an antislavery organ. His *Slavery Discussed in Occasional Essays* (1846) supposedly was the cause of Abraham Lincoln's statement: "If slavery is not wrong, nothing is wrong." Always at the forefront of the controversies concerning the interpretation of Christian doctrine, he did much to strengthen the position of American Congregationalism.

Bacon, Leonard. b. at Solvay, N.Y., May 26, 1887—. American poet. A graduate (1909) of Yale, he was an assistant professor of English (1910–23) at the University of California. Author of *Ulug Beg* (1923), *Animula Vagula* (1926), *Guinea Fowl and Other Poultry* (1927), *The Legend of Quincibald* (1928), *Lost Buffalo* (1930), *Sunderland Capture and Other Poems* (1940, awarded the Pulitzer Prize), *Day of Fire* (1943), and other works. His autobiography is *Semi-Centennial* (1939).

Bacon, Leonard Woolsey. b. at New Haven, Conn., Jan. 1, 1830; d. May 12, 1907. American Congregational clergyman and writer; son of Leonard Bacon (1802–81). He was graduated (1850) from Yale, where he also received his theological degree (1854) and an M.D. (1856). Ordained (1856) as a Congregational minister at Litchfield, Conn., he became (1860) state missionary of the general association of Connecticut, later serving in pastorates at Stamford, Brooklyn, and Baltimore. During a five-year stay abroad he was for a time pastor of the American Church at Geneva, Switzerland, and from 1878 to 1892 was successively pastor of the Park Church, Norwich, Conn.; the Woodland Presbyterian Church, Philadelphia; the Ancient Independent Presbyterian Church, Savannah, Ga.; and the Second Congregational Church, Norwich. He was the author of many religious works, including *An Inside View of the Vatican Council* (1872), *The Simplicity that is in Christ* (1886), *History of American Christianity* (1897), and *Anti-Slavery before Garrison* (1903).

Bacon, Nathaniel. b. 1593; d. 1660. English Puritan lawyer, member of Parliament (1645–60), and master of requests under Oliver Cromwell and Richard Cromwell. He was the author of a *Historical Discourse of the Uniformity of the Government of England* (1647–51).

Bacon, Nathaniel. b. at Friston Hall, Suffolk, England, Jan. 2, 1647; d. in Gloucester County, Va., in October, 1676. American colonial leader, champion of reform in early Virginia, and head of "Bacon's Rebellion" (1676). Educated at Cambridge University and Gray's Inn, he emigrated to Virginia, settling at Curl's Neck on the James River. Although a member of the governor's council, his sympathies were with the social underlings of the colony who labored under inequalities then existing in the colonial laws. Widespread dissatisfaction with Governor John Berkeley's Indian policy caused Bacon to lead an expedition against the Pamunkey Indians; he also compelled Berkeley to call a new assembly for the enacting of reform measures. Lacking a commission from Berkeley authorizing his raids in Indian territory, Bacon, together with some of his followers, was arrested upon his return to Jamestown. He was pardoned and restored to his seat on the council; but fearing for his personal safety, he fled Jamestown, gathered his aroused followers, and forced Berkeley to give him a commission for operations against the Indians. Before Bacon's expedition could get under way, he was proclaimed a rebel by Berkeley. Bacon counterattacked with the capture and burning of Jamestown. He died before he could institute his popular reforms, and with his death the insurrection he led disintegrated.

Bacon, Sir Nicholas. b. at Chislehurst, Kent, England, 1509; d. at London, Feb. 20, 1579. English statesman; father of Francis Bacon. He was graduated (1527) with a B.A. from Corpus Christi College, Cambridge; was called to the bar in 1533; became solicitor of the Court of Augmentations in 1537; attorney of the Court of Wards and Liveries in 1546; and was lord keeper of the great seal from Dec. 22, 1558, to his death, exercising after April 14, 1559, the jurisdiction of lord chancellor.

Bacon, Peggy. b. at Ridgefield, Conn., May 2, 1895—. American satirical artist and writer, probably best known as the author of poems and illustrations, chiefly drypoints and etchings, which caricature with sharpness, rather than bitterness, society in America. She is a writer and illustrator also of books for children. A student of Jonas Lie, Randall Davey, and (at the Art Students League, New York) of John Sloan, Kenneth Hayes Miller, George Bellows, and Andrew Dasburg, she won (1934) a Guggenheim Fellowship and has taught (1935–36; 1948 *et seq.*) at the Art Students League. She is the former wife (1920–40) of the artist Alexander Brook. Represented in the Metropolitan Museum of Art and the Whitney Museum of American Art, New York, among others, she is the author of 12 books illustrated by herself, including *The Lion-Hearted Kitten and Other Stories* (1927) and *Off With Their Heads* (1934).

Bacon, Phanuel. b. at Reading, England, Oct. 13, 1700; d. at Balden, Oxfordshire, England, Jan. 10, 1783. English divine, comic dramatist, and poet. He received degrees in art (1719, 1722) and divinity (1731, 1735) from Oxford University; served as vicar of Bramber, Sussex, and rector of Balden. He was the author of *The Kite* (1719), a mock-heroic poem; *The Snipe*, a humorous ballad; and *A Song of Similies*. The latter two appeared in the *Oxford Sausage* (1764), a collection of college verse. He also wrote five comedies, all dated 1757, published in one volume, *Humorous Ethics*.

Bacon, Robert. b. at Jamaica Plain, Mass., July 5, 1860; d. May 29, 1919. American banker, diplomat, and soldier. After graduation (1880) from Harvard, he joined the financial house of Lee, Higginson and Company, became a partner (1883) in E. Rollins Morse and Brother, and joined (1894) J. P. Morgan and Company as a partner. He participated in the organization of the U. S. Steel Corporation and the Northern Securities Company; resigning (1903) from the Morgan firm, he served (1905–09) as assistant secretary of state to Elihu Root, and as full secretary for a brief period in 1909; he was ambassador (1909–12) to France. Before the U.S. entered World War I, he was a vigorous supporter of preparedness, and during the war served as chief of the American military mission at British headquarters.

Bacon, Roger. [Called **Doctor Mirabilis,** Anglicized as the **"Admirable Doctor."**] b. at or near Ilchester, Somersetshire, England, c1214; d. probably at Oxford, England, in 1294. English philosopher and scientist. He was educated at Oxford and Paris (whence he appears to have returned (c1250) to England), and joined the Franciscan order. In 1257 he was sent by his superiors to Paris where he was kept in close confinement for several years. He was invited (1266) by Pope Clement IV to write a general treatise on the sciences, in answer to which he composed his chief work, the *Opus majus*. He was in England in 1268. In 1278 his writings were condemned as heretical by a council of his order, in consequence of which he was again placed in confinement. He was at liberty in 1292. Besides the *Opus majus*, his most notable works are *Opus minus*, *Opus tertium*, and *Compendium philosophiae*.

General Appreciation. Bacon was essentially an encyclopedist; that is, he was tormented with the idea of the unity of knowledge, and his life consistently reflected an effort better to grasp and to explain that unity. He denounced violently the evils of scholasticism (too violently, in fact, to obtain practical results within his own age). He realized the urgent need for philosophers and theologians to enlarge their basis of knowledge; they were not acquainted with available scientific data, and their mathematical and linguistic equipment was utterly inadequate. His greatest title to fame, however, was his vindication of the experimental spirit. He was not himself an experimenter any more than he was a mathematician, but he saw better than anyone else in his time that without experimentation and without mathematics, natural philosophy is very soon reduced to verbiage. He also realized the utility of knowledge, and this was even more remarkable than to realize its unity, for the latter had been done instinctively by almost every philosopher. In the *Opus majus* and the *Opus tertium* he insists upon that utility repeatedly. This double point of view, unity (to be discovered experimentally and proved with the help of mathematics) and utility, led him to entirely new conceptions of knowledge, of learning, and of education. His accomplishments fell considerably short of his visions. Yet visions are very important, and we need seers as well as inventors. Bacon made few if any experiments, and no invention, not even gunpowder, can be definitely ascribed to him. He seems to have vaguely foreseen fundamental discoveries and inventions: the possibility of circumnavigating the world, of propelling boats by mechanical means, of flying, of utilizing the explosive property of powder, and of improving sight by the proper adjustment of lenses. It is true that, as opposed to a dogmatic system like Thomism, Bacon's thoughts seem (and are) disconnected, but one should not confuse dogmatism with originality. Bacon's thought was less systematic, but on the whole more original than that of his great contemporaries. And the best proof of this is that he was a true harbinger of modern civilization, while Saint Thomas Aquinas (not to speak of the other great scholastics of the Continent) was destined to become virtually a symbol of medievalism. Bacon founded no schools, but the majority of modern scientists feel more genuinely attracted to him than to any other medieval personality.

Baconian Legends. The experiments suggested by Bacon failed to be appreciated for a considerable time, and there emerged gradually the legend of "Friar Bacon, the wonderworker." All sorts of magical powers were ascribed to him. This legend can be traced back to the 14th century; by 1385 it was already known on the W coast of the Adriatic Sea, in Dalmatia. It was finally established by a play of Robert Greene (*The Honorable Historie of Frier Bacon and Frier Bongay,* played with various "magical" properties; printed 1594 *et seq.*) and by a London chapbook dating from about the same time: "The famous historie of Frier Bacon containing the wonderful things that he did in his life, also the manner of his death with the lives and deaths of the two conjurers Bungey [sic] and Vandermast" (reprinted 1627, 1638, *et seq.*). This aspect of the Baconian legend has been recently reinforced by the discovery "in an ancient castle in Southern Europe" of a manuscript written in cipher and ascribed to Bacon. If it were authentic, Bacon should be credited with the invention and actual use of telescope and compound microscope, and with the discovery of seminiferous tubes, cells with nuclei, spermatozoa, and so forth. Such inventions and discoveries in Bacon's time would have been remarkable indeed, but unfortunately the manuscript cannot possibly be ascribed with any authenticity to Bacon. An entirely different legend dating from comparatively modern times represents Bacon as a martyr of science and of the freedom of thought. This is doubly misleading, for Bacon was a scientist but not a free thinker, as this phrase is generally understood. A very original thinker and a forerunner of modern science, he was both outspoken and incautious, but he was also very orthodox and, in many ways, a fundamentalist. Granted that he suffered for the originality of his mind and the eccentricities of his character, his "martyrdom" is nevertheless not established, and he was not in any sense a forerunner of the modern rationalists. For him, theology was still the crown of all knowledge, and the Bible its repository.

Bacon, Thomas. b. on the Isle of Man, c1700; d. at Frederick, Md., May 24, 1768. Anglican clergyman and educator, notable for his efforts on behalf of education for the Negro and in the cause of popular education. He was also compiler of the *Laws of Maryland at Large* (1765).

Bacon's Rebellion. See under **Bacon, Nathaniel.**

Baconthorpe (bā′kọn.thôrp), **John.** [Also: **Bacon, Bacho;** called the **"Resolute Doctor."**] d. 1346. English Carmelite monk and schoolman; grandnephew of Roger Bacon.

Bacoor (bä.kō.ōr′). Town in Cavite province, S Luzon, Philippine Islands. A military road follows the coast from Bacoor to Manila. 6,276 (1948).

Bácsalmás (bäch′ôl.mäsh). Town in S Hungary, N of the Yugoslav border: a station on the railroad line from Subotica to Baja. There is wine cultivation in the vicinity. The population was formerly (until after World War II) largely German. 13,697 (1948).

Bacsányi (bô′chä.nyē), **János.** b. at Tapolcza, Hungary, May 11, 1763; d. at Linz, Austria, May 12, 1845. Hungarian poet, prose writer, and journalist. He founded (1788), with Ferenc Kazinczy and others, the journal *Magyar Museum.*

Bácska (bôch′kô). Hungarian name of **Bačka.**

Bactria (bak′tri.ạ). In ancient geography, a country in C Asia, N of the Paropamisus Mountains on the upper Oxus River (now the Amu Darya), nearly corresponding to the modern district of Balkh in Afghanistan. The ancient capital was Zariaspa, Baktry, or Bactra (now Balkh). Bactria was the cradle of the Persian religion which Zoroaster reformed c600 B.C. At a very early period it was the center of a powerful kingdom which was conquered first by the Medes, then (as part of the domain of the Medes) by the Persians, and finally by Alexander the Great. It was a part of the kingdom of the Seleucidae (a dynasty of rulers in Asia that stemmed from one of Alexander's generals), and from 256 B.C. for about 100 years an independent Greco-Bactrian kingdom which extended to the Kábul and Indus rivers. Bactria belonged thereafter to the Sassanidae until c640

A.D., and has since been under Moslem rule. Bactria played in ancient times an important cultural role, acting as an intermediary between the civilizations of the Greek world, India, and China.

Bactria Plains. Name often given to a large plains region in Afghanistan, N of the Hindu Kush mountains. It is excellent grazing territory and is traditionally visited by Uzbek and Kirghiz shepherds with their sheep and horses during the summer months.

Bacup (bā'kup). Municipal borough, market town, and small manufacturing center in NW England, in Lancashire, ab. 16 mi. N of Manchester. It has brass and iron foundries and manufactures of cottons and of boots and shoes, especially slippers. 18,374 (1951).

Badagry (bä.dä.grē'). [Also, **Badagri.**] Town in W Africa, in Nigeria, W of Lagos, on the Gulf of Guinea close to the border of Dahomey. It was formerly the capital of a native kingdom and a great slave port.

Badajoz (bä.ᴛʜä.hōth'). Province in W Spain, bounded by Cáceres on the N, Ciudad-Real and Córdoba on the E, Sevilla and Huelva on the S, and Portugal on the W: part of the region of Estremadura. The climate is continental, the surface largely hilly or mountainous. Agriculture, livestock raising, and the mining of iron ore are carried on. Capital, Badajoz; area, 8,349 sq. mi.; pop. 815,780 (1950).

Badajoz. [Latin, **Batallium, Colonia Pacensis, Pax Augusta.**] City in W Spain, the capital of the province of Badajoz, situated on the left bank of the Guadiana River near the Portuguese frontier, ab. 52 mi. SW of Cáceres: seat of a bishopric. It has woolen, leather, terra cotta, and foodstuff industries, distilleries, and a considerable border trade. A bastioned wall with massive outworks is preserved, and also the cathedral, built in 1258, which resembles a fortress. There is a castle of the Moorish period and a local museum. The painter Luis de Morales was born here. A Roman town in ancient times, Badajoz rose to importance under the Moslems, who occupied it during the period 930–1229. The town was later disputed between Castile and Portugal. In the Peninsular War, during the Napoleonic era, it was attacked by the French in 1808 and 1809, and finally taken in 1811; in 1812 it was taken by the British under the Duke of Wellington, with heavy losses, and subsequently sacked. In the Spanish Civil War, Badajoz fell to the Nationalists on Aug. 14, 1936. Pop. 79,291 (1950).

Badakhshan (bä.däch.shän'). [Also, **Badakshan** (-däk-).] Province of NE Afghanistan, bounded by the Amu Darya (formerly the Oxus River) on the N, the Hindu Kush mountains on the S, and Kataghan province on the W: especially noted for its rubies, and for lapis lazuli considered among the best in the world. It is a beautiful region including the little *Pamirs* (high mountain valleys), partially forested and very healthy, inhabited largely by Tajiks. Capital, Faizabad; pop. 100,000 (est.).

Badalocchio (bä.dä.lôk'kyō), **Sisto.** [Called **Sisto Rosa.**] b. at Parma, Italy, 1581; d. at Bologna, Italy, 1647. Italian painter and engraver, a pupil and assistant of Annibale Carracci.

Badalona (bä.ᴛʜä.lō'nä). [Latin, **Baetula, Betulo.**] City in NE Spain, in the province of Barcelona, situated on the Mediterranean Sea, ab. 5 mi. NE of Barcelona, of which it is a suburb. It is a seaport and manufacturing town, with shipyards, glassworks, chemical and textile industries, wine cellars, and sugar and petroleum refineries. There are Roman remains and numerous villas and gardens. 61,654 (1950).

Bad Assmannshausen (bät'äs'mäns.hou.zen). See **Assmannshausen.**

Bad Aussee (ous'zā''). Town in C Austria, in the northernmost part of Styria, in the Salzkammergut region, situated near the headstreams of the Traun River, ab. 38 mi. SE of Salzburg. It is a summer and winter resort and has brine baths and salt mines. 6,014 (1946).

Bad Axe (bad aks). City in C Lower Michigan, county seat of Huron County: agricultural trade; milk processing. 2,973 (1950).

Bad Axe, Battle of the. Engagement (Aug. 2, 1832) in the Black Hawk War, between Sauk and Fox Indians led by Black Hawk and an American mixed force of some 1,300 militia and regular infantry under General Henry Atkinson. The battle took place at the mouth of the Bad Axe River, in Wisconsin. The Indians suffered a total defeat.

Badayev (bä'dä.yif), **Alexey Yegorovich.** b. at Yuryevo, Russia, 1883; d. at Moscow, Nov. 3, 1951. Russian politician, president (chief of the presidium of the supreme soviet) of the Russian Soviet Federated Socialist Republic (1938–44).

Badb (bov). See **Morrigan.**

Bad Blankenburg (bät' bläng'ken.bùrk). See **Blankenburg.**

Bad Brückenau (brük'en.ou). See under **Brückenau.**

Bad Child's Book of Beasts, The. Humorous prose work (1896) by Hilaire Belloc. It was his first book and had several sequels.

Badcock (bad'kok), **John.** fl. early 19th century. English writer on pugilistic and sporting subjects, who published between 1816 and 1830 under the pseudonyms Jon Bee and John Hinds. In 1830 he edited the *Works of Samuel Foote*, with remarks, notes, and a memoir (under the name of Jon Bee).

Baddeck (ba.dek'). Fishing village and summer resort on Cape Breton Island, Nova Scotia, Canada, situated on the N shore of Bras d'Or Lake. It is the capital of Victoria county. The first airplane flight from British soil was made here on Feb. 23, 1909. Pop. ab. 400.

Baddeley (bad'li), **Robert.** b. c1733; d. 1794. English actor. He was originally cook for Samuel Foote, the playwright and actor; went on the stage himself sometime before 1761. He was the original Moses in *The School for Scandal.* In his will he left the revenue of his house in Surrey for the support of an asylum for aged and impoverished actors, and also, from the interest, one hundred pounds a year to provide wine and cake for the actors of the Drury Lane Theater on Twelfth Night.

Baddeley, Sophia. b. at London, 1745; d. at Edinburgh, 1786. English actress and singer; wife of Robert Baddeley.

Bad Dürkheim (bät' dürk'hīm). See **Dürkheim.**

Bad Dürrenberg (dür'en.berk). See **Dürrenberg.**

Bad Dürrheim (dür'hīm). See **Dürrheim.**

Bade (båd). French name of **Baden,** Germany.

Bade (bä'de), **Josse.** See **Badius, Jodocus.**

Badeau (ba.dō'), **Adam.** b. at New York, Dec. 29, 1831; d. at Ridgewood, N.J., March 19, 1895. American soldier, diplomat, and writer, noted as the "court historian" of the Grant administration. Military secretary (1864–69) to General Ulysses S. Grant, and secretary (1869–70) of the U.S. legation at London, he was (1870–81) consul general there and held (1882–84) a similar post at Havana, Cuba, resigning when the administration refused to take action on his charges of corruption in the Havana consulate. He aided in the preparation of Grant's *Memoirs,* and wrote the *Military History of Ulysses S. Grant* (3 vols., 1868, 1881); the intimate political revelations of his *Grant in Peace* (1887), make it a valuable record of the period. Author also of *The Vagabond* (1859), *Conspiracy: A Cuban Romance* (1885), and *Aristocracy in England* (1886).

Badebec (båd.bek). Wife of Gargantua in the romance of *Pantagruel*, by François Rabelais.

Bad-Elster (bät'el'stėr). See **Elster.**

Bad Ems (bät' ems'). See **Ems.**

Baden (bä'den). [Also: **Baden bei Wien;** Latin, **Aquae Pannonicae.**] Town and spa in E Austria, in the province of Lower Austria, situated in the valley of the Schwechat River, or Helenen valley, on the slopes of the Wienerwald, ab. 14 mi. SW of Vienna. There are 14 radioactive sulfur springs, used against rheumatism, neuralgia, and gout. The 19th-century development of Baden is chiefly due to the regular summer visits (1813–34) of the Emperor Francis I of Austria; the place was known throughout Europe by the middle of the 19th century. The town has many parks, gardens, bathing establishments, and theaters, and a museum with prehistoric and ethnographical collections. There is a monument to the composers Joseph Lanner and Johann Strauss. Ludwig van Beethoven lived here in 1816 and 1818. The last Austrian emperor, Charles I, had his residence here during World War I. The town was occupied by the Russians at the end of World War II. 21,382 (1951).

Baden. [French, **Bade.**] *Land* (state) of Germany, French Zone, bounded by France (Alsace), Switzerland, Württemberg-Hohenzollern, and Württemberg-Baden. It consists of the S part of the former free state of Baden. The

Rhine River forms the W and S border; a large part of the territory is covered by the Black Forest mountains. Agricultural pursuits, including viticulture, livestock-raising and forestry, and small industries, comprising chiefly lumber, textile, and metallurgical manufactures, are of equal importance. There is little large-scale property. About two thirds of the population are Catholics, one third Protestants. The decrease of the population between 1939 and 1946 was 3.2 percent. Capital, Freiburg im Breisgau; area, 3,842 sq. mi.; pop. 1,338,629 (1950).

Baden (bā′dẹn). Residential borough in W Pennsylvania, in Beaver County, on the Ohio River ab. 20 mi. NW of Pittsburgh. 3,732 (1950).

Baden (bä′dẹn). [Also: **Oberbaden;** Latin, **Aquae Helveticae.**] Town and spa in N Switzerland, in the canton of Aargau, situated on the Limmat River, NW of Zurich: noted for its hot sulfur springs, known to the Romans and in use ever since. It was the meeting place of the Swiss diet for three centuries. Nearby is Burg (castle) Stein, until 1415 a residence of the Hapsburg princes. 10,388 (1941).

Baden, Jacob. b. at Vordingborg, Denmark, May 4, 1735; d. at Copenhagen, July 5, 1804. Danish philologist and critic, appointed (1780) professor of rhetoric and Latin at Copenhagen. He founded (1768) the *Kritisk Journal,* and published *Grammatica Latina* (1782) and others.

Baden, Treaty of. Treaty between the German Empire and France, concluded at Baden, Switzerland, Sept. 7, 1714, which, with the treaties of Utrecht and Rastatt, ended the War of the Spanish Succession. By the terms of this treaty the peace of Ryswick was ratified, the electors of Bavaria and Cologne were reinstated in their lands and dignities, and Landau was left in the possession of France.

Baden-Baden (bä′dẹn.bä′dẹn). [Also: **Baden;** Latin, **Civitas Aurelia Aquensis.**] City and spa in S Germany, in the *Land* (state) of Baden, French Zone, formerly Baden, free state, situated in the valley of the Oos River, ab. 22 mi. SW of Karlsruhe. A famous and fashionable health resort, it has saline, alkaline, and radioactive thermal springs, which are visited by people suffering from gout, rheumatism, and respiratory diseases; there are parks, playgrounds, hotels, bathing establishments, and a casino. The Kurhaus (pavilion within which the curative waters are drunk) was originally built in 1824, and was enlarged in 1854 with the aid of Parisian artists. There are beautiful hilly and wooded surroundings; above or near the town are the ruins of the castles of Hohenbaden, Ebersteinburg, and Yburg. The German chamber-music festival and the horse races in nearby Iffezheim were once famous. The modern city manufactures cigarettes, precision instruments, furniture, shoes, paper, and knitwear. The bathing facilities were known as early as Roman times. The town belonged to the family of Zähringen, later margraves of Baden, from the 11th century; they resided here until 1689 when the town was destroyed by the French. Baden-Baden's prosperity as a resort dates back to the early 19th century, when it became a meeting ground for the social élite of Europe. It was bombed during World War II, but not so heavily damaged as many other German cities; it is now the headquarters of the French Occupation Zone in Germany. 36,582 (1950).

Baden bei Wien (bä′dẹn bī vēn′). See **Baden,** Austria.

Badeni (bä.dā′nē), Count **Kasimir Felix.** b. at Surochow, in Galicia, Oct. 14, 1846; d. at Krasne, Austria-Hungary, July 9, 1909. Austro-Hungarian statesman. He was governor (1888) of Galicia, and in 1895 became prime minister of Austria-Hungary. He was dismissed (1897) through pressure by the German element in Austria because he was considered to be too friendly in his policies toward the Czechs.

Baden-Powell (bā′dẹn.pō′ẹl), **Baden Fletcher Smyth.** b. 1860; d. Oct. 4, 1937. British soldier; son of Baden Powell (1796–1860). He was educated at Charterhouse; served with the army in New Guinea; served (1884–1885) with the camel corps in the region of the upper Nile; was with the Scots Guards during the Boer War; and was a bombing and camouflage officer during World War I. He pioneered with Sir Hiram Maxim and others in the establishment of military ballooning technique, and conducted aeronautical research, especially on propellers. He invented (1894) man-lifting kites; reëstablished (1897) the Royal Aeronautical Society; and wrote books on aeronautics, travel, and ballooning.

Baden-Powell, Sir **George Smyth.** b. 1847; d. 1898. English politician and publicist. He was appointed (1882) a joint commissioner to inquire into the administration, revenues, and expenditure of the British West India colonies; assisted (1885) Sir Charles Warren in his diplomatic negotiations with the native chiefs of Bechuanaland; spent the winter of 1886–87 in Canada and the U.S., investigating the dispute over joint use of and rights to the fishing banks off the Canadian coast; and was made (1887) joint commissioner with Sir George Bowen to arrange the details of the new Malta constitution. He was British commissioner in the Bering Sea fisheries inquiry of 1891, and British member of the Joint Commission, Washington, D.C., 1892. Author of *New Homes for the Old Country* (1872), *Protection and Bad Times* (1879), *State Aid and State Interference* (1882), and others.

Baden-Powell, Sir **Robert Stephenson Smyth.** b. Feb. 22, 1857; d. 1941. British major general, inspector general of cavalry from 1903–07, especially noted for his defense (1900) of Mafeking, in South Africa, during the Boer War, and as founder of the international Boy Scout movement. With a force of some 1,200 men he was besieged at Mafeking for 215 days, being relieved on May 18, 1900. From 1900 to 1903 he was general of the South African constabulary. In 1908 he was appointed lieutenant general commanding the Northumbrian Territorial Division, and in the same year founded the Boy Scouts. With his sister Agnes he also founded the Girl Guides. Among his publications are *Cavalry Instruction* (1895), *The Matabele Campaign* (1896), *Sport in War* (1900), *Sketches in Mafeking and East Africa* (1907), and *Scouting for Boys* (1908). He was knighted in 1909.

Badenweiler (bä″dẹn.vī′lėr). Village in S Germany, in the *Land* (state) of Baden, French Zone, formerly Baden free state, situated on the slopes of the Black Forest, SW of Freiburg in Breisgau. Beautifully located, it is a health resort with radioactive thermal springs, which are visited by people suffering from disorders of the heart, respiratory organs, and nerves, and from rheumatism; there are hotels, parks, and bathing establishments. The springs at Badenweiler were known to the Romans; ruins of the Roman baths were discovered in 1784. Pop. 2,366 (1946).

Bader (bä′dėr), **Joseph.** b. Feb. 24, 1805; d. 1883. German writer on the history and general background of Baden. He was editor (1839–64) of the periodical *Badenia.*

Bad Frankenhausen (bät frängʹkẹn.hou.zẹn). See **Frankenhausen.**

Bad Gastein (gäs′tīn). [Also: **Badgastein, Gastein.**] Village in C Austria, in Salzburg, in the valley of the Gasteiner Ache, at the point where the valley forms narrow gorges with waterfalls: a station on the Tauern railroad line, between Salzburg and Villach. It has 18 hot radioactive springs, the waters of which are used against certain symptoms of nervous disorders, gout, rheumatism, and debility. It has been known as a spa since the Middle Ages, but gained its greatest popularity in the 19th century. There are many hotels. The tunnel of the Tauern railroad is nearby, to the S. After the conclusion of World War II, numerous DP's were temporarily located here. 7,139 (1946).

Badger (baj′ėr), **George Edmund.** b. at New Bern, N.C., April 17, 1795; d. May 11, 1866. American lawyer, jurist, and politician. He left his private law practice at Raleigh to enter (1841) President William Henry Harrison's cabinet as secretary of the navy, resigning after John Tyler took office. Elected (1846) to the U.S. Senate, he was a member until 1855. He became an organizer of the Constitutional Union party during the secession crisis, and was a delegate to the secession convention in 1861.

Badger, George Percy. b. 1815; d. Feb. 21, 1888. English orientalist, compiler of an English-Arabic lexicon (1881).

Badger, Joseph. b. at Charlestown, Mass., March 14, 1708; d. 1765. American colonial portrait painter. Unknown to art scholars until comparatively recent times, he is thought to have been the painter of some 80 unsigned canvases, including portraits of the clergymen Ellis Gray and Thomas Prince (at the American Antiquarian Society, Worcester, Mass.), James Bowdoin (at Bowdoin College), Mrs. Norton Quincy (at the Worcester Art Museum), and William Cooper (Massachusetts Historical Society). Several works previously designated as from the hands of John Singleton Copley, John Smibert, and Joseph Blackburn have been named as his by the art scholar Lawrence Park. Very little is known of his life, but it is certain that he preceded Copley as Boston's chief portraitist, reaching the high point of his practice from c1748 to c1760.

Badger, Joseph. b. at Wilbraham, Mass., Feb. 28, 1757; d. at Perrysburg, Ohio, April 5, 1846. American Revolutionary patriot, Congregational clergyman, and pioneer missionary, founder of the first church in the Western Reserve. Having enlisted in the Continental army at 18, he served at Bunker Hill and accompanied the force which made the march on Canada. He was graduated (1785) from Yale and ordained (1787) pastor of the Congregational Church at Blandford, Mass.; he left Blandford to become (1800) a pioneer missionary in Ohio, where he founded the first church in the Western Reserve, at Austinburg.

Badger, Oscar Charles. b. at Mansfield, Conn., Aug. 12, 1823; d. June 20, 1899. American naval officer, in the Union navy during the Civil War. He attended the U.S. Naval Academy, participated in expeditions to Africa and the Fiji Islands, and took part in the Mexican War. For a time during the Civil War he commanded (1863) the ironclads *Patapsco* and *Montauk*. Wounded (Sept. 1, 1863) while serving as fleet captain during a naval assault upon Forts Moultrie and Sumter, he was later commandant (1882–85) of the Boston navy yard. The destroyer *Badger*, launched in 1918, was named after him.

Badger, Oscar Charles. b. at Washington, D.C., June 26, 1890—. American naval officer who was appointed (1948) commander of U.S. naval forces in the W Pacific; grandson of Oscar Charles Badger (1823–99). Graduated (1911) from the U.S. Naval Academy, he was awarded the Congressional Medal of Honor in 1914. He served during World War I and World War II, and was appointed a captain in 1938. Assistant chief of naval operations for logistics, he was appointed vice-admiral in 1948.

"Badger State." Nickname of **Wisconsin.**

Bad Gleichenberg (bät' glī'ḥen.berk). Village and spa in E Austria, in Styria, ab. 25 mi. SE of Graz. It has springs considered beneficial to pulmonary and cardiac patients. 1,320 (1946).

Bad Godesberg (gō'des.berk). See **Godesberg.**

Badham (bad'am), **Charles.** b. at London, April 17, 1780; d. there, Nov. 10, 1845. English physician, traveler, and classical scholar. Author of medical works, miscellaneous verse, and translator (1814) of Juvenal's *Satires*.

Badham, Charles. b. at Ludlow, Shropshire, England, July 18, 1813; d. at Sydney, Australia, Feb. 26, 1884. English classical scholar and teacher, appointed professor of classics and logic at the University of Sydney in 1867; son of Charles Badham (1780–1845). He published editions of various Greek classics, *Criticism applied to Shakespeare* (1846), and others.

Badia Calavena (bä.dē'ä kä.lä.vā'nä). Town and commune in NE Italy, in the *compartimento* (region) of Veneto, in the province of Verona, ab. 13 mi. NE of Verona. It is the chief place in the "Tredici Communi," until the middle of the 19th century a largely German-speaking enclave. Pop. of commune, 3,221 (1936); of town, 258 (1936).

Badiali (bä.dyä'lē), **Cesare.** b. at Imola, Italy, c1810; d. there, Nov. 17, 1865. Italian bass singer, popular in his day in Italy and England.

Badia Polesine (bä.dē'ä pō.lā'zē.nä). Town and commune in NE Italy, in the *compartimento* (region) of Veneto, in the province of Rovigo, situated in the Polesine district and on the Adige River, W of Rovigo. Pop. of commune, 12,797 (1936); of town, 3,739 (1936).

Badía y Leblich (bä.thē'ä ē lā.blēch'), **Domingo.** [Also, **Ali Bey.**] b. 1766; d. 1818. Spanish traveler in N Africa and the Orient. He was able to pose successfully as a Mohammedan (in which guise he took an Arabic name now usually shortened in English to "Ali Bey") and was the first Christian definitely known to have visited (1807) Mecca after the establishment of Islam. Author of *Voyages d'Ali Bey en Asie et en Afrique pendant les années 1803–07* (1814).

Ba-Dimma (bä.dim'mä). A former name of the **Gambia River.**

Badin (bȧ.daṅ), **Stephen Theodore.** b. at Orléans, France, July 17, 1768; d. at Cincinnati, Ohio, April 19, 1853. American missionary and first Roman Catholic clergyman to be ordained (1793) on American soil.

Badinguet (bȧ.daṅ.gā). [Later name, **Radot.**] d. 1883. Workman in whose clothes Napoleon III is said to have escaped (1846) from the fortress of Ham; hence, a nickname of Napoleon III.

Badius (bä'dē.us), **Jodocus.** [Latin name of **Josse Bade;** sometimes called **Jodocus Badius Ascensius.**] b. at Asche (the Roman Ascensius), near Brussels, 1462; d. 1535. Flemish printer and writer. He taught Greek at Lyons before taking up printing. He established (c1499) at Paris a printing house, the "Praelum Ascensianum."

Bad Lands or **Badlands.** [French, **Mauvaises Terres.**] Certain lands of the NW U.S., characterized by an almost entire absence of natural vegetation, and by the varied and fantastic forms into which the soft strata have been eroded. At a little distance they appear like fields of desolate ruins. The name was first applied, in its French form *mauvaises terres*, to a Tertiary area (Miocene) E of the Black Hills in South Dakota, along the White River, a tributary of the Upper Missouri. Part of this area was established (1939) as a U.S. national monument.

Badman (bad'man), **The Life and Death of Mr.** A work by John Bunyan, published in 1680.

Bad Mergentheim (bät mer'gent.hīm). See **Mergentheim.**

Badminton (bad'min.ton). The residence of the dukes of Beaufort, in Gloucestershire, England, 15 mi. NE of Bristol. Because of its comparative safety, Queen Mary, mother of King George VI, was sent here from London during World War II to escape heavy bombing raids.

Badminton. Coaching and sporting club established at London in 1876.

Bad Münster am Stein (bät mün'stėr äm shtīn). See **Münster am Stein.**

Bad Oeynhausen (ė'in.hou.zen). Town in W Germany, in the *Land* (state) of North Rhine-Westphalia, formerly in the province of Westphalia, Prussia, on the Werra River near its influx into the Weser River, near Minden. It is a popular health resort, with small industries. After World War II it served as headquarters of the British Zone of Occupation in Germany. 6,652 (1946).

Badoglio (bä.dô'lyō), **Pietro.** [Title, Marquis of **Sabotino.**] b. at Grazzano Monferrato, Italy, Sept. 28, 1871—. Italian general and Fascist politician. After having been named (1890) a second lieutenant of artillery, he took part in the Eritrean campaigns (1896–97), the Libyan War (1911–12), and fought (1915–18) with the Italian Second Army, during which time he achieved the rank of general. In August, 1916, he distinguished himself in the battle of Gorizia and became (1917) deputy chief of staff under Armando Diaz; he succeeded (1919) Diaz and remained at the head of the army until 1921 when he became special envoy to Rumania and subsequently to the U.S.; as chief of staff, he signed the World War I armistice for his country. After serving (1924–25) as ambassador to Brazil, he was named (1926) marshal of Italy; he became (1925) chief of staff of all the armed Italian forces, a rank which he kept until 1940 (and lost because of the Italian reverses in Greece at the beginning of World War II). In the meantime he had also been governor (1928–33) of Libya and viceroy (1936) of Ethiopia, with the title of the duke of Addis Ababa. On July 25, 1943, King Victor Emmanuel III called him to succeed Mussolini as prime minister and chief of state; in this capacity he signed (Sept. 8, 1943) the World War II armistice with the Allies and declared war on Germany. His tenure as prime minister ended when he was succeeded (June 8, 1944) by Bonomi. He was divested (1946) of the senatorial rank which he had held since 1919. He wrote *La Guerra d'Etiopia* (1936).

Badon (bä'don), **Mount.** [Latin, **Mons Badonicus.**] Scene of a battle said to have been gained (c520) by King

Arthur over the Saxon invaders: variously identified with Badbury Rings (in Dorsetshire), a hill near Bath, and Bouden Hill (near Linlithgow).

Badoura (bą.dö'rą). A principal character in the story of the "Amours of Prince Camaralzaman and the Princess Badoura," in *The Arabian Nights' Entertainments.*

Bad Ragaz (bät rä'gäts). See **Ragaz** or **Ragatz.**

Badrinath (bud.rę.nät'). [Also, **Bhadrinath.**] Mountain peak in N India, in the Himalayas, situated in the N part of Garhwal district, Uttar Pradesh (United Provinces), Union of India. On it, at an elevation of 10,294 ft. there is a village centering around a temple which contains a shrine of Vishnu; this is one of the most noted places of pilgrimage in all India. Its remote location and the difficulties entailed in reaching it make a pilgrimage to Badrinath particularly meritorious in the view of pious Hindus. 23,210 ft.

Bad Rippoldsau (bät rip'olt.zou). See **Rippoldsau.**

Badroulboudour (bą.dröl'bö.dör). Wife of Aladdin in the story of "Aladdin or the Wonderful Lamp," in *The Arabian Nights' Entertainments.*

Bad Salzbrunn (bät sälts'brůn). A German name of **Szczawienko.**

Bad Schandau (shän'dou). See **Schandau.**

Baducing (bä'dö.ching), **Biscop.** See **Benedict Biscop,** Saint.

Baduila (bad'wi.lą). See **Totila.**

Baebia gens (bē'bi.ą jenz). In ancient Rome, a plebeian clan or house.

Baecula (bek'ū.lą). Ancient name of **Bailén.**

Baedeker (bā'dę.kėr), **Karl.** b. at Essen, Germany, Nov. 3, 1801; d. at Koblenz, Germany, Oct. 4, 1859. German publisher, noted as the founder of the series of guide books which bears his name.

Baegna (beg'nä). [Norwegian, **Baegna Elv.**] River in S Norway, the chief headstream of the Drammen River.

Baekeland (bāk'ląnd), **Leo Hendrik.** b. at Ghent, Belgium, Nov. 14, 1863; d. at Beacon, N.Y., Feb. 23, 1944. American chemist, notable for the invention (1906) of the thermo-setting plastic substance called Bakelite, and other products. He received a B.S. (1882) from the University of Ghent. Having come (1889) to the U.S., he produced Velox photographic paper and founded (1893) the Nepera Chemical Company, for its manufacture. He was president (1910–39) of the Bakelite Corporation; and joined (1917), as chairman, the committee on patents of the National Research Council.

Baelen (bä.lań), **Jean Gustave Adolphe.** b. at Argenteuil, Seine-et-Oise, France, July 16, 1899—. French diplomat, active in the Free French movement during World War II. He was minister to Sweden (1945 *et seq.*).

Baen (bän), **Jan de.** See **Baan, Jan van der.**

Baena (bä.ä'nä). [Latin, **Baniana, Biniana.**] Town in S Spain, in the province of Córdoba, ab. 32 mi. SE of Córdoba: horse markets, grain and oil trade, linen textile manufactures. There are Roman remains and a castle. 24,830 (1940).

Baer (bãr), **George Frederick.** b. near Lavansville, Pa., Sept. 26, 1842; d. April 26, 1914. American lawyer, notable as a coal and railway magnate. He attended Franklin and Marshall College, Lancaster, Pa., and served with the Union army at the second Battle of Bull Run, Antietam, Fredericksburg, and Chancellorsville, resigning after a year's duty to continue the study of law. Admitted (1864) to the bar, he moved to Reading and became (1870) counsel for the Philadelphia and Reading Railway Company. He became a director of the Reading Company and, as an agent of J. P. Morgan, he was made president in 1901 of the Reading properties. When the United Mine Workers struck in the Pennsylvania hard-coal regions in 1902, he gained a national reputation for his stubborn opposition to the miners' demands, particularly as stated in a letter (dated July 17, 1902) which included the following passage: "The rights and interests of the laboring man will be protected and cared for—not by the labor agitators, but by the Christian men to whom God in his infinite wisdom has given the control of the property interests of the country, and upon the successful management of which so much depends."

Baer, Karl Ernst von. b. in Estonia, Feb. 28, 1792; d. at Dorpat (now Tartu, Estonia), Nov. 28, 1876. German naturalist, especially noted for his researches in embryology. He was appointed extraordinary professor of zoölogy at Königsberg in 1819, and, two years later, ordinary professor, and succeeded Karl Friedrich Burdach as director of the Anatomical Institute. In 1829 he went to St. Petersburg as a member of the Academy, returned to Königsberg in 1830, and again went to St. Petersburg in 1834, as librarian of the Academy. His chief works are *Entwicklungsgeschichte der Tiere* (1828–37) and *Untersuchungen über die Entwicklung der Fische* (1835).

Baer, William Jacob. b. at Cincinnati, Ohio, Jan. 29, 1860; d. 1941. American painter, chiefly of miniatures. He studied at the Cincinnati School of Design and at Munich; his awards included medals from the Paris Exposition (1900), Charleston Exposition (1902), and the Panama-Pacific Exposition (1915). He is represented by *Daphne* in the Brooklyn Museum, *Aurora, Nymph,* and *Phoebe* in the Walters Art Gallery at Baltimore, and others.

Baerle, Gaspard van. See **Barlaeus, Casparus.**

Baerlein (bãr'līn), **Henry.** b. at Manchester, England, April 1, 1875—. English writer. Author of *Rimes of the Diables Bleus* (1917), poetry; *The Raft of Love* (1923), a three-act masque, *The House of the Fighting Cocks* (1923), *Mariposa* (1924), *Here are Dragons* (1925), and *Dreamy Rivers* (1930), novels; and *Mexico, the Land of Unrest* (1913), *Over the Hills of Ruthenia* (1923), *In Search of Slovakia* (1929), *Bessarabia and Beyond* (1935), *Travels Without a Passport* (1st series, 1941; 2nd series, 1942), and *Baltic Paradise* (1943), books of description and travel.

Baert (bå.er), **Alexandre Balthazar François de Paule,** Baron **de.** b. at Dunkerque, France, 1750; d. at Paris, March 23, 1825. French politician and geographer. He was elected (1791) to the Legislative Assembly, in which he vainly exerted himself to save Louis XVI. He wrote *Tableau de la Grande-Bretagne* (1800).

Baertson (bärt'sôn), **Albert.** b. at Ghent, Belgium, Jan. 9, 1866; d. there, June 9, 1922. Belgian landscape painter, pastel artist, draftsman, and water colorist who won many prizes at Brussels and Paris. Schooled in Belgium and France, he painted scenes of these countries on his many trips through them.

Baeterrae (bē.ter'ē). A Latin name of **Béziers.**

Baethgen (bāt'gęn), **Friedrich.** b. 1849; d. 1905. German theologian. He attended the universities of Berlin, Göttingen, and Kiel, and in 1895 became professor of Old Testament exegesis and Semitic languages at the University of Berlin. Author of *Untersuchungen über die Psalmen der Peschita* (1878).

Baetica (bē'ti.ką). In ancient geography, the southernmost division of Hispania (Spain).

Baetula (bet'ū.lą). A Latin name of **Badalona.**

Baeyer (bā'yėr), **Adolf von.** [Full name, **Johann Friedrich Wilhelm Adolf von Baeyer.**] b. at Berlin, Oct. 31, 1835; d. at Munich, Sept. 5, 1917. German organic chemist, winner of the Nobel prize for chemistry (1905); son of Johann Jakob Baeyer. His "strain theory" (1886), with some later modification, is still fundamental in organic chemistry. It states that the stability of an organic ring decreases to the extent that the carbon bonds are forced off their normal symmetrically tetrahedral position. His experimental work includes much that is fundamental to the dye industry: the first synthesis of indigo, the first use of zinc dust distillation for reduction, discovery of the phthaleins, and the first synthesis of nitrosophenol (with Heinrich Caro).

Baeyer, Johann Jakob. b. at Müggelsheim, near Köpenick, Germany, Nov. 5, 1794; d. at Berlin, Sept. 10, 1885. Prussian soldier and geodesist; father of Adolf von Baeyer. He fought as a volunteer in the campaigns of 1813 and 1814, joined the regular army in 1815, and attained the rank of lieutenant general in 1858. He conducted several important geodetic surveys, and in 1870 became president of the Geodetic Institute at Berlin. He published various geodetical works.

Báez (bä'es), **Buenaventura.** b. at Azua, Haiti, c1810; d. in Puerto Rico, March 21, 1884. Dominican statesman, four times president (1849–53, 1856–58, 1865–66, 1868–70) of the Dominican Republic. He coöperated with Pedro Santana in the establishment of the Dominican Republic, and was its president from 1849 to 1853, when he was overthrown and expelled by Santana. He retired to New York, but Santana being driven out (1856), he was called back and again elected president. In June, 1858, he was again supplanted by Santana. Elected a third time in 1865, he was supplanted in 1866 by a triumvirate headed by Cabral. Báez was recalled and made president a fourth time in 1868. After various negotiations, he signed with President Grant two treaties (Nov. 29, 1869), one for the annexation of his country to the U.S., and the other for the cession of the bay of Samaná. The annexation scheme was, ostensibly at least, approved by the Dominican people, but the U.S. Senate refused to ratify it. The failure of this resulted in renewed disorders and the fall of Báez.

Baeza (bä.ā'thä). [Latin, **Beatia.**] Town in S Spain, in the province of Jaén, ab. 22 mi. NE of Jaén: agricultural market town. It has a cathedral, and was formerly the seat of a university, founded in 1533. It was a flourishing Moslem city in the Middle Ages, taken by Ferdinand III (of Castile) in 1239. The ancient fortifications are now in ruins. 18,211 (1940).

Baffin (baf'in), **William.** b. c1584; d. Jan. 23, 1622. English navigator and explorer. He was pilot of the *Discovery*, commanded by Robert Bylot, which was despatched (1615) by the Muscovy Company (of London) to North America in search of the Northwest Passage. The expedition resulted in the discovery (1616) of the bay between Greenland and Canada which has since received the name of Baffin Bay. An account of the expedition, written by Baffin, was printed by Samuel Purchas, who, however, took great liberties with the text. The original manuscript, with map, is in the British Museum, and was edited first for the Hakluyt Society in 1849 (published in *Narratives of Voyages towards the North-west*) and later (1881) by Clements Markham. Baffin was killed while serving in the allied English and Persian armies on the island of Qishm, in the Persian Gulf.

Baffin Bay. Sea passage communicating with the Atlantic Ocean by Davis Strait, and with the Arctic Ocean by Smith Sound, and lying W of Greenland; explored in 1616 by William Baffin.

Baffin Island. [Former name, **Baffin** (or **Baffin's**) **Land.**] Largest of the islands of the Canadian Arctic Archipelago, lying W of Baffin Bay and NE of the Northwest Territories, Canada. Area, 197,754 sq. mi.; pop. ab. 1,600.

Baffo (bäf'fō). [Called **"Baffo the Pure."**] fl. c1580–1600. Venetian lady; sultana and counselor of the Turkish sultan Murad III.

Bafing (bä'fing). River in W Africa, one of the chief headstreams of the river Sénégal. It rises in the highlands NW of Sierra Leone and flows generally N until it joins the main stream in SW French Sudan.

Bafra (bä.frä'). [Also, **Bafira** (bä.fi.rä').] Town in N Turkey, in the *il* (province or vilayet) of Samsun, on the Kizil Irmak (River), ab. 30 mi. NW of Samsun and 12 mi. from the Black Sea, in the center of a fertile plain that has been laid down by the river. The most important crop of the area is tobacco; the Bafra leaf, known for its aroma and flavor, took its name from this town. Pop. ab. 10,000.

Bagacum (bag'ą.kum). Ancient name of **Bavay.**

Bagamoyo (bä.gä.mō'yō). Seaport town in E Africa, until the building of the railway from Dar-es-Salaam the largest commercial center in Tanganyika territory; it is situated S of the Kingani River on the Indian Ocean coast opposite Zanzibar. It is a meeting place of inland roads and caravans. Since the completion (1914) of the railway the town has declined in population and in importance as a port. Pop. ab. 5,000.

Bagaria (bä.gä.rē'ä). See **Bagheria.**

Bagaudae (bą.gô'dē). Name applied to a body of Gallic peasants who were in rebellion against the Romans at intervals from c270 A.D. to the 5th century.

Bağazköy (bä.gäz.kė'i). See **Boğazkale.**

Bagby (bag'bi), **Arthur Pendleton.** b. in Louisa County, Va., 1794; d. at Mobile, Ala., Sept. 21, 1858. American politician and diplomat. He settled (1818) at Claiborne, Ala., where he soon achieved a reputation as a criminal lawyer. After serving as a member of the state legislature (1821–22, 1824, 1834–36) and of the state senate (1825), he was governor of Alabama in the period 1837–41, before acting as U.S. senator (1841–48); subsequently he was also U.S. minister to Russia (1848–49).

Bagby, George William. [Pseudonyms: **Moses Adams, Mozis Addums.**] b. in Buckingham County, Va., Aug. 13, 1828; d. at Richmond, Va., Nov. 29, 1883. American humorist. Abandoning medicine after his writings for the Lynchburg *Virginian* won success, he became a coproprietor of the Lynchburg *Express*, and later was a journalist at Washington, D.C. He was editor (1860–64) of the *Southern Literary Messenger*. In 1865–66 he established himself as a lecturer, gaining thereafter a secure reputation as one of the most popular local humorists of the time. His most popular lectures were "The Virginia Negro" and "The Old Virginia Gentleman"; among his writings, some of which were delivered from the lecture platform, were *John M. Daniels' Latch Key* (1868), *What I Did with My Fifty Millions: by Moses Adams* (1874), *Meekins' Twinses* (1877), and *Canal Reminiscences* (1879).

Bagdad (bag'dad). See **Baghdad.**

Bagé (bą.zhe'). City in S Brazil, in the state of Rio Grande do Sul: center of a farming area and of the *xarque* (dried meat) industry. 35,340 (1950).

Bage (bāj), **Robert.** b. at Darley, England, Feb. 29, 1728, d. at Tamworth, England, Sept. 1, 1801. English novelist. He was a paper manufacturer by trade, and did not begin to publish until the age of 53. Author of *Mount Henneth* (1781), *Barham Downs* (1784), *Hermsprong, or Man as he is not* (1796), and others.

Bagehot (baj'ot), **Walter.** b. at Langport, Somersetshire, England, Feb. 3, 1826; d. there, March 24, 1877. English economist, publicist, social scientist, and journalist. He was graduated (1846) from the University of London, was called to the bar in 1852, later serving (1860–77) as editor of the *Economist* (and is considered by most modern authorities to have been one of the greatest, if not indeed the very greatest, of the brilliant editors who have served that publication during the past century). His published works covered a great diversity of subjects, and were written in a prose style which has caused him to be by many critics among the most admired of English 19th-century writers. His description, and at the same time painstakingly scientific analysis, of the British political system in *The English Constitution* (1867), and of the methods and history of the British banking system in *Lombard Street* (1873), remain even today among the standard works in these fields. The relationship of types of science to one another was enormously interesting to him, and in his *Physics and Politics* (1869) he made what is generally considered to have been a pioneer effort in the application of the theories of natural science (specifically, of evolution) to the working of a social science. His other works include *Literary Studies* (1879), *Economic Studies* (1880), and Biographical Studies (1881).

Bagford (bag'ford), **John.** b. at Blackfriars, London, 1650; d. at Charterhouse, London, May 15, 1716. English bibliophile and shoemaker, collector of *Bagford Ballads*, two volumes of broadside ditties.

Baggara (bäg.gä'rä). Arabic-speaking tribe, probably of Semitic origin and mixed with African Negro, found between Shilluk territory and Dar Nuba, principally in Kordofan, Anglo-Egyptian Sudan. They are nomadic hunters and cattle breeders, and constituted the real fighting force of the Mahdi (Mohammed Ahmed) in 1882. With the Hadendoa, they were named the "Fuzzy-wuzzies" by the British soldiers in the campaigns of 1884–89.

Baggesen (bäg'e.sen), **Jens Emmanuel.** b. at Korsør, Denmark, Feb. 15, 1764; d. at Hamburg, Germany, Oct. 3, 1826. Danish poet, author of *Comic Tales* (1785), *Labyrinthen* (1792), *Parthenais* (1804), and others. He traveled widely, and wrote in several languages. An anti-Romanticist, he carried on a lengthy literary feud with Adam Gottlob Oehlenschläger.

Baggio (bäd'jō), **Anselmo.** Original name of Pope **Alexander II.**

Baghdad or **Bagdad** (bäg.däd', bag'dad). [Eng. trans., *"Gift of God."*]. *Liwa* (province) in C Iraq, in the lower valleys of the Euphrates and Tigris rivers. Capital, Baghdad; area, 7,731 sq. mi.; pop. 805,293 (1947).

Baghdad or **Bagdad.** City in E central Iraq, the capital of the *liwa* (province) of Baghdad and of Iraq, situated on the Tigris River ab. 500 mi. from the Persian Gulf. Formerly a city of great importance and still the seat of considerable commerce, it was known for centuries as a cultural center, for its fine architecture, and for its silks; scene of the tales of *The Arabian Nights' Entertainments*, many of which center around the court of Harun al-Rashid, Abbasside caliph who brought Baghdad to its peak of magnificence in the 8th century. The city is generally said to have been founded in 762 by al-Mansur ("the Victorious"), second caliph of the dynasty of the Abbassides, who formally made it his capital in that year, and it was thereafter the capital of the Abbassides for 500 years (sometimes bearing in Moslem literature the names of Mansurijeh (from al-Mansur) and also Dar-es-Salaam, meaning "Dwelling of Peace"). Under the Abbassides it became a celebrated center of Arabic learning and civilization, and the glory and splendor of the Moslem world. During the height of its prosperity it is said to have harbored a million and a half people within its walls. It declined with the decay of the Abbasside dynasty, and came at the fall of this dynasty, in 1258, into the hands of the Mongols. It was the capital (1638 *et seq.*) of the Turkish province of Mesopotamia. Captured by the British in 1917, it became capital of Iraq, then under British mandate, in 1920. It has manufactures of leather, silk, cotton, and woolen goods. 552,047 (1947).

Baghelkhand (bä.gel.kund'). See **Central India States.**

Bagheria (bä.ge.rē'ä). [Also, **Bagaria.**] Town and commune in SW Italy, on the island of Sicily, situated near Cape Zaffarano between the Gulf of Palermo and the Gulf of Termini Imerese, ab. 8 mi. E of Palermo. Only slight damage was sustained during World War II by the baroque villas of the town, and the Palazzino Cinese, also of interest to tourists, was left intact. Pop. of commune, 25,820 (1936); of town, 23,809 (1936).

Baghirmi (bä.gēr'mē). See **Baguirmi.**

Baghistan (bag.i.stan'). Ancient name of **Behistun.**

Bagida (bä'gē.dä). Seaport on the Bight of Benin, Gulf of Guinea, W Africa, in the French trust territory of Togo, E of Lomé.

Bagimont's Roll (baj'i.monts). List of the ecclesiastical benefices of Scotland and their valuation in the latter part of the Middle Ages. The name is derived from an Italian churchman, Boiamond (or Bajimont, and hence Bagimont) of Vicci, a canon of the cathedral of Asti in Piedmont, sent (1274) by the Pope to Scotland to collect the tithe of all the church livings, in order to furnish the means for a crusade.

Baginsky (bä.gin'skē), **Adolf.** b. at Ratibor (now Racibórz, Poland), May 22, 1843; d. at Berlin, May 15, 1918. German pediatrician, active in school and child hygiene. He became (1892) assistant professor at the University of Berlin. Author of *Handbuch der Schulhygiene* (1877) and *Lehrbuch der Kinderkrankheiten* (1883); editor of *Archiv für Kinderheilkunde.*

Bagirmi (bä.gēr'mē). See **Baguirmi.**

Bagley (bag'li), **John Judson.** b. at Medina, N.Y., July 24, 1832; d. at San Francisco, July 27, 1881. American politician, governor of Michigan (1873–77).

Bagley, William Chandler. b. at Detroit, Mich., March 15, 1874; d. July 1, 1946. American psychologist. He was a professor of education (1908 *et seq.*), and director of the school of education (1909 *et seq.*) at the University of Illinois, and a professor (1917 *et seq.*) of education at Columbia University's Teachers College. He published *Class-room Management* (1907).

Baglivi (bä.lyē'vē), **Giorgio.** b. at Ragusa, Sicily, 1669; d. at Rome, 1707. Italian physician, professor of anatomy and medicine at Rome. He was the founder of the system of "solidism" in medicine, as opposed to Galenism or humorism, maintaining that the origin of illness was in the "solid" tissues of the body rather than in the "fluids." His medical writings were held in high esteem for many years, and were frequently reprinted.

Bagnacavallo (bä"nyä.kä.väl'lō). [Original name, **Bartolomeo Ramenghi.**] b. at Bagnacavallo, near Ravenna, Italy, 1484; d. 1542. Italian painter who studied under Raphael and Francia, and assisted Raphael in the decoration of the Vatican. Among Bagnacavallo's best-known works, most of which were done in close imitation of Raphael's style, are a *Crucifixion* and a *Madonna with Saints* at Bologna, and a *Circumcision* now in the Louvre.

Bagnacavallo. Town and commune in N Italy, in the *compartimento* (region) of Emilia-Romagna, in the province of Ravenna, W of the city of Ravenna: agricultural trade center. The brick Romanesque Church of San Pietro in Silvis sustained some damage during World War II, as did some other buildings of tourist interest. Pop. of commune, 16,596 (1936); of town, 3,886 (1936).

Bagnara Calabra (bä.nyä'rä kä'lä.brä). Town and commune in S Italy, in the *compartimento* (region) of Calabria, in the province of Reggio di Calabria, situated on the N coast of the "toe" of Italy, NE of Reggio di Calabria: agricultural community. Pop. of commune, 12,574 (1936); of town, 9,088 (1936).

Bagne or **Bagnes** (bány'), **Val de.** Alpine valley in SW Switzerland, in the canton of Valais SE of Martigny.

Bagnell Dam (bag'nel). Dam in N central Missouri, on the Osage River in the W part of Miller County, SW of Jefferson City. The dam, completed in 1931, is the site of the largest hydroelectric generating plant in Missouri. Its construction created the Lake of the Ozarks, ab. 120 mi. long. A Missouri state park (16,148 acres) around the lake has cabins and camp sites for tourists and vacationers, and facilities for fishing, boating, and swimming. Height of dam, 148 ft.

Bagnères-de-Bigorre (bå.nyer.de.bē.gôr). [Also: **Bagnères-d'Adour** (bå.nyer.då.dör); Latin, **Aquae Bigerrionum Balneariae.**] Town in SW France, in the department of Hautes-Pyrénées, situated on the Adour River, ab. 13 mi. S of Tarbes. It is a tourist center, particularly for winter sports; is also one of the most frequented health resorts of the Pyrenees, having hot sulfur springs. It has good marble and other stone quarries, and woolen and wood manufactures; has been known for the production of the fabric barège. 9,941 (1946).

Bagnères-de-Luchon (bå.nyer.de.lü.shôn). [Also: **Luchon;** Latin, **Onesiorum Thermae, Balneariae Lixovienses.**] Town in S France, in the department of Haute-Garonne, situated at the falls of the Pique River near its junction with the One River, ab. 71 mi. SW of Toulouse and near the Spanish frontier. Surrounded by high mountains, the "Queen of the Pyrenees," as the town is sometimes called, is a health resort and a tourist center of first rank. Its numerous hot sulfur springs are considered useful in the treatment of arthritis, numerous muscular and nervous diseases, and others. The town has an agreeable mountain climate. The Hôtel de Superbagnères, connected with Luchon by a cable railway, is a winter-sports center. Known since ancient times and mentioned by Strabo, Bagnères-de-Luchon became fashionable toward the end of the 18th century. The modern baths were built in 1848. Pop. 4,105 (1946).

Bagnet (bag'net), **Mr.** and **Mrs. Joseph.** Characters in Charles Dickens's novel *Bleak House.* Bagnet is an ex-artilleryman, devoted to the bassoon. He has a notably high regard for Mrs. Bagnet, a large and indomitable woman, but never says so in her presence, as "discipline must be maintained." Their children Malta, Quebec, and Woolwich are named from the posts of the British army where they were born.

Bagni di Fontecchio (bä'nyē dē fôn.tek'kyō). See under **Città di Castello.**

Bagni di Lucca (lök'kä). Town and commune in C Italy, in the *compartimento* (region) of Tuscany, situated in the valley of the Lima River, ab. 13 mi. NE of Lucca. It is a health resort with thermal springs, used by people suffering from arthritis, rheumatism, and other diseases. Pop. of commune, 12,064 (1936); of town, 1,116 (1936).

Bagnigge Wells (bag'nij). Place of amusement which existed in London in the time of George II. It lay to the E of Gray's Inn Road, nearly opposite what later became Mecklenburg Square, and NE of Saint Andrew's burying ground.

Bagno a Ripoli (bä'nyō ä rē'pô.lē). Town and commune in N central Italy, in the *compartimento* (region) of Tuscany: an eastern suburb of Florence. Buildings of interest to tourists, including the Villa gli Olmi, were undamaged in World War II. Pop. of commune, 17,270 (1936); of town, 564 (1936).

Bagno di Romagna (dē rō.mä'nyä). Town and commune in N Italy, in the *compartimento* (region) of Emilia-Romagna, in the province of Forlì, situated in the upper valley of the Savi River, near the central range of the Apennines, S of Forlì. It is a health resort. Pop. of commune, 10,735 (1936); of town, 1,838 (1936).

Bagnold (bag′nǫld), **Enid.** English novelist, poet, and author of books for children; married (1920) to Sir Roderick Jones, chairman of Reuter's News Agency. Author of *A Diary Without Dates* (1917), *Serena Blandish, or the Difficulties of Getting Married* (1925; published anonymously), also a success as a play, and *National Velvet* (1937), a story about horses, later filmed; *Sailing Ships* (1918), poems; *Alice and Thomas and Jane* (1930), a story for children; and *The Loved and Envied* (1950), a novel.

Bagnoles-de-l'Orne (bȧ.nyol.dę.lôrn). [Also, **Bagnoles.**] Small resort in NW France, in the department of Orne, situated in the valley of the Vée River, NW of Alençon. It is connected with the village of Tessé-la-Madeleine. It has thermal springs considered useful in the treatment of phlebitis and circulatory diseases. 485 (1946).

Bagnolet (bȧ.nyo.le). Town in N France, in the department of Seine. It is an eastern suburb of Paris, situated N of Vincennes. 25,059 (1946).

Bagnols-les-Bains (bȧ.nyol.lā.bañ). Resort in S France, in the department of Lozère, situated on the Lot River, E of Mende. It has sulfur springs considered useful in the treatment of arthritis, scrofula, and heart ailments. 331 (1946).

Bagnols-sur-Cèze (bȧ.nyol.sür.sez). [Also, **Bagnols.**] Town in S France, in the department of Gard, situated on the Cèze River, ab. 25 mi. NE of Nîmes. It has an important regional museum, a library, and a theater. 5,211 (1946).

Bagnuolo (bä.nywô′lō), Count. [Title of **Giovanni Vicenzo Sanfelice.**] b. c1590; d. c1650. Neapolitan soldier.

Bagoas (bą.gō′ąs). fl. second half of 4th century B.C. Favorite eunuch of Alexander the Great.

Bagoas. d. 336 B.C. Egyptian eunuch, originally in the service of Artaxerxes III (of Persia). For a short time he virtually usurped the sovereignty of the empire. He put to death Artaxerxes (338) and his son Arses (336), but was himself compelled to drink a poison which he had intended for Arses's successor Darius III.

Bagobo (bä.gō′bō). A Malayo-Polynesian-speaking pagan tribe living NW of Davao Gulf on Mindanao island (Cotabato and Davao provinces), Philippine Islands.

Bagot (bag′ǫt), Sir **Charles.** b. at Blithfield, Staffordshire, England, Sept. 23, 1781; d. at Kingston, Ontario, Canada, May 18, 1843. British diplomat. He became undersecretary of state for foreign affairs in 1807, minister to France in 1814, ambassador to St. Petersburg in 1820, ambassador to Holland in 1824, and governor general of Canada in 1841. From 1815 to 1820 he was ambassador to the U.S.; during this time he was a negotiator (1817) of the Rush-Bagot Convention.

Bagot, Sir **William.** fl. about the end of the 14th century. English statesman, a minister under Richard II. He was one of the council (with Sir John Bussy and others) left in charge of the kingdom when Richard departed for Ireland in 1399.

Bagotville (bag′ǫt.vil). Town on the Saguenay River, Quebec, Canada, at the head of one of the arms of the river midway between the St. Lawrence River and Lake St. John, ab. 13 mi. E of Chicoutimi. 4,136 (1951).

Bagradas (bą.grā′dąs). Ancient name of the **Medjerda River.**

Bagratidae (bą.grat′i.dē). Dynasty of Armenian monarchs which lasted from the 9th century to the 11th century.

Bagration (bä.grä.tyi.ôn′), Prince **Pyotr Ivanovich.** b. 1765; d. 1812. Russian general; descendant of a Georgian princely family. He served with distinction against the Turks and Poles and in 1799 in Italy (at Cassano) and Switzerland, opposed (Nov. 16, 1805) Joachim Murat at Hollabrunn, served at Austerlitz, Eylau, Friedland, and in Finland, was commander in chief in Turkey in 1809, was defeated (July 23, 1812) near Mogilev, and was mortally wounded (Sept. 7, 1812) at Borodino.

Bagrationovsk (bä.grä.tyi.ô′nǫfsk). [Former name, **Eylau,** officially **Preussisch-Eylau.**] City in W U.S.S.R., in the SW part of Kaliningrad *oblast* (region), ab. 23 mi. S of Kaliningrad (Königsberg). The town was founded in 1336 by the Teutonic Knights, and was the scene (Feb. 8, 1807) of a bitterly contested Napoleonic battle in which the French army met a force of Russians and Prussians and defeated them indecisively. Casualties were ab. 33,000, or a quarter of the total force engaged. On Feb. 10, 1945, Soviet armies occupied the city, which was a key point in the defense system of East Prussia. The town is the center of a farming district producing meat, dairy products, and fruit. 7,485 (1939).

Bagritski (bä.grēt′ski), **Eduard.** [Also: **Bagritzky;** pseudonym of **Eduard Georgiyevich Dzyubin.**] b. at Odessa, Russia, 1895; d. Feb. 16, 1934. Russian poet. Inspired by the Revolution in his mature work, he produced a number of original, if uneven, lyrics and several long poems.

Bagshot (bag′shǫt). Rural district and town in SE England, in Surrey, ab. 32 mi. S of London by rail. It comprised part of the former Chertsey and Windlesham rural districts, now abolished. 14,096 (1951).

Bagshot Heath. Tract of land in S and SE England, on the Berkshire-Surrey border. It contains plantations of fir. Elevation, 463 ft.

Bagstock (bag′stok), **Major Joe.** "A wooden-featured, blue-faced" officer, a friend of Mr. Dombey, in Charles Dickens's novel *Dombey and Son.*

Baguio (bä.gē.ō′). City in the S part of Mountain Province, in NW Luzon, Philippine Islands: summer capital of the republic. 29,262 (1948).

Baguirmi (bä.gēr′mē). [Also: **Baghirmi, Bagirmi.**] African kingdom, SE of Lake Chad on the Shari River, between Bornu and Ouadai, within the Chad territory, French Equatorial Africa. The country is a fertile plain. The population is mixed: the mass is Nigritic, the higher class are pastoral Fulahs and Arab traders. Mohammedanism was introduced in the 16th century, but many inhabitants are still pagan. The language is called "Bagrima"; it is related to Kuka and distinct from Kanuri. Capital, Massénya.

Bahadur (bą.hä′dụr), Sir **Ganga Singhji.** See **Bikaner,** Maharaja of.

Bahadur Shah II (shä). [Original name, **Mohammed Bahadur Shah.**] b. c1768; d. at Rangoon, Burma, 1862. Last ruler of India of the Mogul dynasty. During his reign (1837–57) actual power was exercised by the East India Company. In the Sepoy Mutiny of 1857, whether by choice or under constraint, he sided with the mutineers; upon the suppression of the movement he took refuge at the tomb of Humayun, near Delhi, where he was captured.

Bahai (bä.hä′ē), Sir **Abdul Baha.** See **Abdul Baha.**

Bahaism (bą.hä′iz.ęm). [Also, **Bahai** (-hä′ē).] Religious sect founded in 1863 by Baha Ullah. Bahaism is an outgrowth of (and successor to) Babism, but where the latter was in effect a schismatic variant of Shiite Mohammedanism, Bahaism can claim to be a world religion. The difference between Babism and Bahaism was said by Sir Cecil Spring-Rice, one-time British ambassador to Tehran, to parallel the different concepts of Christianity in Apostolic days, when, to some, Christianity was a variant of Judaism while others envisioned it as the destined universal religion. The core of the Bahaist creed is that the Essence of God, the Primal Divine Unity, can be known by man through, but only through, Manifestations, such as those which took mortal form in Abraham, Moses, David, Jesus, Mohammed, and Baha Ullah. (For all practical purposes, in modern Bahaism, Bab, or "the Bab," is included with these.) The Manifestations, outwardly various, are in fact one Being. When the world outgrows one Manifestation, another appears; divine revelation is continuous and progressive, and human evolution, spiritual and social, advances in cycles of approximately 1,000 years each. Modern Bahaists insist upon the essential unity of all religions, and urge universal education, world peace, and the practical equality of men and women. They advocate adoption of an international language, as an essential preliminary step toward all these ends. They practice simplicity in living and emphasize the duty of service to one's fellow men, especially to those in want or sorrow. Following the death of Baha Ullah, his son Abdul Baha became the acknowledged leader of Bahaism. Today there are Bahaist communities in 40 countries, including 500 in Iran and 90 in North America; perhaps the most impressive of Bahaist temples is one serving Chicago, the cornerstone of which was laid by Abdul Baha. A biennial publication, *The Baha'i World*, keeps the faithful informed of the progress of the movement.

Bahalul (bä.hä.löl'). [Called **al-Megnum,** meaning "the Crazy."] Court fool of Harun al-Rashid.

Bahama (bą.hā'mą, -hä'-), **Grand** (or **Great**). See **Grand Bahama.**

Bahama Bank, Great. Extensive bank, or area of shoal water, between N Cuba and Andros island, Bahama Islands.

Bahama Bank, Little. Bank N of Grand Bahama island and E of SE Florida.

Bahama Channel, Old. [Also, **Gulf of Florida.**] Part of the Atlantic Ocean between NE Cuba and the Great Bahama Bank in the S part of the Bahama Islands.

Bahama Islands or **Bahamas.** [Former name, **Lucayos.**] Archipelago in the Atlantic Ocean, E and SE of Florida and N of Cuba. It is a British colony, comprised of 29 islands, 661 cays, and 2,387 reefs over a distance of 760 mi. The principal islands are Great Abaco, Grand Bahama, Andros, New Providence, Eleuthera, Cat Island, San Salvador (or Watlings Island), Long Island, Great Exuma, Crooked Island, Acklins Island, Mayaguana, and Great Inagua. Prior to 1930, sponge fishing was an important industry; its decline was the result of disease which attacked the sponge beds. The tourist trade and the production of tomatoes are the principal sources of income. The Bahamas were discovered (1492) by Columbus, were occupied (1629) by the British, and finally annexed (1783) by them. The name Lucayos was given the islands by the Spaniards, from the Indians who inhabited them. Capital, Nassau, on New Providence Island; area (land), 4,404 sq. mi.; pop. 68,846 (1943), 80,639 (est. 1948).

Bahar (bą.här'). See **Bihar.**

Baharites (bą.har'īts). [Also, **Baharides** (-īdz).] Mameluke dynasty which reigned over Egypt from the middle of the 13th century to the end of the 14th century.

Baha Ullah (bä.hä' ůl.lä'). [Also: **Bahaullah**; original name, **Hussein** (or **Husayn**) **Ali.**] b. at Tehran, Persia, 1817; d. 1892. Persian religious leader and founder of the movement known as Bahaism. As a follower of Bab, he was imprisoned in 1852, and later exiled to Baghdad, where he effectively preached Babism, and to Constantinople, Adrianople, and Acre. In 1863 he announced that he was the new leader (or "Manifestation") who had been prophesied by Bab for that year, and at this time took the name Baha Ullah, meaning "Splendor of God." During his exile he propagated his faith by preaching and writing. After his death he was succeeded in leadership of the faithful by his son Abdul Baha, later Sir Abdul Baha Bahai.

Bahawalpur (bą.hä.wąl.pör', bä.wąl.pör'). [Also, **Bhawalpur.**] State of Pakistan, one of the Punjab States, its center ab. 400 mi. NE of Karachi, on the E side of the Indus and Sutlej rivers. Most of the state is naturally suited only for herding, but since the British development of irrigation projects a considerable area produces cotton and wheat. Capital, Bahawalpur; area, 15,918 sq. mi.; pop. 1,822,501 (1951).

Bahawalpur. Capital of the state of Bahawalpur, Pakistan, on the Sutlej River, ab. 75 mi. above its junction with the Indus River: trading center and railroad junction. 40,698 (1951).

Bahía (bä.ē'ä). Spanish word for "bay": for geographical entries not found here, see the specific element of the name.

Bahía. See also **Bahía de Caráquez.**

Bahia (bą.ē'ą). See also **Salvador.**

Bahia. [Former spelling, **Baía.**] State in E Brazil, bounded on the E by the Atlantic Ocean. For a short time during the 1940's, the spelling of this name was officially Baía, but it was changed officially, at the request of the people, back to Bahia. Capital, Salvador; area, 217,484 sq. mi.; pop. 4,900,419 (1950).

Bahía (bä.ē'ä), **Islas de la.** Spanish name of **Bay Islands.**

Bahía Blanca (bläng'kä). Arm of the Atlantic Ocean off the coast of Buenos Aires state, E Argentina. The seaport Bahía Blanca is located on it.

Bahía Blanca. City in E Argentina, in Buenos Aires province, ab. 350 mi. SSW of the city of Buenos Aires: naval station and shipping center for wool, hides, and grain. 112,597 (1947).

Bahía de Caráquez (dā kä.rä'kes). [Also, **Bahía.**] City in W Ecuador, in Manabí province, on the Pacific: shipping point for balsa, cacao, coffee, nuts, and rubber. 10,499 (est. 1944).

Bahman (bä'mąn), **Prince.** Eldest son of the Sultan of Persia, a character in the story of "The Two Envious Sisters" in *The Arabian Nights' Entertainments.* Before starting out on his adventures, he gave to his sister a magical knife; as long as it remained bright she would know that he was safe, but if a drop of blood were to appear on it, it would mean that he was dead.

Bahnar (bä.när'). A Mon-Khmer-speaking pagan people of Indochina living in the mountains of Annam, in Viet-Nam, E of Kontum. 70,000 (est. 1942).

Bahoruco (bä.ō.rö'kō). Province in the SW part of the Dominican Republic. Capital, Neiba; area, 564 sq. mi.; pop. 39,655 (1950).

Bahr (bär). Arabic word denoting various bodies of water, usually "sea" or "river," sometimes "gulf" or others. For geographical entries not found here, see the specific element of the name.

Bahr, Hermann. b. at Linz, Austria, July 19, 1863; d. at Munich, Germany, Jan. 15, 1934. Austrian journalist, playwright, and essayist. He was also a theater manager at the Deutsches Theater, Berlin (1892–1912), and the Burgtheater, Vienna. His diaries mirror an entire epoch of European culture. The most important of his numerous essays and critical works are collected in *Studien zur Kritik der Moderne* (Studies toward Criticism of the Modern Spirit, 1890), *Die Überwindung des Naturalismus* (Naturalism Conquered, 1891), *Dialogue vom Tragischen* (A Dialogue on the Tragic, 1903), and *Expressionismus* (1918; Eng. trans., *Expressionism,* 1925). As a dramatist he is best remembered for his gay, swift-moving, sensitive comedy of Vienna *Das Konzert* (1909; Eng. trans., *The Concert,* 1910); it was a success on both the European and the American stages.

Bähr (bār), **Johann Christian Felix.** b. at Darmstadt, Germany, June 13, 1798; d. at Heidelberg, Germany, Nov. 29, 1872. German philologist and historian. He wrote *Geschichte der römischen Literatur* (1828; supplements, 1836–37, 1840), and other works, and edited (1825) fragments of Ctesias.

Bahraich (bä.rīch'). [Also: **Bahreich, Bharech.**] District in the Fyzabad division, Uttar Pradesh, Union of India, ab. 200 mi. NW of Benares, near the borders of Nepal: sugar, wheat, and rice. Area, ab. 2,654 sq. mi.; pop. 1,240,569 (1941).

Bahraich. [Also: **Bahreich, Bharech.**] Town in the district of Bahraich, Uttar Pradesh, Union of India, ab. 65 mi. NE of Lucknow: trading center and road junction. 33,783 (1941).

Bahrdt (bärt), **Karl Friedrich.** b. at Bischofswerda, Saxony, Aug. 25, 1741; d. near Halle, Saxony, April 23, 1792. German theologian, noted for his rationalistic theories. He was professor of Biblical philology at Leipzig (1766–68), of Biblical antiquities at Erfurt (1768–71), and of theology (and pastor) at Giessen (1771–75). He was superintendent-general and pastor at Dürkheim when he was declared (1778) by the imperial aulic council ineligible to hold any ecclesiastical office and forbidden to publish any writing. Taking refuge in Prussia, he lectured on philosophy and philology at Halle (1779–89). He was condemned to one year's imprisonment (1789) for having published the pasquinade *Das Religionsedict, ein Lustpiel* (1788). His remaining years were devoted to the management of a tavern.

Bahrein (bä.rān'). [Also: **Aval Islands, Bahrain** (or **Bahrein**) **Islands**; Arabic, **al-Bahrayn.**] Sultanate comprising a group of islands in the Persian Gulf near the E coast of Arabia. The chief island is Bahrein (formerly Samak; 27 mi. long); the others are Muharraq, Sitra, Nabi Saleh, and small islets. There are very productive oil wells here which yield ab. six million barrels a year. The islands are celebrated for their pearl fisheries. Capital, Manamah; area, ab. 213 sq. mi.; pop. 110,000 (est. 1950).

Bahr-el-Ghazal (bär"el.gä.zäl'). River in N central Africa, one of the chief W tributaries of the White Nile. The many headstreams which unite to form the river rise in the SW part of the Anglo-Egyptian Sudan. The

Bahr-el-Ghazal joins the Bahr-el-Jebel W of Malakal, Anglo-Egyptian Sudan.

Bahr-el-Ghazal. Province (part of Equatoria, 1935–48) of the Anglo-Egyptian Sudan, in NE Africa. The capital is Wau; area, 82,530 sq. mi.; pop. 727,847 (1949).

Bahr-el-Jebel (bär.el.jeb′e̤l). [Also (in its upper course), **Albert Nile.**] River in NE Africa, a branch of the Nile River. It flows from the Belgian Congo-Uganda border, through the S part of the Anglo-Egyptian Sudan, and unites with the Bahr-el-Ghazal at Lake No, ab. 1,400 mi. S of Cairo, to form the White Nile. Length, ab. 600 mi.

Bahu (bä′hö). See under **Jolo** island.

Bahya ben Asher (bȧ′yä ben ash′ėr). [Full name, **Bahya ben Asher ben Halawa.**] b. at Saragossa, Spain, c1260; d. there, 1340. Jewish theologian and moralist, notable as a Bible exegete.

Bahya ibn-Paquda (ib″n.pä.kö′dä). [Also, **Bahya ibn-Pakuda.**] fl. at Saragossa, Spain, in the early 12th century (or, according to some authorities, in the late 11th century). Jewish philosopher and moralist. Of his works (all of which were written in Arabic) the best known is unquestionably the one which was translated into Hebrew in the late 12th century as *Hoboth Halebaboth*, part of which was published in English in 1925 as *Duties of the Heart* (a very close translation of the Hebrew title). This work, which places great emphasis upon the inner duties beyond the requirements of the law and of conventional morality, was not only the first Jewish work of its kind, but also one of the best ethical works of the Middle Ages.

Bai (bä′ē), **Tommaso.** [Also, **Baj.**] b. at Crevalcore, Italy, c1650; d. Dec. 22, 1714. Italian tenor, noted as the composer of a *Miserere* considered of equal merit with the works of Giovanni Palestrina. He was maestro (1713 *et seq.*) at the Vatican after many years as a singer in the chapel choir.

Baía (ba̤.ē′a̤). Portuguese word for "bay": for geographical entries not found here, see the specific element of the name.

Baia (bä′yä). [Ancient name, **Baiae.**] Seaport in SW Italy, in the *compartimento* (region) of Campania, near Cape Misenum on the Gulf of Pozzuoli, W of Naples. It was formerly a great seaport and the leading Roman watering-place, especially in the times of Horace, Nero, and Hadrian. It was famous for its luxury, and contained the villas of many celebrated Romans. It was plundered by the Moslems. Among the antiquities of Baia are: (1) A Temple of Diana, so called, in reality part of a Roman bath. It is octagonal without, circular within, with a pointed dome 97 ft. in diameter. The walls have four ornamental niches. The structure is in *opus incertum* cased in masonry of brick and stone. (2) A Temple of Mercury, so called, in reality part of a Roman bath, three subdivisions of which survive. The chief of these is the *frigidarium*, or cold bath, a circular domed structure 144 ft. in diameter, with a circular opening at the apex, as in the Pantheon at Rome. The two others are rectangular and vaulted, the vault of one having excellent ornament in relief. (3) A Temple of Venus, so called, in fact part of a Roman bath, an octagonal buttressed structure of *opus incertum* cased in brick, and *opus reticulatum*, circular within, 94 ft. in diameter, and domed. It has eight windows above, four doors below, and had lateral chambers containing stairs.

Baía (ba̤.ē′a̤). Former name of **Bahia,** state, and of **Salvador,** both in Brazil.

Baiae (bā′ē). Ancient name of **Baia,** Italy.

Baia-Mare (bä′yä.mä′rā). [Hungarian, **Nagybánya.**] Town in NW Rumania, in the region of Crişana-Maramureş, situated near the Someş River, ab. 68 mi. NW of Cluj: railroad junction; chemical industry; state gold refinery. Close by are gold, silver, and copper mines. 20,959 (1948).

Baiburt (bī.bört′). See **Bayburt.**

Baidar (bī.där′). Village and valley in the S part of the U.S.S.R., near the S extremity of the Crimea.

Baie (be). French word for "bay": for geographical entries not found here, see the specific element of the name.

Baiern (bī′ėrn). A German name of **Bavaria.**

Baie St. Paul (bā″ sānt pôl′; French, be saṅ pol). Capital of West Charlevoix County, Quebec, Canada, situated on the N bank of the St. Lawrence River, ab. 62 mi. E of the city of Quebec. 3,716 (1951).

Baïf (bȧ.ēf), **Jean Antoine de.** b. at Venice, Italy, 1532; d. at Paris, Sept. 9, 1589. French poet, a friend of Pierre de Ronsard, and a member of the group known as the Pléiade.

Baikal (bī.käl′), **Lake.** [Russian, **Ozero Baikal;** Tartar, **Bai-kul;** Eng. trans., "*Rich Sea.*"] Largest fresh-water lake in Asia, situated in S Siberia on the border of Irkutsk *oblast* (region) and the Buryat-Mongol Autonomous Soviet Socialist Republic. The deepest (nearly 5,715 ft.) lake in the world, it contains more water than the Caspian Sea. Its chief tributaries are the upper Angara, Selenga, and Barguzin rivers, and its outlet is the lower Angara River to the Yenisei River. Length, ab. 390 mi.; average width, ab. 45 mi.; area, ab. 12,150 sq. mi.

Baikal Mountains. Range of mountains in the U.S.S.R., in the Irkutsk *oblast* (region) of the Russian Soviet Federated Socialist Republic, W and NW of Lake Baikal. Length, ab. 400 mi.

Baikie (bā′ki), **William Balfour.** b. at Kirkwall, Orkney, Scotland, Aug. 21, 1824; d. in Sierra Leone, Africa, Dec. 12, 1864. Surgeon (assistant surgeon in the royal navy, 1848–51), explorer, and pioneer in the valley of the Niger, Africa. He was appointed surgeon and naturalist of the Niger exploring expedition of 1854, and succeeded to the command of the vessel (the *Pleiad*) on the death of its captain. The expedition ascended the river 250 mi. beyond the highest point before reached. He returned (1857) on a second expedition, in the course of which the *Pleiad* was wrecked; he then founded a native settlement at Lokoja, with himself as its head. He translated parts of the Bible into Hausa and made studies of native African languages.

Bai-kul (bī.köl′). Tartar name of **Baikal, Lake.**

Bailak al-Qabajaqi (bī.läk′ äl.kä.bä.jä′kē). fl. at Cairo, c1242–82. Moslem mineralogist. He wrote a work on precious stones which was derived in large part from another work produced earlier in the 13th century, and which cites some 23 earlier authorities from the Moslem world and also from ancient Greece; for the modern scholar, the most notable fact about this work is perhaps that Bailak gives in it a description of the floating compass and its use by sailors, which he had observed in the E Mediterranean sometime during the period 1242–43.

Bailan (bā.län′). [Also, **Beilan.**] Town in S Turkey in the *il* (province or vilayet) of Hatay, situated near the summit of the Bailan Pass, N of Antakya, on one of the important routes to the Persian Gulf: a trading center. Here, on July 29, 1832, the Egyptians under Ibrahim Pasha defeated the Turks. Pop. ab. 5,000.

Baildon (bāl′do̤n). Urban district and health resort in C England, in the West Riding of Yorkshire, ab. 2 mi. N of Shipley, ab. 210 mi. NW of London by rail. It has had a woolen industry since the 18th century. Baildon is becoming increasingly popular as a moorland health resort. 10,132 (1951).

Baile Átha Cliath (bol ô klē′a̤). An Irish name of **Dublin,** capital of the Irish Republic.

Baile Mhisteala (bol vis.tal′a̤). Irish name of **Mitchelstown.**

Bailén (bī.lān′). [Also: **Baylén;** ancient name, **Baecula.**] Town in S Spain, in the province of Jaén, ab. 20 mi. N of Jaén: center of a horse-breeding district; terra-cotta factories; zinc and lead mines. Scipio Africanus ("the Elder") defeated the Carthaginians here in 209 and 206 B.C. In the vicinity, the famous battle of Las Navas de Tolosa took place in 1212; at that time, great numbers of Moslems are said to have been slain by the Castilians under Alfonso VIII of León and Castile (also known as Alfonso III of Castile). In 1808, the Spaniards defeated the French under Dupont here. 10,045 (1940).

Bailén, Duke of. Title of **Castaños, Francisco Xavier de.**

Băilesti (bī.lāsh′tē). Town in S Rumania, in the province of Oltenia, ab. 135 mi. SW of Bucharest, near the Bulgarian and Yugoslav borders. There are mills, leather factories, and cattle markets. 15,289 (1948).

Bailey (bā′li), Sir **Abe.** b. at Cradock, Cape Colony (now Cape of Good Hope, Union of South Africa), Nov. 6, 1864; d. at Capetown, Union of South Africa, Aug. 10, 1940.

South African financier, politician, and sportsman; a friend of Cecil Rhodes. He acquired a fortune from gold discoveries (1880 *et seq.*) in the Transvaal. Imprisoned in 1896–97 by the Boers for 13 months after Jameson's raid, Bailey served (1899–1902) with the British forces during the Boer War, and aided in forming (1910) the Union of South Africa, after having been a member of the Cape Colony parliament (1907–10) and the Transvaal legislative assembly (1910–24).

Bailey, Ann. [Called the **"White Squaw of the Kanawha"**; maiden name, **Hennis.**] b. at Liverpool, England, 1742; d. Nov. 22, 1825. American frontier heroine. Having come (1761) to America, she married Richard Trotter, a Shenandoah Valley pioneer; after he met his death (1774) at the hands of the Indians during Lord Dunmore's war, she donned frontiersman's garb and became widely known as a border scout and messenger. (At approximately this time she was also married again, to a frontier leader named John Bailey, from which marriage she derived the name by which she is now remembered.) Her most notable feat of daring was performed in 1791, when she made a long dash on horseback to secure the gunpowder which saved the occupants of besieged Fort Lee (now Charleston, W. Va.) from slaughter by the Indians. Another version of her life has it that she was actually born in 1700 and was kidnaped as a child; however, most modern historians discredit this account, if only because it would have made her a woman of some 90 years at the time of her most notable feat of horsemanship.

Bailey, Anna Warner. [Called **"Mother Bailey."**] b. at Groton, Conn., in October, 1758; d. Jan. 10, 1851. American war heroine, noted as the donor of the "martial petticoat" which aided in the defense of Groton, Conn., against British raiding parties during the War of 1812. However, her first exploit was performed in the Revolutionary War during the battle of Groton Heights (Sept. 6, 1781), when she rescued her mortally wounded uncle, Edward Mills, from the field of battle, bringing him to his farm for a last farewell to his family. "Mother Bailey," as she has gone down in legend and song, gave her flannel petticoat to American soldiers at Groton in 1813 when they ran short of cartridge wadding during the British fleet's blockade of the Connecticut coast.

Bailey, Ebenezer. b. June 25, 1795; d. Aug. 5, 1839. American educator, principal of the first high school for girls in Massachusetts. Soon after graduation (1817) from Yale, he became (1823) headmaster of the Franklin Grammar School at Boston. He was principal (1826–27) of the Girls' High School of Boston, a pioneer venture in the U.S., and the first of its kind in the state; the school was closed after what later appeared to have been unfair charges were launched against it by the Boston mayor.

Bailey, Florence Augusta. [Maiden name, **Merriam.**] b. at Locust Grove, N.Y., 1863—. American writer and ornithologist. Author of books on birds, including *Birds Through an Opera Glass* (1889), *A-Birding on a Bronco* (1896), *Birds of Village and Field* (1898), and *Handbook of Birds of Western United States* (1902). She also collaborated on several books with her husband, Vernon Bailey.

Bailey, Francis. b. in Lancaster County, Pa., c1735; d. 1815. American printer, editor, and Revolutionary patriot. Having learned the printer's trade from a Dunker (or Dunkard) printer at Ephrata, Pa., he published (1771 *et seq.*) the series of *Lancaster Almanacs*, a fourth edition of Paine's *Common Sense* (1776), and *The Articles of Confederation and Perpetual Union* (1777). With the Continental army, he served as an officer of state troops at Valley Forge (1777–78). He was copublisher of the *United States Magazine* (January–December, 1779) at Philadelphia, and in 1781 was authorized by the Continental Congress to publish *The Constitutions of the Several Independent States of America, The Declaration of Independence, and the Treaties between His Most Christian Majesty and the United States of America* (followed by other editions in 1783). He was appointed official printer for Congress and the Commonwealth of Pennsylvania, and edited (1781 *et seq.*) *The Freeman's Journal or the North American Intelligencer*, publishing it at his Philadelphia shop. Among its contributors were George Bryan, Philip Freneau, and James Wilson.

Bailey, Frank Harvey. b. at Cranesville, Pa., June 29, 1851; d. in Arizona, April 9, 1921. American marine engineer and naval officer. He was graduated (1875) from the U.S. Naval Academy, and subsequently was a professor of marine engineering (1885–88) at Cornell University. He served at the battle of Manila Bay (May 1, 1898) as chief engineer of the *Raleigh*. His most notable contribution to marine engineering was made as chief designer of the Bureau of Steam Engineering, where he was responsible for the machinery of the *Minneapolis* and the *Columbia*, the fastest big ships of the last decade of the 19th century. Recalled to active service in World War I, he was attached to the design division of the Bureau of Engineering.

Bailey, Gamaliel. b. at Mount Holly, N.J., Dec. 3, 1807; d. at sea, June 5, 1859. American antislavery editor and agitator, coeditor of the Cincinnati *Philanthropist*, the first antislavery journal in the West. He was graduated (1827) from Jefferson Medical College, at Philadelphia, and, after adventures in the U.S. and abroad, established himself as a physician at Cincinnati, where he played a signal part in ministering (1831) to the victims of a cholera epidemic. The Lane Seminary debates on slavery in 1834 aroused his interest in the cause of abolition, and in 1836 he joined J. G. Birney in editing the Cincinnati *Philanthropist*, becoming its sole owner and editor in 1837. His office was assaulted by mobs on three occasions; after the third incident he replied by publishing a daily, the *Herald*. As editor in chief (1847–59) of the *National Era*, the weekly organ of the American and Foreign Anti-Slavery Society at Washington, D.C., he wielded a potent influence; among the contributors during his editorship were Theodore Parker, Harriet Beecher Stowe (who published *Uncle Tom's Cabin* in the journal), and John Greenleaf Whittier.

Bailey, Guy Winfred. b. at Hardwick, Vt., May 7, 1876; d. at Boston, Oct. 22, 1940. American educator and politician. He was graduated (1900) from the University of Vermont and served as its comptroller (1917 *et seq.*) and president (1920 *et seq.*). He was a member (1904–08) of the Vermont legislature before acting as secretary of state (1908–17) of Vermont.

Bailey, Henry Christopher. b. at London, Feb. 1, 1878—. English author of historical novels and detective stories; noted as creator of two fictional detectives: Reggie Fortune and Joshua Clunk. Among his historical novels are *My Lady of Orange* (1901), *The Plot* (1922), and *Bonaventure* (1927). His detective books include *Call Mr. Fortune* (1920), *Mr. Fortune's Practice* (1922), *Clunk's Claimant* (1937), and *Mr. Clunk's Text* (1939).

Bailey, Jacob. b. at Rowley, Mass., 1731; d. at Annapolis Royal, Nova Scotia, March 22, 1818. Pioneer missionary of the Church of England in Maine, and Loyalist emigré. He was graduated (1755) from Harvard; licensed (1758) to preach as a Congregational minister, he voluntarily transferred to the Anglican Church and was ordained (1760) a priest by the bishop of Peterborough after making a trip to England. Appointed (1760) by the Society for Promoting the Gospel in Foreign Parts as an itinerant missionary on the E frontier of Massachusetts (then bounded by Canada on the N), he served in this post for 19 years. An adamant Tory during the Revolution, he was finally permitted to move to Nova Scotia, where he was rector at Annapolis Royal until he died.

Bailey, Jacob Whitman. b. at Ward (now Auburn), Mass., April 29, 1811; d. Feb. 27, 1857. American botanist, chemist, geologist, and teacher, noted as one of the first U.S. scientists to apply the microscope to botanical research. He was graduated (1832) from West Point, and served as assistant professor of chemistry (1834–38) and first professor of chemistry, mineralogy, and geology (1838–57) there. As a botanist, he was the first to discover the diatomaseas in a fossil state in the U.S., and was noted for his investigations among the minor algae and the crystals in plant tissues.

Bailey, James Anthony. b. at Detroit, Mich., 1847; d. at Mount Vernon, N.Y., April 11, 1906. American showman, famed as the partner of P. T. Barnum in the internationally known circus which still bears their names. A founder of the firm of Cooper and Bailey, he soon lifted it to a high place in the circus world; his competition with P. T. Barnum was finally resolved by a combining of the two shows. His most notable achievement as a showman was the purchase of the giant elephant Jumbo from the Royal Zoölogical Society in England.

Bailey, James Montgomery. [Called the **"Danbury News Man."**] b. at Albany, N.Y., Sept. 25, 1841; d. March 4, 1894. American humorous journalist, originator of the newspaper humor column. He served with the Union army in the Civil War. In 1865, together with Timothy Donovan, he bought the Danbury *Times* which, after its consolidation (1870) with the *Jeffersonian*, they conducted as the Danbury *News*. The sole editorship and ownership of the paper was taken over by Bailey in 1878, and a daily, the Danbury *Evening News*, was added in 1883. Bailey's great achievement on the Danbury *News* was a nationally known and quoted column of comments on events real and imagined. He also won success as a lecturer. Author of *Life in Danbury* (1873), *Danbury News Man's Almanac* (1873), *They All Do It* (1877), *England from a Back Window* (1878), *Mr. Phillips' Goneness* (1879), *The Danbury Boom* (1880), and *History of Danbury* (1896, the last (completed by Susan B. Hill.

Bailey, John Eglington. b. 1840; d. 1888. English merchant and antiquary of Manchester. In the firm of Ralli Brothers until 1886, he contributed to the *Dictionary of National Biography* and published antiquarian and other writings.

Bailey, Joseph. b. at Pennsville, Ohio, May 6, 1825; d. near Nevada, Mo., March 21, 1867. American Civil War general, noted for his construction (1864) of wing dams above Alexandria, La., which made possible the passage of the 33-vessel fleet accompanying the Union forces in their retirement (by land march) from the Red River expedition. As a reward for this feat, he was brevetted (June 7, 1864) brigadier general and voted the thanks of Congress. He settled (1865) in Vernon County, Mo., where he was elected sheriff in 1866; in 1867 he was killed while returning two desperadoes to justice.

Bailey, Joseph Weldon. b. at Crystal Springs, Miss., Oct. 6, 1863; d. at Sherman, Tex., April 13, 1929. American politician. A Texas representative (1891–1901) in Congress, he subsequently served as a senator (1901–12).

Bailey, Liberty Hyde. b. at South Haven, Mich., March 15, 1858—. American botanist, horticulturist, and educator, director (1903–13) of the N.Y. State College of Agriculture at Cornell University. He is widely known for his pioneer work in establishing college extension courses for farmers, and for varied contributions to horticulture and botany through research. From 1884 to 1888 he was professor of horticulture and landscape gardening at Michigan State Agricultural College (from which he was graduated in 1882); he served (1888–1903) as professor of horticulture at Cornell University, where he organized the agricultural college of which he became director. He retired from teaching in 1913 to write and to work on his plant collection, the Liberty Hyde Bailey Hortorium, given to Cornell in 1935. Among his numerous works are *The Survival of the Unlike* (1896), *The Principles of Fruit-growing* (1897), *Evolution of Our Native Fruits* (1898), *Cyclopedia of American Horticulture* (1900–02), *The Nature-Study Idea* (1903), *Outlook to Nature* (1905), *Cyclopedia of American Agriculture* (1907–09), textbooks of botany and agriculture, and handbooks of horticultural practice.

Bailey, Loring Woart. b. at West Point, N.Y., Sept. 28, 1839; d. 1925. American geologist. He was a professor (1861–1906) at the University of New Brunswick. Author of *Mines and Minerals of New Brunswick* (1864), *Geology of Southern New Brunswick* (1870), and *Elementary Natural History* (1887).

Bailey, Lydia R. b. Feb. 1, 1779; d. at Philadelphia, Feb. 21, 1869. American woman printer, notable as one of the first in Philadelphia. She married (1798) Robert Bailey, a printer, and after his death (1808) carried on his business. The poet Philip Freneau, some of whose writings had been published by Francis Bailey (the father of Robert Bailey), entrusted to her a new edition of his *Poems* (1809). She was city printer (c1830–c1850) for Philadelphia.

Bailey, Nathan or **Nathaniel.** d. at Stepney (now part of London), June 27, 1742. English lexicographer and schoolmaster, author of *An Universal Etymological English Dictionary*, first published in 1721. A supplement appeared in 1727, and a folio edition in 1730, with the title *Dictionarium Britannicum, collected by several hands . . . revised and improved with many thousand additions by N. Bailey*. The dictionary, based on the works of John Kersey, Elisha Coles, Edward Phillips, Thomas Blount, and others, was often republished, and served as a foundation for other works of the kind, including (to some extent) Samuel Johnson's.

Bailey, Philip James. b. at Nottingham, England, April 22, 1816; d. there, Sept. 6, 1902. English poet. Bailey was the author of a version of the Faust story, *Festus* (composed 1836–39, published anonymously in the latter year; subsequently revised and expanded; 2nd ed., 1845, 11th ed., 1889); his other works include *The Angel World* (1850), *The Mystic* (1855), *The Age* (1858), *The Universal Hymn* (1867), *Nottingham Castle* (1878), and other poems. With Sydney Dobell, Alexander Smith, and others, Bailey belonged to what W. E. Aytoun called the "spasmodic school."

Bailey, Rufus William. b. at North Yarmouth, Me., April 13, 1793; d. April 25, 1863. American Congregational clergyman, writer, and educator. He was graduated (1813) from Dartmouth College, attended Andover Theological Seminary, and was ordained pastor at the Congregational Church, Norwich, Vt. Appointed professor of languages at Austin College, Texas, in 1854, he became its president in 1858 and served in that post until his death. He was a writer of textbooks on spelling and grammar, of which the best-known, the *Scholar's Companion* (1830), sold more than a half-million copies during his lifetime. Editor (1841 *et seq.*) of the *Patriarch*.

Bailey, Solon Irving. b. at Lisbon, N.H., Dec. 29, 1854; d. June 5, 1931. American astronomer. A graduate (1881) of Boston University, he served as assistant professor (1893–98), associate professor (1898–1913), and professor (1913–25) of astronomy at Harvard. On an expedition (1889) to Peru, he selected Arequipa as the location for the southern station of the Harvard Observatory and served as its head (1892 *et seq.*); he was subsequently (1919–22) acting director of the Harvard Observatory. He established (1893) the highest meteorological station in the world on El Misti, in Peru, at 19,000 ft. altitude.

Bailey, Temple. [Full name, **Irene Temple Bailey.**] b. at Petersburg, Va., c1889; d. at Washington, D.C., July 6, 1953. American novelist. Among her books are *Glory of Youth* (1913), *The Tin Soldier* (1919), *The Trumpeter Swan* (1920), *The Gay Cockade* (1921), *Peacock Feathers* (1924), *Silver Slippers* (1928), *Enchanted Ground* (1933), *I've Been To London* (1937), and *Tomorrow's Promise* (1938).

Bailey, Theodorus. b. at Chateaugay, N.Y., April 12, 1805; d. Feb. 10, 1877. American naval officer, with the Union navy in the Civil War. Second in command in the attack on New Orleans in 1862, he was sent by Admiral David Glasgow Farragut to demand the surrender of the city. He was made a commodore in 1862, and in the same year was appointed commander of the eastern Gulf blockading squadron, and was responsible for seizing over 150 blockade runners in 18 months.

Bailey, Vernon. b. at Manchester, Mich., June 21, 1864; d. April 20, 1942. American biologist. He served (1887–1933) as chief field naturalist of the U.S. Biological Survey. Author of *Spermophiles of the Mississippi Valley* (1893), *Pocket Gophers of the Mississippi Valley* (1895), *Biological Survey of Texas* (1905), *Beaver Habits and Beaver Farming* (1923), and *Mammals of Oregon* (1936), and co-author of several books with his wife, Florence Augusta Bailey.

Bailey, William Whitman. b. at West Point, N.Y., Feb. 22, 1843; d. at Providence, R.I., Feb. 20, 1914. American botanist. He was associated (1867–68) with the U.S. Geologic Survey of the 40th parallel, and was an instructor (1877–81) and professor (1881–1906) of botany at Brown University. Author of *Botanical Collector's Handbook* (1881), *Among Rhode Island Wild Flowers* (1885), *Botanical Notebook* (1894), *New England Wild Flowers* (1897), *Botanizing* (1899), and *Poems* (1910).

Bailey, Willis Joshua. b. in Carroll County, Ill., Oct. 12, 1854; d. at Kansas City, Mo., May 19, 1932. American banker, politician, and governor (1903–05) of Kansas. He was graduated (1879) from the University of Illinois, elected (1888) to the Kansas state legislature, elected

(1903) governor of Kansas, and made (1922) governor of the Kansas City Federal Reserve Bank.

Bailey v. Drexel Furniture Co., 259 U.S. 20 (1922). Decision of the U.S. Supreme Court which held unconstitutional the federal Child Labor Act of 1919 placing a tax on articles produced by child labor. The majority opinion delivered by Chief Justice William Howard Taft declared the statute an abuse of the federal taxing power and indicated that the area of regulation at issue was reserved to the states.

Bailleul (bȧ.yėl). City in N France, in the department of Nord, situated near the Belgian border, ab. 17 mi. NW of Lille. It is an industrial center on the railroad line from Lille to Boulogne. The city was almost entirely destroyed during the battle of the Lys (April, 1918). The population dropped from 13,250 before World War I to 6,651 after the war. Bailleul escaped a similar fate in World War II, and the population has begun to rise toward the former level. 11,352 (1946).

Baillie (bā'li), Lady **Grizel.** b. at Redbraes Castle, Berwickshire, Scotland, Dec. 25, 1665; d. Dec. 6, 1746. Scottish poet; married (1692) to a son of Robert Baillie (d. 1684); daughter of Sir Patrick Hume, Scottish patriot, to whom she supplied food when he was in hiding from the English. She was in exile (1686–88) with her parents at Utrecht. One of her best-known songs is *And werena my heart licht I wad dee.*

Baillie or **Bailly, Harry.** Host of the Tabard Inn in Geoffrey Chaucer's *Canterbury Tales.* He is a shrewd, bold, manly, well-informed fellow with a blabbing shrew for a wife. He is sometimes called "Henry Bailif."

Baillie, Joanna. b. at Bothwell, Lanarkshire, Scotland, Sept. 11, 1762; d. at Hampstead, England, Feb. 23, 1851. Scottish dramatist and poet. She wrote *Plays on the Passions* (3 vols., 1798, 1802, and 1812), in which she delineates the principal passions of the mind, each passion being made the subject of a tragedy and a comedy; among them are *De Montfort* (1800) and *Family Legend* (1810). Author of the poems *Lines to Agnes Baillie on her Birthday, The Kitten,* and *To a Child.*

Baillie, Matthew. b. at Shotts, Lanarkshire, Scotland, 1761; d. 1823. Scottish physician, author, and lecturer; brother of Joanna Baillie. He attended Balliol College, Oxford, and in 1787 became a physician at St. George's Hospital, London. His *Morbid Anatomy of Some of the Most Important Parts of the Body,* published in 1795, has been considered the first treatise on pathology as a subject in itself. His *Lectures and Observations on Medicine* was published posthumously in 1825.

Baillie, Robert. b. at Glasgow, Scotland, 1599; d. in July, 1662. Scotch Presbyterian divine and controversialist, chiefly remembered as the author of *Letters and Journals, 1637–62.* This work is of historical value, especially in relation to the assembly of 1638 and the assembly of Westminster.

Baillie, Robert. [Called **Baillie of Jerviswood.**] Executed at Edinburgh, Scotland, Dec. 24, 1684. Scottish patriot, condemned for alleged complicity in the "Rye House Plot."

Baillon (bȧ.yôṅ), **Ernest Henri.** b. at Calais, France, Nov. 30, 1827; d. July 19, 1895. French botanist. He compiled a botanical dictionary, and wrote other books on botany.

Baillot (bȧ.yō), **Pierre Marie François de Sales.** b. at Passy, France, Oct. 1, 1771; d. at Paris, Sept. 15, 1842. French violinist. A pupil of Giovanni Battista Viotti, he became professor of the violin in the conservatory of music at Paris in 1795, and performed in Russia, Holland, and England. He wrote *L'Art du violin* (1835) and composed for the violin.

Baillou (bȧ.yö), **Guillaume de.** [Latinized, **Ballonius.**] b. 1538; d. 1616. French physician. He was appointed (1601) first physician to the dauphin by Henry IV, and is reputed to have been the first to make known the nature of croup. He wrote *Adversaria medicinalia* and other medical books.

Bailly (bȧ.yē), **Antoine Nicolas.** b. June 6, 1810; d. Jan. 1, 1892. French architect. He was appointed to a position in the administration of the city of Paris in 1834, and became architect to the French government in 1844. He built the Molière fountain at Paris, constructed the cathedral at Digne, and erected the Tribunal de Commerce at Paris.

Bailly (bȧ.yē), **Jean Sylvain.** b. at Paris, Sept. 15, 1736; d. there, Nov. 12, 1793. French astronomer and politician. He was a member of the Academy of Sciences, of the Academy of Inscriptions, and of the French Academy, president of the Third Estate and of the National Assembly in 1789, and mayor of Paris (1789–91). He was guillotined as a conspirator by the Jacobins. He wrote *Histoire de l'astronomie* (1775–87), *Essai sur l'origine des fables et des religions anciennes* (1799), and *Mémoires.*

Bailly (bā'li; French, bȧ.yē), **Joseph Alexis.** b. at Paris, Jan. 21, 1825; d. June 15, 1883. American sculptor. He studied at the French Institute and, as a refugee from the European insurrections of 1848, settled at Philadelphia, where he was an instructor (1876–77) at the Pennsylvania Academy of the Fine Arts. Among his works are a marble statue of George Washington (1869), originally at Independence Hall and now at City Hall, Philadelphia, and the bronze statue of John Witherspoon (1876) in Philadelphia's Fairmount Park.

Bailundo (bī.lön'dō). [Also, **Ombalundu.**] Name sometimes given to a country and former kingdom on the high plateau NE of Benguela, Angola, in SW Africa.

Baily (bā'li), **Edward Hodges.** b. at Bristol, England, March 10, 1788; d. at London, May 22, 1867. English sculptor. He is known for his statue *Eve at the Fountain* (1818), done for the British Literary Institution, the statue of Nelson in Trafalgar Square, London, and others. He studied (1807) with John Flaxman, and became a member of the Royal Academy in 1821.

Baily, Francis. b. at Newbury, Berkshire, England, April 28, 1774; d. at London, Aug. 30, 1844. English astronomer, notable for introducing improvements into the *Nautical Almanac* and for revision of star catalogues. He was able to retire to the study of astronomy after making a fortune as a broker. He was the first to describe (1636) in full detail the appearance of bright spots along the moon's edge during a total eclipse of the sun, this phenomenon now being known as "Baily's beads." He wrote a *Journal of a Tour in Unsettled Parts of North America in 1796 and 1797* (edited by De Morgan, 1856), *Tables for the Purchasing and Renewing of Leases* (1802), *Doctrine of Interest and Annuities* (1808), and *Account of the Rev. John Flamsteed* (1835).

Bain (bān), **Alexander.** b. in Caithness, Scotland, 1810; d. 1877. Scottish mechanician, inventor (1843) of the automatic chemical telegraph.

Bain, Alexander. b. at Aberdeen, Scotland, June 11, 1818; d. there, Sept. 18, 1903. Scottish philosopher, psychologist, professor, editor, and biographer. He was educated at the Glasgow Mechanics' Institute and at Marischal College (part of Aberdeen University), graduating with honors in 1840. He visited London in 1842 and 1848, meeting Thomas Carlyle, John Stuart Mill, George Henry Lewes, and George Grote (1794–1871), whose *Aristotle* and other works he later edited, and lecturing at the Bedford College for Women (founded 1849); he was appointed (1860) professor of logic and English at Aberdeen University (a post he held until 1881), after being rejected for many positions because of his liberal religious views; he served as lord rector of the University in the period 1880–87. During Bain's lifetime psychology changed from a philosophical subject to an experimental subject. His psychological texts, *Senses and Intellects* (1855; rev. eds., 1860, 1868, 1894), *Emotions and the Will* (1859; rev. eds., 1865, 1875, 1899), and the combined version of these two books, *Mental and Moral Science* (1868), were the outstanding British texts in the field for 50 years. In 1876 he founded *Mind,* the first psychological journal in any language. He explicitly stated a doctrine of psychophysical parallelism, thus holding a physiological orientation toward psychology, restated the doctrine of association in terms of contiguity and similarity, and answered the problem of will in terms of experience of effort. Author also of *The Study of Character, Including an Estimate of Phrenology* (1861), *Logic* (1870), *Mind and Body* (1872), *Education as a Science* (1879, long a popular volume in the well-known "International Scientific Series"), *James Mill, John Stuart Mill,* biographies (both 1882); his own *Autobiography* appeared in 1904. In addition to these works, Bain also wrote several excellent and once-popular, but now no longer used, texts (1863, 1866, 1872, 1874) on grammar and rhetoric.

Bain, George Luke Scobie. b. at Stirling, Scotland, May 5, 1836; d. Oct. 22, 1891. American merchant and flour manufacturer. Having come (c1851) to Montreal, Canada, he later learned the flour business at Portland, Me. After 1871, when he bought a half interest in the Atlantic Mills at St. Louis, he became a prominent miller in the Midwest and served as president (1875 *et seq.*) of the Millers' National Association.

Bainbridge (bān'brij). City in SW Georgia, county seat of Decatur County, on the Flint River: manufactures include baskets and crates. 7,562 (1950).

Bainbridge, Christopher. b. at Hilton, Westmorland, England, c1464; d. at Rome, July 14, 1514. English prelate. He was made bishop of Durham in 1507, archbishop of York in 1508, ambassador to the Pope in 1509, cardinal (St. Praxedis) in 1511 by Pope Julius II, and legate and commander of a papal army. He was poisoned by one of his own chaplains, probably at the instigation of a rival, the bishop of Worcester.

Bainbridge, John. b. at Ashby de la Zouch, England, 1582; d. at Oxford, England, 1643. English physician and astronomer.

Bainbridge, William. b. at Princeton, N.J., May 7, 1774; d. at Philadelphia, July 27, 1833. American naval officer, noted for his part in the war against the Barbary states. Commander of a merchantman before reaching the age of 20, he was made a "lieutenant commandant" when the U.S. navy was organized (1798), and served in West Indian waters during the undeclared war against the French. In 1800 he became a captain, then the highest naval rank, and was placed in command of a frigate carrying American tribute to the dey of Algiers. During the Tripolitan War he was in command of the frigate *Philadelphia.* Taken prisoner, he was released in 1805 and fully exonerated by a naval court of inquiry. During the War of 1812 Bainbridge, already a commodore, commanded the *Constitution* in leading a squadron in the South Atlantic. An encounter (Dec. 29, 1812) with a large British frigate resulted in his being wounded, and he spent the rest of the war at Boston, where he superintended the building of the *Independence,* which he later commanded abroad.

Bain-de-Bretagne (baṅ.dẹ.brẹ.tȧny'). Town in NW France, in the department of Ille-et-Vilaine, situated between Rennes and Nantes. It is known as a health resort. 4,040 (1946).

Baines (bānz). Surname of the two sisters, Constance and Sophia, whose lives provide the story of Arnold Bennett's *The Old Wives' Tale* (1908).

Baines, Edward. b. at Walton-le-Dale, Lancashire, England, Feb. 5, 1774; d. Aug. 3, 1848. English journalist and politician, proprietor (1801 *et seq.*) and editor of the Leeds *Mercury.* He was a member of Parliament (1834–41) for Leeds and the author of histories of Yorkshire and Lancashire.

Baines, Sir **Edward.** b. at Leeds, England, 1800; d. there, March 2, 1890. English journalist, statesman, and philanthropist; son of Edward Baines (1774–1848). He was a member of Parliament (1859–74) for Leeds and wrote *History of the Cotton Manufacture in Great Britain* (1835).

Baines, Frederick Ebenezer. b. Nov. 10, 1832; d. at Hampstead, London, July 4, 1911. English promoter responsible for post-office control of the British telegraph system. His most important plan (1856) advocating government control of existing telegraphic systems was carried through in 1870. He organized (1883) for England the parcel post system, which was later extended to all British dominions and colonies, and most European countries.

Baines, Matthew Talbot. b. Feb. 17, 1799; d. Jan. 22, 1860. English politician; eldest son of Edward Baines (1774–1848). He was appointed chancellor of the duchy of Lancaster, with a seat in the cabinet, in 1855.

Baines, Thomas. b. at King's Lynn, Norfolk, England, 1822; d. at Durban, Natal (in what is now the Union of South Africa), May 8, 1875. English artist and explorer of Africa. He arrived at Cape Colony in 1842; accompanied (1848–51) the British army throughout the military operation against the Kaffirs; explored (1855–56) NW Australia under Augustus Gregory; was artist and storekeeper to the Livingstone Zambezi expedition in 1858; went from the SW coast of Africa to the Victoria Falls in 1861; lectured in England, 1864–68. He wrote *Explorations in Southwestern Africa* (1864) and *The Gold Regions of Southeastern Africa* (1877).

Baini (bä.ē'nē), **Giuseppe.** b. at Rome, Oct. 21, 1775; d. May 21, 1844. Italian priest, music critic, and composer. He became (1818) maestro di cappella of the Vatican choir. He composed a ten-part *Miserere* (1821), and wrote a two-volume biography (1828) of Giovanni Palestrina.

Bains-les-Bains (baṅ.lā.baṅ). [Also, **Bains-en-Vosges** (-zäṅ.vōzh).] Town in NE France, in the department of Vosges, situated in the valley of the Bagnerot River ab. 16 mi. SW of Épinal. Its hot springs, considered useful in the treatment of arteriosclerosis, phlebitis, and rheumatism, were known to the Romans. 1,732 (1946).

Bainville (baṅ.vēl), **Jacques.** b. at Vincennes, France, 1879; d. at Paris, in February, 1936. French journalist, historian, and editor, associated (1908 *et seq.*) with Charles Maurras in the royalist Action Française movement. His most successful works were *Histoire de deux peuples* (1915), *Histoire de trois générations* (1916), *Histoire de France* (1924), and *Napoléon* (1931). He founded (1920), with Henri Massis, the rightist *Revue universelle,* and was elected to the Academy in 1935.

Baiocum (bā.ō'kum) or **Baiocasses** (bā.ọ.kas'ēz). Medieval names of **Bayeux.**

Baiquirí (bī.kē.rē'). See **Daiquirí.**

Bairam (bī.räm'). [Also, **Beiram.**] The name of two Mohammedan feasts. The great Bairam forms the concluding ceremony of the pilgrimage to Mecca, and is celebrated on the tenth day of the 12th month. Each householder who is able to do so sacrifices a sheep, the flesh of which is divided into three portions, one for the family, one for relatives, and one for the poor. The lesser Bairam is celebrated at the termination of the fast of the month of Ramadan (the ninth month). It is a season of great rejoicing at which presents and visits are exchanged.

Baird (bãrd), **Absalom.** b. at Washington, Pa., Aug. 20, 1824; d. near Relay, Md., June 14, 1905. American general, with the Union army in the Civil War. He was graduated (1849) from West Point, where he served (c1852–58) as an instructor. He was in command of the 1st Division at the battles of Chickamauga and Chattanooga in 1863 and in the Atlanta campaign in 1864, and was brevetted major general of volunteers (Sept. 1, 1864) for his services in these operations.

Baird, Sir **David.** b. at Newbyth, Scotland, 1757; d. Aug. 29, 1829. British general. He served (1780–89) in India, where he was wounded and imprisoned for nearly four years by Haidar Ali, ruler of Mysore, in a war (the Second Mysore War) between Great Britain, on the one hand, and an alliance of France with Mysore and its subordinate states on the other. Returned to India as a lieutenant colonel in 1791, he took Pondicherry in 1793, was made major general in 1798, and led the storming column at the capture of Seringapatam on May 4, 1799. He commanded an expedition to Egypt in 1801, led (as lieutenant general) an army to recapture the Cape of Good Hope in 1806, served in the siege of Copenhagen in 1807, was sent to Spain to reinforce Moore in 1808, and was wounded at La Coruña in 1809, losing his left arm as a result.

Baird, Henry Carey. b. at Bridesburg, Pa., Sept. 10, 1825; d. at Wayne, Pa., Dec. 30, 1912. American publisher and writer on economics. He founded the Philadelphia publishing firm of Henry Carey Baird and Company, which was (1849) the first U.S. publishing concern to specialize in industrial and technical books. Among his works are *Protection of Home Labor* (1860) and *Money and Bank Credit in the United States, France and Great Britain* (1891).

Baird, Henry Martyn. b. at Philadelphia, Jan. 17, 1832; d. at Yonkers, N.Y., Nov. 11, 1806. American Presbyterian clergyman and historian; son of Robert Baird. His most notable works are *The Life of the Rev. Robert Baird* (1866), *The History of the Rise of the Huguenots of France* (2 vols., 1879), *The Huguenots and Henry of Navarre* (2 vols., 1886), *The Huguenots and the Revocation of the*

Edict of Nantes (2 vols., 1895), and *Theodore Beza, the Counsellor of the French Reformation* (1899).

Baird, James. b. at Kirkwood, Scotland, Dec. 5, 1802; d. at Cambusdoon, near Ayr, Scotland, June 20, 1876. Scottish ironmaster, one of the first mass-producers of iron. Baird's father was originally a farmer but later became a coal-owner, interested in the production of iron, and established the first blast furnace in 1830. James Baird inherited and improved on his father's business, increasing production from 60 to 250 tons per furnace per week. By 1842 he owned 16 furnaces, which number was again increased (1852) to 40 or 50 with a total production of 300,000 tons per year, employing 10,000 workers. The land his family owned was also increased to a total which was estimated to be worth around two million pounds.

Baird, John L. [Called the **"Father of Television."**] b. at Helensburgh, Scotland, 1888; d. at Bexhill, Sussex, England, June 14, 1946. Scottish inventor, known for his pioneering work in the development of television. Educated at the Royal Technical College and Glasgow University, he invented an early television mechanism called "Televisor," and was also the inventor of the "Noctovisor," an apparatus for seeing in the dark by means of invisible rays. He gave the first public demonstration (Jan. 27, 1926) of true television in Britain at the Royal Institution at London.

Baird, Robert. b. near Pittsburgh, Pa., Oct. 6, 1798; d. March 15, 1863. American Presbyterian clergyman and writer, active in the cause of popular education in New Jersey.

Baird, Spencer Fullerton. b. at Reading, Pa., Feb. 3, 1823; d. at Wood's Hole, Mass., Aug. 19, 1888. American zoölogist, naturalist, and ornithologist, principal founder of the marine laboratory at Wood's Hole. After graduation (A.B., 1840; M.A., 1843) from Dickinson College, he was appointed (1846) professor of natural history at that institution, where he introduced the system of field study of zoölogy and botany that had been employed by J. L. R. Agassiz. He served as assistant secretary (1850–78) of the Smithsonian Institution, of which he became full secretary in 1878. His appointment (1871) as the first U.S. Commissioner of Fish and Fisheries led to his monumental ichthyological investigations at Wood's Hole, and in Pacific waters. Author of 1,068 titles, among them *Catalogue of North American Birds* (1858), *Review of American Birds* (1864–66), *A History of North American Birds* (1874, in collaboration with T. M. Brewer and R. Ridgway), *North American Reptiles* (1853, in collaboration with Charles Girard), and *Catalogue of North American Mammals* (1857).

Baireuth (bī'roit). See **Bayreuth.**

Bairnsfather (bãrnz'fä"ᴛʜėr), **Bruce.** b. in India, in July, 1888—. English cartoonist and journalist. A member (1911–14) of the Warwickshire militia, he served (1914–16) in France with the rank (1915) of captain, and was attached (1916 *et seq.*) to the War Office for work in foreign countries. His sketches of life in the trenches during World War I won popularity, and were later collected in the six-volume *Fragments from France.* He served as an official war cartoonist (1942–44) with the U.S. army in the European theater. Author also of *The Better 'Ole, Bullets and Billets, From Mud to Mufti, Old Bill, M.P.1., Jeeps and Jests* (1943), and *No Kiddin'* (1944).

Bairu (bā.rö'), **Ato Tedla.** b. c1914—. Eritrean statesman, first chief executive of autonomous Eritrea (1952 *et seq.*) after its union with Ethiopia.

Bairut (bā.röt'). See **Beirut.**

Baisan (bā.sän'). See **Beisan.**

Baïse (be.ēz). [Also, **Bayse.**] River in S France which joins the Garonne River W of Agen. Length, ab. 130 mi.

Baiser au Lépreux (be.zā ō lā.prė), **Le.** Novel (1922; Eng. trans., with *Génitrix* under one title, *The Family,* 1930) by François Mauriac, on the theme of self-sacrifice. It is frequently cited as an example of outstanding recent French Roman Catholic fiction.

Bait al-Faqih (bīt äl.fä'kē). See **Beit-el-Fakih.**

Baitul (bā'töl). See **Betul.**

Baius (bā'yus) or **Bajus** (-jus), **Michael.** [Flemish, **Michel de Bay.**] b. at Mehun, Hainaut, Belgium, 1513; d. 1589. Flemish Roman Catholic theologian, the central figure in a complex theological controversy centering about the problem of Grace. Baius taught (1544–70) at the University of Louvain and later became chancellor of that institution. On several occasions he participated in the deliberations of the Council of Trent. Baianism (as his system of thought was called) had as its core a belief in a degree of perfectibility inherent in human nature, anterior to (or apart from) the effects of the Fall and the Redemption. It was repeatedly condemned by Rome, especially in a bull of Pope Pius V in 1567. After each condemnation Baius abjured his errors, and he died in the Church. Baianism in some respects foreshadowed Jansenism.

Baixo Alentejo (bī'shö ä.lān.tā'zhö). Province of Portugal, bounded by Alto Alentejo on the N, Spain on the E, Algarve on the S, and the Atlantic Ocean on the W: coextensive with the district of Beja. It is chiefly steppe country, and thinly populated. Sheep raising and some agriculture are carried on. Capital, Beja; area, ab. 3,970 sq. mi.; pop. 355,771 (1940).

Baj (bä'ē), **Tommaso.** See **Bai, Tommaso.**

Baja (bô'yô). City in S Hungary, in the county of Bács, near the Danube River ab. 93 mi. S of Budapest. It has commerce in grain, cattle, pigs, and wine; flour mills and distilleries. 28,214 (1948).

Baja California (bä'ʜä kä.lē.fôr'nyä). Spanish name of **Lower California.**

Bajada del Paraná (bä.ʜä'dä del pä.rä.nä') or **Bajada de Santa Fé** (dā sän'tä fā'). See **Paraná,** Argentina.

Baja Verapaz (ʙä.rä.päs'). Department in C Guatemala. Capital, Salamá; area, 1,206 sq. mi.; pop. 65,434 (1950).

Bajazet (bȧ.zhȧ.ze). Tragedy by Jean Baptiste Racine, produced on Jan. 4, 1672.

Bajazet I (baj.ą.zet'). [Also: **Bajasid** (baj.ą.sēd'), **Bayazid;** called **Ilderim** or **Yilderim,** meaning "Lightning."] b. 1347; d. 1403. Turkish sultan (1389–1403); son of Murad I. He was given the name "Ilderim" because of his rapid movements. He conquered Bulgaria and a great part of Asia Minor, Macedonia, Serbia, and Thessaly, defeated the allied Hungarians, Poles, and French at Nicopolis in 1396, but was defeated (1402) by Tamerlane at Angora, and held prisoner by him until his death. He is said to have been carried about in an iron cage, but this is probably an invention of later writers.

Bajazet II. b. 1447; d. 1512. Turkish sultan (1481–1512); son of Mohammed II. He was engaged in almost uninterrupted warfare with Hungary, Poland, Venice, Egypt, and Persia; deposed by his son Selim, he died soon after, probably by poison.

Bajazet, Mosque of. Mosque at Constantinople, finished in 1505, one of the finest examples of Moslem architecture. The forecourt has arcades in the pointed style, made of marble, with capitals of jasper and *verde antico.* There are four doorways of Persian type, and a graceful octagonal fountain in the middle of the court.

Bajer (bī'ėr), **Fredrik.** b. at Vester Egede, Denmark, April 21, 1837; d. at Copenhagen, Jan. 22, 1922. Danish pacifist and writer, best known as president of the International Peace Bureau at Bern, Switzerland, which he helped to found (1891). He had earlier established (1882) the Danish Peace Union. He received (1908) the Nobel peace prize jointly with K. P. Arnoldson. His writings include *Nordisk Nevtralitetsforbund* (1885), *Det skandinavske Nevtralitetssystem* (1906), and *Nordens, særlig Danmarks Nevtralitet under Krimkrigen* (1914).

Bajok (bą.jok'). See **Chokwe.**

Bajpai (bäj'pī), Sir **Girja Shankar.** b. 1891—. Indian civil servant and diplomat, secretary-general (1947 *et seq.*) of the ministry of external affairs, and a representative of India at imperial conferences and in the U.S. before India gained her independence. He was secretary for India at the imperial conference (1921) and at the Washington conference (1922), and agent-general for India (1941–47) in the U.S.

Bajraktari (bī.räk.tä'rē), **Muharrem.** b. at Luma, Albania (then part of Turkey), 1896—. Albanian political leader and supporter (until 1934) of Zog I, active as a guerrilla leader during World War II. He served as commandant general of the gendarmerie from 1929 to 1934, when he broke relations with Zog; he went into exile (1945) after the election victory of the Communist regime.

Bajura (ba.jö'ra). Standard of Mohammed.

Bajza (boi'zô), **József.** b. at Szücsi, Hungary, Jan. 31, 1804; d. March 3, 1858. Hungarian poet, critic, and historian. He was appointed director of the National Theater at Pest in 1837. He became editor of the journal *Ellenőr* in 1847, and of Kossuth's *Hirlap* in 1848.

Bakacs (bô'kôch), **Tamás.** [Also, **Bakocz.**] b. in Hungary, c1442; d. 1521. Hungarian prelate and statesman. He was made chancellor and archbishop of Gran by Ladislas II and later (1500) became cardinal primate of Hungary and papal legate. He received permission from the Pope (1513) to undertake a crusade against the Turks, but the army which he raised was, under the leadership of George Dosa, diverted to an attack on the nobility. It was subdued in 1514 by John Zápolya.

Bakarganj (bak.ar.gunj'). [Also: **Backergunge, Bakerganj.**] District in the Dacca division, East Bengal, Pakistan, in the Ganges delta, bordering on the Bay of Bengal. Rice is the all-important crop in the area. Capital, Barisal; area, ab. 4,000 sq. mi.; pop. 3,549,010 (1941).

Bakau (bä'kou). See **Bacău.**

Bakel (bä.kel'). Fortified town and trading station in Senegal territory, French West Africa, on the Senegal River near the junction of Senegal, Mauritania, and French Sudan territories. It is connected by road with St.-Louis and Dakar on the coast. Pop. ab. 2,000.

Bakeless (bāk'les), **John Edwin.** b. at Carlisle, Pa., Dec. 30, 1894—. American writer and editor. Holding degrees from Williams College (1918) and Harvard (1936), he became (1940) an associate professor of journalism at New York University. He served on the editorial staff (1921–25, 1928–29) of *Living Age*, was managing editor (1926–28) of *The Forum*, and was literary editor (1937–38) of *Literary Digest*. Author of *The Economic Causes of Modern War* (1921), *The Origin of the Next War* (1926), *Magazine Making* (1931), *Christopher Marlowe* (1937), *Daniel Boone, Master of the Wilderness* (1939), and other works.

Baker (bā'kėr). [Former name, **Baker City.**] City in E Oregon, county seat of Baker County, on the Powder River: trading center for a livestock-raising, agricultural, and mining area: grain elevators, flour mills, meat-packing plants, and dairies. It was platted in 1865 and made the county seat in 1868; incorporated as Baker City in 1874 and renamed c1912. Its early industries were lumber and iron. 9,471 (1950).

Baker, Sir **Benjamin.** b. 1840; d. at Pangbourne, Berkshire, England, May 19, 1907. English engineer. His most important works are the Forth Bridge in Scotland and the dam across the Nile at Aswan, both done with Sir John Fowler.

Baker, Benjamin A. b. at New York, April 4, 1818; d. Sept. 6, 1890. American actor, playwright, and manager. His most popular effort, produced (1848) at New York, was *A Glance at New York in 1848*, followed by *New York As It Is*, which opened on April 17, 1848. Baker also wrote *Three Years After*, produced in 1849, and *Mose in China*, produced in 1850.

Baker, Benjamin Franklin. b. at Wenham, Mass., July 16, 1811; d. at Boston, March 11, 1889. American musician, teacher, and composer. A teacher of music (1841–50) in the public schools of Boston, he introduced the course into the schools of Lowell and Lawrence, Mass. He was in charge (1839–47) of the music at the church led by Dr. William Ellery Channing, and conducted (1841–48) a popular series of musical conventions. He was the founder (1857–68) of the Boston Music School, acting as its principal and instructor in voice; he edited the Boston *Musical Journal* and compiled the *Boston Musical Education Society's Collections* (1842) and the *Haydn Collection of Church Music* (1850), the latter in collaboration with L. H. Southard. His compositions include *Death of Osceola* (1846), a vocal quartet, *Stars of the Summer Night* (1865), vocal quartet, and the cantatas *The Storm King* (1856), *The Burning Ship* (1865), and *Camillus the Roman Conqueror* (1865).

Baker, Burtis. [Full name, **Samuel Burtis Baker.**] b. at Boston, Sept. 29, 1882—. American portrait, figure, landscape, and still-life painter. He taught at the Corcoran School of Art, Washington, D.C., and was professor of fine arts at George Washington University. He studied with private instructors in Massachusetts and Connecticut, as well as in Europe, and has exhibited in the U.S., New Zealand, and Italy. He has been awarded many prizes, including the W. A. Clark prize (1921) of 15 hundred dollars from the Corcoran Gallery of Art. His works include many portraits which now hang in schools at Boston, Washington, D.C., and elsewhere, and the painting *Black Mantilla.*

Baker, Daniel. b. at Midway, Ga., Aug. 17, 1791; d. at Austin, Tex., Dec. 10, 1857. American Presbyterian clergyman and educator. He was graduated (1815) from Princeton and, after serving as a minister at Winchester, Va., Harrisonburg, Va., Washington, D.C., Savannah, Ga., and Tuscaloosa, Ala., he set out (1840) as an evangelistic missionary to the newly formed Republic of Texas. There he helped found the first presbytery of his church in Texas. He was instrumental in securing the charter (1849) of Austin College, of which he became (1852) president and general agent.

Baker, Dorothy. [Maiden name, **Dodds.**] b. at Missoula, Mont., April 21, 1907—. American novelist. She is the author of the novels *Young Man With a Horn* (1938), *Trio* (1943), and *Our Gifted Son* (1948).

Baker, Edward Dickinson. b. at London, Feb. 24, 1811; d. in action at Ball's Bluff, Va., Oct. 22, 1861. American legislator, lawyer, and soldier, killed while serving as a colonel in the Union army. He was brought (1815) by his family to Philadelphia, going with them (c1826) to Belleville, Ill. Admitted to the bar (c1830), he established (1835) his law practice at Springfield, Ill., after serving in the Black Hawk War. After a year (1845–46) in Congress as a Whig representative, he resigned his seat to enter the Mexican War. He was again elected (1848) to Congress, and, after moving (1860) to Oregon, was chosen U.S. senator. He was an ardent opponent of secession and the only Republican from the Pacific coast in Congress. He led a brigade in the first year of the Civil War.

Baker, Frank Collins. b. at Warren, R.I., 1867; d. 1942. American zoölogist. He attended Brown University and the Philadelphia Academy of Natural Sciences. He was curator (1894–1915) of the Chicago Academy of Sciences and curator (1918 *et seq.*) of the natural history museum at the University of Illinois.

Baker, George Augustus. b. at New York, in March, 1821; d. April 2, 1880. American portrait and miniature painter. He studied at the National Academy of Design and abroad (1844–46); after his return to New York, he became widely known as a portrait painter in oils. His best canvases are usually considered to be those of women and children. Among his paintings are *Faith* and *Love at First Sight;* his portrait of the artist John F. Kensett is in the Metropolitan Museum of Art, New York.

Baker, George Fisher. b. at Troy, N.Y., March 27, 1840; d. at New York, May 2, 1931. American banker. He was a founder, president (1877–1909), and chairman of the board (1909–31) of the First National Bank, New York. Through his gifts, he aided the Graduate School of Business Administration at Harvard University and gave Baker Field to Columbia University.

Baker, George Fisher. b. at New York, March 19, 1878; d. at Honolulu, May 30, 1937. American banker; son of George Fisher Baker (1840–1931). He succeeded (1931) his father as chairman of the First National Bank, New York, and was in charge (1917) of the American Red Cross Commission to Italy.

Baker, George Pierce. b. at Providence, R.I., April 4, 1866; d. at New York, Jan. 6, 1935. American professor of drama, notable as head of the playwriting course known as the "47 Workshop" at Harvard. After graduation (1887) from Harvard, he taught there as instructor (1888–95), assistant professor (1895–1905), and professor (1905–24); later he was professor (1925–33) of the history and technique of drama at Yale University and head of the university theater. Editor of *Some Unpublished Correspondence of David Garrick* (1907), *The Correspondence of Charles Dickens and Maria Beadnell* (1913), *Plays of the 47 Workshop* (series I–IV), *Yale One-Act Plays*, four volumes of *Yale Long Plays*, and various Elizabethan texts; author of *The Development of Shakespeare as a Dramatist* (1907), *Technique of the Drama* (1915), and

Dramatic Technique (1919). Among his students were Philip Barry, Sidney Howard, Eugene O'Neill, and Thomas Wolfe.

Baker, Harriette Newall Woods. [Pseudonym, Mrs. **Madeline Leslie.**] b. 1815; d. 1893. American writer of children's stories.

Baker, Henry. b. at London, May 8, 1698; d. there, Nov. 25, 1774. English naturalist; son-in-law of Daniel Defoe. He established a system of teaching deaf-mutes. Author of *The Microscope Made Easy* (1743), *Employment for the Microscope* (1753), and a poem on the universe.

Baker, James. b. at Belleville, Ill., Dec. 19, 1818; d. in the valley of the Little Snake River, Wyo., May 15, 1898. American trapper, guide, and pioneer settler, a companion of the famous scout "Jim" Bridger.

Baker, James Hutchins. b. near Harmony, Me., Oct. 13, 1848; d. at Denver, Colo., Sept. 10, 1925. American educator, noted for his work in secondary education. He was appointed (1892) president of the University of Colorado, at Boulder, serving until his retirement in 1914. He proposed the Committee of Ten (1893) of the National Education Association which issued what many have termed the first well-rounded program of secondary education. He was influential in the development of the junior college.

Baker, La Fayette Curry. b. at Stafford, N.Y., Oct. 13, 1826; d. at Philadelphia, July 3, 1868. American soldier, one-time head of the U.S. Secret Service. He arrived at Washington following the outbreak of the Civil War and was sent to Richmond on a mission for General Winfield Scott, escaping from Confederate hands and returning to Washington with the necessary information. This and subsequent feats led to his appointment (1862) as special provost marshal of the War Department, and his promotion (1865) to the rank of brigadier general. He planned and led the operation which resulted in the capture of John Wilkes Booth and D. C. Herold; dismissed by President Johnson for operating a spy system in the White House, he appeared as chief witness against Johnson during the impeachment proceedings. Like his testimony against Johnson, his *History of the United States Secret Service* (1867) is considered by most historians to be highly unreliable.

Baker, Lorenzo Dow. b. at Wellfleet, Mass., March 15, 1840; d. June 21, 1908. American sea captain and merchant, noted as the first bulk importer of bananas into the U.S. Captain of a ship at 21 and in 1870 master of his own schooner, he picked up a cargo of bananas at Jamaica, marketing the then little-known fruit upon his return to Boston; subsequently (1879) he was Jamaica agent of the Atlas Line, meanwhile encouraging banana cultivation in Jamaica. He was an organizer and president (1885 *et seq.*) of the Boston Fruit Company, and following the establishment (1897) of the United Fruit Company, was managing director of its Jamaica division.

Baker, Marcus. b. at Kalamazoo, Mich., Sept. 23, 1849; d. Dec. 12, 1903. American geographer and topographer. He was graduated (1870) from the University of Michigan. His first contribution in the field of geography was a survey (conducted with Dr. W. H. Dall in 1873) of the then scarcely explored Alaskan waters. A member (1886 *et seq.*) of the U.S. Geological Survey, during the Venezuelan boundary dispute he drew up a detailed report for the U.S. Government. He was president of the Philosophical Society of Washington, D.C., and a founder, and for many years manager, of the National Geographic Society.

Baker, Mount. Volcanic peak in the Cascade Mountains, in N Washington, in Whatcom County, near the Canadian frontier. 10,750 ft.

Baker, Newton Diehl. b. at Martinsburg, W.Va., Dec. 3, 1871; d. Dec. 25, 1937. American politician and jurist, practicing law (1897 *et seq.*) at Martinsburg, W.Va., and Cleveland, Ohio. After graduation (1892) from Johns Hopkins University, he received (1894) the degree of LL.B. from Washington and Lee University. He was private secretary, during the first two years (1896–97) of William McKinley's first administration, to the postmaster general, city solicitor (1902–12) and mayor (1912–16) of Cleveland, and secretary of war (1916–21) under Woodrow Wilson. He was appointed (1928) a member of the Permanent Court of Arbitration at The Hague, and was appointed (1929) by Herbert Hoover a member of the U.S. Law Enforcement Commission. In 1933 he was honored "for services to humanity" by the National Institute of Social Sciences.

Baker, Oliver Edwin. b. at Tiffin, Ohio, Sept. 10, 1883; d. 1949. American economic and sociological geographer. A graduate of Columbia (1905) and the University of Wisconsin (1921), he served as an economist (1912–42) with the U.S. Department of Agriculture; he was a professor of economic geography (1942 *et seq.*) at the University of Maryland. Coauthor of *The Climate of Wisconsin and Its Relation to Agriculture* (1912), *Geography of the World's Agriculture* (1917), *Agriculture in Modern Life* (1939), and other works.

Baker, Ray Stannard. [Pseudonym, **David Grayson.**] b. at Lansing, Mich., April 17, 1870; d. July 12, 1946. American journalist and author. A prominent contributor to *McClure's Magazine* during the era of muckraking journalism and a close friend of Woodrow Wilson, he later served as U.S. press director at the Versailles Peace Conference. The authorized biographer of Wilson, he was the author also of *Boys' Book of Inventions* (1899), *Second Boys' Book of Inventions* (1903), *Our New Prosperity* (1900), *Seen in Germany* (1901), *Following the Color Line* (1908), *New Ideals in Healing* (1909), and *Spiritual Unrest* (1910). His major works on Wilson were *Woodrow Wilson and World Settlement* (3 vols., 1922) and *Woodrow Wilson: Life and Letters* (8 vols., 1927–39; vols. 7 and 8 awarded a Pulitzer prize in 1940). Author also of *Native American* (1941), and *American Chronicle* (1945). Under the pseudonym David Grayson he wrote several collections of essays, including *Adventures in Contentment* (1907) and *Adventures in Solitude* (1931). With William E. Dodd, he edited a collection of Wilson's public papers (6 vols., 1925–26).

Baker, Remember. b. at Woodbury, Conn., in June, 1737; d. in a skirmish near St. Johns, Quebec, Canada, in August, 1775. American colonial soldier, one of Ethan Allen's "Green Mountain Boys." He settled (1764) at Arlington, Vt. (then in the territory known as the New Hampshire Grants), and during a jurisdictional contest between the New York and the New Hampshire governments, joined the anti-New York faction led by his cousin Ethan Allen. Leader of a company under Allen, he had a reward of 100 pounds placed on his head by Governor William Tryon of New York. He was killed while with General Philip John Schuyler on a scouting party into Canada.

Baker, Sir **Richard.** b. at Sissinghurst, Kent, England, 1568; d. at London, in the Fleet Prison, Feb. 18, 1645. English writer, author of *Chronicle of the Kings of England* (1643), and of various devotional and other works.

Baker, Sir **Samuel White.** b. at London, June 8, 1821; d. at Newton Abbot, England, Dec. 30, 1893. English traveler; brother of Valentine Baker. He founded (1848) a settlement and sanatorium at Ceylon, was in the Turkish railway service, and left Cairo for the sources of the Nile in 1861. He explored (1861–62) the Blue Nile region and, starting from Khartoum in 1862, discovered (March 14, 1864) Lake Albert. Subsequently he commanded (1869–73) an Egyptian expedition in C Africa for the suppression of the slave trade and annexation of territory to Egypt, and traveled in Cyprus, Syria, India, and elsewhere. Author of *The Rifle and the Hound in Ceylon* (1854), *Eight Years' Wanderings in Ceylon* (1855), *The Albert Nyanza* (1866), *The Nile Tributaries of Abyssinia* (1867), *Ismaïlia* (1874), *Cyprus as I Saw It in 1879*, and *Wild Beasts and Their Ways* (1890).

Baker, Sara Josephine. b. at Poughkeepsie, N.Y., Nov. 15, 1873; d. at New York, Feb. 22, 1945. American pediatrician who directed (1908–23) New York City's first bureau of child hygiene and aided in reducing the infant mortality rate there to a level below that of any other large U.S. city. She received an M.D. degree (1898) from the Women's Medical College of New York Infirmary, was appointed (1902) New York Department of Health medical inspector, and joined (1923) the New York State Department of Health as a consultant. Author of *Healthy Mothers* (1923), *Healthy Babies* (1923), *Child Hygiene* (1925), and other books, including her autobiography, *Fighting for Life* (1939).

Baker, Theodore. b. at New York, June 3, 1851; d. Oct. 13, 1934. American music historian and critic. He was the author of one of the first studies of American Indian music, and the compiler of *Baker's Biographical Dictionary* (1900).

Baker, Thomas. b. at Lanchester, Durham, England, Sept. 14, 1656; d. at Cambridge, England, July 2, 1740. English antiquary. He left a valuable collection of materials in 42 manuscript volumes relating to the history of Cambridge; 23 volumes are in the Harleian collection (British Museum) and the rest in the library of Cambridge University.

Baker, Thomas. fl. 1700–09. British playwright. He was the author of five now nearly forgotten comedies: *Humor of the Age* (1701), *Tunbridge Walks, or the Yeoman of Kent* (1703), *An Act at Oxford* (1704), *Hampstead Heath* (1705), an alteration of the previous play, which was banned by Oxford University authorities, and *The Fine Lady's Airs* (1709), all produced at Drury Lane and Covent Garden theaters in London. He is believed to be the author of the *Female Tatler* (1709), one of the many periodicals that attempted to duplicate the success of the *Spectator* and the *Tatler*. Baker, who did not like Sir Richard Steele, ridiculed him in issue No. 72; Steele retaliated with the character of Nick Doubt (*Tatler*, No. 91, Tuesday, Nov. 8, 1709).

Baker, Thomas Stockham. b. at Aberdeen, Md., March 23, 1871; d. April 7, 1939. American educator, noted for his active interest in world peace.

Baker, Valentine. [Called **Baker Pasha.**] b. 1827; d. at Tell el-Kebir, Egypt, Nov. 17, 1887. English officer; brother of Sir Samuel White Baker. He was a colonel in the British army, was in the Turkish service during the war of 1877–78, served (1883 *et seq.*) as Egyptian commander in the Sudan, and was defeated by Osman Digna at Tokar, on Feb. 4, 1884.

Bakerganj (bak.ėr.gunj'). See **Bakarganj.**

Baker Island (bā'kėr). Coral atoll in the Pacific Ocean near the equator, N of the Phoenix Group and ab. 40 mi. from Howland Island. Before 1935 it was shown as British, but in that year the U.S. laid uncontested claim to the island. Formerly important for its guano deposits, at present it is important because of its position astride the trans-Pacific air routes. Area, less than 1 sq. mi.; pop. 3 (1940).

Baker Lake. Lake in N Canada, in the E part of the Northwest Territories. It is a continuation and expansion of the upper or western portion of Chesterfield Inlet, an arm of N Hudson Bay. Length, ab. 100 mi.; width, ab. 20 mi. (at its widest point); area, 1,029 sq. mi.

Baker's Creek, Battle of. See under **Champion's Hill.**

Bakersfield (bā'kėrz.fēld). City in S California, county seat of Kern County, on the Kern River, NW of Los Angeles: an important oil producing and refining center; manufactures of oil-well machinery. The immediate area produces fruit, grain, and livestock. Pop. of city, 34,784 (1950); of urbanized area, 101,696 (1950).

Bakery and Confectionery Workers' International Union of America. Craft trade union affiliated with the American Federation of Labor, with headquarters at Chicago. Membership, 90,000 (1944).

Bakeu (bä.ke'ö). See **Bacău.**

Bakewell (bāk'wel). Urban district and market town in C England, in Derbyshire, situated on the river Wye, ab. 22 mi. NW of Derby. It has mineral springs and baths, and was one of the early centers of the cotton industry. Chatsworth House, a 17th-century building noted for its art collections and gardens, which belonged to the dukes of Devonshire, and Haddon Hall, seat of the dukes of Rutland, are in the vicinity. 3,350 (1951).

Bakewell, Robert. b. at Dishley, Leicestershire, England, 1725; d. Oct. 1, 1795. English agriculturist, remembered chiefly for his improvements in the breeding of sheep and oxen. His breed of Leicester sheep spread itself within half a century over the United Kingdom, Europe, and America. His method was to concentrate on the increase of roasting pieces, and not boiling pieces, with the result that the quantity of mutton was doubled. His breed of cattle, the Dishley, was aimed at the performance of farm work and army use. He is also remembered for the foundation of the Dishley Society which sought to insure the purity of stocks. His careful breeding led also to advocacy of humane treatment of animals.

Bakhchisarai (bäċh"chę.sä.rī'). [Also, **Bakhtchisarai.**] City in the U.S.S.R., in the Crimean Autonomous Soviet Socialist Republic of the Russian Soviet Federated Socialist Republic, ab. 16 mi. SW of Simferopol. It was the capital of the Tatar khans, and contains their residence. There are many vineyards, orchards, and nut plantations in the area. Pop. ab. 10,000.

Bakhmut (bäċh.möt'). Former name of **Artemovsk.**

Bakhtiari (bäċh.tē.ä'rē). [Also, **Bakhtiyari.**] A nomadic, semi-independent, tribally-organized people in Luristan and Khuzistan, in W Iran. They speak a Persian dialect and are divided into two rival confederations, the Haftlang and Chaharlang (or Cheharlang). Each year they make two long and spectacular migrations between their winter quarters in the coastal lowlands and their summer pastures in the mountains.

Bakhtiari Mountains. [Also, **Bakhtiyari Mountains.**] Range of mountains in W Iran, W of Isfahan. It runs NW to SE and reaches a height of 14,200 ft.

Bakhtishwa (bäċh.tish'wä), **Giabril ben Giurgis ben.** [Also: **Bactishua, Bakhtichuna** (bäċh.tē.shö'nä), **Bocht Jesu.**] d. c828. Greek Nestorian; a member of a family of noted physicians. He became (805) physician to Harun al-Rashid, and was the first to present to the Arabs translations of the Greek works on medicine.

Bakhuyzen (bäk'hoi.zęn), **Ludolf.** See **Backhuysen, Ludolf.**

Bakocz (bô'kōch), **Tamás.** See **Bakacs, Tamás.**

Bakony Forest (bô'kōny'). [Hungarian, **Bakony hegység**; German, **Bakonyerwald** (bä'ko.nyėr.vält").] Hilly volcanic region in Hungary, S and W of the Danube River, SW of Budapest, and N of Lake Balaton. At one time it had extensive forests, and was noted as a bandit stronghold. Its highest point is ab. 2,300 ft.

Bakri (bä.krē'), **al-.** [Also, **al-Bekri.**] b. probably at Huelva, Spain, before 1040; d. 1094. Arab geographer. He was active for most of his professional life at Córdoba, Spain (although probably not born there, despite indications to the contrary in some sources). His geographical works are the oldest of the remarkable Hispano-Moslem materials in this field to remain still extant, and were of great importance to European geographers during the Middle Ages. His chief work (which has a title meaning, in English, "Book of the Roads and the Provinces") was a geographical compilation written in the form of an itinerary, and containing also a certain amount of historical and ethnographical information. He also wrote a dictionary of ancient geography (chiefly of Arabia), and has been credited with a book on the principal plants and trees of Andalusia, in Spain.

Bakst (bäkst), **Léon Nikolayevich.** [Original surname, **Rosenberg.**] b. at St. Petersburg, c1867; d. at Paris, Dec. 27, 1924. Russian painter, scenic artist, and costume designer. He studied art at St. Petersburg and at the Julian Academy, Paris; he was active as a portrait painter at Moscow before settling (1906) at Paris, where he became (1909) scenic artist and costume designer for the Ballet Russe under Diaghilev. He achieved international fame with his décor for productions of *Scheherazade*, *Cleopatra*, *L'Après-midi d'un Faune*, and *Daphnis and Chloë*; he also designed the settings for many operas, including *The Secret of Suzanne*, by Ermanno Wolfe-Ferrari, *Boris Godunov* by Modest Moussorgsky, and *Saint Sebastian* (1921) and *La Pisanella* (1913) written by Gabriele D'Annunzio. His final work appeared in the production (1924) of *Istar* at Paris. His style was known for its richness of color.

Baku (bä.kö'). Former government district of czarist Russia, now a part of the U.S.S.R., in the Azerbaijan Soviet Socialist Republic, on the W shores of the Caspian Sea. The land ranges from hilly to mountainous, and is very rich in oil.

Baku. Seaport in the S part of the U.S.S.R., capital of the Azerbaijan Soviet Socialist Republic, situated on the Caspian Sea, on the S coast of the Apsheron Peninsula: Russia's chief center of petroleum production and refining, and one of the foremost in the world; an important pipeline and rail junction. It has an extensive trade in petroleum, grain, and other commodities, is one of the leading Soviet naval stations, and is connected with Caspian ports and by rail with the Black Sea. From ancient times until quite recently it was a place of some importance in the Zoroastrian religion. It belonged to the Persians and Turks, and was taken by the Russians in 1806. Pop. 809,347 (1939).

Bakunin (bä.kö'nyin), **Michael.** [Russian, **Mikhail Aleksandrovich Bakunin.**] b. at Torzhok, near Tver (now Kalinin), 1814; d. at Bern, Switzerland, July 1, 1876. Russian revolutionary socialist, regarded as the founder of anarchism. He left Russia in 1840 and engaged in political agitation in Germany, Austria, and France. After taking part in the Dresden insurrection of 1849 he was arrested by the police of Saxony and handed over first to the Austrian, then to the Russian, authorities. He was imprisoned at Schlüsselburg prison (at what is now Petrokrepost) and later exiled to Siberia, whence he escaped via Japan to England in 1861. His later years, devoted to incessant but ineffective revolutionary activity, were spent mainly in Italy and Switzerland. He joined the first International, but incurred the enmity of Karl Marx, and was expelled at the congress at The Hague in 1872 on the charge of organizing a secret revolutionary Social-Democratic alliance within the International. He had many disciples, chiefly in Italy and Spain, but, though a prolific pamphleteer, left no coherent exposition of his doctrine. Among his more important writings were *God and the State,* an indictment of religious and political authority, and *The Knouto-Germanic Empire,* an attack on the new Germany, inspired by the Franco-Prussian War.

Bala (bä'la). Urban district, in N Wales, in Merionethshire, situated at the foot of Bala Lake, ab. 20 mi. SW of Denbigh, ab. 206 mi. W of London by rail. It is a cattle-raising district, especially of the Welsh Black breed. 1,508 (1951).

Balaam (bā'lam). In the Bible, a prophet of Pethor, in Mesopotamia, mentioned in the Book of Numbers. The Moabite king Balak sent for him to curse the Israelites, who had already conquered Bashan and the land of King Sihon, and were threatening Moab. In the course of his journey, Balaam was rebuked by the ass on which he rode, and upon arriving among the Israelites, blessed them with a favorable prophecy.

Balaam. Character in John Dryden's satire *Absalom and Achitophel,* intended for the earl of Huntingdon.

Balabac (bä.lä'bäk). Hilly island in the SW Philippines, S of Palawan and belonging to Palawan province. It has several good harbors. Area, 124 sq. mi.; pop. 1,930 (1949).

Balabac Strait. Sea passage separating the island of Borneo from Balabac island, Palawan province, Philippine Islands. It connects the Sulu Sea on the E with the South China Sea on the W.

Balaclava (bal.a.klä'va). See **Balaklava.**

Bala Cynwyd (bal'a kin'wid). Unincorporated community in SE Pennsylvania, in Montgomery County, near Philadelphia. Under the urban definition established for use in the 1950 census, Bala Cynwyd has been counted as part of the "urban fringe" of Philadelphia; its last official enumeration was 4,907 (1940).

Baladan (bal'a.dan). [Probable full name, **Merodach-baladan.**] In the Bible, mentioned in 2 Kings, xx. 12, and in Isa. xxxix. 1, father of Merodach-baladan (Assyrian, *Marduk-abal-iddina*).

Baladhuri (bä.lä.ᴛʜö'rē), **al-.** fl. at Baghdad; d. in 892 or 893. Moslem historian, generally considered to have been one of the greatest of his time. He was born a Persian, but (except for some translations from Persian into Arabic which have been ascribed to him) appears to have identified himself completely with the Arab culture which prevailed at Baghdad. His two great works were a history of the conquests of Mohammed and the early caliphs of Islam (a work based on traditions which al-Baladhuri himself collected in many countries) and a genealogical work dealing with Mohammed and his kinsmen.

Baladi (bä.lä'dē), **al-.** fl. in Egypt during the latter half of the 10th century A.D. Egyptian physician. He is of some interest to historians of medicine for a treatise which he wrote on the hygiene of pregnant women and of babies.

Balafré (bà.là.frā), **Le.** See **Lorraine, François de;** also **Lorraine, Henri de** (1550–88).

Balagansk (bä.lä.gänsk'). Small town in the U.S.S.R., in the Irkutsk *oblast* (region) of the Russian Soviet Federated Socialist Republic, on the Angara River ab. 100 mi. NW of Irkutsk. Near it is a noted cave.

Balaghat (bä.lä.gôt'). District in the Chhattisgarh division of the Central Provinces and Berar (now officially Madhya Pradesh), Union of India, ab. 100 mi. NE of Nagpur. There is some manganese mined in the area. Capital, Balaghat; area, ab. 3,614 sq. mi.; pop. 634,350 (1941).

Balaguer (bä.lä.ger'), **Víctor.** b. at Barcelona, Spain, 1824; d. at Madrid, 1901. Spanish poet, historian, and novelist. He became keeper of the archives at Barcelona in 1854, and shortly thereafter professor of history at the university. Author of *Trovador de Montserrat* (1850), *Don Juan de Serravalle* (5th ed., 1875), and *Historia política y literaria de los trovadores* (1878–80).

Balahissar (bä''lä.hi.sär'). Ruined town in Asia Minor, near the Sangarius (Sakarya) River, ab. 85 mi. SW of Ankara, on (or very near) the supposed site of the ancient Pessinus.

Balak (bā'lak). [Also, **Balac.**] In Old Testament history, a king of the Moabites.

Balak. Character in the satire *Absalom and Achitophel,* intended as a caricature of Dr. Burnet. It is in the second section, which was edited by John Dryden but largely written by Nahum Tate.

Balakhany (bä''lä.chä.nē'). [Also, **Balakhani.**] Small town in the S part of the U.S.S.R., in the Azerbaijan Soviet Socialist Republic, N of Baku, noted for its petroleum springs.

Balakhna (bä.läн'na). [Also, **Balatchna** (-läch'-).] Small town in the U.S.S.R., in the Gorki *oblast* (region) of the Russian Soviet Federated Socialist Republic, situated on the Volga River, ab. 15 mi. NW of Gorki: noted in the past for shoemaking. Pop. ab. 10,000.

Balakirev (bä.lä'ki.ryif), **Mili Alekseyevich.** b. at Nizhni Novgorod (now Gorki), Russia, Jan. 2, 1837; d. at St. Petersburg, in May, 1910. Russian composer and conductor. At 18 he went to St. Petersburg, where he appeared with success as a pianist, and where his compositions attracted the attention of Mikhail Ivanovich Glinka, who regarded him as his successor. With Modest Moussorgsky, Nicolai Rimsky-Korsakov, Aleksandr Borodin, and others, Balakirev in 1861 founded the "New Russian" school of music. Under his leadership this group made a thorough analysis and study of the works of classical and contemporary composers, especially Johann Sebastian Bach, Robert Schumann, Hector Berlioz, and Franz Liszt. He founded the Free Music School in 1862, and directed its concerts for many years. He was conductor of the Royal Russian Musical Society (1867–70), and musical director of the Imperial Chapel (1883–95). His principal compositions are the symphonic poems *Tamara* and *Russia,* music for *King Lear,* a symphony, overtures, songs, and *Islamey* and other piano pieces. Especially notable and influential is his collection of Russian folk songs (1866).

Balaklava (bal.a.klä'va). [Also: **Balaclava;** ancient name, **Symbolon Portus;** medieval name, **Cembalo.**] Small seaport in the U.S.S.R., in the Crimean *oblast* (region) of the Russian Soviet Federated Socialist Republic, ab. 8 mi. SE of Sevastopol. Established in ancient times by Greek colonists, it was long an important Black Sea trading center. Its rulers have included (in addition to the Greeks) the Romans, the Genoese, the Turks, and the Russians. A Greek colony was settled here in comparatively modern times by Catherine II of Russia. It was a headquarters of the coalition (England, France, Turkey, and Sardinia) against Russia in the Crimean war, and the site in late October, 1854, of a series of engagements in the initial phase of the campaign to wrest Sevastopol from the Russians. However, its chief renown (and it is perhaps the most widely known of the battle sites of the Crimean War) stems not from its strategic importance but from the gallant (and unnecessary) British cavalry charge immortalized by Tennyson in *The Charge of the Light Brigade.* The situation on October 25, 1854, when this charge took place, was that certain fortified positions commanding the causeway to Balaklava's port (which was being used by the British for debarkation of men and supplies) were taken from a small force of approximately 250 Turks by a Russian force estimated to number some 12,000. A counterattack by the English Heavy Brigade, under James Yorke Scarlett, deflected the Russian blow, but at the same time this was taking place, and through a tragic misunderstanding of orders, the Light Brigade, under the 7th earl of Cardigan, was sent against the Russian artillery at the end of the northern valley in the plain of Balaklava. The description in Tennyson's poem of the situation faced by the Light Brigade is probably as good as any that can be given:

"Cannon to right of them,
Cannon to left of them,
Cannon in front of them
Volleyed and thundered."

Nevertheless, the charge was not repulsed; the Light Brigade broke through the Russian guns, routed the cavalry behind the gunners, and returned to their starting point "through the jaws of Death, back from the mouth of Hell." Of some 670 horsemen (Tennyson says 600), only 198 are known to have returned from the charge. Pop. ab. 1,300.

Bala Lake (bal'a). Small lake in N Wales, in Merionethshire, ab. 13 mi. NE of Dolgelley. Its outlet is the river Dee. Length, ab. 4 mi.; width, less than 1 mi.; elevation, 530 ft.

Balami (bä.lä'mē). Learned vizier under the Samanid dynasty in Persia. He collected old Iranian traditions, and in 963 wrote a Persian abridgment of the Arabic history of Tabari.

Balan (bà.läṅ). Town in NE France, in the department of Ardennes, situated near the Meuse River S of Sedan. It is an industrial town; has woolen manufactures and ironworks. 7,410 (1946).

Balan (bā'lan). In the *Morte d'Arthur*, the brother of Balin.

Balan (bà.läṅ). Early French version of the romance of *Fierabras*, which appears in English as *The Sowdan of Babylon*. Balan is the Sowdan and the father of the knight Fierabras or Ferumbras.

Balance (bal'ạns), **Justice.** Father of Sylvia in George Farquhar's comedy *The Recruiting Officer*, one of the principal characters.

Balanchine (bal'an.chīn), **George.** [Original name, **Georgi Balanchivadze** (bä.län.chē.vä'dzā).] b. at St. Petersburg, Jan. 9, 1904—. American choreographer. After serving (1924 *et seq.*) as ballet master of the ballet company of Sergei Diaghilev at Paris, he organized (1932), with others, the Ballet Russe de Monte Carlo. Having moved (1933) to New York, he was associated (1934–37) with the Metropolitan Opera House, and subsequently (1946) was one of the organizers of the Ballet Theater, later (1948 *et seq.*) known as the New York City Ballet, of which he was made head. The youngest dancer to have been trained by the Russian Imperial School of the Ballet, he did choreography for such ballets as *The Nightingale* (1925), *Apollon Musagète* (1928), *Mozartiana* (1933), and *Orpheus* (1948). The dances he arranged for musical comedies, beginning with "Slaughter on Tenth Avenue" in *On Your Toes* (1936) by Richard Rogers and Lorenz Hart, originated the trend toward ballet dancing in productions of this kind.

Balante (bä.län'tā). Sudanic-speaking people of W Africa, inhabiting N Portuguese Guinea.

Balarama (bal.a.rä'mạ). In Hindu mythology, the elder brother of Krishna.

Balard (bà.làr), **Antoine Jérôme.** b. at Montpellier, France, Sept. 30, 1802; d. at Paris, March 31, 1876. French chemist. He became professor of chemistry at the Collège de France in 1851. He discovered bromine in 1826, and later invented a method for taking sodium sulfate from sea water.

Balaruc (bà.là.rük). Small resort in S France, in the department of Hérault, on the Étang de Thau.

Balashov (bä.lä.shôf'). [Also, **Balashof.**] Town in the U.S.S.R., in the Saratov *oblast* (region) of the Russian Soviet Federated Socialist Republic, on the Khoper River ab. 120 mi. W of Saratov: major rail junction. 26,846 (1926).

Balasore (bal.ạ.sōr'). [Also: **Balasur** (-sör'), **Baleswar.**] Capital of the district of Balasore, in Orissa state, Union of India, ab. 110 mi. SW of Calcutta. Once a seaport, and supposed to be the site of the English East India Company's first (1634) factory in Bengal, Balasore no longer has important foreign or coastal trade. Sea fish are shipped from there to Calcutta. Pop. ab. 18,000.

Balassa (bô'lôsh.shô), **Bálint.** [Title, Baron of **Kékkő and Gyarmat.**] b. 1551; d. 1594. Hungarian poet. Author of love poems, adaptations from the German and Latin, martial and patriotic songs, and religious hymns.

Balassagyarmat (bô'lôsh.shô.dyôr'môt). [Also, **Balassa-Gyarmat.**] Town in N Hungary, the capital of the county of Nógrád, situated on the Ipoly River (German, Eipel) and the Czechoslovakian border, ab. 42 mi. NE of Budapest. It is the center of a wine and fruit growing district. 10,769 (1948).

Balaton (bô'lô.tōn), **Lake.** [German, **Plattensee.**] Largest lake in Hungary, situated ab. 50 mi. SW of Budapest. It is connected by a system of two rivers and a linking canal to the Danube River. Length, ab. 48 mi.; greatest breadth, ab. 7½ mi.

Balatonfüred (bô'lô.tōn.fü'red). [Also, **Füred.**] Village in W Hungary, in the county of Zala, situated on the N shore of Lake Balaton, S of Veszprém. It is a health resort, with carbonic-acid springs, visited by people with heart ailments. The springs, supposed to have been known to the Romans, were rediscovered in the 16th century. The abbot of Tihany enclosed the spring in stone in 1743.

Balaustion's Adventure (bạ.lôs'ti ọnz). Poem by Robert Browning, published in 1871. Balaustion is a Greek girl of Rhodes. Her story is continued in *Aristophanes' Apology*.

Balázs (bô'läzh), **Béla.** [Pseudonym of **Herbert Bauer.**] b. at Szeged, Hungary, 1884—. Hungarian poet and student of the cinema. He emigrated to Russia in 1919 and became professor at the Moscow Film Academy in 1931. His feeling for stylistic arts is noteworthy. He wrote the libretto to Béla Bartók's opera *Fából faragott királyfi*. Author of *Lélek a háborúban* (Soul in the War, 1916).

Balbi (bäl'bē), **Adriano.** b. at Venice, April 25, 1782; d. at Padua, March 14, 1848. Italian geographer and statistician, author of *Atlas ethnographique du globe* (1826), *Abrégé de géographie* (1832), and others.

Balbi, Gasparo. b. at Venice; fl. in the 16th century. Italian traveler. He spent the years 1597–88 in India. On his return to Venice he published *Viaggio all'Indie Orientali* (1590), which was inserted by the brothers De Bry in their collection of voyages (1606).

Balbinus (bal.bī'nus), **Decimus Caelius.** Killed 238. Roman orator, poet, and statesman, of noble birth, appointed (238) by the senate as joint emperor of Rome with Pupienus Maximus, in opposition to Maximinus, who was shortly after killed by his own soldiers at the siege of Aquileia. Balbinus and his colleague were murdered by the soldiers of the Praetorian Guard at Rome before the beginning of August in the same year, after having reigned from about the end of April.

Balbo (bäl'bō), Count **Cesare.** b. at Turin, Italy, Nov. 21, 1789; d. there, June 3, 1853. Italian statesman and writer, first premier of Piedmont in 1848. He wrote *Storia d'Italia* (1830), *Vita di Dante* (1839), *Delle speranze d'Italia* (1844), and others.

Balbo, Italo. b. at Quartasena, Italy, June 6, 1896; d. at Tobruk, Libya, June 28, 1940. Italian politician and airman; leader (1922) of one of the four Fascist columns whose threat to march into Rome forced the acceptance of Mussolini's terms by King Victor Emmanuel III. After serving (1915 *et seq.*) as a volunteer with the Italian Alpine corps (*Alpini*) in World War I, he founded (1919) the newspaper *L'Alpine* at Udine and was a Fascist leader (1920–22) at Ferrara. He commanded (1923–24) the voluntary militia, and served as undersecretary of state for education (1925) and for air (1926 *et seq.*); he was the first minister for air (1929–33). His mass transatlantic flights of ten planes to Rio de Janeiro (c1930) and 24 planes to Chicago (July–August, 1933) were unique at the time. He was appointed (August, 1933) marshal for air and held (1933–40) the governorship of Libya. He met his death when his plane was hit by Italian anti-aircraft guns over Tobruk. He left the works *La Marcia su Roma: Diario della rivoluzione* (1922), *Stormi in volo sull'oceano* (1931), *La Crociera del decennale* (1933), and others.

Balboa (bäl.bō′ä). Town in E Canal Zone, at the Pacific Ocean entrance to the Panama Canal, located between the canal docks and Ancon Hill, which separates it from Panama City, Panama. Balboa is the U.S. administrative center for the entire Canal Zone. 4,168 (1950).

Balboa (bal.bō′a̤; Spanish, bäl.bō′ä), **Vasco Núñez de.** b. at Jerez de los Caballeros, or at Badajoz, Spain, c1475; d. at Acla, on the Isthmus of Panama (Darien), Jan. 12, 1519. Spanish conquistador and soldier of fortune, discoverer of the "South Sea," later renamed the Pacific Ocean by Ferdinand Magellan. In 1500 he came to America with the expedition of Rodrigo de Bastidas, on which occasion he visited the N coast of South America, in what is now Venezuela and Colombia. At the end of this expedition he withdrew to Salvatierra de Sabana on the island of Española (today called Hispaniola), where he acquired a plantation. In 1510 he joined as a stowaway Alonso de Ojeda's expedition to N South America. Unable to maintain a foothold in this region, Balboa led the settlers to the N coast of the Isthmus of Panama, where the town of Santa María de la Antigua del Darién was founded, the first Spanish settlement on continental America. Balboa was elected as one of the two alcaldes of the new settlement. In 1511 he received from Pasamonte, the king's treasurer at Santo Domingo, a commission to act as provisional governor. Balboa made numerous explorations into the interior, usually succeeding in keeping on good terms with the Indians, and later even married the daughter of a native chieftain. From the Indians he also learned that there was a large body of water to the S of the Isthmus, and that the S coast (of the Isthmus) was very rich in gold. Determined to discover if this were true, he set out from Santa María with part of his force on Sept. 1, 1513, and after an adventurous journey reached on Sept. 25 a mountain from which he first saw the Pacific. The shore itself was attained on Sept. 29, and Balboa, entering the water, took possession in the name of King Ferdinand of Spain. He returned to Santa María on Jan. 19, 1514. In the same year (June 29) Pedrarias Dávila (Pedro Arias de Ávila) arrived from Spain as governor of the colony. The relations of the two men were unfriendly. Nevertheless, Pedrarias granted Balboa permission to explore the South Sea. Cutting the timbers for his ships on the Caribbean side, Balboa transported them with immense labor across the Isthmus, and had launched two vessels when he was arrested by Pedrarias on a charge of treason against the king, and beheaded.

Balbriggan (bal.brig′a̤n). Market town, seaport, and seaside resort in Leinster province, Irish Republic, in County Dublin, ab. 19 mi. N of Dublin. It has manufactures of stockings, textiles, and other items. The town has given its name to a kind of unbleached cotton used in making underwear. 2,920 (1951).

Balbuena (bäl.bwā′nä), **Bernardo de.** b. at Valdepeñas, Spain, c1562; d. at San Juan, Puerto Rico, 1627. Mexican poet and first bishop (1620 *et seq.*) of Puerto Rico. Although he lived many years in Spain, Jamaica, and Puerto Rico, Mexico claims him among her greatest poets, principally because of his epic *La Grandeza mexicana* (1604). His other important works are the pastoral *El Siglo de oro en las selvas de Erífile* (1608) and *Bernardo, o victoria de Roncesvalles* (1624), concerning Bernardo del Carpio.

Balbus (bal′bus), **Lucius Cornelius.** [Called **Lucius Cornelius Balbus Major.**] b. in Gades (now Cádiz, Spain); fl. in the 1st century B.C. Roman politician, surnamed "Major" to distinguish him from his nephew Lucius Cornelius Balbus. He served in Spain in the war against Sertorius, and was made a Roman citizen in 72 B.C. His right to the citizenship was successfully defended (c55 B.C.) by Cicero. He sided with Caesar against Pompey, having been entrusted with the management of the former's affairs at Rome. On the death of Caesar he attached himself to Octavius, under whom he obtained the consulship in 40 B.C.

Balbus, Lucius Cornelius. [Called **Lucius Cornelius Balbus Minor.**] Roman politician. He was quaestor (44–43 B.C.) to the propraetor Asinius Pollio in Spain, where he acquired a large fortune through oppression of the native population. He became subsequently governor of Africa, and enjoyed a triumph (19 B.C.) in consequence of a victory over the Garamantes. He was surnamed "Minor" to distinguish him from his uncle Lucius Cornelius Balbus.

Balcarres (bal.kar′is, -iz), 2nd Baron and 1st Earl of. See **Lindsay, Alexander** (1618–59).

Balcarres, 6th Earl of. See **Lindsay, Alexander** (1752–1825).

Balch (bôlch, bȧlch), **Emily Greene.** b. at Jamaica Plain, Mass., Jan. 8, 1867—. American economist, sociologist, and author; winner, with Dr. John R. Mott, of the Nobel peace prize for 1946. A graduate (1889) of Bryn Mawr College, she served as a professor of economics and sociology (1913–18) at Wellesley College; she was associated (1915 *et seq.*) with the Women's International League for Peace and Freedom, of which she was honorary international president (1936 *et seq.*). Author of *Public Assistance of the Poor in France* (1893), *Our Slavic Fellow-Citizens* (1910), *Approaches to the Great Settlement* (1918), *Refugees as Assets* (1939), and other works.

Balchen (bäl′ke̤n), **Bernt.** b. at Tveit, Norway, Oct. 23, 1899—. American aviator. He was commissioned (1920) as a second lieutenant in the Norwegian army, served as chief test pilot (1926–32) for the Fokker Aircraft Corporation, and accompanied the Amundsen-Nobile expedition to Spitzbergen (1926) and Admiral Byrd on his Antarctic flight (1927). He later served as chief pilot (1929–30) with Byrd in the Antarctic. Naturalized (1931) as a U.S. citizen, he was appointed (1942) a colonel in the U.S. army, and served (1943 *et seq.*) in the European theater during World War II. Coauthor of *War Below Zero* (1944).

Balcic (bäl′chēk). [Also: **Balcik, Baltchik.**] Town in NE Bulgaria, in the department of Varna, situated on the Black Sea, W of Cape Caliacra, ab. 18 mi. NE of Varna: formerly in Rumania. It is a seaside resort, and exports grain. A beautiful residence was built here by Queen Marie of Rumania after World War I. 6,011 (1946).

Balcony, A. Play in three acts by Naomi Royde-Smith, published in 1926.

Bald (bôld), **Book of.** [Also, **Leech Book of Bald.**] Name applied to an Anglo-Saxon manuscript dealing with the medical use of herbs, notable as the earliest extant leech-book written in Anglo-Saxon. It dates from about the first half of the 10th century, and is known to have been kept for a time at the monastery of Glastonbury. The leech who gave his name to the book, and under whose directions it was unquestionably compiled, was probably in touch with King Alfred (Alfred the Great). Indeed, one of the chapters contains prescriptions sent by the Patriarch of Jerusalem to Alfred.

Baldassare (bäl.däs.sä′rā). Character in Gaetano Donizetti's opera *La Favorita;* head of the monastery of Saint Jacopo di Compostella. The part is written for a bass voice.

Baldassarre Calvo (käl′vō). See **Calvo, Baldassarre.**

Baldegg Lake (bäl′dek). [German, **Baldegger See** (bäl′deg.ėr zā).] Small lake in the canton of Lucerne, Switzerland, ab. 11 mi. N of Lucerne. It is traversed by the Aa River.

Baldensperger (bȧl.däṅ.sper.zhā), **Philippe Jules Fernand.** b. at St. Dié, France, May 4, 1871—. French literary historian and regionalist poet. He was a professor (1900–36) at the universities of Lyons, Strasbourg and Paris, and subsequently professor at Harvard, and the University of California (at Los Angeles); he was the cofounder (with Paul Hazard) of the *Revue de littérature comparée* (1921). Author of many studies on German and French literature, he is credited with having played a primary role in the development of comparative literature as a scholarly discipline. His poetry, strongly traditional in character, praises the life in his native Vosges mountains.

Balder (bôl′dėr). [Also, **Baldur;** Old Norse, **Baldr** (bäl′dr).] In Old Norse mythology, a son of Odin, and one of the principal gods. Balder's characteristics are those of a sun god. He is the "whitest" of the gods, and so beautiful and bright that a light emanates from him. His dwelling is Breidablik (Old Norse, *Breidhablik*). His wife is Nanna. He is finally slain, at the instigation of Loki, by a twig of mistletoe (the only material free from oath not to injure Balder) in the hands of the blind god Hoder (Old Norse, *Hödhr*).

Balder. Poem by Sydney Dobell, published in 1854.

Balder Dead. Poem by Matthew Arnold.

Balderston (bôl′dėr.stọn), **John Lloyd.** b. at Philadelphia, Oct. 22, 1889—. American journalist, playwright, and scenarist. Chief London correspondent (1923–31) of the New York *World*. Scenarist for the films *Lives of a Bengal Lancer, Berkeley Square, Gaslight, Prisoner of Zenda,* and others, he also wrote *Genius of the Marne* (1919), *Berkeley Square* (1929), *Chicago Blueprint* (1943), and other plays.

Balderstone (bôl′dėr.stōn), **Caleb.** In Sir Walter Scott's novel *The Bride of Lammermoor,* the old servant of the Master of Ravenswood.

Balderstone, Thomas. [Called **"Uncle Tom."**] In Charles Dickens's tale *Mrs. Joseph Porter,* the uncle of Mrs. Gattleton.

Baldi (bäl′dē), **Bernardino.** b. at Urbino, Italy, June 6, 1553; d. there, Oct. 10, 1617. Italian scholar, mathematician, poet, and writer on general topics.

Baldinucci (bäl.dē.nöt′chē), **Filippo.** b. at Florence, Italy, 1624; d. Jan. 1, 1696. Florentine art critic. He wrote *Notizie de' professori del disegno da Cimabue 1260–1670* (1681–88).

Baldivieso (bäl.dē.ʙyā′sō), **Enrique.** b. at Tupiza, Bolivia, April 15, 1902—. Bolivian lawyer, politician, and writer. He was a professor of law (1932, 1939 *et seq.*) at San Andrés University, La Paz; private secretary (1929–30) to President Hernando Siles of Bolivia; first secretary (1932–33) of the Bolivian legation in Chile; minister of education (1935) under Sorzano, of war (1935–36), and of foreign affairs (1936, 1937, 1944 *et seq.*); Bolivian Socialist Party founder and leader (1936); vice-president (1938) of Bolivia; national deputy (1942); president (1943) of the chamber of deputies. Author of poems, plays, and essays.

Bald Mountain. Peak in the Front Range, N Colorado, in Larimer County. Elevation, 11,435 ft.

Baldo (bäl′dō), **Monte.** Chain of the Tridentine Alps, in N Italy, separating Lake Garda from the Adige River. Length, 25 mi. Height of Cinna Val Dritta, 7,275 ft.

Baldock (bôl′dọk). Urban district in SE England, in Hertfordshire, ab. 5 mi. NE of Hitchin, ab. 37 mi. N of London by rail. 5,967 (1951).

Baldock, Ralph de. d. 1313. Bishop of London (1304) and lord chancellor (April, 1307). He was removed on the accession of Edward II.

Baldock, Robert de. d. 1327. English lord chancellor (c1323) under Edward II. He was overthrown with the Despensers, and died at London as the result of ill-treatment by a mob.

Baldo degli Ubaldi (bäl′dō de′lyē ö.bäl′dē). [Latinized, **Baldus de Ubaldis.**] b. at Perugia, Italy, 1327 (or, according to some authorities, 1319); d. at Pavia, Italy, April 28, 1400. Italian jurist, often considered to have been, next to Bartolus (under whom he studied), the greatest of his time. He taught law in many cities: at Bologna (three years), at Perugia (33 years), at Pisa (one year), at Florence (six years), at Padua (three years), and at Pavia (ten years). Known for his love of polemics and for his talent as a dialectician, he was consulted by Pope Urban VI with regard to action against the antipope Clement VII. He was also frequently consulted by the great merchants of Perugia, and was one of the first jurists to give legal opinions concerning bills of exchange.

Baldomir (bäl.dō.mēr′), **Alfredo.** b. at Montevideo, Uruguay, 1884—. Uruguayan architect, general, and president (1938–43) of the republic; leader of the Colorado party (*Baldomiristas*). During his administration an extensive Nazi underground organization was uncovered (1940) in Uruguay, and Uruguay broke off relations (January, 1942) with the Axis powers.

Baldovinetti (bäl″dō.vē.net′tē), **Alessio.** b. at Florence, Italy, c1425; d. there, Aug. 29, 1499. Florentine painter and worker in mosaics. He executed a series of frescoes for the Church of Santa Trinità at Florence.

Baldovini (bäl.dō.vē′nē), **Francesco.** b. at Florence, Italy, Feb. 27, 1635; d. Nov. 18, 1716. Italian poet, author of *Lamento di Cecco da Varlungo* (1694) and others.

Balducci (bäl.döt′chē), **Francesco.** b. at Palermo, Sicily; d. at Rome, 1642. Italian poet, often considered one of the best of the Anacreontic poets of that country. He wrote *Canzoni Siciliani,* in the Sicilian dialect, and others.

Baldung (bäl′dụng), **Hans.** [Called **Hans Baldung Grien** or **Grün.**] b. at Gmünd, Swabia, c1480; d. at Strasbourg, 1545. German painter and engraver. A friend of Matthias Grünewald and probably a pupil of Albrecht Dürer, he showed in his work (which included book illustrations, stained glass, and portraits as well as religious paintings) some influence of these two painters, but also a distinctly individual treatment of figures, and a predilection for the color green, whence his surname. Working principally at Freiburg im Breisgau and at Strasbourg, he painted for the cathedral of the former city an altarpiece (1516) of the *Coronation of the Virgin,* one of his best-known works.

Baldwin (bôld′win). d. at Acre, in Palestine, Nov. 19, 1190. Archbishop of Canterbury. He became bishop of Worcester in 1180, and was elevated to the see of Canterbury in 1184. He crowned Richard I (of England) in 1189, and set out upon the third Crusade in 1190.

Baldwin. Unincorporated community in SE New York, in Nassau County, on Long Island: residential community. Under the urban definition established for use in the 1950 census, Baldwin has been counted with adjoining urban areas; its last official enumeration was 15,507 (1940).

Baldwin I (of *Constantinople*). [French, **Baudouin;** also, **Baldwin IX** (of *Flanders*).] b. at Valenciennes, France, 1171; d. c1206. Emperor of Constantinople, and count of Flanders. He joined (1201) the fourth Crusade. The Crusaders, supported by the Venetian fleet, at the request of Alexius, son of the Byzantine emperor Isaac II Angelus (who had been dethroned by his brother), captured (1204) Constantinople, and restored Alexius and his father to power. As the emperor was unable to fulfill his compact with the Crusaders, which called for a union of the Greek and Roman churches and the payment of large sums of money, hostilities broke out, and the short-lived "Latin" empire at Constantinople was established, with Baldwin as emperor, in 1204. He was defeated (1205) and made prisoner by the Bulgarians at Adrianople.

Baldwin II (of *Constantinople*). [French, **Baudouin.**] b. 1217; d. 1273. Emperor of Constantinople (1228–61); son of Pierre de Courtenay, and a nephew of Baldwin I of Constantinople. He was deposed by the Byzantine emperor Michael VIII Palaeologus, an event which marked the fall of the "Latin" empire at Constantinople. Until 1237 he ruled under the regency of John of Brienne. He made great efforts to maintain the tottering empire, and sold various state valuables. Despite what can only be described as almost complete futility as a monarch, Baldwin has secured a curious niche in the history of science through an astrological treatise written (c1270) for him by an unknown author. The treatise (with the poem that accompanies it) is interesting for two reasons: (1) that it was written in French in a day when virtually all scholarly work was being done in Latin and (2) because of the remarkable backwardness of both poem and treatise. They do not represent the astronomy of their age, but are a late echo of an obsolete tradition. For example, the author clearly states that Mercury and Venus revolve about the sun, which might seem to be an imperfect anticipation of Copernicus, but is in fact a relic of pre-Ptolemaic astronomy.

Baldwin I (of *Flanders*). [French, **Baudouin;** surnamed **Bras de Fer,** meaning "Iron Arm."] d. c879. First count of Flanders; son-in-law of Charles II (Charles the Bald) of France.

Baldwin II (of *Flanders*). [French, **Baudouin.**] d. 918. Count of Flanders; son of Baldwin I of Flanders. He married Alfrith, daughter of Alfred the Great of England.

Baldwin V (of *Flanders*). [French, **Baudouin;** surnamed **le Débonnaire.**] d. 1067. Count of Flanders; father-in-law of William I (William the Conqueror) of England, whom he accompanied in the invasion (1066) of England. He was regent of France (1060–67).

Baldwin I (of *Jerusalem*). [French, **Baudouin.**] b. c1058; d. in Egypt, in March, 1118. King of Jerusalem. He was a brother of Godfrey of Bouillon, whom he accompanied on the first Crusade (1096–99), and whom he succeeded as king of Jerusalem. He conquered Acre in 1104, Beirut in 1109, and Sidon in 1110.

Baldwin II (of *Jerusalem*). [French, **Baudouin.**] d. Aug. 21, 1131. Count of Edessa and king of Jerusalem (1118–

31). In his reign the military orders of Saint John and the Templars were established for the defense of the Holy Land. He was succeeded by Fulc V of Anjou, his son-in-law.

Baldwin III (of *Jerusalem*). [French, **Baudouin.**] b. c1130; d. at Tripolis, Feb. 10, 1162. King of Jerusalem (1143–62). He lost Edessa to the Moslem ruler of Mosul in 1144, an event which gave rise to the second Crusade (1147–49).

Baldwin IV (of *Jerusalem*). [French, **Baudouin**; called **"Baldwin the Leper."**] King of Jerusalem (1173–83); son of Amalric I. He gained a signal victory over Saladin on the plain of Ramah, on Nov. 25, 1177, and again near Tiberias in the early summer of 1182. He was succeeded by his nephew Baldwin V, who died in 1185.

Baldwin, Abraham. b. at North Guilford, Conn., Nov. 22, 1754; d. at Washington, D.C., March 4, 1807. American politician, educator, and Revolutionary patriot. After graduation (1772) from Yale, he was licensed (1775) as a minister and was a tutor at Yale until 1779, when he became a chaplain in the Continental army. After the war, he was admitted to the bar (1783), and moved (c1783) to Georgia, where he became (1785) a member of the state legislature. He was a pioneer in state educational progress and a moving spirit behind the establishment of Franklin College (now the University of Georgia). He served (1785 *et seq.*) in the Congress of Confederation, was a member of the Federal Convention, was a member (1789–99) of the House of Representatives, and served (1799–1807) in the U.S. Senate, where he was president *pro tempore* during the first session of the Seventh Congress. Baldwin County in Georgia is named after him.

Baldwin, Charles H. b. at New York, Sept. 3, 1822; d. there, Nov. 17, 1888. American naval officer, appointed rear admiral in 1883. He served in the Mexican War on the *Congress*, and during the Civil War was commander of the *Clifton* of the mortar fleet at New Orleans. under David G. Farragut, and at Vicksburg, in 1862 He was later an ordnance inspector at the Mare Island navy yard. He retired Sept. 3, 1884.

Baldwin, Charles Sears. b. at New York, March 21, 1867; d. Oct. 23, 1935. American teacher and writer. He served as a professor (1909–11) at Yale, and was a professor of rhetoric and English composition (1911 *et seq.*) at Columbia University. Author of *The Inflections and Syntax of the Morte d'Arthur of Sir Thomas Malory* (1894), *DeQuincey's Revolt of the Tartars* (1896), *A College Manual of Rhetoric* (1902), *Writing and Speaking* (1909), *Introduction to English Medieval Literature* (1931), and *Three Medieval Centuries of Literature in England* (1932).

Baldwin, Count. Father of Biron and Carlos in Thomas Southerne's *Fatal Marriage*, an unyielding, self-willed man.

Baldwin, Evelyn Briggs. b. at Springfield, Mo., July 22, 1862; d. at Washington, D.C., Oct. 25, 1933. American meteorologist and arctic explorer. He accompanied Robert Edwin Peary to North Greenland as meteorologist in 1893–94, and was second in command of the Walter Wellman expedition to Franz Josef Land, 1898–99. In 1901–02 he organized and led the Baldwin-Ziegler polar expedition (financed by William Ziegler), and established a chain of stations, embracing portable houses and a cargo of equipment, through the Franz Josef Land archipelago in preparation for a sledge journey thence to the North Pole during the proposed second year's work of the expedition. He also established three safety stations on Shannon Island, off the NE coast of Greenland, in accordance with his plan to make the return journey along that unexplored territory. These safety stations embraced three houses filled with an additional cargo of equipment. In addition to an exceptionally large pack of dogs, 15 Siberian horses were used with marked success for drawing the sledges upon the sea ice.

Baldwin, Faith. b. at New Rochelle, N.Y., Oct. 1, 1893—. American novelist, the author of numerous popular novels, magazine serials, and short stories. Her works include *Mavis of Green Hill* (1921), *Those Difficult Years* (1925), *Alimony* (1928), *Garden Oats* (1929), *Office Wife* (1930), *Week-End Marriage* (1932), *White Collar Girl* (1933), *American Family* (1935), *This Man Is Mine* (1936), *Hotel Hostess* (1938), *The High Road* (1939), *Reno* (1941), *You Can't Escape* (1943), and *Woman on Her Way* (1946).

Baldwin, Frank Stephen. b. at New Hartford, Conn., April 10, 1838; d. April 8, 1925. American inventor, noted for his development of a calculating machine. After attending Union College, he secured a number of patents between 1855 and 1874, when he patented his arithmometer, which was among the first adding machines marketed in the U.S. Established in business at St. Louis after 1869, he also devised a three-speed bicycle and a mortar mixer. William S. Burroughs, who later invented his own adding machine, was at one time employed by Baldwin to do model work. The perfection of Baldwin's device was for a time thwarted by financial difficulties; he invented the Baldwin computing engine (1890) and the Baldwin calculator (1902), the latter subsequently becoming the Monroe calculating machine, after Baldwin joined with Jay R. Monroe in establishing the Monroe Calculating Machine Company.

Baldwin, Henry. b. at New Haven, Conn., Jan. 14, 1780; d. at Philadelphia, April 21, 1844. American jurist and legislator. Elected in 1816 to Congress, he took part in the Florida treaty negotiations, and in 1822 resigned his seat because of poor health. A supporter of Andrew Jackson, he was appointed (1830) associate justice of the Supreme Court. Neither a loose nor a strict constructionist, he followed his own lights, achieving some repute for his dissenting opinions. The latter constitute the bulk of Baldwin's *A General View of the Origin and Nature of the Constitution and Government of the United States* (1837).

Baldwin, Henry Porter. b. at Coventry, R.I., Feb. 22, 1814; d. Dec. 31, 1892. American businessman and politician. Settling (1838) at Detroit, he later became the owner of a flourishing wholesale boot and shoe business. He was president (1863–87) of the Second National Bank (which became the Detroit National Bank in 1883), and entered (1861) the state senate, later serving as governor of Michigan (1868 *et seq.*) and as a U.S. senator (1879 *et seq.*), having been appointed to the latter post to fill the vacancy caused by Zachariah Chandler's death.

Baldwin, James Mark. b. at Columbia, S.C., Jan. 12, 1861; d. at Paris, Nov. 8, 1934. American psychologist. He was professor of philosophy and psychology at Johns Hopkins University, Baltimore (1903–09) and at the National University of Mexico (1909 *et seq.*). He was a professor of philosophy at Lake Forest University, Illinois (1887–90) and at Toronto University, Canada (1890–93), and of psychology at Princeton University (1893–1903). He wrote *Handbook of Psychology* (1888–90), *Elements of Psychology* (1893), *Mental Development in the Child and the Race* (1896), *Social and Ethical Interpretations* (1897), *Story of the Mind* (1898), *Fragments in Philosophy and Science* (1902), *Development and Evolution* (1902), *Thoughts and Things* (1906–11), *Darwin and the Humanities* (1909), and *The Individual and Society* (1910); edited the *Dictionary of Philosophy and Psychology* (1901–06). He founded (1894) and edited the *Psychological Review*.

Baldwin, John. b. at North Branford, Conn., Oct. 13, 1799; d. at Baldwin, La., Dec. 28, 1884. American grindstone manufacturer and university founder. After settling (1828) at Berea, Ohio, he discovered (c1842) on his land the sandstone which later became the foundation of the Berea grindstone industry. Long concerned about the exclusion of women from many schools, he donated (1845) a tract of land and a building at Berea to the North Ohio Conference of the Methodist Church which in 1846 opened a coeducational school known as Berea (sometimes Baldwin) Institute (now Baldwin-Wallace College). Going to Kansas in 1858, he gave to the Methodist Conference there a university building he erected on the present site of Baldwin, in Douglas County; this institution, opened in 1859, later became Baker University. In 1867 he bought a tract of land in St. Mary Parish, La., establishing there the Baldwin Seminary (now the Baldwin public school).

Baldwin, Loammi. b. at North Woburn, Mass., Jan. 21, 1740; d. there, Oct. 20, 1807. American engineer and Revolutionary army officer, noted for hybridizing the famous Baldwin apple; father of Loammi Baldwin (1780–1838). Largely self-taught as an engineer and land surveyor, he was active as a civil engineer when he joined the Continental army; as a lieutenant colonel of infantry, he took part in Washington's retreat to the Delaware River, and in the attack on Trenton. Leaving (1777) the military service because of poor health, he served (1778–79, 1800–04) as representative from Woburn in the general court of the state and was high sheriff (1780 *et seq.*) of Middlesex County. It was while serving as chief engineer (1794 *et seq.*) of the Middlesex Canal, which he helped plan, that he came upon a seedling apple tree at Wilmington, Mass., from which he cut the grafts that led to his development of the hardy Baldwin apple.

Baldwin, Loammi. b. at North Woburn, Mass., May 16, 1780; d. June 30, 1838. American civil engineer; son of Loammi Baldwin (1740–1807). He was graduated (1800) from Harvard; admitted to the bar (1804), he practiced at Cambridge, Mass. Having already demonstrated his mechanical bent in 1802, when he designed Groton's first fire engine, he turned from the law in 1807 and devoted himself to engineering, opening an office at Charlestown after study abroad. He became (1819) engineer of improvements for the city of Boston, was active (1817–20) on public works in Virginia, and in 1821 became engineer of the Union Canal linking Reading and Middletown, Pa., where he constructed one of the largest dams of the time. He became (1825) connected with the committee on the erection of the Bunker Hill Monument, and planned and built (1833) large masonry dry docks at the Charlestown, Mass., and Norfolk, Va., navy yards; he also helped plan a naval dry dock at New York harbor that was completed after his death. Noteworthy are his *Report on the Subject of Introducing Pure Water into the City of Boston* (1834) and *Report on the Brunswick Canal and Railroad, Glynn County, Ga.* (1836).

Baldwin, Matthias William. b. at Elizabethtown, N.J., Nov. 10, 1795; d. Sept. 7, 1866. American locomotive manufacturer and philanthropist, noted for his contributions to the development of the locomotive in the U.S. In 1819 he established himself as a manufacturing jeweler at Philadelphia, leaving this business in 1825 to enter partnership with David Mason in the making of tools, hydraulic presses, and stationary engines. Baldwin became (c1827) sole owner of the firm, continuing the innovations which had made Mason fear for the future of the firm. Baldwin displayed (April 25, 1831) in Peale's Museum, at Philadelphia, a dummy locomotive and two cars representing an improvement based upon an English prototype. After constructing *Old Ironsides* (among the first practical U.S. locomotives) for the Philadelphia and Germantown Railroad, he devoted his business in increasing measure to locomotive construction. He took in Matthew Baird as a partner in his works which, by the time of Baldwin's death, had constructed more than 1,500 locomotives. He contributed ten thousand dollars annually to charities, established (1835) a school for Negro children, and allocated ten percent of his company's yearly income to the Civil War Christian Commission.

Baldwin, Robert. b. at York (now Toronto), Canada, May 12, 1804; d. Dec. 9, 1858. Canadian statesman, notable as an advocate of representative government in Canada. After serving (1829–30) as a member of the parliament of Upper Canada, he was appointed (1836) to the executive council (from which body he resigned very shortly, when it became evident to him that virtually none of the reforms he espoused were going to be granted by the British governor). In 1842, however, the reformist position won a degree of acceptance and he formed (with Louis Hippolyte La Fontaine) a coalition government to further his aims. He was again a joint head of the administration in the period 1848–51.

Baldwin, Roger Sherman. b. at New Haven, Conn., Jan. 4, 1793; d. Feb. 19, 1863. American lawyer and politician; son of Simeon Baldwin and Rebecca Sherman (daughter of Roger Sherman). An exponent of antislavery, he is noted for his defense of African Negroes in the *Amistad* mutiny (1841). He was a member of the Connecticut senate and of the general assembly, and (1844–45) governor of Connecticut. He was a member of the U.S. Senate (1847–51) and was a Connecticut delegate to the National Peace Conference (1861) at Washington, D.C. An able lawyer active in the cause of abolition, he successfully defended the African Negroes who mutinied aboard the *Amistad* against Cuban slavers, securing freedom for the Negroes after the U.S. government had taken possession of the vessel.

Baldwin, Simeon. b. at Norwich Conn., Dec. 14, 1761; d. May 26, 1851. American jurist and politician; father of Roger Sherman Baldwin and grandfather of Simeon Eben Baldwin. Clerk (1789–1806) of the U.S. district and circuit courts for Connecticut, he at various times served as collector of revenue, city clerk, alderman, and mayor of New Haven. He was a member (1803–05) of Congress, was elected (1806) a judge of the superior court of Connecticut, and was a judge (1808–18) of the state supreme court of errors.

Baldwin, Simeon Eben. b. at New Haven, Conn., Feb. 5, 1840; d. Jan. 30, 1927. American lawyer, jurist and politician; son of Roger Sherman Baldwin and grandson of Simeon Baldwin. He was graduated (1861) from Yale, was admitted to the bar (1863), and in 1869 joined the faculty of the Yale Law School, retiring (1919) as professor emeritus. He served (1872 *et seq.*) on the commission which made the *Revision of 1875, the General Statutes of the State of Connecticut*, was a member of the New Haven public parks commission and common council and served (1886, 1915–17) on commissions reporting on revisions of taxation methods. He was an associate justice and chief justice of the state supreme court; retiring from this position in 1910, he served (1910 *et seq.*) as Democratic governor of Connecticut. Among his writings are *A Digest of All the Reported Cases . . . of Conn.* (2 vols., 1871, 1882), *American Railroad Law* (1904), and *The Young Man and the Law* (1919).

Baldwin, Stanley. [Title, 1st Earl **Baldwin of Bewdley.**] b. Aug. 3, 1867; d. Dec. 14, 1947. British statesman and writer, remembered for his service in settlement of war debts with the U.S. after World War I and for his association with the abdication of Edward VIII (the Duke of Windsor) in 1936. A Conservative member of Parliament from 1908, he became prime minister in 1923, succeeding Bonar Law. Though succeeded (1924) by Ramsay MacDonald in a short-lived Labour government, he was again prime minister in the period 1924–29 (during which term in office occurred (1926) the general strike). During his third term (1935–37) as prime minister arose the crisis (1936) over the marriage and abdication of Edward VIII. After Baldwin's retirement (1937) from public office, a peerage was bestowed on him. He was chancellor of Cambridge University (1930–47). Author of *The Classics and the Plain Man* (1926), *On England and Other Essays* (1926), *Our Inheritance* (speeches, 1928), *This Torch of Freedom* (1935), *Peace and Goodwill in Industry* (1935), *Service of Our Lives* (1937), and *An Interpreter of England* (1939).

Baldwin, William. d. c1564. English divine, schoolmaster, philosopher, and poet. Author of *A Treatise of Moral Philosophy* (1547), *Canticles or Balades of Salomon* (1549, a verse translation of part of the Scriptures), *The Funeralles of King Edward the Sixt* (1560, an elegy), and *Beware the Cat* (1561, a satirical poem). He was associated with George Ferrers in publishing the famous Elizabethan collection of poems on the fall of great men *A Mirror for Magistrates* (1559; numerous subsequent editions). Baldwin's own work in the *Mirror* consists of four poems on Richard, the earl of Cambridge, Thomas Montague, the earl of Salisbury, William de La Pole, the duke of Suffolk, and Jack Cade.

Baldwin of Bewdley (būd'li), 1st Earl. See **Baldwin, Stanley.**

Baldwin of Redvers (red'vėrz). [Title, 1st Earl of **Devon.**] d. probably at Arreton, c1155. Anglo-Norman warrior. He raised revolts against King Stephen in Devonshire (1136) and, subsequent to this, in Normandy, held Corfe Castle against him (1139), and large tracts of land in Devonshire. He was a benefactor of religious houses.

Baldwin Park. Unincorporated community in S California, in Los Angeles County. Under the urban definition established for use in the 1950 census, Baldwin Park has been counted along with adjoining urban areas; its last official enumeration was 7,572 (1940).

Baldwinsville (bôld'winz.vil). Village in W central New York, in Onondaga County: manufactures include machinery, flour, and cellulose. 4,495 (1950).

Baldy Peak (bôl'di). Peak in the Sangre de Christo range, Colorado.

Baldy Peak. Peak, 12,623 ft. high, NE of Santa Fe, New Mexico, forming a part of the southernmost spur of the Rocky Mountains called the Santa Fe range.

Baldy Peak. See also under **Davis Mountains.**

Bâle (bäl). French name of **Basel.**

Bale (bāl), **John.** [Called **"Bilious Bale."**] b. at Cove, near Dunwich, Suffolk, England, Nov. 21, 1495; d. at Canterbury, England, 1563. English Protestant (originally Roman Catholic) prelate, bishop of Ossory (1552 *et seq.*). He was the author of morality plays and the compiler of a chronological catalogue of British writers, *Illustrium Majoris Britanniae Scriptorum Summarium* (1548). He was popularly called "Bilious Bale" on account of his bad temper.

Baleares (bä.lā.ä'rās). [Also, **Islas Baleares.**] Province of Spain, comprising the Balearic Islands in the Mediterranean Sea, E of Valencia. The major islands are Majorca, Minorca, Iviza, Cabrera, and Formentera. Iviza and Formentera are the ancient Pityusae islands. The climate is Mediterranean, the surface largely mountainous. Grain, wine, oil, and fruit are produced. The group was long a possession of Carthage, was acquired by Rome in 123 B.C., and formed the kingdom of Majorca from 1276 till its union with Aragon in 1343. Capital, Palma; area, 1,936 sq. mi.; pop. 436,427 (1950).

Balearic Islands (bal.ẹ.ar'ik). [Spanish, **Islas Baleares.**] Group of islands in the W Mediterranean, belonging to Spain: they form the province of Baleares, with the capital at Palma. The largest island is Majorca (or Mallorca), with the smaller island of Cabrera to the S. The island of Minorca and three smaller islands are to the E; to the W are Iviza and Formentera, the ancient Pityusae islands. The islands were in early antiquity visited by Phoenician and Greek seafarers who formed there a prehistoric civilization (the so-called Balearic culture). The Balearic Islands came under Carthaginian, then Roman overlordship; after the downfall of the Roman Empire, they were overrun by Vandals, Visigoths, and Franks; in 798 they were occupied by Arabs.

Balearis Major (bal.ē.ar'is mā'jọr). Ancient name of **Majorca.**

Baléchou (bȧ.lā.shö), **Jean Joseph Nicolas.** b. at Arles, France, c1715; d. at Avignon, France, Aug. 18, 1765. French engraver. His best work is a full-length portrait of Augustus III, king of Poland.

Balen (bä'lẹn). Town in N Belgium, in the province of Antwerp, E of Antwerp. 10,793 (1947).

Balen, Hendrik van. b. at Antwerp, 1575; d. there, July 17, 1632. Flemish historical painter.

Bales (bālz), **Peter.** [Latinized, **Balesius** (bạ.lē'zhus).] b. at London, 1547; d. c1610. English calligrapher who devised a system of shorthand known as "Brachigraphie." He presented Queen Elizabeth with a sample of his stenography mounted in a ring in 1575. A teacher of handwriting, he was also employed in transcribing public documents and in copying secret political correspondence.

Balesh (bä'lesh). Arabic name of **Elvas.**

Balestier (bal.ẹs.tir'), **Charles Wolcott.** b. at Rochester, N.Y., Dec. 13, 1861; d. at Dresden, Germany, Dec. 6, 1891. American editor, publisher, and novelist. He was graduated (1880) from the Rochester Free Academy, having worked as a reporter on the Rochester *Post-Express* while attending school. He attended Cornell University, and published his first novel, *A Potent Philtre*, in the New York *Tribune* in 1884, thereafter writing *A Fair Device* and a campaign biography of James G. Blaine (both appearing in 1884), and *A Victorious Defeat* (1886). He became (1885) editor of *Tid-Bits*, a weekly journal that was renamed (1886) *Time* and converted into an illustrated humorous publication. Having gone to England in 1888 on a copyright mission for his publisher, John W. Lovell, he formed a partnership with the London publisher William Heinemann and acted thereafter as managing director of Heinemann and Balestier. He also wrote *The Average Woman* (1892) and *Benefits Forgot* (1894) and collaborated with Rudyard Kipling on *The Naulahka* (1892).

Balestra (bä.les'trä), **Antonio.** b. at Verona, Italy, 1666; d. there, April 21, 1740. Italian painter of the Venetian school.

Baleswar (bal.ẹ.swär'). See **Balasore.**

Bâle-Ville (bäl.vēl). French name of **Basel-Stadt.**

Balfe (balf), **Michael William.** b. at Dublin, Ireland, May 15, 1808; d. at Rowney Abbey, Hertfordshire, England, Oct. 20, 1870. Operatic composer, violinist, and singer. His works include *I Rivali di se stessi* (1830), *Siege of Rochelle* (1835), *The Maid of Artois* (1836), *Catherine Grey* (1837), *Joan of Arc* (1837), *Diadeste* (1838), *Falstaff* (1838), *Keolanthe* (1841), *Le Puits d'amour* (1843), *The Bohemian Girl* (1843), *Les Quatre fils d'Aymon* (1844), *L'Etoile de Séville* (1845), *Maid of Honour* (1847), *Sicilian Bride* (1852), *Rose of Castile* (1857), *Satanella* (1858), and *Il Talismano*, an Italian version of his last opera, *The Knight of the Leopard* (1874). The well-known song *I dreamt I dwelt in marble halls* is from *The Bohemian Girl.*

Balfour (bal'för), **Alexander.** b. at Monikie, Forfarshire, Scotland, March 1, 1767; d. Sept. 12, 1829. Scottish poet and novelist. He wrote *Campbell, or the Scottish Probationer* (1819), *Contemplation and other Poems* (1820), *Farmer's Three Daughters* (1822), *The Foundling of Glenthorn, or the Smuggler's Cave* (1823), and *Highland Mary* (1827).

Balfour, Arthur James. [Title, 1st Earl of **Balfour.**] b. July 25, 1848; d. March 19, 1930. British Conservative statesman, known as the author of The Balfour Declaration; nephew of Robert Arthur Talbot Gascoyne-Cecil, the 3rd marquis of Salisbury. He was president of the Local Government Board (1885–86), secretary for Scotland (1886–87), chief secretary for Ireland (1887–91), first lord of the treasury and leader of the House of Commons (1891–92, 1895–1900, and 1900–06), and prime minister (1902–05). He served as member of Parliament for the eastern division of Manchester (1885–1906), and for the City of London (1906–11). He succeeded (1915) Winston Churchill as first lord of the admiralty. During a term (1916–19) as foreign secretary, he framed (1917) the Balfour Declaration favoring limited Jewish settlements in Palestine; this set the official British attitude on the mandate of Palestine for the next 30 years. He served as chief British delegate (1921–22) to the disarmament conference at Washington. Author of *Defense of Philosophic Doubt* (1879), *Essays and Addresses* (1893, 1905), *The Foundations of Belief* (1895), *Economic Notes on Insular Free Trade* (1903), *Reflections Suggested by the New Theory of Matter* (1904), *Speeches (1880–1905) on Fiscal Reform* (1906), *Criticism and Beauty* (Romanes lecture, 1909), and others.

Balfour, Clara Lucas. [Maiden name, **Liddell.**] b. in the New Forest, Hampshire, England, Dec. 21, 1808; d. at Croydon, England, July 3, 1878. English writer. She lectured on temperance and other topics, and was the author of numerous works designed chiefly to promote the temperance cause.

Balfour, Francis Maitland. b. at Edinburgh, Scotland, Nov. 10, 1851; d. in the Alps, probably on July 19, 1882. British biologist; brother of Arthur James Balfour. Lecturer (1876) on animal morphology and professor (1882) of the same subject at Cambridge, he wrote *Development of Elasmobranch Fishes* (1878) and *Comparative Embryology* (1880–81).

Balfour, Sir James. d. 1583. Scottish judge and political intriguer. He was implicated in the plot to assassinate David Beaton, and after the surrender of the castle of St. Andrew's (June, 1547) was imprisoned in the French galleys, where he had John Knox as a companion. He was also commonly reputed to have drawn up the bond for Darnley's murder, and to have provided the house, which belonged to his brother, in the Kirk o'Field, where the murder was accomplished. In the same year (1567) he was appointed by the queen, Mary Tudor, governor of Edinburgh Castle, which he shortly after betrayed to James Stuart, earl of Murray. He accomplished the destruction of the regent James Douglas, 4th earl of Morton, who was executed, in 1581 for the murder of Darnley. He was one of the authors, if not the chief author, of *Balfour's Practicks*, the earliest textbook on Scottish law.

Balfour, Sir James. b. 1600; d. 1657. Scottish antiquary and historian, author of *Annals of the History of Scotland from Malcolm III to Charles II.*

Balfour, James. b. at Pilrig, near Edinburgh, Scotland, 1705; d. 1795. Scottish philosophical writer, professor of moral philosophy (1754) and of law (1764) at Edinburgh.

Balfour, John Hutton. b. at Edinburgh, Scotland, Sept. 15, 1808; d. there, Feb. 11, 1884. Scottish botanist and physician. He was appointed professor of botany at Glasgow University in 1841, professor at Edinburgh in 1845, and emeritus professor in 1879. Author of a manual of botany (1848), a textbook (1852), *Phyto-Theology* (1851), and others.

Balfour, Mary. Maiden name of **Brunton, Mary.**

Balfour, Nisbet. b. at Dunbog, Fifeshire, Scotland, 1743; d. there, in October, 1823. British soldier, appointed lieutenant general in 1798 and general in 1803, conspicuous for his services in America during the Revolutionary War. He was at the battle of Bunker Hill, the battle of Long Island, the capture of New York, and the battles of Elizabethtown, Brandywine, and Germantown, and was appointed commandant of Charleston in 1779.

Balfour, Robert. b. c1550; d. c1625. Scottish philologist and philosophical writer, professor of Greek at the College of Guienne, Bordeaux, France, and principal (c1586) of that institution. He wrote *Commentaries on the Logic and Ethics of Aristotle* (1618–20) and others.

Balfour-Brown (bal′fėr.broun′, -fôr-), **William Alex Francis.** b. at London, Dec. 27, 1874—. English entomologist. He was a professor (1925–30) of entomology at the Imperial College of Science and Technology. Author of *Keys to the Orders of Insects*, *Textbook of Practical Entomology*, and *British Water-beetles*.

Balfour Declaration (bal′fôr). See under **Balfour, Arthur James.**

Balfour of Burleigh (bėr′li), 6th Baron. [Title of **Alexander Hugh Bruce.**] b. at Kennet, Alloa, Scotland, Jan. 13, 1849; d. at London, July 6, 1921. Scottish administrator. After serving as secretary for Scotland (1895–1904) in the British cabinet, and gaining note for legislation improving Scottish social welfare, he became (1896) lord rector of Edinburgh University. In 1900 he was named chancellor of St. Andrews University, and in 1917 chairman of the Carnegie trust for the universities of Scotland. Author of *An Historical Account of the Rise and Development of Presbyterianism in Scotland* (1911).

Balfour of Burley, John. Covenanter, a character in Sir Walter Scott's novel *Old Mortality*, historically taken from a real John Balfour of Kinloch, but by Scott confused with John Balfour of Burleigh (d. 1688). The latter was not a Covenanter.

Balfrush (bäl.frösh′). Former name of **Babul.**

Balgownie (bal.gou′ni), **Brig o'.** Picturesque structure at Aberdeen, Scotland, built in the form of a single high and wide-pointed arch across the Don, and dating from 1320.

Balhorn (bäl′hôrn), **Johann.** [Also, **Ballhorn.**] b. at Lübeck, Germany, c1530; d. 1603. German printer. His name has been perpetuated in the German verb *balhornisieren* or *verbalhornen*, meaning to change for the worse.

Bali (bä′lē). Mountainous and volcanic island of the Lesser Sunda group, E of Java, in the United States of Indonesia, the *negara* (state) of East Indonesia. Sugar is the most important crop; there are tourist resorts. The religion is a form of Hinduism, the language Malayo-Polynesian. Chief town, Singavadja; length, ab. 90 mi.; breadth, ab. 50 mi.; area, ab. 2,100 sq. mi.; pop. 950,000 (1930).

Bali. In Hindu mythology, a Daitya who had attained sovereignty over the three worlds, but lost it when he promised Vishnu, in his dwarf incarnation, as much land as he could measure with three strides. Vishnu met the condition, and banished Bali to the underworld, where he reigned.

Baliev (bä′lyif), **Nikita.** b. 1877; d. 1936. Russian vaudeville and cabaret producer who became internationally known for his colorful acting company, the *Chauve-Souris*, a revue which he developed from a traveling cabaret troupe in Russia in 1917. Originally at the Moscow Art Theater but in no way to be identified with that theater's realistic style, Baliev gave meticulous attention to an imaginative and tasteful burlesque style which entranced audiences at Paris (1920–22) and New York (1922–23), as well as at Constantinople, London, and many other cities. Baliev made many return tours to different countries. One of the Chauve-Souris numbers, "The Dance of the Wooden Soldiers," impishly satirical, became a favorite with the public on both sides of the Atlantic. Baliev played the role of *conferencier* or master of ceremonies at the Chauve-Souris performances and was, perhaps, the most entertaining member of his own company.

Balikesir (bä″li.ke.sėr′). [Turkish, **Balıkesir.**] *Il* (province or vilayet) in NW Turkey, comprising generally hilly land cut by several rich river valleys. Minerals include silver and gold; the largest crops are cereals, cotton, and fruits. Capital, Balikesir; area, 5,526 sq. mi.; pop. 563,100 (1950).

Balikesir. [Also: **Balikesri** (bä.li.kes′rē); Turkish, **Balıkesir.**] Town in NW Turkey in the *il* (province or vilayet) of Balikesir, ab. 112 mi. SE of Istanbul: an important commercial center served by three railway lines and three highways; exports silver, lead, and zinc. 36,001 (1950).

Balikpapan (bä′lik.pä′pän). Town and seaport in the C part of the United States of Indonesia, in SE Borneo, ab. 225 mi. NE of Bandjermasin: one of the principal export centers of the oil industry in Borneo. In World War II, a naval engagement was fought near here on Jan. 24, 1942, between Allied and Japanese naval units. A few days later the Japanese occupied Balikpapan and held it until July 3, 1945, when it was liberated by Australian forces. Pop. 29,843 (1930).

Balin (bä′lēn). In Hindu mythology, the monkey king of Kishkindhya, who was slain by Rama, and whose kingdom was given to his brother Sugriva, the ally of Rama.

Balin (bā′lin) and **Balan** (-lan). In the *Morte d'Arthur*, two brothers, born in Northumberland, each renowned for valor. Balin was called "Le Sauvage." They finally slew each other "by mishap," and were buried in one tomb.

Balin and Balan. Last of the *Idylls of the King* by Alfred Tennyson. Although written about 1870 it was not published until 1885, when it rounded out the cycle to twelve.

Baline (bạ.lēn′), **Israel.** Original name of **Berlin, Irving.**

Balinese (bä.li.nēz′, -nēs′, bal.i-). Malayo-Polynesian-speaking inhabitants of Bali and parts of Lombok in Indonesia. Their religion is a blending of Shivaistic Hinduism with Buddhist and aboriginal elements. Old Indian influences are strong in other aspects of culture as well. Their number was given in 1930 as 1,111,659.

Balingen (bä′ling.ẹn). Town in S Germany, in the *Land* (state) of Württemberg-Hohenzollern, French Zone, formerly in the Schwarzwald *Kreis* (district) of Württemberg, situated on the Eyach River, ab. 38 mi. SW of Stuttgart: leather, shoe, furniture, and metallurgical factories; grain and cattle trade. Much of the town burned down in 1809; only the late-Gothic *Stadtkirche* (town church) dates from as early as 1443. The population is predominantly Protestant. 6,831 (1946).

Balinghem (bȧ.laṅ.gaṅ). Village in N France, in the department of Pas-de-Calais, near Calais, noted as the place of the "Field of the Cloth of Gold" (1520).

Balintang Channel (bä.lēn.täng′). Sea passage separating the Batan Islands from the Babuyan Islands N of Luzon, Philippine Islands. It connects the South China Sea on the W with the Philippine Sea of the Pacific Ocean on the E.

Baliol (bāl′yọl, bā′li.ọl), **Edward de.** [Also, **Balliol.**] d. 1363. Claimant to the throne of Scotland; eldest son of John de Baliol and Isabel, daughter of John de Warenne, the earl of Surrey. He landed in Scotland in 1332, and after a brilliant campaign of seven weeks was crowned at Scone on Sept. 24, but three months later was surprised at Annan by Archibald Douglas, and driven across the border. He was restored by Edward III of England, through whose assistance he won the battle of Halidon Hill, on July 19, 1333. After 1338, Edward being occupied in war with the French, Baliol maintained a nominal footing in Scotland until the return of David Bruce in 1341.

Baliol, John de. [Also, **Balliol.**] d. c1269. Founder of Balliol College, Oxford. He was a regent of Scotland during the minority of Alexander III, until deprived of the post, on a charge of treason, in 1255, through the influence of Henry III, with whom he sided in the barons' war (1263–65). He gave (c1263) the first lands for the endowment of the college which bears his name, an endowment which was increased by his will, and also by the gifts of his widow Devorguilla.

Baliol, John de. [Also, **Balliol.**] b. 1249; d. 1315. King of Scotland; son of John de Baliol (d. 1269). With Robert the Bruce and John Hastings he became one of the principal claimants to the Scottish crown on the death of Margaret (the Maid of Norway) in 1290, basing his claim upon the right of his maternal grandmother, Margaret, eldest daughter of David, earl of Huntingdon, who was brother of William the Lion and grandson of David I. He was recognized as the rightful heir by Edward I of England, to whom the claims of the disputants were referred for arbitration; he was crowned at Scone on Nov. 30, 1292, and rendered homage to Edward as his feudal superior. He made an alliance with Philip the Fair of France in 1295, ravaged Cumberland in 1296, and renounced his allegiance to Edward. Compelled to renounce his crown to Edward during the latter's invasion of Scotland the same year, he was imprisoned (with his son Edward) in England until 1299, and died in exile.

Balisand (bal.i.sand'). Novel by Joseph Hergesheimer, published in 1924.

Balisarda (bä.lē.sär'dä). In Lodovico Ariosto's *Orlando Furioso*, the sword stolen from Orlando by Brunello and given to Rogero. It could cut through even enchanted objects.

Bali Strait (bä'lē). Strait in Indonesia which separates Java from Bali, and connects the Java Sea with the Indian Ocean. Length, ab. 30 mi.; width, ab. 8 mi.

Baliuag (bä.lē'wäg). Town in Bulacan province, in S central Luzon, Philippine Islands. 3,535 (1948).

Balize (ba.lēz'). See **British Honduras.**

Balkan Crisis of 1908 (bôl'kan). Crisis which culminated in the outright annexation by Austria of Bosnia-Hercegovina. Russia had agreed to this on condition that the straits between the Black Sea and the Mediterranean were opened to its battleships, but got no support for such unilateral settlement from France or Great Britain. Austria refused to bring the matter to mediation and held the provinces, since Serbia was not strong enough itself to withstand the annexation. The crisis, which exacerbated Serbian-Austrian relations, was nevertheless a diplomatic victory for Austria and Germany.

Balkan Entente. Relationship established by the treaty of Feb. 9, 1934, between Turkey, Greece, Yugoslavia, and Rumania. It guaranteed existing frontiers and consolidated common policies.

Balkan Peninsula. In its widest sense, the southeasternmost peninsula of Europe, including the regions S of the Sava and Danube rivers. It comprises Yugoslavia, Albania, Bulgaria, part of Rumania, European Turkey, and Greece, which are sometimes called the Balkan States.

Balkans (bôl'kanz). [Also: **Balkan Mountains;** Bulgarian, **Stara Planina;** Latin, **Haemus.**] Mountain system in SE Europe, chiefly in Bulgaria, which extends from the sources of the Timok River (near the frontiers of Yugoslavia and Bulgaria) generally E to Cape Emine on the Black Sea. It formed the main boundary between Bulgaria proper and Eastern Rumelia (a province under the Ottoman Empire until 1885). The chief passes are the Karnobat, Trevna, Shipka, and Troyan. The Balkans were the scene of severe fighting in the Russo-Turkish wars of 1828–29 and 1877–78. Its highest point is ab. 7,800 ft.

Balkan War (1912–13) (bôl'kan). [Called the **First Balkan War.**] War that commenced in the fall of 1912 between Bulgaria, Greece, Montenegro, and Serbia, on the one hand, and Turkey on the other. The military forces of the allied Balkan nations were able practically to drive the Turks out of Europe. By the terms of the Treaty of London (May 13, 1913), which ended the war, Turkey lost all of her European territories except Constantinople, the Dardanelles, Gallipoli, and immediately surrounding areas.

Balkan War (1913). [Called the **Second Balkan War.**] War that commenced in 1913 between Bulgaria, on the one hand, and Serbia and Greece on the other, with Turkey and Rumania coming in later against Bulgaria. Hostilities broke out initially as a result of territorial rivalry between Serbia and Bulgaria: the Treaty of London (May 13, 1913), which ended the Balkan War (1912–13), had awarded to newly independent Albania territory which cut off Serbian access to the sea, and Serbia thereupon sought a portion of the Macedonian territory awarded to Bulgaria. This and other factors led to a surprise attack (June 30, 1913) by Bulgaria on Serbia and Greece. Bulgaria was, after a few initial successes, unable to withstand the combined forces of the other nations involved, and a peace was signed (Aug. 10, 1913) at Bucharest. By this treaty Bulgaria lost a large part of Dobruja and practically all of Macedonia. Virtually no Balkan problems were solved by this war, or by its predecessor: Bulgaria and Turkey both awaited the day when they could regain lost territory, and Austria-Hungary had been convinced that the threat presented to Austro-Hungarian territory by exponents of "Greater Serbia" would be eliminated only when Serbia had been decisively defeated.

Balkh (bälċh). Mountainous desert region in C Asia, belonging to Afghanistan, S of the Amu Darya (river) and N of the Hindu Kush mountains. It ranges in elevation from 1,000 to 12,000 ft. and corresponds nearly to the ancient Bactria. Its inhabitants are of Uzbek stock.

Balkh. Town in SW Asia, in N Afghanistan, ab. 200 mi. NW of Kabul. Ancient Balkh is supposed by most authorities to have been the capital of the ancient country of Bactria. It was the center of Zoroastrianism, and Zoroaster is said to have died there; later Buddhism became the prevailing religion, and still later Mohammedanism. Balkh, which its natives call "Mother of Cities," anciently rivaled Ecbatana, Nineveh, and Babylon. It was conquered by Cyrus the Great and by Alexander the Great; destroyed by Genghis Khan in the 13th century and by Tamerlane in the 14th century; and yet Marco Polo in the 15th century called it "a noble city and a great." After an epidemic of cholera in the 19th century it dwindled to a village, but just north of the site of this a new town of Balkh has arisen. The caravan route passing through Balkh has been for many centuries and still is an important trade route between Iran and other countries to the west, India to the south and east, and China to the east. There is a small bazaar at Balkh, and farming and grazing are carried on in the vicinity. Pop. variously estimated from 6,000 to 10,000.

Balkhan Mountains (bäl.ċhän'). Group of mountains in the U.S.S.R., in the Turkmen Soviet Socialist Republic, E of the Caspian Sea, near the Trans-Caspian railway. They run NW and SE for ab. 150 mi.

Balkhash (bäl.ċhäsh'). [Also: **Ak-Denghiz, Ala-Denghiz, Balkash, Dengis;** Turkic, **Balqash.**] Lake in the U.S.S.R., in the Kazakh Soviet Socialist Republic, C Asia. Its chief tributary is the Ili River. It has no outlet. The water is saline on the E margins; elsewhere it is suitable for drinking. Elevation, ab. 780 ft.; length, ab. 400 mi.; greatest width, ab. 55 mi.; area, ab. 6,700 sq. mi.

Balkhash. [Turkic, **Balqash.**] City in W Asia, in the SW U.S.S.R., in the E part of the Kazakh Soviet Socialist Republic, in the Russian Soviet Federated Socialist Republic, on the N shore of Lake Balkhash. The terminus of a rail line to Akmolinsk, it serves as a shipping point for products of the copper-smelting works in the vicinity. Pop. ab. 70,000.

Balkis (bal'kis). Arabic name, used in the Koran, of the Queen of Sheba.

Ball (bôl), **Albert.** b. at Boylston, Mass., May 7, 1835; d. at Claremont, N.H., Feb. 7, 1927. American engineer and inventor, noted as patentee of the first cartridge-greasing machine and for his outstanding improvements in quarrying and mining machinery. After serving his apprenticeship as a machinist at Worcester, Mass., he brought out as his first invention (1863) a combined single-loading and repeating rifle. The patent was purchased by E. G. Lamson, of Windsor, Vt., whose plant Ball entered in order to supervise the manufacture of his rifle. He resigned in 1868 to devote himself to the development of a diamond-drill channeling machine for quarrying stone. In 1873 Ball, Upham, and others organized the Sullivan Machine Company, of which Ball served as chief mechanical engineer until his retirement in 1914. Among his approximately 135 inventions are the diamond core-drill, first used in opening the South African gold fields, air-driven coal-picking machines, continuous cutting-chain coal-mining machines, presses for making asphalt paving blocks, and a cloth-measuring machine.

Ball, Ephraim. b. in Lake township, Stark County, Ohio, Aug. 12, 1812; d. Jan. 1, 1872. American manufacturer and inventor. Having joined his brothers in the manufacture of agricultural machinery at Greentown, Ohio, he used his own designs in making his "Blue Plough," which sold so widely that he was able to turn to the manufacture of the "Hussey Reaper" and several threshers. In 1851 he became a partner in Ball, Aultman and Company, and the firm's plant was moved to Canton, Ohio, where Ball contributed to the design of the "Ohio Mower." He sold his interest and patent rights to his partners and, setting up his own establishment, turned out his "New American Harvester," making as many as 10,000 in one year. His principal contribution was in the "Ohio Mower," the initial two-wheeled type with flexible finger bar.

Ball (bäl), **Hugo.** b. at Pirmasens, Germany, Feb. 22, 1886; d. at St. Abbondio, Switzerland, Sept. 14, 1927. German writer on religious subjects. A fervent Catholic, he was the author of *Zur Kritik der deutschen Intelligenz* (1919), *Das byzantinische Christentum* (1923), and *Folgen der Reformation* (1924). He also wrote *Hermann Hesse und sein Werk* (1927). He was active also in dadaism during its early period at Zurich.

Ball (bôl), **John.** [Called the **"Mad Priest."**] d. at St. Albans, England, July 15, 1381. English priest who took a prominent part in Wat Tyler's rebellion in 1381. He accepted, in the main, the doctrines of John Wycliffe, modified by views of his own, and made himself popular, especially by preaching the equality of gentry and villeins. He was several times committed to the archbishop of Canterbury's prison, and was excommunicated by the archbishop Simon Islip. He was committed, probably about the end of April, 1381, to the archbishop's prison at Maidstone, and one of the first acts of the insurgents was to set him at liberty. He preached at Blackheath on the text "When Adam dalf [delved], and Eve span, Who was thanne [then] a gentilman?" After the death of Wat Tyler at Smithfield (now part of London), he fled to the midland counties, but was taken at Coventry, and executed at St. Albans in the presence of the king.

Ball, John. b. at Hoylake, England, 1863; d. at Holywell, Wales, Dec. 2, 1940. English golfer. He won the British amateur championship eight times (1888, 1890, 1892, 1894, 1899, 1907, 1910, 1912). The first amateur to win the open championship (1890) and both the open and amateur championships in one year (1890), he also won the Irish open championship in 1893, 1894, and 1899.

Ball, Mary. b. in Lancaster County, Virginia, 1708; d. August 25, 1789. Second wife of Augustine Washington (married 1730) and the mother of George Washington.

Ball, Sir **Robert Stawell.** b. at Dublin, Ireland, July 1, 1840; d. at Cambridge, England, Nov. 25, 1913. Irish professor, astronomer, and scientific writer. Educated at Trinity College, Dublin, he was professor of mathematics (1867–74) at the Dublin Royal College of Science, professor of astronomy (1874–92) at the University of Dublin, royal astronomer of Ireland (1874–92), and professor of astronomy and geometry (1893–1913) at Cambridge University. He was elected a fellow of the Royal Society in 1873, lectured and traveled in America (1884, 1887, 1901), and was knighted in 1886. Author of scientific works, both popular and technical, including *The Theory of Screws: a Study in the Dynamics of a Rigid Body* (1876), *Story of the Heavens* (1886 and many later editions), *Story of the Sun* (1893), *Great Astronomers* (1895), *A Treatise on the Theory of Screws* (1900), *The Earth's Beginnings* (1901), *Popular Guide to the Heavens* (1905), and *Treatise on Spherical Astronomy.*

Ball, The. Comedy by James Shirley and George Chapman, licensed in 1632 and published in 1639.

Ball, Thomas. b. at Charlestown, Mass., June 3, 1819; d. Dec. 11, 1911. American sculptor, noted for his equestrian statue of George Washington in the Public Garden at Boston. Largely self-taught as an artist, he spent the early part of his career as a painter, beginning his important work as a sculptor after going to Italy in 1854. His execution of the statue of Washington took three years; the monumental model was finished in 1864 but was not cast until 1869. Much of his sculpture was made in Italy, where he modeled *Emancipation,* the statue of Edwin Forrest, and *Eve Stepping into Life.* Among his other works are the Chickering monument (1872) at Mount Auburn Cemetery, Cambridge, Mass., *Saint John the Evangelist* (1875, now the Oliver Ditson monument at Forest Hills Cemetery), the statue of Daniel Webster in Central Park, New York, and the Josiah Quincy statue at Boston. His autobiography is *My Threescore Years and Ten* (1891).

Ball, Valentine. b. at Dublin, Ireland, July 14, 1843; d. June 16, 1895. British geologist and explorer. He was appointed to the staff of the geological survey of India in 1864, was professor of geology and mineralogy at the University of Dublin, 1881–83, and became director of the Science and Art Museum at Dublin in 1883.

Balla (bäl′lä), **Giacomo.** b. at Turin, Italy, 1871—. Italian futurist painter noted chiefly for his *Dog on a Leash.* He worked at Rome and exhibited with the first futurist show at Paris (1911).

Ballachulish (bä.lä.ċhö′lish). [Also, **Ballahulish** (-hö′lish).] Village in C Scotland, in Argyllshire, situated on Loch Leven, ab. 23 mi. NE of Oban, ab. 525 mi. N of London by rail. There are extensive slate quarries nearby. Ballachulish was the scene of the murder of the Macdonalds in 1692 by the Campbells. 727 (1931).

Balladino (bal.ạ.dē′nō), **Antonio.** In Ben Jonson's comedy *The Case is Altered,* a "pageant poet" intended to ridicule Anthony Munday.

Ballad of Bouillabaisse (böl.yạ.bās′), **The.** See **Bouillabaisse, The Ballad of.**

Ballad of Reading Gaol (red′ing jāl), **The.** Poem (1898) by Oscar Wilde. It was written, as evidenced by Wilde's letters, under the impulse of intense emotion and is moving in its expression of sympathy for outcasts from society. Inspired by a term of imprisonment which he served during his later life, the poem is now generally considered to be Wilde's best.

Ballad of the Scottish King. Ballad by John Skelton. It was based on the battle of Flodden (1513) and is thought to have been the earliest printed English ballad.

Ballad of William Sycamore. Poem (1923) by Stephen Vincent Benét.

Ballads and Lyrics. Collection of poems (1891) by Katharine Tynan.

Ballads and Lyrics of Old France. Volume of poems (1872) by Andrew Lang.

Ballads and Other Poems. Collection of poems (1841) by Henry Wadsworth Longfellow.

Ballads and Other Poems. Volume of poems (1880) by Alfred Tennyson.

Ballads and Poems of Tragic Life. Volume of poems (1887) by George Meredith.

Ballads and Songs. Volume of poems (1894) by John Davidson.

Ballads and Sonnets. Volume of poems (1881) by Dante Gabriel Rossetti. It was his last published work.

Ballagi (bôl′lô.gē), **Maurice.** [Original name, **Moritz Bloch.**] b. March 18, 1815; d. Sept. 1, 1891. Hungarian philologist and Protestant theologian, best known for his grammars and dictionaries of the Hungarian language.

Ballam (bäl′ạm). See **Bullom.**

Ballance (bal′ạns), **John.** b. at Glenavy, County Antrim, Ireland, March 27, 1839; d. at Wellington, New Zealand, April 27, 1893. New Zealand political leader and premier. An ironmonger, he spent a period in Australia before going (1865) to New Zealand where he became a shopkeeper and newspaper proprietor at Wanganui. He served in the Maori Wars, and was first elected to the New Zealand Parliament in 1875. He first achieved a cabinet post under Sir George Grey, whose political heir he became. He became leader of the Liberals in 1889; as premier (1891 *et seq.*), he initiated the great period of Liberal social reform that won New Zealand international fame. He died in office.

Ballantine (bal′ạn.tīn), **James.** b. at Edinburgh, Scotland, 1808; d. there, in December, 1877. Scottish poet, painter on glass, and manufacturer of stained glass. He wrote *The Gaberlunzie's Wallet* (1843), *The Miller of Deanhaugh* (1845), *Essay on Ornamental Art* (1847), *Poems* (1856), and others.

Ballantine, William. b. at London, 1812; d. at Margate, England, 1887. English lawyer, chiefly remembered for his conviction of the murderer Franz Müller (1864), his defense of the claimant in the Tichborne trial (1871), and his defense of Mulhar Rao, the Gaekwar of Baroda (1875). His honorarium of ten thousand pounds for winning an acquittal on the charge of attempted poisoning against the Gaekwar ranks with the largest ever paid to a British counsel.

Ballantrae (bal'ạn.trā). Civil parish and fishing village in S Scotland, in Ayrshire, situated at the mouth of the river Stinchar, ab. 12 mi. SW of Girvan. 1,076 (1931).

Ballantyne (bal'ạn.tīn), **James.** b. at Kelso, Scotland, 1772; d. Jan. 17, 1833. Scottish publisher; friend and business associate of Sir Walter Scott. He printed the first two volumes of the *Border Minstrelsy* and subsequently published other works by Scott, who became his secret partner in 1805. He was ruined financially in 1826; he later edited the *Weekly Journal.*

Ballantyne, John. See also **Bellenden, John.**

Ballantyne, John. b. at Kelso, Scotland, 1774; d. at Edinburgh, Scotland, June 16, 1821. Scottish writer and publisher; brother of James Ballantyne (1772–1833). He was an associate of his brother in the Edinburgh publishing and bookselling establishment of John Ballantyne and Company, publishers of novels by Sir Walter Scott.

Ballantyne, Robert Michael. b. at Edinburgh, Scotland, April 24, 1825; d. 1894. British writer of juveniles. He was in the service (1841–47) of the Hudson Bay Company. Among his 80 volumes are *Hudson's Bay* (1848), *Ungava* (1857), and *The Gorilla Hunters* (1862). He was also the author of *Personal Recollections* (1893).

Ballantyne, Thomas. b. at Paisley, Scotland, 1806; d. at London, Aug. 30, 1871. Scottish editor, journalist, and social reformer, active in London. He was the editor at various times of the Bolton *Free Press*, Manchester *Guardian*, Manchester *Examiner*, Liverpool *Journal*, *Mercury*, the London *Leader*, the London *Statesman* (which he founded), and *Old St. James's Chronicle.* Interested in social and political questions, he associated himself with Richard Cobden and John Bright during the 1840's in agitating for repeal of the Corn Laws. Author of various papers; compiler of *Passages Selected from the Writings of Thomas Carlyle, with a Biographical Memoir* (1855, 1870); author of *Ideas, Opinions, and Facts* (1865) and *Essays in Mosaic* (1870). As part of his propaganda activity he wrote the *Corn Law Repealer's Handbook* (1841).

Ballarat (bal.ạ.rat'). City in SE Australia, in the state of Victoria, ab. 66 mi. NW of Melbourne. In its vicinity are celebrated gold mines, discovered in 1851. It has in recent years been surpassed by Geelong as the second largest city of the state. It consists of Ballarat East and Ballarat West. 40,214 (1947).

Ballard (bal'ạrd), **John.** d. at London, 1586. English Jesuit priest, famous for his connection with the Babington conspiracy to assassinate Queen Elizabeth. When his conspiratorial activity was revealed by Gilbert Gifford's betrayal, he was racked and disemboweled.

Ballard, Philip Boswood. b. at Maesteg, Glamorganshire, Wales, Feb. 13, 1865—. British child psychologist. He was an inspector (1906–30) for the education department of the London County Council. Author of *Obliviscence and Reminiscence* (1913), *Mental Tests* (1920), and *Teaching and Testing English* (1939).

Ballari (bạ.lä'rē). See **Bellary.**

Ballenden (bal'ẹn.dẹn), **John.** See **Bellenden, John.**

Ballenstedt (bäl'ẹn.shtet). Town in C Germany, in the *Land* (state) of Saxony-Anhalt, Russian Zone, formerly in Anhalt, situated at the foot of the Lower Harz mountains, ab. 36 mi. SW of Magdeburg. It was formerly a popular place of residence for retired government officials and army officers. There are a number of educational institutions, a museum, and a library. The *Nikolaikirche* (Church of Saint Nicholas) is in the Gothic style; the *Rathaus* (town hall) dates from the 16th century. Ballenstedt has a castle, the former residence of the dukes of Anhalt-Bernburg, erected in the 18th century. 10,538 (1946).

Ballhorn (bäl'hôrn), **Johann.** See **Balhorn, Johann.**

Ballia (bal'i.ạ). District in the Benares division, Uttar Pradesh, Union of India: sugar, rice, and wheat. Area, 1,183 sq. mi.; pop. 1,053,880 (1941).

Ballin (bäl'in), **Albert.** b. at Hamburg, Germany, Aug. 15, 1857; committed suicide there, Nov. 9, 1918. German shipowner. He reorganized the Hamburg-Amerika steamship line, and negotiated many agreements designed to eliminate the intense and wasteful competition then prevalent among the great international shipping lines. A leader in German economic life, and an intimate of Kaiser Friedrich Wilhelm II, he opposed the annexationists during World War I. He committed suicide after Germany's military collapse.

Ballin (bal'in), **Hugo.** b. at New York, March 7, 1879—. American mural painter, author, and motion-picture producer, noted especially for his murals in the state capitol, Madison, Wis., and the B'nai B'rith Temple, Los Angeles. He studied at the Art Students League of New York, and at Rome and Florence. His work has been exhibited in the U.S. and South America, and he has won many prizes. He has written a number of books, including *The First Fifty Years Are the Hardest, Broken Toy,* and *Stigma;* he has produced such films as *Jane Eyre, Journey's End,* and *Vanity Fair;* among his paintings are *The European Sybil, The Lesson, Under the Pergola,* and *The Lute Player.*

Ballina (bal'i.nạ). Urban district, market town, and seaport in Connacht province, Irish Republic, in County Mayo, situated on the river Moy, ab. 2 mi. from its mouth, ab. 19 mi. NE of Castlebar. It exports eggs, livestock, timber, and mineral water, and imports coal and general cargo. Ballina was taken by the French in August, 1798. Pop. 6,225 (1951).

Ballinasloe (bal"i.nạ.slō'). Urban district and market town in Connacht province, Irish Republic, in County Galway, situated on the river Suck, ab. 35 mi. E of Galway City. 5,597 (1951).

Balling (bäl'lēng), **Karl Joseph Napoleon.** b. at Gabrielshütte, Saaz (now Žatec), Bohemia, April 21, 1805; d. at Prague, March 17, 1868. Bohemian chemist.

Ballinger (bal'in.jėr). City in C Texas, county seat of Runnels County, on the Colorado River, SW of Dallas: cotton, grain, and other agricultural products. 5,302 (1950).

Ballinger, Richard Achilles. b. at Boonesboro, Iowa, July 9, 1858; d. at Seattle, Wash., June 6, 1922. American lawyer, politician, and U.S. secretary of the interior, noted for his role in the controversy (1909 *et seq.*) over the conservation of U.S. public lands. He was graduated (1884) from Williams College; admitted to the bar in 1886, he set up a law practice in the newly established state of Washington. He served (1894) as superior judge of Jefferson County, and was mayor (1904–06) of Seattle. He was federal commissioner (1907–08) of the General Land Office and was appointed (1909) secretary of the interior by President Taft. The noted Ballinger-Pinchot Controversy (*q.v.*) was set off by the charge, made by Louis R. Glavis, a Public Land Office field man, that Ballinger was obstructing the examination of allegedly unfair claims by private financial interests to Alaskan lands believed to contain rich coal deposits, and also by an apparent reversal of Gifford Pinchot's conservation program in Wyoming and Montana. When President Taft authorized (1909) Ballinger to remove Glavis from the federal service, the insurgent Republicans converted the case into a *cause célèbre* which, despite its political significance, was at bottom a test of the Taft administration's willingness to continue the conservation policies laid down by Theodore Roosevelt. The battle reached its climax during the hearings before a joint Congressional committee in 1910. The committee, like Taft in 1909, vindicated Ballinger, who nevertheless resigned in March, 1911, and resumed his law practice at Seattle.

Ballinger-Pinchot Controversy (bal'in.jėr.pin'shō). Much publicized and politically significant dispute (1909–11) between Richard A. Ballinger, secretary of the interior under President Taft, and Gifford Pinchot, chief forester of the Department of Agriculture. Public lands containing important water sites in Wyoming and Montana had been withdrawn from sale by Theodore Roosevelt as part of Pinchot's conservation program. Ballinger and Taft reopened them for sale, and were accused by Pinchot of favoring the power interests. At the same time (1909), Louis R. Glavis, an investigator attached to the Public Land Office, was dismissed after accusing Ballinger of favoring the claims of the Cunningham syndicate to Alaskan lands said to contain rich coal deposits. Pinchot defended Glavis and was also dismissed, sharpening the division between progressive and conservative forces within the Republican Party. A Congressional investigating committee exonerated Ballinger, but the weight of general public opinion (which was overwhelmingly in favor at that time of the policies established by Gifford Pinchot, under Theodore Roosevelt) unquestionably had much to do with his resignation in March, 1911.

Ballinrobe (bal.in.rōb'). Market town in Connacht province, Irish Republic, in County Mayo, situated on the river Robe, ab. 17 mi. SE of Castlebar. 1,351 (1936).

Balliol (bāl'yọl, bā'li.ọl), **Edward de.** See **Baliol, Edward de.**

Balliol, John de. See **Baliol, John de.**

Balliol College. College of Oxford University, England, founded between 1263 and 1268 through a gift of land from John de Baliol. The oldest of the existing buildings dates from the 15th century.

Ballivián (bä.yē.Byän'), **Adolfo.** b. at La Paz, Bolivia, Nov. 17, 1831; d. in February, 1874. Bolivian politician; son of General José Ballivián. He was a colonel in the army, but headed the party of opposition to the military rulers who for a long time governed Bolivia, and was kept in exile until his party elected him president in 1873. He died soon after his inauguration.

Ballivián, Hugo. b. c1902—. Bolivian army officer and administrator, president of Bolivia (1951–52). When an army junta took control of the government after an election deadlock in which it appeared that Victor Paz Estenssoro would again become president through the complexities of Bolivian election law, General Ballivián, who had become famous during the Chaco War, was named president. Within less than a year, however, the followers of Paz Estenssoro organized a revolt and, in April, 1952, the junta was overthrown and Ballivián went into exile in Chile.

Ballivián, José. b. at La Paz, Bolivia, in May, 1804; d. at Rio de Janeiro, 1852. Bolivian soldier and politician; father of Adolfo Ballivián. In 1841 he headed the army which defended Bolivia against the invasion of the Peruvian president Agustín Gamarra, winning the battle of Ingavi (Nov. 20, 1841), in which Gamarra was killed; soon after, he was elected president of Bolivia, holding the office until the end of 1847, when he was deposed by the revolutionist Manuel Isidoro Belzú, and exiled.

Ballo in Maschera (bäl'lō ēn mäs'kā.rä), **Un.** [Eng. trans., *"A Masked Ball."*] Opera by Giuseppe Verdi, with a libretto by Antonio Somma, first produced at Rome, Feb. 17, 1859. It was originally called *Gustavo III*, but at the time of its rehearsals Felice Orsini made his attempt (1858) to kill Napoleon III, and the title was thought too topical, since Gustavus III had met his death by assassination.

Ballon d'Alsace (bȧ.lôṅ dȧl.zȧs). [German, **Welscher Belchen.**] Mountain peak in NE France, one of the principal summits of the Vosges Mountains, near the border of Haut-Rhin and Vosges departments, in Alsace, ab. 25 mi. NW of Mulhouse. 4,080 ft.

Ballon de Guebwiller (dẹ geb.vē.ler). [Also: **Vallon de Soultz**; German, **Gebweiler Belchen, Sulzer Belchen.**] Mountain peak in NE France, the highest summit of the Vosges Mountains, in Haut-Rhin department, W of Guebwiller and N of Thann. Elevation, ab. 4,680 ft.

Ballonius (bạ.lō'ni.us). Latinized surname of **Baillou, Guillaume de.**

Balloon Hoax, The. Story by Edgar Allan Poe, published (April 13, 1844) in the New York *Sun*. Although it purported to be a straight news story, *The Balloon Hoax* is actually a fictitious account of eight men who crossed the ocean in a balloon filled with coal gas.

Ballot (bä.lôt'), **Buys-.** See **Buys-Ballot, Christoph Heinrich Diedrich.**

Ballou (bạ.lö'), **Adin.** b. at Cumberland, R.I., April 23, 1803; d. Aug. 5, 1890. American Universalist clergyman, reformer, writer, and founder of the Hopedale Community, noted 19th-century Christian Utopian colony. Displaying an ardent religious nature at an early age, he joined (c1821) the Universalists. In 1823 he was a preacher at Mendon, Bellingham, Medway, and Boston, served with the Universalist society at Milford (1824, 1828 *et seq.*) and with the Prince Street association at New York in 1827. He was one of the founders of the Massachusetts Association of Universal Restorationists (1831–41), whose principles he supported in the *Independent Messenger* (1831–39). In 1841 Ballou, whose social viewpoint was radical, joined 31 like-minded individuals in setting up the Hopedale Community, in the town of Milford. He was Hopedale's first president and edited its publication, *The Practical Christian.* He became pastor when the community was combined (1868) with the Hopedale Paris (Unitarian), holding that post until 1880. His last years were devoted to literary and pastoral efforts. Among his works are *Memoir of Adin Augustus Ballou* (1853), *Practical Christian Socialism* (1854), *Primitive Christianity and its Corruptions* (1870), *History of the Town of Milford* (1882), *Autobiography* (1896), and *History of the Hopedale Community* (1897), the last two edited by W. S. Heywood.

Ballou, Hosea. b. at Richmond, N.H., April 30, 1771; d. June 7, 1852. American Universalist clergyman and editor; great-uncle of Hosea Ballou (1796–1861). The son of a Baptist preacher, he joined (1789) the Baptist Church; in 1791 he was excommunicated because of doctrinal differences and joined the Universalists, becoming an itinerant teacher and preacher. He was ordained (1794) and, settling at Dana, Mass., devoted himself to circuit preaching (1796–1803). He later moved to Barnard, Vt., riding the circuit again from 1803 to 1809. His place in the formative period of Universalism is apparent in his *Notes on the Parables* (1804) and *Treatise on the Atonement* (1805), influential in their day. In 1809 he took a pastorate at Portsmouth, N.H., helped form (1811) a ministerial association at Gloucester, and aided in the founding (1811) of the first Universalist periodical, the *Gospel Visitant.* His most important period began in 1818, when he took the pastorate of the Second Universalist Church on School Street in Boston, a position he held until his death. He was editor (1819–28) of the weekly *Universalist Magazine* and editor (1830 *et seq.*) of a bimonthly, the *Universalist Expositor.*

Ballou, Hosea. b. at Guilford, Vt., Oct. 18, 1796; d. May 27, 1861. American Universalist clergyman, editor, author, and college president; grandnephew of Hosea Ballou (1771–1852). Ordained a pastor (1817) at Stafford, Conn., he became an itinerant preacher and in 1821 became pastor of the New Universalist Church at Roxbury, Mass., a post he held for 17 years, meanwhile conducting a private school for boys. In 1838, he took a pastorate at Medford, Mass., where he directed a similar private school. He helped edit the *Universalist Magazine* (1822), the *Universalist Expositor* (1830–40), and the *Universalist Quarterly and General Review* (1844–56). He was the author of a pioneer work, the *Ancient History of Universalism* (1829), which went through four editions. He served (1854–61) as the first president of Tufts College.

Ballou, Maturin Murray. b. at Boston, Mass., April 14, 1820; d. at Cairo, Egypt, March 27, 1895. American journalist, author, and traveler; son of Hosea Ballou (1771–1852). He began writing (c1839) for the *Olive Branch.* He founded and edited *Gleason's Pictorial* (later named *Ballou's Pictorial*), which was among the first illustrated papers in the U.S.; he was also the first editor and manager (1872–74) of the Boston *Daily Globe.* At one time he was deputy navy agent in the Boston Custom House. He spent much time traveling abroad, and in 1882 circled the globe. Writing under the pseudonym "Lieut. Murray," he produced several novels, among them *Red Rupert, the American Buccaneer* (1845) and *The Spanish Musketeer* (1847). His many travel books include *Due West; or Round the World in Ten Months* (1884), *Due South; or Cuba Past and Present* (1885), and *Under the Southern Cross; or Travels in Australia, Tasmania, New Zealand, Samoa, and Other Pacific Islands* (1888).

Ball's Bluff. Bluff in Virginia, on the Potomac River ab. 33 mi. NW of Washington, D.C. Here, on Oct. 21, 1861, ab. 1,900 Union troops were defeated by the Confederates under General N. G. Evans. Union loss, 894; Confederate loss, 302.

Ballston Spa (bôl'stọn spä). Village in E New York, county seat of Saratoga County, ab. 6 mi. SW of Saratoga Springs: tanneries and knitting mills. It was famous as a health resort in pre-Civil war days. 4,937 (1950).

Bally-. Ab element in many Irish place names, from *baile*, meaning "town."

Ballycastle (bal.i.kȧs'l). Urban district, seaport, and market town in Ulster province, Northern Ireland, in

County Antrim, situated on Ballycastle Bay, ab. 44 mi. NW of Belfast. It is the lawn-tennis center of Northern Ireland, the courts being laid out in what was once a harbor. The Giant's Causeway lies ab. 12 mi. W of here. One of the few coal fields of Ireland is in the vicinity of Ballycastle. 2,208 (1937).

Ballymena (bal.i.mē′nạ). Municipal borough and market town in Ulster province, Northern Ireland, in County Antrim, situated on the river Braid, ab. 23 mi. NW of Belfast. It is an important linen-manufacturing center, and also manufactures woolens, especially tweeds and blankets. Except for Belfast, Ballymena is the largest town in County Antrim. 14,000 (est. 1949).

Ballymoney (bal.i.mō′ni). Urban district and market town in Ulster province, Northern Ireland, in County Antrim, situated on a small tributary of the river Bann, ab. 41 mi. NW of Belfast. 2,903 (1947).

Ballyshannon (bal.i.shan′ọn). Market town, seaport, and customs station in Ulster province, Irish Republic, in County Donegal, situated at the mouth of the river Erne, ab. 11 mi. S of Donegal. Access to the port is very difficult, through a winding channel. The town has no exports and imports only coal and general cargo. 2,811 (1951).

Balmaceda (bäl.mä.sā′ᴛʜä), **José Manuel.** b. at Santiago, Chile, c1840; committed suicide there, Sept. 19, 1891. Chilean statesman, president (1886–91) of Chile. An outspoken liberal, he acquired great popularity as a leader of the "Reform Club," and after 1870 as a deputy to the Chilean congress. In 1878 he was appointed minister to Argentina, and in 1881 Domingo Santa Maria made him foreign minister; he was elected president by a great majority in 1886. He instituted numerous reforms, and began an elaborate system of railroads and other public works. Dissensions in his own party culminated in a war between the president and congress. After numerous engagements he was defeated and, unable to escape from Santiago, remained concealed in the Argentine legation until in a fit of desperation he shot himself.

Balmawhapple (bal.mạ.hwap′l). In Sir Walter Scott's novel *Waverley*, an obstinate Scottish laird, a Jacobite; in fuller form, his name is Falconer of Balmawhapple.

Balmazújváros (bôl′mô.zö.i.vä″rōsh). Town in E Hungary, in the county of Hajdu, the chief place in the Hortobágy Puszta region, one of the largest steppe regions in Hungary. It is a trade center. 17,247 (1948).

Balme (bålm), **Col de.** Notably picturesque Alpine pass on the route between Chamonix in France and Martigny in Switzerland. Elevation, 7,225 ft.

Balmez (bäl′meth) or **Balmes** (-mes), **Jaime Luciano.** b. at Vich, in Catalonia, Aug. 28, 1810; d. there, July 9, 1848. Spanish publicist and philosophical writer. He founded the political journal *El Pensamiento de la Nacion* (an organ of the clerical and monarchical party) at Madrid in 1844.

Balmont (bäl′mọnt), **Konstantin Dmitriyevich.** b. at Gumnishchi, Vladimir, Russia, June 17, 1867; d. in France, c1943. Russian symbolist poet. A master of verse technique, he produced a large number of tuneful, light lyrics, many of them on exotic themes; he translated Shelley and Whitman into Russian. He died an expatriate, after years of insanity.

Balmoral Castle (bal.mor′ạl). Favorite residence of Queen Victoria in Aberdeenshire, Scotland, situated on the river Dee ab. 45 mi. W of Aberdeen. The property was purchased in 1852, and the castle was built (1853–55) in Scottish baronial style. It remains today a favorite residence in Scotland of the British royal family.

Balnaves (bal.nav′ẹs), **Henry.** b. at Kirkcaldy, Fifeshire, Scotland; d. 1579. Scotch Protestant reformer who was imprisoned for alleged connection with the assassination of Cardinal David Beaton. During his stay in prison he wrote *The Confession of Faith: Conteining how the Troubled Man Should Seeke Refuge at his God*, which was revised and prefaced by John Knox, and published in 1584.

Balneariae Lixovienses (bal.nẹ̄.ār′i.ē lik″sọ̄.vi.en′sēz). A Latin name of **Bagnères-de-Luchon.**

Balnibarbi (bal.ni.bär′bi). A land visited by Gulliver in Jonathan Swift's *Gulliver's Travels.*

Balodis (bä′lō.dēs), **Janis.** b. in Latvia, Feb. 20, 1881—. Latvian government official. He served (1918–20) as a general and as supreme commander of the army. He was elected (1925) a member of the Latvian parliament; as minister of war (1931) he displayed great interest and initiative in equipping the army with the latest weapons. He became deputy prime minister in 1934 and vice-president in 1936. After the occupation of Latvia (1940) by Soviet forces, he was deported to Soviet Russia.

Balqash (bäl.käsh′). Turkic name of **Balkhash.**

Balsamo (bäl.sä′mō), **Giuseppe.** See **Cagliostro, Count Alessandro di.**

Balsas (bäl′säs). [Also: **Mercala, Mescala, Mexcala;** Spanish, **Río de las Balsas.**] River in SW Mexico which flows W into the Pacific Ocean between the states of Michoacán and Guerrero. Length, ab. 426 mi.

Balsham (bôl′shạm), **Hugh de.** [Also, **Hugo de Balsham.**] d. 1286. English prelate, bishop of Ely, and founder of Peterhouse, a college of Cambridge University.

Balta (bäl′tạ). City in the U.S.S.R., in the Ukrainian Soviet Socialist Republic, situated on the Kodyma River, ab. 130 mi. NW of Odessa. It has a flourishing trade. Pop. ab. 21,000.

Balta (bäl′tä), **José.** b. at Lima, Peru, 1816; killed there, July 26, 1872. Peruvian soldier and statesman. He retired from the army with the rank of colonel in 1855; he was minister of war for a short time in 1865, but was one of the leaders of the insurrection which drove out the unconstitutional president, Prado, in 1868. He was regularly elected president of Peru (Aug. 2, 1868), and served for four years; he was murdered in a military mutiny.

Balta-Limani (bäl′tä.lē.mä′nē), **Convention of.** Treaty concluded in 1849 at Balta-Limani (on the Bosporus), between Turkey and Russia, granting to the latter certain rights in the region of the lower Danube for seven years.

Baltard (bål.tår), **Louis Pierre.** b. at Paris, July 9, 1764; d. Jan. 22, 1846. French architect and engraver of architectural and other subjects; father of Victor Baltard (1805–74).

Baltard, Victor. b. at Paris, June 19, 1805; d. Jan. 14, 1874. French architect; son of Louis Pierre Baltard (1764–1846). He was government architect of the city of Paris, and designed the general market building there. Author of *Monographie de la Villa Médicis* (1847) and others.

Baltazarini (bäl″tä.tsä.rē′nē) or **Baltagerini** (-jā-). [French, **Balthasard de Beaujoyeulx.**] fl. c1550. Italian musician, the leading violinist of his time. He became intendant of music and first *valet de chambre* to Catherine de' Medici, who gave him the name Beaujoyeulx. He apparently first introduced the Italian ballet into Paris.

Baltchik (bäl′chik). See **Balcic.**

Balthazar or **Balthasar** (bal.thā′zạr). One of the three Magi who came from the East to worship the infant Jesus.

Balthazar. Geoffrey Chaucer's name for Belshazzar in "The Monk's Tale," one of *The Canterbury Tales.*

Balthazar or **Balthasar** (in Shakespeare, bal′thạ.zär). Name of several characters in Shakespeare's plays: **1.** A merchant in *A Comedy of Errors.* **2.** The name assumed by Portia as a doctor of law in the trial scene in *The Merchant of Venice.* **3.** A servant of Portia in *The Merchant of Venice.* **4.** A servant of Don Pedro in *Much Ado About Nothing.* **5.** A servant of Romeo in *Romeo and Juliet.*

Balthazar (bal.thā′zạr). Character in Julius Eichenberg's opera *The Doctor of Alcantara.*

Balthazar Claes (bål.tå.zår kläs). See **Claes, Balthazar.**

Baltia (bal′shi.ạ). In ancient geography, an unidentified island off the coast of Scythia, mentioned by Pliny and other writers. From it derived the name of the Baltic Sea.

Baltic Pact (bôl′tik). Treaty signed on Sept. 12, 1934, by Lithuania, Estonia, and Latvia. It provided for common consultation in matters of foreign policy and for the settlement of disagreements between the signatory nations by amicable methods. As a result, periodic conferences were held by the countries' foreign ministers and premiers.

Baltic Port. See **Paldiski.**

Baltic Provinces. Collective name for the three former (until 1918) governments of Russia on the Baltic coast, known as Estonia, Livonia, and Kurland (or Courland). The territory comprising them was divided between the independent states of Estonia and Latvia after World War I, but again placed under Russian domination during World War II. The term "Baltic Provinces" now has only historical meaning; the most usual modern term is the more inclusive "Baltic States."

Baltic Sea. [Danish, **Østersøen;** German, **Ostsee;** Swedish, **Östersjön;** Latin, **Mare Suevicum.**] Arm of the Atlantic, enclosed by Sweden, Finland, the U.S.S.R., Estonia, Latvia, Lithuania, Poland, Germany, and Denmark. It communicates with the North Sea by the Skagerrack, Kattegat, Øresund, Great Belt, and Little Belt. Its chief islands are Zealand, Fyn, Langeland, Laaland, Falster, Møn, Als, Fehmarn, Bornholm, Rügen, Usedom, Wollin, Öland, Gotland, Saaremaa, Hiiumaa, Stockholm Archipelago, and Ahvenanmaa. Its chief arms are the gulfs of Bothnia, Finland, and Riga, Kurisches Haff, Frisches Haff, Gulf of Danzig, Pomeranian Bay, Lübeck Bay, and Kiel Bay. Its chief tributaries are the Finland lake system, the rivers Neva (with Lake Ladoga), Narva (with Lake Peipus), Dvina, Niemen, Vistula, Oder, Dal, Ljusnan, Ångerman, Ume, Pite, Stora Lule, and Torne. Length, ab. 900 mi.; greatest width, ab. 300 mi.; area, ab. 160,000 sq. mi.

Baltic States. Collective name for the states of Estonia, Latvia, and Lithuania, on the Baltic coast. They acquired status as independent republics after World War I. The first two were formed from territory which had previously been included under Russia's three "Baltic Provinces"; Lithuania was formed from additional Russian territory, at least part of which was (and continues to be) disputed between Poland and Lithuania. The three states are now once again under Russian control, having been occupied (allegedly as a protective measure) by the Russians during World War II, but their loss of independence has never been recognized by the U.S. Historically, the population of the region has always consisted chiefly of native Balts plus a considerable German element, with a comparatively slight admixture of Slavs. The term "Baltic States" is also sometimes taken to include Finland and, very infrequently, Poland; although these extensions of the meaning have some geographical and historical justification, they are largely meaningless from a linguistic or ethnographic point of view, and most modern authorities restrict the term to the meaning here preferred.

Baltiisk (bạl.tyēsk'). Russian name of **Pillau.**

Baltimore (bôl'ti.mōr, -mọr). Small fishing village in Munster province, Irish Republic, in County Cork, situated on Baltimore Bay, near Cape Clear, ab. 6 mi. SW of Skibbereen. It has a small export trade in mackerel and cured herring. 250 (1936).

Baltimore. [Called the **"Monumental City."**] City in N Maryland, in Baltimore County, on the Patapsco River near its entrance into Chesapeake Bay: one of the chief Atlantic seaports, a railroad center, and principal city in the state. Notable for great electrolytic copper refineries, and for an extensive oyster-packing industry, it also has a large import trade in ores, petroleum, and other raw materials. Manufactures include clothing, straw hats, baked goods, refined sugar, chemical products, aircraft, liquor, ships, and electrical equipment. It has been the seat of many national political conventions. A large part of the wholesale business and financial section of the city (over 1,000 buildings) was destroyed by fire on February 7–8, 1904. Baltimore is the seat of a Roman Catholic archbishopric, and of the Johns Hopkins University, Peabody Institute, the University of Maryland Schools of Medicine and Law, St. Mary's Seminary and University, Loyola College, and Goucher College. It is the home of H. L. Mencken and the burial place of Edgar Allan Poe. The Pimlico race track is here. The city was laid out c1730 and incorporated in 1797. It was unsuccessfully attacked by the British in 1814, and was the scene of a conflict, on April 19, 1861, between a Baltimore mob and Union troops (6th Massachusetts and 7th Pennsylvania). Pop. of city, 859,100 (1940), 949,708 (1950); of urbanized area, 1,161,852 (1950).

Baltimore, 1st Baron. Title of **Calvert, George.**

Baltimore, 2nd Baron. Title of **Calvert, Cecilius.**

Baltimore, 3rd Baron. Title of **Calvert, Charles.**

Baltimore and Ohio Railroad, The. [Called **"the B and O."**] Railroad chartered on Feb. 28, 1827, whose original line from Baltimore to the Ohio River was completed in 1853 with its western terminus at Wheeling, then in the state of Virginia. Although original plans called for the employment of horsepower, steam was generally used after 1829. After the Civil War the service of the road was extended as far west as Chicago and St. Louis, and as far north as New York.

Baltimore Incident. Incident developing from the encounter (Nov. 16, 1798), of the U.S. sloop *Baltimore* with a British squadron. The *Baltimore* had under convoy a number of merchant craft bound for Havana; its commander, Captain Isaac Phillips, was under orders to avoid armed contest with the British, and so did not offer opposition when the British mustered his crew and impressed all seamen who lacked documentary proof indicating they were U.S. nationals. Of the 55 seamen removed, however, 50 were finally released by the British. As a result of the incident, Phillips was dismissed from the naval service, and the government issued orders specifying that thereafter, under similar circumstances, American craft would offer resistance.

Baltimore Sun. Nonpartisan daily founded at Baltimore in 1837; another edition, *The Evening Sun*, was added in 1910.

Baltischport (bäl'tish.pōrt) or **Baltiski** (bạl.tyēs'ki) or **Baltiski Port** (pōrt). See **Paldiski.**

Baltistan (bul.ti.stän'). [Also: **Balti** (bäl'tē), **Bulti, Bultistan;** called **"Little Tibet."**] Area under the control of Kashmir, N India, situated on the upper Indus River, N of the geographical unit usually defined as Kashmir. The overwhelming majority of the inhabitants are Moslems. The region is in the Karakoram Range and its chief commercial enterprise is the production of timber. Chief town, Skardu; area, ab. 12,000 sq. mi.

Balto-Slavic (bôl"tọ.slav'ik, -släv'-). A conjectural division of the Indo-European linguistic family. By those who accept it, it is taken to include a Baltic branch (including extinct Old Prussian, Lithuanian, and Lett (Latvian), which is extremely archaic in structure and vocabulary) and a Slavic branch (comprising three groups: Southern Slavic (Macedonian and Bulgarian, Serbo-Croat, and Slovene), Eastern Slavic (including Ukrainian, Great-Russian, and Byelorussian), and Western Slavic, which covers Czech, Polish, Sorb or Wend, and extinct Polabian). Most modern scholars, however, are extremely dubious of this entire hypothesis of Balto-Slavic as a unit, and prefer the grouping of Baltic and Slavic as two major and distinct divisions (although accepting the obvious fact that at one time the two divisions were extremely close and subject to considerable cultural and linguistic interchange).

Baltrum (bäl'trụm). Island in NW Germany, in the *Land* (state) of Lower Saxony, British Zone, formerly in the province of Hanover, Prussia, situated in the North Sea, E of the island of Norderney. It is the fourth from the W of the East Frisian islands. 308 (1946).

Balts (bôlts). Name applied to the oldest ethnic group still in existence in the E coastal area of the Baltic Sea. They comprise a major part of the population of the Baltic States, including the Lithuanians and Letts (or Latvians).

Baltzell (bôlt'sẹl), **Winton James.** b. at Shiremanstown, Pa., Dec. 18, 1864; d. 1928. American composer and teacher.

Baluchi (bạ.lö'chẹ). Language of the Iranian branch of the Indo-Iranian subdivision of Indo-European languages. There is no Baluchi literature, but a considerable body of poetry has been orally transmitted, celebrating heroes and their deeds, and some of this has been collected.

Baluchistan (bạ.lö.chi.stän'). [Also: **Beluchistan, Biluchistan.**] Province of Pakistan, in the SW part, bounded by Afghanistan and the North-West Frontier Province on the N, Sind and the Punjab on the E, the Arabian Sea on the S, and Iran on the W. It is largely a desert, and is traversed by mountain ranges. It is divided into nine states, of which Kalat is the largest. Quetta was the former headquarters of a division of the army. There are ab. 800 mi. of railway. The people are chiefly Brahoes and Afghans; the prevailing religion, Sunnite Mohammedanism. Baluchistan was several times invaded by British forces in connection with the Afghan wars. On Feb. 26, 1949 it became part of Pakistan. Chief city, Quetta; area, 134,139 sq. mi.; pop. 1,154,167 (1951).

Bałucki (bä.löts'kē), **Michał.** [Pseudonym, **Elpidon.**] b. at Kraków, Poland, 1837; d. there, 1901. Polish poet, novelist, and playwright, considered the father of Polish bourgeois comedy. Educated at the University of Kraków; he was the author of the popular lyric, often erroneously regarded as a piece of folk music, *Góralu, czy ci nie żal?"* (Oh, mountaineer, dost thou not grieve?). He also wrote novels, now forgotten, and dramas, mostly comedies, of city and especially of official life, such as *The Counselors of Mr. Councillor* (1867), *Big Fish* (1881), *Open House* (1883), and *Bachelors' Club* (1890).

Balue (bȧ.lü), **Jean de la.** b. at Poitiers, France, 1422; d. at Ancona, Italy, October, 1491. French cardinal and politician, imprisoned (1469–80) for treason by Louis XI, it is said, in an iron cage. He was liberated after 11 years, through the influence of Pope Sixtus IV, went to Rome, and was sent back to France as legate *a latere*. Finally, on the death of the Pope, he again retired to Rome, where he was made bishop of Orléans and of Praeneste.

Baluze (bȧ.lüz), **Étienne.** b. at Tulle, France, Dec. 24, 1630; d. at Paris, July 28, 1718. French historian. He wrote *Francorum Capitularia Regum* (1677), *Epistolae Innocentii papae III* (1682), *Conciliorum nova Collectio* (1683), *Les Vies des Papes d'Avignon* (1693), and *Historia Tutelensis* (1717).

Balzac (bȧl.zȧk; Anglicized, bôl'zak), **Honoré de.** b. at Tours, France, May 20, 1799; d. at Paris, Aug. 18, 1850. French novelist. His father, a lawyer and minor government official, was an eccentric whose ambition was to live to a great age, and who, in middle life, married a highly-strung young Parisienne, who so little cared for Honoré that she placed him in a monastic school at Vendôme, and utterly neglected him for years. Balzac described his school life in his autobiographical novel *Louis Lambert*. He was a refractory pupil, who for punishment was daily imprisoned in the school library, where he read every book it contained. His health failing, he joined his family near Paris and became a lawyer's clerk, but detesting law, determined to become an author. This intention was strongly opposed by his parents, who to discourage it installed him in a Paris attic on meager rations; despite this, Balzac recalled those days of privation as the happiest of his life: he was free in Paris, spent most of his time in the Arsenal Library, and composed a tragedy, *Cromwell*, which received only disapproval from his family. Undaunted, "to get his hand in," he wrote at least a dozen novels, under various pseudonyms, all rather mediocre, but with flashes of genius; these brought little money, and were never openly acknowledged by him. To earn more, he determined to be his own publisher, and engaged in business as a printer and type founder, having borrowed capital from relatives and friends; the concern, under Balzac's mismanagement, failed, and he was burdened with debt for the whole of his life.

First Successful Works. To recoup his losses, he resumed his pen, resolved to succeed as an author, and in 1829 wrote *Les Chouans*, the first work to bear his name Honoré Balzac (the particle *de* he added later). This success was followed by *Physiologie du mariage* (1830) and *La Peau de chagrin* (1831); both created a furor, and his position as writer was secure. Then followed a strenuous career in Parisian journalism, to which Balzac contributed a large number of novels, short stories, and articles. This period is vividly revealed in the second part of his *Illusions perdues: Un grand homme de province à Paris*. Nearly all his work appeared first in periodicals, then in book form with titles and text changed. Therefore, only final titles and dates of first book publication are given below, in the order of their steady flow from his pen.

List of Works. In 1830: *La Maison du chat-qui-pelote, Le Bal de Sceaux, La Vendetta, Une double Famille, La Paix du ménage, Gobseck, Un Épisode sous la Terreur.* In 1831: *Étude de femme, Sarrasine, Jésus-Christ en Flandre, Le Chef-d'oeuvre inconnu, L'Enfant maudit, Le Réquisitionnaire, El Verdugo, L'Elixir de longue vie, Les Proscrits.* In 1832: *La Bourse, Madame Firmiani, Le Message, Le Colonel Chabert, La Grande Bretèche, Le Curé de Tours, Adieu, L'Auberge rouge, Maître Cornélius, Louis Lambert, Contes drolatiques.* In 1833: *Le Médecin de campagne, L'Illustre Gaudissart.* In 1834: *La Grenadière, La Femme abandonnée, Le Contrat de mariage, Eugénie Grandet, Histoire des Treize* (3 parts), *La Recherche de l'absolu, Les Marana.* In 1835: *Le Père Goriot, Melmoth reconcilié, Un Drame au bord de la mer, Séraphita.* In 1836: *Le Lys dans la vallée, L'Interdiction.* In 1837: *Sur Catherine de Médicis, La Messe de l'athée, La Vieille Fille, César Birotteau, Facino Cane, Un Passion dans le désert.* In 1838: *Splendeurs et misères des courtisanes* (4 parts), *La Maison Nucingen, Les Employés.* In 1839: *Une Fille d'Ève, Le Cabinet des antiques, Illusions perdues* (3 parts), *Gambara, Massimilla Doni.* In 1840: *Pierrette, Pierre Grassou, Les Secrets de la princesse de Cadignan.* In 1841: *Le Curé de village, Z. Marcas, Mémoires de deux jeunes mariées, Albert Savarus, La Fausse Maîtresse, La Femme de trente ans, Autre étude de femme, Ursule Mirouët, La Rabouilleuse, Une Ténébreuse Affaire.* In 1843, *La Muse du département.* In 1844: *Modeste Mignon, Un Début dans la vie, Honorine, Un Prince de la Bohème.* In 1845: *Béatrix, Petites misères de la vie conjugale.* In 1846: *Gaudissart II, Les Comédiens sans le savoir, L'Envers de l'histoire contemporaine.* In 1847: *Le Cousin Pons, La Cousine Bette, Un Homme d'affaires, Le Député d'Arcis.* In 1855, *Les Paysans.* In 1856–57, *Les Petits Bourgeois.* The foregoing list of nearly 100 works composes the *Comédie humaine.* In addition, Balzac wrote six plays: *Vautrin* (1840), *Les Ressources de Quinola* (1842), *Paméla Giraud* (1843), *La Marâtre* (1848), *Le Faiseur* (*Mercadet*) (1851), and *L'École des ménages* (1839, published 1907). Only one, *Mercadet*, was successful. In 1834 Balzac first conceived the idea of uniting his works by means of reappearing characters, and in 1842 he named the series *La Comédie humaine*, in a memorable *Avant-propos* (foreword). Balzac's ventures as an editor were financial failures; *La Chronique de Paris* (1835) lived but one year; *La Revue parisienne* (1840) ended with the third number. The complete total of Balzac's writings amounts to more than 350 titles. On March 14, 1850, he married a rich widow, Countess Evelina Hanska, of a noble Polish family, with whom he had corresponded since 1833, and whom he had subsequently met at Geneva, Vienna, and St. Petersburg. He died in Paris, three months after his return from the wedding trip.

Critical Evaluation. Balzac is considered the founder of the realistic school of French novelists. More than this, the consensus of leading critical opinion is that in point of quantity, quality, influence on other writers, and particularly power of creation, Balzac is among the greatest novelists who ever lived. In his *Comédie humaine* he succeeds in giving a panorama of the whole of French society in the first half of the 19th century. Through his device of reappearing characters (about 2,000, and as many as 155 in one novel), he gives an impression of comprehensiveness and reality to his fictional world. Marcel Bouteron, member of the Institut de France, and foremost Balzacian, has declared that three works are indispensable for the study of Balzac: *Histoire des oeuvres de H. de Balzac* (3rd edition, Paris, 1888), by Vicomte Charles de Spoelberch de Lovenjoul, *Répertoire de la Comédie humaine de H. de Balzac* (Paris, 1887), by Anatole Cerfberr and Jules Christophe, and *A Balzac Bibliography . . . writings relative to the life and works of Honoré de Balzac* (University of Chicago Press, 1929), by William Hobart Royce. See also *Vie de Balzac* (Paris, 1944), by André Billy, *Balzac visionnaire* (Geneva, 1946), by Albert Béguin, *Balzac* (Bonn, 1923), by Ernst Robert Curtius, and *Balzac* (New York, 1946), by Stefan Zweig. *Balzac as he should be read* (New York, 1946), by W. H. Royce, gives a logical order of reading the *Comédie humaine* according to time of action.

Balzac, Jean Louis Guez de. [Title, Seigneur **de Balzac.**] b. at Balzac, near Angoulême, France, c1597; d. there, Feb. 18, 1654. French writer. At an early age he was taken under the patronage of Louis, Cardinal de la Valette, who took Balzac to Rome. There he began writing those letters to friends and to personages at the French court which first brought him reputation. The substance of these letters was shallow, but their style was considered to be remarkably good. Richelieu appreciated Balzac's talent and held out promises of preferment (which, however, were not kept to the writer's satisfaction). He was elected a member of the French Academy in 1634. His published works were *Lettres* (1624), *Le Prince*, a eulogy of Louis XIII (1631), *Lettres* (1636), *Recueil de nouvelles lettres* (1637), *Discours* (1644), *Le Barbon* (1648), *Socrate chrétien* (1652), *L'Aristippe ou de la Cour* (1658), and several works on style. Balzac helped to bring to French prose the clarity and precision which have since characterized it, and by his extensive use of idiomatic forms strongly influenced the development of the French language.

Bam (bäm). Town in SE Iran, in the region of Kerman, ab. 115 mi. SE of the city of Kerman: a small desert trading center. Pop. ab. 10,000.

Bamako (bä.mä.kō'). [Also: **Bammakou, Bammaku.**] Former native town on the upper Niger River, W Africa, now the capital of the territory of French Sudan, French West Africa. It is situated on the N bank of the Niger and is connected with Dakar on the W coast of Africa by a railway line ab. 450 mi. long. It is an educational and commercial center for the surrounding area. 70,492 (1946).

Bamana (bä.mä'nä). See **Bambara.**

Bambai (bäm.bī'). Hindu name of **Bombay,** city.

Bambara (bäm.bä'rä). Ethnic region in the French Sudan, in French West Africa, in the upper valley of the Niger River, N of the Ivory Coast. The chief town is Ségou.

Bambara. [Also: **Bamana, Banmana.**] Mande-speaking people of W Africa, inhabiting the SE French Sudan E of Bamako. Their population is estimated at more than 200,000 (by Y. Urvoy, *Petit Atlas Ethno-Demographique du Soudan,* 1942). Two separate Bambara empires, with their capitals at Ségou and Karta, controlled large areas of the W Sudan from the 17th to the 19th centuries. Today they are divided into a number of independent subgroups ruled by hereditary kings. They practice hoe agriculture, and their principal food is millet. The Bambara and Malinke in the west, like the Mossi in the center of the W Sudan, have resisted Mohammedanism, and only about 15 percent have become Mohammedans. Their carved wooden masks are highly regarded in the field of African art. They are not to be confused with the Minianka, their neighbors to the east who are also sometimes called Bamana.

Bambé (bäm.bā'). Malay name of **Bombay,** city.

Bamberg (bäm'berk; Anglicized, bam'bėrg). City in S Germany, in the *Land* (state) of Bavaria, American Zone, in the *Regierungsbezirk* (government district) of Middle and Upper Franconia, situated on the Regnitz River near its entrance into the Main River, ab. 33 mi. NW of Nuremberg. Manufactures include shoes, leather, paper, paperware, ceramics, metallurgical and electrical products, and furniture; there are also flour mills, breweries, and wine, grain, cattle, lumber, and hops markets for the surrounding agricultural region. Bamberg is the seat of an archbishopric and of numerous educational institutions; it has archives, botanical gardens, a theater, and a museum of natural history. 76,180 (1950).

Art and Architecture. The art museum contains works by Franconian painters of the 15th and 16th centuries; the library has valuable incunabula and manuscripts. The *Dom* (cathedral) of Bamberg, begun in 1004, is one of the most remarkable Romanesque church buildings in C Europe. It is known especially for its monumental stone sculptures of the early Middle Ages, such as the figures known as the "Rider of Bamberg" and "Elisabeth," the tomb of the emperor Henry II and his wife, Saint Kunigunde, by Tilman Riemenschneider (c1460–1531), the 13th-century tomb of Pope Clement II, and an altar (1521) by Veit Stoss. There are a number of Renaissance and baroque palaces; the "new residence" is a baroque building, erected (1695–1707) according to plans by J. Dientzenhofer. The old *Rathaus* (town hall), standing on an island in the Regnitz River, and the Boettinger House (1713) are remarkable baroque and rococo structures. Saint Michael's Church, begun in 1009, part of a former Benedictine abbey, has baroque additions. Saint Jacob's Church and Saint Stephen's Church date from the 11th century; Saint Martin's Church was built (1693) for the Jesuit Order by Dientzenhofer.

History. Emperor Henry II created the bishopric of Bamberg in 1007 as a missionary center among the Slavs; it remained for centuries one of the most important independent bishoprics of the empire. Bishop Suitger (bishop of Bamberg 1040–46) became Pope Clement II; Saint Otto (bishop 1102–39) Christianized Pomerania; Lothar Franz von Schönborn (bishop 1693–1729) and Franz Ludwig von Erthal (bishop 1779–95) were known as sponsors of the arts. The town and territory came under Bavarian jurisdiction in 1802. It was temporarily the seat of a Socialist government of Bavaria (in opposition to the Spartacists controlling Munich) in the period of German collapse immediately after World War II. Great damage was done in World War II, though less than in other towns of Franconia. Among the damaged buildings is the old town hall. After 1945 a great influx of Sudeten German refugees took place, swelling the population by 33.9 percent as compared with 1939.

Bamberg (bam'bėrg). Town in C South Carolina, county seat of Bamberg County: shipping center for farm products, including watermelons and livestock. It is the seat of Carlisle Fitting School. 2,954 (1950).

Bamberg (bäm'berk; Anglicized, bam'bėrg), **Bishopric of.** Former bishopric and state of the German Empire, now comprised in N Bavaria. It was founded by the emperor Henry II in 1007, secularized in 1801, and annexed to Bavaria in 1802.

Bamberg Conference. Conference of the states, at that time still independent, of C and S Germany, at Bamberg, on May 25, 1854. Its object was to determine the policy of these states in relation to that of Prussia and Austria with reference to Turkish power in E Europe.

Bamberger (bäm'ber"gėr), **Ludwig.** b. at Mainz, Germany, July 22, 1823; d. at Berlin, March 14, 1899. German politician and economist. He took part in the revolutionary movement of 1848–49, was a member of the National Liberal party in the German Reichstag (1873–80), and, with other disaffected National Liberals, seceded from the party in 1880 to form the Liberal Union. He was an influential supporter of the gold standard for Germany, and was a leader in the founding of the *Reichsbank* (national bank).

Bamboccio (bäm.bôt'chō), **Il.** See **Laar** or **Laer, Pieter van.**

Bambouk (bäm.bök'). [Also, **Bambuk.**] Region in W Africa, in the SW corner of French Sudan, French West Africa, between the upper Senegal and Falémé rivers. The region contains iron and gold. The inhabitants are Mandingoes.

Bamburgh (bam'bur.ọ). [Also, **Bamborough.**] Civil parish and coastal village in NE England, in Northumberland, situated on the North Sea coast, ab. 16 mi. SE of Berwick-upon-Tweed. It is celebrated for its castle, founded by Ida, king of Bernicia, c547, and often noted in medieval wars. 438 (1931).

Bamford (bam'fọrd), **Samuel.** b. at Middleton, Lancashire, England, Feb. 28, 1788; d. at Harpurhey, Lancashire, England, April 13, 1872. English weaver and poet, imprisoned (1819) for agitating for repeal of the Corn Laws. Author of *The Weaver Boy, or Miscellaneous Poetry* (1819), *Homely Rhymes* (1843), *Passages in the Life of a Radical* (1840–44), *The Dialect of South Lancashire* (1854), and *Early Days* (1849).

Bamian (bä.mē.än'). Valley in Afghanistan, NW of Kabul. It is an ancient seat of Buddhist worship, and is famous for its colossal figures carved in the rock (highest, 173 ft.) and other antiquities.

Bammakou or **Bammaku** (bä.mä.kö'). See **Bamako.**

Bamoum (bà.möm). French name of the **Bamum.**

Bampton (bamp'tọn), **John.** b. c1689; d. 1751. English divine, and the founder at Oxford of the "Bampton Lectures" on divinity. The first lecturer was chosen in 1779.

Bampton, Rose. b. at Cleveland, Ohio, Nov. 28, 1909—. American contralto. After studying at the Curtis Institute of Music, Philadelphia, she appeared with the Philadelphia Grand Opera Company and at the Metropolitan Opera House, New York, where she made her debut in 1932.

Bampur (bäm.pör'). Town and region in SE Iran, in Kerman region near the border of Baluchistan. The region is mostly desert and mountains. The town is located on the Bampur River, an intermittent stream. Pop. of town, ab. 10,000.

Bamra (bäm'rä). Former state in the Eastern States, now merged with Orissa, Union of India, between the valley of the Mahanadi River and the Chota Nagpur plateau: coal mining. Capital, Deogarh; area, ab. 2,000 sq. mi.; pop. 178,277 (1941).

Bamum (bä.möm'). [Also: **Mum;** French, **Bamoum.**] Semi-Bantu-speaking people of C Africa, inhabiting W Cameroun. Their population is estimated at ab. 75,000 (by I. Dugast, *Inventaire Ethnique du Sud-Cameroun*, 1949). They are ruled by a hereditary king. They practice agriculture, and their principal crops are bananas, taro, maize, and millet. Like the Vai, they invented their own alphabet, which is partly syllabic and partly hieroglyphic.

Ban (ban). In the Arthurian cycle of romances, a king of Brittany; father of Lancelot, and brother of Bors, king of Gaul.

Banach (bä′näн), **Stefan.** b. at Kraków, Poland, March 30, 1892; d. at Lvov, in the Ukraine, in the autumn of 1945. Polish mathematician, noted particularly for his work in functional analysis, linear operators, and the theory of "Banach spaces." Author of *Théorie des opérations linéaires* (1932) and *Mechanika* (in Polish, 1938).

Banagher (ban′ạ.gėr). Market town in Leinster province, Irish Republic, in County Offaly, situated on the river Shannon, ab. 21 mi. SW of Tullamore. It is to the superiority traditionally assumed for and by this town that the phrase "That bangs Banagher, and Banagher bangs the world" alludes. 720 (1936).

Banahao (bä.nä′hou). [Also: **Banajao** (-ноu), **Majaijai.**] Extinct volcano in the N central Philippines, on the border between Tayabas and La Laguna provinces in the S part of Luzon, SE of Laguna de Bay. Elevation, ab. 7,177 ft.

Banamichi (bä.nä.mē′chē). See under **Batonapa.**

Banana (bä.nä′nä). Seaport in W Africa, in the Belgian Congo, in Léopoldville province at the mouth of the Congo River, on the N bank. Its factories and official buildings are built on a land spit. In 1890, a peak year, 132 ships called at the port, but after steamships began to go straight up to Matadi, the starting point of the railroad, Banana lost most of its commercial importance. Pop. less than 1,000.

Banana Islands (bạ.nan′ạ). Group of small islands off the coast of Sierra Leone, W Africa, belonging to Great Britain. They are situated outside Yawri Bay, S of Freetown.

Bananal (bu.nu.näl′). [Also: **Santa Anna, Sant' Anna;** Portuguese, **Ilha de Santa Anna** (or **Sant' Anna**), **Ilha do Bananal.**] Island in S central Brazil, in the Araguaia River, in NW Goiás state on the border of Mato Grosso. Length, ab. 220 mi.; greatest width, ab. 50 mi.

Banaras (bạ.nä′rạs). See **Benares.**

Banas (bä′nạs). River in Rajputana, N central Union of India, which flows generally NE, and joins the Chambal River. Length, ab. 300 mi.

Banas. [Also, **West Banas.**] River in W India which rises in the Aravalli Range and flows SW into the Rann of Kutch. Length, ab. 150 mi.

Banat (bä.nät′). [Also, **Banat of Temesvar.**] Region formerly in S Hungary, now partly in NE Yugoslavia (Vojvodina province), partly in W Rumania (Banat province). It is E of the Tisza River and stretches toward the Carpathian Mountains. The region, although very fertile, was deserted as a result of the Hapsburg wars against the Turks; it was resettled under the empress Maria Theresa of Austria in the latter half of the 18th century by Magyar, Rumanian, Serbian, and German colonists. The descendants of the German settlers, called Schwaben (Swabians), were expelled after World War II.

Banat. Region and former province in W Rumania, bounded by Yugoslavia on the W and S, and Oltenia and Transylvania on the E, and Crişana-Maramureş on the N. Capital, Timişoara; area, 7,224 sq. mi.; pop. 948,596 (1948).

Banbridge (ban′brij). Urban district and market town in Ulster province, Northern Ireland, in County Down, situated on the river Bann, ab. 22 mi. SW of Belfast. It is an important linen-manufacturing center. 5,747 (1947).

Banbury (ban′bėr.i). Municipal borough and market town in S England, in Oxfordshire, situated on the river Cherwell ab. 22 mi. N of Oxford, ab. 68 mi. NW of London by rail: manufactures farm machinery. An iron-ore field is in the vicinity. The ancient Banbury cross, noted in nursery rhyme, was destroyed in the latter part of the reign of Elizabeth. The town was famous until recent years for its ale and cakes, and for its cheese which was proverbially regarded as consisting of nothing but "parings." Hence the allusions in Shakespeare and other writers to persons thin as a Banbury cheese. Insurgents were defeated here by troops of Edward IV in 1469. It was twice besieged in the civil war. 18,917 (1951).

Banbury Man. Name sometimes used to mean a Puritan. Jonathan Swift speaks of a Banbury saint, meaning a particularly rigid or even hypocritical Puritan. The name or epithet "Banbury" was applied in a depreciatory sense before the Puritan times. Thus Latimer, in a letter (c1528) to Henry VIII, speaks of "laws, customs, ceremonies and Banbury glosses," apparently meaning that they were silly or useless.

Banca (bäng′kä). See **Bangka.**

Banc d'Arguin (bäṅ dàr.gaṅ). See **Arguin.**

Bances Candamo (bän′thās kän.dä′mō), **Francisco Antonio de.** See **Candamo, Francisco Antonio de Bances.**

Banchieri (bäng.kyā′rē), **Adriano.** b. at Bologna, Italy, c1567; d. there, 1634. Italian organist, composer, and writer. His works include much liturgical music as well as incidental interludes for dramatic works; the most important of his writings is *L'organo suonarino* (1605), the first work to discuss figured-bass accompaniment.

Banchs (bänchs), **Enrique.** b. 1888—. Argentine poet. Author of *Las barcas* (1907), *El cascabel del halcón* (1909), and others.

Banco (bäng′kō), **Nani d'Antonio.** b. at Siena, Italy, c1374; d. c1420. Florentine sculptor; a pupil of Donatello. He completed (c1402–08) the Porta della Mandola on the south side of the *Duomo* (cathedral), at Florence, commenced by Niccolò d'Arezzo. The figures of angels on this door are very characteristic of his style.

Bancroft (bang′krôft, ban′-), **Aaron.** b. at Reading, Mass., Nov. 10, 1755; d. Aug. 19, 1839. American Unitarian clergyman and author; father of the historian George Bancroft. In 1825 he helped in organizing the American Unitarian Association, serving as its president until 1836.

Bancroft, Cecil Franklin Patch. b. at New Ipswich, N.H., Nov. 25, 1839; d. Oct. 4, 1901. American educator. After graduation (1860) from Dartmouth, he served (1860–64) as principal of Appleton Academy (later McCullom Institute) before entering the Union Theological Seminary at New York. During the Civil War he was with the Christian Commission, engaged in aiding the wounded. He was graduated (1867) from Andover Theological Seminary, ordained (1867), and selected to assume charge of a newly established school at Lookout Mountain, Tenn., which closed after five years. As principal (1873–1901) of Phillips Academy at Andover, Mass., he contributed much to the improvement of the school plant and the raising of its educational standards.

Bancroft, Edward. b. 1744; d. 1821. English chemist, naturalist, traveler, novelist, and spy in the Revolutionary War. In early life he several times visited North and South America. Later he made some important discoveries in dyeing and calico printing. He published an *Essay on the Natural History of Guiana* (1769), *Charles Wentworth* (a novel, 1770), and a work on colors and calico printing (1794 and 1813). He served (1776–78) as a spy for Benjamin Franklin and Silas Deane during their stay at Paris, but allegedly sold information to the British as well.

Bancroft, Frederic. b. at Galesburg, Ill., Oct. 30, 1860; d. at Washington, D.C., 1945. American librarian and historian and specialist on the American South. He received an A.B. (1882) from Amherst and a Ph.D. (1885) from Columbia, and served as a librarian (1888–92) of the U.S. Department of State. He bequeathed almost two million dollars to Columbia University. Author of *The Negro in Politics* (1885), *The Public Life of Carl Schurz* (1908), *Calhoun and the Nullification Movement in South Carolina* (1928), *Slave Trading in the Old South* (1931), and other works; editor of *Speeches, Correspondence and Public Papers of Carl Schurz* (six vols., 1913).

Bancroft, George. b. at Worcester, Mass., Oct. 3, 1800; d. at Washington, D.C., Jan. 17, 1891. American historian, diplomat, and public official, noted for his *History of the United States*, originally issued in ten volumes (1834–74); son of Aaron Bancroft (1755–1839). He was graduated from Phillips Academy, Exeter, N.H. (1813) and Harvard (1817), remaining at the latter as a theological student before leaving on a scholarship for the University of Göttingen, where he received his Ph.D. in 1820. During 1821 he studied at the University of Berlin under Schleiermacher, Friedrich August Wolf, and Hegel, and made a tour of the Continent, returning to the U.S. in 1822. After a brief period at Harvard as a tutor in Greek, he founded (1823) Round Hill School for boys at Northampton, Mass., with J. G. Cogswell. The school was patterned after the German *gymnasium,* its curriculum built on Pestalozzian principles. In 1827 he married Sarah Dwight, who died in 1837, and in 1838 he married Elizabeth Davis Bliss. He began writing in 1823, publishing a book of poems, three textbooks, and some 30 historical and literary articles for the *North American Review* and other journals before leaving Round Hill in 1831. His series on "German Literature," published in *The American Quarterly Review* from September, 1827, to September, 1828, was the first comprehensive treatment of German literature and philosophy to appear in an American periodical. In 1834 he published the first volume of his *History,* originally called *A History of the United States from the Discovery of the Continent to the Present Time.* A revised six-volume "Centenary Edition" appeared in 1876–79, and his two-volume *History of the Formation of the Constitution of the United States of America* in 1882. The "Author's Last Revision" of 1883–85 combined the "Centenary Edition" and the Constitutional history into six volumes, with a marked tempering of the stylistic floridity of the earlier volumes. Bancroft's historical theory was strongly conditioned by his belief in the essential worth of mankind, his faith in progress, and his intuitive trust in a beneficent Deity. The history of the U.S. he treated as a primary illustration of a divine plan for freedom, equality, and democracy. The twin themes of his *History* were therefore democracy and nationalism. Though his style and approach now seem outmoded, it should be recognized that he was the first to begin publication of a comprehensive history of the U.S., and that in his assembling and use of original material he made pioneer contributions to the later tradition of "scientific" history. After 1826 he was active in politics and government service as a Democrat. A supporter of Andrew Jackson, his party work brought him an appointment (1837) as collector of the port of Boston, where he gave a clerkship to Nathaniel Hawthorne. He was secretary of the navy (1845–46) in James Knox Polk's cabinet, handling naval affairs during the early phases of the Mexican War and establishing the U.S. Naval Academy at Annapolis. He served (1846–49) as U.S. minister to Great Britain, where he negotiated a postal treaty, protested British intervention in Central American politics, and reported to the U.S. state department on the European revolutions of 1848. During the Civil War he supported Abraham Lincoln, and afterward Andrew Johnson, writing the latter's first annual message to Congress in 1865. From 1867 to 1871 he was U.S. minister to Prussia, and from 1871 to 1874 minister to the German Empire, becoming a close friend of Bismarck, and serving as representative in the Oregon boundary negotiations between the U.S. and Great Britain. After his return he settled at Washington, writing and revising his *History.* His other works include *Literary and Historical Miscellanies* (1855), a collection containing his oration "The Office of the People in Art, Government, and Religion," which provides a key to his political, religious, and historical thought; *A Plea for the Constitution of the United States* (1886), occasioned by the paper-money controversy of the period; and *Martin Van Buren to the End of his Public Career* (1889), a reminiscent biography. See *The Life and Letters of George Bancroft,* by M. A. DeWolfe Howe (2 vols., 1908), and *George Bancroft: Brahmin Rebel,* by Russel B. Nye (1945).

Bancroft, Hubert Howe. b. at Granville, Ohio, May 5, 1832; d. March 2, 1918. American publisher and historian, noted for his multivolume history of the North and Central American Pacific coast, a project carried out as a collective enterprise under his direction. Beginning as a bookseller's assistant at Buffalo, N. Y., he went to California in 1852, worked in the gold mines, and in 1858 established the publishing and business firm of H. H. Bancroft and Company at San Francisco. Having collected an extensive library of books and documents relating to the Pacific coast, he projected an encyclopedia which eventually developed into his history of the Pacific coast area. In 1868 he hired a force of librarians and copyists and (c1880) sent out reporters to transcribe dictated accounts by pioneers. He ultimately acquired 60,000 volumes of material, and brought out between 1875 and 1890 the 39 volumes of his history covering the Pacific coast and Rocky Mountain regions, British Columbia, Alaska, Mexico, and Central America. Of these volumes, 28 are devoted to history proper, five to the native races, and six to essays; the entire work came from the hands of Bancroft and some 12 writers, supported in their efforts by a considerable number of researchers and note-takers. Among Bancroft's other works are *Resources of Mexico* (1893), *The New Pacific* (1900), *The Book of Wealth* (1909–10), *Retrospection, Political and Personal* (1910), and *In These Latter Days* (1917).

Bancroft, Richard. b. at Farnworth, Lancashire, England, in September, 1544; d. at Lambeth (now part of London), Nov. 2, 1610. English prelate, a vigorous opponent of Puritanism. He became bishop of London in 1597, and served as archbishop of Canterbury in the period 1604–10. He supervised the translations of the Bible used for the Authorized Version.

Bancroft, Sir **Squire.** [Original surname, **Butterfield.**] b. 1841; d. 1926. English actor, theater manager, and writer. He dropped his family name of Butterfield for his original second name of Bancroft at the time of his marriage. After his first appearance on the stage at Birmingham in 1861 he played the provinces until 1865, when he made his London debut in Wooler's play *A Winning Hazard* at the Prince of Wales's Theatre, under the direction of Marie Effie Wilton. He became this popular actress's leading man and, in 1868, her husband; thereafter they were billed as "The Bancrofts." Jointly they managed the Prince of Wales's Theatre until 1879, specializing in producing and acting in the plays of Thomas William Robertson. At a time when the British stage was largely dominated by plays of a bombastic and oratorical character, the Bancrofts are credited with restoring the vogue of light comedy, realistic in theme and simple in diction. In 1879 the Bancrofts moved to the Haymarket Theatre, where for many years they continued to produce and act in modern drama, including Sardou's *Odette* (in which they starred Helena Modjeska), Sardou's *Fedora,* W. S. Gilbert's *Sweethearts,* and Pinero's *Lords and Commons.* Squire Bancroft was knighted in 1897. He was the author, in collaboration with his wife, of *On and Off the Stage* (1888) and *Recollections of Sixty Years* (1909); in 1925, after his wife's death, he published *Empty Chairs.*

Bancroft, Wilder Dwight. b. at Middletown, R.I., Oct. 1, 1867—. American chemist who was awarded (1933) the William H. Nichols medal of the New York section of the American Chemical Society for his work on the application of colloid chemistry to physiological problems. Having received (1888) an A.B. from Harvard, he taught (1895–1937) physical chemistry at Cornell, as professor after 1903. Founder and editor (1896–1932) of *Journal of Physical Chemistry;* author of *The Phase Rule* (1897), *Applied Colloid Chemistry* (1932), and others.

Banda (bän'dä, ban'dạ). District in the Jhansi division, Uttar Pradesh, NE Union of India, W of Allahabad: rice, wheat, and oilseeds. Capital, Banda; area, ab. 2,913 sq. mi.; pop. 722,568 (1941).

Banda. Capital of the Banda district, NE Union of India, on the Ken River, ab. 97 mi. W of Allahabad: commercial center. 22,415 (1941).

Bandaisan (bän.dī.sän). [Also: **Bandai** (bän.dī), **Bantai.**] Volcano in Japan, on the island of Honshu, in Fukushima prefecture ab. 100 mi. N of Tokyo. It underwent a disastrous eruption on July 15, 1888. Elevation, 5,968 ft.

Banda Islands (bän'dä, ban'dạ). Group of about 10 small islands in the Molucca Archipelago, ab. 70 mi. S of Ceram, E Indonesia. Its chief products are nutmegs and mace. Chief town, Bandanairo; pop. 13,036.

Banda Oriental (bän'dä ō.ryen.täl'). [Eng. trans., "*Eastern Shore.*"] Formerly a common name in the Platine region of South America for the territory now comprehended in Uruguay (*q.v.*), especially the plains in the S part.

Bandar (bun'dạr). See **Masulipatam.**

Bandar Abbas (bän.där' äb.bäs'). [Also: **Bender Abbasi, Bender Abbas**; Eng. trans., "*Harbor of Abbas*"; former name, **Gombroon.**] Seaport in S Iran, in Laristan region, situated on the Strait of Ormuz, opposite Ormuz. It has communication by steamer with Bombay, Basra, and other ports, and exports rugs, cotton, gums, and fruit. It was an important commercial point in the 17th century. Marco Polo ended his return voyage here. Pop. ab. 10,000.

Bandar Shah (shä). Small seaport in N Iran, in the Gurgan region, on the SE point of the Caspian Sea, near the border of the U.S.S.R. It is an important trading center and the northern terminus of the Trans-Iranian railway from Bandar Shahpur, on the Persian Gulf.

Bandar Shahpur (shä.pör′). Seaport in W Iran, in Khuzistan region, at the head of the Persian Gulf: important as the southern terminus of the Trans-Iranian railway, though overshadowed as an oil port by Abadan.

Banda Sea (bän′dạ, ban′dạ). Sea in Indonesia, E of the Flores Sea, NW of Arafura Sea, N of Timor, and S of Boeroe and Ceram. Length, ab. 500 mi.; width, ab. 250 mi.

Bandeira (bun.dā′rạ), **Manuel (Carneiro de Sousa).** b. at Recife, Brazil, April 19, 1886—. One of Brazil's best-known contemporary poets. His books of poetry, which began to appear in 1917, were later (1940) printed in a single volume, *Poesias completas*.

Bandel (bän′dẹl), **Ernst von.** [Full name, **Joseph Ernst von Bandel.**] b. at Ansbach, Germany, May 17, 1800; d. at Neudegg, near Donauwörth, Germany, Sept. 25, 1876. German sculptor, designer of the statue of Arminius near Detmold (completed in 1875).

Ban-de-la-Roche (bäṅ.dẹ.lȧ.rosh). [German, **Steinthal**; Eng. trans., *"Stone Valley."*] Mountainous region in Alsace, NE France, ab. 25 mi. W and SW of Strasbourg.

Bandelier (ban.dẹ.lir′). National monument (established 1916) in Frijoles Canyon, Pajarito Plateau, W of Santa Fe and N of Los Alamos, N.M., notable as one of the centers of Regressive Pueblo culture (1300–1600 A.D.). The area is noted for its artificial cave dwellings, cut out of the soft walls of the canyons. The pottery is of the glaze-paint types. Area, 27,049 acres.

Bandelier, Adolph Francis Alphonse. b. at Bern, Switzerland, Aug. 6, 1840; d. at Seville, Spain, March 18, 1914. American historian, archaeologist, anthropologist, and explorer. Emigrating to Highland, Ill., in 1848, he returned (1855) to Switzerland to study geology at the University of Bern. His first scholarly publications, relating to the Mexican Indians, were *On the Art of War and Mode of Warfare* (1877), *On the Distribution and Tenure of Lands* (1878), and *On the Social Organization and Mode of Government* (1879). From 1880 to 1889 he undertook explorations in New Mexico for the Archaeological Institute of America, living among the Pueblos for a time. His surveys were published as *Final Report of Investigations among the Indians of the Southwestern United States* (2 parts, 1890, 1892), and *Contributions to the History of the Southwestern Portion of the United States* (1890). Beginning in 1892 he carried out extensive investigations in South America, returning (1903) to New York, where he served with the Natural History Museum and was a lecturer on Spanish-American literature at Columbia. He was appointed (1911) a research associate of the Carnegie Institute of Washington for archival research in Spain. He is distinguished for his work with original sources.

Bandello (bän.del′lō), **Matteo.** b. at Castelnuovo, Piedmont, Italy, 1480; d. at Agen, France, 1565. Italian prelate (bishop of Agen 1550) and novelist. His tales (1554–73) furnished subjects for Shakespeare, Philip Massinger, and others.

Bandiera (bän.dyā′rä), **Attilio.** b. at Naples, Italy, 1817; executed at Cosenza, Italy, July 25, 1844. Italian patriot; brother of Emilio Bandiera. He was executed by the Neapolitan government for an attempted rising on the coast of Calabria in behalf of Italian independence. The two brothers had previously joined in an unsuccessful conspiracy for an attack on Sicily.

Bandiera, Emilio. b. at Naples, Italy, 1819; executed at Cosenza, Italy, July 25, 1844. Italian patriot; brother of Attilio Bandiera. He joined his brother in an unsuccessful conspiracy, for which both were executed.

Bandinelli (bän.dē.nel′lē), **Bartolommeo** (or **Baccio**). b. at Florence, c1493; d. there, Feb. 7, 1560. Italian painter and sculptor; son and pupil of a Florentine goldsmith named Michelangelo Bandinelli di Vivano. He made the copy of the *Laocoön* group, in the Uffizi, at Florence, the *Hercules* of the Palazzo Vecchio, and the *Adam and Eve*, also at Florence.

Bandinelli, Orlando. Original name of Pope **Alexander III.**

Bandjermasin (bän.jėr.mä′sin). [Also: **Banjarmasin, Banjermasin, Banjermassin.**] City in Borneo, the chief town of the island, situated near the S coast. It exports rubber, iron, coal, and palm oil. 65,600 (1930).

Bandjermasin. Former name of **Banjar.**

Bandoeng (bän′dủng). [Also, **Bandung.**] City in Java, Indonesia, near the SW corner of the island. The city is in the western highlands of the island; some of the government offices have been moved here from Batavia (Jakarta). There are many rubber, coconut, and rice plantations in the area. 166,900 (1930).

Bandol-sur-Mer (bäṅ.dol.sür.mer). Town in SE France, in the department of Var, situated on the Mediterranean coast between Toulon and La Ciotat. It is a winter resort; has two fine bathing beaches and a fishing port. It was almost completely destroyed in the course of the Allied invasion of S France in 1944. Pop. 2,621 (1946).

Bandon (ban′dọn). [Also: **Bandonbridge** (ban′dọn.brij); Irish, **Droichead Banndan.**] Market town in Munster province, Irish Republic, in County Cork, situated on the river Bandon, ab. 16 mi. SW of Cork. 2,528 (1951).

Bandon (bän′dôn″). Town in S Thailand, on the Malay Peninsula, ab. 325 mi. S of Bangkok: a seaport which ships chiefly tin and rubber.

Bandon River (ban′dọn). Small river in Munster province, Irish Republic, in County Cork. It rises ab. 10 mi. NE of Bantry and flows E to the sea at Kinsale Harbour. Length, ab. 40 mi.

Bandrowski (bän.drôf′skē), **Juljusz Kaden-.** b. at Rzeszów, Poland, 1885; d. 1945. Polish writer. In the late 1930's he was cultural censor and literary arbiter of the Polish state.

Bandtke (bänt′ke), **Jan Wincent.** [Also, **Bandtkie.**] b. at Lublin, Poland, 1783; d. at Warsaw, 1846. Polish jurist; brother of Jerzy Samuel Bandtke.

Bandtke, Jerzy Samuel. [Also, **Bandtkie.**] b. at Lublin, Poland, Nov. 24, 1768; d. at Kraków, Poland, June 11, 1835. Polish historian and grammarian.

Bane (bä′nā). See **Bene.**

Banér (bä.nār′), **Johan.** [Also: **Banier, Banner.**] b. at Djursholm, near Stockholm, June 23, 1596; d. at Halberstadt, Germany, June 20, 1641. Swedish general in the Thirty Years' War. He commanded (Sept. 17, 1631), the right wing at Breitenfeld, was made field marshal after the death of Gustavus Adolphus, and gained the victories of Wittstock (Oct. 4, 1636) and Chemnitz (April 14, 1639).

Banerjea (bä′nėr.jē), Sir **Surendranath.** b. at Calcutta, India, 1848; d. 1925. Indian liberal political leader. He was a consistent champion of constitutional reforms to further Indian participation in the administration and control of the government and to secure adequate representation in the British Commonwealth. He was editor of the *Bengalee*, one of the outstanding early nationalist newspapers, president (1895, 1902) of the Indian National Congress, leader of the fight against the partition of Bengal, and president of the Moderate conference at Bombay in 1919. Author of *A Nation in Making* (1925), an autobiography.

Banes (bä′nās). [Full name, **Puerta de Banes.**] City on the NE coast of Cuba, in Oriente province: export center for sugar and fruits. 14,097 (1943).

Banff (bamf, banf). Village in Alberta, Canada, situated on the Canadian Pacific Railway near the border of British Columbia. It is a pleasure resort and the railway station for the Banff National Park. It has hot sulfur springs and is famous for its vacation facilities. Elevation, 4,500 ft.; pop. 2,357 (1951).

Banff. Royal burgh, market town, and seaport in NE Scotland, county seat of Banffshire, situated at the mouth of the river Deveron on Moray Firth, ab. 11 mi. E of Cullen, ab. 588 mi. N of London by rail. It is a fishing port and health resort. 3,340 (est. 1948).

Banff National Park. Canadian national park, established in 1885, located on the E slopes of the Rocky Mountains in W central Alberta, and including Lake Louise. It is through Kicking Horse Pass (5,339 ft.) in this park that the Canadian National Railway crosses the Rocky Mountains. There are hot mineral springs; the railway has developed two hotels and resorts in the park. Area, 2,585 sq. mi.

Banffshire (bamf′shir, banf′-) or **Banff.** Maritime county in NE Scotland. It is bounded on the N by Moray Firth, on the E and S by Aberdeenshire, and on the W by Inverness-shire and Moray. Its surface is mountainous except near the coast. Ben Machdui (4,296 ft.), the second-highest mountain in the United Kingdom, lies partly in Banffshire and partly in Aberdeenshire. Slate and marble quarrying are carried on. Banff is the county seat; area, ab. 630 sq. mi.; pop. 50,135 (1951).

Bánffy (bän′fē), Baron **Desiderius** (or **Dezsö**) **von.** b. at Klausenburg (now Cluj, Rumania), Oct. 28, 1843; d. at Budapest, May 24, 1911. Hungarian politician. He tried to Magyarize the non-Hungarian minorities within his country. As Hungarian prime minister (1895–99), he opposed the policies of the papal nuncio.

Bang (bäng; Anglicized, bang), **Bernhard Laurits Frederik.** b. at Sorø (on the island of Zealand), Denmark, June 7, 1848; d. at Copenhagen, Denmark, June 22, 1932. Danish veterinarian. He discovered (1897) the bacterium, *Brucella abortus*, the cause of Bang's disease (named after him) which often leads to abortion in cattle and undulant fever in humans infected by drinking the raw milk of animals thus afflicted. He described a method (1900) of preventing the spread of bovine tuberculosis by isolation of the affected cows. Author of *Measures against Animal Tuberculosis in Denmark* (1908).

Bang, Herman Joachim. b. on the island of Als, Denmark, April 20, 1857; d. at Ogden, Utah, Jan. 29, 1912. Danish writer, best known for his novels *Haabløse Slægter* (Generations without Hope, 1880) and *Ved Vejen* (Along the Road, 1886). He stirred up controversy by his eccentric, highly artistic style, which became almost a mannerism, and by his sympathetic descriptions of despair and human suffering.

Bangalore (bang.gạ.lōr′). [Also, **Bangalur** (bäng.gä-lör′).] District in Mysore state, S Union of India. Capital, Bangalore; area, ab. 3,000 sq. mi.; pop. ab. 900,000 (1941).

Bangalore. [Also, **Bangalur.**] Capital of the state of Mysore and of Bangalore district, S Union of India, ab. 180 mi. W of Madras. Its chief manufactures are carpets, cotton textiles, woolen goods, and leather goods. There are also many small industries producing soap, porcelain, shellac, furniture, white lead, cigarettes, and other items. It was fortified by Haidar (or Hyder) Ali, and was taken (1791) from Tipu (or Tippoo) Sahib (by storm) by the British under Cornwallis. 248,334 (1941).

Banganapalle (bung″gạ.nạ.pul′ē). Former state in the S part of the Union of India, now part of Madras, ab. 200 mi. NW of the city of Madras. Millet and indigo are raised here, and the making of rope from jute is an important occupation. Capital, Banganapalle; area, 259 sq. mi.; pop. (mostly Hindus) 44,631 (1941).

Bange (bäṅzh), **Charles Ragon de.** b. at Balignicourt, Aube, France, Oct. 17, 1833; d. at Chesnay, near Versailles, Seine-et-Oise, France, 1914. French artillery officer who improved the accuracy of French gunnery. His siege artillery was used by the French during World War I.

Bangka (bäng′kä, bang′kạ). [Also: **Banca, Banka.**] Island in Indonesia, E of Sumatra and separated from it by the Bangka Strait. It is famous for tin mines. The chief port is Muntok. Length, 135 mi.; area, 4,610 sq. mi.; pop. 205,363 (1930).

Bangka Strait. [Also, **Banca** (or **Banka**) **Strait.**] Strait in Indonesia between the islands of Sumatra and Bangka. It connects the South China Sea with the Java Sea. Length, ab. 100 mi.; width, ab. 15 mi.

Bangkok (bang′kok″). [Former name, **Siayuthia**; Siamese, **Krung Thep.**] Capital and chief commercial city of Thailand, situated on the Chao Phraya River, ab. 15 mi. from its mouth. It became (1782) the capital after the destruction of Ayutthaya. The chief exports include rice, teak, sugar, hides, cotton, silk, ivory, pepper, sesame, and cardamom. Rice mills, teak sawmills, cement mills, and match factories comprise the main industries. The Great Pagoda of Wat-ching at Bangkok is, in its general concave-conoid form, similar to the Burmese pagodas, but is much more polygonal in plan, and is ornamented elaborately in both color and carving. Instead of terminating in a sharp finial, it ends in a tall hexagonal prism with a domical top. At the base and toward the summit there are large rectangular niches with lavish adornment of flame-tongued pinnacles. The old port extends along the river, and near it are the larger commercial establishments; the new port is some miles below the city. About 1,000 steamers call here each year. The modern section of the city is laid out along spacious lines with Western buildings and many Buddhist temples; elsewhere there are narrow streets with the shops of the Chinese traders. The royal palace and the associated buildings are in strikingly beautiful Thai architecture, with varicolored tile roofs. The city was taken by the Japanese in 1941, and underwent frequent bombing attacks in World War II. 800,000 (est. 1940).

Bangor (bang′gôr, -gọr). City in C Maine, county seat of Penobscot County, on the W bank of the Penobscot River, at the head of navigation. It is a lumbering, shipping, and manufacturing center; products include sardines, cheese, textiles, canned blueberries, wood pulp, paper, and canoes. It became a city in 1834. It is the seat of the Bangor Theological Seminary, which was founded in 1814, was opened at Hampden in 1816, and was removed to Bangor in 1819. Pop. 31,558 (1950).

Bangor. Municipal borough, seaport, and seaside resort in Ulster province, Northern Ireland, in County Down, situated on the S bank of Belfast Lough, near its entrance, ab. 11 mi. NE of Belfast. It is the principal yachting center in Ireland. There are ruins of Bangor Castle and of an abbey nearby. 19,500 (est. 1949).

Bangor. Borough in E Pennsylvania, in Northampton County, ab. 23 mi. NE of Allentown: slate-quarrying center. It was established in 1773, and named for Bangor, Wales. 6,050 (1950).

Bangor. Municipal borough, railway junction, educational and tourist center, and market town in N Wales, in Caernarvonshire, situated at the N entrance to Menai Strait, ab. 9 mi. NE of Caernarvon, ab. 239 mi. NW of London by rail. It contains a restored cathedral, and is the seat of the University College of North Wales and four other colleges. 12,822 (1951).

Bangor. [Also: **Bangor-Isycoed** (bang′gôr.is′i.koid), **Bangor-Iscoed** (-is′koid).] Civil parish in Overton rural district, N Wales, in Flintshire, situated on the river Dee, ab. 5 mi. SE of Wrexham. It was formerly famous for its monastery. 533 (1931).

Bangorian Controversy (bang.gō′ri.ạn). Controversy stirred up by a sermon preached before George I (of England) on March 31, 1717 by Benjamin Hoadley, Bishop of Bangor, in Wales, from the text "My kingdom is not of this world." He argued that Christ had not delegated judicial and disciplinary powers to the Christian ministry. Supporters of ecclesiastical authority in the Church of England sharply disputed Hoadley's points, and hundreds of pamphlets were published on both sides of the question during the ensuing several years.

Bangs (bangz), **John Kendrick.** b. at Yonkers, N.Y., May 27, 1862; d. Jan. 21, 1922. American humorist, editor, and lecturer. Graduated (1883) from Columbia, where he edited *Acta Columbiana*, he served (1884–88) as associate editor of the humor magazine *Life*, and from 1888 to 1899 was on the staff of *Harper's Magazine*, heading its humor department and also that of *Harper's Bazaar*. For a brief time, in 1889, he was the first editor of *Munsey's Weekly*, and subsequently contributed to other periodicals. He was editor (1899–1903) of *Harper's Weekly*, editor (1903–04) of the *New Metropolitan Magazine*, and editor (1904 *et seq.*) of *Puck*. After 1907 he devoted himself to free-lancing and lecturing; his most noted lecture was called *Salubrities I Have Met*. His first book, *The Lorgnette* (1886; written with S. W. Van Schaick), was followed by more than 30 volumes of verse and humor published up until 1910. Among the better known ones are *Tiddledywink Tales* (1891), *Coffee and Repartee* (1893), *The Idiot* (1895), and *A Houseboat on the Styx* (1896). He wrote also *Three Weeks in Politics* (1894), a humorous account of his unsuccessful bid for the mayoralty of Yonkers, *Uncle Sam, Trustee* (1902), a commentary on Cuban affairs, and a play, *Lady Teazle*, in which Lillian Russell took the title role.

Bangued (bäng.gād′). Town in the Philippine Islands, the capital of Abra province, in NW Luzon. 5,663 (1948).

Bangui (bäng′gē). Capital of the Ubangi-Shari territory, French Equatorial Africa, on the Ubangi River, near the NW corner of the Belgian Congo and almost on the border between the Middle Congo and Ubangi-Shari territories. It is an important river port, trading with points on both the lower and upper reaches of the river. Pop. ab. 23,000.

Bangweulu (bang.wē.ō′lō). [Also: **Bangweolo** (-ō′lō), **Bemba.**] Lake in C Africa, in the NW part of Northern Rhodesia, near the Belgian Congo border. It is formed by the headstreams of the Congo River. The Luapula River, the only stream flowing out of it, emerges from its S point, and is ab. 1 mi. wide at the place of exit. The lake was discovered (1868) by David Livingstone, who died near its shore in 1873.

Baní (bä.nē′). City in the S part of the Dominican Republic, in Trujillo province. 10,048 (1950).

Baniana (ban.i.ā′na). A Latin name of **Baena.**

Banier (bä.nēr′), **Johan.** See **Banér, Johan.**

Banim (bā′nim), **John.** b. at Kilkenny, Ireland, April 3, 1798; d. near Kilkenny, Aug. 13, 1842. Irish novelist, dramatist, and poet. He wrote the tragedies *Damon and Pythias* (produced 1821) and *The Prodigal*, the *Tales of the O'Hara Family* (somber stories of Irish peasant life, written in collaboration with his brother Michael), *The Nowlans* (a novel), and others.

Banim, Michael. b. at Kilkenny, Ireland, Aug. 5, 1796; d. at Booterstown, near Dublin, Ireland, Aug. 30, 1874. Irish novelist; brother of John Banim (1798–1842). He collaborated with his brother in writing the *Tales of the O'Hara Family* (6 vols., 1825–26), a work portraying in grim colors the life of the Irish peasantry. Author of *The Ghost Hunter* (1833), *Father Connell* (1842), and *The Town of the Cascades* (2 vols., 1864).

Banister (ban′i.ster), **John.** b. at London, 1630; d. there, Oct. 3, 1679. English violinist, noted for organizing the first public concerts advertised (1672) at London. He was a protegé of Charles II until he disagreed with that monarch's preference for Italian violins.

Banister, John. b. at Twigworth, Gloucestershire, England, 1650; d. in Virginia, in May, 1692. American colonial botanist; grandfather of John Banister (1734–88). He was graduated (B.A., 1671; M.A., 1674) from Magdalen College, Oxford, where he subsequently served as clerk and chaplain. After a visit to the West Indies, he settled (1678) in Virginia. He became minister of what was later Bristol Parish, but spent most of his time in scientific work. He studied the flora and fauna of the region and drew up catalogues of Virginia plants, which appeared in Ray's *Historia Plantarum* and *Petiver's Memoirs*, and wrote entomological and botanical articles, several of which were published in the *Philosophical Transactions* after his death. His *Natural History of Virginia* was interrupted by his death.

Banister, John. b. in Bristol Parish, Va., Dec. 26, 1734; d. Sept. 30, 1788. American Revolutionary patriot; grandson of John Banister (1650–92). He studied law in England, where he was admitted to the bar in 1753. A member of the Virginia Convention of 1776, he served (1777) in the Virginia House of Burgesses and was a delegate (1778–79) to the Continental Congress, where he helped frame the Articles of Confederation. He served (1778–81) as a lieutenant colonel of cavalry, winning Washington's esteem, and in 1781 took part in beating off the British invasion of Virginia.

Banister, Zilpah Polly. [Maiden name, **Grant.**] b. at Norfolk, Conn., May 30, 1794; d. Dec. 3, 1874. American educator, notable as a pioneer in schooling for women. She attended (until 1821) the Byfield (Mass.) Seminary before serving as principal (1824 *et seq.*) of Adams Female Academy, Derry, N.H., which she transferred (1828) to Ipswich. She gave up the school in 1839 because of poor health. Mary Lyon was for some time her assistant, and founded Mt. Holyoke Seminary (now Mt. Holyoke College) on the Ipswich pattern.

Baniyas (bä.nē.yäs′). [Also: **Banias** (-äs′), **Paneas**; ancient name, **Caesarea Philippi.**] Village in SW Syria, at the foot of Mount Hermon, ab. 40 mi. SW of Damascus: said to have been named by the Greeks for the God Pan.

Baniyas. [Also, **Banias.**] Fishing village in W Syria, ab. 25 mi. S of Latakia. Pop. ab. 2,000.

Banja Luka (bä′nyä lö′kä). Town in C Yugoslavia, in the federative unit of Bosnia-Hercegovina, the principal town of the former *banovina* (province) of Vrbaska, situated near the junction of the Vrbas and Krbanja rivers, NW of Sarajevo. It is an important commercial center, particularly as a market for cattle and grain. It was, in earlier periods, the site of several battles between the Austrians and the Turks. 33,191 (1948).

Banjar (bän′jar). [Former name, **Bandjermasin, Banjarmasin, Banjarmassin,** or **Banjermassin** (bän.jėr-mä′sin).] *Daerah* (autonomous area), formerly a Dutch residency, in SE Borneo, once a sultanate, now part of the United States of Indonesia. It lies in the lowlands on the S part of the island. Its chief crops are palm oil and rubber; there are also deposits of coal in the area. Chief town, Bandjermasin.

Banjarmasin, Banjermasin, or **Banjermassin** (bän-jėr.mä′sin). See **Bandjermasin.**

Banjo. Poem (1929) by Claude McKay. Its theme is that the Negro, by realizing fully his racial consciousness, may make his finest contribution to the national culture.

Banjoemas (bän′yö.mäs). [Also: **Banjumas, Banyumas.**] Town in the Republic of Indonesia, near the S coast of the island of Java. Coal and phosphate mining are important in the area, and the town has a sugar refinery. Pop. ab. 7,000.

Banjoewangi (bän.yö.wäng′gē). [Also: **Banyuwangi, Banjuwangi.**] Seaport in the United States of Indonesia, in the *negara* (state) of East Java, on the E coast of Java, across Bali Strait from the island of Bali: an important port for the export of sugar. 25,185.

Banka (bäng′kä). See **Bangka.**

Banker's Daughter, The. Drama (1878) by Bronson Crocker Howard.

Bankette of Sapience, The. [Also, **The Banquet of Sapience.**] Collection of wise and moral sayings by Sir Thomas Elyot. It was printed as "newely augmented" in 1539, and was popular enough to have had at least five editions.

Bank for International Settlements. World bank established (1929) at Basel, Switzerland, in response to the need for an agency to transfer German reparation payments under the Young Plan. It conceived for itself the wider mission of aiding in the clearance of currency exchanges and maintaining currency stability during economic declines, but this hopeful aim failed to achieve practical realization. Its authorized capital was about one hundred million dollars, to which the U.S., Great Britain, France, Italy, Germany, Japan, and Belgium were the largest subscribers. It had no authority to issue bank notes. Although, strictly speaking, the U.S. did not directly participate in the operations of the bank, it played an influential role in determining the unit's affairs.

Bankhead (bangk′hed), **John Hollis.** b. at Moscow (now Sulligent), Ala., July 8, 1872; d. at Bethesda, Md., June 12, 1946. American politician, a U.S. senator (1931–46) from Alabama, known for his support of New Deal agricultural measures; brother of William Brockman Bankhead. The Bankhead Cotton Act of 1934 (*q.v.*) was largely the work of himself (in the Senate) and his brother (in the House of Representatives). As a member (1903–07) of the Alabama legislature, he drafted the present Alabama election law. In private life he practiced law and operated coal mines.

Bankhead, Tallulah (Brockman). b. at Huntsville, Ala., Jan. 31, 1903—. American actress; daughter of William Brockman Bankhead. She made appearances during most of her early career (1923–31) at London, where she gained great popularity. On the New York stage (1933 *et seq.*) she played both dramatic and comedy roles; the former included leading parts in *The Green Hat* and *Rain;* Thornton Wilder's *The Skin of Our Teeth* (1942) furnished her with one of her best-known comic parts. After appearing (1947) in Jean Cocteau's *The Eagle has Two Heads*, she toured (1948–50) in a revival of *Private Lives* by Noel Coward. She was engaged (1950) as mistress of ceremonies for a weekly radio comedy show. She has also acted in films, including *Lifeboat* (1943). Author of *Tallulah: My Autobiography* (1952).

Bankhead, William Brockman. b. at Moscow, Ala., April 12, 1874; d. at Washington, D.C., Sept. 15, 1940. American politician, speaker of the House of Representatives (1936–40); brother of John Hollis

Bankhead (1872–1946) and father of Tallulah Bankhead (1903—). He was graduated (1893) from Alabama University and received (1895) his law degree from the Georgetown University Law School. After a brief career on the stage, he was admitted to the bar (1895) and established his law practice at Huntsville, Ala. He was a member (1900–01) of the Alabama legislature, served as city attorney for Huntsville for four years, and was circuit solicitor (1910–14) of the 14th Judicial District. He became (1917) a Democratic member of Congress from Alabama, serving in that capacity until his death. He became (1934) chairman of the rules committee and was elected (June 3, 1936) speaker of the House of Representatives. It was in this latter post that he led the unsuccessful battle for the passage of President Roosevelt's Supreme Court reorganization plan. Among the legislative measures sponsored by him was the Cotton Control Act.

Bankhead Cotton Act. Act of the U.S. Congress, approved (April 21, 1934) as a supplement to the restrictions on cotton production already stipulated by the Agricultural Adjustment Act (May 12, 1933). It was drafted and guided through Congress largely by the Bankhead brothers: John Hollis Bankhead (in the Senate) and William Brockman Bankhead (in the House of Representatives). By it farmers were encouraged to restrict cotton production voluntarily (thereby raising prices to "parity" level) by the designation of a national cotton quota. A tax of 50 percent of the central market price (at a minimum of five cents per pound) was to be levied on all cotton processed in excess of the quota. The act was repealed (Feb. 10, 1936) by Congress following the Supreme Court's invalidation of the Agricultural Adjustment Act.

Bankhead-Jones Act of 1937. Measure passed by the U.S. Congress in 1937 for the purpose of extending federal aid to farm tenants, sharecroppers, and farm laborers. Under the administration of the Farm Security Administration until 1946, and thereafter under the Farmers Home Administration, the act provided for long-term credits enabling the purchase of farms, agricultural supplies, and equipment.

"Bank Holiday." Name applied to the culmination of the national banking crisis of 1933 in the U.S. The "holiday" was the result of mounting bank moratoriums declared by the various states between Feb. 14 and March 4, 1933. By most frequent usage, the term refers to the period between the latter date (the occasion of Franklin D. Roosevelt's first inaugural) and March 14, 1933, when not a single bank was publicly functioning in the U.S.

Banking Act. Name applied to two measures passed by the U.S. Congress: **1.** The Banking Act of June 16, 1933, which widened the credit-control functions of the Federal Reserve Board, sanctioned bank-deposit insurance under the Federal Deposit Insurance Corporation, and forbade the operation of investment affiliates by commercial banks and the operation of deposit-banking facilities by investment houses. **2.** The Banking Act of Aug. 23, 1935, two of the three titles of which were amendments to the Banking Act of 1933, while the remaining title provided for the reorganization of the Federal Reserve Board, whose official designation was changed to the Board of Governors of the Federal Reserve System.

Bank of Augusta v. Earle, 13 Peters 519 (1839). U.S. Supreme Court decision, rendered by Chief Justice Roger Brooke Taney, notable for its definition of the position of foreign corporations in American law. The decision upheld the right of the Bank of Augusta to recover on a bill of exchange it had bought in Alabama on the ground that the laws of Alabama did not specifically forbid foreign corporations from selling such bills. The court pointed out that in the absence of positive action on the part of the state it could be assumed that foreign corporations could enter into contracts; but the court recognized the right of a state to bar or control by statute the entry of a foreign corporation within its boundaries.

Bank of England. [Called the **"Old Lady of Threadneedle Street."**] Principal bank in Great Britain, since 1946 formally owned by the British government, originally a private joint-stock institution incorporated by charter on July 27, 1694. Formed at the outset for the purpose of advancing a loan of 1,200,000 pounds to the government, it still has the management of the national debt, acts as the government's banker, and administers the exchange-control regulations. It also acts as banker for many leading British banks, and has branches in various parts of the country. It enjoys the monopoly of issuing paper currency, popularly known as Bank of England notes. The Bank of England was formally nationalized (March 1, 1946) under the Labour government of Clement R. Attlee by the terms of legislation passed in the previous year. Its building in London stands on Threadneedle Street opposite the Mansion House; hence it is often called the "Old Lady of Threadneedle Street."

Bank of France. Principal bank in France, since 1945 owned by the French government, an institution acting as banker for the government, founded Feb. 13, 1800, with the support of Napoleon I. Its building at Paris, which has undergone many alterations, was formerly a private mansion called the Hôtel de Toulouse. The bank has branches and offices throughout the country. It was established for the purpose of advancing national and other loans at a moderate rate and promoting national trade and industries. It has the exclusive right to issue French paper currency. Since 1890 it has practiced the making of small loans on moderate security. It also receives jewels, plate, and other valuables at a fixed charge for safe deposit. In international importance and repute the Bank of France ranked for many years next to the Bank of England. It has had (since 1857) a fixed capital of 182,500,000 francs. A law passed in 1945 nationalized the Bank of France, which originally had been a private joint-stock venture.

Bank of North America. First government-incorporated bank in the U.S., formed by Robert Morris and chartered (1781) by the Continental Congress. It began operations in 1782 at Philadelphia, and played an important financial role in the closing phase of the Revolutionary War. Among those associated with its early history were Benjamin Franklin, John Jay, Alexander Hamilton, and Thomas Jefferson.

Bank of the United States, First. Bank established (1791) by act of the U.S. Congress for a period of 20 years. One-fifth of its capitalization of ten million dollars was subscribed by the U.S. government and the balance by private individuals. The bank, with headquarters at Philadelphia, was managed by a board of 25 directors chosen by the shareholders; shareholders were limited to a maximum of 30 votes; foreign shareholders were forbidden to vote by proxy, and could not serve as directors. The bank was authorized to conduct commercial banking operations and issue circulation notes not exceeding its capitalization. It commenced operations on Dec. 12, 1791, and by 1811, when its charter expired, had eight branches. It acted as a fiscal agency for the national government and performed its functions creditably, but questions concerning its constitutional status played an important role in its failure to secure renewal of its charter.

Bank of the United States, Second. Bank incorporated (1816) by act of the U.S. Congress, with a charter which did not differ substantially from that of the First Bank of the United States except for the authorization of capital and note issue up to but not exceeding 35 million dollars, a clause permitting the government to name five of the 25 directors, and a provision requiring the bank to pay 1,500,000 dollars to the government for its franchise. The Second Bank of the United States, a measure promoted by the Madison administration, came after a five-year period of state banking which failed to meet the financial and currency demands created by the War of 1812. Under its first president, William Jones, who served from 1816 until his resignation in 1819, the administration of the bank was marked by fraud, manipulation, and mismanagement. Jones was succeeded by Langdon Cheves, who did much to restore the bank to a sound footing. Nicholas Biddle, who became president in 1823, was responsible for a period of efficient and capable management. Under his regime, however, the bank was popularly attacked as a "capitalistic monster" by those who believed that through its main office and 25 branches the institution controlled, under the hand of one man, the economic fortunes of the nation. The climax of the so-called "Bank War" between President Andrew Jackson and Biddle came after the bank figured as the chief issue in the presidential campaign of 1832. In July of that year

Jackson had vetoed the bill for the recharter of the bank, assailing the "rich and powerful" who "bend the acts of Government to their selfish purposes," and the attempt to pass the bill over Jackson's veto failed. In September, 1833, Jackson ordered the removal of the government deposits from the bank, thus causing a sharp decline in its operations and a contraction of credit. The bank's charter expired in 1836.

Bankrupt, The. Comedy by Samuel Foote, produced in 1773.

Banks (bangks), **George Linnaeus.** b. at Birmingham, England, March 2, 1821; d. at London, May 3, 1881. English editor, song writer, dramatist, and social reformer; husband of Isabella Banks, the novelist and poet. He was the author of *The Slave King,* written for the Negro tragedian Ira Frederick Aldridge, and two burlesques, *Old Maids and Mustard,* and *Ye Doleful Wives of Windsor.* He also wrote *What I Live For,* a humanitarian poem, *Dandy Jim of Caroline,* a Negro song, and *Warwickshire Will,* a song in tribute to Shakespeare. He edited (1848–64) the Harrogate *Advertiser,* Birmingham *Mercury,* Dublin *Daily Express,* Durham *Chronicle,* Sussex *Mercury,* and other journals. Author also of a life of Blondin, the famous French tightrope walker, published in 1862.

Banks, Isabella. [Often called **Mrs. Linnaeus Banks;** maiden name, **Varley.**] b. at Manchester, England, March 25, 1821; d. at Dalston, England, May 5, 1897. English novelist and poet; married (1864) George Linnaeus Banks. Her works include the novels *God's Providence House* (1865), *Stung to the Quick* (1867), and *The Manchester Man* (1876); also the collection of poems entitled *Ripples and Breakers* (1878).

Banks, John. b. c1650; d. after 1696. English dramatist of the period of the Restoration. He wrote *The Rival Kings* (1677), *The Destruction of Troy* (acted 1678, printed 1679), *The Unhappy Favorite* (1682), *The Innocent Usurper* (1683, published 1694), *The Island Queens* (1684, acted 1704 as *The Albion Queens), Virtue Betrayed* (1692), and *Cyrus the Great* (1696).

Banks, Sir **Joseph.** b. at London, Feb. 13, 1743; d. at Isleworth, England, June 19, 1820. English naturalist (especially known as a botanist) and patron of science. He equipped the ship *Endeavour,* and accompanied Cook's first expedition (1768–71), visited Iceland (1772), and served as president of the Royal Society (1778–1820). His herbarium and library became after his death the property of the British Museum. He wrote *A Short Account of the Causes of the Disease called the Blight, Mildew, and Rust* (1805) and others.

Banks, Nathan. b. at Roslyn, N.Y., 1868—. American entomologist. He was graduated (M.S., 1890) from Cornell, served (1900–16) as an assistant entomologist with the U.S. Department of Agriculture, and was curator of insects (1916–41) and head curator of recent insects (1941–45) at the museum of comparative zoölogy at Harvard, where he was also associate professor of zoölogy (1928–36). He assembled the largest single collection in the U.S. of the *Neuroptera* and *Arachnida.* Author of *Treatise on the Acarina* (1904), *How to Collect and Preserve Insects* (1909), and *Catalogue of Nearctic Spiders* (1910).

Banks, Nathaniel Prentiss. [Called the **"Bobbin Boy."**] b. at Waltham, Mass., Jan. 30, 1816; d. there, Sept. 1, 1894. American politician and general. In early life he was a machinist, editor, and lawyer; thereafter he served in the Massachusetts legislature. He was a member (1853–57) of the U.S. Congress from Massachusetts, elected first as a coalition Democrat, then as a Know-Nothing, and later as a Republican. He served as speaker of the House of Representatives in the period 1856–57, before serving as Republican governor of Massachusetts (1858–61). In 1861 he was commissioned a major general of volunteers; he commanded a corps on the upper Potomac and in the Shenandoah Valley in 1862, commanded at the Battle of Cedar Mountain, Aug. 9, 1862, and succeeded Butler in command at New Orleans at the end of 1862; invested Port Hudson and captured it in July, 1863, commanded the Red River expedition in 1864, was defeated at Sabine Cross Roads, and gained a victory at Pleasant Hill. He was a Republican member of Congress from Massachusetts again in 1865–73, 1875–77, and 1889–91, and was defeated as Liberal-Republican candidate for Congress in 1872.

Banks, Thomas. b. at Lambeth (now part of London), England, Dec. 29, 1735; d. at London, Feb. 2, 1805. English sculptor. He began his career as a carver of ornaments, and studied later at the Royal Academy, where he received a prize, and at Rome (1772–79). He spent some time (1781–82) in Russia, his *Cupid Catching a Butterfly* being bought by Catherine the Great. Among his notable works is also *Shakespeare Attended by Painting and Poetry,* which is now at Stratford-on-Avon.

Bankside (bangk'sīd). Name applied to that portion of the Thames bank which lies on the S side between Blackfriars and Waterloo bridges, London. In the time of the Tudors it consisted of a single row of houses, built on a dike, or levee, higher both than the river at high tide and the ground behind the bank. At one end of "Bank Side" (as it was then spelled) stood the Clink Prison, Winchester House, and Saint Mary Overies Church. A little to the W of the Clink and behind the houses stood the Globe Theatre. The Festival of Britain (1951) was situated on this area.

Banks Island (bangks). [Former name, **Banks Land.**] Large island in NE Canada, in the Arctic Archipelago, in the Arctic Ocean NW of Victoria Island and SW of Melville Island. Area, 25,675 sq. mi.

Banks Islands. Group of small islands in the South Pacific, NE of the New Hebrides; named for Sir Joseph Banks (1743–1820), English naturalist. Politically, they are part of the British-French New Hebrides Condominium.

Banks Peninsula. Peninsula on the E coast of the South Island of New Zealand, separating Pegasus Bay from Canterbury Bight. The city of Christchurch is situated on its N side.

Banks Strait. Strait separating Tasmania from the Furneaux Group to the NE, both S of Australia.

Banks Strait. Former name of **McClure Strait.**

Bankura (bäng'kö.rä). District of the Burdwan division, West Bengal, E Union of India, NW of Calcutta: rice, jute, and sugar. Capital, Bankura; area, ab. 2,646 sq. mi.; pop. 1,289,640 (1941).

Bankura. Capital of the Bankura district, E Union of India, on the Dhalkisor River, ab. 100 mi. NW of Calcutta: important trading center and road junction. 31,703 (1941).

Banmana (bän.mä'nä). See **Bambara.**

Bann (ban). River in Ulster province, Northern Ireland. It is divided into the Upper Bann, a river which rises in the Mourne Mountains and flows NW into Lough Neagh, and the Lower Bann, a river which flows NW from Lough Neagh to the Atlantic Ocean, ab. 5 mi. NW of Coleraine. Length of Upper Bann, ab. 25 mi.; of Lower Bann, ab. 33 mi.

Bannalec (bà.nà.lek). Town in NW France, in the department of Finistère, between Lorient and Quimper. It has an old castle. 6,098 (1946).

Bannatyne (ban'ą.tīn), **George.** b. in Scotland, 1545; d. c1608. Collector of early Scottish poetry. His manuscript collection was printed in part by Allan Ramsay and David Dalrymple, Lord Hailes, and completely by the Hunterian Club; the manuscripts relate to the poetry of the 15th and 16th centuries.

Bannatyne, John. See **Bellenden, John.**

Bannatyne Club. Scottish literary club, named for George Bannatyne (1545–c1608), founded under the presidency of Sir Walter Scott in 1823, and dissolved in 1859. It was devoted to the publication of works on Scottish history and literature.

Banner (bä.ner'), **Johan.** See **Banér, Johan.**

Banner (ban'ėr), **Peter.** b. in England; fl. 1794–1828. American architect. He arrived in the U.S. from England at Boston in 1794, proceeding shortly to New York (his name is found in the *New York Directory* of the years 1795–98, with his profession given as house carpenter and master-builder). When he returned to Boston is not known, but he was listed as an architect in the *Boston Directory* for 1806. Apparently he lived at Boston from that time until 1828; there is no known reference to him after that year, and it is not known when or where he died. Peter Banner (whose name sometimes appears in the records, erroneously, as Baner and as Bonner) influenced the development of American architecture through the Eben Crafts house at Roxbury, Mass., erected in 1805, and the Park Street Church at Boston, finished in 1809. Both of these structures are noted for a largeness of conception and excellence of design combined with grace and delicacy in the details, and meticulous workmanship. They brought a kind of freshness and, it has been said, a new beauty to New England architecture. The spire of the Park Street Church, though it combines superimposed architectural orders and is thought by some to derive in part from the spire of Christopher Wren's Saint Bride's church at London, is considered Peter Banner's masterwork. Other structures known to have been of his design were the Old South parsonage houses, long since demolished, and the first home of the American Antiquarian Society at Worcester, Mass., which stood until 1910.

Banner Hill. Unincorporated community in E Tennessee, in Unicoi County. 2,873 (1950).

Banners, Feast of. See **Feast of Banners** or **Flags.**

Banning (ban'ing). City in S California, in Riverside County, E of Los Angeles, in a fruit-producing area. 7,034 (1950).

Banning, Margaret Culkin. b. at Buffalo, Minn., March 18, 1891—. American novelist. A graduate (1912) of Vassar, she is the author of *This Marrying* (1920), *Half Loaves* (1921), *Spellbinders* (1922), *Prelude to Love* (1929), *The First Woman* (1935), *Too Young to Marry* (1938), *Out in Society* (1940), *Women for Defense* (1942), *Conduct Yourself Accordingly* (1942), *The Clever Sister* (1947), and other works.

Bannister (ban'is.tėr), **Charles.** b. in Gloucestershire, England, c1738; d. at London, Oct. 26, 1804. English actor and bass singer.

Bannister, John. b. at Deptford, England, May 12, 1760; d. at London, Nov. 7, 1836. English comedian; son of Charles Bannister. He created (1779) the original interpretation of the role of Don Ferolo Whiskerandos in *The Critic* by Richard Brinsley Sheridan. He served (1802–03) as manager of the Drury Lane.

Bannister, Nathaniel Harrington. b. Jan. 13, 1813; d. at New York, Nov. 2, 1847. American playwright and actor.

Bannock (ban'ọk). North American Indian tribe, formerly mainly distributed in N Nevada but now nearly extinct. The language is of the Uto-Aztecan family.

Bannockburn (ban'ọk.bėrn). Town in C Scotland, in Stirlingshire, ab. 3 mi. SE of Stirling, ab. 415 mi. N of London by rail. Here, on June 24, 1314, the Scots (ab. 30,000) under Robert the Bruce totally defeated the English (ab. 100,000) under Edward II. The loss of the English was ab. 30,000. At Sauchieburn, in the vicinity, James III of Scotland was defeated and slain by rebellious nobles in 1488. Pop. of electoral division, 4,522 (1931).

Bannock War (ban'ọk). Indian uprising (1878) in the U.S. Northwest, touched off by the discontent of the Bannock Indians, and others, over the government's policies concerning reservations in Oregon and Idaho. Some 1,500 tribesmen under Chiefs Egan and Buffalo Horn opposed U.S. regulars under General O. O. Howard; the Indians lost about 80 to some 50 for their opponents. Most of the surviving Indians were taken (1879) to the Yakima Reservation, in what was then the Washington Territory.

Bannu (bä'nö). [Also, **Banu.**] District in the North-West Frontier Province, Pakistan, ab. 250 mi. NW of Lahore. Sheep raising and subsistence farming are the chief occupations of the people. Capital, Bannu; area, ab. 1,670 sq. mi.; pop. 295,930 (1941).

Banquet of Sapience, The. See **Bankette of Sapience, The.**

Banquo (bang'kwō). Thane of Lochaber in Shakespeare's tragedy *Macbeth*. He is a general in the king's army, with the same rank as Macbeth, and with the same ambitions, but is of a quieter nature and more discretion. The Weird Sisters, who appear to Macbeth and Banquo, prophesy the crown for Macbeth, but promise Banquo that his offspring shall reign thereafter. Macbeth, in an effort to avert this prophecy, sends murderers to kill Banquo and his only son, Fleance. The boy, however, escapes. In one of the most powerful scenes of the play Banquo's ghost appears to the guilty Macbeth, unseen by the other banqueters.

Bansda (bänz'dä). Former state in the Union of India, one of the Gujarat states, now merged with Bombay, ab. 200 mi. N of the city of Bombay. Manganese is mined here, and tobacco and cotton are the important crops. Capital, Bansda; area, 215 sq. mi.; pop. 54,764 (1941).

Banse (bän'zẹ), **Ewald.** b. at Brunswick, Germany, May 23, 1883—. German geographer, author of works on geopolitics and psychological warfare. It is said that Hitler was influenced by his theories. His most important book is *Landschaft und Seele* (1928).

Banshee and Other Poems, The. Volume of poems (1888) by John Todhunter.

Baňská Belá (bän'skä be'lä). See under **Baňská Štiavnica.**

Baňská Bystrica (bēs'trē.tsä). [German, **Neusohl;** Hungarian, **Beszterczebánya.**] Town in Czechoslovakia, in C Slovakia, situated on the Hron River E of Kremnica. It has a number of noteworthy modern buildings, including the National House, the National Bank, and the National Forestry and Estates administration. A Slovak rising against the Germans took place here in 1944. Pop. 12,230 (1947).

Baňská Štiavnica (shtyäv'nē.tsä). [German, **Schemnitz;** Hungarian, **Selmeczbánya.**] Town in Czechoslovakia, in C Slovakia, between Nitra and Zvolen, ab. 67 mi. N of Budapest. It is an old mining town. In the 15th and 16th centuries gold and silver mining was controlled by the Fugger financial house of Augsburg. Silver, iron, and lead are still mined in the vicinity. There is a mining academy and various textile, wood, and iron industries. Buildings of interest include the town hall, built in 1488, a Piarist monastery, a castle (now a local museum), and a mining museum. The town of Baňská Belá is incorporated into Baňská Štiavnica. 11,870 (1947).

Banstead (ban'sted). Urban district in SE England, in Surrey, ab. 3 mi. E of Epsom, ab. 15 mi. SW of Victoria station, London. It is between 400 and 700 ft. above sea level and possesses great scenic beauty. A considerable area of the urban district lies within the London "Green Belt" scheme (a program of planned housing and industrial development designed to combine the advantages of the country with accessibility to the city). 33,526 (1951).

Banswara (bän.swä'rạ). Former state in the Union of India, now merged with Rajasthan, in the S tip of Rajputana, ab. 330 mi. N of the city of Bombay. Grazing is important here, some nickel is mined, and the main crops are jute, cotton, wheat, and forest products. Capital, Banswara; area, 1,946 sq. mi.; pop. 258,760 (1941).

Bantai (bän.tī). See **Bandaisan.**

Bantam (bän.täm', ban'tạm). [Also, **Bantan** (-tän').] Small seaport in W Java, Indonesia, ab. 61 mi. W of Batavia, formerly of great commercial importance.

Bantayan (bän.tä.yän'). One of the Visayan group of islands in the Philippines, NE of Cebu: fisheries. Area, ab. 47 sq. mi.; pop. 28,602 (1939).

Bantayan. Port in the SW part of Bantayan island, province of Cebu, Philippine Islands. 4,816 (1948).

Banti (bän'tē), **Guido.** b. at Montebicchieri, Italy, June 18, 1852; d. at Florence, Jan. 8, 1925. Italian pathologist. He described typhoid septicemia, leukemia, and pneumococcic infection; made notable descriptions of splenic anemia (1882; named Banti's disease, after him) and splenomegalia (1894).

Bantia (ban'shi.ạ). In ancient geography, a town in S Italy, SE of Venusia and NE of the modern Potenza.

Banting (ban'ting), Sir **Frederick Grant.** b. at Alliston, Ontario, Canada, Nov. 4, 1891; d. in an army airplane crash on the E coast of Newfoundland on the way to England, in February, 1941. Canadian research physician, who, with Charles H. Best, a sophomore medical student, experimenting on depancreatized dogs at the University of Toronto, discovered (July 30, 1921) the hormone now employed as a specific remedy for diabetes. The discovery was made during the absence on summer vacation of J. J. R. Macleod, professor of physiology. After the discovery of insulin by Banting and Best, Professor Macleod and J. P. Collip collaborated in purifying and assaying insulin so that it could be used in human diabetes. Banting was educated at Alliston High School and the University of Toronto; served (1915–19) in World War I; was appointed (1919) resident surgeon at the Hospital for Sick Children at Toronto; was an instructor in physiology (1920) at the University of Western Ontario, London, Ontario; returned (1921) to the University of Toronto to begin research on internal secretion of the pan'creas; and served (1923–41) as professor of medical research at the University of Toronto. In 1923, with J.J.R. Macleod he received the Nobel prize for physiology, in recognition of their contributions to the discovery of insulin; Banting shared his part of the prize with Charles H. Best, and Professor Macleod shared his portion with J. P. Collip. Banting served as a major in the medical corps of the Canadian army and as chairman of the medical section of the National Research Council of Canada, during World War II.

Banting, William. b. 1797; d. at Kensington (now part of London), March 16, 1878. London undertaker who, in 1863, in a pamphlet entitled *A Letter on Corpulence*, recommended a course of diet for the reduction of corpulence, which has sometimes been called "banting," after him. The diet recommended was originally prescribed for Banting by William Harvey, and consists of the use of lean meats principally and abstinence from fats, starch, and sugar.

Bantock (ban'tọk), Sir **Granville.** b. at London, Aug. 7, 1868; d. 1946. English composer and conductor. He made (1894–95) a tour of the world as conductor of a musical comedy company, and subsequently led various orchestras in England, also conducting concerts at Antwerp. He introduced many new works by English composers; his own compositions are numerous and include symphonic poems, suites, overtures, and vocal and chamber music, many of them based on Oriental themes. He was principal of the school of music at Birmingham, and succeeded Edward Elgar as professor at Birmingham University in 1908, serving in the latter post until 1934.

Bantry (ban'tri). [Irish, **Beanntraighe.**] Market town and seaport in Munster province, Irish Republic, in County Cork, situated near the head of Bantry Bay, ab. 45 mi. SW of Cork. 2,316 (1951).

Bantry Bay. Inlet of the Atlantic Ocean in Munster province, Irish Republic, in County Cork. Length, ab. 25 mi.; width, ab. 5 mi.

Bantu (ban'tö). Large and homogeneous group of related African languages spoken, with the exception of Khoisan in SW Africa, throughout S, E, and C Africa. The N boundary of the Bantu-speaking peoples is defined approximately by a line drawn from just E of Calabar in SE Nigeria, across the N Belgian Congo between the Congo and the Wele rivers, to the N shores of Lake Victoria, and then SE to Dar-es-Salaam in E Tanganyika. According to the conventional classification, Bantu is one of the five language families of Africa, along with Khoisan, Sudanic, Semitic, and Hamitic. However, in recent years (since 1945), J. H. Greenberg has shown the relationship between Bantu and the W Sudanese languages, and has grouped them together as the Niger-Congo family, in which Bantu is a member of one of 15 subfamilies. The most characteristic feature of Bantu is the agreement of words in a sentence, based on a system of noun classes with associated noun prefixes. Thus for the Gogo, we have *Wa-gogo* (plural), the Gogo people; *Mu-gogo* (singular), a Gogo person; *Ki-gogo* (singular) the Gogo language; and *U-gogo* (singular), the Gogo country. The term *Ba-ntu* itself, first applied in this sense in 1862 by W. H. Bleek, is a widespread word meaning "the people" found also in the forms *aba-ntu*, *awa-ntu*, *a-tu*, *ba-tu*, and *ova-ndu*. The prefixes of most frequent occurrence (for people) are *Ba-*, *Wa-*, *Ova-*, *A-*, *Ma-*, *Ama-;* seldom *I-*, *Tu-*, *Eshi-*, *Bashi-*, or *Akua-*. For a person the most frequent are *Mu-*, *Um-*, *Mo-*, *M-;* seldom *Ki-*, *Tshi-*, *Ka-*, *Mushi-*, *Mukua-*. For a language the prefixes of most frequent occurrence are *Ki-*, *Tshi-*, *Shi-*, *Si-*, *Se-;* seldom *U-*, *Lu-*, *Di-*. For the country the most frequent are *Bu-* and *U-;* seldom *Le-*.

Examples	Person	People	Language	Land
Ganda	*Mu-ganda*	*Ba-ganda*	*Lu-ganda*	*Bu-ganda*
Luba	*Mu-luba*	*Ba-luba*	*Ki-luba*	*U-luba*
Suto	*Mo-suto*	*Ba-suto*	*Se-suto*	*Le-suto*
Mbangala	*Ki-mbangala*	*I-mbangala*	*U-mbangala*	
Mbundu	*O-tishi-mbundu*	*Ovi-mbundu*	*U-mbundu*	

The Bantu languages are also characterized by class gender rather than sex gender, prepositional genitive, polysyllabic roots, both semantic and grammatical tone, and a system of verb suffixes which distinguish between passive, neuter, causative, applied, reciprocal, intensive, reversive, extensive, diminutive, associative, perfective, stative, contactive, and other derivative forms. The term *Bantu* is sometimes used to denote a "race," but this usage is questionable; the differences in physical type between the Bantu of SE Africa and of W Congo, not to mention the Bantu-speaking Pygmies, are no less than those between the Bantu-speaking peoples as a group and the non-Bantu Negroes of W Africa. Culturally the Bantu-speaking peoples are even more diverse.

Banu (bä'nö). See **Bannu.**

Banvard (ban'värd), **John.** b. at New York, Nov. 15, 1815; d. at Watertown, S.D., May 16, 1891. American painter and writer. Barred by poor health from outdoor sports in childhood, he dabbled in scientific experiments, drawing, and versifying. When he was 15 years of age, at Louisville, Ky., he became a drug clerk but was discharged for spending his time drawing caricatures on the walls. He then set up an art gallery on a flatboat, and, starting at New Harmony, Ind., floated down the Ohio River, disposing of his wares for potatoes, eggs, fowl, and other edibles more often than for cash, until navigational troubles and malaria put an end to the adventure. Banvard, who had a lifelong passion for bigness, next painted a panorama of Venice, a city which he had never seen. He purchased a museum at St. Louis and lost his capital in the venture. After recouping his fortunes by peddling merchandise on the Ohio, he set out on the voyage which brought him fame and fortune. Alone in an open skiff he journeyed thousands of miles up and down the Mississippi River, diligently sketching the scenes and characters which became the material of his gigantic painting *Panorama of the Mississippi*. This was advertised to cover three miles of canvas (and actually was half a mile long). Mississippi River captains and pilots praised the accuracy with which Banvard depicted the life they knew; no critic, however, conceded any artistic merit to this or any of his other paintings. After exhibiting this panorama at New Orleans, Natchez, Cincinnati, and other American cities, the painter took it to England, where it aroused much interest, especially as Queen Victoria admired it. Banvard then traveled extensively in Europe, Asia, and Africa, painting scenes in Palestine and a *Panorama of the Nile*. From his work *The Orison*, painted in 1861, was made the first American chromolithograph, a species of picture which in time was to be seen in millions of American homes. John Banvard wrote something like 1,700 poems, of which some were printed in periodicals. His published books were *Description of the Mississippi River* (1849), *Pilgrimage to the Holy Land* (1852), *Amasis, or the Last of the Pharaohs* (1864), *The Private Life of a King, Embodying the Suppressed Memoirs of the Prince of Wales, afterwards George IV* (1876), and *The Tradition of the Temple* (1883). Banvard also wrote two dramas: *Amasis*, which was performed at the Boston Theatre at Boston (1864), and *Carrinia*, produced at the Broadway Theatre at New York (1875).

Banville (bäṅ.vēl), **Théodore Faullain de.** b. at Moulins, France, March 14, 1823; d. at Paris, March 13, 1891. French poet, dramatist, and novelist. The son of an officer in the navy, he early devoted himself to literature, publishing in 1842 two volumes of verse, entitled *Les Cariatides*. He also wrote *Odes Funambulesques* (1857) and others. His most successful play, *Gringoire*, was published in 1866. In *Mes Souvenirs* (1882) he portrayed some of his contemporaries.

Banyuls-sur-Mer (bäṅ.yül.sür.mer). [Also, **Banyules-sur-Mer.**] Seaport in S France, in the department of Pyrénées-Orientales, situated on the Mediterranean Sea near the Spanish frontier, ab. 20 mi. SE of Perpignan. It produces fine Roussillon wine. Pop. ab. 4,000.

Banyumas (bän'yö.mäs). See **Banjoemas.**

Banyuwangi (bän.yö.wäng'gē). See **Banjoewangi.**

Bao-Daï (bä'ō.dä'ē). [Also: **Bao Dai**; personal name, **Nguyen-vinh-Thuy.**] b. Oct. 22, 1913—. Emperor of Annam (1926–45) and of Viet-Nam (1949 *et seq.*). Educated in France, he abdicated (Aug. 26, 1945) under pressure from Ho Chih-minh. He then went (February, 1946) to China, Hong Kong, and France. He returned (April, 1949) to Annam as ruler, under French sponsorship, of Viet-Nam, consisting finally of Annam, Tonkin, and Cochin-China, all former provinces of French Indo-China.

Baoni (bä.ō′nē). Former state in the Union of India, one of the Central India states, now merged with Vindhya Pradesh, ab. 50 mi. SW of Cawnpore: rice, wheat, and sugar. Capital, Baoni; area, 121 sq. mi.; pop. 25,256 (1941).

Baoule (bä.ö′lā). See **Baule.**

Bapaume (bȧ.pōm). Town in N France, in the department of Pas-de-Calais, ab. 14 mi. S of Arras. Here, on Jan. 2 and 3, 1871, the Germans under August von Goeben gained a victory over the French under Louis Léon César Faidherbe. The scene of heavy fighting in World War I, Bapaume was severely damaged. Pop. ab. 2,800.

Baphomet (baf′ọ.met). Imaginary idol or symbol which the Templars were accused of worshiping. This speculation has never had the general acceptance of scholars. Indeed, the word may be simply a manipulated form of "Mahomet," a name which took strange shapes in the Middle Ages.

Baps (baps), **Mr.** In Charles Dickens's novel *Dombey and Son*, a dancing-master, "a very grave gentleman."

Bapst (bäpst), **John.** b. at La Roche, Fribourg, Switzerland, Dec. 17, 1815; d. Nov. 2, 1887. Jesuit missionary and educator in America. Ordained (1846) in Switzerland, he served as a missionary among the Abnaki Indians at Oldtown, Me. As a priest (after 1850) at Ellsworth, Me. (a center of the "Know-Nothing" party), he sued the local school-committee for requiring Catholic children to participate in Protestant religious ceremonies and was driven from the town by a mob. He served (1860–69) as rector of a Jesuit training school which under his direction became Boston College.

Baptista (bap.tis′tạ). In Shakespeare's *Taming of the Shrew*, a rich gentleman of Padua, the father of Katharina, the "Shrew."

Baptista (bä.tēs′tä), **Mariano.** b. 1832; d. 1907. Bolivian conservative politician and newspaperman; president of Bolivia (1892–96). During his administration two treaties were signed (1895) with Chile, including one promising Tacna and Arica, won by Chile in the "War of the Pacific," to Bolivia in the event that a referendum in these territories was favorable to Chile rather than Peru. The treaties, which would have given Bolivia a corridor to the Pacific, were never carried out.

Baptistery of San Giovanni (sän jō.vän′nē). Baptistery at Florence, Italy, remodeled by Arnolfo di Cambio in the 13th century. It is octagonal in plan (108 ft. in diameter); the exterior is in white and black marble, with arcades and inlaid panels, and the interior is domed, with a small lantern. It is famous for its three magnificent double gates in bronze, of which that on the south (1330) is by Andrea Pisano, and those on the north and east (1403–24) by Lorenzo Ghiberti. Andrea's gate has a beautiful wreathed framing of leaves, flowers, and birds, and 28 panel-reliefs of the story of John the Baptist. The north Ghiberti gate has also 28 reliefs, mostly of the life of Christ; and the chief gate, that toward the east, has in richly ornamented framing ten reliefs from the Old Testament. The Baptistery escaped serious damage in World War II.

Ba Quan Am (bä′ kwän′ äm′). [Also, **Quan Am.**] The Viet-Namese (specifically, Annamese) name for the Buddhist goddess of mercy and the protectress of children. She is invoked by sterile women.

Baquedano (bä.kä.ᴛʜä′nō), **Manuel.** b. at Santiago, Chile, 1826; date of death not known. Chilean soldier. He began the Peruvian campaign of 1879 as a brigadier general under Escala, and in 1880 succeeded that general in command of the army of invasion, conducting the Tacna and Lima campaigns with an almost uninterrupted series of victories, the Peruvian forces being inferior. For his services he was made generalissimo of the Chilean army.

Baquerizo Moreno (bä.kä.rē′sō mō.rā′nō), **Alfredo.** b. at Guayaquil, Ecuador, June 27, 1861; d. at New York, March 19, 1951. Ecuadorian political leader. He was president (1916–20) of Ecuador, and again (1931–32) provisional president.

Bar (bär). Former territory in E France, whose capital was Bar-le-Duc. It was a county and later a duchy, was united with the duchy of Lorraine in 1473, was annexed by France in 1659, and was restored in 1661 to Lorraine.

Bar. Town in the U.S.S.R., in the Ukrainian Soviet Socialist Republic, situated on the Roff River, a tributary of the Bug River: center of a large wheat-growing area. It was founded by Sigismund I of Poland. No official or reliable population figures have been made available since World War II, and estimates have ranged from ab. 6,000 to as high as ab. 25,000.

Bar. [Italian, **Antivari.**] Town and harbor in SW Yugoslavia, in the federative unit of Montenegro, in the former *banovina* (province) of Zetska, situated near the Adriatic Sea, SE of Kotor and SW of Lake Scutari. It was under Venetian sovereignty in the Middle Ages. In 1878, it was conquered by Montenegro and was ceded by Turkey in the same year. In 1919 it was incorporated into the kingdom of Yugoslavia. 5,541 (1931).

Bar, Confederation of. Name applied to a league of Polish nobility and gentry formed in 1768 at Bar, then a part of Poland, now included in the Ukrainian Soviet Socialist Republic. The circumstances leading to this movement were complex. Pressure was being applied by other states to compel the Polish government to grant to religious dissidents rights equal to those enjoyed by Roman Catholics, who formed the majority of the Polish population. The aggressive demands of Russia, as presented by that country's representative at Warsaw, Prince Nicholas Repnin, were especially resented. The dissidents having set up a confederation at Radom in 1766, the Polish Diet in 1767 conceded to them all rights except that of the Crown. The church authorities at Rome thereupon made known their view that Polish Catholics should act in defense of the faith, and the Confederation of Bar took the field against dissidents and foreign aggressors alike. The prime movers of the Confederation were Adam Krasinski, bishop of Kamenets, Michael Krasinski, and Count Osip Pulawski (or Joseph Pulaski), father of the man who was to achieve fame in U.S. history as General Casimir Pulaski of the Continental Army in the Revolutionary War. The confederates promptly began military operations against Russia, defeated Polish King Stanislaus's attempts to curb them, and, ignoring Stanislaus, entered into negotiations with France, Austria, and Turkey, with the aim of forming a league against Russia. The French government actually sent a commander to organize the Confederation's armed forces, which won many victories. These forces, however, operating in comparatively small bands, were in the end no match for the Russian armies, and by 1772 the Confederation of Bar was suppressed, though some of its adherents struggled on until 1776.

Bara (bä′rä), **Jules.** b. Aug. 31, 1835; d. June 26, 1900. Belgian liberal politician. He was minister of justice (1865–70, 1878–84).

Bara (bãr′ạ), **Theda.** [Original name, **Theodosia Goodman.**] b. at Cincinnati, Ohio, c1890—. American motion-picture actress. She was a popular star of the silent films, the apotheosis of the heavy-lidded, languorous siren popular with the audiences of that time. Among her starring vehicles were *Cleopatra*, *The Vampire*, and *A Fool There Was*.

Bara Banki (bä′rạ bung′kē). District of the Fyzabad division, Uttar Pradesh, Union of India: wheat, rice, and sugar. Area, ab. 1,722 sq. mi.; pop. 1,162,508 (1941).

Barabas (bạ.rab′ạs). Central character in Christopher Marlowe's *The Jew of Malta*.

Baraba Steppe (bä.rä.bä′). [Russian, **Barabinskaya Step** (bä.rä.bēn′skạ.yạ styep).] Steppe in W Siberia, situated between the rivers Ob and Irtysh, in the Novosibirsk *oblast* (region) of the Russian Soviet Federated Socialist Republic.

Barabbas (bạ.rab′ạs). [Also, **Barrabas.**] In the Bible, a robber and insurrectionary leader whose release from prison instead of that of Jesus was demanded of Pilate by the Jews.

Baraboo (bar′ạ.bö). City in S Wisconsin, county seat of Sauk County, on the Baraboo River, ab. 35 mi. NW of Madison: trading center for a farming region. It was the original headquarters of the Ringling Brothers' circus. The name was taken from that of Jean Baribault, a French trader. 7,264 (1950).

Baracaldo (bä.rä.käl′dō). Town and commune in N Spain, in the province of Vizcaya, situated near the mouth of the Bilbao River, NW of Bilbao. Originally a river port and an agricultural commune covering a wide area, it has become industrialized in recent decades; there are large iron and steel works and metallurgical industries. 36,165 (1940).

Baracoa (bä.rä.kō′ä). City in E Cuba, in Oriente province: tropical fruits, cacao, and coffee. The oldest town of Cuba, it was founded in 1512. Pop. 10,395 (1943).

Barada (bä.rä′dä). [Also: **Amana;** Biblical name, **Abana;** Greek, **Chrysorrhoas.**] Small river in Syria, flowing through the plain and city of Damascus. In modern times, it has been important in irrigation, but in Biblical times it was probably chiefly known, in conjunction with the river Pharphar, for the sacredness of its waters. 2 Kings, v. 12.

Baraga (bar′ạ.gạ), **Frederic.** b. near Döbernig, in Slovenia, June 29, 1797; d. Jan. 19, 1868. Roman Catholic missionary in America. Ordained in 1823, he arrived (1831) in America as a missionary to the Ottawa Indian village of Arbre Croche (now Harbor Springs, Mich.). He founded (1833) a mission at the site of Grand Rapids, Mich., and transferred (1835) it to La Pointe, on Madeline Island. He founded (1843) a mission at L'Anse (in what is now Baraga County, Mich.). He was consecrated (1853) bishop of Upper Michigan.

Baraguay d'Hilliers (bà.rà.gā dē.lyā), **Achille.** b. at Paris, Sept. 6, 1795; d. at Amélie-les-Bains, France, June 6, 1878. French marshal; son of Louis Baraguay d'Hilliers.

Baraguay d'Hilliers, Louis. b. at Paris, Aug. 13, 1764; d. at Berlin, Jan. 6, 1813. French soldier, notable for his service under Napoleon.

Barahona (bä.rä.ō′nä). Province in the SW part of the Dominican Republic. Capital, Barahona; area, 1,341 sq. mi.; pop. 62,032 (1950).

Barahona. City in SW Dominican Republic, capital of Barahona province. 14,690 (1950).

Barak (bạ.räk′). Name given to the upper course of the Surma, a river in Assam, NE Union of India.

Baramba (bạ.rum′bạ). Former state in the Union of India, one of the Eastern States, now merged with Orissa, ab. 90 mi. W of Cuttack: timber and other wood products. Capital, Baramba; area, 142 sq. mi.; pop. 52,924 (1941).

Baramula (bä.rạ.mö′lạ). Town in W Kashmir, N India: the river port of the state, on the Jhelum River, W of Srinagar. Near it is the famous gorge of the Jhelum. The town was almost destroyed by earthquake in 1885. Pop. ab. 5,900.

Baranof Island (bar′ạ.nôf, bä.rä′nọf). [Also, **Sitka Island.**] Island in the Alexander Archipelago, off the coast of SE Alaska, containing the town of Sitka. Length, ab. 95 mi.

Baranov (bä.rä′nọf), **Aleksandr Andreyevich.** b. 1746; d. 1819. Russian trader, first governor of Alaska as a Russian possession. He founded a trading colony on Bering Strait in 1796, and took possession (1799) of the island in the Sitka group which was afterward named, after him, Baranof Island, founding there a factory and fortress.

Baranovichi (bä.rä.nô′vē.chē). [Polish, **Baranowicze** (bä.rä.nô.vē′che).] City in the W U.S.S.R., in the Byelorussian Soviet Socialist Republic, ab. 85 mi. SW of Minsk, ab. 500 mi. S of Leningrad, and ab. 485 mi. SW of Moscow. Baranovichi is an important railroad center. During World War I it was the site of major battles between German and Russian armies in June and July, 1916. In World War II it was captured by the German forces in July, 1941 and held until July 8, 1944. Pop. 30,119 (est. 1939).

Baranquila (bä.räng.kē′lä). See **Barranquilla.**

Barante (bà.ränt), **Aimable Guillaume Prosper Brugière,** Baron **de.** b. at Riom, France, June 10, 1782; d. Nov. 22, 1866. French statesman and historian. He was an official under Napoleon I and Louis XVIII of France, and was ambassador to Turin and St. Petersburg under Louis Philippe. Among his works are *Tableau de la littérature française au dix-huitième siècle* (1808), translations of Schiller's dramatic works and of *Hamlet, Histoire des ducs de Bourgogne de la maison de Valois* (1824–26), *Histoire de la convention nationale* (1851–53), and *Histoire du Directoire* (1855).

Bárány (bä′räny′), **Robert.** b. at Vienna, April 22, 1876; d. at Uppsala, Sweden, April 8, 1936. Austrian otologist. He was the recipient (1914) of a Nobel prize in medicine for his work on the physiology and pathology of the vestibular apparatus. His name is associated with the caloric differential test (1906) for the function of the labyrinth, and with the pointing test (1906) for circumscribed lesions of the cerebellum. In 1911 he described a syndrome characterized by vertigo, pain in the occipital region, and unilateral deafness. A special chair for testing air pilots has received his name.

Barataria (bä.rạ.tä′rē.ạ). Island city over which Sancho Panza, in Cervantes' *Don Quixote,* was made governor. At his inauguration feast every dish was snatched away untasted, so that he starved in the midst of abundance. Disgusted with the joys of government, after a short trial, he abjured his ephemeral royalty, preferring his liberty.

Barataria Bay (bar.ạ.tãr′i.ạ). Inlet of the Gulf of Mexico, on the SE coast of Louisiana, in Plaquemines Parish, W of the Mississippi River. Length, ab. 18 mi.

Barathron (bar′ạ.thron). Steep ravine on the W slope of the Hill of the Nymphs, at Athens, Greece, outside of the ancient walls, rendered more precipitous by ancient use of it as a quarry. In antiquity this was the "pit" into which the bodies of criminals were thrown after execution, or in some cases while still living.

Baratier (bà.rà.tyā), **Albert Ernest Augustin.** b. at Belfort, France, July 11, 1864; d. in a front-line trench near Reims, France, Oct. 17, 1917. French army commander, best known for his exploration (1896) of the route from the Congo River valley to Fashoda, near the head of the Nile, and as a member of the military mission to Fashoda under Captain Jean Baptiste Marchand. The expedition, and subsequent French occupation (1898) of Fashoda, precipitated a crisis in Anglo-French relations because of British fears that French interests might threaten the British position in Africa. Baratier subsequently commanded (1917) a division during World War I.

Baratier (bä.rä.tēr′), **Johann Philipp.** b. at Schwabach, in Anspach, Germany, 1721; d. 1740. German scholar noted for his extraordinary precociousness. He is said to have been able to read and write German and French at four years of age, Latin at five, and Greek and Hebrew at seven. He compiled a Hebrew dictionary at 12, and published a French translation of the itinerary of Benjamin of Tudela at 13.

Baratieri (bä.rä.tyā′rē), **Oreste.** b. at Condino, in the Italian Tyrol, Nov. 13, 1841; d. at Vipiteno (formerly Sterzing), Italy, Aug. 7, 1901. Italian soldier and follower (1860) of Garibaldi. He joined (1866) the Italian regular army, in which he became (1872) a captain; as a colonel of the Bersaglieri he served (1887–88) in Eritrea, where he later (1891) became governor. In the war in Abyssinia (now Ethiopia) he was victorious in his battles (1894–95) against the lesser native chieftains, but after the entry (1895) of Menelik II, the emperor of Abyssinia, into the conflict he suffered a defeat (March 1, 1896) at Aduwa that resulted in complete rout. As a result, he was court-martialed for negligence, but was acquitted and subsequently retired. He wrote *Memorie d'Africa* (1897).

Baraya (bä.rä′yä), **Antonio.** b. 1791; executed at Bogotá, Colombia, July 20, 1816. New Granadan general and Spanish-American patriot. He joined the revolutionists against Spain in 1810, and was one of the members of the first independent junta. He was captured and shot as a rebel.

Baraza (bä.rä′sä) or **Barax** (bà.rà), **Cypriano.** b. in France, 1642; d. in Mojos, Bolivia, Sept. 16, 1702. Jesuit missionary who, in 1674, was the first to visit the Mamoré region, in what is now N Bolivia. He founded the celebrated missions of Loreto and Trinidad, and was murdered by Indians in the forests E of the Mamoré River.

Barbacena (bär.bạ.sā′nạ). City in E Brazil, in the state of Minas Gerais. 25,768 (1950).

Barbacena, Marquês **de.** Title of **Caldeira Brant Pontes, Felisberto** (or **Feliberto**).

Barbacoas (bär.bä.kō′äs). Town in SW Colombia, in Nariño department. Pop. under 5,000 (1938).

Barbados (bär.bā′dōz). [Also: **Barbadoes, Barbudoso** (bär.bụ.dō′sō); sometimes called **"Little England."**] Island in the Lesser Antilles, Caribbean Sea, NE of Trinidad near the Windward Islands: a British colony. It is famous for its molasses; sugar, margarine, cotton, and rum are also important exports. The population density of Barbados, 1,200 to the square mile, is the highest in all of Latin America. The island was colonized c1627. Capital, Bridgetown; area, 166 sq. mi.; pop. 192,841 (1946), 211,682 (est. 1950).

Barbalho Bezerra (bär.bä′lyọ̈ bẹ.zer′rạ), **Luiz.** b. at Pernambuco (now Recife), Brazil, 1601; d. at Rio de Janeiro, 1644. Leader of the Portuguese in the hostilities (1630–40) with the Dutch at Pernambuco and Bahia. For illegal acts he was called to Portugal in 1640 and for a time imprisoned, but was subsequently pardoned and employed in war against Spain. In 1643 he returned to Brazil as governor of Rio de Janeiro.

Barbara (bär′bạ.rạ), Saint. fl. 3rd or 4th century. Christian martyr and saint of the Greek and Roman Catholic churches, martyred possibly at Nicomedia, in Bithynia, c235 A.D. (or c306). The earliest mention of her in surviving records occurs in *Martyrologium Romanum parvum*, which is dated about the year 700; thus it is known that she has been venerated at least since the 7th century. The Acts of her martyrdom are not authentic. According to the legend she was the daughter of Dioscorus, a wealthy noble of Nicomedia. He built a white marble bath for her, and when she first entered this building she made the sign of the cross on the marble; the mark remained in the stone, and when the report of this was spread, many came to see the marvel, and many who kissed it were healed of their sicknesses. Learning by these occurrences that his daughter was a Christian, Dioscorus delivered her to Marrianus, governor of the city, who caused her to be scourged, torn with iron implements, beaten with hammers, and driven naked through the streets. Throughout these tortures the girl remained steadfast in her faith, and it is said that when she was cast into a cell Christ came to her, assuaged her sufferings, and promised her salvation in heaven. When Marrianus condemned her to be beheaded, her father obtained permission to do the deed: but after he had struck off her head, it is related that he was struck by lightning. By a curious process, originating in the legend of her father's death by lightning, Saint Barbara came in time to be the patroness of makers and users of firearms and fireworks.

Barbara Allen's Cruelty. Old ballad, given in Thomas Percy's *Reliques*, relating the cruelty to her lover, and subsequent remorse, of Barbara Allen. There is another version called *Bonny Barbara Allan*, or simply *Barbara Allan*, which was also included in Percy's collection.

Barbara Frietchie (frich′i). American Civil War ballad by John Greenleaf Whittier, first published in the *Atlantic Monthly* (October, 1863) and reprinted in *In War Time and Other Poems* (1864). Based upon an allegedly historic occurrence at Frederick, Md., on Sept. 2, 1862, it describes the patriotic act of Barbara Frietchie, an aged woman who raised a Union flag when Confederate troops under "Stonewall" Jackson occupied the town. It contains the familiar lines:

> "Shoot, if you must, this old gray head
> But spare your country's flag," she said.

Touched by her courage, the Confederate soldiers pass by, leaving both flag and heroine unharmed. Whittier later learned that Mrs. Mary A. Quantrell, a younger woman, had raised the flag. Mrs. Frietchie, however, followed her example several days afterward.

Barbara Frietchie. Play (1899) by Clyde Fitch.

Barbaro (bär′bä.rō), **Monte.** Modern name of **Gaurus.**

Barbarossa (bär.bạ.ros′ạ), **Frederick.** See **Frederick I** (of the *Holy Roman Empire*).

Barbarossa, Khair ed-Din. [Also: **Barbarossa II**; original prename, **Khizr.**] b. c1483; d. at Constantinople, 1546. Mohammedan corsair; brother of Koruk Barbarossa, whom he succeeded (1518) as ruler of Algiers. Having surrendered the sovereignty of Algiers to the Turkish sultan Selim I in order to gain support against the Spaniards, he was appointed governor general, and received (1519) a reinforcement of 2,000 Janizaries. He made himself master of Tunis in 1534, but in 1535 forces of the emperor Charles V besieged and captured the city. He was appointed (1537) high admiral of the Ottoman fleets, and in conjunction with Francis I captured Nice in 1543.

Barbarossa, Koruk. [Also: **Barbarossa I**; prename also written **Arooj, Aruch, Horuc, Horuk,** or **Uruj.**] b. c1474; d. 1518. Mohammedan corsair. He was at one time in the service of the Mamelukes, at Cairo, Egypt, but turned to operations in the Mediterranean on his own behalf and (with his brother, Khair ed-Din Barbarossa) raided many coastal towns in Spain and North Africa. He was slain in a battle against the Spaniards. After 1515, the brothers were in effective control of Algiers, and their exploits against the various Christian rulers of the Mediterranean area made them heroic figures in contemporary Islamic history. They were probably of Albanian descent (although their father is known to have lived on the Greek island Mytilene, and for this reason they are given as Greeks by some sources), and the derivation of their surname "Barbarossa" has been the subject of considerable conjecture. Some authorities follow the traditional etymology (i.e., that they had red beards), and others have seen in it a development of one of Koruk Barbarossa's names (Baba Arooj).

Barbaroux (bår.bå.rö), **Charles Jean Marie.** b. at Marseilles, France, March 6, 1767; guillotined at Bordeaux, France, June 25, 1794. French orator and politician, a member of the Girondist party during the French Revolution. A lawyer by profession, he led the Marseilles battalion in the attack on the Tuileries (Aug. 10, 1792), and was a Girondist deputy to the National Convention. However, he was proscribed (May 31, 1793) as a royalist and enemy of the republic.

Barbary (bär′bạ.ri). [French, **Barbarie** (bår.bå.rē).] General name for the regions along or near the N coast of Africa, W of Egypt, comprising Morocco, Algeria, Tunisia, and sometimes Libya.

Barbary Coast. Name popularly, but unofficially, given after 1849 to a waterfront area of San Francisco, noted for its gaudy eating, drinking, and sporting establishments especially designed to win the patronage of men coming in from the mining areas with an abundance of gold.

Barbary Wars. In U.S. history, the wars (1801–05, 1815) between the U.S. and the Barbary states (Algiers, Morocco, Tunis, and Tripoli). The latter, following their traditions of piracy, exacted tribute as the condition for permitting merchant vessels peaceful and uninterrupted passage through the Mediterranean; after the American Revolution the U.S. joined the maritime nations of Europe in meeting the levy. A succession of incidents, including one involving the vessel *George Washington* in 1800, led to a declaration of war (1801) by Tripoli. The ensuing conflict was almost wholly naval. The "Derna Expedition" (1805) led by William Eaton was the only land action of the war, and its success played an important role in bringing Tripoli to agree to peace negotiations. The treaty of peace, concluded on June 4, 1805, provided for the abolition of all future levies. However, tribute continued to be paid to the other Barbary states until 1815, when the depredations carried out upon American merchantmen led to the dispatch to Algiers of a strong naval force under Stephen Decatur. Algiers thereupon agreed to a treaty abolishing the payment of tribute, and Tripoli and Tunis soon followed suit.

Barbason (bär′bạ.son). Fiend referred to in Shakespeare's *Henry V*, act ii, scene 1, and *Merry Wives of Windsor*, act ii, scene 2.

Barbate (bär.bä′tā). Town in S Spain, in the province of Cádiz, situated on the Atlantic Ocean, near the mouth of the Barbate River, E of Cape Trafalgar: chiefly a fishing port. 10,660 (1940).

Barbauld (bär′bôld), **Anna Letitia.** [Maiden name, **Aikin.**] b. at Kibworth-Harcourt, Leicestershire, England, June 20, 1743; d. at Stoke Newington (now part of London), March 9, 1825. English poet and essayist. She wrote *Poems* (1773), *Hymns in Prose for Children* (1781), *The Female Spectator* (1811), *Eighteen Hundred and Eleven* (1812), and others.

Barbazan (bår.bå.zäṅ), **Arnaud Guillaume de.** [Called **le chevalier sans reproche,** meaning "the knight without reproach" or "the blameless knight."] b. 1360; d. c1432. French general in the service of Charles VII. He defeated (1430) the combined English and Burgundian army at La Croisette, in consequence of which he was made governor of Champagne and Brie, with the title of "Restorer of the Kingdom and Crown of France."

Barbe-Bleue (bàrb.blė). [Eng. trans., "*Bluebeard.*"] Musical comedy by Michel Jean Sedaine, with music by A. E. M. Grétry, produced at Paris in 1789.

Barbe-Bleue. [Eng. trans., "*Bluebeard.*"] Opéra bouffe, words by Henri Meilhac and Ludovic Halévy, music by Jacques Offenbach, produced in 1866.

Barbe-Bleue. French name of **Bluebeard.**

Barbellion (bär.bel′yon), **Wilhelm Nero Pilate.** [Pseudonym of **Bruce Frederick Cummings.**] b. at Barnstaple, Devonshire, England, Sept. 7, 1889; d. at Gerrard's Cross, London, Oct. 22, 1919. English biologist, known chiefly as a diarist. Published under the title of *The Journal of a Disappointed Man,* the extracts of his journal reveal his sensitive, courageous, and critical personality, ambitious and greedy of life, but thwarted by limited opportunity and bad health. He was a frequent contributor to *The Countryside, The Zoölogist,* and *Proceedings* of the Zoölogical Society, *Journal of Botany,* and *Science and Progress.* His other writings include *Enjoying Life and Other Literary Remains* (1919), and *A Last Diary* (1920).

Barbé-Marbois (bàr.bā.màr.bwà), Marquis **François de.** b. at Metz, 1745; d. at Paris, 1837. French statesman. In 1803 he negotiated the treaty by which Louisiana was ceded to the U.S. He served as minister of justice under Louis XVIII, after the fall of Napoleon.

Barber (bär′bėr), **Amzi Lorenzo.** b. at Saxton's River, Vt., June 22, 1843; d. April 17, 1909. American businessman who formed (1888) the Trinidad Asphalt Company, leasing from the British government 42-year rights to the 114-acre pitch lake on the West Indies island of Trinidad. By 1896 his company had laid one-half of the asphalt pavement in the U.S.

Barber, Donn. b. at Washington, D.C., Oct. 19, 1871; d. May 29, 1925. American architect, known for his designs for the Department of Justice Building at Washington, D.C., the Travelers Insurance Building at Hartford, Conn., the Cotton Exchange at New York, and many other buildings. President of the Architectural League of New York (1925) and of the Society of Beaux Arts Architects (1909, 1910), he was also a member of other American and foreign architectural societies.

Barber, Edwin Atlee. b. at Baltimore, Md., Aug. 13, 1851; d. Dec. 12, 1916. American archaeologist, noted for his work in the field of ceramics. His classification of ceramics made him a leading authority in this sphere. Author of *The Pottery and Porcelain of the United States* (1893), *Maiolica of Mexico* (1908), *Hispano-Moresque Pottery* (1915), and some 200 articles on archaeology.

Barber, Francis. b. at Princeton, N.J., 1751; d. at Newburgh, N.Y., Feb. 11, 1783. American officer (lieutenant colonel) in the Revolutionary War and, earlier, a teacher. He taught at Elizabethtown (1769–76), having Alexander Hamilton among his pupils. In 1781 he was selected by Washington to quell the mutiny of the New Jersey and Pennsylvania troops. He commanded a battalion at Yorktown in the last major operation of the war.

Barber, John Warner. b. at Windsor, Conn., Feb. 2, 1798; d. June 22, 1885. American historical writer and engraver. Author of *History and Antiquities of New England, New York, and New Jersey* (1841) and others, illustrated with his own engravings.

Barber, Mary. b. probably in Ireland, c1690; d. 1757. English poet, best known as a friend of Jonathan Swift.

Barber, Samuel. b. at West Chester, Pa., March 9, 1910—. American composer. He began to study music at the age of six, and first tried his hand at composing when he was seven. From 1923 to 1932 he studied at the Curtis Institute of Music at Philadelphia, which conferred on him the degree of Doctor of Music in 1945. His compositions include *Serenade for String Quartet* (1929), *Dover Beach,* voice and string quartet (1931), *Sonata* for cello and piano (1932), *Overture* to *School for Scandal,* for orchestra (1932), *Music for a Scene from Shelley,* for orchestra (1933), *The Virgin Martyrs,* choral (1935), *String Quartet in B minor, Adagio for Strings,* and *Symphony in One Movement* (all 1936), *Essay for Orchestra* (1937), *Concerto for Violin and Orchestra* (1940), *Second Essay* (1942), *Second Symphony, Capricorn Concerto,* and *Four Excursions,* for piano (all 1944), *Ballet for Martha Graham* (1946), *Piano Sonata* (1948), and many songs, particularly *A Stopwatch and an Ordnance Map,* for men's chorus and drums, *Reincarnations,* for mixed chorus, and *Let Down the Bars, O Death.* The first American musical work ever heard at the Salzburg Festival was Barber's *Symphony in One Movement,* which was performed there under the baton of Artur Rodzinski in 1937. Barber's works are now included in the repertories of most American symphony orchestras and have been performed at Rome and at Moscow. He was first included in a program of the Berkshire Festival in 1941. Among the awards he has received are the Prix de Rome (1935), the Pulitzer prize for music (1935 and 1936), the Guggenheim Award (1945), and the New York Music Critics' Award (1946). He was the first composer to receive the Pulitzer prize for music in two successive years.

Barberek (bär′be.rek), Baron **von.** Title of **Alvinczy** or **Alvinzi, Josef.**

Barberini (bär.bā.rē′nē). Italian princely family named from what is now Barberino di Mugello, in Tuscany near Florence. Its power and wealth were established by Carlo Maffeo Barberini (later Pope Urban VIII), who made his brother Antonio and two nephews Francesco and Antonio cardinals, and gave to a third nephew, Taddeo, the principality of Palestrina. The family established a magnificent palace and library at Rome.

Barberini, Francesco. b. at what is now Barberino di Mugello, in Tuscany, 1264; d. 1348. Italian poet and jurist, author of *Del Reggimento e Costumi di Donna* and *Documenti d'Amore* (printed 1640), both informative documentations of 13th-century Italian mores.

Barberini Faun. Ancient statue now belonging to the collection of the Glyptothek, Munich. It formerly belonged to the Barberini family at Rome.

Barberini Palace. Palace at Rome, near the Quirinal, begun by Pope Urban VIII, and finished in 1640. It is noted for the art treasures in its collection. The palace and collection escaped serious damage in World War II.

Barberino di Mugello (bär.bā.rē′nō dē mö.jel′lō). Town and commune in C Italy, in the *compartimento* (region) of Tuscany, in the province of Firenze, situated on the Stura River near the central range of the Appenines, ab 17 mi. N of Florence. It is the center of a wine-producing district. Pop. of commune, 11,791 (1936); of town, 2,585 (1936).

Barbero (bär.bā′rō), **Andrés José Camilo.** b. at Asunción, Paraguay, 1877—. Paraguayan physician, educator, and administrator; dean of medical sciences (1906 *et seq.*) at the Asunción medical school. Director (1906, 1917) of the national board of health, and founder (1919) and president (1919–39) of the Paraguayan Red Cross, he was appointed (1937) minister of agriculture, and served (1938–39) as minister of national economy. Author of *Instrucción técnica* (1908), *Higiene municipal y rural* (1917), *Plantas medicinales del Paraguay* (1917), and other books.

Barber of Bagdad (bag′dad), **The.** Opera in two acts by Peter Cornelius, with libretto by the composer, first performed at Weimar, Germany, on Dec. 15, 1858.

Barberton (bär′bėr.ton). City in NE Ohio, in Summit County, ab. 7 mi. SW of Akron: manufactures matches, rubber articles, and other products. 27,820 (1950).

Barberton. Town in the Transvaal, Union of South Africa, situated on the railway ab. 136 mi. W of Lourenço Marques, Mozambique, and ab. 283 mi. E of Pretoria. It is in the heart of the De Kaap gold fields, discovered in 1875. With the decline of the gold fields, agriculture has increased in importance especially in the De Kaap valley. 5,279 (1946).

Barbey d'Aurevilly (bàr.bā dōr.vē.yē), **Jules Amédée.** b. at St.-Sauveur-le-Vicomte, France, Nov. 2, 1808; d. at Paris, April 23, 1889. French critic and novelist. He went to Paris in 1851, and founded (with Granier de Cassagnac) *Le Réveil.* He wrote *Une vieille maîtresse* (1851), *L'Ensorcelée* (1854), and *Le Prêtre marié* (1865).

Barbezieux (bàr.bẹ.zyė). Town in SW France, in the department of Charente, situated on a hill near the junction of the Trèfle and Condéon rivers, ab. 20 mi. SW of Angoulême. It is the center of a district known for its wines, and has manufactures of agricultural machinery. 4,243 (1946).

Barbican (bär′bi.kan). In historical geography, a locality in London, so called from a former watchtower of which nothing now remains.

Barbié du Bocage (bár.byā dü bo.kàzh), **Jean Denis.** b. at Paris, April 28, 1760; d. there, Dec. 28, 1825. French geographer and philologist.

Barbier (bár.byā), **Antoine Alexandre.** b. at Coulommiers, Seine-et-Marne, France, Jan. 11, 1765; d. at Paris, Dec. 6, 1825. French bibliographer; author of a *Dictionnaire des ouvrages anonymes et pseudonymes* (1806–08).

Barbier, Henri Auguste. b. at Paris, April 28, 1805; d. at Nice, France, Feb. 13, 1882. French poet. His best-known work is *Les Iambes* (1831), a series of satires, political and social, occasioned by the revolution of 1830 and the subsequent reign of Louis Philippe. The most famous is *La Curée*, a satire on the scramble for place under that government.

Barbier, Paul Jules. b. at Paris, March 8, 1825; d. there, Jan. 16, 1901. French dramatic poet and librettist. He published the drama *Un Poëte* in 1847, and from 1850 worked much in collaboration with Michel Carré, as in *Cora ou l'esclavage* (1866).

Barbier de Séville (dẹ sä.vēl), **Le.** [Eng. title, **"The Barber of Seville."**] Comedy by Pierre Augustin Caron de Beaumarchais, first composed in 1772 as a comic opera. It was at first rejected, and in 1775, after various vicissitudes, appeared in its present form as a comedy. It is in this play, the basis for Rossini's opera *Il Barbiere di Siviglia*, and others of the same name, that Figaro makes his first appearance.

Barbiere di Siviglia (bär.byā'rā dē sē.vē'lyä), **Il.** [Eng. title, **"The Barber of Seville."**] *Opéra bouffe* by Giovanni Paisello, based on the comedy *Le Barbier de Séville* by Pierre Augustin Caron de Beaumarchais, first performed at St. Petersburg in 1780.

Barbiere di Siviglia, Il. [Eng. title, **"The Barber of Seville."**] *Opéra bouffe*, after Pierre Augustin Caron de Beaumarchais's play *Le Barbier de Séville*, with music by Gioacchino Antonio Rossini, presented at Rome in 1816 and at Paris in 1819.

Barbieri (bär.byā'rē), **Francisco Asenjo.** b. at Madrid, Aug. 3, 1823; d. there, in February, 1894. Spanish composer, notably of zarzuelas (a type of dance), such as *Jugar con fuego* (1851), *Pan y toros* (1864), and *El Barberillo de Lavapiés* (1874).

Barbieri, Paolo Antonio. b. 1596; d. 1640. Bolognese painter of animals, fruits, and flowers; brother of Guercino (Giovanni Francesco Barbieri).

Barbier v. Connolly (bär.bir'; kon'ọl.i), **113 U.S. 27 (1885).** Decision of the U.S. Supreme Court upholding a San Francisco ordinance forbidding night work in laundries. Important as one of the early interpretations of that part of the first section of the 14th Amendment relating to "the equal protection of the laws," it recognized the power of government to classify and regulate business enterprise.

Barbirolli (bär.bi.rō'li), **Sir John.** b. at London, Dec. 2, 1899—. Orchestra conductor. He studied music with his father and at the Trinity College of Music (1911, 1912); organized his own chamber orchestra after World War I; was a violoncellist and soloist in the Queen's Hall Orchestra; played with the Kutcher and the International string quartets; was appointed (1936) for three years as conductor of the New York Philharmonic Orchestra, succeeding Arturo Toscanini; and conducted (1938) radio concerts with the Ford Symphony Orchestra. Subsequently he became the regular conductor of the Hallé Orchestra at Manchester, England.

Barbizon (bär'bi.zon; French, bàr.bē.zôṅ). Small village in N France, in the department of Seine-et-Marne, near the forest of Fontainebleau. It is noted as having been one of the favorite haunts of what is known as the Barbizon, or Fontainebleau, school of painters.

Barbizon School. [Also, **Fontainebleau School.**] Name given to an informal, unorganized group of French painters which flourished c1830–70, working for the most part in and about the town of Barbizon and nearby Fontainebleau in N France, in the department of Seine-et-Marne. The prime movers in the rise of the Barbizon or Fontainebleau School, sometimes referred to also as the "Men of 1830," were Théodore Rousseau (1812–67) and Jean François Millet (1814–75), both of whom lived and died at Barbizon. It was their letters to other artists, and their ardent pleas for a new approach of art to nature, which caused so many painters to take their brushes and palettes to Barbizon. Most noted among those who gathered there, in addition to Rousseau and Millet, were Jean Baptiste Camille Corot (1796–1885), Narcisso Virgilio Diaz de la Peña (1808–76), Constant Troyon (1810–65), Jules Dupré (1812–89), Charles Émile Jacque (1813–94), Charles François Daubigny (1818–67), and Henri Joseph Harpignies (1819–1916). Although Millet is best known for his pictures of peasants, while Troyon and Jacque were noted for their paintings of animals, the Barbizon School was a landscape school, and may truly be said to have created French landscape painting. At the time of its rise the long ascendancy of the Classicists in French art had been overthrown by the Romanticists. Neither of these schools was much concerned with landscape, nor much given to the study of nature. A growing acquaintance with the work of English landscapists, especially following a showing of paintings by Constable at the Paris Salon of 1824, awakened an interest in landscape among French painters, and Millet called for an art which, instead of relying on cleverness (with which he asserted that decadence began), would "lean directly and naïvely upon impressions made by nature." At Barbizon French artists for the first time used trees and fields, rocks and pools, not merely as backgrounds for ruined temples or for violent action, but with the purpose of producing "impassioned portraits of their native land." This new program encountered academic scorn and public indifference. In the end, however, all of the Barbizon masters were recognized and honored, and the best collection of paintings of the Barbizon School can now be seen in the Louvre at Paris; they are also well represented in the Metropolitan Museum of Art at New York.

Barbo (bär.bō), **Pietro.** Original name of Pope **Paul II.**

Barbon (bär'bōn), **Nicholas.** b. at London, c1640; d. 1698. English economist, writer, and originator of fire insurance in England; probably the son of Praisegod Barbon (c1596–1679). He received (1661) an M.D. at Utrecht and became an honorary fellow of the College of Physicians and Surgeons in 1664; he was a member of Parliament for Bramber in 1690 and 1695. After the great London fire of 1666, he helped to rebuild London, wrote two treatises on raising the value of coinage, and participated (c1695) in land-bank speculations.

Barbon (bär'bon) or **Barebone** (-bōn) or **Barebones** (-bōnz), **Praisegod.** b. c1596; d. 1679. English Baptist preacher, leather dealer, and politician. He became a member of Cromwell's "little parliament" of 1653, named, by its enemies, for him, "Barebone's Parliament." He is said (probably erroneously) to have had two brothers named respectively "Christ-came-into-the-world-to-save," and "If-Christ-had-not-died-thou-hadst-been-damned" (familiarly abbreviated to "Damned").

Barbosa (bạr.bô'zạ), **Domingos Caldas.** b. at Rio de Janeiro, c1738; d. at Lisbon, Nov. 9, 1800. Brazilian poet who achieved great success in Portugal with his songs and guitar.

Barbosa, Rui (or **Ruy**). b. at Salvador, Brazil, Nov. 5, 1849; d. at Petrópolis, Brazil, March 1, 1923. Brazilian jurist, statesman, orator, journalist, and essayist, eminent as the most indefatigable advocate of human and civil liberties in Brazil and one of the most powerful prose writers in the Portuguese language. Forced into exile (1895), he wrote in England his famous *Cartas de Inglaterra*, which appeared regularly in a Rio de Janeiro newspaper. He held many important elective posts in Brazil, was the chief architect of its first republican constitution, and represented his country at the Hague Peace Conference (1907), where he defended the rights of the small nations. He served (1921–23) as a member of the Permanent Court of International Justice. Among his numerous works are *O Papa e o Concílio* (1877), *Réplica ás defesas da redação do Código Civil* (1903), *Contra o militarismo* (1910), and *Queda do Império* (1921). The Brazilian government acquired his house in Rio de Janeiro, with his rich private library, transforming it (1928) into a national shrine devoted to his memory, and undertook the publication of his complete works.

Barbosa du Bocage (dö bö.kä'zhẹ), **Manuel Maria.** See **Bocage, Manuel Maria Barbosa du.**

Barbotan (bàr.bo.täṅ). [Also, **Barbotan-les-Thermes** (-lā.term).] Small resort in SW France, in the department of Gers, situated near the Douze River, ab. 38 mi.

SW of Agen. It has hot sulfur springs and mud baths, which have been known since antiquity. The population is included in that of Cazaubon. 1,856 (1946).

Barbou (bär.bö). Noted French family of printers which flourished from c1540 to 1808. The most famous were Jean, the founder of the family; Hugues, his son; and Joseph Gérard.

Barbour (bär'bėr), **Clarence Augustus.** b. at Hartford, Conn., April 21, 1867; d. at Providence, R.I., Jan. 16, 1937. American Baptist clergyman and educator. After graduation (1888) from Brown University, he received (1891) a degree from the Rochester Theological Seminary and was ordained. He served as pastor (1891–1909) of the Lake Avenue Church at Rochester, N.Y., was president (1915–29) and professor of homiletics at the Rochester Theological Seminary, and was president (1929 *et seq.*) of Brown University.

Barbour, James. b. in Orange County, Va., June 10, 1775; d. near Gordonsville, Va., June 7, 1842. American statesman; brother of Philip Pendleton Barbour. He was admitted to the bar in 1794, became (1815) U.S. senator from Virginia, resigned (1825) from the Senate on being appointed secretary of war by President John Quincy Adams, and served (1828–29) as minister to England.

Barbour, John. b. c1316; d. March 13, 1395. Scottish poet, archdeacon of Aberdeen, and an auditor of the exchequer. His chief poem is *The Brus* (1375; edited by Skeat, 1870–77; edited by Mackenzie, 1909) on the subject of Robert the Bruce of Scotland. He is believed to be the author of *Legends of the Saints* (edited by Metcalfe, 1887–96).

Barbour, Oliver Lorenzo. b. at Cambridge, Washington County, N.Y., July 12, 1811; d. at Saratoga Springs, N.Y., Dec. 17, 1889. American legal writer.

Barbour, Philip Pendleton. b. in Orange County, Va., May 25, 1783; d. at Washington, D.C., Feb. 25, 1841. American politician and jurist; brother of James Barbour. He served as a member of Congress from Virginia, 1814–25, was speaker of the House of Representatives, 1821–23, and was again a member of Congress 1827–30. One of the candidates for the Democratic nomination for vice-president in 1832, he was an associate justice (1836–41) of the U.S. Supreme Court.

Barbour, Ralph Henry. [Pseudonym, **Richard Stillman Powell.**] b. at Cambridge, Mass., Nov. 13, 1870; d. at Pass Christian, Miss., Feb. 19, 1944. American author, especially of books for boys. Among his works are *Kitty of the Roses* (1904), *The Crimson Sweater* (1906), *Four Afloat* (1907), *Harry's Island* (1908), *Double Play* (1909), *Metipom's Hostage* (1921), *Comrades of the Key* (1928), *Boys' Book of Dogs* (1928), and others.

Barbourville (bär'bėr.vil). City in SE Kentucky, county seat of Knox County, on the Cumberland River ab. 90 mi. SE of Lexington: seat of Union College. 2,926 (1950).

Barbox Brothers (bär'boks), and **Barbox Brothers and Co.** Story and its sequel by Charles Dickens, included in "Mugby Junction," an extra Christmas number of Dickens's own magazine, *All the Year Round*, in 1866.

Barboza (bär.bō'sä), **Francisco Villela.** See **Villela Barboza, Francisco.**

Barbuda (bär.bö'dạ). Island in the Caribbean Sea, E of Puerto Rico, part of the British colony of Leeward Islands, in the presidency of Antigua. Cattle breeding, farming, and fishing are the major economic activities. It was long owned (1691–1872) by the Codrington family. Area, 62 sq. mi.; pop. 900 (1938).

Barbusse (bȧr.büs), **Henri.** b. at Asnières, France, 1873; d. at Moscow, 1935. French editor, novelist, and poet. Although the protegé and son-in-law of Catulle Mendès, he remained relatively unknown until, having left (1914) a Swiss tuberculosis sanatorium to enlist in the French army, he quit the army to write the disillusioned *Le Feu* (1916; Eng. trans., *Under Fire*, 1917). Earlier he had worked on the *Siècle* and other papers, edited the *Je sais tout* magazine, and published a collection of poems, *Pleureuses* (1895), and two novels, *Les Suppliants* (1903) and *L'Enfer* (1908; Eng. trans., *The Inferno*, 1917). After the success of *Le Feu* he devoted himself largely to social problems and antiwar propaganda.

Barby (bär'bē). Town in C Germany, in the *Land* (state) of Saxony-Anhalt, Russian Zone, formerly in the province of Saxony, Prussia, situated on the Elbe River, near the mouth of the Saale River, ab. 17 mi. SE of Magdeburg: center of a sugar-beet growing district; agricultural trade. The Church of Saint Mary and the Church of Saint John date from the 12th century. 7,788 (1946).

Barca (bär'kạ). In ancient geography, a city in Cyrenaica, N Africa, situated near the coast: one of the cities of the Pentapolis.

Barca. Former vilayet of the Turkish empire (1879–1912), in N Africa, bounded by the Mediterranean on the N, Egypt on the E, and the Gulf of Sidra on the W: a part of ancient Cyrenaica. A small part of the region is very fertile, the remainder largely a desert. It later formed part of the Italian province of Libya. The capital was Bengasi. Area, ab. 20,000 sq. mi.

Barca. District in NE Africa, N of Ethiopia, near the upper course of the Barca River, part of the former Italian colony of Eritrea.

Barca, Conde de. Title of **Araujo de Azevedo, Antônio de.**

Barca (bär'kä), **Frances Inglis Calderón de la.** See **Calderón de la Barca, Frances Inglis.**

Barca, Pedro Calderón de la. See **Calderón de la Barca, Pedro.**

Barca River (bär'kạ). River in E Africa which flows N into the Red Sea S of Suakin. It rises near the N border of Ethiopia, entering the sea near the S end of the Red Sea coast of the Anglo-Egyptian Sudan.

Barcellona Pozzo di Gotto (bär.chel.lō'nä pōt'tsō dē gôt'tō). [Also, **Barcellona.**] Town and commune in SW Italy, on the island of Sicily, in the province of Messina, situated on the Longano River near the Gulf of Patti on the N shore of the island, ab. 20 mi. W of Messina. It is a summer resort. The town has cattle markets; there are citrus and olive orchards and vineyards in the surrounding region. Pop. of commune, 27,134 (1936); of town, 8,454 (1936).

Barcelona (bär.sẹ.lō'nạ; Spanish, bär.thā.lō'nä). Province in NE Spain, bounded by Gerona on the N and NE, by the Mediterranean Sea on the SE and S, and by Tarragona and Lérida on the W: part of the region of Catalonia. The province is fertile; mixed farming and horticulture are highly developed. The metropolitan region of Barcelona has the largest concentration of industry in Spain; it is the seat of the separatist Catalan movement. Capital, Barcelona; area, 2,942 sq. mi.; pop. 2,236,719 (1950).

Barcelona. [Phoenician, **Barcino, Barcelo**; Latin, **Julia Faventia, Colonia Faventia Julia Augusta Pia Barcino**; medieval name, **Barcinona, Barchinona**; Arabic, **Barchaluna.**] City in NE Spain, the capital of the province of Barcelona, situated on the Mediterranean Sea between the mouths of the Llobregat and Besos rivers, ab. 315 mi. NE of Madrid: the second largest city in Spain and its largest commercial and industrial center. 1,285,920 (1950).

Commerce and Industry. The city has an inner and an outer harbor, lined with warehouses; exports consist mainly of wine, oil, cork, textiles, and leather articles; among the chief imports are grain, coal, cotton, and a number of manufactured goods. Industries include cotton, linen, and silk textile factories, cloth, shawl, and lace manufactures; also important metallurgical industries, iron foundries, railroad shops, and shipyards. There are numerous commercial establishments, banking and insurance institutions, and a stock exchange.

Chief Buildings. Barcelona has many scientific and educational institutions. The university, founded in 1430 and confirmed by Pope Nicholas V in 1450, was suppressed in 1714, but restored in 1841; it includes an academy of natural sciences and a large library. There are various other libraries, archives, and theaters. Barcelona grew rapidly during the 19th and 20th centuries; many of the villages formerly surrounding the city are now incorporated in it, and new suburbs are expanding. It is the seat of a bishopric. The cathedral, erected 1298–1448, is in the Gothic style; in the same style are the churches of Santa María del Mar and Santa María del Pino. San Pablo del Campo dates from the 10th century; other churches are of the baroque period. The 13th-century palace of the kings of Aragon contains the archives of the crown of Aragon and archaeological collections; there are numerous other palaces, and a 14th-century city hall. The Pedralbes Palace was presented to King Alfonso on the occasion of his visit to the city in 1924. The Teatro del Liceo is one of the most important in Spain.

History. Founded, according to tradition, by the Carthaginian leader Hamilcar Barca and named in his honor, it later became a Roman colony. It was captured by the Visigoths in 415, and by the Moslems in 713, but reconquered by the Franks in 801, and became the capital of the Hispanic March, then a frontier area of Christendom against Islam; in 1131 it was incorporated, together with all Catalonia, into Aragon; in 1479, along with Aragon, it became part of Castile. In the 12th, 13th, and 14th centuries the city developed its municipal self-government and its commercial hegemony over the entire seaboard of Aragon; it became one of the leading mercantile centers on the W Mediterranean; its maritime code was widely recognized as authoritative. However, under Castilian rule, its position was jeopardized by the dominance of Andalusia in American trade, and regionalistic sentiments found expression. Municipal and regional self-government were abolished after 1714. Barcelona was occupied by the British in 1705, and by the French in 1809. In the 19th and 20th centuries (from 1815 on) the history of Barcelona was one of increasing prosperity but also of social and political unrest. It became the center of a regionalistic movement aiming at an autonomous regime for Catalonia, the birthplace of the Spanish trade-union movement, and the center of Spanish Syndicalism and socialism. There was a strong element of anticlericalism in all these movements. In the uprisings of 1835 and of 1909 numerous churches and convents were burnt down. Revolutionary committees were formed in 1916 and 1923. On Aug. 2, 1936, following the outbreak of the civil war in Spain, Barcelona became the seat of an autonomous Catalonian government and from 1938 was the capital of the Loyalist cause. Nationalist superiority in artillery and air power overcame the city's defenses on Jan. 26, 1939, foreshadowing the final surrender of the Republican government in the following March.

Barcelona (bär.sā.lō′nä). City in N Venezuela, capital of Anzoátegui state, near the Caribbean Sea, ab. 160 mi. E of Caracas: trading center for coal, salt, petroleum, livestock, coffee, sugar, and cacao. 26,446 (1950).

Barcelona (bär.thā.lō′nä), Count of. See **Borbón y Battenberg, Juan de.**

Barcelona Transit Conference. Meeting sponsored by the League of Nations in 1921 to clarify principles of free navigation on international rivers. It issued a series of conventions, the most important of which were a statute affirming free navigation, making maintenance a duty of riparian states, and limiting charges to maintenance costs, a statute on "freedom of transit," and a protocol providing for reciprocal agreements on national rivers and canals.

Barcelonnette (bȧr.se̦.lo̦.net). Town in SE France, in the department of Basses-Alpes, situated on the Ubaye River, ab. 32 mi. SE of Gap: winter resort and climatological station; has flour mills and produces perfumes. It suffered severely in the wars of the frontier. 3,007 (1946).

Barchaluna (bär.cha̦.lö′na̦). Arabic name of **Barcelona,** Spain.

Barchester Towers (bär′che̦s.tėr). Novel by Anthony Trollope, published in 1857. It is the second in the so-called Barsetshire series of six novels, all dealing with the inhabitants of the imaginary cathedral town of Barchester in the imaginary county of Barsetshire.

Barcia (bär.thyä), **Andres Gonzalez.** b. at Madrid, 1670; d. there, Nov. 4, 1743. Spanish historian. He was one of the founders of the Spanish Academy, and held various honorary offices. He wrote *Ensayo cronológico para la historia general de la Florida* (Madrid, 1723), and edited an extensive series of historical works relating to America, with the general title *Historiadores primitivos de Indias.*

Barcino (bär′si.nō) or **Barcelo** (-se.lō). Phoenician names of **Barcelona,** Spain.

Barcinona (bär.si.nō′na̦) or **Barchinona** (-chi-). Medieval names of **Barcelona,** Spain.

Barclay (bär′kli), **Alexander.** b. probably in Scotland, c1475; d. at Croydon, England, 1552. British poet, author of *The Shyp of Folys* (The Ship of Fools), regarded as being in part a translation of, and in part an imitation of, the *Narrenschiff* of Sebastian Brant; he was the author also of *Egloges* (Eclogues), among the earliest eclogues in English. He was a monk of Ely and Canterbury, priest at the College of Ottery St. Mary, vicar of Much Badew in Essex, and rector of All Hallows, Lombard Street, London.

"Barclay, Captain." See **Allardice, Robert Barclay.**

Barclay, Edwin. b. 1882—. Liberian statesman. He was attorney general (1914–20), secretary (1919–30) for foreign affairs, and twice president (1930–34, 1936 *et seq.*) of Liberia.

Barclay, Florence Louisa. [Maiden name, **Charlesworth.**] b. in Surrey, England, Dec. 2, 1862; d. at Norfolk, England, March 10, 1921. English novelist and lecturer. In 1909 she visited the U.S., lecturing on Palestine, and again visited the U.S. in 1910. Author of religious and sentimental novels, including *The Wheels of Time* (1908), *The Rosary* (1909, her best-known and most successful work, over a million copies having been sold before she died), *The Mistress of Shenstone* (1910; also popular as a moving picture), *The Following of the Star* (1911), *Through the Postern Gate* (1912), *The Broken Halo* (1913), *My Heart's Right There* (1914), and *The White Ladies of Worcester* (1917).

Barclay, Sir George. fl. 1696. British army officer and chief agent in the assassination plot (1696) against William III of England. Acting on a commission from James II (who was, of course, no longer in power) "to . . . make war upon the Prince of Orange . . . ," he gathered together a group of conspirators who were to attack William as he returned from hunting; the plot detected, Barclay fled to France, the only principal to escape.

Barclay, John. b. at Pont-à-Mousson, France, Jan. 28, 1582; d. Aug. 15, 1621. Scottish poet; son of William Barclay. His verse, which is satirical in nature, is exemplified in the *Satyricon* (1603; second part, 1607). He also wrote *Sylvae* (Latin poems; 1606), *Apologia* (1611), *Icon Animorum* (1614), and the *Argenis* (1621).

Barclay, John. b. at Muthill, Perthshire, Scotland, 1734; d. at Edinburgh, July 29, 1798. Clergyman of the Church of Scotland, founder of the sect known as Barclayites, or Bereans. His principles were set forth in *Without Faith, Without God* (1769).

Barclay, John. b. in Perthshire, Scotland, Dec. 10, 1758; d. Aug. 21, 1826. Scottish anatomist, lecturer on anatomy at Edinburgh; nephew of John Barclay (1734–98).

Barclay, Robert. b. at Gordonstown, Morayshire, Scotland, Dec. 23, 1648; d. at Ury, Kincardineshire, Scotland, Oct. 3, 1690. Scottish writer, a member of the Society of Friends. He wrote *Apology for the True Christian Divinity* (Latin ed., 1676; English ed., 1678), a standard exposition of the doctrines of the sect. He was nominal governor (1682–88), and, with William Penn, one of the proprietors of East New Jersey.

Barclay de Tolly (bär.klī′ de̦ tô′lyi), Prince **Mikhail Andreas.** b. at Luhde-Grosshoff, Livonia, on the Baltic Sea (in what is now Estonia and Latvia), Dec. 27, 1761; d. May 26, 1818. Russian field marshal, of Scottish descent. He served in the wars with Turkey, Sweden, and Poland, commanded the advance guard at Pultusk, was wounded (1807) at Eylau, served (1808–09) with distinction in the war with Sweden, led an expedition across the Gulf of Bothnia on the ice in 1809, became minister of war in 1810, and commanded against Napoleon in 1812. His policy of steady withdrawal before the French, in order to lead them further and further from their base of supply, resulted in the loss of vast areas of Russia and caused him to become greatly unpopular. Following his defeat at Smolensk, in the late summer of 1812, he was replaced by Kutusov, who not only continued to use the tactics originated by Barclay de Tolly, but was able through their use finally to entrap the French and to destroy their armies in their disastrous retreat from Moscow. This strategy of withdrawal and attrition before the enemy (often credited to Kutusov) was again used by the Russians (this time against the Germans) in World War II. Barclay de Tolly later served at Borodino and at Bautzen; conquered Thorn in 1813; became commander of the Russian contingent of the European force ranged against Napoleon in 1813; and served at Dresden and Leipzig, and in France.

Barclay Sound (bär'klā). Inlet of the Pacific Ocean on the SW coast of Vancouver Island, British Columbia, Canada.

Bar Cocheba (bär kok'ẹ.bạ), **Bar Cochba,** or **Bar Kokba** (kok'bạ), **Simon.** [Also: **Barcochebas** (bär.kok'ẹ.bạs) or **Bar Coziba** (bär kō.zē'bạ).] Killed at Bethar, near Caesarea, 135 A.D. Leader of the Jewish insurrection (132–135 A.D.) against the Romans. He was believed by many Jews to be the Messiah, was proclaimed king, and maintained his cause against Hadrian for two years, but is said to have been overthrown amid the slaughter of over half a million Jews and the destruction of 985 villages and 50 fortresses. Jerusalem was destroyed, and Aelia Capitolina founded on its ruins. After his failure his name was interpreted by his detractors to mean "son of lies."

Barcroft (bär'kroft), Sir **Joseph.** b. 1872; d. at Cambridge, England, March 21, 1947. English physiologist, noted for his work on the action of the blood as an oxygen carrier. He was educated at Cambridge, served as a professor (1923–26) at The Royal Institution, and was a professor of physiology (1926–37) at Cambridge. An authority on defense against gas attack, he was a member of the chemical warfare committee of the British war office during World War II. He used himself as a subject for physiological experiments. His works include *The Respiratory Function of the Blood, Features in the Architecture of Physiological Function,* and *The Brain and Its Environment.*

Barcynska (bär.sin'skạ), Countess. See **Sandys, Oliver.**

Bard (bȧr). See **Bardo.**

Bard (bärd), **John.** b. at Burlington, N.J., Feb. 1, 1716; d. at Hyde Park, N.Y., March 30, 1799. American physician, one of the first to employ dissection of the human body as a method of instruction, the first to report a case of extrauterine pregnancy, and a pioneer advocate of sanitation. He studied medicine at Philadelphia, where he became a lifelong friend of Benjamin Franklin, but during most of his life practiced at New York. He was the first president (1788) of the Medical Society of the State of New York. As a quarantine officer, he persuaded New York to purchase Bedloe Island for a quarantine station.

Bard, Samuel. b. at Philadelphia, April 1, 1742; d. at Hyde Park, N.Y., May 24, 1821. American physician and medical writer; son of John Bard. He was physician to George Washington after the Revolutionary War. President of the College of Physicians and Surgeons at New York in the period 1813–21, he took a leading part in founding the New York Hospital.

Bard, The. Poem by Thomas Gray, published in 1758, beginning with the phrase "Ruin seize thee, ruthless King." It is a Pindaric ode, based on a medieval legend.

Bard, William. b. at Philadelphia, April 4, 1778; d. on Staten Island, N.Y., Oct. 17, 1853. American businessman, a pioneer in life insurance; grandson of John Bard and son of Samuel Bard. He organized (1830) the New York Life Insurance and Trust Company, the first American company of its kind to specialize in life insurance, and by skillful propaganda overcame public indifference to, and distrust of, its service. He also established the agency system.

Bardamu (bȧr.dȧ.mü), **Louis.** Central character and narrator of *Voyage au bout de la nuit* (1932; Eng. trans., *Journey to the End of Night,* 1934), novel by the French writer Louis Fuch Destouches, writing under the pseudonym of Louis-Ferdinand Céline.

Bardas (bär'dạs). d. at Kepos, in Caria, Asia Minor, April 21, 866. Byzantine politician. He was the brother of the empress Theodora, and, on the death of her husband, the emperor Theophilus, was appointed one of the tutors of her son Michael III. He killed his colleague Theoctistes, confined Theodora in the monastery of Gastria, and persuaded Michael to confer on him the title of Caesar. Superseded in the favor of the emperor by Basil the Macedonian, he was assassinated.

Bardeen (bär.dēn'), **Charles William.** b. at Groton, Mass., Aug. 28, 1847; d. Aug. 24, 1924. American publisher, author, and educator. He served as an agent (1873 *et seq.*) at Syracuse, N.Y., for Clark and Maynard's educational publications, and was editor (1874 *et seq.*) of the *School Bulletin.* His *Common School Law* was printed in a number of editions. Author also of *History of Educational Journalism* (1896), *Teaching as a Business* (1897), and *A Dictionary of Educational Biography* (1901).

Bardejov (bär'de.yôf). [Hungarian, **Bártfa;** German, **Bartfeld.**] Town in Czechoslovakia, in E Slovakia, ab. 40 mi. N of Košice, on the Joplá River, in the Carpathian Mountains S of the Vychodny Bekydy range and the Polish frontier. The town was once an important center for the trade between Hungary and Poland and has ceramics industries and a brewery. There is a Gothic church and town hall. Bardejov-Lažne, a health resort, is nearby. 6,394 (1947).

Bardeleben (bär'dẹ.lā.bẹn), **Henry Fairchild De.** See **De Bardeleben, Henry Fairchild.**

Bardeleben, Marie von. Maiden name of **Kremnitz, Marie.**

Bardell (bär.del'), **Mrs. Martha.** In Charles Dickens's *Pickwick Papers,* an accommodating landlady who let lodgings to Mr. Pickwick and brought a suit for breach of promise against him.

Bardera (bär.de'rä). [Also, **Barderah.**] Town in Somaliland, E Africa, on the Juba River at the head of navigation. It is connected by steamship with Kismayu at the mouth of the river. Pop. ab. 1,500.

Bardesanes (bär.dẹ.sā'nēz). [Also, **Bardaisan** (-dī.sän').] b. at Edessa, in Mesopotamia, 154 A.D.; d. in Armenia, 222. Syrian scholar, poet, astrologer, and Christian theologian. He was the author of mystic hymns of a Gnostic character (some authorities classify him as the last of the Gnostics), which were employed by the Syrian Christians for more than two centuries, until they were driven out of use by the more orthodox work of Ephraem Syrus. He was also the earliest Syriac writer (except for the translators of the Bible), and is generally considered to have been the founder of Syriac poetry. In a treatise on astronomy (now lost) he sought to prove that the total duration of the world was 6,000 years. Apparently, in his later life, he lost faith in many of his Gnostic and astrological theories, as evidenced by a dialogue on destiny written sometime after 196, which lacks any trace of Gnosticism and reveals a greatly diminished interest in astrology. It is possible that this work (a sort of Platonic dialogue, in which Bardesanes is the chief speaker) was not written by himself, but by one of his disciples; nevertheless, it undoubtedly reflects his teaching.

Bardhwan or **Bardwan** (bur.dwän'). See **Burdwan.**

Bardi (bär'dē). Town and commune in N Italy, in the *compartimento* (region) of Emilia-Romagna, in the province of Parma, ab. 32 mi. SW of Parma. Excellent wines are made in the vicinity. Buildings of interest to tourists were undamaged in World War II. Pop. of commune, 7,985 (1936); of town, 1,190 (1936).

Bardi, Bardo di. In George Eliot's novel *Romola,* a blind Florentine scholar, the father of Romola.

Bardia (bär.dē'ä). [Also, **Porto Bardia.**] Town in N Africa, in NE Libya, in Cyrenaica near the Egyptian border. It has a good harbor, an airfield, a radio station, and a military supply depot. Bardia saw severe fighting and changed hands several times during World War II, being finally captured by the British on Nov. 13, 1942. Pop. 2,370.

Bardili (bär.dē'lē), **Christoph Gottfried.** b. at Blaubeuren, Württemberg, Germany, May 28, 1761; d. at Stuttgart, Germany, June 5, 1808. German philosopher. He was professor of philosophy at the *gymnasium* at Stuttgart, and the expounder of a system of rational realism which exerted considerable influence upon later metaphysical speculation, including that of Schelling, and Hegel. His *Grundriss der ersten Logik* (1800) is notable for its criticism of Kant's theories.

Bardo (bär'dō). [Also, **Bard.**] Village in NW Italy, in the *compartimento* (region) of Piedmont, in the province of Torino, situated on the Dora Baltea River, ab. 38 mi. N of Turin. Its fort commands the St. Bernard passes, and resisted Napoleon's passage of the Alps in 1800.

Bardolph (bär'dolf). Character in Shakespeare's plays *Henry VI,* parts I and II, *Henry V,* and *Merry Wives of Windsor.* He is a sharper and hanger-on, one of Falstaff's dissolute and amusing companions, called "The Knight of the Burning Lamp" by Falstaff on account of his red nose; a fellow, like Nym and Pistol, without conventional honor or principle.

Bardolph, Lord. Character in Shakespeare's *Henry IV*, part II.

Bardonnechia (bär.dôn.nek'kyä). [French, **Bardonnèche** (bȧr.do.nesh).] Town and commune in NW Italy, in the *compartimento* (region) of Piedmont, in the province of Torino, situated at the Italian entrance to the Mont Cenis tunnel, W of Turin. It is a winter-sports resort in the Susa valley; dominated by the castle of the counts of Bardonnechia. Pop. of commune, 2,409 (1936); of town, 630 (1936).

Bardoux (bȧr.dö), **Agénor.** b. 1829; d. 1897. French politician and writer; father of Jacques Bardoux. He was minister of public instruction, ecclesiastical affairs, and fine arts from Dec. 14, 1877, until the resignation of President Marie Edme Patrice Maurice de MacMahon, and in 1882 was appointed senator for life. Author of *Les Légistes et leur influence sur la société française* (1878).

Bardoux, Jacques. b. at Versailles, France, May 27, 1874—. French political leader and journalist, chairman (1936) of the state reform commission; son of Agénor Bardoux. He became (1901) foreign editor of the *Journal des Débats*, and was named (1908) a lecturer at the École de Hautes Études Politiques. He served as political secretary (1919) to Marshal Ferdinand Foch, as a senator (1938–40) and as a deputy (1945 *et seq.*); member of the Academy of Moral and Political Sciences.

Bardowiek (bär'dō.vēk). Small town in N Germany, in the *Land* (state) of Lower Saxony, British Zone, situated on the Ilmenau River, ab. 24 mi. SE of Hamburg. It has a ruined cathedral. Bardowiek was important in the early Middle Ages, was taken by Henry the Lion in 1189, and later became the chief trading town in northern Germany. The Abbey Church, famous for its late-Gothic altarpiece, as well as the rest of the town, escaped damage in World War II.

Bardsey (bärd'zi). [Welsh, **Ynys-Enlli.**] Small island in N Wales, in Caernarvonshire. It lies off the SW point of that county, at the entrance to Cardigan Bay, separated from the mainland by Bardsey Sound. Area, less than 1 sq. mi.

Bardstown (bärdz'toun''). [Former name, **Salem.**] City in C Kentucky, county seat of Nelson County. It was settled in 1778. Pop. 4,154 (1950).

Barduli (bär'dụ.lī). Ancient name of **Barletta.**

Barebone (bãr'bōn) or **Barebones** (-bōnz), **Praisegod.** See **Barbon, Praisegod.**

Barebone's Parliament. See **Little Parliament.**

Barefoot Boy, The. Poem in tetrameter couplets by John Greenleaf Whittier, published in *The Panorama and Other Poems* (1856). It describes innocent adventures in the course of a happy boyhood in the country.

Barèges (bȧ.rezh). [Also, **Barèges-les-Bains** (bȧ.rezh-lā.baṅ).] Village and spa in SW France, in the department of Hautes-Pyrénées, ab. 23 mi. S of Tarbes, near Bagnères-de-Bigorre. It is a summer resort noted for its mineral (sulfate of soda) baths.

Bareilly (bạ.rā'lẹ). [Also, **Bareli.**] District of the Rohilkhand division, Uttar Pradesh, W Union of India, ab. 135 mi. E of Delhi: rice, wheat, sugar, and barley. Capital, Bareilly; area, ab. 1,591 sq. mi.; pop. 1,176,197 (1941).

Bareilly. [Also, **Bareli.**] Capital of the Bareilly district, N Union of India, near the Ramganga River, ab. 135 mi. E of Delhi: important rail and road junction and trading center. It was held (1857–58) by Sepoy mutineers. Pop. 192,688 (1941).

Barel (bȧ.rel), **Virgile.** b. at Drap, Alpes-Maritimes, France, Dec. 17, 1889—. French political leader. He was a Communist deputy (1936–39, 1946 *et seq.*) and was imprisoned (1939–43) during World War II.

Bareli (bạ.rā'lẹ). See **Bareilly.**

Barentin (bȧ.räṅ.taṅ). Town in N France, in the department of Seine-Inférieure, ab. 11 mi. NW of Rouen. It has various industries. Most of the town was destroyed (1944) in World War II. 5,490 (1946).

Barents (bä'rẹnts), **Willem.** d. in the arctic regions, June 20, 1597. Dutch navigator and explorer, commander of several exploring expeditions (1594–97) to Novaya Zemlya and Spitzbergen. His first voyage was an attempt to discover a passage to China through the Arctic Ocean. He discovered Spitzbergen in 1596. The Barents Sea and an island in the Spitzbergen group (or Svalbard) are named for him.

Barents Sea (bar'ẹnts, bä'rẹnts). That part of the Arctic Ocean which lies between Novaya Zemlya, Svalbard, Franz Josef Land, and the mainland of Europe. Named for Willem Barents.

Barère de Vieuzac (bȧ.rer dẹ vyė.zȧk), **Bertrand.** b. at Tarbes, France, Sept. 10, 1755; d. Jan. 13, 1841. French lawyer, politician, and agitator. He was deputy to the Constitutional Assembly in 1789 and to the Convention in 1792. He was president of the Convention during the trial of Louis XVI. As a member of the Committee of Public Safety, he supported the Terror, but later opposed Robespierre. He served as a deputy in the Hundred Days of 1815 and was exiled from France until the general amnesty under Louis Philippe in 1830.

Baret or **Barret** (bar'ẹt), **John.** d. c1580. English lexicographer. He received an M.A. from Trinity College, Cambridge, in 1558, and the degree of M.D. at Cambridge in 1577. In 1574 he published *An Alvearie, or Triple Dictionarie in English, Latin, and French.*

Baretti (bä.rāt'tē), **Giuseppe Marc' Antonio.** b. at Turin, April 25, 1719; d. at London, May 6, 1789. Italian writer and lexicographer. He lived for many years at London, where he was a friend of David Garrick, Samuel Johnson, and Edmund Burke. He wrote *Lettere famigliari* (1762), and compiled an English-Italian and Italian-English dictionary (1760), a Spanish-English dictionary (1778), and others.

Barfleur (bȧr.flėr). Small seaport in NW France, in the department of Manche, ab. 15 mi. E of Cherbourg. It was an important port in the Middle Ages.

Barfod (bär'fōᴛʜ), **Paul Frederik.** b. April 7, 1811; d. at Copenhagen, June 16, 1896. Danish historian. He was a member (1848–69) of the Rigsdag, and was assistant (1861–66) in the Royal Library at Copenhagen. Author of *Förtällinger af Fädrelandets Historie* (1853; 4th ed., 1874), *Danmarks Historie 1319-1536, 1536-1670* (1885–93), and others.

Barfrush (bär.frösh') or **Barfurush** (-fö.rösh'). Former name of **Babul.**

Barfuss (bär'fös), Count **Hans Albrecht von.** b. 1635; d. near Beeskow, Prussia, Dec. 27, 1704. Prussian field marshal. He fought with distinction in the European army that defeated the Turks at Slankamen on Aug. 19, 1691.

Barga (bär'gä). Town and commune in C Italy, in the *compartimento* (region) of Tuscany, in the province of Lucca, ab. 17 mi. NE of Lucca: metallurgical industry. The Collegiate Church dates from the 12th century; in the Church of San Francesco are sculptures by della Robbia. Considerable damage was suffered during World War II by the cathedral and several other churches of tourist interest, but repairs have now been completed or are being carried out. Pop. of commune, 11,708 (1936); of town, 2,362 (1936).

Bargello (bär.jel'lō). A 13th-century palace at Florence, Italy, originally the residence of the imperial governor of the city, but subsequently a prison and the headquarters of the municipal police. In 1857 it was remodeled as a repository for treasures of medieval and Renaissance art, and it now ranks with the other museums which give Florence its unique artistic eminence. In its courtyard are exhibited Renaissance sculptures including Michelangelo's *David*, Verocchio's *David* and his relief of the death mask of Francesca Pitti Tornabuoni, and several of the works of Donatello, including his *David* and his *Saint George*. The Bargello also houses work by Benvenuto Cellini, Giovanni da Bologna (including his *Mercury*), Jacopo Sansovino, and Antonio Pollajuolo. The collection of reliefs is particularly notable, including two rooms containing work by Luca and Andrea della Robbia, and by Ghiberti and Brunelleschi. The chapel is adorned by Giotto's frescoes (in which, among others, Dante is portrayed).

Bargiel (bär'gēl), **Woldemar.** b. at Berlin, Oct. 3, 1828; d. there, Feb. 23, 1897. German composer. He was appointed professor at the Conservatory of Cologne in 1859, Kapellmeister and director of the school of music at Rotterdam in 1865, and teacher at the royal high school of music at Berlin in 1874. His compositions included chamber music, a symphony, and others.

Bargrave (bär′grāv), **Mrs.** Woman to whom the ghost of Mrs. Veal appears in Daniel Defoe's narrative of *The True Relation of the Apparition of One Mrs. Veal* (1706).

Bargu (bär′gö). [Also: **Bariba, Borgu, Bussa.**] Sudanic-speaking people of W Africa, inhabiting N Dahomey and W Nigeria. Their population is estimated at ab. 50,000 (based on Y. Urvoy, *Petit Atlas Ethno-Demographique du Soudan*, 1942, and C. K. Meek, *The Northern Tribes of Nigeria*, 1925). Like the Gurma and Mossi to their NW, they have a well-organized and powerful kingdom. They are almost entirely non-Mohammedan.

Barguzin (bär.gö.zēn′). See under **Baikal, Lake.**

Bargwe (bär′gwā). [Also: **Rgwe, Wabarwe.**] Subgroup of the Bantu-speaking Shona in SE Africa, inhabiting C Mozambique.

Bargylus (bär.jī′lus). See **Casius.**

Barham (bar′ạm), 1st Baron. Title of **Middleton,** Sir **Charles** (1726–1813).

Barham (bär′ạm), **Richard Harris.** [Pseudonym, **Thomas Ingoldsby.**] b. at Canterbury, England, Dec. 6, 1788; d. at London, June 17, 1845. English clergyman and poet. He wrote *The Ingoldsby Legends* (1840), a collection of burlesque poems originally published (1837 *et seq.*) in *Bentley's Miscellany;* a second series was published in 1847, and a third, edited by his son, in the same year. His other works include *Baldwin* (1819) and *My Cousin Nicholas* (1841).

Bar Harbor (bär′ här′bọr). Unincorporated community in E Maine, in Hancock County: noted summer resort on the island of Mount Desert. In the path of forest fires, the community was extensively damaged in the fall of 1947. Pop. 2,572 (1950).

Bar-Hebraeus (bär′hē.brē′us). [Popular name, meaning "Son of the Hebrew," of **Abulfaraj;** Latinized, **Abulfaragius.**] b. at Malatya, in Turkish Armenia, 1226; d. at Maragheh, Persia, 1286. Syriac scholar and historian. He was made bishop of Aleppo in 1253, and was the author of the Syriac *Chronicle*, supposedly comprising secular history from creation down to his own time, especially that of SE Europe and W Asia, and church history, especially of Antioch and the Eastern Syrian Church. He also wrote *Ausar Raze*, a scriptural commentary, as well as commentaries on Aristotle and an autobiography.

Bari (bä′rē). Province in the *compartimento* (region) of Apulia, SE Italy. Capital, Bari; area, ab. 1,980 sq. mi.; 1,010,997 (1936).

Bari. [Also: **Bari delle Puglie;** ancient name, **Barium.**] Town and commune in SE Italy, in the *compartimento* (region) of Apulia, the capital of the province of Bari, situated on the Adriatic Sea, NW of Brindisi. It is a seaport, which carries on trade with various European countries and the Near East; has local commerce in cereals, wine, olive oil, and almonds; it has important flour mills, woolen and cotton textile industries, and manufactures of oriental rugs, polygraphic materials, soap, glass, tobacco, liquor, and various food products. Bari is the seat of an archbishopric and of a university. It has well-known fairs and commercial exhibits. The old city contains a number of monuments from the early Middle Ages, including the cathedral and the Church of San Nicola, both dating from the 11th century and showing Norman and Byzantine influences, the Romanesque Church of San Gregorio, built in the 12th and 13th centuries, and the castle; there is a provincial museum. A well-known city in ancient times, Bari became more important in the Middle Ages, when it was successively dominated by Goths, Lombards, Moslems, and Byzantines. It fell into the hands of the German emperor Otto I in 982; it suffered thereafter from Arabic and Byzantine invasions as well as domestic rivalries and became entirely depopulated. The castle and harbor were reconstructed under the emperor Frederick II (as Frederick I, king of Sicily) but after the downfall of the Hohenstaufen regime the city was again subject to frequent changes of rulers, particularly the French, Venetians, and Spaniards; it declined under the Bourbons. The modern development of Bari started in 1813 when Marshal Joachim Murat, appointee of Napoleon and successor of the Bourbons on the throne of Naples (as Joachim I Napoleon), authorized the construction of the new city. Its growth was accelerated after 1860 when it was incorporated into Italy. In World War II, it was occupied by the British in September, 1943. Some war damage was sustained by buildings of tourist interest, including the cathedral and San Nicola. Pop. of commune, 197,918 (1936), 273,143 (1951); of town, 162,238 (1936).

Bari. Nilo-Hamitic-speaking people of S Anglo-Egyptian Sudan in NE Africa, inhabiting the province of Mongalla on both banks of the White Nile. Their population is estimated at ab. 30,000 (by M. A. Bryan, *Distribution of the Nilotic and Nilo-Hamitic Languages of Africa*, 1948). They call themselves Bari, which is said to mean "strangers," and are known by the same name among their neighbors. They are divided into a number of independent districts headed by hereditary rainmakers. The Bari have patrilineal clans, some of which are composed of exogamous lineages, and age grades. They are also divided into a class of serfs and a class of freemen, and these classes do not intermarry. They practice hoe agriculture and herding, with the cattle complex.

Baria (bä′ri.ạ). Former state in the W Union of India, one of the Gujarat States, now merged with Bombay, ab. 250 mi. N of the city of Bombay: wood products, tobacco, and wheat; the growing and processing of jute is also important. Capital, Devgad Baria; area, 879 sq. mi.; pop. 202,055 (1941).

Bariba (bä′rē.bä). See **Bargu.**

Bari delle Puglie (bä′rē del.lā pö′lyā). See **Bari,** city.

Barinas (bä.rē′näs). [Former name, **Zamora.**] State in NW Venezuela. Capital, Barinas; area, 13,591 sq. mi.; pop. 80,503 (1950).

Barinas. Town in NW Venezuela, capital of Barinas state. 8,672 (1950).

Baring (bãr′ing), **Alexander.** [Title, 1st Baron **Ashburton.**] b. at London, Oct. 27, 1774; d. at Longleat, Wiltshire, England, May 13, 1848. English merchant and statesman; second son of Sir Francis Baring (1740–1810). He was president of the Board of Trade in the period 1834–35, and as special commissioner to the U.S. negotiated the Webster-Ashburton Treaty in 1842.

Baring, Evelyn. [Title, 1st Earl of **Cromer.**] b. Feb. 26, 1841; d. Jan. 29, 1917. English financier and diplomat; grandson of Sir Francis Baring (1740–1810). He was appointed one of the comptrollers general representing England and France in Egypt in 1879. As British agent and consul general (1883–1907) in Egypt, he aided in modernizing that country in many ways, promoting land, educational, legal, and railroad reforms. Author of *Modern Egypt* (1908), *Ancient and Modern Imperialism* (1910), *Abbas II* (1915), and *Political and Literary Essays* (1908–16).

Baring, Sir **Francis.** b. at Larkbear, near Exeter, England, April 18, 1740; d. at Lee, Kent, England, Sept. 11, 1810. English financier, chief founder of the British banking house of Baring Brothers and Company. He wrote *Observations on the Establishment of the Bank of England* (1797) and other works.

Baring, Sir **Francis Thornhill.** [Title, Baron **Northbrook.**] b. at Calcutta, April 20, 1796; d. Sept. 6, 1866. English statesman; grandson of Sir Francis Baring (1740–1810); created Baron Northbrook on Jan. 4, 1866. He was a lord of the treasury (November, 1830–June, 1834), chancellor of the exchequer (August, 1839–September, 1841), and first lord of the admiralty (1849–52).

Baring, Maurice. b. at London, April 27, 1874; d. at Beaufort Castle, Beauly, Scotland, Dec. 14, 1945. English novelist, essayist, dramatist, poet, war correspondent, traveler, and diplomat; a member of the Baring family of financial and commercial note. Educated at Eton, in Germany and Italy, where he studied languages, and at Trinity College, Cambridge, he served (1893–1904) in the British diplomatic service at Paris, Copenhagen, Rome, and London. He spent several years in Russia, covering the Russo-Japanese War and writing weekly articles (1904–12) for the *Morning Post;* as a special correspondent (1912) for the London *Times*, he covered the First Balkan War. Author of the novels *Passing By* (1921), *A Triangle* (1923), *C* (1924), *Cat's Cradle* (1925), *Daphne Adeane* (1926), *Tinker's Leave* (1927), *Friday's Business* (1933), *The Lonely Lady of Dulwich* (1934), and *Darby and Joan* (1936), many of which have been translated into several European languages; *Poems* (1899; several eds., 1905–30), *Pastels* (1891), *Triolets* (1893), *The Black Prince* (1903), *Sonnets* (1914), and *Fifty Sonnets* (1915); the dramas

Gaston de Foix (1903), *Mahasena* (1905), *The Grey Stocking* (1911), and *Manfroy* (1920); essays on Russian literature (1910, 1914) and on French literature (1927). *The Puppet Show of Memory* (1922) is an autobiography.

Baring, Thomas George. [Title, 1st Earl of **Northbrook.**] b. Jan. 22, 1826; d. Nov. 15, 1904. English politician; son of Sir Francis Thornhill Baring. He was viceroy of India (1872–76) and first lord of the admiralty (1880–85). He was created earl of Northbrook in 1876.

Baring, William Bingham. [Title, 2nd Baron **Ashburton.**] b. in June, 1799; d. near Alresford, England, March 23, 1864. English politician; son of Alexander Baring (1774–1848). He served as secretary of the board of control (until 1845) and as paymaster general (1845–46) under Sir Robert Peel. He married (1823) Lady Harriet Mary Montagu, who became a well-known hostess to political figures and men of letters.

Baring-Gould (bãr′ing.göld′), **Sabine.** b. at Exeter, England, 1834; d. Jan. 2, 1924. English clergyman and writer. His works include *Iceland* (1861), *The Book of Werewolves* (1865), *Post-Medieval Preachers* (1865), *Curious Myths of the Middle Ages* (1866–68), *The Origin and Development of Religious Belief* (1869–70), *Lives of the Saints* (1872–77), *Some Modern Difficulties* (1874), and *Mehalah* (1880), *John Herring* (1883), and other novels. He also wrote the hymn *Onward Christian Soldiers* which was subsequently set to music by Sir Arthur Sullivan.

Baringo (bä.ring′gō), **Lake.** Small lake in E Africa, in Kenya NE of Lake Victoria. The lake, which has no outlet, was discovered by Joseph Thomson in 1883.

Barisal (bu.rē.säl′). Capital of the district of Bakarganj, Pakistan, ab. 125 mi. E of Calcutta: river port; rope is made from jute here. 89,278 (1951).

Barito (bä.rē′tō). River in N central Republic of Indonesia, in SE Borneo. It rises in the E range of the Muller Mountains, flowing S into the Java Sea. Around the lower course of this river there is a broad region of marshes, and cross branches of the Barito connect through this with other streams. The Barito is one of the largest rivers in Borneo, ab. 550 mi. in length, and it is navigable for steam vessels of moderate draft for ab. 250 mi. from its mouth.

Barium (bãr′i.um). Ancient name of **Bari,** city.

Barjols (bår.zhol). Town in SE France, in the department of Var, ab. 30 mi. N of Toulon, called the "Tivoli of Provence" on account of its picturesque surroundings. It has a leather industry. 2,390 (1946).

Barjot (bår.zhō), **Pierre.** [Pseudonym, **Pierre Belleroche.**] b. at Le Blanc, Indre, France, Oct. 13, 1899—. French naval commander, commander (1947 *et seq.*) of the French naval forces in Morocco. He was assistant chief of staff (1943) of the Free French navy in World War II, and assistant chief of staff (1944–46) of the ministry of national defense in the French Fourth Republic.

Barkal (bär′käl). Hill with noted inscriptions, in N Anglo-Egyptian Sudan, in Northern Province, situated on the Nile below the fourth cataract, near the ancient Meroë or Napata.

Barker (bär′kėr), **Albert Smith.** b. at Hanson, Mass., March 31, 1843; d. Jan. 29, 1916. American naval officer, commissioned a rear admiral in 1899. He was graduated from the U.S. Naval Academy in 1861. An officer in the Union navy during the Civil War, he served aboard the *Mississippi* during the bombardment of Forts Jackson and St. Philip and the capture of New Orleans; transferred (1863) to the *Monongahela,* he participated in the capture of Port Hudson. He ran a line of deep-sea soundings around the world while in command (1883–86) of the *Enterprise;* was a member of the board of strategy at the opening of the Spanish-American War; commanded the *Newark* in the bombardment (July 1, 1898) of Santiago de Cuba, and later the *Oregon;* relieved Admiral Dewey at Manila on May 29, 1899. From 1900 to 1903 he was commandant of the New York navy yard, and was named commander in chief of the North Atlantic fleet. He retired in 1905.

Barker, Benjamin Fordyce. b. at Wilton, Franklin County, Me., May 2, 1818; d. at New York, May 30, 1891. American gynecologist and medical writer. He became professor of gynecology at the New York Medical College in 1850 and professor of clinical gynecology at Bellevue Hospital in 1860.

Barker, Edmund Henry. b. at Hollym, England, 1788; d. at London, 1839. English classical scholar. He edited Greek and Latin works, ranging from the fables of Aesop to speeches of Demosthenes. He was cast into Fleet prison after an unsuccessful lawsuit (c1827), undertaken to prove his father's legitimacy, had impoverished him; he became involved in rash financial adventures following his release and died penniless. Compiler, with Professor George Dunbar of Edinburgh, of a Greek and English lexicon.

Barker, Ernest. b. at Woodley, Cheshire, England, Sept. 23, 1874—. English historian. He was successively a fellow and lecturer (1898–1905) of Merton College at Oxford, and a lecturer at Wadham College (1899–1909), lecturer at St. John's College (1909–13), at New College (1913–20), principal (1920–27) of King's College at London, and a professor (1928–39) of political science at Cambridge. Author of *The Political Thought of Plato and Aristotle* (1906, revised as *Greek Political Theory,* 1915), *Political Thought in England from Herbert Spencer to Today* (1915), *The Crusades* (1923), *National Character* (1927), *Oliver Cromwell and the English People* (1927), *Ideas and Ideals of the British Empire* (1941), *Britain and the British People* (1942), and essays collected in *Church, State, and Study* (1930) and *The Citizen's Choice* (1937).

Barker, Eugene Campbell. b. near Riverside, Texas, Nov. 10, 1874—. American historian and educator. After receiving the degrees of B.A. in 1899 and M.A. in 1900 from the University of Texas, he was an instructor in history at that institution (1901–06), a Harrison fellow at the University of Pennsylvania (1906–07), an Austin Scholar at Harvard University, and an assistant in history at Radcliffe College (1907–08). He received the degree of Ph.D. from the University of Pennsylvania in 1908. In 1940 Transylvania College conferred upon him the degree of LL.D. Since 1908 he has taught history at the University of Texas, going on modified service in 1945. The regents of the University of Texas have honored him by the establishment of the Eugene C. Barker Texas Historical Center in connection with the university. He is a member of the American Historical Association, of the Texas State Historical Association, and of the Mississippi Valley Historical Association, which he served as president in 1923. He is the author of *Life of Stephen F. Austin* (1925), *Mexico and Texas (1821–1835)* (1928), *Readings in Texas History* (1929), *The Father of Texas* (1935), and coauthor of *A School History of Texas* (1912), *Growth of a Nation* and *Story of Our Nation* (1928–40). He edited *The Austin Papers* (1924–28) and is coeditor of *With the Makers of Texas* (1912) and *The Writings of Sam Houston* (1938–43). From 1910 to 1937 he was managing editor of the *Southwestern Historical Quarterly.*

Barker, George Frederic. b. July 14, 1835; d. May 24, 1910. American physician and chemist. He became professor of natural sciences at the Western University of Pennsylvania (now the University of Pittsburgh) in 1864, professor of physiological chemistry and toxicology at the Yale Medical School in 1867, and was professor of chemistry and physics at the University of Pennsylvania in the period 1873–1900.

Barker, Sir Herbert Atkinson. b. at Southport, England, April 21, 1869; d. July 21, 1950. English manipulative surgeon. He was a specialist in correcting muscular damage (particularly of knee cartilages) without surgical operation or the use of orthopedic appliances. He was appointed (1941) to the staff of Noble's Hospital on the Isle of Man.

Barker, Jacob. b. on Swans Island, Me., Dec. 17, 1779; d. at Philadelphia, Dec. 26, 1871. American financier and politician. He was employed by the U.S. government, on the outbreak of the War of 1812, to raise a loan of five million dollars.

Barker, James Nelson. b. at Philadelphia, June 17, 1784; d. at Washington, D.C., March 9, 1858. American politician, poet, and playwright. His play *The Indian Princess* (1808) was the first American play to deal with the American Indian (its titular heroine was Pocahontas), and the first American play to be produced in England after a production in the U.S. He also achieved success with his stage adaptation (1812) of Sir Walter Scott's

Marmion. His political posts included the mayoralty (1819 *et seq.*) of Philadelphia, collector (1829–38) of the port of Philadelphia, and comptroller (1838–58) of the U.S. treasury. He also combined his political and literary interests in writing odes and songs for public patriotic occasions.

Barker, James William. b. at White Plains, N.Y., Dec. 5, 1815; d. June 26, 1869. American dry-goods merchant and politician, who, as New York mayoral candidate of the Know-Nothing Party, was defeated (1854) by Fernando Wood. A member later of the Republican party, he participated in Lincoln's campaign of 1860. He was one of the founders of the "Order of the Star Spangled Banner," a secret society dedicated to preventing foreign-born Americans from holding political office.

Barker, Jeremiah. b. March 31, 1752; d. Oct. 4, 1835. American physician and medical writer. Author of *Vade Mecum* (a medical reference book), *A Book of Anatomy*, and several medical papers.

Barker, John. b. at Smyrna (now Izmir), Turkey, March 9, 1771; d. Oct. 5, 1849. British consul in Syria, and consul general in Egypt. He is best known, aside from his political services, for his attempts, as a horticulturist, to promote the cultivation of Western fruits in the East.

Barker, Joseph. b. at Bramley, near Leeds, England, May 11, 1806; d. at Omaha, Neb., Sept. 15, 1875. Anglo-American preacher and political agitator. He was expelled from the Methodist New Connexion in 1841, on theological grounds, and established a sect known as Barkerites. Later he adopted deistical opinions, but finally returned to the orthodox point of view. In 1847 he visited America, on his return supported the Chartist agitation, was arrested (1848) at Manchester, and at the same time was elected to Parliament. In 1851 he emigrated to the U.S., where he identified himself with the Abolition movement. He was a lecturer and a voluminous writer.

Barker, Josiah. b. at Marshfield, Mass., Nov. 16, 1763; d. at Charlestown, Mass., Sept. 23, 1847. American shipbuilder. He was the constructor of the *Frolic*, the *Vermont*, the *Virginia*, and the *Cumberland*, master carpenter on the *Independence*, rebuilder (1834) of the *Constitution*, and designer (1843) of the sloop *Portsmouth*.

Barker, Lewellys Franklin. b. at Norwich, Ontario, Canada, Sept. 16, 1867; d. at Baltimore, Md., July 13, 1943. American physician. A graduate (1890) of the University of Toronto, he studied also at Leipzig, Munich, and Berlin. He served as a professor and head of the department of anatomy (1900–05) at Rush Medical College, professor of medicine (1905–13) at Johns Hopkins University, and chief physician (1905–13) at Johns Hopkins Hospital. Author of *The Nervous System and Its Constituent Neurones* (1899), *The Clinical Diagnosis of Internal Diseases* (1916), *The Young Man and Medicine* (1927), *Psychotherapy* (1940), and an autobiography, *Time and the Physician* (1942).

Barker, Matthew Henry. b. at Deptford, England, 1790; d. June 29, 1846. English journalist and novelist, best known for his sea tales. He wrote *Land and Sea Tales* (1836), *Topsail-sheet Blocks* (1838), *Life of Nelson* (1836), *The Victory, or the Wardroom Mess* (1844), and others.

Barker, Thomas. b. near Pontypool, Monmouthshire, England, 1769; d. at Bath, England, Dec. 11, 1847. English painter of landscapes and historical subjects. His best-known picture is *The Woodman*.

Barker, Thomas Jones. b. 1815; d. 1882. English painter; son of Thomas Barker (1769–1847). He specialized in military subjects and in portraits.

Barker, Wharton. b. at Philadelphia, May 1, 1846; d. April 8, 1921. American financier and politician. He was graduated (1866) from the University of Pennsylvania before becoming a member of the banking firm of Barker Brothers and Company. He was a special U.S. financial agent (1878) for the Russian government, and an economic advisor (1879) in Russia, where he was given a title by Alexander II. He organized the Investment Company and the Finance Company at Philadelphia. In 1895 he visited China on the invitation of Li Hung-chang. He was the publisher (1880–91; 1894–1900) of the *American*, a weekly magazine of political and economic opinion. A prominent member (until 1896) of the Republican Party, actively supporting Garfield and Harrison, he was a Bryan supporter in 1896. Named a "middle of the road" Populist candidate (1900) for president, he received 50,232 votes against the 7,207,923 votes cast for William McKinley.

Barkhausen (bärk'hou.zen), **Heinrich Georg.** b. at Bremen, Germany, Dec. 2, 1881—. German electrical engineer and physicist, noted as the discoverer (1920) of the Barkhausen effect in magnetics. Author of *Das Problem der Schwingungserzeugung* (1907) and *Elektronenröhren* (1923).

Barking (bär'king). [Also: **Barking Town;** Middle English, **Berkyng;** Anglo-Saxon, **Beorcingas.**] Municipal borough in SE England, in Essex, situated on the river Roding, ab. 8 mi. E of Fenchurch Street station, London. It has a nonferrous metals industry. It was celebrated in the Middle Ages for its abbey for Benedictine nuns, founded c670. Pop. 78,197 (1951).

Barkis (bär'kis), **Mr.** In Charles Dickens's *David Copperfield*, a bashful carrier who marries Peggotty. He conveys his intentions to her by sending her, by David, the message "Barkis is willing'."

Barkla (bär'kla), **Charles Glover.** b. at Widnes, Lancashire, England, June 7, 1877—. English physicist. Educated at the Liverpool Institute, at University College, Liverpool, and at Trinity and King's Colleges, Cambridge, he became in 1902 an Oliver Lodge fellow of Liverpool University, in 1905 a demonstrator and assistant lecturer in physics, and in 1907 a lecturer in advanced electricity. In 1909 he went to King's College, University of London, as Wheatstone professor of physics, a post he filled until 1913, when he was appointed professor of natural philosophy at Edinburgh University, with which he has been associated since that time. In 1916 he was Bakerian lecturer at the Royal Society, and in 1917 was Hughes medallist of that scientific body. In 1917 also he was the recipient of the Nobel prize in physics. He is the author of numerous contributions to scientific periodicals on electric waves, x-rays, and secondary rays.

Barkley (bär'kli), **Alben William.** b. on a farm in Graves County, Ky., Nov. 24, 1877—. American politician. 35th vice-president of the U.S. He has been a senator from Kentucky (1926–49) and Senate majority leader (1937–46). Notable for Democratic Party loyalty, he espoused the repeal of Prohibition in 1932, though he himself was a bone-dry Methodist; he effectively supported many administration measures not wholly pleasing to him, and is said to have accepted the 1948 vice-presidential nomination as a matter of party loyalty rather than personal desire. He broke once (1944) with F. D. Roosevelt over the latter's tax veto message of that year, resigning as majority leader, but was promptly reëlected and a few months later, as Democratic national convention chairman, led the movement for Roosevelt's unprecedented fourth-term nomination. He took office as vice-president in 1949, having been elected (1948) on the Democratic ticket as Harry S. Truman's running mate.

Barkly (bär'kli), Sir **Henry.** b. 1815; d. at South Kensington, London, Oct. 20, 1898. English colonial administrator. He served (1848–53) as commander in chief and governor of British Guiana, and was governor successively of Jamaica (1853–56), Victoria (1856–63), Mauritius (1863–70), and Cape of Good Hope Colony (1870–77). He opposed a scheme then current for enforced federation of the Cape Colony, believing this development should be allowed to come about naturally.

Barkly Tableland. Highland region in N Australia S of the Gulf of Carpentaria. The general elevation is over 1,000 ft. and the area is used for sheep and cattle raising.

Barksdale (bärks'dāl), **William.** b. in Rutherford County, Tenn., Aug. 21, 1821; killed at Gettysburg, Pa., July 3, 1863. American politician and soldier, with the Confederate army in the Civil War. He was a Democratic member of Congress from Mississippi (1853–61), joined the Confederate army at the outbreak of the Civil War, and rose to the rank of brigadier general. He fell while leading an assault of his brigade on the Federal position at the Peach Orchard in the battle of Gettysburg.

Barksteed (bärk'stēd) or **Barksted** (-sted), **William.** fl. c1611. English actor and poet. His name appears instead of John Marston's on some copies of *The Insatiate Countess*. He was the author of *Hiren, or the Faire Greeke* (1611).

Barlaam (bär′lạ.ạm). [Also, **Bernardo of Seminara.**] b. at Seminara, in Calabria, Italy, toward the end of the 13th century; d. probably in 1350. Italian theologian, humanist, logician, and mathematician. He went to Constantinople sometime shortly after 1328, while still a young man, and acquired considerable favor at the Byzantine court, particularly with that faction (including the empress) which sought a reconciliation of the Orthodox and Roman churches. In 1333 he engaged in preliminary discussions toward this end with legates from Rome, and was sent (1339) to Avignon to negotiate, in the emperor's name, with Pope Benedict XII. The aim of these negotiations was twofold: to explore the possibilities of religious union and to obtain Latin help against the Turks. The mission was a failure, and Barlaam returned to Constantinople, where he continued (until his cause was defeated in 1341) to struggle against that faction in the Orthodox Church which opposed union with Rome. In 1341 he returned to Italy, where (at Naples) he met Boccaccio, and proceeded thence to Avignon, where he met Petrarch. In 1346 he was sent to Constantinople to seek again for some means of reconciliation between the two churches, but was again defeated. He is known to have surrendered his bishopric in 1348, and died shortly thereafter (probably in 1350).

Barlaam, Saint. Eremite of Sinai, counselor of Josaphat, in the romance *Barlaam and Josaphat.*

Barlaam and Josaphat (jos′ạ.fat). Romance, sometimes attributed to Saint John of Damascus (a Syrian monk of the 8th century), translated into Latin before the 13th century. It recounts the adventures of Barlaam, a monk of the wilderness of Sinai, in his successful attempt to convert Josaphat (or Joasaph), the son of a king of India, to Christianity and asceticism. The incidents of the story were probably taken from an Indian source. That part of the plot of Shakespeare's *Merchant of Venice* which relates to the choosing of the casket is said to have come originally from this romance, through the *Speculum Historiale* of Vincent of Beauvais (c1290), the *Cento Novelle Antiche* (65th tale), Boccaccio's *Decameron,* the *Golden Legend,* and the *Gesta Romanorum.* An English translation of this was printed (c1510–15) by Wynkyn de Worde, which contained the "Story of the Three Caskets." It is considered probable that Shakespeare read one of Richard Robinson's reissues (there were six between 1577 and 1601). Rudolf von Ems wrote a poem of the same name and subject in the 13th century, probably based on the original.

Barlach (bär′läċh), **Ernst.** b. at Wedel, Germany, Feb. 2, 1870; d. at Rostock, Germany, Oct. 24, 1938. German sculptor, graphic artist, and playwright, an exponent of German expressionism. As a sculptor working in wood, bronze, and stone he is best characterized by his figures in monumental works, depicting people overwhelmed by suffering, or engaged in battle. His *Ehrenmal* (1927) in the cathedral at Güstrow, Germany, and his war monuments at Magdeburg (1929) and Hamburg (1930) are among his greatest works. His woodcuts, lithographs, and etchings deal with the same subjects as his sculpture. After attaining fame at sculpture he turned, when more than 40 years old, to writing, chiefly of dramas such as *Der tote Tag* (1912), *Der arme Vater* (1918), *Die echten Sedemunds* (1920), *Der Findling* (1922), and *Die Sündflut* (1924).

Bârlad (bėr.läd′). [Also, formerly, **Bêrlad.**] Town in NE Rumania, in the province of Moldavia, situated ab. 60 mi. NW of Galaţi on the Bârlad River: a railroad junction, with grain markets, flour mills, and factories for hosiery and foodstuffs. 24,035 (1948).

Barlaeus (bär.lē′us), **Casparus.** [Latinized name of **Gaspard van Baerle.**] b. at Antwerp, Feb. 12, 1584; d. at Amsterdam, Jan. 14, 1648. Dutch historian. He was a professor of logic at the University of Leiden in 1617, and of philosophy and rhetoric at the Athenæum at Amsterdam in 1631. His *Rerum per octennium in Brasilia et alibi nuper gestarum* (Amsterdam, 1647; 2nd ed., with additions by Piso, Cleves, 1660) has been one of the standard authorities on the wars between the Dutch and Portuguese in Brazil.

Barlaymont or **Barlaimont** (bär.lā.môṅ′), **Charles,** Count **of.** d. 1579. Dutch statesman in the service of Philip II (of Spain) in The Netherlands. He was a member of the *consulta,* a council of state headed by Cardinal Antoine Perrenot de Grenvelle, for the purpose of supervising and advising the actions of Margaret of Parma during her service as regent (1559–67) of The Netherlands under her half-brother Philip II.

Bar-le-Duc (bår.lẹ.dük). [Also, **Bar-sur-Ornain.**] Town in E France, the capital of the department of Meuse, situated on the Ornain River, SW of Verdun; a station on the railroad line from Paris to Strasbourg. It consists of two parts, the commercial lower town and the more picturesque upper town. It has cotton textile, hosiery, machine, and construction industries. Bar-le-Duc is famous for its wines, its preserves, and its cooking; has an ethnographical and commercial museum, old ramparts, and a castle of the dukes of Bar. It was the birthplace of Jules Henri Poincaré and of André Maginot, whose name is connected with the line of fortifications erected along France's E border after World War I. 15,460 (1946).

Barletta (bär.let′tä). [Ancient name, **Barduli.**] City and commune in SE Italy, in the *compartimento* (region) of Apulia, in the province of Bari, situated on the Ofanto River, ab. 35 mi. NW of Bari. It is a seaport and shipping center, with coastwise trade; has agricultural industries. The city is rich in art treasures. The Cathedral of Santa Maria Maggiore, erected in the 12th century in Romanesque style, has Gothic additions from the 14th century; also in Romanesque style is the Church of Sant' Andrea; there is a medieval castle, various palaces from the Renaissance and baroque periods, and an art museum. After the downfall of the Roman Empire, the city was under Gothic, Byzantine, Lombard, and Hohenstaufen rule; it had from an early period important trade with the Near East. It declined under the French and the Spaniards. The modern development started in 1860, after its incorporation into the kingdom of Italy. Buildings of interest to tourists were undamaged in World War II. Pop. of commune, 52,386 (1936); of city, 51,597 (1936).

Barletta, Gabriello. fl. second half of 15th century. Dominican friar of Naples, noted as a preacher. He preached in the manner of Abraham a Sancta Clara, endeavoring to correct by ridicule which, however, sometimes degenerated into vulgarity.

Barley (bär′li), **Clara.** In Charles Dickens's novel *Great Expectations,* a pretty girl who marries Herbert Pocket.

Barley, Old Bill. Drunken and gouty old man, the father of Clara Barley, in Charles Dickens's novel *Great Expectations.*

Barleycorn (bär′li.kôrn), **John** (or **Sir John**). Personification of malt liquor, as being made from barley. There is an English ballad in which he appears as a person.

Barlow (bär′lō), **Francis Channing.** b. at Brooklyn, N.Y., Oct. 19, 1834; d. Jan. 11, 1896. American lawyer and soldier, with the Union army in the Civil War. He joined the Federal volunteer service at the outbreak of the Civil War, and became a brigadier general in 1862 and a major general in 1865. He participated (as a colonel) in the battles of Fair Oaks and Antietam, and commanded a division in the battles of the Wilderness and Spottsylvania Court House and in the assault on the defenses of Petersburg. He headed (1871) the prosecution against the Tweed Ring.

Barlow, George. b. at London, June 19, 1847; d. in January, 1914. English poet. He was educated at Harrow and at Exeter College, Oxford. Author of *Poems and Sonnets* (3 vols., 1871), *A Life's Love* (1873), *Under the Dawn* (1874), and *Pageant of Life* (1888). At the invitation of Charles François Gounod, who was in London during the Franco-Prussian War, Barlow added English words to the French composer's *Ave Maria.*

Barlow, Henry Clark. b. at Newington Butts, Surrey, England, May 12, 1806; d. at Salzburg, Austria, Nov. 8, 1876. English physician and scholar, noted as a student of Dante. He wrote *Critical, Historical, and Philosophical Contributions to the Study of the "Divina Commedia"* (1864) and others.

Barlow, Jane. b. at Clontarf, Ireland, Oct. 17, 1860; d. April 17, 1917. Irish novelist and poet. Among her works, which deal mainly with peasant life in Ireland, are *Bogland Studies* (1892), *Irish Idylls* (1892), *Kerrigan's Quality* (1893), *The End of Elfintown* (1894), *Strangers at Lisconnel* (1895), *A Creel of Irish Stories* (1897), *At the Back of Beyond* (1902), *By Beach and Bog Land* (1905), *Irish Neighbors* (1907), *Irish People in Irish Places* (1909), and *Flaws* (1911).

Barlow, Joel. b. at Redding, Conn., March 24, 1754; d. near Kraków, Poland, Dec. 24, 1812. American poet and diplomat, one of the group of American writers known as the "Hartford Wits." He resided abroad for many years, chiefly (1788–1805) in France, where he associated himself with the Girondist party. He was consul (1795–97) to Algiers, arranging treaties with the native rulers of Tripoli, Algiers, and Tunis, and was U.S. minister (1811–12) to France. He died en route to a conference with Napoleon I, under orders from President James Madison. Author of the epic poem *The Vision of Columbus* (1787; enlarged as *The Columbiad*, 1807), *Advice to the Privileged Orders* (1792), and *Hasty Pudding* (1796).

Barlow, John Whitney. b. at Perry, Wyoming County, N.Y., June 26, 1838; d. at Jerusalem, Feb. 27, 1914. American army engineer. A graduate (1861) of the U.S. Military Academy, he served as an artillery lieutenant and later with the engineer corps during the Civil War. He was the leader of the government exploration (1871) of what became (1872) Yellowstone National Park, was chief engineer (1886–90) on the Muscle Shoals project, and served as commander (1892–96) of the U.S. engineers who, with members of the Mexican engineer corps, plotted the international boundary from El Paso to the Pacific. He retired (1901), as chief of engineers, with the rank of brigadier general.

Barlow, Peter. b. at Norwich, England, in October, 1776; d. March 1, 1862. English mathematician, optician, and physicist, deviser of a system for correcting errors made by ships' compasses. He wrote *An Elementary Investigation of the Theory of Numbers* (1811), *A New Mathematical and Philosophical Dictionary* (1814), *New Mathematical Tables* (1814), *An Essay on the Strength of Timber and other Materials* (1817), *Essay on Magnetic Attractions* (1820), and others. He was the inventor of a lens which bears his name.

Barlow, Samuel Latham Mitchill. b. at Granville, Hampden County, Mass., June 5, 1826; d. at Glen Cove, Long Island, N.Y., July 10, 1889. American lawyer. He collected an important library of Americana (which was sold at auction in 1890) and edited, with Henry Harrisse, *Notes on Columbus* (1866; privately printed).

Barlow, William. d. 1568. English Protestant prelate and controversialist, bishop successively of St. Asaph, St. David's, Bath and Wells, and Chichester; father of William Barlow (d. 1625). A violent opponent of Cardinal Thomas Wolsey, he also attacked the church in a series of pamphlets which he afterward repudiated.

Barlow, William. b. at St. David's, Wales; d. 1625. English ecclesiastic, archdeacon of Salisbury; son of William Barlow (d. 1568). He wrote *The Navigators' Supply* (1597), a work on navigation treating largely of compasses. He contributed some marked improvements to the method of hanging compasses at sea, and discovered the difference between iron and steel for magnetic purposes, the proper way of touching magnetic needles, and the proper method of cementing loadstones.

Barlowe (bär'lō), **Arthur.** [Also, **Barlow.**] b. c1550; d. c1620. English navigator, who, with Philip Amadas, reached islands off the coast of what is now North Carolina in two ships fitted out by Sir Walter Raleigh. Barlowe's account of this voyage was a factor in persuading Queen Elizabeth to lend her aid to the establishment of a permanent colony, named Virginia (she was often called the "Virgin Queen") in her honor.

Bärmann (ber'män), **Heinrich Joseph.** b. at Potsdam, Germany, in February, 1784; d. at Munich, June 11, 1847. German clarinetist, court musician at Munich; father of Karl Bärmann (1811–85). He composed many works for the clarinet, including concertos, sonatas, and chamber works.

Bärmann, Karl. b. at Munich, 1811; d. May 24, 1885. German clarinetist; son of Heinrich Joseph Bärmann (1784–1847) and father of Karl Bärmann (1839–1913). He composed various works for the clarinet.

Bärmann, Karl. b. at Munich, July 9, 1839; d. at Boston, Jan. 17, 1913. Concert pianist and music teacher; son of Karl Bärmann (1811–85). He studied under Franz Liszt and, after attaining success as a concert pianist, became a teacher (later professor) at the royal music school at Munich. In 1881 he left for America; planning to stay for two years, he remained for 24, settling at Boston and appearing with many symphony orchestras. He is remembered today chiefly as a teacher.

Barmbeck (bärm'bek). Town in NW Germany, in the *Land* (state) of Hamburg, British Zone. It is a suburb of Hamburg.

Barmecides (bär'mẹ.sīdz). [Also, **Barmekids** (-kidz).] Family of the Persian nobility, established under the Abbasside caliphate. The family gained great wealth and influence. Khaled ibn-Barmak rose to be a member of the government of Abu-al-Abbas, and his son was vizier to the caliph al-Mahdi. The son, Yahya, was also tutor to Harun al-Rashid, later becoming his friend, as did his two sons. However, Harun al-Rashid so feared the power of this family that he had them all assassinated, only one child escaping. The Barmecides figure largely in several tales in *The Arabian Nights' Entertainments*.

Barmecide's Feast. Feast where the dishes were empty and everything was imaginary; hence, any tantalizing illusion. The allusion is to the story of "The Barber's Sixth Brother" in *The Arabian Nights' Entertainments*, in which a rich Barmecide gives a dinner of this description to a starving wretch, and obliges him to pretend that he eats what is not before him. However, when it comes to pretending to drink wine, the guest feigns drunkenness and knocks the Barmecide down and the latter, displaying a sense of humor, not only forgives him but heaps benefits upon him.

Barmen (bär'mẹn). Former city in W Germany, in the *Land* (state) of North Rhine-Westphalia, British Zone, formerly in the Rhine Province, Prussia, situated on the Wupper River, ab. 24 mi. NE of Cologne. It is incorporated into the city of Wuppertal, which includes the former twin cities of Elberfeld and Barmen. Pop. under 200,000.

Barmouth (bär'muth). Urban district, seaport, seaside resort, and market town in N Wales, in Merionethshire, situated near the estuary of the river Mawddach (or Maw), on Cardigan Bay, ab. 9 mi. W of Dolgelley, ab. 233 mi. NW of London by rail. It has a wide bathing beach; nearby is the famous Cader Idris mountain range. 2,466 (1951).

Barmstedt (bärm'shtet). Small town in N Germany, British Zone, in the former province of Schleswig-Holstein, situated on the Krückau River, ab. 21 mi. NW of Hamburg.

Bärn (bern). German name of **Beroun,** Moravia.

Barnabas (bär'nạ.bạs), Saint. d. at Cyprus, c61 A.D. Surname (from Aramaic, meaning "Son of Prophecy") of the Cyprian Levite Joses, or Joseph, an apostle of the Christian church. He was one of the first to sell his land for the benefit of the common fund. He introduced Paul after the latter's conversion, taught, with Paul, at Antioch, undertook with him a missionary journey to Cyprus and various cities in Asia Minor, and was sent with him to Jerusalem by the church at Antioch to consult the apostles and elders on the question of circumcision. When about to undertake a second missionary journey with Paul, Barnabas separated from him, owing to a difference arising out of Barnabas's determination to take his sister's son, Mark, with him. He was, according to the legend, martyred at Cyprus in 61 A.D. His day is celebrated by the Greek, Roman, and Anglican churches on the 11th of June, and his symbol is a rake, as his day comes in the time of the hay harvest. It was formerly a great feast among the English people.

Barnabas, The Epistle of. Anonymous epistle, containing no mention of the readers for whom it was intended, dating from an early period of the Christian church. It was intended for persons in danger of being Judaized, and emphasizes the separation of Christianity from Judaism. Its authorship was ascribed to Barnabas (the apostle) in the early church; but some later critics have assigned it to a post-apostolic writer, perhaps a converted Jew of Alexandria.

Barnabas of Reggio (red′jō). [Also, **Barnabas de Reatinis** (or **Riathinis**) (rē.ą.tī′nis).] b. at Reggio nell' Emilia, Italy; d. at Venice, c1365. Italian physician. He practiced first at Mantua (where he wrote, in 1331, a short treatise entitled *De conservanda sanitate*, based almost entirely on Arabic sources), but was called (c1334) to Venice by the medical college in that city, and there spent the rest of his life. He was the author of *De naturis et qualitatibus alimentorum* (1338), which is a discussion, in alphabetical order, of the natures and qualities of various foods, and of *De conservanda sanitate oculorum* (1340), a collection of aphorisms and general statements on the care of the eyes, based on the works of Galen and others.

Barnabee (bär′ną.bē), **Henry Clay.** b. at Portsmouth, N.H., Nov. 14, 1833; d. Dec. 16, 1917. American actor, singer, and producer. His early roles were Toby Winkle in *All that Glitters is not Gold* and Cox in Gilbert and Sullivan's *Cox and Box*. With a company known as the Boston Ideals, he staged one of the first performances (1879) of *H.M.S. Pinafore*, by Gilbert and Sullivan, and with another company, known as the Bostonians, which he helped organize (1887), he produced Reginald De Koven's *Robin Hood*, appearing in it himself more than 1,900 times as the Sheriff of Nottingham.

Barnaby Brittle (bär′ną.bi brit′l). See **Brittle, Barnaby.**

Barnaby Bunch (bunch). See **Bunch, Barnaby.**

Barnaby Rudge (ruj). Novel by Charles Dickens which came out in parts, and was published in book form in 1841. It is based on the anti-Catholic riots of the London populace in June, 1780, which were instigated and abetted by Lord George Gordon. Barnaby, a half-witted fellow, the friend of Grip the raven, becomes ignorantly involved in the riots, and is condemned to death but pardoned.

Barnacle (bär′ną.kl), **Lord Decimus Tite.** Pompous and windy peer, with a high position in the Circumlocution Office, in Charles Dickens's *Little Dorrit*. Clarence, an empty-headed youth, and Ferdinand, a well-dressed and agreeable young man, his sons, are also employed in the office.

Barnadine (bär′ną.din). Character in Shakespeare's *Measure for Measure;* a savage and sullen prisoner, "careless, reckless, and fearless of what's past, present, or to come."

Barnard (bär′nąrd), Lady **Anne.** [Maiden name, **Lindsay.**] b. Dec. 8, 1750; d. May 6, 1825. Scottish poet; daughter of James Lindsay, the fifth Earl of Balcarres; married (1793) to Andrew Barnard, a British colonial official in South Africa. She wrote the ballad *Auld Robin Gray* (1772) and a sequel to it.

Barnard, Charles. b. at Boston, Feb. 13, 1838; d. April 11, 1920. American author. He was editor of *Vox Humana*, department head (1875–84) of "World's Work" in *Scribner's Magazine*, and author of books on small-scale agriculture, music, weather, and electricity, several novels, and numerous plays. *The County Fair* (1889; written with Neil Burgess) and *The Forest Ring* (1901; written with William C. De Mille) were two of his successful dramas. He was a contributing editor to the *Century Dictionary* for terms on tools and machines.

Barnard, Charles Francis. b. at Boston, April 17, 1808; d. at Somerville, Mass., Nov. 8, 1884. American Unitarian clergyman, humanitarian, and philanthropist. He was ordained in 1834. An associate (1832) of Dorothea Lynde Dix in teaching underprivileged children, he founded (1836) the Warren Street Chapel, at Boston, for the instruction of children.

Barnard, Charlotte Alington. [Pseudonym, **"Claribel."**] b. Dec. 23, 1830; d. at Dover, England, Jan. 30, 1869. English ballad composer. Many of her songs, such as *Come back to Erin*, were very popular in the 19th century.

Barnard, Daniel Dewey. b. in Berkshire County, Mass., Sept. 11, 1796; d. at Albany, N.Y., April 24, 1861. American politician and diplomat. He was a member of Congress from New York (1827–29, 1839–45) and U.S. minister to Prussia (1850–53).

Barnard, Edward Emerson. b. at Nashville, Tenn., Dec. 16, 1857; d. Feb. 6, 1923. American astronomer. He was graduated from Vanderbilt University in 1886, and made a number of astronomical discoveries which were reported in the *Sidereal Messenger*, *Observatory*, *Science Observer*, and *Astronomische Nachrichten*. His most notable discovery was that of the fifth satellite of Jupiter, made at the Lick Observatory, on Sept. 9, 1892. He also discovered 16 comets, and was known for celestial photography. He was astronomer of the Yerkes Observatory from 1895.

Barnard, Frederick Augustus Porter. b. at Sheffield, Mass., May 5, 1809; d. at New York, April 27, 1889. American educator, scientist, and author; brother of John Gross Barnard. He was a professor (1837–54) at the University of Alabama, president (1856–61) of the University of Mississippi, and president (1864–89) of Columbia College. He served as U.S. commissioner at the Paris Exposition of 1867, and assistant commissioner general at that of 1878. He was an advocate of educational opportunities for women equal to those for men. Barnard College, opened at New York some months after his death, was named for him.

Barnard, George Grey. b. at Bellefonte, Pa., May 24, 1863; d. 1938. American sculptor. He was educated at the Art Institute of Chicago, and at the École des Beaux Arts, Paris (1884–87). He was awarded gold medals at the Paris Exposition (1900), the Pan-American Exposition, Buffalo (1901), and the Louisiana Purchase Exposition, St. Louis (1904). His head of Lincoln and a marble statue of the *Two Natures* are in the Metropolitan Museum of Art, New York, and his *God Pan* at Columbia University, New York. Among his other works are *Work and Fraternity* and *The Burden of Life*, sculptural groups designed for the capitol at Harrisburg, Pa., first exhibited at the Paris Salon in the spring of 1910. Barnard's interest in the art of the Middle Ages led him to amass a notable collection of French Gothic remains. This was purchased by John D. Rockefeller, Jr. in 1925 and presented by him to the Metropolitan Museum of Art. It forms the nucleus of the Cloisters, a museum of medieval art at New York.

Barnard, Henry. b. at Hartford, Conn., Jan. 24, 1811; d. there, July 5, 1900. American educator, coleader, with Horace Mann, in the 19th-century movement to develop a high standard of popular education in the U.S. He left politics and the law (1839) to direct the reorganization of Connecticut's public school system, later (1843) doing similar work for Rhode Island. He served as chancellor (1858–60) of the University of Wisconsin, president (1866–67) of St. John's College, Annapolis, Md., and first U.S. commissioner of education (1867–70). His effective public speaking did much to further the cause of popular education. He edited the monumental 32-volume *American Journal of Education* and published a 52-volume *Library of Education*.

Barnard, John. fl. 17th century. English clergyman. Canon of Saint Paul's Cathedral under Charles I, he is remembered as the editor of the first English collection of cathedral music, which appeared in 1641 under the title *The First Book of Selected Church Musick . . . Collected out of divers approved Authors*.

Barnard, John. b. at Boston, Mass., Nov. 6, 1681; d. Jan. 24, 1770. American Congregational clergyman, minister at Marblehead, Mass., 1716–70. He published numerous sermons, *A History of the Strange Adventures of Philip Ashton* (1725), and others.

Barnard, John Gross. b. at Sheffield, Mass., May 19, 1815; d. at Detroit, Mich., May 14, 1882. American military engineer and general; brother of Frederick Augustus Porter Barnard. He served in the Mexican War (brevetted major in May, 1848). He surveyed the isthmus of Tehuantepec in 1850, and the mouths of the Mississippi River in 1852. Thereafter he served as superintendent (1855–56) of the U.S. Military Academy before acting as chief engineer of the Army of the Potomac in 1862 and 1864; he was brevetted major general at the close of the Civil War. Author of numerous scientific and military papers.

Barnard Castle. Urban district and market town in NE England, in Durham, situated on the river Tees, ab. 21 mi. SW of Durham, ab. 249 mi. N of London by rail.

It is a holiday resort. Charles Dickens is said to have been inspired to write *Nicholas Nickleby* and *Master Humphrey's Clock* during sojourns in the vicinity. The town is named from its ruined castle, founded 1180, which is the chief scene of Sir Walter Scott's poem *Rokeby*. 4,433 (1951).

Barnardo (bär.när′dō), **Thomas John.** b. in Ireland, 1845; d. at Surbiton, England, Sept. 19, 1905. British philanthropist, noted for his labors in rescuing and training destitute children. He began his work in London, c1866, established a home for destitute children in 1867, founded a village for girls at Ilford in 1873 and a hospital for sick waifs in 1887, and formed the "Young Helpers' League" in 1891. About 150 branch schools (now generally known as "Dr. Barnardo's Homes") were opened at London and in the provinces. The institutions were incorporated in 1899 as "The National Institution for the Reclamation of Destitute Waif Children."

Barnard's Inn. One of the inns of Chancery in Holborn, London. The society is of very great antiquity; the hall itself was certainly in existence in 1451, and probably much earlier. The house began to be used as an inn of Chancery c1454. In 1894 the Mercers' Company erected two buildings here for the Mercers' Schools. The old hall of the inn was preserved as a dining-room for the boys. The area suffered considerable damage in World War II.

Barnato (bär.nä′tō), **Barnett.** [Original name, **Barnett Isaacs;** called **"Barney" Barnato** and **"the Kaffir King."**] b. at London, 1852; drowned June 14, 1897. English speculator and capitalist. He was the son of poor Jewish parents, and, according to report, as a young man supported himself as a peddler and billiard-marker. In 1872 or 1873 he left London for South Africa where he made a large fortune in the Kimberley diamond mines and the gold mines around Johannesburg. In 1888 his diamond-mining interests were joined with those of Cecil Rhodes. In the same year he was elected to the legislative assembly of Cape Colony as member for Kimberley, and was reëlected in 1894. In 1895 he returned to London, and was the center of the speculation in South African mining stocks known as the "Kaffir Circus." The failure of the so-called Barnato Banking Company in October, 1895, subsequent financial losses, and great mental strain are supposed to have affected his reason. He committed suicide by jumping into the sea from the steamship *Scot* near Funchal.

Barnaul (bär.nä.öl′). City in the U.S.S.R., in the Altai *oblast* (region) of the Russian Soviet Federated Socialist Republic, situated on the Turkistan-Siberia railroad and the Barnaulka and Ob rivers, ab. 240 mi. SW of Tomsk. It is the chief cotton-textile manufacturing center in W Siberia, and also has sawmills and machinery and food-processing industries. It has a school of mines and a meteorological observatory. 148,129 (1939).

Barnave (bȧr.nȧv), **Antoine Pierre Joseph Marie.** b. at Grenoble, France, Oct. 22, 1761; guillotined at Paris, Nov. 29, 1793. French revolutionist and orator. He was a Jacobin deputy of the Third Estate in 1789, and president of the National Assembly in 1790. One of the group who conducted Louis XVI on his return to Paris from Varennes in 1791, he became a constitutional monarchist. He was arrested for alleged treason in 1792, and executed.

Barnay (bär′nī), **Ludwig.** b. at Budapest, Feb. 11, 1842; d. 1924. German actor. He first appeared on the stage at Trautenau in 1860, and thereafter played chiefly in German cities. He visited the U.S. in 1882. In 1906 he became director of the Royal Theater at Berlin.

Barnburners (bärn′bėr″nėrz). Name popularly applied (c1843 *et seq.*) to a wing of the Democratic Party in New York state which opposed the conservative faction. Originally called Radicals, they came to be known as Barnburners after the tale of the farmer who burned his barn to rid it of rats; like this farmer, the Barnburners were considered to be adopting methods of cure which might result in the destruction of the object under treatment. In local affairs they called for a direct state tax, a ceiling on the state debt, and a termination of additional appropriations for canals. On the national scene, they were aligned against the extension of slavery and supported the Wilmot Proviso. In 1847 they broke away from the Democratic state convention, and in 1848 from the national convention, nominating in the latter year Martin Van Buren for president and joining the Free Soil Party in the national electoral contest. Although some of the Barnburners found their way back to the Democratic ranks, most of them later joined the new Republican Party.

Barnby (bärn′bi), Sir **Joseph.** b. at York, England, Aug. 12, 1838; d. at London, Jan. 28, 1896. English organist, composer, and conductor. He was made director of musical instruction at Eton College in 1875, and in 1886 was made conductor at the Royal Academy of Music; he was knighted in 1892. Among his works are songs (including *Sweet and Low*), anthems, and the oratorio *Rebekah*.

Barne (bärn), **Cape.** Steep, rocky bluff in Antarctica, lying on the W coast of Ross Island between Cape Royds and Cape Evans, in ab. 77°35′ S., 166°13′ E. It was discovered by the National Antarctic Expedition (1901–04), under the leadership of Captain Robert F. Scott, who named this feature for Lieutenant Michael Barne, a member of the expedition. Elevation, ab. 300 ft.

Barnegat Bay (bär′nẹ.gat). Bay E of New Jersey, communicating with the Atlantic Ocean by Barnegat Inlet. Length, ab. 30 mi.

Barnegat Inlet. Strait off the E coast of New Jersey connecting Barnegat Bay with the Atlantic Ocean.

Barnes (bärnz). Municipal borough in SE England, in Surrey, situated on the river Thames, ab. 7 mi. SW of Waterloo station, London. 40,558 (1951).

Barnes, Albert. b. at Rome, N.Y., Dec. 1, 1798; d. at Philadelphia, Dec. 24, 1870. American Presbyterian clergyman and Biblical commentator, pastor of the First Presbyterian Church at Philadelphia (1830–67). He is best known for his *Notes* on the New Testament, Job, Psalms, Isaiah, and other Biblical material.

Barnes, Albert Coombs. b. at Philadelphia, 1873; d. near Philadelphia, July 24, 1951. American art collector and physician, notable among scientists for the discovery of argyrol and in the world of art for his outstanding collection of modern French paintings. He studied medicine at the University of Pennsylvania, receiving the degree of M.D. in 1892. After a year as resident physician in a sanitarium he went to Berlin in 1894 to study physiological chemistry, and in 1899 he enrolled at the University of Heidelberg. After returning to the U.S. he formed, in 1902, the firm of A. C. Barnes Company, which manufactured argyrol and other medical preparations originated by him. The success of this business made him, by the time he was 35 years of age, a millionaire, and afforded him the means to begin assembling what was to become one of the most notable collections of art in the U.S. Beginning in 1913 he gave virtually all of his time and attention to his art interests. Although his collection included distinguished examples of older periods, his particular enthusiasm was for modern French paintings. The works of Monet, Renoir, and Degas were already widely known and esteemed when he began to acquire them, but the names of Cézanne, Matisse, and Picasso were little known, and their works neglected, at that time, and his belief in them did much to establish their fame. Barnes was also a collector of sculpture, furniture, and the native handicrafts of Pennsylvania. In 1922 he established the Barnes Foundation at Merion, Pa., with an endowment of ten million dollars, to afford free instruction in the arts to students showing promise. In the early years of the Foundation he was one of its lecturers. He was the author of *The Art in Painting* (1925), and coauthor of *French Primitives and Their Forms from their Origin to the End of the Fifteenth Century* (1931), *The Art of Henri Matisse* (1933), *The Art of Renoir* (1935), and *The Art of Cézanne* (1939). His services to French art were recognized by his appointment as an officer of the Legion of Honor of France.

Barnes, Barnabe. b. in Yorkshire, England, c1569; d. 1609. English poet. In 1593 he published a collection of love poems, sonnets, and madrigals, entitled *Parthenophil and Parthenophe*. He also wrote a book of sonnets (1595) and *The Divil's Charter* (1607), a tragedy.

Barnes, Charles Reid. b. Sept. 7, 1858; d. Feb. 24, 1910. American botanist. A graduate (1877) of Hanover College, Ind., he received a Ph.D. in 1887. He was professor of natural science at Purdue University, a professor (1887–98) at the University of Wisconsin, and plant physiologist (1898–1910) at the University of Chicago. Coeditor with John Merle Coulter of the *Botanical Gazette*.

Barnes, Earl. b. at Martville, N.Y., July 15, 1861; d. May 29, 1935. American educator, lecturer, and writer; husband of Mary Downing Barnes. Professor (1891–97) of education at Stanford University, he was the author of *Studies in Education* (2 vols., 1897), *Where Knowledge Fails* (1907), *Women in Modern Society* (1912), and *Psychology of Childhood and Youth* (1914).

Barnes, Ernest William. b. at Altrincham, Cheshire, England, April 1, 1874—. English mathematician and clergyman, bishop of Birmingham (1924 *et seq.*). He has written articles and monographs on mathematics, as well as *Should Such a Faith Offend?* (1928) and *Scientific Theory and Religion* (1933).

Barnes, George Nicoll. b. near Dundee, Scotland, 1859; d. at Herne Hill, London, April 22, 1940. British labor leader, known as a member (1917) of David Lloyd George's World War I cabinet. He served (1896–1908) as general secretary of the Amalgamated Society of Engineers. A Labour member of Parliament (1906–22), he was a delegate (1919) to the Paris Peace Conference where he helped draft the constitution of the International Labor Organization. He was also a delegate (1919) and vice-president of the International Labor Conference at Washington, D.C. Among his books are *From Workshop to War Cabinet* (1923), *Industrial Conflict* (1924), and *The History of the International Labour Organization* (1926).

Barnes, Harry Elmer. b. at Auburn, N.Y., June 15, 1889—. American educator, sociologist, editorial writer, and author. After graduation from Syracuse University (1914) and Columbia University (1918), he became a professor at Clark University (1920–23) and Smith College (1923–30), and served (1929–40) on the Scripps-Howard newspapers editorial staff. Author of *Sociology Before Comte* (1917), *Social History of the Western World* (1921), *Progress of American Penology* (1922), *Sociology and Political Theory* (1923), *The Genesis of the World War* (1926), *The Twilight of Christianity* (1929), *History of Western Civilization* (2 vols., 1935), *An Economic History of the Western World* (1937), *An Intellectual and Cultural History of the Western World* (1937), *Prisons in Wartime* (1944), and other works.

Barnes, Howard Turner. b. at Woburn, Mass., July 21, 1873—. American physicist and engineer. A professor at McGill University, Canada, he introduced ice-removal techniques to U.S. cities. He is known for researches on the temperature of the Hudson River and Lake Champlain, and for breaking up ice jams by use of thermit.

Barnes, James. b. at Boston, Dec. 28, 1801; d. at Springfield, Mass., Feb. 12, 1869. American soldier, with the Union army in the Civil War. He commanded the brigade which covered the Rappahannock retreat (May 2–4, 1863).

Barnes, James. b. at Annapolis, Md., Sept. 19, 1866; d. April 30, 1936. American writer and editor. He served on the staff of *Scribner's Magazine* (1891–93), *Harper's Weekly* (1894–95), and D. Appleton and Company (1905–08). Author of *For King or Country* (1895), *Naval Actions of 1812* (1896), *A Princetonian* (1896), *The Hero of Erie* (1898), *With the Flag in the Channel* (1902), *The Unpardonable War* (1904), *The Blockaders* (1905), *Commodore Perry* (1912), *Rifle and Caravan* (1912), and *Through Central Africa from Coast to Coast* (1915).

Barnes, John Gorell. [Title, 1st Baron **Gorell of Brampton.**] b. 1848; d. 1913. English jurist; father of Ronald Gorell Barnes. Educated at Cambridge, he was called to the bar in 1876 and subsequently became a leading figure in English law.

Barnes, Joseph K. b. at Philadelphia, July 21, 1817; d. at Washington, D.C., April 5, 1883. American surgeon. He became the Surgeon General of the U.S. army in 1863, received the brevet rank of brigadier general in 1865, and was placed on the retired list in 1882.

Barnes, Joshua. b. at London, Jan. 10, 1654; d. Aug. 3, 1712. English classical scholar and antiquarian, appointed professor of Greek at Cambridge in 1695. He was a voluminous writer, but was not highly regarded as a scholar. His *Gerania, or the Discovery of a Better Sort of People, anciently discoursed of, called Pygmies*, is his best-known work. He published an edition of Homer (1710).

Barnes, Margaret Ayer. b. at Chicago, April 8, 1886—. American playwright and novelist. She was graduated from Bryn Mawr in 1907. Her writings include a volume of short stories, *Prevailing Winds* (1928); a dramatization of Edith Wharton's *The Age of Innocence* (1928); the plays *Jenny* (1929) and *Dishonored Lady* (1930), both written with Edward Sheldon; and the novels *Years of Grace* (1930, Pulitzer prize), *Westward Passage* (1931), *Within This Present* (1933), *Edna, His Wife* (1935), and *Wisdom's Gate* (1938).

Barnes, Mary Downing. [Maiden name, **Sheldon.**] b. at Oswego, N.Y., Sept. 15, 1850; d. Aug. 27, 1898. American educator; wife of Earl Barnes and daughter of Edward A. Sheldon (1823–97), the educator, from whom she gained her enthusiasm for better teaching methods. One of the first American women to be graduated (1874) from a coeducational college, the University of Michigan, she became (1891) the first woman member of the Stanford University faculty.

Barnes, Ronald Gorell. [Title, 3d Baron **Gorell of Brampton.**] b. April 16, 1884—. English poet, editor, journalist, and soldier; son of John Gorell Barnes (1848–1913). He was educated at Winchester, Harrow, and Oxford. He wrote (1910–15) for the London *Times* and saw service in World War I, attaining the rank of major; he held industry and government posts after the war. He edited (1933–39) the *Cornhill Magazine*, and produced several volumes of verse, including *Babes in the African Wood* (1911), *Love Triumphant* (1913), *Days of Destiny* (1917), *Pilgrimage* (1920), *Many Mansions* (1926), *Unheard Melodies* (1934), *In the Potter's Field* (1936), and *Last of the English* (1939); his *London to Paris by Air* is considered one of his best poems.

Barnes, Thomas. b. 1785; d. May 7, 1841. English journalist. He was editor (1817–41) of the London *Times*.

Barnes, William. b. in Dorsetshire, England, Feb. 22, 1800; d. at Winterbourne Came, England, in October, 1886. English poet, philologist, and clergyman. He is best known for his three series of *Poems of Rural Life in the Dorsetshire Dialect* (1844, 1847, and 1862). He wrote also various philological works, including a *Philological Grammar* (1854).

Barnes, William, Jr. b. at Albany, N.Y., Nov. 17, 1866; d. June 25, 1930. American politician and publisher (1889 *et seq.*) of the Albany *Journal*. He was a member (1892–1914) and chairman (1911–14) of the Republican state committee, and a delegate (1912 and 1916) to the Republican national committee.

Barnesboro (bärnz'bur.ō). Borough in W Pennsylvania, in Cambria County, in a bituminous-coal mining area: manufactures of shirts. It was platted in 1891. Pop. 3,442 (1950).

Barnesville (bärnz'vil). City in W Georgia, county seat of Lamar County: cotton and lumber mills; furniture factories. It is the seat of Gordon Military College. 4,185 (1950).

Barnesville. City in E Ohio, in Belmont County, in a coal-mining region. 4,665 (1950).

Barnet (bär'net). [Also, **Chipping Barnet.**] Urban district and market town in SE England, in Hertfordshire, ab. 11 mi. N of London by rail. A victory was gained here, on April 14, 1471, by the Yorkists under Edward IV over the Lancastrians under Richard Neville, earl of Warwick. Warwick and many Lancastrians were slain, and Edward IV was reëstablished on the throne. 25,017 (1951).

Barnett (bär.net'), **Eugene Epperson.** b. at Leesburg, Fla., Feb. 21, 1888—. American official of welfare organizations, general secretary (1941 *et seq.*) of the national committee and international council of the Y.M.C.A. A graduate (1907) of Emory University, he was a founder (1910) and general secretary (1910–21) of the Y.M.C.A. at Hangkow, China, before serving as a member (1921–37) of the Y.M.C.A. secretariat for China.

Barnett (bär'net, -net), **John.** b. at Bedford, England, July 15, 1802; d. in England, April 17, 1890. English music director, singing teacher, and composer. Author of numerous songs and operettas, he is best known for his operas *The Mountain Sylph* (1834) and *Farinelli* (1838). In 1841 he retired to Cheltenham and devoted himself to vocal training. His father, a Prussian immigrant, changed his name to Barnett from Beer; his mother was Hungarian.

Barnett, John Francis. b. at London, Oct. 16, 1837; d. there, Nov. 24, 1916. English composer, nephew of John Barnett (1802–90). He taught at the Guildhall School of Music and at the Royal College of Music, London. His first work to attract public attention was a *Symphony in A Minor*, performed in 1864. He also composed the cantatas *The Ancient Mariner* (1867), *Paradise and the Peri* (1870), the oratorio *The Raising of Lazarus* (written 1873; produced at Hereford, 1876), and others.

Barnett, Morris. b. 1800; d. 1856. English comedian and music critic. He also acquired some reputation as a writer of plays, particularly *The Serious Family* (which he adapted from a French original entitled *Le Mari à la Campagne*) and *Monsieur Jacques*.

Barnett, Samuel Augustus. b. at Bristol, England, Feb. 8, 1844; d. 1913. English clergyman and social worker. He was educated at Wadham College, Oxford University. He was vicar of Saint Jude's, Whitechapel, London, in the period 1872–94. Appointed canon of Bristol in 1893, he was made canon of Westminster in 1906. He was one of the founders of Toynbee Hall, a settlement in London's Whitechapel district, and was its warden until 1906, and its president after 1906. He published *Practicable Socialism* (1893; written in collaboration with his wife), *Service of God* (1897), *Religion and Progress* (1907), and *Towards Social Reform* (1909).

Barnett (bär.net'), **Samuel Jackson.** b. in Kansas, Dec. 14, 1873—. American physicist. He served as an instructor and, subsequently, assistant professor and professor of physics at Colorado College (1898–1900), and as professor at Stanford University (1900–05), Tulane University (1905–11), and Ohio State University (1911–18). In 1918 he accepted the post of physicist at the Carnegie Institute of Washington, but in 1926 was named professor of physics at the University of California at Los Angeles, where he has continued since that time (as professor emeritus since 1944). He has also been a research associate of the California Institute of Technology since 1924. He served on the National Research Council and on that body's committee on theories of magnetism and electromagnetic induction (1922–24). For the discovery of magnetization by rotation, Dr. Barnett received the Comstock prize for electricity, magnetism, and radiation of the National Academy of Sciences (1918). He is a fellow of the American Association for the Advancement of Science and a member of the American Physical Society, the American Academy of Arts and Sciences, the American Geophysical Union, and the Philosophical Society of Washington. He is the author of *Elements of Electro-Magnetic Theory* (1903), and a coauthor of *Theories of Magnetism* (1922) and *Le Magnestisme* (1940).

Barneveld (bär'nę.velt). Town in the E part of the Netherlands, in the province of Gelderland, ab. 17 mi. NW of Arnhem: agricultural trade center; largest fowl and egg markets in the Netherlands. 20,058 (est. 1951).

Barneveldt or **Barneveld** (bär'nę.velt), **Jan van Olden.** b. at Amersfoort, Netherlands, Sept. 25, 1547; beheaded at The Hague, May 13, 1619. Dutch statesman. He became grand pensionary of Holland in 1586, and negotiated the treaty with Spain in 1609. He sided with the Remonstrants (an Arminian sect) against their Calvinist opponents and Maurice of Nassau, by whom he was arrested for treason in 1618. He was condemned to death by a court now generally believed to have been "packed" against him. A tragedy was written on this subject and acted in August, 1619; it was first printed from manuscript by Bullen and announced by him as a play of John Chapman's, but afterward as by John Fletcher and Philip Massinger.

Barney (bär'ni). In Charles Dickens's novel *Oliver Twist*, a waiter, with a cold in his head, at the "Three Cripples."

Barney, Joshua. b. at Baltimore, Md., July 6, 1759; d. at Pittsburgh, Pa., Dec. 1, 1818. American naval officer, who served in the Revolutionary War and the War of 1812. He became a lieutenant in 1776. On April 8, 1782, he captured, while in command of the *Hyder-Ally*, the British sloop of war *General Monk*. Later in the same year he was sent to France with dispatches for Benjamin Franklin. He was a commodore (1796–1802) in the French service. He commanded in Chesapeake Bay in 1814, and was taken prisoner by the British at Bladensburg in the same year.

Barnfield (bärn'fēld), **Richard.** b. at Norbury, Shropshire, England, 1574; d. 1627. English poet. Author of *The Affectionate Shepherd* (1594), *Cynthia* (1595), and *Poems in Divers Humors* (1598). In the last are the poems "If Music and Sweet Poetry Agree" and "As it Fell Upon a Day," which were long thought to be by Shakespeare.

Barni (bår.nē), **Jules Romain.** b. at Lille, France, June 1, 1818; d. 1878. French republican politician and writer on philosophy. His chief works are *Histoire des idées morales et politiques en France au XVIII*ᵉ *siècle* (1866), and translations from Immanuel Kant.

Barnim (bär'nim). Ancient name of a region in the *Mittelmark* (middle district) of Brandenburg, E Germany, N and NE of Berlin.

Barnivelt (bär'ni.velt), **Esdras, Apothecary.** Pseudonym under which a key to *The Rape of the Lock* was published shortly after the poem itself. It was attributed to Alexander Pope, and also to John Arbuthnot.

Barnoldswick (bär.nōldz'wik). Urban district in C England, in the West Riding of Yorkshire, ab. 9 mi. SW of Skipton, ab. 233 mi. NW of London by rail: cotton manufactures. 10,282 (1951).

Barnsley (bärnz'li). County borough and coal-mining center in C England, in the West Riding of Yorkshire, situated on the river Dearne, ab. 13 mi. N of Sheffield, ab. 173 mi. N of London by rail. The Barnsley coal seam is a very rich one, located in the center of the South Yorkshire coal field, part of the larger Yorkshire, Derbyshire, and Nottinghamshire coal field. Barnsley was for many years one of the centers of the British linen trade. 75,625 (1951).

Barnstable (bärn'stą.bl). Town in SE Massachusetts, county seat of Barnstable County, on Cape Cod Bay, ab. 69 mi. SE of Boston. It is a popular summer resort. 10,480 (1950).

Barnstaple (bärn'stą.pl). Municipal borough, market town, and seaport in SW England, in Devonshire, situated on the river Taw, ab. 35 mi. NW of Exeter, ab. 188 mi. SW of London by rail. It is a tourist center and an administrative center for the area. Barnstaple has been called the "Metropolis of North Devon." It has an annual fair, held in September. During the 17th and 18th centuries it was in the serge trade, importing high-grade wools from Ireland and Spain. 13,302 (1951).

Barnum (bär'num), **Frances Baylor.** See **Baylor, Frances Courtenay.**

Barnum, Henry A. b. at Jamesville, Onondaga County, N.Y., Sept. 24, 1833; d. at New York, Jan. 29, 1892. American soldier, with the Union army in the Civil War.

Barnum, Phineas Taylor. b. at Bethel, Conn., July 5, 1810; d. at Bridgeport, Conn., April 7, 1891. American showman. He became proprietor of the American Museum at New York in 1842, exhibiting, as one of his major attractions, the midget Charles S. Stratton, known as "General Tom Thumb," with whom he also toured in the U.S. and in Europe. He also managed Jenny Lind's concert tour (1850–51) through America. He established his circus in 1871, billing it as "The Greatest Show on Earth"; his success in this venture was in some part the result of his liberal use of advertising. In 1881 he joined with a rival, J. A. Bailey, in forming the Barnum and Bailey circus, and they imported at great expense, from London, Jumbo, a very large elephant. Barnum was a member of the Connecticut legislature (1865–69), and was elected mayor of Bridgeport in 1875. Besides lecturing on temperance and other popular subjects, he wrote *The Humbugs of the World* (1865), *Struggles and Triumphs, or Forty Years' Recollections* (1869), and left the autobiographical material published in *Barnum's Own Story* (1927).

Barnum, William H. b. at Boston Corners, N.Y., Sept. 17, 1818; d. at Lime Rock, Conn., April 30, 1889. American politician. He was a Democratic member of Congress from Connecticut (1867–76), U.S. senator from Connecticut (1876–79), and chairman of the Democratic national committee (1880 and 1884).

Barnum, Zenus. b. near Wilkes-Barre, Pa., Dec. 9, 1810; d. April 5, 1865. American hotel keeper, railroad president, and capitalist. During the period in the 19th century when Baltimore, Md., was the chief convention city of America, Barnum's Hotel was its most popular gathering place for delegates. Barnum organized a Washington-New York telegraph service that merged (1852) with Samuel F. B. Morse's company, Barnum being chosen as president; he was again made president when a further merger with the American Telegraph Company took place in 1859. He also headed the Baltimore Central Railroad, and brought it out of insolvency.

Barnwell (bärn'wel), **Robert Woodward.** b. at Beaufort, S.C., Aug. 10, 1801; d. at Columbia, S.C., Nov. 25, 1882. American politician. He was a member of Congress from South Carolina (1829-33), a U.S. senator (1850-51), a commissioner from South Carolina to confer with the federal government regarding the secession of that state (1860), a member of the provisional congress of the Confederate States of America (1861-62), and a senator from South Carolina in the Confederate Congress (1862-66).

Baroach (bą.rōch'). See **Broach.**

Barocchio (bä.rôt'chō), **Giacomo.** See **Vignola.**

Barocci (bä.rôt'chē) or **Baroccio** (-chō), **Federigo.** b. at Urbino, Italy, c1528; d. there, in September, 1612. Italian painter of the Roman school. Among his many works are *Crucifixion*, at Genoa, and *Madonna del popolo*, belonging to the collection of the Uffizi, Florence.

Baroche (bȧ.rosh), **Pierre Jules.** b. at Paris, Nov. 18, 1802; d. on the island of Jersey, in the English Channel, Oct. 29, 1870. French lawyer and statesman. An adherent of Napoleon III, he was minister of the interior (1850), minister of foreign affairs (1851), president of the council of state (1852), and minister of justice and public worship (1863-69).

Baroda (bą.rō'dą). Former native state in W India, one of the most important of the states N of Bombay, ruled by a Mahratta gaekwar: now part of Bombay state, Union of India. Cotton, millet, and tobacco are grown here. Capital, Baroda; area, 8,236 sq. mi.; pop. 2,855,010 (1941).

Baroda. District of Baroda state, W Union of India, ab. 80 mi. SE of Ahmedabad: cotton, millet, and tobacco. Capital, Baroda; area, 1,887 sq. mi.; pop. 644,071.

Baroda. Capital of the state and district of Baroda, W Union of India, on the Viswamitri River, ab. 80 mi. SE of Ahmedabad. It has considerable trade, manufactures pottery and textiles, and contains a college and several schools. 153,301 (1941).

Baroja y Nessi (bä.rō'нä ē ne'sē), **Pío.** b. at San Sebastián, Spain, 1872—. Spanish novelist, considered by some to be Spain's leading contemporary writer in this form. His novels, largely devoid of plot in the ordinary sense, are written in a style that is abrupt and humorless, but are noteworthy for their descriptions. Of the 50 volumes he has written, perhaps the best are the following, written in sets of trilogies: *La casa de Aizgorri, El Mayorazgo de Labraz*, and *Zalacaín el adventuero; Aventuras, inventos y mixtificaciones de Silvestre Paradox, Camino de perfección*, and *Paradox rey; La dama errante, La ciudad de la niebal* and *El árbol de la ciencia. Memorias de un hombre de acción* is the title of a series of historical novels on the first Carlist war, patterned after *Episodios nacionales* of Benito Pérez Galdós.

Baron (bȧ.rôṅ), **Michel.** [Original name, **Michel Boyron.**] b. at Paris, Oct. 8, 1653; d. at Paris, Dec. 3, 1729. French actor, in his day a leading star of the French stage (which he abandoned from 1691 to 1720). He wrote, it is said in collaboration with others, seven comedies, the best of which are generally considered to be *L'Audrienne* and *L'Homme à bonnes fortunes* (1686).

Baron de Hirsch Fund (bar'ǫn dẹ hėrsh'). Fund established in the 19th century by Baron Maurice de Hirsch of Austria to provide schools at New York and elsewhere for Jewish immigrants to the U.S. from Russia, Rumania, and Galicia. The purpose of the schooling was to give instruction in elementary English and the principles of the Constitution, and to inculcate improved sanitary habits. It had as its primary object the Americanization of the immigrants in order that they might become useful citizens and adapt themselves as speedily as possible to their new country.

Barondess (bar.ǫn.des'), **Joseph.** b. at Kamenets Podolski, Russia, 1867; d. at New York, 1928. Jewish labor organizer and Zionist leader. After having come to the U.S. in 1888, he became a labor organizer, aiding in the establishment of the International Ladies' Garment Workers' Union, the Cloakmakers' Union, the Hebrew Actors' Union, and others; he was active (c1903 *et seq.*) in the Zionist movement and pioneered in the founding of the American Jewish Congress. He served as honorary vice-president of the American Zionist Organization.

Baronius (bą.rō'ni.us) or **Baronio** (bä.rô'nyō), **Cesare.** b. at Sora, in Campania, Oct. 30, 1538; d. June 30, 1607. Roman Catholic church historian. He became a cardinal in 1596, and was librarian of the Vatican. His chief work is *Annales ecclesiastici a Christo nato ad annum 1198* (1588-93).

Barons (bä'rōns), **Krisjanis.** b. in Latvia, Oct. 31, 1835; d. at Riga, Latvia, March 8, 1923. Latvian scholar, teacher and collector of Latvian folksongs. Barons studied (1856-60) mathematics and astronomy at the University of Tartu, was editor (1862-65) of the Latvian progressive newspaper *Peterburgas Awihzes*, and served (1867-93) as a high-school teacher at Moscow. He went (1893) to Riga, where he began his great project, lasting 21 years, of collecting Latvian folksongs. *Dainas*, the product of this work, was published in eight volumes by the Russian academy of sciences at St. Petersburg.

Barons' War. Insurrection (1263-65) of English barons under Simon de Montfort against the arbitrary government of Henry III. Its chief incidents were the victory of Montfort at Lewes in 1264 and the capture of the king, and the defeat and death of Montfort by the forces of Prince Edward (later Edward I) at Evesham in 1265. The discontent began in 1261, when Henry refused to delegate the power of appointing councilors, but did not develop into open revolt until 1263, when Montfort returned to England from France. Before the battle of Lewes, Louis the IX of France, in his capacity of arbitrator, pronounced in favor of Henry, a decision the barons refused to accept. In 1267, the barons officially submitted to the king.

Barons' Wars, The. Poem in six cantos, by Michael Drayton. It was first published in 1596 under the title *Mortimeriados*, and republished with many alterations in 1603 under its present title.

Barotseland (bą.rot'sẹ.land). [Also, **Njenji.**] Region in S central Africa, in the W part of Northern Rhodesia, N of the Zambezi River; formerly Northwestern Rhodesia. In 1911 Northwestern Rhodesia and Northeastern Rhodesia were united into Northern Rhodesia and in 1924 the entire area passed from the British South Africa Company to the British crown, under which it has been governed since. Area, 182,000 sq. mi. (est.).

Barozzi (bä.rôt'tsē), **Giacomo.** See **Vignola.**

Barquisimeto (bär.kē.sē.mā'tō). City in NW Venezuela, capital of Lara state, ab. 155 mi. W of Caracas: trading center for coffee, fiber, cacao, sugar, and copper. It was severely damaged by an earthquake in 1812. Pop. 105,080 (1950).

Barr (bȧr). Town in E France, in the department of Bas-Rhin (formerly Lower Alsace), situated at the foot of the Vosges Mountains, ab. 18 mi. SW of Strasbourg. It is one of the most important centers of the French leather industry. Most of the town was destroyed toward the end of World War II. Nearby is the convent of Sainte Odilie, patron saint of Alsace. 4,430 (1946).

Barr (bär), **Amelia Edith.** [Maiden name, **Huddleston.**] b. at Ulverston, Lancashire, England, March 29, 1831; d. March 10, 1919. American novelist. She came to the U.S. in 1853, lived in Texas, and settled (1868) at New York. She was the author of historical novels which enjoyed a wide popularity. Her works include *Romance and Reality* (1872), *Jan Vedder's Wife* (1885), *The Bow of Orange Ribbon* (1886), *Remember the Alamo* (1888), *The Maid of Maiden Lane* (1900), *The Belle of Bowling Green* (1904), *The House on Cherry Street* (1909), *The Paper Cap* (1918), and an autobiography, *All the Days of My Life* (1913).

Barr, Charles. [Sometimes called **"Wee Charlie."**] b. at Gourock on the Firth of Clyde, Scotland, July 11, 1864; d. Jan. 24, 1911. American yachtsman, naturalized (1889) as a citizen of the U.S. In the *Shamrock* he won the Lipton Cup for Frederick Thompson; later, commanding Wilson Marshall's *Atlantic*, he won (1905) the German Emperor's Cup for trans-ocean racing. He later served as commander of August Belmont's *Mineola*, Cornelius Vanderbilt's *Rainbow*, and Alexander Smith Cochran's *Westward*.

Barr, Robert. [Pseudonym, **Luke Sharp.**] b. at Glasgow, Scotland, Sept. 16, 1850; d. at Woldingham, Surrey, England, Oct. 21, 1912. British novelist and editor. He was educated at Toronto, Canada, and taught in Canada until 1876, when he joined the editorial staff of the Detroit *Free Press*. He established the weekly English edition of the *Free Press* at London in 1881, and in 1892 founded, with Jerome K. Jerome, the *Idler* magazine, of which he was coeditor until 1895. Among his works are *In a Steamer Chair* (1892), *From Whose Bourne* (1893), *In the Midst of Alarms* (1894, 1900), *The Face and the Mask* (1895), *The Countess Tekla* (1899), *The Strong Arm* (1900), *The Unchanging East* (1900), *Over the Border* (1903), *The O'Ruddy* (1904; with Stephen Crane), *The Woman Wins* (1904), *A Chicago Princess* (1904), *Speculations of John Steele* (1905), *The Triumph of Eugene Valmont* (1906), *A Rock in the Baltic* (1907), *Cardillac* (1909), and *The Swordmaker* (1910).

Barra (bär′ạ). [Also, **Barr.**] Former petty kingdom in W Africa, near the mouth of the Gambia River. The Mandingos are the chief inhabitants; the chief town, Barrinding.

Barra (bar′ạ). Island and civil parish, in N Scotland, in Inverness-shire, ab. 150 mi. NW of Glasgow. The parish comprises several islands, some of which are uninhabited. The inhabitants are chiefly Gaelic Roman Catholics. Length, ab. 8 mi.; greatest width, ab. 5 mi.; pop. 2,250 (1931).

Barrabas (bạ.rab′ạs). See **Barabbas.**

Barrackpore (bar′ạk.pōr). [Also, **Barrackpur** (-pör).] Town and military station in West Bengal, E Union of India, on the Hooghly River, ab. 15 mi. N of Calcutta.

Barrack-Room Ballads. Volume of poems (1892) by Rudyard Kipling. They were published originally by W. E. Henley in *The National Observer*, and in their collected form added greatly to the fame which had come to Kipling in 1886 with the publication of *Departmental Ditties*.

Barradall (bar′ạ.dôl), **Edward.** b. 1704; d. at Williamsburg, Va., June 19, 1743. American lawyer. He emigrated from England to Virginia, where he practiced law at Williamsburg. He was legal adviser (1734 *et seq.*) to Thomas Fairfax, 6th baron Fairfax, attorney general (1737 *et seq.*) of Virginia, and a member (1738, 1740, 1742) of the General Assembly. Author of *Cases Adjudged in the General Court of Virginia from April 1733* to *October 1741*, a collection of notes valuable for the historical study of Virginia law.

Barradas (bär.rä′ᴛʜäs), **Isidro.** b. in the Canary Islands, c1775; d. at New Orleans, La., c1841. Spanish general. In 1824 he commanded the Spanish land forces assembled at Havana with the object of reconquering Mexico. In July, 1829, he landed, with 3,000 men, on the Mexican coast at Tampico. They were attacked by Antonio Lopéz de Santa Anna, and after several engagements were forced (Sept. 11, 1829) to capitulate.

Barra do Piraí (bär′rạ dö pē.rạ.ē′). [Also, **Barra do Pirahy.**] City in E Brazil, in the state of Rio de Janeiro. 20,254 (1950).

Barra do Rio Negro (rē′ö nā′grö). Former name of **Manaus.**

Barrafranca (bär.rä.fräng′kä). Town and commune in SW Italy, on the island of Sicily, in the province of Enna, situated in the interior of the island, ab. 14 mi. S of Enna. Sulfur mines are in the vicinity. Pop. of commune, 13,111 (1936); of town, 13,054 (1936).

Barragan (bär.rä.gän′), **Miguel.** b. at Valle del Mais, San Luis Potosí, Mexico, 1789; d. at Mexico City, March 1, 1836. Mexican general. In 1821 he was one of the officers who supported Augustín de Iturbide's movement for independence. As commandant of Vera Cruz, he forced the capitulation (Nov. 18, 1825) of San Juan de Ulúa, the last Spanish fort in Mexico. He was vice-president of Mexico under Antonio Lopéz de Santa Anna in 1835, and, during Santa Anna's absence, acted as president; he held this position until his death.

Barra Isles (bar′ạ). [Also, **Barra Islands.**] Group of small islands in the S part of the Outer Hebrides, N Scotland, in Inverness-shire, comprising a civil parish. The chief island of the group is Barra (*q.v.*).

Barrande (bȧ.räṅd), **Joachim.** b. at Saugues, Haute-Loire, France, c1799; d. Oct. 5, 1883. French paleontologist, author of *Système silurien du centre de la Bohème* (1852) and others. The greatest portion of his work was done in Austria and Bohemia.

Barranquilla (bär.räng.kē′yä). [Also, **Baranquila.**] City in N Colombia, capital of Atlántico department, near the mouth of the Magdalena River: the chief port of Colombia, handling half its foreign commerce; its industries include numerous mills and factories; air service. It is the site of a cathedral. 278,269 (1951).

Barraquer (bär.rä.ker′), **Ignacio A.** b. 1884—. Spanish ophthalmologist at Barcelona. He was the first to describe (1906) progressive lipodystrophy, and devised (1917) a procedure for extracting cataract.

Barras (bȧ.rȧs), **Paul Jean François Nicolas,** Comte **de.** b. at Echempoux, in Provence, France, June 30, 1755; d. at Chaillot, near Paris, Jan. 29, 1829. French revolutionist. He was a deputy to the Third Estate in 1789, and to the Convention in 1792. He commanded a division at the capture of Toulon in 1793, and took a leading part in the overthrow of Robespierre on July 27, 1794. He was a member of the Committee of Public Safety, and, as commander in chief of the government forces during the uprising on the 13th Vendémiaire (1795), he summoned Napoleon Bonaparte to Paris and placed him in charge of the troops. He became a member of the Directory in 1795, dictator in 1797, and retired from office in 1799. His memoirs were published in 1895.

Barratt (bar′ạt), Sir **Arthur Sheridan.** b. at Peshawar, India, Feb. 25, 1891—. English air force officer. Educated at Woolwich and Camberley for the army, he served (1914–18) with the Royal Flying Corps in France during World War I before joining (1919) the Royal Air Force. He was chief instructor, and later commandant (1936–39), of the Royal Air Force staff college at Andover. He commanded (1931–32) the First Indian Group at Peshawar; was senior air staff officer (1932–34) at Royal Air Force headquarters in India; served (1939–45) in World War II as head (1940) of the British air forces in France, commander in chief (1940-43) of the Army Co-operation Command, and commander in chief (1943–45) of the Technical Training Command; was inspector general (1945–47) of the Royal Air Force; and was named (1946) an air chief marshal.

Barrault (bȧ.rō), **Jean-Louis.** b. 1911—. French actor and director. In 1935 he directed his first play, an adaptation of William Faulkner's novel *As I Lay Dying*. In 1940, he joined the Comédie Française and played many classical roles. Between World Wars I and II, he opened his own theater, the Marigny, and here he produced classic revivals, and new plays by Paul Claudel and Albert Camus. He directed several of the plays presented by a French-language company at New York in 1952.

Barre (bar′i). Town in C Massachusetts, in Worcester County, ab. 22 mi. NW of Worcester: processing and shipping point for dairy, woolen, and iron products. 3,406 (1950).

Barre. [Called the **"Granite Center"**; former name, **Wildersburgh.**] City in C Vermont, in Washington County, ab. 5 mi. SE of Montpelier: notable as a granite-quarrying center. 10,922 (1950).

Barre (bȧr), **Antoine le Fevre de la.** b. c1605; d. at Paris, May 4, 1688. French general and author. In 1667 he was appointed a lieutenant general and sent against the English in the West Indies, where he was generally successful. From 1682 to 1685 he was governor of Canada. Author of *Description de la France équinoxiale*.

Barré (bar′i), **Isaac.** b. at Dublin, Ireland, 1726; d. at London, July 20, 1802. British officer and politician, of French descent. He served with distinction under Wolfe in the battle for Quebec in 1759. In Parliament, which he entered in 1761, he gained a considerable reputation as an orator, especially for his use of invective. He has sometimes been suggested as the possible author of the letters of Junius, a series of vituperative articles which appeared (1769–72) in the London *Public Advertiser;* the letters, signed with the pseudonym Junius, expressed Whig policies. He opposed taxation of the American colonies.

His name is commemorated in the names of Wilkes-Barre, Pa., and Barre, Vt.

Barreda Laos (bär.rā'ᴛʜä lä'ōs), **Felipe.** b. at Lima, Peru, Aug. 16, 1884—. Peruvian lawyer, diplomat, and author. He was professor of history (1912–19) at the University of San Marcos, editor (1926–30) of Lima's *La República*, ambassador (1930–38) to Argentina and to Uruguay, organizer (1933) of the Pan-American Institute of Economics and Finance, and a delegate to the Permanent Court of International Justice at The Hague. Author of *La Reforma de la instrucción pública en el Perú* (1919), *América latina ante la crisis mundial* (1932), and other books.

Barre des Écrins (bȧr dā zā.kraṅ). [Also, **Pic des Écrins.**] Highest peak of the Pelvoux range, in the Alps of Dauphiné, France. 13,462 ft.

Barreiro (bạr.rā'rö). Town and *concelho* (commune) in W Portugal, in the province of Estremadura, in the district of Setubal, situated on the Mar da Palha, a bay at the mouth of the Tejo (or Tagus) River, opposite Lisbon: a seaport, with wine trade and fisheries. The Church of Palhais dates from the early Middle Ages. Pop. of concelho, 26,172 (1940); of town, 22,000 (1940).

Barrelier (bȧ.rẹ.lyā), **Jacques.** b. at Paris, 1606; d. Sept. 17, 1673. French botanist. He wrote *Plantae per Galliam, Hispaniam et Italiam observatae* (1714) and other botanical works.

Barrell (bar'ẹl), **Joseph.** b. at New Providence, N.J., Dec. 15, 1869; d. May 4, 1919. American geologist and mining engineer. He served as a professor of geology (1903–19) at Yale, after having taught at Lehigh University. He is known for his publications on the subjects of igneous intrusions, regional geology, geological processes, geological time, isostasy, evolution, and the earth's genesis.

Barren. [Also, **Big Barren.**] River in Kentucky, in Allen, Barren, Butler, and Warren counties, which joins the Green River NW of Bowling Green. Length, ab. 120 mi.

Barren Ground. Novel by Ellen Glasgow, published in 1925. Dorinda Oakley, dismissing her plans to help her father rebuild his farm, decides to marry Jason Greylock. When Jason breaks his engagement to her, Dorinda goes to New York to start a new life. Later she returns to reclaim the farm and by the application of scientific principles puts it on a paying basis. She cares for her family, marries Nathan Pedlar, and cares for his motherless children; after his death, she takes care of Jason until his death. The barren farmland becomes fertile, but Dorinda's life remains stark and devoid of warmth.

Barrère (bȧ.rer), **Camille Eugène Pierre.** b. at La Charité-sur-Loire, Nièvre, France, Oct. 23, 1851; d. at Paris, Oct. 9, 1940. French diplomat who, as ambassador to Italy (1897–1924), brought about closer relations between France and Italy, and was one of those largely responsible for Italian entry into World War I on the side of the allies. He had previously been ambassador (1894–97) to Switzerland.

Barrère, Georges. b. at Bordeaux, France, Oct. 31, 1872; d. at New York, 1944. American flutist and ensemble leader. After playing (1897–1905) with the Colonne Concerts at Paris, he came to the U.S., where he joined the New York Symphony Orchestra; in 1930 he became a staff member of the Juilliard School of Music. He founded (1910) the Barrère Ensemble, which he expanded (1914) into the Barrère Little Symphony.

Barrère, Pierre. b. at Perpignan, France, c1690; d. there, Nov. 1, 1755. French naturalist and traveler. He studied medicine and botany, from 1722 to 1725 traveled in French Guiana, and after his return was professor of botany at Perpignan. He wrote several works on the natural history and geography of French Guiana.

Barrère Ensemble. [Later called **Little Symphony.**] Wind instrument group established (1910) by Georges Barrère; expanded in 1914, it toured in the U.S. as the Little Symphony.

Barrès (bȧ.res), **Maurice.** b. at Charmes, in Lorraine, France, Sept. 22, 1862; d. at Neuilly, France, Dec. 4, 1923. French novelist, journalist, and nationalist politician. Author of *Sous l'oeil des barbares* (1888), *Un homme libre* (1889), *Le Jardin de Bérénice* (1891), *Du Sang, de la volupté et de la mort* (1894), *Les Deracinés* (1897), *L'Appel au soldat* (1900), *Leurs figures* (1902), *Amori et dolori sacrum* (1903), *Colette Baudoche* (1909; Eng. trans., 1918), *La Colline inspirée* (1913; Eng. trans., *The Sacred Hill*, 1929) and others. His early work records a period of intense egocentrism and lyricism, followed by a middle period of discovery that the self meant to him little apart from the selves of other Frenchmen, and eventually by complete commitment to the doctrines of French nationalism, which he did much to elaborate. Elected deputy from Nancy in 1889, he remained prominent in politics from then until his death, favoring the dictatorship during the Boulanger campaign, the anti-Dreyfus party during the Dreyfus affair, and the strong-army, anti-German *revanchards* of the years before World War I. His literary following, originally very large, dwindled after 1918.

Barret (bar'ẹt), **John.** See **Baret** or **Barret, John.**

Barreto (bạr.rā'tö), **(Afonso Henriques de) Lima.** b. at Rio de Janeiro, May 13, 1881; d. there, Nov. 1, 1922. Brazilian novelist who created characters of great realism. Among his works are *Recordações do escrivão Isaías Caminha* (1909), *Triste fim de Policarpo Quaresma* (1913), *Vida e morte de M. J. Gonzaga de Sá* (1919), and *Os Bruzundangas* (1922).

Barreto, Tobias. [Full name, **Tobias Barreto de Menezes.**] b. at Campos, Sergipe, Brazil, June 7, 1839; d. at Recife, Brazil, June 20, 1889. Brazilian poet, critic, jurist, and thinker, who introduced into his country new European theories in the fields of criticism, law, and philosophy. Among his books are *Ensaios e estudos de filosofia e crítica* (1875), *Estudos alemães* (1880), *Dias e noites* (poetry, 1881), and *Menores e loucos* (1883).

Barreto de Menezes (dẹ̄ mẹ.nā'zēs), **Francisco.** b. c1600; d. after 1663. Portuguese soldier. In 1647 he was appointed chief of the Portuguese forces in Pernambuco. He gained brilliant victories in 1648 and 1649, and finally forced the capitulation of Pernambuco's capital city (now called Recife, then still called Pernambuco) on Jan. 27, 1654. From April, 1648, to August, 1656, he was governor of Pernambuco, and from the latter date to June 24, 1663, captain general of Brazil.

Barretos (bạr.rā'tös). City in SE Brazil, in the state of São Paulo. 23,683 (1950).

Barrett (bar'ẹt), **Benjamin Fiske.** b. at Dresden, Me., June 24, 1808; d. at Germantown, Pa., Aug. 6, 1892. American New Church clergyman and writer. Ordained in 1840, he served ministries at Cincinnati and Philadelphia, and later edited *New Christianity* at Philadelphia. Author of *Life of Emanuel Swedenborg* (1841), *Lectures on the New Dispensation* (1842), *Beauty for Ashes* (1855), *The Question* (*What Are the Doctrines of the New Church?*) *Answered* (1883), and *Maximus Homo* (1892).

Barrett, Charles Simon. b. in Pike County, Ga., Jan. 28, 1866; d. April 4, 1935. American farm-labor organizer. He was president of the Georgia Farmers' Union (1905) and of the National Farmers' Union (1906–28). A member (1917) of the U.S. price fixing commission for wheat, he was a delegate (1918–19) from the National Board of Farm Organizations and the National Farmers' Union to the Peace Conference at Paris after World War I, before serving as a member (1924) of the President's Agricultural Commission.

Barrett, Elizabeth. See **Browning, Elizabeth Barrett.**

Barrett, George Horton. [Called **"Gentleman George."**] b. at Exeter, England, June 9, 1794; d. at New York, Sept. 5, 1860. American actor, famous for light comedy roles. He played in August Friedrich Ferdinand von Kotzebue's *The Stranger* (c1798), in *The West Indian* (1822), Richard Brinsley Sheridan's *The School for Scandal* (1848), and a stage version of Charles Dickens's *Dombey and Son.*

Barrett, John. b. at Grafton, Vt., Nov. 28, 1866; d. at Bellows Falls, Vt., Oct. 17, 1938. American diplomat, notable as the founder of the Pan-American Foundation. He was graduated (1889) from Dartmouth College, and served as American minister to Siam (1894–98), Argentine (1903–04), Panama (1904–05), and Colombia (1905–06). Director general (1907–20) of the Pan American Union at Washington, D.C., he was the founder (1912) of the Pan American Society of the U.S. Author of *Admiral George Dewey* (1899), *Pan American Union—Peace, Friendship, Commerce* (1911), *Panama Canal—What It Is, What It Means* (1913), *Pan American Commerce—Past,*

Present, Future (1919), *Pan American and Pan Americanism* (1922), and *The Call of South America* (1924).

Barrett, Lawrence. b. at Paterson, N.J., April 4, 1838; d. at New York, March 20, 1891. American tragic actor. He first appeared on the stage at Detroit in 1853 as Murad in *The French Spy*, and first appeared at New York on Jan. 19, 1857, as Clifford in *The Hunchback*. He was a leading actor in the Boston Museum in 1858. He enlisted in the Union army in 1861, and served for a time as captain of Company B, 28th Massachusetts Volunteers. He was a partner (1863–64) of Lewis Baker in the management of a theater at New Orleans, and from that time continued as a star actor and manager. From 1886 until his death he was closely associated with Edwin Booth, playing Shakespearean roles with him. He also produced a number of new plays. He published a biography of Edwin Forrest in 1881, and one of Edwin Booth in *Actors and Actresses of the Time*.

Barrett, Sir William Fletcher. b. at Jamaica, in the British West Indies, 1844; d. 1925. British physicist, for many years (1873–1910) a professor at the Royal College of Science, Dublin. In 1882 he joined in founding the Society for Psychical Research. He is noted for his technical developments in electrical engineering, and for his research in the fields of magnetism, radiant heat, sound, and vision. He was coauthor of *Introduction to Practical Physics* (1892), *On Swedenborg* (1912), and others.

Barrett, Wilson. [Original name, **William Henry Barrett.**] b. at Chelmsford, Essex, England, Feb. 18, 1846; d. at London, July 22, 1904. English actor, manager, and dramatist. He made his first appearance (1864) at the Halifax Theatre Royal; in 1866 he married Caroline Heath (1835–87), an actress, with whom he traveled and acted until her health forced her to give up the stage. He operated several theaters at Hull, Leeds, and London, and played throughout England, in Australia (1898, 1902), and in the U.S., which he visited six times. He introduced the Polish actress Helena Modjeska to English audiences, playing Mercutio to her Juliet in Shakespeare's *Romeo and Juliet*. Some of his outstanding successes were as Hamlet, Othello, Wilfred Denver in *The Silver King*. Lemuel in *Daughters of Babylon*, Pete in *The Manxman*, Tom Robinson in *It's Never Too Late To Mend*, and roles in *East Lynne*, *Lights o' London*, *The Romany Rye*, and in his own popular success *The Sign of the Cross* (1895). Author of the plays *Nowadays* (1889), *Daughters of Babylon* (1897), *Quo Vadis?* (1900; from the novel by Henryk Sienkiewicz), *Lucky Durham* (1905); coauthor of *Hoodman Blind* (1885), *Lord Harry* (1886), both with Henry Arthur Jones; *Sister Mary* (1886), with Clement Scott; *Clito* (1886), with Sydney Grundy; *The Golden Ladder* (1887), with George Robert Sims; *Ben-My-Chree* (1888), *The Good Old Times* (1889), both with Hall Caine; *The People's Idol* (1890), with Victor Widnell; and *Man and His Makers* (1899), with Louis N. Parker.

Barretto (ba̤.ret'ō), **Larry.** [Full name, **Laurence Brevoort Barretto.**] b. at Larchmont, N.Y., May 30, 1890—. American novelist. He served (1917–19) in the U.S. army and was a war correspondent during World War II in the Caribbean area (1943) and the China-Burma-India (1944) theater. Author of *A Conqueror Passes* (1924), *To Babylon* (1925), *Old Enchantment* (1928), *Horses in the Sky* (1929), *The Indiscreet Years* (1931), *Children of Pleasure* (1932), *Tomorrow Will Be Different* (1936), *Journey Through Time* (1940), *The Great Light* (1947), and other novels.

Barretts of Wimpole Street (bar'ets; wim'pōl), **The.** Play (1931) by Rudolph Besier, produced in the U.S., based on the courtship of Robert and Elizabeth Barrett Browning. The revelation on the stage of Mr. Barrett's transparently incestuous feelings toward his daughter, which provides the climax in the play, is based on no valid evidence from real life and, in the opinion of many authorities, does a considerable disservice to the actual story of both Browning and the Barretts.

Barrhead (bär.hed'). Police burgh and industrial town in S Scotland, in Renfrewshire, ab. 7 mi. SW of Glasgow, ab. 407 mi. N of London by rail: manufactures plumbing equipment. 13,055 (est. 1948).

Barrias (bȧ.ryȧs), **Félix Joseph.** b. at Paris, Sept. 13, 1822; d. there, in January, 1907. French painter, especially known for historical scenes; brother of Louis Erneste Barrias.

Barrias, Louis Erneste. b. at Paris, April 3, 1841; d. there, Feb. 4, 1905. French sculptor; brother of Félix Joseph Barrias. He was a pupil of Pierre Jules Cavelier, Léon Cogniet, and François Jouffroy, and studied also at the École des Beaux Arts. He was awarded the grand prix de Rome in 1865, the first medal at the Salon of 1872, and its medal of honor in 1878. In 1884 he was elected a member of the French Institute. He produced a large number of decorations for buildings and on other structures. Among the more important of his independent works may be mentioned the *Oath of Spartacus* (1872), *Religion and Charity* (1873), and the *Defense of Paris* at Courbevoie, France.

Barricades, Days of the. In French history, a name given to several insurrections at Paris (May 12, 1588; Aug. 26–27, 1648; 1830; 1848; and others).

Barrie (bar'i). Town in Ontario, Canada, county seat of Simcoe County, situated on the W shore of Lake Simcoe. 12,514 (1951).

Barrie, Sir James Matthew. b. at Kirriemuir, Forfarshire, Scotland, May 9, 1860; d. June 19, 1937. Scottish playwright and novelist, noted for his deft use of whimsy to illustrate the value of simple emotions. His most popular work is now probably *Peter Pan* (1904), a fairy-tale play in which Maude Adams, Jean Arthur, and others have appeared with great success in America. His other plays include *The Professor's Love Story* (1895), *Quality Street* (1901), *The Admirable Crichton* (1903), *Alice Sit-by-the-Fire* (1905), *What Every Woman Knows* (1908), *Der Tag* (1914), *The Old Lady Shows Her Medals* (1917), *Dear Brutus* (1917), and *Shall We Join the Ladies?* (1922); outstanding among his prose works are *The Little Minister* (1891), which he also adapted for the stage, *A Window in Thrums* (1889), *Sentimental Tommy* (1896), the biographical *Margaret Ogilvie* (1896), *Tommy and Grizel* (1900), and *Peter and Wendy* (1911).

Barrientos (bär.ryen'tōs), **Álamos de.** See **Álamos de Barrientos.**

Barrière (bȧ.ryer), **Théodore.** b. at Paris, 1823; d. there, Oct. 16, 1877. French dramatist. A prolific writer, he collaborated on many plays.

Barrier Reef, Great. See **Great Barrier Reef.**

Barriers, Battle of the. Victory gained over the French, by the forces ranged against Napoleon, under the walls of Paris, in March, 1814.

Barriers Burned Away. Novel by Edward Payson Roe, published in 1872. Denis Fleet, in his effort to support his mother and family, performs such tasks as shoveling snow and serving as a porter. His love for Christine, his employer's daughter, is not returned at first, but eventually her indifference is overcome when he rescues her during the Chicago fire of 1871, and when she realizes that he is a man of refinement.

Barrier Treaty. Treaty signed at Antwerp, Nov. 15, 1715, by Austria, Great Britain, and the Netherlands, determining the relations of the Dutch and the Austrians in the strategic towns of the Low Countries. The term was later given general application to any treaty which had as its principal purpose the fixing of a frontier or boundary.

Barrili (bär.rē'lē), **Antonio Giulio.** b. 1836; d. Aug. 15, 1908. Italian writer. He served with Giuseppe Garibaldi in the Tyrol in 1866, participated in the Roman campaign of 1867, and became editor of *Il Movimento* in 1860, and of *Il Caffaro* at Genoa in 1872. Author of the novels *Il Capitan Dodèro* (1865), *I Rossi e i Neri* (1871) and other books.

Barrinding (bär'in.ding). See under **Barra, W Africa.**

Barringer (bar'in.jėr), **Daniel Moreau.** b. near Concord, N.C., July 30, 1806; d. at White Sulphur Springs, W.Va., Sept. 1, 1873. American lawyer, congressman, and diplomat. He served as a representative (1829–35) in the North Carolina House of Commons, was a Whig member (1843–49) of Congress, and acted as minister (1849–53) to Spain. Although he opposed secession, he loyally served the Southern cause once the Civil War had begun. He approved President Andrew Johnson's administration of reconstruction policies after the Civil War.

Barringer, Rufus. b. in Cabarrus County, N.C., Dec. 2, 1821; d. Feb. 3, 1895. American lawyer, politician, and Confederate army soldier. Although personally hopeful that the Union might remain whole, he accepted his state's decision to secede, and served in the army throughout the Civil War. After the war he joined the Republican party and approved the U.S. government's reconstruction policies. Active politically, he was a candidate (1880) for lieutenant governor.

Barrington (bar'ing.tọn). Village in NE Illinois, in Cook and Lake counties: residential community; processing point for coffee and tea; manufactures tableware. 4,209 (1950).

Barrington. Borough in W New Jersey, in Camden County near Camden. 2,651 (1950).

Barrington. Town in E Rhode Island, in Bristol County, on the Barrington River: brick, shipbuilding, and fish-processing industries. Founded in 1632 and incorporated in 1677, as Swansea, it was separated from Swansea in 1717. Pop. 8,246 (1950).

Barrington, Daines. b. 1727; d. March 14, 1800. English lawyer, naturalist, and antiquary; fourth son of John Shute Barrington. He wrote *Observations on the Statutes* (1766), *The Naturalist's Calendar* (1767), and others.

Barrington, E. A pseudonym of **Beck, Lily Adams.**

Barrington, George. [Original name, **George Waldron.**] b. at Maynooth, Ireland, May 14, 1755; d. c1840. Irish writer on Australian topics. He was transported to Australia as a pickpocket in 1790, and emancipated in 1792. His most notable exploit as a thief was the robbing of one of the Russian princes of the Orlov family, at Covent Garden Theatre, of a snuffbox said to be worth about 150 thousand dollars. When the play, *The Revenge*, by Edward Young, was presented at Sydney by a group of actors most of whom were convicts, it was probably Barrington who wrote the prologue containing the lines: "True patriots we, for be it understood, we left our country for our country's good." He also wrote *A Voyage to Botany Bay* (1801), *The History of New South Wales* (1802), *The History of New Holland* (1808), and other works.

Barrington, John Shute. [Title, 1st Viscount **Barrington.**] b. at Theobalds, Hertfordshire, England, 1678; d. at Becket, Berkshire, England, Dec. 14, 1734. English lawyer and polemical writer; father of Daines Barrington, Samuel Barrington, Shute Barrington, and William Wildman Barrington. He was created Baron Barrington and Viscount Barrington (in the Irish peerage) in 1720. As a result of his favoring civil rights for Protestant dissenters he was sent to Scotland to gain Presbyterian backing for the union of Scotland with England. In 1723 he was expelled from the House of Commons for his connection with a lottery. His expulsion was thought by many to have been the result of personal malice on the part of Robert Walpole. He wrote *The Rights of Protestant Dissenters* (1704; second part 1705), *A Dissuasive to Jacobitism* (1713), *Miscellanea Sacra* (1725), and others.

Barrington, Sir **Jonah.** b. in Ireland, 1760; d. at Versailles, France, April 8, 1834. Irish judge. He was the author of *Personal Sketches* (1827; 3rd vol., 1832), *Historic Memoirs of Ireland* (1832), and *The Rise and Fall of the Irish Nation* (1833).

Barrington, Samuel. b. 1729; d. 1800. English admiral; fifth son of John Shute Barrington. He served with distinction in the West Indies.

Barrington, Shute. b. at Becket, Berkshire, England, May 26, 1734; d. March 25, 1826. English prelate; sixth son of John Shute Barrington. He was bishop of Llandaff, and later of Salisbury and of Durham.

Barrington, William Wildman. [Title, 2nd Viscount **Barrington.**] b. Jan. 15, 1717; d. Feb. 1, 1793. English statesman; eldest son of John Shute Barrington. He was secretary of war (1755–61, 1765–78) and chancellor of the exchequer (1761–62).

Barrio (bär'ryō), **Diego Martínez.** b. at Seville, Spain, 1887—. Spanish politician and journalist. At first a printer and owner of a small press, he started his political career as a member of the government of Seville. In the provisional government of 1931 which replaced the monarchy, he was made minister of communications, and continued in the republic as minister of the interior under Alcalá Zamora. He was chosen to be prime minister of the republic in October, 1933. During his career in the Cortes he had shifted from the center right to the radical party of Lerroux, in whose cabinet he functioned (1933) as minister of war. In the difficult days of 1933 he characterized the Spanish Republic as one of "mud, blood and tears," which, indeed it became when, despite his attempts to reconcile General Emilio Mola in 1936, the Spanish Civil War broke out. In this same year he was again for a brief period prime minister, at the appointment of President Manuel Azaña. Barrio subsequently went into exile at Paris, and failed to return to Spain in 1939, although he would have been in line to succeed the retiring President Azaña as speaker of the Cortes. From 1940 to 1945 he was considered president of the Spanish government in exile in Mexico, leaving for Paris again at the end of that period.

Barrios (bär'ryōs), **Eduardo.** [Full name, **Eduardo Barrios y Hudtwalcker.**] b. at Valparaiso, Chile, Oct. 25, 1884—. Chilean author of psychological novels, notable also as a dramatist and short-story writer. His style is simple and his character delineation skillful. He is the author of the novels *El niño que enloqueció de amor* (1915), *Un perdido* (1917), *El hermano asno* (1922), and *Páginas de un pobre diablo* (1923); his plays include *Lo que niega la vida*, *Vivir*, and others.

Barrios, Gerardo. b. at San Salvador, El Salvador, c1810; executed there, Aug. 29, 1865. Salvadorian general, president of El Salvador (1860–63). He was an adherent of Francisco Morazán, and took part in the war in Nicaragua in 1844. In 1857 he commanded the Salvadorian troops sent to Nicaragua against the filibustering expedition of William Walker. In the same year he returned and fomented an unsuccessful revolution against Campos, then president of El Salvador. In 1860 he became president of El Salvador by regular election, but was deposed in 1863 by Rafael Carrera, president of Guatemala. In 1865 he attempted a war against Dueñas, his successor, whom Carrera had put in office, but was captured and shot.

Barrios, Justo Rufino. b. at San Marcos, Quezaltenango, Guatemala, c1835; killed near Chalchuapa, El Salvador, April 2, 1885. Guatemalan statesman and general, president of Guatemala (1873–85). After 1867 he opposed President Cerna, and in 1871 took a prominent part in his overthrow. He was supreme commander (1871–73) of the army and from June 4, 1873, until his death was, by successive elections, president of Guatemala. In the period 1882–83 he visited the U.S. and Europe. His scheme of forcing a confederation of the Central American states led to a war with El Salvador. Barrios invaded that country, and was killed in an assault on Chalchuapa.

Barron (bar'ọn), **Clarence Walker.** b. at Boston, July 2, 1855; d. Oct. 2, 1928. American financial editor. He served on the staff (1875–84) of the Boston *Transcript*, was the founder (1887) and president of the Boston News Bureau, founded (1897) the Philadelphia News Bureau, and was the editor (1921 *et seq.*) of *Barron's Financial Weekly*. In 1901 he was the manager and in 1902 became president, of Dow, Jones and Company, at New York, publishers of the *Wall Street Journal*. He was also chairman (1911) of the Massachusetts Inland Waterways Commission. Author of *The Federal Reserve Act* (1914), *The Audacious War* (1915), *The Mexican Problem* (1917), *War Finance* (1919), and *A World Remaking* (1920).

Barron, James. b. in Virginia, 1769; d. at Norfolk, Va., April 21, 1851. American naval officer; brother of Samuel Barron (1765–1810), and uncle of Samuel Barron (1809–88). While in command of the *Chesapeake* (1807) he refused, on June 22, to surrender three alleged British deserters demanded by Captain Humphreys of the British ship *Leopard*, and was attacked (at a time when the U.S. and Great Britain were, however uneasily, still at peace) and his vessel boarded. The *Chesapeake* was taken unprepared, and fired only one gun during the action. The incident represented a culminating point in the British insistence on their right to board and search American vessels for deserters, and intensified the popular American resentment of Great Britain which was to contribute to the outbreak of the War of 1812. Barron was court-martialed, found guilty of failure to anticipate the possibility of the action, and deprived of his rank and pay (as commodore) for five years. On his return to duty he was refused an active command; as a result, a duel was fought (1820) between him and Commodore Stephen Decatur (who had opposed him at the court martial) and the latter was killed.

Barron, Samuel. b. at Hampton, Va., 1765; d. Oct. 29, 1810. American naval officer; brother of James Barron. He commanded a squadron in the war against the Barbary states in 1805.

Barron, Samuel. b. at Hampton, Va., Nov. 28, 1809; d. Feb. 26, 1888. American naval officer, with the Confederate navy in the Civil War; nephew of James Barron. He withdrew (April 22, 1861) from the U.S. navy at the outset of the Civil War, and organized the distribution of ordnance and naval defenses for the Confederate navy; in command (1861) at Fort Hatteras, he was taken prisoner when the fort surrendered, but was exchanged after less than a year. As a ranking Confederate naval officer in Europe (1863–65), with headquarters at Paris, he aided in the purchase and operation of the commerce raiders *Stonewall* and *Georgia*.

Barros (bär′rōsh), **João de.** b. at Viseu, Portugal, 1496; d. near Pombal, Portugal, 1570. Portuguese writer, generally considered the most outstanding historian in Portugal in the 16th century. His chief work, *Ásia*, was divided into several *Décadas* (Decades), of which only three appeared during his lifetime (the first in 1552, the second in 1553, and the third in 1563). He also wrote *Gramática da língua portuguesa* (1540), which was the second Portuguese grammar ever published, and *O Imperador Clarimundo*, a romance of chivalry.

Barros Arana (bär′rōs ä.rä′nä), **Diego.** b. at Santiago, Chile, 1830; d. Nov. 4, 1907. Chilean historian. After studying law, he served at Santiago as a professor of the history of literature. His first treatise was *Estudios historicos sobre Vicente Benavides y las campañas del sur* (1850). Later he published a succession of important works, among them *Historia de la independencia de Chile* (Santiago, 4 vols., 1854–58), *El General Freire*, *Vida y viages de Hernando de Magallanes*, and *Historia general de Chile* (16 vols., 1884 *et seq.*). He edited the *Coleccion de historiadores primitivos de Chile*, and the *Puren indómito*, a historical poem of the Spanish war against the Araucanian Indians.

Barros Jarpa (ħär′pä), **Ernesto.** b. at Chillán, Chile, July 7, 1894—. Chilean jurist and statesman. After graduation (1915) from the University of Chile, he served as minister of foreign affairs (1921; 1925; 1942), of finance (1932) and of the interior (1932). He was a professor of international public law (1933 *et seq.*) at the University of Chile; he also served as president of the Chilean Electricity Company. Author of *Hacia la solución* (1921), *Derecho internacional* (1932), *La conferencía de la paz y el convenio sobre arreglo pacífico de los conflictos internacionales*, and others.

Barroso (bạr.rō′zö), **Gustavo.** b. at Fortaleza, Brazil, Dec. 29, 1888—. Brazilian historian, novelist, and folklorist. Among his works are *Terra de sol* (1912), *Heróis e bandidos* (1917), and *Através do folclore* (1927), as well as novels and works on South American history.

Barrot (bȧ.rō), **Camille Hyacinthe Odilon.** b. at Villefort, France, July 19, 1791; d. at Bougival, France, Aug. 6, 1873. French lawyer and statesman; brother of Victorin Ferdinand Barrot. He was a leader of the "dynastic" opposition to the "July Monarchy" of Louis Philippe. He served as premier and minister of justice (1848–49), and later for a time as president of the council of state.

Barrot, Victorin Ferdinand. b. at Paris, Jan. 10, 1806; d. there, Nov. 12, 1883. French Bonapartist politician; brother of Camille Hyacinthe Odilon Barrot. He was elected a senator for life in 1877.

Barrow (bar′ō). See also **Barrow-in-Furness.**

Barrow. River in Leinster province, Irish Republic. It rises in the Slieve Bloom Mountains, in County Laoighis, and flows E to the County Kildare-County Laoighis boundary, whence it flows S, forming the boundary of these counties. It forms ab. 5 mi. of the County Carlow-County Laoighis boundary before crossing the W portion of County Carlow to the County Carlow-County Kilkenny boundary, of which it forms ab. 20 mi. It continues southward, forming the County Kilkenny-County Wexford boundary, to Waterford Harbour, ab. 5 mi. E of Waterford. Length, ab. 119 mi.

Barrow, Cape. Headland on the N coast of the Mackenzie District, Northwest Territories, Canada, projecting into Coronation Gulf. It was named for Sir John Barrow, British geographer.

Barrow, Frances Elizabeth. [Maiden name, **Mease;** pseudonym, **Aunt Fanny.**] b. at Charleston, S.C., Feb. 22, 1822; d. at New York, May 7, 1894. American writer of books for children. She wrote the following series: *Little Pet Books* (1860), *Good Little Hearts* (1864), *Nightcap Series*, *The Pop-Gun Stories*, and *The Six Mitten Books*.

Barrow or **Barrowe** (bar′ō), **Henry.** Hanged at Tyburn (in what is now London), April 6, 1593. English religious reformer, sometimes regarded as one of the founders of Congregationalism. He held many of the views of the Brownists (a group of early English Separatists, followers of Robert Browne) and, with John Greenwood, a nonconformist clergyman, was imprisoned for rejecting the authority of ecclesiastical and legal authorities; he was hanged, together with Greenwood, at Tyburn for publishing what the law of that day considered seditious literature.

Barrow, Isaac. b. at London, 1630; d. there, in April, 1677. English theologian, classical scholar, and mathematician; a teacher of Isaac Newton. He was educated at Cambridge (scholar of Trinity, 1647, and fellow, 1649), traveled on the Continent (1655–59), was appointed professor of geometry at Gresham College, and in 1663 became the first Lucasian professor of mathematics at Cambridge (a post from which he resigned in 1669 in favor of Newton). He served as chaplain to Charles II; in 1672 he became master of Trinity College. Among his works are *Lectiones Opticae et Geometricae* (1669, 1670–74) and the posthumously published *Treatise on the Pope's Supremacy* (1680). The best edition of his theological works is that of Alexander Napier (1859).

Barrow, Sir **John.** b. near Ulverston, Lancashire, England, June 19, 1764; d. at Camden Town, now part of London, Nov. 23, 1848. English writer, geographer, and traveler. He was secretary to the British ambassador to China (1792–94) and to the governor of the Cape of Good Hope (1796–98). While in Africa he was sent on missions into the interior and secured valuable information on that area. Following his return to England in 1803 he was second secretary of the admiralty (1804–06, 1807–45). He was a promoter of Arctic exploration (Barrow Straits, Cape Barrows, and Point Barrow were named for him), and a chief founder of the Royal Geographical Society. He was made a baronet in 1835. Among his works are *Travels in South Africa* (1801–04), *Travels in China* (1804), *Voyage to Cochin-China* (1806), *History of Arctic Voyages* (1818), *Voyages of Discovery and Research Within the Arctic Regions* (1846), an autobiography, and others.

Barrow, Point. Headland on the N coast of Alaska, projecting into the Arctic Ocean. It was named for Sir John Barrow, the English geographer.

Barrow, Washington. b. in Davidson County, Tenn., Oct. 5, 1817; d. at St. Louis, Oct. 19, 1866. American politician and newspaper editor. At first a Jacksonian Democrat, he later joined the Whig Party during its early days in Tennessee. After having been appointed (1841) American chargé d'affaires at Lisbon, he was elected (1847) to Congress. He was an editor (1844 *et seq.*) of the Nashville, Tenn., *Republican Banner*. As a Tennessee state senator, he was a member of the commission which negotiated (1861) an agreement with the Confederacy.

Barrow-in-Furness (bar′ō.in.fėr′nẹs) or **Barrow.** County borough, seaport, and manufacturing town in NW England, in Lancashire, situated at the S end of Furness peninsula, opposite the island of Walney (which is included in the county borough), between the estuaries of the rivers Duddon and Leven, ab. 50 mi. NW of Liverpool, ab. 265 mi. NW of London by rail. It has an open-hearth steel industry, producing steel rails and constructional steel. Locomotives were formerly built here, but Barrow-in-Furness is now only a repair center. It has some of the largest shipyards in the country, specializing in the building of submarines, but also building cargo craft, yachts, dredges, and metal pontoons. As a seaport on the Irish Sea, it imports mainly iron ore and exports iron and steel products. The town has grown rapidly since the mid-19th century. 67,473 (1951).

Barrows (bar'ōz), **David Prescott.** b. at Chicago, June 27, 1873—. American educator, ethnologist, and soldier. A graduate of Pomona College (1894), the University of California (1895), and Columbia University (1896), he served as director of education (1903–09) in the Philippine Islands. He was successively a professor of education (1910) and political science (1911), dean of faculties (1913), and president (1919–23) at the University of California. He was also a major general (1926–37) in the U.S. Army. Author of *The Ethno-Botany of the Coahuilla Indians* (1900), *A History of the Philippines* (1903), *Berbers and Blacks* (1927), and other works.

Barrows, Elijah Porter. b. at Mansfield, Conn., Jan. 5, 1817; d. at Oberlin, Ohio, Sept. 14, 1888. American religious writer. He was a professor (1853–66) of Hebrew at Andover Seminary, and accepted (1872) a similar appointment at Oberlin Theological Seminary.

Barrows, John Henry. b. near Medina, Mich., July 11, 1847; d. June 3, 1902. American clergyman, president (1898–1902) of Oberlin College. He was pastor of a Congregational church (1875 *et seq.*) at Lawrence, Mass., and of Chicago's First Presbyterian Church (1881–96). As chairman of the Committee on Religious Congresses of the World's Columbian Exposition (1893) at Chicago, he organized the Parliament of Religions which was attended by some 150,000 persons. He delivered (1895–1901) the Haskell lectures on comparative religion at the University of Chicago and the Haskell-endowed Barrows lectures on Christianity in India and Japan.

Barrows, Katherine Isabel Hayes Chapin. b. at Irasburg, Vt., April 17, 1845; d. Oct. 25, 1913. American editor, first woman stenographer in the Department of State at Washington, D.C.; wife of Samuel June Barrows. For a period of 20 years she edited the *Proceedings* of the National Conference of Charities and Corrections, for 16 years she served as assistant editor of the *Christian Register*, and was secretary and editor for 17 years of the Lake Mohonk Conference. Coauthor with her husband of *The Shaybacks in Camp* (1887).

Barrows, Samuel June. b. at New York, May 26, 1845; d. April 21, 1909. American Unitarian clergyman, editor, and reformer; husband of Katherine Isabel Hayes Chapin Barrows. He is noted chiefly for his work toward the passage of New York's first probation law and the federal parole law, but he was active also in Negro and Indian welfare, woman suffrage, prohibition, international coöperation and other movements. Having started to work at the age of nine, he learned shorthand and telegraphy, operating the first private telegraph line in New York; he became a reporter for the New York *Tribune* at 21, later spending summers (on vacation from attending Harvard Divinity School) as a correspondent on the Western plains with Henry Morton Stanley and George Armstrong Custer. He edited (1880–96) the *Christian Register*, a Unitarian national weekly. In 1896 he was elected to Congress for one term. He was international prison commissioner for the U.S. and president (1905) of the international prison congress. He was the author of various penological reports, including *The Prison Systems of the United States*.

Barrow Strait (bar'ō). Channel in the Arctic region of North America, communicating with Viscount Melville Sound on the W, Lancaster Sound on the E, Prince Regent Inlet on the SE, and Peel Sound on the S: discovered by Sir William Edward Parry in 1819, and named for Sir John Barrow, English geographer. Width, ab. 50 mi.

Barrundia (bär.rön'dyä), **José Francisco.** b. in Guatemala, 1779; d. at New York, Aug. 4, 1854. Central American statesman, president (1829–30) of the Central American Confederation. He took an early and prominent part in the movement for political independence from Spain, and in 1813 was condemned to death, but escaped and concealed himself for six years. He was a member of the constitutional convention of Central America (1823–24), and introduced the decree by which slavery was abolished there. From June 25, 1829, to Sept. 16, 1830, he was president of the Central American Confederation. In 1851, when Honduras, El Salvador, and Nicaragua attempted to form a confederation, Barrundia was chosen president, but the union was dissolved in the following year. In 1854 Barrundia came to the U.S. as envoy from Honduras, with the avowed object of offering the annexation of that country to the authorities at Washington, but he died before any action could be taken.

Barry (bar'i). Municipal borough, seaport, and seaside resort in S Wales, in Glamorganshire, situated on Bristol Channel, ab. 7 mi. SW of Cardiff, ab. 154 mi. W of London by rail. It owes its origins to the South Wales coal trade and is a large exporter of coal. The town has grown rapidly in the last 50 years. 40,979 (1951).

Barry, Ann. [Maiden name, **Street.**] b. at Bath, England, 1734; d. Nov. 29, 1801. English actress; wife of Spranger Barry. When very young she married an actor named Dancer, and first appeared (c1756) on the stage under his name. She married Barry in 1768. After his death she remained on the stage until 1798, marrying in 1778 a Mr. Crawford. She was considered good in tragedy and superb in comedy. She is buried near her husband in the cloisters of Westminster Abbey.

Barry, Sir **Charles.** b. at Westminster, London, May 23, 1795; d. at Clapham, London, May 12, 1860. English architect, designer of the Houses of Parliament (1840–46), London; father of Edward Middleton Barry and of John Wolfe Wolfe-Barry. He also designed the buildings of the Travellers' Club (1831), the Reform Club (1837), and others.

Barry (bá.rē), Comtesse **du.** See **du Barry,** Comtesse.

Barry (bar'i), **Edward Middleton.** b. at London, June 7, 1830; d. there, Jan. 27, 1880. English architect; son of Sir Charles Barry. He designed the Covent Garden Theatre (as it was rebuilt in the latter half of the 19th century) and others.

Barry, Elizabeth. b. 1658; d. Nov. 7, 1713. English actress. She went on the stage under the patronage of the poet John Wilmot, 2nd earl of Rochester, and was the creator of more than 100 roles, mostly those of tragedy. Her Monimia (in Thomas Otway's *The Orphan*) and Belvidera (in Otway's *Venice Preserved*) made her highest reputation; another of her popular parts was the comic one of Lady Brute in *The Provoked Wife* by John Vanbrugh. She retired from the stage in 1710, and was buried at Acton, now part of London. She (not Mrs. Ann Barry) was usually known as "the great Mrs. Barry."

Barry, James. b. at Cork, Ireland, Oct. 11, 1741; d. at London, Feb. 22, 1806. Irish painter of historical and mythological subjects; a protégé of Edmund Burke. He was notorious for his violent temper (which led to his being deprived of his professorship of painting at the Royal Academy and his expulsion from that body) and erratic views. He carried his theory of the classical in art so far as to represent nude all the figures in his *Death of General Wolfe*. Among his other well-known paintings are *Adam and Eve* and *Venus Rising from the Sea*.

Barry, John. b. at Tacumshane, County Wexford, Ireland, 1745; d. at Philadelphia, Sept. 13, 1803. American naval commander who distinguished himself in the Revolutionary War. He settled (c1760) at Philadelphia; on the outbreak of the war he was given command of the *Lexington*, and captured (1776) the British tender *Edward*, first British ship to be taken by American arms. In 1778 he took command of the *Raleigh*, which was captured, a few days after sailing, by the British ship *Experiment*, but Barry escaped and returned to America. In command of the *Alliance* (1781), he captured the British ships *Atalanta* and *Trepassy*, and later in the same year conveyed Lafayette and Louis Marie de Noailles to France. He was given the rank of commodore in 1794.

Barry, John Arthur. b. at Torquay, Devonshire, England, 1850; d. at Sydney, New South Wales, Australia, Sept. 23, 1911. Australian cattle dealer, newspaper correspondent, journalist, and novelist. He served (1864–70, 1877–80) in the British merchant service before beginning his writing career in 1880. He contributed to magazines and newspapers in Australia, England, and America, and was a staff member (1896–1900) of the Sydney *Town and Country Journal* and an editorial writer (1900 *et seq.*) for the Sydney *Evening News*. Author of *Steve Brown's Bunyip* (1893), *In the Great Deep* (1895), *The Luck of the Native-Born* (1898), *A Son of the Sea* (1899), *Against the Tides of Fate* (1899), *Red Lion and Blue Star* (1902), all novels of

Australian life, and *Old and New Sydney* (1903), and *Sea Yarns* (1910).

Barry, John Stetson. b. at Boston, March 26, 1819; d. at St. Louis, Mo., Dec. 11, 1872. American Universalist clergyman and historical writer. He wrote *History of Massachusetts* (1855–57).

Barry, John Stewart. b. at Amherst, N.H., Jan. 29, 1802; d. Jan. 14, 1870. American politician, governor of Michigan (1842–46; 1850–52). A member (1835) of the state constitutional convention, he was elected (1841) as Democratic governor following a financially disastrous Whig administration, and reëlected eight years later.

Barry, Sir **John Wolfe Wolfe-.** b. Dec. 7, 1836; d. Jan. 22, 1918. English civil engineer; son of Sir Charles Barry. The builder of the Tower bridge, the Barry docks, and other structures, he was appointed to the Royal Commission on Irish Public Works (1886) and to the Western Highlands and Islands Commission (1889). Author of *Railway Appliances* (1874–92), *The Tower Bridge* (1904) and others.

Barry, Martin. b. at Fratton, Hampshire, England, March 29, 1802; d. at Beccles, Suffolk, England, April 27, 1855. English physician, noted as an embryologist. He made (1843) the discovery of the penetration by spermatozoa of the ovum.

Barry, Patrick. b. in Ireland, May 24, 1816; d. at Rochester, N.Y., June 23, 1890. American horticulturist and pomologist. He was editor of the *Genesee Farmer* (1844–52) and of the *Horticulturist* (1852–54). He also prepared the catalogue of the American Pomological Society and published *A Treatise on the Fruit Garden* (1851).

Barry, Philip. b. at Rochester, N.Y., June 18, 1896; d. at New York, Dec. 3, 1949. American playwright. After receiving (1919) an A.B. from Yale, he studied (1919–22) at Harvard under George Pierce Baker, and won (1922) a prize at Harvard for his play *You and I*, which was later (1923) produced on Broadway. His other plays include *In a Garden* (1925), *White Wings* (1926), *Paris Bound* (1927), *Cock Robin* (1928, with Elmer Rice), *Holiday* (1929), *Hotel Universe* (1930), *Tomorrow and Tomorrow* (1931), *The Animal Kingdom* (1932), *Bright Star* (1935), *Here Come the Clowns* (1938), *The Philadelphia Story* (1939), *Liberty Jones* (1941), *Without Love* (1942), and *Foolish Notion* (1945). *Second Threshhold* (1950), which he had left unfinished at his death, was produced posthumously after having been completed by Robert E. Sherwood.

Barry, Spranger. b. at Dublin, Ireland, 1719; d. at London, Jan. 10, 1777. Irish actor, a rival of David Garrick; husband of Ann Barry. He first appeared on the stage on Feb. 15, 1744, at Dublin. He was generally considered one of the best actors of his time, and excelled in tragedy, though he occasionally played in comedy. Among his roles were Hamlet and Macbeth (in which he alternated with Garrick), Romeo (with Mrs. Cibber, the wife of Theophilus Cibber, as Juliet), and Othello (the part in which he made his London debut, at the Drury Lane Theatre). He is buried, near his wife, in the cloisters of Westminster Abbey.

Barry, William Farquhar. b. at New York, Aug. 18, 1818; d. at Fort McHenry, Baltimore, Md., July 18, 1879. American soldier, with the Union Army in the Civil War. He was chief of artillery (1861–62) in the Army of the Potomac, participating in the siege of Yorktown and in the engagements at Gaines's Mill, Mechanicsville, Charles City Cross-Roads, Malvern Hill, and Harrison's Landing. He held a similar post (1864–66) under General W. T. Sherman, taking part in the siege of Atlanta and in the northern Georgia, Alabama, and Carolina campaigns. His services were rewarded with the brevet of brigadier general.

Barry, William Taylor. b. at Lunenburg, Va., Feb. 5, 1785; d. at Liverpool, England, Aug. 30, 1835. American politician and jurist. He was a member of Congress (1810–11), served in the War of 1812, and was a U.S. senator (1815–16). He became a judge of the Kentucky supreme court in 1816, and as postmaster general (1829–35) was the first incumbent of that office invited to sit in the cabinet. He was appointed minister to Spain in 1835, but died before reaching his post.

Barry, William Taylor Sullivan. b. in Mississippi, Dec. 10, 1821; d. at Columbus, Miss., Jan. 29, 1868. American politician and Confederate leader. He was president (1861) of the Mississippi secession convention, a delegate to the Montgomery convention to form the Confederate government, a member of the provisional Confederate congress, and colonel of a Mississippi infantry regiment.

Barry Island. Islet in Antarctica, lying in the center of the Debenham Islands group, off the Fallières Coast in Marguerite Bay; in 68°08′ S., 67°06′ W. It was charted and named by members of the British Graham Land Expedition of 1934–37, who used it for a base in 1936 and 1937.

Barry Island. Name given to a small area of land, formerly an island, in S Wales, in Glamorganshire, situated on the S coast, on Bristol Channel, ab. 7 mi. SW of Cardiff. The narrow channel which formerly separated it from the mainland has now been filled.

Barry Leroy (lē.roi′). Historical novel by Henry Christopher Bailey, published in 1919. It is set in England and on the Continent, and takes place in the period 1793–1800.

Barry Lyndon (lin′dọn), **Memoirs of.** Novel by William Makepeace Thackeray, first published serially in *Fraser's Magazine*, beginning in 1844, as *The Luck of Barry Lyndon*. It portrays a scoundrel of extreme rascality.

Barrymore (bar′i.mōr), **Ethel.** b. at Philadelphia, Aug. 15, 1879—. American actress; daughter of Maurice Barrymore (1847–1905) and Georgiana Emma Drew Barrymore (1856–93). She made her debut (1894) substituting for Elsie DeWolfe in *The Bauble Shop*. Popularity and success came to her with her first starring role, in *Captain Jinks of the Horse Marines* (1901). She appeared with Henry Irving; her other starring vehicles include Ibsen's *A Doll's House* (1905), J. M. Barrie's *Alice-Sit-by-the-Fire* (1906) and *The Twelve Pound Look* (which she played for several seasons in vaudeville), Somerset Maugham's *The Constant Wife* (1926), and Emlyn Williams' *The Corn is Green* (1942); she has appeared also in films including *Rasputin and the Empress*, *None But the Lonely Heart*, *Portrait of Jenny*, and *Pinky*. She married Russell Griswold Colt in 1909, and was divorced from him in 1923.

Barrymore, Georgiana Emma Drew. b. 1856; d. at Santa Barbara, Calif., July 2, 1893. American comic actress; daughter of John Drew (1827–62), and Louisa Lane Drew (1820–97), wife of Maurice Barrymore (1847–1905), and mother of John Barrymore, Lionel Barrymore, and Ethel Barrymore. While with Augustin Daly's company, she played in *Pique*, *The Serious Family*, *Weak Women*, *As You Like It*, *Frou Frou*, *Divorce*, *Life*, *The School for Scandal*, and *The Princess Royal*. Having joined Albert Marsham Palmer's stock company, she played in *Diplomacy*, *The Wages of Sin*, *Moths*, *L'Abbé Constantin*, *Mr. Wilkinson's Widow*, *Settled Out of Court*, and *The Sportsman*. She played occasionally opposite her husband, and sometimes with Helena Modjeska.

Barrymore, John. [Full name, **John Blythe Barrymore.**] b. at Philadelphia, Feb. 15, 1882; d. at Hollywood, Calif., May 29, 1942. American actor; son of Maurice Barrymore (1847–1905) and Georgiana Emma Drew Barrymore (1856–93). After making his theatrical debut (1903) in *Magda*, he appeared with his brother Lionel Barrymore in *The Jest* (1919). He won acclaim for his performance in *Richard III* (1920), and his performance in *Hamlet* (1924–25) was very highly regarded. He also appeared in the comedies *The Royal Family* (1927–28) and *My Dear Children* (1939), both of which were to some extent based on characteristics of the Barrymore family. In his later years he acted mostly in films, including *Beau Brummel*, *Don Juan*, *Moby Dick*, and *Rasputin and the Empress*.

Barrymore, Lionel. b. at Philadelphia, April 28, 1878—. American actor; son of Maurice Barrymore (1847–1905) and Georgiana Emma Drew Barrymore (1856–93). He made his theatrical debut in *The Rivals* (1893), playing with his grandmother Louisa Lane Drew; subsequently he starred in *Squire Kate*, *Arizona*, and other plays. He left the stage to appear in such films as *Grand Hotel*, *Rasputin and the Empress*, *Reunion in Vienna*, and the *Doctor Kildare* series. He played (1934 *et seq.*) Scrooge in an annual radio broadcast at Christmas of Charles Dickens's *Christmas Carol*.

Barrymore, Maurice. [Original name, **Herbert Blythe.**] b. at Fort Agra, India, 1847; d. March 26, 1905. English actor, celebrated on British and American stages as a leading man with Madame Helena Modjeska, Lily Langtry, Olga Nethersole and Mrs. Minnie Maddern Fiske, though he was never starred; husband of Georgiana Emma Drew Barrymore, and father of Ethel Barrymore, John Barrymore, and Lionel Barrymore. Before entering the theater in 1872, he won the Queensberry cup and the British amateur boxing championship. He was noted for his wit, grace, rich voice, and personal magnetism. He was married (1876) to the comedienne Georgiana Emma Drew, daughter of the well-known actors John and Louisa Lane Drew, and a year after her death (1893) to Mary Floyd.

Barsac (bȧr.sȧk). Town in SW France, in the department of Gironde, situated on the Garonne River ab. 21 mi. SE of Bordeaux. It is noted for its wine.

Barse (bärs), **George Randolph, Jr.** b. at Detroit, Mich., July 31, 1861; d. Feb. 25, 1938. American figure and portrait painter, notable for his series of eight panels in the Library of Congress, Washington, D.C. He studied at Paris, under Alexandre Cabanel and Jules Joseph Lefebvre, and exhibited at Paris, and throughout the U.S. He became a member of the National Academy of Design in 1900. His work is now in permanent collections at Chicago, Pittsburgh, Minneapolis, Kansas City, and Philadelphia. *Literature* and *Night and the Decline of Day* are two of his better-known works.

Barsetshire (bär′sẹt.shir). Imaginary county in S England which is the scene of six novels by Anthony Trollope (*The Warden*, 1855; *Barchester Towers*, 1857; *Doctor Thorne*, 1858; *Framley Parsonage*, 1861; *The Small House at Allington*, 1864; *The Last Chronicle of Barsetshire*, 1867), collectively known as *The Chronicles of Barsetshire*. Barsetshire resembles parts of the counties of Southampton in S England and Somersetshire in SW England, but its county seat, Barchester, is usually identified with Winchester in the county of Southampton. The 20th-century English novelist Angela Margaret Thirkell has used this same region as the scene of some of her novels.

Barsotti (bär.sôt′tē), **Charles.** b. at Bagni di San Giuliano, Italy, Jan. 4, 1850; d. March 30, 1927. American editor, publisher, and philanthropist, noted for the statues of famous Italians he and the subscribers of his newspaper *Il Progresso* erected at New York. His was the first (founded 1880) Italian daily in the U.S. and enjoyed a great success from the beginning. Barsotti, who came to America in 1872, contributed generously to charitable causes in Italy, and gave 250 thousand dollars for a tunnel to be built through the mountain separating Pisa from Lucca.

Barssel (bär′sẹl). Town in NW Germany, in the *Land* (state) of Lower Saxony, British Zone, formerly in Oldenburg, situated near the Hunte-Ems Canal, W of Oldenburg: agricultural commune, located on land reclaimed from former moors; sawmills. 10,450 (1947).

Barstow (bär′stō). Town in SE California, in San Bernardino County, ab. 90 mi. NE of Los Angeles. It is a division point on the Atchison, Topeka and Santa Fe, and Union Pacific railroads, and was a noted frontier town in the early days of mining in California. 6,135 (1950).

Barstow, William Augustus. b. in Connecticut, Sept. 13, 1813; d. Dec. 13, 1865. American politician, governor (1854–56) of Wisconsin. Upon his supposed reëlection (1855), his opponent contested the result and had himself also sworn in as governor. However, after fraud in the election returns had been proved before the courts, Barstow was declared governor for a second term.

Bar-sur-Aube (bȧr.sür.ōb). Town in E France, in the department of Aube, situated on the right bank of the river Aube, ab. 30 mi. E of Troyes. An agricultural trade center, it is surrounded by vineyards and has a number of flour mills. Its church of St. Pierre dates from the 12th century. It is the site also of an 18th-century château in which Czar Alexander I of Russia and King Frederick William III of Prussia stayed from February to March, 1814, after the battle of Bar-sur-Aube. In World War I Marshal Joffre had his headquarters here in 1914. Pop. 3,921 (1946).

Bar-sur-Aube, Battle of. Victory over the French by the forces ranged against Napoleon I, on Feb. 27, 1814, near the community of Bar-sur-Aube, in NE France.

Bar-sur-Ornain (bȧr.sür.ôr.naṅ). See **Bar-le-Duc.**

Bar-sur-Seine (bȧr.sür.sen). Town in NE France, in the department of Aube, situated on the Seine River ab. 18 mi. SE of Troyes. It was the scene in 1814 of conflicts between the French and forces of the countries allied against Napoleon. Pop. 2,105 (1946).

Bart or **Barth** (bärt; French, bȧr), **Jean.** [Also, **Baert.**] b. at Dunkerque, France, 1651; d. there, April 27, 1702. French naval hero. He served first with the Dutch under Michel Adriaanszoon de Ruyter, but entered the French service at the beginning of the war with Holland. As his humble birth prevented promotion in the regular navy, he became captain of a privateer, but so distinguished himself against the Dutch and English that Louis XIV appointed him successively a lieutenant, captain, and (in 1697) commander of a squadron.

Bart (bärt), **Lily.** Heroine of *The House of Mirth* (1905), novel by Edith Wharton. An almost impecunious member of high society, Lily sees salvation for herself only in an advantageous marriage; but her natural instinct against scheming and toward romance, coupled with great honesty but very little financial sense, lead her inevitably to a situation of social and monetary ruin.

Bartas (bȧr.tȧs), **Guillaume de Salluste,** Seigneur **du.** b. at Montfort, near Auch, France, 1544; d. 1590. French Huguenot poet who served under Henry of Navarre in war and diplomacy, and died from wounds received at the battle of Ivry. His most noted work is *La Semaine ou La Création*, an epic poem describing the Creation. It passed through 30 editions in a few years, and was translated into English by Joshua Sylvester. Author also of *Judith*, *Uranie*, *La Seconde Semaine*, and others.

Bart Bank (bärt). Former name of **Barth Bank.**

Bartel (bär′tel), **Kazimierz.** b. at Lvov, in the Ukraine, c1882; d. cAug. 27, 1941. Polish mathematician and one-time prime minister. He studied at Munich and later became a professor, rector, and principal at the University of Lvov. In 1919 he took the post of minister for Polish railways and communications in the first government of Ignace Jan Paderewski, resigning in 1922. In 1926 he became prime minister and then deputy prime minister under Jozéf Pilsudski. He retired from politics in 1930, and resumed his academic interests at Lvov. In World War II, he was executed by the Germans for alleged coöperation with the Russians.

Bartels (bär′tẹls), **Adolf.** b. at Wesselburen, Germany, 1862—. German poet and literary historian. He wrote poems, a regional historical novel (*Die Dithmarscher*, 1898), and dramas (*Martin Luther*, *Trilogie*, 1903), but he is known mostly for the violent anti-Semitism of his critical writings, notably in *Geschichte der deutschen Literatur*, which appeared in numerous editions after 1901.

Bartels, Hans von. b. at Hamburg, Germany, Dec. 25, 1856; d. at Munich, Germany, Oct. 5, 1913. German landscape and marine painter and water colorist. He was appointed (1891) professor of painting at Munich. He executed many storm scenes, and a list of his works includes *Lonely Beach*, *Storm-Bornholm*, and *Moonlight on Zuyder-Zee*. His work was exhibited in his day throughout Europe and won prizes at Paris and New York.

Bartenstein (bär′tẹn.shtīn). German name of **Bartoszyce.**

Bartenstein, Baron **Johann Christoph von.** b. at Strasbourg, 1689; d. at Vienna, Aug. 6, 1767. Austrian statesman. He was among the statesmen chiefly instrumental in securing the consent of Europe to the Pragmatic Sanction (1713) of the emperor Charles VI (an arrangement by which the traditional Salic law of succession, which permitted only males to inherit the throne, was set aside to allow the family dominions to pass to Charles's eldest daughter, Maria Theresa). He was appointed (1751) by Maria Theresa tutor to her son, who later ascended the Austrian throne as Joseph II.

Bartered Bride, The. [Czech title, **Prodaná Nevěstá;** German title, **Die Verkaufte Braut.**] Opera by Friedrich Smetana, produced at Prague in 1866. The comedy, introduced by a popular overture, deals with the uniting of Marzhenka and Yenik in spite of parental obstacles.

Bártfa (bärt′fô). Hungarian name of **Bardejov.**

Bartfeld (bärt'felt). German name of **Bardejov.**

Barth (bärt). Town in NE Germany, in the *Land* (state) of Mecklenburg, Russian Zone, formerly in the province of Pomerania, Prussia, situated on the Baltic Sea, ab. 15 mi. W of Stralsund: seaport, with shipyards. Before World War II it had jute spinning and weaving mills, sugar refineries, machine and furniture factories, and some agricultural trade. Its Church of Mary, in the Gothic style, dates from the 13th century. The town was colonized by German settlers in the 13th century, and was famous in the Middle Ages for its breweries and shipyards. It passed to Pomerania in 1325, to Sweden in 1630, and to Prussia in 1815. Pop. 13,794 (1946).

Barth, Heinrich. b. at Hamburg, Germany, Feb. 16, 1821; d. at Berlin, Nov. 25, 1865. German traveler. He was educated at Berlin; traveled (1845–48) through Algeria, Tunis, Tripoli, Egypt, Syria, Asia Minor, Greece, and elsewhere; visited (1850–55), many others, the Sahara region, Bornu, Adamawa, Kanem, Baghirmi, Sokoto, Timbuktu; discovered the Binue River (June 18, 1851); and traveled later in Asia Minor, Turkey, and Greece. Among his works are *Wanderungen durch die Küstenländer des Mittelmeers* (1849; Eng. trans., *Journeys through the Border Lands of the Mediterranean*), *Reisen und Entdeckungen in Nord- und Centralafrika* (1855–58; Eng. trans., *Journeys and Discoveries in Northern and Central Africa*), and works on the dialects of C Africa (1862–64).

Barth, Jean. See **Bart, Jean.**

Barth, Karl. b. at Basel, Switzerland, Oct. 5, 1886—. Swiss Protestant Reformed theologian and educator, noted as an advocate of "crisis" and "dialectical" theology. He was educated at the universities of Bern, Berlin, Tübingen, and Marburg, became (1909) a vicar at Geneva, served (1911–21) as pastor at Safenwil, Switzerland, was named (1930) professor of systematic theology at the University of Bonn, and became (1935) a professor at the University of Basel. His philosophical views, which became very influential after World War I, hold that the divine is a contradiction of the knowable, that man cannot apprehend God by either reason or works, and that the alternatives to faith in the scheme of divine salvation are ruin and chaos. Author of *Der Römerbrief* (1919), *Die Auferstehung der Toten* (1924), *Das Wort Gottes und die Theologie* (1925), *Kirchliche Dogmatik* (1932 *et seq.*), and *Die grosse Barmherzigkeit* (1935).

Barth, Kaspar von. b. at Küstrin, in Brandenburg, June 21, 1587; d. at Leipzig, Sept. 17, 1658. German classical philologist. He is said to have read and elucidated nearly all the Greek and Roman authors. He published *Adversaria* in 60 books.

Barth, Paul. b. c1857; d. 1922. German philosopher, and a founder of the historical philosophical school in Germany. In *Die Philosophie der Geschichte als Soziologie* (1897) he rejected the division of science and the humanities, and identified sociology with the philosophy of history.

Barth, Theodor. b. at Duderstadt, in Hanover, Germany; July 16, 1849; d. at Baden-Baden, Germany, June 2, 1909. German publicist. He practiced law (1871–72), was a magistrate at Bremerhaven (1872–76), and was executive secretary of the Bremen Chamber of Commerce (1876–83). He became a Liberal member of the Reichstag in 1881. He edited (1883–1907) *Die Nation*, a weekly paper, and published *Amerikanisches Wirtschaftsleben* (1887) and *Amerikanische Eindrücke* (1896).

Barth Bank. [Former name, **Bart Bank.**] Submarine bank in Antarctica, lying SE of the South Orkney Islands, in the northernmost reaches of the Weddell Sea; in ab. 62°58′ S., 41°15′ W. Named for Einar Barth, a Norwegian whale gunner who discovered the bank in 1937.

Barthe (bärth), **Richmond.** b. at Bay St. Louis, Miss., Jan. 28, 1901—. American Negro sculptor, noted for his expressive figures, portraits, and larger works in public buildings and collections in the U.S., England, Germany, Virgin Islands, Austria, Rumania, and Africa. He studied at the Art Institute of Chicago, the Art Students League, New York, and received an M.A. degree at Xavier University. His work has been extensively exhibited, and he has won many prizes and awards. His works include *Toussaint L'Overture*, *Henry Tanner*, *Booker T. Washington*, *Paul Lawrence Dunbar*, *The Devil Crab Man*, *The Blackberry Woman*, *The Harmonica Player*, *African Dancer*, and *John Gielgud as Hamlet*.

Barthel (bär'tel), **Max.** b. at Loschwitz, near Dresden, Germany, Nov. 17, 1893—. German poet and novelist.

Barthélemy (bȧr.tāl.mē), **Auguste Marseille.** b. at Marseilles, 1796; d. there, Aug. 23, 1867. French satirical poet and author. He wrote many works, chiefly in collaboration with Joseph Méry, as *La Villéliade* (1827), *Napoléon en Égypte* (1828), and others. Also with Méry, he founded (1831) the periodical *Némésis*, in which the authors wrote against the existing French government.

Barthélemy, François, Marquis **de.** b. at Aubagne, France, Oct. 20, 1747; d. at Paris, April 3, 1830. French diplomat and politician. At the beginning of the French Revolution he was minister to Switzerland, and negotiated (1795) the treaties of Basel (one with Prussia and one with Spain). In 1797 he became a member of the Directory, but was deposed later in the same year, and was sent to French Guiana, where he remained for a period of two years. He later became a senator under Napoleon I. After Napoleon's fall he supported the Bourbons and was made a peer under Louis XVIII.

Barthélemy, Jean Jacques. b. at Cassis, near Marseilles, Jan. 20, 1716; d. at Paris, April 30, 1795. French antiquarian and man of letters.

Barthélemy, Joseph. b. at Toulouse, France, June 9, 1874; d. in May, 1945. French politician and professor of law (1913) at the University of Paris. A member (1919–28) of the Chamber of Deputies, he headed a moderate democratic group. He served also as a delegate (1922) to the League of Nations. Minister of justice (Jan. 27, 1941–March 26, 1943) during World War II in the Vichy government, he died while awaiting trial for treason.

Barthélemy Saint-Hilaire (saṅ.tē.ler), **Jules.** b. Aug. 19, 1805; d. Nov. 24, 1895. French statesman, philosopher, and Orientalist, a professor at the Collège de France and member of the French Institute. He became a member of the Assembly in 1848, refused to recognize the coup d'état of 1851, and under the French Third Republic was a deputy and senator, and minister of foreign affairs (1880–81). Among his works are a translation of Aristotle (1839–44), *Sur les Védas* (1854), *Du Bouddhisme* (1855), *Mahomet et le Coran* (1865), *Pensées de Marc Aurèle* (1876), *Philosophie des deux Ampères* (1866), and *Étude sur François Bacon* (1890).

Barthez (bȧr.tez) or **Barthès** (-tes), **Paul Joseph.** b. at Montpellier, France, Dec. 11, 1734; d. at Paris, Oct. 15, 1806. French physician and scientific writer. He was a believer in vitalism, a theory maintaining that the life force is separate and distinct from both mind and body (in effect, a "third quantity" of being). Author of *Nouveaux éléments de la science de l'homme* (1778) and *Nouvelle mécanique des mouvements de l'homme et des animaux* (1798).

Barthold (bär'tolt), **Friedrich Wilhelm.** b. at Berlin, Sept. 4, 1799; d. Jan. 14, 1858. German historian. He became a professor of history at Greifswald, Germany, in 1834. Among his works are *Der Römerzug König Heinrichs von Lützelburg* (1830–31), *Geschichte von Rügen und Pommern* (1839–45), *Geschichte des grossen deutschen Kriegs vom Tode Gustav Adolfs ab* (1843), and *Geschichte der deutschen Städte* (1850–52).

Bartholdi (bȧr.tol.dē), **Frédéric Auguste.** b. at Colmar, in Alsace, April 2, 1834; d. at Paris, Oct. 4, 1904. French sculptor. Best known among his works is the statue of *Liberty Enlightening the World* (*Liberté Éclairant le Monde*; commonly called the Statue of Liberty) on Bedloe's Island in New York harbor, presented (1885) to the people of the U.S. by the people of France; it was dedicated in 1886. Other notable examples of his work include a statue of Lafayette in Union Square, New York, and the *Lion of Belfort* (*Le Lion de Belfort*), marking the historic defense (1870–71) of Belfort in the Franco-Prussian War.

Bartholdt (bär'tōlt), **Richard.** b. at Schleiz, Germany, Nov. 2, 1855; d. at St. Louis, Mo., March 19, 1932. American editor and politician. He arrived (1872) in America as a boy. He was editor in chief (1885–92) of the St. Louis *Tribune*. A member (1888–92) and president (1891–92) of the St. Louis school board, he served also as a representative (1893–1915) from the tenth Missouri district to Congress. Author of *From Steerage to Congress* (1930).

Bartholdy (bär.tol′dē), **Jakob Salomon.** b. at Berlin, May 11, 1779; d. at Rome, July 27, 1825. German diplomat, art collector, and patron of art. For his house at Rome he commissioned various works by the so-called Nazarene school of classical and historical painters. Author of *Der Krieg der Tiroler Landleute* (1814) and others.

Bartholin (bär′tō.lēn), **Kaspar.** b. at Malmö, Sweden, Feb. 12, 1585; d. at Copenhagen, July 13, 1629. Danish physician and scholar; father of Thomas Bartholin. He became professor of oratory at the University of Copenhagen in 1611, of medicine in 1615, and of theology in 1624. His textbook on anatomy, *Institutiones anatomicae* (1611), was highly regarded in the 17th century.

Bartholin, Thomas. b. Oct. 20, 1616; d. Dec. 4, 1680. Danish physician and scholar; son of Kaspar Bartholin (1585–1629), and father of Kaspar Bartholin (1655–1738). He was a professor of mathematics at the University of Copenhagen in 1646, and of medicine in the period 1647–61. He wrote on anatomy and medicine, and revised (1641) his father's *Institutiones anatomicae.* He also described his observations on the lymph glands.

Bartholo (bår.to.lō). In Beaumarchais's comedy *Le Barbier de Séville*, an old doctor who has become the type of the jealous guardian. He proposes to marry his ward Rosine, who is enamored of Count Almaviva. As Bartolo, he appears in Rossini's opera, *The Barber of Seville.* Again as Bartolo, he also appears as a less important character, and furnishes the part of comic bass, in Mozart's *Le Nozze di Figaro* (*The Marriage of Figaro*).

Bartholomaeus Anglicus (bär.thol.ǫ.mē′us ang′gli.kus), or **Bartholomew the Englishman** (bär.thol′ǫ.mū). fl. 1230–50. English Franciscan friar, and professor of theology at Paris and later in Saxony. He is frequently confused with another English Franciscan, Bartholomew de Glanville, who lived in the next century. He is noted as the author of *De proprietatibus rerum*, an encyclopedia widely used and translated throughout Europe, and still current in the late 16th century. Shakespeare is believed to have been well acquainted with it. This work, although remarkably comprehensive and methodical, represented, nonetheless, a state of knowledge which had already been superseded at the time of its writing. For example, its astronomy was in the early medieval tradition (specifically, of the 5th century), and for this reason included allusions to a geo-heliocentrical system which had long since lost currency in the world of science. The geography and natural history were more advanced, and the herbal was by far the most notable work of its kind written by an Englishman in the Middle Ages. Also, the political geography contains a quantity of information which had never previously been collected in one work. Its account of the division of time was curious: the day is divided into 24 hours, the hour into four points or 40 moments, the moment into 12 ounces, the ounce into 47 atoms (and thus there are 22,560 atoms in an hour, as compared with our 3,600 seconds). The work was translated from Latin into Italian (1309), into French (1372), into Provençal (before 1391), into English (1397 or 1398), and into Spanish (sometime in the 15th century).

Bartholomäussee (bär″tō.lō.mā′ūs.zā). See **Königssee.**

Bartholomé (bår.to.lo.mā), **Paul Albert.** b. at Thiverval, France, Aug. 29, 1848; d. at Paris, Nov. 2, 1928. French painter and sculptor who was president (1921–24) of the Société Nationale des Beaux Arts. Many honors were bestowed upon him, including the Grand Prix for sculpture at the Exposition Universelle (1900), designation as an officer of the Legion of Honor (1911), and election as a corresponding member of the Academies in England, Spain, and Belgium. In the field of sculpture, his *Monument aux Morts* (1899) in the Père-Lachaise cemetery, Paris, is considered his greatest work; among his better-known works in painting and sculpture are *Jeune Fille se Lamentant*, a bust of Jean Jacques Rousseau, *La Douleur*, and *Enfant Pleurant.*

Bartholomew (bär.thol′ǫ.mū), Saint. One of the Twelve apostles of Jesus Christ, mentioned in Matt. x. 3; Mark, iii. 18; Luke, vi. 14; Acts, i. 13; not mentioned in John, but it is widely believed that he was identical with Nathanael, referred to in John i. 45–51 and xxi. 2. The name, in the Aramaic language, means "son of Talmai." Little is known of his work. According to Eusebius he went as an evangelist to India, but that term may have been applied to a region more or less W of India as known today; it is also said that he preached in Mesopotamia, Persia, Egypt, Armenia, Lycaonia, and Phrygia. There is also a tradition that he suffered martyrdom by flaying in Armenia. Pictorially he has been shown (for instance, in Michelangelo's *Last Judgment*) flayed and holding his own skin in his hands. In the early Christian period there was current a gospel attributed to Saint Bartholomew.

Bartholomew, Massacre of Saint. See **Saint Bartholomew, Massacre of.**

Bartholomew Bayou. River which rises in Arkansas, near Pine Bluff, and joins the Ouachita River in N Louisiana. Length, ab. 265 mi.

Bartholomew Cokes (kōks). See **Cokes, Bartholomew.**

Bartholomew de Glanville (dę glan′vil). fl. 14th century; d. 1360. English Franciscan friar. Virtually nothing is known about either his life or his accomplishments, but he has acquired a curious niche in history through the fact that he has long been confused with Bartholomaeus Anglicus (who actually lived a century earlier); indeed, some modern reference works actually cite Bartholomaeus Anglicus as a variant name of Bartholomew de Glanville.

Bartholomew Fair. Fair formerly held at Smithfield, London, beginning on St. Bartholomew's day, in August, and lasting for about two weeks. It was first held by royal charter in 1133; in 1691 it was shortened from 14 to 4 days; in 1753, owing to the change to the New Style calendar, it opened on Sept. 3; in 1840 it was removed to Islington; and in 1855 it came to an end. It was originally the great cloth fair of England and a market for all kinds of goods. Its provision for popular amusements, however, gradually destroyed its character as a market, and it became simply an occasion for merrymaking. The Bartholomew pig, often alluded to by past writers, was a chief dainty at the fair.

Bartholomew Fair. Comedy by Ben Jonson, acted first in 1614 and published in 1631. It is a satire on Puritanism, and roused considerable opposition in the period between its first performance and the English Civil War. After the Restoration, however, it was received with applause.

Bartholomew of Bologna (bǫ.lōn′yą). b. at Bologna, Italy, toward the end of the 13th century; d. probably at what is now called Erzurum, in Turkey, Aug. 15, 1333. Italian ecclesiastic, a member of the Dominican order, notable as the first scholar from Western Europe to acquire an intimate knowledge of Armenian (the next Armenologists did not appear until the 17th century). He translated a considerable amount of religious literature into Armenian (he has been credited with the Bible, the Dominican breviary, missal, ritual, and much of the work of Saint Thomas Aquinas in Armenian, but there is considerable doubt as to how much he actually did), and was for many years bishop of Maragha (or Maragheh), in what is now Iran. The fact that both the place of his bishopric (Maragha) and probable place of his death (Erzurum) are not, from their present names, obviously Armenian may give rise to some confusion; actually, both are in areas which were then (and still are, to a greater or lesser extent) possessed of a considerable Armenian population.

Bartholomew of Bruges (brözh). [Latinized, **Bartholomaeus de Brugis.**] d. c1354–56. Flemish physician, philosopher, and commentator on the works of Aristotle. Little is known about a great part of his life (and nothing at all about his early years), but he is known to have obtained a medical degree at Montpellier sometime before 1315. From c1330 to 1342 he was physician to the count of Blois and was occasionally consulted by members of the French royal family. Many writings have been ascribed to him, perhaps the most interesting of which is a medical work entitled *Remedium epydimie*, which may have been composed at the time of the Black Death (although this is unproven) and which asserts that dying people are more infectious than others.

Bartholomew of Messina (me.sē′nạ). fl. 1258–66. Italian scholar, notable for his translations from Greek into Latin of various Aristotelian and pseudo-Aristotelian works, and also of a treatise by Hierocles on the veterinary art. Some authorities have thought that *Lu libru de la maniscalchia di li cavalli*, a treatise on the veterinary art in 50 chapters, written in Sicilian dialect, may actually be Bartholomew's translation of Hierocles' work, but this is as yet unproven.

Bartholomew of Parma (pär′mä). b. at Parma, Italy; fl. at Bologna, Italy, 1286–97. Italian astrologer and geomancer. His best-known work, *Ars geomantiae*, was the most elaborate treatise on geomancy written in that age. It attracted considerable attention, and a few years later, in 1294, he wrote an abridgment of it for two German friends, and in 1295 he composed another abridgment. One of these texts was translated into French before the end of the 14th century.

Bartholomew of Salerno (sä.ler′nō). [Latinized, **Bartholomaeus Salernitanus.**] fl. first half of the 12th century. Italian writer on medicine. He was the author of a treatise (*Practica*) on pathology and therapeutics which, judging from the number of commentaries and translations into various vernaculars, enjoyed great popularity in Western Europe (although some of the translations appear to be based on other texts as well as his).

Bartholomew's Hospital. Hospital at Smithfield, London, founded in 1123.

Bartholomew-the-Great, Saint. Church at Smithfield, London, founded in 1123, and chiefly Norman in its style. It shares with the chapel of the Tower of London a claim to be the oldest church in the city. The existing church (which was not damaged in World War II) consists of the choir, transepts, and one bay of the nave; the remainder of the nave, which was probably later, was destroyed by Henry VIII. The handsome Lady chapel in decorated Gothic style was long used as a factory, but was later restored. The church was founded by Rahere, a jester of Henry I of England, who became a monk. His tomb, on the north side of the sanctuary, is of a later date than his effigy, which is placed upon it.

Bartholow (bär′thọ.lō), **Roberts.** b. at New Windsor, Md., Nov. 28, 1831; d. at Philadelphia, May 10, 1904. American physician. He performed an experimental operation for a brain tumor which, although valuable to science, hastened the death of the patient (who, knowing that he was hopelessly ill, had given his consent). Bartholow's moral right in the matter was the center of violent controversy (1874), but he was ultimately vindicated. He received his M.D. (1852) from the University of Maryland, served as an assistant surgeon (1855 *et seq.*) in the U.S. army, and was a professor of medical chemistry (1864 *et seq.*) at Ohio Medical College and a professor (1879 *et seq.*) at Jefferson Medical College. He was founder and editor of the *Clinic*, a medical journal, and author of *Practical Treatise on Materia Medica and Therapeutics* (1876) and *Treatise on the Practise of Medicine* (1880).

Barthou (bȧr.tö), **Louis.** [Full name, **Jean Louis Firmin Barthou.**] b. at Oloron-Ste.-Marie, France, Aug. 25, 1862; assassinated at Marseilles, France, Oct. 9, 1934. French statesman and lawyer, slain, while foreign minister of France, at the side of King Alexander I of Yugoslavia whom he had gone to Marseilles to welcome to France. He was elected to the Chamber of Deputies in 1889 and to the Senate in 1922. Named minister of public works in the Dupuy cabinet (1894), he subsequently held the following ministries: interior (1898), public works (1906–09), justice (1909, 1913, 1922, 1926), war (1921–22), and foreign affairs (1934). As premier and minister of education (March 21–Dec. 9, 1913), he forced through the Chamber of Deputies a law establishing a three-year term of military service, as a result of which the French army entered World War I with expanded reserves. As foreign minister in the Doumergue cabinet, he sought to strengthen France's military alliances. He was elected (1918) to the French Academy.

Bartin (bär.tin′). [Also, **Bartan** (-tän′).] Town in N Turkey, in the *il* (vilayet) of Zonguldak, near the Black Sea ab. 48 mi. NE of Ereğli, ab. 120 mi. NW of Ankara: important lumber industry, with pine, oak, box, and chestnut the most important trees; sawmills. Pop. ab. 9,000.

Bartleby the Scrivener: A Story of Wall Street (bär′-tl.bi). Allegorical tale by Herman Melville, published anonymously in 1853 and included in *The Piazza Tales* (1856).

Bartlesville (bär′tlz.vil). City in NE Oklahoma, county seat of Washington County, on the Caney River, ab. 30 mi. SW of Coffeyville, Kansas, in a petroleum-producing and agricultural region: processing center for zinc; manufactures ceramic retorts. The city lies in the Coowee-scoo-wee district, formerly owned by the Cherokees. 19,228 (1950).

Bartlet (bärt′lẹt), **William.** b. at Newburyport, Mass., Jan. 31, 1748; d. Feb. 8, 1841. American merchant, textile manufacturer, and philanthropist, a benefactor of Andover Theological Seminary.

Bartlett (bärt′lẹt), **Elisha.** b. at Smithfield, R.I., Oct. 6, 1804; d. there, July 19, 1855. American physician. He was professor of materia medica and medical jurisprudence (1851–55) at the College of Physicians and Surgeons at New York.

Bartlett, Frederic Charles. b. 1886—. English psychologist, and anthropologist, chiefly noted for experimental work on the processes of thinking and memory. He was educated at Cambridge University, and the University of London, where he received (1909) a B.A. degree. In 1931 he was appointed a professor at Cambridge. He was elected (1947) a member of U.S. National Academy of Sciences. His works include *Psychology and Primitive Culture* (1923) and *The Problem of Noise* (1934).

Bartlett, Frederic Clay. b. at Chicago, June 1, 1873; d. at Beverly, Mass., June 25, 1953. American painter, best known for his murals. He studied with Whistler at Paris, and has exhibited in the U.S. and Europe. He became a member of the Royal Academy at Munich, and won many prizes in the U.S. Some of his better-known works are *Blue Blinds*, *Evening White*, *Roman Afternoon*, and *Canton Street*.

Bartlett, Homer Newton. b. at Olive, Ulster County, N.Y., Dec. 28, 1845; d. at Hoboken, N.J., April 3, 1920. American musician and composer, organist at the Marble Collegiate Church, New York, for 12 years and at the Madison Avenue Baptist Church for 31 years. A prolific composer, he wrote what is considered his most profound work, *Opus I*, *Grand Polka de Concert* (1867), as a birthday present to his fiancée. His opus numbers in the publisher's catalogue had risen to 269 before his death.

Bartlett, Ichabod. b. at Salisbury, N.H., July 24, 1786; d. Oct. 19, 1853. American lawyer and politician. He was a member (1819 *et seq.*) of the New Hampshire legislature (several times speaker of the house), and served as counsel for Woodward in the Dartmouth College case (1817); in 1822 he was elected to Congress.

Bartlett, John. b. at Plymouth, Mass., June 14, 1820; d. at Cambridge, Mass., Dec. 3, 1905. American publisher and editor. He became a member of the publishing house of Little, Brown and Company, at Boston, in 1863, and was the senior partner in the period 1878–89. At that time he had already completed the work with which he is now identified, the compilation *Familar Quotations: Being an Attempt to Trace to their Sources Passages and Phrases in Common Use* (1855: the most recent major revision, by Christopher Morley and Louella D. Everett, appeared in 1937). He also compiled a concordance to Shakespeare (1894).

Bartlett, John Russell. b. at Providence, R.I., Oct. 23, 1805; d. there, May 28, 1886. American antiquarian and historian. After engaging (1837–49) in business as a bookseller at New York, he was appointed (1850) one of the commissioners to establish the boundary line between the U.S. and Mexico. He served later (1855–72) as secretary of state for Rhode Island. He wrote a *Dictionary of Americanisms* (1850; revised edition, 1877), a *Bibliography of Rhode Island* (1864), *Literature of the Rebellion* (1866), *Primeval Man* (1868), and others.

Bartlett, John Sherren. b. in Dorsetshire, England, 1790; d. Aug. 23, 1863. American journalist. A surgeon in the British navy during the War of 1812, he was captured and decided to remain in America. He established (1822) the *Albion*, a newspaper devoted to acquainting Americans with news of England.

Bartlett, Joseph. b. at Plymouth, Mass., June 10, 1762; d. at Boston, Oct. 20, 1827. American satirical poet, author of *Physiognomy*, recited before the Harvard Phi Beta Kappa Society in 1799.

Bartlett, Josiah. b. at Amesbury, Mass., Nov. 21, 1729; d. May 19, 1795. American patriot and statesman. He was a member of the committee of safety of New Hampshire in 1775, a member of the Continental Congress and a signer of the Declaration of Independence in 1776, chief justice of New Hampshire (1778–90), and "president" and first governor of New Hampshire (1790–94). He was a physician by profession.

Bartlett, Paul Wayland. b. at New Haven, Conn., Jan. 24, 1865; d. at Paris, Sept. 20, 1925. American sculptor, noted especially for such heroic portraitures as *Lafayette* in the Louvre, *Benjamin Franklin* at Waterbury, Conn., *Alexander Agassiz* at Boston, and *Robert Morris* at Philadelphia. He studied and worked for much of his life in France, where he received many honors; in the U.S. he served as president (1918) of the National Sculpture Society. A romantic who eschewed contemporary subjects, Bartlett carefully documented his work; to all his monumental statues may be applied the phrase he used to refer to his *Lafayette:* "as a fact and as a symbol."

Bartlett, Robert Abram. [Called **"Captain Bob Bartlett."**] b. at Brigus, Newfoundland, 1875; d. 1946. American arctic explorer. He sailed to the Arctic with Peary in 1897–98, and was master of Peary's ship, the *Roosevelt,* on the expeditions of 1905–06 and 1908–09 (on the last of these expeditions, which led to Peary's announcement of discovery of the North Pole, Bartlett accompanied Peary as far as latitude 80° 47′ N.). In the Canadian government expedition of 1913–14, under Stefansson, Bartlett commanded the *Karluk,* which was frozen in near Point Barrow and drifted until crushed in the ice near Wrangel Island. Bartlett, accompanied by an Eskimo, made his way to Siberia, where he enlisted help and returned to rescue 13 of the *Karluk's* party. Bartlett commanded the third Crocker Land Relief Expedition to N Greenland (1917), and expeditions to NW Alaska (1925), N Greenland and Ellesmere Island (1926), Baffin Island (1927), Siberia (1928), Labrador (1929), and Greenland (1930). He was the author of *The Last Voyage of the Karluk* (1916), *The Log of Bob Bartlett* (1928), and *Sails Over Ice* (1934).

Bartlett, Samuel Colcord. b. at Salisbury, N.H., Nov. 25, 1817; d. Nov. 16, 1898. American educator and Congregational clergyman. He was professor of philosophy and rhetoric at Western Reserve College (1846–52), professor of Biblical literature at the Chicago Theological Seminary (1858–77), and president of Dartmouth College (1877 *et seq.*). He wrote *From Egypt to Palestine* (1879) and several religious works.

Bartlett, Vernon. b. at Westbury, Wiltshire, England, April 30, 1894—. English novelist and radio broadcaster. A special correspondent (1919–22) for the London *Times,* and a regular broadcaster (1928–34) on foreign affairs, he is known as the founder and publisher of the *World Review.* Author of *Mud and Khaki* (1916), *Topsy Turvy* (1927), *No Man's Land* (1930), *If I Were Dictator* (1935), *This is My Life* (1938), and *Tomorrow Always Comes* (1943).

Bartlett, William Henry. b. at London, March 26, 1809; d. Sept. 13, 1854. English draftsman, traveler, writer, and editor. He illustrated works on Palestine, Switzerland, and America, and was the author and illustrator of *Walks about Jerusalem* (1844), *Forty Days in the Desert* (1848), *The Nile Boat* (1849), *Pictures from Sicily* (1853), *The Pilgrim Fathers* (1853), and others.

Bartley (bärt'li), **Elias Hudson.** b. at Bartleyville, N.J., Dec. 6, 1849; d. Jan. 12, 1937. American physician and professor of chemistry. He was professor (1875–78) of chemistry at Swarthmore College, instructor (1880–86) and professor (1886–1915) at Long Island College Hospital, and chief chemist (1882–88) of the Brooklyn Health Department. Author of *Textbook of Medical and Pharmaceutical Chemistry* (7th ed., 1909) and *Manual of Clinical Chemistry* (3rd ed., 1907).

Bartley, Mordecai. b. in Fayette County, Pa., Dec. 16, 1783; d. at Mansfield, Ohio, Oct. 10, 1870. American politician. He served as a member of Congress from Ohio (1823–31) and governor of Ohio (1844–46).

Bartning (bärt'ning), **Otto.** b. at Karlsruhe, Germany, April 12, 1883—. German architect, best known for his attempt to introduce the principles and forms of modern industrial design into church architecture. Director (1926–30) of the state academy of architecture at Weimar, he was afterwards active at Berlin. He wrote *Vom neuen Kirchenbau* (1918).

Bartók (bôr'tōk; Anglicized, bär'tok), **Béla.** b. at Nagyszentmiklós, Hungary (now in Yugoslavia), March 25, 1881; d. at New York, Sept. 26, 1945. Hungarian composer and pianist, noted for the incorporation of folk tunes into his concert works. After making his first public appearance (1891) as a pianist and composer, he studied piano at Pressburg (now Bratislava) during the period 1893–99 with Lászlό Erkel, and at Budapest (1899–1903) with Stephan Thoman. His programmatic *Kossuth* symphony (1903), using the strains of the Austrian national anthem, was the first indication of his special interest in folk music; realizing that very little of what had popularly come to be regarded as Magyar music was ethnologically correct, he collaborated with Zoltan Kodály in an investigation of the various Slavic strains of music, published *Hungarian Folk Music,* the standard work in the field, and collected over 6,000 Slavic folk-tunes. Professor (1907–12) of piano at the Royal Hungarian Musical Academy at Budapest, he first received recognition as a composer in Hungary with his ballet *The Wooden Prince* (1917) and the opera *Duke Bluebeard's Castle* (1911), performed first in 1918; with the performance (1918) of his *Second String Quartet* he became the chief figure in the world of Hungarian music. The orchestral *Deux Images* (Opus 10) was the first of his works to be performed (1919) in America. In 1940 he moved to America, where he thereafter performed and composed. His compositions in every musical form include *The Miraculous Mandarin* (1919), a ballet long banned for its overt portrayal of basic passions; *Concerto for Orchestra* (1944); concertos for piano (1926, 1931, 1945) and violin (1938); five string quartets (1908, 1917, 1927, 1928, 1934); many works for piano, such as the collection of *Mikrokosmos* (1935); and vocal works for both solo voices and chorus.

Bartol (bär.tol'), **Cyrus Augustus.** b. April 30, 1813; d. Dec. 16, 1900. American Unitarian clergyman, pastor (1861–87) of the West Church at Boston. He was the author of *Discourses on the Christian Spirit and Life* (1850), *Pictures of Europe* (1855), *Radical Problems* (1872), and of various other works on ethical and religious topics.

Bartoli (bär'tō.lē), **Adolfo.** b. in Tuscany, Italy, Nov. 19, 1833; d. at Genoa, May 16, 1894. Italian historian of literature. He was associated (1856–59) with the editorial management of the *Archivio storico italiano,* and became (1874) a professor at the Instituto dei Studii Superiori at Florence. Author of *Storia della litteratura italiana* (1877).

Bartoli, Daniello. b. at Ferrara, Feb. 12, 1608; d. at Rome, Jan. 12, 1685. Italian priest, historian, and physicist, for many years rector of the College of Jesuits at Rome. He wrote the important 27-volume *Istoria della compagnia di Gesù* (1630–73), and various treatises on physics (*Del Suono,* 1680; *Della tensione e pressione,* 1677).

Bartoli, Pietro Santi. [Called **Il Perugino.**] b. c1635; d. at Rome, Nov. 7, 1700. Italian engraver and painter; pupil of Nicolas Poussin. His engravings after Renaissance monuments have now been for the most part lost or destroyed. In spite of nickname, there is no relationship between Bartoli and the painter always referred to as Perugino (the name merely indicates residence or birth at Perugia).

Bartolini (bär.tō.lē'nē), **Lorenzo.** b. at Vernio, in Tuscany, Italy, 1777; d. at Florence, 1850. Italian sculptor. In 1797 he went to Paris, where he studied painting under Desmarets and sculpture under F. F. Lemot. He executed a colossal bust of Napoleon, who sent him to Carrara to set up a school of sculpture. He lived the rest of his life at Carrara and Florence. The Demidoff monument in the latter city is usually considered his masterpiece, but other noted works are a *Charity* in the Pitti Palace, Florence, a *Macchiavelli* in the Uffizi Gallery, Florence, and *Faith in God,* now in the Poldi-Pezzoli Museum, Milan.

Bartolo (bär'tō.lō). See also **Bartolus.**

Bartolo. Name of a character in two operas: *Il Barbiere di Siviglia* (*The Barber of Seville*), by Rossini, and *Le Nozze di Figaro* (*The Marriage of Figaro*), by Mozart. See also under **Bartholo.**

Bartolommeo (bär.tō.lôm.mā'ō), Fra. [Also: **Bartolomeo**; original name, **Bartolommeo di Pagholo del Fattorino**; called **Baccio della Porta.**] b. at Savignano, Tuscany, Italy, March 28, 1472; d. near Florence, Oct. 31,

1517. Italian painter of the Florentine school. He was a pupil of Cosimo Rosselli, and was greatly influenced by his study of the works of Leonardo da Vinci, and also by Giovanni Bellini and Giorgione, whose works he saw while at Venice. An adherent of Girolamo Savonarola, he retired in 1500 to a monastery at Florence after destroying all his previous works. In 1504 he resumed his art, and founded (1509) a school at Florence; he was a friend of Raphael. Among his paintings are *St. Mark*, *Marriage of St. Catherine* (Pitti Palace, Florence), and others done in partnership with Mariotto Albertinelli, such as *The Last Judgment* (Uffizi, Florence). He was given the name Baccio della Porta because he lived close to the Porta Romana.

Bartolommeo da Pisa (dä pē′zä). d. 1401. Italian physician, a member of the Franciscan order. The date of his birth has not yet been ascertained, but it is known that he was a centenarian at the time of his death. He was the author of *Epitoma medicinae*, a summary of medical knowledge.

Bartolommeo da Varignana (vä.rē.nyä′nä). b. at Bologna, Italy; d. there, 1318. Italian physician. His practice of medicine at Bologna brought him fame and wealth at a comparatively young age, and it is known that he was employed by the city to teach medicine. The earliest post-mortem examination of which we have formal record was made by him, assisted by another physician and three surgeons.

Bartolommeo Veneto (ve.nā′tō). b. c1480; d. 1555. Italian painter. It is known that he was a pupil of Gentile Bellini at Venice, and later painted in the manner of the Milanese school; he is known to have lived at Cremona and Ferrara. His earliest known extant work is a *Madonna* dated 1502; a *Madonna and Child* painted in 1505 exhibits a remarkable landscape. Examples of his work have been included in the collections of the Fitzwilliam Museum, Cambridge, England; the Staedel Institut, Frankfort on the Main, Germany; the Ambrosiana, Milan; the Albertina, Vienna; and in private collections in Italy, England, and the U.S.

Bartolozzi (bär.tō.lôt′tsē), **Francesco.** b. at Florence, Sept. 21, 1727; d. at Lisbon, Portugal, March 7, 1813. Italian engraver; grandfather of the singer and actress Lucia Elizabeth Mathews, known professionally as Madame Vestris. He studied engraving for six years in Italy, before going (1764) to London, where he was appointed engraver to the king; he became an original member of the Royal Academy in 1769. In 1802 he went to Lisbon to take charge of the Portuguese Royal Academy. Among his works is a series of engravings after paintings by Guercino. He was for many years associated with Giovanni Battista Cipriani.

Bartolus (bär′tǫ.lus). [Italian, **Bartolo da Sassoferrato.**] b. at Sassoferrato, in what is now the *compartimento* (region) of Marches, Italy, in 1314; d. at Perugia, Italy, in July, 1357. Italian jurist, generally considered to have been one of the greatest of the Middle Ages. He studied law (1327 *et seq.*) at Perugia and Bologna, and was a professor of law at Perugia from 1343 until his death. Considering the comparatively brief span of his life, his activity was prodigious. He wrote a commentary on the Justinian Code (*Corpus juris civilis*), and many treatises on legal questions. His influence continued to be felt until the 17th century, not only in Italy and Germany, but wherever Roman law was cultivated.

Bartolus. In John Fletcher and Philip Massinger's play *The Spanish Curate*, a greedy, unprincipled lawyer, the husband of Amaranta.

Barton (bär′tǫn). Town (in Vermont the equivalent of township in many other states) and village in NE Vermont, in Orleans County, in a summer resort area. Pop. of town, 3,298 (1950); of village, 1,267 (1950).

Barton, Amos. See **Amos Barton.**

Barton, Andrew. d. Aug. 2, 1511. Scottish naval commander in the service of James IV of Scotland. He announced his success in clearing the Scottish coast of Flemish pirates by sending the monarch three barrels filled with pirates' heads. He obtained letters of marque (documents authorizing him to capture and confiscate vessels) against the Portuguese, but, as his capture of Portuguese merchantmen inflicted damage on the trade of London, he was attacked by Sir Thomas Howard and Sir Edward Howard, acting for Henry VIII of England, and killed in an engagement in the Downs, in the English Channel off the coast of Kent. The incident is celebrated in the ballad *Sir Andrew Barton*.

Barton, Benjamin Smith. b. at Lancaster, Pa., Feb. 10, 1766; d. at Philadelphia, Dec. 19, 1815. American physician, naturalist, and ethnologist, father of Thomas Pennant Barton, and uncle of William Paul Crillon Barton. He wrote *New Views on the Origin of the Tribes of America* (1797), *Elements of Botany* (1803), the first American elementary botany text, and others.

Barton, Bernard. [Called the **"Quaker Poet."**] b. at Carlisle, England, Jan. 31, 1784; d. at Woodbridge, England, Feb. 19, 1849. English poet, known as a friend of Charles Lamb. Author of *Metrical Effusions* (1812), *Poems by an Amateur* (1818), and *Poems and Letters* (1849).

Barton, Bruce. b. at Robbins, Tenn., Aug. 5, 1886—. American advertising executive, politician, and author; son of William Eleazar Barton. A graduate (1907) of Amherst, he was managing editor (1909–11) of *The Housekeeper* and editor (1914–18) of *Every Week*, before becoming (1918) the head of what became the advertising firm of Batten, Barton, Durstine and Osborn, Inc.; he was also a congressman (1937–41) from New York. Author of *More Power to You* (1917), *It's a Good Old World* (1920), *Better Days* (1924), *The Man Nobody Knows* (1925), *The Book Nobody Knows* (1926), *What Can a Man Believe?* (1927), *On the Up and Up* (1929), and others.

Barton, Clara. [Full name, **Clarissa Harlowe Barton.**] b. at Oxford, Mass., Dec. 25, 1821; d. at Glen Echo, Md., April 12, 1912. American philanthropist, an organizer of the American Red Cross. She entered the Union military hospital service at the beginning of the Civil War, and was placed in charge of the hospitals at the front of the Army of the James in 1864. At the beginning of the Franco-Prussian War she assisted the Grand Duchess of Baden in the organization of military hospitals. Subsequently she superintended the supplying of work to the poor of Strasbourg in 1871, and the distribution of supplies to the destitute in Paris in 1872. She organized the American Red Cross Society in 1881, and was its president in the period 1882–1904. In 1883 she was appointed superintendent of the reformatory for women at Sherborn, Mass. As president of the Red Cross Society, she superintended the expedition of relief to the sufferers from the overflow of the Ohio and Mississippi rivers in 1884, and in 1893 was put in charge of the relief for the sufferers from a cyclone on the South Atlantic coast. As president of the American National Red Cross Society she also went from the U.S. to Constantinople to administer (Jan. 22–Sept. 12, 1896) the funds of the National Armenian Relief Committee. She superintended relief work during the Spanish-American War (1898) and the Boer War (1899–1902), and conducted Red Cross work at Galveston, Texas, in August, 1900. She wrote *History of the Red Cross in Peace and War* (1898) and others.

Barton, Sir **Edmund.** b. at Sydney, Australia, Jan. 18, 1849; d. at Medlow Bath, New South Wales, Australia, Jan. 7, 1920. Australian statesman, political figure, and leading advocate of Australian federation, first prime minister of the Commonwealth of Australia and first high court judge. He was educated at the University of Sydney (B.A. 1868, M.A. 1870), and called to the Sydney bar in 1871. He entered (1877) politics in New South Wales, and until 1894 served variously as a member of the legislative assembly, its speaker, and occasionally as a minister. A federated Australia was his chief political interest from c1890. A member of the constitutional conventions (1891, 1897–98), he influenced the drafting of the constitution and took a leading part in getting the electorate of New South Wales to accept it, and was a member of the committee to watch the bill through the Imperial parliament in 1900. He formed the first federal ministry, and was confirmed in office at the first federal election on March 20, 1901. Having resigned as prime minister on Sept. 23, 1903, he was immediately appointed as original judge of the newly constituted high court, a post in which he continued until his death.

Barton, Elizabeth. [Called **the "Nun of Kent," the "Maid of Kent."**] b. c1506; executed at Tyburn, London, April 20, 1534. English religious figure and mystic. In 1525, while in domestic service at Aldington, Kent, she was stricken with what appeared to be a nervous illness, accompanied by religious mania and trances. She was admitted to the priory of St. Sepulchre, at Canterbury, in 1527, and began to make prophecies regarding political questions and to denounce the opponents of the Roman Catholic Church, gaining great influence even in high quarters. She inveighed against the marriage of Henry VIII with Anne Boleyn, and after the marriage declared that, like Saul in the Old Testament, Henry was no longer king in the sight of God. This caused her arrest in 1533, and she was executed at Tyburn with Edward Bocking, a Roman Catholic priest, and several others convicted of "treasonable conspiracy."

Barton, Frances. Maiden name of **Abington, Frances.**

Barton, George Aaron. b. at East Farnham, Quebec, Canada, 1859; d. at Weston, Mass., June 28, 1942. American educator and writer. He was graduated (1882) from Haverford College, was professor of biblical literature and Semitic languages (1891–1922) at Bryn Mawr, professor of Semitic languages (1922 *et seq.*) at the University of Pennsylvania, and in 1921 was named director of the American School of Oriental Study and Research at Baghdad. Author of *A Sketch of Semitic Origins, Social and Religious* (1902), *The Heart of the Christian Message* (2nd ed., 1912), *The Religion of Israel* (1918), and *Royal Inscriptions of Sumer and Akkad* (1929).

Barton, George Hunt. b. at Sudbury, Mass., July 8, 1852; d. Nov. 25, 1933. American geologist. He was assistant professor (1884–1904) of geology at the Massachusetts Institute of Technology and at Boston University, and director (1904 *et seq.*) of the Teachers' School of Science. He assisted (1881–83) with the Hawaiian Government Survey at Honolulu; subsequently he was a member (1896) of the sixth Peary expedition to Greenland. Author of *Outline of Elementary Lithology* (1900) and others.

Barton, John Rhea. b. at Lancaster, Pa., in April, 1794; d. at Philadelphia, Jan. 1, 1871. American surgeon, notable as a pioneer in modern orthopedics. He received an M.D. degree (1818) from the University of Pennsylvania Medical School, and became (1823) a member of the surgical staff of Pennsylvania Hospital.

Barton, Port. Bay on the W coast of Palawan, Philippine Islands. It is safe for large vessels in all weather.

Barton, Robert Thomas. b. at Winchester, Va., Nov. 24, 1842; d. Jan. 17, 1917. American lawyer and publisher of colonial documents. Admitted (1865) to the bar, he practiced law at Winchester. He prepared and edited a collection of colonial records published (1909) under the title *Virginia Colonial Decisions: The Reports by Sir John Randolph and Edward Barradall of Decisions of the General Court of Virginia 1728–1741.*

Barton, Seth Maxwell. b. at Fredericksburg, Va., Sept. 8, 1829; d. at Washington, D.C., April 11, 1900. American army officer, with the Confederate army during the Civil War. A graduate (1849) of the U.S. Military Academy, he was at the siege of Vicksburg in the Civil War. He was relieved of his rank of brigadier general following criticism of his part in the defense of Richmond (1864).

Barton, Thomas Pennant. b. at Philadelphia, 1803; d. there, April 5, 1869. American book collector; son of Benjamin Smith Barton. He collected a valuable Shakespearian library, which after his death was acquired by the public library of Boston.

Barton, William. b. at Warren, R.I., May 26, 1748; d. at Providence, R.I., Oct. 22, 1831. American Revolutionary officer. He planned and, with 38 men, executed the capture of the British general Robert Prescott, on July 10, 1777, at the general's headquarters in a farmhouse near Newport, R.I.

Barton, William Eleazar. b. at Sublette, Ill., June 28, 1861; d. at Brooklyn, N.Y., Dec. 7, 1930. American Congregationalist clergyman and writer; father of Bruce Barton. He served as pastor (1899–1924) of the First Church at Oak Park, Ill., and founded (1928) and preached at the Collegeside Church at Nashville, Tenn. He was editor in chief (1913–17) of *The Advance*, and served on the staff (1900–17, 1925 *et seq.*) of *The Youth's Companion.* His writings include *Life of the Hills of Kentucky* (1889), *Pocket Congregational Manual* (1910), *The Parables of Safed the Sage* (1917), *Abraham Lincoln and His Books* (1920), and *The Great Good Man* (1927).

Barton, William Paul Crillon. b. at Philadelphia, Nov. 17, 1786; d. there, Feb. 29, 1856. American botanist; a nephew of Benjamin Smith Barton. He wrote *Flora of North America* (1821–23), *Lectures on Materia Medica and Botany* (1823), and others.

Barton-upon-Humber (bär'tọn.u.pon''hum'bėr). [Also, **Barton-on-Humber.**] Urban district and market town in C England, in Lincolnshire, in the Parts of Lindsay, situated on the river Humber, ab. 7 mi. SW of Kingston-upon-Hull, ab. 174 mi. N of London by rail. 6,235 (1951).

Barton-upon-Irwell (bär'tọn.u.pon''ėr'wel). [Also, **Barton-on-Irwell.**] Former rural district, now incorporated in Worsley urban district, in NW England, in Lancashire, situated on the river Irwell, ab. 5 mi. W of Manchester. The Worsley Canal crosses the river Irwell here on a viaduct. 15,712 (1931).

Bartoszyce (bär.tô.shi'tse). [German, **Bartenstein.**] Town in N Poland, in the *województwo* (province) of Olsztyn, formerly in East Prussia, situated on the Lyna (or Alle) River, ab. 34 mi. SE of Kalingrad. It is located immediately S of the new border between Poland and the U.S.S.R., running through the former East Prussia. Before World War II it was a flour-milling center. It was assigned to Poland at the Potsdam Conference in 1945. Most of the German-speaking inhabitants have now left. 12,912 (1939); 3,449 (1946).

Bartow (bär'tō). City in C Florida, county seat of Polk County, E of Tampa. It was the site of Fort Blount, built during the Seminole War. 8,694 (1950).

Bartow, Edward. b. at Glenham, N.Y., Jan. 12, 1870—. American chemist, professor at the University of Illinois from 1906, and director of the Illinois state water survey from 1905. His publications relate chiefly to the water supply of Illinois and other states. He taught (1920–40) at the University of Iowa, serving at the same time as head of its department of chemistry and chemical engineering.

Bartram (bär'trạm), **John.** b. in Chester County, Pa., March 23, 1699; d. at Kingsessing, Pa., Sept. 22, 1777. American botanist; father of William Bartram. Self-educated, he founded (1728), at Kingsessing, near Philadelphia, the first botanical garden in America. This garden is still in existence as part of the park system of Philadelphia. He corresponded with Linnaeus, and was appointed honorary American botanist to George II of England.

Bartram, William. b. at Kingsessing, Pa., Feb. 9, 1739; d. there, July 22, 1823. American botanist and ornithologist; son of John Bartram. He spent about five years in investigating the animals and plants of the Carolinas, Georgia, and Florida, and prepared the most complete list of American birds in existence before the publication (1808–13) of *American Ornithology* by Alexander Wilson. Author of *Travels through North and South Carolina, Georgia, East and West Florida* (1791).

Bartsch (bärch). German name of the **Barycz.**

Bartsch, Johann Adam Bernhardt, Ritter **von.** b. at Vienna, Aug. 17, 1757; d. there, Aug. 21, 1821. Austrian engraver and historian of engraving. He was a librarian of the Imperial Library and a member of the Academy of Art at Vienna, and in 1816 was appointed custodian of the engravings collection of the library. His most important publication is the monumental *Le Peintre-graveur* (21 vols., 1802–21), a catalogue of engravers and engravings from periods before the 19th century.

Bartsch, Karl. b. at Sprottau, in Silesia, Feb. 25, 1832; d. Feb. 19, 1888. German philologist. He was appointed professor of German and Romance philology at Rostock in 1858, and a professor at Heidelberg in 1871. In addition to his other works, he translated and edited the *Nibelungenlied*, Wolfram von Eschenbach's, *Parzival* and other medieval German works, and compiled chrestomathies (selections) of Provençal and Old French literature, including the *Chrestomathie de l'ancien français.*

Bartsch, Rudolf Hans. b. at Graz, Austria, Feb. 11, 1873—. Austrian novelist. He is also a gifted short-story writer, but has been less successful as a dramatist and lyric poet.

Bartsch, Paul. b. at Tuntschendorf, in Silesia, Aug. 14, 1871—. American zoölogist and authority on malacology. He received his B.S. degree (1896) and his Ph.D. degree (1905) from the State University of Iowa. He was a professor of zoölogy (1899–1939) at George Washington

University, before being associated with the U.S. National Museum, in the division of mollusks (1896–1914, 1920 *et seq.*), and marine invertebrates (1914–20). During World War II, he was a consultant on health problems for the U.S. armed forces.

Baruch (bā'ruk; bãr'uk). In the Old Testament, a Jew who repaired a part of the wall of Jerusalem c446 B.C., after the return of the Jews from the Babylonian Exile, when there was much opposition to the reconstruction of the wall. Neh. iii. 20.

Baruch. In the Old Testament, the amanuensis and faithful friend of the prophet Jeremiah. Jer. xxxii. 13. He is also the nominal author of the book of Baruch in the Apocrypha.

Baruch (bą.rök'), **Bernard Mannes.** b. at Camden, S.C., Aug. 19, 1870—. American stock broker, presidential adviser, and holder of various appointive public offices; son of Simon Baruch. A graduate (1889) of the College of the City of New York, he became a member of the New York Stock Exchange and was appointed (1916) by President Woodrow Wilson to the advisory commission of the National Defense Council. Subsequently he was chairman of the Committee on Raw Materials, Minerals and Metals, chairman (1918–19) of the War Industries Board, and economic adviser (1919) to the American Peace Commission, serving also as a member of the Supreme Economic Council. He was a member of President Wilson's Conference for Capital and Labor (1919) and President Warren G. Harding's Agricultural Conference (1922). Appointed (1934) by President F. D. Roosevelt as a committee chairman to suggest legislation to forestall war profiteering, he recommended (1937) to the Senate military affairs committee a plan for wartime industrial mobilization. During World War II he was again influential, taking the part of "elder statesman." He was chairman (1942) of a special commission appointed by President Roosevelt to study the U.S. rubber situation, an adviser (1944) to the Army ordnance department and House of Representatives Postwar Planning Committee, and U.S. representative (1946–47) to the United Nations Atomic Energy Commission. The American plan for control of atomic weapons, which came to be called the "Baruch plan," was the subject of much debate both in the U.S. and in the United Nations. Author of *Making of Economic and Reparation Sections of Peace Treaty* (1920) and others.

Baruch (bā'ruk, bãr'uk), **Book of.** Apocryphal book of the Old Testament bearing the name of the friend and amanuensis of Jeremiah. It is assigned by some critics to the later part of the Maccabean period.

Baruch (bä'ruċh), **Löb.** Original name of **Börne, Ludwig.**

Baruch (bą.rök'), **Simon.** b. near Posen (now Poznań, in Poland), July 29, 1840; d. June 3, 1921. American physician; father of Bernard Mannes Baruch. He emigrated to America and received his M.D. from the Medical College of Virginia; after serving in the Confederate army as a surgeon, he practiced medicine at Camden, S.C., and New York. He introduced European methods of hydrotherapy into America, and popularized the Brand treatment of typhoid fever. He was appointed a member of the Saratoga Commission following the New York State purchase of the Saratoga mineral springs.

Barus (bãr'us), **Carl.** b. at Cincinnati, Ohio, Feb. 19, 1856; d. at Providence, R.I., Sept. 20, 1935. American physicist, professor of physics at Brown University from 1895, where he was also dean (1903–26) of the graduate section. He was a physicist of the U.S. Geological Survey in the period 1880–92, professor of meteorology of the U.S. Weather Bureau in the period 1892–93, and physicist of the Smithsonian Institution in the period 1893–95. The Rumford medal of the American Academy of Sciences was awarded to him in 1900 for his research in the field of heat. He published numerous scientific papers.

Baruth (bä'röt). Small town in E Germany, Russian Zone, in the former province of Brandenburg, Prussia, ab. 33 mi. S of Berlin.

Barwala (bur.wä'lą). Former state of the Union of India, one of the Western India states, just S of the Rann of Kutch: cotton and cattle raising. Capital, Barwala; area, 45 sq. mi.; pop. 7,000 (1941).

Bärwalde (ber'väl''dę), **Treaty of.** See **Brandenburg, Treaty of.**

Barwan (bär'wän) or **Barwon** (-won). See **Darling.**

Barwani (bur.wä'nē). Former state of the Union of India, one of the Central India states, merged (1948) with the Gwalior-Indore-Malwa Union, ab. 130 mi. SE of the city of Cawnpore: rice, wheat, and sugar. Capital, Barwani; area, ab. 1,178 sq. mi.; pop., 176,666 (1941).

Bary (bä.rē'), **Heinrich Anton de.** See **De Bary, Heinrich Anton.**

Baryatinsky (bă.ryä'tyin.ski), Prince **Aleksandr Ivanovich.** b. 1815; d. at Geneva, Switzerland, March 9, 1879. Russian field marshal. He served in the Caucasus and in the Crimean War, distinguishing himself as a commander in the Caucasus by the final defeat of the tribal leader, Shamyl, in 1859.

Barycz (bä'rich). [German, **Bartsch.**] River in W Poland which joins the Oder River near Głogów in Silesia. Length, ab. 100 mi.

Barye (bá.rē), **Antoine Louis.** b. at Paris, Sept. 24, 1795; d. there, June 25, 1875. French sculptor, especially of animals. He was the son of a master silversmith from Lyons. Conscripted into the French army in 1812, he served as a topographical engineer, and is said to have modeled several relief maps afterward preserved in the French War Office. In 1819 he presented himself at a competition of the École des Beaux-Arts, with *Milo di Crotona*, which won the second prize. In 1820 he again entered, but lost the second prize. From 1823 to 1831 he worked for Fauconnier, jeweler to the duchess of Angoulême. At this time he began to devote himself more particularly to sculpting animals. In the exhibition of 1831 Barye exhibited his celebrated *Tiger Devouring a Crocodile.* Hector Martin Lefuel, who succeeded Lodovico Tullio Gioacchino Visconti as architect of the Louvre, employed Barye to make four groups for the pavilion on the Place du Carrousel. Barye was an officer of the Legion of Honor, a member of the French Institute, and a professor at the Jardin des Plantes.

Barygaza (bar.i.gā'zą). Ancient name of **Broach.**

Barzillai (bär.zil'ā.ī, bär.zil'ī). In the Old Testament, a wealthy Gileadite who aided David when he fled from Absalom. 2 Sam. xvii. 27.

Barzillai. The name given to the character representing James Butler, 1st Duke of Ormonde, the friend of Charles II, in John Dryden's *Absalom and Achitophel.*

Barzun (bär'zun), **Jacques.** b. at Paris, Nov. 30, 1907—. American historian and educator. He came to the U.S. in 1919 and was naturalized in 1933. He became a lecturer in history at Columbia University in 1927, instructor in 1929, associate professor in 1942, and professor in 1945. Author of *The French Race: Theories of its Origins* (1932), *Race: A Study in Modern Superstition* (1937), *Of Human Freedom* (1939), *Darwin, Marx, Wagner* (1941), *Teacher in America* (1945), and *Berlioz* (1950).

Barzu-Nameh (bär'zö.nä'me). Persian epic poem, modeled on the *Shahnamah.* The name of its author is unknown.

Barzyński (bä.zhin'skē), **Vincent.** b. in Poland, Sept. 20, 1838; d. May 2, 1899. American Catholic priest. He was ordained in 1861; emigrated (1866) to Texas following the failure of a Polish insurrection in that year; and served as pastor (1874 *et seq.*) of St. Stanislaus Kostka, Chicago's first Polish church. A leader of Polish groups in Chicago, he enlarged his parish, founded a school and an orphanage, and aided in the establishment of Polish newspapers in that city.

Bas (bä). See **Batz.**

Bas (bas), **William.** See **Basse** or **Bas, William.**

Basa (bä'sä). [Also, **Bassa.**] Bantu-speaking people of C Africa, inhabiting a large area in E French Cameroons, in the vicinity of Edea. Their population is estimated at ab. 157,000 (by I. Dugast, *Inventaire Ethnique du Sud-Cameroun*, 1949).

Basantello (bä.sän.tel'lō). [Also, **Basentello.**] Small place near Taranto, Italy. Its name is sometimes used in connection with the battle in which Otto II (of the Holy Roman Empire) was overthrown by the Greeks and Moslems on July 13, 982, although later investigations show that the battlefield lay in some unidentified locality S of Crotone.

Basauri (bä.sou'rē). Town and commune in N Spain, in the province of Vizcaya, SE of Bilbao: an agricultural community belonging to the metropolitan region of Bilbao. 10,605 (1940).

Basch (bäsh), **Victor.** b. at Budapest, Hungary, Aug. 18, 1863; d. near Lyons, France, Jan. 10 or 11, 1944. French educator, best known as a leader of the League of the Rights of Man. A professor of aesthetics and art history at the Sorbonne, he sought to promote better relations between France and Germany during the period between World Wars I and II. He and his wife were killed by militia of the Vichy government.

Baschi (bäs'kē), **Matteo.** [Also, **Bassi.**] b. at Bascio, near Urbino, Italy, 1495; d. at Venice, 1552. Italian friar and visionary, founder of the order of the Capuchins.

Bascom (bas'kọm), **Fort.** U.S. military post built (1868) on the Canadian River, in New Mexico, as a safeguard against frontier raids by Indians of the Southwest. It was garrisoned until 1870.

Bascom, Henry Bidleman. b. at Hancock, N.Y., May 27, 1796; d. at Louisville, Ky., Sept. 8, 1850. American bishop (1850) of the Methodist Episcopal Church (of the South), and president of Transylvania University, Kentucky, in the period 1842–50.

Bascom, John. b. at Genoa, N.Y., May 1, 1827; d. Oct. 2, 1911. American educator and philosophical writer. He was president (1874–87) of the University of Wisconsin, and professor of political science (1891–1903) at Williams College. He wrote *Political Economy* (1859), *Aesthetics* (1862), *Philosophy of Rhetoric* (1865), *Principles of Psychology* (1869), *Science, Philosophy, and Religion* (1871), *Philosophy of English Literature* (1874), *Problems in Philosophy*, and others.

Basedow (bä'zẹ.dō), **Johann Bernhard.** b. at Hamburg, Germany, Sept. 11, 1723; d. at Magdeburg, Germany, July 25, 1790. German teacher and educational reformer. He became a teacher in an academy at Sorø, in Denmark, in 1753, and in the gymnasium at Altona, near Hamburg, in 1761; published the *Elementarwerk* (4 vols., 1774; with 100 copper engravings, mostly by Chodowiecki), containing the exposition of a new system of primary education, and opened a model elementary school, called the Philanthropinum, at Dessau in 1774, retiring from its management in 1778.

Basel (bä'zẹl). [Also: **Basle**; French, **Bâle.**] Canton of Switzerland, divided into the two half-cantons of Basel-Stadt (approximately coextensive with the city of Basel) and Basel-Land (capital, Liestal). It was admitted into the confederation in 1501 and sends 12 representatives to the Swiss national council. Area, 179 sq. mi.; pop. 304,051 (1950).

Basel. [Also: **Basle**; French, **Bâle**; Latin, **Basilia.**] City in NW Switzerland, approximately coextensive with the half-canton of Basel-Stadt, the second largest city in Switzerland, situated in the N bend of the Rhine River, comprising Grossbasel (Great Basel) on the left and Kleinbasel (Little Basel) on the right bank of the river, in the immediate vicinity of the German and French borders. It is Switzerland's chief railway junction, river port, and gateway of foreign trade; also a large industrial and commercial center. Silk-ribbon weaving is the oldest industry; there are other textile manufactures and chemical, electrical, and machine industries. Basel has numerous philanthropic and educational institutions, among which the university, founded in 1460 by Pope Pius II, is outstanding; it was the center of European humanism in the 16th century, when Erasmus of Rotterdam taught there. Basel was the birthplace of the 19th-century historian Jakob Burckhardt, who taught (1844–93) at the university; the philosopher Friedrich Nietzsche was (1869–79) also a professor there. The painters Hans Holbein (the younger), Arnold Boecklin, and others lived at Basel. There are fine art collections in the historical and art museums; there is also a natural history museum and an ethnological museum. The *Münster* (cathedral), with colored roof and two towers, has Romanesque sections (notably the Saint Gallus Portal) dating from the 11th and 12th centuries, and Gothic parts which were added in the 14th century. Other noteworthy buildings include a picturesque cloister and patrician residences. The *Rathaus* (town hall), with interior court, belfry, and stained-glass windows, was erected in 1508. Basel was part of the German Empire in the Middle Ages but joined the Swiss Confederation in 1501 and took part early in the Protestant Reformation. Separation of church and state was instituted in 1910. Many international conferences have taken place at Basel, of which the First Zionist Congress (1897), where Theodor Herzl proclaimed the Jewish State, is the most famous of recent years. The Bank for International Settlements is located at Basel. 183,742 (1950).

Basel, Confession of. A statement of principles of the Reformation, drafted by Oecolampadius, and revised by Oswald Myconius, published in 1534.

Basel, Confession of. [Also, **First Helvetic Confession.**] Statement (1536) of the views of Zwingli on the Reformation, especially as they differed from those of Luther, drawn up after Zwingli's death by Heinrich Bullinger and others.

Basel, Council of. Council held at Basel from July 23, 1431, to May 7, 1449, the last of the three great reforming councils of the 15th century. It was called by Pope Martin V and by his successor Eugenius IV. Its main objects were the union of the Greek and Latin churches, the reconciliation of the Bohemians, and the reformation of the church. It deposed (June 25, 1439) Eugenius IV, who refused to acknowledge its authority, and replaced him as Pope (Oct. 30, 1439) with Amadeus, duke of Savoy, who took the name of Felix V (resigned 1449). The ultramontanes reject this council altogether, while the Gallican Church acknowledges the first 25 of its 45 sessions.

Basel, Treaty of. Treaty concluded on April 5, 1795, between France and Prussia. Prussia agreed to withdraw from the coalition against France; France was to continue in possession of the Prussian territory W of the Rhine until peace should be concluded with the empire, while a line of demarcation fixed the neutrality of N Germany. In a secret article it was stipulated that, on conclusion of a general peace, if the empire should cede to France the principalities W of the Rhine, Prussia would cede its territory in that district, and receive compensation elsewhere.

Basel, Treaty of. Treaty concluded on July 22, 1795, by which Spain ceded the island of Hispaniola, in the West Indies, to France.

Basel-Land (bä'zẹl.länt''). Half-canton in NW Switzerland, bounded by France (Alsace) on the NW, Germany (Baden), separated by the Rhine River, on the N, the canton of Aargau on the E, and the cantons of Solothurn and Bern on the S. The majority of the population uses the German language and professes the Protestant religion. It was separated from the half-canton of Basel-Stadt in 1833, after an armed revolt in 1831. Capital, Liestal; area, 165 sq. mi.; pop. 107,393 (1950).

Basel-Stadt (bä'zẹl.shtät''). [French, **Bâle-Ville.**] Half-canton in NW Switzerland, composed of the city of Basel and three villages on the right bank of the Rhine River. The language of the majority is German, the prevailing religion Protestant. Capital, Basel; area, 14 sq. mi.; pop. 196,658 (1950).

Basentello (bä.zen.tel'lō). See **Basantello.**

Basento (bä.sen'tō). [Also: **Basiento**; Latin, **Casuentus.**] River in S Italy which flows into the Gulf of Taranto ab. 27 mi. SW of Taranto. Length, ab. 90 mi.

Baserac (bä.sä.räk'). Village in NW Mexico, in Sonora state, on the upper Yaqui River, S of Babispe. A settlement of Opata Indians, it contains the ruins of a once important Jesuit mission, founded about 1642.

Basevi (bä.sä'vē), **George.** b. at London, 1794; d. at Ely, England, Oct. 16, 1845. English architect. His chief work, the Fitzwilliam museum at Cambridge, was begun by him in 1837, continued by R. C. Cockerell, and completed by E. M. Barry in 1874. He was accidentally killed while inspecting the western bell tower of Ely Cathedral.

Basford (bas'fọrd). Rural district and small manufacturing town in C England, in Nottinghamshire, situated on the river Lene, ab. 3 mi. NW of Nottingham, ab. 128 mi. N of London by rail. It is a suburb of Nottingham. 50,302 (1951).

Bashahr (bu'shạr). [Also: **Bassahir, Bussahir.**] One of the former Simla Hill States of the Punjab, British India, now merged with Himachal Pradesh, Union of India. Area, 3,439 sq. mi.; pop. 111,459 (1941).

Bashan (bā'shạn). In Biblical geography, a district of Palestine, E of the Jordan, reaching from the river Arnon in the S to Mount Hermon on the N, and bounded on the W by the Hauran. At the time of the entrance of the Israelites into Canaan the whole of this region was inhabited by the Amorites. It was conquered by the Israelites and allotted to the tribe of Manasseh (Num. xxxii. 33, Deut. iii. 13, Josh. xiii. 29 ff.), and afterward its inhabitants were deported to Assyria (2 Kings, xv. 30). During the Roman period the country was divided into five provinces; Ituraea and Gaulonitis (later Jaulan), and to the E of these Batanea, to the NE Trachonitis (later Lajah) and Auranitis. The fertility of the country is proverbially mentioned in the Old Testament (Deut. xxxii. 14, Ps. xxii. 12, Jer. l. 19, Micah vii. 14).

Bashford (bash'fọrd), **Coles.** b. in New York, Jan. 24, 1816; d. at Prescott, Ariz., April 25, 1878. American politician, governor (1856–57) of Wisconsin. In the 1855 election, he was defeated by his Democratic opponent, William A. Barstow, but the supreme court declared Bashford governor after hearing his charges of fraud in the election returns. His administration became involved in the railroad land-grant scandals, and he retired to Arizona where he held office under the territorial government.

Bashford, Henry Howarth. b. at London, 1880—. English novelist and physician. He was a medical officer (1933–43) with the English post office department, and medical adviser (1943–45) to the treasury. Author of *The Corner of Harley Street*, *The Happy Ghost*, *The Harley Street Calendar*, *Lodgings for Twelve*, and *Fisherman's Progress*.

Bashford, James Whitford. b. at Fayette, Wis., May 29, 1849; d. at Pasadena, Calif., March 18, 1919. American college president, Methodist bishop, and missionary, noted for his knowledge of China. Offered the presidencies of 11 colleges while still a pastor at Buffalo, N.Y., he chose Ohio Wesleyan and served there (1889–1904) until his election as bishop of the China "area." During 11 years of work in the Orient, he personally urged (1912) President William Howard Taft to recognize the Chinese republic, and when Japan made (1915) her secret "21 Demands" on China, he learned their militaristic import, and informed President Woodrow Wilson and Secretary of State William Jennings Bryan, pointing out the dangers of the Japanese policy. Author of *Wesley and Goethe* (1903), *China and Methodism* (1906), *Christian Missions* (1906), *God's Missionary Plan for the World* (1907), *China: an Interpretation* (1916), and *The Oregon Missions* (1918).

Bashful Lover, The. Play by Philip Massinger, licensed in 1636. In some old catalogues it is ascribed to B. J., or Ben Jonson.

Bashi Islands (bä'shē). See **Batan Islands.**

Bashkir (bäsh.kēr'). Turkic people, numbering some 843,000 (1939), inhabiting the SW slopes of the Ural Mountains of the U.S.S.R. They migrated to their present homes from C Asia as part of the "Golden Horde" of the Mongols in the 13th century A.D. In the 14th century they adopted Islam, which is still the predominant religion. They began paying tribute to the Russian government in 1553–58, and thereafter came under increasing Russian control. Originally herdsmen, they long ago adopted grain agriculture.

Bashkir Autonomous Soviet Socialist Republic. [Also: **Bashkir, Bashkiria** (bäsh.kir'i.ạ), **Bashkir Republic.**] Autonomous republic of the U.S.S.R., in the Russian Soviet Federated Socialist Republic, centered ab. 600 mi. NE of the N shores of the Caspian Sea, on the W side of the Urals. The surface of the area is mostly very hilly. There are extensive deposits of iron ore, oil, and aluminum, but the chief occupation of the people is farming, with cereal crops the most important. The republic was formed on March 23, 1919 and its capital placed at Ufa. Area 54,253 sq. mi.; pop. 3,144,713 (1939).

Bashkirtsev (bäsh.kēr'tsif), **Marie.** [Russian, **Maria Konstantinovna Bashkirtseva** (-tsẹ.vạ).] b. at Gavrontsi, in the government of Poltava, Russia, Nov. 23, 1860; d. at Paris, Oct. 31, 1884. Russian artist and author. A member of a wealthy family of the nobility, she studied painting at Paris, where she became widely known in French society. She left many studies and some finished pictures, some of which show the influence of her teacher and close friend, Jules Bastien-Lepage. Parts of her *Journal* were published in 1887 (Eng. trans., 1890), and evoked wide interest. Her *Letters* (a correspondence with Guy de Maupassant) were published in 1891.

Basidu (bä.sē.dö'). [Also, **Bassadore.**] Town in S Iran, in Laristan, at the W end of the island of Qishm, at the entrance to the Persian Gulf. Its port was first built as a haven for British ships that were being terrorized along the "Pirate Coast" of Oman.

Basiento (bä.syen'tō). See **Basento.**

Basil (baz'il, bā'zil). See also **Vasili.**

Basil, Saint. [Called **"Basil the Great"**; Latin, **Basilius.**] b. at Caesarea, in Cappadocia, 329 A.D.; d. there, Jan. 1, 379. Bishop of Caesarea and metropolitan of Cappadocia (370–379), notable as one of the fathers of the Greek Church. He studied at Constantinople under Libanius, and at Athens in the schools of philosophy and rhetoric, and then returned to Caesarea as a rhetorician. About 361 he retired to Pontus and entered upon the monastic life. In 364 he was made presbyter, and in 370 elevated to a bishopric. He was a vigorous supporter of the orthodox faith in the struggle against Arianism, and a distinguished preacher. His works include commentaries on the Scriptures, five books against Eunomius, homilies, and others. Several Oriental liturgies (or at least several anaphora) are attributed to him.

Basil. [Latin, **Basilius.**] fl. in the 12th century; put to death by burning, 1118. Bulgarian physician and monk, a leader of the Bogomils, a Christian sect that derived its creed from the Paulicians, with some modifications, and was, like that group, branded as heretic by the established Church. They were a political as well as a religious force, and displayed during the several centuries of their existence a fierce sense of nationalism.

Basil I. [Called **Basil the Macedonian**; Latin, **Basilius.**] b. c813; d. 886. Byzantine emperor (867–886), the founder of the Macedonian dynasty. He was of obscure origin, but succeeded in winning the favor of Michael III, who raised him to the dignity of coemperor in 866, and entrusted him with the administration of the empire. In the meantime, Michael acquired another favorite, and Basil (who saw his fortunes beginning to wane) contrived to bring about Michael's death, and ascended the throne as sole ruler in 867. Despite his ruthless method of acquiring power, he was one of the most intelligent and effective of the Byzantine emperors. He improved the administration of the empire, drove the Saracens out of Italy in 885, and began the collection of laws called *Constitutiones Basilicae*, or simply *Basilica*, which was completed by his successor, Leo VI (legally his son, but believed by many to have been actually the son of Michael). Basil is also remembered for his earnest, although unsuccessful, efforts to end the separation of the Church in the West and the East.

Basil II. [Surnamed **Bulgaroktonos**, meaning "slayer of Bulgarians"; Latin, **Basilius.**] b. c958; d. 1025. Byzantine emperor (976–1025); elder son of Romanus II of the Macedonian dynasty. He succeeded, with his brother Constantine VIII, the usurper Joannes Zimisces, and is notable as one of the greatest generals of the time. He began (c987) a war with Bulgaria, which resulted (1018) in the incorporation of that kingdom into the Byzantine empire.

Basilan (bä.sē'län). Group of islands in the S Philippines, in the Sulu Archipelago S of the W peninsula of Mindanao: part of Zamboanga province. The largest island in the group is also called Basilan. Area of the group, ab. 500 sq. mi.

Basilan. Largest of the Basilan islands, Philippines, in the Sulu Archipelago, W of Mindanao. It is part of Zamboanga province. It is mountainous, wooded, and fertile, and has, at Isabela de Basilan, on the NW coast, a harbor safe in all weather for large vessels. Length, 41 mi.; area, 493 sq. mi.; pop. 48,086 (1939).

Basilan Strait. Strait which separates Basilan island from Mindanao, in the S Philippines, and connects the Sulu Sea with the Celebes Sea. Width, ab. 8 mi.

Basile (bá.zēl). Slanderer who figures in Pierre Beaumarchais's comedies *Le Barbier de Séville* and *Le Mariage de Figaro*. His name has become proverbial in some contexts for this type of character.

Basilia (bạ.zil'i.ạ). Latin name of **Basel.**

Basilica of Saint Mark (sānt märk'). See **Mark, Basilica of Saint.**

Basilicata (bä.sē.lē.kä'tä). [Also, **Lucania.**] *Compartimento* (region) in S Italy, containing the provinces of Matera and Potenza, and comprising the E part of the former region of Lucania. It is bounded by the *compartimenti* (regions) of Apulia, Campania, and Calabria and has short shore lines on the Gulf of Taranto and the Tyrrhenian Sea. The region is largely mountainous, suffers from extensive erosion, and is exceedingly poor. Agriculture and livestock-raising produce little that is exportable; the land is in the hands of feudal overlords; there are few industries; internal as well as overseas emigration was heavy during the 19th and 20th centuries. In ancient times, the region was part of the Roman Empire; in the Middle Ages it shared the fate of the neighboring regions, experiencing a short-lived prosperity in the reign of the emperor Frederick II. It was part of the Kingdom of Naples and of the Two Sicilies and, together with the entire kingdom, incorporated into modern Italy in 1860. Capital, Potenza; area, 3,856 sq. mi.; pop. 543,262 (1936), 627,700 (1951).

Basilides (bas.i.lī'dēz). d. c138 A.D. Gnostic of the 2nd century, probably a Syrian, the founder of the Basilidians, a heretical Christian sect. About his life little is known. He appears to have taught at Alexandria and elsewhere in Egypt, and perhaps in Persia. He claimed to be a disciple of Glaucias, an interpreter of Saint Peter, and to be in possession of the secret traditions of that apostle. He wrote commentaries on the Gospel in 24 books, extracts from which have been preserved.

Basilidians (bas.i.lid'i.ạnz). Followers of Basilides, a teacher of Gnostic doctrines at Alexandria, Egypt, in the 2nd century A.D. They discouraged martyrdom, kept their doctrines as secret as possible, and were much given to magical practices, and soon declined from the asceticism of their founder into gross immorality.

Basilikon Doron (bạ.sil'i.kon dō'ron). [Also, **Basilicon Doron.**] Work on the divine right of kings, written by James I of England. The work, which was written by James while he was king of Scotland (as James VI), but before he ascended the throne of England, was designed to instruct his son Henry in effective methods of kingly rule, and reflects James's great irritation with what he considered to be improper assumption of authority by his ministers (hence the emphasis on "divine right" and, by extension, absolute rule by the king). The work was published in 1599; Henry, to whom it was addressed, died in 1612, before his father, and therefore never ruled.

Basilisco (bas.i.lis'kō). Boastful character in the old play *Soliman and Perseda*, referred to in Shakespeare's *King John.*

Basiliscus (bas.i.lis'kus). Emperor of the Eastern Roman Empire, 475–c477 A.D. He was the brother-in-law of Leo I, by whom he was appointed (468) commander of the expedition to Carthage against Genseric, king of the Vandals. He was defeated, and was thereupon banished by the emperor to Thrace. He dethroned Zeno, Leo's successor, but was himself deposed by Zeno, and died in prison. In his reign the great library of Constantinople was destroyed by fire.

Basiliskos (bas.i.lis'kos). Ptolemy's name for the first-magnitude white star α Leonis, now ordinarily known as Regulus, a Latin translation of Basiliskos.

Basilius (bạ.sil'i.us). The lover of Quiteria in Miguel de Cervantes' *Don Quixote.* He gets her away from Camacho by a stratagem.

Basilius. Prince of Arcadia in love with Zelmane, in Sir Philip Sidney's pastoral romance *Arcadia.*

Basilius. Latin form of **Basil.**

Basilius Valentinus. fl. about the beginning of the 15th century. German alchemist. He is supposed to have made important discoveries in chemistry, notably antimony and muriatic acid. *Currus triumphalis Antimonii* (1604) by Johannes Thölde was claimed as a translation from a work by Basilius; however, some critics are inclined to doubt Basilius's existence, believing the name to have been merely a pseudonym of Thölde himself.

Basille (bā'zil), **Theodore.** See under **Becon, Thomas.**

Basil of Ancyra (baz'il, bā'zil; an.sī'rạ), Saint. **Basil of Ancyra,** Saint. b. at Ancyra, in Cappadocia, d. c363 A.D. Bishop of Ancyra. Some sources say (incorrectly) that he was a leader of the semi-Arians. Actually, he condemned the Arians, and was martyred under Julian the Apostate, probably at Constantinople (although some sources suggest Illyricum).

Basing (bā'zing), Baron. A title of **Paulet, Sir Charles** (1685–1754).

Basing House. Former country residence of the marquises of Winchester, situated E of Basingstoke, England. It became famous for its long defense by the Royalists against the Parliamentarians, in the English Civil War. It was taken by Cromwell in October, 1645, and destroyed.

Basingstoke (bā'zing.stōk). Municipal borough and market town in S England, in Southampton (an administrative county in the geographical county of Hampshire), ab. 48 mi. SW of London by rail. It is being developed as an industrial center and now has, among others, a clothing industry. Basingstoke still lies beyond the area of continuous urban development surrounding London. 16,979 (1951).

Basingstoke Canal. Canal in S and SE England, in Southampton (an administrative county in the geographical county of Hampshire) and Surrey. It extends from Basingstoke to the vicinity of Weybridge. The canal, which no longer carries commercial traffic, has been purchased by a group interested in its preservation for its recreational and scenic values. Length, 37 mi.

Basin Ranges (bā'sin). Name given (1907) by the U.S. Geographic Board to all those ranges in the W U.S. which lie between the plateau region on the E, the Sierra Nevada and Cascade Range on the W, and the Blue Mountains of Oregon on the N, including the Wasatch and associated ranges.

Baskerville (bas'kėr.vil), **Charles.** b. at Deer Brook, Miss., June 18, 1870; d. Jan. 28, 1922. American chemist and author, professor (1904 *et seq.*) in the College of the City of New York. He was a member of the faculty of the University of North Carolina in the period 1892–1904. The discovery of two supposed new elements, berzelium and coralinium, was announced by him.

Baskerville, John. b. at Wolverley, Worcestershire, England, Jan. 28, 1706; d. at Birmingham, Jan. 8, 1775. English printer and type founder. In early life he followed various pursuits (footman, stonecutter, calligrapher, teacher, and maker of japanned ware), but about 1750 he turned his attention to typography and printing, and was elected (1758) printer to the University of Cambridge for ten years. His type faces were based on those of William Caslon, then universally accepted as the best; Baskerville's designs made a distinction in thickness between upstrokes and downstrokes, and refined the serifs. In his day, although subjected to considerable ridicule, they nevertheless also found immediate supporters among thoughtful users of type, and served as models for many later innovations in type design. His fonts were sold, after his death, to Pierre Augustin Caron Beaumarchais, who used them to print a 70-volume edition of the works of Voltaire. Baskerville's own first work was a famous edition of Vergil (1757); other noted specimens of his art are editions of Milton (1758 and 1759), the Prayer-Book (1760; four editions, and others in subsequent years), Juvenal (1761), Horace (1762), the Bible (1763), and a series of Latin authors (1772–73).

Basket Maker. Collective term for a number of North American Indian cultures known through archaeological evidence in the area surrounding the common meeting-point of the states of Utah, Colorado, Arizona, and New Mexico. The remains are dated at 100–700 A.D. and include round houses in caves and in the open, storage pits, a variety of weapons and implements, clothing, clear evidences of agricultural pursuits as well as hunting, and much basketry of various styles (whence the name), but no pottery in the earlier horizons. The culture of the Basket Makers was ancestral to the later Pueblo culture found in the same area among a number of tribes.

Basle (bäl). See **Basel.**

Basnage de Beauval (bá.názh dẹ bō.vál), **Henri.** b. at Rouen, France, Aug. 7, 1656; d. in Holland, March 19, 1710. French jurist; a brother of Jacques Basnage de Beauval. He was a lawyer at Rouen, and (as a Huguenot) took refuge in Holland after the revocation of the Edict of Nantes. Author of *Histoire des ouvrages des savants* (1687) and others.

Basnage de Beauval, Jacques. b. at Rouen, France, Aug. 8, 1653; d. at The Hague, Holland, Dec. 22, 1723. French Protestant theologian and historian, diplomat, and pastor (after the revocation of the Edict of Nantes) at Rotterdam and The Hague; brother of Henri Basnage de Beauval. His chief historical works are *Histoire de l'église depuis Jésus-Christ jusqu' à présent* (1699), *Histoire des Juifs* (1706), *Dissertation historique sur les duels et les ordres de chevalerie* (1720), and *Histoire de la religion des églises réformées* (1690).

Basoche (bȧ.zosh), **La.** See **Bazoche, La.**

Basoeto (bą.sö'tō). See **Suto.**

Basque Provinces (bask). [Also: **Biscay Provinces;** Spanish, **Vascongadas.**] Region in N Spain, comprising the provinces of Guipúzcoa, Vizcaya, Álava, and parts of Navarra. The Basque district in France comprises the arrondissements of Bayonne and Mauléon, in the department of Basses-Pyrénées.

Basques (basks). People of unknown origin inhabiting parts of Spain in the neighborhood of the Pyrenees, and part of the department of Basses-Pyrénées, France. They are the oldest people in Europe and still speak their ancient language, which defies linguistic classification. It is unrelated to any other language in the world. The Basques have been Christians since the 5th century A.D.

Basra (baz'rą, bus'-). [Also, **Basrah.**] *Liwa* (province) in the SE corner of Iraq, at the head of the Persian Gulf, crossed by the Tigris and Euphrates rivers, three railway lines, several highways, and an oil pipe line. Its cities have several large oil refineries. Capital, Basra; area, 4,758 sq. mi.; pop. 352,039 (1947).

Basra. [Also: **Basrah, Bassora, Bassorah, Busra, Bussorah.**] City in SE Iraq, capital of the *liwa* (province) of Basra, situated on the Shatt-al-Arab ab. 55 mi. from the Persian Gulf. It was founded c635, was an important medieval market town and Arabic literary center, and has increased in importance since the development of steam navigation. During World War II it was a supply port after 1941 for the U.S.S.R. and the Near East. Its chief export is dates, some 75 percent of the world's supply being produced in the vicinity. Legendary port of Sinbad the Sailor in the story in *The Arabian Nights' Entertainments,* where it is called Bassorah. 206,302 (1947).

Bas-Rhin (bä.raṅ). [German, **Unter-Elsass.**] Department in NE France, bounded by the department of Moselle on the W, Germany (Baden and Rhine Palatinate) on the N and E, the department of Haut-Rhin on the S, and the department of Vosges on the SW. It is separated from Germany (Baden) by the Rhine. It is the N part of the ancient region of Alsace, which was part of the Holy Roman Empire of the German nation until the 17th century and, as far as some subterritories are concerned, until the 18th century. The main part of the department went to France in the reign of Louis XIV. It was ceded to Germany in 1871 and incorporated into Alsace-Lorraine (German, Elsass-Lothringen), returned to France in 1918, reincorporated into Germany in 1940, and again returned to France in 1945. The population speaks an Alemannic dialect of High German, but French is the official language, spoken in public and among the educated classes. A large part of the population, evacuated at the beginning of World War II, has returned. The department has three distinct regions: the plain of the Rhine, the hill country to the N, and the Vosges Mountains to the W. It is rich in historical monuments, particularly from the Middle Ages, and in mountain scenery attractive to tourists. The plain country is among the richest agricultural regions of France, producing abundant harvests of grain, vegetables, fruits, wine, and tobacco. There are good pasture lands, large forests, stone quarries, and petroleum wells. Industrial production is diversified. Iron and steel mills, mechanical, metallurgical, and construction industries, textile, leather, lumber, chemical, and food industries are the most important in the manufacturing field. Among the food industries are brewing, distilling, canning, candy manufacturing, and the production of sauerkraut and of pâté de foie gras. The printing establishments of Strasbourg are among the oldest in Europe. Capital, Strasbourg; area, 1,848 sq. mi.; pop. 673,281 (1946).

Bass (bas), **Edward.** b. at Dorchester, Mass., Nov. 23, 1726; d. Sept. 10, 1803. American Episcopal bishop, consecrated (1797) first bishop of Massachusetts after the American Revolution; great-great-grandson of John and Priscilla Alden. He was first elected (1789) because his colonial sympathies during the war might mitigate any bad feeling over the connection of the Episcopal Church with the Church of England, but his consecration was delayed eight years owing to criticism of his second marriage (1789) less than six months after his first wife's death.

Bass, George. b. at Asworthy, near Sleaford, Lincolnshire, England; d. c1812. English navigator. He discovered Bass Strait (separating Australia from Tasmania) in 1798, and in the same year circumnavigated Tasmania.

Bass, Michael Arthur. [Title, 1st Baron **Burton.**] b. at Burton-on-Trent, England, Nov. 12, 1837; d. Feb. 1, 1909. English brewer. A member of Parliament (1865–86), Bass was frequent host to Edward VII (at that time Prince of Wales), and a personal friend of William Ewart Gladstone, though he opposed (1886) Gladstone's home-rule policy. He was a benefactor of Burton-on-Trent, where he built a ferry bridge and several churches; his art collection included pictures by Thomas Gainsborough, George Romney, and Joshua Reynolds.

Bass, Sam. b. near Mitchell, Ind., July 21, 1851; killed at Round Rock, Texas, July 21, 1878. American desperado. With four others he robbed (Sept. 19, 1877) a Union Pacific train of 65 thousand dollars at Big Springs, Neb. He later (1878) robbed four other Western trains and attempted a hold-up of the Round Rock, Tex., bank. A former member of the band informed the Texas Rangers, and Bass was mortally wounded in the skirmish.

Bass, William Capers. b. at Augusta, Ga., Jan. 13, 1831; d. at Macon, Ga., Nov. 15, 1894. American educator, president of Methodist Wesleyan Female College at Macon, Ga.

Bassa (bä'sä). See also **Basa.**

Bassa. [Also: **Bassah, Gbasa.**] Sudanic-speaking people of W Africa, inhabiting the coastal and interior region of C Liberia. They are divided into a number of subgroups ruled by independent hereditary kings, and they have exogamous patrilineal clans. They practice hoe agriculture, and their principal staple food is rice.

Bassadore (bas.ą.dōr'). See **Basidu.**

Bassae (bas'ē). Place in Arcadia, Greece, near Phigalia. It is noted for its ruined temple of Apollo Epicurius, built in the second half of the 5th century B.C., probably by Ictinus, the architect of the Parthenon. It is a Doric peripteros of 6 by 15 columns, in plan 41 by 125 ft., the cella with pronaos and opisthodomos of two columns *in antis.* In the interior of the cella six piers project from each side wall, their faces formed by Ionic three-quarter columns. A portion toward the back of the cella has no piers, and has a door in the side wall facing the east; it is probable that this was the cella proper, and that the main part of the cella was merely a monumental court, open to the sky—a unique arrangement. The famous frieze, ab. 2 ft. high (often called the Phigalian Marbles; since 1814 in the British Museum), surrounded the interior of the cella, above the architrave; it is in high relief, and represents combats of Greeks with Amazons and of Lapithae with Centaurs.

Bassahir (bus'ą.hir). See **Bashahr.**

Bassam (bä.säm'). See **Grand Bassam.**

Bassanes (bas'ą.nēz). Jealous nobleman in John Ford's tragedy *The Broken Heart.* He exhibits traces of basic strength and shrewdness through a cloud of indecision and weak raving.

Bassani (bäs.sä'nē), **Giovanni Battista.** b. at Padua, Italy, c1657; d. in Italy, Oct. 1, 1716. Italian violinist and composer, presumed to have been the teacher of Arcangelo Corelli. He was conductor (c1680 *et seq.*) of cathedral music at Bologna. His works include secular and liturgical compositions for voice, as well as violin sonatas.

Bassanio (bą.sä'ni.ō). In Shakespeare's *Merchant of Venice,* a Venetian nobleman, the friend of Antonio, and Portia's successful suitor. It is on Bassanio's account that Antonio obligates himself to Shylock.

Bassano (bäs.sä'nō), **Francesco.** [Original name, **Francesco da Ponte.**] b. at Bassano del Grappa, Italy, c1550; d. at Venice, July 4, 1591. Italian painter of the Venetian school; eldest son of Jacopo Bassano.

Bassano, Jacopo. [Original name, **Jacopo** (or **Giacomo**) **da Ponte.**] b. at Bassano del Grappa, Italy, 1510; d. there, Feb. 13, 1592. Italian painter of the Venetian school, noted as one of the earliest of Italian genre painters, given the name Bassano after his native town. His works include also Biblical scenes and portraits. Perhaps his best-known single painting is the one based on Christ's expulsion of the money changers from the temple at Jerusalem, now in the National Gallery, London. His frescoes in the Piazza Ponte Vecchio at Bassano del Grappa escaped damage in World War II.

Bassano, Leandro. [Original name, **Leandro da Ponte.**] b. at Bassano del Grappa, Italy, 1558; d. at Venice, 1623. Italian portrait painter; third son of Jacopo Bassano.

Bassano del Grappa (bäs.sä′nō del gräp′pä). [Also, **Bassano.**] City and commune in NE Italy, in the *compartimento* (region) of Veneto, in the province of Vicenza, situated on the Brenta River, ab. 20 mi. NE of Vicenza. It has manufactures of leather goods, ceramics, and straw hats, and is a summer resort. It has a famous wooden bridge, medieval ramparts, a 13th-century castle, the Romanesque Church of San Francesco, the baroque Church of San Giovanni Battista, and an art museum. It is the birthplace of the Bassano, or da Ponte, family of painters. Known as early as 998, during the Middle Ages the city was the object of contention between local families; it became part of the Venetian republic c1404. Under Venetian rule it developed crafts and industries and became a celebrated resort for wealthy Venetians, artists, and literary personalities in the 17th, 18th, and 19th centuries; numerous villas date from this period. Napoleon I defeated the Austrians here in 1796. After 1797 Bassano was a duchy under French overlordship; from 1814 to 1866 it was under Austrian rule. Some damage was suffered during World War II by structures of tourist interest, including the wooden bridge and the roof and cloisters of San Francesco, but repairs have been completed or are being carried out. San Giovanni was not damaged. Pop. of commune, 23,106 (1936); of city, 11,911 (1936).

Bassantin (bas′ạn.tin), **James.** d. 1568. Scottish astronomer and mathematician, author of an *Astronomique Discours* (1557).

Bassas da India (bä′sạzh dạ ēn′dyạ). Small island in the C part of the Mozambique Channel, W of Madagascar and E of Mozambique, SE Africa: a French possession, administered as a dependency of Madagascar.

Basse (bas), **Jeremiah.** d. 1725. English colonial governor in North America, commissioned (1697) governor of East and West Jersey. He found the West Jersey proprietors disputing his authority and thus shaped his policy to favor the antiproprietary party in East Jersey. Although he was removed from office, the "East Jersey Revolution" was successful, and a royal government was formed with Basse as secretary.

Basse or **Bas, William.** d. c1653. English poet, best known for his *Epitaph on Shakespeare*, a sonnet first attributed to John Donne. His *Angler's Song* is quoted by Izaac Walton in *The Compleat Angler*.

Bassée (bȧ.sā), **La.** See **La Bassée.**

Bassein (bäs.sēn′). [Also, **Bassim.**] District in the Irrawaddy division, S Burma, situated on the E coast of the Bay of Bengal, SW of Rangoon, and containing the mouths of the Irrawaddy. The area is mostly covered with mangrove swamps. Chief town, Bassein; area, 4,127 sq. mi.; pop. ab. 500,000.

Bassein. [Also, **Bassim.**] Chief town of the district of Bassein, S Burma, situated on the Bassein River, ab. 90 mi. W of Rangoon. It has an important trade in rice. 45,662 (1931).

Bassein. Capital of Thana district, Bombay state, Union of India, ab. 28 mi. N of the city of Bombay, on land that was formerly an island. A prosperous center under the Portuguese (16th and 17th centuries), it was known as the "Court of the North." Pop. ab. 13,000.

Bassein River. One of the mouths of the Irrawaddy, in Burma, emptying into the Andaman Sea, ab. 100 mi. SW of Rangoon.

Basselin (bȧs.laṅ), **Olivier.** b. in the Val-de-Vire, Normandy; d. c1418. French poet, a fuller by trade, who wrote a large number of gay songs. Only a few have survived. They were called *Vaux de Vire* (whence the modern word *vaudeville*), from their place of origin.

Bassenthwaite (bas′ẹn.thwāt), **Lake.** Lake in NW England, in Cumberland, ab. 3 mi. NW of Keswick. Length, 4 mi.; width, ¾ mi.; elevation, 223 ft.

Bassermann (bäs′ėr.män), **Albert.** b. at Mannheim, Germany, Sept. 7, 1867; d. May 15, 1952. German actor. While a member of Max Reinhardt's company, he achieved a great reputation in such classical roles as Lear, Shylock, and Mephistopheles, and with his own company he toured in the plays of Friedrich Schiller. In 1933 he left the German stage and moved to Austria; in 1938 he went to Switzerland, and in 1940 he went to Hollywood to appear in *Dr. Ehrlich's Magic Bullet.* He then appeared in numerous motion pictures, such as *Foreign Correspondent* (1940), *Dispatch From Reuters* (1940), *Escape* (1941), and *The Moon and Sixpence* (1942). He made his New York stage debut (1944) in *Embezzled Heaven*, a Theatre Guild production, and played in a German language production (1948) of *Faust* at New York.

Bassermann, Ernst. b. at Wolfach, Germany, July 24, 1854; d. at Baden-Baden, Germany, July 24, 1917. German politician. He was a leader of the National Liberal party, of which he was chairman (1904 *et seq.*), and a member of the Reichstag (1893 *et seq.*). An opponent of the Junkers, he favored the liberal element in his party.

Basses (bas′ẹz), **Great.** Ledge of rocks situated ab. 6 mi. off the SE coast of Ceylon.

Basses, Little. Ledge of rocks ab. 4 mi. off the SE coast of Ceylon, and NE of the Great Basses.

Basses-Alpes (bäs.zȧlp). Department in SE France, bounded by the department of Drôme on the NW, the department of Hautes-Alpes on the N, Italy and the department of Alpes-Maritimes on the E, the department of Var on the S, and the department of Vaucluse on the W. It once formed part of Provence, afterward of Savoy, but went to France through the Treaty of Utrecht, in the reign of Louis XIV. The region is mountainous and sparsely populated; agriculture and livestock-raising are the main sources of income. Mulberries, olives, and wines are produced. There are stone quarries, magnesium and coal mines, and a number of minor industries. The scenery is outstanding, and the department has a number of tourist centers and health resorts. The population has declined by more than one-third since the beginning of the century. Capital, Digne; area, 2,697 sq. mi.; pop. 83,354 (1946).

Basses-Pyrénées (bäs.pē.rā.nā). Department in SW France, bounded by the department of Landes on the N, the department of Gers on the NE, the department of Hautes-Pyrénées on the E, Spain on the S and SW, and the Bay of Biscay on the W. It was formed from Béarn and part of the Basque region, including the territories of Soule, Navarre, Labourd, and Bayonne. It went to the crown of France under Henry IV, who was born here. The terrain is largely mountainous, sloping down toward the N, the climate healthy and moderate. The lower parts of the valleys produce fruits and wine; in the highlands horses, cattle, and sheep are raised, with the sheep's-milk cheeses going to Roquefort in Aveyron. Grain is produced in the plains. There are stone quarries and coal mines. Dairy, distillery, chocolate, and other food industries, iron and steel manufactures, and shipyards are among the more important industries. The chief port is Bayonne; Saint-Jean-de-Luz has important sardine and anchovy fisheries. Capital, Pau; area, 2,977 sq. mi.; pop. 415,797 (1946).

Basset (bas′ẹt). Swindler in Colley Cibber's *Provoked Husband.*

Basset (bȧ.se), **René.** b. at Lunéville, France, July 24, 1855; d. at Algiers, Jan. 4, 1924. French Orientalist. He served (1894 *et seq.*) as director of the École Supérieure des Lettres at Algiers. Author of books on the Berber language, also of *La Poésie arabe antéislamique* (Pre-Islamic Arabic Poetry, 1880), *Le Tableau des Cébès* (1898), and *Arab-Faqih* (1897–1909).

Basseterre (bäs″ter′). City in SE St. Christopher (St. Kitts), Leeward Islands, British West Indies, in St. Christopher and Nevis presidency: capital and chief seaport of the presidency. 29,142 (1948).

Basse-Terre (bäs.ter). [Also, **Basseterre;** Eng. trans., *"Low Land."*] City in SW Guadeloupe, French West Indies, on the Caribbean Sea: capital of Guadeloupe department. 10,086 (1946).

Basse-Terre. See also under **Guadeloupe.**

Bassett (bas'ęt), **James.** b. at Mundus, near Hamilton, Ontario, Canada, Jan. 31, 1834; d. at Los Angeles, Calif., March 10, 1906. American Presbyterian missionary. He was graduated (1859) from Lane Seminary. Appointed (1871) a missionary to Persia, he opened a mission (1872) and a girls' boarding school (1874) at Tehran, and headed (1881) the mission schools for boys at Tehran. Author of *Persia, the Land of the Imams* (1886) and *Persia, Eastern Mission* (1890).

Bassett, John Spencer. b. at Tarboro, N.C., Sept. 10, 1867; d. at Washington, D.C., Jan. 27, 1928. American historian, editor, and social critic, noted for his *Life of Andrew Jackson* (1911). He served as professor of history (1894–1906) at Trinity College (now Duke University), where he became first editor (1902) of the *South Atlantic Quarterly.* An editorial (1903) comparing the past rise of submerged classes with the rise of the American Negro evoked great resentment in North Carolina and led to a demand for his resignation. Removing (1906) to Smith College, he began that institution's first learned publication, the *Smith College Studies in History.* He was elected (1919) secretary of the American Historical Association. Author of a *Short History of the United States* (1913), *The Plain Story of American History* (1916), *Our War with Germany* (1919), *Expansion and Reform* (1926), *The League of Nations, a Chapter in World Politics* (1928), and other works.

Bassett, Richard. b. in Delaware, April 2, 1745; d. Sept. 15, 1815. American politician. He was a member of the Constitutional Convention (1787), U.S. senator from Delaware (1789–93), and governor of Delaware (1798–1801).

Basset-Table (bas'ęt.tā"bl), **The.** Comedy by Susannah Centlivre, first acted in 1705, and published the next year. It is a witty treatment of the fashionable gambling habit of the day.

Bassetts (bas'ęts). Unincorporated community in S Virginia, in Henry County, ab. 10 mi. NW of Martinsville. 3,421 (1950).

Bassi (bäs'sē), **Laura Maria Caterina.** b. at Bologna, Italy, Oct. 29, 1711; d. Feb. 20, 1778. Italian scholar, noted for her attainments in experimental philosophy and languages.

Bassi, Fra Ugo. [Original prename, **Giovanni.**] b. 1801; d. Aug. 8, 1849. Italian preacher. He entered the order of Saint Barnabas in 1818, and began his public ministry in 1833. His sermons produced a great effect, people throwing down their garments for him to walk on. In 1848 he joined Alessandro Gavazzi and a party of *Crociati,* a liberal religious movement, and later joined Garibaldi at Rieti, where he continued preaching until he was taken prisoner by the Austrians, tortured, and shot. He was buried where he fell.

Bassianus (bas.i.ā'nus). In *Titus Andronicus,* attributed to Shakespeare, a brother of Saturninus and son of the late Emperor of Rome.

Bassianus. Original name of **Caracalla.**

Bassianus, Alexianus. Original name of **Alexander Severus, Marcus Aurelius.**

Bassigny (bä.sē.nyē). Small former division of France, lying partly in Lorraine and partly in Champagne, in the neighborhood of Langres.

Bassim (bäs.sēm'). See **Bassein,** Burma.

Bassin (bá.sañ). French word for "basin" or, more freely, "inlet": see the specific element of the name.

Bassin (bas'in). See **Christiansted.**

Bassini (bäs.sē'nē), **Edoardo.** b. at Pavia, Italy, April 14, 1844; d. at Padua, Italy, July 19, 1924. Italian surgeon. He served in the army of Giuseppe Garibaldi, studied in the laboratory of G. Bizzozero at Turin, and became professor of surgery at the universities of Pavia, Genoa, and Padua. He is known especially for the operation on inguinal hernia (1889) that bears his name, and also devised useful operations for the extirpation of humeroscapular sarcoma, ileo-caecal resection, and nephropexy (1882). Author of *Un caso di rene mobile fissato col mezzo dell'operazione cruenta* (1882), *Nuovo metodo operativo per la cura dell'ernia inguinale* (1889), and *Nuovo metodo operativo per la cura radicale dell'ernia crurale* (1893).

Bassino (ba.sē'nō). "The perjured husband" in Susannah Centlivre's play of that name.

Bassiolo (bas.i.ō'lō). "The gentleman usher" in George Chapman's play of that name, a foolish, conceited busybody.

Basso (bas'ō), **(Joseph) Hamilton.** b. at New Orleans, La., Sept. 5, 1904—. American journalist, novelist, and editor. He attended Tulane University, became (1927) a reporter for the New Orleans *Tribune,* subsequently serving with the *Item* and *Times-Picayune* in the same city, and was an associate editor (1935–37) of the *New Republic.* In 1944 he became an associate editor of the *New Yorker,* for which he also writes occasional book reviews. His novels include *Relics and Angels* (1929), *Cinnamon Seed* (1934), *In Their Own Image* (1935), *Courthouse Square* (1936), *Days Before Lent* (1939), *Wine of the Country* (1941), *Sun in Capricorn* (1942), and *The Greenroom* (1949). He is also the author of two historical studies, *Beauregard, the Great Creole* (1933) and *Mainstream* (1943).

Bassompierre (bá.sôñ.pyer), Baron **François de.** b. at the Château d'Harouel, in Lorraine, France, April 12, 1579; d. Oct. 12, 1646. French diplomat and soldier who became marshal of France in 1622. He served in the imperial army against the Turks in 1603, at the siege of Château-Porcien in 1617, was wounded at Rethel, and took part in the sieges of St.-Jean-d'Angely, Montpellier, and La Rochelle. He served as ambassador to Spain, later to Switzerland, and carried out a mission to London. Through the enmity of Cardinal de Richelieu he was thrown into the Bastille, where he remained until 1643. He was noted for his amours, and, on his arrest, is said to have destroyed 6,000 love letters. Author of *Mémoires du Maréchal de Bassompierre* (1665), which have been considered valuable by historians of the period.

Bassora or **Bassorah** (bas'ǫ.rą). See **Basra.**

Bass Rock (bas). Islet, ab. 1 mi. in circumference, at the entrance of the Firth of Forth, Scotland, near North Berwick. It was held (1691–94) by the Jacobites against William III.

Bass Strait. Channel between Australia and Tasmania, named for George Bass, English navigator, who discovered it in 1798. Length, ab. 200 mi.; breadth, ab. 140 mi.

Bassville or **Basseville** (bäs.vēl), **Nicolas Jean Hugon** (or **Husson**) **de.** d. at Rome, Jan. 13, 1793. French journalist and diplomat. He was editor of the *Mercure National* when he became (1792) secretary of the French legation at Naples. Summoned to Rome soon after, he was killed by the populace for attempting, under orders from the French government, to display the republican cockade.

Bast (båst). [Also, **Pasht.**] In Egyptian mythology, a lioness-headed goddess of life and fecundity. In her special city, Bubastis, she appears to have held a supreme place like that of Neith at Saïs. In a cat-headed aspect she was called Pasht.

Bastable (bas'tą.bl), **Charles Francis.** b. at Charleville, County Cork, Ireland, 1855; d. 1945. Irish economist and political scientist. He was professor of political economy at the University of Dublin from 1882, of jurisprudence and international law from 1902, and regius professor of laws from 1908. He wrote *The Commerce of Nations* (1892), *Public Finance* (1892), *The Theory of International Trade* (1897), and others.

Bastán (bäs.tän'). See **Baztán.**

Bastar (bus'tąr). Former state of the Union of India, one of the Eastern States, now merged with Madhya Pradesh (Central Provinces and Berar), ab. 220 mi. SE of Nagpur: forest products, linseed, and millet. Chief town, Jagdalpur; area, ab. 13,701 sq. mi.; pop. 633,888 (1941).

Bastardella (bä.stär.del'lä) or **Bastardina** (-dē'nä), **La.** Epithet of **Agujari, Lucrezia.**

"Bastard of Orléans" (ôr.lēnz'). See **Dunois, Jean.**

Bastarnae (bas.tär'nē) or **Basternae** (-tėr'-). Germanic tribe. They appear in history in the 2nd century B.C., as auxiliaries of Perseus against the Romans in the third Macedonian war, in the region about the Black Sea N of the Danube, whither they had come from their original seat, apparently on the upper Vistula. During the succeeding centuries they were in frequent conflict with the Romans, but disappear in the 3rd century A.D. They appear to have been among the first Germanic people to leave their old homes in the north, and were the forerunners, accordingly, of the movement southward that afterward became general.

Bastei (bäs'tī). Rocky height in E Germany, in the region called the "Saxon Switzerland," situated on the Elbe River ab. 6 mi. E of Pirna. Elevation, ab. 750 ft.

Basti (bus'tē). District of the Gorakhpur division, Uttar Pradesh (United Provinces), Union of India, ab. 100 mi. N of Benares: wheat, rice, and sugar. Area, ab. 2,822 sq. mi.; pop. 2,185,641 (1941).

Basti (bas'tī). Ancient name of **Baza.**

Bastia (bä.stē'ä; French, bȧs.tyȧ). Seaport on the island of Corsica, in the French department of Corse, situated on the NE coast of the island. Its port exports fruit, wine, hides, and olive oil; it is the seat of the island military establishment. The town (formerly the capital of Corsica) has a citadel dating from the 16th and 17th centuries, and a number of old churches. Much damage, both in the town and in the harbor, was done by aerial bombardment during World War II. Among the damaged buildings are the churches of Saint Jean Baptiste and Notre-Dame-de-Lourdes. 49,327 (1946).

Bastian (bäs'tē.än), **Adolf.** b. at Bremen, Germany, June 26, 1826; d. at Port of Spain, Trinidad, Feb. 3, 1905. German ethnologist. He studied law, medicine, and the natural sciences at various German universities, became a surgeon, and traveled (1851–66) in Australia, New Zealand, Peru, Colombia, Central America, remote parts of China, India, and Persia, Syria, Egypt, Arabia (penetrating to Mecca), the Cape of Good Hope and West Africa, Norway, India (a second time), the Malay Islands, China, N Asia, the Caspian and Black seas, and the Caucasus. In 1866 he was appointed professor of ethnology at Berlin, and administrator of the ethnological museum there. He succeeded Rudolf Virchow as president of the Berlin Anthropological Society, and was the principal organizer and president of the African Society, which gave a great impetus to German explorations in Africa. Among his important published works are *Der Mensch in der Geschichte* (Man in History, 3 vols., 1860), *Sprachvergleichende Studien* (Studies in Comparative Linguistics, 1870), *Die Culturländer des Alten Americas* (The Cultural Countries of Ancient America, 1878), and numerous papers for scientific societies. He was cofounder of the *Zeitschrift für Ethnologie* in 1869.

Bastian (bas'chan), **Henry Charlton.** b. at Truro, Cornwall, England, April 26, 1837; d. 1915. English physician and biologist. He was professor of pathological anatomy (1867–87) and the principles and practice of medicine (1887–95) at University College, London, and was noted as a defender of the doctrine of spontaneous generation. He wrote *Origin of Lowest Organisms* (1871), *Beginnings of Life* (1872), *Evolution and the Origin of Life* (1874), *The Brain as an Organ of Mind* (1880), and others.

Bastiana (bas.ti.ā'na). Medieval name of **Baza.**

Bastiat (bȧs.tyȧ), **Frédéric.** b. at Bayonne, France, June 29, 1801; d. at Rome, Dec. 24, 1850. French political economist, deputy to the Constituent and Legislative assemblies (1848). He was an influential opponent of the protective system and of socialism. Among his works are *De l'influence des tarifs français et anglais sur l'avenir des deux peuples* (in the *Journal des Économistes*), *Sophismes économiques* (1846), *Propriété et loi, Justice et fraternité* (1848), *Protectionnisme et communisme* (1849), *Capital et rente* (1849), and *Harmonies économiques* (1849).

Bastid (bȧs.tēd), **Paul.** b. at Paris, May 17, 1892—. French educator and politician, a leader of the Radical-Socialist party. Minister of commerce in the first Popular Front cabinet of Léon Blum (June, 1936–June, 1937), he had been a deputy since May, 1924. He was a professor at the University of Lyons and a member of the Second Constituent Assembly (1946) and the National Assembly (1947).

Bastidas (bäs.tē'ᴛʜäs), **Rodrigo de.** b. c1460. Spanish navigator and explorer. After the discoveries of Christopher Columbus he joined Juan de la Cosa in an expedition to the New World. During the early 16th century, he visited the shores of the Caribbean Sea, including the site of Cartagena, Colombia.

Bastide (bȧs.tēd), **Jules.** b. at Paris, Nov. 22, 1800; d. there, March 3, 1879. French journalist and politician, a leader in the unsuccessful insurrection of 1832. He was condemned to death for taking part in the riot (June 5, 1832) on the occasion of the funeral of Maximilien Lamarque, but escaped to London. In 1834 he returned, and in the revolution of 1848 was made minister of foreign affairs. He wrote *La République francaise et l'Italie en 1848* (1858) and *Guerres de religion en France* (1859).

Bastien and Bastienne (bȧs.tyaṅ'; bȧs.tyen'). One-act opera by Wolfgang Amadeus Mozart, written early in his career. It was first performed at Vienna in 1768.

Bastien-Lepage (bȧs.tyaṅ' le.pȧzh), **Jules.** b. at Damvillers, Meuse, France, Nov. 1, 1848; d. at Paris, Dec. 10, 1884. French painter. At 16 years of age he went to Paris, where he partly supported himself by entering the postal service, and entered the studio of Alexandre Cabanel, with whom he remained until 1870. During the Franco-Prussian War he enlisted in a company of francs-tireurs. After the war was over he returned to Damvillers to paint. On returning to Paris he supported himself by working for the illustrated papers. Again in Damvillers in the summer of 1873, he painted his grandfather's portrait, which was one of the successes of the Salon of 1874, winning him a third-class medal. In the Salon of 1875 his *First Communion* gained a second-class medal. In 1880 he exhibited his well-known picture of Joan of Arc, now in the Metropolitan Museum at New York.

Bastille (bas.tēl'). Celebrated prison at Paris. The first stone is said to have been laid on April 22, 1370; Hugh Aubriot, provost of Paris under Charles V, is generally considered to have been the original builder. There were at first only two round towers 75 ft. high, flanking the city gate. Afterward two more were added to the north and south and a parallel line was built to the west; four others were afterward added to these. These towers were united by walls of the same height and a moat dug around the whole, forming a quadrangle, the inner court of which was 162 ft. long and 72 ft. wide. The terrors of the Bastille as a state prison reached a culmination during the ministry of Richelieu (1624–42), when François Le Clerc du Tremblay (usually referred to as Father Joseph) was commandant. In the reign of Louis XI cages of iron had been constructed, and the vaults beneath the towers, being on a level with the water in the moat, were especially dreaded. From the beginning of the French Revolution the Bastille was an especial mark for the fury of the populace. On July 14, 1789, it was attacked by a mob which, after several unsuccessful attempts, forced it to surrender. The Commandant, Bernard René Jordan de Launay, was disarmed and conducted toward the Hôtel de Ville; at the Place de Grève he was killed and his head mounted on a pike. After the first anniversary of the fall of the Bastille (July 14, 1790) the old building was razed (demolition completed May 21, 1791).

Bastille Day. French national holiday, falling on July 14, commemorating the storming of the Bastille on July 14, 1789, during the French Revolution. Bastille Day has for the average Frenchman somewhat the same significance as Independence Day, or the Fourth of July, for a citizen of the U.S.: it symbolizes the overthrow of tyranny and the establishment of a government which would derive its power from the people rather than from royal heritage.

Basto (bäsh'tö), Marquis of. A title of **Coelho, Duarte de Albuquerque.**

Bastogne (bȧs.tony'). Town in SE Belgium, in the province of Luxembourg, situated in the Ardennes region near the border of the grand duchy of Luxembourg, ab. 45 mi. S of Liége: a railroad and road junction. In World War II, during the German offensive called the "Battle of the Bulge," the American 101st Airborne Division was surrounded here Dec. 22–26, 1944; the position was held with severe losses until the start of the Allied counter-offensive on January 16, 1945. The town suffered great damage. Saint Peter's Church, which dated from the 12th–15th centuries, with Romanesque tower and ancient murals, was completely destroyed. Pop. ab. 4,500.

"Bastogne, Battle of." See under **Battle of the Bulge.**

Baston (bas'ton), **Robert.** b. near Nottingham, England, toward the close of the 13th century. English poet. He was a Carmelite monk, and prior of the abbey of Scarborough. He followed Edward II on a campaign to Scotland, and was captured. Author of *Metra de Illustri de Bannockburn*, a panegyric upon Robert the Bruce, written at the request of the Scots.

Bastos (bäs'tös), (**Aureliano Cândido**) **Tavares.** b. at Maceió, Brazil, April 20, 1839; d. at Nice, France, Dec. 3, 1875. Brazilian journalist and sociologist, a progressive thinker, and a defender of civil liberties. Among his best-known works are *Cartas do solitário* (1862), *O vale do Amazonas* (1866), and *A provincia* (1870).

Bastrop (bas'trop). Town in N Louisiana, parish seat of Morehouse Parish: manufactures include paper, carbon black, and bricks. 12,769 (1950).

Bastrop. City in S central Texas, county seat of Bastrop County, on the Colorado River ab. 25 mi. SE of Austin. Poultry and cotton are raised and lignite is mined in the surrounding region. 3,176 (1950).

Bastuli (bas'tū.lī). Ancient people in S Spain, identified by Strabo with the Bastetani.

Bastwick (bast'wik), **John.** b. at Writtle, Essex, England, 1593; d. 1654. English physician and Protestant theological controversialist. He was imprisoned and fined by the Star Chamber in 1634 on account of his *Flagellum Pontificis*, and in 1637 for his *Letanie of Dr. John Bastwicke*, in which he roundly denounced episcopacy. He was released in 1640 and the amount of his fine returned to him.

Basuto (bä.sö'tō). See **Suto.**

Basutoland (ba.sö'tō.land). Native colony in S Africa, geographically within the Union of South Africa but under the direct administration of the British government, as one of the High Commission Territories. It is bounded by the Orange Free State on the W and N, Natal on the E, and Cape of Good Hope province on the S. Its surface is mountainous, and it is traversed by the Orange River. The inhabitants are Basutos. It is governed by a British resident commissioner under the high commissioner for Basutoland, the Bechuanaland protectorate, and Swaziland. In 1868 it was taken under British protection, was annexed to Cape Colony in 1871, was at war with the British 1880–82, and was returned to direct British control in 1884. Capital, Maseru; area, 11,716 sq. mi.; pop. 556,390, including 1,678 Europeans (1946).

Bata (bä'tä). Chief town in Río Muni, Spanish Guinea, on the W coast of Africa, about the middle of the coast-line of the small territory.

Bát'a (bä'tyä; Anglicized, bā'ta). Shoe-producing family and firm in Czechoslovakia. The factory is located at Zlín, in Moravia, and before World War II had reached an output of some 70,000 shoes per day. The enterprise was based on the most modern principles of mass production and has been distinguished by its labor policy, including employee ownership of stock, the erection of a model town, and the furnishing of a variety of recreational and cultural facilities. The firm was founded by Thomas Bát'a (1876–1932) and carried on by his brother Jan Bát'a (1898—), who achieved renown as the author of numerous books on modern industrial processes, efficiency, exploitation of natural resources, and transportation facilities. The Bát'a company was incorporated, after World War II, into the nationalized industrial framework of Czechoslovakia, and is a chief instrument in the Czechoslovak drive to export commodities throughout Europe.

Bataan (bä.tä.än'; Anglicized, ba.tan'). Peninsular province in SW Luzon, Philippine Islands, S of Zambales and Pampanga provinces, and between Manila Bay on the S and E and the South China Sea on the W. Two groups of mountains, continuations of the Zambales range, culminate in the Four Peaks, or Mariveles group, the loftiest of which is Mount Bataan, an extinct truncated volcano (4,700 ft.). Mariveles Bay, on the S coast, is a safe harbor in all weather. The province is watered by many small streams, and produces sugar cane, tobacco, rice, and indigo. The native inhabitants are chiefly Tagalogs. Capital, Balanga; area, 480 sq. mi.; pop. 92,901 (1948).

Bataan, Mount. [Former name, **Mount Mariveles.**] Extinct truncated volcano, the highest of the Four Peaks, or Mariveles group, in the S end of Bataan province, Luzon, Philippine Islands. 4,700 ft.

Bataan Campaign. Campaign involving Japanese and U.S.-Philippine forces during the early period of World War II. Bataan, a rocky peninsula on the N side of Manila harbor, and guarded at its tip by the fort of Corregidor, was the scene of the U.S. forces' last stand on Luzon island. From Jan. 2 to April 9, 1942, troops, first under Douglas MacArthur, then under Jonathan Wainwright, held out, though lacking planes, artillery, and rations. Finally, weakened by malaria and lack of food, they were completely outflanked by troops under Japanese General Homma and surrendered Corregidor on April 9.

Batac (bä'täk). Town in Ilocos Norte province, in NW Luzon, Philippine Islands. 6,218 (1948).

Bataille (bå.täy'), **Félix Henry.** b. at Nîmes, France, April 4, 1872; d. at Malmaison, France, March 2, 1922. French poet and playwright. He entered (1890) the École des Beaux Arts to study painting, but turned to the theater with *La Belle au bois dormant* (1894, with Robert d'Humières). He established his reputation with *L'Enchantement* (1900), *Le Masque* (1902), and *Maman Colibri* (1905); from that time until 1914 plays like *La Femme nue* (1908) and other dramas of passion kept his name constantly before the public. Later he essayed the "theater of ideas," in plays like *La Chaire humaine* (1922), but with diminishing success.

Batak (bä'täk). A Malayo-Polynesian-speaking people living in N Sumatra around Lake Toba, divided into five tribes (Toba, Mandailing, Karo, Pakpak, Timur); they number 1,207,514 (1930). They were the only people in Indonesia to practice cannibalism. Some 29 percent are now Moslems, and another 25 percent are Christians (Protestants).

Batak (bä'täk, bä.täk'). A Malayo-Polynesian-speaking Negrito tribe of Palawan, Philippine Islands.

Batalha (ba.tä'lya). Town and *concelho* (commune) in C Portugal, in the province of Beira Litoral, in the district of Leiria, situated on the Liz River, NE of Lisbon. The former Dominican monastery of Santa María da Victoria was erected here by King John I in memory of his victory over Castile, which preserved the independence of Portugal (Battle of Aljubarrota, Aug. 14, 1385); declared a national monument in 1840. The monastery buildings, begun in 1388 and finished in 1515, are among the most splendid examples of the Romanesque and Gothic styles in Portugal. Pop. of concelho, 11,153 (1940); of town, 4,370 (1940).

Batallium (ba.tal'i.um). A Latin name of **Badajoz,** city.

Batalpashinsk (ba.tal.pa.shinsk'). A former name of **Cherkessk.**

Batam (bä.täm'). [Also, **Batang.**] Small island in Indonesia, in the Strait of Singapore, ab. 20 mi. SE of Singapore.

Batan (bä.tän'). One of the Batan Islands, N of Luzon, Philippine Islands. It belongs to Batanes province. Its coal deposits are of good quality, and were in part developed by the U.S. for transport supply. Area, ab. 25 sq. mi.; pop. ab. 6,000.

Batanea (ba.tā'nē.a). See under **Bashan.**

Batanes (bä.tä'näs). Province of the Philippine Islands, composed of the Batan Islands off the N coast of Luzon. The province is bordered by the Bashi Channel on the N, by the Balingtang Channel on the S, by the South China Sea on the W, and the Philippine Sea of the Pacific Ocean on the E. The main islands are Itbayat, Batan, and Sabtang. Basco, the capital, is situated on the W coast of Batan island. Area, 74 sq. mi.; pop. 10,705 (1948).

Batang (bä.täng'). See **Batam.**

Batanga (bä.täng'gä). Region on the W coast of Africa, bordering on the Bight of Biafra. It was divided between France and Germany until 1920, but since then it has formed part of the French mandate of Cameroun.

Batangas (bä.täng'gäs). Province of the Philippine Islands, the southernmost of the W provinces of Luzon. It is bounded by Cavite (separated by the Tagatay Mountains) and Laguna on the N; Laguna, Tayabas, and Tayabas Bay on the E; and Mindoro island (separated by Verde Island Passage) on the S. The native population is Tagalog. The mountains are wooded and the valleys fertile, producing coffee, maize, pineapples, rice, and sugar cane. The province is rich in mineral springs and streams, the waters of which are considered beneficial in cutaneous diseases and in rheumatism. The N central part of Batangas is occupied by Lake Taal, in which is situated Taal volcano. Capital, Batangas; area, 1,192 sq. mi.; pop. 510,224 (1948).

Batangas. Seaport on SW Luzon, Philippine Islands. It is the capital of Batangas province and is situated on Batangas Bay across from the island of Mindoro. 10,326 (1948).

Batan Islands (bä.tän'). [Also: **Batanes, Bashi Islands.**] Group of small islands between Formosa and Luzon in the Philippines. They are coextensive with Batanes province. The main islands are Itbayat, Batan, and Sabtang. Area, 74 sq. mi.; pop. ab. 9,500 (1949).

Batara Guru (bạ.tä'rạ gö'rö). "The divine teacher," the name by which the Hindu deity Shiva is known in the literature and folk belief of various (now Moslem) peoples of Indonesia (Javanese, Malays, Batak, Buginese, and others). He is regarded as the creator of earth and mankind.

Bátaszék (bä'tô.sāk). [Also, **Báttaszék.**] Town in S Hungary, in the county of Tolna, situated near the Danube River W of the city of Baja. Wine and nuts are grown in the vicinity. The population is largely German. Pop. ab. 10,000.

Batava Castra (bạ.tā'vạ kas'trạ). Name of a Roman fort on the site of the modern Passau, in Bavaria.

Batavi (bạ.tā'vī). Germanic tribe, a branch of the Chatti. The Batavi inhabited the Insula Batavorum (between the Rhine, Waal, and Meuse rivers) in Roman times, were subjugated, probably by Drusus, and became the allies of the Romans (serving in the Roman armies, especially as cavalry). Later they took part in the rising under their own countryman, Civilis. They were ultimately merged in the Salic Franks.

Batavia (bạ.tā'vi.ạ). In ancient geography, originally a name for the island of the Batavi (Insula Batavorum), then the entire region inhabited by the Batavi; later, Holland, and then the kingdom of the Netherlands.

Batavia. City in NE Illinois, in Kane County, on the Fox River, ab. 32 mi. W of Chicago: manufactures farm machinery. 5,838 (1950).

Batavia. [Malay, **Jakarta.**] Seaport and the capital of the Republic of Indonesia, situated on the N coast of Java, near its W end: the chief commercial city in the East Indies, with some 2,400 ships entering its harbor in 1939. It comprises the old city, long notorious for its unhealthfulness, and the suburbs (best known of which are Weltevreden, the residential section, and Tandjoengpriok, the port). It exports coffee, rice, sugar, spice, rubber, and other East Indian products. It was settled in the beginning of the 17th century, and was briefly held (1811–14) by the British. The name was officially changed to Jakarta in 1949. Pop. 470,700 (1940), 2,500,000 (est. 1951).

Batavia. City in W New York, county seat of Genesee County, on Tonawanda Creek, ab. 36 mi. E of Buffalo; manufactures include farm machinery, brass and aluminum castings, shoes, shoe dyes, paper boxes, and flavoring extracts. 17,799 (1950).

Batavian Republic (bạ.tā'vi.ạn). Republic formed by France out of the Netherlands in **1795**. It existed until 1806.

Batavorum (bat.ạ.vō'rum), **Insula.** In ancient geography, in the time of Tacitus, a name given to an island in the Low Countries, formed by the Rhine, Waal, and Meuse rivers, inhabited by the Batavi.

Batbie (bȧ.bē), **Anselme Polycarpe.** b. at Seissan, France, May 31, 1828; d. at Paris, June 30, 1887. French politician, economist, and legal writer. He became professor of administrative law at the University of Paris in 1862, and senator for the department of Gers in 1871. Author of *Doctrine et jurisprudence en matière d'appel comme abus* (1852), *Précis du cours de droit public et administratif* (4th ed., 1876), and *Nouveau cours d'économie politique* (1864–65).

Batchelder (bach'el.dėr), **John Putnam.** b. at Wilton, N.H., Aug. 6, 1784; d. at New York, April 8, 1868. American surgeon, distinguished for his rhinoplastic operations, facial surgery, and inventions of surgical instruments.

Batchelder, Samuel. b. at Jaffrey, N.H., June 8, 1784; d. at Cambridge, Mass., Feb. 5, 1879. American inventor, cotton manufacturer, and writer, chiefly remembered for his dynamometer (1837) for measuring the power of belt-driven machinery. He also invented (1832) a stop-motion for the drawing frame in cotton manufacture. He managed cotton mills at Exeter, Peterboro, and New Ipswich, N.H. Author of *Introduction and Early Progress of Cotton Manufacture in the United States* (1836), *Responsibility of the North in Relation to Slavery* (1856), and *Young Men of America* (1860).

Batcheller (bach'ẹ.lėr), **George Sherman.** b. at Batchellerville, N.Y., July 25, 1837; d. at Paris, July 2, 1908. American jurist and Union soldier, known best as U.S. judge (1876–85, 1898–1908) on the international tribunal administering the laws of Egypt. He rose to the rank of lieutenant colonel in the Civil War; afterwards as inspector general (1865–68) he reorganized the New York National Guard. He was appointed assistant secretary (1889) of the U.S. treasury and minister to Portugal (1891).

Batchelor (bach'ẹ.lọr, bach'lọr), **George.** b. at Southbury, Conn., July 3, 1836; d. June 21, 1923. American Unitarian clergyman and editor. He was a pastor at Salem, Mass. (1866–82), Chicago (1882–85), and Lowell, Mass. (1889–93), and editor (1897–1911) of *The Christian Register*. Author of *Social Equilibrium* (1887).

Batchelor's Banquet, The. Pamphlet by Thomas Dekker, first published in 1603, and four or five times reprinted. It is based on an old French satire of the 15th century, *Les Quinze Joyes de Mariage*, but is so treated as to be almost an original work.

Batchian (bä.chän'). See **Batjan.**

Batchopi (bä.chō'pē). See **Chopi.**

Bate (bāt), **William Brimage.** b. at Bledsoe's Lick (now Castalian Springs), Tenn., Oct. 7, 1826; d. March 9, 1905. American Confederate soldier and politician, governor (1882 *et seq.*) of Tennessee. He served in the Mexican War, was elected (1854) attorney general of the Nashville, Tenn., district, supported secessionist forces in Tennessee, and served in the Civil War, rising through the ranks to a major-generalship. He participated in postwar Tennessee politics, opposing the Brownlow administration; as governor he settled the state-debt problem. While serving (1886–1905) in the U.S. Senate, he was the author of the law (1893) repealing all federal supervision of local elections.

Bateman (bāt'mạn), **Harry.** b. at Manchester, England, May 29, 1882; d. en route to New York, Jan. 21, 1946. Mathematician who wrote numerous papers and books on geometry, differential equations, integral equations, and the theory of functions. He studied at Cambridge, Göttingen, and Paris, and taught at Liverpool and Manchester. In 1910 he moved to the U.S., where he taught at Bryn Mawr (1910–12), Johns Hopkins (1913–17), and the California Institute of Technology (1917 *et seq.*). His books include *The Mathematical Analysis of Electrical and Optical Wave Motion* (1915), *Differential Equations* (1918), and *Partial Differential Equations of Mathematical Physics* (1932).

Bateman, Henry Mayo. b. at Sutton Forest, Australia, Feb. 15, 1887—. British caricaturist. He has contributed to *Punch* and other leading magazines and designed numerous theatrical posters. He studied at the Westminster and New Cross art schools and in the studio of Charles van Havenmaet. His publications include *Burlesques*, *A Book of Drawings*, and *Suburbia*.

Bateman, Hezekiah Linthicum. b. at Baltimore, Md., Dec. 6, 1812; d. at London, March 22, 1875. Actor and theatrical manager; husband of Sidney Frances Bateman and father of Kate Josephine Bateman. He was the lessee of the Lyceum Theatre at London from 1871 until his death; it was at his theater that Henry Irving made his first appearance (1871) in one of his most popular roles, in *The Bells*.

Bateman, Kate Josephine. b. at Baltimore, Md., Oct. 7, 1843; d. April 8, 1917. American actress; daughter of Hezekiah Linthicum Bateman and Sidney Frances Bateman. She and her younger sister appeared on the stage (c1851) as "the Bateman Sisters." In 1863 she began to play in *Leah* at the Adelphi Theatre, London; in 1866 she married George Crowe, but returned to the stage in 1868 under her maiden name, playing Lady Macbeth opposite Henry Irving, Medea, Juliet, and Queen Mary in Tennyson's drama (in 1876).

Bateman, Newton. b. at Fairton, Conn., July 27, 1822; d. at Galesburg, Ill., Oct. 21, 1897. American educator, active (1858 *et seq.*) in the founding of Illinois Normal University. He served as state superintendent of public instruction (1859–63, 1865–75) in Illinois. A cofounder and sometime editor of the *Illinois Teacher*, he was a member of the three-man committee which drafted the bill organizing the U.S. Bureau of Education. President (1874–92) of Knox College; editor of the *Historical Encyclopedia of Illinois*.

Bateman, Sidney Frances. [Maiden name, **Cowell.**] b. March 29, 1823; d. Jan. 13, 1881. American playwright, actress, and theater manager; wife of Hezekiah Linthicum Bateman and mother of Kate Josephine Bateman. After her husband's death, she was manager (1871 *et seq.*) of the Lyceum Theatre, London. Author of the plays *Self* (1856), *Geraldine* (1859), a dramatization (1860) of Henry Wadsworth Longfellow's *Evangeline*, and others.

Bateman, Virginia. Maiden name of **Compton, Virginia.**

Baten Kaitos (bä′tẹn kī′tos). The third-magnitude star ζ Ceti.

Bates (bāts). A soldier in the king's army, in Shakespeare's *Henry V*.

Bates, Arlo. b. at East Machias, Me., Dec. 16, 1850; d. Aug. 24, 1918. American author and journalist. With his wife, Harriet L. Vose, who wrote under the pseudonym Eleanor Putnam, he wrote *Prince Vance* (1888). He was editor (1880–86) of the *Boston Sunday Courier*, and was professor of English (1893 *et seq.*) at the Massachusetts Institute of Technology. Author of *Mr. Jacobs* (1883), *The Pagans* (1884), *A Wheel of Fire* (1885), *Sonnets in Shadow* (1887), *The Philistines* (1889), *Talks on Writing English* (1896–1901), *The Puritans* (1898), *Talks on Teaching Literature* (1906), *The Intoxicated Ghost* (1908), and *A Mother's Meeting* (1909).

Bates, Barnabas. b. at Edmonton, England, 1785; d. at Boston, Mass., Oct. 11, 1853. American advocate of postal reform, and an organizer of the movement for cheap postage. Brought to America as a child, he later served as a Baptist minister at Bristol, R.I., until his views as a Freemason and his Unitarian leanings caused antagonism in the community. He moved to New York, where he served as assistant postmaster; in 1840 he published an article, "Post-Office Reform—Cheap Postage," and subsequently organized public meetings which petitioned Congress to standardize postage rates at five cents an ounce and repeal franking privileges. An act passed (1846) reducing postage to five cents for 300-mi. distances was unsatisfactory to him, and he organized (1848) the New York Cheap Postage Association, of which he became first corresponding secretary. An act was passed (1851) reducing rates to three cents a half-ounce for 3,000-mi. distances.

Bates, Blanche. b. at Portland, Ore., 1873; d. at San Francisco, Dec. 25, 1941. American stage and operatic actress. She made her debut (1894) in Stockwell's Theater at San Francisco, played (1898) Shakespearian parts in Augustin Daly's company, and starred in *The Great Ruby*, *The Musketeers*, and *Madame Butterfly* (1900). She acted the leading role in the first performances of *Under Two Flags*, *The Darling of the Gods*, and *The Girl of the Golden West*. She retired in 1926 but acted again for a short period in 1933.

Bates, Charley. Cheerful young thief in the employ of Fagin, in Charles Dickens's novel *Oliver Twist*.

Bates, Charlotte Fiske. [Married name, **Rogé.**] b. at New York, Nov. 30, 1838; d. Sept. 1, 1916. American poet; she married (1891) Adolphe Rogé (d. 1896). At one time an associate of and collaborator with Henry Wadsworth Longfellow, she edited the *Cambridge Book of Poetry and Song* (1882), and wrote *Risk, and Other Poems* (1879).

Bates, Daisy. b. c1860; d. 1951. Irish welfare worker in Australia. She arrived (1899) in Australia as a London *Times* correspondent, to investigate living conditions of Australian aborigines; she subsequently engaged in welfare work and lived among the aborigines for more than 30 years. She conferred (1933) at Canberra about native problems with representatives of the commonwealth government, and was made (1934) a commander of the Order of the British Empire. Author of *The Passing of the Aborigines* (1938).

Bates, Daniel Moore. b. at Laurel, Del., Jan. 28, 1821; d. at Richmond, Va., March 28, 1879. American jurist; father of George Handy Bates. He was admitted (1842) to the bar, and appointed (1849) commissioner to revise Delaware state laws. He served as U.S. district attorney for Delaware (1852 *et seq.*), commissioner (1861) at the Washington peace conference, and chancellor (1865–73) of Delaware. He published (1876, 1878) *Reports of Cases Adjudged and Determined in the Court of Chancery of the State of Delaware*.

Bates, David. b. c1810; d. at Philadelphia, Jan. 25, 1870. American poet. He wrote the poem "Speak Gently." His poems were published in book form under the title *The Eolian* (1848).

Bates, Edward. b. at Belmont, Goochland County, Va., Sept. 4, 1793; d. at St. Louis, Mo., March 25, 1869. American statesman and jurist. He was a member of Congress from Missouri (1827–29), unsuccessful candidate for the Republican nomination for President in 1860, and attorney general (1861–64) under Lincoln.

Bates, Ernest Sutherland. b. at Gambier, Ohio, Oct. 14, 1879; d. Dec. 4, 1939. American author and teacher. He received the degrees of A.B. (1902) from the University of Michigan and Ph.D. (1908) from Columbia University, served as professor (1908–15) of English at the University of Arizona, and was professor of English (1915–21) and of philosophy (1921–25) at the University of Oregon. Later he was associate editor (1933–36) of *The Modern Monthly*. Editor of *The Four Gospels* (1932) and *The Bible Designed to Be Read as Living Literature* (1936); author of *Study of Shelley's The Cenci* (1908), *The Friend of Jesus* (1928), *This Land of Liberty* (1930), *The Story of Congress* (1936), *The Story of the Supreme Court* (1936), and *Biography of the Bible* (1937).

Bates, Frederick. b. June 23, 1777; d. near Chesterfield, Mo., Aug. 4, 1825. American territorial administrator and governor (1824–25) of Missouri; brother of Edward Bates. He was associate judge of the Michigan Territory, and assisted in drafting the first territorial code.

Bates, George Handy. b. at Dover, Del., Nov. 19, 1845; d. Oct. 31, 1916. American lawyer and special diplomatic agent; son of Daniel Moore Bates. Admitted (1869) to the bar, he became prominent in the Democratic Party in Delaware, and was appointed (1886) special agent to investigate conditions in Samoa. His report recommended a native government under the supervision of executives appointed by the U.S., Great Britain, and Germany. He attended the tripartite conference (1889) at Berlin, and the resultant treaty embodied many of his suggestions.

Bates, H. E. [Full name, **Herbert Ernest Bates.**] b. at Rushden, England, May 16, 1905—. English novelist and author of many widely anthologized short stories. His novels include *The Two Sisters* (1926), *Charlotte's Row*, *The Poacher*, *A House of Women* (all 1936), *Spella Ho* (1938), *Fair Stood the Wind for France* (1944), and *The Scarlet Sword* (1951).

Bates, Henry Walter. b. at Leicester, England, Feb. 18, 1825; d. at London, Feb. 16, 1892. English naturalist and traveler. In 1848 he went to the Amazon with A. R. Wallace; at first with him, and afterward alone, he traveled over all parts of the Brazilian Amazon. Returning to England in 1859, with some 8,000 new species, he published *The Naturalist on the River Amazon* (1863). He also wrote a handbook of Central and South America, and others.

Bates, John Coalter. b. in St. Charles County, Mo., Aug. 26, 1842; d. at San Diego, Calif., Feb. 4, 1919. American army officer, best remembered for the "Bates Treaty" with the Sultan of Sulu (1899) during the insurrection of Emilio Aguinaldo in the Philippines, under which the Sultan acknowledged U.S. sovereignty in return for a monthly subsidy. He served throughout the Civil, Spanish-American, and Philippine wars, retiring (1906) as a lieutenant general.

Bates, Joshua. b. at Weymouth, Mass., Oct. 10, 1788; d. at London, Sept. 24, 1864. American banker, connected with the house of Baring Brothers and Company. His activities on behalf of the Boston Public Library during the period 1852–58 have caused him to be known as its chief founder.

Bates, Katharine Lee. b. at Falmouth, Mass., Aug. 29, 1859; d. March 28, 1929. American writer and educator, best remembered as the author of *America The Beautiful.* She was graduated from Wellesley College in 1880 and taught there from 1885, becoming professor of English literature in 1891. She wrote *Rose and Thorn* (1889), *English Religious Drama* (1893), *American Literature* (1898), *Spanish Highways and By-Ways* (1900), as well as collections of verse.

Bates, Ralph. b. at Swindon, Wiltshire, England, Nov. 3, 1899—. English writer. He served in World War I, and was an officer (1936–37) in the International Brigade of the Spanish Loyalist army during the Spanish Civil War. His books include *Sierra* (1933), *Lean Men* (1934), *Schubert* (1934), *The Olive Field* (1936), *Rainbow Fish* (1937), *The Fields of Paradise* (1941), *The Undiscoverables* (1942), and *The Journey to the Sandalwood Forest* (1947); he also published the collections of stories *Sirocco* (1939) and *The Miraculous Horde* (1939).

Bates, Samuel Penniman. b. at Mendon, Mass., Jan. 29, 1827; d. July 14, 1902. American educator and historian, author of the *History of Pennsylvania Volunteers* (1869–70). He was appointed (1860) deputy state superintendent of public instruction in Pennsylvania.

Bates, Walter. b. at what is now Darien, Conn., March 14, 1760; d. Feb. 11, 1842. American Loyalist during the Revolutionary War. He settled (1783) in Nova Scotia. Author of *Kingston and the Loyalists of the "Spring Fleet" of 1783*, a valuable source (first published 1889) on Connecticut Loyalism, and *The Mysterious Stranger; or Memoirs of Henry More Smith* (1816), a work of fiction.

Batesburg (bāts′bėrg). Town in W South Carolina, in Lexington and Saluda Counties: manufactures include coffins, boxes, and crates. 3,169 (1950).

Bateson (bāt′sọn), **Thomas.** b. c1570; d. at Dublin, 1630. English composer and organist, remembered for his madrigals, published in two groups (1604, 1618). His best-known piece is the *Oriana* madrigal.

Bateson, William. b. at Whitby, England, 1861; d. Feb. 8, 1926. English naturalist, fellow (1908–09) of St. John's College, Cambridge. In 1910 he was appointed director of the John Innes Horticultural Institution at Merton, Surrey. Besides numerous papers on biological topics, he published *Materials for the Study of Variation* (1894) and *Mendel's Principles of Heredity* (1902).

Batesville (bāts′vil). City in N Arkansas, county seat of Independence County: marketing center for fruits, poultry, and dairy products. It is the seat of Arkansas College. 6,414 (1950).

Batesville. City in SE Indiana, in Ripley County: furniture-manufacturing center. 3,194 (1950).

Bath (bȧth). [Latin, **Aquae Solis** (or **Sulis**) meaning "Springs," or "Baths, of the Sun"; sometimes **Aquae Calidae,** meaning "Hot Springs."] City and county borough in SW England, in Somersetshire, situated on the river Avon, ab. 12 mi. SE of Bristol, ab. 107 mi. W of London by rail. It is an ancient health resort, one of the leading spas of England, noted for its saline and chalybeate hot springs. In the Roman period it was an important watering place, noted for its splendid buildings, its temples, its buildings for public amusement, and still more so for its medicinal baths. Remains of the Roman bathing-houses have been discovered in the course of modern excavations. It was the site of a magnificent temple dedicated to Minerva, who is supposed to have been the patron goddess of the place. The Roman town was destroyed by the Saxons. The redevelopment of Bath in the 17th and especially in the 18th century came about in part through the influence of Richard ("Beau") Nash. It engaged in cloth manufacture in the Middle Ages, during which time its function as a health resort was interrupted; while woolens were being manufactured, Fullers' earth was worked in the vicinity. Bath limestone, quarried nearby, is important as a building stone, having the virtue that it can be cut in any direction. Bath has manufactures of boots and shoes, electrical machinery, paints, and other items. The abbey church of Bath, an excellent example of the Perpendicular style, was begun c1500. It has been called "the Lantern of England," from the number and size of its traceried windows. The plan presents a square chevet and narrow transepts. The W window is considered noteworthy, as is the restored fan-vaulting of the interior. The church is 225 ft. long, the central tower 162 ft. high. Of the Roman thermae five large halls remain, one of them 68 by 110 ft., and several smaller ones, with the arrangements for heating beneath the floors. One of the *piscinae* (basins) retains its ancient lining of lead. Pop. of county borough, 79,275 (1951).

Bath. City in SW Maine, county seat of Sagadahoc County, on the W bank of the Kennebec River: a shipbuilding center for small craft and light cruisers; formerly one of the principal producers of sailing vessels. It has a fine harbor. It was incorporated in 1781. Pop. 10,644 (1950).

Bath. Village in S New York, county seat of Steuben County, on the Cohocton River, ab. 56 mi. SE of Rochester, in an agricultural area: manufactures include ladders, saddlery, and knit goods. 5,416 (1950).

Bath, Earl of. Title of **Pulteney, William** (1684–1764).

Bath. Official name of **Berkeley Springs.**

Bath, Colonel. An inflexibly punctilious but kind-hearted character in Henry Fielding's novel *Amelia.*

Bath, Order of the. Order of British knighthood, now conferred for outstanding services either military or civil. The "most honourable Order of the Bath" was established by George I in 1725, ostensibly as a revival of an order supposedly originated by Henry IV at his coronation in 1399. The Order of the Bath is now limited in membership to the sovereign, the royal princes, distinguished foreigners, and 55 military and 27 civil knights of the grand cross (G.C.B.), 145 military and 108 civil knights commanders (K.C.B.), and 705 military and 298 civil companions (C.B.). The officers of the Order are the dean, who is the Dean of Westminster, the Bath King of Arms, the registrar, and the usher of the Scarlet Rod. In the gradations of knighthood in Great Britain, the Order of the Bath yields precedence only to the Order of the Garter.

Batha (bä′tä). [Also: **Ba Tha, Bat-ha.**] River in C Africa, the chief river of Ouadai district, Chad territory, French Equatorial Africa. It flows westward into Lake Fitri.

Bath Club. London club established in 1894 for social and athletic purposes.

Bathgate (bȧth′gạt). Police burgh and market town in S Scotland, in West Lothian, ab. 5 mi. S of Linlithgow, ab. 412 mi. N of London by rail. 10,747 (est. 1948).

Báthory or **Báthori** (bä′tọ.rē), **Christoph.** b. 1530; d. 1581. Prince of Transylvania; brother of Stephen Báthory (1533–86). He became ruler of Transylvania in 1576, in succession to Stephen, who had ascended the throne of Poland. He invited the Jesuits into Transylvania, which intensified the religious strife already existing in the land. He is perhaps best remembered as the father of Sigismund Báthory, who was elected prince in 1581, just before his father's death.

Báthory or **Báthori, Elizabeth.** d. 1614. Hungarian princess, notorious for her crimes; niece of Stephen Báthory or Báthori, king of Poland, and wife of a Hungarian count Nádasdy. She is alleged, by contemporary accounts, to have been a werewolf. From time to time, with the aid of her attendants, she killed young girls (said in different accounts to number from 80 to more than 600) in order to use their blood as a bath which would, she hoped, renew her youth. She was imprisoned for life, and her accomplices were maimed and burned.

Báthory or **Báthori, Gabriel.** b. 1589; d. 1613. Prince of Transylvania; son of Stephen Báthory (1533–86). Possessed of an inclination toward cruelty that was notable even in a family that included the infamous Elizabeth Báthory, his ferocious excesses led to a revolt by which he was driven from the country.

Báthory or **Báthori, Sigismund.** [Hungarian, **Zsigmond Báthory.**] b. 1572; d. at Prague, in Bohemia, 1613. Prince of Transylvania (1581–98): nephew of Stephen Báthory, king of Poland.

Báthory or **Báthori, Stephen.** b. 1533; d. 1586. Hungarian noble, prince of Transylvania (1571–76) and king of Poland (1575–86). He was crowned in 1576.

Bath-sheba (bath.shē′bạ or bath′shē.bạ). In the Bible, the wife of Uriah the Hittite, sinfully loved by David; afterward the wife of David and the mother of Solomon. (2 Sam. xi.)

Bathsheba. Character in John Dryden's *Absalom and Achitophel,* intended to represent Louise Kerouaille, duchess of Portsmouth, a favorite of Charles II of England.

Baths of Caracalla (kar.ạ.kal'ạ). Baths in ancient Rome, begun by the emperor Lucius Septimius Severus in 206 A.D. The thermae proper occupied a space of 720 ft. by 375 ft., in a large square enclosure, bordered by porticos and connected foundations. The remains include walls, arches, and vaults, which are among the most imposing ruins of ancient Rome, and portions of the figured mosaic pavements.

Baths of Diocletian (dī.ọ.klē'shạn). Baths in ancient Rome, begun by the emperor Diocletian in the late 3rd century A.D. They were not opened, however, until 306 A.D., the year after the abdication of Diocletian.

Baths of Leuk (loik). English name of **Leukerbad.**

Baths of Titus (tī'tus). Baths in ancient Rome, constructed in the 1st century A.D. by the emperor Titus, situated NE of the Colosseum.

Bathurst (bȧth'ėrst). Town in SE Australia, in the state of New South Wales, ab. 100 mi. NW of Sydney; the central point of a gold-producing district. 11,889 (1947).

Bathurst. Capital of Gambia colony and protectorate, W Africa, situated on St. Mary's island near the mouth of the Gambia River. Its commerce is mostly in the form of transshipment from river boats to ocean vessels. 21,152 (1946).

Bathurst. Seaport and county town of Gloucester County, New Brunswick, Canada, situated on Chaleur Bay in the N part of the province: paper mills. It is on the main line of the Canadian National Railway from Quebec. 4,453 (1951).

Bathurst, Allen. [Title, 1st Earl **Bathurst.**] b. at Westminster, England, Nov. 16, 1684; d. at Cirencester, England, Sept. 16, 1775. English statesman, a friend of Alexander Pope, Jonathan Swift, Matthew Prior, William Congreve, and Laurence Sterne. To him Pope addressed the third of his "Moral Essays." After serving (1705-12) as the member from Cirencester in the House of Commons, he was created a peer (1712), and raised (1772) to the rank of earl.

Bathurst, Sir **Charles.** See **Bledisloe,** 1st Viscount.

Bathurst, Henry. [Title, 2nd Earl **Bathurst;** additional title, Baron **Apsley.**] b. May 2, 1714; d. Aug. 6, 1794. English politician; son of Allen Bathurst. He was lord chancellor of England (1771-78), and lord president of the council (1779-82).

Bathurst, Henry. [Title, 3rd Earl **Bathurst.**] b. May 22, 1762; d. 1834. English statesman; son of Henry Bathurst (1714-94). He was president of the Board of Trade (1809-12), secretary for war and the colonies (1812-27), and president of the council (1828-30).

Bathurst Inlet. Inlet of the Arctic Ocean, extending S from Coronation Gulf into the Mackenzie District of the Northwest Territories, Canada.

Bathurst Island. Large island of the Arctic Archipelago, in the Arctic Ocean N of Canada, N of Prince of Wales Island. It is now believed to be the location of the North Magnetic Pole.

Bathurst Island. Island N of Australia, and W of Melville Island. It belongs to the Northern Territory of Australia. Area, 786 sq. mi.

Bathycles or **Bathykles** (bath'i.klēz). b. at Magnesia (now Manisa, in Turkey); fl. c560 B.C. Greek sculptor. Having been commissioned to do so by the Spartans, he constructed a throne for the colossal statue of the Amyclaean Apollo in Laconia.

Bathyllus of Alexandria (bạ.thil'us). fl. c20 B.C. Freedman of Maecenas, noted as a comic dancer in the *pantomimi,* a popular dramatic form of the Hellenistic period.

Bathys (bath'is). See under **Batum.**

Batiffol (bȧ.tē.fol), **Pierre Henri.** b. at Toulouse, France, Jan. 27, 1861; d. at Paris, Jan. 13, 1929. French educator and church historian, appointed (1898) rector of the Catholic institute at Toulouse. Author of *Histoire de littérature grecque chrétienne* (History of Greek Christian Literature, 1897).

Batignolles (bȧ.tē.nyol). Quarter of Paris, France, situated in the NW part of the city.

Batista y Zaldívar (bä.tēs'tä ē säl.dē'ʙär), **Fulgencio.** b. at Banes, Cuba, Jan. 16, 1901—. Cuban military leader, president (1940-44) of Cuba. A former agricultural worker, mechanic, and railway employee, he joined the national army in 1921; after serving a two-year enlistment, he joined again later as a private, then as a sergeant first class. A member of the ABC revolutionary secret society, he took part in the revolution (1933) against President Gerardo Machado. Made a colonel and chief of staff (September, 1933) of the Constitutional army by the Government of Five, he reorganized the army, and developed it into a powerful force. He brought about the impeachment (1936) of President Miguel Mariano Gómez and the selection of Laredo Brú to succeed him. The coalition candidate (1940) for president, he was elected and served until 1944. In 1952, by a coup d'état, he again obtained control of the government of Cuba.

Batiste (bȧ.tēst), **Antoine Édouard.** b. at Paris, March 28, 1820; d. there, Nov. 9, 1876. French organist, composer, and teacher. As a student at the Paris Conservatory he won many prizes, and in 1840 was awarded the second Prix de Rome. He became organist at the church of Saint Nicolas des Champs, and was organist (1854-76) at the church of Saint Eustache. He composed many pieces for the organ, but is best known for his solfeggio method.

Batjan (bä.chän'). [Also: **Bachan, Bachian, Batchian.**] One of the Molucca islands, Indonesia, SE of Halmahera, and separated from it by the Patientie Strait. Length, ab. 40 mi.; width, ab. 25 mi.; pop. ab. 8,000.

Batley (bat'li). Municipal borough and manufacturing town in C England, in the West Riding of Yorkshire, ab. 8 mi. SW of Leeds, ab. 184 mi. N of London by rail. It is a center of the heavy woolen trade, having manufactures of woolens and shoddy. Batley has grown rapidly during recent years. 40,192 (1951).

Batlle (bät'yä), **Lorenzo.** b. at Montevideo, Uruguay, 1812; d. c1875. Uruguayan general and statesman, president of Uruguay in the period 1868-72. During the nine-year siege of Montevideo by Manuel Oribe, Batlle belonged to the *Defensa,* or Montevidean party, commanding one of the bodies of infantry in the garrison, and leading various raids into the interior. He was minister of war under Venancio Flores, provisional president (1866-68), and was elected president on Feb. 28, 1868. During his term there were frequent revolts and a great financial crisis. He gave up the office in 1872 and resumed his duties as general.

Batlle y Ordóñez (ē ôr.ᴛʜō'nyes), **José.** b. at Montevideo, Uruguay, May 21, 1856; d. there, Oct. 20, 1929. Uruguayan statesman and journalist; twice (1903-07, 1911-15) president of Uruguay; son of Lorenzo Batlle. As a youth, he interrupted his law studies at Montevideo to go to Paris, where he became deeply interested in liberal ideas of government. Returning to Montevideo, he founded the newspaper *El Dia,* which remained throughout his life his chief medium for advancing his political and social principles. Entering politics in 1887 as a leader of the Colorado (Liberal)Party, he denounced the incumbent president of Uruguay as a dictator. For this he was jailed, exiled, and threatened with death, but he nevertheless took part thereafter in several insurrectionary movements against various dictators. When the Colorados returned to power he sought, contrary to the practice then usual in many Latin American countries, to prevent the police from persecuting members of the opposition party. When, as an advocate of reform in government, he was first elected to the presidency in 1903, the opposition organized a revolution; he suppressed it, but gave the rebels unusually easy terms of surrender. At the end of his first presidential term, in 1907, he went to Switzerland, and studied in some detail that country's democratic methods of government. Again elected (1911) president of Uruguay, he endeavored to put these methods into operation in his own country. After his retirement in 1915, many of his principles were embodied in the new Uruguayan Constitution of 1918, especially provisions for social insurance and for setting up state corporations to conduct banking and a variety of other businesses when private capital failed to do so. The core of his political thought was that the state is obligated to help all its citizens by promoting prosperity, security, and a better distribution of the fruits of industry and labor. He pleaded for understanding, not hatred, between classes. In the opinion of many historians, the present character of

Uruguay as a progressive and democratic country is in large part due to his achievements.

Batman (bat'mạn), **John.** b. at Parramatta, New South Wales, Australia, Jan. 21, 1801; d. at Melbourne, Australia, May 6, 1839. Australian colonist, considered a founder of Melbourne. A cattle grazer, he settled in Tasmania in 1821 and prospered. About 1825 he became interested in unoccupied country near Port Phillip Bay on the mainland, and organized (1835) the Port Phillip Association and crossed to the new country to explore and purchase land from the aborigines (the purchases were, however, later disallowed). In the meantime another party from Tasmania, sent by John Pascoe Fawkner, actually erected the first buildings at Melbourne in August, 1835; Batman himself arrived to settle in November of that same year.

Batn el Hajar (bä'tn el hä'jär). Name applied at one time to a region in Nubia, Anglo-Egyptian Sudan, on both sides of the Nile River above the second cataract.

Batoe (bä'tö). [Also: **Batu;** Dutch, **Batoe Eilanden.**] Group of small islands in Indonesia, W of Sumatra, near the equator, inhabited by Malays. The largest is 45 mi. in length. Formerly under Dutch rule, they are now a part of the Republic of Indonesia.

Batonapa (bä.tō.nä'pä). Hill in NW Mexico, in Sonora state, a few miles S of the village of Banamichi on the Sonora River, overgrown with dense thickets, but covered with the remains of ancient Indian fortifications consisting of rude parapets of stone. They were reared in ancient times by the Opatas of the valley of Banamichi, as a place of refuge in case of attack.

Batoni (bä.tō'nē), **Pompeo Girolamo.** b. at Lucca, Italy, 1708; d. 1787. Italian painter. He is said to have portrayed 22 sovereigns and equivalent notables, including Emperor Joseph II and Popes Benedict XIV, Clement XIII, and Pius VI. His *Magdalen*, now in the Louvre at Paris, is the best known of his works, of which other examples are an *Achilles* in the Uffizi gallery, Florence, a *John the Baptist* at Dresden, a *Marriage of Cupid and Psyche* in the Berlin Museum, a *Marriage of Saint Catherine* in the Quirinal Palace, Rome, and a *Hercules* in the Pitti Palace, Florence.

Baton Rouge (bat'ọn rözh). [Eng. trans., *"Red Staff."*] City in SE Louisiana, capital of the state and parish seat of East Baton Rouge Parish, on the Mississippi River ab. 75 mi. NW of New Orleans: manufactures include refined oil and alkali. It is the seat of Louisiana State University and Agricultural and Mechanical College. It was captured by Union troops on May 12, 1862; on Aug. 5 following, the Union brigadier general Thomas Williams, with less than 2,500 men, repulsed an attack by the Confederate major general John C. Breckinridge, with ab. 2,600 men; Union loss in killed, wounded, and missing 383, the Confederate, 456. The city is said to have been named from a red boundary mark which separated the lands of the Indians from those of the whites. It was the capital of Louisiana from 1849 to 1862, and again became the capital in 1880. In the decade between the last two U.S. censuses, the city's population more than doubled (although the higher figure is due in part to the new urban definition used by the census bureau in 1950). Pop. of city, 34,719 (1940), 125,629 (1950); of urbanized area, 138,864 (1950).

Batoum (bä.töm'). See **Batum.**

Batrachomyomachia (bat"rạ.kọ.mī"ọ.mā'ki.ạ). [English, **The Battle of the Frogs and Mice.**] Ancient Greek mock epic, in hexameters, of which 316 lines are extant. Although its authorship is, at best, a matter of conjecture, it was formerly attributed to Homer, and by some critics to Pigres, brother of Artemisia, queen of Caria. It tells the story of a war between frogs and mice.

Batrachus (bat'rạ.kus) or **Batrachos** (-kos). Greek architect and sculptor at Rome in the time of Augustus.

Batschka (bäch'kä). German name of **Bačka.**

Batshioko (bä.chō'kō) or **Batshiokwe** (-chōk'we). See **Chokwe.**

Batt (bat), **William Loren.** b. at Salem, Ind., 1885—. American engineer and industrialist. He received his M.E. (1907) and Eng. D. (1933) degrees from Purdue; after having been associated (1941–42) with the U.S. Office of Production Management, he was vice-chairman (1942–45) in charge of international supply for the U.S. War Production Board.

Battambang (bat'ạm.bang). City in Indochina, in W Cambodia, ab. 280 mi. NW of Saigon. There are several sulfur mines in the area; in the city itself the leading industries are fish packing, cigarette manufacturing, and hand weaving of cotton and silk. Pop. ab. 20,000.

Battani (bät.tä'nē), **al-.** [Latinized, **Albategnius, Albatenius.**] b. at or near what is now Haran, Turkey, sometime before 858; d. near Samarra (in what is now Iraq), in 929. Arab astronomer, generally considered to have been the greatest of his time and one of the greatest in the entire history of Islam. Various astrological writings, including a commentary on Ptolemy's *Tetrabiblon*, are ascribed to him, but his main work was an astronomical treatise with tables, which remained extremely influential until the Renaissance. From 877 until the time of his death, he made astronomical observations of a range and accuracy astounding in that day. He found that the longitude of the sun's apogee had increased by 16°47′ since the time of Ptolemy; that implied the discovery of the motion of the solar apsides and of a slow variation in the equation of time. He proved the possibility of annular eclipses of the sun, and did not believe in the trepidation of the equinoxes (although Copernicus, many years later, still did). In the third chapter of his treatise on astronomy he concerned himself with trigonometry, and used sines regularly with a clear consciousness of their superiority to the Greek chords. He completed the introduction of the functions *umbra extensa* and *umbra versa* (whence our cotangents and tangents) and gave a table of cotangents by degrees. This work was translated into Latin in the 12th century, and a century later (at the order of Alfonso X) into Spanish.

Báttaszék (bät'tô.sāk). See **Bátaszék.**

Battenberg (bät'ẹn.berk; Anglicized, bat'ẹn.bėrg). Town in W Germany, in the *Land* (state) of Hessen, American Zone, formerly in the province of Hesse-Nassau, Prussia, situated on the Eder River, ab. 44 mi. SW of Kassel: lumber trade; furniture manufacture. It was the seat of the Battenberg family. The original family ended in 1314; the title was revived by the grand duke of Hesse in 1858 when he conferred it upon the descendants of Prince Alexander of Hesse and the Polish countess Julia von Haucke. The British line of the family changed the name to Mountbatten in 1917. Battenberg lace (also called Renaissance lace), a characteristic pattern of braid and lace stitches, is named for this town.

Battenberg. Family of European nobility, originally (until 1314) comprised of German counts, but recreated in the middle of the 19th century as a princely family stemming from the morganatic marriage of Alexander, one of the younger sons of the house of Hesse-Darmstadt, with a Polish countess. They had three sons: Louis Alexander (the eldest son, and progenitor of the present Mountbatten family of Great Britain), Alexander (who became Alexander I of Bulgaria), and Henry (who married a daughter of Queen Victoria, and was the father by her of the last queen of Spain). Louis Alexander of Battenberg, the eldest son, was naturalized as a British subject in 1868, became an admiral in the Royal Navy, married (1884) Victoria (a granddaughter of Queen Victoria), and was elevated to the British peerage in 1917 as 1st Marquis of Milford Haven. During World War I, he changed his name to "Mountbatten" (involving actually only a simple translation of the German word *berg*, which means "mount" or "mountain" in English) and the English members of the family (including Lord Louis Mountbatten) have since used this name. One of his daughters married a member of the Greek royal house, and was the mother of Philip (elevated to the British peerage in 1947 as the Duke of Edinburgh), who is the consort of Queen Elizabeth II.

Battenberg, Prince **Alexander of.** See **Alexander I** (of *Bulgaria*).

Battenberg (bat'ẹn.bėrg), Prince **Henry Maurice of.** b. Oct. 5, 1858; d. Jan. 21, 1896. Younger brother of Prince Louis Alexander of Battenberg. He married (1885) Princess Beatrice, Queen Victoria's youngest daughter. He died of a fever while on the way home from service with a British expeditionary force fighting the Ashanti.

Battenberg, Prince **Louis Alexander of.** [Additional title, 1st Marquis of **Milford Haven.**] b. at Gratz, Austria, May 24, 1854; d. 1921. English admiral; the eldest son of Prince Alexander of Hesse-Darmstadt, and the brother of Alexander I of Bulgaria, and Prince Henry of Battenberg. In 1868 he was naturalized a British subject and entered the Royal Navy as naval cadet. He served in the Egyptian campaign of 1882. In 1884 he married Princess Victoria of Hesse, granddaughter of Queen Victoria. He served (1904) with the navy as a vice-admiral, commanded (1908–10) the Atlantic fleet, and was made an admiral in 1919. He was given the title Marquis of Milford Haven in 1917.

Battenberg, Prince **Louis Francis Albert Victor Nicholas of.** See **Mountbatten,** Lord **Louis.**

Battersea (bat′ėr.sē). Metropolitan borough in W London, in the County of London, situated on the S side of the river Thames, opposite Chelsea, ab. 1 mi. W of Victoria station. The name of Battersea is derived from Peter's Eye or Island, which was originally a part of the ancient patrimony of Saint Peter's Abbey at Westminster. Battersea was once famous for its asparagus beds. 117,130 (1951).

Battersea Park. One of the parks of London. It faces Chelsea Hospital, and is on the Surrey side of the Thames.

Batterson (bat′ėr.sọn), **James Goodwin.** b. at Wintonbury (now Bloomfield), Conn., Feb. 23, 1823; d. Sept. 18, 1901. American businessman, best known as a founder (1863) of the Travelers Insurance Company. At the time of its founding, his company was the only accident-insurance organization of its kind in the U.S. He was also a scholar, interested in sociology, economics, geology, and mineralogy, and devoted much time to the study of both classical and modern languages.

Battery (bat′ėr.i). [Also, **Battery Park.**] Park of ab. 20 acres at the S extremity of New York City, on or near the site of an old Dutch fort. It was at one time a fashionable quarter, but now lies within an area devoted to shipping and commerce. Here is the Manhattan terminus of the Brooklyn-Battery Tunnel (10,500 ft. long); ferries run from near the Battery to Staten Island, Governor's Island, Bedloe's Island, and Ellis Island. See also **Castle Garden.**

Batteux (bȧ.tė), **Charles.** b. near Vouziers, France, May 6, 1713; d. at Paris, July 14, 1780. French man of letters, chiefly noted as a writer on aesthetics. Author of *Parallèle de la Henriade et du Lutrin* (1746), *Les Beaux-Arts réduits à un même principe* (1746), *Cours des belles-lettres* (1747–50; his principal work), *La construction oratoire* (1764), and *Histoire des causes premières* (1769).

Battey (bat′i), **Robert.** b. at Augusta, Ga., Nov. 26, 1828; d. at Rome, Ga., Nov. 8, 1895. American physician and surgeon. He was professor of obstetrics at the Atlanta Medical College (1873–75) and editor of the *Atlanta Medical and Surgical Journal* (1873–76). He performed in 1872 what has since been known as "Battey's operation" for the removal of the ovaries.

Batthyány (bôt′tyäny′) or **Batthyányi** (-tyä.nyē), Prince **Karl von.** [Hungarian, **Károly József Batthyány.**] b. c1697; d. April 15, 1772. Hungarian field marshal, in the service of Austria. He played a prominent part in the War of the Austrian Succession, and distinguished himself by the victory over the French and Bavarians at Pfaffenhofen, on April 15, 1745.

Batthyány or **Batthyányi,** Count **Louis von.** [Hungarian, **Lajos Batthyány.**] b. at Pressburg (now Bratislava, Czechoslovakia), April 9, 1806; d. at Budapest, Oct. 6, 1849. Hungarian statesman. He was premier of Hungary (March–September, 1848). After his resignation he took part in public affairs, chiefly as a member of the Hungarian Diet, with great moderation, seeking to avoid a break with Austria. Nevertheless, when the tension between Austria and Hungary reached the point of armed conflict, and the Austrians entered Budapest, he was arrested by them and, at the end of the war, executed.

Battiadae (bạ.tī′ạ.dē). Dynasty of Greek rulers in Cyrene, which reigned from the 7th to the 5th century B.C. They have been classified as follows: Battus I (631–591), founder of the city; Arcesilaus I (591–75), his son; Battus II (the Happy, his son, 575–555); Arcesilaus II (the Ill-tempered, his son, c555–c540); Battus III (the Lame, his son, c540–c530); Arcesilaus III (his son, c530–c515); Pheretima, regent c515–c514; Battus IV (the Fair, son of Arcesilaus III, c514–c470); Arcesilaus IV (his son) ascended the throne c470, gained a Pythian victory in 466, and lived perhaps until nearly 431.

Battisti (bät.tēs′tē), **Cesare.** b. at Trent (then in Austria, now in Italy), Feb. 4, 1875; d. July 13, 1916. Italian nationalist politician and newspaper editor. As founder (1895) of the *Rivista popolare trentina*, a socialist periodical, he campaigned for the autonomy of Trentino; he founded (1900) the daily *Il Popolo* and was imprisoned (1904) for its anti-Austrian policy. He moved (Aug. 12, 1914) to Italy where he led (1914–15) the Interventionists and enlisted (1915) in the *alpini* (Alpine troops). Still an Austrian citizen, he was hanged as a traitor following his capture (July 10, 1916) by the Austrians.

Battistini (bät.tēs.tē′nē), **Mattia.** b. at Rome, Feb. 27, 1857; d. Nov. 7, 1928. Italian concert baritone, famous for his rendition of the old-school Italian bel canto. He first appeared (1878) at the Teatro Argentina at Rome in *La Favorita*, sang (1883) at Covent Garden, became famous as Wolfram in *Tannhäuser* while in Russia, and gave (1922) vocal recitals at Queen's Hall. His most successful performances included leading roles in *Rigoletto, Don Giovanni*, and *Eugène Onegin*.

Battle (bat′l). Rural district and market town in SE England, in East Sussex, ab. 7 mi. NW of Hastings, ab. 56 mi. SE of London by rail. It contains an abbey (Battle Abbey), founded (1067) by William I (the Conqueror) in gratitude for his victory at Hastings. The remains include considerable portions of the monastic buildings (in part fitted as a residence of the Duke of Cleveland), fragments of the cloisters and refectory, and the ruins of the large church. The entrance is by a splendid fortified medieval gate. 30,400 (1951).

Battle, Cullen Andrews. b. at Powelton, Ga., June 1, 1829; d. at Greensboro, N.C., April 8, 1905. American politician and soldier, with the Confederate army in the Civil War. An ardent secessionist, he campaigned (1860) throughout Alabama. During the war, he commanded forces at Fredericksburg, at Gettysburg, in the Battle of the Wilderness, and in the Shenandoah Valley campaign.

Battle, George Gordon. b. at Cool Spring Plantation, near Rocky Mount, in Edgecombe County, N.C., Oct. 26, 1868; d. at Fredericksburg, Va., April 29, 1949. American lawyer. He was educated at Hanover Academy, the University of Virginia, and Columbia Law School. Affiliated with Tammany Hall, the New York Democratic organization, he was named president of the New York Parks and Playgrounds Association (later called the Park Association). He was active in interfaith religious groups.

Battle, Kemp Plummer. b. in Franklin County, N.C., Dec. 19, 1831; d. Feb. 4, 1919. American educator, president (1876–91) of the University of North Carolina. He was the author of *History of the University of North Carolina* (2 vols., 1907 and 1912).

Battle, Mrs. A character in Charles Lamb's *Essays of Elia*.

Battle above the Clouds. Name often given to the military engagement in the Civil War, on Nov. 24, 1863, between Union forces under General Joseph Hooker and Confederate forces under General James Longstreet, on the high ridge near Chattanooga, Tenn., known as Lookout Mountain.

Battle at Sea. Painting by Tintoretto, acquired by the Prado museum at Madrid, representing an attack on Christian ships by Moslem corsairs. In the foreground a strenuous hand-to-hand combat rages around a beautiful female figure. The coloring is rich and strong.

Battle Bridge. In old London, a locality marked by a bridge across the Upper Fleet or Holborn, at what is now King's Cross, supposed to have derived its name from a battle between Suetonius and Boadicea, or between Alfred and the Danes.

Battle Creek. [Called the **"Health City."**] City in S Lower Michigan, in Calhoun County, ab. 108 mi. W of Detroit, on the Kalamazoo River: widely known as a manufacturing center of breakfast foods; other industrial products include farm machinery, printing presses, and gas stoves. The Battle Creek Sanatarium (founded in 1866 as the Western Health Reform Institute) is known for its medical and surgical appliances, and for its contributions to the field of dietetics. Points of interest include the Kingman Memorial Museum of Natural History, Leila Arboretum, Fort Custer, and Kellogg Field, a U.S. air base. 48,666 (1950).

Battlefield, The. Poem (1837) by William Cullen Bryant. It was prompted by the attacks made upon him for his active interest in liberal movements of the time (most notably those for free trade and for abolition), and contains one of his most famous quatrains:

Truth, crushed to earth, shall rise again;
Th' eternal years of God are hers,
But Error, wounded, writhes in pain,
And dies among his worshippers.

Battleford (bat'l.fọrd). Town in W Saskatchewan, Canada, situated at the junction of the Battle and Saskatchewan rivers. It was formerly the capital of the Northwest Territories, and today is a suburb of the more important town of North Battleford. 1,319 (1951).

Battle Harbour. Unofficial capital of Labrador, Canada, situated on a small island near the entrance to the Strait of Belle Isle in the S part of the territory.

Battle Hill. Height in Greenwood Cemetery, Brooklyn, the scene of a part of the Battle of Long Island.

Battle Hymn of the Republic, The. American patriotic song of the North in the Civil War, written by Julia Ward Howe during a visit to the Union army camps near Washington in 1861. It is sung to the same tune as *John Brown's Body*. The opening line is "Mine eyes have seen the glory of the coming of the Lord." It was first published anonymously in the *Atlantic Monthly* for February, 1862.

Battle Monument. Memorial structure at Baltimore, Md., built (1815) to commemorate the soldiers who were engaged in the defense of the city against the British troops in September, 1814. The total height of the monument is 72 ft.

Battle of Alcazar (al.kaz'ạr), **The.** Play by George Peele, acted c1588 and printed in 1594. Under this title Peele writes of a battle fought in Barbary between Sebastian, king of Portugal, and Abdelmelek, king of Morocco, which really took place on Aug. 4, 1578, at what is now the city of Alcázarquivir, in Spanish Morocco.

Battle of Amazons. Painting by Peter Paul Rubens, in the collection of the old Pinakothek at Munich. The subject is the victory of Theseus over the Amazons on the Thermodon. The chief struggle is on a bridge, upon which the Greeks are charging, while the Amazons begin to flee at the opposite end. Horses and riders, dead and wounded, are falling in confusion into the stream.

"Battle of Berlin." Name given to the year-long struggle between the Western powers (France, Great Britain, and the U.S.) and the U.S.S.R. for control of Berlin, which began on June 24, 1948, when the Russians shut off all railway and water traffic into the city from the zones of Germany outside of Berlin occupied by the three Western powers. This effort to evict the Western powers from Berlin by cutting their lines of supply was defeated by an unremitting Allied "airlift," which carried in supplies and food by air over a year's time. Efforts to end the blockade, which included conferences by the Western ambassadors with Joseph Stalin, were unsuccessful until negotiation by United Nations representatives of the four powers at New York during the spring of 1949.

Battle of Blenheim (blen'ẹm), **The.** Poem by Robert Southey (1774–1843).

Battle of Brooklyn, The. Anonymous play (1776). It is a satire written by a Tory who sought to turn the tables against the rebellious American colonists.

Battle of Bunkers Hill, The. Tragedy in blank verse by Hugh Henry Breckenridge, published in 1776. It was probably acted by his students at the school in Maryland, where he taught.

Battle of Dorking (dôr'king), **The.** Prose work (1871) by Sir George Chesney. It was a warning, published in pamphlet form, of the German threat and possible invasion of England after the victory of Prussia over France in 1870–71. The alarm it created soon subsided and the traditional enmity with France again loomed larger than any other in the contemporary British consciousness, if only because of the intense rivalry then existing between France and England in Africa.

Battle of Hastings. First tragedy written by Richard Cumberland, produced in 1778.

Battle of Hastings, The. Poem by Thomas Chatterton, written c1768. He wrote two poems of this name, the first of which he acknowledged, but perversely insisted that the second and very much longer one was by Thomas Rowley, a fictitious 15th-century monk created as a by-product of Chatterton's own imagination.

Battle of Issus (is'us). Ancient mosaic from the House of the Faun at Pompeii, now in the Museo Nazionale, Naples. It is ab. 17 by 8 ft., formed of small cubes of marble, and represents with much life and vigor the armies of kings Alexander and Darius in active combat, both on horse and on foot.

Battle of Life, The. Story by Charles Dickens, published in 1846.

Battle of Lovell's Pond (luv'ẹlz), **The.** Poem by Henry Wadsworth Longfellow. His first published poem, it appeared in the Portland *Gazette* on Nov. 17, 1820, when he was not yet 14. The subject matter, which he used again in a later poem, *Ode* (1825), concerns a skirmish between the settlers and the Indians.

Battle of Niagara. Poem (1818) by John Neal, published under the name of Jehu O'Cataract. It consists of a highly idealized account of the Battle of Niagara, in the War of 1812.

Battle of the Books. Satirical work by Jonathan Swift, written in 1697. It is his contribution to the Bentley and Boyle controversy, and his first prose composition. The literary dispute began when Charles Boyle, 4th Earl of Orrery, published *Epistles of Phalaris*, supposedly an ancient work, which Sir William Temple praised extravagantly; but Richard Bentley proved the spuriousness of the manuscript and ridiculed Temple for his admiration of the work. In Swift's satire, the argument is between ancient and modern learning, and the outcome is a draw.

Battle of the Bulge. [Also, **Ardennes Offensive.**] German offensive (December, 1944) in the region of the Ardennes, chiefly in Belgium, during World War II, the last major German effort to wrest the initiative from the Allies on the Western Front. The German forces were commanded by Karl Rudolf Gerd von Rundstedt and included a considerable air force as well as 14 infantry and 10 *panzer* (armored) divisions. An armored unit equipped with captured American equipment headed the initial assault and endeavored, with some success, to spread confusion in and behind the American front line. The Germans sought to break through to the Meuse River, to take Liége (a major Allied supply depot), and finally to capture Antwerp, which would have separated the British and some American armies on the north from the French and remaining American forces on the south. It was the German hope that, even if all of these objectives were not attained, the offensive would nevertheless disorganize the Allied drive in the west to such an extent that German units might then be diverted to counter the Russians in the east, that supplies (particularly oil and gasoline) would be captured, and that negotiations for a separate peace might thereupon be opened with one or more of the Allied nations. The assault began on Dec. 16, 1944, and had a considerable initial success: a break some 45 mi. wide was made in the Allied line between Monschau and Echternach, and German troops were able to operate, because of fog, without serious hindrance from the air. In order to counter the attack, which had split the American forces under General Omar Bradley, General Dwight Eisenhower assigned temporary operational command of all ground troops N of the break to the British General Bernard Law Montgomery, and gave Bradley command S of the break. Units in the path of the German drive were reinforced as speedily as possible, while mounting pressure was exerted on the German flanks. It was during this period that the American 101st Airborne Division was surrounded by the Germans and fought the engagement since known as the "Battle of Bastogne"; the fact that such key points as Bastogne and St.-Vith did not fall according to the German schedule had much to do with halting the advance. On Dec. 22, units of General George Patton's Third Army opened a counterattack on the Germans' S flank and on Dec. 26 the offensive was halted; it had covered ab. 60 mi., reaching the town of Celles ab. 4 mi. from the Meuse River. On Jan. 16,

1945, units of the American First Army from the N met the Third Army drive from the S, thus cutting the salient. Final collapse of the positions won by the Germans in the early period of their assault came with an offensive (Jan. 20, 1945) in S Alsace by the American 6th Army Group under General Jacob Loucks Devers.

Battle of the Frogs and Mice, The. See **Batrachomyomachia.**

Battle of the Giants. Epithet applied to the battle of Marignano or Melegnano, Sept. 13 and 14, 1515, in which Francis I of France defeated the Duke of Milan and the Swiss: so called from the obstinacy with which it was fought, and the great military ability of the troops on both sides.

Battle of the Horizons, The. Novel by Sylvia Thompson, published in 1928.

Battle of the Kegs. Mock-heroic poem (1778) by Francis Hopkinson, occasioned by the use of mines in the Revolutionary War.

Battle of the Spurs. [Also, **Battle of the Golden Spurs.**] Battle (1302) near Courtrai, Belgium, between an army representing the Flemish cities and the forces of Philip IV of France. The name derived from the quantity of gilt spurs found on the field after the struggle (which is therefore sometimes also called the Battle of the Golden Spurs). The historical background of the battle was that the Flemish weavers, being dependent on supplies of wool from England, had constrained Guy of Dampierre, who became Count of Flanders in 1280, to enter an alliance with Edward I, king of England, against the French. Philip IV (Philip the Fair) of France thereupon overran Flanders, making prisoners of Guy, his sons, and numerous nobles. The harshness of French rule caused the Flemings to rebel, and after they had massacred the French garrison at Bruges on May 19, 1302, Philip led a large punitive force into the country, but was disastrously defeated on July 11. Nevertheless, when peace was concluded in 1305, the French were able to impose severe terms because they held Count Guy and the other captives at their mercy.

Battle of the Spurs. Battle (1513) near Guinegate, France, between the English under Henry VIII and the French under Louis XII. The battle was an incident of the long-drawn-out contest arising in that epoch from the conflicting interests of England and France. Maximilian I, the emperor-elect of the Holy Roman Empire, was one of Henry VIII's allies, and led a contingent when the English forces closed with the French near the town of Guinegate, in what is now Pas-de-Calais department, on August 16, 1513. The hasty flight of the French cavalry is said to have caused the English to name the event the Battle of the Spurs.

Battle of the Summer Islands, The. Mock-epic poem by Edmund Waller (1606–87). It is about an ineffectual attempt by the Bermudians to capture two stranded whales.

Battle-Pieces and Aspects of the War. Poems by Herman Melville, on the Civil War, published in 1866.

Battles of Crescey and Poictiers (kres'i; pwä'tyā), **The.** Narrative poem (1631) by Charles Aleyn.

Battonya (bôt'tō.nyô). Town in SE Hungary, in the vicinity of the Rumanian border, situated on the Szaraz River between Arad and Szeged. Grain and tobacco are cultivated in the vicinity. 12,651 (1948).

Batts-Fallam Expedition (bats'fal'ạm). Expeditionary party (1671) dispatched from Fort Henry (at what is now Petersburg, Va.) by Colonel Abraham Wood for the purpose of finding trans-Allegheny water routes leading to the "South sea." The group, numbering five persons, takes its name from its leader, Captain Thomas Batts, and from Robert Fallam, who kept a daily record of its activities. The expedition reached (Sept. 17, 1671) the junction of New River and what is now the West Virginia boundary.

Battus (bat'us). Name of four kings of Cyrene, in the dynasty of the Battiadae. The first one, a Greek from the island of Thera (now Santorin), in the Aegean Sea, was the leader of a colony that settled at Cyrene c630 B.C.

Batu (bä'tö). See **Batoe.**

Batu Khan (bä'tö kän'). d. c1255. Mogul ruler of Kipchak; grandson of Genghis Khan. He defeated Henry, the duke of Lower Silesia, at Wahlstadt in 1241, and Béla IV, king of Hungary, on the Sajó in 1242, and held Russia in subjection for ten years.

Batum (bä.töm'). [Also: **Batoum, Batumi** (-tö'mē).] Seaport in the S part of the U.S.S.R., capital of the Adzhar Autonomous Soviet Socialist Republic, in the Georgian Soviet Socialist Republic, situated on the Black Sea. It is an oil producing and refining center, also a major pipe-line, rail, and road junction. It has the best harbor on the E coast of the Black Sea, and is the chief commercial port in Transcaucasia, exporting timber, hides, oil, and other products. It is connected by railway with Tiflis. The modern city stands near the site of the ancient Petra, earlier Bathys. It was ceded by Turkey to Russia in 1878. Pop. 70,807 (1939).

Baty (bȧ.tē), **Gaston.** b. at Pelussin, France, 1885; d. Oct. 13, 1952. French director and playwright. His company became notable for its unified, ensemble production and for making production more important than the playwrights' texts. For his theater, Baty made many free dramatizations of novels, all intended to serve as the basis for ingeniously contrived and imaginative tours de force of the director's art. Among the best known of these were *Madame Bovary* (1936) and *Manon Lescaut* (1938).

Batyushkov (bä'tūsh.kọf), **Konstantin Nikolayevich.** b. 1787; d. 1855. Russian poet, essayist, and translator.

Batz (bäts). [Also: **Bas**; French, **Île de Batz.**] Island in NW France, in the department of Finistère, situated in the English Channel, ab. 14 mi. NE of Morlaix. It has a beach and grows early vegetables. 1,172 (1946).

Batz (bȧts), **Bourg-de-.** See **Bourg-de-Batz.**

Batz, Baron **Jean de.** b. in Gascony, France, Dec. 6, 1761; d. at Chadieu, France, Jan. 10, 1822. French royalist, notable for his attempts to rescue Louis XVI and Marie Antoinette from the guillotine. In 1789 he was chosen to be a deputy of the nobility of Nerac to the States General. He became a member of the Constituent Assembly and served on the committee on finance, in which he opposed the issue of assignats. On Jan. 21, 1793, as Louis XVI was being taken to the guillotine, Batz tried in vain to rescue him, and in June of the same year he organized a conspiratorial, and futile, attempt to liberate Marie Antoinette. Batz was a party to the counterrevolutionary conspiracy of French conservatives and foreign interventionists, but it was not until June 14, 1794, that he was publicly accused before the Convention, the charge being that he was associated with men who were seeking to restore the Bourbon dynasty and who were also speculating with public funds. Arrested along with a number of others, he alone escaped the guillotine. It is supposed that he served in Condé's counterrevolutionary army until its dissolution in 1800.

Bauan (bä'wän). Town in Batangas province, in SW Luzon, Philippine Islands. 2,975 (1948).

Baubo (bô'bō). In Greek mythology, a personage connected with the Eleusinian myth of Demeter, developed chiefly under the influence of Orphism. According to the myth, Demeter, in search of her daughter, came to Baubo, who offered her something to drink, which she refused. Thereupon Baubo, indignant, made a vulgar gesture which caused Demeter to smile, despite her grief, and accept the gift. In a fragment of an Orphic hymn the same act is attributed to a servant, Iambus. Baubo came to have a place in the nocturnal mysteries of Eleusis. Goethe makes her symbolize gross sensuality in the second part of his *Faust.*

Bauchant (bō.shäṅ), **André.** b. at Châteaurenault, France, April 24, 1873—. French painter of landscapes and mythological scenes. He started to paint as an avocation, but gave art his full attention after he achieved success. The Salon d'Automne included his work in its exhibits from 1921 to 1928, and he has exhibited at other important salons at Paris; prizes were awarded him at London and Paris. A list of his paintings includes *Death of Lucretia, Battle of Marathon, Spring, The Storm, Eve Imploring Adam,* and a décor for Igor Stravinsky's ballet *Apollon Musagète.*

Baucher (bō.shā), **François.** b. at Versailles, France, 1796; d. at Paris, March 14, 1873. French trainer of horses. He invented a method of training saddle horses, of which the chief feature was a method of suppling the horse's neck and jaw by a progressive series of flexions of the muscles, so that the animal ceased to bear or pull on the bit. He wrote *Méthode d'équitation* (1842).

Bauchi (bou'chē). Town in W Africa, an important mining center and the administrative center of Bauchi province, Northern Provinces, Nigeria. It is situated in the highlands in the heart of a tin-mining area, and is connected by road with Jos, a town on the railroad line to Port Harcourt, from which the tin is shipped. Pop. ab. 10,000.

Baucis (bô'sis). Greek poetess of Tenos, a friend of Erinna and a disciple of Sappho. An epitaph upon her by Erinna is extant.

Baucis. In Greek legend, a Phrygian woman who, with her husband Philemon, showed hospitality to Zeus and Hermes when everyone else had refused them admission. They were saved from an inundation with which the country was visited by the gods, and were made priests in the temple of Zeus. Wishing to die together, they were changed at the same moment into trees. Goethe wrote a poem on this subject.

Baucis and Philemon (fi.lē'mon, fī-). Poem by Jonathan Swift, published in 1707. It is a poetic rendering, in a new style, of Ovid's *Baucis and Philemon.* There is a savage undertone in his attitude towards the village "Pack of churlish Boors," who may be thought to represent average mankind.

Baudelaire (bōd.ler), **Charles Pierre.** b. at Paris, April 9, 1821; d. there, Aug. 31, 1867. French poet and critic. His only volume of verse, *Les Fleurs du Mal* (1857), exerted an influence perhaps without parallel in French literature, first on the French symbolists and later on such modern poets as Paul Valéry and T. S. Eliot. His earliest works were brochures on the art salons of 1845 and 1846, followed by brilliant essays on Eugène Delacroix, Honoré Daumier, Constantin Guys, and other artists little appreciated or completely unknown at the time. He was an ardent and early champion of Richard Wagner's music (*R. Wagner et Tannhaeuser à Paris,* 1861). His literary criticism, including articles on Victor Hugo, Théophile Gautier, and Gustave Flaubert, was collected posthumously, together with his art criticism, under the titles of *Art Romantique* and *Curiosités esthétiques* (1868–69). A treatise on excitants (*Paradis artificiels,* 1860) is, in part, an adaptation of De Quincey's *Confessions of an English Opium Eater*. Baudelaire is considered to have created a literary genre with his *Petits Poèmes en Prose* (*Spleen de Paris*), collected posthumously in 1869. His translation of the more important prose works of Edgar Allan Poe (5 vols., 1856–65) did much to establish that author's European reputation. *Fusées* and *Mon Coeur mis à nu,* often referred to under the factitious title of *Journaux intimes,* first appeared in 1887. The standard modern edition of his works is that of Jacques Crépet (Paris, 1922–50).

Baudelocque (bōd.lok), **Jean Louis.** b. at Heilly, in Picardy, 1746; d. at Paris, 1810. French surgeon, an obstetrician at the Hospital de la Maternité, Paris. Author of *L'Art des accouchements* (1781).

Baudens (bō.däṅ), **Jean Baptiste Lucien.** b. at Aire, Pas-de-Calais, France, April 3, 1804; d. at Paris, Dec. 3, 1857. French surgeon. He became (1830) a surgeon in the French army in Algeria, where he founded a hospital in which he taught surgery and anatomy for nine years. He returned to France in 1841, becoming director of the military hospital of Val-de-Grâce, and serving as a member of the sanitary commission of the army in the Crimean War. He wrote *Nouvelle méthode des amputations* (1842) and *La Guerre de Crimée* (1857).

Baudin (bō.daṅ), **Nicolas.** b. on Île de Ré, in the Bay of Biscay, 1750; d. on Mauritius, in the Indian Ocean, Sept. 16, 1803. French naturalist, and a captain in the French navy. He conducted an expedition to Australia, an account of which was published in *Voyage aux terres australes par les corvettes Géographe et le Naturaliste* (1807).

Baudin des Ardennes (dā.zȧr.den), **Charles.** b. at Sedan, France, 1792; d. on the island of Ischia, in the Tyrrhenian Sea, June 7, 1854. French naval officer. He served (1808–12) with distinction against the English. After the "Hundred Days" he engaged in trade, but returned (1830) to the navy on account of financial reverses. In 1838 he was sent to the island of Hispaniola with the commissioners who were to demand indemnity for the losses there sustained by French subjects, and, shortly after, with the rank of rear admiral, he was empowered to secure a similar indemnity from Mexico. His demands being refused, he bombarded (Nov. 27, 1838) the fort of San Juan de Ulúa, Vera Cruz, forced its abandonment the next day, and, on Dec. 5, occupied Vera Cruz after a hot fight, but soon withdrew; he then blockaded the port until the French demands were settled by a treaty. On his return to France he was made vice-admiral. He commanded (1840) a French naval force off the South American coast, and was prefect of Toulon (1840–47), and president of the Bureau of Longitude after 1848. Shortly before his death he became a full admiral.

Baudissin (bou'di.sin), Count **Wolf Heinrich (Friedrich Karl) von.** b. at Copenhagen, Jan. 30, 1789; d. at Dresden, Germany, April 4, 1878. German writer and translator, contributor to the German translation of Shakespeare edited by August Wilhelm von Schlegel and Ludwig Tieck. The plays translated by him are *Henry VIII, Much Ado about Nothing, The Taming of the Shrew, A Comedy of Errors, Measure for Measure, All's Well That Ends Well, Antony and Cleopatra, Troilus and Cressida, The Merry Wives of Windsor, Love's Labor's Lost, Titus Andronicus, Othello,* and *King Lear*. He also published *Ben Jonson und seine Schule* (1836), translations of a number of old English dramas, and translations of works by Molière and others.

Baudissin, Wolf Wilhelm. b. at Sophienhof, Holstein, 1847; d. 1926. German theologian. After serving as professor at the universities of Strasbourg and Marburg, he became (1900) professor at the University of Berlin. Author of *Studien zur semitischen Religionsgeschichte* (1870–78) and *Einleitung in die Bücher des Alten Testamentes* (1901).

Bauditz (bou'dits), **Sophus Gustav.** b. at Aarhus, Denmark, Oct. 23, 1850; d. at Copenhagen, Aug. 16, 1915. Danish writer of widely-read novels (especially *Hjortholm,* 1896), short stories, and plays.

Baudobrica (bô.dob'ri.ka). A Latin name of **Boppard.**

Baudouin (bōd'win; French, bō.dwaṅ). See also **Baldwin.**

Baudouin I (of *Belgium*). b. Sept. 7, 1930—. King of Belgium (1951 *et seq.*); son (by his first marriage, to Astrid of Sweden) of Leopold III. Baudouin formally acceded to the throne of Belgium on July 17, 1951, the day after the abdication of his father, although he had exercised the prerogatives of rule under the Belgian constitution since Aug. 11, 1950, when the Belgian parliament formally accepted Leopold's offer (Aug. 1, 1950) to delegate these powers to him.

Baudoin (bō.dwaṅ), **Paul.** b. at Paris, Dec. 19, 1894—. French banker and politician, first foreign minister (June–October, 1940) of the Vichy government. He was long associated with the Bank of Indochina as director and manager (1926–44). Sentenced to prison (March, 1947) as a collaborator, he was later (January, 1948) paroled.

Baudricourt (bō.drē.kör), **Jean de.** d. at Blois, France, May 11, 1499. French marshal. He served successively under Charles the Bold, Louis XI, and Charles VIII, was sent as ambassador to the Swiss cantons in 1477, was made governor of Burgundy and Besançon in 1481, and became a marshal of France in 1486.

Baudrillart (bō.drē.yȧr), **Henri Joseph Léon.** b. at Paris, Nov. 28, 1821; d. there, Jan. 24, 1892. French political economist; son of Jacques Joseph Baudrillart. He became editor of the *Constitutionnel,* and later of the *Journal des économistes.* Among his works are *Manuel d'économie politique* (1857), *Des rapports de la morale et de l'économie politique* (1860), *Publicistes modernes* (1862), and *Histoire du luxe* (1878–90).

Baudrillart, Henri Marie Alfred. b. at Paris, Jan. 6, 1859; d. 1942. French prelate and historian, for many years rector of the Catholic university at Paris; grandson of Jacques Joseph Baudrillart. Author of *Philippe V et la cour de France* (Philip V and the French Court, 1890–1901) and *L'Allemagne et les alliés devant la conscience chrétienne* (Germany and the Allies in the Presence of Christian Conscience, 1917).

Baudrillart, Jacques Joseph. b. at Givron, in Ardennes, France, May 20, 1774; d. at Paris, March 24, 1832. French writer on forestry.

Baudry (bō.drē), **Paul Jacques Aimé.** b. at La Roche-sur-Yon, Vendée, France, Nov. 7, 1828; d. at Paris, Jan. 17, 1886. French painter of mythological subjects and portraits, and also of decorative works. Of the last the best-known are at Paris in the foyer of the Grand Opéra (1866–74) and the Palais de Justice. He became a member of the Institute in 1870.

Bauer (bou'ėr), **Anton.** b. at Marburg, Germany, Aug. 13, 1772; d. at Göttingen, Germany, June 1, 1843. German jurist. He became professor at Göttingen in 1813, and privy judiciary councilor in 1840. Among his works is *Grundsätze des Kriminalprozesses* (1805), a revised edition of which was published under the title of *Lehrbuch des Strafprozesses* (1835).

Bauer, Bruno. b. at Eisenberg, in Saxe-Altenburg, Sept. 6, 1809; d. at Rixdorf, near Berlin, April 15, 1882. German philosophical, theological, and historical writer of the Hegelian school, noted as an exponent of extreme rationalism; brother of Edgar Bauer. His Bible criticism lost him his job as a professor at Bonn. He was the author of *Religion des Alten Testaments* (1838), *Kritik der evangelischen Geschichte des Johannes* (1840), *Das entdeckte Christenthum* (1843), *Geschichte der Französischen Revolution* (1847), *Geschichte der Politik, Kultur und Aufklärung des 18. Jahrhunderts* (1843–45), *Die Apostelgeschichte* (1850), *Kritik der Paulinischen Briefe* (1850), *Christus und die Cäsaren* (1877), and others.

Bauer, Edgar. b. at Charlottenburg, Prussia, Oct. 7, 1820; d. at Hanover, Aug. 18, 1886. German publicist; brother of Bruno Bauer. He was the author of numerous historical and polemical works considered by the authorities of his day to be dangerously radical, and was imprisoned (1843–48) on account of his *Streit der Kritik mit Kirche und Staat.*

Bauer, Georg. Original name of **Agricola, Georg.**

Bauer, Gustav. b. at Darkehmen, Germany, Jan. 6, 1870; d. 1944. German statesman, president (1908 *et seq.*) of the general committee of the trade unions of Germany. He served (1912–18) as a Social Democratic member of the Reichstag and was appointed (1918) state secretary of labor in the last imperial cabinet, under Prince Max of Baden. He was minister of labor (February, 1919–June, 1919) under the German republic and succeeded Philipp Scheidemann as *Reichskanzler* (chancellor). He signed the Versailles Treaty, and was minister of the treasury (May, 1921–November, 1922). He retired as chancellor after the "Kapp Putsch," an unsuccessful monarchist uprising (1920) led by Wolfgang Kapp.

Bauer, Harold. b. at New Malden, England, April 28, 1873; d. March 12, 1951. Anglo-American pianist. At nine he made his debut as a violinist, and toured England for the next nine years; thereafter (1892 *et seq.*) he devoted himself to the study of the piano, on which he was largely self-taught, although he received some instruction from Ignace Jan Paderewski. He first appeared in the U.S. at Boston, on Dec. 1, 1900, and thereafter made many American tours. He is especially known for his playing of the works of Brahms, Schumann, and the modern French composers.

Bauer, Herbert. See **Balázs, Béla.**

Bauer, Karoline. b. at Heidelberg, Germany, March 29, 1807; d. at Zurich, Switzerland, Oct. 18, 1877. German actress; morganatic wife (1829) of Leopold (later king of Belgium) under the name of Countess Montgomery. She returned to the stage when Leopold became king, but finally abandoned the theater in 1844; in the same year she married a Polish count. She was famous both in comedy and tragedy. Her memoirs, denouncing Leopold and his adviser Baron Christian Friedrich von Stockmar, were published posthumously.

Bauer, Louis Agricola. b. at Cincinnati, Ohio, Jan. 26, 1865; committed suicide April 12, 1932. American physicist and astronomer, director (1904 *et seq.*) of the department of terrestrial magnetism of the Carnegie Institution. He was chief of the division of terrestrial magnetism of the U.S. Coast and Geodetic Survey in the period 1899–1906.

Bauer, Marius Alexandre Jacques. [Pseudonym, **Rusticus.**] b. at The Hague, Jan. 25, 1864; d. 1932. Dutch painter, water-colorist, and etcher, most noted for his exotic engravings of such subjects as Ali Baba, Aladdin, and the Queen of Sheba. He studied in the Netherlands, then traveled a great deal, especially to the Near East. He was awarded several prizes and had paintings on exhibit at Paris, London, New York, and Amsterdam.

Bauer, Otto. b. at Vienna, Sept. 5, 1881; d. at Paris, July 4, 1938. Austrian statesman. A brilliant socialist theoretician, he collaborated on Kautsky's *Neue Zeit* and Victor Adler's *Kampf.* He was a prisoner of war in Russia at the time of the October revolution (1917). Austrian foreign secretary from 1918 to 1919, he was leader of the Social Democratic party, and author of the party program of 1926. He was a member of parliament from 1929 until the uprising of 1934, when he went into exile, first in Czechoslovakia and later in France. His most important works are *Nationalitätenfrage und Sozialdemokratie* (1907), *Bolschewismus oder Sozialdemokratie* (1920), *Sozialdemokratische Agrarpolitik* (1926), and *Zwischen zwei Weltkriegen?* (1936).

Bauer, Rudolf. b. at Lindenwald, Germany, 1889—. German nonobjective painter and writer, one of the leaders, with Vasily Kandinsky, of the abstractionist movement. He received his schooling at the Academy of Fine Arts at Berlin; very early in his career, he did many humorous sketches and cartoons. He began as an academic painter, developing through the stages of impressionism, expressionism, and cubism into a nonobjective artist. He has exhibited widely in Europe and in the U.S., and was the founder of the Geistrich, a private museum of nonobjective painting, at Berlin (1929). Among his writings are *The Cosmic Movement* (1918) and *Das Geistrich* (1931).

Bauer, Walter. b. at Merseburg, Germany, 1904—. German writer of verse and fiction. A schoolteacher closely associated with the proletariat, he takes the part of the latter in his verses in *Kameraden, zu euch spreche ich* and *Stimmen aus dem Leunawerk.* His novel *Ein Mensch zog in die Stadt* (1931) deals with the great drift from the country to industrial centers, individualized here in one farmer who moved to town.

Bäuerle (boi'ėr.lẹ), **Adolf.** [Occasional pseudonym, **Otto Horn.**] b. at Vienna, April 9, 1786; d. at Basel, Switzerland, Sept. 20, 1859. Austrian dramatist and novelist. He founded (1806) the *Wiener Theaterzeitung,* and was the author of the comedies *Die falsche Primadonna* (1818) and *Der Freund in der Noth,* and of various novels, including *Therese Krones* (1854) and *Ferdinand Raimund* (1855), both of which appeared under the pseudonym Otto Horn.

Bauernfeind (bou'ėrn.fīnt), **Karl Maximilian von.** b. at Arzberg, Bavaria, Nov. 18, 1818; d. at Munich, Bavaria, Aug. 2, 1894. German geodesist and engineer. He became professor of geodesy and engineering at the school of engineering at Munich in 1846, and was the inventor of a prism for measuring distances, which bears his name. Author of *Elemente der Vermessungskunde* (1856–58) and others.

Bauernfeld (bou'ėrn.felt), **Eduard von.** b. at Vienna, Jan. 13, 1802; d. Aug. 9, 1890. Austrian dramatist. Among his works are *Die Bekentnisse* (The Confessions, 1834), *Bürgerlich und Romantisch* (Bourgeois and Romantic, 1835), *Grossjährig* (Fullgrown, 1846), and *Moderne Jugend* (Modern Youth, 1869).

Baugé (bō.zhā). Town in W France, in the department of Maine-et-Loire, situated on the Couesnon River ab. 22 mi. NE of Angers. It was the scene of a French victory by Marshal Gilbert Motier de La Fayette over the English in 1421. Pop. ab. 2,800.

Bauges (bōzh), **Les.** See **Les Bauges.**

Baugher (bou'ėr), **Henry Louis.** b. at Abbottstown, Pa., July 18, 1804; d. April 14, 1868. American Lutheran clergyman and educator, president (1850 *et seq.*) of the Pennsylvania College of Gettysburg (now Gettysburg College).

Bauhaus (bou'hous). Institute of art study, design, and research in Germany, continued in the U.S. as the New Bauhaus and, later, as the Chicago Institute of Design. "Das Staatliche Bauhaus Weimar" was founded at Weimar, Germany, in 1919, when the architect Walter Gropius merged the Weimar academy of art with a school of crafts. The central principle from which this most influential of modern art institutions took form was that architecture, the fine arts, and the applied arts must be correlated and, moreover, brought into fruitful relationship with modern industry and modern methods of production, since, the several arts all having their roots in man's creative urge, their separation had had disastrous results. Gropius expressed his ideal as "the composite but inseparable work of art, the great building." The name Bauhaus was derived from the German word *bauen* (building). Assisted by a faculty which included the painter-designers Paul Klee, Vasily Kandinsky, Lyonel Feininger, and László Moholy-Nagy and the architect Marcel Breuer, Gropius undertook to persuade industry of the practical value of the arts, and to make artists and craftsmen realize that in the modern world they must co-operate with industry. Students at the Bauhaus were given instruction not only in the arts and crafts but in such diverse fields as biology, sociology, and accounting, as their equipment for persuading industrialists of the possibilities for profit in mass production of articles of artistic quality. With a view to the development of creative talents in harmony with the forces shaping modern society, Gropius and his colleagues gave their followers manual as well as intellectual training, set them to evolving designs suited to modern production methods, and placed advanced students as workmen in factories where articles of Bauhaus design were turned out. Implicit in these ideas was the suggestion of social and cultural changes, which incurred the antagonism both of academic artists and of politicians. The atmosphere of Weimar became so unfriendly that in 1925 the school moved to Dessau, which offered municipal support. There it was housed in buildings especially designed by Gropius. Upon his resignation in 1928, the directorship fell to the architect Hannes Meyer, who was succeeded in 1932 by Miës van der Rohe. In 1932 the city of Dessau withdrew its support, and the Bauhaus moved to Berlin, where in the following year it was closed by the German government, then under Nazi control. Many Bauhaus instructors and graduates came to the U.S., where their influence as architects, designers, and instructors has been great. The New Bauhaus, established (1937) at Chicago, failed after a year. Its successor, the Chicago Institute of Design, founded by Moholy-Nagy and directed by him until his death, especially carried on the work of the Bauhaus, whose synthesis of craftsmanship with mass-production techniques has been applied to buildings, to furniture, tableware, and carpets, to typography, and, perhaps most notably, to many household articles of modest price.

Bauhin (bō.aṅ), **Gaspard.** b. at Basel, Switzerland, Jan. 17, 1560; d. there, Dec. 5, 1624. Swiss botanist and anatomist, of French descent; brother of Jean Bauhin. He was professor of anatomy and botany, and later of medicine, at the University of Basel. Author of *Pinax theatri botanici.*

Bauhin, Jean. b. at Basel, Switzerland, 1541; d. at Montgéliand, Switzerland, 1613. Swiss physician and naturalist; brother of Gaspard Bauhin. He compiled a botanical history.

Bauld (bôld), **Cape.** Northernmost point of Newfoundland, separated from the Labrador mainland by the Strait of Belle Isle.

Baule (bä.ö'lā). [Also, **Baoule.**] Largest and most important group of the Anyi, in Africa, inhabiting the SE Ivory Coast. They are divided into the following independent subgroups: the Agba, Atue, Atutu, Fafwe, Nanafwe, Ngba, Nzipuri, Sa, and Warebo.

Baule-sur-Mer (bōl.sür.mer). [Also, **La Baule.**] Town in W France, in the department of Seine-Inférieure, situated on the Atlantic Ocean, near the estuary of the Loire River, W of St.-Nazaire. It is a fashionable seaside resort. 4,011 (1946).

Baum (boum), **Friedrich.** d. at Bennington, Vt., Aug. 18, 1777. German officer in the British service in the Revolutionary War. He was defeated by General John Stark and fatally wounded in the battle of Bennington, Aug. 16, 1777.

Baum (bôm), **Lyman Frank.** [Pseudonyms: **Schuyler Staunton, Floyd Akers,** and **Edith Van Dyne.**] b. at Chittenango, N.Y., May 15, 1856; d. at Hollywood, Calif., May 6, 1919. American writer and playwright, remembered chiefly for his *Oz* books and plays. Having started as a newspaper reporter and trade-paper editor, he had his first success (1899) with a children's book called *Father Goose: His Book*, followed by the *Wonderful Wizard of Oz* (1900), which was staged (1901) at Chicago. He also wrote 13 other *Oz* stories that have acquired a lasting place in children's literature. Temporarily popular (but now little read) were two novels under the pseudonym Schuyler Staunton, six boys' books by Floyd Akers, and 24 girls' books by Edith Van Dyne.

Baum (boum), **Vicki.** b. at Vienna, Jan. 24, 1896—. American novelist and scenarist. She has worked as a magazine editor (1926 *et seq.*) at Berlin, and a scenarist (1932 *et seq.*) at Hollywood. Author of *Grand Hotel* (1931), *And Life Goes On* (1932), *Men Never Know* (1935), *A Tale From Bali* (1937), *Shanghai* (1939), *Grand Opera* (1942), *The Weeping Wood* (1943), *Mortgage on Life* (1946), *Danger from Deer* (1951), and other works.

Baumann (bō.màn), **Émile.** b. at Lyons, France, 1868—. French Catholic novelist and biographer, author of *L'Immolé* (1908), *La Fosse aux lions* (1911), *Saint-Paul* (1925), *Abel et Caïn* (1930), and others.

Baumann (bou'män), **Oskar.** b. at Vienna, June 25, 1864; d. there, Oct. 12, 1899. Austrian explorer and traveler in Africa. In 1885 he accompanied Oskar Lenz to Stanley Falls on the Congo, in 1890 explored Usambara, and explored (1891–93) the regions south and west of Lake Victoria. He was honorary consul (1896 *et seq.*) in Zanzibar.

Baumannshöhle (bou'mäns.hė.lẹ). Stalactite cave in the lower Harz Mountains, in Brunswick, C Germany, ab. 5 mi. SE of Blankenburg, near the Bode River.

Baumbach (boum'bäċh), **Rudolf.** [Pseudonym, **Paul Bach.**] b. at Kranichfeld, Germany, Sept. 28, 1840; d. at Meiningen, Germany, Sept. 22, 1905. German lyric poet. He is best known for his poetic rendering of popular legends. Among his works are *Zlatorog* (1877), *Horand und Hilde* (1878), *Lieder eines fahrenden Gesellen* (1878), *Frau Holde* (1881), *Thüringer Lieder* (1891), *Neue Märchen* (1896), and *Bunte Blätter* (1897). His *Sommermärchen* (1881) have gone through numerous editions.

Baumé (bō.mā), **Antoine.** b. at Senlis, France, Feb. 26, 1728; d. Oct. 15, 1804. French chemist and pharmacist. He was the inventor of a hydrometer (now known as the Baumé hydrometer) and a process of making sal ammoniac. Author of *Éléments de pharmacie* (1762), *Chimie expérimentale et raisonnée* (1773), and other books.

Baumeister (bou'mīs"tėr), **Johann Wilhelm.** b. at Augsburg, Germany, April 27, 1804; d. at Stuttgart, Germany, Feb. 3, 1846. German veterinary surgeon, painter of animals, and writer on the care and training of domestic animals. He was a professor (1839–46) at the veterinary school at Stuttgart.

Bäumer (boi'mėr), **Gertrud.** b. at Hohenlimburg, Germany, Sept. 12, 1873—. German feminist leader, teacher, and popular writer. She was a collaborator of the feminist Helene Lange (1848–1930) and of Friedrich Naumann (1860–1919), with whom she was coeditor of the periodicals *Die Frau* and *Die Hilfe.* She was president (1910–19) of the Union of German Women's Associations, a Democratic member of the Weimar Constitutional Assembly, and of the Reichstag (1920–33), counselor in charge of education in the ministry of the interior, and second chairman (1916–20) of the Democratic party. From 1933 to 1945 she wrote historical studies and fiction, but returned to political activities after the end of World War II.

Baumes (bô'mẹs), **Caleb Howard.** b. at Bethlehem, N.Y., March 31, 1863; d. Sept. 25, 1937. American lawyer, politician, and penologist. After having been admitted (1898) to the New York bar, he practiced at Newburgh, N.Y. He was a member (1909–13) of the N.Y. State General Assembly, and served (1919–37) in the state senate. As chairman (1926) of a joint legislative committee, he helped draft the penal amendments in which one of the statutes, known as the "Baumes Law," specifies life imprisonment for those convicted for the fourth time of a felony. Although Baumes's original legislation applied only to the state of New York, similar laws now exist in other states.

Baumes Law. Statute of the state of New York passed (1926) by the legislature as an amendment to the state penal code for the purpose of countering the increase in crime after World War I. It provides for a life term of imprisonment for fourth offenders. The measure takes its name from its sponsor, State Senator Caleb H. Baumes.

Baumgarten (boum'gär"tẹn), **Alexander Gottlieb.** b. at Berlin, July 17, 1714; d. at Frankfort on the Oder,

Germany, May 26, 1762. German philosopher, appointed professor of philosophy at Frankfort on the Oder in 1740. He is regarded by some authorities as the founder of the modern science of aesthetics, and exerted a lasting influence upon the terminology of metaphysics, especially in the German language. Immanuel Kant held him in great esteem as a metaphysician, and for a long time employed Baumgarten's works as a foundation for his lectures. Baumgarten wrote *De nonnullis ad poema pertinentibus* (1735), *Aesthetica Acromatica* (1750–58), *Metaphysica* (1739), and others.

Baumgarten, Hermann. b. April 28, 1825; d. June 19, 1893. German historian and publicist, professor of history (1872–89) at the University of Strasbourg. He wrote *Geschichte Spaniens zur Zeit der Französischen Revolution* (1861), *Geschichte Spaniens vom Ausbruch der Französischen Revolution bis auf unsere Tage* (1865–71), *Karl V und die Deutsche Reformation* (1889), and others.

Baumgarten, Konrad. In the William Tell legend, one of the Unterwalden patriots.

Baumgarten, Michael. b. at Haseldorf, in Holstein, March 25, 1812; d. at Rostock, in Mecklenburg, July 21, 1889. German Protestant theologian, professor of theology at Rostock (1850–58). He was elected to the Reichstag in 1874, 1877, and 1878.

Baumgarten, Moritz Julius Maximilian Paul Maria. b. at Ritterhausen, Germany, July 25, 1860—. German clergyman and historian. Author of *Die katholische Kirche unserer Zeit* (The Catholic Church of Our Time, 1899–1902).

Baumgarten, Sigmund Jakob. b. at Wolmirstedt, near Magdeburg, Germany, March 14, 1706; d. at Halle, Germany, July 4, 1757. German Protestant theologian, professor at Halle (1730–57).

Baumgarten-Crusius (boum'gär"tẹn.krö'zē.ůs), **Ludwig Friedrich Otto.** b. at Merseburg, Saxony, July 31, 1788; d. at Jena, Saxony, May 31, 1843. German Protestant theologian, a professor (1812 *et seq.*) at Jena. He was the author of *Lehrbuch der Dogmengeschichte* (1831–32), *Kompendium der Dogmengeschichte* (1840–46), and others.

Baumgartner (boum'gärt"nėr), Baron **Andreas von.** b. at Friedberg, Bohemia, Nov. 23, 1793; d. near Vienna, July 30, 1865. Austrian scholar and politician. He became professor of physics at the University of Vienna in 1823, was minister of commerce, trade, and public works (1851–55), and became president of the Academy of Sciences at Vienna in 1851.

Baumgartner, Gallus Jakob. b. at Altstätten, Switzerland, Oct. 15, 1797; d. at St. Gallen, Switzerland, July 12, 1869. Swiss historian and politician. He wrote *Die Schweiz in ihren Kämpfen und Umgestaltungen von 1830–50* (1853–66) and others.

Baumgärtner (boum'gert"nėr), **Karl Heinrich.** b. at Pforzheim, Baden, Oct. 21, 1798; d. at Baden-Baden, Baden, Dec. 11, 1886. German physiologist, professor of clinical medicine (1824–62) at Freiburg im Breisgau. He was the author of *Beobachtungen über die Nerven und das Blut* (1830), *Lehrbuch der Physiologie* (1853), and others.

Baumgartner (bōm.gårt.ner), **Wilfred.** b. May 21, 1902—. French banker, elected (January, 1949) governor of the Bank of France. After a career as a finance ministry official (1928–36), he served (1937–49) as chairman and manager of the Crédit National. Arrested by the Gestapo and deported (1943) to Germany, he remained there until 1945.

Bäumler (boim'lėr), **Joseph Michael.** Original name of **Bimeler, Joseph Michael.**

Baumstark (boum'shtärk), **Anton.** b. at Sinzheim, Baden, April 14, 1800; d. March 28, 1876. German classical philologist, professor of philology (1836–71) at Freiburg im Breisgau; brother of Eduard Baumstark.

Baumstark, Eduard. b. at Sinzheim, Baden, March 28, 1807; d. April 8, 1889. German political economist and politician; brother of Anton Baumstark.

Baur (bour), **Albert.** b. at Aachen, Germany, July 13, 1835; d. May 7, 1906. German historical painter of the Düsseldorf school (so called from the style characteristic of the works of faculty members of the art academy at Düsseldorf), professor of historical painting at Weimar, 1872–76.

Baur, Erwin. b. at Ichenheim, Baden, April 16, 1875; d. at Berlin, Jan. 13, 1933. German botanist and experimental geneticist. He was trained in medicine at the universities of Strasbourg and Kiel; having secured (1900) his M.D., he was granted (1903) a Ph.D. in botany at the University of Freiburg im Breisgau. He was named (1911) professor of botany at the Agricultural School of Berlin, where he established the Institut für Vererbungsforschung (Institute for Researches into Heredity), and later founded a similar institute at Dahlem-Berlin. He was the founder (1908) and editor of *Zeitschrift für inductive Abstammungs- und Vererbungslehre.* He was appointed (1929) director of the Institut für Züchtungsforschung at Müncheberg.

Baur, Ferdinand Christian. b. at Schmiden, near Cannstatt, Germany, June 21, 1792; d. at Tübingen, Germany, Dec. 2, 1860. German Protestant theologian and Biblical critic, the founder of the "Tübingen School" of theology, professor at Blaubeuren, and, after 1826, professor of theology at Tübingen. He was noted for his profound scholarship, constructive criticism, and boldness in innovation. His theories of apostolic and post-apostolic Christianity were revolutionary in their time, resolving the history of Christianity into a speculative process of conflicting tendencies (Petrinism and Paulinism) from which the supernatural and miraculous are eliminated. Among his works are *Das manichäische Religionssystem* (1831), *Die christliche Gnosis* (1835), *Die christliche Lehre von der Versöhnung* (1838), *Die christliche Lehre von der Dreieinigkeit* (1841–43), *Der Gegensatz des Katholizismus und Protestantismus, Paulus* (1845), *Lehrbuch der christlichen Dogmengeschichte* (1847), *Kritische Untersuchungen über die kanonischen Evangelien* (1847), *Das Markus-Evangelium* (1851), and *Das Christenthum und die christliche Kirche der drei ersten Jahrhunderte* (1853).

Baur, Gustav Adolf Ludwig. b. at Hammelbach, Germany, June 14, 1816; d. at Leipzig, Germany, May 22, 1889. German Protestant theologian. He became professor of theology at the University of Leipzig in 1870.

Baur (bōr), **Harry.** b. at Marseilles, 1883; d. at Paris, April 9, 1943. French stage and screen actor. He started working at the Marseilles docks at 12 years of age, but attended the Conservatoire there, preparing himself for an acting career at Paris. Although well known on the stage for his fine character performances, it was in films that he made his international reputation; among those in which he appeared were *David Golder* (1932), *Poil de Carotte* (1933), *Life and Loves of Beethoven* (1938), and *Rasputin* (1939). In 1942, he was arrested at Paris by the Nazis for having "forged" papers to prove his Aryan ancestry. He died the next year under mysterious circumstances, and it is believed he was executed for underground activities.

Baures (bou'rās). River in E Bolivia, in Santa Cruz and Beni departments, flowing NW to join the Guaporé River on the border between Brazil and Bolivia. Length, ab. 300 mi.

Baurú (bou.rö'). City in SE Brazil, in the state of São Paulo. 53,126 (1950).

Bausch (boush), **Carl Louis.** b. at Syracuse, N.Y., June 20, 1887—. American mechanical engineer, vice-president of the Bausch and Lomb Optical Company in charge of research and engineering; grandnephew of John Jacob Bausch. After entering the company as a machinist (1909), he became manager of research and engineering (1926) and a director (1930).

Bausch, Edward. b. at Rochester, N.Y., Sept. 26, 1854; d. there, July 30, 1944. American optical manufacturer and inventor; son of John Jacob Bausch. He studied engineering at Cornell before becoming associated (1874) with the optical firm of Bausch and Lomb, of which he later served as chairman of the board. Author of *Manipulation of the Microscope* (1885), which became a standard textbook.

Bausch, John Jacob. b. at Süssen, Württemberg, Germany, July 25, 1830; d. Feb. 14, 1926. American optical manufacturer. Having come to America in 1849, he established (1853), with Henry Lomb, and headed (1853–1926) the Bausch and Lomb Optical Company at Rochester, N.Y.

Bausch, William. b. at Rochester, N.Y., March 25, 1861; d. near there, Oct. 19, 1944. American optical manufacturer; son of John Jacob Bausch (1830–1926). He joined (1875) the Bausch and Lomb Optical Company, and served as secretary (1909–35), vice-president (1935 *et seq.*), and chairman of the board (1944). He founded (1915) the optical-glass plant at the Bausch and Lomb factory.

Bause (bou'zẹ), **Johann Friedrich.** b. at Halle, Germany, Jan. 5, 1738; d. at Weimar, Germany, Jan. 3, 1814. German engraver on copper. He was for a time professor of this art in the Academy of Art at Leipzig.

Bausman (bous'mạn), **Benjamin.** b. near Lancaster, Pa., Jan. 28, 1824; d. at Reading, Pa., May 8, 1909. American German-Reformed clergyman. Ordained in 1853, he edited the *Guardian* (1867–81), a religious magazine for young people, and *Der Reformierte Hausfreund* (1866–1903), a religious magazine with wide circulation among Pennsylvania Germans. Author of *Sinai and Zion* (1861), *Wayside Gleanings in Europe* (1875), and editor of *Harbaugh's Harfe* (1902), poems written in the dialect-German known as Pennsylvania-Dutch by Henry Harbaugh.

Bausset (bō.se), **Louis François de.** b. at Pondichéry, India, Dec. 14, 1748; d. at Paris, June 21, 1824. French ecclesiastic and man of letters. He became bishop of Alais in 1784, and a cardinal in 1817. He was the author of *Histoire de Fénelon* (1808–09), *Histoire de Bossuet* (1814), and others.

Bautzen (bout'sẹn). [Wendish, **Budissin** (the official name until 1868).] City in C Germany, in the *Land* (state) of Saxony, Russian Zone, formerly in the state of Saxony, the capital of the former *Kreis* (district) of Bautzen and of Upper Lusatia, situated on the Spree River, ab. 30 mi. E of Dresden. Before World War II it had metalworking, machine, cloth, leather, and paper factories. There are a number of educational institutions, a theater, archives, and a library; also a museum of Wendish antiquities and a municipal museum containing prehistoric, folklore, and natural history collections. It is the seat of a Roman Catholic bishopric (titular bishop of Meissen). Above the city is the Ortenburg, founded in 957, rebuilt in the 15th and in the 19th century, formerly a seat of the governors of Bohemia. There are remains of medieval fortifications and numerous churches; the Cathedral of Saint Peter and the *Michaeliskirche* (Church of Saint Michael) date from the 15th century; other notable buildings include the Church of Our Lady and a number of secular buildings, chiefly in the baroque style. Originally a Slavic fort, it was occupied by the Germans in the 11th century; it was later vainly besieged by the Hussites. Lutheranism was introduced in 1523; however, an agreement in 1560 insured the continuation of the Roman Catholic diocese. The Saxons took the town in 1620 and in 1634; it passed definitely to Saxony in 1635. Napoleon I defeated the Prussians and Russians here in 1813. The city was occupied by the Russians in 1945, after heavy fighting and much destruction. 38,524 (1946).

Bautzen, Battle of. Victory gained by Napoleon I, on May 20 and 21, 1813, with ab. 140,000 troops (under Michel Ney, Nicolas Charles Oudinot, Nicolas Jean de Dieu Soult, and others; Ney with his 40,000 men was not present on May 20) over some 90,000 troops of the allied Russians and Prussians. The loss of the French was ab. 20,000; that of the Russians and Prussians, ab. 13,000.

Baux (bō), **Les.** See **Les Baux.**

Bauzanum (bô.zā'num). Ancient name of **Bolzano,** city.

Bavaria (bạ.vãr'i.ạ). [German, **Bayern, Baiern**; French, **Bavière.**] *Land* (state) in S Germany, American Zone, bounded by Austria, Czechoslovakia, Saxony, Thuringia, Hessen, Württemberg-Baden, and Württemberg-Hohenzollern. It corresponds to the former free state of Bavaria, except for the Rhenish Palatinate and the town and district of Lindau. Capital, Munich; area, 27,119 sq. mi.; pop. 9,126,010 (1950).

Economic and Cultural Description. Of the gainfully employed, 37.2 percent are engaged in agriculture, livestock raising, and forestry, 47.1 percent in industry, trade, commerce, and transport. The most fertile soils are along the Danube River and immediately S of it, and in the Main River valley. There are large harvests in grain and fruit. Wine is produced in Lower Franconia, hops in the Holledau district S of Regensburg and near Nuremberg. Pasture lands, which support a considerable dairy industry, prevail in the region N of the Alps. The soils in the C and NE parts of the country are less fertile; large areas, particularly in the Bohemian and Bavarian forests, the Fichtelgebirge, the Spessart Mountains, and Upper Bavaria, are densely forested. There are few mineral resources, except kaolin, lignite, and salt. Industries are diversified: machine and metallurgical industries, cotton textile, paper, and woodenware manufactures are of importance; brewing and the manufacture of porcelain and precision instruments are specialties. About 71 percent of the population are Roman Catholics, 26 percent Protestants; the Roman Catholics are most numerous in the S and E and in the Main valley, the Protestants in the center and N. The increase in population between 1939 and 1946, largely due to the influx of *Volksdeutsche* (German nationals) expelled from Poland, Czechoslovakia, Hungary, and Yugoslavia, was 24.9 percent.

History. The early inhabitants were Celts, then the German Boii, transmigrants from Bohemia. The S part belonged to the Roman Empire. Bavaria was ruled by its dukes, the Agilolfinger, c560–788. It came under the supremacy of the Franks, and in 788 its duke, Tassilo III, was deposed and it was incorporated with the Frankish empire. Later it was one of the four great duchies composing the German Empire of the early Middle Ages, extending across the Alps into N Italy and toward the E and SE into what is now Austria. The country E of the Enns River was at that time colonized from Bavaria. On the other hand, Franconia was not then included in Bavaria. The duchy of Bavaria passed to Welf IV in 1070. In 1180, after the fall of Henry the Lion, it was granted by Frederick Barbarossa to Count Otto of Wittelsbach, the founder of the dynasty which ruled Bavaria until 1918. The country was frequently subdivided among various branches of the house of Wittelsbach; members of the same line ruled also in the Rhenish Palatinate and occupied the bishoprics of Trier and Cologne. Duke Maximilian I received the dignity of prince-elector in 1623, in recognition of his services to the Catholic cause. The Upper Palatinate was incorporated in 1628. The country suffered much during the Thirty Years' War and during the War of the Spanish Succession. The Bavarian house of Wittelsbach became extinct in 1777 and the Palatinate branch combined the Palatinate and Bavaria. In 1806 Bavaria joined the Napoleonic Confederation of the Rhine and became a kingdom. It was obliged to cede territory by the *Reichsdeputationshauptschluss* (imperial delegations enactment) of 1803, but received Würzburg, Bamberg, Augsburg, and in 1805, Tirol and other territories. It received Salzburg in 1809, but was obliged to cede Tirol and Salzburg in 1815. In 1813 it joined the Allies against Napoleon I. As a result of the changes that had taken place during the Napoleonic period, the predominantly Protestant Franconian districts were definitely joined to the Bavarian domain. The country received a constitution in 1818. It sided with Austria in 1866. It was obliged to enter into military and economic agreements with Prussia, but the Bavarian diet decided, with only a one-vote majority, in favor of entering the war on the Prussian side when the Franco-Prussian War broke out in 1870. Bavaria entered the German empire in 1871, reserving a number of privileges, such as an independent postal administration, and command over its own army in peace time. King Louis II (German, Ludwig) of Bavaria drowned in the Starnbergersee in 1886. Louis III was deposed by the Bavarian revolution in 1918. The country was temporarily split in the spring of 1919 when a left-socialist and communist government took over in Munich while the right-socialist and moderate government had its official seat in Bamberg. Soon afterward, the government was assumed by a coalition of clerical and nationalist groups largely dominated by military leaders and the semi-military *Freikorps.* In the fall of 1923, Adolf Hitler, at the head of the National-Socialist movement, attempted the unsuccessful *Bierkeller* (Beerhall) Putsch. He was sent to the Landsberg prison, but was soon paroled. The headquarters of the Nazi movement was the *Braunes Haus* (Brown House) at Munich, while the annual party conventions were held in Nuremberg.

Bavaria. Bronze statue, 67 ft. high, in the Theresienwiese, near Munich, designed by Ludwig von Schwanthaler. It was built by order of Louis I (German, Ludwig) of Bavaria, and was finished in 1850. It stands before the *Ruhmeshalle* (Hall of Fame) and holds a wreath above its head. There is an interior ascent by a spiral iron staircase of 60 steps to the head.

Bavaria, Lower. See **Lower Bavaria.**

Bavarian Alps (bą.vãr′i.ąn). That part of the Alps which lies in S Bavaria and in the adjoining lands of Austria.

Bavarian Circle. [German, **Bayrischer Kreis.**] One of the ten circles, or districts, of the old German Empire, now included in Bavaria and neighboring parts of Austria.

Bavarian Forest. [German, **Bayrischer Wald, Bayerwald.**] Mountainous region in the E part of Bavaria, S Germany, N of the Danube River, noted for its forests. It is a part of the Bohemian Forest.

Bavarian Succession, War of the. War (1778–79) between Austria on one side, and Prussia, Saxony, and Mecklenburg on the other. It exemplified the 18th-century political wars which consisted more of secret correspondence than of actual fighting. On the death (1777) of Maximilian Joseph without issue, the electorate of Bavaria fell to the legal heir, Charles Theodore of Wittelsbach, elector of the Palatinate. Austria, however, made certain claims and, on making several concessions to Charles Theodore, persuaded him to give parts of the Palatinate and all of Lower Bavaria to Austria, and Austrian troops occupied this territory. Frederick II of Prussia incited Charles Augustus Christian (Charles Theodore's heir apparent) to declare formally his rights to Bavaria. Saxony and Mecklenburg joined Prussia in their support of Charles Augustus Christian. Although the German provinces drew up their armies, no battle took place in this short war; Bohemia was invaded, but, except for a few minor skirmishes, the hostilities took the form of a siege. Maria Theresa of Austria began a correspondence with Frederick II, and the Treaty of Teschen (May 13, 1779) was arranged, at which Austria renounced all claims to Bavaria except for the Innviertel, which it retained.

Bavay or **Bavai** (bȧ.ve). [Ancient name, **Bagacum.**] Town in N France, in the department of Nord, ab. 14 mi. E of Valenciennes. It is built on the site of the ancient capital of the Nervii. Pop. ab. 1,500.

Baveno (bä.vā′nō). Town and commune in NW Italy, in the *compartimento* (region) of Piedmont, in the province of Novara, situated on the W shore of Lago Maggiore, opposite the Borromean Islands. It is a resort, and has granite quarries and cotton textile manufactures. Pop. of commune, 3,028 (1936); of town, 921 (1936).

Baviad (bā′vi.ad), **The.** Satire on the so-called Della Cruscans, a group of English poets, by William Gifford, published in 1794, and republished (1797) with Gifford's *The Maeviad* (originally published 1795). The latter also attacked some of the minor dramatists of the time. The titles of these works have allusion to the Roman poets Bavius and Maevius, both of whom wrote against Vergil and Horace.

Bavian (bä.vē.än′). Place in N Iraq, in Mosul province, NE of Khorsabad (ancient name, Dur Sharrukin), near the ancient Mesopotamian city of Nineveh. Near it was discovered a rock with an inscription containing a record of Sennacherib's battle (691 B.C.) against the Elamite-Babylonian coalition at Halule, a city on the lower Tigris River.

Bavieça (bä.ʙyā′thä). [Also, **Babieça.**] Favorite horse of the Cid, Spanish hero.

Bavier (German, bä.fēr′; French, bȧ.vyā), **Simon.** b. at Chur, Graubünden, Switzerland, Sept. 16, 1825; d. at Basel, Switzerland, Jan. 28, 1896. Swiss statesman. He served (1882) as federal president, and became (1883) minister to Rome. Author of *Die Strassen der Schweiz* (1878).

Bavière (bȧ.vyer). French name of **Bavaria.**

Bavius (bā′vi.us). d. in Cappadocia, 35 B.C. Roman poet, an enemy of Vergil and Horace. His name is always associated with that of Maevius, who shared his vindictive feelings toward those greater poets and his lack of poetical ability.

Bavo (bä′vō). An ancient name of **Čiovo.**

Bawdwin (bôd′win). Town in E Burma, in the Shan State, ab. 100 mi. NE of Mandalay. There are several silver, lead, zinc, and copper mines in the vicinity. In 1933 lead production reached 72,000 tons, placing Burma as eighth country in the world for the production of lead. Silver production in the same year was 5,000,000 ounces.

Bawean (bä′vä.än). [Also, **Bawian** (-vē-).] Small island in Indonesia, in the Java Sea between Java and Borneo, ab. 80 mi. N of Surabaya, Java. Formerly a colonial possession of the Netherlands, it is now part of the Republic of Indonesia.

Bawr (bour), **Alexandrine Sophie Goury de Champgrand,** Baroness **de.** [Also, Comtesse **de Saint-Simon.**] b. at Stuttgart, Germany, 1776; d. at Paris, 1861. French novelist and dramatist. She wrote *Argent et Adresse* (1802), *Le Rival obligeant* (1805), *L'Argent du voyage* (1809), *Le Double Stratagème* (1813), *Auguste et Frédéric* (1817), *Histoire de la musique* (1823), and others.

Bax (baks), Sir **Arnold Edward Trevor.** b. at London, Nov. 6, 1883—. English composer; brother of Clifford Bax. He entered (1900) the Royal Academy of Music, where he studied under Frederick Corder. Many of his works are based on Celtic legends. His compositions include the symphonic poems *The Garden of Fand* (1916), *In Memoriam* (1917), *Tintagel* (1917), and *November Woods* (1917); among his symphonies are *Romantic Overture, Symphony No. 1, E-Flat Minor and Major* (1921–22), and *London Pageantry* (1937). He was knighted in 1937.

Bax, Clifford. b. July 13, 1886—. English playwright and poet; brother of Sir Arnold Edward Trevor Bax. His plays include *The Poetasters of Ispahan* (1912), *Polly* (1923), *Midsummer Madness* (1924), *Mr. Pepys* (1926), *Waterloo Leave* (1928), *Socrates* (1930), *The Venetian* (1931), *The Immortal Lady* (1931), *The Rose without a Thorn* (1932), and *The House of Borgia* (1935). Author also of *Twenty-five Chinese Poems* (1910), *Many a Green Isle* (1927), *Pretty Witty Nell* (1932) concerning Nell Gwyn, *Farewell My Muse* (1932), *Ideas and People* (1936), and *Golden Eagle* (1946).

Bax, Ernest Belfort. b. at Leamington, Warwickshire, England, July 24, 1854; d. at London, Nov. 26, 1926. English socialist, economist, and philosopher. As a young man he went to Germany to study music, but became interested in radical economic and philosophical theories, and, upon returning to England, joined William Morris in establishing the Socialist League, becoming (1885) with Morris a coeditor of the League's organ, *The Commonweal.* Later, objecting to the developing anarchist tendencies of the Socialist League, he joined the Social Democratic Federation and edited its paper, *Justice.* He was the author of *The Problem of Reality* (1893), *The Roots of Reality* (1907), *The Real, the Rational and the Alogical* (1920), and a volume of reminiscenses (1908); coauthor with William Morris of *Socialism, Its Growth and Outcome* (1894); editor of Kant's *Prolegomena* (1882) and of *Handbook to the History of Philosophy* (1884).

Baxar (buk′sąr). See **Buxar.**

Baxley (baks′li). City in SE Georgia, county seat of Appling County: marketing and shipping point for pecans, naval stores, lumber, tobacco, and syrup. 3,409 (1950).

Baxley, Henry Willis. b. at Baltimore, Md., June, 1803; d. March 13, 1876. American physician and surgeon, cofounder (1839) of the Baltimore College of Dental Surgery, the first U.S. dental college. He received his M.D. in 1824, and became a demonstrator in anatomy (1834) at the University of Maryland Medical School. He involved himself in a fight between the trustees and the faculty, allying himself with the trustees. Upon his appointment (1837) as president, the entire faculty resigned, and the school operated with two faculties and campuses for several years. He is said to have been one of the first surgeons to operate for strabismus.

Baxter (baks′tėr), **Andrew.** b. at Aberdeen, Scotland, c1686; d. at Whittingham, near Edinburgh, April 23, 1750. Scottish metaphysician. His chief work is an *Enquiry into the Nature of the Human Soul* (1733).

Baxter, Elisha. b. in Rutherford County, N.C., Sept. 1, 1827; d. May 31, 1899. American politician, governor (1873 *et seq.*) of Arkansas. He was elected (1864) to the U.S. Senate, but the passage by Congress of the Wade-Davis Reconstruction Bill prevented his admission. A circuit judge (1868 *et seq.*) under the Reconstruction government, he was inaugurated (1873) as reform governor of Arkansas.

Baxter, Gregory Paul. b. at Somerville, Mass., March 3, 1876—. American chemist and specialist in atomic weights. He received the degrees of A.B. (1896), A.M. (1897), and Ph.D. (1899) from Harvard, where he was professor of chemistry (1915–44). He served also as chairman of the International Committee on Atomic Weights. Author of *Researches upon the Atomic Weights* (1910) as well as scientific papers on the subject.

Baxter, Henry. b. at Sidney Plains, N.Y., Sept. 8, 1821; d. at Jonesville, Mich., Dec. 30, 1873. American soldier, with the Union army in the Civil War. He commanded troops at Gettysburg, where he captured nearly an entire Confederate brigade; he also participated in the battles of Antietam, Fredericksburg, Dabney's Mill, Five Forks, and the Wilderness. He was U.S. minister (1869–72) to Honduras.

Baxter, James Phinney. b. at Gorham, Me., March 23, 1831; d. at Portland, Me., May 8, 1921. American historian and public official; grandfather of James Phinney Baxter (1893—). He served six terms as mayor of Portland, and endowed that city with a public library. Author of numerous historical works, including *George Cleeve of Casco Bay* (1885), *Sir Ferdinando Gorges and His Province of Maine* (1890), *The Pioneers of New France in New England* (1894), and *A Memoir of Jacques Cartier with a New Translation of his Voyages* (1905).

Baxter, James Phinney. b. at Portland, Me., Feb. 15, 1893—. American educator and historian; grandson of James Phinney Baxter (1831–1921). A graduate of Williams College (1914) and Harvard (1926), he was professor of history (1936–37) at Harvard, and president (1937 *et seq.*) of Williams College. In World War II, he was deputy director (1942–43) of the Office of Strategic Services, and historian (1943–46) of the Office of Scientific Research and Development. Author of *The Introduction of the Ironclad Warship* (1933) and *Scientist Against Time* (1946).

Baxter, John. b. March 5, 1819; d. April 2, 1886. American lawyer and Unionist politician in East Tennessee. He campaigned against secession in spite of his proslavery sympathies, and published (1862 *et seq.*) a Unionist newspaper. After the Civil War, he attempted unsuccessfully, with Thomas A. R. Nelson, to form a political party less extremist than either the Democratic or Republican. He served as a delegate (1870) to the state constitutional convention and chairman of the judiciary committee. He was a supporter of William G. Brownlow. In 1877 he was named a U.S. circuit judge.

Baxter, Mount. Truncated cone in Antarctica, rising between Mount Levick and Mount Mackintosh, in Victoria Land, in ab. 74°20′ S., 162°30′ E. It was discovered and named by the National Antarctic Expedition (1901–04), under the command of Captain Robert F. Scott. Elevation, ab. 8,600 ft.

Baxter, Richard. b. at Rowton, Shropshire, England, Nov. 12, 1615; d. at London, Dec. 8, 1691. English nonconformist divine. He was ordained in 1638, was chosen lecturer at Kidderminster in 1641, and became (c1645) a chaplain in Cromwell's army. He subsequently favored the Restoration, and on the accession of Charles II in 1660 was appointed chaplain to the king, but left the Church of England on the passage of the Act of Uniformity in 1662, when he retired to Acton. In May, 1685, he was tried by George Jeffries on the charge of libeling the established church, and was fined a considerable sum, for nonpayment of which he was detained in prison until November, 1686. His chief works are *The Saint's Everlasting Rest* (1650), *A Call to the Unconverted* (1657), *Methodus Theologiae* (1674), and *Reliquiae Baxterianae* (1696).

Baxter, Robert Dudley. b. at Doncaster, England, Feb. 3, 1827; d. May 20, 1875. English economist and statistician. He became a solicitor in 1842, and a partner in the law firm of Baxter, Rose, and Norton at Westminster in 1860. He wrote *The National Income* (1868), *The Taxation of the United Kingdom* (1869), *The National Debts of the Various States of the World* (1871), *Local Government and Taxation* (1874), and others.

Baxter, Sylvester. b. at West Yarmouth, Mass., Feb. 6, 1850; d. at San Juan, Puerto Rico, Jan. 28, 1927. American journalist, noted for his proposal to organize a municipal park system at Boston. He served on the staff of the Boston *Advertiser* (1871–75) and *Herald* (1879–83, 1887–1905), was editor of the *Mexican Financier* (1883–84) and *Outing Magazine* (1885–86), and acted as foreign correspondent in Germany (1875–77) for the Boston *Advertiser* and in Mexico (1883–84) for the Boston *Herald* and the New York *Sun*. Author of *Berlin—A Study in Municipal Government* (1890), *Greater Boston* (1891), *Spanish Colonial Architecture in Mexico* (1902), and *The Quest of the Holy Grail* (1904).

Baxter, William. b. at Leeds, Yorkshire, England, July 6, 1820; d. at New Castle, Pa., Feb. 11, 1880. American evangelical clergyman and educator. Brought (1828) to America, he became a member of the Christian Church (Disciples of Christ). He served pastorates in Pennsylvania, Mississippi, and Louisiana before being appointed (1860) president of Arkansas College. Because of his Union sympathies, the townspeople burned (1863) the college. He was later (1865–75) pastor of the Christian Church, Lisbon, Ohio. Author of *Pea Ridge and Prairie Grove, or Scenes and Incidents of the War in Arkansas* (1864) and *Life of Elder Walter Scott* (1874).

Baxter, William Edward. b. at Dundee, Scotland, 1825; d. at London, Aug. 10, 1890. British politician, traveler, and author. He became secretary to the admiralty under William Ewart Gladstone in 1868, and was secretary of the treasury in the period 1871–73. Author of *America and the Americans* (1855).

"Baxter's Call." See **Call to the Unconverted.**

Baxter Springs. City in SE Kansas, in Cherokee County: center of a lead and zinc mining area; formerly a cattle-shipping point. 4,647 (1950).

Bay (bā). [Also, **Bay Village.**] Village in NE Ohio, in Cuyahoga County: residential community. 6,917 (1950).

Bay (bī), **Laguna de.** Lake in the S part of Luzon, Philippine Islands, lying within the provinces of Rizal and Laguna. It contains several small islands, the largest being Talim. Its outlet is the Pasig River, which connects it with Manila Bay. Greatest depth, ab. 20 ft.

Bay (bā), **Michel de.** Flemish name of **Baius** or **Bajus, Michael.**

Bayamo (bä.yä′mō). Town in E Cuba, in Oriente province, ab. 25 mi. E of Manzanillo: cattle raising and agricultural industries. 16,161 (1943).

Bayamón (bä.yä.mōn′). Town in N Puerto Rico, in San Juan department, on the Bayamón River: coffee, sugar, fruits, and tobacco. 20,171 (1950).

Bayamón River. River in C Puerto Rico, flowing N to the Bay of San Juan.

Bayan Kara Shan (bä.yän′ kä.rä′ shän′). See **Bayen Kala Shan.**

Bayard (bā′ąrd; French, bȧ.yȧr). Legendary horse given by Charlemagne to the four sons of Aymon. He possessed magical powers, including the remarkable facility of being able to lengthen himself so as to accommodate all four of his masters at once. He is, according to French legend, still alive in the Forest of Ardennes, where he can be heard neighing on Midsummer Day.

Bayard, Chevalier **de.** [Original name, **Pierre Terrail.**] b. near Grenoble, France, c1475; killed at the river Sesia, Italy, April 30, 1524. French national hero, called *le chevalier sans peur et sans reproche* ("the knight without fear and without reproach"), who distinguished himself in the Italian campaigns of Charles VIII, Louis XII, and Francis I. He was especially renowned for his bravery at the battles of Guinegate (1513) and Marignano (1515), and in the defense of Mézières (1521).

Bayard (bī′ąrd), **James Asheton.** b. at Philadelphia, July 28, 1767; d. at Wilmington, Del., Aug. 6, 1815. American statesman. At the time of the disputed presidential election of 1800 he arranged the understanding whereby Thomas Jefferson gave certain assurances of his intentions, if elected, which secured a shift of votes from Aaron Burr to him. He was a member of Congress from Delaware (1797–1803), a U.S. senator (1805–13), and a commissioner to negotiate the treaty of Ghent (1814) which terminated the War of 1812. He was the father of James Asheton Bayard (1799–1880).

Bayard, James Asheton. b. at Wilmington, Del., Nov. 15, 1799; d. there, June 13, 1880. American politician; son of James Asheton Bayard (1767–1815). He was a U.S. senator from Delaware in 1851–64 and 1867–69.

Bayard (bȧ.yȧr), **Jean François Alfred.** b. at Charolles, Saône-et-Loire, France, March 17, 1796; d. at Paris, Feb. 19, 1853. French dramatic writer, said to have written, partly in conjunction with Augustin Eugène Scribe and others, some 225 separate works. Among them are *La Reine de seize ans* (1828) and *Le Gamin de Paris* (1836).

Bayard (bī'ärd), **John Bubenheim.** b. at Bohemia Manor, Md., Aug. 11, 1738; d. Jan. 7, 1807. American merchant and patriot; uncle of James Asheton Bayard (1767–1815) and father of Samuel Bayard (1767–1840). A member of the Sons of Liberty and of the Provincial Convention (1774), he presided (1776) over meetings called to reorganize the Pennsylvania state government. After serving as a major and colonel with the Continental forces in the Revolutionary War, he was a member (1785 *et seq.*) of the Continental Congress.

Bayard, Nicholas. b. at Alphen, Holland, 1644; d. at New York, 1707. American colonial officer, secretary of the Province of New York in 1673 (under the Dutch), and mayor of the city of New York (under Governor Thomas Dongan). He was a member of the governor's council, and drew up the Dongan Charter.

Bayard, Richard Henry. b. at Wilmington, Del., Sept. 26, 1796; d. at Philadelphia, March 4, 1868. American Whig politician; a son of James Asheton Bayard (1767–1815). He twice served as a U.S. senator from Delaware (1836–39, 1839–45), and was chargé d'affaires at Brussels (1850–53).

Bayard, Samuel. b. at Philadelphia, Jan. 11, 1767; d. May 11, 1840. American jurist; son of John Bubenheim Bayard (1738–1807). During his service (1794 *et seq.*) as prosecuting attorney before the British admiralty courts, awards of more than ten million dollars were made on U.S. claims.

Bayard, Thomas Francis. b. at Wilmington, Del., Oct. 29, 1828; d. Sept. 28, 1898. American statesman; son of James Asheton Bayard (1799–1880) and father of Thomas Francis Bayard (1868–1942). He was a U.S. senator from Delaware (1869–85), president *pro tempore* of the Senate (1881), and member of the Electoral Commission (1877); unsuccessful in obtaining the nomination as Democratic candidate for the Presidency in 1880 and 1884, he served as U.S. secretary of state in the period 1885–89. He was appointed U.S. ambassador to England in 1893, the first to hold that diplomatic post (earlier U.S. representatives in England had had only ministerial rank).

Bayard, Thomas Francis. b. at Wilmington, Del., June 4, 1868; d. there, July 12, 1942. American politician, notable as the fifth of his family to hold a seat in the U.S. Senate; son of Thomas Francis Bayard (1828–98). Long active (1896 *et seq.*) in the Democratic Party, he was elected (1922) senator from Delaware but was defeated for reëlection (1928) by Josiah Wolcott.

Bayard and Wife v. Singleton, 1 Martin (North Carolina Reports) 5 (1787). Decision of the state supreme court of North Carolina invalidating a statute requiring the court to dismiss on motion any suit brought by a person whose property had been confiscated by the state during the American Revolution, against the purchasers, on affidavit of the defendants that they were purchasers from the commissioners of confiscated property. The decision of the court is one of the earliest discussions of the right of a court to declare a legislative act void.

Bayard-Chamberlain Treaty (-chām'bėr.lin). Treaty drawn up (Feb. 15, 1888) at Washington, D.C., by an Anglo-American commission for the purpose of defining the jurisdiction of Great Britain and the U.S. in Canadian waters off Newfoundland and surrounding areas. The provisions related chiefly to fishing privileges. The treaty was rejected (Aug. 21, 1888) by the U.S. Senate, but some of its important clauses comprised the basis of the North Atlantic fisheries settlement made (Sept. 7, 1910) by the Hague Permanent Court of Arbitration.

Bayardelle (bȧ.yȧr.del), **André.** b. at Martinique, in the French West Indies, Feb. 18, 1896—. French colonial administrator. He was appointed (1943) governor general of French Equatorial Africa.

Bayazid (bä.yä.zēd'). See **Bajazet I.**

Bayazid or **Bayazit** (bä.yä.zēt'). See **Doğubayazit.**

Baybay (bī.bī'). Town in the Philippine Islands, on the W coast of the island and province of Leyte, on Ormoc Bay. 9,414 (1948).

Bayburt (bī.bört'). [Also, **Baiburt.**] Town in NE Turkey, in the *il* (vilayet) of Gümüşane, ab. 66 mi. NE of Erzurum, on the Çoruh River. It has an important strategic and commercial position. Pop. ab. 10,000.

Bay City. City in C Lower Michigan, on the Saginaw River near its mouth, ab. 110 mi. NW of Detroit, the county seat of Bay County: largest port on Lake Huron; shipbuilding, beet-sugar refining, coal mining, and manufactures of automobile parts. In the 1870's and 1880's Bay City was a booming lumber town. 52,523 (1950).

Bay City. City in E Texas, county seat of Matagorda County, SW of Houston: shipping center for oil, rice, and cotton. 9,427 (1950).

Bayen Kala Shan (bä.yen' kä.lä' shäṅ'). [Also, **Bayan Kara Shan.**] Range of mountains in China, in the province of Tsinghai. It runs NW to SE for ab. 300 mi. and joins the Kunlun Shan in the NW. Elevation, up to 18,000 ft.

Bayer (bī'ėr), **August von.** b. at Rorschach on Lake Constance, in Switzerland, May 3, 1803; d. at Karlsruhe, Germany, Feb. 2, 1875. German painter of historical and architectural subjects.

Bayer, Gottlieb Siegfried. b. 1694; d. at St. Petersburg, Feb. 21, 1738. German Orientalist. He became professor of Greek and Roman antiquities at St. Petersburg in 1726.

Bayer, Johann. b. at Rain, Bavaria, c1572; d. at Augsburg, Bavaria, March 7, 1625. German astronomer and Protestant preacher, surnamed from his eloquence "*Os Protestantium*" ("the Protestants' mouth[piece]"). He was the author of *Uranometria* (1603), enlarged and reprinted under the title *Coelum stellatum christianum* (1627). This work was the first complete and convenient chart of the heavens, representing the then-existing state of astronomical knowledge. Bayer was the first to adopt the method of designating the stars by Greek and Latin characters, in the order of their magnitude.

Bayer, Karl Robert Emmerich von. [Pseudonym, **Robert Byr.**] b. at Bregenz, Austria, April 15, 1835; d. June 30, 1902. Austrian novelist, notable both for works of fiction and for nonfiction on military subjects. He entered the military academy at Neustadt in 1845, became lieutenant in a regiment of hussars at Milan in 1852, and retired from military service in 1862. Among his works are *Kantonierungsbilder* (1860), *Österreichische Garnisonen* (1863), *Anno Neun und Dreizehn* (1865), a number of social-political novels, such as *Der Kampf ums Dasein* (1869), and the dramas *Lady Gloster* (1869) and *Der wunde Fleck* (1875).

Bayern (bī'ėrn). German name of **Bavaria.**

Bayerwald (bī'ėr.vält). A German name of the **Bavarian Forest.**

Bayes (bāz). Character in the farce *The Rehearsal* (1671), presumed to be, at least in part, by George Villiers, 2nd Duke of Buckingham. A dramatic coxcomb, the character was at first called Bilboa, and was intended to ridicule Sir Robert Howard; but the piece having been laid aside for several years, and Sir Robert having meanwhile become a very good friend of Buckingham, the character was altered to fit John Dryden, who at this time appeared to Buckingham to be a fit object for satire. The name "Bayes" is a play on words in reference to the poet laureateship, which Dryden received in 1670. The satirical portrait of Monmouth which Dryden made so important a part of his *Absalom and Achitophel* (1681) is usually considered to have been inspired in large part by his resentment of this satirical treatment.

Bayes, Nora. [Stage name of **Dora Goldberg.**] b. at Los Angeles, 1880; d. at Brooklyn, N.Y., March 19, 1928. American actress; married (1925) Benjamin Friedland. She was very popular in musical-comedy and vaudeville roles, where she introduced or featured such popular songs as *Take Me Out to the Ball Game, Over There,* and *Japanese Sandman.*

Bayes's Troops, Like. Phrase referring to the foot-soldiers and hobby-horses who fight a battle in *The Rehearsal* (1671), presumed to be, at least in part, by George Villiers, 2nd Duke of Buckingham. When all are killed it is a question of how they are to go off the stage. Bayes suggests, "as they came on, upon their legs." Whereupon they are obliged to revive and walk off.

Bayeux (bȧ.yė). [Latin, **Augustodorus**; medieval name, **Baiocum** or **Baiocasses.**] Town in NW France, in the department of Calvados, situated on the Aure River, ab. 17 mi. NW of Caen. It was the chief town of the Gallic, or Celtic, tribe of the Baiocasses, and capital of the medieval district of Bessin. It has cattle markets, dairies, and a porcelain industry. It is an archbishopric, a tourist center, and one of the most interesting cities in Normandy; has an art museum and a number of churches. There are two main attractions: the so-called Bayeux Tapestry (actually embroidered linen), supposedly the work of Queen Matilda, depicting the history of the conquest of England by the Normans under her husband William I (the Conqueror); and the cathedral of Notre Dame, a structure in Norman style dating from the 12th and 13th centuries, having a magnificent interior with richly ornamented Romanesque arcades. Although the town is situated in the region where the Allied beachhead was established in the first days of the World War II invasion (August, 1944) of France, the city was bypassed and thus saved from destruction. 10,246 (1946).

Bayeux Tapestry. Strip of linen c230 ft. long and 20 in. wide, preserved in the Museum at Bayeux, France, embroidered with episodes of the Norman conquest of England from the visit of Harold II to the Norman court until his death at Senlac, each with its title in Latin. The work is of great archaeological interest from its details of costume and arms. It is traditionally ascribed to Matilda, wife of William I (the Conqueror), but is believed by many experts to be of a somewhat later date.

Bayezid (bä.ye.zēd′). See **Doğubayazit.**

Bay Fight, The. Poem (c1863) by Henry Howard Brownell. It deals with the battle of New Orleans, during the Civil War, and was actually written while Brownell was a member of Admiral Farragut's staff aboard the flagship *Hartford.*

Bayındır (bä.yin.dir′). Modern Turkish name of the **Caÿster.**

Bay Islands (bā). [Spanish, **Islas de la Bahía.**] Group of islands N of Honduras, in the Gulf of Honduras near the Caribbean Sea, comprising the Honduran department of Islas de la Bahía. Chief islands are Roatán, the largest, Guanaja, Elena, Utila, and Morat. Chief city, Roatán.

Bay Islands. English name of **Islas de la Bahía,** department.

Bayle (bel), **Gaspard Laurent.** b. at Vernet, in Provence, France, Aug. 8, 1774; d. at Paris, May 11, 1816. French physician and medical writer.

Bayle, Pierre. b. at Carlat, in Foix, France, Nov. 18, 1647; d. at Rotterdam, Dec. 28, 1706. French rationalist philosopher and critic. He was appointed professor of philosophy at Sedan in 1675, and at the Protestant academy of Rotterdam in 1681, and was removed (because his skeptical opinions seemed to the authorities dangerously close to religious unbelief) from his professorship in 1693. He is generally considered to have been the progenitor of 18th-century rationalistic philosophy, and is known as the compiler of the famous *Dictionnaire historique et critique* (1697), in which that point of view found clear expression. Among his other works are *Cogitationes rationales de Deo, anima, et malo, Pensées sur la comète, écrites à un docteur de la Sorbonne* (1682), and *Commentaire philosophique sur ces paroles de l'Évangile* (1686). In 1684 he established a sort of journal of literary criticism, *Nouvelles de la république des lettres,* which was maintained for several years.

Baylén (bī.lān′). See also **Bailén.**

Baylén, Capitulation of. Capitulation (July 22, 1808) by which the French general Pierre Antoine Dupont de l'Étang and his army surrendered to the Spaniards under Francisco Xavier de Castaños, and the French forces were to be allowed to leave Spain. The Junta of Seville refused to ratify the capitulation, and all the French except the superior officers were sent to the galleys at Cádiz.

Bayley (bā′li), **James Roosevelt.** b. at New York, Aug. 23, 1814; d. at Newark, N.J., Oct. 3, 1877. American Catholic prelate. He was made first bishop of Newark in 1853, and was archbishop of Baltimore in the period 1872–77. He wrote a *History of the Catholic Church in New York* (1853) and others.

Bayley, Sir **John.** b. at Elton, Huntingdonshire, England, Aug. 3, 1763; d. near Sevenoaks, Kent, England, Oct. 10, 1841. English jurist, and legal and religious writer. He became judge of the King's Bench in 1808, was removed to the Court of Exchequer in 1830, and resigned from the bench in 1834. He wrote *A Short Treatise on the Law of Bills of Exchange, Cash Bills, and Promissory Notes* (1789) and other works.

Bayley, Richard. b. at Fairfield, Conn., 1745; d. on Staten Island, N.Y., Aug. 17, 1801. American physician, appointed professor of anatomy at Columbia College in 1792, and of surgery in 1793. He studied in England with William Hunter, with whom he remained in correspondence after his return to New York; it is in a letter to Hunter that Bayley set forth (1781) his findings differentiating diphtheria from other throat infections, based on examinations of patients during an epidemic (1774) of fatal croup.

Bayley, William Shirley. b. at Baltimore, Md., Nov. 10, 1861; d. 1943. American geologist. He was graduated (Ph.D., 1886) from Johns Hopkins University, served as a geologist with the U.S. Geological Survey, and headed the geology department at the University of Illinois.

Baylies (bā′liz), **Francis.** b. at Taunton, Mass., Oct. 16, 1783; d. there, Oct. 28, 1852. American politician, a member of Congress from Massachusetts (1821–27). He wrote *Memoir of the Colony of New Plymouth.*

Bayliss (bā′lis), Sir **William Maddock.** b. at Wolverhampton, England, May 2, 1860; d. at London, Aug. 27, 1924. English physiologist. Entering University College, London, as a medical student in 1881, he presently decided upon a career as a scientist and specialist rather than as a medical practitioner. In 1885 he went to Oxford to study physiology, and in 1888 returned to University College, London, where from that time until 1924 he lectured on physiology (holding the rank of professor from 1912) and conducted experiments in the college's physiological laboratories. The son of an iron manufacturer, he possessed independent means and was able to devote himself entirely to science. Recognized as one of the ablest physiologists of his time, he made important discoveries, notably in the fields of electromotive phenomena affecting the action of the heart, the nervous mechanisms involved in the control of the viscera and the circulation, and the physiological effects of surface phenomena. His name, however, is particularly associated with the discovery, jointly with Ernest Henry Starling, of "secretin," the hormone governing the functioning of the pancreas, and with the saline injection treatment of wound-shock which he devised during World War I. In 1919 he received the Copley Medal of the Royal Society, and in 1922 he was knighted. He was the author of *The Nature of Enzyme Action* (1908), *Principles of General Physiology* (1914), and *The Vaso-motor System* (1923). For a time he edited *Physiological Abstracts.*

Bayliss, Sir **Wyke.** b. at Madeley, Shropshire, England, Oct. 21, 1835; d. at London, April 6, 1906. British artist, most of whose paintings portrayed cathedral and church interiors. He was president of the Royal Society of British Artists from 1888. He was knighted in 1897.

Baylor (bā′lọr), **Frances Courtenay.** [Married name, **Barnum.**] b. at Fayetteville, Ark., Jan. 20, 1848; d. Oct. 19, 1920. American novelist. She wrote "The Perfect Treasure" and "On This Side," two short magazine stories, which were published in book form as one narrative under the title *On Both Sides* (1886). Her other works include *Behind the Blue Ridge* (1887), *Claudia Hyde* (1894), *Miss Nina Barrow* (1897), and *Juan and Juanita* (1897).

Baylor, Robert Emmet Bledsoe. b. in Bourbon (or Lincoln) County, Ky., probably on May 10, 1793; d. Dec. 30, 1873. American lawyer, politician and Baptist preacher, best remembered for the university, now at Waco, Texas, which bears his name. He served one term as a Congressman from Alabama (21st Congress). Subsequently he was associate justice (1841–45) of the supreme court of the Texas republic and, when Texas entered the Union, remained on the bench (1845–61) as a Federal district judge. He drew up and helped obtain passage of the charter for the first Baptist college in Texas, subsequently named for him.

Bayly (bā'li), **Ada Ellen.** [Pseudonym, **Edna Lyall.**] b. at Brighton, England; d. at Eastbourne, England, Feb. 8, 1903. English novelist. Among her works are *Won by Waiting* (1879), *Donovan* (1882), *Autobiography of a Slander* (1887), *Knight Errant* (1887), and *A Hardy Norseman* (1889).

Bayly, Sir Lewis. b. Sept. 22, 1857; d. May 17, 1938. British naval officer who served (1915–19) during World War I as commander in chief of the western approaches. He was appointed (1917) admiral in the British navy, welcomed (1917) the first U.S. naval contingent to reach European waters during World War I, and helped to promote closer ties between Great Britain and the U.S. Author of a book of memoirs entitled *Pull Together!* (1939).

Bayly, Thomas Haynes. b. at Bath, England, Oct. 13, 1797; d. at Cheltenham, England, April 22, 1839. English songwriter, dramatist, and novelist. He wrote *Perfection* and other plays, many popular songs (among them *The Soldier's Tear, I'd be a Butterfly, We met—'twas in a Crowd*), and such novels as *The Aylmers* and *A Legend of Killarney*.

Bayly, Thomas Henry. b. at Mount Custis, near Accomac, Va., Dec. 11, 1810; d. June 22, 1856. American politician who served as a member of the Virginia House of Delegates (1836–42) and as a congressman from Virginia (1844–56).

Bayma (bī'mä), **Joseph.** b. at Ciriè, near Turin, Italy, Nov. 9, 1816; d. in California, Feb. 7, 1892. Jesuit priest, philosopher, mathematician, and physicist. He was ordained in 1847, taught (1858 *et seq.*) philosophy at Stonyhurst College, England, was ordered (1869) to the new California mission, and was made president of St. Ignatius College, San Francisco. Author of *De studio religiosae perfectionis excitando* (1852), *Philosophia Realis* (1861), and *Elements of Molecular Mechanics* (1866); coeditor of *Il Ratio studiorum adattato ai tempi presenti.* He outlined a theory of modern dynamics contending that the attractive or repulsive nature of elements was inherent rather than dependent upon distance.

Bay Minette (bā mi.net'). Town in SW Alabama, county seat of Baldwin County, ab. 25 mi. NE of Mobile: railroad junction; hunting and fishing resort. 3,732 (1950).

Baynard's Castle (bā'nardz). Strong fortification on the Thames just below Blackfriars, London, founded by Baynard, a follower of William I (the Conqueror), and forfeited to the crown by one of his successors. It was burned in the London fire of 1666.

Bayne (bān), **Peter.** b. at Fodderty, Scotland, Oct. 19, 1830; d. Feb. 12, 1896. Scottish author and journalist. He edited newspapers at Edinburgh, Glasgow, and London. Among his works are *Christian Life* (1855), *Hugh Miller* (1871), and *Luther* (1887).

Baynes (bānz), **Thomas Spencer.** b. at Wellington, Somersetshire, England, March 24, 1823; d. at London, May 30, 1887. British philosophical writer, appointed professor of logic, rhetoric, and metaphysics at the University of St. Andrews in 1864. He was assistant editor of the London *Daily News*, and editor of the ninth edition (1873–87) of the *Encyclopædia Britannica.*

Baynham (bān'am), **William.** b. Dec. 7, 1749; d. Dec. 8, 1814. American physician and surgeon, one of the first to perform a successful operation for extrauterine pregnancy.

Bay of Biscay (bis'kā). See **Biscay, Bay of.**

Bay of Islands. See **Islands, Bay of.**

Bay of Winds. Embayment in Antarctica, ab. 25 mi. wide between Cape Dovers and Delay Point, indenting the Queen Mary Coast ab. 12 mi.; in ab. 66°35′ S., 97°28′ E. It was discovered by the Australasian Antarctic Expedition (1911–14), under the leadership of Sir Douglas Mawson, and was so named because of the almost constant outflow of cold, dense air from the plateau into and down this bay.

Bayombong (bä.yôm.bông'). Town in the Philippine Islands, the capital of Nueva Vizcaya province, in N central Luzon. It is situated on the Magat River. 6,929 (1948).

Bayonne (bȧ.yon; Anglicized, bā.on', bā.yōn'). [Ancient name, **Lapurdum.**] City in SW France, in the department of Basses-Pyrénées, situated at the junction of the Nive and Adour rivers, near the Bay of Biscay, E of Biarritz. It is a seaport, with fortifications designed by Vauban. The bayonet was first made here. The cathedral of Bayonne dates from the 13th and 14th centuries, but has modern spires. There are beautiful medieval stained-glass windows, and two fine sculptured portals. The 13th-century cloister has been in part enclosed and transformed into an additional aisle in the church. The city has armament, textile, liquor, and candy factories, ship-repair yards, and an active import trade. The hams of Bayonne are famous. It is said that an interview was held here between Charles IX of France, Elizabeth of Spain, the duke of Alba, and Catherine de' Medici, in which the Saint Bartholomew massacre was planned. Later, in 1808, King Charles IV of Spain was forced here by Napoleon I to abdicate in favor of Joseph Bonaparte. The British captured the city in 1814 after a prolonged defense. The harbor, which was once obstructed by sand bars, has been improved, and trade is on the increase. 32,620 (1946).

Bayonne (bā.yōn'). City in NE New Jersey, in Hudson County, on the Kill Van Kull between New York and Newark Bays, ab. 6 mi. SW of New York: oil-refining center; has a U.S. naval supply depot. The Bayonne Bridge (1,675 ft. long) connects it with Staten Island. 77,203 (1950).

Bayonne, Convention of. Convention concluded May 10, 1808, between France and the grand duchy of Warsaw.

Bayonne, Treaty of. Treaty concluded at Bayonne, France, in May, 1808, between Napoleon I and Charles IV of Spain. By it the latter renounced his right to the Spanish throne.

Bayonne Decree. Decree issued by Napoleon I at Bayonne, France, on April 17, 1808, directing the seizure of all American vessels then in the ports of France.

Bayou Folk. Collection of 23 stories and sketches of Louisiana life by Kate Chopin, published in 1894.

"Bayou State." Occasional nickname of **Mississippi.**

Bay Path. Name variously given to three separate routes used by colonists in 17th-century New England for travel within Massachusetts and Connecticut or between the two colonies. The precise direction and terminal points of the routes have been disputed by authorities, but it is likely that the trails followed for a considerable distance the east bank of the Connecticut River, and linked what are now Springfield, Mass., and Hartford, Conn.

Bayport (bā'pōrt). Village in SE Minnesota, in Washington County, on the Mississippi River: woodworking plants; seat of Minnesota state prison. 2,502 (1950).

Bay Psalm Book, The. Earliest New England version of the Psalms. Its title is *The Whole Booke of Psalmes Faithfully Translated into English Metre.* It was printed by Stephen Daye in 1640 at Cambridge, Mass., and was the first book published in English in the British American colonies, though not in the New World. It was the joint production of Richard Mather, Thomas Welde, and John Eliot. Eleven copies are known to be extant. Its bibliographic importance has misled critics into giving it a literary notoriety it does not deserve, and its clumsy verses have been cited as typical of Puritan poetry, whereas they are actually completely accurate translations of the Psalms which could be sung to familiar tunes.

Bayreuth (bī.roit'). [Also, **Baireuth.**] Former German burgraviate and principality, now in the N part of Bavaria. It was united to Ansbach in 1769, acquired by Prussia in 1791–92, lost by Prussia in 1805, and was ceded to Bavaria in 1810.

Bayreuth. [Also, **Baireuth.**] Town in S Germany, in the *Land* (state) of Bavaria, American Zone, in the *Kreis* (district) of Middle and Upper Franconia, situated on the Red Main River, ab. 40 mi. NE of Nuremberg: cotton-textile spinning and weaving mills; metallurgical, electrical, and foodstuff industries; manufactures of precision instruments, rubber goods, toys, and pianos. The older part of the town has largely the architectural character of the baroque and rococo periods. The old castle dates from the 16th and 17th centuries, the new castle from the 18th century; the opera house is also in the baroque style. The *Stadtkirche* (town church) dates from the 15th century, and there are several notable 18th-century churches. 58,800 (1950).

History. Bayreuth was founded in 1194 by Bishop Otto II of Bamberg; it passed to the burgrave Frederick III of Nuremberg, of the Hohenzollern family, in 1248, and remained with one or the other branch of the house of Hohenzollern until 1806 when it was ceded to Napoleon I who, in turn, ceded it to Bavaria in 1810. The increase of the population from 1939 to 1946 amounted to 29.6 percent, largely due to the influx of East-German and Sudeten-German refugees.

Bayreuth Festival. Music festival held at fairly regular intervals (usually every two years, except for wartime) at Bayreuth, Germany, for the presentation of Richard Wagner's works in the *Opernfestspielhaus* (Opera-Festival House), which was opened by Wagner in 1876. Music lovers from every part of the world have flocked to this festival for many years.

Bayrhoffer (bīr'hof.ėr), **Karl Theodor.** b. at Marburg, Germany, 1812; d. at Jordan, Wis., Feb. 3, 1888. German philosophical writer, publicist, and politician. He was professor of philosophy at Marburg (1838–46), a member of the *Landtag* (diet) of the state of Hesse (1848), and later (1850 *et seq.*) president of the chamber. He subsequently went to the U.S. and settled in Wisconsin.

Bayrischer Kreis (bī'rish.ėr krīs). German name of the **Bavarian Circle.**

Bayrischer Wald (vält). German name of the **Bavarian Forest.**

Bayse (bez). See **Baïse.**

Bay Shore (bā' shōr'). Unincorporated community in SE New York, in Suffolk County, on Great South Bay, S Long Island: residential community. 9,665 (1950).

"Bay State." Nickname of **Massachusetts.**

Bay St. Louis (bā' sānt lö'is). [Former name, **Shieldsborough.**] City in S Mississippi, county seat of Hancock County, on St. Louis Bay. 4,621 (1950).

Bayswater (bāz'wô"tėr). Part of London lying immediately N of Kensington Gardens, in W London, in Kensington and Paddington metropolitan boroughs. The original Bayswater was a hamlet near what is now Gloucester Terrace.

Baytown (bā'toun). City in E Texas, in Harris County, SE of Houston: oil refining and shipping; chemical plants. 22,983 (1950).

Bay Village. See **Bay.**

Baza (bä'thä). [Ancient name, **Basti**; medieval name, **Bastiana.**] City in S Spain, in the province of Granada, situated in the Sierra de Baza, ab. 53 mi. NE of Granada: linen, hat, and pottery manufactures; agricultural trade. The ancient Collegiate Church of San Maximo occupies the site of a church founded by the Visigothic King Reccared c600 and later converted into a mosque. An important Moslem city, it was captured by Isabella of Castile in 1489. It was the scene of a victory (1810) of the French under Nicolas Soult over the Spaniards. 20,772 (1940).

Bazaine (bȧ.zen), **Achille François.** b. at Versailles, France, Feb. 13, 1811; d. at Madrid, Spain, Sept. 23, 1888. French marshal. He served in Algeria, and in Spain against the Carlists; commanded the Foreign Legion in the Crimean War; commanded a division in the Italian war of 1859, and distinguished himself at Solferino; took part in the Mexican expedition, and became commander in chief in Mexico in 1863; was made marshal in 1864; withdrew from Mexico in 1867, and was made commander of the Imperial Guard in 1869. He commanded a corps at the beginning of the Franco-Prussian war, was made commander of the Army of the Rhine in August, 1870, and was besieged at Metz, which he surrendered, with 173,000 men, on Oct. 27, 1870. For this surrender he was tried before a tribunal under the presidency of Henri Eugène Philippe Louis d'Orleans, Duc d'Aumale, and condemned to degradation and death. The sentence was commuted to 20 years' imprisonment, and he was imprisoned (December, 1873) near Cannes, whence he escaped (Aug. 9–10, 1874). He resided later at Madrid, and wrote several works on the Metz episode.

Bazalgette (baz'al.jet), Sir **Joseph William,** b. 1819; d. 1891. English civil and sanitary engineer. As chief engineer for the Metropolitan Board of Works he designed and executed (1858–65) the system of drainage which is the basis of that now in operation at London. He was also largely responsible (1863–74) for the Victoria, the Albert, and the Chelsea embankments along the Thames.

Bazan (bȧ.zäṅ), **Don César de.** See **Don César de Bazan.**

Bazard (bȧ.zȧr), **Saint-Amand.** b. at Paris, Sept. 19, 1791; d. at Courtry, near Montgermeil, France, July 29, 1832. French socialist. He was an organizer of Carbonarist societies, and an adherent of Claude Henri de Rouvroy, Comte de Saint-Simon.

Bazargic (bä.zär'jēk). Rumanian name of **Tolbukhin,** Bulgaria.

Bazarov (bä.zä'rof). Brutal but intelligent medical student in Ivan Turgenev's *Fathers and Sons*. He is the representative of young Russia of the 19th century, with aspirations toward progress. In him is first formulated the theory of nihilism. He takes pride in absolute negation.

Bazas (bȧ.zȧs). Town in SW France, in the department of Gironde, picturesquely situated on a hill above the Beuve River, ab. 33 mi. SE of Bordeaux. A Roman city and the old capital of the province, it has preserved numerous vestiges of former times, such as ramparts, houses, and arcades. The Cathedral of Saint Jean, dating from the 13th century, has a 15th-century bell tower. 4,290 (1946).

Bazeilles (bȧ.zey'). Village in NE France, in the department of Ardennes, SE of Sedan, near the Meuse River. It was taken by the Bavarians on Sept. 1, 1870.

Bazin (bȧ.zaṅ). Lackey of Aramis in the novel *The Three Musketeers*, by the elder Alexandre Dumas.

Bazin, Antoine Pierre Louis. b. 1799; d. 1863. French Orientalist. He was the author of *Théâtre chinois* and *Grammaire mandarine*.

Bazin, François Emmanuel Joseph. b. at Marseilles, Sept. 4, 1816; d. at Paris, July 2, 1878. French composer of comic operas, the cantata *Loyse de Montfort* (1840), which won the Prix de Rome, religious music, and part songs.

Bazin, Jacques Rigomer. b. in France, 1771; d. Jan. 20, 1820. French publicist, man of letters, and politician. He was the author of pamphlets published under the title *Le Lynx* (1814) and *Suite du Lynx* (1817); also wrote *Jacqueline d'Olysbourg* (1803), a melodrama, *Charlemagne*, (1817), a tragedy, and *Séide* (1816), a novel.

Bazin, René François Nicolas Marie. b. at Angers, France, Dec. 23, 1853; d. at Paris, July 20, 1932. French novelist. Educated at the Catholic university of Angers and subsequently (1875 *et seq.*) professor of law there, he began his literary career as a regionalist with *Stephanette* (1884), *Une Tache d'encre* (1888; Eng. trans., *A Blot of Ink*, 1892; also, *Ink Stain*, 1905), and others. He exploited the problem of the urban movement, as it affected rural communities, in novels like *La Terre qui meurt* (1899) and *Le Blé qui lève* (1907; Eng. trans., *The Coming Harvest*, 1908). He wrote a series of novels on the problem of Alsace-Lorraine, *Les Oberlé* (1901; Eng. trans., *The Children of Alsace*, 1912), *Les Nouveaux Oberlé* (1919), and *Baltus le Lorrain* (1926). An urbane traditionalist, he was elected to the Academy in 1903.

Bazoche (bȧ.zosh), **La.** [Also, **La Basoche.**] Association of clerks connected with the parliament of Paris. It watched over the interests of its members, and performed farces satirizing the parliament. It arose at the beginning of the 14th century, and was suppressed in 1791, but was later revived.

Baztán (bäth.tän'). [Also, **Bastán.**] Valley in the Pyrenees, in the N part of the province of Navarra, Spain. It is traversed by the Bidassoa River.

Baztán. Town and commune in NE Spain, in the province of Navarra, situated in the Pyrenees, N of Pamplona: center of a livestock-raising district. 10,326 (1940).

Bazzard (baz'ard), **Mr.** In Charles Dickens's *Mystery of Edwin Drood*, a clerk to Mr. Grewgious, and author of a tragedy which gives him a baleful influence over his master.

Bazzini (bäd.dzē'nē), **Antonio.** b. at Brescia, Italy, March 11, 1818; d. at Milan, Feb. 10, 1897. Italian composer and violin virtuoso. His works include the opera *Turandot* (1867, not to be confused with Giaccomo Puccini's opera of the same title), string quartets, religious cantatas, and two overtures for symphony orchestra.

Beach (bēch), **Alfred Ely.** b. at Springfield, Mass., Sept. 1, 1826; d. Jan. 1, 1896. American inventor and science editor, notable for his contributions to the development of the typewriter, cable railways, pneumatic tubes for mail and passengers, and a tunneling shield. He was an editor and co-owner with Orson D. Munn and Salem H.

Wales of the *Scientific American*. He was a nephew of Benjamin H. Day, who founded the New York *Sun*, and son of Moses Yale Beach, who later bought the paper.

Beach, Amy Marcy. [Maiden name, **Cheney.**] b. at Henniker, N.H., Sept. 5, 1867; d. 1944. American pianist and composer. Her compositions include the *Gaelic Symphony*, a concerto for piano and orchestra, a sonata for piano and violin, and a mass; among her best-known songs is her setting of Browning's verses, *The Year's at the Spring*.

Beach, Charles Fisk. b. at Hunter (now Jewett), N.Y., Sept. 5, 1827; d. May 25, 1908. American Presbyterian clergyman and legal writer. He served as pastor (1854–73) of various churches and was editor (1873–95) of the *National Presbyterian*. Author of *The Muzzled Ox* (1866), *The Christian Worker* (1869), *Commentaries on the Law of Trusts and Trustees* (1897), and *Monopolies and Industrial Trusts* (1898).

Beach, Chester. b. at San Francisco, May 23, 1881—. American sculptor and coin designer. He has done several portrait busts for the Hall of Fame, and larger works for Saint Mark's Cathedral, the American Academy of Arts and Letters, New York, and the Panama-Pacific Exposition (San Francisco, 1915). He studied at Paris and Rome, and has exhibited in the U.S. and France. He has won many prizes; in 1924 he was made a member of the National Academy of Design, and also the American Academy of Arts and Letters. Among his better-known works are *The Sacred Fire, Cloud Forms, Dawn, Beyond, Service to the Nation;* the portraits *Peter Cooper, Asa Gray, Eli Whitney, Walt Whitman, Adolph Lewisohn, S.F.B. Morse,* and *William H. Harrison;* and designs for the Monroe-Adams half dollar, Hawaiian half dollar, and the Lexington-Concord half dollar.

Beach, David Nelson. b. at South Orange, N.J., Nov. 30, 1848; d. at Southington, Conn., Oct. 18, 1926. American Congregational clergyman, active in campaigns against saloons at Cambridge, Mass. He held (1876–1902) various pastorates before serving as president (1903–21) and professor of homiletics at Bangor Theological Seminary. Author of *Plain Words on Our Lord's Work* (1886), *The Newer Religious Thinking* (1893), *How We Rose (A Resurrection Parable)* (1895), *The Intent of Jesus* (1896), *Statement of Belief* (1897), and *A Handbook of Homiletics* (1917).

Beach, Frederick Converse. b. at Brooklyn, N.Y., March 27, 1848; d. June 18, 1918. American publisher, patent solicitor, and photographer; son of Alfred Ely Beach (1826–96) and grandson of Moses Yale Beach (1800–68). He was a director (1896 *et seq.*) of the Scientific American Company, cofounder and editor (1889 *et seq.*) of the magazine *American Amateur Photographer* (later *American Photography*), and editor-in-chief (1902 *et seq.*) of the *Encyclopedia Americana*.

Beach, Harlan Page. b. at South Orange, N.J., April 4, 1854; d. at Winter Park, Fla., March 4, 1933. American Congregational missionary and teacher. He was a missionary (1883–90) in China, a teacher (1892–95) and head of the School for Christian Workers at Springfield, Mass., professor (1906–21) of the theory and practice of missions at the Yale Divinity School, and a lecturer (1921–28) at Drew Theological Seminary. Author of *The Cross in the Land of the Trident* (1895), *Dawn on the Hills of Tang* (1898), *Renaissant Latin America* (1916), and *Missions as a Cultural Factor in the Pacific* (1927).

Beach, Miles. b. in Saratoga County, N.Y., 1840; d. 1902. American jurist. He was a judge (1879–94) of the New York court of common pleas until his election (1894) to the state supreme court.

Beach, Moses Sperry. b. at Springfield, Mass., Oct. 5, 1822; d. July 25, 1892. American journalist and inventor, connected (1845–68) with the New York *Sun*, which his father, Moses Yale Beach, purchased from a brother-in-law, Benjamin H. Day, founder of the paper. He was a liberal, enterprising publisher, aiming his paper at the working man. His mechanical contributions to newspaper production included a device for feeding paper into presses from a roll, one for dampening paper before printing and another for cutting it after printing, and a method of printing both sides of the sheet at once.

Beach, Moses Yale. b. at Wallingford, Conn., Jan. 15, 1800; d. there, July 19, 1868. American inventor and journalist, proprietor (1838–48) of the New York *Sun* until he turned its management over to his sons Moses Sperry Beach and Alfred Ely Beach.

Beach, Rex (Ellingwood). b. Sept. 1, 1877; d. Dec. 7, 1949. American novelist. Among his works are *Pardners* (1905), *The Spoilers* (1906), *The Barrier* (1907), *Going Some* (1910), *The Ne'er-do-Well* (1911), *The Net* (1912), *The Auction Block* (1914), *Oh, Shoot* (1921), *The Goose Woman* (1925), *Don Careless* (1928), *Son of the Gods* (1929), *Alaskan Adventures* (1933), *Jungle Gold* (1935), *Personal Exposures* (1941), and *The World in His Arms* (1946). He also collaborated in preparing stage and moving-picture versions of *The Spoilers, Going Some,* and others of his books.

Beach, Thomas Miller. [Pseudonym, **Henry le Caron.**] b. at Colchester, England, Sept. 26, 1841; d. at London, April 1, 1894. English spy notable for his reports on the Fenian organization in the U.S. and Canada. A Union soldier (1861–65) during the Civil War, he enlisted under the name "Henri le Caron" and attained the rank of major. After informing (1866) the English government of a Fenian plan for the invasion of Canada, he returned (1867) to the U.S. as a paid agent. Under cover of active Fenian membership, he informed (1868, 1869, 1870, 1871) English and Canadian authorities of Fenian plans and campaigns. He practiced medicine at Detroit and Braidwood (near Wilmington, Del.) until he left America in 1888. In 1889 he gave evidence in an investigation of Irish agitators. Author of *Twenty-five Years in the Secret Service* (1892).

Beach, William Augustus. b. at Saratoga Springs, N.Y., Dec. 9, 1809; d. June 21, 1884. American lawyer. He was admitted to the bar in 1833, and represented Cornelius Vanderbilt in the Erie Railroad case.

Beach, Wooster. b. at Trumbull, Conn., 1794; d. Jan. 28, 1868. American writer of books on medicine, author of *The American Practice of Medicine* (3 vols., 1833), a widely read and often reprinted textbook. Founder (1836) of the *Eclectic Medical Journal* and president (1855 *et seq.*) of the National Eclectic Medical Association, he was an advocate of the medicinal use of herbs and roots and a crusader against bloodletting and mercurial purgatives.

Beachy Head (bē'chi). Chalk headland on the coast of SE England, in Sussex, ab. 3 mi. SW of Eastbourne, projecting into the English Channel. Elevation, ab. 530 ft.

Beachy Head, Battle of. Naval victory gained in the English Channel, off Beachy Head, by the French under Anne Hilarion de Cotentin, Comte de Tourville, over the allied English and Dutch under Arthur Herbert, Earl of Torrington, on June 29–30, 1690.

Beacon (bē'kọn). City in SE New York, in Dutchess County, on the Hudson River: manufactures include bricks and paper cartons. Mount Beacon (1,602 ft.) is nearby. The city was formed (1913) from the villages of Fishkill Landing and Matteawan. 14,012 (1950).

Beacon Hill. Elevation N of Boston Common, in Boston, Mass. It was named from the beacon fires which were formerly lighted upon it.

Beaconsfield (bē'kọnz.fēld). Urban district and market town in S central England, in Buckinghamshire, situated on the N bank of the river Thames, ab. 23 mi. NW of London by rail. It still lies beyond the area of continuous urban development surrounding London. It was the home and burial-place of Edmund Waller and of Edmund Burke. 7,909 (1951).

Beaconsfield, 1st Earl of. Title of **Disraeli, Benjamin.**

Beacon Street. Street in Boston, Mass., which extends from Tremont Street along the N side of the Common and Public Gardens westward. It was noted in the 19th and early 20th centuries as a street of residences, and its name became a synonym for the wealth and culture of the city.

Beadle (bē'dl), **Erastus Flavel.** b. at Pierstown, N.Y., Sept. 11, 1821; d. Dec. 18, 1894. American publisher, especially of dime novels. Beadle began his publishing career by issuing ten-cent song books and game manuals. In 1859, with his brother, Irvin P. Beadle, and Robert Adams he organized the firm of Beadle and Adams to publish "dollar books for a dime." From the start this venture was phenomenally successful. Of the first of these dime novels, *Malaeska, or the Indian Wife of the White Hunter*, 65,000 copies were sold, and within a year other numbers of the series sold as many as 500,000 copies in this country and 100,000 in Great Britain, where (until 1866) all Beadle and Adams books were also issued. Although the success of the Beadle and Adams dime novels caused many competitors to appear, the "Beadle books," as they were sometimes called, remained easily the most successful and influential. They were praised by Abraham Lincoln, Henry Ward Beecher, and other civic and religious leaders, and their strongly patriotic tendency had its part in disseminating a sense of national pride. These dime novels also gave rise to the "Westerns" which in recent times have been popularized by the motion pictures, the radio, and television. Among Beadle and Adams's early authors (nominally or actually) were William F. ("Buffalo Bill") Cody, S. M. Ellis, and the novelist Mayne Reid. But in the 1880's, under pressure of competition and of a dwindling of interest in the Western adventure story, the Beadle and Adams publications became more lurid and found their subjects more and more in train robberies, and tales of city life in its more sordid and criminal aspects. By the 1890's "Beadle books" were being widely denounced as unfit reading matter for the young. The firm of Beadle and Adams underwent various reorganizations, was finally absorbed by another firm, and eventually publication of the typical dime novel was discontinued. However, because of their authentic status as Americana (if not as great literature), they have recently attracted the interest of many scholars and collectors, and a collection of Beadle and Adams dime novels is now in the New York Public Library.

Beadle, William Henry Harrison. b. in Parke County, Ind., Jan. 1, 1838; d. at San Francisco, Nov. 13, 1915. American educator who served (1879 *et seq.*) as superintendent of public instruction in the Dakota Territory. He was responsible for a provision included (1889) in the state constitution that ten dollars an acre should be the minimum price for school lands.

Beagle (bē′gl). Ship in which Darwin made his voyage as a naturalist. She was a 10-gun brig of 235 tons, commanded by Captain Robert Fitzroy. She sailed from England on Dec. 27, 1831, and returned almost five years later, on Oct. 2, 1836, having in the meantime circumnavigated the globe. The vessel had previously been used in surveying work along the South American coast. The scientific results of the expedition given in Darwin's diary of the voyage were published as Volume III of the official *Voyage of H.M.'s Ships Adventure and Beagle*, edited by Robert Fitzroy (1839). It was issued separately later in the same year. The zoölogy and botany of the expedition were published by Darwin and assistants in eight volumes (1840–46). The definitive edition is *Charles Darwin's Diary of the Voyage of H.M.S. "Beagle,"* edited by Nora Barlow (1934).

Beagle, Sir Harry. Fox-hunting English squire in the elder George Colman's comedy *The Jealous Wife*.

Beagle Channel. Strait in the archipelago of Tierra del Fuego, which extends E and W, at the S extremity of South America, between Tierra del Fuego, Argentina, and a part of Tierra del Fuego, Chile.

Beal (bēl), **Gifford Reynolds.** b. at New York City, Jan. 24, 1879—. American painter and etcher, at first chiefly of marine subjects, later also of figure groups, often set along parts of the Massachusetts coast. A student of William M. Chase and, at the Art Students League of New York, of Frank V. DuMond and Henry Ward Ranger, he was the recipient of awards at the Panama-Pacific Exposition (1915), and from the National Arts Club (1918) and the National Academy of Design (1931). He is represented in the Metropolitan Museum of Art, New York, the Art Institute of Chicago, the Syracuse Museum of Art, and others.

Beal, Samuel. b. at Devonport, England, 1825; d. 1889. English clergyman and scholar of Chinese. Between the years of 1856 and 1858, he served as naval chaplain and interpreter on the China station. In 1877 he was appointed professor of Chinese at University College, London. He published translations from the Chinese, and other works.

Beal, William James. b. at Adrian, Mich., March 11, 1833; d. at Amherst, Mass., May 12, 1924. American botanist and teacher, pioneer of the "new botany." Boyhood observation of the waste of Michigan forests influenced him to become a conservationist; studying under Louis Agassiz at Harvard he became a naturalist, and under Asa Gray a systematic botanist. He taught (1871–1910) at Michigan Agricultural College and is said to have had more than 1,200 publications, notably *The New Botany* (1881), *Grasses of North America* (1887), and *Seed Dispersal* (1898).

Beale (bēl), **Dorothea.** b. March 21, 1831; d. at Cheltenham, Gloucestershire, England, Nov. 9, 1906. English educator. In 1857 she was head teacher of the Clergy Daughters' School at Casterton, in Westmorland (an institution which is famous as the model of "Lowood," in Charlotte Bronte's novel *Jane Eyre*). In 1858 she became principal of the Cheltenham Ladies' College, which was at that time in difficulties that actually threatened its existence, but Miss Beale made it one of the best institutions of its kind in England, and continued to guide it until 1906. In 1885 she was one of the founders of Saint Hilda's College, for women teachers in secondary schools, at Cheltenham, and in 1893 she was instrumental in establishing Saint Hilda's Hall for women teachers at Oxford. She also taught mathematics at Queen's College for Ladies, at London, of which she had been one of the earliest students. She was the author of *Reports on the Education of Girls* (1869).

Beale, Edward Fitzgerald. b. at Washington, D.C., Feb. 4, 1822; d. there, April 22, 1893. American naval lieutenant and courier, who brought east the first authentic news (1848) of the California gold strikes. He traveled many thousand miles for the government, crossing from ocean to ocean six times in one two-year period.

Beale, Lionel Smith. b. Feb. 5, 1828; d. March 28, 1906. English physiologist and microscopist. He was professor of medicine, physiology, and morbid anatomy (1853–69), and later (1869–76) of pathological anatomy at King's College, London. He was the author of *How to Work with the Microscope, Protoplasm, or Life, Matter, and Mind, On Life and on Vital Action in Health and Disease*, and others.

Beale, Mary. [Maiden name, **Cradock.**] b. in Suffolk, England, 1632; d. at London, Dec. 28, 1697. English artist, noted as a portrait painter.

Beale, Truxtun. b. at San Francisco, March 6, 1856; d. June 3, 1936. American diplomat. He served as minister to Persia (1891–92) and to Greece, Rumania, and Serbia (1892–94), and as envoy extraordinary and minister plenipotentiary (1893–94). He traveled (1894–96) in Siberia, C Asia, and Chinese Turkestan.

Beales (bēlz), **Edmond.** b. 1803; d. 1881. English reformer. He achieved celebrity in the 19th century by his connection with the Polish Exiles' Friends Society, Circassian Committee, Emancipation Society, Garibaldi Committee, and the Reform League, over which he presided at the time of the Hyde Park Riots (1866); four years later he became a county-court circuit judge.

Beall (bēl), **John Yates.** b. in Virginia, Jan. 1, 1835; d. on Governor's Island, N.Y., Feb. 24, 1865. American Confederate soldier, spy, and guerrilla. He commanded a body of men who, disguised as passengers, seized the Lake Erie steamer *Philo Parsons* on Sept. 19, 1864, and subsequently captured and sank another boat, the *Island Queen*. He was arrested at Suspension Bridge, N.Y., on Dec. 16, 1864, was tried at Fort Lafayette by a military commission and, in spite of a proclamation by Jefferson Davis, dated Dec. 24, 1864, in which the Confederate government assumed the responsibility for Beall's action, was convicted and hanged for spying.

Beall, Samuel Wootton. b. in Montgomery County, Md., Sept. 26, 1807; shot in an argument at Helena, Mont., Sept. 26, 1868. American politician and territorial official. A receiver (1827 *et seq.*) for the sale of northwestern lands at Green Bay, Wis., he was active in the movement for Wisconsin statehood, and was lieutenant governor (1850–52) of Wisconsin. He was the leader (1859) of the Pike's Peak, Colo., exploratory expedition. During the Civil War, he served as a lieutenant colonel with the Union army.

Beals (bēlz), **Carleton.** b. at Medicine Lodge, Kan., Nov. 13, 1893—. American journalist, lecturer, and author. A graduate of the University of California (1916) and Columbia University (1917), he served as a correspondent in Italy (1920–22), Central America (1927–28), Europe (1929), Cuba (1932–33, 1935), South America (1934, 1946) and intermittently in Mexico (1923–37).

He was president (1933–37) of *Latin-American Digest*, and a lecturer (1925–28, 1930–31) in a seminar on relations with Mexico. His works include *Rome or Death—The Story of Fascism* (1923), *Mexico—An Interpretation* (1923), *Brimstone and Chili* (1927), *Mexican Maze* (1931), *Banana Gold* (1932), *Fire on the Andes* (1934), *America South* (1937), *American Earth: The Biography of a Nation* (1939), *Pan America, a Program for the Western Hemisphere* (1940), and *Rio Grande to Cape Horn* (1943); he also wrote the autobiographical *Glass Houses* (1938) and *The Great Circle* (1940).

Beals, Edward Alden. b. at Troy, N.Y., April 23, 1855; d. Dec. 26, 1931. American meteorologist. He was head of U.S. Weather Bureau stations at New York (1883), Atlanta (1883), Mount Washington, N.H. (1884–85), Chattanooga, Tenn. (1886–87), La Crosse, Wis. (1887–90), Minneapolis (1891–95), Cleveland (1896–99), Portland, Ore. (1900–17), and San Francisco (1917–24); he was also in charge (1924–26) of the Hawaiian weather service.

Bealtaine (bal'toin). See **Beltane.**

Bealwood (bēl'wůd). Unincorporated community in W Georgia, in Muscogee County, near Columbus. Under the urban definition established for use in the 1950 census, Bealwood was counted with adjoining urban areas. The last official enumeration was 4,793 (1940).

Beaman (bē'mạn), **Charles Cotesworth.** b. at Houlton, Me., May 7, 1840; d. at New York, Dec. 15, 1900. American lawyer and expert on international law. He studied the "Alabama Claims" controversy between the U.S. and Great Britain and, following his publication (1871) of *The National and Private "Alabama Claims" and Their "Final and Amicable Settlement,"* was appointed U.S. sclicitor at the Geneva Arbitration Tribunal. Author of *The Rights of Insurance Companies under the Geneva Award* (1876).

Bean (bēn), **Tarleton Hoffman.** b. at Bainbridge, Pa., Oct. 8, 1846; d. Dec. 28, 1916. American ichthyologist and one-time (1895–98) director of the New York Aquarium, most distinguished ichthyologist of his time in the U.S. Curator (1880–95) of the department of fisheries in the U.S. National Museum, and head fish culturist (1906–16) of New York State, he was a pioneer in the national movement to preserve native fish; he made important scientific discoveries and uncovered information of great commercial value on fish migrations. Author of *Fishes of Pennsylvania* (1893), *Fishes of Long Island* (1901), *Fishes of New York* (1903), *Fishes of Bermuda* (1906); coauthor with G. B. Goode of *Oceanic Ichthyology* (1895).

Beanntraighe (ban'tri). Irish name of **Bantry.**

Bear (bãr). River in N Utah, S Wyoming, and S Idaho, which flows into Great Salt Lake. Its waters are used at various points for irrigation. Length, 350 mi.

Beard (bird), **Charles Austin.** b. near Knightstown, Ind., Nov. 27, 1874; d. at New Haven, Conn., Sept. 1, 1948. American historian and educator, known for his economic interpretation of history; husband (married 1900) of Mary Ritter Beard. A graduate of DePauw (1898) and Columbia (1904), he was professor (1915–17) of politics at Columbia until he resigned in protest against the dismissal of two other faculty members because of their antiwar position in World War I. He was a founder of the New School for Social Research, and director (1917–22) of the Training School for Public Service, New York. Author of *The Office of Justice of the Peace* (1904), *American Government and Politics* (1910), *American City Government* (1912), *Economic Interpretation of the Constitution* (1913), *Economic Basis of Politics* (1922), *American Party Battle* (1928), *The Republic* (1943), *American Foreign Policy in the Making: 1932–1940* (1946), *President Roosevelt and the Coming of War: 1941* (1948), and other works; coauthor, with James Harvey Robinson, of *Development of Modern Europe* (1907), with W. C. Bagley, of *History of the American People* (1918), and, with Mary Ritter Beard, of *American Citizenship* (1913), *History of the United States* (1921), *The Rise of American Civilization* (1927), *The Making of American Civilization* (1937), *America in Midpassage* (1939), *The American Spirit: A Study of the Idea of Civilization in the United States* (1942), and *A Basic History of the United States* (1944).

Beard, Daniel Carter. [Called **"Dan" Beard.**] b. at Cincinnati, Ohio, June 21, 1850; d. June 11, 1941. American writer and illustrator, notable for organizing (1910) the first Boy Scout group in America; son of James Henry Beard. A student (1880–84) at the Art Students League of New York, he was the teacher (1893–1900) of the first animal-drawing class in the world, at the Woman's School of Applied Design, and was the organizer (1911) and head (1911–15) of the department of woodcraft at Culver (Ind.) Military Academy. Mount Beard, the peak adjoining Mount McKinley, was named for him. Author of *American Boys' Handy Book* (1882), *Moonlight and Six Feet of Romance* (1890), *Outdoor Handy Book* (1900), *Boy Pioneers and Sons of Daniel Boone* (1909), *Shelters, Shacks and Shanties* (1914), *Signs, Signals and Symbols* (1918), *American Boys' Book of Camplore and Woodcraft* (1920), *Wisdom of the Woods* (1927), and *Buckskin Book for Buckskin Men and Boys* (1929).

Beard, George Miller. b. at Montville, Conn., May 8, 1839; d. at New York, Jan. 23, 1883. American physician, known for research on nervous diseases, including the study of electrotherapeutics. Author of *Stimulants and Narcotics* (1871), *Eating and Drinking* (1871), *Hay Fever* (1876), *American Nervousness* (1881), and others.

Beard, James Carter. b. at Cincinnati, Ohio, June 6, 1837; d. at New Orleans, La., Nov. 15, 1913. American illustrator and editor; son of James Henry Beard and brother of Daniel Carter Beard. Now known chiefly as the author of illustrated articles on plant and animal life, he was for many years an editor of D. Appleton and Company. Author of *The Adventures of Little Fantasy among the Water Devils* (1871), *Little Workers* (1871), *Painting on China* (1882), *Curious Homes and their Tenants* (1897), and *Billy Possum* (1909); illustrator of *Hunting Trip of a Ranchman*, by Theodore Roosevelt.

Beard, James Henry. b. at Buffalo, N.Y., May 20, 1812; d. at Flushing, N.Y., April 4, 1893. American artist; brother of William Holbrook Beard. He is best known as a painter of animals and for his portraits of such noted Americans as John Quincy Adams, Henry Clay, and William Henry Harrison. His sons James Carter Beard, Daniel Carter Beard, and Thomas Francis Beard were also, in addition to their other activities, artists of some repute.

Beard, Mary Ritter. b. at Indianapolis, Ind., Aug. 5, 1876—. American historian and feminist; wife (married 1900) of Charles Austin Beard. She was graduated from DePauw University in 1897. Author of *Woman's Work in Municipalities* (1915), *Women as a Force in History* (1946), and other works; coauthor, with Charles Austin Beard, of *American Citizenship* (1913), *History of the United States* (1921), *The Rise of American Civilization* (1927), *The Making of American Civilization* (1937), *America in Midpassage* (1939), *The American Spirit: A Study of the Idea of Civilization in the United States* (1942), and *A Basic History of the United States* (1944).

Beard, Thomas Francis. [Called **"Frank" Beard.**] b. Feb. 6, 1842; d. Sept. 28, 1905. American illustrator, cartoonist, lecturer, and editor; son of James Henry Beard and brother of Daniel Carter Beard. At 18 he was assigned by *Harper's Weekly* and *Leslie's Weekly* to do cartoons of the Army of the Potomac. After the Civil War he began a career as a public lecturer, illustrating his talks with extemporaneous chalk sketches. He held a chair of aesthetics and painting (1881–84) at Syracuse University, and was editor of *Judge* during the James G. Blaine campaign (1884). Later he became interested in the Chautauqua movement and Sunday schools; he devoted himself (1890 *et seq.*) to a Chicago religious weekly, the *Ram's Horn*.

Beard, William Holbrook. b. April 13, 1825; d. Feb. 20, 1900. American painter, chiefly of humorous animal pictures; brother of James Henry Beard.

Beardie (bir'di), **Earl.** See **Lindsay, Alexander** (d. 1454).

Beardmore Glacier (bird'mōr). One of the largest known valley glaciers in the world, in Antarctica, descending from the south polar plateau to the Ross Shelf Ice; in 83°30′ S., 173°00′ E. It was discovered (1908) and traversed by Sir Ernest H. Shackleton and his party in their Antarctic expedition of 1908–09, and named for Sir William Beardmore (later Lord Invernairn), who helped support Shackleton's expedition. It passes between sandstone mountains from 10,000 to 15,000 ft. in height. These walls force the ice-stream into a winding route. Its surface is broken into ridges and crevasses which constitute a constant peril to the explorer. Area, ab. 1,200 sq. mi.

Beardshear (bird′shir), **William Miller.** b. Nov. 7, 1850; d. Aug. 5, 1902. American United-Brethren minister and educator, president (1881–89) of Western College, Toledo, Iowa, and president (1891–1902) of Iowa State College of Agriculture and Mechanic Arts.

Beardslee (birdz′li), **Lester Anthony.** b. at Little Falls, N.Y., Feb. 1, 1836; d. near Augusta, Ga., Nov. 11, 1903. American naval officer, commissioned (1895) rear admiral. He was in the Union navy during the Civil War, and was commander in chief (1894–97) of the naval forces in the Pacific. He discovered and surveyed (1879–80) Glacier Bay while in command of the USS *Jamestown;* as a survivor of Commodore Perry's visit (1853) to Japan, he was instrumental (1900–01) in the erection of a commemorative monument in Japan.

Beardsley, Aubrey Vincent. b. at Brighton, England, Aug. 24, 1872; d. at Menton, France, March 16, 1898. English illustrator (in black and white) and draftsman. He had little special training and at first divided his time between business and an architect's office. From this he turned to book illustration, in which he found extensive employment. His work is full of caprices which suggest Pre-Raphaelitism, the Japanese convention, and the French art of the 18th century. Among the works which he illustrated were *Volpone,* Oscar Wilde's *Salomé,* the *Rape of the Lock,* and *Morte d'Arthur.* He became the art editor of the *Yellow Book* in 1894.

Beardsley, Eben Edwards. b. at Stepney, Conn., Jan. 8, 1808; d. at New Haven, Conn., Dec. 21, 1891. American Protestant Episcopal clergyman and historical writer. He became rector of Saint Thomas's Church, New Haven, Conn., in 1848, and was the author of *History of the Episcopal Church in Connecticut* (1865).

Beardsley, Samuel. b. at Hoosic, N.Y., Feb. 6, 1790; d. at Utica, N.Y., May 6, 1860. American politician and jurist. He was a Democratic member of Congress from New York (1831–36, 1843–44), served as associate judge of the Supreme Court of New York (1844–47), and was appointed chief justice in 1847.

Beardstown (birdz′toun). City in W Illinois, in Cass County, on the Illinois River: shipping point for farm products, especially canteloupes and watermelons; clam fishing; flour and glove manufactures. 6,080 (1950).

Beare and Ye Club (thẹ bãr′ ạn thẹ klub′), **Ye.** First play in the English language to be performed in America, written in 1665 by three Virginians, Cornelius Watkinson, Philip Howard, and William Darby.

Bear Flag Battalion. Name given to a group of U.S. citizens which provided the chief military backing of the Bear Flag Revolt (1846) in California.

Bear Flag Revolt. Uprising (1846) by the community of U.S. citizens in N central California which led to the establishment of the Republic of California. The revolt was the product of differences between the Mexican officials and the U.S. settlers, and was undertaken by the latter in the belief that the Mexicans, at the first opportunity, would expel them from California. The revolt takes its name from the republic's flag, designed by William Todd; the standard bore a grizzly bear and a red star. The life of the republic was short, for with the outbreak of the Mexican War, the authority of the U.S. government was officially established (July 10, 1846) in the area.

Bear Island. [Norwegian, **Bjørnøya.**] Small Norwegian island in the Arctic Ocean, S of Spitsbergen, ab. 240 mi. N of Norway. It has a weather station. Area, ab. 69 sq. mi.

Bear Islands. [Russian, **Medvezhi Ostrova.**] Group of islands in the NE part of the U.S.S.R., in the East Siberian Sea, an arm of the Arctic Ocean, N of Siberia and W of Wrangel Island.

Bear Lake. Lake on the border of SE Idaho and NE Utah. Length, ab. 20 mi.; width ab. 7 mi.

Bear Lake, Great. See **Great Bear Lake.**

Bear Mountain. Peak in NW Connecticut, ab. 44 mi. NW of Hartford. It is the highest point in the state, and a local center for winter sports. 2,355 ft.

Bear Mountain. Peak in SE New York, ab. 40 mi. N of New York City, overlooking the Hudson River. It is located in a 1,000-acre section of Palisades Interstate Park named after the mountain. 1,314 ft.

Bear Mountain. Hill in the NE part of Dauphin County, E central Pennsylvania. There are coal deposits in its vicinity. Elevation, ab. 750 ft.

Bear Mountain Bridge. Highway toll bridge in SE New York, ab. 40 mi. N of New York City. It is a suspension bridge over the Hudson River, with a central span 1,632 ft. long. The bridge was opened in November, 1924, under private ownership, and acquired by the state of New York in 1940. Height above river, 135 ft.

Béarn (bā.ȧr, bā.ȧrn). [Latin, **Beneharnum.**] Region and former province in SW France, corresponding nearly to the department of Basses-Pyrénées. In the Middle Ages it was a viscounty. It passed to the Albret family of Navarre in 1465, and came with Henry of Navarre to France. It was formally incorporated with France in 1620. The capital was at Pau.

Bear River, Battle of. Engagement (Jan. 29, 1863) at Bear River, Utah, between a party of Californians, led by Colonel P. E. Connor, and Indians who had been carrying out raids upon the Overland Mail Route. Although the Indians outnumbered the whites by 3 to 2, the Californians subdued their opponents, killing more than 200 of the Indian force of 300.

Beas (bē′äs). [Also: **Beypasha, Bias;** ancient Greek, **Hyphasis.**] River in the Punjab, N Pakistan, which joins the Sutlej River ab. 50 mi. SE of Lahore: one of the "five rivers" of the Punjab. Length, ab. 290 mi.

Beas de Segura (bā′äs dā sä.gö′rä). Town in S Spain, in the province of Jaén, situated in mountainous surroundings, ab. 55 mi. NE of Jaén: center of a wine, oil, and fruit producing district. 14,953 (1940).

Beasley (bēz′li), **Frederick.** b. near Edenton, N.C., 1777; d. at Elizabethtown, N.J., Nov. 2, 1845. American clergyman and philosophical writer. He was professor of mental and moral philosophy at the University of Pennsylvania, 1813–28.

Beasley, Mercer. b. at Philadelphia, March 27, 1815; d. Feb. 19, 1897. American jurist, chief justice (1864–97) of New Jersey.

Beasts, Men, and Gods. Semifictional account (1922) by the Polish writer Ferdynand Antoni Ossendowski of his flight across Asia following the Russian Revolution of 1917. The veracity of the work was seriously questioned by Sven Hedin in *Ossendowski und die Wahrheit* (1925).

Beatenberg (bā.ä′tẹn.berk). See **St. Beatenberg.**

Beatia (bẹ.ā′shạ). Latin name of **Baeza.**

Beatitudes. Name applied to the enumerated blessings of Jesus Christ, being the opening sentences of the Sermon on the Mount. By Roman Catholics they are commonly called the Eight Beatitudes. The designation is derived from the Latin *beati,* the first word of each of the sentences in the Vulgate. The complete text is found in Matthew, v. 1–12. Four of the Beatitudes, in slightly different phraseology, occur in Luke, vi. 22. The Beatitudes as given in the Authorized (King James) Version of the Bible, with the introductory passage, read:

"1 And seeing the multitudes, he went up into a mountain: and when he was set, his disciples came unto him: 2 And he opened his mouth, and taught them, saying,

"3 Blessed are the poor in spirit: for theirs is the kingdom of heaven.

"4 Blessed are they that mourn: for they shall be comforted.

"5 Blessed are the meek: for they shall inherit the earth.

"6 Blessed are they which do hunger and thirst after righteousness: for they shall be filled.

"7 Blessed are the merciful: for they shall obtain mercy.

"8 Blessed are the pure in heart: for they shall see God.

"9 Blessed are the peacemakers: for they shall be called the children of God.

"10 Blessed are they which are persecuted for righteousness' sake: for theirs is the kingdom of heaven.

"11 Blessed are ye, when men shall revile you, and persecute you, and shall say all manner of evil against you falsely, for my sake. 12 Rejoice, and be exceeding glad: for great is your reward in heaven: for so persecuted they the prophets which were before you."

In the Douay (Roman Catholic) Version, these passages are given thus:

"1 And seeing the multitudes, he went up into a mountain, and when he was set down, his disciples came unto him.

"2 And opening his mouth, he taught them, saying:

"3 Blessed are the poor in spirit: for theirs is the kingdom of heaven.

"4 Blessed are the meek: for they shall possess the land.

"5 Blessed are they that mourn: for they shall be comforted.

"6 Blessed are they that hunger and thirst after justice: for they shall have their fill.

"7 Blessed are the merciful: for they shall obtain mercy.

"8 Blessed are the clean of heart: for they shall see God.

"9 Blessed are the peacemakers: for they shall be called the children of God.

"10 Blessed are they that suffer persecution for justice' sake: for theirs is the kingdom of heaven.

"11 Blessed are ye when they shall revile you, and persecute you, and speak all that is evil against you, untruly, for my sake:

"12 Be glad and rejoice, for your reward is very great in heaven. For so they persecuted the prophets that were before you."

It has been said that the central thought of the Beatitudes is that the Messianic kingdom is a spiritual realm. Of all the sayings of Jesus reported in the Gospels, the Beatitudes alone are poetic in their phrasing.

Beaton (bē'tọn), **Cecil Walter Hardy.** b. at London, Jan. 14, 1904—. English photographer, writer, and designer. He held his first exhibit of photographs at New York in 1929; in 1930 his photographs were first exhibited at London. During the next decade his work in this medium became known to millions through reproduction in American and British magazines, and he came to be especially noted as a photographer of beautiful women. In 1939 he made a series of photographic portraits of Queen Elizabeth of Great Britain, and became official photographer to the British royal family. In World War II he served with the British Ministry of Information, and his books of photographs, *Air of Glory, History Under Fire, Bomber Command,* and *Wings on Her Shoulders* were produced through this organization. He has also published *The Book of Beauty* (1930), *Cecil Beaton's Scrap Book* (1937), *Cecil Beaton's New York* (1939), *My Royal Past* (1939), *Winged Squadrons* (1942), *Near East* (1943), *British Photographers* (1944), *Far East* (1945) *Time Exposure* (1946; in 1941 he published in collaboration with Peter Quennell another book also entitled *Time Exposure*), *Ballet as Seen by Cecil Beaton,* and *Photobiography* (1951).

Beaton, David. [Also, **Bethune.**] b. 1494; murdered at the castle of St. Andrew's, in Scotland, May 29, 1546. Scottish Catholic prelate and statesman. He was several times ambassador to France, was made bishop of Mirepoix by Francis I in 1537, became a cardinal in 1538, and was appointed archbishop of St. Andrew's and primate of Scotland in 1539, lord privy seal in 1528, and chancellor in 1543. He negotiated the marriage of James V of Scotland with Magdalen, daughter of Francis I, and also his second marriage, with Mary of Guise. After the death of James he was arrested, but later regained liberty and power. He strongly opposed the proposed English marriage of Mary Stuart. He was a violent opponent of the Reformation, and it was by his order that George Wishart, a well-known Protestant preacher of the time, was arrested, tried, and burned at the stake.

Beaton, James. [Also, **Bethune.**] d. 1539. Scottish Catholic prelate; uncle of David Beaton. He became archbishop of Glasgow in 1509, and of St. Andrew's in 1522, and was lord treasurer from 1505, and chancellor in the period 1513–26. He played a conspicuous part in Scottish politics during the minority of James V, and, like his nephew, bitterly opposed the Reformation. He is said to have had much to do with the political alignment of Scotland with France rather than England.

Beaton, James. [Also, **Bethune.**] b. 1517; d. April 30, 1603. Scottish Catholic prelate; nephew of David Beaton. He became archbishop of Glasgow in 1552, and was Scottish ambassador to France for many years.

Beatrice (bẹ.at'ris). City in SE Nebraska, county seat of Gage County, on the Big Blue River: manufactures include mirrors, steel tanks, showcases, cultivators, irrigation machinery, and gasoline engines; it is a trading center for dairy products. 11,813 (1950).

Beatrice (bē'ạ.tris). Gay and wayward niece of Leonato, and rebellious lover of Benedick, in Shakespeare's comedy *Much Ado About Nothing;* a character of intrigue, gaiety, wit, and diversity of humor.

Beatrice. In John Marston's play *The Dutch Courtezan,* an innocent, modest girl, the antithesis of her gay sister Crispinella.

Beatrice. Principal character in Nathaniel Hawthorne's story *Rappacini's Daughter.* Her poison-fed beauty fills her lover with passion, horror, and finally despair when he sees that he himself has imbibed some of her fatal charm.

Beatrice Cenci (bā.ä.trē'chā chen'chē). Portrait by Guido Reni, in the Corsini Gallery, Rome. It is a three-quarter face seen over the shoulder, with golden hair confined by a white turban; the expression is of grief and gentle resignation.

Beatrice di Tenda (dē ten'dä). Opera by Vincenzo Bellini, first performed at Venice in 1833.

Béatrice et Bénédict (bā.å.trēs ā bā.nā.dēkt). Opera by Hector Berlioz, based on Shakespeare's *Much Ado About Nothing;* first performed on Aug. 9, 1862, and now chiefly known for its overture.

Beatrice-Joanna (bē'ạ.tris.jō.an'ạ). Heroine of Thomas Middleton and William Rowley's play *The Changeling.* She is a headstrong, unscrupulous, unobservant girl, intent on putting an unwelcome lover out of the way. She induces De Flores, whom she loathes, to murder him (expecting thus to become free to marry Alsemero, whom she loves), and is astounded when her maidenly virtue is demanded as a reward instead of money. Unable to escape De Flores, she yields. In the meantime, her wedding with Alsemero has been arranged; Beatrice-Joanna induces her maid Diaphanta to take her place on the wedding night; De Flores, intent on removing any witnesses to his crime, kills Diaphanta. When the double crime is discovered, De Flores kills Beatrice-Joanna and himself.

Beatrice of Venice (bē'ạ.tris). Historical novel by Sir Max Pemberton, published in 1904. Set in Venice and Verona in 1796, it includes among its characters Napoleon I, his secretary Andoche Junot, and General Jean Victor Moreau.

Beatrice Portinari (bā.ä.trē'chā pōr.tē.nä'rē). b. 1266; d. June 9, 1290. Italian lady, celebrated by Dante chiefly in his *Vita Nuova* and also in the *Divina Commedia* (Divine Comedy). Dante first saw her, in Florence, when he was nine years old; she represented to him ideal beauty and goodness. She married Simone de' Bardi, a Florentine, sometime before 1287.

Beatrix (bē'ạ.triks). Maid and confidante of the two sisters Theodosia and Jacintha in John Dryden's comedy *An Evening's Love, or The Mock Astrologer.*

Beatrix. Novel by Honoré de Balzac, begun in 1839 and finished in 1844.

Beattie (bē'ti), **Francis Robert.** b. at Guelph, Ontario, Canada, March 31, 1848; d. Sept. 3, 1906. American Presbyterian clergyman and educator. A graduate (1878) of Knox Theological College, he was professor of apologetics (1884 *et seq.*) at Columbia Seminary, in South Carolina, and professor of apologetics and systematic theology (1893–1906) at the Presbyterian Theological Seminary, Louisville, Ky. Author of *Presbyterian Standards* (1898), *Apologetics* (1903), and others.

Beattie (bā'ti), **George.** b. at St. Cyrus, Kincardineshire, Scotland, 1786; d. there by suicide, Sept. 29, 1823. Scottish poet and attorney. He practiced law successfully at Montrose, Forfarshire, Scotland, but is now better known as the author of short poems including "John o'Arnha" (1815), "The Murderit Mynstrell" (1818), "The Bark" (1819), and "The Dream" (1820), all published in the Montrose *Review.*

Beattie, James. b. at Laurencekirk, Kincardineshire, Scotland, Oct. 23, 1735; d. at Aberdeen, Scotland, Aug. 18, 1803. Scottish poet, essayist, and philosophical writer. He was professor of moral philosophy and logic at Marischal College, Aberdeen. An opponent of David Hume, he advocated a philosophy of common sense. He wrote *Original Poems and Translations* (1761), *Judgment of Paris* (1765), *The Minstrel* (1771–74), *Essay on the Nature and Immutability of Truth* (1770), *Dissertations* (1783), and *Elements of Moral Science*.

Beatty (bē′ti), **David.** [Title, 1st Earl of the **North Sea** and of **Brooksby.**] b. in England, Jan. 17, 1871; d. March 10, 1936. British naval officer, chiefly noted for leading his cruiser squadron in an attack (1916) against the bulk of the German fleet off the coast of Jutland during World War I. He entered (1884) the Royal Navy, and was made successively rear admiral (1910), vice-admiral (1915), admiral (1919), admiral of the fleet (1919), and first sea lord of the admiralty (1919–27).

Beatty, Sir **Edward Wentworth.** b. at Therold, Ontario, Canada, 1877; d. at Montreal, March 23, 1943. Canadian lawyer and businessman. He was president and chairman of the board (1918–42) of the Canadian Pacific Railway Company. A graduate of Toronto University, he was admitted (1901) to the bar and became chancellor of McGill University, and honorary vice-president of the Canadian National Council of Education. He was appointed (1939) representative in Canada of the British Ministry of Shipping.

Beatty, John. b. at Neshaminy, Pa., Dec. 19, 1749; d. April 30, 1826. American Revolutionary soldier. Captured (1776) by the British in the battle of Fort Washington, he spent two years in prison; he was appointed (1778) commissary general of prisoners after his exchange, but resigned (1780) from the army when charged with trading with the enemy. He was a delegate (1784–85) to the Continental Congress, and a member (1793–95) of the Third Congress. He served also as secretary of state (1795–1805) of New Jersey.

Beatty, John. b. near Sandusky, Ohio, Dec. 16, 1828; d. Dec. 21, 1914. American banker, Union army soldier, and congressman (1868–73). He was a banker (1854) at Cardington, Ohio before serving as a brigadier general in the Civil War, commanding troops at Lookout Mountain. He was president (1873–1903) of the Citizens' Savings Bank, Columbus, Ohio. Republican nominee (1884) for the governorship of Ohio, he was defeated by J. B. Foraker. Author of *The Citizen Soldier* (1879), *The Belle o' Becket's Lane* (1883), *High or Low Tariff, Which?* (1894), and *Answer to "Coin's Financial School"* (1896), the last-named published during the free silver campaign.

Beatty, William Henry. b. at Monclova, Ohio, Feb. 18, 1838; d. at San Francisco, Aug. 4, 1914. American jurist, chief justice (1888–1914) of California.

Beatus (bē.ā′tus), Saint. [Also, **Beatus Libaniensis** (or **Livaniensis**).] b. c730; d. 798. Spanish ecclesiastic and geographer. The map of the world (*Mappa mundi*, 776) illustrating a work produced by him is one of the earliest maps to be made in the Christian world. Some ten later maps were based upon it.

Beau and the Lady, The. One of five historical narratives in *The Gallants* (1927), by Lily Adams Beck, writing under the pseudonym E. Barrington.

Beau Brummell (bō′ brum′ẹl). See **Brummell, George Bryan.**

Beau Brummel, the King of Calais (bō brum′ẹl; ka.lā′). Play by William Blanchard Jerrold, produced at the Lyceum Theatre, on April 11, 1859. A play called *Beau Brummell* by Clyde Fitch was also produced at New York in 1891 by Richard Mansfield. George Bryan Brummell, called "Beau" Brummell, was a celebrated London dandy of the 18th century.

Beaucaire (bō.ker). [Latin, **Ugernum, Belli Quadrum.**] Town in S France, in the department of Gard, situated at the junction of the Rhone River, the Beaucaire Canal, and the Canal du Rhône à Sète; it is opposite the town of Tarascon, with which it is connected by a bridge, and ab. 14 mi. E of Nîmes. The fair of Beaucaire, famous since 1217, has lost its importance. There are various old churches and, on a rock above the town, the ruins of a medieval castle which was dismantled by Richelieu. The town was almost entirely destroyed in World War II. 9,343 (1946).

Beauce (bōs). Region in N central France, included within the departments of Eure-et-Loir and Loir-et-Cher, famous for its production of wheat. Its chief town is Chartres.

Beauchamp (bō.shäṅ), **Alphonse de.** b. at Monaco, 1767; d. at Paris, June 1, 1832. French historian and man of letters, charged with the supervision of the press under the Directory. He wrote *Le Faux Dauphin* (1803), *Histoire des guerres de la Vendée* (1806), *Histoire de la conquête et des révolutions du Péron* (1808), *Histoire du Brésil depuis sa conquête en 1500 jusqu'an 1810* (1815), and *Vie de Louis XVIII* (1821).

Beauchamp (bē′chạm), **Richard de.** [Title, Earl of **Warwick.**] b. at Salwarp, Worcestershire, England, Jan. 28, 1382; d. at Rouen, France, April 30, 1439. English soldier and statesman, prominent in affairs of state during the reign of Henry V. In the service of Henry IV, he defeated Owen Glendower in Wales and opposed the Percys at Shrewsbury in 1413. Lord high steward at the coronation (1413) of Henry V, he followed that monarch in his French campaigns (1415) after having been a member of the English delegation at the Council of Constance (1414). In 1429 he was appointed tutor to Henry VI, a post he held until his appointment (1437) as lord lieutenant of France and Normandy.

Beauchamp, Thomas de. [Title, Earl of **Warwick.**] d. 1401. English statesman; father of Richard de Beauchamp (1382–1439). He was with John of Gaunt on his French campaign (1373), and followed Richard II on his Scottish campaign in 1385. One of the governors of Richard II during that monarch's minority, in 1387 Beauchamp allied himself with the nobles who opposed the king. When Richard reasserted himself in 1389, Thomas de Beauchamp retired from public life, but in 1397 Richard had him arrested and imprisoned in the Tower of London. (The Beauchamp Tower in that building commemorates his place of incarceration.) After the accession (1399) of Henry IV Beauchamp was set free.

Beauchamp, Viscount. Title given by the Jacobites to Sir Frederick Vernon in Sir Walter Scott's novel *Rob Roy*.

Beauchamp, William Martin. b. at Coldenham, N.Y., March 25, 1830; d. Dec. 13, 1925. American archaeologist and historian of the Iroquois Indians. Associated with the New York State Museum, he was the author of *The Iroquois Trail* (1892), *Indian Names in New York* (1893), *History of the New York Iroquois* (1905), *Iroquois Folk-lore* (1922), and others.

Beauchampe or, The Kentucky Tragedy (bē′chạm). Novel by William Gilmore Simms, published in 1842. It is one of his series of "Border Romances," and based on a sordid but widely discussed incident at Frankfort, Ky., in 1825. Solomon P. Sharp had seduced Anne Cooke, some years before her marriage to Jeroboam Beauchamp (spelled "Beauchampe" in the novel), and she demanded that her husband kill her betrayer. He challenged Sharp who refused to fight and Beauchamp stabbed him. The pair were convicted of murder, attempted suicide in prison, and Beauchamp was executed. The events were dramatized by Edgar Allan Poe, Charlotte Barnes, and others who laid the scene elsewhere, but Simms used the locality and some of the real names and followed events closely, as did Robert Penn Warren in *World Enough and Time* (1950), the most recent treatment of the material.

Beauchamp's Career (bē′chạmz). Novel by George Meredith, serialized in 1875 and published in book form in 1876. A work with a political theme, it deals with the career of Nevil Beauchamp, whose radical views and love affairs furnish the chief interest of the novel. He was drawn from one of Meredith's friends, and the program of state control, universal suffrage, limitation of private wealth, and provision for future generations is that of the radicals of the period.

Beauclerc (bō′klãr), **Henry.** Name given to Henry I of England in recognition of his achievements as a scholar.

Beauclerk (bō′klärk, -klãr), **Topham.** b. Dec. 17, 1739; d. at London, March 11, 1780. English gentleman, notable chiefly as an intimate friend of Samuel Johnson, and for his library of 30,000 volumes (sold at auction in 1781), which was rich in works relating to the English stage and English history. His wife Diana, the granddaughter of the 1st duke of Marlborough, was an artist who achieved some renown for her illustrations in John Dryden's *Fables*.

Beaucourt (bō.kör), Marquis **de.** [Title of **Gaston du Fresne.**] b. at Paris, June 7, 1833; d. 1902. French historian. He founded (1866) the *Revue des questions historiques.* Author of *Histoire de Charles VII* (History of Charles VII, 1881–91) and *Captivité et derniers moments de Louis XVI* (Captivity and Last Moments of Louis XVI, 1892).

Beaufort (bō.fôr). [Also, **Beaufort-en-Vallée** (-täṅ.và-lā).] Town in W France, in the department of Maine-et-Loire, ab. 18 mi. E of Angers. It has a church dating from the 14th century, numerous old houses, a ruined castle, and a local museum. 3,306 (1946).

Beaufort (bō'fọrt). [Former name, **Fishtown.**] Town in SE North Carolina, county seat of Carteret County, on an inlet of the Atlantic Ocean: port of entry; fisheries. It was platted in 1722. Pop. 3,212 (1950).

Beaufort (bū'fọrt). [Former name, **Port Royal.**] City in S South Carolina, county seat of Beaufort County, on Port Royal island: second oldest city in the state; has canneries for vegetables and seafood, and considerable tourist trade. Parris Island, the U.S. Marine Corps training base, is nearby. A settlement was attempted here by the French under Jean Ribaut in 1562; another was made by the English c1680. The present city was founded in 1710. It was captured (1861) by Union forces in the Civil War. 5,081 (1950).

Beaufort (bō'fọrt), **Edmund.** [Titles: Earl of **Dorset,** 2nd Duke of **Somerset.**] d. 1455. English politician; son of John Beaufort (c1373–1410) and grandson of John of Gaunt. He succeeded his brother, John Beaufort (1403–44) as duke of Somerset. English commander (1431 *et seq.*) in France, he recaptured (1440) Harfleur from the French. He relieved Calais and was elevated to the earldom of Dorset in 1442. Later (1449 *et seq.*) he was unsuccessful in resisting French attacks on English positions in France, and Normandy was lost to the French. He was appointed lord high constable of England on his return in 1450, and became chief minister of Henry VI. In 1453, when the king was stricken with insanity, Somerset supported Queen Margaret in her contest for the regency with the duke of York, the heir presumptive to the throne. York triumphed, and Somerset was imprisoned. Somerset was, however, released and restored to office on the recovery of the king in 1455, but fell at the battle of St. Albans in the same year.

Beaufort, Sir **Francis.** b. in Ireland, 1774; d. at Brighton, England, Dec. 17, 1857. English rear admiral and man of science, hydrographer to the navy (1829–55); known as the originator of a method for indicating the velocity of wind. He wrote *Karamania, or a Brief Description of the South Coast of Asia Minor* (1817) and others.

Beaufort (bō.fôr), **François de Vendôme,** Duc **de.** b. 1616; d. June 15, 1669. French politician and soldier; grandson of Henry IV (Henry of Navarre). In 1642 he joined in a conspiracy against Cardinal Richelieu, as a result of which he was exiled until the latter's death in that same year. Returning to Paris, he became the principal personage in a group called the "Importants," which included many personages attached to the French court. At the death of Louis XIII this faction sought to become dominant in French affairs, but Cardinal Mazarin balked their plans, and Beaufort was imprisoned on a charge of being involved in a plot to assassinate Mazarin. He escaped on May 31, 1648, and became a leader of the Fronde, an insurrection which began chiefly as a movement for redress of grievances. In 1652 Beaufort was again exiled from France, but permitted to return in 1654, after which he was a loyal supporter of Louis XIV. He rose to high command in the French navy, and was killed while participating in the defense of Crete against the Turks. Because of his popularity with the Parisian masses and his coarse and audacious manner of speech, Beaufort was nicknamed "Roi des Halles" ("King of the Markets")

Beaufort (bō'fọrt), **Henry.** b. at Beaufort Castle, Anjou, France, c1377; d. at Winchester, England, April 11, 1447. English prelate and statesman; natural son of John of Gaunt by Catherine Swynford (but legitimized by an act of Richard II), brother of John Beaufort (c1373–1410), and half brother of King Henry IV. He became bishop of Winchester in 1404 and a cardinal in 1427, and was chancellor (1403–05, 1413–17, 1424–26).

Beaufort, Henry. [Title, 3rd Duke of **Somerset.**] b. cApril, 1436; executed on battlefield at Hexham, England, May 14, 1464. English leader of Lancastrian forces during the War of the Roses; son of Edmund Beaufort (d. 1455). He was defeated (April, 1460) by a Yorkist army at Newnham Bridge, but later defeated the Yorkists (December, 1460) at Wakefield and at the second battle of St. Albans (February, 1461). Attainted (1461) by Parliament, he was pardoned (1463), and rejoined (1464) the Lancastrian army; he was taken prisoner at Hexham and executed on the battlefield.

Beaufort, John. [Titles: Earl of **Somerset,** Marquis of **Dorset.**] b. c1373; d. at London, March 16, 1410. English soldier and nobleman; son of John of Gaunt (1340–99) and half brother of Henry IV. He served (1390) in the English expedition against Barbary, took the part of Richard II against Gloucester in the revolution of 1397, and was appointed (1398) admiral of the Irish fleet and of the northern fleet. Under the rule of Henry IV he became (1399) chamberlain, in 1401, privy councillor and captain of Calais, in 1403, lieutenant of South Wales, and in 1404, deputy-constable of England.

Beaufort, John. [Title, 1st Duke of **Somerset.**] b. 1403; d. 1444. English military commander of Henry VI's forces in France; son of John Beaufort (c1373–1410) and brother of Edmund Beaufort (d. 1455). He became (1419) earl of Somerset upon the death of his brother Henry, and was created duke in 1443. He was a captain-general in Aquitaine and Normandy. It is said that he committed suicide.

Beaufort, Margaret. [Title, Countess of **Richmond and Derby.**] b. 1441; d. 1509. Daughter of John Beaufort, 1st Duke of Somerset, and wife successively of Edmund Tudor, Earl of Richmond (half brother of Henry VI), of Henry Stafford (son of the duke of Buckingham), and of Thomas Stanley (who was later made earl of Derby), and mother by her first marriage of Henry VII. A member of the Lancastrian party, she was held in honorable confinement at Pembroke, in Wales (to which she had voluntarily retired) after the ascendancy (1461) of the Yorkists, during the Wars of the Roses. She took a leading part in the scheme to unite the two factions by the marriage of Elizabeth of York, daughter of Edward IV, to her son Henry. She endowed Christ's and St. John's Colleges, Cambridge, and founded divinity professorships at both Oxford and Cambridge. She was among the early patrons of the printers William Caxton and Wynkyn de Worde.

Beaufort, Sir **Thomas.** [Title, Duke of **Exeter.**] d. at Greenwich, England, cJan. 1, 1427. English military commander created (1416) duke of Exeter; third son of John of Gaunt by Catherine Swynford, brother of John Beaufort (c1373–1410) and Henry Beaufort (c1377–1447). Made (1403) admiral of the fleet in the north, he became (c1408) admiral of the northern and western seas for life. He commanded (1405) the royal forces in the rebellion of Richard Scrope, whose execution he helped to bring about. In 1407 he was captain of Calais. He became (1410) the only lay chancellor, a position from which he resigned in 1412. He accompanied Henry V, engaging (1412–27) in wars with the French. He was appointed to the council under Gloucester's protectorate, and was appointed justice of North Wales.

Beaufort Sea. Part of the Arctic Ocean, lying N of Alaska and the Canadian Yukon and Northwest territories, and W of Banks Island.

Beaugard (bō'gärd), **Captain.** Principal character in Thomas Otway's *The Soldier's Fortune* and its sequel *The Atheist.*

Beaugard, Old. A wild, extravagant man, father of Captain Beaugard in *The Atheist,* by Thomas Otway.

Beaugency (bō.zhäṅ.sē). Town in N central France, in the department of Loiret, situated on the Loire River ab. 16 mi. SW of Orléans. It suffered severely in the Huguenot wars. Pop. ab. 3,000.

Beau Geste (bō' zhest'). Novel by P. C. Wren, published in 1924. It deals with the adventures in the French Foreign Legion of a dashing young Englishman and his brothers, accused of a crime which they did not commit, but loyal to each other and to their family to the end. It has been widely popular as a book, play, and film.

Beauharnais (bō.ȧr.ne), **Alexandre,** Vicomte **de.** b. in Martinique, May 28, 1760; guillotined at Paris, July 23, 1794. French politician and general; husband of Joséphine (later the wife of Napoleon Bonaparte). He served with distinction on the American side in the Revolutionary War and, after his return to France, was a deputy for the nobility in the General Assembly. As commander in chief of the army of the Rhine, he was held responsible by a French revolutionary tribunal for the surrender at Mainz, and condemned to death for treason.

Beauharnais, Eugène de. [Titles, Duke of **Leuchtenberg** and Prince of **Eichstädt.**] b. at Paris, Sept. 3, 1781; d. at Munich, Feb. 21, 1824. French soldier and statesman; son of Alexandre and Joséphine de Beauharnais. He served with Napoleon I in Egypt in 1798. Appointed viceroy of Italy in 1805, he married the princess Augusta Amelia of Bavaria in 1806, was adopted by Napoleon, and made heir apparent to the crown of Italy in 1806. He won the battle of Raab (1809). He commanded an army corps in the Russian campaign in 1812, taking charge of the broken forces after the departure of Napoleon and the flight of Joachim Murat; he decided the victory of Lützen in 1813, and, when deprived of his viceroyalty by the campaigns of 1813 and 1814, retired to Bavaria, where he obtained, with the principality of Eichstädt, the title of duke of Leuchtenberg.

Beauharnais, Eugénie Hortense de. b. at Paris, April 10, 1783; d. at Arenenberg, Switzerland, Oct. 5, 1837. Daughter of the empress Joséphine, wife of Louis Bonaparte, and mother of Napoleon III.

Beauharnais, François, Marquis **de.** b. at La Rochelle, France, Aug. 12, 1756; d. at Paris, 1823. French Royalist politician; brother of Alexandre de Beauharnais.

Beauharnais, Joséphine de. [Maiden name, **Marie Joséphine Rose Tascher de la Pagerie.**] b. at Trois-Ilets, in Martinique, June 23, 1763; d. at Malmaison, near Paris, May 29, 1814. Empress of the French; first wife of Napoleon I. She removed to France in 1778, married (Dec. 13, 1779) Alexandre, Vicomte de Beauharnais (who died in 1794), and became the wife of Napoleon on March 9, 1796. She was crowned empress in 1804, and was divorced by Napoleon in 1809.

Beauharnois (bō.här′nwä; French, bō.ȧr.nwȧ). Capital of Beauharnois County, Quebec, Canada, situated on the St. Louis River at the point where that river enters Lake St. Louis of the St. Lawrence River. It is a few miles E of the E end of the Beauharnois Canal. 5,694 (1951).

Beauharnois, Fort. French colonial establishment in North America, consisting of a military post and a Jesuit mission, built (1727) on Lake Pepin, on the upper Mississippi, for the purpose of safeguarding from the Sioux Indians the French communications route between Lake Superior and the western regions. It ceased to be of importance after 1728.

Beauharnois Canal. Power canal in SW Quebec, on the S side of the St. Lawrence River ab. 40 mi. SW of Montreal. The canal was originally completed in 1845 as a navigation canal, being at that time ab. 11½ mi. long, with 9 locks. Because the upper entrance was dangerous, another canal was built for navigation purposes on the N side of the river in 1899. After a long period of disuse, the Beauharnois Canal was put into operation as a power canal in 1932. It is capable of delivering 742,000 horse power to the hydroelectric station it serves, which makes it the second largest power source of its kind in Canada. Length, ab. 15 mi.; total fall, 83 ft.

Beau Ideal (bō ī.dē′ạl). Novel by P. C. Wren, published in 1928. Like its predecessor, *Beau Geste,* it is a story of adventure in the French Foreign Legion.

Beaujeu (bō.zhė). Town in E central France, in the department of Rhône, situated on the Ardière River ab. 31 mi. NW of Lyons. 2,021 (1946).

Beaujeu. Historical novel by Henry Christopher Bailey, published in 1905. It is set against a background of London and Oxford in the late 17th century.

Beaujeu, Anne de. See **Anne de France.**

Beaujeu, Hyacinthe Marie Lienard de. b. at Montreal, Canada, Aug. 9, 1711; d. July 9, 1755. French officer in North America. He became commander of Fort Duquesne in 1755, and planned the ambuscade which resulted in the defeat (July 9, 1755) of Edward Braddock, but fell at the first fire of the British.

Beaujolais (bō.zho.le). Historical region in E central France, in the government of Lyonnais, now comprised in the departments of Rhône and Loire. Its chief towns were Beaujeu and Villefranche. It was a barony and county, and was united to the crown by Francis I. It was later in the possession of the Orléans family. It is noted for its wines.

Beaujoyeulx (bō.zhwȧ.yė), **Balthasard de.** French name of **Baltazarini.**

Beaulieu (bū′li). [Also, **Bewley.**] Civil parish and village in S England, in Southampton (an administrative county within the geographical county of Hampshire), ab. 6 mi. NE of Lymington. Bewley Abbey is located here. 1,201 (1931).

Beaulieu (bō.lyė), Baron **Jean Pierre de.** b. at Namur, Belgium, Oct. 26, 1725; d. near Linz, Austria, Dec. 22, 1819. Austrian general. He served in the Seven Years' War, commanded at Jemappes in 1792, and as Austrian commander in chief in Italy was defeated (1796) by Napoleon I at Montenotte, Millesimo, Montesano, Mondovì, and Lodi.

Beaulieu-Marconnay (bō.lyė′mȧr.ko.nā′), Baron **Karl Olivier von.** b. at Minden, Germany, Sept. 5, 1811; d. at Dresden, Germany, April 8, 1889. German government official and historical writer.

Beaulieu-sur-Dordogne (bō.lyė.sür.dôr.dony′). [Also, **Beaulieu.**] Town in S central France, in the department of Corrèze, situated on the Dordogne River ab. 20 mi. S of Tulle. It has an old Benedictine monastery. 2,053 (1946).

Beauly (bū′li). Village and ruined priory in N Scotland, in Inverness-shire, situated on the river Beauly, ab. 9 mi. W of Inverness, ab. 569 mi. N of London by rail. The priory was founded in 1230. Pop. of special district (including the village and responsible, in Scottish administrative phraseology, for "water, drainage, lighting, and scavenging"), 799 (1931).

Beauly Firth. [Also, **Beauly Basin.**] Inlet of Moray Firth in N Scotland, lying between Inverness-shire and the county of Ross and Cromarty, ab. 2 mi. NW of Inverness. Length, ab. 9 mi.; width, ab. 2 mi.

Beaumanoir (bō.mȧ.nwȧr), **Jean de.** b. in Brittany; fl. in the middle of the 14th century. French knight. He is celebrated as the French commander in the Battle of the Thirty (1351), in which 30 Bretons are said to have defeated 30 Englishmen between the castles of Ploërmel and Josselin in Brittany.

Beaumanoir, Philippe de Rémi, Sire **de.** b. c1250; d. Jan. 7, 1296. French jurist. He was *bailli* (bailiff, or royal steward) at Senlis in 1273, and at Clermont in 1280, and presided at assizes held in various towns. His chief work, highly esteemed in the study of old French law, is *Coutumes de Beauvoisis* (edited by De la Thaumassière 1690, and by Beugnot 1842).

Beaumanoir, Sir Lucas de. In Sir Walter Scott's novel *Ivanhoe,* the grand master of the Knights Templar. He seizes Rebecca and tries her as a witch.

Beaumarchais (bō.mär.shā′; French, bō.mȧr.she), **Pierre Augustin Caron de.** b. at Paris, Jan. 24, 1732; d. there, May 18, 1799. French polemic writer and dramatist. He was the seventh child of Charles Caron, a master clockmaker. After an elementary schooling, he joined his father in the trade. Subsequently he assumed the name of Beaumarchais, in accordance with a usage prevalent in France during that century. His claim to the invention of a new escapement in clockwork being disputed, young Caron appealed to the Academy of Sciences and to public opinion, thereby attracting also the attention of the court. On the death in 1770 of the financier Duverney, who had taken Beaumarchais into partnership, a question of inheritance occasioned litigation. Beaumarchais conducted his own case, and to vindicate himself published (1774–75) four *Mémoires* replete with wit and eloquence, which made him famous. In the meantime, his attempts to write for the stage, *Eugénie* and *Les Deux Amis, ou le négociant de Lyon,* had been failures. Moreover, *Le Barbier de Séville* (which was to bring him fame as a dramatist) waited two years to be presented to the public, and the first performance, on Feb. 23, 1775, was not very successful. He subsequently altered and greatly improved it. *Le Mariage de Figaro,* begun in 1775 and completed in 1778, was suppressed for four years by the censure of Louis XVI.

It was given for the first time on April 27, 1784, and was immediately successful. During the war of American independence, Beaumarchais sent to the U.S. a fleet of his own, carrying a cargo of weapons and ammunition for the American colonists. His poverty during the latter part of his life was largely due to the difficulty he experienced in recovering payment for this from the U.S. He also spent a great deal of money in the publication of a 70-volume edition of the works of Voltaire, which he brought out in 1895–90. Beaumarchais is the hero of one of Goethe's plays, *Clavigo.*

Beaumaris (bō.mar'is). [Former name, **Bornover.**] Municipal borough, seaport, and seaside resort in N Wales, in Anglesey, situated on Beaumaris Bay, ab. 7 mi. NE of Bangor. It has no direct rail connections for passengers, being reached by rail to Bangor, ab. 239 mi. NW of London. Beaumaris has the ruins of a castle, a large 13th-century fortress built by Edward I of England. The long, low line of the interior walls is impressive, with their many towers, surmounted by the huge cylindrical towers of the main structure. The central court is particularly picturesque, surrounded by ruins of the chapel and the great hall, with finely traceried windows, and of the interesting residential buildings profusely overgrown with ivy. 2,128 (1951).

Beaumaris Bay. Inlet of the Irish Sea in N Wales. It lies at the N end of Menai Strait, which separates Anglesey from Caernarvonshire on the mainland. Length, ab. 12 mi.; width, ab. 7 mi. across the entrance.

Beaumelle (bō.mel'). Heroine of Philip Massinger and Nathaniel Field's play *The Fatal Dowry.* She is married to Charalois, who kills her when he suspects her of being unfaithful.

Beaumelle (bō.mel), **Laurent Angliviel de la.** b. at Valleraugue, Gard, France, Jan. 28, 1726; d. at Paris, Nov. 17, 1773. French man of letters, professor (1749–51) of French literature at Copenhagen. In 1751 he went to Berlin, and in 1752 to Paris. His works brought him two periods of imprisonment in the Bastille and the active enmity of Voltaire.

Beaumont (bō'mont). City in S California, in Riverside County, ab. 80 mi. SE of Los Angeles in the foothills of the San Bernardino Mountains. Nuts and fruit are grown in the surrounding region. 3,152 (1950).

Beaumont (bō.môṅ). [Also: **Beaumont-en-Argonne** (-täṅ.nȧr.gon); Latin, **Bellus Mons, Belmontium.**] Town in N France, in the department of Ardennes, situated on the Meuse River ab. 14 mi. SE of Sedan. Here, on Aug. 30, 1870, the Germans under the crown prince of Saxony defeated a division of MacMahon's army. 620 (1946).

Beaumont (bō'mont). City in E Texas, county seat of Jefferson County, on the Sabine-Neches canal, NE of Houston: an inland port and shipping center for East Texas oil, lumber, timber, and rice; it has shipbuilding yards. It was platted in 1835. The noted Spindletop oil pool, where a gusher in 1901 marked the opening of the Texas oil industry, is nearby. 94,014 (1950).

Beaumont (bō.môṅ), **André.** See **Conneau, Jean.**

Beaumont (bō'mont), **Basil.** b. 1669; d. 1703. English rear admiral. He perished in the Downs, in the English Channel off the coast of Kent, in a terrible storm which destroyed 13 vessels, with 1,500 seamen.

Beaumont, Francis. b. at Grace-Dieu, Leicestershire, England, 1584; d. March 6, 1616. English dramatist and poet. He was educated at Oxford and entered (1600) the Inner Temple, but apparently did not pursue his legal studies. In 1602 he published *Salmacis and Hermaphroditus,* a poem after Ovid. His friendship for Ben Jonson probably began shortly after this, and from 1607 to 1611 his commendatory poems were prefixed to several of Jonson's plays. In 1613 Beaumont produced *A Masque for the Inner Temple,* and about that time he married Ursula, daughter of Henry Isley of Sundridge in Kent. His close personal and literary intimacy with John Fletcher dated from c1606. They lived together not far from the Globe Theatre on the Bankside, and collaborated until c1616. *The Woman Hater* (printed 1607), is believed to have been written by Fletcher alone. Among the plays (approximately 50) by Beaumont and Fletcher are *The Knight of the Burning Pestle* (printed 1613), *The Scornful Lady* (printed 1616), *The Maid's Tragedy* (printed 1619), *Philaster* (printed 1620), and *The Coxcomb* (printed 1647). Beaumont is buried in Westminster Abbey.

Beaumont, Sir George Howland. b. at Dunmow, Essex, England, Nov. 6, 1753; d. Feb. 7, 1827. English patron of art, connoisseur, and landscape painter one of the founders of the National Gallery at London. He was a close friend of Sir Joshua Reynolds and acquainted with Sir Walter Scott, William Wordsworth, Byron, S. T. Coleridge, and other notables of his day.

Beaumont, Sir John. b. probably at Grace-Dieu, Leicestershire, England, 1583; d. April 19, 1627. English poet; brother of Francis Beaumont. He wrote poetical works including *Metamorphosis of Tobacco* (1602) and *Bosworth Field* (1629).

Beaumont, Joseph. b. at Hadleigh, Suffolk, England, March 13, 1616; d. at Cambridge, England, Nov. 23, 1699. English divine, Royalist, poet, professor, and master of two Cambridge colleges. He was the author of *Psyche* (1648), an epic poem in 30,000 lines dealing with spiritual tribulation. He took his master's degree (1638) from Peterhouse (St. Peter's) College, Cambridge, but was ejected (1644) from Peterhouse because of his Royalist sympathies. For the latter he was rewarded (1660) at the Restoration by being made a doctor of divinity and appointed chaplain to the king. He was master (1662) of Jesus College and master (1663–99) of Peterhouse; in 1674 he was appointed regius professor of divinity at Cambridge. He engaged in a long controversy (1665 *et seq.*) with Henry More, the Cambridge Platonist.

Beaumont, Robert de. [Title, Earl of **Leicester.**] b. 1104; d. 1168. Anglo-Norman justiciary and feudal statesman. With his twin brother Waleran (1104–66) he took sides with Stephen (of Blois) upon his return (1137) to England, and in the civil war (1139). He secured his interests with the Plantagenet party after the Battle of Lincoln in 1141. He was appointed chief justiciar (1155 and 1156); during the absences (1158–63 and 1165) of Henry II, he was vice-regent, with Richard Lucy, of the kingdom; he sought (1164) unsuccessfully to reconcile Thomas à Becket with the king.

Beaumont, Waleran de. [Title, Count of **Meulan.**] b. 1104; d. 1166. Anglo-Norman warrior and feudal statesman. He fought for (1119–21), then against (1121–35) Henry I; with his twin brother Robert (1104–68) he advised and supported Stephen (of Blois) against the adherents of Henry II until the battle of Lincoln (1141), after which he joined (1143) Geoffrey of Anjou. Upon his return from a pilgrimage (1145) to Palestine, he assisted (1150) Matilda against Stephen.

Beaumont, William. b. Nov. 21, 1785; d. April 25, 1853. American surgeon, celebrated for his observations of the exposed stomach of Alexis St. Martin, a feat which has often been called the greatest individual contribution to that branch of science which is concerned with the study of digestion and digestive processes. After serving (1812–15) as surgeon's mate during the War of 1812 with the American forces at Plattsburg, N.Y., Beaumont again (1818) joined the army and was sent to Fort Mackinac (on the site of what is now the resort village of Mackinaw City, in Upper Michigan); it was there that he met the patient Alexis St. Martin, who had received (June 6, 1822) an accidental gunshot wound. Although the nature of the wound seemed fatal, the patient survived and recovered without, however, being healed. The freak accident had ripped away several ribs and the outer wall of the stomach, leaving that organ exposed; it remained in this state, thus affording a unique opportunity for the study of digestive functions. Although Beaumont personally cared for St. Martin from the first, he did not begin regular experiments upon him until 1825. In these experiments, which he performed almost continuously until 1833 (when St. Martin refused to submit to further treatment, preferring to live a normal life, for which he was by this time quite adequately recovered), Beaumont proved conclusively the presence of gastric juices and their active function in the digestive process; his analyses also proved these juices to be composed in great part of hydrochloric acid. The experiments (over 235) and their results are detailed in *Experiments and Observations on the Gastric Juice and the Physiology of Digestion* (1833), which promptly became a standard authority.

Beaumont de la Bonnière (bō.môṅ dẹ là bo.nyer), **Gustave Auguste.** b. at Beaumont-la-Châtre, Sarthe, France, Feb. 16, 1802; d. at Tours, France, Feb. 6, 1866. French politician and man of letters. He was the author of *Du système pénitentiaire aux États-Unis* (1832), *De l'esclavage aux États-Unis* (1840), and *L'Irlande, politique, sociale, et religieuse* (1839).

Beaumont-de-Lomagne (bō.môṅ.dẹ.lo.màny'). Town in S France, in the department of Tarn-et-Garonne, situated on the Gimone River ab. 22 mi. SW of Montauban, in a fertile agricultural region. 3,183 (1946).

Beaumont-sur-Oise (bō.môṅ.sür.wàz). Town and river port in N France, in the department of Seine-et-Oise, situated on the Oise River, ab. 18 mi. N of Paris. It has Portland cement works and rubber factories. 5,444 (1946).

Beau Nash (bō' nash'). Three-act comedy in prose by Douglas Jerrold, produced at the Haymarket Theatre, London, and published in 1825. Richard Nash, called "Beau" Nash, was in real life an 18th-century dandy, master of ceremonies at Bath.

Beaune (bōn). [Latin, **Belna.**] Town in E France, in the department of Côte-d'Or, ab. 24 mi. SW of Dijon. It has an extensive trade in Burgundy wines, produces equipment for vintage and wine-making, and has other small industries. The hospital building of Beaune remains almost precisely as when it was completed in 1443; it has a picturesque doorway, a court with two tiers of galleries, and a steep roof; tapestries hang in the interior. The collegiate church of Notre Dame and its adjacent buildings date from the 10th and 12th centuries; there is a 15th-century castle. 11,990 (1946).

Beaune-la-Rolande (bōn.là.rô.läṅd). Village in N central France, in the department of Loiret, ab. 19 mi. NE of Orléans. Here, on Nov. 28, 1870, the Prussians defeated the French under Aurelle de Paladines. The French loss was ab. 6,700.

Beauport (bō'pōrt; French, bō.por). Town in Quebec, Canada, on the N side of the St. Lawrence River, ab. 3 mi. E of the city of Quebec, of which it is a residential suburb. 5,390 (1951).

Beaupré (bō.prā'), **Arthur Matthias.** b. at Oswego, Ill., July 29, 1853; d. Sept. 13, 1919. American diplomat and lawyer. He was consul general and secretary (1897–99) of the U.S. legation to Guatemala and Honduras, arbitrator (1899) in a dispute between Great Britain and Honduras, U.S. consul general and secretary (1899–1903) of the Colombian legation and minister (1903–04) to Colombia during the Panama crisis, minister (1904–08) to Argentina and (1908 *et seq.*) to Luxembourg and The Netherlands, a member (1908 *et seq.*) of the administrative council of the Permanent Court of Arbitration, and minister (1911–13) to Cuba.

Beaupréau (bō.prā.ō). [Eng. trans., *"fair meadow."*] Town in W France, in the department of Maine-et-Loire, situated on the Evre River ab. 29 mi. SW of Angers. It was the scene of a Vendéan victory in 1793.

Beauregard (bō'rẹ.gärd), **Pierre Gustave Toutant.** b. near New Orleans, La., May 28, 1818; d. there, Feb. 20, 1893. American general, with the Confederate army in the Civil War. He was graduated from West Point (1838), and served with distinction in the Mexican War, being brevetted a captain for gallant and meritorious conduct at Contreras and Churubusco, and a major for similar conduct at Chapultepec. Appointed superintendent of West Point in 1860, with the rank of colonel, he resigned in 1861, on the secession of Louisiana from the Union, to accept an appointment as brigadier general in the Confederate army. He bombarded and captured Fort Sumter on April 12–13, 1861; in immediate command (under Joseph E. Johnston) at the first battle of Bull Run on July 21, he was raised in consequence of his services in this battle to the rank of general; he assumed command of the army at Shiloh, on the fall of General A. S. Johnston, on April 6, 1862, commanded at Charleston (1862–64), and defeated Benjamin Franklin Butler at Drury's Bluff (May 16, 1864), but surrendered with Johnston in 1865. He was president (1865–70) of the New Orleans and Jackson Railroad Company, and became adjutant general of Louisiana in 1878.

Beaurepaire (bō.rẹ.pãr'). Castle celebrated in Arthurian legend.

Beaurepaire-Rohan (bōr.per.ro.äṅ), **Henrique de.** b. 1818; d. July, 1894. French general and geographer. He wrote a *Descripcão de uma viagem de Cuyabá ao Rio de Janeiro* (1846), a topography of Mato Grosso and other regions, and was chief of the commission which prepared the map of Brazil published in 1878. In 1864 he was Brazilian minister of war.

Beau Sabreur (bō' sa.brėr'). Novel by P. C. Wren, published in 1926. It is a sequel to his popular *Beau Geste* (1924).

Beau's Duel, or A Soldier for the Ladies, The. Comedy by Susannah Centlivre, produced and printed in 1702. It was in part based on Jasper Mayne's *City Match.*

Beauséjour (bō.sā.zhör'), **Fort.** [Also, **Fort Cumberland.**] Military fort in SE New Brunswick built by the French in 1751 to command the isthmus between New Brunswick and Nova Scotia. It was captured in 1755 by the British and renamed Fort Cumberland. It was abandoned after the War of 1812. In 1926 it was made a Canadian national park. Area, 81 acres.

Beausobre (bō.sobr), **Isaac de.** b. at Niort, France, March 8, 1659; d. at Berlin, June 6, 1738. French Protestant theologian, pastor of a French church at Berlin. He was the author of an *Essai critique de l'histoire de Manichée et du Manichéisme* (2 vols., 1739, 1744), and a translation of the New Testament into French from the original Greek.

Beausoleil (bō.so.ley'). Town in SE France, in the department of Alpes-Maritimes, situated near the Mediterranean coast, E of Monte Carlo, of which it is virtually a part. It is a resort; has hotels and a casino. 10,865 (1946).

Beautemps-Beaupré (bō.täṅ.bō.prā), **Charles François.** b. at Neuville-au-Pont, Marne, France, 1766; d. 1854. French hydrographer.

Beauties of English Poesy, The. Compilation (2 vols., 1767) by Oliver Goldsmith.

Beauties of Santa Cruz (san'tạ kröz), **The.** Poem by Philip Freneau, published in 1786.

Beautiful and Damned, The. Novel (1922) by F. Scott Fitzgerald. It was his second novel.

Beautiful Years, The. Autobiographical novel by Henry Williamson, published in 1921. It is the first volume of a tetralogy under the general title *The Flax of Dream.*

Beauty and the Beast. [French title, **La Belle et la bête** (là bel ā là bet).] Story in which a daughter (Beauty), Zémire, to save her father's life, becomes the guest of a monster (Azor, or the Beast), who, by his kindness and intelligence, wins her love, whereupon he regains his original form, that of a handsome young prince. The original French version was published in 1757. It probably derived its plot from Giovanni Straparola's *Piacevoli Notti*, a collection of the Italian stories published in 1550. There have been many English versions, of which one of the most noteworthy is that by Anne Isabella Ritchie, daughter of W. M. Thackeray. The story gave Grétry the subject for his opera *Zémire and Azor* and was recently the subject (although so greatly altered from the original as to be virtually unrecognizable) for Jean Cocteau's film *La Belle et la bête.*

Beauvais (bō.vā'; French, bō.ve). [Ancient names, **Caesaromagus, Bellovacum, Belvacum.**] City in N France, the capital of the department of Oise, situated on the Thérain River, ab. 43 mi. NW of Paris. It was the capital of the Bellovaci, a Belgic tribe, whence its name Bellovacum or Belvacum. Beauvais has important ceramic, glass, and woolen industries. The national tapestry factory, founded by Colbert in the 17th century and located at Beauvais until World War II, maintained the ancient art of tapestry-making. In the Middle Ages, Beauvais was defended against the English (1433), and against Charles the Bold of Burgundy by citizens led by Jeanne Hachette (1472). Many church councils have taken place here. The cathedral of Beauvais is a fragment consisting merely of a choir and transept; it was begun c1225 with the intention of surpassing in height all other churches, but the plan failed because the foundations proved too weak for the stupendous superstructure. The choir has beautiful 13th-century vaulting and tracery. The area surrounding the cathedral retained the general appearance of its medieval past until recent years. The

10th-century Church of Notre-Dame-de-la-Basse-Oeuvre, residences dating from the 12th to the 17th centuries, the Place de l'Hôtel de Ville, and the Place St. Pierre were all in this area, which was completely leveled as a result of combat action in World War II; only the cathedral itself and the Palais de Justice remained. 23,156 (1946).

Beauvais, Charles Théodore. b. at Orléans, France, Nov. 8, 1772; d. at Paris, 1830. French general and writer. He compiled *Victoires et conquêtes des français,* and edited *Correspondance de Napoléon avec les cours étrangères.*

Beauval (bō.vål), **Basnage de.** See **Basnage de Beauval.**

Beauvallet (bō.vå.le), **Léon.** b. at Paris, 1829; d. there, March 22, 1885. French littérateur; son of Pierre François Beauvallet (1801–73).

Beauvallet, Pierre François. b. at Pithiviers, France, Oct. 13, 1801; d. at Paris, Dec. 21, 1873. French actor and dramatic writer; father of Léon Beauvallet.

Beauvan (bō.väṅ), **René François de.** b. 1664; d. Aug. 4, 1739. French prelate, bishop of Bayonne, and later (1707) of Tournai, where he distinguished himself during the siege of 1709.

Beauvau (bō.vō), **Charles Juste de.** b. at Lunéville, France, Sept. 10, 1720; d. May 2, 1793. Marshal of France, who distinguished himself in the Seven Years' War.

Beauvoir (bō.vwår), **Simone de.** b. 1908—. French existentialist novelist, collaborator and wife of the existentialist philosopher, novelist, and dramatist Jean Paul Sartre. Her reputation as a novelist stems from one book, *Le Sang des autres* (1945; Eng. trans., *The Blood of Others,* 1948), a fictionalized treatise on the subject of human responsibility.

Beaux (bō), **Cecilia.** b. at Philadelphia, 1863; d. 1942. American painter. She was a pupil (in America) of William Sartain, and (at Paris) of Adolf William Bougereau, Jean Joseph Benjamin Constant, and others. She is chiefly remembered as a portraitist of children and women. *Last Days of Infancy* and *A New England Woman* (Pennsylvania Academy of the Fine Arts) are among her well-known works. Her paintings are in major U.S. galleries as well as in the Gallery of the Uffizi at Florence and the Luxembourg Gallery at Paris.

Beaux-Arts (bō.zår), **Académie des.** See **Academy of Fine Arts,** Paris.

Beaux-Arts, École des. See **École des Beaux-Arts.**

Beaux' Stratagem, The. Comedy by George Farquhar, produced March 8, 1707. Considered by many to be his best play, it tells its story with ease and high spirits. The fortune-hunters, Archer and Aimwell, win the audience's sympathies and their success, though somewhat accidental, is most pleasing. Lady Bountiful, with relatively few lines, lives perfectly as a type, and so do other minor persons.

Beauzée (bō.zā), **Nicolas.** b. at Verdun, France, May 9, 1717; d. at Paris, Jan. 23, 1789. French grammarian and man of letters.

Beaver (bē'vėr). [Also, **Beaver City.**] Town in NW Oklahoma, in the Panhandle, county seat of Beaver County: shipping center for wheat. The former capital of the "Territory of Cimarron," it was a supply point along the cattle trail to Dodge City, Kan. 1,495 (1950).

Beaver. Borough in W Pennsylvania, county seat of Beaver County, on the Ohio River: residential community. It was founded in 1778, and was the home of the politician and senator Matthew S. Quay (1833–1904). 6,360 (1950).

Beaver, James Addams. b. at Millerstown, Pa., Oct. 21, 1837; d. Jan. 31, 1914. American politician and general, in the Union army in the Civil War. He was colonel and brigade commander in the Army of the Potomac in the Civil War, was the (unsuccessful) Republican candidate for governor of Pennsylvania in 1882, and was Republican governor of Pennsylvania in the period 1887–91.

Beaver, Philip. b. at Lewknor, Oxfordshire, England, Feb. 28, 1766; d. at Table Bay, South Africa, April 5, 1813. English naval officer, a captain in the Royal Navy. He attempted unsuccessfully (1792–93) to colonize the island of Bolama, off the coast of West Africa.

Beaverbrook (bē'vėr.brůk), 1st Baron. [Title of **William Maxwell Aitken.**] b. at Maple, near Toronto, Ontario, Canada (but spent boyhood at Newcastle, New Brunswick), May 25, 1879—. British newspaper publisher and politician. He acquired the basis of his original fortune by the consolidation of cement mills in Canada. He served as an observer (1915) with the Canadian military forces, and was an official Canadian government representative (1916) at the front; after a period in charge (1917) of Canadian war records, he was British minister of information (1918). In World War II, he was minister for aircraft production (1940–41), of state (1941), and of supply (1941–42), British representative (February, 1942) in America for the supervision of British supply agencies, and lord privy seal (1943–45). Publisher of several newspapers, the most important of which is the London *Daily Express;* author of *Canada in Flanders* (2 vols., 1916, 1917), *Success* (1921), *Politicians and the Press* (1925), *Politicians and the War* (2 vols., 1928, 1932), and *Resources of the British Empire* (1934).

Beaver Creek (bē'vėr). River in NW Kansas and S Nebraska, a tributary of the Republican River. Length, ab. 200 mi.

Beaver Dam. City in E central Wisconsin, in Dodge County, ab. 59 mi. NW of Milwaukee: manufactures include shoes, soap, stoves, farm equipment, cheese boxes, water heaters, confections, beverages, canned goods, and cream cheese. 11,867 (1950).

Beaver Dam Creek. See under **Mechanicsville,** Va.

Beaver Dams, Battle of. Engagement (June 24, 1813) in the War of 1812, near what is now Merritton, in SE Ontario, Canada, involving a force of some 600 Americans dispatched from Fort George, a Canadian post seized in May, 1813. The Americans, who had been ordered to deal with a mixed force of British and Indians, surrendered after falling into an ambush.

Beaver Falls. [Former name, **Brighton.**] City in W Pennsylvania, in Beaver County, near the confluence of the Beaver and Ohio rivers, ab. 26 mi. NW of Pittsburgh: manufactures include china, and metal and cork products. It is the seat of Geneva College. Platted in 1806, it was incorporated in 1868, and chartered as a city in 1930. Pop. 17,375 (1950).

Beaver Islands. Group of islands in the N part of Lake Michigan, belonging to Charlevoix County, Mich. The length of the largest, Beaver or Big Beaver, is ab. 24 mi.

Beaver River. See also **Churchill River.**

Beaver River. River in W Pennsylvania, in Lawrence and Beaver counties, formed by the union of the Mahoning and Shenango rivers. It joins the Ohio near Beaver Falls.

"Beaver State." Nickname of **Oregon.**

Beaverton (bē'vėr.tọn). City in NW Oregon, in Washington County, ab. 5 mi. SW of Portland. 2,512 (1950).

Beazley (bēz'li), Sir **Charles Raymond.** b. at Blackheath, Kent, England, April 3, 1868—. English geographer and historian. A Master of Arts (1893) from Oxford, he was professor (1909–33) of history at the University of Birmingham and also lectured at various American universities. Author of *James of Aragon* (1890), the three-volume *Dawn of Modern Geography* (1897, 1901, 1906), *Voyages and Travels: 16th–17th Centuries* (1902), *Friar Travellers, 1245–1255* (1903), *Notebook of Mediæval History* (1917), *History of Russia* (1918), *The Road to Ruin in Europe* (1932), and *Beauty of the North Cotswolds* (1945).

Beazley, John Davidson. b. at Glasgow, Sept. 13, 1885—. Scottish archaeologist. He was a tutor (1908–25) at Christ Church and was appointed professor of classical archaeology at Oxford in 1925. Author of *Attic Red-figured Vases in American Museums* (1918), *Greek Vases in Poland* (1928), *Der Berliner Maler* (1930), *Potter and Painter in Ancient Athens* (1945), and *Etruscan Vase-painting* (1947).

Beazley, Samuel. b. at London, 1786; d. at Tunbridge Castle, Kent, England, Oct. 12, 1851. English architect and dramatist, noted as a designer of theaters.

Bebedouro (bā.bẹ.dō'rö). City in SE Brazil, in the state of São Paulo. 11,642 (1950).

Bebek (be.bek'). Place in NW Turkey, on the Bosporus ab. 6 mi. from Istanbul: minor trading center.

Bebel (bā'bel), **Ferdinand August.** b. at Cologne, Germany, Feb. 22, 1840; d. at Passugg, Switzerland, Aug. 13, 1913. German labor politician and writer, one of the leaders of the Social-Democratic Party in Germany. He joined the German labor movement which began under the leadership of Ferdinand Lassalle, and which resulted in the formation of the Social-Democratic Party. Bebel was one of the founders of the new party. He was chosen (1867) deputy from the district of Glauchau-Meerane, in Saxony, to the constituent assembly of North Germany. and in 1871 was elected to the first Reichstag of the German empire. An opponent of Bismarck, he was sentenced (1872) to two years' imprisonment on a charge of high treason against the German empire, and to nine months' imprisonment on a charge of lese-majesty against the German emperor; in addition he was deprived of his seat in the Reichstag. He was reëlected in 1873 to the Reichstag, in which, with interruptions, he represented various constituencies until his death. Author of *Unsere Ziele* (1870), *Der deutsche Bauernkrieg* (1876), *Die Frau und der Sozialismus* (1883), *Christentum und Sozialismus* (1892), *My Life* (Eng. trans., 1913), and others.

Bebel, Heinrich. b. at Ingstetten, Germany, 1472; d. at Tübingen, Germany, 1518. German humanist, professor (1497 *et seq.*) at Tübingen. One of the greatest Latinists of his time, he collected and translated into Latin German proverbs (1508), wrote a Latin history of the ancient Germans (1508), and in his collection of anecdotes, *Facetiae* (1506), turned his sharp wit on human follies, chiefly of the clergy. His lengthy poem *Triumphus Veneris* (1509) attacks immorality. He was crowned poet by the emperor Maximilian I in 1501.

Bebenhausen (bā'bẹn.hou.zẹn). Romanesque and Gothic Cistercian abbey, 3 mi. N of Tübingen, Württemberg, founded c1185.

Bebington (beb'ing.tọn). Municipal borough, manufacturing town, and suburban area in W England, in Cheshire, situated on the Wirral Peninsula, on the estuary of the river Mersey, opposite Liverpool, ab. 192 mi. NW of London by rail. It has a chemical and soap industry, the world-famous industrial area of Port Sunlight being located wholly within the borough. Bebington forms part of the Port of Liverpool, having a frontage of 5½ mi. on the river Mersey. The town itself, however, is very largely residential, a quite recent development. 47,742 (1951).

Bebra (bā'brä). Village in W Germany, in the *Land* (state) of Hessen, American Zone, formerly in the province of Hesse-Nassau, Prussia, situated near the Fulda River, ab. 26 mi. SE of Kassel: an important railroad junction, with lumber mills and electrochemical and knitwear factories. 6,922 (1946).

Bebriacum (bē.bri'ạ.kum). See **Bedriacum.**

Bebutov (bi.bö'tọf), Prince **Vasili Osipovich.** b. 1792; d. at Tiflis, in the Transcaucasus, Russia, March 22, 1858. Russian general, of Armenian descent. During the Crimean War, he defeated the Turks at Kadiklar, on Dec. 1, 1853, and at Kuruk-Dere, on Aug. 5, 1854.

Bec (bek). Ruined abbey at Bec-Helloin, near Brionne, in the department of Eure, NW France, famous as a seat of learning in the 11th century under the rule of Lanfranc and Saint Anselm.

Beccafumi (bāk.kä.fö'mē), **Domenico di Pace.** [Called **Il Meccherino.**] b. near Siena, Italy, 1486; d. at Siena, May 18, 1551. Italian painter. His best-known works are his designs for scenes from the Old Testament for the decorations of the pavement in the cathedral at Siena, and frescoes for the city hall at Siena.

Beccari (bāk.kä'rē), **Odoardo.** b. at Florence, Nov. 19, 1843; d. 1920. Italian botanist, explorer in New Guinea, the East Indies, and East Africa. He founded the *Nuovo giornale botanico italiano* (1869), which, together with the *Bollettino della Società geografica italiana*, contains most of his descriptions of travel and botanical discoveries.

Beccaria (bāk.kä.rē'ä), **Cesare Bonesano, Marchese di.** b. at Milan, March 15, 1735; d. there, Nov. 28, 1794. Italian economist, jurist, and philanthropist, a professor at Milan. He was one of the earliest opponents of the death penalty in Italy. His most famous work is *Tratto dei delitti e delle pene* (Essay on Crimes and Punishments, 1764; revised 1781), which was written from a humanitarian point of view and was very influential. His written work and published lectures, which anticipated to some extent the social theories of Malthus and the economic theories of Adam Smith, are said to have influenced Voltaire and Jeremy Bentham.

Beccaria, Giovanni Battista. b. at Mondovi, Piedmont, Italy, Oct. 3, 1716; d. at Turin, May 27, 1781. Italian mathematician and physicist, professor of physics at Turin, especially noted for his researches in electricity, which led him to a study (and circulation in Italy) of Benjamin Franklin's printed findings in the field.

Beccles (bek'lz). Municipal borough and market town in E England, in East Suffolk, situated on the river Waveney ab. 17 mi. SE of Norwich, ab. 109 mi. NE of London by rail. It has a printing and bookbinding industry. 6,869 (1951).

Bečej (be'chā). See **Stari Bečej.**

Bech (bek), **Joseph.** b. at Diekirch, Luxembourg, Feb. 17, 1887—. Luxembourg statesman. He studied at the University of Paris, where he received (1912) the doctorate of law. He began his career as a lawyer and has been a member of parliament since 1914. His posts include minister of justice (1921–25), prime minister and minister of foreign affairs (1926–37), foreign minister (1937 *et seq.*), delegate to the League of Nations (1925–39), chairman (1945) of the Luxembourg delegation to the United Nations Conference at San Francisco, and chairman (1946 *et seq.*) of the Luxembourg delegation to the assembly of the United Nations.

Béchamp (bā.shäṅ), **Pierre Jacques Antoine.** b. at Bassing, near Dieuze, Meurthe-et-Moselle, France, Oct. 16, 1816; d. at Paris, April 15, 1908. French chemist, especially noted for his researches in organic, and particularly in biological, chemistry (e.g. fermentation).

Beche (besh), Sir **Henry Thomas de la.** b. near London, 1796; d. at London, April 13, 1855. English geologist. He wrote *The Geological Observer* (1851), and others.

Becher (beċh'ėr), **Johannes Robert.** b. at Munich, 1891—. German expressionist poet, generally considered to be the most violent and persistently revolutionary of his country's expressionist group. He fled to Russia in 1932 and did not return home until after the defeat of Germany in 1945. There have been periods when his verse was less wild, as in *Gedichte an Lotte* (1919) or in *Um Gott* (1921), and some have seen in his work since 1932 a semblance of classic form. Most critical readers, however, find the greater part of his enormous output of verse to be truculent, clouded with passion, and warped by propaganda, as in *Verbrüderung* (1916), *Ewig im Aufruhr* (1920), *Am Grabe Lenins* (1925), and *Maschinenrhythmen* (1925).

Becher, Johann Joachim. b. at Speyer, Bavaria, 1635; d. probably at London, in October, 1682. German chemist, economist, and physician. He was the author of numerous treatises, the most noted of which is the *Actorum laboratorii chymici Monacensis, seu physicae subterraneae libri duo* (1669). Of the three elements recognized by him in the composition of metals (and in general of minerals), a vitrifiable earth, a volatile earth, and an igneous principle, the last served as the foundation of the theory of Georg Ernst Stahl.

Becher, Siegfried. b. in Bohemia, Feb. 28, 1806; d. March 4, 1873. Austrian economist and statistician. He became (1835) professor of history and geography at the polytechnical institute at Vienna.

Bechstein (beċh'shtīn), **Friedrich Wilhelm Carl.** b. at Gotha, Germany, June 1, 1826; d. at Berlin, March 6, 1900. German piano maker, the founder (1856) at Berlin of a well-known piano-manufacturing house.

Bechstein, Johann Matthäus. b. at Waltershausen, Gotha, Germany, July 11, 1757; d. at Meiningen, Germany, Feb. 23, 1822. German naturalist and forester, author of *Die Forst- und Jagdwissenschaft* (1818–27), and others.

Bechstein, Ludwig. b. at Weimar, Germany, Nov. 24, 1801; d. at Meiningen, Germany, May 14, 1860. German poet, folklorist, and novelist; nephew of Johann Matthäus Bechstein. His collections of fairy tales were published in *Deutsches Märchenbuch* (1846) and *Neues deutsches Märchenbuch* (1853).

Bechuanaland (bech.ö.ä'nạ.land). Region in S Africa, between the Transvaal and the Orange River, Union of

South Africa, on the S, South-West Africa on the W, and the Rhodesias on the N and NE. The region includes the present Bechuanaland protectorate and the former colony (also known as British Bechuanaland), which is now part of the Union of South Africa, in Cape of Good Hope province.

Bechuanaland. [Official name, **Bechuanaland Protectorate.**] British protectorate in S Africa, bounded on the W by South-West Africa, on the S by the Union of South Africa, on the E by the Union of South Africa and Southern Rhodesia, and on the N by Northern Rhodesia and South-West Africa. The Molopo River in the S and the Zambezi River in the N form part of the boundaries. The protectorate was proclaimed in 1885 and until 1895 was administered as part of the crown colony of Bechuanaland, but when the latter became part of Cape Colony in 1895, the protectorate was given a separate administration. Today it is administered by a resident commissioner, stationed at Mafeking (which is in Cape of Good Hope Province, Union of South Africa), who is responsible to the high commissioner for Basutoland, Bechuanaland protectorate, and Swaziland, the High Commission Territories. Cattle raising and dairying are the chief industries; there is some mining of gold and silver. Capital, Mafeking; area, 275,000 sq. mi.; pop. 294,000 (1946).

Beck (bek), Sir **Adam.** b. at Baden, Ontario, Canada, June 20, 1857; d. at London, Ontario, Canada, Aug. 15, 1925. Canadian politician and financier. After serving as mayor of London, Ontario (1902–04), he was elected to the provincial legislative assembly in 1905, and remained a member of that body until 1919. He introduced the legislation which set up the Hydro-Electric Power Commission of Ontario, and served as its chairman from 1906 until his death. He was knighted in 1914.

Beck, Carl. b. at Neckargemünd, Germany, April 4, 1856; d. at Pelham, N.Y., June 9, 1911. American surgeon. He received an M.D. (1879) from the University of Jena before settling (1881) at New York, where he became a professor of surgery at New York Post-Graduate Medical School and president of St. Mark's Hospital. He was an early student of x-ray diagnosis and therapy and its application to surgery.

Beck, Charles. b. at Heidelberg, Germany, Aug. 19, 1798; d. March 19, 1866. American classical scholar. After receiving his Ph.D. (1823) at Tübingen, he came (1824) to New York and later served as professor of Latin (1832–50) at Harvard. The author of a *Latin Syntax* (1838), he is also remembered for his editions of Seneca's *Medea* (1834), Cicero's *Brutus* (1837), and Seneca's *Hercules Furens* (1845), and for his collection of the manuscripts of Petronius Arbiter's *Satyricon* (1863).

Beck, Christian Daniel. b. at Leipzig, Germany, Jan. 22, 1757; d. Dec. 13, 1832. German classical philologist He was professor (1825–32) of Greek and Roman literature at the University of Leipzig, and editor of the *Allgemeine Repertorium der neuesten in- und ausländischen Literatur* (1819–32). He published editions of Pindar, Aristophanes, Euripides, Apollonius Rhodius, Plato, Cicero, and Calpurnius, *Commentarii historici decretorum religionis christianae*, and other works.

Beck, James Burnie. b. in Dumfriesshire, Scotland, Feb. 13, 1822; d. at Washington, D.C., May 3, 1890. American politician. He was a Democratic member of Congress from Kentucky (1867–75) and U.S. senator (1877–90).

Beck, James Montgomery. b. at Philadelphia, July 9, 1861; d. at Washington, D.C., April 12, 1936. American politician and lawyer. He was U.S. attorney (1896–1900) for the eastern district of Pennsylvania, assistant U.S. attorney general (1900–03), solicitor general (1921–25) of the U.S., and a representative (1927–34) to Congress. Author of *The Evidence in the Case* (1914), *War and Humanity* (1916), *The Passing of the New Freedom* (1920), *The Constitution of the United States* (1922), and *Our Wonderland of Bureaucracy* (1933).

Beck, Johann Heinrich. b. at Cleveland, Ohio, Sept. 12, 1856; d. there, May 26, 1924. American composer, violinist, and conductor. His compositions include several overtures, an orchestral tone poem, a cantata, and chamber music.

Beck, Johann Ludwig Wilhelm. b. at Leipzig, Germany, Oct. 27, 1786; d. there, Feb. 14, 1869. German jurist; son of Christian Daniel Beck. He became professor of law at Königsberg in 1812, and president of the court of appeals at Leipzig in 1837.

Beck, Johann Tobias von. b. at Balingen, Württemberg, Feb. 22, 1804; d. Dec. 28, 1878. German Protestant theologian, appointed professor of theology at Tübingen in 1843.

Beck, John Brodhead. b. at Schenectady, N.Y., Sept. 18, 1794; d. April 9, 1851. American physician, teacher, and expert in medical law; brother of Lewis Caleb Beck and Theodric Romeyn Beck. His contributions to the latter's *Elements of Medical Jurisprudence* (1823), perhaps most notably in connection with infanticide, were of such importance that many consider him to have been actually a collaborator in the work.

Beck, Jozef. b. 1899; d. 1944. Polish diplomat. He served in the Polish Legion (1914–18), was military attaché at Paris (1924), and department chief in the war ministry under Jozef Pilsudski; later transferred to the ministry of foreign affairs, he became (1930) vice-minister and served (1932–39) as foreign minister. He concluded a nonaggression pact (1934) with Hitler, denounced (1934) the minority treaties of the League of Nations as unacceptable to Poland, and sided with Germany and Italy in the Ethiopian and Spanish conflicts; at the same time, however, he tried to improve Poland's relations with England and France and rejected all German plans for making war against the U.S.S.R. After the dismemberment of Czechoslovakia by Germany, he was instrumental in seizing from Czechoslovakia the city of Cieszyn, mostly populated by Poles. After the German and Soviet attack on Poland (1939), he escaped to Rumania and was interned there until his death. Author of *Przemówienia, deklaracje, wywiady* (1937) and *Beiträge zur europäischen Politik* (1939).

Beck, Karl. b. at Baja, Hungary, May 1, 1817; d. at Währing, near Vienna, April 10, 1879. Austrian poet. Author of *Nächte: Gepanzerte Lieder* (1838), *Der Fahrende Poet* (1838), *Stille Lieder* (1839), *Saul* (1841, a drama), *Janko* (1842), *Lieder vom armen Manne* (1846), *Aus der Heimat* (1852), *Mater Dolorosa* (1853), and *Jadwiga* (1863).

Beck, Lewis Caleb. b. at Schenectady, N.Y., Oct. 4, 1798; d. April 20, 1853. American physician, author, and teacher in the fields of botany, chemistry, and mineralogy; brother of John Brodhead Beck and Theodric Romeyn Beck. He was successively appointed a professor at the Vermont Academy of Medicine (1826), Rutgers University (1830), New York University (1836), and Albany Medical College (1840). Author of *Gazetteer of the States of Illinois and Missouri* (1823), *Manual of Chemistry Containing a Condensed View of the Present State of Science* (1831), and *Mineralogy of New York* (1842).

Beck, Lily Adams. [Pseudonyms: **E. Barrington** and **Louis Moresby.**] d. at Kyoto, Japan, Jan. 3, 1931. English romantic novelist, traveler, and mystic; daughter and granddaughter of two British admirals, John Moresby and Sir Fairfax Moresby. Before 1919 she traveled with her father in India, Ceylon, China, Java, Egypt, Japan, and Burma; from 1919 to 1930, she lived in Canada, and resided in Japan from 1930 until her death. Writing under three names, she was the author of a large body of miscellaneous work; as Louis Moresby she wrote works on the East, *The Treasure of Ho* (1924), *The Glory of Egypt* (1926), *Rubies* (1927), and *Captain Java* (1928); as L. Adams Beck she was the author of *The Ninth Vibration and Other Stories* and *The Key of Dreams* (both 1922), *Perfume of the Rainbow* (1923), *Dreams and Delights* (1926), *Story of Oriental Philosophy* (1928), *Joyous Story of Astrid* (1931), and *A Beginner's Book of Yoga* (1937); as E. Barrington she wrote a series of historical romantic novels and stories, among them *The Ladies!* (1922, which includes the tales "My Lady Mary," "The Golden Vanity," and "A Bluestocking at Court"), *The Chaste Diana* (1923), *The Divine Lady* (1924), *Glorious Apollo* (1925), *The Exquisite Perdita* (1926), *The Thunderer* (1927), *The Gallants* (1927, a volume of historical tales, including "The King and the Lady," "Her Majesty's Godson," "The Prince's Pawns," "The Pious Coquette," and the "Beau and the Lady"), *The Empress of Hearts* (1928), *The Laughing Queen* (1929), *The Irish Beauties* (1931), and *Anne Boleyn* (1932).

Beck, Madame. One of the principal characters in Charlotte Brontë's novel *Villette*.

Beck, Theodric Romeyn. b. at Schenectady, N.Y., Aug. 11, 1791; d. Nov. 19, 1855. American physician, teacher, and author, known best for his *Elements of Medical Jurisprudence* (1823); brother of John Brodhead Beck and Lewis Caleb Beck. He practiced (1811–17) at Albany, N.Y., then was principal (1817–53) of the Albany Academy. President of the state medical society of New York for three successive terms, he also served on the board of managers of the state lunatic asylum and for a four-year term edited the *American Journal of Insanity*.

Becke (bek'ẹ), **Friedrich.** b. at Prague, Dec. 31, 1855; d. at Vienna, June 18, 1931. Austrian mineralogist and geologist. He served as professor (1882 *et seq.*) at the universities of Czernowitz, Prague, and Vienna, and edited Gustav Tschermak's *Lehrbuch der Mineralogie* and *Mineralogische und etrographische Mitteilungen*.

Beckenham (bek'ẹn.ạm). Municipal borough in SE England, in Kent, ab. 2 mi. W of Bromley, ab. 9 mi. SE of Victoria station, London. 74,834 (1951).

Becker (bek'ėr), **Albert Ernst Anton.** b. at Quedlinburg, Germany, June 13, 1834; d. Jan. 10, 1899. German composer, notably of religious music. His work also includes a symphony, the opera *Loreley*, songs, and chamber music.

Becker, August. b. at Darmstadt, Germany, Jan. 27, 1821; d. at Düsseldorf, Germany, Dec. 19, 1887. German landscape painter.

Becker, Carl Heinrich. b. at Amsterdam, April 12, 1876; d. at Berlin, Feb. 10, 1933. German Orientalist and statesman. He served as professor at Hamburg, Bonn, and Berlin, and also (1921, 1925–30) as a government minister of science, arts, and education, making notable reforms in the universities. Author of *Islamstudien* (Islamic Studies, 1924, 1932) and *Das Problem der Bildung* (The Problem of Education, 1930).

Becker, Carl Lotus. b. in Lincoln township, Blackhawk County, Iowa, Sept. 7, 1873; d. at Ithaca, N.Y., April 10, 1945. American author and historian. He was graduated (1896) and received (1907) a Ph.D. degree from the University of Wisconsin. He served as professor (1917–41) of European history at Cornell, and was president of the American Historical Association. Among his books are *Beginnings of the American People* (1915), *Our Great Experiment in Democracy* (1924), *Modern History* (1931), *Progress and Power* (1936), *The Declaration of Independence* (1942), and *How New Will the Better World Be?* (1944).

Becker, Christiane Luise Amalie. [Maiden name, **Neumann.**] b. at Krossen, Germany, Dec. 15, 1778; d. at Weimar, Germany, Sept. 27, 1797. German actress; daughter of the actor Johann Christian Neumann, and wife of an actor, Heinrich Becker. She acted in both comedy and tragedy, and was much admired by Goethe who, after her death, memorialized her in the elegy *Euphrosine*.

Becker, George Ferdinand. b. at New York, Jan. 5, 1847; d. at Washington, D.C., April 20, 1919. American geologist, mathematician, and physicist. He did important work on surveys along the 40th parallel, of the Comstock Lode, of Pacific Coast quicksilver deposits, of South African gold fields, and of Philippine Islands mineral resources. He was graduated from Harvard (A.B.), then did graduate work at Heidelberg (Ph.D.) and the Royal Academy of Mines at Berlin. A pioneer in research on mineral deposits, he was the author of many monographs in his field.

Becker, Hans. b. at Strasbourg, May 12, 1860; d. 1917. German violist and violinist; son of Jean Becker (1833–84). He taught violin at the Leipzig Conservatory.

Becker, Hugo. b. at Strasbourg, Feb. 13, 1864; d. 1941. German violoncello virtuoso; son of Jean Becker (1833 84), who was his first teacher. He studied the cello with Jules De Swert and others, and made his debut at Leipzig. Widely known as a concert player, he made his first appearance in the U.S. at Boston, Jan. 12, 1901. He composed a concerto and other pieces for his instrument.

Becker, Jakob. b. at Dittelsheim, near Worms, Germany, March 15, 1810; d. at Frankfort on the Main, Germany, Dec. 22, 1872. German genre painter.

Becker, Jean. b. at Mannheim, Germany, May 11, 1833; d. there, Oct. 10, 1884. German violinist. He was a member of the Florentine Quartet. His children, Hans, Hugo, and Jeanne, were also musicians.

Becker, Jeanne. b. at Mannheim, Germany, June 9, 1859; d. there, April 6, 1893. German pianist; daughter of Jean Becker (1833–84).

Becker, Johann Philipp. b. at Frankenthal, Germany, March 19, 1809; d. at Geneva, Switzerland, Dec. 9, 1886. German political agitator and socialist; a friend of Karl Marx.

Becker, Julius Maria. b. at Aschaffenburg, Germany, March 29, 1887—. German poet. A man of good will, he has consistently tried to stress the mystic values in a materialistic age, as with such plays as *Das Friedensschiff* (about Henry Ford's peace ship), *Das letzte Gesicht* (1919), and *Der Schächer zur Linken*.

Becker, Karl Ferdinand. b. at Liser, near Trier, Germany, April 14, 1775; d. at Offenbach, Germany, Sept. 5, 1849. German philologist and physician. He wrote *Ausführliche deutsche Grammatik*, *Handbuch der deutschen Sprache*, and others.

Becker, Karl Ferdinand. b. at Leipzig, July 17, 1804; d. there, Oct. 26, 1877. German organist and writer on music. His chief works are *Systematisch-chronologische Darstellung der musikalischen Literatur* (1836–39) and *Die Hausmusik in Deutschland* (1840).

Becker, Karl Friedrich. b. at Berlin, 1777; d. there, March 15, 1806. German historian. He wrote *Weltgeschichte für Kinder und Kinderlehrer* (1801–05), *Erzählungen aus der Alten Welt* (1801–03), and others.

Becker, Lydia Ernestine. b. 1827; d. 1890. English suffrage leader. Secretary (1867) of the Manchester National Society for Women's Suffrage, she edited (1870–90) the *Women's Suffrage Journal* and published pamphlets on women's suffrage.

Becker, May Lamberton. b. at New York, Aug. 26, 1873—. American critic, editor, and author. She was departmental editor (1915–24) for the New York *Evening Post* book section, where she edited "The Reader's Guide," a feature which she subsequently continued in the *Saturday Review of Literature* from 1924 to 1933 and after 1933 in *Books*, the weekly literary section of the New York *Herald Tribune*. She is the author or compiler of *A Reader's Guide Book* (1923), *Adventures in Reading* (1927), *Golden Tales of Our America* (1929), *Books as Windows* (1929), *Golden Tales of the Old South* (1930), *Golden Tales of New England* (1931), *Golden Tales of the Prairie States* (1932), *Under Twenty* (1932), *Golden Tales of the Far West* (1935), *First Adventures in Reading* (1936), *Choosing Books for Children* (1937), *Golden Tales of Canada* (1938), *Golden Tales of the Southwest* (1939), *Introducing Charles Dickens* (1940), *Growing Up With America* (1941), and *The Home Book of Christmas* (1941).

Becker, Nikolaus. b. at Bonn, Germany, Jan. 8, 1809; d. Aug. 28, 1845. German poet. He was author of the popular *Rheinlied* (Rhine song) *Sie sollen ihn nicht haben, den freien deutschen Rhein* (They shall not have it, the free German Rhine), written in 1840, which brought him a rich reward from Frederick William IV of Prussia, and has often since been set to music; it also, however, called forth Alfred de Musset's poem in reply, *Nous l'avons eu, votre Rhin allemand* (We have had it, your German Rhine).

Becker, Oskar. b. at Odessa, Russia, June 18, 1839; d. at Alexandria, Egypt, July 16, 1868. German medical student at the University of Leipzig who attempted to assassinate William I of Prussia at Baden-Baden, on July 14, 1861. At the subsequent trial he gave as the reason for his act the opinion that the king was unequal to the task of uniting Germany. He was sentenced to 20 years' imprisonment, but, at the intercession of the king, was released (1866) on the condition that he leave Germany.

Becker, Wilhelm Adolf. b. at Dresden, Germany, 1796; d. at Meissen, Germany, Sept. 30, 1846. German classical archaeologist; son of Wilhelm Gottlieb Becker. He was a professor at the University of Leipzig. Among his works are *Gallus* (1838) and *Charikles* (1840), both on ancient Greek and Roman life, and *Handbuch der römischen Alterthümer* (Manual of Roman Antiquities, 1843–46; continued by Theodor Mommsen, 1849–64).

Becker, Wilhelm Gottlieb. b. at Oberkallenberg, Saxony, Nov. 4, 1753; d. at Dresden, Germany, June 3, 1813. German archaeologist and man of letters. His chief work is *Augusteum, Dresden's antike Denkmäler enthaltend* (1805–09).

Beckerath (bek'ėr.ät), **Hermann von.** b. at Krefeld, Germany, Dec. 13, 1801; d. there, May 12, 1870. Prussian politician, a member of the Frankfort parliament, and minister of finance (1848–49).

Beckers (bek'ėrs), **Hubert.** b. at Munich, Nov. 4, 1806; d. there, March 11, 1889. German philosophical writer, appointed professor of philosophy at the University of Munich in 1847. He wrote extensively upon the philosophy of Schelling.

Becket (bek'ẹt). Tragedy (1879) by Alfred Tennyson. It was the last in a series of three, the other two being *Queen Mary* (1875) and *Harold* (1877), in which Tennyson sought to dramatize the story of "the Making of England." Of these plays, only *Becket* had a successful run and then only after it had been much revised by Sir Henry Irving.

Becket, Thomas à. See **Thomas à Becket.**

Beckett (bek'ẹt). See **à Beckett.**

Beckford (bek'fọrd), **Peter.** b. at Stapleton, Dorsetshire, England, 1740; d. there, Feb. 18, 1811. English sportsman, author of hunting treatises, and student of classical and modern literature. His works include *Thoughts upon Hare and Fox Hunting: also an Account of the most Celebrated Dog Kennels in the Kingdom* (1781), historically important as the first English work to give a complete and accurate account of the sport, *Essays on Hunting, containing a Philosophical Inquiry into the Nature and Properties of Scent, on Different Kinds of Hounds, Hares, etc., with an Introduction describing the Method of Hare-hunting among the Greeks* (1781), and *Familiar Letters from Italy to a Friend in England* (2 vols., 1805), an account of his travels in 1787, during which he met Voltaire, Jean Jacques Rousseau, and Laurence Sterne.

Beckford, William. b. on the island of Jamaica, in the British West Indies, 1709; d. at London, June 21, 1770. English politician. He became lord mayor of London in 1762, and again in 1769. He was a friend and supporter of John Wilkes. During his second mayoralty he acquired celebrity by a fearless impromptu speech made before George III, on May 23, 1770, on the occasion of his presenting an address to the king, in which Beckford voiced his belief that false returns had been published in an election in Middlesex.

Beckford, William. b. at Fonthill, Wiltshire, England, Sept. 29, 1759; d. May 2, 1844. English man of letters, connoisseur, and collector; son of William Beckford (1709–70). He was for many years a member of Parliament, but is best known as the author of *Vathek* (1784), an Oriental tale written in French. He wrote also *Letters* (1834), and two burlesques, *The Elegant Enthusiast* (1796) and *Amezia* (1797). His villa at Fonthill, upon which he expended more than a million dollars, was famous in its day as an instance of eccentric extravagance and fanciful splendor.

Beckham (bek'ạm), **John Crepps Wickliffe.** b. near Bardstown, Ky., Aug. 5, 1869; d. at Louisville, Ky., Jan. 9, 1940. American politician. A member (1894, 1896–98) of the Kentucky legislature, he was elected (1899) lieutenant governor of Kentucky, served as governor (1900–07) of the state, and was a U.S. senator (1915–21) from Kentucky.

Beckington (bek'ing.tọn), **Thomas.** [Also, **Bekyinton.**] b. in Somerset, England, c1390; d. 1465. English prelate and statesman. He was a fellow (1408–20) of Oxford University; during and after service as prolocutor of convocation (c1433–38), he accompanied embassies to France (1432–42); he was appointed king's secretary (c1439), lord privy seal (c1443), and bishop of Bath and Wells (1443), adorning the latter place with many fine buildings.

Beckley (bek'li). City in S West Virginia, county seat of Raleigh County, in an agricultural and coal-mining area. It was settled in 1838 and made county seat in 1850. It is the seat of Beckley College. 19,397 (1950).

Beckman (bek'män), **Ernst Otto.** b. at Solingen, Germany, 1853; d. at Berlin-Dahlem, 1923. German chemist. He first made useful, and developed extensively, the fundamental cryoscopic and ebullioscopic methods for determining molecular weights (1888 *et seq.*). Moreover, he discovered the important Beckman rearrangement of oximes. Professor at Giessen (1891), Erlangen (1892–96), and Leipzig (1897–1912), he was the first director of the Kaiser Wilhelm institute for chemistry (1912–21).

Beckmann (bek'män), **Max.** b. at Leipzig, Germany, Feb. 12, 1884; d. Dec. 27, 1950. German painter and engraver. He studied at Florence and Paris, came (1937) to the U.S., and participated in the exposition of contemporary German painters at Paris in 1929. Among his works are *The Bridge, Woman Reclining,* and *Portrait of Richard Piper* (lithograph). His triptych *Departure* (1937), in the Museum of Modern Art, New York, contains figures reminiscent of medieval art.

Becknell (bek'nẹl), **William.** b. c1790; d. c1832. American pioneer, chiefly remembered for laying cut the Santa Fe Trail on a wagon expedition in 1822.

Beckum (bek'ụm). Town in W Germany, in the *Land* (state) of North Rhine-Westphalia, British Zone, formerly in the province of Westphalia, Prussia, situated on the Werse River, ab. 22 mi. SE of Münster: agricultural trade center; metallurgical, electrical, chemical, and paperware manufactures. There is a Gothic *Rathaus* (town hall); the Church of Saint Stephen dates from the 12th century. During World War II the town suffered no serious damage. The population is predominantly Roman Catholic. 17,551 (1950).

Beckwith (bek'with), Sir **George.** b. 1753; d. at London, March 20, 1823. English military commander and colonial official. He entered the army in 1771, and served (1776–82) in the war in North America. From 1787 to 1791 he was diplomatic agent of England in the U.S., and he was successively governor of Bermuda (April, 1797), and of St. Vincent, in the Windward Islands (October, 1804). From October, 1808, to June, 1814, he was governor of Barbados, with command of the British forces in the Windward and Leeward islands, and during this time he was successful in military expeditions against the French islands of Martinique (Jan. 30–Feb. 24, 1809) and Guadeloupe (Jan. 28–Feb. 5, 1810). He subsequently commanded in Ireland.

Beckwith, James Carroll. b. at Hannibal, Mo., Sept. 23, 1852; d. at New York, Oct. 24, 1917. American portrait and genre painter, a pupil of Carolus-Duran. He shared a studio at Paris with John Singer Sargent. Among his paintings are portraits of Mrs. R. H. McCurdy, Mark Twain, Theodore Roosevelt, and Paul du Chaillu. He taught for many years at the Art Students League of New York. He became a member of the National Academy in 1894.

Beckwith, John Charles. b. 1789; d. 1862. English army officer; nephew of Sir George Beckwith (1753–1823) and Sir Thomas Sydney Beckwith (1772–1831). He lost a leg at the Battle of Waterloo (1815), after which he was made lieutenant colonel; in 1846 he became a major general. From 1827 he had made his home in Piedmont, at a house called La Torre, where he spent many years among the Waldenses, attempting to rekindle in them the strong evangelical faith which had been a notable characteristic of the Waldensian sect in earlier days.

Beckwith, Sir **Thomas Sydney.** b. 1772; d. at Mahabaleshwar, India, in January, 1831. English military commander; brother of Sir George Beckwith (1753–1823) and uncle of John Charles Beckwith (1789–1862). He served (1807) in Denmark, where his regiment fought at the battle of Kioge, and took part (1808–11) in the Peninsular Campaign. Appointed (1829) commander in chief at Bombay, India, he was made a lieutenant general in 1830.

Beckx (beks), **Pierre Jean.** b. at Sichem, near Louvain, Belgium, Feb. 8, 1795; d. at Rome, March 4, 1887. Roman Catholic ecclesiastic, general of the order of Jesuits from 1853 to 1883.

Becky Sharp (bek'i shärp'). Central character in William Makepeace Thackeray's novel *Vanity Fair:* a friendless girl, "with the dismal precocity of poverty," whose object it is to rise in the world. She is agreeable, cool, selfish, and entirely unmoral; "small and slight of person, pale, sandy-haired, and with green eyes, habitually cast down, but very large, odd, and attractive when they looked up."

Becon (bē'kọn), **Thomas.** [Pseudonym, **Theodore Basille.**] b. in Norfolk, England, c1511; d. at London, 1567. English ecclesiastic and writer. He was for a time a supporter of the Reformation in books written under the name of Theodore Basille, the doctrines of which, however, he was obliged to recant. He was chaplain to Lady Jane Seymour and to Thomas Cranmer under Edward VI, and rector of Saint Stephen's, Walbrook. His best-known work is *The Governaunce of Vertue.*

Becque (bek), **Henry François.** b. at Paris, April 9, 1837; d. there, May 12, 1899. French dramatist and critic. His works include *L'Enfant prodigue, Michel Pauper, L'Enlèvement, La Navette, Les Honnêtes Femmes, Les Corbeaux, La Parisienne, Le Départ, Veuve, Le Domino à quart,* and *Une Exécution;* the libretto of an opera, *Sardanapale,* with music by Victorin de Jonciers; a volume of memoirs; and *Querelles Littéraires.* He received the decoration of the Legion of Honor in 1886.

Bécquer (bā'ker), **Gustavo Adolfo Dominguez.** b. at Seville, Spain, Feb. 17, 1836; d. at Madrid, Dec. 22, 1870. Spanish poet and writer of tales. He was orphaned at the age of ten, and was subsequently set adrift by his guardian because he would not prepare himself for a career in any of the professions. At the age of 18 he went to Madrid, where for the rest of his brief life he lived on the scant earnings of hack writing and translating novels from other languages into Spanish. His short *Leyendas Españolas* have been likened to tales by Poe and Hoffman, and his lyrical poems have been compared with those of Heine. His books of poetry were entitled *Volverán las Oscures Golondrinas, Olas Gigantes que Os Rompéis Bramando,* and *Cuando Me Lo Contaron Sentí el Frío.* A collection of Becquer's works was published at Madrid in 1885, and an enlarged edition in 1904. A selection from his books in an English translation has been issued under the title *Legends, Tales and Poems.*

Becquerel (bek.rel), **Alexandre Edmond.** b. at Paris, March 24, 1820; d. there, May 13, 1891. French physicist; son of Antoine César Becquerel. He was noted for researches on the electric light, photography, and magnetism.

Becquerel, Antoine César. b. at Châtillon-sur-Loing, Loiret, France, March 7, 1788; d. at Paris, Jan. 18, 1878. French physicist, noted for his discoveries in electricity and in electrochemistry. His chief works are *Traité expérimental de l'électricité et du magnétisme* (1834–40), *Traité d'électro-chimie* (1843), and *Traité de physique.* He served (1810–12) with the French army in Spain, but abandoned his military career in 1815, and thereafter devoted himself exclusively to science.

Becquerel, Antoine Henri. b. at Paris, Dec. 15, 1852; d. at Paris, Aug. 25, 1908. French physicist, professor (1895 *et seq.*) at the École Polytechnique; son of Alexander Edmond Becquerel. In 1896 he discovered the radiation from uranium which bears his name (Becquerel rays). His investigations were concerned chiefly with phosphorescence, ultrared radiation, and spectroscopy. In 1903 he received, with Pierre and Marie Curie, the Nobel prize in physics. In 1908 he was made life secretary of the Academy of Sciences.

Bécu (bā.kü), **Marie Jeanne.** Original name of **du Barry,** Comtesse.

Beczwa (bech'vä). See **Betschwa.**

Beda (bē'dạ). See **Bede.**

Bedamar (bed.ạ.mär'). Spanish statesman in the Abbé de Saint-Réal's *Conjuration des Espagnols contre la république de Venise,* from which Thomas Otway took his *Venice Preserved.* The character (based on the Marqués de Bedmar, in real life) is a noble one in Saint-Réal's work, but is reduced to small proportions in Otway's play.

Bédarieux (bā.dȧ.ryė). Town in S France, in the department of Hérault, situated on the Orb River, ab. 36 mi. W of Montpellier. It has manufactures of leather and textiles. 7,033 (1946).

Bedaux (bẹ.dō'), **Charles Eugène.** b. in France, 1887; d. Feb. 19, 1944. Efficiency engineer and industrialist. He arrived (c1908) in the U.S. He originated the so-called Bedaux (or point) system of wage payment, and controlled companies in 21 countries which provided efficiency surveys for industries throughout the world.

Bedawin (bed'ạ.win). See **Bedouin.**

Beddington and Wallington (bed'ing.tọn; wol'ing.tọn). Municipal borough in SE England, in Surrey, ab. 2 mi. W of Croydon, ab. 9 mi. S of Victoria Station, London. 32,751 (1951).

Beddoes (bed'ōz), **Thomas.** b. at Shiffnal, Shropshire, England, April 13, 1760; d. Dec. 24, 1808. English physician and scientist; brother-in-law of Maria Edgeworth. He was a reader in chemistry at the University of Oxford (1788–92), and established at Bristol in 1798 a "Pneumatic Institute" for the treatment of disease by inhalation, employing as his assistant Humphry Davy. Author of *Isaac Jenkins* (1793), *Hygeia, or Essays Moral and Medical* (1801–02), and others.

Beddoes, Thomas Lovell. b. at Clifton, England, July 20, 1803; d. at Basel, Switzerland, Jan. 26, 1849. English poet and physician and anatomist; son of Thomas Beddoes (1760–1808). His early poems *The Improvisatore* (1821) and *The Bride's Tragedy* (1822), which he published while an Oxford undergraduate, met with no success. Isolated from English literary society and influenced by a profound melancholy which made him skeptical of the value of literary effort, he published no more works. His most famous work, *Death's Jest-Book, or the Fool's Tragedy* (1850), was begun about 1825 and for almost a quarter of a century he tinkered with it, revising, deleting, and expanding. A selection from the mass of Beddoes' writings (*Poems*) was published (1851) posthumously by a devoted friend, Thomas Kelsall. In youth Beddoes was one of the earliest admirers of Shelley. Beddoes' fondness for sinister and spectral imagery probably owes something to Shelley but he was also influenced by tales of terror and Jacobean tragedies, for Beddoes was at the very center of the Elizabethan revival. Beddoes was aware of the new scientific speculation and experiment in the dim regions of physiology and psychology. He was the first among the English poets to use the discoveries of paleontology as material for poetry and there are passages in his poetry that suggest that he believed in the evolution of the species. Beddoes is memorable for scattered lines and passages, cadences of haunting beauty, and images of arresting grandeur.

Bede (bēd) or **Baeda** (bē'dạ). [Also: **Beda;** called **"Baeda Venerabilis,"** meaning the **"Venerable Bede."**] b. at or near Jarrow, Durham, England, c673; d. there, May 26, 735. English historian, theologian, and scientist, considered to have been the greatest master of chronology in the Middle Ages. Probably the most learned Western European scholar of his period, he is generally assumed to have been the father of English history. He was educated at the monastery of Saint Peter's (at Wearmouth, now called Sunderland) and that of Saint Paul's (at Jarrow), where he spent the rest of his life. (Both Wearmouth and Jarrow were small towns in the NE part of England, near to Newcastle and to each other; some sources, for this reason, and because Bede's own statement in the matter is anything but explicit, cite Wearmouth as Bede's place of birth.) He was ordained a deacon in his 19th year, and became a priest 11 years later. The greater part of his life, however, was spent in teaching and writing rather than in carrying out what are now ordinarily thought of as priestly duties (this was not unusual, of course, in the time of Bede, when virtually all of European scholarship was confined to the monasteries). He understood Greek and had some acquaintance with Hebrew (in addition, obviously, to Latin). His main work, *Historia ecclesiastica gentis Anglorum libri quinque,* is an ecclesiastical history of England which has been for centuries invaluable to historians concerned with the sequence of events in England between the latter part of the 6th century and 731 (the year in which Bede completed it). His other historical and biographical works include *Historia abbatum,* concerning the abbots of the monasteries at Wearmouth and Jarrow, and biographies of various outstanding figures in the Church. His *De natura rerum* is concerned with the physical sciences, as they were understood in his day, and is based chiefly on Pliny and Isidore of Seville. It deals with various phenomena, which are referred to natural causes; for example, the earth is a sphere surrounded by a watery heaven. The *De loquela per gestum digitorum* (or *De indigitatione*) is our main source for the study of medieval finger-reckoning or symbolism. One of the most important of Bede's works on arithmetic and chronology is *De temporum ratione.* This work contains a remarkable theory of tides based upon Pliny, and also upon personal observation (Bede was curiously close to modern science and scholarship in the matter of making actual observations, where possible, and of citing his sources). The first collected edition of Bede's writings appeared at Paris in 1544–45, and was reprinted in 1554. Both of these editions are now extremely rare. The latest edition is in two volumes, edited by Charles Plummer, and published in 1896. English translations have appeared often in the past several centuries, one of the most recent having been made in 1870.

Bede, Adam. Principal character in George Eliot's novel of the same name, a young carpenter, a keen and clever workman, somewhat sharp-tempered, and with a knowledge of some good books. He has an alert conscience, good common sense, and "well-balanced shares of susceptibility and self-control." He loves Hetty Sorrel, but finally marries Dinah Morris. He is said to be in part a portrait of George Eliot's father.

Bede, Cuthbert. Pseudonym of **Bradley, Edward.**

Bede, Lisbeth. Mother of Adam and Seth in George Eliot's novel *Adam Bede.*

Bede, Seth. Tender-hearted mystical brother of Adam, in George Eliot's novel *Adam Bede.*

Bedeau (bẹ.dō), **Marie Alphonse.** b. at Vertou, near Nantes, France, Aug. 10, 1804; d. there, Oct. 30, 1863. French general. He served in Algeria, and later failed in an attempt to suppress the rising (February, 1848) at Paris. He became vice-president of the Constituent and Legislative assemblies, and was taken prisoner in the coup d'état of 1851.

Bedel (bẹ.del), **Maurice.** b. at Paris, 1883—. French novelist. Author of *L'Amour camarade* (1931), *Une enquête sur l'amour* (1931), and others.

Bedel (bē'dẹl), **Timothy.** b. at Salem, N.H., c1740; d. at Haverhill, N.H., 1787. American officer in the Revolutionary War. He was in command of the force which was attacked by Indians under the Mohawk chief (and captain in the British army) Joseph Brant, at the Cedars, near Montreal, and which was surrendered without resistance by a Captain Butterfield, the subordinate officer in command. The blame for this affair was placed by General Benedict Arnold on Bedel, although at the time of the attack the latter lay ill at Lachine.

Bedell (bẹ.del'), **Frederick.** b. at Brooklyn, N.Y., April 12, 1868—. American physicist who invented the cathode-ray oscilloscope and bone-conduction hearing aids. A graduate of Yale (1890) and Cornell (1892), he has served as professor (1904–37) of applied electricity at Cornell, managing editor (1913–22) of *The Physical Review,* and consulting physicist (1937 *et seq.*) for the R. C. Burt Scientific Laboratories, Pasadena, Calif. Author of *Alternating Currents* (1892), *Airplane Characteristics* (1917), *The Airplane* (1920), and other works.

Bedell, Gregory Thurston. b. at Hudson, N.Y., Aug. 27, 1817; d. at New York, March 11, 1892. American bishop of the Protestant Episcopal Church; son of Gregory Townsend Bedell. He was rector (1843–59) of the Church of the Ascension at New York. Consecrated assistant bishop of Ohio on Oct. 13, 1859, he became bishop of that diocese in 1873, but resigned the office in 1889 on account of illness. Author of *Canterbury Pilgrimage to the Lambeth Conference* (1878), *The Pastor* (1880), and *Centenary of the American Episcopate* (1884).

Bedell, Gregory Townsend. b. on Staten Island, N.Y., Oct. 28, 1793; d. at Baltimore, Md., Aug. 30, 1834. American Protestant Episcopal clergyman and hymn writer.

Bedell, William. b. in Essex, England, 1571; d. Feb. 7, 1642. English prelate. He became provost of Trinity College, Dublin, in 1627, and bishop of the united sees of Kilmore and Ardagh in Ireland in 1629, but resigned the see of Ardagh in 1633, in disapproval of pluralities. Having been imprisoned during the Irish uprising against the English in 1641, he died as a result of the treatment which he received.

Beder (bed'ėr). See **Bedr.**

Bedford (bed'fọrd). See also **Bedfordshire.**

Bedford. Municipal borough in C England, county seat of Bedfordshire, situated on the river Ouse, ab. 50 mi. NW of London by rail. It has manufactures of farm machinery, pumps, engines, and electrical equipment, and tanneries. Bedford was the scene of a battle between the Britons and Saxons in 571. It had a castle in the Middle Ages, and has in the course of its history withstood many attacks and sieges. In Bedford jail John Bunyan was imprisoned (1660–72 and 1675–76) and wrote *Pilgrim's Progress.* 53,065 (1951).

Bedford. City in S Indiana, county seat of Lawrence County, ab. 65 mi. SW of Indianapolis. The quarries in the vicinity produce the building stone known as Indiana or Bedford limestone. 12,562 (1950).

Bedford. Town (in Massachusetts the equivalent of township in many other states) and unincorporated village in E Massachusetts, in Middlesex County: seat of the Convent of Saint Thérèse of Lisieux and the Maryknoll Seminary. Pop. of town, 5,234 (1950); of village, 1,407 (1950).

Bedford. City in NE Ohio, in Cuyahoga County: residential suburb of Cleveland. Its factories manufacture china, chairs, and other articles. It was settled in 1813. Pop. 9,105 (1950).

Bedford. [Former name, **Raystown.**] Borough in S Pennsylvania, county seat of Bedford County, on the Raystown branch of the Juniata River, ab. 34 mi. S of Altoona: residential community. There are mineral springs at nearby Bedford Springs. Fort Bedford was built here c1757. Pop. 3,521 (1950).

Bedford. [Former name, **Bedford City.**] Town in C Virginia, county seat of Bedford County: manufactures include asbestos, tires, and military uniforms. It was incorporated in 1890. Pop. 4,061 (1950).

Bedford, Fort. Military post of the American colonial period, originally erected (1757) as Fort Raystown (on the site of what is now Bedford, Pa.). It became known as Fort Bedford in 1759, and during subsequent operations in the French and Indian War was the chief base for troops and supplies between Fort Pitt and Carlisle. It was besieged, but did not yield, during the period of war with Indians under the Ottawa chief, Pontiac. It fell into disuse before the Revolutionary War.

Bedford, Francis. b. at Paddington, London, June 18, 1799; d. at Shepherd's Bush, London, June 8, 1883. English bookbinder. In 1817 he was apprenticed to a binder and later became assistant to Charles Lewis (1786–1836). He was considered the best English binder of his time.

Bedford, Gunning. b. April 7, 1742; d. in September, 1797. American soldier and politician; cousin of Gunning Bedford (1747–1812). He was a colonel at the battle of White Plains (Oct. 22, 1776), delegate (1783–85) to the Continental Congress from Delaware, and governor (1796–97) of Delaware.

Bedford, Gunning. b. at Philadelphia, 1747; d. March 30, 1812. American politician; cousin of Gunning Bedford (1742–97). He served as delegate to the Continental Congress (1785–86), the Annapolis Convention (1786), and the Federal Convention (1787). He was an advocate of states' rights.

Bedford, Gunning S. b. at Baltimore, Md., 1806; d. at New York, Sept. 5, 1870. American physician. He was professor of obstetrics at the University of New York, 1840–62. He wrote *Diseases of Women and Children, Principles and Practice of Obstetrics,* and others.

Bedford, Randolph. b. at Sydney, Australia, July 28, 1868—. Australian journalist, mining engineer, and miscellaneous writer. His works include *True Eyes, The Whirlwind* (1903), and *Snare of Strength* (1905), all fiction; he also wrote *After Victory—What?* and *Naught to Thirty-Three,* autobiography (both 1944), and was a contributor to various newspapers, magazines, and reviews.

Bedford City. Former name of **Bedford,** Va.

Bedford Coffee House. Coffee house which formerly stood in Covent Garden, London, a resort of David Garrick, Samuel Foote, Henry Fielding, and others.

Bedford Cut Stone Company v. Journeymen Stone Cutters' Association, 274 U.S. 37 (1927). Decision of the U.S. Supreme Court upholding an injunction against a labor union which had sanctioned a secondary boycott. It lent broad approval to the use of the injunction in cases involving the violation of antitrust laws, and is notable as one of the decisions which vitiated the labor provisions of the Clayton Antitrust Act.

Bedford House. Mansion which formerly stood in Belgrave Square, London, the residence of the dukes of Bedford.

Bedford Level. Flat tract of land on the E coast of England, extending from Milton in Cambridgeshire to Toynton in Lincolnshire, and from Peterborough in Northamptonshire to Brandon in Suffolk. It comprises nearly all the marshy district called the Fens and the Isle of Ely. It gets its name from Francis Russell, 4th Earl of Bedford, who in 1634 undertook to drain it. Extensive drainage works have since been established, and the district affords rich grain and pasture lands. Length, ab. 60 mi.; breadth, ab. 40 mi.; area, 450,000 acres.

Bedfordshire (bed′fọrd.shir). [Also: **Bedford, Beds** (always written without a period).] Midland county of England, bounded by Northamptonshire on the NW, Huntingdonshire on the NE, Cambridgeshire on the E, Hertfordshire on the SE, and Buckinghamshire on the S and W. The surface is generally level, but is hilly in the S and NW parts. The chief industries include tanneries and the manufacture of automobiles. The greater part of the land is under cultivation and produces wheat and barley; it is also an important market-gardening county. County seat, Bedford; area of administrative county, ab. 473 sq. mi.; pop. 311,844 (est. 1951).

Bedford Springs. See under **Bedford,** Pa.

Bedford Square. Square in London, situated W of the British Museum, from which it is divided by Gower Street.

Bédier (bā.dyā), **(Charles Marie) Joseph.** b. at Paris, 1864; d. 1938. French author, and scholar in the field of medieval French literature; successor of Gaston Paris at the Collège de France. He elaborated, in *Les Légendes épiques* (4 vols., 1908–13), the now widely accepted theory that French epic songs like *The Song of Roland* are not of Frankish origin but developed in monasteries during the Crusades, where they were sung for the edification of pilgrims. He was elected to the Academy in 1920.

Bedivere (bed′i.vir), **Sir.** In the Arthurian cycle of romance, a knight of the Round Table. It was he who brought the dying Arthur to the barge in which the three queens bore him to the Vale of Avalon.

Bedlam (bed′lạm). The hospital of Saint Mary of Bethlehem (slurred in popular usage in Middle English to "Bethlem" or "Bedlem," and thence to "Bedlam") at London, originally a priory (founded c1247), but afterward used as an asylum for lunatics. It has been known in modern times as the Bethlehem Royal Hospital, and its facilities were moved (1930) from their original location in Lambeth, a densely populated borough of London, to the suburban community of Croydon.

Bedlington (bed′ling.tọn). Civil parish and town in NE England, in Northumberland, situated on the river Blyth, ab. 11 mi. N of Newcastle-upon-Tyne, ab. 285 mi. N of London by rail. It is in a coal-mining region. 7,148 (1931).

Bedlingtonshire (bed′ling.tọn.shir). Urban district in NE England, in Northumberland, ab. 11 mi. N of Newcastle. The Port of Blyth lies partly within the urban district, which includes Bedlington parish. Industries include coal mining, coal export, and brickmaking; some agriculture; Bedlington terriers are raised here. 28,836 (1951).

Bedloe (bed′lō), **William.** b. at Chepstow, England; d. at Briston, England, 1680. English adventurer remembered for his "exposé" of the fictitious "Popish Plot" invented (1678) by Titus Oates. After years of fraud, broils, and intrigues, he became notorious by "confessing," in his "revelations," *A Narrative and Impartial Discovery of the Horrid Popish Plot* (1679), his part in the plot, and "exposing" the intention of Catholics to burn London, assassinate the king, and massacre the Protestants.

Bedloe's Island (bed′lōz). [Indian name, **Minissais;** former names, **Bedloe Island, Great Oyster Island.**] Small island in Upper New York Bay, within New York City's harbor, slightly more than 1 mi. from the Battery. The island was bought (1758) from private owners by New York City, and some 42 years later was transferred to U.S. ownership. Fort Wood was erected in 1841, its foundations later serving as the base for Frédéric Auguste Bartholdi's statue of *Liberty Enlightening the World,* popularly known as the "Statue of Liberty," which was erected in 1884. The island, which is under the supervision of the National Park Service of the Department of the Interior, is visited annually by more than 500,000 persons who come to view the statue. It is named after Isaac Bedloe, the earliest white owner.

Bedmar (bāᴛʜ.mär′), Marqués **de.** [Title of **Alfonso de la Cueva.**] b. 1572; d. Aug. 2, 1655. Spanish diplomat and prelate who, while an ambassador of Philip III to Venice, was the leader in an unsuccessful conspiracy (1618) to destroy that republic. He became a cardinal in 1622. His conspiracy is said to have suggested the plot of Thomas Otway's *Venice Preserved.*

Bednur (bed.nör′) or **Bednore** (-nōr′). Town in W Mysore, Union of India. It was taken by Hyder Ali in 1763, and by Tippu Sahib in 1783. Formerly it was the seat of a rajah.

Bedny (byed′ni), **Demyan.** [Pseudonym of **Yefim Alexeyevich Pridvorov.**] b. at Gubovka, Kherson, Russia, April 1, 1883; d. 1945. Russian author who was for many years a prolific writer for various Soviet newspapers.

Bed of Roses, A. Novel by W. L. George, published in 1911. It shows the same heightened interest in sex and its problems that marks his *Second Blooming* (1914) and *Blind Alley* (1919).

Bedouin (bed′ọ̈.in). [Also, **Bedawin.**] General term designating the camel-breeding, pastoral nomads of the Arabian peninsula and adjacent regions. True Bedouins are of Semitic stock, speak Arabic, are Mohammedans, and are organized into tribes and confederations. The Bedouins are distinguished from the Raiyyi, who pasture sheep and goats and occasionally practice agriculture. In North Africa the term is more loosely used to cover both these categories.

Bedouin Tribes of the Euphrates. Travel book (1879) by Lady Anne Blunt. In it she recounts the journeys on which she accompanied her husband, Wilfrid Scawen Blunt.

Bedr (bed′ẹr). [Also, **Beder.**] Village in W Arabia, between Medina and Mecca. It was the scene of the first victory of Mohammed over the Koraishites, about the beginning of 624 A.D.

Bedreddin Hassan (bed.red.dēn′ has′ạn). Son of Noureddin Ali in the story of that name in *The Arabian Nights' Entertainments.* Having been carried off by a genie and adopted by a pastry cook, he is discovered by the superior quality of the cheese cakes he makes, arrested on a false charge of putting no pepper in them, and restored to his family.

Bedriacum (bẹ.drī′ạ.kum). [Also, **Bebriacum.**] In ancient geography, a village in N Italy, E of Cremona. The exact location is undetermined. Here the forces of Vitellius, under Cecina and Valens, defeated (April, 69 A.D.) the forces of Otho; later in the same year, the forces of Vespasian, under Antonius, defeated the forces of Vitellius.

Beds (bedz). See **Bedfordshire.**

Bedwas and Machen (bed′wạs; mak′ẹn). Urban district in W England, in Monmouthshire, ab. 2 mi. NE of Caerphilly, ab. 144 mi. W of London by rail. 8,712 (1951).

Bedwell (bed′wẹl), **William.** b. c1561; d. 1632. Originator of Arabic studies in England and one of the translators of the King James Bible (1604–11). Rector (1601 *et seq.*) of Saint Ethelburgh's, London, he published the Epistles of Saint John in English and Arabic at Leiden (1612), and Arabic and mathematical works, including an explanation of the use of the carpenter's square (*Mesolabium Architectonicum,* 1631). He left the manuscript of an Arabic lexicon, used in Edmund Castell's *Lexicon Heptaglotton.*

Bedwellty (bed.wel′ti). Urban district in W England, in Monmouthshire, ab. 6 mi. S of Tredegar, ab. 4 mi. SW of Abertillery. 28,826 (1951).

Bedwin (bed′win), **Mrs.** "A motherly old lady," Mr. Brownlow's housekeeper, who is kind to Oliver, in Charles Dickens's novel *Oliver Twist.*

Bedworth (bed'wėrth). Urban district in C England, in Warwickshire, ab. 4 mi. S of Nuneaton, midway between there and Coventry, ab. 100 mi. NW of London by rail. 24,866 (1951).

Będzin (ben'jēn). [German, **Bendzin**; Russian, **Bendin.**] Town in SW Poland, in the *województwo* (province) of Katowice, formerly in Russian Poland, situated near the former German border, on the Czarna Przemsza River, ab. 38 mi. NW of Kraków: a coal-mining town; it has metallurgical (zinc sheets, chains, and other metal products), food, ceramic, and chemical industries. 27,754 (1946).

Bee (bē), **Bernard Elliott.** b. in February or March, 1824; killed at Bull Run, July 22, 1861. American Confederate brigadier general in the Civil War. He commanded a brigade of South Carolina troops at Bull Run, where he fell.

Bee, Hamilton Prioleau. b. at Charleston, S.C., July 22, 1822; d. Oct. 2, 1897. American soldier, with the Confederate army in the Civil War. He was secretary of the U.S.-Texas boundary commission (1839), served in the Mexican War, and was a brigadier general (1862 *et seq.*) at Brownsville, Texas, in charge of the boundary exchange of cotton from the South for munitions from Mexico.

Bee, The. English periodical which first appeared on Oct. 6, 1759; only eight weekly numbers were published. Oliver Goldsmith was the author of nearly all the essays.

Beebe (bē'bē), (**Charles**) **William.** b. at Brooklyn, N.Y., July 29, 1877—. American naturalist, author, and explorer; husband (married 1927) of Elswyth Thane. A graduate (1898) of Columbia University, he was curator of ornithology (1899 *et seq.*) and director of the scientific research department of the New York Zoölogical Society. He originated the collection of living birds at New York Zoölogical Park, and led scientific expeditions to Nova Scotia, Mexico, South America, the Himalayas, Borneo, and other places. His investigations of land and water vertebrates in these places and his oceanographic surveys in Bermuda waters are well known; he designed a bathysphere for underwater exploration. Author of *Two Bird Lovers in Mexico* (1905), *Jungle Peace* (1918), *Galápagos, World's End* (1923), *Jungle Days* (1925), *The Arcturus Adventure* (1925), *Pheasants—Their Lives and Homes* (1926), *Beneath Tropic Seas* (1928), *Half Mile Down* (1934), *Book of Bays* (1942), *High Jungle* (1949), and other books.

Beebe, Lucius (**Morris**). b. at Wakefield, Mass., Dec. 9, 1902—. American journalist. He was graduated (A.B., 1927) from Harvard, became (1929) a member of the staff of the New York *Herald Tribune*, and conducted intermittently after 1933 a syndicated column under the title, "This New York." His works include *Fallen Stars* (1921), *Edwin Arlington Robinson and the Arthurian Legend* (1927), *Boston and the Boston Legend* (1935), *High Iron, A Book of Trains* (1938), *Highliners, A Railroad Album* (1940), *Highball, A Pageant of Trains* (1945), and, with Charles M. Clegg, *Mixed Train Daily, A Book of Short Line Railroads* (1947), *U.S. West* (1949), and *Hear the Train Blow* (1952).

Beecham (bē'chąm), Sir **Thomas.** b. at St. Helens, Lancashire, England, April 29, 1879—. English conductor; son of Sir Joseph Beecham (1848–1916), wealthy manufacturer of Beecham's pills. Educated at Rossall School and Wadham College, Oxford, he established (1906) the New Symphony Orchestra, giving concerts of old music at Wigmore Hall. In 1908 he founded the Beecham Symphony Orchestra with which he performed (1910) Delius's *Village Romeo and Juliet*, later giving the first performance of concert works by Delius. He produced some 120 operas of which about 60 were new to England or revived, including Richard Strauss's *Salomé* and *Ariadne auf Naxos;* was instrumental in introducing (1911) the Russian ballet to England; produced (1913) *Boris Godounov, Khovantchina*, and *Ivan the Terrible*, in which Feodor Ivanovich Chaliapin made his first English appearance; and added (1914) *The Magic Flute, Prince Igor, Coq d'Or*, and *Daphnis and Chloë* to the English operatic and ballet repertoire. In 1920 he suspended operatic productions, but reappeared (1923) as orchestral conductor in Manchester and London. He has toured extensively, first appearing at New York (1928) with the Philharmonic Symphony.

Béeche Argüello (bā'ā.chā är.gwā'yō), **Octavio.** b. at San José, Costa Rica, July 16, 1866—. Costa Rican jurist and diplomat. A professor (1894–99) of penal law, he was twice (1902, 1935) candidate for president. He served as minister (1920–22) to the U.S., minister of foreign relations (1930–31), and president (1935) of the supreme court.

Beecher (bē'chėr), **Catharine Esther.** b. at East Hampton, L.I., N.Y., Sept. 6, 1800; d. at Elmira, N.Y., May 12, 1878. American educator and writer; daughter of Lyman Beecher. She conducted a female seminary at Hartford, Conn. (1822–32) and was the author of *An Appeal to the People, Common Sense applied to Religion, Domestic Service, Physiology and Callisthenics*, and others.

Beecher, Charles. b. at Litchfield, Conn., Oct. 7, 1815, d. at Georgetown, Mass., April 21, 1900. American clergyman and writer; son of Lyman Beecher.

Beecher, Charles Emerson. b. at Dunkirk, N.Y., Oct. 9, 1856; d. at New Haven, Conn., Feb. 14, 1904. American paleontologist and geologist, professor of paleontology and curator of the geological collection at Yale University. He published *Studies in Evolution* (1901) and various scientific papers.

Beecher, Edward. b. at East Hampton, L.I., N.Y., Aug. 27, 1803; d. July 28, 1895. American Congregational clergyman and theological writer; son of Lyman Beecher. He was a founder (1849) of *The Congregationalist*, which he edited (1849–53).

Beecher, Henry Ward. b. at Litchfield, Conn., June 24, 1813; d. at Brooklyn, N.Y., March 8, 1887. American Congregational clergyman, lecturer, reformer, and author; son of Lyman Beecher. He was graduated from Amherst College in 1834 and studied theology at Lane Theological Seminary; subsequently he served as pastor at Lawrenceburg, Ind. (1837–39), of a Presbyterian church at Indianapolis (1839–47), and of the Plymouth Congregational Church at Brooklyn (1847–87). He was one of the founders and early editors of the *Independent*, the founder of the *Christian Union* and its editor (1870–81), and one of the most prominent of antislavery orators, speaking also in favor of female suffrage. He delivered Union addresses in Great Britain on subjects relating to the Civil War in the U.S. in 1863. He was the defendant in a suit brought (1874) by Theodore Tilton, accusing him of committing adultery with Mrs. Tilton. After a six-month trial the jury failed to reach an agreement, and the shadow of the scandal hung over Beecher's last years, during which, however, his Brooklyn church remained steadfastly loyal to him. He published *Lectures to Young Men* (1844), *Star Papers* (1855), *Freedom and War* (1863), *Eyes and Ears* (1864), *Aids to Prayer* (1864), *Norwood* (1867), *Earlier Scenes, Lecture Room Talks, Yale Lectures on Preaching, A Summer Parish, Evolution and Religion* (1885), and others.

Beecher, Lyman. b. at New Haven, Conn., Oct. 12, 1775; d. at Brooklyn, N.Y., Jan. 10, 1863. American Congregational clergyman and theologian; father of 13 children, including Henry Ward Beecher and Harriet Beecher Stowe. He was pastor at East Hampton, Long Island (1799–1810), Litchfield, Conn. (1810–26), and Boston (1826–32), and president of Lane Theological Seminary (1832–51). He was noted as a temperance and antislavery reformer and controversialist, often clashing with more conservative elements.

Beecher, Thomas Kinnicut. b. at Litchfield, Conn., Feb. 10, 1824; d. at Elmira, N.Y., March 14, 1900. American Congregational clergyman; son of Lyman Beecher. He served as pastor at Elmira, N.Y., in the period 1854–1900, where he was active in promoting the "institutional church."

Beecher, Willis Judson. b. at Hamden, Ohio, April 29, 1838; d. May 10, 1912. American Presbyterian clergyman, teacher, and author. After ordination (1864) he was pastor at Ovid, N.Y. (1864–65) and Galesburg, Ill. (1869–71), professor (1865–69) of moral science and belles-lettres at Knox College in Illinois, professor (1871–1908) of Hebrew language and literature at the Auburn, N.Y., Theological Seminary, and president (1904) of the Society of Biblical Literature and Exigesis. Author of *Farmer Tompkins and His Bibles* (1874), *The Prophets and the Promise* (1905), *The Teaching of Jesus Concerning* *the Future Life* (1906), *The Dated Events of the Old Testament* (1907), and *Reasonable Biblical Criticism* (1911).

Beecher Island, Battle of. Nine-day engagement (Sept. 17, 1868 *et seq.*) on the bank of the Arickaree River, in what is now the state of Colorado, between 50 U.S. scouts under Colonel George A. Forsyth and some 1,000 Sioux and Cheyenne Indians under Roman Nose. In the face of the superior Indian force, the scouts withdrew to a small island, where they improvised defensive positions; the initial Indian charge cost the lives of Roman Nose and a U.S. lieutenant named Beecher. After a nine-day siege, additional U.S. forces arrived and drove off the Indians. The U.S. casualties were five dead and 18 wounded.

"Beecher's Bibles." In U.S. history, an epithet applied to Sharps Rifles during the era of "bleeding Kansas" before the Civil War, when free-state and proslavery forces contested the territory. The term had its basis in an address (March, 1856) made at New Haven, Conn., by Henry Ward Beecher, who on that occasion declared that a Sharps Rifle had, as a weapon against slavery men in Kansas, more moral force than a Bible.

Beechey (bē′chi), **Frederick William.** b. at London, Feb. 17, 1796; d. there, Nov. 29, 1856. English rear admiral and geographer; son of Sir William Beechey. He distinguished himself in arctic exploration with Sir John Franklin (1818), with Sir William Edward Parry (1819), and as commander of an expedition in 1825–31. He later explored the North African and Irish coasts. He wrote *Voyage of Discovery toward the North Pole* (1843) and others.

Beechey, Sir **William.** b. at Burford, Oxfordshire, England, Dec. 12, 1753; d. at Hampstead, now part of London. Jan. 28. 1839. English portrait painter; father of Frederick William Beechey. He was appointed portrait painter to Queen Charlotte in 1793.

Beech Grove (bēch grōv). City in C Indiana, in Marion County, near Indianapolis. 5,685 (1950).

Beechwood (bēch′wu̇d). Unincorporated community in SE Pennsylvania, in Delaware County. Under the urban definition established for use in the 1950 census, Beechwood was counted with adjoining urban areas. The last official enumeration was 4,966 (1940).

Beeding (bē′ding), **Francis.** [Joint pseudonym of the English authors **John Palmer** and **Hilary Aidan St. George Saunders.**] Under this name they wrote many mystery and adventure novels, including *The Seven Sleepers* (1925), *The Little White Hag* (1926), *The Six Proud Walkers* (1928), *Pretty Sinister* (1929), *The Three Fishers* (1931), *Death Walks in Eastrepps* (1931), *The Nine Waxed Faces* (1936), *The Ten Holy Horrors* (1939), *Eleven Were Brave* (1941), and *Twelve Disguises* (1942).

Beefeaters or **Beef Eaters.** In English history, a name given to the Yeomen of the Guard, whose function it has been, ever since 1485, when they first appeared in the coronation procession of Henry VII, to attend the sovereign at banquets and other state occasions. The warders of the Tower of London are also sometimes called Beefeaters, 15 having been sworn in as Yeomen Extraordinary of the Guard during the reign of Edward VI. The uniform differs slightly, the Tower warders having no cross-belt; both groups wear flat hats, red, frogged coats, and breeches.

Beefington (bē′fing.tọn), **Milor.** Fictitious English nobleman exiled by royal tyranny before the granting of the Magna Charta. He is introduced in *The Rovers*, a verse printed in the *Anti-Jacobin*, a periodical established in 1797 by George Canning with the purpose of ridiculing the French Revolution, its doctrines, and its sympathizers in England.

Beefsteak Club. English club founded in the reign of Queen Anne (it was called a "new society" in 1709), believed to be the earliest club with this name. It was composed of the "chief wits and great men of the nation" and its badge was a gridiron. The "Society of Beefsteaks," established some years later, which has been confused with this, scorned being called a club: they designated themselves "the Steaks." "The Sublime Society of the Steaks" was founded at Covent Garden Theatre in 1735. It is said to have originated in a dinner taken by Charles Mordaunt, 3rd Earl of Peterborough, with John Rich, the manager, in his private room at the theater. The latter cooked a beefsteak so appetizingly that Lord Peterborough proposed repeating the entertainment the next Saturday at the same hour. After the fire at Covent Garden in 1808 the Sublime Society met at the Bedford Coffee House, whence they removed to the Old Lyceum in 1809. When this was burned in 1830, they returned to the Bedford. When the Lyceum Theatre was rebuilt in 1838, a magnificent and appropriate room was provided for them, and they met there until 1867, when the dwindling society was dissolved. A Beefsteak Club was established (c1749) at the Theatre Royal, at Dublin, by Richard Brinsley Sheridan, with Peg Woffington as its president. There were also other clubs of the kind, one of the most recent being that founded by J. L. Toole, an English actor, in 1876.

"Beef Trust." In U.S. history, a popular designation of the National Packing Company, a trade body created in 1902 by the three large meat-packing firms of Armour, Morris, and Swift. The attempts of this organization to secure monopoly control of the meat industry led to a government suit (1904–05) during the "trust-busting" campaign initiated under President Theodore Roosevelt.

"Beef Trust Cases." In U.S. history, a term used to describe a series of Supreme Court cases involving allegedly monopolistic practices within the U.S. meat-packing industry. Although the unanimous decision of the U.S. Supreme Court in *Swift and Co.* v. *U.S., 196 U.S. 375 (1905)*, upheld an injunction issued against a meat-packing combination in restraint of trade, the federal government did not order the dissolution of the National Packing Company, popularly called the "Beef Trust." Prosecution under the Sherman Antitrust Law was made a virtual impossibility when a federal district court at Chicago held, in the case of *United States* v. *Armour and Co., 142 Fed. 808 (1906)*, that the rendering of testimony for a government bureau made individuals immune to punishment under the antitrust law. Additional attempts were made in 1910 to restrain monopoly practices in the packing industry, but the issue was not finally decided until the Supreme Court upheld the Packers and Stockyards Act of 1921 in the case of *United States* v. *Swift and Co., 286 U.S. 106 (1932)*. Chief Justice William H. Taft held that livestock and packing enterprises were endowed with a public interest and were engaged in interstate commerce.

"Beehive State." Nickname of **Utah.**

Beel (bāl), **Louis Joseph Maria.** b. at Roermond, the Netherlands, April 12, 1902—. Dutch author, educator, and statesman. He received the degree of LL.D. (1935) at the University of Nijmegen, and served thereafter in various capacities in municipal and provincial administration. These posts have included minister of the interior (1945) in the cabinet of Pieter S. Gerbrandy and also in the cabinet of Schermerhorn-Drees, member (1946) of the second chamber of the states general, minister-president, minister of the interior, and minister of general affairs (1947–48), and high representative of the crown in Indonesia (1948–49). He also served as professor of administrative law at the Catholic University of Nijmegen. He was vice-premier (1952 *et seq.*) in the Drees cabinet.

Beelaerts van Blokland (bā′lärts vän blôk′länt), **F.** b. at The Hague, Jan. 21, 1872—. Dutch lawyer and statesman. He studied at Leiden and served in the ministry of foreign affairs. The posts he has held include envoy extraordinary and minister plenipotentiary to China (1909–19), delegate to the Washington disarmament conference (1922), envoy to Belgium (1927), minister of foreign affairs (1927–33), minister of state (1936), chairman of the extraordinary advisory council at London (1942–44), and member (1944–46) of the control commission, League of Nations.

Beelzebub (bẹ.el′zẹ.bub). [Also, **Belzebub.**] Name given to a god of the Philistines, who had a famous temple at Ekron. The name is ordinarily explained as having been a compound of "Baal" with "zebub," to mean, literally, "lord of flies." For obvious political as well as theological reasons, his worship was abhorrent to the Jews, and it was probably originally through them that the name became one of the appellations of the Devil.

Beelzebub. In demonology, one of the Gubernatores (rulers) of the Infernal Kingdom, under Lucifer.

Beelzebub. In Milton's *Paradise Lost*, one of the fallen angels, second only to Satan himself.

Beer (bār), **Adolf.** b. at Prossnitz, in Moravia, Feb. 27, 1831; d. at Vienna, May 7, 1902. Austrian historian. His works include *Geschichte des Welthandels* (1860-64), *Holland und der österreichische Erbfolgekrieg* (1871), *Die erste Teilung Polens* (1873-74), and various works on Austrian history.

Beer (bir), **George Louis.** b. on Staten Island, N.Y., July 26, 1872; d. March 15, 1920. American historian and publicist, an authority on the British colonial system. A one-time tobacco merchant (1893-1903), he was a delegate to the Paris Peace Conference and head of the mandates division of the League of Nations. Author of *British Colonial Policy, 1754-65* (1907), *The Origins of the British Colonial System, 1578-1660* (1908), *The Old Colonial System, Part I* (1912), *The English-Speaking Peoples* (1917), and others.

Beer (bār), **Michael.** b. at Berlin, Aug. 19, 1800; d. at Munich, March 22, 1833. German dramatist; brother of Giacomo Meyerbeer. His chief work is the tragedy *Struensee* (1829).

Beer (bir), **Thomas.** b. at Council Bluffs, Iowa, Nov. 22, 1889; d. April 18, 1940. American writer. A graduate (1911) of Yale University, he studied (1911-13) law at Columbia University before serving in World War I as a private (1917) and as a first lieutenant (1918) with an infantry division in France. His publications include *Fair Rewards* (1922), *Stephen Crane* (1923), *Sandoval* (1924), *The Mauve Decade* (1926), *The Road to Heaven* (1928), *Hanna* (1929), and *Mrs. Egg and Other Barbarians* (1933), as well as short stories in the *Century, Saturday Evening Post, Smart Set,* and elsewhere.

Beer (bār), **Wilhelm.** b. at Berlin, Jan. 4, 1797; d. there, March 27, 1850. German banker and astronomer; brother of Giacomo Meyerbeer. He published (1836) a map of the moon.

Beerberg (bār′berk). Highest mountain of the Thüringerwald, S central Germany, ab. 15 mi. NE of Meiningen. Elevation, ab. 3,400 ft.

Beerbohm (bir′bōm), Sir **Max.** b. at London, Aug. 24, 1872—. English writer, critic, and caricaturist; half brother of Sir Herbert Beerbohm Tree (1853-1917) and husband (1910 *et seq.*) of Florence Kahn, originally of Memphis, Tenn. He studied at Merton College, Oxford, living later (1910 *et seq.*) at Rapallo, Italy. He was successor (1898) to George Bernard Shaw as dramatic critic on the *Saturday Review*, at London. His caricature portraits of contemporary literary and political figures have been collected in *Twenty-five Gentlemen* (1896), *The Poet's Corner* (1904), *Rossetti and His Circle* (1922), and *Observations* (1925). He was knighted in 1939. His only novel, *Zuleika Dobson* (1911), is a satirical account of a visit to Oxford University by a beautiful woman, and her effect upon the students; in *A Christmas Garland* (1912) he presents a series of parodies of contemporary writers; his essay collections include *The Happy Hypocrite* (1897), *More* (1899), *And Even Now* (1920), *Variety of Things* (1928), and *Mainly on the Air* (1947). Author also of *Seven Men* and *The Dreadful Dragon of Hay Hill.*

Beerenberg (bār′ẹn.bėrg). See under **Jan Mayen.**

Beer Hall Putsch (pu̇ch). Name given to an abortive attempt to overthrow the Bavarian government, made at Munich by Adolf Hitler and a group of his followers on Nov. 9, 1923. Hitler was arrested and imprisoned after the failure of this effort to achieve a coup d'état, but the organization of the Nazi party was not seriously interfered with as a result of it. The *putsch*, despite its ignominious outcome, was later treated as an episode of almost heroic proportions by the historians of the Nazi party.

Beer-Hofmann (bār′hōf′män), **Richard.** b. at Vienna, July 11, 1866; d. at New York, Sept. 26, 1945. Austrian poet, playwright, and novelist. He was a member of the *Jung-Wien* (Young-Vienna) group of writers, and a well-known representative of the neo-romantic movement in the Austrian drama. The most important of his works are the play *Der Graf von Charolais* (The Count of Charolais, 1904) and the verse drama *Jaakobs Traum* (Jacob's Dream, 1918). His poem *Schlaflied für Mirjam* (Lullaby for Miriam, 1898) has been widely anthologized.

Beernaert (bār′närt), **Auguste Marie François.** b. at Ostend, Belgium, July 26, 1829; d. at Lucerne, Switzerland, Oct. 6, 1912. Belgian statesman. He was minister of labor (1873-78), minister of agriculture (1884), and subsequently minister of finance and president of the national council. Head of the Catholic party, he initiated various reforms in taxation, promoted the interests of the Congo state, and supported the claims of the Flemish people, as against the Walloons, in Belgium. In 1894 he resigned, but acted as president (1895-1900) of the Chamber of Deputies. He was a member of the peace conferences at The Hague in 1899 and 1907, and in 1909 was a joint recipient of the Nobel prize for his services in the cause of peace.

Beers (birz), **Clifford Whittingham.** b. at New Haven, Conn., March 30, 1876; d. 1943. American founder of the mental hygiene movement. A graduate of the Sheffield Scientific School of Yale University, he was in business at New York until 1906, when he suffered a mental breakdown. He was able to study his own case and the steps toward his recovery, and in 1908 he published *A Mind that Found Itself*, a book which subsequently went through many editions. In that same year he founded the Connecticut Society for Mental Hygiene, the first such organization anywhere in the world. In 1909 he formed the National Committee for Mental Hygiene and became its secretary. In 1923 he visited Britain, France, and Belgium, interesting many influential leaders, including King Albert and Cardinal Mercier of Belgium, in the subject of mental hygiene. Following the establishment in 1928 of the American Foundation for Mental Hygiene, of which he remained secretary until his death, he organized and served as secretary general of the first International Congress on Mental Hygiene, held in the U.S. in 1930. In that year he also established the International Committee for Mental Hygiene, and in 1931 he set up the International Foundation for Mental Hygiene, becoming secretary of both of these groups. In 1933 the government of France made Beers a chevalier of the Legion of Honor, and the National Institute of Social Sciences awarded him a gold medal "for distinguished services for the benefit of mankind."

Beers, Ethel Lynn. [Maiden name, **Ethelinda Eliot.**] b. at Goshen, Orange County, N.Y., Jan. 13, 1827; d. at Orange, N.Y., Oct. 11, 1879. American poet. She is best known as the author of the poem "All Quiet Along the Potomac," which originally appeared in *Harper's Weekly* for Nov. 30, 1861, under the title "The Picket Guard"; it was reprinted in *All Quiet Along the Potomac, and Other Poems* (1879).

Beers, Henry Augustin. b. at Buffalo, N.Y., Jan. 2, 1847; d. Sept. 7, 1926. American man of letters, appointed professor of English at the Sheffield Scientific School of Yale University in 1880. He edited *A Century of American Literature* (1878), and wrote *Sketch of English Literature* (1886), *Nathaniel Parker Willis* (1885, in the *American Men of Letters* series), and others.

Beersheba (bir.shē′bạ, bir′shē.bạ). Subdistrict of the Gaza district in SW Palestine, in Israel: a very dry, flat to hilly area where the chief occupations are subsistence farming from irrigated oases and migratory herding. Capital, Beersheba; area, 4,855 sq. mi.

Beersheba. [Hebrew, **B'eyr Sheva'**; Arabic, **Bir-es-Saba, Bir-es-Seba.**] Town in Israel, ab. 44 mi. SW of Jerusalem. It was referred to in the Old Testament as a seat of idolatry (Amos, v. 5; viii. 14), and was reinhabited after the return from the captivity (Neh. xi. 27). In the period of the Roman Empire it was the seat of a garrison, and later of a bishopric. It was mentioned in the Middle Ages, and was then identified with the ruins surrounding seven large wells called by the Arabs Bir-es-Saba, "Well of Seven" or "Well of the Oath." It is one of the oldest places in Palestine. Because it was at the S extremity of ancient Palestine, it is familiar in the phrase "from Dan to Beersheba," that is, from one end of the land to the other. British forces won a victory over the Turks here in 1917. Pop. 8,300 (1950).

Beeskow (bā′skō). Town in NE Germany, in the *Land* (state) of Brandenburg, Russian Zone, formerly in the province of Brandenburg, Prussia, situated on the Spree River, ab. 43 mi. SE of Berlin: small industries; agricultural trade. Medieval town walls are preserved; the

Marienkirche (Church of Mary), in the Gothic style, dates from the 13th century. The population is predominantly Protestant. 7,571 (1946).

Beeston (bēs′tǫn), Sir **William.** b. at Tichfield, Hampshire, England, 1636; fl. 1693–1702. British colonial administrator. While lieutenant governor of Jamaica (1693–1702) he resisted, as commander in chief, an attempted French invasion (1694); for refusing to account for money he allegedly appropriated, he was superseded (1702). He left topographical and other manuscripts.

Beeston and Stapleford (stā′pl.fǫrd). Urban district and small manufacturing town in N central England, in Nottinghamshire, situated near the river Trent, ab. 3 mi. SW of Nottingham, ab. 123 mi. N of London by rail. Beeston has small manufactures of lace, and is a satellite of Nottingham. The district has developed rapidly in recent years. 48,849 (1951).

Beethoven (bā′tō.vẹn), **Ludwig van.** b. at Bonn, Prussia, probably Dec. 16, 1770 (although through some confusion in the birth registry, Beethoven himself believed for a time that he was born in 1772); d. at Vienna, March 26, 1827. German composer, considered by many to have been the greatest composer in the history of music. He was the eldest surviving son of a tenor singer attached to the chapel of the electoral archbishop of Cologne, in a family which may be traced to a 17th century origin in a village near Louvain, Belgium (hence the "van" in his name; it is not a sign of nobility, as some have thought). The father had some knowledge of both violin and piano, and gave Ludwig lessons on both. In 1778 the teaching was taken over by the court organist, in 1779 by a singer (and friend of his father) newly arrived from Berlin, and some two years after this by Christian Gottlieb Neefe, successor as court organist to Beethoven's first teacher. Neefe was a very competent musician, composer, and director; that he recognized the talent of his young pupil is evidenced by a statement he published in 1783: "This young genius deserves help, to enable him to travel. He will certainly be a second Mozart, if he goes on as he has begun." From this time until 1792 Beethoven filled various positions, including that of teacher, court organist, and (in orchestra rehearsals) a place at the piano which was equivalent at that time to the position of conductor today. In November, 1792, Beethoven was sent at the elector's expense to study music under Haydn at Vienna. It was in this city, in 1795, that he may be said to have begun what is often called "the First Period" of his career as a composer, and from that time on each year brought wider recognition of his greatness. In 1802 his deafness, which had caused him some trouble since c1798, began to be really serious. In 1814 lawsuits and other anxieties commenced, and these difficulties on top of his deafness (which was by that time total), clouded all his later years. An attempt to conduct in 1822 proved a complete failure, and in 1824 occurred one of the most pathetic and moving incidents in the history of any composer's life: at the close of the first performance of his great Ninth Symphony, the audience broke into a storm of applause which shook the concert hall; however, Beethoven, who had shared the platform with the conductor, was now so deaf he could not hear it, and had to be turned around to see with his eyes the acclaim his ears could no longer detect. Two years later, on Dec. 2, 1826, his last illness began.

The First Period. This span of Beethoven's career as a composer is generally accepted as extending from 1795, the year of the three Trios dedicated to Haydn, until the end of 1802, when the *Pastoral* Sonata and the String Quintet (Op. 29) appeared, and the Violin Sonatas (Op. 30) were in course of publication. Beethoven still showed at the beginning of this period little indication of the enormous impact he was to have on music; the first unmistakable revelation of the revolutionary Beethoven is found in the *Sonate Pathétique*. Familiarity has blinded many of us to the originality of this work, but at the time of its composition this was evident to all. With the six String Quartets (Op. 18) we see a sureness and imagination so obvious that there can no longer be question of dependence on the past, and the certainty of mind which he had now acquired gave him the courage to attempt the more crucial task of writing a symphony. In the First Symphony (Op. 21) we have the first of those nine universally acclaimed works which provide the surest evidence of Beethoven's greatness.

The Second Period. This period is usually considered to have begun with Op. 31. It includes by far the greater volume of his whole work, and represents him at the very height of his confidence in his revolutionary principles of music. The Second Symphony (Op. 36) was finished before the end of 1802 and belongs to the period of transition, but the Third Symphony (the *Eroica*, Op. 55), finished in August, 1804, is wholly representative not only of the second period but of the prophet of the new faith. (It is this symphony which was, according to most accounts, originally dedicated to Napoleon. The story is told that when Beethoven heard that Napoleon had so completely surrendered his democratic ideals as to have himself proclaimed emperor, he (Beethoven) tore off the title page in a fury, saying: "He is no better than other men.") The Fourth Symphony (Op. 60), completed in 1806, is one of the most serene of Beethoven's works, but now also one of the least popular of his symphonies with most listeners. The Fifth Symphony (Op. 67), which was begun in 1805 and finished in 1808, is unquestionably the most popular orchestral work ever written. So far as it may be characterized in the few words which space here permits, it may be said that it represents a more kinetic, affirmative sense of exalted human purpose even than the *Eroica*. (It gained in modern times, during World War II, even greater currency through the use of its opening phrase as a radio signal used by the Allies to reach the various underground movements on the Continent.) The *Pastoral* Symphony (Op. 68) is the sixth of Beethoven's symphonic works, and expresses his deep love of nature. The Seventh Symphony (Op. 92), completed in 1812, is perhaps the most enigmatic of Beethoven's symphonic works. It is now generally considered to indicate the changing mental attitude of the composer in the year of its composition, and this is confirmed to some extent by the Eighth Symphony (Op. 93), which was also written in 1812, and which reveals a subject or idea clearly no longer epic in breadth.

The Third Period. In 1812 there occurred a very definite change in Beethoven's creative activity, which may be attributable in large part to personal difficulties of various kinds. However, it was in this third and last period that he produced the Ninth Symphony (Op. 125), employing some six years (1817–23) to complete what was for the composer perhaps the most important project of his life. The *Finale* of this work, for the first time since the symphony had become a purely instrumental form, employs a chorus; and the text is that of Schiller's *Ode to Joy*, which Beethoven had determined many years before, while still a boy at Bonn, to set someday to music. The first three movements are in the nature of a prologue to this imposing *Finale*. There has been much debate as to the success of this last movement. Undoubtedly Beethoven demands too much of the voices; undoubtedly the movement is too long. But when all is said and done, the symphony remains still the most colossal effort of its kind in the 19th century, and an eloquent revelation of the undying human sympathies of its creator. However, many critics believe that the noblest music of all is to be found in the last Quartets (Op. 130 to 135), in which the whole later development of 19th-century music seems to be foreshadowed. That freedom of form toward which Beethoven was striving in the last Piano Sonatas seems in these works to be fully attained. Each idea seems to create its own form; and while the listener's effort in adjusting his expectations to a constantly changing musical order is at first so great that the music seems hardly intelligible, repeated experience only increases our certainty that in these Quartets Beethoven has attained the highest ambition of the creative artist: to make form and thought indissoluble.

Beethoven Quartet. [Also, **Beethoven Quintet.**] Ensemble founded (1873) at Boston by Charles N. Allen, violinist, with Wulf Fries, cellist, Gustave Dannreuther, and H. Heindl. It was active for 20 years.

Beethoven Society. Mixed choral group organized (1873) at Chicago with Carl Wolfsohn as conductor; it was active until 1884.

Beets (bāts), **Nikolaas.** [Pseudonym, **Hildebrand.**] b. at Haarlem, Netherlands, Sept. 13, 1814; d. at Utrecht, Netherlands, March 14, 1903. Dutch poet. His works include the poems *Kuser* (1835), *Ada van Holland* (1840), *Korenbloemen* (1853), and *Guy de Vlaming* (1857); among his prose writings are *Camera Obscura* (1839), *Verscheidenheden* (1858), and *Stichtelijke Uren* (1848–60).

Beeville (bē′vil). City in S Texas, county seat of Bee County, NW of Corpus Christi: center of a petroleum area. 9,348 (1950).

Befana (bā.fä′nä), **the.** In Italian folklore, an old woman who is a sort of Santa Claus, but sometimes also a means of frightening children who have misbehaved. She is the good fairy who fills the children's stockings with presents on Twelfth Night, or the feast of the Epiphany, Jan. 6. If the children have been naughty she fills the stockings with ashes or coals; but she is compassionate, and will sometimes relent and return to comfort the little penitents with gifts. Tradition says that she was too busy sweeping to come to the window to see the Three Wise Men of the East when they passed by on their way to offer homage to the newborn Saviour, but said she could see them when they came back. For this lack of reverence she was duly punished, as they went back another way and she has been watching ever since. At one time her effigy was carried about the streets on the eve of the Epiphany, but the custom has now fallen into disuse. She has also sometimes been used as a bugbear by Italian mothers. The name is a corruption of *Epiphania* (Epiphany), the feast on which she makes her appearance.

Before Adam. Novel by Jack London, published in 1906.

Before the Bombardment. Novel by Sir Osbert Sitwell, published in 1926.

Before the Curfew. Volume (1887) of verse by Oliver Wendell Holmes.

Béfort (bā.fôr). See **Belfort.**

Beg (beg), **Callum.** Minor character in Sir Walter Scott's novel *Waverley*, the foot-page of Fergus MacIvor, in the service of Waverley.

Bega (bā′gä). [Also, **Begeiski.**] River and canal in W Rumania, in Banat province, a tributary of the Tisza River.

Bega (bē.gä′), **El.** See **Bika, El.**

Begas (bā′gäs), **Karl.** b. at Heinsberg, near Aachen, Germany, Sept. 30, 1794; d. at Berlin, Nov. 24, 1854. German painter of historical subjects and portraits who studied at Paris and in Italy. He was court painter to the king of Prussia, and professor at the Berlin Academy. He began as a Nazarene (or German Pre-Raphaelite), went on to paint in the romantic vein, and ended by painting realistically. *Christ on the Mount of Olives* is among his best-known works.

Begas, Karl. b. at Berlin, Nov. 23, 1845; d. at Köthen, Germany, Feb. 2, 1916. German sculptor; son of the painter Karl Begas (1794–1854) and youngest brother and pupil of Reinhold Begas (1831–1911). His combination of baroque trends with a gentle naturalism followed the artistic tradition of his family. He is known for his portrait busts and figure groups; among the latter, his best-known work is *Silenus with Young Bacchus.*

Begas, Oskar. b. at Berlin, July 31, 1828; d. there, Nov. 10, 1883. German historical and portrait painter, son of Karl Begas (1794–1854).

Begas, Reinhold. b. July 15, 1831; d. Aug. 3, 1911. German sculptor, son of Karl Begas (1794–1854). In Berlin he studied under Christian Daniel Rauch; later he studied also in Italy. A Schiller memorial, *Mercury and Psyche,* and *Borussia,* all at Berlin, are among his most notable works. He also did portrait busts of Helmuth von Moltke, Alexander von Humboldt, and several of the Hohenzollerns.

Begbie (beg′bi), **Harold.** [Pseudonym, **A Gentleman With a Duster.**] b. at Fornham St. Martin, Suffolk, England, 1871; d. Oct. 8, 1929. English novelist, journalist, and biographer. He was at various times on the staffs of the *Daily Chronicle, Globe, Times,* and *Daily Mail.* Author of *The Handy Man* (1900), *The Fall of the Curtain* (1901), *Master Workers* (1905), *The Priest* (1906), *The Cage* (1909), *Broken Earthenware* (1909; American title, *Twice-Born Men,* 1910), *Souls in Action* (1911), *The Distant Lamp* (1912), *The Ordinary Man and the Extraordinary Thing* (1912), *The Rising Dawn* (1913), *The Ways of Laughter* (1921), *Punishment and Personality* (1927), *Black Rent* (1928), and biographies of Kitchener (1915) and William Booth (1920). Other novels by him are *The Vigil* (1907), *The Challenge* (1911), *Millstone* (1915), and *The Convictions of Christopher Sterling* (1919); as "A Gentleman With a Duster" he wrote *Mirrors of Downing Street* (1920), *The Glass of Fashion* (1921), *The Conservative Mind* (1924), *The Great World* (1925), *The Howling Mob* (1927), an attack on democracy, and two novels, *Julius* (1927) and *The Laslett Affair* (1928). *Fighting Lines* (1914) is a volume of poetry, and *Painted Windows* (1922) contains studies of contemporary religious figures.

Begeiski (be.gā′skē). See **Bega.**

Begg (beg), **Alexander.** b. at Quebec, Canada, July 19, 1840; d. 1898. Canadian pioneer and historian. Going west as a young man, he became one of the earliest settlers of the then remote region of Manitoba, where he established himself as a merchant. During the rebellion of 1869 he was an advocate of representative government. From 1878 to 1884 he served as deputy treasurer of the province of Manitoba. He was the author of *The Creation of Manitoba* (1871), *Ten Years in Winnipeg* (1879), the three-volume *History of the North-West* (1894–95), and also of *Dot It Down, A Story of the Saskatchewan,* and *A Practical Guide to Manitoba.*

Beggar of Bethnal Green (beth′nal), **The.** Comedy by J. Sheridan Knowles, produced in 1834. It was abridged from *The Beggar's Daughter of Bethnal Green* (1828), which was based on a popular ballad.

Beggar on Horseback. Satirical play by George S. Kaufman and Marc Connelly, with music by Deems Taylor, produced in 1924. Most critics consider it one of the most effective dream satires on the excessive regimentation sometimes characteristic of highly organized business.

Beggar's Bush, The. Tragicomedy by John Fletcher and others (William Rowley and Philip Massinger), performed at court in 1622 and printed in 1647. It was long popular. Several alterations have appeared: one, *The Royal Merchant,* an opera, in 1767, and another in 1815, under the title of *The Merchant of Bruges.*

Beggar's Daughter of Bethnal Green (beth′nal), **The.** Popular ballad preserved in Thomas Percy's *Reliques,* in *Ancient Poems,* and in other collections of old ballads. It is the story of "pretty Bessee," the daughter of "the Blind Beggar." The latter is in reality Henry, the son of Simon de Montfort, who assumes this disguise to escape the spies of King Henry III. Bessee is wooed by a merchant, an innkeeper, a gentleman, and a knight; all but the knight, however, say farewell to her on learning that her father is a beggar. The knight marries her, and her father reveals his true fortune and character at the wedding.

Beggars of Life. Autobiographical narrative by Jim Tully, published in 1924.

Beggar's Opera, The. Opera by John Gay, first produced at Lincoln's Inn Fields, London, on Jan. 29, 1728. It is said to have been suggested by a remark of Jonathan Swift to Gay "that a Newgate pastoral might make . . . a pretty sort of thing." Gay was also said to have been induced to produce this opera from spite at having been offered an unacceptable appointment at court. It was intended as a satire on the elaborate style, dealing always with wealthy and highborn characters, then recently imported from Italy. Its great success led a wit to remark that the work had "made Gay rich, and Rich, gay" (John Rich was manager of the theater at Lincoln's Inn Fields). The songs were written for popular English and Scottish tunes, and were arranged and scored by John Christopher Pepusch, who composed the overture. The characters are highwaymen, pickpockets, and like characters, satirizing the corrupt political conditions of the day. The satire was blunt enough so that there was some danger that *The Beggar's Opera* might be closed by Robert Walpole, who was the British prime minister at the time and one of the characters attacked in it; this did not happen, but *Polly,* a sequel written in 1729, was shut at the order of the lord chamberlain. *The Beggar's Opera* served as the basis for the modern *Dreigroschen Oper* by Bert Brecht and Kurt Weill, and *Beggar's Holiday* by John Latouche and Duke Ellington.

Beggar's Ride, The. Tragedy in six scenes, by Edward Shanks, published in 1926.

Beghards (beg'ąrdz). See **Beguins.**

Bègles (begl). Town in SW France, in the department of Gironde, situated on the left bank of the Gironde River, S of Bordeaux. It belongs to the suburban region of Bordeaux and has various industries. 22,590 (1946).

Bégon (bā.gôṅ), **Michel.** b. at Blois, France, 1638; d. at Rochefort, France, March 4, 1710. French magistrate and administrator. He was a naval officer and, successively, intendant of the French West Indies, of Canada, and of Rochefort and La Rochelle. He was noted for his love of science, and the genus of plants *Begonia* was named in his honor.

Beg-Shehr (bā.sher'). See **Beyşehir.**

Begtrup (bek'trůp), **Bodil Locher.** b. at Nyborg, Denmark, Nov. 12, 1903—. Danish political leader and diplomat, minister (1948 *et seq.*) to Iceland. She has also been (1939–48) national film censor. She is a leader in the Danish women's movement and has represented Denmark at sessions of the League of Nations and United Nations.

Béguine (bā.gēn), **Michel Léonard.** b. at Uxeau, Saône-et-Loire, France, Aug. 9, 1855; d. in April, 1929. French sculptor. His statues and monuments generally follow an academic style; among them are an allegorical statue (1899) representing Greek art, on the façade of the Grand Palais on the Champs Elysées, Paris, and the monument (1899) to the painter Jean Baptiste Camille Corot at the Père Lachaise cemetery, Paris. He exhibited at the Paris Salon, and at Chicago, St. Louis, and Brussels.

Beguines (beg'inz). [Also, **Beguins.**] Name given to the members of various religious communities of women who, professing a life of poverty and self denial, went about in coarse gray clothing (of undyed wool), reading the Scriptures and exhorting the people. They originated in the 12th or 13th century, and flourished for centuries in Germany, the Netherlands, France, and Italy. Communities of the type (called *beguinages*) still exist in Belgium and the Netherlands.

Beguins (beg'inz). [Also, **Beghards.**] Community of men founded on the same general principle of life as that of the female religious communities of the Beguines. They were condemned as heretics by Pope John XXII in the early part of the 14th century. The faithful Beguins thereupon joined themselves in numbers with the different orders of friars. The sect, generally obnoxious to, and the object of severe measures by the established Church, had greatly diminished by the following century, but continued to exist till perhaps the beginning of the 16th century.

Behaghel (bę.hä'gęl), **Otto.** b. at Karlsruhe, Germany, May 3, 1854; d. at Munich, Oct. 9, 1936. German philologist, editor of *Germania* and *Literaturblatt für germanische und romanische Philologie*, and of the *Heliand* and Heinrich von Veldeke's *Eneït*, both medieval epics. Among his original works, the *Geschichte der deutschen Sprache* (1898) and *Deutsche Syntax* (1923–28) are usually considered to be the most important.

Behaim (bā'hīm), **Martin.** [Also: **Behem, Boeheim, Böheim.**] b. at Nuremberg, about the middle of the 15th century; d. at Lisbon, July 29, 1506. Navigator and cosmographer. He was in the service (c1484 *et seq.*) of Portugal, taking part in the expedition (1484) of Diogo Cam and others on the African coast. He was a friend of Christopher Columbus. The Nuremberg globe, still preserved in that city, was constructed by him in 1492, during a visit to his family, and is interesting as showing the idea of the world entertained by the first cosmographers, just previous to the discovery of America. Behaim was one of the inventors of the astrolabe.

Behaim, Michael. b. at Sulzbach, Germany, 1416; d. there, 1474. German Meistersinger.

Béhal (bā.àl), **Auguste.** b. at Lens, France, 1859; d. at Mennecy, France, 1941. French organic chemist. He investigated the complex acetylenic hydrocarbons, camphoric compounds, glycol and phenyl ethers, B-diketones, and other compounds. His introduction of thionyl chloride for making acid chlorides is of considerable importance in organic chemistry. Professor at the École de Pharmacie (1905–35).

Beham (bā'häm), **Barthel.** b. at Nuremberg, Germany, 1502; d. at Venice, 1540. German engraver and painter, one of the "Little Masters"; brother of Hans Sebald Beham. He served as court painter at Munich.

Beham, Hans Sebald. b. at Nuremberg, Germany, c1500; d. at Frankfort on the Main, Germany, 1550. German painter and engraver, one of the "Little Masters"; brother of Barthel Beham. Among his notable works are a series of *Village Weddings*, a group of religious miniatures for prayer books, and scenes from the life of David (painted on a table top).

Behar (bę.här'). See **Bihar.**

Behechio (bā.e.chē'ō). d. c1502. Indian cacique of Xaraguá, on the island of Hispaniola, at the time of its discovery by Christopher Columbus. In 1495 he joined his brother-in-law, Caonabo, and other chieftains in war against the Spaniards. After the defeat of the Indians at the battle of the Vega Real (April 25, 1495) he retired to his own province, where he ruled conjointly with his sister, Anacáona. Influenced by her, he made peace with the brother of Christopher Columbus, Bartholomew Columbus, in 1498.

Beheim-Schwarzbach (bā'bīm.shvärts'bäch), **Martin.** b. at London, April 27, 1900—. German author. Among his works are *Lorenz Schaarmanns unzulängliche Busse* (1928), *Der kleine Moltke und die Rapierkunst* (1929), and the story of a children's crusade on the Lüneburg Heath, *Die Michaelskinder* (1930).

Beheira (be.hā'rą). Province of Lower Egypt, NE Africa, in the N end of the delta W of the Rosetta Branch of the Nile River, NE of Alexandria. Capital, Damanhur; settled area, 1,719 sq. mi.; pop. 1,242,487 (1947).

Behem (bā'hem), **Martin.** See **Behaim, Martin.**

Behind the Veil. Volume of poems (1863) by Roden B. W. Noel. In his poems Noel expresses the transition from pessimistic realism to religious faith.

Behistun (bā.his.tön'). [Also: **Bisitun, Bisutun;** ancient name, **Baghistan.**] Town in W Iran, ab. 23 mi. E of the city of Kermanshah: a trading center. It is the site of a monument of Darius the Great, called the "Rosetta Stone of Asia," consisting of bas-reliefs and trilingual inscriptions on the face of a high cliff. The inscriptions, deciphered (c1840) by Sir Henry Rawlinson, provided the first key to ancient Assyrian writings.

Behm (bām), **Ernst.** b. at Gotha, Germany, Jan. 4, 1830; d. there, March 15, 1884. German geographer and statistician. He was an editor of *Petermann's Mitteilungen* (from 1856; editor in chief after 1878), of the statistical parts of the *Almanac de Gotha*, and of the *Geographisches Jahrbuch* (1866–78).

Behmen (bā'męn), **Jakob.** See **Böhme** or **Böhm** or **Behmen, Jakob.**

Behn (bān), **Aphra** or **Afra** or **Aphara.** [Maiden name, **Johnson.**] b. at Wye, Kent, England, 1640; d. at London, April 16, 1689. English dramatic writer and novelist. She was the daughter of a barber, John Johnson, and wife of a Dutch merchant named Behn, who died before 1666. After her husband's death she served as a spy for the British government, at Antwerp; later, far from being rewarded by her government, she was imprisoned for debt. In her youth she spent several years in Surinam, where she made the acquaintance of the chieftain who served as the model of her famous romance *Oroonoko, or The Royal Slave* (c1678). She wrote much, and is said to have been the first female writer who lived by her pen in England. Her writings are generally regarded as gay and witty, but marked by the earthy vulgarity, if not actual coarseness, of the period. Among her dramatic works are *The Forc'd Marriage* (1671), *The Amorous Prince* (1671), *The Dutch Lover* (1673), *Abdelazar* (1677), *The Rover* (1677), *The Debauchee* (1677), *The Town Fop* (1677), and *The False Count* (1682). She also published *Poems* (1684).

Behncke (bāng'kę), **Paul L. Gustav.** b. at Süsel, Germany, Aug. 13, 1866—. German naval commander. He led a squadron in the Battle of Jutland (May 31, 1916) and in an attack on the Baltic islands. As chief of naval affairs in the war ministry (1920–24), he organized a new German fleet.

Behold the Bridegroom. Play (1927) by George Kelly.

Behr (bār), **Wilhelm Joseph.** b. at Sulzheim, Germany, Aug. 26, 1775; d. at Bamberg, Germany, Aug. 1, 1851. German publicist and liberal politician. He was professor of public law (1799–1821) at the University of Würzburg, and was twice elected to the Bavarian diet. He suffered imprisonment (1833–48) for alleged lese majesty, and became a member of the Frankfort parliament in 1848.

Behram (be.räm') or **Behramköy** (be.räm.kė'i). Modern Turkish names of **Assos.**

Behrend (bãr'ẹnd), **Bernard Arthur.** b. at Villeneuve, Switzerland, May 9, 1875; committed suicide March 25, 1932. American electrical engineer and inventor of electrical devices. As a consulting engineer of Allis-Chalmers Company, advisory engineer for Westinghouse Company, and chief engineer for Bullock Electric Manufacturing Company, he designed or invented many electric devices. Author of *The Induction Motor—Its Theory and Design* (1900), *Engineering Education* (1907), and *The Work of Oliver Heaviside* (1928).

Behrends (bãr'ẹndz), **Adolphus Julius Frederick.** b. at Nijmegen, Netherlands, Dec. 18, 1839; d. May 22, 1900. American clergyman, writer, and lecturer. He was a member of the Baptist ministry (1865–76) and the Congregational ministry (1876 *et seq.*). Author of *Counting the Cost* (1881), *The World For Christ* (1896), *The Old Testament Under Fire* (1897), and *Sursum Corda, a Book of Praise* (1898).

Behrendt (bā'rẹnt), **Walter Curt.** b. 1884; d. 1945. German art historian and critic, particularly of modern architecture. After being for some years associated with the Prussian ministry of finance as an adviser on architecture and building, he came to the U.S. in 1934 and became a member of the faculty of Dartmouth College at Hanover, N.H. He was the author of *Alfred Messel* (1910), *Der Sieg des neuen Baustils* (1927), *Die holländische Stadt* (1928), and *Modern Building* (1937).

Behrens (bãr'ẹnz), **Henry.** b. at Munstadt, Hanover, Germany, Dec. 10, 1815; d. Oct. 17, 1895. American Jesuit priest. Forced to flee (1847) from Switzerland during the persecution of the Jesuits, he voyaged first to America, but returned to Europe and took up work in Germany until the Jesuits were expelled from that country. He arrived (1872) at Buffalo, N.Y., where he was superior (1872–78, 1886–92) of a mission; he also founded (1886) St. Ignatius College (now John Carroll University) at Cleveland, Ohio.

Behrens (bā'rẹns), **Peter.** b. at Hamburg, Germany, April 14, 1868; d. at Berlin, Feb. 27, 1940. German architect and artist, one of the pioneers of modern architecture. Striving for monumental form, he developed his principles from decorative and applied arts, moving toward a moderate functionalism. Most typical of his work are the buildings of the AEG (1910) at Berlin, one of the first modern industrial plants, and the German embassy building (1912; now demolished) at Leningrad. He was director (1903–07) of the *Kunstgewerbeschule* (Academy of Applied Arts) at Düsseldorf, Germany, and later taught architecture at the academies of Düsseldorf, Vienna, and Berlin.

Behring (bā'ring), **Emil von.** b. at Hansdorf, Germany, March 15, 1854; d. at Marburg, Germany, March 31, 1917. German physiologist, appointed (1895) professor of hygiene and director of the hygienic institute at Marburg. In 1890 he announced his discovery of the antidiphtheria serum, and from that time on devoted himself chiefly to the study of disease immunization. He received the Nobel prize for medicine in 1901. Among his works are *Die Blutserumtherapie* (1892), *Die Geschichte der Diphtherie* (1893), *Therapie der Infektionskrankheiten* (1899), and *Beiträge zur Experimentellen Therapie* (1900).

Behring, Vitus. See **Bering, Vitus.**

Behring Island (bir'ing, ber'-). See **Bering Island.**

Behring Sea. See **Bering Sea.**

Behring Strait. See **Bering Strait.**

Behrman (bãr'mạn), **Samuel Nathaniel.** b. at Worcester, Mass., June 9, 1893—. American playwright and scenarist. Graduate of Harvard (1916) and Columbia (1918). His plays, chiefly drawing-room comedies, include *The Second Man* (1927), *Serena Blandish* (1928; adapted from the novel by Enid Bagnold), *Meteor* (1929), *Brief Moment* (1932), *Biography* (1933), *Love Story* (1934), *End of Summer* (1936), *Wine of Choice* (1938), *No Time for Comedy* (1939), *The Talley Method* (1940), and *The Pirate* (1942). He has also been scenarist for such films as *Queen Christina* and *Tale of Two Cities*. *Duveen* (1951) is a biography of the art dealer Joseph Duveen, 1st Baron Duveen of Millbank.

Beïd (bā'id). The fourth-magnitude very white star *o* Eridani.

Beijerland (bī'ėr.länt). [Also: **Beyerland, Hoeksche-waard, Hoeksche Waard.**] Island in the province of South Holland, Netherlands, lying between the Oude Maas River and the Hollandsch Diep and Haringvliet channels.

Beila (bā'lạ). See **Bela.**

Beilan (bī.län'). See **Bailan.**

Beilan Pass. See **Cilician Gates.**

Beilngries (bīln'grēs). Small town in S Germany, in the *Land* (state) of Bavaria, American Zone, in the *Regierungsbezirk* (government district) of Middle and Upper Franconia, situated on the Ludwigscanal, near the Altmühl River, ab. 29 mi. W of Regensburg.

Beilstein (bīl'shtīn), **Friedrich Konrad.** b. at St. Petersburg, Russia, 1838; d. at Baden-Baden, Germany, 1906. Russian organic chemist. His *Handbuch der Organischen Chemie* (1881 *et seq.*), is still an indispensable reference work in organic chemistry. In 1900 its further compilation passed from Beilstein to the German Chemical Society. He was a professor at St. Petersburg (1866–81) and a member of the Russian Academy of Sciences (1881–1906).

Being a Boy. Collection of essays (1878) by Charles Dudley Warner.

Beinn an Oir (ben an oir'). See under **Jura, Paps of.**

Beir (bā'ėr). [Also: **Ajiba, Molen.**] Nilotic-speaking people of NE Africa, occupying an area in the S part of the province of Upper Nile, in the S Anglo-Egyptian Sudan. Linguistically and culturally they are closely related to the Didinga people of E Africa.

Beira (bā'rạ). Town in SE Africa, an important railway terminus and seaport in Mozambique, on the Mozambique Channel, ab. 100 mi. SW along the coast from the mouth of the Zambezi River. It serves as the port for Southern and Northern Rhodesia, and for Nyasaland protectorate, and is connected by rail with these places. The port exports sugar, cotton, maize, and rubber. It is also the administrative center of the province of Manica and Sofala. 12,988 (1940).

Beira. Region and former province in N central Portugal, subdivided in 1835 to form the modern provinces of Beira Alta, Beira Baixa, and Beira Litoral. The region was inhabited in ancient times by Celtic tribes, conquered by the Romans in the 2nd century B.C., and subsequently invaded by the Suevi, and later by the Goths. After a brief period of Moorish occupation, it was incorporated into Portugal in the 12th century. Later, parts of it were lost to Castile, but recovered in the 14th century. The region is traversed by the highest mountain range in Portugal (peak elevation, 6,533 ft.) and is largely mountainous and hilly. Principal products are wheat, wine, vinegar, olives, chestnuts, salt, marble, and beef cattle. Area, 9,216 sq. mi.; pop. 1,900,946 (1940).

Beira Alta (äl'tạ). Province of Portugal, bounded by Tráz-os-Montes e Alto Douro on the N, Douro Litoral on the NW, Beira Litoral on the SW, Beira Baixa on the S, and Spain on the E. It comprises the districts of Viseu and Guarda. A mountainous area, its chief products are cork oak, chestnuts, and wine. Capital, Viseu; area, ab. 4,050 sq. mi.; pop. 662,616 (1940).

Beira Baixa (bī'shạ). Province of Portugal, bounded by Beira Alta on the N, Beira Litoral and Ribatejo on the W, Alto Alentejo on the S, and Spain on the SE and E. Part of the Spanish border is formed by the river Tejo (or Tagus). The province contains the district of Castelo Branco. It is a thinly settled steppe country. Capital, Castelo Branco; area, 2,588 sq. mi.; pop. 334,788 (1940).

Beira Litoral (lē.tö.räl'). Province of Portugal, bounded by Douro Litoral on the N, Beira Alta and Beira Baixa on the E, Ribatejo and Estremadura on the S, and the Atlantic Ocean on the W. It is divided into the districts of Aveiro, Coimbra, and Leiria. Flat alluvial country along the coast, and hilly farther inland, it has fertile soils and is richly cultivated. Capital, Coimbra; area, ab. 3,920 sq. mi.; pop. 896,719 (1940).

Beiram (bī.räm'). See **Bairam.**

Beira Railway (bā'rạ). Railway in SE Africa, running from Beira, Mozambique, to the Southern Rhodesia frontier at Umtali. As the Beira-Mashonaland railway, it was begun in 1891 under a 99-year concession from Portugal. At Umtali the railway is connected with the Southern Rhodesia railway system and by the latter with Northern Rhodesia and the Belgian Congo to the N, and with the Union of South Africa to the S. Distance to points in Southern Rhodesia: Umtali, 204 mi.; Salisbury, 374 mi.; Bulawayo, 674 mi. The railway has been the incentive for the development of the port of Beira and provides the mining regions of the interior with an outlet to the markets of the world.

Beirut (bā.röt'). [Also: **Bairut, Beyrout;** French, **Beyrouth;** ancient name, **Berytus.**] Capital and chief city and port of Lebanon, situated on the Mediterranean Sea, ab. 80 mi. N of Haifa. Also the chief seaport for Syria, it has a considerable commerce with Great Britain, France, Egypt, and other countries. It was an ancient Phoenician town, and later a Roman colony (Augusta Felix), a noted seat of learning under the later empire, twice devastated by earthquakes. The Crusaders held it for many years; later it was occupied by Druses. It was conquered from the Turks by a Russian fleet in 1772, was held by the Egyptians in 1840, and was bombarded by the British fleet (Sept. 10–14). It is the seat of an American and a French university. Exports include fruits and vegetables, madder, silk, wool, olive oil, tobacco, and gums. 201,451 (est. 1949).

Beisan (bā.sän'). [Also: **Baisan;** in the Old Testament, **Beth-shean** or **Beth-shan;** ancient Greek name, **Scythopolis.**] Town in NE Palestine, in Israel, ab. 4 mi. W of the Jordan River and ab. 55 mi. NE of Jerusalem: a trading center served by a railway and three highways. It was one of the ten cities of the Decapolis and was captured by Joshua. Archaeological excavations here have produced finds dating from c1500 B.C. Pop. ab. 3,000.

Bei-Shehr (bā.sher'). See **Beyşehir.**

Beissel (bī'sel), **Johann Konrad.** [Religious name, **Father Friedsam.**] b. at Eberbach, Germany, 1690; d. at Ephrata, Pa., 1768. German baker, religious leader, and writer of hymns. He fled religious intolerance in his native Palatinate in 1720 and became, as Father Friedsam, the founder (c1730) and first prior of a brotherhood of Seventh-Day Baptists or German Dunkers at Ephrata on the Cocalico River in Pennsylvania.

Beit (bīt), **Alfred.** b. at Hamburg, Germany, 1853; d. July 16, 1906. British financier and South African diamond magnate. He went to Kimberley, South Africa, in 1875, acquired interests in the diamond fields of that region, and accumulated a great fortune. He was closely associated with Cecil Rhodes, and collaborated with him in amalgamating various diamond-mine interests to form De Beers Consolidated Mines, Ltd., in 1889. He was also one of the original directors of the British South Africa Company, and together with Rhodes was censured by the Commission of Inquiry set up by the British House of Commons to investigate the Jameson Raid. Under Cecil Rhodes's will, Alfred Beit and his brother, Sir Otto Beit, were named trustees to carry out Rhodes's South African bequests. Alfred Beit established a chair for colonial history at Oxford University, and at his death provided bequests of 200,000 pounds for the establishment of a university at Johannesburg, South Africa, and 100,000 pounds for a similar institution at his native city of Hamburg.

Beit-el-Fakih (bāt'el.fä'kē). [Also, **Bait al-Faqih.**] Town in Yemen, SW Arabian peninsula, near the Red Sea, ab. 80 mi. N of Mocha: noted for its coffee trade. Pop. ab. 8,000.

Beith (bēth). Civil parish and market town in S Scotland, in Ayrshire, ab. 7 mi. NE of Kilwinning, ab. 405 mi. N of London by rail. 5,977 (1931).

Beith, John Hay. [Pseudonym, **Ian Hay.**] b. at Manchester, England, April 17, 1876; d. at Petersfield, England, Sept. 22, 1952. English novelist and playwright. He served in the Argyll and Sutherland Highlanders with the British Expeditionary Force in World War I; he was also director (1938–41) of public relations at the British War Office during the early part of World War II. His early novels are *Pip* (1907), *The Right Stuff* (1908), *A Man's Man* (1909), and *A Safety Match* (1911), but he is better known for *Carrying On* (1917), *The Last Million* (1918), and *Paid, with Thanks* (1925); among his plays are *Tilly of Bloomsbury* (1919), *The Happy Ending* (1922), *Housemaster* (1936), and *Little Ladyship* (1939).

Beitin (bā.tēn'). Arabic name of **Bethel,** Palestine.

Beit Jibrin (bāt ji.brēn'). Arabic name of **Eleutheropolis.**

Beit Lahm (bāt' läm'). Arabic name of **Bethlehem,** Palestine.

Beit Likia (lē'kē.ạ). Arabic name of **Eltekeh.**

Beit Ur el-Fokha (ör' el.fō'ċhạ) and **Beit Ur el-Tahta** (-tä'tạ). Arabic names of **Beth-horon, Upper** and **Nether.**

Beitzke (bīts'kẹ), **Heinrich Ludwig.** b. at Muttrin, in Pomerania, Feb. 15, 1798; d. at Berlin, May 10, 1867. German historian. His works include *Geschichte der deutschen Freiheitskriege* (1855), *Geschichte des russischen Kriegs im Jahre 1812* (1856), *Geschichte des Jahres 1815* (1865), and others.

Beja (bā'zhạ). District in S Portugal, in the province of Baixo Alentejo. Capital, Beja; area, ab. 3,970 sq. mi.; pop. 288,411 (1950).

Beja. [Latin, **Pax Julia.**] City and *concelho* (commune) in S Portugal, capital of the province of Baixo Alentejo and of the district of Beja, ab. 85 mi. SE of Lisbon: center of a wheat-growing and livestock-raising region; trades in cork and olive oil, and has tanneries and majolica manufactures. It is the seat of a bishopric, with baroque and Renaissance churches; the Chapel of Santo Amaro is an ancient Latin basilica. There is a remarkable medieval castle. The archaeological museum contains Roman, Visigothic, and Moorish antiquities. Once a Roman colony, it was later under Visigothic and Arab domination; it passed to the crown of Portugal in 1102. Pop. of concelho, 42,113 (1940); of city, 14,745 (1940).

Béja (bā.zhȧ). [Ancient name, **Vacca.**] Town in N Africa, in Tunisia, ab. 70 mi. from Tunis, with which it is connected by rail. It is situated in the middle of the very fertile Medjerda valley and is the commercial center for the surrounding rich agricultural area. Pop. 22,208, including 1,832 Europeans (1946).

Beja (bā'jạ). [Also, **To-Bedawie.**] Group of predominantly Caucasoid peoples of NE Africa, inhabiting a region between the Nile and the Red Sea in SE Egypt, NE Anglo-Egyptian Sudan, and N Eritrea. By certain of the older sources they are classified as Hamitic. Their combined population may be estimated at more than 150,000, including the Abadba, Amarar, Beni-Amer, Bisharin, Hadendowa, and other subgroups. The Amarar, Bisharin, and Hadendowa speak a Cushitic language; the Beni-Amer speak both a Cushitic and a Semitic language; while the Ababda have lost their Cushitic language and now speak Arabic. The Beja are nomadic or seminomadic pastoralists, whose herds include camels, cattle, and sheep. Although they were still pagan and matrilineal at the beginning of the 15th century, they have become fanatic Mohammedans.

Bejapur (bē.jä'půr). See **Bijapur.**

Béjar (bā'ʜär). Town in W Spain, in the province of Salamanca, situated in the Sierra de Béjar, ab. 47 mi. S of Salamanca: cloth manufacture. 12,518 (1940).

Béjart (bā.zhȧr). Name of a family of French comedians who played in Molière's comedies and belonged to his troupe. The best known were Armande and Madeleine.

Béjart, Armande. b. 1642; d. 1700. French actress; a member of the Béjart family of actors. She was brought up by Madeleine Béjart, whose sister she probably was. She played many leading parts in plays by Molière, whose wife she became in 1662. After his death she married Guérin d'Étriché, an actor, and carried on the management of Molière's acting troupe.

Béjart, Madeleine. b. 1618; d. 1672. French actress; a member of the Béjart family of actors, and probably the sister of Armande Béjart. She first met Molière c1640, and it is sometimes supposed that it was his attraction to her that made him become an actor. After returning (1658) to Paris after touring in the provinces, she took parts in many of Molière's plays, playing usually the part of a soubrette (a pert young woman, by tradition a lady's maid completely aware of, and able to exploit, her mistresses' follies).

Bek (bek). Architect of Ikhnaton (Amenhotep IV), king of Egypt. He supervised the building of the city which was the progenitor of the later Tel-el-Amarna. The inscription on his tombstone has been preserved and deciphered.

Bek, Antony. d. c1310. English prelate and commander. He was consecrated (c1285) bishop of Durham and joined Edward I in his expeditions (1296 and 1298) against Scotland. In the latter expedition he reduced the castle of Dirleton, and commanded the second division of the English in a battle at Falkirk, in S Scotland, on July 22, 1298.

Békásmegyer (bā'käsh.me.dyer). [German, **Krottendorf.**] Town in N central Hungary, a northwestern suburb of Budapest, situated on the right bank of the Danube River between Óbuda and Szentendre. 13,936 (1948).

Bek-Budi (bek.bö'di). Former name of **Karshi.**

Beke (bēk), **Charles Tilstone.** b. at Stepney, now part of London, Oct. 10, 1800; d. at London, July 31, 1874. English traveler and geographer. After traveling through Palestine, he explored Shoa and other regions of Ethiopia, returning via Massawa, and received, in 1846, a gold medal for his travels in Ethiopia. From 1847 to 1860 he published a series of works on the languages of Ethiopia and the sources of the Nile. He made a second expedition to Bible lands, and wrote several books on Bible geography.

Beke (bā'kẹ), **Joos van der.** See **Cleve** or **Cleef, Joos van.**

Békés (bā'kāsh). Town in E Hungary, situated at the junction of the Black and White Körös rivers, SE of Szolnok, in one of the richest agricultural regions of Hungary. 28,095 (1948).

Békéscsaba (bā'kāsh.chô'bô). [Also, **Csaba.**] City in E Hungary, S of the town of Békés. It is a station on the railroad line from Szolnok to Arad, has silk, hosiery, and pottery manufactures and flour mills, and produces sausages. The population is largely Slovakian in origin and Protestant in religion. 45,904 (1948).

Békés-Gyula (bā'kāsh.dyö'lô). See **Gyula.**

Bekhterev (byeн'tyi.rif), **Vladimir Mikhailovich.** b. at Ssarali, Russia, Jan. 20, 1857; d. at Moscow, Dec. 24, 1927. Russian neuropathologist. He studied at St. Petersburg, where he became (1878) a member of the staff of the psychiatric clinic and was named (1881) privatdocent of neurology and psychiatry; in 1884 he went to Leipzig, where he studied under W. M. Wundt and P. E. Flechsig; he also studied under J. M. Charcot at Paris. He became (1885) a full professor of psychiatry at Kazan, and in 1893 succeeded J. P. Mershjewsky at St. Petersburg, where he founded a psychoneurological institute which later became the Psychoneurological Academy. He perfected cerebral localization, classified insanity (1891), and contributed in the field of experimental psychology. He described the following: a layer of fibers in the cerebral cortex (called Bekhterev's fibers) in 1891, ankylosing spondylitis (called Bekhterev's disease) in 1892, the superior nucleus of the vestibular nerve (called Bekhterev's nucleus) in 1908, a reaction in tetany, also named for him, and various kinds of reflexes (all subsequently called Bekhterev's reflexes). He founded a number of scientific societies and journals and wrote *Die Leitungsbahnen im Gehirn und Rückenmark* (1894), *Die Bedeutung der Suggestion im socialen Leben* (1905), *Die Persönlichkeit und die Bedingungen ihrer Entwicklung und Gesundheit* (1906), *Die Grundlagen der Lehre von den Hirnfunktionen* (1908–11), *Psyche und Leben* (1908), *Das Verbrechertum im Lichte der objektiven Psychologie* (1914), and *General Principles of Human Reflexology* (1932). In his *Objektive Psychologie oder Psychoreflexologie* (1913), he applied the Pavlovian principles of the conditioned reflex to psychological problems. This work, through its direct influence on John B. Watson, influenced the development of behaviorism in the U.S.

Bekker (bek'ėr), **August Immanuel.** b. at Berlin, May 21, 1785; d. there, June 7, 1871. German classicist and philologist, professor of philology at Berlin. He edited critical editions of Plato, the Attic orators, Aristotle, Sextus Empiricus, Thucydides, Theognis, Aristophanes, Herodotus, Pausanias, Polybius, Livy, Tacitus, and other Greek writers, and also of Byzantine, Provençal, and old French authors. Author of *Anecdota graeca* (1814–21) and other works.

Bekker, Balthazar. b. at Metslanier, in Friesland, March 30, 1634; d. there, June 11, 1698. Dutch theologian. He was pastor (1679–92) of a Reformed congregation at Amsterdam. His book *De betoverde wereld* caused his dismissal from his pastorate on a charge of Cartesianism. In the book, he had expressed theories denying the actuality of demoniacal possession, along the same lines as those developed at a later date by the rationalists.

Bekker, Elisabeth. [Married name, **Wolff.**] b. at Vlissingen, Netherlands, July 24, 1738; d. at The Hague, Nov. 4, 1804. Dutch novelist; wife of Adrian Wolff. She wrote (conjointly with Agatha Deken) *De Historie van Mejuffrouw Sara Burgerhart* (1782), *De Historie van Willem Leevand* (1784), *Cornelia Wildschut* (1793–96), and others.

Bek Pak (bek pak). See **Golodnaya Step.**

Bekri (bek'rē), **al-.** See **Bakri, al-.**

Beku (bā'kö). One of the western pygmy groups of C Africa, inhabiting the province of Gabon in French Equatorial Africa.

Bekyinton (bek'ing.tọn), **Thomas.** See **Beckington, Thomas.**

Bel (bel). One of the most important of the ancient Babylonian gods, of Semitic origin, cognate with Baal. In the enumeration of the 12 great gods of Babylonia he holds the second place in the first triad. His importance in Babylonia was about the same as that of Baal among the Canaanites, but he had no solar character. To him is ascribed the creation of the world, and especially of mankind; thus, the kings called themselves "governors of Bel," and "rulers over Bel's subjects." He is also often entitled "father of the gods," and his spouse, Belit, is called "the mother of the great gods." It is Bel who brings about the deluge and destroys mankind. His name occurs in Isa. xlvi. 1, and Jer. 1, 2. The principal seat of his worship was Nippur, while the tutelar deity of the city of Babylon was Merodach (or Marduk), who is often called Bel-Merodach, or simply Bel, and is alluded to in the passages of the Old Testament cited above. Bel being known as the supreme god of Babylonia, Herodotus considered the great Nebo temple of Borsippa as that of Bel.

Bél (bāl), **Karl Andreas.** b. at Pressburg (now Bratislava, Czechoslovakia), July 13, 1717; d. at Leipzig, Germany, April 5, 1782. Hungarian historian. He was the author of *De vera origine et epocha Hunnorum, Avarorum,* and editor of the *Acta Eruditorum* and the *Leipziger gelehrte Zeitung* (1753–81).

Bél (or **Belius**), **Matthias.** b. at Ocsova, March 24, 1684; d. at Pressburg (now Bratislava, Czechoslovakia), Aug. 29, 1749. Hungarian historian. His works include *Hungariae prodromus, Adparatus ad historiam Hungariae,* and *Notitia Hungariae.*

Bela (bā'lạ). [Also, **Beila.**] Town in W Pakistan, the capital of the state of Las Bela, Baluchistan, ab. 110 mi. NW of the city of Karachi: trading center. Pop. ab. 4,000.

Béla I (bā'lô). King of Hungary (1061–63); member of the Árpád dynasty. He strengthened the royal authority, suppressed the last pagan uprising, and introduced financial and commercial reforms.

Béla II. King of Hungary (1131–41); member of the Árpád dynasty. He took away self-government from Bosnia, which had been acquired (1091) by Ladislas I.

Béla III. d. 1196. King of Hungary (c1172–96); member of the Árpád dynasty. He married a sister of Philip Augustus of France. He fought against Venice over possession of Dalmatia.

Béla IV. b. 1206; d. 1270. King of Hungary (1235–70); a member of the Árpád dynasty. His attempts to regain for Hungary some of the lands lost in the previous reign were frustrated by the devastating Mongol invasion under Batu Khan; this came to a halt on the death of Genghis Khan, but not before it had laid waste the entire country. He later, however, defeated (1246) Frederick of Austria, the last Babenberg duke, and carried on war with Ottokar II of Bohemia. His son succeeded him as Stephen V.

Beladori (bel.ä.dō'ri), **Abul Hassan Ahmed al-.** [Also, **Albeladory.**] d. at Baghdad, c895. Arab historian, author of a history of the conquest of Syria, Cyprus, Mesopotamia, Armenia, Egypt, Spain, Nubia, and the islands of the Mediterranean by the Arabs. He describes the condition of the conquered countries and various towns founded by the Moslems, among them Baghdad.

Bel Air (bel ãr'). Town in NE Maryland, county seat of Harford County, ab. 20 mi. NE of Baltimore in a rich farming section: commercial center. 2,578 (1950).

Béla Kun (bā'lô kön). See **Kun, Béla.**

Belalcázar (bā.läl.kä'thär), **Sebastián de.** See **Benalcázar, Sebastián de.**

Beland (bē'lạnd), **Henri Sévérin.** b. at Louisville, Quebec, Canada, 1869; d. at Eastview, near Kingston, Ontario, Canada, April 22, 1935. Canadian physician and legislator. Graduated (1893) from Laval University, he began (1897) his political career with his election to the Quebec legislative assembly. He served as a member of Canadian House of Commons, a cabinet minister, and a member of the Canadian senate.

Bel and the Dragon (bel). One of the books of the Apocrypha.

Belardo d'Ascoli (bā.lär'dō däs'kō.lē). [Also, **Belardus de Esculo** (bẹ.lär'dus dē es'kụ.lō).] fl. 1112–20. Italian ecclesiastic. He was the author of a Latin description of the Holy Land which has brought him mention, if not fame, in the history of geography as a science.

Belarius (bẹ.lãr'i.us). Banished lord disguised under the name of Morgan in Shakespeare's play *Cymbeline.* He steals Arviragus and Guiderius, Cymbeline's sons, out of revenge, passing them off, under false names, as his own sons. When Cymbeline is made prisoner by the Roman general, Belarius comes to his rescue, is reconciled, and restores the princes.

Belasco (bẹ.las'kō), **David.** b. at San Francisco, July 25, 1853; d. May 14, 1931. American producer and playwright, noted both for his effective staging techniques and for his ability to build and present successfully the talents of actors. After a period as stage manager (c1873) of Baldwin's Theater, Grand Opera House, and the Metropolitan Theater at San Francisco, he was stage manager (1880–87) of the Madison Square Theater at New York, and was subsequently manager of the Lyceum Theater and owner and manager of the Belasco Theater at New York. He featured E. H. Sothern in *Lord Chumley* (1887) and *Accused* (1925), Mrs. Leslie Carter in *The Heart of Maryland* (1895), Blanche Bates in *Naughty Anthony* (1899), David Warfield in *The Music Master* (1904) and *The Merchant of Venice* (1922), and Ina Claire in *The Gold Diggers* (1919). Author of *May Blossom* (1884), *Lord Chumley* (1887), *The Heart of Maryland* (1895), *The Girl of the Golden West* (1905), *The Return of Peter Grimm* (1911), and *Van der Decken* (1915); coauthor of *The Darling of the Gods* (1920), *Adrea* and *Laugh, Clown, Laugh* (1923), and *Fanny* (1926).

Bela-Slatina (byä'lä.slä'tē.nä). [Also, **Byala Slatina.**] Town in NW Bulgaria, in the department of Vratsa, situated on the Skota River, ab. 28 mi. NE of Vratsa. 9,357 (1946).

Belaúnde (bā.lä.ön'dā), **Víctor Andrés.** [Full name, **Víctor Andrés Belaúnde y Diez Canseco.**] b. at Arequipa, Peru, Dec. 15, 1883—. Peruvian diplomat, lawyer, and professor, notable as an exponent of Pan-American coöperation. He was a delegate (1945) to the United Nations Conference at San Francisco.

Belaya (bye'lạ.yạ). River in the W central part of the U.S.S.R., traversing the Bashkir Autonomous Soviet Socialist Republic, and joining the Kama River inside the NE corner of the Tatar Autonomous Soviet Socialist Republic, ab. 620 mi. E of Moscow. It rises in the S Urals, flows SW and W through the mountains, and then bends NW through a hilly region. The head of river navigation is at Sterlitamak. The Belaya is linked to the Volga waterway system by the Kama. Length, ab. 885 mi.; drainage basin area, ab. 55,000 sq. mi.

Belaya Tserkov (tser'kọf). [Also: **Bielatserkof, Bielaya-Tserkoff, Tserkov.**] City in the U.S.S.R., in the Ukrainian Soviet Socialist Republic, ab. 55 mi. S of Kiev by rail. It has extensive commerce. Pop. ab. 43,000.

Belbeis (bel.bās'). See **Bilbeis.**

Belbek (bel.bek'). Small river in the S part of the U.S.S.R., in the Crimean *oblast* (region) of the Russian Soviet Federated Socialist Republic, NE of Sevastopol.

Belch (belch), **Sir Toby.** Uncle of Olivia in Shakespeare's comedy *Twelfth Night;* he is a roistering knight, fond of drinking and singing, and not averse to promoting Malvolio's downfall.

Belchen (bel'ċhẹn). German word used as an element in the names of various summits of the Vosges (for example, Gebweiler Belchen). It is the equivalent of the French "ballon," which is now more generally used for these mountains (for example, Ballon de Guebwiller). It is a descriptive word in both languages for a certain type of peak, and not, by itself, a proper name.

Belcher (bel'chėr), Sir **Edward.** b. in Nova Scotia, 1799; d. March 18, 1877. British admiral and explorer. He commanded an unsuccessful expedition (1852–54) in search of Sir John Franklin. Author of *Narrative of a Voyage round the World* (1843) and *Last of the Arctic Voyages* (1855).

Belcher, Jonathan. b. at Cambridge, Mass., Jan. 8, 1682; d. at Elizabethtown, N.J., Aug. 31, 1757. American merchant and politician. He was governor of Massachusetts and New Hampshire in the period 1730–41, and was appointed governor of New Jersey in 1747.

Belcher Islands. Group of rocky, treeless islands in SE Hudson Bay, ab. 70 mi. W of the coast of NW Quebec. They belong to the Keewatin district of the Northwest Territories, and are inhabited by about 150 Eskimos. Area, ab. 1,100 sq. mi.

Belchertown (bel'chėr.toun). Town in C Massachusetts, in Hampshire County, in an apple-growing and dairy-farming region. 4,487 (1950).

Bełcikowski (bel.chē.kôf'skē), **Adam.** b. at Kraców, Poland, 1839; d. 1909. Polish essayist and playwright, author of historical dramas of slight account in themselves but important in their influence on the development of this form in Poland. He contributed articles on Polish literature to the London *Athenæum.*

Belcourt (bel.kör), **George Antoine.** b. at Bay du Febvre, Quebec, Canada, April 22, 1803; d. at Shediac, New Brunswick, Canada, May 31, 1874. Catholic missionary among the Chippewa Indians in W Canada and in the Minnesota Territory.

Belcredi (bel.krā'dē), Count **Richard von.** b. Feb. 12, 1823; d. Dec. 2, 1902. Austrian politician. He served (1865–67) as prime minister.

Belding (bel'ding). City in C Lower Michigan, in Ionia County: silk textiles. 4,436 (1950).

Beleaguered City, A. Novel (1880) by Margaret Oliphant. It is a story of the occult.

Beled el Jerid (be'led el je.rēd'). [Also, **Beled el Djerid.**] Region in N Africa, in Tunisia and Algeria, lying S of the Atlas range, and N of the Sahara, in the neighborhood of the Chott Djerid (Djerid Salt Lake).

Belém (bẹ.lāñ'; Anglicized, bẹ.lem'). [Also: **Pará;** full name, **Santa Maria de Belém do Grão Pará.**] Capital of the state of Pará, a seaport in NE Brazil: the principal Amazon port for rubber, cacao, lumber, nuts, and other inland products. Founded in 1616, it has an 18th-century cathedral. Flood-control and drainage systems have been constructed in recent years. 230,181 (1950).

Belém. Western suburb of Lisbon, Portugal. It contains a monastery of Saint Hieronymus, founded in 1500, in commemoration of the voyage of Vasco da Gama, and later used as an orphan asylum. The church contains the tombs of Luiz Vaz de Camões, Vasco da Gama, and many Portuguese sovereigns. The tower of Belém, erected 1515–21, serves now as a prison. The Palacio de Belém, built in 1700, is the seat of the president of the republic.

Belen (bẹ.len'). Village in W New Mexico, in Valencia County: trading and shipping center for a corn, oats, cereal, and alfalfa producing section of the Rio Grande valley. 4,495 (1950).

Beleño (bā.lā'nyō). Pseudonym of **Azuela, Mariano.**

Belerium (bē.lē'ri.um). Ancient name of **Cornwall** and of **Lands End,** England.

Belesme (bẹ.lem'), **Robert of.** [Also: **Robert of Bellême;** title, Earl of **Shrewsbury.**] fl. c1077–1112; d. at Wareham, England. Anglo-Norman rebel warrior and statesman. He was active in the rebellions of Robert II of Normandy against William I (1077) and William Rufus (1088), whom he joined after the fall of Rochester (1088); for turning coat, he was imprisoned by Robert, but was soon released and, with his brothers, rejoined Robert, this time (1101) in a conspiracy against Henry I. Defeated at Shrewsbury, in the center of his earldom, by Henry, he returned to Normandy and vainly sought to ally the lords against the king; he again fought the king, lost, and made peace (1106). While acting as French ambassador (1112) to Henry, he was taken, tried for old crimes, and confined until death.

Belesta (be.les.tà). Town in S France, in the department of Ariège, ab. 18 mi. E of Foix. A tourist resort, noted for the intermittent spring of Fontestorbe. It has woolen manufactures and marble quarries. 1,341 (1946).

Belev (bye'lyif). [Also, **Bielef.**] Town in the W part of the U.S.S.R., in the Tula *oblast* (region) of the Russian Soviet Federated Socialist Republic, ab. 180 mi. SE of Smolensk by rail.

Belfagor (bel'fā.gôr), **Story of.** [Italian, **Novella di Belfagor arcidiavolo** (nō.vel'lä dē bel.fä.gôr' är.chē-dyä'vō.lō).] Satirical tale by Niccolò Macchiavelli (published in 1549) of the devil who takes refuge in hell to avoid a scold. It has frequently been translated, and was remodeled by Jean de La Fontaine.

Belfast (bel'fåst). City in S Maine, county seat of Waldo County, on the W side of Penobscot Bay: resort community. It was settled c1770, and incorporated in 1853. Pop. 5,960 (1950).

Belfast. City and county borough, seaport, market town, and manufacturing center in Ulster province, Northern Ireland, in County Antrim, situated at the influx of the river Lagan to Belfast Lough. It is the capital of Northern Ireland; the actual seat of the government is at Stormont, a suburb ab. 5 mi. outside the city. The Parliament buildings were opened here, in 1932, by Edward VIII, then Prince of Wales. Stormont Castle, nearby, is the official residence of the prime minister. Belfast is the principal port of Northern Ireland, and a port of call for transatlantic liners to Glasgow and Liverpool. Its imports are chiefly coal, pig iron and steel, and flax and linen yarn; exports include livestock, meat, farm produce, and linen, cotton, and woolen textiles. Belfast is the leading center of linen manufacture in the United Kingdom. It achieved its first importance as a linen center in the 17th century with the influx of French Huguenot refugees who brought the skill with them. The first flax-spinning machine was erected here in 1828. Heavy industries include shipbuilding (which, however, has declined), ship-repair, locomotive-building, and textile-machinery manufactures. Other industries include woolen manufactures (especially of tweeds and blankets), cotton-spinning, rope-making, distilleries, carbonated-water manufactures, soap manufactures, and tobacco-processing. Belfast is the seat of Queen's University (founded 1908, and replacing Queen's College, opened 1849), the Belfast Academy, Academical Institution, Presbyterian College, and others. It shares with Cork the epithet "Athens of Ireland." The population of the city has increased sevenfold within the last 100 years. 455,000 (est. 1949).

Belfast Lough (loċh). [Also, **Carrickfergus Bay.**] Inlet of the Irish Sea, in Ulster province, Northern Ireland, lying between County Antrim and County Down. The city of Belfast is at its head. The lough provides a very good anchorage for ships. Length, ab. 13 mi.; width, ab. 3 mi.

Belfield (bel'fēld). Character in Fanny Burney's *Cecilia*, said to have been drawn from the "animated, ingenious, and eccentric Percival Stockdale."

Belfond (bel'fond). Courteous, good-tempered, and accomplished gentleman in Thomas Shadwell's comedy *The Squire of Alsatia*. He is extremely dissipated and nearly ruined by women. His elder brother is a vicious, obstinate, and clownish boor.

Belford (bel'fọrd). The intimate friend of Lovelace in Samuel Richardson's *Clarissa Harlowe*.

Belfort (bel.fôr). [Also, **Béfort.**] Town in E France, the capital of the Territoire de Belfort, situated on the Savoureuse River, between Mulhouse and Besançon. It has great strategic importance because it commands the Trouée de Belfort (Belfort Gap) and is the junction of various routes between France, Germany, and Switzerland. It is dominated by the citadel, near which is the granite statue of the *Lion of Belfort* executed by Frédéric Auguste Bartholdi. In the center of the town are the churches of Saint Christopher and Saint Joseph. Belfort was united to France in 1648, and was fortified by Vauban. It resisted the Allies in 1814–15, and was besieged and bombarded by the Germans in 1870, the garrison surrendering with honors of war on Feb. 16, 1871. It reverted to France by the treaty of 1871. Belfort has a number of vocational schools and many industries, particularly metallurgical industries of great variety (including blast furnaces), and also textile and food factories. 37,387 (1946).

Belfort, Battle of. [Sometimes called the **"Battle of Héricourt."**] Battle between the French and Germans, on Jan. 15–17, 1871, during the Franco-Prussian War.

Belfort, Territoire de. Department in E France, called a territory, and bounded by the department of Haut-Rhin on the N and E, the departments of Haute-Saône and Doubs on the W and SW, and by Switzerland on the S. It was constituted after the Franco-Prussian War of 1870–71 when the department of Haut-Rhin, of which it had formed a part, was ceded to Germany. It remained a separate territory when Alsace was returned to France and the department of Haut-Rhin was re-formed in 1945. The agriculture is similar to that of Haut-Rhin. Belfort is an important center for the metallurgical industry; it has blast furnaces, iron and steel mills, and factories producing railroad equipment, ovens, shutters, bolts, screws, grates, and machine tools and instruments of various kinds; there are also textile and lumber mills. Capital, Belfort; area, 235 sq. mi.; pop. 86,648 (1946).

Belfort, Trouée de. [English, **Belfort Gap.**] Depression near Belfort, E France, between the S limit of the Vosges Mountains and the N slope of the Jura. It is of great strategic importance.

Belfrage (bel'frāj), **Cedric.** b. at London, Nov. 8, 1904—. Anglo-American journalist and author. He attended Cambridge University, came (1926) to the U.S., worked as a journalist and scenario reader at Hollywood, and was a staff member (1931 *et seq.*) of the London *Daily Express*. He made (1934 *et seq.*) a global cruise and in 1945 was a member of a Supreme Headquarters Allied Expeditionary Forces psychological-warfare team which, after World War II, established newspapers in German cities occupied by the Allies. He is the author of biographies, travel books, and novels, including *Away From It All: An Escapologist's Notebook* (1937), *Promised Land: Notes For a History* (1938), *Let My People Go* (1940), *South of God* (1941), *They All Hold Swords* (1941), and *Abide With Me* (1948).

Belfry of Bruges (brözh), **The.** Poem by Henry Wadsworth Longfellow, the title-piece of a volume published in 1845.

Belgae (bel'jē). In ancient history, a people in northern Gaul, mainly of Celtic origin, occupying the area that now comprises Belgium, Luxembourg, NE France, the S part of the Netherlands, and part of W Germany.

Belgae. Personification of Holland in Edmund Spenser's *Faerie Queene*. She has 17 sons (the 17 provinces of Holland).

Belgard (bel'gärd). German name of **Białogard.**

Belgarde (bel.gärd'). Poor and proud captain, in Philip Massinger's play *The Unnatural Combat*, who, when told not to appear at the governor's table in his shabby clothes, arrives in full armor.

Belgaum (bel.goum'). [Also, **Belgam.**] District in the S division of Bombay state, W Union of India, ab. 275 mi. SE of the city of Bombay: cotton, sugar, millet, and rice. Chief town, Belgaum; area, ab. 4,600 sq. mi.; pop. 1,225,428 (1941).

Belgaum. [Also, **Belgam.**] Chief town of the district of Belgaum, W Union of India, ab. 50 mi. NE of Goa: silk and cotton center and important trading place. 58,319 (1941).

Bel Geddes (bel ged'ẹs), **Norman.** See **Geddes, Norman Bel.**

Belgian Congo (bel'jan kong'gō). [Flemish, **Belgisch Congo** (bel'gis kông'gō); French, **Congo Belge;** former name, **Congo** (or **Kongo**) **Free State.**] Belgian colony in W and C Africa, recognized and defined by the conference of powers at Berlin in 1885. It lies mostly S of the lower Congo and Ubangi rivers, extending to the NE watershed of the Congo basin, and E to the line of lakes (Lakes Albert, Edward, Kivu, and Tanganyika). It is bounded by the Atlantic Ocean on the W, by French Equatorial Africa on the W, NW, and N, by the Anglo-Egyptian Sudan on the N and NE, by Uganda, Tanganyika, and Northern Rhodesia on the E, and by Northern Rhodesia and Angola on the S. Capital, Léopoldville; area, ab. 902,082 sq. mi.; pop. 11,390,950 (1950).

History. The Belgian Congo is the successor of the International African Association, founded by Leopold II of Belgium and organized by Stanley. This company established stations, annexed lands, hoisted its own flag (first recognized by the U.S.), and became so aggressive as to enter into conflicts with Portugal, France, and England. The Berlin conference constituted (Feb. 26, 1885) the Congo Free State, with Leopold II as sovereign. The conditions under which it received most of the Congo basin as its sphere of influence were that all nations and religions should have equal privileges within its borders, and that free trade should prevail. The latter clause was modified by the Brussels conferences of 1890 so as to enable the Congo Free State and other countries concerned in the Congo Free Trade Basin to levy certain import duties. By will, dated Aug. 2, 1889, Leopold II bequeathed to Belgium all his sovereign rights, and by the convention of July 3, 1890 (continued Aug. 10, 1901), he gave Belgium the right to annex the Congo Free State after a period of ten years. It was annexed to Belgium in October, 1908, and the name changed to the Belgian Congo. The territory was divided for administrative purposes into 14 districts, which, by decree of March 28, 1912, were changed into 22 districts. In 1914 the Belgian Congo was divided into four provinces to which a trust territory, Ruanda-Urundi, was added in 1925 from territory formerly part of German East Africa. In 1933 another redivision was made, this time into seven provinces including Ruanda-Urundi, which remained unchanged as a trust territory administered as a province.

Government. The provinces are divided into a total of 20 administrative districts which, in turn, divide into 122 administrative territories. The capital of each province bears the name of the province (Léopoldville, Coquilhatville, Lusambo, Stanleyville, Costermansville, and Elisabethville). Government is in the hands of a governor general at Léopoldville; he is the personal representative of the Belgian crown and is assisted by a vice-governor general, a secretary general, and the provincial governors; he also represents bureaus at Brussels, under the supervision of the Belgian crown.

Economic Geography. The chief exports are mineral products, especially copper from the Katanga region. The Congo leads in world production of industrial diamonds and cobalt, is second in the production of tantalite, and is important for uranium, copper, and tin. Agricultural products include cotton and palm oil.

Belgica (bel′ji.ka̤). [Also, **Gallia Belgica.**] In ancient geography, a province of the Roman Empire in E and NE Gaul, extending NE of the province of Lugdunensis. The frontier here was the lower Seine River, and followed nearly the line of the Marne River.

Belgioioso (bel.jō.yō′zō), Principessa **di.** [Title of **Cristina di Trivulzio.**] b. at Milan, Italy, June 28, 1808; d. there, July 15, 1871. Italian author and patriot, exiled for participation in the revolution of 1848. From Paris, where she had lived since 1830, she financed Giuseppe Mazzini's march (1834) into Savoy. Among her works are *Histoire de la maison de Savoie* (1860) and *Della presente condizione delle donne e del loro avvenire* (1866).

Belgium (bel′jum). [Official names: (French) **Royaume de Belgique,** (Flemish) **Koninkrijk België;** Dutch, **België** (bel′gē.e̤); French, also, **Belgique** (bel.zhēk); German, **Belgien** (bel′gē.e̤n).] Country in NW Europe, bounded on the E by Germany and the Grand Duchy of Luxembourg, on the SW by France, on the NW by the North Sea, and on the N and NE by the Netherlands. With the exception of the small frontage on the North Sea, the country is devoid of natural frontiers. Capital, Brussels; area, 11,775 sq. mi.; pop. 8,512,195 (1947).

Terrain and Climate. The physical features of Belgium present no extremes. Three, or even four, distinct regions can, however, be distinguished. About one fifth of the country was reclaimed from the sea between the 8th and 13th centuries. This is the fertile stretch of land along the North Sea coast and the Schelde River estuary. Behind this fringe lies the great N plain, comprising Flanders, the Kempen, Limbourg, and part of the Hainaut. It is flat country, with partly loamy and clayey and partly sandy soils. The C part of the country is a slightly higher plateau of undulating hills, covering part of Hainaut, of Brabant, of Namur, and a small part of Liége. The S part, including the Ardennes, is a comparatively high plateau of between 600 and 2,100 ft.; it contains caves and a number of streams cut deep through the limestone rocks. This section has a large share in the country's coal fields, which extend also into part of the C zone. The climate is oceanic in character, with cool summers and mild winters. Only the Ardennes region, because of its higher elevation, presents sharper contrasts.

Agriculture, Industry, Trade. Less than 20 percent of the population are engaged in agriculture, but cultivation is most intensive. Grain, potatoes, and sugar beets prevail, but some parts of the country specialize in growing flax, hops, and tobacco. Market gardening and horticulture flourish particularly aroung Brussels and Ghent. There is ample pasturage, although not as much as in the N Netherlands. Formerly horses, particularly of the heavy type, were the chief product of Belgian livestock-raising endeavors. Now, cattle, pigs, and fowl are of increasing importance. The density of population in the rural districts of Belgium is among the greatest in Europe. There are fisheries on the coast. Forests are found mainly in the C and S parts of the country, where soils are less favorable to agriculture. Belgium is one of the foremost industrial nations of Europe. Arts and crafts, organized in vigorous guilds, flourished in Flanders, Brabant, and the Hainaut as early as the Middle Ages, with linen weaving prevailing in Flanders, lacemaking in Brabant, and iron working in the Hainaut. Many of these crafts survived until the 19th century, when they were industrialized. Flanders, Brabant, and Kempen are still the chief seats of textile manufacture, while the Walloon provinces lead in the metallurgical industries. In the 19th century, the linen and woolen industries expanded and cotton spinning and weaving were added. The S industrial belt has seen a growth in the production of iron, steel, and zinc, in glassmaking in all its branches (mirrors, plate glass, bottles, pitchers), the chemical industry, and various kinds of machine and construction industries, including railroad equipment, bicycles, automobiles, tractors, and ornaments. Among the plants for processing agricultural products breweries and sugar refineries are most important. Lacemaking and paper manufacture are specialties in Flanders and Brabant, glove manufacture in Brussels, and diamond polishing in Antwerp. Belgium has a dense network of highways, railroads, and canals. By way of canals, inland cities such as Bruges, Ghent, and Brussels can be reached by seagoing vessels. The chief seaport of the country and one of the most important ports of the whole European continent is Antwerp. It serves not only the needs of the Belgian economy, but those of the hinterland in Alsace-Lorraine and in Rhineland-Westphalia.

Early History. In ancient times the territory of the Celtic Belgae was conquered by the Romans; the native population was Romanized. Later, the Germanic Franks invaded the N part of the country and stopped only at the Great Coal Forest which was organized as a Roman frontier zone. For 1,400 years, the two ethnic groups inhabiting Belgium today, the Romanized Celtic Walloons and the Germanic Flemings, have lived in the territory they occupied in the 5th century. Apart from the inroads of French speech as a more fashionable tongue into the upper layers of society in some Flemish towns, the language frontier has remained practically unchanged.

French and Spanish Domination. The medieval history of Belgium is divided into the history of Flanders, Hainaut, Liége, and other parts of the country as separate entities. After 1384 the French house of Burgundy unified these various regions under one scepter. The heiress, Mary of Burgundy, married Archduke Maximilian of Hapsburg in 1477. After her death, her son, Philip the Handsome, married Joanna the Mad, daughter of the sovereigns of Aragon and Castile, and became ruler of these two kingdoms. His son, Charles of Hapsburg, born at Ghent in 1500, became king of the Spanish countries and emperor of the Holy Roman Empire; he was recognized as sovereign by the states-general of the United Provinces of the Low Countries, which included Belgium. Here was the center of the immense empire of Charles V (in the Netherlands, Charles I). Under his son, Philip II, the Low Countries became a tool of Spain. A revolution broke out, but during the protracted struggle a break occurred between the Catholic South and the Protestant North; the South was kept by Spain. In 1598, Philip's daughter, Isabella, who shortly afterward married the archduke Albert of Austria, was given the provinces of the Low Countries, but they soon fell back to Spain. Subsequently, the region was the goal of the expansionist tendencies of France under Louis XIV; Artois and parts of Flanders and Hainaut were joined to France. In the Peace of Utrecht, which was concluded in 1713, the region was ceded to Austria. Under the rule of the Hapsburgs Charles VI, Maria Theresa, and Joseph II a period of peace was conducive to economic recovery. The French revolutionary generals Dumouriez and Jourdan conquered the country; Austria renounced the sovereignty formally in the peace of Campo Formio, on Oct. 17, 1797. Belgium was under French rule from 1797 to 1814, in the period 1804-14 as part of the French Empire. After the downfall of Napoleon, the Congress of Vienna decided that the country should be annexed to the Netherlands. Commercial competition, religious differences, and administrative rigidity created discontent. The news of the July Revolution in France aroused the Belgians. On Aug. 25, 1830, disturbances started in Brussels. The Dutch had to leave the country. A Belgian constitution was ratified on Feb. 17, 1831. On June 4, 1831, the Belgian Congress elected Prince Leopold of Saxe-Coburg-Gotha as King of the Belgians. However, actual fighting and diplomatic controversy continued until, on April 19, 1839, the treaties establishing the international status of Belgium were signed in London by Belgium, the Netherlands, and the Great Powers of Europe. Belgium was declared neutral and the Great Powers promised to protect Belgian integrity and independence.

19th-20th Centuries. The history of Belgium in its present geographical sense is a history of hardly more than one century, during which Leopold I, Leopold II, Albert I, and Leopold III ruled the country as constitutional monarchs, sometimes with Catholic, sometimes with liberal cabinets and since 1914 with coalition cabinets, variously composed of Catholics, Liberals, and Socialists. An unprecedented economic prosperity aided the country. The most remarkable of the rulers was Leopold II, a man of sharp business acumen and boundless energy, the creator of the empire of the Congo. Throughout the 19th century the Flemish movement, striving for linguistic equality with the French-speaking elements in the country, made slow but consistent headway. In 1930 the University of Ghent was definitely established as a Flemish university, with instruction offered in the Flemish language. According to the law of July 15, 1932, elementary and secondary instruction was to be given in the language most widely used in the district in which the child lived, with the proviso that classes in the second national language might be organized when a minimum number of students requested them; in areas where at least 20 percent of the population spoke a language not the one of the majority, bilingual instruction was to be organized.

World War I. Violating the treaties guaranteeing Belgian neutrality, the German armies invaded Belgium on Aug. 4, 1914. The heavily fortified towns of Liége and Namur were subdued with the aid of superior artillery fire; this was the opening of World War I. Almost all of Belgium was overrun, the exception being a corner of West Flanders around the town of Ypres, which was laid in ruins. Belgium was administered by German governors until Belgian sovereignty was restored in 1918. The Treaty of Versailles abrogated the international agreement of 1839 as no longer conforming to the requirements of the situation.

World War II. The German army invaded Belgium once more on May 10, 1940. The country was occupied after a campaign of 18 days. King Leopold III of Belgium surrendered and spent the remainder of the war as a prisoner in Germany. The country was almost entirely liberated by September, 1944, but fighting continued on the NW and E frontiers until the beginning of November. New fighting occurred in the SE provinces from mid-December, 1944, to mid-January, 1945, on account of the unsuccessful von Rundstedt offensive. The damage done to the country in these years was appalling: of 2,173,031 buildings existing in 1939 about one fourth, or 540,634, had been destroyed or damaged; fully one third of those were totally destroyed or heavily damaged. The damage done to shipping and railroad rolling stock amounted to 60 percent. Among the historical monuments which were completely or almost completely destroyed are the church of Nivelles, public buildings and old houses in the center of Tournai, the archives of Tournai and Mons, and the churches of Saint Gertrude and Saint Michael in Louvain. The universities of Liége and Louvain suffered heavily. The library of the University of Louvain, already once destroyed in 1914 and rebuilt with American donations, was again burnt down on May 17, 1940; more than 900,000 volumes, manuscripts, incunabula, and precious documents were lost. However, other treasures, such as the van Eycks' *Adoration of the Lamb* from Ghent, which the Germans had looted, were recovered after the war. The toll in human lives among the civilian population amounted to 28,000 killed during military operations, and 12,000 who died as political prisoners, slave workers, or executees; 20,000 more persons were East and Central European Jews, living in Belgium. In spite of the heavy damage, postwar reconstruction proceeded more speedily in Belgium than in many other European countries. An agreement envisaging the gradual achievement of an economic union, including a customs union between Belgium, the Netherlands, and Luxembourg, called "Benelux," was concluded in London in 1944. In view of the detention of King Leopold III in Germany, the Belgian parliament elected Prince Charles, Count of Flanders, brother of the king, as regent in 1944. A plebiscite concerning the return of the king, who then resided in Switzerland, was held in the spring of 1950, with 57 percent of the voters declaring themselves in favor of return; however, no parliamentary majority was available to put the plebiscite into effect. The Catholic party favored return, the Socialist party opposed it, and the Liberal party was split; the majority of the Flemish voters favored return but the majority of the Walloon voters opposed it. In 1951 Leopold abdicated and his son was crowned as Baudoin I.

Government. According to the constitution of 1831, Belgium is a constitutional, representative, and hereditary monarchy. The legislative power is vested in the king, the senate, and the chamber of representatives. The king convokes, prorogues, and dissolves the chambers but needs the countersignature of one of his ministers for any act that he undertakes. Elections are according to the principle of universal suffrage of both sexes. The minimum age of voters is fixed at 21 years. There is proportional representation. The majority of the senators are elected by the provincial councils; they must be 40 years of age. The provinces and communes have a large measure of autonomous government.

Education and Culture. The majority of the population is Roman Catholic, but no inquiry as to profession of faith is made in the censuses. There are six Roman Catholic dioceses. The Evangelical Church is under a synod. There is a central Jewish consistory. Elementary education is free and compulsory, but there are many private schools, mostly under ecclesiastical care. There are universities at Louvain, Brussels, Ghent, and Liége. The Belgian contribution in the fields of painting, sculpture, architecture, literature, and music comes from Flemish as well as Walloon sources but has a flavor of its own. The enjoyment of life in all its aspects, as depicted on the canvases of Breughel and Rubens, is an essential part of it. Historical experience as well as economic reasons make Belgium an essential factor in the unification of Europe.

Belgoraj (bel.gô'rī). See **Biłgoraj.**

Belgorod (byel'go.ro̧t). [Also, **Bielgorod.**] City in the SW part of the U.S.S.R., in the Kursk *oblast* (region) of the Russian Soviet Federated Socialist Republic, situated on the Donets River ab. 46 mi. N of Kharkov: rail and road junction. Pop. ab. 26,000.

Belgorod-Dnestrovski (byel'go̧.ro̧d.dnyi.strôf'ski). [Also: **Belgarod-Dnestrovsky;** Rumanian, **Cetatea Albă;** former name, **Akerman, Akkerman,** or **Akyerman;** ancient name, **Tyras.**] Seaport in the SW part of the U.S.S.R., in the Ukrainian Soviet Socialist Republic, situated on the estuary of the Dniester River, on the Black Sea. It is probably on the site of the ancient Milesian colony of Tyras. It was occupied by the Venetians and Genoese in the later Middle Ages, taken (1484) by the Turks, then, as part of Bessarabia, became Russian early in the 19th century, for a time (1918–40) Rumanian, and again (1940) Russian. Pop. ab. 19,000 (est. 1940).

Belgrade (bel'grād). [Serbo-Croatian, **Beograd**; Latin, **Singidunum.**] City in NE Yugoslavia, the capital of the former kingdom of Serbia and now of Yugoslavia. Situated at the junction of the Sava and Danube rivers, on a high bank overlooking the Danubian plain, it occupies a most strategic location. It is an important river port, has a number of light industries, and is the foremost commercial center in the country. A railroad and passenger bridge across the Sava River connects Belgrade with the city of Zemun, and with the W provinces and regions of Yugoslavia and the countries of C Europe, particularly Hungary and Austria. There are connections S and SE to Skoplje and Salonika, the Black-Sea port of Varna, and Istanbul (Constantinople). All the offices of the central departments of the government, including the supreme court and the general staff of the army, are situated here. Many important public buildings, such as the former royal palace, the parliament building, the national theater, the academy of arts and sciences, the archaeological and ethnographic museum, the Greek-Orthodox cathedral, and others, were entirely or partially destroyed by German bombardment during World War II. An ancient city of the Romans, it belonged at later times successively to the domains of the Byzantines, Avars, Bulgars, and Serbs. Conquered by the Turkish Sultan Suleiman II in 1521, it was occupied in 1688 by Maximilian of Bavaria and in 1717 by Eugene of Savoy, who were both commanders of the Hapsburg armies. Under Austrian rule from 1718 to 1739, and subsequently returned to Turkey, it became early in the 19th century the capital of the independent kingdom of Serbia, and after 1918 capital of the kingdom, now the republic, of Yugoslavia. In the period 1918–41 it was the seat of the prefecture of Belgrade, not included in the *banovine* (provinces) of Dunavska and Moravska, but is now the capital of the federative unit of Serbia. Many violent chapters of internal Serbian and Yugoslav history have been enacted here. 388,246 (1948).

Belgrade, Battle of. Victory of the Hungarians, under their national hero, János Hunyadi, over the Turks, under the sultan Mohammed II, in 1456, which compelled the latter to withdraw from their attack on the city of Belgrade. Hunyadi himself died of the plague shortly after the victory.

Belgrade, Battle of. Decisive victory by Eugene of Savoy, the Austrian general, who was besieging Belgrade, over a relieving army of 200,000 Turks, on Aug. 16, 1717. In consequence, Belgrade surrendered (Aug. 18, 1717), and the peace of Passarowitz (now Požarevac, in Yugoslavia) was concluded on July 21, 1718, between Turkey, Venice, and Austria.

Belgrade, Sieges of. Term applied to several historically important sieges involving what is now the capital of Yugoslavia: **1.** By the Turkish sultan Murad II c1442. **2.** By the successor to Murad II, the Turkish sultan Mohammed II, 1456. (See **Belgrade, Battle of.**) **3.** By the Turkish sultan Suleiman I (Suleiman the Magnificent), 1521; captured and annexed. **4.** By the forces of the Holy Roman Empire under the elector Maximilian of Bavaria, 1688; taken from the Turks. **5.** By the Turks, 1690; taken from the realm of the Holy Roman Emperor. **6.** By the Austrians under Eugene of Savoy, 1717; stormed and taken. (See **Belgrade, Battle of.**) **7.** By the Austrians under Laudon, 1789; taken, but restored to the Turks in 1791.

Belgrade, Treaty of. Treaty concluded at Belgrade, in September, 1739, between Turkey, Austria, and Russia. Russia renounced naval rights in the Black Sea, and restored to Turkey conquests in Moldavia and Bessarabia; Austria yielded territory in Wallachia, Bosnia, and Serbia, including Belgrade.

Belgrano (bel.grä'nō), **Manuel.** b. at Buenos Aires, June 3, 1770; d. there, June 20, 1820. Argentine general in the war for independence. He was sent (1810) with a small army to free Paraguay, but was unsuccessful. In 1812 he led an army against Upper Peru (the present Bolivia), defeating the Spaniards at Tucumán (Sept. 24, 1812) and Salta (Feb. 20, 1813), and advancing to Potosí, but was twice defeated and soon after was superseded by José de San Martín.

Belgrave (bel'grāv). Ward of Leicester, in C England, in Leicestershire, situated on the river Soar. It is a suburb in the N section of Leicester. 18,890 (1931).

Belgrave Square. Residential square at London, designed originally by George Basevi. It is some 684 ft. long by 637 ft. wide, and is named from Belgrave in Leicestershire, the estate of the dukes of Westminster (who once owned not only the square, but all the land immediately surrounding it).

Belgravia (bel.grā'vi.ạ). Fashionable district in the West End of London. It is bounded approximately by Hyde Park, Green Park, Sloane Street, and Pimlico. More or less SW of Mayfair, it was originally marshy ground, and occupies in great part what was once known as the Ebury Farm. In 1825 it was filled up with earth obtained in excavating St. Katharine's Docks, and residences were built. It derives its name from Belgrave Square, which is included in it.

Belhaven (bel.hā'vẹn). Town in E North Carolina, in Beaufort County, on an arm of Pamlico Sound ab. 120 mi. SE of Raleigh: fishing and lumbering. 2,528 (1950).

Belhaven, 2nd Baron. Title of **Hamilton, John** (1656–1708).

Belial (bē'li.ạl, bēl'yạl). In the Bible, the spirit of evil personified; the devil; Satan; in Milton's *Paradise Lost*, one of the fallen angels, distinct from Satan. In *Faust's Book of Marvels* (1469) he is called the Viceroy of the Infernal Kingdom under Lucifer or Satan.

Belianis of Greece (bel.i.ā'nis). One of the continuations of the romance *Amadis of Gaul*. It first appeared, in Spanish, in 1547, and was written by Jeronimo Fernández. In 1586 an Italian version appeared; in 1598 it was translated into English, and in 1625 into French.

Bel-Ibni (bel''ib'ni). Governor of Babylonia under Assurbanipal, king of Assyria (668–626 B.C.).

Belibus (bel'i.bus). King of Babylonia, appointed by Sennacherib, king of Assyria (705–681 B.C.).

Bélidor (bā.lē.dôr), **Bernard Forest de.** b. in Catalonia, 1693 or 1697; d. at Paris, Sept. 8, 1761. French engineer. His works include *Architecture hydraulique* (1737–51), *Le Bombardier français* (1731), and *Traité des fortifications* (1735).

Believe as You List. Play attributed to Philip Massinger. It was licensed for performance at London on May 7, 1631. This play and a later one, *The Maid of Honor* (c1632), introduced propaganda in behalf of the unfortunate brother-in-law of Charles I, the elector Frederick V of the Palatinate, briefly (1619–20) king of Bohemia, who was one of the outstanding victims of Spanish diplomacy and of the Thirty Years' War (1618–48).

Believe Me, if All Those Endearing Young Charms. Song by Thomas Moore, one of his *Irish Melodies* (published intermittently between 1807 and 1834). It is still often sung (as a tenor solo).

Bel Inconnu (bel aṅ.ko.nü), **Le.** [Eng. trans., *"The Fair Unknown."*] One of the secondary Arthurian romances. It is said to have been written by a certain Renauld de Beaujeu. The hero is a young knight who appears before the Round Table and, on being questioned, says he has no name, his mother having always called him Beau-fils, whereupon Arthur commands that he be called Le Bel Inconnu. The romance was printed for the first time in Paris in 1860.

Belinda (bẹ.lin'dạ). One of the principal characters in George Etherege's comedy *The Man of Mode.*

Belinda. Character in Charles Shadwell's comedy *The Fair Quaker of Deal:* a rich woman.

Belinda. Character in John Vanbrugh's comedy *The Provok'd Wife.*

Belinda. Character in William Congreve's comedy *The Old Bachelor.*

Belinda. Principal character in Alexander Pope's mock-heroic poem *The Rape of the Lock.*

Belinda. Character in Arthur Murphy's comedy *All in the Wrong:* a proud but tender-hearted girl in love with Beverley.

Belinda. Novel by Maria Edgeworth, published in 1801.

Béline (bā.lēn). Mercenary second wife of Argan in Molière's comedy *Le Malade imaginaire*. She pretends to love him, but her falsehood is discovered when he pretends to be dead and she bursts into exclamations of joy.

Belinsky (byi.lyēn'ski), **Vissarion Grigoryevich.** [Also, **Bielinski.**] b. c1811; d. at St. Petersburg, Russia, 1848. Russian critic and journalist. He became editor of the Moscow *Observer*, which ceased to appear in 1839, and was one of the principal contributors to the *Annales de la patrie*. At first an adherent of romanticism, he became interested in didactic and realistic literature. His criticism had a profound effect on later critical writing in Russia. He was also an expounder of liberalism in the fields of politics and sociology.

Bélisaire (bā.lē.zer). See also **Bélissaire.**

Bélisaire. Political romance by Jean François Marmontel, published in 1767.

Belisario (bā.lē.sä'ryō). Opera by Gaetano Donizetti, in three acts, produced at Venice, Feb. 7, 1836, at London, April 1, 1837, and at Paris, Oct. 24, 1843.

Belisarius (bel.i.sãr'i.us). b. in Illyria, or possibly Dardania, c505; d. March 13, 565. Byzantine soldier, perhaps the greatest general of the Eastern Roman Empire. He was commander, under Justinian I, of the eastern armies in the period, 529–532, and rescued Justinian by the suppression of the "Green" faction at Constantinople in 532. He overthrew the Vandal kingdom in Africa in 533–534, won famous victories over the Goths in Italy in 534–540, conquered Sicily in 535, and S Italy in 536–537, and conquered Ravenna in 540. He conducted the war against the Persians in the period 541–542, and again took command against the Goths in Italy in 544, but was superseded by Narses in 548. In 559 he rescued Constantinople from northern (Bulgarian) invaders. He was imprisoned (c563) for a short time by Justinian. The tale that in old age he was blind and obliged to beg his bread from door to door is believed to be untrue.

Bélise (bā.lēz). Sister of Philaminte in Molière's comedy *Les Femmes savantes*. She is gifted with remarkable self-appreciation, and thinks every man is in love with her.

Bélissaire (bā.lē.ser). Tragicomedy by Jean de Rotrou, produced in 1643.

Belit (be.lit'). One of the prominent female deities of the Babylonian pantheon, wife of Bel. She is called "lady of the nations" and "mother of the great gods."

Belitoeng (be.lē'tụng). Dutch name of **Billiton.**

Belitong (be.lē'tông). See **Billiton.**

Beliza (be.lē'zą). The waiting-woman of Doralice in John Dryden's comedy *Marriage à la Mode*.

Belize (bẹ.lēz'). See also **British Honduras.**

Belize. City in E British Honduras, on the Caribbean Sea: seaport and capital of the colony; also export point for Quintana Roo territory, Mexico. 17,289 (1941).

Beljak (be'lyäk). Slovenian name of **Villach.**

Beljame (bel.zhȧm), **Alexandre.** b. at Villiers-le-Bel, France, 1842; d. at Domont, France, 1906. French educator, the first to become professor of English literature and language at the Sorbonne. Author of *Le Public et les hommes de lettres en Angleterre au XVIIIe siècle* (The Public and Men of Letters in England During the 18th Century, 1881), and also of critical text editions and of translations into French of Shakespeare (1902).

Belkin (byel'kin), **Ivan.** Character represented as the narrator in Aleksandr Sergeyevich Pushkin's *Tales of Belkin*, a collection of five of his prose tales.

Belknap (bel'nap), **George Eugene.** b. at Newport, N.H., Jan. 22, 1832; d. at Key West, Fla., April 7, 1903. American naval officer, with the Union navy in the Civil War. He was commander of the monitor *Canonicus* in the attack on Fort Fisher (December, 1864–January, 1865), and commander in chief (c1885 *et seq.*) on the Asiatic station. While president (c1885–94) of the Board of Inspection and Survey, he was appointed rear admiral (1889).

Belknap, Jeremy. b. at Boston, Mass., June 4, 1744; d. there, June 20, 1798. American historian and Congregational clergyman. He wrote a *History of New Hampshire* (1784–92), *American Biographies* (1794–98), *The Foresters, an American Tale* (1796), and others. He was a founder of the Massachusetts Historical Society.

Belknap, William Worth. b. at Newburgh, N.Y., Sept. 22, 1829; d. at Washington, D.C., Oct. 13, 1890. American politician and general. He served as a volunteer with the Union army throughout the Civil War, participating in the Shiloh, Vicksburg, and Georgia campaigns, and obtaining the rank of major general in 1865. He was later collector of internal revenue in Iowa (1865–69) and secretary of war (1869–76) under President Grant. He resigned from the latter post as the result of charges of official corruption, and impeachment proceedings against him were then halted.

Bell (bel). City in S California, in Los Angeles County, SE of Los Angeles. 15,430 (1950).

Bell, Acton. Pseudonym of Anne Brontë; see **Brontë Family.**

Bell, Adam. English outlaw, celebrated for his skill in archery, said to have lived in the time of Robin Hood's father. About him nothing certain is known. He is the hero of several old ballads, notably *Adam Bell, Clym of the Cloughe, and Wyllyam of Cloudeslee*, printed without date by William Copland c1550. There are several allusions to him in dramatic literature. Shakespeare alludes to him in *Much Ado about Nothing* and in *Romeo and Juliet*, as does William Davenant in a poem called *A Long Vacation in London*. Ben Jonson speaks of Clym o' the Clough in *The Alchemist*. Thomas Percy and Joseph Ritson both adhere mainly to Copland's text, and Francis James Child reprints from Ritson with some improvements. However, the real person or persons of the name were thought by Child to have no connection with the hero of the ballads.

Bell, Alexander Graham. b. at Edinburgh, Scotland, March 3, 1847; d. in Nova Scotia, Aug. 2, 1922. American physicist, noted chiefly as the inventor of the telephone; son of Alexander Melville Bell. He developed his father's system of "visible speech" and came (1871) to the U.S. to use it in teaching the deaf. He became (1873) a professor of vocal physiology at Boston University. His apparatus for the transmission of sound by electricity, the telephone, was first exhibited in 1876. He later invented the photophone, and later still shared in the development of a method of recording sound on wax disks. He contributed a vast amount of experiment to the early science of aviation (1896–1910). He helped establish (1890) the American Association to Promote the Teaching of Speech to the Deaf, and was prominent in the work of the National Geographic Society, the Smithsonian Institution, and the American Association for the Advancement of Science.

Bell, Alexander Melville. b. at Edinburgh, March 1, 1819; d. at Washington, D.C., Aug. 7, 1905. Scottish-American educator, inventor of a method of phonetic notation called by him "visible speech," because the characters indicate by their form and position the physiological formation of the sounds; father of Alexander Graham Bell. He wrote *Visible Speech: the Science of Universal Alphabetics*, *Principles of Phonetics*, works on elocution and shorthand and "World-English," an adaptation of the Roman alphabet to the phonetic spelling of English.

Bell, Andrew. b. at St. Andrew's, Scotland, March 27, 1753; d. at Cheltenham, England, Jan. 27, 1832. Clergyman of the Church of England, noted as the founder of the so-called "Madras system," or monitorial system, of popular education. From 1774 until 1781 he lived in Virginia, and from 1787 till 1796 in India, where as superintendent of the Madras Male Orphan Asylum he developed his educational system, in which the older pupils, under the direction of a master, were enabled to teach those younger than themselves. His originality was disputed by Joseph Lancaster, and the contest between their systems assumed, in its day, considerable public importance. He wrote *An Experiment in Education made in the Asylum of Madras*.

Bell, Aubrey FitzGerald. b. at Muncaster, Cumberland, England, Aug. 20, 1881—. English writer and critic, a specialist in Spanish and Portuguese literature. Among his works are *The Magic of Spain* (1912), *Portuguese Literature and Bibliography* (1922), *Contemporary Spanish Literature* (1925), and *Cervantes* (1947). Editor of the *Oxford Book of Portuguese Verse* (1925).

Bell, Sir **Charles.** b. at Edinburgh, in November, 1774; d. at Hallow Park, near Worcester, England, April 28, 1842. British physiologist and anatomist, noted as the discoverer of the distinct functions of the sensory and motor nerves. He served as professor of surgery at Edinburgh, and studied injuries of men wounded at La Coruña and at Waterloo, in order to advance his knowledge of gunshot wounds. He was the author of *Anatomy of Expression* (1806), *Anatomy of the Brain* (1811), *System of Comparative Surgery* (1807), *Nervous System of the Human Body* (1830), and others.

Bell, Charles Frederic Moberly. b. at Alexandria, Egypt, April 2, 1847; d. at London, April 5, 1911. English journalist, correspondent, and publisher. He began (1865) his career as a journalist in Egypt, as correspondent (1865–90) for the London *Times;* he founded (1880) the *Egyptian Gazette,* and returned (1890) to London to become manager of the *Times.* During the period 1897–1901 he conducted, as a special section of the paper, *Literature,* which later became the *Times Literary Supplement;* thereafter he served as managing editor (1908–11) of the *Times.* Author, during his residence in Egypt, of *Khedives and Pashas* (1884), *Egyptian Finance* (1887), and *From Pharaoh to Fellah* (1889); publisher of the *Times Atlas* (1895), the *Encyclopedia Britannica* (9th ed., 1898), and *History of the South African War* (9 vols., 1900–09).

Bell, Clark. b. at Whitesville, N.Y., March 12, 1832; d. at New York, Feb. 22, 1918. American expert on medical jurisprudence. He was president (1872 *et seq.*) of the New York Medico-Legal Society, a founder (1884) of the *Medico-Legal Journal,* which he edited, and the founder (1900) of the American Congress on Tuberculosis. Author of *Judicial History of the Supreme Court of the United States and Provinces of North America* (1895), *Spiritism, Telepathy and Hypnotism* (1902), and *Medico-Legal Studies* (11 vols., 1889 *et seq.*).

Bell, Clive. [Full name, **Arthur Clive Howard Bell.**] b. 1881—. English art critic and writer; husband of Vanessa Bell, and father of Julian Bell. The publication of his *Art* (1914) is now considered to have been an event of considerable importance in winning wide recognition of "modern art" defined as the work of the post-impressionists, cubists, futurists, *fauves,* and other innovators since the 1880's. Bell maintained that form and design are the important matters in painting and sculpture, and that some people have a special sensitiveness to these characteristics, while others do not. The effect of this doctrine was virtually to eliminate subject matter and realism from among the criteria of excellence in a work of art. Bell's *Since Cézanne* (1922), *Landmarks in Nineteenth-Century Painting* (1929), and *An Account of French Painting* (1932) further argued the case for modernism. Bell's command of an excellent English prose style was a contributing factor to the influence of his books. He is also the author of *Peace at Once* (1915), *Pot Boilers* (1918), *The Legend of Monte della Sibilla* (1920), *Poems* (1921), *On British Freedom* (1923), *Civilization* (1928), *Proust* (1929), and *Enjoying Pictures* (1934).

Bell, Currer. Pseudonym of Charlotte Brontë; see **Brontë Family.**

Bell, Ellis. Pseudonym of Emily Brontë; see **Brontë Family.**

Bell, George. b. 1814; d. at Hampstead, London, Nov. 27, 1890. English publisher, founder of the London firm of G. Bell and Sons. Educated at Richmond (Yorkshire) Grammar School, he went (1820) to London, later entering the employ of Whitaker and Company; in 1838 he established his own business, and was associated with J. R. Daldy, and with Deighton and Company, publishers for Cambridge University Press. The firm founded by him was originally known as Bell and Daldy; in 1864 he purchased the business and the *Libraries* of H. G. Bohn, an outstanding figure in the history of English publishing. Bell is remembered especially for his editions, in many volumes, of the English poets. After his death, the business was carried on by his son Edward Bell (1844–1926).

Bell, George Joseph. b. at Fountain Bridge, near Edinburgh, March 26, 1770; d. 1843. Scottish jurist; brother of Sir Charles Bell. He was appointed professor at Edinburgh, 1822, and served on various commissions on legal proceedings. He published several works on the laws of Scotland.

Bell, Gertrude Margaret Lowthian. b. 1868; d. 1926. English traveler, archaeologist, and official of various Near Eastern governments; granddaughter of Sir Isaac Lowthian Bell (1816–1904). A graduate (1888) of Oxford, she traveled (1905) from Jerusalem to Konya in Asia Minor; she reached Haïl in an unsuccessful attempt (1913) to visit the interior of Arabia. Appointed (1915) to the Arab intelligence bureau at Cairo, she was later an assistant political officer (1916) at Basra, and aided (1921) the postwar faction which made Faisal king of Iraq. Author of *The Desert and the Sown* (1907), *Amurath to Amurath* (1911), and *The Palace and Mosque of Ukhaidir* (1914).

Bell, Henry. b. at Torphichen Mill, near Linlithgow, Scotland, 1767; d. at Helsburgh, Scotland, 1830. Scottish engineer. He is famous as the builder of the steamship *Comet* which began (January, 1812) to ply on the Clyde, and thus as the originator of steam navigation in Europe. It has been asserted that Robert Fulton derived his ideas for steam navigation from Bell.

Bell, Henry Glassford. b. at Glasgow, Nov. 8, 1803; d. there, Jan. 7, 1874. Scottish lawyer and poet, ardent defender of the name and reputation of Mary Stuart (Queen of Scots). He founded (1828) and edited the *Edinburgh Literary Journal* for three years. He was the author of *Summer and Winter Hours* (1830), poetry, and *My Old Portfolio* (1832), prose selections, of which two stories, "The Dead Daughter" and "The Living Mummy" are sometimes believed to have inspired Edgar Allan Poe.

Bell, Henry Haywood. b. in North Carolina, April 13, 1808; drowned in the Osaka River, Japan, Jan. 11, 1868. American rear admiral. He became fleet-captain to David Glasgow Farragut in 1862, and commanded a division of the Union fleet in the attack on the defenses of New Orleans, April 18–25.

Bell, Sir **Isaac Lowthian.** b. at Newcastle, England, 1816; d. Dec. 20, 1904. English manufacturer and politician; grandfather of Gertrude Margaret Lowthian Bell. He founded (1852), with his brothers Thomas and John Bell, the Clarence Iron Works on the Tees, and was member of Parliament for Hartlepool (1875–80). Author of *The Chemical Phenomena of Iron Smelting* (1872), and *Report on the Iron Manufacture of the United States, and a Comparison of it with that of Great Britain* (1877).

Bell, James. b. 1825; d. March 31, 1908. English chemist. He was principal of the Somerset House Laboratory (1875 *et seq.*) and the author of *Chemistry of Foods.*

Bell, James Franklin. b. near Shelbyville, Ky., Jan. 9, 1856; d. Jan. 8, 1919. American soldier. He was graduated from the U.S. Military Academy in 1878, served on the plains of the West until 1894, and was an aide (1894–97) to the commanding general in California. He took part in the campaign in the Philippine Islands in 1898, and was awarded a medal of honor by Congress for gallantry in action near Porac, Luzon. A brigadier general of volunteers (1899–1901), he was provost marshal general of Manila until 1901, when he was made a brigadier general in the regular army. In 1903 he was appointed commandant of the infantry and cavalry school, signal school, and staff college at Fort Leavenworth, Kansas, and was chief of the general staff of the U.S. army (1906–10), succeeding Lieutenant General John C. Bates. He was made a major general in 1907. He headed (1911–14) the Philippine Department, and was named (1917) commander of the Eastern Department.

Bell, James Montgomery. b. at Williamsburg, Pa., Oct. 1, 1837; d. Sept. 17, 1919. American soldier, promoted to the rank of brigadier general in 1901. He entered the army in 1862 and served with the Union army in the Civil War, and subsequently in various campaigns against the Indians, on the frontiers, and in the Philippine Islands (1900–01). He retired in 1901.

Bell, James Stroud. b. at Philadelphia, June 30, 1847; d. April 5, 1915. American merchant and miller, a pioneer in the advertising and marketing of a large variety of cereals.

Bell, John. b. at Antermony, Scotland, 1691; d. there, July 1, 1780. Scottish traveler in European and Asiatic Russia, China, and Turkey. His *Travels* were published in 1763.

Bell, John. b. at Edinburgh, May 12, 1763; d. at Rome, April 15, 1820. Scottish surgeon and anatomist; brother of Sir Charles Bell. Author of *Principles of Surgery* (1801–07) and *Anatomy of the Human Body* (1793–1802).

Bell, John. b. near Nashville, Tenn., Feb. 15, 1797; d. at Cumberland Iron Works, in Tenn., Sept. 10, 1869. American politician. He was member of Congress from Tennessee (1827–41), speaker (1834–35), Whig secretary of war (1841), U.S. senator (1847–59), and candidate of the Constitutional Union Party for President of the U.S. in 1860. He received 39 electoral votes (those of Tennessee, Kentucky, and Virginia) and 589,581 popular votes.

Bell, John. b. at Hopton, Suffolk, England, 1811; d. in March, 1895. English sculptor. His works include *Eagle Slayer*, *Andromeda*, the Guards' memorial (at Waterloo Place, London), *United States Directing the Progress of America* (on the Albert Memorial; copy at Washington), and others.

Bell, John Joy. b. May 7, 1871; d. 1934. Scottish journalist, humorist, and dramatist. Educated at Scottish academies and Glasgow University; the author of humorous stories and novels of simple Scottish life, told in dialect, he is best known for his creation of the character of Wee Macgreegor. His works are *New Noar's Ark* (1898), *Wee Macgreegor* (1902; dramatized in 1912), *Mistress McLeerie* (1903), *Wee Macgreegor Again* (1904), *Mr. Pennycook's Boy* (1905), *Clyde Songs* (1906–11), *Oh Christina Coortin' Christina* (1913), *A Kingdom of Dreams* (1914), *Wee Macgreegor Enlists* (1915), *Johnny Pryde* (1918), *Secret Cards* (1922), *The Invisible Net* (1924), *Mr. and Mrs. Craw* (1926), *Exit Mrs. McLeerie*, *Betty* (1927), and *Hoots!* (1929).

Bell, Julian. [Full name, **Julian Heward Bell.**] b. 1908; d. 1937. English poet and pacifist; son of Clive Bell. He wrote *Winter Movement* (1930) and *Work for the Winter* (1936), both volumes of poetry. He was killed during the Spanish Civil War while driving an ambulance for the Loyalists; like his father, he was a confirmed pacifist. He edited, with an introduction, *We Did Not Fight, 1914–18. Experiences of War Resisters* (1935), a collection of essays by prominent English pacifists.

Bell, Lilian. [Married name, **Bogue.**] b. at Chicago, 1867; d. July 18, 1929. American author. Among her works are *A Little Sister to the Wilderness* (1895), *As Seen by Me* (1900), *Abroad with the Jimmies* (1902), *At Home with the Jardines* (1904), *Carolina Lee* (1906), *Angela's Quest* (1910), *The Story of the Christmas Ship* (1915), and *Last of the Romanoffs* (1926).

Bell, Louis. b. Dec. 5, 1864; d. June 14, 1923. American physicist and engineer. He was graduated (1884) from Dartmouth College, and attended (until 1888) Johns Hopkins University, where he did research in solar spectrum wave lengths; he served as chief engineer (1893 *et seq.*) of the General Electric Company's power transmission department. A three-phase electric-power transmission plant at Redlands, Calif., was made possible as a result of his researches in multiphase transmission.

Bell, Mackenzie. [Full name, **Henry Thomas Mackenzie Bell.**] b. at Liverpool, England, March 2, 1856; d. at Bayswater, London, Dec. 13, 1930. English biographer, poet, and traveler. He studied in France, Italy, Spain, and Portugal. He was the author of biographical and critical studies, including *A Forgotten Genius: Charles Whitehead* (1884) and *Christina Rossetti* (1898); he also wrote *Pictures of Travel and Other Poems* (1898), *Poems* (1909), and *Poetical Pictures of the Great War* (1917).

Bell, Peter Hansborough. b. near Fredericksburg, Va., March 11, 1808; d. March 8, 1898. American soldier and politician, governor (1849 *et seq.*) of Texas. At the outset of the Texas Revolution (1836), he joined Sam Houston's army and later held offices in the Texas government. He served as lieutenant colonel with the Rangers during the Mexican War. Elected governor (1849) during the Wilmot Proviso crisis, he was later elected to Congress, where he served two terms.

Bell, Robert. b. at Glasgow, Scotland, c1732; d. at Richmond, Va., Sept. 23, 1784. American publisher and book auctioneer. Having come to America c1766, he instituted book auctions at Philadelphia and sold books in most of the major urban centers of the eastern seaboard. He published the first edition of Thomas Paine's *Common Sense* (1776) and an American edition of William Blackstone's *Commentaries*.

Bell, Sir Robert. b. at Cork, Ireland, Jan. 16, 1800; d. at London, April 12, 1867. British journalist, compiler, and general writer. His chief work is an *Annotated Edition of the British Poets* (24 vols., 1854–67), covering poets from Geoffrey Chaucer to William Cowper. He contributed to Dionysius Lardner's *Cabinet Cyclopaedia*.

Bell, Robert. b. at Toronto, Canada, June 3, 1841; d. June 20, 1917. Canadian geologist, associated from 1857 with the Geological Survey of Canada, of which he was for many years the director. He was naturalist and geologist of the *Neptune* (1884) and *Alert* (1885) expeditions to Baffin Bay, and of that of the *Diana* (1897) to the S coast of Baffin Island; he made important geological and topographical surveys in many parts of the Dominion of Canada. From 1863 to 1867 he was professor of chemistry at Queen's University, Kingston, Ontario.

Bell, Samuel. b. at Londonberry, N.H., Feb. 8, 1770; d. Dec. 23, 1850. American lawyer and politician, governor (1819–23) of New Hampshire. Admitted to the bar in 1796, he held offices in New Hampshire as a Jeffersonian Republican, and was a U.S. senator (1823 *et seq.*).

Bell, The. Inn at Edmonton, in Middlesex, not far from London. It was to this spot that John Gilpin pursued his mad career in Cowper's ballad *John Gilpin*.

Bell, The. Noted old inn in Warwick Lane, London. The Scottish prelate and scholar Robert Leighton died there in 1684.

Bell, Thomas. b. at Poole, Dorsetshire, England, Oct. 11, 1792; d. at Selborne, Hampshire, England, March 13, 1880. English dental surgeon and zoölogist. He was professor of zoölogy at King's College, London (1836–80), a secretary of the Royal Society (1848–53), president of the Linnaean Society (1853–61), and president of the Ray Society (1843–59). His works include a *Monograph of Testudinata* (1832–36), *History of British Quadrupeds* (1837), *History of British Reptiles* (1839), and *History of British Stalk-Eyed Crustacea* (1853), an edition of the *Natural History of Selborne* (1877), and others.

Bell, Vanessa. [Maiden name, **Stephen.**] English woman of letters; eldest daughter of Sir Leslie Stephen (1832–1904), sister of Virginia Woolf (1882–1941), wife (1907 *et seq.*) of Clive Bell; and mother of the poet Julian Bell (1908–37).

Bell, William Melvin. b. in Whitley County, Ind., Nov. 12, 1860; d. Oct. 6, 1933. American clergyman of the United Brethren in Christ. Ordained in 1882, he was pastor (1879–92) at various churches in Indiana, before serving as general secretary (1893–1905) of the department of home and foreign missions. After his election as bishop (1905) and senior bishop (1921), he was head (1917–29) of the eastern district of the Gulf and Atlantic states. Author of *The Love of God* (1902), *Torches Aloft* (1913), and *Biography of Bishop Nicholas Castle* (1923).

Bella (bel′lä). Town and commune in S Italy, in the *compartimento* (region) of Calabria, in the province of Potenza, ab. 18 mi. NW of Potenza. Pop. of commune, 5,103 (1936); of town, 3,919 (1936).

Bella, Isola. [Eng. trans., "*Fair Island.*"] One of the two chief islands of the Borromean Islands, in Lago Maggiore, Italy. The other is Isola Madre.

Bella, Stefano della. b. at Florence, May 18, 1610; d. there, July 12, 1664. Italian engraver. He was commissioned by Cardinal Richelieu to execute designs of the principal military events of the minority of Louis XIII, and to make engravings from these. His works number more than 1,400 pieces.

Bella Bella (bel′ą bel′ą). North American Indian language, spoken on the coast of British Columbia N of Vancouver Island, belonging to the Wakashan linguistic stock.

Bellac (be.låk). Town in W central France, in the department of Haute-Vienne, situated on the Vincou River, ab. 23 mi. NW of Limoges. It has an old church, partly in Romanesque and partly ogival style; manufactures leather goods. 4,327 (1946).

Bella Coola (bel′ą kö′lą). North American Indian tribe inhabiting the coast of British Columbia, Canada. The language is of the Salishan family.

Bellafront (bel′ą.frunt). Principal female character in John Middleton and Thomas Dekker's *Honest Whore*. She gives its name to the play, but turns out a true penitent, resisting the temptations of Hippolito.

Bellagio (bel.lä′jō). Town and commune in NW Italy, in the *compartimento* (region) of Lombardy, in the province of Como, situated at the separation of Lake Como into two arms, ab. 15 mi. NE of Como. It is a resort, known since ancient times. The Villa Serbelloni, one of the most beautiful in Italy, has famous gardens. Pop. of commune, 3,643 (1936); of town, 864 (1936).

Bellah (bel'ạ), **James Warner.** b. at New York, Sept. 14, 1899—. American novelist and short-story writer. He served with the Royal Canadian Air Force in World War I and was an officer in the U.S. army during World War II. He was graduated (A.B., 1923) from Columbia University, where he also served (1923–26, 1936–37) as an instructor in English. Among his works are *Sketch Book of a Cadet from Gascony* (1923), *Those Frantic Years* (1927), *Gods of Yesterday* (1928), *Dancing Lady* (1932), *The Brass Gong Tree* (1936), *The Bones of Napoleon* (1940), *Ward Twenty* (1945), and *Irregular Gentleman* (1948).

Bellaigue (be.leg), **Camille.** b. at Paris, May 24, 1858; d. 1930. French musicologist and biographer. Reviewer (1885 *et seq.*) for the *Revue des Deux Mondes,* he was the author of *Psychologie musicale* and *Souvenirs de musique et de musiciens* (1921); his biographies of composers include *Mozart* (1906), *Mendelssohn* (1907), and *Gounod* (1910).

Bellair (bel.ãr'), **Count.** Character originally in George Farquhar's *The Beaux' Stratagem,* a French officer, a prisoner at Lichfield. This part was cut out by the author after the first night's representation, and the words added to the part of Foigard.

Bellair, Old. Amorous old man who imagines he disguises his love for women, in George Etherege's comedy *The Man of Mode, or Sir Fopling Flutter.*

Bellair, Young. In *The Man of Mode, or Sir Fopling Flutter,* the son of Old Bellair, a well-bred, polite youth of the period; a character in which the author, George Etherege, is said to have drawn his own portrait.

Bellaire (bel.ãr'). City in E Ohio, in Belmont County, on the Ohio River, ab. 5 mi. S of Wheeling: coal mining; manufactures of glass and enamelware. 12,573 (1950).

Bellaire. City in SE Texas, in Harris County: a western suburb of Houston. In the decade between the last two U.S. censuses its population grew from 1,124 (1940) to 10,173 (1950).

Bellamira, her Dream, or the Love of Shadows (bel.ạ.mē'rạ). Tragicomedy in two parts by Thomas Killigrew. It is in the folio edition of his works published in 1664.

Bellamira, or The Mistress. Comedy by Charles Sedley, produced in 1678. The play was partly founded on the *Eunuchus* of Terence; in it Sedley mirrored the frailty of Barbara Villiers, Countess of Castlemaine, and the audacity of John Churchill, 1st Duke of Marlborough.

Bellamont (bel'ạ.mont), 1st Earl of. See **Coote, Richard.**

Bellamy (bel'ạ.mi). In John Dryden's play *An Evening's Love, or the Mock Astrologer,* a young, lively gallant, a friend of Wildblood. He disguises himself as an astrologer, and thus gives the subtitle to the play.

Bellamy, Edward. b. at Chicopee Falls, Mass., March 26, 1850; d. there, May 22, 1898. American author, noted for his once widely popular *Looking Backward: 2000–1887* (1888), a Utopian romance written from a socialist point of view. His other works include *Dr. Heidenhoff's Process* (1880), *Mrs. Ludington's Sister* (1884), *Equality* (1897, a not particularly successful sequel to *Looking Backward*), and *The Blind Man's World and Other Stories* (1898).

Bellamy, George Anne. b. at Fingal, Ireland, c1731; d. at London, cFeb. 16, 1788. English actress. She was the illegitimate daughter of a Mrs. Bellamy and James O'Hara, 2nd Baron Tyrawley, who acknowledged her and supported her. She first appeared on the stage in *Love for Love* at Covent Garden (1742) and later as Monimia in *The Orphan* (1744). Thereafter she rose rapidly in her profession. In 1750 she played Juliet to David Garrick's Romeo, while Mrs. Cibber and Spranger Barry were playing the same roles in a rival performance. In 1785 her *Apology* was brought out in five volumes, to which a sixth was later added. Alexander Bicknell is believed to have written it from her material. The name George Anne was given her, apparently by mistake for Georgiana, in her certificate of birth.

Bellamy, Jacobus. b. at Flushing, Netherlands, Nov. 12, 1757; d. March 11, 1786. Dutch poet. He wrote patriotic and anacreontic poems, and was the author of the ballad *Roosje.*

Bellamy, Joseph. b. at North Cheshire, Conn., Feb. 20, 1719; d. at Bethlehem, Conn., March 6, 1790. American Congregational clergyman and theologian, author of *True Religion Delineated* (1750) and others.

Bellamy, Lord. Character in Thomas Shadwell's comedy *Bury Fair.*

Bellano (bel.lä'nō). Town and commune in NW Italy, in the *compartimento* (region) of Lombardy, in the province of Como, situated on the E shore of Lake Como, ab. 18 mi. NE of Como. It is a resort and produces cotton and silk textiles and ironware. Good wines are grown in the vicinity. Pop. of commune, 3,700 (1936); of town, 2,381 (1936).

Bellaria (bẹ.lãr'i.a). Wife of Pandosto in Robert Greene's *Pandosto, or the Triumph of Time.* She is the character on which is based Hermione in Shakespeare's *The Winter's Tale.*

Bellario (bẹ.lãr'i.ō). In Beaumont and Fletcher's play *Philaster,* a page. She is Euphrasia in disguise, who follows the fortunes of Philaster with romantic tenderness and fidelity.

Bellario, Doctor. Erudite lawyer of Padua, as whose substitute Portia appears in the trial scene in Shakespeare's *Merchant of Venice.* He makes no stage appearance.

Bellarmine (bel'ạr.min). Name applied to a drinking jug with the face of Cardinal Robert Bellarmine on it, and the shape of which was supposed to resemble him: originated by the Protestants of Holland to ridicule him.

Bellarmine. Character, impertinent fine gentleman, in Henry Fielding's *Joseph Andrews.* He is the mercenary lover of Leonora.

Bellarmine, Robert Francis Romulus. [Italian, **Roberto Francesco Romolo Bellarmino** (bel.lär.mē'nō).] b. at Montepulciano, Tuscany, Oct. 4, 1542; d. at Rome, Sept. 17, 1621. Italian cardinal, and Jesuit theologian and controversialist. His theological disputes with James I of England and the Scottish theologian William Barclay, over the power of the Pope in political (as opposed to religious) spheres, were famous in their day. He was professor at Louvain and in the Roman College, and archbishop of Capua. His works include *Disputationes de Controversiis, fidei . . .* (1581), *Tractatus de potestate summi pontificis in rebus temporalibus,* and *Christianae doctrinae applicatio* (1603).

Bellary (be.lä'rē). [Also, **Ballari.**] District of Madras state, S Union of India, between Hyderabad on the N and Mysore on the S. Cotton and sugar raising, and manganese and gold mining are important here. Capital, Bellary; area, 5,870 sq. mi.; pop. 1,051,235 (1941).

Bellary. [Also, **Ballari.**] Capital of the district of Ballari, S Union of India, ab. 260 mi. NW of Madras: refineries for manganese ore. 56,148 (1941).

Bellasis (bel'ạ.sis), **Edward.** b. at Basildon, Berkshire, England, Oct. 14, 1800; d. at Hyères, France, Jan. 24, 1873. English parliamentary lawyer and magistrate of Middlesex and Westminster, who supported (1833–45) the Tractarian movement. He published anonymous pamphlets in the period 1850–72 remonstrating with the Anglicans; in 1850 he took Catholic communion. Cardinal Newman called him ". . . one of the best men I ever knew."

Bellaston (bel'ạs.tọn), **Lady.** Fashionable demirep in Henry Fielding's *Tom Jones.* She is a sensual, profligate, and imperious woman.

Bellatrix (bel'ạ.triks). A very white glittering star of the second magnitude, in the left shoulder of Orion. It is γ Orionis.

Bellay (be.lā'; French, be.le), **Guillaume du.** See **Langey,** Seigneur **de.**

Bellay, Jean du. b. 1492; d. at Rome, Feb. 16, 1560. French cardinal and diplomat; brother of Seigneur de Langey (Guillaume du Bellay). He became bishop of Bayonne in 1526, bishop of Paris in 1533, and cardinal in 1535. He was a friend of letters, and is noted as the patron of François Rabelais.

Bellay, Joachim du. [Called **"the French Ovid"** and **"Prince of the Sonnet."**] b. at the Château de Liré, near Angers, France, c1524; d. at Paris, Jan. 1, 1560. French poet, one of the most noted members of the group of poets known as the Pléiade. He was a relative of Jean du Bellay, and for a time served as his secretary. He wrote *L'Olive* (sonnets to his mistress, Mademoiselle de

Viole, of whose name Olive is an anagram), 47 sonnets upon the antiquities of Rome (1558; translated into English by Edmund Spenser as *The Ruins of Rome*, 1611), *Les Regrets* (sonnets), *Discours de la Poésie*, *Défense et illustration de la langue française* (a notable work in prose that outlines the principles of the Pléiade), and others.

Belle (bel), **Jean François Joseph de.** b. at Voreppe, Isère, France, May 27, 1767; d. in June, 1802. French general. He served in the Italian campaign of 1799, and subsequently under Charles Victor Emmanuel Le Clerc on the island of Hispaniola, where he fell in battle.

Belle-Alliance (bel.å.lyäṅs), **La.** In the history of the Napoleonic wars, a farm ab. 13 mi. from Brussels, between Waterloo and Genappe, in Belgium. It was occupied by the center of the French infantry at the battle of Waterloo (June 18, 1815), Napoleon I himself being stationed in the vicinity. By this name the Prussians designate the battle of Waterloo.

Belleau (be.lō), **Rémy.** b. at Nogent-le-Rotrou, in Maine, France, 1528; d. at Paris, March 16, 1577. French poet, a member of the Pléiade. His life was spent in the service of Rémy de Lorraine, marquis d'Elbeuf, and of his son, Charles, duc d'Elbeuf, whose tutor he was. He wrote *Petites inventions* (1557, short descriptive poems), *Bergerie* (1565, a mixture of prose and poetry), *Amours et nouveaux eschanges de pierres précieuses* (1576), and various translations.

Belleau Wood (bel'ō''), **Battle of.** World War I operation in France, notable for its demonstration of the fighting qualities of the 2nd Division of the American Expeditionary Forces. The action (June 2–July 7, 1918) began as part of a general operation aimed against the German Marne salient but continued as a local offensive until more than a month after the general enemy drive had been stemmed. American forces made their initial attack on June 6 and after intense fighting seized the entire wood by June 21. Outstanding in this action was the 4th Marine Brigade (2nd Division), which was relieved for a short time by the 7th Infantry Regiment (3rd Division). The action was brought to a close when the 2nd Division was relieved by the 26th Division on July 9.

Belleau Wood American War Memorial. American war memorial at Belleau Wood, France, 5 mi. NW of Château-Thierry, which is maintained by the U.S. government in commemoration of all U.S. troops who fought in World War I. The memorial site, consisting of shell holes, trenches, and war relics, is in the area captured by American forces after bitter fighting in June and July, 1918.

Belle Dame Sans Merci (bel dåm säṅ mer.sē), **La.** [Eng. trans., "*The Fair Lady without Mercy.*"] French poem by Alain Chartier. It was translated into English by Sir Richard Ros, and not by Geoffrey Chaucer, although the translation has been attributed to him. Perhaps the best-known poem of this title, however, is the ballad (1819) by John Keats.

Belle et la bête (bel ā lå bet), **La.** French title of **Beauty and the Beast.**

Bellefontaine (bel.fon'tạn). First permanent community established (1779) by English-speaking settlers in what was then called "the Northwest." It took its name from a spring near what is now Waterloo, Ill. At the beginning of the 19th century it ranked as the third largest community in the Illinois territory, but subsequently lost its standing as a separate settlement.

Bellefontaine (bel.foun'tạn, -fon'tạn). City in W Ohio, county seat of Logan County, ab. 52 mi. NW of Columbus: rail and trading center for an agricultural area where rye and alfalfa are important crops. It was settled in 1806 and became the county seat in 1820. It occupies the site of a former Shawnee village. 10,232 (1950).

Bellefontaine (bel.fon.ten'), **Benedict.** In the poem *Evangeline* (1847), by Henry Wadsworth Longfellow, a wealthy farmer of Grand Pré, the father of the heroine. He died of a broken heart when starting on his exile, and was buried on the seashore.

Bellefontaine (bel.fon'tạn), **Fort.** U.S. military post established (1805) on the S bank of the Missouri River, near its junction with the Mississippi. It was the military headquarters for the Middle West until the construction (1826) of Jefferson Barracks.

Bellefonte (bel'font). Borough in C Pennsylvania, county seat of Centre County, on Spring Creek, at the base of Bald Eagle Mountain, in an agricultural and limestone-quarrying area: commercial center for farm products. It was the birthplace of George Grey Barnard (1863–1938). It was settled c1769. 5,651 (1950).

Belle Fourche (bel försh). City in W South Dakota, county seat of Butte County, on the Belle Fourche River in the N foothills of the Black Hills, ab. 50 mi. NW of Rapid City. In an extensive sheep and cattle raising region, it has wool markets and stockyards. The irrigated surrounding area produces sugar beets, which are processed here. Bentonite is mined nearby. 3,540 (1950).

Belle Fourche River. River in NE Wyoming and W South Dakota, which flows into the Cheyenne River. On it is Belle Fourche Dam (1911), 112 ft. high.

Bellegarde (bel.gârd). Small town in S France, in the department of Gard, ab. 10 mi. SE of Nîmes.

Bellegarde. Fortress on the Spanish frontier, in the department of Pyrénées-Orientales, France, ab. 18 mi. S of Perpignan on the Col de Pertuis.

Bellegarde, Gabriel du Bac de. b. at the Château de Bellegarde, near Carcassonne, France, Oct. 17, 1717; d. at Utrecht, Netherlands, Dec. 13, 1789. French Jansenist theologian.

Bellegarde, Count **Heinrich Joseph Johannes von.** b. at Dresden, Aug. 29, 1756; d. at Vienna, July 22, 1845. Austrian general.

Bellegarde, Jean Baptiste Morvan de. b. at Piriac, near Nantes, France, Aug. 30, 1648; d. at Paris, April 26, 1734. French man of letters and member of the community of priests of Saint Francis de Sales. Authorship of the *Histoire universelle des voyages* (1707) is attributed to him.

Bellegarde, Val de. French name of the **Jaun Valley.**

Bellegarde-sur-Valserine (bel.gârd.sür.vål.sẹ.rēn). Town in E France, in the department of Ain, situated at the junction of the Valserine and Rhone rivers, ab. 16 mi. SW of Geneva. The waters of the two rivers form cascades called Perte du Rhône and Perte de la Valserine. The Génissiat Dam, completed in 1949, is nearby; the water power serves a number of industries. The town was severely damaged in World War II. 5,407 (1946).

Belle Glade (bel' glād''). Town in S Florida, in Palm Beach County, NW of Miami, on Lake Okeechobee: trading and shipping center for an agricultural region producing especially tomatoes, peppers, and green beans. It was severely damaged by a hurricane in 1928. Pop. 7,219 (1950).

Belle Hélène (bel ā.len), **La.** Comic opera, with words by Henri Meilhac and Ludovic Halévy, and music by Jacques Offenbach, produced at Paris on Dec. 17, 1864.

Belle-Île-en-Mer (bel.ēl.äṅ.mer). [Breton, **Guerveur.**] Island in NW France, in the department of Morbihan, situated in the Bay of Biscay, ab. 8 mi. S of Quiberon. It has high cliffs. The chief place is Le Palais. At one time privately owned, it was taken by the British in 1761, restored to France in 1763. Pop. 5,646 (1946).

Belle Isle (bel īl). Island at the E entrance of the Strait of Belle Isle, NE of Cape Bauld, Newfoundland: lighthouse. It belongs to Newfoundland, Canada.

Belle Isle. Island in the James River, opposite Richmond, Va., used (1861–63) by the Confederacy as a prison for holding enlisted men of the Union forces. The establishment had some 10,000 captives by the close of 1863, when they were transferred to the stockade at Andersonville, Ga.

Belle-Isle (bel.ēl), **Charles Louis Auguste Fouquet,** Duc **de.** b. at Villefranche, Aveyron, France, Sept. 22, 1684; d. Jan. 26, 1761. French marshal and politician; grandson of Nicolas Fouquet. He shared with François Marie de Broglie the command of the French forces in the War of the Austrian Succession, and captured (Nov. 26, 1741) Prague, but was forced by the treaty of peace between Austria and Prussia at Breslau to retreat (Dec. 17, 1742) to Cheb (German, Eger). He became commander in chief of the French army in Italy in 1746, and was minister of war from 1757 to his death.

Belle-Isle, Marquis **de.** Title of **Fouquet, Nicolas.**

Belle Isle (bel'' īl'), **Strait of.** Sea passage separating Newfoundland from Labrador, and connecting the Gulf of St. Lawrence with the Atlantic Ocean. Width, 10–15 mi.

Belle Jardinière (bel zhår.dē.nyer), **La.** Madonna and Child with Saint John, by Raphael, painted in 1507 in his Florentine manner, in the collection of the Louvre, Paris. A fair-haired Madonna is seated amid a conventionalized garden-landscape, and the children stand and kneel at her knee. It has often been reproduced.

Bellême (bẹ.lem). Small town in NW France, in the department of Orne, ab. 22 mi. E of Alençon. Pop. ab. 2,000.

Bellême (be.lem'), **Robert of.** See **Belesme, Robert of.**

Belle Meade (bel' mēd'). City in N central Tennessee, in Davidson County: a southwestern suburb of Nashville. 2,831 (1950).

Belle Mignonne (bel mē.nyon), **La.** Name given in France in the 18th century to a skull illuminated with tapers and highly decorated, which was an accepted furnishing of a devout lady's boudoir. One of the French queens is said to have prayed before the skull of Anne Lenclos (Ninon de Lenclos).

Bellenden (bel'ẹn.dẹn), **Edith.** Heiress of Tillietudlem in Sir Walter Scott's novel *Old Mortality*.

Bellenden, John. [Also: **Ballantyne, Ballenden, Bannatyne.**] b. at Haddington (or Berwick), Scotland, c1490; d. perhaps at Rome, in 1550 or 1587. Scottish poet, scholar, clergyman, and translator. Educated at the universities of St. Andrews and Paris, he received his Doctor of Divinity degree from the latter. He was attached to the court of King James V of Scotland, at whose suggestion he translated into Scots the Latin chronicle-history of Hector Boece, *Historia Gentis Scotorum* (1527), for which he received 78 pounds. His translation (1530–33) was published at Edinburgh in 1536. He also translated the first five books of Livy's Roman history, for which he received 36 pounds. This work, however, was not published until 1822. Bellenden was also the author of two poems, *Proem of the Cosmographie* and *Proem of the History*, and a prose *Epistle*, all of which were published in 1536. Bellenden was archdeacon of Moray and canon of Ross; opposed to the Reformation, he is said to have fled to Rome and to have died there in 1550, but Thomas Maitland, Lord Dundrennan, who edited Bellenden's Livy, declared that he was living in 1587.

Bellenden, Sir **John.** d. 1577. Scottish lawyer and privy councillor (1561) to Mary Stuart (Queen of Scots). He was implicated in the murder of David Rizzio (1566), but was soon restored to favor. He joined the nobles against Mary and James Hepburn, 4th Earl of Bothwell, and continued in office after Mary was imprisoned; he helped frame the pacification of Perth (1573).

Bellenden, William. d. c1633. Scottish classical scholar, employed as a diplomatic agent in France by James VI of Scotland and Mary Stuart (Queen of Scots).

Bellenz (bel'ẹnts). German name of **Bellinzona.**

Belle Plaine (bel' plān'). [Former name, **Gwinsville.**] City in E Iowa, in Benton County, ab. 42 mi. NW of Iowa City. It was renamed in 1862. Pop. 3,056 (1950).

Bellerby (bel'ėr.bi), **John Rotherford.** b. at York, England, May 25, 1896—. English economist. He studied at the University of Leeds and at Harvard before serving (1921–27) on the staff of the International Labor Office of the League of Nations. He was a technical adviser (1927) to the British delegation to the International Economic Conference at Geneva, a professor (1930–32) of economic science at the University of Liverpool, and was engaged at the services secretariat (1943) of the British Ministry of Food during World War II. Author of *Monetary Stability* (1925), *A Contributive Society* (1931), *The Conflict of Values* (1933), and *Economic Reconstruction* (1943).

Bellermann (bel'ėr.män), **Ferdinand.** b. at Erfurt, Germany, March 14, 1814; d. at Berlin, Aug. 11, 1889. German landscape painter. He was employed (1842–46) by Alexander von Humboldt in Venezuela.

Bellermann, Johann Gottfried Heinrich. b. March 10, 1832; d. at Potsdam, Germany, April 10, 1903. German music theorist and composer. He was a professor (1866 *et seq.*) at Berlin University, and the author of *Die Mensuralnoten* (1858) and a work (1862) on counterpoint; composer mainly of vocal music.

Bellermann, Ludwig. b. 1836; d. 1915. German educator and historian of literature. He was the author of a standard biography (1900) of Friedrich Schiller and a three-volume study, *Schillers Dramen*. He was also editor of the most useful all-purpose edition, *Schillers Werke* (Bibliographisches Institut).

Belleroche (bel.rosh), **Pierre.** Pseudonym of **Barjot, Pierre.**

Bellerophon (bẹ.ler'ọ.fon) or **Bellerophontes** (bẹ.ler.ọ.fon'tēz). In Greek legend, a son of Glaucus, king of Corinth (or, in some accounts, of Poseidon), and grandson of Sisyphus. He was the rider of Pegasus, the slayer of the monster Chimera, and a conqueror of the fabulous Amazons. His exploits gained for him the daughter and one half the kingdom of Iobates, king of Lycia, but he later fell under the displeasure of the gods. According to Pindar his pride so increased with his good fortune that he attempted to mount to heaven on Pegasus, but Zeus maddened the horse with a gadfly, and Bellerophon fell and perished. He was worshiped as a hero at Corinth.

Bellérophon (be.lā.ro.fôṅ). Opera by Jean Baptiste Lully, with words by Thomas Corneille, Bernard le Bovier de Fontenelle, and Nicolas Boileau-Despréaux, produced in 1679.

Bellerophon (bẹ.ler'ọ.fon). Name of two famous British war vessels: **1.** British line-of-battle ship of 74 guns and 1,613 tons. She served in the Channel squadron of 1793 and 1794, and was disabled at the battle of the Nile, Aug. 1, 1798, but was repaired and fought in the battle of Trafalgar, Oct. 21, 1805. **2.** One of the first armored warships, built according to the designs of Sir Edward James Reed, chief constructor of the British navy, and launched in 1866. Length, 300 ft.; breadth, 56 ft.; draught, 26.7 ft. She had an armored belt at the water line 10 ft. wide, and a high-decked central citadel with armored bulkheads at each end, mounting ten 12-ton guns. She had two 6½-ton guns behind armor in the bows, and one 6½-ton gun behind armor in the stern. The armor was 6 inches of iron on 16 inches of wood backing.

Bellerus (be.lē'rus). Cornish giant in old English legend. Belerium was the name given to Lands End, supposed to be his home.

Belle's Stratagem, The. Comedy by Hannah Cowley, produced in 1780.

Belleval (bel.vål), **Pierre Richer de.** b. at Châlons-sur-Marne, France, 1558; d. at Montpellier, France, 1623 or 1625. French physician and botanist, the inventor of an unsuccessful system of Greek botanical nomenclature. The genus *Richeria* was named for him.

Belleville (bel.vēl). Town in E central France, in the department of Rhône, situated on the Rhone River ab. 26 mi. N of Lyons. Pop. ab. 3,000.

Belleville (bel'vil). Manufacturing city in S Illinois, county seat of St. Clair County, ab. 15 mi. SE of St. Louis. It developed in the first half of the 19th century as a coal-mining and brickmaking center. The Air Forces base Scott Field is in the vicinity. 32,721 (1950).

Belleville. City in N Kansas, county seat of Republic County: agricultural trade. It was settled in 1869. Pop. 2,858 (1950).

Belleville. Town in NE New Jersey, in Essex County, on the Passaic River, near Newark, of which it was formerly a part. 32,019 (1950).

Belleville. County city of Hastings County, Ontario, Canada, situated on the Bay of Quinte, Lake Ontario. It is a port of entry, and the seat of Albert College. 19,519 (1951).

Belleville. Former name of **Colfax.**

Bellevue (bel'vū). City in N Kentucky, in Campbell County: suburb of Cincinnati and Covington. 9,040 (1950).

Bellevue. Village in E Nebraska, in Sarpy County, on the Missouri River ab. 6 mi. S of Omaha. Site of an Indian agency (1823 *et seq.*), trading post (1827 *et seq.*), and an agency (established c1830) of the American Fur Company, it is the oldest town in Nebraska, having been incorporated in 1855. Pop. 3,858 (1950).

Bellevue. City in N Ohio, in Huron and Sandusky counties, ab. 14 mi. SW of Sandusky: railroad and manufacturing center. 6,906 (1950).

Bellevue. Borough in SW Pennsylvania, in Allegheny County; residential suburb of Pittsburgh. Settled in 1802, it was incorporated in 1867. Pop. 11,604 (1950).

Bellevue (bel.vü). Former royal castle, SW of Paris, near Sèvres, built by Jeanne Antoinette Poisson, Marquise de Pompadour, and destroyed in the French Revolution.

Bellevue. [Eng. trans., "*Beautiful View.*"] Castle near Kassel in Germany, noted for its picture-gallery. It has contained works by Holbein, Rembrandt, Van Dyck, Rubens, Dürer, Teniers, Wouwerman, Titian, Guido Reni, Carlo Dolce, Murillo, and many others. Most of these were not accessible to the general public till 1866.

Bellevue Hospital (bel'vū). Public hospital at New York, situated at the foot of East 26th Street, overlooking the East River. One of the oldest general hospitals in North America, it is affiliated with the medical schools of New York, Cornell, and Columbia universities. Its first services were established in 1736, and the present site occupied in 1816; the first ambulance service in the world (1869) and the first bacteriological laboratory in the U.S. (1892) were founded here. The large modern establishment (about 12 city blocks square) includes a psychiatric hospital, a nurses' training school (founded 1873) which was a pioneer in its field, and the New York City morgue.

Bellevue War. Armed clash (April 1, 1840) between law-enforcement officers and a group led by W. W. Brown, operator of a hotel at Bellevue, Jackson County, Iowa. It was thought that Brown was the chief of an outlaw band. The clash resulted in Brown's death and in the capture of 13 of his followers. The local citizenry, by public vote, designated flogging as the mode of punishment for the alleged outlaws, who were expelled from the town after being whipped.

Belley (be.le). Town in E France, in the department of Ain, ab. 40 mi. E of Lyons. It is a tourist center; has a cathedral and Roman antiquities. There are quarries of stone used for lithography, in the vicinity. 5,308 (1946).

Bellflower (bel.flou'ėr). Unincorporated community in S California, in Los Angeles County. 18,572 (1950).

Bell for Adano (ä.dä'nō), **A.** Novel by John Hersey, published in 1944 and awarded the Pulitzer prize the following year. It was dramatized and filmed. The action takes place during the American occupation of southern Italy during World War II.

Bell Gardens. Unincorporated community in S California, in Los Angeles County. 17,134 (1950).

Belli (bel'lē), **Giuseppe Gioacchino.** b. at Rome, Sept. 10, 1791; d. Dec. 21, 1863. Italian poet. Belli wrote some 2,000 sonnets, many of which conveyed a picture of the life of the common people of Rome in the later years of the Papal temporal power, while others were sharp political satires in poetic form. A collection of his works was published under the title *I Sonetti Romaneschi* (1886–89).

Belliard (be.lyår), Count **Augustin Daniel.** b. at Fontenay-le-Comte, Vendée, France, March 25, 1769; d. at Brussels, Jan. 28, 1832. French lieutenant general, who distinguished himself in the Napoleonic campaigns, particularly at Borodino (1812). He took part in the Egyptian campaign, and, as governor of Cairo, surrendered it to the English on June 27, 1801.

Bellicent (bel'i.sent). Half sister of King Arthur, in the Arthurian romances. Tennyson also tells her story, in somewhat altered form, in "Gareth and Lynette," one of the *Idylls of the King*.

Bellicourt War Memorial (be.lē.kör'). American war monument N of Bellicourt, France, ab. 9 mi. N of St.-Quentin and ab. 13 mi. S of Cambrai, erected in commemoration of the combat operations of American units which served with the British forces in France during World War I. The monument stands on a ridge over the St.-Quentin Canal tunnel, a part of the Hindenburg Line penetrated by American troops at this point in 1918.

Bellin (be.laṅ), **Jacques Nicolas.** b. at Paris, 1703; d. at Versailles, France, March 21, 1772. French geographer and cartographer. He was officially charged by the French government with the preparation of maps of the coasts of the known seas. His work appeared in the *Neptune français* (1753; the French coasts), *Hydographie française* (1756; maps of all known coasts), *Petit atlas maritime, Mémoires sur les cartes des côtes de l'Amérique septentrionale* (1755), *Essais géographiques sur les Îles Britanniques* (1763), and similar works on Guiana, the Antilles, Hispaniola, and other places.

Bellincioni (bel.lēn.chō'nē), **Gemma.** b. at Como, Italy, in August, 1866—. Italian opera singer. She first appeared on the stage (1881) at the Fiorentini Theatre, Naples, in *Tutti in Maschera*. She sang (1895) at Covent Garden, after having played (1890) Santuzza in the first production of *Cavalleria Rusticana* at the Costanzi Theatre, Rome; she also created the chief soprano parts in *Fedora, A Santa Lucia, Lorenza, La Cabrera,* and *Sapho*. Her tours have included Germany, Austria, Portugal, England, France, Russia, and South America. She married Roberto Stagno, with whom she sang in *Cavalleria Rusticana*.

Belling (bel'ing), **Rudolf.** b. at Berlin, Aug. 26, 1886—. German expressionist sculptor. He is best known for his composition in wood, *Dreiklang* (1918), in which he abstracts the human form, and for his figure of the German boxer Max Schmeling. Some of his work emphasizes expression of the specific qualities of the material employed, as in *Head in Mahogany* and *Head in Brass;* in his full-length figure of the *Miner* he turned more towards naturalism. His work was shown at New York in 1935.

Belling, Wilhelm Sebastian von. b. at Paulsdorf, in East Prussia, Feb. 15, 1719; d. at Stolp, in Pomerania, Nov. 28, 1779. Prussian cavalry general who distinguished himself in the Seven Years' War.

Bellingham (bel'ing.ham). Town in SE Massachusetts, in Norfolk County, near the border of Rhode Island: manufactures include leather and textiles. 4,100 (1950).

Bellingham. [Former name, **Whatcom.**] City in NW Washington, county seat of Whatcom County, on Bellingham Bay, ab. 50 mi. SE of Vancouver: lumber mills and salmon canneries; the surrounding area produces vegetables, fruits, and dairy products. Bellingham is the seat of the Western Washington College of Education. The region was settled c1846, and the present city was formed by the union of Whatcom, New Whatcom, Sehome, and Fairhaven and renamed in 1903. Pop. 34,112 (1950).

Bellingham (bel'ing.ạm, -ham), Sir **Edward.** d. 1549. English lord deputy of Ireland (1548–49), who there suppressed a rebellion in King's and Queen's counties. He served with Thomas Seymour in Hungary, and with Thomas Howard, Earl of Surrey, at Boulogne and on the Isle of Wight (1545); he became (c1546) privy councilor to Edward VI of England.

Bellingham, Richard. b. in England, c1592; d. in Massachusetts, Dec. 7, 1672. Colonial governor of Massachusetts. He emigrated to America in 1634, and was governor of the Massachusetts Colony in 1641, 1654, and 1665–72. In 1641 he contracted a second marriage, performing the marriage ceremony himself, without proclamation of banns. He was presented by the great inquest for breach of the order of court, but, as he refused to vacate the bench, the other magistrates were at a loss how to proceed, and he thus escaped official censure.

Bellingshausen (bel'ingz.hou.zẹn), **Mount.** [Also, **Mount Bellinghausen** (-ing-).] Steep, conspicuous cone in Antarctica, lying on the S side of Larsen Glacier, on the coast of Victoria Land, in ab. 75°10′ S., 162°18′ E. It was discovered by the National Antarctic Expedition (1901–04), commanded by Captain Robert F. Scott, who named this peak for Admiral Thaddeus von Bellingshausen, commander of the Russian expedition of 1819–21. Elevation, ab. 3,200 ft.

Bellingshausen Sea. One of the large marginal seas surrounding Antarctica, an arm of the South Pacific Ocean between Alexander I Island and Thurston Peninsula, which terminates in approximately 71°20′ S., 98°00′ W. It was named for Admiral Thaddeus von Bellingshausen, commander of the Russian Antarctic expedition (1819–21).

Bellini (bel.lē'nē), **Gentile.** b. c1427; d. Feb. 22, 1507. Italian painter of the Venetian school, known as a portraitist as well as a painter of processions and pageants; son of Jacopo Bellini. He was called to the court at Constantinople in 1479, remaining there until 1480. With his more famous brother, Giovanni Bellini, he worked on frescoes in the ducal palace, now destroyed, at Venice. One of his best-known paintings is *Preaching of Saint Mark*.

Bellini, Giovanni. b. after 1427; d. Nov. 29, 1516. Italian painter of the Venetian school, known chiefly for his magnificent altarpieces; son of Jacopo Bellini. His works are in virtually all the principal art galleries of the world. Among his pupils were Titian and Giorgione. His self-portrait, at Rome, is considered by most authorities to be one of the outstanding examples of portraiture in oil, and is a fine example of the work of the Venetian school, older than the portrait in the Uffizi at Florence.

Bellini, Jacopo. b. c1400; d. c1464. Italian painter, the first of a famous family of Venetian painters; father of Giovanni Bellini and Gentile Bellini, and father-in-law of Andrea Mantegna. He studied with Gentile da Fabriano, and is considered, with his sons, to be among the founders of the Venetian School of Renaissance painting. Many of his paintings are no longer in existence, but a *Crucifixion*, an *Annunciation*, and some sketchbooks may still be seen as examples of his work.

Bellini, Lorenzo. b. at Florence, Sept. 3, 1643; d. Jan. 8, 1704. Italian physician and anatomist, professor of philosophy and afterward of anatomy at Pisa. His collected works were published in 1708.

Bellini, Vincenzo. b. at Catania, Sicily, Nov. 1, 1801; d. at Puteaux, France, Sept. 24, 1835. Italian operatic composer. His works include *Bianca e Fernando* (1826), *Il Pirata* (1827), *La Straniera* (1829), *Zaira* (1829), *I Capuletti ed i Montecchi* (1830), *La Sonnambula* (1831), *Norma* (1831), *Beatrice di Tenda* (1833), and *I Puritani* (1835). Of all these, *La Sonnambula*, *Norma*, and *I Puritani* are the only ones to be given any popular 20th-century performances.

Bellinzona (bel.lēn.tsō′nä). [German, **Bellenz.**] Town in S Switzerland, the capital of the canton of Ticino, situated on the Ticino River, E of the N end of Lago Maggiore. It occupies an important position on the St. Gotthard route across the Alps, and is near the terminus of the San Bernardino route. Numerous industrial establishments and the repair shops of the St. Gotthard railway are located here. 10,948 (1941).

Belli Quadrum (bel′ī kwod′rum). A Latin name of **Beaucaire.**

Bellisant (bel′i.sant). In the Charlemagne cycle of romance, the mother of Valentine and Orson. She was banished by her husband Alexander, emperor of Constantinople, for supposed infidelity, and her sons were born in a wild forest.

Bellisant. One of the principal female characters in Philip Massinger's *The Parliament of Love.*

Bell Island. Island in Conception Bay, SE Newfoundland, Canada, the iron-mining center of the province, near St. John's. The mines have been worked since 1893 and are of major importance to the economy of Newfoundland. 7,200 (1945).

Bell Island. Island situated NE of Newfoundland near the entrance to White Bay. (It should not be confused with Bell Island in Conception Bay, SE Newfoundland.) Length, ab. 8 mi.

Bellius (bel′i.us), **Martinus.** The pseudonym under which was published a book entitled *De haereticis, an sint persequendi, etc.*, at "Magdeburg" (false for Basel), in 1554. It was published soon after Calvin's defense of the execution of the Spanish theologian, Michael Servetus, and was a plea for religious toleration. The authorship was ascribed to Sebastianus Castellio, a French Protestant theologian, who in fact wrote a part of the book under the pseudonym Basilius Montfortius.

Bellman (bel′män), **Karl Mikael.** b. at Stockholm, Feb. 4, 1740; d. Feb. 11, 1795. Swedish humorous and lyric poet. Chief among his works are *Fredman's Epistlar* (Epistles, 1790) and *Fredman's Sänger* (Songs, 1791). His writings include drinking songs, love songs, comic poems, religious poems, and parodies.

Bellman (bel′man), **The.** Literary review (1906–19) published by William C. Edgar.

Bellman of London, The. Satirical work by Thomas Dekker, published in 1608. It is founded on the *Ground Work of Coney Catching*, which some believe to have been also written by Dekker. The latter was taken largely from Harman's *Caveat for Cursitors.* In the same year Dekker published a second part called *Lanthorne and Candlelight, or The Bellman's Second Night's Walke.* In 1612 a fourth or fifth edition of the second part appeared, called *O per se O, or a new cryer of Lanthorne and Candlelight, Being an addition or lengthening of the Bellman's Second Night's Walke.* A number of editions of the second part were published before 1648, all with differences. They are amusing descriptions of London rogues.

Bellman of Paris, The. Play by Thomas Dekker and John Day, licensed in 1623, but not printed.

Bellmawr (bel.mär′). Borough in SW New Jersey, in Camden County, ab. 6 mi. S of Camden. In the decade between the last two U.S. censuses its population more than quadrupled. 1,250 (1940); 5,213 (1950).

Bellmore (bel′mōr). Unincorporated community in SE New York, in Nassau County, on Long Island. Under the urban definition established for use in the 1950 census, Bellmore was counted with adjoining urban areas. The last official enumeration was 6,793 (1940).

Bellmour (bel′mör). The lover of Belinda, in William Congreve's comedy *The Old Bachelor.*

Bellmour. Faithful friend of Jane Shore, in Nicholas Rowe's *The Tragedy of Jane Shore.*

Bello (bā′yō), **Andrés.** b. at Caracas, Venezuela, Nov. 29, 1781; d. at Santiago, Chile, Oct. 15, 1865. South American poet, scholar, and journalist. Honored by the king of Spain before his native country's revolt, he sought aid for the insurgents at London, where he remained (1810–29) as an official of (successively) Venezuela, Colombia, and Chile. He founded *El repertorio americano*, which first published his *Silva a la agricultura de la zona tórrida* (1826), which is considered by some to be the greatest of Spanish American poems. From 1829 on he lived in Chile, where he became editor of *El araucano*, first president of the national university, and codifier of the country's civil law. His *Gramática de la lengua castellana* (1847) is old-fashioned but still influential. As a classicist and humanist he engaged in a celebrated controversy with the Argentine writers of the romantic school. The 15 volumes of his complete works, published (1881–93) by the Chilean government, include *Principios de derecho internacional* (1832) and *La oración pro todos* (1843).

Belloc (bel′ok), **Hilaire.** [Full name, **Joseph Hilaire Pierre Belloc.**] b. at St.-Cloud, Paris, July 27, 1870; d. at Guildford, Surrey, England, July 16, 1953. English essayist, historian, novelist, journalist, and poet. He was educated at the Oratory School, Edgbaston, England, and at Balliol College, Oxford. He became a naturalized British subject (1902) and was a member (1906–10) of the House of Commons for Salford. He published *The Bad Child's Book of Beasts* (1896), *More Beasts for Worse Children* (1897), *The Modern Traveller* (1898), *Danton* (1899), *Robespierre* (1901), *The Path to Rome* (1902), *Caliban's Guide to Letters* (1903), *Esto Perpetua* (1906), *The Historic Thames* (1907), *On Nothing* (1908), *The Pyrenees* (1909), *Hills and the Sea* (1910), *Pongo and the Bull* (1910), *The Servile State* (1912), *The Book of the Bayeux Tapestry* (1913), *Europe and the Faith* (1920), *The Jews* (1922; 2nd ed., 1937), *History of England* (4 vols., 1925–31), *Many Cities* (1928), *Belinda* (1928), *The Missing Masterpiece* (1929), *Richelieu* (1930), *Wolsey* (1930), *A Conversation with a Cat* (1931), *Napoleon* (1932), *Charles I* (1933), *Cromwell* (1934), *Characters of the Reformation* (1936), *The Great Heresies* (1938), and *The Last Rally* (1940).

Bello Codecido (or **Codesido**) (bā′yō kō.ᴛʜā.sē′ᴛʜō), **Emilio.** b. at Santiago, Chile, July 31, 1868—. Chilean politician, president (1925) of the governing junta. He has served as undersecretary of war and navy. He organized (1892) the *Partido Liberal Democrático* (Liberal Democratic Party), was national deputy (1894, 1897) for Valparaíso, and served as minister of industry and public works (1898), of justice (1900), of foreign affairs (1901, 1904, 1919), of the interior (1905), of state (1924), and of national defense (1932–38). Other posts have included minister to Mexico (1901) and to Bolivia (1919), councillor of state (1909–12), and arbitrator (1930) in the Guatemala-Honduras frontier dispute.

Bello Horizonte (be″lô.rē.zōn′tẹ). See **Belo Horizonte.**

Bellona (bẹ.lō′nạ). In Roman mythology, the goddess of war, regarded sometimes as the wife and sometimes as the sister of Mars. She was, probably, originally a Sabine divinity, and her worship appears to have been introduced at Rome by a Sabine family, the Claudii. She is represented as armed with shield and lance.

Bellona. An asteroid (No. 28) discovered by R. Luther at Düsseldorf, Germany, March 1, 1854.

Bellonte (be.lônt), **Maurice.** b. c1893—. French aviator. With Dieudonné Coste, he made the first westbound flight from Paris to New York (Sept. 1–2, 1930), in 37 hours and 18½ minutes. He copiloted the *Question Mark*, a Bréguet-Hispano craft.

Bellot (be.lō), **Joseph René.** b. at Paris, 1826; d. 1853. French naval officer, a volunteer on English expeditions to arctic regions, on one of which, in 1853, he met his death by falling through a hole in the ice-sheet.

Bellot Strait. Strait in the arctic regions of North America, between the Boothia peninsula and the island of Somerset.

Bellotto (bāl.lôt′tō), **Bernardo.** See under **Canaletto, Antonio.**

Bellovaci (be.lov′ą.sī). [Also, **Belovaci.**] In ancient history, an important tribe of the Belgian Gauls, occupying a territory corresponding to the later dioceses of Beauvais and Senlis, France; they were subdued (57 B.C.) by Julius Caesar. Their chief town was on the site of what is now Beauvais.

Bellovacum (be.lov′ą.kum). An ancient name of **Beauvais.**

Bellow (bel′ō), **Saul.** b. at Lachine, Quebec, Canada, July 10, 1915—. American novelist. He was graduated (B.S., 1937) from Northwestern University and was a teacher (1938–42) at Pestalozzi-Froebel Teachers College, Chicago. In 1943 he became a member of the editorial department of the *Encyclopaedia Britannica.* Author of the novels *Dangling Man* (1944) and *The Victim* (1947).

Bellows (bel′ōz), **Albert Fitch.** b. at Milford, Mass., Nov. 29, 1829; d. at Auburndale, Mass., Nov. 24, 1883. American painter. In 1845 he found employment in the office of a Boston architect, whose partner he became when he was only 19 years of age. A few years later his interest in painting led him to devote his career entirely to that art. He studied in Belgium, France, and England, and became the principal of the New England School of Design. His earlier pictures were in oils, but in later years he worked chiefly in water colors, and his work in that medium became particularly well known. He also executed large etchings. In 1861 he became a National Academician, and in 1868 was made an honorary member of the Royal Belgian Water Color Society. He was most successful with landscape subjects, and examples of his work are to be seen in the Chicago Museum of Art, the New York Public Library, and other public institutions. He was the author of *Water Color Painting* (1868).

Bellows, George Wesley. b. at Columbus, Ohio, Aug. 12, 1882; d. Jan. 8, 1925. American painter and lithographer. An athlete and a prolific artist, he became noted for his depictions of figures engaged in pastimes popular in America, ranging from prize fights and circuses to family picnics. After attending Ohio State University, he was a student (1904 *et seq.*) at New York of Robert Henri, Kenneth Hayes Miller, and H. G. Maratta; he was made (1909) at 27 an associate of the National Academy. One of the organizers of the Armory Show (1913), he also taught at the Art Students League of New York (1910, 1918, 1919) and at the Chicago Art Institute (1919); among his students were many later to be noted as "American Scene" painters. Among the best known of his paintings are *Stag at Sharkey's* (1907; Cleveland Museum of Art), *Love in Winter* (1913), *Padre* (1917), *Spring*, and *Gramercy Park* (1920). His illustrations include those for Donn Byrne's *The Wind Bloweth* and H. G. Wells's *Men Like Gods.* He is represented in the Metropolitan Museum of Art, New York, the Boston Museum of Fine Arts, the Corcoran Gallery of Art, Washington, D.C., and elsewhere.

Bellows, Henry Whitney. b. at Walpole, N.H., June 11, 1814; d. Jan. 30, 1882. American Unitarian divine and writer, pastor of All Souls Church, New York. He was organizer and president of the U.S. Sanitary Commission, which he set up for the care of the wounded and ill during the Civil War.

Bellows Falls. [Former name, **Great Falls.**] Village in S Vermont, in Windham County, at the falls of the Connecticut River, ab. 41 mi. SE of Rutland: manufactures include paper, farm machinery, and maple-sugar-making equipment; shipping center for milk. It was at one time the home of Hetty Green (1834–1916). 3,881 (1950).

Belloy (be.lwå), **Pierre Laurent Buyrette de.** b. at St. Flour, Cantal, France, Nov. 17, 1727; d. at Paris, March 5, 1775. French dramatist and actor. He was among the first to introduce native heroes on the French stage, rather than classical heroes. His works include *Titus* (1759), *Zelmire* (1762), *Le Siège de Calais* (1765), *Gaston et Bayard* (1771), *Pierre le Cruel* (1772), and others.

Bell Rock. [Also: **Inchcape Rock, Inch Cape.**] Rock in the North Sea, off the Firth of Tay (E Scotland), ab. 11 mi. SE of Arbroath. It is marked by a lighthouse.

Bells, The. Poem of four stanzas by Edgar Allan Poe, published in 1849. Utilizing onomatopoeia, the poem suggests the sounds of sleigh bells, wedding bells, alarm bells, and funeral bells, and the human emotions evoked by them.

Bells, The. Dramatization by Leopold Lewis from Erckmann-Chatrian's novel *Le Juif Polonais;* produced in 1871. Henry Irving created and was successful in the role of Mathias, the leading character.

Bells and Pomegranates. Series of eight pamphlets by Robert Browning, published between 1841 and 1846. They contained many of his famous poems, as well as six dramas.

Bell Savage or **Belle Sauvage** (bel sav′ąj). London tavern which formerly stood on Ludgate Hill. Its inn yard was one of those used in the 16th century as a theater and for bearbaiting and other spectacles. A printing house later occupied the site.

Bell-Smith (bel′smith′), **Frederick Marlett.** b. at London, 1846; d. at Toronto, Canada, 1923. Canadian painter, chiefly of urban scenes. He studied at London, and then at Paris under Gustave Claude Etienne Courtois, Alexander Harrison, and others. He helped to found the Society of Canadian Artists in 1867 and served as president of the Ontario Society of Artists from 1905 to 1908; he became a member of the Royal Canadian Academy in 1886 and of the Royal British Colonial Society of Artists in 1908. He was awarded a gold medal at Halifax in 1881, and received prizes for water colors at the Montreal Art Association in 1892 and 1909. His principal works include *Lights of a City Street* and *Tower Bridge, London.*

Bells of Shoreditch (shōr′dich″), **The.** Novel by Ethel Sidgwick, published in 1928.

"Bell-the-Cat." Nickname of **Douglas, Archibald** (c1449–1514). At a deliberation of the nobles for the purpose of effecting the removal of Robert Cochrane, Earl of Mar, James III's obnoxious favorite, their predicament was compared to that of the mice which determined to hang a bell around the cat's neck, and the question was asked who would be brave enough to perform the act. To this Douglas replied: "I will bell the cat."

Bellune (bel.lün), Duc **de.** Title of **Victor** or **Victor-Perrin, Claude.**

Belluno (bel.lö′nō). Province in NE Italy, in the *compartimento* (region) of Veneto. Capital, Belluno; area, ab. 1,300 sq. mi.; pop. 216,333 (1936).

Belluno. [Latin, **Belunum.**] Town and commune in NE Italy, in the *compartimento* (region) of Veneto, the capital of the province of Belluno, situated on the Piave River, in the Venetian Alps, ab. 50 mi. NW of Venice: has textile manufactures and is a center for the local wine and lumber trade. It is the seat of a bishopric; the cathedral dates from the 16th century, and has a famous bell tower. There are a number of palaces from the Renaissance period; the civic museum contains prehistoric and Roman antiquities. The town became Roman in 180 B.C., was in the Middle Ages successively a Lombard duchy, a Frankish county, a bishopric, and a free city. It joined the republic of Venice in 1420, was under Austrian rule during part of the 19th century, and has been Italian since 1866. In World War I it was occupied by the Austro-German army after the battle of Karfreit, Nov. 10, 1917. Buildings of interest to tourists were undamaged in World War II. Pop. of commune, 25,547 (1936); of town, 10,083 (1936).

Bellus Mons (bel′us monz). Latin name of **Beaumont,** France.

Bell Ville (bel vēl′; Spanish, bey′ bē′yā). City in C Argentina, in Córdoba province, ab. 280 mi. NW of Buenos Aires. 15,796 (1947).

Bellvue (bel′vū), **West.** Former name of **Avalon, Pa.**

Bellwood (bel′wůd). Village in NE Illinois, in Cook County, near Chicago: residential community. 8,746 (1950).

Bellwood. Borough in C Pennsylvania, in Blair County. 2,559 (1950).

Belly (bel′i). River in NW Montana and SW Alberta, Canada, rising in Glacier National Park, and flowing NE to join the Oldman River. Length, ab. 75 mi.

Belmar (bel′mär). Borough in C New Jersey, in Monmouth County, on the Atlantic Ocean: resort and residential community. 4,636 (1950).

Bélmez (bel′meth). Town in S Spain, in the province of Córdoba, situated on the Guadiato River, ab. 35 mi. NW of Córdoba. It has a medieval castle. Iron, coal, copper, and lead mines are in the vicinity. 10,440 (1940).

Belmont (bel′mont). City in W California, in San Mateo County, ab. 10 mi. S of San Francisco. In the decade between the last two U.S. censuses its population more than quadrupled. 1,229 (1940); 5,567 (1950).

Belmont. Town in E Massachusetts, in Middlesex County: residential community near Boston, Watertown, and Waltham. 27,381 (1950).

Belmont. Village in SE Missouri, in Mississippi County, on the Mississippi River, ab. 17 mi. S of Cairo, Ill. Here, on Nov. 7, 1861, occurred an indecisive battle between Union forces under Ulysses S. Grant and Confederates under Gideon Johnson Pillow. The Union loss was 485, that of the Confederates, 642.

Belmont. Town in W North Carolina, in Gaston County. It is the seat of Belmont Abbey College. 5,330 (1950).

Belmont, August. b. at Alzey, Germany, Dec. 2, 1816; d. at New York, Nov. 24, 1890. American banker and politician. He was Austrian consul at New York (1844–50), U.S. minister to The Netherlands (1855–58), and chairman of the Democratic National Committee (1860–72); he aided the Union in the Civil War. He was notable as a patron of the turf and as an art collector.

Belmont, August. b. at New York, Feb. 18, 1853; d. at New York, Dec. 10, 1924. American banker; son of August Belmont (1816–90) and successor to his father as head of August Belmont and Company. He was chairman of the board of various transportation enterprises. He was married (1910) to the actress Eleanor Elise Robson.

Belmont, Charles. Rakish young fellow in Edward Moore's play *The Foundling*. The part was played with great success by David Garrick.

Belmont, Perry. b. at New York, Dec. 28, 1850; d. May 25, 1947. American banker and politician; son of August Belmont (1816–90). He was a Democratic member of Congress from New York (1881–89).

Belmonte (bel.mōn′tā), **Juan.** b. at Seville, Spain, 1892—. Spanish bullfighter, considered by many to be the greatest of the modern period. He made his first appearance in the ring at Madrid in 1913, and before long became one of the popular heroes of the Spanish national sport by virtue of his courage, adroitness, and style. Belmonte's story of his life and career, as told to Manuel Chaves Nogales, was translated into English in 1937.

Belmonte (bel.mōn′tę), **Rio Grande do.** See **Jequitinhonha.**

Belmontet (bel.môṅ.te), **Louis.** b. at Montauban, France, March 25, 1799; d. at Paris, Oct. 14, 1879. French poet and dramatist. His works include *Les Tristes* (1824), *Le Souper d'Auguste* (1828), and *Une fête de Néron* (1829), a tragedy written with Alexandre Soumet.

Belmont Heights (bel′mont). Unincorporated community in W Florida, in Hillsborough County, near Tampa. Under the urban definition established for use in the 1950 census, Belmont Heights was counted with adjoining urban areas. The last official enumeration was 2,836 (1940).

Belmontium (bel.mon′shum). Latin name of **Beaumont,** France.

Belna (bel′nạ). Latin name of **Beaune.**

Bel-Nirari (bel′nē.rä′rē). King of Assyria, c1380 B.C. He conquered part of Babylonia.

Belo (bē′lō), **Alfred Horatio.** b. at Salem, N.C., May 27, 1839; d. April 19, 1901. American newspaper publisher and soldier, with the Confederate army in the Civil War. Employed (1865) by the Galveston, Texas, *News*, in which he bought (1875) a dominant interest, he made the *News* a popular Texas newspaper by distributing the papers by special mail car throughout the state; in 1885 he instituted a duplicate edition at Dallas. He was a cofounder and twice vice-president of the Associated Press.

Beloch (bā′loċh), **Karl Julius.** b. at Petschendorf, in Silesia, Jan. 21, 1854; d. at Rome, Feb. 1, 1929. German historian. He served as a professor (1879 *et seq.*) at the universities of Rome and Leipzig. Author of *Die Bevölkerung der griechisch-römischen Welt* (The population of the Greek-Roman World, 1886), *Griechische Geschichte* (Greek History, 1893–1904), and *Römische Geschichte bis zum Beginn der punischen Kriege* (Roman History to the Beginning of the Punic Wars, 1926).

Beloe (bē′lō), **William.** b. at Norwich, England, 1756; d. at London, April 11, 1817. English clergyman and writer. He was a founder (1793) with Robert Nares of the *British Critic*. He became rector of All Hallows, at London, in 1796, and was keeper (1803–06) of printed books in the British Museum. He wrote *The Sexagenarian, or Recollections of a Literary Life* (1817).

Beloeil (be.lėy′). Town in W Belgium, in the province of Hainaut, ab. 11 mi. NW of Mons. It contains a castle of the princes of Ligne.

Belogorsk (bye.lo̩.gôrsk′). [Former name, **Karasubazar, Karasu-Bazar.**] Town in SW U.S.S.R., in the Crimean *oblast* (region) of the Russian Soviet Federated Socialist Republic, ab. 28 mi. NE of Simferopol. Pop. over 10,000 (1951).

Belo Horizonte (be″lô.rē.zōn′tę). [Also, **Bello Horizonte.**] Capital of the state of Minas Gerais, in E Brazil: second largest of the country's inland cities, important for agricultural and mining industries. It was founded (c1890) expressly as the seat of government. 346,207 (1950).

Beloit (bę.loit′). City in N Kansas, county seat of Mitchell County, on the Solomon River: agricultural trade; flour mills. It was settled in 1868. Pop. 4,085 (1950).

Beloit. [Former names, **Turtle, Blodgett's Settlement, New Albany.**] City in S Wisconsin, in Rock County, on the Rock River, ab. 68 mi. SW of Milwaukee: manufactures include farm engines, papermaking machines, pumps, stokers, fireworks, automobile radiators, electric brakes, refrigerating units, x-ray tubes, powdered milk, and hosiery. It is the seat of Beloit College, which is noted for its work in anthropology and archaeology. Logan Museum, on the campus, houses important artifacts from the Cro-Magnon period. 29,590 (1950).

Belon (bę.lôṅ), **Pierre.** b. at Soulletière, near Mans, Sarthe, France, 1517; d. at Paris, in April, 1564. French naturalist and traveler (1546–49) in the Orient. He wrote *Histoire naturelle des estranges poissons marines* (1551) and *L'Histoire de la nature des oyseaux* (1555), as well as accounts of his travels. Epicures associate him with the particularly succulent French oyster which bears his name.

Belopolsky (bye.lo̩.pôl′ski), **Aristarch Apolonovich.** b. at Moscow, July 1, 1854; d. May 16, 1934. Russian astrophysicist, associated with Pulkovo Observatory from 1891, and its director from 1919. His broad spectroscopic studies were largely directed toward variable and binary stars.

Beloretsk (bye.lo̩.retsk′). City in the W central part of the U.S.S.R., in the E Bashkir Autonomous Soviet Socialist Republic, on the Belaya River, ab. 800 mi. E of Moscow. The city owes its growth to the early establishment (1762) of a considerable metallurgical industry based on regional resources of iron ore and pyrites. The plant has been much expanded in recent years, and is an important producer of high-quality alloy steels, using regional manganese and chrome ores for production. During World War II special types of metal were made here for the war effort. 19,870 (1926); 31,500 (est. 1933).

Belorussia (bye.lo̩.rush′ạ). See **Byelorussian Soviet Socialist Republic.**

Belorussians (bye.lo̩.rush′ạnz). See **Byelorussians.**

Belos (bē′los). See **Belus.**

Belostok (bye.lo̩.stôk′). Russian name of **Białystok.**

Belot (bę.lō), **Adolphe.** b. at Pointe-a-Pitre, on the island of Guadeloupe, Nov. 6, 1829; d. at Paris, Dec. 17, 1890. French novelist and dramatist. Among his works are the novel *Mademoiselle Giraud, ma femme* (1870), the plays *Le Testament de César Girodot* (1859; written in collaboration), *Miss Multon* (1867; with Eugène Nus), and *L'Article 47* (1871; from a novel).

Belotto (bā.lôt′tō), **Bernardo.** See under **Canaletto, Antonio.**

Belovaci (be.lov′ạ.sī). See **Bellovaci.**

Beloved Vagabond, The. Novel by William John Locke, published in 1906. Its central character, the "vagabond" of the title, is Berzelius Nibbidard Paragot, a Quixotic hero, one of the author's favorite types.

Below (bā′lō), **Otto von.** b. at Danzig, Jan. 1, 1857; d. 1944. German general. He defended East Prussia (1914) against the Russian invasion, and was commander (1916) of an army group in Macedonia, and on the Italian front (1917–18). After the end of World War I he organized the defense of German frontiers.

Belpasso (bel.päs′sō). Town and commune in SW Italy, on the island of Sicily, in the province of Catania, situated on the slope of Mount Etna, ab. 8 mi. NW of Catania. It was destroyed by an eruption of Etna in 1669, and rebuilt N of the old site. Pop. of commune, 10,281 (1936); of town, 9,482 (1936).

Belper (bel′pėr). Urban district and market town in C England, in Derbyshire, situated on the river Derwent, ab. 7 mi. N of Derby, ab. 136 mi. N of London by rail. It is a cotton-spinning center, and has had manufactures of hosiery and silk. 15,716 (1951).

Belphegor (bel′fẹ.gôr). Archdemon who undertook an earthly marriage, but who fled, daunted, from the horrors of female companionship. His name derives from the Baal-peor mentioned in the Bible. The story in its modern form, with merely a difference of names, was originally told in an old Latin manuscript, which is now lost, but which, till the period of the civil wars in France, remained in the library of Saint Martin de Tours. There has been some dispute as to whether Brevio or Niccolò Machiavelli (who spelled the name "Belfagor") first exhibited the tale in an Italian garb. It was printed by Brevio during his life, and under his own name, in 1545; and with the name of Machiavelli in 1549, which was about 18 years after that historian's death. It is believed that both writers borrowed the incidents from the Latin manuscript. Jean de La Fontaine treated this subject in one of his *Contes*, and Arthur Wilson printed an English tragicomedy called *Belphegor, or the Marriage of the Devil* in 1691.

Belphegor. Translation and adaptation of *Palliasse*, a French play by Adolphe Philippe Dennery and Marc Fournier, made (1856) by Charles Webb.

Belphoebe (bel.fē′bē). Huntress in Edmund Spenser's *Faerie Queene*, intended to represent Queen Elizabeth as a woman, as Gloriana represented her as a queen. She is the twin sister of Amoret and the daughter of the nymph Chrysogone.

Belsen (bel′zẹn). See under **Bergen-Belsen.**

Belsham (bel′shạm), **Thomas.** b. at Bedford, England, April 26, 1750; d. at Hampstead, now part of London, Nov. 11, 1829. English Unitarian divine; brother of William Belsham. He published a number of theological books.

Belsham, William. b. at Bedford, England, 1752; d. near Hammersmith, now part of London, Nov. 17, 1827. English historian and political essayist; brother of Thomas Belsham. He was the author of numerous works supporting the Whigs.

Belshazzar (bel.shaz′ạr). [Babylonian, **Bel-shar-uzur** (bel.shär′ö′zör).] d. 538 B.C. In the Bible, according to the book of Daniel (v.), the son of Nebuchadnezzar, and the last king of Babylonia. According to the cuneiform inscriptions this was Nabonidus, while Belshazzar was his eldest son. He was governor of southern Babylonia and chief of the army in the last struggle, and coregent with his father. When the latter fled to Borsippa, after being defeated by Cyrus, Belshazzar assumed the command in Babylonia, and was killed in the sack of the city by Cyrus. According to the scriptural narrative he was warned during a feast of his coming doom by handwriting on the wall, which was interpreted by Daniel (Dan. v., vii. 1, viii. 1; Bar. i. 11, 12).

Belshazzar. Oratorio by George Frederick Handel, first performed at the King's Theater at London in 1745.

Belshazzar. Tragedy by Henry Hart Milman, published in 1822.

Belsunce de Castel Moron (bel.zėṅs dẹ kȧs.tel mo.rôṅ), **Henri François Xavier de.** b. at the Château de la Force, in Périgord, France, Dec. 4, 1671; d. at Marseilles, June 4, 1755. French Jesuit, bishop of Marseilles, and opponent of Jansenism, noted for his heroism during a pestilence (1720–21) at Marseilles. He was a voluminous writer.

Belt, Great. [Danish, **Storebælt.**] Middle sea passage between the Kattegat and the Baltic Sea, separating Zealand and Fyn islands, in Denmark. Width, ab. 9–20 mi.

Belt, Little. [Danish, **Lillebælt.**] Western sea passage between the Kattegat and the Baltic Sea, separating Fyn island from the mainland, in Denmark. Average width, ab. 7–10 mi.

Beltane (bel′tạn). [Also, **Bealtaine.**] **1.** The first day of May (O.S.); old May day, one of the four quarter days (the others being Lammas, Hallowmạs, and Candlemas) anciently observed in Scotland. **2.** An ancient Celtic festival or anniversary formerly observed on Beltane or May day in Scotland, and in Ireland on June 21. Bonfires were kindled on the hills, all domestic fires having been previously extinguished, only to be relighted from the embers of the Beltane fires. This custom is supposed to derive its origin from the worship of the sun, or fire in general, which was formerly in vogue among the Celts as well as among many other heathen nations.

Belteshazzar (bel.tẹ.shaz′ạr). Babylonian name of **Daniel.** Dan. i. 7, ii. 26, iv. 5.

Belton (bel′tọn). Town in NW South Carolina, in Anderson County, near Anderson: cotton mills. 3,371 (1950).

Belton. City in C Texas, county seat of Bell County, on Nolan Creek, ab. 57 mi. NE of Austin. It is the seat of Mary Hardin-Baylor College. A Spanish expedition explored the area (1721) for gold and silver. 6,246 (1950).

Belton Estate, The. Novel (1866) by Anthony Trollope.

Beltraffio (bel.träf′fē.ō), **Giovanni Antonio.** See **Boltraffio, Giovanni Antonio.**

Beltramelli (bel.trä.mel′lē), **Antonio.** b. at Forlì, Italy, Jan. 11, 1879; d. at Rome, March 15, 1930. Italian writer and nationalist. At first an adherent of Gabriele D'Annunzio, he was later a member of the Fascist Party. He was elected (1929) to the Italian academy. His works include a life of Mussolini entitled *L'Uomo nuovo* (1923) and the political *Cavaliere Mostardo* (1921), as well as novels, plays, and poetry.

Beltrami (bel.trä′mē), **Eugenio.** b. at Cremona, Italy, Nov. 16, 1835; d. at Rome, Feb. 18, 1900. Italian scientist and mathematician, president of the Accademia dei Lincei; known for research in the field of non-Euclidean geometry. He was the author also of scores of papers on algebra, optics, and elasticity. He was originally a civil engineer, and became professor successively at Bologna, Pisa, Rome, Pavia, and again at Rome. His *Opere matematiche* appeared in four volumes at Milan, 1902–20.

Beltrán de Guzmán (bel.trän′ dā göth.män′), **Nuño** (or **Nuñez**). See **Guzmán, Nuño** (or **Nuñez**) **Beltrán de.**

Beltrán-Espejo Expedition (bel.trän′es.pā′hō). Spanish expedition (November, 1582 *et seq.*) from what is now the S part of Chihuahua, Mexico, into the Pueblo region of "New Mexico," led by Bernardino Beltrán, a Spanish Roman Catholic friar, with the intent of securing the safety of two missionaries who had gone to the Pueblo area on an earlier expedition. Although the expedition did not succeed in carrying out its primary purpose, its encouraging reports of the resources and inhabitants of the Pueblo country were instrumental in causing the Spanish authorities to penetrate the area with settlements and missions. One of the outstanding figures of the expedition, and a writer of one of its chief reports, was a soldier named Espejo.

Beltrán y Masses (bel.trän′ ē mä′sās), **Federico.** b. at Guira de Malena, Spain, July 8, 1885—. Spanish portraitist and landscape artist, whose sitters have included King Alfonso XIII of Spain, a shah of Persia, Rudolph Valentino, Pola Negri, and a princess of Denmark. He studied in Spain, exhibited at Barcelona, and then went to Paris (1916), where he had a showing at the Petit Palais and the Société Nationale des Beaux-Arts. In addition to exhibiting his work at Paris, London, New York, Brussels, Madrid, and Munich, he organized several important exhibitions in Spain and France, and won prizes in both countries. *Women of the Sea*, *Towards the Stars*, *The Pearl*, and *Blue Night* are among his more popular works.

Beluchistan (bę.lö.chi.stän'). See **Baluchistan.**

Belukha (bye.lö'ʜą). [Also: **Byelukha;** English, **White Mountain.**] Mountain in the U.S.S.R., in the Kazakh Soviet Socialist Republic, in the Altai range. Six glaciers radiate from this peak, one of them 5 mi. long. It is the highest peak in the range. Elevation, ab. 14,783 ft.

Belunum (be.lö'num). Latin name of **Belluno.**

Belus (bē'lus). In ancient geography, a river of Palestine flowing into the Mediterranean at Acre. It is the reputed place of the discovery of glass by the Phoenicians.

Belus (bē'lus) or **Belos** (-los). In classical mythology, a son of Poseidon and Libya (or Eurynome), regarded as the ancestral hero and divinity of various earlier nations.

Belus or **Belos.** In classical legend, the father of Dido, and conqueror of Cyprus.

Belvacum (bel'vą.kum). An ancient name of **Beauvais.**

Belvedere (bel.vę.dir'). Township in S California, in Los Angeles County. 46,667 (1950).

Belvedere (bel.vę.dir'; Italian, bel.vā.dā'rā). A portion of the Vatican Palace at Rome. Its *Apollo* and the *Laocoön* are among the best-known pieces in its valuable collection of classical art.

Belvedere Gardens. Unincorporated community in S California, in Los Angeles County. Under the urban definition established for use in the 1950 census, Belvedere Gardens was counted with adjoining urban areas. The last official enumeration was 33,502 (1940).

Belvedere Lake. See **Ennell, Lough.**

Belvidera (bel.vē.dā'rą). Daughter of Priuli, the senator, and the wife of Jaffier, the conspirator, in Thomas Otway's tragedy *Venice Preserved.* Jaffier conspires to murder all the senators, and is persuaded by his wife to divulge the plot to her father, on condition that all the conspirators are forgiven. The promise is not kept, and Jaffier, his friend Pierre, and all the other conspirators are condemned to death on the wheel. Belvidera, on learning the result of her interference, goes mad and dies. The part was a favorite one with the English actresses of the 18th century.

Belvidere (bel.vi.dir'). City in N Illinois, county seat of Boone County, on the Kishwaukee River ab. 64 mi. NW of Chicago: manufactures sewing machines; market town for a corn-producing area. 9,422 (1950).

Belville (bel'vil). The lover of Peggy in David Garrick's *The Country Girl,* an adaptation of William Wycherley's *The Country Wife.*

Belvoir Castle (bē'vėr). In English history, the seat of the dukes of Rutland, in Leicestershire, England.

Bely (bye'li), **Andrey.** [Also: **Belyi;** pseudonym of **Boris Nikolayevich Bugayev.**] b. at Moscow, Oct. 26 or 27, 1880; d. there, Jan. 8, 1934. Russian man of letters. He has to his credit literary studies, works on prosody and aesthetics, a number of esoteric poems in the symbolist manner, and several remarkable novels couched in a highly original style. His last years were devoted to the writing of a voluminous autobiography, considered to be a work of great literary and documentary merit.

Belyaev (byi.lyä'yif), **Mitrofan Petrovich.** b. at St. Petersburg, in February, 1836; d. Jan. 10, 1904. Russian music publisher, noted as a supporter of the Russian music of his day.

Belz (belts). Town in E Poland, in the *województwo* (province) of Lublin, formerly in Galicia, Austria, situated on the Sotokija River, ab. 41 mi. N of Lvov: an agricultural market town. It was formerly the seat of a chassidic rabbi. It became Polish in 1462, Austrian in 1772, and part of the newly established republic of Poland in 1919. The new border between Russia and Poland, as designated after World War II, is in the vicinity. 11,694 (1946).

Belzebub (bel'zē.bub). See **Beelzebub.**

Belzig (bel'tsiċh). Town in NE Germany, in the *Land* (state) of Brandenburg, Russian Zone, formerly in the province of Brandenburg, Prussia, situated in the Fläming hills, ab. 43 mi. SW of Berlin: agricultural trade, lumber mills, and brickyards. 7,597 (1946).

Belzoni (bel.zō'ni). City in W Mississippi, county seat of Humphreys County, on the Yazoo River. 4,071 (1950).

Belzoni (bel.tsō'nē), **Giovanni Battista.** b. at Padua, Italy, 1778; d. at Gato, in Benin, West Africa, Dec. 3, 1823. Italian traveler and explorer, the son of a barber of Padua. He was endowed with great physical strength, and earned a living for a time in London (at Astley's Theatre) and elsewhere as a vaudeville athlete. As a hydraulic engineer he visited Egypt in 1815, and devoted himself until 1819 to the study of Egyptian antiquities. He published in English, in 1820, *A Narrative of the Operations and Recent Discoveries within the Pyramids. . . .* In 1823 he started for central Africa, but died on the way.

Belzú (bel.sö'), **Manuel Isidoro.** b. at La Paz, Bolivia, 1808; killed there, in March, 1865. Bolivian revolutionist. In 1847 he headed a revolution which overthrew José Ballivián and put José Miguel de Velasco in his place; next year he rebelled against Velasco, usurped the presidency, and retained the post until 1855. After some years in Europe he returned and headed the revolt against Mariano Melgarejo. The latter attacked him at La Paz and, after a bloody street battle, killed him with his own hand.

Bem (bem), **Józef.** b. at Tarnów, in Galicia, 1795; d. at Aleppo, in Syria, Dec. 10, 1850. Polish general. He served in the Polish insurrection of 1830. Having fled to Vienna, where he joined the Hungarians, he conquered Transylvania for the Hungarian insurgents and drove the Austrian and Russian allies into Walachia in 1849. He also conquered the Banat, but was defeated by the Russians at Schässburg (now Sighişoara, in Rumania), on July 31, 1849. He took part in the battle of Temesvar, on Aug. 9, 1849. On his defeat, he escaped to Turkey and took service in the Turkish army.

Beman (bē'mąn), **Nathaniel Sydney Smith.** b. at New Lebanon, N.Y., Nov. 26, 1785; d. at Carbondale, Ill., Aug. 6, 1871. American Presbyterian clergyman.

Beman, Wooster Woodruff. b. at Southington, Conn., May 28, 1850; d. Jan. 18, 1922. American professor of mathematics. He was an instructor (1871–74), assistant professor (1874–82), associate professor (1882–87), and professor (1887 *et seq.*) of mathematics at the University of Michigan. Author of *Continuity and Irrational Numbers* and a translation from the German of *Nature and the Meaning of Numbers* (1901); coauthor with David Eugene Smith of *Plane and Solid Geometry* (1895), *Elements of Algebra* (1900), *A Brief History of Mathematics* (1900; from the German), and *Academic Algebra* (1902).

Bemba (bem'bä). [Also: **Awemba, Babemba, Wabemba, Wawemba.**] Bantu-speaking people of C Africa, inhabiting NE Northern Rhodesia and SE Belgian Congo between the Luapula River and Lake Tanganyika. Their population is estimated at ab. 140,000 (by A. I. Richards in *African Political Systems,* edited by M. Fortes and E. E. Evans-Pritchard, 1940). They live in small, scattered villages ruled by village chiefs under district chiefs and an autocratic hereditary king. They have exogamous matrilineal clans. The Bemba practice hoe agriculture, moving their villages when the land has been exhausted. Their principal food is millet.

Bemba, Lake. See **Bangweulu.**

Bembatoka (bem.bą.tō'ką), **Bay of.** See **Bombetoka, Bay of.**

Bemberg (bem'bėrg), **Herman.** b. at Buenos Aires, March 29, 1861—. French musical composer. He was a student of Théodore Dubois and Jules Émile Frédéric Massenet at the Paris Conservatoire. His opera *Elaine* was performed (1892) at Covent Garden. He also composed a cantata, *La Mort de Jeanne d'Arc* (1886), and the comic opera, *Le Baiser de Suzon* (1888); among his songs is *Nymphes et silvains.*

Bembo (bem'bō), **Pietro.** b. at Venice, May 20, 1470; d. at Rome, Jan. 18, 1547. Italian cardinal (1539 *et seq.*) and man of letters of the Renaissance period. He was the author of poems, epistles, a history of Venice, and *Gli Asolani* (dialogues on Platonic love).

Bemelmans (bem'ęl.mąnz), **Ludwig.** b. at Meran, in the Austrian Tirol, April 27, 1898—. American author, painter, and illustrator, best known as the author of witty and satirical books, which he also illustrates. He was educated at Rothenburg and Regensburg in Bavaria, emigrated to the U.S. in 1914, and became a U.S. citizen in 1918. Among his better-known books are *Hansi, Madeline, Golden Basket, My War with the U.S.A.* (describing his experiences in the U.S. army during World War I), *Life Class, Small Beer, I Love You, I Love You, I Love You, Hotel Splendide,* and *Dirty Eddie;* his articles and illustrations have appeared in *The New Yorker,*

Vogue, Stage, Town and Country, and other magazines. His novel *Now I lay Me* was dramatized in 1949.

Bement (bẹ.ment', bē'mẹnt), **Caleb N.** b. 1790; d. at Poughkeepsie, N.Y., Dec. 22, 1868. American agriculturist and inventor of farm implements. A breeder and exhibitor of livestock, he was the inventor of an expanding corn cultivator and a turnip drill. Editor of two short-lived agricultural journals; author of *American Poulterer's Companion* (1844) and *The Rabbit Fancier* (1855).

Bement, Clarence Sweet. b. at Mishawaka, Ind., April 11, 1843; d. Jan. 27, 1923. American bibliophile, numismatist, and collector of minerals. His library of rare books forms part of the Widener Library at Harvard; his collection of minerals, considered one of the best in America, was bought by J. P. Morgan for New York's American Museum of Natural History. He also amassed a wide selection of Greek and Roman coins.

Bemidji (bẹ.mij'i). City in N Minnesota, county seat of Beltrami County, on Bemidji Lake, ab. 140 mi. NW of Duluth: a trading and resort center; dairy products. At one time a lumber town, Bemidji has a statue of Paul Bunyan. 10,001 (1950).

Bemini (bem'i.ni), **Straits of.** See **Florida, Straits of.**

Bemini Islands. See **Bimini Islands.**

Bemis (bē'mis). Unincorporated community in W Tennessee, in Madison County: manufactures bags. 3,248 (1950).

Bemis, Edward Webster. b. at Springfield, Mass., April 7, 1860; d. Sept. 25, 1930. American economist. He was professor (1889–92) of history and political economy at Vanderbilt University, associate professor (1892–95) of political economy at the University of Chicago, and professor (1897–99) of economics and history at Kansas State Agricultural College. Subsequently he served as superintendent (1901–09) of water, gas, and electricity supply at Cleveland, Ohio, and as deputy commissioner (1910) of New York utilities. Author of *Gas Works in the United States* (1891) and *Municipal Monopolies* (1899).

Bemis, Samuel Flagg. b. at Worcester, Mass., Oct. 20, 1891—. American historian and educator. A graduate of Clark University (1913) and Harvard (1916), he served as professor of history at George Washington University (1924–34) and Yale (1935 *et seq.*). Author of *Jay's Treaty, A Study in Commerce and Diplomacy* (1923), *Pinckney's Treaty, A Study of America's Advantage from Europe's Distress* (1926), *A Diplomatic History of the United States* (1936), *The Latin-American Policy of the United States* (1942), *John Quincy Adams and the Foundations of American Foreign Policy* (1949; awarded the Pulitzer prize in biography, 1950), and other works.

Bémont (bā.môṅ), **Charles.** b. at Paris, 1848; d. 1939. French historian. He served as professor at the École des Hautes Études, also as a member of l'Académie des Inscriptions. Author of *Simon de Montfort* (1885); editor of *Chartes des libertés anglaises* (1892).

Bempe (bem'pẹ). See **Limpopo.**

Bemrose (bem'rōz), **William.** b. at Derby, England, Dec. 30, 1831; d. at Bridlington, Yorkshire, England, Aug. 6, 1908. English publisher, author, and school official. Educated at King William's College, on the Isle of Man, he became a member of a printing and publishing business at Derby, established by his father, and became its head in 1857. From 1886 to 1902 he was chairman of the Derby school board; a fellow of the Society of Antiquaries, he wrote several authoritative works on woodcarving and china, such as *Manual of Woodcarving* (1862) and *Longton Hall Porcelain* (1906). Author also of a biography of the Derby artist Joseph Wright.

Ben (ben). A gay, simple, but somewhat incredible sailor in William Congreve's comedy *Love for Love*. He is designed to marry Miss Prue.

Benaco (bā.nä'kō), **Lake** or **Lago.** See **Garda, Lake.**

Benacus (be.nā'kus), **Lacus.** Latin name of **Garda, Lake.**

Benaduci (bā.nä.dö'chē), **Lorenzo Boturini.** See **Boturini Benaduci, Lorenzo.**

Benaiah (bẹ.nā'ạ). Name of several persons mentioned in the Old Testament, of whom the most notable was the son of Jehoiada, the chief priest. He slew Adonijah and Joab, and succeeded the latter, under Solomon, as commander in chief of the army.

Benaiah. Character in John Dryden and Nahum Tate's second part of *Absalom and Achitophel*, intended for George Edward Sackville, who was called General Sackville and was devoted to the duke of York. See 1 Kings, ii. 35 for the Biblical character.

Benalcázar (bā.näl.kä'thär), **Sebastián de.** [Also: **Belalcázar, Velalcázar**; original name, **Sebastián Moyano.**] b. at Benalcaz, Estremadura, Spain, c1499; d. at Popayán, Colombia, 1550. Spanish conqueror of Quito and Popayán. He joined the expedition of Pedro Arias de Avila (Pedrarias) to Darien, and in March, 1532, joined Francisco Pizarro on the coast at Portoviejo with 30 men. Incited by the Cañaris Indians, who promised to join him, he undertook the conquest of Quito. Marching over the mountains, he defeated the Inca general Rumi-ñaui on the plains of Riobamba, and entered (1533) Quito. He invaded Popayán in 1533, and in the following year carried his conquests still farther north, to the country of the Chinchas Indians. After founding many Spanish towns, Benalcázar went to Spain in 1537, and in 1538 he was appointed governor of Popayán, a district which comprised what is now southwestern Colombia.

Ben-Ami (ben.ä'mē, -am'i), **Jacob.** b. at Minsk, Russia, 1890—. Russian actor and director. After attracting favorable notice when he appeared (1918–19) at New York with the Jewish Art Theater, he was put under contract by Arthur Hopkins. He made his debut on the English-speaking stage in 1920 and played important roles in *The Idle Inn* (1921), *Johannes Kreisler* (1922), *The Failures* (1923), *Welded* (1924), *Man and Masses* (1924), *John* (1927), and *Diplomacy* (1928). From 1929 to 1931 he was with Eva Le Gallienne's Civic Repertory Company, playing in *The Sea Gull, The Cherry Orchard, The Living Corpse*, and *Camille*. He appeared in the film *The Wandering Jew* (1933) and the play *The Eternal Road* (1935), and in 1939 produced and acted in *Chaver Nachman*, a dramatic version of Israel J. Singer's novel *East of Eden.*

Benares (bẹ.nä'rez). Division of Uttar Pradesh (the United Provinces), N Union of India: sugar, wheat, rice, and silk. Capital, Benares; area, ab. 10,000 sq. mi.; pop. 5,545,257 (1941).

Benares. District of the division of Benares, N Union of India, ab. 400 mi. NW of Calcutta. Area, ab. 1,960 sq. mi.; pop. 1,218,629 (1941).

Benares. [Hindi, **Banaras**; Sanskrit, **Kashi, Varanasi.**] Capital of the division of Benares, Uttar Pradesh (United Provinces), N Union of India, on the N side of the Ganges River. It is one of the largest cities in N India, and the principal Hindu holy city, famous as a resort for pilgrims. It has hundreds of religious buildings, best known of which is probably the mosque of Aurangzeb. Its chief commercial activity is silk weaving; it also manufactures brasswares and the like, and has important trade. It is the seat of a Hindu university. The Ganges is crossed here by the Dufferin Bridge. Benares was founded c1200 B.C., was for many years a Buddhistic center, was conquered by the Mohammedans c1193, and was ceded to the East India Company in 1775. It was the scene of an outbreak of the Indian mutiny of 1857. Pop. 263,100 (1941).

ben Asher (ben ash'ėr), **Aaron ben Moses.** See **Aaron ben Moses ben Asher.**

Benavente (be.nạ.vān'tẹ). Small town and *concelho* (commune) in S central Portugal, in the province of Ribatejo, Santarém district, situated on the Zatas River, ab. 28 mi. NE of Lisbon. Pop. of concelho, 10,500 (1940); of town, 5,150 (1940).

Benavente y Martínez (bā.nä.ᴃen'tā ē mär.tē'neth). **Jacinto.** b. at Madrid, 1866—. Spanish playwright, considered the foremost dramatist of the "generation of 1898." Influenced by the works of other European writers, his plays were a departure from the Spanish dramatic school; they depend on social satire, characterization, and clever dialogue rather than powerful plots. In 1922 he received the Nobel prize for literature. His plays have been translated into many languages and have been produced in many countries. *La Malquerida* (The Passion Flower) and *Los intereses creados* (The Bonds of Interest) have been presented successfully in the U.S.

Benavides (ben.ạ.vē'ᴛʜẹs). City in S Texas, in Duval County, SW of Corpus Christi, in an oil-producing region. It was incorporated in 1936. Pop. 3,016 (1950).

Benavides (bā.nä.ᴃē′ᴛʜās), **Alonso de.** b. c1580; date of death not known. Spanish Franciscan friar who in 1621 was appointed "Father Custodian" of the missions of New Mexico. He arrived on the Rio Grande in 1622 and labored indefatigably to convert the Indians of the region, assisted by 26 others of his order, till 1629, when he was relieved. In 1630 he went to Spain and presented to the king the now world-famous *Memorial* containing the record of his work, travels, the natives, and their towns. This was published in 1630 at Madrid and was soon translated into other languages. The work forms the foundation of the history of New Mexico for that period. In 1632 he published another book on the opening to commerce of the rivers of the Bay of Espíritu Santo. He became assistant bishop in Portuguese India, and on the death of the archbishop of Goa succeeded him.

Benavides, Óscar Raimundo. b. at Lima, Peru, March 15, 1876; d. July 2, 1945. Peruvian soldier and politician, president (1933–39) of Peru. He was educated (1890–94) at the national military school, served five years with the French army, and was chief of the Peruvian military expedition (1911) to Yquitos, in the Amazon region. Appointed (1913) Peruvian chief of staff, he led the military coup (1914) which deposed Guillermo Enrique Billinghurst, and served as head of the provisional government which followed. He later held the posts of minister to Italy (1917–21), Spain (1930), and England (1932–33), and was appointed (1933) chief of national defense. Elected president after the assassination of Luis M. Sánchez Cerro, he was opposed by a socialistic group known as *Apra;* he took measures such as a public works program and the building of model homes for laborers, to offset the Aprista influence. In 1940 he was appointed ambassador to Spain.

Benavides y de la Cueva (bā.nä.ᴃē′ᴛʜās ē dā lä kwā′ᴃä), **Diego de.** [Title, Count of **Santistevan.**] b. c1600; d. at Lima, Peru, March 17, 1666. Spanish soldier and administrator. He was appointed viceroy of Peru in 1659, reaching Lima on July 31, 1661. He held the office until his death.

Benavides y Díez Canseco (ē dē′es kän.sā′kō), **Alfredo.** b. at Lima, Peru, May 30, 1881—. Peruvian diplomat. He was appointed chancellor of the consulate at Antwerp (1907) and consul at Le Havre (1909), Bordeaux (1909), and Bremen (1911). He was acting chief of the consular bureau in the ministry of foreign affairs in 1913, and chief of the diplomatic bureau (1914–20). Appointed (1931) minister of the navy and aviation, he was also minister plenipotentiary (1933–41) to Great Britain, and ambassador (1944 *et seq.*) to Canada. Author of *Escalafón diplomático del Perú* (1914), *Recopilación de los tratados del Perú* (1918), and other books.

Benbecula (ben.bek′ū̟.lạ). Island of the Outer Hebrides, belonging to Inverness-shire, Scotland, between North Uist and South Uist. The soil of the island is sandy and barren. Length, ab. 8 mi.

Benbecula Sound. Narrow sea passage between Benbecula island and South Uist island. Outer Hebrides, in N Scotland, in Inverness-shire. Length, ab. 5 mi.; width, ab. 1 mi.

Benbow (ben′bō), **John.** b. at Shrewsbury, England, March 10, 1653; d. at Port Royal, Jamaica, Nov. 4, 1702. British admiral. He early ran away to sea, served in various merchant and government vessels, and after 1689 was continuously in the royal navy. He became captain in 1689, rear admiral in 1696, and vice-admiral in 1701. In 1692 and 1693 he was engaged in various unsuccessful attacks on the French coast; in 1696 he served as squadron commander at Dunkerque; in 1699 and again in 1701 he commanded squadrons in the West Indies. From Aug. 19 to Aug. 24, 1702, he had a running fight with a section of the French fleet. On the last day his leg was shattered by a ball, but he continued to direct the battle. Benbow claimed that his failure to capture this fleet was the result of the poor conduct of his officers, much of his squadron having deserted him.

Benbow, William. fl. 1825–40. English publisher, considered by some to have been the originator of the labor tactic now called the general strike. Of William Benbow's life and career, singularly little is known. He had a publishing house in London, belonged to the National Union of Working Classes, was active but relatively inconspicuous in the Chartist movement, and was sent to prison more than once; such is the scanty record of his life. However, he wrote and published one book of very considerable importance. This was entitled *Grand National Holiday; or, Congress of the Productive Classes*, and in it the theory of the general strike was first formulated.

Benc (bents), **Adolf.** Czech architect. He designed (1947) the Prague High School for Art and Industry.

Benchley (bench′li), **Robert Charles.** b. at Worcester, Mass., Sept. 15, 1889; d. at New York, Nov. 21, 1945. American journalist and humorist. After receiving an A.B. degree (1912) from Harvard, he joined the staffs of the Curtis Publishing Company of Philadelphia (1912), the New York *Tribune* (1916), and the Sunday *Tribune Graphic* (1917). He was managing editor (1919–20) of *Vanity Fair*, contributing columnist (1920–21) with the New York *World*, drama editor of *Life* until 1929, and theatrical writer for the *New Yorker* until 1940. He appeared in motion-picture shorts (1929, 1937 *et seq.*) and on the radio (1937 *et seq.*). His short, humorous essays are collected in *Of All Things* (1921), *Love Conquers All* (1922), *Pluck and Luck* (1925), *The Early Worm* (1927), *The Treasurer's Report* (1930), *No Poems* (1932), *From Bed to Worse* (1934), *My Ten Years in a Quandary* (1936), *After 1903, What?* (1938), *Inside Benchley* (1942), *Benchley Beside Himself* (1943), *Chips Off the Old Benchley* (1949), and other books.

Bencius Alexandrinus (ben′shi.us al″ek.san.drī′nus). Latinized name of **Benzo d'Alessandria.**

Ben Cleuch (ben klöċh′). See under **Ochil Hills.**

Bencoelen or **Bencoolen** (ben.kö′lẹn). See **Benkoelen.**

Bencovazzo (ben.kō.vät′tsō). Italian name of **Benkovac.**

Ben Cruachan (ben krö′ạ.ċhạn). Mountain in W central Scotland, in Argyllshire, situated near the N end of Loch Awe, ab. 14 mi. N of Inveraray. 3,689 ft.

Benczur (ben′tsůr), **Gyula Julius de.** b. at Nyíregyháza, Hungary, Jan. 28, 1844; d. 1920. Hungarian portraitist and genre painter. He was educated at Munich and at Budapest and was strongly influenced by his teacher, Karl Piloty. From 1876 to 1883 he was a professor at the academy at Munich; later he painted *The Baptism of Vajk*, for which he was awarded a bronze medal at Paris. He was given other prizes for his portraits of the count and countess Karolyi, King Ferdinand I of Bulgaria, and the countess Andrassy.

Bend (bend). City in C Oregon, county seat of Deschutes County, on the Deschutes River, in a tourist resort area: lumber mills. Agriculture in the surrounding region is served by a large irrigation project. 11,409 (1950)

Benda (ben′dä), **Franz.** b. at Altbenatek, in Bohemia, Nov. 25, 1709; d. at Potsdam, Germany, March 7, 1786. Bohemian violinist in Germany; the founder of a school of violin-playing.

Benda, Friedrich Ludwig. b. at Gotha, Germany, 1746; d. at Königsberg, March 27, 1792. Composer and director (1789 *et seq.*) of concerts at Königsberg; son of Georg Benda (1722–95). His works include liturgical compositions, operas, and works for the violin.

Benda, Friedrich Wilhelm Heinrich. b. at Potsdam, Germany, July 15, 1745; d. there, June 19, 1814. German violinist and composer; son of Franz Benda (1709–86). He served (1765–1810) as royal chamber musician. His works include *Alceste* (1786) and *Orpheus* (1789), both operas, concertos and oratorios, a considerable body of chamber music, and an operetta, *Das Blumenmädchen* (The Flowergirl).

Benda, Georg. b. in Bohemia, June 30, 1722; d. at Köstritz, in Thuringia, Nov. 6, 1795. Bohemian composer and violinist in Germany; brother of Franz Benda (1709–86). He wrote the operas *Ariadne auf Naxos* (1774), *Medea*, and others.

Benda, Joseph. b. 1724; d. at Berlin, 1804. Bohemian violinist in Germany; brother of Franz Benda (1709–86). He was head of the orchestra of Frederick II of Prussia.

Benda (baṅ.dȧ), **Julien.** b. at Paris, Dec. 26, 1867—. French philosopher, novelist, and critic, of strongly marked rationalist leanings, author of *Belphégor* (1919; Eng. trans., 1929), *La Trahison des clercs* (1927; Eng. trans., *The Great Betrayal*, and also *The Treason of the Intellectuals*, both 1928), and *La France Byzantine* (1946). Ranked since World War I as a leader of the antiromantic movement in French criticism, he had earlier delivered a distinguished attack on the philosophy of Henri Bergson in *Le Bergsonisme, ou une philosophie de la mobilité* (1912), *Une Philosophie pathétique* (1913), and *Sur le succès du Bergsonisme* (1914). Implicit in all his criticism is the belief that emotion has replaced reason as the chief motivation of French life. He has also written novels and two volumes of autobiography.

Benda (ben'dä), **Karl Hermann Heinrich.** b. in May, 1748; d. 1836. German composer and violinist; son of Franz Benda (1709–86). He was leader of the Prussian royal opera orchestra and music instructor to Friedrich Wilhelm III. Composer of chamber works.

Benda, Władysław Theodor. b. at Poznań (Posen), Poland, 1873; d. at New York, Nov. 30, 1948. Painter, designer, lecturer, writer, and illustrator, who originated the Benda masks, used in theatrical productions. He studied at Kraców, Vienna, San Francisco, and New York. In 1899 he settled in the U.S., where he worked as a painter and illustrator. His Benda masks were originally made as a hobby, but later were found useful in the production of plays and moving pictures, and as decorative works of art. They were used in the *Greenwich Village Follies* (1920) and in the original production of Eugene O'Neill's *The Hairy Ape*. He wrote the book *Masks* (1945) and an article on masks for the *Encyclopaedia Britannica*. His works include the masks *Golden Beauty, American Soldier, Long Eyes, Sad Negro, Dolorosa,* and *Beelzebub*, and the painting *Oriental Dance*.

Ben David or **Bendavid** (ben.dä'fit), **Lazarus.** b. at Berlin, Oct. 18, 1762; d. there, March 28, 1832. German philosophical writer and mathematician. He was the author of *Versuch über das Vergnügen* (Essay on Pleasure), *Vorlesungen über die Kritik der reinen Vernunft* (Lectures on the Critique of Pure Reason), *Zur Berechnung des judischen Kalenders* (Toward the Calculation of the Jewish Calendar), and others.

Bendemann (ben'dẹ.män), **Eduard.** b. at Berlin, Dec. 3, 1811; d. at Düsseldorf, Germany, Dec. 27, 1889. German painter of portraits and historical scenes. A professor of art at the Dresden Academy of Art (1838 *et seq.*), he later served as director of the Düsseldorf Academy. Among his works are *Die trauernden Juden* (1832), *Jeremias auf den Trümmern von Jerusalem* (1837), and *Die Wegführung der Juden in die Babylonische Gefangenschaft* (1872).

Bendemeer (ben'dẹ.mir). River in Thomas Moore's poem *Lalla Rookh*.

Bender (ben'dėr), **Harold Herman.** b. at Martinsburg, W.Va., April 20, 1882; d. in August, 1951. American philologist. He received (1903) the A.B. degree from Lafayette College, and was awarded (1907) a Ph.D. degree by Johns Hopkins University; he studied for a time also in Germany. He served as a member of the faculty (1909 *et seq.*), as professor of Indo-Germanic philology (1918 *et seq.*), and as chairman of the department of Oriental languages and literature (1927 *et seq.*) at Princeton University. He was a writer of etymologies and special editor for philology and linguistics for *Webster's New International Dictionary* (2nd ed.). His works include *On the Lithuanian Word-Stock as Indo-European Material* (1920), *A Lithuanian Etymological Index* (1921), *The Home of the Indo-Europeans* (1922), and *The Selection of Undergraduates* (1926).

Bender Abbas (ab.bäs') or **Bender Abbasi** (ab.bä'sē). See **Bandar Abbas.**

Bender Family. Family which settled (1871) in the SE part of Kansas where, in a prairie hut, they lodged travelers, of whom they would occasionally kill and rob one. Mounting suspicion caused the Benders and their son and daughter to flee (May, 1873) into Indian territory, where their pursuers lost them; nothing further is known of their fate. The area around their cabin yielded at least 11 bodies.

Bendery (bin.dye'rē). [Rumanian ,**Tighina**; Turkish, **Bender.**] Town and former fortress in the U.S.S.R., in the Moldavian Soviet Socialist Republic, situated on the Dniester River ab. 61 mi. NW of Odessa: a rail and road junction and trading center. Near it was the residence (1709–13) of Charles XII of Sweden. It was stormed by the Russians under Piotr Ivanovich Panin in 1770, and under Grigori Aleksandrovich Potemkin in 1789, and was again taken by the Russians in 1806 and 1811. As part of Bessarabia, it was Rumanian between World Wars I and II. Pop. ab. 31,800 (1940).

Bendigo (ben'di.gō). [Former name, **Sandhurst.**] City in SE Australia, in the state of Victoria, ab. 90 mi. NW of Melbourne: the site of extensive gold-mining operations. 30,778 (1947), 32,000 (est. 1950).

Bendin (byen'dyin). Russian name of **Będzin.**

Bending of the Bough, The. Adaptation by George Moore of *The Tale of a Town* (1902) by Edward Martyn.

Bendish (ben'dish), **Bridget.** b. c1650; d. 1726. Daughter of General Henry Ireton, and granddaughter of Oliver Cromwell, famous for her resemblance to the latter. She is supposed to have been involved in the Rye House Plot (1683).

Bendish: A Study in Prodigality. Historical novel by Maurice Hewlett, published in 1913. It is set against a background of London in the 1830's.

Bendix (ben'diks), **Max.** b. at Detroit, Mich., March 28, 1866; d. at Chicago, Dec. 6, 1945. American orchestra conductor. He served as concertmaster (1886) at the Metropolitan Opera House, New York, and as assistant conductor and concertmaster (1886–96) of the Theodore Thomas Orchestra, succeeding (1893) Thomas at the Columbian Exposition at Chicago. After a series of tours (1897–1903) with the Bendix Quartet, he conducted (1904) an orchestra at the St. Louis World's Fair. He was also concertmaster (1904–05) for the Wagnerian performances at the Metropolitan Opera House at New York, concertmaster and conductor (1906) at the Manhattan Opera House, and conductor (1915) of the Exposition Orchestra at the San Francisco Panama-Pacific Exposition. His compositions include *Pavlowa*, a valse caprice for orchestra, and *The Sisters*, a ballad for soprano and orchestra.

Bendl (ben'dl), **Karel.** b. at Prague, April 16, 1838; d. there, in September, 1897. Bohemian composer, chiefly of operas such as *Lejla, Břetislav and Jitka, Stary Zenich, Indicka Princezna,* and *The Montenegrins* (in Czech, *Černahorci*). His other works include choral compositions and chamber music.

Bendorf (ben'dôrf). Town in W Germany, in the *Land* (state) of Rhineland-Palatinate, French Zone, formerly in the Rhine Province, Prussia, situated on the right bank of the Rhine River, ab. 5 mi. N of Koblenz: a river port, it has sawmills, and metallurgical, ceramics, paperware, and furniture industries. The population is predominantly Roman Catholic. 11,980 (1950).

Bend-the-Bow (bend'ᴛʜẹ.bō'). English archer in Sir Walter Scott's *Castle Dangerous*.

Bendzin (ben'tsēn). German name of **Będzin.**

Bene (bā'nā). [Also, **Bane.**] Subgroup of the Bantu-speaking Pangwe of C Africa, inhabiting an area S of Yaounde in SW Cameroun. Their population is estimated at ab. 58,000 (by I. Dugast, *Inventaire éthnique du Sud-Cameroun*, 1949).

Beneath Tropic Seas. Prose work (1928) by William Beebe. One of Beebe's informal books written for the purpose of popularizing scientific research for untrained readers, it stands out for vividness of impression and novelty of subject.

Benedek (bā'nẹ.dek), **Ludwig von.** b. at Sopron (German, Ödenburg), Hungary, July 14, 1804; d. at Graz, Austria, April 27, 1881. Austrian general. He served with distinction in the Italian and Hungarian campaigns (1848–49) and at Solferino in 1859. He was made governor of Hungary in 1860, commanded the northern Austrian army in 1866, and was defeated by the Prussians at Sadowa (German, Königgrätz) on July 3, 1866. He was removed from his command after this defeat.

Beneden (bẹ.nā'dẹn), **Edouard van.** b. 1846; d. 1910. Belgian biologist and teacher. He taught at the University of Liége, received the Prix quinquennal des Sciences Naturelles on three separate occasions, and was awarded the Prix Serres by the Institute of France. He exerted a great influence upon the development of biology during the 19th century. He was a cofounder (1880) of the *Archives de Biologie*.

Benedetti (bā.nā.det'tē), Count **Vincent.** b. at Bastia, Corsica, April 29, 1817; d. at Paris, March 28, 1900. French diplomat. He was envoy at Turin in 1860, and French ambassador (1864–70) at Berlin. His interviews with William I of Prussia at Ems (July 9–13, 1870), in which he sought formal disavowal by William of any intent to support a Hohenzollern for the Spanish throne, were so inauspiciously timed and so clumsily carried out that it was possible for Otto von Bismarck to make of them a seeming insult to Germany and thus by his intentionally inflammatory "dispatch from Ems" set the stage for the outbreak of the Franco-Prussian War.

Benedetto da Majano (or **Maiano**) (bā.nā.det'tō dä mä-yä'nō). [Original name, **Benedetto di Leonardo.**] b. at Florence, 1442; d. there, 1497. Italian sculptor and architect; member of a family which for generations had been stone masons and builders. His altarpiece in the church of Monte Oliveto at Naples is generally considered his masterwork in sculpture, but connoisseurs of Renaissance art admire the moving beauty of all the works of his maturity. The Metropolitan Museum of Art at New York has a polychrome sketch by him in terra cotta of the figure of the Virgin in the Monte Oliveto altarpiece. The pulpit he executed for the Church of Santa Croce at Florence is considered by many to be the supreme achievement of Italian sculpture in pictorial relief in marble. In the same city the Palazzo Vecchio is adorned by many of Benedetto's most notable works, but the Palazzo Strozzi may be called his principal monument.

Benedick (ben'ę.dik). Character in Shakespeare's comedy *Much Ado About Nothing.* He is a young gentleman of Padua, of inexhaustible humor, wit, and raillery, a ridiculer of love. He engages in a great deal of spirited bickering with Beatrice, and avows again and again his determination to die a bachelor. But a very simple maneuver brings him and Beatrice together in mutual affection. His name has become a byword for a newly married man, and is in this connection frequently written Benedict.

Benedicks (bā'nę.diks), **Carl Axel Fredrik.** b. at Stockholm, May 27, 1875—. Swedish physicist. He was educated at the University of Uppsala, where he became (1904) a lecturer. Later he served (1911–22) as professor of physics at the University of Stockholm, and was director (1920–35) of the Metallographical Institute at Stockholm. He received the Bergstedt and Englund prizes, the Bessemer gold medal, and the Carnegie gold medal.

Benedict (ben'ę.dikt). d. 1193. English ecclesiastic, abbot of Peterborough (1177–93). He wrote a history of the passion, and another of the miracles of Saint Thomas à Becket, but is not, as has been commonly supposed, the author of the *Gesta Henrici Secundi.*

Benedict I. [Surnamed **Bonosus.**] d. July 30, 579. Pope from 575 to 579. During his pontificate the Langobards extended their conquests in Italy, and threatened Rome.

Benedict II, Saint. d. May 8, 685. Pope from 684 to 685. He is said to have prevailed upon the emperor Constantine IV to renounce the right of confirming papal elections.

Benedict III. d. April 17, 858. Pope from 855 to 858. His election was contested by the ambitious Anastasius. In his pontificate Ethelwulf, king of the West Saxons and Kentishmen, visited Rome (whither he had previously sent his son Alfred), and rebuilt the school or hospital for English pilgrims.

Benedict IV. d. 903. Pope from 900 to 903. He crowned Louis, king of Provence, as Holy Roman emperor in 901.

Benedict V. [Surnamed **Grammaticus.**] d. July 4, 966. Pope from 964 to 966. He was elected Pope by the Romans in 964, in opposition to Leo VIII, whom the emperor Otto I supported after the deposition of the unworthy John XII. The emperor attacked Rome, and secured the person of Benedict, who was kept till his death in confinement at Hamburg.

Benedict VI. d. in August, 974. Pope from 973 to 974. He was elected in 972, under the influence of the emperor Otto I, on whose death in 974 he was deposed and put to death by a Roman faction which subsequently elected the antipope Boniface VII.

Benedict VII. d. 983. Pope from 974 to 983. He excommunicated the antipope Boniface VII in a council held at Rome in 975.

Benedict VIII. d. April 9, 1024. Pope from 1012 to 1024. He ousted the antipope Gregory with the aid of Henry II, whom he crowned Holy Roman emperor in 1014. He decisively defeated the Saracens in Tuscany in 1016.

Benedict IX. d. 1056. Pope from 1032 to 1044. He obtained his elevation to the papacy by simony and, on account of the opposition aroused by his profligacy, resigned in 1044. He seized the papal throne twice subsequently, once in 1045, after expelling Sylvester III, and again in 1047 after the death of Clement II. He is said to have spent his last years in penitence in the monastery of Grottaferrata.

Benedict X. [Original name, **Giovanni di Velletri.**] An antipope elected in 1058. He reigned nine months, when he was compelled to give way to Nicholas II.

Benedict XI. [Original name, **Nicolo Boccasini.**] b. at Treviso, Italy, 1240; d. at Perugia, Italy, July 7, 1304. Pope from 1303 to 1304. He annulled the bulls of Boniface VIII against Philip IV (the Fair) of France. He was beatified in 1773.

Benedict XII. [Original name, **Jacques Fournier.**] b. at Saverdun, in Toulouse province, France; d. at Avignon, France, April 24, 1342. Pope from 1334 to 1342. Earlier a Cistercian monk and abbot of Montfroide, he was the third of the Avignon pontiffs. He was a friend of Petrarch, and a severe ecclesiastical reformer, who endeavored, unsuccessfully, to return the papacy to Rome.

Benedict XIII. [Original name, **Pedro de Luna.**] b. in Aragon, Spain; d. at Peñiscola, Valencia, Spain, 1424. An antipope elected by the French cardinals on the death of Clement VII in 1394. The Italian cardinals had chosen Boniface X in 1389. Benedict was deposed by the Councils of Pisa (1409) and Constance (1417), in spite of which he retained the support of Aragon, Castile, and Scotland till his death.

Benedict XIII. [Original name, **Pietro Francesco Orsini.**] b. at Rome, Feb. 2, 1649; d. Feb. 23, 1730. Pope from 1724 to 1730. He became in his youth a Dominican, and was created cardinal in 1672 by Clement X, to whom he was related. As archbishop of Manfredonia he was known for his zeal and ecclesiastical reforms. When he was first elevated to the papal chair he took the name of Benedict XIV, but changed it almost at once to Benedict XIII in view of the fact that there had been no legitimate Benedict XIII; the title had been borne earlier by an antipope. He made an ineffectual attempt to reconcile the Roman, Greek, Lutheran, and Calvinist churches.

Benedict XIV. Antipope in 1424; successor to the antipope Benedict XIII. One successor to the antipope Benedict XIII, Clement VIII, submitted to Pope Martin V in 1429; Benedict XIV, the other antipope (who had been elected by only one cardinal) was excommunicated by Martin V, and soon lost what small following he had.

Benedict XIV. [Original name, **Prospero Lambertini.**] b. at Bologna, March 31, 1675; d. May 3, 1758. Pope from 1740 to 1758. Author of the monumental work *De Servorum Dei Beatificatione et de Beatorum Canonizatio,* still used in the canonization process. He was a scholar, a patron of the arts, and a promoter of peace. He prohibited in two bulls, *Ex quo singularis* (1742) and *Omnium solicitudinem* (1744), the practice, extensively adopted by the Jesuits in their Indian and Chinese missions, of accommodating Christian language and usage to native cultures.

Benedict XV. [Original name, **Giacomo della Chiesa.**] b. at Pegli, near Genoa, Italy, 1854; d. Jan. 22, 1922. Pope from 1914 to 1922. Elected to the papal chair on Sept. 3, 1914, shortly after the outbreak of World War I, he made a number of attempts to promote peace. He also encouraged the revival in Thomistic theology, and in 1918 promulgated the new *Codex Juris Canonici* (Code of Canon Law).

Benedict, Erastus Cornelius. b. at Branford, Conn., March 19, 1800; d. at New York, Oct. 22, 1880. American admiralty lawyer and educator. As a member (1850–63) of the New York City board of education he helped found the Free Academy (now City College). Author of *American Admiralty* (1850) and *A Run Through Europe* (1860); translator of *The Hymn of Hildebert and Other Medieval Hymns* (1861).

Benedict, Francis Gano. b. at Milwaukee, Wis., Oct. 3, 1870—. American chemist noted for metabolic studies of humans and animals. A graduate (1893) of Harvard he was director (1907–37) of the nutrition laboratory, Carnegie Institution, Washington, D.C.

Benedict, Sir Julius. b. at Stuttgart, Germany, Nov. 27, 1804; d. at London, June 5, 1885. British composer, conductor, and pianist, resident in England after 1835. He was director of music (1840) at the Drury Lane Theatre, and accompanied Jenny Lind to America in 1850. His works include the operas *The Gipsy's Warning* (1838), *The Bride of Venice* (1843), *The Crusaders* (1846), and *The Lily of Killarney* (1862); the cantatas *Undine* (1860) and *Richard Coeur de Lion* (1863); and the oratorios *Saint Cecilia* (1866) and *Saint Peter* (1870).

Benedict, Ruth Fulton. b. at New York, June 5, 1887; d. there, Sept. 17, 1948. American anthropologist and humanist. For several years after graduating from Vassar College at Poughkeepsie, N.Y., in 1909, she taught the humanities, wrote poetry and biographies, and studied the art of the dance. In her mid-thirties, an interest in anthropology was aroused in her by Franz Boas, and after acquiring the degree of Ph.D. from Columbia University in 1923, she became a lecturer in anthropology at that institution. In 1930 she was named an assistant professor, in 1936 an associate professor, and in 1948 a full professor of anthropology at Columbia. Granted leave (1943–46) to serve with the Bureau of Overseas Intelligence, Office of War Information, she wrote *The Chrysanthemum and the Sword: Patterns of Japanese Culture.* This study of Japanese mores and ways of thought (published in 1946) is considered to have been of great value in helping to shape American policy toward the Japanese people during and after World War II. She was also the author of *Patterns of Culture* (1934), *Zuni Mythology* (1935), *Race, Science and Politics* (1940), and (with Gene Weltfish) *The Races of Mankind* (1943). She served as editor of *Journal of American Folklore* and of *Columbia University Contributions to Anthropology.*

Benedict, Wayland Richardson. b. at Rochester, N.Y., Jan. 9, 1848; d. July 21, 1915. American professor of philosophy. He was executive officer (1875–76), professor (1875–1907) of various fields of philosophy, and dean (1890–91) at the University of Cincinnati, Ohio. Author of *Nervous System and Consciousness* (1885), *Theism and Evolution* (1886), *Outlines of the History of Education* (1888), *Ethics and Evolution* (1889), *New Studies in the Beatitudes* (1890), *Psychological Table* (1889, 1900), *Religion as an Idea* (1903), and *Greek Thought Movements and Their Ethical Implication* (1905).

Benedict Bellefontaine (bel.fon.ten′). See **Bellefontaine, Benedict.**

Benedict Biscop (bis′kọp), Saint. [Also called **Biscop Baducing.**] b. c628; d. at Wearmouth, England, Jan. 12, 690. English ecclesiastic, the founder of the monasteries of Wearmouth (674) and of Jarrow (682). He was an Angle of noble birth, thane of the king of Northumbria. He entered the church, and in 669 was made abbot of Saint Peter's in Canterbury, and is noteworthy as the guardian of Bede, who when only seven years old was placed under his charge. He introduced into England artisans to construct stone churches and glass windows. He was canonized, and his festival is celebrated in the Roman Catholic and Anglican churches on Jan. 12.

Benedictines (ben.ẹ.dik′tinz, -tēnz, -tīnz). Roman Catholic monastic order. Saint Benedict of Nursia about the year 500 turned from the luxury and corruption of Rome to become a hermit. Other religious devotees gathered around his cave at Subiaco, and in this manner the precursor of the Benedictine monastery came into existence. In c529 Benedict established the celebrated monastery at Monte Cassino. When this was sacked by the Lombards, about 580, Pope Pelagius II established the monks at Rome, where for 140 years they had their principal house, and from which numerous missionaries went out to all parts of Western Europe and to England. The Christianization of the Germans in particular is credited largely to the "black monks," as Benedictines are often called from the color of their habit. Where the "black monks" established themselves in regions already partly Christianized by Irish and other Celtic missionaries, the very strict Celtic monasticism in many cases was softened by adaptation to the milder "Rule of Saint Benedict," which in the 8th century largely prevailed throughout Western Europe. Charlemagne patronized the Benedictines, and in 817 his son Louis the Pious caused minute regulations in conformity with the Benedictine Rule to be imposed on all monasteries in the newly revived Holy Roman Empire, but this attempt at compulsory uniformity in all details was not very successful. Benedictine monasticism took no root in eastern Europe, except in parts of Poland, Bohemia, Bavaria, and Austria. It is generally supposed that Saint Benedict had no intention of founding an order, but the increasing numbers of religious who put themselves under his guidance and the multiplication of monastic establishments on the model of Monte Cassino caused him, about the year 530, to commit to writing the Rule which thereafter guided this first monastic order of the Western Church. The Benedictine Order is probably unique in that it has never had an actual centralized authority and no general superior but the Pope. As Benedictine houses multiplied, they became grouped in so-called congregations, each administratively autonomous, united only by allegiance to the Rule, with considerable latitude, however, for modification of that Rule to meet conditions peculiar to a particular congregation or house. Union of individual houses in congregations was positively directed by the Fourth Lateran Council in 1215, which also ordered that the abbots of all houses in a congregation should meet every three years with power to pass regulations binding on all such houses. During the next century this directive was seriously followed only in England, but following publication of the Bull *Benedictina* of Pope Benedict XII in 1336, this reform was generally effected, and almost all Benedictine monasteries today are grouped in congregations. During the early years of the Reformation, most Benedictine establishments in Protestant countries were suppressed. Today, however, the Benedictine Order is flourishing, with houses in most parts of the world including the U.S. While Saint Benedict was at Monte Cassino his sister Scholastica presided over a religious community of women nearby. It is surmised that this community was under Benedict's spiritual direction and that such regulations as he made for them must have conformed closely to those which he embodied in his Rule.

Benedict of Aniane (à.nyàn), Saint. b. in Languedoc, France, c750; d. 821. French ecclesiastic, noted as a reformer of monastic discipline. Being entrusted by Louis the Pious with the superintendence of the convents of western France, he attempted to bring them all under one rule by joining to the rule of Benedict of Nursia, so far as practicable, all other rules, with the result that the "Concordia Regularum" of Benedict of Aniane became hardly less celebrated than the original rule of Benedict of Nursia.

Benedict of Nursia (nėr′shi.ạ), Saint. b. at Nursia, near Spoleto, in Umbria, c480; d. March 21, 543. Italian monk who founded the order of the Benedictines (*q.v.*), at Monte Cassino, c529. He established a set of rules for monastic living, and the monasteries established according to these rules are now considered by many authorities to have been the chief civilizing agencies in Western Europe during the 6th, 7th, 8th, and 9th centuries. His feast is commemorated on March 21, and in the Greek calendar on March 14.

Benediktbeuern (bā″nẹ.dikt.boi′ėrn). Village in S Germany, in the *Land* (state) of Bavaria, American Zone, in the *Kreis* (district) of Upper Bavaria, situated in the foothills of the Alps, ab. 30 mi. SW of Munich. Near it is the mountain Benediktenwand. It is the seat of a former Benedictine abbey, founded in 733 and secularized in 1803; the buildings, in the Renaissance and baroque styles, date from the 17th century. 2,200 (1946).

Benediktsson (ben′e.dikts.sôn), **Bjarni.** b. at Reykjavik, Iceland, April 30, 1908—. Icelandic political leader and educator, known especially for his leadership (1936 *et seq.*) of the Independence party. He was (1932–40) professor of constitutional law at the University of Reykjavik, was elected (1934) to the Reykjavik city council, became (1940) mayor of Reykjavik, and obtained (1942) a seat in the *Althing* (parliament). Chairman of the parliament's foreign relations committee (1946–47), he became (1947) Iceland's foreign minister.

Benedix (bā′nẹ.diks), **Roderich Julius.** b. at Leipzig, Germany, Jan. 21, 1811; d. there, Sept. 26, 1873. German dramatist and miscellaneous writer, author of numerous comedies.

Benefactor (bā.nā.fäk.tōr′). Province in the C part of the Dominican Republic. Capital, San Juan de la Maguana; area, 1,343 sq. mi.; pop. 107,060 (1950).

Benefield (ben′ẹ.fēld), **(John) Barry.** b. at Jefferson, Texas, 1880—. American journalist and writer. After receiving (1902) a B.Litt. degree from the University of Texas, he worked on the staffs of the Dallas *News*, the Brooklyn *Standard Union*, and the New York *Times*. He served on the editorial staff of D. Appleton-Century Company, and was an associate editor of Reynal and Hitchcock Company. Among his books are *The Chicken-Wagon Family* (1925), *Short Turns* (1926), *Bugles in the Night* (1927), *Valiant is the Word for Carrie* (1935), and *April Was When It Began* (1939).

Beneharnum (ben.ẹ.här′num). Latin name of **Béarn.**

Bene Israel or **Beni Israel** (bā′nē iz′rā̤.ẹl). Jewish community in India. The people of this isolated Jewish community (the term means "sons of Israel" or "children of Israel" in Hebrew, and has usage among speakers of Hebrew as a general term referring to the Jews as a group) are found in the Kolaba, Bombay, and Shana districts and the state of Janjira; they resemble the Jews of Yemen, and by some are thought to have come to India from that country, perhaps in the 6th century. Other students of the matter believe they were refugees from Persian persecution at a much earlier date. First observed by Europeans in the 1840's, they were found to have retained for at least 1,500 years their ethnic integrity, the essence of the Jewish religion, and many Jewish customs. They keep the Sabbath and some, but not all, of the traditional holidays, wear long side curls, eat the flesh of sheep, goats, and fowl, but of no other animals, and continue the rite of circumcision. However, they retain little knowledge of the Hebrew tongue excepting the prayer "Hear, O Israel," which occurs in all of their religious ceremonies. Numbering perhaps 15,000, the Bene Israel are mainly engaged in agriculture and crafts, but they also in the past frequently served as soldiers of Indian princes.

Beneke (bā′nẹ.kẹ), **Friedrich Eduard.** b. at Berlin, Feb. 17, 1798; d. there, March 1, 1854. German empirical psychologist and philosopher.

Benelli (bā.nel′lē), **Sem.** b. c1875; d. 1949. Italian dramatic poet. Benelli's romantic dreams and comedies are marked by strong dramatic qualities and by opulence of speech and setting. Best known among his works are *Rosamunda, Orfeo and Proserpina, The Jest*, and *The Love of Three Kings*. These have been translated into various languages including English, and the two last named have been made the libretti of operas which have been produced in the U.S., where *The Love of Three Kings* is a part of the permanent repertoire of the Metropolitan Opera Company of New York.

Benelux (ben′ẹ.luks). Name applied to a customs union established in September, 1944, between Belgium, the Netherlands, and Luxembourg. Completely successful operation of the scheme was hampered, however, by different currency exchange values, import quotas, and price subsidies, and a further agreement was made in June, 1948, with a view to full economic union by Jan. 1, 1950 (this last development was later postponed for six months). Benelux has become a generic term to describe the three nations which are members of the customs union.

Benengeli (be.nen.gē′lē; Spanish, bā.neng.ʜā′lē), **Cid Hamet.** See **Cid Hamet Benengeli.**

Beneš (be′nesh), **Eduard.** b. at Kožlany, in Bohemia, May 28, 1884; d. near Prague, Czechoslovakia, Sept. 3, 1948. Czechoslovak statesman. Born in humble surroundings, he studied at the University of Prague, the Sorbonne, and the École des Sciences Politiques at Paris, and received the LL.D. degree from Dijon in 1908. He began as a teacher, serving as professor at the Prague Commercial Academy in 1909, and as lecturer (1912) and later professor at Charles University. He was active in the Czech national movement and instrumental in organizing resistance to Austria-Hungary in 1914. He left Bohemia in 1915 to become secretary-general of the Czechoslovak National Council and was, with T. G. Masaryk and M. Štefaník, a leader of the independence movement. In 1918 he became foreign minister of Czechoslovakia and served in this post until 1935. He headed the Czechoslovak delegation to the peace conference in 1919–20, served as prime minister (1921–22), and in 1923 and 1925 served on the League of Nations Council. He founded the Little Entente and in 1924 was coauthor of the Geneva Protocol. He was a strong advocate of collective security, of the rights of small states, and of the League generally. In December, 1935, he succeeded T. G. Masaryk as president of Czechoslovakia, but resigned in October, 1938, in protest against German pressure on Czechoslovakia and the terms of the Munich pact. He served as president (1940–45) of the government in exile at London and in 1946, following the Nazi defeat, was reëlected president at Prague. He followed a policy of Slavic coöperation and of friendship with Russia and the West, and sanctioned a progressive policy of nationalization. He resigned office in June, 1948, after Communists had seized the bulk of power in the government, and died shortly thereafter. See *Beneš, Statesman of Central Europe* by Pierre Crabites (London, 1935).

Benešov (be′ne.shôf). [German, **Beneschau** (bā′nẹ-shou).] Town in Czechoslovakia, in C Bohemia, S of the Sazava River, between Prague and Jabos, ab. 24 mi. S of Prague: breweries, distilleries, tanneries, and a shoe factory. The Gothic church dates from the 13th and 14th centuries. Nearby is the castle of Konopiště, with a park; it belonged formerly to Archduke Francis Ferdinand, whose murder at Sarajevo initiated World War I, but is now state property, 8,241 (1947).

Benét (be.nā′), **Stephen Vincent.** b. at Bethlehem, Pa., July 22, 1898; d. March 13, 1943. American poet, novelist, and story writer; brother of William Rose Benét (1886–1950). He received the degrees of B.A. (1919) and M.A. (1920) from Yale University, and was awarded a Guggenheim fellowship in 1926. Author of *Five Men and Pompey* (1915), *Young Adventure* (1918), *Heavens and Earth* (1920), *The Beginning of Wisdom* (1921), *Jean Huguenot* (1923), *Tiger Joy* (1925), *Spanish Bayonet* (1926), *Ballads and Poems* (1931), *The Devil and Daniel Webster* (1937), *Thirteen O'Clock* (1937), *Tales Before Midnight* (1939), *Western Star* (1943; posthumously published and unfinished, received the 1944 Pulitzer prize for poetry), *America* (1944), and other books; his *John Brown's Body* (1928), a narrative poem on the American Civil War, received the Pulitzer poetry prize in 1929.

Benét, William Rose. b. at Fort Hamilton, N.Y., Feb. 2, 1886; d. May 4, 1950. American poet, novelist, and editor; brother of Stephen Vincent Benét (1898–1943), and husband (1923 *et seq.*) of Elinor Morton Wylie (1885–1928), his second wife. A graduate (1907) of Yale, he served as a staff member of the *Century Magazine* (1911–18), the New York *Evening Post Literary Review* (1920–24), and the *Saturday Review of Literature* (1924 *et seq.*). His volumes of poetry include *Merchants from Cathay* (1913), *The Falconer of God* (1914), *The Great White Wall* (1916), *Moons of Grandeur* (1920), *Man Possessed* (1927), *Starry Harness* (1933), *Golden Fleece* (1935), *The Dust Which Is God* (1941; Pulitzer prize for poetry, 1942), and *The Stairway of Surprise* (1947); his novels include *The First Person Singular* (1922) and *The Flying King of Kurio* (1926); he edited *The Reader's Encyclopedia* (1948).

Benetnasch (bẹ.net′nash). [Also, **Alkaid.**] The bright second-magnitude star η Ursae Majoris, at the extremity of the tail of the animal.

Benevento (ben.ẹ.ven′tō). Province in S Italy, in the *compartimento* (region) of Campania. Capital, Benevento; area, ab. 1,000 sq. mi.; pop. 349,707 (1936).

Benevento. [Latin, **Beneventum** (ben.ẹ.ven′tum), originally **Maleventum.**] City and commune in S Italy, in the *compartimento* (region) of Campania, the capital of the province of Benevento, situated between the Sabato and Calore rivers, ab. 35 mi. NE of Naples. It is an agricultural trade center, has metallurgical, gold and silver plating, leather, and foodstuff industries, particularly distilleries and candy manufactures. It is the seat of an archbishopric. The city is rich in Roman and medieval architecture, the most remarkable Roman monument being the Arch of Trajan, built in 114 A.D.; there are Roman bridges. The cathedral, begun in 1114, is in the Norman Romanesque style and has bronze doors dating from the 12th century. There are numerous other churches and monasteries, and a medieval castle and ramparts. The ancient Samnite town became a Roman colony c269 B.C., after the victory over Pyrrhus which took place there; it was pillaged by Hannibal after his victory at Cannae in 216 B.C. Destroyed by the Goths and rebuilt under the Byzantines, it became a flourishing commercial and cultural center under Lombard rule, trading with Franks, Germans, and Moslems. It became part of the States of the Church under Pope Leo IX in 1049. In a decisive battle which was fought near Benevento in 1266, Manfred of Hohenstaufen, king of Sicily, lost throne and life against Charles of Anjou, who fought for the papacy. The city remained under papal control, except during the Napoleonic era, until 1860. Considerable damage was suffered during World War II by the cathedral and other buildings of tourist interest, but repairs have been completed or are being carried out. Pop. of commune, 37,865 (1936); of city, 26,692 (1936).

Benevento, Battle of. [Also, **Battle of Grandella.**] Victory gained (February, 1266) by Charles of Anjou over Manfred of Hohenstaufen, king of Sicily. Manfred was killed, and the kingdom of Sicily passed to Charles.

Benevento, Duchy of. Former Lombard duchy in S Italy, in and near Benevento, established in 571. It was divided in 840, passed to the States of the Church under Pope Leo IX in 1049, came under the power of the Normans in 1053, and was acquired by Pope Gregory VII in 1077.

Benevenutus de Rambaldis (ben″e̜.ve.nū′tus de̜ ram-bal′dis). Latinized name of **Benvenuto de' Rambaldi.**

Benevolus (bē̜.nev′ǫ.lus). See also **Benlowes, Edward.**

Benevolus. Character in William Cowper's *Task*, meant for John Courtney Throckmorton of Weston Underwood.

Benezet (ben.e̜.zet′), **Anthony.** b. at St.-Quentin, France, Jan. 31, 1713; d. at Philadelphia, May 3, 1784. American philanthropist and teacher. His family moved to London, where they joined the Society of Friends, and to Philadelphia in 1731. He wrote several pamphlets against the slave trade (1762–71), and in behalf of the American Indians.

Benfeld (ben′feld; French, bañ.feld). Small town in NE France, in Bas-Rhin department, situated on the Ill River ab. 17 mi. S of Strasbourg. Pop. ab. 2,700.

Benfey (ben′fī), **Theodor.** b. at Nörten, near Göttingen, Germany, Jan. 28, 1809; d. there, June 26, 1881. German Orientalist, professor at Göttingen (1848–81). His works include *Vollständige Grammatik der Sanskritsprache* (1852), *Sanskrit-English Dictionary* (London, 1866), *Geschichte der Sprachwissenschaft und orientalischen Philologie in Deutschland* (1860), and others.

Benfleet (ben′flēt). Urban district in SE England in Essex, adjoining the county borough of Southend-on-Sea on the E. 19,881 (1951).

Bengal (ben.gôl′, beng-). Region in N India, a former province and presidency of British India, in the E part, with its capital at Calcutta: now divided for the most part into East Bengal, which is part of Pakistan, and West Bengal, which belongs to the Union of India. It was conquered by Mohammedans c1199, became independent of Delhi in 1336, and was under the Moguls from 1576 to 1765. The early settlements of the East India Company were made in the first part of the 17th century. It became a lieutenant-governorship in 1854. It once comprised Bengal Proper (Lower Bengal), Bihar, Chota Nagpur, and Orissa. In 1905 the divisions of Dacca, Chittagong, and Rajshahi (except Darjeeling), the district of Malda, and the state of Hill Tipperah were transferred from it to the newly formed province of Eastern Bengal and Assam. An imperial announcement at Delhi, in December, 1911, decreed the political reconstitution of Bengal with the status of a presidency, the establishment of a new lieutenant-governorship for Bihar, Chota Nagpur, and Orissa, and the consequent disappearance of Eastern Bengal and Assam as a separate lieutenant-governorship. Bengal was made an autonomous province in 1937. Under the Indian Independence Act (1947) the Dacca and Chittagong divisions and the predominantly Mohammedan parts of the Rajshahi and Presidency divisions went to Pakistan. The chief products of the region are rice, opium, jute (it has long been classified as the world's leading jute-producing region), indigo, tea, and oilseeds. There are also extensive coal fields. The leading religions are Hinduism and Mohammedanism, and the chief language is Bengali (although there is a Hindustani-speaking minority).

Bengal, Bay of. [Also: **Gulf of Bengal**; Latin, **Gangeticus Sinus.**] Name applied to that part of the Indian Ocean which lies between the Union of India and Burma, from the Ganges delta S to the S end of Ceylon. It receives the waters of the Kistna, Godavari, Mahanadi, Ganges, Brahmaputra, and Irrawaddy rivers. The name now includes what used to be known as the Sea of Bengal.

Bengal, East. See **East Bengal.**

Bengal, Sea of. Name formerly given to the S part of the Bay of Bengal.

Bengal, West. See **West Bengal.**

Bengali (ben.gô′li, beng-). Indo-European language, spoken by ab. 53 million people in E India, mainly in the Ganges delta and adjoining areas of the region of Bengal. It has its own script, examples of which have been found dating from the 11th century A.D. Since that time there has been a continuing production of written works in Bengali.

Bengal Presidency (ben.gôl′, beng-). One of the three former chief political divisions of British India, of which it comprised at one time nearly all the N portion. The term was used only for purposes of political administration; it now has no ethnic or important regional significance (except insofar as it gave rise to the name "Presidency division" for one of the parts of Bengal which was partitioned in 1947 between Pakistan and the Union of India). See also **Bengal.**

Bengal Proper or **Lower Bengal.** Name given to the S part of the former Bengal Presidency in E British India, now divided between the Union of India (West Bengal) and Pakistan (East Bengal). See also **Bengal.**

Bengasi (ben.gä′zē). [Also: **Bengazi, Benghazi**; ancient names, **Berenice, Hesperides.**] Seaport in N Africa, the capital of the former Italian province of Bengasi, in Cirenaica territory, Libya, situated on the NE corner of the Gulf of Sidra. It was the scene of fierce fighting between the Germans and the British Eighth Army during World War II and changed hands many times. 64,641 (1938).

Bengel (beng′e̜l), **Johann Albrecht.** b. at Winnenden, Württemberg, June 24, 1687; d. at Stuttgart, Württemberg, Nov. 2, 1752. German Protestant theologian and Biblical scholar, the founder of the so-called Biblical realism. The earliest to classify the manuscripts of the New Testament into African and Asiatic families, he was the author of a critical edition of the New Testament (1734), *Gnomon Novi Testamenti* (1742), and others.

Benger (beng′gėr), **Elizabeth Ogilvy.** b. at Wells, Somersetshire, England, 1778; d. at London, Jan. 9, 1827. English author. She wrote novels including *Marian* and *The Heart and the Fancy*, and poems and dramas. She is chiefly known as the compiler of memoirs, among which are those of Elizabeth Hamilton, John Tobin, Anne Boleyn, Mary Queen of Scots, and Elizabeth of Bohemia.

Bengough (ben′gō), **John Wilson.** b. at Toronto, Canada, 1851; d. 1923. Canadian cartoonist and newspaper man, whose on-the-scene drawings of the Spanish-American War were widely published during the last years of the 19th century. He also wrote the article "A Chalk Talk" for the *Canadian Magazine*, painted *An Evening at the Hotel, Tampa, Florida*, published two books of poetry, *Verses Grave and Gay* (1895) and *In Many Keys* (1902), and wrote several political pamphlets, including *The Gin Mill Primer* (1898) and *The Whole Hog Book* (1911).

Bengtson (bengt′so̜n), **Nels August.** b. at Morkhult, Sweden, May 22, 1879—. American geographer and geologist. A graduate of the University of Nebraska (1908) and Clark University (1927), he became (1918) professor of geography at the University of Nebraska. He was also U.S. trade commissioner (1919) to Norway, and a geologist in Honduras (1920), Ecuador (1922), and Venezuela (1928). Author of *Physical Geography Manual* (1913), *Norway—Commercial and Industrial Handbook* (1920), and other works; senior author of *Economic Geography Manual* (1937).

Bengtsson (bengts′sôn), **Frans Gunnar.** b. at Tossjö, Skåne, Sweden, 1894—. Swedish prose writer, critic, and poet. He went to college at Kristianstad, and later studied at the University of Lund. A learned and witty writer who has developed his own technique for using historical material in a new and amusing way, he has, as with his half-humorous, half-serious *Karl XII:s levnad* (The Life of Charles XII, 1935–36), caused considerable controversy in Sweden, which is not accustomed to having its national heroes used for purposes of entertainment. Bengtsson is especially noteworthy as an essayist, having what is considered a very fine style. Of his poems, *En ballad om franske kungens spelmän* (A Ballade of the French King's Bandsmen) is probably best known. It has been set to music by Gunnar Turesson. Other works include *Tärningskast* (Throw of the Dice, 1923), *Legenden om Babel* (The Legend of Babel, 1925; poetry), *Litteratörer och militärer* (Literati and Soldiers, 1929), and *De långhåriga merovingerna* (The Long-haired Merovingians, 1933; essays). Bengtsson has also made a well-known Swedish translation of *Paradise Lost* (1926).

Benguela (beng.gel′a̤). [Also, **Benguella.**] Province of Angola, in SW Africa, between the provinces of Luanda and Huila; it includes six *concelhos* (communes). 1,100,546 (1940).

Benguela. [Also: **Benguella, São Filipe de Benguela.**] Seaport in SW Africa, the capital of the province of Benguela, Angola. Founded in 1617, it was once an important slave-trading station, and was the most important port of the colony until the completion in recent times of the Benguela Railway and the establishment of Lobito as the port of entry. 14,243 (1940).

Benguela Railway. Railway in C Africa, running from Lobito, Angola, to Beira, Mozambique. At Tenke, Belgian Congo, it connects with the Cape-Congo railway. The journey from Lobito to Elisabethville, Belgian Congo, takes three days. The railway is an important artery for trade and the main outlet for the mineral products of the rich Katanga region of the Belgian Congo. The sparse European settlement in Angola has tended to follow the railway, which is playing a vital role in the opening up and development of C Africa. Total length, 2,920 mi.

Benguet (beng.get′). Former inland province of the Philippine Islands, in W Luzon. It now forms the SW corner of the Mountain Province. The area is traversed by the Agno River, which rises in the mountains in the N part of Luzon and flows generally S into Pangasinan province. The surface is irregular, and indicates former great volcanic activity. For centuries gold and copper have been mined in small quantities by the Igorrotes, who form ab. 95 percent of the population.

Ben-Gurion (ben.gö′ri.o̤n), **David.** b. at Płońsk, Poland, Oct. 16, 1886—. Israeli statesman, prime minister of Israel (1948 *et seq.*). He came to Palestine in 1906, became active in the labor movement, helped to organize defense units for the Jewish settlers against the raids of the Arabs, and, as an opponent of Turkish rule in Palestine, was exiled by the Turkish government in 1915, going to the U.S., where he acted as an organizer for the Jewish Legion of World War I and as a recruiting agent for the Palestinian pioneer movement. He fought in the Jewish Legion under Allenby against the Turks. Active in the socialist General Federation of Jewish Labor (*Histadruth*) and in the Zionist movement after World War I, he became (1933) an executive of the Jewish Agency for Palestine, later serving as its chairman. With the declaration of Israel's independence (1948), Ben-Gurion became prime minister and minister of defense of the provisional government of the new country and organized its resistance to the troops of the neighboring Arab countries. After the constitution was adopted and Chaim Weizmann was elected president, Ben-Gurion, head of the socialist Mapai Party, remained as premier.

Benha (ben′hä). City in NE Africa, in Lower Egypt, the capital of Qalyubiya province, situated on the Damietta Branch of the Nile River, ab. 32 mi. N of Cairo. It is on the main railway line from Alexandria to Cairo and is the junction point of the line from Ismailia and Zagazig. It occupies the site of the ancient city of Athribis. 35,245 (1947).

Benhadad I (ben.hā′dad). [Also, **Ben-Haddad.**] fl. c900 B.C. In Biblical history, a king of Syria, father of Benhadad II. He was a contemporary and ally of Asa, king of Judah, with whom he fought against Baasha of Israel. 1 Kings, xv. 18.

Benhadad II. [Also, **Ben-Haddad.**] fl. c854 B.C. In Biblical history, a king of Syria; son of Benhadad I. Successively an antagonist and ally of Ahab, king of Israel (1 Kings, xx. 22, 34), he was murdered and succeeded by Hazael. Shalmaneser III, king of Assyria (c860–c824), claims in his annals that in the sixth year of his reign (c854) he defeated at Karkar (near the river Orontes) 12 allied kings of Hatti and the sea coast, among them the king Dadda-idri of Damascus, and Ahab of Israel, but it is now believed by many scholars that the battle was indecisive, if not an outright defeat for Shalmaneser. Two other victories over Dadda-idri are recorded in the annals of 849 and 846. Dadda-idri is considered to be the same as Benhadad, for in both the inscriptions and the Old Testament (1 Kings, xx. 34 *et seq.*) he figures as an ally of Ahab and as the predecessor of Hazael (Assyrian, Haza-ilu), whose murder of Benhadad II enabled him to gain the throne of Syria. His full name was probably Bin-addu-idri, the son of the storm god (called in Assyrian, Ramman), and was shortened to Benhadad by the Hebrews and to Dadda-idri by the Assyrians.

Benhadad III. [Also, **Ben-Haddad.**] fl. c800 B.C. In Biblical history, a king of Syria; son of Hazael. 2 Kings, xiii. 3.

Benham (ben′a̤m), **Andrew Ellicott Kennedy.** b. at New York, April 10, 1832; d. at Lake Mahopac, N.Y., Aug. 11, 1905. American naval officer, promoted to the rank of rear admiral in 1890. He entered the service in 1847, and was a member of the Union navy throughout the Civil War. In 1894 he was in command of the U.S. squadron at Rio de Janeiro, and forced the insurgent Brazilian vessels to raise the blockade of that port.

Benham, Henry Washington. b. at Quebec, Canada, April 8, 1813; d. June 1, 1884. American soldier and military engineer. He was appointed (1861) chief engineer of the Ohio department of the U.S. army, headed (1863 *et seq.*) the engineer brigade of the Army of the Potomac, and organized (1865–82) the construction of Boston and New York harbor defenses.

Benham, Sir **William Gurney.** b. 1859; d. 1944. English compiler, and author of guide and travel books. The author of *A Pilgrimage to Cymbeline's Town and Constable's Country* (1903), *Elmstead Parish Church—Its Monuments and Relics* (1931), *Colchester—A History and a Guide* (1946), and many similar works, he is also widely known for *Cassell's Book of Quotations, Proverbs, and Household Words* (1907, 1913, 1914, 1936) and *Cassell's Classified Quotations* (1921), both of which he compiled.

Ben Hur (ben″hėr′). [Full original title, **Ben-Hur: A Tale of the Christ.**] Novel by Lew Wallace, published in 1880, named after its principal character, Judah Ben-Hur, a young Jew. The scene is laid in the time of Christ. Few books in English have had greater popularity: by 1911 a million copies had been sold, and in 1913 one million copies of a special 39-cent edition were printed for a mail-order house. It was dramatized in 1899, and in 1925 it was adapted to the screen as one of the most expensive (and profitable) motion pictures made up to that time.

Beni (bā′nē). [Full name, **El Beni.**] Department in N Bolivia. Capital, Trinidad; area, 80,005 sq. mi.; pop. 119,770 (1950).

Beni-Amer (bā′nē.a′mėr). One of the predominantly Caucasoid Beja peoples of NE Africa, inhabiting N Eritrea and NE Anglo-Egyptian Sudan. Their population is estimated at more than 30,000 (based on S. F. Nadel, *Notes on Beni-Amer Society, Sudan Notes,* 1945). Linguistically they are divided into those speaking a Semitic language (Tigre), those speaking a Cushitic language (Beja), and those who are bilingual.

Benicia (be̤.nish′a̤). [Former name, **Santa Francisca.**] City in C California, in Solano County on the Strait of Carquinez, ab. 25 mi. NE of San Francisco. It contains a U.S. arsenal, and was once the capital of the state. In the decade between the last two U.S. censuses, its population more than tripled. 2,419 (1940); 7,284 (1950).

Beni-Hassan (bā′nē.hä′sän). [Also, **Beni Hasan.**] Village in Middle Egypt, situated on the E bank of the Nile River, opposite the ancient Hermopolis. It is famous for its rock tombs, and for its grottoes (sometimes called the caves of Artemis). The chief groups of rock-cut sepulchers occupy a terrace in the limestone cliff bordering at a little distance the E bank of the Nile. The tombs date from the beginning of the XIIth dynasty (3000–2500 B.C.), and consist of a rock-cut vestibule preceding a chamber in which is sunk a shaft, at the bottom of which lies the tomb itself. The walls of the chambers are covered with remarkable paintings of scenes of ancient life, but the tombs are especially notable for the celebrated so-called proto-Doric columns of many of their vestibules. These are set, usually two placed opposite each other, in the rectangular rock-openings, and support an architrave on their thin square abaci; there is no echinus. Some of the rock-cut shafts are shaped in prismatic forms; others have shallow channels with sharp arrises.

Beni Israel (bā′nē iz′rā.el). See **Bene Israel.**

Benin (be.nēn′). Former name of the E part of Upper Guinea, W Africa, and now the name of one of the Western Provinces of Nigeria.

Benin. [Former name, **Great Benin.**] Province of Nigeria, W Africa, a former Negro kingdom extending from the W part of the Niger River delta to Yoruba on the NW. Today it is one of the Western Provinces of Nigeria, occupying the territory immediately W of the Niger delta. The principal city is Benin. The people of the thickly settled area are the Binis, and their ancient kingdom probably reached its height c1600, when it became the dominant power in the S part of what is now Nigeria. The kingdom came under British rule with the capture of the city of Benin in 1897.

Benin. [Former name, **Benin City.**] Town in W Africa, capital of the province of Benin, Western Provinces, Nigeria, situated on the Benin River (a W mouth of the Niger River), ab. 70 mi. from the Gulf of Guinea. It is now small, although in former days it was the capital of the powerful native kingdom of Benin and known for the cruelty and violence of its people. Pop. ab. 15,000.

Benin, Bight of. Arm of the Atlantic Ocean off W Africa, that part of the Gulf of Guinea which lies W of the Niger River delta and S of the French territories of Dahomey and Togo and part of Nigeria.

Beni River (bā′nē). [Also: **Vení, Paro.**] River in N Bolivia which rises near La Paz, unites with the Mamoré River, and flows NE to form the Madeira River. Length, ab. 1,000 mi.

Beni-Saf (bā′nē.säf′). Town and artificial port in NW Africa, on the Mediterranean coast of Oran department, Algeria. It was built by the French in the last decade of the 19th century for the shipment of the iron ore found in its surrounding hills. The trade of the port is dominated by the mineral activities in the area. 13,747 (1936).

Beni Suef (bā′nē swef′). Province of Upper Egypt, NE Africa, occupying, on both sides of the Nile River, the cultivable land about the city of Beni Suef and between the provinces of Faiyum and Minya. Capital, Beni Suef; settled area, 413 sq. mi.; pop. 613,365 (1947).

Beni Suef. City in NE Africa, the capital of the province of Beni Suef, Upper Egypt, on the W bank of the Nile River, ab. 72 mi. S of Cairo: a cotton center. 57,464 (1947).

Benítez (bā.nē′tes), **Justo Pastor.** b. at Asunción, Paraguay, 1896—. Paraguayan journalist, politician, and diplomat. He served as president (1927–30) of the Paraguayan exchange bureau, was minister (1930–34) of justice and public instruction, interior, finance, war, and foreign affairs, and held the diplomatic posts of minister to Brazil (1935–38) and Bolivia (1938–39). He served as minister of finance in the period 1939–40. Editor of the newspapers *El Liberal* and *El Diario;* author of *Ideario político* (1919), *Jornadas democráticas* (1921–22), *La Vida solitaria del doctor José Gaspar de Francia, dictador del Paraguay* (1937), *La Revolución de los comuneros* (1938), and other books.

Benito Cereno (bā.nē′tō sā.rā′nō). Story by Herman Melville, published in *The Piazza Tales* (1856). It is considered by some critics to be the best of Melville's fiction, next to *Moby Dick*.

Benjamin (ben′ja.min). In the Old Testament, the youngest son of Jacob; ancestor of one of the 12 tribes of Israel. He was named Benoni (meaning "son of my sorrow") by his mother, Rachel, who died in giving him birth, but this was changed to Benjamin (meaning "son of the right hand") by Jacob. The tribe of Benjamin occupied a territory ab. 26 mi. long and 12 mi. wide between Ephraim (on the N) and Judah, containing Jerusalem and Jericho. Gen. xlii. 4, xliv. 20.

Benjamin, Arthur. b. at Sydney, Australia, Sept. 18, 1893—. British pianist and composer. He was professor of piano at the Sydney State Conservatory (1919–21) and at the Royal College of Music (1921 *et seq.*) in England. Awarded (1924) the Carnegie prize for his *Pastoral Fantasia* string quartet, he composed also the operas *The Devil Take Her* (1931) and *Prima Donna* (1934), a concerto for violin, viola, and orchestra (1937), a piano suite (1927), and works for the violin, solo voice, and chorus.

Benjamin, Asher. b. at Greenfield, Mass., 1773; d. 1845. American architect. He designed houses and churches in many New England communities, but his very important influence on the architecture of that region developed chiefly from two of his books: *The Elements of Architecture, Town and Country Builder's Assistant* (1797), which is believed to have been the first book on architecture published in the U.S., and *The American Builder's Companion* (1806), of which he was coauthor with Daniel Reynard. Both works included many architectural plates, and several editions were published of each. One result of this was that the late colonial design, which they favored and illustrated, was widely adopted in New England, with lasting effects upon architectural standards and preferences throughout the U.S. In later publications, *The Rudiments of Architecture* (1814) and *The Practical House Carpenter* (1830), Benjamin laid greater emphasis on design derived from classic Greek examples.

Benjamin, Judah Philip. b. on the island of St. Thomas, in the West Indies, Aug. 6, 1811; d. at Paris, May 6, 1884. American lawyer and Confederate statesman. After attending Yale (1825–27), he entered a commercial firm at New Orleans, where he gave English lessons in addition to his regular job. Working as a clerk for a notary, he acquired legal training, established a practice, and soon gained a national reputation as a lawyer. A member of the Whig Party, he entered (1842) the Louisiana state legislature, was a delegate (1844–45) to the state constitutional convention, and was elected (1852) to the U.S. Senate. An advocate of economic expansion for the South, he came to believe in the need for political independence for that part of the country; he transferred (May 2, 1856) his allegiance from the collapsing Whig organization to the Democratic Party, and was one of the first Southern politicians to advise secession. When Louisiana did secede, he resigned (1861) from the Senate, and was appointed a few weeks later attorney general of the Confederacy; he held this position for only a few months, being named (November, 1861) Confederate secretary of war (his formal appointment came two months after he actually assumed the duties of secretary). Military reverses early in 1862 caused Benjamin to be attacked as inefficient and his resignation was demanded; it is now believed, however, that he cannot be held responsible for the Confederate loss of Roanoke Island, nor for any of the other events of those months, the true fault lying with the lack of equipment from which the Confederate forces suffered. Nevertheless, Jefferson Davis removed Benjamin from the department of war, naming him instead secretary of state, a position he held until the fall of the Confederacy in 1865. Although he continued to enjoy Davis's friendship and trust, he never regained popularity with the people, who continued to blame him for the losses of 1862. He aroused further opposition with his scheme for arming slaves and using them to supplement the dwindling military man-power of the South, with the understanding that emancipation would follow; while the Confederate legislature was not averse to using Negro troops, they refused to pass any bills which would jeopardize the institution of slavery. After the Northern victory, Benjamin escaped capture and fled to England. There he enrolled (1866) as a law candidate at Lincoln's Inn, at London; later in the same year, he was called to the bar, and began to practice in the northern circuit of England. Highly successful from the outset, he was named (1872) a queen's counsel, and continued to practice until his retirement in 1883. He was the author of *Treatise on the Law of Sale of Personal Property* (1868).

Benjamin, Lewis Saul. [Pseudonym, **Lewis Melville.**] b. at London, March 30, 1874; d. 1932. English author, editor, biographer, and actor. After a short career (1896–

1901) on the London stage, he turned to writing, producing a large number of books in various fields of literary and state history, and biography. Among his works are lives of W. M. Thackeray (1909), Laurence Sterne (1911), William Cobbett (1913), and Tobias Smollett (1926). He was the author also of *Victorian Novelists* (1906), *Farmer George* (2 vols., 1907), *Beaux of the Regency* (1908), *Some Aspects of Thackeray* (1911), *Memoirs of Lady Craven* (1913); *London Scene* (1926), *Stage Favorites* (1928–29), and an edition (1901–07) of the works of Thackeray. He also wrote *The First Gentleman of Europe* (1906), *Bath Under Beau Nash* (1907), *Brighton—Its History, Follies, and Fashions* (1909), *Beau Brummell* (1924), *Famous Duels and Assassinations* (1929), and *Horace Walpole* (1930).

Benjamin, Marcus. b. at San Francisco, Jan. 17, 1857; d. Oct. 22, 1932. American chemist, editor (1896 *et seq.*) for the U.S. National Museum. He was graduated (1878) from the School of Mines at Columbia University, was a chemist at the U.S. laboratory of the New York appraiser's stores (1883–85), and was a sanitary engineer of the New York Board of Health in 1885. He contributed scientific articles to many publications, and was a member of the editorial staffs of various encyclopedias and dictionaries.

Benjamin, Park. b. at Demerara, British Guiana, Aug. 14, 1809; d. at New York, Sept. 12, 1864. American journalist and poet; father of Park Benjamin (1849–1922). He was associated with Charles Fenno Hoffman as editor (1837–38) of the *American Monthly Magazine*, established (1839) the *New World* (in connection with E. Sargent and R. W. Griswold), and was connected with various other journals.

Benjamin, Park. b. at New York, May 11, 1849; d. Aug. 21, 1922. American patent lawyer and writer; son of Park Benjamin (1809–64). He was graduated from the U.S. Naval Academy in 1867 (resigning from the navy in 1869) and from the Albany Law School in 1870. He served as associate editor (1872–78) of the *Scientific American*, and was the author of *The Age of Electricity* (1886), *The Voltaic Cell* (1892), *Intellectual Rise in Electricity* (1895), and *The United States Naval Academy* (1900); he also edited *Appleton's Cyclopedia of Applied Mechanics* (1892), and wrote extensively on naval subjects.

Benjamin (baṅ.zhà.maṅ), **René.** b. at Paris, March 20, 1885; d. 1948. French novelist, playwright, and essayist. His reputation is based on a novel, *Gaspard* (1915), which celebrates the heroism of a typical "little man" during the German invasion of France during World War I. He wrote much later fiction, which did not increase his fame, but his series of popular biographies on Honoré de Balzac (1922), Joffre (1929), Molière (1936), and Marie Antoinette (1940) have been widely read.

Benjamin (ben'ja.min), **Samuel Greene Wheeler.** b. at Argos, Greece, Feb. 13, 1837; d. July 19, 1914. American author and artist; the son of an American missionary. He was graduated from Williams College in 1859, subsequently studied law, seamanship, and art, and served as first U.S. minister to Persia (1883–85). His works include *Contemporary Art in Europe* (1877), *Art in America* (1879), *The Multitudinous Seas* (1879), *Troy, Its Legend and Literature* (1880), *Persia and the Persians* (1887), and numerous paintings.

Benjamin Allen (al'en). See **Allen, Benjamin.**

Benjamin 'Anav (ä'näf). [Full name, **Benjamin ben Abraham 'Anav;** Italian, **Benjamin delli Mansi** (del'lē män'sē).] fl. at Rome in the last quarter of the 13th century. Jewish scholar. He is of some importance to modern historians of the Middle Ages for his *shelihot* (messages) which contain information on the defamation of the Talmud (1239), on its burning (1244), on the distinctive badges or garments which Jews were obliged to wear (1257), and on the desecration of tombs in the Jewish cemetery at Rome (1267).

Benjamin Backbite (bak'bīt), **Sir.** See **Backbite, Sir Benjamin.**

Benjamin ben Isaac of Carcassonne (ben ī'zak; kär-kȧ.son). fl. in the 2nd half of the 14th century. Jewish scholar and translator. He is now remembered chiefly for his translation from Latin into Hebrew of a treatise on the plague and on the corruption of the air, written at Liége in 1362 or 1365. The exact date of the translation is not known, but was probably shortly after 1370. A manuscript of the original work is preserved in the Bibliothèque Nationale, at Paris.

Benjamin Britain. See **Britain, Benjamin** (or **Little**).

Benjamin Nahawendi (nä.hä.ven'di). [Full name, **Benjamin ben Moses Nahawendi** (or **Nahavendi**).] fl. at what is now Nehavend, Iran, in the late 8th and early 9th centuries. Jewish scholar and theologian, a member of the Karaite sect. He is considered to have done much to advance the Karaite doctrine that theological inquiry is a duty, and that errors occasioned by inquiry do not constitute sins. He wrote commentaries on the Bible, most of which are in Arabic but some of which are in Hebrew.

Benjamin of Tudela (tö.dā'lä). d. 1173. Jewish rabbi, scholar, and traveler. His fame now rests chiefly on an account he wrote in Hebrew of his travels over a period of some 13 years, which took him to France, Italy, Sicily, Greece, Constantinople, Egypt, Palestine, and Assyria. (By some authorities he is said to have gone still further east, through Persia and even into China. If this is true, he was probably the first traveler of the Middle Ages to reach China, but most modern historians believe that his accounts of the regions east of Baghdad are based on hearsay rather than his own knowledge from first-hand experience.) It has been translated into Latin (1575), into French (1734), and on several occasions into English. The most recent English translation of his writings is a critical edition, by Marcus Nathan Adler, published in 1907.

Ben Jochanan (ben jō.kā'nan). In the second part of *Absalom and Achitophel*, by John Dryden and Nahum Tate, a character intended for Samuel Johnson (1649–1703), a clergyman who upheld the right of private judgment and was persecuted therefor.

Ben Jonson Entertains a Man from Stratford. Dramatic monologue in blank verse by Edwin Arlington Robinson, published in *The Man Against the Sky* (1916).

Benjowsky (ben.yôf'ski), Count **Moritz August von.** b. at Verbó, Hungary, 1741; killed in Madagascar, May 23, 1786. Hungarian adventurer. He was involved in intrigues in Kamchatka and Madagascar.

Benkoelen (ben.kö'len). [Also: **Bencoelen, Bencoolen, Benkulen.**] City in the Republic of Indonesia, situated on the SW coast of Sumatra. Rubber is the main commercial item. It was settled (c1685) by the English, and ceded to the Dutch in 1825. Now of comparatively little commercial importance, it had formerly a considerable trade. 13,418.

Benkovac (beng'kô.väts). [Italian, **Bencovazzo.**] Town in W Yugoslavia, in the federative unit of Croatia, in the region of Dalmatia, former *banovina* (province) of Primorska, situated SE of Zadar: a road junction. 15,575 (1931).

Ben Lawers (ben lô'ėrz). Mountain in C Scotland, in Perthshire, ab. 3 mi. N of Loch Tay. A 20-foot cairn has been built on its summit. 3,984 ft.

Ben Ledi (led'i). Mountain in C Scotland, in Perthshire, ab. 5 mi. NW of Callander. 2,875 ft.

Benlliure y Gil (ben.lyö'rā ē hēl), **José.** b. at Cañamelas, Spain, Oct. 1, 1855; d. sometime after 1914. Spanish religious painter and portraitist whose painting *L'Accueil de Chefs Germains par le Cardinal Adrian*, done at the age of 19, caused a sensation at its first showing at Valencia. He studied in Spain and went to Rome as a professor at the Spanish Academy. Many of his works were awarded prizes at Paris, London, New York, and Madrid. Among his better known works are *Vision of Martyrs in Rome*, *Saint Francis*, and a portrait of the prince of Asturias.

Ben Lomond (ben lō'mond). Mountain in W central Scotland, in Stirlingshire, ab. 28 mi. NW of Glasgow, ab. 1 mi. E of Loch Lomond. It is noted for its extended view. 3,192 ft.

Benlowes (ben'lōz), **Edward.** [Called **Benevolus.**] b. in Essex, England, c1603; d. at Oxford, England, Dec. 18, 1676. English poet. In 1620 he matriculated at St. John's College, Cambridge. He inherited his father's estate, and squandered it in foolish generosity (whence the name by which he was called, Benevolus, almost an anagram of his own name). He was the author of many poems in Latin, including *Theophila, or Love's Sacrifice, a Divine Poem* (1652, in 13 cantos, setting forth the victorious struggle of Theophila, the Soul, against sin) and *The Summary* *of Divine Wisdom* (1657). Samuel Butler, Alexander Pope (in his *Dunciad*), and Bishop William Warburton ridiculed Benlowes and his work.

Ben Macdhui (ben mak.dö'i). [Also, **Ben Muichdhui** (muċh.dö'i).] Mountain in N central Scotland, situated on the Aberdeenshire-Banffshire boundary, ab. 26 mi. N of Pitlochry. It is the second highest mountain in Great Britain (only Ben Nevis being higher). 4,296 ft.

Ben More (mōr'). Mountain in W Scotland, in Argyllshire, situated on the island of Mull, ab. 21 mi. W of Oban. It is the highest mountain on the island. 3,169 ft.

Ben More Assynt (a̤.sint'). [Also, **Ben More.**] Mountain in N Scotland, in Sutherland, situated ab. 18 mi. NW of Lairg. 3,273 ft.

Benmore Head (ben'mōr). See **Fair Head.**

Benn (ben), **Alfred William.** b. in County Westmeath, Ireland, 1843; d. Sept. 16, 1916. British classical scholar and historian. He was the author of *The Greek Philosophers* (1882), *The Philosophy of Greece* (1898), *A History of English Rationalism in the Nineteenth Century* (1906), *Modern England* (1908), *Revaluations* (1909), and others.

Benn, Gottfried. b. at Mansfeld, Germany, May 2, 1886—. German critic, physician, and expressionistic writer. He is the author of poems, predominantly pessimistic, collected under the titles *Morgue* (1912), *Fleisch* (1916), and *Schutt* (1924), of stories published under the title *Gehirne* (1917), the drama *Vermessungsdirigent* (1919), the critical works *Nach dem Nihilismus* (1932), *Kunst und Macht* (1934), and others. In 1931 he wrote the text for Paul Hindemith's oratorio *Das Unaufhörliche.*

Benn, William Wedgwood. [Title, 1st Viscount of **Stansgate.**] b. May 10, 1877—. British politician. He was a member of Parliament (1906–27, 1928–31, 1937–42), at first (1906–27) as a Liberal and thereafter (1928 *et seq.*) as a member of the Labour Party, and served (1929–31) also as secretary of state for India. He was made a viscount in 1941. Author of *In the Side Shows* and (with his wife) of *Beckoning Horizon* (1935).

Bennaskar (ben.nas'ka̤r). A magician in Ridley's *Tales of the Genii.*

Benndorf (ben'dôrf), **Otto.** b. at Greiz, Germany, Sept. 13, 1838; d. at Vienna, Jan. 2, 1907. German archaeologist. He served as a professor (1869 *et seq.*) at the universities of Zurich, Munich, Prague, and Vienna, and directed excavations at Ephesus. He was coauthor of *Die antiken Bildwerke des lateranischen Museums* (The Antique Sculptures of the Lateran Museum, 1867), and author of *Griechische und sizilianische Vasenbilder* (Greek and Sicilian Vase Pictures, 1869–83).

Bennet (ben'e̤t), **Elizabeth.** Heroine of Jane Austen's novel *Pride and Prejudice.* The second in a family of five daughters, her intelligence is constantly required to cope with problems created by her mother's single-minded matchmaking, her older sister Jane's sentimental helplessness, and her younger sister Lydia's wild precociousness. Her pride comes in conflict with that of Fitzwilliam Darcy; she is turned against him by his imperiousness at a local ball, and by stories that have reached her of his ruthlessness; he, on the other hand, is irritatingly conscious of the superiority of his social position as compared to hers. Nevertheless, they are strongly attracted to each other, and Darcy makes Elizabeth a proposal, which she rejects absolutely. He then lets her know that the rumors against him have been completely untrue, thus disabusing Elizabeth of her prejudice against his moral character. Finally, in spite of his arrogant aunt, Lady Catherine de Bourgh, Darcy comes to realize that Elizabeth is in every way his equal, and his second proposal to her is accepted.

Bennet, Henry. See **Arlington,** 1st Earl of.

Bennet, Jane. Sister of Elizabeth Bennet, a character in Jane Austen's *Pride and Prejudice.* In love with Charles Bingley, she is separated from him by the design of Bingley's sisters, who consider Jane too vulgar to marry into their family. At the end of the book, however, the lovers are happily reunited.

Bennet, John. fl. c1600. English composer of madrigals. He is best known for "All creatures now are merry minded," which he contributed to the collection *The Triumphes of Oriana.*

Bennet, Lydia. Sister of Elizabeth Bennet, a character in Jane Austen's *Pride and Prejudice.* Her high spirits and emotional susceptibility get her into various difficulties, which are all, however, righted in the end.

Bennet, Sanford Fillmore. b. at Eden, N.Y., June 21, 1836; d. June 11, 1898. American physician and hymn writer, chiefly remembered for *In the Sweet By and By.* He was the author of a hymnal anthology, *The Signet Ring* (1871), and of *The Pioneer, an Idyll of the Middle West* (1898).

Bennett (ben'e̤t), **Albert Arnold.** b. at Yokohama, Japan, June 2, 1888—. American mathematician. A graduate of Brown (1911) and Princeton (1914), he was a mathematics and dynamics expert (1919–21) in the U.S. army ordnance department. Later he held posts as professor (1925–27) of mathematics and department head at Lehigh University, and as professor of mathematics (1927 *et seq.*) at Brown. Author of *Introduction to Ballistics* (1921) and *Tables for Interior Ballistics* (1922); coauthor with C. A. Bayliss of *Formal Logic* (1939).

Bennett, Arnold. [Full name, **Enoch Arnold Bennett.**] b. in Staffordshire, England, May 27, 1867; d. March 27, 1931. English novelist. He studied law, but turned to journalism, serving (1893–1900) as assistant editor and subsequently editor of *Woman.* He resigned his editorial post to devote his full time to writing. Besides several plays and miscellaneous writings he published a number of novels. He is best known for *The Old Wives' Tale* and his "Five Towns" books, all set against his native pottery-making region of the five towns which form now, together with a sixth, the county borough of Stoke-on-Trent, England. *Anna of the Five Towns* (1902), *Leonora* (1903), and *Sacred and Profane Love* (1905; revised ed., *The Book of Carlotta,* 1911) comprise the first "Five Towns" trilogy; the second—sometimes also called the "Clayhanger" series—consists of *Clayhanger* (1910), *Hilda Lessways* (1911), and *These Twain* (1916), brought out collectively as *The Clayhanger Family* (1925). His other works include *A Man from the North* (1898), *The Grand Babylon Hotel* (1902), *Buried Alive* (1908), *Your United States* (1912), *The Pretty Lady* (1918), *The Roll-Call* (1919), *Lilian* (1922), *Riceyman Steps* (1923), *Lord Raingo* (1926), *Accident* (1929), and *Imperial Palace* (1930). *The Great Adventure* (1913) was a dramatization of his *Buried Alive;* he collaborated with Edward Knoblock on the play *Milestones* (1912).

Bennett, Caleb Prew. b. Nov. 11, 1758; d. at Wilmington, Del., May 9, 1836. American Revolutionary soldier and politician. In 1833 he became governor of Delaware.

Bennett, Charles Edwin. b. at Providence, R. I., April 6, 1858; d. May 2, 1921. American classical scholar, notable for research in Latin syntax and metrics. Professor of Latin (1892–1921) at Cornell, he was editor (1895–1905) of the *College Latin Series,* author of *A Latin Grammar* (1895), *Appendix to Bennett's Latin Grammar* (1895), *A Latin Composition* (1896), and *Syntax of Early Latin* (1910–14), and translator of *Frontinus, The Stratagems and the Aqueducts of Rome* (1925) and others.

Bennett, Constance. b. at New York, Oct. 22, 1905—. American motion-picture actress; daughter of Richard Bennett (1872–1944). After her debut in *Cytherea* (1924), she appeared in *The Goose Hangs High, Moulin Rouge, Topper, Tailspin, Paris Underground,* and other films and plays.

Bennett, Edmund Hatch. b. at Manchester, Vt., April 6, 1824; d. Jan. 2, 1898. American jurist, teacher, and legal writer. Dean (1876 *et seq.*) of Boston University law school, he was the author of *Fire Insurance Cases, being a Collection of All Reported Cases in England, Ireland, Scotland and America to Date* (1872–77) and *Farm Law* (1880).

Bennett, Emerson. b. at Monson, Mass., March 16, 1822; d. at Philadelphia, May 11, 1905. American novelist, poet, and short-story writer, contributor to popular magazines. Some of his works were serialized in the *Saturday Evening Post* and the New York *Ledger.* Author of the novel *The Prairie Flower* (1849) and others.

Bennett, Enoch Arnold. See **Bennett, Arnold.**

Bennett, Floyd. b. near Warrensburg, N.Y., Oct. 25, 1890; d. at Quebec, Canada, April 25, 1928. American aviator. He went with Richard Evelyn Byrd on the MacMillan expedition to Greenland (1925) and the Spitsbergen-North Pole flight (1926); with Bernt Balchen he undertook the incomplete Detroit-Greenly Island flight

(1928) which caused his death through pneumonia. Floyd Bennett Field, at New York, was named after him.

Bennett, Henry Gordon. b. in Australia, April 15, 1887—. Australian army officer. After service (1915–18) in World War I, he headed (1926–31) the 2nd division of the Australian military forces. Commander (1940) of the 8th division of the Australian Imperial Force, he was general officer (1941–42) in command of Australian forces in Malaya; he made his escape (February, 1942) from Singapore after its fall to the Japanese, and was commissioned a lieutenant general in March, 1942.

Bennett, James Gordon. b. at New Mill, Banffshire, Scotland, 1795; d. at New York, June 1, 1872. American journalist, founder (1835) of the New York *Herald;* father of James Gordon Bennett (1841–1918). He emigrated to America in 1819, and was thereafter at various times a journalist, teacher, and lecturer. He founded the New York *Herald* on May 6, 1835, at a price of one cent per copy. The *Herald* pioneered in publishing daily financial reports, and with the development of the telegraph he secured extensive general news coverage over a wide area. The paper achieved a tremendous circulation for its day, Bennett remaining as its editor until late in life, when he turned its control over to his son James Gordon Bennett.

Bennett, James Gordon. b. at New York, May 10, 1841; d. at Beaulieu, France, May 14, 1918. American journalist, proprietor of the New York *Herald;* son of James Gordon Bennett (1795–1872). He took control (1867) of the *Herald* upon his father's retirement, becoming its owner in 1872. Perhaps his most spectacular single journalistic exploit was his dispatch of Henry M. Stanley in 1869 to find the missing African explorer, David Livingstone; the *Herald's* running account of the search for and final discovery of Livingstone (at Ujiji, on the shore of Lake Tanganyika, on Nov. 10, 1871) was one of the most shrewdly handled news stories of the 19th century. Under his auspices also (and those of the London *Telegraph*) Stanley made his later, and equally important, journey of exploration across Africa (1874–77). Bennett also fitted out the *Jeannette* polar expedition (1879–81). Together with John W. Mackay he established (1883) the Commercial Cable Company, which broke Jay Gould's monopoly in the field. He organized the New York *Evening Telegram* and founded (1887) the Paris edition of the *Herald.* (A person of many strong likes and dislikes, not all of them admirable, Bennett had for France an affection quite devoid of self-interest. His establishment of the Paris *Herald* actually brought him financial loss, but the result was a paper which enormously helped Franco-American relations.) A leading yachtsman of his time, he also took a keen interest in balloon, airplane, and automobile racing, establishing trophies in his name for champions in these fields.

Bennett, James William. b. at Mitchell, Ind., 1891—. American novelist and short-story writer. Among his collections of short stories are *Plum Blossoms and Blue Incense* (1926) and *Dragon Shadows* (1928); his novels include *Manchu Cloud* (1927), *The Yellow Corsair* (1927), *Son of the Typhoon* (1928), *Chinese Blake* (1930), and *Spinach Jade* (1939).

Bennett, Joan. b. at Palisades, N.J., Feb. 27, 1910—. American actress; daughter of Richard Bennett (1872–1944). She made her stage debut in *Jarnegan* (1928) and starred in the play *Stage Door* (1938). She has appeared in films including *Bull Dog Drummond, Disraeli, Little Women, Private Worlds, Man Hunt, The Woman in the Window, Scarlet Street, The Macomber Affair,* and *Father of the Bride.*

Bennett, John Hughes. b. at London, Aug. 31, 1812; d. at Norwich, England, Sept. 25, 1875. British physician and physiologist, an early advocate of the use of the microscope in medical research. He is notable also for a description of leukemia published (1845) at the same time as Rudolf Virchow's. He received (1837) his M.D. at Edinburgh, lectured (1841) on histology at Edinburgh, and later (1843–74) served there as professor of medicine.

Bennett, Richard. b. at Deacon Mills, Ind., May 21, 1872; d. at Los Angeles, Oct. 22, 1944. American actor and producer; father of Constance Bennett and Joan Bennett. Associated (1896–1908) as a producer with Charles Frohman, he also acted in *Charley's Aunt, The Lion and the Mouse, What Every Woman Knows, He Who Gets Slapped, The Royal Family, Jarnegan, The Barker,* and other plays. He was starred in such films as *Arrowsmith, This Reckless Age,* and *The Magnificent Ambersons.*

Bennett, Richard Bedford. [Title, Viscount **Bennett.**] b. at Hopewell, Canada, July 3, 1870; d. 1947. Canadian statesman. A member (1911–17, 1925–39) of the Canadian House of Commons, he was also minister of justice and attorney general (1921), and minister (1926–30) of finance. As head of the Conservative Party, he became prime minister in 1930, a position which he relinquished in 1935 when his party lost the general election. While in office he took part in the imperial conference (1930) at London, the Ottawa empire conference (1932), and the world economic conference (1933) at London.

Bennett, Sir **William Sterndale.** b. at Sheffield, England, April 13, 1816; d. at London, Feb. 1, 1875. English composer. An intimate friend of Mendelssohn and Schumann, he became (1839) a teacher at the Royal Academy of Music, conducted (1856–66) the London Philharmonic orchestra, and was named (1866) principal of the Royal Academy of Music. He founded (1849) the Bach Society, and was knighted in 1871. His works include *The Naiads* (1837), *The May Queen,* a cantata (1858), *Paradise and the Peri* (1862), *The Woman of Samaria,* an oratorio (1867), and others.

Bennettsville (ben'ẹts.vil). Town in NE South Carolina, county seat of Marlboro County: vegetable canneries, lumber yards, and manufactures of yarn, tire fabric, furniture, and fertilizer. 5,140 (1950).

Ben Nevis (ben nē'vis, nev'is). Mountain of the Grampians, in N Scotland, in Inverness-shire, situated near the head of Loch Linnhe, ab. 27 mi. SW of Fort-Augustus: highest mountain in Great Britain. There is a meteorological observatory on its summit. 4,406 ft.

Bennewitz (ben'ẹ.vits), **Peter.** See **Apianus, Petrus.**

Bennigsen (ben'iċh.sẹn), Count **Alexander Levin.** b. at Zakret, near what is now Vilna, Lithuania, July 21, 1809; d. Feb. 27, 1893. Hanoverian statesman; son of Count Levin August Theophil Bennigsen.

Bennigsen, Count **Levin August Theophil.** b. in Brunswick, Germany, Feb. 10, 1745; d. near Hanover, Germany, Oct. 3, 1826. Hanoverian general in the Russian service; father of Alexander Levin Bennigsen. He was a leader in the murder of Czar Paul I of Russia in 1801, and served with distinction against Napoleon I at Pułtusk (1806) and Eylau (1807), and in the campaigns of the period 1812–14.

Bennigsen, Rudolf von. b. at Lüneburg, Hanover, Germany, July 10, 1824; d. Aug. 7, 1902. German statesman, a cofounder and leader of the National Liberal party. He was a member of the Hanoverian chamber (1857–66), where he led the opposition, of the Prussian Landtag (1867–83), the North German Reichstag (1867–70), and the German Reichstag (1871–83, 1887–97). At first a supporter of Bismarck, he subsequently disagreed with him on economic policies and on his attitude toward the Socialists.

Benning (ben'ing), **Henry Lewis.** b. in Columbia County, Ga., April 2, 1814; d. July 10, 1875. American jurist and political leader. A supporter of secession, he also advocated the complete political unification of Southern slavery interests. As an associate judge (1853 *et seq.*) of the Georgia supreme court, he delivered an opinion in the case of Padleford v. Savannah, enunciating the principle that a state supreme court was legally coequal with the U.S. Supreme Court and therefore not bound by its decisions.

Bennington (ben'ing.tọn). Town (in Vermont the equivalent of township in many other states) and village in S Vermont, county seat (with Manchester) of Bennington County, ab. 34 mi. NE of Albany, N.Y., in a granite-quarrying area: various manufactures, including textiles, machinery, plastics, furniture, and paper; tourist resort. Bennington College for women, known for its experiments in educational method, is here. Settled in 1761, Old Bennington was during the colonial period the headquarters of the Green Mountain Boys. Near here, on Aug. 16, 1777, American troops under Colonel John Stark defeated the British forces under Colonel Baum. Pop. of town, 12,411 (1950); of village, 8,002 (1950).

Benno (ben'ō), Saint. b. at Hildesheim, Germany, 1010; d. June 16, 1106. German monk, abbot of Hildesheim, and bishop of Meissen (1066 *et seq.*). He is noted as a supporter of Pope Gregory VII in his struggle with the emperor Henry IV, and for his missionary labors among the Slavs. He was canonized in 1523 (an event which brought a bitter attack from Martin Luther in his *Wider den neuen Abgott und Alten Teuffel*), and in 1576 his remains were deposited at Munich; since then he has been regarded as the patron saint of that city.

Benois (be.nwä'), **Aleksandr Nikolayevich.** b. at St. Petersburg, 1870—. Russian historical painter and art critic, who painted many scenes of the times of Louis XIV and Catherine II. He studied law in Russia, but turned to art when he went to Paris. His books include *A History of Russian Art*, which he also illustrated. He has also worked with the Russian Ballet at Paris, with Sergei Pavlovich Diaghilev and Leon Bakst, and is known especially for scenery painted for *Petroushka*, the Igor Stravinsky ballet.

Benoît (bẹ.nwȧ), **Pierre.** b. at Albi, France, 1886—. French novelist, author of colorful romances, of which *L'Atlantide* (1920), reminiscent of Rider Haggard's *She*, attracted international attention. Much traveled, he has placed the scenes of his tales in widely diverse locales: *Le Lac salé* (1921) takes place in Utah, *Le Chausée des géants* (1922) in Ireland, *Le Puits de Jacob* (1925) in the Levant; other exotic settings include the New Hebrides, scene of his *Erromango* (1929). His production has averaged better than one novel a year. Since 1931 he has been a member of the French Academy.

Benoît, Pierre Léonard Léopold. b. at Harelbeke, Belgium, Aug. 17, 1834; d. at Antwerp, March 8, 1901. Belgian author and composer. He studied music at the Brussels Conservatory and in Germany. Initiator of the Flemish music movement, he was the founder (1867) and first director of the Royal Flemish Conservatory at Antwerp. His musical compositions in many forms include operas, oratorios, cantatas, masses, and songs. His books, pamphlets, and articles supported a strictly national school of music.

Benoît de Sainte-Maure (dẹ saṅt.mōr). [Also, **Sainte-More.**] b. at Sainte-Maure, in Touraine, France; fl. in the 12th century. French trouvère. Little is known of his life beyond the brief autobiographical notices contained in his works. His royal patron, Henry II of England (1154–89), charged him to write the history of the Normans. Benoît accordingly composed *La Chronique des ducs de Normandie*, a poem of 45,000 lines, written c1180. Benoît de Sainte-Maure is also known by his *Roman de Troie*, a poem of over 30,000 lines, written c1160 and dedicated to Eleanor of Aquitaine, wife of Henry II of England. Two other works are sometimes ascribed to this trouvère: *Aeneas*, a poem of some 10,000 verses, and *Le Roman de Thèbes*, in 15,000 lines.

Benoîton (bẹ.nwȧ.tôṅ), **La Famille.** Comedy by Victorien Sardou, produced in 1865. Madame Benoîton is conspicuous by her absence, and has been the bane of her family because of her neglect. She is constantly inquired for, and has always gone out. Hence the saying "to play the part of Madame Benoîton."

Benoni (bẹ.nō'ni). City in S Africa, in Transvaal province, Union of South Africa, situated in the Witwatersrand area, ab. 19 mi. E of Johannesburg. Some of the richest gold deposits in the world are located here; many of the inhabitants are engaged in gold mining. There are also ironworks and a brass foundry. 74,238 (1946).

Benozzo Gozzoli (bā.nôt'tsō gōt'tsō.lē). See **Gozzoli, Benozzo.**

Benrath (ben'rät). Town in W Germany, in the *Land* (state) of North Rhine-Westphalia, British Zone, formerly in the Rhine Province, Prussia, NW of Cologne: incorporated into the city of Düsseldorf. A river port, it has chemical, metallurgical (machines), and other industries. The castle, erected in 1757–60, is in the rococo style; it was severely damaged during World War II, but is not beyond repair. Pop. ab. 26,000.

Bensenville (ben'sẹn.vil). Village in NE Illinois, in Du Page County ab. 16 mi. NW of Chicago. 3,754 (1950).

Benserade (baṅs.rȧd), **Isaac de.** b. at Paris, 1613; d. there, Oct. 17, 1691. French dramatic and lyric poet. He was the author of a famous sonnet on Job which accompanied a paraphrase of several chapters of Job. A protégé of the cardinal Richelieu, he found himself in competition with the court poet Vincent Voiture, the merits of whose poem *Urania* were placed against those of *Job*. For some time the entire court was divided into two factions—called respectively Uranists and Jobelins—over this issue. His other works include *Cléopâtre* (1635) and other tragedies, masques, and ballets.

Bensheim (bens'hīm). City in W Germany, in the *Land* (state) of Hessen, American Zone, formerly in the province of Starkenburg, Hesse, situated on the Lauter River, ab. 15 mi. S of Darmstadt: aluminum and cement works, canneries, and manufactures of paper, paperware, toys, and costume jewelry. It is the center of a wine and fruit growing district. Bensheim is an old city, with a number of churches and houses of the 16th, 17th, and 18th centuries, and the remains of medieval fortifications. The majority of the population is Roman Catholic, with a large Protestant minority. The increase of the total population between 1939 and 1946 was 29.3 percent. 20,207 (1946), 22,279 (1950).

Bensley (benz'li), **Robert.** b. c1738; d. c1817. English actor, much admired by Charles Lamb.

Benson (ben'sọn) or **Bensington** (-sing.tọn). Civil parish and village in S England, in Oxfordshire, ab. 12 mi. SE of Oxford. Here, in 775 A.D., Offa, king of Mercia, defeated Cynewulf, king of Wessex. 1,264 (1931).

Benson. City in SW Minnesota, county seat of Swift County, on the Chippewa River: shipping point for livestock; grain elevators. 3,398 (1950).

Benson, Arthur Christopher. b. April 24, 1862; d. June 17, 1925. English educator and author; son of Edward White Benson. He was a fellow and lecturer of Magdalene College, Cambridge, and a master at Eton College (1885–1903). Appointed (1911) professor of English fiction at the Royal Society of Literature, at London, he became (1915) a master of Magdalene College. He published *Archbishop Laud* (1887), *Rossetti* (1904), *The Upton Letters* (1905), *Walter Pater* (1906), *From a College Window* (1906, critical writings on Rossetti, FitzGerald, and Pater), *Selections from the Correspondence of Queen Victoria* (edited, with Viscount Esher, 1907), *The Silent Isle* (1910), *Ruskin, a Study in Personality*, *The Leaves of the Tree*, and others.

Benson, Carl. Pseudonym of **Bristed, Charles Astor.**

Benson, Edward Frederic. b. in Berkshire, England, July 24, 1867; d. Feb. 29, 1940. English novelist; son of Edward White Benson. He was the author of *Dodo* (1893), *The Babe* (1897), *Mammon and Co.* (1900), *Scarlet and Hyssop* (1902), *The Challoners* (1904), *The Angel of Pain* (1906), *The Blotting Book* (1908), *The Climber* (1908), *The Osbornes* (1910), *Mezzanine* (1926), and *Final Edition* (1940), an autobiography. Best known among his novels are the series of gentle satires centered around the heroine Lucia.

Benson, Edward White. b. at Birmingham, England, July 14, 1829; d. at Hawarden, Flintshire, Wales, Oct. 11, 1896. English prelate; father of Arthur Christopher Benson, Edward Frederic Benson, and Robert Hugh Benson, and uncle of Frank Robert Benson. After having received his B.A. at Trinity College, Cambridge, in 1852, he served (1859–72) as the first headmaster of Wellington College. He became bishop of Truro in 1877, and was consecrated archbishop of Canterbury in 1883. As archbishop of Canterbury he delivered (1890) the important and precedent-setting judgment on the charges of ritual offenses made against Dr. Edward King, bishop of Lincoln; by his refusal to impose any penalty or constraint on the latter, he tacitly allowed variations in the ritual procedures. His works include *Boy-Life* (1874), *Single-heart* (1877), *The Cathedral* (1879), and several volumes of sermons.

Benson, Egbert. b. at New York, June 21, 1746; d. at Jamaica, L.I., N.Y., Aug. 24, 1833. American jurist and historian.A Revolutionary patriot in New York, he was an adherent of Alexander Hamilton, with whom he attended the Annapolis Convention of 1786; he was named (1794) a justice of the supreme court of New York. A founder (1804) of the New York Historical Society, he was its president from 1805 to 1815. He wrote *Vindication of the Captors of Major André* (1817), *Memoir on Dutch Names of Places* (1835), and other works.

Benson, Ezra Taft. b. at Whitney, Idaho, Aug. 4, 1899—. American administrator, U.S. secretary of agriculture (1953 *et seq.*) under Eisenhower. An agricultural agent (1929–30) and marketing specialist (1930–38) for the extension service of the University of Idaho, he was the executive secretary (1939–44) of the National Council of Farmer Coöperatives and an executive of the board of trustees (1943 *et seq.*) of the American Institute of Coöperatives. A Mormon, he served as a missionary in Great Britain and Europe (1921–23) and has been a member of the Quorum of Twelve Apostles (the church's board of governors) since 1943.

Benson, Sir Frank (or Francis) Robert. b. at Alresford, Hampshire, England, Nov. 4, 1858; d. Dec. 31, 1939. English actor; nephew of Edward White Benson and brother of Godfrey Rathbone Benson, 1st Baron Charnwood. While at Oxford he superintended the production of Greek plays at that university. In 1882 he appeared at the Lyceum at London under the management of Henry Irving, and in 1889 undertook the production of Shakespearian plays by a specially selected company of his own. From 1887 he superintended the staging of the annual Shakspearian performance at Stratford on Avon.

Benson, Frank Weston. b. March 24, 1862; d. Nov. 14, 1951. American figure painter, teacher at the Boston Museum of Fine Arts (1889 *et seq.*). He painted a series of decorations, *The Three Graces* and *The Seasons*, for the Congressional Library, at Washington, D.C. Benson was also noted for his etchings of waterfowl, especially wild ducks.

Benson, Godfrey Rathbone. See **Charnwood,** 1st Baron.

Benson, Joseph. b. at Kirk-Oswald, Cumberland, England, Jan. 26, 1749; d. Feb. 16, 1821. British Methodist clergyman and controversialist.

Benson, Louis FitzGerald. b. at Philadelphia, 1855; d. 1930. American Presbyterian clergyman and hymnologist, noted as editor of *The Hymnal.* He was the author of *Hymns and Verses* (1897) and *The English Hymn* (1915).

Benson, Robert Hugh. b. Nov. 18, 1871; d. Oct. 19, 1914. English Catholic priest and author; son of Edward White Benson. He was converted (1903) to Roman Catholicism, being ordained as a priest in 1904; subsequently he was made privy chamberlain to Pope Pius X, with the title of monsignor. His works include *The Light Invisible, By What Authority?, The Queen's Tragedy, The Religion of the Plain Man, Lord of the World,* and *The Cost of a Crown.*

Benson, Stella. b. at Much Wenlock, Shropshire, England, Jan. 6, 1892; d. in China, Dec. 6, 1933. English novelist, short-story writer, poet, and dramatist; wife (1921 *et seq.*) of John C. O'Gorman Anderson. Author of the novels *I Pose* (1915), *This Is the End* (1917), *Living Alone* (1919), *The Poor Man* (1922), *Goodbye, Stranger* (1926), *The Far-Away Bride* (1930; published in England as *Tobit Transplanted,* 1931; awarded the 1931 Femina-Vie Heureuse Prize); *The Awakening* (1925), *The Man Who Missed the 'Bus* (1928), *Hope Against Hope* (1931), *Christmas Formula* (1932), collections of short stories; *The Little World* (1925) and *Worlds Within Worlds* (1928), travel books, both illustrated by herself; *Kwan-Yin* (1922), a play; and *Twenty* (1918) and *Poems* (1935), volumes of poetry.

Benson, William Shepherd. b. near Macon, Ga., Sept. 25, 1855; d. at Washington, D.C., May 20, 1932. American naval officer. A graduate (1877) of the U.S. Naval Academy at Annapolis, he was promoted successively to ensign (1881), lieutenant (1893), lieutenant commander (1900), captain (1909), and rear admiral (1915). He was head (1913–15) of the Philadelphia navy yard, was named (1915) chief of naval operations, and served as a member (1917–19) of various commissions to confer with the Allied powers and to negotiate peace terms; in 1919 he retired from naval service. He was appointed chairman (1920) and commissioner (1921) of the U.S. Shipping Board.

Bent (bent), **Charles.** b. at Charleston, Va. (now West Va.), Nov. 11, 1799; d. at Taos, N.M., Jan. 19, 1847. American pioneer and a founder (1828) of Bent's Fort (near what is today La Junta, Colo.), a famous southwestern trading post; brother of William Bent (1809–69) and Silas Bent (1820–87). He was appointed (1846) civil governor of New Mexico by General Stephen Watts Kearny.

Bent, James Theodore. b. 1852; d. 1897. English explorer and archaeologist, known for archaeological researches on the coast of Asia Minor (1888–89), in the Bahrein islands (1889), Ethiopia (1893), Arabia, notably in the Hadramaut region (1893–97), and elsewhere. He was the author of *The Cyclades: or Life Among the Insular Greeks* (1885), *The Ruined Cities of Mashonaland* (1892), and *The Sacred City of the Ethiopians* (1893).

Bent, Josiah. b. at Milton, Mass., April 26, 1771; d. April 26, 1836. American manufacturer. He was the founder of a widely known water-cracker bakery.

Bent, Silas. b. at what is now South St. Louis, Mo., Oct. 10, 1820; d. on Shelter Island, in Long Island Sound, N.Y., Aug. 26, 1887. American naval officer and oceanographer; brother of Charles Bent (1799–1847) and William Bent (1809–69). He made hydrographic surveys (1852–54) on Matthew Calbraith Perry's Japan expedition, and served (1860–61) with the hydrographic division of the coast survey.

Bent, William. b. at St. Louis, Mo., May 23, 1809; d. May 19, 1869. American pioneer, considered the first permanent white resident of Colorado; brother of Charles Bent (1799–1847) and Silas Bent (1820–87). He was a builder (1828–32) of Bent's Fort, the first southwestern trading post, and its sole owner after 1848. He is said to have attempted unsuccessfully to sell Bent's Fort to the government; another fort, which he built ab. 40 miles away, was leased to the government in 1859.

Bentan (ben′tän). Dutch name of **Bintan.**

Bentham (ben′thạm), **George.** b. Sept. 10, 1800; d. 1884. English botanist; nephew of Jeremy Bentham. He became interested, while living at Montpellier, France, in the study of botany, and began collecting material for his first book, *Catalogue des plantes indigènes des Pyrénées et du Bas Languedoc* (1826). During a six-year period (1826–32) as secretary to Jeremy Bentham, he studied for the bar and wrote *Outline of a New System of Logic, with a Critical Examination of Dr. Whateley's Elements of Logic* (1827), as well as articles on legal subjects. However, upon coming into considerable inheritances from his father and uncle, he returned to his earlier interest and thereafter devoted himself to his herbarium and his botanical library. In 1854 these had grown too great for his means to support, and were offered to the government on condition that they should be used in connection with research in the Royal Botanic Gardens at Kew, near London. He was long active in the work of the Royal Horticultural Society and of the Linnaean Society. He published his *Handbook of the British Flora* in 1858. Meanwhile, in 1857, the government had agreed to assist in the preparation of a series of works on the flora of the British colonies and possessions, and in this connection Bentham compiled *Flora Hongkongensis* (1861) and *Flora Australiensis* (7 vols., 1863–78). His crowning achievement, however, was *Genera Plantarum,* written in collaboration with Joseph Hooker and published in 3 volumes (1862–83).

Bentham, Jeremy. b. at London, Feb. 4, 1748; d. there, June 6, 1832. English reformer and utilitarian philosopher. He took the degree of B.A. at Queen's College, Oxford, in 1763, and of A.M. in 1766, and was subsequently admitted to the bar at Lincoln's Inn. He shortly gave up the practice of law in order to devote himself wholly to publishing and correspondence directed to the accomplishment of reform, and to the development of philosophical, political, and legal theories found necessary to that end. In this he was aided by a corps of zealous disciples, both in England and abroad, whose names included many of the most famous of the era. Bentham's accomplishments were so great, in all fields of government and law, that it may be said that the total body of English law existing in 1875 bore a closer resemblance to Bentham's proposals than it did to the body of law existing a century earlier, before he commenced publication. He advocated the principles of associationist psychology, and was the first to formulate the theory of utilitarianism in ethics. The inaccessibility and unreadability of his later works, and the literary vogue of John Stuart Mill (his indirect disciple) and his associates, caused Bentham's philosophical merits and his practical achievements to be almost forgotten until a revival of interest which started about a century after his death. Bentham's chief works are *Introduction to the Principles of Morals* *and Legislation* (1789), *Fragment on Government* (1776), *Theory of Legislation* (1802), *Rationale of Judicial Evidence* (1825), and *Constitutional Code* (1830).

Bentham, Thomas. b. at Sherburn, Yorkshire, England, 1513; d. at Eccleshall, Staffordshire, England, Feb. 21, 1578. English Protestant bishop. He was one of the translators of the "Bishops' Bible."

Bentheim (bent'hīm). Town in NW Germany, in the *Land* (state) of Lower Saxony, British Zone, formerly in the province of Hanover, Prussia, situated near the Dutch border, ab. 30 mi. NW of Münster: livestock markets, cotton-weaving mills, and an agricultural school. There is a castle of the princes of Bentheim, which was undamaged during World War II. 5,797 (1946).

Bentinck (ben'tingk), **Henry.** [Title, 1st Duke of **Portland.**] b. 1680; d. 1724. English nobleman; son of William Bentinck (c1649–1709). He was created Duke of Portland in 1716.

Bentinck, William. [Title, 1st Earl of **Portland.**] b. in Holland, c1649; d. at Bulstrode, near Beaconsfield, Buckinghamshire, England, Nov. 23, 1709. Companion, confidential adviser, and diplomatic agent of William III of England, by whom he was created Earl of Portland; father of Henry Bentinck (1680–1724). He was the son of a Henry Bentinck of Diepenheim, in Overyssel, Holland. He became a personal attendant of William, the Prince of Orange (who was to be William III of England), went with him to England, and rose there to a high position in the service of the state (serving as a privy councillor) and in the army. In 1697 he helped negotiate the treaty of Ryswick.

Bentinck, Lord **William Cavendish.** b. Sept. 14, 1774; d. at Paris, June 17, 1839. English statesman and general; second son of William Henry Cavendish Bentinck. He was governor (1803–07) of Madras, and in the period 1811–14 was envoy to Sicily, commander in chief of the British forces there, and practically governor of the island. He was appointed governor general of Bengal in 1827, and governor general of India in 1833, his administration extending from 1828 (when he took his seat) to 1835. He abolished suttee in 1829, and made attempts at suppression of the Thugs.

Bentinck, William George Frederick Cavendish. [Commonly called Lord **George Bentinck.**] b. at Welbeck Abbey, England, Feb. 27, 1802; d. there, Sept. 21, 1848. English politician and sportsman; grandson of William Henry Cavendish Bentinck. He was the leader of the protectionist opposition, in support of the corn laws, to Sir Robert Peel in the period 1846–47.

Bentinck, William Henry Cavendish. [Title, 3rd Duke of **Portland.**] b. 1738; d. at Bulstrode, near Beaconsfield, Buckinghamshire, England, Nov. 30, 1809. English Whig statesman; father of William Cavendish Bentinck and grandfather of William George Frederick Cavendish Bentinck. He was prime minister (April–December, 1783, and 1807–09) and home secretary (1794–1801).

Bentinck's Act (ben'tingks), **Lord George.** English statute of 1845, restricting unlawful gaming and wagers. It derives its name from the fact that it was introduced in the House of Commons by William George Frederick Cavendish Bentinck, who was commonly called "Lord George Bentinck."

Bentivoglio (ben.tē.vô'lyō), **Cornelio.** b. at Ferrara, Italy, 1668; d. at Rome, Dec. 30, 1732. Italian ecclesiastic and man of letters. He was archbishop of Carthage, papal nuncio to France, cardinal (1719), and legate *a latere* in Rumania. He was also the author of sonnets, a translation of the *Thebaid* of Statius, and other works.

Bentivoglio, Ercole. b. c1512; d. 1573. Italian poet and diplomat; grandson of Giovanni Bentivoglio.

Bentivoglio, Giovanni. b. at Bologna, Italy, c1438; d. at Milan, Italy, 1508. Italian nobleman, virtual ruler of Bologna (1462–1506); grandfather of Ercole Bentivoglio.

Bentivoglio, Guido. b. at Ferrara, Italy, 1579; d. 1644. Italian cardinal, noted as a diplomat and historian. He was papal nuncio to Flanders and France, and author of *Della Guerra di Fiandra* (1633–39), letters, and memoirs.

Bentivolio and Urania (ben.ti.vō'li.ō; ū.rā'ni.ạ). Romance (1660–64) by Nathaniel Ingelo. It went through four editions by 1682, possibly aided by the fact that the title page advertises that "all the Obscure Words throughout the Book are interpreted in the Margin."

Bentley (bent'li), **Edmund Clerihew.** b. at London, July 10, 1875—. English writer of detective fiction; father of Nicholas Clerihew Bentley (1907—). He devised a form of witty quasi-biographical verse, sometimes called clerihews, consisting of four lines of unequal length, short ones alternating with long ones, and rhyming as couplets. Author of *Biography for Beginners* (1905), *Trent's Last Case* (1912), *Trent Intervenes* (1938), *Those Days* (1940), and *Elephant's Work* (1950).

Bentley, John Francis. b. at Doncaster, England, 1839; d. at Clapham, now part of Wandsworth, London, March 2, 1902. English architect. He was especially known for the designing and decoration, in modified Gothic or Byzantine styles, of Roman Catholic churches in England. In 1894 he was commissioned to design the new Roman Catholic cathedral of Westminster, at London, of which the structural part alone was finished at his death.

Bentley, Nicolas Clerihew. b. at London, June 14, 1907—. English humorous writer and illustrator; son of Edmund Clerihew Bentley (1875—). His works include *Die? I Thought I'd Laugh* (1936), *Ballet Hoo* (1937), *Le Sport* (1939), *Second Thoughts* (1939), and *Animal, Vegetable, and South Kensington* (1940). He has also written the detective stories *The Tongue-tied Canary* (1949) and *The Floating Dutchman* (1951).

Bentley, Phyllis. [Full name, **Phyllis Eleanor Bentley.**] b. at Halifax, Yorkshire, England, Nov. 19, 1894—. English novelist, best known for works set against a Yorkshire background. She has done much lecturing in the U.S. and in the Netherlands. She was employed (1942–44) in the American division of the Ministry of Information during World War II. Author of *The World's Bane* (1918), *Pedagomania* (1918), *The Spinner of the Years* (1928), *The Partnership* (1928), *Carr* (1929), *Trio* (1930), *Inheritance* (1932), *A Modern Tragedy* (1934), *Freedom, Farewell!* (1936), *Take Courage* (1940), *Manhold* (1941), *The Rise of Henry Morcar* (1946), and *Quorum* (1951).

Bentley, Richard. b. at Oulton, near Wakefield, Yorkshire, England, Jan. 27, 1662; d. July 14, 1742. English cleric, classical scholar, and critic. He received the B.A. degree at St. John's College, Cambridge, in 1680, and was appointed master of Trinity College, Cambridge, in 1700, after taking orders in 1690. Although generally conceded to have been one of the greatest of all English classical scholars, he is perhaps more vividly remembered for the violence of his temper and the tyranny of his administration of Trinity College (which last resulted in trial and near-expulsion by his fellow scholars). He was the author of scholarly works including *Epistola ad Millium* (*Letter to Dr. John Mill*, 1691), on the Greek writer Malelas, which first won him note as a classical scholar; *Boyle Lectures* (1692), which he delivered at Oxford; and *Dissertation on the Epistles of Phalaris* (1697, 1699), in which he proved these epistles a forgery (precipitating the literary Battle of the Books).

Bentley, Richard. b. at London, 1794; d. at Ramsgate, Kent, England, Sept. 10, 1871. English printer and publisher. He learned the printing business from his uncle John Nichols, author of *History and Antiquities of Leicester*, and entered (1819) a printing establishment owned by his brother Samuel; in 1829 he entered into partner ship with Henry Colburn, publisher of novels, continuing the business after Colburn withdrew in 1832. He founded (1837) *Bentley's Miscellany* (with Charles Dickens as editor) in which *Oliver Twist* first appeared (January, 1837–March, 1839). He also published the works of R. H. Barham, T. C. Haliburton, Isaac and Benjamin D'Israeli, George Cruikshank, and many others, and brought out 127 volumes in the *Library of Standard Novels.*

Bentley, Robert. b. at Hitchin, Hertfordshire, England, March 25, 1821; d. in December, 1893. English botanist. His works include *Manual of Botany* and *Medicinal Plants.*

Bentley, William. b. at Boston, June 22, 1759; d. at Salem, Mass., Dec. 29, 1819. American Unitarian clergyman and linguist, whose diary of the period 1784–1819 is a storehouse of Salem history and antiquities. He held a ministry (1783–1819) at Salem, Mass.

Bentley Dock. A former name of **Tottenville.**

Bentleyville (bent′li.vil). Borough in SW Pennsylvania, in Washington County. 3,295 (1950).

Bentley with Arksey (bent′li; ärk′si). Urban district in N central England, in the West Riding of Yorkshire, situated on the river Don, ab. 2 mi. N of Doncaster. It has no direct rail connections for passengers, being reached by rail to Doncaster, ab. 156 mi. N of London. 19,826 (1951).

Benton (ben′tọn). City in C Arkansas, county seat of Saline County, the most important bauxite-mining county in the U.S. The city has furniture and pottery factories. 6,277 (1950).

Benton. City in S Illinois, county seat of Franklin County, in a coal-mining and farming region. 7,848 (1950).

Benton. In the Civil War, an ironclad gunboat of 1,000 tons, altered in 1861 from a vessel used to remove snags and other large objects from the channels of the Mississippi River and its major tributaries. She belonged to the Mississippi flotilla, and took part in the fighting at Island No. 10, Fort Pillow, Vicksburg, and on the Yazoo and Red River expeditions.

Benton, Guy Potter. b. at Kenton, Ohio, May 26, 1865; d. June 28, 1927. American educator, awarded the Distinguished Service Medal for his service (1917–19) as chief educational director for the American army of occupation in Europe during and after World War I. A professor (1896–99) at Baker University, he was subsequently president of Upper Iowa University (1899–1902), Miami University (1902–11), and the University of Vermont (1911–19); he also served as educational consultant (1921–24) to the University of the Philippines. Author of *The Real College* (1909).

Benton, James Gilchrist. b. at Lebanon, N.H., Sept. 15, 1820; d. Aug. 23, 1881. American army officer, and ordnance and gunnery expert.

Benton, Thomas Hart. [Called **"Old Bullion."**] b. at Hillsboro, N.C., March 14, 1782; d. at Washington, D.C., April 10, 1858. American politician. He first entered politics as a member (1809) of the Tennessee state senate, before being admitted (1811) to the bar. While in Tennessee, he became involved in a quarrel with Andrew Jackson, and the friendship between the two men was broken off for several years. After having moved (1815) to St. Louis, where for a time he edited the *Missouri Enquirer*, Benton was elected (1821) to the U.S. Senate. During the entire period (1821–51) of his senatorship (the longest term to that date ever served consecutively by one man), his greatest interest lay in legislation favoring gold and silver currency as opposed to paper money (whence his epithet, in which he delighted). He became reconciled to Jackson and furthered the latter's campaign for the presidency in 1828; after Jackson's election, Benton was his chief spokesman in the Senate. In this capacity, he took a leading part in the opposition (1831) to the Second Bank of the United States. In an effort to make more effective the use of "hard money," Benton revised the ratio of gold to silver from 15 to 1 to 16 to 1; he also sponsored the proposition that public lands be paid for in gold or silver. (In addition to this, however, he proposed a reduction in the price of such lands, and advocated the wider use of homesteading, thus making land more easily available to settlers.) He was against national expansion to the extent demanded by the "54–40 or fight" slogan (he believed the U.S. had no justifiable claim north of the 49th parallel), but when war with Mexico came about, he supported the government. He took an interest in the annexation of California, partly because John Charles Frémont was his son-in-law. He also became an opponent of slavery, although he urged its elimination by means more gradual than were advocated by the extreme abolitionists. His opposition to the Compromise of 1850 probably cost him his seat in the Senate; and because most of his Missouri constituents favored the Compromise, and because of increasing differences with the Democratic Party, he lacked the backing for successful reëlection. He did serve one term (1853–55) in the House of Representatives, but opposed the Kansas-Nebraska Bill, and was not reëlected. In his retirement he wrote the two-volume autobiographical work *Thirty Years' View* (1854–56) about his 30 years as a member of the U.S. Senate.

Benton, Thomas Hart. b. at Neosho, Mo., April 15, 1889—. American painter, lithographer, and writer whose name (with those of John Steuart Curry and Grant Wood) figured prominently in the 1920's and 1930's in publicity given the "American Scene," or regional, trend in U.S. painting. A grandnephew and namesake of the Missouri senator Thomas Hart Benton (1782–1858), he covered on trips with his father, also a politician, the Midwestern region which he later decided to portray in most of his painting. He worked as a cartoonist (1905) for a Joplin, Mo., newspaper before attending the Art Institute of Chicago; at Paris he studied (1908 *et seq.*) various modern movements and early Italian painters; he was an architectural draftsman for the Navy during World War I. After instructorships at Bryn Mawr College, Dartmouth College, and the Art Students League of New York, he made a ten-year trip, particularly through the South and West, one product of which was his book *An Artist in America* (1937). He was appointed (1935) director of painting at the Kansas City Art Institute. Among the best-known of his works are the murals *Contemporary America* for the New School for Social Research, at New York, *The Arts of Life in America* for the library of the Whitney Museum of American Art, *History of Indiana* for the Indiana building at the Century of Progress Exposition (1933; later acquired by Indiana University), and a series for the Missouri state capitol at Jefferson City. *Huck Finn and Nigger Jim*, in the last-named series, and such paintings as *The Jealous Lover of Lone Green Valley* (1930) are typical of his use of American themes and folk-legend. *Louisiana Rice Field* (1939) and *Threshing Wheat* (1941) exemplify his linear treatment of design. He is interested also in texture studies, as shown in *Pussy Cat and Roses* (1939) and *Persephone* (1939). He is represented in the Metropolitan Museum of Art and the Museum of Modern Art, at New York, and elsewhere.

Benton Harbor. City in S Lower Michigan, on Lake Michigan, in Berrien County, twin city of St. Joseph: fruit markets and manufactures of silk products, automobile parts, and iron products. A religious group popularly known as the House of David, brought here in 1903, now has its center in a section, on the edge of Benton Harbor, called the City of David. 18,769 (1950).

Benton Heights. Unincorporated community in S Lower Michigan, in Berrien County. 6,160 (1950).

Bentonville (ben′tọn.vil). City in NW Arkansas, county seat of Benton County, near the Missouri line, in the Ozarks: shipping point for apples, poultry and dairy products raised in the vicinity. It was founded in 1837. Pop. 2,942 (1950).

Bentonville, Battle of. Victory gained (March 19–20, 1865) at Bentonville, S of Raleigh, N.C., by Union forces under W. T. Sherman over the Confederates under Joseph Eggleston Johnston. Union loss, 1,646; Confederate loss, 2,825.

Bent's Fort (bents). Fur-trading post built (1828–32) along the mountain route of the Santa Fe trail, on the N bank of the Arkansas River, E of what is now La Junta, Colo. Originally known as Fort William, it was established by William Bent and his brothers and associates, and became the most prominent post of its kind in the American Southwest. Bent abandoned the adobe structure in 1849, and built (1853) Bent's New Fort along the river ab. 40 mi. distant from the site of the first one. It came under U.S. government operation in 1859, was named Fort Wise in 1860 and Fort Lyon in 1861, and was abandoned in 1866, when Fort Lyon was moved to a different location.

Bent Twig, The. Novel by Dorothy Canfield Fisher, published in 1915.

Bentzel-Sternau (ben′tsẹl.shter′nou), Count **Christian Ernst zu.** b. at Mainz, Germany, April 9, 1767; d. near Zurich, Switzerland, Aug. 13, 1849. German politician, humorous novelist, and miscellaneous writer. He was minister of finance (1812 *et seq.*) to the grand duke of Frankfurt. His written works include *Das goldene Kalb* (1802), *Der steinerne Gast* (1808), and *Der alte Adam* (1819–20).

Benue (bā′nwā). [Also, **Binue.**] River in W Africa, chiefly in Nigeria, the largest affluent of the Niger River. It rises in Adamawa, N of Ngaundere, French Equatorial Africa, flows N, makes a bend to the W, and joins the

Niger at Lokoja in Nigeria. It was explored principally by W. B. Baikie and Robert Flegel. Length, ab. 870 mi.; navigable for ab. 620 mi., from May to January.

Ben Venue (ben vẹ.nū'). Mountain in C Scotland, in Perthshire, situated ab. 3 mi. SW of the Trossachs, ab. 10 mi. SW of Callander. It rises from the S shore of Loch Katrine. 2,393 ft.

Benvenuto Cellini (ben.vā.nö'tō chel.lē'nē). Opera by Hector Berlioz, produced at Paris in 1838 and at London in 1853.

Benvenuto de' Rambaldi (dā räm.bäl'dē). [Also: **Benvenuto da Imola** (ē'mô.lä); Latinized, **Benevenutus de Rambaldis.**] b. at Imola, Italy, c1336; d. probably at Ferrara, Italy, 1390 (not 1380, as indicated by some sources). Italian humanist, now considered to have been the most important early commentator on Dante. In 1364 he met Petrarch, at Bologna; in 1365 he was sent to Avignon, as one of the members of a mission to Pope Urban V (it was here that he renewed his acquaintance with Boccaccio, who, jointly with Petrarch, served as a main guide to his thought for the rest of his life). In 1375 (following the example of Florence, which had established Boccaccio in 1373 as the first holder of a city-supported lectureship on Dante) Bologna invited Benvenuto to lecture on Dante. His interest in Dante had already been clearly evidenced by the completion, in 1373, of a first draft of his elaborate *Commentum* (Commentary). His was the most learned early commentary, and has remained important in all later discussions of Dante's work; moreover, such a piece of writing is bound to be as encyclopedic as Dante himself, and hence Benvenuto's commentary has come to be also an important source of information about 14th-century thought. Indeed, it contains information of interest even to historians of science; for example, in connection with *Inferno XXIX*, Benvenuto takes occasion to discuss alchemical theories, and points out that, as all metals are derived (in alchemical theory) from mercury and sulfur, their differences are accidental, not essential; every metal is imperfect except gold and sulfur, and, although transmutation may not be theoretically impossible, nevertheless all those who have tried to accomplish it have failed. Possibly even more important than this (and surely more unexpected) is a discussion of probabilities in connection with *Purgatorio VI*, which constitutes the earliest mention of probabilities in world literature. It concerns the throwing of three dice: the lowest and highest throws (3 and 18) can occur in only one way, and this is true (according to Benvenuto) also of the next to the lowest and highest (4 and 17), which can occur only in the combinations (1–1–2) and (6–6–5). This latter is incorrect to the extent that it does not distinguish between permutations and combinations: there are actually three ways (1–1–2, 1–2–1, and 2–1–1) of throwing the next to the highest and lowest, and the permutations are what count here. However, the comment remains extremely interesting and important in its early recognition of what was later to develop as a point of major scientific importance.

Benvolio (ben.vō'li.ō). Friend of Romeo and nephew of Montague, in Shakespeare's tragedy *Romeo and Juliet*.

Ben Vorlich (ben vôr'lich). [Also, **Ben Voirlich.**] Mountain in C Scotland, in Perthshire, situated ab. 2 mi. S of Loch Earn, ab. 7 mi. N of Callander. 3,224 ft.

Benwood (ben'wůd). City in N West Virginia, in Marshall County, on the Ohio River, ab. 5 mi. SW of Wheeling: steel mills and coal mining. One of the country's most serious mine disasters occurred here in 1924 when 119 miners were killed by an explosion. 3,485 (1950).

Benz (bents), **Karl.** b. at Karlsruhe, Germany, Nov. 26, 1844; d. 1929. German engineer and automobile manufacturer. He was among the first to build a motor-powered highway vehicle, and is credited with the invention of the differential and the system of battery ignition with spark induction. He established Benz and Company at Mannheim, Germany, for the manufacture of motor vehicles. Having built his first car in 1885 (patented in 1886), he took out a patent on a triple-axle steering gear in 1893. His firm later (1926) merged with that of the engine designer Gottlieb Daimler, and manufactured the automobile known as the Mercedes-Benz.

Benz, Richard. b. 1884—. German historian of literature. His controversy (1915–16) with the philologist Konrad Burdach established him as a leading protagonist of the view that literary values are not merely the creation of outstanding individuals but one aspect of the multi-faceted cultural life of the people as a whole. His studies include *Alte deutsche Legenden* (1909), *Die deutschen Volksbücher* (1913), *Die Renaissance, das Verhängnis der deutschen Kultur* (1915), *Die Stunde der deutschen Musik* (1923–27), *Reformation und Revolution* (1928), and *Die deutsche Romantik* (1937), with its characteristic subtitle, "Geschichte einer geistigen Bewegung."

Benzayda (ben.zā'dạ). In John Dryden's play *The Conquest of Granada*, the daughter of the sultan. She loves Ozwy, the son of her father's deadliest foe, and exhibits heroic courage and endurance while following her lover through the hardships and perils of civil war.

Benzert (ben.zert'). See **Bizerte.**

Benzo d'Alessandria (bān'tsō dä.läs.sän'drē.ä). [Also: **Benzo Cona** (kō'nä); Latinized, **Bencius Alexandrinus.**] b. at Alessandria, in Piedmont, in the second half of the 13th century; d. at Verona, c1335. Italian historian and humanist, chancellor to the bishop of Como (1312–22) and to the ruling family of Verona (1325–35). He is considered by many scholars to have been, in the matter of humanism, the most genuine Italian forerunner of Petrarch. While serving the bishop of Como he prepared a three-part literary encyclopedia entitled *Chronicon* (or *Historia de moribus et vita philosophorum*). This work, of which only the first part is still extant, was based upon a great variety of classical and medieval sources, and reveals the painstaking care of a researcher and archivist in some ways far ahead of his time.

Benzoni (bān.dzō'nē), **Girolamo.** b. at Milan, Italy, 1519; d. sometime after 1566. Italian traveler. In 1542 he went to Spanish America, traveling over much of the area then known, and sometimes joining the Spaniards in their raids against the Indians. Returning to Italy in 1556, he published an account of his travels, with the title *Historia del mondo nuovo* (Venice, 1565).

Ben-Zvi (ben.tsvē'), **Itzhak.** b. at Poltava, Russia, c1884—. Israeli statesman, second president (1952 *et seq.*) of Israel. He came to Palestine in 1904 and was one of the organizers of the defense groups against Arab attacks on the Jewish settlers. He fought against the Turks in World War I and afterward became prominent in political life during the British mandate. A leading Mapai (socialist) Party member, he was chosen by the Israeli parliament as successor to Chaim Weizmann.

Beograd (be.ô'gräd). Serbo-Croatian name of **Belgrade.**

Beothuk (bā'ọ.thůk). North American Indian tribe, extinct since the early 19th century, which formerly inhabited Newfoundland. The language may have formed an independent linguistic family, though some scholars believe it was distantly related to Algonquian.

Beöthy (bė'tē), **Zsolt.** b. at Komorn (now Komárno, Czechoslovakia), Sept. 4, 1848; d. April 18, 1922. Hungarian educator and literary historian. He served as a professor (1882 *et seq.*) at the University of Budapest. Author of *A magyar irodalom kis-tükre* (The Little Mirror of Hungarian Literature, 1896) and *A poetika útja és célja* (Methods and Goals of Poetics, 1892).

Beowulf (bā'ọ.wůlf). Eighth-century English epic poem, 3,182 lines long, in alliterative verse. The poem is named after its hero, represented as a champion (later king) of the Geatas, a Scandinavian tribe living north of the Danes (i.e., in what is now a part of Sweden). The action of the poem falls into two main parts. In part one (about two-thirds of the whole) the youthful hero goes to Denmark to rid the Danish royal hall of Grendel, a troll who for years had haunted it at night, and succeeds in slaying both Grendel and Grendel's mother (a creature fully as fearsome as her offspring). In part two, the aged hero defends the Geatas against a dragon, which he kills at the cost of his own life. The action of part one takes about a week; that of part two, a day. The unknown but presumably clerical author was an Englishman learned not only in the traditional heroic lore of the Germanic peoples but also in the Latin writings current in the England of his day; in particular, he knew the *Aeneid*. Like Vergil, the English poet set his scene in a past which he thought of as remote and heroic. Through his hero he sought to glorify the courtly ways of Germanic antiquity and the ideals of heroism which made part of the moral and poetic heritage common to the English and the other Germanic nations. He succeeded so well that his poem is reckoned among the masterpieces of world literature.

Beppo (bep′ō). [Full title, **Beppo: A Venetian Story.**] Poem by Byron, written at Venice in 1817 and published in 1818. It is in mock-heroic style, relating the happy reconciliation of Beppo with his wife after a long absence.

Béranger (bā.rän.zhā), **Pierre Jean de.** b. at Paris, Aug. 19, 1780; d. there, July 16, 1857. French lyric poet, author of political, amatory, satirical, and philosophical songs. He was the son of a notary's clerk. In 1804 necessity compelled him to seek aid from Lucien Bonaparte; he received a clerkship in the office of the Imperial University, which he held until 1821. The first collection of his songs was published in 1815. In 1848 he was elected to the Constituent Assembly from the department of the Seine. His political sympathies were republican and Bonapartist, and for expressing them he was twice (1821, 1828) prosecuted by the government. His songs have had great popularity, partly perhaps because they were set to popular tunes. The earliest piece to win him acclaim was *Le Roi d'Yvetot*.

Berar (bā.rär′). [Former official name, **Hyderabad Assigned Districts.**] Division of Madhya Pradesh (formerly Central Provinces and Berar), Union of India, in the C part of the peninsula, W of Nagpur. It is generally level and fertile, and produces cotton and grain. It formed part of the dominions of the Mahratta Rajah of Nagpur, was ceded to Hyderabad in 1803, and was assigned (hence its former official name) by the Nizam of Hyderabad to the British government in 1853 and 1861. In 1902 an agreement was reached with the Nizam by which Berar was leased in perpetuity to India, and in 1903 it was transferred to the administration of the Central Provinces, which became Madhya Pradesh under the constitution of India in 1950. Area, 17,808 sq. mi.; pop. 3,604,866 (1941).

Bérard (bā.rär), **Christian.** b. at Paris, 1902; d. Feb. 12, 1949. French portraitist and designer. He created the settings for many operas, ballets, and dramas, including *The Madwoman of Chaillot*, by Jean Giraudoux, *Poetic Works*, by Jean Cocteau, and *Renaud and Armide*. His painting *Nude in an Armchair* won a prize (1944) at Paris, and his *Portrait of René Creval* is in the collection of the Museum of Modern Art at Paris.

Bérard, Joseph Frédéric. b. at Montpellier, France, Nov. 8, 1789; d. April 16, 1828. French physician and psychologist.

Bérard, Léon. b. at Sauveterre-de-Béarn, Basses-Pyrénées, France, Jan. 6, 1876—. French politician and lawyer, known especially for his efforts, as minister of public instruction (1917, 1919–20, 1926–28), to stress the study of the classics in the French educational system. He entered politics as secretary (1901–10) to Raymond Poincaré, was a deputy (1910–27) and a senator (1927 *et seq.*), held (1931–32) the ministry of justice, was elected (1935) to the French Academy, and was ambassador (1944–45) to the Vatican from the Vichy government. After World War II, he refused (1945) to return to France to face trial.

Bérard, Pierre Honoré. b. at Lichtenberg, in Alsace, 1797; d. 1858. French surgeon and physiologist. He was for many years professor of physiology at Paris.

Bérard, Victor. b. at Morez, France, 1864—. French scholar and publicist. He served as member of the École Française at Athens. Author of books on Homeric problems such as *Les Phéniciens et l'Odyssée* (The Phoenicians and the Odyssey, 1902–03), he also wrote voluminously on French foreign policy, as in *France et Guillaume II* (France and William II, 1907).

Berat (be.rät′). [Also, **Berati** (-rä′tē); ancient name, **Antipatrea** or **Antipatria.**] Town in S central Albania, chief town of Berat prefecture, situated on the Seman River. 10,403 (1930).

Béraud (bā.rō), **Henri.** b. at Lyons, France, 1885—. French poet, novelist, and political essayist. Originally a symbolist poet, he is the author of *Poèmes ambulants* (1903); subsequently he became a literary, art, and drama critic. He is the author also of novels, including *Le Martyre de l'obèse* (1922) and *Au Capucin gourmand* (1925), as well as of books on foreign affairs, such as *Ce que j'ai vu à Moscou* (1925).

Béraud, Jean. b. at St. Petersburg, Russia, Dec. 31, 1849; d. 1936. French portrait, religious, and genre painter, who was one of the founders of the Société Nationale des Beaux-Arts at Paris. He was a pupil of L. J. R. Bonnat, and began to exhibit at the Salon in 1873; his mixture of Biblical subjects with contemporary scenes provoked much criticism and discussion. From 1910 to 1929, he exhibited at the Société Nationale. He became an officer of the Legion of Honor, and received many other awards and prizes during his career. Most of the important galleries in France and Belgium own paintings by him. *Study of a Woman, The Cardinal Café, Christ Crowned with Thorns, The Way of the Cross,* and *Descent from the Cross* are among his best-known works.

Beraun (bā′roun). German name of **Beroun,** Bohemia.

Beraun. German name of the **Berounka.**

Berber (bėr′bėr). Region of Nubia, Anglo-Egyptian Sudan, in NE Africa, near the junction of the Atbara River with the Nile. It was, until 1945, a province of the Anglo-Egyptian Sudan; it is now part of Northern Province.

Berber. [Also, **El Mekheir.**] Town in NE Africa, in Northern Province, Anglo-Egyptian Sudan, on the E bank of the Nile River between the mouth of the Atbara River and the fifth cataract. It was an important point on the caravan routes to Cairo, Khartoum, and Suakin, and a station on the railway between Wadi Halfa and Khartoum. It was taken by Mahdists in 1884. Pop. 16,550 (est. 1949).

Berber. Group of related languages of NW Africa, spoken by peoples inhabiting the C Sahara and a coastal strip of NW Africa, in N French West Africa, S Algeria, Morocco, and Río de Oro. Berber is one of the two subgroups of Hamitic, Cushitic being the other.

Berbera (bėr′bėr.ạ). Seaport and former capital of British Somaliland, Africa, on the Gulf of Aden. It is a market place for inland tribes and has a good climate. It was annexed by Egypt in 1875, and by England in 1884. Berbera has the only good harbor on the S side of the Gulf of Aden. Italian forces occupied it from 1940 to 1941. Its population fluctuates from the hot season (ab. 15,000) to the cold season (ab. 30,000).

Berbers (bėr′bėrz). North African peoples who speak various Berber languages or dialects. Separated in many cases by areas of Arabic speech, they are culturally adapted to their various environments. Most (such as the Riffians, Soussis, Kabyles, and Shawia) are mountain farmers; some (such as the Middle Atlas Berbers and the Mzabites) are oasis farmers and merchants; still others, such as the Tuareg, are camel nomads. Physically, they vary considerably, but the majority belong to the Mediterranean race in some form. All are nominally Moslems. Some, such as the Mzabites and Jerbans, belong to the heterodox sects. The Tuareg alone have preserved a knowledge of the old Libyan writing.

Berbice (bėr.bēs′). County in E British Guiana. It was a Dutch colony in the 17th and 18th centuries. Capital, New Amsterdam; area, 16,920 sq. mi.; pop. 75,919 (1931).

Berbice. Former name of **New Amsterdam,** British Guiana.

Berbice River. River in E British Guiana, in Berbice County. It flows N to the Atlantic Ocean. Length, ab. 300 mi.

Berchem (ber′ċhẹm). Town in N Belgium, in the province of Antwerp, S of Antwerp, of which it is a suburb. 45,401 (1947).

Berchem or **Berghem** (ber′ċhẹm), **Nicolaes.** b. at Haarlem, the Netherlands, 1620; d. Feb. 18, 1683. Dutch landscape painter and etcher.

Berchem-Ste.-Agathe (-sant.ȧ.gȧt). [Flemish, **St. Agatha-Berchem.**] Town in C Belgium, in the province of Brabant, ab. 2 mi. E of Brussels. 11,180 (1947).

Berchet (ber.ket′), **Giovanni.** b. at Milan, Italy, Dec. 23, 1783; d. at Turin, Italy, Dec. 23, 1851. Italian poet. He was a leader of the Romantic Movement in Italy, and his *Lettera Semiseria di Grisostomo* (1816) is considered by many to have been virtually its manifesto. He escaped the imprisonment which many of the Romantics suffered (for their political activities) at the hands of the Austrian authorities in Italy by going into exile, living in England, France, and Germany from 1821 to 1847. In the latter year he returned to Italy and became a member of the parliament of Piedmont. Berchet's poetry, uneven in quality but exhibiting great beauty at its best, was popular and patriotic, and was counted an influence toward the liberation and unification of Italy. His published volumes of poetry include *I Profughi di Parga* (Refugees from Parga), *Il Romito del Cenisio* (The Hermit of the Mount Cenis Pass), and *Il Rimorso* (Remorse).

Berchta (berċh'tä). Fairy in S German legends. She corresponds to the Hulda of N Germany, and was originally gracious and beautiful. She has, however, largely lost this character in modern times, and, like the Befana of Italy, is now sometimes portrayed almost as a witch, particularly by mothers who seek, through frightening them, to discipline their children.

Berchtesgaden (berċh'tes.gä.den). Alpine district in S Germany, in the SE corner of Bavaria, near the town of Berchtesgaden.

Berchtesgaden. Town in S Germany, in the *Land* (state) of Bavaria, American Zone, in the *Kreis* (district) of Upper Bavaria, situated on the Achen River, ab. 15 mi. S of Salzburg: a summer resort in the Bavarian Alps. It has saline thermal springs, which are visited by people suffering from intestinal and heart diseases. The town has salt works and lumber trade, and specializes in the manufacture of wood-carved articles. There is a school of wood carving and a museum. Berchtesgaden was founded in 1102 by members of the Augustinian order; it remained an independent principality until 1803, and passed to Salzburg in 1803, to Austria in 1805, and to Bavaria in 1810. Adolf Hitler had a summer residence on top of the nearby Obersalzberg, where he frequently held conferences of great political importance; he directed from here the annexation of Austria in 1938. Berchtesgaden and Obersalzberg were subjected to bombardment in March, 1945, and occupied by Allied troops on May 7 of the same year. A great part of the adjoining region was set aside as a recreation area for U.S. occupation troops after the end of the war, and the ruins of Hitler's residence became a much visited point of tourist interest for soldiers and civilians. 5,732 (1946).

Berchtold (berċh'tolt), Count **Leopold von.** b. at Vienna, April 18, 1863; d. at Ödenburg (now Sopron), Hungary, Nov. 21, 1942. Austro-Hungarian statesman. He served (1906–11) as ambassador to Russia. As foreign minister (1912–15) he sent (July, 1914) the ultimatum to Serbia which helped touch off World War I. He retired (January, 1915) because he could not obtain a declaration from Italy that she would fulfill her treaty obligations of alliance with Austria-Hungary. In 1916 he was appointed lord high steward to the heir of the throne, and later served as lord high chamberlain. After the revolution of 1918 he withdrew from public life.

Berck (berk). [Also, **Berck-sur-Mer** (-sür.mer).] Town in N France, in the department of Pas-de-Calais, situated on the English Channel, N of the Bay of Authie and ab. 22 mi. S of Boulogne. It consists of Berck-Ville and Berck-Plage; has a fishing port and is a seaside health resort renowned for its wholesome climate. 11,529 (1946).

Bercovici (bėr.kō.vē'sē, ber'kō.vēch), **Konrad.** b. at Brăila, Rumania, June 22, 1882—. American novelist and short-story writer. Among his works are *Around the World in New York* (1918), *Ghitza* (1919), *Ileana—The Marriage Guest* (1925), *The Story of the Gypsies* (1928), *That Royal Lover* (1931), *Against the Sky* (1932), and *The Incredible Balkans* (1933).

Bercy (ber.sē). Former commune in N central France, situated on the right bank of the Seine; now a southeastern quarter of Paris, annexed in 1860.

Berdanier (bėr.dan.ir'), **Paul Frederick.** b. at Frackville, Pa., March 7, 1879—. American painter, etcher, cartoonist, and designer of historical costumes and stage settings. He studied at the St. Louis School of Fine Arts, and at Paris, and has exhibited in the U.S. and France. He has been awarded several prizes and his work is in permanent collections in both countries. Some of his works are *On the Canal at Moret*, *Charon*, *Summer Showers*, and *Ambition.*

Berdichev (bir.dyē'chif). [Also, **Berdichef.**] City in the W part of the U.S.S.R., in the Ukrainian Soviet Socialist Republic: a major industrial town with several large chemical plants. 66,306 (1939).

Berdyaev (bir.dyä'yif), **Nikolai Aleksandrovich.** b. at Kiev, Russia, March 6, 1874; d. 1948. Russian philosopher, champion of a Christian-apocalyptic philosophy. He was the founder (1919), at Moscow, of a free academy for spiritual culture. As an anti-Communist, he was exiled from Russia, and moved to Paris where he founded a religious-philosophical academy. Author of the following works (written in Russian, translated into English): *Christianity and Class War* (1933), *Dostoievsky* (1934), *The Destiny of Man* (1937), *Spirit and Reality* (1939), and *Dream and Reality* (1951).

Berea (be.rē'a). Town in E central Kentucky, in Madison County, ab. 35 mi. S of Lexington. It is the seat of Berea College, opened in 1855. Both town and college produce handmade articles of a wide variety, of which perhaps the hand-woven materials are best known. 3,372 (1950).

Berea. City in NE Ohio, in Cuyahoga County, near Cleveland, in a sandstone-quarrying region. It is the seat of Baldwin-Wallace College. In the decade between the last two U.S. censuses, the city's population doubled. 6,025 (1940); 12,051 (1950).

Berea College v. Kentucky, 211 U.S. 45 (1908). Decision of the U.S. Supreme Court which upheld the constitutionality of a Kentucky law forbidding the education of whites and Negroes at the same private school. The case involved an interpretation of the 14th Amendment.

Berend (bā'rent), **Alice.** b. at Berlin, 1878—. German novelist, known for her humorous, light fiction. Her works include *Die Reise des Herrn Sebastian Wenzel* (1912), *Die Bräutigame der Babette Bomberling* (1927), and *Der Herr Direktor* (1928).

Berengar I (ber'en.gär). [Italian, **Berengario** (bā.reng-gä'ryō); Latin, **Berengarius** (ber.en.gãr'i.us).] d. 924. King of Italy (888–924) and titular Holy Roman emperor (915–924); a son of Eberhard, the marquis of Friuli, grandson of Louis I (the Pious), and grandfather of Berengar II. He was chosen king of Italy in opposition to Guido, the duke of Spoleto. He was crowned (915) as Holy Roman Emperor by Pope John X, but he was never able to assert his claim to imperial authority against Conrad I of Franconia and Henry I of Germany (Henry the Fowler), who successively held (911 *et seq.*) title as kings of Germany, and thus, by tradition, could claim also to be the heirs of Charlemagne as Holy Roman Emperors; perhaps more important than either tradition or legality, however, was the fact that both Conrad and Henry were rulers of powerful realms and could make their claims respected by all. Nevertheless, in some chronologies Berengar is listed as a sort of "phantom emperor," paralleling, but not replacing, Conrad and Henry. He was defeated by Rudolph, king of Burgundy, in a decisive battle at Firenzuola on July 29, 923. He was assassinated in the following year.

Berengar II. [Italian, **Berengario;** Latin, **Berengarius.**] d. at Bamberg, Germany, Aug. 6, 966. King of Italy (950–961), jointly with his son; a grandson of Berengar I. On Italy's being invaded by the emperor Otto I, Berengar became a feudatory of Germany. He was eventually dethroned, and died in prison.

Berengaria (ber.en.gãr'i.a). d. c1230. Queen of England as wife of Richard I (Richard Coeur de Lion); daughter of Sancho VI of Navarre and Blanche of Castile. She married Richard at Limassol, Cyprus, in 1191. While Richard warred against the Saracens, she lived at Acre, in Palestine; during his imprisonment in Germany, she made her residence at Poitou, in France. It is possible that she became estranged from him after his release, since the records do not show that she lived near him thereafter. She is buried at Le Mans, France.

Bérenger (bā.räṅ.zhā). [Latin, **Berengarius** (ber.en.gãr'-i.us).] b. at Tours, France, c998; d. near Tours, France, 1088. French ecclesiastic and dialectician. He was a pupil of Fulbert of Chartres, and became (1040) archdeacon of Angers. His attack (c1045 *et seq.*) on the dogmas of transubstantiation and the real presence, caused him to be condemned at (among other synods) Vercelli (1050) and Rome (1059, 1079).

Bérenger, Henry. [Full name, **Victor Henry Bérenger.**] b. in France, April 22, 1867; d. May 18, 1952. French political leader and writer, in charge of the gasoline and fuel supply system in France during World War I. A senator from 1912, he served as ambassador (1925–26) to the U.S. and as president (1935–38) of the International Diplomatic Academy.

Berenger (ber′ẹn.jėr), **Lady Eveline.** Resolute, somewhat impatient woman in Sir Walter Scott's novel *The Betrothed.*

Berenguer (bā.reng.ger′), **Dámaso.** b. in Cuba, c1873; d. May 18, 1953. Spanish general and politician. He was minister of war (1918–19) and high commissioner of Morocco (1919–20). He headed (1926–30) the *casa militar* (military household) of Alfonso XIII, and upon the fall of the dictator Primo de Rivera was appointed his successor. He functioned thereafter for 15 months as president of the royal council and minister of war, and continued to serve in the cabinet of Admiral Aznar, but the monarchy could no longer be saved and upon the establishment of the republic, in 1931, Berenguer was imprisoned. He was released in 1933.

Berenice (ber.ẹ.nī′sē). d. 246 B.C. Daughter of Ptolemy II (Philadelphus) of Egypt and wife of Antiochus II (Theos), king of Syria.

Berenice. fl. 1st century B.C. Sister of Cleopatra, slain by the Romans in 55 B.C.

Berenice. fl. 6 B.C. Jewish princess; a niece of Herod the Great. Berenice was married to her cousin Aristobulus (a son of Herod), by whom she was the mother of Herod Agrippa I, and was accused of complicity in the murder (on Herod's orders) of Aristobulus in 6 B.C. Her second husband, Theudion, an uncle of Herod the Great, was put to death for conspiring against him. Her third husband, Archelaus, was briefly king of Egypt. Berenice's later years were spent with him at Rome, where she was befriended by the imperial household.

Berenice. b. c28 A.D.; d. after 79 A.D. Jewish princess; daughter of Herod Agrippa I, king of Judea (41–44 A.D.). A woman of remarkable beauty (events from her life provide the theme of Racine's *Bérénice*), she married, as her second husband, her uncle Herod, king of Chalcis in Lebanon. After his death she lived with her brother Herod Agrippa II (the possibility, or probability, of an incestuous relationship was generally accepted by many of her contemporaries). She subsequently married Polemon, king of Cilicia, but abandoned him soon and returned to her brother. Josephus Flavius declares that she endeavored to stop the cruelties of Florus, the last and worst of the Roman governors in Judea (*Jewish Wars*, II. 15, 1). However, in the last struggle of her country she, like her brother, was on the side of Rome. She played some part in Roman politics, supporting the elevation of Vespasian as emperor. For some time Titus was attracted by her beauty and grace, and it was believed that he would marry her. She followed the conqueror of her country to Rome, but Titus was compelled, by the low repute in which Jews were held among the Romans, to repudiate her. In the New Testament she is mentioned as coming with her brother to welcome Festus at Caesarea, and as being present at the audience which Paul had with this governor (Acts, xxv. 13, 23; xxvi. 30).

Berenice. In ancient geography, a town in Egypt, situated on the Red Sea, founded by Ptolemy II. It was an important trading center.

Bérénice (bā.rā.nēs). Tragedy by Thomas Corneille, produced in 1657. The subject was taken from Madeleine de Scudéry's romance *Artamène, or the Grand Cyrus.* Although there is similarity in the titles of all three, this play is in no way connected with the much better known *Bérénice*, by Jean Baptiste Racine, and *Tite et Bérénice*, by Pierre Corneille (Thomas's more famous brother).

Bérénice. Tragedy by Jean Baptiste Racine, produced on Nov. 21, 1670, founded on the story of the Roman emperor Titus and the Jewish princess Berenice. The subject is said to have been proposed to Racine and Pierre Corneille at the same time by Henrietta Anna, daughter of Charles I of England, who perhaps wished to see her own secret history on the stage (her own position at the French court was in some respects similar to that of Berenice at Rome). Corneille was beaten by a week in the production of the plays (his was entitled *Tite et Bérénice*), and Racine's play was considered on the whole more successful.

Berenice (ber.ẹ.nī′sē). Tale by Edgar Allan Poe, published (1835) in the *Southern Literary Messenger*, and subsequently included in *Tales of the Grotesque and Arabesque* (1840).

Berenice. An ancient name of **Bengasi.**

Berenice I. fl. 4th and 3rd centuries B.C. Wife of Ptolemy I (Soter) of Egypt and the mother of Ptolemy II (Philadelphus).

Berenice II (of *Cyrene*). fl. 3rd century B.C. Egyptian princess; wife of Ptolemy III (Euergetes). She is said to have dedicated her hair in the temple of Arsinoë at Zephyrium for the safe return of her husband from an expedition to Syria. The astronomer Conon of Samos reported that her hair had been transformed into the constellation called *Coma Berenices.*

Berenices (ber.ẹ.nī′sēz), **Coma.** See **Coma Berenices.**

Berenson (ber′ẹn.sọn), **Bernhard** (or **Bernard**). b. at Vilna, Lithuania, June 26, 1865—. American art critic and writer, generally regarded as one of the world's outstanding authorities on Italian art of the Renaissance; married (1900) Mary Logan Smith, daughter of Hannah Whitall Smith and sister of Logan Pearsall Smith. After receiving his A.B. at Harvard, he went to Italy, in which country he has spent a great part of his life. He is the author of *Venetian Painters of the Renaissance* (1894), *Lorenzo Lotto, an Essay in Constructive Art Criticism* (1895), *Florentine Painters of the Renaissance* (1896; revised ed., 1909), *Central Italian Painters of the Renaissance* (1897), *The Study and Criticism of Italian Art* (1901, 1902, 1915), *The Drawings of the Florentine Painters* (1903), *North Italian Painters of the Renaissance* (1906), *A Sienese Painter of the Franciscan Legend* (1910), *Essays in Mediaeval Art* (1930), *Aesthetics and History in the Visual Arts* (1949), *Rumor and Reflection* (1952), and shorter contributions to various magazines and reviews.

Berent (be′rent), **Wacław.** b. at Warsaw, Poland, 1873; d. there, 1940. Polish fiction writer. He was the author of a series of novels which, taken together, offer a revealing portrait of the Polish soul from the time of the three partitions of the country (1772, 1793, 1795) to 1918. Among the most notable are *The Expert* (1898), *Dry Rot* (1901), *Winter Wheat* (1911), and the cycle *The Current* (1934–39). He was greatly influenced by Friedrich Nietzsche.

Beresford (ber′ẹz.fọrd), Lord **Charles William de la Poer.** [Title, 1st Baron **Beresford.**] b. in Ireland, Feb. 10, 1846; d. Sept. 6, 1919. English admiral and parliamentarian. He entered the navy in 1859, and rose to the rank of rear admiral (1897), vice-admiral (1902), and admiral (1906). He was rear admiral in the Mediterranean (1900–02), commanded the Channel squadron (1903–05) and the Mediterranean fleet (1905–07), and was commander in chief of the Channel fleet (1907–09). He was a Conservative member of Parliament for various terms. In the bombardment of Alexandria in 1882 he commanded the *Condor*, and in the Nile expedition of 1884–85 was a member of Wolseley's staff, and subsequently commanded the naval brigade at the battles of Abu-Klea, Abu-Kru, and Metamneh, in the Sudan. He wrote *Nelson and his Times* (1898; with W. H. Wilson), *The Break-up of China* (1899), *The Betrayal* (1912), and others. He was retired in February, 1911.

Beresford, Frank Ernest. b. at Derby, England, Aug. 30, 1881—. English painter of portraits and sporting subjects, noted primarily for his likenesses of members of the British royal family. He studied at the Derby School of Art (1895–1900), St. John's Wood Art School (1900–01), and the Royal Academy Schools (1901–06); later he won a British Institute scholarship. In 1906 he began to exhibit at the Royal Academy; thereafter he exhibited also at Glasgow and Toronto. During World War II he painted with the armed services for four years. In 1947 he founded the Beresford Press, Limited. Among his principal works are portraits of Queen Mary of England, King George VI of England, the Duke of Norfolk, and Viscount Wakefield.

Beresford, James. b. at Upham, Hampshire, England, May 28, 1764; d. at Kibworth Beauchamp, Leicestershire, England, Sept. 29, 1840. English clergyman. He was the author of a prose satire entitled *The Miseries of Human Life* (1806–07), and of other works.

Beresford, John Davys. b. at Castor, England, March 7, 1873; d. 1947. English novelist and architect. He first achieved prominence with a trilogy dealing with the life of an architect, the separate volumes of which were entitled *The Early History of Jacob Stahl* (1911), *A Candidate for Truth* (1912), and *The Invisible Event* (1915). Author also of *The Mountains of the Moon* (1915), *God's Counterpoint* (1918), *The Monkey Puzzle* (1925), *Love's Illusion* (1930), *Cleo* (1937), *Snell's Folly* (1939), *Strange Rival* (1940), *A Common Enemy* (1942), *The Riddle of the Tower* (1944), and *The Prisoner* (1945).

Beresford, William Carr. [Title, Viscount **Beresford.**] b. Oct. 2, 1768; d. at Bedgebury, Kent, England, Jan. 8, 1854. English general. He served with distinction in the Peninsular War, organized the Portuguese army, and commanded at the battle of La Albuera, on May 16, 1811.

Berettyó (be'ret.tyō). River in W Rumania and E Hungary, a N tributary of the Kőrös River.

Berettyóújfalu (be'ret.tyō.ö'i.fô.lö). Town in E Hungary, situated on the Berettyó River S of Debrecen. 11,696 (1948).

Berezina (bi"ri.zē.nä'). [Also, **Beresina.**] River in the U.S.S.R., in the Byelorussian Soviet Socialist Republic, a tributary of the Dnieper River. It was the scene of fighting, near Borisov, during Napoleon's retreat (1812) from Moscow. The area was also a battleground for Russian and German troops in World War II. Length, ab. 350 mi.

Berezina, Passage or **Battle of the.** Passage of Napoleon's army over the Berezina River on the retreat from Moscow, Nov. 26–29, 1812. It was opposed by the Russians near Studyanka. Many thousands of the French were slain and drowned, and about 16,000 were made prisoners.

Berezniki (bi.ryôz'nyi.ki). [Former name, **Usolye-Solikamskoye.**] City in the U.S.S.R., in the Molotov *oblast* (region) of the Russian Soviet Federated Socialist Republic, ab. 89 mi. N of Molotov: site of one of the largest chemical plants in the Soviet Union, and of a large electrical power plant which burns coal and peat. Salt and potash are mined from underground deposits. 63,575 (1939).

Berezovo (bi.ryô'zǫ.vǫ). [Also: **Berezof, Berezov** (-zǫf).] Town in the U.S.S.R., in the Omsk *oblast* (region) of the Russian Soviet Federated Socialist Republic, situated on the Sosva River in the center of the swamplands of the Ob River. It has trade in furs and other products of the region; formerly known as a place of banishment for political offenders. Pop. ab. 4,700.

Berezovski (bi.ryô'zǫf.ski). [Also, **Berezofsk** (-zofsk).] Town in the U.S.S.R., in the Sverdlovsk *oblast* (region), situated in the Urals N of Sverdlovsk, in an important industrial region. There are gold fields in the vicinity.

Berfon (bėr'fon). See **Birifo.**

Berg (berk). Former European duchy in W Germany, on the E bank of the Rhine opposite Cologne. First mentioned as a county in the 11th century, it became a duchy in 1380. It became associated with Jülich in 1423, and with Cleve in 1511. In the 17th century it was incorporated into the Palatinate holdings. In 1766 Karl Theodore, ruler of the Palatinate, obtained Bavaria, and Berg became a part of the Bavarian Rhineland. Napoleon I of France took Berg from Bavaria in 1806, and made it a grand duchy with Joachim Murat as its ruler. It was greatly enlarged by annexations in 1807–09. The original duchy and nearly all of the annexed territory were incorporated into Prussia in 1815. Area of duchy, ab. 1,150 sq. mi.; of grand duchy, ab. 6,700 sq. mi.

Berg. Village in S Germany, in the *Land* (state) of Bavaria, American Zone, in the *Kreis* (district) of Upper Bavaria, situated on the Lake of Starnberg (Starnbergersee), SW of Munich. It has a castle and a chapel, erected in 1896–99, memorializing Louis II, king of Bavaria, who was drowned here on June 13, 1886. Pop. 1,848 (1946).

Berg. Former town in S Germany, in the *Land* (state) of Württemberg-Baden, American Zone, formerly in the Neckar *Kreis* (district) of Württemberg. It is incorporated into the city of Stuttgart.

Berg, Alban. b. at Vienna, Feb. 9, 1885; d. there, Dec. 24, 1935. Austrian composer, one of the leading members of the modern school. He studied (1904 *et seq.*) under Arnold Schönberg and, like his teacher, composed in the 12-tone scale. His compositions include the operas *Wozzeck* (1914–21) and the unfinished *Lulu* (1928–34), as well as *Pianoforte Sonata* (1908), *String Quartet* (1909–10), and *Der Wein* (1929), a concert aria. *Wozzek* had its first performance at Berlin in 1925, and was revived at the Salzburg music festival in 1951. *Lulu* was given at Zurich in 1937.

Berg (berg), **Chresten** (or **Christen**) **Poulsen.** b. at Fjaltring, Denmark, Dec. 18, 1829; d. at Copenhagen, Nov. 28, 1891. Danish political leader and teacher, known for his advocacy of advanced democratic ideas. He was elected (1865) to the *Folketing* (lower chamber of the Danish parliament), of which he served (1883–87) as president; in 1887 he founded a radical reform party to oppose the conservative government in office at that time.

Berg (berk), Count **Friedrich Wilhelm Rembert.** [Russian, **Feodor Feodorovich Berk.**] b. in Livonia, c1790; d. at St. Petersburg, Jan. 18, 1874. Russian field marshal and diplomat. He was lieutenant general of Poland (1863–74).

Berg, Hans Heinrich. b. at Itzehoe, in Schleswig-Holstein, Nov. 19, 1889—. German physician. He served as assistant to Gustav von Bergmann at Altona, was a military surgeon during World War I, became a member of the staff of the Hospital of Clinical Medicine at Marburg in 1920, served (1920–27) at Frankfort on the Main, and joined (1927) the staff of the Charité Hospital at Berlin. He became (1926) privatdocent of clinical medicine and roentgenology at the University of Frankfort on the Main, was named (1929) professor at the University of Berlin, and became (1930) physician in chief of the department of clinical medicine at the municipal hospital at Dortmund. He worked on x-ray diagnosis of the digestive canal, and is known for his studies of mucosal relief of the stomach and a duodenum spot film device. Author of *Beitrag zur Klinik der Haemochromatose* (1920) and *Röntgenuntersuchungen am Innenrelief des Verdauungskanals* (1930).

Berg (bėrg), **Joseph Frederic.** b. at Antigua, in the British West Indies, June 3, 1812; d. July 20, 1871. American Dutch-Reformed clergyman. Ordained (1835) at the German Reformed Church, at Harrisburg, Pa., he taught (1862–67) theology at Rutgers College (now Rutgers University). Author of *Lectures on Romanism* (1840), *Papal Rome* (1841), and *The Inquisition; Church and State; or, Rome's Influence upon the Civil and Religious Institutions of our Country* (1851).

Bergamasca (ber.gä.mä'skä). District in N Italy, in the N part of the province of Bergamo, comprising the Brembo, Serio, and Scalve valleys. It is mountainous and picturesque.

Bergamasco (ber.gä.mäs'kō), **Il.** See **Castello, Giovanni Battista.**

Bergamo (ber'gä.mō). Province in the *compartimento* (region) of Lombardy, NW Italy. Capital, Bergamo; area, 1,065 sq. mi.; pop. 605,810 (1936).

Bergamo. [Latin, **Bergomum.**] City and commune in NW Italy, in the *compartimento* (region) of Lombardy, the capital of the province of Bergamo, situated at the junction of the Serio and Brembo rivers in the foothills of the Alps, ab. 28 mi. NE of Milan. It is the seat of a bishopric, and has an art academy (Accademia Carrara) and an important library. There are textile, cement, and other industries and considerable trade. The old city contains beautiful medieval monuments, such as the 12th-century Church of Santa Maria Maggiore, containing murals painted by Tiepolo in the 18th century, the cathedral which dates from the 14th–16th centuries, the Capella Colleoni (Colleoni Chapel), and a number of other churches and palaces. Bergamo played an important role in the development of music in the 16th–18th centuries; Gaetano Donizetti lived here. The town, a Gallic settlement, became a Roman *municipium* under Julius Caesar; it was destroyed by Attila. In the Middle Ages a member of the Lombard federation, it was later allied to the Ghibellines, and fell to the pro-Guelph Milan in 1264; it was ruled by the Visconti of Lombardy (1296–1428), by the republic of Venice (1428–1797); belonged to the Cisalpine Republic (1797–1814) and to Austria (1814–59). Buildings of interest to tourists were undamaged in World War II. Pop. of commune, 86,043 (1936), 105,399 (1951); of city, 70,717 (1936).

Bergamo Alps. Division of the Alps in N Italy which extends from Lake Como E to the Oglio River and Lake Iseo, and S from the Valtellina (valley of the Adda River).

Bergara (ber.gä'rä), **Convention of.** [Also, **Convention of Vergara.**] Term applied to a capitulation of Spanish Carlist forces, on Aug. 31, 1839, which virtually put an end to the first phase of the 19th-century civil war between the Carlists (supporters of Don Carlos as the rightful king of Spain) and the adherents of Queen Isabella II, who was the niece of Don Carlos and who could not (under the Salic law forbidding women to inherit the throne) justify her rule in the eyes of many of her subjects.

Berg Bay (bėrg). Bay in Antarctica, lying between Islands Point and the promontory terminating in Birthday Point, along the W coast of Robertson Bay, in N Victoria Land; in ab. 71°27′ S., 169°23′ E. It was surveyed and named in 1911 by the Northern Party of the British Antarctic Expedition (1910–13). Width, ab. 3 mi.

Berge (bėrj), **Edward.** b. at Baltimore, 1876; d. there, Oct. 12, 1924. American sculptor. He studied at Baltimore and at Paris, won a medal at the Pan-American Exposition (Buffalo, 1901), and received a prize from the American Art Association at Paris. His work has been exhibited in the U.S., France, and Hawaii. Best known are his fountains, garden sculpture, and various monuments to historical figures.

Bergen (ber'ċhe̩n). See also under **Alkmaar.**

Bergen (ber'ge̩n). Town in NE Germany, in the *Land* (state) of Mecklenburg, Russian Zone, formerly in the province of Pomerania, Prussia, the chief place on the island of Rügen, situated in the C part of the island: agricultural and livestock trade; fisheries. The Romanesque church dates from the 12th century. The town came under Sweden in 1648, under Prussia in 1815. Pop. 8,748 (1946).

Bergen (bėr'ge̩n; Norwegian, ber'ge̩n). City in SW Norway, capital of the *fylke* (county) of Hordaland and itself a separate administrative unit, situated on the Pudde Fjord, which is the innermost part of the By Fjord; the Hardanger Fjord and the Sogne Fjord, the longest fjords in Norway, are in the vicinity. It is the second largest city in Norway, a seaport, and a commercial center; imports grain, coal, and colonial products, and exports fish and fish products. There are fisheries, shipyards, cordage and wood industries, and distilleries. Bergen is the seat of a Lutheran bishopric and of a university, opened in 1948, and has astronomical, nautical, and oceanographic stations. There is a maritime museum, fishery museum, industrial art museum, natural history and cultural history collections, an art gallery, theater, and library. The picturesque fish market is one of the points visited by tourists. Haakon's Hall, built in the 13th century and long used as stables, was restored in the 20th century. Founded in the 11th century, Bergen became a bishopric in the 12th century. Around 1530, the Hanseatic League opened here one of its chief branch offices, called Tyske Bryggen (German Bridge), which dominated the commercial life of the town at that time; some of the privileges were lost in 1559, and the office passed into Norwegian hands in 1630. In World War II, Bergen was occupied by the Germans in 1940; it was heavily bombed by the Allied forces on Oct. 4 and 29, 1944, with numerous casualties; many acts of sabotage were committed against the Germans during the war period. 109,320 (1946).

Bergen. Flemish name of **Mons,** Belgium.

Bergen (bėr'ge̩n), **Edgar (John).** b. at Chicago, Feb. 16, 1903—. American ventriloquist and comedian, known especially for radio performances with the dummies "Charlie McCarthy" and "Mortimer Snerd." He was a performer on Chautauqua summer circuits (1922–25), and later in American and European vaudeville and supper clubs (1926–36). He made his first radio appearance on Dec. 17, 1936. He has since had a regular radio show, and has had parts in motion pictures and on television.

Bergen-Belsen (ber'ge̩n.bel'ze̩n). Name applied to a community, technically two villages, but now grouped as a single unit, in NW Germany, in the *Land* (state) of Lower Saxony, British Zone, formerly in the province of Hanover, Prussia, situated in the Lüneburger Heide, N of Hanover. During the Nazi regime it was the site of a huge concentration camp where numerous prisoners were put to death for political offenses or for alleged racial undesirability. Pop. of Bergen, 2,626 (1946); of Belsen, 222 (1946).

Bergenfield (bėr'ge̩n.fēld). Borough in NE New Jersey, in Bergen County. 17,647 (1950).

Bergengruen (ber'ge̩n.grün), **Werner.** b. at Riga, Latvia, Sept. 16, 1892—. German novelist and poet. His novels include *Das Gesetz des Atum* (1923), *Das grosse Alkahest* (1926), *Herzog Karl der Kühne* (1930), and *Die Schnur um den Hals* (1935). He is a leading representative of the German lyrical renaissance which followed World War II, as evidenced in his *Dies Irae* (1947).

Bergen-op-Zoom (ber'ċhe̩n.ôp.zōm'). Town in S Netherlands, in the province of North Brabant, situated on the Zoom River, a small stream flowing into the East Schelde bay, ab. 15 mi. N of Antwerp. The port is accessible to large vessels only at high tide; there are oyster and lobster fisheries, agricultural markets, a sugar refinery, distilleries, and metallurgical establishments. The town has an old castle, and at one time had extensive fortifications; it was taken by the Netherlanders in 1576 and successfully defended against the Spaniards and others in 1588, 1597, 1605, and 1622; in 1747 and 1795 it was conquered by the French. The British, under Thomas Graham, attempted to storm the fortress in 1814. Pop. 30,326 (est. 1951).

Bergenroth (ber'ge̩n.rōt), **Gustav Adolf.** b. at Oletzko, in East Prussia, Feb. 26, 1813; d. at Madrid, Feb. 13, 1869. Student of history, noted for his researches in English history among the Spanish national archives at Simancas, Spain.

Berger (ber'gėr), Baron **Alfred von.** b. at Vienna, April 30, 1853; d. there, Aug. 23, 1912. Austrian dramatist and writer of short stories.

Berger (bėr'gėr), **Bessie.** Character in the play *Awake and Sing*, by Clifford Odets. She is the mother of a daughter Hessie and a son Ralph, and the action of the play centers around her and her inability to understand her children's predicaments.

Berger (ber'gėr), **Hans.** b. at Neuses, near Coburg, Bavaria, Germany, May 21, 1873; d. at Bad Blankenburg, Thuringia, Germany, June 1, 1941. German psychiatrist. Assistant to Otto L. Binswanger at Jena, he was appointed assistant professor (1901), associate professor (1906), *oberarzt* (head physician) of the hospital (1912), and professor *ordinarius* of psychiatry (1919) at the University of Jena, where he was Binswanger's successor as director of the psychiatric hospital of the medical school. He opened a new field of electrophysiology by discovering the correlation between the electrical activity of the cortex and psychic functions, introducing the electroencephalograph (1929). Author of *Über das Elektrenkephalogramm des Menschen* (1929).

Berger, Ludwig. b. at Berlin, April 18, 1777; d. there, Feb. 16, 1839. German composer and piano teacher, resident (1815 *et seq.*) at Berlin. Among his works are 27 piano études; his pupils included Mendelssohn, Adolf von Henselt, and Fanny Hensel.

Berger (ber.zhā), **Philippe.** b. at Beaucourt, in Alsace, 1846; d. at Paris, 1912. French Orientalist. He served as professor of Hebrew at the Collège de France, and also as successor to Joseph Ernest Renan at the Académie des Inscriptions. He was the author of *Histoire de l'écriture dans l'antiquité* (History of Writing in Ancient Times, 1892), and editor of *Corpus inscriptionum semiticarum.*

Berger (bėr'gėr), **Victor Louis.** b. at Nieder-Rehbach, in Transylvania (in what is now part of Rumania), Feb. 28, 1860; d. Aug. 7, 1929. American socialist politician and editor. He studied at Budapest and Vienna, but before he took his degree his family emigrated to America. After working in the U.S. at various trades, he was for a time a teacher in the public schools. In 1892 he was made editor of the Milwaukee *Daily Vorwärts,* of the *Wahrheit,* and of the *Social Democratic Herald,* and was soon recognized as a prominent advocate of the socialist cause. He was one of the organizers of the group known as the Social Democracy (1897) and of the Social Democratic Party (1898, known since 1900 as the Socialist Party), and except for a short interval, was a member of the national executive committee of that party from the time of its origin until his death. He was a representative in Congress from Wisconsin (1911–13), the first Socialist member of that legislative body. Indicted (1918) because of his antiwar statements and judged guilty of sedition under the statutes of the World War I Espionage Act, he was sentenced to 20 years in prison, but the sentence was reversed (1921) by the U.S. Supreme Court. Although he was twice reëlected to Congress during the period of his indictment and appeal, the House prevented him from taking his seat. When reëlected in 1922, however, he was finally reseated, serving thereafter as a representative until his death.

Bergerac (ber.zhe̜.råk). Town in SW France, in the department of Dordogne, situated on the Dordogne River, ab. 51 mi. E of Bordeaux. It is an ancient Huguenot stronghold and has become famous because of Edmond Rostand's play *Cyrano de Bergerac*. The Church of Saint Jacques dates from the 12th century, the castle of Henry IV from the 16th and 17th centuries. The Church of Notre Dame is a modern building in 13th-century style. There are a museum and a town library. The town has metallurgical industries, canning factories, and distilleries. It is a center for the trade in truffles, grain, and the red and white wines of the region. 22,525 (1946).

Bergerac, Cyrano de. See **Cyrano de Bergerac.**

Bergerac, Treaty of. [Also, **Treaty of Poitiers.**] In French history, a treaty concluded between the Huguenots and Roman Catholics in 1577. It brought a temporary halt to open warfare between the two religious groups, but no important issues were resolved to the complete satisfaction of either party and the treaty was disregarded by Henry III of France. Hostilities on a limited scale were reopened in 1580, and in 1584 the two factions became involved in the last major phase of the religious wars prior to the issuance in 1598 of the Edict of Nantes, which granted the Huguenots religious and civil rights under the French crown. (In those chronologies which enumerate the religious wars of France, the Treaty of Bergerac is taken as ending the sixth distinguishable period of hostilities.)

Bergerat (ber.zhe̜.rå), **Auguste Émile.** [Pseudonym, **Caliban.**] b. at Paris, April 29, 1845; d. 1923. French journalist, novelist, and dramatic writer; son-in-law and biographer of Théophile Gautier.

Bergersen (bėr'gėr.se̜n), **Mount.** Massive northward projection of the Southern Escarpments at the edge of the polar plateau in Princess Ragnhild Coast in Antarctica; in ab. 72°08′ S., 24°35′ E. It was discovered and photographed from the air on Feb. 6, 1937 by members of a Norwegian expedition under Lars Christensen, and named for Birger Bergersen, chairman of the Norwegian Whaling Board.

Berges (berzh), **Aristide.** b. at Toulouse, France, 1833; d. at Lancey, Isère, France, 1904. French paper manufacturer. He developed a system for the utilization of waterfalls near his paper mill at Lancey to produce hydroelectric power, and is known from this in France as the inventor of *la houille blanche* (white coal).

Bergey (bėr'gi), **David Hendricks.** b. in Montgomery County, Pa., Dec. 27, 1860; d. Sept. 5, 1937. American bacteriologist. After graduating (1884) from the University of Pennsylvania, he served there as assistant professor (1903–26) and professor (1926–31) of hygiene and bacteriology, acting professor (1931–32) of hygiene, and director (1928–31) of the laboratory of hygiene; he was subsequently (1931 *et seq.*) director of research in biology for the National Drug Company. Author of *Handbook of Practical Hygiene* (1899) and *The Principles of Hygiene* (1901).

Bergh (bėrg), **Christian.** b. near Rhinebeck, N.Y., April 30, 1763; d. at New York, June 24, 1843. American shipbuilder famed for the speed and durable construction of his products; father of Henry Bergh. His New York shipyard on the East River was opened in the 1780's and was the yard that built the U.S.S. *President*, used in the War of 1812.

Bergh, Henry. b. at New York, Aug. 29, 1811; d. there, March 12, 1888. American philanthropist, notable as a founder (1866) and first president of the American Society for the Prevention of Cruelty to Animals; son of Christian Bergh (1763–1843). He was also influential in organizing (1875) the Society for the Prevention of Cruelty to Children. He was secretary of the legation and acting vice-consul at St. Petersburg (1862–64). Author of the play *Love's Alternative*, produced at the Union League Theater, Baltimore, in 1881.

Berghaus (berk'hous), **Heinrich.** b. at Cleve, Prussia, May 3, 1797; d. at Stettin, Prussia, Feb. 17, 1884. German geographer. He was professor of applied mathematics (1824–55) at the Academy of Architecture at Berlin, and editor (1825–29) of the periodical *Hertha*. Author of *Atlas von Asien* (1833–43), *Physikalischer Atlas* (1837–52), and others.

Berghem (ber'ċhe̜m), **Nicolaes.** See **Berchem** or **Berghem, Nicolaes.**

Bergisch-Gladbach (ber'gish.glät'bäċh). Town in W Germany, in the *Land* (state) of North Rhine-Westphalia, British Zone, formerly in the Rhine Province, Prussia, ab. 8 mi. NE of Cologne: manufactures stoves, tools, instruments, bicycles, steel wool, and wire; has construction works, iron foundries, and leather, woolen textile, and chemical industries. It is a weekend excursion place for the people of Cologne. The population is predominantly Roman Catholic; the increase in population between 1939 and 1947 was 35.8 percent. 30,230 (1946), 32,681 (1950).

Bergius (ber'ge̜.ůs), **Friedrich.** b. at Goldschmieden, in Silesia, 1884; d. 1949. German industrial chemist. He shared (1931) with Karl Bosch the Nobel prize for chemistry. He developed the fundamentals and the technology of the "Bergius process" for hydrogenating coal to oil, important to the Germans in World War II, and of great potential world importance if, as now seems probable, petroleum production should exhaust existing oil fields more rapidly than new fields can be discovered. He established his residence at Madrid after the collapse of Germany in World War II.

Bergman (bėrg'ma̜n), **Ingrid.** b. at Stockholm, Aug. 29, 1911—. Swedish stage and screen actress. As a student at the Royal Dramatic Theater at Stockholm, she showed great promise and played many leading roles; as a result she was signed immediately upon graduation by Svensk Films, a Swedish company. She appeared in 12 motion pictures and in two stage plays during this period. In 1937, her film *Intermezzo*, in which she co-starred with Leslie Howard, was such a success that she was put under contract by the Hollywood producer David O. Selznick. In Hollywood, she became one of the most successful screen actresses, playing in such films as *Rage in Heaven* (1942), *Casablanca* (1942), *Gaslight* (1944, in which she won the Academy of Motion Picture Arts and Sciences award for the best actress of the year), *Spellbound* (1945), *Saratoga Trunk* (1946), *Arch of Triumph* (1947), and *Joan of Arc* (1949). She made her New York stage debut in a revival of *Liliom* (1940), and won acclaim with her appearance in Maxwell Anderson's stage play *Joan of Lorraine* (1946). In 1949, she went to Italy to play the leading role in the motion picture *Stromboli*, under the direction of Roberto Rossellini, whom she married in 1950.

Bergman (bery''män), **Torbern Olof.** b. in Sweden, March 20, 1735; d. July 8, 1784. Swedish chemist and naturalist, appointed (1758) professor of physics at Uppsala. He is said to have been the first to refine (1775) nickel to its pure state.

Bergmann (berk'män; Anglicized, bėrg'ma̜n), **Carl.** b. at Ebersbach, Saxony, Germany, 1821; d. at New York, Aug. 10, 1876. Conductor (1855 *et seq.*) of the New York Philharmonic Society. He shared the podium until he became (1866) sole leader of the orchestra, serving in that post until his death. His programs included many works by Richard Wagner.

Bergmann (berk'män), **Ernst von.** b. at Ruhen, in Livonia, Dec. 16, 1836; d. at Wiesbaden, Germany, March 25, 1907. German surgeon, appointed (1882) professor of surgery and director of the surgical clinic of the University of Berlin; father of Gustav von Bergmann. He was especially noted for his work in aseptic surgery.

Bergmann, Gustav von. b. at Würzburg, Germany, Dec. 24, 1878—. German physician; son of Ernst von Bergmann (1836–1907). He conducted researches on the functional pathology of the liver (1927), on ulcers of the stomach, on the "epiphrenale syndrome" in connection with angina pectoris and with cardiospasm (1932), and on hypertonia in relation to the vegetative nervous system. Author of *Die Erkrankungen des Magens* (1926) and *Die korrelativen Funktionen des autonomen Nervensystems* (1930); coeditor of *Handbuch der normalen und pathologischen Physiologie* (1925) and *Handbuch der inneren Medizin* (1925–31).

Bergmann, Julius. b. at Opherdicke, Germany, April 1, 1840; d. at Marburg, Germany, Aug. 24, 1904. German philosopher. He served as a professor at the universities of Königsberg and Marburg. Author of *Geschichte der Philosophie* (1892) and *System des objektiven Idealismus* (1903).

Bergner (bėrg′nėr), **Elisabeth.** b. at Vienna, Aug. 22, 1900—. Austrian actress. She studied acting (1915–19) at the Vienna Conservatory, made her debut (1919) at Zurich, and the next year played Rosalind in *As You Like It* with great success. Having joined (1920) Max Reinhardt's company, she added Juliet, Viola, and Queen Katharine of Aragon to her Shakespearian repertoire. Her performance in Shaw's *St. Joan* (1924) won her an international reputation. She also performed successfully in *Camille* (1924), *The Circle of Chalk* (1925), *The Constant Nymph* (1927), *The Merchant of Venice* (1928), *Strange Interlude* (1929), and *Amphitryon 38* (1938). Her English debut was made at Manchester in November, 1933, in *Escape Me Never*, and in 1936 she repeated her performance at New York for the Theatre Guild. Her other Broadway productions included *The Two Mrs. Carrolls* (1943–45), *The Duchess of Malfi* (1946), and *Cup of Trembling* (1948). She toured the American summer theaters with *Escape Me Never* in 1948, and with *Amphitryon 38* in 1949. She started a film career in 1931, and appeared on the screen in such motion pictures as *Catherine the Great* (1934), *Escape Me Never* (1935), *As You Like It* (1936), and *Dreaming Lips* (1937).

Bergognone (ber.gō.nyō′nā), **Ambrogio.** See **Borgognone, Ambrogio.**

Bergomum (bėr′gǫ.mum). Latin name of **Bergamo,** city.

Bergonzi (ber.gôn′tsē), **Carlo.** b. c1685; d. 1747. Italian maker of musical instruments; father of Michel Angelo Bergonzi and grandfather of Carlo and Zosimo Bergonzi. A pupil of Antonio Stradivarius, he was particularly known for his violins and violoncellos.

Bergonzi, Carlo. fl. in the second half of the 18th century. Italian violin-maker; grandson of Carlo Bergonzi (c1685–1747).

Bergonzi, Michel Angelo. b. c1726; d. c1765. Italian violin-maker; son of Carlo Bergonzi (c1685–1747), and father of Nicola Bergonzi.

Bergonzi, Nicola. fl. in the second half of the 18th century. Italian violin-maker; son of Michel Angelo Bergonzi.

Bergonzi, Zosimo. fl. in the second half of the 18th century. Italian violin-maker; grandson of Carlo Bergonzi (c1685–1747).

Bergsøe (berk′sė), **Jørgen Wilhelm.** b. at Copenhagen, Feb. 8, 1835; d. there, June 26, 1911. Danish naturalist, novelist, and poet. Best known of his works are the romances *Fra Piazza del Popolo* (1866), *Fra den gamle Fabrik*, and *I Sabinerbjergene*.

Bergson (bėrg′sǫn), **Alexandra.** Heroine of *O Pioneers!* (1913), a novel by Willa Cather.

Bergson (bėrg′sǫn; French, berg.sôṅ), **Henri Louis.** b. at Paris, Oct. 18, 1859; d. there, Jan. 4, 1941. French philosopher, a professor at the Collège de France from 1900 to 1921. Bergson became a member of the Academy of Moral and Political Science in 1901, and received (1927) the Nobel prize for literature (but world renown had already come to him with the publication of *L'Évolution créatrice* in 1907). Published in English in 1911, under the title *Creative Evolution*, this book, according to William James, marked "one of the great turning-points in the history of thought. . . . It tells of reality itself . . . new horizons loom on every page." The reason for Bergson's influence lay in the originality of his attack on mechanistic materialism. Reality, he argued, cannot be revealed by intelligence alone, since concepts are always relative to practical needs. Philosophy must begin with the intuitions of the inmost reality of consciousness, which is experienced time, or duration, as evidenced, for example, in the phenomenon of memory. In human personality is found the freest expressions of what Bergson terms the *élan vital*, the creative force operative in nature, through the process of evolution. Other important works include *Essai sur les données immédiates de la conscience* (1889; Eng. trans., 1910), *Matière et mémoire* (1897; Eng. trans., 1929), *Le Rire* (1900; Eng. trans., 1911), and *Les Deux Sources de la morale et de la religion* (1932; Eng. trans., 1935).

Bergstrasse (berk′shträs″ẹ). Region in S Germany, in the S part of Hessen, reaching into the N part of Württemberg-Baden. It takes its name from the road connecting Darmstadt with Heidelberg, leading along the Odenwald Mountains in the plain of the upper Rhine. It is distinguished by its mild climate, producing fruits, vegetables, wine, and tobacco.

Bergstrøm (berk′strėm), **Hjalmar Julius.** b. at Copenhagen, Aug. 1, 1868; d. there, March 27, 1914. Danish playwright. His best-known plays, *Lynggaard and Co.* (1905) and *Karen Bornemann* (1907), show a humorous, unsentimental effort at honest description.

Bergthórsson (berg′tôr.sǫn), **Bjarni.** See **Bjarni Bergthórsson.**

Bergues (berg). [Also, **Bergues-St.-Winoc** (berg.saṅ.vē.nok).] Town in N France, in the department of Nord situated at the junction of three canals, ab. 7 mi. SE of Dunkerque. It was fortified by Vauban, and unsuccessfully besieged by the British in 1793. A tower dating from the middle of the 16th century, the museum, and many other buildings in the town were destroyed in World War II. 3,257 (1946).

Berhampore (bėr′ạm.pōr). Town in the NE part of the Union of India in N central West Bengal state, ab. 116 mi. by rail N of Calcutta in the Ganges delta region. The first mutiny of the Sepoy Rebellion took place here in 1857. Industries include brickyards and an oilseed-processing mill. 41,558 (1941).

Berhampur (bėr′ạm.pör). Town in the E central part of the Union of India, in S central Orissa state, ab. 375 mi. by rail SW of Calcutta. The town is a center for silk weaving, rice milling, and oilseed milling, and has an export trade in sugar through its port of Gopalpur, ab. 9 mi. SE on the coast. 43,536 (1941).

Beria (byā′ri.yạ), **Lavrenti Pavlovich.** [Also, **Beriya.**] b. March 28, 1899—. Russian Communist leader, chief of the Russian secret police (1938–53) as minister of internal affairs and public security. He became a Communist in 1917 and fought in the revolution. He was a member of the presidium of the supreme soviet (1946 *et seq.*) and a member of the Politburo (1946 *et seq.*) and of the central committee of the Communist Party. Beria, who was mentioned prominently as a leading candidate as Stalin's successor, is said to be largely responsible for the Russians' development of the atom bomb. In the Malenkov government that succeeded (1953) that of Stalin, he remained minister of interior and security until July, 1953, when he was dismissed and charged with treason.

Bering (bā′ring), **Vitus.** [Also, **Behring.**] b. at Horsens, Jutland, Denmark, 1680; d. on Bering Island, in the Bering Sea, 1741. Danish navigator, in the Russian service, noted for his discoveries in the North Pacific Ocean. Under orders from Peter I of Russia, he explored (1725 *et seq.*) the N coast of Siberia. On a second voyage he set out from Kamchatka, and traversed (1728) Bering Strait (named after him, as were also Bering Island and Bering Sea), thus proving that Asia and America are separated. He also explored (1741) the W coast of America to latitude 69° N. A victim of scurvy, he died before this voyage was completed.

Beringhen (ber′ing.gẹn), **De.** Gourmand in Edward Bulwer-Lytton's *Richelieu;* he is banished by the cardinal.

Bering Island (bir′ing; ber′-). [Also, **Behring Island;** Russian, **Ostrov Bering.**] Island off the E coast of Kamchatka peninsula, NE Asia, belonging to the U.S.S.R., situated in the N Pacific Ocean opposite the Aleutian Islands. It is one of the Komandorski group.

Bering Sea. [Also: **Behring Sea, Sea of Kamchatka.**] That part of the North Pacific Ocean which lies between Bering Strait and the Aleutian Islands, and between the NE part of the U.S.S.R. (Siberia) and Alaska. It was named for the Danish navigator Vitus Bering.

Bering Sea Arbitration Treaty. Treaty between the U.S. and Great Britain, signed at Washington, D.C., on Feb. 29, 1892, which led to the decision (1893) of a seven-man mixed tribunal supporting the British position on pelagic-sealing rights in the Bering Sea. The controversy began in 1886, when U.S. revenue cutters seized Canadian schooners in Bering Sea waters, and reached its climax in the talk of war following the exchange (1890) of notes between U.S. Secretary of State James G. Blaine and British Foreign Secretary Lord Salisbury.

Bering Strait. [Also: **Behring Strait;** called by early geographers **Straits of Anian.**] Sea passage which connects the Arctic Ocean with the Pacific Ocean, and separates Alaska (Cape Prince of Wales) from Siberia (East Cape). The Diomede Islands are about midway. The strait was named for the Danish explorer Vitus Bering, who first traversed it in 1728. The name Straits of Anian, of uncertain origin, was applied first in the 16th century. Mercator (1569), Ortelius (1570), and other geographers of the period give the strait under this name, which by some is supposed to have been derived from an Asiatic province of Ania. Ortelius, in 1570, indicates this province in NE Siberia. Width, in the narrowest part, 36 mi.; average, ab. 53 mi.

Berington (ber′ing.tọn), **Joseph.** b. in Shropshire, England, 1746; d. at Buckland, Berkshire, England, Dec. 1, 1827. English Roman Catholic priest and author. He wrote *History of the Lives of Abeillard and Heloisa* (1787), *History of the Reign of Henry II* (1790), *Literary History of the Middle Ages* (1814), and numerous other works, many of which (because of their author's faith and because of their allegedly anti-Protestant bias) aroused some controversy in their day.

Berinthia (bẹ.rin′thi.ạ). Young and dissolute widow in Sir John Vanbrugh's comedy *The Relapse;* she also appears in Richard Brinsley Sheridan's adaptation, *A Trip to Scarborough.* It is she who, in the former play, lures Loveless away from the habits of marital fidelity which he has for a short time maintained.

Berinthia. [Called **"Berry."**] Niece of Mrs. Pipchin in Charles Dickens's novel *Dombey and Son;* she is much afflicted with boils on her nose.

Bériot (bā.ryō), **Charles Auguste de.** b. at Louvain, Belgium, Feb. 20, 1802; d. there, April 20, 1870. Belgian violinist and composer; father of Charles Wilfrid de Bériot (1833–1914).

Bériot, Charles Wilfrid de. b. at Paris, Feb. 12, 1833; d. 1914. French pianist and composer of piano works and chamber music; son of Charles Auguste de Bériot (1802–70).

Berislav (bi.ri.släf′). [Also, **Kakhovka.**] Town in the U.S.S.R., in the Ukrainian Soviet Socialist Republic, situated on the Dnieper River ab. 46 mi. E of Kherson: famous for its horses; also a wheat and barley center.

Beristaín y Souza (bā.rēs.tä.ēn′ ē sō′sä), **José Mariano.** b. at Puebla, Mexico, 1756; d. at Mexico City, March 23, 1817. Mexican bibliographer, rector of the College of San Pedro. His best-known work is *Biblioteca hispano-americana sententrional,* a catalogue of Spanish North American authors, with a list of their works.

Beriya (byā′ryạ), **Lavrenti Pavlovich.** See **Beria, Lavrenti Pavlovich.**

Berja (ber′ʜä). Town in E Spain, in the province of Almería, situated in the Sierra de Gador, ab. 20 mi. W of Almería: metallurgical and textile industries; wine trade. 12,480 (1940).

Berk (byerk), **Feodor Feodorovich.** Russian name of **Berg,** Count **Friedrich Wilhelm Rembert.**

Berkeley (bėrk′li). City in C California, in Alameda County, NE of San Francisco: residential, industrial, and business center in the "East Bay" area (the E shore of San Francisco Bay). It is the seat of one of the two main branches of the University of California. 113,805 (1950).

Berkeley (bėrk′li, bärk′li). [Middle English, **Berkley** (berk′lā); Anglo-Saxon, **Bercleā, Beorcleā.**] Civil parish and market town in W England, in Gloucestershire, situated on the river Avon, ab. 15 mi. SW of Gloucester, ab. 140 mi. W of London by rail. 664 (1931).

Berkeley (bėrk′li). City in E Missouri, in St. Louis County: incorporated in 1937. In the decade between the last two U.S. censuses, the city's population slightly more than doubled. 2,577 (1940); 5,268 (1950).

Berkeley (bėrk′li, bärk′li), **Elizabeth.** b. 1750; d. at Naples, Italy, Jan. 13, 1828. English writer. Her autobiography was published in 1825 and *Letters to the Margrave of Anspach* (her second husband) in 1814.

Berkeley, George. [Title, 1st Earl of **Berkeley.**] b. 1628; d. 1698. English nobleman. He was created first earl of Berkeley in 1679. In 1688, he was a member of the provisional government (set up after the flight of James II) which confirmed William III (William of Orange) as the ruler of England.

Berkeley, George. b. at Dysert Castle, in County Kilkenny, Ireland, March 12, 1685; d. at Oxford, England, Jan. 14, 1753. Irish prelate (of English descent) of the established church (Church of England), known for his philosophical writings. He is especially famous for his theory of vision, the foundation of the later psychophysiological investigation of that subject, and for the extreme subjective idealism of his metaphysical views, his major tenet being expressed in *Three Dialogues between Hylas and Philonous* (1713), Socratic discussions in which Berkeley sets out to prove the nonexistence of matter except as it is perceived (and thus, of course, finally to confirm the existence of God). He was graduated from Trinity College, Dublin, where he held (1707–24) various offices; in the period 1713–20 he traveled in England and on the Continent. He became dean of Derry in 1724, and bishop of Cloyne in 1734. In 1725 he obtained the patent for a college in Bermuda, of which he was appointed first president, but which was never established; he sailed for Newport, R.I., on Sept. 4, 1728, landing there in January, 1729, and remaining in America until the end of 1731. In 1752 he retired. His other works include *Essay toward a New Theory of Vision* (1709; 3rd edition bound with *Alciphron* in 1732), *A Treatise concerning the Principles of Human Knowledge* (1710 and 1734), *Alciphron, or the Minute Philosopher* (1732), and *Siris, a Chain of Philosophical Reflections and Inquiries concerning the Virtues of Tar-water* (1744; the title *Siris* was first used in the edition of 1746). He was an enthusiastic advocate of the use of tar water as an almost universal remedy. His firm belief in the desirability of settlement in America is reflected in his poem containing the familiar line "Westward the course of Empire takes its way."

Berkeley, Sir **George.** b. at London, April 26, 1821; d. there, Dec. 20, 1893. English engineer, an associate of Robert Stephenson (son of the great railway builder, George Stephenson) in various experiments in the building of railways. He succeeded (1859) Robert Stephenson as engineer of the Great India Peninsular Railway, and was president (1892) of the Institute of Civil Engineers.

Berkeley, George Charles Grantley Fitzhardinge. b. Feb. 10, 1800; d. at Poole, Dorsetshire, England, Feb. 23, 1881. English writer and sportsman. He was a member of Parliament from 1832 to 1852. He wrote *Berkeley Castle,* a novel (1836), *Sandron Hall, or the Days of Queen Anne* (1840), *The English Sportsman on the Western Prairies* (1861), *Anecdotes of the Upper Ten Thousand* (1867), and *Tales of Life and Death* (1870).

Berkeley, John. [Title, 1st Baron **Berkeley of Stratton.**] d. 1678. English soldier, a Royalist officer during the English Civil War. He surrendered (April 13, 1646) Exeter to Parliamentary forces under Ferdinando Fairfax on honorable terms. Placed upon the staff of the admiralty at the time of the Restoration, he was appointed (1670) lord lieutenant of Ireland, a position which he held for two years; he was also appointed (1676) ambassador at the Congress of Nijmegen, but he was forced to leave (1677) because of bad health. In 1664 he was named a proprietor of New Jersey.

Berkeley, Miles Joseph. b. in Northamptonshire, England, 1803; d. at Sibbertoft, Leicestershire, England, July 30, 1889. English botanist. A clergyman of the Anglican Church, he became vicar of Sibbertoft, near Market Harborough, in 1868. He is generally considered to have been the first English mycologist and, in his day, the most authoritative of English writers on fungi and plant pathology (he is credited with identification of some 6,000 species of fungi). He was also among the earliest investigators of potato murrain, grape mildew, hop mildew, wheat rust, and diseases of cabbage, pears, onions, and coffee. The herbarium he established at Kew, near London, containing 9,000 specimens, is an important source for the study of plant problems. He was the author of *Gleanings in British Algae* (1833), *Introduction to Cryptogamic Botany* (1857), *Outlines of British Fungology* (1860), and papers on vegetable pathology printed (1854 *et seq.*) in *Gardeners' Chronicle.* He also contributed the account of British fungi to Hooker's *British Flora* (1836).

Berkeley, Norborne. See **Botetourt,** Baron **de.**

Berkeley, Sir **William.** b. at or near London, 1606; d. in England, July 9, 1677. Royal governor of Virginia in the periods 1642–51 and 1660–76. His dictatorial policies and inability to defend his colony against Indian attacks brought on Bacon's Rebellion (a popular revolt headed by Nathaniel Bacon) in 1676.

Berkeley Castle. Norman fortress and baronial hall between Bristol and Gloucester, England. It was founded soon after the Conquest. Edward II of England was murdered at Berkeley Castle in 1327.

Berkeley House. See under **Devonshire House.**

Berkeley Springs (bėrk'li). [Official name, **Bath.**] Town in NW West Virginia, county seat of Morgan County, ab. 30 mi. E of Cumberland: mineral-spring resort. Settled c1740, it is one of the oldest resorts of its kind in the U.S. An elm planted here by George Washington, who was one of the first to popularize the spa, is still standing. 1,213 (1950).

Berkeley Square (bėrk'li, bärk'li). Three-act play (1928) by J. C. Squire and John L. Balderston. The central character, in the 1920's, gets his wish to live back in the 18th century; he takes the place of an earlier namesake, but cannot altogether fit himself into the older pattern of life.

Berkenhead (bėr'kẹn.hed), Sir **John.** See **Birkenhead,** Sir **John.**

Berkey (bėr'ki), **Charles Peter.** b. at Goshen, Ind., March 25, 1867—. American geologist. He received the degrees of B.S. (1892), M.S. (1893), and Ph.D. (1897) from the University of Minnesota. Associate professor and professor of geology (1903–41) at Columbia University, he was also named (1922) chief geologist of the American Museum of Natural History's Central Asiatic expeditions; his other posts include geologist of the Port of New York Authority, and consulting geologist to the New York Board of Water Supply (1906 *et seq.*) and to other agencies in various cities. Author of *Geology of the St. Croix Dalles, Minnesota* (1898), *A Geological Reconnaissance of Porto Rico* (1913), *Engineering Geology of the City of New York* (1933), and other works.

Berkey, Russell Stanley. b. at Goshen, Ind., Aug. 4, 1893—. American naval officer. A graduate (1916) of the U.S. Naval Academy, he was commissioned an ensign (1916), and advanced through the grades to rear admiral (1943). He was commander of the gunboat *Panay* (1933–34) in the Yangtze River, of the *Santa Fe* (1942–43) in the Pacific area, and of cruisers of the 7th fleet and Task Forces 74 and 75 (1943–45). In the battle of Suriago Strait, during the defense of Leyte beachhead, he commanded the U.S. right-flank forces.

Berkhamsted (bėrk'ạm.sted, bärk'-). [Also: **Great Berkhamsted, Great Berkhampstead.**] Urban district and market town in E central England, in Hertfordshire. It is located on the Grand Union Canal, ab. 28 mi. NW of London by rail. 10,777 (1951).

Berkhey (berk'hī), **Jan Lefrancq van.** b. at Leiden, Netherlands, Jan. 23, 1729; d. there, March 13, 1812. Dutch naturalist and poet. His chief works are *Natuurlijke historie van Holland* (1769–79), and the poem *Het verheerlijkt* (1774).

Berkley (bėrk'li). City in S Lower Michigan, in Oakland County: suburb of Detroit. In the decade between the last two U.S. censuses, the city's population more than doubled. 6,406 (1940); 17,931 (1950).

Berkman (bėrk'mạn), **Alexander.** b. at Vilna (now in Lithuania), c1870; committed suicide at Nice, France, June 28, 1936. Anarchist; colleague of Emma Goldman. He arrived in the U.S. in 1887. For having shot and stabbed the head of the Carnegie Steel Company, Henry Clay Frick, during the Homestead, Pa., strike (1892), he was confined (1892–1906) to a penitentiary. He published with Emma Goldman the anarchist magazines *Mother Earth* and *Blast.* After his conviction (1917) with Emma Goldman for obstructing conscription, he was imprisoned (1917–19), and deported (1919) to Russia; later he quarreled with Lenin and Trotsky and moved to France; he committed suicide in his home at Nice.

Berkshire (bärk'shir, bėrk'-). [Also: **Berks** (bärks, bėrks); Middle English, **Berkschire** (berk'shi.rẹ); Anglo-Saxon, **Bearrucscire, Barrucscire, Barrocscir.**] Royal county in S central England, lying inland between Gloucestershire, Oxfordshire, and Buckinghamshire on the N, Surrey on the SE, Hampshire on the S, and Wiltshire on the W. The chief occupation is farming, much of it stock or dairy farming; noted for Berkshire hogs. Industries include the manufacture of automobiles, agricultural implements, malt, and whiting. There is a large biscuit factory at Reading. County seat, Reading; area of administrative county, ab. 711 sq. mi.; pop. 288,763 (1951).

Berkshire Festivals of Chamber Music (bėrk'shir). Presentations of chamber music originated (1918) by Mrs. Elizabeth Sprague Coolidge at Pittsfield, Mass. The festivals, held annually until 1924 and irregularly thereafter, have presented many new works and several unknown instrumental groups to the public, and since 1924 have commissioned composers to write special works.

Berkshire Hills. [Called **"the Berkshires."**] Mountains in Berkshire County, W Massachusetts, noted as a summer and autumn resort. Mount Greylock is the highest point.

Berkshire Music Festival. Annual series of public concerts of Stockbridge, Mass. The concerts are sponsored by the Berkshire Symphonic Festival, Inc., a nonprofit corporation founded in 1934. The present and permanent site of the concerts is the Tanglewood estate, in Stockbridge, where a music shed has been erected. Among the conductors who have been active in the Berkshire Music Festival are Serge Koussevitzky, Leonard Bernstein, and Aaron Copland. Audiences of considerable size are drawn from all parts of Canada and the U.S.

Berkshire String Quartet. [Former name, **Kortschak Quartet of Chicago.**] Ensemble reëstablished (1917) at Pittsfield, Mass., with Mrs. Elizabeth Sprague Coolidge as patroness. Composed of Hugo Kortschak and Sergei Kotlarsky, violinists, Clarence Evans, violist, and Emmeran Stoeber, cellist, the group participated in the first and second Berkshire Festivals of Chamber Music.

Bêrlad (bėr.läd'). See **Bârlad.**

Berlage (ber'lä.chẹ), **Hendrik Petrus.** b. at Amsterdam, June 21, 1856; d. there, Aug. 12, 1934. Dutch architect, one of the pioneers in modern architecture. His principles of design were based upon a structure's function and the maintenance of harmony with the materials employed. Before opening (1889) his own office at Amsterdam, he studied in Switzerland, Italy, Austria, and Germany. He designed many commercial and office buildings and private residences in the Netherlands and Germany; best known among the former is the commodity exchange building (1898–1903) at Amsterdam. His last work, the *Gemeindehaus* (civic center) at The Hague, was completed after his death. Regarded as a leader by the younger Dutch architects, he introduced into his country an understanding of Frank Lloyd Wright's architecture. He published *Gedanken über Stil in der Baukunst* (1905).

Berle (bėr'lẹ), **Adolph Augustus, Jr.** b. at Boston, Jan. 29, 1895—. American lawyer and diplomat. He received the degrees of A.B. (1913), A.M. (1914), and LL.B. (1916) from Harvard. He served at Paris (1918–19) as a U.S. adviser and consultant to the Peace Commission, after World War I, and in 1938 became assistant U.S. secretary of state, a post he held until 1944. Thereafter he was president (1944) of the International Civil Aviation Conference at Chicago, U.S. ambassador (1945–46) to Brazil, and professor (1946 *et seq.*) at Columbia University Law School. Author of *Studies in the Law of Corporation Finance* (1928), *Cases and Materials in the Law of Corporation Finance* (1930), and *New Directions in the New World* (1940); coauthor, with G. C. Means, of *The Modern Corporation and Private Property* (1932) and, with Victoria J. Pederson, of *Liquid Claims and National Wealth* (1934).

Berlichingen (ber'lich.ing.ẹn), **Götz** (or **Gottfried**) **von.** [Sometimes called **"Götz with the Iron Hand."**] b. at Jagsthausen, Württemberg, Germany, c1480; d. at Hornberg Castle, on the Neckar River, Germany, July 23, 1562. German feudal knight. His right hand, lost at the siege of Landshut (1504) was replaced by an artificial one made of iron. He was one of the leaders of the peasant revolt in 1525, and subsequently served under the emperor Charles V against the Turks under the sultan Suleiman (the Magnificent), and also against Francis I of France. The literary revolution of the 18th century from the artificial to the realistic style was foreshadowed by Goethe's *Götz von Berlichingen* (1772), a drama which he constructed from the autobiography of the original robber-knight, who represented himself as an honest but much misunderstood person.

Berlin (bėr′lin). Town in C Connecticut, in Hartford County, on a branch of the Connecticut River, SE of New Britain: manufactures include lacquer, hardware, and industrial jewels. The first tin goods in the U.S. were manufactured here in 1740, and Berlin-made tin utensils were widely sold by peddlers. 7,470 (1950).

Berlin (bėr.lin′; German, ber.lēn′). City in NE Germany, capital of Eastern Germany and the former capital of the German Empire, the Weimar Republic, and the Third Reich, as well as of Prussia; situated on the Spree River, near its influx into the Havel River, midway between the Elbe and the Oder rivers. It is the largest city in Germany and was, prior to World War II, the largest on the European continent. It was the hub of the North German railroad system and one of Europe's chief traffic centers. Next to Duisburg-Ruhrort the largest inland port of Germany, it was the focal point of a system of canals and waterways connecting with the North Sea and Baltic ports, particularly Hamburg and Stettin, with the industrial regions of the Rhine and Ruhr, Middle Germany, and Silesia, and with the agrarian districts to the E. It has a system of subways, and a large airport at Tempelhof. Area of Russian Sector, 145.5 sq. mi.; of American, British, and French sectors combined, 188.0 sq. mi.; pop. of Russian Sector, 1,174,582; of American Sector, 979,846; of British Sector, 605,287; of French Sector, 427,755 (1946). Preliminary figures for the 1950 census were: Russian Sector, 1,189,523; Western Berlin, 2,146,952.

Industry and Commerce. Berlin was, and to some extent still is, the seat of Germany's largest banking and insurance institutions and of the leading stock exchange in Germany. It was one of the world centers of industry and commerce. The most important of Berlin's industries were the production of metallurgical, machine, and electrotechnical items, garment making, and the printing and publishing trades. About two fifths of the workers of Berlin were occupied at the huge firms of Borsig, Schwarzkopff, Ludwig Löwe, A.E.G., Siemens and Halske, Bergmann, and others, producing locomotives, railroad rolling stock and equipment, bridges, vehicles of all sorts, motors, machines, instruments, electrical apparatus, and construction materials. More than 40 percent of all German workers in the electrotechnical industry were in Berlin; more than 80 percent of all those producing electric bulbs and related articles were employed by Berlin enterprises, particularly the Osram Works. About 25 percent of German garment and lingerie production was concentrated in Berlin's numerous establishments in these fields. A similar percentage held true in the printing, publishing, and editing trades. There were also important factories producing lumber products and cigarettes, and processing furs, and a number of distilleries and breweries, among them one of the largest breweries in the world, the Schultheiss-Patzenhofer A.G. Commercially, Berlin was the leading center in Germany for the trade in textiles, grain, foodstuffs, liquors, tobacco, iron and steel products, scrap metals, and art objects, and in the fashion trade. In retail merchandising it was a pioneer in the field of department stores, such as Tietz, Wertheim, and Karstadt.

Art and Culture. Berlin has numerous educational, cultural, and scientific institutions. It is the seat of a Roman Catholic and a Lutheran bishopric, of a university, now in the Russian Sector, and of a free university in the Western Sector, with many attached institutions. There is an institute of technology; schools of commerce, agriculture, veterinary medicine, administrative science, politics, and physical culture; an art academy, conservatory of music, and numerous institutions for adult education. Berlin is the seat of a number of scientific and learned societies, such as the Akademie der Wissenschaften, Akademie der Künste, and the former Kaiser Wilhelm Gesellschaft zur Förderung der Wissenschaften. There were botanical and zoölogical gardens before World War II. Many vocational schools are located at Berlin, particularly in the metallurgical, electrotechnical, textile, and garment trades, as well as in tailoring, millinery, market gardening, and other fields. The Public Library of Berlin contains more than 2,000,000 volumes, manuscripts, and incunabula, and important collections of maps and musical documents. The university library, the municipal library, the library of the geographical society, and others are also outstanding. There are many public libraries and reading rooms in various sections of the city. What has become of the large library of the former German General Staff is not known. Berlin has a number of famous art collections: that of the Kaiser Friedrich Museum contains paintings and sculptures of the first rank and of many periods, as well as Byzantine and Islamic works; the Pergamon Museum building used to stand nearby. The National Gallery was devoted to German masters and modern art; the Old and the New Museum contained chiefly Greek, Roman, and Egyptian art and the "Kupferstich Kabinett," a collection of prints and engravings. There were museums of ethnology, of arts and crafts, of the armed forces (*Zeughaus*), of natural history, of botany, and others. Most of these collections have survived the holocaust of World War II, although the museum buildings were destroyed. Berlin has always been known for its theaters and musical culture and to some extent continues the tradition. Before World War I it was competing with Munich in this respect, and after the war was clearly in the lead. Before World War II Berlin had three opera houses and many theaters, most of which were destroyed; postwar theatrical enterprise had to start from scratch. The Berlin Philharmonic Orchestra, the orchestra of the State Opera, the *Dom-Chor* (cathedral choir), the Singakademie, and other musical groups have been able in part to regain their high level of performance.

Architecture. Pre-World War II Berlin was a sprawling city, with drab working-class sections and fashionable residential areas, busy commercial districts, and a number of remarkable examples of modern architecture, but few monuments of historical significance. Almost all of the latter are now either severely damaged or completely in ruins. Among them are the former castle of the electors of Brandenburg and kings of Prussia, the main part of which was built in the 18th century according to plans of Andreas Schlüter and Eosander von Göthe and constituted one of the best examples of German baroque and rococo architecture. Also destroyed were the Charlottenburg Castle and Castle Monbijou, also built in the 18th century, the French Church, the Hedwig-Church, the Opera House of the same period, the Central Cathedral (*Dom*), with a huge cupola of 19th-century derivation, the Neo-Romanesque Kaiser Wilhelm *Gedächtniskirche* (memorial church), the building of the German Reichstag, the Brandenburg Gate, and other structures.

History. In the early Middle Ages there were scattered Wendish and Slavic fishing villages in the region; the C part of the territory now covered by the city of Berlin was colonized by German settlers in the 13th century; their original twin cities of Berlin and Kölln are first mentioned in records dating from 1237 and 1244. The town became a member of the Hanseatic League and of local confederations of towns; from 1432 on it was subjected to the rule of the margraves of Brandenburg, of the house of Hohenzollern. It became (1486) the residence of the prince-electors of Brandenburg, under whom it accepted the Protestant Reformation. It was repeatedly occupied by Swedes and Imperialists in the Thirty Years' War. The city began to grow rapidly in the reign of Frederick William (1620–88), called the "Great Elector" of Brandenburg, and his successors in the 18th century who had accepted the title of kings of Prussia; it received an influx of Viennese Jews in 1670, of French Huguenots in considerable numbers in 1685, and later refugees from Holland, Switzerland, Bohemia, and Salzburg in addition to rural migrants from surrounding territories. New industrial and commercial activities were thus transferred to the city; numerous suburbs were added. The military occupations (1757 and 1760) during the Seven Years' War by the Austrians and Russians hardly retarded this growth. At the end of the 18th century, Berlin was the largest German city, excluding Vienna, the seat of the German enlightenment and of its counterpart, the school of Romanticism. After the battle of Jena, Napoleon I occupied (1806–08) the city; in 1810 the university was founded and became immediately the rallying ground of Prussian patriotism and German nationalism; Lessing,

Moses Mendelssohn, the Schlegel and the Humboldt brothers, Ludwig Tieck, the theologian Schleiermacher, and the philosophers Hegel and Fichte lived in Berlin in these decades of change. The prominence of Berlin among the large cities of Germany became more pronounced in the 19th century as Prussia became the dominant power among the German states. Berlin took part vigorously in the frustrated revolutionary movement of 1848. It led the opposition against the crown in the Prussian constitutional conflict of 1862–66, but its people grew enthusiastic when Bismarck's aggressive policy led to the victories of 1866 and 1870; in 1871 it was made the capital of the newly founded empire. The city again grew rapidly, and became the undisputed leader in industry, commerce, politics, and the arts and sciences. In 1878 it housed the Berlin Congress which settled the differences between England and Russia in the Near East. In 1918 it became the capital of the German Republic; it witnessed in 1919 and 1920 first communist upheavals, then the nationalist insurrection of the Kapp-Putsch, but until the end of the Republic remained true to its liberal and socialist voting traditions. Hitler's rise to power was marked by the engineered Reichstag fire of 1933. From 1933 to 1945 Berlin was the capital of the Third Reich; building activity in this period produced, among others, the huge complex of the Reichs-Chancellery and the Sport Stadium. Frequently bombed in the period 1941–45, the city became a battleground in the spring of 1945; in bitter street fighting the Russian army finally subdued and occupied the ruined city in May, 1945. Hitler, Goebbels, and other leading National Socialists had met their deaths previously. Berlin was under four-power Allied government (*Kommandantura*) until July 1, 1948, when the Russians withdrew from the administrative organization. The traffic by rail, road, and waterway of the three Western Sectors of Berlin with the Western Zones of Germany was stopped on June 18, 1948; from that date until May 12, 1949, the food and industrial supply of the Western sectors was maintained by the airlift organized by the U.S. and British governments. Two different city administrations were set up, in the Western and in the Russian sectors, and Berlin became a focal point in the "cold war." West Berlin signed the Bonn constitution, but had not yet been permitted (1951) to join the German Federal Republic. The Berlin population is unique in Germany because of its mixture of many elements. Slavic, Dutch, French Huguenot, and Jewish components played an important role in the growth of the population in the 17th, 18th, and 19th centuries; from the middle of the 19th century on, Germans from all parts of the Reich flocked to Berlin, while the foreign colonies continued to grow. Because of this background, the Berliner is said by many to combine openness of mind and quickness of wit with the preciseness and orderliness which are inherent in the Prussian tradition. The laboring people of Berlin, the majority of them organized in the Social-Democratic Party and in well-administered trade unions, are among the most industrious and reliable workers in the Western world. Under the strains caused by the destruction of war and by international tension the population decreased by 26.5 percent between 1939 and 1947.

Berlin (bėr′lin). City in N New Hampshire, in Coos County, on the Androscoggin River, ab. 90 mi. NE of Concord: manufactures include paper, especially newsprint, and artificial leather. It is a winter ski resort, and a summer center for vacationers in the White Mountains. 16,615 (1950).

Berlin. City in E Wisconsin, in Green Lake and Waushara counties. 4,693 (1950).

Berlin. Former name of **Kitchener,** Ont.

"Berlin (bėr.lin′), **Battle of."** See **"Battle of Berlin."**

Berlin, Congress of. Congress consisting of the representatives of the German Empire, Austria-Hungary, France, England, Italy, Russia, and Turkey, held at Berlin in the period of June 13–July 13, 1878, for the purpose of settling the affairs of the Balkan Peninsula. Occasioned by the dissatisfaction of England and Austria with the peace of San Stefano, concluded between Russia and Turkey on March 3, 1878, it convened at the invitation of Prince Otto von Bismarck, who was chosen president. Its most influential members were Prince Aleksandr M. Gorchakov (Russia), Count Gyula Andrássy (Austria-Hungary), Benjamin Disraeli (Great Britain), William Henry Waddington (France), Count Corti (Italy), and Karatheodori Pasha (Turkey). The outcome of the meeting was the Treaty of Berlin.

Berlin, Ellin Mackay. b. at Roslyn, Long Island, N.Y., March 22, 1903—. American novelist; wife (1926 *et seq.*) of the American composer Irving Berlin. Her novels include *Land I Have Chosen* (1944) and *Lace Curtain* (1948).

Berlin, Irving. [Original name, **Israel Baline.**] b. in Russia, May 11, 1888—. American song writer; husband (married 1926) of Ellin Mackay Berlin. He first made a hit with the song *Alexander's Ragtime Band* (1911); among his other outstandingly popular tunes are *Always*, *God Bless America*, *White Christmas*, *Easter Parade*, and *Blue Skies*. In 1918 he composed the revue *Yip Yip Yaphank*, which was performed by army personnel and was revived in 1942 under the title *This is the Army;* in it, Berlin himself sang *Oh, How I Hate to Get Up in the Morning*. Among other revues and musical comedies for which Berlin has furnished the score are several *Music Box Revues* and *Ziegfeld Follies*, *Annie Get Your Gun* (1946), and *Call Me Madam* (1950). He has also written songs for such films as *Top Hat* (1935) and *Blue Skies* (1946).

Berlin, Public Library of. [German, **Öffentliche Wissenschaftliche Bibliothek.**] Library founded by Frederick William, called the "Great Elector," and opened in 1661. Originally known as the Royal Library of Berlin, it was later called the Prussian State Library. It has been said to contain upwards of two million volumes, and collections of maps, manuscripts, and incunabula.

Berlin, Treaty of. Treaty concluded July 13, 1878, between the powers represented at the Congress of Berlin (June 13–July 13, 1878). By this treaty (1) the N part of Bulgaria was constituted an independent, autonomous, and tributary principality; (2) the S part of Bulgaria (Eastern Rumelia) was retained under the direct rule of Turkey, but was granted administrative autonomy; (3) Turkey retained the right of garrisoning the frontiers of Eastern Rumelia, but with regular troops only; (4) Turkey agreed to apply to Crete the organic law of 1868; (5) Montenegro was declared independent, and the seaport of Antivari (now Bar) was allotted to it; (6) Serbia was declared independent, and received an accession of territory; (7) Rumania was declared independent, and received some islands on the Danube in exchange for Bessarabia; (8) Kars, Batum, and Ardahan were ceded to Russia; (9) Turkey undertook to carry out without further delay the reforms required in Armenia; (10) in the event of the Greeks and the Turks not being able to agree upon a suggested rectification of frontier, the powers reserved to themselves the right of offering their mediation.

Berlin, Treaty of. Peace treaty (1921) between the U.S. and Germany signed after the U.S. Senate had rejected the Treaty of Versailles. Known as an "index-treaty," it merely referred to provisions of the Versailles Treaty. Features retained from the Versailles Treaty governed disposition of colonies, reparations agreements, disarmament, and fixed German responsibility for the war. Provisions were not included regarding boundary decisions, the International Labor Organization, and the League of Nations.

Berlin, University of. [Sometimes called the **"Friedrich Wilhelm University."**] German university founded in 1810. The largest of the German universities, it has faculties of medicine, law, theology, mathematical and natural sciences, philosophy, economics, agricultural economics, education, and forestry.

Berlin—American Sector. American-administered sector of Berlin, Germany, established after World War II, including the administrative districts of Kreuzberg, Neukölln, Tempelhof, Schöneberg, Zehlendorf, and Steglitz. Area, 81.3 sq. mi.; pop. 1,052,903 (1950).

Berlin—British Sector. British-administered sector of Berlin, Germany, established after World War II, including the administrative districts of Tiergarten, Charlottenburg, Wilmersdorf, and Spandau. Area, 63.8 sq. mi.; pop. 644,848 (1950).

Berlin Conference. Conference of the European powers, held at Berlin in the summer of 1880, to settle the boundary dispute between Turkey and Greece.

Berlin Conference. Congress of representatives from all the European nations (except Switzerland), and from the U.S., which met at Berlin in the period of Nov. 15, 1884–Jan. 30, 1885. It provided for a free-trade zone in the Congo Basin, regulated the navigation of the Niger, and laid down rules regarding the partition of Africa. It also sanctioned the International Congo Association (the later Congo Free State).

Berlin Declaration. Document signed on June 5, 1945, by General Dwight D. Eisenhower (U.S.), Marshal Georgi Konstantinovich Zhukov (U.S.S.R.), Field Marshal Bernard Law Montgomery (Great Britain), and General de Lattre de Tassigny (France), announcing the quadrupartite assumption of supreme authority over Germany. It announced also the complete cessation of hostilities and the unconditional surrender of the Germans, and ordered the disarmament of enemy troops, ships, and planes, the apprehension of designated war criminals, the release by the Germans of all prisoners of war, and the evacuation of all Germans from all territories conquered by Adolf Hitler.

Berlin Decree. Decree issued (November, 1806), by Napoleon I at Berlin, prohibiting commerce and correspondence with Great Britain, which was declared to be in a state of blockade. The decree also declared all English property forfeited, and all Englishmen in a state occupied by French troops prisoners of war.

Berliner (bėr'li.nėr), **Emile.** b. in Hanover, Germany, May 20, 1851; d. Aug. 3, 1929. American inventor. He arrived in America in 1870. His inventions and developments include the microphone, or loose-contact telephone transmitter (1877); the use (1878) of the induction coil in telephone transmitters; a gramophone (1887), also known as the Victor Talking Machine, in which the motion of the record groove propels the stylus; a method of reproducing disk records; a lightweight internal-combustion engine (1908) for airplanes; and acoustic tiles (1925) for the soundproofing of interiors.

Berlin—French Sector (bėr.lin'). French-administered sector of Berlin, Germany, established after World War II, including the administrative districts of Wedding and Reinickendorf. Area, 42.7 sq. mi.; pop. 449,201 (1950).

Berlin-Köpenick (ber.lēn'kė'pe.nik). Full name of **Köpenick.**

Berlin Memorandum (bėr.lin'). Memorandum drawn up at Berlin, on May 13, 1876, by the governments of Austria-Hungary, Russia, and Germany (which had united in presenting to Turkey, on Jan. 31, 1876, the Andrássy Note). It was approved by France and Italy, but rejected by England. It imposed an armistice of two months on Russia and Turkey, provided that the reforms promised by Turkey in accordance with the Andrássy Note should be carried out under the superintendence of the representatives of the European powers, and threatened force if before the end of the armistice Turkey should not have assented to these terms.

Berlin—Russian Sector. Russian-administered sector of Berlin, Germany, established after World War II, including the administrative districts of Mitte, Friedrichshain, Prenzlauer Berg, Pankow, Weissensee, Lichtenberg, Treptow, and Köpenick. Area, 145.5 sq. mi.; pop. 1,189,523 (1950).

Berlin to Baghdad Railway. Name now commonly given to a trans-European and Near Eastern transportation project which has had a long history and been the occasion of much international rivalry between the major powers of Europe. A railway from the Bosporus to Baghdad was first proposed by British interests around the middle of the 19th century, but the project was allowed to lapse when the British government acquired effective control of the Suez Canal. In 1889, a group of German financiers, aided by the Deutsche Bank and with official approval, revived the scheme by their formation of the Anatolian Railway Company. A line was completed (1896) to what is now Konya, Turkey, and in 1903 the Germans organized the Imperial Ottoman Baghdad Railway Company and commenced building toward Baghdad. The project was far from completed when World War I broke out in 1914, and at the close of that conflict there was still a gap of 300 miles between the line running generally SE from Konya and the terminus of the 84-mile stretch running generally N from Baghdad. The French, the Russians, and the British regarded the German operations in Anatolia and beyond with great hostility from the outset, and protested against them to the Turkish government. The British, especially, viewed the prospect of a continuous rail connection between Germany and any point in Asia as a threat to their dominant position in that region, a position secured by control of the Suez Canal which such a railway would circumvent. The rivalries, suspicions, and enmities centering around this Berlin to Baghdad rail route, which the Germans considered an essential part of their struggle for "a place in the sun," were among the causes of World War I, and among its results was the immediate suppression of the German concessions for the project. British capital thereupon took over, in the main, but the situation in the years following the war was very complex: the line was divided into sections under Turkish, Syrian, and Iraqi control, with French capital backing Syria and British capital operating through Iraq. Despite these complications the last link, connecting Basra in Iraq with the Bosporus opposite Istanbul, was completed in 1940. Thus the Middle East sections of the line are a physical reality, but the complex political situation in the countries between Berlin and Istanbul still inhibits anything like the continuously busy flow of trade which fired the imagination and enterprise of the early projectors of the project.

Berlioz (ber.lyoz; Anglicized, ber'li.ōs), **Hector.** [Full name, **Louis Hector Berlioz.**] b. at La-Côte-St.-André, Isère, France, Dec. 11, 1803; d. at Paris, March 8, 1869. French composer of great originality, noted for his contributions to the form and substance of dramatic instrumental music. Although his several works bear different subtitles, they exemplify the genre he created, which is known as the "dramatic symphony" and whose influence on later composers is not yet exhausted. Especially fruitful were his innovations in rhythm, melody, instrumentation, and structure. In addition to some half a dozen overtures and numerous songs, his chief works are, for orchestra, the *Symphonie Fantastique* (1830), *Harold in Italy* (1834), *Romeo and Juliet* (1839), and the *Funeral and Triumphal* Symphony (1840); for sacred occasions, the *Requiem* (1837), *Te Deum* (1849), and the Christmas oratorio *The Infant Christ* (1854); on dramatic themes drawn from Goethe, Shakespeare, Benvenuto Cellini, and Vergil, the *Damnation of Faust* (1846), *Beatrice and Benedict* (1862), *Benvenuto Cellini* (1838), and the monumental music drama *Les Troyens* (1858). For 30 years a music critic and theorist, he left four volumes of essays, including the lively *Evenings with the Orchestra* (1852), two volumes of *Memoirs* (1870), and the epoch-making *Treatise on Orchestration* (1844). He married (1883) the Irish actress Harriet Constance Smithson (1800–54).

Berman (ber.mäṅ; Anglicized, bėr'mạn), **Eugène.** b. at St. Petersburg, Nov. 4, 1899—. Russian painter and theatrical designer; brother of Léonide Berman. Resident in France (1919 *et seq.*) and the U.S. (1937 *et seq.*), and a leader of the neoromantic movement at Paris (1925 *et seq.*), he studied at St. Petersburg, Berlin, Munich, Paris, and in Italy. He designed settings for *The Beggar's Opera* (Paris, 1937), *Le Bourgeois Gentilhomme* (1944), and the Ballet Russe de Monte Carlo (1938). His work is in permanent New York collections (Metropolitan Museum of Art and Museum of Modern Art) and has been exhibited at the Whitney Museum (1937), Painters and Sculptors Annual (1938, Art Institute of Chicago), and elsewhere.

Berman, Léonide (or **Léonid**). b. at St. Petersburg, 1896—. Russian landscape and marine painter, residing in France; brother of Eugène Berman. He exhibited at the Salon d'Automne between 1923 and 1926, and later won prizes for *The Boats* (1927), *Port* (1929), *Portrait of a Woman* (1929), and other works. In order to avoid confusion with his brother, he often dispenses with his surname in signing his work.

Bermejo (ber.mā'hō). [Also: **Vermejo, Río Grande**; Spanish **Río Bermejo.**] River in S central S America, a W branch of the Paraguay River, rising in Bolivia, flowing SE through the Gran Chaco plains of Argentina, and joining the Paraguay River shortly above the junction of the latter with the Paraná River. The middle and lower portions spread out in swamps in which the channel is nearly lost. Length, ab. 1,000 mi.

Bermeo (ber.mā′ō). Town in N Spain, in the province of Vizcaya, situated on the Bay of Biscay, ab. 15 mi. NE of Bilbao: a fishing port with large-scale fisheries and fish-canning industries. 11,739 (1940).

Bermondsey (bėr′mọn.zi, -mọnd-). Metropolitan borough in SE London, in the County of London, situated on the S side of the river Thames, opposite the borough of Stepney. It is a crowded district chiefly occupied by tanners and is London's market place for hides and skins; it also has extensive wharves and wool storehouses. Bermondsey suffered heavily from aerial bombardment in World War II. Out of 19,529 buildings existing in 1939, only 730 remained undamaged at the end of the war. Among the buildings destroyed or seriously damaged were the Bermondsey Town Hall, the Rotherhithe Library building, and the Rotherhithe Museum. Bermondsey formerly contained a royal country palace, which was occupied by Henry II, and a Cluniac abbey founded in 1082. Portions of this abbey were still standing at the beginning of the 19th century. Before the Norman Conquest Bermondsey belonged to Harold, and was a royal domain until 1094, when William Rufus gave it to the priory of Saint Mary. 60,661 (1951).

Bermondsey Spa Gardens. Place of entertainment, at London, in the time of George II, about two miles from London Bridge.

Bermoothes (bėr.mö′ᴛʜez). An old name for Bermuda. It is the name of the island in Shakespeare's *The Tempest.*

Bermuda (bėr.mū′dạ). [Also: **Bermuda Islands, Bermudas**; former names, **Bermoothes, Somers** (or **Summers** or **Summer**) **Islands.**] Group of islands in the Atlantic Ocean, extending over a distance of 22 mi., ab. 650 mi. SE of Cape Hatteras, N.C., and ab. 700 mi. SE of New York: a British colony. The chief islands are Bermuda (or Great Bermuda), Somerset, Ireland, and St. George. The chief enterprise is the tourist trade; flowers, bananas, vegetables, and lily bulbs are exported. The islands were discovered by Juan Bermudez before 1515, and settled by the English about 100 years later. The shipwreck (1609) here of Sir George Somers and a group of colonists may have been used by Shakespeare as material for *The Tempest.* The English crown took over the colony from a private company in 1684. The U.S. leased air and naval bases here in 1940 and 1941. Capital: Hamilton; area, ab. 20 sq. mi.; pop. 37,254 (est. 1950).

Bermuda Agreement. Anglo-American agreement on commercial air transport services between Great Britain and the U.S. concluded at Bermuda on Feb. 11, 1946. It represented a compromise between the British protectionist and the American free-trade theories of the development of air services, which had clashed earlier at the Chicago Civil Aviation Conference. The Bermuda agreement provided for fixed air routes, joint rate approval by the two governments, and standards for review of competitive conditions.

Bermuda Hundred. Village on a bend of the James River in Virginia, near City Point. The peninsula was occupied by part of the Union army under Butler in the summer of 1864 as a base of operations. For part of the time the troops were hemmed in within the lines ("bottled at Bermuda Hundred").

Bermudas (bėr.mū′dạz). Name given to a group of alleys and courts between the bottom of St. Martin's Lane, Half Moon, and Chandos Street, in London; a resort and refuge of thieves, fraudulent debtors, and prostitutes in the 16th and 17th centuries. The area was also called (in the 17th century) the Streights and the Caribbee (corrupted into Cribbee) Islands, and the names were often applied to other localities of similar character.

Bermúdez (ber.mö′ᴛʜeth) or **Bermudes** (-ᴛʜes), **Geronimo.** b. in Galicia, c1530; d. c1589. Spanish Dominican friar (professor of theology at Salamanca), poet, and dramatist. He wrote *Nise Lastimosa* (1577), *Nise Laureada* (in both of these "Nise" is an anagram of "Ines"), and other works.

Bermúdez (ber.mö′ᴛʜes), **José Francisco.** b. at Cumaná, Venezuela, Jan. 23, 1782; assassinated there, Dec. 15, 1831. Venezuelan general in the war for independence. He defended Cartagena against Pablo Morillo in 1815, until forced by famine to withdraw. In May, 1820, he took Caracas, and on Oct. 16, 1821, occupied Cumaná after a bloody siege. He subsequently commanded at Cumaná and elsewhere.

Bermúdez, José Manuel. b. at Tarma, Peru, c1760; d. at Lima, Peru, 1830. Peruvian ecclesiastic, historian, philologist, and orator. He was vicar of Huánuco, and after 1803 held various Church offices at Lima; from 1819 he was chancellor of the University of San Marcos. In 1821 he was a member of the *junta de pacificación,* appointed with the hope of conciliating the revolutionists.

Bermúdez, Pedro Pablo. b. at Tacna, Peru, 1798; d. at Lima, Peru, 1852. Peruvian general. In 1833 he was Augustín Gamarra's candidate for president, and, having lost the election, joined Gamarra in a revolt (Jan. 4, 1834), but was defeated and driven into Bolivia. He then joined Andréz Santa Cruz, and, on the formation (1836) of the short-lived Peru-Bolivian confederation, was elected vice-president of North Peru.

Bermúdez, Remijio Morales. See **Morales Bermúdez, Remijio.**

Bern (bėrn; German, bern). [French, **Berne** (bern); Italian, **Berna** (ber′nä).] Canton in W and C Switzerland, bounded by France (Belfort and Haut-Rhin departments) on the N, Basel, Solothurn, Aargau, Lucerne, Unterwalden, and Uri on the E, Valais on the S, and Vaud, Fribourg, Neuchâtel, and again France (Doubs department) on the W. It is traversed by the Jura and Alps, and contains the Bernese Oberland in the S. It is the largest canton in point of population, and sends 33 representatives to the Swiss national council. The prevailing religion is Protestant, the prevailing language German. It entered the Swiss Confederation, as the eighth canton, in 1353. Capital, Bern; area, 2,658 sq. mi.; pop. 798,264 (1950).

Bern. [French, **Berne;** Italian, **Berna.**] City in W Switzerland, the capital of the canton of Bern and the seat of the government of the Swiss Confederation, situated on both banks of the Aare River. The old part has a picturesque situation and medieval appearance; there are numerous old fountains and the streets are flanked with arcades. Bern is a trade center for cheese, wine, coal, and cattle; it also has weaving and spinning industries and manufactures machinery and chocolate. The Gothic *Münster* (cathedral) was built in 1421–1596, its tower finished in 1893; it has a celebrated organ. The *Rathaus* (town hall), dating from 1406, was later restored; the *Bundespalast* (palace of the federal council) is a modern building. Bern has a theater, a university, an industrial school, and municipal and university libraries. One of the chief tourist attractions is a pit in which bears (Bern's heraldic symbol) are kept. There are splendid views of the Alps from various points in the city. Bern was founded by Duke Berchthold V of Zähringen in 1191, granted self-government by the German emperor Frederick II in 1218, and joined the Swiss Confederation in 1353. It embraced the Reformation in 1528; became the seat of the Swiss government and the federal assembly in 1848. Headquarters of the International Telegraphic Union have been at Bern since 1869, those of the International Postal Union since 1874; the Bern Convention on international copyright was signed in 1886. Pop. 145,740 (1950).

Bern (bern), **Dietrich von.** See **Dietrich von Bern.**

Bernabei (ber.nä.bā′ē), **Ercole.** b. at Caprarola, Italy, c1620; d. at Munich, Germany, 1687. Italian composer and *Kapellmeister* (choir leader); father of Gioseffo Antonio Bernabei (c1649–1732). He served at the Lateran at Rome, and at Munich under the Bavarian Elector. Among his compositions are operas, church music, and many madrigals.

Bernabei, Gioseffo Antonio. b. at Rome, c1649; d. March 9, 1732. Italian composer, notably of operas; son of Ercole Bernabei (1620–87), whom he followed as court musician at Munich.

Bernacchi (ber.näk′kē), **Antonio.** b. at Bologna, Italy, in June, 1685; d. in March, 1756. Italian singer and teacher, noted for his performances in Handel's works, first appearing (1717) as Goffredo in *Rinaldo.* He later (1736) founded a music school in Italy, where Joseph Joachim Raff was among his pupils.

Bernacchi, Cape. Low rocky promontory in Antarctica, forming the N entrance point to New Harbor, on the coast of Victoria Land, in ab. 77°30′ S., 163°45′ E. It was discovered by the National Antarctic Expedition (1901–04), under the leadership of Captain Robert F. Scott, who named this cape for Louis C. Bernacchi, physicist with the expedition.

Bernacchi Bay. Bay in Antarctica, lying between Marble Point and Cape Bernacchi along the coast of Victoria Land, in ab. 77°28′ S., 163°47′ E. The bay takes its name from Cape Bernacchi, S entrance to the bay, which was named by the National Antarctic Expedition (1901–04), commanded by Captain Robert F. Scott, for Louis C. Bernacchi, physicist with the expedition. Width, ab. 3 mi.

Bernacchi Head. Precipitous cliff in Antarctica, forming the SE extremity of Franklin Island, in the Ross Sea, in ab. 76°07′ S., 168°20′ E. Franklin Island was discovered and named by Sir James Clark Ross in 1841. The island was visited again in February, 1900, by the *Southern Cross*, under the command of C. E. Borchgrevink, who named this point for Louis C. Bernacchi, a member of the expedition.

Bernadette (bėr.nạ.det′; French, ber.nȧ.det), Saint. [Also: **Bernadette of Lourdes** (lörd, lördz; French, lörd); original name, **Marie Bernarde Soubirous** (or **Soubiroux**); in religion, Sister **Marie-Bernard.**] b. at Lourdes, Hautes-Pyrénées, France, Jan. 7, 1844; d. at Nevers, Nièvre, France, April 16, 1879. Roman Catholic saint, a French girl who reported visions of the Virgin Mary at Lourdes. The first apparition of the Virgin reported by this pious French maiden was on Feb. 11, 1858, when she was 14 years of age. The total number of apparitions was 18, the last occurring on July 16, 1858. The Virgin, Bernadette reported, appeared to her in a hollow of the rock known as Massabielle, as a "young and beautiful lady." Others accompanied Bernadette to the rock but could not see the apparition, nor could any but she hear it speak. Bernadette, who often manifested ecstasy during her interviews with the apparition, declared that the Virgin instructed her to make known that the waters of a fountain in the grotto would, by the Virgin's grace, possess miraculous powers of healing human illnesses and infirmities. It is said that the existence of such a fountain was previously entirely unknown, but that it gushed forth when the Virgin spoke. Bernadette, on the Virgin's instructions, told the priests at Lourdes of her visions and transmitted the Virgin's instructions that they should build a chapel at the grotto. In 1862 the bishop of the diocese declared that the faithful could believe in the reality of the apparition. A church was built, and later replaced by a much larger structure when the pilgrims, who began coming to Lourdes in 1873, became very numerous. In 1866 Bernadette became a novice of the Sisters of Charity at Nevers, and took perpetual vows in 1878. She was beatified in 1925 and canonized in 1933. Her feast day is celebrated on Feb. 11, the anniversary of her first vision of the Virgin Mary.

Bernadotte (ber.nä.dôt′; Anglicized, bėr′nạ.dot), Count **Folke.** [Full name, Count **Folke Bernadotte of Wisborg.**] b. at Stockholm, Jan. 2, 1895; assassinated at Jerusalem, Sept. 17, 1948. Swedish statesman, a member of the Swedish royal family; nephew of King Gustaf V of Sweden. He is best known for his role (May 20–Sept. 17, 1948) as United Nations mediator in Palestine. He was assassinated by Jewish terrorists while seeking to end Jewish-Arab hostilities. He served (1915–39) in the Swedish army, rising to the rank of major, was named (1939) Swedish commissioner to the New York World's Fair, and was active (1943 *et seq.*) in the Swedish Red Cross, becoming its president in 1946. As a Red Cross official, he arranged for the exchange of ill and disabled prisoners of war between Britain and Germany, as well as the release of Danish and Norwegian nationals from German concentration camps. In the final months of World War II, he acted (February–May, 1945) as a peace emissary, transmitting German surrender offers from Heinrich Himmler to the British and Americans. Among his publications are *Slutet* (1945; Eng. trans., *The Curtain Falls*, 1945), *Människor jag mött* (1947), and *I Stället för vapen* (1947).

Bernadotte, Jean Baptiste Jules. Original name of **Charles XIV** (of *Sweden and Norway*).

Bernál (bėr.näl′), **Peak of.** [Also, **Bernal Hill.**] Steep truncated cone which rises above the outlet of the upper Pecos River valley in C New Mexico. It also bears the name of "Starvation Peak," from a tradition that several Spanish soldiers were starved to death on its summit by the Apaches.

Bernalda (ber.näl′dä). Town and commune in S Italy, in the *compartimento* (region) of Calabria, in the province of Matera, ab. 33 mi. SW of Taranto. It is the center of a grain-exporting district. Pop. of commune, 8,380 (1936); of town, 7,735 (1936).

Bernaldez (ber.näl′deth) or **Bernal** (ber.näl′), **Andres.** [Called **"El Cura de Los Palacios,"** meaning "the curate of Los Palacios."] b. c1450; d. probably at Los Palacios, near Seville, Spain, c1513. Spanish historian. Having taken orders, he was chaplain to the Archbishop of Seville, and from 1488 to 1513 curate of the village of Los Palacios near Seville. He was a friend of Christopher Columbus, and in 1496 entertained him at his house. It appears that the admiral gave him much information, orally and in writing, which Bernaldez used in his *Historia de los Reyes Católicos*. His work, particularly valuable with regard to Columbus and his voyages, was long used by historians in manuscript copies. It was first printed at Granada in 1856.

Bernalillo (bėr.nạ.lē′yō). Village in C New Mexico, county seat of Sandoval County, on the Rio Grande, ab. 18 mi. N of Albuquerque: cattle trading and shipping center. There were several villages of the Tigua Indians on or about the site, all of which were later abandoned. The first white settlement (1698) was made by descendants of Bernal Díaz del Castillo, soldier and historian of the conquest of Mexico, at or near the site of the headquarters (1540–42) of Coronado. 1,922 (1950).

Bernal Osborne (bėr′nạl oz′bọrn), **Ralph.** b. March 26, 1808; d. in England, June 21, 1880. English politician noted for his wit.

Bernanos (ber.nȧ.nōs), **Georges.** [Full name, **Paul Louis Georges Bernanos.**] b. at Paris, May 5, 1888; d. there, July 5, 1948. French novelist and essayist. Educated in Jesuit schools and at the Catholic Institute at Paris, he served with distinction throughout World War I, and became an insurance inspector, but wrote little until 1926, when he published *Sous le soleil de Satan* (Eng. trans., *The Star of Satan*, 1940). Five subsequent novels, of which the most widely known is *Journal d'un curé de campagne* (1936; Eng. trans., *Diary of a Country Priest*, 1937), are spiritual dramas of sin and salvation. Angered by the support which French Catholics gave to General Francisco Franco during the Spanish Civil War, he also published *Les Grands Cimetières sous la lune* (1938; Eng. trans., *A Diary of My Times*, 1938), which critics have called a masterpiece of moral indignation.

Bernard (bėr′nạrd, bėr.närd′), Saint. See Saint **Bernard of Clairvaux,** Saint **Bernard of Menthon,** and Saint **Berward.**

Bernard (bėr′nạrd). Sheep in *Reynard the Fox.*

Bernard (bėr.närd′). An old man in *The Waves*, by Virginia Woolf.

Bernard (ber.nȧr), **Claude.** [Called **"The Poor Priest."**] b. at Dijon, France, 1588; d. March 23, 1640. French monk who devoted his fortune and his life to the service of the poor.

Bernard, Claude. b. at St.-Julien, Rhône, France, July 12, 1813; d. at Paris, Feb. 10, 1878. French physiologist. He was a pioneer in certain chemical phenomena of medicine, particularly in connection with digestion, and studied the glycogenic function of the liver, the function of the pancreas, and the workings of the sympathetic nervous system. He published *Recherches sur les usages du pancréas*, *Recherches d'anatomie et de physiologie comparées sur les glandes salivaires*, *Recherches sur les fonctions du nerf spinal*, *Mémoire sur le suc gastrique et son rôle dans la digestion*, and other works.

Bernard (bėr′nạrd), **Edward.** b. at Perry St. Paul, Northamptonshire, England, May 2, 1638; d. at Oxford, England, Jan. 12, 1697. English scholar. He was Savilian professor of astronomy at Oxford in the period 1673–91.

Bernard, Sir Francis. b. in England, in July, 1712; d. at Aylesbury, England, June 16, 1779. English lawyer and politician, colonial governor of the New Jersey (1758–60) and of the Massachusetts Bay (1760–69) colonies; father of Sir Thomas Bernard (1750–1818). He was recalled

(1769) to England after arousing much colonial hostility by his rigorous execution of British government policy.

Bernard (ber.när), **Jacques.** b. at Nions, in Dauphiné, France, Sept. 1, 1658; d. April 27, 1718. French Protestant clergyman and scholar. On the revocation of the Edict of Nantes he retired to Holland, and founded at The Hague a school of belles-lettres, philosophy, and mathematics. He continued the publication of the *Bibliothèque Universelle* of Jean Le Clerc, and succeeded Pierre Bayle as editor of *République des Lettres.* He wrote *Recueil de traités de paix, de trêves, de neutralité, . . . et d'autres actes publics faits en Europe* (1700), *Actes et mémoires des négociations de la paix de Ryswick* (1725), and others.

Bernard, Jean Jacques. b. at Enghien-les-Bains, France, July 30, 1888—. French playwright and novelist of the "theater of silence" group; son of Tristan Bernard (1866–1947). His plays, quiet comedies which leave the audience to infer much that is left unexpressed, include *La Maison épargnée* (1919), *Le Feu qui reprend mal* (1921), *Invitation au voyage* (1924; Eng. trans., *Glamour*, 1927, also *Invitation to a Voyage*, 1939), *L'Ame en peine* (1926; Eng. trans., *The Unquiet Spirit*, 1932), *National 6* (1935), and *Louise de la Vallière* (1945).

Bernard (bėr'nạrd), **John.** b. at Portsmouth, England, 1756; d. at London, 1828. English actor; father of William Bayle Bernard (1807–75). He made his first appearance in England in 1773. In 1797 he came to America, where he remained as an actor and manager until 1819.

Bernard, Mountague. b. in Gloucestershire, England, Jan. 28, 1820; d. at Overross, England, Sept. 2, 1882. English lawyer, first professor of international law (1859–74) at Oxford University. One of the high commissioners who negotiated the Treaty of Washington (1871), at which it was decided to submit the Alabama claims to the Geneva tribunal, he was in the following year one of the counsels of the British government at Geneva.

Bernard (ber.när; Anglicized, bėr.närd'), **Simon.** b. at Dôle, France, April 28, 1779; d. Nov. 5, 1839. French general and engineer, in the service of Napoleon I, and later (1816–31) of the U.S. He was minister of war (1836–39) under Louis Philippe. His chief work in the U.S. is Fort Monroe; he had a part in other important engineering works, notably the Chesapeake and Ohio Canal.

Bernard (bėr'nạrd), Sir **Thomas.** b. at Lincoln, England, April 27, 1750; d. July 1, 1818. English philanthropist and lawyer; son of Sir Francis Bernard (1711–79). Treasurer (1795–1806) and vice-president (1806 *et seq.*) of the Foundling Hospital at London, he established (1805) the Institution for the Promotion of Fine Arts in the United Kingdom, and founded (1808) the Barrington School for teachers.

Bernard (ber.när), **Tristan.** [Original name, **Paul Bernard.**] b. at Besançon, France, Sept. 7, 1866; d. 1947. French playwright and novelist, noted for his melancholy and sometimes sardonic humor; father of Jean Jacques Bernard. Although he began his career as a contributor, with Léon Blum and others, to the serious *Revue blanche*, his first successes were a light novel, *Les Mémoires d'un jeune homme rangé*, and a comedy, *L'Anglais tel qu'on le parle* (both 1899). Subsequent comedies, all exploiting stock comic situations and immensely popular, include *Daisy* (1902), *Triplepatte* (1905), *Le Petit Café* (1911), and *Le Prince charmant* (1921), and have overshadowed his less hilarious novels, such as *Le Mari pacifique* (1901).

Bernard (bėr'nạrd), **William Bayle.** b. at Boston, Mass., Nov. 27, 1807; d. at Brighton, England, Aug. 5, 1875. English dramatist; son of John Bernard (1756–1828). His chief plays are *Rip Van Winkle* (1832), *The Nervous Man* (1833), *The Boarding School* (1841), and *The Round of Wrong.*

Bernard Délicieux (ber.när dā.lē.syė). [Latinized, **Bernardus Deliciosus.**] b. at Montpellier, France, in the latter half of the 13th century; d. 1320. French ecclesiastic, a member of the Franciscan order. He early became an opponent of the methods of the Inquisition (at the very outset this was probably a phase of the fierce rivalry between the Dominicans, who controlled the Inquisition, and the Franciscans) and during the papal interregnum of 1304–05 he led in petitioning the college of cardinals and the king of France against the excesses of the inquisitors. Obtaining no help, he negotiated for Aragonese help against the French. This was treason, and Bernard owed his life for years thereafter largely to the mercy of Pope Clement V, who tried vainly to repress the inquisitors. However, after the election of Pope John XXII in 1316, Bernard's fate was sealed. Accused (among other things) of having killed Pope Benedict XI in 1304 by poison or sorcery, he was thrown into prison, formally tried, and twice tortured. (In connection with this last, it is interesting to note that he is said to have asserted publicly that "Saints Peter and Paul would not be able to defend themselves from heresy if they were now alive and they were examined in the fashion followed by the inquisitors.") Nevertheless, it would be a mistake to think of Bernard as a defender of free thought in the modern sense; he was a bitter opponent of inquisitorial arbitrariness, injustice, and cruelty, but in all other matters involving his faith he was orthodox and obedient.

Bernardes (bėr.när'dẹs), **Artur** (or **Arthur**) **da Silva.** b. at Viçosa, Minas Gerais, Brazil, Aug. 18, 1875—. Brazilian politician, president (1922–26) of Brazil. He received the degree of LL.B. (1900) from the University of São Paulo. Having served as federal deputy (1909) and, later, as a federal senator, he became secretary of finance and later (1918–22) was president of the state of Minas Gerais. Exiled (1932–34) from Brazil, he was named (1934) professor of Brazilian studies at the University of Lisbon.

Bernardes (bėr.när'dẹsh), **Diogo.** [Full name, **Diogo Bernardes Pimenta.**] b. at Ponte de Lima, Portugal, c1530; d. c1605. Portuguese poet. Attaching himself in his youth to the poet and playwright Sá de Miranda, Bernardes later became one of the most productive poets of the Renaissance in Portugal. His poems are mostly of bucolic character and are notably melodious. His best-known books are *Varias Rimas ao Bom Jesús* (Various Rhymes of the Good Jesus, 1594), *O Lima* (The Lima, 1596), and *Rimas Varias: Flores do Lima* (Various Rhymes: Flowers from the Banks of the Lima, 1596). From his devotion to the small stream flowing through his native place, he has been called "The Sweet Singer of the Lima." In his later years Bernardes was the beneficiary of a pension from Philip II of Spain.

Bernardes, Padre Manuel. b. at Lisbon, Portugal, Aug. 20, 1644; d. there, Aug. 17, 1710. Portuguese prose writer, regarded by many critics as the supreme master of Portuguese ascetic literature. Among his most famous works were *Luz e Calor* (1696), *Nova floresta* (5 vols., 1706–28), *Sermoes e práticas* (1st part, 1711; 2nd part, 1733), and *Os últimos fins do homem* (uncompleted; posthumously published, 1728).

Bernard Horne (bėr'nạrd hôrn), **Mount.** See **Horne, Mount.**

Bernardin de Saint-Pierre (ber.när.dañ dẹ sañ pyer), **Jacques Henri.** b. at Le Havre, France, Jan. 19, 1737; d. at Éragny-sur-Oise, France, Jan. 21, 1814. French author. He was an engineer in Russia, and on the Île de France (now known as Mauritius) in the period 1767–71, before settling at Paris in 1771. A friend of Jean Jacques Rousseau, he was much influenced by him. His chief works are *Voyage à l'Île de France*, *Études de la nature* (1784–88), the romantic novel *Paul et Virginie* (1788), *La Chaumière indienne* (1791), and *Harmonies de la nature* (1815).

Bernardino of Siena (ber.när.dē'nō; sye'nä), Saint. b. at Massa di Carrara, in Tuscany, 1380; d. 1444. Franciscan monk, famous as a preacher. He was made vicar-general of the order in 1438, and restored the rigid rule of Saint Francis of Assisi.

Bernardo (bėr.när'dō). Danish officer in Shakespeare's *Hamlet.* It is he, with Marcellus, who first sees the murdered king's ghost.

Bernardo del Carpio (ber.när'dō del kär'pyō). fl. 9th century. Legendary Spanish hero. A nephew of Alfonso II (the Chaste), he is said to have fought with great distinction against the Moors, and, according to one tradition, defeated Roland at Roncesvalles. His exploits are celebrated in many Spanish ballads, and form the subject of several dramas by Lope de Vega.

Bernard of Chartres (bėr'nạrd, bėr.närd'; French, ber-när; shär'trẹ; French, shärtr). b. in Brittany, in the latter part of the 11th century; d. probably at Chartres, France, c1126. French philosopher, teacher, and ecclesiastic, notable as the first great master of the school at Chartres. His works are now all lost, yet such was his influence that he remains still famous (one of his pupils said of him that he was the "most abounding spring of letters in Gaul in modern times" and the "most perfect Platonist of his age"; the latter statement may seem odd, considering that Bernard's knowledge of Plato was of necessity very limited, and yet it is true in a deeper sense: what little we know of his life has a genuinely Platonic ring, and because of his gentleness he may be said to be closer to Plato than any other medieval philosopher). Bernard and his followers sought to reconcile Plato and Aristotle, but their attempt was based on a double misunderstanding (their knowledge of the former was essentially restricted to the *Timaeus*, and that of the latter to his logic). Nevertheless, and imperfect as it is, this philosophy is perhaps the most impressive episode in the history of Platonism between the Byzantine renaissance of the second half of the 11th century and the Florentine revival in the second half of the 15th century. One of the statements attributed to Bernard is of particular interest to modern historians of science: "In comparison with the ancients we stand like dwarfs on the shoulders of the giants." A similar saying is ascribed to Newton, and the attitude it implies in the case of Bernard is, however vaguely, some understanding of the cumulative nature of science.

Bernard of Clairvaux (kler.vō), Saint. b. at Fontaines, near Dijon, France, 1090; d. at Clairvaux, France, Aug. 20, 1153. French monastic reformer, scholar, and Doctor of the Church (so named by Pope Pius VIII). He entered the Cistercian monastery of Cîteaux in 1113, and in 1115 became abbot of Clairvaux, near Langres, which post he continued to fill until his death. Refusing all offers of preferment, he nevertheless exercised a profound influence on the ecclesiastical politics of Europe, and was the chief instrument in prevailing upon France and England to recognize Innocent II as Pope in opposition to the rival claimant, Cardinal Peter of León. He procured the condemnation of Abelard's writings at the Council of Sens in 1140, and preached on behalf of the second Crusade in 1146.

Bernard of Cluny or **of Morlaix** (klö'ni; môr.lā'). fl. 12th century. French Benedictine monk, author of a Latin poem *De Contemptu Mundi* popularly known through John Mason Neale's translations into the three hymns: *The World Is Very Evil, Jerusalem the Golden,* and *For Thee, O Dear, Dear Country.*

Bernard of Menthon (mäṅ.tôṅ), Saint. [Called the **"Apostle of the Alps."**] b. in Savoy, 923; d. at Novara, in Piedmont, May 28, 1008. Roman Catholic priest, archdeacon of Aosta. He labored among the people of the Pennine Alps, founded the Hospices of the Little and Great St. Bernard passes (which derived their names from him), and established a community of Hospitallers to give aid to travelers in the Alps. He is the patron saint of mountain climbers.

Bernard of Treviso (trā.vē'zō). [Assumed title, Count of the **March of Treviso.**] b. at Padua, Italy, 1406; d. 1490. Italian alchemist. After many years of study and experiment, he is said to have declared that the secret of the philosopher's stone lay in the adage "To make gold one must have gold." He was the author of many works on alchemy.

Bernardone (ber.när.dō'nā), **Giovanni Francesco.** See Saint **Francis of Assisi.**

Bernardo of Seminara (ber.när'dō; sem.i.nä'rä). See **Barlaam.**

Bernard Silvester (bėr'nąrd, bėr.närd'; sil.ves'tėr). [Also: **Silvestris, Sylvester,** or **Sylvestris.**] fl. at Tours, France, c1145–53. French philosophical poet. His chief work is the *De mundi universitate* (or *Cosmographia*), written in mixed verse and prose. The fact that this work is based chiefly on Plato's *Timaeus,* and certain Neoplatonic writings, has caused its writer to be confused in some sources with the much more famous Bernard of Chartres (who lived at approximately the same time and was also known for his interest in Platonic thought).

Bernardsville (bėr'nąrdz.vil). [Original name, **Vealtown.**] Borough in N New Jersey, in Somerset County, W of Newark, near Mine Mountain. 3,956 (1950).

Bernau (ber'nou). Town in NE Germany, in the *Land* (state) of Brandenburg, Russian Zone, formerly in the province of Brandenburg, Prussia, NE of Berlin. It belongs to the metropolitan region of Berlin; has glove manufactures and other industries. The Gothic *Marienkirche* (Church of Mary) was consecrated in 1519. Pop. 12,984 (1946).

Bernauer (ber'nou.ėr), **Agnes.** Killed at Straubing, Bavaria, Oct. 12, 1435. The daughter of an Augsburg tradesman, who was secretly married to Albert, son of Duke Ernest of Bavaria. She was thereupon drowned in the Danube as a witch by order of the enraged duke. Her story forms the subject of many tragedies and poems in German literature.

Bernay (ber.ne). Town in N France, in the department of Eure, situated on the Charentonne River, ab. 35 mi. SW of Rouen. It is the center of the dairy and textile industries of the region; holds an annual horse fair. 8,174 (1946).

Bernays (ber'nīs), **Michael.** b. at Hamburg, Germany, Nov. 27, 1834; d. at Karlsruhe, Germany, Feb. 25, 1897. German historian of literature, professor (1873–90) at the University of Munich. He was especially known as a Goethe scholar, and was the editor of the standard three-volume source work, *Der junge Goethe* (1875).

Bernburg (bern'bůrk). City in C Germany, in the *Land* (state) of Saxony-Anhalt, Russian Zone, situated on the Saale River, ab. 44 mi. NW of Leipzig. It owes its importance to the salt and potash mines in the vicinity, and to the chemical industries based on these materials. Before World War II it was the seat of the German Solvay Works, and also had a number of metallurgical industries, large-scale airplane production, stone quarries, and a number of small industries. On the right bank of the Saale River is a 17th-century castle and castle church; on the left bank is the town hall and the former monastery of the Servants of Mary; founded in the 14th century as a Catholic institution, it was transformed into a hospital when the town adopted (1535) Protestantism; there are also the Gothic *Marienkirche* (Church of Mary; 11th–15th centuries) and the *Nikolaikirche* (Church of Saint Nicholas; 14th–15th centuries). The city has various educational institutions, a library, theater, and local museum. Founded in the 12th century by the princes of Anhalt on the site of an earlier settlement, Bernburg remained their residence until 1468 and served the same function in the period 1603–1863. It was of commercial importance because of its location at the crossing of the navigable Saale River and the road leading from Leipzig via Halle to Magdeburg. It was twice occupied by the Swedes in the Thirty Years' War. During World War II the city was subjected to frequent bombardments, and considerable damage was done. The increase of population between 1939 and 1946 amounted to 31 percent. 53,367 (1946).

Bern Conference (bėrn; German, bern). International socialist meeting in February, 1919. It was the first full post-war conference of the Second International, with delegates from 26 countries. The concrete accomplishments of the meeting were sparse because of the sharp feeling which still existed against the Germans, who were the traditional bulwark of the organization, and broad divisions as to the nature of political tactics that should be pursued.

Berndorf (bern'dôrf). Town in E Austria, in the province of Lower Austria, situated on the Triesting River, in the hills of the Wienerwald, SE of Vienna. It has a large silverplating factory, the Berndorfer Metallwarenfabrik A.G., formerly belonging to the Arthur Krupp Werke in Essen, Germany, and after World War II put under government control. 9,117 (1946).

Berne (bern). French name of **Bern.**

Berne-Bellecour (bern.bel.kör), **Étienne Prosper.** b. at Boulogne, France, June 29, 1838; d. at Paris, Nov. 29, 1910. French painter, especially of military subjects.

Berneker (ber'ne.kėr), **Erich.** b. at Königsberg, Germany, Feb. 3, 1874—. German Slavic scholar. He served as professor (1902 *et seq.*) at the universities of Prague, Breslau, and Munich. Author of *Russische Grammatik* (Russian Grammar, 1897; 3rd ed., 1927), *Graf Leo Tolstoy* (Count Leo Tolstoy, 1900), and *Slavisches etymologisches Wörterbuch* (Slavic Etymological Dictionary, 1908–14).

Berner Oberland (ber'nėr ō'bėr.länt). German name of the **Bernese Oberland.**

Berners (bėr′nėrz), 2nd Baron. Title of **Bourchier, John.**

Berners, 14th Baron. Title of **Tyrwhitt-Wilson, Gerald Hugh.**

Berners (bėr′nėrz) or **Bernes** (bėrnz), **Juliana.** [Also, **Barnes.**] b. c1388; date of death not known. English-woman, said to have been a prioress of Sopwell Nunnery, near St. Albans, England, and reputed author of *The Boke of St. Albans* (printed 1486; 2nd ed., 1496), a rhymed treatise on hunting and fishing.

Berner Seeland (ber′nėr zā′länt). German name of the **Bernese Seeland.**

Bernese Oberland (bėr.nēz′, -nēs′, ō′bėr.länt). [Also: **Bernese Alps;** German, **Berner Oberland;** sometimes called the **Oberland.**] Mountainous region in the S part of the canton of Bern, Switzerland, famous for its picturesque scenery. It contains such tourist centers as Interlaken, Grindelwald, and Meiringen, and the Jungfrau, Finsteraarhorn, and other peaks.

Bernese Seeland (zā′länt). [Also: **Bernese Zealand** (zē′lạnd); German, **Berner Seeland.**] Name given to a district in W Switzerland, in the canton of Bern, situated between the Lake of Neuchâtel and the canton of Solothurn.

Bernetti (ber.nāt′tē), **Tommaso.** b. at Fermo, Italy, Dec. 29, 1779; d. there, March 21, 1852. Italian cardinal and papal statesman. He was secretary of state from 1828 to 1836.

Bernhard (bern′härt). [Title, Duke of **Saxe-Weimar.**] b. at Weimar, Germany, Aug. 16, 1604; d. at Neuenburg, Germany, July 18, 1639. German general who served on the side of the Protestants in the Thirty Years' War. Having at first served under Christian IV of Denmark, he joined (1631) Gustavus Adolphus of Sweden, after whose death (Nov. 16, 1632) during the Battle of Lutzen he assumed command and is credited by many with the victory won on that day. Commander of a Swedish army in S Germany, he captured (1633) Regensburg, but was defeated (1634) at Nördlingen; in consequence of this defeat, he lost the duchy of Franconia (which he had held under the Swedish crown). In 1635 he joined the French, with the expectation of being given another duchy in Alsace. He was twice victorious in 1638, at Rheinfelden and at the capture of Breisach.

Bernhard, Georg. [Pseudonyms: **Plutus, Gracchus.**] b. at Berlin, Dec. 20, 1875; d. in exile, 1944. German journalist. At Berlin, he was editor-in-chief (1914–30) of the *Vossische Zeitung* and professor of economics at a school of commerce. He was a member (1928–30) of the Reichstag. Forced to emigrate after 1933, he edited the German-language emigré *Tageblatt* at Paris until 1940. Author of *Die Börse* (1906) and *Wirtschaftsparlamente* (1926).

Bernhard, Karl. [Pseudonym of **Andreas Nicolai de Saint-Aubin.**] b. Nov. 18, 1798; d. at Copenhagen, Nov. 25, 1865. Danish novelist. He was the author of *A Year in Copenhagen* (1835) and others.

Bernhardi (bern.här′dē), **Friedrich von.** b. at St. Petersburg, Nov. 22, 1849; d. at Kunnersdorf, Germany, July 10, 1930. German army officer and military writer. A follower of Heinrich von Treitschke (1834–96), he was in charge of the military history department of the German general staff at Berlin. His chief book, *Deutschland und der nächste Krieg* (1912; Eng. trans., *Germany and the Next War*, 1914), was accepted abroad as proof of Germany's aggressive plans. Bernhardi is considered the spiritual leader of Pan-Germanism. During World War I he served on both the eastern and western fronts, and took part in the battle of Armentières, in April, 1918.

Bernhard of Lippe-Biesterfeld (bern′härt; lip′ẹ.bē′stėr-felt), Prince. [Full name, **Bernhard Leopold Friedrich Eberhard Julius Kurt Gottfried Peter.**] b. at Jena, Germany, June 29, 1911—. Husband of Queen Juliana of the Netherlands; married at The Hague, Jan. 7, 1937. During the German occupation of the Netherlands in World War II, he acted as chief Dutch liaison officer with the Allied forces. He became (1945) chief inspector of the Royal Netherlands army.

Bernhardt (bėrn′härt; French, ber.nȧr), **Sarah.** [Original name, **Rosine Bernard;** called **"the Divine Sarah."**] b. at Paris, 1844; d. there, March 26, 1923. French actress. Born of a Dutch and Jewish family which had embraced Catholicism, she was brought up in a convent. At 13 she began her theatrical training at the Paris Conservatoire and made her debut at the Comédie Française in 1862. She soon left the company to try her career in burlesque, but failed because she could not sing in tune. Her first success came six years later at the Odéon in Jean Racine's *Athalie.* During the Franco-Prussian War, while the theaters were closed, she worked as an ambulance nurse. She returned to the Odéon in 1872 and played Cordelia in Shakespeare's *King Lear* and the Queen in Victor Hugo's *Ruy Blas.* Two years later, she went back to the Comédie Française and scored a triumph in Racine's *Phèdre;* three years later she won acclaim with her playing of Doña Sol in Hugo's *Hernani.* She made a first American tour in 1880 and five more by 1906. She found some of her most successful roles in Victorien Sardou's *Tosca, Froufrou* by Henri Meilhac and Ludovic Halévy, and the younger Alexandre Dumas's *La Dame aux Camélias;* she also played the male leads in Edmond Rostand's *L'Aiglon* and in *Hamlet.* In 1912, she made a short film, *Queen Elizabeth,* and became the first great actress to appear in the at that time infant medium of the motion picture. In 1915 one of her legs was amputated because of an old stage injury, but she went on acting, even going to the front to play for the French soldiers in World War I. Her final American tour was in 1918, and her last continental tour was in 1922.

Berni (ber′nē), **Francesco.** [Also: **Berna** (-nä), **Bernia** (-nē.ä).] b. at Lamporecchio, in Tuscany, c1497; d. at Florence, May 26, 1535. Italian poet, author of *Rime burlesche,* and a *rifacimento* (new version) of the *Orlando Innamorato* by Matteo Maria Boiardo (1541). His poetry is marked by a tone of "light and elegant mockery," for which his name has furnished the descriptive adjective "bernesque."

Bernice (bėr.nēs′). Play (1920) by Susan Glaspell. It contains an ingenious analysis of a woman who has died before the beginning of the action, her character being reflected in the gestures and the speeches of her relatives and friends.

Bernicia (bėr.nish′i.ạ). Anglian kingdom of the 6th century, located along the coast of the North Sea in NE England and SE Scotland. It extended from the Tees to the Forth, and was united with Deira to form Northumbria. The capital was at what is now Bamburgh.

Bernier (ber.nyā), **François.** b. at Angers, France; d. at Paris, Sept. 22, 1688. French physician, philosophical writer, traveler in the East (Syria, Egypt, India), and court physician to Aurangzeb, one of the Mogul emperors of India. He was the author of *Abrégé de la philosophie de Gassendi* (1678; enlarged 1684), *Voyages de Bernier* (1699), and other books.

Bernina (ber.nē′nä). Group of the Alps in the S part of the canton of Graubünden, Switzerland, on the Italian border. The highest point is the Piz Bernina (13,295 ft.).

Bernina Pass. Pass over the Alps, traversed by a road and railroad, leading from Samaden in the Engadine valley, Switzerland, to Tirano in the Valtellina, Italy. Elevation, 7,645 ft.

Berninghaus (bėr′ning.hous), **Oscar Edmund.** b. at St. Louis, Mo., Oct. 2, 1874; d. at Taos, N.M., April 27, 1952. American painter, notably of the Southwest. He studied at the St. Louis School of Fine Arts, and has exhibited throughout the U.S., winning prizes at the National Academy of Design (New York), at St. Louis, and at Chicago. Many of his paintings hang in permanent collections, including those of the City Art Museum at St. Louis, the Fort Worth Museum, the Los Angeles Museum, the San Diego Museum, and several libraries and schools. He executed a series of lunettes on the Missouri state capitol, and murals in the U.S. post office at Phoenix, Ariz.

Bernini (ber.nē′nē), **Giovanni Lorenzo.** b. at Naples, Italy, Dec. 7, 1598; d. at Rome, Nov. 28, 1680. Italian architect, sculptor, and painter, patronized particularly by Pope Urban VIII and King Louis XIV of France. On the death of Carlo Maderna, he was appointed (1629) architect of Saint Peter's Church at Rome. Between 1629 and 1667 he designed the forecourt and four rows of colonnades adorning the piazza in front of the church, and for the high altar in the nave. In 1665 he visited France at the request of Louis XIV and Colbert, and made designs for the east front of the Louvre. Construction was begun but abandoned. He made the Versailles bust of Louis XIV. In the pontificate of Clement IX he completed the southern porch of the cortile of Saint Peter's and the parapet and statues of the bridge of Sant'Angelo. Under Clement X he was made architect to the palace of the Quirinal. One of his best-known sculptures is *Apollo and Daphne* (Borghese Gallery, Rome).

Bernis (ber.nēs), **François Joachim de Pierre de.** b. at St.-Marcel, Ardèche, France, May 22, 1715; d. at Rome, Nov. 2, 1794. French cardinal, statesman, diplomat, and poet. Under Louis XV of France, he was ambassador (1752) to Venice, before serving (1757–58) as foreign minister. He was held responsible by some influential persons for the unfortunate political position in which France found itself, and was sent into exile in 1758, not being recalled until 1764. In 1769 he was made ambassador to Rome; there he effected the suppression of the Jesuits in France. His verses were admired by Voltaire.

Bernoulli (French, ber.nö.yē; German, ber.nö'lē), **Christophe.** [Also, **Bernouilli.**] b. at Basel, Switzerland, May 15, 1782; d. Feb. 6, 1863. Swiss technologist; grandnephew of Daniel Bernoulli (1700–82). He was professor of natural history at the University of Basel in the period 1817–61.

Bernoulli, Daniel. [Also, **Bernouilli.**] b. at Groningen, Netherlands, Jan. 29, 1700; d. March 17, 1782. Swiss mathematician and physicist; son of Jean Bernoulli (1667–1748), and great-uncle of Christophe Bernoulli (1782–1863). He became professor of anatomy and botany at the University of Basel in 1733, and professor of physics in 1750. His chief work is a treatise on hydrodynamics.

Bernoulli, Jacques. [Also, **Bernouilli.**] b. at Basel, Switzerland, Dec. 27, 1654; d. there, Aug. 16, 1705. Swiss mathematician, professor of mathematics at the University of Basel in the period 1687–1705; brother of Jean Bernoulli (1667–1748). He improved the differential calculus invented by Gottfried Wilhelm von Leibnitz and Isaac Newton, solved the isoperimetrical problem, and discovered the properties of the logarithmic spiral.

Bernoulli, Jean. [Also, **Bernouilli.**] b. at Basel, Switzerland, July 27, 1667; d. there, Jan. 1, 1748. Swiss mathematician and physicist known for his work on calculus; brother of Jacques Bernoulli (1654–1705), and father of Jean Bernoulli (1710–90). He became professor of mathematics at Groningen in 1695, and at the University of Basel in 1705.

Bernoulli, Jean. [Also, **Bernouilli.**] b. at Basel, Switzerland, May 18, 1710; d. there, July 17, 1790. Swiss jurist and mathematician; son of Jean Bernoulli (1667–1748). He was professor of rhetoric at Basel in the period 1743–48, and later of mathematics.

Bernoulli, Johann Jakob. b. at Basel, Switzerland, Jan. 18, 1831; d. there, July 22, 1913. Swiss archaeologist. He served as professor (1895 *et seq.*) at the University of Basel. Author of *Römische Ikonographie* (Roman Iconography, 1882–91) and *Griechische Ikonographie* (Greek Iconography, 1901).

Bernoulli, Karl Albrecht. b. at Basel, Switzerland, 1868—. Swiss scholar and author writing in German. He studied theology, and became professor of church history at the University of Basel. The long list of his publications includes scholarly works and short stories, novels, poems, and patriotic plays such as *Ulrich Zwingli* (1905) and *Der Meisterschütze* (1915).

Bernstein (bern'shtīn), **Eduard.** b. at Berlin, Jan. 6, 1850; d. there, Dec. 18, 1932. German socialist and author. He was a political revisionist who advocated the evolutionary (rather than revolutionary) path to Marxian socialism. Resident for a time in Switzerland while Germany's laws forbade the activities of Socialists, he edited (until 1888) at Zurich the periodical *Sozial-Demokrat.* Having moved to London, he encountered the policies of Fabianism, and was influenced by them toward his revisionist standpoint. After the repeal of the German antisocialist legislation he returned there, to serve (1902–06) as a member of the Reichstag. He founded *Dokumente des Sozialismus,* and wrote *Sozialismus und Demokratie in der englischen Revision* (2nd ed., 1908), *Entwicklung eines Sozialisten* (1930), and others.

Bernstein (bern.sten), **Henry Léon Gustave Charles.** b. at Paris, 1876—. French dramatist, known especially for violent plays about cynical, brutal characters. After the dramas responsible for his reputation, such as *La Rafale* (1905), *La Griffe* (1906), and *Samson* (1907), he turned to dramas of character analysis, like *Le Secret* (1913) and *La Galerie des glaces* (1924). In still later plays, such as *Espoir* (1934), he explores social problems.

Bernstein (bėrn'stīn), **Herman.** b. at Neustadt-Scherwindt, Russia, Sept. 21, 1876; d. at Sheffield, Mass., Aug. 31, 1935. American journalist and author, noted for publishing (1918) the so-called Willy-Nicky telegrams (which comprised a secret correspondence between the German kaiser and the Russian czar). Having been a special correspondent in Europe (1908, 1909, 1911, 1912) for the New York *Times,* he went to Russia (1917, 1918) and Paris (1919) for the New York *Herald;* he was a founder (1914) and editor (1914–16) of *The Day,* a Jewish newspaper at New York, and editor of *The American Hebrew* (1916–19) and *The Jewish Tribune* (1923–28). As envoy extraordinary and minister plenipotentiary (1930–33) from the U.S. to Albania, he negotiated a naturalization treaty (1931) and an extradition treaty (1932) with that country. Author of *The Flight of Time* (1899), a book of poems, and of *In the Gates of Israel* (1902), *Contrite Hearts* (1905), *Celebrities of Our Time* (1925), consisting of interviews, and *The History of a Lie* (1921), which exposed the forgery of the *Protocols of the Wise Men of Zion;* translator of Russian works and adapter of Russian and German plays.

Bernstein (bėrn'stēn), **Theresa Ferber.** b. at Philadelphia, 1903—. American painter of portraits, figures, and landscapes. She studied at Philadelphia and at the Art Students League of New York, and has exhibited her paintings throughout the U.S. Her work has won several prizes, and is represented in many permanent collections. She has lectured on art and on mural painting, and has written articles for newspapers and museum bulletins. A list of her better known works includes portraits of several justices of the U.S. Supreme Court (H. F. Stone, Felix Frankfurter, and Owen Roberts), as well as *Portrait of Albert Einstein, First Orchestra in America, Home of James Monroe, Gloucester Wharves, Girl in Cap, Girlhood,* and *Garnersville—July 4.*

Bernstorff (bern'shtôrf), Count **Andreas Peter von.** b. at Gartow, near Lüneburg, Germany, Aug. 28, 1735; d. at Copenhagen, June 21, 1797. Danish statesman; nephew of Johann Hartwig Ernst von Bernstorff. He served as minister of foreign affairs (1773–80) and as prime minister (1784–97). In the latter post, he supported many reforms, including the abolition of laws which maintained the right of Danish landowners to hold their peasants in serfdom. During his term as foreign minister, he concluded agreements with Russia and other European powers; his temporary dismissal from all office in the period from 1780 to 1784 was a political measure designed to win Russian approval (his lack of enthusiasm as foreign minister for any diplomatic agreement which might tend to jeopardize Danish freedom of action had run counter to Russian ambitions in the area of the Baltic Sea).

Bernstorff, Count **Johann Hartwig Ernst von.** b. at Hanover, Germany, May 13, 1712; d. at Hamburg, Germany, Feb. 18, 1772. Danish statesman, minister of foreign affairs (1751–70), called by Frederick II of Prussia (Frederick the Great) "the Oracle of Denmark"; uncle of Andreas Peter von Bernstorff. He entered the service of Denmark and was sent (1744) as ambassador to Paris; he was later (1751) appointed foreign minister, serving in this capacity until 1770. He maintained a neutral policy for Denmark, preventing the country from involvement in the Seven Years' War. His dismissal was accomplished by Johann Friedrich von Struensee.

Bernstorff, Count **Johann Heinrich von.** b. at London, Nov. 14, 1862; d. at Geneva, Switzerland, Oct. 6, 1939. German diplomat. He entered the German foreign service in 1899, and served at Belgrade, Dresden, St. Petersburg, and Munich, and then as counselor at the German embassy at London. He came (1908) to Washington as German ambassador, remaining there until the U.S. entered World War I. He unsuccessfully warned his government against the initiation of an unrestricted submarine campaign. After the American declaration of war (1917) he was sent as ambassador to Constantinople. From 1920 to 1928 he was a Democratic member of the Reichstag. He was active in postwar disarmament negotiations, and was chairman of the German League of Nations Union until Adolf Hitler's rise to power, when he went into exile.

Berntsen (bernt'sen), **Klaus.** b. at Eskilstrup, Denmark, June 12, 1884; d. at Copenhagen, March 27, 1927. Danish political leader and educator, whose premiership (1910–13) ended when he failed to obtain the passage of democratic election reforms. Elected (1873) to the *Folketing* (lower chamber of the Danish parliament), he served (1908–09) as minister of the interior; he also held (1920–22) the post of minister of defense, and was (1922–24) minister without portfolio.

Bernward (bėrn'wạrd), Saint. See Saint **Berward.**

Berodach-baladan (bẹ.rō'dak.bal'ạ.dan, ber'ọ.dak-). See under **Merodach-baladan.**

Beroea (bẹ.rē'ạ). Ancient name of **Aleppo.**

Berosus (bẹ.rō'sus) or **Berossus** (-ros'us). fl. early 3rd century B.C. Babylonian priest and historian, author of a history of Babylonia (in Greek), fragments of which have been preserved by later writers, including Eusebius and Josephus.

Beroun (be'rōn). [German, **Beraun.**] Town in Czechoslovakia, in W central Bohemia, situated at the junction of the Litavka and Berounka rivers, ab. 15 mi. SW of Prague, between Prague and Plzen. It has textile, machine, and sugar factories, a sawmill, and a flour mill. There are medieval architectural remains. 12,345 (1947).

Beroun. [Also: **Moravský Beroun;** German, **Bärn.**] Town in Czechoslovakia, in N Moravia, ab. 16 mi. NE of Olomouc. 1,957 (1947).

Berounka (be'rōng.kä). [German, **Beraun.**] River in Bohemia, Czechoslovakia, which joins the Vltava (Moldau) River S of Prague. Length, ab. 100 mi.

Berquin (ber.kaṅ), **Arnaud.** [Called the **"Friend of Children."**] b. at Langoiran, near Bordeaux, France, c1749; d. at Paris, Dec. 21, 1791. French man of letters, especially noted as a prolific writer of works for children. Best-known of his works are *L'Ami des enfants* (24 vols., 1782–83) and *Le Petit Grandison* (1807).

Berra (ber'rä). Town and commune in N Italy, in the *compartimento* (region) of Emilia-Romagna, in the province of Ferrara, situated on the Po Grande River, NE of Ferrara: center of an agricultural district in the Po delta. Pop. of commune, 11,397 (1936); of town, 1,774 (1936).

Berredo e Castro (ber.rā'dö ē käsh'trö), **Bernardo Pereira de.** b. at Serpa, Alentejo, Portugal, c1688; d. at Lisbon, March 13, 1748. Portuguese soldier, statesman, and historian. From 1718 to 1722 he was governor of Maranhão, which at that time included all of N Brazil; he was later captain-general of Mazagão, in Africa. His *Annaes historicos do estado de Maranhão* (Lisbon, 1749; 2nd ed., Maranhão, 1849) is a principal source of historical information for that part of Brazil.

Berre-L'Étang (ber.lā.täṅ). [Also, **Berre** (ber).] Port town in SE France, in the department of Bouches-du-Rhône, situated on the N shore of the Étang-de-Berre (a lagoon of the Gulf of Lions), between Marseilles and Arles. It has an oil refinery. Salt is found nearby. 5,859 (1946).

Berrettini (ber.rāt.tē'nē), **Pietro.** Original name of **Cortona, Pietro da.**

Berri (ber'i; French, be.rē). See **Berry.**

Berrien (ber'i.ẹn), **John Macpherson.** b. in New Jersey, Aug. 23, 1781; d. at Savannah, Ga., Jan. 1, 1856. American lawyer and politician. He was attorney general of the U.S. (1829–31), and a U.S. senator from Georgia (1825–29, 1841–52).

Berro (ber'rō), **Bernardo Prudencio.** b. at Montevideo, Uruguay, c1800; killed there, in April, 1868. Uruguayan politician and journalist. He was president of the country in the period 1860–64.

Berruguete (ber.rö.gā'tā), **Alonso.** b. c1481; d. 1561. Spanish sculptor, painter, and architect. As a young man he studied under Michelangelo at Rome. Upon his return to Spain he became court painter and sculptor to Charles V. Berruguete did much to make Spanish art responsive to the influence of the Italian Renaissance, and yet, in the opinion of most critics, his own work, vigorous and strong and highly individual, is thoroughly Spanish. He is best remembered for his sculpture in wood, especially such works as the altar screens he executed for the Church of San Benito el Real, which are now in the museum at Valladolid, and the choir stalls of the Toledo cathedral. His marble tomb of Cardinal Tavera at Toledo is also famous.

Berry (ber'i; French, be.rē). [Also: **Berri;** ancient name, **Biturica.**] Region and former government in C France, the land of the Gallic Bituriges. It was bounded by Orléanais on the N, Nivernais on the E, Bourbonnais on the SE, Marche on the S, Poitou on the W, and Touraine on the NW, and is chiefly included in the modern departments of Indre and Cher. It was formerly a county and duchy, and was frequently an appanage of the king's younger son. It was united to the crown in 1465 and again in 1601.

"Berry" (ber'i). See **Berinthia.**

Berry (ber'i), **Agnes.** b. at Kirkbridge, Yorkshire, England, 1764; d. 1852. English literary figure; sister, and close companion for 48 years, of Mary Berry (1763–1852). Horace Walpole bequeathed (1797) to the sisters a building on his famous estate of Strawberry Hill (at Twickenham, England), volumes of his published works, and manuscripts of his unpublished works.

Berry (be.rē), **Charles,** Duc **de.** b. Dec. 28, 1446; d. May 24 or 28, 1472. Duke of Berry, Normandy, and Guienne; second son of Charles VII of France and Marie of Anjou.

Berry, Charles, Duc **de.** b. Aug. 31, 1686; d. at Marly, France, May 4, 1714. Third son of Louis, the Grand Dauphin. He was selected as successor to the Spanish throne in case the duke of Anjou, named his successor by Charles II of France, should become king of France.

Berry, Charles Ferdinand, Duc **de.** b. at Versailles, France, Jan. 24, 1778; assassinated at Paris, Feb. 13. 1820. French royalist; second son of the Comte d'Artois (later Charles X of France), and father of Henri, Comte de Chambord. He emigrated during the Revolution, and served in the army of Louis Joseph de Bourbon, Prince de Condé, and later in that of Russia. He went to England in 1801, and there married a wife whom he afterward repudiated. On his return to France, he married the princess Caroline Ferdinande Louise of Naples.

Berry, Duchesse **de.** [Maiden name, Princess **Caroline Ferdinande Louise** of Naples.] b. Nov. 5, 1798; d. April 17, 1870. Wife of Charles Ferdinand, Duc de Berry, and mother of Henri, Comte de Chambord. She promoted an unsuccessful attempt at revolution in favor of her son in 1832.

Berry (ber'i), **Edward Wilber.** b. at Newark, N.J., Feb. 10, 1875; d. Sept. 20, 1945. American paleontologist. He was appointed associate professor of paleontology at the Johns Hopkins University, Baltimore, in 1913, and professor in 1917. He was associated as a geologist with the U.S. Geological Survey from 1910 to his death, and was assistant state geologist of Maryland from 1917 to 1942. In 1901 he was awarded the Walker prize of the Boston Society of Natural History. He served terms as president of the Paleontological Society of America and of the Geological Society of America, and was a member of other American and foreign scientific groups. In addition to contributing more than 500 articles on paleontological, biological, and geological subjects to scientific periodicals, he was the author of *Lower Cretaceous of Maryland* (1911), *Eocene Floras of Southeastern North America* (1916), *Tree Ancestors* (1923), and *Paleontology* (1929).

Berry, Hiram Gregory. b. at or near what is now Rockland, Me., Aug. 27, 1824; killed in action at Chancellorsville, Va., May 3, 1863. American army officer, with the Union army in the Civil War. He served as a brigadier general at the battles of Williamsburg (May 5, 1862) and Fair Oaks (May 31–June 1, 1862), as a major general (1862) at Fredericksburg, and as commander of a division (1863) at Chancellorsville.

Berry, James Henderson. b. in Jackson County, Ala., May 15, 1841; d. Jan. 30, 1913. American politician. He was governor (1882 *et seq.*) of Arkansas and later (1885–1907) a U.S. senator.

Berry, Sir John. b. at Knoweston, Devonshire, England, 1635; d. at Portsmouth, England, c1690. English naval officer. At first an officer in the merchant service, he entered the royal navy in 1663, and attained the rank of vice-admiral. In 1667 he defeated the French and Dutch fleets off the island of Nevis, in the West Indies. In 1682 he commanded the *Gloucester*, which was wrecked with the duke of York and his entourage on board; however, the duke escaped harm, and Berry was exonerated of blame for the disaster.

Berry (be.rē), **Marie Louise Elisabeth d'Orléans,** Duchesse **de.** b. Aug. 20, 1695; d. July 21, 1719. Eldest daughter of Philippe d'Orléans, and wife of the duke of Berry, the grandson of Louis XIV.

Berry (ber'i), **Martha McChesney.** b. near Rome, Ga., Oct. 7, 1866; d. in Georgia, Feb. 27, 1942. American educator, founder of the Berry Schools for poverty-stricken children of mountain districts in and around Georgia. Her first school, opened in 1902, for five pupils with two teachers, has since developed into a group of three schools and a college, occupying more than 30,000 acres near Rome, Ga., where students work for their tuition. She received more than one million dollars in donations from Henry Ford, was awarded (1925), by President Coolidge, the Roosevelt memorial medal for patriotic services, was voted (1931) one of the 12 greatest American women by a nationwide poll, and received (1940) a humanitarian award from the Variety Clubs of America.

Berry, Mary. b. at Kirkbridge, Yorkshire, England, March 16, 1763; d. at London, Nov. 20, 1852. English literary figure. She and her sister Agnes (1764–1852) were friends of Horace Walpole, and she was one of his literary executors. Her chief work is *Social Life in England and France, 1660–1830* (2 vols., 1828, 1831).

Berry, Nathaniel Springer. b. at Bath, Me., Sept. 1, 1796; d. April 27, 1894. American politician, governor (1861–63) of New Hampshire. Identified first with the Democratic Party, he later joined the Free Soil Party, and finally the Republican Party, as a local leader in the antislavery movement.

Berry, Richard James Arthur. b. at Upholland, Lancashire, England, May 30, 1867—. British anatomist. He was professor (1905–29) of anatomy at the medical school of the Royal College at Edinburgh, and wrote *A Cerebral Atlas of Normal and Defective Brains* (1938), *Your Brain and Its Story* (1939), and *Brain and Mind, or the Nervous System of Man* (1928).

Berry, William. b. 1774; d. at Brixton, England, July 2, 1851. English genealogist. He published *Introduction to Heraldry* (1810), *Genealogia Antiqua* (1816), *Encyclopædia Heraldica* (1828–40), and others.

Berryer (be.ryā), **Pierre Antoine.** b. at Paris, Jan. 4, 1790; d. Nov. 29, 1868. French lawyer and political orator. He was one of the lawyers who defended Marshal Ney after the fall of the regime of Napoleon I, but is now perhaps best known for his lifelong espousal of the so-called Legitimist cause (the faction in 19th-century French politics that supported the descendants of Louis XVIII as the rightful rulers of France).

Bersimis (ber.sē.mē'). River in S central Quebec, Canada, flowing from the interior plateau S and SE to the St. Lawrence estuary ab. 200 mi. NE of Quebec city. It is navigable to the first falls, 35 mi. from its mouth. There is salmon and sea trout fishing in the lower river. Length, ab. 240 mi.

Bert (ber), **Paul.** b. at Auxerre, Yonne, France, Oct. 17, 1833; d. in Tonkin, in Indochina, Nov. 11, 1886. French physiologist and politician, minister of public instruction and worship in Gambetta's cabinet (1881–82). He was resident governor of Annam (which then included Tonkin for administrative purposes) in 1886. He wrote *Revue des travaux d'anatomie et de physiologie, 1864* (1866), *Notes d'anatomie et de physiologie comparées*, and others.

Berta (ber'tä). African people inhabiting W Ethiopia and the SE part of Blue Nile province in E Anglo-Egyptian Sudan, in NE Africa, E and S of the Blue Nile River. A second group of Berta dialects is found in the area of the Blue Nile province.

Bertaut (ber.tō), **Jean.** b. at Caen, France, 1552; d. June 8, 1611. French ecclesiastic and poet. He served at various times as secretary to the king, bishop of Séez, and almoner to Marie de' Médici.

Bertha (bėr'thą) or **Berthrada** (bėr.thrā'dą). [Italian and Spanish, **Berta** (ber'tä); French, **Berthe** (bert); nicknamed **Berthe au grand pied** (ō grän pyā), meaning "Bertha with the large foot."] d. at Choisy, France, 783, at an advanced age. Frankish queen; daughter of Caribert, count of Laon; one of her feet was larger than the other. She was the wife of Pepin the Short and the mother of Charlemagne. She has been celebrated by many poems and Carolingian legends. Some romances have made her the daughter of an emperor of Constantinople; others make her descend from Flore, a king of Hungary, and his queen, Blanche-Fleur. One, by Adenet ("le Roi"), is rhymed, and was written in the second half of the 13th century from popular legends which go back to the 8th century.

Bertha (bėr'thą). [Known as **Gertrude.**] Daughter of the Duke of Brabant in *The Beggar's Bush*, a comedy by John Fletcher and others.

Bertha, Big. See **Big Bertha.**

Berthelot (ber.tę.lō), **Henri Mathias.** b. at Feurs, Loire, France, Dec. 7, 1861; d. at Paris, Jan. 29, 1931. French army officer who took a leading part in drawing up the plan of operations ("Plan 17") followed by the French army at the outbreak of World War I. He reorganized (1917) the Rumanian army as chief of a French mission, commanded (1918) a French army, and after the war was named French governor of Strasbourg and a member of the superior war council.

Berthelot, Marcelin Pierre Eugène. b. at Paris, 1827; d. there, 1907. French chemist and statesman; father of Philippe Berthelot. He accomplished many of the very early syntheses of organic chemistry, being the first to synthesize (from inorganic sources) methane, acetylene, formic acid, ethanol, benzene, and others. He was a professor at the École supérieure de Pharmacie (1859–61) and at the Collège de France (1861–1907). He served also as life senator (1881–1907), minister of public instruction (1886–87), and minister of foreign affairs (1895–96). He was winner of the Davy medal in 1900.

Berthelot, Philippe. b. at Sèvres, Seine-et-Oise, France, Oct. 9, 1866; d. at Paris, Nov. 22, 1934. French diplomat; son of Marcelin P. E. Berthelot. He entered the diplomatic service in 1889, served (1904–23, 1925–32) at the Quai d'Orsay (the French foreign office), and was named (1920) general secretary of the foreign ministry.

Berthier (ber.tyā), **Louis Alexandre.** [Titles: Duke of **Valangin,** Prince of **Neuchâtel** and of **Wagram.**] b. at Versailles, France, Nov. 20, 1753; d. at Bamberg, Germany, June 1, 1815. French soldier, marshal of the French empire, and confidential friend of Napoleon I. He served in the American Revolution under Lafayette, and in Egypt and Italy with Napoleon; later (1814) he supported Louis XVIII. His *Mémoires* were published in 1827.

Berthold of Lokkum (or **Loccum**) (ber'tolt). [Called the **"Apostle of Livonia."**] d. July 24, 1198. Abbot of the Cistercian monastery of Loccum who was consecrated (1196) bishop of the Livonians, to succeed Meinhard, the first missionary in Livonia. He raised an army in Lower Germany for the purpose of converting the heathen by force of arms, and was killed in battle near the mouth of the Dvina River.

Berthold of Ratisbon (rat'is.bon). b. c1220; d. at Ratisbon (Regensburg), Germany, Dec. 13, 1272. German Franciscan preacher and missionary in Austria, Moravia, Thuringia, and elsewhere.

Bertholet (ber.to.le), **Alfred.** b. at Basel, Switzerland, Nov. 9, 1868—. Swiss Protestant theologian. Educated at the universities of Basel, Strasbourg, and Berlin, he became (1928) professor and, later, professor emeritus at the University of Berlin. Known for his commentaries on the Old Testament, he edited *Die Heilige Schrift des Alten Testaments* (1922). Author of *Die Stellung des Israeliten und der Juden zu den Fremden* (1896), *Kulturgeschichte Israels* (1911), *Das Geschlecht der Gottheit* (1934), and *Über kultische Motivverschiebungen* (1938).

Berthollet (ber.to.le), **Claude Louis,** Comte. b. near Talloire, in Savoy, Dec. 9, 1748; d. near Paris, Nov. 6, 1822. French chemist, professor in the normal school at Paris. He was among those who, with Antoine Lavoisier, worked out the system of chemical nomenclature which forms the basis of the system used today. He made studies in the relationship of chemical affinity to the speed of chemical reactions, discovered the composition of ammonia, and developed one of the earliest bleaching solutions. He joined Napoleon's Egyptian expedition, returning in 1799. His works include *Essai de statique chimique*, *Éléments de l'art de la teinture*, and *Méthode de nomenclature chimique* (1787; with Lavoisier).

Berthoud (ber.tö). French name of **Burgdorf,** Switzerland.

Berthoud, Ferdinand. b. at Neuchâtel, Switzerland, March 19, 1727; d. June 20, 1807. Swiss mechanician, noted for the accuracy of his chronometers. He was the author of *Essai sur l'horlogerie* (1765), *Traité des horloges marines* (1773), *Longitudes par la mesure du temps . . .* (1775), and others.

Bertie (bär'ti), **Francis Leveson.** [Title, 1st Viscount **Bertie of Thame.**] b. at Wytham Abbey, Berkshire, England, Aug. 17, 1844; d. at London, Sept. 26, 1919. English diplomat. Attached (1863–1903) to the British Foreign Office, Bertie served as senior clerk (1889–94), and as assistant under-secretary of state (1894–1903) for foreign affairs. Thereafter he was ambassador (1903–04) to Rome, and (1906–18) to Paris, and was influential in preserving the Anglo-French alliance. The diary which he kept while in Paris was edited and published (1924) under the title *The Diary of Lord Bertie of Thame 1914–1918*.

Bertie, Peregrine. [Title, Baron **Willoughby de Eresby.**] b. at Cleve, Germany, Oct. 12, 1555; d. June 25, 1601. English soldier and statesman. He served (1586–89) with distinction against the Spanish in the Low Countries, being appointed Sir Philip Sidney's successor as governor of Bergen-op-Zoom in March, 1586, and succeeding Robert Sidney, 1st Earl of Leicester, as commander in chief in November, 1587. Later he served under Henry IV of France (Henry of Navarre).

Bertie, Willoughby. [Title, 4th Earl of **Abingdon.**] b. Jan. 16, 1740; d. Sept. 26, 1799. English liberal statesman and political writer. He opposed his country's participation in the Revolutionary War, and the policy which led to it, and sympathized with the French Revolution. He wrote *Thoughts of Mr. Burke's Letter to the Sheriffs of Bristol on the Affairs of America* (1777) and others.

Bertillon (ber.tē.yôn; Anglicized, bėr.til'yon), **Alphonse.** b. at Paris, April 22, 1853; d. there, Feb. 3, 1914. French anthropologist, chief of the department of identification in the prefecture of police of the Seine, at Paris. He devised the so-called Bertillon system, a method of identifying criminals by means of anthropometric measurements. He wrote *L'Anthropométrie judiciaire* (1890), *Identification anthropométrique* (1893), *La Comparison des écritures et l'identification graphique* (1897), *Anthropologie métrique et photographique* (1909, with Dr. A. Chervin), and others.

Bertin (ber.tañ), **Édouard François.** b. at Paris, 1797; d. there, Sept. 13, 1871. French journalist and artist; son of Louis François Bertin (1766–1841). He succeeded his brother Louis Marie Armand Bertin (1801–54) in the editorship (1854–71) of the *Journal des Débats*.

Bertin, Louise Angélique. b. at Roche, France, Feb. 15, 1805; d. at Paris, April 26, 1877. French singer and composer; daughter of Louis François Bertin. She composed the operas *Le Loup-garou* (1827), *Faust* (1831), and *La Esméralda* (1836).

Bertin, Louis François. b. at Paris, Dec. 14, 1766; d. there, Sept. 13, 1841. French journalist; father of Édouard François Bertin, Louise Angélique Bertin, and Louis Marie Armand Bertin. He was the founder (1800), with his brother, Louis François Bertin de Veaux (1771–1842), of the *Journal des Débats*, changed (1801) by Napoleon I into the *Journal de l'Empire*, but given back its former name in 1814.

Bertin, Louis Marie Armand. b. at Paris, Aug. 22, 1801; d. Jan. 11, 1854. French journalist, successor to his father Louis François Bertin (1766–1841) in the editorship of *Journal des Débats*.

Bertini (ber.tē.nē), **(Jérôme) Henri.** b. at London, Oct. 28, 1798; d. at Meylan, France, Oct. 1, 1876. French pianist, and composer for the piano.

Bertinoro (ber.tē.nō'rō). Town and commune in N central Italy, in the *compartimento* (region) of Emilia-Romagna, in the province of Forlì, situated ab. 18 mi. S of Ravenna. The town, center of a wine-producing district, has preserved its medieval character. In the vicinity is the Church of San Donato, founded in the 11th century, which is famous because of an ode by Giosuè Carducci, *Alla chiesa di Polenta*. The cathedral sustained some damage during World War II. Pop. of commune, 9,341 (1936); of town, 1,580 (1936).

Bertoldo (ber.tôl'dō). Hero of an Italian comic romance *Bertoldo Della Lyra*, written near the end of the 16th century by Giulio Cesare Croce. Its popularity was very great and long continued.

Bertolini (ber.tō.lē'nē), **Francesco.** b. at Mantua, Italy, 1836; d. at Bologna, Italy, Dec. 30, 1909. Italian historian. He served as a professor at the University of Bologna. Author of *Storia romana* (Roman History, 1886) and *Storia del risorgimento* (History of the Risorgimento, 1888).

Berton (ber.tôn), **(Henri) François Montan.** b. at Paris, May 3, 1784; d. in July, 1832. French operatic composer; son of Henri Montan Berton (1767–1844). He was appointed (1821) professor of singing at the Paris Conservatoire.

Berton, Henri Montan. b. at Paris, Sept. 17, 1767; d. there, April 22, 1844. French operatic composer, notably of *Montano et Stéphanie* (1799); son of Pierre Montan Berton (1727–80), and father of François Montan Berton (1784–1832). He taught harmony (1795 *et seq.*) and composition (1818 *et seq.*) at the Paris Conservatoire. Composer of ballets and vocal works.

Berton, Pierre Montan. b. at Maubert-Fontaines, France, Jan. 7, 1727; d. at Paris, May 14, 1780. French conductor and composer. He was director (1759 *et seq.*) of the orchestra at the Paris Opera.

Bertoni (ber.tō'nē), **Ferdinando Giuseppe.** b. at Salo, Italy, Aug. 15, 1725; d. at Desenzano del Garda, Italy, Dec. 1, 1813. Italian composer, notably of operas. He was organist and later (1785 *et seq.*) conductor at Saint Mark's Church at Venice. His best-known works are the operas *Orfeo* and *Quinto Fabio*, but he was the composer also of many oratorios and some chamber works.

Bertonio (ber.tō'nyō), **Ludovico.** b. near Ancona, Italy, 1555; d. probably at Lima, Peru, Aug. 3, 1625. Italian Jesuit missionary. He joined the order in 1575, was sent to Peru in 1581, and spent the remainder of his life laboring among the Indians, principally the Collas or Aymarás of Upper Peru. Bertonio left several works on the Aymará language.

Bertram (bėr'tram). Count of Rousillon, hero of Shakespeare's *All's Well that Ends Well*.

Bertram. Tragedy by Charles Robert Maturin, produced in 1816. The character of Bertram is an incarnation of a burning desire for revenge combined with passionate love, but with a considerable element of pathos. Edmund Kean created the part.

Bertram. Aged minstrel who is the companion and protector of Lady Augusta de Berkely in Sir Walter Scott's novel *Castle Dangerous*.

Bertram, Charles. [Pseudonym, **Charles Julius.**] b. at London, 1723; d. 1765. English literary figure, a professor of English at the Royal Marine Academy, grammarian, and literary forger. He pretended, like James Macpherson and Thomas Chatterton, to have discovered an old manuscript on Roman antiquities which he claimed was by Richard of Cirencester, a 14th-century monk and chronicler; he deceived William Stukeley, an eminent antiquary of the day, and many others, who accepted his work as genuine, a reputation it generally held until 1866, when it was completely exposed as a forgery by Benjamin B. Woodward in the *Gentleman's Magazine*. Stukeley published Bertram's work in good faith in 1757, and Bertram himself published it at Copenhagen in the same year. His other works, all published at Copenhagen, are *An Essay on the Excellency of the English Tongue* (1749), *Rudimenta Grammaticae Anglicanae* (1750), *Ethics from Various Authors* (1751), *Royal English-Danish Grammar* (1753), *On the Great Advantages of a Godly Life* (1760, trans. from English into Danish), and other works in both German and Danish.

Bertram (ber'träm), **Ernst.** b. at Elberfeld, Germany, July 27, 1884—. German professor and poet, one of the group around Stefan George. He has published several volumes of poems (*Gedichte*, 1913; *Strassburg*, 1920; *Das Nornenbuch*, 1925), and has written on Hugo von Hofmannstahl, Adalbert Stifter, Theodore Fontane, C. F. Meyer, Thomas Mann, and Heinrich von Kleist. With his book on Nietzsche (*Versuch einer Mythologie*, 1918) in particular, he has found many readers.

Bertram (bėr'tram), **Godfrey.** Laird of Ellangowan in Sir Walter Scott's novel *Guy Mannering*. He is a man of weak character, anxious for political preferment, plundered and ruined by Glossin.

Bertram, Harry. Son of Godfrey Bertram in Sir Walter Scott's novel *Guy Mannering;* one of the principal characters, and the lover of Julia Mannering.

Bertram, Lucy. Daughter of Godfrey Bertram in Sir Walter Scott's novel *Guy Mannering*.

Bertrand (ber.träṅ), **Alexandre.** b. at Paris, 1820; d. 1902. French archaeologist, notable for his studies of prehistoric Gaul. He served (1862 *et seq.*) as curator of the Museum at St.-Germain, and was the author of *Cours d'archéologie nationale; la Gaule avant les Gaulois* (Course of National Archaeology; Gaul Before the Gauls, 1884–86), and *Les Celtes dans les vallées du Pô et du Danube* (The Celts in the Valleys of the Po and the Danube, 1894; with Salomon Reinach).

Bertrand, Gabriel Émile. b. at Paris, May 17, 1867—. French biochemist and bacteriologist. He joined (1900) the Pasteur Institute, Paris, at which he became chief of the biochemistry section; he was elected (1923) to the French Academy of Sciences. Among his works are *La Vaccination antivénimeuse, La Bactérie du Sorbose*, and *Conservation du lait*.

Bertrand, Count **Henri Gratien.** b. at Châteauroux, Indre, France, March 28, 1773; d. there, Jan. 31, 1844. French general, a companion of Napoleon I in exile on the islands of Elba and St. Helena. He served with distinction under Napoleon at Austerlitz, Spandau, and Friedland, in the campaign of Wagram, in Russia, at Leipzig, and at Waterloo. He succeeded Géraud Christophe Michel Duroc as grand marshal of the palace.

Bertrand, Joseph Louis François. b. at Paris, March 11, 1822; d. there, April 5, 1900. French mathematician and, in his lifetime, perpetual secretary of the Académie des Sciences. He was educated at the École Polytechnique, and in 1862 he succeeded Jean Baptiste Biot as professor at the Collège de France. He contributed especially to the study of arithmetic, algebra, infinitesimal analysis, and the theory of functions. His works include *Sur la convergence des séries* (1842), *Sur la propagation du son* (1846), *Sur la théorie des phénomènes capillaires* (1848), *Traité de calcul différentiel et intégral* (1864–70), *Thermodynamique* (1887), *Calcul des probabilités* (1889), and *Leçons sur la théorie mathématique de l'électricité* (1890).

Bertrand, Louis Jacques Napoléon Aloïsius. b. at Ceva, in Piedmont, April 20, 1807; d. at Paris, May, 1841. French poet and journalist. He was the author of *Fantaisies à la manière de Rembrandt et de Callot* (published posthumously in 1842) and of *Gaspard de la Nuit*, a set of prose poems.

Bertrand, Louis Marie Émile. b. at Spincourt, France, March 20, 1866; d. 1941. French novelist, biographer, and writer of travel books. Originally a poet, he published *À la Tour de Clovis* in 1884; he essayed the novel with *Le Cina* (1901), *Le Rival de Don Juan* (1903), and *La Mue* (1904); later he turned to biography and literary studies. He is considered an expert on Flaubert, about whom he wrote *Gustave Flaubert* (1912), *Flaubert à Paris ou le mort vivant* (1921), and *Madame Bovary* (1921).

Bertrand, Marcel. b. at Paris, July 2, 1847; d. Feb. 13, 1907. French geologist, professor of geology at the French National School of Mines. In 1896 he was elected a member of the Académie des Sciences, as successor to Louis Pasteur.

Bertrand d'Agoust (dȧ.gö). Original name of Pope **Clement V.**

Bertrand de Born (dẹ bôrn). See **Born, Bertrand de.**

Bertrand de Got (dẹ gō). Original name of Pope **Clement V.**

Bertrand of Brittany (bėr'trạnd; brit'ạ.ni). Historical novel by Warwick Deeping, published in 1908. It deals with the adventures of Bertrand Du Guesclin (c1320–80), who, as a constable of France, won himself the epithet "Eagle of Brittany" with his exploits against the English at Rennes (1356–57) and elsewhere.

Bertuch (ber'tůċh), **Friedrich Justin.** b. at Weimar, Germany, Sept. 30, 1747; d. there, April 30, 1822. German writer and publisher. An expert in Spanish literature, he translated *Don Quixote* (1775), put out a *Spanisches Lesebuch* (1790), and published *Magazin der spanischen und portugiesischen Literatur* (1780–82). He was involved in many successful publishing ventures. His *Geographische Ephemeriden* (1798–1824) stimulated interest in geography, but it is in large measure to his *Bilderbuch für Kinder* (1790–1822) that he owes his lasting fame.

Berward (bėr'wạrd), Saint. [Also: **Bernard, Bernward.**] b. in Saxony; d. at Hildesheim, in Hanover, Nov. 20, 1022. German Roman Catholic bishop, a member of the Benedictine order. He was court chaplain and tutor to the Holy Roman Emperor Otto III. Consecrated (993) bishop of Hildesheim, he built the monastery of Saint Michael, and adorned the cathedral at Hildesheim with monuments of considerable artistic merit.

Berwick (bėr'wik). Town in S Louisiana, in St. Mary Parish, on the Atchafalaya River ab. 50 mi. S of Baton Rouge: oyster and shrimp fisheries and canning plants; shipyards. 2,619 (1950).

Berwick. Borough in E Pennsylvania, in Columbia County, on the Susquehanna River, ab. 23 mi. SW of Wilkes Barre: manufactures include steel railroad cars, silk textiles, clothing, and machinery. Established in 1786, it was named for Berwick-upon-Tweed, England. 14,010 (1950).

Berwick and Alba (ber'ik; al'bạ), Duke of. [Title of **Jacobo Carlos Fitz-James Stuart Falcó.**] b. 1878—. Spanish diplomat, politician, and historian, one of the wealthiest noblemen of modern Spain. He was a deputy and senator during the regime of Alfonso XIII and minister of foreign affairs in the Berenguer cabinet (1930–31). He functioned under the republic as a counselor of the Bank of Spain in connection with agrarian reform efforts. At the outbreak of the Spanish Civil War he was ambassador at London and remained there during the conflict as representative of General Francisco Franco. From 1939 to 1945 he was again Spanish ambassador to Great Britain, and from 1943 he was also a member of the Cortes. On the basis of his historical work he has been made a member of many learned societies and academies. The rich archives of the earlier dukes of Alba (or Alva) have been the basis for most of his publications.

Berwickshire (ber'ik.shir) or **Berwick** (ber'ik). Maritime county in SE Scotland. It is bounded on the N by East Lothian, on the E by the North Sea, on the SE by Northumberland (England), on the S by Roxburghshire, and on the W by Midlothian. Its divisions are the Merse, Lammermuir, and Lauderdale. The coastline is cliffed and rocky and provides few harbors. Eyemouth is the principal port. Practically all of the N portion of the county is occupied by the Lammermuir Hills. The S portion comprises the Merse of Berwick, a fertile lowland, sloping SE to the river Tweed. Lauderdale, in the W, is mainly upland. Principal activities are agriculture, stock farming, fishing, and manufactures of woolens and linen. Duns is the county seat; area, ab. 457 sq. mi.; pop. 25,060 (1951).

Berwick-upon-Tweed (ber'ik; twēd). [Also: **Berwick, Berwick-on-Tweed.**] Municipal borough, seaport, and fishing town in NE England, in Northumberland, situated on the N side of the small estuary of the river Tweed, ab. 67 mi. NW of Newcastle-upon-Tyne, ab. 336 mi. N of London by rail. In the 13th century it was the chief seaport in Scotland, and it changed hands several times during the 14th and 15th centuries. Today it has fisheries for salmon and herring. 12,550 (1951).

Berwyn (bėr'win). City in NE Illinois, in Cook County: residential suburb of Chicago. It was incorporated in 1902. Pop. 51,280 (1950).

Beryn (ber'in), **History of.** Middle English poem formerly ascribed to Geoffrey Chaucer as *The Merchant's Second Tale*, but no longer considered as such. The author is unknown.

Berytus (bę.rī'tus). Ancient name of **Beirut.**

Berzelius (bėr.zē'li.us; Swedish, ber.sā'lę.ůs), Baron **Jöns Jakob.** b. at Westerlösa, near Linköping, Östergötland, Sweden, Aug. 20, 1779; d. at Stockholm, Aug. 7, 1848. Swedish chemist. He was appointed (1807) professor of medicine and pharmacy at Stockholm, became (1818) perpetual secretary of the Academy of Sciences at Stockholm, was created (1835) a baron, and became (1838) a royal councilor. He introduced a new nomenclature for chemistry; discovered selenium, thorium, and cerium; first exhibited calcium, barium, strontium, columbium (or tantalum), silicium, and zirconium as elements; was one of the originators of the electrochemical theory; and contributed much toward the perfection of the atomic theory after John Dalton. His most important work is now usually considered to have been *Lärebok i Kemien* (1808–28), a handbook on chemistry, which has been translated into many languages.

Berzeviczy (ber'ze.vē.tsē), **Albert de.** b. at Berzevicze, Hungary, June 7, 1853; d. 1936. Hungarian politician and writer. He became (1881) a Liberal member of parliament, and was minister of culture and education (1903–05), and subsequently president of the Hungarian Academy of Science at Budapest. He served as president (1910–12) of the house of deputies. Author of *Der Absolutismus in Ungarn*, 1848–65 (2 vols., 1924–26).

Besançon (bę.zäṅ.sôṅ). [Latin, **Vesontio.**] Industrial city in E France, the capital of the department of Doubs, situated on a peninsula nearly surrounded by the Doubs River. The city has a number of industries, producing watches, precision instruments, rubber and plastic articles, articles of artificial silk, chocolate and other types of candy, as well as other items. The French watchmaking industry originated here in the 17th century. Besançon is an old city. The Porte Noire and the Porte Tailée date from Roman times; the Cathedral of Saint Jean reflects the styles of various centuries, mainly the 12th, 15th, and 16th; the Hôtel de Ville and the Palais Granvelle date from the 16th century. There are large military barracks, a school of medicine, an archaeological and arts museum, and a natural history museum. The city also has thermal baths considered useful in the treatment of rheumatism and other ailments. Founded by the Gauls, the city was later defended by Julius Caesar against Germanic tribesmen under Ariovistus; it was given the status of a free imperial city by the German emperor Frederick I (Frederick Barbarossa). It belonged afterward to the counts of Burgundy and to the Spanish Hapsburgs until it was brought to France by the treaty of Nijmegen in 1678. The city was fortified by Vauban and escaped the invasions of 1814–15, 1870, and 1914, as well as major destruction in the course of the liberation of France (1944) in World War II. It is the birthplace of the cardinal Antoine Perrenot de Granvelle, the poet Victor Hugo, the author Pierre Joseph Proudhon, and the chemists Auguste-Marie Lumière and Louis-Jean Lumière, inventors of an early moving-picture camera. 63,508 (1946).

Besant (bez'ąnt), **Annie.** [Maiden name, **Wood.**] b. at London, Oct. 1, 1847; d. Sept. 20, 1933. English political radical, theosophist, and writer on philosophical topics. In 1867 she married Frank Besant, a clergyman, and was legally separated from him in 1873. She was influential in the radical free-thought movement represented by Charles Bradlaugh, and in 1877 was tried with him on charges of immorality, as a result of their joint publication of a pamphlet explaining and advocating birth control. In 1889 she became prominent as a pupil of Madame Helena Petrovna Blavatsky and a member of the Theosophical Society. By her long residence (1889 *et seq.*) in India, and her championship of the cause of home rule for India, she became an outstanding figure in Indian political life. She was equally renowned for her extensive writings and lectures on religious and philosophical subjects and was instrumental in acquainting English readers with Hindu philosophical speculation and thought. Her early efforts in India were dedicated to establishing (1898) a Hindu university, the Central Hindu College at Benares; her later career was devoted to agitation for home rule for India within the framework of the British Commonwealth. Among her best-known works on religion and philosophy are *Karma* (1895), *Four Great Religions* (1897), *Theosophy and the New Psychology* (1904), and *Wisdom of the Upanishads* (1906); among her other writings are *Autobiography* (1893), *How India Wrought for Freedom* (1915), and *India, Bond or Free* (1926).

Besant (bę.zant'), Sir **Walter.** b. Aug. 14, 1836; d. June 9, 1901. English novelist, knighted in 1895. He was appointed a professor at the Royal College of Mauritius, but returned to England on account of ill health. From 1871 to 1882 he wrote in collaboration with James Rice, producing such novels as *Ready-Money Mortiboy* (1872) and *The Seamy Side* (1881). It was due to his novel *All Sorts and Conditions of Men* (1882), that the "People's Palace," a public hall in the East End of London, was built. Among his other works are *French Humorists* (1873), and an autobiography (1902).

Besborodko (biz.bo.rôt'kǫ), Prince **Aleksandr Andreyevich.** See **Bezborodko,** Prince **Aleksandr Andreyevich.**

Bescherelle (besh.rel), **Louis Nicolas.** b. at Paris, June 10, 1802; d. at Auteuil, France, Feb. 4, 1883. French grammarian, lexicographer, and librarian. His works include *Grammaire nationale* (1834–38), and *Dictionnaire national* (1843–46); he was coauthor of *Les Classiques et les romantiques* (1838), and *La Grammaire de l'Académie* (1825).

Beseler (bā'zę.lėr), **Hans Hartwig von.** b. at Greifswald, Germany, April 27, 1850; d. at Neubabelsberg, Germany, Dec. 20, 1921. German general. He occupied Antwerp on Oct. 9, 1914, later commanded on the eastern front, and was governor general of Poland from August, 1915, until the end of World War I. His attempt, while in authority in Poland, to organize a Polish state under German domination was unsuccessful.

BeSHT or **BeShT** (besht). See **Baal Shem-Tob.**

Besicovich (be.zē'kǫ.vich), **Abram Samoilovich.** b. in Russia, Jan. 24, 1891—. Mathematician who is known, through his many papers in periodicals, chiefly for his work on almost-periodic functions. He was educated at the University of St. Petersburg, and emigrated from Russia to England in 1925. He taught at Liverpool, and was elected to the Royal Society in 1934.

Besika Bay (be.sē.kä'). Small bay on the NW coast of Turkey, near the entrance to the Dardanelles.

Beskids (bes'kidz, bes.kēdz'). Mountain ranges of the NW Carpathians, ab. 190 mi. S of Warsaw, extending along the border between Poland and Czechoslovakia, and into the W part of the Ukrainian Soviet Socialist Republic, U.S.S.R. The western Beskids are higher (peak, 5,659 ft.) and much dissected by deep, well-populated valleys opening N into the Galician foothills. The eastern Beskids consist of parallel wooded ridges, with few peaks over 3,000 ft., and are thinly populated. The mountains are composed chiefly of sandstones and shales. Total length, ab. 250 mi.

Beskow (bes'kôv), Baron **Bernhard von.** b. at Stockholm, April 19, 1796; d. there, Oct. 17, 1868. Swedish dramatist and poet. His chief dramas are *Erik den Fjortonde* (1827), *Torkel Knutsson, Birger och hans Ätt, Gustav Adolf i Tyskland* (1838).

Beskow, Elsa Maartman. b. at Stockholm, Feb. 11, 1874—. Swedish writer and illustrator of books for children. She studied (1889–95) at the Technical School and at the College of Industrial Arts, Stockholm, and was subsequently employed as a teacher of drawing. The best known of her children's books is the *Bland Tomtar och Troll* (Among Pixies and Goblins) series, which is considered by some to be unsurpassed in Swedish children's literature. She married a Swedish theologian, Natanael Beskow.

Besnard (bā.nȧr), **Paul Albert.** b. at Paris, June 2, 1849; d. there, Dec. 4, 1934. French painter, known especially for his impressionistic style. He studied at the École des Beaux-Arts and with the painter Aléxandre Cabanel. His decorations of the École de Pharmacie are considered notable by many critics in the field of art. He headed (1919 *et seq.*) the École Nationale des Beaux-Arts.

Bessaraba (bes.sä.rä'bä). Family of Walachian *voivodes* (princes) prominent in the politics of SE Europe from the 13th to the 18th century, which has given the name of Bessarabia to the region between the Prut and Dniester rivers.

Bessaraba, Constantine Brancovan. d. Aug. 26, 1714. *Voivode* (prince) of Walachia (1688–1714). He acted as the secret agent of Leopold I of Austria in the war which was terminated (1699) by the Treaty of Karlowitz, while ostensibly supporting his lawful sovereign, the sultan of Turkey. He served (1711) as an ally of Peter the Great in a war of the Russians against the Turks, with the result that he and his four sons were put to death by order of the sultan. With his death the Bessaraba dynasty was extinguished.

Bessarabia (bes.a.rā′bi.a). Region in the SW part of the U.S.S.R., lying E and NE of Rumania between the Prut and Dniester rivers and the Black Sea, formerly a government district of Russia, with its capital at Kishinev, now divided between the Moldavian Soviet Socialist Republic and the Izmail *oblast* (region) of the Ukrainian Soviet Socialist Republic. It was overrun by nomadic races from the 2nd to the 13th century, part of the Turkish empire from the Middle Ages to the 19th century, ceded to Russia by Turkey in 1812, ceded in part to Moldavia in 1856, and restored to Russia in 1878. Annexed by Rumania in 1918, restored to the U.S.S.R. in 1940, and again occupied by Rumania during World War II, it was finally ceded to Russia by the Russo-Rumanian treaty of 1947.

Bessarion (be.sā′ri.on), **Johannes** or **Basilius.** b. at Trebizond (now Trabzon, Turkey), c1395–1403; d. at Ravenna, Italy, Nov. 19, 1472. Greek scholar and Roman Catholic ecclesiastic, notable as a patron of learning and a collector of manuscripts. He entered the order of Saint Basil in 1423, studied under the Platonic scholar George Gemistus Pletho, became archbishop of Nicaea in 1437, and accompanied John Palaeologus to Italy, in 1438, to assist in effecting union between the Greek and Latin churches. He supported the Roman Church at the councils of Ferrara and Florence, whereby he gained the favor of Pope Eugenius IV, by whom he was made cardinal in 1439 and successively invested with the archbishopric of Siponto and the bishoprics of Sabina and Tusculum. He received the title of (Latin) Patriarch of Constantinople in 1463. He wrote *Adversus Calumniatorem Platonis* and other works.

Bessèges (be.sezh). Town in S France, in the department of Gard, situated on the Cèze River, ab. 33 mi. NW of Nîmes. It is in the heart of a coal-mining region; has blast furnaces and iron and steel works. 5,648 (1946).

Bessel (bes′el), **Friedrich Wilhelm.** b. at Minden, Prussia, July 22, 1784; d. March 17, 1846. Prussian astronomer, director (1810 *et seq.*) of the observatory at Königsberg. In 1804 he calculated the course of Halley's comet, and, by his own system, determined the parallax of the star 61 Cygni. He was thus enabled to announce in 1838 what was not formally recognized until three years later: the first authenticated calculation of a star's distance from the earth. His works include *Fundamenta Astronomiae deducta ex observationibus J. Bradley* (1818), *Messungen der Entfernung des 61 Sterns im Sternbilde des Schwans* (1839), *Astronomische Untersuchungen* (1841–42), and *Populäre Vorlesungen über wissenschaftliche Gegenstände* (1848).

Besselia (be.sē′li.a). The sweetheart of Captain Crowe, in Tobias Smollett's *Sir Launcelot Greaves.*

Bessemer (bes′e.mėr). City in C Alabama, in Jefferson County, ab. 11 mi. SW of Birmingham. It is a railroad center, and contains blast furnaces, machine shops, foundries, and steel mills. Iron and coal mining are of great importance in the area of this city. Founded in 1887, it was named for Sir Henry Bessemer. 28,445 (1950).

Bessemer. City in the W upper peninsula of Michigan, county seat of Gogebic County, in a major hematite-producing area. 3,509 (1950).

Bessemer, Sir **Henry.** b. at Charlton, Hertfordshire, England, Jan. 19, 1813; d. at London, in March, 1898. English engineer, inventor (1856–58) of the Bessemer process for making steel by using a blast of air to force carbon from melted iron. The American patent (1857) was contested by William Kelly, and the two processes were combined, retaining Bessemer's name.

Bessemer City. Town in W North Carolina, in Gaston County, near Whetstone Mountain: textile manufactures. It was named for Sir Henry Bessemer. 3,961 (1950).

Bessenyei (be′shen.yā), **György.** b. 1747; d. 1811. Hungarian dramatist. A member of an aristocratic family, he was enrolled in his youth in a guard regiment of the imperial court at Vienna. It was at this time that he encountered the influence of Voltaire and the French Encyclopedists, and decided upon a literary career. His works are of indifferent quality, but extremely important from the fact that they used the Hungarian language (which had long been neglected in the literature of the country), and thus opened the door for modern, native Hungarian writing. His tragedy *Agis* and his comedy *The Philosopher* seem to have been the first works of their kind written in that country. Bessenyei also wrote a *Life of John Hunyadi* and a *Philosophical History of Hungary.*

Bessey (bes′i), **Charles Edwin.** b. at Milton, Ohio, May 21, 1845; d. Feb. 25, 1915. American botanist, professor at the University of Nebraska from 1884, notable as a pioneer in the use of simple laboratory methods in the teaching of botany. He published botanical textbooks, *Plant Migration Studies* (1905), *Synopsis of Plant Phyla* (1907), and various technical papers.

Bessie (bes′i), **Alvah Cecil.** b. at New York, June 4, 1904—. American writer. He received an A.B. degree (1924) from Columbia University, and was awarded (1935) a Guggenheim fellowship. He fought in the Abraham Lincoln battalion during the Spanish Civil War. In 1947 he was cited with nine other writers, all employed in Hollywood as scenarists, for contempt of Congress for refusing to admit or deny, to a congressional investigating committee, membership in the Communist Party. In 1950 he was fined and sentenced to a year in jail. Author of *Dwell in the Wilderness* (1935), *Bread and a Stone* (1941), and other novels, he also published a personal account of combat in the Spanish Civil War, *Men in Battle* (1939), and translated René Maran's *Batouala* and Mirbeau's *Torture Garden* (1948).

Bessie Berger (bėr′gėr). See **Berger, Bessie.**

Bessières (be.syer), **Jean Baptiste.** [Title, Duke of **Istria.**] b. at Preissac, Lot, France, Aug. 5, 1768; killed near Lützen, Germany, May 1, 1813. Marshal (1804 *et seq.*) of the French empire under Napoleon I. He served with distinction at Acre, Abukir, Marengo, Austerlitz, Jena, Eylau, Friedland, and Essling, and commanded at the victory of Medina del Rio-Seco, in Spain, on July 14, 1808.

Bessin (be.saṅ). Historical district in the NW part of Normandy, France, bordering on the English Channel E of the Cotentin. Its chief town is Bayeux.

Bess of the Woods. Novel by Warwick Deeping, published in 1906. It is a story of English rustic life in the middle of the 18th century.

Bessus (bes′us). fl. 331–330 B.C. Persian soldier and satrap of Bactria. He commanded the left wing of the Persian army at the battle of Arbela in 331 B.C. He murdered Darius III in 330, but was captured shortly thereafter by Alexander the Great, and delivered to Oxathres, the brother of Darius, by whom he was executed.

Bessus. Blustering, swaggering coward in Beaumont and Fletcher's play, *King and No King.*

Best (best), **Charles Herbert.** b. at West Pembroke, Me., Feb. 27, 1899—. Canadian physiologist, noted as one of the discoverers (1921), with F. G. Banting and others, of insulin. He was head (1922–41) of insulin production at the Connaught Laboratories of the University of Toronto, where he was also appointed (1929) head of the department of physiology.

Best, William Thomas. b. at Carlisle, England, Aug. 13, 1826; d. at Liverpool, England, May 10, 1897. English organist. He became (1868) organist of the Liverpool Musical Society and was associated (1871 *et seq.*) with the Handel Festivals. He edited the organ works of Johann Sebastian Bach and Georg Frederick Handel.

Bestiaires (bes.tyer), **Les.** Novel (1926; Eng. trans., *The Bullfighters,* 1927) by the French writer Henry de Montherlant (1896—), the story of a French youth who becomes a matador. It reflects the author's deep disdain for modern French life, his delight in sports, and his interest in such atavisms as Mithra worship.

Bestiary. Poem (c1120) by the earliest known Anglo-Norman poet, Philippe de Thaün. In it highly fanciful characteristics of animals are made the basis of a rather forced moral.

Bestiary. Middle English poem (c1250). It is a poem of some 800 short lines made up of descriptions (all more or less fabulous) of the lion, eagle, serpent, ant, hart, fox, spider, whale, mermaid, elephant, turtle-dove, panther, and the culver (or dove), followed in each case by a Christian application or moral.

Bestuzhev (bis.tö'zhif), **Aleksandr Aleksandrovich.** [Pseudonym, **"Cossack Marlinsky."**] b. Nov. 3, 1797; killed near Ekaterinodar (now Krasnodar), in the Caucasus, Russia, June, 1837. Russian soldier, poet, and novelist. The best-known of his books is *Ammalat Bek*.

Bestuzhev-Ryumin (bis.tö'zhif.ryö'min), Count **Aleksey Petrovich.** b. at Moscow, in June, 1693; d. April 21, 1766. Russian diplomat and statesman. In the reign of Elizabeth Petrovna, he became (1744) imperial chancellor. In this post he advocated an alliance of Russia with England, Austria, and Saxony to check the combined power of France and Prussia. On Elizabeth's death he fell from grace but was recalled (1762) by Catherine II. He invented, in 1725, a medicinal preparation of iron, *tinctura tonico-nervina Bestusewi.*

Besze (bez), **Théodore de.** See **Bèze, Théodore de.**

Besztercze (bes'ter.tse). Hungarian name of **Bistrița.**

Beszterczebánya (bes'ter.tse.bä'nyô). Hungarian name of **Baňská Bystrica.**

Betancourt (bā.täng.kör'), **Agustín de.** [Also: **Vetancour, Vetancur, Vetancurt.**] b. at Mexico City, 1620; d. there, 1700. Mexican monk and historian, of the Franciscan order, curate of the parish of San José. His principal work, *Teatro mejicano* (1697–98), is an ethnographical and historical account of New Spain. Author also of biographies, theological treatises, and a grammar of the Nahuatl language.

Betanzos (bā.tän'thōs). Town in NW Spain, in the province of La Coruña, situated near the mouth of the Mandeo River, SE of the city of La Coruña: sardine fisheries. 10,504 (1940).

Betanzos (bā.tän'thōs), **Domingo de.** [Also, in some older sources, **Betanços.**] b. in León, Spain; d. at Valladolid, Spain, 1549. Spanish missionary on the island of Hispaniola, and in Mexico and Guatemala. His representation of the cruelty of the Spaniards to the natives occasioned the promulgation (1537) of the bull *Veritas ipsa* by Pope Paul III, in which all Christians are commanded to treat the heathen as brothers.

Betanzos, Juan José de. fl. in the 16th century. Spanish soldier who went to Peru, probably with Francisco Pizarro in 1532. He settled at Cusco, and married a daughter of the Inca King Atahualpa. He became fluent in the Quichua language, and wrote in it a *doctrina* and two vocabularies, now lost. By order of the viceroy, Antonio de Mendoza, he wrote an account of the Incas and of the conquest. It was finished in 1551, but remained in manuscript until 1880, when it was printed for the *Biblioteca Hispano-Ultramarina*, with the title *Suma y Narracion de los Incas.*

Betchwa (bech'vä). See **Betschwa.**

Betelgeuse (bet'ẹl.jėz; bē'tẹl.jöz). [Also: **Betelgeuze, Betelgeux.**] The first-magnitude, red, slightly variable star α Orionis, in the right shoulder of the constellation. It is sometimes called Mirzam, from *al-mirzam*, the roarer.

Betham (beth'ạm), Sir **William.** b. at Stradbrooke, Suffolk, England, May 22, 1779; d. Oct. 26, 1853. English antiquary, Ulster king-of-arms. His works include *Irish Antiquarian Researches* (1827), *Origin and History of the Constitution of England, and of the early Parliaments of Ireland* (1834; a reissue, with a new title, of an earlier work), and *The Gael and the Cymbri* (1834).

Betham-Edwards (beth'ạm.ed'wạrdz), **Matilda Barbara.** b. at Westerfield, Suffolk, England, March 4, 1836; d. at Hastings, Essex, England, Jan. 4, 1919. English novelist, poet, editor, autobiographer, and author of books on France. She was educated chiefly by travel in France and Germany. A prolific author, she wrote the novels *The White House by the Sea* (1857), *John and I* (1862), *Dr. Jacob* (1864), *Kitty* (1869), *A Dream of Millions* (1891), *Lord of the Harvest* (1899), *A Suffolk Courtship* (1900), *Barham Brockleband, M.D.* (1904). *The Golden Bee* (1860), poetry published by Dickens in his periodical, *All the Year Round*, and *Poems* (1885 and 1907) are included in her verse works. *France of To-Day* (1892–94), *The Roof of France, or Travels in Lozère* (1899), *East of Paris* (1902), *Home Life in France* (1905), *Literary Rambles in France* (1907), *French Men, Women, and Books* (1910), *In French Africa* (1913), *Hearts of Alsace* (1916), and *Twentieth Century France* (1917) give evidence of her interest in France. Her autobiographical works include *Reminiscences* (1898), *Anglo-French Reminiscences* (1899), and *Mid-Victorian Memories* (1919). In 1889 and 1898, respectively, she edited Arthur Young's *Travels in France* and *Autobiography and Correspondence.*

Bethany (beth'ạ.ni). City in NW Missouri, county seat of Harrison County: marketing and shipping point for poultry, livestock, and dairy products. 2,714 (1950).

Bethany. City in C Oklahoma, in Oklahoma County, near Oklahoma City: seat of Bethany-Peniel College. It was incorporated in 1931. In the decade between the last two U.S. censuses its population more than doubled. 2,590 (1940); 5,705 (1950).

Bethany. [Modern name, **El-Azariyeh.**] In the New Testament, a village in Palestine near Jerusalem, on the road to Jericho, SE of the Mount of Olives. It is often mentioned in the New Testament as the home of Lazarus, Martha, and Mary, and of Simon the Leper (Mat. xxi. 17, xxvi. 6; Mark, xi. 1 ff.; Luke, xix, 29; John, xi. 1; A.V.).

Beth-Arbel (beth.är'bel). [Modern name, **Irbid.**] In Biblical geography, a place mentioned in Hos. x. 14 as the scene of a sack and massacre by Shalman; probably identical with the modern Irbid, E of the Jordan. Shalman may be either Shalmaneser III, king of Assyria (782–772 B.C.), who made a campaign against Damascus, or Salaman, king of Moab, who is mentioned in the Assyrian inscriptions as having paid tribute to Tiglath-Pileser III, king of Assyria (745–727 B.C.).

Bethe (bā'tẹ), **Hans Albrecht.** b. at Strasbourg, July 2, 1906—. Physicist, noted for work in nuclear physics and astrophysics. After having received (1928) a Ph.D. degree from Munich, he taught in Germany until 1933, and then for two years (1933–35) taught in England. Arrived (1935) in the U.S., he was named acting assistant professor (1935) and professor (1937) of physics at Cornell; during World War II, he was chief of the theoretical physics division at the Los Alamos laboratory of the Manhattan project (atomic bomb); he has also been visiting professor of physics at Columbia. An article on the hydrogen bomb by Bethe, written for a widely circulated magazine and containing only what the editors asserted were well-known facts, caused a furor in 1950 when the Atomic Energy Commission ordered its suppression in the interests of national security, with the result that thousands of copies of the issue were destroyed.

Bethel (beth'ẹl). Town (in Connecticut the equivalent of township in many other states) and unincorporated village in SW Connecticut, in Fairfield County: hat factories. Pop. of town, 5,104 (1950); of village, 4,145 (1950).

Bethel. [Eng. trans., *"House of God"*; original name, **Luz**; modern name, **Beitin.**] In Biblical geography, a town in Palestine, ab. 12 mi. N of Jerusalem, the resting place of the ark, and, later, a seat of idolatrous worship.

Bethel. Suburb of Pittsburgh, in SW Pennsylvania, in Allegheny County. 11,324 (1950).

Bethell (beth'ẹl), **Richard.** [Title, 1st Baron **Westbury.**] b. at Bradford-on-Avon, England, June 30, 1800; d. at London, July 20, 1873. English jurist and statesman, created 1st Baron Westbury in 1861. He became attorney general in 1856, and was lord chancellor in the period 1861–65.

Béthencourt (bā.täṅ.kör), **Jean de.** d. c1425. French adventurer, conqueror of the Canary Islands. He organized an expedition which sailed from La Rochelle, France, on May 1, 1402, in quest of adventure. Having arrived in the Canaries, he built a fort on the island of Lanzarote, which he left in charge of his second-in-command while he returned to the Continent for reinforcements. He came again to the islands with the official title of seigneur of the Canary Islands; he converted the king of the islands in 1404, an event which was followed by the baptism of most of the natives; in 1406 he returned to France, after deputizing his nephew as governor. His exploits are recorded in *Histoire de la premiere descouverte et conqueste des Canaries, faite des l'an 1402 par messire Jean de Bethencourt, escrite du temps mesme par F. Pierre Bontier . . . et Jean le Verrier* (1630).

Bethesda (bę.thez′dạ). [Eng. trans., "*House of Mercy.*"] In Biblical history, an intermittent spring near the sheep-gate at Jerusalem; commonly identified with the modern Birket Israil.

Bethesda. Unincorporated community in C Maryland, in Montgomery County, near the Potomac River: suburb of Washington, D.C. It is the site of the U.S. Naval Hospital and (since the early part of World War II) of the main research facilities of the National Cancer Institute. 45,807 (1950).

Bethesda. Urban district in N Wales, in Caernarvonshire, ab. 5 mi. SE of Bangor, ab. 244 mi. NW of London by rail. Near it are the great Penrhyn slate quarries. 4,436 (1951).

Bethge (bāt′gę), **Hans.** b. at Dessau, Germany, 1876—. German poet of the neo-romantic group, much of whose work tends toward the delicate and esoteric (*Die chinesische Flöte,* 1907). His anthology of modern verse, *Deutsche Lyrik seit Liliencron* (1905), has been very popular.

Beth-horon (beth.hō′rọn), **Upper** and **Nether.** [Eng. trans., "*Place of the Hollow*"; modern names, **Beit Ur el-Fokha** and **Beit Ur el-Tahta.**] In Biblical geography, two villages in Palestine, ab. 12 mi. NW of Jerusalem. At the pass between them Joshua defeated the kings of the Amorites. It is also the scene of a victory of Judas Maccabaeus in the 2nd century B.C.

Bethlehem (beth′lē.ẹm, -lę.hem). [Eng. trans., "*House of Bread*"; modern Arabic name, **Beit Lahm.**] Town in Palestine, ab. 5 mi. S of Jerusalem: a dwellingplace of David and (according to Matthew, Luke, and John) the birthplace of Jesus Christ. The Convent of the Nativity at Bethlehem is a complex body of structures distributed between the Greek and Latin creeds, and grouped around the church, a basilica of five naves, with apse and apsidal transepts, built by the empress Helena and the emperor Constantine. There are four long ranges of monolithic Corinthian columns 19 ft. high, above which rise the walls of the nave with round-arched windows. The choir is richly ornamented with attributes of the Greek rite; beneath it is the tortuous Grotto of the Nativity. The apse and parts of the walls bear beautiful Byzantine mosaics. The church measures 86 by 136 ft. 9,140 (est. 1946).

Bethlehem. City in E Pennsylvania, in Lehigh and Northampton counties, on the Lehigh River, ab. 50 mi. N of Philadelphia: noted for the production of iron and steel. The predecessor of the modern Bethlehem Steel Corporation, using local anthracite, began its production of iron and steel here during the Civil War. It is the seat of the Moravian College for Women, the Moravian College and Theological Seminary, and Lehigh University. Founded (1741) by Moravians, the city has long been noted as a music center. 66,340 (1950).

Bethlehem, Synod of. [Sometimes called **Synod of Jerusalem.**] Synod of the Greek Church held (1672) at Bethlehem, in Palestine. It condemned Calvinism and Lutheranism, and defended the memory of Cyril Lucaris (patriarch of Alexandria and afterward of Constantinople, who had died c1638) against the imputation of Calvinism.

Bethlehem Bach Choir (of *Bethlehem, Pa.*). Mixed choral group organized (1900) by Ruth Porter Doster and John Frederick Wolle, conductor. The choir holds an annual two-day festival of Johann Sebastian Bach's choral works, always including the B Minor Mass.

Bethlehemites (beth′lē.ẹm.īts). Religious order founded in Guatemala in 1653, extended to Mexico a few years later, and ultimately to other parts of Spanish America. The members lived according to the monastic rules of the Augustinians.

Bethlen (bet′len), **Gabriel.** b. 1580; d. 1629. Prince of Transylvania and, for a brief period, king of Hungary. Member of a leading Protestant family of upper Hungary, having extensive estates in Transylvania, he was attached as a young man to the court of Sigismund Báthory, prince of Transylvania. He later served Gabriel Báthory, from 1608 to 1613. It is supposed that Gabriel Báthory's jealousy of Bethlen was the cause of the latter's flight to Turkey. The Turkish sultan, to whom the principality of Transylvania was subordinate, named Bethlen prince and provided him with an army. The murder of Gabriel Báthory cleared the way for Bethlen's succession to the throne in 1613. Bethlen proceeded to organize Hungarian resistance to the Austrians, and, invading Austrian territory, seemed about to entrap the imperial army, when his Turkish troops insisted on going home for the winter, and the approach of an army under the count of Tilly caused him to withdraw. But he was again drawn into the Thirty Years' War, in defense of the liberties of the north Hungarian provinces, which in 1620 elected him king. In alliance with the German Protestants he continued at war until peace was made on Dec. 31, 1621. At this time Bethlen relinquished his claim to the crown of Hungary in return for confirmation of religious liberty in that country, and was made a prince of the Holy Roman Empire and granted estates in Hungary and Silesia. Following his marriage in 1625 to Catherine of Brandenburg, he was again for a time involved in the religious wars. Bethlen is considered to have been one of the greatest Magyars of his time. His force of character impressed his contemporaries and his correspondence, which was extensive, reveals an original turn of mind. He was an able ruler, and patronized literature and the sciences. He is said to have taken part in 42 battles, and it was his boast that he had read the Bible 25 times. He was an ardent Calvinist but free of the persecuting spirit, and is known to have helped the Jesuit Father Kaldy to translate and print the Scriptures.

Bethlen, Count Stefan. b. at Gernyeszag, Hungary, Oct. 8, 1874; reported dead in a Russian prison camp, 1951. Hungarian statesman. He became (1901) a member of the national parliament, and in 1919 organized the opposition against the communistic Hungarian government of Béla Kun. In 1920 he was one of the delegates who signed the Treaty of Trianon; he became prime minister in 1921 and held this office until 1931, longer than any other modern Hungarian statesman. During his term of office he declared (1921) the end of the Hapsburg dynasty, and, with a loan from the League of Nations, succeeded in reorganizing the Hungarian economy; he allied Hungary with Italy in 1927.

Bethmann-Hollweg (bāt′män.hol′vāk), **Theobald von.** b. at Hohenfinow, Germany, Nov. 29, 1856; d. there, Jan. 2, 1921. German statesman, chancellor (1909–17) of the empire. After serving as Prussian minister of the interior (1905 *et seq.*) and secretary of state (1907 *et seq.*), he succeeded (1909) Bernhard von Bülow as chancellor. A Liberal, he obtained (1911) greater autonomy for Alsace-Lorraine, then a part of the German empire. An opponent at the time of its outbreak of World War I, he nevertheless characterized the Belgian guarantee as "a scrap of paper," a phrase which gained wide notoriety. He had previously worked, unsuccessfully, for a German-British agreement. His continued efforts for peace caused his resignation (July, 1917) under pressure from Paul von Hindenburg and Erich Friedrich Wilhelm Ludendorff. Author of *Betrachtungen zum Weltkriege* (2 vols., 1919–21).

Bethnal Green (beth′nạl). Metropolitan borough in E London, in the County of London, situated on the N bank of the river Thames, ab. 1 mi. NE of Liverpool Street station. It forms a part of the East End of London and is among the smallest of the London boroughs in area. A large proportion of the inhabitants live in small tenements under crowded conditions. Furniture manufacture and tobacco processing are of some importance here. It was once populated chiefly by silk weavers, partly descended from Huguenot refugees. It is noted as the locality mentioned in the old ballad *The Beggar's Daughter of Bednal Green.* The beggar's house is still shown. The Bethnal Green Museum is a branch of the Victoria and Albert Museum, and was opened in 1872 in Victoria Park Square, Cambridge Road, for the inhabitants of East London. The district was heavily bombed (1940–41) during World War II. 58,374 (1951).

Béthouart (bā.twȧr), **(Marie) Émile.** b. at Dôle, Jura, France, Dec. 17, 1889—. French army commander, French high commissioner (1946 *et seq.*) in Austria. In 1945 he was named commander in chief of the French army of occupation in Austria. He commanded (1940) the French forces in the Allied expedition to Narvik, Norway. Arrested (1942) by the Vichy regime, he subsequently served (1943–44) in the Free French forces, and assumed command (1944) of the French First Army Corps.

Bethphage (beth'fą.jē, beth'fāj). [Eng. trans., "*House of Unripe Figs.*"] In Biblical geography, a village in Palestine, situated on the Mount of Olives, E of Jerusalem and near Bethany. The exact site is in dispute. Traditionally it was situated halfway between Bethany and the top of the mountain.

Bethsaida (beth.sā'i.dą). [Eng. trans., "*Fishing Place.*"] In Biblical geography, a place in Palestine, probably situated on the shore of the Sea of Galilee between Capernaum and Magdala.

Beth-shean (beth.shē'ąn) or **Beth-shan** (-shan'). Old Testament name of **Beisan.**

Beth-shemesh (beth.shē'mesh). [Also: **Ir-shemesh;** Arabic, **Ain Shems.**] Ancient city in C Judea, now E central Israel, Palestine, ab. 16 mi. W of Jerusalem. It lies in the western hill-country near the W border of the ancient Hebrew kingdom of Judah, and belonged to the tribe of Dan. In Solomon's time it was the seat of a royal officer. In the 8th century B.C., Beth-shemesh was conquered by the Philistines, and lost its importance. Excavations have revealed that there were also Egyptian and Assyrian cities here.

Béthune (bā.tün). Town in N France, in the department of Pas-de-Calais, situated on the Brette River, NW of Arras, at the junction of the river Tawe and the Canal d'Aire. It is a river port, the administrative center of an arrondissement, and was the seat of an ancient barony. It has shoe and tobacco manufactures, is a center for the local grain trade, and has been known for coal mines. It was taken by John Churchill, 1st Duke of Marlborough, and Prince Eugene of Savoy in 1710, but was united with France in 1713. It suffered from bombardments during World War I and was severely damaged in World War II. Most of its medieval and Renaissance monuments have been destroyed. 22,081 (1946).

Bethune (bē'tun), **David.** See **Beaton, David.**

Bethune (bę.thūn'), **George Washington.** b. at New York, March 18, 1805; d. at Florence, April 28, 1862. American Dutch-Reformed clergyman and poet, who issued (1846) the first American edition of Izaak Walton's *Complete Angler*, containing the most complete bibliography on angling ever published up to that time. Author also of *Lays of Love and Faith* (1848).

Bethune (bē'tun), **James.** See **Beaton, James.**

Bethune (bę.thūn'), **Mary.** [Maiden name, **McLeod.**] b. at Mayesville, S.C., July 10, 1875—. American Negro educator. A teacher (1895–1904) in Florida and Georgia mission schools, she was the founder (1904) and president (1904–23) of Daytona Normal and Industrial School for Girls (which was later expanded and is now Bethune-Cookman College). She was also director (1936–44) of the National Youth Administration's Division of Negro Affairs, special assistant (1942) to the secretary of war in choosing selectees for the first Women's Army Corps Officers' Candidate School, and founder and president of the National Council of Negro Women.

Béthune (bā.tün), **Maximilien de.** See **Sully, Duc de.**

Betie (bā'tē.ā). [Also, **Bettie.**] One of the Sudanic-speaking Anyi peoples of W Africa, inhabiting the SE part of the Ivory Coast.

Bet-Pak-Dala (bet'päk'dä.lä'). See **Golodnaya Step.**

Betrothed, The. Novel (1825) by Sir Walter Scott, classed as one of the *Tales of the Crusaders*. It should not be confused with *The Betrothed*, the English title of Alessandro Manzoni's *I Promessi Sposi*.

Betschwa or **Betchwa** or **Beczwa** (bech'vä). River in E Moravia, Czechoslovakia, a tributary of the Morava River.

Betsileo (bet.si.lā'ō). Malayo-Polynesian-speaking tribe living in the mountain plateaus of C Madagascar. 513,697 (1934).

Betsimisaraka (bet''si.mi.sä'rą.ką). Malayo-Polynesian-speaking tribe of NE Madagascar. 510,029 (1934).

Betsy Thoughtless. Novel (1751) by Eliza Haywood.

Bettendorf (bet'ęn.dôrf). City in E Iowa, in Scott County: industrial suburb of Davenport. A factory opened here (1910) under the direction of William P. Bettendorf to make steel frames for railroad cars has been succeeded by large plants manufacturing farm machinery and other items. 5,132 (1950).

Bettendorf, William Peter. b. at Mendota, Ill., July 1, 1857; d. June 3, 1910. American manufacturer and inventor of farm implements and railway-car parts. He opened (1886) a machine plant at Davenport, Iowa, and later (1910) a large factory to make steel frames for railroad cars at what is now Bettendorf, a suburb of Davenport. He devised a power-lift sulky plow, a metal wheel and a steel gear for farm wagons, a railway-car bolster, a steel side-frame truck, and an integral journal box.

Betterton (bet'ėr.tǫn), **Thomas.** b. at London, c1635; d. there, April 28, 1710. English actor and dramatist; son of an under-cook of Charles I. He was apprenticed to a bookseller, but other than this little is known of his early life. It is supposed that he began to act in 1659 or 1660, and it is known that he joined Sir William Davenant's company at the Lincoln's Inn Fields Theatre in 1661. Samuel Pepys, who saw him at the beginning of his career, and Alexander Pope, who saw him at the end, spoke of him as the best actor they had ever seen. After Davenant's death, Betterton headed the acting company, and with it moved (1671) to a different theater. He joined his company with that of the Theatre Royal, but broke with this group in 1695. Thereafter he reopened the Lincoln's Inn Fields Theatre with a production of William Congreve's *Love for Love*, and remained there until 1705, when he moved to the Haymarket Theatre, a new house especially constructed for him by John Vanbrugh. Although active also in Restoration drama, he excelled in Shakespearian roles, both comic and tragic. He was intimate with John Dryden and with many other notable men of his time.

Betti (bet'tē), **Enrico.** b. at Pistoia, Italy, Oct. 21, 1823; d. at Pisa, Italy, Aug. 11, 1892. Italian mathematician, contributor to analysis situs and mathematical physics, best known for the "Betti numbers" in spaces of many dimensions. He was the author of *Teorica delle forze Newtoniane e sue applicazioni all'elettrostatica e al magnetismo* (1879) and *Lehrbuch der Potentialtheorie* (1885). His *Opere matematiche* appeared in two volumes in the period 1903–13.

Bettie (bet'tē.ā). See **Betie.**

Bettris (bet'ris). Country girl who loves the titular hero in the play *George-a'-Greene, The Pinner of Wakefield*, attributed to Robert Greene.

Betts (bets), **Louis.** b. at Little Rock, Ark., Oct. 5 1873—. American portrait painter. He was educated at the Pennsylvania Academy of the Fine Arts, at Philadelphia, and has exhibited throughout the U.S. Many prizes have been awarded to him, including a St. Louis Exposition prize (1904), a Carnegie Institute award (1910), a prize from the Art Institute of Chicago (1920), and awards from the National Academy of Design (1918 and 1923). Some of his better-known works are the portraits *George Eastman, Dr. William Mayo, Dr. Charles Mayo, Charles E. Hutchinson, Martin L. Ryerson, C. A. Hamill*, and *Dr. Augustus Gonsalus*.

Betts, Samuel Rossiter. b. at Richmond, Mass., June 8, 1786; d. Nov. 3, 1868. American congressman, jurist, and authority on admiralty law. He served (1815–17) as a congressman from New York; later (1826–67) he presided over the federal court for the southern district of New York.

Bettws-y-Coed (bet'ůs.i.koid'). Urban district in N Wales, in Caernarvonshire, situated at the confluence of the rivers Llugwy and Conway, ab. 4 mi. S of Llanrwst, ab. 239 mi. NW of London by rail. It is a tourist center. 776 (1951).

Betty (bet'i), **William Henry West.** [Called **"Master Betty"** and the **"Young Roscius."**] b. at Shrewsbury, England, Sept. 13, 1791; d. at London, Aug. 24, 1874. English actor, especially famous for his precocity. He made his first appearance, on Aug. 19, 1803, as Oswyn in *Zara*, and played Douglas, Rolla, Romeo, Tancred, and Hamlet within two years with great success. At the height of his popularity, the younger William Pitt got a motion passed in the House of Commons that an adjournment should be made to allow the members of that body to attend a performance of Betty as Hamlet. His popularity, however, faded as quickly as it had grown; he left the stage in 1808 to attend Cambridge, returned to it in 1812, and finally abandoned it in 1824.

Betul (bā.töl'). [Also, **Baitul.**] District of the Nagpur division, Madhya Pradesh (Central Provinces), Union of

India, ab. 100 mi. NW of Nagpur. Coal is mined in the area. 438,342 (1941).

Betulius (bẹ.tū'li.us), **Xystus.** Latinized name of **Birk, Sixt.**

Betulo (bet'ų.lō). A Latin name of **Badalona.**

Betwa (bet'wä). River in the N part of the Union of India, in the state of Madhya Bharat. It flows NE into the Jumna. Length, ab. 240 mi.

Between the Acts. Novel (1941) by Virginia Woolf. It was published posthumously (the authoress had died earlier in the same year) and represents a return to the essentially poetic technique which had marked *To the Lighthouse* (1927) and *The Waves* (1931).

Betz (bets), **Franz.** b. at Mainz, Germany, March 19, 1835; d. at Berlin, Aug. 11, 1900. German operatic baritone. His performance (1859) as Don Carlos in Giuseppe Verdi's *Ernani* at Berlin led to his immediate engagement by the Royal Opera, where he remained until 1897; he was the first Hans Sachs in Richard Wagner's *Die Meistersinger* (1868), the original Falstaff in the Berlin production of Verdi's *Falstaff*, and played (1876) Wotan in Wagner's *Ring of the Nibelungen* at Bayreuth.

Beudant (bė.däñ), **François Sulpice.** b. at Paris, Sept. 5, 1787; d. there, Dec. 10, 1850. French mineralogist and physicist. He became professor of mathematics at Avignon in 1811, professor of physics at Marseilles in 1813, and professor of mineralogy on the faculty of sciences at Paris in 1818.

Beuel (boi'ẹl). Town in W Germany, in the *Land* (state) of North Rhine-Westphalia, British Zone, formerly in the Rhine Province, Prussia, situated opposite Bonn, ab. 15 mi. SE of Cologne: chemical and cement works, canneries, and manufactures of lingerie, paper, and leather goods. 24,730 (1950).

Beuerland (bė'ėr.länt), **Hadrianus.** b. in the Netherlands, c1653; d. after 1712. Dutch scholar. He studied law, and was later interested in natural history. He was the author of *De peccato originali* (1678), an erotic book which caused his banishment from Leiden University, and of satires (in English).

Beulah (bū'lạ). In the Old Testament, the name of the land of Israel when it shall be "married." Isa. lxii. 4.

Beulah. A land of rest, "where the sun shineth night and day," in John Bunyan's *Pilgrim's Progress.* The Pilgrims stay here till the time comes for them to go across the river of Death to the Celestial City.

Beulé (bė.lā), **Charles Ernest.** b. at Saumur, in Anjou, France, June 29, 1826; d. April 4, 1874. French archaeologist and politician.

Beumelburg (boi'mẹl.bůrk), **Werner.** b. at Traben-Trarbach, Germany, Feb. 19, 1899—. German journalist and novelist. Of his half-dozen war stories, *Sperrfeuer um Deutschland* (1929) and *Gruppe Bosemüller* (1930) are best known. In the latter the ripening effect of comradeship in arms is shown as it affects one individual; the former attempts to give an impression of the war in its entirety. *Deutschland in Ketten* (1931) deals with defeated Germany. His later novels draw on history for object lessons in German nationalism (*Mont Royal,* 1936; *Kaiser und Herzog,* 1936; *Reich und Rom,* 1937).

Beuningen (bė'ning.ẹn), **Daniel George van.** b. at Utrecht, the Netherlands, March 4, 1877—. Dutch industrialist. He was educated at Leipzig, and employed by companies in Germany, England, and the Netherlands.

Beurnonville (bėr.nôñ.vēl), **Pierre de Ruel,** Marquis **de.** b. at Champignolle, Aube, France, May 10, 1752; d. at Paris, April 23, 1821. French general and politician. He was made a marshal of France in 1816. After serving as minister of war, he was sent (1800) to Berlin as ambassador, and later (1803) to Madrid. He served in the provisional government set up after Napoleon's abdication, and supported Louis XVIII, by whom he was made a marquis.

Beust (boist), Count **Friedrich Ferdinand von.** b. at Dresden, Germany, Jan. 13, 1809; d. at Altenberg, near Vienna, Oct. 24, 1886. Saxon and Austrian statesman and diplomat. He became minister of foreign affairs in Saxony in 1849, and during the decade preceding the Austro-Prussian War was the chief opponent of Otto von Bismarck in German politics. His object was to form a league of the minor German states strong enough to hold the balance of power between Austria and Prussia, and it was chiefly through his efforts that Saxony was allied with Austria in the Austro-Prussian War of 1866. Having entered the Austrian service as minister of foreign affairs in October, 1866, he succeeded Richard Belcredi as prime minister on Feb. 7, 1867, and on June 23, 1867, was created chancellor of the Austrian empire. He reorganized the empire, in 1868, on the basis of a dualistic union between Austria and Hungary. He was dismissed from his leading position in the government on Nov. 8, 1871, and was thereafter ambassador to London (1871–78) and to Paris (1878–82).

Beutenmüller (boi'tẹn.mül.ėr), **William.** b. at Hoboken, N.J., March 31, 1864; d. Feb. 24, 1934. American entomologist. He was editor of the *Journal* (vols. I–XI) of the New York Entomological Society, and was curator of the department of entomology at the American Museum of Natural History, at New York, in the period 1889–1909.

Beuthen (boi'tẹn). German name of **Bytom.**

Beuve-Méry (bėv.mā.rē), **Hubert.** b. at Paris, Jan. 5, 1902—. French journalist, director general (1944 *et seq.*) of the Paris newspaper *Le Monde.* He was diplomatic correspondent (1934–38) of *Le Temps* at Prague, and was active (1942–44) in the Resistance movement in France during World War II.

Beuzeval-Houlgate (bėz.vàl.öl.gàt). Resort in NW France, in the department of Calvados, situated on the English Channel ab. 15 mi. SW of Le Havre.

Bevan (bev'ạn), **Aneurin.** b. at Tredegar, Monmouthshire, England, in November, 1897—. English politician, a Labour member (1929 *et seq.*) of Parliament; husband of Jenny Lee, also a Labour member of Parliament. The son of a coal miner, he went into the mines himself at an early age, and became prominent in the South Wales Miners' Federation. In 1945 he was named minister of health in Clement Attlee's cabinet. On April 22, 1951, Bevan resigned from the cabinet over a policy split in the Labour government (but retained his membership and influence in the Labour Party). Author of *In Place of Fear* (1952).

Beveland (bā'vẹ.länt), **North.** [Dutch, **Noord-Beveland.**] Island in SW Netherlands, in C Zeeland province, in the Scheldt estuary, ab. 40 mi. NW of Antwerp. The island is reclaimed polder land, diked on all sides. Area, 35 sq. mi.; pop. 7,755 (1947).

Beveland, South. [Dutch, **Zuid-Beveland.**] Island in SW Netherlands, in C Zeeland province, in the Scheldt estuary, ab. 30 mi. NW of Antwerp. Originally a small island, it was much expanded by polder reclamation in 1809 and 1874. It is traversed by the railroad from Vlissingen (Flushing) to Rosendaal, which passes through the principal town of Goes. Intensive farming and livestock raising are practiced. In World War II the island was the scene of a sharp battle between British and German forces, in October, 1944. Area, 135 sq. mi.; pop. ab. 58,000 (1947).

Beveren (bā'vėr.ẹn). Town in NW Belgium, in the province of East Flanders, ab. 6 mi. W of Antwerp: manufactures lace; agricultural trade. 13,510 (1947).

Beveridge (bev'ėr.ij), **Albert Jeremiah.** b. on a farm on the border of Adams and Highland counties, Ohio, Oct. 6, 1862; d. April 27, 1927. American politician. He was a U.S. senator from Indiana (1899–1911), and a noted public speaker, but is now best known as author of *The Life of John Marshall* (1916–19). A leader in Senate debates, in 1906 he was the center of a bitter fight over legislation providing for closer supervision of the meat-packing industry. Defeated (1910) for the Senate by a Democrat, he switched (1912) to the Progressive Party, serving as chairman of the national convention and running unsuccessfully for governor.

Beveridge, William. b. at Barrow, Leicestershire, England, 1637; d. at Westminster, now part of London, March 5, 1708. English prelate. He became archdeacon of Colchester in 1681, president of Sion College in 1689, and bishop of St. Asaph in 1704.

Beveridge, Sir **William Henry.** [Title: 1st Baron **Beveridge of Tuggal.**] b. at Rangpur, India (in the part that is now Pakistan), March 5, 1879—. English economist, originator (1942) of the "Beveridge plan" for social security for Great Britain. Graduated (1902) from Oxford, he was an editorial writer (1906–08) for the London

Morning Post; in 1909 he became director of labor exchanges for the Board of Trade, and served as second secretary (1916–18) and permanent secretary (1919) in the Ministry of Food. He was director (1919–37) of the London School of Economics and Political Science, and master (1937–45) of University College at Oxford. He headed (1934–44) the Unemployment Insurance Statutory Committee, and was chairman (1941–42) of the Interdepartmental Committee on Social Insurance and Allied Services. Author of *A Problem of Industry* (1909), *Insurance for All* (1924), *Changes in Family Life* (1932), *Full Employment in a Free Society* (1944), and *India Called Them* (1947).

Beverlacensis (bev″ėr.lą.sen′sis), **Alredus** (or **Aluredus**). Latinized name of **Alfred of Beverley.**

Beverley (bev′ėr.li). [Also, **Beverly.**] Municipal borough and market town in NE England, in the East Riding of Yorkshire, ab. 7 mi. N of Hull, with which it has canal connections, and ab. 205 mi. N of London by rail. It was formerly noted for its fine woolen manufactures. Today it has a small shipbuilding industry, building trawlers for the fishing industry at Hull. It is the county seat of the East Riding. Beverley contains Saint Mary's Church, and the Church of Saint John, or Beverley Minster. The minster is a church of the 13th and 14th centuries, with double transepts, and a Perpendicular façade, flanked by two towers, resembling that of York. The fine nave dates from about 1350; the choir is in Early English style, with a modern sculptured screen and handsome old stalls. The minster is interesting for the Frid Stool, a stone chair which was a place of sanctuary from the law in early times, still preserved there. The building measures 334 by 64 ft. 15,499 (1951).

Beverley. Titular hero of Edward Moore's tragedy *The Gamester.* David Garrick first played the part. Mrs. Beverley was a favorite character with the actresses of the time.

Beverley. Jealous lover of Belinda in Arthur Murphy's play *All in the Wrong.*

Beverley, Constance de. Perjured nun in Scott's poem *Marmion.* She loves Marmion, and

"... bows her pride
A horseboy in his train to ride."

She is walled alive in the dungeons of a convent as a punishment for her broken vows.

Beverley, Ensign. The character assumed by Captain Absolute, in Richard Brinsley Sheridan's comedy *The Rivals,* to win the love of the romantic Lydia, who will not marry any one so suitable as the son of Sir Anthony Absolute.

Beverley, Robert. b. in Middlesex County, Virginia, c1673; d. 1722. American historian. He became (c1696) clerk of the Council of Virginia, an office previously held by his father, and published *History and Present State of Virginia* (1705).

Beverly (bev′ėr.li). City in NE Massachusetts, in Essex County, ab. 17 mi. NE of Boston. Formerly important for shipping, it now has one of the largest shoe-machinery factories in the world. Beverly, settled c1625, is said to have had the first navy yard in the country, which launched the first U.S. naval vessel, the *Hannah,* in 1775. Pop. 28,884 (1950).

Beverly. City in C New Jersey, in Burlington County. 3,084 (1950).

Beverly Hills. City in S California, in Los Angeles County, contiguous to the W boundary of Los Angeles: noted as a residential colony of motion-picture actors, directors, and producers. 29,032 (1950).

Beverwijk (bā′vėr.wīk). Town in W Netherlands, in the province of North Holland, situated near the Noord Zee Canal, NW of Amsterdam: horticultural center; vegetables, flowers, and strawberries are shipped from here. There is a paper factory. 28,328 (est. 1951).

Bevil (bev′il). Character in Thomas Shadwell's comedy *Epsom Wells.*

Bevil. Model of everything becoming a gentleman, in Richard Steele's play *The Conscious Lovers.*

Bevin (bev′in), **Ernest.** b. at Winsford, Somersetshire, England, March 9, 1881; d. April 14, 1951. English trades-union leader and statesman, for many years a prominent figure in the Labour Party. After working as farm laborer, shop clerk, and truck driver, he began (c1909) the organization of labor unions; he became prominent (1920) through a lengthy speech on the standard minimum wage for dockers before the Transport Workers' Court of Inquiry. In 1922 he consolidated 45 unions into the national Transport and General Workers' Union, of which he served as general secretary (1922–40); he also organized and led (1910–21) the Dockers' Union, and was a member (1925–40) and chairman (1936–37) of the Trades Union Congress. A member (1940 *et seq.*) of Parliament, he served as minister (1940–45) of labor and national service. When the Labour Party came to power he was made (1945) secretary of state for foreign affairs; in this capacity he attended such important international meetings as the Potsdam Conference (1945) and the second meeting of the United Nations General Assembly (1946, at New York).

Bevis (bē′vis). Horse of Lord Marmion in Sir Walter Scott's poem *Marmion.*

Bevis Marks. Thoroughfare in St. Mary Axe, near Houndsditch, London. It is referred to in Charles Dickens's *Old Curiosity Shop.*

Bevis of Hampton (hamp′tọn). [Also, **Sir Southhampton.**] Knight whose bravery and adventures are celebrated in Arthurian romance and by Michael Drayton in *Polyolbion.* An old English poem on Bevis was in the 15th or 16th century turned into a prose romance and printed c1650. He was originally called Beuves d'Antone, from the Italian *Buovo d'Antona,* a name adapted as *d'Hantone* in French and *Hampton* in English.

Bewdley (būd′li), 1st Earl **Baldwin of.** See **Baldwin, Stanley.**

Bewick (bū′ik), **Thomas.** b. at Cherryburn, near Newcastle, England, in August, 1753; d. at Gateshead, near Newcastle, Nov. 8, 1828. English wood engraver. He was apprenticed at the age of 14 to Ralph Bielby, a copperplate engraver at Newcastle; after 1770 he did most of Bielby's wood-engraving business. At the expiration of his apprenticeship he went to London, but returned shortly to Newcastle, where he entered into partnership with Bielby and occupied his old shop in Saint Nicholas Churchyard until a short time before his death. Among his chief works are the illustrations for John Gay's *Fables* (1779), *Select Fables* (1784), a *General History of Quadrupeds* (1790), and his best-known work, which was never completely finished, *The History of British Birds* (2 vols., 1797–1804), in which he showed the knowledge of a naturalist combined with the skill of an artist. His best-known (and perhaps his finest) single block is *The Chillingham Bull* (1789), after a painting by Landseer. His last complete work was the illustrations for *Aesop's Fables* (1818), upon which he was engaged six years. He was assisted by his son Robert Elliot Bewick, and by some of his pupils.

Bewley (bū′li). See also **Beaulieu.**

Bewley, Anthony. b. in Tennessee, May 22, 1804; hanged by a mob at Fort Worth, Texas, Sept. 13, 1860. American Methodist clergyman. He joined (1843) the Missouri Conference, but refused (1845) to join the Methodist Episcopal Church of the South. He was associated with missions in Arkansas and Texas in spite of his antislavery sympathies. A letter published (1860) in newspapers and church publications connected him with abolitionists and saboteurs, and he fled into Missouri. He was captured by a Texas posse, returned to Fort Worth, and killed.

Bex (be). Small town in SW Switzerland, in the canton of Vaud, near the Rhone River, S of Villeneuve. A tourist and health resort, it has brine baths. 4,264 (1941).

Bexar Territory or **District** (bãr, bā′är). Former name of a region in W Texas adjoining New Mexico, and bounded by the Pecos River on the SW. Area, ab. 25,000 sq. mi.

Bexhill (beks′hil). Municipal borough and seaside resort in SE England, in East Sussex, situated on the English Channel ab. 5 mi. SW of Hastings, ab. 62 mi. SW of London by rail. It has an interesting old church, dating back to 1070. Pop. 25,668 (1951).

Bexley (beks′li). Municipal borough in SE England, in Kent, situated on the river Cray, ab. 4 mi. W of Dartford, ab. 14 mi. SE of Charing Cross station, London. 88,767 (1951).

Bexley. City in C Ohio, in Franklin County, near Columbus: residential community. It is the seat of Capital University. 12,378 (1950).

Beyen (bī'ęn), **Johan Willem.** b. at Utrecht, Netherlands, May 2, 1897—. Dutch industrialist and financier. He studied law at Utrecht before being attached to the ministry of finance (1918–23). He became a director of several banks, business organizations, and airlines, and was vice-president (1935–37) of the Bank for International Settlements at Basel, and its president from 1937 to 1940. A financial director (1940–46) of Lever Brothers and Unilever, and financial adviser (1940 *et seq.*) to the Netherlands government, he was named (1946) an executive director of the International Monetary Fund. In 1952 he and M. A. H. Luns shared the portfolio of foreign affairs in the Drees coalition cabinet.

Beyerland (bī'ėr.länt). See **Beijerland.**

Beyerlein (bī'ėr.līn), **Franz Adam.** b. at Meissen, Germany, March 22, 1871—. German novelist and dramatist. He has attained his greatest success with two works that have to do with military life: *Jena oder Sedan* (1903), a realistic novel that evoked great interest in Germany and abroad, and has run into hundreds of printings; and *Zapfenstreich* (1904), a play attacking the evils of the Prussian military system. Other works are *Ein Winterlager* (1906), *Stirb und werde* (1910), *Die Siebenschläfer* (1924), and *Kain und Abel* (1925).

Beylerbeg Serai (bā.lėr.beg' se.rī'). Summer-palace at Constantinople, finished in 1865 by Abdul-Aziz, on the Bosporus. The water façade displays great purity and harmony of design, and the grand staircase and ceremonial saloons, decorated in a Turkish modification of the Moorish style, are outstanding examples of their type.

Beyoğlu (bā.ôg.lö'). [Also, **Pera.**] Northern quarter of Istanbul, Turkey. It is situated on the opposite side of the Golden Horn from the old part (Stambul) of the city, and is inhabited chiefly by Europeans. Pop. ab. 230,000.

Beyond the Horizon. Play by Eugene O'Neill, produced and published in 1920 and awarded a Pulitzer prize in the same year. Robert Mayo, who finds farm work distasteful, gives up his romantic dreams of going to sea, in order to marry Ruth Atkins. Robert settles down as a farmer while his brother Andrew, who had also wanted to marry Ruth, becomes a sailor. The farm is a failure, and Ruth's love for Robert is weakened by the increasing hardship of their life. Hardened by his worldly experience, Andrew returns to find Robert dying of tuberculosis. Ruth, who has transferred her affection to Andrew, finds him cold toward her. The play ends with the dying Robert seeking his old dream of a life "beyond the horizon."

Beypasha (bā.pash'ä). See **Beas.**

Beyrich (bī'rich), **Heinrich Ernst.** b. at Berlin, Aug. 31, 1815; d. there, July 9, 1896. German geologist and paleontologist, professor (1856 *et seq.*) at the University of Berlin. He was associate director of the Geological Survey of Prussia, and published a number of important paleontological works.

Beyrout (bā.röt'). See **Beirut.**

Beyrouth (bā.röt). French name of **Beirut.**

Beyschlag (bī'shläk), **Franz.** b. at Karlsruhe, Germany, Oct. 5, 1856—. German geologist who served (1903–23) as director of the Preussische Geologische Landesanstalt; son of Willibald Beyschlag. He was the author of *Die Lagerstätten der nutzbaren Mineralien und Gesteine* (2nd edition, 1914; Eng. trans., 1914–16).

Beyschlag, Willibald. b. at Frankfort on the Main, Germany, Sept. 5, 1823; d. at Halle, Germany, Nov. 25, 1900. German Protestant theologian; father of Franz Beyschlag. He was educated at the universities of Bonn and Berlin, and as court chaplain at Karlsruhe became prominent through his opposition to the liberal movement within the church. Professor of practical theology (1860 *et seq.*) at the University of Halle, he was the leader of the *Mittelspartei* (moderate wing) of theologians; he took part in founding the Evangelical Alliance and the *Deutsch-evangelische Blätter*.

Beyşehir (bā.she.hėr'). [Also: **Beg-Shehr, Bei-shehr, Bey-Shehr** (bā.sher').] Town in S Turkey in the *il* (province or vilayet) of Konya, situated near the E shore of Lake Beysehir, ab. 75 mi. NE of Antalya: a trading center served by three roads; small exports of opium and rugs. Pop. ab. 3,000.

Beyşehir, Lake. [Also: **Lake Beg-Shehr** (or **Bei-Shehr** or **Bey-Shehr**); Turkish, **Beyşehir Gölü** (gė.lü).] Lake in S central Turkey, ab. 65 mi. N of Antalya. It is a salt lake with no outlet. Length, ab. 25 mi.

Bezaleel (bę.zal'ę.el). In the Old Testament, the artificer who executed the works of art on the tabernacle. Ex. xxxi. 2–6.

Bezaliel (bę.zal'i.el). In the second part of the satire *Absalom and Achitophel* by John Dryden and Nahum Tate, a character meant for Henry Somerset, marquis of Worcester, afterward Duke of Beaufort. He was noted for his devotion to learning.

Bezborodko (biz.bo.rôt'ko), Prince **Aleksandr Andreyevich.** b. at Stolnoi, Russia, March 25, 1747; d. at St. Petersburg, Aug. 9, 1799. Russian statesman. He was appointed secretary of foreign affairs in 1780, and imperial chancellor in 1796.

Bèze (bez), **Théodore de.** [Also: **Théodore de Besze;** Latinized, **Theodorus Beza.**] b. at Vézelay, France, June 24, 1519; d. at Geneva, Oct. 13, 1605. French Protestant theologian, successor (1564) to John Calvin as leader of the Reformed Church at Geneva. He studied (1528–35) the classics under the humanist Melchior Wolmar at Orléans and Bourges, and then studied (1535–39) law at the University of Orléans; in 1539 he went to the University of Paris, where he eventually devoted himself to humanistic studies. In 1548 he published a collection of poems, *Juvenilia;* in the same year he fled to Geneva, where he abjured Catholicism. After having become (1549) professor of Greek in the academy at Lausanne, he accepted (1559) the rectorship of the academy at Geneva and a pastorate in Geneva; he participated in the Colloquy of Poissy in 1561, and in that of St.-Germain in 1562. He succeeded Calvin at Geneva on the latter's death in 1564, and thereafter presided at the synods of the French Protestants at La Rochelle in 1571, and Nîmes in 1572, and participated (1586) in the Colloquy at Mompelgard. He wrote *De haereticis a civili magistratu puniendis,* in which he defends the execution of Servetus, and other works.

Bezerra (bę.zer'rą), **Luiz Barbalho.** See **Barbalho Bezerra, Luiz.**

Bezhitsa (bye'zhi.tsą). [Former name, **Ordjonikidzegrad,** or **Ordzhonikidzegrad.**] City in the U.S.S.R., in the Orel *oblast* (region) of the Russian Soviet Federated Socialist Republic, across the Desna River from Bryansk, halfway between Moscow and Kiev: important locomotive works; also has wood and paper industries. 82,331 (1939).

Béziers (bā.zyā). [Latin, **Biterra Septimanorum, Baeterrae.**] City in S France, in the department of Hérault, situated on the Orb River and the Canal du Midi near the Mediterranean Sea, between Montpellier and Narbonne. The center of a wine-making region, it produces agricultural and vineyard tools, textiles, liquors, and other items. It is famous for the theatrical performances in its arenas. The Church of Saint-Nazaire dates from the 12th, 13th, and 14th centuries. There are a museum, a theater, and beautiful promenades. Béziers was the scene of massacres in the Albigensian wars. 64,561 (1946).

Bezold (bā'tsolt), **Wilhelm von.** b. at Munich, June 21, 1837; d. at Berlin, Feb. 17, 1907. German meteorologist, named (1885) professor of meteorology and director of the Meteorological Institute at Berlin. He is best known for his studies in the physics of the atmosphere and in terrestrial magnetism. He published numerous scientific works and papers.

Bezonian (bę.zō'ni.ąn). Name given to a beggar; a mean, low person. According to John Florio a *bisogno* was "a new leuied souldier such as comes needy to the war." Randle Cotgrave defines *bisongne* as "a filthie knave, or clowne, a raskall, a bisonian, basehumoured scoundrel." Its original sense is a raw recruit; hence, as a term of contempt, a beggar, a needy person. The word is used by Shakespeare in *Henry IV, Part II,* and derives from the Italian noun *bisogno* (need).

Bezons (bę.zôn̂). Town in N France, in the department of Seine-et-Oise, situated on the Seine River, W of Argenteuil. An industrial town, and a suburb of Paris, it was largely destroyed during World War II. It has been known for its automobile, airplane, and chemical factories. 12,684 (1946).

Bezwada (bez.wä'dạ). [Also: **Vijayavada, Vizayawada.**] City in the SE part of the Union of India, in NE Madras state, ab. 268 mi. by rail N of the city of Madras, located on the N bank of the Kistna River at the head of its delta. An ancient river-crossing trade center, Bezwada has old shrines dating back at least to the 7th century. It is important today as a railroad junction and trade center, with rice-milling and cotton-processing industries. Just E of the city is a great irrigation dam 3,715 ft. long, built in 1855, which waters ab. 1,250 sq. mi. of delta farming land. Rocky hills tower above the city on the N, W, and S. 86,184 (1941).

Bhaca (bä'kä). [Also, **Amabaca.**] One of several regroupings of heterogeneous Nguni refugees from the Zulu wars of the early 19th century, in S Africa, inhabiting the E part of Cape Province and S Natal, in the Union of South Africa.

Bhadrinath (bud.rẹ.nät'). See **Badrinath.**

Bhagalpur (bä'gạl.pör). Division of Bihar state, NE Union of India, ab. 250 mi. NW of Calcutta. The chief crops in the area are rice, wheat, sugar, and tobacco. Capital, Bhagalpur; area, ab. 19,000 sq. mi.; pop. 9,598,025 (1941).

Bhagalpur. District of the Bhagalpur division, Bihar, NE Union of India. Capital, Bhagalpur; area, 4,226 sq. mi.; pop. 2,408,879 (1941).

Bhagalpur. Chief city of Bhagalpur division, Bihar state, NE Union of India, on the Ganges River, ab. 220 mi. NW of Calcutta: important trading center. 93,254 (1941).

Bhagavad-Gita (bä"gạ.vạd.gē'tä). In Sanskrit literature, "the song of Bhagavat," that is, the mystical doctrines sung by "the adorable one," a name of Krishna when identified with the Supreme Being. The author is unknown. He is supposed to have lived in India in the 1st or 2nd century of our era. The poem was at an early date dignified by a place in the *Mahabharata*, the Sanskrit epic of India, but is of a much later date than the main body of that epic. Its philosophy is eclectic, combining elements of the Sankhya, Yoga, and Vedanta systems with the later theory of Bhakti, or "faith." The whole composition is skilfully thrown into the form of a dramatic poem or dialogue, characterized by great loftiness of thought and beauty of expression. The speakers are the two most important personages of the *Mahabharata*, Arjuna and Krishna. In the great war Krishna refused to take up arms on either side, but consented to act as Arjuna's charioteer and to aid him with counsel. At the commencement of the *Bhagavad-Gita* the two armies are in battle array, when Arjuna is struck with compunction at the idea of fighting his way to a kingdom through the blood of his kindred. Krishna's reply is made the occasion of the dialogue which in fact constitutes the *Bhagavad-Gita*, the main design of which is to exalt the duties of caste above all other obligations, including the ties of friendship and affection, but at the same time to show that the practice of those duties is compatible with the self-mortification of the Yoga philosophy as well as with the deepest devotion to the Supreme Being, with whom Krishna claims to be identified.

Bhagavata-Purana (bä"gạ.vạ.tạ.pọ.rä'nạ). Epic poem (one of the 18 included in the *Puranas*) of Bhagavata, or Vishnu, a work of great celebrity in India, exercising a more powerful influence upon the opinions of the people than any of the other *Puranas*. It consists of 18,000 verses, and is ascribed by Henry Thomas Colebrooke to the grammarian Vopadeva, of about the 13th century A.D. Its most popular part, the tenth book, which narrates the history of Krishna, has been translated into many of the vernaculars of India.

Bhagirathi (bä.gē'rạ.ti). Name of the **Ganges** in its upper course.

Bhamo (bä'mō). Town in NE Burma, situated on the Irrawaddy River ab. 175 mi. NE of Mandalay: famous for its trade in rubies that are found in the area. Rubber and rice are the important crops. 7,827.

Bhandara (bun.dä'rạ). District of the Chhattisgarh division, in Madhya Pradesh (Central Provinces), Union of India, just W of Nagpur: important manganese mines. Area, 3,965 sq. mi.; pop. 963,225 (1941).

Bhandarwa (bun.där'wạ). Former state of the Union of India, in the Central India states, now merged with Vindhya Pradesh, ab. 160 mi. SW of the city of Benares: silk and rice. Capital, Bhandarwa; area, 27 sq. mi.; pop. 13,520 (1941).

Bharat (bä'rät). See **India, Union of.**

Bharatpur (bu'rut.pör). [Also: **Bhartpur** (burt'pör), **Bhurtpore** (-pōr).] Former state in the NW part of the Union of India, in Rajputana, now merged with Rajasthan, ab. 100 mi. SE of Delhi: rice, wheat, cotton, and barley. Capital, Bharatpur; area, 1,972 sq. mi.; pop. 575,625 (1941).

Bharech (bä.rech'). See **Bahraich.**

Bharoch (bạ.rōch'). See **Broach.**

Bhaskara (bäs'kạ.rạ). [Surnamed **Acarya** (or **Acharya**), meaning the "Learned."] b. 1114; date of death not known. Hindu astronomer and mathematician. He wrote *Siddhantasiromani*, which contains treatises on algebra, arithmetic, and geometry.

Bhatnagar (but.nug'ạr), Sir **Shanti Swarup.** b. 1895—. Indian scientist, director (1947 *et seq.*) of industrial and scientific research in India, a member of the Indian scientific mission (1945) to the U.S. and England. Professor of chemistry (1921–24) at Benares University and at Lahore University (1924–40), he was knighted in 1941, and served as president (1945) of the Indian Scientific Congress. Author of *Principles and Applications of Magneto Chemistry* (1935).

Bhatpara (bät.pä'rạ). City in the E part of the Union of India, in E West Bengal state, on the E bank of the Hooghly River, ab. 22 mi. N of Calcutta. Long famous as a center of Sanskrit learning, Bhatpara is now a modern industrial city, with many large jute mills along the river, and a paper mill. 117,044 (1941).

Bhattikavya (bät.ti.kä'vyạ). In Sanskrit literature, "the poem of Bhatti," an artificial epic poem by Bhatti, celebrating the exploits of Rama, and illustrating Sanskrit grammar by the employment of all possible forms and constructions. By some it is ascribed to Bhartrihari.

Bhaunagar (bou.nug'ạr). See **Bhavnagar.**

Bhavabhuti (bä.vạ.bö'ti). fl. 8th century. Sanskrit poet, author of the three dramas *Malatimadhava*, *Mahaviracharita*, and *Uttararamacharita*. The first of these is sometimes referred to as "the Hindu Romeo and Juliet."

Bhavnagar (bou.nug'ạr). [Also, **Bhaunagar.**] Former state in the W part of the Union of India, one of the Western India states, now merged with Saurashtra, across the Gulf of Cambay from Surat: one of the largest dairying areas in the Union of India; cotton also is important. Capital, Bhavnagar; area, 2,961 sq. mi.; pop. 618,429 (1941).

Bhavnagar. [Also, **Bhaunagar.**] City in the W part of the Union of India, in E Saurashtra state, ab. 200 mi. N of Bombay. Founded in 1723, the city is modern, and has developed a small deep-water port on the Gulf of Cambay, trading in cotton, cotton textiles, iron, and other goods. The chief manufactures are cotton and silk textiles, hosiery, matches, salt, and iron products. 102,851 (1941).

Bhawalpur (bä'wạl.pör). See **Bahawalpur.**

Bhil (bēl). Tribe of W India, now numbering about two million, whose language is of the Indo-European family. The word *Bhil* means "bowman," and some of the tribe still are forest dwellers who live by the hunt and by shifting cultivation. Others of the tribe have become cultivators, or act as village watchmen. They are found from Bombay through the Rajputana region and into C India.

Bhil States. Former group of small states in the Union of India, in the Vindhya and Satpura Mountains.

Bhima (bē'mạ). [Also: **Bhimasena** (bē.mạ.sā'nạ), **Vrikodara.**] In Hindu mythology, the reputed second son of Pandu, but in reality the son of his wife Pritha or Kunti by Vayu, the god of the wind. He was remarkable for his vast size and strength and voracious appetite.

Bhir (bir). See **Bir.**

Bhoja (bō'jạ). Name borne by a number of Hindu kings. A king Bhoja, ruler of Malwa, who dwelt at Dhar and Ujjain, and who, according to an inscription, lived between c1040 and c1090 A.D., is said by tradition to have been the Vikrama at whose court the "nine gems" flourished.

Bholan (bō.län'). See **Bolan.**

Bhopal (bō.päl'). [Also, **Bhopal Agency.**] Former political agency in the Central India Agency of British India, ab. 200 mi. NW of Nagpur. It included, among others, the native state Bhopal, later one of the Central India states, and made a "centrally administered area" under the Constitution of the Union of India.

Bhopal. State of the Union of India, in the N central part of the Deccan. Cattle, wheat, and tobacco growing and the mining of manganese are the important occupations. Formerly one of the Central India states, Bhopal became (1949) a "centrally administered area" under the Constitution of the Union of India, with one seat in the Council of States. Capital, Bhopal; area, 6,921 sq. mi.; pop. 838,107 (1951).

Bhopal. Capital of the state of Bhopal, in the C part of the Union of India: road and railroad junction and trading center. 75,228 (1941).

Bhor (bōr). Former state in W India, one of the Deccan States, now part of Bombay state, Union of India, located ab. 40 mi. SE of the city of Bombay. Teakwood is one of the important exports of this region; its carvings are famous. Capital, Bhor; area, 910 sq. mi.; pop. 155,961 (1941).

Bhubaneswar (bö.vä.ne'swär). See **Bhuvaneswar.**

Bhurtpore (burt'pōr). See **Bharatpur.**

Bhutan (bö.tän'). [Also, **Bootan.**] Country in Asia, lying between Tibet on the N, Sikkim on the W, Assam on the E, and the Union of India on the S, occupied largely by the Himalaya Mountains. Chief crops are rice, millet, and corn; guns, swords, and cloth are manufactured; elephants and ponies are raised. Until 1907 power was held by the *Deb Raja* (secular head), and the *Dharma Raja* (spiritual head). Government is now vested in a maharajah. The predominant religion is Buddhism. Part of the country was annexed by Great Britain in 1866. Under the terms of a treaty signed in 1949, the Union of India agreed to return ab. 32 sq. mi. to Bhutan and to continue the guidance of Bhutanese external affairs formerly undertaken by the British Indian government. Capital, Bumthang; area, ab. 18,000 sq. mi.; pop. 300,000 (est. 1941).

Bhuvaneswar (bö.vä.nes'wär). [Also: **Bhubaneswar, Bhuvaneshwar** (-nesh'wär).] Town in the E central part of the Union of India, in E central Orissa state, ab. 272 mi. SW of Calcutta by rail: the new capital of Orissa state. It was the capital of the Kesari kings of Orissa from the 5th to the 10th century, and it is believed that 7,000 shrines once surrounded its sacred lake; now there are only about 500 decaying relics, of various styles of Buddhist and Hindu architecture. The Great Temple dates from the 7th century A.D. and is considered one of India's finest Hindu temples. The foundation stone of the new government center was laid in April, 1948, by Prime Minister Nehru.

Biafra (bē.ä'frạ). Small district of Cameroun, W Africa, situated on the Bight of Biafra.

Biafra, Bight of. Eastern part of the Gulf of Guinea, on the W coast of Africa, between the mouths of the Niger River and Cape Lopez, S of Nigeria and W of Cameroun.

Biała Krakowska (byä'lä krä.kôf'skä). [Also, **Biała.**] Town in S Poland, in the *województwo* (province) of Kraków, formerly in Austrian Galicia, situated on the Biała River in the foothills of the Carpathian Mountains, ab. 43 mi. SW of Kraków: agricultural markets, particularly for livestock; textile manufactures. It had formerly a considerable German-speaking minority. 19,564 (1946).

Biała Podlaska (pôd.lä'skä). [Also, **Biała.**] Town in E Poland, in the *województwo* (province) of Lublin, situated on the Krzna River, ab. 60 mi. NE of Lublin: agricultural market town. 15,007 (1946).

Bialik (byä'lik), **Chaim Nachman.** [Also, **Byalik.**] b. at Radi, in Volhynia, in territory now controlled by the U.S.S.R., Jan. 9, 1873; d. at Vienna, July 4, 1934. Hebrew poet. He attended a *yeshiva* (Talmudic academy) before publishing his first book of poems at Warsaw in 1901; he attained standing as a Hebrew poet of the first rank with his poem *Beir Haharegah* (In the City of Slaughter), which was included in his volume of pogrom poems *The Songs of Wrath.* It was inspired by his anger against the Kishinev massacres of April, 1903. He became (1905) a partner in a publishing house at Odessa, but left the U.S.S.R. in 1921 to live at Berlin and, later, Hamburg; he settled in Palestine in 1924, and visited the U.S. in 1926. He made Hebrew translations of Cervantes' *Don Quixote* and Schiller's *Wilhelm Tell.* Among his works are *Halachah Veagadah* (Eng. trans., 1933) and *Safiah* (Eng. trans., 1939). Two of his best-known poems are *Megillath Haesh* (The Scroll of Fire) and *Methe Hidbar* (The Dead of the Wilderness).

Białogard (byä.lô'gärt). [German, **Belgard.**] City in NW Poland, in the *województwo* (province) of Szczecin, formerly in Pomerania, Germany, situated on the Persante River, ab. 72 mi. NE of Stettin: agricultural market town and an important railroad junction; has had lumber, leather, and machine industries. The city came under Polish administration in 1945; the former German population has left, and has been replaced by Polish settlers. 16,456 (1939); 12,211 (1946).

Biały Kamień (byä'li kä'myen). [German, **Weisstein.**] Town in SW Poland, in the *województwo* (province) of Wrocław, formerly in Silesia, Germany, situated in the Silesian Mountains, NW of Wałbrzych, of which it is a suburb. It is a coal-mining town; the former German population is now supplanted by Polish immigrants. 17,348 (1939); 18,717 (1946).

Białystok (byä.li'stôk). [Also: **Byalistock;** German, **Bjelostock;** Russian, **Belostok, Bielostok.**] *Województwo* (province or voivodship) in NE Poland, bordering on the U.S.S.R. (Byelorussia) on the E, Lublin on the S, Warszawa and Olsztyn on the W, and Lithuania on the N. Capital, Białystok; area, ab. 11,410 sq. mi.

Białystok. [Also: **Byalistock;** German, **Bjelostock;** Russian, **Belostok, Bielostok.**] City in E Poland, in the *województwo* (province) of Białystok, situated on the Biała River, a tributary of the Narew River, ab. 105 mi. NE of Warsaw: important railroad junction in a wheat-raising area; has textile and machinery industries. Founded in the 14th century, Białystok remained a village until 1749 when a *hetman* (chieftain) named Branicki established his residence there; it was part of Prussia 1795–1807, passed (1814) to Russia, and was restored (1919) to Poland. In World War I, it was occupied by the Germans on Aug. 26, 1915. In World War II, it was once more occupied on Sept. 16, 1939; the Russians reconquered the town in July, 1944, and it was for a time part of the Byelorussian Soviet Socialist Republic. The city suffered heavy damage in World War II; 70 percent of all buildings were destroyed; however, reconstruction got under way after the war and new settlements were begun. The factories were reconstructed, as was the theater building, and the city transport (buses) was put back into operation. The majority of the population, prior to World War II, was Jewish; they were deported to death camps during the German occupation. 56,759 (1946).

Bianca (bi.ang'kạ). Woman of Cyprus, in Shakespeare's *Othello.*

Bianca. Sister of Katharina, in Shakespeare's *The Taming of the Shrew.* She is wooed and won by Lucentio.

Bianca. Venetian beauty, in Thomas Middleton's play *Women Beware Women,* married to Leontio and tempted by a shameless woman to become the duke's mistress.

Bianca. The Duchess of Pavia, in John Ford's play *Love's Sacrifice;* a gross and profligate woman who has the art of appearing innocent by denying the favors she means to grant.

Bianca. A pathetic and beautiful girl, the titular heroine of *The Fair Maid of the Inn,* by Philip Massinger, William Rowley, and John Fletcher.

Bianca. Wife of Fazio, in Henry Hart Milman's play *Fazio* (1815).

Biancavilla (byäng.kä.vēl'lä). [Ancient name, **Inessa.**] Town and commune in S Italy, on the island of Sicily, in the province of Catania, situated on the Simeto River in the interior of the island, ab. 9 mi. NW of Catania. Center of a grain and fruit producing district. Pop. of commune, 16,644 (1936); of town, 16,076 (1936).

Bianchi (byäng'kē). Political faction which arose in Tuscany c1300. The Guelph family of the Cancellieri at Pistoia having banished the Ghibelline family of the Panciatichi, a feud for power arose between two distantly related branches of the former, who were distinguished from each other by the names of Bianchi and Neri (the whites and the blacks). In the period 1296–1300, the two factions became so violent that Florence, in order to bring peace to Pistoia, required that city to banish the whole family of the Cancellieri, but at the same time opened its own gates to them. In Florence the Neri allied themselves with Corso Donati and the violent Guelphs, and the Bianchi with Vieri de' Cerchi and the moderate Guelphs, and subsequently with the Ghibellines and the Panciatichi. Pope Boniface VIII espoused the party of the Neri, and sent, nominally to bring about a reconciliation, Charles de Valois to Florence in 1301, with the result that the Bianchi, among whom was Dante, were exiled.

Bianchi, Francesco. b. at Cremona, Italy, c1752; d. at Hammersmith, London, Nov. 27, 1810. Italian composer, conductor, and teacher, notable chiefly for his operas, which include *Semiramide, Acige e Galatea, Merope,* and *Alzira.* He was a conductor in Italy and England (1793 *et seq.*).

Bianchi, Luigi. b. at Parma, Italy, Jan. 18, 1856; d. at Pisa, Italy, June 6, 1928. Italian mathematician, who contributed especially to differential geometry and the Lie theory of groups. He took his doctorate at the University of Pisa in 1877, and later taught there. He was the author of numerous papers in the *Rendiconti della R. Accademia dei Lincei* and other journals. His books include *Lezioni di geometria differenziale* (1894), *Lezioni sulla teoria dei gruppi* (1900), *Lezioni sulla teoria delle funzioni* (1901), and *Lezioni sulla teoria dei numeri algebrici* (1923).

Bianchini (byäng.kē'nē), **Francesco.** b. at Verona, Italy, Dec. 13, 1662; d. at Rome, March 2, 1729. Italian astronomer and antiquary. He was named, by Pope Clement XI, secretary of a commission engaged in calendar reform. His astronomic discoveries include three comets.

Bianco or **Biancho** (byäng'kō), **Andrea.** fl. early 15th century. Venetian cartographer. He left a collection of hydrographical charts anterior to the discovery of the Cape of Good Hope and of America. In a chart dated 1436 he shows two islands west of the Azores, named "Antillia" and "De laman Satanaxio," which some scholars have claimed as evidence of a knowledge of the two Americas prior to the voyage of Christopher Columbus.

Bianco (byäng'kō), **Margery.** [Maiden name, **Williams.**] b. at London, July 22, 1881; d. at New York, Sept. 6, 1944. English novelist and author of books for children. Educated in the U.S., where she lived for many years, she also resided in France, Italy, and England. Author of *The Late Returning* (1902), *The Price of Youth* (1904), *The Bar* (1906), novels; and books for children, including *The Velveteen Rabbit* (1922), *Poor Cecco* (1925), *The Little Wooden Doll* (1925) and *The Skin Horse* (1927), the latter two illustrated by her daughter, Pamela, *The Adventures of Andy* (1927), *Candlestick,* and *All About Pets* (both 1929).

Bianco, Monte. Italian name of **Blanc, Mont.**

Biandrata (byän.drä'tä), **Giorgio.** See **Blandrata, Giorgio.**

Biard (byàr), **Auguste (François).** b. at Lyons, France, c1800; d. near Fontainebleau, France, 1882. French genre painter.

Biard, Pierre. b. at Grenoble, France, c1567; d. at Avignon, France, Nov. 17, 1622. French Jesuit missionary in what is now the SE part of Canada and the N part of Maine. Having joined (1583) the Society of Jesus, he taught theology and Hebrew at Lyons, France, until appointed (1608) head of a mission to Acadia. In 1611 he sailed for Acadia, reaching Port Royal on May 22, 1611, and there setting up religious services. He won the confidence of natives all the way S to the Kennebec River. In 1613 he was a cofounder of a settlement at St. Sauveur (now Bar Harbor, Me.), but this was soon attacked by English plunderers, and Biard with another priest was carried off as a prisoner to Virginia. Having narrowly escaped hanging, he was sent back to Port Royal, there to witness the destruction of the settlement. Finally sent back to France, he went back to teaching. Author of *Relation de la Nouvelle France* (1616).

Biarritz (bē'ą.rits; French, byà.rēts). Town in SW France, in the department of Basses-Pyrénées, situated on a high cliff overlooking the Gulf of Gascogne (the southernmost part of the Bay of Biscay), ab. 5 mi. SW of Bayonne. It is one of the most famous and fashionable resorts in France; has an excellent beach and saline thermal baths; it is visited the year round by more than half a million guests. The two principal seasons are in the periods August–September and March–April; during the winter months English visitors predominate. The town was developed during the Second Empire; Napoleon III contributed much to the initial success. It has numerous hotels, casinos, and bathing establishments. 22,022 (1946).

Bias (bē'äs). See also **Beas.**

Bias (bī'ąs). b. at Priene, in Ionia, fl. middle of the 6th century B.C. One of the "Seven Sages" of Greece, noted for his apothegms.

Bibb (bib), **George Mortimer.** b. in Prince Edward County, Va., Oct. 30, 1776; d. April 14, 1859. American jurist, U.S. senator (1811–14, 1829–35), and cabinet member. He was also chief justice (1809–10, 1827–28) of the Kentucky court of appeals, and U.S. secretary of the treasury (1844–45).

Bibb, William Wyatt. b. in Amelia County, Ga., Oct. 2, 1781; d. in Autauga County, Ala., July 10, 1820. American politician, notable as the first (1817) governor of Alabama (established in that year as a U.S. territory; it acquired statehood two years later). Granted (1801) a medical degree from the University of Pennsylvania, he established a practice at Petersburg, Ga. After having served in the state legislature, he was elected to the U.S. Congress, taking his seat in 1805 and serving until 1813, when he resigned. Elected to the U.S. Senate to fill the seat of a deceased member, he again resigned, after having served for three years. Having been named (1817) governor of the territory of Alabama by President James Monroe, he continued in that position after the territory acquired statehood, and held the post until his death.

Bibbiena (bēb.byä'nä). See also **Bibiena.**

Bibbiena. Town and commune in C Italy, in the *compartimento* (region) of Tuscany, in the province of Arezzo, situated in the Casentino valley, near the confluence of the Archiano and Arno rivers, N of Arezzo. It has woolen manufactures and a school for electricians. In the Church of San Lorenzo are sculptures in terra cotta by Andrea and Giovanni della Robbia; these were undamaged during World War II, although the roof of the church was partly destroyed. Pop. of commune, 10,214 (1936); of town, 2,320 (1936).

Bibbiena, Bernardo Dovizio da. [Also called **Bernardo di Tarlatti.**] b. at Bibbiena, Arezzo, Italy, Aug. 4, 1470; d. Nov. 9, 1520. Italian poet and humorist; an intimate friend of Raphael. The private secretary of Cardinal Giovanni de' Medici (later Pope Leo X), he was himself made a cardinal in 1513. He wrote the comedy *Calandria* (1521) and others.

Biber (bē'bėr), **Heinrich Johann Franz von.** b. at Wartenburg, in Bohemia, Aug. 12, 1644; d. at Salzburg, Austria, May 3, 1704. German violinist, notable as the originator of the German school of violin playing. He was the composer of sonatas, church music, and a musical drama.

Biberach (bē'bėr.äċh). Town in S Germany, in the *Land* (state) of Württemberg-Hohenzollern, French Zone, formerly in the Danube *Kreis* (district) of Württemberg, situated on the Riss River, ab. 22 mi. SW of Ulm. It is a center for agricultural and livestock trade, and manufactures canned goods, agricultural machinery, shoes, and leather articles. The town has preserved its medieval character; the parish church dates from the 12th century, the Church of Magdalene from the 15th century; there are also remains of old fortifications. 14,984 (1950).

Bibesco (bē.bes'kō), **Barbo Demetrius.** [Rumanian, **Bibescu;** title, Prince **Stirbey.**] b. 1799; d. at Nice, France, April 13, 1869. Walachian politician; brother of George Demetrius Bibesco, hospodar of Walachia. He was adopted by Barbo Stirbey and took his name.

Bibesco, George Demetrius. [Rumanian, **Bibescu.**] b. 1804; d. at Paris, June 1, 1873. Walachian politician, hospodar of Walachia in the period 1842–48; brother of Barbo Demetrius Bibesco. The revolutionary movement of 1848 brought him into disfavor, forcing his resignation.

Bibiena (bē.byä'nä), **Allesandro Galli da.** [Also, **Bibbiena.**] b. 1687; d. c1769. Italian painter and architect;

son of Ferdinando Galli da Bibiena. His most notable work was done when he was architect and painter at the court of the elector of the Palatinate. His best known creations are the right wing of the *Schloss* (castle) at Mannheim and the Jesuit church in the same city.

Bibiena, Antonio Galli da. [Also, **Bibbiena.**] b. 1700; d. 1744. Italian architect and designer; son of Ferdinando Galli da Bibiena. He was employed at the imperial court at Vienna, but his best remembered works are the Academia Virgiliana at Mantua, Italy, and the Teatro Communale at Bologna, Italy.

Bibiena, Ferdinando Galli da. [Also, **Bibbiena.**] b. at Bologna, Italy, Aug. 18, 1657; d. there, Jan. 3, 1743. Italian painter and architect. A member of a family of architects, he is noted for his theater constructions and designs.

Bibiena, Giuseppe Galli da. [Also, **Bibbiena.**] b. at Parma, Italy, Jan. 5, 1696; d. at Berlin, 1756. Italian designer, considered the most distinguished member of his family; son of Ferdinando Galli da Bibiena. As a youth he accompanied his father to Barcelona and to Vienna. He remained in the latter capital, where he became attached to the imperial court and found opportunity for his talents in the organization of imposing court functions, festivities, plays, and gala entertainments. Other royal and princely courts sought his services; he went to Munich in 1722 and to Prague the following year. Back in Vienna, he designed the decorations of the opera in 1742; but in 1747 he went to Dresden, in 1748 to Bayreuth, and in 1751 to Berlin, where he remained until his death. In 1740 he published a series of architectural designs, entitled *Architettura e Prospettive.*

Bible, The Bishops'. See **Bishop's Bible, The.**

Bible Christians. See **Bryanites.**

Bible Commonwealth. Designation used by recent historians for the Massachusetts and New Haven colonies settled by the Puritans, deriving from use of Scripture as support for provisions of the legal code and the confinement of the franchise to church members.

Bible of Amiens (am′i.ęnz; French, à.myaṅ), **The.** Prose work (1885) by John Ruskin.

Bible of Forty-two Lines. Edition of the Vulgate, printed between 1450 and 1455 by Gutenberg and his companions. The book proper consists of 1,282 printed pages, two columns to the page, and, for the most part, with 42 lines to the column (whence the name).

Bible of the Poor. [Also, **Biblia Pauperum.**] Illustrated manuscript copies of the Scriptures, said by some authorities to date from the latter part of the 12th century, in their original form, and also to have been originally a book of pictures only. Numerous transcriptions of it were made during the Middle Ages.

Bible of Thirty-six Lines. Edition of the Vulgate, said to have been printed by Gutenberg and considered by some to be the oldest edition of the Latin Bible in printed form. A copy was given by Gutenberg to a monastery near Mainz. It contains 1,764 pages, which are made up, for the most part, in sections of 10 leaves, and usually bound in three volumes. Each page has 2 columns of 36 lines each (whence the name).

Bibliander (bib.li.an′dėr), **Theodore.** [Original name, **Theodor Buchmann.**] b. at Bischoffszell, Switzerland, c1504; d. at Zurich, Switzerland, Sept. 26, 1564. Swiss divine and Orientalist. He was successor to Huldreich Zwingli as professor of theology, and professor also of Oriental philology, at the University of Zurich from 1532 to 1560, when, on account of his opposition to the Calvinistic doctrine of predestination, he was removed from the faculty. He wrote a Latin translation of the Koran, and made many valuable contributions to the history of Islam.

Biblical Repertory. Presbyterian periodical, published, with interruptions, during the period 1825–88. It was renamed (1878) *The Princeton Review*, ceased publication in 1884, and was reissued (1886–88) as *The New Princeton Review.*

Bibliographical Society of America. Organization founded in 1904 (incorporated 1927) for the purpose of promoting bibliographical research and publications. It maintains headquarters at New York and issues a *News Sheet* (irregularly) and *Papers* (annually).

Bibliographisches Institut (bē″blē.ō.gräf′ish.ęs ēn.stē-töt′). German publishing firm founded (1826) by Joseph Meyer.

Bibliophile Jacob (bē.blē.*o*.fēl zhà.k*o*b), **Le.** Novel by Honoré de Balzac, written in 1830.

Bibliothèque de Ste. Geneviève (bē.blē.*o*.tek dę saṅt zhęn.vyev). Originally, the library of the Abbey of Ste.-Geneviève, at Paris, founded in 1624. The modern structure and organization date from 1850. The library is especially rich in incunabula, fine works from the Aldine and Elzevir presses, and other impressions of early printers. It has also a fine collection of manuscripts, and contains some 800,000 volumes.

Bibliothèque Mazarine (mà.zà.rēn). Library of ab. 350,000 volumes and 16,000 manuscripts, founded by Cardinal Mazarin. It is rich in bibliographic curiosities. In 1945 it was attached to the French Institute.

Bibliothèque Nationale (nà.syo.nàl). French national library at Paris. It has been called successively La Bibliothèque du Roi, Royale, Nationale, Impériale, and again Nationale. The Bibliothèque du Roi was originally in the Palais de la Cité, consisting of the library of the kings of France. Charles V removed it and collected a library of 910 volumes in the old Louvre. This was sold to the duke of Bedford. Louis XI partly repaired this loss and added the first results of the new invention of printing. Louis XII established it at Blois, incorporating it with the Orléans library. The Gruthuyse collection was next added to it. Francis I transferred the library to Fontainebleau, and placed it in charge of Jean Budié. Henry II made obligatory the deposit of one copy of every book published in the kingdom. Henry IV brought it back to Paris, where it changed in location frequently before resting in quarters in the Palais Mazarin, Rue Richelieu. Napoleon I increased the government grant, and under his care the library was much enlarged. It contains about five million volumes, 130,000 manuscripts, 3,100,000 prints and engravings, and 240,000 coins and medals. It is especially rich in Oriental manuscripts.

Biblis (bib′lis). [Also, **Byblis.**] In Greek legend, a nymph of Miletus who fell in love with her brother and was changed into a fountain.

Bibra (bē′brä), **Ernst von.** b. at Schwebheim, Bavaria, June 9, 1806; d. at Nuremberg, Bavaria, June 5, 1878. German chemist, naturalist, traveler, and novelist. Among his numerous works are *Reisen in Südamerika* (1854), *Die narkotischen Genussmittel und der Mensch* (1855), *Erinnerungen aus Südamerika* (1861), and *Reiseskizzen und Novellen* (1864).

Bibracte (bi.brak′tē). In ancient geography, a town in C Gaul, the capital of the Aedui, on the site of the small community of Mont Beuvray, ab. 8 mi. W of Autun, with which it was formerly identified. Near it Caesar defeated (58 B.C.) the Helvetii.

Bibrax (bī′braks). [Also, **Bibracte.**] In ancient geography, a town of the Remi, in N Gaul, probably at or near what is now Laon.

Bibulus (bib′ṵ.lus), **Marcus Calpurnius.** d. near Corcyra, on the island now known as Corfu, Greece, 48 B.C. Roman politician. He was Julius Caesar's colleague in the consulship in 59 B.C., having been elected through the efforts of the aristocratic party. After an ineffectual attempt to oppose Caesar's agrarian law, he shut himself up in his own house, whence he issued edicts against Caesar's measures. Pompey appointed him commander of the fleet in the Ionian Sea, in 49 B.C., to prevent Caesar from crossing over into Greece. His vigilance was, however, eluded by the latter in January of the following year.

Bicêtre (bē.setr). Village in N central France, ab. 1½ mi. S of Paris, containing a celebrated hospital, founded by Louis XIII in 1632, for invalid officers and soldiers. The foundation was greatly enlarged by Louis XIV and turned into a general hospital. It is now devoted to the destitute aged and incurable, and to the insane.

Bichat (bē.shà), **Marie François Xavier.** b. at Thoirette, Jura, France, Nov. 11, 1771; d. at Paris, July 22, 1802. French physiologist and anatomist, considered by some to have been the founder of scientific histology and pathological anatomy. His chief works are *Traité des membranes* (1800), *Recherches sur la vie et la mort* (1800), and *Anatomie générale* (1801).

Bickell (bik'ẹl), **Gustav Wilhelm Hugo.** b. at Kassel, Germany, 1838; d. at Vienna, 1906. German theologian and Orientalist. Converted (1865) to Catholicism, he was ordained a priest in 1867, and, after holding posts at the universities of Münster and Innsbruck, became (1891) professor of Oriental languages at the University of Vienna. He compiled a Hebrew grammar and wrote numerous theological studies.

Bickerdyke (bik'ėr.dīk), **Mary Ann Ball.** [Called **"Mother Bickerdyke."**] b. near what is now Mount Vernon, Ohio, July 19, 1817; d. at Bunker Hill, Kan., Nov. 8, 1901. American Civil War nurse, famous for her service (1861–65) with the Union armies in the West; a favorite of Ulysses S. Grant and William T. Sherman.

Bickerstaff (bik'ėr.ståf), **Isaac, Astrologer.** Pseudonym adopted by Jonathan Swift in 1708 during his controversy with the cobbler John Partridge, and borrowed (1709) by Richard Steele for his use as editor of *The Tatler.* The Swift-Partridge encounter began when Partridge published astrological predictions in an almanac; Swift, to prove these nonsensical, retorted with the parody *Predictions for the ensuing year, by Isaac Bickerstaff;* in this pamphlet he foretold Partridge's death on March 29; on March 30, he published a fulsome account of Partridge's demise; when the cobbler protested vigorously, Swift published a *Vindication,* in which he purported to prove Partridge's death beyond doubt. The joke became very popular, and when Steele wanted a pseudonym for himself, he adopted the name of Bickerstaff, as did Benjamin West (1730–1813).

Bickerstaffe (bik'ėr.ståf), **Isaac.** b. in Ireland, c1735; d. c1812. British dramatic writer. As a boy he was one of the pages to Lord Chesterfield, at that time lord lieutenant of Ireland. He attained an honorable position in the society of men of letters, but in 1772 was suspected of a capital crime, and fled to St.-Malo, France, where he lived under an assumed name. He wrote *Leucothoe,* a tragic opera (1756), *Love in a Village,* a comic opera, acted with great success in 1762 (printed in 1763), *The Maid of the Mill* (1765), *The Hypocrite* (1769), an adaptation of Colley Cibber's *The Non-Juror,* and others.

Bickerstaffe-Drew (bik'ėr.ståf.drö'), Monsignor Count **Francis Browning Drew.** [Pseudonym, **John Ayscough.**] b. at Headingly, Leeds, England, Feb. 11, 1858; d. at London, July 3, 1928. English novelist, essayist, and Roman Catholic priest. He was educated at Lichfield, at St. Chad's College, Denstone, and at Oxford University. The son of a Church of England clergyman, he became a Roman Catholic in 1879 and added his mother's maiden name, Drew, to his own name, in 1897; ordained in 1884, he was acting Catholic chaplain (1886–92) and chaplain (1892–99) to the British forces at Plymouth, and served (1914–15) in World War I; he was made a papal count in 1909. Under his pseudonym he wrote several novels, tales, and collections of essays, among them *Marotz* (1908), *Dromina and San Celestino* (1909), *Mezzogiorno* (1910), *Hurdcott* (1911), *Faustula* (1912), *Gracechurch* (1913), *Monksbridge* (1914), *French Windows* (1917), *Jacqueline* (1918), *Abbotscourt* (1919), *First Impressions in America* (1921), *Pages from the Past* (1922), and *Dobachi* (1923).

Bickersteth (bik'ėr.steth), **Edward.** b. at Kirby Lonsdale, England, March 19, 1786; d. at Walton, England, Feb. 28, 1850. English clergyman; father of Edward Henry Bickersteth. He is notable as the compiler of an anthological work containing more than 700 hymns. Author of *Help to the Study of the Scriptures* (1814) and others.

Bickersteth, Edward Henry. b. Jan. 25, 1825; d. May 16, 1906. English clergyman and poet; son of Edward Bickersteth. He was the author of *Yesterday, To-day, and For Ever* (1866) and others. He became bishop of Exeter in 1885.

Bickersteth, Henry. [Title, Baron **Langdale.**] b. at Kirkby Lonsdale, England, June 18, 1783; d. at Tunbridge Wells, England, April 18, 1851. English jurist. He became master of the rolls in January, 1836.

Bickmore (bik'mōr), **Albert Smith.** [Called the **"Father of the Museum."**] b. at Tenant's Harbor, Me., March 1, 1839; d. at Nonquitt, Mass., Aug. 12, 1914. American naturalist, active in the founding (1869) of the American Museum of Natural History at New York. Graduated (1864) from Harvard, he traveled (1865–67) through the Malay Archipelago, the Dutch East Indies, and parts of China and Japan, before serving as professor of natural history (1868–69) at Madison (now Colgate) University. He was superintendent (1869–84) of the American Museum of Natural History and curator (1884 *et seq.*) of its department of public instruction. He published *Travels in the East Indian Archipelago* (1868), among others.

Bicknell (bik'nẹl). City in SW Indiana, in Knox County, in a coal-mining district. 4,572 (1950).

Bicknell, Frank Alfred. b. at Augusta, Me., Feb. 17, 1866; d. April 7, 1943. American landscape painter and sculptor. He studied at Malden, Mass., and at the Julian Academy, Paris. He exhibited at Paris and in the U.S., and became a member of the American Art Association, at Paris, and, in 1913, an associate of the National Academy of Design. A list of his better-known works includes *October Morning, Spring, Mountain Laurel, Pirate's Cove, November,* and *The Beech and the Birch.*

Bicknell, George Augustus. b. at Batsto, N.J., May 15, 1846; d. at New Albany, Ind., Jan. 27, 1925. American naval officer, appointed (1907) a rear admiral. As an officer (1867–80) on the *Iroquois,* he was present at the opening (1868) of the ports of Kobe and Osaka in Japan. He commanded (until 1898) the USS *Niagara,* was commandant (1902–04) of the naval station at Key West, Fla., and served as commandant (1907–08) of the Portsmouth, N.H., navy yard.

Bicknell, Thomas Williams. b. at Barrington, R.I., Sept. 6, 1834; d. at Providence, R.I., Oct. 6, 1925. American educator and writer. He was the founder of a normal school (1871) in Rhode Island, the New England Bureau of Education (1876), the National Council of Education (1880), of which he was president (1880–84), and of the *New England Journal of Education, Education,* and *Primary Teacher* (1875), all of which he edited (1875–87). Author of *Biography of William L. Noyes* (1867), *Barrington in the Revolution* (1898), and *The Story of Dr. John Clarke, Founder of Civil and Religious Liberty in Rhode Island, 1638* (1915).

Bicocca (bē.kôk'kä). See **La Bicocca.**

Bicol (bē.kōl'). See also **Bikol.**

Bicol (bē'kōl). [Also, **Inaya.**] River in the N central Philippines, the chief river of Camarines-Sur province, SE Luzon. It flows from Lake Bato NW to San Miguel Bay, and is navigable by steamers of 9-ft. draft to Nueva Caceres, a distance of 15 mi.

Bicorne (bī'kôrn). See under **Chichevache.**

Bida (bē'dä). Town in W Africa, in Niger province, Northern Provinces, Nigeria, situated N of the Niger River. It is a center for glass-bead work, copper and brass manufactures, and weaving, carried on by the native peoples.

Bida (bē.då), **Alexandre.** b. 1813; d. Jan. 2, 1895. French designer and painter, noted chiefly for his treatments of scriptural and Oriental subjects. Designs illustrating the works of the Evangelists (1873) were his chief work.

Bidar (bē'dạr). District of the Gulbarga division, Hyderabad, Union of India, centered ab. 100 mi. NW of the city of Hyderabad. Of chief importance are millet, wheat, tobacco, and forest products. Area, ab. 4,000 sq. mi.; pop. 874,000 (est. 1941).

Bidasoa (bē.ᴛʜä.sō'ä). [Also, **Bidassoa.**] River in N Spain which flows into the Bay of Biscay at Fuenterrabia. It is, for ab. 12 mi., the boundary between France and Spain. The duke of Wellington passed the Bidasoa on Oct. 7, 1813, defeating the French under Soult. Length, ab. 50 mi.

Bidault (bē.dō), **Georges.** b. at Moulins, Allier, France, Oct. 5, 1899—. French statesman, notable as a leader of the French Resistance movement during World War II, and subsequently as foreign minister and premier under the French Fourth Republic. A leader in the Catholic youth movement after World War I, he received (1925) a university degree in history, and taught (1925–39) at Valenciennes, Reims, and Paris. He was active in the Parti Démocrate Populaire, writing editorials for the Catholic daily *L'Aube.* He served as an infantry sergeant (1939–40) until taken (May, 1940) prisoner of war. After his release (July, 1941), he was assigned to a teaching post at Lyons, where he joined (Feb. 28, 1942) the

Resistance movement, "Combat." He then became a member of the Conseil National de la Résistance. As its president (August, 1943–September, 1944), he helped lead the Paris insurrection (August, 1944) against the Germans. He served (Sept. 9, 1944–Jan. 26, 1946) as foreign minister under Charles De Gaulle, later as president of the provisional government, and again as foreign minister (June 24–Nov. 29, 1946). He was foreign minister in the cabinets of premiers Paul Ramadier and Robert Schuman (Jan. 22, 1947–July 19, 1948), and subsequently himself was premier (Oct. 28, 1949–June 24, 1950). Afterward he held (1951 *et seq.*) the post of vice-premier in several cabinets and was foreign minister in the Pleven (1951) and Mayer (1952) cabinets. Bidault is recognized as the leader of the MRP (Mouvement Républicain Populaire).

Biddeford (bid'ę.fǫrd). City in SW Maine, in York County, on the Saco River, ab. 17 mi. SW of Portland: twin city of Saco. It has manufactures of cotton textiles, and of textile machinery. 20,836 (1950).

Biddenden Maids (bid'ęn.dęn). b. at Biddenden, Kent, England, early in the 12th century. Two sisters joined in the manner of Siamese twins. They were the reputed donors of the "Bread-and-Cheese-land," Biddenden, for the defrayal of the cost of a yearly distribution of bread and cheese at Easter.

Biddle (bid'l), **Anthony Joseph Drexel.** b. at Philadelphia, Oct. 1, 1874; d. at Syosset, L.I., N.Y., May 27, 1948. American publisher and writer, who was prominent in U.S. military physical training programs during World Wars I and II. Educated at Philadelphia and Heidelberg, he was editor (1895) of the Philadelphia *Sunday Graphic*, and headed the Philadelphia publishing house of Drexel Biddle. His books include *An Allegory and Three Essays* (1894), *The Froggy Fairy Book* (1896), *Shantytown Sketches* (1898), *The Madeira Islands* (1900), *The Land of Wine* (1901), and *Do or Die: Military Manual of Advanced Science in Individual Combat* (1937).

Biddle, Clement. [Called the **"Quaker Soldier."**] b. at Philadelphia, May 10, 1740; d. there, July 14, 1814. American Revolutionary officer; father of Clement Cornell Biddle. He was one of the signers of the nonimportation resolutions framed at Philadelphia in 1765, and, although a Quaker, joined the Revolutionary army on the outbreak of hostilities, serving as colonel in the battles of Trenton, Princeton, Brandywine, and Monmouth. He was a personal friend and correspondent of George Washington.

Biddle, Clement Cornell. b. at Philadelphia, Oct. 24, 1784; d. Aug. 21, 1855. American lawyer and political economist; son of Clement Biddle. He fought in the War of 1812.

Biddle, Francis. b. at Paris, May 9, 1886—. American lawyer and public official, U.S. attorney general (1941–45); brother of George Biddle (1885—). He was graduated (1909) from Harvard, where he also received (1911) his law degree. He served (1911–12) as private secretary to U.S. Supreme Court Justice Oliver Wendell Holmes, and was admitted (1912) to the Pennsylvania bar, becoming an associate member of the Philadelphia law firm of Biddle, Paul and Jayne. He served briefly in the U.S. army during World War I, and from 1917 to 1939 was a member of the Philadelphia law firm of Barnes, Biddle and Myers. He served (1922–26) as special assistant U.S. attorney for the eastern district of Pennsylvania, was admitted (1927) to practice before the U.S. Supreme Court, and was chief counsel (1938–39) of the joint committee to investigate the Tennessee Valley Authority. He was a judge (1939–40) of the third circuit, federal circuit court of appeals, and became (1940) solicitor general of the U.S. He was U.S. attorney general from September, 1941 to June 30, 1945. In 1951 he was appointed to the Permanent Court of Arbitration. Author of *The Llanfear Pattern* (1927), *Mr. Justice Holmes* (1942), *Democratic Thinking and the War* (1944), and *The Fear of Freedom* (1951).

Biddle, George. b. at Philadelphia, Jan. 24, 1885—. American painter and sculptor; brother of Francis Biddle (1886—). He received the degrees of A.B. (1908) and LL.B. (1911) from Harvard. Instrumental in founding (1933) the Federal Arts Projects, he was commissioned (1935) to paint five fresco panels in the Department of Justice Building, Washington, D.C.; he was also commissioned (1942) with his wife, Helene Sardeau, to decorate the national library at Rio de Janeiro. In 1943 he was chairman of the War Department Art Advisory Committee. His work is represented in the Metropolitan Museum of Art, the Whitney Museum, and national museums at Berlin and Mexico City, among others. Author of *Adolphe Borie* (1937), *Boardman Robinson* (1937), *American Artist's Story* (1939), and *Artist at War* (1944); author and illustrator of *Green Island* (1930) and *George Biddle's War Drawings* (1944).

Biddle, James. b. at Philadelphia, Feb. 28, 1783; d. there, Oct. 1, 1848. American naval commander, distinguished in the War of 1812. He commanded the *Wasp*, the *Hornet* (which fought and captured the British brig *Penguin* off the island of Tristan da Cunha on March 23, 1815), and the *Ontario*, a sloop sent (1817) to the mouth of the Columbia River to claim the Oregon region for the U.S. He later was charged with protecting American ships in South American waters, and negotiated (1846) the first treaty between China and the U.S.

Biddle, John. [Called the **"Father of English Unitarianism."**] b. at Wotton-under-Edge, Gloucestershire, England, 1615; d. at London, Sept. 22, 1662. English Unitarian divine. He became master of the free school at Gloucester in 1641. Suspected of heresy, he was called before Parliament in 1645 and committed to custody, remaining in prison until 1652. During this period he published (1647) *Twelve Questions or Arguments*, a work directed against belief in the Anglican concept of the Holy Ghost. He was banished (1655) by Oliver Cromwell to the Scilly islands for his *Twofold Catechism* (1654), but was recalled three years later. He was again arrested under Charles II, and died in prison. He also wrote *Confession of Faith touching the Holy Trinity* (1648) and others.

Biddle, Nicholas. b. at Philadelphia, Sept. 10, 1750; killed at sea, March 7, 1778. American naval commander, distinguished in the Revolutionary War. He was blown up with his ship, the *Randolph*, in an action against the British ship *Yarmouth*.

Biddle, Nicholas. b. at Philadelphia, Jan. 8, 1786; d. there, Feb. 27, 1844. American financier; brother of Richard Biddle (1796–1847). After having been the editor of a literary magazine and a state senator, he was selected (1819) by President James Monroe, with four others, to serve as a director of the Second Bank of the United States. Three years later (1822) he succeeded Langdon Cheves as president of the Bank, a post which he held until the institution was dissolved (1836) through nonrenewal of its charter. He was thereafter, until 1839, president of a successor institution under a Pennsylvania charter.

Biddle, Richard. b. at Philadelphia, March 25, 1796; d. at Pittsburgh, July 7, 1847. American lawyer and author; brother of Nicholas Biddle (1786–1844). He wrote *Memoir of Sebastian Cabot* (1831) and other works.

Biddle, William Phillips. b. at Philadelphia, Dec. 17, 1853; d. at Nice, France, Feb. 26, 1923. American Marine officer, appointed (1911) a major general, and commandant of the U.S. Marine Corps.

Biddulph (bid'ulf). Urban district in C England, in Staffordshire, ab. 4 mi. SE of Congleton. It has no direct rail connections for passengers, being reached by rail to Congleton, ab. 157 mi. NW of London. 10,898 (1951).

Biddy (bid'i). Mr. Wopsle's "great-aunt's granddaughter," in Charles Dickens's *Great Expectations;* an orphan who for a time is in love with Pip, she is afterward married to Joe Gargery.

Biddy, Miss. Comic character in David Garrick's farce *Miss in her Teens.*

Bideford (bid'ę.fǫrd). Municipal borough, small seaport, and manufacturing and fishing town in SW England, in Devonshire, situated on the river Torridge near its mouth, ab. 9 mi. SW of Barnstaple, ab. 221 mi. SW of London by rail. The town is built on both sides of the river. It is one of the scenes of Kingsley's novel *Westward Ho!* 10,100 (1951).

Bidlack (bid'lak), **Benjamin Alden.** b. at Paris, N.Y., Sept. 8, 1804; d. in New Granada (now Colombia), Feb. 6, 1849. American politician and diplomat. As U.S. chargé d'affaires in New Granada (1845–49), he negotiated (1846) the Bidlack-Mallarino Treaty with New

Granada, which abolished differential duties and permitted a U.S. right of way across the Isthmus of Panama. He was a member of Congress from 1841 to 1845.

Bidlack-Mallarino Treaty (bid'lak.mä.yä.rē'nō). Treaty (1846) between the U.S. and New Granada (later Colombia), insuring the latter's sovereign rights over the Isthmus of Panama, guaranteeing the neutral status of the Isthmus, and eliminating discriminatory tariffs against U.S. commerce. The treaty was of significance after the Panama revolution of 1903, when the U.S. government claimed that it had a "vested . . . property right" in the Isthmus under the covenant.

Bidloo (bid'lō), **Godfried.** b. at Amsterdam, March 12, 1649; d. at Leiden, in April, 1713. Dutch surgeon and anatomist. He was successively professor of anatomy at The Hague, professor of anatomy and chemistry at Leiden, and physician to William III of England. His chief work is *Anatomia corporis humani* (1685).

Bidou (bē.dö), **Henry Louis Auguste Gabriel.** b. at Givet, Ardennes, France, June 28, 1873; d. 1943. French dramatic and literary critic, author of numerous prefaces and, after 1909, theatrical reviewer for such conservative reviews as the *Revue des deux mondes* and the *Revue critique des idées et des livres*. He also specialized in reporting the reception speeches of new members of the Academy.

Bidpai (bid'pī). See under **Kalilah and Dimnah.**

Bidwell (bid'wel), **John.** b. in Chautauqua County, N.Y., Aug. 5, 1819; d. near Sacramento, Calif., April 4, 1900. American pioneer and politician in California. A member of the first wagon train to reach California (1841) from Missouri, he was also the first to find gold in the region of the Feather River. An associate of John Augustus Sutter, particularly in connection with the uprising (1844) against local Mexican authorities, he later served on the committee of independence after the Bear Flag Revolt (1846). A member of Congress (1864–66) from California, he was the Prohibition Party's candidate (1892) for president of the U.S.

Bidwell, Marshall Spring. b. at Stockbridge, Mass., Feb. 16, 1799; d. at New York, Oct. 24, 1872. American lawyer and politician who became one of the leaders of the "Reform Party" in Canada. Elected (1824) to the Canadian House of Assembly, he served until 1836, several times as speaker of the House. Although he took no part in the "Upper Canada Rebellion," he was forced (1837) to leave Canada. He settled at New York, where he thereafter practiced law. He participated, on behalf of James Fenimore Cooper, in the libel suit brought by Cooper against William L. Stone.

Bidwell, Shelford. b. at Thetford, Suffolk, England, March 6, 1848; d. Dec. 18, 1909. English barrister and amateur scientist, known for his research regarding electricity, magnetism, and optics, and as a pioneer in telephotography. He was the author of *Curiosities of Light and Sight* (1899).

Bidyogo (bid.yō'gō). See **Bisago.**

Bieber (bē'bėr), **Hugo.** b. 1883—. German historian of literature, author of a "cultural history" of German literature from 1830 to 1880 under the title *Der Kampf um die Tradition* (1928).

Bieberbach (bē'bėr.bäċh), **Ludwig.** b. at Goddelau, Germany, Dec. 4, 1886—. German mathematician, noted for his work in differential equations, differential geometry, group theory, and the theory of functions. He studied at Heidelberg and Göttingen, and taught at Zurich, Königsberg, Basel, Frankfort on the Main, and Berlin. His many books include *Einführung in die konforme Abbildung* (1915), *Lehrbuch der Funktionentheorie* (2 vols., 1921–27), *Theorie der Differentialgleichungen* (1923), *Zur Geschichte der Logik* (1927), *Differential- und Integralrechnung* (3rd ed., 2 vols., 1928), *Analytische Geometrie* (1930), *Differentialgeometrie* (1932), and *Einleitung in die höhere Geometrie* (1933).

Bieberstein (bē'bėr.shtīn), Baron **Adolf Hermann von Marschall von.** See **Marschall von Bieberstein,** Baron **Adolf Hermann von.**

Biebrich (bē'briċh). Town in W Germany, in the *Land* (state) of Hessen, American Zone, formerly in the province of Hesse-Nassau, Prussia, situated on the Rhine River, ab. 3 mi. S of Wiesbaden. A former residence of the dukes of Nassau, it is now incorporated into the city of Wiesbaden. Pop. ab. 22,000.

Bieda (byā'dä). [Ancient name, **Blera.**] Town and commune in C Italy, in the *compartimento* (region) of Latium, in the province of Viterbo, situated near Viterbo. It is an agricultural trade center and contains an extensive Etruscan necropolis of rock-cut tombs. Pop. of commune, 4,462 (1936); of town, 2,722 (1936).

Biedermann (bē'dėr.män), **Felix.** See **Dörmann, Felix.**

Biedermann, Friedrich Karl. b. Sept. 25, 1812; d. March 5, 1901. German publicist, politician, and historian. He was professor extraordinary of philology at Leipzig in the period 1838–54. A proponent of German unification under Prussia, he was imprisoned in 1854, as editor of the *Deutschen Annalen*, for political reasons, and lost his professorship, but was reinstated in 1865. Active in the politics of Saxony and of the German empire, he was a member of the Saxon parliament, and sat (1871–74) in the German Reichstag.

Biedermann, Baron **Woldemar von.** b. at Marienberg, Germany, March 5, 1817; d. at Dresden, Germany, Feb. 6, 1903. German Goethe scholar, editor of *Goethes Gespräche* (1889 *et seq.*) in ten volumes.

Biedermeier (bē'dėr.mī.ėr). Comic figure in the poems of Ludwig Eichrodt in the German weekly *Fliegende Blätter*, and thence a term applied to the period in Germany between the Napoleonic wars and 1850. It designates small-town simple-heartedness and naïveté, marked, particularly in art, by very limited imagination and ornamentation.

Bièfve (byev), **Édouard de.** b. at Brussels, Dec. 4, 1809; d. there, Feb. 7, 1882. Belgian historical painter. His chief work is *Compromise of the Nobles at Brussels, Feb. 16, 1566*.

Biel (bēl). [French, **Bienne.**] City in W Switzerland, in the canton of Bern, situated at the NE end of Lake Biel: seat of the Technical Institute for Western Switzerland and of the Schwab Museum, which has relics from ancient lake dwellings, the iron age, and the Celtic and Roman periods. Watchmaking is an important industry. The population is about two-thirds German, one-third French. 48,342 (1950).

Biel, Gabriel. [Also, **Byll.**] b. at Speyer, Germany, c1425; d. at Tübingen, Germany, 1495. German scholastic philosopher, professor of theology and philosophy at the University of Tübingen; sometimes called "the last of the schoolmen." A nominalist, his chief work was *Epitome et Collectorium ex Occamo* (1508), derived from the teachings of William of Ockham.

Biel, Lake. [Also: **Lake of Bienne**; German, **Bieler See.**] Lake in NW Switzerland, ab. 3 mi. NE of Lake Neuchâtel. It is traversed by the Zihl (French, Thièle) Canal. Length, ab. 9½ mi.; breadth, ab. 2½ mi.

Biela (bē'lä), Baron **Wilhelm von.** b. at Rosslau, Germany, March 19, 1782; d. at Venice, Feb. 18, 1856. Austrian astronomer and army officer, noted for his observations (Feb. 27, 1826 *et seq.*) of a comet, named for him, at what was then Josephstadt, in Bohemia. It was later discovered, by astronometric computation, to be identical with a comet observed on three earlier occasions (1772 *et seq.*), and to have separated (1846) into two parts. The comet, in part or in whole, has not been seen since 1852.

Bielatserkof (bye.lą.tser'kǫf). See **Belaya Tserkov.**

Bielawa (bye.lä'vä). [German, **Bielau** (bē'lou), **Langenbielau.**] Town in SW Poland, in the *województwo* (province) of Wrocław, formerly in Silesia, Germany, situated at the foot of the Eulengebirge, ab. 33 mi. SW of Wrocław (Breslau): textile center, particularly for linens. The former German population has been supplanted by Polish immigrants. 20,116 (1939); 17,269 (1946).

Bielaya-Tserkoff (bye'lą.yą.tser'kǫf). See **Belaya Tserkov.**

Bielef (bye'lyif). See **Belev.**

Bielefeld (bē'lę.felt). City in W Germany, in the *Land* (state) of North Rhine-Westphalia, British Zone, formerly in the province of Westphalia, Prussia, E of Münster. The center of the Westphalian linen industry, which was founded by immigrants from the Netherlands in the 16th century, it has linen spinning and weaving mills, and manufactures lingerie, hosiery, knitwear, lace, umbrellas, and men's and boys' garments. There are also dyeing and bleaching works, important metallurgical industries (producing bicycles, sewing machines, and fireproof safes), canneries, shoe and tobacco factories, and sugar refineries. The city has numerous educational institutions, a municipal museum, ethnological museum, theater, and music conservatory. Its hospitals for epileptics, called Bethel and Sarepta, are well known. There is a medieval castle, as well as various medieval churches and houses. During World War II the old part of the city was severely damaged, the *Nikolaikirche* (Church of Saint Nicholas) destroyed, and the *Marienkirche* (Church of Mary) damaged. Bielefeld received town privileges in 1250 and became a member of the Hanseatic League in 1270. It was incorporated into Prussia in 1609. Pop. 153,613 (1950).

Bieler See (bē'lėr zā). German name of **Biel, Lake.**

Bielgorod (byel'gǫ.rǫt). See **Belgorod.**

Bielgrad (byil.grät'). See **Bolgrad.**

Bielinski (byi.lyēn'ski), **Vissarion Grigoryevich.** See **Belinsky, Vissarion Grigoryevich.**

Bielitz (bē'lits). German name of **Bielsko.**

Biella (byel'lä). Town and commune in NW Italy, in the *compartimento* (region) of Piedmont, in the province of Vercelli, situated on the Cervo River in the foothills of the Alps, ab. 39 mi. NE of Turin. It is a tourist center and a center of the Italian woolen industry; cotton textile, leather, and paper factories, and trade schools for the textile industry are also situated at Biella. First mentioned in 826 A.D., the town came under the house of Savoy in 1379, but was at various times occupied and plundered by the Spaniards and the French during the 16th, 17th, and 18th centuries (plundered by the Spanish army in 1647). Buildings of interest to tourists were undamaged in World War II. Pop. of commune, 38,115 (1936); of town, 24,328 (1936).

Bielostok (bye.lǫ.stôk'). Russian name of **Białystok.**

Bielschowsky (bēl.shôf'skē), **Alfred.** b. at Namslau, in Silesia, Dec. 11, 1871; d. at Brooklyn, N.Y., Jan. 5, 1940. German ophthalmologist. He was a member of the staff of the ophthalmological clinic of the University of Leipzig, where he became a privatdocent (1900) and professor (1906); appointed (1912) professor at Marburg, he later (1923–34) served as professor of ophthalmology at the University of Breslau. In 1934 he resigned and went to the Ames Clinic at Hanover, N.H., where he served as director of the eye institute at the Dartmouth medical school. He is known for his work on the physiology and pathology of the sense of space and the movements of the eyes.

Bielshöhle (bēls'hė''lẹ). Stalactite cavern in C Germany, in the Harz Mountains, Brunswick, near the Bode River, discovered in 1762. Length, over 600 ft.

Bielski (byel'skē), **Marcin.** b. at Biała, near Sieradz, Poland, c1495; d. there, 1575. Polish historian. His chief works (the first historical writings in the Polish language) are *Kronika swiata* (1550) and *Kronika polska* (a history of Poland, continued by his son Joachim Bielski from 1576 to 1597; published in 1597).

Bielsko (byel'skô). [German, **Bielitz.**] Town in SW Poland, in the *województwo* (province) of Śląsk (Silesia), formerly in Austria, situated at the foot of the Carpathian Mountains, ab. 30 mi. S of Katowice. An important center of the woolen textile industry, it also has metallurgical (smelting, machinery, and tools) and chemical industries and produces alcohols, liqueurs, and wines. Founded in the 13th century, it belonged to Austrian Silesia until 1919. A concentration camp was established at Bielsko by the German occupation forces during World War II. 25,725 (1946).

Bien (bēn), **Julius.** b. at Naumburg, near Kassel, Germany, Sept. 27, 1826; d. Dec. 21, 1909. American map engraver and pioneer, in the U.S., in the science of cartography. He engraved an early standard map of the Mississippi-Pacific territory during the Franklin Pierce administration (1853–57), and prepared maps for the 9th to 12th U.S. census reports (1870–1900). His other projects included *Atlas to Accompany the Official Records of the Union and Confederate Armies* (1891–95) and *Atlas of the Metropolitan District Around New York City* (1891).

Bienewitz (bē'nẹ.vits), **Peter.** See **Apianus, Petrus.**

Biên Hoa (byen hō'ä). [Also, **Bienhoa.**] Town in Indochina, SE Asia, in Cochin-China (South Viet-Nam), ab. 12 mi. NE of Saigon. It is a trading center, served by a railway line and two major roads. There are several rice mills. Pop. ab. 20,000.

Bienne (byen). French name of **Biel.**

Bienne, Lake of. See **Biel, Lake.**

Bienville (byen'vil; French, byañ.vēl), **Jean Baptiste Le Moyne, Sieur de.** b. at Longueuil, France, Feb. 23, 1680; d. in France, 1768. French governor of Louisiana (1701–13, 1718–26, 1733–43). After serving (1692–97) in the French navy, he accompanied an expedition sent to America for the purpose of rediscovering the mouth of the Mississippi and establishing a French settlement there. In 1699 he was left as second in command, becoming head in 1701, of the colony founded at Old Biloxi, which served as headquarters for the exploring party. Deciding that a better site was needed for the colony, he built (1702) Fort Louis, and removed (1710) to what is now Mobile, Ala. Louisiana was granted (1712) by the king of France to a private company, and put under the authority of Cadillac, but Bienville remained there and served in various administrative posts. In 1718, when he was again governor, he founded New Orleans, which became the capital of the colony in 1722 (and where he developed and put in force a code of behavior for and toward Negroes which exercised considerable influence on the later cultural development of the area). Accused (1724) of inefficiency, he was recalled (1725) to France, but was invited to resume his governorship in 1732.

Bier (bēr), (**Karl Gustav**) **August.** b. at Helsen, Germany, Nov. 24, 1861; d. at Sauen, near Beeskow, Germany, March 14, 1949. German surgeon. He served as a professor at the universities of Kiel (1894 *et seq.*), Greifswald (1899 *et seq.*), and Bonn (1903 *et seq.*), and in 1907 succeeded Ernst von Bergmann at the University of Berlin. He introduced (1899) intraspinal anesthesia with cocaine, which he first tried on himself; a vein anesthesia (1908), known as Bier's local anesthesia; a new method of treating amputated stumps (1900); and active and passive hyperemia as a treatment of chronic infection (1893), recommending (1904) its use also in cases of acute infection. Author of *Behandlung chirurgischer Tuberkulose der Gliedmassen mit Stauungshyperämie* (1893), *Behandlung der Gelenkstuberkulose mit Stauungshyperämie* (1895), and *Hyperämie als Heilmittel* (1903; Eng. trans., *Hyperemia as a Therapeutic Agent*, 1905); editor of *Chirurgische Operationslehre* (together with H. F. W. Braun and Hermann Kümmel, 1912).

Bierbaum (bēr'boum), **Otto Julius.** b. at Grünberg, in Silesia, June 28, 1865; d. Feb. 1, 1910. German editor, critic, poet, and novelist, one of the most versatile of modern German men of letters. His journalistic achievements are notable: he took over (1892) the editorship of *Die freie Bühne*, rechristening it *Die Neue Deutsche Rundschau;* together with Meier-Graefe he founded (1894) the de luxe art and literary journal *Pan;* and with A. W. Heymel he founded the excellent critical magazine *Die Insel* (1899–1902) from which developed the Insel-Verlag, a publishing house noted for its attractive inexpensive reprints. He also edited *Der moderne Musenalmanach* (1891–94) and collected the *Überbrettl* poems in *Deutsche Chansons* (1901). Among his own writings should be mentioned the critical work *Detlev von Liliencron* (1892), and also art monographs on Fritz von Uhde and Franz von Stuck, as well as his poems *Nemt, Frouwe, disen Kranz* (1894) and *Irrgarten der Liebe* (1901).

Bierce (birs), **Ambrose Gwinett.** [Pseudonym, **Dod Grile.**] b. near Chester, Meigs County, Ohio, June 24, 1842; d. c1914. American short-story writer and journalist, noted for his bitter irony and incisive prose style. He served with distinction in the Civil War (9th Indiana Infantry), was twice wounded, and emerged a brevet major, cited for conspicuous gallantry under fire. He edited belligerent gossip columns in several San Francisco journals (*News Letter, Argonaut, Wasp*), from 1868 to 1887, and thereafter, until 1899, in the San Francisco *Examiner*. For three and a half years (1872–76), he lived and wrote in England, where he published three volumes of satirical sketches under the pseudonym "Dod Grile." In 1899 he removed to Washington, D.C., where he continued to write for the *Examiner* and other Hearst newspapers. His principal books are *Tales of Soldiers and Civilians* (1891; reissued as *In the Midst of Life*) and *Can Such Things Be?* (1893), which include most of his brilliant and mordant short stories. Other notable works are *Fantastic Fables* (1899) and *The Cynic's Word Book* (1906; reissued as *The Devil's Dictionary*). With a collaborator, Gustav Adolf Danziger, he translated *The Monk and the Hangman's Daughter* (1892) from the German of Richard Voss. His *Collected Works* (1909–12) bring together these and many lesser writings, including considerable satirical verse. Late in 1913, Bierce disappeared in Mexico and no certain information concerning his death ever has come to light. Many picturesque and romantic legends have grown up around his disappearance, but there is no good reason to suppose that he long survived his arrival in Mexico.

Biernatzki (bēr.nät'skē), **Johann Christolph.** b. at Elmshorn, Germany, Oct. 17, 1795; d. at Friedrichstatt, Germany, May 11, 1840. German Pietist, pastor, and writer of poems and narratives. Two of the latter, *Die Hallig, oder die Schiffbrüchigen auf dem Eiland in der Nordsee* (1836) and *Der braune Knabe* (1839), have been unusually popular.

Bierstadt (bir'stat, bēr'shtät), **Albert.** b. at Solingen, near Düsseldorf, Germany, Jan. 7, 1830; d. at New York, Feb. 18, 1902. American landscape and historical painter. Among his paintings are *Sunshine and Shadow* (1857), *Lander's Peak* (1863), *Domes of the Yosemite*, and *Mount Hood*.

Bierut (bye'röt), **Bolesław.** [Original name, **Krasnodebski.**] b. 1892—. President of Poland after World War II. A Communist from his early youth, he was twice arrested in Poland for subversive activities, went to the U.S.S.R. to receive special political training, and was designated (1943) by the Comintern to become chairman of the Moscow-sponsored Polish National Council. He became (1947) president of Poland and general secretary of the United Workers (Communist) Party in that country. After the adoption of a new Polish constitution abolishing the presidency, Bierut was chosen premier (1952).

Biesbosch (bēs'bôs). Marshy lake in SW Netherlands, on the border of South Holland and North Brabant provinces, SE of Dordrecht. Its outlet to the North Sea is the Hollandsch Diep. It was formed in 1421 by an inundation of the Maas (Meuse) River.

Biet (bye), **Antoine.** fl. middle of the 17th century. French missionary who accompanied the 600 colonists sent by France to the island of Cayenne in 1652. He remained there 18 months, and published an account of the region and its people in *Voyage de la France Équinoxiale* (Paris, 1664).

Bietigheim (bē'tiċh.hīm). Town in S Germany, in the *Land* (state) of Württemberg-Baden, American Zone, situated on the Enz River, N of Stuttgart. It has wine and livestock markets; there are also linoleum works, lumber mills, shoe factories, and factories making toys and musical instruments. The parish church dates from the 12th century, the *Rathaus* (town hall) from the 16th century. Town privileges date back to 1364. The population is chiefly Protestant. 12,289 (1950).

Bifrost (biv'rost). [Also: **Asbru;** Old Norse, **Ásbrú.**] In Norse mythology, the rainbow, the bridge of the gods which reached from heaven to earth. Every day the gods rode over it to their judgment-place under the tree Yggdrasil, near the sacred well of the Norns.

Big Barren. See **Barren.**

Big Beaver. See under **Beaver Islands.**

Big Ben. Name given to the bell in the clock tower of the houses of Parliament, London. It was cast in 1856 and is said to have been the largest bell to that date in England. It is the second of the name, the first having been defective. During World War II, the sound of Big Ben was made a symbol of British resistance, and its striking was broadcast nightly at 9 P.M. over the British Broadcasting network.

Big Bend National Park. Park in SW Texas, in the big bend of the Rio Grande ab. 250 mi. SE of El Paso. It occupies a great wilderness of dry mountain and plateau country, dissected by deep canyons. The Rio Grande here flows through three great canyons over 1,500 ft. deep. Numerous rare plant forms are found, and animal life includes deer, black bear, antelopes, and javelinas. The former state park was incorporated into the national park in 1944. Area, 1,081 sq. mi.

Big Bertha. Name popularly applied to a type of long-range 8.26-inch gun used by the Germans in shelling Paris in the spring of 1918, during the latter part of World War I. The name was derived from that of Bertha Krupp von Bohlen, heiress of the Krupp works at Essen, Germany, where the gun was manufactured. (The name was originally coined as "Die dicke Bertha" by German soldiers; it was picked up in translation by members of the Allied forces.)

Big Bethel (beth'ẹl). Village in E Virginia, ab. 10 mi. NW of Fort Monroe. Here, on June 10, 1861, Union forces (2,500) under General Ebenezer Peirce were defeated by the Confederates (1,800) under General John B. Magruder.

Big Black Mountain. [Also, **Black Mountain.**] Mountain in SE Kentucky and western Virginia, in the Cumberlands. It is a lofty, winding wooded ridge ab. 45 mi. long, running E from Harlan, Ky. to the state line, thence NE along the boundary, and E into Virginia. The peak elevation of 4,150 ft. is on the state boundary, ab. 4 mi. SE of Lynch, Ky., and is the highest point in Kentucky.

Big Black River. River in W Mississippi which joins the Mississippi River at Grand Gulf. It was noted in Ulysses S. Grant's campaign before Vicksburg, in May, 1863. Length, over 200 mi.; navigable ab. 50 mi.

Big Bone Lick. Salt spring in Boone County, Kentucky, situated ab. 20 mi. SW of Cincinnati: noted for its fossil deposits.

Big Bottom Massacre. Assault (Jan. 2, 1791) by Shawnee Indians upon a settlement of whites along the Muskingum River in the Ohio country. The Indians killed 14 whites (including one woman and two children) and carried away three as captives.

Big Brother Movement. Interdenominational and international organization founded (1904) in the U.S. for the purpose of guiding youth and preventing juvenile delinquency. In 1948 the movement, with headquarters at New York, had 970 participating volunteer organizations.

Bigelow (big'ẹ.lō), **Edward Fuller.** b. at Colchester, Conn., Jan. 14, 1860; d. at Greenwich, Conn., in July, 1938. American editor, naturalist, and lecturer. He became (1883) editor of the first daily newspaper in Fairfield County, Conn., the Middletown *Herald;* later he founded the Middletown *Tribune*, the Stamford *Telegram*, and the Stamford *Bulletin*. The recipient of M.A. and Ph.D. degrees from Taylor University, he served as nature instructor and lecturer at county teachers' institutes throughout the U.S., and at university summer schools. He organized and was president of the Connecticut Editorial Association, and was curator of the Bruce Museum at Greenwich, Conn.

Bigelow, Erastus Brigham. b. at West Boylston, Mass., April 2, 1814; d. at Boston, Dec. 6, 1879. American inventor and economist, notable for the development of power looms used in the production of Brussels, Wilton, tapestry, and velvet carpetings. He also invented power looms for the manufacture of coach lace (1837), as well as counterpanes and ginghams, silk brocatel, pile fabrics, and wire cloth. Author of *The Self-Taught Stenographer* (1832), *The Tariff Question Considered in Regard to the Policy of England and the Interests of the United States* (1862), and *The Tariff Policy of England and the United States Contrasted* (1877).

Bigelow, Frank Hagar. b. Aug. 28, 1851; d. at Vienna, March 2, 1924. American meteorologist. A graduate (1873) of Harvard, he served as assistant astronomer (1873–76, 1881–83) at Córdoba Observatory, in Argentina. He was chief (1906–10) of the U.S. Weather Bureau's department of climatology, and professor (1894–1910) of solar physics at George Washington University.

Bigelow, Henry Jacob. b. at Boston, March 11, 1818; d. Oct. 30, 1890. American surgeon, considered to have been one of the greatest in the history of the profession in New England; son of Jacob Bigelow (1786–1879). He was associated with the first use of surgical anesthesia, and was the first surgeon in America to excise a hip joint (1852). Author of *Manual of Orthopedic Surgery* (1884) and *Medical Education in America* (1871).

Bigelow, Jacob. b. at Sudbury, Mass., Feb. 27, 1786; d. Jan. 10, 1879. American physician and botanist; father of Henry Jacob Bigelow (1818–90). His *Florula*

Bostoniensis (1st ed., 1814) served as the standard botanical manual in New England until 1848; his *Discourse on Self-limited Diseases* (1835) was praised by Oliver Wendell Holmes. His other works include *American Medical Botany* (1817–20), *Treatise on the Materia Medica* (1822), *The Useful Arts* (1840), and *Modern Inquiries* (1867). He was president (1847–63) of the American Academy of Arts and Sciences.

Bigelow, John. b. Nov. 25, 1817; d. at New York, Dec. 19, 1911. American author and diplomat; father of John Bigelow (1854–1936) and Poultney Bigelow (1855—). He was an editor (1849–61) and one of the proprietors (1848–61), with William Cullen Bryant, of the New York *Evening Post;* later he served as consul at Paris (1861–65), and minister to France (1865–66). He edited (1868) Benjamin Franklin's autobiography and wrote *Jamaica in 1850, Life of Frémont* (1856), *Les États-Unis d'Amérique en 1863*, a monograph on *Molinos the Quietist* (1882), *Life of Samuel J. Tilden* (1895), and *Retrospections of an Active Life* (1909–12).

Bigelow, John. b. at New York, May 12, 1854; d. Feb. 29, 1936. American military officer and writer; son of John Bigelow (1817–1911). He served in the Spanish-American War. A professor (1894–98) at the Massachusetts Institute of Technology, he later (1917–18) taught military science at Rutgers. Author of *Mars-la-Tour and Gravelotte* (1884), *Principles of Strategy* (1894), *American Policy* (1914), *World Peace* (1915), and *Breaches of Anglo-American Treaties* (1917).

Bigelow, Marshall Train. b. at South Natick, Mass., Oct. 5, 1822; d. at Cambridge, Mass., Dec. 28, 1902. American editor and stylist. He was associated (1843 *et seq.*) with the university press at Cambridge, Mass., which was named (1859–79) Welsh, Bigelow and Company. Author of *Punctuation and Other Typographic Matters* (1881) and *Mistakes in Writing English and How to Avoid Them* (1886).

Bigelow, Maurice Alpheus. b. at Milford Center, Ohio, Dec. 8, 1872—. American biologist. A graduate of Ohio Wesleyan (1894), Northwestern (1896), and Harvard (1901) universities, he was professor of biology (1907–39) and director of the School of Practical Arts (1914–35) of Teachers College, Columbia University. Author of *Early Development of Lepas* (1902), *Sex Education* (1916), *Adolescence, Educational and Hygienic Problems* (1924), and other works; coauthor, with Anna N. Bigelow, of *Applied Biology* (1911).

Bigelow, Melville Madison. b. near Eaton Rapids, Mich., Aug. 2, 1846; d. at Boston, May 4, 1921. American authority on legal history. His *Elements of the Law of Torts* (1878) became a standard American textbook in the field, and his *Law of Fraud on its Civil Side* (1888–90) was considered in its time the greatest American contribution to that study. His other works include *Reports of all the Published Life and Accident Insurance Cases, American Courts* (1871–77), *The Law of Estoppel and its Application in Practice* (1872), *History of Procedure in England from the Norman Conquest: The Norman Period 1066–1204* (1880), and *Papers on the Legal History of Government; Difficulties Fundamental and Artificial* (1920).

Bigelow, Poultney. b. at New York, Sept. 10, 1855—. American journalist and historian; son of John Bigelow (1817–1911). He was graduated from Yale University in 1879, and was admitted to the bar in 1882, but abandoned law for journalism and traveled extensively. He edited (1885–87) *Outing*, a pioneer American magazine in the field of amateur outdoor sport, and later served as foreign correspondent for *Harper's Weekly* and, in the Spanish-American War, for the London *Times*. In 1892 his political writings caused his expulsion from Russia, and he became a close friend of Kaiser Wilhelm II of Germany. His publications include *The German Emperor and his Eastern Neighbors* (1891), *Borderland of Czar and Kaiser* (1893), *White Man's Africa* (1897), *Children of the Nations* (1901), *History of the German Struggle for Liberty* (4 vols., 1896; new ed., 1912), *Prussian Memories* (1915), *Japan and Her Colonies* (1923), and *Seventy Summers* (1925).

Bigelow, Robert Payne. b. at Baldwinsville, N.Y., July 10, 1863—. American zoölogist. A graduate of Harvard (1887) and Johns Hopkins (1892) universities, he was professor (1922–33) of zoölogy and parasitology at the Massachusetts Institute of Technology. Author of *Stomatopoda of the Albatross* (1894), *Stomatopoda of Porto Rico* (1900), *Directions for the Dissection of the Cat* (1935), and other works; he also contributed to W. T. Sedgwick's and M. W. Tyler's *A Short History of Science* (1939).

Bigelow, Samuel Lawrence. b. at Boston, Feb. 23, 1870—. American chemist. He was graduated from Harvard and the Massachusetts Institute of Technology, and in 1901 became acting director of the chemistry laboratory at the University of Michigan, where he was named (1907) professor of chemistry. Author of *Denatured Alcohol* (1907) and *Theoretical and Physical Chemistry* (1912).

Big-endians (big'en'di.ạnz). In Jonathan Swift's *Gulliver's Travels*, a religious sect (intended to satirize the Catholic party) of Lilliput, who considered it a matter of duty to break eggshells at the big end. They were considered heretics by the Little-endians (intended for the Protestants), who broke their eggshells in what was for them the orthodox manner, at the little end.

Big Four Railroad Brotherhoods. Chief labor organizations of American railway workers, originally formed as insurance benefit associations to protect the families of workers killed or injured in the performance of their duties. Independent organizations, they include the Grand International Brotherhood of Locomotive Engineers (founded at Detroit, March, 1863), the Order of Railway Conductors (founded at Chicago in 1868), the Brotherhood of Locomotive Firemen and Enginemen (founded at Port Jervis, N.Y., in 1873), and the Brotherhood of Railroad Trainmen (founded by workers of the Delaware and Hudson Railroad in 1883). By 1940 the brotherhoods had a total membership of approximately 300,000.

Bigg (big), **John Stanyan.** b. at Ulverston, Lancashire, England, July 14, 1828; d. there, May 19, 1865. English poet, dramatist, novelist, and journalist. Editor of the Ulverston *Advertiser* and later, during his stay in Ireland, of the *Downshire Protestant*, he was finally editor and proprietor (1860 *et seq.*) of the *Advertiser*. His works are *The Sea King* (1828), a metrical tale; *Night and the Soul* (1854), a poetic drama; *Shifting Scenes and other Poems* (1862); and *Alfred Staunton* (1860), a novel. With Gerald Massey, Alexander Smith, Sydney Dobell, and Philip James Bailey, Bigg was a member of what William E. Aytoun called the "spasmodic school" of English writers.

Biggers (big'ėrz), **Earl Derr.** b. at Warren, Ohio, Aug. 26, 1884; d. at Pasadena, Calif., April 5, 1933. American novelist and playwright, noted chiefly for his creation of the character Charlie Chan, a fictional Chinese detective whom he used in several novels which were later adapted for stage and motion-picture presentation. He was the author of the plays *If You're Only Human* (1912) and *Inside the Lines* (1915), and of *See-Saw* (1919), a musical comedy. His novels include *Seven Keys to Baldpate* (1913, subsequently dramatized), *Love Insurance* (1914), *The Agony Column* (1916), *The House Without a Key* (1925), *The Chinese Parrot* (1926), *Behind That Curtain* (1928), *The Black Camel* (1929), and *Charlie Chan Carries On* (1930).

Biggers, John David. b. at St. Louis, Mo., Dec. 19, 1888—. American glass manufacturer who served (1941) as production director of the U.S. Office of Production Management. A graduate (1909) of the University of Michigan, he was associated (1914–26) with the Owens Bottle Company at Toledo, Ohio, and was president (1930 *et seq.*) of the Libby-Owens-Ford Glass Company. In 1941 he was a special emissary to Great Britain, in charge of war-production coördination.

Biggleswade (big'lz.wād). Urban district and market town in E central England, in Bedfordshire, situated on the river Ivel, ab. 9 mi. SE of Bedford, ab. 41 mi. NW of London by rail. The surrounding region specializes in fruit and vegetable production. 7,280 (1951).

Biggs (bigz), **Asa.** b. at Williamston, N.C., Feb. 4, 1811; d. at Norfolk, Va., May 6, 1878. American jurist and politician. Elected to Congress (1846) and to the U.S. senate (1856) from North Carolina, he was also appointed (1851) a codifier of the state laws. He presided as state district judge (1858–61) and Confederate district judge (1861–65).

Biggs, Herman Michael. b. at Trumansburg, N.Y., Sept. 29, 1859; d. June 28, 1923. American pathologist and bacteriologist, notable for the introduction (1894) of diphtheria antitoxin in the U.S. He was professor at New York University and Bellevue Hospital Medical College from 1887, and chief medical officer of the Health Department of the city of New York from 1902. In 1892, he established the bacteriological laboratories of the Health Department of New York city, the first municipal institution of the kind, and served for a time (1901 *et seq.*) as director of the Rockefeller Institution for Medical Research. In 1914 he was made state director of health for New York, and in this post pioneered in establishing the state's facilities for maternity care and child health.

Bighorn (big'hôrn). River in Fremont County, Wyo., and Treasure and Yellowstone counties, Mont., formed by the junction of the Popo Agie and Wind rivers and flowing into the Yellowstone River. Length, ab. 450 mi.

Big Horn Mountains. Range of the Rocky Mountains in C and N Wyoming, extending N into Montana. The highest point is Cloud Peak (13,165 ft.).

Big House, The. Play, with the subtitle *Four Scenes in its Life*, by Lennox Robinson, produced in 1926 and published in 1928.

Bight of Benin (be.nēn'). See **Benin, Bight of.**

Bight of Biafra (bē.ä'frą). See **Biafra, Bight of.**

"Big Knives." [Also, **"Long Knives."**] Name applied by the Indians of colonial America to characterize the English settlers. For a time (1750 *et seq.*) it was employed only in reference to the Virginia colonists, but subsequently was used by the Indians as a term for any white American.

Bigler (big'lėr), **William.** b. at Shermansburg, Pa., Jan. 1, 1814; d. Aug. 9, 1880. American politician. He was governor (1851–54) of Pennsylvania, and a U.S. senator (1857–61).

Big Lick. Early name of **Roanoke,** Va.

Big Loch Broom (loċh bröm). See **Broom, Big Loch and Little Loch.**

Biglow Papers (big'lō), **The.** Humorous political poems in a form of New England dialect by James Russell Lowell, published in two series (1848, relating chiefly to slavery and the Mexican War, and 1867, relating chiefly to the Civil War and Reconstruction). The latter also appeared serially (1862–65) in the *Atlantic Monthly.* Many were published under the pseudonym of Hosea Biglow.

Big Money, The. Novel by John Dos Passos, published in 1936; it is the last volume in the trilogy *U.S.A.* (1937), of which the other volumes are *The 42nd Parallel* (1930) and *1919* (1932). As in the other two volumes, Dos Passos employs several styles in *The Big Money* to convey his theme of economic and social change within a framework of the shifting standards of the 1920's. The chapters of narrative are separated by the objective "newsreel" (listings in newspaper style of contemporary events), "the camera eye" (interior monologues), and impressionistic biographies of notables of the day, including Henry Ford, Isadora Duncan, the Wright brothers, and Thorstein Veblen. The fictional narrative itself takes up in broken sections the lives of a group of people representing different social and regional viewpoints; some of them meet toward the end of the book. Chief among these are Mary French, called "Daughter," a spoilt only-child, who after graduation from Vassar becomes interested in social work and extends her sympathies further and further toward the political left; and Dick Savage, a brilliant opportunist, one-time poet and pacifist. Many of the other characters also appeared in the two previous volumes.

Bignon (bē.nyôṅ), **Jérôme.** b. at Paris, Aug. 24, 1589; d. there, April 7, 1656. French jurist. He was the author of *Traité de la grandeur de nos rois et de leur souveraine puissance* (1615; published under the name of Théophile du Jay), and other works.

Bignon, Louis Pierre Édouard. b. Jan. 3, 1771; d. at Paris, Jan. 5, 1841. French diplomat and historian. As Napoleon's minister plenipotentiary at Kassel he played an important part in establishing the Confederation of the Rhine in 1806, and after the Prussian defeat at Jena he was appointed administrator of public lands and finances of that country. In 1809 Napoleon assigned him to a similar office in Austria, and in 1810 he became French resident at Warsaw. After Waterloo he served as minister of foreign affairs of the interim regime, and as such signed the agreement of July 3, 1815, which yielded Paris to the Allies. In 1817 Bignon was elected to the French Chamber of Deputies, where he sat until 1830, vigorously opposing the reactionary trends of government under the restored Bourbons. In the first government of Louis Philippe he served short terms as minister of foreign affairs and as minister of public instruction. In 1839 he became a member of the Chamber of Peers. Bignon wrote a number of polemics dealing with aspects of the political struggles in post-Waterloo years, but his principal achievement was the *Histoire de France sous Napoleon*, a work which the ex-emperor had designated to him in his will. The first ten volumes of this work were published between 1829 and 1838, under the title *Histoire de France depuis le 18-Brumaire jusqu'en 1812*, and four additional volumes appeared after the author's death, between 1847 and 1850.

Bigod (bī'god), **Hugh.** [Title, 1st Earl of **Norfolk.**] d. c1176. English nobleman; father of Roger Bigod, 2nd Earl of Norfolk. Created (1135) earl of Norfolk by Stephen of Blois, he subsequently opposed him, as he did Henry II.

Bigod, Hugh. d. 1266. English nobleman; father of Roger Bigod, 5th Earl of Norfolk. He was made chief justiciar in 1258.

Bigod, Roger. [Title, 2nd Earl of **Norfolk.**] d. 1221. English nobleman; son of Hugh Bigod, 1st Earl of Norfolk.

Bigod, Roger. [Title, 4th Earl of **Norfolk.**] d. 1270. English nobleman; uncle of Roger Bigod, 5th Earl of Norfolk. He was appointed earl marshal of England in 1246.

Bigod, Roger. [Title, 5th Earl of **Norfolk.**] b. 1245; d. Dec. 11, 1306. English nobleman; son of Hugh Bigod (d. 1266), and nephew of Roger Bigod, 4th Earl of Norfolk.

Bigordi (bē.gôr'dē), **Domenico.** Original name of **Ghirlandajo, Domenico.**

Bigorre (bē.gôr), **L'Abbé.** Name under which Voltaire wrote his *History of the Parlement of Paris* (Amsterdam, 1769).

Big Rapids. City in C Lower Michigan, on the Muskegon River, county seat of Mecosta County, in a large natural-gas field: seat of Ferris Institute. It was formerly a vacation resort. 6,736 (1950).

Big River. See **Fort George River.**

Big Sandy Creek. River in E Colorado which joins the Arkansas River near the Kansas boundary. Length, nearly 200 mi.

Big Sandy River. River forming the boundary between NE Kentucky and W West Virginia, and emptying into the Ohio River at Catlettsburg, Ky. It is formed at Louisa, Ky. by the junction of Tug Fork and Levisa Fork. Length, ab. 22 mi.

Big Sioux (sö). River in E and SE South Dakota, and NW Iowa. It rises in E South Dakota and flows generally S through a broad, gently rolling plain to join the Missouri River at Sioux City, Iowa. Its lower course forms the boundary between Iowa and South Dakota. Length, ab. 400 mi.

Big Spring. City in W Texas, county seat of Howard County, S of Lubbock. It is a distributing center for natural gas, a cattle-shipping point, and the site of petroleum refineries and cotton gins. A Cowboy's Reunion and an Old Settlers' Reunion are held here annually. 17,286 (1950).

"Big Stick" Policy. Name given by Theodore Roosevelt to his aggressive methods of handling diplomatic problems during his two presidential administrations (1901–09). At one time he was quoted as saying "I have always been fond of the West African proverb: 'Speak softly and carry a big stick, you will go far.' "

Big Stone Gap. [Former names, **Three Forks, Imoden, Mineral City.**] Town in SW Virginia, in Wise County, on the Powell River: a coal-mining town in the Cumberland Mountains. It was for a time the home of the novelist John Fox, Jr., author of *The Little Shepherd of Kingdom Come.* 5,173 (1950).

Big Town, The. Novel (1921) by Ring Lardner. It was his first novel.

Bihar (bē.här'). [Also: **Bahar, Behar.**] State of the Union of India, between West Bengal and Uttar Pradesh (the United Provinces), in the basin of the Ganges River. It produces opium, indigo, rice, grain, and sugar, and has various manufactures. Capitals: Patna (winter), Ranchi (summer); area, 70,368 sq. mi.; pop. 40,218,916 (1951).

Bihar. [Also: **Bahar, Behar.**] City in Bihar state, E Union of India, ab. 155 mi. E of Benares: trading center; formerly the residence of a governor. 54,551 (1941).

Bihari (bē.hä′rē). An Indo-European language spoken by about 37 million people in E central India, mainly in the state of Bihar and in Uttar Pradesh (the United Provinces). Its literature dates from the 15th century A.D.

Biisk (bēsk). See **Bisk.**

Bijago (bē.zhä′gö). See **Bisago.**

Bijagos or **Bijagoz** (bē.zhä′gösh), **Arquipélago** (or **Ilhas) dos.** See **Bissagos.**

Bijapur (bē.jä′pör). [Also, **Bejapur.**] Town in the S part of the Union of India, in Bombay state, ab. 240 mi. SE of the city of Bombay, formerly of great importance as capital of a medieval Moslem state. It contains the Jumma Musjid, and the tomb of Mahmud Shah. The latter dates from c1600. It is 135 ft. in interior diameter; this is somewhat less than the Roman Pantheon, but being square in plan, the total area is greater. Like the Pantheon it is covered by a great dome, which here is 124 ft. in diameter, resting on an ingeniously combined system of pendentives which diminish the area to be covered by the dome and by their weight counteract its outward thrust. At each corner of the building rises an octagonal domed tower of eight stages. The decoration, inside and out, is of great intricacy. 39,747 (1941).

Bijeljina (bē.ye′lyē.nä). [Also, **Bjeljina.**] Town in N Yugoslavia, in the federative unit of Bosnia-Hercegovina, in the former *banovina* (province) of Drinkska, situated near the junction of the Sava and Drina rivers, between Belgrade and Brod. 13,830 (1948).

Bijnor (bij′nôr). District of the Rohilkhand division, Uttar Pradesh (United Provinces), N Union of India, ab. 145 mi. E of Delhi: rice, wheat, sugar, and barley. Area, ab. 1,800 sq. mi.; pop. 910,223 (1941).

Bijns (bīns), **Anna.** [Also, **Byns.**] b. at Antwerp, c1494; d. there, April 10, 1575. Flemish poet, accounted by some to have been one of the principal Flemish writers of the 16th century.

Bika (bē.kä′), **El.** [Also: **El Bega, El Bukaa**; ancient name, **Coele-Syria** or **Cele-Syria.**] Valley in Syria and Lebanon, lying between the Lebanon and the Anti-Lebanon mountains and watered by the Orontes River. In this valley Shalmaneser III fought the armies of 12 Syrian kings; his account of the battle helps determine Biblical chronology.

Bikaner (bik.ạ.nir′), Maharaja of. [Title of Sir **Ganga Singhji Bahadur.**] b. 1880; d. 1943. Indian soldier and statesman. A prominent spokesman in behalf of the interests of the Indian princes, and a participant in imperial and world diplomatic conferences, he was ruler of the state of Bikaner (1898 *et seq.*), represented the Indian states at the peace conference (1919) after World War I, and was leader (1930) of the Indian delegation to the League of Nations. He was general-secretary (1916–21) of the Indian princes' conference, chancellor (1921–26) of the chamber of princes, and delegate to the Round Table Conferences (1930–32).

Bikaner. [Also, **Bikanir.**] Former state of the Union of India, now merged with Rajasthan, ab. 250 mi. W of Delhi. Most of the state is located in the Thar desert, and the people are herders; camels, cattle, and horses are the chief products. In the N and W sections there are ab. 1,500,000 acres of land irrigated by waters from the Sutlej River, which reach the area through the Gang Canal, the longest cement-lined canal in the world (length of main canal, 84.7 mi.; length including all feeder and distributary canals, 850.8 mi.). Capital, Bikaner; area, 23,181 sq. mi.; pop. 1,292,938 (1941).

Bikaner. [Also, **Bikanir.**] City in NW Union of India, former capital of Bikaner state, ab. 250 mi. W of Delhi. A prosperous town with much trade, it is noted for its manufacture of camel-hair goods and carpets. 127,226 (1941).

Bikelas (vē.ke′läs), **Demetrios.** b. at Hermoupolis, on the island of Syros, 1835; d. at Athens, July 20, 1908. Greek poet and essayist. Among his best-known works is the novel *Lukis Laras* (1879), a story of the Greek war of independence. A collection of his poems was published in 1862 (2nd ed., 1885). He also translated a number of Shakespeare's plays into modern Greek.

Bikini (bi.kē′ni). Small coral atoll in the Ralick Chain of the Marshall Islands, Pacific Ocean. In the lagoon of this atoll the U.S. tested in 1946 the effect of the atom bomb on naval armament and equipment and on certain forms of animal life. The inhabitants (ab. 180) were removed by the U.S. government to Rongerik and later to Kili, where a mission of the U.N. Trusteeship Council in 1950 found them making a difficult transition from their past life as fishermen to an economy based on agriculture.

Bikol (bē.kōl′). [Also, **Bicol.**] Malayo-Polynesian-speaking, Christian people of the Philippine Islands, dwelling in S Luzon, and on the islands of Catanduanes, Burias, Ticao, and Masbate.

Bilac (bē.läk′), **Olavo** (**Braz Martins dos Guimares**). b. at Rio de Janeiro, Dec. 16, 1865; d. there, Dec. 28, 1918. Brazilian poet, journalist, and lecturer, generally regarded as the greatest representative of the group called the Parnassians. Some of his poems are considered to be among the most perfect ever written in Portuguese. He was the author of *Poesias* (1888; 2nd ed., enlarged, 1902), *Sagres* (1898), *Poesias infantís* (1904), and *Tarde* (1919). Among his prose writings are *Crônicas e novelas* (1894), *Crítica e fantasia* (1904), *Conferências literárias* (1906), and *Últimas conferências e discursos* (1924).

Bilaspur (bē.läs.pör′). [Also. **Kahlur.**] State in the E Punjab, in N Union of India, formerly a feudatory state. It holds a seat in the Indian Council of States jointly with Himachal Pradesh. Capital, Bilaspur; area, 453 sq. mi.; pop. 127,566 (1951).

Bilaspur. District of the Chhattisgarh division, Madhya Pradesh (Central Provinces), Union of India, ab. 200 mi. NE of Nagpur. There is some coal mining in the area, but forest products and general agriculture are also important. Area, ab. 8,000 sq. mi.; pop. 1,549,509 (1941).

Bilauktaung Range (bē.louk′toung). Range of mountains between Thailand and Burma on the Malay Peninsula. It runs N and S for ab. 300 mi. and reaches a height of ab. 5,000 ft.

Bilbao (bil.bä′ō). City in N Spain, the capital of the province of Vizcaya, situated on both banks of the Nervion River, ab. 7 mi. from its influx into the Bay of Biscay. A large commercial and manufacturing city, it is the second largest seaport of Spain, exporting chiefly iron ore, pig iron, wine, and codfish, and importing coal, timber, and other materials. 229,091 (1950).

Commerce and Industry. Bilbao is the seat of shipping companies, has docks and shipyards, and an inner and outer harbor. Iron mining has declined somewhat, owing to exhaustion of ore deposits, competition of North African mines, and the crisis in the British iron industry. There are considerable metallurgical and construction industries, and also breweries, distilleries, flour mills, tanneries, and cotton textile, glass, paper, and soap industries.

Cultural Institutions. Bilbao has a Jesuit university, a museum, a theater, and a number of learned societies. The old town contains a number of churches and convents. The Basque language is widely spoken.

History. The city, founded c1300, became an important commercial port in the 15th and 16th centuries. The commercial code of Bilbao, covering both land and sea trade, became the basis of Spanish commercial law and of several codes in Latin American countries. Bilbao suffered from sieges by the Carlists in the period 1835–36 and in 1874. In the civil war of 1936–37, the Basques put up strong resistance to the Nationalist armies, which, however, because of superior artillery and air power, captured the city on June 19, 1937.

Bilbao, Francisco. b. at Santiago, Chile, Jan. 9, 1823; d. at Buenos Aires, Feb. 19, 1865. Latin American journalist and propagandist. Banished from Chile in 1845, he went to Paris where he took part in the revolution of 1848; returning to Chile, he was a leader in the disturbances of 1851, but was again forced to flee his country, going first to Peru, and later to Ecuador and Buenos

Aires. His death is said to have been due to exposure incurred while saving a drowning woman.

Bilbeis (bil.bās'). [Also: **Belbeis, Belbeys.**] Town in NE Africa, in Lower Egypt, ab. 30 mi. NE of Cairo, on the Ismailia Canal. It was besieged (1163–64) by Crusaders under Amalric, who later (1168) took the town. Pop. ab. 15,000.

Bilbilis (bil'bi.lis). See under **Calatayud.**

Bilbo (bil'bō), **Theodore Gilmore.** b. at Juniper Grove, Miss., Oct. 13, 1877; d. at New Orleans, La., Aug. 21, 1947. American politician. At the age of 17 he became a religious worker, and was a licensed Baptist preacher at 19. He entered politics in 1903 as a candidate for circuit judge, but was defeated. Thereafter he took up the study of law and was admitted to the bar in 1908, meanwhile having been elected to the state senate of Mississippi in 1907. In 1910 he was acquitted of a charge of having accepted a bribe while a member of the legislature; in 1912 he was elected lieutenant governor, and in 1916 governor of Mississippi. At the end of his first term as governor he was defeated in his bid for reëlection, in 1920. Shortly thereafter he was sentenced to ten days in prison for refusing to testify in a case involving his successful rival for the governorship. In 1928 he was again elected governor, holding office until 1932, and being the first man ever to fill that office twice in Mississippi. Early in Franklin D. Roosevelt's first term as president of the U.S., Bilbo was an official of the Agricultural Adjustment Administration, but in 1935 he was elected to the U.S. Senate from Mississippi after a campaign which was widely considered demagogic in its use of the issue of states' rights and inflammatory in its insistence on "white supremacy." These two issues were Bilbo's main reliance in his political campaigns, which won him reëlection to the Senate in 1940 and 1946. Following his third election to the Senate, that body refused to seat him pending investigation of charges of alleged improprieties in office. Hearings were postponed because of Bilbo's illness, and his death put an end to the proceedings.

Bildad (bil'dad). [Called **"Bildad the Shuhite."**] In the Old Testament, one of the three friends of Job. He is called the "Shuhite," after a territory identified by some with the Sakaia of Ptolemy, E of Bashan, by others with Suhu of the cuneiform inscriptions, situated on the Euphrates S of Carchemish.

Bilderdijk (bil'dėr.dīk), **Willem.** b. at Amsterdam, Sept. 7, 1756; d. at Haarlem, Netherlands, Dec. 18, 1831. Dutch poet, grammarian, and critic. His works include *Buitenleven* (1803), *De ziekte der geleerden* (1807), *De Mensch* (1808), and *De ondergang der eerste wereld* (1820).

Bildt (bilt), **De.** See **De Bilt.**

Bilecik (bē.le.jēk'). *Il* (province or vilayet) in NW Turkey: a hilly upland cut by the valley of the Sakarya River. Mineral resources include rich chromite mines; chief crops are wheat, cotton, and tobacco. Capital, Bilecik; area, 1,826 sq. mi.; pop. 136,844 (1950).

Bilfinger (bil'fing.ėr), **Georg Bernhard.** [Also, **Bülffinger.**] b. at Kannstadt, Württemberg, Jan. 23, 1693; d. at Stuttgart, Württemberg, Feb. 18, 1750. German philosopher (of the Leibnitz-Wolffian school) and mathematician. He was professor of theology at Tübingen, and privy councilor at Stuttgart. Author of *Dilucidationes de Deo, anima humana* (1725).

Biłgoraj (bēl.gô'rī). [Also, **Belgoraj.**] Town in E Poland, in the *województwo* (province) of Lublin, situated on the Lada River, ab. 72 mi. S of Lublin. Before World War II, it had agricultural trade and manufactured hats. The majority of the population was Jewish. 23,320 (1946).

Bilguer (bil'gwėr), **Paul Rudolf von.** b. at Ludwigslust, in Mecklenburg-Schwerin, Sept. 21, 1815; d. at Berlin, Sept. 10, 1840. Prussian army officer, noted as a chess player. He wrote *Handbuch des Schachspiels* (1843) and other works.

Bilhah (bil'hạ). In the Old Testament, Rachel's handmaid and Jacob's concubine, by Rachel's wish. She was the mother of Dan and Naphtali and thus ancestress of two of the 12 tribes of Israel. Subsequently she sinned with Reuben. References to Bilhah are found in Gen. xxix. 29; xxx. 1–8; xxxv. 22, and in 1 Chron. vii. 13.

Bílina (bē'lē.nä). [German, **Bilin.**] Town in Czechoslovakia, in N Bohemia, ab. 42 mi. NW of Prague, situated on the Biela River, between Teplice and Most. Glass and carpets are manufactured here. In the vicinity are lignite mines. From springs at the nearby spa of Bílina Kyselka, mineral water and digestive tablets are produced. The population declined from 8,551 (1930) to 7,915 (1947).

Bilioso (bil.i.ō'sō). Comic diplomat, in John Marston's play *The Malcontent.*

Biliran (bē.lē'rän). Island of the Philippines, off the N coast of Leyte and belonging to Leyte province. Its surface is mountainous. The highest peak is Mabui (4,267 ft.). Area, 230, sq. mi.; pop. 47,867 (1939).

Bilitis (bi.lī'tis; French, bē.lē.tēs). Putative singer of *Les Chansons de Bilitis* (1894) by the French writer Pierre Louÿs (1870–1925), a collection of erotic lyrics originally published as a "translation from the Greek" and accepted as authentic by several contemporary scholars.

Bilkha (bil'kạ). Former state of the Union of India, one of the Western India states, now merged with Saurashtra, S of the Gulf of Kutch. There are several small towns of minor industrial importance in the region, but the main occupation of the inhabitants is cotton and cattle raising. Capital, Bilkha; area, 167 sq. mi.; pop. 45,000 (1941).

Billaud-Varenne (bē.yō.vȧ.ren), **Jacques Nicolas.** b. at La Rochelle, France, April 23, 1756; d. at Port-au-Prince, Haiti, June 3, 1819. French politician, active in the French Revolution. A member of the Convention and of the Committee of Public Safety, he conspired against Danton, also against Robespierre, whom he, for a time, backed. He was deported to Guiana in 1795, and, refusing an amnesty offered by Napoleon I, remained in exile, moving (1816) to Haiti.

Billaut (bē.yō), **Adam.** b. 1602; d. 1662. French poet, most familiarly known as Maître Adam or Master Adam.

Bill Barley (bär'li), **Old.** See **Barley, Old Bill.**

Bille (bil'ẹ), **Steen Andersen.** b. Aug. 22, 1751; d. at Copenhagen, April 15, 1833. Danish admiral and minister of state; father of Steen Andersen Bille (1797–1883). He distinguished himself in an attack on Tripoli in 1798, and in the battle of Copenhagen in 1807.

Bille, Steen Andersen. b. at Copenhagen, Dec. 5, 1797; d. there, May 7, 1883. Danish admiral and minister of marine; son of Steen Andersen Bille (1751–1833). He took part (1840) in an expedition to South America, and, in the corvette *Galatea*, commanded (1845–47) a scientific expedition round the world, of which he gave an account in *Beretning om Corvetten Galatheas Reise omkrung jorden 1845–46 og 47* (1849–51).

Billerica (bil'ri.kạ). Town in NE Massachusetts, in Middlesex County, on the Concord River. It has railroad car shops and woolen manufactures, and is a marketing point for strawberries, apples, and cherries. 11,101 (1950).

Billericay (bil'ri.kā). Urban district in SE England, in Essex, ab. 5 mi. E of Brentwood, ab. 25 mi. E of Liverpool Street station, London. The town is noted for its High Street, which contains many ancient and interesting buildings. The Norsey Woods, site of an ancient camp, and the Langdon Hills, including the highest point in Essex, are contained within the urban district. 43,352 (1951).

Billickin (bil'i.kin), **Mrs.** Keeper of lodgings in Charles Dickens's *Mystery of Edwin Drood.* Her distinguishing characteristics are "personal faintness and an overpowering personal candor."

Billinge and Winstanley (bil'inj; win'stạn.li). [Locally called **Billinge.**] Urban district in NW England, in Lancashire, ab. 5 mi. SW of Wigan. It has no direct rail connections for passengers, being reached by rail to Wigan, ab. 194 mi. NW of London. 6,157 (1951).

Billinger (bil'ing.ẹr), **Richard.** b. at St. Marienkirchen, near Schärding, on the Inn River, Austria, July 20, 1893—. Austrian author, considered by many to be the most original and forceful dramatist of modern Austria. He has also written several volumes of poetry. His most important works are the two dramas *Das Perchtenspiel* (The Perchten Play, 1926) and *Rauhnacht* (1931). Rauhnacht is the night of December 23 when, according to folk tradition, pagan spirits are loosed to plague humanity.

Billingham or **Billingham-on-Tees** (bil'ing.ạm; tēz). Urban district and manufacturing town in NE England, in Durham, situated on the N bank of the river Tees, ab. 3 mi. NE of Stockton-on-Tees, ab. 240 mi. N of London by rail. It has a large chemical industry. 23,944 (1951).

Billings (bil'ingz). City in S Montana, county seat of Yellowstone County, on the Yellowstone River, ab. 202 mi. E of Butte. The site of beet-sugar-refining, oil-refining, meat-packing, and canning plants, it is also a marketing point for cattle and horses. It is the seat of Rocky Mountain College (formerly Billings Polytechnic Institute) and of a state teachers college. Founded in 1882, it was named for Frederick Billings (1823–90). 31,834 (1950).

Billings, Frank. b. at Highland, Wis., April 2, 1854; d. at Chicago, Sept. 20, 1932. American physician. He was a demonstrator (1882–86) in anatomy, and a professor (1886–98) at Northwestern University, before serving as a professor (1898 *et seq.*) and dean (1900 *et seq.*) at Rush Medical College at Chicago. Later (1905–24) he was professor of medicine at the University of Chicago. In 1917 he headed the American Red Cross mission to Russia.

Billings, Frederick. b. at Royalton, Vt., Sept. 27, 1823; d. Sept. 30, 1890. American lawyer and railroad promoter, president (1879–81) of the Northern Pacific Railroad. He emigrated (1849) to California and opened law offices at San Francisco. Financially interested after 1866 in the Northern Pacific, he directed its land department and after the panic of 1873 took part in reorganizing the company.

Billings, Henry. b. at New York, July 13, 1901—. American painter, designer, and decorator; grandson of John Shaw Billings (1838–1913). After apprenticeship in architectural offices, he studied at the Art Students League of New York under Boardman Robinson and Kenneth Hayes Miller, and at the Woodstock, N.Y., art colony. His pictures (many of which are based on themes involving a background of modern industry or machinery) include a group owned by the New York Museum of Science and Industry and a mural originally a part of the Ford Building at the New York World's Fair (1939). He is a painter also of such socially critical works as *Arrest No. 2* (1936), and has done murals for the Radio City Music Hall, and the Lake Placid, N.Y., and Medford, Mass., post offices. He is represented in the Museum of Living Art and the Whitney Museum of American Art, at New York.

Billings, John Shaw. b. in Switzerland County, Ind., April 12, 1838; d. at New York, March 11, 1913. American librarian, director of the New York Public Library from 1896; grandfather of Henry Billings (1901—). He was graduated from Miami University in 1857 and from the Ohio Medical College in 1860, and served in the Union army as a surgeon during the Civil War. In 1864 he was transferred to the surgeon general's office at Washington, and took charge of the medical library there. From 1893 to 1896 he was professor of hygiene at the University of Pennsylvania. Among his publications are the index-catalogue of the library of the Surgeon General's office, and the reports on vital and social statistics for the 11th census of the U.S. While at the New York Public Library, he supervised the consolidation of its three separately endowed parts into the main body; he re-catalogued the entire collection, and set up the city's system of branch libraries.

Billings, Joseph. fl. in the second half of the 18th century. English navigator in the Russian service, engaged (1785–91) in arctic exploration. He was also a companion of Captain James Cook on his last voyage.

Billings, Josh. See **Shaw, Henry Wheeler.**

Billings, William. b. at Boston, Oct. 7, 1746; d. there, Sept. 26, 1800. American composer. He is said to have been the first professional musical composer in America, and to have introduced into New England the spirited style of church music. He also introduced the use of the pitch pipe. At Stoughton, Mass., he organized (1774) a singing class which developed into the first American musical society. He published *The New England Psalm Singer* (1770), *The Singing-Master's Assistant* (1778), *The Psalm-Singer's Amusement* (1781), and *The Continental Harmony* (1794).

Billingsgate (bil'ingz.gāt). Gate, wharf, and fish-market in London, on the N bank of the Thames, near London Bridge. There may have been a water gate here from the earliest times. The market was established in 1559, in the reign of Queen Elizabeth, and was made a free market in 1699. It was at first a general landing place for merchandise of all kinds. It was burned down in 1715 and rebuilt. In 1852 new buildings were erected, and again in 1856. The present buildings were finished in 1874. The coarse language once used by the fishwives and others in the neighborhood gave the name of Billingsgate to such speech.

Billington (bil'ing.tọn), **Elizabeth.** [Maiden name, **Weichsel.**] b. at London, c1768; d. at Venice, Aug. 25, 1818. English singer. She retired from the stage in 1811.

Billiton (bēl'lē.ton). [Also: **Belitong;** Dutch, **Belitoeng.**] Island in the Republic of Indonesia, E of Bangka and SW of Borneo. In the temporary federation (1946–50), it comprised, with several small islands to the W, a *negara* (state) of the United States of Indonesia. It has important tin mines. Area, 1,866 sq. mi.; pop. ab. 70,000.

Bill of Rights. Name applied to one of the most important of the statutes which, taken collectively and with a considerable body of tradition, may be said to comprise the constitution of what is now the United Kingdom of Great Britain and Northern Ireland. When William of Orange and his consort Mary were offered the crown of England, the tender was conditional upon their acceptance of the Declaration of Rights of 1688. This Declaration, with the addition of an article barring the crown to Roman Catholics, was given the force of law by enactment as the Bill of Rights in 1689, the full title being "An Act declaring the Rights and Liberties of the Subject, and settling the Succession to the Crown." The Bill declares in effect: that laws and their execution cannot be suspended or dispensed with by royal authority without the consent of Parliament; that commissions and courts to deal with ecclesiastical issues, and all commissions and courts of like nature, are illegal; that levying money for use of the crown without grant of Parliament or for other use or longer time than granted by Parliament, is illegal; that subjects have the right to petition the king and shall not be committed or prosecuted for so doing; that raising or keeping a standing army within the kingdom in time of peace, without the consent of Parliament, is illegal; that Protestant subjects may keep arms for their defense; that "elections of members of Parliament ought to be free"; that speech, debate, and proceedings in Parliament should not be impeached or questioned anywhere outside of Parliament; that excessive bail should not be required, nor excessive fines imposed, nor cruel and unusual punishments be inflicted; that "jurors should be duly empanelled and returned" and jurors in trials for high treason should be freeholders; "that all grants and promises of fines and forfeitures" of particular persons before conviction are illegal and void; and that Parliament should be convened "frequently." The spirit, if not always the letter, of this statute has influenced the constitutional development and framework of law in every country in the British Commonwealth of Nations, as well as in the U.S., and (with the Magna Charta) it is often cited as part of the political heritage of the world's English-speaking democracies.

Bill of Rights. Name applied to the first ten amendments to the Constitution of the U.S. The amendments, drafted by James Madison and based upon the Virginia Declaration, were submitted to the states after the ratification of the Constitution had evoked widespread criticism pointing out that the organic law did not include proper safeguards for existing and inalienable individual rights. The Bill of Rights, declared ratified on Dec. 15, 1791, guarantees such fundamental rights as freedom of speech, press, assembly, and religion, among others, and is binding upon the central government, but not upon the states. Similar provisions in the constitutions of the several states are also called Bills of Rights. Their underlying doctrine owes much to the concepts of natural law prevailing in the late 18th century.

Billotte (bē.yot), **Gaston Henri Gustave.** b. at Sommeval, Aube, France, Feb. 10, 1875; d. at Ypres, Belgium, May 28, 1940. French army commander, best known for his campaigns in the French colonies. He was a member (1935 *et seq.*) of the superior war council, military governor (1937 *et seq.*) of Paris, and commander of an army group during World War II. He died from injuries incurred in an automobile accident while on active duty.

Billoux (bē.yö), **François.** b. at St.-Romain-Lamotte, Loire, France, May 21, 1903—. French political leader, a member (1939 *et seq.*) of the political bureau of the French Communist party. A deputy since 1936, he was arrested (1940) and interned (1940–43). After his release, he held office (1944) in the Free French government at Algiers, and served subsequently (1945–47) on various occasions as minister of national economy, reconstruction, and national defense.

Billroth (bil′rōt), **Theodor.** b. at Bergen, on the island of Rügen, in the Baltic, April 26, 1829; d. at Abbazia (now in Yugoslavia), Feb. 6, 1894. Austrian surgeon, noted for his work in pathology and military surgery. An accomplished pianist, he was a friend of Johannes Brahms.

Billy Budd (bil′i bud′). [Original full title, **Billy Budd, Foretopman.**] Novelette by Herman Melville, written a short time before he died and not published until 1924. Many literary scholars and critics, including E. M. Forster (in his *Aspects of the Novel*), consider it one of Melville's most significant works. It was dramatized in 1950.

Billy-Montigny (bē.yē.môṅ.tē.nyē). Coal-mining town in N France, in the department of Pas-de-Calais, between Lens and Douai. 9,371 (1946).

Billy the Kid. [Real name, **William H. Bonney.**] b. at New York, Nov. 23, 1859; killed at Fort Sumner, N.M., July 15, 1881. American desperado, one of the most notorious of the American Southwest. Having moved to the West with his family, he early abandoned schooling for gambling. It was said that at the age of 12 he stabbed a man to death. By the time he was 18, he had a record of 12 supposed killings; at this time he went to the Pecos Valley, in what is now New Mexico, and there became an employee of a cattleman. In 1878, after he had seen his employer killed in the opening skirmish of the Lincoln County cattle war, he made himself leader of the McSween faction which killed (April 1, 1878) a sheriff and his deputy, and took a large part in the battle at Lincoln. When General Lew Wallace, later in the same year, came to the Territory of New Mexico as governor, he extended a general amnesty; Billy the Kid refused to avail himself of it, maintaining that if he surrendered he would be killed, and thereafter he engaged extensively in cattle stealing. Several cattlemen, including John S. Chisum, a former friend of the Kid, prevailed upon Pat Garrett, another of the Kid's former acquaintances, to take over the job of sheriff. Garrett went gunning for Billy the Kid, and forced him to surrender (in December, 1880) at Fort Sumner. Imprisoned at Mesilla under sentence of death, Billy the Kid made his escape by killing his two guards; but a few months later Garrett again cornered him, and shot him. In all, 21 deaths were attributed to him.

Biloxi (bi.lok′si). [Eng. trans. of Indian name, "*first people.*"] City in SE Mississippi, in Harrison County, on Mississippi Sound near the Gulf of Mexico. A fishing and packing center for oysters and shrimp, it also has a shipbuilding industry and is a tourist resort. The first French settlement in the lower Mississippi Valley was made on the Bay of Biloxi in 1699 by a party under Pierre Le Moyne, Sieur d'Iberville (1661–1706). Biloxi was the capital (1719–23) of the French colony of Louisiana. It is the seat of a U.S. Coast Guard Air Base, and the Air Forces' Keesler Field is nearby. In the decade between the last two U.S. censuses, the city's population more than doubled. 17,475 (1940); 37,425 (1950).

Biloxi. North American Indian tribe formerly inhabiting the SE portion of Mississippi. Their language was of the Siouan family.

Bilson (bil′sọn), **Thomas.** b. at Winchester, England, 1546; d. at Westminster, England, June 18, 1616. English prelate and author, consecrated bishop of Worcester in 1596, and of Winchester in 1597.

Bilston (bil′stọn). Municipal borough, market town, and manufacturing center in N central England, in Staffordshire, ab. 3 mi. SE of Wolverhampton, ab. 121 mi. NW of London by rail. It was formerly a coal-mining center, but the coal field on which it was located is now exhausted. It now has manufactures of heavy metal goods and steel pipe and tubing. 33,464 (1951).

Bilt (bilt), **De.** See **De Bilt.**

Biluchistan (bi.lö.chi.stän′). See **Baluchistan.**

Bilwana (bēl.wä′nä). Northern subgroup of the Bantu-speaking Nyamwezi of E Africa, inhabiting W Tanganyika.

Bimani (bim′ạ.ni). See **Bimini.**

Bimeler (bī′mẹ.lėr), **Joseph Michael.** [Original name, **Joseph Michael Bäumler.**] b. probably in Württemberg, Germany, c1778; d. Aug. 27, 1853. American religious leader, founder of the Separatist Society of Zoar in Ohio. Having led (1817) a group of 300 Separatists from Württemberg, Bavaria, and Baden to Philadelphia, he headed the Society's communal settlement until his death.

Bimini (bim′i.ni). [Also, **Bimani.**] Name formerly given by West Indian natives to an island or region N of the West Indies, where, according to legend, there was a fountain whose waters conferred perpetual youth. The island or islands meant may have been the small group now called Bimini Islands or the Biminis, in the Bahamas; but the name was given in the early maps to the peninsula of Florida. About the middle of the 16th century Bimini was sometimes supposed to be in Mexico.

Bimini Islands. [Also: **Bemini Islands, Bimini,** the **Biminis.**] Two small islands in the Atlantic Ocean, ab. 50 mi. E of Miami, Fla.: the westernmost islands of the Bahamas. Area, 9 sq. mi.; pop. 800.

Binche (baṅsh). Town in S Belgium, in the province of Hainaut, ab. 10 mi. SE of Mons. The so-called *fleurs à plat*, used in the manufacture of Brussels lace, are produced here as a specialty; there are also glass and shoe industries and cattle and horse markets. 10,623 (1947).

Binchois (baṅ.shwȧ), **Gilles** or **Egidius.** b. near Mons, Belgium, c1400; d. at Lille, France, 1460. Flemish composer and churchman, noted for his three-part secular songs set to French words. His work also includes religious music.

Binda (bēn′dä). [Also: **Cabinda, Kabinda, Mangoio, Ngoyo.**] Bantu-speaking people of C Africa, inhabiting the Portuguese territory of Cabinda N of the mouth of the Congo River. Their kingdom bordered on those of Loango to the N, Yombe to the W, and the great empire of Kongo to the SE.

Binding (bin′ding), **Rudolf G.** b. at Basel, Switzerland, Aug. 13, 1867; d. at Starnberg, Germany, 1938. German poet and story writer. Following in the footsteps of his father, Karl Binding, a professor of law, he first tried law, but was unsuccessful. He was no happier in medicine and soon gave it up for literature. He was an officer in World War I and wrote about it in *Aus dem Kriege* (1925; Eng. trans., *A Fatalist at War*, 1929). Although not very politically minded he greeted the united Germany of 1933 with enthusiasm. Binding's work reveals a deep love of adventure and romance, shown chiefly in stories like *Waffenbrüder* (1910), *Angelucia* (1911), *Der Opfergang* (1911), and *Unsterblichkeit* (1921). His first work, *Legenden der Zeit* (1909), continues the tradition made famous by Gottfried Keller's *Sieben Legenden.* His autobiography, *Erlebtes Leben*, appeared in 1928.

Binet (bē.ne; Anglicized, bē.nā′), **Alfred.** b. at Nice, France, July 8, 1857; d. at Paris, Oct. 18, 1911. French psychologist, famous for his development (with Théodore Simon) of the intelligence test known as the Binet, or Binet-Simon test, which first appeared in 1905, and which, with revisions, has been widely used, especially in the U.S., in schools, the armed forces, and industrial concerns. With Henri Beaunis he founded the first French journal of psychology, *L'Année psychologique* (1895), and the first psychology laboratory in France (1889) at the University of Paris. Other men (Sir Francis Galton in Great Britain, and James McKeen Cattell and Lewis M. Terman in the U.S.) had attempted to devise mental tests, but these men concerned themselves with simple capacities (such as ability to judge visual length), while Binet attempted to measure complex functions. His life work was outlined in *La Psychologie du raisonnement* (1886; Eng. trans., 1899). His chief work is *L'Étude expérimentale de l'intelligence* (1903).

Binet-Valmer (bē.ne.vȧl.mer), **Jean.** [Called **Jean Binet de Valmer.**] b. at Geneva, Switzerland, 1875; d. 1940. French novelist. He was the author of some 35 novels, which include *Le Coeur en désordre* (1912), *La*

Passion (1914), *Une Femme a tué* (1924), and others. In 1914 he became a citizen of France.

Bing (bing), **Paul Robert.** b. at Strasbourg, May 8, 1878—. Swiss neurologist.

Bingen (bing'ęn). [Latin, **Bingium.**] City in W Germany, in the *Land* (state) of Rhineland-Palatinate, French Zone, formerly in the province of Rhine-Hesse, Hesse, situated at the junction of the Nahe and Rhine rivers, ab. 16 mi. W of Mainz. A center of the Rhenish wine trade, it has distilleries, as well as metallurgical, electrical, and chemical industries. It is the seat of a technical institute. Bingen is located at the major bend of the Rhine, where the river enters, between the Hunsrück and Taunus mountains, the narrow valley which has been mentioned so often in saga and song. Notable structures include the Bridge of Drusus, the Klopp castle, now serving as town hall and museum, a Romanesque parish church with baroque altar, the 17th-century Church of the Capuchins, and various ruined castles in the vicinity. A Roman colony, Bingen became an important town in the Middle Ages; it belonged to the Federation of Rhenish cities, before coming under the jurisdiction of the archbishop of Mainz; destroyed (1689) by the French, it passed to France in 1797 and to Hesse-Darmstadt in 1816; it suffered damage in World War II. The population is mixed, the majority being Roman Catholic. 16,803 (1950).

Binger (bań.zhā), **Louis Gustave.** b. at Strasbourg, Oct. 14, 1856—. French officer and African explorer. Working for the French government, he connected the French possessions on the upper Niger River with the Ivory Coast. In 1892 he returned to West Africa as French commissioner for the settlement of the Ashanti boundaries with England. He was governor of the Ivory Coast (1893–96), and director of African affairs in the ministry of colonies (1896–1907). Bingerville, for a time capital of the Ivory Coast, was named for him.

Bingerville (bań.zhā.vēl). Former capital of the Ivory Coast, French West Africa. It is situated on a lagoon near the coast, a few miles from the present capital at Abidjan, and is connected by road with the latter and with Grand Bassam, the chief port. It was named for the French explorer and administrator Louis Gustave Binger. Pop. ab. 800.

Bingham (bing'ąm), **Amelia.** [Maiden name, **Smiley.**] b. at Hicksville, Ohio, March 20, 1869; d. at New York, Sept. 1, 1927. American actress famous for melodramatic roles. She made her debut in *The Struggle for Life* (1893), and subsequently (1897) starred under Charles Frohman's management in *The White Heather*. In 1901 she produced and acted in *The Climbers*. Later appearances were made in *Great Moments from Great Plays* (1909) and in *Trelawny of the Wells* (1925).

Bingham, Anne. [Maiden name, **Willing.**] b. Aug. 1, 1764; d. in Bermuda, May 11, 1801. American leader of the Federalist society; wife of William Bingham.

Bingham, Caleb. b. at Salisbury, Conn., April 15, 1757; d. at Boston, April 6, 1817. American textbook writer. He published the second English grammar to appear in America, *The Young Lady's Accidence or a Short and Easy Introduction to English Grammar: Designed Principally for the Use of Young Learners, more especially of the Fair Sex, though Proper for Either* (1785). His other books include *The American Preceptor* (1794), *The Columbian Orator* (1797), and *Astronomical and Geographical Catechism* (1803).

Bingham, George. b. at Melcombe, Dorsetshire, England, Nov. 7, 1715; d. at Pimperne, Dorsetshire, England, Oct. 11, 1800. English divine and antiquarian. He was rector of Pimperne.

Bingham, George Caleb. b. 1811; d. 1879. American genre and portrait painter. After studying at the Pennsylvania Academy of Fine Arts at Philadelphia, and at Düsseldorf, Germany, he began his career in Missouri, where he set up his studio first at Jefferson City, later moving to St. Louis and then to Kansas City. In 1877 he became professor of art at the University of Missouri in the city of Columbia. Bingham obviously took a zestful pleasure in the scenes and characters of the Middle West, and his genre pieces have held their place chiefly by their vitality and veracity, as well as by their humor. In recent years reproductions of such Bingham pictures as *Stump Speaking, Jolly Flatboatmen, Raftsmen Playing Cards*, and *Emigration of Daniel Boone* have had a new popularity.

Bingham, George Charles. [Title, 3rd Earl of **Lucan.**] b. at London, April 16, 1800; d. Nov. 10, 1888. British general and field marshal. He became a major general in 1851. Commander of a cavalry division in the Crimean War, in 1854 he directed the charge of the heavy brigade, and used it to cover the retreat of the light brigade at Balaklava.

Bingham, Hiram. b. at Bennington, Vt., Oct. 30, 1789; d. at New Haven, Conn., Nov. 11, 1869. American missionary (1820–40) at Honolulu; father of Hiram Bingham (1831–1908). With associates he devised a Hawaiian alphabet and translated (1839) the Bible. He was the author of *First Book for Children* (1831), *Scripture Catechism* (1831), and *Residence of Twenty-one Years in the Sandwich Islands; or The Civil, Religious, and Political History of Those Islands* (1847).

Bingham, Hiram. b. at Honolulu, Hawaii, Aug. 16, 1831; d. at Baltimore, Md., Oct. 25, 1908. American missionary (1857–64, 1873–75) to the Gilbert Islands who translated the Bible into Gilbertese (1890); son of Hiram Bingham (1789–1869), and father of Hiram Bingham (1875—). Author of a Gilbertese hymn and tune book (1880), as well as a Gilbertese dictionary (1908) and *Gilbert Islands Bible Dictionary* (1895).

Bingham, Hiram. b. at Honolulu, Hawaii, Nov. 19, 1875—. American politician, explorer, and historian; son of Hiram Bingham (1831–1908). He served as a U.S. senator (1925–33) from Connecticut. He lectured on South American geography and history at Yale (1907–08), and on diplomatic history at Johns Hopkins University (1910), and was adviser (1910 *et seq.*) on Latin American collections at Yale University. In the period 1906–07 he explored Simon Bolívar's route through Venezuela and Colombia, and in the next two years the Spanish trade route from Buenos Aires to Lima. As assistant professor (1909–15) and professor (1915–24) of Latin American history at Yale, he headed three expeditions to Peru which discovered important Inca ruins. In 1951 he was nominated to preside over the loyalty review board of the U.S. Civil Service Commission. He has published *Journal of an Expedition Across Venezuela and Colombia* (1909), *The Monroe Doctrine, An Obsolete Shibboleth* (1913), and *Lost City of the Incas* (1948), among others.

Bingham, John Armor. b. at Mercer, Pa., Jan. 21, 1815; d. at Cadiz, Ohio, March 19, 1900. American lawyer and politician in Ohio. He was a member (1854 *et seq.*) of Congress before serving as minister (1873 *et seq.*) to Japan. He is remembered for his participation as special judge advocate in the trial of Abraham Lincoln's assassins, and for his three-day speech at the impeachment trial of Andrew Johnson.

Bingham, Joseph. b. at Wakefield, England, in September, 1668; d. at Havant, near Portsmouth, England, Aug. 17, 1723. English divine and writer on church history. His chief work is *Origines Ecclesiasticae or Antiquities of the Christian Church* (1708–22).

Bingham, Robert Worth. b. in Orange County, N.C., Nov. 8, 1871; d. Dec. 18, 1937. American diplomat, and publisher of the Louisville (Ky.) *Courier-Journal* and *Times*. An attorney (1904–07) in Jefferson County, Ky., he was mayor (1907) of Louisville, before serving as ambassador (1933–37) to Great Britain.

Bingham, Theodore Alfred. b. at Andover, Conn. May 14, 1858; d. Sept. 6, 1934. American engineer and army officer. An engineer officer (1879–90), he was a military attaché with the legations at Berlin (1890–92) and Rome (1892–94); he was promoted (1904) to brigadier general on his retirement from the army. He served as police commissioner (1906–09) of New York, and later (1911–15) as consulting engineer for the department of bridges at New York.

Bingham, William. b. at Philadelphia, April 8, 1752; d. Feb. 6, 1804. American banker and politician who founded (1781) the Bank of North America, the first bank in the U.S.; husband of Anne Bingham. He was a member of the Continental Congress (1786–89), the Pennsylvania Assembly (1790–95), and the U.S. Senate (1795–1801). Considered by tradition to have been a founder of Binghamton, N.Y. (in 1786 he purchased the land which now comprises it), he was also the first president of the Philadelphia and Lancaster Turnpike Corporation, which built the earliest turnpike in America. Author of *Description of Certain Tracts . . . in the District of Maine* (1793).

Bingham Canyon. Town in N Utah, in Salt Lake County: noted for its open-pit copper mines. Settled (1848) by Mormons named Thomas and Sanford Bingham as a farming community, it was mined for gold in the 1860's, for lead and silver from 1880 to 1896, and subsequently for copper. 2,569 (1950).

Bingham Purchase. In U.S. history, a term applied to certain land tracts in Maine (at that time part of Massachusetts) purchased (1786) by a Philadelphia banker, William Bingham, who drew the purchase rights by lottery. His original holding of one million acres was later enlarged by an equivalent amount. As a term applicable to a specific tract of land, "Bingham Purchases" is used only in connection with the Bingham holding in Maine, although Bingham also owned considerable areas in New York (perhaps most notably that on which the city of Binghamton was founded).

Binghamton (bing'ạm.tọn). City in S New York, county seat of Broome County, at the confluence of the Chenango and Susquehanna rivers: manufactures include shoes, machinery, cameras, and photographic film; seat of a state mental hospital. It was settled c1787 on land purchased by William Bingham (1752–1804), a Philadelphia banker. 80,674 (1950).

Bingium (bin'ji.um). Latin name of **Bingen.**

Bingley (bing'li). Urban district, market town, and manufacturing center in N England, in the West Riding of Yorkshire, situated on the river Aire, ab. 5 mi. NW of Bradford, ab. 212 mi. NW of London by rail. It has textile mills, and manufactures textile machinery. 21,566 (1951).

Bingöl (bēng.gėl'). *Il* (province or vilayet) in E Turkey: very rugged, mountainous country. Herding and subsistence agriculture are the chief occupations; the principal cash crop is opium. Capital, Bingöl; pop. 97,225 (1950).

Bini (bē'nē). [Also, **Edo.**] Subgroup of the Sudanic-speaking Edo peoples of W Africa, inhabiting an area in the vicinity of the town of Benin, Nigeria. Their population is estimated at ab. 70,000 (by P. A. Talbot, *The Peoples of Southern Nigeria*, 1926). Their great kingdom of Benin, with its capital at what was then known as Benin City, once extended from the Niger River into Dahomey, and was the most powerful empire on the Guinea Coast when the first Portuguese arrived in 1472. According to tradition, this kingdom was founded by Yoruba people from Ife, in what are now the Western Provinces of Nigeria. Benin has achieved fame because of its remarkable bronze castings, also derived from Ife (according to Benin tradition), and other art forms, and for its mass human sacrifices in honor of its former kings. In 1897 Benin was sacked and burned by a British punitive expedition; its king was exiled, and its art treasures were carried to Europe.

Biniana (bin.i.ā'nạ). A Latin name of **Baena.**

Binmaley (bēn.mä.lā'). Town in Pangasinan province, W Luzon, Philippine Islands. 2,081 (1948).

Binnen Alster (bin'ẹn äl'stėr). See under **Alster.**

Binney (bin'i), **Amos.** b. at Boston, Mass., Oct. 18, 1803; d. at Rome, Feb. 18, 1847. American naturalist and patron of science. He wrote *Terrestrial and Air-breathing Mollusks* (1851) and others.

Binney, Horace. b. at Philadelphia, Jan. 4, 1780; d. there, Aug. 12, 1875. American lawyer and legal writer. He was graduated from Harvard College in 1797, and admitted to the Philadelphia bar in 1800. A Whig member of Congress (1833–35), he was a director and defender of the Second Bank of the United States, and, as such, an opponent of Andrew Jackson.

Binney, Thomas. b. at Newcastle, England, in April, 1798; d. at Clapton, England, Feb. 24, 1874. English Congregational divine and controversialist.

Binns (binz), **Archie.** b. at Port Ludlow, Wash., in July, 1899—. American writer. He served (1918) in the U.S. army, and was later a sailor and newspaper reporter. His books include *Maiden Voyage* (1931), *Lightship* (1934), *Backwater Voyage* (1936), *The Laurels are Cut Down* (1937), *The Land is Bright* (1939), *The Roaring Land* (1942), and *You Roaring River* (1947).

Binns, Charles Fergus. b. at Worcester, England, Oct. 4, 1857; d. Dec. 4, 1934. American ceramist. He served on the staff (1872–96) of the Royal Porcelain Works at Worcester, England. In the U.S., he was principal (1897–1900) of the Technical School of Science and Art at Trenton, N.J., and director (1900–31) of the New York state college of ceramics (a part of Alfred University) at Alfred, N.Y. Author of *Ceramic Technology* (1896), *The Story of the Potter* (1897), and *The Potter's Craft* (1909).

Binns, John Alexander. b. in Loudoun County, Va., c1761; d. 1813. American agriculturalist whose experiments (1784–1803) with gypsum, clover, and deep plowing improved farming in Virginia and Maryland. The Loudoun system, praised by Thomas Jefferson, was expounded in Binns's *Treatise on Practical Farming* (1803).

Binondo (bē.nōn'dō). Division of the city of Manila, Luzon, Philippine Islands.

Binswanger (bins'väng.ėr), **Otto Ludwig.** b. at Münsterlingen, Switzerland, Oct. 14, 1852; d. at Kreuzlingen, Switzerland, July 15, 1929. Swiss psychiatrist. He was assistant to L. Meyer at the insane asylum at Göttingen, to E. Ponfick at the Pathological Institute at Breslau, and to C. F. O. Westphal at the Charité Hospital at Berlin. He became (1879) privatdocent of psychiatry at the University of Berlin, and a professor (1882) at the University of Jena. He is one of the founders of the modern theory of hysteria. He introduced (1896) the W. S. Playfair treatment by rest and feeding in cases of neurasthenia (also called Binswanger's treatment), and described chronic, progressive encephalopathy with presenile dementia and loss of memory (Binswanger's dementia).

Bintan (bin'tän) or **Bintang** (-täng). [Dutch, **Bentan.**] Island in the Republic of Indonesia, in the Riouw Archipelago, situated ab. 50 mi. SE of Singapore, in the South China Sea. Area, ab. 455 sq. mi.

Binue (bin'wē). See **Benue.**

Binyon (bin'yọn), **Laurence.** b. at Lancaster, England, Aug. 10, 1869; d. 1943. English poet and Orientalist. He served (1893–95) as assistant in the department of printed books of the British Museum, and in the museum's department of prints and drawings (1895 *et seq.*), where he became (1913) chief of Oriental works. Among his publications are *Lyric Poems* (1894), *Poems* (1895), *London Visions* (1895, 1898), *The Praise of Life* (1896), *Porphyrion and Other Poems* (1898), *Odes* (1900), *The Death of Adam* (1903), *Penthesilea* (1905), *Paris and Oenone* (1906), and *Attila* (1907). He also wrote a number of works on art, including *Painting in the Far East* (1908) and *The Drawings and Engravings of William Blake* (1922), compiled a catalogue of English drawings in the British Museum, and translated the first two parts of Dante's *Divine Comedy.*

Binz (bints), **Karl.** b. at Bernkastel, Germany, July 1, 1832; d. at Bonn, Germany, Jan. 12, 1913. German physician and pharmacologist. He was a pupil of Rudolf Virchow and F. T. Frerichs, and was professor of pharmacology at the University of Bonn, where he founded (1869) the Pharmacological Institute. He wrote extensively on the action of quinine, ethereal oils, alcohol, and anesthetics, and described a test for quinine in urine. Author of *Grundzüge der Arzneimittellehre* (1866) which went through 14 editions, *Vorlesungen über Pharmakologie* (1883–86), *Experimentelle Untersuchungen über das Wesen der Chininwirkung* (1868), and an important history of anesthesia, *Der Aether gegen den Schmerz* (1896).

Bío-Bío (bē'ō.bē'ō). Province in C Chile. Capital, Los Angeles; area, 4,343 sq. mi.; pop. 123,295 (est. 1950).

Bío-Bío River. Largest river in Chile; it flows into the Pacific at Concepción. Length, ab. 238 mi.

Biographia Literaria (bī.ọ.graf'i.ạ lit.ẹ.rãr'i.ạ). Prose work (2 vols., 1817) by Samuel Taylor Coleridge.

Biography. Play (1932) by Martin Flavin.

Bion (bī'ọn). b. at Phlossa, near Smyrna, Asia Minor; fl. c280 B.C. (or, according to some authorities, in the 2nd century B.C.). Greek bucolic poet. His chief extant poem is the *Epitaphios Adōnidos* ("Lament for Adonis").

Biondello (bē.on.del'ō). Servant to Lucentio, in Shakespeare's *The Taming of the Shrew.*

Biondi (byōn′dē), Sir **Giovanni Francesco.** b. on the island of Lesina (now Hvar), in the Adriatic Sea, 1572; d. at Aubonne, near Lausanne, Switzerland, 1644. Italian novelist and historian, long resident in England, where he became a gentleman of the king's privy chamber. He published three romances of chivalry, in Italian, which were translated into English as *Eromena, or Love and Revenge* (1631), *Donzella desterrada, or The Banish'd Virgin* (1635), and *Coralbo* (1655), a sequel to the preceding.

Biorra (bir′ạ). Irish name of **Birr.**

Biot (bē.ō), **Jean Baptiste.** b. at Paris, April 21, 1774; d. there, Feb. 3, 1862. French physicist and chemist, noted for his discoveries in optics, particularly concerning the polarization of light. His chief works are *Essai de géometrie analytique* (1805), *Traité élémentaire d'astronomie physique* (1805), *Traité de physique expérimentale* (1816), *Traité élémentaire de physique expérimentale* (1818–21), and works on ancient Egyptian, Indian, and Chinese astronomy.

Bir (bir). See also **Birecik.**

Bir. [Also: **Bhir, Birh.**] District of the Aurangabad division, Hyderabad, S central Union of India, centered ab. 200 mi. E of Bombay. The important crops of the area are cotton, millet, fruits, tobacco, and sugar. Area, ab. 4,500 sq. mi.; pop. 634,000 (est. 1941).

Birch (bėrch), **Harvey.** Hero of *The Spy* (1821), a novel by James Fenimore Cooper.

Birch, Jonathan. b. at London, 1783; d. at Berlin, 1847. English timber merchant, the first translator into English of both parts of Goethe's *Faust* (1839–43). He served (1803–12) in the Memel office of the timber merchant John Argelander. An intimate of Frederick William IV of Prussia, he dedicated the second part of *Faust* to him; while in Berlin, he also translated the *Nibelungenlied* (1848).

Birch, Samuel. b. at London, Nov. 3, 1813; d. there, Dec. 27, 1885. English archaeologist. He published *Gallery of Antiquities* (1842), *Introduction to the Study of Egyptian Hieroglyphs* (1857), *History of Ancient Pottery* (1858), and others.

Birch, Thomas. b. at London, Nov. 23, 1705; d. near London, Jan. 9, 1766. English writer on history and biography. He wrote nearly all the English biographies in the *General Dictionary, Historical and Critical* (1734–41), edited *Thurloe's State Papers* (1742), and compiled *Memoirs of the Reign of Queen Elizabeth* (1754).

Birchard Letter (bėr′chạrd). Open letter (June 29, 1863) by President Abraham Lincoln to 19 Ohio Democrats, one of whom was named Birchard, justifying the national government's treatment of those in the North who publicly opposed the Civil War. Lincoln noted that if a majority of the 19 Democrats supported specific pledges in regard to the furthering of the war effort, he would release the Copperhead leader, Clement L. Vallandigham.

Birches. Poem in blank verse by Robert Frost, published in his *Mountain Interval* (1916). The author, nostalgically recalling his childhood joy in climbing birches, recaptures a vision of soaring freedom and develops it into a philosophical concept.

Birch-Pfeiffer (birċh′pfī′fėr), **Charlotte Katharina.** b. at Stuttgart, Germany, June 23, 1800; d. at Berlin, Aug. 25, 1868. German actress and playwright. Her stage career began when she was 13 and lasted until her death. She was for a time (1837–43) manager of a Zurich theater. Nearly all of her 71 plays are adaptations of narratives, notably *Dorf und Stadt* (1847) from Auerbach's *Die Frau Professorin, Die Waise von Lowood* (1855) from Charlotte Brontë's *Jane Eyre*, and *Der Glöckner von Notre-Dame* from Victor Hugo's *Notre Dame de Paris.*

Bird (bėrd), **Arthur.** b. at Cambridge, Mass., July 23, 1856; d. 1923. American composer, resident (1886 *et seq.*) at Berlin. He composed a symphony and other orchestral works, a comic opera, *Daphne*, and many piano pieces.

Bird, Charles. b. at Wilmington, Del., June 17, 1838; d. there, March 22, 1920. American army officer. Brevetted (1867) a captain and major in recognition for service in the Union army during the Civil War, he served (1882–1902) in the volunteers, and was named (1902) a brigadier general before his retirement.

Bird, Cyril Kenneth. b. Dec. 17, 1887—. English illustrator and cartoonist, who became art editor of *Punch* in 1937. He studied at Cheltenham College and King's College, London. Among his publications are *The Luck of the Draw* (1936), *Stop and Go* (1938), *Running Commentary* (1941), and *A School of Purposes* (1946).

Bird, Frederic Mayer. b. at Philadelphia, June 28, 1838; d. at South Bethlehem, Pa., April 2, 1908. American Lutheran and Episcopal clergyman, hymnologist, and writer. He published *Charles Wesley Seen in His Finer and Less Familiar Poems* (1867) and *The Story of Our Christianity* (1893), and compiled *Hymns for the Use of the Evangelical Lutheran Church* (1865) with Beale Melancthon Schmucker, and *Hymns of the Spirit* (1871) with Bishop Oldenheimer. Author of the novels *A Pessimist in Theory and Practice* (1888) and *An Alien from the Commonwealth* (1889), he also contributed hymnological articles to Julian's *Dictionary of Hymnology* and edited (1893–98) *Lippincott's Magazine.*

Bird, Golding. b. in Norfolk, England, Dec. 9, 1814; d. at Tunbridge Wells, England, Oct. 27, 1854. English physician and medical writer. He was appointed lecturer on natural philosophy at Guy's Hospital in 1836, and lecturer on materia medica at the College of Physicians in 1847. His chief work is *Elements of Natural Philosophy* (1839).

Bird, James. b. at Earl's Stonham, Suffolk, England, Nov. 10, 1788; d. at Yoxford, Suffolk, England, 1839. English poet and dramatist. An unsuccessful miller from 1814 to 1820, and a stationer from 1820 until his death, he began to write before he was 16, some of his juvenile efforts later appearing in the *Suffolk Chronicle.* Author of *The Vale of Slaughden* (1819), a narrative of the Danish invasion of East Anglia; *The White Hats* (1819), a mock-heroic satire on radicals; *Machin, or the Discovery of Madeira* (1821), *Dunwich, a Tale of the Splendid City* (1828), *Framlingham, a Narrative of the Castle* (1831), and *The Emigrant's Tale* (1833), poems; and the dramas *Cosmo, Duke of Florence* (1822) and *The Smuggler's Daughter* (1836).

Bird, Robert Montgomery. b. at Newcastle, Del., Feb. 5, 1806; d. at Philadelphia, Jan. 23, 1854. American physician, playwright, and novelist. He wrote several plays for Edwin Forrest, among them *The Gladiator* (1831), *Oralloosa* (1832), and *The Broker of Bogota* (1834). His novels, which achieved great popularity, include *Calavar* (1834), *The Infidel* (1835), *The Hawks of Hawk-Hollow* (1835), *Nick of the Woods; or, The Jibbenainosay* (1837), *Peter Pilgrim; or, a Rambler's Recollections* (1838), and *The Adventures of Robin Day* (1839).

Bird, Theophilus. Hero of William John Locke's novel *The Kingdom of Theophilus* (1927).

Bird, William. See **Byrd** or **Byrde** or **Bird, William.**

Birdcage Walk. Walk on the S side of St. James's Park, London. It is so named from the aviaries which were ranged along its side as early as the time of the Stuarts.

Bird in a Cage, The. Play by James Shirley, printed in 1633.

Bird Islands. See also **Aves.**

Bird Islands. [Also, **Chaos Islands.**] Group of small islands off the S coast of Africa, in Algoa Bay, Cape of Good Hope province, Union of South Africa.

Birdlime (bėrd′līm). Disreputable character in John Webster and Thomas Dekker's *Westward Hoe.*

Bird of Dawning. Novel (1933) by John Masefield. It is considered by most critics to be one of his best novels.

Birds, The. Comedy by Aristophanes, produced in 414 B.C.

Birds, Beasts and Flowers. Collection (1923) of poems by D. H. Lawrence.

Birdsboro (bėrdz′bur.ō). Borough in SE Pennsylvania, in Berks County: manufactures steel castings. It was founded in 1740. Pop. 3,158 (1950).

Birds' Christmas Carol, The. Christmas story for children by Kate Douglas Wiggin, published in 1887.

Birdseye (bėrdz′ī), **Clarence.** b. at Brooklyn, N.Y., Dec. 9, 1886—. American executive and inventor, who developed (1923 *et seq.*) a method of quickly freezing (and thereby preserving) perishable foods. He engaged also in research in processing foodstuffs by means of extremely rapid water removal; he was granted over 250 patents by the U.S. and foreign countries in the fields of food preservation and incandescent lighting. The trademark "Birds Eye" on one company's frozen food products is derived from his name.

Birds in London. Prose work (1898) by W. H. Hudson. Although Hudson is, and unquestionably will continue to be, best known as the author of the novel *Green Mansions*, he had a considerable knowledge of ornithology, and his writings on the subject still maintain a reputation among people interested in birds (Hudson's own great interest in the subject is clearly reflected even in his fiction; it is more than coincidence that the heroine of *Green Mansions* should be capable of what is virtually metamorphosis between woman and bird).

Birds of America. Study of birds by John James Audubon, containing colored illustrations, engraved from Audubon's paintings, of approximately 500 species, published in England in serial form, the first installment appearing in 1827. The text gives an account of bird behavior, the observations being based upon investigations conducted by Audubon while touring the North American continent.

Birds of Killingworth (kil'ing.wėrth), **The.** Narrative poem in *Tales of a Wayside Inn* (1886), by Henry Wadsworth Longfellow.

Birdwood (bėrd'wůd), Sir **William Riddell.** [Title, Baron **Birdwood of Anzac and of Totnes.**] b. in India, Sept. 13, 1865; d. May 16, 1951. British military officer. A lieutenant colonel, he was military secretary (1902, 1905) in South Africa to Horatio Herbert Kitchener. Later he was a general officer commanding the Australian and New Zealand army corps (1914–18), and the Australian Imperial Force (1915–20); with the latter group he took part in actions at Gallipoli and the Western front during World War I. He was commander in chief of the Northern army (1920–24) and of the entire army (1925–30) in India with the rank (1925 *et seq.*) of field marshal.

Birecik (bē.re.jēk'). [Also: **Bir, Birejik, Birijik**; ancient name, **Birtha** or **Bithra.**] Town in S Turkey, in the *il* (province or vilayet) of Urfa, situated on the Euphrates River near the border of Syria, ab. 150 mi. E of Adana. It is at the junction of three important trade routes. Pop. ab. 9,000.

Biren (bē'rẹn), **Ernst Johann.** See **Biron, Ernst Johann.**

Bireno (bē.rā'nō). Husband of the deserted Olimpia, in Lodovico Ariosto's *Orlando Furioso.*

Bir-es-Saba (bir'es.sä'bạ) or **Bir-es-Seba** (-se'bạ). Arabic name of **Beersheba.**

Birge (bėrj), **Edward Asahel.** b. at Troy, N.Y., Sept. 7, 1851; d. at Madison, Wis., June 9, 1950. American zoölogist, limnologist, and president (1918–25) of the University of Wisconsin, later president emeritus; uncle of Raymond Thayer Birge. A graduate of Williams College (1873) and Harvard (1878), he was professor (1879–1911) of zoölogy at the University of Wisconsin. Director (1897–1919) of the Wisconsin Geological and Natural History Survey, he was also president (1893–1909) of the Madison Free Library.

Birge, Henry Warner. b. at Hartford, Conn., Aug. 25, 1825; d. at New York, June 1, 1888. American army officer, in the Union army in the Civil War. Appointed (1862) colonel of the 13th Connecticut infantry, he took part in the campaigns of Port Hudson (1863) and Red River (1864). At the war's end he was assigned to command the Savannah district.

Birge, Raymond Thayer. b. at Brooklyn, N.Y., March 13, 1887—. American physicist; nephew of Edward Asahel Birge (1851–1950). In 1933 he was named head of the physics department at the University of California.

Birgida (bir.gē'dä), **Birgit** (bir'gēt), or **Birgitta** (bir-gēt'tä). See **Bridget** (of *Sweden*), Saint.

Birh (bir). See **Bir.**

Birifo (bē.rē'fō). [Also: **Berfon, Birifor** (-fōr).] Sudanic-speaking people of W Africa, inhabiting the E part of the Ivory Coast, near the NW border of the Gold Coast. Their population is estimated at ab. 40,000 (by H. Labouret, *Les Tribus du Rameau Lobi*, 1931). Linguistically, they resemble the Lobi to the W. They have exogamous matrilineal clans, and chiefs were lacking before the establishment of French rule. They practice hoe agriculture, and their principal food is millet. They are non-Mohammedans.

Birijik (bē.rē.jēk'). See **Birecik.**

Birk (birk), **Sixt.** [Latinized, **Xystus Betulius.**] b. at Augsburg, Germany; d. there, 1554. German dramatist and schoolteacher. His plays, in the spirit of the time of the Reformation, were on Biblical themes and either written in Latin or later turned into Latin. The most famous was *Susanna* (1532; Latin, 1537), which served Rebhun as a model for his drama of the same name.

Birkbeck (bėrk'bek), **George.** b. at Settle, Yorkshire, England, Jan. 10, 1776; d. at London, Dec. 1, 1841. English physician and educational reformer. With others, he founded the Glasgow Mechanics' Institute in 1823, a similar institution at London (later called the Birkbeck Institute) in 1824, and University College, London, in 1827.

Birkbeck, Morris. b. at Settle, Yorkshire, England, Jan. 23, 1764; drowned in Fox River, near Harmony, Ind., June 4, 1825. American pioneer and author of travel books which influenced western colonizing. He settled (1817) in Edwards County, Ill., founded (1818) Wanborough, Ill. (nonexistent today), and was appointed (1824) Illinois secretary of state. His works include *Notes on a Journey through France* (1814), *Notes on a Journey in America from the Coast of Virginia to the Territory of Illinois* (1817), and *Letters from Illinois* (1818), all widely read in their day.

Birkeland (bir'kẹ.län), **Olaf Kristian.** b. at Oslo, Dec. 13, 1867; d. at Tokyo, June 18, 1917. Norwegian physicist. He served (1918 *et seq.*) as professor at the University of Oslo, and collaborated with Samuel Eyde in developing the Birkeland-Eyde process of nitrogen fixation. Also noted for his investigations in the field of terrestrial magnetism, he played a leading role in setting up magnetic observatories in arctic regions.

Birkenfeld (bir'kẹn.felt). Former principality and district of Oldenburg, Germany, situated E of Trier: an enclave in Rhenish Prussia. It became part of Prussia in 1937.

Birkenfeld. Town in W Germany, in the *Land* (state) of Rhineland-Palatinate, French Zone, formerly the capital of Birkenfeld district, Oldenburg, ab. 26 mi. E of Trier: agricultural trade and lumber mills. It is the site of the castle of the grand dukes of Oldenburg. Until 1733 it was the seat of the palatinate of Zweibrücken-Birkenfeld; ceded to Oldenburg (exclave) in 1816. Pop. 3,802 (1946).

Birkenhead (bėr'kẹn.hed), 1st Earl of. [Title of **Frederick Edwin Smith.**] b. 1872; d. 1930. English statesman and lord chancellor. As a Conservative member of Parliament (1906–18), he opposed David Lloyd George's budget plan (1909), the Parliament Bill of 1911, and bills (1914) for Irish Home Rule and the disestablishment of the Welsh Church. He served as attorney-general (1915), lord chancellor (1919–22), and secretary of state for India (1924–28). He was noted for many legal reform measures.

Birkenhead, 2nd Earl of. [Title of **Frederick Winston Furneaux Smith.**] b. Dec. 7, 1907—. English author; son of Frederick Edwin Smith, 1st Earl of Birkenhead. He was appointed (1938) parliamentary private secretary to foreign minister Viscount Halifax. Author of biographies of his father, *The First Phase* (1933) and *The Last Phase* (1935), and of a study of Strafford.

Birkenhead. County borough, seaport, and manufacturing and shipbuilding city in W England, in Cheshire, situated on the S bank of the estuary of the river Mersey, opposite Liverpool, ab. 194 mi. NW of London by rail. Its principal industries are shipbuilding and the manufacture of machinery; it has large docks. As a seaport it engages principally in the import of iron ore and pig iron; chief exports are iron and steel products. Birkenhead is in many ways a suburb of Liverpool, with which it is connected by tunnel under the river, and by ferries. 142,392 (1951).

Birkenhead. English troop steamer which was wrecked off the Cape of Good Hope on Feb. 26, 1852. The troops formed at the word of command and went down at their posts, having put the women and children in the boats. More than 400 men were drowned.

Birkenhead, Sir **John.** [Also, **Berkenhead.**] b. near Northwich, Cheshire, England, March 24, 1616; d. at London, Dec. 4, 1679. English satirist and journalist. He was the editor of the *Mercurius Aulicus* during the English Civil War.

ket el Kurun (bir'ket el kö.rön'). [Also: **Birket run, Lake Karun.**] Brackish lake in NE Africa, in yum province, Egypt, fed by the Nile River: thought be the modern remainder of Lake Moeris, a large gation basin of ancient Egypt described by Herodotus. igth, ab. 34 mi.; greatest breadth, ab. 6½ mi.

ket el Mariut (or **Maryut**) (mär.yöt'). Modern name **Mareotis, Lake.**

ket Israil (ēs.rä'il). See under **Bethesda,** Jerusalem.

ket-Smith (bir'ket.smēt'), **Kaj.** b. at Copenhagen, . 20, 1893—. Danish ethnologist. He was educated at University of Copenhagen, where he was appointed 45) reader in ethnology. He carried out (1918) ethno-ical studies in Greenland, investigated Eskimo culture ethnologist with a polar expedition (1921–23), and also died (1933) Eskimo life in Alaska. He became (1940) ef keeper of the ethnological department at the tional Museum, Copenhagen.

khoff (bėrk'hôf), **George David.** b. at Overisel, Mich., rch 21, 1884; d. at Cambridge, Mass., Nov. 12, 1944. erican mathematician and dean of the faculty of s and sciences at Harvard University. He published nost 200 papers on various aspects of mathematics and ence, including dynamics, differential equations, thetics, and the theory of relativity. He graduated 05) from Harvard University, received (1907) the D. degree from the University of Chicago, and taught the University of Wisconsin (1907–09), Princeton 09–12), and Harvard (1912 *et seq.*). He was the ipient of numerous awards and honorary degrees. His ks include *Relativity and Modern Physics* (with R. E. nger, 1923), *The Origin, Nature, and Influence of ativity* (1925), and *Aesthetic Measure* (1933).

a (bēr'lạ), **Ghanshyamdas.** b. in Jaipur state, India, 4—. Indian industrial magnate and business leader, naging director of Birla Brothers, Limited, an All-lia group of industries. He served as a member (1921) he Indian fiscal commission, sat on the royal committee labor (1930), and was a member (1927–30) of the lian legislative assembly. One of the drafters of the mbay Plan of economic development for India, he is chairman of the All-India Harijan Sevak Sangh, a iety formed to better the conditions of India's un-chables. He has been a benefactor of many public itutions. Author of *The Present Depression and netary Reform* (1931) and *Indian Prosperity: A Plea Planning* (1934).

ningham (bėr'ming.ham). [Called the **"Pittsburgh the South."**] City in C Alabama, county seat of ferson County, in Jones Valley: largest city in the state, nded in 1871. It is the chief iron and steel manu-turing city in the South. There are large supplies of l, limestone, and iron in the neighborhood. Birming-n is also an important railroad center, and has large ton mills, metallurgical industries (stoves, machinery, e, castings), and chemical and furniture factories. It he seat of Birmingham-Southern, Miles, and Howard eges. On Red Mountain, a height on the outskirts the city, stands a 53-ft. statue in pig iron of Vulcan, de for the St. Louis Exposition (1904). 326,037 (1950).

ningham (bėr'ming.ạm). [Also: **Brummagem** (see ow); Middle English, **Bermingham;** Anglo-Saxon, bably, **Beormingaham.**] Manufacturing city and nty borough in C England, in Warwickshire, situated the river Tame and its tributaries, the rivers Cole and , ab. 111 mi. NW of London by rail. It is the second-king city in the United Kingdom in the order of ulation, and is one of the very few large urban centers he world actually on or near a water divide. Birming-n is not on a navigable stream, but has well-developed al communications. Located in what is probably the atest metalworking area in the world, the Black intry of England, it has some 1,500 industries. It is chief center in the country for the nonferrous metals ustry, making articles of copper, brass, bronze, zinc, l, silver, aluminum, and other metals, and for the ber industry. From the large manufacture of cheap tal articles and of coins, one of the old variants of the 's name, Brummagem, came to be used to mean nething showy but cheap, or something counterfeit. mingham began industrially as a saddlery center. It had a long history in the iron industry, beginning before the 16th century, but its production has essentially shifted from heavy iron and steel manufactures to the lighter metal trades. There are automobile factories specializing in commercial vehicles. Other manufactures include electrical equipment, radios, machine tools, weighing and measuring devices, chemicals, rayon, and clothing. Birmingham suffered heavily from aerial bombardment during World War II, but many of the buildings which were destroyed are now being rebuilt or replaced. The city operates the largest municipal bus service in the country. It has large libraries, including the Shakespeare Memorial Library, which contains 33,000 volumes by and relating to Shakespeare in 61 languages, and is the seat of a university. Birmingham is believed to have been built on the site of an ancient Roman station. In Norman times it was a village in a clearing of the Forest of Arden. It is mentioned in the Domesday Book. In 1643 it was taken by Prince Rupert. It was the scene of riots against Joseph Priestley in 1791, and of Chartist riots in 1839. Pop. 1,112,340 (1951).

Birmingham (bėr'ming.ham). City in S Lower Michigan, in Oakland County: residential suburb of Detroit and Pontiac. 15,467 (1950).

Birmingham Festival (bėr'ming.ạm). Musical festival held triennially at Birmingham, England; established in 1768, it remained active until 1912. George Frederick Handel's music originally formed the main part of the programs. The proceeds of the festivals were given to the funds of the General Hospital.

Birmingham University. University at Birmingham, England, incorporated by royal charter on March 24, 1900. An outgrowth of Mason University College, Birmingham (founded in 1875), it includes faculties of science, arts, medicine, and commerce, and grants degrees to both men and women. Its library contains ab. 313,000 volumes.

Birnam Hill (bėr'nạm). Hill in C Scotland, in Perthshire, ab. 1 mi. SE of Dunkeld. It was formerly part of a royal forest which is referred to in Shakespeare's *Macbeth* as Birnam Wood. The ruins of a fort, known as Duncan's Camp, are here. Elevation, 1,324 ft.

Birnam Wood. See under **Birnam Hill.**

Birnbaumer Wald (birn'bou.mėr vält). In European history, the name applied to a plateau in the NW part of what is now Yugoslavia, NE of Trieste, near the river Frigidus, the scene of the victory of Theodosius in 394. It contains the Roman station Ad Pirum, on the main road across the Alps into Italy.

Birney (bėr'ni), **David Bell.** b. at Huntsville, Ala., May 29, 1825; d. at Philadelphia, Oct. 18, 1864. American brigadier general, with the Union army in the Civil War; son of James Gillespie Birney. He served (1862–64) with distinction in the Army of the Potomac, especially at Chancellorsville and at Gettysburg.

Birney, James. b. at Danville, Ky., June 7, 1817; d. May 8, 1888. American lawyer and diplomat; son of James Gillespie Birney. Elected (1859) to the Michigan state senate, he later (1876) acted as Michigan's commissioner to the Philadelphia Centennial Exposition, and served (1876–82) as minister to The Hague. He was the founder (1871) of the Bay City (Mich.) *Chronicle.*

Birney, James Gillespie. b. at Danville, Ky., Feb. 4, 1792; d. at Perth Amboy, N.J., Nov. 25, 1857. American antislavery leader and politician, candidate (1840 and 1844) of the Liberty Party for president; father of David, James, and William Birney. In 1837 he was elected executive secretary of the American Anti-Slavery Society; in this post he advocated the abolition of slavery by political action, as opposed to William Lloyd Garrison's policy of seeking abolition by means not involving direct political action.

Birney, William. b. in Madison County, Ala., May 28, 1819; d. Aug. 14, 1907. American lawyer, soldier, and religious writer; son of James Gillespie Birney. He was a student barricade-commander during the February, 1848, revolt at Paris. During the Civil War, he superintended Negro enlistments and aided (1864) in the recovery of Florida from the Confederates; he became a major general in 1865. He was the author of *James G. Birney and His Times* (1890), *Functions of the Church and State Distinguished: A Plea for Civil and Religious Liberty* (1897), and *Creeds not for Secularists* (1906).

Birni (bēr′nē). [Also, **Old Birni.**] Town in W Africa, the former capital of Borgou, Dahomey, French West Africa. It is situated in the N part of the territory, near the border of Togo.

Birnirk (bēr.nērk′). Archaeological culture associated with the Eskimo populations of NE Siberia and NW Alaska, and dated c600–1000 A.D. The remains suggest a relationship with the Thule culture known archaeologically in the E Eskimo area.

Biró (bē′rō), **Lajos.** b. at Vienna, 1880—. Hungarian novelist, publicist, and dramatist. He earned his worldwide reputation as a scriptwriter at Hollywood, where he settled. His published writings attack the conservative groups of Hungarian society. His best-known novels are *A diadalmas asszony* (The Victorious Woman, 1924) and *Hotel Imperial.* His plays include *Sárga liliom* (Yellow Lily) and *A czárnő* (The Czarina, 1912).

Birobidzhan (bir″o̩.bi.jän′). [Also, **Jewish Autonomous Oblast.**] Autonomous *oblast* (region) in the SE part of the U.S.S.R., in the bend of the Amur river ab. 400 mi. N of Vladivostok. It was established in 1928 to provide a national home for the Jews of the U.S.S.R., and became an autonomous oblast in 1934. The Trans-Siberian railroad crosses the area, and there is a branch line south to the Amur. The NW part of Birobidzhan is a wild, hilly to mountainous, forested region, in which iron-ore mining, lumbering, and granite quarrying are carried on. The SE area is largely lowland, with large swamps, and some agricultural settlements, producing wheat, oats, soybeans, and vegetables. Capital and chief city, Birobidzhan; area, ab. 13,820 sq. mi.; pop. 108,419 (1939), 150,000 (est. 1948).

Biron (bī′ro̩n; French, bē.rôṅ). Lord attending on the king of Navarre, in Shakespeare's *Love's Labour's Lost.* He is gay and eloquent.

Biron (bī′ro̩n). Husband of Isabella in Thomas Southerne's play *The Fatal Marriage.* Supposedly killed in battle, he returns after seven years to find his wife married to another as the result of the machinations of his younger brother Carlos. He is killed in a fray instigated by Carlos.

Biron (bē.rôṅ), **Armand de Gontaut,** Baron (later Duc) **de.** b. c1524; killed at Épernay, France, July 26, 1592. French soldier, a marshal of France; father of Charles de Gontaut, Duc de Biron (1562–1602). He fought in the Catholic army in the battles of Dreux, St.-Denis, and Moncontour, became grand master of artillery in 1569, and negotiated the peace of St.-Germain. He became marshal of France in 1577, was one of the first to recognize Henry IV, contributed to the victories of Arques and Ivry, and was killed at the siege of Épernay.

Biron, Armand Louis de Gontaut. [Titles: **Duc de Lauzun**; later, **Duc de Biron.**] b. at Paris, April 15, 1747; guillotined there, Dec. 31, 1793. French general and politician. He led a successful expedition against the British colonies of Senegal and Gambia, in Africa, in 1779. Having joined Lafayette in America in 1780, he commanded an unsuccessful expedition to capture New York from the British in 1781. He became general in chief of the French army of the Rhine in 1792, and of the army of the coast at La Rochelle in 1793. However, in spite of his capture of Saumur and his defeat of the counter-revolutionary forces of the Vendée, he was executed by order of the revolutionary tribunal of Antoine Quentin Fouquier-Tinville.

Biron, Charles de Gontaut, Duc **de.** b. 1562; d. at Paris, July 31, 1602. French admiral, marshal of France; son of Armand de Gontaut, Baron de Biron (c1524–92). He was the friend and a trusted officer of Henry IV, by whom he was made admiral of France in 1592, marshal in 1594, governor of Burgundy in 1595, and a duke and peer in 1598. He was executed for plotting with Savoy and Spain to dismember France.

Biron (bē′rôn), **Ernst Johann.** [Also: **Biren**; probable original name, **Ernst Johann Bühren**; title, Duke of **Courland.**] b. Dec. 1, 1690; d. Dec. 28, 1772. Russian statesman; a favorite of Anna Ivanovna. The son of noble parents in Courland (according to some authorities, however, the son of a groom or shoemaker), he was educated at the University of Königsberg, and in 1724 became permanently associated with the court of the widowed duchess of Courland, Anna Ivanovna, niece of Peter the Great. He accompanied her to Russia wher ascended the throne, in defiance of the pact of the empress with the Russian nobles who gave her empire, which included an express stipulation exclu him from Russia; he was created by Anna heredi duke of Courland. As her chief favorite, hated by al his cruelty and arrogance, he ruled Russia during entire reign (1730–40) of Anna Ivanovna, and his ep regarded by some as the worst in the history of Russian empire, is known as the "Bironovshtchi Having made the infant Ivan Antonovich (listed an the czars as Ivan VI) her heir, the empress appoi Biron regent of Russia during the emperor's mino but he had ruled only a few weeks when he and his fa were exiled (1741) to Siberia. The empress Eliza allowed (1742) him to live at Yaroslavl, on the V Peter III summoned him to St. Petersburg, restorin orders and property; in 1762 Catharine II restore him the duchy of Courland, and he reigned at Jel until 1769, when he abdicated in favor of his son P

Birr (bėr). [Also: **Parsonstown**; Irish, **Biorra.**] Ma town in Leinster province, Irish Republic, in Co Offaly, situated on the river Little Brosna, ab. 21 mi. of Tullamore. Birr Castle contains a famous telesc 3,296 (1951).

Birrell (bir′e̩l), **Augustine.** b. at Wavertree, near L pool, England, Jan. 19, 1850; d. Nov. 20, 1933. En essayist, lecturer, and statesman. He studied at C bridge before being admitted to the bar in 1875, an in Parliament as Liberal member for Fifeshire West (1 1900) and for Bristol North (1906–18), also servin professor of law at University College, London, in period 1896–99. In 1903 he was a bencher of the I Temple; he was president of the board of education, a seat in the cabinet, from December, 1905, to 1907, he was appointed chief secretary for Ireland, a pos held until after the Easter Rebellion of 1916.

Birs Nimrud (birs nim.röd′). See under **Bab** (Mesopotamia) and under **Borsippa.**

Birstall (bėr′stôl). Former urban district in N ce England, in the West Riding of Yorkshire, ab. 7 mi of Leeds, ab. 215 mi. N of London by rail. The tov now in Batley municipal borough. 7,204 (1931).

Birth. Novel (1918) by Zona Gale. Dramatized by author, it was produced (1924) under the title *Mr.*

Birtha (bėr′tha̩). An ancient name of **Birecik.**

Birth of Merlin (mėr′lin), **The,** or **The Child Has a Father.** Tragicomedy published in 1662, then tributed to Shakespeare and William Rowley. It is thought to be a refashioning by Rowley of an old The present title is Rowley's; the original auth unknown.

Birú (bē.rö′). fl. early 16th century. Indian chief ruled a small region in the extreme NW corner of S America, adjacent to the isthmus of Darien. The Sp called this region the province of Birú, and extende appellation to a rich region farther south, of which had vague reports; it is probably the origin of the r Peru. The territory proper of Birú was traverse Pascual de Andagoya in 1522.

Biruni (bē.rö′nē), **al-.** [Also, **al-Bairuni.**] b Khwarizm (now Khiva, in Iran), 973; d. at Gh (now Ghazni, in Afghanistan), 1048. Moslem phi pher, mathematician, astronomer, geographer, anc cyclopedist. He was by birth a Persian and a memb the Shiite sect (although his religious belief was temp by a considerable agnosticism), and is now consider have been one of the very greatest scientists not on Islam, but of all time. His critical spirit, fair-minded love of truth (he insisted that the sentence "All omniscient" did not justify ignorance), and intelle courage were almost without parallel in medieval t His main works were (1) the "Chronology of an nations" or "Vestiges of the past," written in 1000 dealing chiefly with the calendars and eras of va peoples, (2) an account of India, which was comp c1030 at Ghazna (Ghazni), in Afghanistan, (3 astronomical encyclopedia, dedicated in 1030 to the of Ghazna, (4) a summary of mathematics, astron and astrology. His description of India was based a deep study of the country and its people. Gr interested in the Hindu philosophy (and particularly i agavad-Gita), he translated several works from nskrit into Arabic. He gave a clear account (in fact, e best account of the Middle Ages) of Hindu numerals, d dealt with such problems as the trisection of the angle, ich cannot be solved by the ruler and compass alone om him, such problems have since often been called e "Albirunic problems"). He discussed the question whether or not the earth revolves around its axis, but ched no definite conclusion, and made numerous ntributions to contemporary understanding of the tural sciences.

žiška (bir.zhēsh'kä), **Mykolas.** b. at Viekšniai, thuania, Aug. 24, 1882—. Lithuanian scholar and blic figure, one of the signers of the Lithuanian declaran of independence on Feb. 16, 1918, and minister of ucation in the first independent Lithuanian governnt. He was a cofounder of the Lithuanian academy of ences and is considered to have laid the foundations much contemporary work in early Lithuanian literare. He has been a resident of the U.S. since 1949.

žiška, Vaclovas. b. at Viekšniai, Lithuania, Dec. 2, 84—. Lithuanian bibliographer, considered to be the remost in the history of Lithuanian scholarship; other of Mykolas Biržiška. He was editor-in-chief of a tional Lithuanian encyclopedia (1932–44), and the thor of many studies of Lithuanian cultural history. was the editor also of *Knygos* (Books, 1922–24), *bliografijos žinios* (Bibliographical News, 1928–44), and *ūsu senove* (Our Heritage, 1937–40). He has been a sident of the U.S. since 1949.

a (bē'sä). [Also: **Abisa, Babisa, Wabisa, Wisa.**] ntu-speaking people of SE Africa, inhabiting an area of Lake Bangweulu, in E Northern Rhodesia. Culrally they resemble the Bemba, their northern neighrs. It was at Chitambo, in the N part of their territory, at the explorer David Livingstone died (1873).

ago (bi.sä'gō). [Also: **Bidyogo, Bijago, Bissago.**] danic-speaking people of W Africa, inhabiting the ssagos islands, off Bissau in Portuguese Guinea.

aya (bē.sä'yä) or **Bisayans** (-yanz). See **Visaya** or **sayans.**

bee (biz'bē). City in SE Arizona, in Cochise County, . 84 mi. SE of Tucson. Center of one of the largest pper-mining areas in the U.S., its mines and copper elters are principally owned by the Phelps Dodge rporation. The area was prospected for silver as early 1875, but copper is today its most important product. ilt on the sides of two steep canyons, Bisbee is one of e most precipitously located cities in the country. 301 (1950).

bee, William Henry. b. at Woonsocket, R.I., n. 28, 1840; d. at Brookline, Mass., June 11, 1942. merican soldier in the Civil and Spanish-American wars. ommissioned (1862) a second lieutenant in the Union my, he was brevetted a first lieutenant for bravery at urfreesboro; he fought in 13 battles during the Atlanta mpaign, and was brevetted a captain after the battle Jonesboro, Ga. He fought in the Battle of San Juan Hill 898) as a lieutenant colonel during the Spanish-Amern War, and served (1899 *et seq.*) in the Philippines. ppointed (October, 1901) a brigadier general, he was, his death, the oldest retired U.S. army officer.

cay (bis'kā), **Bay of.** [Latin, **Aquitanicus Sinus, ntaber Oceanus, Sinus Cantabricus;** sometimes lled the **Aquitanian Sea.**] Arm of the Atlantic W of ance and N of Spain. Its limits are the island of Ushant, ar Brest, France and Cape Ortegal, Spain. It is noted its storms. The chief tributaries are the Loire and aronne rivers.

cay Provinces. See **Basque Provinces.**

ceglie (bē.shä'lyä). City in SE Italy, in the *compartinto* (region) of Apulia, in the province of Bari, situated the Adriatic Sea between Bari and Trani, ab. 22 mi. W of Bari. It is a center for the production of table apes and has small agricultural industries and a fishing rt. The cathedral and the Church of Santa Margherita, ilt in the 11th and 12th centuries, are in the Apulian omanesque style; the castle dates from the Hohenaufen period. These and other buildings of interest to urists were undamaged in World War II. 33,552 (1936).

chheim (bē.shem; German, bish'hīm). Town in E ance, in the department of Bas-Rhin (formerly Lower Alsace), situated on the Marne-Rhine Canal, ab. 4 mi. N of Strasbourg. A suburb of Strasbourg, it has a number of industries. 10,740 (1946).

Bischof (bish'of), **Karl Gustav.** b. at Wörd, near Nuremberg, Bavaria, Jan. 18, 1792; d. at Bonn, Prussia, Nov. 30, 1870. German chemist and geologist. He was professor of chemistry at Bonn.

Bischof, Marie. Original name of **Brandt, Marianne.**

Bischoff (bish'of), **Joseph Eduard Konrad.** [Pseudonym, **Konrad von Bolanden.**] b. at Niedergaillbach, in the Rhine Palatinate, Germany, Aug. 9, 1828; d. 1910. German novelist. He was ordained a priest in the Roman Catholic Church in 1852, and in 1872 was appointed by Pope Pius IX acting privy chamberlain. His works include *Franz von Sickingen* (1859), *Barbarossa* (1862), *Die Aufgeklärten* (1864), *Angela* (1866), *Deutsche Kulturbilder* (1893–94), and *Die Säule der Wahrheit* (1907).

Bischoff, Theodor Ludwig Wilhelm. b. at Hanover, Germany, Oct. 28, 1807; d. at Munich, Germany, Dec. 5, 1882. German anatomist and physiologist. He was professor of physiology and anatomy at Heidelberg, and did important research in the field of embryology.

Bischofshofen (bish'ofs.hō.fen). Market village in C Austria, in Salzburg province, situated on the Salzach River, in the Pongau region, S of the city of Salzburg. The railroad lines reaching Salzburg from Graz, from Villach, and from Innsbruck are joined here. It is a tourist center. 7,685 (1946).

Bischofswerda (bish'ofs.ver.dä). Town in C Germany, in the *Land* (state) of Saxony, Russian Zone, formerly the free state of Saxony, E of Dresden. Before World War II, it had metallurgical, glass, and ceramics manufactures and a linen industry. 10,835 (1946).

Bischofszell (bish'ofs.tsel). Town in NE Switzerland, in the canton of Thurgau, at the junction of the Sitter and Thur rivers S of Konstanz. An industrial town, it is known mainly for weaving and embroideries. 3,000 (1941).

Bischwiller or **Bischwiler** (bēsh.vē.ler). [German, **Bischweiler** (bish'vī.lėr).] Town in E France, in the department of Bas-Rhin (formerly Lower Alsace), situated near the Rhine River, SE of Haguenau. It has numerous woolen, jute, and other manufactures. The town was severely damaged in World War II. 7,581 (1946).

Biscop Baducing (bis'kôp bä'dö.ching). See **Benedict Biscop,** Saint.

Biserta (bē.zer'tä). See also **Bizerte.**

Biserta. Capital of King Agramante, in Lodovico Ariosto's *Orlando Furioso.* It was besieged and taken by Orlando, Astolfo, and Brandimarte.

Bisharin (bē.shä.rēn'). Cushitic-speaking Beja peoples of NE Africa, inhabiting NE Anglo-Egyptian Sudan in the area NE of Khartoum. Their population is estimated at ab. 15,000 (by G. E. R. Sandars, *The Bisharin, Sudan Notes,* vol. 16, 1933). They are predominantly Caucasoid in physical type.

Bishop (bish'op). Town in E California, in Inyo County, near the Owens River, ab. 85 mi. NE of Fresno. It is a trade center for a cattle-raising region and a starting point for trips into the Sierras. Tungsten is mined nearby. 2,891 (1950).

Bishop. Town in S Texas, in Nueces County ab. 20 mi. SW of Corpus Christi, in an oil and cotton producing region. In the decade between the last two U.S. censuses, its population more than doubled. 1,329 (1940); 2,731 (1950).

Bishop, Ann. [Called **"Madame Anna Bishop";** maiden name, **Rivière.**] b. at London, Jan. 9, 1810; d. at New York, March 18, 1884. English soprano singer in oratorio and opera. She married Sir Henry Rowley Bishop in 1831, and in 1839 eloped with the harpist Robert N. C. Bochsa. She appeared first on the concert stage in 1837, and for the last time in 1883.

Bishop, Sir **Henry Rowley.** b. at London, Nov. 18, 1786; d. there, April 30, 1855. English musician, composer of operas, songs, cantatas, and incidental music. His numerous works include *The Miller and His Men* (1813), *The Slave* (1816), *Maid Marian* (1823), *Clari* (containing Payne's *Home, Sweet Home,* 1822), and his setting of Shakespeare's *Lo! Here the Gentle Lark.* He was one of the founders of the London Philharmonic Society.

Bishop, Isabella Lucy. [Maiden name, **Bird.**] b. at Boroughbridge Hall, Yorkshire, England, Oct. 15, 1831;

d. at Edinburgh, Oct. 7, 1904. English traveler, travel writer, and founder of hospitals. She traveled in America and Canada (1854), Australia and New Zealand (1872), the Hawaiian Islands, and the Rocky Mountains (1873), Japan (1878), various parts of India and Armenia (1889–90), and in Japan, Korea, and China (1894–97). In China and India she founded five hospitals and an orphanage in memory of her parents, her sister, and her husband. Elected (1892) a fellow of the Royal Geographical Society, she was the first woman to be so honored. Author of *The Englishwoman in America* (1856), *Notes on Old Edinburgh* (1869), *The Hawaiian Archipelago* (1875), *A Lady's Life in the Rocky Mountains* (1879), *Unbeaten Tracks in Japan* (1880), *Journeys in Persia and Kurdistan* (1891), *Among the Tibetans* (1894), *Korea and Her Neighbors* (1898), and *The Yangtze Valley and Beyond* (1899).

Bishop, John. b. 1665; d. at Winchester, England, Dec. 19, 1737. English organist. He served on the staff of Winchester College (1695–1729) and Winchester Cathedral (1729 *et seq.*).

Bishop, John Peale. b. at Charles Town, W. Va., May 21, 1892; d. at Hyannis, Mass., April 4, 1944. American writer. A graduate (1918) of Princeton, where he was a friend of Edmund Wilson and F. Scott Fitzgerald, he served in Europe during World War I as a first lieutenant. After residence (1922–33) in France, he returned to the U.S., where he was appointed (1942) a fellow of the Library of Congress. Author of the poetry collections *Green Fruit* (1917), *Now With His Love* (1933), *Minute Particulars* (1936), and *Selected Poems* (1941), he wrote fiction including *Many Thousands Gone* (1931) and *Act of Darkness* (1935); *The Collected Essays of John Peale Bishop* and *The Collected Poems of John Peale Bishop* were published in 1948.

Bishop, Joseph Bucklin. b. at Seekonk, Mass. (now East Providence, R.I.), Sept. 5, 1847; d. Dec. 13, 1928. American journalist, author, and government representative. After serving on the editorial staff (1870–83) of the New York *Tribune*, he was a writer (1883–1900) for the New York *Evening Post*, and chief (1900–05) of the editorial staff of the New York *Globe*. He was later (1905–14) secretary of the Isthmian Canal Commission. Author of *Cheap Money Experiments* (1892), *The Panama Gateway* (1913), *A Chronicle of One Hundred and Fifty Years* (1918), *Theodore Roosevelt and His Time* (2 vols., 1920), *Life of A. Barton Hepburn* (1923), and *Notes and Anecdotes of Many Years* (1925).

Bishop, Louis Faugères. b. at New Brunswick, N.J., March 14, 1864; d. Oct. 6, 1941. American physician, a specialist in diseases of the heart. He was a resident physician (1889–92) at St. Luke's Hospital, New York, and a professor at Fordham University. His publications in his special field include *Heart Troubles, Their Prevention and Relief* (1920), *Arteriosclerosis* (1914), *Heart Disease, Blood Pressure and the Nauheim Treatment* (1914), and *History of Cardiology.*

Bishop, Seth Scott. b. at Fond du Lac, Wis., Feb. 7, 1852; d. Sept. 6, 1923. American laryngologist. A professor (c1887) at Loyola University and at the Chicago Post-Graduate medical schools, he was also a surgeon at the Jefferson Park Hospital and an editor (1912–23) of the New York *Medical Times.* Author of *Diseases of the Ear, Nose, and Throat and their Accessory Cavities; a Condensed Textbook* (1897) and *The Ear and Its Diseases, a Textbook for Students and Physicians* (1906).

Bishop, William Avery. b. at Owen Sound, Ontario, Canada, Feb. 8, 1894—. Canadian air force officer. Trained at the Royal Military College at Kingston, he went (1914) to France with the Canadian Expeditionary Force in World War I, and transferred (1915) to the Royal Flying Corps. He was officially credited with the destruction of 72 enemy planes, for which he was awarded the Victoria Cross. He has since held the posts of group captain (1931) in the Royal Canadian Air Force, air vice-marshal (1936), air marshal (1938), and director (1940–44) of recruiting for the air service.

Bishop, William Darius. b. at Bloomfield, N.J., Sept. 14, 1827; d. Feb. 4, 1904. American railroad executive, president (1866–79) of the New York and New Haven Railroad. He was also president (1855–66, 1883–1903) of the Naugatuck Railroad.

Bishop, William Henry. b. at Hartford, Conn., Jar 1847; d. Sept. 26, 1928. American novelist. He graduated from Yale University in 1867, studied ar tecture, became proprietor and editor of the Milwau *Commercial Times,* and was instructor in modern l guages (1893–1902) at Yale. In 1903 he was appoir U.S. consul at Genoa, and he served later (1905–10) consul at Palermo. His novels include *Detmold* (1879), *House of a Merchant Prince* (1885), *The Golden Ju* (1887), *A Pound of Cure* (1894), *Writing to Rosina* (18 *Tons of Treasure* (1902), and *Anti-Babel* (1919).

Bishop-Auckland (bish'ọp.ôk'lạnd). Urban district market town in NE England, in Durham, situated or elevation near the confluence of the rivers Wear Gaunless, ab. 10 mi. SW of Durham, ab. 245 mi. N London by rail. It has long been famous for its excel coking coal, which is the best of all English coals for i smelting, but the coal field in which it is found is r exhaustion. Bishop-Auckland contains the palace of Bishop of Durham. 36,350 (1951).

Bishop Blougram's Apology (blog'rạmz). Dram monologue in verse by Robert Browning, publishe *Men and Women* (1855).

Bishops' Bible, The. Folio edition of the Bible, p lished in October, 1568. It was a revision of the G Bible of 1539, organized by Archbishop Matthew Pa and undertaken in 1563 by himself, 11 bishops, and deans and prebendaries. It was not reprinted after 1

Bishop's Corners. Former name of **Granville,** N.Y

Bishopscote (bish'ọps.kōt) or **Bishopscott** (bish'ọps.k Old variations of *Pejebscot,* an early name of the **droscoggin.**

Bishopsgate (bish'ọps.gāt). The principal entra through the N wall of old London. The only entra in the N wall of Roman times was near this point. N here Ermyn Street and the Vicinal Way entered the c Bishopsgate Street is the street which goes over the of the old gate, and is divided into "Bishopsgate witl and "Bishopsgate without." The gate was destroye the reign of George II. The foundations of the old Ro gate have been found.

Bishop's Hatfield (bish'ọps hat'fēld). See **Hatfield.**

Bishop's Stortford (stôrt'fọrd). Urban district market town in E central England, in Hertfordsh situated on the river Stort, ab. 14 mi. NE of Hertf ab. 30 mi. NE of London by rail. It was formerly center of a silk industry. 12,772 (1951).

Bishopville (bish'ọp.vil). Town in N South Carol county seat of Lee County. 3,076 (1950).

Bisitun (bē.sē.tön'). See **Behistun.**

Bisk (bēsk). [Also: **Biisk, Biysk.**] City in the U.S.S in the Altai territory of the Russian Soviet Federa Socialist Republic, on the Katun River. A flax-proces and linen-manufacturing city, it is also an import highway junction and the center of a wheat and su beet growing area. 80,190 (1939).

Biskra (bis'krạ). [Also, **Biskara** (bis'kạ.rạ).] Oasis in the department of Constantine, Algeria, in NW Afr on the Biskra River, ab. 150 mi. SW of the city of C stantine. Biskra is the main commercial center for surrounding area. It was taken by the French in 1 Pop. 36,422 (1948).

Bisley (biz'li). Village in S England, in NW Surrey, 30 mi. SW of London. It has been the location of ranges of the National Rifle Association since 1 Pop. 1,151 (1931).

Bismarck (biz'märk). City in S North Dakota, on E bank of the Missouri River: capital of North Dak and county seat of Burleigh County. It is a distribu point for spring wheat, and has grain elevators, f mills, creameries, and seed houses. Settled in 1872, named for Otto von Bismarck, the town became ca of the Dakota Territory in 1883. Pop. 18,640 (1950).

Bismarck. German battleship prominent in W War II. Early in the war the newly commissioned 45, ton ship, eight 15-inch guns and thick armor ma her the most powerful naval vessel afloat, broke into Atlantic Ocean accompanied by the *Prinz Eugen.* threat to British control of the Atlantic sea lanes serious. The German ships were brought to battle in Denmark Strait on the morning of May 24, 1941, the British battleships *Hood* and *Prince of Wales,* but smarck sank the *Hood* by means of a well-aimed volley to her magazine. The *Prince of Wales* also suffered hits. the other hand, the British *Prince of Wales* inflicted mage on the *Bismarck*, forcing the German ship to try the port of Brest. In this attempt she was intercepted the naval squadron, under Admiral James Fownes merville, which came steaming north from Gibraltar. the evening of May 26 airplanes from the British k *Royal* attacked and disabled the *Bismarck*. Continued stroyer attacks during the night, gunfire from the ttleships *Rodney* and *King George V*, and finally torpedo tacks by light cruisers on the morning of May 27 entually sank Hitler's "pride of the German Navy."

marck (biz'märk; German, bis'-) or **Bismarck-hönhausen** (-shen'hou.zen), Prince **Herbert Nikolaus n.** b. at Berlin, Dec. 28, 1849; d. at Friedrichsruh, rmany, Sept. 18, 1904. German statesman; son of ince Otto von Bismarck (1815–98). He was occupied iefly with diplomatic affairs and was secretary of state foreign affairs (1886–90).

marck or **Bismarck-Schönhausen,** Prince **Otto luard Leopold von.** [Sometimes called the **"Iron ancellor."**] b. at Schönhausen, Prussia, April 1, 15; d. at Friedrichsruh, Prussia, July 30, 1898. Prussn statesman, famous as the creator and first chancellor the German Empire. He studied at the Universities of ttingen and Berlin. In the Prussian United Diet in 47 and in the House of Representatives in the period 49–51, he became known as an outspoken opponent of eral and of German national measures, and a vigorous pporter of a reactionary Prussian monarchy. In 1851 was appointed Prussian ambassador to the Diet of e Germanic Confederation at Frankfort on the Main, iere he matured from a narrow *Junker* to a statesman European vision and caliber. In 1859 he was sent as nister to Russia and in 1862 as ambassador to France. became president of the Council of Ministers on pt. 22, 1862, and took over the foreign office as well on t. 8 of the same year. He continued the conflict with e House of Representatives over the reorganization of e army and successfully maintained the prerogatives the crown. To the budget committee, he declared that e great questions of the time are settled "not by speeches d majority votes . . . but by iron and blood." His reign policy, amoral but successful, was simple in its ns but dazzlingly versatile in execution. It led to torious war in 1864, in alliance with Austria, against nmark for the possession of Schleswig-Holstein; in 66, in alliance with Italy, against Austria for supremacy Germany; and in the period 1870–71, in alliance with e south German states, against France (called the anco-Prussian War).

Formation of the German Empire. After the war of 1866, ussian territory was rounded out by the annexation of anover, Hesse-Cassell, Frankfort, and Schleswig-olstein. The North German Confederation, formed in 67 under Prussian dominance and with Bismarck as ancellor, became the German Empire in 1871 with the try of the south German states and the annexation of sace-Lorraine. After this, Bismarck considered Ger-any one of the "saturated" states. Although he did give e colonial movement some support in the 1880's and cured colonies in Africa and the South Seas, his primary n was not to expand, but to consolidate and safeguard, creation. Until 1878 he worked in general harmony th the National Liberal Party and engaged in the *ulturkampf*, a protracted struggle with the "Ultra-ontanes" (organized politically in the Center Party) iich resulted from fear that the Roman Catholic ctrine of papal infallibility represented a threat of erference in German domestic and foreign affairs by e Catholic Church. After 1878 he gradually broke off e conflict, in part because the rise of the Socialist Party emed a greater threat to state and society, and in part cause he wanted the support of the powerful Center rty when the National Liberals were unwilling to cept tariff protection for industry and agriculture.

Later Years. In the 1880's he continued his policies of onomic and social reform, especially in the enactment the first comprehensive system of workmen's insurance ainst the disabilities of sickness, accident, and old age. isolate France and thus to protect Germany against a war of revenge for 1870–71, Bismarck built up a complicated system of alliances, at first informal, but after the Congress of Berlin of 1878 (over which he presided) formal and written in treaties. The German-Austrian alliance (1879–1918) against Russia was followed by the "Three Emperors' Alliance" (1881–87) of Germany, Austria, and Russia, the Triple Alliance (1882–1915) of Germany, Austria, and Italy, later joined by Rumania, and the German-Russian "reinsurance" treaty (1887–90). In consequence of differences with the young Emperor William II, especially over foreign and social policy, Bismarck gave up office in March, 1890. He had been raised to the rank of count in 1865, that of prince in 1890, and was made Duke of Lauenburg in 1890, a title which did little to console him for his loss of power. His 80th birthday (April 1, 1895) was made the occasion for extraordinary ovations in his honor, in which the emperor joined.

Bismarck or **Bismarck-Schönhausen,** Prince **Otto von.** b. at Schönhausen, Germany, Sept. 25, 1897—. German diplomat; eldest son of Herbert von Bismarck. He was a representative of the *Deutsch-Nationale Partei* (German National People's Party) in the Reichstag from 1924 to 1928. In 1927 he went to Sweden to serve as a secretary with the German embassy at Stockholm, and later served at London in the same capacity.

Bismarck Archipelago. [Former name, **New Britain Archipelago.**] Group of volcanic islands in the Pacific Ocean E of New Guinea, comprising New Britain (German, Neu-Pommern), New Ireland (German, Neu-Mecklenburg), Lavongai (formerly New Hanover), the Admiralty and Duke of York islands, and some smaller neighboring islands, formerly (1884–1918) a German possession. The present name, in honor of Otto von Bismarck, was substituted for the name New Britain Archipelago in 1885. The islands were included in the Territory of New Guinea mandate to Australia by the League of Nations in 1920. They were occupied by the Japanese in World War II and retaken by Allied forces in the period 1943–44. Area, 19,200 sq. mi.; pop. 140,759 (counted 1940; est. total, 155,759).

"Bismarck of Asia." See **Li Hung-chang.**

Bismarck Sea. Arm of the S Pacific Ocean lying between the island of New Guinea and the Bismarck Archipelago. An important victory of Allied air forces over Japanese naval forces occurred here in 1943.

Bispham (bis'fam), **David Scull.** b. at Philadelphia, Jan. 5, 1857; d. at New York, Oct. 2, 1921. American baritone. He studied (1886–89) in Italy under Francesco Lamperti, and made his debut at London in 1891. He was a member (1897 *et seq.*) of grand-opera companies at New York and London.

Bissago (bi.sä'gō). See **Bisago.**

Bissagos (bi.sä'gōs). [Portuguese, **Arquipélago** (or **Ilhas**) **dos Bijagos** (or **Bijagoz**).] Group of islands in the Atlantic Ocean, W of Portuguese Guinea, W Africa, belonging to Portugal.

Bissau (bi.sou'). [Also, **Bissão** (bē.soun').] Town in W Africa, the capital and chief port of Portuguese Guinea. It was made the capital in 1942, replacing Bolama. Pop. ab. 1,000.

Bissell (bis'el), **Clayton Lawrence.** b. at Kane, Pa., July 29, 1896—. American army officer. He was graduated (LL.B., 1917) at the Valparaiso Law School, entered (1917) the U.S. Signal Corps as an enlisted man, and rose to the rank (1943) of major general. He served in World War I and in the army of occupation, was assistant (1921–24) to General William Mitchell, was commander (1942–43) of the 10th Army Air Force, and from 1944 to 1945 was assistant chief of staff in charge of intelligence, U.S. Army. He served (1946–48) as military air attaché at the U.S. embassy at London. Author of *History of the U.S. Army Air Corps* (1923).

Bissell, Edwin Cone. b. at Schoharie, N.Y., March 2, 1832; d. April 10, 1894. American Congregational clergyman and Biblical scholar. After serving intermittently as a pastor in Massachusetts (1859–73) and in California (1864–69), he worked as a missionary (1873–78) in Austria. Author of *The Historic Origin of the Bible* (1873), *The Pentateuch, Its Origin and Structure* (1885), and *Biblical Antiquities* (1888); translator of *The Apocrypha of the Old Testament* (1880).

Bissell, George Henry. b. at Hanover, N.H., Nov. 8, 1821; d. Nov. 19, 1884. American oilman who helped organize (1854) the Pennsylvania Rock Oil Company, the first oil company in the U.S. He was a pioneer also in the technique of obtaining petroleum through drilled wells.

Bissell, Wilson Shannon. b. in Oneida County, N.Y., Dec. 31, 1847; d. Oct. 6, 1903. American lawyer and U.S. postmaster general (1893–95); a friend and legal associate of Grover Cleveland. He was chancellor (1902) of the University of Buffalo.

Bissen (bis'ẹn), **Hermann Wilhelm.** b. near Schleswig (now in Germany), Oct. 13, 1798; d. at Copenhagen, March 10, 1868. Danish sculptor; a student of Bertel Thorvaldson. He was director of the academy at Copenhagen after 1850. His chief works are at Copenhagen.

Bissing (bis'ing), Baron **Moritz Ferdinand von.** b. at Bellmannsdorf, Germany, Jan. 30, 1844; d. at Brussels, Belgium, April 18, 1917. German general, governor general of occupied Belgium (1914 *et seq.*) during World War I. Bissing worked ceaselessly, though unsuccessfully, to force the Flemish-speaking section of the population to collaborate with the German occupation authorities.

Bissolati-Bergamaschi (bēs.sō.lä'tē.ber.gä.mäs'kē), **Leonida.** b. at Cremona, Italy, Feb. 20, 1857; d. at Rome, March 6, 1920. Italian statesman and party leader. He became (1891) a republican-socialist, was among the founders (1892) of the Italian Socialist Party, and edited (1896 *et seq.*) *Avanti*, a socialist daily. He was elected (1897) to the chamber of deputies, where he led the revisionist group of the Socialist Party, a position which caused (1898) his arrest during the Milan riots. Opposition (1902–03) by revolutionary socialists forced him to abandon the editorship of *Avanti* until 1908; he then led the reformists and organized (1912) the Reformist Socialist Party. Strongly in favor of intervention on the side of the Allies in World War I, he enlisted (1915) in the Italian army and was badly wounded. He was appointed a minister without portfolio (June, 1916) and minister of military assistance and pensions (Nov. 1, 1918); his opposition to the annexationist policy (which advocated that certain parts of the Tyrol should be given to Italy) led to his resignation (Dec. 31, 1918) from the government.

Bissot (bē.sō), **François Marie.** See **Vincennes, Sieur de.**

Bistrița (bēs'trē.tsä). [Also: **Bistritsa;** German, **Bistritz** (bis'trits); Hungarian, **Besztercze.**] City in NW Rumania, in the region of Transylvania, situated on the Bistrița River, ab. 50 mi. NE of Cluj. Settled in the 12th century by colonists from Germany, the city was in the Middle Ages the main trading center between Danzig and the Levant. It has a stately 16th-century church. There are agricultural markets, mills, distilleries, and manufactures of wood, leather, shoes, and ceramics. 15,801 (1948).

Bisutun (bē.sü.tön'). See **Behistun.**

Bitche (bēch). [German, **Bitsch;** former name, **Kaltenhausen.**] Town in NE France, in the department of Moselle, on the N slope of the Vosges Mountains, E of Sarreguimines. It has a historic fortress situated on an isolated hill, which was besieged without success by the Prussians (1793) and by the Germans (1870). The town was severely damaged in World War II. 3,479 (1946).

Biterra Septimanorum (bi.ter'ạ sep"ti.mạ.nō'rum). A Latin name of **Béziers.**

Bithra (bith'rạ). An ancient name of **Birecik.**

Bit Humri (bēt höm'ri). Name of the country of Israel in the Assyrian inscription, named after Omri, the founder of the 4th dynasty in the kingdom of Israel. It was the Assyrian fashion to name countries after the founders of their reigning houses.

Bithynia (bi.thin'i.ạ). In ancient geography, a division of Asia Minor, lying between the Propontis (Sea of Marmara), Bosporus, and Euxine (Black Sea) on the N, Mysia on the W, Phrygia and Galatia on the S, and Paphlagonia on the E. Its inhabitants were of Thracian origin. Nicomedes I became (c278 B.C.) its first independent king; and Nicomedes III bequeathed (74 B.C.) the kingdom to Rome. It was governed by Pliny the Younger. The chief cities were Chalcedon, Heraclea, Prusa, Nicaea, and Nicomedia.

Bitlis (bēt.lēs'). *Il* (province or vilayet) in E Turkey. It is a dry, mountainous area where sheep raising and rug weaving are the principal occupations. Capital, Bi[tlis]; pop. 88,422 (1950).

Bitlis. City in SE Turkey, capital of the *il* (province[e] vilayet) of Bitlis, in a narrow valley in the Anato[lian] Taurus Mountains ab. 12 mi. SW of Lake Van. It [is a] trade center for products of the region, including w[ool,] gallnuts, fruit, and tobacco. Industries include manu[fac]ture of weapons and textiles, and dyeing, with some g[old] and silver work. Cotton is imported through Iran. T[here] are numerous mosques, and also convents of the [Ar]menian Church. Elevation, ab. 4,750 ft.; pop. 10,[...] (1945).

Bitola (bē'tô.lä). [Also: **Bitolj** (-tôly'); Bulgar[ian,] **Bitolya** (-tô.lyä); Greek, **Monasterion;** Italian, **Bit[...]** (-tō.lyä); Turkish, **Monastir.**] City in S Yugoslavia[,] the federative unit of Macedonia, in the former *bano[vina]* (province) of Vardarska and once the capital of [the] former Turkish vilayet of Monastir, situated immedia[tely] N of the Greek border and not far from the Alba[nian] border, SW of Skopje. It is a station on a local railr[oad] connecting with the main line running from Belgrad[e to] Salonika. An important commercial and strategic cen[ter,] it is claimed by the Bulgarians as the historic capita[l of] Bulgarian Macedonia. It was occupied by the Turks [for] several centuries, captured by the Serbians in 1912, [by] the Germans and Bulgarians in 1915 and again in 1[941,] and by the Allies under Maurice Paul Emmanuel Sa[rrail] in 1916. It was incorporated into Yugoslavia in 1919. [The] majority of the population is now Serbian, but there [are] still a large Albanian and smaller Bulgarian, Greek, [and] Turkish minorities. 31,131 (1948).

Biton and Cleobis (bī'tọn; klē'ọ.bis). In Greek leg[end,] the sons of Cydippe, priestess of Hera at Argos. Du[ring] a festival, the priestess had to ride to the temple i[n a] chariot, and, as the oxen were not at hand, Biton [and] Cleobis dragged the chariot forty-five stadia to [the] temple. There they fell asleep; in answer to a praye[r of] their mother to Hera to reward this act of filial piety [with] the greatest boon possible for mortals, they were gi[ven a] painless and swift death in their sleep. Herodotus ma[kes] Solon relate this story to Croesus.

Bitonto (bē.tōn'tō). [Ancient name, **Bituntum.**] [City] and commune in SE Italy, in the *compartimento* (regi[on]) of Apulia, in the province of Bari, situated ab. 11 mi [W] of Bari. It is the center of a fertile agricultural reg[ion,] particularly noted for the quality of its oil. The cit[y is] still more famous for its cathedral, built in the 12th [cen]tury, which represents one of the finest examples of [the] Apulian Romanesque style, with strong Byzantine [and] Saracenic influence. The history of this part of Italy is [one] of many battles; in 1734, the Spaniards defeated [the] Austrians here, thereby gaining the kingdom of Nap[les.] Buildings of interest to tourists were undamaged [in] World War II. Pop. of commune, 30,622 (1936); of c[ity,] 27,342 (1936).

Bitsch (bich). German name of **Bitche.**

Bitter (bit'ėr), **Karl Theodore Francis.** b. at Vien[na,] Dec. 6, 1867; d. in 1915. American sculptor. He [was] educated at the Academy of Art in Vienna, and cam[e to] New York in 1889. His work was chiefly monumental, [the] best examples being decorations for the expositions [at] Chicago (1893), Buffalo (1901), and St. Louis (19[04).] He was elected a member of the National Academy [of] Design in 1902.

Bitter Creek. Novel by James Boyd, published in 1[939.]

Bitterfeld (bit'ėr.felt). City in C Germany, in the *L[and]* (state) of Saxony-Anhalt, Russian Zone, formerly in [the] province of Saxony, Prussia, situated on the M[ulde] River, ab. 20 mi. N of Leipzig. It is the seat of the giga[ntic] Leuna Works of the I.G. Farbenindustrie, producing s[yn]thetic chemicals, mostly coal derivatives; it also [has] lignite mines and metallurgical and ceramics industr[ies.] The city was founded in 1153, conquered by Co[unt] Dietrich of Meissen in 1476, and belonged to Sax[ony] until it was incorporated into Prussia in 1815. The po[pu]lation is predominantly Protestant; the increase betw[een] 1939 and 1946 was 37.1 percent. 32,833 (1946).

Bitterroot Range (bit'ėr.röt, -růt). Range of mount[ains] between Idaho and Montana, extending from Clark F[ork] of the Columbia River, on the NW, to Monida, the cr[oss]ing of the Oregon Short Line Railroad.

terroot River. River in W Montana, flowing from the aho border N to join Clark Fork near Missoula, Mont. flows through a scenic valley, and supplies water for igation farming. Length, ab. 110 mi.

ter Sweet. Musical play (1929) by Noel Coward.

tinger (bit′in.jėr), **Charles.** b. at Washington, D.C., ne 27, 1879—. American historical, landscape, and ıral painter. He studied at the Art Students League of ɜw York, and at the École des Beaux-Arts, Paris. His ɒrk has been exhibited in the U.S. and France, and he s been awarded many prizes. In 1912 he was made an sociate, and in 1937 an academician, of the National ademy of Design. He served in the camouflage section the U.S. Navy in World Wars I and II. His work is in e collections of such museums as the Metropolitan useum of Art at New York, the City Art Museum at . Louis, and the Montgomery, Ala., Museum of Fine t. Some of his better-known paintings are *The Boudoir*, *brary of the Dauphin*, *The Boston Atheneum*, *Solar ectrum*, *Room in Arlington Where Lee Married*, *Entrance the Hall of Mirrors*, and *Ultra-Violet Mural* (Franklin stitute, Philadelphia).

tner (bit′nėr), **Julius.** b. at Vienna, April 9, 1874; d. ere, Jan. 10, 1939. Austrian composer; a student of sef Labor and Bruno Walter. His most important works clude the operas *Die Rote Gret* (1907), *Der Musikant* 910), *Der Bergsee* (1911), and *Das Veilchen* (1934). He o composed chamber music, songs, and orchestral orks.

untum (bi.tun′tum). Ancient name of **Bitonto.**

urica (bi.tū′ri.ka̧). Ancient name of **Berry.**

Yakin (bēt yä.kēn′). In ancient geography, a prin- pality in the extreme S part of Babylonia, on the sea- ast, named for its ruling family, from which Merodach- aladan, king (721 B.C. *et seq.*) of Babylonia, descended. e last king of this powerful family was subdued by surbanipal, king (c669–626 B.C.) of Assyria.

zer (bit′sėr). Schoolboy under Mr. M'Choakum, ought up on the Gradgrind system, in Charles Dickens's ry *Hard Times*.

zius (bēt′sē.ůs), **Albert.** See **Gotthelf, Jeremias.**

ar (bē.ʙär′), **Rodrigo** (or **Ruy**) **Díaz de.** Original me of **Cid, the.**

va (bē.wä). [Also, **Omi.**] Lake in W central Honshu, pan, ab. 6 mi. E of Kyoto. Surrounded by mountain nges, it is famous for its scenic beauty, and is known Japanese legends. It is the largest lake in Japan. evation, 139 ft.; area, 260 sq. mi.

by (biks′bi), **Horace Ezra.** b. at Geneseo, N.Y., May 1826; d. at Maplewood, Mo., Aug. 1, 1912. American er pilot, one of the most famous on the Mississippi ver; friend of Samuel Langhorne Clemens (Mark vain), whom he accepted (1858) as a partner. He was ot of the steamboat *Olivia* (1846 *et seq.*) and of the nboat *Benton* during the Civil War, and was later ptain of the *City of Baton Rouge*. He was also chief of e Union River Service during the Civil War. He was owner of the Anchor Line. The association between xby and Mark Twain is described in the latter's *e on the Mississippi*.

by, James Thompson. b. at Barre, Mass., July , 1843; d. Dec. 26, 1921. American Unitarian minister d theologian. He was pastor of First Parish, Water- wn, Mass. (1870–74), the Independent Congregational urch, Belfast, Me. (1874–78), and the Unitarian urch, Yonkers, N.Y. (1887–1903). Author of *Similar- es of Physical and Religious Knowledge* (1876), *Religion d Science as Allies* (1889), *The Crisis in Morals* (1891; vised in 1900 as *the Ethics of Evolution*), *The New World d the New Thought* (1902), *Biliotheca Sacra* (1916), and *blical World* (1920).

by, William Herbert. b. at Charlestown, Mass., c. 27, 1849; d. Sept. 29, 1928. American civil and litary engineer. He was graduated from the U.S. ilitary Academy in 1873, and became a brigadier neral in 1910. He was chief engineer of the Department the Lakes, Dakota, and Missouri (1907–08), presi- nt of the Mississippi River Commission (1908–10), and ief of engineers for the U.S. army (1910–13).

sk (bēsk). See **Bisk.**

erte (bē.zert′; Anglicized, bi.zėr′tē). [Also: **Benzert, serta, Bizerta** (bē.zer′tä); ancient names, **Hippo Zaritus, Hippo Zarytus.**] Seaport in N Africa, in W Tunisia E of Cape Blanc. It is one of the chief ports for Tunisia and is connected by rail with the city of Tunis and the other important centers of French North Africa. In World War II British and American forces took (1943) the city from Italy. It is the most important French naval base along the Mediterranean Sea, except for Toulon. Pop. 39,237, including 9,893 Europeans (1946).

Bizet (bē.zā′; French, bē.ze), **Georges.** [Original name, **Alexandre César Léopold Bizet.**] b. at Paris, Oct. 25, 1838; d. there, June 3, 1875. French composer, best known for his opera *Carmen* (1875). His other works include the operas *Les Pêcheurs de Perles* (1863) and *La Jolie Fille de Perth* (1867), *L'Arlésienne* (1872; originally composed as incidental music to a play by Alphonse Daudet, and subsequently arranged as two orchestral suites), and a symphony.

Bjarni Bergthórsson (byär′nē berg′tôr.so̧n). d. 1173. Icelandic mathematician and astronomer, believed by some to have written the earliest Icelandic treatise on the computus (*rím*). It dealt with such subjects as the length of the months, the date of Easter, and other matters of chronology. It is based in large part on Bede's *De temporum ratione*.

Bjeljina (bye′lyē.nä). See **Bijeljina.**

Bjelostock (bye′lo.stok). German name of **Białystok.**

Bjerknes (byerk′nȩs), **Jakob Aall Bonnevie.** b. at Stockholm, Nov. 2, 1897—. Norwegian meteorologist, naturalized a U.S. citizen; son of Vilhelm Bjerknes (1862–1951). Educated at the universities of Leipzig and Oslo (Ph.D., 1924), he became (1918) meteorologist at the Bergen observatory, directed (1920) the weather service for western Norway, was professor of meteorology (1931–40) at the Geophysical Institute at Bergen, and became (1940) professor of meteorology at the University of California. During World War II he served with the U.S. air force in Europe.

Bjerknes, Vilhelm. b. at Oslo, March 14, 1862; d. there, April 9, 1951. Norwegian physicist. Well known in the field of hydrodynamics, he was the founder of the so-called Bergen school of meteorology, which proposed the electric wave theory of cyclones; during his earlier career he advanced (c1895) a theory of electric resonance which extended the development of wireless telegraphy. He served as professor of mechanics and mathematical physics at the University of Stockholm (1895–1907) and at the University of Oslo (1907–12); he was professor of geophysics (1913–17) at the University of Leipzig and held the same post (1917–26) at the Bergen Geophysical Institute; he again (1926–32) served as a professor at the University of Oslo. Author of *Fields of Force* (1906) and *Dynamic Meteorology and Hydrography* (2 vols., 1910–11).

Bjerregaard (byer′ȩ.gôr), **Carl Henrik Andreas.** b. at Fredericia, Denmark, May 24, 1845; d. Jan. 28, 1922. American librarian and mystical philosopher. He was a staff member (1879–1922) of the Astor Library (now incorporated in the New York Public Library). Among his works are *Lectures on Mysticism and Talks on Kindred Subjects* (1896), *Lectures on Mysticism and Nature Worship, Second Series* (1897), *Sufi Interpretations of the Quatrains of Omar Khayyam and Fitzgerald* (1902), *The Inner Life and the Tao-Teh-King* (1912), and *The Great Mother: a Gospel of the Eternally Feminine* (1913).

Bjerrum (byer′ům), **Niels.** b. at Copenhagen, 1879—. Danish physical chemist. He has contributed particularly to theories of electrolytes in solution, having put forth the first 100 percent dissociation theory (1918) and suggested a possibly significant extension of the Debye-Hückle theory. He was appointed (1914) a professor at the Veterinary and Agricultural School, Copenhagen.

Björkman (byėrk′ma̧n), **Edwin August.** b. at Stockholm, Oct. 19, 1866; d. at Asheville, N.C., Nov. 16, 1951. American writer and translator. He came to the U.S. in 1891. Among his translations are the play *The Bridal Crown* by August Strindberg, and the novel *Suzanne* by Johannes Buchholtz.

Björkö (byėrk′ė″), **Treaty of.** [Also, **Treaty of Byörkö.**] Treaty signed (July 24, 1905) between William II of Germany and Nicholas II of Russia at a personal meeting at Björkö (Finnish, Koivisto), a fortress off the Finnish coast, shortly after the Japanese defeat of the Russian fleet at Tsushima Strait. The two rulers were unaccompanied by their political advisers. The treaty, which was to go into effect at the conclusion of the Russo-Japanese War, promised mutual military aid in Europe if either signatory was attacked by another European power, and that neither would conclude a separate peace with a common adversary. Nicholas II was soon persuaded that the treaty was incompatible with the Franco-Russian alliance and the treaty never went into effect.

Björling (byėr′ling), **Gunnar Olof.** b. at Helsinki, Finland, 1887—. Finnish poet and aphorist, writing in Swedish. A member of an upper-middle-class family, Björling studied at the university at Helsinki. During World War II, Björling's often bizarre and fragmentary poetry attracted considerable attention in Scandinavia. His broken imagery and cinematic abruptness are characteristic of the modern tempo; his "sprung rhythms," vaguely reminiscent of the style of Gerard Manley Hopkins, have meant a renewal of certain aspects of Swedish poetic language. Among his works are *Vilande dag* (Resting Day, 1922), *Kirira!* (1930), *Solgrönt* (Sun-Green Stuff, 1933), *Men blåser violer på havet* (But if Violets Blow over the Sea, 1936), *Att syndens blåa nagel* (That Sin's Blue Nail, 1936), and *Björling-urval* (Selections From Björling, 1937).

Bjørnøya (byėrn′ė″yä). Norwegian name of **Bear Island.**

Bjørnson (byėrn′sôn), **Bjørnstjerne.** b. at Kvikne, Hedmark, Norway, Dec. 8, 1832; d. at Paris, April 26, 1910. Norwegian poet, novelist, and dramatist who took an active part in the political life of Norway. In 1903 he received the Nobel prize for literature. His father was a clergyman in the Østerdal region and later held the living at Næs in the Romsdal. After attending the grammar school at Molde, Bjørnson went to the university at Christiania (now Oslo), and was subsequently at Uppsala and Copenhagen. In 1857 he returned from abroad, and was first director of the theater at Bergen, and afterward (1859) for a short time editor of the journal *Aftenbladet* in Christiania. In 1860 he went abroad; upon his return, in 1863, the *Storthing* (the Norwegian parliament) voted him a yearly stipend. From 1865 to 1867 he was director of the Christiania theater, and editor, during the same time, of the journal *Norske Folkeblad*. In 1880 he traveled in America. Later he lived at his estate Olestad, in the Gausdal. His first novel, *Synnöve Solbakken*, appeared in 1857. It was followed by *Arne* (1858), *En Glad Gut* (A Happy Boy, 1860), and later (1868) by *Fiskerjenten* (The Fisher Maiden); these are all collections of stories of Norwegian peasant life, to which were to be added at various times in subsequent editions a number of shorter tales in the same vein. *Magnhild* (1877) and *Captain Manzana* followed, the one a tale of middle-class life in Norway, the other an Italian story. His later novels, *Det Flager i Byen og paa Havnen* (Flags are Flying in the Town and Harbor), and *Paa Guds Veie* (In God's Way), are tendential novels. He was the author, besides, of numerous dramas whose material was taken from the sagas, from recent history, and from modern life. They are *Mellem Slagene* (Between the Battles) and *Halte Hulda* (Lame Hulda, 1858), *Kong Sverre* (King Sverre, 1861), the trilogy *Sigurd Slembe* (1862), *Maria Stuart i Skotland* (Mary Stuart in Scotland, 1863), *De Nygifte* (The Newly Wedded Pair, 1865), *Sigurd Jorsalfar* (Sigurd the Crusader, 1873), *En Fallit* (A Bankruptcy) *Redaktören* (The Editor, 1875), *Kongen* (The King, 1877), *Leonardo*, and *Det nye System* (The New System, 1879). There are a number of less important dramas, including *En Hanske*, *Geografi og Kjaerlighed*, and *Over Ævne*. The earlier works, like *Arne*, contain a number of lyrics. An epic poem, *Arnljot Gelline*, appeared in 1870.

Bjørnsson (byėrs′sôn), **Sveinn.** b. at Copenhagen, Feb. 27, 1881; d. at Reykjavík, in the republic of Iceland, Jan. 25, 1952. Icelandic statesman and diplomat, elected (June 17, 1944) the first president of Iceland. He had previously served (1941–44) as regent of Iceland during the German occupation of Denmark. He practiced (1920 *et seq.*) law before the Icelandic supreme court, and held (1920–24, 1926–41) the post of Icelandic minister to Denmark. He was also chairman of the board of directors (1914–20, 1924–26) of the Icelandic Steamship Company, and director of numerous industrial, fishing, and insurance firms. He sat (1914–16, 1920 *et seq.*) in the *Althing* (parliament), represented Iceland as a special envoy the U.S. and Great Britain during World War I, headed the Icelandic delegation to the Genoa confere (1922) and the London monetary and economic con ence (1933). In 1945 and again in 1949 he was reëlec president.

Björnstjerna (byėrn′sher.nä), Count **Magnus Fred Ferdinand.** b. at Dresden, Germany, Oct. 10, 17 d. at Stockholm, Oct. 6, 1847. Swedish diplomat, l tenant general, and political writer. He was mini plenipotentiary to Great Britain in the period 1828-

Blacas d'Aulps (blȧ.kȧs dōp). b. at Aulps or France, c1160; d. 1229. French troubadour.

Black (blak). See also **Black River.**

Black, Adam. b. at Edinburgh, Feb. 20, 1784; d. th Jan. 24, 1874. Scottish book publisher and politic Having begun a bookselling business in his own nam 1808, he established (1834) at Edinburgh the hous Adam and Charles Black by taking his nephew i partnership. He acquired the copyright to the *Ency pædia Britannica* on the failure of Archibald Const and Company in 1827. He was a member (1856–65 Parliament for Edinburgh.

Black, Frank Swett. b. at Limington, Me., Marc 1853; d. March 22, 1913. American lawyer and politic

Black, Greene Vardiman. b. near Winchester, Aug. 3, 1836; d. Aug. 31, 1915. American dentist author of books and articles on dentistry. He served lecturer (1870–80) at Missouri Dental College, profe of dental pathology (1883–89) at the Chicago Colleg Dental Surgery, professor of dental pathology and teriology (1890–91) at the University of Iowa, and fessor (1891 *et seq.*) and dean (1897 *et seq.*) at the No western University Dental School. He originate method of making dental amalgam alloys which is widely used.

Black, Hugh. b. at Rothesay, Buteshire, Scotland, M 26, 1868—. American Presbyterian clergyman, note a preacher and church writer. He was appointed (1 professor of practical theology at Union Theolog Seminary, New York.

Black, Hugo La Fayette. b. at Harlan, Clay Cou Ala., Feb. 27, 1886—. American jurist and politic one-time (1926–37) senator from Alabama, and s Aug. 17, 1937, an associate justice of the U.S. Supr Court. His belief in public power projects, a 30-hour w week, and the right of government to intervene for public good in private enterprise made him a loyal porter of the New Deal under Franklin D. Roose The fact that he had been a member (although appare never active) of the Ku Klux Klan caused a wav protest when he was appointed to the Supreme Court radio speech repudiating the Klan (made on Oct. 1, 1 to an estimated audience of 50 million) was the instance in which a Supreme Court justice had discu on the air a controversial subject while still in office.

Black, James. b. at Lewisburg, Pa., Sept. 23, 1 d. Dec. 16, 1893. American temperance advocate, fou of the National Prohibition Party. He joined (1840) Washington Temperance Society, organized local tem ance leagues in Pennsylvania, and introduced (186 plan for a national publishing house to handle prohibi literature. He was nominated (1872) for president on first National Prohibition Party ticket.

Black, Jeremiah Sullivan. b. at the Glades, Some County, Pa., Jan. 10, 1810; d. at Brockie, York Cou Pa., Aug. 19, 1883. American jurist and statesn attorney general (1857–60) in the cabinet of Ja Buchanan, and secretary of state (1860–61). As atto general, he uncovered frauds regarding California titles.

Black, John. b. near Dunse, Berwickshire, Scotl 1783; d. at Scotland, near Maidstone, Kent, Engl June 15, 1855. Scottish reporter, journalist, editor, translator. He was a pupil at the Dunse parish sc and attended classes at the University of Edinb while serving as a clerk in an accountant's office. In he went to London and became a reporter, and transl of foreign correspondence, on the *Morning Chronicl* which he became editor in 1817. Requested to resig 1843, he spent the rest of his life in retirement. Au of essays on Italian and German literature, contribut

807–09) to the London *Universal Magazine*, and *Life Tasso* (1810).

ack, John Charles. b. at Lexington, Miss., Jan. 27, 39; d. Aug. 17, 1915. American lawyer, soldier, and litician. He served with the Union army during the vil War. He practiced law in Illinois, and was a U.S. ngressman-at-large (1892 *et seq.*); he was also a member 903–13), and for a time president, of the U.S. Civil rvice Commission.

ack, Joseph. b. at Bordeaux, France, 1728; d. at linburgh, Dec. 6, 1799. Scottish chemist, noted for his scoveries in relation to carbon dioxide and latent heat. e became professor of medicine at the University of asgow in 1756, and of medicine and chemistry at linburgh in 1766.

ck, William. b. at Glasgow, in November, 1841; d. at ighton, England, Dec. 10, 1898. British novelist and urnalist. In 1864 he went to London, and was attached the staff of the London *Morning Star* in 1865. He was so for some years assistant editor of the London *Daily ews*. His works include *In Silk Attire* (1869), *A Daughter Heth* (1871), *The Strange Adventures of a Phaeton* (1872), *Princess of Thule* (1873), *The Maid of Killeena, and er Stories* (1876), *Three Feathers* (1875), *Madcap Violet* 876), *Lady Silverdale's Sweetheart, and other Stories* 876), *Green Pastures and Piccadilly* (1877), *Macleod Dare* (1878), *White Wings* (1880), *Sunrise* (1880), *hite Heather* (1885), and *In Far Lochaber* (1888).

ck, William Murray. b. at Lancaster, Pa., Dec. 8, 55; d. at Washington, D.C., Sept. 24, 1933. American my engineer, engaged mainly in river and harbor improvement, and inventor of the aerating method of purifyg sewage. Named (1898) chief engineer and lieutenant lonel of U.S. volunteers, he was appointed (1916) a igadier general. He was an engineer (1898–1901) in ıba during the Spanish-American War and the subseent engineering work carried on there; he was later 909–16) division engineer of the eastern division, River d Harbor Improvements.

ckacre (blak'ā"kėr), **Jerry.** In William Wycherley's *e Plain Dealer*, a raw booby, not of age and still under s mother's care, trained by her to the law, or at least a glib use of its terms.

ckacre, Widow. In William Wycherley's *The Plain ealer*, a petulant, litigious woman, always with a law se on hand. She is considered one of the author's best d most amusing characters, and is taken from the untess in Jean Baptiste Racine's *Les Plaideurs*.

ck Act, The. English statute of 1722, so called cause designed originally to suppress associations of wless persons who called themselves blacks. It made onies of certain crimes against game laws, the sending anonymous letters demanding money, and others.

ack Agnes." See **Dunbar, Agnes.**

ckall (blak'ôl) or **Blackhall** (-hôl), **Offspring.** b. at ndon, 1654; d. at Exeter, England, Nov. 29, 1716. glish prelate and controversialist, made bishop of eter in 1708. He engaged in controversies with John land, whom he accused of having denied the genuiness of the Scriptures in his *Life of Milton*, and with shop Benjamin Hoadly (or Hoadley), against whom he pported the cause of Charles I and high-church inciples.

ck April. Novel by Julia Peterkin, published in 1927.

ck Armour. Collection of poems by Elinor Wylie, blished in 1923.

ck Assize. Name given to the Oxford assize of 1577, which year Oxford was ravaged by jail fever.

ck Ball Line. Popular name applied to the New rk-to-Liverpool packet line of sailing vessels, so called cause of the figure of a black ball which appeared on e standard of the house and on the fore-topsails of its ft. Regular monthly crossings were announced in 1817.

ck Bateman of the North (bāt'mạn). Play (1598) Thomas Dekker, in collaboration with Michael Drayn and others.

ckbeard (blak'bird). [Original name, **Edward Teach Thach** or **Thatch**).] d. Nov. 22, 1718. English ate. All that is known of him before 1716 is that he s a privateer under English letters of marque during the ar of the Spanish Succession, and that he turned to wless adventure after peace was concluded in 1714. Operating out of the Bahamas he sailed the Spanish Main and the Atlantic as far north as the coast of the Carolinas in a captured French merchantman which he armed with 40 guns, and renamed *Queen Anne's Revenge*. It has always been suspected that the colonial governor of North Carolina at that time afforded him protection, for a price. His audacity and ferocious cruelty won him the name of "the scourge of the Spanish Main," but his career was brought to an end when his pirate craft was attacked by two sloops sent after him by the governor of Virginia.

Black Beetles in Amber. Collection of satirical verse (1892) by Ambrose Bierce.

Black Belt. Prairie area of highly fertile black soil, occupying some 5,000 sq. mi. running along the Alabama River in Alabama to the Tombigbee River in the NE section of Mississippi. Its extraordinary fertility is caused by the layer of decomposed limestone rock under the soil. The first settlers in the Black Belt made their homes in Alabama, which contains about 75 percent of the belt.

Black Book, The. Prose satire by Thomas Middleton, a coarse, humorous attack on the vices and follies of the time, published in 1604. It was suggested by Thomas Nash's *Pierce Pennilesse*.

Black Boy. Novel (1945) by Richard Wright. It is autobiographical.

Black Boys, The. Group of frontier settlers in colonial Pennsylvania who banded together (1763, 1765, 1769) under James Smith for the purpose of safeguarding the frontier against the Indians. In 1765 they destroyed a supply train belonging to whites who were trading with the Indians.

Black Brunswickers (brunz'wik.ėrz). [Also, **Death's Head Corps.**] Corps of 2,000 horsemen equipped by Frederick William, Duke of Brunswick, to operate against Napoleon I in Germany. It vainly attempted to coöperate with the Austrians in 1809.

Blackburn (blak'bėrn). County borough and manufacturing town in NW England, in Lancashire, ab. 11 mi. E of Preston, ab. 208 mi. NW of London by rail. Its chief industry is cotton manufacture, formerly specializing in cheap cloths for the Oriental trade, and known for several centuries for Blackburn checks and Blackburn grays. Other industries include textile-machinery manufacture, rayon weaving, and flour milling. Blackburn was the center of the fustian industry in the 17th century. It was the birthplace of James Hargreaves. 111,217 (1951).

Blackburn, Colin. [Title, Baron **Blackburn.**] b. in Selkirkshire, Scotland, 1813; d. in Ayrshire, Scotland, 1896. British jurist. He was the author of *Treatise on the Effect of the Contract of Sale on the Legal Rights of Property and Possessions in Foods, Wares, and Merchandise* (1845), a standard text for many years. He became puisne judge (1859) and lord of appeal in ordinary (1876).

Blackburn, Helen. b. at Kingstown (now Dún Laoghaire), Ireland, May 25, 1842; d. at Westminster, England, Jan. 11, 1903. English pioneer in the field of women's suffrage. Secretary (1875–95) to the National Society for Woman's Suffrage, she was also editor (1881–1903) of the *Englishwoman's Review* and author of *Woman's Suffrage* (1902), for many years a standard work on the movement.

Blackburn, Joseph. [Sometimes called **Jonathan B. Blackburn.**] b. in Connecticut, c1700; d. at Boston, Mass., c1765. American portrait painter who worked in England and America, and painted portraits of many prominent Boston families. He may have been a teacher of John Singleton Copley.

Blackburn, Joseph Clay Styles. b. near Spring Station, Ky., Oct. 1, 1838; d. Sept. 12, 1918. American lawyer, soldier, and politician. He fought as a lieutenant under Leonidas Polk in the Civil War. Having served as a congressman (1875–85) and U.S. senator (1885–97) from Kentucky, he was appointed governor of the Canal Zone by Theodore Roosevelt, and resident commissioner of the Lincoln Memorial (1914) by Woodrow Wilson.

Blackburn, Luke Pryor. b. in Fayette County, Ky., June 16, 1816; d. at Frankfort, Ky., Sept. 14, 1887. American physician and governor (1879 *et seq.*) of Kentucky. He organized the control of a cholera epidemic at Versailles, Ky. (1835) and of yellow fever epidemics in the lower Mississippi Valley (1848, 1854), Long Island, N.Y. (1856), Memphis, Tenn. (1875), and Hickman, Ky. (1878). He served during the Civil War with the Confederate forces as surgeon to the staff of General Sterling Price.

Blackburn, William Maxwell. b. at Carlisle, Ind., Dec. 30, 1828; d. Dec. 29, 1898. American Presbyterian clergyman, educator, and religious historian. He was pastor of the Park Presbyterian Church at Erie, Pa. (1857–63) and of the Central Presbyterian Church at Cincinnati, Ohio (1881–84), professor (1868–81) of Biblical and ecclesiastical history at the Seminary of the Northwest (later to be called McCormick Theological Seminary), and president (1885–98) of Pierre University (later to be called Huron College, at Huron, S.D.). Among his works are *The Holy Child* (1859), *History of the Christian Church from its Origin to the Present Time* (1879), and a translation of Johann Gerhard's *Sacred Meditations.*

Black Butte. See under **North Dakota.**

Black Canyon of the Gunnison (gun′i.sọn). [Also, **Gunnison Canyon.**] Canyon of the Gunnison River, in W Colorado, near Montrose. The river has cut a 50-mile gorge through granite and other dark-colored rocks, at some points to a depth of 3,000 ft. Part of the canyon is now a national monument (established 1933; area, 13,176 acres).

Black Cat, The. Story by Edgar Allan Poe, published in 1843, and included in his volume *Tales* (1845).

"Black Christ." See under **Esquipulas.**

Black Codes. Legislation, enacted (1865–66) by former states of the Southern Confederacy, which fixed the social and economic status of the emancipated Negro slaves. The codes, regarded by the South as necessary measures for preventing the collapse of its social order, were viewed by the North as a disguised revival of slavery. They played an important part in spurring on the reconstruction program of the Radical Republicans.

Black Country. Manufacturing region in C England, occupying all the area in S Staffordshire and adjacent NW Warwickshire within a radius of 10 mi. centered upon Birmingham. It is the oldest of the machinery-manufacturing regions, long associated with the bituminous coal from the South Staffordshire coal field (now largely exhausted in this region). The iron mining formerly carried on here has also been largely abandoned, but the Black Country remains an important industrial region, having a wide variety of industries. Automobiles and other finished steel products are manufactured in this section, and it is the center of the nonferrous metals industry and of the rubber industry. The Black Country early became the focal point of a well-developed canal system, now largely in disuse, however, more goods being moved by rail.

Blackcraig Hill (blak′krāg). See under **Ayrshire.**

Black Crom (krom). Idol worshiped in Ireland at the time of Saint Patrick's arrival there. Irish folklore designates a Sunday in early August as "Cromfudd Sunday."

Black Current. See **Japan Current.**

Black Death. In European history, the name given to the epidemic which swept across the world in the middle of the 14th century and is considered by many to have been probably the most terrible calamity in the recorded annals of mankind. There had been earlier plagues (the earliest one of this nature was almost certainly not the one described by Thucydides as occurring at Athens in the period 430–425 B.C., but there were many outbreaks of disease in Europe during the ten centuries immediately preceding the 14th which were unquestionably of the same type as the Black Death), but the Black Death was enormously more disastrous than any of the others. There can be no doubt as to its nature; it was the true Oriental plague, whether bubonic or pulmonary (indeed, axillary, inguinal, and pulmonary lesions were witnessed and duly recorded). The Black Death, so far as we can ascertain, began in India in 1332; epidemics occurring in Russia in 1341 and in Styria in 1342 may have been its forerunners in Europe. By the latter part of 1347 it had progressed, via Constantinople, as far as Sicily, Naples, and Genoa. Venice was visited by the pestilence early in 1348, and from that great commercial center it spread rapidly (one of the reasons for its severity may have been, indeed, that international commerce had vastly increased over early centuries and thus multiplied the chances of contagion, while there had been no corresponding devel- ment in scientific means of combating it). It reached climax in central Europe and England in 1349, and Russia in 1352 (which was a recurrence, if the epide of 1341 had been, indeed, the Black Death). The clim in each region lasted from about four to six months. it broke out during the winter, it assumed the pulmona form, and kept it or became the bubonic type in the spri We now know that the disease was spread by fleas a rats, but nobody suspected that at the time, and prophylactic measures were therefore irrelevant (exce insofar as cleanliness tended to keep down every sort parasite, and segregation restricted contagion). It is i possible to estimate with any precision how many peo were its victims, although some have thought that quarter of the population of the civilized world was wip out. In any case, it had enormous social, political, mor and religious impact. For example, probably because th were more exposed to contagion than the wealthy a powerful, there was a very high incidence of deaths amo the poor, and this led to a shortage of labor which, turn, gave rise in all probability to an atmosphere m favorable to the laborer than had ever before been p sible. One particularly hideous consequence of the plag was that a great many people threw the responsibil for the common miseries upon the Jews, whom th accused of having poisoned wells in order to destr Christians. This terrible delusion became very prevale in central Europe, particularly in Germany. In fa violent anti-Semitism reached such a point in that count that there were left in Germany, by the end of the 1 century, only three considerable Jewish communities. is perhaps a relief, in view of crimes so unspeakable, turn to Pope Clement VI, who sought vigorously to sh the absurdity of the accusation made against the Je and took them under his own protection. It is even p sible that the plague may have been felt in the field linguistics, in that it favored the diffusion of the Europe vernaculars over Latin. It is certain that the diffusion English (in England) as opposed to French increa materially during the second half of the 14th centu It is possible, even probable, that the Black Death h something to do with this, for it delivered such a form able blow to the whole of society that everything affected by it.

Black Domino, The. Comic opera produced in 18 an English version of Augustin Eugène Scribe's *Le D ino noir* (1837).

"Black Douglas (dug′lạs), **The."** See **Douglas, Arc bald,** and **Douglas,** Sir **James.**

Black Dwarf, The. Novel by Sir Walter Scott, p lished in 1816. "The Black Dwarf" was a name gi in parts of Scotland to a most malicious, uncanny creat considered responsible for all mischief done to flocks a herds; hence the name was applied in the novel to Edward Mauley, who was deformed and gnomish-looki

Black Elster (el′stėr). See **Schwarze Elster.**

Black Esk (esk). See under **Esk,** S Scotland and N England.

Blackett (blak′ẹt), **Patrick Maynard Stuart.** b. London, Nov. 18, 1897—. English physicist, one of discoverers of the positive electron, and winner of Nobel prize in physics for 1948. He was a lecturer (19 33) at Cavendish Laboratory, Cambridge, and a profes at Birkbeck College (1933–37) of the University of L don, before being named (1937) a professor at the U versity of Manchester. In World War II he served as adviser on atomic energy to the British government. investigations have centered on the improvement of Wilson cloud chamber (a device allowing the photogra ing of radioactive particles), on cosmic rays, and mesons. He is the author of *The Methodology of Operat Research* (1943) and *The Military and Political Co quences of Atomic Energy* (1948), the latter carryin defense of the Russian rejection of the U.S. proposal international control of atomic energy; *Fear, War,* *the Bomb* (1949) continues his attack on the Baruch p for control of atomic weapons.

Black-eyed Susan. [Full name, **Sweet William's Fa well to Black-eyed Susan.**] Ballad by John Gay, p lished in 1720 in a collection of his poems. The m to it was written by Richard Leveridge.

ack-eyed Susan, or All in the Downs. Comedy by)ouglas Jerrold, produced on June 8, 1829. It was played 00 times in that year alone.

ack Flags. Name given in the late 19th century to the ands of irregular soldiers which infested the upper valley f the Red River in Tonkin. They were originally survivors of the Taiping Rebellion in China. With their ranks ncreased by the accession of various adventurers, they ought against the French in their conquest of Annam uring the latter half of the 19th century.

ackfoot (blak′fůt). City in SE Idaho, in Bingham County: beet-sugar refineries. It is the site of a state ental hospital. 5,180 (1950).

ackfoot. North American Indian tribe, formerly ranging chiefly over SE Alberta, Canada. The language was f the Algonquian family.

ackfoot. See also **Sihasapa**; also **Siksika.**

ack Forest. [German, **Schwarzwald**; ancient names: **bnoba, Silva Marciana, Montes Rauraci.**] Mountainous region in SW Germany, in the E part of Baden and ne W part of Württemberg-Hohenzollern, containing the ources of the Danube. Small parts of the range, around aden-Baden and Wildbad, are in Württemberg-Baden, etween the valleys of the Rhine and Neckar rivers. It divided by the Kinzig River into the Lower Black orest in the N, and the Upper Black Forest in the S. he region has many tourist resorts, and produces clocks, ats, wooden articles, textiles, and precision instruments. he highest summit is the Feldberg (ab. 4,900 ft.); among ther peaks are the Belchen and Hornisgrinde.

ackfriars (blak′frī.ąrz). Name given to the locality t the SW angle of old London city, on the Fleet, from s association with the "Black Friars," or mendicant nonks of the Dominican order. Members of this order ade their appearance in London in 1221 under the atronage of Hubert de Burgh, and were located in Iolborn. In 1285 they moved to the site of the old Montchett tower, which had been given them for a monastery. he tower itself was destroyed and the material used building the church. From Ludgate to the river the ty wall was pulled down and moved W to the Fleet, ll the added space being devoted to the monastery. he original site was given by Gregory Rokesley "in a treet of Baynard Castle." The monastery was endowed ith a privilege of asylum, which attached itself to the ocality even after the dissolution.

ackfriars Bridge. One of the great stone bridges of ondon, the third bridge from the Tower of London, riginally called Pitt Bridge, but soon named after the ocality. After much discussion its construction was enrusted to a man named Mylne, of Edinburgh. The first ile was driven in June, 1760, and the structure was ompleted on Nov. 19, 1769, at a total cost of 300,000 ounds. It was ab. 995 ft. long, ab. 42 ft. wide, and ab. 2 ft. high. The central span was ab. 100 ft. wide. It as demolished in 1864, and rebuilt a few years later, rom the designs of Joseph Cubitt, at a cost of 320,000 ounds.

ackfriars Theatre. Famous London theater, the site f which came later to be occupied by the London *Times* ffice and Playhouse Yard. Some time in 1596 Sir William Iore conveyed to James Burbage, the father of Richard urbage the actor, part of a large house in Blackfriars, onsisting of "seaven greate upper romes." This he conerted into a theater. The first tenants were an acting roupe known as the Children of the Chapel, afterward alled the Children of Her Majesty's Revels. Shakespeare nd his colleagues, Richard Burbage, John Lowin, and Ienry Condell, acted in Blackfriars. In it there were hree tiers of galleries, and beneath them rooms or boxes. he orchestra was seated in a balcony at the side of the tage, and played at the beginning and between the acts. t a triple flourish of trumpets the curtain opened and isclosed the stage, which was strewn with rushes and, a tragedy was to be presented, hung with black. hakespeare wrote exclusively for the Globe and Blackriars, and almost all of the great dramas of the time ere performed here. The building was pulled down in 655.

ack Friday. Good Friday; so called because on that ay, in many Christian sects, the vestments of the clergy nd altar are black.

Black Friday. Any Friday marked by a great calamity, with two special references in England: to Friday, Dec. 6, 1745, the day on which news reached London that the Young Pretender, Charles Edward, had reached Derby; or to the commercial panic caused by the failure of the house of Overend and Gurney, on May 11, 1866. In the U.S. the name is applied to the sudden financial panic and ruin caused by reckless speculation in gold on the stock exchange at New York on Friday, Sept. 24, 1869, or to another similar panic there which began on Sept. 18, 1873. (For a similar expression referring to the stock-market crash of October, 1929, see **Black Thursday.**)

Black Hand. [Italian, **Mafia.**] Secret society which originated in Sicily and was later active in the U.S., after some of its members arrived there in the late 19th century. The Black Hand enforced a ruthless code of discipline which made its own members as liable to punishment by death as its enemies. Italian regimes, even as recently as that under Benito Mussolini, made attempts to suppress the Black Hand; in the U.S. its power had waned before the outbreak of World War I.

"Black Hat." See **Karakalpak.**

Black Hawk. b. at what is now Kaskaskia, Ill., 1767; d. near the Des Moines River, in Iowa, Oct. 3, 1838. American Indian, chosen chief of the Sacs (or Sauks) c1788, and leader in the revolt of the Sacs and Foxes in 1832 known as the Black Hawk War. He was the author of *Autobiography of Black Hawk* (1833).

Black Hawk Purchase. Treaty (Sept. 21, 1832) between the U.S. government and the Sac (or Sauk) and Fox Indians, signed at Fort Armstrong on Rock Island, in the Mississippi River. It concluded the Black Hawk War and provided for the cession of six million acres of land by the Indians, for which they were paid 14 cents an acre. Black Hawk, who was held in confinement at Jefferson Barracks, Mo., did not sign the treaty. The Black Hawk Purchase ushered in the era of legal settlement for Indian lands in Iowa.

Black Hawk War. War (1832) between the U.S. and a group of Fox and Sac (or Sauk) Indians under the leadership of Black Hawk. The cause of the war lay in differences over a cession of 50 million acres of land which had been made over (1804) to the U.S. government by representatives of the two tribes. Black Hawk refused to recognize any cession, and the dispute was brought to a head when squatters placed a claim (1831) upon the locality of Black Hawk's village near what is now Rock Island, Ill. Black Hawk's threat of retaliation was stemmed by the formation of a force of U.S. regulars and Illinois militia (in which Abraham Lincoln served), and the Indian chieftain retreated to the west bank of the Mississippi. The war began when Black Hawk crossed to the Illinois side in 1832, and operations were confined largely to Illinois and Wisconsin. Despite offers of peace made by Black Hawk, his opponents pursued him into Wisconsin, where, on Aug. 3, 1832, the Indian force was virtually wiped out at the mouth of the Bad Axe River. Black Hawk was taken captive and confined at Jefferson Barracks, Mo., and the treaty concluding the war was signed on Sept. 21, 1832.

Blackheath (blak′hēth). Name given to a locality in S London, once an open common of considerable extent, ab. 5 mi. S of Saint Paul's Cathedral. The Danes were defeated here in 1011. It was the scene of Wat Tyler's rebellion in 1381, and of Jack Cade's uprising in 1450. The Cornish rebels were also defeated (June 22, 1497) here by the royalists.

Black Hills. Group of mountains in SW South Dakota and NE Wyoming, noted for their mineral wealth. The chief towns in the region (all in South Dakota) are Belle Fourche, Spearfish, Deadwood, Lead, Rapid City, and Custer. The highest point is Harney Peak (7,242 ft.). Gold was discovered here in 1874 and is still mined, as are tungsten, silver, lead, oil, and coal. Area, ab. 6,000 sq. mi.

Black Hole of Calcutta. Garrison strongroom, or "black hole," at Calcutta, measuring ab. 18 ft. square, in which 146 British prisoners were confined, on June 20, 1756, during the Sepoy Rebellion in India. The next morning all but 23 were dead.

Blackhope Scar (blak′hōp). See under **Moorfoot Hills.**

Black-Horse Cavalry. Epithet applied (c1875–c1900) to Republican and Democrat members of the New York State legislature who used corrupt means to extract funds from corporate interests. They submitted bills aimed against the corporations, and then withdrew the proposed legislation upon the payment of money by the intended victims.

Blackie (blak'i), **John Stuart.** b. at Glasgow, in July, 1809; d. at Edinburgh, March 2, 1895. Scottish philologist and poet, professor of Greek at Edinburgh from 1852 to 1882. He translated the works of Aeschylus in 1850, and later *Faust,* and the *Iliad,* and wrote *Four Phases of Morals* (1871), *Lays of the Highlands* (1872), *Horae Hellenicae* (1874), and others.

Black Isle. [Also: **Ardmeanach, Mullbuie.**] Peninsula in N Scotland, in the county of Ross and Cromarty, situated between Cromarty Firth on the N, Moray Firth on the E, and Beauly Firth on the S. Length, ab. 19 mi.; greatest width, ab. 8 mi.

Black is My Truelove's Hair. Novel (1938) by Elizabeth Roberts. In it Dena Janes loves Will Langtry but cannot gain his final loyalty and transfers her affections to a merrier and better-hearted fellow, Cam Elliott, the miller's son, who is, however, a less vivid lover.

Black Jack, Battle of. Opening action (June 2, 1856) of the Kansas Border War, fought at Black Jack, near Baldwin, Kan., between a force led by John Brown and a band which had crossed into Kansas from Missouri. The action of the proslavery forces was taken in retaliation for the massacre perpetrated by Brown at Potawatomie Creek.

Black Knight. In medieval romances, a son of Oriana and Amadis of Gaul; he is so called because of his black armor.

Black Knight. Disguise under which, in Sir Walter Scott's *Ivanhoe,* Richard Coeur de Lion wanders in Sherwood Forest, performs feats of valor, and feasts with Friar Tuck.

Black Lamb and Grey Falcon. Prose work (1941) by Rebecca West. It is an account of a visit to Yugoslavia in 1937, two and a half years after the assassination, at Marseilles, of Alexander I of Yugoslavia, and two years before the outbreak of World War II. It is written in a style that appears at first to be rambling, if not actually casual (as one critic has put it, the book has "divagations anthropological, cultural, literary, philosophical, and emotional"), and was greeted even before publication in book form in the U.S. (it was partly serialized in the *Atlantic Monthly* in 1940) as Rebecca West's greatest achievement.

Black Laws. Laws passed (1804, 1807) by the Ohio State legislature requiring, among other provisions, the registration of all Negroes residing in the state and the posting of a 500-dollar bond for any free Negro resident to prevent his becoming a public charge. They were repealed in the session of 1848–49, after the Free Soil Party had led the opposition against them. Similar laws prevailed in several other Northern states, and were aimed in particular at the status of the free Negro.

Black Legion. Secret organization which arose (c1936) in Michigan and practiced terrorism in that and nearby states. The killing of Charles A. Poole of Detroit by some of its members in 1936 led to a criminal trial for the latter and public exposure of the Legion's activities.

Blacklock (blak'lok), **Thomas.** b. at Annan, Scotland, Nov. 10, 1721; d. at Edinburgh, July 7, 1791. Scottish poet. Having lost his sight at the age of six months through an attack of smallpox, he was given an education, including a course at the University of Edinburgh, by Dr. Stevenson, a physician of Edinburgh, and was licensed to preach in 1759. He became (c1762) minister of Kirkcudbright, but resigned in 1764. He enjoyed the friendship and patronage of David Hume and Joseph Spence. An edition of his poems appeared in 1756, with an introduction by Spence.

Blacklock, William James. b. at Cumwhitton, near Carlisle, England, c1815; d. at Dumfries, Scotland, March 12, 1858. Scottish landscape painter.

Black Man, The. Epithet sometimes applied to the devil.

Blackmar (blak'mär), **Frank Wilson.** b. at West Springfield, Pa., Nov. 3, 1854; d. March 30, 1931. American sociologist. He was professor (1889 *et seq.*) and dean (1896–1922) of the graduate school at the University of Kansas. Among his works are *Federal and State Aid Higher Education in the United States* (1890), *Span Colonization* (1890), *Spanish Institutions in the Southw* (1891), *History of Higher Education in Kansas* (190 *The Elements of Sociology* (1905), *Justifiable Individuali* (1922), and *History of Human Society* (1926).

Black Mesa. See under **Oklahoma.**

Black Mischief. Satirical novel by Evelyn Waugh, pu lished in 1932. Its hero, Basil Seal, goes to Azania, th to help the local king (with whom he had been at Oxfo modernize his country. The locale is thought to be bas on Abyssinia.

Black Monday. Easter Monday; so called from a terri storm which occurred on Easter Monday, 1360, causi the English army before Paris to suffer severely.

Blackmore (blak'mōr), Sir **Richard.** b. at Corsha Wiltshire, England, c1650; d. at Boxsted, Essex, Englar Oct. 9, 1729. English physician, poet, and prose writ physician in ordinary to William III. His best-kno work is *The Creation* (1712).

Blackmore, Richard Doddridge. b. at Longwor Berkshire, England, June 7, 1825; d. at Teddingt Middlesex, England, Jan. 20, 1900. English noveli poet, and translator, best known as the author of *Lor Doone* (1869). Educated at Blundell's School at Tivert in Devonshire, and at Exeter College, Oxford, he tri teaching and the practice of law for a time, but ga up both on coming into an inheritance. Author of *Poe by Melanter* (1853), *Epullia* (1853), *The Bugle of the Bl Sea* (1855), *The Fate of Franklin* (1860), and *Fring* (1895), all poetry, he also translated the *Hero and Lean* of Musaeus, the *Georgics* of Virgil, and the *Idylls* of Th critus. He is remembered for the novel *Lorna Doo A Romance of Exmoor* (1869); his other novels inclu *Clara Vaughan* (1864), *Cradock Nowell* (1866), *The M of Sker* (1872), *Alice Lorraine* (1875), *Erema, or Father's Sin* (1877), *Mary Anerley* (1880), *Christou* (1882), *The Remarkable History of Tommy Upmore* (188 *Springhaven* (1887), *Kit and Kitty* (1889), *Perlycr* (1894), and *Dariel* (1897).

Black Mountain. See **Big Black Mountain.**

Black Mountains. Group of mountains in W Nor Carolina (chiefly in Yancey County), the highest in t Appalachian system. The chief peak is Mount Mitch (6,684 ft.).

Black Opal, The. Novel by Katharine Susannah Pri ard, published in 1921.

Black Oxen. Novel (1923) by Gertrude Atherton.

Black Patch War. Name given to the struggle of Te nessee and Kentucky tobacco growers to throw off t domination of markets and prices by the "tobacco trus deriving from the "Black Patch" region in SW Kentuc and adjacent areas in Tennessee. The association form by the growers sometimes employed violent measu against those who refused to join; the so-called Sil Brigade carried out night-rides against their oppone in the years 1907–08, and brought violence in retu Robert Penn Warren's novel *Night Rider* (1938) is bas on the events of the Black Patch War.

Blackpool (blak'pöl). [Called **"Britain's Playground.** County borough, seaport, and seaside resort in NW E land, in Lancashire, situated on the Irish Sea, ab. 15 NW of Preston, ab. 230 mi. NW of London by rail. It the most famous of all Lancashire seaside resorts, a is especially popular with holidaymakers from Liverpo it is estimated that approximately seven million visit per year visit Blackpool. The Tower, 500 ft. high, amusement center, is a famous landmark. Blackpool i former fishing village which owes its present developme to the railroad. 147,131 (1951).

Blackpool, Stephen. In Charles Dickens's *Hard Tim* a power-loom weaver of upright character tied to a mis able, drunken wife. He cannot see the propriety of livi with her and giving up a better woman whom he lov and in his own words "'t is a' a muddle." He dies a ling ing death from a fall into an abandoned mine, and appears that his goodness and integrity have met wi a poor return in this world.

Black Pope. Name sometimes applied to the general head) of the Jesuit order. It derives partly from the f that members of the order wear black vestments, a partly also from the fact that at various times in the h ory of the Roman Catholic Church the head of the ociety of Jesus has had power so great as to rival in ertain respects that of the Pope himself.

ack Prince, The. Tragedy by Roger Boyle, 1st Earl Orrery, acted in 1667.

ack Prince, the. See **Edward** (1330–76).

ack Range. See **Mimbres Mountains.**

ack Riders and Other Lines, The. Collection of free erse by Stephen Crane, published in 1895. The poems flect the author's philosophical determinism and indi- ate his stylistic affinity with the later work of the nagists.

ack Ridge. Narrow dividing ridge in Antarctica, with arp peaks ab. 3,500 ft. high, between Corner Glacier nd Priestley Glacier, in Victoria Land; in ab. 74°37′ S., 53°28′ E. First explored by the Northern Party of the ritish Antarctic Expedition (1910–13), it was so named ecause of its appearance.

ack River. River in E central Louisiana, formed by the inction of the Tensas and Ouachita rivers ab. 25 mi. W Natchez, Miss., and following a winding course S on e broad flood plain of the Mississippi to join the Red iver. Length, ab. 70 mi.

ack River. River in SE Missouri and NE Arkansas, sing in the E central Ozarks, and flowing SE into rkansas through a hilly region, then SW along the margin the hill country to join the White River ab. 3 mi. W of Newport, Ark. The lower river is open to naviga- on except in periods of low water, but it was formerly uch more used than it is today. Length, ab. 300 mi.

ack River. River in N New York which empties into ake Ontario near Watertown. Length, ab. 120 mi.

ack River. River in W central Wisconsin, flowing S nd SW to join the Mississippi near La Crosse. It was rmerly important in lumbering. Length, ab. 200 mi.

ack River, Big. See **Big Black River.**

ack River Falls. City in C Wisconsin, county seat Jackson County, on the Black River. Site of one of e earliest sawmills (1819) in Wisconsin, the town was lumbering center for nearly a century. 2,824 (1950).

lackrobe" (blak′rōb). See **De Smet, Pierre Jean.**

ackrock (blak′rok). [Also, **Black Rock.**] Town in unster province, Irish Republic, in County Cork, situ- ed at the mouth of the river Lee, ab. 3 mi. E of Cork. 915 (1946).

ack Rock. District within the municipality of Buffalo, .Y., situated on the Niagara River: the scene of severa gagements (1812–14) between the Americans anc ritish.

ack Rock, The. Collection (1928) of poems by John ould Fletcher.

ack Rod. Title of a gentleman usher, with special ities, in the English houses of Lords and Commons. e carries a black rod of office surmounted with a gold on.

ack Roses. Novel by Francis Brett Young, published 1929. It is set in Italy during the latter part of the 19th ntury. The hero is Paul Ritchie, an artist, son of an nglish father and an Italian mother.

ck's and White's. Former name of **Blackstone,** Va.

ack Saturday. In Scottish history, Aug. 4, 1621, when e Parliament at Edinburgh passed certain acts favor- g Episcopacy.

acksburg (blaks′bėrg). Town in SW Virginia, in Mont- mery County ab. 25 mi. W of Roanoke: seat of Virginia olytechnic Institute. 3,358 (1950).

ack Sea. [Also: **Euxine Sea**; Russian, **Chernoe More**; urkish, **Karadeniz**; Latin, **Pontus Euxinus.**] Inland a in SE Europe and W Asia, bounded by the U.S.S.R. on e N and E, Asiatic Turkey on the S, and European Tur- y, Bulgaria, and Rumania on the W. It communicates th the Mediterranean by the Bosporus, the Sea of Mar- ara, and the Dardanelles. Its chief arms are the Sea of zov and the Gulf of Karkinitsk (or Perekop); its chief ibutaries, the rivers Danube, Dniester, Bug, Dnieper, on, Kuban, Çoruh, Yesil Irmak, Kizil Irmak, and Sak- ya. On it are situated the cities of Burgas, Varna, Con- anța, Odessa, Sevastopol, Novorossisk, Sukhumi, Poti, atum, Trabzon, Samsun, and Sinop. The Black Sea was utralized by the treaty of Paris (1856), no warships being rmitted in its waters, and no military or naval arsenals its coasts. Russia in 1870 abrogated the provisions relating to her warships and arsenals. Length, ab. 740 mi.; greatest width, ab. 390 mi.; estimated area, 168,500 sq. mi.

Blacksod Bay (blak′sod). Bay in Connacht province, Irish Republic, in County Mayo, lying between the Mullet Peninsula and the Irish mainland. Length, ab. 10 mi.; greatest width, ab. 6 mi.

Black Soul, The. Novel by Liam O'Flaherty, published in 1924.

Blackstairs Mountain (blak′stãrz). Mountain in Leinster province, Irish Republic, situated near the County Carlo- County Wexford boundary, ab. 11 mi. NW of Enniscorthy. 2,409 ft.

Blackstone (blak′stōn). Town (in Massachusetts the equivalent of township in many other states) and unincorporated village in SE Massachusetts, in Worcester County, ab. 35 mi. SW of Boston, at the Massachusetts-Rhode Island border: textile mills. Pop. of town, 4,968 (1950); of village, 1,815 (1950).

Blackstone. [Former name, **Black's and White's.**] Town in S Virginia, in Nottoway County: marketing center for tobacco. It is the seat of Blackstone College. 3,536 (1950).

Blackstone, William. d. near Providence, R. I., May 26, 1675. English colonist in America, believed to have been the first white settler (c1623) at what is now Boston. He is said to have built a cabin on what was later named Beacon Hill.

Blackstone, Sir William. b. at London, July 10, 1723; d. there, Feb. 14, 1780. English teacher, judge, and writer on common law whose famous work, *Commentaries on the Laws of England* (4 vols., 1765–69), has exerted more influence than any other treatise on law in the English language. Of humble parentage and educated at Oxford and the Middle Temple, he attracted attention through his lectures on the common law at Oxford, where he subsequently held the first Vinerian professorship. His fame as a legal scholar led to a successful law practice in London and to election (1761) to Parliament, where he supported George III. In 1770 he was appointed to the Court of King's Bench and knighted. Most of his time as judge was devoted to appeals and he became an advocate of prison reform. The *Commentaries* rescued English common law from Latin and provided a convenient means for its transmission to the British colonies. Some 35 editions and numerous abridgments of the work have been published, and it has been translated into several foreign languages. The first American edition was published at Philadelphia (1771–72). For more than a century after Blackstone's death the *Commentaries* were widely read by law students, and they are still cited by courts and writers of legal history.

Blackstone River. River which rises in Worcester County, Massachusetts, and joins the Providence River near Providence, Rhode Island. Length, ab. 75 mi.

Black Thursday. Name commonly applied to Thursday, Oct. 24, 1929, when more than twelve million shares were sold on the New York Stock Exchange. The prices of virtually all stocks dropped sharply, and by Oct. 29 the stock-market crash of 1929 was an accomplished fact of disastrous proportions. By the end of that year the average value of stocks had dropped almost 50 percent (to the value of 15 billion dollars). The crash was the culmination of the feverish speculation in the stock market which reached its peak in the months after December, 1928. In the U.S. it is regarded as the abrupt termination of the boom of the 1920's, and as marking the threshold of the great depression of the 1930's.

Black Warrior. River in Alabama which joins the Tombigbee River near Demopolis. Length, ab. 178 mi.; navigable to Tuscaloosa.

Black Watch. Body of Scotch Highlanders employed by the English government to watch the Highlands in 1725, and enrolled as a regiment in the regular army in 1739. The adjectival epithet black is occasioned by their dark (but not actually black) tartan uniform.

Blackwater (blak′wô″tėr, -wot″ėr). [Also, in its upper course, **Pant.**] River in SE England, in N central Essex, winding SE into a tidal estuary ab. 15 mi. long bearing the same name. Length, ab. 40 mi.

Blackwater. River in Munster province, in the Irish Republic. It rises near the County Cork-County Kerry boundary and flows SE ab. 13 mi. along the boundary, then flows E across County Cork to the County Cork-County Waterford boundary ab. 22 mi. NE of Cork. It continues E across County Waterford to Cappoquin, thence flowing S into Youghal Harbour ab. 28 mi. E of Cork. It is the largest river in Munster province. Length, ab. 100 mi.

Blackwater. River in Ulster province, flowing mostly in Northern Ireland, but forming also ab. 10 mi. of the Irish Republic-Northern Ireland border, between County Tyrone in Northern Ireland, and County Monaghan in the Irish Republic. It rises in County Tyrone ab. 11 mi. SE of Omagh and flows generally E to the SW corner of Lough Neagh ab. 11 mi. NE of Armagh. Near here, on Aug. 14, 1598, the Irish defeated the English under Sir Nicholas Bagnal. Length, ab. 50 mi.

Blackwater, Battle of. Engagement (Dec. 18, 1861) in the American Civil War, between Union forces under Colonel J. C. Davis and Confederate elements under General Sterling Price, fought at the mouth of Clear Creek, near Milford, Mo. The Confederates were surrounded and defeated.

Blackwelder (blak'wel''dėr), **Eliot.** b. at Chicago, June 4, 1880—. American geologist. He received the degrees of A.B. (1901) and Ph.D. (1914) from the University of Chicago. After serving as a professor (1911–16) at the University of Wisconsin, he was professor of geology and department head at the University of Illinois (1916–19) and at Stanford (1922–45). Author of *Regional Geology of the United States* (1912); coauthor, with B. Willis, of *Research in China* (1906) and, with H. H. Barrows, of *Elements of Geology* (1911).

Blackwell (blak'wel). City in N Oklahoma, in Kay County, on the Chikaskia River, in an agricultural area. A marketing center for wheat, and a processing center for petroleum, zinc, and meat, it also manufactures glass, bricks, cheese, and cabinets. 9,199 (1950).

Blackwell, Alice Stone. b. at East Orange, N.J., Sept. 14, 1857; d. at Cambridge, Mass., March 15, 1950. American suffragette leader and editor; daughter of Lucy Stone and Henry Brown. She was a leader in the struggle which brought (1920) women the right to vote in U.S. elections. An editor of *Woman's Journal*, she also published collections of poetry from various countries.

Blackwell, Antoinette Louisa. [Maiden name, **Brown.**] b. at Henrietta, N.Y., May 20, 1825; d. Nov. 5, 1921. American prohibitionist, social reformer, and Congregationalist preacher. Appointed pastor (1852) of the Congregational Church at South Butler, N.Y., she resigned in 1854 and became a Unitarian. A delegate (1853) to the World's Temperance Convention at New York City, she was denied permission to speak. Author of *Shadows of Our Social System* (1855), *Studies in General Science* (1869), *A Market Woman* (1870), *The Making of the Universe* (1914), and *The Social Side of Mind and Action* (1915).

Blackwell, Elizabeth. b. at Bristol, England, Feb. 3, 1821; d. at Hastings, England, May 31, 1910. American physician, the first woman doctor of medicine in the modern era, and the first woman to obtain a medical diploma in the U.S. Her family emigrated to the U.S. in 1832. In 1849 she was graduated from the Geneva Medical College at Geneva, N.Y. After two years of study abroad she began the practice of medicine at New York City, opening (1853), with the help of her sister Emily, and others, a dispensary, the New York Infirmary for Women and Children, which in 1857 was incorporated as the New York Infirmary and College for Women. In 1869 she returned to England, where she was a professor of gynecology (1875–1907) at the London School of Medicine for Women. She was the author of numerous books and papers in the field of health and the education of the young.

Blackwell, Emily. b. at Bristol, England, 1826; d. at York Cliffs, Me., Sept. 8, 1910. American physician; sister of Elizabeth Blackwell, with whom in 1853 she founded the New York Infirmary for Women and Children, the first hospital for women in America. She was at first refused admission to several medical colleges, but finally was allowed to take her degree at Cleveland, after which she completed her medical studies at Edinburgh, Paris, and London, and returned to practice in America.

Blackwell, Henry Brown. b. at Bristol, England, May 4, 1825; d. Sept. 7, 1909. American editor and suffragist; brother of Elizabeth and Emily Blackwell, husband [of] Lucy Stone, and father of Alice Stone Blackwell. On t[he] day of their wedding (May 1, 1855), he and Lucy Sto[ne] published a joint condemnation of inequalities in [the] marriage law. He was associated (1869 *et seq.*) with [the] American Woman Suffrage Association, and edited (c18[..]) the Boston *Woman's Journal*.

Blackwell, Thomas. b. at Aberdeen, Scotland, 17[..]; d. at Edinburgh, 1757. Scottish classical scholar a[nd] educator. He took (1718) an M.A. degree at Marisc[hal] College, Aberdeen, where he later was professor of Gr[eek] (1723–57) and principal (1748–57). His chief works [are] *An Enquiry Into the Life and Writings of Homer* (17[..]) and *Memoirs of the Court of Augustus* (1753–55); the th[ird] volume of these memoirs was published posthumou[sly] (1764).

Blackwood (blak'wůd), **Adam.** b. at Dunfermline, Sc[ot]land, 1539; d. 1613. Scottish writer, and champion [of] Mary Stuart, Queen of Scots. He studied, taught, [and] wrote at Paris, dedicating (1612) a volume of La[tin] didactic poetry to Mary Stuart; during her captivity, [he] continued to pay her visits and homage. He publis[hed] *De Vinculo* (1575) and another work condemning heret[ics]. His work denouncing John Knox and Queen Elizabet[h of] England, *Martyre de la Royne d'Escosse, Douairiere [de] France*, was printed at Paris (1587) and Antwerp (1[...]) and 1589), and appears in Jebb's collection (1725); [he] also wrote eulogies of Charles IX of France and James [...] of Scotland, and pious prose and verse.

Blackwood, Algernon. b. in Kent, England, 18[..]; d. Dec. 10, 1951. English author known for tales of [the] weird and supernatural. Before he began (1906) his writ[ing] career, he was a farmer in Canada, operated a Toro[nto] hotel, was on the staff of the New York *Sun* and *Ti[mes]*, and worked in the dried-milk industry. Author of [*The*] *Empty House* (1906), *The Listener* (1907), *John Sile[nce]* (1908), *The Human Chord* (1910), *The Centaur* (19[..]), *The Wave* (1916), *The Bright Messenger* (1921), *The Fr[..]* *Stoners* (1934), *Shocks* (1935), and *The Doll and One O[..]* (1946).

Blackwood, Frederick Temple Hamilton-Tem[ple]. [Title, 1st Marquis of **Dufferin and Ava**; additi[onal] (earlier) title, Baron **Clandeboye.**] b. at Florence, J[une] 21, 1826; d. Feb. 12, 1902. English statesman and di[plo]mat, created marquis of Dufferin and Ava in 1888. [He] was governor general of Canada (1872–78), ambassa[dor] to Russia (1879–81), ambassador to Constantin[ople] (1881–18), governor general of India (1884–88), amba[ssa]dor to Italy (1888–91), and ambassador to France (18[..]–96). He published *Letters from High Latitudes* (18[..]), *Contributions to an Inquiry into the State of Ireland* (18[..]), *Irish Emigration and the Tenure of Land in Irel[and]* (1867), *Mill's Plan for the Pacification of Ireland Exam[ined]* (1868), *Speeches and Addresses* (1882), and others.

Blackwood, John. b. at Edinburgh, Dec. 7, 1818; d. [at] Strathtyrum, near St. Andrews, Scotland, Oct. 29, 1[..]. Scottish publisher who brought out the works of Ge[orge] Eliot; son of William Blackwood (1776–1834), and fri[end] of W. M. Thackeray. Manager (1840–45) of the Lon[don] branch of Blackwood's Edinburgh firm, he was su[bse]quently editor (1845–79) of *Blackwood's Magazine* [and] head (1852 *et seq.*) of Blackwood's, both of which w[ere] founded by his father. The first to recognize Ge[orge] Eliot's genius, he published (1857) her first work, *Sc[enes] of Clerical Life*, in his magazine. Until his death he [was] her friend, critic, and publisher.

Blackwood, William. b. at Edinburgh, Nov. 20, 1[..]; d. there, Sept. 16, 1834. Scottish publisher and bo[ok]seller; father of John Blackwood. He was the foun[der] (1817) and editor of *Blackwood's Edinburgh Magaz[ine]*, later *Blackwood's Magazine*, and founder (c1816) of [the] publishing firm of William Blackwood and Sons.

Bladen (blā'dẹn), **Frank Murcott.** b. at Hanley, ([now] part of Stoke-on-Trent), England, Dec. 23, 1858; d. 1[..]. Australian librarian, historian, and poet. Educated [at] Sydney University, New South Wales, where he [won] medals for English verse and prose compositions, he [was] head (1895–1905) of the New South Wales public lib[rary] and, later, chief state librarian. He was the autho[r of] *China*, a poem, and of authoritative works on Austra[lian] history, among them *The Growth and Development of [the]* *Australian Colonies and their Relation to the Mother C[ountry]* y, *European Archives, Peopling Australia,* and *Early* overnors *of Australia,* dealing with the period of settle-ent, 1762–1811; he also edited *Historical Records* (7 vols., 893–1901) of New South Wales.

adensburg (blā′dẹnz.bėrg). Village in Maryland, ab. mi. NE of Washington, D.C. Here, on Aug. 24, 1814, he English under General Robert Ross defeated the mericans. In the decade between the last two U.S. ensuses the population of this residential suburb more han doubled. 1,220 (1940); 2,899 (1950).

adud (blā′dud). Mythical British king, reputed founder the city of Bath, England.

aenavon (blīn.av′ọn). Urban district in W England, Monmouthshire, ab. 6 mi. NW of Pontypool, ab. 150 i. W of London by rail. It was a center of the iron dustry in the 19th century. 9,777 (1951).

aeu (blou), **Willem Janszoon.** b. at Amsterdam, 571; d. there, Oct. 21, 1638. Dutch geographer and artographer; a pupil and friend of Tycho Brahe. He ounded a publishing firm at Amsterdam which, while it rought out a variety of works in several fields, was est known for its geographical publications.

agoev (blä.gō′ef), **Dimitr.** b. at Zagorichane, Bulgaria; . 1924. Bulgarian socialist. A founder of the socialist ovement in Bulgaria, he was the leader of the Social-emocrat Party, and, after 1919, of the Communist arty. He was educated in Russia, and was the author of number of works popularizing Marxism.

agoveshchensk (blä.gọ.vyesh′chinsk). City in the .S.S.R., in the Bashkir *krai* (subdivision) of the Russian oviet Federated Socialist Republic, on the Amur River. Iachine construction and metalworking are important dustries. It is in the center of a grain-growing area. 3,761 (1939).

áha-Mikeš (blä′hä.mē′kesh), **Záboj.** b. at Prague, ov. 22, 1887—. Czech pianist and composer. Among is works are a setting for the *Song of Solomon,* piano ieces, and songs.

aich (blīċh), **Hans Erich.** [Pseudonym, **Dr. Owlglass.**] . at Leutkirch, Germany, January 19, 1873—. German uthor of light verse and tales, contributor (after 1896) , and editor (1912–24) of, the Munich periodical *Sim-icissimus.* His pseudonym (in German, "Doktor Eulen-ass") combines an allusion to his being a practicing hysician with an expression of his high esteem for Till ulenspiegel.

aikie (blā′ki), **William.** b. at York, N.Y., May 24, 843; d. at New York, Dec. 6, 1904. American lawyer, nd writer on physical training. He was graduated from arvard in 1866 and from the Harvard Law School in 868, and accompanied the Harvard crew to England 1869. He wrote *How to Get Strong and How to Stay So* .879), *Sound Bodies for Our Boys and Girls* (1883), and thers.

aine (blān), **James Gillespie.** b. at West Browns-lle, Pa., Jan. 31, 1830; d. at Washington, D.C., Jan. 27, 893. American statesman. He was a Republican mem-er of the House of Representatives (1863–76) and its peaker (1869–75), U.S. senator from Maine (1876–81), nd secretary of state (March 4–Dec. 19, 1881, and 1889–2). He was the unsuccessful Republican candidate for resident in 1884. In the course of his campaign for the residency, a New York clergyman made a speech in his ehalf, characterizing the Democratic Party as the party "rum, Romanism, and rebellion"; this speech lost laine many votes, particularly among the Irish residents the state of New York. Although he was still anxious r the Republican presidential nomination in 1888, he as persuaded at that time to make way for Benjamin arrison. Blaine's influence was most deeply felt in the eld of foreign policy, where as a brilliant, though not ways popular, secretary of state, he planned and pre-ded over the first Pan-American Congress, promoted e theory of reciprocity in tariffs, and advocated pro-ection of the Bering Sea seal-fishing grounds, securing treaty with Great Britain whereby the question of U.S. nd British rights was to be submitted to arbitration. e wrote *Twenty Years of Congress* (1884–86).

ainville (blaṅ.vēl), **Henri Marie Ducrotay de.** See **ucrotay de Blainville, Henri Marie.**

air (blãr). City in E Nebraska, county seat of Wash-gton County, on the Missouri River: marketing and canning center for corn. Dana College is nearby. 3,815 (1950).

Blair, Andrew George. b. at Fredericton, Canada, 1844; d. Jan. 25, 1907. Canadian statesman, remembered chiefly as chairman of the Railway Commission of 1904, appointed by act of Parliament. He also served (1903) as minister of railways and canals.

Blair, Austin. b. at Caroline, N.Y., Feb. 8, 1818; d. in Michigan, Aug. 6, 1894. American politician and governor (1860–65) of Michigan. A member of the Free-Soil Party, he participated (1854) in organizing the Republican Party. He led the Michigan delegation at the Chicago presidential convention (1860) that nominated Abraham Lincoln. After serving in Congress (1867–73), he was regent (1882–90) of the University of Michigan.

Blair, Eric. See **Orwell, George.**

Blair, Francis Preston. b. at Abingdon, Va., April 12, 1791; d. at Silver Spring, Md., Oct. 18, 1876. American journalist and politician; father of Francis Preston Blair (1821–75) and Montgomery Blair (1813–83). A graduate (1811) of Transylvania University, he studied law and was admitted (1817) to the bar. In the War of 1812, he served under George Madison, his uncle, who at that time was governor of Kentucky; subsequently he entered upon his political career in that state. With Amos Kendall, he became an editor of the *Argus of Western America* and the *Patriot,* for both of which he wrote political editorials. Many of these supported Andrew Jackson, who, in 1830, asked Blair to establish the *Globe* at Washington. From 1832 to 1841, the *Globe* was one of the chief supporters of the administration, and was extremely influential. He retired (1844) from the *Globe* at the insistence of Polk, whom he had opposed on the question of the annexation of Texas. Considering himself disillusioned in the Democratic Party, he was one of the organizers of the Republican Party; he supported Lincoln, and, after the latter's election, was one of his advisors. A participant in the Hampton Roads Conference, he rejoined the Democratic Party after Lincoln's death.

Blair, Francis Preston. b. at Lexington, Ky., Feb. 19, 1821; d. at St. Louis, Mo., July 9, 1875. American politician; son of Francis Preston Blair (1791–1876). He early contributed to his father's publication, the Washington *Globe,* and was graduated from Princeton in 1841. A graduate of the law school of Transylvania University, he settled at St. Louis in 1842. He served under George Bent in the Mexican War, and became attorney general for the new territory of New Mexico. A member of the Free-Soil Party, he organized it in the state of Kentucky and was its leader in Missouri in the election of 1848. In 1856 he was elected to Congress, where he proved himself an enemy of those advocating the extension of slavery. A supporter of Lincoln, he raised troops for, and took part in, the Civil War. From 1871 to 1873 he served in the U.S. Senate.

Blair, Henry William. b. at Campton, N.H., Dec. 6, 1834; d. March 14, 1920. American lawyer and political figure. He served as a U.S. congressman (1875 *et seq.*) and senator (1879–91).

Blair, Hugh. b. at Edinburgh, April 7, 1718; d. there, Dec. 27, 1800. Scottish Presbyterian divine and author. He was a lecturer on rhetoric and belles-lettres at Edinburgh in the period 1762–83. He wrote *Sermons* (1777), *Lectures on Rhetoric* (1783), and others.

Blair, James. b. in Scotland, 1655; d. in Virginia, April 18, 1743. American clergyman and educator. He was instrumental in founding William and Mary College (chartered in 1693), whose first president he became, entering formally on his duties in 1729. He was also president of the Virginia council from 1740 to 1741, and in this post served as acting governor of the colony.

Blair, John. b. at Edinburgh; d. June 24, 1782. Scottish chronologist. He published a *Chronological History of the World* (1754), was elected a fellow of the Royal Society in 1755, became mathematics tutor to the Duke of York in 1757, and held various ecclesiastical appointments.

Blair, John. b. at Williamsburg, Va., 1732; d. there, Aug. 31, 1800. American jurist. A representative (1776) to the constitutional convention of the Virginia commonwealth, he was elected (1778) a judge and, later, chief justice of the state general court; he also served (c1780) as judge of the first state court of appeals. He was a member of the Constitutional Convention of 1787, and served (1789–96) as associate justice of the U.S. Supreme Court.

Blair, John Insley. b. near Belvidere, N.J., Aug. 22, 1802; d. Dec. 2, 1899. American banker and railroad owner, associated with Oakes Ames (1804–73) in building the Union Pacific. He opened (1821) a merchandising business at Blairstown, N.J., and was the founder and president of the Belvidere National Bank. As president or stockholder in 20 railroads, he owned an interest in the largest mileage held by any individual in his day. At the beginning of the Civil War, he lent over one million dollars to the U.S. government.

Blair, Montgomery. b. in Franklin County, Ky., May 10, 1813; d. at Silver Spring, Md., July 27, 1883. American politician and lawyer; son of Francis Preston Blair (1791–1876). He served (1861–64) as postmaster general in Lincoln's cabinet. Previously he had made a name for himself as counsel for Dred Scott before the Supreme Court. He had also been mayor (1842–43) of St. Louis.

Blair, Robert. b. at Edinburgh, 1699; d. at Athelstaneford, East Lothian, Scotland, Feb. 4, 1746. Scottish clergyman and poet. His best-known poem is *The Grave* (1743), a lengthy work in blank verse. It was illustrated by William Blake.

Blairgowrie and Rattray (blãr.gou′ri; rat′rā). Municipal burgh in C Scotland, in Perthshire, situated on the river Ericht, ab. 9 mi. NE of Dunkeld, ab. 461 mi. N of London by rail. Fruit and flax are raised in the vicinity. 5,261 (est. 1948).

Blairsville (blãrz′vil). Borough in SW Pennsylvania, in Indiana County, on the Conemaugh River, in a coal and clay mining and stone-quarrying area. It has manufactures of enamelware and store fixtures, and railroad shops. It was settled in 1792. Pop. 5,000 (1950).

Blaisois (ble.zwȧ). See **Blois,** county.

Blaize or **Blaise** (blāz), Saint. See Saint **Blasius.**

Blake (blāk), **Cape.** Cape in Antarctica, lying ab. 4 mi. SW of Cape Wild on the George V Coast, in 68°22′ S., 148°58′ E. It was discovered in 1912 by the Australasian Antarctic Expedition (1911–14), under the leadership of Sir Douglas Mawson, who named this point for L. R. Blake, geologist and cartographer to the Macquarie Island party of the expedition.

Blake, Francis. b. at Needham, Mass., Dec. 25, 1850; d. at Weston, Mass., Jan. 19, 1913. American physicist, inventor (1878) of an early form of telephone transmitter.

Blake, Frederic Columbus. b. at Decatur, Ill., Oct. 30, 1877—. American physicist. He was graduated (Ph.D., 1905) from Columbia University, studied at Cambridge and Berlin, and in 1912 became full professor of physics at Ohio State University. He has conducted investigations in curved crystal spectrographs and x-ray diffraction.

Blake, George. b. at Greenock, Scotland, Oct. 28, 1893—. British novelist and journalist. He served as an editorial staff member of *John o' London's Weekly* (1924–28) and of the *Strand Magazine* (1928–30). His novels include *Vagabond Papers* (1922), *The Shipbuilders* (1935), *David and Joanna* (1936), *Late Harvest* (1938), *The Valiant Heart* (1940), *The Westering Sun* (1946), and *The Five Arches* (1947).

Blake, John Lauris. b. at Northwood, N.H., Dec. 21, 1788; d. at Orange, N.J., July 6, 1857. American Episcopal clergyman and writer of textbooks and reference books. He was rector of Saint Paul's Parish, Pawtucket, R.I. (1815–20), and Saint Matthew's, Boston (1824–32), and was editor (c1824 *et seq.*) of the *Gospel Advocate.* Author of *General Biographical Dictionary* (1835), *A Family Encyclopedia of Useful Knowledge* (1852), and *A Family Text-Book for the Country, or the Farmer at Home, Being a Cyclopaedia of the More Important Topics in Modern Agriculture* (1853).

Blake, Lillie. [Maiden name, **Devereux.**] b. at Raleigh, N.C., Aug. 12, 1835; d. Dec. 30, 1913. American suffragist, novelist, and publicist. President of the New York State Woman's Suffrage Association, she was the founder (1900) of the National Legislative League, and was president (1886–1900) of the New York City Suffrage League. Author of the novel *Fettered for Life, or Lord and Master* (1874) and the lecture series *Woman's Place Today* (1883).

Blake, Lyman Reed. b. at South Abington, Mass., Aug. 24, 1835; d. Oct. 5, 1883. American inventor and pioneer in the field of modern shoe manufacture. [He] patented (1858) what is known as the McKay mach[ine] for sewing soles of shoes to uppers, essentially the mod[ern] process.

Blake, Mary Elizabeth McGrath. b. at Dungarv[an,] Ireland, Sept. 1, 1840; d. at Boston, Feb. 26, 1907. Am[er]ican poet and writer. She wrote the poetry collecti[ons] *Poems* (1882), *The Merry Months All* (1885), *Youth* [in] *Twelve Centuries* (1886), *Verses along the Way* (18[90]) and *In the Harbour of Hope* (1907); her other works incl[ude] the travel books *On the Wing* (1883) and *A Sum[mer] Holiday in Europe* (1890), and the antimilitarist pampl[et] *The Coming Reform* (1887).

Blake, Robert. b. at Bridgewater, Somersetshire, E[ng]land, in August, 1599; d. at sea near Plymouth, Engla[nd,] Aug. 17, 1657. English admiral. He held Taunton agai[nst] the Royalists for the Parliamentarians in the per[iod] 1644–45. As commander of the British fleet (1649 *et se[q.]*) he chased Prince Rupert's fleet to the Mediterrane[an,] where he destroyed the bulk of it. He was made war[den] of the Cinque Ports in 1651, commanded against [the] Dutch in the period 1652–53 (defeating De Witt, De R[uy]ter, and Tromp, and thereby ending Dutch claims [to] naval supremacy), commanded in the Mediterranean [in] the period 1654–56, and defeated the Spaniards off Sa[nta] Cruz, on Tenerife, in the Canary Islands, on April [20,] 1657.

Blake, William. b. at London, Nov. 28, 1757; d. [at] London, Aug. 12, 1827. English poet, engraver, pain[ter,] and mystic. His works are noted for their lyrical [and] metaphysical power. Many of them are based on a myt[ho]logical structure evolved by Blake. Apprenticed (1771) [as] an engraver, he later illustrated his own works w[ith] copperplate engravings colored by hand. He was [the] author of *Poetical Sketches by W.B.* (1783), *Songs [of] Innocence* (1789), *Songs of Experience* (1794), and [the] so-called "Prophetical Books," including *The Book of T[hel]* (1789), *The Marriage of Heaven and Hell* (1790), *[The] Gates of Paradise* (1793), *The Vision of the Daughters [of] Albion* (1793), and *The Song of Los* (1795); he also wr[ote] *Jerusalem* (1804), *The Emanation of the Giant Alb[ion]* (1804), and *Milton* (1804). He illustrated works by M[ary] Wollstonecraft (1791), Edward Young's *Night Thou[ghts]* (1793–1800), Robert Blair's *The Grave* (1805), and [the] Book of Job (1826).

Blake, William Phipps. b. at New York, June 21, 18[33;] d. May 22, 1910. American mineralogist and geolog[ist.] He edited (1859–60) the *Mining Magazine,* which [he] changed to the *Mining Magazine and Journal of Geol[ogy,] Mineralogy and Metallurgy, Chemistry and the Arts.* [Em]ployed (1861–63) as a mining engineer by the Japan[ese] government, he was later appointed (1873) U.S. comm[is]sioner to the Vienna International Exposition, and sup[er]vised a government exhibit at the Philadelphia Centen[nial] Exposition (1876), the exhibit becoming the basis of [the] New National Museum's collections begun in 1870.

Blake, William Rufus. b. at Halifax, Nova Sco[tia,] Canada, 1805; d. at Boston, Mass., April 22, 1863. Am[er]ican actor and manager. He went on the stage c18[..] and first appeared at New York in 1824. He excelled [in] the portrayal of old men.

Blakelock (blāk′lok), **Ralph Albert.** b. at New Yo[rk,] Oct. 15, 1847; d. Aug. 9, 1919. American landsc[ape] painter. He was destined for the medical profession, [but] became instead an artist and musician, largely self-taug[ht.] He traveled in the Far West and embodied his study [of] Indian life in his work. The National Academy of Des[ign] elected him to full membership in 1916. His paintin[gs,] many of which are of moonlit scenes, are rich in li[ght] and shadow contrasts and in color, and romantic in feeli[ng.] *Sunset, Canoe Builders,* and *Moonrise,* at the Natio[nal] Gallery, Washington, D.C., *Colorado Plains,* at the C[or]coran Gallery, Washington, D.C., and *From St. Ives[,] Lelant,* at the St. Louis Museum, are among his works.

Blakely (blāk′li). City in SW Georgia, county seat [of] Early County. It has sawmills, and is a marketing po[int] for lumber. Peanuts are raised in the vicinity. 3,234 (195[0]).

Blakely. Borough in NE Pennsylvania, in Lackawan[na] County, on the Lackawanna River, ab. 5 mi. NE [of] Scranton, in an anthracite coal area; residential suburb [of] Scranton. 6,828 (1950).

Blakely, Johnston. b. near Seaford, Ireland, in October, 1781; lost at sea, in October, 1814. American naval officer. During the War of 1812 he served in the Mediterranean squadron aboard the vessels *President*, *John Adams*, and *Congress*. Commander (1811–13) of the brig *Enterprise*, which captured the schooner *Fly*, he also commanded (1813–14) the sloop of war *Wasp*, which sank the brigs *Reindeer* and *Avon* during separate engagements, and captured the brig *Atalanta*. After October, 1814, he was reported missing with his ship on which he had been serving as captain.

Blakeney (blāk′ni), **William.** [Title, Baron **Blakeney.**] b. at Mount Blakeney, County Limerick, Ireland, 1672; d. Sept. 20, 1761. British military commander. He became (1747) lieutenant governor of Minorca; failing to receive reinforcements from George Byng, the admiral who was sent to his relief, he was compelled to surrender the island to the French in 1756.

Blakeslee (blāks′lē), **Albert Francis.** b. at Geneseo, N.Y., Nov. 9, 1874—. American botanist. A graduate of Wesleyan University, Conn. (1896) and Harvard University (1904), he served as professor of botany at Connecticut Agricultural College (1907–15) and Smith College (1942–43). In 1912 he became a member of the Carnegie Station for Experimental Evolution, at Cold Spring Harbor, N.Y., and for a time (1936–41) was director of the department of plant genetics there. Author of *Sexual Reproduction in the Mucorineae* (1904); coauthor, with C. D. Jarvis, of *New England Trees in Winter* (1911) and *Trees in Winter* (1913).

Blakeslee, George Hubbard. b. at Geneseo, N.Y., Aug. 27, 1871—. American university professor, and authority on international affairs. A graduate of Wesleyan University, Conn. (1893) and Harvard (1903), he served as professor (1933–43) of diplomacy and international politics at the Fletcher School of Law and Diplomacy, professor of history and international relations at Clark University, and consultant (1942–43) to the U.S. state department; he held a military rank in the period 1943–45. Author of *The Recent Foreign Policy of the United States* (1925), *The Pacific Area—An International Survey* (1929), and *Conflicts of Policy in the Far East* (1934).

Blakey (blā′ki), **Robert.** b. at Morpeth, Northumberland, England, May 18, 1795; d. Oct. 26, 1878. English philosopher and miscellaneous writer. He was professor of logic and metaphysics at Queen's College, Belfast, and wrote *History of the Philosophy of Mind* (1848), books on angling, and others.

Blameless Prince, The. Narrative poem (1869) by Edmund C. Stedman. It is a Tennysonian tale of the secret love of a prince for a lady of lesser degree.

Blamey (blā′mi), Sir **Thomas Albert.** b. at Wagga, Australia, Jan. 24, 1884; d. May 27, 1951. Australian soldier. In World War I he rose to the rank of brigadier general on the staff, and chief of staff, serving with the Australian Imperial Forces at Gallipoli and in France. He was the Australian military representative at London (1922–24), chief commissioner of police in Victoria (1925–36), aide-de-camp to the governor general of Australia (1927–31), commander of the third division Australian forces (1931–37), controller-general of the recruiting secretariat (1938), and chairman of the manpower committee (1939). In World War II he served as deputy commander in chief in the Middle East (1939–42); later in the war he held the posts of commander in chief of the Australian military forces, and commander of the Allied land forces in the SW Pacific (1942–45). He was knighted in 1935 and made a baron in 1950.

Blamire (blą.mīr′), **Susanna.** [Called the **"Muse of Cumberland."**] b. at Cardew Hall, near Carlisle, Cumberland, England; d. at Carlisle, April 5, 1794. English poet and song writer. Her poems and songs appeared, unsigned, in various magazines; no collection of her work appeared until almost half a century after her death, when Henry Lonsdale, a Carlisle physician and man of letters, publisher her *Poetical Works* (1842). Her first poem, *Written in a Churchyard on Seeing a Number of Cattle Grazing in It*, composed when she was 19, shows the influence of Thomas Gray. *Stoklewath, or the Cumbrian Village* is suggestive of Oliver Goldsmith's *Deserted Village*. Her *Epistle to Friends at Gartmore* is a picture of the simple life she led with her aunt and of her physical suffering from rheumatic attacks. *What Ails this Heart o'Mine?*, *The Nabob*, *And Ye Shall Walk in Silk Attire*, *The Traveller's Return*, and *The Waefu' Heart*, all in Scottish dialect, are regarded as some of her loveliest songs.

Blanc (bläṅ), **Anthony.** b. near Lyons, France, Oct. 11, 1792; d. June 20, 1860. Roman Catholic prelate, bishop of New Orleans (1835–50), and its first archbishop (1850–60).

Blanc, Auguste Alexandre Philippe Charles. b. at Castres, Tarn, France, Nov. 15, 1813; d. at Paris, Jan. 17, 1882. French art critic; brother of Louis Blanc. He wrote *Grammaire des arts du dessin* (1867) and other works, and was the chief contributor to *Histoire des peintres de toutes les écoles* (1849–76).

Blanc (blängk, blangk; French, bläṅ), **Cape.** [Also: **Cape Blanco**; French, **Cap Blanc.**] Headland in W Africa, on the Atlantic coast at the NW corner of Mauritania, French West Africa, and the SW corner of Rio de Oro, Spanish Sahara.

Blanc (bläṅ), **Le.** See **Le Blanc.**

Blanc, Louis. [Full name, **Jean Joseph Charles Louis Blanc.**] b. at Madrid, Oct. 29, 1811; d. at Cannes, France, Dec. 6, 1882. French politician, historian, political writer, and socialist, prominent in the revolution of 1848; brother of Auguste Alexandre Philippe Charles Blanc. He studied law at Paris, and from 1832 to 1834 was a private tutor at Arras, France. On his return to Paris he wrote for newspapers, including the *National*, the *Revue républicaine*, and the *Nouvelle Minerve*. He became (January, 1837), editor of the *Bon sens* and after 18 months founded a new organ, *La Revue du progrès*, in which appeared his review of the *Idées napoléoniennes* of Louis Napoleon, and his own *L'Organisation du travail* (1840). He also wrote an account of the decade 1830–40 entitled *Histoire de dix ans* (5 vols., 1841 *et seq.*), and began his 12-volume *Histoire de la révolution*, the first two volumes of which appeared in 1847. In 1848 he became a member of the provisional government of the French Republic. He advocated state socialism, and introduced such measures as the establishment of social workshops, where workers would be supported by the state; this was in line with the socialist policy already outlined in his work of 1840. However, his written attacks on Louis Philippe turned the people against him and he was forced to seek refuge in England, where he wrote *Appel aux honnêtes gens* (1849), *Pages de l'histoire de la révolution de Février 1848* (1850), and a couple of polemic pamphlets entitled *Plus de Girondins* (1851) and *La République une et indivisible* (1851). He ended his history of the revolution with the dissolution of the National Convention, and issued the 12th and final volume of the work in 1862. His *Historical Revelations ascribed to Lord Normanby* were written originally in English, but translated by the author into French under the title *Histoire de la révolution de 1848* (1870). From 1857 to 1870 Blanc wrote a weekly letter, at first to the *Courier de Paris*, and afterward to the *Temps*. These articles on the political and parliamentary life of Great Britain were later collected in ten volumes entitled *Dix années de l'histoire d'Angleterre* (1879–81). In 1870 he returned to France and took part in several political assemblies. In 1876 he founded and directed a daily journal, *L'Homme libre*. His articles from this paper and from the *Rappel* fill five volumes entitled *Questions d'aujourd'hui et de demain* (1873–84).

Blanc, Marie Thérèse. [Pseudonym, **Thérèse Bentzon**; maiden name, **de Solms.**] b. at Seine-Port, Seine-et-Marne, France, Sept. 21, 1840; d. Feb. 5, 1907. French novelist, journalist, and critic. She was for a number of years on the staff of the *Revue politique et littéraire* (*Revue bleue*) and the *Revue des deux mondes*. She wrote many novels, among them *Un Remords* (1878) and *Tony* (1884), both of which were awarded prizes by the French Academy; a number of her contributions to the *Revue des deux mondes* were collected and published under the titles *Nouveaux romanciers américains* (1885), *Littérature et moeurs étrangères* (1887), and *Les Américaines chez elles* (1895).

Blanc, Mont. [Italian, **Monte Bianco**; Latin, **Mons Albus.**] Highest mountain of the Alps, situated on the frontier of France (department of Haute-Savoie) and Italy (Piedmont). The summit is crossed by the French-

Italian boundary line. The Mont Blanc massif is sometimes classed with the Pennine Alps, but more generally as a group by itself. The mountain was first ascended in 1786. A French observatory was erected on its summit in 1893. Its largest glacier is the Mer de Glace, and the valley of Chamonix is at its foot. 15,781 ft.

Blanca Peak (blang'kạ). [Also, **Mount Blanca.**] Peak in S Colorado ab. 70 mi. SW of Pueblo. It is the highest point in the Sangre de Cristo Mountains, and consists of a twin jagged peak rising abruptly from the floor of San Luis valley. 14,363 ft.

Blanch (blanch), **Arnold.** b. at Mantorville, Minn., June 4, 1896—. American painter, etcher, lithographer, illustrator, and author. He gained his art education partly at the Arts Students League of New York and the Minnesota School of Art, and has exhibited extensively in the U.S. He has taught at the Art Students League, the Colorado Springs Fine Arts Center, and the California School of Fine Arts. His awards have included a Guggenheim Fellowship (1933), and examples of his work are in the Metropolitan Museum of Art, New York, the Whitney Museum of American Art, New York, the Palace of the Legion of Honor, San Francisco, and elsewhere. He has also done murals for several U.S. post offices (Norwalk, Conn., Fredonia, N.Y., and Columbus, Wis.). Among his books are *Gouache* and *The Humboldt River*. A list of his paintings includes *Carolina Low Country, Man and Wife, Midsummer Landscape, Little Girl, Miss Columbine, Painter of Birds, Legend,* and *People.*

Blanchan (blan'chän), **Neltje.** Pseudonym of **Doubleday, Neltje.**

Blanchard (blän.shär), **Alain.** d. 1418. French citizen of Rouen, who played a prominent part in the defense of that city during the siege (1418) by Henry V of England. After the capitulation of the city, he was executed by the order of Henry.

Blanchard (blan'chạrd), **Amy Ella.** b. at Baltimore, 1856; d. on Bailey Island, Me., July 5, 1926. American writer, mainly of novels for younger readers. Her works include *An Independent Daughter* (1898), *Kittyboys' Christmas* (1898), *A Girl of '76* (1898), *The Four Corners* (1906), *A Journey of Joy* (1908), *Elizabeth, Betsy and Bess* (1913), *Nancy First and Last* (1917), *The Awakening of Martha* (1923), *An Everyday Girl* (1924), and *The House That Jack Built* (1925).

Blanchard, Edward Litt Laman. b. at London, Dec. 11, 1820; d. there, Sept. 4, 1889. English journalist, dramatist, critic, novelist, and author of pantomimes, songs, and variety entertainments. He edited (1841) the *London Journal*, before establishing and editing (1845) *The Astrologer and Oracle of Destiny*. Author of travel and railway guides and of two novels, *Temple Bar* and *Brave Without a Destiny*, for 37 years he wrote pantomimes for Drury Lane and for other theaters at London and elsewhere; he was also engaged as a dramatic critic for the *Sunday Times*, the *Weekly Dispatch*, the *Illustrated Times*, the London *Figaro*, the *Observer*, and the *Daily Telegraph*.

Blanchard (blän.shär), **Émile.** b. at Paris, March 6, 1819; d. there, Feb. 10, 1900. French naturalist, especially noted as an entomologist. He was the author of many scientific works, including *Recherches sur l'organisation des vers* (1837), *Histoire naturelle des insectes orthoptères . . .* (1837–40), and *Histoire des insectes* (1843–45).

Blanchard, François. b. at Andelys, Eure, France, 1753; d. March 7, 1809. French aeronaut. His first balloon ascent was made in 1784, and in 1785, with John Jeffries, he crossed the English Channel from Dover to Calais in a balloon (the first crossing of the Channel by air). Later he visited the U.S. In all he made more than 50 ascents. He is sometimes credited with the invention of the parachute.

Blanchard, Henri Pierre Léon Pharamond. b. near Lyons, France, Feb. 27, 1805; d. at Paris, Jan. 19, 1874. French painter.

Blanchard (blan'chạrd), **Newton Crain.** b. in Rapides Parish, La., Jan. 29, 1849; d. June 22, 1922. American politician and lawyer. He was elected to six terms as a congressman from the fourth Louisiana district, and appointed (1893) to fill out an unexpired term in the U.S. Senate. He subsequently served (1897–1904) as associate justice of the Louisiana supreme court, and was elected (1904) to a four-year term as governor of Louisiana. At the outset of his career, he was charged by the federal government with intimidating Negroes who wished to vote, but was acquitted.

Blanchard, Samuel Laman. b. at Great Yarmouth, England, May 15, 1804; d. at London, Feb. 15, 1845. English poet and journalist. He was acting editor of the *Monthly Magazine* (1831), editor of *The True Sun* (1832), *The Constitutional* (1836), *The Court Journal* (1837), *The Courier* (1837–39), and other periodicals, and author of *Lyric Offerings* and *Sonnets*.

Blanchard, Thomas. b. at Sutton, Mass., June 24, 1788; d. at Boston, April 16, 1864. American inventor. He invented a machine for cutting and heading tacks by a single operation, and a lathe for turning irregular forms.

Blanche (blänsh), **August Theodor.** b. at Stockholm, Sept. 17, 1811; d. there, Nov. 30, 1868. Swedish poet, dramatist, and novelist.

Blanche (bläṅsh), **Jacques Émile.** b. at Paris, Feb. 1, 1861; d. 1942. French still-life painter and portraitist, who painted many notables of his day at Paris. A pupil of Henri Gervex, he was strongly influenced by the English masters of the 17th century. He was a regular contributor to the exhibitions of the Société Nationale from its earliest days; he won many prizes at Paris and London, and his works were acquired for collections at Brussels, Dieppe, Paris, Rouen, and elsewhere. He was made a commander of the Legion of Honor. Among his more important works are *The Painter Thaulow and his Family, Still Life, Flowers in a Vase*, and the portraits *The Artist's Mother, James Joyce*, and *Nijinski*.

Blanche Amory (blanch ā'mọ.ri). See **Amory, Blanche.**

Blanchelande (bläṅsh.läṅd), **Philibert François Roussel de.** b. at Dijon, France, 1735; d. at Paris, April 11, 1793. French general. In 1779 he was sent as a lieutenant colonel to the West Indies, and commanded at St. Vincent, where he repulsed an English attack. In 1790 he became acting governor of Haiti. He returned to France in 1792, and was executed by the revolutionary tribunal.

Blanche of Bourbon (blanch, bör'bọn; French, bläṅsh, bör.bôṅ). b. in France, c1338; d. at Medina Sidonia, Spain, 1361. French princess; daughter of Pierre, Duc de Bourbon, and wife of Pedro of Castile (Pedro the Cruel), by whom she was abandoned shortly after the marriage on a charge of infidelity, and imprisoned. Her death was ascribed to poisoning. Her fate produced a profound impression, and has furnished the subject matter for a number of poems.

Blanche of Castile (kas.tēl'). b. c1187; d. Dec. 1, 1252. Queen of France; daughter of Alfonso IX of Castile and Eleanor of England, and wife of Louis VIII of France. She acted as regent (1226–36) during the minority of her son Louis IX, and again (1248–52) during his absence on a crusade in the Holy Land.

Blanche of Devan (blanch; dev'ạn). Name of the demented Lowland bride in Sir Walter Scott's poem *The Lady of the Lake*.

Blanchet (bläṅ.she), **François Norbert.** b. Sept. 3, 1795; d. June 18, 1883. Catholic missionary in Canada and the American Far West. Ordained in 1819, he engaged in missionary work first in New Brunswick, next in the area of Montreal, and finally in the Columbia River region; in 1846 he was made an archbishop, with his seat at what is now Oregon City.

Blanc-Mesnil (bläṅ.mā.nēl), **Le.** See **Le Blanc-Mesnil.**

Blanco (bläng'kō), **Cape.** See **Blanc, Cape.**

Blanco, José Félix. b. in Venezuela, Sept. 24, 1782; d. at Caracas, Venezuela, Jan. 8, 1872. Venezuelan priest, soldier, statesman, and historian. He was one of the leaders in the revolution at Caracas on April 19, 1810, and was the first editor of the great historical work *Documentos para la historia de la vida publica del Libertador . . .*, which was published after his death (Caracas, 14 vols., 1875–77).

Blanco, Otilio Ulate. See **Ulate Blanco, Otilio.**

Blanco, Pedro. b. at Cochabamba, Bolivia, Oct. 19, 1795; shot at Sucre, Bolivia, in January, 1829. Bolivian army officer and president of Bolivia (1828). He served (1812) in the Spanish army, but transferred his sympathies to the successful revolutionary movement, and rose to general. In 1828 he succeeded Antonio José de Sucre as president of Bolivia, but was deposed by a revolution on Dec. 31 of the same year.

Blanco Encalada (eng.kä.lä'ᴛʜä), **Manuel.** b. at Buenos Aires, Sept. 5, 1790; d. at Santiago, Chile, Sept. 5, 1876. Chilean general and naval commander, who distinguished himself in the Chilean war for independence. In July, 1826, he was elected president of Chile, but resigned soon after. Made a general of the army, he led an unsuccessful invasion of Peru in 1837, and was allowed to retire only after signing a treaty of peace. The Chilean government annulled this treaty, and Blanco Encalada was court-martialed, but exonerated. He was intendant of Valparaíso in 1847, and minister to France in the period (1853–58).

Blanco Fombona (fōm.bō'nä), **Rufino.** b. at Caracas, Venezuela, 1874; d. 1944. Venezuelan modernist poet, novelist, political writer, critic, and publisher. Exiled (1910) for opposition to the regime of Juan Vicente Gómez, he held European consular posts under various Latin-American nations, and established (1915) a small publishing house at Madrid, before returning (1935) to Venezuela. He was a leader in the campaign for Spanish-American union against North American "tyranny." Author of *Cuentos americanos* (1904), *El hombre de hierro* (1907), *Tragedias grotescas* (1928), *El secreto de la felicidad* (1932), and others.

Blancos (bläng'kōs) or **Blanquillos** (bläng.kē'yōs). In Uruguayan history, the name given to one of the two major political parties into which Uruguayan politics were originally divided. It had its origin c1835, when the adherents of Manuel Oribe took the name of Blancos, and those of José Fructuoso Rivera that of Colorados. Both parties have had various leaders, and have differed, ostensibly at least, on many important questions. From 1842 to 1851 the Colorados held Montevideo (whence they were also known as the Defensa Party, or Partido de la Defensa), and the Blancos, under Oribe, kept the city in a state of continuous siege.

Blanco y Arenas (bläng'kō ē ä.rā'näs), **Ramón.** [Title, **Marqués de Peña Plata.**] b. at San Sebastián, Spain, c1832; d. April 4, 1906. Spanish general, governor general (1897–98) of Cuba, where he opposed the U.S. invasion. He fought in the Carlist war, served in Cuba during the rebellion of 1868 *et seq.*, and was captain-general of that island (1880–81), of Catalonia (1877–79, 1882, 1887–93), and of the Philippines (1894). He also took part in the Spanish conquest of Santo Domingo.

Bland (bland), **Edith Nesbit.** [Pen name, **E. Nesbit.**] b. at London, Aug. 19, 1858; d. May 4, 1924. English writer; wife of Hubert Bland. A founder (1883) of the Fellowship of New Life, a predecessor of the Fabian Society, she is now, however, chiefly remembered as a writer of books for children. Her original contribution was the use as characters in her books of realistic young people behaving like ordinary youngsters, in place of the previously traditional heroes or moral dummies. Author of *The Would-be Goods* (1901), *Five Children and It* (1902), *The Red House* (1903), and others.

Bland, Hubert. d. 1914. English socialist writer; husband of Edith Nesbit Bland.

Bland, John Otway Percy. b. at Whiteabbey, County Antrim, Ireland, Nov. 15, 1863—. English diplomat, journalist, and author. Educated in Switzerland, and at Trinity College, Dublin, he joined the Chinese imperial maritime customs in 1883, and, from that time until 1910, served in various diplomatic and commercial posts. He was a London *Times* correspondent at Shanghai (1897–1907) and at Peking (1907–10), before leaving China in 1910. Author of *Lays of Far Cathay* (1900), *Houseboat Days in China* (1902), *China under the Empress Dowager* (1910), *Annals and Memoirs of the Court of Peking* (1913), *Men, Manners, and Morals in South America* (1920), and *China, Japan and Korea* (1921). In 1917 he published the translation *The Schemes of the Kaiser* from the French of Juliette Adam's *Guillaume II.*

Bland, Richard. b. May 6, 1710; d. Oct. 26, 1776. American politician, who served as Virginia delegate to the First and Second Continental congresses. He was the author of *A Letter to the Clergy of Virginia* (1760), *The Colonel Dismounted, or the Rector Vindicated* (1764), and *An Inquiry into the Rights of the British Colonies* (1766).

Bland, Richard Parks. b. near Hartford, Ky., Aug. 19, 1835; d. near Lebanon, Mo., June 15, 1899. American politician. Admitted to the Utah bar in 1860, he was a Democratic member of the U.S. Congress from Missouri, 1873–95 and 1897–99. Throughout his congressional career he was a conspicuous champion of the free coinage of silver, and he was an author of the Bland-Allison Act (1878). In 1896 he was given considerable support in the early balloting for the Democratic presidential nomination, but the voting went finally to William Jennings Bryan (whom Bland loyally and vigorously, but in the end vainly, supported throughout the ensuing campaign).

Bland, Theodorick. b. in Prince George County, Va., March 21, 1742; d. at New York, June 1, 1790. American patriot. He joined the Continental army in 1777, was a delegate from Virginia to the Continental Congress in the period 1780–83, and was a representative (1789–90) from Virginia to the first Congress under the federal constitution. He left memoirs of the Revolutionary period, which were published (1840) under the title *The Bland Papers.*

Bland-Allison Act (bland'al'i.sọn). Act passed (1878) by the U.S. Congress, reëstablishing as legal tender the silver dollar containing 412½ grains troy of standard silver. Its special feature was a clause requiring the U.S. treasury to purchase every month, at the prevailing market price, not less than two million nor more than four million dollars' worth of silver bullion and to coin it into dollars. The bill introduced by Representative Richard Parks Bland of Missouri provided for free coinage, but an amendment sponsored by Senator W. B. Allison of Iowa incorporated the limited purchase feature. The act, which represented a compromise between the silver interests of the West and the gold-standard East, was unsatisfactory to both groups alike. It was vetoed by President Hayes, but passed over his veto. The act is important as a chapter in the quarter century of agitation for the free and unlimited coinage of silver which followed the demonetization of silver in 1873.

Blandamour (blan'dä.mör), **Sir.** Fickle and vainglorious knight, in Edmund Spenser's *The Faerie Queene.* He was defeated by Britomart, and won the false Florimel from Paridel.

Blandiman (blan'di.mạn). Attendant of Bellisant, in the early French romance *Valentine and Orson.*

Blandina (blan.dī'nạ), Saint. Female slave who, during a persecution of the Christians, was put to death at Lyons in 177. She is commemorated on June 2.

Blandrata (blän.drä'tä), **Giorgio.** [Also, **Biandrata.**] b. at Saluzzo, Italy, c1515; d. in Transylvania, c1588. Italian physician, now chiefly known as a propagator (especially in Poland and Transylvania) of anti-Trinitarian Protestant doctrines, and later (according to some sources) of Socinianism and Arianism. He was thrown into prison at Pavia by the Inquisition, but escaped to Geneva, where it is said he was finally forced to profess Calvinism (his anti-Trinitarianism was, of course, as much opposed by the Calvinists as by the Roman Catholics).

Bland-Sutton (bland'sut'ọn), Sir **John.** b. at Enfield Highway, Middlesex, England, April 21, 1855; d. at London, Dec. 20, 1936. English surgeon and author. In 1887 he was appointed a professor at the Royal College of Surgeons; he was also president of the Medical Society of London (1914) and of the Royal Society of Medicine (1919). Author of *Evolution and Disease* (1890), *Tumours, Innocent and Malignant* (1893), *Man and Beast in Eastern Ethiopia* (1911), *The Story of a Surgeon* (1930), and other works.

Blandy (blan'di), **William Henry Purnell.** b. at New York, June 28, 1890—. American naval officer. Commissioned an ensign (1913) after graduation from the U.S. Naval Academy, he advanced through the grades to reach (1947) the rank of admiral. He was chief (1941–43) of the navy ordnance bureau, commander (1944–45) of Amphibious Group One, and deputy chief of naval operations for special weapons (1945–46). He planned and commanded (1946) the Bikini atom-bomb tests before he was named (1947) commander in chief of the Atlantic fleet. After his retirement (1950) he became president of the Health Information Foundation.

Blane (blān), Sir **Gilbert.** b. at Blanefield, Ayrshire, Scotland, Sept. 8, 1749; d. at London, June 26, 1834. Scottish physician, known for the introduction of lime juice in the British navy as a method of preventing scurvy. He had the medical charge (1779–81) of the West Indian fleet under George Brydges, 1st Baron Rodney, and was later (1785) appointed physician extraordinary to the Prince of Wales. He was influential in putting sanitary measures for the navy into effect, and was the author of *Elements of Medical Logic* (1819) and others.

Blane, Niel. Popular landlord of the Howff, in Sir Walter Scott's novel *Old Mortality*. He is also town piper.

Blangini (blän.jē′nē), **Giuseppe Marco Maria Felice.** b. at Turin, Italy, Nov. 18, 1781; d. at Paris, Dec. 18, 1841. Italian tenor and composer of operatic works. He wrote *Chimère et réalité*, *Encore un tour de Caliphe*, *Romances* (in 34 numbers), and others.

Blankenberghe (blän′kẹn.ber.ċhẹ). [Also, **Blankenberge.**] Town in NW Belgium, in the province of West Flanders, situated on the North Sea, ab. 9 mi. NW of Bruges. A fashionable seaside resort, it also has a fishing port and a fishing fleet. It is connected with the Bruges-Ostende Canal. Occupied by the Germans in World Wars I and II, the town sustained considerable war damage. 8,344 (1946).

Blankenburg (blän′gkẹn.bu̇rk). Town in C Germany, in the *Land* (state) of Saxony-Anhalt, Russian Zone, situated in the Harz Mountains, ab. 9 mi. SW of Halberstadt: summer resort and center for excursions in the Harz Mountains. It has a large iron foundry, formerly belonging to the Bergbau A. G. Lothringen, and stone quarries, and trades in lumber and seeds. The *Rathaus* (town hall) and the Church of Saint Bartholomew date from the 13th century; above the town is the 18th-century castle of the former dukes of Brunswick. The population is predominantly Protestant. 18,445 (1946).

Blankenburg. [Also, **Bad Blankenburg.**] Town in C Germany, in the *Land* (state) of Thuringia, Russian Zone, situated on the Schwarza River in the Thuringian Mountains, ab. 21 mi. S of Weimar. A summer resort, it has sport facilities which formerly belonged to the *Verband der Turnerschaften* (athletic union) of the German universities; there are also sanitariums for nervous diseases. At Blankenburg Friedrich Froebel founded (1840) the first kindergarten. 6,601 (1946).

Blankenburg (blangk′ẹn.bėrg), **Rudolph.** [Called the **"Old War Horse of Reform"** and **"Old Dutch Cleanser."**] b. at Barntrup, Germany, Feb. 16, 1843; d. April 12, 1918. American businessman and one-time independent mayor of Philadelphia. Though a Republican in national affairs, he was successful in opposing the city and state Republican organizations and was the organizer of the Citizens' Permanent Relief Committee in the interest of public charity.

Blankenstein (bläng′kẹn.stīn), **Marcus van.** b. at Ouderkerk, the Netherlands, June 13, 1880—. Dutch journalist. Graduated (Litt.D., 1911) from the University of Leiden, he studied literature at Leiden, Copenhagen, and Berlin. After serving as a traveling correspondent for many Dutch and East Indian newspapers, he was editor (1940–46) of *Vrij Nederland* at London, and correspondent (1946 *et seq.*) for *Het Parool*.

Blanketeers (blang.kẹ.tirz′). Name given to a body of Manchester mill-workers who met at St. Peter's Field, Manchester, England, on March 10, 1817. Each man was provided with provisions and a blanket, and their purpose was to walk to London to petition for some legislative remedy against what they conceived to be the willful injustices imposed upon them by their employers, and also for the great panacea of parliamentary reform. The leaders of the group were seized and imprisoned, as were some of their followers. The marchers never reached London.

Blankfort (blangk′fọrt), **Michael.** b. at New York, Dec. 10, 1907—. American novelist and scenarist. He was graduated from the University of Pennsylvania and from Princeton, and served in the U.S. Marine Corps during World War II. Among the motion pictures for which he prepared scenarios are *Blind Alley*, *Adam Had Four Sons*, and *An Act of Murder*. His novels include *I Met A Man* (1937), *The Brave and the Blind* (1940), *A Time to Live* (1943), and *The Widow-Makers* (1946). He is also the author of *The Big Yankee* (1947), a biography of Evans F. Carlson.

Blank Verse. Collection of poems by Charles Lamb in collaboration with Charles Lloyd, a Quaker. This contains Lamb's best-known poem, "Old Familiar Faces," which in its gentle pathos and nostalgia for the past is characteristic of the author.

Blanqui (bläṅ.kē), **Jérôme Adolphe.** b. at Nice, France, Nov. 21, 1798; d. at Paris, Jan. 28, 1854. French political economist; brother of Louis Auguste Blanqui. His works include *L'Histoire de l'économie politique en Europe* (1837–38) and *Voyage en Angleterre* (1824).

Blanqui, Louis Auguste. b. at Puget-Théniers, Alpes-Maritimes, France, Feb. 7, 1805; d. at Paris, Jan. 1, 1881. French socialist and political agitator, believed to have been the originator of the phrase "dictatorship of the proletariat"; brother of Jérôme Adolphe Blanqui. He took part in the French insurrectionary movements of 1839, 1848, and 1871. Thirty-four of the 50 years he devoted to politics were spent in prison, including one term shortly before the announcement of the Commune of Paris, when Thiers had Blanqui imprisoned for his connection with it.

Blantyre (blan.tīr′). Town in Nyasaland protectorate, SE Africa, in the Shiré Highlands, ab. 355 mi. N of Beira, Mozambique, with which it is connected by rail. It is the chief commercial center in Nyasaland, and is the headquarters of several missionary societies. Pop. 4,459, including 379 Europeans (1945).

Blanzy (bläṅ.zē). Town in E central France, in the department of Saône-et-Loire, situated on the Bourbince River, ab. 19 mi. S of Autun. It is in the center of a coal-mining region; has glassworks and horse markets. The town was largely destroyed in World War II. 4,284 (1946).

Blarney (blär′ni). Town in Munster province, Irish Republic, in County Cork, situated on the Blarney stream, ab. 5 mi. NW of Cork. It contains a noted castle built in 1446 by Cormac McCarthy, and now forming a picturesque ivy-clad ruin centered about a high, square, battlemented and machicolated keep. The fame of the castle is due to its possession of the wonder-working Blarney Stone, a block bearing a Latin inscription that includes the name of the castle's builder and the date, originally built into the S angle of the keep ab. 20 ft. below the top. It is now possible for a tourist to kiss the stone by leaning head down over the parapet while someone holds his feet. An iron grating is provided as a safeguard. 723 (1936).

Blarney, Lady. In Oliver Goldsmith's *Vicar of Wakefield*, one of the two town ladies, or rather ladies of the town, who make the acquaintance of the vicar's innocent family under false pretenses. The other lady is named Miss Carolina Wilhelmina Skeggs.

Blarney Stone. See under **Blarney.**

Blaschke (bläsh′kẹ), **Wilhelm.** b. at Graz, Austria, Sept. 13, 1885—. German professor of mathematics. He took his doctorate at Vienna in 1908, and has taught at Bonn, Prague, Leipzig, Königsberg, Tübingen, Hamburg, and elsewhere. His most important work is *Vorlesungen über differential Geometrie* (3 vols., 1921–29).

Blasco Ibáñez (bläs′kō ē.ʙä′nyeth), **Vicente.** b. in Valencia, Spain, 1867; d. in exile in France, 1928. Spanish journalist, short-story writer, and novelist of the naturalistic school. As a result of his socialistic conspiracies and his written attacks on the Spanish monarchy, he suffered imprisonment and long years in exile. He was a prolific writer, whose novels have been widely translated; among them are *La Barraca* (1898), *Cañas y barro* (1902), *La Catedral* (1903; *The Shadow of the Cathedral*), *Sangre y arena* (1908; *Blood and Sand*), *Mare Nostrum* (1918). *Los Cuatro Jinetes del Apocalipsis* (1916; *The Four Horsemen of the Apocalypse*, 1918) won him international fame during World War I.

Blasdell (blaz′dẹl). Village in W New York, in Erie County ab. 6 mi. S of Buffalo. 3,127 (1950).

Blaserna (blä.zer′nä), **Pietro.** b. 1836; d. Feb. 26, 1918. Italian physicist and government official. He served as professor of experimental physics at the University of Rome, and was president of the Italian senate. Author of special studies on the conservation of force, acoustics, and the dynamic theory of heat.

Blashfield (blash′fēld), **Edwin Howland.** b. at New York, Dec. 15, 1848; d. Oct. 12, 1936. American painter. In 1867 he went to Paris and entered the atelier of Léon Bonnat, coming also under the influence of Jean Léon Gérôme and H. M. A. Chapu. He was especially successful in the execution of monumental decorations, among which are a dome in the Manufactures and Liberal Arts Building at the Chicago Exposition in 1893, the central dome of the Congressional Library in Washington, and a large picture in the state capitol, Des Moines, Iowa. He was a member of the National Academy of Design from 1888.

Blasius (blā′zi.us) or **Blaize** or **Blaise** (blāz), Saint. [Also, **Blase.**] A physician, and bishop of Sebaste, Armenia, martyred c316. He was adopted by the wool combers as their patron saint, apparently because iron combs were used in tearing his flesh when martyred. His festival is celebrated on Feb. 3 by the Roman and Anglican churches, and on Feb. 11 by the Greeks. The wool combers' procession is still held on Feb. 3 in England.

Blasius (blȧ.zyüs), **Docteur.** Pseudonym of **Grousset, Pascal.**

Blasket Islands (blȧs′kẹt). [Also: **Blasquet Islands, Ferriter Islands.**] Group of small, rocky islands in Munster province, Irish Republic, in County Kerry. They lie immediately offshore from Slea Head, in the Atlantic Ocean, ab. 10 mi. W of Dingle. The largest of the islands, Great Blasket, has an area of ab. 2 sq. mi.

Blass (bläs), **Friedrich.** b. at Osnabrück, Germany, Jan. 22, 1843; d. at Halle, Germany, March 6, 1907. German philologist, appointed (1892) professor of classical philology at Halle. He was especially distinguished for his studies of the Greek language and his work upon Greek texts.

Blas Urrea (bläs ör.rā′ä), **Lic.** Pseudonym of **Cabrera, Luis.**

Blatant Beast, The. In Edmund Spenser's *The Faerie Queene*, the personification of slander. He is a foul monster with a hundred tongues.

Blatch (blach), **Harriot.** [Maiden name, **Stanton.**] b. at Seneca Falls, N.Y., Jan. 20, 1856; d. at Greenwich, Conn., Nov. 20, 1940. American leader in the woman-suffrage movement; daughter of Elizabeth Cady Stanton (1815–1902). President (1907–15) of the Women's Political Union, she headed (1917) the speakers' bureau of the U.S. Food Administration. Author of *Mobilizing Woman Power* (1918), *A Woman's Point of View* (1919), and *Elizabeth Cady Stanton as Revealed in Her Reminiscenses, Letters and Diary* (1921).

Blatchford (blach′fọrd), **Robert.** b. at Maidstone, Kent, England, March 17, 1851; d. in Sussex, England, Dec. 17, 1943. English journalist, socialist, and author. A soldier (1871–78), and later a clerk at Northwich, he went into journalism, joining the staff of Bell's *Life* in 1884 and serving (1885–91) on the *Sunday Chronicle;* in 1891 he founded and edited *The Clarion*, which he published as a Socialist organ until World War I. He was the author of *God and My Neighbor* (1903), *Not Guilty: A Plea for the Bottom Dog* (1905), *My Life in the Army, Shadow Shapes*, and *My Eighty Years* (1931), but is best known for two propaganda works, *Merrie England*, which sold several million copies, both in England and the U.S., swelling the ranks of the Socialist movement, and *Britain for the British.* In 1910 he contributed several papers to the London *Daily Mail*, in which he was one of the first to call attention to the evil of German militarism and its danger to England.

Blatchford, Samuel. b. at New York, March 9, 1820; d. at Newport, R.I., July 7, 1893. American lawyer and jurist, who served (1882–93) on the U.S. Supreme Court. He founded (1854) the law firm of Blatchford, Seward, and Griswold, in which he became an expert in international and maritime law. Appointed (1867) a judge of the federal court of the southern district of New York, he was named (1872) a circuit judge for the second judicial district.

Blathers (blaᴛʜ′ėrz). Bow-street officer in Charles Dickens's *Oliver Twist.*

Blätter für die Kunst (blet′ėr für dē kůnst′). An esoteric German journal (1892–1919) devoted to the art of poetry, put out by Stefan George and his circle. Hugo von Hofmannsthal, Max Dauthendey, and others concerned with aestheticism were among its contributors. The title was obviously suggested by the French symbolist publication, *Écrits pour l'art.* Selections (*Auslese aus den Jahren 1892–1898; 1898–1904; 1904–1909*) were reprinted in 1929.

Blattergowl (blat′ėr.goul). Prosy Scotch minister, in Sir Walter Scott's novel *The Antiquary.*

Blaubart (blou′bärt). German name of **Bluebeard.**

Blaubeuren (blou′boi.rẹn). Town in S Germany, in the *Land* (state) of Württemberg-Baden, American Zone, formerly in the Danube *Kreis* (district) of Württemberg, situated on the Blau River, ab. 10 mi. W of Ulm. It has livestock markets, cement works, and metallurgical and leather manufactures; there are also various vocational institutions. The town grew around a convent founded in 1095, which was transformed into a Protestant school in 1534. The town church and the municipal hospital date from the 15th century, the town hall from the 16th century. 6,951 (1946).

Blauen (blou′ẹn). One of the chief summits of the Black Forest, in S Germany, near Müllheim. 3,830 ft.

Blaumanis (blou′mä.nēs), **Rudolfs.** b. in Latvia, Jan. 1, 1863; d. in Finland, Sept. 4, 1908. Latvian poet, playwright, short-story writer, and editor. He achieved a leading rank in Latvian literature with his masterly depiction (in 15 plays and some 50 stories) of the psychological conflicts and situations of contemporary Latvian farmers. He was for several years editor of *Zeitung für Stadt und Land*, and edited the Latvian progressive newspapers *Dienas Lapa* (1898–1901), *Peterburgas Awihzes* (1901–03), and *Latwija* (1906–08).

Blauvelt (blô.velt′), **Lillian Evans.** b. at New York, March 16, 1873—. American concert soprano. She studied under Jacques Bouhy at the National Conservatory at New York, and made her operatic debut (1893) at Brussels in *Mireille.* She sang with orchestras conducted by Walter Damrosch, Theodore Thomas, and Anton Seidl, sang (1899) before Queen Victoria, was soloist (1900) at the Handel Festival in the Crystal Palace, London, sang (1902) the Coronation Ode for Edward VII, and appeared (1903 *et seq.*) at Covent Garden.

Blavatsky (blạ.vat′ski), Madame **Helena Petrovna Hahn-Hahn.** [Often called **Madame Blavatsky.**] b. at Ekaterinoslav (now Dnepropetrovsk), Russia, 1831; d. at London, May 8, 1891. Russian theosophist and traveler in the U.S., the East and elsewhere; one of the chief founders at New York of the Theosophical Society in 1875. The daughter of a German nobleman and granddaughter of the Russian Princess Dolgorouki, she went to Tibet and to India, where she was active in exhibiting her alleged supernatural powers. These psychic demonstrations were deemed unsatisfactory by the Society for Psychical Research. She wrote *Isis Unveiled* (1876), *The Secret Doctrine* (1888), *Key to Theosophy* (1889), and others.

Blavia (blā′vi.ạ). Latin name of **Blaye.**

Blaydon (blā′dọn). [Also **Blaydon-on-Tyne.**] Urban district and manufacturing town in NE England, in Durham, situated on the river Tyne, ab. 5 mi. W of Newcastle, ab. 273 mi. N of London by rail: iron, steel, and bricks are manufactured. 30,791 (1951).

Blaye (blȧy′). [Also, **Blaye-Ste.-Luce** (blȧy′.saṅt.lüs); Latin, **Blavia.**] Town and river port in SW France, in the department of Gironde, situated on the right bank of the Gironde River, ab. 21 mi. NW of Bordeaux. It is the center of a wine-making region. The town suffered damage from aerial bombardment in the late stages of World War II. 3,788 (1946).

Blaze (blȧz), **François Henri Joseph.** [Called **Castil-Blaze.**] b. at Cavaillon, France, Dec. 1, 1784; d. at Paris, Dec. 11, 1857. French writer on music, music critic, and operatic composer; father of Blaze de Bury. From 1822 to 1832 he was music critic of the *Journal des Débats.* He wrote *De l'opéra en France* (1820) and others.

Blaze de Bury (dẹ bü.rē). [Original name, **Ange Henri Blaze;** pseudonyms, **Henri Blaze, F. de Lagenevais, Hans Werner.**] b. at Avignon, France, May 17, 1813; d. at Paris, March 15, 1888. French author; son of François Henri Joseph Blaze. He wrote for the *Revue des Deux Mondes*, and later lived for some time at the court of Weimar. His works include *Écrivains et poètes de l'Allemagne* (1843) and *Les Poésies de Goethe* (1843).

Blazed Trail, The. Novel (1902) by Stewart Edward White.

Bleak House. Novel by Charles Dickens, published in the period 1852–53 in 20 monthly numbers. It was named from a dreary-looking house which was his summer residence at Broadstairs. It was aimed at the delays of the

Court of Chancery, and is generally considered one of the most impressive of Victorian novels.

Blease (blēs), **Coleman Livingston.** b. in Newberry County, S.C., Oct. 8, 1868; d. Jan. 19, 1942. American politician and lawyer. He served as a representative (1890–98) in the South Carolina legislature, state senator (1904–08), governor (1911–15) of South Carolina, and a member (1925–31) of the U.S. Senate.

Blech (blech), **Leo.** b. at Aix-la-Chapelle (now Aachen, Germany), April 21, 1871—. German conductor and composer. He studied under Woldemar Bargiel at the Hochschule für Musik at Berlin, and from 1895 to 1898 studied intermittently with Engelbert Humperdinck. Appointed (1899) first *Kapellmeister* (meaning, in this use, director of the chorus, rather than choir leader in the ordinary American sense) of the German *Landestheater* (national theater); he was made (1906) *Kapellmeister* of the Berlin Opera, where he became general musical director in 1913. His works include the operas *Das War Ich* (1902) and *Cinderella* (1905). He also composed three symphonic poems, choral works, and songs.

Bled (bled). [German, **Veldes.**] Village and spa in NW Yugoslavia, in the federative unit of Slovenia, in the former *banovina* (province) of Dravska, situated on the E bank of the Lake of Bled in beautiful Alpine surroundings. It is a railroad junction and a summer resort, and has thermal springs. The Yugoslav royal family used to spend its summers here. 2,753 (1931).

Bledisloe (bled'is.lō), 1st Viscount. [Title of Sir **Charles Bathurst.**] b. Sept. 21, 1867—. British statesman. A barrister (1894–1910) and member (1910–18) of Parliament, he served as parliamentary secretary (1924–28) in the ministry of agriculture. After having been governor general and commander in chief (1930–35) of New Zealand, he was president (1937–45) of the "Empire Day" movement.

Bledow (blā'dō), **Ludwig.** b. July 27, 1795; d. at Berlin, Aug. 6, 1846. German chess player, founder (1837) of the so-called Berlin chess school. His collection of works on chess was purchased by the Royal Library of Berlin.

Bledsoe (bled'sō), **Albert Taylor.** b. Nov. 9, 1809; d. at Alexandria, Va., Dec. 8, 1877. American editor, author, and official in the Confederate government, known for his stand against industrialism and the democratic theories of Thomas Jefferson. A graduate (1830) of the U.S. Military Academy, he was professor of mathematics at the University of Mississippi (1848–54) and at the University of Virginia (1854–61). Appointed assistant secretary of war in the Confederate government, he later (1867) founded and edited the *Southern Review*, which he used as a vehicle for the glorification of the Confederate cause. Author of *Is Davis a Traitor?, or Was Secession a Constitutional Right Previous to the War of 1861?* (1866) and others.

Bleeding-heart Yard. Name applied to a part of London not far distant from the lower end of Fleet Street. It was once the property of the family of Sir Christopher Hatton, a member of the government under Queen Elizabeth. About the origin of its title there are various traditions. It was introduced by Charles Dickens in *Little Dorrit* as the residence of the Plornishes, Daniel Doyce, and others.

Bleek (blāk), **Friedrich.** b. at Ahrensbök, Germany, July 4, 1793; d. at Bonn, Germany, Feb. 27, 1859. German Biblical critic. He served (1829–59) as professor of theology at Bonn.

Bleek, Wilhelm Heinrich Immanuel. b. at Berlin, March 8, 1827; d. at Capetown, South Africa, Aug. 17, 1875. German linguist, noted for his work on African languages. He went to Natal, South Africa, in 1855, and in 1856 to Capetown, where he was appointed librarian of Sir George Grey's library. In this capacity he wrote *Catalogue of Sir George Grey's Library* (3 vols., 1858–63), *Hottentot Fables* (1864), and *Comparative Grammar of South African Languages* (1862–69). He died while working on a dictionary of the Bushman language.

Blefuscu (ble.fus'kū). Island described in Jonathan Swift's *Gulliver's Travels*. It was separated from Lilliput by a channel, and was intended to satirize France. The inhabitants were pygmies, like those of Lilliput. Gulliver waded across the channel and carried off the entire fleet of Blefuscu.

Blei (blī), **Franz.** b. at Vienna, Jan. 18, 1871—. Austrian writer living in Germany, especially effective in his essays on German literature.

Bleibtreu (blīp'troi), **Georg.** b. at Xanten, Rhenish Prussia, March 27, 1828; d. at Berlin, Oct. 16, 1892. German painter of battle scenes. His chief paintings include *Battle of Katzbach* (1857) and *Battle of Waterloo* (1858).

Bleibtreu, Karl. b. at Berlin, Jan. 13, 1859; d. at Locarno, Switzerland, 1928. German critic, novelist, and journalist; son of Georg Bleibtreu.

Blekinge (blā'king.e). *Län* (county) in S Sweden. Capital, Karlskrona; area, 1,173 sq. mi.; pop. 145,664 (1950).

Blemyes or **Blemmyes** (blem'i.ēz). In ancient history, a nomadic Ethiopian tribe, inhabiting Nubia and Upper Egypt. They were frequently at war with the Romans, and were defeated under Aurelian, Probus, and Diocletian. They were the subjects of fabulous accounts by early writers, who represented them as headless and as having their eyes, noses, and mouths in their breasts.

Bléneau (blā.nō), **Battle of.** Victory (1652) gained at Bléneau (in the department of Yonne, France) by the Spaniards under Condé over Turenne. In another battle on the next day Turenne gained the advantage.

Blenerhasset (blen.ėr.has'et), **Thomas.** b. c1550; d. c1625. English poet and historian. His best-known work is *The Second Parte of the Mirrour for Magistrates* (1578).

Blenheim (blen'im). [German, **Blindheim.**] Village in S Germany, in the *Land* (state) of Bavaria, American Zone, situated on the Danube River, ab. 23 mi. NW of Augsburg. Near here, on Aug. 13, 1704, the allied English, Germans, Dutch, and Danes, under John Churchill, the 1st Duke of Marlborough, and Prince Eugene of Savoy, defeated the French and Bavarians under Marshal Tallard and the prince-elector Max Emanuel of Bavaria. The battle is called by French and Germans the battle of Höchstädt. It is the subject of Robert Southey's poem *The Battle of Blenheim*. 969 (1946).

Blenheim. Historical work by George Macaulay Trevelyan, published in 1930. It is the first part of his three-volume *England under Queen Anne* (1930–34; the other two are *Ramelies and the Union with Scotland* and *The Peace and the Protestant Succession*); the work as a whole is now generally recognized as one of the standard references for English history in that period.

Blenheim, The Battle of. See **Battle of Blenheim, The.**

Blenheim Palace. Palladian mansion at Woodstock, Oxfordshire, England, built for John Churchill, the 1st Duke of Marlborough, by John Vanbrugh at the national expense in the period 1705–16. Located on an estate given by Queen Anne to the victor of the Battle of Blenheim, it measures ab. 320 ft. east and west, and ab. 190 ft. north and south. The chief façade presents a projecting entrance-portico between two prominent wings, whose inner faces sweep in a curve toward the entrance. The columns are so large as almost to dwarf even the enormous building. The park façade and the two lesser façades are of interest; each has a large bow-window in the middle, and is flanked by end pavilions. The interior has many large rooms.

Blenheim Park. Estate in S central England, in C Oxfordshire, at Woodstock, ab. 8 mi. NW of Oxford. It was given by the English government to John Churchill, the 1st Duke of Marlborough, for his victory at Blenheim. It is the site of Blenheim Palace. Area of park, ab. 2,700 acres.

Blenk (blengk), **James Hubert.** b. at Neustadt, Bavaria, July 28, 1856; d. April 20, 1917. American Catholic clergyman who became (1906) archbishop of New Orleans. He served as president (1891) of Jefferson College, La., and was named (1899) bishop of Puerto Rico.

Blenkinsop (bleng'kin.sop), **John.** b. near Leeds, England, 1783; d. at Leeds, Jan. 22, 1831. English pioneer in locomotive engineering, remembered chiefly for his improvement on Richard Trevithick's locomotive by combining its mechanism with a new plan intended to overcome the presumed difficulty of securing adhesion between the engine wheels and rails. The result was the first commercially successful engine on the rails. It was on Blenkinsop's pattern that George Stephenson, the railway engineer, built his first locomotive.

Blennerhasset or **Blennerhassett** (blen.ėr.has′ẹt), **Harman.** b. in Hampshire, England, Oct. 8, 1765; d. on Guernsey, in the Channel Islands, Feb. 2, 1831. Englishman noted in connection with Aaron Burr's conspiracy. He settled about 1798 on a small island (later to be called Blennerhassett Island) in the Ohio River, near Marietta, where he erected a mansion which he surrounded with gardens and conservatories, and furnished with a library and other facilities. He was persuaded in 1805 by Aaron Burr to join his enterprise for colonization in the Southwest, probably without knowing its true character; he was arrested and indicted for treason, but was released in 1807 on Burr's acquittal, his home having in the meantime been sold to satisfy his creditors. Tradition has it that his last years were spent in poverty, but some authorities have doubted this.

Blennerhassett Island. [Also, **Blennerhasset** (or **Blennerhassett's**) **Island.**] Small island in the Ohio River, ab. 2 mi. below Parkersburg, Wood County, West Virginia: so called from the fact that it was once the residence of Harman Blennerhasset, noted in connection with Aaron Burr's conspiracy.

Blera (blē′rạ). Ancient name of **Bieda.**

Blériot (blā.ryō), **Louis.** b. at Cambrai, France, July 1, 1872; d. at Paris, Aug. 3, 1936. French inventor and aviator. He crossed (July 25, 1909) the English Channel in a monoplane of his own invention, starting from Calais, France, and landing at the Shakespeare Cliff, near Dover, England. The time occupied by the flight was ab. 40 minutes. He was awarded the prize of one thousand pounds offered by the London *Daily Mail* to the first aviator to make an unbroken daylight-flight across the Channel.

Blesae (blē′sē). An ancient name of **Blois.**

Blésois (blā.zwȧ). See **Blois,** county.

Blessed Damozel, The. Poem (1847–48) by Dante Gabriel Rossetti. In it he resolved the conflict between the early Pre-Raphaelite realism and the visionary world of dreams (into which latter, of course, the poet moved ever more deeply during the rest of his life). The poem was one of those which were circulated in manuscript and which established Rossetti as a new force in poetry long before he became generally known to the public.

Blessing of the Bay. Thirty-ton bark launched at Mistick (later Medford), Mass., in 1631. It was the second seaworthy craft constructed in what is now the U.S.

Blessington (bles′ing.tọn), **Marguerite,** Countess of. [Original name, **Marguerite Power.**] b. near Clonmel, County Tipperary, Ireland, Sept. 1, 1789; d. at Paris, June 4, 1849. Irish beauty and woman of letters. Born Marguerite Power, the daughter of a small farmer, she was married at the age of 14 to an army officer, Maurice St. Leger Farmer, whose intemperance and bad temper caused her to leave him. Farmer was killed in 1817, and the following year his widow became the wife of Charles John Gardiner, the 1st Earl of Blessington, a widower. He was wealthy and fond of lavish living, a taste which his second wife fully shared. Their house at London became a gathering place for the intellect, wit, and fashion of the day. In 1822 the count d'Orsay became an intimate of the family, and in 1827 married Blessington's daughter by his first wife (it was probably a loveless, and certainly an unsuccessful, marriage; separation came a few years later). Blessington died in 1829, and in 1831 his widow took a house in Mayfair. In 1833 she began her literary career as a means of adding to an income which, though large, was not sufficient to sustain the extravagant scale of living to which she had become accustomed. In 1836 she acquired Gore House, where d'Orsay lived with her for the next 13 years, during which her activity in the intellectual and fashionable worlds continued. In April, 1849, d'Orsay fled to avoid arrest at the demand of his creditors. Marguerite followed him to Paris in May, where she died less than a month later. Her novels include *The Two Friends* (1835), *Confessions of an Elderly Gentleman* (1836), *Confessions of an Elderly Lady* (1838), *The Governess* (1839), *Lottery of Life* (1842), *Strathern* (1843), *Memoirs of a Femme de Chambre* (1846), and *Marmaduke Herbert* (1847). She and Blessington had become well acquainted with Byron in 1823, and in 1834 she published what is now her best-known book, *Conversations with Lord Byron.* For a time after 1834 she edited *The Book of Beauty*, and from 1841 to the year of her death she was editor of *The Keepsake.*

Blest Gana (blest′gä′nä), **Alberto.** b. at Santiago, Chile, 1830; d. 1920. Chilean novelist, among the earliest of that country. Educated abroad and long in the diplomatic service, he spent more than half his life in the U.S., England, and France. His works, largely social or historical, include *La aritmética en el amor* (1860, which won the first prize ever offered in Chile for a work of prose fiction), *Martín Rivas* (1862), *El ideal de un calavera* (1863), and *Durante la reconquista* (1897).

Blesum (blē′sum). An ancient name of **Blois.**

Bletchley (blech′li). Urban district in S central England, in Buckinghamshire, ab. 47 mi. NW of London by rail. It is an important railway junction. 10,916 (1951).

Bleuler (bloi′lėr), **Paul Eugen.** b. at Zollikon, Zurich canton, Switzerland, April 4, 1857; d. there, July 15, 1939. Swiss psychiatrist and neurologist. He served (1898–1927) as professor at the University of Zurich. In 1911 he made an important contribution to the study of dementia praecox, introducing the term "schizophrenia," which denotes a cleavage or fissuration of the mental functions; he also described (1914) the phenomenon of "relative idiocy." Author of *Der geborene Verbrecher. Eine kritische Studie* (1896), *Affektivität, Suggestibilität, Paranoia* (1906), *Dementia praecox oder Gruppe der Schizophrenien* (1911; Eng. trans., *Dementia Praecox*, or, *Group of the Schizophrenias*), *The Theory of Schizophrenic Negativism* (1912), *Lehrbuch der Psychiatrie* (1916; Eng. trans., *Textbook of Psychiatry*, 1924), and *Naturgeschichte der Seele und ihres Bewusstwerdens. Mnemistische Biopsychologie* (1921); co-editor (with Sigmund Freud and C. G. Jung) of the *Jahrbuch für psychoanalytische und psychopathologische Forschungen* (1909–13).

Bleyle (blī′lẹ), **Karl.** b. at Feldkirch, Vorarlberg, Austria, May 7, 1880—. Austrian composer. He studied under Hugo Wehrle and Samuel de Lange, and after having attended (1897–99) the conservatory at Stuttgart, settled at Munich. His works include choral and orchestral selections, a violin concerto, and piano pieces.

Blgariya (bul.gä′rē.yä). Bulgarian name of **Bulgaria.**

Blicher (blē′kėr), **Steen Steensen.** b. at Vium, Jutland, Denmark, Oct. 11, 1782; d. at Spentrup, March 26, 1848. Danish lyric poet and novelist. His works include the novels *Jydske Romanzer* and *Nationalnoveller* (published collectively with others, 1833–36).

Blickling Homilies (blik′ling). Collection of 19 sermons recorded on manuscript c970 and named by modern scholars after the English village of Blickling, the former home of the manuscript. They antedate the homilies of Ælfric and Wulfstan, and are considered to be more significant for their antiquity than for their literary merit.

Blida (blē′dä). City in the department of Algiers, Algeria, in NW Africa, ab. 25 mi. SW of the city of Algiers; also the name of a commune in the same department. Oranges are grown in the surrounding region. Pop. of city, 61,607 (1948).

Blifil (blī′fil), **Captain John.** In Henry Fielding's novel *Tom Jones*, a hypocritical coxcomb, of "pinchbeck professions and vamped up virtues."

Blifil, Doctor. Elder brother of Captain John Blifil, in Henry Fielding's novel *Tom Jones.*

Bligger (or **Blikker**) **von Steinach** (blig′ėr; blik′ėr; fon shtīn′äċh). Middle High German poet who seems to have lived somewhere along the Neckar River, and is documented as early as 1165 and as late as 1209. Some of his minnesongs have come down to us, but his longer work, *Der Umbehang* ("the tapestry"), which is supposed to have been a collection of verse narratives, is lost. Gottfried von Strassburg, in his *Tristan und Isolde*, has warm praise for Bligger.

Bligh (blī), **William.** b. at Tyntan, Cornwall, England, 1754; d. at London, Dec. 7, 1817. English admiral. He was appointed commander of H.M.S. *Bounty* in 1787; after a mutiny of his crew, he and 18 others were cast adrift (1789) near the Friendly Islands in an open boat; they reached Timor after sailing close to 4,000 mi. He later served as governor of New South Wales; there he antagonized the soldiers, and was arrested by them. In 1814 he became a vice-admiral. He is an important figure in the novels *Mutiny on the Bounty* (1932) and its sequel *Men Against the Sea* (1933) by James Norman Hall and

Charles Bernard Nordhoff. He published a narrative of the mutiny in 1790.

Blight (blīt), **Young.** Mr. Mortimer Lightwood's office-boy in Charles Dickens's novel *Our Mutual Friend.* He is of a peculiarly depressing aspect.

Blimber (blim'ėr), **Cornelia.** Daughter of Doctor Blimber in Charles Dickens's *Dombey and Son.* She wore short hair and spectacles and was "dry and sandy with working in the graves of deceased languages."

Blimber, Doctor. Principal of the boarding school in Charles Dickens's *Dombey and Son,* to which little Paul Dombey is sent. He is an unimpassioned, grave man with an appearance of learning.

Blind (blint), **Karl.** b. at Mannheim, Germany, Sept. 4, 1826; d. at London, May 31, 1907. German political agitator and writer; stepfather of Mathilde Blind. His written works dealt chiefly with German folklore, and with politics, literature, and history. A participant in the German revolution of 1848, he later lived in England.

Blind (blīnd), **Mathilde.** b. at Mannheim, Germany, March 21, 1841; d. at London, Nov. 26, 1896. English poet; stepdaughter of Karl Blind. She published *Poems by Claude Lake* (1867), *The Prophecy of Saint Oran* (1881), *The Heather on Fire* (1886), *The Ascent of Man* (1888), *Dramas in Miniature* (1891), *Songs and Sonnets* (1893), and *Birds of Passage* (1895). She translated Strauss's *The Old Faith and the New* (1873–74) and *The Journal of Marie Bashkirtseff* (1890), and wrote biographies of George Eliot (1883) and Madame Roland (1886).

Blind Alley. Novel by W. L. George, published in 1919, and similar in its theme and purpose to his *Bed of Roses* (1911) and *Second Blooming* (1914).

Blind Beggar of Alexandria, The. Comedy by George Chapman, first acted in February, 1596, and printed in 1598.

Blind Beggar of Bednall Green, with the Merry Humors of Tom Stroud (bed'nạl; stroud), **The.** Play by Henry Chettle and John Day, written before May, 1600, but not printed till 1659. It was based on the popular ballad called *The Beggar's Daughter of Bednal Green.*

Blinder (blin'dėr), **Mrs.** Keeper of a chandler's shop in Charles Dickens's *Bleak House.* She has "a dropsy or an asthma, or perhaps both."

Blind Harry (or **Hary**). [Also, **Henry the Minstrel.**] d. c1492. Scottish minstrel, putative author of a poem on Sir William Wallace. The only known manuscript of the poem, dated 1488, is a copy made by John Ramsay. The poem, in rhyming couplets, has more than 11,000 lines, and recounts the heroic deeds of the Scottish patriot who was finally captured and executed by the English in 1305.

Blindheim (blint'hīm). German name of **Blenheim.**

Blind Man, The. Short story by D. H. Lawrence. Considered by most critics to be one of Lawrence's finest short stories, it appeared in *England, My England* (1922).

Blind River. Town in Ontario, Canada, on the N shore of the North Channel, Georgian Bay, Lake Huron. It is situated ab. 87 mi. SE of Sault Ste. Marie. It is the starting point for the ferry to Manitoulin Island, and a fishing and vacation resort; has lumber mills. 2,512 (1951).

Blindtown (blīnd'toun). Former name of **Larksville.**

Blinn (blin), **Holbrook.** b. at San Francisco, Jan. 23, 1872; d. at Croton-on-Hudson, N.Y., June 24, 1928. American actor. He made his debut as a child in *The Streets of New York* (1878), and acted with Maurice Barrymore in *The Battle of the Strong* (1900), and, from 1908 to 1911, with Minnie Maddern Fiske in *The Pillars of Society, The Green Cockatoo,* and *Becky Sharpe.* His later appearances were made in *The Challenge* (1919), *The Bad Man* (1920–23), *The Dove* (1925–26), and *The Play's the Thing* (1926–28), among others.

Bliss (blis). Volume of short stories by Katherine Mansfield, published in 1920. Among the stories are "The Escape," "The Little Governess," "Psychology," "Pictures," and "Prelude," as well as the title story, a delicate study of moods.

Bliss, Aaron Thomas. b. at Peterboro, N.Y., May 22, 1837; d. Sept. 16, 1906. American politician who served as governor (1900–04) of Michigan. He was elected (1882) to the Michigan state senate, and was a member of Congress (1889–91) from Michigan.

Bliss, Arthur. b. at London, Aug. 2, 1891—. English composer. After graduation (1913) from Pembroke College, Cambridge, he attended (1914) the Royal College of Music, London, where his teachers included Sir Charles Villiers Stanford, Ralph Vaughan Williams, and Gustav Holst. During World War I he served in France with the Royal Fusiliers. Appointed (1921) professor at the Royal College of Music, he settled later (1923) at Santa Barbara, Calif., where he wrote scores for motion pictures. Chief among his works are the ballets *Checkmate* (1937) and *Miracle in the Gorbals* (1944) for the Sadler's Wells company, *Hymn to Apollo* (1926), *The Women of Yueh* (1923), and *Pastoral* (1929).

Bliss, Cornelius Newton. b. at Fall River, Mass., Jan. 26, 1833; d. at New York, Oct. 9, 1911. American merchant and cabinet officer. He was treasurer of the Republican national committee in 1892, 1896, 1900, and 1904, and was U.S. secretary of the interior in the period 1897–99.

Bliss, Daniel. b. at Georgia, Vt., Aug. 17, 1823; d. July 27, 1916. American Protestant missionary and educator; father of Howard Sweetser Bliss and Frederick Jones Bliss. He founded Syrian Protestant College (chartered in 1864, later to be called American University) at Beirut, and served as its first president (1864–1902).

Bliss, Edwin Elisha. b. at Putney, Vt., April 12, 1817; d. Dec. 20, 1892. American Protestant missionary, who edited (1865–92), at Constantinople, the *Avedaper* (Messenger), printed in Turkish and Armenian. He worked in Asiatic Turkey at Trabzon (1843–51) and Merzifon (1851–56) before transferring (1856) to Constantinople. Author of a Bible handbook in Armenian.

Bliss, Edwin Munsell. b. at Erzurum, Turkey, Sept. 12, 1848; d. Aug. 6, 1919. American missionary, editor, and author. He was intermittently (1873–88) an assistant agent for the Bible Society, editor (1889–91) of the *Encyclopaedia of Missions* (1891), associate editor (1891–1901) of the New York *Independent,* and special assistant (1907–19) in the Bureau of the Census as an expert on religious bodies. Author of *The Turk in Armenia, Crete, and Greece* (1896), *Turkey and the Armenian Atrocities* (1896), *Concise History of Missions* (1897), and *The Missionary Enterprise* (1908).

Bliss, Eleanor Albert. b. at Jamestown, R.I., Aug. 16, 1899—. American bacteriologist, discoverer of the hemolytic streptococcus known as Group F. A graduate of Bryn Mawr (1921) and Johns Hopkins (1925), she became (1940) assistant professor of preventive medicine at Johns Hopkins. During World War II, she was a consultant (1942–45) to the secretary of war on the Board for Control of Epidemic Diseases, and began (1944) to serve as a civilian consultant with the Chemical Warfare Service. Coauthor, with Perrin H. Long, of *Clinical and Experimental Use of Sulfanilamide, Sulfapyridine and Allied Compounds* (1939).

Bliss, Frederick Jones. b. in Syria, Jan. 23, 1859; d. at White Plains, N.Y., June 4, 1937. American archaeologist under the Palestine Exploration Fund (London) in the period 1891–1900; son of Daniel Bliss (1823–1916). He excavated the site of the ancient Palestinian city of Lachish, and directed archaeological work at Jerusalem and other localities. His publications include *A Mound of Many Cities* (1894), *Excavations at Jerusalem 1894–97* (1898), *Excavations in Palestine 1898–1900* (1902), and *The Development of Palestine Exploration* (1906).

Bliss, George. b. at Springfield, Mass., May 3, 1830; d. at Wakefield, R.I., Sept. 2, 1897. American lawyer and legal codifier. He drafted the New York City charter of 1873, while serving as U.S. attorney for the southern district (1872–77); he also was a member of the commission which drafted (1879–80) *The Special and Local Laws Affecting Public Interests in the City of New York,* and helped draft (c1881) the *New York City Consolidation Act.*

Bliss, Howard Sweetser. b. in Syria, Dec. 6, 1860; d. at Saranac Lake, N.Y., May 2, 1920. American Protestant missionary; son of Daniel Bliss (1823–1916). He served (1894–1902) as pastor of the Union Congregational Church, at Upper Montclair, N.J., before succeeding (1903) his father as president of Syrian Protestant College (later to be known as American University) at Beirut. In 1919 he attended the Paris peace conference as an expert on Syrian and Near Eastern affairs.

Bliss, Philip. b. at Chipping Sodbury, England, 1787; d. at Oxford, England, 1857. English antiquary and registrar of Oxford University (1824–53), remembered for his four-volume edition (1813–20) of Anthony à Wood's *Athenae Oxonienses and Fasti.* Educated at Oxford, he became (1809) a fellow there, and was ordained a priest in 1818. He served as under-librarian of the Bodleian Library (1822–28), keeper of archives (1826–57), principal of St. Mary's Hall (1848–57), and deputy professor of civil law. He also edited *Reliquiae Hearnianae* (1857), and compiled other antiquarian works.

Bliss, Philip Paul. b. in Clearfield County, Pa., July 9, 1838; d. Dec. 29, 1876. American singing evangelist. He sang (c1865 *et seq.*) at concerts throughout Illinois, before being appointed a chorister of the First Congregational Church at Chicago; he traveled (1874–76) through the West and South as an evangelist with Major D. W. Whittle. *Gospel Songs* (1874), which he brought out with Ira Sankey, contains the well-known songs "Hold the Fort," "Only an Armor Bearer," "Let the Lower Lights Be Burning," and "Pull for the Shore." He was author also of the song books *The Charm* (1871), *The Song Tree* (1872), *The Sunshine* (1873), and *The Joy* (1873).

Bliss, Porter Cornelius. b. on the Seneca Indian Reservation, Cattaraugus, N.Y., Dec. 28, 1838; d. at New York, Feb. 2, 1885. American journalist, explorer, and author. Commissioned (1862) by the Argentine government to explore the Gran Chaco desert region, he was later (1866) commissioned by Francisco Solano López, president of Paraguay, to write a history of that country. Accused by the Paraguayans of conspiring against López, he was imprisoned and tortured, but was cleared of the charges by a U.S. government investigation; he served (1870–74) as secretary of the U.S. legation in Mexico. Biographical editor (1874 *et seq.*) of *Johnson's New Universal Cyclopaedia,* editor (1877) of the literary periodical *Library Table,* and a correspondent (1878 *et seq.*) for the New York *Herald;* coauthor with L. P. Brockett of *The Conquest of Turkey* (1878).

Bliss, Tasker Howard. b. at Lewisburg, Pa., Dec. 31, 1853; d. at Washington, D.C., Nov. 9, 1930. American army officer. Graduated (1875) from the U.S. Military Academy at West Point, N.Y., he was later promoted to brigadier general (1902) and major general (1915), and was brevetted (1917) general. During the Spanish-American War, he served (1898) in the Puerto Rican campaign and was a member (1898) of the board appointed to choose camp sites for American troops in Cuba. He served as chief (1898–1902) of the Cuban customs service, as chief of staff (1917), as a member (1917) of the Allied conference and of the supreme war council in France, and as one of the American commissioners (1917–18) to negotiate peace in World War I.

Bliss, William Dwight Porter. b. at Constantinople, Turkey, Aug. 20, 1856; d. at New York, Oct. 8, 1926. American sociologist. He was graduated from the Hartford Theological Seminary in 1882, and held pastorates in the Congregational and Protestant Episcopal churches. In the period 1907–09 he acted as an investigator for the U.S. Bureau of Labor, and subsequently (1909 *et seq.*) directed the Social Science Library Bureau. In 1889 he organized the first Christian Socialist society in the U.S., and in 1899 became president of the National Social Reform Union. Author of *Handbook of Socialism* (1895) and *Directory of Social Thought and Work* (1910).

Blister (blis'tėr). Apothecary in Henry Fielding's *Old Man Taught Wisdom, or The Virgin Unmasked.*

Blithedale Romance (blīth'dāl), **The.** Novel by Nathaniel Hawthorne, published in 1852. It was based on the Brook Farm experiment in communal living, and in Miles Coverdale Hawthorne described much of his own character. The character Zenobia, an attractive and intellectual woman, is said to have been modeled after Margaret Fuller. The story is concerned with the confusions and difficulties encountered by impractical idealists.

Blitz (blits). Shortened form of the word "Blitzkrieg," widely used during and after World War II as both noun and verb. It may be said to have meaning as a proper name in its application to the extremely heavy bombing of London during the latter part of 1940 (and intermittently thereafter until 1944, when the German tactical effort in the air shifted to the use of the jet-propelled, pilotless aircraft usually called "buzz bombs"). In English usage, the terms "Blitz" or "London Blitz" are usually restricted to the bombings of 1940–41, and the later assaults are called "the Little Blitz."

Blitzkrieg (blits'krēg). German word meaning "lightning war." It was used by the Germans to describe the technique of sudden attack in overwhelming force by tanks, planes, and motorized infantry which was a basic part of their tactical scheme during the initial phase of World War II. It may be said to have meaning as a proper name in its application to the German conquest of Poland, in the fall of 1939, and of France, in the early summer of 1940.

Bliven (bliv'ẹn), **Bruce (Ormsby).** b. at Emmetsburg, Iowa, July 27, 1889—. American journalist and author. A graduate (1911) of Stanford University, he was a member of the editorial staffs of the San Francisco *Bulletin* (1909–12), *Printers' Ink* (1916–18), and the New York *Globe* (1919–23); thereafter he served as managing editor (1923–30) and editor (1930–46) of the *New Republic,* before becoming (1946) one of its editorial directors. Author of *Mr. Ware and the Peasants* (1925), *The Jewish Refugee Problem* (1938), *The Men Who Make the Future* (1942); coeditor, with A. G. Mezerik, of *What the Informed Citizen Needs to Know* (1945).

Blix (bliks). Novel by Frank Norris, published in 1899.

Blixen (Finecke) (blek'sẹn fē'nek"ẹ), Baroness **Karen.** See **Dinesen, Isak.**

Bloch (bloċh), **Bruno.** b. at Ober-Endingen, Aargau, Switzerland, Jan. 19, 1878; d. at Zurich, Switzerland, April 10, 1933. Swiss dermatologist. He was a staff member of the dermatological clinics at Vienna, Berlin, and Paris, and a pupil of J. Jadassohn at Bern. He became privatdocent (1909) of dermatology and syphilology, and professor (1913) at the University of Basel, and served also (1916–33) at the University of Zurich. Known for his studies in biology, biochemistry, and functional pathology of the skin, he introduced dynamic dermatology into medicine through his researches, chiefly on cutaneous allergy, pigment-formation (Bloch's reaction), endocrine dysfunction, and carcinogenesis. Author of *Die allgemein-pathologische Bedeutung der Dermatomykosen* (1913), *Das Pigment* (1927), and *Allgemeine und experimentelle Biologie der durch Hyphomyceten erzeugten Dermatomykosen* (1928).

Bloch (blok), **Claude Charles.** b. at Woodbury, Ky., July 12, 1878—. American naval officer who served (1938–40) as commander in chief of the U.S. fleet. He was graduated (1899) from the U.S. Naval Academy, after having been honored (1898) for meritorious service in the Spanish-American War; he was appointed chief of the ordnance bureau (1923) with the rank of rear admiral, and commander in chief of the U.S. fleet (1938) as a full admiral. He was commandant (1940–42) of the 14th naval district in Hawaii, a member (1942 *et seq.*) of the general board of the U.S. navy, and was awarded the Legion of Merit (1946) for his services as chairman of the navy board for production awards.

Bloch, Ernest. b. at Geneva, Switzerland, July 24, 1880—. American composer and teacher. After studying with Émile Jaques-Dalcroze and Eugène Ysaye, he came to the U.S. in 1916, and acquired American citizenship in 1924. He was a director of the Cleveland Institute of Music (1920) and of the San Francisco Conservatory of Music (1925–30). In 1929 he was named an honorary member of the Academy of Santa Cecilia, Rome. Many of his compositions are based on Jewish themes; among these are *Trois Poèmes Juifs* (1913), and the rhapsody *Schelomo* (1916); among his other works are the operas *Macbeth* (1903; first performed at Paris, 1910) and *Jezebel* (1918), symphonic poems, sonatas, and a violin concerto.

Bloch, Felix. b. at Zurich, Switzerland, Oct. 23, 1905—. American physicist. He served as associate professor (1934–36) and professor (1936 *et seq.*) of physics at Stanford. During World War II he was connected with Los Alamos and other research projects. He shared with E. M. Purcell the 1952 Nobel prize in physics for their discoveries, made independently, in the measurement of nuclear magnetic fields.

Bloch (blok), **Jean de.** b. 1836; d. 1902. Polish financier and economist, known as an ardent pacifist. In his seven-volume work *The Future of War*, he attempted to prove that the development of modern weapons and resources, as well as economic complications, would make future wars impossible. To illustrate the horrors of modern war, he founded the War and Peace Museum at Lucerne, Switzerland. His works on economics, published in several languages by his own research institute, deal with problems of railroad and tax policy. Author of *Wplyw dróh żelaznych na stan ekonomiczny Rosji* (1878), *Finanse Rosji* (1882), *Przyszła wojna* (7 vols., 1898; abridged and translated as *Is War Now Impossible?*, 1899), *The Future of War in its Technical, Economic, and Political Relations* (1899), *Modern Weapons and Modern War* (1900), and *Zur gegenwärtigen Lage in China* (1900).

Bloch, Jean Richard. b. at Paris, May 25, 1884; d. there, 1947. French novelist and playwright, editor of literary reviews. He was the author of *Et Cie* (1918; Eng. trans., *And Company*) and *La Nuit Kurde* (1925).

Bloch (bloċh), **Moritz.** See **Ballagi, Maurice.**

Block (blôk), **Adriaen.** fl. 1610–1624. Dutch explorer in America. The earliest fact known about him is that he made a voyage up the Hudson River in 1610; in 1614 he retraced this route, leading five Dutch vessels. He later sailed through what is now Hell Gate into Long Island Sound, entered the harbor on which New Haven was later located, and went up the Connecticut River. He also discovered Block Island (which is named for him), explored the coasts of what are now Buzzards Bay, Massachusetts Bay, and Nahant Bay, and furnished the data used in compiling the *Figurative Map* (1616), the first detailed map of the S New England coast.

Block (blok), **Maurice.** b. at Berlin, Feb. 18, 1816; d. at Paris, Jan. 9, 1901. French political economist and statistician. A naturalized French citizen, he served in the French ministry of agriculture (1844–52) and in the department of statistics (1852–62). His works include *Des charges de l'agriculture* (1850) and *Puissance comparée des divers états de l'Europe*. He edited (1856 *et seq.*) *L'Annuaire de l'économie politique et de la statistique*.

Blockade, The. Unpublished play by John Burgoyne, British general and dramatist. It was performed at Boston during the Revolutionary War, in the period of British occupation.

Blockheads or the Affrighted Officers, The. Prose farce (1776), of unknown authorship. Erroneously attributed at one time to Mercy Warren, it was a retort to General John Burgoyne's *The Blockade*.

Block Island (blok). [American Indian, **Manisees.**] Island in the Atlantic Ocean, ab. 10 mi. SW of Point Judith in Rhode Island: coextensive with the township of New Shoreham in Newport County, R.I. A noted summer resort, it has many fresh-water ponds as well as seaside beaches. Points of interest include the old harbor, with its fishing fleet, a large new harbor, a U.S. Coast Guard station, and two lighthouses. It was discovered (c1614) by the Dutch navigator Adriaen Block and first settled in 1661. Length, ab. 7 mi.; width, 3½ mi.

Blocksberg (bloks'berk). See **Brocken.**

Blockx (bloks), **Jan.** b. at Antwerp, Belgium, Jan. 25, 1851; d. there, May 26, 1912. Belgian composer. He was director (1902 *et seq.*) of the Royal Flemish Conservatory, and the composer of several operas, such as *Iets vergeten*, *Maître Martin* (1892), and *Herbergprinses* (1896), and of other stage works, as well as of cantatas, orchestral pieces, and chamber music.

Bloc National (blok nà.syo.nàl). [Eng. trans., "*The National Bloc.*"] Alliance of conservative French political parties, in power from 1919 until 1924. It was formed (October, 1919) to oppose the Leftist parties. Soon after its inception the Radical-Socialist and Republican-Socialist parties withdrew from it. It was victorious in the national election of Nov. 16, 1919, but was defeated in the election of 1924. It followed a policy of conservatism on social and financial questions, and sought to enforce upon Germany strict observance of the Versailles Treaty.

Bloc Populaire Canadien (blok po.pü.ler kà.nà.dyaṅ). Canadian political party representing the interests of the French-Canadian nationalists of Quebec.

Blodget (bloj'ẹt), **Lorin.** b. May 25, 1823; d. March 25, 1901. American physicist and statistician. He was the author of *Climatology of the United States* (1857) and others.

Blodget, Samuel. b. at Woburn, Mass., April 1, 1724; d. at Derryfield, Mass., Sept. 1, 1807. American manufacturer and canal builder. He manufactured (c1760 *et seq.*) potash and pearl ash at and around Boston, and constructed (1794–1807) a canal around the Amoskeag Falls of the Merrimack River, for which he also designed the locks.

Blodgett (bloj'et), **Benjamin Colman.** b. at Boston, March 12, 1838; d. at Seattle, Wash., Sept. 22, 1925. American musician who founded the Smith College School of Music, of which he was principal until 1903. At various times he served as organist at Eliot Church, Newton, Mass., Park Street Church, Boston, and Essex Street Church, Boston. He was music master (1865) at Maplewood Institute, Pittsfield, Mass., and director (1860) of a music school there, before being appointed (1878) professor of music at Smith College, Northampton, Mass.; he was also organist and choir director (1904) at Stanford University. His works include a cantata, songs, and piano pieces.

Blodgett, Henry Williams. b. at Amherst, Mass., July 21, 1821; d. Feb. 9, 1905. American politician and jurist. A member of the Illinois house of representatives (1852–54) and senate (1859–63), he was appointed a U.S. district judge (1869) and a member of the circuit court of appeals (1891) of Illinois. He served (1892) as a U.S. counsel in the Bering Sea arbitration.

Blodgett, Katharine Burr. b. at Schenectady, N.Y., Jan. 10, 1898—. American physicist who discovered (1939) a method for making nonreflecting glass. Graduated from Bryn Mawr, she received an M.A. degree from the University of Chicago, and was the first woman to be awarded (1926) a Ph.D. degree from the Cavendish Institute of Oxford University, England. She collaborated with Irving Langmuir in physical and chemical research at the research laboratory of the General Electric Company.

Blodgett's Settlement. A former name of **Beloit,** Wis.

Bloem (blöm), **Jacques C.** b. 1887—. Dutch poet. Melancholy and pessimism, resulting from frustrated love of life and mankind, dominate his delicate poetry. His works include *Het Verlangen* (Longing, 1921), *Media Vita* (1931), *De Nederlaag* (Defeat, 1937), and *Sintels* (Cinders, 1945); his *Collected Works* were published in 1948.

Bloem (blėm), **Walter.** b. at Elberfeld, Germany, June 20, 1868—. German novelist, playwright, and theater director. He is decidedly a popular author, whose books sell in Germany by the hundred thousands. He dropped the practice of law to write plays (*Caub*, 1897; *Heinrich von Plauen*, 1902; *Schnapphähne*, 1902) with such success that he was made dramaturgist at the Stuttgart Court Theater (1910–14), but he found novel writing more profitable. His trilogy from the time of the Franco-Prussian War, *Das eiserne Jahr* (1911), *Volk wider Volk* (1912), and *Die Schmiede der Zukunft* (1913), put him in the van of contemporary German best sellers.

Bloemaert (blö'märt), **Abraham.** b. at Gorkum, Netherlands, 1564; d. at Utrecht, Netherlands, 1651. Dutch painter of landscapes and historical pieces, noted as a colorist.

Bloemen (blö'mẹn), **Jan Frans van.** [Called **Orizzonte.**] b. at Antwerp, c1656; d. at Rome, c1748. Flemish landscape painter, called Orizzonte from the horizons of his landscapes; brother of Pieter van Bloemen.

Bloemen, Pieter van. [Called **Standaert.**] b. 1651; d. 1720. Flemish painter of battle scenes; brother of Jan Frans van Bloemen.

Bloemendaal (blö'mẹn.däl). Town in W Netherlands, in the province of North Holland, N of Haarlem, separated from the North Sea by dunes. It is a summer resort, and has horticultural establishments. 20,515 (est. 1951).

Bloemfontein (blöm'fon.tān). City in S Africa, the capital of Orange Free State province, Union of South Africa, situated in the W central section of the province. It is the geographical center of the Union's rail system, ab. 750 mi. NE of Capetown and ab. 263 mi. SW of Johannesburg. It is a beautiful city possessing many unusually fine buildings and monuments of interest. In 1910 it became the seat of the supreme court of the Union of South Africa. 82,322 (1946).

Blois (blwä). [Also: **Blaisois, Blésois.**] Medieval county of France, included in the government of Orléanais, and comprised in the modern department of Loir-et-Cher; the capital was Blois. It became a possession of the crown in 1498.

Blois. [Ancient names, **Blesae, Blesum.**] City in W France, the capital of the department of Loir-et-Cher, situated on the right bank of the Loire River and dominated by a magnificent medieval castle. In medieval times it was the capital of the county of Blois. The château is a former royal palace, purchased by Louis of Orléans, and was the residence of Louis XII. The E front was built by Louis XIII; another wing was built by Francis I; the apartments in the interior date from the 13th to the 17th centuries. Other important buildings in the city include the Cathedral of Saint Louis, in flamboyant Gothic style, with a 12th-century tower and a Renaissance portal; the Church Saint-Nicholas-Saint-Laumer, built 1138–1210, part of a former Benedictine abbey; the Hôtel d'Alluye, a charming Renaissance mansion; the museum of ancient art, the museum of modern art, and the museum of archaeology and natural history. From Blois some of the most impressive feudal castles of the royal period of France, such as those of Chambord, Cheverny, Chaumont, Bury, and Beauregard, are easily accessible. The printing establishments of Blois, as well as its chocolate and candy manufactures, are widely renowned. The cheese known as crême de St.-Gervais is manufactured nearby. 26,774 (1946).

Blois, Charles de. [Also, **Charles de Châtillon.**] b. 1319; killed at the battle of Auray, 1364. Duke of Brittany; nephew of Philip VI of France. He laid successful claim to the duchy of Brittany, and was given the title in 1341.

Blok (blôk), **Aleksandr Aleksandrovich.** b. at St. Petersburg, Nov. 28, 1880; d. there, Aug. 7, 1921. Russian poet. A writer of symbolist verse, he greeted the seizure of power by the Bolsheviks with an enthusiasm that had an element of mysticism in it. In 1918 he composed *The Twelve*, generally held to be the outstanding poem of the Russian Revolution. One of several English translations of this poem and a number of his lyrics appear in Avrahm Yarmolinsky's *A Treasury of Russian Verse* (1949).

Blok, Petrus Johannes. b. at Den Helder, Netherlands, Jan. 10, 1855; d. at Leiden, Oct. 24, 1929. Dutch historian. He served as professor (1884 *et seq.*) at the universities of Groningen and Leiden. Author of *Een Hollandsche stad in verschillende tijden* (1883), and *Geschiedenis van het Nederlandsche volk* (History of the Dutch People, 1892).

Blokland (blôk'länt), **F. Beelaerts van.** See **Beelaerts van Blokland, F.**

Blomberg (blom'berk), **Werner von.** b. at Stargard, Germany, Sept. 2, 1878; d. 1946. German general. A member of the general staff in World War I, he was appointed (1925) chief of the training department in the ministry of defense, and served as military expert for the German disarmament commission with the League of Nations. He was defense minister (1933–35) under Hitler, and became minister of war and commander in chief in 1935. He was retired in 1939.

Blome (blōm), **Richard.** d. 1705. English publisher and compiler of many books said to have been written by impoverished authors for a pittance, and for which he obtained subscriptions from wealthy persons. Among these are a large work on heraldry, and two books relating to the British colonies in America.

Blomefield (blōm'fēld), **Francis.** b. at Fersfield, England, 1705; d. at London, 1752. English topographer and clergyman who chronicled the history of Norfolk. After taking a B.A. degree (1727) at Cambridge, he served as rector of Hargham (1729–30). On a private press that he had bought in 1736, he began to publish (1739) numbers of his *History of Norfolk* (based chiefly on an earlier collection), containing accounts of Norwich and Thetford; his death left the third volume unfinished. The work was continued by Charles Parkin, and ultimately completed by a bookseller's hack; the whole work was republished at London in 11 octavo volumes (1805–10).

Blomfield (blōm'fēld), Sir **Arthur William.** b. at London, March 6, 1829; d. at Broadway, Worcestershire, England, Oct. 30, 1899. English architect; son of Charles James Blomfield, and uncle of Sir Reginald Blomfield. He was articled for three years (1853–56) to Philip Charles Hardwick, architect of the Bank of England, whom he succeeded in this office in 1883. He was especially identified with the Gothic revival of the middle of the 19th century, his best buildings being churches. At various times he had charge of restorations at the cathedrals of Salisbury, Canterbury, Lincoln, and Chichester. His reconstruction of the Church of Saint Mary Overie at London is especially notable; he also designed the Fleet Street law courts building at London.

Blomfield, Charles James. b. at Bury-St.-Edmunds, England, May 29, 1786; d. at Fulham, London, Aug. 5, 1857. English prelate, bishop of London in the period 1828–56; brother of Edward Valentine Blomfield (1788–1816), whose translation of Matthiae's *Greek Grammar* he edited, and father of Arthur William Blomfield. He edited various plays of Aeschylus and others.

Blomfield, Edward Valentine. b. at Bury-St.-Edmunds, England, 1788; d. at Cambridge, England, 1816. English classical scholar. His chief work, a translation of Matthiae's *Greek Grammar*, appeared posthumously, edited by his brother, Charles James Blomfield (1786–1857). He studied at Caius College, Cambridge (B.A., 1811), where he was chancellor's classical medallist; fellowships in his own college being full, he was elected to a classical lectureship and fellowship at Emmanuel, a post which he retained until his death.

Blomfield, Sir **Reginald.** b. Dec. 20, 1856; d. 1942. English architect and writer; nephew of Sir Arthur William Blomfield. He designed many memorials and public buildings, and also worked on residential architecture and gardens. Among his published works are *The Formal Garden in England* (1892), *History of Renaissance Architecture in England* (1897), *Studies in Architecture* (1906), and numerous contributions to architectural periodicals.

Blomidon (blom'i.dọn), **Cape.** Cape in N central Nova Scotia, on the NW coast ab. 57 mi. NW of Halifax. It is a high promontory of crystalline rock projecting into Minas Basin. Elevation, ab. 670 ft.

Blommaert (blom'ärt), **Philipp.** b. at Ghent, Belgium, c1808; d. there, Aug. 14, 1871. Flemish historian, poet, and reviver of old Flemish literature. His chief work is *Aloude geschiedenis der Belgen of Nederduitschers* (1849).

Blondel (blon'dẹl; French, blôn.del). [Also, **Blondel de Nesle** (dẹ nel).] b. at Nesle, Picardy, France; fl. in the second half of the 12th century. French trouvère; attendant and friend of Richard Coeur de Lion. According to the traditional account, probably legendary, he discovered the presence of the imprisoned Richard in the castle of Dürrenstein by singing a song which the two had composed, and to which the king responded.

Blondel (blôn.del), **Charles A.** b. 1876; d. 1939. French social psychologist. Strongly influenced by the collective determinism of Emile Durkheim and by Bergsonian philosophy, he sought to develop a genuinely social theory of emotions and sentiments, and explored areas of feelings, will, and mental disorders. His important works were *La Conscience morbide* (1914) and *Introduction à la psychologie collective* (1928).

Blondel, François. [Title, Sieur **des Croisettes.**] b. 1617; d. 1686. French architect. His most noted work was the triumphal arch erected at the Porte St.-Denis, Paris, in 1672. In the same year he became director of the French Academy of Architecture.

Blondel, Jacques François. b. at Rouen, France, Jan. 8, 1705; d. Jan. 9, 1774. French architect. He executed several important works at Paris, and in 1773 designed an extensive scheme of reconstruction in the city of Metz, according to which were built the Hôtel de Ville (1765), the Place d'Armes, and the portal of the cathedral (1771). He also designed similar improvements at Strasbourg. In 1739 he opened an architectural school at Paris, which was merged in 1756 with the Académie d'Architecture, in which he became a professor. He is also known for his books *De la distribution des maisons de plaisance* (1737–38), *L'Architecture française* (known familiarly as the "*Grand Blondel*," 1752–56), and *Cours d'architecture civile* (the "*Petit Blondel*," 1771–77).

Blondel, Maurice. b. at Dijon, France, Nov. 2, 1861—. French philosopher. He served as a professor (1896 *et seq.*)

at the University of Aix-Marseilles, and was the author of *L'Action, essai d'une critique de la vie et d'une science de la pratique* (1893), *L'Illusion idéaliste* (1898), *Les Principes élémentaires d'une logique de la vie morale* (1903), and *La Pensée* (1934).

Blondin (blôn.dañ; Anglicized, blon'din), **Charles.** [Original name, **Jean François Gravelet.**] b. at St.-Omer, France, Feb. 28, 1824; d. at Ealing, London, Feb. 22, 1897. French acrobat, famous as a tightrope walker. He three times (1855, 1859, and 1860) crossed the Niagara River on a tightrope.

Blood (blud), **Benjamin Paul.** b. at Amsterdam, N.Y., Nov. 21, 1832; d. Jan. 15, 1919. American poet and philosopher. He was the author of the long poems *The Bride of the Iconoclast* (1854) and *The Colonnades* (1868), and the philosophical works *The Philosophy of Justice* (1851), *Optimism* (1860), and *Pluriverse* (1920). His last known writing was an introduction to the anonymous *A Capitalist's View of Socialism* (1916).

Blood, Council of. See **Council of Blood.**

Blood, Thomas. [Called **"Colonel Blood."**] b., probably in Ireland, c1618; d. Aug. 24, 1680. Irish adventurer. He is now chiefly remembered for his remarkable (and nearly successful) attempt to steal the crown jewels of England, which were then guarded with a casualness that seems unbelievable today. His scheme entailed an elaborate preliminary campaign to win the friendship and confidence of the keeper of the jewels (some accounts have it that he posed as a clergyman), and he had actually almost reached safety when he was caught with the royal crown under his coat. He then demanded, and got, an interview with Charles II of England, who appears to have pardoned him and even to have shown him royal preferment (some historians have suggested that the sheer audacity of Blood's scheme aroused Charles's admiration and amusement). In his earlier life, Blood had been the leader in an unsuccessful attempt to seize (1663) Dublin Castle and the person of James Butler, the 1st duke of Ormonde, who was then lord lieutenant of Ireland under Charles II. Blood escaped capture, and remained for a time in Ireland, but finally fled to Holland. He later made his way to England, where he joined the Fifth Monarchy men (a religious group that became prominent in England during the middle of the 17th century. Its members believed in the imminent return of Christ to rule the earth as the world's fifth great monarchy, in succession to the empires of Assyria, Persia, Greece, and Rome. Their objections to the established church and their readiness to assert their views by force, if necessary, caused the civil authorities to hang or imprison many of them.) Blood forsook this group to go to Scotland, where he associated himself with the Covenanters, remaining with them until their defeat on Pentland Hills, on Nov. 27, 1666; he then revisited England and Ireland. In 1670 he led another assault on Ormonde, and in 1671 made his famous attempt to steal the crown jewels from the Tower of London. Sir Walter Scott introduces him in *Peveril of the Peak.*

Bloodless Revolution. See **Glorious Revolution.**

Blood Money. Poem by Walt Whitman published on a political issue of the day in the New York *Tribune* (1850). It is of some importance in the history of American literature from the fact that it gave one of the first published indications of the Biblical source of Whitman's style of free verse. It begins with these lines:

Of olden time, when it came to pass
That the beautiful god, Jesus, should finish
his work on earth,
Then went Judas, and sold the divine youth,
And took pay for his body.

Bloody Angle. In the Civil War, a salient at the battle of Spotsylvania Court House, which received this name from the severe fighting which followed the capture there by General Winfield Scott Hancock of about 4,000 Confederate soldiers under General Edward Johnson, on May 12, 1864.

Bloody Assizes. Popular name for the trials for participation in the rising (1685) by which the Duke of Monmouth (the illegitimate son of Charles II) sought to take the throne of England from James II. The trials were held in the western counties of England and presided over by George Jeffreys, 1st Baron Jeffreys of Wem. Over 300 persons are supposed to have been executed, and Jeffrey's name has ever since been a byword for extreme or unnecessary brutality in a court of law.

Bloody Brook. Brook ab. 1 mi. NW of Deerfield, Mass., the scene of an Indian massacre in 1675.

Bloody Brother, The. [Full title, **The Bloody Brother, or Rollo, Duke of Normandy.**] Tragedy by John Fletcher and others (probably William Rowley and Philip Massinger), printed in 1639. The date of production is uncertain.

Bloody Chasm, The. Novel (1881) by John W. De Forest. It is considered to give authentic glimpses of the life and manners of South Carolina in that day.

Bloody Island. Sand bar in the Mississippi River, off St. Louis, Mo., which made its first above-water appearance in 1798 and later became known as a dueling ground. In 1837 U.S. army engineers, following a plan drawn up by Captain Robert E. Lee, carried out the construction of works which in time made the island a part of the Illinois shore.

Bloody Marsh, Battle of. Engagement (July 7, 1742) in the War of Jenkins' Ear (1739–43), fought in Georgia between the invading Spaniards and the English defenders under James Edward Oglethorpe. Some 400 Spaniards were ambushed when they advanced into a marsh; half of them were killed and the rest withdrew. The action was the chief one of the war, and decided it in favor of the English.

Bloody Monday. Name applied to the riots on Aug. 6, 1855, which accompanied elections held at Louisville, Ky. The differences which culminated in violence had their roots in the antagonism between the nativistic Know-Nothing Party and the Democratic Party. The nativists spread unfounded reports that Catholics and aliens had attempted to influence the voting, and the resulting riots took a toll of 22 persons killed and considerable destruction of property.

Bloody Pond, Battle of. Engagement (Sept. 8, 1755) in the French and Indian War, fought between the British and a Canadian and Indian force near the southernmost point of Lake George in New York. After ambushing the British and attacking their camp, the Canadians and Indians paused near a forest pool, where they were assaulted by a British scouting expedition and withdrew. The name Bloody Pond was given to the pool into which the British threw the enemy dead.

Bloody Run, Battle of. Engagement (July 31, 1763) in Pontiac's War (or Pontiac's Conspiracy), fought between a British force under Captain James Dalzel and Indians under the leadership of Pontiac. The action occurred at Parent's Creek (subsequently called Bloody Run) where the British, en route from their base at Detroit in a projected attack against Pontiac's camp at what is now Grand Marais, a small village in Michigan, were severely beaten and compelled to return to Detroit. Dalzel was among those killed.

Bloody Tenent yet More Bloody, The. Tract by Roger Williams, published at London in 1652. It is a sequel to his *The Bloudy Tenent of Persecution* and reaffirms the position of religious tolerance for which Williams is now chiefly remembered, and which so greatly infuriated the Puritans of his day.

Bloom (blöm), **Leopold.** A Dublin Jew, the central character of James Joyce's novel *Ulysses* (1922). An advertising solicitor for a newspaper, he represents a combination of man and myth. The book takes Bloom through the 24 hours of an ordinary day, and parallels all his encounters with events in the travels of Ulysses; this correspondence is worked chiefly by implication. Bloom is sought out as a father symbol by Stephen Dedalus, who corresponds to Telemachus, while Molly, Bloom's wife, is comparable to Penelope. Bloom also appears as a counterpart of the Wandering Jew.

Bloom, Milly. Character in James Joyce's novel *Ulysses* (1922), the daughter of Leopold and Molly Bloom. She never appears in the book, but is the subject of many thoughts and conversations.

Bloom, Molly. In James Joyce's novel *Ulysses* (1922), the wife of Leopold Bloom. Although presented as unfaithful to her husband, she is yet made to correspond to Penelope in the *Odyssey,* and is presented as the embodiment of the elemental and the feminine. The stream-of-consciousness section which closes the novel voices her thoughts in a single, unbroken sentence (which is perhaps the longest in all recorded English literature).

Bloom, Sol. b. at Pekin, Ill., March 9, 1870; d. at Bethesda, Md., March 7, 1949. American politician, congressman (1923 *et seq.*) from New York. Before he entered politics he was at various times a play producer, fight promoter, theater builder, and child actor. As chairman of the House foreign affairs committee, he was, under F. D. Roosevelt, a leader in the fight against neutrality legislation during the early period of World War II. Upon the establishment (May 15, 1947) of the state of Israel, Bloom urged President Truman to give it U.S. recognition, and strongly criticized U.S. failure to permit the export of arms to Israel in subsequent months.

Bloom, Ursula. b. at Chelmsford, Essex, England. English writer. She married (1916) Arthur Brownlow Denham-Cookes and, after his death (1918), became (1925) the wife of Charles Gower Robinson. Author of *The Great Beginning* (1924), *Vagabond Harvest* (1925), *The Driving of Destiny* (1925), *Tarnish* (1929), *Pastoral* (1934), *These Roots Go Deep* (1939), *The Flying Swans* (1940), *No Lady with a Pen* (1946), *Four Sons* (1946), and *Adam's Daughter* (1947).

Bloomer (blö'mėr). City in W Wisconsin, in Chippewa County, ab. 20 mi. N of Eau Claire. 2,556 (1950).

Bloomer, Amelia. [Maiden name, **Jenks.**] b. May 27, 1818; d. at Council Bluffs, Iowa, Dec. 30, 1894. American reformer who wrote and lectured on temperance and the rights of women. She became chiefly known, however, for her adoption of a reformed dress for women, consisting of Turkish trousers and a dress with short skirts (which was actually first introduced to American women by Elizabeth Smith Miller, but which gained its first great currency through Amelia Bloomer, and hence came to be called the "bloomer costume."

Bloomfield (blöm'fēld). Town (in Connecticut the equivalent of township in many other states) and unincorporated village in N Connecticut, in Hartford County, NW of Hartford. The production of tobacco for cigar-wrappers is the principal industry. Pop. of town, 5,746 (1950); of village, 1,205 (1950).

Bloomfield. City in SE Iowa, county seat of Davis County: distributing center for livestock, particularly sheep. It was the home of James B. Weaver. 2,688 (1950).

Bloomfield. Town in NE New Jersey, in Essex County, ab. 11 mi. NW of New York City: residential and industrial suburb of Newark. It is the seat of Bloomfield College and Seminary. 49,307 (1950).

Bloomfield, Joseph. b. at Woodbridge, N.J., Oct. 18, 1753; d. at Burlington, N.J., Oct. 3, 1823. American soldier and politician, governor (1801, 1805–12) of New Jersey. A major and judge advocate of the northern army during the Revolutionary War, he was the commander of an infantry brigade during the Whiskey Rebellion, and a brigadier general during the War of 1812. He served as New Jersey attorney general (1783–92), and as a congressman (1817–21) from New Jersey.

Bloomfield, Leonard. b. at Chicago, April 1, 1887; d. at New Haven, Conn., April 18, 1949. American linguist active in the spread of the scientific study of language in the first half of the 20th century. In 1906 he received his A.B. degree from Harvard and went to the University of Wisconsin as assistant in German and to do graduate work. There he met Eduard Prokosch, who influenced Bloomfield to work in the field of linguistics. After two years of teaching and study at Wisconsin, Bloomfield went to the University of Chicago, where he continued both activities under the direction of Professor Francis A. Wood. He received his doctorate from the University of Chicago in 1909. In 1913 and 1914 he further extended his knowledge of linguistics through study at the universities of Leipzig and Göttingen; among the scholars with whom he worked in Germany were August Leskien, Karl Brugmann, and Herman Oldenberg. Bloomfield's teaching positions were: instructor in German, University of Cincinnati (1909–10); the same, University of Illinois (1910–13); assistant professor of Comparative Philology and German, University of Illinois (1913–21); professor of German and Linguistics, Ohio State University (1921–27); professor of Germanic Philology, University of Chicago (1927–40); and Sterling Professor of Linguistics, Yale University (1940–49). Bloomfield's scholarly writings were at first concerned with Indo-European phonology and morphology. In 1914 he published his first inclusive survey of the field of language, *An Introduction to the Study of Language.* Working increasingly in languages outside the Indo-European orbit, he published in 1917 *Tagalog Texts with Grammatical Analysis,* in which he described and analyzed the chief language of the Philippines for the first time. Five years later, in a review of Truman Michelson's work on Fox in the American Journal of Philology, Bloomfield wrote the first of his many contributions to the descriptive and comparative study of the Algonquian languages. Bloomfield's masterpiece is unquestionably his book *Language* (1933), a work without an equal as an exposition and synthesis of linguistic science. He called it, in the preface, "a revision of the author's *Introduction to the Study of Language*"; but it is in fact a new work in every detail of its plan and execution. Even the author's fundamental point of view is wholly different in the two books: in 1914 Bloomfield had viewed language from the position of Wilhelm Wundt; by 1933, partly as a result of his association with the psychologist Albert Paul Weiss, he had become a behaviorist. More important, however, than the shift of his psychological point of view was his position that linguistic facts should be stated "without reference to any one psychological doctrine." *Language* was far in advance of the current theory and practice of linguistics, and its unfamiliar plan seemed to many scholars a needless flouting of tradition. The book, however, summarized and clarified the main results of linguistic research up to the time of its publication, and pointed the direction that linguistics was to take in the immediate future. Today its innovations have become commonplace and the book approaches the status of a standard text. Bloomfield was also concerned with the practical applications of linguistics. He wrote a beginning book in German (*First German Book,* 1923; 2nd ed., 1928) and a complete course for teaching schoolchildren to read (*Children's Reader,* 1939), based on the true relation of writing to speech and carefully planned to illustrate all regular spellings before proceeding to the irregular. In 1942 he wrote a booklet, *Outline Guide for the Practical Study of Foreign Languages,* which was a brief but lucid statement of how a linguist works with an informant. The principles set forth in this booklet were utilized by trained linguists in the construction of a series of practical manuals giving instruction in strategically important languages for use by the armed services in World War II. Bloomfield was one of the founders of the Linguistic Society of America; he himself wrote the call for the organization meeting, as well as the first published article in the Society's scholarly publication, *Language.* Bloomfield's greatness as a scholar was not limited to any one branch or aspect of linguistics. Trained as an Indo-Europeanist in the great tradition of the neo-grammarians, he had also a specialist's knowledge of at least four groups within the general field: Germanic, Indic, Slavic, and Greek. He appreciated not only the value of comparative and historical grammar but that of descriptive grammar as well. His interest in the latter subject, and the depth of insight that he brought to it —both stemming from his intimate study of Panini—are notably reflected in his book *Language.* Bloomfield's greatest contribution to the study of language was to make a science of it. Others before him had worked scientifically in linguistics; but no one had so uncompromisingly rejected all prescientific methods, or had been so consistently careful, in writing about language, to use terms that would imply no tacit reliance on factors beyond the range of observation. Bloomfield taught linguists the necessity of speaking about language in the style that every scientist uses when he speaks about the object of his research: impersonally, precisely, and in terms that assume no more than actual observation discloses to him. Other works by Bloomfield in addition to those mentioned above are *Menomini Texts* (1928), *Plains Cree Texts* (1934), *Linguistic Aspects of Science* (1939), *Colloquial Dutch* (1944), and *Spoken Dutch* (vol. 1, 1944; vol. 2, 1945).

Bloomfield, Maurice. b. at Bielitz (now Bielsko, Poland), Feb. 23, 1855; d. June 13, 1928. American scholar, professor of Sanskrit and comparative philology at Johns

Hopkins University; uncle of Leonard Bloomfield. He was graduated from Furman University, Granville, S.C., in 1877. He edited (1890) the *Kangika-Sutra* from the original manuscripts, translated the hymns of the *Atharva-Veda* (in Max Müller's *Sacred Books of the East*), and edited, with Professor Richard von Garbe of Tübingen, the Kashmirian *Paippalada-Veda* (1901). Among his other publications are *The Atharva-Veda and the Gopatha-Brāhmaṅa* (1899), *Cerberus, the Dog of Hades* (1905), a concordance to Vedic literature (1907), and numerous technical articles.

Bloomfield, Robert. b. at Honington, Suffolk, England, Dec. 3, 1766; d. at Shefford, Bedfordshire, England, Aug. 19, 1823. English poet and shoemaker. His best-known work is *The Farmer's Boy* (1800). He also wrote *Rural Tales* (1802) and *The Banks of the Wye* (1811).

Bloomfield, Samuel Thomas. b. 1790; d. at Wandsworth, London, Sept. 28, 1869. English scholar and Biblical critic. He edited (1832) the Greek Testament.

Bloomgarden (blöm'gär.dęn), **Solomon.** [Pseudonym, **Yehoash.**] b. at Wertzblowo, Lithuania, in March, 1870; d. at New York, Jan. 10, 1927. American writer and poet in Yiddish. He came to the U.S. in 1890, lived briefly (1914) in Palestine, and returned (1915) to New York, where he lived until his death. He translated into Yiddish *The Song of Hiawatha* (1910), *Sayings of the Fathers* (1912), and large sections of the Jewish Bible, and compiled, with Charles D. Spivak, *Yiddish Dictionary Containing all the Hebrew and Chaldaic Elements of the Yiddish Language* (1911). Author of *Gezamelte Lieder* (1907), *Neie Shriften* (2 vols., 1910), *From New York to Rehoboth and Return* (3 vols., 1917), *In Geweb* (2 vols., 1919–21), and others.

Bloomingdale (blöm'ing.dāl). Borough in N New Jersey, in Passaic County. 3,251 (1950).

Blooming Grove. Town in S Wisconsin, in Dane County. 5,428 (1950).

Bloomington (blöm'ing.tọn). Unincorporated community in S California, in San Bernardino County E of Los Angeles. Under the urban definition established for use in the 1950 census, Bloomington was counted with adjoining urban areas; the last official enumeration was 2,726 (1940).

Bloomington. City in C Illinois, county seat of McLean County, in the center of a corn-growing and coal-mining region: sister city of Normal. It is the seat of Illinois Wesleyan University, and a commercial and manufacturing center. Here, on May 29, 1856, Lincoln delivered his "lost speech" denouncing slavery. 34,163 (1950).

Bloomington. City in S Indiana, county seat of Monroe County, ab. 46 mi. SW of Indianapolis. It has extensive quarrying interests, chiefly in limestone, and manufactures of furniture. It is the seat of Indiana University. 28,163 (1950).

Bloomington. Former name of **Muscatine,** Iowa.

Bloomsburg (blömz'bėrg). Town in E Pennsylvania, county seat of Columbia County, on Fishing Creek, ab. 35 mi. SW of Wilkes-Barre: manufactures include silk textiles, carpets, and mouse traps. It is the seat of a state teachers college. Platted in 1802, it is the only area in the state incorporated as a town, rather than as a borough or city. 10,633 (1950).

Bloomsbury (blömz'bėr.i). Ward of Holborn metropolitan borough, in W central London, in the County of London. The district, which is chiefly residential, lies N of Oxford Street between Euston Road, Gray's Inn Road, and Tottenham Court Road, and contains the British Museum. A favorite residential section with artists and writers, Bloomsbury gave its name to an intellectual group of the 1920's and 1930's which included Virginia Woolf, Clive Bell, Roger Fry, and Lytton Strachey. 4,979 (1931).

Bloomsbury Gang. In English history, the name given to a political clique which had considerable influence in the politics of the late 18th century. It was led by Francis Russell, 5th Duke of Bedford (whose activities in various ministries of the day caused Burke to characterize him as "the leviathan of the creatures of the crown") and had its headquarters at Bloomsbury House, London.

Bloomsbury Square. Square at London, N of Oxford Street, and E of the British Museum.

Blooms of the Berry. Volume (1887) of poems by Madison Cawein. Although generously praised by William Dean Howells in *Harper's*, Cawein's poetry did not find public favor, and the bulk of it was soon forgotten.

Bloor (blōr), **Ella Reeve.** [Sometimes called **"Mother Bloor."**] b. on Staten Island, N.Y., July 8, 1862; d. in August, 1951. American socialist leader, writer, and trade-union organizer, identified with the U.S. Communist Party from its beginning. Arrested 36 times before her 74th birthday for her activities on the picket line and elsewhere, she was at one time associated with Eugene Debs and Daniel De Leon, but broke with both. Her work on behalf of Sacco and Vanzetti, of the Passaic strikers in the period 1926–27, and of the miners in the period 1927–28 made her a heroine of the left wing of the U.S. labor movement.

Blore Heath (blōr). Heath situated near Market Drayton, Shropshire, England. Here the Yorkists under the Earl of Salisbury defeated (Sept. 23, 1459) the Lancastrians under Lord Audley.

Blos (blōs), **Wilhelm.** b. at Wertheim, Germany, Oct. 5, 1849; d. at Degerloch, Germany, July 6, 1927. German politician. He was a Social-Democratic member of the Reichstag (1881–1918), and *Ministerpresident,* or head of the state, of Württemberg (1918–20). He published historical studies, plays, and novels. His memoirs are a valuable source of data concerning the history of the Weimar Republic.

Blossius Aemilius Dracontius (blos'i.us ē.mil'i.us drakon'shus). See **Dracontius, Blossius Aemilius.**

Blossom (blos'ọm), **Henry Martyn.** b. at St. Louis, Mo., May 10, 1866; d. March 23, 1919. American dramatist. His plays include *Checkers* (from his story of the same name), *The Yankee Consul, Baron Trenck, The Only Girl, The Princess Pat,* and *Eileen.* He also wrote the comic operas *Mlle. Modiste* and *The Slim Princess,* the musical comedies *The Red Mill* and *The Man from Cooks,* and an opera, *Prima Donna.*

Blostman (blōst'män). [Meaning, in Modern English, "Blossoms."] Prose work (c898) by King Alfred of England (Alfred the Great). The selections in it were taken chiefly from the *Soliloquies* of Saint Augustine.

Blot on the 'Scutcheon, A. Tragedy by Robert Browning, brought out in England in 1843. The cause of a bitter quarrel between Browning and the actor William Charles Macready, it was afterward produced in America by Lawrence Barrett. The plot (a melodramatic quarrel between two noble houses in the 18th century) is of Browning's invention, but it has points of resemblance to *Romeo and Juliet.*

Bloudy Tenent of Persecution (blud'i), **The.** Tract by Roger Williams, published at London in 1644, arguing the cause of freedom of conscience.

Blouet (blö.e), **Paul.** [Pseudonym, **Max O'Rell.**] b. in Brittany, France, March 2, 1848; d. at Paris, May 24, 1903. French author and lecturer. He published works translated into English as *John Bull and His Island* and *Jonathan and His Continent* (dealing, respectively, with Great Britain and the U.S.).

Blount (blunt), **Charles.** [Title, 5th Baron **Mountjoy.**] d. 1545. English nobleman, noted as a patron of learning.

Blount, Charles. [Titles: 8th Baron **Mountjoy;** created Earl of **Devonshire** in 1603.] b. 1563; d. at London, April 3, 1606. English nobleman. He was a favorite of Queen Elizabeth, and a friend and supporter of Essex, whom he succeeded in Ireland. He defeated Hugh O'Neill, 2nd Earl of Tyrone, and, with Sir George Carew, obtained military possession of nearly the whole of Ireland.

Blount, Charles. b. at Upper Holloway, England, April 27, 1654; d. a suicide, in August, 1693. English deist and pamphleteer. He wrote against the censorship of the press, and, having fallen in love with his deceased wife's sister, published a defense of marriage between persons so connected (at that time proscribed in England). He wrote *Anima mundi* (1679), *The Two Books of Philostratus, or the Life of Apollonius of Tyanaeus, from the Greek* (1680), and others.

Blount or **Blunt** (blunt), **Edward.** fl. 1588–1632. English printer, publisher, and translator. He was an intimate friend of Christopher Marlowe, whose *Hero and Leander* he published (1598). He also issued John Florio's translation of Montaigne's *Essays,* translated Lorenzo Ducci's

Ars Aulica, or the Courtier's Arte, published (1620) Thomas Shelton's first English translation of *Don Quixote,* and produced (1623) with Isaac Jaggard, under the direction of John Heming and Henry Condell, the first great folio of Shakespeare's works. He made (1632) the first collection of John Lyly's *Sixe Court Comedies;* in the same year Blount translated *Christian Police* from the Spanish of Juan de Santa Maria.

Blount, Harry. Lord Marmion's page, in Sir Walter Scott's poem *Marmion.*

Blount, James Henderson. b. in Jones County, Ga., Sept. 12, 1837; d. March 8, 1903. American lawyer, congressman, and diplomat, whose report to President Cleveland is said to have decided U.S. policy against formal annexation at that time of Hawaii. A member (1872–93) of Congress from Georgia, he was appointed special commissioner (1893) and minister (1893) to Hawaii. After the establishment of the unofficial protectorate of Hawaii, he considered that Queen Liliuokalani of Hawaii had been wronged, and ordered the American flag lowered to indicate the end of the U.S. protectorate. This act of opposition was reported to Cleveland, who supported it.

Blount, Martha. b. probably near Reading, England, June 15, 1690; d. in Berkeley Row, Hanover Square, London, 1762. Englishwoman, an intimate friend of Alexander Pope. He left her by his will 1,000 pounds, many books, all his household goods, and made her residuary legatee. He had previously dedicated to her his *Epistle on Women.*

Blount, Sir Frederick. Poor but well-dressed fortune hunter, in Edward Bulwer-Lytton's play *Money.* He is quite unable to pronounce the letter *r,* considering it "wough and wasping."

Blount, Thomas. b. at Bordesley, Worcestershire, England, 1618; d. at Orleton, Herefordshire, England, Dec. 26, 1679. English writer on law. He studied law at the Inner Temple, and was admitted to the bar, but as a Roman Catholic in a country at that time strongly anti-Catholic, he found it difficult to practice his profession; he retired to his estate at Orleton, and continued his study of the law as an amateur. His most famous work is *Glossographia* (1656), the first English dictionary to include etymologies and to list the authorities consulted. In making the *Glossographia,* Blount utilized freely the English dictionary of Bullokar (1616) and the Latin-English dictionaries of Thomas Thomas and Francis Holyoke. However, Blount introduced new words into the dictionary and defended the practice by citing their use by current authors. The Glossographia was not a complete dictionary of English as native words and words from "poetical stories" were omitted, but the dictionary went through five editions (1656, 1661, 1670, 1674, 1681) and must have been fairly popular. Among his other works are the *Academie of Eloquence* (1654), *A Law Dictionary* (1670), and *Fragmenta Antiquitatis, Ancient Tenures of Land* (1679).

Blount, Sir **Thomas Pope.** b. at London, Sept. 12, 1649; d. at Tittenhanger, Hertfordshire, England, June 30, 1697. English statesman, member of Parliament, and critic and essayist. Made a baronet by Charles II, he was a member of Parliament for St. Albans. Author of *Criticism on Celebrated Authors* (1690), recording in a chronological system what various famous writers have thought about each other; *A Natural History, Containing Many not common Observations* (1693); *Remarks upon Poetry, with Characters and Censures of the most considerable Poets* (1694), dealing with poetry as an art, types of poetry, and the poetry of England, France, Italy, and Spain; and *Essays on Several Subjects* (1692), a collection of essays on such subjects as self-interest, popery, and the dangers of learning.

Blount, Sir Walter. Killed July 23, 1403. English soldier. He accompanied (1367) Edward (the Black Prince) and John of Gaunt to Spain with the intent of restoring Peter the Cruel to the throne of León and Castile, and probably went (1386) to Castile with John of Gaunt, on an expedition to assert the latter's claim to the throne. He was killed by Archibald, 4th Earl of Douglas, who mistook him for Henry IV of England during the battle of Shrewsbury. In Shakespeare's *Henry IV, Part I,* the character Sir Walter Blunt appears and his military accomplishments are lauded by Hotspur and Henry IV.

Blount, William. [Title, 4th Baron **Mountjoy.**] d. in Staffordshire, England, 1534. English nobleman and patron of learning, who brought (1498) Erasmus to England. He studied (c1496) at Paris under Erasmus. An intimate of Henry Tudor, later Henry VIII of England, he fought against Perkin Warbeck in 1497, was bailiff of Tournai (1514–17), and served as an attendant of Henry VIII at the meeting of the Field of the Cloth of Gold (1520) and at a meeting with Charles V at Dover (1522). Erasmus lamented his patron's death in his dedications to *Ecclesiastes* (1535) and to *Adagia* (1536 edition). Blount also befriended Richard Whytforde and Richard Sampson.

Blount, William. b. in North Carolina, March 26, 1749; d. at Knoxville, Tenn., March 21, 1800. American politician. During the Revolutionary War, he served with the forces of North Carolina, and during the period 1780–89 with that state's legislature. He was a delegate (1782–83, 1786, 1787) to the Continental Congress, and one of the signers (1787) of the Constitution. He was appointed (1790), by George Washington, governor of the territory south of the Ohio; when this area was incorporated (1796) into the U.S. as the state of Tennessee, he was elected its first U.S. senator. While still governor of the territory, he sought to obtain help with certain personal financial difficulties by engaging in a scheme whereby a group of Tennessee frontiersmen, plus Creek and Cherokee Indians, would aid the British in conquering the Spanish territory of West Florida; when his part in this plot was discovered, he was expelled (1797) from the Senate, but impeachment proceedings against him were not carried through. In 1798 he was elected to the Tennessee state legislature.

Blow (blō), **John.** b. at Collingham, Nottinghamshire, England, c1648; d. at Westminster, London, Oct. 1, 1708. English composer, organist of Westminster Abbey, and later of the Chapel Royal. He was the teacher of Henry Purcell, who, in 1679, succeeded him for a time as organist at Westminster Abbey.

Blow, Susan Elizabeth. b. at St. Louis, Mo., June 7, 1843; d. March 26, 1916. American educator and author. She established at St. Louis the first American public kindergarten (1873) and a training school (1874). A student of the theories of Friedrich Froebel, she lectured and conducted study classes (1895) at Boston, and was associated with the New York Kindergarten Association. Her works include *Symbolic Education* (1894), *The Mottoes and Commentaries of Froebel's Mother Play* (1895), *Letters to a Mother on the Philosophy of Froebel* (1899), and *Kindergarten Education* (1900).

Blowers (blō'ėrz), **Sampson Salter.** b. at Boston, March 10, 1742; d. at Halifax, Nova Scotia, Oct. 25, 1842. American Loyalist jurist, remembered for his successful defense of the British soldiers involved in the "Boston Massacre." Proscribed by the American revolutionary government, he emigrated to Nova Scotia where he practiced law and held various political offices, including chief justice and president of the council (1797 *et seq.*).

Blowitz (blō'vits), **Henry Georges Stephane Adolphe Opper de.** b. at Blowitz, near Pilsen (now Plzeň), in Bohemia, Dec. 28, 1825; d. at Paris, Jan. 18, 1903. French journalist, and Paris representative of the London *Times.* Of Austrian parentage, he adopted the name of his birthplace and was naturalized a Frenchman in 1870.

Blowzelinda (blou.zę.lin'dą) or **Blowsalinda** (-zą-). Country girl in John Gay's pastoral poem *The Shepherd's Week.* She is not the traditional rustic maiden of such poetry, but a physically strong, approximately true-to-life milkmaid, who feeds the hogs and does other necessary (but unromantic) chores.

Bloxham (blok'sąm), **William Dunnington.** b. in Florida, July 9, 1835; d. March 15, 1911. American politician. He was governor (1881–85, 1897–1901) of Florida.

Bloy (blwȧ), **Léon Marie.** b. at Périgueux, France, July 11, 1846; d. at Bourg-la-Reine, France, Nov. 3, 1917. French novelist, literary critic, and Catholic pamphleteer, considered an instigator of the French "Catholic Renaissance" movement. He was the author of novels, including *Le Pal* (1885) and *La Femme pauvre* (1897; Eng. trans., *The Woman who Was Poor,* 1939), of a 7-volume

Journal (1918), of many polemic pamphlets, and of a voluminous correspondence, *Lettres de jeunesse* (1920) and *Lettres à la fiancée* (1922; Eng. trans., 1937).

Blubo (blö'bō). See **Blut und Boden.**

Blücher (blü'ċhėr; Anglicized, blö'chėr, -kėr), **Gebhard Leberecht von.** [Title, Prince of **Wahlstatt;** called **Marschall Vorwärts,** meaning "Marshal Forward."] b. at Rostock, in Mecklenburg-Schwerin, Dec. 16, 1742; d. at Krieblowitz, in Silesia, Sept. 12, 1819. Prussian field marshal, noted as one of Napoleon's outstanding military adversaries. While still a youth he entered (1756) the Swedish military service and was captured (1760) by the Prussians in the Pomeranian phase of the Seven Years' War; he was induced by the Prussians to enter the Prussian service as a lieutenant of hussars. Disgruntled at his slow rise in rank, he resigned from the Prussian army, thereby incurring the displeasure of Frederick the Great. However, after about 15 years of farming, during which he became an estate owner, he rejoined his regiment as a major, taking part (1787) in the Netherlands campaign, and the French campaign of 1793–94. In the last-named year he was promoted to major general; he became a lieutenant general in 1801. He commanded (Oct. 14, 1806) at Auerstädt, and was forced (November, 1806) to surrender to the French near Lübeck, but was soon exchanged for the French general Victor. When the War of Liberation of the Prussians against the French broke out in 1813, Blücher, already an elderly man, was placed in a high military post, and served with distinction at Lützen, Bautzen, Katzbach, Möckern, Leipzig, and elsewhere, and received the rank of field marshal. Although routed several times by Napoleon in 1814, Blücher defeated him at Laon, on March 9, 1814, occupying Paris on March 31, and for these triumphs received the title Prince of Wahlstatt (Wahlstatt was part of the Katzbach battlefield). Following the Allied rulers to England he was honored there for his achievements. He retired to his property in Silesia, remaining there until the return of Napoleon in 1815, when he was given command of the Prussian army. He was severely defeated (June 16, 1815) by Napoleon at Ligny, almost losing his own life in this battle; however, having gone to the aid of Wellington at La Belle Alliance, the battlefield of Waterloo, on June 18, 1815, he helped turn the tide of that battle against Napoleon, and occupied Paris for a second time. He was awarded the Iron Cross (created to honor service in the War of Liberation) by Frederick William III.

Blücher, Vasily Konstantinovich. [Surname assumed in China, **Galen** or **Galin.**] b. 1889—. Russian general. He served in the Russian army during World War I as an enlisted man. He took part in the initial phase (1917) of the Russian Revolution, being identified from the outset with the Bolshevik followers of Lenin, and was quickly promoted to high command when the Bolsheviks became the dominant faction in the Russian government. In the period 1919–20 he led armies against the counterrevolutionary forces of Kolchak and Wrangel, serving immediately thereafter (1921–22) as chief Russian commander in the Far East (he is generally credited with having driven the Japanese out of Vladivostok in 1922). From 1924 to 1928, he headed an advisory military mission to the Kuomintang, in China, but returned to Moscow when Chiang Kai-shek repudiated further Communist help in his campaign to unite all of China under the Kuomintang. Blücher was thereafter for seven years the chief Russian commander in the Far East; in 1938 he mysteriously disappeared and no word about him has since come out of the U.S.S.R. Like many revolutionary figures in Russia, he took an assumed name; in his case, unlike those of Molotov and Stalin (whose original names are known), no one has yet been able to determine (except, presumably, the Russian secret police) what his original name was. He assumed another name (Galen or, sometimes, Galin) while he was in China (and is referred to under this name in the novel *Man's Fate,* by André Malraux).

Bludenz (blö'dents). Town in W Austria, in Vorarlberg province, situated on the Ill River, near the borders of Liechtenstein and Switzerland, ab. 24 mi. S of Bregenz. It is a station on the railroad from Vienna to Paris, the first major stop W of the Arlberg tunnel. There are textile, chocolate, stove, and watchmaking factories. 10,130 (1951).

Bludov (blö'dǫf), Count **Dmitry Nikolayevich.** b. in the government of Vladimir, Russia, April 16, 1785; d. at St. Petersburg, March 2, 1864. Russian statesman and diplomat. He was appointed minister of the interior in 1837, minister of justice in 1839, and president of the council of the empire and council of the ministry in 1861. He was active in improving the conditions of the serfs, and in the official abolishment (1861) of serfdom in Russia.

Blue (blö), **Rupert.** b. in Richmond County, N.C., May 30, 1868; d. at Charleston, S.C., April 12, 1948. American public health authority, noted for campaigns against bubonic plague and other communicable diseases. He served until 1920 as a staff member and acted (1912–20) as surgeon general of the U.S. Public Health Service; he also participated (1928) in the revision of quarantine rules. He retired from active service in 1932.

Blue, Victor. b. in Richmond County, N.C., Dec. 6, 1865; d. en route to Washington, D.C., Jan. 22, 1928. American naval officer. Graduated (1887) from the U.S. Naval Academy, he served in the Spanish-American War, during which he volunteered for two scouting expeditions on the Cuban mainland, the first (June 11–13, 1898) to determine the position of the Cervera fleet in the Santiago harbor, and the second (June 25–27, 1898) to locate the position of enemy ships in preparation for a torpedo attack. He was chief of staff (1910 *et seq.*) of the Pacific fleet, and chief (1913 *et seq.*) of the Bureau of Navigation; in 1919 he was made a rear admiral.

Blue and the Gray, The. Names applied, respectively, to the Union and Confederate armies during the American Civil War. As a rule, the uniforms of the Union troops were blue, while those worn by their opponents were gray. The expression "The Blue and the Gray" now carries connotations of sectional reunion and mutual understanding displacing the hatreds of the Civil War and Reconstruction periods.

"Bluebeard" (blö'bird). See also **Barbe-Bleue.**

Bluebeard. [French, **Barbe-Bleue;** German, **Blaubart.**] Nickname of the chevalier Raoul (an imaginary personage), celebrated for his cruelty. The historic origin was, perhaps, Gilles de Laval, Baron de Retz (b. 1396; d. 1440). He is the subject of works by Charles Perrault, André Ernest Modeste Grétry, Jacques Offenbach, Ludwig Tieck, and others. In Perrault's story, he is a rich man who, in spite of his hideous blue beard, has had six wives and marries a seventh, a young girl named Fatima. He leaves the keys of the castle with her while he goes on a journey, telling her that she may enter any room but one. She disobeys, enters the forbidden chamber, and discovers the bodies of his former wives. A bloodstain on the key reveals her disobedience, and her husband gives her five minutes to prepare for death. Her sister Anne mounts to the top of the castle to watch for aid, and at last sees their brothers coming. They arrive and kill Bluebeard as he is about to dispatch Fatima. Perrault's story was written (c1697) in French, and translated into English in the 18th century.

Blue Beard. Comic opera by Michel Jean Sedaine, with music by André Ernest Modeste Grétry, produced in 1797.

Blue Beard, or Female Curiosity. Musical play by the younger George Colman, produced in 1798.

Blue Bird, The. [French title, **L'Oiseau bleu.**] Fairy tale by Marie Catherine d'Aulnoy. Flora and Troutina, daughters of a king, are rivals for the hand of Prince Charming. He loves Flora, who is good and beautiful, but the queen insists that he shall marry Troutina, who is ill-tempered and hideous. In consequence of his refusal, he is condemned to wear the form of a bluebird for seven years. The superior powers of a friendly enchantress and a fairy enable them to restore him to his own form and unite him to the lovely Flora.

Blue Bird, The. [French title, **L'Oiseau bleu.**] Drama by the Belgian poet Maurice Maeterlinck. It was first published, under its French title, in 1909. It was intended by its author to convey symbolically a number of mystical ideas. In the English-speaking world, however, it has achieved its chief fame as one of the most popular children's plays in existence.

Blue Boy, The. Oil painting (1779) by Thomas Gainsborough, in the Huntington Art Gallery, at San Marino, Calif. It is a full-length portrait of a boy, wearing a 16th-century costume of blue satin, set against a landscape background.

Bluecher (blü'ċhėr). See **Blücher.**

Blue Coat School. See **Christ's Hospital.**

Blue Division. Spanish "volunteer" military unit, consisting mostly of Falangists, sent by Francisco Franco to aid Hitler in his attack upon Russia during World War II. First active on the Russian front in July, 1942, the unit was officially disbanded after protests by the U.S. ambassador, Carlton J. H. Hayes, and the British ambassador, Sir Samuel Hoare, that it constituted a violation of Franco's professed "nonbelligerency." The first elements of the unit returned to Spain in 1943, but a proclamation of Generalissimo Franco had meanwhile urged its members to join the German army, and many men came back later than the official date set for their return.

Blue Eagle. Blue thunderbird emblem, captioned "We Do Our Part," proclaimed (July 20, 1933) as the symbol of the National Recovery Administration by its chief administrator, Hugh S. Johnson. All industries or establishments conforming to the "blanket code" (the President's Reëmployment Agreement) or individual codes of fair competition were entitled to display the emblem. It was abolished (Sept. 5, 1935) following invalidation by the U.S. Supreme Court of the government-sponsored code system.

Blue Earth. City in S Minnesota, county seat of Faribault County, on the Blue Earth River. A trading center for an agricultural area, it produces canned goods (especially peas and corn) and dairy products. 3,843 (1950).

Bluefield (blö'fēld). Town in SW Virginia, in Tazewell County, adjoining Bluefield, West Virginia. 4,212 (1950).

Bluefield. City in S West Virginia, in Mercer County, ab. 70 mi. W of Roanoke, in the Pocahontas coal field. A distributing center for coal, it also manufactures flour, lumber, mattresses, and electrical and mechanical mine equipment. It is the seat of the Bluefield State Teachers College. The state line separates it from Bluefield, Va. 21,506 (1950).

Bluefields (blö'fēldz). Town and *municipio* (administrative unit equivalent to a county) in SE Nicaragua, capital of Zelaya department, in the Mosquito Reserve, near the mouth of the Escondido River: export center for bananas, hardwoods, and gold. Pop. of municipio, 20,278 (est. 1947); of town, 7,463 (1950).

Bluefields River. See **Escondido River.**

Blue Glacier. Glacier in Antarctica, flowing into the Bowers Piedmont Glacier ab. 10 mi. S of New Harbor, in Victoria Land; in ab. 77°52′ S., 164°10′ E. It was discovered by the National Antarctic Expedition (1901–04), under the command of Captain Robert F. Scott, who gave it this name because of its clear blue ice at the time of discovery. Length, ab. 20 mi.; width, 2–4 mi.

Blue-gowns. In Scottish history, the name given to certain bedesmen who received alms from the kings of Scotland. They wore a blue gown with a pewter badge, and were allowed to beg in any part of Scotland.

Bluegrass Region. Popular name given to that part of C Kentucky which abounds in blue grass (*poa pratensis*); known for its race horses.

"Bluegrass State." Nickname of **Kentucky.**

Blue Grotto. Cavern on the shore of Capri island, in the Bay of Naples, S Italy.

"Blue Hen State." A nickname of **Delaware.**

Blue Hills. Range of hills in Norfolk County, Massachusetts, near Milton, S of Boston. The height of Great Blue Hill is 635 ft.

Blue Hotel, The. Short story (c1898) by Stephen Crane.

Blue Island. City in NE Illinois, in Cook County, ab. 10 mi. SW of Chicago: residential and industrial suburb, and canning center. 17,622 (1950).

Blue Knight. In Arthurian legend, Sir Persaunt of India, overthrown by Sir Gareth. He is described in Thomas Malory's *Morte d'Arthur* and in Tennyson's idyll *Gareth and Lynette.*

Blue Laws. In U.S. history, a term applied to statutory enactments prohibiting work or recreation on the Sabbath, or forbidding certain personal indulgences (such as the imbibing of spirituous liquors or the smoking of cigarettes). Although Blue Laws are perhaps best known in association with the Puritan colonies in New England, they did not originate there. The term gained currency after the publication of Samuel A. Peters's description of the Connecticut Blue Laws in *A General History of Connecticut, by a Gentleman of the Province* (1781), and at first was confined to characterizing the statutes of the New Haven Colony.

Blue Licks, Battle of. Engagement (Aug. 19, 1782) between Kentucky frontier settlers and a British force of Canadians and Indians, fought near the Lower Blue Lick Springs on the Middle Fork of Licking River. Although the Kentuckians were compelled to retreat, this action was the last major invasion of Kentucky carried out by the Indians.

Blue Lights. In U.S. history, a term originating in the War of 1812, when Stephen Decatur saw blue lights burning at the mouth of the Thames River near New London, Conn., and regarded them as signals to the British blockaders informing them of the imminent departure of his frigates. The presence of the lights caused Decatur to abandon his scheme to run the blockade. The term "Bluelight Federalist" was subsequently applied to Federalists who opposed the war and were suspected of being in league with the British.

Blue Lodges. In U.S. history, a term applied to the clandestine proslavery bodies organized (1854) in the western areas of Missouri to oppose the efforts of Northern free soilers to make Kansas a free territory. They facilitated the settlement of proslavery adherents in Kansas and sometimes went across the border to take part in electing men of their own party to offices in the territorial government.

Blue Mountains. See also **Kittatinny Mountains.**

Blue Mountains. Name given to a boldly warped portion of the earth's crust in E New South Wales, Australia, NW of Sydney. Average elevation, ab. 3,000–4,000 ft.

Blue Mountains. Range of mountains in the E part of Jamaica, British West Indies, in Portland, St. Andrew, and St. Thomas parishes. The highest point is Blue Mountain Peak (ab. 7,360 ft.).

Blue Mountains. Mountains of NE Oregon, with the exception of the Wallowa Mountains, extending into Washington to the bend of the Snake River.

Blue Nile. [Also: **Gezira**; Arabic, **El Jezira.**] Province of the Anglo-Egyptian Sudan, in NE Africa, bounded on the N by Khartoum province, on the W by Kordofan and Upper Nile provinces, on the S by Ethiopia, and on the E by Kassala province. The province is mainly contained by the Blue Nile River on the E and the White Nile River on the W, and is one of the more fertile and prosperous sections of the country. Sennar in the center of the province is the junction of the railway lines connecting Kassala and El Obeid with Khartoum. Created in 1935, this province contains the old provinces of Blue Nile, Fung, and White Nile. Capital, Wad Medani; area, 54,775 sq. mi.; pop. 1,779,756 (est. 1949).

Blue Nile. [Arabic, **Bahr el Azraq, Bahr el Azrak.**] River in NE Africa, one of the branches of the Nile River. It drains Lake Tana in the Ethiopian highlands and joins the White Nile (Bahr-el-Abyad) at Khartoum, Anglo-Egyptian Sudan. Length, ab. 900 mi.

Blue Ridge. Easternmost of the chains of the Appalachian system of mountains, chiefly in Virginia and North Carolina, extending from Harpers Ferry, W.Va., to N Georgia. It is a continuation of the South Mountain of Pennsylvania and Maryland, which is also often called the Blue Ridge. It is famous for its picturesque scenery; two national highways, the Skyline Drive and Blue Ridge Parkway, attract many tourists. In Virginia it separates the Piedmont region from the Shenandoah Valley. Highest point, in North Carolina, Mount Mitchell (6,684 ft.).

Blue Ridge Tunnel. Tunnel through Rockfish Gap linking Waynesboro and Afton, Va., built (1850–58) by the state of Virginia, the Blue Ridge Railroad, and the Virginia Central Railroad. It was for some time the longest tunnel in the U.S. It became (1870) the property of the Chesapeake and Ohio Railroad.

Blue River City. Former name of **Crete,** Neb.

Bluestocking at Court, A. One of three historical tales in *The Ladies!* (1922), by Lily Adams Beck, published under the pseudonym E. Barrington. Its central character is Fanny Burney.

Bluestocking Clubs. Name applied to assemblies held in London c1750 at the houses of Elizabeth Montagu and other ladies, in which literary conversation and other intellectual enjoyments were substituted for cards and gossip. These meetings were characterized by a studied plainness of dress on the part of some of the guests. Among these was Benjamin Stillingfleet, who always wore blue stockings (rather than white ones, as would have been more usual on a formal occasion in that day), and in reference to whom the coterie was called in derision the "Bluestocking Society" or the "Bluestocking Club." The members, especially the ladies, were called "bluestockingers," "bluestocking ladies," and later simply "bluestockings" or "blues." The term "bluestocking" came later to be applied, usually derisively, to any woman who gave evidence of an affected (rather than real) interest in intellectual or literary matters.

Bluet d'Arbères (blü.e dȧr.ber), **Bernard de.** b. c1560; d. at Paris, 1606. French professional fool. He assumed the title of Comte de Permission, and published crackbrained prophecies and eulogies on his patrons. His *Œuvres*, consisting of about 180 numbered pieces, are extremely rare, and are highly prized by bibliophiles.

Bluff (bluf). [Former name, **Campbelltown.**] Borough at the S tip of South Island, New Zealand, ab. 17 mi. S of Invercargill, which it serves as a port. It has a natural deep-water harbor, opening to Foveaux Strait. 2,170 (est. 1948).

Bluff, Colonel. Character in Henry Fielding's *The Intriguing Chambermaid.*

Bluffton (bluf'tọn). City in NE Indiana, county seat of Wells County, in a farming region. 6,076 (1950).

Bluffton Movement. South Carolina program (1844), under the leadership of Robert Barnwell Rhett, for invoking "separate state action" as a means of securing a rectification of the tariff of 1842. Calhoun's disapproval of the movement was one of the chief reasons for its collapse.

Blum (blöm), **Alex Aladar.** b. at Budapest, Hungary, Feb. 7, 1889—. American painter, etcher, and teacher. He studied at the National Academy of Design, New York, and has exhibited etchings and paintings there and at the Metropolitan Museum of Art, New York, the Pennsylvania Academy of the Fine Arts, and elsewhere. In 1924, he won an award at the National Academy of Design. His work is in the collections of the Boston Museum of Fine Arts, the Metropolitan Museum, the Library of Congress, and others.

Blum, Ernest. b. at Paris, Aug. 15, 1836; d. there, Sept. 19, 1907. French journalistic writer.

Blum, Karl Ludwig. b. 1786; d. 1844. German operatic composer. As stage manager of the Berlin Opera, he introduced vaudeville from France into Germany.

Blum, Léon. b. at Paris, April 9, 1872; d. near Versailles, France, March 30, 1950. French statesman, journalist, and man of letters, leader of the French Socialist Party from 1919, and three times premier of France. While taking university degrees in law and literature, he began an active career as a literary critic and writer of short stories and essays. A member (1895–1919) of the Conseil d'État, the highest administrative tribunal in France, he entered the Socialist movement under the guidance of Jean Jaurès, contributing to Jaurès's journal, *L'Action Socialiste*, in 1900. In 1902 he joined the "French Socialist Party" organized (1902) by Jaurès, and became (1904) a member of the editorial staff of *L'Humanité*, the newspaper established by Jaurès. In the next few years, his work as a man of letters (1906–14) drew more attention than his political activity. He contributed literary criticism to *Gil Blas*, *L'Humanité*, *La Grande Revue*, and *Comoedia*. At the outbreak of World War I he was named by Marcel Sembat, Socialist minister of public works and supply, as chief of his executive staff (August, 1914–December, 1916). Upon election (1919) to the Chamber of Deputies from a Paris constituency, he assumed leadership of the Socialist Party, heading the Socialist group after the split between the Socialists and Communists at the Tours Congress (1921) of the Socialist Party. *L'Humanité* having passed into Communist hands, Blum, with Jean Longuet, organized another Socialist newspaper, *Le Populaire*, of which he became editor. Reëlected as a deputy in 1924, he was defeated four years later, but won back a seat at a by-election (1929) at Narbonne, and was returned by that constituency in the elections of 1932 and 1936. He helped to form (1934) the Popular Front. On Feb. 13, 1935, he was assaulted and severely injured by extremist opponents of socialism in France. With the victory of the Popular Front in the elections of May, 1936, he served as premier from June 4, 1936 to June 21, 1937. He followed a policy of social reform, monetary devaluation, and "nonintervention" in the Spanish Civil War. The French senate having refused (June, 1937) to grant him full powers to govern by decree, he resigned as premier, served (1937–38) as vice-premier under Camille Chautemps, and returned briefly (March 13–April 8, 1938) as premier. After the defeat of France in World War II, he voted (July 12, 1940) against the grant of dictatorial powers to Henri Pétain; arrested (Oct. 16, 1940) by the Vichy government, he was interned, and brought to trial (Feb. 19–April 11, 1942) at Riom. Turned over to the Germans with his codefendants in March, 1943, he was held at the Buchenwald concentration camp until April, 1945. After having been moved from camp to camp in the following month, he was liberated (May, 1945) by U.S. troops at Dobbiaco, Italy. He returned at once to Paris, where he resumed leadership of the Socialist Party and *Le Populaire.* He was head of an interim government (Dec. 12, 1946–Jan. 17, 1947) pending the election of the first president of the Fourth Republic, and was later named vice-premier in the cabinet of André Marie (July 24–Aug. 21, 1948). As special ambassador to the U.S., he negotiated (February–May, 1948) a Franco-American trade treaty and loan agreement. Among his works are *Les Nouvelles conversations de Goethe avec Eckermann* (1901), *Du mariage* (1907), and *Stendhal et le Beylisme* (1914).

Blum, Robert. b. at Cologne, Prussia, Nov. 10, 1807; executed at Vienna, Nov. 9, 1848. German political agitator and writer, leader of the Liberal Party in Saxony in the revolution of 1848.

Blum, Robert Frederick. b. at Cincinnati, Ohio, July 9, 1857; d. at New York, June 8, 1903. American painter, illustrator, and etcher. Having been commissioned by *Scribner's Magazine* to illustrate Sir Edwin Arnold's *Japonica*, he spent (1890–93) three years in Japan, where he developed his technique of pastel drawing. Many of his works are in the Cincinnati Art Museum, and one, *The Ameya*, is in the Metropolitan Museum of Art, New York.

Blume (blöm), **Peter.** b. in Russia, Oct. 27, 1906—. American surrealist painter who is considered by some critics to be one of the leaders of modernism in art in the U.S. He came to the U.S. in 1911, and studied at the Art Students League of New York; he won Guggenheim Fellowships in 1932 and 1936, and a first prize at the Carnegie International Exhibition of 1934. He has exhibited extensively in the U.S., and his work has provoked much discussion. His output of work is extremely limited because of the meticulosity of his technique. His paintings are now in collections of the Museum of Modern Art, the Whitney Museum of American Art, and the Metropolitan Museum of Art, New York, the Museum of Fine Arts, Boston, and other large institutions. Among his better-known works are *Interior*, *South of Scranton*, *Eternal City*, *Light of the World*, *The Rock*, *The White Factory*, *Parade*, and a mural for the U.S. post office at Cannonsburg, Pa.

Blumenau (blö.mẹ.nou'). River port in SE Brazil, on the Itajaí River, in the state of Santa Catarina: marketing center for grains, vegetables, fruits, and sugar; tobacco, maté, and butter are the principal exports. 22,919 (1950).

Blumenbach (blö'mẹn.bäċh), **Johann Friedrich.** b. at Gotha, Germany, May 11, 1752; d. at Göttingen, Germany, Jan. 22, 1840. German naturalist and physiologist, the originator of the science of physical anthropology. He was professor of medicine and anatomy (1776–1835) at the University of Göttingen, and editor (1780–94) of the *Medizinische Bibliothek.* He was the first to teach natural history on the basis of comparative anatomy, and proposed the division of the human species into five races: the Caucasian, Mongolian, Malay, American, and

African or Ethiopian. His works include *Handbuch der vergleichenden Anatomie und Physiologie* (1804), *Über den Bildungstrieb und das Zeugungsgeschäft* (1781), and *Institutiones physiologicae* (1787).

Blumenfeld (blö'mẹn.felt), **Feliks Mikhailovich.** b. April 19, 1863; d. at Moscow, Jan. 21, 1931. Russian conductor, composer, and pianist. He studied under Rimsky-Korsakov at the St. Petersburg conservatory, before being appointed a professor there. From 1898 to 1912 he conducted the Imperial Opera at St. Petersburg. His works include songs, preludes, a quartet, a symphony, and numerous selections for the piano.

Blumenschein (blö'mẹn.shīn), **Ernest Leonard.** b. at Pittsburgh, Pa., May 26, 1874—. American painter and illustrator, noted especially for his portraits; husband of Mary Shepard Blumenschein. He first studied music, then went on to study art at the Art Students League of New York, and the Julian Academy, Paris. From 1896 to 1908, his chief work consisted of illustrations for the *Scribner's*, *Century*, *Harper's* and *American* magazines, and for other periodicals as well as for books. His work has been exhibited throughout the U.S., and has won important prizes and awards. He is represented in the Kansas City, Mo., Museum and Library, the National Museum, Washington, D.C., the Metropolitan Museum of Art, New York, the Brooklyn Museum, the Museum of Modern Art, New York, the Milwaukee Art Institute, and others. He was made an academician of the National Academy of Design in 1927.

Blumenschein, Mary Shepard. [Maiden name, **Greene.**] b. at New York, Sept. 26, 1869—. American painter, illustrator, and craftsman; wife of Ernest L. Blumenschein. She studied at the Adelphi Academy and Pratt Institute, both at Brooklyn, and at Paris. Her work has been exhibited at Paris and in the U.S., and she won prizes at the Paris Salon (1902), the St. Louis Exposition (1904), and the National Academy of Design (1915). In 1913 she was made an associate of the National Academy of Design. She has also done magazine illustrations.

Blumenthal (blö'mẹn.täl), **Jacob.** b. at Hamburg, Germany, Oct. 4, 1829; d. in England, May 17, 1908. German piano teacher and composer. Pianist (1848 *et seq.*) to Queen Victoria at London, he composed pieces for piano, voice, and violin and cello.

Blumenthal, Count **Leonhard von.** b. July 30, 1810; d. Dec. 22, 1900. Prussian general. He became chief of the general staff of the army in Schleswig-Holstein in 1849, and served as chief of staff of the combined German forces against Denmark in 1864. He won added distinction in the Austro-Prussian War (Seven Weeks War) in 1866, becoming a lieutenant general in October of that year, and in the Franco-Prussian War, as chief of staff in the army of the German crown prince. He was made general field-marshal in 1888.

Blumenthal, Oskar. b. at Berlin, March 13, 1852; d. there, 1917. German dramatist. He founded the Lessing Theater at Berlin in 1888 and conducted it until 1897. His works include a large number of comedies, many of which were successful in their day. Among the best known are *Die grosse Blocke*, *Der schwarze Schleier*, *Ein Tropfen Gift*, and two written with Gustav Kadelburg, *Als ich wiederkam* and *Im weissen Rössl.* He was famous also for his witty epigrams (*Gesammelte Epigramme*, 1890).

Blümlisalp (blüm'lēs.älp). Mountain group in the Bernese Oberland, Switzerland, W of the Jungfrau. Its highest peak is the Blümlisalphorn (ab. 12,040 ft.).

Blunck (blủngk), **Hans Friedrich.** b. at Altona, Germany, Sept. 3, 1888—. German novelist, most prominent among the writers of regional fiction in the Low Saxon part of Germany. After serving with the German armed forces in World War I, he became syndic of the new University of Hamburg. On the advent of Hitler he was made (1933) president of the *Reichsschriftumskammer* (office of government documents), a post he held until 1935.) Since then he has retired to his farm in Holstein. He has traveled extensively, in Africa, South America, and elsewhere. A voluminous writer, his works, some of them in Low German, fill more than 40 volumes. They include fairy stories peopled with the sprites of the northern coast country (*Märchen von der Niederelbe*, 1923; *Von Klabautern*, 1926; *Geschichten in der Dämmerung*, 1933); several plays (among them *Kampf um Neuyork*, 1939); and ballads and other verse (collected 1937). But his chief fame is based on his many novels in which he has tried to depict the evolution of the Germans from the earliest times to the present (*Urvätersaga*, trilogy completed 1934; *Werdendes Volk*, trilogy completed 1933; and *Volkswende*, 1931). His advocacy of strong-man leadership and of "Nordic" superiority brought him due recognition in the Third Reich.

Blundell (blun'dẹl), **Francis.** [Pseudonym, **Mary E. Francis;** maiden name, **Sweetman.**] b. at Dublin, Ireland; d. in North Wales, March 9, 1930. English writer of children's books, dramatist, and novelist. She wrote stories of North Lancashire and Dorset life and character. Author of *Whither* (1892), *In a North Country Village* (1893), *The Song of Dan* (1894), *Town Mice in the Country* (1894), *Daughter of the Soil* (1895), *Among the Untrodden Ways* (1896), *The Duenna of a Genius* (1898), *Pastorals of Dorset* (1901), *The Manor Farm* (1902), *Dorset Dear* (1905), *Simple Annals* (1906), *Margery o' the Mill* (1907), *Galatea of the Wheatfield* (1909), *Molly's Fortunes* (1914), *Dark Rosaleen* (1915), *A Maid o' Dorset* (1917), and many others, popular in America as well as England. Her plays include *The Widow Woos* (1904) and *The Third Time of Asking* (1906).

Blundell, Peter. b. at Tiverton, Devonshire, England; d. 1601. English merchant and founder (1604) of Blundell's School. Of humble origin, he accumulated great wealth as a merchant and manufacturer in the kersey trade, and bequeathed his fortune toward the establishment and endowment of Blundell's School, near Tiverton, and the benefaction of London hospitals, and various institutions of the Devonshire cities of Tiverton and Exeter. Blundell's School is mentioned in Richard Doddridge Blackmore's novel *Lorna Doone*, as the place where its hero was educated.

Blunden (blun'dẹn), **Edmund Charles.** b. at London, Nov. 1, 1896—. English poet and critic. He served as professor (1924–27) of English literature at Tokyo University, and fellow and tutor (1931–43) in English literature at Merton College, Oxford. He published *Poems 1914–1930* and *Poems 1930–40;* his prose works include *The Bonadventure* (1922), *Undertones of War* (1928), *Life of Leigh Hunt* (1930), *The Face of England* (1932), *Charles Lamb and his Contemporaries* (1934), *The Mind's Eye* (1934), *Keats's Publisher* (1936), and *Shelley, a Life-Story* (1946).

Blunderbore (blun'dėr.bōr). Giant in the *Jack the Giant Killer* cycle of folk tales, who imprisoned Jack. Jack threw a noose out the window and strangled him. In another version, Jack scuttled his boat, and he was drowned.

Blunderstone Rookery (blun'dėr.stōn rủk'ėr.i). Residence of David Copperfield, senior, in Charles Dickens's novel *David Copperfield.*

Blundevill (blun'dẹ.vil), **Randulph de.** [Title, Earl of **Chester.**] d. at Wallingford, England, 1232. English feudal warrior and statesman; son of Hugh of Cyveiliog (1147–81); married into Henry II's family (1187) and William of Scots' (1200). He led the armies against the Welsh (1210 *et seq.*), and under John, and later under Henry III, against the barons (1215); after a crusade to the Holy Land (1218), he aided Henry in the siege of Nantes (1230), and remained in France a year in charge of the armies. His name occurs frequently in *Piers Plowman.*

Blundeville (blun'dẹ.vil), **Thomas.** fl. 2nd half of the 16th century. English author. On the death of his father, he inherited (1568) an estate at Newton Flotman, Norfolk. He is supposed to have been educated at Cambridge. In 1571 he erected, in the church of Newton Flotman, a monument under which he was later buried. He wrote, besides a number of treatises on horsemanship and other subjects, *A Briefe Description of universal Mappes and Cardes and of their use; and also the use of Ptholemeny his Tables . . .* (London, 1589), *M. Blundeville his Exercises* (six treatises on cosmography, astronomy, geography, and the art of navigation; London, 1594), *The Arte of Logike . . .* (1599), and *The Theoriques of the Planets, together with the making of two instruments for seamen to find out the latitude without seeing sun, moon, or stars, invented by Dr. Gilbert* (London, 1602).

Blunt (blunt), **Colonel.** Character in Sir Robert Howard's *The Committee.* Like Benedick, in Shakespeare's *Much Ado About Nothing,* he was a confirmed bachelor.

Blunt, Edmund. b. at Newburyport, Mass., Nov. 23, 1799; d. at Brooklyn, N.Y., Sept. 2, 1866. American hydrographer; son of Edmund March Blunt.

Blunt, Edmund March. b. at Portsmouth, N.H., June 20, 1770; d. at Sing Sing (now Ossining), N.Y., Jan. 4, 1862. American hydrographer, author of the *American Coast Pilot* (1796), and other works; father of Edmund Blunt and of George William Blunt.

Blunt, George William. b. at Newburyport, Mass., March 11, 1802; d. at New York, April 19, 1878. American hydrographer and publisher of nautical books and charts, who pioneered in the establishment of the U.S. Hydrographic Office; son of Edmund March Blunt. He served (1833–78) as first assistant of the U.S. Coast Survey, was a member of the Board of Pilot Commissioners, served for the rest of his life, except for a period of six months, as pilot commissioner (1845–78) of New York, and was commissioner (1852–54) of immigration. His firm published under his editorship *The Young Sea Officer's Sheet Anchor* (1843), *Memoir of the Dangers and Ice of the North Atlantic Ocean* (1845), *The Way to Avoid the Center of our Violent Gales* (1868), and *Pilot Laws, Harbor and Quarantine Regulations of New York* (1869).

Blunt, James Gillpatrick. b. at Trenton, Me., July 21, 1826; d. July 25, 1881. American soldier, who, during the Civil War, thwarted (Oct. 28, 1864) a Confederate invasion of Missouri led by General Sterling Price. He commanded a brigade of Kansans and Cherokees at the battle of Old Fort Wayne (Oct. 22, 1862), defeated General Marmaduke at Cane Hill (Nov. 28, 1862), captured Van Buren on the Arkansas River (Dec. 28, 1862), and defeated General Cooper at Honey Springs (July 16, 1863).

Blunt, John James. b. at Newcastle-under-Lyme, Staffordshire, England, 1794; d. at Cambridge, England, June 18, 1855. English divine, and ecclesiastical writer.

Blunt, Major-General. Old cavalier, rough but honest, in Thomas Shadwell's play *The Volunteers.*

Blunt, Sir Walter. See under **Blount, Sir Walter.**

Blunt, Stanhope English. b. at Boston, Sept. 29, 1850; d. at Palm Beach, Fla., March 22, 1926. American army officer and small-arms expert. He headed (1897–1907) the Rock Island, Ill., arsenal, and was commander (1907–12) of the Springfield, Mass., armory. Author of *Rifle and Carbine Firing* (1885) and *Firing Regulations for Small Arms* (1889).

Blunt, Wilfrid Scawen. b. at Crawley, Sussex, England, in August, 1840; d. at London, Sept. 10, 1922. English poet, prose writer, diplomat, traveler, and anti-imperialist. The son of a wealthy Roman Catholic family, he was educated at Stonyhurst and St. Mary's College, Oscott. His diplomatic duties (1858–70) took him to Greece, Turkey, France, Spain, Germany, and South America; a strong defender of freedom for minority national groups within the British empire, he frequently attacked his government's Eastern policies; he also favored Egyptian, Indian, and Irish independence, being sent to prison (1888) for advocating the latter. He was the author of *Future of Islam* (1882), *Ideas About India* (1885), *India Under Ripon* (1909), *Gordon at Khartoum* (1911), *The Land War in Ireland* (1912), *My Diaries* (1919–20; it created a sensation and was taken off the market by the publisher because it revealed state secrets), and of *Love Sonnets of Proteus* (1880), *The Wind and the Whirlwind* (1883), *Esther* (1892), *Stealing of the Mare* (1892), *Griselda* (1893), *Seven Golden Odes of Pagan Arabia* (1905), and other volumes of poetry. *On the Shortness of Time, The Two Highwaymen, The Desolate City, Farewell,* and *Laughter and Death* are some of his best-known short poems.

Bluntschli (blůnch'lē), **Johann Kaspar.** b. at Zurich, Switzerland, March 7, 1808; d. at Karlsruhe, Germany, Oct. 21, 1881. Swiss political economist and statesman, one of the founders of the Institute of International Law at Ghent. He was a professor at Zurich (1833–48), Munich (1848–61), and Heidelberg (1861). He compiled several works on the law of Zurich; in his *Allgemeines Staatsrecht* (1852) he was the first to develop the theory of the state as an integral organism, and paralleled the life of a state to human life. In his later writings, he examined German law, and professed himself as preferring the Germanic elements of it to the Roman ones. Author also of *Das deutsche Privatrecht* (1853) and *Das moderne Völkerrecht* (1868).

Blurt, Master Constable (blėrt). Play by Thomas Middleton and William Rowley, produced in 1602. "Blurt, Master Constable," is equivalent to "A fig for Master Constable," and is a proverbial phrase. Blurt is also the name of the constable in the play; he is a sort of Dogberry, imbued with a tremendous sense of his own and his master the duke's importance.

Blut und Boden (blöt' ůnt bō'dẹn). [Abbreviation, **Blubo;** Eng. trans., "*Blood and soil.*"] German designation of the racial and nativistic quality of certain writings of the Hitler period which sought to make a grass-roots appeal through the expression of a mystic relationship between the peasant and his soil. *Neuadel aus Blut und Boden* (1930) by Walter Darré did much to give the term widespread acceptance.

Blyth (blīᴛʜ, blīth). Municipal borough and seaport in NE England, in Northumberland, situated at the mouth of the river Blyth, ab. 9 mi. SE of Morpeth, ab. 284 mi. N of London by rail. It ranks as the fourth coal-exporting port in the United Kingdom; also has fisheries and shipyards. 34,742 (1951).

Blyth, Port of. See under **Bedlingtonshire.**

Blythe (blīᴛʜ). City in SE California, in Riverside County, near the Arizona border, ab. 200 mi. E of Los Angeles. In the irrigated surrounding region, near the Colorado River, agricultural produce, especially cotton, is raised. 4,089 (1950).

Blythe, Herbert. Original name of **Barrymore, Maurice.**

Blythe, Vernon. See **Castle, Vernon Blythe.**

Blytheville (blīᴛʜ'vil). City in NW Arkansas, county seat (with Osceola) of Mississippi County: important as a cotton-ginning and cotton-shipping center. 16,234 (1950).

Bo (bō). Chief town in the Sierra Leone protectorate, W Africa, ab. 105 mi. E of Freetown, on the main railroad line. It is connected by road with the mining areas in the N and the oil-bearing region in the S. It is the seat of a government school for boys and a teachers college.

Boa Bahia (bō'ạ bạ.ē'ạ). Old Portuguese name of **Bombay, city.**

Boabdelin (bō.ab'dẹ.lin), **Mahomet.** Name given to the last king of Granada in John Dryden's play *The Conquest of Granada.* He is one of the principal characters in the work.

Boabdil (bō.äb.dēl'). [Arabic, **Abu Abdullah;** called (in Spanish) **El Chico** (meaning "the little") and **El Zogoybi** (meaning "the unfortunate").] d. in the middle of the 16th century. Last Moorish king of Granada. He revolted against his father Abu-al-Hasan, and seized the throne in 1482. In the period 1491–92 he was attacked and defeated by Ferdinand and Isabella of Spain, and made a prisoner. He was set at liberty on condition of being a vassal of Spain.

Boac (bō'äk). Town in the Philippine Islands, the capital of Marinduque province, situated in the NW part of the island of Marinduque, S of Luzon. 21,000 (1939).

Boaco (bō.ä'kō). Department in C Nicaragua. Capital, Boaco; area, 2,085 sq. mi.; pop. 50,039 (1951).

Boaden (bō'dẹn), **James.** b. at Whitehaven, Cumberland, England, May 23, 1762; d. Feb. 16, 1839. English dramatist and biographer. His works include *The Secret Tribunal* (1795), *An Italian Monk* (1797), *Aurelio and Miranda* (1799), and lives of the actresses Sarah Siddons, Dorothea Jordan, and Elizabeth Inchbald. In one of his works he exposed (1796) the Ireland Shakespeare forgeries, and in an edition (1837) of Shakespeare's *Sonnets,* he sought to identify W. H., to whom they had been dedicated, with William Herbert, 3rd Earl of Pembroke.

Boadicea (bō"ạ.di.sē'ạ). [Also, **Boudicca.**] d. 62 A.D. Queen of ancient Britain; wife of Prasutagus, king of the Iceni, a tribe in eastern Britain. Thinking to secure his kingdom and family from molestation, Prasutagus, who died c60 A.D., bequeathed his great wealth to his daughters jointly with the Roman emperor. However, the will was used by the Roman officials as a pretext for appropriating the whole property. Boadicea was flogged, her daughters subjected to various outrages and indignities, and other members of the royal family treated as slaves, with the result that the Iceni joined the Trinobantes in a revolt under Boadicea against the Romans, in 62 A.D., which was put down by Suetonius Paulinus. Boadicea thereupon killed herself by taking poison. She has been made the subject of a tragedy by John Fletcher (see *Bonduca*). Richard Glover produced a play on the subject in 1735, and William Mason also wrote one, called *Caractacus*, in 1759. Both William Cowper and Tennyson have made Boadicea the subject of poems.

Boae (bō'ē). An ancient name of **Čiovo.**

Boa Esperança (bō'ą ēsh.pę.ruṅ'są), **Cabo de.** Portuguese name of **Good Hope, Cape of.**

Boanerges (bō.ą.nėr'jēz). In the New Testament, a surname, explained as meaning "sons of thunder," given to James and John, the sons of Zebedee. Mark, iii. 17.

Boardman (bōrd'mąn), **George Dana.** b. at Livermore, Me., in February, 1801; d. near Tavoy, Burma, Feb. 11, 1831. American Baptist missionary in Burma; father of George Dana Boardman (1828–1903).

Boardman, George Dana. b. at Tavoy, Burma, Aug. 18, 1828; d. at Atlantic City, N.J., April 28, 1903. American Baptist clergyman; son of George Dana Boardman (1801–31). His works include *Studies in the Creative Week* (1878) and *Epiphanies of the Risen Lord* (1880).

Boardman, Harold Sherburne. b. at Bangor, Me., 1874—. American educator, president (1926–34) of the University of Maine. He was graduated (B.C.E., 1895) from the Maine State College, and in 1901 joined the faculty of the University of Maine, where he was professor of civil engineering and head of the department (1904–26), dean of the college of technology (1910–26), acting president (1925–26), and president (1926–34).

Boardman, Henry Augustus. b. at Troy, N.Y., Jan. 19, 1808; d. at Philadelphia, June 15, 1880. American Presbyterian divine and religious writer.

Board of Economic Welfare. U.S. federal unit established on July 30, 1941, under the title of the Economic Defense Board, which developed policies and programs designed to reinforce U.S. economic relations and to regulate the export of vital defense materials during World War II. It was renamed on Dec. 17, 1941, became part of the Foreign Economic Administration in 1943, and was eventually incorporated into the state department.

Board of Trade and Plantations. Chief British colonial agency (1696–c1783) for the administration of British interests and policy in the American colonies. Much of the board's machinery was devoted to the supervision of trade and commerce, but its domain also extended to colonial legislation and government in relation to imperial policies. Among those who were members of the board were William Petty, 2nd Earl of Shelburne, Charles Townshend, James Grenville, and the historian Edward Gibbon. The body consisted of five paid members, and ex-officio members drawn from among high state officials.

Boar's Head. Tavern in Eastcheap, London, celebrated by Shakespeare as the scene of Falstaff's carousals. It was destroyed in the great fire of London (September, 1666), afterward rebuilt, and again demolished to make room for one of the approaches to London Bridge. A statue of William IV was later erected on the spot.

Boas (bō'az), **Franz.** b. at Minden, Westphalia, Germany, July 9, 1858; d. at New York, Dec. 21, 1942. American anthropologist. In the period 1883–84, as a member of a German scientific expedition to Baffin Island and adjoining arctic regions, he first became interested in the type of ethnological research which was to be a chief part of his professional career. Upon returning to Germany he was appointed assistant at the Royal Ethnological Museum at Berlin and instructor in geography at the University of Berlin. In 1886 he began a series of investigations of the Indians of North America (including Mexico) and Puerto Rico which were continued until 1931. He served as instructor in anthropology at Clark University, Worcester, Mass., from 1888 to 1892. From there he went to Chicago as a lecturer in anthropology at the Chicago Natural History Museum, and thence, in 1896, to Columbia University, at New York. From 1899 to 1937 he was professor of anthropology (the first ever appointed to the Columbia faculty), and thereafter until his death, professor emeritus. From 1901 to 1905 he was curator of anthropology at the American Museum of Natural History, at New York, an institution in which he continued to be interested throughout his life. As a scientist, Franz Boas's interests ranged from the primitive customs of the Eskimos and the Indians of the Canadian Northwest to the anthropometric evolution of immigrant stocks in American cities. To an extent unusual before his time, he pursued his anthropological studies in the field. He was a leader in the analysis of anthropometric data on a mass scale and in the study of the effects on the human physique of environment, social conditions, and the mixture of races. He served as president of the American Anthropological Society (1907–08) and as president of the New York Academy of Sciences (1910). He was a member or honorary member of numerous learned societies in many countries. More than 600 of his scientific papers were published, and his many books include *The Growth of Children* (1896), *Changes in Form of Body of Descendants of Immigrants* (1911), *The Mind of Primitive Man* (1911), *Kultur und Rasse* (1913). *Primitive Art* (1927), *Anthropology and Modern Life* (1928), *Materials for the Study of Inheritance in Man* (1928), and *Race, Language and Culture* (1940). He edited the results of the Jessup North Pacific Expedition, edited and contributed extensively to the original *Handbook of American Indian Languages* (2 vols., 1911–22), and for many years edited *Columbia University Contributions to Anthropology.*

Boas, Frederick S. b. at Belfast, Ireland, July 24, 1862—. English literary historian. He was professor (1901–05) of history and English literature at Queen's College, Belfast, before serving as inspector (1905–27) for the London County Council education department. His works include *Shakespeare and his Predecessors* (1896), *University Drama in the Tudor Age* (1914), *Shakespeare and the Universities* (1922), *Richardson to Pinero* (1936), *Marlowe and his Circle* (1929), and *An Introduction to Stuart Drama* (1946).

Boas (bō'äs), **Ismar Isidor.** b. at Exin, Germany, March 28, 1858; d. at Vienna, March 15, 1938. German physician. He worked under C. A. Ewald on the physiology and pathology of digestion. He founded (1886) at Berlin the first polyclinic for gastro-intestinal diseases in Germany, devised with Ewald the test breakfast and the expression method for the examination of the gastric juice (called the Ewald-Boas procedure), and discovered the frequent occurrence of lactic acid in the stomach of patients suffering from cancer of this organ. Boas furnished also a new test for the presence of free hydrochloric acid. His greatest discovery was the occurrence of occult blood in peptic ulcers and cancer of the gastro-intestinal tract.

Boatswain's Mate, The. Opera in two acts by Ethel Smyth, based on a story by W. W. Jacobs and first produced at the Shaftesbury Theatre at London in 1916.

Boat Yard, the. A former name of **Kingsport.**

Boa Vista (bō'ą vēs'tą). Capital of Rio Branco territory, in N Brazil. Pop. under 5,000 (1940).

Boa Vista. [Also, **Bonavista.**] Island in the Atlantic Ocean, off W Africa, the easternmost of the Cape Verde Islands. It belongs to Portugal.

Boaz (bō'az). Town in NE Alabama, in Marshall County, ab. 60 mi. NE of Birmingham, in a cotton-raising region. 3,078 (1950).

Boaz. [Also, **Booz.**] In the Old Testament, a wealthy Bethlehemite, kinsman of Elimelech and husband of Ruth. Ruth, ii, iii, iv.

Boaz. In the Old Testament, the name of one of the two brazen pillars erected in the porch of Solomon's temple. The other was Jachin. 1 Kings, vii. 21.

Bob Acres (bob' ā'kėrz). See **Acres, Bob.**

Bobadil (bob'ą.dil), **Captain.** In Ben Jonson's *Every Man in His Humour*, a Paul's man (that is, a man who lounged in the middle aisle of London's old Saint Paul's Cathedral, which was destroyed in the great fire of 1666. In Jonson's day the middle aisle of this cathedral was the resort of sharpers, gulls, and loafers of every kind.) His cowardice and bragging are made comic by his intense gravity and the serious manner in which he regards himself.

Bobadilla (bō.bä.ᴛʜē'lyä), **Francisco de.** d., probably at sea, July 1, 1502. Spanish officer. In 1500, he was sent to Hispaniola, in the West Indies, to investigate the affairs of that colony, and especially to inquire into charges made against Christopher Columbus, whom he succeeded (1499) as viceroy of the Indies. On his arrival (Aug. 23, 1500) at Santo Domingo, he summoned Columbus before him, imprisoned him and his brothers, and sent them to Spain. Bobadilla remained as governor of the colony until the arrival of Nicolás de Ovando, on April 15, 1502, when he was himself sent under arrest to Spain.

Bob Brierly (brī'ėr.li). See **Brierly, Bob.**

Bobbs (bobz), **William Conrad.** b. in Montgomery County, Ohio, Jan. 25, 1861; d. Feb. 11, 1926. American publisher. Associated (1879 *et seq.*) with, and director (1890–95) of, Merrill, Meigs and Company, booksellers at Indianapolis, Ind., he became (1895) the first president of Bobbs-Merrill Company, publishers.

Bobchev (bôp'chef), **Stefan Savov.** b. at Elena, Turkey (in territory now part of Bulgaria), 1853—. Bulgarian lawyer, scholar, and public figure. He served as minister of education (1911), and ambassador at St. Petersburg (1912). Professor of law (1902 *et seq.*) at the University of Sofia, he wrote numerous works on the history of Bulgarian and canon law.

Bob Cratchit (krach'it). See **Cratchit, Bob.**

Bobigny (bo.bē.nyē). Town in N France, in the department of Seine; a northeastern suburb of Paris, between Drancy and Noisy-le-Sec. 16,547 (1946).

Bobillier (bo.bēl.yā), **Étienne.** b. 1797 or 1798; d. at Châlons-sur-Marne, France, 1832. French mathematician. He contributed (1827–28) important papers on homogeneous coördinates and abridged notation in algebraic geometry to J. D. Gergonne's *Annales.* His name has been attached to the "theorem of Bobillier" in geometry. He was director of the École des Arts et Métiers de Châlons and author of *Principes d'algèbre* (1825), and *Cours de géométrie* (1832) which appeared in more than a dozen editions.

Bobillier, Marie. See **Brenet, Michel.**

Böblingen (bėb'ling.ẹn). Town in S Germany, in the *Land* (state) of Württemberg-Baden, American Zone, formerly in the Neckar *Kreis* (district) of Württemberg, SW of Stuttgart. It manufactures knitwear, paperware, and ceramics, and has a large airport. The population is predominantly Protestant. 12,601 (1950).

Bobo (bō'bō). Sudanic-speaking people of W Africa, inhabiting the N part of the Ivory Coast. Their population is estimated at ab. 239,000 (by Y. Urvoy, *Petit Atlas Ethno-Demographique du Soudan,* 1942). They are divided into four subgroups, the Nienige, Kian, Tara, and Bua.

Bobo-Dioulasso (bō'bō.dū.läs'ō). Town in the reconstituted territory of Upper Volta, French West Africa, formerly in the Ivory Coast territory. It is situated in the SW part of Upper Volta and is the terminus of the railway line from Abidjan, ab. 494 mi. away on the Guinea Coast. 24,000 (1943).

Bobo-fing (bō'bō.fing'). See under **Bua.**

Boboli Gardens (bō'bō.lē). Gardens in the rear of, and adjacent to, the Pitti Palace at Florence. They are open to the public, and are filled with fountains, grottoes, and statues, some of the latter by John of Bologna (Jean Bologne). From the terrace there is a magnificent view of Florence. The land was bought in 1549 by Eleanora of Toledo, the Spanish wife of Cosimo I, Duke of Tuscany. The laying out was commenced by the sculptor Il Tribolo, who died in 1550, and finished by Buontalenti.

Bobolina (bō.bō.lē'nä). d. 1825. Greek heroine, the widow of a Spetsai shipowner who was assassinated by order of the sultan of Turkey in 1812. She equipped three vessels in the revolution of 1821, one of which she commanded, and participated in the siege of Tripolis, in September, 1821.

Bobriki (bôb'ryi.ki). Former name of **Stalinogorsk.**

Bobruisk (bo.brö'ẹsk). City in the U.S.S.R., in the Byelorussian Soviet Socialist Republic, ab. 60 mi. S of Minsk. Specializing in wood and paper industries, it also has food industries. It contained an important fortress. 84,107 (1939).

Bobrzyński (bô.bzhin'skē), **Michał.** b. 1849; d. 1935. Polish statesman and historian. Professor of history and public law at the University of Kraków from 1876, he was the founder of a school of historical theory which explained the partitions of Poland as a result of Polish disunity and the weakness of its governments. He was a member of the Austrian parliament and a leader of the Polish Conservative Party in Austrian Poland before World War I, and worked for a reëstablishment of Poland within the framework of the Austro-Hungarian monarchy. As Austrian lieutenant governor in Polish Galicia (1908–13), he sought to reconcile the Poles and the Ukrainians and to introduce democratic election reforms. In 1917 he was nominated Austrian minister for Galicia and prepared an autonomous Polish regime for that province. He retired from political life in independent Poland, devoting himself to his scientific work and serving as a government expert on state administration. He was author of many books on public law, and wrote a history of Poland in three volumes, which was reprinted four times.

Bob Sawyer (sô'yėr). See **Sawyer, Bob.**

Boca de Dragón (bō'kä dā drä.gōn'). A Spanish name of the **Dragon's Mouth.**

Boca de la Sierpe (lä syer'pā). Spanish name of the **Serpent's Mouth.**

Bocage (bo.kȧzh), **Jean Denis Barbié du.** See **Barbié du Bocage, Jean Denis.**

Bocage, Le. See **Le Bocage.**

Bocage (bö.kä'zhẹ), **Manuel Maria Barbosa du.** b. at Setúbal, Portugal, Sept. 15, 1765; d. at Lisbon, Dec. 21, 1805. Portuguese poet, his country's most celebrated of the 18th century, who has been looked upon as a precursor of romanticism in Portugal. Three volumes of his *Rimas* appeared during his lifetime (I, 1793; II, 1799; III, 1804). His other poetical works were published after his death. His sonnets rank among the most perfect in the Portuguese language.

Bocanegra (bō.kä.nā'grä), **Simone.** See **Boccanera** or **Bocanegra, Simone.**

Bocardo (bō.kär'dō). Old gate (N gate) of Oxford, England, near the Church of Saint Michael, destroyed in 1771. The room over it was used as a prison.

Bocas del Dragón (bō'käs del drä.gōn'). A Spanish name of the **Dragon's Mouth** (or **Mouths**).

Bocas del Toro (tō'rō). Province in NW Panama, bordering on the Caribbean Sea and Costa Rica. Bananas are the principal crop. Capital, Bocas del Toro; area, 3,508 sq. mi.; pop. 22,047 (1950).

Boca Tigris (bō'kä tē'gris). [Also: **Bocca Tigris,** the **Bogue;** Chinese, **Hu Mun.**] Narrow passage in the Canton River, ab. 40 mi. SE of Canton, China. The Bogue forts were stormed by the British in 1841 and 1857.

Boccaccio (bọ.kä'chẹ.ō; Italian, bōk.kät'chō), **Giovanni.** b. at Paris, 1313; d. at Certaldo, near Florence, Italy, Dec. 31, 1375. Italian writer and humanist. Brought as a youth to Florence by his father, a merchant of that city, he was sent during the late 1320's to Naples in order to learn the trade of a merchant. Commercial work proved extremely distasteful to him (as did also canonical law, to which he also turned for a time), and he was persuaded by his great affection for learning and literature that he should devote his life to study and writing. In the early 14th century, Naples was a city of active life, rich, cheerful, and gay, and Boccaccio seems to have entered wholeheartedly into the pleasures of youth. Like many other poets, he had one great love, in his case for Maria d'Aquino, daughter of Robert, the king of Naples, and wife of a Neapolitan nobleman; it was this woman to whom Boccaccio gave the name Fiammetta in his imaginative writing. In Boccaccio's case, there was a real enough love affair, in which Fiammetta yielded to his desires fairly soon, but she proved inconstant and as unfaithful to her lover as she had been to her husband. Boccaccio's disillusionment and bitterness was great, and found reflection in various of his works. This affair with Fiammetta is usually ascribed to the middle 1330's, and from this Neapolitan period and immediately thereafter date most of his lesser works in Italian. During the 1330's Boccaccio's father was evidently in fairly comfortable financial circumstances, but economic reverses at the end of the decade made it necessary for Boccaccio to return to Florence, and from 1340 onward his permanent base was at that city.

Middle Years. Our information about Boccaccio's life in the 1340's is extremely scanty, and nearly all that can be said is that he lived in obscurity and apparently in considerable want and discomfort. He seems to have traveled at least somewhat in central Italy in this decade, and more in the 1350's. He became a fervent admirer of Petrarch, whose works he read and with whom he perhaps corresponded in the 1340's; he met Petrarch in 1350, when the latter passed through Florence, and saw him again several times afterwards. In the 1350's Boccaccio began to emerge from obscurity, and was sent on several occasions as Florentine ambassador to Avignon and Ravenna. It is doubtful whether Boccaccio was in Florence in 1348, when the Black Death reached that city, although he graphically describes its effects in the introduction to the *Decameron.* During this time, he was gradually turning away from his youthful dissipations to a more serious and ascetically inclined attitude. He never married; his youthful excesses had given him an antipathy towards marriage and towards the female sex in general, which found its expression especially in the *Corbaccio.* In his mature years, Boccaccio devoted more and more time to the study of the Latin classics and of Dante; in his old age, he took up the study of Greek, for which he succeeded in having a chair established at the University of Florence.

Later Years. Despite increasing recognition, Boccaccio's financial position was still precarious, and he apparently entertained hopes of returning to a happier situation at Naples. Finally, in 1362, he did return, hoping to find a home with a former friend who had risen to the position of grand seneschal to the king of Naples; however, Boccaccio was treated as a mere mendicant and hanger-on, and soon returned, in disgust, to Florence. In following years he took further trips, to visit Petrarch at Venice in 1367, and again to Naples in 1370–71. Boccaccio's poor financial position eventually excited some degree of public sympathy and a willingness to render assistance, and he was granted a professorship at Florence in 1373 for the public reading and exposition of Dante. However, his poor health forced him to end his lectures in 1374, and he died in the following year.

Written Works and Evaluation. Boccaccio's first long novel, *Il Filocolo,* was written at the request of Fiammetta; and his early lyrics as well as his two long poems in *ottava rima,* the *Filostrato* and the *Teseida* (which were later to be used as sources by Geoffrey Chaucer), make use of this early experience in "polite" love, as do also his *Elegy of Madonna Fiammetta,* the *Ameto,* and the *Amorosa Visione.* Some of these works were finished at Florence, shortly after his recall to that city from Naples by his father in 1340. It was at Florence that he wrote his mythological poem *Il Ninfale Fiesolano,* in which are already evident a new objectivity and a freedom from autobiographical themes pointing to the full maturity of his narrative art. This was realized in the *Decameron,* his very famous collection of 100 tales written (according to most authorities) between 1348 and 1353. His works of erudition in Latin, all compiled in the last years of his life, include *De casibus virorum illustrium, De claris mulieribus,* and *De genealogiis deorum gentilium.* Any estimate of Boccaccio's personality must depend entirely upon what can be deduced from his written works. He must obviously have been a man of considerable intellectual ability, both in the extent of his learning and in his observation of the life of his times. That Boccaccio had a very keen understanding of human psychology is evident from the tales of the *Decameron.* His nature must have been intensely emotional and strongly sexed, as we can tell both from the history of his youth and his earlier works, and from his later ascetic revulsion against his youthful excesses (although the inclination on the part of some to regard the bulk of his stories, particularly those in the *Decameron,* as essentially lascivious, if not actually immoral, is surely an error; it was his intent simply to represent the world as it was (and, in certain basic respects, as it still is), rather than to concern himself with what might be considered the world that should be). It is also certainly true that Boccaccio did not have as complicated a personality as either Dante or Petrarch, having neither the ability of the former to analyze and organize, nor the latter's wide range of emotional perception and forward-looking attitude toward knowledge, particularly of the Latin classics. In his studies, Boccaccio was essentially a man of the Middle Ages, accepting and assimilating traditional knowledge without broadening its horizon or making new discoveries or interpretations; his originality consisted primarily in bringing new content and new technique to vernacular literature.

Boccanera (bōk.kä.nā'rä) or **Bocanegra** (bō.kä.nā'grä), **Simone.** b. c1300; poisoned at Genoa, 1363. The first doge of Genoa. He was elected in 1339, abdicated in 1344, and was reëlected in 1356.

Boccardo (bōk.kär'dō), **Girolamo.** b. at Genoa, March 16, 1829; d. at Rome, March 20, 1904. Italian political economist, and writer on history and geography, professor of political economy at the University of Genoa. He became a senator in 1877, and after 1888 lived at Rome. His works include *Trattato teorico pratico di economia politica* (1853), and *I principii della scienza e dell'arte delle finanze* (1887).

Boccasini (bōk.kä.sē'nē), **Nicolo.** Original name of Pope **Benedict XI.**

Bocca Tigris (bok'ą tē'gris). See **Boca Tigris.**

Boccherini (bōk.ke.rē'nē), **Luigi.** b. at Lucca, Italy, Feb. 19, 1743; d. at Madrid, May 28, 1805. Italian composer of chamber music. He was engaged as cellist at the court of Madrid from 1768. His compositions include almost 100 string quartets.

Bocchoris, Bochchoris, or **Bokkhoris** (bok.kō'ris). fl. probably at the end of the 8th century B.C. Egyptian king given by Manetho as the sole king of the XXIVth dynasty: identified as King Wah-ka-re Bekenranef of the monuments (but both identification and name are considered by some scholars to be far from certain). According to a tradition of Greek times, which is probably correct, he reformed the laws of his country, and Greek (and Roman) laws were probably influenced by this legislation.

Boccioni (bōt.chō'nē), **Umberto.** b. at Reggio, Italy, Oct. 19, 1882; d. at Sorte, Italy, Aug. 16, 1916. Italian sculptor and painter, who was one of the leaders of the Italian futurist movement from its inception. He studied at Rome with Giacomo Balla, then traveled to France and Russia, finally returning to Italy, where he met the poet Filippo Tommaso Marinetti in 1909, and was interested by him in futurism. He exhibited his work in all the futurist shows at Paris, Brussels, London, and Berlin; his best-known piece of sculpture, *Movement of Forms in Space,* was acquired by the Museum of Modern Art at New York. Another of his more important works is the painting *Those Who Go Away.* The artist was killed during World War I, when he fell from a horse.

Boccone (bōk.kō'nā), **Paolo.** b. at Palermo, Sicily, April 24, 1633; d. near Palermo, Dec. 22, 1704. Sicilian naturalist, professor of botany at Padua, and later a Cistercian monk.

Bochart (bo.shȧr), **Samuel.** b. at Rouen, France, May 30, 1599; d. at Caen, France, May 16, 1667. French Orientalist and Biblical scholar. He was a Huguenot pastor at Caen.

Bochchoris (bok.kō'ris). See **Bocchoris.**

Bôcher (bō.shā'), **Maxime.** b. at Boston, Mass., Aug. 28, 1867; d. Sept. 12, 1918. American mathematician, noted particularly for his work on algebra, linear differential equations, and potential theory. He graduated from Harvard (1888), took his Ph.D. degree at Göttingen (1891), and taught at Harvard (1891 *et seq.*). He held numerous offices, including that of president of the American Mathematical Society. His books include *Reihenentwickelungen der Potentialtheorie* (1891), *Leçons sur les méthodes de Sturm* (1913), and a well-known textbook, *Introduction to Higher Algebra* (1907).

Bóchica (bō'chē.kä). Important god and culture hero of the Chibcha Indians of the Andean region. He is described as being a preacher and teacher who, among other things, instructed the Chibcha in the art of spinning, weaving, and painting cloth.

Bochnia (bôн'nyä). Town in S Poland, in the *województwo* (province) of Kraków, formerly in Galicia, Austria, situated on the Raba River, ab. 30 mi. E of Kraków. It has large salt mines and gypsum quarries, as well as agricultural trade. The town was conquered by Charles XII of Sweden in 1702. Pop. 10,072 (1946).

Bocholt (boċh'olt). [Also: **Bochold, Bockholt.**] City in W Germany, in the *Land* (state) of North Rhine-

Westphalia, British Zone, formerly in the province of Westphalia, Prussia, situated on the Bocholter Aa River, near the Dutch border, W of Münster. It has cotton-textile spinning and weaving mills, and manufactures of pharmaceutical cotton garments, ironware, and fireproof safes. Educational institutions include an agricultural and horticultural school, and a school for the textile trades. The Church of Saint George, built in the 15th century, is in the Gothic style; the *Rathaus* (town hall), erected in the 16th century, is in the Renaissance style. Both buildings, as well as the whole city, were heavily damaged during World War II. 37,674 (1950).

Bochsa (bok.sȧ), **Robert Nicolas Charles.** b. at Montmédy, France, Aug. 9, 1789; d. at Sydney, Australia, Jan. 6, 1856. French harpist and operatic composer.

Bochum (bō′chụm). City in W Germany, in the *Land* (state) of North Rhine-Westphalia, British Zone, formerly in the province of Westphalia, Prussia, situated N of the Ruhr River, between Essen and Dortmund. It is located in the center of the Ruhr coal-mining district; S of the city the coal-bearing strata are near the surface and easy to exploit; N of the city they must be mined by means of deep shafts. The coal-mining industry has been organized by huge enterprises (Vereinigte Stahlwerke, Harpener Bergbau, Krupp A.G., Bergbau A.G. Lothringen, Gewerkschaft Constantin, and others); there are also organizations for the sale of the byproducts of the coal industry, such as ammonia, benzol, and synthetic resins. There are in addition large iron and steel works, iron foundries, and blast furnaces; metallurgical, chemical, electrical, and machine tool factories; and canneries and other food industries, breweries, tobacco factories, and construction and garment industries. Bochum has a number of educational institutions, including schools of mining and of metallurgy, a school of administration belonging to the University of Münster, and others. There are museums of mining and geology, a folklore museum, an art gallery, libraries, and a theater. Notable buildings include a few old churches and monuments; most of the public buildings, including the administrative buildings of the large industries, date from the 20th century; there are large parks. Bochum, first mentioned in the 10th century, came in the 13th century under the countship of Mark. Large-scale modern industry started only in the middle of the 19th century. The city was occupied by French troops from January, 1923 to August, 1925. It was frequently bombed during World War II and suffered severe damage. The population is predominantly Roman Catholic. 289,804 (1950).

Bock (bok), **Fedor von.** [Full name, **Moritz Albert Franz Friedrich Fedor von Bock.**] b. at Küstrin, Brandenburg, Germany, Dec. 3, 1880; d. near Hamburg, Germany, cMay 1, 1945. German field marshal. During World War I, in which he held the ranks of lieutenant and captain, he received the Order Pour le Merite and the Hohenzollern Order. He was a particular friend of Crown Prince Wilhelm. After the Treaty of Versailles he remained with the Reichswehr, becoming a lieutenant general in 1931 and one of three group commanders in 1935. During this period he founded the so-called Black Reichswehr, a secret army which was distributed throughout Upper Silesia close to the Polish border. In 1938 he commanded the forces which occupied Austria, and later those which seized the Sudetenland. When World War II began in September, 1939, Bock commanded the Northern Army Group which destroyed a large Polish force along the Vistula. Later he led the German armies which overran the Netherlands and Belgium, and in 1940 he commanded the central sector in the invasion of France. When the Germans attacked the U.S.S.R. in 1941 Bock, who had been made a field marshal, was commander of the forces assigned to take Moscow, and was removed from command for failing to do so. In 1942, however, he was put in command of German forces in southern Russia, but later in the same year, after the German failure at Stalingrad, he was again relieved and placed on the retired list. An aristocrat and monarchist, Bock's ruthlessness caused his soldiers to call him *Der Sterber*, meaning "the Preacher of Death." On May 6, 1945, his body was found near Hamburg, in a condition indicating death several days earlier.

Bock, Franz. b. at Burtscheid, Prussia, May 3, 1823; d. at Aix-la-Chapelle (now Aachen, Germany), April 30, 1899. German writer on ecclesiastical archaeology. He became an honorary canon of the cathedral at Aix-la-Chapelle in 1864.

Bock, Karl Ernst. b. at Leipzig, Germany, Feb. 21, 1809; d. at Wiesbaden, Germany, Feb. 19, 1874. German anatomist and medical writer. He was appointed professor extraordinary at the University of Leipzig in 1839

Bockelmann (bok′ẹl.män), **Rudolf.** b. at Bodenteich, Germany, April 2, 1892—. German baritone, notable for his interpretation of such Wagnerian characters as Hans Sachs and Wotan. He has appeared with the Hamburg opera company (1926), the Chicago Civic Opera (1930–31), and in the Bayreuth festivals of 1933 and 1934.

Bockenheim (bok′ẹn.hīm). Town in W Germany, in the *Land* (state) of Hessen, American Zone, formerly in the province of Hesse-Nassau, Prussia. In 1895 it was incorporated with Frankfort on the Main, of which it is a northeastern suburb.

Böckh (bėk), **August.** b. at Karlsruhe, Baden, Germany, Nov. 24, 1785; d. at Berlin, Aug. 3, 1867. German archaeologist and philologist. He was appointed a professor at Heidelberg in 1807, and at Berlin in 1811, and was five times rector of the University of Berlin.

Bockholt (bok′holt). See **Bocholt.**

Bockhorn (bok′hôrn). [Former name, **Friesische Wehde.**] Commune in NW Germany, in the *Land* (state) of Lower Saxony, British Zone, formerly in the free state of Oldenburg, situated near the Jade Bay, ab. 20 mi. N of Oldenburg: agricultural commune, consisting of several settlement units (*Bauernschaften*); the district produces grain, livestock, and dairy products. 16,973 (1946).

Böcking (bėk′ing), **Eduard.** b. at Trarbach, Rhenish Prussia, May 20, 1802; d. at Bonn, Prussia, May 3, 1870. German jurist, professor of Roman law at Bonn (1829–70).

Böcklin (bėk′lin), **Arnold.** b. at Basel, Switzerland, Oct. 16, 1827; d. near Fiesole, Italy, Jan. 16, 1901. Swiss painter. He studied in Italy, and lived there, in Switzerland, and in Germany. He is known for his allegorical landscapes, embodying classical subjects with a romantic overtone; typical of his style is *Die Toteninsel* (The Island of the Dead).

Bocksberger (boks′ber.gėr) or **Bocksperger** (boks′per.gėr), **Hans** or **Hieronymus.** b. at Salzburg, Austria, 1540; d. c1600. German painter, noted especially for hunting scenes and battle pictures.

Bockum-Hövel (bok′ụm.hė′fẹl). Town and commune in W Germany, in the *Land* (state) of North Rhine-Westphalia, British Zone, formerly in the province of Westphalia, Prussia, situated N of the Lippe River opposite Hamm: agricultural trade, coal mines, and small industries. 21,716 (1950).

Bocock (bō′kok), **Thomas Stanley.** b. in that part of Buckingham County now in Appomattox County, Va., May 18, 1815; d. near Appomattox Courthouse, Va., Aug. 5, 1891. American politician who was speaker (1861 *et seq.*) of the Confederate house of representatives in its first and second congresses. He had served (1847 *et seq.*) as a U.S. congressman from Virginia, and after the Civil War was a member (1869–70) of the Virginia general assembly.

Bocskay (bôch′kī), **István.** b. at Cluj, Transylvania, 1557; d. Dec. 29, 1606. Prince of Transylvania. Bocskay was an adviser of Sigismund Báthory while the latter was prince of Transylvania, but Sigismund's successors deprived Bocskay of his estates and he fled to Vienna to seek redress from the imperial authorities. When the emperor Rudolf II suppressed the constitution of Hungary and banned religious liberty in that country, Bocskay, who was one of the Protestant leaders, sought Turkish aid, and helped the Turkish armies to drive the imperial forces out of Transylvania. The Hungarian diet elected him prince of Transylvania and the Sultan sent him a crown of great magnificence, but he refused to assume the title of king. When Rudolf was deposed and superseded by his brother Matthias as Holy Roman Emperor, Matthias made peace with Bocskay by the Treaty of Vienna, which reëstablished the rights of Hungarian Protestants, in 1606. It was believed that Bocskay's death before the close of that same year was caused by poison given to him by his chancellor Mihály Katay, who was thereupon torn limb from limb by the populace.

Bodanzky (bō.dänts′kē), **Artur.** b. at Vienna, Dec. 16, 1877; d. at New York, Nov. 23, 1939. Austrian conductor, active in Europe and America. He first conducted operetta at Budweis, Bohemia, in 1900; later he assisted (1903 *et seq.*) Gustav Mahler at the Vienna Opera, and conducted (1914) the London première of Richard Wagner's *Parsifal* at Covent Garden. In 1915 he succeeded Alfred Hertz and Arturo Toscanini as conductor of German opera at the Metropolitan Opera House, New York, and later (1918–31) also led the Society of the Friends of Music at New York.

Bode (bōd), **Boyd Henry.** b. at Ridott, Ill., Oct. 4, 1873; d. at Gainesville, Fla., March 29, 1953. American philosopher. He taught philosophy at the universities of Wisconsin and Illinois, and became (1921) professor of education at Ohio State University. Author of *Progressive Education at the Crossroads* and other books on education.

Bode (bō′dẹ), **Johann Elert.** b. at Hamburg, Germany, Jan. 19, 1747; d. at Berlin, Nov. 23, 1826. German astronomer. He founded (1776) the *Berliner Astronomisches Jahrbuch*, and was named (1786) director of the observatory at Berlin. He is now best known for his work *Uranographia* (1801), in which he mapped and listed upwards of 12,000 more stellar bodies than had appeared in previous compilations of its type. Bode's law, a formula expressing the relative distances of the planets from the sun, was independently stated by him in 1772, and bears his name although, in its essence, it had been stated previously.

Bode, Johann Joachim Christolph. b. at Brunswick, Germany, Jan. 16, 1730; d. at Weimar, Germany, Dec. 13, 1793. German publisher, translator, and musician. Self-educated son of a day laborer, he became editor of the *Hamburger Korrespondent* (1762), founded with Lessing a short-lived publishing house, and through the good offices of Countess Bernstorff settled at Weimar in 1778. He helped to make English literature better known in Germany by translating Sterne's *Sentimental Journey* (1768) and *Tristram Shandy* (1774), Goldsmith's *Vicar of Wakefield* (1776), and Fielding's *Tom Jones* (1786). He was also an instrumentalist and composer.

Bode, Wilhelm von. b. at Calvörde, Brunswick, Germany, Dec. 10, 1845; d. at Berlin, March 1, 1929. German critic and historian of art.

Bodel (bo.del), **Jean** (or **Jehan**). b. at Arras, France, c1165; d. c1210. French trouvère. He is now probably best remembered as the author of the earliest known miracle play in French, *Le Jeu de saint Nicolas*, which is considered to have excellent dramatic quality as well as sharp characterization, and is valuable for its depiction of details of French life in those times. Bodel was probably the author also of the chanson de geste or epic poem known as *Chanson des Saisnes*, a celebration of Charlemagne's conquest of the Saxons, but this has been disputed. It is thought, however, that he was the author of eight fabliaux which are attributed to a Jean Bedel, of whom history holds otherwise no trace. It is certain that Bodel wrote four pastorals which, like his other works, are characterized by skilled and intricate rhyming and opulent tropes. In his later life, the poet resolved to join the fourth Crusade, but before he could set forth he was stricken by leprosy, and in what is perhaps his best poem, *Les Congés*, he bids a touching farewell to the world and to his friends and patrons before entering a lepers' refuge.

Boden (bö′dẹn). Town in N Sweden, in the *län* (county) of Norrbotten, situated on the Lule River, ab. 22 mi. NW of Luleå. The Finnish border is in the vicinity. It is a railroad junction; the town was fortified in the 19th century. 10,926 (1949).

Bodenbach (bō′dẹn.bäċh). German name of Podmokly; see under **Děčín-Podmokly.**

Bodenheim (bō′dẹn.hīm), **Maxwell.** b. at Hermanville, Miss., 1895—. American writer. He is the author of *Minna and Myself* (1918), *Against This Age* (1925), *Bringing Jazz* (1930), and other books of poetry. His prose works include *Blackguard* (1923), *Crazy Man* (1924), *Replenishing Jessica* (1925), *Georgie May* (1927), *Sixty Seconds* (1929), *Virtuous Girl* (1930), and *Naked on Roller Skates* (1931). He has also published several volumes of essays.

Boden See or **Bodensee** (bō′dẹn.zā). German name of **Constance, Lake.**

Bodenstedt (bō′dẹn.shtet), **Friedrich Martin von.** b. at Peine, Hanover, Germany, April 22, 1819; d. at Wiesbaden, Germany, April 19, 1892. German poet, author, and journalist. He studied at Göttingen, Munich, and Berlin, and went to Moscow as a tutor, then to Tiflis, where he taught at the gymnasium, and later traveled extensively through the Caucasus and the East. He was subsequently a newspaper editor at Trieste and at Bremen. In 1854 he was made professor at the University of Munich, a position from which he resigned in 1866 to undertake the direction of the theater at Meiningen, where he remained until 1870. He was ennobled in 1867. The Berlin journal *Tägliche Rundschau* appeared under his direction in the period 1880–88. Among his many prose works are *Tausend und ein Tag im Orient* (1849–50) and *Shakespeares Zeitgenossen und ihre Werke* (3 vols., 1858–60). In collaboration with Paul Heyse, Hermann Kurz, and others he made a new translation of Shakespeare's dramatic works (9 vols., 1868–73), and he himself translated the sonnets. A journey to the U.S. in 1881 is described in *Vom Atlantischen zum Stillen Ozean* (1882). His most celebrated poetic work is *Lieder des Mirza-Schaffy.*

Bodenstein (bō′dẹn.shtīn), **Andreas Rudolf.** Original name of the reformer **Karlstadt.**

Bodenstein, (Ernst August) Max. b. at Magdeburg, in Saxony, Germany, 1871; d. 1942. German physical chemist. He did extensive experimentation on the kinetics of gas reactions, particularly photochemical ones, and introduced (1916) the chain reaction concept to explain very high quantum yields. He was a professor at Berlin (1923 *et seq.*), and at Johns Hopkins University (1929 *et seq.*).

Boderg (bō′dėrg), **Lough.** Lake in Connacht province, Irish Republic, through which passes the County Leitrim-County Roscommon boundary: an expansion of the river Shannon. The lake extends SW into County Roscommon. Lough Bofin forms an extension of it (and a continuation of the river Shannon) to the SE. Length, of Lough Boderg, ab. 7 mi.; width, ab. 1 mi.

Bodhisattva (bō.di.sat′vạ). In Buddhist theology, term applied to one who has reached the point where perfect knowledge may be said to be the essence of his being. He is one who is so far on his way to the full attainment of perfect knowledge that he has only one birth (or a certain few births) to undergo before reaching the state of a supreme Buddha; thus he is a future Buddha, or Buddha elect.

Bodichon (bō.di.shon′), **Barbara Leigh Smith.** b. at Wathington, Sussex, England, April 8, 1827; d. at Scalands Gate, Sussex, England, 1891. English benefactress who endowed Girton College (for women), Cambridge, and whose pamphlet on the legal status of women contributed to the enactment in Parliament of married women's property legislation. A friend of George Eliot, she was the original in real life of the heroine in *Romola.*

Bodin (bo.dañ), **Jean.** b. at Angers, France, 1530; d. at Laon, France, 1596. French publicist and political economist. His works include *Six livres de la république* (1576), *Methodus ad facilem Historiarum Cognitionem* (1566), and *Réponse aux paradoxes de Malestroit* (1568). The first-named is considered a leading work on the science of politics before the 18th century.

Bodincomagus (bō.din.kom′ạ.gus). Latin name of **Casale Monferrato.**

Bodio (bō′dyō), **Luigi.** b. at Milan, Italy, Oct. 12, 1840; d. at Rome, Nov. 2, 1920. Italian statistician and political economist. He served (1872 *et seq.*) as director of the Italian statistical bureau at Rome, and also as a professor at Leghorn, Milan, and Venice. Author of *Della statistica nei suoi rapporti coll' economia politica e colle altre science affini* (On Statistics in its Relation to Economics and other Homogeneous Sciences, 1869).

Bodländer (bōt′len″dėr), **Guido.** b. at Breslau, Germany (now Wrocław, Poland), 1855; d. at Brunswick, Germany, 1904. Germany physical chemist. He experimented on the optical properties of solid solutions, mixed crystals, affinities from electromotive forces, complexions, and others. In 1899 he was named a professor at Brunswick. He invented a gas baroscope and a gas gravimeter (1894).

Bodleian Library (bod.lē′ạn, bod′lẹ.ạn). Library of Oxford University, England, which was originally established in 1445 and actually opened in 1488. Reëstablished by Sir Thomas Bodley in the period 1597–1602 (it had been destroyed during the troubled reign of Edward VI), it was formally reopened on Nov. 8, 1603, and in 1604 James I of England granted letters of patent styling it by Bodley's name. The library (which has had a new building since 1946) later absorbed the quadrangle and buildings of the old Examination Schools, whose Jacobean entrance tower, with its columns of all five classical orders, remains to this day one of the chief architectural curiosities of Oxford. The library contains almost two million volumes and ab. 40,000 manuscripts, as well as many portraits, models of ancient buildings, literary antiquities, and coins.

Bodley (bod′li), **George Frederick.** b. at Hull, Yorkshire, England, March 14, 1827; d. 1907. English architect. He was considered in his time the most eminent ecclesiastical architect in England, especially in the 14th-century English Gothic style. He was the architect also for cathedrals at Hobart Town, Tasmania, San Francisco, Calif., and Washington, D.C. He also designed a number of official buildings and residences in England. He was made an associate of the Royal Academy in 1881 and a member of the same body in 1902. He was a connoisseur of art, published a volume of poems, designed wallpapers, and was a friend of the pre-Raphaelites.

Bodley, Sir **Thomas.** b. at Exeter, England, March 2, 1545; d. at London, Jan. 28, 1613. English diplomat and scholar. He is now chiefly remembered for his reëestablishment of the library at Oxford, now universally known as the Bodleian Library.

Bodley Homilies. Collection of Middle English prose pieces. They are almost wholly made up of pieces from Ælfric's homilies and *Lives of the Saints,* and from Wulfstan, and other Old English homilists.

Bodmer (bōd′mėr), **Johann Georg.** b. at Zurich, Switzerland, Dec. 6, 1786; d. there, May 30, 1864. Swiss mechanic. He invented (1803) the screw- and cross-wheels, and made improvements in firearms and industrial machinery, especially in the machinery for wool-spinning.

Bodmer, Johann Jakob. b. at Greifensee, Switzerland, July 19, 1698; d. at Zurich, Switzerland, Jan. 2, 1783. Swiss author and critic writing in German. He was for many years professor of history at the *Gymnasium* (in Europe, an advanced school preparatory to study at a university) at Zurich. Although his many attempts at creative writing were, on the whole, unsuccessful, he became one of the most influential literary critics in the German-speaking world of his time. His translation of John Milton's *Paradise Lost* into German (1732) and his essays *Von dem Einfluss und Gebrauche der Einbildungs-Kraft* (1727) and *Kritische Abhandlungen von dem Wunderbaren in der Poesie* (1740) paved the way for a deeper appreciation of English poetry, and especially of Shakespearian drama, in Germany and Switzerland. He also propagated his critical theories in the weekly *Die Discours der Mahlern,* which he founded and edited (1721–23) with Jakob Breitinger. He discovered and edited a number of Middle High German manuscripts. He was most generous in his assistance to such younger figures as Christoph Martin Wieland, Friedrich Gottlieb Klopstock, and Johann Heinrich Pestalozzi.

Bodmer, Karl. b. at Zurich, Switzerland, 1805; d. at Paris, Oct. 31, 1893. Swiss landscape-artist and etcher.

Bodmin (bod′min). Municipal borough in SW England, county seat of Cornwall (although most of its own municipal affairs are now conducted at nearby Truro), ab. 29 mi. NW of Plymouth, ab. 256 mi. SW of London by rail. It was one of the five coinage towns (communities which had, by royal patent, the right to produce coins of the realm) in Cornwall during the Middle Ages, and was in a major copper-producing area until Cornish copper mining declined c1860. Sheep are pastured on Bodmin Moor nearby. 6,058 (1951).

Bodø (bō′dė). Seaport in W Norway, capital of the *fylke* (county) of Nordland: the chief place in the region of the Salten Fjord. Pop. ab. 5,000.

Bodo (bō′dō). Name of a group of tribes dwelling in the valleys and mountains of SE Bengal and Assam; pop. in Assam 531,450 (1931). They are the most westerly situated of the Tibeto-Burman-speaking peoples. Some tribes, such as the matrilineal, head-hunting Garo, have retained their old customs, but for the most part the Bodo have been Hinduized in varying degrees.

Bodobriga (bọ.dob′ri.gạ). A Latin name of **Boppard.**

Bodoni (bō.dō′nē), **Giambattista.** b. at Saluzzo, Italy, Feb. 16, 1740; d. probably at Parma (some authorities cite Padua), Nov. 23, 1813. Italian type-designer and printer. He is now usually considered to have been one of the pioneers in the designing of the so-called modern type faces. In point of strict chronology, John Baskerville (1706–75), in England, and possibly François Ambroise Didot (1730–1804), in France, may be said to have preceded him, but his contribution was nonetheless enormous. His faces (which are still very widely used in various modified forms) differ from the so-called old-style designs of William Caslon and other earlier designers by their sharply contrasting dark and light lines, and by their level serifs. The Bodoni (and other modern faces) were so popular during the first half of the 19th century as virtually to replace Caslon and the other old-style faces, although these have now regained considerable favor. It should be pointed out about Bodoni himself that he was what might be called a "printer's printer," a type designer and user whose chief concern was with typographical appearance rather than content (the number of typographical errors and editorial slips in some of his books is staggering, by modern standards of book making). He made many editions of Homer, Vergil, and other classic authors. His two-volume *Manuale Tipografico,* which constituted what was, in effect, a catalogue of his faces, was published in 1818.

Bodrum (bō.dröm′). Modern name of **Halicarnassus.**

Bødtcher (bėt′ċhėr), **Ludwig Adolph.** b. at Copenhagen, 1793; d. there, 1874. Danish poet. Most of his life was spent at Copenhagen. In 1824 he went to Italy and lived for 11 years in close association with the sculptor Bertel Thorvaldsen at Rome. A number of his poems, which are wholly lyric, are on Italian subjects.

Body of Liberties. Code of laws, drawn up for the Massachusetts Bay Colony by Nathaniel Ward in 1641. It was the first such code in New England.

Body of This Death. Volume (1923) of short lyrics by Louise Bogan.

Bodza (bō′dzô). Hungarian name of **Buzău.**

Boece (bō.ēs′) or **Boethius** (bō.ē′thi.us) or **Boetius** (bō.ē′shus), **Hector.** [Also: **Bois, Boyce, Boyis.**] b. at Dundee, Scotland, c1465; d. at Aberdeen, Scotland, c1536. Scottish humanist and historian. His family name was *Boyce* (also spelled *Boys, Bois, Boyis*), *Boyis* being an adaptation of *Boetius* (corresponding to the later *Boice,* and the modern *Boyce*). He studied and later taught at Paris, where he attracted the interest and friendship of Erasmus, and subsequently served as a chief adviser to William Elphinstone, bishop of Aberdeen, in the founding of the University of Aberdeen. He was appointed (c1498) to be the first principal of the university, and is known to have been at the university when lectures were given for the first time in 1500. The work for which he is now best known is a history of Scotland (which had the full title *Scotorum Historiae a prima gentis origine cum aliarum et rerum et gentium illustratione non vulgari*) first published in 17 books in 1527 (a later edition, published in 1574, contains an 18th book and part of a 19th). Boece's primary purpose in this work was not to prepare a chronicle of events, but to tell the story of the Scottish people as reflected in their legends (despite the obviousness of which, many historians on the Continent and England used it as a source of what they took to be actual facts. Holinshed took much from it, and thus, coincidentally, provided Shakespeare (who read Holinshed) with the plot for *Macbeth.*) During the 16th century the work was twice translated from its original Latin: first, into Scottish verse, and later (between 1530 and 1533) by John Bellenden into Scottish prose. An edition of the latter of these versions was last published during the first quarter of the 19th century. Boece also wrote a Latin account of the lives of two Scottish bishops (one of whom was William

Elphinstone, of Aberdeen) which was first published at Paris in 1522.

Boeckh (bėk), **Richard.** b. at Berlin, March 28, 1824; d. at Grunewald, near Berlin, Dec. 6, 1907. German statistician, professor of statistics (1852–92) and director (1875–92) of the city statistical department at Berlin. He edited the Berlin *Jahrbuch* and published numerous technical works and papers.

Boehe (bė'ẹ), **Ernst.** b. at Munich, Germany, Dec. 27, 1880; d. 1938. German conductor and composer. His works include songs, selections for orchestra, and four symphonic poems based on the Ulysses legend.

Boeheim (bė'hīm), **Martin.** See **Behaim, Martin.**

Boehler (bė'lėr), **Peter.** b. at Frankfurt on the Main, Germany, 1712; d. at London, 1775. German Moravian missionary and colonizer. He was ordained to the Moravian ministry in 1737 and went to America in 1738 to minister to Moravian colonists at Savannah, Georgia, and in North Carolina, and to conduct missions among the slaves in those colonies. A threat of invasion by the Spanish caused the Moravians to leave Savannah for Pennsylvania, where in 1740, under Boehler's leadership, they established a settlement and called it Bethlehem. After this Boehler went to England, where he organized another group of Moravian emigrants, whom he led to Pennsylvania, where they founded Nazareth, near Bethlehem. Boehler returned to Germany, but, in 1747, became superintendent of the Moravian Church in England, was consecrated bishop in 1748, and was until 1753 in charge of all Moravian congregations in America, England, Wales, and Ireland. In 1753 he again visited America, remaining until 1764.

Boehm (bām), Sir **Joseph Edgar.** b. at Vienna, 1834; d. Dec. 12, 1890. English sculptor. In 1859 he went from Vienna to Paris, and thence in 1862 to London, where he exhibited a bust in the Royal Academy. His most important works include busts of John Ruskin, William Ewart Gladstone, Thomas Huxley, and Garnet Joseph Wolseley; his full-length figures include those of Thomas Carlyle (on the Thames Embankment, at London), Arthur Penrhyn Stanley (in Westminster Abbey), and Sir Francis Drake (at Tynemouth). He also made equestrian statues of Thomas George Baring (at Calcutta), Prince Albert (at Windsor, near London), and others. Among his works are also various statues and statuettes of unmounted horses.

Boehm, Martin. b. Nov. 30, 1725; d. March 23, 1812. American bishop of the United Brethren. Consecrated (1759) a bishop of the Mennonite Church, he is said to have been excluded from this group for theological views considered to be too liberal, if not actually heretical. With William Otterbein, he became (1800) one of the first bishops of the United Brethren Church, which he had helped organize (1789). He had previously been affiliated (1775 *et seq.*) with the Methodists.

Boekelman (bůk'ẹl.mạn), **Bernardus.** b. at Utrecht, Netherlands, June 9, 1838; d. 1930. American pianist, composer, and teacher. Educated (1857–60) at the Leipzig Conservatory, he settled (1866) in the U.S., to which he came from Mexico. He was music director (1897 *et seq.*) at Miss Dow's School, at Briarcliff, N.Y., and taught privately at New York. Among his best-known works are *Festival March* and *Concert Polonaise.*

Boelcke (bėl'kẹ), **Oswald.** b. 1891; d. 1916. German aviator. One of the leading German aces of World War I, he was credited with 40 victories.

Boëllmann (bo.el.mȧn), **Léon.** b. at Ensisheim, in Alsace, Sept. 25, 1862; d. at Paris, Oct. 11, 1897. French composer, organist at the church of Saint Vincent de Paul at Paris. As a composer he is best known for his *Symphonic Variations* for cello and orchestra, but he also wrote many other compositions for organ, orchestra, piano, and strings.

Boeotia (bē.ō'shạ). In ancient times, a district in C Greece, bounded by the land of the Locri Opuntii on the N, Attica and the strait of Evripos on the E, Attica, Megaris, and the Gulf of Corinth on the S, and Phocis on the W. Its surface was generally level, forming a basin in which was Lake Copais, now drained. According to ancient Greek tradition, the inhabitants of this district were all extremely stupid (but this, like most other Greek traditions, has come down to us through Athenian sources, and the Athenians had little love for the people or cities of Boeotia). The chief city of Boeotia was Thebes, which with other cities formed the Boeotian League.

Boeotia. [Modern Greek, **Voiotia.**] *Nomos* (department) in C Greece. Capital, Levadia; area, 1,300 sq. mi.; pop. 106,662 (1951).

Boeotian League or **Confederacy** (bẹ.ō'shạn). League of independent cities in Boeotia, supposed to have been at various times from 11 to 14 in number, with Thebes at the head (although Theban leadership was always resented, to some extent, by certain of the member cities). Its common sanctuaries were the temple of the Itonian Athene near Coronea, where the Pamboeotia were celebrated, and the temple of Poseidon in Onchestus. Its chief magistrates were called *boeotarchs,* and were elected annually, two for Thebes and one for each of the other cities. It was finally dissolved, in 171 B.C. or in 146 B.C.

Boerhaave (bör'hä.vẹ), **Hermann.** b. at Voorhout, near Leiden, Netherlands, Dec. 31, 1668; d. at Leiden, Sept. 23, 1738. Dutch physician, professor of botany, medicine, and chemistry at Leiden (1701–29). His works include *Elementa chemiae.*

Boeroe or **Buru** (bö'rö). [Also, **Bouro.**] Island in the Moluccas, Republic of Indonesia, in the Banda Sea E of Celebes. Under the federation (1946–50) known as the United States of Indonesia, Boeroe belonged to the *negara* (state) of East Indonesia. Nickel is mined on the island, and coconuts are an important crop. Area, ab. 3,500 sq. mi.; pop. 19,625 (1930).

Boers (börz). South Africans of Dutch descent. The Dutch term *boer* is the equivalent of the German word *bauer* and the English word *boor* in its original meaning of farmer or husbandman (which is what most of the Boers were in their original South African settlements). The Boers first settled in South Africa, in the vicinity of the Cape of Good Hope, in 1652. Through all the vicissitudes which drove them from the Cape Colony to Natal and across the Vaal and Orange rivers, and finally brought them under British rule, they have retained their language and, to a remarkable degree, their characteristics of courage, industry, piety, and stubborn resistance to cultural Anglicization.

Boer War *(1880–81)* (bör). Name sometimes applied to the brief period of hostilities which followed the proclamation of the Transvaal Republic, in December, 1880, between that country and Great Britain. Its chief events were the defeat of the British at Laing's Neck, on Jan. 28, 1881, and at Majuba Mountain, on Feb. 27, 1881 (the British commander, George Pomeroy Colley, being killed). By a treaty signed in April, 1881, the basic autonomy of the Transvaal Republic was recognized, but the Boers acknowledged the suzerainty of Queen Victoria. By some historians this period of Anglo-Boer hostilities is called the "Revolt of the Boers," and the term "Boer War" is applied only to the more serious conflict of 1899–1902.

Boer War *(1899–1902).* [Also: **South African War, Anglo-Boer War.**] Name usually applied to the conflict of 1899–1902 between Great Britain and the joint forces of the Transvaal Republic and the Orange Free State. In its essence, the war may be said to have been the culmination of the conflict between British commercial and territorial interests in W and S Africa (as specifically expressed by the great influx of British gold-hunters into the Witwatersrand area of the Transvaal after 1886, and bluntly emphasized by the Jameson Raid of 1895) and the desire of the Boers to carry out in their own fashion and for their own profit the development of South Africa. However, the immediate *casus belli* was not expressed in terms as general as this: hostilities began on Oct. 12, 1899, with a joint declaration by the Transvaal Republic and the Orange Free State that British refusal to withdraw troops stationed in the Transvaal constituted a basic violation of Boer autonomy (the British case was that troops were necessary in order to protect British nationals against Boer assaults, and that the Transvaal Republic had acknowledged British suzerainty in April, 1881). The Boers had a considerable initial success, but were overwhelmed in the end by the vastly greater military resources of Great Britain; with the fall of Pretoria (June 5, 1900) organized Boer resistance virtually disappeared (although pockets of Boer strength still existed, and peace was not formally arrived at until May 31, 1902). Major events in the war included the siege and relief of Ladysmith (Oct. 29, 1899–Feb. 28, 1900), the siege and relief of Kimberley (Oct. 14, 1899–Feb. 15, 1900), the siege and relief of Mafeking (Oct. 15, 1899–May 16, 1900), the capture of the chief Boer army at the Modder River on February 27, 1900, and the aforementioned capture of Pretoria on June 5, 1900.

Boesset (bwe.se), **Antoine.** [Also, **Boisset**; title, Sieur **de Villedieu.**] b. c1585; d. at Paris, in December, 1643. French court musician, and composer of nine books of *Airs de cour*, part songs; father of Jean Baptiste Boesset.

Boesset, Claude Jean Baptiste. fl. in the 17th century. French court musician and composer; son of Jean Baptiste Boesset. He composed *Fruits d'automne* (1684).

Boesset, Jean Baptiste. b. c1613; d. at Paris, Dec. 27, 1685. French court musician; son of Antoine Boesset, and father of Claude Jean Baptiste Boesset. He composed songs and ballets.

Boethius (bō.ē'thi.us). Translation by King Alfred of the famous treatise *De Consolatione Philosophiae* (On the Consolation of Philosophy), by Anicius Manlius Severinus Boethius. It is generally considered from the literary point of view to have been King Alfred's major work.

Boethius. Early Provençal poem of 258 decasyllabic verses, consisting mainly of moral reflections taken from the *De Consolatione Philosophiae* of Anicius Manlius Severinus Boethius. It is believed to have been composed in the 11th century or possibly at the beginning of the 12th, but is thought to be a rehandling of another poem which may have been written as much as two centuries earlier.

Boethius, Anicius Manlius Severinus. b. c480 A.D.; d. 524 or 525 A.D. Medieval philosopher, sometimes described as a transmitter of classical thought and also as the first of the scholastics. Of a patrician family, he was married to Rusticiana, daughter of Symmachus, the guardian of his childhood; he and his sons in turn became consuls, and he was also *magister officiorum* under Theodoric the Goth. For political reasons, and also because he belonged to the Catholic party, he incurred the displeasure of this Arian king, who had him put to death on a charge of treason. He was early regarded as a martyr, and his cult as Saint Severinus has in modern times been sanctioned for the diocese of Pavia. During the greater part of his life his efforts as a scholar were given to the preparation of various commentaries and a translation of Aristotle's logical works, and he also wrote on music and geometry, and apparently on astronomy. It was his version of Aristotle that formed the basis for education during a great part of the Middle Ages. The ardor and significance of his religious life are clear in his several theological treatises, in which he argues for trinitarian views. His greatest work, however, is the essay in five books of prose and verse, *De Consolatione Philosophiae*, written when he was facing death at Pavia. Here, in a dialogue with Lady Philosophy, who sets him straight about the ways of the goddess Fortuna, he uses material from Aristotle, Plato, and the Neoplatonists, to discuss the problem of moral responsibility. The essay had a profound influence on Dante, and was translated by King Alfred, Geoffrey Chaucer, Queen Elizabeth, and others. It was often imitated, and its material has been borrowed by countless writers.

Boethius or **Boetius** (bō.ē'shus), **Hector.** See **Boece** or **Boethius** or **Boetius, Hector.**

Boethius of Dacia (dā'shą). fl. at Paris, c1277. Danish philosopher. He is known to have been one of the chief defenders of Averroism at the University of Paris, and to have been condemned for this in 1277. He wrote commentaries on Aristotelian logic, a treatise on speculative grammar (*De modis significandi*), and other works.

Boëthus (bō.ē'thus). b. at Chalcedon (or Carthage, according to Pausanias); fl. in the 2nd century B.C. Greek sculptor of the Alexandrian school, famous in antiquity for genre work of a high character. Pliny mentions a bronze figure of a boy strangling a goose, of which there is a replica in the Louvre. The boy extracting a thorn, found in replica in many museums, is supposed to represent Boëthus's statue of the same subject.

Boetoeng (bö'tüng). [Also: **Boeton, Bouton, Buton.**] Island in the Republic of Indonesia, SE of Celebes, and separated from it by the Tiworo Strait. Under the federation (1946–50) known as the United States of Indonesia, it was part of the *negara* (state) of East Indonesia. Area, ab. 1,700 sq. mi.

Boffin (bof'in), **Nicodemus.** [Called **"Noddy"** or the **"Golden Dustman."**] In Charles Dickens's *Our Mutual Friend*, a faithful retainer of the elder Mr. Harmon.

Boffin's Bower (bof'inz). Residence of the Boffins, in Charles Dickens's *Our Mutual Friend.* Mrs. Boffin, not liking its former name, Harmon's Jail, given it from its late owner's habits of life, gave it this cheerful appellation. Miss Jennie Collins established a successful charity for working-girls at Boston in 1870 under this name.

Bofin (bō'fin), **Lough.** See under **Boderg, Lough.**

Bogalusa (bō.gą.lö'są). City in SE Louisiana, in Washington Parish. It produces paper, tung oil, and lumber. Located in a region heavily forested with yellow pine and kept productive by reforestation, it has one of the largest sawmills in the world and is the seat of a state college of forestry. 17,798 (1950).

Bogan (bō'gan), **Gerald Francis.** b. on Mackinac Island, Mich., July 27, 1894—. American naval officer. He was commissioned an ensign (1916) after graduation from the U.S. Naval Academy, and advanced to vice-admiral (1946). After commanding fighting squadrons on the USS *Langley* (1925–28) and USS *Saratoga* (1931–32), he was in command (1942–43) of the *Saratoga.* He was task group commander in Task Force 58/38 until 1945, and became (1946) commander of the Atlantic fleet air force.

Bogan, Louise. b. at Livermore Falls, Me., Aug. 11, 1897—. American poet. She is a poetry reviewer for the *New Yorker*, and was appointed (1945) a consultant in poetry to the Library of Congress. Her collections of verse include *Body of This Death* (1923), *Dark Summer* (1929), *The Sleeping Fury* (1927), and *Poems and New Poems* (1941).

Bogardus (bǫ.gär'dus), **Emory Stephen.** b. near Belvidere, Ill., Feb. 21, 1882—. American sociologist. A graduate of Northwestern University (1909) and the University of Chicago (1911), he was named (1915) professor of sociology at the University of Southern California, and became (1927) editor of the *Journal of Sociology and Social Research.* He is the author of *The Relation of Fatigue to Industrial Accidents* (1912), *Introduction to the Social Sciences* (1913), *Introduction to Sociology* (1913), *Sociology* (1934), *Democracy by Discussion* (1942), *Dictionary of Cooperation* (1943), *History of Cooperation* (1946), and other works.

Bogardus, Everard. b. in the Netherlands; drowned in Bristol Channel, off the coast of England, Sept. 27, 1647. Dutch clergyman at New Amsterdam (now New York). He owned a farm which came to be known as "the Dominie's Bouwerie." The property which once comprised it is now owned by the Trinity Church corporation at New York; its location in the financial section of modern New York makes it one of the most valuable "farms" on the face of the earth.

Bogardus, James. b. at Catskill, N.Y., March 14, 1800; d. April 13, 1874. American inventor. His numerous inventions include a ring-spinner for cotton-spinning (1828), an engraving machine (1831), and the first dry gas meter (1832).

Bogart (bō'gärt), **Ernest Ludlow.** b. at Yonkers, N.Y., March 16, 1870—. American economist and teacher. He was graduated (A.B., 1890; A.M., 1896) from Princeton and received the Ph.D. degree (1897) from the University of Halle. He has been professor of economics at several American universities, including Princeton (1905–09) and New York University (1941–46), and served (1922–23) as an adviser on currency and banking to the Persian government. Among his works are *The Finances of the American States* (1897), *Economic History of the United States* (1907, and later editions), *Direct and Indirect Costs of the Great World War* (1919), *Economic History of Agriculture of the United States* (1923), *Economic History of the American People* (1930, and later editions), and *Economic History of Europe, 1760–1939* (1942).

Bogart, John. b. at Albany, N.Y., Feb. 8, 1836; d. April 25, 1920. American civil engineer notable for his construction of a 60,000-h.p. hydroelectric plant on the Tennessee River near Chattanooga. An advisory engineer for the original New York Rapid Transit Commission, he drafted plans for Hudson River tunnels to Jersey City and

Hoboken, and for a subway between New York and Queens. He was a U.S. delegate to the Navigation congresses at Düsseldorf, Germany (1902), Milan, Italy (1905), and St. Petersburg, Russia (1908).

Boğazkale (bō.gäz.kä.le'). [Also: **Bağazköy, Bogazköy** (-kė'i), **Boghazkeui, Boghasköi, Hattushash;** ancient name, **Pteria.**] Village in C Turkey, ab. 90 mi. E of Ankara: capital of the Hittite empire in the 13th century B.C. Its ruins include a Hittite palace, placed on an artificial terrace, and otherwise analogous to Assyrian monuments. The foundations are of polygonal masonry, and measure 138 by 187 ft.; the superstructure was of brick. The chief gate is a great tower 59 ft. deep. There are also Hittite sculptures consisting of a long frieze on the walls of two rock-hewn chambers and a corridor. They consist of processions of personages, men and women in semi-Assyrian costume, winged and animal-headed divinities, animals, and two-headed eagles. The figures range in height from 3 to 11 ft.

Bogdanovich (bog.dä.nô'vich), **Ippolit Fyodorovich.** b. Dec. 23, 1743; d. near Kursk, Russia, Jan. 18, 1803. Russian poet. His chief work is *Dushenka*, a romantic poem, published in 1775.

Bogert (bō'gėrt), **George H.** b. at New York, 1864; d. 1944. American painter of landscapes (often sunsets or moonlight scenes) in Venice, France, the Netherlands, England, and elsewhere. A student at the National Academy of Design, New York, of Puvis de Chavannes, and of Aimé Nicolas Morot and Eugène Louis Boudin at Paris, he was the recipient of medals for his paintings at the Paris Exposition (1900) and the St. Louis Exposition (1904), of a first prize from the National Academy (1899), and others. His *Surf and Wind, Rouen, October Moonlight*, and *Chale Church, Isle of Wight, England*, are in the Metropolitan Museum of Art, New York; he is represented also in the Art Institute of Chicago, the Pennsylvania Academy of the Fine Arts, galleries at Edinburgh and Shanghai, and others.

Bogert, Marston Taylor. b. at Flushing, N.Y., April 18, 1868—. American chemist, professor of chemistry at Columbia University from 1904 to 1939, when he became professor emeritus. He was adjunct professor there in the period 1901–04. During World War I, he was connected with several government agencies, and during World War II was associated (1942–45) with the War Production Board. He has published papers upon various topics in organic chemistry.

Bogey (bō'gi), **Colonel.** See **Colonel Bogey.**

Boggs (bogz), **Charles Stuart.** b. Jan. 28, 1811; d. April 22, 1888. American rear admiral. He was commander of the gunboat *Varuna* which, in David Glasgow Farragut's attack on the defenses of New Orleans in 1862, destroyed six Confederate gunboats before she was herself disabled and sunk.

Boggs, Frank Myers. b. at Springfield, Ohio, Dec. 6, 1855; d. at Meudon, France, Aug. 11, 1926. American painter, at one time a student of Gérôme at the École des Beaux-Arts, Paris. In 1882 the French government acquired his *Place de la Bastille* for the Luxembourg Museum, and the following year bought his *Isigny* for the Niort Museum. In 1885 the American Art Gallery awarded Boggs a prize of 2,500 dollars for his marine painting *A Rough Day, Honfleur*. The *Rough Day* was acquired by the Boston Museum of Art, and his *On the Thames* is in the Metropolitan Museum of Art at New York. Others of his works hang in the museums at Le Havre, Nantes, and Dieppe in France, and in many French private collections.

Boggs, Lillburn W. b. at Lexington, Ky., Dec. 14, 1792; d. in the Napa Valley, Calif., March 14, 1860. American politician. As governor (1836–40) of Missouri, he is now held to have been chiefly responsible for the expulsion of the Mormons from that state. During his administration, the Bank of Missouri was chartered, a state university founded, and the first public-school law passed. He served (1842–46) in the state senate. During his later years he moved to California, where, for a short time after the breakdown of Mexican control, he served as the chief *alcalde* of N California.

Bøgh (bég), **Erik.** b. at Copenhagen, Jan. 17, 1822; d. there, Aug. 17, 1899. Danish dramatist, poet, and miscellaneous writer.

Boghazkeui or **Boghasköi** (bō.gäz.kė'i). See **Boğazkale.**

Bognor Regis (bog'nọr rē'jis). Urban district and seaside resort in SE England, in West Sussex, situated on the English Channel, ab. 7 mi. SE of Chichester, ab. 67 mi. SW of London by rail. It owes its name "Regis" to George V of England, who convalesced there in 1929. Pop. 25,624 (1951).

Bog of Stars, The. Collection (1893) of short stories by Standish James O'Grady.

Bogomils (bog'ǫ.milz). [Also, **Bogomilians** (bog.ǫ.mil'-yạnz).] Heretical sect of the 10th–15th centuries, thought by some to have been founded by Basil, a monk of Philippopolis, who was put to death at Constantinople in 1118. They were held to be Manichaean and Docetist in their doctrine, and were probably an offshoot of the Paulician sect. They flourished in Bulgaria, and spread thence to Bosnia and Serbia.

Bogomolets (bo.go.mô'lyits), **Aleksandr Aleksandrovich.** b. at Kiev, Russia, June 23, 1881; d. in Russia, July 19, 1946. Russian endocrinologist and physiologist. A pupil of E. I. I. Metchnikov, he was appointed (1911) professor of pathological physiology at the University of Saratov, and served (1925–30) as professor of pathological physiology at one of the Moscow universities. He founded and became director (1930) of the Kiev Institute of Experimental Biology and Pathology. He is regarded in Russia as the "father of longevity," having investigated various possible means of combating the ravages of old age. He has also made studies of infectious diseases, of acute neuromuscular fatigue in horses, and of the effect of special diets on fatigue curves. He worked on various problems of blood transfusion and helped found (1924) the Central Institute of Blood Transfusions, where he promulgated the theory of colloidoclasia to explain the medical effect of blood transfusions. He advanced and developed the thesis of the active elements of the connective tissue in the process of aging, resistance to infection, and predisposition to cancer. He developed his antireticular cytotoxic serum for the improvement of the health of patients and prolongation of life. Author of *Histology and Physiology of the Adrenal Glands* (1909), *Crisis of Endocrinology* (1927), *Vegetative Centers of Metabolism, Constitution and the Mesenchume, Prolongation of Life* (1938; Eng. trans., 1946), and *The Influence of the Antireticular Cytotoxic Serum upon the Healing of Bone Fractures* (1944).

Bogong (bō'gong), **Mount.** See under **Victoria,** Australia.

Bogoraz (bo.go.räs'), **Vladimir Germanovich.** [Pseudonym, **"Tan."**] b. at Ovruch, Volhynia (now under control of the U.S.S.R.), April 27, 1865; d. en route to Rostov, Russia, May 10, 1936. Russian ethnographer and novelist. Deported in his youth to Russia's far north for revolutionary activities, he became interested in the life of the aborigines and was thus launched on his scientific career. In the period 1901–04 he was in the U.S., where he wrote a novel, *Beyond the Ocean,* about the experiences of Russian immigrants in America. He signed his fiction with the pseudonym "Tan." He visited the U.S. again in 1928, later publishing a book of American impressions.

Bogorodsk (bo.go.rôtsk'). Former name of **Noginsk.**

Bogoslof (bō'gọ.slôf). Small volcanic island in the Aleutian group, off the coast of Alaska, ab. 35 mi. NW of Unalaska. The volcano was discovered during the last decade of the 18th century by a Russian expedition under the command of a naval officer named Bogoslof (or Bogoslov). A second island, ab. 2½ mi. distant, appeared in the winter of 1886–87, and became connected with the original island. Since then various changes have occurred, new peaks having appeared and disappeared.

Bogotá (bō.gō.tä'). [Full name, **Santa Fé de Bogotá.**] Capital of Colombia, in the C part, in Cundinamarca department, on a plateau ab. 8,670 ft. high. A trading center, it has a cathedral, university, museums, a rich library, and an observatory; there is air service. Founded by the Spaniards in 1538. Pop. 643,187 (1951).

Bogota (bọ.gō'tạ). Borough in NE New Jersey, in Bergen County. 7,662 (1950).

Bogotá River (bō.gō.tä'). [Spanish, **Río Bogotá.**] River in C Colombia, a tributary of the Magdalena River. At one point there is a 400-ft. drop in the river, called the Falls of Tequendama.

Bogra (bog′rạ). District of the Rajshahi division, East Bengal, Pakistan. Jute and tobacco growing are important. Area, ab. 1,359 sq. mi.

Bogue (bōg). See **Bell, Lilian.**

Bogue, the. See **Boca Tigris.**

Bogue, Virgil Gay. b. at Norfolk, N.Y., July 20, 1846; d. at sea en route to New York, Oct. 14, 1916. American civil engineer notable for his work on the development of North and South American railroads. After working in Peru as an assistant engineer (1869–77) on the construction of the Oroya Railway across the Andes, and as manager (1877–79) of the Trajilo Railway, he was assistant engineer (1880–86) for the Northern Pacific, chief engineer (1886–91) for the Union Pacific, and vice-president and chief engineer (1905–09) during the construction of the Western Pacific.

Bogurodzica (bô″gö.rô.jē′tsä). Thirteenth-century Polish hymn to the Mother of God, of unknown authorship, used in medieval times as a battle song. It is of great importance in the history of the Polish language.

Bogusławski (bô.gö.släf′skē), **Wojciech.** b. at Glinno, near Poznań, Poland, c1760; d. at Warsaw, July 23, 1829. Polish dramatist and actor.

Boguszów (bô.gö′shöf). [German, **Gottesberg.**] Town in SW Poland, in the *województwo* (province) of Wrocław, formerly in Silesia, Germany, situated in the Silesian Mountains, W of Waldbrzych: coal-mining. The town became part of Poland in 1945, and the former German population has been replaced by Poles. 11,011 (1939); 10,862 (1946).

Bohain-en-Vermandois (bo.an̈.nän̈.ver.män̈.dwȧ). [Also, **Bohain.**] Town in N France, in the department of Aisne, ab. 31 mi. NW of Laon: manufactures textiles, hosiery, embroidery, and electrical cables. It has been besieged in many wars. In World War I, from 1914 to 1918, it was occupied by the Germans; it was heavily damaged in World War II. 6,246 (1946).

Böheim (bė′hīm), **Martin.** See **Behaim, Martin.**

Bohême (bo.em). French name of **Bohemia.**

Bohème (bo.em), **La.** Opera in four acts by Giacomo Puccini, with a libretto by Giuseppe Giacosa and Illica based on Henri Murger's *Scènes de la vie de Bohème*, first produced at Turin on Feb. 1, 1896.

Bohème, La. Opera by Ruggiero Leoncavallo, first performed at Venice on May 6, 1897. The libretto is taken from Henri Murger's *Scènes de la vie de Bohème.* Produced a year after Giacomo Puccini's work on the same subject, Leoncavallo's opera is now seldom performed.

Bohemia (bō̤.hē′mi.ạ). Former crownland in the Cisleithan division of Austria-Hungary, and the northernmost portion of the empire: now part of Czechoslovakia. It was bounded by the kingdom of Saxony on the NW and N, Prussian Silesia on the NE, Moravia and Lower Austria on the SE, Upper Austria on the S, and Bavaria on the SW. It had 130 representatives in the Austrian Reichsrat, and a landtag of 242 members. The language of the majority was Czech, but about 35 percent spoke German. The capital was at Prague.

Bohemia. [Czech, **Čechy**; French, **Bohême**; German, **Böhmen**; Latin names, **Boihaemum, Boiohaemum.**] Historical country in E central Europe: the westernmost territorial unit (until 1948 a province) of the Czechoslovak republic, bounded on the NW, W, and SW by Germany (Saxony and Bavaria), on the S by Austria, on the SE and E by Moravia and Moravia-Silesia, and on the NE by the Polish province of Śląsk (formerly Prussian Silesia). Capital, Prague; area, 20,101 sq. mi.; pop. 7,109,376 (1930), 5,626,566 (1947).

Terrain. The boundaries are almost entirely marked by mountains, the principal ranges being the Erzgebirge, the Bohemian Forest, and the Riesengebirge, while the interior consists of fertile plains and rolling hills. The main rivers are the Vltava, Labe, and Ohrě, which empty their waters into the North Sea.

Agriculture, Industry, and Trade. Agriculture is highly developed. The barley and hops of Bohemia are famous. Rye, wheat, sugar beets, potatoes, and flax are also important crops, and cattle, horses, hogs, and fowl are raised. There are many fishponds. The mountains have large stands of forests. Many industries are based on agricultural and forest products, particularly brewing, sugar refining, flour and lumber milling, paper and furniture manufacture, and a large part of the highly developed Bohemian textile industry. There are also iron, machine, and metal industries; the ceramics and glass industries, a Bohemian specialty, are based on natural resources. Coal, lignite, and graphite mines are located mainly in the W parts of Bohemia. Kaolin, granite, sandstone, and basalt are produced in various districts of the country. There are numerous mineral springs and world-famous spas. The commercial position of the country between E and W Europe is favorable.

Culture. In religion the majority of the population is Roman Catholic, but Hussite sympathies are widespread and have led to a strong freethinking movement. Ethnically, Bohemia has been contested between Germans and Czechs since the dawn of history. At the beginning of the 20th century, the situation seemed settled, with the Germans prevailing in the border regions to the N and E, and to a lesser degree to the W and S, and Czechs prevailing in the interior. But after 1945, with the departure of the German population, Bohemia became ethnically an almost homogeneous Czech country.

History. Bohemia was originally inhabited by the Boii, and was settled by a Germanic tribe, the Marcomanni, who moved westward at the time of the great migrations. Slavic tribes, the ancestors of the present Czech people, occupied the deserted territory. The first native dynasty was the Přemyslides who, however, in the 10th century recognized the sovereignty of the German kings and emperors and admitted German settlers, particularly merchants and craftsmen. At the same time, the country was Christianized. The Přemyslides were succeeded by the house of Luxembourg in 1310. The rulers from this house also gained the crown of the Holy Roman Empire and made Bohemia one of the most highly developed parts of the ancient *Reich* and the cornerstone of the imperial domain. Charles IV united Brandenburg and Bohemia, furthered commerce, industry, art, and science, and founded the University of Prague as a German university in 1348. However, the Hussite movement represented a Czech nationalist reaction against this development, albeit in a religious garb. The Hussite wars devastated the country and only an uneasy peace was finally restored. The Luxembourg house ceased to exist in 1437. There followed an interim period during which the Slavic inflence prevailed. George of Poděbrad, the leader of the Hussite Utraquists, was elected king in 1457; his successor was Ladislas II, a son of Casimir IV of Poland, who combined for a short while the crowns of Bohemia and Hungary. When Ladislas's son, Ludwig II, fell in battle against the Turks in 1526, Archduke Ferdinand of Austria was elected king. Bohemia was from then on until 1918 under Hapsburg rule, but remained a strife-torn country. The old Hussite feeling expressed itself in Protestant leanings. The Bohemian estates elected the Protestant prince-elector of the Palatinate, Frederick V, in preference to the strictly Catholic Ferdinand II of Austria, but the battle of the White Mountain in 1620 decided the issue in favor of the Hapsburgs. The Bohemian aristocracy was decimated and dispossessed, a new ruling class created, and the Counter Reformation enforced. Bohemia suffered severely during the Thirty Years' War and had to be defended also in the Wars of the Austrian Succession and in the Seven Years' War. Economic and cultural recovery started at the end of the 18th century, and in the 19th century Bohemia rose to a prominent position not only in the Austro-Hungarian monarchy but also within Europe as a whole because of her rapid economic development. On the other hand, while the religious battle had died down, the ethnic battle commenced. In the revolution of 1848 Germans and Czechs at first seemed to be united, but the Germans aimed at incorporation into a united Germany while the Czechs participated in the Slav Congress which took place in Prague. Both movements were suppressed. The Czechs backed the subsequent Austrian governments which opposed German unity but on the other hand fought for the restoration of a separate Bohemian kingdom, which was not granted, nor could the Austrian government find a solution to the administrative and cultural problems which divided the Germans and the Czechs in Bohemia. When the Czechs gained the majority in the Bohemian diet in 1882, the Germans began to demand the partition of Bohemia into German and Czech units while the Czechs insisted on the unity of the country. In 1897 all governmental offices became bilingual, but the indignation of the Germans forced the resignation of the Badeni cabinet. The attempt to go back to the former rule, which assured the prevalence of the German language, led to Czech riots in 1899. From then on until the outbreak of World War I, the Bohemian issue deadlocked the parliamentary machine, both in Bohemia and in Austria as a whole. No solution was acceptable to both groups or sure of attaining a majority in the central parliament. During World War I, Czech troops in the Austro-Hungarian army deserted to the Russians while Czech politicians in exile worked in Switzerland, France, England, and the U.S. for the dissolution of the Austro-Hungarian monarchy. All Czech parties demanded an independent state of the Czechs and Slovaks on Jan. 6, 1918. The independent republic was declared on Oct. 28 of the same year. (For recent history, see under **Czechoslovakia.**)

Bohemia. Name for a place, or section, as of a city, where people, especially artists and writers, lead an unconventional or somewhat irregular life; or the group collectively (often called Bohemians) who lead such a life. This usage was taken, probably by W. M. Thackeray (it occurs in chapter two of *Vanity Fair*), from the French, who had incorrectly associated the historical country of Bohemia with the Gypsies (who led what the French considered to be very irregular lives indeed).

Bohemian Brethren. Religious sect in Bohemia, in the 15th to 17th centuries, a branch of the Hussites.

Bohemian Club. Theatrical organization at San Francisco presenting (1878 *et seq.*) the musical Grove Plays.

Bohemian Forest. [German, **Böhmerwald, Oberpfälzerwald;** Czech, **Šumava, Český Les.**] Mountain region extending ab. 150 mi. along the border between Bavaria, Germany and Bohemia, Czechoslovakia, ab. 80 mi. SW of Prague. It is heavily wooded with coniferous forests, and farming is carried on only in the lower valleys. It is crossed by only one rail line, and by several highways. Peak elevation, 4,780 ft.

Bohemian Girl, The. Opera in three acts by Michael William Balfe, produced at London in 1843. The libretto was by Alfred Bunn from a ballet which was taken from Miguel de Cervantes. It was brought out again at London in 1858 as *La Zingara.* It was translated into French, Italian, and German, and had a great success. The opera appeared at Hamburg as *La Gitana,* at Vienna as *Die Zigeunerin,* and at Paris as *La Bohémienne* (which should not be confused with Puccini's four-act opera *La Bohème*). Among its ballads are *I Dreamt I Dwelt in Marble Halls* and *Then You'll Remember Me.*

Bohemians. Musicians' club established (1907) at New York. The membership, restricted to men, was set at 500.

Bohemian String Quartet. [Also, **Czech String Quartet.**] Ensemble established (1892) at Prague with Karel Hoffmann and Joseph Suk, violins, Oskar Nedbal, viola, and Otto Berger, cello. The group, with varying membership, toured Russia (1895–96), Italy (1895), France (1896), Belgium (1897), Holland and England (1898), and the Balkans (1901 and 1902).

Bohemund I (bō′ẹ.mund). [Also: **Bohemond;** French, **Bohémond** (bo.ā.môṅ).] b. c1056; d. at Canossa, Italy, 1111. Crusader; son of Robert Guiscard. He became prince of Tarentum in 1085, joined the first Crusade in 1096, and led in the capture of Antioch in 1098 (it was he who conceived the strategy whereby the Crusaders were able to capture it, and it is he who is often held responsible for their atrocities immediately after its fall). As self-styled Prince of Antioch (1099–1111), he incurred the enmity of the Byzantine emperor Alexius I Comnenus, to whom he had previously sworn fealty at Constantinople. He was captured (1100) by the Moslems, and after his release (1103) returned to Europe. After his marriage to Constance, daughter of Philip I of France, he again went to the East, to wage war against Alexius; he was defeated, and thereafter Antioch was ruled as a vassal state of Alexius.

Bohio (bō′yō). An Indian name of **Hispaniola.**

Böhlau (bė′lou), **Helene.** b. at Weimar, Germany, Nov. 22, 1859—. German novelist and short-story writer. When she went with a married man to Turkey, and then (when he became a Moslem) married him, she allied herself with the advocates of women's rights and started a lifelong fight for these rights. However, it was not as al-Rasbid Bey (her husband's Turkish name and title) but as Helene Böhlau that she wrote. The charm of her *Ratsmädelgeschichten* (1888) is largely due to Weimar reminiscences. It was in *Rangierbahnhof* (1895), *Das Recht der Mutter* (1897), *Halbtier* (1899), and *Isibies* (1911) that man's world is flayed.

Bohlen (bō′lẹn), **Peter von.** b. at Wüppels, Oldenburg, Germany, March 9, 1796; d. at Halle, Germany, Feb. 6, 1840. German Orientalist, professor of Oriental languages at Königsberg.

Böhler (bė′lėr), **Lorenz.** b. at Wolfurt, Vorarlberg, Austria, Jan. 15, 1885—. Austrian orthopedist. He has worked at the clinic of J. Hochenegg at Vienna, at hospitals at Bolzano and Tetschen, and at the Mayo Clinic at Rochester, Minn. Most recently, he has been director of the *Unfallkrankenhaus* (hospital for accidents) at Vienna. He has made possible considerable improvements in the treatment of fractures with such of his many inventions as the "skin-tight" plaster, the Böhler screw traction apparatus, the reduction of fractures under local anesthesia, and many different splints. He has also devised an operation for slipping patella (1918), and a walking iron for the ambulatory treatment of leg fractures. Author of *Technik der Knochenbruchbehandlung* (1929; Eng. trans., *The Treatment of Fractures,* 1929), *Diagnosis, Pathology and Treatment of Fractures of the Os Calcis* (1931), *Entstehung, Erkennung und Behandlung der Fersenbeinbrüche* (1933), and *Medullary Nailing of Küntscher* (1948).

Böhler, Peter. b. at Frankfort on the Main, Germany, Dec. 31, 1712; d. at London, April 27, 1775. German clergyman, a bishop of the Moravian Church in America and England.

Böhlitz-Ehrenberg (bė′lits.ā′rẹn.berk). Town in C Germany, in the *Land* (state) of Saxony, Russian Zone, formerly in the free state of Saxony, W of Leipzig, of which it is an industrial suburb. Before World War II it was the seat of large firms manufacturing musical instruments. 10,453 (1946).

Böhl von Faber (bėl fon fä′bėr), **Cecilia.** Maiden name of **Caballero, Fernán.**

Böhm (bėm), **Georg.** b. at Goldbach, near Gotha, Germany, in September, 1661; d. at Lüneburg, Germany, May 18, 1733. German organist, clavichordist, and composer of many liturgical works and pieces for the clavier.

Bohm (bōm), **Max.** b. at Cleveland, Ohio, Jan. 21, 1868; d. at Provincetown, Mass., 1923. American marine, figure, and mural painter. He studied at the Cleveland Art School, and was a pupil of J. P. Laurens and of Benjamin Constant at Paris. His work was extensively exhibited in the U.S. and France, and won a number of awards. He was a member of the Association of American Artists at Paris, the National Academy of Design, and art clubs in England and the U.S. Some of his better-known paintings are *Nature and Imagination, Evening Meal, Governor Lind,* and mural decorations for the Cleveland courthouse.

Böhm (bėm), **Theobald.** b. at Munich, April 9, 1794; d. there, Nov. 25, 1881. German flutist and composer. He was the inventor of several improvements in the flute, especially of a new system of fingering.

Böhm-Bawerk (bėm′bä′verk) or **Böhm von Bawerk** (bėm fon bä′verk), **Eugen.** b. at Brünn, Austria, Feb. 12, 1851; d. at Vienna, Aug. 27, 1914. Austrian political economist and government official, professor at the University of Vienna. In 1884 he was appointed professor at Innsbruck; in 1889 he entered the ministry of finance at Vienna, and was minister of finance in 1895 and in the periods 1897–98 and 1900–04. He was a founder and one of the leading figures of the so-called Austrian school, which propounded an economic doctrine based on the concept of final utility. He published *Kapital und Kapitalzins* (1884–89), *Einige strittige Fragen der Kapitalstheorie* (1900), and others.

Böhme (bė′mẹ), **Herbert.** b. at Frankfort on the Oder, Germany, 1907—. German author of numerous patriotic songs and poems in the era of the Third Reich. His poems *Der Führer* and *Morgenrot, Deutschland* were missing from no major German anthology of the Nazi era. His collections include *Morgenrot* (1932), *Des Blutes Gesänge* (1934), and *Gesänge unter der Fahne* (1935). He is the author of numerous occasional plays and editor of the anthology *Rufe in das Reich, heldische Dichtung von Langemarck bis zur Gegenwart* (1933).

Böhme (bė′mę) or **Böhm** (bėm) or **Behmen** (bā′mẹn), **Jakob.** b. at Altseidenberg, Silesia, 1575; d. at Görlitz, Prussia, Nov. 17, 1624. German mystic. His works include *Aurora* (1612), *Der Weg zu Christo* (1624), and others. He was a shoemaker at Görlitz, where he also published his writings; these were considered heretical and were suppressed, but had great influence, especially in England. Böhme's mysticism leads to a kind of pantheism, according to which God is the source of all things, including good and evil.

Böhmen (bė′mẹn). German name of **Bohemia.**

Böhm-Ermolli (bėm′er.mōl′lē), Baron **Eduard von.** b. at Ancona, Italy, Feb. 21, 1856—. Austrian general. During World War I he lifted the siege of Lemberg (June, 1915), commanded (1916) the Carpathian-Pripet army, and in 1917 defended Galicia against Russian attacks.

Böhmerwald (bė′mėr.vält). A German name of the **Bohemian Forest.**

Böhmisch-Brod (bė′mish.brōt′). German name of **Český Brod.**

Böhmisch-Kamnitz (bė′mish.käm′nits). German name of **Česká Kamenice.**

Böhmisch-Leipa (bė′mish.lī′pä). German name of **Česká Lípa.**

Böhmisch-Skalitz (bė′mish.skä′lits). German name of **Česká Skalice.**

Bohn (bōn), **Henry George.** b. at London, Jan. 4, 1796; d. at Twickenham, England, Aug. 22, 1884. English publisher and bookseller. He is best known for his editions of standard works in various "libraries" issued under his name.

Böhner (bė′nėr), **Johann Ludwig.** b. at Töttelstedt, Gotha, Germany, Jan. 8, 1787; d. March 28, 1860. German composer and performer, who served as the model for the central character of E. T. A. Hoffmann's novelette *Kapellmeister Kreisler.* His compositions include an opera, orchestral and chamber music, and sonatas, up to Opus 120.

Bohol (bô.hôl′). Province of the Philippine Islands, situated between Cebu and Leyte, and consisting of numerous islands, the largest of which is Bohol. Most of the rivers are unimportant for navigation; a few are navigable by boats of light draft for distances of from 3 to 12 mi. The population is chiefly Visayan. The capital, Tagbilaran, is on Bohol, on the SW coast opposite Panglao island. Area of Bohol island, 1,492 sq. mi.; of province, ab. 1,536 sq. mi.; pop. of province, 553,407 (1948).

Bohol Strait. Sea passage in the Philippine Islands separating Bohol and Cebu islands and connecting Mindanao Sea with Camotes Sea.

Bohort (bôrt), **Sir.** See **Bors, Sir.**

Bohr (bōr), **Niels.** [Full name, **Niels Henrik David Bohr.**] b. at Copenhagen, Oct. 7, 1885—. Danish physicist, noted for his contributions to the theory of atomic structure. He was awarded (1922) the Nobel prize in physics. He received his Ph.D. at the University of Copenhagen, studied at Cambridge under Sir Joseph John Thomson, and held faculty status (1914–16) as a reader in mathematical physics at the University of Manchester, where he studied under Sir Ernest Rutherford. He was appointed (1916) professor of theoretical physics at the University of Copenhagen, became (1920) director of the Copenhagen Institute for Theoretical Physics, was named (1939) president of the Danish Academy of Science, and served as an adviser (1944–45) to the scientific staff of the Manhattan Project at Los Alamos, New Mexico. By his application (1913) of Max Planck's quantum theory to Rutherford's nuclear concept of the atom, he formulated the Bohr theory of atomic structure which laid the groundwork for modern atomic physics and the atom bomb; this was supplemented (1939) by his theory (in collaboration with John A. Wheeler) of nuclear fission. Bohr's original hypothesis stated that electrons rotate in nonradiating orbits around a nucleus, but are capable of leaping between different orbits, emitting radiation in the jump to an orbit possessing less energy. He is the author of *On the Application of the Quantum Theory to Atomic Structure* and *Theory of Spectra and Atomic Constitution.*

Bohrod (bō′rod), **Aaron.** b. at Chicago, Nov. 21, 1907—. American painter and illustrator, best known for his scenes of Chicago. He was educated at the Art Institute of Chicago and at the Art Students League of New York. Many museums and galleries in the U.S. have exhibited his work, and he has won a number of awards, including two Guggenheim fellowships (1936 and 1937). The Metropolitan Museum of Art and the Whitney Museum of American Art, both at New York, the Art Institute of Chicago, the Boston Museum of Fine Arts, and the Kansas City, Mo., Museum, among others, include his works in their collections. He executed murals for the post offices at Vandalia, Clinton, and Galesburg, Ill., a series of pictures on Chicago for *Life* magazine, and a series on Kansas City for the Missouri Documentary Art Project; a World War II correspondent (1943–45) for the U.S. government and *Life* magazine, he has had his works reproduced in *Time, Life, Fortune, Esquire,* and *Coronet* magazines. He illustrated *The Illinois,* by James Gray, and is artist in residence at the Southern Illinois Normal University.

Böhtlingk (bėt′lingk), **Otto von.** b. at St. Petersburg, June 11, 1815; d. at Leipzig, Germany, April 1, 1904. Russian Orientalist. His chief work is *Sanskrit-Wörterbuch* (with Rudolf Roth; published 1855–75).

Bohun (bō′hun), **Edmund.** b. at Ringsfield, Suffolk, England, March 12, 1645; d. in Carolina, Oct. 5, 1699. English publicist and miscellaneous writer, appointed chief justice of the colony of Carolina c1698. His chief work is *Geographical Dictionary* (1688).

Bohun (bön), **Henry de.** [Title, 1st Earl of **Hereford.**] b. 1176; d. on a pilgrimage to the Holy Land, June 1, 1220. English nobleman. He was created 1st Earl of Hereford in April, 1199, and was constable of England. He was one of the chief opponents of the effort made by King John of England to restrict the powers and rights of the English nobility, and a leader among the barons who forced John to sign (1215) the Magna Charta.

Bohun, Humphrey III de. d. 1187. Anglo-Norman warrior, a supporter of Henry II in the rebellion of 1173. Although he was in 1140 a chief retainer of Stephen of Blois, he fought against him under Matilda's banner in the following year. In 1164 he attended the council at Clarendon.

Bohun, Humphrey V de. [Titles: 2nd Earl of **Hereford,** 1st Earl of **Essex.**] d. Sept. 24, 1274. English nobleman. He was constable of England. In 1258 he joined the barons under Simon de Montfort in their confederation for the redress of grievances, but went over to the king in 1263, during the Barons' War (War of the Barons), and was taken prisoner by Montfort in the battle of Lewes, on May 14, 1264.

Bohun, Humphrey VII de. [Titles: 3rd Earl of **Hereford,** 2nd Earl of **Essex.**] d. 1298. English nobleman, constable of England. He was associated with Roger Bigod, Earl of Norfolk, and other barons in their opposition to what they considered to be unfair taxation by Edward I of England.

Bohun, Humphrey VIII de. [Titles: 4th Earl of **Hereford,** 3rd Earl of **Essex.**] b. 1276; killed at the battle of Boroughbridge, March 16, 1322. English nobleman, constable of England. He joined the barons in their opposition to Edward II's favorites, Piers Gaveston, and also to the Despensers. He was taken prisoner at the battle of Bannockburn, on June 24, 1314, but was exchanged for the wife of Robert Bruce.

Boiardo (bō.yär′dō), **Matteo Maria.** [Also: **Bojardo;** title, Count of **Scandiano.**] b. at Scandiano, near Reggio nell' Emilia, Italy, 1440 (or 1441); d. there, in December, 1494. Italian lyric poet. His best-known work, entitled *Orlando Innamorato* (Roland in Love), is a chivalric romance now generally recognized as one of the major achievements of Italian literature. Himself a man of truly noble and knightly character, he grew to maturity in what was perhaps the best place in the Italy of that day for such a nature: the court of Ferrara, where the tradition of feudalism and the true spirit of chivalry had lingered longer than elsewhere in Italy. Both his character and the atmosphere of that court are reflected in the *Orlando Innamorato*, which comes closer, perhaps, to the spirit of medieval chivalry than any other Italian work. In its immediate sources, it is a Carolingian epic, but he reworked the material from these sources in the spirit of the Arthurian romances. The old unity of the Carolingian epic, its nationalistic and religious enthusiasm, has been replaced by a new unity based on the principles of chivalry and courtly love, and the portrayal of its effect on different natures. The work is in three books, of which the third remained unfinished at the time of Boiardo's death (he died just as the French were invading Italy, and the last lines of the poem, which are translated into English below, refer in pathetic and prophetic fashion to this: "While I sing, O God our Saviour, I see all Italy set on fire and in flames by these Gauls, who come with great fury, to devastate I know not what region."). As a narrator, Boiardo is extremely able and rich in invention. He developed to a very high point of excellence the technique of concurrent narration of several different threads of the action, with skillful use of cutting at high points of suspense and of the flashback to take up an action left off at some previous point. In this way, he keeps several narratives going at once, and maintains the reader's interest in all of them without letting the action flag or become dull. The various adventures and tales are further knit together by interlocking characters and actions, so that each episode has its beginning in previous events of the story, and eventually dissolves into new episodes. The *Orlando Innamorato* strikes an almost perfect balance between merit of narrative technique and interest of content, with good understanding of psychology (according to the conventions of romantic legend) and motivation of action. The one respect in which it is deficient (and to the readers and critics of 15th-century Italy it was a most important respect) is that of polished language and style. Boiardo's versification is facile and his words flow easily, but his usage is far from that demanded by Tuscan purism. The modern reader, especially if he has not been brought up in the Italian puristic tradition, finds this unimportant, but Boiardo's 15th-century Italian readers placed such great emphasis on it that as soon as Ariosto's *Orlando Furioso* (a continuation of *Orlando Innamorato* which had a diction and style which were acceptably Tuscan) appeared, the *Orlando Innamorato* fell into an undeserved oblivion. The disrepute of Boiardo's work was further increased by the unfortunate distortions which it underwent at various times through the efforts of well-intentioned, but inept, editors to bring it up to the Tuscan purity of Ariosto. However, the discovery in the 19th century of the original manuscript by Boiardo enabled readers once more to evaluate his work without the impediment of intervening bowdlerization, and it may be safely said that Boiardo has now been restored to his proper position as a great poet and teller of stories.

Boie (boi'ẹ), **Heinrich Christian.** b. at Meldorf, Germany, July 19, 1744; d. there, 1806. German writer belonging to the fraternity of poets known as the *Hainbund* or the *Göttinger Dichterbund*, early precursors of the romantics. As a student at Göttingen, Boie founded (1770) with Friedrich Wilhelm Gotter the *Musenalmanach*, which became the organ of the *Hainbund*. He also edited (1776–91) *Das Deutsche Museum*.

Boieldieu (bwȧl.dyė), **Adrien Louis Victor.** b. Nov. 3, 1815; d. July 9, 1883. French composer of comic operas; son of François Adrien Boieldieu (1775–1834).

Boieldieu, François Adrien. b. at Rouen, France, in December, 1775; d. Oct. 8, 1834. French composer of comic operas; father of Adrien Louis Victor Boieldieu (1815–83). He lived at Paris and St. Petersburg. His works include *La Famille suisse* (1797), *Beniowski* (1800), *Le Calife de Bagdad* (1800), *Ma tante Aurore* (1803), *Jean de Paris* (1812), *La Dame blanche* (1825), and *Les Deux Nuits* (1829).

Boies (boi'ẹz), **Horace.** b. at Aurora, N.Y., Dec. 7, 1827; d. April 4, 1923. American lawyer and politician, notable as Iowa's first Democratic governor after the Civil War. First elected in 1889 on an antiprohibition platform, he was reëlected in 1891 as an opponent of the protective tariff on behalf of the farmers. In 1896 he was defeated for the Democratic presidential nomination by William Jennings Bryan, having earlier (1893) declined an appointment by President Grover Cleveland to the post of secretary of agriculture, preferring to remain governor of Iowa.

Boihaemum (bō.i.hē'mum). A Latin name of **Bohemia.**

Boii (bō'i.ī). Ancient Celtic people who entered Italy from Gaul c400 B.C. and settled between the Po and the Apennines. They were overcome by the Romans in 282 B.C., continued to struggle against them, but after 191 B.C. were not heard of again in Italy. It is thought that they migrated to what is now Bohemia, to which they gave their name. They disappeared from there also, c50 B.C. Another group of Boii joined the Helvetii in their invasion of Gaul in 58 B.C.; to them Caesar assigned land in the territory of the Aedui.

Boileau (bwä.lō'), **Philip.** b. at Quebec, Canada, 1864; d. at New York, Jan. 18, 1917. American portrait and landscape painter, and illustrator. He painted portraits of many fashionable women of his time, and was the originator of the "Peggy Head," typifying his idea of feminine beauty. He lived at Baltimore until 1902, and then at New York. His work was exhibited (1920–23) at the Salon d'Automne, Paris, and in the U.S. Besides his portraits, his paintings *The Fortune Teller* and *Eyelets* are well known.

Boileau-Despréaux (bwȧ.lō.dā.prā.ō), **Nicolas.** b. at Paris, Nov. 1, 1636; d. there, March 13, 1711. French critic and poet. He studied law, and was admitted to the bar in December, 1656. His first satire dates from 1660 or 1661, and was the forerunner of a series of seven, completed in 1665. To this same period belong his *Dissertation sur Joconde* and his *Dialogue des héros de roman*. His satires were published without his sanction by a Dutch bookseller, who issued the book under the title *Recueil contenant plusieurs discours libres et moraux, en vers* (1665). Boileau issued his own corrected version in 1666, and within a period of two years there had appeared some 20 additional editions, both authorized and unauthorized. Boileau was attacked from many quarters, and framed his reply in two satires, published in 1669. Little is known of his life between 1670 and 1677. During that interval, however, he wrote his second and third *Épîtres*, translated the *Treatise on the Sublime* of Longinus, published fragments of *Lutrin* (1673), and finally gave out his fourth and fifth *Épîtres*, the first four books of the *Lutrin*, and *L'Art poétique*, in the first edition of the *Oeuvres du sieur D . . .* (1674). This publication raised Boileau to the first rank among French writers. In 1677 he received a pension of 2,000 livres, and was invited with Jean Racine to compile the history of Louis XIV. In the same year he composed his seventh, eighth, and ninth *Épîtres*. In 1684, despite his enemies' opposition, Boileau entered the French Academy on the expressed desire of the king. In 1693 he published his *Réflexions critiques sur Longin*, in answer to Perrault's *Dialogues sur les anciens et les modernes*. The first five editions of Boileau's works are dated 1666, 1674, 1694, 1701, and 1713. The last edition revised throughout by Boileau himself, that of 1701, is generally taken as the standard for the tenth and eleventh satires, and the last three *Épîtres*. A twelfth satire was published after Boileau's death in the edition of 1716.

Boiling Springs Township. Former name of **East Rutherford.**

Boinn (boin). Irish name of the river **Boyne.**

Boiohaemum (boi.ọ.hē'mum). A Latin name of **Bohemia.**

Boiro (boi'rō). Town in NW Spain, in the province of La Coruña, situated on the Ria de Arosa, a bay of the Atlantic Ocean, ab. 54 mi. SW of the city of La Coruña. It has fisheries and sardine canneries; cattle are raised in the district. 11,668 (1940).

Bois (bwä), **Guy Pène du.** See **duBois, Guy Pène.**

Bois (bois), **Hector.** See **Boece** or **Boethius** or **Boetius, Hector.**

Bois, Jaques de. See **Jaques.**

Bois, John. b. at Nettleshead, Suffolk, England, Jan. 3, 1561; d. Jan. 14, 1644. English clergyman and Biblical scholar, one of the translators and revisers of the Bible under James I.

Bois (bwä), **Raoul Henri Pène du.** See **duBois, Raoul Henri Pène.**

Bois (bois), **William Edward Burghardt Du.** See **Du Bois, William Edward Burghardt.**

Boisard (bwȧ.zȧr), **Jean Jacques François Marie.** b. at Caen, France, 1743; d. there, 1831. French fabulist. He was the author of *Fables nouvelles* (1773), *Fables et poésies diverses* (1804), *Mille et une fables* (1806), and others.

Boisbaudran (bwä.bō.drän), **Paul Émile Lecoq de.** b. at Cognac, France, 1838; d. at Paris, 1912. French inorganic chemist. He discovered the elements gallium (1875), samarium (1879), and dysprosium (1886), and helped found the science of spectroscopy. He worked in a private laboratory, supported by his family.

Bois-Colombes (bwä.ko.lônb). Town in N France, in the department of Seine, situated within the bend of the Seine River, NW of Paris, between Aspères and Colombes. It is a suburb of Paris. 25,754 (1946).

Bois de Boulogne (bwä dẹ bö.lony'). Park in Paris. With an area of 2,158 acres, it contains the race courses of Longchamps and Auteuil, and is famous for its turf, trees, and ornamental sheets of water. The present park was ceded to the city and laid out in 1853.

Bois de Vincennes (van.sen). Public park in Paris, somewhat larger than the Bois de Boulogne. It contains "La Faisanderie" (a farm for agricultural experiments), a drill ground, a race course, and a famous zoo.

Boise (boi'si, -zi). [Former name, **Boisé City.**] City in SW Idaho, capital of the state and county seat of Ada County, on the Boise River. The largest city in the state, in a farming, dairying, and mining region, it is a marketing center and manufactures candy and furniture. Arrowrock Dam, near here on the Boise River, is one of a series in a large irrigation project which serves ab. 400,000 acres. 34,393 (1950).

Boisé, Fort. Fur trading establishment erected in Idaho by the Hudson's Bay Company. The first post of this name was constructed (1834) several miles from the mouth of the Boise River; in 1838 another site was chosen at the confluence of the Snake and Boise rivers. The second post became one of the important points along the Oregon Trail. It fell into disuse after 1855.

Boise (boiz), **James Robinson.** b. at Blandford, Mass., Jan. 27, 1815; d. at Chicago, Feb. 9, 1895. American educator. He was professor of Greek at Brown University (1843–50), at the University of Michigan (1852–68), and at the University of Chicago (1868 *et seq.*). He wrote *Greek Syntax* and others.

Boise, Otis Bardwell. b. at Oberlin, Ohio, Aug. 13, 1844; d. at Baltimore, in December, 1912. American organist, and teacher of organ, music theory, and composition. He was active at Cleveland (1865–70), New York (1870–77), Berlin (1888–1901), and Baltimore (1901 *et seq.*).

Boisé City (boi'si, -zi). Former name of **Boise.**

Boise River. River in W central Idaho, rising in three forks in the mountains E of Boise, and flowing NW and W to join the Snake River at the Oregon border. Over 600 sq. mi. of land are irrigated by its waters, which are impounded by two great dams, Arrowrock Dam, and Anderson Ranch Dam (on the South Fork). Length, ab. 60 mi.

Boisgobey (bwȧ.go.bā), **Fortuné Abraham du.** [Original surname, **Castille.**] b. at Granville, Manche, France, Sept. 11, 1824; d. Feb. 26, 1891. French novelist, known during the 19th century for "police" stories not unlike the detective stories of today. He served (1844–88) as a paymaster with the French army in Algeria. His works include *Les Gredins* (1873), *Le Chevalier Casse Cou* (1873), *Le Demi-monde sous la Terreur* (1877), *La Main coupée* (1880), *La Revanche de Fernande* (1882), *La Bande rouge* (1886), and others.

Bois-Guilbert (bwä'gēl.ber'), **Brian de.** Knight Templar, a preceptor of the order, in Sir Walter Scott's novel *Ivanhoe.* Having fallen in love with Rebecca and been repulsed by her, he carries her off to his preceptory. Compelled to accuse her of witchcraft, he meets her defender Ivanhoe in the lists, and falls dead at the beginning of the encounter.

Boisguilbert (bwȧ.gēl.ber), **Pierre Le Pesant,** Sieur **de.** [Also, **Boisguillebert.**] b. at Rouen, France, 1646; d. 1714. French statesman and economist. Unlike Colbert, who theorized that a country is wealthy if there is an abundance of money, Boisguilbert arrived at the conclusion that the keys to wealth are the production of goods and their exchange in commerce. These ideas, which so strikingly foreshadowed some of the principal theses of major economists of the 18th century and later, were set forth in his principal work, *Le Détail de la France, la cause de la diminution de ses biens, et la facilité du remède,* published in 1695. In 1705 or 1706 he published a recapitulation of his theses and proposals under the title *Factotum de la France.* In substitution for customs duties and other burdensome levies, he proposed a single tax of one tenth of the revenue of any property. The influence of the "tax-farmers" (people who bought from the king the right to collect and keep the taxes in a particular area), who had a heavy stake in the prevailing system, was sufficient to keep such proposals from being adopted.

Bois-Reymond (bwä.rā.môn), **Emil Du.** See **Du Bois-Reymond, Emil.**

Bois-Reymond, Paul David Gustav Du. See **Du Bois-Reymond, Paul David Gustav.**

Boisserée (bwä.sẹ.rā'), **Johann Sulpiz.** b. at Cologne, Germany, Aug. 2, 1783; d. at Bonn, Germany, May 2, 1854. German art collector, whose achievements had a decisive influence on the Romantic Movement in Germany. Together with his younger brother Melchior Hermann Josef Boisserée (b. 1786), he salvaged some 200 paintings of the Cologne school of the 14th to 16th centuries which French secularization edicts had thrown on the antique market. The Boisserée collection awakened Friedrich Schlegel's appreciation of German art of the Middle Ages; it aroused Goethe's enthusiasm, and became the most precious unit in the possession of the Alte Pinakothek at Munich. His autobiography appeared in 1862.

Boisset (bwȧ.se), **Antoine.** See **Boesset, Antoine.**

Boissevain (bwä.sẹ.van'), **Inez.** [Maiden name, **Milholland.**] b. at New York, Aug. 6, 1886; d. Nov. 25, 1916. American suffragist and reformer, identified with many women's rights organizations. She took part (1912) in the Philadelphia suffrage convention, and later, at Washington, D.C., organized a parade of women which, from her seat on the back of a white horse, she proceeded to lead down Pennsylvania Avenue.

Boissier (bwȧ.syā), **Gaston.** [Full name, **Marie Louis Gaston Boissier.**] b. at Nîmes, France, Aug. 15, 1823; d. at Paris, June 10, 1908. French classical scholar, historian, and critic, life secretary (1895 *et seq.*) of the French Academy. He became professor of Latin literature in the Collège de France in 1861, and was elected (1876) to the French Academy; he was also named (1886) to the Academy of Inscriptions and Belles-Lettres. Among his works are *Cicéron et ses amis* (1865), *La Religion romaine d'Auguste aux Antonins* (1874), *L'Opposition sous les Césars* (1875), *Promenades archéologiques* (1880), *La Fin du paganisme* (1891), *Saint Simon* (1892), *L'Afrique romaine* (1895), *Tacite* (1903), and *La Conjuration de Catilina* (1905).

Boissieu (bwȧ.syė), **Jean Jacques de.** b. at Lyons, France, 1736; d. there, 1810. French painter and engraver.

Boisson (bwȧ.sôn), **Pierre François.** b. at St.-Launeuc, Côtes-du-Nord, France, June 19, 1894; d. at Le Vésinet, Seine-et-Oise, France, July 21, 1948. French colonial administrator. As governor of French West Africa (1939–40), he supported the Henri Pétain government, becoming head of French North Africa. He joined the governments of Jean Darlan and Henri Giraud, and was again (Feb. 6–July 1, 1943) governor of French West Africa.

Boissonade (bwȧ.so.nȧd), **Jean François.** b. at Paris, Aug. 12, 1774; d. at Passy, France, Sept. 8, 1857. French classical scholar, professor of Greek literature in the faculty of letters of the University of Paris.

Boissy d'Anglas (bwȧ.sē dän.glȧs), **François Antoine,** Comte **de.** b. at St.-Jean-Chambre, Ardèche, France, Dec. 8, 1756; d. at Paris, Oct. 20, 1826. French statesman and publicist. He became a member of the assembly of the States-General in 1789, of the National Convention of 1792 (which set up the first French Republic), of the Committee of Public Safety in 1794, of the Council of Five Hundred in 1795, of the Senate in 1805, and of the Chamber of Peers in 1814. He wrote *Essai sur la vie, les écrits, et les opinions de M. de Malesherbes* (1819).

Boisterer (bois'tėr.ėr). One of Fortunio's servants in Marie Catherine d'Aulnoy's fairy tale *Fortunio*. His breath had the power of a tremendous wind.

Boito (bō'ē.tō), **Arrigo.** b. at Padua, Italy, Feb. 24, 1842; d. at Milan, Italy, June 10, 1918. Italian poet and composer. His first opera, *Mefistofele*, was produced with his own libretto at Milan, on March 5, 1868. It was first played in a revised form in 1875. He wrote many librettos (among which are *Othello* and *Falstaff*, for Giuseppe Verdi), a volume of poems, and other works.

Boizenburg (boi'tsẹn.bürk). Town in NE Germany, in the *Land* (state) of Mecklenburg, Russian Zone, formerly in the free state of Mecklenburg, situated on the Elbe River, SE of Hamburg. A river port, it has lumber mills and grain markets. The town was first mentioned in 1255, and belonged subsequently either to the counts of Schwerin or to the prince-electors of Hanover. 10,609 (1946).

Bojardo (bō.yär'dō), **Matteo Maria.** See **Boiardo, Matteo Maria.**

Bojer (boi'ėr), **Johan.** b. at Orkdalsøra, Norway, March 6, 1872—. Norwegian novelist and playwright. His novels *Troens Magt* (1903; Eng. trans., *The Power of a Lie*, 1938), and *Den store hunger* (1916; Eng. trans., *The Great Hunger*, 1918) have won him an international circle of readers, but he is considered by many critics to be at his most effective level when describing the humble fisher folk whom he knows best, as in *Den siste Viking* (1921; Eng. trans., *The Last of the Vikings*, 1923).

Bok (bok), **Edward William.** b. at Den Helder, Netherlands, Oct. 9, 1863; d. at Lake Wales, Fla., Jan. 9, 1930. American editor and writer. Resident in the U.S. from 1869, he worked during his young manhood as a stenographer, being employed by the publishing houses of Henry Holt and Company and Charles Scribner's Sons. Editor (1882) of *The Brooklyn Magazine*, he founded (1886) and headed (1886–91) the Bok Syndicate Press, originally established for the purpose of publishing Henry Ward Beecher's sermons, and was also editor in chief (1889–1919) of *The Ladies' Home Journal.* He gave (1923) 100,000 dollars for the American Peace Award, as a prize for the best plan toward universal peace. Author of *Successward* (1895), *Why I Believe in Poverty* (1915), *The Americanization of Edward Bok* (1920; awarded the Pulitzer prize), *Two Persons* (1922), *A Man from Maine* (1923), *Twice Thirty* (1924), *Dollars Only* (1926), and *Perhaps I Am* (1928).

Bokanowski (bo.kȧ.nof.skē), **Maurice.** b. at Le Havre, France, Aug. 31, 1879; d. in an airplane accident at Toul, France, Sept. 2, 1928. French politician and lawyer. Elected to the Chamber of Deputies in 1914, he served under Premier Paul Poincaré as navy minister (1924) and minister of trade and aeronautics (1926).

Bokenham or **Bokenam** (bok'ẹn.ạm), **Osbern.** b. possibly at Bokeham (or Bookham), Surrey, England, Oct. 6, 1393; d. c1447. English dialect poet and member of the Augustinian order. He was the author of a collection of 13 poems dedicated to 12 holy women, including Saint Anne, Saint Magdalene, and Saint Elizabeth, and the 11,000 virgins. The first poem in the series, to Saint Margaret, begun on September 6, 1443, was composed for his friend Thomas Burgh, a Cambridge monk. Bokenham was familiar with Greek and Latin authors and was influenced by Geoffrey Chaucer and John Lydgate. His work, important as an example of 15th-century Suffolk dialect, was published (1835) by the Roxburghe Club.

Boker (bō'kėr), **George Henry.** b. at Philadelphia, Oct. 6, 1823; d. there, Jan. 2, 1890. American poet, dramatist, and diplomat. He was U.S. minister to Turkey (1871–75) and to Russia (1875–79). His works include the dramas *Calaynos* (1848), *Anne Boleyn* (1850), *The Bethrothal* (1850), *Leonor de Guzman* (1853), *Francesca da Rimini* (1855), and *Widow's Marriage*, and *Poems of War* (1864), *Plays and Poems*, *Street Lyrics* (1865), and *The Book of the Dead* (1882).

Bokerly Dyke (bō'kėr.li dīk). Name applied to the ruins of Roman entrenchments in the neighborhood of Farnham, England, the site of the ancient Vindogladia.

Bokhara (bō.kä'rạ). See **Bukhara.**

Bokkhoris (bok.kō'ris). See **Bocchoris.**

Bokn Fjord (bô'kün). [Also, **Bukn Fjord.**] Arm of the North Sea in SW Norway, N of Stavanger. Length, ab. 35 mi.

Boksburg (boks'bėrg). City in S Africa, an important mining center in the Transvaal, Union of South Africa, situated on the main railway line, ab. 14 mi. E of Johannesburg. There are very rich gold mines in the area, and as in all the other towns on the Witwatersrand, its economy is largely dependent on the mines. 53,432 (1946).

Bokstel (bôks'tẹl). See **Boxtel.**

Bol (bôl), **Ferdinand.** b. at Dordrecht, Netherlands, 1616; d. at Amsterdam, 1680. Dutch painter. He studied under Rembrandt, of whom he is said to have been the favorite pupil. His best-known painting, *Portrait of Saskia* (Saskia was Rembrandt's wife), is now in the Brussels Museum. His other works include *Regents of the Leprosy Hospital* in the Town Hall, and *Portrait of Admiral de Ruyter* in the Rijks Museum, both at Amsterdam, *Joseph Presenting Jacob to Pharaoh*, in the Dresden Gallery, and *The Women at the Sepulcher*, in the Copenhagen Museum. Like Rembrandt, Bol also executed many etchings.

Bolama (bö.lä'mạ). [Also, **Bulama.**] Island in the Atlantic Ocean, off W Africa, the easternmost of the Bissagos islands, Portuguese Guinea. Chief town, Bolama.

Bolama. [Also, **Bulama.**] Town in W Africa, a port and former capital of Portuguese Guinea, situated on the island of Bolama about the middle of the coast of the colony. It served as the capital until 1942, when Bissau on the mainland replaced it as administrative center. Pop. ab. 5,000.

Bolan (bō.län'). [Also: **Bholan, Bolan** (or **Bholan**) **Pass**; former official name, **Bolan Pass and Nushki Railway District.**] Subdivision of Baluchistan, W Pakistan, in the N part of the state. In it is the Bolan Pass, on the railway between Sind and Afghanistan. 6,009 (1941).

Bolanden (bō'län.dẹn), **Konrad von.** Pseudonym of **Bischoff, Joseph Eduard Konrad.**

Bolandshahr (bō.lạnd.shär'). See **Bulandshahr.**

Bolan Pass (bō.län'). [Also, **Bholan Pass.**] Gorge in the mountains of NE Baluchistan, W Pakistan. It is traversed by a railway, built (1885–86) for the British army, which connects Sind, by way of Quetta, with Afghanistan. Elevation, 5,800 ft.; length, ab. 54 mi.

Bolbec (bol.bek). Town in N France, in the department of Seine-Inférieure, situated at the junction of four valleys, ab. 18 mi. NE of Le Havre. It is an industrial town, with a number of cotton spinning and weaving mills. 10,779 (1946).

Bolbitinic Mouth of the Nile (bol.bi.tin'ik). [Also: **Bolbitine** (bol.bi.tī'nē), **Bolbitic** (bol.bit'ik).] One of the principal ancient mouths of the Nile River, Egypt, partly represented by the modern Rosetta Branch.

Boldini (bōl.dē'nē), **Giovanni.** b. at Ferrara, Italy, 1845; d. in January, 1931. Italian painter. He was trained at the Academy of Fine Arts at Florence, and made his initial success at London. In 1872 he established himself at Paris and produced many portraits and easel pictures. He was a brilliant colorist and technician.

Boldon (bōl'dọn). Urban district in NE England, in Durham, ab. 4 mi. NW of Sunderland, ab. 269 mi. N of London by rail. It includes part of the former South Shields rural district. 16,692 (1951).

Boldrewood (bōl'dėr.wůd), **Rolf.** Pseudonym of **Browne, Thomas Alexander.**

Bold Stroke for a Husband, A. Comedy by Hannah Cowley, brought out in 1783.

Bold Stroke for a Wife, A. Comedy by Susannah Centlivre, produced in 1718.

Boldt (bōlt), **George C.** b. April 25, 1851; d. Dec. 5, 1916. American hotel executive. He worked as a steward in hotels and restaurants in New York and Philadelphia, before becoming manager of New York's Waldorf Hotel when it opened in 1893, and subsequently president of the Waldorf-Astoria Hotel Company. He was active in building the Bellevue-Stratford Hotel at Philadelphia.

Bolerium (bọ.lir'i.um). Ancient name of **Lands End.**

Bolero (bō.lā'rō). Orchestral composition by Maurice Ravel, first performed as a ballet at the Paris Opera on Nov. 20, 1928; it received its first New York performance on Nov. 14, 1929.

Boleslav I (bō′lę.slav, bol′ę-). [Also: **Boleslas** (-slas, -släs), **Boleslaus** (-slôs); Polish, **Bolesław** (bô.le′släf); surnamed **Chrobry,** meaning "Brave" or "Mighty."] b. c966; d. 1025. Duke and king of Poland (992–1025). An able soldier, he united and enlarged the Polish domain by taking over those parts of it which had been left to his two brothers and by seizing territories from the Hungarians, Bohemians, and Pomeranians, and holding them against the emperors Otto III and Henry II. He had the title of duke of Poland from 992 to 1000; in the latter year Otto III granted him the title of king (which, however, he seems not to have used until 1024). In 1000, also, he persuaded Otto III to make the bishopric of Gniezno a metropolitan see, which freed the Polish church from German domination. With Henry II he concluded in 1018 a treaty favorable to Poland. Because of his zeal in building schools and monasteries (and possibly also because of his capacity for territorial aggrandizement) he has sometimes been called "the Charlemagne of Poland."

Boleslav II. [Also: **Boleslas, Boleslaus;** Polish, **Bolesław;** surnamed **Śmiały,** meaning "Bold."] b. c1039; d. 1081 or 1083. King of Poland (1058–79); son of Casimir I. Although he succeeded to the royal title upon his father's death, he was not crowned until 1076. He was frequently at war with Hungary and Bohemia, and he annexed Ruthenia to the Polish territories, but subsequently had to relinquish it. Although he consistently followed the counsel of the Pope in his foreign policy, he became involved in a bitter controversy with the Church over the right of investiture, and, upon a charge of having caused the murder of Bishop Stanislav of Kraków, he was excommunicated and deposed by Pope Gregory VII in 1079. He went into exile in Hungary, where he died.

Boleslav III. [Also: **Boleslas, Boleslaus;** Polish, **Bolesław.**] b. 1085 or 1086; d. 1138. King of Poland (1102–38). The inheritance of the kingdom of Poland having been divided between him and a bastard half-brother, Boleslav (with the backing of the Russians and Hungarians) reunited the domain by defeating the other heir, who had the assistance of Pomerania, Bohemia, and the forces of the Holy Roman Empire. He seized Pomerania, took steps to complete its Christianization, held it against the emperors Henry V and Lothair II, and in 1135, by the terms of a treaty with Lothair III, was confirmed in possession of that territory as well as of Rügen, as fiefs of the Holy Roman Empire. Boleslav III changed the law governing succession to the Polish crown, leaving the kingdom as a unit to the oldest surviving member of his family instead of allowing it to be divided among his sons. In this way he sought to remedy a weakness which had more than once destroyed the unity of Poland, but his reform was not permanently effective.

Boleslavsky (bō.lę.släf′ski), **Richard.** b. at Warsaw, 1889; d. at Hollywood, Calif., Jan. 17, 1937. Russian actor, producer and director. He was a member (1906–15) of the Moscow Art Theatre, and became famous for his portrayal of Toby Belch in Shakespeare's *Twelfth Night.* He came to New York in 1920 and staged a series of productions including *Revue Russe* (1922), *The Vagabond King* (1925), *White Eagle* (1927), *Ballyhoo* (1927), *Mr. Moneypenny* (1928), and *Judas* (1929). In 1928 he founded, with Maria Ouspenskaya, the American Laboratory Theatre, an experimental group which set out to "harmonize all aspects of production as a form of collective education." In its year of operation the company produced *Granite, The Big Lake, Bridal Veil,* and *Dr. Knock.* In 1930 he became a Hollywood director; among his best-known films were *Woman Pursued* (1931), *Men in White* (1934), and *Clive of India* (1935).

Bolesławiec (bô.le.slä′vyets). [German, **Bunzlau.**] Town in S Poland, in the *województwo* (province) of Wrocław, formerly in Silesia, Germany, situated on the Bobr River, ab. 25 mi. NW of Legnica. It has been famous for its pottery industry since the 16th century. Before World War II there were also woolen-textile and glass manufactures and an iron foundry. The town hall dates from 1525, the parish church from the period 1482–92; there is a local museum. The poet Martin Opitz was born here. The settlement of the Moravian Brethren (Herrnhut Community) at nearby Gnadenberg was transferred to Germany after 1945, when the town was taken over by the Polish administration. Bolesławiec was taken by the Russians on Feb. 13, 1945, in World War II. Its population declined from 22,455 (1939) to 3,145 (1946).

Boleyn (bu̇l′in), **Anne.** b. c1507; beheaded at London, May 19, 1536. English queen; second wife of Henry VIII of England, whom she married on or about Jan. 25, 1533, and mother by him of Queen Elizabeth. She was the daughter of Sir Thomas Boleyn, later earl of Wiltshire and Ormond, and was Henry's acknowledged mistress for some time before he gained his divorce from Catherine of Aragon. She was condemned to death on a charge of adultery and incest, and decapitated. It is now generally believed that she was certainly not guilty of all the crimes of which she was accused, but her entire innocence has never been established. She has been the subject of various works of literature, including in recent times Maxwell Anderson's play *Anne of the Thousand Days* (1948).

Bolgary (bul′gą.ri). [Also: **Bolgari, Bulgary, Bulgar the Great.**] Ruins of the ancient capital of the Bolgarian state of the 10th–14th centuries are situated near Spassky Zaton, S of Kazan, in the C part of the U.S.S.R. Arab travelers of the 10th century mention the wooden buildings of Bolgary, and state that its inhabitants spent the summer in tents outside the city. The remaining ruins are made of white stone and date from the last period of the Bolgarian state (which became subject to Tartar rule in 1236). The buildings are of Moslem architecture, which was probably introduced here in the 10th century, together with Mohammedanism. It is possible that Bolgar art had some influence on the Old-Russian art, since there is evidence that Bolgary furnished some building material to the Vladimir-Suzdal region. Thus it is possible that Bolgary served as a path along which the Oriental tent form (an octagonal base placed on a cube) was introduced into the Old-Russian architecture.

Bolgolam (bol′gǫ.lam). Character in David Garrick's play *Lilliput.*

Bolgrad (bol.grät′). [Also, **Bielgrad.**] Town in the SW part of the U.S.S.R., in the Izmail *oblast* (region) of the Ukrainian Soviet Socialist Republic, formerly in Rumania. Food processing and textiles are important. Pop. ab. 13,000.

Bolin (bö.lēn′), **Andreas Wilhelm.** b. at St. Petersburg, Aug. 2, 1835; d. at Helsinki, Finland, June 16, 1924. Finnish philosopher, of Swedish descent, who served as professor and as librarian at the University of Helsinki. He opposed the philosophy of Hegel, and was a proponent of the theories of Spinoza and of Ludwig Feuerbach. Author of *Europas statslif* (1868–71), *Studier och föredrag* (1888–95), and biographies of Leibnitz, Spinoza, and Feuerbach.

Bolingbroke (bol′ing.bru̇k). Conjurer, in the second part of Shakespeare's play *Henry VI.*

Bolintineanu (bō.lēn.tē.nyä′nö), **Dimitri.** b. at Bolintina, Rumania, 1826; d. at Bucharest, Sept. 1, 1872. Rumanian poet and politician. He published a French translation of his poems under the title *Brises d'Orient* (1866).

Bolitho (bǫ.lī′thō), **Hector.** [Full name, **Henry Hector Bolitho.**] b. at Auckland, New Zealand, May 28, 1898—. English writer of fiction and biography, resident (1922 *et seq.*) in England. He is the author of *The Islands of Wonder* (1920), *Thistledown and Thunder* (1928), *The New Zealanders* (1928), *The New Countries* (1929), *The Glorious Oyster* (1929), *Albert the Good* (1932), *The Prince Consort and his Brother* (1934), *Victoria, the Widow and her Son* (1934), *Older People* (1935), *The House in Half Moon Street* (1936), *Edward VIII* (1937), *Royal Progress* (1937), *George VI* (1937), *Victoria and Albert* (1938), *A Century of British Monarchy* (1951), and the novels *Solemn Boy* (1927) and *Judith Silver* (1929).

Bolitho, William. [Full name, **William Bolitho Ryall.**] b. at Capetown, South Africa, 1890; d. at Avignon, France, June 2, 1930. English newspaper correspondent, columnist, and author. During his service in World War I, he was the only one of a group of 16 who survived a mine explosion on the Somme front; after recovering, he became Paris correspondent for the Manchester *Guardian,* and European correspondent for the New York *World.* He was the author of political and biographical studies including *Leviathan* (1924), *Italy Under Mussolini* (1926), *Murder for Profit* (1926), and

Twelve Against the Gods (1929). He also wrote a play, *Overture* (produced after his death), essays published in *Camera Obscura* (1931), and an unfinished novel, published by his wife, Sybil Bolitho, in her own novel, *My Shadow As I Pass.*

Bolívar (bō.lē′bär). See also **Ciudad Bolívar.**

Bolívar. Department in N Colombia. Capital, Cartagena; area, 22,981 sq. mi.; pop. 1,047,300 (est. 1950).

Bolívar. Province in C Ecuador. Capital, Guaranda; area, 1,246 sq. mi.; pop. 110,270 (est. 1944).

Bolivar (bol′i.vạr). City in SW Missouri, county seat of Polk County. 3,482 (1950).

Bolivar. Town (in New York the equivalent of township in many other states) and village in S New York, in Allegany County, in a petroleum-producing area: oil refineries. Pop. of town, 2,680 (1950); of village, 1,490 (1950).

Bolívar (bō.lē′bär). State in E Venezuela. Capital, Ciudad Bolívar; area, 91,892 sq. mi.; pop. 122,114 (1950).

Bolívar (bol′i.vạr; Spanish, bō.lē′bär), **Simón.** [Called **"El Libertador,"** meaning "the Liberator."] b. at Caracas, Venezuela, July 24, 1783; d. at San Pedro, near Santa Marta, Colombia, Dec. 17, 1830. Venezuelan general and statesman, hero of the South American independence movement in the early 19th century. He took an active part in the revolution against Spain at Caracas in 1810, served under Francisco de Miranda in 1812, captured Caracas (Aug. 4, 1813), was there named general of the Venezuelan forces and temporary dictator, and received (Oct. 13, 1813) the title *Salvador de la Patria, Libertador de Venezuela* ("Savior of the Country, Liberator of Venezuela"). After subsequent losses, he left Venezuela for Cartagena, Colombia, and captured (1814) Bogotá. Military setbacks in 1815 forced him to take refuge for a time in Jamaica, in the British West Indies. He made an unsuccessful descent upon the Venezuelan coast in May, 1816, and a second, successful attempt in December, and took Angostura (now Ciudad Bolívar) in July, 1817. A patriot congress there confirmed Bolívar as dictator. In 1819 he marched into New Granada, and there increased his forces by a union with Francisco de Paula Santander. The victory of Boyacá (Aug. 7, 1819) made him master of Bogotá and New Granada and brought him the additional title of "Liberator of New Granada." A congress at Angostura now decreed the union of Venezuela and New Granada in the original republic of Colombia (comprising finally what is now Colombia, Venezuela, Panama, and Ecuador), and Bolívar was elected (Dec. 17, 1819) president. He completely routed the Spanish army in Venezuela in the battle of Carabobo (June 24, 1821), and entered Quito on June 16, 1822, thus adding the region of what is now Ecuador to Colombia. On Sept. 1, 1823, he was made dictator of Peru, at Lima (San Martín, the other great South American patriot of the day, withdrew from Peru at this time for reasons which still remain unascertained). He defeated José Canterac at Junín, Aug. 6, 1824, and on Dec. 9, 1824 Antonio José de Sucre's great victory at Ayacucho ended the Spanish power in South America. At this time he was given a third title, "Liberator of Peru." In June, 1825, Bolívar visited Upper Peru (comprising the territory of what is now Bolivia); a congress met there in August, decreed the formation of the republic of Bolivia (named in his honor), invited Bolívar to frame the constitution, and named him perpetual protector. But Peru declared against him in 1826, and Bolivia soon followed. Shortly thereafter Venezuela and Ecuador withdrew from Colombia, and in 1830, the year of his death, he relinquished the presidency of what was left.

Bolivia (bọ.liv′i.ạ). [Official Spanish name, **República de Bolivia;** former names (in colonial times), **Charcas, Upper Peru.**] Republic in W central South America, bounded by Brazil on the N and E, the Argentine Republic and Paraguay on the S, and Chile and Peru on the W. The W part is a plateau traversed by the Andes. In the SE is the Gran Chaco, and in the NE the plains of the Madeira. It produces coca, rubber, cinchona, coffee (some of the best coffee in the world comes from the Bolivian highlands), wheat, maize, gold, silver, copper, and tin. It has nine departments, and is governed by a president and a congress consisting of a senate and chamber of deputies. Bolivia formally achieved independence from Spain in August, 1825, was united to Peru in the period 1836–39, and has since undergone frequent political revolutions. Attacked by Chile in the period 1879–83, it was defeated, and was forced to cede its seaboard and districts containing important nitrate deposits (in 1950, however, Chile formally offered to give Bolivia a corridor to the sea). In November, 1903, the republic ceded to Brazil the territory of Acre for ten million dollars. In March, 1905, a treaty was negotiated between Bolivia and Chile whereby Chile agreed to build a railway from Arica to La Paz and Bolivia was to have free transit to the Pacific ports. The question of the boundary with Peru was submitted to the president of Argentina for arbitration in 1908 and settled in 1909. In the period 1936–38 there were intermittent hostilities with Paraguay over the region of the Gran Chaco. Capitals, La Paz (administrative), Sucre (constitutional); area, ab. 414,364 sq. mi.; pop. 3,019,031 (1950).

Bolkhov (bol.ʜôf′). [Also, **Bolkhof.**] Town in the U.S.S.R., in the Orel *oblast* (region) of the Russian Soviet Federated Socialist Republic, ab. 75 mi. NE of Bryansk. Food processing is the local industry; corn and wheat are grown in the area. Pop. ab. 17,500.

Boll (bol). German name of **Bulle.**

Bolland (bôl′änt), **Gerardus Johannes Petrus Josephus.** b. at Groningen, Holland, June 9, 1854; d. at Leiden, Feb. 11, 1922. Dutch philosopher, propagandist in Holland for Hegelian philosophy. Author of *Zuivere Rede en hare Werkelijkheid* (1904) and *Collegium Logicum* (1905).

Bolland (bôl′änt; Anglicized, bol′ạnd), **Johann van.** [Latinized surname, **Bollandus.**] b. at Julemont, in Brabant, Aug. 13, 1596; d. at Antwerp, Sept. 12, 1665. Jesuit martyrologist. He edited the early volumes of the great *Acta Sanctorum,* begun by Heribert Rosweyde (d. 1629), a work which was continued by his collaborators and successors, the so-called Bollandists.

Bollandists (bol′ạn.dists). Name given to the collaborators and successors of Johann van Bolland, the first editor of *Acta Sanctorum,* the most authoritative and comprehensive work in existence on the lives of the Roman Catholic saints. Among them may be mentioned Georg Henschen (d. 1681), Daniel Papebroeck (d. 1714), Konrad Janning (d. 1723), Peter Booch (d. 1736), Suyskens (d. 1771), Hubers (d. 1782), Dom Anselmo Berthod (d. 1788), and Joseph Ghesquière (d. 1802).

Boller (bō′lėr, bol′ėr), **Alfred Pancoast.** b. at Philadelphia, Feb. 23, 1840; d. Dec. 9, 1912. American civil engineer notable for his construction of a bridge over the Harlem River, at New York, the Thames River Bridge, at New London, Conn., the Municipal Bridge, at St. Louis, and a bridge over the Connecticut River, near its mouth, at Saybrook, Conn. His firm (including Henry M. Hodge and Howard C. Baird) served also as consulting engineers for the steel frameworks of New York's Singer and Metropolitan Life Insurance buildings. Author of *Practical Treatise on the Construction of Iron Highway Bridges, for the Use of Town Committees* (1876).

Bolles (bōlz), **Albert Sidney.** b. at Montville, Conn., March 8, 1846; d. at Williamstown, Mass., May 8, 1939. American lawyer and writer on finance. He was professor of mercantile law and banking at the Wharton School of Finance and Economy in the University of Pennsylvania, chief of the Bureau of Industrial Statistics of the State of Pennsylvania, and editor of the *Bankers' Magazine.* His works include *Conflict Between Labor and Capital* (1876), *Industrial History of the United States* (1878), *Practical Banking* (1884), *A History of Pennsylvania* (1899), and *American Finance* (1901).

Bolles, Frank. b. at Winchester, Mass., Oct. 31, 1856; d. Jan. 10, 1894. American nature writer and secretary (1887 *et seq.*) of Harvard University. He was the author of collections of sketches entitled *The Land of the Lingering Snow* (1891), *At the North of Bearcamp Water* (1893), and *From Blomidon to Smoky, and Other Papers* (1894). He also wrote the volume of verse *Chocorua's Tenants* (1895), and published (with others) *A Collection of Important English Statutes* (1880).

Bolley (bol′i), **Henry Luke.** b. at Manchester, Ind., Feb. 1, 1865—. American plant pathologist, noted for devising methods of preventing diseases of potatoes, flax, and cereal grains. He was graduated (B.S., 1888; M.S., 1889) from Purdue University, and in 1890 became professor of zoölogy and botany at the North Dakota Agricultural College, and botanist and plant pathologist of the North Dakota experiment station. He served (1909–29) as state seed commissioner for North Dakota, and drafted that state's pure seed laws and barberry eradication act.

Bolligen (bol′i.gen). Town in W central Switzerland, in the canton of Bern. It has a flourishing dairy industry. 8,434 (1941).

Bollington (bol′ing.ton). Urban district in W England, in Cheshire, ab. 3 mi. NE of Macclesfield, ab. 168 mi. NW of London by rail. 5,313 (1951).

Bollman (bōl′man), **Justus Erich.** b. at Hoya, Hanover, Germany, 1769; d. in Jamaica, British West Indies, Dec. 9, 1821. American profiteer, confidential agent (1806–07) of Aaron Burr during the Bastrop land-grant conspiracy. Arrested in possession of Burr's cipher, he was called before the Supreme Court but later released; he reported (1807) the plans to Thomas Jefferson, but denied Burr's disloyalty, and at Burr's trial testified in his favor. In 1805 he was offered the Indian agency at Natchitoches, La., by Jefferson.

Bollstädt (bol′shtet), Count **von.** See **Albertus Magnus,** Saint.

Bologna (bō.lō′nyä; Anglicized, bo.lōn′ya). Province in N central Italy, in the *compartimento* (region) of Emilia-Romagna. Capital, Bologna; area, ab. 1,440 sq. mi.; pop. 714,705 (1936).

Bologna. [Etruscan, **Felsina;** Roman **Bononia.**] City in N central Italy, in the *compartimento* (region) of Emilia-Romagna, the capital of the province of Bologna, situated at the foot of the Apennines, between the Savena, Aposa, and Reno rivers: one of the most important cities of Italy, linking the N and the C provinces. It is a railroad junction and has numerous industries, among which the manufacture of a type of sausage (locally called *mortadella,* but known throughout the U.S. as "bologna") has become particularly known. There are also macaroni factories, distilleries, and metallurgical, glass, leather, linen, and silk industries. Pop. of commune, 349,326 (1951).

Cultural History. Bologna is famous for its educational institutions. It contains the oldest university in Europe, founded during the latter part of the 11th century; the school of law was outstanding in the 12th and 13th centuries, and the study of anatomy was introduced in the 14th century; the university is still one of the most renowned in Italy, with an important library. There are numerous other institutions of higher learning, including a school of art (which is connected with one of the best art collections in Italy), a school of engineering, and the famous school of music (*Liceo Filarmonico*), founded in 1805, but based upon a much older tradition. The *museo civico* (municipal museum) contains a collection of antiquities; there are a number of theaters and opera houses of long standing, some of them dating back to the 16th and 17th centuries. In the latter period, the city was also the seat of a school of painting led by Guido Reni, Domenichino, and others.

Architecture. Architecturally, Bologna is among the most distinguished of Italian cities; its medieval churches, towers, and palaces are characteristic features of the city even today. Particular mention should be made of the Basilica of San Petronio, the Gothic Cathedral of San Pietro, and the churches of San Domenico, San Giaccomo Maggiore, San Francesco, and Santa Maria della Vita. The palaces of Bologna date from many periods, with Gothic and Renaissance styles prevailing. The leaning towers (Garisenda and Asinelli) are considered by some to equal the one at Pisa.

Political History. Built on the site of an ancient Etruscan town, Bologna became a Roman military colony in 189 B.C.; in the early Middle Ages it belonged to the Byzantine exarchate of Ravenna and to the Lombard kingdom; then, as a free city, it was one of the most powerful members of the Lombard League and of the Guelph party. The victory of Fossalta (1249) brought Emperor Frederick II's son Enzio as prisoner to Bologna, where he was kept until his death in 1272; he was the last of the house of Hohenstaufen. In 1278 the city came under the control of the papacy but, torn by feuds among the great families, it was not definitely incorporated into the States of the Church until 1506. Emperor Charles V was crowned here in 1530, the last time that a German emperor was crowned in Italy. After the French occupation in 1796, Bologna was made capital of the Cispadane Republic; it came again under the States of the Church in 1815, revolted against papal rule in 1831, 1843, and 1848, and was finally united to the kingdom of Italy in 1860. In World War II, it was controlled by the Germans from September, 1943 to April, 1945, when the Allied armies entered the city. There had been fighting going on in the area immediately S of Bologna from September, 1944, in the course of which considerable damage was sustained by the cathedral, the Church of San Francesco, several of the palaces, and other buildings of tourist interest, but repairs have been completed or are being carried out.

Boloko (bō.lō′kō). See **Lomami.**

Bolonia (bo.lō′ni.a). Medieval name of **Boulogne.**

Bolor-Tagh (bō.lôr′täg′). Range of mountains in the U.S.S.R., in the Uzbek Soviet Socialist Republic, C Asia, on the border of the Pamir plateau, running NW and SE. Maximum elevation, ab. 18,000 ft.

Bölsche (bėl′she), **Wilhelm.** b. at Cologne, Germany, Jan. 2, 1861; d. 1939. German author. He helped lay the theoretical foundations of the naturalistic school of German literature with his essay *Die naturwissenschaftlichen Grundlagen der Poesie* (1887). His novel *Die Mittagsgöttin* (1891) marks his shift to scientific subjects in the wake of Darwin, Haeckel, and others. His popularizations of such matters include *Das Säugetier und seine Entstehung, Das Pferd und seine Geschichte, Was ist Natur?,* and *Das Liebesleben in der Natur* (1898 *et seq.;* translated as *Love Life in Nature,* 1929).

Bolsena (bôl.sā′nä). Town and commune in C Italy, in the *compartimento* (region) of Latium, in the province of Viterbo, situated on the Lake of Bolsena, ab. 7 mi. SW of Orvieto: probably the site of the ancient Volsinii. The Church of Santa Cristina, built in the 11th century, has a Renaissance façade added in 1500. The Miracle of Bolsena (a vision, by a doubting priest, of a flow of blood from the Host at Mass), which occurred in 1263, gave rise to the institution by Pope Urban IV of the festival of Corpus Christi. Some damage was sustained during World War II by Santa Cristina and other buildings of tourist interest. Pop. of commune, 3,996 (1936); of town, 3,063 (1936).

Bolsena, Lake of. [Italian, **Lago di Bolsena;** Latin, **Lacus Volsiniensis.**] Lake in C Italy, ab. 52 mi. NW of Rome. It occupies the crater of an extinct volcano. Length, ab. 8 mi.

Bolshaya (bol.shä′ya). Russian name of **McKinley, Mount.**

Bolsheviks (bōl′she.viks). See under **Bolshevism.**

Bolshevism (bōl′she.viz.em). Name originally applied to the theory and practice of the majority group (Russian, *Bolsheviki,* "those of the majority") at the conference (1902–03) of the Russian Social Democratic Labor Party at London and Brussels, and now more usually to political ideology of the successors to that group. The effective leader of the group at the London-Brussels conference was Nikolai Lenin, whose ascendancy among the Bolsheviks continued until his death. In the course of a conference at Paris in 1910 the breach between the Bolsheviks and the Mensheviks (Russian, *Mensheviki,* "those of the minority") became irreconcilable, and at the Prague conference in 1912 the Bolsheviks severed relations with the Mensheviks and adopted the name *Russian Social Democratic Labor Party* (*Bolsheviks*), the parenthesized word being in common practice abbreviated to (*B*). In 1918 this was succeeded by the *Russian Communist Party* (*B*), and in 1925 by the *All-Union Communist Party* (*B*). (The italicized terms above are, of course, all English translations of the actual Russian names.) In October and November, 1917, the Bolsheviks secured control of the revolutionary movement in Russia and came into power with the overthrow of the Kerensky government. The intense factional struggles which marked the evolution of Bolshevism from 1902 to 1918 were echoed in the decade beginning in 1927 when a number of leading veterans of the movement were expelled by the party, and tried and sentenced to execution or imprisonment by the Russian government (which was actually controlled, of course, by their own erstwhile colleagues in the party).

Ideology of Bolshevism. This is a complex subject, the

occasion of extensive controversy and the theme of a very voluminous literature. It may be said that remotely from Hegel, and directly from Marx and Engels, Bolshevism took the concept of inevitable class struggle. From Marx and Engels and from the pronouncements, in the 1880's, of the Group for the Emancipation of Labor, it derived the conviction that the proletariat, defined as the urban wage-workers, or workers in industries other than agriculture, must take (and indeed, alone can take) the lead in the class struggle, both because it is more sharply evident to them and because, being concentrated in smaller areas, they can be more readily activated. The chief contribution of Lenin to Bolshevism was perhaps his dogged insistence on the organization of the proletariat into a compact, disciplined party (the term "monolithic" has been used to describe the quality of this party structure). Lenin envisaged this group as wholly independent, and able to make temporary alliances with liberal, utopian, and bourgeois groups without losing its independence, keeping always in view the goal of revolutionary seizure of power when circumstances offered the propitious moment. Bolshevism, as thus shaped by Lenin, rejected the theory of other schools of socialism that the proletariat should concede leadership to the bourgeois liberals who proposed to gain their social and economic objectives by parliamentary and other legal means.

Bolshoi Kavkaz (bol.shoi' käf.käs'). Russian name of the **Caucasus Mountains.**

Bolshoi Lyakhov (lyä'ʜọf). See **Lyakhov.**

Bolshoi Teatr (tä'ä.tėr). [Eng. trans., *"Big Theater."*] Russian theater, founded at Moscow in 1825, the second of the two imperial theaters, the Maly, or Little, Theatre (1824) being the other. A huge opera house on Theatre Square, it became famous for the staging of conventional operas. It continued this function under the Soviet government, and *Boris Godunov, Prince Igor, Carmen,* and *Lohengrin* were typical operas in its repertoire.

Bolsón de Mapimí (bōl.sōn' dā mä.pē.mē'). See **Mapimí, Bolsón de.**

Bolsover (bol'sō"vėr, bou'zėr). Urban district in C England, in Derbyshire, ab. 6 mi. E of Chesterfield, ab. 161 mi. N of London by rail. 10,815 (1951).

Bolsover Castle. Castle near Bolsover, in Derbyshire, England, ab. 23 mi. NE of Derby. The original structure was built shortly after the Norman Conquest, and fell to the forces of king John in the short civil war that immediately followed the signing of the Magna Charta in 1215. A new castle was built on the site in 1613, and fell to the Parliamentary forces in 1644; it is this latter structure which remains standing.

Bolswert (bôl'swert), **Boetius van.** b. at Bolswert, Friesland, Netherlands, 1580; d. at Antwerp, c1634. Dutch engraver, noted for his engravings based on the paintings of Peter Paul Rubens; brother of Schelte van Bolswert.

Bolswert, Schelte van. b. at Bolswert, Friesland, Netherlands, c1586; d. at Antwerp, in December, 1659. Dutch engraver; brother of Boetius van Bolswert. He made engravings based on the paintings of Peter Paul Rubens and Anthony Vandyke.

Bolt (bōlt), **Ithuel.** Character in *Wing-and-Wing* (1842), a novel by James Fenimore Cooper.

Bolt Court. Name of a short alley at London, ab. $\frac{1}{16}$ mi. long, leading N off Fleet Street into Gough Square. Dr. Samuel Johnson passed the last years of his life here, dying at Number 8, in 1784.

Bolté (bōl'tā), **Charles L.** b. at Chicago, May 8, 1895—. American infantry officer. A graduate (1917) of the Armour Institute of Technology, he served (1918 *et seq.*) with the 4th division in France. In World War II he was chief of staff (1942) of U.S. forces in Great Britain, and chief of staff for the European theater (1942). He commanded (1944) the 34th infantry division from the crossing of the Arno River to the Axis surrender in Italy. In 1946 he became chief of staff of the army ground forces. He was named (1951) deputy chief of staff.

Bolte (bol'tẹ), **Johannes.** b. 1858; d. 1937. German historian of literature and folklorist. He was coauthor (with Polivka) of the useful annotations to Grimm's *Household Tales,* the *Anmerkungen zu den Grimmschen Märchen* (1913 *et seq.*).

Bolton (bōl'tọn) or **Bolton-le-Moors** (bōl'tọn.lẹ.mörz'). County borough and manufacturing town in NW England, in Lancashire, situated on the river Croal, ab. 11 mi. NW of Manchester, ab. 194 mi. NW of London by rail. It is one of the oldest centers of English woolen and cotton manufacture (the manufacture of woolen textiles was introduced (c1337) by Flemings). It was a center of the fustian trade in the 17th century; today it spins worsted yarns and fine cotton yarns. Other industries include quilt weaving, the manufacture of fine cotton fabrics, the making of spinning machines and looms for the textile industry, and coal mining. Bolton developed rapidly during the early days of the industrial revolution, and today is the fourth largest town in Lancashire. 167,162 (1951).

Bolton, Duchess of. Title of **Fenton, Lavinia.**

Bolton, Duke of. Title held by various members of the **Paulet** family.

Bolton, Charles Knowles. b. at Cleveland, Ohio, Nov. 14, 1867—. American antiquary, known as an authority on heraldry. He served (1898–1933) as librarian of the Boston Athenaeum, and was the author of *Private Soldier Under Washington, The Real Founders of New England,* and other books.

Bolton or **Boulton** (bōl'tọn), **Edmund.** b. c1575; d. c1633. English historian and poet who was a fellow-contributor (1600) with Sir Philip Sidney, Edmund Spenser, and Sir Walter Raleigh to *England's Helicon.* He formulated a scheme (1617) for a royal academy of letters and science, which, although favorably received by James I, was never carried out. Among his writings are *Elements of Armouries* (1610), *Life of King Henry II* (originally intended for Speed's *Chronicle,* but rejected as too favorable to Thomas à Becket), *The Roman Histories of Lucius Iulius Florus* (translated 1618), *Hypercritica* (c1618), *Nero Caesar* (1624), *An Historical Parallel* (at the end of some copies of *Nero Caesar*), *Commentaries Roial,* and Latin verses prefacing William Camden's *Britannia* and Ben Jonson's *Volpone* (1605). He was once thought to be the "E.B." who first published Christopher Marlowe's *Hero and Leander,* but it is now generally accepted that these initials identify Edward Blount.

Bolton, Guy. b. at Broxbourne, Hertfordshire, England, Nov. 23, 1887—. American playwright and scenarist. A practicing architect at New York, he began writing for the stage and motion pictures after 1913. Author of such plays and musical comedies as *Sally, Kissing-Time, The Dark Angel, Lady Be Good, Grounds for Divorce, Polly Preferred,* and *Swing Along,* he also collaborated (with P. G. Wodehouse and others) on *Polly with a Past, Rio Rita, Anything Goes, Girl Crazy,* and others; his scenarios include *The Love Parade, The Camels are Coming, The Murder Man, Weekend at the Waldorf,* and *Till the Clouds Roll By.*

Bolton, Henry Carrington. b. at New York, Jan. 28, 1843; d. at Washington, D.C., Nov. 19, 1903. American chemist, bibliographer, and folklorist. He was a professor (1877–87) of chemistry at Trinity College, at Hartford, Conn. Author of *Scientific Correspondence of Joseph Priestley* (1892), *Evolution of the Thermometer, 1592–1743* (1900), and *The Follies of Science at the Court of Rudolph II, 1576–1612* (1904), and of the bibliographies *Annals of the New York Lyceum of Natural History* (1870), *Catalogue of Scientific and Technical Periodicals, 1865–82* (1885), and *Select Bibliography of Chemistry* (Part I, 1893). He also published *The Counting Out Rhymes of Children* (1888).

Bolton, Herbert Eugene. b. at Wilton, Wis., July 20, 1870—. American historian. A graduate of the University of Wisconsin (1895) and the University of Pennsylvania (1899), he was professor of American history at Stanford University (1909–11), and professor (1911–40) and head of the department (1919–40) of American history at the University of California. Author of *Guide to Materials for United States History in the Archives of Mexico* (1913), *Texas in the Middle Eighteenth Century* (1915), *The Spanish Borderlands* (1921), *Anza's California Expeditions* (1930), *Wider Horizons of American History* (1939), *Cultural Coöperation with Latin America* (1940), and *Coronado* (1949).

Bolton, Sarah Knowles. b. at Farmington, Conn., Sept. 15, 1841; d. Feb. 21, 1916. American poet, writer of popular biographies, and reformer. She was associated

(1874) with the Woman's Temperance Crusade in Ohio, and was an editor (1878–81) of the Boston *Congregationalist.* Her biographies include *Poor Boys Who Became Famous* (1885), *Girls Who Became Famous* (1886), *Famous American Statesmen* (1888), and *Famous Men of Science* (1889). She was author also of *Orlean Lamar and Other Poems* (1864) and *The Inevitable and Other Poems* (1895), and coauthor of *From Heart and Nature* (1887).

Bolton, Sarah Tittle Barrett. b. at Newport, Ky., Dec. 18, 1814; d. Aug. 4, 1893. American poet. She was associated with Robert Owen in support of women's property rights at the Constitutional Convention of 1850. Her published works include *Poems* (1865), *The Life and Poems of Sarah T. Bolton* (1880), and the selections *Songs of a Life Time* (1892).

Bolton Castle. Castle in N Yorkshire, England, in the West Riding, ab. 15 mi. NNW of Bradford. It was the place of Mary Queen of Scots' imprisonment in the period 1568–69.

Boltraffio (bōl.träf'fyō), **Giovanni Antonio.** [Also, **Beltraffio.**] b. at Milan, Italy, 1467; d. 1516. Italian painter. A pupil of Leonardo da Vinci, Boltraffio, like his master, was distinguished as a religious painter and a portraitist. His masterpiece is often considered to be the *Madonna and Child* now in the National Gallery, London. His *Madonna Casio* is to be seen in the Louvre at Paris. His native city is particularly rich in examples of his work, which is to be found in the Borromean Palace, the Brera and Frizzoni galleries, and the Poldi-Pezzoli collection, while a great many of his drawings are preserved in the Ambrosian Gallery.

Bolts of Melody. Volume of poetry by Emily Dickinson. It consists of more than 650 new poems or fragments collected and edited by Mabel L. Todd and her daughter, Millicent Todd Bingham.

Boltwood (bōlt'wu̇d), **Bertram Borden.** b. at Amherst, Mass., July 27, 1870; d. in Maine, Aug. 15, 1927. American chemist, professor of radiochemistry at Yale University from 1910. He was assistant professor of physics there in the period 1906–10. Among his major contributions to modern physics was the discovery that radium is produced by the disintegration of uranium by way of an intermediate element which he named ionium (radium itself, although not an intermediate element, holds an intermediate position in the disintegrative process of uranium, which finally terminates with lead). Boltwood's work with the intermediate element ionium has been carried further by later researchers, who used his discovery that ionium and thorium, as a combination, could not be separated from each other (by any process then known) as a lead toward recognition of what are now called isotopes. He published various papers on radioactivity.

Boltzmann (bolts'män), **Ludwig.** b. at Vienna, Feb. 14, 1844; d. Sept. 5, 1906. Austrian physicist who contributed to the probability theory and the partition of energy in connection with the kinetic theory of gases. He is known especially for the Stefan-Boltzmann law of black-body radiation. He became professor of mathematics and physics at Gratz in 1869; of mathematics at Vienna in 1873; of experimental physics at Gratz in 1876; of physics at Munich in 1890, at Vienna in 1895, and at Leipzig in 1900. His works include *Vorlesungen über Maxwells Theorie der Elektrizität und des Lichtes* (1891–93) and *Vorlesungen über Gastheorie* (1895, 1898).

Bolu (bō.lö'). *Il* (province or vilayet) in NW Turkey, consisting of a rolling plain near the Black Sea and a hilly inland area. It is crossed by an important Istanbul-Ankara highway. Capital, Bolu; area, 4,300 sq. mi.; pop. 302,805 (1950).

Bolus (bō'lus), **Dr.** Name of the apothecary of the younger George Colman's poem *The Newcastle Apothecary,* published in a volume of humorous verse entitled *Broad Grins.* It was Dr. Bolus's practice to write his prescriptions in rhyme, one of which ("When taken, To be well shaken") was too literally applied to the patient instead of to the dose.

Bolyai (bō'yô.ē), **Farkas.** b. at Bolya, Hungary, Feb. 9, 1775; d. Nov. 20, 1856. Hungarian mathematician, professor (1802–49) at the Reformed College of Maros-Vásárhely, father of János Bolyai. His chief work was *Tentamen juventutem studiosam in elementa matheseos purae introducendi* (1832–33).

Bolyai, János. b. at Klausenburg (now Cluj, Rumania), Dec. 15, 1802; d. at Maros-Vásárhely, Hungary (now Târgu-Mureş, Rumania), Jan. 27, 1860. Hungarian mathematician; son of Farkas Bolyai. His most famous work is an appendix to the first volume of the *Tentamen* of his father, entitled *Appendix scientiam spatii absolute veram exhibens,* in which he develops the idea of a geometry which is independent of Euclid's axiom of parallels.

Bolza (bol'tsä), **Oskar.** [Pseudonym, **F. H. Marneck.**] b. at Bergzabern, Germany, May 12, 1857; d. probably at Freiburg im Breisgau, Germany, July 5, 1942. German mathematician. A contributor to the theory of hyperelliptic functions and integral equations, he is best known for his work on the calculus of variations. He received the Ph.D. degree at Göttingen in 1886 and taught at Johns Hopkins University (1888–89), Clark University (1889–92), the University of Chicago (1893–1910), and the University of Freiburg (1910–33). His most important work is *Lectures on the Calculus of Variations* (1904). He also wrote, under the pseudonym F. H. Marneck, *Glaubenlose Religion* (1930).

Bolzano (bōl.tsä'nō). [German, **Bozen.**] Province in NE Italy, in the *compartimento* (region) of Trentino-Alto Adige. The population includes a large number of German-speaking Tyrolese. Capital, Bolzano; pop. 277,720 (1936).

Bolzano. [German, **Bozen;** ancient name, **Bauzanum.**] City and commune in NE Italy, in the *compartimento* (region) of Trentino-Alto Adige, the capital of the province of Bolzano, situated at the junction of the Talfero and Isarco rivers, near their confluence with the Adige River, ab. 32 mi. NE of Trent. The largest city between the Brenner Pass and the Venetian plain, it is a center for tourists in the Italian Alps, with many hotels. It is also a marketing center for the wines and fruits of the district; there are metallurgical, aluminum, automobile, and other new industries, which were transplanted here after 1919. The picturesque old town, which had preserved much of its medieval character, including the Franciscan monastery and the Gothic parish church, was heavily damaged during World War II, but repairs have been completed or are being carried out. An old Roman town, it fell to the Lombards in 680 A.D., to the Franks in 740, to the bishop of Trent in 1027, and later to the counts of Tyrol; from 1363 it belonged to the Hapsburg domain; it was incorporated into Italy in 1918. The population, before 1918 overwhelmingly German, now includes a large Italian element consisting mainly of industrial workers and executives. Pop. of commune, 45,505 (1936); of city, 41,722 (1936).

Bolzano, Bernhard. b. at Prague, Oct. 5, 1781; d. there, Dec. 18, 1848. Austrian mathematician, philosopher, and Roman Catholic theologian, who contributed to the arithmetization of mathematics through his rigorous definitions of the basic terms used in infinite series and the calculus. He is remembered also for pointing out that for infinite classes of elements a part can be put into one-to-one correspondence with the whole. His liberal views in philosophy and theology led him into occasional conflicts with the Church, although his basic loyalty to it was never in doubt. He wrote a number of short but important books on mathematics, including *Rein analytischer Beweis* (1817) and *Paradoxien des Unendlichen* (1848), but his work on the calculus was largely overlooked until the publication of his *Schriften* (4 vols., 1930–35).

Boma (bō'mä). Town in W Africa, former capital of the Belgian Congo. It is built on the N bank of the Congo River, ab. 50 mi. from its mouth. Until 1876 Boma was the extreme inland post for Dutch and Portuguese traders. In 1923 it was replaced as the capital by Léopoldville. Pop. ab. 10,000.

Bomarsund (bō'mär.su̇nd). Formerly a Russian fortress in the Ahvenanmaa islands, in the Baltic Sea: now part of Finland. It was taken by the English and French, on Aug. 16, 1854.

Bomba (bōm'bä), **King.** Nickname given in Italy to Ferdinand II, king of the Two Sicilies, from his bombardment of Messina and other cities during the revolutionary troubles of 1849.

Bombardinian (bom.bär.din'i.an), **General.** General of the king's forces in Henry Carey's burlesque *Chronon-*

hotonthologos. He has become proverbial for burlesque bombast.

Bombastes Furioso (bom.bas'tēz fū.ri.ō'sō). Burlesque opera by William Barnes Rhodes, produced in 1790. It takes its name from the principal character, a victorious general, who returns from the wars with his army, which consists of four unprepossessing warriors. He discovers his king, Artaxominous, visiting Distaffina, his betrothed, and resolves to go mad. His howling, despairing, bombastic rant caused his name to become proverbial. He fights and kills his king for a pair of jackboots which he had hung up as a challenge, and is in his turn killed by Fusbos, the minister of state. The farce is a burlesque of Lodovico Ariosto's *Orlando Furioso*.

Bombay (bom.bā'). State of the Union of India, lying between Rajasthan on the N, Rajasthan, Madhya Bharat, Madhya Pradesh, and Hyderabad on the E, Madras and Mysore on the SE and S, and the Arabian Sea, Saurashtra, and Kutch on the W. Cotton, tea, sugar, rice, millet, and wheat are grown; coconut products are important, and there is some iron mining. A number of formerly separate states were merged with Bombay for administrative purposes in 1948 and 1949, including Baroda and the Gujarat States. Capital, Bombay; area, 76,443 sq. mi. (1941), 115,570 sq. mi. (1951); pop. 20,849,840 (1941), 35,943,559 (1951).

Bombay. [Hindi, **Bambai;** Malay, **Bambé;** old Portuguese name, **Boa Bahia,** meaning "good harbor."] Capital of the state of Bombay, Union of India, on an island near the N end of the W coast of the Indian peninsula. It is the second largest city of India, a seaport, a leading city in commerce, and an important terminus of the Indian railway system. Bombay University (founded 1857) has affiliated colleges including 20 art schools and 17 professional schools. There are some 75 cotton spinning and weaving mills, many oilseed crushing and refining plants, dyeing and bleaching works, and metal-stamping factories. The largest hydroelectric plant in the country is S of the city. Bombay was acquired by the Portuguese c1530, and was ceded to England in 1661, and to the East India Company in 1668. Pop. 1,489,883 (1941).

Bombay Plan. Name applied to an ambitious plan of economic development for India, formulated in 1944 by Indian business interests. It urged a huge investment program, especially for the development of industry, and called for doubling agricultural production and quintupling industrial output over a period of 15 years, through the working out of three successive five-year plans.

Bomberg (bôm'berċh), **Daniel.** b. at Antwerp; d. at Venice, 1549. Dutch printer, noted for his editions of the Hebrew Bible and the Talmud.

Bomberger (bom'bėr.gėr), **John Henry Augustus.** b. at Lancaster, Pa., Jan. 13, 1817; d. Aug. 19, 1890. American clergyman of the German-Reformed Church, and ecclesiastical writer, who was the first president (1869–90) of Ursinus College, at Collegeville, near Norristown, Pa. Pastor (1854–70) of Old Race Street Church at Philadelphia, he was the founder and editor of the *Reformed Church Monthly* (1868–76). His published works include *The Protestant Theological and Ecclesiastical Encyclopedia* (1858–60) and *Kurtz's Text-Book of Church History* (1860–62).

Bombetoka (bom.be.tō'kạ), **Bay of.** [Also: **Bay of Bembatoka;** French, **Baie de Bombetoka.**] Large inlet of Mozambique Channel, on the NW coast of Madagascar.

Bombois (bôn.bwȧ), **Camille.** b. at Vuarey-les-Laumes, Gold Coast, Feb. 3, 1883—. French painter. He is what is known as a primitive (which means, in this case, that he was entirely self-taught) and his work bears a strong similarity to that of Henri Rousseau (also a primitive) in the naïveté of its conception. He started to paint as a hobby during World War I, and in 1925 was finally able to devote himself fully to art. The charm, simplicity, and sincerity of his work make up for any possible lack of technical skill. Fritz von Uhde and others encouraged him and helped to spread his fame. He won several prizes in France, where his work hangs in many important collections, and has also exhibited in the U.S. Among his better-known compositions are *On Entering the Ring, Promenade, Cathedral at Albi, Bridge on the Yonne, The Farm,* and *The Lake*.

Bombonon (bōm.bō.nōn'), **Port.** See **Bonbonon, Port.**

Bomby (bom'bi), **Hope-on-High.** Puritan, in John Fletcher's play *Women Pleased*, intended to ridicule the sect to which he belonged. He denounces worldly pleasures, but joins in them.

Bomford (bum'fọrd), **George.** b. at New York, 1782; d. at Boston, March 25, 1848. American military officer. He was a colonel and chief of ordnance (1832), and the inventor of a muzzle-loading gun called the "columbiad."

Bomilcar (bọ.mil'kạr). fl. at the end of the 4th century B.C. Carthaginian general. He commanded (310 B.C.) the Carthaginians against Agathocles, the tyrant of Syracuse. Possibly impressed by the example of Agathocles, he conspired in 308 to make himself tyrant of Carthage with the aid of 500 citizens and a number of mercenaries, but was captured and crucified.

Bomokandi (bō.mō.kän'dē). River in C Africa, the left (or S) affluent of the Uele River, in Stanleyville province, NE Belgian Congo.

Bomoseen (bō.mọ.sēn', bom'ọ.zēn), **Lake.** Lake in W Vermont, ab. 13 mi. W of Rutland, surrounded by rocky, wooded hills. It is important as a summer resort. Area, ab. 3½ sq. mi.

Bomtempo (bōn.tām'pö), **João Domingos.** b. at Lisbon, Dec. 28, 1775; d. there, Aug. 18, 1842. Portuguese composer. His works include an opera, a requiem, piano concertos, a piano quintet, and various religious pieces.

Bomu (bō'mö). [Also, **M'bomu.**] River in C Africa forming a part of the boundary between N Belgian Congo and E French Equatorial Africa. It flows westward across the NE portion of the Congo plateau, and unites with the Uele at Yakoma (elevation, 1,325 ft.) to form the Ubangi River. Its course is broken by seven great rapids. Length, ab. 550 mi.

Bomvana (bōm.vä'nä). [Also, **Amabomvana.**] Bantu-speaking people of the S Nguni group of S Africa, inhabiting the E part of Cape Province, Union of South Africa, and resembling the Xhosa in culture.

Bon (bôn). Primitive pre-Buddhist cult of Tibet.

Bon. [Also, **Obon.**] Buddhist festival in Japan. It is held July 13 to 16, when the souls of the dead are believed to return to earth. Family graves are cleaned, the household shrine is decorated and special offerings are placed before it, and lanterns are hung at graves and house gates to guide the souls. For this reason outsiders sometimes call it the Feast of Lanterns.

Bon (bon; French, bôṅ), **Cape.** [Arabic, **Ras Addar.**] Peninsula and headland in NE Tunisia, North Africa, with the extreme NE tip projecting into the Mediterranean Sea ab. 52 mi. NE of the city of Tunis. It is a hilly region, with wheat and olive cultivation. In ancient times it was one of the richest areas of North Africa. In World War II remnants of the German forces in North Africa surrendered to the Allies here in May, 1943. Length, ab. 60 mi.

Bona (bō'nạ). See also **Bonda** and **Bône.**

Bona. Sister of the Queen of France, in Shakespeare's *Henry VI, Part III*.

Bonacca (bō.nä'kä). See **Guanaja.**

Bonacieux (bo.nȧ.syė). Sordid, avaricious old rascal in the novel by the elder Alexandre Dumas *The Three Musketeers*. He sacrifices his young wife in his desire to gain favor with the cardinal.

Bona Dea (bō'nạ dē'ạ). In Roman mythology, the goddess of fecundity, worshiped only by women. She was the female counterpart of Faunus (in various accounts, she is called his sister, wife, or daughter) and bore, in this relationship, the name Fauna. However, she was so exclusively a woman's goddess that the name used by women (Bona Dea) has come to be her usual name.

Bonaire (bō.nãr'). [Also: **Buen Aire, Buen Ayre.**] Island in the Caribbean Sea, N of Venezuela: a possession of the Netherlands. The major economic activities are goat grazing and the marketing of aloes, a medicinal plant. Chief town, Kralendijk; area, 95 sq. mi.; pop. 5,079 (est. 1951).

Bonald (bo.nȧl), **Louis Gabriel Ambroise,** Vicomte de. b. at Monna, near Millau, France, Oct. 2, 1754; d. there, Nov. 23, 1840. French politician and publicist. He became (1815) a member of the council of public instruction and served (1815–22) as a deputy. He was made a member of the French Academy in 1816, and in 1822 was named minister of state. A noted traditionalist, he was the author of *Théorie du pouvoir politique et religieux* (3 vols., 1796).

Bonald, Louis Jacques Maurice de. b. at Millau, France, Oct. 30, 1787; d. at Lyons, Feb. 25, 1870. French Ultramontaine ecclesiastic; son of Louis Gabriel Ambroise, Vicomte de Bonald. He became bishop of Puy in 1823, archbishop of Lyons in 1839, and cardinal in 1841.

Bonampak (bō.näm'päk). Small early Maya center, discovered in 1946, in the state of Chiapas, Mexico. It is notable for the many polychrome frescoes, some of them excellently preserved, on the interior walls of the temple.

Bonaparte (bō'na.pärt; French, bo.na.pȧrt). [Italian, **Buonaparte.**] Corsican family, said to have been of Italian origin. Members of the family have ruled in France (Napoleon I, emperor 1804–14; Napoleon III, emperor 1852–70), Spain (Joseph, king 1808–13), Holland (Louis, king 1806–10), Naples (Joseph, king 1806–08), and Westphalia (Jérôme, king 1807–13). A number of persons bearing this name figured in the history of Padua, Florence, San Miniato, and other Italian cities, in the Middle Ages, although the connection between them and the Corsican family cannot with certainty be established. One Gabriel Bonaparte rose to a position of some eminence at Ajaccio, Corsica, c1567. His descendant, Carlo Bonaparte (1746–85), was the father of Napoleon I.

Bonaparte. Former name of **Galax.**

Bonaparte, Carlo. b. at Ajaccio, Corsica, March 29, 1746; d. at Montpellier, France, Feb. 24, 1785. Corsican lawyer; father of Napoleon I. He was for a time a partisan of Pasquale Paoli, with whom he fought for Corsican liberty against the Genoese. He married Maria Laetitia Ramolino in 1765.

Bonaparte, Charles Joseph. b. at Baltimore, June 9, 1851; d. near Baltimore, June 28, 1921. American lawyer and cabinet officer; grandson of Jérôme Bonaparte. He was graduated from Harvard University in 1871 and from the Harvard Law School in 1874. He was prominent in reform movements, and served as secretary of the navy (1905–06), and attorney general (1906–09).

Bonaparte, Charles Louis Napoléon. See **Napoleon III.**

Bonaparte, Charles Lucien Jules Laurent. [Title, Prince of **Canino and Musignano.**] b. at Paris, May 24, 1803; d. there, July 29, 1857. French naturalist; son of Lucien Bonaparte by his second wife. He lived at Philadelphia for some years. His chief works are *American Ornithology* (1825–33) and *Iconografia della fauna Italica* (1832–41).

Bonaparte, Elizabeth. [Also: **Bonaparte-Patterson;** maiden name, **Patterson.**] b. at Baltimore, Feb. 6, 1785; d. there, April 4, 1879. American woman, daughter of a Baltimore merchant, who married Jérôme Bonaparte, brother of Napoleon I, on Dec. 24, 1803. Napoleon refused to recognize the marriage, and prevented her from landing on the Continent when she went to Europe with her husband. She accordingly sought refuge in England, while Jérôme went to Paris and finally yielded to his brother's demand for an annulment of the marriage.

Bonaparte, Jérôme. b. at Ajaccio, Corsica, Nov. 15, 1784; d. near Paris, June 24, 1860. Brother of Napoleon I; made king of Westphalia in 1807. He married Elizabeth Patterson of Baltimore on Dec. 24, 1803. After this marriage was annulled, he married Princess Catherine of Württemberg in 1807. Early in his career he served in the navy, and later took part in the battle of Waterloo. He lived in Italy after Napoleon I's abdication, but returned to France to live at the court of Napoleon III.

Bonaparte, Joseph. b. at Corte, Corsica, Jan. 7, 1768; d. at Florence, Italy, July 28, 1844. Eldest brother of Napoleon I. He became a member of the Council of Five Hundred in 1798, and a councilor of state in 1799. Napoleon named him king of Naples in 1806, and king of Spain in 1808. He lived (1815 *et seq.*) in the U.S. under the name of Comte de Survilliers.

Bonaparte, Louis. b. at Ajaccio, Corsica, Sept. 2, 1778; d. at Leghorn, Italy, July 25, 1846. Brother of Napoleon I, and father of Napoleon III. He married Hortense Beauharnais on Jan. 4, 1802, became king of Holland in 1806, and abdicated in 1810, assuming the title of Comte de St. Leu. He wrote *Documents historiques et réflexions sur le gouvernement de la Hollande* (1820).

Bonaparte, Louis. [Called **"Prince Louis";** full French name, **Napoléon Louis Joseph Jérôme Bonaparte.**] b. at Meudon, Seine-et-Oise, France, July 16, 1864; d. at Prangins, Switzerland, Oct. 14, 1932. Member of the house of Bonaparte; son of Victor Bonaparte. He served as a lieutenant general in the Russian czarist army.

Bonaparte, Louis Lucien. b. at Thorngrove, near Worcester, England, Jan. 4, 1813; d. at Fano, Italy, Nov. 4, 1891. French philologist; the fourth son of Lucien Bonaparte. He lived chiefly in Italy until 1848, when he went to France. He was made a senator in 1855, and received from his cousin Napoleon III the title of prince in 1863. After 1870 he lived chiefly in England. His scientific reputation rested principally on his investigations of Basque. His collection of books in and about many languages of the world is now in the Newberry Library at Chicago.

Bonaparte, Louis Napoleon. See **Napoleon III.**

Bonaparte, Lucien. [Title, Prince of **Canino.**] b. at Ajaccio, Corsica, May 21, 1775; d. at Viterbo, Italy, June 30, 1840. Brother of Napoleon I. He became a member of the Council of Five Hundred in 1798, and its president in 1799; in this office, he was instrumental in helping Napoleon to the consulship. He was minister of the interior in 1799, and ambassador to Spain in 1800. Having come to disagree with Napoleon, he went to live in Italy, where he became prince of Canino in 1814. On his way to Italy, he was captured (1810) by the British, and held for a time as a prisoner of state in England. He was an art connoisseur and poet.

Bonaparte, Maria Anna Elisa. b. at Ajaccio, Corsica, Jan. 3, 1777; d. near Trieste, Aug. 6, 1820. Sister of Napoleon I. She married (1797) Felice Pasquale Bacciocchi (or Bacciochi), who was, at the time of his marriage, an obscure infantry officer, but whose career was thereafter considerably aided by his spouse's close relationship to the most powerful man in France. Napoleon made Maria Anna Elisa princess of Lucca and Piombino (1805), and grand duchess of Tuscany (1809).

Bonaparte, Maria Annunciata. [Later called **Carolina.**] b. at Ajaccio, Corsica, March 25, 1782; d. at Florence, Italy, May 18, 1839. Sister of Napoleon I. She married Joachim Murat in 1800, and became queen of Naples in 1808. She was known as the Countess Lipona after 1815.

Bonaparte, Maria Letizia (or **Laetitia**). [Maiden name, **Ramolino.**] b. at Ajaccio, Corsica, Aug. 24, 1750; d. at Rome, Feb. 2, 1836. Mother of Napoleon I. She married Carlo Bonaparte in 1764, joined her son at Paris in 1799, and on the elevation of Napoleon to emperor in 1804 received the title of Madame Mère.

Bonaparte, Maria Paulina. [Also: **Marie Pauline;** originally, **Carlotta;** after 1803, Duchess of **Guastalla.**] b. at Ajaccio, Corsica, Oct. 20, 1780; d. at Florence, June 9, 1825. Sister of Napoleon I. She married Prince Camillo Borghese on Aug. 28, 1803.

Bonaparte, Mathilde Laetitia Wilhelmine. b. at Trieste, May 27, 1820; d. at Paris, Jan. 2, 1904. Daughter of Jérôme Bonaparte and Catherine, Princess of Württemberg.

Bonaparte, Napoleon. See **Napoleon I** and **Napoleon III.**

Bonaparte, Napoléon Eugène Louis Jean Joseph. b. at Paris, March 16, 1856; killed in Zululand, South Africa, June 1, 1879. Prince imperial of France; son of Napoleon III.

Bonaparte, Prince **Napoléon Joseph Charles Paul.** [Called **"Prince Napoleon"** and **"Plon-Plon."**] b. at Trieste, Sept. 9, 1822; d. at Rome, March 17, 1891. French politician and soldier; son of Jérôme Bonaparte. He was made prince in 1852, served as general in the Crimean War, and in 1879, on the death of the prince imperial in Zululand, became the chief of the Bonapartist party and pretender to the French throne. He married Clotilde, daughter of Victor Emmanuel II.

Bonaparte, Pierre Napoléon. b. at Rome, Oct. 11, 1815; d. at Versailles, France, April 7, 1881. Son of Lucien Bonaparte; made a prince after 1852. In a quarrel, he shot the journalist Victor Noir on Jan. 10, 1870, but was acquitted of a murder charge.

Bonaparte, Roland Napoléon. b. at Paris, May 19, 1858; d. there, April 14, 1924. French scientist; son of Pierre Napoléon Bonaparte (1815–81). He published numerous works on geography, ethnography, and botany, and held membership in several scientific societies, including the Geographical Society of Paris, of which he was president.

Bonaparte, Victor. [Called **"Prince Victor"**; full name, **Napoléon Victor Jérôme Frédéric Bonaparte.**] b. at Meudon, Seine-et-Oise, France, July 18, 1862; d. at Brussels, May 2, 1926. Son of Napoléon Joseph Charles Paul Bonaparte (1822–91); and father of Louis Bonaparte (1864–1932). With his father he was expelled (1866) from France. He married Princess Clémentine (b. 1872) of Belgium.

Bonaparte-Patterson (bō′nạ.pärt.pat′ẹr.sọn), **Jérôme Napoléon.** b. at Camberwell, England, July 7, 1805; d. at Baltimore, June 17, 1870. Eldest son of Jérôme Bonaparte.

Bonaparte-Patterson, Jérôme Napoléon. b. at Baltimore, Nov. 5, 1832; d. at Pride's Crossing, Essex County, Mass., Sept. 4, 1893. Son of Jérôme Napoléon Bonaparte-Patterson. He entered the French military service in 1854, and served with distinction in the Crimean and Italian campaigns.

Bonar (bon′ạr), **Horatius.** b. at Edinburgh, Dec. 19, 1808; d. there, July 31, 1889. Scottish clergyman, lyric poet, and writer. While pastor at Kelso in the period 1837–66, he joined with his congregation in the Free-Church movement of 1843. In 1866 he became pastor of the Grange Free Church at Edinburgh. He wrote *Hymns of Faith and Hope* (1857–66).

Bonassus (bọ.nas′us). Imaginary beast with whom the Scottish poet James Hogg (called the "Ettrick Shepherd") pretended in one of his works to have had an adventure.

Bonaventura (bon″ạ.ven.tū′rạ). In John Ford's play *'Tis Pity She's a Whore,* a friar of a kindly, pliable nature, obviously modeled on Shakespeare's Friar Lawrence in *Romeo and Juliet.*

Bonaventure (bon.ạ.ven′ṭūr). River in E Quebec, in the S central part of the Gaspé peninsula, rising in the mountainous interior and flowing generally S through a forested region into Chaleur Bay. It has trout and salmon fishing. Length, ab. 75 mi.

Bonaventure or **Bonaventura** (bon″ạ.ven.tū′rạ; Italian, bō″nä.ven.tö′rä), Saint. [Called the **"Seraphic Doctor"**; original name, **Giovanni di Fidanza.**] b. at Bagnorea, Italy, 1221 (or 1222); d. at Lyons, France, July 15, 1274. Scholastic philosopher. He became professor of theology at Paris in 1253, general of the Franciscans in 1256, bishop of Albano in 1273, and cardinal in 1274. He was canonized in 1482. He was the author of *Breviloquium* and *Centiloquium* (manuals of doctrinal theology), *Itinerarium mentis ad Deum, Reductio artium in theologiam, Biblia Pauperum,* and others.

Bonavista (bon.ạ.vis′tạ). See also **Boa Vista,** Cape Verde Islands.

Bonavista. Town on the island of Newfoundland, near the end of the peninsula which separates Bonavista Bay and Trinity Bay. A prosperous fishing town, it is the terminus of a railway line which connects with the main line to St. John's. 3,636 (1945).

Bonavista Bay. Large indentation of the Atlantic Ocean on the E coast of Newfoundland, separated from and N of Trinity Bay, and bounded by Cape Bonavista on the S and Cape Freels on the N.

Bonbonon (bōm.bō.nōn′), **Port.** [Also, **Port Bombonon.**] Bay and port on the S coast of Negros island, in the Philippines. It is safe for large vessels in all weather.

Bonchamp (bôṅ.shäṅ), Marquis **Charles Melchior Artus de.** b. at Jouverdeil, France, May 10, 1760; d. near Chollet, France, Oct. 18, 1793. French general. He was a leader of the Vendeans.

Bonci (bōn′chē), **Alessandro.** b. at Cessena, Italy, 1870; d. at Milan, Italy, 1940. Italian tenor. Having begun his career as a church singer, he made his operatic debut at Parma as Fenton in *Falstaff.* He sang in most of the large cities of the world, and spent his winters in America from the fall of 1906, singing in opera and concert. His principal roles included Rodolfo in *La Bohème,* Ottavio in *Don Giovanni,* the Duke in *Rigoletto,* and Alfredo in *Lucia di Lammermoor.*

Bond (bond), **Carrie.** [Maiden name, **Jacobs.**] b. at Janesville, Wis., 1862; d. 1946. American song writer. Her songs (1903 *et seq.*), which she published herself, include the popular *A Perfect Day, Just a-Wearyin' For You,* and *I Love You Truly.*

Bond, Sir **Edward Augustus.** b. at Hanwell, England, Dec. 31, 1815; d. at Bayswater, London, Jan. 2, 1898. English librarian. He was principal librarian of the British Museum in the period 1878–88. In 1833 he entered the Records Office of the British government as an assistant, and was transferred to the British Museum in 1838. In conjunction with Sir E. Maunde Thompson he founded the Palaeographical Society in 1873. He was knighted a few days before his death.

Bond, Elizabeth Powell. b. in Dutchess County, N.Y., Jan. 25, 1841; d. March 29, 1926. American author and educator, notable for her efforts on behalf of coeducation in American colleges. She was dean (1890–1906) of Swarthmore College, Swarthmore, Pa., after having been an instructor (1866–70) in calisthenics at Vassar College, Poughkeepsie, N.Y. She was a lifelong member of the Society of Friends (Quakers), and also a friend of Ralph Waldo Emerson and William Lloyd Garrison. Author of *Words by the Way* (1895, 1901).

Bond, George Phillips. b. at Dorchester, Mass., May 20, 1825; d. at Cambridge, Mass., Feb. 17, 1865. American astronomer; son of William Cranch Bond. He was director (1859 *et seq.*) of the observatory at Harvard University. He pioneered in the use of photography for such ends as the preparation of stellar maps, a more exact study of the surface of the moon, determination of double stars, and the measurement of the comparative brightness of stellar bodies in general. He was associated for much of his professional career with his father, William Cranch Bond (it was during their joint investigation of Saturn that he discovered the existence of Hyperion, Saturn's eighth satellite). Although it was itself soon demonstrated to be incorrect, his hypothesis that the ring around Saturn was comprised of semifluid (or actually fluid) matter did advance his science insofar as it enabled more or less final repudiation of the erroneous (but long generally accepted) theory that the rings were solid. Author of *On the Construction of the Rings of Saturn* and others.

Bond, Hugh Lennox. b. at Baltimore, Dec. 16, 1828; d. Oct. 24, 1893. American jurist. As a judge (1870 *et seq.*) of the fourth circuit court of the U.S., he imposed fines and prison sentences which effectively ended the Ku Klux Klan terrorism of that day in South Carolina. From the same bench, in 1876, he released, on a writ of habeas corpus, a number of South Carolina canvassers who had been (and thereafter continued to be) active in the presidential campaign of Rutherford B. Hayes (the canvassers' imprisonment had earlier been sustained by the state supreme court, allegedly in order to make it impossible for the Republicans to wage an effective campaign in the state. In view of the fact that South Carolina, with Florida, Louisiana, and Oregon, was one of the disputed states in the extremely close election of 1876, and that the loss of any one of these states would have given the presidency to Hayes's Democratic opponent, Samuel J. Tilden, it is possible to say that Bond contributed, in a very real sense indeed, to the election of a president of the U.S.). In 1868, before his appointment to the federal bench, Bond was active at Baltimore in the establishment (under the auspices of a group known as the "Association for the Improvement of Colored People") of schools for Negro children.

Bond, Sir **Robert.** b. at St. John's, Newfoundland, Canada, Feb. 25, 1857; d. March 16, 1927. Canadian statesman. He was elected to the Newfoundland house of assembly in 1882, became speaker of that body in 1884, was colonial secretary (1859–97), and was premier and colonial secretary of Newfoundland in the period 1900–09. In 1902 he negotiated the Hay-Bond treaty in the interest of reciprocal trade between the U.S. and Canada, but it was never put into effect. He was knighted in 1902. In 1913 he retired from politics.

Bond, Shadrach. b. in Baltimore County, Md., c1773; d. April 13, 1832. American politician, notable as the first governor (1818–22) of Illinois. Elected (1812) the first Illinois territorial delegate to Congress, he is considered to have been influential in the passage of the preemption law of 1813 (which considerably clarified the rights of many Western settlers to their land). He was appointed receiver of public moneys (1814) and register of the land office (1825) at Kaskaskia, Ill.

Bond, Thomas. b. in Calvert County, Md., 1712; d. March 26, 1784. American physician. With Benjamin Franklin, he founded (c1751) what was later to be the hospital served by the University of Pennsylvania's medical school (and considered by many to be, in point of continuous operation, the oldest hospital of its kind in the U.S.). He devised a splint for fractures of the lower extremity of the radius, was credited by Benjamin Rush with introducing the general medical use of mercury in Philadelphia, and established (1766) the first clinical lecture course in the U.S. Associated with the founding (1765) of what is now the University of Pennsylvania's medical school, he contributed "An account of a Worm bred in the Liver" and "A letter to Doctor Fothergill on the use of the Peruvian Bark in Scrofula" to *Medical Observations and Inquiries by a Society of Physicians in London* (1754).

Bond, William Cranch. b. at Portland, Me., Sept. 9, 1789; d. at Cambridge, Mass., Jan. 29, 1859. American astronomer; father of George Phillips Bond. He superintended the building of the Harvard observatory in 1839, becoming its director upon its completion, and became noted (with his son) for his observations of Saturn and the fixed stars, as well as for his operations in celestial photography.

Bonda (bōn′dä). [Also, **Bona.**] One of the Sudanic-speaking Anyi peoples of W Africa, inhabiting the SE part of the Ivory Coast.

Bond and Free. Poem by Robert Frost, published in his collection *Mountain Interval* (1916).

Bondeno (bōn.dā′nō). Town and commune in N Italy, in the *compartimento* (region) of Emilia-Romagna, in the province of Ferrara, situated near the Panaro and Po rivers, W of Ferrara. It is the center of a rich agricultural district, and has a sugar refinery. Pop. of commune, 27,192 (1936); of town, 3,463 (1936).

Bondfield (bond′fēld), **Margaret Grace.** b. in Somerset, England, 1873; d. in Surrey, England, June 16, 1953 English labor leader and cabinet member. She was assistant secretary (1898–1908) of the Shop Assistants Union, and national officer (until 1938) of the National Union of General and Municipal Workers. A member (1923–24, 1926–31) of Parliament, she was parliamentary secretary (1924) to the ministry of labor; her appointment (1929) to the labor minister's post made her the first woman to hold a ministerial position in the British government.

Bondi (bôn′dē), **Clemente.** b. at Mezzana, near Parma, Italy, June 27, 1742; d. at Vienna, June 20, 1821. Italian poet. He was a member of the Jesuit order, professor of oratory in the Royal Seminary at Parma, and later instructor of history and literature at the court of Vienna.

Bondman, The. Tragedy by Philip Massinger, licensed in 1623, and first acted in 1624. It was dedicated to Philip Herbert, 1st Earl of Montgomery, and satirized the "amateur-admiral" George Villiers, 1st Duke of Buckingham, the young and powerful favorite of James I of England.

Bondman, The. Opera by Michael William Balfe, produced at Drury Lane Theatre, London, in 1846.

Bond Street. Thoroughfare between Oxford Street and Piccadilly, at London. It was formerly a popular promenade, and is now filled with fashionable shops. Laurence Sterne, Jonathan Swift, and James Boswell at one time or other all lived on this street. The section near Piccadilly is known as Old Bond Street, while New Bond Street is the end nearest Oxford Street.

Bondu (bon.dö′). See **Boundou.**

Bonduca (bon.dū′ka̧). Tragedy by John Fletcher, produced before 1619. An alteration of Fletcher's play was brought out in 1696 by George Powell, an actor, and another alteration by the elder George Colman was acted in 1778. A third alteration was made by J. R. Planché and acted in 1837 it was called *Caractacus.* The title character of the play is the British queen now usually known as Boadicea, the name Bonduca being an early variant of her name.

Bondy (bôn.dē). Town in N France, in the department of Seine, a northeastern suburb of Paris, traversed by the Canal d'Ourcq, and the railroad line from Paris to Metz. It has been known for its chemical products. 19,487 (1946).

Bône (bōn). [Also, **Bona.**] Seaport in NW Africa, in the department of Constantine, Algeria, on the Gulf of Bône NE of the city of Constantine, near the site of the ancient city of Hippo, or Hippo Regius. It was occupied by the French in 1832. Fourth largest town of the country, it is the major port and commercial center of E Algeria. Bône is also the name of an *arrondissement* (administrative division) in Constantine department. Pop. of city, 102,823 (1948).

Bone (bōn), **David William.** b. at Patrick, near Glasgow, Scotland, 1874—. Scottish sailor, captain, and novelist of the sea; brother of Sir Muirhead Bone (1876—). He joined the British merchant marine in 1889, and in 1899 entered the service of the Anchor Line, being made captain (1915) of the *Columbia,* a passenger steamer. In 1900 he began writing sea sketches for magazines. He is the author of *The Brassbounder* (1910), *Merchantmen-at-Arms* (1919; revised 1929; illustrated by his brother), *The Lookoutman* (1923), and *Capstan Bars* (1931).

Bone, Henry. b. at Truro, Cornwall, England, 1755; d. 1834. English enamel painter. Employed by jewelers at London to execute designs in enamel, the distinction of his work brought him an appointment as associate of the Royal Academy in 1800, and to full membership in 1811. Some of his miniatures were larger than anything of that sort ever attempted previously in England. (For example, a series of portraits which he made of Elizabethan personages ranged in size from five by four inches to thirteen by eight inches. This series is now at Kingston Lacey, Wimborne, Dorsetshire.) Examples of Bone's exquisite work are to be seen in many English collections, including the Wallace Collection at London.

Bone, Sir **Muirhead.** b. at Patrick, near Glasgow, Scotland, March 23, 1876—. Scottish painter in oil and water color, and etcher, known chiefly for his topographical views; brother of David William Bone (1874—). He studied at the Glasgow School of Art; later he became a member of the International Society of Painters and Engravers, the New English Art Club, and the Society of Twelve; he has served also as a trustee of the National Gallery of British Art and the Imperial War Museum. His work has been exhibited frequently at Paris, London, Glasgow, and New York. He has done many illustrations for books and magazines, and a series of drawings made at the front in France during World War I. Among his principal works are *The Port of Naples, Picadilly Circus,* and *The Fair of Saint Gilles at Oxford.*

Bonelli (bo̧.nel′i), **Richard.** [Original surname, **Bunn.**] b. 1894—. American operatic baritone. He first appeared (1923) in opera at Modena, Italy; subsequently he sang at Monte Carlo, at the Milan La Scala, and with the Franco-American Opera at Paris. He was named (1925) to the roster of the Chicago Civic Opera Company, and later joined (1932) the Metropolitan Opera Company of New York.

Boner (bō′nėr), **Edmund.** See **Bonner, Edmund.**

Boner, Ulrich. fl. first half 14th century. Swiss Dominican friar who collected, at the request of a Bern patrician, 100 fables (mostly from Latin sources) which he retold in popular language under the title *Der Edelstein.* It was, so far as we now know, the first German collection of fables and possibly also the first German book ever to be printed (it was first issued in 1461, at Bamberg, Germany). *Der Edelstein* was republished by Johann Jakob Breitinger in 1751.

Bo'ness (bō.nes′). [Official name, **Borrowstounness and Carriden.**] Police burgh, seaport, and large industrial center in S Scotland, in West Lothian, situated on the S bank of the Firth of Forth, ab. 16 mi. W of Edinburgh, ab. 422 mi. N of London by rail. The town exports coal from the Clackmannanshire coal field; imports include pit props for the coal mines, and iron and steel for local industries. 10,411 (est. 1948).

Bonesteel (bon′stēl), **Charles Hartwell.** b. at Fort Sidney, Neb., April 9, 1885—. American army officer. A graduate (1908) of the U.S. Military Academy, he served in France during World War I with the 7th division. Appointed colonel (1937), brigadier general (1940), and major general (1941), he was named commander of U.S. forces (1941) and Allied forces (April, 1942) in Iceland.

He was commanding general (1943–44) of the infantry school at Fort Benning, Ga., until his appointment (1944) as Western defense commander.

Bonfire. Novel (1933) by Dorothy Canfield Fisher.

Bonggren (bong'grẹn), **Olof Jakob.** b. at Bergane, Dalsland, Sweden, 1854; d. in the U.S., 1944. Swedish-American poet and writer. With Elmblad, Bonggren was a leading poet of the golden age of Swedish-American literature (c1870–1900). He attended college at Vänersborg, Sweden, before emigrating to America in 1882 and settling in the Middle West. His poetry is characterized by great mastery of form, and preoccupation with religion, philosophy, and culture.

Bongo (bông'gō). [Also, **Obong.**] Sudanic-speaking people of SW Anglo-Egyptian Sudan, in NE Africa. Their population is estimated at less than 5,000 (by E. E. Evans-Pritchard, in C. G. and B. Z. Seligman's *Pagan Tribes of the Nilotic Sudan*, 1932), having declined, as a result of raids by the Azande and Arab traders and slaves, from 100,000 (G. A. Schweinfurth, *The Heart of Africa*, 1873). The remnants of this once-important group are concentrated in an area SE of Wau, the capital of the province of Bahr-el-Ghazal. They are divided politically into numerous independent local groups headed by chiefs with little authority. Rain makers, who are not necessarily chiefs, are important. They have exogamous patrilineal clans, and since Schweinfurth's visit have adopted circumcision and age grades from the Zande to the south. They practice agriculture and hunting. They are not to be confused with the Bongo (or Bongou, Mobongo, Mombongo) of the NW Belgian Congo, who occupy an area S of the Ubangi River and N of the Congo River.

Bongo. [Also: **Abongo, Obobongo.**] One of the western pygmy groups of C Africa, inhabiting the province of Gabon in French Equatorial Africa.

Bonham (bon'ạm). City in E Texas, county seat of Fannin County, NE of Dallas: manufactures include cotton textiles, gasoline pumps, and dairy products. It was named for James Butler Bonham, a hero of the Alamo. It served as the Civil War Headquarters of the Union general Henry E. McCulloch. 7,049 (1950).

Bonheur (bo.nėr), **François Auguste.** b. at Bordeaux, France, Nov. 4, 1824; d. at Paris, Feb. 23, 1884. French painter of landscapes and animal life; brother of Rosa Bonheur.

Bonheur, Jules Isidore. b. at Bordeaux, France, May 15, 1827; d. 1901. French sculptor; brother of Rosa Bonheur.

Bonheur, Juliette. [Married name, **Peyrol.**] b. July 19, 1830; d. July 19, 1891. French painter; sister of Rosa Bonheur.

Bonheur, Rosa. [Full name, **Marie Rosalie Bonheur.**] b. at Bordeaux, France, March 16, 1822; d. at Fontainebleau, France, May 25, 1899. French painter of animal life and landscapes; sister of François Auguste Bonheur, Jules Isidore Bonheur, and Juliette Bonheur. She was a pupil of her father and of Léon Cogniet. She received medals of the first class at the Paris Salons of 1848 and 1855. At the Exposition Universelle of 1855 she exhibited *La Fenaison en Auvergne*, which established her reputation. From 1849 she was the directress of the Free School of Design for Young Girls. Among her noted works are *Labourage nivernais* in the Luxembourg museum, Paris, *Etudes d'animaux* (Musée de Bordeaux), *Paysage et animaux* (Musée d'Orléans), and *The Horse Fair* (Metropolitan Museum of Art, New York).

Bonhomme (bo.nom), **Col du.** One of the chief passes over the Vosges Mountains, NE France, on the border of Alsace SW of Markirch. Elevation, 3,084 ft.

Bonhomme, Col du. Pass in the Alps, S of Mont Blanc, on the route between Chamonix and Courmayeur (in Italy). Elevation, 7,680 ft.

Bonhomme, Jacques. See under **Cale, Guillaume.**

Bonhomme Richard (bo.nom rē.shàr). One of a fleet of five vessels prepared by the French government, on the advice of Benjamin Franklin, and placed under the command of John Paul Jones. It was a merchantman changed to a man-of-war and originally named *Duras* (and then renamed *Bonhomme Richard*, or *Poor Richard*, at Jones's suggestion, in honor of Franklin). The fleet sailed from L'Orient, Aug. 14, 1779, passed along the west Irish coast around Scotland, and, on Sept. 23, 1779, reduced to three ships, encountered the English North Sea merchant fleet under convoy of the *Serapis* (44 guns) and *Countess of Scarborough* (20 guns) off Flamborough Head. The *Bonhomme Richard* engaged the *Serapis* at 7:30 P.M. by moonlight, in the presence of thousands of spectators. The *Serapis* struck her colors at 10:30, but the victorious *Bonhomme Richard* had suffered greater damage (particularly at and just below the water line) and on Sept. 25, from the deck of the captured *Serapis*, Jones watched her sink. It was during this battle, when the English commander observed how seriously the *Bonhomme Richard* had been damaged and asked if Jones was prepared to surrender, that Jones made the statement "Sir, I have not yet begun to fight." (There was more than a grain of truth in this brave statement, as evidenced by the fact that Jones thereupon closed with the *Serapis*, lashed the *Bonhomme Richard* to her side, boarded her, and carried out the most decisive phase of his battle on the decks of the enemy vessel.)

Boni (bō'nī), **Albert.** b. at New York, Oct. 21, 1892—. American publisher and inventor. He attended Cornell and Harvard universities, helped found (1915) the Washington Square Players (later to be named the Theatre Guild), took part in organizing (c1917) the publishing firm of Boni and Liveright at New York, and was president (1923 *et seq.*) of the publishing house of Albert and Charles Boni, Inc. Inventor of microprint and the Readex reading projector, he became (1940) president of the Readex Microprint Corporation. He edited *The Modern Book of French Verse* (1920) and *A Guide to the Literature of Photography and Related Subjects* (1943).

Boni (bō'nē), **Giacomo.** b. at Venice, April 25, 1859; d. 1925. Italian architect and archaeologist. He had charge (September, 1898 *et seq.*) of excavations in the Roman Forum by which the conditions of ancient Roman life were revealed to an extent never before possible. He also superintended the reconstruction of the Campanile at Venice.

Boniface (bon'i.fās). See also **Bonifacius.**

Boniface, Saint. See also Saint **Bruno.**

Boniface, Saint. [Called the **"Apostle of Germany"**; original name, **Winfrid, Winfrith, Wynfrith.**] b. at Kirton, or Crediton, Devonshire, England, c680; d. near Dokkum, Friesland, June 5, c755. English missionary. From 716 he labored among the Friesians and among the German tribes. He was made a bishop in 723, and archbishop in 732. He founded (c743) the abbey of Fulda, where his remains were later laid. From 746 to 754 he occupied the see of Mainz. He was murdered in 755. He is said to have enforced his missionary teaching by cutting down with his own hand the sacred oak at Geismar, in what is now Hesse, Germany. According to the most generally accepted account of this exploit, Boniface not only felled the oak (thus demonstrating the utter powerlessness of the god to whom it was sacred) but also used its wood to build a Christian chapel. There can be no doubt that this story, in its main outlines, is substantially true, and its effectiveness in converting the people of the area to Christianity was enormous. His festival is celebrated in the Roman and Anglican churches on June 5.

Boniface. Landlord in George Farquhar's *The Beaux' Stratagem.* He was in league with the highwaymen, and prided himself on his diet of ale. From him the name has been applied to innkeepers in general.

Boniface I, Saint. d. 422. Pope from 418 to 422. His pontificate was contested by the turbulent antipope Eulalius. He is commemorated on Oct. 25.

Boniface II. fl. 6th century. Pope from 530 to 532. He was nominated to the papacy by his predecessor, Saint Felix IV (or, in some chronologies, Felix III), which aroused the anger of Roman priests. These elected the antipope Dioscorus, who died 14 days afterward.

Boniface III. fl. 7th century. Pope from February to November, 607. He influenced the emperor Phocas to decree that the title Universal Bishop should be given only to the Bishop of Rome. He also forbade the choice of a successor to a pope or bishop during the lifetime of the incumbent.

Boniface IV, Saint. fl. 7th century. Pope from 608 to 615. He received permission from the emperor Phocas to convert the Pantheon erected by Agrippa, at Rome, into a Christian church under the name of Sancta Maria Rotunda.

Boniface V. b. at Naples; d. Oct. 25, 625. Pope from 619 to 625. He enacted the decree by which churches became places of asylum.

Boniface VI. fl. 9th century. Pope in 896. He was of an abandoned character, and was seated in the papal chair by a mob after the death of Formosus. He died (or was ejected) 15 days later.

Boniface VII. [Also, **Boniface Franco.**] fl. 10th century. Antipope in 974 and again in the period 984–985. He attained the papal throne in a popular tumult in 974, was driven from Rome in 975, and returned and deposed John XIV in 984. He probably died by violence.

Boniface VIII. [Original name, **Benedetto Gaetani.**] b. at Anagni, Italy, c1228; d. at Rome, Oct. 11, 1303. Pope from Dec. 24, 1294, to Oct. 11, 1303. He issued (Feb. 25, 1296) the bull *Clericis laicos*, which was directed against Philip IV of France (Philip the Fair), who had imposed taxes on the French clergy, and which forbade the clergy of any country to pay tribute to the secular government without the papal permission; but was forced by an enactment of Philip, which stopped the exportation of money from France, to concede that the French clergy might render voluntary contributions. He opened at Rome on Oct. 30, 1302 (as the result of a quarrel with Philip over the imprisonment of an insolent papal legate, the bishop of Pamiers), a synod, in which he promulgated (Nov. 18, 1302) the bull *Unam sanctam*, asserting the temporal as well as spiritual supremacy of the papacy. He was made prisoner at Anagni on Sept. 7, 1303, by Nogaret, vice-chancellor to Philip, and Sciarra Colonna; and although shortly released by the populace, died at Rome of a fever.

Boniface IX. [Original name, **Pietro Tomacelli.**] b. at Naples; d. at Rome, Oct. 1, 1404. Pope from 1389 to 1404. He quarreled with Richard II of England on the subject of the collation of benefices, established the perpetual annates, and during his reign made vain attempts to secure the submission of Avignon.

Boniface, Abbot. Head of the monastery of Saint Mary, in Sir Walter Scott's novel *The Monastery*.

Boniface of Savoy (sa̤.voi'). d. 1270. A younger son of Thomas I, Count of Savoy, nominated archbishop of Canterbury in 1241, confirmed by the Pope in 1243, and consecrated in 1245.

Bonifacio (bō.nē.fä'chō). Town on the island of Corsica, in the French department of Corse, situated at the S extremity of the island. It is a picturesque old town, founded c828, with a citadel and a fishing port. The Church of Santa Maria Maggiore dates from the 12th and 13th centuries. 2,048 (1946).

Bonifácio (bō.nē.fä'syō), **José.** [Full name, **José Bonifácio de Andrada e Silva**; pseudonym, **Américo Elisío.**] b. at Santos, Brazil, June 13, 1765; d. at Niterói, Brazil, April 6, 1838. Brazilian statesman, scientist, and poet. He lived and studied for many years in several European countries. For his contribution to the political emancipation of his country he became known as the "Patriarch of Brazilian Independence." A leader of the opposition in the first Parliament, he was arrested and lived in exile (1824–29) in France, where he published under the pseudonym of "Américo Elísio" his book of poems, *Poesias avulsas* (1825), thus linking his name to the introduction of Romanticism in Brazilian literature. He also wrote several scientific and political papers.

Bonifacio (bō.nē.fä'chō), **Strait of.** Strait in the Mediterranean Sea which separates Corsica from Sardinia. Width, ab. 7 mi.

Bonifacius (bon.i.fā'shus) or **Boniface** (bon'i.fās). b. in Thrace; d. 432 A.D. Roman general in the time of Honorius and Placidia; a rival of Aëtius and a friend of Saint Augustine. He served with distinction against the Goths and the Vandals in France (defending Marseilles against Ataulf, king of the Goths, in 413) and Spain, and in Africa. Through the plotting of Aëtius he was led to revolt against Galla Placidia and ally himself with the Vandals in Africa. He soon, however, returned to his allegiance, and attacked Genseric, but was defeated and besieged for 14 months at Hippo. On returning to Italy, he met and conquered Aëtius, but died from wounds received in the battle.

Bonifacius. Essay by Cotton Mather, published in 1710.

Bonin (bō.nēn'), **Adolf von.** b. Nov. 11, 1803; d. at Berlin, April 16, 1872. Prussian infantry general. He was governor of Dresden (1866–67) and of Lorraine (1870–71).

Bonin, Eduard von. b. at Stolpe, Prussia, March 7, 1793; d. at Koblenz, Prussia, March 13, 1865. Prussian infantry general. He distinguished himself in the Schleswig-Holstein war (1848–50).

Bonington (bon'ing.to̤n), **Richard Parkes.** b. at Arnold, near Nottingham, England, Oct. 25, 1801; d. at London, Sept. 23, 1828. English painter of coast and street scenes, and of genre subjects. He studied in France, at the École des Beaux-Arts and under Gros, and spent much of his short life in that country, though he made visits to England. A friend of Eugène Delacroix, he introduced into France the theories of J. M. W. Turner and John Constable (who were primarily landscape painters), receiving in turn the French ideas of the period on the painting of historical subjects.

Bonin Islands (bō'nin). [Japanese: **Bu-nin-to, Ogasawara Gunto, Ogasawarajima, Ogasawara Sima.**] Group of 15 islands of volcanic formation in the North Pacific, ab. 550 mi. S of Tokyo. Marcus Island (Japanese, Minamitori Shima), further to the W, is sometimes classified as one of the Bonins. They were known to the Japanese by c1593 (although not then known to the Western world, and thus in some sources said to have been "discovered" either by the Spanish (c1543) or by Tasman (1675); however, if the Japanese did know of their existence in the late 16th century, as now seems fairly certain, the later "discoveries" were genuine only insofar as they made it possible for the islands to be shown on European charts), and formally annexed by Japan between 1875 and 1880. Area, 40 sq. mi.; pop. ab. 7,000 (1940).

Bonivard (bo.nē.vår), **François de.** See **Bonnivard** or **Bonivard, François de.**

Bonjour Brothers (bôṅ.zhör'). fl. c1775–90. b. at Pont d'Ain, France; d. in exile at Lausanne, Switzerland. Two French heretics who became curé and vicar of the parish of Fareins. They founded a sect called the "flagellants Fareinistes."

Bonn (bon; German, bon). [Latin, **Bonna, Castra Bonnensia.**] City in W Germany, in the *Land* (state) of North Rhine-Westphalia, British Zone, formerly in the Rhine Province, Prussia, situated on the W bank of the Rhine River, ab. 15 mi. SE of Cologne. It is the seat of the government and parliament of the West-German Federal Republic which was recognized by the governments of the U.S., Great Britain, and France on May 8, 1949; the former teachers' seminary now serves as parliament building. Bonn is a river port; manufactures include ceramics, plate glass and mirrors, flags, musical and precision instruments, tobacco, and foodstuffs.

Educational Institutions and Culture. It has a university, founded in 1784, with several faculties of high standing, formerly known socially as the seat of the *Verbindung* (student association) Saxo-Borussia, to which belonged the princes of the house of Hohenzollern who were students here. The university is housed in the castle of the former ecclesiastical prince-electors of Cologne; erected in the period 1697–1723, it was taken over by the university in 1818; it is surrounded by a large park. There are schools of agriculture, administration, and education, a conservatory of music, botanical gardens, well-known clinics, numerous scholarly societies, good libraries (including the university library, Borromaeus Library, and municipal library), and a theater. Various museums house zoölogical, anatomical, and art collections; the *Landesmuseum* (provincial museum) contains prehistoric relics, antiquities, and medieval and modern art. The birthplace of Beethoven, Bonn has also a Beethoven Museum.

Architecture. The *Münster* (cathedral) is a remarkable Romanesque basilica of the 11th and 12th centuries, rebuilt after the bombardment of Bonn by the French in 1689. The Church of Saint Remigius dates from the 15th century, the Church of the Jesuits from the 16th century, the *Rathaus* (town hall) from the 18th century. Bonn is notable for its parks, gardens, villas, and views of the surrounding hills, especially the Siebengebirge; the Rhine River leaves its narrow valley here and enters into the North Rhenish plain.

History. Bonn, originally a Roman military camp on

the Rhine frontier, was destroyed by the Franks in the 4th century, and by the Normans in the 9th century. From 1273 to 1794 it was the residence of the archbishops of Cologne, who were among the prince-electors of the German Empire. The emperors Frederick III (1314) and Charles IV (1346) were crowned here. The city was occupied by the French in 1689; annexed by France in 1801, by Prussia in 1814. From 1919–26 Bonn was occupied by British and French troops; it was bombed several times in 1944–45 and the cathedral, the Church of Saint Remigius, the Kreuzkirche, and the zoölogical institute were badly damaged, while the Landesmuseum and the university were almost completely destroyed; the Beethoven House, however, remained intact. The Allied armies entered on May 7th and 8th, 1945. The population is predominantly Roman Catholic. 115,394 (1950).

Bonn (bon), **Moritz Julius.** b. at Frankfort on the Main, Germany, June 28, 1873—. German economist. He served (1910 *et seq.*) successively as professor at Munich, Berkeley (University of California), Madison (University of Wisconsin), Ithaca (Cornell University), Berlin, London, and, for a second time, at the University of California. Author of *The Crisis of European Democracy* (1925), *The American Experiment* (1930, 1933), *Prosperity, Myth and Reality in American Business Life* (1932), and *The Crumbling of Empire* (1938).

Bonna (bon'ạ). A Latin name of **Bonn.**

Bonnard (bo.nàr), **Abel.** b. at Poitiers, France, Dec. 19, 1883—. French poet and novelist. His collections of poems include *Les Familiers* (1906), *Les Royautés* (1908), and *La France et ses morts* (1919). He is the author also of a novel, *La Vie et l'amour* (1913), and of various incidental books, including a continuation (1928) of Stendhal's *De l'Amour* and a study (1929) of Saint Francis of Assisi.

Bonnard, Pierre. b. at Fontenay-aux-Roses, France, Oct. 3, 1867; d. at Le Cannet, near Cannes, France, Jan. 23, 1947. French landscape and still-life painter, who furthered the tradition of the impressionist school, and paved the way for Fauvism. At the insistence of his father, he studied law, but his interest in painting superseded his law studies. In his spare time he attended classes at the École des Beaux-Arts and the Julian Academy, where he met Jean Édouard Vuillard, Maurice Denis, Sérusier, and Valloton; the men formed a group known as the Nabis, their purpose being to formulate a theoretical background for their work. Bonnard began to earn his living by drawing lithographs and posters; he first exhibited (1891) at Paris in the Salon des Indépendents, and after that exhibited fairly regularly at the Indépendents and the Durand-Ruel gallery. He lived at Paris for a short time but preferred the country to the city, and therefore spent much of his time traveling and living in the provinces. Japanese prints had an important influence on his work, as did the art of Paul Gauguin, Toulouse-Lautrec, and the impressionist school. The work of Vuillard is quite close to that of Bonnard; both were interested in the use of an overall pattern or design, in color, and in the expression of light as atmosphere. Bonnard was a very prolific artist, and won several hundred prizes; his work is included in the collections of almost every important museum in Europe and in North and South America. Among his more prominent works are *Woman with Crossed Legs* (1919), *Dancers* (1922), *Woman with Dog* (1924), *Torso of a Girl* (1927), *Fishing Boats* (1929), *Open Window on the Sea* (1933), *The Red Corsage* (1936), *Boulevard des Batignolles* (1939), *Vase of Flowers* (1942), and *The Breakfast* (1943).

Bonnat (bo.nà), **Léon Joseph Florentin.** b. at Bayonne, France, June 20, 1833; d. 1922. French painter of historical pieces and portraits. A pupil of Léon Cogniet, he won the second prix de Rome in 1851. He made his debut at the Paris Salon of 1857 with three portraits, won a medal of the second class in 1867 and a medal of honor in 1869, and became a member of the French Institute in 1874.

Bonnel Town (bon'ẹl). Former name of **Chatham,** N.J.

Bonner (bon'ėr), **Edmund.** [Also, **Boner.**] b. at Hanley, Worcestershire, England, c1495; d. at London, Sept. 5, 1569. English prelate, made bishop of London in 1539, noted for his persecution of Protestants in the reign of Mary of England, in the period 1553–58. On the accession of Elizabeth he refused to take the oath of supremacy, and was committed to the Marshalsea prison, where he died.

Bonner, Robert. b. near Londonderry, Ireland, April 28, 1824; d. at New York, July 6, 1899. American publisher, founder (1851) of the New York *Ledger*. He expanded the paper, which he established at the printing plant of a previous newspaper, the *Merchant's Ledger*, into a family weekly with a wide circulation. He paid high rates to his contributors, and excelled in novel and successful advertising methods. After his death, the *Ledger* ceased publication. He was also known in his day as the owner of a number of excellent race horses.

Bonnet (bo.ne), **Charles.** b. at Geneva, Switzerland, March 13, 1720; d. near Lake Geneva, Switzerland, May 20, 1793. Swiss naturalist and philosophical writer, who first described parthenogenesis as observed in aphids. His works include *Traité d'insectologie* (1745), *Traité de l'usage des feuilles* (1754), *Essai analytique sur les facultés de l'âme* (1760), *Considérations sur les corps organisés* (1762), *Contemplation de la nature* (1764), and *Palingénésie philosophique* (1769).

Bonnet, Georges. b. 1889—. French politician and diplomat, foreign minister of France during the years leading up to World War II and the German invasion of France. In the period of World War I, as an official of the Conseil d'État, the supreme administrative tribunal, he was in charge of demobilization (1919) and became a delegate to numerous international conferences, including that which formulated (1919) the Covenant of the League of Nations. He was French delegate (1924 *et seq.*) to the League, was chief French delegate to the Lausanne conference (1932), and presided over the Stresa conference (1935). Elected to the Chamber of Deputies in 1924, he served as a member of numerous cabinets, and as minister of finance, trade, public works, mails, and pensions. In September, 1935, as minister of trade and French delegate to the League of Nations, he called for a return by the nations of the world to free trade and stable currencies. He was named (February, 1937) ambassador to the U.S., but soon returned to France to serve as finance minister in the Chautemps cabinet (June, 1937–March, 1938) and as foreign minister in the last Daladier cabinet. As foreign minister, he sought to reach an adjustment with Germany, and strongly supported the Munich agreement (1938); he followed the British lead in declaring war on Germany (1939), and continued to direct French foreign policy until the German invasion (May, 1940). During the Vichy régime, he did not participate in the government, but sought to maintain good relations with both the German occupation authorities and American representatives. He was expelled (June, 1944) from the Radical-Socialist Party, and established residence in Switzerland.

Bonnet, Henri. b. at Paris, May 26, 1888—. French diplomat, first ambassador to the U.S. from the Fourth French Republic. He was a member (1919–30) of the Secretariat of the League of Nations. During World War II, he fled from France to London in June, 1940, and proceeded thence to the U.S.; he was named (1941) a professor of political science at the École des Hautes-Études at New York. He became (September, 1944) minister of information in the provisional French government, and was appointed (Nov. 29, 1944) French ambassador to the U.S.

Bonnet (Anglicized, bo.nā'), **Joseph Élie Georges Marie.** b. at Bordeaux, France, March 17, 1884; d. in Quebec, Aug. 2, 1944. French organist. He studied under Félix Alexandre Guilmant at the Paris Conservatoire, before serving as organist (1906 *et seq.*) of St. Eustache, Paris. After touring England and the U.S., he was appointed professor of organ at the University of Rochester. He published several volumes of organ pieces.

Bonnétable (bo.nā.tàbl). Town in W France, in the department of Sarthe, situated on the Triboulin River, ab. 16 mi. NE of Le Mans. It has a castle built in 1478 and restored at the beginning of the 20th century. 3,470 (1946).

Bonne Terre (bon ter'). City in SE Missouri, in St. Francois County: lead-mining center. 3,533 (1950).

Bonneval (bon.vàl). Town in N central France, in the department of Eure-et-Loir, situated on the Loir River ab. 18 mi. SW of Chartres. Pop. ab. 3,000.

Bonneval, Claude Alexandre, Comte **de.** [Called in Turkey, **Achmet Pasha.**] b. at Coussac, Limousin, France, July 14, 1675; d. at Constantinople, March 27, 1747. French soldier of fortune, at various times in the military service of the French, the Austrians, and the Turks. He served under Prince Eugene of Savoy in Italy, Provence, and in the campaigns of the period 1710–12. In 1708 he commanded an army corps in the Papal States, and served under Austria against the Turks in 1715.

Bonneville (bon.vēl). Town in E France in the department of Haute-Savoie, situated on the Arve River ab. 16 mi. SE of Geneva. 2,452 (1946).

Bonneville (bon′e.vil), **Benjamin Louis Eulalie de.** b. in France, April 14, 1796; d. at Fort Smith, Ark., June 12, 1878. American soldier and explorer. He fought with distinction in the war with Mexico, commanded an expedition to the Gila River in 1857, and in the Civil War was commandant (1862–65) of Benton Barracks at St. Louis. He became a colonel in 1855, and brevet major general in 1865. While a captain he engaged in explorations (1831–36) of the Rocky Mountains and California. His journal was amplified by Washington Irving, and published under the title *Adventures of Capt. Bonneville, U.S.A., in the Rocky Mountains of the Far West* (1837).

Bonneville Dam. Large power and navigation dam in NW Oregon, ab. 40 mi. E of Portland in the Columbia river. The dam and power plant were constructed in the period 1933–43. There is a navigation lock and a special system of ladders to enable the spawning salmon to go upstream. The dam has a head of 67 ft. at low water, and creates a reservoir ab. 45 mi. long. Installed capacity of power station, 518,000 kilowatts.

Bonnevue (bon.vü), **Louis Hector de Callières.** See **Callières Bonnevue, Louis Hector de.**

Bonney (bon′i), **Charles Carroll.** b. at Hamilton, N.Y., Sept. 4, 1831; d. at Chicago, Aug. 23, 1903. American lawyer whose efforts on behalf of an international court of justice led to the founding of the Permanent Court of Arbitration at The Hague. President (1882 *et seq.*) of the Illinois bar association, he was the founder (c1883) and first president of the Citizens' Law and Order League, and was associated with the founding of the Parliament of Religions at the Chicago Columbian Exposition (1893). Author of *Rules of Law for the Carriage and Delivery of Persons and Property by Railway* (1864) and *Summary of the Law of Marine, Fire and Life Insurance* (1865); contributor of addresses to *World's Congress Addresses* (1900).

Bonney, William H. See **Billy the Kid.**

Bonnibel (bon′i.bel). In old pastoral poetry, a common name for a young girl. It is adapted from the French *bonne et belle,* meaning "good and beautiful."

Bonnie Blue Flag, The. Title of a Confederate ballad which achieved wide popularity throughout the South during the Civil War. Its authorship is disputed. The "blue flag" has been said to refer to the blue field of the U.S. flag (initially carrying a sole star for South Carolina) employed before an official standard was adopted by the Confederate States of America.

Bonnière (bo.nyer), **Gustave Auguste Beaumont de la.** See **Beaumont de la Bonnière.**

Bonnivard or **Bonivard** (bo.nē.vàr), **François de.** b. at Seyssel, Switzerland, c1493; d. at Geneva, 1570. Swiss prelate and politician, the hero of Byron's poem *The Prisoner of Chillon.* He became (1514) prior of St. Victor, Switzerland, and was a conspicuous opponent of Charles III, Duke of Savoy, who endeavored to obtain control of Geneva. He was largely instrumental in bringing about an alliance (1518) between Geneva and Fribourg, and in 1519 was captured by the duke and imprisoned for 20 months. In 1530 he obtained a safe-conduct from the duke to visit his aged parents at Seyssel, but was arrested (May 26, 1530) at Lausanne, and confined in the castle of Chillon, where, after a visit (1532) from the duke, he was placed in a subterranean dungeon and, according to the local tradition, fastened to a pillar. He was liberated (March 29, 1536) upon the capture of Chillon by the Bernese. He was the author of *Les Chroniques de Genève* (edited by Dunant, Geneva, 1831), which was written at the instance of the magistracy of Geneva.

Bonny (bon′i). River in W Africa, an arm of the Niger River delta, flowing into the Bight of Biafra, Gulf of Guinea.

Bonnyrigg and Lasswade (bon′i.rig; las′wād). Municipal burgh in S Scotland, in Midlothian, situated on the river North Esk, ab. 6 mi. SE of Edinburgh, ab. 391 mi. N of London by rail. It has carpet and paper manufactures. 5,535 (est. 1948).

Bono (bō′nō), **Emilio De.** See **De Bono, Emilio.**

Bonomi (bō.nô′mē), **Giuseppe.** b. at Rome, Jan. 19, 1739; d. at London, March 9, 1808. Italian architect resident in England, a leader in the revival of Greek style; father of Joseph Bonomi. Among his principal works is Roseneath Hall, in Dumbartonshire, Scotland.

Bonomi (bō.nô′mē), **Ivanoe.** b. at Mantua, Italy, Oct. 18, 1873; d. at Rome, April 20, 1951. Italian socialist statesman. Trained as a teacher, he became (1898), together with Leonida Bissolati-Bergamaschi, a leader of the reform branch of the Socialist Party. Elected (1909) a deputy, he was expelled (1912) from the party for his reformist convictions. He volunteered (1915) in the army, where he served as a second lieutenant. His subsequent career included the posts of minister of public works (1916–17, 1919), minister of war (1920–21), and minister of the treasury (1921), before he became (1921) prime minister; in this capacity he was one of the signers of the Rapallo pact. His defeat (1924) as a candidate for the chamber of deputies as an antifascist caused his retirement, until he headed (1943) the national antifascist groups and served (1944–45) for a second time as prime minister. He was appointed (1948) a senator, and president of the senate.

Bonomi (bō.nô′mē), **Joseph.** b. at Rome, Oct. 9, 1796; d. at London, March 3, 1878. English sculptor and draftsman; son of Giuseppe Bonomi. He made a large number of drawings of Assyrian and especially Egyptian remains for the works of various archaeologists, and published *Nineveh and its Palaces* (1852) and others.

Bononcini (bō.nôn.chē′nē) or **Buononcini** (bwō-), **Giovanni Battista.** b. at Modena, Italy, c1672; d. probably at Venice, c1750. Italian composer of operas, and a rival, at London, of George Frederick Handel; son of Giovanni Maria Bononcini.

Bononcini or **Buononcini, Giovanni Maria.** b. at Modena, Italy, 1640; d. there, in November, 1678. Italian court musician and composer; father of Giovanni Battista Bononcini and Marc Antonio Bononcini.

Bononcini or **Buononcini, Marc Antonio.** b. at Modena, Italy, 1675; d. at Rome, July 8, 1726. Italian operatic composer; son of Giovanni Maria Bononcini.

Bononia (bō.nō′ni.ạ). Roman name of **Bologna,** city.

Bononia Gessoriacum (jes.ō.ri′ạ.kum). Latin name of **Boulogne.**

Bonorva (bō.nôr′vä). Town and commune on the island of Sardinia, Italy, ab. 25 mi. SE of Sassari. It is an agricultural trade center. Roman and prehistoric remains are in the vicinity. Pop. of commune, 7,443 (1936); of town, 7,076 (1936).

Bonpland (bôn.plän), **Aimé Jacques Alexandre.** [Original surname, **Goujaud.**] b. at La Rochelle, France, Aug. 22, 1773; d. at San Borja, Uruguay, May 4, 1858. French naturalist and traveler. From 1799 to 1805 he traveled with Alexander von Humboldt in America, and on his return published *Plantes équinoxiales* and other botanical works. In 1816 he went to Buenos Aires, and in 1821 attempted a journey from Buenos Aires to Bolivia. Passing the frontiers of Paraguay, he was seized by order of the dictator José Gaspar Rodríguez Francia, and was not allowed to leave the country until 1830. After his release he resided on a small plantation near Brazil.

Bonsal (bon′sạl), **Stephen.** b. at Baltimore, March 29, 1865; d. at Washington, D.C., June 8, 1951. American journalist and author. He was special corespondent of the New York *Herald* in the Bulgarian-Serbian conflict of 1885, in the Macedonian uprising (1890), in the Sino-Japanese War (1895), in the Cuban insurrection (1897), in the Spanish-American War (1898), with the China relief expedition (1900), in the Philippine Islands (1901), in Venezuela (1903), in the Balkans (1904), in Russia (1907), and in Mexico (1910–11). He became (1913) secretary to the governor general of the Philippines, served (1918) with the U.S. army in France, and was a member of the post-war inter-Allied mission to the Balkans. He was in the diplomatic service of the U.S. as secretary of legation and chargé d'affaires (1891–96) at

Peking, Madrid, and Tokyo, and in Korea. Author of *Morocco as It Is* (1892), *The Real Condition of Cuba* (1897), *The Fight for Santiago* (1899), *The Golden Horseshoe* (1900), *The American Mediterranean* (1912), *Heyday in a Vanished World* (1933), and *Unfinished Business* (1944; awarded a Pulitzer prize).

Bonsels (bōn′zẹls), **Waldemar.** b. at Ahrensburg, Germany, Feb. 2, 1881; d. 1952. German novelist. His most widely read book is *Die Biene Maja* (1912; Eng. trans., *Maya*, 1922), a novel in which bees are humanized and idealized. He wrote a number of stories about vagabonds (*Notes of a Vagabond*, 1931). His attempted escape from reality leads to travels that are described in *Indienfahrt* (1916; Eng. trans., *An Indian Journey*, 1928), *Brasilianische Tage und Nächte* (1931), and *Der Reiter in der Wüste, eine Amerikafahrt* (1935).

Bonset (bôn′set), **I. K.** A pseudonym of **Doesburg, Theo van.**

Bonstetten (bon.ste.ten), **Charles Victor de.** [Also, **Karl Victor von Bonstetten** (bōn′shtet.ẹn).] b. at Bern, Switzerland, Sept. 3, 1745; d. at Geneva, Feb. 3, 1832. Swiss man of letters and philosophical writer. His works include *Recherches sur la nature et les lois de l'imagination* (1807) and *Études sur l'homme* (1821).

Bontemps (bôṅ.täṅ), **Roger.** [Pseudonym of **Roger de Collerye.**] b. at Paris, c1470; d. c1540. French poet. He was of a lively, gay, and carefree temperament. Pierre Jean de Béranger popularized this type in one of his famous songs, and the name is proverbially given to any jovial fellow.

Bonthe (bon′tē). Town in W Africa, the second largest port in Sierra Leone, situated on the E end of Sherbro Island. It is a collecting center and shipping point for the edible oils and other products which are brought down the numerous rivers to the coast. Pop. ab. 4,500.

Bontok (bon.tok′) or **Bontoc Igorot** (ig.ọ.rōt′). Malayo-Polynesian-speaking, pagan mountain tribe of NW Luzon (Bontok subprovince), Philippine Islands. 20,909 (1939).

Bon Ton (bôṅ tôṅ). Comedy by John Burgoyne, produced in 1760. David Garrick shortened it, and produced it in 1775 as *Bon Ton, or High Life above Stairs.*

Bonus March. March of a veterans' "Bonus Army" on Washington, D.C., in 1932, resulting from agitation among U.S. ex-servicemen for the immediate cash payment of a deferred bonus sanctioned by the Adjusted Compensation Act of 1924, which provided for payment in 1945. The primary aim of the "Bonus Army" (also known as the "Bonus Expeditionary Force" or "BEF") was to secure the passage of the Patman Bill providing for immediate payment to eligible veterans. Some 15,000 men from throughout the country who gathered at Washington finally dispersed, after earlier rioting had been quelled by federal troops and Washington police.

Bonvalot (bôṅ.và.lō), **Pierre Gabriel Édouard.** b. at Épagne, Aube, France, 1853; d. 1933. French explorer and author. He explored (1880–82) the interior of Asia, and in 1886 became the first to traverse the Pamirs. After traveling (1889–90) through Tibet and Siberia, he went (1897) on a government mission to Antoto, Ethiopia. Author of *De Moscou en Bactriane* (1884), *De Paris au Tonkin à travers Tibet inconnu* (Eng. trans., 1891), and *L'Asie inconnue* (1896).

Bonvin (bôṅ.vaṅ), **François.** b. at Vaugirard, Seine, France, 1817; d. 1887. French painter. He produced genre pictures in the style of the Flemish school.

Bonvin (bon′vin), **Ludwig.** b. at Siders, Switzerland, Feb. 17, 1850; d. 1939. American composer and Jesuit priest, a noted authority on the Gregorian chant. He studied in the Netherlands, where he became a choirmaster and organist, and was director (1887–1907) of the orchestra and choir at Canisius College, Buffalo, N.Y. His compositions include six masses, as well as smaller liturgical choral works; cantatas such as *Wittekind* (Opus 28), *In the Summer Night* (Opus 39), and *Bretagne* (Opus 60); the *Reminiscences* symphony in G Minor (Opus 67) for strings; *Johanna d'Arc vor dem Scheiterhaufen* for orchestra and soprano; and chamber music, tone poems, and songs.

Bonwill (bon′wil), **William Gibson Arlington.** b. Oct. 4, 1833; d. Sept. 24, 1899. American dentist. He was the inventor of the electromagnetic mallet (1873), and several other innovations in 19th-century dental equipment.

Bonython (bon′i.thon), **John.** Character in *Mogg Megone* (1836), by John Greenleaf Whittier. The character was based upon an actual person of the same name, the son of Richard Bonython, who lived a turbulent and violent life in colonial Maine during the middle years of the 17th century. He was finally outlawed for contempt of court.

Bonython, Richard. b. in England, 1580; d. c1650. English soldier. He received a grant of a tract of land on the east side of the Saco River, in Maine, and settled there in 1631. He was commissioner for the government of Maine under Ferdinando Gorges in 1636, and later (1640–47) one of his council. His son, John Bonython, was introduced by John Greenleaf Whittier in *Mogg Megone.*

Booby (bö′bi), **Lady.** In Henry Fielding's novel *Joseph Andrews*, a woman no longer young, but with unabated interest in carnal pleasure, who tries to seduce Joseph Andrews, her footman. She dismisses him when he refuses her advances.

Boodle's (bö′dlz). London club established in 1762. It was kept by one Boodle, and was a famous resort for country squires and masters of foxhounds.

Book about Myself, A. Autobiographical sketch (1922) by Theodore Dreiser.

Bookman, The. American journal of literature and criticism founded in 1895 and published monthly. It suspended publication in 1933.

Book of Ahania (ạ.hā′ni.ạ), **The.** Volume (1795) of poetry by William Blake. It is the sequel to *The Song and Book of Los*, also published in 1795. In these two works, and in *Europe* (1794), Blake's use of symbolic characters and the actions he attributes to them have defied the interpretative ingenuity of all the commentators on Blake's works.

Book of Americans, A. Volume (1933) of poems by Stephen Vincent Benét and Rosemary Benét. It consists of a group of more than 50 poems about famous characters and was primarily designed for children.

Book of Annandale (an′ạn.dāl). Narrative in blank verse by Edwin Arlington Robinson, published in *Captain Craig* (1902).

Book of Common Order. Liturgy of the Church of Scotland. In 1562 the Book of Common Order, commonly termed "Knox's Liturgy," was partially introduced in place of the Book of Common Prayer, and in 1564 its use was authoritatively ordained in all the churches in Scotland. This liturgy was taken from the order or liturgy used by the English church at Geneva.

Book of Common Prayer. [Popularly called the **Prayer Book.**] Service book of the Church of England, or a similar book authorized by one of the other branches of the Anglican Church. The first Book of Common Prayer was issued in 1549. It was almost entirely taken from medieval liturgical books. English was substituted for Latin, and a uniform use was established for the whole Church of England. Revisions were made in 1552, 1559, and 1662. The American Prayer Book was authorized in 1789; a revision was begun in 1880, and issued in 1892. Another revision was issued in 1928.

Book of Faith, The. Treatise (c1456) by Reginald Pecock. In it Pecock defends the authority of the Church even though he admits that she can err.

Book of Hours, A. Prose work (1937) by Donald Culross Peattie. It is a sequel to his *An Almanac for Moderns*, and contains 24 chapters for the hours of the day. In it he displays again the great range of knowledge and feeling which had been first revealed in *An Almanac for Moderns.*

Book of Kells (kelz). See under **Kells.**

Book of Leinster (len′stėr, lin′-). See under **Tain Bo Cuailgne.**

Book of Margery Kempe (kemp), **The.** Autobiography by Margery Kempe of Lynn (d. c1438). The manuscript of this work was discovered in 1934, a modernized version was published in 1936, and the original text in 1940. Both as a human document and for its many glimpses of medieval life, it has great interest for students of English literature and history.

Book of Martyrs, The. History of the persecution of various Protestant reformers in England, by John Foxe. It was finished in 1559, and was written in Latin. It was published on March 20, 1563, and called *Actes and Monu-*

ments, but was popularly known as *The Book of Martyrs.* Foxe himself translated it into English from the Latin in which he originally wrote it.

Book of Nonsense, The. Collection (1848) of humorous verse by Edward Lear.

Book of Sentences. [Latin, **Sententiarum libri IV.**] Collection of opinions of the Church Fathers, by Peter the Lombard, who was for two years (1158–60) the bishop of Paris, and who is, on account of this work, sometimes called *Magister Sententiarum* (Master of the Sentences). Published in the 12th century, the work was long a theological textbook, and was influential in formulating the official clerical doctrine of the sacraments. The questions are decided by the authority of Scripture and of the Fathers of the Church, and are divided into four books. The first book contains questions concerning God and the doctrine of the Trinity in particular; the second concerns the Creation; the third concerns Christ and the Christian religion; and the fourth deals with religious and moral duties.

Book of Snobs, The. A series of sketches by William Makepeace Thackeray on one of his favorite subjects, snobbery in all its branches. The sketches first came out (1843) in *Punch* as "The Snob Papers."

Book of St. Albans (sānt ôl′bạnz). Rhymed treatise on hawking, hunting, and similar sports, printed in English in 1486. It was reprinted by Wynkyn de Worde in 1496. It has been attributed to Juliana Berners, and some of it was certainly written by her. The second edition contains the popular *Treatyse on Fysshynge with an Angle.* It was reprinted many times. The original edition was reprinted in facsimile by Eliot Stock in 1881.

Book of the Dead, The. Collection of prayers, hymns, and magical chants believed to comprise, among other things, the funeral ritual of ancient Egypt. It described the adventures of the soul after death, and the incantations by which it might avoid the lower world's torments. Consisting of 106 chapters, it is the chief extant monument of the religious literature of ancient Egypt. Portions of it were inscribed on mummy cases and tombs, or on papyri which were laid in the grave for the dead to carry with them. It is largely a literary reflection of the Osiris myth, and grew along with the latter. A hieratic text of the XIth dynasty gives two varying versions of the 64th chapter, but only the essence of the work went back to the Old Empire. The rest consisted of additions and glosses, and glosses of glosses, which continued to be made up to the time of the Persians. The oldest portion, of a practical and moral character, contrasts with the mystical tone of the later portions, where the doctrine of justification by faith in Osiris has taken the place of that of good works.

Book of the Duchess. Poem by Geoffrey Chaucer, known also as *The Death of Blanche the Duchess.* The earliest of Chaucer's original poems of any length, it was probably written near the end of 1369, as Blanche, the wife of the duke of Lancaster, died on Sept. 12, 1369. The poem represents the inconsolable grief of the duke, and embodies the story of Ceyx and Alcyone. The duke, John of Gaunt, married again, however, in 1372. The broader outlines of the plot come from Guillaume de Machault's tales, *Dit du Lion* and *Dit de la Fontaine Amoureuse.*

Book of the Dun Cow. See under **Tain Bo Cuailgne.**

Book of Thel (thel), **The.** Prose work by William Blake, published in 1789. The first of his so-called Prophetical Books, it is a mystical treatment of vanity, death, and redemption.

Book of Vices and Virtues, The. Middle English translation in the East Midland dialect of Friar Lorens's *Somme.*

Book of Wonder, The. Narrative (1912) by Lord Dunsany. Like many of his other stories, it is a fantasy laid against a background of the mythology which he had himself invented.

Books. Essay (1858) by Ralph Waldo Emerson. In it he regretted that there was, as such, no professor of books in the colleges of the day and presented his three famous rules for reading: "1. Never read any book that is not a year old. 2. Never read any but famed books. 3. Never read any but what you like."

Books and Characters. Prose work (1922) by Lytton Strachey. It contains a miscellaneous collection of articles originally printed in various periodicals as well as some brilliant sketches of various French personages of the 18th century.

Books and Men. Collection (1888) of essays by Agnes Repplier.

Boole (böl), **Ella Alexander.** b. at Van Wert, Ohio, July 26, 1858; d. at New York, March 13, 1952. American temperance advocate. She headed the New York state Women's Christian Temperance Union (1909–26) and the national W.C.T.U. (1925–33); after serving (1928–31) as vice-president of the world W.C.T.U., she was its president from 1931 until she retired in 1947.

Boole, George. b. at Lincoln, England, Nov. 2, 1815; d. near Cork, Ireland, Dec. 8, 1864. English mathematician and logician, who was professor of mathematics at Queen's College, Cork. His chief works are *Mathematical Analysis of Logic* (1847), *An Investigation of the Laws of Thought* (1854), *Treatise on Differential Equations* (1859), and *Treatise on the Calculus of Finite Difference* (1860).

Boom (bōm). Town in N Belgium, in the province of Antwerp, situated at the junction of the Canal of Brussels and the Rupel River, ab. 10 mi. S of Antwerp: shipyards and brick factories. 19,614 (1947).

Boone (bön). City in C Iowa, county seat of Boone County, ab. 36 mi. NW of Des Moines, in a coal and clay mining area. It is a railroad center; manufactures include building materials, paving brick, reinforced concrete pipe, machinery, brooms, brushes, hosiery thread, and flour. Boone Biblical College is here. The town was laid out (1865) as a rival of Boonesboro, settled in the 1850's, which later became part of Boone. 12,164 (1950).

Boone. Town in NW North Carolina, county seat of Watauga County, in the Blue Ridge Mountains ab. 85 mi. W of Winston-Salem. It is the seat of a state teachers college. 2,973 (1950).

Boone, Daniel. b. in Berks County (near Reading), Pa., Nov. 2, 1734; d. near La Charette, Mo., Sept. 26, 1820. American pioneer in Kentucky. While he was still a boy he was taken by his father to settle on the Yadkin River, in what is now Davidson County, North Carolina. He made explorations of Kentucky in 1764 and 1769, and built (1775) a fort at what was later to be called Boonesboro. He emigrated to Missouri, then a possession of Spain, about 1799. He had great influence in extending American settlement, and in the defense of the Revolutionary frontier.

Boonesboro (bönz′bur″ọ). Village in E central Kentucky, on the Kentucky River ab. 18 mi. SE of Lexington. Here once stood a fort founded by Daniel Boone and his party in April, 1775. The pioneer village was the chief settlement in the region then known as Transylvania, and was frequently besieged by Indian attacks. Only a graveyard remains from this settlement. The modern village is a resort on the river. 167 (1940).

Booneville (bön′vil). Town in NE Mississippi, county seat of Prentiss County, ab. 95 mi. SE of Memphis, Tenn. 3,295 (1950).

Boonsboro (bönz′bur″ọ), **Battle of.** See under **South Mountain.**

Boonton (bön′tọn). Town in N New Jersey, in Morris County, ab. 25 mi. NW of New York: manufactures include hosiery, plastics, dynamite, and gunpowder. It is the site of the reservoir that supplies Jersey City with water. 7,163 (1950).

Boonville (bön′vil). City in SW Indiana, county seat of Warrick County: center of a coal-mining and farming area. 5,092 (1950).

Boonville. City in C Missouri, county seat of Cooper County, on the Missouri River, ab. 43 mi. NW of Jefferson City: seat of Kemper Military School. Nearby was the scene of a battle (June 17, 1861) in which Union forces under Captain Nathaniel Lyon defeated Confederate troops under Colonel John S. Marmaduke. 6,686 (1950).

Boonville. Town (in New York the equivalent of township in many other states) and village in C New York, in Oneida County: distributing center for a dairy-farming area. Pop. of town, 3,593 (1950); of village, 2,329 (1950).

Boorlos (bör′los), **Lake.** See **Burullus, Lake.**

Boosey and Hawkes Limited (bö′si; hôks). Firm of English music publishers and instrument makers, established (1816) by Thomas Boosey under the name of Boosey and Company; the present title dates from a merger (1930) with the firm of Hawkes and Son.

Bootan (bö.tän′, -tan′). See **Bhutan.**

Boötes (bǫ.ō′tēz). Northern constellation containing the first-magnitude star Arcturus, situated behind the Great Bear. It is supposed to represent a man holding a crook and driving the Bear. In modern times the constellation of the Hounds has been interposed between Boötes and the Bear.

Booth (böth). Husband of Amelia, a prominent character in Henry Fielding's novel *Amelia.* Fielding intended, in this character, partly to represent his own follies, improvidence, and weakness.

Booth, Agnes. [Full maiden name, **Marian Agnes Land Rookes.**] b. at Sydney, Australia, Oct. 4, 1846; d. Jan. 2, 1910. American actress. She played with Edwin Forrest in *Richelieu* (c1865), starred in *The Sporting Duchess* (1895–96), and played in Augustus Thomas's dramas, *Afterthought* and *Alabama* (c1891), before making her last appearance in *L'Arlésienne* (1897).

Booth, Ballington. b. at Brighouse, Yorkshire, England, July 28, 1859; d. Oct. 5, 1940. English reformer, founder (1896) and general-in-chief of the Volunteers of America; second son of William Booth and husband of Maud Ballington Booth. He was active (1885–87) in the Salvation Army in Australia and served with it in the U.S. until he left it to establish the Volunteers of America.

Booth, Barton. b. in Lancashire, England, 1681; d. at London, May 10, 1733. English tragedian noted for Shakespearian parts. He first appeared at London in 1700, having previously played in Ireland. He played with Thomas Betterton and with Robert Wilks.

Booth, Catherine. [Called the **"Mother of the Salvation Army"**; maiden name, **Mumford.**] b. at Ashbourne, Derbyshire, England, Jan. 17, 1829; d. at Clacton-on-Sea, Essex, England, Oct. 4, 1890. English woman preacher; wife of William Booth. She is remembered chiefly for her work in defining the position of women in the Salvation Army, and for developing many of its methods. Born of a family of Wesleyans, she was excommunicated (1848) by the Wesleyan Church for being a "reformer." She met and married (1855) William Booth, who was then a minister at Gateshead. In 1860 she published a pamphlet maintaining women's right to preach, and first appeared in her husband's pulpit. Meanwhile, William Booth had resigned his ministry to take up the work of the Revivalist movement, his wife participating everywhere. After the foundation at a London meeting of the Salvation Army (1865) under the name of the Christian Revival Association, Catherine Booth directed her preaching at the wealthy, with a consequent great improvement in the standing of the movement both socially and financially. Author of *Papers on Practical Religion* (1879), *Papers on Aggressive Christianity* (1881), *Papers on Godliness* (1882), *The Salvation Army in Relation to Church and State and Other Addresses* (1883), and *Popular Christianity: a Series of Lectures Delivered in Princes Hall, Piccadilly* (1887).

Booth, Charles. b. at Liverpool, England, March 30, 1840; d. at Whitwick, Leicestershire, England, Nov. 23, 1916. English businessman, shipowner, social reformer, and author of sociological works. Educated at the Liverpool Royal Institution School, he joined, after a short apprenticeship, his brother's firm, Alfred Booth and Company, as a partner, later becoming chairman of the Booth Steamship Company, a post he held until 1912. He began to write when he was 45, and produced books on sociological topics, some of which were instrumental in effecting such social reforms as old-age pensions. Author of *Occupations of the People* (1886), *Labour and Life of the People* (1889), *Life and Labour of the People in London* (17 vols., 1891–1903), *Old Age Pensions* (1899), *Poor Law Reform* (1910), and *Industrial Unrest and Trade Union Policy* (1913).

Booth, Edwin Thomas. b. at Bel Air, Md., Nov. 13, 1833; d. at New York, June 7, 1893. American tragedian; son of Junius Brutus Booth (1796–1852). His first stage appearance as a professional was as Tressel to his father's Richard III, on Sept. 10, 1849. In 1857 he first appeared as a star, at Boston, in the part of Sir Giles Overreach. In 1861 he went to London and played an engagement there. The assassination of Abraham Lincoln by his brother John Wilkes Booth led to his temporary retirement from the stage, but he reappeared as Hamlet on Jan. 3, 1866, at New York, and acted in Shakespearian plays at the Winter Garden Theater until its destruction by fire in 1867. He then erected a theater of his own at New York, which was opened on Feb. 3, 1869, but was financially a failure. In 1880 he again went to London. In 1883 he acted in Germany. In 1886 he began his engagement to play under the management of Lawrence Barrett, and continued to play with him until Barrett's death in 1891. His last appearance was at Brooklyn, on April 4, 1891, in the part of Hamlet. In 1888 he founded, at New York, The Players, a club designed to promote social intercourse between the dramatic and kindred professions, and in its clubhouse he died.

Booth, Evangeline Cory. b. 1865; d. at Hartsdale, N.Y., July 17, 1951. General (1934–39) of the international Salvation Army; daughter of William Booth (1829–1912). She was head of the Army for five years at London and nine years in Canada, before serving as commander (1904–34) in the U.S.; she retired in 1939. Author of the words and music of many Salvation Army songs, she published *Love is All* (1925), *Songs of the Evangel* (1927), *Towards a Better World* (1928), and *Woman* (1930), and was coauthor, with Grace Livingstone Hill, of *The War Romances of the Salvation Army* (1919).

Booth, Florence Eleanor. [Maiden name, **Soper.**] b. at Blaina, Monmouthshire, Wales, Sept. 12, 1861—. British Salvation Army worker; wife of William Bramwell Booth (1856–1929), whom she married in 1882. She began to work for the Army in 1880, and organized the Women's Social Work in 1883.

Booth, George. [Title, 1st Baron **Delamere** or **de la Mer.**] b. 1622; d. at Dunham Massey, England, 1684. English political and military leader, on the side of Parliament during the English Civil War; father of Henry Booth.

Booth, Henry. [Titles: 2nd Baron **Delamere** or **de la Mer,** 1st Earl of **Warrington.**] b. 1652; d. at London, 1694. English politician, chancellor of the exchequer under William III; son of George Booth (1622–84). He was imprisoned (1683) on suspicion of being connected with the Rye House plot, but released on bail; again imprisoned, he was again released in 1685; charged with implication in Monmouth's rebellion, he was committed to the Tower a third time, but acquitted (1685). He fought for William of Orange (1688), and, upon his accession (1689) to the English throne as William III, was appointed chancellor of the exchequer.

Booth, James Curtis. b. at Philadelphia, July 28, 1810; d. March 21, 1888. American chemist. A founder (1878) of the firm of Booth, Garrett and Blair, which gave practical training instruction to analytical chemists, he was professor of applied chemistry at the Franklin Institute, Philadelphia (1836–45) and at the University of Pennsylvania (1851–55). He was appointed (1849) melter and refiner at the Philadelphia mint, and was president (1883–84) of the American Chemical Society. One of the first to analyze sugar and molasses with a polariscope, he was the author of *Our Recent Improvements in the Chemical Arts* (1851). Editor of Belton's translation of Regnault's *Elements of Chemistry* (1852); collaborator on *Encyclopaedia of Chemistry, Practical and Theoretical* (1850).

Booth, John Wilkes. b. at Bel Air, Md., 1838; shot near Bowling Green, Va., April 26, 1865. American actor; son of Junius Brutus Booth (1796–1852), and brother of Edwin Booth. He is remembered as the assassin of Abraham Lincoln at Ford's Theater, Washington (April 14, 1865), although he had been a popular actor. Having made his stage debut at the age of 17, he became a star in 1860, specializing in Shakespearian roles; his acting was acclaimed both by audiences and by other actors. In 1863 he retired from the stage because of a bronchial condition, making only occasional appearances thereafter. His final appearance was in *The Apostate,* on March 18, 1865, at Ford's Theater. Less than a month later, he successfully carried out his plan for the assassination of the president. Having learned that Lincoln was to attend a performance of *Our American Cousin* on the night of April 14, he arranged the plot in the course of that same afternoon. It was provided that two of his accomplices were to kill Vice-President Johnson and Secretary of State Seward on the same evening, but only Booth saw his task to completion. Having prepared the President's box, he entered it shortly after ten o'clock, shot Lincoln through the head, and jumped away from Lincoln's companions, onto the stage, where he shouted, *"Sic semper tyrannis!* The South is avenged!" In his leap, he broke his leg, but managed to escape the theater and ride away on a prearranged route. His broken leg hampered him, and he was discovered, on April 26, 1865, by Union troops, where he and an accomplice were hidden in the barn of a man named Richard H. Garrett, near Rappahannock. The accomplice surrendered immediately, but Booth refused. In the subsequent turmoil, he met his death in a manner that has never been clearly ascertained; he definitely died of a bullet wound, but whether it was self-inflicted or fired by one of the Union men is not known. That the body was indeed that of Booth was proven without a doubt. The overt reason for Booth's assassination of Lincoln was one of patriotism, the killing being to his mind the courageous act of a Southern sympathizer. It has also been suggested, however, that Booth was emotionally unstable, verging on the insane, and was driven to his action by exhibitionism.

Booth, Junius Brutus. b. at London, May 1, 1796; d. on a Mississippi steamboat, Nov. 30, 1852. American actor; father of Edwin Thomas Booth, John Wilkes Booth, and Junius Brutus Booth (1821–83). His first professional appearance was as Campillo, in *The Honeymoon,* in 1813 at Peckham, England; his last, as Sir Edward Mortimer in *The Iron Chest,* Nov. 19, 1852, at New Orleans. His career was brilliant though erratic. His rivalry with Edmund Kean (whom he somewhat resembled) resulted in his departure for America in 1821. On Jan. 13 of that year he married Mary Anne Holmes. He played in America with great success. In 1822 he bought a farm in Harford County, Md., where his family lived, and to which he retired when not acting.

Booth, Junius Brutus. b. at Charleston, S.C., 1821; d. at Manchester, Mass., 1883. American actor; eldest son of Junius Brutus Booth (1796–1852). He was active in the theater both as a manager and as an actor.

Booth, Mary. b. at Hadley Wood, Barnet, England. English Salvation Army worker, who commanded (1924–29) Salvation Army activities in Germany; daughter of William Bramwell Booth. Jointly responsible for Salvation Army work in France during World War I, she was also in charge of that organization's operations in the West Indies, Denmark, and Belgium. She was interned (1940–43) by German authorities during World War II.

Booth, Mary Louise. b. at Yaphank, L.I., N.Y., April 19, 1831; d. March 5, 1889. American translator, historian, and editor, whose *History of the City of New York* (1859) was the first complete account of that subject. She translated from the French *The Marble-Workers' Manual* (1856), *New and Complete Clock and Watch-Makers' Manual* (1860), *The Uprising of a Great People* (1861), *Results of Slavery* (1863), and *Results of Emancipation* (1863); for these books she was commended by President Lincoln and Charles Sumner. She also was editor (1867–88) of *Harper's Bazaar.*

Booth, Maud Ballington. [Maiden name, **Charlesworth.**] b. at Limpsfield, Surrey, England, Sept. 13, 1865; d. at Great Neck, N.Y., Aug. 26, 1948. English writer and welfare worker; wife of Ballington Booth, and his successor as president of the Volunteers of America. She served with the Y.M.C.A. in France and Germany during World War I, and was a founder of the Parent-Teachers Association. Author of *Branded* (1897), *Look Up and Hope, Sleepy Time Stories* (1889), *After Prison—What?* (1905), and others.

Booth, William. [Called **"General Booth."**] b. at Nottingham, England, April 10, 1829; d. near London, Aug. 20, 1912. English preacher, founder of the Salvation Army; husband of Catherine Mumford Booth, and father of Ballington Booth, Evangeline Cory Booth, William Bramwell Booth, and Emma Moss Booth-Tucker. He became a minister of the Methodist New Connexion in 1850, and organized (1865) the Christian Revival Association which, when it had become a large organization formed on military lines, was renamed (1878) the Salvation Army. He established (1880) the *War Cry,* and published *In Darkest England* (1890).

Booth, William Bramwell. b. at Halifax, England, March 8, 1856; d. 1929. English reformer; eldest son of William Booth, husband of Florence Eleanor Booth, and father of Mary Booth. He succeeded his father as head of the Salvation Army in 1912.

Boothauk (böt'hôk). See **Butkhak.**

Boothby (böth'bi), **Guy Newell.** b. at Adelaide, South Australia, Oct. 13, 1867; d. at Bournemouth, England, Feb. 26, 1905. Australian novelist and short-story writer. He lived in England (1874–83), in Australia (1883–94), and again (1894–1905) in England. Among his works are *A Lost Endeavor* (1895), *A Bid for Fortune, or Dr. Nikola's Vendetta* (1895), *A Beautiful White Devil* (1896), *Dr. Nikola* (1896), *Billy Banks, Hero, and other Stories* (1898), *Dr. Nikola's Experiment* (1899), *Farewell, Nikola* (1901), and *On the Wallaby* (1894), a travel book.

Boothia (bö'thi.ạ), **Gulf of.** Continuation of Prince Regent Inlet, N of Canada. It lies between Baffin Island on the E and Boothia Peninsula on the W. Length, 310 mi.

Boothia Peninsula. [Former name, **Boothia Felix** (fē'liks).] Peninsula in the district of Franklin, Northwest Territories, Canada, between Victoria Island and Baffin Island, discovered by John Ross in 1829, and named by him for Sir Felix Booth, who promoted the expedition responsible for its discovery. The north magnetic pole, which Ross believed he had located here, has lately been proven to be on Bathurst Island, to the NW.

Booth-Tucker (böth'tuk'ėr), **Emma Moss.** b. at Gateshead, England, June 8, 1860; d. at Dean Lake, Kan., Oct. 29, 1903. Salvation Army worker; daughter of William Booth. She was in charge of training homes for the Salvation Army from 1880 until her marriage in 1888 to Frederick St. George de Latour Tucker, who at that time assumed also the name of Booth. After some years of missionary work in the Far East, they jointly commanded the Salvation Army in the U.S. from 1896 until Mrs. Booth-Tucker's death in a railroad accident in 1903.

Booth-Tucker, Frederick St. George de Latour. [Original surname, **Tucker.**] b. at Monghyr, India, March 21, 1853; d. 1929. Commander (1896–1905) of the Salvation Army in the U.S. He married Emma Moss Booth (d. 1903), a daughter of William Booth, and prefixed her surname to his own. He established the Salvation Army in India in 1882.

Bootle (bö'tl). County borough in NW England, in Lancashire, situated at the mouth of the river Mersey, ab. 204 mi. NW of London by rail: a suburb of Liverpool, adjoining it on the NW. It has a tin-smelting industry. 74,302 (1951).

Boott (böt), **Francis.** b. at Boston, 1813; d. there, 1904. American composer. His works include a mass, a *Te Deum,* an a capella *Miserere,* a cantata, string quartets, and various sacred and secular songs. He bequeathed 10,000 dollars to Harvard for an annual award for the best choral work in four voices composed by a Harvard graduate.

Boott, Kirk. b. Oct. 20, 1790; d. at Boston, April 11, 1837. American canal builder and pioneer cotton manufacturer. He enlarged (c1796) the Pawtucket Canal, and was later (c1821) an agent of the Merrimack Manufacturing Company. He opened a machine shop which pioneered in American-built locomotives.

Booz (bō'oz). See **Boaz.**

Bo-Peep (bō.pēp'), **Little.** Small shepherdess, in a popular nursery story, who lost her sheep. The term "bo-peep" appears to have been connected at a very early period with sheep. An old ballad of the time of Queen Elizabeth, in a manuscript in the library of Corpus Christi College, Cambridge, has the following lines:

Halfe Englande ys nowght now but shepe,
In everye corner they playe a boe-pepe.

Bopp (bop), **Franz.** b. at Mainz, Germany, Sept. 14, 1791; d. at Berlin, Oct. 23, 1867. German linguist, notable as a founder of the science of comparative philology. He studied Sanskrit at Paris (1812) and published in 1816 his first pioneering work, *Über das Conjugationssystem der Sanskritsprache in Vergleichung mit jenem der griechischen, lateinischen, persischen und germanischen Sprache.* His numerous critical editions, textbooks, and monographs are, however, overshadowed in their importance by his monumental comparative grammar in six parts (1833–52), entitled *Vergleichende Grammatik des Sanskrit, Zend, Griechischen, Lateinischen, Litthauischen, Altslavischen, Gothischen, und Deutschen*, an English translation of which by E. B. Eastwick began to appear in 1845.

Boppard (bop′ärt). [Latin, **Baudobrica, Bodobriga.**] Town in W Germany, in the *Land* (state) of Rhineland-Palatinate, French Zone, formerly in the Rhine Province, Prussia, situated on the Rhine River, ab. 9 mi. S of Koblenz: the center of a district of market gardens, orchards, and vineyards. Because of its beautiful location it is much frequented by tourists; it has the remains of medieval walls and a castle. The Church of Saint Severus (12th–13th centuries) is in the Romanesque style; the Church of the Carmelites (14th century) is in the Gothic style. Originally a Roman military camp (the station of the XIIIth Legion), it was a free imperial city in the Middle Ages; various assemblies of the Diet and of the prince-electors took place here. 7,189 (1946).

Bora (bō′rä), **Katharina von.** b. at Löben, near Merseburg, Germany, Jan. 29, 1499; d. at Torgau, Germany, Dec. 20, 1552. Cistercian nun (1515–23) at Nimptschen, Saxony; wife of Martin Luther, whom she married on June 13, 1525.

Borachia (bō.rä′cha̤). A woman given to drink, a comic and unwholesome character, in the play *A Very Woman*, ascribed to Philip Massinger.

Borachio (bō.rä′chō). A villain, a follower of Don John, in Shakespeare's *Much Ado about Nothing.* Borachio is the Spanish name for a leathern wine-bottle (whence the name is frequently given in old works of literature, either as a proper name or as a mark of opprobrium, to drunkards).

Borah (bō′ra̤), **Mount.** [Also, **Borah Peak.**] Mountain peak in E central Idaho, highest point in Idaho. 12,655 ft.

Borah, William Edgar. b. at Fairfield, Ill., June 29, 1865; d. at Washington, D.C., Jan. 19, 1940. American statesman and lawyer, remembered chiefly as an opponent of America's entrance into the League of Nations and the formation of the World Court, and as instigator (1920–21) of the disarmament conference. After having been admitted (1889) to the bar, he practiced (1891 *et seq.*) law at Boise, Idaho; as a senator (1907–40) from Idaho, he was chairman (1924 *et seq.*) of the Senate Foreign Relations Committee, and served on the Judiciary Committee, the Education and Labor Committee, and the Expenditures in Department of Justice Committee.

Boraq (bō′räk), **al-.** See **Al Borak.**

Borås (bö.rōs′). City in SW Sweden, in the *län* (county) of Älvsborg, ab. 35 mi. E of Göteborg, founded by Gustavus Adolphus in 1632. It has numerous cotton, woolen, and rayon factories; vocational schools, a theater, and a museum. The Caroli Church dates from the 17th century. 58,076 (1950).

Borbeck (bôr′bek). Town in W Germany, in the *Land* (state) of North Rhine-Westphalia, formerly in the Rhine Province, Prussia. It is a northwestern suburb of Essen.

Borberg (bôr′berg), **William.** b. at Copenhagen, Nov. 3, 1885—. Danish diplomat, appointed (1947) permanent delegate to the United Nations. He held (1928–40) the same post at the League of Nations, after having served (1921–26) as secretary of the Danish Legation at London.

Borbón (bôr.bōn′). Spanish spelling of Bourbon, to which house belonged rulers of Spain from Philip V through Alfonso XIII. Other members of this branch included the several princes known as Don Carlos, and Carlota of Portugal.

Borbón y Battenberg (ē bät′e̤n.berk), **Jaime de.** [Title, Duke of **Segovia.**] b. at San Ildefonso, Spain, 1908—. Eldest living son of Alfonso XIII of Spain. Though born a deaf mute, he was in line for succession to the throne until he renounced (1933) his claim to the title in favor of his brother Juan de Borbón y Battenberg (Don Juan). He has lately renewed his claim in behalf of the eldest son of his first marriage, Alfonso Jaime de Borbón y Segovia, while his second wife, a German commoner, has offered to be divorced in order to make possible the reëstablishment of his claim for himself. Don Jaime has some following among monarchists in Spain, and was enthusiastically hailed in Madrid in 1947, when he was the first member of the exiled royal family to set foot on Spanish soil after 1931.

Borbón y Battenberg, Juan de. [Title, Prince of **Asturias**; used title of Count of **Barcelona** until 1933.] b. at San Ildefonso, Spain, 1913—. Pretender to the Spanish throne; third son of Alfonso XIII. He made his first speech as pretender on March 8, 1941. Of his two elder brothers, Alfonso, Prince of Asturias, died of hemophilia in 1938, having renounced his claim to the succession upon his marriage to a Cuban commoner, and Jaime de Borbón y Battenberg (Don Jaime), second son of Alfonso XIII, renounced his claim in 1933, but later changed his mind. "Juan III" (as he is now hailed by his supporters) is undoubtedly the strongest candidate among the pretenders to the Spanish throne. Sharing his family's exile in 1931, he served in the British navy, intrigued briefly with General Mola in 1936, took up headquarters in Switzerland during World War II and, in 1945, moved to Estoril in Portugal. From there he has continued intermittently to criticize the Franco regime. In 1935 he married the infanta Maria Mercedes of Bourbon Sicily, and the marriage produced two sons and two daughters. In 1947 Don Juan met Generalissimo Francisco Franco aboard a yacht off the coast of Galicia and reached an agreement regarding the education of his eldest son, Juan Carlos de Borbón y Borbón, at Madrid. No agreement regarding the restoration of the monarchy resulted, and in 1950 the policy of the Spanish government appeared to be still one of keeping the monarchists divided and of persecuting them wherever they were too strong (although, in the next year, Franco made a cautious, very much qualified offer of the throne to Juan Carlos).

Borbón y Borbón (bôr.bōn′ ē bôr.bōn′), **Juan Carlos de.** [Title, Prince of **Asturias.**] b. 1938—. Eldest son and heir apparent of Don Juan de Borbón y Battenberg, pretender to the Spanish throne. In 1950 he was being educated at Madrid under the terms of an agreement between his father and Generalissimo Francisco Franco. In 1951, Franco indicated, with many qualifications, that the throne might be made available to him.

Borchard (bôr′cha̤rd), **Edwin.** b. at New York, Oct. 17, 1884; d. at Hamden, Conn., July 22, 1951. American expert in international law. He was appointed (1917) a professor in the Yale Law School. He also served as a U.S. technical adviser (1930) at the Conference on Codification of International Law, and U.S. member on the Committee of Experts for the Inter-American Codification of International Law. His works include *Guide to Law and Legal Literature of Germany* (1911), *The Diplomatic Protection of Citizens Abroad* (1915), *Convicting the Innocent* (1932), and *Bibliography of International Law and Continental Law;* coauthor, with W. P. Lage, of *Neutrality for the United States* (1937).

Borchardt (bôr′ċhärt), **Ludwig.** b. at Berlin, Oct. 5, 1863; d. at Paris, Aug. 12, 1938. German Egyptologist. He served (1906 *et seq.*) as director of the German institute of Egyptian archaeology at Cairo. Author of *Die ägyptische Pflanzensäule* (The Egyptian Plantiform Column, 1897), and of books describing Egyptian tombs excavated under his direction.

Borchardt, Rudolf. b. at Königsberg, in East Prussia, June 9, 1877; d. 1945. German poet and translator. Although he was not in the circle surrounding Stefan George, he was in touch with its members and had much the same aims as a writer. The range of his translations was remarkable: from Latin, Tacitus' *Germania* (1914); from the Greek, *Altionische Götterlieder* (1924) and *Pindarische Gedichte* (1930); from Old French, *Die grossen Trobadors* (1924); from Middle High German, *Der arme Heinrich* of Hartmann von Aue (1925); from Italian, the *Divina Commedia* (1930); from English, Swinburne's poems. He set forth his ideas on style in *Gespräch über Formen* (1905) and *Rede über Hofmannsthal* (1918). Particularly worthy of mention are his medieval epic *Der Durant* (1921), his *Vermischte Gedichte* (1924), and his essays.

Borchert (bôr′ċhert), **Wolfgang.** b. at Hamburg, Germany, 1921; d. in Switzerland, 1947. German story writer and poet. His career as an actor was cut short by World War II, in which he served in the Russian campaign. From imprisonment (to which he was twice condemned for criticism of the German government) he was released by American troops in 1945, but, broken in health, he died soon afterward. His lyrics are contained in *Laterne, Nacht und Sterne* (1946); his one play was *Draussen vor der Tür* (1947); his stories are collected in *Die Hundeblume* and *An diesem Dienstag* (both 1947).

Borchgrevink (bôrk'grā''vingk), **Carsten Egeberg.** b. at Christiania (now Oslo), Norway, 1864; d. 1934. Norwegian antarctic explorer. He emigrated (1888) to Australia and worked there for several years as a surveyor and teacher; in 1894 he made a voyage to the antarctic seas on a whaler, and commanded (1898–1900) an antarctic expedition (in the *Southern Cross*) which attained lat. 78°50′ S. (in King Edward VII Land), the southernmost point which had been reached up to that time. He also determined the approximate position of the south magnetic pole. He wrote *First on the Antarctic Continent: an Account of the British Antarctic Expedition 1898–1900* (1901).

Borchhorst (bôrċh'hôrst). See **Borghorst.**

Borcke (bôr'kẹ), **Caspar Wilhelm von.** b. at Gersdorf, in Pomerania, Germany, Aug. 30, 1704; d. March 8, 1747. Prussian diplomat (at one time ambassador to London) who is now remembered chiefly for the fact that he was the first to translate a play of Shakespeare's into German. His translation of *Julius Caesar* in Alexandrines appeared in 1741. It was reviled by Johann Christoph Gottsched, the literary arbiter of the day, but it served to make Shakespeare known in Germany. Gottsched's attack was against Shakespeare, not against the translator or manner of translation.

Borda (bôr.dȧ), **Jean Charles.** b. at Dax, Landes, France, May 4, 1733; d. at Paris, Feb. 20, 1799. French mathematician and naval officer, known for his researches in nautical astronomy and hydrodynamics.

Bordeaux (bôr.dō). [Latin, **Burdegala, Burdigala, Bordigala.**] Industrial and commercial seaport city in SW France, the capital of the department of Gironde, situated on both banks of the Garonne River at the point where the river forms a vast estuary. It is the fifth largest city of France and the country's third largest seaport. It has a large harbor, with quays, shipyards, ship-repair shops, and a famous bridge. The commerce of the port is carried on chiefly with the Atlantic and Baltic ports of Europe, with India, Africa, and the Americas. Its trade is in wines (for which Bordeaux is especially known), liquors, metals, grain, coal, timber, and colonial products; Bordeaux has also been known for the manufacture of dyes, pottery, textiles, drugs, and rope. The part of the city surrounding the Place de la Bourse and particularly the harbor installations were heavily damaged by air raids made in preparation for the Allied invasion of France in 1944. As a result, the traffic of the harbor fell from 5,354 vessels carrying 7,318,463 tons (1938) to 1,675 vessels and 4,160,348 tons (1946). There are various industries among which machine factories (including airplane construction works) and food-processing plants are predominant. There are several notable medieval churches, the ruins of a Gallo-Roman amphitheater, an art museum, a museum of antiquities, a library, and a theater dating from the 18th century. Bordeaux, once the leading Roman city in Gaul, passed through the period of the barbaric invasions and flourished under British rule. The kings of France rescinded the town's privileges, and the ensuing revolt was cruelly repressed. Ever since that time, Bordeaux has remained a seat of regionalistic sentiment in France. It participated in the Fronde, opposed Louis XIV, and revolted (1793) against the revolutionary convention in the period of the Gironde. Conversely, Bordeaux served several times as a refuge for the national government in periods of stress. It was the seat of a provisional government in 1870–71, and again from September to December, 1914; in 1940 it witnessed the abortive attempt of the cabinet of Paul Reynaud to establish a center of resistance against the advance of the German armies. 253,751 (1946).

Bordeaux, Duc de. See **Chambord,** Comte de.

Bordeaux, Henry. b. at Thonon-les-Bains, France, Jan. 9, 1870—. French novelist and critic, of strong Catholic and conservative views. His works include the novels *Jeanne Michelin* (1896), *La Peur de vivre* (1902; Eng. trans., *The Fear of Living,* 1913), *Les Roquevillard* (1906; Eng. trans., *The Will to Live,* 1915), *La Croisée des chemins* (1909; Eng. trans., *The Parting of the Ways,* 1911), and *La Neige sur les pas* (1912; Eng. trans., *The Footprints Beneath the Snow,* 1913), as well as many volumes of essays, children's stories, books about events of World War I, and much dramatic criticism. He was drama critic (1910–21) for the *Revue hebdomadaire,* and was elected to the French Academy in 1920.

Bordelais (bôr.dẹ.le). [Latin, **Burdigalensis** (from *Burdigala,* Bordeaux).] Historical subdivision of France, now comprised in the departments of Gironde and Landes.

Bordelon (bôr.dẹ.lôṅ), **Laurent.** b. at Bourges, France, 1653; d. at Paris, April 6, 1730. French dramatist and theologian.

Borden (bôr'dẹn), Sir **Frederick William.** b. at Cornwallis, Nova Scotia, Canada, May 14, 1847; d. at Canning, Nova Scotia, Jan. 6, 1917. Canadian statesman who served as minister of militia and defense (1896–1911). During his regime the last British troops were withdrawn (1901) from Canada, and the practice of appointing a British general officer to command the militia ceased. He was also a Canadian Liberal member of Parliament (1874–82; 1887–1911), and a physician, educated at Harvard University.

Borden, Gail. b. at Norwich, N.Y., Nov. 9, 1801; d. at Borden, Texas, Jan. 11, 1874. American surveyor and inventor, who developed (c1851) a meat biscuit and a process (1853) for condensing milk. He superintended (c1833) the surveys of Stephen Fuller Austin's Texas colony, and drew the first topographical map of the Republic of Texas. He also surveyed and laid out (c1839) the city of Galveston, Texas. To produce his condensed-milk product, he opened (1861) the first American condensing plant at Wassaic, N.Y.; he also received (1862) patents for concentrating cider, juices, and fruits.

Borden, Lizzie Andrew. b. 1860; d. June 2, 1927. Daughter of a wealthy banker of Fall River, Mass., who was accused of murdering her father and stepmother. After the discovery (Aug. 4, 1892) of their bodies bludgeoned to death with an ax, she became the central figure in a celebrated trial, and was finally acquitted (June 20, 1893); the murder remains still unsolved. The fame of this case inspired the play *Nine Pine Street* (1933), the novel *A Study in Conjecture* (1939) by Mrs. Belloc Lowndes, and the ballet *Fall River Legend* (1948) by Agnes de Mille.

Borden, Richard. b. at Freetown, Mass., April 12, 1795; d. Feb. 25, 1874. American manufacturer. A cofounder (1821) of the Fall River Iron Works, he was also influential in the organization of the Fall River-Providence (1827) and the Fall River-New York (1847) steamship lines, and of several railroad lines which served to connect Fall River more closely with other New England centers.

Borden, Sir **Robert Laird.** b. at Grand Pré, Nova Scotia, Canada, June 26, 1854; d. June 10, 1937. Canadian lawyer and statesman, prime minister of Canada from 1911 until 1920. He was a member of Parliament for Halifax and for Carleton, and became leader of the Conservative Party in the House of Commons in 1901. After representing (1919) Canada at the Paris Peace Conference after World War I, he served on the League of Nations Council.

Borden, Simeon. b. at Fall River, Mass., Jan. 29, 1798; d. Oct. 28, 1856. American civil engineer, inventor, and surveyor. He constructed (1830) a base bar for base-line measurement, used in an official map survey of the city of Boston (of which he was chief surveyor in the period 1834–41). He surveyed the line between Rhode Island and Massachusetts to settle a boundary dispute between these states that reached the Supreme Court in 1844. Author of *A System of Useful Formulae* (1851).

Borden Island. Northernmost island of the Parry island group, in the Arctic Archipelago, N Canada, named for Sir Robert Laird Borden, one-time prime minister of Canada. It is N of Melville Island. Area, 4,068 sq. mi.

Bordentown (bôr'dẹn.toun). City in C New Jersey, in Burlington County, on the Delaware River, ab. 6 mi. SE of Trenton: manufactures include bricks, dyes, ice cream, and overalls. Bordentown was an important river port and transportation center in the 18th and 19th centuries. It was at one time the residence of Thomas Paine; Joseph Bonaparte lived here (1816–39) as the Comte de Survilliers. It is the seat of Bordentown Military Institute. 5,497 (1950).

Border. Name usually applied to the region along both sides of the boundary between England and Scotland; sometimes the term is used to mean the area on the Scottish side only. From earliest historic times different peoples and nationalities, different languages and customs, and different sovereignties have met along the Border, with a consequent high incidence of violence and warfare. The actual boundary line, which now begins N of Berwick on the E coast and runs generally SW along the Tweed and other rivers and the watershed of the Cheviot Hills to the Solway Firth, was not officially fixed until 1552. The distance in a direct line between its NE and SW ends is only 70 miles, but numerous irregularities make the actual boundary 108 miles long. The counties of Northumberland and Cumberland in England, and of Berwickshire, Roxburghshire, and Dumfriesshire in Scotland, lie along the Border, and in addition Selkirkshire and Peeblesshire in Scotland are traditionally considered as part of the Border. The region S of the boundary consists largely of high moors with many wild glens, a terrain suitable for cattle and sheep, but to the N there are broad valleys and many fertile areas. In both English and Scottish literature, the Border has been a fertile source of legend, romance, and balladry. Formerly, it was divided into East, West, and Middle Marches, and for some centuries both before and after the union of the English and Scottish crowns, there was in each march an English warden and a Scots warden, who met periodically (and generally in an amicable spirit) to confer on measures for keeping the peace. In the late 18th century, and for much of the 19th, the Border was the scene of another sort of romance, being much resorted to by eloping couples who found it convenient to be married at Gretna Green and other Border towns. Sir Walter Scott's *Minstrelsy of the Scottish Border* and *Border Antiquities of England and Scotland* are two among many books which preserve a record of the exciting history and legendry of this famous region.

Border Antiquities of England and Scotland, The. Prose work (1817) by Sir Walter Scott. It describes the scenery and architecture of the region known as the Border.

Border Beagles, a Tale of Mississippi. Romance by William Gilmore Simms, published in 1840 as a sequel to *Richard Hurdis* (1838). It is one of his series of Border Romances.

Borderers, The. Play by William Wordsworth. Written in the period 1796–97, it was not published until 1842, and no early draft exists to show how much it may have been revised in the meantime (although a preface, long believed to be lost, has now been recovered). The work is of slight moment as a drama but of great importance as a milestone in Wordsworth's life both as a poet and as a person who had taken more than a passing interest in the rationalist philosophies of 18th-century France; this play clearly reflects the transition in Wordsworth's point of view which took place in the autumn of 1795, when he began to turn away from France and Godwinism to a political philosophy more in harmony with Burke, and to the loveliness of the natural world. Its story of the villain Oswald who, after committing a crime, banishes remorse by condemning all human feeling as weakness, and thus becomes a malignant moral skeptic, is intended to demonstrate that though the attempt to live by the light of reason may be a noble aspiration, yet to discard affections and "prejudices" leaves not reason but the passions supreme.

Border Romances. Series of novels by William Gilmore Simms, including *Guy Rivers* (1834), *Richard Hurdis* (1838), *Border Beagles* (1840), and *Voltmeier; or, The Mountain Men* (1869).

Border Slave State Convention. See **Conference Convention.**

Border States. Formerly the slave states of Delaware, Maryland, Virginia, Kentucky, and Missouri, situated near the free states; in a wider meaning the name comprised also North Carolina, Tennessee, and Arkansas.

Border War. In U.S. history, the name applied to the armed clashes (1854–59) between proslavery and antislavery elements in the Kansas Territory. Although differences over land claims also played their part, the slavery controversy was never absent. Guerrilla bands and associations of regulators were formed on both sides, and were responsible for individual and group murders, lynchings, robbery, and plundering. Among the best-known episodes of the war are the "sack of Lawrence" (May 21, 1856), and the Potawatomie massacre (May 24–25, 1856) perpetrated by John Brown. Proslavery inhabitants of western Missouri who actively intervened in Kansas for the establishment there of the institution of slavery were popularly called "border ruffians." The last massacre of the era of "bleeding Kansas" was the murder (May 19, 1858) of nine (some authorities say eleven) free-state men at Marais des Cygnes, near Ottawa, Kan.

Bordes (bôrd), **Charles.** b. at La Roche-Corbon, France, May 12, 1863; d. at Toulon, France, Nov. 8, 1909. French composer, organist, and cofounder (1894) of the Schola Cantorum at Paris. He was appointed organist at Nogent-sur-Marne (1887), and at Saint Gervais at Paris (1890) where he established (1892) the "Chanteurs de Saint Gervais." He wrote orchestral works, piano pieces, and songs.

Bordet (bôr.de), **Jules Jean Baptiste Vincent.** b. at Soignies, France, June 13, 1870—. Belgian bacteriologist. Graduated (1892) from the University of Brussels, he conducted important studies (1894–1901) at the Pasteur Institute at Paris, and in 1907 became full professor at the University of Brussels; at Brussels he was also founder and director of the Institut Pasteur de Brabant. He became a pioneer in the theory of serology and immunity reactions, discovered (1898) bacterial hemolysis, described phagocytosis (1895), anaphylaxis (1913), and fixation of the complement (1900, together with Octave Gengou), and in a classical work (1895) described the properties of sera of immunized animals. He also discovered (1906) the bacillus pertussis, the etiologic agent of whooping cough, and won the Nobel prize in medicine (1919) for his discoveries in the field of immunity. Author of *Studies in Immunity* (1909), *Traité de l'immunité* (1920), *Traité de l'immunité dans les maladies infectieuses* (1920), *The Theories of Blood Coagulation* (1921), and *Infection et immunité* (1947).

Bordewijk (bôr'dẹ.wīk), **Frans.** b. 1884—. Dutch novelist and lawyer. His early writing was influenced by the works of Edgar Allan Poe. In the Poe vein he wrote *Fantastische Vertellingen* (Fantastic Stories, 3 vols., 1919–24). In an abrupt and yet magical style he wrote *Blokken* (1931), a satire on collectivism; *Knorrende Beesten* (Grunting Beasts, 1933), on auto races; and *Bint* (1934), all revealing the essence of relations between men. The same is true of the more realistic novels *Karakter* (Character, 1938), *Rood Paleis* (Red Palace, 1937), *Noorderlicht* (Northern Light, 1948), and in collaboration, *Sumbo N.V., spel van olie, dood en leven* (Sumbo Inc., a Play of Oil, Life and Death, 1938).

Bordigala (bôr.dig'ạ.lạ). A Latin name of **Bordeaux.**

Bordighera (bôr.dē.gā'rä). Town and commune in NW Italy, in the *compartimento* (region) of Liguria, in the province of Imperia, situated on the Riviera di Ponente, between San Remo and Ventimiglia: one of the most frequented winter resorts on the Ligurian coast, owing to its mild climate. It has many date palms, and exports young palm trees and palm leaves for use on Palm Sunday. Pop. of commune, 7,347 (1936); of town, 5,978 (1936).

Bordone (bôr.dō'nā), **Paris.** b. at Treviso, Italy, c1500; d. at Venice, c1571. Italian painter of the Venetian school; a pupil of Titian. His best-known painting is *The Fisherman Extending a Ring to the Doge.*

Boré (bô.rā'), **Jean Étienne.** b. Dec. 27, 1741; d. Feb. 2, 1820. American sugar planter, who pioneered (1795 *et seq.*) in the sugar industry in the Louisiana region. He was the first mayor (1803) of New Orleans, after the transfer of Louisiana from Spain to France.

Boreas (bō'rẹ.ạs). In Greek mythology, the personification of the north wind. He was a son either of Aeolus or of Astraeus and Eos, and brother of Hesperus, Zephyrus, and Notus. He was identified by the Romans with their Aquilo.

Borel (bo.rel), **Félix Édouard Émile.** b. at St.-Affrique, Aveyron, France, Jan. 7, 1871—. French mathematician, professor at Paris, laureate of the Académie des Sciences, and author of books on the theory of functions. He has also been active politically, serving (1924–36) in the Chamber of Deputies as a Radical-Socialist; in 1937, he became minister of the navy. Under the Vichy regime he was arrested (c1940). His works include *Leçons sur la théorie des fonctions* (1898), *Leçons sur les séries divergentes* (1901), *Leçons sur les fonctions mésomorphes* (1903), *Leçons sur les fonctions de variables réelles* (1905), *Eléments de la théorie des probabilités* (1909), and *Méthodes et problèmes de la théorie des fonctions* (1922).

Borel, Pétrus. [Full name, **Joseph Pétrus Borel d'Hauterive.**] b. at Lyons, France, June 28, 1809; d. at Mostaganem, Algeria, July 14, 1859. French journalist and man of letters. He was the author of *Campavert*, a collection of stories, and of *Madame Putiphar*, a novel with a preface in verse.

Borelli (bō.rel'lē), **Giovanni Alfonso.** b. at Castelnuovo, near Naples, Italy, Jan. 28, 1608; d. at Rome, Dec. 31, 1679. Italian astronomer, professor of mathematics at Messina and later at Pisa. He was a founder of the so-called iatrophysical (or iatromathematical) school in Italian medicine (this was a group that sought to explain disease in terms of physics rather than chemistry). He is believed to have been the first to describe the parabolic path of comets. His chief work is *De motu animalium* (1680–81).

Boreman (bōr'man), **Arthur Ingram.** b. July 24, 1823; d. April 19, 1896. American lawyer and political leader, first governor of West Virginia. Admitted (1845) to the bar, he was a member of the Virginia House of Delegates, and present at the secession convention (1861). When Virginia voted to secede, he met with followers at Wheeling to reorganize the Virginia government. West Virginia was shortly afterwards admitted as a separate state and he served (1862–68) as its governor, and thereafter (1869–75) as a U.S. senator.

Borger (bôr'chėr). Town in NE Netherlands, in the province of Drenthe, SE of Assen: agricultural community. 10,129 (1939).

Borger (bôr'gėr). City in NW Texas, in Hutchinson County, in the Panhandle near Oklahoma, NE of Amarillo: produces oil, natural gas, and petroleum byproducts. 18,059 (1950).

Borgerhout (bôr'chėr.hout). Town in N Belgium, in the province of Antwerp, E of Antwerp, of which it is a suburb: has establishments for the polishing of diamonds, textile mills, and other industries. 50,877 (1947).

Borges (bôr'hās), **Jorge Luis.** b. at Buenos Aires, 1899—. Argentine poet who brought (1921) the exotic modernism of *ultraísmo* home with him from Spain, where he had participated (1918) in that short-lived movement. His poetry is marked by unique descriptiveness and intense patriotism. He is the author of *Fervor de Buenos Aires* (1923) and *Luna de enfrente* (1925).

Borgese (bôr.jā'zā), **Giuseppe Antonio.** b. at Polizzi Generosa, Palermo, Sicily, Nov. 12, 1882; d. at Fiesole, Italy, Dec. 4, 1952. Italian scholar and author, a naturalized citizen of the U.S. after 1938. He married (1939) Elizabeth Mann, daughter of Thomas Mann. A graduate (1903) of the University of Florence, he was professor (1910–17) of German literature at the University of Rome, before serving as head (1917–18) of the Italian Press and Propaganda Bureau. He served as professor of German literature (1917–25) and of esthetics and the history of criticism (1926–31) at the University of Milan, but left Italy because he refused Fascist allegiance, and came (1931) to the U.S., where he became (1936) professor of Italian literature at the University of Chicago. In 1945 he was named secretary of the Committee to Frame a World Constitution. He was author of poetry, fiction, literary criticism, and books on history and philosophy, including *Storia della Critica Romantica* (1905), *Rubè* (1921), *On Dante Criticism* (1936), *Goliath, the March of Fascism* (1937), and *Common Cause* (1943).

Borghese (bôr.gā'zā). Name of a family famous at Rome during the period of the Renaissance. Of Sienese origin, they first appear in the records in 1238. Marcantonio Borghese, a jurisconsult who became attached to the papal court early in the 16th century, established the family at Rome, where one of his sons, Camillo, became Pope under the name of Paul V, and another, Francesco, was commander of the papal troops. The Pope secured important titles of nobility for his nephew Marc Antonio, and by his influence another nephew, Scipione, became a cardinal. Marc Antonio's son Paolo married Olimpia, the heiress of the important family of Aldobrandini, Paolo's son Giovanni Battista was ambassador of Philip V to Rome, and Giovanni Battista's son Marc Antonio was for a time viceroy of Naples. A later Marc Antonio Borghese was a noted art collector. Camillo Filippo Ludovico Borghese married Maria Paulina Bonaparte, sister of Napoleon I, and sold to the latter much of the Borghese collection of Italian art.

Borghese, Prince **Camillo Filippo Ludovico.** b. at Rome, July 19, 1775; d. at Florence, May 9, 1832. Italian nobleman. By his marriage (Aug. 28, 1803) to Maria Paulina Bonaparte he was a brother-in-law of Napoleon I.

Borghese, Scipione. [Original name, **Scipione Caffarelli.**] d. 1633. Italian cardinal. He was a nephew of Camillo Borghese, who became Pope Paul V, and it was by his influence that Scipione was made a cardinal. He is best remembered for having built the Villa Borghese at Rome and for beginning the collection of art treasures which it housed. Many of these were removed to France c1803 after being sold to Napoleon I by Camillo Filippo Ludovico Borghese, who married one of Napoleon's sisters, but these were subsequently returned. The Villa Borghese recently became known also as the Villa Umberto I, and is the property of the government of Italy. Many paintings formerly displayed in the Borghese Palace are now housed in the Villa Borghese.

Borghese, Villa. See under **Borghese, Scipione.**

Borghese Gladiator. [Also: **Borghese Warrior, Fighting Gladiator.**] Ancient Greek statue by Agasias of Ephesus, representing a warrior or an athlete. It is in the collection of the Louvre, Paris, having formerly been in the collection of the Villa Borghese, Rome. It dates from about the beginning of the Christian era. The vigorous figure, undraped, is in an attitude of rapid advance, the left arm, encircled by the shield-strap, raised above the head, and the right (restored) extended downward and backward in the line of the body, grasping the sword.

Borghese Mars. Antique statue of Mars in the collection of the Louvre, at Paris.

Borghese Palace. Palace of the Borghese family at Rome, in the Via della Fontanella, noted for its art collections. It was built toward the end of the 16th century by Martino Lunghi and Flaminio Ponzio. Its galleries contained originally the most important art treasures of Rome, save those of the Vatican; many of them were later removed to the Villa Borghese, Rome, which became the property of the government.

Borghesi (bôr.gā'zē), Count **Bartolommeo.** b. at Savignano, near Rimini, Italy, July 11, 1781; d. at San Marino, Italy, April 16, 1860. Italian numismatist and epigraphist. He wrote *Nuovi frammenti dei fasti consolari capitolini* (1818–20) and others.

Borghi-Mamo (bôr'gē.mä'mō), **Adelaide.** b. at Bologna, Italy, Aug. 9, 1829; d. there, Sept. 29, 1901. Italian opera singer. A mezzo-soprano, she performed at London, Paris, Lisbon, Madrid, and many Italian cities.

Borghorst (bôrk'hôrst). [Also, **Borchhorst.**] Town and commune in W Germany, in the *Land* (state) of North Rhine-Westphalia, British Zone, formerly in the province of Westphalia, Prussia, N of Münster: agricultural community. 14,723 (1950).

Borgia (bôr'jä). [Spanish, **Borja.**] Spanish-Italian family of great prominence in Europe from the late 14th through the early 16th centuries. Its best-known members were: Alfonso (1378–1458), who became Pope under the title of Calixtus III (1455–58); Alfonso's nephew Rodrigo (c1431–1503), better known as Pope Alexander VI (1492–1503); and Alexander's children, Giovanni (d. 1497), Cesare (c1476–1507), cardinal and soldier, and Lucrezia (1480–1519).

Borgia, Alfonso. Original name of Pope **Calixtus III.**

Borgia, Cesare. [Title, Duke of **Valentinois.**] b. c1476; killed before the castle of Viana, Spain, March 12, 1507. Italian ruler; natural son of Rodrigo Lenzuoli Borgia (Pope Alexander VI). He was created (1492) a cardinal by his father. In 1497 he procured the murder of his brother Giovanni Borgia, Duke of Gandia. Having resigned (1497) the cardinalate, he was invested (1498) with the duchy of Valentinois by Louis XII, and married

(1499) Charlotte d'Albret, daughter of Jean d'Albret, king of Navarre. He was created (1501) duke of Romagna by his father, after having reduced by force and perfidy the cities of Romagna, which were ruled by feudatories of the Papal See; with the assistance of his family, he endeavored to found an independent hereditary power in central Italy, including Romagna, Umbria, and the Marches. His father having died in 1503, he was detained in captivity by Pope Julius II (1503–04) and by Ferdinand of Aragon (1504–06), until he escaped to the court of Jean d'Albret of Navarre, in whose service he fell before the castle of Viana. Handsome in person, educated, eloquent, a patron of learning, and an adept in the cruel and perfidious politics in vogue in his day, his methods are described with approval by Machiavelli in his *Principe*.

Borgia, Saint **Francesco.** [Spanish, **Francisco de Borja;** title, Duke of **Gandia.**] b. at Gandia, Spain, c1510; d. at Rome, 1572. General of the Society of Jesus (1565–72); great-grandson of Pope Alexander VI. He entered (1527) the service of Charles V of Spain, and was vice-regent (1539–40) of Catalonia. His correspondence with Ignatius Loyola aroused his interest in the Jesuit order, which he entered in 1546, renouncing his secular connections, and making large gifts to the Society of Jesus. Before becoming its general, he was active in Spain, where he won many converts.

Borgia, Lucrezia. [Title, Duchess of **Ferrara.**] b. 1480; d. June 24, 1519. Daughter of Pope Alexander VI, and sister of Cesare Borgia. She married Giovanni Sforza, lord of Pesaro, in 1493. This marriage was annulled by Alexander, who found (1498) a more ambitious match for her in Alfonso of Aragon, a natural son of Alfonso II of Naples. Alfonso having been murdered by Cesare Borgia in 1500, she married (1501) Alfonso of Este, who subsequently succeeded to the duchy of Ferrara. She was a woman of great beauty and ability, a patron of learning and the arts. She was long accused of the grossest crimes, but later writers have cleared her reputation of the worst charges brought against her.

Borgia, Rodrigo Lanzol y. Original name of Pope **Alexander VI.**

Borgia, Stefano. b. at Velletri, Italy, Dec. 3, 1731; d. at Lyons, France, Nov. 23, 1804. Italian cardinal, statesman, historian, and patron of science. He was secretary of propaganda in the period 1770–88.

Borglum (bôr'glum), **Gutzon.** [Full name, **John Gutzon de la Mothe Borglum.**] b. March 25, 1867; d. 1941. American sculptor and painter; brother of Solon Hannibal Borglum. He was educated at the school of the Art Association at San Francisco, and at the Julian Academy and the École des Beaux-Arts at Paris. His bronze group *The Mares of Diomedes* won a gold medal at the Louisiana Purchase Exposition in 1904, and was purchased by the Metropolitan Museum of Art, New York. His works include a massive head of Lincoln for the Capitol, Washington, D.C., a Sheridan monument, Washington, D.C., figures for the Cathedral of Saint John the Divine, New York, and the Mount Rushmore memorial group, in South Dakota (federally authorized, financed by the state), consisting of portraits of Washington, Jefferson, Lincoln, and Theodore Roosevelt carved in the mountain stone (and actually finished after his death by his son). A Civil War memorial begun on Stone Mountain, Georgia, was abandoned because of various disagreements between Borglum and the association which had commissioned the memorial.

Borglum, Solon Hannibal. b. 1868; d. 1922. American sculptor; brother of Gutzon Borglum. His subjects were chiefly the people and animals of the old West. His *On the Border of the White Man's Land* is in the Metropolitan Museum of Art, New York; *Lassoing Wild Horses* is in the Cincinnati Museum.

Borgne (bôrn), **Lake.** Bay in SE Louisiana, the continuation of Mississippi Sound. It communicates with the Gulf of Mexico on the E, and with Lake Pontchartrain, by the Rigolets Pass, on the NW. Width, ab. 25 mi.

Borgo (bōr'gō). [German, **Burgen;** ancient name, **Ausugum.**] Town and commune in NE Italy, in the *compartimento* (region) of Trentino-Alto Adige, in the province of Trento, situated on the Brenta River, ab. 17 mi. E of Trent. It is one of the chief places in the Val Sugana district and a summer resort; a number of feudal castles are in the vicinity. Pop. of commune, 9,597 (1936); of town, 4,056 (1936).

Borgogna (bôr.gō'nyä). Italian name of **Burgundy.**

Borgognone (bôr.gō.nyō'nā), **Ambrogio.** [Also: **Bergognone;** original surname **Stefani** (or **di Stefano**) **da Fossano.**] b. 1455; d. 1535. Italian painter. He is known today chiefly for his decorations in the Certosa, a Carthusian monastery at Pavia, Italy, the most admired of these being a *Crucifixion.* Examples of his work may also be seen in the Louvre at Paris, the National Gallery at London, and the Berlin Museum, but more numerous works have remained in Italy, and are especially to be found at Pavia, Milan, Lodi, and Bergamo.

Borgomanero (bōr"gō.mä.nā'rō). Town and commune in NW Italy, in the *compartimento* (region) of Piedmont, in the province of Novara, situated near the S end of Lago Maggiore and Lago di Orta, ab. 19 mi. NW of Milan. It has silk and cotton textile, metallurgical, and ceramics industries. Pop. of commune, 13,434 (1936); of town, 7,669 (1936).

Borgoña (bôr.gō'nyä). Spanish name of **Burgundy.**

Borgo San Donnino (bōr'gō sän dōn.nē'nō). Former name of **Fidenza.**

Borgo San Lorenzo (lō.ren'tsō). Town and commune in C Italy, in the *compartimento* (region) of Tuscany, in the province of Firenze, situated in the Apennines, on the Sieve River, NE of Florence. It is a station on the railroad line from Florence to Faënza. The town produces artistic majolica and glassware; it is a summer resort, with sulfur springs in the vicinity. Walls and towers have been preserved from medieval times. The Church of San Giovanni Maggiore has an altar which is one of the oldest examples of Florentine Romanesque art. Pop. of commune, 16,805 (1936); of town, 5,555 (1936).

Borgosesia (bōr.gō.se'zyä). Town and commune in NW Italy, in the *compartimento* (region) of Piedmont, in the province of Vercelli, situated in the valley of the Sesia River, NE of Turin. It manufactures woolen and cotton textiles and paper articles, and has metallurgical industries and stone quarries. Pop. of commune, 10,956 (1936); of town, 5,788 (1936).

Borgo Val di Taro (bōr'gō väl dē tä'rō). [Former names, **Albareto di Borgotaro, Borgotaro** (bōr.gō.tä'rō).] Town and commune in N Italy, in the *compartimento* (region) of Emilia-Romagna, in the province of Parma, situated in the valley of the Taro River, in the Apennines between Parma and Genoa. Lignite mines are in the vicinity. Pop. of commune, 15,209 (1936); of town, 3,655 (1936).

Borgu (bôr'gö). See **Bargu** and **Borkou.**

Borgundsund (bôr'gůn.sůn). See under **Alesund.**

Bori (bō'rē), **Lucrezia.** [Original name, **Lucrecia Borja González de Riancho.**] b. at Valencia, Spain, c1888—. American operatic soprano. She made her debut (1908) at Rome as Micaela in Georges Bizet's *Carmen;* her American première (Nov. 11, 1912) was in *Manon Lescaut;* with the Metropolitan Opera Company at New York, she has appeared (1912–15, 1921–36) in such roles as Fiora in *L'Amore dei Tre Re* (1914), Lucinda in *L'Amore Medico* (1914) by Ermanno Wolf-Ferrari, Ah-Yoe in *L'Oracolo* (1915), the title role of Pietro Mascagni's *Iris* (1915), and Mimi in Giacomo Puccini's *La Bohème* (1921).

Borie (bo.rē), **Pierre Rose Ursule Dumoulin.** b. at Beynat, Corrèze, France, Feb. 20, 1808; beheaded in Tonkin, Indochina, Nov. 24, 1838. French missionary in Tonkin (1832–38).

Borinage (bo.rē.nàzh). Coal-mining region in W central Belgium, adjoining Mons and extending SW ab. 8 mi. to the French border. Its coal mines have been active since the 13th century, and in the last 100 years coke ovens and briquette plants, as well as metal, ceramic, and glass industries, have developed in the region. Coal is still the major product, and it moves out by rail and by canal and river barges. Area, ab. 35 sq. mi.; pop. 128,626 (1947).

Boring (bō'ring), **Edwin Garrigues.** b. at Philadelphia, Oct. 23, 1886—. American psychologist. He received the degrees of M.E. (1908) and Ph.D. (1914) from Cornell University, before serving as professor (1919–22) of experimental psychology at Clark University, and professor (1928 *et seq.*) of psychology at Harvard; he was also coeditor (1925–46) of the *American Journal of Psychology.*

His writings include *A History of Experimental Psychology* (1929), *The Physical Dimensions of Consciousness* (1933), *Sensation and Perception in the History of Experimental Psychology* (1942). He was coeditor of *Psychology for the Fighting Man* (1943), *Psychology for the Armed Services* (1945), and other works.

Boring, William Alciphron. b. at Carlinville, Ill., Sept. 9, 1859; d. May 5, 1937. American architect. He was educated at the University of Illinois, Columbia University, and the École des Beaux-Arts, Paris. He designed buildings for the University of Southern California, the U.S. Immigrant Station at Ellis Island, the Jacob Tome Institute at Port Deposit, Md., and many other public structures in various parts of the U.S.

Boris I (bō′ris). d. 903 or 907. Ruler of Bulgaria (c852–c890). After military defeats early in his reign by the Germans and the Serbs, he effected a treaty with the Byzantine emperor Michael III (Michael the Drunkard) in 864, and in that or the following year was baptized a Christian. At first he acknowledged the primacy of Rome in religious matters, but when the promise apparently held out by Pope Nicholas I to grant Bulgaria an independent patriarchate was not fulfilled, Boris at the Council of Constantinople (870) adhered to the Byzantine Church and adopted the Greek rite. In 889 he abdicated and retired to a monastery, but in 893 took power again briefly in order to depose his eldest son and successor, whose brief reign was characterized by cruelty and disorders. He thereupon proclaimed his youngest son Simeon czar, the title he himself had taken. In the calendar of the Orthodox Church, Boris I appears as a saint.

Boris III. b. at Sofia, Bulgaria, Jan. 30, 1894; d. there, Aug. 28, 1943. King of Bulgaria (1918–43). He established a thinly veiled personal dictatorship in 1935, and led Bulgaria into the Axis camp in 1941. He participated as a staff officer in the Balkan wars and World War I. By his marriage (1930) to Princess Giovanna of Savoy, he was the father of Simeon II, who was king until 1946.

Boris Godunov (go.dö.nôf′; Russian, bo.rēs′). See also **Godunov, Boris Fyodorovich.**

Boris Godunov. Opera by Modest Moussorgsky, first performed at St. Petersburg on Jan. 24, 1874. The work is taken from a play by Pushkin.

Boris Godunov. [Also: **Boris Godonof, Boris Godounoff.**] Tragedy by Aleksandr Pushkin, founded on that episode in Russian history known as the Interregnum. It is the basis of Modest Moussorgsky's opera of the same name. Lope de Vega also wrote a play on this subject, called *El Gran Duque de Muscovia.*

Borislav (bo.rē′sla̤f). [Polish, **Borysław.**] City in the W part of the U.S.S.R., in W Ukrainian Soviet Socialist Republic, in the Carpathian foothills ab. 45 mi. SW of Lvov. It is a center for oil and natural gas production, and has had a rapid industrial growth since the discovery of the oil fields in the early 20th century. The city was in Galicia, a province of the Austro-Hungarian empire. In 1919 it passed to Poland, and in 1945 was annexed by the U.S.S.R. 40,000 (1940).

Borisoglebsk (bo.rē.so̤.glyepsk′). [Also, **Borissogliebsk.**] City in the U.S.S.R., in the Voronezh *oblast* (region) of the Russian Soviet Federated Socialist Republic, ab. 150 mi. E of Sartov. Located in the center of a wheat and sugar-beet area, the city has important food industries. 52,055 (1939).

Borisov (bo.rē′so̤f). [Also, **Borrissoff.**] Town in the U.S.S.R., in the Byelorussian Soviet Socialist Republic, ab. 50 mi. NE of Minsk: wood and paper industries. Pop. 34,800 (1933).

Borja (bôr′hä), Doña **Ana de.** b. c1640; d. Sept. 23, 1706. Vice-queen of Peru; daughter of the duke of Béjar, and the third wife of the count of Lemos, whom she accompanied to Peru in 1667. During the absence of the viceroy in Charcas she was left in charge (1668 and 1669) of the government. This is almost the only instance of its kind in Spanish America.

Borja, Francisco de. See **Borgia,** Saint **Francesco.**

Borja y Arragón (ē är.rä.gōn′), **Francisco de.** b. at Madrid, 1582; d. there, 1658. Spanish statesman. By his marriage he became prince of Esquilache or Squillace in Calabria, Italy. From December, 1615, to December, 1621, he was viceroy of Peru.

Börjeson (bėr′ye.sôn), **Johan Laurentius Helenus.** b. at Tölö, Halland, Sweden, Dec. 30, 1835; d. at Stockholm, in January, 1910. Swedish sculptor, noted for his monumental works. After studies in his native country, and at Rome and Paris, he settled at Stockholm, where he taught at the art academy. Among his works are statues of Nils Ericson (1893) and of Axel Oxenstjerna (1890) at Stockholm and an equestrian statue of Charles XI of Sweden, at Göteborg.

Börjesson (bėr′yes.sôn), **Johan.** b. at Tanum, Bohus (now included in the *län* (county) of Göteborg), Sweden, March 22, 1790; d. at Uppsala, Sweden, in May, 1866. Swedish dramatic poet. His chief drama is *Erik XIV* (1846).

Borkou (bôr′kö). [Also: **Borgu, Borku.**] Group of oases in the Sahara, N central Africa, between Fezzan territory, Libya, and Ouadai in the NW part of Chad territory, French Equatorial Africa, S of the Tibesti highlands. It is an important meeting place of commercial routes; inhabited chiefly by a Berber tribe.

Borkovec (bôr′kô.vets), **Pavel.** b. at Prague, June 10, 1894—. Czech composer. His works include a symphony in D flat Major (1927), two symphonic poems (1920, 1929), two string quartets (1924, 1928), a sonata for viola solo (1931), and a piano suite (1930).

Borku (bôr′kö). See **Borkou.**

Borkum (bôr′kům). Island in NW Germany, in the *Land* (state) of Lower Saxony, British Zone, formerly in the province of Hanover, Prussia, situated in the North Sea, between the Wester Ems and Oster Ems (mouths of the Ems River), NW of Emden. It is the westernmost of the East Frisian islands; a popular seaside resort. There is a local museum. Livestock raising is a principal occupation. Length, ab. 6 mi.; width, ab. 2 mi.; pop. 5,499 (1946).

Borland (bôr′la̤nd), **Solon.** b. near Suffolk, Va., Sept. 21, 1808; d. at or near Houston, Texas, in January, 1864. American politician and diplomat. Appointed (1853) minister to Nicaragua and the other Central American states, he was injured while intervening in a dispute between the Accessory Transit Company and the authorities of Greytown, Punta Arenas; the subsequent shelling of the city by the U.S.S. *Cyane* was carried out (July 13, 1854) with the approval of President Franklin Pierce.

Borlänge (bör′leng″e̤). Town in C Sweden, in the *län* (county) of Kopparberg, situated on the Västerdal River, SW of Falun. It is a railroad junction and now includes the steel mills of Domnarvet. 20,947 (1950).

Borlase (bôr′la̤s), **Edmund.** [Also, **Burlace.**] d. at Chester, England, c1682. English physician, and writer on Irish history.

Borlase, William. b. at Pendeen, Cornwall, England, Feb. 2, 1695; d. Aug. 31, 1772. English antiquary and naturalist. His chief works are *Antiquities of Cornwall* (1754) and *Natural History of Cornwall* (1758).

Bormann (bôr′män), **Martin Ludwig.** b. at Halberstadt, Germany, June 17, 1900; reported to have been killed in action at Berlin, April 30, 1945. German politician. He was in charge (1930 *et seq.*) of the relief funds of the Nazi party, in which he held the office of *Stabsleiter* (chief of staff) after 1933; he succeeded Rudolf Hess as vice-führer in 1941. Alleged to have been killed by the Russians during the capture of Berlin, he was tried *in absentia* at the Nuremberg war crimes trial (1946), and sentenced to death.

Bormio (bôr′myō). Town and commune in NW Italy, in the *compartimento* (region) of Lombardy, in the province of Sondrio, situated at the head of the Valtellina, on the Adda River, near the frontier of Switzerland. It is a tourist center, and has preserved the architectural character of the 15th century. Pop. of commune, 2,276 (1936); of town, 2,231 (1936).

Bormio, District of. Territory around Bormio, in NW Italy, whose history was largely connected with that of the Valtellina.

Born (bôrn), **Bertrand de.** b. at Born, in Périgord, France, c1140; d. c1215. French troubadour and soldier. He took part in the struggles of the sons of Henry II of England against their father.

Born, Ignaz von. b. at Karlsburg, in Transylvania, Dec. 26, 1742; d. at Vienna, July 24, 1791. Austrian mineralogist and metallurgist.

Born, Max. b. at Breslau, Dec. 11, 1882—. German physicist, noted for his studies in the quantum theory, atomic structure, and the theory of relativity. He became (1909) lecturer in physics at the University of Göttingen, and was professor of theoretical physics at the University of Berlin (1915 *et seq.*), the University of Frankfort on the Main, and the University of Göttingen. Dismissed from his post by the Nazi regime, he became (1933) a British subject, was Stokes Lecturer in mathematics at Cambridge from 1933 to 1936, and was named (1936) Tait Professor of Natural Philosophy at the University of Edinburgh, where he subsequently became head of the department of mathematical physics. He is the author of *Die Relativitätstheorie Einsteins und ihre physische Grundlagen* (1922), *Probleme der Atomdynamik* (1926), *Vorlesungen über Atommechanik* (1930), *Atom Physics* (1935), *The Restless Universe* (1935), and *Experiment and Theory in Physics* (1944).

Borna (bôr′nä). City in E Germany, in the *Land* (state) of Saxony, Russian Zone, formerly in the free state of Saxony, situated on the Wybra River, ab. 16 mi. SE of Leipzig. It has lignite mines, machine shops, and piano factories. The Church of Saint Kunigunde is a Romanesque basilica, erected about 1200. The town was looted by the Hussites in 1430, and belonged to the house of Wettin from 1484. The population is predominantly Protestant. 18,425 (1946).

Borne (bôr′nẹ). Town in E Netherlands, in the province of Overijssel, SE of Zwolle: small industries. 10,283 (1939).

Börne (bėr′nẹ), **Ludwig.** [Original name, **Löb Baruch.**] b. at Frankfort on the Main, Germany, May 6, 1786; d. at Paris, Feb. 12, 1837. German satirist and political writer. Primarily a journalist and politician, he fished in the troubled waters of revolution, often from the vantage point of Paris. His collected writings were published 1829–34.

Borneil (bôr.ney′), **Guiraut** (or **Giraud**) **de.** fl. in the latter part of the 12th century. French troubadour, many of whose poems have survived. Dante mentions him in the *Divina Commedia.*

Borneo (bôr′nẹ.ō). [Also: **Brunai, Bruni, B'rni**; Malay, **Burni**; native name, **Pulo Kalamantin** (or **Kalimanten**).] Largest island of the East Indies, W of Celebes, N of Java, and E of Sumatra. A large part of it is mountainous. It has rubber plantations, and also exports coconut products, palm oil, petroleum, and coal. It is divided into the former Dutch possessions and (British) North Borneo, Brunei, and Sarawak. "Dutch Borneo" was divided (1946) into five *daerahs* (autonomous areas) of the United States of Indonesia (Banjar, East Borneo, Great Dayak, Southeast Borneo, and West Borneo), formed with the intention of later merging into a *negara* (state) to be known as Kalimanten; with the abolishment (1950) of the federal system in Indonesia, Borneo became a province of the independent Republic of Indonesia. The inhabitants are Dayaks, Malays, Negritos, Bugis, and Chinese. Borneo was first visited by the Portuguese c1518. Length, 830 mi.; breadth, 600 mi.; area, ab. 287,000 sq. mi.; area of Borneo province, ab. 206,100 sq. mi.; pop. ab. 3 million (1951); area of North Borneo, 29,387 sq. mi.; pop. 333,752 (1951); area of Sarawak and Brunei, ab. 49,226 sq. mi.; pop. 587,042 (1947).

Borneo, East. See **East Borneo.**

Bornet (bôr.ne), **Jean Baptiste Édouard.** b. 1828; d. 1911. French botanist. He studied medicine and botany at Paris, and collaborated with Gustave Adolphe Thuret at Cherbourg in the study of marine flora. Among his works are *Recherches sur la structure de l'éphèbe pubescens* (1852), *Recherches sur les gonidies des lichens* (1873), and *Les Algues de Schonsboe* (1892).

Bornholm (bôrn′hôlm). Island in the Baltic Sea, the easternmost territory belonging to Denmark, between S Sweden and NW Poland. It forms the Danish *amt* (county) of Bornholm (*q.v.*).

Bornholm. *Amt* (county) of Denmark, identical with the island of Bornholm. Capital, Rønne; area, 228 sq. mi.; pop. 47,337 (1945).

Bornier (bôr.nyā), **Henri,** Vicomte **de.** b. at Lunel, Hérault, France, Dec. 25, 1825; d. at Paris, Jan. 29, 1901. French poet and dramatist, who succeeded Xavier Marmier as a member of the French Academy in 1893. Among his works are *Les Premières feuilles* (1848), a volume of poems, and the plays *Le Mariage de Luther* (1845), *Dante et Béatrix* (1853), *Le Mond renversé* (1853), *La Fille de Roland* (1875), *Les Noces d'Attila* (1879), *La Moabite* (1880), *L'Apôtre* (1881), *Mahomet* (1890), *Le Fils de l'Arétin* (1895), and *France d'abord!* (1899). He published his collected verse, *Poésies complètes,* in 1888.

Born in Exile. Novel (1892) by George Gissing. In it Gissing tells of the efforts of a young man to rise above his own social class.

Borno (bôr.nō′), **Louis Eustache Antoine François Joseph.** b. at Port-au-Prince, Haiti, Sept. 20, 1865; d. there, July 29, 1942. Haitian lawyer and statesman, president (1922–30) of Haiti. He practiced law at Port-au-Prince, served as minister of foreign affairs, supported American intervention following the Haitian revolt (1915), and was a member (1919 *et seq.*) of the Permanent Court of International Justice at The Hague. He resigned (1930) from the presidency on the recommendation of U.S. President Hoover's investigating commission.

Bornover (bôrn′ō″vėr). Former name of **Beaumaris.**

Bornu (bôr′nö). Region in W Africa, in NE Nigeria, SW of Lake Chad. Its inhabitants are Negroes (Kanuris), Tuaregs, Arabs, and mixed races; the prevailing religion is Mohammedanism. Bornu formed part of the Kanem monarchy in the Middle Ages, and became a separate kingdom in the 15th century. It was conquered by Fulahs at the beginning of the 19th century, and is now in large part within the British protectorate of Nigeria. One of the Northern Provinces of Nigeria bears the name of Bornu today and is mainly occupied by the Kanuri people, numbering ab. 931,000. These people were one of the few groups able to resist the Fulahs in the early 19th century and became the dominant people in the Bornu kingdom. Administrative center of the province, Maiduguri.

Borny (bôr.nē), **Battle of.** See under **Colombey.**

Boro (bō′rō). [Also, **Miranha.**] South American Indian tribe, living in the area latitude 1°–2° S., longitude 71°–73° W. Their language is of the Witoto linguistic family.

Borobudur (bō″rō.bö.dör′). [Eng. trans., "*Innumerable Buddhas.*"] Greatest of all Indonesian Buddhist monuments, a stupa erected in C Java at the time of the first Mataram empire. Its main building dates from c800 A.D. Its 505 statues and nearly 2,000 reliefs make it the great focal point of early Hindu-Javanese sculpture. It is a solid, terraced stone pyramid with a natural hill as its core. Three concentric, circular top levels rise from six steplike quadrangular terraces and support a bell-shaped, pagodalike shrine (called a *dagoba*). The total height is ab. 40 meters (ab. 131 ft.); the base is ab. 120 meters (ab. 394 ft.) square. Its original purpose is unknown, but it is an embodiment and a symbolic materialization of the entire world of Mahayana Buddhism. As a pyramid, descending through various levels from apex to base, it expresses the material world as the unfolding of emanations of the one divinity; in reverse, ascending to the top, it symbolizes the return to the abstract parity and all-unity of Nirvana. The simple, circular top levels carry 72 statues of Buddha, enshrined in open-work stone bells.

Borodin (bō′rọ.dēn, bô′-; Russian, bọ.ro.dyēn′), **Aleksandr Porfiryevich.** b. at St. Petersburg, Nov. 12, 1834; d. there, in February, 1887. Russian composer, a member of the young national school founded by Mili Alekseyevich Balakirev. He studied medicine and chemistry, becoming assistant professor of chemistry in the Academy of Medicine at St. Petersburg in 1862, but from that time devoted his leisure time to music. He composed three symphonies (the third of which remains unfinished), string quartets, piano pieces and songs, the orchestral tone poem *In the Steppes of Central Asia,* and an opera, *Prince Igor* (unfinished, but completed by Rimsky-Korsakov and Glazunov, and published in 1889).

Borodino (bọ.rọ.dyē.nô′; Anglicized, bō.rọ.dē′nō). Town in the U.S.S.R., in the Moscow *oblast* (region) of the Russian Soviet Federated Socialist Republic, situated near the Moskva River ab. 70 mi. W of Moscow. Near here, on Sept. 7, 1812, Napoleon I's army (ab. 140,000) gained a victory over the Russians under Mikhail Kutuzov (ab. 140,000). The loss of Napoleon's army was 30,000; that of the Russians, nearly 50,000. This engagement is also called the "battle of the Moskva," and is described in Leo Tolstoy's *War and Peace.*

Boroimhe (bǫ.rō′, -rō′), **Brian.** See **Brian Boru.**

Borojević von Bojna (bô′rô.ye.vich fon boi′nä), Baron **Svetozar.** b. at Batumetić, in Croatia, Dec. 13, 1856; d. at Klagenfurt, Austria, May 23, 1920. Austrian general. In World War I he attempted to lift the siege of Przemysl; as commander (1915 *et seq.*) on the Isonzo front, he contained the attacks of Italian armies superior in numbers to his forces.

Borondon (bǫ.ron′dǫn), Saint. See **Brendan** or **Brenainn,** Saint.

Bororó (bō.rō.rō′). Group of South American Indian tribes, now nearly extinct, living near the headwaters of the Paraguay River in S and C Brazil. The Bororó languages form an independent linguistic stock.

Borotra (bo.ro.trȧ; Anglicized, bǫ.rō′trą), **Jean.** b. in France, Aug. 13, 1898—. French lawn-tennis player and one-time engineer. From 1922 to 1935 he was ten times winner of the French covered-court championship. He was a member (1925–33) of the French Davis Cup team that won the cup in 1927 and defended it until 1932. Founder (1929) of the International Lawn Tennis Club of France, he was also president (1931 *et seq.*) of the Tennis Club of Paris. He was named (1940) secretary general for sports by the Vichy government of France, and was accused, after the end of World War II, of having collaborated with the Germans.

Borough (bur′ǫ), **Stephen.** [Also: **Borrows, Burrough, Burrowe.**] b. at Northam, Devonshire, England, Sept. 25, 1525; d. July 12, 1584. English navigator. He was master of one of several English ships which set out to reach Russia by the northern route. The vessels became separated and the *Edward Bonaventure*, under Borough's command, alone completed the voyage in 1553. It was thus the first English ship to round the North Cape, to which Borough gave its English name. Thereafter English merchant adventurers formed the Muscovy Company, in whose service Borough sailed in 1556–57, reaching Novaya Zemlya and the passage south of it into the Kara Sea. In 1560 he was in command of three English merchantmen which may be credited with having actually initiated direct maritime commerce between England and Russia. Accounts of some of Stephen Borough's voyages appear in Richard Hakluyt's *The Principal Navigations, Voyages, and Discoveries of the English Nation.*

Borough, The. Poem by George Crabbe, published in 1810.

Borough, William. [Also: **Borrows, Burrough, Burrowe.**] b. at Northam, Devonshire, England, 1536; d. 1599. English naval officer; brother of Stephen Borough. He was with his brother when the latter commanded the first English ship to round the North Cape, in 1553. He thereafter entered the employ of the Muscovy Company of English merchant adventurers and made several voyages to Russia before becoming an officer of the English navy. In that capacity he commanded the *Lion* in Drake's fleet when the latter attacked Cádiz, in 1587, and in the following year he was master of one of the English warvessels that harassed the Spanish Armada. Some of William Borough's charts are still preserved at the British Museum, and accounts of several of his voyages are found in Richard Hakluyt's *The Principal Navigations, Voyages, and Discoveries of the English Nation.* Borough was the author of *A Discourse of the Variation of the Compas, or Magneticall Needle* (1581).

Boroughbridge (bur′ǫ.brij). Civil parish and market town in N central England, in the West Riding of Yorkshire, situated on the river Ure, ab. 17 mi. NW of York, ab. 210 mi. N of London by rail. Here, on March 16, 1322, Edward II defeated the earl of Lancaster. 862 (1931).

Borovichi (bo.ro.vē.chē′). Town in the U.S.S.R., in the Leningrad *oblast* (region) of the Russian Soviet Federated Socialist Republic, situated on the Msta River: textile mills. Pop. ab. 28,000.

Borovsk (bô′rǫfsk). City in the U.S.S.R., in the Moscow *oblast* (region) of the Russian Soviet Federated Socialist Republic, ab. 85 mi. S of Moscow: textile mills and machine shops.

Borowlaski (bô.rô.vlä′skē) or **Boruwlaski** (bô.rö-), **Joseph.** b. at Halicz, in Galicia, 1739; d. near Durham, England, Sept. 5, 1837. Polish dwarf, erroneously called a "count," who traveled from place to place as part of a freak show giving concerts. His height was a little under 39 inches. He published (1788) an autobiography.

Borowski (bǫ.rôf′ski), **Felix.** b. at Burton, England, March 10, 1872—. American composer, teacher, and music critic. In 1897 he came to the U.S., where he joined the staff of the Chicago Musical College, of which he was later (1916–25) president; he also headed (1926–32) the Chicago Civic Music Association, and was professor (1937 *et seq.*) of musicology at Northwestern University. He was music critic for the Chicago *Evening Post* and *Record-Herald*, and the *Christian Science Monitor*. His compositions include *Adoration* for violin and piano, three symphonies, program music including several tone poems, a string quartet in G Major (1930), a ballet, and an opera.

Borrás (bôr.räs′), **Enrique.** b. at Badalona, near Barcelona, Spain, 1862—. Spanish actor. After playing in amateur groups, he joined (1886) the company of Antonio Vico and appeared in many plays by Angel Guimerá and other Catalonian playwrights. He transferred (1904) his activities to Madrid and made Catalonian drama widely known through his successful productions. Endowed with an impressive voice and expressive gestures and facial play, he came to be regarded as one of Spain's leading modern actors.

Borre (bôr), **Sir.** [Also, **Sir Bors.**] In the Arthurian legends, a natural son of King Arthur.

Borren (bôr′ẹn), **Charles-Jean-Eugène Van Den.** b. at Ixelles, near Brussels, Nov. 17, 1874—. Belgian musicologist. He obtained (1897) the degree of doctor of laws, but abandoned his law practice to devote himself to music. He has been music critic for *L'Art Moderne*, professor of the history of music at Liége and associate professor at the University of Brussels, librarian of the Royal Conservatory at Brussels, and laureate of the Royal Academy of Belgium and of the French Institute. His works include *L'Oeuvre dramatique de César Franck* (1907) and *Les Origines de la musique de clavier en Angleterre* (1912).

Borrioboola-gha (bor″i.ǫ.bö′lą.gä′). Imaginary place in Africa, on the left bank of the Niger River, selected by Mrs. Jellyby (in Charles Dickens's *Bleak House*) as a field for her missionary philanthropic exertions, to the neglect of all home duties.

Borrissoff (bo.rē′sǫf). See **Borisov.**

Borromean Islands (bor.ǫ.mē′ąn). [Italian, **Isole Borromee** (ē′zō.lā bōr.rō.me′ā).] Group of four islands in Lago Maggiore, in the province of Novara, N Italy, near the W shore. The two most noted, Isola Bella and Isola Madre, belonged to the Borromeo family, and were converted into pleasure gardens by Count Federigo Borromeo in the 17th century.

Borromeo (bōr.rō.mā′ō), Saint **Carlo.** b. at Arona, on Lago Maggiore, Italy, Oct. 2, 1538; d. at Milan, Nov. 3, 1584. Italian cardinal (1560 *et seq.*), archbishop of Milan, noted as an ecclesiastical reformer and a philanthropist. He was canonized in 1610. His death is commemorated on Nov. 4.

Borromeo, Count **Federigo.** b. at Milan, 1564; d. 1631. Italian cardinal, and archbishop of Milan, founder of the Ambrosian Library at Milan in 1609. He was a cousin of Saint Carlo Borromeo.

Borromeo, San Carlo. Colossal statue on a hill near Arona, on Lago Maggiore, Italy. It stands ab. 70 ft. high, on a pedestal measuring 42 ft., and was finished in 1697. The figure, bareheaded, is in the act of blessing the town. The head, hands, and feet are of bronze, the remainder of welded sheets of beaten copper, braced with iron, and supported on a central pier of stone.

Borromeo, Sisters of San Carlo. Religious order founded (1652) by the Abbé d'Estival. Its chief seat is at Nancy, France.

Borromini (bōr.rō.mē′nē), **Francesco.** b. at Bissone, Italy, Sept. 25, 1599; d. at Rome, Aug. 2, 1667. Italian architect and sculptor. He was for a time architect of Saint Peter's, under Bernini's direction, and became official architect of the city of Rome. Borromini had an important influence on the evolution of Italian architecture, being a leader of the movement toward the baroque style, with its wide departures from the conventions of the Renaissance, and one of the ablest practitioners of that style. He is perhaps now best known for the façade of the Church of Sant'Agnese in the Piazza Navone,

Rome, in which city also the Church of La Sapienza is an example of his design. He died by his own hand. Engravings of his chief designs were posthumously published in 1727.

Borrow (bor′ō), **George.** b. at East Dereham, Norfolk, England, in July, 1803; d. at Oulton, Suffolk, England, in July, 1881. English philologist, traveler, and novelist, noted for his works on Gypsies and the Romany language. His works include *Targum, or Metrical Translations from thirty Languages . . .* (1835), *The Bible in Spain* (1843), *The Zincali, or an Account of the Gypsies in Spain* (1841), *Lavengro, the Scholar, the Gypsy, and the Priest* (1851), *The Romany Rye, a sequel to Lavengro* (1857), *Wild Wales . . .* (1862), and *Romano Lavo-Lil, or Word-book of the Romany* (1874).

Borrowdale (bor′ǫ.dāl). Valley in NW England, in Cumberland. It is in the Lake District, S of Derwentwater.

Borrows (bor′ōz, bur′-). See **Borough, Stephen,** and **Borough, William.**

Borrowstounness and Carriden (bō.nes′, bor″ǫ.stō.nes′; kar′i.dẹn). Official name of **Bo'ness.**

Bors (bôrs). In Arthurian legend, a king of Gaul; uncle of Lancelot. He and his brother went to King Arthur's assistance when he first mounted the throne.

Bors, Sir. See also **Borre, Sir.**

Bors, Sir. [Also: **Sir Bohort, Sir Bort.**] Knight of the Round Table, called Sir Bors de Ganis, nephew of Sir Lancelot. He was one of the few who were pure enough to see the vision of the Holy Grail.

Borsippa (bôr.sip′ạ). Ancient city of Babylonia, probably a suburb of Babylon. It contained a temple of Nebo, its tutelar deity, called *Ezida* ("eternal house"), which was constructed in the form of a pyramid consisting of seven stories, which are termed in the inscriptions "the seven spheres of heaven and earth." The imposing ruins of the mound Birs Nimrud NE of Babylon are identified as the site of Borsippa and its celebrated temple.

Bort (bôrt), **Sir.** See **Bors, Sir.**

Borthwick (bôrth′wik), **Algernon.** [Title, 1st Baron **Glenesk.**] b. at Cambridge, England, Dec. 27, 1830; d. at London, Nov. 24, 1908. English statesman, journalist, and owner of the London *Morning Post;* son of Peter Borthwick. Educated at Paris, and in London at King's College School, he became associated with his father's paper, the *Morning Post,* as Paris correspondent (1850), editor (1852), and proprietor (1876–95). Conservative member of Parliament (1885–95) for South Kensington, he was knighted in 1880, made a baronet in 1887, and named Baron Glenesk in 1895, at which time he transferred control of the *Post* to his son, Oliver (1873–1905). It was in the pages of the *Post* in 1883 that Borthwick suggested forming the Primrose League, an English political group dedicated to Conservative principles.

Borthwick, Peter. b. at Cornbank, Borthwick Parish, Midlothian, Scotland, Sept. 13, 1804; d. at London, Dec. 18, 1852. British editor and politician; father of Algernon Borthwick. He was editor (1850–52) of the London *Morning Post,* and member of Parliament for Evesham (1835–47). He sponsored the "Borthwick Clause," under which old married couples entering a poorhouse were no longer required to be separated. He was the author of theological works, and of speeches (published 1832, 1833, 1836) defending the institution of slavery.

Bort-les-Orgues (bôr.lā.zôrg). Town in C France, in the department of Cher, situated on the Dordogne River, NE of Tulle. Interesting basalt formations are located in the vicinity. 5,086 (1946).

Bortnyansky (bort.nyän′ski), **Dmitri Stepanovich.** b. at Glukhov, Chernigov, Russia, c1752; d. at St. Petersburg, Oct. 9, 1825. Russian composer; pupil of Baldassare Galuppi. He was director of the imperial choir, and composed much music for the Russian Church.

Boru or **Borumha** (bǫ.rō′, -rö′), **Brian.** See **Brian Boru.**

Bory de Saint Vincent (bo.rē dẹ saṅ vaṅ.säṅ), **Jean Baptiste Georges Marie.** b. at Agen, France, c1780; d. at Paris, in December, 1846. French naturalist and traveler. He wrote *Essai sur les îles fortunées et l'antique Atlantide* (1803) and *L'Homme, essai zoölogique* (1827).

Borysław (bô.ri′släf). Polish name of **Borislav.**

Borysthenes (bǫ.ris′thẹ.nēz). An ancient name of the **Dnieper.**

Bos (bō), **Charles du.** See **du Bos, Charles.**

Bos (bôs), **Jerom.** See **Bosch, Hieronymus.**

Bos, Willem Hendrik van den. b. at Rotterdam, Netherlands, Sept. 25, 1896—. Dutch astronomer. He has concentrated exclusively on visual binary star measures and orbit determinations, first at Leiden and, since 1930, at Johannesburg, South Africa.

Bosa (bō′sä). Town and commune in W Italy, on the island of Sardinia, in the province of Nuoro, situated near the W coast of the island, between Oristano and Sassari. It is the seat of a bishopric and has a seaport. Pop. of commune, 7,138 (1936); of town, 6,828 (1936).

Bosanquet (bō′zạn.ket), **Bernard.** b. at Alnwick, England, 1848; d. Feb. 8, 1923. English idealist philosopher, professor of moral philosophy at St. Andrews (1903–08). He was graduated from Oxford, and was lecturer (1871–81) at University College there. Among his publications are *Logic, or Morphology of Knowledge* (1888), *A History of Aesthetics* (1892), *The Philosophical Theory of the State* (1899), and a translation of Lao-Tze's *System of Philosophy.*

Bosanski Brod (bô′sän.skē brôd). [German, **Bosnisch Brod.**] Town in N Yugoslavia, in the federative unit of Bosnia-Hercegovina, in the former *banovina* (province) of Vrbaska, situated on the Sava River opposite the town of Brod. It is a railroad station and river port, and has many mosques. 7,386 (1931).

Bosanski Petrovac (pe.trô′väts). Town in C Yugoslavia, in the federative unit of Bosnia-Hercegovina, in the former *banovina* (province) of Vrbaska, situated SW of Banja Luka. 15,347 (1931).

Bosboom (bôs′bōm), **Johannes.** b. Feb. 18, 1817; d. Sept. 14, 1891. Dutch painter; husband (1851 *et seq.*) of Anna Louisa Geertruida Bosboom-Toussaint.

Bosboom-Toussaint (bôs′bōm.tö.saṅ′), **Anna Louisa Geertruida.** [Maiden name, **Toussaint.**] b. at Alkmaar, Netherlands, Sept. 16, 1812; d. at The Hague, April 13, 1886. Dutch historical novelist; wife (1851 *et seq.*) of the painter Johannes Bosboom. Her works include *Het Huis Lauernesse, Leycester in Nederland, De Vrouwen van het Leycestersche Tijdperk,* and *Gideon Florenoz.*

Bosc (bosk), **Louis Augustin Guillaume.** b. at Paris, Jan. 29, 1759; d. there, July 10, 1828. French naturalist. He wrote *Histoire naturelle des coquilles* (1801) and *Histoire naturelle des crustacés* (1802).

Boscán Almogaver (bōs.kän′ äl″mō.gä.ʙer′), **Juan.** b. at Barcelona, Spain, c1493; d. near Perpignan, France, 1542. Spanish poet, considered the founder of the Italian poetical school in Spain. He was engaged at the court of Charles V of Spain. His collected works were published in 1543.

Boscawen (bos.kō′ẹn), **Edward.** b. in Cornwall, England, Aug. 19, 1711; d. near Guildford, Surrey, England, Jan. 10, 1761. English admiral. He commanded at the taking of Louisburg (1758), and defeated the French at Lagos Bay, off Lagos, Portugal, Aug. 18, 1759. Previously, he had taken part in naval actions off Portobelo, in what is now Panama (1739), Cartagena, in what is now Colombia (1741), and Cape Finisterre, Spain (1747).

Bosch (bosh), **Carl.** b. at Cologne, Germany, 1874; d. at Heidelberg, Germany, 1940. German industrial chemist and industrialist. With Friedrich Bergius he won the Nobel prize in chemistry in 1931. He was largely responsible for the adaptation of the Haber process to extremely large-scale production (1907–17) of artificial fertilizers and explosives from atmospheric nitrogen, and was later active in the industrial adaptation of the Bergius process for catalytically hydrogenating coal and oil. He was a director of Badische Anilin und Sodafabrik (1919–25), chairman of the board of a German dye trust (1925), and president and general director of I. G. Farbenindustrie (1935–40).

Bosch (bôs), **Hieronymus.** [Also: **Jerom Bos;** family surname, **van Aeken.**] b. at 's Hertogenbosch, Netherlands, c1450; d. there, 1516. Dutch painter, popularly known for the fantastic figures that appear in many of his works. A painter also of satirical genre pictures, Bosch excelled in large representations of religious subjects. In such works as *The Temptation of Saint Anthony* and *The Last Judgment,* he surrounded his central characters with nightmarish creatures representing evil and torture. His work is said to have been especially pleasing to Philip II of Spain; many of his paintings were acquired by Spanish collections. His keen perception was applied equally to nature and the human character; master of a precise brush technique and a luminous treatment of color, Bosch achieved in his compositions a unity between background and figures new at that time to Dutch art.

Bosch, Count **Jan van den.** b. 1780; d. 1844. Dutch governor of Batavia (1830–33). He introduced into the Netherlands East Indies the infamous "culture system" under which the production of export crops was multiplied on behalf of a Netherlands monopoly by forcing the peasants either to pay a land rent of about two fifths of the crop raised or to devote one fifth of the area under cultivation (previously mostly planted with rice for domestic consumption) to a crop designated by and deliverable to the government, such as sugar, indigo, or coffee. In 1833 he was appointed Dutch minister of colonies.

Bosch (bosh), **Robert (August).** b. at Albeck, Germany, Sept. 23, 1861; d. at Stuttgart, Germany, March 12, 1942. German industrialist. He studied in England and in the U.S., and later founded (1886) at Stuttgart a firm manufacturing electrical appliances for cars, which in 1936 employed ab. 19,000 workers. Bosch was on the administrative boards of the Krupp A.-G. and of the I. G. Farben firms; he was regarded as one of the most liberal and socially progressive German industrialists.

Bosco (bôs'kō), Saint **John.** [Italian name (as a priest), Don **Giovanni Bosco.**] b. in Piedmont, Italy, 1815; d. 1888. Italian priest, notable as the founder of the order now known as the Salesians. His work as a priest lay with boys and young men, and in 1842 he founded the oratory at Turin for the care and education of youth. The Salesian Society developed (1844) out of this. He founded a similar society of sisters (of Mary Auxiliatrice) for the care of girls. He was canonized in 1929.

Boscobel (bos'kọ.bel). Farmhouse near Shiffnal, in Shropshire, England, noted in connection with the escape of Charles II of England, in September, 1651. The "royal oak" (in which Charles hid) was in the vicinity.

Boscoreale (bôs''kō.rā.ä'lā). Town in S central Italy, in the *compartimento* (region) of Campania, in the province of Napoli, at the foot of Mount Vesuvius ab. 13 mi. SE of Naples. The site of the ancient city of Pompeii is just S of the town, and two Roman villas have been unearthed at Boscoreale. The modern town is in the commune of Torre Annunziata. 11,082 (1931).

Boscovich (bôs'kō.vēch), **Ruggiero Giuseppe.** b. at Ragusa, in Dalmatia (now Dubrovnik, Yugoslavia), May 18, 1711; d. at Milan, Feb. 12, 1787. Italian mathematician, scientist, and philosopher. He was a member of the Jesuit order, and an early supporter of the Newtonian theory. He traveled extensively, often on diplomatic missions. During a stay in England he was elected a fellow of the Royal Society. He published extensively on astronomical problems and on aspects of mathematics, philosophy, and literature. The definition of the conic sections in terms of the ratio of distances from a focus and a directrix is often known as "Boscovich's definition," although this property had been known to the ancient Greeks. Among his most important works are *De maculis solaribus* (1736), *Elementa universae matheseos* (3 vols., 1754), and *Theoria philosophiae naturalis* (1758).

Bose (bōs), Sir **Jagadis Chandra** (or **Chunder**). b. 1858; d. 1937. Indian physicist and plant physiologist. He was a delegate to numerous international scientific congresses, and a member of the committee of intellectual coöperation of the League of Nations. He attended the International Scientific Congress (Paris, 1900) and was a scientist member of the Indian deputation to Europe and America (1907, 1914, 1919). Author of *The Movement of Plants, Plant Response, Response in the Living and the Non-Living,* and *Electro-Physiology of Plants.*

Bose, Sarat Chandra. b. 1889; d. Feb. 20, 1950. Indian lawyer and politician; brother of Subhas Bose. Founder (1947) of the Socialist Republican Party in Bengal, he became (1949) a member of the West Bengal legislative assembly. He was a member for works, mines, and power in the Indian interim government of 1946.

Bose, Subhas Chandra. b. 1897; d. (reported killed in an airplane crash) 1945. Indian nationalist leader, commander, in World War II, of the Indian revolutionary army, who secured German and Japanese support for an Indian provisional government and led a military campaign against India; brother of Sarat Chandra Bose (1889–1950). He was said to have been killed in an airplane accident while on a military mission, but persistent rumors held that he was still alive. A prominent leader of the left-wing forces in the Indian National Congress, he was president of that body in 1938, and was reëlected in 1939, but resigned because of opposition from Gandhi and members of the Working Committee. An uncompromising foe of British rule in India, he organized (1940) the Forward Bloc, which declared for drastic action against Britain and immediate resort to civil disobedience. One of the most internationally-minded of Indian leaders, he studied and wrote on world political developments, and predicted that Indian nationalism would benefit from imperialist rivalries which would lead to war. He sought to unite Hindus and Moslems in the nationalist struggle by advancing a program of social and economic revolution in which religious differences would be subordinated to class interests. Chief executive (1924–27) of the Calcutta municipality, he served (1926–29) as a member of the Bengal legislative council, and as president (1927–31) of the Bengal Congress Party. He was the author of *The Indian Struggle 1920–1934.*

Boselli (bō.zel'lē), **Paolo.** b. at Savona, Italy, June 8, 1838; d. at Rome, March 10, 1932. Italian statesman and economist. After having acquired (1860) a law degree at Turin, he was elected (1870) a deputy of the right center faction, and served as minister of education (1888–91, 1906), agriculture (1893–94), and finance (1894–96); as secretary of the treasury (1899–1900), he reorganized the Bank of Italy. For his service before and during World War I he was given (1916) the order of Annunciation which carried the appellation "Cousin to the King." As prime minister (1916–17) he was unable to maintain his cabinet after the disastrous defeat (1917) at Caporetto; in 1921 he was named to the senate. He was for many years president of the Dante Alighieri Society, and wrote several historical works.

Bosher (bō'shėr), **Kate Lee Langley.** [Pseudonym, **Kate Cairns.**] b. at Norfolk, Va., Feb. 1, 1865; d. at Richmond, Va., July 27, 1932. American novelist. She was the author of *Mary Cary* (1910), *Miss Gibbie Gault* (1911), *The House of Happiness* (1912), *The Man in Lonely Land* (1913), *How It Happened* (1914), *People Like That* (1915), *Kitty Canary* (1917), and *His Friend, Miss McFarlane* (1918).

Bosio (bō'zyō), **Angiolina.** b. at Turin, Italy, Aug. 22, 1829; d. at St. Petersburg, April 12, 1859. Italian opera singer.

Bosio (bo.zyō), Baron **François Joseph.** b. at Monaco, c1769; d. at Paris, July 29, 1845. French sculptor. Among his best-known works are the bas-reliefs of the Vendôme column, and an equestrian statue of Louis XIV, both at Paris. He was in the employ of Napoleon I, and executed portrait busts of several members of the emperor's family.

Bosjesmans (bôsh'yẹs.mäns). Dutch name for **Bushmen.**

Bosley (boz'li), **Frederick Andrew.** b. at Lebanon, N.H., Feb. 24, 1881; d. 1942. American painter. A student of Edmund Charles Tarbell and Frank Weston Benson at Boston, he won the Paige Scholarship of the School of the Boston Museum of Fine Arts for two years in Europe; later he was the winner of prizes from the Panama-Pacific Exposition (1915), the Carnegie International Exhibition (1920), and the Pennsylvania Academy of the Fine Arts (1925). He resided at Boston, maintaining his summer studio in New Hampshire. He is represented in the Boston Museum of Fine Arts (*The Dreamer*), the Locust Club at Philadelphia, and other collections.

Bosnia (boz'ni.ạ). [Serbo-Croatian and Turkish, **Bosna** (bôs'nä); French, **Bosnie** (boz.nē); German, **Bosnien** (bos'nẹ.ẹn).] Territory in SE Europe, the major part of the federative unit of Bosnia-Hercegovina in the republic of Yugoslavia. Bosnia was a part of the Roman Empire, was governed by native rulers in the Middle Ages under the sovereignty of the kings of Hungary, and belonged to the kingdom of Serbia in the 14th century. The separate kingdom of Bosnia originated in 1376; it was subjugated by the Turks in 1463. Bosnia was the theater of many revolts against Turkish rule, and of many conflicts between Austria and Turkey. It was provided in the treaty of Berlin (1878) that Bosnia and Hercegovina be occupied by Austria-Hungary. The Moslems of Bosnia, however, could be subdued only after a bloody conflict (1878). There was a popular revolt in 1881. The region was annexed to Austria-Hungary in 1908, to Yugoslavia in 1919. It was a center of partisan resistance against the Germans during World War II.

Bosnia-Hercegovina (boz'ni.ạ.hėr''tsẹ.gọ.vē'nạ). [Also: **Bosnia and Herzegovina**; Serbo-Croatian, **Bosna i Hercegovina** (bôs'nä ē her.tse.gô'vē.nä); Turkish, **Bosna-Hersek** (bôs'nä.her.sek').] Federative unit of the republic of Yugoslavia, formed in 1945 from the former *banovina* (province) of Vrbaska and parts of the *banovine* (provinces) of Drinska, Zetska, and Primorska; it coincides with the former Turkish, later Austrian, administrative units of Bosnia and Hercegovina. It is bounded on the N and NW by Croatia, on the E by Serbia and Montenegro, and on the S and W by the former Austrian crownland of Dalmatia (now largely a part of the federative unit of Croatia). A narrow strip near Hercegnovi and Metković borders on the Adriatic Sea. The surface is mountainous, densely wooded in the E part, badly eroded in the W part. In the N the unit has a share in the fertile basin of the Sava River. The inhabitants are mainly engaged in agriculture and stock raising, but there are also copper and coal mining districts and an iron-smelting industry. A number of other minerals are also found. Members of the Serbian-Orthodox faith predominate, but there is a considerable Mohammedan minority, particularly around Sarajevo and Mostar. The Jewish population has all but disappeared as a result of the Nazi extermination policy. The mountains and forests of Bosnia-Hercegovina were the center of Yugoslav partisan resistance in World War II. Capital, Sarajevo; area, ab. 19,900 sq. mi.; pop. 2,565,277 (1951).

Bosnisch Brod (bos'nish brōt). German name of **Bosanski Brod.**

Bosola (bo.sō'lạ). Character in John Webster's tragedy *The Duchess of Malfi.* An ex-galley slave, he is hired by the Duchess's brothers to spy on their sister while ostensibly in her employ. He betrays her, and joins with her brother Ferdinand in torturing her and, finally, in murdering her, after killing her lover Antonio. He turns remorseful and kills the cardinal, the other brother, and is himself killed by Ferdinand.

Bosporus (bos'pọ.rus). See also **Cimmerian Bosporus.**

Bosporus. [Also: **Bosphorus** (bos'fọ.rus); Turkish, **Karadeniz Boğazı**; ancient name, **Bosporus Thracius** (thrā'shi.us), **Thracian Bosporus.**] Strait which connects the Black Sea and Sea of Marmara, and separates Europe from Asia. On it are Istanbul and Üsküdar. The name means "ox-ford": so named from the legend that Io, transformed into a heifer, swam across it. Length, ab. 20 mi.; greatest width, ab. 2½ mi.; narrowest, ab. 800 yds.

Bosporus Cimmerius (si.mir'i.us). See **Cimmerian Bosporus** and **Kerch Strait.**

Bosquet (bos.ke), **Pierre François Joseph.** b. at Mont-de-Marsan, Landes, France, Nov. 8, 1810; d. at Toulouse, France, Feb. 5, 1861. French soldier, marshal of France. He served with distinction in Algeria, and, in the Crimean War, at the battles of the Alma River and Inkerman (1854), and of the Malakhov fortress (1855).

Bosra (boz'rạ). [Also: **Bozrah, Busra**; Latin, **Bostra.**] Village in SW Syria, on the site of an ancient town of Bashan and of a Roman city, notable for several examples of Roman and Moorish architecture. Under Trajan it became the capital of the Roman province of Arabia, under Alexander Severus (222–235) a Roman military colony, and under Philip (244–249) the seat of a bishopric (metropolitan). Later it became the seat of an archbishopric. On its site are many ruins. The cathedral, built in 512 A.D., is square on the exterior; the interior is a circle 91 ft. in diameter, with an apse in each of the four angles. The circle was covered with a wooden dome. On the E side projects a choir flanked by *parabemata* (the sacristy, and the chapel in which the Eucharist is prepared), outside of which are two large chapels. The Mosque of Omar el-Ketab, an example of a very early type, resembles an open cloister. It has on two sides a vaulted double gallery with fine columns, having monolithic shafts of green cipolin marble and antique white marble capitals of various orders. The walls bear a rich frieze of arabesques. The handsome square minaret is 150 ft. high. The Roman triumphal arch has three openings, besides a transverse archway. The chief opening is ab. 40 ft. high. The arch is ornamented with pilasters. The Roman theater is in great part covered by a strong, square-towered Arabian castle. Several tiers of seats of the *cavea* (auditorium) are exposed in the castle court. The cavea, ab. 250 ft. in diameter, is supported on vaulted foundations. Flights of steps ascend from outside to the landing between the tiers of seats and there was a gallery with Doric columns above the cavea. The stage structure is unusually perfect. The stage itself is ab. 25 ft. deep.

Boss (bôs, bos), **Lewis.** b. at Providence, R.I., Oct. 26, 1846; d. at Albany, N.Y., Oct. 5, 1912. American astronomer. He was director of the Dudley Observatory, at Albany, N.Y., from 1876, and also director of the department of meridian astronomy at the Carnegie Institution from 1906. He was graduated from Dartmouth College in 1870, was astronomer of the northern boundary commission (1872–76), and was chief of the U.S. government expedition sent to Chile in 1882 to observe the transit of Venus. He published *Declinations of Fixed Stars* (1878), *Catalogue of 8,241 Stars* (1890), *Positions and Motions of 627 Principal Standard Stars* (1904), *Preliminary General Catalogue of 6,188 Stars* (1910), and numerous scientific papers. He was awarded the gold medal of the Royal Astronomical Society of London in 1905.

Boss, The. Play by Edward Sheldon, produced in 1911 and published in 1917.

Bosse (bos'ẹ), **Robert.** b. at Quedlinburg, Germany, July 12, 1832; d. at Berlin, July 3, 1902. German statesman. As undersecretary of state in the ministry of the interior, he was instrumental in drafting Germany's social security laws. From 1892 to 1899 he served as Prussian minister of cultural affairs.

Bosshart (bos'härt), **Jakob.** b. at Stürzikon, Switzerland, 1862; d. at Clavadel, Switzerland, 1924. Swiss author writing in German. He was a high-school principal at Zurich. In his stories and novels he combined traditional Swiss realism with a searching psychological insight into, and great concern for, the moral disintegration of European society. His *Ein Rufer in der Wüste* (1921) is considered by most critics to be a novel of lasting artistic and philosophical significance.

Bossi (bôs'sē), **Giuseppe.** b. at Busto-Arsizio, Italy, in August, 1777; d. at Milan, Dec. 15, 1815. Italian painter, and writer on art. He organized the Brera Gallery at Milan, and was the author of *Del cenacolo di Leonardo da Vinci* (1810) and other works.

Bossi, Baron **Giuseppe Carlo Aurelio, de'.** b. at Turin, Italy, Nov. 15, 1758; d. at Paris, Jan. 20, 1823. Italian lyric poet and diplomat. His chief poems include *Independenza Americana* (1785), *Monaca* (1787), and *Oromasia* (1805).

Bossi, Count **Luigi.** b. at Milan, Feb. 28, 1758; d. there, April 10, 1835. Italian historian, archaeologist, and writer on art.

Bossi, Marco Enrico. b. at Salo, Italy, April 25, 1861; d. at sea, in February, 1925. Italian composer, organist, and teacher. He was choirmaster and organist (1881–91) at Como Cathedral, director (1896–1902) of the Liceo Benedetto Marcello at Venice, head (1902–12) of the Liceo Musicale at Bologna, and was in charge (1916–23) of the Academy of Saint Cecilia at Rome. His works include *L'Angelo della notte,* a four-act melodramatic opera; short orchestral works; *Il Paradiso Perduto* (1903) for chorus and orchestra; a large body of organ works; and a string and a piano trio. He was coauthor of *Metodo di studio per l'organo moderno* (1893).

Bossier City (bo.sir'). Town in N Louisiana, in Bossier Parish, near Shreveport: oil refineries and railroad shops; manufactures include cotton-oil, grease, and fertilizer. In the decade between the last two U.S. censuses its population more than doubled. 5,786 (1940); 15,470 (1950).

Bossuet (bo.sü.e), **Jacques Bénigne.** b. at Dijon, France, Sept. 27, 1627; d. at Paris, April 12, 1704. French prelate, historian, and theological writer, noted as a pulpit orator. He was preceptor (1670–81) to the dauphin (father of Louis XV), and became bishop of Meaux in 1681. His chief works are *Exposition de la doctrine catholique* (1671), *Discours sur l'histoire universelle* (1681), *Histoire des variations des églises protestantes* (1688), and funeral orations (*Oraisons funèbres*).

Bossut (bo.sü), **Charles.** b. at Tarare, near Lyons, France, Aug. 11, 1730; d. at Paris, Jan. 14, 1814. French mathematician. His chief work was *Essai sur l'histoire générale des mathématiques* (1802).

Boston (bôs'tọn, bos'-). [Original name, **Ikanho;** later name, **Botolphstown.**] Municipal borough and seaport in E England, in Lincolnshire, in the Parts of Holland, situated on the river Witham, ab. 30 mi. SE of Lincoln, ab. 107 mi. N of London by rail. It is the headquarters of a deep-sea fishery, and as a seaport exports pig iron, made in Leicestershire and Northamptonshire, to Scotland and to the Continent. It has a riverside quay 2,440 ft. long, opened in 1938. Boston is in the chief early-potato producing area in England; the region is also important for the raising of peas and beans. It is located in the Fens, and an ancient sea dike from Wainfleet to King's Lynn runs through here. Boston was an important trading town in the Middle Ages. Much of its former importance as a port has been lost as a result of the silting up of the approaches. It was here, while the community was still known as Ikanho, that Saint Botolph founded his famous monastery in 654. From Saint Botolph, the town became known as "Botolphstown," and through contraction of this its modern name of "Boston" was derived. The parish church of Saint Botolph's, which may still be seen at Boston, is a long, low building in Decorated style, with a high tower in Perpendicular style, surmounted by an octagonal lantern, locally known as "Boston Stump." The tower is ab. 300 ft. high. The light and spacious interior has very lofty arches resting on slender pillars, a small clerestory, and a fine east window. Boston is the place where the Pilgrim Fathers, among them William Brewster, were tried (1607) for attempting to flee the country. Boston, Mass., was named for it. 24,453 (1951).

Boston. [Original name, **Trimountain.**] City in E Massachusetts, the capital of Massachusetts and county seat of Suffolk County, on Massachusetts Bay, at the mouths of the Charles and Mystic rivers. It is the largest city in New England, and one of the chief commercial cities and literary centers in the country. It has an extensive foreign and coastwise trade, and is the terminus of many railroad and steamship lines. In terms of annual tonnage, it may be justly called the leading fishing port of the U.S. (although in very recent years it has been surpassed by Los Angeles); it is also one of the four principal Atlantic seaports, importing cacao, coffee, bananas, sugar, paper pulp, and hides. It is the site of a U.S. navy yard. Historical landmarks include Faneuil Hall, the Old North Church (or Christ Church), and the old State House. It was the residence of such notable literary figures as Ralph Waldo Emerson, Nathaniel Hawthorne, Louisa May Alcott, and William Dean Howells, and was called the "Athens of America." The city now contains various annexed districts (including Roxbury, Dorchester, Neponset, and Charlestown). Boston was founded by English colonists (some of them from Boston, England) under John Winthrop in 1630, according to tradition on the recommendation of William Blackstone, who had built on Beacon Hill some years before. It was first named Trimountain, from the three summits of Beacon Hill, and later received its present name in honor of John Cotton, a clergyman who had been settled at Boston in Lincolnshire. It expelled Governor Edmund Andros in 1689, was involved in the witchcraft delusion in 1692, was the scene of the Boston Massacre in 1770 and of the Boston Tea Party in 1773, was besieged (1775–76) by the American army under Washington, and was evacuated by the British on March 17, 1776. It was incorporated as a city in 1822. It suffered from fires in 1676, 1679, 1711, 1760, and especially in the period of Nov. 9–11, 1872 (loss about 80 million dollars). It annexed Roxbury in 1868, and Charlestown, Brighton, Dorchester, and West Roxbury in 1874. It is the seat of Boston University, Northeastern University, Emmanuel College, Simmons College, the New England Conservatory of Music, the Massachusetts College of Pharmacy, Harvard Medical School, the Boston Public Latin School, and the Roxbury Latin School. 801,444 (1950).

Boston. Novel (2 vols., 1928) by Upton Sinclair. It was Sinclair's contribution to the literature of protest against the Sacco-Vanzetti execution and documents the story of the two Italians by showing them through the eyes of an old lady, Cornelia Thornwell, who runs away from her rich family and lives by the work of her own hands among the poor people of the suburbs. In her eyes, they are saints and the judge at their trial is a sinner against every human law.

Boston, Thomas. b. at Dunse, Scotland, March 17, 1677; d. at Ettrick, Scotland, May 20, 1732. Scottish Presbyterian divine. He wrote *Human Nature in Its Fourfold State* (1720) and other works. He was one of 12 clergymen known as "Marrow Men" because they based their views on a book (written anonymously) entitled *The Marrow of Modern Divinity*.

Boston Conservatory of Music. Music school established (1867) and reorganized (1920) at Boston, offering courses in all branches of the field.

Boston Daily Advertiser. New England daily newspaper (1813–1929), the first successful journal in that region.

Boston Daily Evening Transcript. Newspaper (1830–1941) noted among historians interested in American journalism for its undeviating adherence to 19th-century standards of conservative good taste long after these had gone out of fashion in the editorial offices of most American newspapers.

Boston Evening Post. Newspaper (1735–75) which succeeded the *Weekly Rehearsal;* its first editor was Thomas Fleet.

Boston Gazette, The. America's second newspaper, published in the period 1719–41.

Bostonians (bos.tō'ni.ạnz), **The.** [Original name, **Boston Ideal Opera Company.**] Organization established (1879) for the presentation of light operas, the first of which was Gilbert and Sullivan's *Pinafore*. It subsequently toured with Reginald de Koven's *Robin Hood* and Victor Herbert's *The Serenade*, among others. The company's name was changed to its present form in 1887.

Bostonians, The. Novel by Henry James, published in 1886.

Boston Massacre. Incident at Boston, Mass., March 5, 1770, involving the British soldiers stationed there and a small group of citizens. It was occasioned by the prejudices excited against a squad of soldiers who, provoked by words and blows, fired at the crowd, killing three and wounding eight (two mortally). The members of the squad, together with their captain, Thomas Preston, were tried (defended by John Adams and Josiah Quincy) and acquitted, except two, who were convicted of manslaughter and punished lightly. The "massacre," which was greatly exaggerated and has become legendary in the popular conception of American history, contributed to the formation of anti-British sentiment in the era preceding the outbreak of the Revolutionary War.

Boston Miscellany of Literature and Fashion. Magazine of criticism, published (1842–43) monthly. Among its contributors were Nathaniel Hawthorne, James Russell Lowell, and Edgar Allan Poe.

Boston Mountains. [Also, **Ozark Mountains.**] Mountain region in NW Arkansas, ab. 70 mi. NW of Little Rock. It is a very rugged, wooded area, with river valleys from 500 to 1,500 ft. deep, and peak elevations up to ab. 2,500 ft.; the roughest part of the Ozark Plateau. Length, ab. 150 mi.; greatest width, ab. 50 mi.

Boston Music Company. Music-publishing firm established (1885) by Gustave Schirmer, with offices at Boston and at New York.

Boston News-Letter. Colonial newspaper (1704–76) initially issued as a hand-written report sent to colonial governors in New England. It was later published as *The Boston Weekly News-Letter and New-England Chronicle*, and subsequently as *The Massachusetts Gazette and Boston News-Letter*.

Boston Port Act. Bill introduced by Frederick North, and passed by the British Parliament, in March, 1774, closing the port of Boston, Mass., after June 1, 1774. It was designed as a punitive measure in retaliation for the Boston Tea Party, and is known as one of the Coercive Acts, or "Intolerable Acts."

Boston Public Library. Building at Boston Mass., in the Roman Renaissance style, situated on the W side of Copley Square. It was erected in the period 1888–95, at a cost of 2,486,000 dollars, from the designs of the architectural firm of McKim, Mead, and White. It is ab. 228 ft. long, 225 ft. wide, and 68 ft. high (to the cornice), and encloses an open court ab. 136 ft. long and ab. 100 ft. wide. The decorations include sculpture by Frederick William MacMonnies, Augustus Saint-Gaudens, and Louis Saint-Gaudens, and paintings by Puvis de Chavannes, Edwin A. Abbey, John Singer Sargent, and others. Among its valuable collections are the Ticknor collection of Spanish and Portuguese books, the Barton library (containing Shakespeariana), the Prince library (manuscripts and early New England books), and the Barlow library (Americana).

Boston Quarterly Review, The. Review founded and edited by Orestes Brownson and published at Boston, Mass., in the period 1838–42. It was noted for its receptivity to new ideas.

Boston Society of Natural History. Organization founded in 1830 (incorporated 1831) at Boston, Mass., for the purpose of encouraging and promoting the science of natural history. It maintains a library of 6,000 volumes and 4,000 pamphlets, and issues publications including *Memoirs* (irregularly) and the *New England Naturalist* (quarterly).

"Boston Stump." See under **Boston,** England.

Boston Symphony Orchestra. Ensemble established (1881) at Boston, Mass., by Henry Lee Higginson with Sir George Henschel as first conductor. Among its later conductors have been Artur Nikisch (1889–93), Pierre Monteux (1918–24), Serge Koussevitzky (1924–49), and Charles Munch (1949 *et seq.*).

Boston Tea Party. Demonstration by colonial patriots at Boston, Mass., on Dec. 16, 1773, as a protest against the attempted importation of tea into the colonies. A large popular assembly met at the Old South Church to voice their grievances. As their protest was ineffectual, the same evening a body of about 50 men, disguised more or less as Indians, boarded the three British tea-ships in the harbor, and threw 342 chests of tea (valued at 18,000 pounds) into the water. The incident marked the rising influence of the radical wing in the colonies, and helped initiate the open break between Great Britain and the American colonists.

Bostra (bos′trạ). Latin name of **Bosra.**

Boström (bö′strėm), **Erik Gustaf Bernhard.** b. at Stockholm, Feb. 11, 1842; d. there, Feb. 21, 1907. Swedish political leader, twice premier (1891–1900, 1902–05) during the period of sharp crisis in Sweden's relations with Norway, prior to the dissolution of the Swedish-Norwegian union. His policy of mediation, which failed to prevent Norwegian independence, was also applied to questions of tariff, military service, and suffrage. Elected to parliament in 1876, he was a Conservative leader, but moved toward the Liberals after the fall of his first cabinet.

Bostwick (bost′wik), **Arthur Elmore.** b. at Litchfield, Conn., March 8, 1860; d. Feb. 13, 1942. American scientific writer, librarian of the St. Louis Public Library from 1909. He was librarian of the New York Free Circulating Library (1895–99) and of the Brooklyn Public Library (1899–1901), and was chief of the department of circulation of the New York Public Library (1901–09).

Boswell (boz′wel, -wẹl), **Alexander.** [Title, Lord **Auchinleck.**] b. 1706; d. 1782. Scottish judge; father of James Boswell (1740–95). Appointed (1754) lord of session, he served in that capacity until his death, while also serving (1755–80) as lord justiciary. His son, in *Journal of A Tour to the Hebrides,* tells of Samuel Johnson's visit to him at Auchinleck.

Boswell, Sir **Alexander.** b. at Auchinleck, Scotland, 1775; d. of a collarbone wound inflicted in a duel, at Balmuto, Scotland, 1822. Scottish antiquary and poet; son of James Boswell (1740–95). After an education at Oxford, he settled (1795) at the family home at Auchinleck. In 1818 and 1820 he represented Plympton, Devonshire, in Parliament. At his home he established a private press and issued series of reprints of old poems, entitled *Frondes Caducae* (1816–18). He originated the idea of erecting a monument to Robert Burns on the banks of Doon, published poetical and antiquarian writings and edited several reprints of ancient works, and was poet laureate of the Harveian Society of Edinburgh.

Boswell, James. b. at Edinburgh, Scotland, Oct. 29, 1740; d. at London, May 19, 1795. An English man of letters, notable as a diarist and biographer of Dr. Samuel Johnson. He was the son of Alexander Boswell, a judge of the Court of Session at Edinburgh, who took the style of Lord Auchinleck from the ancient estate of the Boswell family in Ayrshire. James Boswell was admitted to the Scots bar in 1766, succeeded to Auchinleck in 1782, was called to the English bar in 1786 (removing his family to London in that year), and was elected Recorder of Carlisle in 1788. For upwards of 20 years he practiced law with complete regularity and a fair degree of assiduity; had plenty of business so long as he remained in Scotland, but never won distinction in his profession. In 1765, while traveling on the Continent, he went to Corsica, then in a state of armed revolt from the Republic of Genoa, and established an intimacy with General Paoli. This adventure he exploited in 1768 in *An Account of Corsica, the Journal of a Tour to that Island, and Memoirs of Pascal Paoli,* a book which had a considerable contemporary success in England and America, and was widely translated. In 1763 he made the acquaintance at London of Dr. Johnson, whom he accompanied on a journey to the Hebrides in 1773, and whom he managed to attend at London nearly every year during the vacations of the Scots courts. He began keeping a private journal as early as 1758. From this he drew the most valuable portion of his book on Corsica; and in 1785, a year after Johnson's death, he published a particularly brilliant segment as *The Journal of a Tour to the Hebrides with Samuel Johnson, LL.D.* In 1791 appeared his famous *Life of Samuel Johnson.* The journal again furnished the parts of the work that make it unique—Johnson's casual conversations, dramatically rendered. Boswell's voluminous papers, which for a century were supposed to have perished, became (1950) the property of Yale University. Though Boswell was vain and had the more serious weaknesses of incontinence and intemperance, he was a wellborn, cultured, and intelligent man, and in his own special fields of self-analysis and the imaginative recording of familiar history, especially as revealed in conversation, he stands without a peer in English letters. The standard biographies are *Young Boswell* (1922), by C. B. Tinker, and *A New Portrait of Boswell* (1927), by C. B. Tinker and F. A. Pottle; see also *The Hooded Hawk* (1947), by D. B. Wyndham Lewis.

Boswell, James. b. 1778; d. at London, 1822. Scottish lawyer and Shakespeare scholar; son of James Boswell (1740–95). Educated at Oxford (B.A. 1801 and M.A. 1806), he was elected a fellow on the Vinerian foundation. In 1805 he was called to the bar of the Inner Temple, London, and he was afterwards appointed a commissioner of bankrupts. He assisted Edmund Malone in collecting and compiling the materials for his second edition of Shakespeare, and upon Malone's death-bed request, completed it; he edited (1821) the third variorum Shakespeare.

Bosworth (boz′wėrth). See **Market Bosworth.**

Bosworth, Francke Huntington. b. at Marietta, Ohio, Jan. 25, 1843; d. Oct. 17, 1925. American laryngologist. He took his M.D. degree in 1868, and was a professor (1881 *et seq.*) at Bellevue Hospital Medical College. His publications include *Handbook upon Diseases of the Throat for the Use of Students* (1879), *Manual of the Diseases of the Throat and Nose* (1881), and *A Treatise on Diseases of the Nose and Throat* (2 vols.; vol. 1, 1889; vol. 2, 1892).

Bosworth, Joseph. b. in Derbyshire, England, 1789; d. May 27, 1876. English philologist, appointed Rawlinson professor of Anglo-Saxon at Oxford in 1858. His chief work is *Dictionary of the Anglo-Saxon Language,* published in 1838. In 1848 he published an abridgment of it under the title *A Compendious Dictionary of Anglo-Saxon.* The larger work was edited after its author's death by Thomas Northcote Toller (part I, 1882; part II, 1898; supplement, 1908).

Bosworth, William Welles. b. at Marietta, Ohio, 1869—. American architect who designed the American Telephone and Telegraph Company Building, New York, buildings for the Massachusetts Institute of Technology, and many buildings for the Rockefeller family. He studied at the Marietta Academy, the Massachusetts Institute of Technology, and the École des Beaux-Arts, Paris. He supervised restorations at Versailles and Fontainebleau, and of the cathedral at Reims. He also designed Letchworth Village for New York State and the monument to Pierre Charles L'Enfant in Arlington National Cemetery. In 1928 he was made an academician of the National Academy; he is also a commander of the Legion of Honor.

Bosworth Field. Battlefield in C England, in W Leicestershire, ab. 13 mi. N of Coventry, the site of the last battle in the Wars of the Roses, in 1485, when Richard III was killed and the crown passed to Henry VII (Henry Tudor).

Botanical Society of America, Inc. Organization originally set up (1894) as the Botanical Society of America for the purpose of advancing knowledge in all fields of plant science. It issues the *American Journal of Botany* (monthly).

Botany Bay (bot'ạ.ni). Inlet in SE Australia, ab. 6 mi. S of the center of Sydney, opening E to the Pacific Ocean. Captain Cook made the first landing in Australia here in 1770, and the settlement of Australia was begun here in 1788. The suburban areas of the city of Sydney have grown out to reach the bay. In English and Australian history, its name has long been connected with the penal colony which once existed in Australia (and which was actually situated on the site of what is now Sydney). Length, ab. 10 mi.; greatest width, ab. 6 mi.

Bote and Bock (bō'tẹ; bok). Music-publishing firm established (1838) at Berlin by Eduard Bote and Gustav Bock, noted especially for its editions of sacred music.

Botein (bō.tẹ̄.in'). A name given to the two stars δ and ϵ Arietis.

Botetourt (bot'ẹ.tört, bot'ẹ.tot), Baron **de.** [Title of **Norborne Berkeley.**] b. in England, c1718; d. at Williamsburg, Va., Oct. 15, 1770. English politician, governor of Virginia in the period 1768–70. He dissolved the House of Burgesses in 1769 for passing resolutions condemning parliamentary taxation and the trial of Americans in England. He attempted to influence the home government to abandon the principle of parliamentary taxation, and failing in this he resigned.

Botha (bō'tä), **Louis.** b. at Greytown, Natal, Sept. 27, 1862; d. Aug. 27, 1919. South African general and statesman. During the Boer War (1899–1902), he commanded the Boer forces during part of the siege of Ladysmith (Oct. 29, 1899 *et seq.*), at Colenso (Dec. 15, 1899), and at Spion Kop (Jan. 22–24, 1900); on the death of Petrus Jacobus Joubert, he became chief commander of the Boer forces. When the war ended he became a vigorous advocate of Boer political cooperation with the British. In 1907 when the crown colony of the Transvaal became a self-governing unit within the British Empire, he became its first prime minister; in 1910 he became premier of the Union of South Africa (which was established in that year as a British dominion comprising the four provinces of the Transvaal, Natal, Orange Free State, and Cape of Good Hope). At this time, and thereafter until he died, his chief political supporter and loyal coworker in the South African government was Jan Christiaan Smuts, who shared Botha's conviction that wholehearted Anglo-Boer cooperation was now essential to the development of South Africa. Many Boers, embittered by their memories of the war of 1899–1902, and still clinging to the dream of a completely independent and ethnically homogeneous Boer state, considered Botha to be virtually a traitor to their country; at the outbreak of World War I, when Botha unhesitatingly aligned the Union of South Africa with the other British dominions in a common military effort against the Central Powers, these anti-British sentiments crystallized (with, unquestionably, a certain amount of clandestine encouragement from Berlin) into an actual revolt, which Botha's government promptly suppressed. Thereafter, Botha himself took a leading part in the war in Africa, and was the actual commander of the troops which wrested what is now the territory of South-West Africa (under the Union of South Africa) from the German colonial forces who had held it up to that time.

Bothie of Tober-na-Vuolich (bō'ᴛʜi; tō'bėr.nạ.vwô'lich), **The.** Novelette (1848) in hexameters by Arthur Hugh Clough.

Bothmer (bōt'mėr), Count **Felix von.** b. at Munich, Germany, Dec. 10, 1852; d. there, March 18, 1937. German general, in charge of the German southern army and of the 19th army in World War I. He commanded the German defense during the Brussilov offensive in the summer and fall of 1916.

Bothnia (both'ni.ạ). Former province of Sweden, E and W of the Gulf of Bothnia; partly in what is now Finland.

Bothnia, Gulf of. Northern extension or arm of the Baltic Sea, between Finland on the E and Sweden on the W. Length, 400 mi.; breadth, ab. 100 mi.

Bothwell (both'wel, -wẹl; boᴛʜ'-), 4th Earl of. [Title of **James Hepburn.**] b. c1536; d. 1578. Scottish noble, husband of Mary, Queen of Scots. He took no part in the murder of Rizzio, and aided Mary, after that event, in her flight from Holyrood, and was her chief supporter. He was the principal in the assassination of Darnley, was tried for the murder, under circumstances which made his conviction practically impossible, and was acquitted. On April 24, 1567, while the queen was returning to Edinburgh, she was met by Bothwell, who, with a show of force, carried her to his castle of Dunbar. He obtained a divorce from his wife early in May, and married the queen soon after (May 15, 1567). They were divorced in 1570. He became a pirate and died insane.

Bothwell. Civil parish in S Scotland, on the river Clyde SE of Glasgow, ab. 395 mi. N of London by rail. The ruins of Bothwell Castle and of a 13th-century priory are in the vicinity. At Bothwell Bridge, near here, in 1679, a battle was fought in which the Scottish Covenanters were defeated by an English army under the Duke of Monmouth. 60,660 (1931).

Bothwell. Tragedy by Algernon Charles Swinburne, published in 1874. It is the second part of a trilogy on Mary, Queen of Scots.

Bothwell Bridge, Battle of. Battle fought near Bothwell, Scotland, in which the Scottish Covenanters were decisively defeated by an English army under the Duke of Monmouth, on June 22, 1679. (The Covenanters were Scottish Presbyterians who had made a pledge (or "covenant") of mutual support against any attack on Presbyterianism). From 1638, when Archbishop William Laud attempted to make them accept the Anglican Book of Common Prayer, to the fall of James II of England in 1688, they were intermittently in revolt against or under attack by the English. In 1650, in order to get their support in his effort to gain the crown, Charles II of England had committed himself not to violate their religious liberty, but when he actually acceded to the throne his actions were guided by immediate expediency rather than his promise, and he alternately harried and sought to pacify the Covenanters. In 1675 he sent James Scott, the Duke of Monmouth (whom he had acknowledged as his illegitimate son in 1663) to subdue them, and the Battle of Bothwell Bridge was the final and decisive encounter in this particular phase of the 17th-century conflict between the Scottish Presbyterians and the government of Great Britain.)

Both Your Houses. Play by Maxwell Anderson, produced in 1933 and published in the same year. It was awarded the Pulitzer prize. The plot revolves around the political battles waged against graft and corruption by a young U.S. congressman, Alan McClean.

Botocudo (bō.tō.kö'dō). [Also, **Aimoré.**] South American Indian tribe, now virtually extinct, which formerly inhabited the adjacent inland areas and portions of the coast of Brazil between ab. latitudes 15° and 22° S. Their name is derived from the Portuguese word *botoque,* (plug), and refers to the large wooden disks worn in the lips and ears by members of the tribe as ornaments. The Botocudo resisted fiercely the colonial efforts of Portuguese settlers until well into the 19th century. Their language comprised an independent linguistic stock.

Botolph (bọ.tolf') or **Botolphus** (-tol'fus), Saint. [Also, Saint **Botulf.**] fl. 7th century. English monk. According to Old English chronicles, he founded (654) a monastery at Ikanho in Lincolnshire, which is now called Boston (contracted from Botolphstown). He instituted the rule of Saint Benedict there. His death is commemorated on June 17.

Botolphstown (bot'ọlfs.toun). See **Boston,** England.

Botoşani (bō.tō.shän′, -shä′nē). [Also: **Botoshan** (bō.to.shän′), **Botushani.**] Town in NE Rumania, in Moldavia, ab. 60 mi. NW of Iaşi. It has agricultural markets, mills, wheat and oil markets, and clothing factories. 29,145 (1948).

Bo Tree (bō). See under **Buddha.**

Botrel (bo.trel), **Théodore.** b. at Dinan, France, Sept. 14, 1868; d. at Pont Aven, France, 1925. Breton poet and dramatist. He was the author of *Chansons de chez nous* (1898), *Les Chansons de Jean-qui-chante*, and others.

Botsford (bots′fo̤rd), **George Willis.** b. at West Union, Iowa, May 9, 1862; d. at New York, Dec. 13, 1917. American historian. He served as professor of Greek at Kalamazoo College (1886–90) and Bethany College (1891–95), and as professor of ancient history (1910–17) at Columbia University. He was the author of *The Development of the Athenian Constitution* (1893), *A History of Greece for High Schools and Academies* (1899), *A History of Rome for High Schools and Academies* (1901), *An Ancient History* (1902), *The Roman Assemblies* (1909), *History of the Ancient World* (1911), and *Hellenic History* (1922); coauthor, with Lillie S. Botsford, of *A Source-book of Ancient History* (1912) and, with E. G. Sihler, of *Hellenic Civilization* (1915).

Bott (bot), **Jean Joseph.** b. 1826; d. 1895. German composer and violinist. He was *Kapellmeister* (choir leader) at Meiningen and Hanover (1865). His compositions include two operas, symphonies, songs, piano works, and violin concertos.

Botta (bôt′tä, bot′a̤), **Anne Charlotte Lynch.** b. at Bennington, Vt., Nov. 11, 1815; d. at New York, March 23, 1891. American writer. In 1855 she married Vincenzo Botta, and their house at New York became a literary center. She wrote *Leaves from the Diary of a Recluse* (1845), and *Poems* (1848).

Botta (bôt′tä), **Carlo Giuseppe Guglielmo.** b. at San Giorgio del Canavese, Piedmont, Italy, Nov. 6, 1766; d. at Paris, Aug. 10, 1837. Italian historian; father of Paul Émile Botta. His works include *Storia della guerra dell'independenza degli Stati Uniti d'America* (1809), *Storia d'Italia dal 1789 al 1814* (1824), and *Storia d'Italia continuata da quella del Guicciardini* (1832).

Botta (bo.tà), **Paul Émile.** b. at Turin, Italy, Dec. 6, 1802; d. at Archères, near Poissy, France, March 29, 1870. French archaeologist and traveler; son of Carlo Giuseppe Guglielmo Botta. He was noted for his archaeological discoveries in Assyria. His work, which included the excavation of a palace near Khorsabad, is described in *Monument de Ninive découvert et décrit par Botta* (5 vols., 1847–50).

Botta (bôt′tä, bot′a̤), **Vincenzo.** b. at Cavallermaggiore, Italy, Nov. 11, 1818; d. at New York, Oct. 5, 1894. American educator; husband (married 1855) of Anne Charlotte Lynch Botta. He was graduated at the University of Turin and subsequently held the post of professor of philosophy there. In 1849 he was elected to the Sardinian parliament. For more than 30 years he was professor of Italian language and literature at the University of the City of New York (later to be called New York University). He wrote *Discourse on the Life, Character, and Policy of Cavour* (1862), *Dante as Philosopher, Patriot, and Poet* (1865), and others.

Bottari (bōt.tä′rē), **Giovanni Gaetano.** b. at Florence, Jan. 15, 1689; d. at Rome, June 3, 1775. Italian prelate and archaeologist.

Bottesini (bōt.tā.zē′nē), **Giovanni.** b. at Crema, Italy, c1822; d. at Parma, Italy, July 7, 1889. Italian virtuoso on the double bass, and conductor and composer, noted as the most celebrated contrabassist of his time. He wrote several operas and symphonies.

Böttger (bėt′ċhėr), **Adolf.** b. at Leipzig, Germany, May 21, 1815; d. at Gohlis, near Leipzig, Nov. 16, 1870. German poet. He translated poems of Byron, Goldsmith, Pope, Milton, and others, and wrote *Habaña* (1853), *Der Fall von Babylon* (1855), *Till Eulenspiegel* (1850), and a drama, *Agnes Bernauer* (1845). His fairy tales are usually considered his best work (*Das Galgenmärchen*, 1870).

Böttger, Johann Friedrich. [Also: **Böttcher** (bėt′ċhėr), **Böttiger** (-i.gėr).] b. at Schleiz, Germany, Feb. 4, 1682; d. at Dresden, Germany, March 13, 1719. German chemist, noted as the discoverer of the process by which Dresden china is made. His porcelains were widely esteemed, and when Sweden invaded Dresden in 1706, he was removed from the city in order to safeguard the formula.

Botticelli (bōt.tē.chel′lē), **Sandro.** [Original name, **Alessandro di Mariano dei Filipepi.**] b. at Florence, c1444; d. there, May 17, 1510. Italian painter. He was a pupil of Filippo Lippi, and was influenced by Antonio Pollaiuolo and Andrea Castagno. Among his earliest works are *Fortitude*, a series of circular pictures in the Uffizi at Florence, and madonnas now in the collection of the Uffizi and at London. In 1478 he painted, for the Villa di Castello, *Spring* and *Birth of Venus* (both in the Uffizi). Among his notable pictures is a reconstruction of the *Calumny* of Apelles from the description of Lucian. For Pier Francesco de' Medici he made a series of illustrations to the *Divina Commedia* of Dante, 84 of which were later acquired by the Kaiser Friedrich Museum at Berlin, and eight of which were acquired by the Vatican. In 1482 he was invited by Pope Sixtus IV to assist in the decoration of the Sistine Chapel. He became one of the followers of Savonarola, and changed the subject-matter and style of his work to conform to his new religious attitude.

Bötticher (bėt′i.ċhėr), **Karl.** b. at Nordhausen, Germany, May 29, 1806; d. at Berlin, June 21, 1889. German archaeologist, assistant director (1854–68) and director (1868–76) of the sculpture gallery of the Berlin Museum. His chief work, *Tektonik der Hellenen* (1844–52), was considered an important contribution to the knowledge of Greek architecture.

Böttiger (bėt′i.gėr), **Karl August.** b. at Reichenbach, Saxony, Germany, June 8, 1760; d. at Dresden, Germany, Nov. 17, 1835. German archaeologist, director (1791–1804) of the *Gymnasium* (advanced secondary school) at Weimar. After 1804 he lived at Dresden. He wrote *Sabina, oder Morgenscenen im Putzzimmer einer reichen Römerin* (1803), *Griechische Vasengemälde* (1797–1800), and others.

Böttiger, Karl Vilhelm. b. at Westrås, Sweden, May 15, 1807; d. at Uppsala, Sweden, Dec. 22, 1878. Swedish poet. His collected writings were published in 1856.

Bottineau (bot.in.ō′), **Pierre.** b. c1817; d. July 26, 1895. American frontier guide. He led (1837) James Dickson and companions from Selkirk settlement to Fort Snelling, led Pacific Railway (1853) and Northern Pacific (1869) expeditions to Fort Benton, guided (1862) the James L. Fisk expedition to the Montana mining country, and served as a scout (1863) with General Henry H. Sibley in pursuit of the Sioux Indians.

Bottom (bot′o̤m), **Nick.** In Shakespeare's *A Midsummer Night's Dream*, an Athenian weaver who plays the part of Pyramus in the interpolated play. He is ambitious and enthusiastic, and in his eagerness wants to take all the parts in the play. While rehearsing the play in the forest, he has an ass's head put on him by Puck. In this guise he meets Titania; she has been put under a spell by Oberon to love the first person she sees on waking; when this is Bottom with his ass's head, she is deluded into thinking him beautiful, until Oberon releases her from the magic.

Bottome (bo.tōm′), **Margaret McDonald.** b. at New York, Dec. 29, 1827; d. Nov. 4, 1906. American writer, founder and president of the International order of the King's Daughters and Sons, a society for the study and spread of Christian principles. She was an editor of the *Ladies' Home Journal*, and contributed many articles to religious and other papers. Among her publications are *Crumbs from the King's Table, A Sunshine Trip to the Orient*, and *Heart to Heart Letters*.

Bottome, Phyllis. b. at Rochester, England, May 31, 1884—. English novelist; daughter of an American clergyman; wife (1917 *et seq.*) of Ernan Forbes Dennis. She published *Raw Material*, her first novel, in 1905, and used her experiences as a relief worker (1919 *et seq.*) at Vienna in *Old Wine*. Her other works include *Wind in His Fists* (1931), *Private Worlds* (1934), *Level Crossing* (1936), *The Mortal Storm* (1937), *Danger Signal* (1939), *London Pride* (1941), *Within the Cup* (1943), *From the Life* (1944), *Life-Line* (1946), and *Under the Skin* (1950).

Bottomley (bot′o̤m.li), **Gordon.** b. at Keighley, Yorkshire, England, Feb. 20, 1874—. English playwright, poet, and Elizabethan scholar. He has written the plays

King Lear's Wife (1915) and *Gruach* (1921), on Shakespearean themes. His one-act tragedy *The Riding to Lithend* (1909) is based on Icelandic sagas. The three dramatic eclogues collected as *A Vision of Giorgione* (1910) have their source in Renaissance Italy. The one-act plays published under the title *The White Widow* (1936) are of Scottish origin. His other works include the two-volume *Chambers of Imagery* (1907, 1912), *The Crier by Night* (1902), *Poems of Thirty Years* (1925), *Lyric Plays* (1932), and *Kate Kennedy* (1945).

Bottomley, Horatio William. b. 1860; d. at London, May 26, 1933. English businessman, editor, politician, and orator. Educated at Mason College, at Birmingham, he went to London, where he engaged in business and journalism. He founded (1888) the *Financial Times,* a London daily, and established (1906) *John Bull,* a political and satirical weekly of which he was owner and editor. In its pages he exposed various forms of fraud in business; frequently involved in lawsuits in which he acted as his own lawyer, he was found guilty of fraudulent practices and was imprisoned (1922–27). As a Liberal member of Parliament for South Hackney (1906–12, 1918–22), he criticized the administration and constantly advocated a "business government" as the country's great need. He died a pauper.

Bottom the Weaver (bot'om), **The Merry Conceited Humours of.** Farce made from the comic scenes of *A Midsummer Night's Dream,* published in 1672, attributed to Robert Cox, a comedian of the time of Charles I of England.

Bottrop (bot'rop). City in W Germany, in the *Land* (state) of North Rhine-Westphalia, British Zone, formerly in the province of Westphalia, Prussia, situated near the Rhine-Herne Canal, ab. 5 mi. NW of Essen. It belongs to the Ruhr coal district, and has numerous coal mines, coke furnaces, cement works, and metallurgical, electrical, machine, leather, and rubber manufactures. The majority of the population is Roman Catholic. 93,268 (1950).

Botts (bots), **Charles Tyler.** b. in Virginia, 1809; d. at Oakland, Calif., 1884. American agriculturist and editor. He established (1841) the *Southern Planter,* an agricultural journal, and in 1848 emigrated to California, where he became publisher of the Sacramento *Standard.*

Botts, John Minor. b. at Dumfries, Va., Sept. 16, 1802; d. in Culpeper County, Va., Jan. 7, 1869. American politician, a member of Congress in the periods 1839–43 and 1847–49. An anti-secessionist, he wrote *The Great Rebellion, Its Secret History* (1866) and others.

Botucatú (bö.tö.ka.tö'). City in SE Brazil, in the state of São Paulo. 23,692 (1950).

Botulf (bō.tulf'), Saint. See **Botolph** or **Botolphus,** Saint.

Boturini Benaduci (bō.tö.rē'nē bä.nä.dö'chē), **Lorenzo.** b. at Milan, c1680; d. at Madrid, 1740. Italian antiquary.

Botushani (bō.tö.shä'nē). See **Botoşani.**

Botvinnik (bôt'vē.nyik), **Mikhail.** b. in Russia, April 17, 1911—. Russian chess master and world chess champion (1948 *et seq.*). He held the U.S.S.R. championship for many years. His principal tournament successes have been first prizes at Leningrad (1931, 1934), Moscow (1935; equal first), Nottingham (1936; equal first), Groningen (1946), and Moscow (1948).

Botzaris (bôt'sä.rēs), **Markos.** See **Bozzaris** or **Botzaris, Marco** (or **Markos**).

Bouaké (bwä'kā). [Also, **Bwake.**] Town in the Ivory Coast territory, French West Africa, in about the center of the territory on the railway line between Abidjan and Bobo-Dioulasso, ab. 200 mi. N of Abidjan. 16,000 (1943).

Bouchard (bö.shär), **Charles Jacques.** b. at Montier-en-Der, France, Sept. 6, 1837; d. at Lyons, France, Oct. 28, 1915. French physician and biologist. He was a pupil of J. M. Charcot, with whom he collaborated in describing (1866) the fulgurent pains of ataxia. The first to call attention to autointoxication (1887) and to diseases caused by diminished nutrition (1879–80), he also wrote a treatise on general pathology (1899) which was popular as a students' textbook. Author of *Étude sur quelques points de la pathogénie des hémorrhagies cérébrales* (1866), *De la pathogénie des hémorrhagies* (1869), *Secondary Degeneration of the Spinal Cord* (1869), *A Study of some Points in the Pathology of Cerebral Haemorrhage* (1872), *Les Microbes pathogènes* (1892), *Traité de médecine* (1891–94), *Lectures on Autointoxication in Disease, or Self-poisoning of the Individual* (1894), and *Traité de radiologie médicale* (1904).

Bouchard, Henry. b. at Dijon, France, Dec. 13, 1875—. French sculptor, best known for his statues and bas-reliefs for the International Monument of the Reformation at Geneva, Switzerland. He studied under Louis Ernest Barrias at Paris, won (1901) a Prix de Rome, and was a professor (1929–45) at the École des Beaux-Arts, Paris.

Bouchardon (bö.shär.dôn), **Edme.** b. at Chaumont, France, May 29, 1698; d. at Paris, July 27, 1762. French sculptor of the late baroque period. He executed statues, portrait busts, and groups for parks and churches at Paris and its environs.

Bouché (bö.shā'), **Louis.** b. at New York, 1896—. American painter, known particularly for his murals. Son of a French jewelry-designer, he studied (1910–15) at Paris and for the next year at the Art Students League of New York, with Frank V. DuMond. He established himself during the 1920's as a publicity consultant to artists, directed Wanamaker's Gallery of Decorative Arts, and later formed a firm of mural painters. He was awarded a Guggenheim Fellowship (1933), won a purchase prize in the Metropolitan Museum of Art's "Artists for Victory" Exhibition (1942–43), and became (1943) an instructor at the Art Students League. His murals are in the Radio City Music Hall, New York, the Department of Justice and Department of Interior buildings, Washington, D.C., and in the post office, Ellenville, N.Y. Easel paintings are in the Metropolitan Museum of Art and the Whitney Museum of American Art, New York, and others.

Bouché-Leclercq (bö.shā.le.kler), **Louis Théodore Auguste.** b. at Francières, France, 1842; d. at Nogent-sur-Marne, France, July 18, 1923. French historian. He served as a professor (1879 *et seq.*) at Paris, and was the author of *Histoire des Lagides* (1903–07) and *Histoire des Séleucides* (1913–14).

Boucher (bö.shā), **André.** b. at Nogent-sur-Seine, Aube, France, Sept. 23, 1850; d. at Aix, Bouches-du-Rhône, France, 1934. French sculptor, best known for his bronze group *Au but* (1886) in the Luxembourg Gardens. He studied with Paul Dubois at Paris, received numerous awards, and exhibited in the Paris Salon from 1874.

Boucher, François. b. at Paris, Sept. 29, 1703; d. there, May 30, 1770. French painter of historical and pastoral subjects and genre pieces. The special strength of Boucher lay in his grouping and decorative treatment of women and children. A popular artist in his day, he was a favorite of Madame de Pompadour. His style was in the tradition of Jean Antoine Watteau, under whom he had studied.

Boucher (bou'chėr), **Jonathan.** b. at Blencogo, near Wigton, Cumberland, England, March 12, 1738; d. at Epsom, England, April 27, 1804. English clergyman and writer. He collected materials for a *Glossary of Archaic and Provincial Words,* a part of which (the letter A) was published in 1807, and another part (as far as "Blade") in 1832; it was originally planned as a supplement to Samuel Johnson's dictionary.

Boucher (bö.shā), **Pierre.** b. in Perche, France, 1622; d. at Boucherville, Canada, April 20, 1717. French pioneer in Canada. He was the author of *Histoire véritable et naturelle des mœurs et des productions de la Nouvelle France* (1663).

Boucher de Crèvecoeur de Perthes (de krev.kėr de pert), **Jacques.** b. at Rethel, Ardennes, France, Sept. 10, 1788; d. at Amiens, France, Aug. 5, 1868. French archaeologist and man of letters. He was the first to prove the existence of man in the Pleistocene epoch. His works include *De la création* (1839–41) and *Antiquités celtiques et antédiluviennes* (1847–65).

Boucher-Desnoyers (bö.shā.dā.nwä.yā). See **Desnoyers, Auguste Gaspard Louis Boucher,** Baron.

Bouches-du-Rhône (bösh.dü.rōn). Department in S France, bounded by the department of Vaucluse on the N, the department of Var on the E, the Mediterranean Sea on the S, and the department of Gard on the W. The region was colonized in ancient times by Phoenicians and Greeks, and later annexed by the Romans; it was subject to Moorish and Saracen invasions. In the Middle Ages it was part of Provence, coming under the French crown in the reign of Louis XI. After centuries of peace, it again saw war and destruction in World War II. In some of the cities of the department, remnants of Roman and medieval architecture have been preserved. The population is of Mediterranean stock, the product of many mixtures. Agriculture likewise is of the Mediterranean type. Industry, commerce, and navigation, however, are more important in the economic life of the department; they are concentrated in Marseilles, with chemical, textile, and food industries predominating. Nine tenths of the soap production of France comes from Marseilles. There are lignite mines which produce two thirds of the total French output. Capital, Marseilles; area, 2,025 sq. mi.; pop. 976,220 (1946).

Bouchor (bö.shôr), **Joseph Félix.** b. at Paris, Sept. 15, 1853—. French landscape painter, illustrator, and pastel artist, notable for his Oriental scenes as well as his studies of the French countryside. He was a pupil of Benjamin Constant and Jules Joseph Lefebvre, and first exhibited at the Salon des Artistes Français in 1878. He won several prizes at Paris, and became a Chevalier of the Legion of Honor in 1900. Among his better-known works are *Oasis*, *Farm Road*, *Spring and Autumn*, and *Sahara Camp*.

Bouchor, Maurice. b. at Paris, 1855; d. there, 1929. French poet, playwright, and translator of Shakespeare. He was the author of much light verse under such titles as *Contes parisiens en vers* (1880), and of parlor drama for amateurs, including *Théâtre pour les jeunes filles* (1906).

Boucicault (bö′sẹ.kō), **Dion.** [Also: **Bourcicault**; original name, **Dionysius Lardner Boursiquot.**] b. at Dublin, Dec. 26, 1820 (some sources say 1822); d. at New York, Sept. 18, 1890. American dramatist, manager, and actor. Existing accounts of his early life reveal a considerable amount of confusion, both as to dating and to actual episodes. However, he is now usually believed to have been only nominally the son of Boursiquot, the French refugee who was married to his mother; a certain Dionysius Lardner, who boarded in their house, is held to have been his actual father, and this is given some credence both by the similarity in names and by the fact that Lardner is known to have paid for Boucicault's education at London. He was first married to Agnes Robertson, the adopted daughter of Charles Kean, who was herself an actress of some note. (Some accounts have it that he separated from her many years later, declaring that he had never been legally married.) He toured extensively in the U.S. His plays include *London Assurance* (1841), *Old Heads and Young Hearts* (1843), *Colleen Bawn* (1860), *Arrah-na-Pogue* (1865), a version of *Rip Van Winkle* (1865), and *The Shaughraun* (1874).

Boucicaut (bö.sẹ.kō), **Jean.** [Also: **Bouciquaut**; original name, **Jean le Meingre.**] b. c1366; d. 1421. French marshal. His life was spent in warfare and he was already a veteran of several campaigns when he was captured by the Turks in 1396. Having been ransomed from this captivity he returned to the Turkish wars in 1399, commanding a fleet and an army of 1,400 men which rendered valuable and perhaps decisive service to the Byzantine emperor Manuel II Palaeologus in the defense of Constantinople. Boucicaut scattered the Turkish naval forces at Gallipoli and defeated them at the Golden Horn. He returned to France with the purpose of raising additional forces for the war against the Turks, but was sent to govern Genoa, then under French rule. This post he held for several years, but during his absence the Genoese successfully revolted in 1409. Continuing in his king's service, he fought at Agincourt, and on that day of disaster for the French was taken prisoner, and detained in England until his death. Renowned for his skill in knightly tournaments, Boucicaut originated the medieval order known as "Dame blanche à l'écu vert," dedicated to the defense of wives and daughters of absent knights.

Boudet (bö.de), Count **Jean.** b. at Bordeaux, France, Feb. 19, 1769; d. at Budweis (now České Budějovice, Czechoslovakia), Sept. 14, 1809. French general. He was sent, in 1794, to the West Indies, where he recovered Guadeloupe from the English and aided in the attacks on St. Vincent and Grenada. On his return (1796), he was made general of a division, fought in Holland and Italy, and in 1802 commanded under Leclerc in the Santo Domingo expedition. He subsequently served under Napoleon I until 1809, distinguishing himself at Essling and Aspern.

Boudicca (bö.dik′ạ). See **Boadicea.**

Boudin (bö.dañ), **Eugène Louis.** b. at Honfleur, France, July 12, 1824; d. at Deauville, France, Aug. 8, 1898. French painter. The son of a pilot, this self-taught painter devoted his art chiefly to the depiction of marine scenes and subjects which had been familiar to him from childhood in and about his native Norman city of Harfleur. He lived and worked, however, mostly at Paris. His pictures are in many public and private collections, and a typical example, *On the Beach at Trouville*, is to be seen at the Metropolitan Museum of Art, New York.

Boudinot (bö′di.not), **Elias.** b. at Philadelphia, May 2, 1740; d. at Burlington, N.J., Oct. 24, 1821. American patriot and philanthropist, president of the Continental Congress in 1782. A member (1777, 1778, 1781–84) of the Continental Congress, he was a vigorous supporter of the Constitution and did much to obtain its ratification by New Jersey (which state he later (1789–95) represented in Congress). He was named (1795) director of the U.S. Mint, and held the post for ten years. He took great interest in missionary work among the Indians and served as first president of the American Bible Society during the last five years of his life.

Boudinot, Elias. [Original name, **Galagina.**] b. in Georgia, c1803; murdered in Indian Territory, June 22, 1839. American Indian editor. A Cherokee, he took his name from Elias Boudinot (1740–1821), benefactor of the Cornwall, Conn., mission school which he attended. Editor (1828–35) of the *Cherokee Phoenix*, established 1824, he joined John Ridge and others in signing (1835), with questionable authority, a treaty permitting removal by the U.S. government of the Cherokees to lands west of the Mississippi River. Author of *Poor Sarah or the Indian Woman* (1833), written in Cherokee characters.

Boué de Lapeyrère (bö.ā dẹ lȧ.pā.rer), **Auguste.** b. at Castéra-Lectourois, Gers, France, 1852; d. at Pau, Basses-Pyrénées, France, Feb. 17, 1924. French naval officer, commander of the French Mediterranean fleet during World War I. He served (1909–10) as minister of the navy.

Bouet-Willaumez (bö.e.vē.yō.mez), **Louis Édouard,** Comte **de.** b. near Toulon, France, April 24, 1808; d. at Paris, Sept. 9, 1871. French admiral. He published *Description nautique des côtes comprises entre le Sénégal et l'équateur* (1849).

Boufarik (bö.fä.rēk′). Town in NW Africa, in the department of Algiers, Algeria, ab. 16 mi. SW of the city of Algiers: founded by the French in 1836. It is situated in the middle of the very fertile Mitidja plain, and is the vineyard center of this region. 21,526 (1948).

Boufflers (bö.fler), **Louis François, Duc de.** [Called **Chevalier de Boufflers.**] b. Jan. 10, 1644; d. at Fontainebleau, France, Aug. 20, 1711. French soldier, marshal of France. He served with distinction in the campaigns in the Low Countries, defended Lille (1708), and commanded in a successful retreat (1709) from the battlefield of Malplaquet.

Boufflers, Stanislas Jean, Marquis **de.** [Called **Chevalier de Boufflers.**] b. at Nancy, France, May 31, 1738; d. at Paris, Jan. 18, 1815. French courtier and man of letters. He was the author of *Voyage en Suisse* (1770).

Boufflers-Rouvrel (bö.fler.rö.vrel), **Marie Charlotte Hippolyte,** Comtesse **de.** b. at Paris, 1724; d. c1800. Frenchwoman, a leader in Parisian literary circles.

Bouffons (bö.fôñ), **Guerre des.** Name applied to the quarrel carried on (c1750) at Paris between French encyclopedists and writers including Denis Diderot and Jean Jacques Rousseau, who were in favor of the Italian comic opera as exemplified by Giovanni Battista Pergolesi, and the adherents of Jean Philippe Rameau and French serious opera.

Bougainville (bö′gạn.vil; French, bö.gañ.vēl). Largest of the Solomon Islands, in the S Pacific, S of New Ireland and E of New Guinea. It is part of the Australian-mandated Territory of New Guinea. The Japanese established a military and naval base at Buin and an airfield at Kahili during their occupation of the island in World War II. Length, ab. 180 mi.; width, ab. 30 mi.; area, 3,880 sq. mi.; pop. 49,067 (counted 1940); 54,067 (est. 1940).

Bougainville, Louis Antoine de. b. at Paris, Nov. 11, 1729; d. there, April 31, 1811. French navigator, head of the first French naval force to circumnavigate the globe. He entered the army in 1754, went to Canada in 1756 during the latter part of the French and Indian Wars as an aide-de-camp to Louis Joseph de Montcalm, and took part in the battle for Quebec, on the Plains of Abraham, by which France lost her position as a major power in North America. In 1763 he left the army for the navy, and shortly thereafter was given command of a fleet which was intended to establish a French colony on the Falkland Islands (a small colony was actually set up, but it fell to the Spanish within a few months), and thence to circumnavigate the globe. After leaving the Falkland Islands he explored the Straits of Magellan, visited a great number of the Pacific islands, some of which he discovered and some of which he rediscovered (including Bougainville, which is named for him), skirted the coasts of New Ireland and New Guinea, touched at the Moluccas, and returned to France by the Cape of Good Hope in 1769. His *Voyage autour du monde*, a description of the circumnavigation, was published in 1771. In 1781 Bougainville commanded under François Joseph Paul, Comte de Grasse, in the expedition to America, and had an engagement with a British squadron under Admiral Samuel Hood off Martinique. On his return he left the navy and rejoined the army as a field marshal. He retired in 1790.

Bougainville Campaign. American campaign in World War II. This operation, begun on Oct. 26, 1943, by U.S. Marines, regained for the Allies domination over the Solomon Islands. It was supported by cruisers, destroyers, land-based bombers, and infantry reinforcements, and brought Bougainville effectively under American control by late November of the same year. Thereafter, by cutting their lines of logistic support, the pockets of Japanese strength still remaining in the area were gradually liquidated.

Boughton (bou'to̤n), **George Henry.** b. near Norwich, England, c1833; d. at London, Jan. 19, 1905. English genre and landscape painter. His family emigrated to the U.S. in 1839, and settled at Albany, N.Y. He went to London in 1853 to study art, went to Paris in 1860, and fixed his residence near London in 1862. He was named a royal academician in 1896. Besides painting easel pictures, he illustrated books by Washington Irving.

Boughton, Martha Arnold. b. at Corunna, Mich.; d. May 18, 1928. American poet and biographer. She taught (1880–84) in various public schools in Michigan, and was a delegate (1895, 1906) to the World Congress of the Women's Christian Temperance Union at London. Author of *Memoir of J. M. Arnold, D.D.* (1885), *The Quest of a Soul and Other Verse* (1911), and *Mystery and Other Poems* (1926).

Boughton, Rutland. b. at Aylesbury, England, Jan. 23, 1878—. English composer, noted as an advocate of music drama. He taught (1904–11) at the Midland Institute at Birmingham. Wishing to establish in England an institution similar to the Bayreuth festivals, he organized (1914) at Glastonbury a group to perform works based on the Arthurian and other legends. His compositions, some of which were first performed by the Glastonbury Players, include the operas *The Immortal Hour* (1914), the choral dramas *The Birth of Arthur, Bethlehem,* and *Alkestis* (1922), and other works for chorus, orchestra, and chamber players.

Bougie (bö.zhē'). [Arabic, **Bujayah;** Latin, **Saldae.**] Seaport in NW Africa, in the department of Constantine, Algeria, on the W side of the Gulf of Bougie. It was an important medieval city. Bougie is the fifth largest port of Algeria and the outlet for one of the most densely populated regions of the country. It is also the name of an *arrondissement* (administrative division) in Constantine department. Pop. of city, 28,547 (1948).

Bouguer (bö.ger), **Pierre.** b. at Croisic, in Brittany, France, Feb. 16, 1698; d. at Paris, Aug. 15, 1758. French mathematician and hydrographer, inventor of a heliometer. He made some of the first photometric measurements.

Bouguereau (bög.rō), **Adolphe William.** b. at La Rochelle, France, Nov. 30, 1825; d. there, Aug. 20, 1905. French painter, a pupil of the historical painter, François Édouard Picot, and of the École des Beaux-Arts. He was awarded a Prix de Rome in 1850. On his return to Paris, he was entrusted with important decorative works in public buildings, and in 1866 painted *Apollo and the Muses* in the foyer of the municipal opera at Bordeaux. He received medals of the second class in 1855, first class in 1857, and medals of honor in the period 1878–85. He became a member of the French Institute in 1876.

Bouilhet (bö.ye), **Louis.** b. at Cany, Seine-Inférieure, France, May 27, 1822; d. at Rouen, France, July 18, 1869. French lyric and dramatic poet. He wrote *Meloenis* (1851), *Fossiles* (1854), *Hélène Peyron* (1858), *Festons et astragales* (1859), and others.

Bouillabaisse (bö.yȧ.bes'), **The Ballad of.** Ballad by William Makepeace Thackeray celebrating the charms of a type of fish chowder (called bouillabaisse) which has long been identified with Marseilles and adjoining coastal regions in the S part of France.

Bouillé (bö.yā), **François Claude Amour,** Marquis **de.** b. at Cluzel, Auvergne, France, Nov. 19, 1739; d. at London, Nov. 14, 1800. French general. From 1768 to 1782 he was governor in the Antilles, and not only defended himself against the English, but took several islands from them. Promoted to lieutenant general, he was commander at Metz when the French Revolution broke out. In 1790 he quelled a mutiny of his soldiers, and soon after suppressed the uprising of the garrison at Nancy. In June, 1791, he secretly arranged to get Louis XVI out of the country; when the plan failed, Bouillé fled to England. He published an account of the revolution.

Bouillon (bö.yôṅ). Former duchy in W Europe, now comprised in the province of Luxembourg, Belgium. It became a duchy about the time of Godfrey of Bouillon, who sold it to the Bishop of Liége in 1095. In later times it belonged, always under French suzerainty, to the houses of La Marck and La Tour d'Auvergne, and specifically to the descendants of Louis XIV's great military leader, Henri de La Tour d'Auvergne, Vicomte de Turenne.

Bouillon. Town in S Belgium, in SW Luxembourg province, in the valley of the Semois, ab. 2 mi. NE of the French border. In the 11th century it was the capital of a small duchy, and passed to Liége in 1095, and to the La Marck territories in the 15th century. It was annexed to France in 1678, and was assigned to the United Netherlands in 1815, and to Belgium in 1830. Bouillon was the first Belgian town liberated in World War II, being occupied by the 1st American Army in September, 1944. Pop. 2,818 (1947).

Bouillon, Duc **de.** [Family name, **Henri de La Tour d'Auvergne.**] b. in Auvergne, France, Sept. 28, 1555; d. March 25, 1623. Marshal of France, and diplomat; father of Frédéric Maurice de La Tour d'Auvergne, Duc de Bouillon, and Henri de La Tour d'Auvergne, Vicomte de Turenne.

Bouillon, Duc **de.** [Family name, **Frédéric Maurice de La Tour d'Auvergne.**] b. at Sedan, France, c1605; d. at Pontoise, France, Aug. 9, 1652. French general; son of Henri de La Tour d'Auvergne, Duc de Bouillon, and brother of Henri de La Tour d'Auvergne, Vicomte de Turenne.

Bouilly (bö.yē), **Jean Nicolas.** b. at Coudraye, near Tours, France, Jan. 24, 1763; d. at Paris, April 14, 1842. French dramatist and novelist. He wrote *Pierre le Grand* (1790, a comic opera), *La famille américaine* (1796), *Jean Jacques Rousseau à ses derniers moments* (1791) and other plays designed to glorify French celebrities, *Contes populaires* (1844), and others.

Bouisson (bwē.sôṅ), **Fernand.** b. at Constantine, Algeria, June 16, 1874—. French politician, president (1927–36) of the Chamber of Deputies, and a member of the Vichy regime. A deputy since 1909, he was premier for five days (May 31–June 4, 1935).

Boulainvilliers (bö.laṅ.vē.lyā), **Henri,** Comte **de.** b. at St.-Saire, Seine-Inférieure, France, Oct. 11, 1658; d. at Paris, Jan. 23, 1722. French historian. He was the author of *Histoire de l'ancien gouvernement de la France* (1727), *Histoire des Arabes* (1731), and *Histoire de la prairie de France et du parlement de Paris* (1753).

Boulanger (bö.läṅ.zhā), **Georges Ernest Jean Marie.** [Called the **"Man on Horseback."**] b. at Rennes, France, April 29, 1837; d. at Brussels, Belgium, Sept. 30, 1891. French soldier and political adventurer, now chiefly remembered for his nearly successful attempt to become dictator of France. He entered the army in 1856, took part in the Kabyle expedition in 1857, and was with the expedition to Cochin-China in 1861. He served as chief of battalion in the army that defended Paris during the Franco-Prussian War (1870–71), and took command (1884) of the French army of occupation in Tunis, with the rank of a general of division. He became minister of war in the cabinet formed by Charles Louis de Saulces de Freycinet on Jan. 7, 1886, retaining that post during the ministry of René Goblet, and bringing about certain worthwhile reforms in the French army. At the same time, however, he began to make himself heard as the self-appointed leader of those Frenchmen who most greatly desired revenge against Germany. In a country which had prided itself for centuries on its military prowess, and which was still smarting under the humiliating defeat of 1871, Boulanger's violently anti-German position quickly brought him widespread popular support. However, it was obvious from the very outset to most responsible French politicians that his real motives were not those of a simple patriot, but rather those of a man whose hunger for absolute power was so great as to be a possible source of danger to the entire framework of republican government in France. Unquestionably this conviction contributed in part to the decision to leave him out of the ministry formed by Pierre Maurice Rouvier on May 30, 1887, despite the great outcry of popular disapproval which this could be expected to bring. However, now that he was out of the government, Boulanger began to seek the support of such various and extremist groups as the so-called Intransigeants of Victor Henri Rochefort, the League of Patriots of Paul Deroulède, the anarchists, and the Orleanist supporters of the Comte de Paris. While his more or less secret negotiations with these diverse groups (probably the only thing they had in common was their opposition to the French Third Republic) were being carried out, Boulanger continued to make his dramatic appearances on horseback before crowds of his supporters (the phrase "Man on Horseback" was first applied to him, and has now come into fairly wide usage as a term to describe any political figure who may be said to seek, or to have acquired, dictatorial power by methods resembling those of Boulanger). Now clearly committed to the goal of making himself dictator, he adopted the cry for revision of the constitution, and, partly by means of money furnished by the Duchesse d'Uzès and the Comte de Paris, was elected (1888) a deputy by a large majority in the department of Nord. In a duel (July, 1888), with the then Premier Floquet, he was severely wounded. In January, 1889, he was elected by the city of Paris, and later by a number of departments. The Boulangist movement had now grown to such proportions that the cabinet of Pierre Emmanuel Tirard was formed with suppression of Boulangism as possibly its chief objective. Thereupon, frightened by the determined attitude of Jean Antoine Ernest Constans, the minister of the interior, Boulanger fled to Brussels on April 2, 1889. Tried *in absentia* by the French Senate for conspiracy, he was sentenced *in contumaciam* to deportation. He passed his exile in Belgium and on the island of Jersey, and shot himself on the grave of his mistress, Madame Bonnemain, at Brussels.

Boulanger, Gustave Rodolphe Clarence. b. at Paris, April 25, 1824; d. there, Sept. 22, 1888. French painter, noted especially for his paintings of Oriental subjects. Among his works are *Les Kabyles en déroute* (1863) and *Cavaliers sahariens* (1864).

Boulanger, Louis. b. at Vercelli, Piedmont, Italy, May 11, 1806; d. at Dijon, France, March 5, 1867. French painter. He was director (1860–67) of the Imperial School of Fine Arts, at Dijon. A painter of the romantic school, Boulanger executed historical, religious, and genre works, but is now best remembered for his portraits of some of the noted French literary men of his time, including Victor Hugo, Honoré de Balzac, and the elder Alexandre Dumas. He also illustrated many books, including Hugo's *Notre Dame de Paris.*

Boulanger, Nadia (Juliette). b. at Paris, Sept. 16, 1887—. French musician. She was professor of harmony, counterpoint, and the history of music at the École Normale at Paris before joining the staff of the American Conservatory at Fontainebleau. She has also for many years given private instruction. Many of the younger American composers and musicians have been her pupils, including George Gershwin, Aaron Copland, Theodore Chanler, Roy Harris, and Virgil Thomson. She was the first woman to conduct the Paris Philharmonic Orchestra, and in 1936 was also the first woman to conduct the Royal Philharmonic Society Orchestra of London. In 1938 she appeared as guest conductor at a performance of the Boston Philharmonic, and in the following year made similar appearances with the New York Philharmonic Symphony Society and with the Philadelphia Orchestra. She had visited this country previously, appearing as organist with the New York Symphony Society in 1924. During her stay in 1939 she taught at Wellesley College and the Longy School and lectured at Radcliffe College and the Juilliard School of Music. She has composed orchestral and piano pieces and songs, one of her best-known works being incidental music, for orchestra, for D'Annunzio's *The Dead City.*

Boulangism (bö.lan'jiz.ẹm, bö.läṅ'zhiz.ẹm). In the political history of France, a term applied originally to a widespread popular movement during the late 1880's for military revenge against Germany. Although the movement had no possible chance of seeing its goal immediately achieved (no sane French politician in the 1880's believed that France could then hope to win a war with Germany) the sentiment which motivated it had a considerable effect on French politics even until the outbreak of World War I. For additional information about its leader, see **Boulanger, Georges Ernest Jean Marie.**

Boulder (bōl'dėr). City in N Colorado, county seat of Boulder County, ab. 30 mi. NW of Denver, in a mining region. A summer resort, it is also the seat of the University of Colorado. 19,999 (1950).

Boulder City. [Also, **Boulder.**] Unincorporated community in SE Nevada, in Clark County, near Hoover Dam. It was built (1931) by the Federal government and serves as the administrative headquarters for the regional Reclamation and National Park Service. 3,903 (1950).

Boulder Dam. Former name (1933–47) of **Hoover Dam.**

Boulder Rock. Rock in Antarctica, lying along the W coast of the Cape Adare peninsula just S of Ridley Beach, in N Victoria Land, in ab. 71°19′ S., 170°14′ E. It was surveyed and named in 1911 by the Northern Party of the British Antarctic Expedition (1910–13).

Boule (böl), **Pierre Marcellin.** b. at Montsalvy, France, Jan. 1, 1861; d. 1942. French paleontologist. He served as a professor (1915 *et seq.*) at the Musée Nationale d'Histoire Naturelle, and as director of the Institut de Paléontologie Humaine, at Paris. Author of *Les Hommes fossiles* (Fossil Men, 1921).

Boulea (bö.lā'ä). See **Builsa.**

Boulger (bōl'jėr), **Demetrius Charles.** b. at London, July 14, 1853; d. Dec. 15, 1928. English historian and writer on Asiatic affairs. In 1885, with Sir Lepel Griffin, he founded the *Asiatic Quarterly Review*, of which he was editor for several years. His works include *England and Russia in Central Asia* (1879), *Central Asian Portraits* (1880), *History of China* (1881), *Central Asian Questions* (1885), *The Story of India* (1897), *The Congo State* (1898), *India in the Nineteenth Century* (1904), and *Life of Sir Halliday Macartney* (1908).

Boulle or **Boule** (böl), **Charles André.** [Also, **Buhl.**] b. at Paris, Nov. 11, 1642; d. there, Feb. 29, 1732. The leading member of a large family of French cabinetmakers. He learned his trade from his father, Jean Boulle, and in 1672 was granted quarters in the Louvre palace, where he built up an establishment for the manufacture of fine furniture and inlaid work, which in 1720 was destroyed by fire. He was a protégé of Louis XIV of France, for whom his best work was done. His characteristic effects were secured by inlaying metals, tortoise-shell, mother-of-pearl, and other colored materials on ebony or ebonized wood. Modern buhl (the German spelling of the name) is an imitation of this.

Boulliau (bö.lyō), **Ismaël.** [Latinized surname, **Bullialdus.**] b. at Loudun, France, Sept. 28, 1605; d. at Paris, Nov. 25, 1694. French ecclesiastic and astronomer. Born into a Protestant family, he became a Roman Catholic and entered the Order of Saint Victor. He traveled widely and was the friend and advisor of Christian Huygens and of Johannes Hevelius. He gave the name "evection" to the second inequality of the moon's motion. Among his principal works are *De Natura Lucis* (1638), *Philolaus sive dissertatio de vero Systemate Mundi* (1639; a defense of the Copernican system), and *Astronomica Philolaica* (1645; a treatise in defense of Johannes Kepler's elliptic law). In 1667 he published a small book which is considered a classic in the history of astronomy, *Ad Astronomos Monita Duo*. The first event taken up in this book is the long-period variable star *o* (Mira) Ceti, for which Boulliau suggested a period of 333 days; he published his own observations of the star and those of others, and attempted to give an explanation of stellar variability. The second event mentioned is the Andromeda nebula, which had been recently rediscovered and which was thought in the 17th century to be a variable star. Many of Boulliau's observations are published in A.C. Pingré, *Annales célestes du dix-septième siècle* (Paris, 1901).

Boullom (bůl′ọm). See **Bullom.**

Boulogne (bů.lōn′; French, bö.lony′). [Also: **Boulogne-sur-Mer**; Latin, **Gesoriacum, Bononia Gessoriacum**; medieval name, **Bolonia.**] City in N France, in the department of Pas-de-Calais, situated on the Strait of Dover at the mouth of the Liane River. The lower city is the commercial quarter; the upper city, surrounded by medieval ramparts, is the administrative and religious center. Boulogne is an important fishing port and the terminus of a steamship line crossing the English Channel to Folkestone, England. It has a bathing beach and tourist establishments. Boulogne was an ancient Roman seaport in Gaul. In 1808 it was the gathering place for Napoleon's projected expedition against England. The harbor installations and a large part of the lower city were destroyed in World War II. 34,885 (1946).

Boulogne, Bois de. See **Bois de Boulogne.**

Boulogne-Billancourt (bö.lony′.bē.yän.kör). [Former name, **Boulogne-sur-Seine** (-sür.sen).] Town in N France, in the department of Seine, a southwestern suburb of Paris, situated on the right bank of the Seine River, which flows in a huge bend around it. To the N, it borders on the Bois de Boulogne and the Hippodrome de Longchamps. It has been known for the manufacture of chemical products, airplanes, and automobiles. Many buildings were destroyed in World War II. 79,410 (1946).

Boulou (bö.lö). French name of the **Bulu.**

Boult (bōlt). Servant in *Pericles, Prince of Tyre*, attributed to Shakespeare.

Boulton (bōl′tọn), **Edmund.** See **Bolton** or **Boulton, Edmund.**

Boulton, Matthew. b. at Birmingham, England, Sept. 3, 1728; d. Aug. 18, 1809. English manufacturer, engineer, and inventor. Now remembered chiefly as a partner of James Watt in the development and marketing of the steam engine, he was also an intimate of Benjamin Franklin, Joseph Priestley, Darwin (the elder), Wedgwood, and Richard Lovell Edgeworth. Born of a family of Birmingham merchants who manufactured and sold a silver stamper and piercer, Boulton improved on the technique of its mass production. He also improved the copper coinage of his day by his development of a steam-operated press (for which he was granted a patent in 1790).

Bouncer (boun′sėr), **Mr.** Friend of Mr. Verdant Green in Cuthbert Bede's novel *Verdant Green.* He is a good-hearted little fellow, whose dogs Huz and Buz are a feature of the book.

Boundary Peak. Mountain peak in SW Nevada, ab. 140 mi. SE of Reno. It is a rugged, thinly wooded peak, the highest point in Nevada, ab. 1 mi. E of the California-Nevada state line. 13,145 ft.

Bound Brook. Borough in N New Jersey, in Somerset County: manufactures include paint and chemicals. It was the scene of a raid (1777) by British forces under General Charles Cornwallis. 8,374 (1950).

Bound East for Cardiff (kär′dif). One-act play by Eugene O'Neill, produced and published in 1916. The seaman Yank, who lies dying aboard the English tramp steamer *Glencairn*, is comforted by his shipmates. Despite their assurances that he will recover, Yank knows himself near death, and is not too sorry to leave his drab and harsh existence as a sailor.

Bounderby (boun′dėr.bi), **Joseph.** Character in Charles Dickens's *Hard Times:* "a rich man, banker, merchant, manufacturer, and what not . . . a self-made man . . . the Bully of humility." He marries Mr. Gradgrind's daughter Louisa.

Boundou (bön.dö′). [Also, **Bondu.**] Former kingdom, and now a region in Senegal territory, French West Africa, in the SE portion of the territory, E of Gambia.

Bountiful. [Former name, **Sessions Settlement.**] City in N Utah, in Davis County near Salt Lake City: residential community, in a region of farms and orchards. Established originally by a man named Peregrine Sessions in 1847, it was renamed for a country in the Book of Mormon. 6,004 (1950).

Bountiful, Lady. In George Farquhar's comedy *The Beaux' Stratagem*, a kind-hearted country gentlewoman. Her name has become proverbial for a charitable woman.

Bounty. English ship whose crew, after leaving Tahiti, mutinied on April 28, 1789, under the lead of Fletcher Christian. The captain, William Bligh, and 18 of the crew were set adrift in a small boat and made their way over approximately 4,000 mi. of open sea to Timor, whence (by way of Batavia) they were able to make their way back to England. Of the mutineers, one group returned to Tahiti, on which island some of them were later captured; another group, under the leadership of John Adams (or possibly Fletcher Christian), settled on Pitcairn Island. Here, according to some accounts, they mingled with the natives, and eventually formed a curiously isolated but civilized community, in sharp contrast to the earlier violence of their mutiny; according to other accounts, they were all killed by the natives, except for one man (and it is true that at the beginning of 1829, only John Adams was left alive out of the original group). A fictional trilogy (but based on facts, so far as these could be ascertained) was written by James Norman Hall and Charles Nordhoff about the *Bounty* and the various members of its crew.

Bounty of Sweden, The. Essay (1925) by William Butler Yeats. It was inspired by the award of the Nobel prize for literature to Yeats in 1923.

Bouquet (bö.kā′), **Henry.** b. at Rolle, Switzerland, 1719; d. at Pensacola, Fla., 1765. English officer in America. During the French and Indian Wars in America, he was appointed (1754) lieutenant colonel of the Royal American regiment which distinguished itself in Virginia and Pennsylvania. Sent (1763) from Carlisle, Pa., by Jeffrey Amherst with military stores for the relief of Fort Pitt, he defeated en route a body of Indians at Bushy Run (near what is now the town of Turtle Creek). This was the first successful engagement in the remarkable colonial campaign since called Bouquet's Expedition (*q.v.*). He later became a brigadier general and commandant of all British troops in the southern colonies of America.

Bouquet de la Grye (bö.ke dẹ lȧ grē), **Jean Jacques Anatole.** b. at Thiers, France, 1827; d. 1909. French hydrographic engineer. As engineer in chief (1866 *et seq.*) of the French government's office of hydrographic engineering, he suggested the construction of a ship canal from Paris to the sea. He also invented and perfected several astronomical instruments.

Bouquet's Expedition (bö.kāz′). British expedition (1763–65) under Colonel Henry Bouquet which, at the beginning of that portion of the French and Indian Wars known as Pontiac's War, was dispatched from Carlisle, Pa., with orders to go to the relief of Fort Pitt. At Bushy Run, Bouquet inflicted a defeat (Aug. 5–6, 1763) upon the Indians, but inadequate forces prevented him from undertaking operations against Indians in the Ohio country. In October, 1765, having received fresh accessions of troops and supplies, he advanced to the Muskingum River, where Indian emissaries asked for peace and delivered to him more than 200 white prisoners. Bouquet then made his way back to Fort Pitt, his expedition having brought an end to the Indian menace on the Pennsylvania frontier.

Boura (bö′rä). See **Bura.**

Bourassa (bö.rȧ.sȧ), **Henri.** b. at Montreal, 1868; d. Aug. 31, 1952. French-Canadian politician; grandson of Louis Joseph Papineau (1786–1871). A member (1896–99, 1900–07, 1925, 1926) of the Dominion House of Commons, he contributed (1897 *et seq.*) to Montreal's *Le Nationaliste*. At one time (1899) he resigned his seat in the House because of his opposition to Canadian entry into the Boer War, but was reëlected almost at once. Leader (1900 *et* *seq.*) of the Nationalist Party, and founder (1910) and editor of the independent *Le Devoir*, he also opposed the Canadian entry into World War I. Bourassa retired in 1935, but returned to public life in 1942 to oppose conscription by the Canadian government in World War II.

Bourassa, Napoléon. b. at L'Acadie, Quebec, Canada, Oct. 21, 1827; d. in Canada, Aug. 27, 1916. French-Canadian author and architect who designed the Church of Nôtre Dame de Lourdes, at Montreal. He studied in Canada and Italy, and worked mostly in his native country. Two of his books are *Jacques and Marie* and *Our Grandmothers*.

Bourbaki (bör.bà.kē), **Charles Denis Sauter.** b. at Pau, France, April 22, 1816; d. at Bayonne, France, Sept. 22, 1897. French general. In the Crimean War he fought with distinction at Alma and Inkerman (1854), and at Malakhov (1855); he was present at Solferino (1859), and, in the Franco-Prussian War, in the battles (Aug. 16, 31, 1870) at Metz, commanded the Imperial Guard which he left (Sept. 25, 1870) on a secret mission to the empress Eugénie in England. In the period of Jan. 15–17, 1871, he endeavored to break through the Prussian line, which was held by troops under General August von Werder, at Belfort, but was compelled to retreat to Switzerland; after an attempt at suicide (Jan. 26, 1871), he was relieved of his command. In July, 1871, he was given the command of the 6th army corps, and in 1873 that of the 14th army corps and the government of Lyons. He retired in 1881.

Bourbon (bör′bọn; French, bör.bôṅ). French family which held royal and ducal power in France, Spain, and Italy. The historical record of the family begins with Adhemar or Aimar, who late in the 9th century became baron of Bourbon l'Archambault in central France. Four centuries later, Beatrix, a Bourbon heiress, became the wife of Robert, Count of Clermont, a son of Louis IX, king of France, and their son Louis in 1327 was given the title of Duke of Bourbon. In 1505 Suzanne, heiress of this line, was married to Charles of the Montpensier branch of the family, who assumed the ducal title in 1505, was named constable of France in 1515, plotted with the emperor Charles V and with Henry VIII of England against his sovereign Francis I, and was killed while leading an army of Germans and Spaniards against Rome in 1527. It was another branch of the family, however, which eventually came to the throne of France. Antoine de Bourbon (Anthony of Bourbon) in 1548 married Jeanne d'Albret, of the house of Navarre, and became king of Navarre in 1554. The son of this union was the renowned Henry of Navarre, who became Henry IV of France, reigning from 1589 to 1610. The later Bourbon kings of France were Louis XIII (b. 1601; d. 1643), Louis XIV (b. 1638; d. 1715), Louis XV (b. 1710; d. 1774), Louis XVI (b. 1754; d. 1793), Louis XVIII (b. 1755; d. 1824), Charles X (b. 1757; d. 1836), and Louis-Philippe (of the Orléans branch of the family, b. 1773; d. 1850). The son of Louis XVI, reputedly put to death in childhood by the revolutionists, was to royalists nominally Louis XVII. The revolutionary and Napoleonic eras intervened between the execution of Louis XVI in 1793 and the resumption of the throne by Louis XVIII in 1814.

The Spanish and Italian Bourbons. King Charles II of Spain, dying in 1700, named as his successor the duke of Anjou, who as Philip V was the first Bourbon to wear the Spanish crown; he was also a Hapsburg. The Bourbon (or Borbón) line ruled in Spain until 1931 when, the Spanish people having voted for a republic, Alfonso XIII abdicated (for living members of this line, see also Borbón y Battenberg). Philip V succeeded in placing his son Charles on the throne of Naples and Sicily, where he reigned from 1735 to 1759, when he became Charles III of Spain, while his son Ferdinand succeeded him in Naples and Sicily, and changed the name of that kingdom to the Two Sicilies. The last Bourbon monarch of this kingdom was dethroned in 1861 by the revolution which made the Two Sicilies part of a united Italy. In 1748 Philip, youngest son of Philip V of Spain, became ruler of the duchy of Parma and Piacenza. In Napoleon's rearrangement of Italian affairs, this duchy was annexed to France in 1801, its Bourbon ruler, Duke Louis, being made king of Etruria. This title Louis' son Charles Louis had to surrender in 1807, but in 1815 the Congress of Vienna gave him the duchy of Lucca. A later Bourbon-Parma, also named Charles Louis, in 1847 ceded Lucca to Tuscany but was restored to the throne of Parma and Piacenza. This was finally abolished in 1859, in the course of the unification of Italy. The Bourbons are now probably remembered by many people chiefly for the luxurious and extravagant mode of living of Louis XIV and Louis XV, and for their alleged stubborn resistance to political progress, which gave rise to the saying that "a Bourbon never learns and never forgets."

Bourbon, Antoine de. See **Antoine de Bourbon.**

Bourbon, Charles, Duc **de.** [Called **Connétable de Bourbon,** meaning literally "Constable of Bourbon," but usually taken to convey the sense that he was the "Bourbon Constable," as opposed to other constables of France.] b. Feb. 17, 1490; d. at Rome, May 6, 1527. French general. He was descended from a younger branch of the house of Bourbon (being a son of a count of Montpensier), and married Suzanne, an heiress of Bourbon, through whom he obtained the title of duke. In 1515 he was created constable of France. In 1522 (on the death of Suzanne) he concluded a private alliance with the emperor Charles V and Henry VIII of England. In return, he was promised, by the emperor, that he would receive the emperor's sister Eleonora in marriage, with Portugal as a jointure, and an independent kingdom which was to include Provence, Dauphiné, Bourbonnais, and Auvergne. He fled from France in 1523, aided in expelling the French from Italy in 1524, and contributed to the victory of Pavia in 1525, in spite of which his interests were neglected in the treaty of peace between Spain and France in 1526. He was one of the commanders of the army of Spanish and German mercenaries which stormed Rome on May 6, 1527, and fell in the assault.

Bourbon, Charles, Cardinal **de.** b. c1520; d. May 9, 1590. French nobleman and ecclesiastic; brother of Antoine of Navarre and uncle of Henry IV (Henry of Navarre). He was one of the leaders of the Catholic League, by which he was proclaimed king (1589) with the title of Charles X, in opposition to Henry IV (who was opposed by the Catholic League because of the Protestantism which he did not formally renounce until 1593).

Bourbon, Henri de. See **Condé,** Prince **de.**

Bourbon, Louis Antoine de. See **Angoulême,** Duc **d'.**

Bourbon, Louis de. See **Condé,** Prince **de.**

Bourbon, Louise Adelaïde de. See **Condé,** Princesse **de.**

Bourbon, Louis François de. See **Conti,** Prince **de** (1717–76).

Bourbon, Louis François Joseph de. See **Conti,** Prince **de** (1734–1814).

Bourbon, Louis Henri, Duc **de.** b. at Versailles, France, 1692; d. at Chantilly, France, Jan. 27, 1740. French nobleman. He was prime minister to Louis XV of France from 1723 to 1726.

Bourbon, Louis Henri Joseph de. See **Condé,** Prince **de** (1756–1830).

Bourbon, Louis Joseph de. See **Condé,** Prince **de** (1736–1818).

Bourbon, Marie Thérèse Charlotte de. See **Angoulême,** Duchesse **d'.**

Bourbon-Condé (bör.bôṅ.kôṅ.dā), **Anne Geneviève de.** See **Longueville,** Duchesse **de.**

Bourbon-Lancy (bör.bôṅ.läṅ.sē). [Latin, **Aquae Nisinei.**] Town in E central France, in the department of Saône-et-Loire, ab. 22 mi. E of Moulins. It is a health resort, with thermal springs containing chlorine, sodium, and iron, which are considered useful in the treatment of rheumatism and other ailments. 4,559 (1946).

Bourbon-l'Archambault (bör.bôṅ.lär.shäṅ.bō). [Latin, **Aquae Bormonis.**] Town in C France, in the department of Allier, situated on the Burge River, ab. 14 mi. W of Moulins. It is a health resort. Until the 16th century it was the capital of one of the largest fiefs of the French crown, that of the Bourbon family. 4,774 (1946).

Bourbonnais (bör.bo.ne). Medieval duchy and former province in C France. It was bounded by Berry on the W and N, Nivernais on the N, Burgundy on the E, Lyonnais on the SE, Auvergne on the S, and Marche on the W. Its capital was Moulins. It corresponds mainly to the modern department of Allier and part of Cher. The duchy of Bourbon was united to the crown c1525.

Bourbonne-les-Bains (bör.bon.lā.baṅ). [Latin, **Aquae Borvonis.**] Town in E France, in the department of Haute-Marne, situated on a hill between the valleys of the Apance and Montlétang rivers, between Langres and Épinal. It is a health resort known for its thermal springs, which are considered useful in the treatment of rheumatism and other ailments. The park of the casino contains ruins of Roman buildings. 2,709 (1946).

Bourbon-Vendée (bör.bôṅ.väṅ.dā). A former name of **La-Roche-sur-Yon.**

Bourboule (bör.böl), **La.** See **La Bourboule.**

Bourbourg (bör.bör), **Charles Étienne Brasseur de.** See **Brasseur de Bourbourg, Charles Étienne.**

Bourchier (bou'chėr), **John.** [Title, 2nd Baron **Berners.**] b. 1467; d. at Calais, France, March 16, 1533. English statesman and author. He was chancellor of the exchequer in 1516. He translated Froissart's *Chronicle* (1523–25), and *Arthur of Lytell Brytayne, Huon of Burdeux, The Castell of Love,* and others.

Bourchier, Thomas. b. c1404; d. at Knowle, near Sevenoaks, England, 1486. English ecclesiastic, archbishop of Canterbury in the period 1454–86. Originally a Lancastrian, he crowned Edward IV (1461) and Richard III (1483), and officiated (1486) at the marriage of Henry VII to Elizabeth of York. He drew up the terms of agreement (1458) between the Lancastrians and Yorkists, and was one of the arbiters (1475) at the peace of Amiens. He was nominated (1467) and installed (1473) as cardinal.

Bourcicault (bůr'si.kō), **Dion.** See **Boucicault, Dion.**

Bourdaloue (bör.dȧ.lö), **Louis.** b. at Bourges, France, Aug. 20, 1632; d. at Paris, May 13, 1704. French theologian. He was a member of the order of Jesuits, professor of rhetoric, philosophy, and theology in the Jesuit college at Bourges, court preacher (1670), and one of the most illustrious pulpit orators of France. His sermons have been published in editions of 16 volumes (1707–34), and 17 volumes (1822–26).

Bourdeau (bör.dō), **Louis.** b. at Rochechouart, France, 1824; d. at Paris, 1900. French philosopher and sociologist. He was the author of *Théorie des sciences . . .* (1882), *Le Problème de la mort* (1892), and *Le Problème de la vie* (1901).

Bourdeilles (bör.dey'), **Pierre de.** See **Brantôme, Pierre de Bourdeilles,** Seigneur **de.**

Bourdelle (bör.del), **Émile Antoine.** b. at Montauban, Tarn-et-Garonne, France, Oct. 30, 1861; d. at Le Vésinet, Seine-et-Oise, France, Oct. 1, 1929. French sculptor and pastel painter.

Bourdet (bör.de), **Édouard.** b. at St.-Germain-en-Laye, France, Oct. 26, 1887; d. 1945. French dramatist, author of *L'Heure du Berger* (1922), *L'Homme enchainé* (1923), *La Prisonnière* (1926), *Vient de paraître* (1928), *Le Sexe faible* (1931), and others. Condemned by some critics as a sensationalist, he has been hailed by others for his talent as a satirist, and for his exploitation of unusual themes.

Bourdillon (bo̤r.dil'yo̤n), **Francis William.** b. March 22, 1852; d. Jan. 13, 1921. English poet. He wrote *Among the Flowers, and other Poems* (1878), *Ailes d'Alouette* (1890), *A Lost God* (1891), *Sursum Corda* (1893), *Nephelé* (1896), *Minuscula* (1897), *Preludes and Romances* (1908), and others. Bourdillon also edited and translated *Aucassin and Nicolette* (1887).

Bourdon (bör.dôṅ), **Louis Pierre Marie.** b. at Alençon, France, July 16, 1799; d. at Paris, March 15, 1854. French mathematician. He was the author of *Éléments d'algèbre* and other mathematical works.

Bourdon, Sébastien. b. at Montpellier, France, 1616; d. 1671. French historical painter. It is supposed that he came of a family poor in worldly goods, for as a youth he became a soldier. But he found means to study painting and to visit Italy for that purpose, and it is known that he was a pupil of Poussin and of Claude Lorrain. When he returned from Italy he set up his studio in Paris and won recognition, especially with his *Martyrdom of Saint Peter,* which is now in the Louvre in that city. When the religious controversies which beset France at that time caused him to go into exile in 1652, his reputation and abilities secured him an appointment as painter to Queen Christina of Sweden. In more peaceful times he returned to France and continued to command attention with paintings of historical and Biblical subjects. His standing among the artists of his day is attested to by the fact that he was one of the founding members of the Academy of Painting, and became its rector. He was also a master of copperplate engraving. His death occurred while he was engaged in the decoration of the Tuileries Palace at Paris.

Bourg (bör). See **Bourg-en-Bresse.**

Bourgade (bör.gȧd), **François.** b. at Ganjou, France, July 7, 1806; d. 1866. French Orientalist, a missionary in Algeria. He wrote *Toison d'or de la langue phénicienne* (1852), and *Soirées de Carthage* (1852).

Bourgas (bör.gä). French name of **Burgas.**

Bourgault-Ducoudray (bör.gō.dü.kö.drā), **Louis Albert.** b. at Nantes, France, Feb. 2, 1840; d. at Vermouillet, France, July 4, 1910. French musicologist and composer. Professor (1878 *et seq.*) of music history and aesthetics at the Paris Conservatoire, he published collections of folk songs from Greece and Brittany. His compositions include operatic, orchestral, and choral works.

Bourg-de-Batz (bör.de̤.bȧts). [Also, **Batz.**] Village in W France, in the department of Loire-Inférieure, situated on the coast ab. 14 mi. W of St.-Nazaire. It has saltworks.

Bourg-de-Péage (bör.de̤.pā.ȧzh). Town in SE France, in the department of Drôme, near Romans, of which it is a suburb. It has a number of factories; the chief manufacture is felt hats. 6,633 (1946).

Bourgelat (bör.zhe̤.lȧ), **Claude.** b. at Lyons, France, 1712; d. Jan. 3, 1779. French veterinarian, said to have been the founder of the first veterinary school in Europe. Bourgelat was an attorney, but veterinary matters were his first interest. His *Éléments d'hippiatrique, ou nouveaux principes sur la connaissance et sur la médecine des chevaux* appeared in the period 1750–53. He succeeded in persuading the French government to establish a veterinary school, which opened at Lyons in 1762, and later another school at Alfort, near Paris. His *Traité de la conformation extérieure du cheval* was published in 1776, and his *Réglement sur les écoles vétérinaires de France* in 1777.

Bourg-en-Bresse (bör.käṅ.bres). [Also, **Bourg.**] Town in E France, the capital of the department of Ain, situated on the Reyssouze River, ab. 36 mi. NE of Lyons. It was the capital of Bresse; has a good regional museum. The Church of Notre Dame de Brou is one of the most richly decorated and graceful old churches in France; it was built (1506–32) by Marguerite of Austria. Bourg-en-Bresse has important cattle markets, and manufactures cotton goods, hosiery, and linen goods. 25,944 (1946).

Bourgeois (bör.zhwȧ), **Dominique François.** b. at Pontarlier, France, 1698; d. at Paris, June 18, 1781. French inventor, especially noted in his day for his improvements in regard to lanterns.

Bourgeois, Léon Victor Auguste. b. at Paris, in May, 1851; d. at Château d'Oger, near Épernay, France, Sept. 29, 1925. French statesman and lawyer, a member of numerous cabinets for more than a quarter of a century, and head of the first French delegation to the League of Nations. After a brief but successful career as a lawyer, he was a member (1877–87) of the government service, was elected (1888) to the Chamber of Deputies, and served (1902–04) as its president, and was elected (1905) to the Senate, of which he was president in the period 1920–23. Named to a subordinate ministry in 1888, he was premier (1895–96), also occupying the ministry of the interior. He also held the following ministries: interior (1890, 1895), public instruction (1890, 1898), justice (1893), foreign affairs (1906, 1914), labor (1912, 1917), and minister without portfolio (1914–17). He supported the arbitration of international disputes and formation of a world court at the Hague Peace Conferences (1899, 1907). At the League of Nations, where he was chief French delegate (1919–24), he advocated (with no success) that the League be given the means by which to enforce its decisions. He was chosen as first chairman of the League. In 1920 he was awarded the Nobel peace prize. His writings include *Des Travaux publics communaux* (1877) and *Les Chemins de fer économiques à voie étroite et les accotements* (1878).

Bourgeois Gentilhomme (zhäṅ.tē.yom), **Le.** Comedy by Molière, with incidental music by Jean Baptiste Lully, produced in 1670. An orchestral suite by Richard Strauss also has this name.

Bourges (börzh). [Latin, **Avaricum.**] City in C France, the capital of the department of Cher, situated at the junction of the Yèvre and Auron rivers and the Canal du Berry. It is an archbishopric and one of the centers of medieval art in France. The Cathedral of Saint Étienne, built 1192–1324, is a Gothic structure with beautifully sculptured portals, and stained-glass windows; the Maison de Jacques Cœur, built 1443–51, is one of the masterworks of Gothic secular architecture. The Musée du Berry has art collections. The city, capital of the Bituriges, a Gallic tribe, was ravaged by Julius Caesar during his expeditions in Gaul; it was later the capital of Berry, and, in the reign of Charles VII, of France. Bourges has important metallurgical and armament industries; has also been known for manufactures of leather, iron products, and textiles. 51,040 (1946).

Bourget (bör.zhe), **Lake.** [Also: **Lake Châtillon;** French, **Lac du Bourget.**] Lake in E France, in the department of Savoie. Length, ab. 11 mi.

Bourget, Le. See **Le Bourget.**

Bourget, Paul. b. at Amiens, France, Sept. 2, 1852; d. at Paris, Dec. 25, 1935. French psychological novelist and literary critic. He was the author of *L'Irréparable* (1884), *Cruelle énigme* (1885), *André Cornélis* (1886), *Mensonges* (1887), *Le Disciple* (1889), *L'Etape* (1902), *L'Emigré* (1907), *Nos Actes nous suivent* (1927) and many other novels, and of literary criticism, *Essais de psychologie contemporaine* (1883), *Nouveaux essais de psychologie* (1885), and others, as well as many short stories and accounts of travels in England, Italy, and the U.S. Originally a disciple of Taine, he was converted to Catholicism in the middle 1880's and tended from that time to assume an extreme rightist position in politics and social matters; his later books were increasingly devoted to developing his own social theses. He was elected to the French Academy in 1894. The discrediting of his political associates did much to submerge his literary reputation in the years directly following his death.

Bourg-la-Reine (bör.lȧ.ren). Town in N France, in the department of Seine, a southern suburb of Paris. 10,244 (1946).

Bourg-lès-Valence (bör.lā.vȧ.läṅs). Town in SE France, in the department of Drôme, situated on the Rhone River. It is a northern industrial suburb adjoining Valence. 6,772 (1946).

Bourgogne (bör.gony'). French name of **Burgundy.**

Bourgoin (bör.gwaṅ). Town in SE France, in the department of Isère, situated on the Bourbre River, between Lyons and Chambéry. It has textile manufactures and paperware factories. 7,699 (1946).

Bourguignon (bör.gē.nyôṅ), **Louis Dominique.** See **Cartouche.**

Bourignon (bö.rē.nyôṅ), **Antoinette.** b. at Lille, France, Jan. 13, 1616; d. at Franeker, Netherlands, Oct. 30, 1680. Flemish religious enthusiast, a believer in quietism. She assumed the Augustinian habit, traveled in France, Holland, England, and Scotland (where she gained special influence), and became the founder of a sect, the Bourignonists, which maintained that Christianity does not consist in faith and practice, but in inward feeling and supernatural impulse. Her works were published in 19 volumes by her disciple Poiret as *Toutes les œuvres de Mlle. A. Bourignon* (1679–84).

Bourignonists (bö.rin'yọn.ists). Sect of quietists founded in the 17th century by Antoinette Bourignon (1616–80). She claimed to be inspired by God; her doctrines were essentially quietistic.

Bourinot (bö'ri.nō), Sir **John George.** b. at Sydney, Cape Breton Island, Nova Scotia, Oct. 24, 1837; d. at Ottawa, Canada, Oct. 13, 1902. Canadian parliamentary official, editor, and historical and political writer. Educated at Trinity College, Toronto, he founded and edited (1860) the *Halifax Herald,* and served as chief reporter (1861 *et seq.*) for the Nova Scotia Assembly and head clerk (1880 *et seq.*) of the Canadian House of Commerce. He was the author of *Intellectual Development of the Canadian People* (1881), *Parliamentary Procedure and Practice in Canada* (1884), *Local Government in Canada* (1887), *Manual of the Constitutional History of Canada* (1888; considered a standard work), *Federal Government in Canada* (1889), *How Canada is Governed* (1895), *The Story of Canada* (1897), *Canada Under British Rule* (1900), *Builders of Nova Scotia* (1900), and of many historical papers contributed to the *Transactions* of the Royal Society of Canada, of which he was president and one of the first members.

Bourke-White (bėrk'hwīt'), **Margaret.** b. at New York, June 14, 1906—. American photographer and author, noted for her photographs taken in every corner of the world. She studied at Columbia University, the University of Michigan, and Cornell University, and early in her career was an industrial photographer for American, Canadian, German, and South American firms. She photographed the progress of Russia's Five-Year Plan, and produced the movies *Eyes on Russia* and *The Red Republic* in 1934. She has been on the editorial staffs of *Fortune* and *Life* magazines, and was for a time the chief photographer for the newspaper *PM*. Her work has been exhibited at the Museum of Modern Art, Brooklyn Museum, Library of Congress, and the Cleveland Museum of Art, among others. She has also done photomurals for Rockefeller Center at New York, and the Aluminum Company of America. She was the wife (1939–42) of the writer Erskine Caldwell. Her books include *Eyes on Russia, U.S.S.R., A Portfolio of Photographs,* and, in collaboration with Erskine Caldwell, *You Have Seen Their Faces, North of the Danube,* and *Say! Is this the U.S.A.?;* she illustrated with photographs *The Story of Steel* and other books. *Halfway to Freedom* (1949) is about India and Pakistan.

Bourmont (bör.môṅ), **Louis Auguste Victor de.** [Title, Comte **de Ghaisne.**] b. at Bourmont, Maine-et-Loire, France, Sept. 2, 1773; d. there, Oct. 27, 1846. French soldier and politician. Commander (1815) of a Napoleonic division in the Hundred Days, he deserted Napoleon and joined the Bourbon faction a few days before the battle of Waterloo. He was minister of war in 1829, and commander in chief of the Algerian expedition in 1830. On the outcome of the revolution of 1830, he was exiled, but returned under an amnesty in 1840.

Bourne (bōrn, bôrn). [Original name, **Monument.**] Town in SE Massachusetts, in Barnstable County, near Buzzards Bay and the Cape Cod Canal. Formerly important for the manufacture of freight cars, it is now a resort and agricultural community. 4,720 (1950).

Bourne (börn, bōrn, bôrn), **Edward Gaylord.** b. at Strykersville, N.Y., June 24, 1860; d. at New Haven, Conn., Feb. 24, 1908. American historian and educator, professor of history at Yale University from 1895. He was graduated from Yale in 1883 and was professor of history at Adelbert College in the period 1890–95. His works include *The History of the Surplus Revenue of 1837* (1885), *Essays in Historical Criticism* (1901), a historical introduction to *The Philippine Islands* (1903), *Spain in America* (1904), *Discovery, Conquest, and Early History of the Philippine Islands* (1907), *Travels of Jonathan Carver* (1907), and editions of the narratives of the explorations of De Soto, Champlain, and Columbus.

Bourne, Francis. b. at Clapham, London, March 23, 1861; d. at London, Jan. 1, 1934. English Roman Catholic prelate. Ordained in 1884, he served (1884–89) as a curate at orphan schools. He was appointed bishop of Southwark (1897), archbishop and metropolitan of Westminster (1903), and, as cardinal (1911), head of the Roman Catholic Church in England. Author of *Ecclesiastical Training* (1926) and *Occasional Sermons* (1930).

Bourne, George. b. at Westbury, England, June 13, 1780; d. Nov. 20, 1845. American Presbyterian and Dutch Reformed clergyman, abolitionist, and author, whose *The Book and Slavery Irreconcilable* (1816) was one of the first American arguments for immediate emancipation. He served as pastor (1825–28) of two Presbyterian churches at Quebec, Canada, pastor (1833 *et seq.*) of the Dutch Reformed church at Houston Street, New York, and delegate (1833) to the Anti-Slavery Society convention. His works include *The History of Napoleon Bonaparte* (1806), *The Spirit of the Public Journals; or Beauties of the American Newspapers for 1805* (1806), *The Picture of Quebec* (1829), *Picture of Slavery in the United States of America* (1834), and *A Condensed Anti-Slavery Bible Argument* (1845).

Bourne, Hugh. b. at Stoke-on-Trent, Staffordshire, England, April 3, 1772; d. at Bemersley, Staffordshire, England, Oct. 11, 1852. English clergyman. He was the founder (1810) of the first society of the so-called Primitive Methodists.

Bourne, Jonathan, Jr. b. at New Bedford, Mass., Feb. 23, 1855; d. at Washington, Sept. 2, 1940. American politician and lawyer. He was a member (1885, 1886, 1892) of the Oregon legislature, and a U.S. senator in the period 1907–13. As chairman of the Senate Post Office Committee, he took a leading part in formulation of the act that established the present mailing service known as parcel post.

Bourne, Randolph Silliman. b. at Bloomfield, N.J., May 30, 1886; d. at New York, Dec. 22, 1918. American pacifist and essayist, whose contributions, before America's entry into World War I, to the periodicals *The Masses* and *Seven Arts* influenced literary and political radicalism. His *Untimely Papers* (1919) contain his articles on the pacifistic argument of the period; the published fragments of his uncompleted work upon the state are considered to constitute one of the finest analyses of its kind. His other works include *Youth and Life* (1913), *The Gary Schools* (1916), *Education and Living* (1917), and *The Education of a Literary Radical* (1920).

Bourne, Vincent. b. 1695; d. Dec. 2, 1747. English writer of Latin verse. He was the author of *Poemata . . .* (1734) and other works.

Bournemouth (bōrn′muth, bôrn′-, börn′-). County borough and seaside resort in S England, in Southampton (an administrative county of the geographical county of Hampshire), situated at the mouth of the river Bourne on the English Channel ab. 22 mi. SW of the city of Southampton, ab. 107 mi. SW of London by rail. One of the principal seaside resorts of the S coast of England, it was a fishing village before the advent of the railroad. Bournemouth has been called the youngest large town in Britain. It was incorporated in 1890. Pop. 144,726 (1951).

Bournville (bōrn′vil, bôrn′-, börn′-). Planned model town in C England ab. 4 mi. SW of Birmingham, now part of the county borough of Birmingham. It was founded by George Cadbury in 1879 as a residential garden-city for the workers in his chocolate factory, and was annexed by Birmingham in 1911.

Bouro (bö′rö). See **Boeroe.**

Bourrienne (bö.ryen), **Louis Antoine Fauvelet de.** b. at Sens, France, July 9, 1769; d. at Caen, France, Feb. 7, 1834. French diplomat. He was private secretary to Napoleon I in Egypt and, during the consulate, served as minister plenipotentiary (1804) at Hamburg. After the fall of Napoleon, under Louis XVIII, he was, for a time, minister of state. He wrote *Mémoires sur Napoléon, le directoire, le consulat, l'empire et la restauration* (1829).

Bourru Bienfaisant (bö.rü byaṅ.fe.zaṅ), **Le.** [Eng. trans., "*The Benevolent Misanthrope.*"] Comedy by Carlo Goldoni, written in French at Paris, first played on Nov. 4, 1771.

Boursault (bör.sō), **Edmé.** b. at Mussy-l'Évêque, in Burgundy, France, in October, 1638; d. at Paris, Sept. 15, 1701. French dramatic poet and miscellaneous writer. His works include *Le Mercure galant* (considered his chief play), *Ésope à la ville*, *Ésope à la cour*, and *Phaéton*. His dramatic works were published in 1725 (enlarged edition in 1746). Several of his plays were imitated by John Vanbrugh.

Bourse (börs), **La.** [Eng. trans., "*The Purse.*"] Novel by Honoré de Balzac, written in 1832.

Bouscat (bös.kȧ), **Le.** See **Le Bouscat.**

Boussansi (bö.sän′sē). See **Busansi.**

Bousset (bö.sā′), **Wilhelm.** b. at Lübeck, Germany, 1865; d. 1920. German theologian. He served (1896 *et seq.*) as professor of New Testament exegesis at the University of Göttingen, and was editor of the *Teologische Rundschau* and *Forschungen zur Religion und Litteratur des alten und neuen Testaments.* Author of *Jesu-Predigt in ihrem Gegensatz zum Judentum* (1892), *Antichrist* (1894), and *Die Religion des Judentums im neutestamentlichen Zeitalter* (1903).

Boussingault (bö.saṅ.gō), **Jean Baptiste Joseph Dieudonné.** b. 1802; d. 1887. French chemist, a specialist in agricultural chemistry. As a young man he went to South America, where he served in the revolutionary forces against Spain under Simon Bolívar. After his return to France he became professor of chemistry at Lyons. The relationship of chemistry to agriculture attracted his special attention, and is dealt with in his *Économie rurale* (1844), which later, in revised form, was entitled *Agronomie, chimie agricole et physiologie* and was translated into English and other languages. The French government recognized his services to the science of agriculture by naming him a grand officer of the Legion of Honor.

Boussu (bö.sü). Town in S Belgium, in the province of Hainaut, situated immediately W of Mons. A manufacturing town, it has metallurgical and other industries. Coal mines are in the vicinity. 12,325 (1947).

Bouteiller (bö.te.yā), **Sophie de.** See **Browne, Henriette.**

Boutelle (bou.tel′), **Charles Addison.** b. at Damariscotta, Me., Feb. 9, 1839; d. May 21, 1901. American naval officer, journalist, and congressman (1882 *et seq.*) from Maine. In the Civil War, he was an acting volunteer lieutenant (1864–65) in the Union navy during the Mobile operations. He was the principal owner (1874 *et seq.*) of the Bangor *Whig and Courier.*

Boutelleau (bö.te.lō), **Jacques.** See **Chardonne, Jacques.**

Boutens (bou′tẹns), **Pieter C.** b. 1870; d. 1943. Dutch poet, whose lyric poetry is considered to represent a high point in modern Dutch literature. He is also a scholar of note in the field of classic languages. He expressed a strong Platonic idealism in his melodious and intense poetry: *Praeludiën* (1902), *Stemmen* (Voices, 1907), *Vergeten Liedjes* (Forgotten Songs, 1909), *Carmina* (1912), *Lentemaan* (Spring Moon, 1917), *Liederen van Isoude* (Songs of Isoude, 1919), *Sonnetten* (1920), and *Zomerwolken* (Summer Clouds, 1922). Love of his country is expressed in *Bezonnen Verzen* (Verses Long Thought Of, 1931), *Hollandsche Kwatrijnen* (1932), and *Tusschenspelen* (Interplays, 1940). He also made translations of Aeschylus, Sophocles, Homer, and others. Some of his verses were translated into English by Herbert Grierson (*Three Poems, The Flute*).

Bouterwek (bö′tėr.vek), **Friedrich.** b. at Oker, near Goslar, Prussia, c1766; d. at Göttingen, Germany, Aug. 9, 1828. German writer on philosophy and the history of literature, appointed professor at Göttingen in 1797. His chief work is *Geschichte der neuern Poesie und Beredsamkeit* (1801–19).

Boutet de Monvel (bö.te dẹ môṅ.vel), **Charles Louis André Bernard.** b. at Paris, Aug. 10, 1884; killed in an airplane crash in the Azores, Oct. 28, 1949. French painter, landscape artist, and water colorist; son and pupil of Louis Maurice Boutet de Monvel. A member of the Société Nationale des Beaux-Arts and the Salon d'Automne, he exhibited (1910) at the Exposition at Brussels, and the Exposition of Humorists at Copenhagen.

Boutet de Monvel, Louis Maurice. b. at Orléans, France, 1851; d. 1913. French painter and illustrator; father of Charles Louis André Bernard Boutet de Monvel. He first exhibited in the Salon of 1874. Between 1876 and 1880 he made several visits to Algeria, and painted numerous portraits and Algerian subjects, but was best known as an illustrator. His colored drawings for books, especially those for children, have a peculiar simplicity and naïveté.

Bouteville (böt.vēl), **François de Montmorency,** Seigneur **de.** [Additional title, Comte **de Suxe.**] b. 1600; d. at Paris, June 27, 1627. French soldier, celebrated as a duelist. He served with distinction at the taking of St.-Jean-d'Angély and the siege of Montauban, but was condemned to death and executed for his dueling escapades.

Boutmy (böt.mē), **Émile.** b. at Paris, 1835; d. there, 1906. French educator and writer. He served (1865 *et seq.*) as professor of the history of civilization at the École Spéciale d'Architecture, and founded (1872) the École Libre des Sciences Politiques, for political and administrative education. Author of *Essai d'une psychologie politique du peuple américain* (Essay on a Political Psychology of the American People).

Bouton (bö′tôn). See **Boetoeng.**

Bouton (bou′tọn), **John Bell.** b. at Concord, N.H., March 15, 1830; d. Nov. 18, 1902. American editor and author. He was editor of the New York *Journal of Commerce* and of *Appleton's Annual Cyclopedia*, and author of essays and books on travel.

Boutroux (bö.trö), **Étienne Émile Marie.** b. at Montrouge, France, July 28, 1845; d. at Paris, Nov. 22, 1921. French philosopher and educator, a member (1898 *et seq.*) of the Académie des Sciences Morales. In 1902 he was named director of the Fondation Thiers. Author of a thesis concerning the laws of nature, he published it in *De la contingence des lois de la nature* (On the Contingency of the Laws of Nature, 1874).

Bouts (bouts), **Dierick** or **Dierik** or **Dirk** or **Thierry.** b. c1410; d. at Louvain, Belgium, May 6, 1475. Dutch painter. It is surmised that he worked for a time at Brussels, for evidence of the influence of Roger van der Weyden is seen in his work, which, however, exhibits an even stronger affinity for that of the Van Eycks. One of his masterpieces is an altarpiece in panels, in the church of Saint Peter at Louvain. The Johnson collection at Philadelphia includes his *Moses and the Burning Bush*, a prime example of his great qualities, and one of his portraits hangs in the Metropolitan Museum of Art at New York.

Boutwell (bout'wel), **George Sewall.** b. at Brookline, Mass., Jan. 28, 1818; d. at Groton, Mass., Feb. 27, 1905. American politician. He was Democratic governor of Massachusetts (1852–53), commissioner of internal revenue (1862–63), a Republican member of Congress (1863–69), secretary of the treasury (1869–73), and a Republican U.S. senator from Massachusetts (1873–77). He was one of the organizers of the impeachment of Andrew Johnson. As secretary of the treasury under Grant, he concerned himself, almost to the exclusion of every other problem, with reduction of the national debt; technically, it was he who broke the famous attempt to corner the gold market on Black Friday (Sept. 24, 1869), but the threat need never have reached the point it did, if he had been willing to act sooner.

Bouvard or **Bouvart** (bö.vår), **Alexis.** b. in Haute-Savoie, France, June 27, 1767; d. June 7, 1843. French astronomer, author of *Nouvelles tables des planètes Jupiter et Saturne* (1808), and other works. He discovered a total of eight comets, and described irregularities in the course of Uranus which he thought might be attributable to the influence of an additional planet, at that time still undiscovered (this possibility was sustained by the investigations of Urbain Jean Joseph Leverrier, which led to the discovery of the planet Neptune in 1846).

Bouvard (bö.vår), **Joseph Antoine.** b. at St.-Jean-de-Bournay, Isère, France, Feb. 19, 1840; d. at Paris, Nov. 5, 1920. French architect. Most of his work was done for the city of Paris. He was the collaborator of, and successor to, Jean Charles Adolphe Alphand as commissaire général des fêtes and architecte de l'administration central. His best-known work is the pavilion for the city of Paris at the Paris World Exposition (1878).

Bouveret (böv.re), **Pierre.** b. at Le Mans, France, Feb. 16, 1905—. French financier and insurance company executive, director general (1943 *et seq.*) of the Mutuelle du Mans. In 1947 he was named president of its board.

Bouvet (bö.vā'), **Marie Marguerite.** b. at New Orleans, La., Feb. 14, 1865; d. May 27, 1915. American writer of books for children, most of them with European settings and characters. Her works include *Sweet William* (1890), *Little Marjorie's Love Story* (1891), *Prince Tip Top* (1892), *My Lady* (1894), *A Child of Tuscany* (1895), *A Little House in Pimlico* (1897), and *The Smile of the Sphinx* (1911).

Bouvet Island. [Norwegian, **Bouvet-Øya** (bö'vā.ė''yä).] Island in the S Atlantic Ocean, ab. 1,600 mi. SW of the Cape of Good Hope. Discovered in 1739 by the French explorer Pierre Bouvet, it has been a possession of Norway since 1927. Area, ab. 23 sq. mi.

Bouvier (bö.vir'), **John.** b. at Condognan, Gard, France, 1787; d. at Philadelphia, Nov. 18, 1851. American jurist, appointed associate judge of the Court of Criminal Sessions at Philadelphia in 1838. He compiled *Law Dictionary* (1839), *Institutes of American Law* (1851), and others.

Bouvier-O'Cottereau (bö.vyā.*o*.kot.rō), **Jean Marie.** b. at Laval, Mayenne, France, Dec. 7, 1896—. French political leader, a deputy (1945 *et seq.*) representing the Parti républicain de la liberté (PRL). He operated (1919–39) leading agricultural enterprises in French Morocco, and served (1940–44) as a Free French military commander in North Africa and Europe.

Bouvines (bö.vēn). [Also, **Bovines.**] Village in N France, in Nord department, ab. 7 mi. SE of Lille. Here, on July 27, 1214, the French under Philip II of France defeated the army of the Holy Roman Emperor Otto IV (100,000–150,000 Germans, Flemings, and English). The loss of Otto was ab. 30,000.

Bovard (bō̦.värd'), **George Finley.** b. at Alpha, Ind., Aug. 8, 1856; d. Sept. 24, 1932. American Methodist Episcopal clergyman and educator. Ordained in 1883, he was president (1903–21), and later president emeritus, of the University of Southern California.

Boveri (bō.vā'rē), **Theodor.** b. at Bamberg, Germany, Oct. 12, 1862; d. at Würzburg, Germany, Oct. 15, 1915. German zoölogist, noted for his investigations in the field of cytology. He was among the first to explore the possibility that chromosomes were of significance in transmitting hereditary traits. Author of *Zellenstudien* (1887–1907) and *Das Problem der Befruchtung* (1902).

Boves (bō'ʙās), **José Tomas.** b. at Gijón, in Asturias, Spain, c1770; killed at the battle of Urica, near Maturín, Venezuela, Dec. 5, 1814. Venezuelan partisan chief. In 1809 he was imprisoned at Puerto Cabello, Venezuela, as a contrabandist. Banished to Calabozo, he was again imprisoned there. On his release in 1812 he declared against the revolution, drew about him an irregular guerrilla band, and carried on, until his death, a war in the interior with horrible cruelties.

Bovey (bō'vi), **Wilfrid.** b. at Montreal, Canada, Dec. 13, 1882—. Canadian lawyer and writer. Admitted in 1906 to the English bar and in 1907 to the bar of the province of Quebec, he practiced (1907–14, 1921) at Montreal. In 1942 he was named to the legislative council of Quebec. He is the author of *The French-Canadians Today* (1930) and other works.

Bovianum (bō.vi.ā'num). In ancient geography, a city in Samnium, Italy.

Bovino ((bō.vē'nō). Town and commune in SE Italy, in the *compartimento* (region) of Apulia, in the province of Foggia, ab. 17 mi. SW of the town of Foggia. It is the seat of a bishopric. The cathedral, of Byzantine origin (11th century), was reconstructed in the 13th century. The nearby valley of Bovino was until the middle of the 19th century a brigand stronghold. Pop. of commune, 8,248 (1936); of town, 7,843 (1936).

Bow (bō). See also **Bow River.**

Bow. [Also, **Stratford-le-Bow.**] District in E London, in Poplar metropolitan borough, ab. 5 mi. NE of the Houses of Parliament, on the W bank of the river Lea. Formerly a town in Middlesex, Bow was noted for its dye works, established in the 17th century, and for porcelain, which was made here from 1744 to 1775. During the 19th century many factories were established in Bow, and it grew rapidly. It was annexed to London in 1888. Pop. 37,003 (1931).

Bow Church. See **Saint Mary le Bow.**

Bowdich (bou'dich), **Thomas Edward.** b. at Bristol, England, June 20, 1791; d. at Bathurst, on the island of St. Mary, Gambia, Jan. 10, 1824. English traveler in Africa, and scientific writer. He went to Cape Coast Castle (now Cape Coast, in Gold Coast colony) in 1814, and in 1815 went on a mission, for the African Company, to Ashanti. He published an account of this expedition, *A Mission from Cape Coast Castle to Ashantee*, in 1819.

Bowditch (bou'dich), **Charles Pickering.** b. Sept. 30, 1842; d. June 1, 1921. American archaeologist notable for his pioneer studies of Maya hieroglyphics; grandson of Nathaniel Bowditch (1773–1838) and brother of Henry Pickering Bowditch (1840–1911). He was president (1917–19) of the American Academy of Arts and Sciences, and presented Harvard's Peabody Museum with voluminous library material relating to Mexican and Central American languages. Author of *The Numeration, Calendar Systems and Astronomical Knowledge of the Mayas* (1910); translator of Landa's *Relación de las Cosas de Yucatán* and Avendaño's *Relación*.

Bowditch, Henry Ingersoll. b. at Salem, Mass., Aug. 9, 1808; d. Jan. 14, 1892. American physician, abolitionist, and pioneer in the development of American public health services; son of Nathaniel Bowditch (1773–1838). He was a member of the committee which edited (1842–43) the *Latimer Journal* and *North Star* in honor of the runaway slave, George Latimer. He demonstrated (1851) the safe usage of a trocar and suction pump for removing pleural effusions from the chest, and served as an original member (1869–79) of the Massachusetts State Board of Health. Author of *A Brief Plea for an Ambulance System for the Army of the United States; as drawn from the Extra Sufferings of the Late Lieut. Bowditch and a Wounded*

Comrade (1863), *The Young Stethoscopist* (1846), and *Public Hygiene in America* (1877).

Bowditch, Henry Pickering. b. at Boston, April 4, 1840; d. at Jamaica Plain, Mass., March 13, 1911. American physiologist; grandson of Nathaniel Bowditch (1773–1838) and brother of Charles Pickering Bowditch (1842–1921). He was a professor (1871–1906) and dean of the medical faculty (1883–93) in the medical school of Harvard University. His numerous contributions to the science of physiology include the establishment (1871) of the first physiological laboratory in the U.S.

Bowditch, Nathaniel. b. at Salem, Mass., March 26, 1773; d. at Boston, March 17, 1838. American mathematician and astronomer; father of Henry Ingersoll Bowditch (1808–92), and grandfather of Charles Pickering Bowditch (1842–1921) and Henry Pickering Bowditch (1840–1911). Almost entirely self-educated, he interested himself at an early age in mathematical calculations; this interest he applied to a revision of *The Practical Navigator*, a contemporary English work by J. H. Moore. Bowditch's third revision of this work appeared as *The New American Practical Navigator* (1802), bore his name only, and is without any question the most famous work on navigation ever written by an American (in its later editions, pubplished by an agency of the U.S. government, it is still in use). In 1823 he became actuary of the Massachusetts Hospital Life Insurance Company, and held this position to the end of his life; he still found time, however, to write various papers on astronomic calculations. Among his most popular papers was one embodying speculations (1807) concerning a meteor which had exploded over Weston, Conn.; his most important contribution to astronomy was his translation (1829–38), with commentary, of sections of Pierre Simon de Laplace's *Mécanique céleste*.

Bowditch's Navigator. See **American Practical Navigator.**

Bowdler (boud'lėr, bōd'-), **Thomas.** b. at Ashley, near Bath, England, July 11, 1754; d. at Rhyddings, near Swansea, Wales, Feb. 24, 1825. English editor of Shakespeare. He published *The Family Shakespeare* (1818), and his method of expurgating the text gave rise to the term "bowdlerize." He prepared, on similar lines, an edition of Edward Gibbon's *History of the Decline and Fall of the Roman Empire* (completed 1825 and published 1826).

Bowdoin (bō'dọn), **James.** b. at Boston, Aug. 7, 1726; d. there, Nov. 6, 1790. American politician; father of James Bowdoin (1752–1811). While governor of Massachusetts (1785–87), he suppressed Shays's Rebellion. Bowdoin College, at Brunswick, Me., was named in his honor.

Bowdoin, James. b. at Boston, Sept. 22, 1752; d. at Naushon Island, Mass., Oct. 11, 1811. American diplomat; son of James Bowdoin (1726–90). He served as minister to Spain in the period 1804–08. He was a benefactor of Bowdoin College, at Brunswick, Me.

Bowdoin College. Nonsectarian college for men at Brunswick, Maine. Petitions were presented in 1788 to the General Court of Massachusetts (at that time the District of Maine was a part of the Commonwealth of Massachusetts) for the foundation and endowment of a college but favorable action was delayed because of the rivalry between James Bowdoin and his successor in office as governor, John Hancock. When Samuel Adams succeeded John Hancock as governor the bill establishing Bowdoin College was signed on June 24, 1794. The single munificent donor was James Bowdoin, the son of the late governor. At the first meeting of the Board of Trustees on July 19, 1796 the site for the college was selected. On Sept. 2, 1802, the first president and a single professor were inducted and on the following day eight candidates for instruction presented themselves, were duly enrolled, and the college was in operation. Among the noted alumni are Jacob Abbott, William Pitt Fessenden, Franklin Pierce, Nathaniel Hawthorne, Henry W. Longfellow, Melville W. Fuller, Thomas B. Reed, and Admiral Robert E. Peary.

Bowell (bō'ẹl), Sir **Mackenzie.** b. at Rickinghall, England, Dec. 27, 1823; d. at Belleville, Ontario, Canada, Dec. 11, 1917. Canadian statesman. Brought to Canada as a child, he grew up in Belleville and made it his home throughout his life. His political career, which began with his election to the Canadian Parliament in 1867, was aided by his ownership of *The Intelligencer*, which he also edited, and his growing influence in the Conservative Party led to his becoming, in 1878, a member of Sir John Alexander MacDonald's cabinet, in which he sat until 1891. He also served in the cabinet of Sir John Sparrow Thompson (1892–94), and in 1894 succeeded Thompson as prime minister of Canada, his government lasting into 1896. From that time until 1906 he was Conservative Party leader in the Dominion Parliament. In 1895 he was knighted.

Bowen (bō'ẹn), **Charles Synge Christopher.** [Title, Baron **Bowen.**] b. at Woolaston, England, 1835; d. 1894. English jurist, notable as junior counsel against the claimant in the Tichborne case (1871–72; in which an impostor, Arthur Orton, sought to eject Henry, Baronet Tichborne, as the heir to Henrietta, Lady Tichborne, on the claim that he, Orton, was her son Roger, presumed lost at sea). Appointed (1857) a fellow at Oxford while still an undergraduate, he became a bencher and a judge of the queen's bench (1879), and lord of appeal in ordinary (1893). Bowen published (1887) verse translations of Vergil's *Eclogues* and the first six books of the *Aeneid*.

Bowen, Elizabeth (Dorothea Cole). b. at Dublin, June 7, 1899—. British novelist and short-story writer; wife (married 1923) of Alan Charles Cameron. Her novels include *The Hotel* (1927), *To the North* (1932), *The House in Paris* (1935), *The Death of the Heart* (1938), and *The Heat of the Day* (1949). Among her collections of short stories are *The Cat Jumps* (1934), *Look At All Those Roses* (1941), *Ivy Gripped the Steps* (1946), and *Early Stories* (1950). Author also of a family biography, *Bowen's Court* (1942), *The Shelbourne Hotel* (1951), and essays published in *Collected Impressions* (1950).

Bowen, Francis. b. at Charlestown, Mass., Sept. 8, 1811; d. at Cambridge, Mass., Jan. 21, 1890. American idealist philosopher, and writer on philosophy and political economy. He was editor and proprietor of the *North American Review* (1843–54), and became Alford professor of natural religion, moral philosophy, and civil polity at Harvard University in 1853. He wrote *American Political Economy* (1870) and *Modern Philosophy, from Descartes to Schopenhauer and Hartmann* (1877), and compiled and edited *Documents of the Constitutions of England and America from Magna Charta to the Federal Constitution of 1789*, with notes (1854), and others.

Bowen, George. [Called the **"White Saint of India."**] b. at Middlebury, Vt., April 30, 1816; d. at Bombay, India, Feb. 5, 1888. American missionary in India. A religious skeptic after reading (1833) the works of Edward Gibbon, he was "converted" (1844) by William Paley's *Natural Theology*. He was a missionary at Bombay (1848–53), and edited (1854–88) the *Bombay Guardian*. In 1873 he joined the Methodist Church. Author of *Daily Meditations, The Amens of Christ*, and *Love Revealed*.

Bowen, Sir **George Ferguson.** b. in Ireland, Nov. 2, 1821; d. at Brighton, England, Feb. 21, 1899. English colonial official. He served successively as first governor (1859 *et seq.*) of Queensland, governor (1868–72) of New Zealand (where his conferences with native chiefs did much to reconcile the Maoris to British rule), governor (1872–79) of Victoria, Australia, governor (1879–82) of Mauritius, and governor (1882–87) of Hong Kong. Author of *Ithaca in 1850* (1850), *Mount Athos, Thessaly, and Epirus* (1852), and other works.

Bowen, Herbert Wolcott. b. at Brooklyn, N.Y., Feb. 29, 1856; d. May 29, 1927. American diplomat. Appointed (1901) envoy extraordinary and minister plenipotentiary to Venezuela, he secured the release of all foreign nationals during the revolt (1902) against the dictator Cipriano Castro, but was discharged (1905) from the diplomatic corps for his connection with certain incriminating documents found at Caracas. He had previously served as consul general at Barcelona (1895–99) and in Persia (1899–1901).

Bowen, Ira Sprague. b. at Seneca Falls, N.Y., Dec. 21, 1898—. American physicist and astronomer. A graduate of Oberlin College (1919) and the California Institute of Technology (1926), he was professor (1931–45) of physics at the University of Chicago, before his appointment (1946) as director of the Mount Wilson Observatory in California. He is also director (1948 *et seq.*) of the Palomar

Observatory. His publications include articles on cosmic rays, atomic structure, and spectra of gaseous nebulae.

Bowen, Mount. Mountain of stratified sandstone in Antarctica, capped by a sharp black peak and lying on the N side of Davis Glacier and S by SW of Mount Howard, in Victoria Land; in ab. 75°46′ S., 161°02′ E. Elevation, ab. 4,100 ft.

Bower (bou′ėr), **Archibald.** b. at or near Dundee, Scotland, Jan. 17, 1686; d. at London, Sept. 3, 1766. English historian. He was for a time a member of the Society of Jesus (Jesuits), and secretary of the Court of the Inquisition at Macerata, Italy, but later joined the Church of England. He published *History of the Popes* (7 vols., 1748–66).

Bower, Frederick Orpen. b. at Ripon, Yorkshire, England, Nov. 4, 1855—. English botanist. He served as regius professor (1885–1925) of botany at the University of Glasgow. His works include *Practical Botany for Beginners* (1894), *Botany of the Living Plant* (1919), *Size and Form in Plants* (1930), and *Primitive Land Plants* (1935).

Bower or **Bowmaker** (bō′mā″kėr), **Walter.** b. at Haddington, Scotland, c1385; d. 1449. Scottish cleric and writer. He is believed to have been one of the authors of *Scotichronicon*, a primary source for early Scottish history.

Bower of Bliss, The. Garden of the enchantress Armida, in Torquato Tasso's *Gerusalemme Liberata* (*Jerusalem Delivered*).

Bower of Bliss, The. Enchanted home of Acrasia, in Edmund Spenser's *The Faerie Queene*.

Bowers (bou′ėrz), **Claude Gernade.** b. in Hamilton County, Ind., Nov. 20, 1878—. American journalist, historian, and diplomat. He was an editorial writer (1923–31) on the New York *World* and a political columnist (1931 *et seq.*) on the New York *Journal* (serving in both capacities as a spokesman for, and consistent upholder of, the Democratic Party). He was later U.S. ambassador to Spain (1933–39) and Chile (1939 *et seq.*). Author of *Irish Orators* (1916), *Life of J. Worth Kern* (1918), *The Party Battles of the Jackson Period* (1922), *Jefferson and Hamilton—The Struggle for Democracy in America* (1925), *The Tragic Era —The Revolution After Lincoln* (1929), *Jefferson in Power* (1936), *Spanish Adventures of Washington Irving* (1940), *The Young Jefferson* (1945), and other works.

Bowers, Elizabeth Crocker. b. at Stamford, Conn., March 12, 1830; d. Nov. 6, 1895. American actress and manager.

Bowers, Lloyd Wheaton. b. at Springfield, Mass., March 9, 1859; d. Sept. 9, 1910. American lawyer, notable for his many successes while U.S. solicitor general (1909–10). He served (1893–1909) as general counsel of the Chicago and North Western Railway.

Bowers, Theodore Shelton. b. at Hummelstown, Pa., Oct. 10, 1832; d. at Garrison, N.Y., March 6, 1866. American soldier who accompanied General Ulysses S. Grant throughout all his campaigns in the Civil War. Assigned (1862) as an aide to Grant, he was captured and escaped (December, 1862) during Van Dorn's raid on Holly Springs, Miss.; he became Grant's adjutant general after the capture of Vicksburg.

Bowers Piedmont Glacier. [Also: **Butter Point Piedmont, Butter Point Piedmont Glacier.**] Piedmont glacier in Antarctica, lying S of New Harbor and merging with the Blue Glacier on its S extremity, along the W coast of McMurdo Sound; in ab. 77°45′ S., 164°25′ E. Area, ab. 25 sq. mi.

Bowery (bou′ėr.i). Thoroughfare in New York City, running parallel to Broadway, from Chatham Square to about 7th Street, where it divides into Third and Fourth avenues. It received its name from the fact that it ran through Peter Stuyvesant's farm or *bouwerij*. In the 1860's and 70's the theatrical center of New York, it later became notorious as a haunt of lawless persons ("Bowery Boys"). It is now known chiefly for its saloons, shabby lodging houses, small retail stores, and pawnshops.

Bowes (bōz), Sir **Jerome.** d. 1616. English diplomat, appointed (1583) ambassador to the Russian court by Queen Elizabeth.

Bowes-Lyon (bōz′lī′ọn). Family name of Elizabeth, queen of George VI of England. The family's nobility derives from the marriage (1376) of Sir John Lyon to a daughter of Robert II of Scotland; the 9th earl in line of descent created the hyphenated form by attaching his wife's name, Bowes, to his own.

Bowge of Court (böj), **The.** Poem (c1499) by John Skelton. Like Skelton's *Garland of Laurel*, it is a dream allegory in rime royal. In it, the hazards of one who lives at court are powerfully pictured in the growing terror of a young man, Dread, who believes himself at sea with a gang of ruffians and awakes at the moment when he is about to leap overboard to escape their malign whisperings.

Bowides (bō′i.dēz). See **Buyides.**

Bowie (bö′i). City in C Texas, in Montague County, NW of Dallas: distributing point for poultry and eggs. 4,544 (1950).

Bowie, James. b. in Burke County, Ga., 1799; killed at the Alamo, Tex., March 6, 1836. American soldier. He became notorious in 1827 from a duel which resulted in a general melee, in the course of which he killed Major Norris Wright with a weapon which had been made from a large file or rasp. After the fight it was made by a cutler into the kind of knife which is still known as a bowie knife. He took part in the Texas revolution, and was made a colonel in 1835. He died in the battle of the Alamo.

Bowie, William. b. at Annapolis Junction, Md., May 6, 1872; d. 1940. American geodesist, chief of the division of geodesy in the U.S. Department of Commerce Coast and Geodetic Survey. He served in the Coast and Geodetic Survey from 1895 to 1937, and was named (1933) president of the International Geodetic and Geophysical Union. Author of *Isostasy* (1927).

Bowker (bou′kėr), **Richard Rogers.** b. at Salem, Mass., Sept. 4, 1848; d. at Stockbridge, Mass., Nov. 12, 1933. American publisher, editor, and writer. As president of R. R. Bowker and Company, publishers, he issued *The Library Journal* (1876 *et seq.*), *Publisher's Weekly* (1884 *et seq.*), *The Reader's Guide in Economics, Social and Political Science* (1891) with George Iles, and *The Economic Fact-Book* (1885). Author of *Work and Wealth* (1883), *Primer for Political Education* (1886), *Electoral Reform* (1889), *Of Business* (1901), *Of Politics* (1901), *Of Education* (1903), *Of Religion* (1903), and *Economic Peace* (1923).

Bowles (bōlz), **Chester (Bliss).** b. at Springfield, Mass., April 5, 1901—. American politician, public administrator, and diplomat. A graduate (1924) of Yale, he was an advertising executive before serving as Connecticut state director (1942–43), general manager (1943), and head (1943–46) of the Office of Price Administration. In 1946 he was director of the Economic Stabilization Board, and a delegate to the United Nations Educational, Scientific and Cultural Organization Conference. He was elected governor of Connecticut in 1948 and appointed U.S. ambassador to the Union of India on Sept. 12, 1951. He has been a member of the *Encyclopaedia Britannica* board of directors, and wrote *Tomorrow Without Fear* (1946).

Bowles, Francis Tiffany. b. at Springfield, Mass., Oct. 7, 1858; d. Aug. 3, 1927. American naval officer, chief constructor of the U.S. navy, with the rank of rear admiral (1901–03). He was graduated from the U.S. Naval Academy in 1879, and was engaged in the construction of the new navy of the U.S. from its foundation. In 1903 he resigned from the navy to engage in private shipbuilding.

Bowles, Samuel. b. at Hartford, Conn., June 8, 1797; d. Sept. 8, 1851. American newspaper publisher and editor; father of Samuel Bowles (1826–78). A publisher (1819–22) of the Hartford *Times*, he founded (1824) the Springfield, Mass., *Republican*, originally a weekly, published daily after 1844.

Bowles, Samuel. b. at Springfield, Mass., Feb. 9, 1826; d. there, Jan. 16, 1878. American journalist and author; son of Samuel Bowles (1797–1851) and father of Samuel Bowles (1851–1915). He was editor (1844–78) of the Springfield, Mass., *Republican*, and built it into one of the leading papers of the day, in which he advocated, among other measures, the founding of the Republican Party. He wrote *Across the Continent* (1865), *The Switzerland of America* (1869), and *Our New West* (1869).

Bowles, Samuel. b. Oct. 15, 1851; d. Mar. 14, 1915. American newspaper editor who assumed control (1878) of the Springfield, Mass., *Republican* after the death of his father, Samuel Bowles (1826–78). Previously, he had served on its staff as an editorial assistant (1873) and as business manager (1875). He founded (1878) the Springfield *Sunday Republican,* and became (1913) a director of the Associated Press.

Bowles, William Augustus. b. in Frederick County, Md., Oct. 22, 1763; d. in confinement, in the Morro Castle, at Havana, Cuba, Dec. 23, 1805. American adventurer and Indian agent who attempted several times to incorporate Florida into the British Empire. He served in the Maryland Loyalist Corps, and became a trading agent in Florida among the Creek Indians. Arrested (1792) by the Spanish, he escaped and again attempted to complete his scheme of taking Florida for England; arrested again (1803), he died in prison.

Bowles, William Lisle. b. at King's Sutton, Northamptonshire, England, Sept. 24, 1762; d. at Salisbury, England, April 7, 1850. English poet, antiquary, and clergyman. He was vicar of Bremhill in Wiltshire, and became canon residentiary of Salisbury in 1828. His works include *Fourteen Sonnets* (1789), which brought praise from Samuel Taylor Coleridge, William Wordsworth, and Robert Southey, *Coombe Ellen* (1798), *St. Michael's Mount* (1798), *Battle of the Nile* (1799), *Sorrows of Switzerland* (1801), *The Picture* (1803), *The Spirit of Discovery* (1804), *Ellen Gray* (1823), and various prose works, including *Hermes Britannicus* (1828). His assertion, in an edition (1806) of Alexander Pope's works, that Pope was an inferior writer led to a heated controversy with Byron.

Bowley (bō'li), **Albert Jesse.** b. at Westminster, Calif., Nov. 24, 1875; d. in Northumberland County, Va., May 22, 1945. American artillery officer. Graduated (1897) from the U.S. Military Academy, he served in the Spanish-American War (1898), in the Philippines, and in World War I. He was a member (1920–21) of the general staff corps, was appointed (1939) a lieutenant general, and retired (November, 1939) from active duty.

Bowley (bou'li), **Sir Joseph.** In Charles Dickens's story *The Chimes,* a very stately gentleman, "the poor man's friend," with a very stately wife.

Bowling (bō'ling), **Lieutenant Tom.** In *Roderick Random* by Tobias Smollet, a sailor, uncle of Roderick, the titular hero of the novel.

Bowling, Tom. Hero of a song by Charles Dibdin, celebrated in the line "Here, a sheer hulk, lies poor Tom Bowling."

Bowling Green. City in SW Kentucky, county seat of Warren County, on the Barren River, in a former petroleum-producing area: marketing center for agricultural produce including burley tobacco and strawberries. Horses are raised in the vicinity. It is the seat of the Western Kentucky State Teachers College and of Bowling Green Business University. It was settled in 1780, and was an important strategic point (1861–62) during the Civil War. 18,347 (1950).

Bowling Green. Small open space in New York City, at the foot of Broadway, in what was once the governmental and aristocratic center of the city. Part of a cattle market in the 17th century, the plot was set apart for bowling in 1732.

Bowling Green. City in NW Ohio, county seat of Wood County: manufactures include glass and canned vegetable products. It was formerly (1886 *et seq.*) important for its petroleum production, and some of its wells were still being pumped more than a half century later. It is the seat of Bowling Green State University. The city was platted in 1835. Pop. 12,005 (1950).

Bowmaker (bō'mā"kėr), **Walter.** See **Bower** or **Bowmaker, Walter.**

Bowman (bō'mạn), **Edward Morris.** b. at Barnard, Vt., July 18, 1848; d. at Brooklyn, N.Y., Aug. 27, 1913. American organist. He was active at St. Louis (1867–72, 1874–87), Newark, N.J. (1887–94), Brooklyn (1895–1906), and New York (1906 *et seq.*). A founder (1884) and president (1884–93) of the American College of Musicians, he also taught (1891–95) at Vassar.

Bowman, Isaiah. b. at Waterloo, Ontario, Canada, Dec. 26, 1878; d. at Baltimore, Jan. 6, 1950. American geographer and educator. A graduate of Harvard (1905) and Yale (1909), he taught (1905–15) in the geography department at Yale, and led (1907–13) Yale expeditions to South America. He was director (1915–35) of the American Geographical Society, before becoming (1935) president of the Johns Hopkins University. He also served as a special adviser (1943–45) to the secretary of state during the latter part of World War II. Author of *Forest Physiography* (1911), *South America* (1915), *The Andes of Southern Peru* (1916), *Geography in Relation to the Social Sciences* (1934), *Design for Scholarship* (1936), and *The Graduate School in American Democracy* (1939).

Bowman, John Gabbert. b. at Davenport, Iowa, May 18, 1877—. American educator. He was president (1911–14) of the University of Iowa, and director, for six years, of the American College of Surgeons, and was appointed chancellor (1921) and president (1945) of the University of Pittsburgh. He is the author of *The World that Was, Thoughts Along the Way,* and a volume of verse, *Happy All Day Through.*

Bowman, Thomas. b. at Berwick, Pa., July 15, 1817; d. March 3, 1914. American Methodist Episcopal bishop and educator. He served as principal (1848–58) of Dickinson Seminary, Williamsport, Pa. As president (1858–72) and chancellor (1884–99) of Indiana Asbury (later to be called De Pauw) University, he was influential in securing Washington Charles De Pauw's donations to the university. In 1872 he was elected a bishop.

Bowman, Sir **William.** b. at Nantwich, England, July 20, 1816; d. near Dorking, England, March 29, 1892. English surgeon. He is known especially for his work in ophthalmology and for his investigations relating to the mucous membranes, muscular fiber, and the structure of the kidney.

Bowman Peninsula. Peninsula in Antarctica, lying between Nantucket Inlet and Gardner Bay, at the S end of Richard Black Coast, in ab. 74°45′ S., 62°15′ W. It was discovered by the Ronne Antarctic Research Expedition (1947–48), under the leadership of Commander Finn Ronne, who named this feature for Isaiah Bowman, then president of the Johns Hopkins University, and former director (1915–35) of the American Geographical Society.

Bowmanville (bō'mạn.vil). Manufacturing town in SE Ontario, Canada, situated a few miles inland from the N shore of Lake Ontario, ab. 43 mi. E of Toronto. 5,430 (1951).

Bowne (boun), **Borden Parker.** b. at Leonardville, N.J., Jan. 14, 1847; d. April 1, 1910. American educator and author. He studied at Halle, Paris, and Göttingen, and from 1876 was professor of philosophy and dean of the Graduate School of Arts and Sciences at Boston University. He made a tour (1905–06) of the world, lecturing in India, China, and Japan. Bowne evolved a theory of "personalism," according to which the ultimate essence may be said to consist of independent, separate beings. Among his philosophical and religious works are *The Philosophy of Herbert Spencer* (1874), *The Philosophy of Theism* (1888), *The Theory of Thought and Knowledge* (1897), and *The Essence of Religion* (1910).

Bowness (bou.nes') and **Bowness-on-Windermere** (-win'dėr.mir). Ward of Windermere urban district, in NW England, in Westmorland, situated on the E side of Lake Windermere, in the Lake District. Bowness is the name of the ward of Windermere; Bowness-on-Windermere is the name of a civil parish. They are coextensive. 3,304 (1931).

Bowring (bou'ring), Sir **John.** b. at Exeter, England, Oct. 17, 1792; d. there, Nov. 23, 1872. British philologist economist, and author of 36 works. A member of Parliament in the periods 1835–37 and 1841–49, he traveled extensively to promote British trade. He was superintendent of trade with China and consul at Hong Kong (1849–53), and was knighted and appointed (1854) governor of Hong Kong. He aroused protests in England in 1856 by ordering the bombardment of Canton in retaliation for Chinese police action against pirates on the *Arrow,* a ship under British registry. In 1855 he visited Siam and concluded a commercial treaty which opened up that country to extensive British trade by lowering export duties, placing opium on the free list, and reducing restrictions on the movement of British subjects in Siam. In 1858 he visited the Philippines. His accounts of the Philippines and of Siam are among the earliest accurate first-hand descriptions of these countries in the English language. His translations and anthologies of poetry from Oriental and European languages are also highly regarded.

Bow River (bō). River in S Alberta, Canada. Rising in the Rocky Mountains, it flows SE through a beautiful scenic valley in Banff National Park, and then across the plains to join the Oldman River ab. 46 mi. W of Medicine Hat. Calgary is the principal city on the Bow. Length, ab. 315 mi.

Bows (bōz). Little old humpbacked violin player, the family friend of the Costigans, in William Makepeace Thackeray's *Pendennis.* He has taught the actress "the Fotheringay" (Emily Costigan) all she knows, and loves her devotedly, although he knows her to be self-centered and heartless.

Bowser (bou'zėr), **Edward Albert.** b. at Sackville, New Brunswick, Canada, June 18, 1837; d. 1910. American mathematician and engineer. A professor (1871 *et seq.*) at Rutgers University, he was appointed (1875) to head the Geodetic Survey of New Jersey. He was the author of *Analytical Geometry* (1880), *Differential and Integral Calculus* (1880), *Analytical Mechanics* (1884), *Academic Algebra* (1888), *Treatise on Trigonometry* (1892), and *Roofs and Bridges* (1898).

Bow Street (bō). Street in London, by Covent Garden, forming the connecting link between Long Acre and Russell Street, in which is located one of the principal police courts of the city, established there in 1749. In the 17th and 18th centuries it was a fashionable quarter, and was the site of "Will's" also called the "Wits' Coffee House."

Bowyer (bō'yėr), **Fort.** Former fort near Mobile, Ala. It was attacked on Sept. 15, 1814, by a British land force of 730 troops and 200 Creek Indians, assisted by a naval force. The garrison, which consisted of 134 men, repelled the attack with the loss of 5 killed and 4 wounded. The British lost 162 killed and 70 wounded.

Bowyer, Sir George. b. at Radley Park, Berkshire, England, Oct. 8, 1811; d. at London, June 7, 1883. English jurist. His works include *Commentaries on the Constitutional Law of England* (1841) and *Commentaries on Modern Civil Law* (1848).

Bowyer, William. b. at London, 1663; d. there, Dec. 27, 1737. English printer; father of William Bowyer (1699–1777). He established (1699) his printing business in London, and there brought out his first book, *A Defence of the Vindication of King Charles the Martyr Justifying His Majesty's Title to Eikon Basilike,* a small quarto volume of 96 pages. He later moved to Gowell Court, in the Whitefriars district of London, where his son was born. In 1700 he was made a liveryman or freeman of the City of London by the Stationers' Company, and appointed one of the 20 printers allowed by the Star Chamber. His home, business, and many books and rare manuscripts were destroyed in the fire of 1712. Bowyer resumed business (October, 1713), aided by charitable subscriptions and by contributions from friends and fellow printers.

Bowyer, William. [Called the **"Learned Printer."**] b. at Gowell Court, Whitefriars, London, Dec. 19, 1699; d. there, Nov. 18, 1777. English printer, classical scholar, author, editor, and translator; son of William Bowyer (1663–1737). Made a partner (1722) in his father's business, he took charge of the editorial and scholarly work involved in publishing. He served as printer for both houses of Parliament, for the Royal Society, and for the Society of Antiquaries. Author of many papers and pamphlets on classical subjects, and editor of Jonathan Swift's works, he is best known for his edition (1763) of the New Testament in Greek, and for his own work, *The Origin of Printing, in Two Essays* (1774). His edition of Bentley's *Phalaris* and a reprint of the famous *Domesday Book* were not published until after his death.

Bowzybeus (bou.zi.bē'us). Musical Silenus in John Gay's *The Shepherd's Week.*

Box and Cox. Play (1847) by John M. Morton. The chief characters are two men with these names who occupy the same room, though neither knows it, one being employed all night, the other all day. This play should not be confused with the operetta on the same theme by Sir Arthur Sullivan and Sir Francis Cowley Burnand, entitled *Cox and Box.*

Box Elder. Former name of **Brigham,** Utah.

Boxer Rebellion (bok'sėr). Uprising (1899–1900) in China by a group of anti-foreign Chinese ("Boxers"). Several hundred foreigners were killed in the ensuing hostilities, and many more were besieged in Peking. A joint military expedition of American, English, Russian, German, French, and Japanese troops was sent to the rescue. Fearing the expedition might be used as an excuse for further foreign encroachment upon Chinese territory, U.S. Secretary of State John Hay issued a note declaring the U.S. intention to preserve the territorial integrity of China and to safeguard the principles of equal and impartial trade. After the insurgents had been defeated, an indemnity of 332 million dollars was levied on the Chinese government, but a good portion of the American share was returned.

Boxers (bok'sėrz). Name popularly applied in the U.S. and Great Britain to a Chinese patriotic society, the members of which took a prominent part in the attack upon foreigners and native Christians in China in the period 1899–1900. The Chinese name of the society was *I Ho-chuan,* meaning "League of United Patriots"; but since the last part of the name could be so accented as to mean "fists," and since athletic exercises were much practiced by members of the society, the name "Boxers" was given to them by foreigners.

Boxing Day. In Great Britain, the name given to the first weekday after Christmas, when gratuities or gifts are traditionally given to employees.

Boxtel (bôks'tel). [Also, **Bokstel.**] Town in S Netherlands, in North Brabant province, ab. 12 mi. E of Tilburg: damask and linen manufactures; furniture and cigar factories. 11,151 (1939).

Boy. Novel by James Hanley, published in 1931.

Boyacá (bō.yä.kä'). Department in E central Colombia, bordering on Venezuela. Capital, Tunja; area, 24,928 sq. mi.; pop. 791,300 (est. 1950).

Boyacá. Village in N Colombia, in Boyacá department, ab. 12 mi. S of Tunja. Here, on Aug. 7, 1819, Simon Bolívar defeated the superior Spanish force of Barreiro, taking him prisoner with more than half of his army. This victory decided the independence of Colombia and Venezuela. Pop. under 5,000 (1938).

Boy at Mugby (mug'bi), **The.** Story by Charles Dickens, originally published (1866) as the third part of a special Christmas issue of *All the Year Round* entitled "Mugby Junction." It satirizes, by a comparison with facilities available in France, the refreshment counters of English railway stations: "French refreshmenting comes to this; and, oh, it comes to a nice total! First, eatable things to eat, and drinkable things to drink. . . ."

Boyce (bois), **Hector.** See **Boece** or **Boethius** or **Boetius, Hector.**

Boyce, James Petigru. b. at Charleston, S.C., Jan. 11, 1827; d. at Pau, France, Dec. 28, 1888. American Baptist clergyman. He was pastor (1851 *et seq.*) of the Baptist Church at Columbia, S.C., and professor of theology (1855 *et seq.*) at Furman University, Greenville, S.C. He organized (1859) the Southern Baptist Theological Seminary at Greenville (its location was changed after the Civil War to Louisville, Ky.).

Boyce, William. b. at London, 1710; d. at Kensington (now part of London), Feb. 7, 1779. English composer of church music, noted as the compiler of three volumes of the once widely used *Cathedral Music* series. He was named (1755) master of the king's music and was appointed (1758) organist at the chapel royal. He composed sonatas, anthems, masques and odes, and Te Deums.

Boyce Thompson Institute for Plant Research, Inc. Organization incorporated in 1919 for the purpose of conducting research and the diffusion of knowledge concerning living plants and plant products, including insecticides and fungicides. It has an endowment of about ten million dollars, maintains headquarters at Yonkers, N.Y., and publishes *Contributions* (quarterly) and *Professional Papers* (irregularly).

Boycott (boi'kot, -kot), **Charles Cunningham.** b. 1832; d. 1897. English army officer. He is, however, known in history not for his military exploits but for the events that took place during his service (after retirement from the army) as agent for the owner of a large estate in County Mayo, Ireland. In 1880, when he refused to accept rents lower than those to which his employer was legally entitled, he was subjected to an organized campaign of abuse and calculated ostracism (his servants left him, and efforts were even made to prevent him from getting food. Some idea of the intensity of local feeling against him may be obtained from the fact that when the time arrived for harvesting his employer's crops, some 600 British soldiers had to be brought in to protect the harvesters—who were themselves imported from the north of Ireland.) From his experience, the word "boycott" has come to have very wide usage, as both verb and noun, to describe a policy or practice of abstention, as a punitive or retaliatory measure, from commerce of any sort with a person, group, or country.

Boyd (boid), **Andrew Kennedy Hutchinson.** b. at Auchinleck Manse, Ayrshire, Scotland, Nov. 3, 1825; d. at Bournemouth, England, March 1, 1899. Scottish Presbyterian divine, and author of essays and religious works. He received a D.D. degree (1864) from Edinburgh University and an LL.D. degree (1889) from St. Andrews. After serving other parishes, he became (1865) minister of St. Andrews, holding that post until his death. His works include *Recreations of a Country Parson* (3 vols., 1859, 1861, 1878), *Graver Thoughts of a Country Parson* (1862, 1865, 1875), *Twenty-Five Years at St. Andrews* (1896), and several volumes of sermons. Through his articles and essays in *Fraser's Magazine* he became known to a large reading public, not only in Scotland but in the U.S.

Boyd, Augusto Samuel. b. at Panama City, Panama, Aug. 1, 1879—. Panamanian surgeon and politician, president (1939–40) of Panama; son of Federico Boyd (1851–1924) and brother of Jorge Eduardo Boyd (1886—). He was a resident surgeon (1899–1901) at the City Hospital, New York, and chief surgeon (1905–36) of Santo Tomás Hospital, Panama. He later served as vice-president (1936–39) and president (1939–40) of Panama. Author of *Esplenectomía para hiperplasia del bazo* (1915), *Calecistectomía versus calecistostomía* (1925), *20,000 casos de anastesia raquídea* (1930), and other books.

Boyd, Belle. [Married name, **Hardinge.**] b. May 9, 1843; d. June 11, 1900. American Confederate spy. In her book, *Belle Boyd in Camp and Prison* (1865), she relates her adventures during the Civil War, which included conveying secret information to Stonewall Jackson. She was imprisoned for a month during 1862; sufficient evidence was not then available to hold her longer, but in 1863 Union forces again imprisoned her, and held her for about six months. She was entrusted with letters from Jefferson Davis to Confederate agents at London, which she managed to deliver. While in England, she attempted a few stage performances. The success of these encouraged her to do the same in the U.S., and she continued touring until her death, presenting a narrative of her own exploits.

Boyd, Ernest. b. at Dublin, June 28, 1887; d. at New York, Dec. 30, 1946. American critic, essayist, and translator. He joined (1910) the editorial staff of the Dublin *Irish Times*, and later wrote (1920–22) editorials for the New York *Evening Post.* He also wrote frequent articles of criticism for the *American Mercury*, edited by his close friend, Henry Louis Mencken, and helped to found the *American Spectator* (discontinued in February, 1935). His writings include *Appreciations and Depreciations* (1917), *Ireland's Literary Renaissance* (1922), *Studies in Ten Literatures* (1925), *Literary Blasphemies* (1927), and *The Pretty Lady* (1934). Among his translations are *Opium* by Jean Cocteau, *Der Untertan* by Heinrich Mann, and *Les Propos d'Anatole France.*

Boyd, Federico. b. 1851; d. 1924. Panamanian political leader, prominent in the independence movement (1903); father of Augusto Samuel Boyd and Jorge Eduardo Boyd.

Boyd, James. b. in Dauphin County, Pa., July 2, 1888; d. at Princeton, N.J., Feb. 25, 1944. American author of historical novels. A graduate (1910) of Princeton, he served, during World War I, in the U.S. army as a first lieutenant, participating in the St.-Mihiel and Meuse-Argonne offensives. Author of the novels *Drums* (1925), *Marching On* (1927), *Long Hunt* (1930), *Roll River* (1935), and *Bitter Creek* (1939), he also published the volume of verse entitled *Eighteen Poems* (1944).

Boyd, John Parker. b. at Newburyport, Mass., Dec. 21, 1764; d. Oct. 4, 1830. American soldier. Arrived (1789) in India to offer his military services, he was employed by various Indian princes, among them the rulers of Hyderabad and Poona. He returned to the U.S. to enter the army, and fought in the battle of Tippecanoe (1811), and commanded forces in the capture of Fort George (1813) and at the battle of Chrystler's Farm. Discharged (1815) from the army, he later became naval officer for the port of Boston.

Boyd, Jorge Eduardo. b. at Panama City, Panama, March 14, 1886—. Panamanian diplomat, jurist, and author; son of Federico Boyd and brother of Augusto Samuel Boyd. He served as Panamanian delegate, representative, or counsel at various international conferences (1911–36), and several times (1916–38) as associate justice of the supreme court, and was attorney general (1924–26) of Panama. Subsequently he was named ambassador to the U.S. (1939) and to Mexico (1943). His works include *Emisión bancaria* (1909) and *El Tratado del canal Hay-Bunau-Varilla* (1913).

Boyd, Lynn. b. at Nashville, Tenn., Nov. 22, 1800; d. Dec. 17, 1859. American politician. He assisted in the "Jackson Purchase," from the Chickasaw Indians, of Kentucky lands west of the Tennessee River. Having settled (1826) in that region, he was elected (1835; 1839 *et seq.*) to Congress, where he was speaker of the House (1851–55). He opposed the Bank of the United States and supported the annexation of Texas and the Compromise of 1850.

Boyd, Mark Alexander. b. in Galloway, Scotland, Jan. 13, 1563; d. at Penkill Castle, Ayrshire, Scotland, April 10, 1601. Scottish writer of Latin verse. He studied civil law in France and Italy, and was an accomplished classical scholar. Though a Protestant, he fought with the Catholic League in France in the period 1587–88. He was the author of *M. Alexandri Bodii Epistolae Heroides, et Hymni* (1592), and others.

Boyd, Robert. [Title, Lord **Boyd.**] d. at Alnwich, England, c1469. Scottish statesman, now chiefly remembered as the abductor (1466) of the young James III of Scotland. After his kidnapping of the king he assumed sole governorship of the realm, by act of Parliament, and he was appointed in 1467 chamberlain for life. Despite a rule that was in most ways satisfactory, jealous Scottish nobles forced him to face trial (1469) for the abduction; found guilty, he fled to Alnwich, in Northumberland, below the Border.

Boyd, Robert. [Title, 4th Lord **Boyd.**] d. 1590. Scottish statesman and soldier. He assisted the regent James Hamilton, 2nd Earl of Arran, in quelling Lennox's rebellion (1554), sided with the lords in their war (1559) against the queen regent, and was perhaps party to the murder of Henry Stewart, Lord Darnley. A member of the packed jury that acquitted (1567) Bothwell of the murder, he joined the nobles to protect the young prince against Bothwell after the marriage of the former to Mary; later he defended Bothwell against his calumniators. Between appointments to the privy council (1567) and to Mary's council (1569), he served with her forces at Langside (1568), following vain negotiations with Murray for her release. He was suspected of complicity in Murray's murder in 1570, the year he became privy councillor of the regent's party. He was lord of session in 1573. Banished (1583) for his participation in the Raid of Ruthven, he was restored to the bench in 1586.

Boyd, Thomas Alexander. b. at Defiance, Ohio, July 3, 1898; d. Jan. 27, 1935. American writer. He was the author of *Through the Wheat* (1923), *The Dark Cloud* (1924), *Points of Honor* (1925), *Samuel Drummond* (1925), *Simon Girty, The White Savage* (1928), *Shadow of the Long Knives* (1928), *Mad Anthony Wayne* (1929), and *Lighthorse Harry Lee* (1931).

Boyd, William. [Title, 4th Earl of **Kilmarnock.**] b. 1704; executed at Tower Hill, London, 1746. English Jacobite nobleman. Influenced by his Catholic wife, he deserted the Hanoverian cause and joined (1745) Prince Charles Stuart, and fought at Falkirk and Culloden (1746). Captured after the destruction of the Jacobite army, he was executed chiefly because the duke of Cumberland erroneously believed him responsible for the "no quarter to the English" order.

Boyd, William. b. near Cambridge, Ohio, June 5, 1895—. American actor, identified with the cowboy character Hopalong Cassidy. A leading man in silent films, his motion-picture career having begun in 1919, he made the first of his "Hoppy" pictures in 1934; these pictures, based on the Bar-20 novels of Montgomery Mulford, were shown on television beginning in 1949 and rapidly reached a position of top popularity, especially with the juvenile television audience. A fad of Hopalong Cassidy toys (costumes, cap pistols, belts, and other paraphernalia) was matched by the spread of the cowboy hero into syndicated comic strips, comic books, and other popular media. When the original series of motion pictures was exhausted, Boyd began making pictures specially for release on television.

Boydell (boi'del), **John.** b. at Dorrington, Shropshire, England, Jan. 19, 1719; d. at London, Dec. 12, 1804. English engraver and print publisher. He founded the Shakespeare Gallery at London, where were housed prints by a group of artists, illustrating various scenes in Shakespeare's plays, which Boydell had previously commissioned and published. He was elected lord mayor of London in 1790.

Boyden (boi'dẹn), **Roland William.** b. at Beverly, Mass., Oct. 18, 1863; d. there, Oct. 25, 1931. American lawyer and government official. Admitted (1888) to the bar, he practiced at Boston. He was an unofficial representative (1921–24) of the U.S. on the Reparations Commission after World War I.

Boyden, Seth. b. at Foxborough, Mass., Nov. 17, 1788; d. at Hilton, N.J., March 31, 1870. American inventor, called by Thomas Alva Edison "one of America's greatest inventors"; brother of Uriah Atherton Boyden (1804–79). He originated machines for manufacturing nails and cutting files, and a leather-splitting machine; duplicated (1819) a European process for applying lacquer to leather, and established the first patent-leather factory in America; cast (1826) malleable iron, patenting his process for doing so in 1831; manufactured locomotives and stationary steam engines; and invented a hat-shaping machine and an inexpensive process for making sheet iron.

Boyden, Uriah Atherton. b. at Foxborough, Mass., Feb. 17, 1804; d. Oct. 17, 1879. American engineer and inventor; brother of Seth Boyden (1788–1870). He supervised (1836–38) the construction of the Nashua and Lowell Railroad, was an engineer for the Amoskeag Manufacturing Company, designing hydraulic works at Manchester, N.H.; and designed for the Appleton cotton mills at Lowell, Mass., a water-driven turbine of 175-horsepower (1844) and three turbines of 190-horsepower (1846).

Boyd Orr (boid' ôr'), Sir **John.** See **Orr,** Sir **John Boyd.**

Boyd's (boidz). Name given to a tavern at Edinburgh, formally called the White Horse Inn, in Boyd's Close, St. Mary's Wynd, Canongate. The tavern and most of the buildings in the immediate vicinity were later demolished. Samuel Johnson stopped at this inn on his arrival (1773) at Edinburgh.

Boye (bô'yẹ), **Karin Maria.** b. at Göteborg, Sweden, 1900; d. at Alingsås, Sweden, 1941. Swedish novelist and poet. Of a middle-class family, she went to college at Stockholm. Later she studied at the University of Uppsala, and worked as a teacher of psychology at the Viggbyholm school outside Stockholm. The life of Karin Boye mirrored a tragic internal conflict, and ended in suicide. Her themes were always a search for the true sources of life, a rejection of the conventional and sterile, and a hatred of political tyranny, poignantly expressed in her most famous prose work, *Kallocain* (1940). This work is considered by many to be the Swedish counterpart of Aldous Huxley's *Brave New World,* and a forerunner of George Orwell's *Nineteen Eighty-Four.* Her verse works include *Moln* (Clouds, 1922), *Gömda land* (Hidden Lands, 1924), *Härdarna* (The Hearths, 1927), and *För Trädets skull* (For the Tree's Sake, 1925). She was the author also of the prize-winning novel *Astarte* (1931).

Boyé (bô.yē'), **Martin Hans.** b. at Copenhagen, Dec. 6, 1812; d. March 5, 1909. American chemist and geologist. He arrived at New York in 1836. Associated (1838) with Henry D. Rogers in a geological survey of Pennsylvania, he found nickel in iron pyrites ores in Lancaster County, Pa. Boyé discovered ethyl perchlorate and methyl perchlorate, and refined (1845) an oil product from cottonseed, obtaining cottonseed oil, valuable in cooking and in soap manufacture.

Boy-Ed (boi'āt'), **Ida.** [Maiden name, **Ida Ed.**] b. at Bergedorf, near Hamburg, Germany, April 17, 1852; d. at Travemünde, Germany, May 13, 1928. German novelist. She enjoyed throughout her life great popularity with such novels as *Fast ein Adler* (1908) and other works such as *Aus alten und neuen Tagen* (1925), a collection of her short stories. Her son, Carl von Boy-Ed, was German naval attaché at Washington during the early period of World War I.

Boy Emigrants, The. Novel for children by Noah Brooks, published in 1876.

Boyer (bwȧ.yā'), **Abel.** at Castres, France, June 24, 1667; d. at Chelsea, London, Nov. 16, 1729. English lexicographer and historical writer. He compiled (1702) a French-English dictionary which had many subsequent editions.

Boyer (bwȧ.yā), Baron **Alexis de.** b. at Uzerche, in Limousin, France, c1757; d. at Paris, Nov. 25, 1833. French surgeon. He was the son of a tailor, and rose to the rank of baron of the empire during the reign of Napoleon I, who also made him his first surgeon. He wrote *Traité complet d'anatomie* (1797–99), *Traité des maladies chirurgicales* (1814–22), and other works.

Boyer, Jean Baptiste Nicolas. b. at Marseilles, Aug. 5, 1693; d. April 2, 1768. French physician and philanthropist. He wrote *Relation historique de la peste de Marseille* (1721), and other works.

Boyer, Jean Pierre. b. at Port-au-Prince, Haiti, Feb. 28, 1776; d. at Paris, July 9, 1850. Haitian insurgent; president (1820–43) of Haiti. A free mulatto, he joined in the attempt to set up a republic, which was made by Toussaint L'Ouverture, Henri Christophe, and the Negro slaves in the insurrection of 1791–93. After the accession (1799) of Toussaint L'Ouverture, Boyer, with Alexandre Sabès Pétion and others, retired to France; returning in 1802 as a captain in the French army, he was made a general. On Pétion's death (1818), Boyer became his successor as president of the southern part of the country. By the death (1820) of Christophe, and Boyer's conquest of the Spanish territory soon after, the latter brought the whole island under his rule, practically as dictator. He was expelled by a revolution in 1843, and took refuge in Jamaica.

Boyer d'Agen (dȧ.zhaṅ), **Augustin.** [Original name, **Jean Auguste Boyer.**] b. at Agen, France, 1859—. French writer, expert on religious questions. He wrote numerous studies of church art and of the lives of churchmen.

Boyertown (boi'ėr.toun). Borough in SE Pennsylvania, in Berks County: agricultural center; manufactures include leather goods, metal goods, textiles, lumber products, and coffins. It was founded in 1834. Pop. 4,074 (1950).

Boyesen (boi'ẹ.sẹn), **Hjalmar Hjorth.** b. at Frederiksvärn, Norway, Sept. 23, 1849; d. Oct. 4, 1895. American novelist, poet, and critic. He was graduated from the University of Christiania (now Oslo) in 1868, came to America in 1869, was professor of German (1874–80) at Cornell University, and became a professor at Columbia College in 1880. His works include *Gunnar: a Tale of Norse Life* (1874) and *The Golden Calf* (1892).

Boyet (bwȧ.yā'). Mocking, mirthful lord attending on the Princess of France, in Shakespeare's *Love's Labor's Lost.*

Boyis (bois), **Hector.** See **Boece** or **Boethius** or **Boetius, Hector.**

Boyle (boil). Market town in Connacht province, Irish Republic, in County Roscommon, situated on the river Boyle, ab. 25 mi. NW of Roscommon. It contains an abbey, a fine ivy-clad medieval ruin. The spacious church has a well-proportioned W front with a single large window in early Pointed style, and a square chevet, also with a large window. The N side of the nave is also early Pointed; the S side is in Norman style, with curiously sculptured capitals. The crossing, surmounted by a tower, is very fine, and the transepts mingle Norman and Early English forms. Much remains of the secular buildings, especially the kitchen and the guest house. 1,935 (1951).

Boyle, Charles. [Titles: 4th Earl of **Orrery,** 1st Baron **Marston.**] b. at Chelsea, London, 1676; d. Aug. 28, 1731. English statesman, soldier, and author; grandson of

Roger Boyle (1621–79) and father of John Boyle (1707–62). He edited (c1695) the *Epistles of Phalaris*, which the classicist Richard Bentley proved spurious, and thus became involved in a controversy leading to Jonathan Swift's *Battle of the Books*. After fighting at Malplaquet, he was appointed (1709) a major general, and subsequently took part in preliminary negotiations for the Treaty of Utrecht (1713). He was imprisoned (1721) for his connection (which Swift denied) with Layer's Jacobite Plot. An astronomical instrument, the orrery, was named after him (in gratitude for his patronage) by George Graham, the instrument's inventor.

Boyle, John. [Titles: 5th Earl of **Cork,** 5th Earl of **Orrery.**] b. Jan. 2, 1707; d. at Marston, Somerset, England, Nov. 16, 1762. British nobleman; son of Charles Boyle, 4th Earl of Orrery. He published *Remarks on the Life and Writings of Jonathan Swift* (1751), and others.

Boyle, Kay. b. at St. Paul, Minn., Feb. 19, 1903—. American short-story writer, novelist, and poet. Some of her early work appeared in Eugene Jolas's magazine, *transition;* subsequently she became a contributor to the *New Yorker.* For many years she lived in France, and, after World War II, moved to Germany where her husband was active with the U.S. military administration. Her novels *Primer for Combat* (1942), *Avalanche* (1943), and *A Frenchman Must Die* (1943) are laid in France during World War II; her impressions of post-war Germany are given in the short stories collected under the title *The Smoking Mountain* (1951). Her other novels include *Plagued by the Nightingale* (1931), *Year Before Last* (1932), *Gentlemen, I Address You Privately* (1933), *My Next Pride* (1934), *Monday Night* (1938), and *His Human Majesty* (1949). Her short stories have been collected in *Wedding Day* (1930), *First Lover* (1933), *The White Horses of Vienna* (1936), and *The Crazy Hunter* (1940). She has also published the poetry collections *A Glad Day* (1938) and *American Citizen* (1944).

Boyle, Richard. [Title, 1st Earl of **Cork.**] b. at Canterbury, England, Oct. 13, 1566; d. Sept. 15, 1643. English politician, created 1st Earl of Cork in 1620, and commonly called "the great Earl of Cork." He became lord treasurer of Ireland in 1631. After he had acquired Sir Walter Raleigh's Irish holdings, he came into conflict with Thomas Wentworth, 1st Earl of Strafford, whom he was instrumental in having removed from office.

Boyle, Richard. [Titles: 3rd Earl of **Burlington,** 4th Earl of **Cork.**] b. April 25, 1695; d. in December, 1753. British nobleman, noted as an architect and as a patron of the arts.

Boyle, Robert. b. at Lismore Castle, Ireland, Jan. 25, 1627; d. at London, Dec. 30, 1691. British chemist and physcist; seventh son of Richard Boyle, 1st Earl of Cork. He studied at Eton and Geneva (which he left in 1641), settled at Oxford in 1654. The dons at Oxford are said to have tried to dissuade him from the study of chemistry by arguing that it was not a study for gentlemen. Boyle was a member of a small inner group at Oxford (later, in 1663, to be chartered as the Royal Society) devoted to the study of the new philosophy and using the experimental methods of Francis Bacon. Boyle regarded the acquisition of knowledge as an end in itself, and so he gained a wider view of the aims of scientific inquiry than shown by most of his predecessors. He protested against considering chemistry simply with a view to the preparation of medicines, as physicians did, or to the improvement of metals, as alchemists did. Our present-day chemical concepts of element, compound, and decomposition go back to him. He was the first really to state that it is needful to investigate the elementary constituents into which the substances found in nature can be decomposed. Boyle thus brought into being our present concept of an element but a further hundred years were necessary before Lavoisier finally carried out Boyle's program and put the system of elements on a true basis, for until then an error, the phlogiston theory of Stahl, had led investigation astray. In 1660, Boyle announced the so-called gas law (Boyle's law) which states that the pressure of a gas is proportional to the number of molecules present in a given space and to their temperature, that is the average value of their energy of motion. Boyle knew the difference between a mixture and a compound and called for quantitative statements showing the exact quantity of A that combined with B. Boyle knew the effect of atmospheric pressure on the boiling point of water, isolated methyl alcohol (1661), collected hydrogen over water, and prepared phosphorus. In 1668 he moved to London. Elected president of the Royal Society in 1680, he declined the honor because he did not want to take an oath. He was also the founder of the Boyle Lectures. His ideas are set forth in *The Sceptical Chemist* (1661) where he questioned "the experiments whereby vulgar Spagyrists" (i.e. the followers of Paracelsus) "are wont to endeavor to evince their Salt, Sulphur, and Mercury to be the true principles of things." He was also the author of *New Experiments* (1665, 1669, and 1682), *Hydrostatical Paradoxes* (1666), *Discourse of Things Above Reason* (1681), *Memoirs for the Natural History of the Human Blood* (1684), and other works.

Boyle, Roger. [Titles: Baron **Broghill,** 1st Earl of **Orrery.**] b. at Lismore, Ireland, April 25, 1621; d. Oct. 16, 1679. British statesman, soldier, and dramatist; third son of Richard Boyle, 1st Earl of Cork, and grandfather of Charles Boyle (1676–1731). He was created Baron Broghill in 1627, and 1st Earl of Orrery in 1660. Though a Royalist, he served under Oliver Cromwell in the conquest of Ireland, and continued to support him and his son Richard. His dramatic works include *Henry V* (acted in 1664, published in 1668), *Mustapha* (acted in 1665), *The Black Prince* (acted in 1667), *Tryphon* (acted in 1668), *Guzman*, a comedy, and *Mr. Anthony*, a comedy (published in 1690). He also wrote a number of poems and a romance, *Parthenissa* (1654).

Boyle, Thomas. b. probably at or near Marblehead, Mass., c1776; d. c1825. American sea captain and privateersman. He commanded the privateer schooner *Comet* (1812) and the *Chasseur* (1814), captured some 80 ships during the War of 1812, among them the British schooner *St. Lawrence*, and became a merchant seaman after the war.

Boyle, Virginia Frazer. b. near Chattanooga, Tenn.; d. Dec. 13, 1938. American poet and novelist on regional themes. She was named (1910) poet laureate of the United Confederate Veterans Association; her poems for special occasions include the Tennessee centennial ode (1896), the Jefferson Davis centennial ode (1908), and *Abraham Lincoln* (1909), on the centenary of the Philadelphia Brigade Association. Author of *Brokenburne* (1897) and *Serena* (1905), both novels, and of *The Other Side* (1893) and *Bugle Calls* (1906), collections of verse.

Boyle Lectures. Course of eight lectures in defense of Christianity, instituted by Robert Boyle, commenced in 1692 and delivered annually, originally at Saint Mary-le-Bow Church, London.

Boylesve (bwȧ.lev), **René.** [Original name, **René Tardivaux.**] b. at La Haye-Descartes, France, April 14, 1867; d. at Paris, Jan. 14, 1926. French novelist whose works deal with provincial life. He was the author of *La Becquée* (1901), *L'Enfant à la balustrade* (1903), *La Jeune Fille bien élevée* (1909), and a series of stories, *Les Leçons d'amour dans un parc* (3 vols., 1902, 1924, 1925). Critics value his work for its trenchant psychological analysis.

Boylston (boil'stọn), **Zabdiel.** b. at Brookline, Mass., March 9, 1679; d. March 1, 1766. American physician, the first in the U.S. to inoculate against smallpox. During a Boston smallpox epidemic (1721), he obtained permission from Cotton Mather to inoculate the people. The colony, unfamiliar with such practice, abusively attacked both men, and a hand grenade was thrown into Mather's study. Many books and pamphlets were written in defense of inoculation, among them Boylston's *An Historical Account of the Small-pox inoculated in New England* (1726).

Boyne (boin). [Irish, **Boinn.**] River in Leinster province, in the Irish Republic. It rises near the County Kildare-County Meath boundary, in the Bog of Allen, and flows generally NE to Drogheda Bay, ab. 4 mi. E of Drogheda. It is the largest river in Leinster province. On its banks, ab. 3 mi. W of Drogheda, on July 1, 1690, was fought the Battle of the Boyne in which the army of William III (36,000) defeated that of James II (26,000). The loss of William was 500; that of James, 1,500. Length, ab. 70 mi.

Boyne City. City in N Lower Michigan, in Charlevoix County: resort community; manufactures of leather soles.

The smelt-fishing season here is inaugurated by a three-day Smelt Festival. 3,028 (1950).

Boynton (boin'tọn), **Henry Walcott.** b. at Guilford, Conn., April 22, 1869; d. at Providence, R.I., May 11, 1947. American writer and literary editor; brother of Percy Holmes Boynton (1875–1946). He received the degrees of B.A. (1891) and M.A. (1893) from Amherst College, and was head (1892–1901) of the department of English literature at Phillips Academy, Andover, Mass., and chief book reviewer (1901–04) for the *Atlantic Monthly*. His works include *Life of Washington Irving* (1901), *Bret Harte* (1903), and *James Fenimore Cooper* (1931). He also prepared editions of Tennyson's *The Princess*, Milton's *Paradise Lost*, Goldsmith's *The Vicar of Wakefield*, and other classics.

Boynton, Percy Holmes. b. at Newark, N.J., Oct. 30, 1875; d. 1946. American teacher and author; brother of Henry Walcott Boynton (1869–1947). He was graduated from Amherst (1897) and from Harvard (M.S., 1898), became (1902) a member of the faculty of the University of Chicago, where he was later named professor of English literature, and was dean of its college of arts, literature, and science from 1912 to 1923. His works include *London in English Literature* (1913), *History of American Literature* (1919, 1923), *The Rediscovery of the Frontier* (1931), *Literature and American Life* (1936), and *America in Contemporary Fiction* (1940).

Boynton Beach. City in SE Florida, in Palm Beach County, on the Atlantic coast ab. 10 mi. S of Palm Beach. It is a seaside resort. 2,542 (1950).

Boyron (bwȧ.rôṅ), **Michel.** Original name of **Baron, Michel.**

Boys (bois), **Jaques de.** See **Jaques.**

Boy Scouts of America. Organization for boys and young men, dedicated to the development of ideals of manly character, civic spirit, and public service. It grew out of the movement known as the Woodcraft Indian Scouts, was incorporated in 1910, and secured a charter from the U.S. Congress in 1916. Its national headquarters are at New York. In 1951 it had a national membership of more than 2,900,000.

Boy's King Arthur, The. Adaptation (1880) by Sidney Lanier of the story of King Arthur and his court. Edited for the use of children, it was, in his own lifetime, the most successful of Lanier's works (although he is now more usually cited for his poetry).

Boys Town. Village in E Nebraska, in Douglas County ab. 11 mi. W of Omaha. It was founded in 1917 by Monsignor Edward J. Flanagan (1886–1948) as a home for abandoned boys, and was incorporated as a village in 1936. 975 (1950).

Boy's Will, A. Volume (1913) of verse by Robert Frost.

Boythorn (boi'thôrn), **Lawrence.** Boisterously energetic and handsome old man of sterling qualities, a friend of Mr. Jarndyce, in Charles Dickens's *Bleak House*. The character was intended as a portrait of Walter Savage Landor.

Boz (bōz, boz). Pseudonym assumed by Charles Dickens in his *Sketches by Boz*, first published together in 1836. He first used the name in the second part of "The Boarding House," which appeared in *The Monthly Magazine* (August, 1834). He himself says: "Boz was the nickname of a pet child, a younger brother (Augustus), whom I had dubbed Moses in honour of the Vicar of Wakefield; which being facetiously pronounced through the nose became Bōses, and being shortened became Bōz." Through ignorance of the derivation, the pronunciation boz, based on the nearest analogy, sprang up, and is now very widely heard.

Bozeman (bōz'mạn). City in S Montana, county seat of Gallatin County, ab. 80 mi. SE of Helena: marketing and canning point for agricultural produce, particularly peas and string beans. It is in a mountainous region, and situated at an altitude of ab. 4,773 ft. It was founded by John M. Bozeman in 1864, and is the seat of Montana State College. 11,325 (1950).

Bozeman, John M. b. in Georgia, 1835; killed by Indians, April 20, 1867. American miner and trail-maker. He was a placer miner (1862 *et seq.*) at Virginia City, Mont., and, in order to find a direct route to the Montana mining fields, made several expeditions with his partner through the Indian country, finally crossing the Continental Divide at what is now Bozeman Pass (elevation, 6,003 ft.) between the Yellowstone and Gallatin rivers. He was killed by Indians in that region.

Bozeman Pass. See under **Bozeman, John M.**

Bozeman Trail. Most convenient route used by emigrants bound west for the gold fields at Virginia City, Mont. It was traced (1863–65) by John M. Bozeman, who started out from Julesburg, on the South Platte River. After 1877 the trail was used for cattle herds brought from Texas to Montana and Wyoming.

Bozen (bō'tsẹn). German name of **Bolzano.**

Bozman (boz'mạn), **John Leeds.** b. at Oxford, Md., Aug. 25, 1757; d. there, April 20, 1823. American jurist and historian. He wrote *History of Maryland, 1633–60* (1837) and others.

Bozrah (boz'rạ). See also **Bosra.**

Bozrah. [Probably the same as the modern village of **El Buseira.**] In Biblical geography, a city of Edom, located in the mountains SE of the S end of the Dead Sea, in what is now Transjordan. It is mentioned several times in the Bible.

Bozzaris (bọ.zar'is, -zär'is; Greek, bôt'sä.rēs) or **Botzaris** (bôt'sä.rēs), **Marco** (or **Markos**). b. c1788; d. near Missolonghi, Greece, Aug. 20, 1823. Greek patriot. A member (1813 *et seq.*) of the Hetaeria (a secret society of political opponents to Turkish rule), he joined Ali Pasha against Turkey in 1820, was made a general in the army of Western Hellas in 1823, and is especially noted for his desperate defense of Missolonghi in the period 1822–23. His death, in a successful night attack on a superior Turkish force near Carpenisi, was made the subject of a poem by Fitz-Greene Halleck.

Bra (brä). Town and commune in NW Italy, in the *compartimento* (region) of Piedmont, in the province of Cuneo, between Turin and Cuneo, ab. 28 mi. S of Turin. It has flour mills, distilleries, and leather and textile manufactures; excellent wines are grown in the vicinity. The Sanctuary of the Madonna dei Fiori is a place of pilgrimage. Nearby is the former royal castle of Pollenzo. Buildings of interest to tourists were undamaged in World War II. Pop. of commune, 19,849 (1936); of town, 11,651 (1936).

Braak (bräk), **Menno ter.** b. 1902; d. 1940. Dutch essayist and scholar, particularly in the field of history. He committed suicide after the German invasion of the Netherlands. Seeking always for a clear and unbiased judgment of life, he unmasked in his penetrating essays the empty, conventional idealism of many of his fellow men. He was influenced by Friedrich Nietzsche. His essays are collected in *Het Carnaval der burgers* (Bourgeois Carnival, 1930), *Afscheid van Domineesland* (Farewell to Dominee's Land, 1931), *Man tegen man* (Man Against Man, 1931), *Démasqué der Schoonheid* (Unmasking of Beauty, 1932), *Politicus zonder Partisj* (Politician Without a Party, 1934), and *Van oude en nieuwe Christenen* (Of Old and New Christians, 1937). He also wrote some novels. English translations of some of his works may be found in *Harvest of the Lowlands*, edited by Jan Greshoff.

Brabançonne (brȧ.bäṅ.son), **La.** Belgian national song, with music by François van Campenhout, composed in the revolution of 1830, and so named from the province of Brabant. In 1848 new words for it were written, and in 1852 Louis Hymans wrote still others, all appropriate to their respective contemporary political situations.

Brabant (brạ.bant'; Dutch and Flemish, brä.bänt'; French, brȧ.bäṅ). Former county and duchy in W Europe, which corresponded to the modern provinces of North Brabant (in the Netherlands) and Antwerp and Brabant (in Belgium). It was at first a county, and became a duchy c1190. Limbourg was united with it in 1288. Philip the Good of Burgundy succeeded to Brabant in 1430, and it followed the fortunes of Burgundy and of the house of Hapsburg.

Brabant. Province of Belgium, bounded by Antwerp on the N, Limbourg on the E, Namur and Hainaut on the S, and East Flanders on the W. It is a densely populated agricultural and manufacturing province, containing Brussels, the capital of the country and the seat of the provincial administration. In its N part it is a level and fertile plain, in the S part hill country; it is watered by the Senne, Dyle, and Demer rivers. The N part is inhabited by Flemings, the S part by French-speaking Walloons;

the capital city itself contains both ethnic and linguistic groups. The province was formerly part of the duchy of Brabant. Capital, Brussels; area, 1,267 sq. mi.; pop. 1,822,834 (est. 1949).

Brabantio (bra̤.ban'shi.ō). In Shakespeare's *Othello*, a Venetian senator, father of Desdemona. He violently denounces Othello for his marriage with the latter.

Brač (bräch). [Also: **Brach**; full Serbo-Croatian name, **Ostrvo Brač**, meaning "Brač Island"; Italian, **Brazza**; Latin, **Brattia.**] Island in W Yugoslavia, in the Adriatic Sea, in the federative unit of Croatia, off the Dalmatian coast S of Split. 17,331 (1931).

Bracara Augusta (brak'a̤.ra̤ ô.gus'ta̤). Latin name of **Braga,** city.

Bracciano (brät.chä'nō). Town and commune in C Italy, in the *compartimento* (region) of Latium, in the province of Rome, situated on the Lake of Bracciano, ab. 21 mi. NW of Rome. A resort, frequented especially by people from Rome, it has a large medieval castle of the Orsini family. Pop. of commune, 5,319 (1936); of town, 4,360 (1936).

Bracciano, Duchess of. See **Accoramboni, Vittoria.**

Bracciano, Lake of. [Latin, **Lacus Sabatinus.**] Lake in C Italy, in the *compartimento* (region) of Latium, in the province of Rome, ab. 20 mi. NW of Rome. Length, ab. 6 mi.

Braccio da Montone (brät'chō dä mōn.tō'nä), **Andrea.** b. at Perugia, Italy, 1368; d. 1424. Italian condottiere. He took Rome in 1417, and fought in the service of Naples against Giacomuzzo Attendolo Sforza.

Bracciolini (brät.chō.lē'nē), **Francesco.** b. at Pistoia, Italy, Nov. 26, 1566; d. at Florence, Aug. 31, 1645. Italian poet and ecclesiastic. His works include the mock epic *Lo Scherno degli Dei* (1618), and the serious epic *La Croce racquistata* (1605), as well as *L'Elezione di papa Urbano VIII* (1628), *La Rocella espugnato* (1630), and the tragedies *L'Evandro, L'Arpalice,* and *La Pentesilea.*

Brace (brās), **Charles Loring.** b. at Litchfield, Conn., June 19, 1826; d. in the Tyrol, Aug. 11, 1890. American traveler, author, and philanthropist. He devoted himself to aiding the underprivileged at New York, becoming the chief founder of the Children's Aid Society in 1853. Besides books of travel, he wrote chiefly on sociological subjects.

Brace, Gerald Warner. b. at Islip, Long Island, N.Y., Sept. 23, 1901—. American novelist and teacher. He was graduated from Amherst (B.A., 1922) and from Harvard (M.A., 1924; Ph.D., 1930), and has taught English at Radcliffe, Williams, Dartmouth, Amherst, and Boston University. His novels include *The Islands* (1936), *The Wayward Pilgrims* (1938), *Light on a Mountain* (1941), *The Garretson Chronicle* (1947), *A Summer's Tale* (1949), and *The Spire* (1952).

Brace, Julia. b. at Newington, Conn., June 13, 1806; d. at Bloomington, Conn., Aug. 12, 1884. American blind deaf-mute, noted in the history of the instruction of those similarly handicapped.

Bracebridge Hall, or The Humorists: A Medley (brās'brij"). Collection of sketches by Washington Irving, published in 1822 under the pseudonym Geoffrey Crayon. The scenes of some of the sketches were laid at Bracebridge Hall. The sequel to the English sketches in the *Sketch Book,* it is charming in its style and quiet humor, as shown in the chapter in which Irving pokes fun at the scholarship of the Literary Antiquary who searches all his life for trifles.

Bracegirdle (brās'gėr"dl), **Anne.** b. c1663; d. at London, 1748. English actress. It was said at one time that she played the page in *The Orphan* before she was six years old, but *The Orphan* was not produced until 1680. She was on the stage till 1707, when a trial of skill with Mrs. Anne Oldfield took place, both playing the part of Mrs. Brittle in Thomas Betterton's *The Amorous Widow* on alternate nights. The preference was given to Mrs. Oldfield, and Mrs. Bracegirdle (in disgust, according to some accounts) left the stage. (However, she played once more, in 1709, at Thomas Betterton's benefit.) Both William Rowe and William Congreve were devoted to her, and she was suspected of being married to the latter.

Brach (bräch). See **Brač.**

Brachet (brȧ.she), **Albert.** b. at Liége, Belgium, 1869; d. at Brussels, 1930. Belgian teacher. He taught at the University of Brussels and was widely known for his researches in anatomy and embryology. The success of a series of lectures given by him at the Collège de France in 1915 led him to publish *L'Œuf et les facteurs de l'ontogenèse.*

Brachiano (brä.chē̤.ä'nō), **Duke of.** In John Webster's tragedy *The White Devil,* the husband of Isabella and the lover of the "white devil," Vittoria Corombona. He kills his wife, and, having rescued Vittoria from prison, marries her. He is killed by the duke of Florence, Isabella's brother.

Bracht (brächt), **Eugen Felix Prosper.** b. in Switzerland, June 3, 1842; d. 1921. German landscape painter, known especially for his scenes of Syria, Egypt, and Palestine. He studied in Germany, at Düsseldorf and Karlsruhe, and later taught art at Berlin. In 1884, he became a member of the academy of art there; his work was honored in Berlin and Munich. Among his better-known works are *The Tomb of Cecil Rhodes, Desert with Resting Caravan, The Kidron, Near Jerusalem,* and *Mount Sinai.*

Brachvogel (brä̆ch'fō"ge̤l), **Adalbert Emil.** b. at Breslau, April 29, 1824; d. at Berlin, Nov. 27, 1878. German novelist and playwright. He went from sculpture to acting before he entered newspaper work and, finally, free-lance writing. His most successful play was *Narziss* (1857). He wrote many novels about poets, musicians, and artists, of which *Friedemann Bach* (1858) is the best-known. He also published a history of *Das königliche Theater zu Berlin* (1877–78).

Brachvogel, Udo. b. at Herren-Grebin, near Danzig, 1835; d. at Chicago, 1913. German-American journalist and businessman. He came to the U.S. in 1867, edited for a time the newspaper *Westliche Post,* at St. Louis, then edited *Das New Yorker belletristische Journal,* and afterwards went into the insurance business at Omaha and Chicago. He published his *Jugendgedichte* in 1860 and *Gedichte* in 1912.

Brachylogus (bra.kil'ǭ.gus). Name given in the 16th century to a manual of Roman law, *Corpus legum,* composed, probably, in the 11th and 12th centuries (published at Berlin, 1829, as *Brachylogus juris civilis*).

Bracidas (bras'i.da̤s). See **Amidas and Bracidas.**

Bracken (brak'e̤n), **Brendan.** b. 1901—. British politician and newspaper publisher. He was chairman (1928–40) of the *Financial News,* and managing director (1928–40) of the *Economist.* A member of Parliament from North Paddington (1929–45) and Bournemouth (1945 *et seq.*), he served as private secretary (1940–41) to Prime Minister Winston Churchill, minister (1941–45) of information, and first lord (1945) of the admiralty.

Bracken, John. b. at Ellisville, Ontario, Canada, June 22, 1883—. Canadian politician, premier (1922–42) of Manitoba. He was elected (1922, 1927, 1932, 1936, and 1940) to the Manitoba legislature. Leader (1942) of the Dominion Progressive Conservative Party, he was chosen (1945) leader of the opposition in the Canadian House of Commons.

Brackenberry or **Brakenbury** (brak'e̤n.ber.i, -bėr.i), Sir **Robert.** Killed at Bosworth Field, England, 1485. English courtier, constable (1483 *et seq.*) of the Tower of London under Richard III. He helped to suppress the rebellion (1484) of Henry Stafford. Though he refused to obey Richard's order to kill the little princes Edward and Richard, sons of Edward IV, he delivered the keys of the Tower of London, where they were held, to Sir James Tyrrell, who committed the murders.

Brackenridge (brak'e̤n.rij). Borough in W Pennsylvania, in Allegheny County, on the Allegheny River near Pittsburgh: manufactures include coke, stainless steel, mirrors, and beer. It was incorporated in 1901. Pop. 6,178 (1950).

Brackenridge, Henry Marie. b. at Pittsburgh, May 11, 1786; d. Jan. 18, 1871. American lawyer and author; son of Hugh Henry Brackenridge (1748–1816). Admitted (1806) to the bar, he practiced law (1810–14) in Missouri and Louisiana. During the War of 1812, he sent information to the government on British plans to invade Louisiana. He recommended recognition of South American nations, and was appointed (1817) secretary of a commission to study the South American political situation. He served in Florida under Andrew Jackson in the period 1821–32. His *Views of Louisiana* (1814) contains a journal of a Missouri River trip used by Washington Irving in the writing of *Astoria* (1836). He was the author also of *History of the Late War* (1816), *South America, A Letter on the Present State of that Country to James Monroe* (1817), *Voyage to South America* (1819), *Letters to the Public* (an attack on Andrew Jackson, 1832), *Recollections of Persons and Places in the West* (1834), and *History of the Western Insurrection in Western Pennsylvania* (1859).

Brackenridge, Hugh Henry. b. in Scotland, 1748; d. at Carlisle, Pa., June 25, 1816. American author, jurist, and political leader; father of Henry Marie Brackenridge (1786–1871). A writer of Revolutionary propaganda, champion of the federal constitution, and leader of the Republican (as opposed to Federalist) Party in the West, he edited (1799) at Philadelphia the *United States Magazine.* He was a cofounder of the Pittsburgh *Gazette* (1786) and of the Pittsburgh Academy (1787), and served as a justice (1799 *et seq.*) of the supreme court of Pennsylvania. Author of two patriotic plays, *The Battle of Bunker's Hill* (1776) and *The Death of General Montgomery* (1777), the satirical novel *Modern Chivalry* (in several parts, 1792–1815), and *Law Miscellanies* (1814).

Brackett (brack'ẹt), **Anna Callender.** b. May 21, 1836; d. March 9, 1911. American educator. She was a graduate (1856) of the state normal school at Framingham, Mass., which later made her assistant principal for two years. She served as vice-principal (1860–61) of the Charleston, S.C., normal school, and principal of the St. Louis normal school. In 1870 she founded, with Ida M. Eliot, a New York private school for girls. She was the author of *The Education of American Girls* (1874) and *Woman and the Higher Education* (1893), and editor of a regular feature in *Harper's Bazaar.*

Brackett, Frank Parkhurst. b. at Provincetown, Mass., June 16, 1865—. American astronomer and mathematician. He was graduated (B.A., 1887; M.A., 1890) from Dartmouth College, and was professor of mathematics (1890–1924), director of the observatory (1908–33), and professor of astronomy (1924–33) at Pomona College, Calif. He was a member of several astronomical expeditions, including that to Mount Whitney in 1913.

Brackett, John Quincy Adams. b. at Bradford, N.H., June 8, 1842; d. at Arlington, Mass., April 6, 1918. American lawyer and politician. He practiced law (1868 *et seq.*) at Boston. A representative (1877–82, 1884–87) to the Massachusetts legislature, he was also lieutenant governor (1887–90) and governor (1890–91) of the state.

Brackley (brak'li), Viscount. A title of **Egerton, Francis** (1800–57), and of **Egerton,** Sir **Thomas.**

Brackman (brak'mạn), **Robert.** b. at Odessa, Russia, Sept. 25, 1898—. American romantic painter and portraitist who has been teaching at the Art Students League of New York since 1933, and at the Brooklyn Institute of Art since 1936. He came to the U.S. as a child. Trained at the National Academy of Design, New York, and a student of Robert Henri and George Bellows, he has exhibited with great success in the U.S. Among his better-known works are *Life and Still Life, Self-Portrait, Still Life, After the Masque, Roberta and Celia, Market Woman, Reclining Nude, Arrangement 6,* and the portraits *Charles and Ann Lindbergh, Mrs. John D. Rockefeller, J. D. Rockefeller, Jr.,* and *Henry Stimson.*

Brackwede (bräk'vā.dẹ). Town in W Germany, in the *Land* (state) of North Rhine-Westphalia, British Zone, formerly in the province of Westphalia, Prussia, situated ab. 35 mi. E of Münster near Bielefeld. 21,486 (1950).

Bracq (bråk), **Jean Charlemagne.** b. at Cambrai, France, May 3, 1853; d. Dec. 18, 1934. American professor of French. In 1871 he arrived in the U.S., where he served as associate professor (1891–92) and professor (1892–1918) of romance languages at Vassar College, Poughkeepsie, N.Y. His paper on French rights in Newfoundland, read at the meeting of the Academy of Moral and Political Sciences at Paris, served as a basis for the settlement of certain minority problems which had beset Newfoundland. Among his writings on French Protestantism, Anglo-French relations, and French imperialism are *France Under the Republic* (1910), *The Provocation of France* (1916), and *The Evolution of French Canada* (1924).

Bracquemond (bråk.môṅ), **Félix Joseph Auguste.** b. at Paris, May 22, 1833; d. 1914. French painter, etcher, ceramist, and ornamenter. He was a pupil of Joseph Guichard, who had been a pupil of Jean Auguste Dominique Ingres. He exhibited first in the Salon of 1852. His chief successes were his etchings.

Bracton (brak'tọn) or **Bratton** (brat'ọn) or **Bretton** (bret'ọn), **Henry de.** d. 1268. English ecclesiastic and jurist. In 1264 he was named chancellor of the cathedral of Exeter. He was the author of *De legibus et consuetudinibus Angliae* (printed in part in 1567, and entire in 1569), the first systematic and practical treatment of the body of English law. With regard to most of the facts of his life there is great uncertainty.

Bracy (brā'si), **Maurice de.** In Sir Walter Scott's novel *Ivanhoe,* a handsome and not ungenerous mercenary, a follower of Prince John. He carries off Rowena, but she is soon rescued.

Bradamante (brä.dä.män'tā). [Also: **Bradamant** (brad'ạ.mant), **Brandiamante.**] Sister of Rinaldo, in Matteo Maria Boiardo's *Orlando Innamorato* and Lodovico Ariosto's *Orlando Furioso.* She is a Christian but loves Ruggiero, and after incredible adventures in which her prowess, assisted by her enchanted spear, is equal to that of a knight, she marries Ruggiero after he has been baptized. Robert Garnier wrote a tragicomedy with this name; it was produced in 1580. Thomas Corneille produced (1695) a tragedy (his last play) with the same name. There have been several other plays on the same subject, notably one by Gautier de Costes de La Calprenède written in 1637.

Bradbury (brad'bėr.i), Sir **John Swanwick.** [Title, 1st Baron **Bradbury of Winsford.**] b. Sept. 23, 1872; d. May 3, 1950. English financier, whose signature on World War I treasury notes caused them to be called "Bradburies." He was joint permanent secretary (1913–19) of the treasury, chief British delegate (1919–25) to the Reparations Commission at Paris, and chairman (1925–29) of the National Food Council.

Bradbury (brad'ber"i), **William Batchelder.** b. at York, Me., Oct. 6, 1816; d. at Montclair, N.J., Jan. 7, 1868. American organist and composer of hymns. He was organist (1840 *et seq.*) at the New York Baptist Tabernacle, where he established annual singing festivals. He collaborated with Thomas Hastings in publishing *The Young Choir* (1841). His many music collections include *The Jubilee* (1858).

Braddock (brad'ọk). Borough in SW Pennsylvania, in Allegheny County, on the Monongahela River near Pittsburgh: manufactures steel, machinery, and plaster. It was the scene of an engagement (July 9, 1755) between French and Indians, and colonial and British troops under General Edward Braddock, which ended in disaster for Braddock's force. 16,488 (1950).

Braddock, Edward. b. in Perthshire, Scotland, 1695; d. July 13, 1755. British general. He entered the Coldstream Guards in 1710, served in Holland in the period 1746–48, and in 1753 became colonel of a regiment stationed at Gibraltar. He was promoted to major general in 1754, and in the same year was appointed to the command in America, with a view to expelling the French from their recent encroachments west of the Allegheny Mountains. The plan of a general campaign against the French, which was to include several independent expeditions, having been agreed upon with the colonial governors, he marched, from a spot known as Little Meadows, with an army of 1,200 chosen men, regulars and provincials, against Fort Duquesne, on June 18, 1755. He crossed the Monongahela River on July 8, and on the following day, when about ten miles from the fort, near what is now Braddock, Pa., fell into an ambuscade of French and Indians, who put his army to rout after two hours' fighting. He was mortally wounded while trying to re-form his men, and died at a place called Great Meadows, ab. 60 mi. from Fort Duquesne (the site of the present Pittsburgh).

Braddock's Road (brad'ọks). Road (c1752 *et seq.*) linking the Potomac River, at what is now Cumberland, Md., to the Monongahela River at Turtle Creek, near Pittsburgh, Pa. It was constructed under the auspices of the Ohio Company, was improved (1754) by George Washington, who brought it to within several miles of what is now Uniontown, Pa., and in 1755 was used by the expedition led by General Edward Braddock, who built an extension with its terminal point near Fort Duquesne. Subsequently a portion of the road became part of the National Road.

Braddon (brad'ọn), Sir **Edward Nicholas Coventry.** b. in Cornwall, England, June 11, 1829; d. Feb. 3, 1904. English colonial administrator, notable as premier (1894–99) of Tasmania, brother of Mary Elizabeth Braddon. After service (1854–77) in India, Braddon retired (1878) to Tasmania. He was elected (1901) senior member for Tasmania in the first parliament of the Australian Commonwealth. Author of *Life in India* (1872) and *Thirty Years of Shikar* (1895).

Braddon, Mary Elizabeth. [Married name, **Maxwell**; pseudonym, **Babington White.**] b. at London, Oct. 4, 1837; d. at Richmond, Surrey, England, Feb. 4, 1915. English novelist, dramatist, poet, and editor; sister of Sir Edward Nicholas Coventry Braddon, and wife (1874 *et seq.*) of John Maxwell, a London publisher. She was educated at home by private tutors, and began to write while still in her teens, contributing to *Punch, The World*, the Paris *Figaro*, to the Christmas issues of various periodicals, and to *Robin Goodfellow* and the *Sixpenny Magazine;* she edited *Temple Bar*, *Belgravia*, and other magazines. She was the author of 80 novels, including *Three Times Dead, or the Secret of the Heath* (1856; rev. ed., 1861, as *The Trail of the Serpent*), *The Lady Lisle* (1861), *Lady Audley's Secret* (1862, her best-known work, a sensational murder-story, immensely popular in its own day and still popular almost a century later), *Aurora Floyd* (1863), *John Marchmont's Legacy* (1863), *Henry Dunbar* (1864), *The Doctor's Wife* (1864), *Birds of Prey* (1867), *Charlotte's Inheritance* (1868), *Robert Ainsleigh* (1872), *Strangers and Pilgrims* (1873), *Dead Men's Shoes* (1876), *Joshua Haggard's Daughter* (1876), *Vixen* (1879), *Asphodel* (1881), *Mount Royal* (1882), *Phantom Fortune* (1883), *Ishmael* (1884), *All Along the River* (1893), *Sons of Fire* (1895), *London Pride* (1896), *Rough Justice* (1896), *The Rose of Life* (1905), and *The Green Curtain* (1911); she also wrote short stories, plays, and *Garibaldi and Other Poems* (1861).

Braden (brā'dẹn), **Spruille.** b. at Elkhorn, Mont., March 13, 1894—. American diplomat and businessman, now possibly best known for his outspoken stand against the government of Juan Perón in a U.S. State Department controversy (1945) over Argentina. As American ambassador to Colombia (1938–41), Cuba (1941), and Argentina (1945), and as assistant secretary of state for American republic affairs (1945–47), he energetically opposed what he considered to be dangerously reactionary influence in Latin America. Like his father, William Braden, who founded several copper-mining companies in Chile, he was engaged first in South American mining developments, but returned to the U.S. in the mid-1920's for a business career that varied from real estate to oil.

Bradenton (brā'dẹn.tọn). City in W Florida, county seat of Manatee County, on the Manatee River and Tampa Bay, S of Tampa. A winter resort, it is also a shipping point for citrus fruits, and for winter vegetables including celery, tomatoes, eggplant, and cabbage. 13,604 (1950).

Bradford (brad'fọrd). [Old English, **Bradanford** (brä'dän.fōrd).] County borough and manufacturing city in N central England, in the West Riding of Yorkshire, ab. 9 mi. W of Leeds, ab. 192 mi. N of London by rail. It is the headquarters of the English woolen-textile industry, possessing the largest mills in Britain, and manufacturing both worsteds and woolens. Bradford is also the chief wool-combing center in the United Kingdom, and has almost a monopoly in the alpaca and mohair trades; there are also cotton and silk mills, as well as a considerable dyeing industry and clothing and rug factories. It is situated on a coal field which produces good smelting coal, used in the manufacture of a high-grade wrought iron of great purity known as "Best Yorkshire." The city also has automobile factories and produces electrical equipment. It is the seat of the United Yorkshire College. Its cathedral, the Church of Saint Peter, was erected c1458 on the site of an early Norman church. 292,394 (1951).

Bradford. City in NW Pennsylvania, in McKean County, in a petroleum-producing area: manufactures include paper boxes, steel couplings, furniture, and cutlery. It was incorporated in 1879. Pop. 17,354 (1950).

Bradford, Alden. b. at Duxbury, Mass., Nov. 19, 1765; d. at Boston, Oct. 26, 1843. American historical writer and journalist, originally a Congregational clergyman. He was secretary of state for Massachusetts in the period 1812–24, and edited the *Boston Gazette* in 1826. He wrote *History of Massachusetts to 1820.*

Bradford, Amory Howe. b. at Granby, N.Y., April 14, 1846; d. Feb. 18, 1911. American Congregational minister. He was a pastor (1870 *et seq.*) at Montclair, N.J., and served as associate editor (1897–99) of *Outlook.* His books include 15 volumes, some of them collections of his sermons and addresses.

Bradford, Andrew. b. 1686; d. Nov. 24, 1742. American printer and newspaper publisher; son of William Bradford (1663–1752) and uncle of William Bradford (1722–91). He moved (1712) from New York to Philadelphia, where his press issued *The Laws of the Province of Pennsylvania* (1714), and where he was appointed official "Printer to the Province." He founded (1719) and published the *American Weekly Mercury*, the first newspaper in Pennsylvania. Imprisoned for criticism of the provincial government, he was later freed. He was the founder (1741) of a short-lived *American Magazine.*

Bradford, Augustus Williamson. b. at Bel Air, Md., Jan. 9, 1806; d. at Baltimore, March 1, 1881. American politician, governor of Maryland during the Civil War. Admitted (1827) to the bar, he practiced law at Bel Air and Baltimore. He was elected (1861) Union Party governor of Maryland, a nationally sponsored army intervention having precluded any possibility of a secessionist administration; in the election of 1863, he unsuccessfully opposed a repetition of this practice. He called (1864) a state convention which abolished slavery constitutionally and prevented federal intervention.

Bradford, Edward Hickling. b. at Roxbury, Mass., June 9, 1848; d. May 7, 1926. American orthopedic surgeon. Graduated (M.D., 1873) from the Harvard Medical School, he practiced (1875 *et seq.*) at Boston. He taught (1881–1912) at the Harvard Medical School, attaining (1903) the rank of full professor, and was its dean (1912–18). Founder (1893) of the Boston Industrial School for Crippled and Deformed Children, he was also influential in the establishment (1904) of a state hospital school at Canton, Mass. He was coauthor of the textbook *Orthopaedic Surgery* (1890).

Bradford, Francis Scott. b. at Appleton, Wis., Aug. 17, 1898—. American mural painter. His best-known murals were done for the International Telephone and Telegraph Company Building at New York, the Milwaukee County Courthouse (25 panels), the Cranbrook, Mich., Cathedral, and the New York World's Fair (10 murals). He studied at the National Academy of Design, the American Academy at Rome, and at the University of Wisconsin, and won a Prix de Rome in painting (1932), and a scholarship from the National Academy of Design (1923). He is an academician of the National Academy, and a trustee of the American Academy at Rome. He taught at the National Academy of Design from 1932 to 1937, and served (1942–44) on the U.S. Army Chemical Warfare Board.

Bradford, Gamaliel. b. at Boston, Jan. 15, 1831; d. at Hartford, Conn., Aug. 20, 1911. American banker and writer; father of Gamaliel Bradford (1863–1932). He was the author of *The Lesson of Popular Government* (1898) and others.

Bradford, Gamaliel. b. at Boston, Oct. 9, 1863; d. at Wellesley Hills, near Boston, April 11, 1932. American author, noted for his biographies; son of Gamaliel Bradford (1831–1911). He was educated at Harvard. His first published work was *Types of American Characters* (1895); others include *Lee, the American* (1912), *Confederate Portraits* (1914), *Union Portraits* (1916), *Damaged Souls* (1923), *Darwin* (1926), *D. L. Moody—A Worker in Souls* (1927), *Daughters of Eve* (1930), *The Quick and the Dead* (1931), and *As God Made Them.* He developed a biographical form which he called the "psychograph." His poetry includes *A Prophet of Joy* and *Shadow Verses.*

Bradford, John. b. at Manchester, England, c1510; d. July 1, 1555. English Protestant preacher and martyr. He became chaplain to Edward VI in 1552. Arrested in 1553, shortly after the accession of Queen Mary of England, on a charge of sedition and heresy, he was tried before a commission consisting of the bishops Stephen Gardiner and Edmund Bonner, and of other prelates; with a young man named John Leaf, he was burned at the stake at Smithfield in London.

Bradford, John. [Called the **"Kentucky Franklin."**] b. in what is now Fauquier County, Va., June 6, 1749; d. March 20, 1830. American pioneer printer and publisher in Kentucky. He moved (c1779) to Kentucky County, Va., and was persuaded (1786) to settle as a printer in the Kentucky territory. He published the *Kentucke Gazette* (1787 *et seq.*, its spelling was changed to *Kentucky Gazette* in 1789) and the *Kentucke Almanac* (1788 *et seq.*). He also published the first book in the territory.

Bradford, Roark. b. in Lauderdale County, Tenn., Aug. 21, 1896; d. at New Orleans, Nov. 13, 1948. American novelist and short-story writer. He was Sunday editor (c1924–26) of the New Orleans *Times Picayune*, and author of *Ol' Man Adam an' His Chillun* (1928; dramatized by Marc Connelly as *Green Pastures*, 1930). His other works include *This Side of Jordan* (1929), *Ol' King David and the Philistine Boys* (1930), *Let the Band Play Dixie* (1934), and *The Three-Headed Angel* (1937). He dramatized (1940) his *John Henry* (1931), with music by Jacques Wolfe.

Bradford, Royal Bird. b. at Turner, Me., July 22, 1844; d. at Washington, D.C., Aug. 4, 1914. American naval officer, commissioned (1904) a rear admiral. He was a naval attaché (1898) to the U.S. peace commission at Paris, and head (1897–1903) of the navy bureau of equipment.

Bradford, Thomas. b. May 4, 1745; d. May 7, 1838. American printer and publisher; son of William Bradford (1722–91). He worked (1762 *et seq.*) on one of his father's papers, the *Pennsylvania Journal and Weekly Advertiser*, and founded (1797) the *Merchant's Daily Advertiser*, which published news of the business world. He published William Cobbett's political pamphlets.

Bradford, William. b. at Austerfield, Yorkshire, England, c1590; d. at Plymouth, Mass., in May, 1657. English pioneer in America, one of the "Pilgrim Fathers." Having joined, as a boy, a nonconformist congregation, he went with the group to Amsterdam in 1609; this move was brought about by the need of the nonconformists for a residence where their belief would not be persecuted. He became a citizen of Leiden, there made arrangements to join the Pilgrim expedition to America, and was a signer of the Mayflower Compact in November, 1620, on the day the *Mayflower* reached Cape Cod. He was one of the 20 who, under Miles Standish, were the first to land and explore for a settling place. In April, 1621, he was elected governor of the colony. He served in this capacity for 30 years (except for five isolated years in which he was assistant governor). During his governorship, trading and fishing developed, the Plymouth colony became consolidated, and the debt to the English company was paid off (1648). Although he believed in maintaining his colony in compact isolation, he interested himself in other settlements springing up in New England. He wrote *History of Plimmoth Plantation*, which is the most valuable source on the settlement to 1646; the full manuscript was not published until 1856.

Bradford, William. b. in Leicestershire, England, May 20, 1663; d. at New York, May 23, 1752. American printer, the founder (1725) of the New York *Gazette*, the first newspaper in New York; father of Andrew Bradford (1686–1742) and grandfather of William Bradford (1722–91). He sailed with William Penn for America on Sept. 1, 1682, returned to England, and again sailed for America in 1685. He became printer for Pennsylvania, New York, New Jersey, and Rhode Island, and, in 1702, for Maryland. The first book (1685) issued from his press was an almanac, *America's Messenger*, for 1686.

Bradford, William. [Called the **"Patriot Printer of 1776."**] b. at New York, Jan. 19, 1722; d. Sept. 25, 1791. American printer and publisher; grandson of William Bradford (1663–1752), father of Thomas Bradford (1745–1838), and nephew of Andrew Bradford (1686–1742). At first a partner (1739–40) of his uncle Andrew, he opened (1742) a printing shop and bookstore at Philadelphia. In the same year he founded the *Weekly Advertiser, or Pennsylvania Journal;* he also published the short-lived *American Magazine and Monthly Chronicle* (1757–58) and *The American Magazine, or General Repository* (1769). In 1762 he established, with John Kidd, the Philadelphia Insurance Company. He was active in the press and on committees in opposition to the British during the pre-Revolutionary period, and served with distinction in the Continental Army during the Revolutionary War.

Bradford, William. b. at Philadelphia, Sept. 14, 1755; d. Aug. 23, 1795. American lawyer. He was attorney general of the U.S. in the period 1794–95.

Bradford, William. b. at Fairhaven, Mass., c1823; d. at New York, April 25, 1892. American artist, painter of coast scenes, and especially of the scenery of the arctic regions. Among his works are *The Land of the Midnight Sun*, *Crushed by Icebergs*, *Arctic Wreckers*, and *Sunset in the North*.

Bradford-on-Avon (ā'vọn, av'ọn). Urban district and market town in S England, in Wiltshire, situated on the river Avon, ab. 9 mi. SE of Bath, ab. 99 mi. W of London by rail. It is noted for its manufactures of worsteds. During the course of excavation for new housing in 1945, a burial ground believed to date back to the Bronze Age (c2000 B.C.) was discovered here. 5,627 (1951).

Bradlaugh (brad'lô), **Charles.** b. at London, Sept. 26, 1833; d. Jan. 30, 1891. English radical politician and advocate of secularism. He served (1850–53) with the 7th Dragoon Guards, before becoming a lawyer's clerk at London. He founded the *National Reformer* in 1860. Having been elected to Parliament from Northampton in 1880, he refused to take the parliamentary oath on the Bible, on atheistic grounds, and was not allowed to take his seat, even on an affirmation, which he was willing to make. Though several times reëlected, and though he kept on asserting his willingness to express affirmation, he was excluded from his seat till 1886, when objection was no longer offered to his taking his form of the oath. He wrote *A Few Words about the Devil, and other Biographical Sketches and Essays* (1873), *The True Story of my Parliamentary Struggle* (1882), and others. An advocate of social reform, he is remembered also for his connection with Annie Besant in a celebrated 19th-century trial involving the dissemination of literature on birth control.

Bradley (brad'li). Village in NE Illinois, in Kankakee County: manufactures include Venetian blinds, farm implements, and furniture. 5,699 (1950).

Bradley, Andrew Cecil. b. at Cheltenham, Gloucestershire, England, March 26, 1851; d. Sept. 2, 1935. English lecturer, professor, and Shakespearian critic; brother of Francis Herbert Bradley (1846–1924). He was educated at Cheltenham College, and at Balliol College, Oxford, of which he was made a fellow (1874) and at which he lectured (1876–81). He was later professor of modern literature (1881–89) at Liverpool, of English language and literature (1889–1900) at Glasgow, and of poetry (1901–06) at Oxford. Author of *Utopias—Ancient and Modern* (1875), *Commentary on Tennyson's In Memoriam* (1901), and *Oxford Lectures on Poetry* (1909). He is remembered chiefly for his *Shakespearean Tragedy* (1904, and many subsequent editions), criticism dealing with the nature of tragedy in general and especially with *Hamlet*, *Othello*, *Lear*, and *Macbeth*.

Bradley, Arthur Granville. b. Nov. 11, 1850; d. 1943. English historian and writer. Among his publications are *Life of Wolfe* (1895), *Highways and Byways of North Wales* (1898), *Highways and Byways of the English Lake District* (1901), *Owen Glyndwr* (1901), *Highways and Byways of South Wales* (1903), *Marches of South Wales* (1905), and *The Romance of Northumberland* (1908).

Bradley, Charles Henry. b. at Johnson, Vt., Feb. 13, 1860; d. Jan. 30, 1922. American educator. He was an instructor and assistant superintendent (1885 *et seq.*) at the State Primary School, Palmer, Mass. As head (1888 *et seq.*) of the Farm and Trades School on Thompson's Island in Boston Harbor, he instituted the first sloyd (manual training in woodworking) classes held in America. He also started a boys' government plan known as "Cottage Row City." In 1905 he established a meteorological observatory.

Bradley, Charles Schenck. b. at Victor, N.Y., April 12, 1853; d. 1929. American inventor. His patents include an aluminum-producing process, the three-phase transmission of power, a rotary converter, and a method for the fixation of atmospheric hydrogen.

Bradley, Edward. [Pseudonym, **Cuthbert Bede.**] b. at Kidderminster, England, 1827; d. 1889. English author. He was rector of Denton, Huntingtonshire (1859–71) and of Stretton, Rutlandshire (1871–83), and became vicar of

Lenton in 1883. He wrote *Adventures of Mr. Verdant Green* (1853), *The Curate of Cranston* (1861), *A Tour in Tartanland* (1863), *The Rook's Garden* (1865), and *Matins and Muttons* (1866).

Bradley, Francis Herbert. b. at Glasbury, Brecknockshire, South Wales, Jan. 30, 1846; d. at Oxford, England, Sept. 18, 1924. English philosopher; brother of Andrew Cecil Bradley (1851–1935). Educated at Cheltenham and Marlborough, and at University College, Oxford, he won a fellowship at Merton College (1876) which he held until his death. He contributed many articles to the psychological quarterly *Mind*, and was the author of *Presuppositions of Critical History* (1874), *Ethical Studies* (1876), *Mr. Sidgwick's Hedonism* (1877), *The Principles of Logic* (1883, a criticism of, and a reply to, John Stuart Mill), and *Essays on Truth and Reality* (1914); his outstanding work, *Appearance and Reality* (1893), aroused keen interest and was hailed as "the greatest thing since Kant" by the Scottish philosopher Edward Caird. An opponent of utilitarianism, Bradley expounded a philosophy of absolute idealism.

Bradley, Harold Cornelius. b. at Oakland, Calif., Nov. 25, 1878—. American physiological chemist. A graduate of the University of California (1900) and of Yale University (1905), he became (1910) research director of the Woods Hole Marine Biological Laboratory. In 1919 he was named professor of physiological chemistry at the University of Wisconsin.

Bradley, Henry. b. at Manchester, England, Dec. 3, 1845; d. at Oxford, England, May 23, 1923. English lexicographer, historian, and philologist. He was educated at Oxford and Heidelberg, and was employed as a clerk and foreign correspondent at Sheffield until 1884, when he moved to London. He was president of the Philological Society in the periods 1891–93 and 1900–03. In 1889 he became joint editor with James Augustus Henry Murray of *The New English Dictionary* (which was later renamed *The Oxford English Dictionary*), and in 1915 succeeded to the post of editor in chief. His publications include *The Story of the Goths* (1888) and *The Making of English* (1904). He was made a fellow of the British Academy in 1907.

Bradley, James. b. at Sherbourn, Gloucestershire, England, in March, 1693; d. at Chalford, Gloucestershire, England, July 13, 1762. English astronomer. He became Savilian professor of astronomy at Oxford in 1721, lecturer on experimental philosophy at Oxford in 1729, and astronomer royal in 1742. He is especially famous for his discovery of the aberration of light, and his demonstration of the nutation of the earth's axis. His observations were published in two volumes, the first in 1798, the second in 1805.

Bradley, Joseph P. b. at Berne, N.Y., March 14, 1813; d. at Washington, D.C., Jan. 22, 1892. American jurist, appointed an associate justice of the U.S. Supreme Court in 1870. He was a member of the electoral commission in 1877.

Bradley, Katherine Harris. [Pseudonym (with Edith Emma Cooper), **Michael Field.**] b. at Birmingham, England, Oct. 27, 1848; d. at Richmond, Surrey, England, Sept. 26, 1914. English dramatic and lyric poet; aunt of Edith Emma Cooper. From the ages of 16 and 3, respectively, to their deaths nine months apart in 1914, aunt and niece lived, traveled, and subsequently worked together. The collaboration under the name Michael Field, which began in 1879, was so close that it is impossible to distinguish the work of one from the other. It resulted in eight volumes of poetry, 27 poetic tragedies, a masque, and a journal and letters. Under the joint pseudonym they wrote *Long Ago* (1889, imitations of Sappho), *Sight and Song* (1892), *Underneath the Bough* (1893), *Wild Honey* (1908), *Poems of Adoration* (1912), *Mystic Trees* (1913), all poetry; and the dramas *Calirrhoe* (1884), *Fair Rosamund* (1884), *The Father's Tragedy* (1885), *William Rufus* (1886), *Canute the Great* (1887), *The Tragic Mary Queen of Scots* (1890), *Borgia* (1905), and *The Accuser and Other Plays* (1911).

Bradley, Omar Nelson. b. at Clark, Mo., Feb. 12, 1893—. American army officer. In World War II, he was commander of U.S. ground forces in Europe (1943–44) and of the 12th Army Group (1944–45). A graduate (1915) of the U.S. Military Academy, he commanded the 2nd Corps in the northern Tunisian campaign (1943) and the Sicilian campaign (1943), commanded (1944) the 1st Army in the Normandy campaign, and was commissioned a full general (March, 1945). He was administrator (1945–48) of veterans' affairs. In 1948 he succeeded Dwight D. Eisenhower as chief of staff of the U.S. Army; in August, 1949, he became the first chairman of the joint chiefs of staff, answerable directly to the department of defense. In 1950 he was granted a fifth general's star by Congress and named general of the army by President Truman. Author of *A Soldier's Story* (1951).

Bradley Beach. Borough in C New Jersey, in Monmouth County, on the Atlantic Ocean, S of Asbury Park: residential and resort community. 3,911 (1950).

Bradley Quarters. Unincorporated community in S Arkansas, in Bradley County. 2,880 (1950).

Bradman (brad'mạn), Sir **Donald George.** b. at Cootamundra, New South Wales, Australia, August 27, 1908—. Australian cricketer and businessman, considered the outstanding cricket batsman of his generation. He left school at the age of 14, entered first-class cricket (1927) for New South Wales, and first played for Australia in England in 1930. He is the holder of innumerable cricket records. He retired from cricket in 1949. At various times a real estate salesman and journalist, he is now a member of the stock exchange of Adelaide. He was knighted in 1949.

Bradshaw (brad'shô), **George.** b. near Pendleton, Lancashire, England, July 29, 1801; d. 1853. English printer and engraver, notable as the originator of a type of railway timetable now standard throughout Great Britain and much of Europe. As a boy he was apprenticed to an engraver, and in time became proprietor of his own printing and engraving shop, specializing in maps. His first venture was the publication of *Bradshaw's Maps of Inland Navigation*, but he perceived the growing importance of railways, and in 1839 gave England and the world the first railway timetables. In 1841 he began issuing timetables every month under the name of *Bradshaw's Monthly Railway Guide*, and in 1847 he extended his service beyond the shores of England with the publication of *The Continental Railway Guide*. Subsequently a collocation of American timetimes was undertaken, but the Bradshaw technique of combining timetables has never won wide public acceptance in the U.S. (although monthly guides not unlike those of Bradshaw may be found in most U.S. travel agencies and railroad ticket offices).

Bradshaw, Henry. b. at Chester, England, c1450; d. 1513. English Benedictine monk and poet. He wrote *De Antiquitate et Magnificentia Urbis Cestriae*, and a life of Saint Werburgh, in English verse, mainly a translation of a Latin work by an unknown author.

Bradshaw, Henry. b. 1831; d. 1886. English scholar, antiquary, and librarian who was prominent in exposing (1863) Simonides' forgeries. At Cambridge, he became a B.A. (1854), and fellow (1853), and served as assistant in the university library (1856–58), supervisor of manuscripts and early printed books (1859), and university librarian (1867–86). He published treatises of typographical and antiquarian interest, some describing original discoveries. The Henry Bradshaw Society for editing rare liturgical texts was established (1890) in his memory.

Bradshaw, John. b. at Stockport, Cheshire, England, 1602; d. at Westminster, London, Oct. 31, 1659. English judge and politician, famous as one of the regicides. He was judge of the sheriff's court at London in the period 1643–49, and became chief justice of Chester in 1647. He was president of the High Court of Justice which tried and condemned Charles I, in January, 1649. He was president of the Council of State in the period 1649–52, and became chancellor of the duchy of Lancaster and attorney general of Cheshire and North Wales in 1649. Opposed to the dissolution of the Long Parliament by Oliver Cromwell in 1653, he refused to sign the "recognition" pledging the members of Parliament to sustain the government in 1654. His memory was attainted by Parliament, on May 15, 1660, and his body hanged in its coffin, on Jan. 30, 1661.

Bradstreet (brad'strēt), **Anne.** [Maiden name, **Dudley.**] b. at Northampton, England, c1612; d. at Andover, Mass., Sept. 16, 1672. American colonial poet; daughter of Thomas Dudley, governor of the colony of Massachusetts. She was married in 1628 to Simon Bradstreet, who was afterward also to be a governor of Massachusetts, and with him she emigrated to New England in 1630. A collection of her poems was published at London in 1650, under the title *The Tenth Muse*, the second edition of which (Boston, 1678) contains what is often considered the best of her poems, "Contemplations."

Bradstreet, John. b. c1711; d. at New York, Sept. 25, 1774. British officer, active in the French and Indian Wars. A member of the British forces, he was captured (1744) and imprisoned at Louisburg; after his exchange he communicated his knowledge of the Louisburg defenses to his superior officers (and is thus often credited with having been responsible for Pepperell's attack and victory over that fort). In 1746 he was named lieutenant governor of St. John's, Newfoundland. He attempted (1747) to purchase Pepperell's entire regiment, but, failing, accepted (1751) a commission as a captain in Pepperell's new regiment. He was instrumental in the capture of Frontenac (1758), as the officer responsible for the destruction of fortifications and boats. He also took part in Pontiac's War (1764).

Bradstreet, Simon. b. at Horbling, Lincolnshire, England, in March, 1603; d. at Salem, Mass., in March, 1697. American politician; husband of Anne Bradstreet (1612–72), and grandfather of Simon Bradstreet (1671–1741). He was governor's assistant (1630–79), and governor (1679–86 and 1689–92) of Massachusetts. Previously he had been secretary (1630–36) of the colony, and had been instrumental in the formation (1643) of the New England Confederation, of which he was named (1646) a commissioner.

Bradstreet, Simon. b. at New London, Conn., March 7, 1671; d. at Charlestown, Mass., Dec. 31, 1741. American clergyman; grandson of Simon Bradstreet (1603–97).

Bradwardine (brad'wạr.dēn), **Baron.** In Sir Walter Scott's *Waverly*, an old man, the master of Tully Veolan. He was a scholar, and of a very ancient family, a circumstance of which he was inordinately proud. He had been trained for the bar, and had served in the army. He had been in arms for the Stuarts, and was in concealment after the rebellion of 1745 till released by pardon.

Bradwardine, Rose. In Sir Walter Scott's *Waverly*, the daughter of Baron Bradwardine; "the Rose of Tully Veolan." She saves Waverly's life, and he marries her.

Bradwardine, Thomas. [Surnamed **"Doctor Profundus."**] b. at Hartfield, Sussex, England, c1290; d. at Lambeth (now part of London), Aug. 26, 1349. English prelate, theologian, and mathematician. He was appointed archbishop of Canterbury in 1349. His works include *De causa Dei*, *De quadratura circuli*, *Geometria speculativa*, and *Ars memorativa*.

Bradwell (brad'wel), **Myra.** [Maiden name, **Colby.**] b. at Manchester, Vt., Feb. 12, 1831; d. at Chicago, Feb. 14, 1894. American lawyer and editor. After studying law (but before being admitted to the bar) at Chicago, she established (1868) and edited the *Chicago Legal News;* a special act of the legislature stipulated that copies of the *News* containing state laws and supreme court opinions would be considered legal evidence. She passed (1869) her bar examinations and applied for admission to the bar, but was refused twice, on the grounds of being a woman, by the state supreme court, with the U.S. Supreme Court upholding the decision; she secured (1882) an act of the legislature which gave freedom of choice of profession to all persons irrespective of sex, and was thereupon admitted (1885) to practice. She was also active in the suffragist movement.

Brady (brā'di). City in C Texas, county seat of McCulloch County, on Brady Creek, NW of Austin: shipping point for turkeys and other poultry, and for wool, mohair, and cotton. 5,944 (1950).

Brady, Alice. b. at New York, Nov. 2, 1892; d. Oct. 28, 1939. American actress; daughter of William A. Brady (1863–1950). In the years after her debut in *The Balkan Princess*, she appeared in Gilbert and Sullivan operettas, in plays, and in motion pictures produced by her father. She won acclaim for her stage performance in the leading role of *Forever After*.

Brady, Cyrus Townsend. b. at Allegheny, Pa., Dec. 20, 1861; d. at Yonkers, N.Y., Jan. 24, 1920. American clergyman and author. Although he was graduated originally from the U.S. Naval Academy, at Annapolis, in 1883 his basic interests were religious rather than military, and he was ordained a priest of the Protestant Episcopal Church in 1890. He served as archdeacon of Kansas (1892–95) and of Pennsylvania (1895–99), and was rector of the church at Overbrook, Philadelphia (1899), of Trinity Church, Toledo, Ohio (1905–09), and of Saint George's Church, Kansas City (1909–13). He served as chaplain of the First Pennsylvania Volunteers during the Spanish-American War. Author of *Recollections of a Missionary in the Great West* (1900), the *American Fights and Fighters* series, and some 70 volumes of fiction and biography.

Brady, Edwin J. b. at Carcoar, New South Wales, Australia, August 7, 1869—. Australian poet and journalist. He was editor of the *Australian Workman* (1892) and the *Australian Worker* (1904), and became the owner (1901) of the newspaper *Grip* at Grafton, New South Wales. His books include *The Ways of Many Waters* (1899), *The Earthen Floor* (1902), *River Rovers* (1911), *The King's Caravan* (1912), *Bells and Hobbles* (1912), *Australia Unlimited* (1918), *The House of the Winds* (1919), *The Land of the Sun* (1924), and *Two Frontiers* (1944).

Brady, James Buchanan. [Called **"Diamond Jim" Brady.**] b. at New York, 1856; d. 1917. American speculator, financier, bon vivant, and philanthropist. As a youth he was a bellboy in a New York hotel. His later employment with the New York Central Railroad led to his becoming a salesman for a firm dealing in railway supplies, which put him on the road to fortune and fame, for his ability to sell either his wares or his schemes appears to have been almost irresistible. Early in his successful business career he became noted for wearing many valuable diamonds and other gems, and when he began to be called "Diamond Jim" he recognized the soubriquet as an asset and played up to it, letting it be known that he had a separate complete set of jewelry for each day of the month. It has been estimated that, at the height of his career, he possessed jewelry to a value of about two million dollars. His liking for precious stones was paralleled by a prodigious appetite for good food and for social gaiety, and he became one of the best-known figures in the night life of New York's Broadway. His acquaintanceship was very extensive, and among his friends were, on the one hand, many of the country's ablest businessmen, and, on the other hand, famous actresses, beautiful women, and men of the sporting fraternity. In 1912 he established, with a liberal endowment, the James Buchanan Brady Urological Institute at Johns Hopkins University in Baltimore.

Brady, James Henry. b. in Indiana County, Pa., June 12, 1862; d. Jan. 13, 1918. American politician. He was governor (1909–11) of Idaho, and a U.S. senator (1913–18).

Brady, James Topham. b. at New York, April 9, 1815; d. there, Feb. 9, 1869. American civil and criminal lawyer. He was appointed New York City's district attorney (1843) and corporation counsel (1845). He first acquired a measure of renown as junior counsel to Daniel Webster in the Goodyear v. Day case (1836), and for the Parish and Allaire will cases and the Cole murder trial. Author of "A Christmas Dream," published (1846) in *New World*.

Brady, Mathew B. b. in Warren County, New York, c1823; d. 1896. American photographer. In 1839, while still a boy lacking several years of his majority, he became interested in the then still new Daguerre technique of photography. After mastering this, and adding certain improvements to it, he set up (c1842) a photographic portrait studio at the corner of Broadway and Fulton Street, at New York. The enterprise was successful from its start, and among the many who crowded his establishment, eager to have their portraits done by this quick modern process, were contemporary leaders of the political, business, and intellectual worlds, so that in 1850 Brady was able further to excite public interest by exhibiting a "Gallery of Illustrious Americans." In 1851 and 1853 his exhibits won prizes at the World's Fairs at New York and at London. In 1855 Brady began using the then new wet-plate process, and established a second studio at New York, as well as one in Washington. Upon the outbreak of the Civil War, he received permission to accompany the Union armies for the purpose of making a photographic record. With the cumbersome equipment required by the wet-plate process, Brady and his assistants followed the armies throughout the war, not only into camp but to the very battlefields, taking all told more than 3,500 photographs, the first such record ever made of a war. An extensive selection of his work was published in 1870 under the title of *Brady's National Photographic Collection of War Views and Portraits of Representative Men.* Brady suffered severe financial reverses in the early 1870's, and in 1875 the U.S. government purchased many of his plates, while others were widely dispersed. Not only is his record of the Civil War of great historical value, but his simple, clearcut portraits reveal a great deal concerning the mid-19th-century generations of Americans.

Brady, Nicholas. b. at Bandon, County Cork, Ireland, Oct. 28, 1659; d. at Richmond, Surrey, England, May 20, 1726. English divine and poet. He collaborated with Nahum Tate in *New Version of the Psalms of David* (1696).

Brady, William A. b. at San Francisco, June 19, 1863; d. at New York, Jan. 6, 1950. American theater manager and producer; husband of Grace George and father of Alice Brady. He began his career at San Francisco in 1882, leased (1896) the Manhattan Theatre at New York, built (1910) William A. Brady's Playhouse and the Forty-Eighth Street Theatre in 1912, and was for a time the head of the World Film Company. In addition to producing more than 250 plays at New York, he was the manager of such sports figures as James J. Corbett and James J. Jeffries. He was president (1915–20) of the National Association of the Motion Picture Industry. Among the noted players who have appeared under his management have been Grace George (whom he married in 1899), Douglas Fairbanks, Florence Reed, Alice Brady, and Tallulah Bankhead.

Braekeleer (brä'kẹ.lär), **Ferdinand de.** b. at Antwerp, Belgium, 1792; d. there, 1883. Belgian painter. In 1819 he won the grand prize of the Antwerp Academy, which financed his further studies in art at Rome. There, and elsewhere in Italy, he studied for three years and painted historical and legendary subjects, his style showing a marked influence by Jacques Louis David, leader of the classical school. Upon his return to Antwerp he turned to the execution chiefly of small genre pictures; he also did a number of historical paintings, on subjects drawn from Belgian history.

Braekeleer, Henri de. b. c1840; d. 1888. Belgian painter; son of Ferdinand de Braekeleer. His instruction in art was chiefly at the hands of his father, and, like the latter, he was successful and highly esteemed in his time. Examples of his work are numerous in the museums of Antwerp, Brussels, and Amsterdam.

Braeme (brām), **Charlotte Monica.** See **Clay, Bertha M.**

Brag (brag), **Jack.** See **Jack Brag.**

Braga (brä'gạ). District in N Portugal, in the province of Minho. Capital, Braga; area, 1,054 sq. mi.; pop. 544,891 (1950).

Braga. [Latin, **Bracara Augusta.**] City and *concelho* (commune) in NW Portugal, capital of the province of Minho and of the district of Braga, situated on the Este River, NE of Pôrto. Formerly famous for its goldsmiths' craft and its production of arms, it is now a wine and livestock marketing center and has cotton and woolen textile industries. It is the seat of an archbishopric; the cathedral, begun in the 11th century as a Romanesque structure, was finished largely in the Gothic style, with Renaissance and baroque additions; it contains the tomb of Henry of Burgundy, the crusader and adventurer whose son Alfonso became (1139) the first king of Portugal. The city has numerous other churches and ecclesiastical buildings, among them the Church of the Holy Cross, the Hospital of Saint Mark, and the archiepiscopal palace, most of them in the baroque style of the 17th and 18th centuries; hence the name "Portuguese Rome." There is a medieval castle and an archaeological museum. The chapel of São Fructuoso in the nearby village of Montelios is an Arabic building of the 11th century; the Sanctuary of Bom Jesus do Monte is also in the vicinity. Once a Roman colony, Braga became a residence of the kings of Portugal in the 12th century. Pop. of concelho, 75,846 (1940); of city, 29,362 (1940).

Braga (brä'gä), **Gaetano.** b. 1829; d. 1907. Italian cellist and composer of operas, and vocal and instrumental music; noted for his song *Angel's Serenade.*

Braga (brä'gạ), **(Joaquim) Teófilo (Fernandes).** b. at Ponta Delgada, the Azores, Feb. 24, 1843; d. at Lisbon, Jan. 28, 1924. Portuguese critic, poet, historian, journalist, and social and political thinker. One of the most prolific writers in Portugal, he is considered the first systematic critic of her literature. *Visão dos tempos* and *Tempestades sonoras* (1864) are his best-known books of poems. His prose writings include *História da literatura portuguesa, História da Universidade de Coimbra, As modernas idéias na literatura portuguesa, Camoes e o sentimento nacional,* and many other works. He became the head of the provisional government when the Portuguese republic was proclaimed (1910).

Bragado (brä.gä'ᴛʜō). City in E Argentina, in Buenos Aires province, ab. 120 mi. SW of the city of Buenos Aires. 16,104 (1947).

Bragaglia (brä.gä'lyä), **Anton Giulio.** b. Feb. 11, 1890—. Italian actor, stage director, and manager. He founded the Independent Theater at Rome (1924), where he produced experimental plays by Savoir, Georg Kaiser, and others; among his most impressive productions was a treatment of Eugene O'Neill's *The Hairy Ape.* The theater lasted for nine seasons, but appealed only to a special public. In 1936 he established another theater, The Arts, at Rome, and in 1937 he toured South America.

Bragança (brạ.guṅ'sạ). City in SE Brazil, in the state of São Paulo. 16.456 (1950).

Bragança. [Also, **Braganza** (brạ.gan'zạ).] District in N Portugal, in the province of Tráz-os-Montes e Alto Douro, forming the NE corner of the country. Capital, Bragança; area, 2,526 sq. mi.; pop. 229,422 (1950).

Bragança. [Also, **Braganza.**] Town and *concelho* (commune) in N Portugal, in the province of Tráz-os-Montes e Alto Douro, the capital of the district of Bragança, situated near the Spanish border, NE of Pôrto: formerly an important center of the silk textile industry. The town is the seat of a bishopric; it has a huge early medieval castle, built in the Romanesque style, now largely in ruins, which originally belonged to the dukes of Bragança (members of a Portuguese royal house generally known in history under the spelling Braganza). There are various Renaissance churches, and the Church of Santa María in rich baroque style. The town was frequently sacked, destroyed, and rebuilt during the centuries of struggle between the Moslems and the Christians for control of the Iberian Peninsula. The duchy of Braganza was created in 1442; a member of the house of Braganza first ascended the throne of Portugal in 1640. The fortifications were razed by the Spaniards in 1740. Pop. of concelho, 34,295 (1940); of town, 6,595 (1940).

Braganza (brạ.gan'zạ), House of. [Also, **Bragança** (brạ.guṅ'sạ).] Reigning family of Portugal from 1640 until 1910, and, until 1889, of Brazil. In 1385 the Portuguese crown was attained by John I, bastard son of Pedro I of Portugal (Pedro the Severe), and his illegitimate son Alfonso was created duke of Braganza in 1442. In 1640 a duke of this house headed the revolution by which Portugal was separated from Spain; he assumed the crown as John IV, and it was retained by the family, with some changes in the line, until 1910, when the republic was founded. Pedro I of Brazil was the son of John VI, and, as Pedro IV of Portugal, was heir to the Portuguese throne; Pedro II of Brazil was his son; a daughter became queen of Portugal in 1834.

Braganza, Catherine of. See **Catherine of Braganza.**

Bragdon (brag'dọn), **Claude (Fayette).** b. at Oberlin, Ohio, Aug. 1, 1866; d. at New York, Sept. 17, 1946. American architect, designer, and writer. He practiced architecture (1901–23) at Rochester, N.Y. He was stage designer (1923 *et seq.*) for productions starring Walter Hampden, and was appointed (1934) special lecturer on architecture at Princeton. One of his best-known buildings is the New York Central Railroad station at Rochester. He was the author of works on theosophy including *Four-Dimensional Vistas, The Beautiful Necessity,* and *Delphic Woman.*

Bragg (brag), **Aristabulus.** Character in *Home as Found* (1838), a novel by James Fenimore Cooper.

Bragg, Braxton. b. at Warrenton, N.C., March 22, 1817; d. at Galveston, Tex., Sept. 27, 1876. American soldier; brother of Thomas Bragg (1810–72). He served with distinction in the Mexican War, and as a member of the Confederate forces in the Civil War. After graduation (1837) from the U.S. Military Academy, he was assigned to active duty in the Seminole War, which had begun in 1835 and was to continue for some six years longer. In the Mexican War, having joined (1845) Zachary Taylor's forces in Texas, Bragg participated (1846) in the battles at Fort Brown and Monterey, and was promoted to a captaincy. He was brevetted a lieutenant colonel for his bravery at the battle of Buena Vista (Feb. 23, 1847). He resigned from the U.S. army in 1856, and retired to a plantation in Louisiana until 1861, when he was appointed a colonel in the Louisiana militia. Commissioned (Feb. 23, 1861) a brigadier general in the Confederate army, he first commanded the Confederate forces in the coastal area between Mobile, Ala., and Pensacola, Fla. After promotion (1862) to major general, he suggested that some of his forces should be sent to Kentucky; on the way to that destination, he was given command of General Albert Sidney Johnston's 2nd Corps, which he led in the battle of Shiloh (which was usually called, in the Confederacy, the battle of Pittsburg Landing). On the death of Johnston, and having been named (April 12, 1862) a full general, Bragg assumed charge of the Army of Tennessee. On advice that Federal troops were planning to take Chattanooga, he moved his forces there, reaching Chattanooga ahead of the enemy. However, his effort to drive the Union forces out of Kentucky was a failure, and he was forced to fall back (October, 1862) to his bases in Tennessee. At Murfreesboro, he was forced back (Jan. 2, 1863) still further by a Union force under William Starke Rosecrans; later, Rosecrans maneuvered him out of Chattanooga (September, 1863), but he won at Chickamauga, and laid siege to the Union forces at Chattanooga. However, in December, 1863, he was forced to retreat again, and was ordered to turn over his command to Joseph Eggleston Johnston. He served (1864) as adviser to Jefferson Davis, with the nominal rank of commander in chief (and commanded briefly against Sherman in North Carolina); in 1865, he was captured and paroled. After the Civil War, he practiced as a civil engineer.

Bragg, Edward Stuyvesant. b. in New York, Feb. 20, 1827; d. at Fond du Lac, Wis., June 20, 1912. American soldier and congressman (1877–83, 1885–87) from Wisconsin. He is remembered as the coiner of the epigram used in Grover Cleveland's campaign of 1884: "We love him for the enemies he has made." In the Civil War, he was an officer in the Union army. He served (1902–06) as U.S. consul general at Hong Kong.

Bragg, Thomas. b. at Warrenton, N.C., Nov. 9, 1810; d. Jan. 21, 1872. American lawyer and politician who served (1861–62) as Confederate attorney general; brother of Braxton Bragg (1817–76). Twice elected (1854, 1856) governor of North Carolina, he also served (1859 *et seq.*) as a senator from North Carolina.

Bragg, Sir **William Henry.** b. at Wigton, England, July 2, 1862; d. March 12, 1942. English physicist who in 1915 won, with his son William Lawrence Bragg, the Nobel prize in physics for work on x-rays and crystals. He attended King William's College on the Isle of Man, and Trinity College, Cambridge. He was professor of mathematics and physics (1886–1908) at Adelaide University, in South Australia, Cavendish professor (1909–15) at Leeds University, and professor of physics (1915–23) at the University of London. Appointed (1923) professor of chemistry at the Royal Institution and director of the Davy-Faraday research laboratory, he also became director of the Royal Institution. He shared with his son in the development of an x-ray spectrometer which aided in elucidating arrangements of atoms and crystals. His works include *Studies in Radioactivity* (1912), *X-Rays and Crystal Structure* (with his son; 1915), *The World of Sound* (1920), *Concerning the Nature of Things* (1925), and *The Universe of Light* (1933).

Bragg, Sir **William Lawrence.** b. at Adelaide, Australia, March 31, 1890—. English physicist; son of Sir William Henry Bragg (1862–1942). Educated at St. Peter's College, Adelaide, and at Cambridge, he was named Langworthy professor (1919) at Manchester University, and Cavendish professor (1938) of experimental physics at Cambridge. In 1915 he shared with his father the Nobel prize in physics. He is the author of *The Crystalline State* (1934) and *Atomic Structure of Minerals* (1937), and coauthor, with his father, of *X-Rays and Crystal Structure* (1915).

Braggadocchio (brag.ą.dō′chi.ō). In Edmund Spenser's *The Faerie Queene*, a big bragging fool. He personifies Cowardice, and is the comic element in the book. It is thought that he was taken from Martano, a similar character in Lodovico Ariosto's *Orlando Furioso.*

Bragi (brä′gē). In Old Norse mythology, a son of Odin, and the god of poetry. He is Odin's principal skald, or poet, in Valhalla. His wife is Idun.

Bragmardo (brag.mär′dō; French, brâg.mår.dō), **Janotus de.** Character in François Rabelais's *Gargantua and Pantagruel.* He was sent by the citizens of Paris to Gargantua to voice their objection to Gargantua's hanging the bells of Notre Dame around the neck of his horse.

Braham (brā′ąm), **John.** [Original surname, **Abraham.**] b. at London, c1774; d. there, Feb. 17, 1856. English tenor singer and composer of popular songs, among them *The Death of Nelson.* He toured Italy, France, and the U.S.

Brahe (brä; Danish, brä′ę), **Tycho.** b. at Knudstrup, in Skåne, Denmark (now in Sweden), Dec. 14, 1546; d. at Prague, Oct. 24, 1601. Danish astronomer. He built, under the patronage of Frederick II of Denmark, an observatory, the Uranienborg (completed 1580), on the island of Hven, off the SW coast of Sweden. Having entered the service of the emperor Rudolf II, he settled (1599) at Prague. He discovered (1572) a new star in the constellation Cassiopeia, discovered the variation of the moon and the fourth inequality of the motion of the moon, and is said never to have been surpassed as a practical astronomer, although he rejected the Copernican system.

Brahm (bräm), **Otto.** [Original surname, **Abrahamsohn.**] b. at Hamburg, Germany, Feb. 5, 1856; d. at Berlin, Nov. 28, 1912. German literary historian and theater director. The quality of his critical judgment may be seen in his monographs *Das deutsche Ritterdrama des 18. Jahrhunderts* (1880), *Gottfried Keller* (1883), *Heinrich von Kleist* (1884), and *Ibsen* (1887). In his choice of plays, very often from abroad, he exercised a decisive and liberalizing influence on the new generation in the German theater. Brahm functioned as a dramatic critic for ten years, and distinguished himself as a defender of Ibsen and Bjørnson, laying the foundations for a realistic stage technique in Germany. His critical comments on acting demanded "naturalness, immersion in the role, and consciousness of ensemble." With Theodor Wolff and Maximilian Harden, he became one of the founders and the first director of the *Freie Bühne* (Free Stage), a small theater at Berlin, which opened with Ibsen's *Ghosts* on Sept. 29, 1889. Because the theater was a private subscription organization, it was possible to produce all the new plays which were forbidden in Germany. Brahm became the foremost exponent of naturalism among the world's director-managers, and established a superb acting company of naturalistic performers, among them Frank Reicher and Albert Basserman. In the first season of the Freie Bühne, Brahm also produced Gerhart Hauptmann's *Before Sunrise,* Bjørnson's *The Gauntlet,* and Tolstoy's *The Power of Darkness.* The theater failed to finish out its third season because there were not enough good naturalistic plays to produce, and because Brahm found it impossible to hold his acting group together. Brahm then became manager of the chief Berlin theater, the Deutsches Theater, in 1894. He made the Deutsches Theater the stronghold of naturalism, developing a style of production and acting that became known as the "Brahm style." He remained in charge of this theater until 1905, and was succeeded by Max Reinhardt, who had acted for him but was able to adapt himself to nonnaturalistic styles more easily than his master.

Brahma (brä′mą). One of the major gods of the Hindu pantheon, "the creator." Although Brahma is believed to be the creator of the universe, he is rarely worshiped, and there are only a few temples to him. He is portrayed as having four arms, holding a sceptre, a bow, beads, and the scripture called *Veda*. His vehicle is a swan or a goose.

Brahma. Poem by Ralph Waldo Emerson, published in 1857.

Brahmagupta (brä.mạ.göp'tạ). b. c598; d. c660. Hindu mathematician and astronomer. He was the greatest Hindu scientist of his time, and one of the greatest of all time. To him is credited a work which has been called *Ahargana*, changed by the Arabs into *Arkand*. This *Arkand*, the *Sindhends* (i.e., the five *Siddhantas*), and the system of Arjabahr (Aryabhata) were the works which were principally studied and in part translated by the Arabs in the 8th and 9th centuries.

Brahmana (brä'mạ.nạ). Dicta on matters of Hindu faith and worship; especially as a designation of one of a class of Vedic writings which contain these dicta. Their object is to connect the songs and sacrificial formulas of the *Vedas* with the rites. They contain the oldest rituals, linguistic explanations, traditional narratives, and philosophical speculations we have. They originated from the priests and individual sages, imparted by oral tradition, and preserved as well as supplemented in their families and by their disciples. A comparatively large number of *Brahmanas* is still extant, owing to their being each annexed to a particular *Veda*, as well as to a sort of jealousy among the families in which the study of the different *Vedas* was hereditarily transmitted.

Brahmans (brä'mạnz). [Also, **Brahmins.**] Hindus of the highest or priestly caste.

Brahmapurana (brä"mạ.pö.rä'nạ). In Sanskrit literature, one of the 18 epic poems known as *Puranas*, so called as revealed by Brahma to Daksha. This *Purana* is sometimes placed first, and therefore called *Adipurana*.

Brahmaputra (brä.mạ.pö'trạ). [Also: in Tibet, **Matsang, Tamchok, Tsangpo**; in Assam, **Dihang, Dihong**; in East Bengal, **Jamuna**; ancient names, **Dyardanes, Oedanes.**] River in S Asia, in S Tibet and NE India. It rises near Lake Manasarowar and flows E and S. The name (Brahmaputra) is sometimes given to the stream formed by the main river, the Dihang, with the Dibong and Brahmakunda. It turns S, then SW, and flows through Assam, in the E part of the Union of India, and East Bengal, in Pakistan. It sends part of its water (as the Jamuna) to the Ganges, and part to the Meghna, and forms with these rivers a vast delta at the head of the Bay of Bengal. The section between the junctions with the Ganges and the Meghna is sometimes called the Padma. In 1908 Sven Hedin announced that he had determined in Tibet the true sources of the river. Its valley in Assam is second only to Ceylon as one of the world's largest tea-producing areas. The waters rise some 30–40 ft. during the rainy season, and flood the adjoining fields, making irrigation unnecessary. Length, ab. 1,800 mi.; navigable to Dibrugarh, in NE Assam, ab. 800 mi.

Brahmasamaj (brä"mạ.sạ.mäj'). [Bengali, **Brahmosomaj** (-mō.sō-); former names, **Brahmasabha** (brä.mạ.säb'hạ), **Brahmiyasamaj** (brä"mẹ̄.yạ.sạ.mäj').] "The society of believers in God." Theistic church founded (1830) at Calcutta by the Hindu religious and social reformer Rammohun Roy. It was joined in 1841 by Debendranath Tagore, who undertook the task of organizing it with properly appointed officers and teachers, a settled form of worship, and a fixed standard of faith and practice. This was completed by the end of 1843. The year 1844 may be given as the date of the real commencement of the first organized theistic church of India. Its history has been marked by various schisms, but it has exercised a powerful influence against idolatry and greatly promoted social reform.

Brahma-Veda (brä'mạ.vā'dạ). See under **Atharva-Veda.**

Brahmins (brä'minz). See **Brahmans.**

Brahms (brämz; German, bräms), **Johannes.** b. at Hamburg, Germany, May 7, 1833; d. at Vienna, April 3, 1897. German composer. He was the son of a jolly, sturdy, not particularly cultured double-bass player, and it was taken for granted that Johannes would become a musician, in the footsteps of his father, but there was no parental dreaming about the child's genius. However, of all the instruments, the boy loved the piano best, and he was sent to one Otto Friedrich Willibald Cossel, a man with a passion and a genius for teaching, who guided with a sure hand the astonishingly rapid development of the boy's talent both for playing and for composition. Although he had appeared but three times in public by the time he was ten, his playing had attracted the attention of musical circles at Hamburg, and a proposal was made that the boy be taken on a concert tour which might even extend to America. Cossel, aghast at this proposed exploitation of one so young, and whom he already believed to be a genius, sent Johannes to the most eminent of Hamburg teachers and theorists, Eduard Marxsen, whose reluctant acceptance of the pupil put a stop to the project of the tour. Marxsen, a thorough classicist, would have nothing to do with such "adventurers" as Schumann and Chopin, and gave his pupil only the music of Bach and Beethoven. Brahms, susceptible to the romantic fever of the day, continued his lessons with Cossel; but he was also a docile follower of Marxsen's precepts, and learned from him what many of his contemporaries never learned: the real purport and substance of the classical style. When Mendelssohn died in 1847, Marxsen was bold enough to say: "A master of the art has gone; a greater arises in Brahms." By all this labor, Brahms acquired an extraordinary power of self-discipline. Playing for pittances in cafés and bars, giving poorly paid lessons, he yet managed to read extensively and to compose, without thought of publication, inordinate quantities of music (he set, for instance, almost the whole of Heine's *Buch der Lieder* to music, and this, with all the rest of his work of the period, he one day complacently consigned to the furnace). None but a great mind could have preserved its elasticity under such discipline, but Brahms's survived.

First Ventures into the World, and Schumann's Prophecy. In 1853 Brahms joined Edouard Reményi, a noted Hungarian violinist, on a concert tour, and it was through an introduction by Reményi that Brahms met the violinist Joseph Joachim, whose friendship was to be so enormously valuable to Brahms during the rest of his life. It was through Joachim that Brahms met Schumann, whose enthusiasm for the young man's work was so great (and who may also have sensed the tragic end which was so immediately in store for himself) that he wrote an article for the *Neue Zeitschrift* which contained the words "[here was] one who would not show us his mastery in a gradual development, but like Athene, would spring fully armed from the head of Zeus." This article was published in October, 1853, and its effect was unfortunate indeed: an unknown young man was exalted above older and more experienced artists; his actual production was too meager to support the contention made in his behalf; and by implication the whole "futuristic" movement of Liszt and Wagner was condemned. Brahms turned at once to the task of mastering the classics; the strong romantic impulse apparent in the works which he had submitted to Schumann he now set himself not wholly to suppress, but to curb. The next few years were difficult ones: they saw Schumann's suicide in 1854, the need to sustain (and the self-imposed impossibility of marrying) Schumann's widow, and the actual hissing (in January, 1859) of Brahms's own first major appearance, at Leipzig. Nevertheless, Brahms had completed, by 1860, three piano sonatas, the *Scherzo* in E flat minor, four *Ballades*, three sets of variations (all for piano), two *Serenades* for orchestra, the piano concerto in D minor, and several other works.

The Choral Decade, and the German Requiem. The decade 1860–70 saw more disappointments and also a measure of deep sorrow following the death (1865) of his mother. In some measure, however, the fruit of this sorrow was the *German Requiem*, a work which soon established the truth of Schumann's prophecy. Also, several other large choral works were completed during this decade: *Rinaldo* (a cantata, set to Goethe's text), the *Harzreise Rhapsodie* for alto solo, male chorus, and orchestra, the *Song of Destiny* (to a poem by Hölderlin), and finally the *Triumphlied* (1870, after the great victory of the Germans over the French at Sedan in the Franco-Prussian War). At the end of the decade, as recognition increased, his life also gained a degree of happiness which had hitherto been lacking.

The Symphonies and Last Works. Brahms approached the composition of the symphony, instrumental music for full orchestra, with some trepidation; he had a vast respect for the symphony, little use for the symphonic attempts of some of his contemporaries, and the memory that his first attempt at a symphony had ended as a piano concerto. However, in the C-minor symphony, which finally appeared in 1876, he triumphed over his doubts. In this gnarled structure (as rigid in its logic as any Bach fugue) there is to be seen the very essence of Brahms's philosophy up to this time—his utter rejection of all triviality; his conscientious devotion to the fundamentals of art as he understood them; and (in the last movement) a strong sense of the final achievement of his goal. The symphony that appeared in the following year is in strong contrast to the first, but its structure is equally perfect; it may be taken as a kind of pastoral symphony, but without the literalness of Beethoven's, in its suggestion of the well-being that comes from true contact with nature. In 1883 appeared the third symphony, and in 1884–85 came the contrast to it—the wonderful E-minor symphony, under whose quiet exterior many hearers believe they finally come to find more suggestion of mature feeling than is perhaps to be found in any other symphonic work. In this period also, Brahms produced the contrasting *Academic Festival Overture* and *Tragic Overture*, his two very popular *Rhapsodies* (Op. 76), and a great body of chamber music (which was perhaps his chief passion, as it had finally been Beethoven's).

Braid (brād), **James.** b. in Fifeshire, Scotland, c1795; d. at Manchester, England, March 25, 1860. British medical writer, especially noted for his investigation of hypnotism (named by him originally "neurohypnotism").

Braidwood (brād'wůd), **Thomas.** b. 1715; d. at Hackney, London, 1806. Scottish teacher of deaf-mutes. Educated in the schools of Edinburgh, he opened a school of mathematics there, and, subsequently, a school for deaf-mutes (removed in 1783 to London). The first school in the British Isles for the deaf and dumb, it was visited and praised by Samuel Johnson in 1773.

Brăila (bru.ē'lä). [Also: **Braïla, Ibraïl**; Russian, **Braïlov** (brä.ē'lǫf).] City in SE Rumania, in the region of Muntenia, situated on the Danube River, ab. 20 mi. S of Galaţi. It is a railroad station and Danube port of transshipment for oil products, and has agricultural markets, mills, shipyards, and factories producing iron goods and wire. It was formerly a fortress. It was taken by the Russians in 1770 and in 1828. Pop. 95,514 (1948).

Braille (brāl; French, bräy'), **Louis.** b. at Coupvray, France, c1806 or c1809; d. 1852. French teacher and musician, notable as the man who developed the system of writing and printing which has since been used by the blind. Himself blind from the age of three, he nevertheless studied music to such effect that he came to be considered one of the best organists in Paris, and a master of the cello as well. A system of writing that depended on combinations of raised points, devised by Charles Barbier, made Braille's musical and other studies possible, but he set himself to simplify and improve Barbier's method, and the system which he evolved is now used throughout the world and is known by his name.

Braille System. See under **Braille, Louis.**

Brailowsky (brī.lôf'ski), **Alexander.** b. at Kiev, Russia, Feb. 16, 1896—. Russian concert pianist, particularly known for his renditions of works by Chopin. His first New York appearance (1924) was followed by a Chopin series (1938) at Town Hall at New York. He has repeatedly played at New York since, and has toured in America.

Brailsford (brāls'fǫrd), **Henry Noel.** b. at Mirfield, Yorkshire, England, 1873—. English journalist and author. A member (1913) of the Carnegie International Commission in the Balkans, he was later (1922–26) editor of *The New Leader*, and became a staff member of *The New Republic*. His books include *Macedonia* (1906), *How the Soviet Works* (1927), *Rebel India* (1932), *Property or Peace?* (1934), *Voltaire* (1935), *America Our Ally* (1940), and *Our Settlement With Germany* (1944).

Brainard (brā'nąrd), **Daniel.** b. in Oneida County, N.Y., May 15, 1812; d. at Chicago, Oct. 10, 1866. American surgeon, notable for his writings on clinical surgery. A founder (1843) of Rush Medical College, Chicago, he was professor of surgery (1843–66) there. He served also as president (1854 *et seq.*) of the Illinois State Medical Society. Among his best-known papers is "An Essay on a New Method of Treating Ununited Fractures and Certain Deformities of the Osseous System," published in *Transactions of the American Medical Association* (1854).

Brainard, David Legge. b. at Norway, Herkimer County, N.Y., Dec. 21, 1856; d. March 22, 1946. American arctic explorer. He enlisted in the U.S. army in 1876, was promoted to sergeant, and fought in the Indian campaigns of 1877–78 under General Nelson Appleton Miles. He was a member of Adolphus Washington Greely's expedition (1881–84) to Lady Franklin Bay. With Lieutenant J. B. Lockwood he reached lat. 83°24′ N. (the northernmost point attained up to that time) in May, 1882, and with him in 1883 explored Grinnell Land and the northwestern coast of Greenland. In 1886 he was commissioned a second lieutenant in the U.S. army "for distinguished and meritorious services in connection with the Arctic Expedition 1881–1884," and was promoted to lieutenant colonel in the army's subsistence department in 1905.

Brainard, John Gardiner Calkins. b. at New London, Conn., Oct. 21, 1796; d. there, Sept. 26, 1828. American poet and journalist. He was editor of the *Connecticut Mirror* (1822–27). He published a volume of poems (1825), a second enlarged edition of which appeared (1832) with a sketch of the author by John Greenleaf Whittier, under the title of *Literary Remains.*

Braine-l'Alleud (bren.lå.lė). [Also: **Braine-la-Leude** (-lå.lėd); Flemish, **Eigenbrakel.**] Town in C Belgium, in the province of Brabant, ab. 12 mi. S of Brussels: glass manufactures. It was the scene of part of the operations of the battle of Waterloo. 12,026 (1947).

Braine-le-Comte (bren.lẹ.kônt). [Flemish, **'s Gravenbrakel.**] Town in W Belgium, in the province of Hainaut, ab. 14 mi. NE of Mons. 10,040 (1947).

Brainerd (brā'nėrd). City in C Minnesota, county seat of Crow Wing County, on the Mississippi River, ab. 105 mi. SW of Duluth. It is a shipping point for dairy products, and has railroad shops and manufactures wallpaper. A week-long festival is held here in July of each year in honor of Paul Bunyan. 12,637 (1950).

Brainerd, David. b. at Haddam, Conn., April 20, 1718; d. at Northampton, Mass., Oct. 9, 1747. American missionary among the Indians. His biography was written by Jonathan Edwards (1749; enlarged edition, 1822), and included parts of his diary, others having been published previously.

Brainerd, Ezra. b. at St. Albans, Vt., Dec. 17, 1844; d. Dec. 8, 1924. American botanist and educator, famous for his studies of hybridism in the genus *viola*. From 1885 to 1906 he was president of Middlebury College in Vermont. Among his works is *Blackberries of New England* (1900). His *Violets of North America* and *Some Natural Violet Hybrids of North America* were published as Bulletins 224 and 239, respectively, of the Vermont Experimental Station.

Brainerd, Thomas. b. at Leyden, N.Y., June 17, 1804; d. at Scranton, Pa., Aug. 21, 1866. American Presbyterian clergyman and editor. Pastor (1831–33) of the Fourth Church, at Cincinnati, Ohio, he was later (1837–66) a member of the New School Presbyterian Church. He served as associate editor (c1833) of the Cincinnati *Journal*, editor of *Youth's Magazine*, and assistant editor of the *Presbyterian Quarterly Review*.

Braintree (brān'trē). Town in E Massachusetts, in Norfolk County, ab. 10 mi. S of Boston: industrial and residential suburb. 23,161 (1950).

Braintree and Bocking (bok'ing). Urban district, comprising the former urban district of Braintree and parts of Braintree and Halstead rural districts, in SE England, in Essex, situated on the river Blackwater ab. 11 mi. NE of Chelmsford, ab. 45 mi. NE of London by rail. Braintree is an East Anglian market town, supplying farm necessities. It has silk and rayon industries, and was a woolen-textile center in the 16th century. 17,430 (1951).

"Brain Trust." In U.S. history, an epithet applied originally to the group of Columbia University professors, among them Raymond Moley, Rexford Guy Tugwell, and Adolph A. Berle, Jr., who served Franklin D. Roosevelt as advisers before his nomination and during his campaign for the presidency in 1932, and as officials in the government after his inauguration (March 4, 1933).

Moley was appointed to the state department, Tugwell to the department of agriculture, and Berle to the Reconstruction Finance Corporation. Much of the research that preceded the legislation of the early New Deal was done under their direction. The term was expanded to apply to all scholars and university personnel who joined the administration. Roosevelt's political opponents used the epithet indiscriminately to derogate the application of academic research to governmental problems, a process it considered to be the essence of New Deal experimentation.

Brainworm (brān'wėrm). In Ben Jonson's *Every Man in His Humour,* a servant of old Knowell, witty and shrewd, whose various disguises contribute to the perplexities and elaboration of the plot.

Braithwaite (brā'thwāt), **William Stanley Beaumont.** b. at Boston, Dec. 6, 1878—. American Negro poet, critic, and anthologist. He served as professor of literature at Atlanta University, and was awarded the Spingarn medal in 1918. His books of poetry include *Lyrics of Life and Love* (1904), *The House of Falling Leaves* (1908), and *Selected Poems* (1948). Among his anthologies are *The Book of Elizabethan Verse* (1906), *The Book of Georgian Verse* (1908), *The Book of Restoration Verse* (1909), and *The Book of Modern British Verse* (1919). He wrote an autobiography, *The House Under Arcturus* (1941).

Brake (brä'kẹ). Town in NW Germany, in the *Land* (state) of Lower Saxony, British Zone, formerly in Oldenburg, situated on the Weser River, ab. 22 mi. NW of Bremen: river port. For several centuries, until the port of Bremerhaven was built in 1830, it was the port for Bremen; grain and phosphates are shipped from here. It has shipyards, lumber yards, and canneries. 15,641 (1950).

Brakenbury (brak'ẹn.ber.i, -bėr.i), Sir **Robert.** See **Brackenbury** or **Brakenbury,** Sir **Robert.**

Bräker (brā'kėr), **Ulrich.** b. at Näbis, Switzerland, Dec. 22, 1735; d. at Wattwil, Switzerland, Sept. 11, 1798. Swiss author writing in German. His autobiography, *Lebensgeschichte und natürliche Ebentheuer des armen Mannes im Tockenburg* (1789), is an account of his experiences, first as a poor farm boy, then as a soldier (against his will) under Frederick II of Prussia, and finally as a cotton-wool weaver in his native mountain valley. In spite of his neglected schooling he was able to grasp the greatness of Shakespeare, on whose plays he commented with insight and enthusiasm in *Etwas über William Shakespeares Schauspiele,* posthumously published in 1877.

Braklond (brak'lọnd), **Long** and **Little.** Two ancient streets in St. Edmundsbury (now Bury St. Edmunds), England.

Brakpan (brak'pan). City in S Africa, in the Witwatersrand region, Transvaal, Union of South Africa, situated ab. 23 mi. E of Johannesburg. It was formerly part of Benoni but was made a separate municipality in 1919; has gold mines, a power-generating station, and ironworks. 83,456 (1946).

Braley (brā'li), **Berton.** b. at Madison, Wis., Jan. 29, 1882—. American writer. He has published novels, collections of verse, and the autobiography *Pegasus Pulls a Hack* (1934).

Bramah (brä'mạ), **Ernest.** [Full name, **Ernest Bramah Smith.**] b. c1869; d. in Somersetshire, England, June 27, 1942. English author of detective stories, and an expert on medals. He was the author of short stories in which he created two original characters, Kai Lung, a Chinese story-teller, and Max Carrados, a blind detective. His works include *The Wallet of Kai Lung* (1900), *The Mirror of Kung Ho* (1905), *Kai Lung's Golden Hours* (1922; dramatized 1931), *Kai Lung Unrolls His Mat* (1928), *The Moon of Much Gladness* (1932; American title, *The Return of Kai Lung*), and *Kai Lung Beneath the Mulberry-Tree* (1940). In the second series are *Max Carrados* (1914), *The Eyes of Max Carrados* (1923), and *Max Carrados Mysteries* (1927). Bramah also wrote a humorous autobiography, *English Farming and Why I Turned It Up* (1894), and *Guide to the Varieties and Rarity of English Regal Copper Coins: Charles II-Victoria* (1929), a standard work in its field, as well as publishing *Short Stories of Today and Yesterday* (1929).

Bramah (bram'ạ, brä'mạ), **Joseph.** b. at Stainborough, Yorkshire, England, April 13, 1748; d. at Pimlico, London, Dec. 9, 1814. English mechanician and engineer. He patented the Bramah lock in 1784, and a hydraulic press in 1796.

Bramante (brä.män'tā), **Donato d'Agnolo.** b. at Monti Asdrualdo, near Urbino, Italy, c1444; d. March 11, 1514. Italian architect. He studied painting before architecture, and established himself (c1472) at Milan, living in northern Italy the greater part of his life. He abandoned Milan for Rome in 1499, and became the greatest master of the architectural style then developing on a basis of study of the ruins of ancient Rome. His works at the Vatican are the long gallery connecting the old palace with the Belvedere, the court of the loggia finished by Raphael, containing the frescoes of Raphael, and the first plan (which was later followed to a large extent) of Saint Peter's. Bramante's design was considered by Michelangelo the best of the many which were made for this church. It was a Greek cross with a dome and two spires, and instead of the single great order of the interior employed two orders superimposed, as in the Ospidale Maggiore. The first stone was laid on April 18, 1506. As a military engineer, Bramante assisted Pope Julius II in the sieges of Bologna and Mirandola, and built the fort at Civita Vecchia near Rome.

Bramantino (brä.män.tē'nō). [Also: **Il Bramantino,** meaning "the Little Bramante"; original name, **Bartolommeo Suardi.**] b. c1455; d. c1535. Italian architect and painter. He studied and worked with Bramante, and was called Il Bramantino or "the Little Bramante" from his close adherence to his master's style, which seems to have been not a matter of imitation but of natural affinity. Like Bramante, he had a powerful influence on the Lombard school of painters. As a young man he went to Rome, where Pope Julius II commissioned him to execute various frescoes. His work, however, was mostly done, and mostly remains, in northern Italy. He became court architect at Milan to the duke Francesco Maria Sforza in 1525, and his architectural interest is evidenced in many of his paintings of this period, in which the buildings depicted share interest with the human figures. His work is considered notable for excellent draughtsmanship as well as for composition and for delineation of character. His frescoes in the Brera Gallery and in the church of Santa Maria delle Grazie at Milan are among the most admired examples of his work, which at its best has been compared to the masterpieces of Leonardo da Vinci. Apart from the frescoes, the Brera contains other Bramantino paintings, and there is a notable altarpiece of his execution in the Ambrosiana, also at Milan; outside that city, some of his best work is to be seen at Venice, Pavia, and Locarno. There are also many Bramantinos in England, some being in the Victoria and Albert Museum. The Metropolitan Museum of Art at New York counts 12 Bramantino panels among its works of the Italian Renaissance, and the New York Historical Society possesses a *Calvary.*

Brambilla (bräm.bēl'lä), **Marietta.** b. c1807; d. 1875. Italian operatic contralto. She sang at London, Vienna, and Paris, and in Italy.

Bramble (bram'bl), **Frederick.** In the younger George Colman's play *The Poor Gentleman,* the nephew of Sir Robert Bramble. He is generous and enthusiastic; he insults Emily's abductor "with all the civility imaginable," and saves her.

Bramble, Matthew. In Tobias Smollett's novel *Humphry Clinker,* a hot-tempered, kind-hearted, gouty squire, whose opinions are supposed to represent Smollett's.

Bramble, Sir Robert. In the younger George Colman's play *The Poor Gentleman,* a kindly but choleric squire.

Bramble, Tabitha. In Tobias Smollett's novel *Humphry Clinker,* the sister of Matthew Bramble. She is a prying and ugly old maid, "exceedingly starched, vain and ridiculous," who finally ensnares "the immortal Lismahago."

Bramhall (bram'hôl), **John.** b. at Pontefract, Yorkshire, England, 1594; d. in Ireland, in June, 1663. English prelate in Ireland, and controversialist. He became bishop of Derry (Londonderry) in 1634. Impeached by the Irish House of Commons on March 4, 1641, and arrested on the charge of complicity in the alleged treason of Thomas Wentworth, 1st Earl of Strafford, he was liberated (1641), without acquittal, through the exertions of James Ussher with the king. He became archbishop of Armagh in 1661, and in the same year became speaker of the Irish House of Lords. He induced the Church of Ireland to embrace the Thirty-nine Articles, and disputed with Thomas Hobbes on liberty and necessity.

Brampton (bramp'tọn). Industrial town in S Ontario, Canada, the county seat of Peel County, situated on the main highway, ab. 12 mi. N of Lake Ontario and ab. 32 mi. NW of Toronto. 8,389 (1951).

Brampton, Lady. Character in Richard Steele's play *The Funeral.*

Bramwell (bram'wel, -wẹl), **George William Wilshere.** [Title, Baron **Bramwell.**] b. at Cornhill, England, 1808; d. at Edenbridge, England, 1892. English jurist who (with Sir James Shaw Willes) drafted the Common Law Procedure Act (1852) and the Companies Act (1862). Elevated to the bench (1856) and to lord justice of the court of appeal (1876), he retired in 1881, and thereafter waged a persistent campaign for freedom of contract, both in the House of Lords and in columns of the London *Times.*

Bramwell-Booth (bram'wel.böth', -wẹl-), **Catherine.** b. at London, 1883—. English Salvation Army worker; daughter of William Bramwell Booth (1856–1929). She supervised (1926) the women's social work of the Salvation Army in Great Britain and Ireland.

Bran (bran). Name of Fionn mac Cumhail's (Finn MacCool's) dog.

Bran. [Called **"The Blessed."**] In Brythonic mythology, a son of Llyr, the sea, and a king of Britain whose head was buried outside London, facing France, to protect the country from invasion. Later he was regarded as a saint.

Brancaleone (bräng"kä.lā.ō'nā), **Dandolo.** d. at Rome, 1258. Italian statesman of Bolognese origin. He was elected by the people *podestà* (which means mayor, or chief city official) of Rome in 1253, with the power of enforcing justice, and the command of the military forces. He repressed the nobles and forced Pope Innocent IV to recognize the power of the people, but he exercised his power with such severity that he was driven from the city. Two years later, however, he was recalled.

Branch (brȧnch), **Anna Hempstead.** b. at New London, Conn., March 18, 1875; d. Sept. 8, 1937. American lyric poet and social worker. After her graduation (1897) from Smith College, she was the first recipient (1898) of the *Century* prizes for college graduates for her poem *The Road 'Twixt Heaven and Hell.* She was the author of *The Heart of the Road* (1901), *The Shoes That Danced* (1905), and *Nimrod, and Other Poems* (1910).

Branch, John. b. at Halifax, N.C., Nov. 4, 1782; d. at Enfield, N.C., Jan. 4, 1863. American politician and governor (1817–20) of North Carolina. He also served as state senator (1811, 1813–17, 1822, 1834), speaker of the state senate (1815–17), U.S. senator (1823–29), secretary of the navy (1829–31), congressman (1831–33), and governor of the Florida Territory (1834–45).

Branchidae (brang'ki.dē). In ancient geography, a small town in Sogdiana, said to have been built by priests from the temple of Apollo Didymaeus, near Miletus; it was destroyed by Alexander the Great.

Branco (brung'kö). [Portuguese, **Rio Branco.**] River in N Brazil which flows SW to join the Rio Negro. Length, ab. 350 mi.

Branco, Camilo Castelo. See **Castelo Branco, Camilo.**

Branco, Manoel Alves. See **Alves Branco, Manoel.**

Brancuşi (bräng'kösh), **Constantin.** b. at Pestisani-Gorque, Rumania, 1876—. Rumanian abstract sculptor, active for most of his life at Paris. His best-known work, *Bird in Space* (now in the Museum of Modern Art, New York), was involved in a lawsuit when the U.S. Customs Service held that it was not a work of art, and attempted to impose an import duty on it as scrap metal; Brancuşi won the case, setting a precedent for subsequent import of such works of art. He won (c1900) the first prize at the Academy of Bucharest; although a pupil of Rodin, he early abandoned all naturalistic devices, and progressively turned to the abstraction of natural forms. Among his works are *The Miracle* (1936) in marble, *L'Oiseau* (1940) in polished bronze, and a bronze head, *Mlle. Pogany.*

Brand (brand), Sir **Henry Bouverie William.** [Titles, 1st Viscount **Hampden of Glynde,** 23rd Baron **Dacre.**] b. Dec. 24, 1814; d. at Pau, France, March 14, 1892. English statesman; father of Henry Robert Brand. He was Liberal member of Parliament for Lewes (1852–68) and for Cambridgeshire (1868–84), was parliamentary secretary to the treasury (1859–66), and was speaker of the House of Commons (1872–84). He was knighted in 1881, was created Viscount Hampden of Glynde in 1884, and succeeded to the title of Lord Dacre in 1890.

Brand, Henry Robert. [Titles: 2nd Viscount **Hampden of Glynde,** 24th Baron **Dacre.**] b. at Devonport, England, May 2, 1841; d. at London, Nov. 22, 1906. British politician and administrator; son of Sir Henry Bouverie William Brand (1814–92). He served (1858–65) in the Coldstream Guards, was a member of Parliament (1868–74, 1880–86), and served as governor (1895–99) of New South Wales.

Brand, John. b. at Washington, Durham, England, Aug. 19, 1744; d. at London, Sept. 11, 1806. English antiquary and topographer, rector of the parishes St. Mary-at-Hill and St. Andrew Hubbard in the City of London. He published *Observations on Popular Antiquities; including the whole of Mr. Bourne's "Antiquitates Vulgares"* (1777), and other works.

Brand, Sir **John Henry.** [Also: **Jan Hendrik Brand, Johannes Henricus Brand.**] b. at Capetown, Cape Colony, in South Africa, Dec. 6, 1823; d. 1888. South African politician. He was admitted to the English bar in 1849, practiced at Capetown, and in 1858 accepted appointment as a professor of law in South Africa. He was elected president of the Orange Free State in 1863, and reëlected in 1869, 1874, 1879, and 1884. Under his leadership, the Orange Free State defeated the Basutos in a prolonged struggle. In 1871 Brand was offered the presidency of the Transvaal Republic, to be held simultaneously with the presidency of the Orange Free State. This proposal was clearly intended to prepare the way for a union of the two Boer republics, an eventuation which the British opposed, and Brand opposed any policy which might add to the tension which was even then beginning to be obvious in Anglo-Boer relations. He therefore declined the offer. In 1882 he accepted knighthood from the British crown.

Brand, Millen. b. at Jersey City, N.J., Jan. 19, 1906—. American novelist, poet, and short-story writer. He was graduated (1929) from Columbia University, was a publicity writer for the New York Telephone Company, and during World War II was attached to the Office of Civilian Defense at Washington, D.C. His novels include *The Outward Room* (1937), *The Heroes* (1939), and *Albert Sears* (1947).

Brandan (bran'dạn), Saint. See **Brendan** or **Brenainn,** Saint.

Brande (brand), **William Thomas.** b. at London, Feb. 11, 1788; d. at Tunbridge Wells, England, Feb. 11, 1866. English chemist. He became professor of chemistry to the Apothecaries' Company in 1812, professor of materia medica in 1813, and master of the company in 1851. He was professor of chemistry at the Royal Institution in the period 1813–54, became superintendent of the die department of the mint in 1825, and of the coining department in 1854, and edited (1816–36), with Michael Faraday, the *Quarterly Journal of Science and Art.*

Brandegee (bran'dẹ.jē), **Frank Bosworth.** b. at New London, Conn., July 8, 1864; d. at Washington, D.C., Oct. 14, 1924. American politician. A congressman (1902–05) and senator (1905–24) from Connecticut, he was at various times a member of the Foreign Relations, Judiciary, Library, and Patents committees. He voted against the League of Nations, income tax, federal regulation of child labor, the Federal Reserve system, popular election of senators, and votes for women.

Brandegee, Townshend Stith. b. at Berlin, Conn., Feb. 16, 1843; d. at Berkeley, Calif., April 7, 1925. American botanist. In 1886 he visited Santa Cruz island, off SW California, to obtain rare timbers. He was a volunteer in the California Academy of Sciences expedition (1889) to Magdalena Bay, Baja California, Mexico. Author of *Plantae Mexicanae Purpusianae* (1909–24), issued by University of California Publications.

Brandeis (bran'dīs), **Louis Dembitz.** b. at Louisville, Ky., Nov. 13, 1856; d. at Washington, D.C., Oct. 5, 1941. American jurist. Granted an LL.B. degree (1877) from Harvard, he practiced law (1879–1916) at Boston, where he earned the name "the people's counsel" for his activities on both local and national levels in the public interest. He devised a sliding scale of rates and dividends for gas utility regulation, opposed the New Haven Railroad merger and monopoly, fostered the system of savings-bank life insurance, and created a protocol of labor-management relations in the New York garment industry. Nationally, he acted as counsel in the investigation of Secretary of the Interior Richard Achilles Ballinger, and served as counsel to the Interstate Commerce Commission in rate investigations. As advocate for the validity of social legislation, notably minimum wage laws, he prepared documented factual arguments (the "Brandeis brief") that have become models in similar causes. He was appointed (1916) by Woodrow Wilson to the U.S. Supreme Court as associate justice, a post from which he retired in 1939. His judicial opinions are distinguished for their hospitality toward state and federal economic experiments, solicitude for the powers of the states in the American federal system, and close scrutiny of restraints on freedom of expression. Combining high technical proficiency with strong social vision, he was described by Chief Justice Charles Evans Hughes as "master of the microscope and telescope." He was the author of *Other People's Money* (1914), *Business, A Profession* (1914), and *The Curse of Bigness* (miscellaneous papers, edited by O. K. Fraenkel, 1934).

Brandeis an der Adler (brän'dīs än dėr äd'lėr). German name of **Brandýs nad Orlici.**

Brandeis an der Elbe (el'bę). German name of **Brandýs nad Labem.**

Brandenburg (bran'dęn.bėrg; German, brän'dęn.bůrk). Former margravate and electorate of the German empire, the nucleus of the kingdom of Prussia. The Nordmark (northern mark, or tract; later called Altmark) was granted in 1134 to Albert I of Brandenburg (Albert the Bear), who subdued the Slavic Wends, Christianized the region and colonized it with Germans, and took the title of Margrave of Brandenburg, making the town of Brandenburg his capital. Brandenburg was recognized as one of the seven electorates in the Golden Bull of 1356. It was united with Bohemia in the period 1373–1415. In 1415 Frederick of Hohenzollern (Burgrave of Nuremberg) received the mark and electorate of Brandenburg, and was formally invested with it in 1417. The mark consisted then mainly of the Altmark, Priegnitz, and the Mittelmark; the Ukermark was added (mainly) in the period 1415–40, the Neumark (mainly) c1450. Brandenburg early embraced the Reformation. It acquired the additional territories of Cleve, Mark, and Ravensberg in 1614 (formally 1666), and the duchy of Prussia was united with it in 1618. During the reign of Frederick William, the Great Elector (1640–88), it became an important military power. In 1648 it acquired eastern (or Further) Pomerania, and the bishoprics of Halberstadt, Minden, and Kamin, and in 1680 the archbishopric of Magdeburg. It became the kingdom of Prussia in 1701.

Brandenburg. *Land* (state) in E Germany, Russian Zone, bounded by Poland, Saxony, Saxony-Anhalt, Lower Saxony, and Mecklenburg. It comprises the former province of Brandenburg, Prussia, W of the Oder and Neisse rivers, excluding Berlin, and includes the Mittelmark, Ukermark, Priegnitz, and most of the Neumark. The soil is largely sandy and covered with pine forests, but some parts are fertile. There are numerous metallurgical, textile, lumber, and other manufactures, particularly in the area surrounding Berlin; the formerly leading textile centers of Cottbus, Guben, and Forst have declined. The population is predominantly Protestant; the increase between 1939 and 1946 was 4.7 percent. A margravate in the Middle Ages, Brandenburg became the nucleus of the Prussian monarchy. The connection with the remainder of the former Prussian provinces was severed in 1945. Capital, Potsdam; area, 10,412 sq. mi.; pop. 2,514,700 (1946).

Brandenburg. [Also: **Brennaburg;** Slavic, **Brennabor.**] City in NE Germany, in the *Land* (state) of Brandenburg, Russian Zone, formerly in the province of Brandenburg, Prussia, situated on the Havel River, ab. 35 mi. SW of Berlin. It is a river port and industrial center known particularly for its iron foundries (formerly belonging to Mitteldeutsche Stahlwerke); the Brennabor works produce automobiles and bicycles. Before World War II there were also metallurgical, cotton textile, chemical, and leather industries. The city has a number of educational institutions, including vocational schools, a library, and a local museum. Many medieval buildings are preserved, such as the Romanesque Church of Saint Nicholas (1200), the Romanesque and Gothic Church of Saint Gotthard (1350), the Church of Saint Catherine (1400), a brick building in the North German Gothic style, and the Gothic Church of Saint Paul (1286); there are two town halls, one of the 14th and one of the 15th century; the Prince-Electors' House dates from 1543. The most remarkable building is the cathedral, located on an island in the Havel River; a Romanesque basilica built in 1165, it was rebuilt in the Gothic style in the 14th century. Originally a Slavic fortress, Brandenburg was conquered by Henry I in 928; a bishopric was established by Otto I in 948; the town was reconquered by the Wendish tribesmen in 983, and resettled by Germans in 1138. It later became the seat of the margraves of Brandenburg. The bishopric was abolished in 1598, after the bishop Mathias had accepted Lutheranism. The Prussian National Assembly gathered here in 1848. In World War II the city was occupied by the Russians in May, 1945. Pop. 70,632 (1946).

Brandenburg (brän'dęn.bůrk), **Erich.** b. at Stralsund, Germany, July 31, 1868—. German historian who served (1899 *et seq.*) as professor at the University of Leipzig. Author of *Die Reichsgründung* (The Foundation of the Reich, 1916), and *Die Ursachen des Weltkrieges* (The Causes of the World War, 1925).

Brandenburg, Count **Friedrich Wilhelm von.** b. at Berlin, Jan. 24, 1792; d. Nov. 6, 1850. Prussian general and statesman; son of Frederick William II of Prussia by his morganatic wife, the Countess von Doenhoff. He became the head of a strongly reactionary minority, on Nov. 2, 1848, and represented Prussia at Warsaw, on Oct. 29, 1850, before the Czar of Russia, who acted as arbiter between Prussia and Austria in the difference arising out of Austria's interference in the politics of Hesse-Cassel.

Brandenburg (bran'dęn.bėrg), **Treaty of.** [Also, **Treaty of Bärwalde.**] Treaty made on Jan. 13, 1631, between France and Gustavus Adolphus of Sweden. Gustavus was to receive an annual subsidy of 1,200,000 livres from France, in return for which he was to maintain, at his own expense and under his own direction, an army of 30,000 infantry and 6,000 horse in the war against the emperor. He also received an advance of 300,000 livres, exclusive of the annual subsidy, as compensation for past expenses. The treaty was to stand for five years.

Brandenburg Concertos. Set of six *concerti grossi* (concertos with more than one solo instrument, against the background of a chamber orchestra) by Johann Sebastian Bach, completed on March 24, 1721, and dedicated to Christian Ludwig, Margrave of Brandenburg.

Brandenburger (brän'dęn.bůr.gėr), **Clemens.** b. at Fulda, Germany, July 10, 1879—. German historian, resident of Brazil (1909 *et seq.*). He has served as a professor at Rio de Janeiro. Author of *Mythen, Sagen und Märchen brasilianischer Indianer* (Myths, Legends, and Fairy Tales of the Brazilian Indians, 1919), and *Brasiliens Geschichte und Literatur im Überblick* (Brazilian History and Literature in a Survey, 1929).

Brandes (brän'dęs), **Carl Edvard.** [Original surname, **Cohen.**] b. 1847; d. 1931. Danish critic, novelist, dramatist, and politician; brother of Georg Morris Brandes. In his earlier years he had some fame as an Orientalist, but his lively interest in contemporary literature and life led him into the field of criticism, particularly dramatic criticism, from which he went on to the writing of plays and novels, and to active participation in political life. In 1880 he became a member of the lower house of the Danish parliament; in 1906 he was elected to the upper house. He was an associate editor of the *Morgenblad*, a leading Copenhagen newspaper, in which his political articles appeared before publication in book form. His first play appears to have been *En Forlovelse* (A Betrothal, 1884), which was followed by *Under Loven* (Under a Vow, 1891), and *Et Besøg* (A Visit, 1892). His first novel, *A Politician*, appeared in 1889; his second, *Young Blood* (1899), was suppressed.

Brandes, Georg Morris. [Original surname, **Cohen.**] b. at Copenhagen, Feb. 4, 1842; d. there, Feb. 19, 1927. Danish writer on esthetics and the history of literature; brother of Carl Edvard Brandes. Between 1865 and 1871 (time spent principally in France and Germany) he published *Ästhetiske Studier* (Esthetic Studies), *Kritiker og Portraeter* (Criticisms and Portraits), and *Den franske Ästhetik i vore Dage* (French Esthetics in Our Day, 1870). Returning to Denmark, he became a docent at the University of Copenhagen. His lectures, which afterward appeared under the title *Hovedströmninger i det 19de Aarhundredes Literatur* (Principal Tendencies in the Literature of the Nineteenth Century, 1872–75), brought upon him the charge of radicalism and free-thinking, and accordingly, in 1877, he left Denmark for Germany, and settled at Berlin. In the same year he published *Sören Kjerkegaard* and *Danske Diktere* (Danish Poets). At Berlin appeared *Esaijas Tegnér* and *Benjamin d'Israeli,* both in 1878.

Brandiamante (brän.dyä.män'tā). See **Bradamante.**

Brandimarte (brän.dē.mär'tā). [Also, **Brandimart** (bran'di.märt).] Husband of Fiordiligi, and the king of the Distant Islands, in Matteo Maria Boiardo's *Orlando Innamorato* and Lodovico Ariosto's *Orlando Furioso.* He is killed by Gradasso.

Brandis (brän'dis), **Christian August.** b. at Hildesheim, Germany, Feb. 13, 1790; d. at Bonn, Germany, July 21, 1867. German philosophical writer and historian, professor at Bonn (1821). He wrote *Handbuch der Geschichte der griechisch-römischen Philosophie* (1835–66), *Geschichte der Entwickelungen der griechischen Philosophie* (1862–64), and others.

Brandis, Sir **Dietrich.** b. at Bonn, Germany, March 31, 1824; d. there, May 28, 1907. German botanist and authority on forestry. In 1856 he went to India and was placed in charge of the teak forests of Burma, and in 1864 was appointed the first inspector general of the forests of India. He retired to Bonn in 1883, and was knighted in 1887.

Brandl (brän'dl), **Alois.** b. at Innsbruck, Austria, June 21, 1855; d. at Berlin, Feb. 5, 1940. Austrian Anglicist and literary historian. He was a professor (1895 *et seq.*) at the University of Berlin. Author of *Shakespeare* (1894), *Quellen des weltlichen Dramas in England vor Shakespeare* (Sources of Secular Drama in England Prior to Shakespeare, 1898), and *Lebendige Sprache* (Living Language, 1930–32).

Brandon (bran'dọn). Manufacturing city in S Canada, the county seat of Brandon County and the third largest city in Manitoba. It is situated in the SW part of the province on the Assiniboine River, ab. 140 mi. W of Winnipeg. Brandon is chiefly a grain center, although the raising of cattle and hogs is important in the surrounding region. It is the seat of an industrial school for Indians. 20,598 (1951).

Brandon. Character in Shakespeare's *King Henry VIII.*

Brandon, Charles. [Title, 1st Duke of **Suffolk.**] d. at Guildford, England, Aug. 24, 1545. English nobleman, created Duke of Suffolk in February, 1514. He was a favorite of Henry VIII, and served him in various diplomatic missions, on one of which he secretly married Henry's sister, the widow of Louis XII of France, after getting a papal annulment of his first marriage. He accompanied (1520) Henry to the Field of the Cloth of Gold, and commanded the armies which invaded France in 1523 and 1544. In the latter year he captured Boulogne.

Brandon, Richard. d. at London, 1649. English executioner of Charles I and of his followers. He received thirty pounds for decapitating the king. His father, Gregory Brandon, had been hangman of London.

Brandon and Byshottles (bī'shot''lz). Urban district in NE England, in Durham, ab. 3 mi. SW of Durham. It has no direct rail connections for passengers, being reached by rail to Durham, ab. 254 mi. N of London. It is a coal-mining center. Brandon Hill (875 ft.) is within the district. 19,751 (1951).

Brandt (bränt), **Marianne.** [Original name, **Marie Bischof.**] b. at Vienna, Sept. 12, 1842; d. there, July 9, 1921. Austrian operatic singer. She was particularly successful as Brangäne in Richard Wagner's *Tristan und Isolde,* and as Leonore in Ludwig van Beethoven's *Fidelio.*

Brandts-Buys (bränts'bois'), **Jan.** b. at Zutphen, Netherlands, Sept. 12, 1868; d. at Salzburg, Austria, Dec. 8, 1933. Dutch composer. His first piano concerto (c1897) attracted wide attention; his other works include the orchestral *Oberon Romancero* (Opus 27), and operas.

Brandts-Buys, Johann Sebastian. b. 1879. Dutch musicologist. He became a reviewer for the *Utrechtsch Dagblad.* For many years a resident of Java, he has written extensively on its native music.

Brandýs nad Labem (brän'dēs näd lä'bem). [German, **Brandeis an der Elbe.**] Town in Czechoslovakia, in C Bohemia, situated on the Labe (German, Elbe) River between Nymburk and Melník, NE of Prague. It has an old castle, and machine industries. 6,904 (1947).

Brandýs nad Orlici (ôr'lē.tsē). [German, **Brandeis an der Adler.**] Town in Czechoslovakia, in E Bohemia, situated on the Orlice River E of Pardubice. It was the main seat of the sect of Bohemian Brethren and the asylum of their bishop John Amos Comenius. 1,534 (1947).

Brandywine Creek (bran'di.wīn). River in SE Pennsylvania which joins the Christina River near Wilmington, Del. Here, on Sept. 11, 1777, General Howe defeated the Americans under Washington. The force of the British was about 18,000; that of the Americans, 11,000. British losses were over 1,000; American, about 1,000.

Branford (bran'fọrd). Town (in Connecticut the equivalent to township in many other states) and borough in S Connecticut, in New Haven County, on the Branford River, E of New Haven: fishing and salt processing. Pop. of town, 10,944 (1950); of borough 2,552 (1950).

Branford, Frederick Victor. b. at London, 1892—. English poet, editor, and soldier. He lived in Scotland during his childhood, and has been resident there since 1918; he was educated at the universities of Edinburgh and Leiden. He served in World War I as an officer in the air force, and was wounded. Founder of the magazine *Voices,* he is also the author of *Titans and Gods* (1922), *Five Poems* (1923), and *The White Stallion: Poems* (1924). "Any Daisy" and two sonnets, "Shakespeare" and "Secret Treaties," are anthology favorites.

Brangäne (brän'gā.nẹ). In Richard Wagner's opera *Tristan und Isolde,* the confidante of Isolde. It is a mezzo-soprano part. The character is taken from the legend of Tristram and Isolde, where her name appears most commonly as Brangwaine.

Brangtons (brang'tọnz), **The.** In Fanny Burney's novel *Evelina,* a family of the middle class. Their name was for a time proverbial for vulgar, malicious jealousy.

Brangwaine or **Brangwayne** (brang'wān) or **Brengwin** (breng'win). The confidante of Isolde (Iseult) in the romance of *Tristram and Isolde.*

Brangwyn (brang'win), Sir **Frank.** b. at Bruges, Belgium, May 13, 1867—. English mural painter and etcher, noted primarily for his exotic scenes. He studied at the South Kensington Museum in 1877; five years later he worked under William Morris, making designs for tapestries; subsequently he traveled around the world. His work was exhibited by the most important art associations at London beginning in 1885. His panels were purchased by Lloyd's Registry, the Royal Exchange, and Skinner's Hall, all at London, and by Rockefeller Center at New York, among others, as well as by many museums in England and on the Continent. In addition, he illustrated several books, including *The Arabian Nights' Entertainments.* He became a member of the Royal Academy in 1919; he is also a member of organizations of artists in France, Italy, Germany, Japan, Austria, Belgium, the U.S., and Spain. Among his best-known works are *The Buccaneers, The Stations of the Cross,* and *The Bridge of Sighs.*

Branicki (brä.nē'tskē), **Jan Klemens.** b. 1688; d. at Białystok, Poland, Oct. 9, 1771. Polish politician, leader of the republican party. He was the champion of the nobility against Augustus II (Augustus the Strong), and after the death of Augustus III put himself, with Charles Stanislas Radziwill, at the head of the republican party, which offered him the crown. The monarchical party, under the brothers Czartoryiski, triumphed in the diet of 1764, however, and he was banished, remaining in exile till the accession of Stanislas II Augustus.

Branicki, Xavery. [Original surname, **Branetzki** (brä-nets'kē).] d. 1819. Polish politician, of the Russian party. He was the agent of Catherine II of Russia in her dealings with Stanislas II Augustus, and in 1771 became grand general of the kingdom of Poland. He was convicted (1794) of treason, and spent the rest of his life in the Ukraine.

Braniewo (brä.nye'vô). [German, **Braunsberg.**] Town in N Poland, in the *województwo* (province) of Olsztyn, formerly in East Prussia, situated on the Passarge River near its mouth on the Frisches Haff, ab. 35 mi. SW of Kaliningrad. Before World War II it had cigar and leather manufactures and breweries. 21,142 (1939).

Branly (brän.lē), **Édouard.** b. 1846; d. 1940. French physicist. He devised (1890) the coherer which enabled the development of wireless telegraphy. He served in the department of physics at the Sorbonne, and was professor of physics at the Catholic Institute at Paris.

Brannan (bran'ạn), **Charles Franklin.** b. at Denver, Colo., Aug. 23, 1903—. American lawyer and government official, at one time (1948 *et seq.*) secretary of agriculture of the U.S. After graduating from the law school of the University of Denver in 1929, he practiced law in his native city until 1935, when he became an assistant regional attorney to the Resettlement Administration, U.S. Department of Agriculture. From 1937 to 1941 he was regional attorney in the Denver office of the solicitor of the Department of Agriculture, and from 1941 to 1944, regional director of the Farm Security Administration of that department. In 1944 he was appointed assistant secretary of agriculture. This post he held until 1948, when he entered President Truman's cabinet as secretary of agriculture. He had also served in 1945 as agricultural adviser to the U.S. delegation to the San Francisco conference which established the United Nations.

Brannan, Samuel. b. at Saco, Me., March 2, 1819; d. at Escondido, Calif., May 5, 1889. American pioneer. He headed a group of Mormon settlers which sailed (Feb. 4, 1846) from New York. On arrival (July 31, 1846) in California the group found itself the first body of Anglo-Americans to reach the territory after American possession. He published (1847 *et seq.*) the California *Star*, the first San Francisco paper, and maintained (1847–49) a store at Sutter's Fort. He was an organizer of the San Francisco Committee of Vigilance of 1851.

Branner (bran'ėr), **John Casper.** b. at Newmarket, Tenn., July 4, 1850; d. at Stanford, Calif., March 1, 1922. American geologist and educator. He was a professor at Stanford University from 1891, and its vice-president (1899–1913), president (1913–16), and president emeritus (1916 *et seq.*). He was graduated from Cornell University in 1874, and served as geologist of the Imperial Geological Commission of Brazil (1875–77), and as an agent of the U.S. Department of Agriculture in Brazil (1882–83). He was connected with the geological survey of Pennsylvania (1883–85), was professor of geology at the University of Indiana (1885–91), was state geologist of Arkansas (1887–93), and conducted an expedition to Brazil in 1899. He published numerous scientific reports and papers.

Branscombe (brans'kọm), **Gena.** b. at Picton, Ontario, Canada, Nov. 4, 1881—. Canadian composer. Her compositions include the orchestral works *Quebec* (a suite), *Festival Prelude*, and *Elegie*, a sonata (1920) for piano and violin, and *Pilgrims of Destiny* (1927, a choral drama) and other choral works.

Brant (brant), **Joseph.** [Indian name, **Thayendanegea.**] b. in what is now Ohio, 1742; d. near the shores of Lake Ontario, in Canada, Nov. 24, 1807. Mohawk chief, in the British service during the Revolutionary War. After accompanying Sir William Johnson in the campaign of 1755 against the French at Crown Point, he entered (c1761) Moor's Charity School, at Lebanon, Conn. (under Eleazar Wheelock), where he remained until 1763, when he left to act as interpreter to a missionary. However, shortly thereafter, he joined the Iroquois in their alliance with the whites against Pontiac. When Guy Johnson (possibly a nephew of Sir William Johnson, although this has never been definitely established) became (1774) superintendent of Indian affairs, he named Brant his secretary. When the Revolutionary War broke out, he joined the English in his capacity as Mohawk chief. Having been made a captain, he was sent to England, where he was received with great acclaim. After his return to America, he took part in many engagements, including the battle of Oriskany (Aug. 6, 1777); he led his Indian troops in raids in the Mohawk Valley, in S New York, and in N Pennsylvania; he is also held responsible for the Cherry Valley massacre of 1778. After the end of the war, he attempted to get lands in the U.S. for the settlement of his followers, but, failing this, settled with them in Canada. He spent some years translating religious documents into the Mohawk language.

Brant (bränt), **Sebastian.** b. at Strasbourg, 1457; d. there, May 10, 1521. German satiric poet. He studied law at Basel, and was city scribe (1503 *et seq.*) at Strasbourg. He is now best remembered for *Das Narrenschiff*, a long didactic poem in which he comments on human weaknesses and contemporary manners; it was first published in 1494, and subsequently appeared in many editions. Alexander Barclay based *The Shyp of Folys* on Brant's work.

Brantford (brant'fọrd). City in Ontario, Canada, situated on the Grand River, ab. 23 mi. SW of Hamilton. It is the 23rd city of Canada in size, the county seat of Brant County, and an industrial center. Pop. of city, 36,727 (1951); with suburbs, 52,231 (1951).

Branting (brän'ting), **Hjalmar.** [Full name, **Karl Hjalmar Branting.**] b. at Stockholm, Nov. 23, 1860; d. there, Feb. 25, 1925. Swedish statesman and journalist, founder of the Swedish Social-Democratic Labor Party and three times (1920, 1921–23, 1924–25) premier. He joined (1884) the staff of the newspaper *Tiden*, later (1886) going to the newspaper *Socialdemokraten*, on whose staff he remained until 1908. He served (1887–90, 1892–96) as parliamentary reporter for the newspaper *Dagens nyheter*. He was a leader in the foundation (1889) of the Swedish Social-Democratic Labor Party, became (1897) its first member of parliament, advocated the Entente cause during World War I, was finance minister (1917–18) in the Edén government, shared (1921) the Nobel peace prize with Christian Lange, and served (1923 *et seq.*) as Swedish representative on the League of Nations Council. Among his diplomatic achievements was the neutralization of the Åland Islands (now part of Finland and called Ahvenanmaa).

Brantôme (brän.tōm). Town in S central France, in the department of Dordogne, situated on the Dronne River ab. 13 mi. NW of Périgueux. There is a remarkable dolmen in its vicinity. Pop. ab. 1,000.

Brantôme, Pierre de Bourdeilles, Seigneur **de.** b. in Périgord, France, c1535; d. July 15, 1614. French chronicler. He was made Abbé de Brantôme at the age of 16, without taking orders. He served in the army against the Huguenots, and traveled extensively. His *Mémoires* (1665–66) are valued for their lively description of the chief historical persons and events of his time.

Brant Pontes (brunt' pōn'tẹs), **Felisberto** (or **Feliberto**) **Caldeira.** See **Caldeira Brant Pontes, Felisberto** (or **Feliberto**).

Branville (bran'vil), **Sir Anthony.** In Frances Sheridan's play *The Discovery*, a pedantic and solemn lover. He talks most passionately, without showing a spark of meaning in his action or features, and has made love in this manner to eight women in 13 years. David Garrick first played the part.

Braose (brōz), **William de.** d. at Corbeil, France, 1211. Anglo-Norman baron who led a rebellion (1210) in Wales against King John of England. Earlier, he had accompanied Richard I (1195), then John (1200), to Normandy, where John promised him land in Wales. He obtained the honor of Limerick in 1201, and a grant of the city in 1203; following his fall from royal favor, he raised (1210) an insurrection against the king, was outlawed, and fled to France.

Braque (bråk), **Georges.** b. at Argenteuil, France, 1882—. French cubist painter, collage and papier collé artist, illustrator, and designer, one of the originators and leaders of the cubist movement in France. He studied at Le Havre, where his work was influenced by the post-impressionists. In 1904 he went to Paris, where he became a member of the Fauves, under Matisse; then he met Pablo Picasso, and, with him, formed the cubist movement in the period 1907–08. He exhibited in the Salon d'Automne and the Salon des Indépendants, and since that time has exhibited frequently, and has had several important one-man shows at Paris, New York, and elsewhere. Most of his work consists of still-life paintings and papiers collés, as well as some nude studies and landscapes. He has adapted cubism into a highly individual style, more three-dimensional in appearance than strict cubism, but still abstract; in his later works, objects are clearly recognizable, but are often placed in startling perspective, and have their shadows sharply defined. In 1924 he designed the setting for Sergei Pavlovich Diaghilev's ballet, *The Angry Ones;* he also illustrated Erik Satie's lyric comedy, *Medusa's Trap*. Many prizes were awarded him in the U.S. and France. Among his more important works are *Nude* (1908), *Still Life with Playing Cards* (1913), *Composition* (1913), *Music* (1914), *Still Life, Plums and Lemons* (1928), *Landscape* (1928), and several harlequins.

Braschi (brä'skē), **Giovanni Angelo.** Original name of Pope **Pius VI.**

Bras d'Or (brä''dôr'), **Lake.** Arm of the sea in NE Nova Scotia, in the C part of Cape Breton Island. Two elongated tidal channels known as the Great Bras d'Or and the Little Bras d'Or connect the lake with the Atlantic Ocean on the NE. At the SE corner of the lake a canal ab. ½ mi. long has been constructed to open the lake for through deep-water navigation. Greatest length, ab. 60 mi.; total area, 360 sq. mi.

Brasenose College (brāz'nōz). College of Oxford University, England, founded (c1509) by Bishop William Smith of Lincoln and Sir Richard Sutton, upon the site of an old academical institution named Brasenose Hall (it is thought from its doorknocker, in the shape of a brass nose). The foundation stone was laid on June 1, 1509, and the charter was granted in 1512. The quadrangle is very picturesque; the Tudor gate tower and hall remain unaltered. The library and chapel are of a later period.

Brashear (bra̤.shir'), **John Alfred.** b. Nov. 24, 1840; d. April 8, 1920. American optical manufacturer, famous for his astronomical lenses and precision instruments. He began his business career in 1881, and was active in the manufacture of speculum-metal plates for Rowland diffraction gratings and in the preparation of surfaces for the Rowland ruling engine. He also designed and developed an astronomical spectroscope. He was associated with the founding of the Carnegie Institute of Technology, and planned the organization of the Frick Educational Commission.

Brashear City. Former name of **Morgan City.**

Brasher (brash'ėr), **Rex.** b. at Brooklyn, N.Y., July 31, 1869—. American ornithologist and artist, noted for his paintings of birds made under natural conditions. A series of these were collected in 874 reproductions and published as *Birds and Trees of North America* (12 vols., 1934).

Brashov (brä.shôv'). See **Braşov.**

Brasidas (bras'i.da̤s). Killed at Amphipolis, Macedonia, 422 B.C. Spartan general, distinguished in the Peloponnesian war. He captured Amphipolis in 424, and defeated Cleon there in 422.

Brasil. Portuguese (bra̤.zēl') and Spanish (brä.sēl') name of **Brazil.**

Braslau (bras'lou), **Sophie.** b. at New York, Aug. 16, 1892; d. there, Dec. 22, 1935. American dramatic contralto with the Metropolitan Opera Company of New York (1913 *et seq.*).

Braşov (brä.shôv'). [Also: **Brashov;** officially, **Stalin;** Hungarian, **Brassó;** German, **Kronstadt.**] City in C Rumania, in the region of Transylvania, ab. 100 mi. N of Bucharest, on the slopes of the Transylvanian Alps: the commercial and manufacturing center of Transylvania. It has a university of commerce, and manufactures chemicals, leather, sugar, chocolate, furniture, steel, pianos, weapons, airplanes, and munitions. It was founded (13th century) by Teutonic settlers and was the center of the Reformation in Transylvania in the 16th century. The best-known building is the Protestant "Black" Church; other notable structures include the Protestant Church of Saint Bartholomew (13th century), a Gothic church (1385–1425), the city hall (15th century), and the Orthodox Church of Saint Nicholas (16th century). In 1689 the city was almost totally destroyed by fire. In 1920 it became part of Rumania by the terms of the Peace of Trianon. 82,984 (1948).

Brass (brås). In John Vanbrugh's comedy *The Confederacy,* the knavish companion of Dick Amlet, passing for his servant; a clever valet.

Brass, Sally. Sister and partner of Sampson Brass in Charles Dickens's *Old Curiosity Shop*. She has a very red nose and suspicions of a beard, and devotes herself "with uncommon ardor to the study of the law."

Brass, Sampson. Harsh-voiced "attorney of no very good repute," in Charles Dickens's *Old Curiosity Shop;* the legal adviser of Quilp.

Brass Ankle, The. Play (1931) by DuBose Heyward, on the theme of miscegenation. As in much of his work, Heyward here skilfully utilized a knowledge of Negro ways which he had acquired while working on the Charleston waterfront.

Brasschaat (brä.sċhät'). [Also, **Brasschaet.**] Town in N Belgium, in the province of Antwerp, N of the city of Antwerp. It is a railroad junction and has agricultural markets. 16,333 (1947).

Brass Check, The. Tract by Upton Sinclair, published in 1919. The author accuses newspapers and fact-gathering agencies of undemocratic aims and advocates the founding of an unslanted national weekly.

Brasseur de Bourbourg (brå.sėr dȩ bör.bör), **Charles Étienne.** b. at Bourbourg, Nord, France, Sept. 8, 1814; d. at Nice, France, Jan. 8, 1874. French clergyman, ethnologist, and author. From 1845 to 1848 he was a teacher and priest in Canada and the U.S. He was almoner (1848–51) of the French legation at Mexico City, and, from 1854 to 1863, traveled extensively in Mexico and Central America, studying Indian antiquities and ancient manuscripts. In 1864 he was appointed archaeologist to the French scientific expedition in Mexico. He was the author of *Histoire des nations civilisées du Mexique et de l'Amérique Centrale* (4 vols., 1857–58), and various other works on the ancient history of Mexico and its monuments.

Brassey (bras'i), **Anna** (or **Annie**). [Maiden name, **Allnutt.**] b. 1839; d. at sea, Sept. 14, 1887. English traveler; married Thomas (later 1st Earl) Brassey in 1860. She accompanied her husband on his tours in the yacht *Sunbeam,* of which she wrote interesting accounts. Author of *A Voyage in the Sunbeam, our Home on the Ocean for Twelve Months* (1878), *Sunshine and Storm in the East, or Cruises to Cyprus and Constantinople* (1879), *In the Trades, the Tropics, and the Roaring Forties* (1884), and others.

Brassey, Thomas. b. at Aldford, Cheshire, England, Nov. 7, 1805; d. at Hastings, Sussex, England, Dec. 8, 1870. English railway contractor; father of Thomas Brassey (1836–1918). He supervised the construction of a great part of the Grand Trunk Railway in Canada, as well as many other lines.

Brassey, Thomas. [Title, 1st Earl **Brassey.**] b. at Stafford, England, Feb. 11, 1836; d. Feb. 23, 1918. English political economist and naval writer; son of Thomas Brassey (1805–70) and husband of Anna Brassey. He became a lord of the admiralty under William Ewart Gladstone in 1880, secretary of the admiralty in 1884, and was created a baron in 1886 and an earl in 1911. His works include *Work and Wages* (1872) and *Lectures on the Labor Question* (1878). He was president of the Institute of Naval Architects in the period 1893–95, and was governor of Victoria, Australia, in the period 1895–1900. He was the founder and first editor of the *Naval Annual*. Among his later works are *The British Navy* (1881), *Sixty Years of Progress,* and *New Fiscal Policy* (1904).

Brassin (brå.san̈'), **Gerhard.** b. at Aix-la-Chapelle (now Aachen, Germany), June 10, 1844; d. c1885. Violinist and conductor; brother of Leopold Brassin and Louis Brassin. He was concertmaster at Göteborg, Sweden, a professor (1874–75) at the Berlin Stern Conservatory, and subsequently conductor at Breslau. He was also active (1880 *et seq.*) at St. Petersburg and Constantinople.

Brassin, Leopold. b. at Strasbourg, May 28, 1843; d. at Constantinople, in May, 1890. Pianist to the court at Coburg, Germany; brother of Gerhard Brassin and Louis Brassin.

Brassin, Louis. b. at Aix-la-Chapelle (now Aachen, Germany), June 24, 1840; d. at St. Petersburg, May 17, 1884. Pianist and composer; brother of Gerhard Brassin and Leopold Brassin. He was an instructor at Berlin (1866 *et seq.*), at Brussels (until 1879), and at St. Petersburg. His compositions include two operettas, and piano works.

Brassó (brôsh'shō). Hungarian name of **Brasov.**

Brasstown Bald (bras'toun bôld). [Also, **Mount Enotah.**] Mountain in N Georgia, ab. 41 mi. N of Gainesville and ab. 7 mi. S of the state line, in the southern Appalachians. It is the highest point in Georgia. 4,784 ft.

Brathwaite or **Brathwait** or **Brathwayte** (brath'wāt), **Richard.** [Pseudonym, **Corymbaeus.**] b. at Burneside, near Kendal, Westmorland, England, c1588; d. at East Appleton, Catterick, Yorkshire, England, May 4, 1673. English poet and satirist. He studied at Oxford and Cambridge before going to London to devote himself to literature. He returned to Westmorland in 1610, after his father's death, and became justice of the peace for the county after his brother's death in 1618. Among his works are *The Golden Fleece* (1611), poetry; *The Poet's Willow* (1614), *The Prodigal's Tears* (1614), *The Scholar's Medley* (1614), and *A Strappado for the Devil* (1615), satires, derived from George Wither's *Abuses Whipt and Stript;* and *Essays upon the Five Senses* (1620). His most important work, *Barnabae Itinerarium, or Barnabee's Journall* (1638), a combination of Latin and English doggerel, is a lively account of Barnaby's four journeys to the north of England, and was published under the pseudonym of Corymbaeus.

Brătianu (bru.tē.ä'nö), **Dimitri.** b. 1818; d. 1892. Rumanian politician; brother of Ioan Brătianu (c1821–91). He accompanied his brother into exile following the failure of the revolt of 1848, and returned with him to Rumania in 1857, but thereafter opposed his political policies. Following Ioan Brătianu's retirement from the prime ministry, Dimitri Brătianu was appointed to that post in 1888.

Brătianu, Ioan or **Ion.** b. at Pitesci, in Walachia, June 2, 1821 (or 1822); d. May 16, 1891. Rumanian political leader. At the time of Ioan Brătianu's birth, his native Walachia (now part of Rumania) was under a kind of joint rule, the suzerain Turks having granted the Russian government a role as protector of that province and of Moldavia. Brătianu entered the Walachian army in 1838, and in 1841 went to Paris to study, but returned to Walachia and participated in the revolt of 1848, which was suppressed by the Turks and Russians jointly. Brătianu thereupon fled to Paris, and from this time on worked for a union of the two provinces. This hope was realized when a conference of the European powers in 1858 decreed the union of Walachia and Moldavia in the autonomous principality of Rumania, effective in 1859. Brătianu, who had returned in 1857, became one of the principality's chief political leaders. He was arrested on suspicion of being implicated in an attempted rebellion in 1870, but was soon released. He had served as premier in 1867–68, and in 1876 returned to that post, which he held until 1888. From the first his efforts were directed with inflexible purpose toward the independence of Rumania. A Rumanian revolt in 1877, taking advantage of the war then raging between Russia and Turkey, led to the realization of that objective when the Congress of Berlin decreed the independence of Rumania, effective in 1878. Not without reason, Ioan Brătianu is regarded as a principal founder of an independent Rumania.

Brătianu, Ion. b. in Rumania, 1864; d. there, 1927. Rumanian statesman and head of the Liberal Party; son of Ioan Brătianu. He served as prime minister for 12 years during the period 1909–27.

Brătianu, Vintilă. b. 1867; d. 1930. Rumanian politician; son of Ioan Brătianu (c1821–91) and brother of Ion Brătianu. He succeeded Ion Brătianu as premier of Rumania in 1927, but his tenure in this office came to an end in 1928 when the Peasant Party came into control of the government.

Bratislava (brä'tē.slä.vä). Administrative region or county in S Czechoslovakia, in the former province of Slovakia, created by decree of Dec. 21, 1948, which came into effect in 1949. Capital, Bratislava; area, 2,903 sq. mi.; pop. 838,134 (1948).

Bratislava. [German, **Pressburg;** Hungarian, **Pozsony;** Latin, **Posonium.**] City in S Czechoslovakia, the capital until 1949 of the province of Slovakia and since then of the administrative region of Bratislava, situated on the left bank of the Danube River at the extreme W edge of Slovakia, ab. 50 mi. E of Vienna. It is a commercial center, the hub of Slovakia's railroad system, Czechoslovakia's chief Danube port, and the seat of a university. 172,664 (1947).

Industry and Trade. The yearly turnover of the port is over one million tons. The city's industries produce leather goods, kitchen utensils, and other metal products; there are textile, paper, and cement works, a flour mill, a chocolate factory, a paint factory, and an oil refinery.

History. Bratislava was inhabited from the 9th century on and was incorporated in 1291. In 1536, it became the capital of Hungary; in 1563 it was declared the coronation city of the Hungarian kings; from 1526 to 1848 it was the seat of the Hungarian diet. The first Slovak newspaper was published here in 1722. In 1805, after the battle of Austerlitz, the emperor Francis II of Austria and Napoleon I concluded here the treaty of Pressburg. In 1848 the Hungarian revolution started here. The city became part of Czechoslovakia in 1918; thereafter it acquired importance for its chemical, electrical, and paper industries and its harbor works, and as the seat of the international Danube commission of the League of Nations. It became the capital of the German puppet state of Slovakia in 1938, but was returned to Czechoslovakia in 1945. It once had considerable German, Hungarian, and Jewish minorities, but these have all now disappeared.

Bratsberg (bräts'bery'). Former name of **Telemark.**

Brattia (brat'i.ạ). Latin name of **Brač.**

Brattle (brat'l), **Thomas.** b. at Boston, June 20, 1658; d. there, May 18, 1713. American merchant, and writer on astronomical topics. In 1692 he protested (in a private letter printed in the *Massachusetts Historical Collections*) against the proceedings of the court in the "witchcraft cases."

Brattle, William. b. Nov. 22, 1662; d. Feb. 15, 1716 or 1717. American Congregational clergyman and educator. He was a fellow (1696–1700, 1703 *et seq.*) of the Harvard College Corporation, and a pastor (1696 *et seq.*) at Cambridge, Mass. Author of *Compendium Logicae Secundum Principia D. Renati Cartesii,* the first American text in logic.

Brattleboro (brat'l.bur.ọ). Town (in Vermont the equivalent of township in many other states) and unincorporated village in S Vermont, in Windham County, on the Connecticut River. Manufactures include multi-manual pipe organs, autos, sporting goods, cotton textiles, brush handles, lacquer, heels, hardware, finished woods, toys, overalls, paper, soft drinks, and granite monuments. The painter William Morris Hunt and the architect Richard Morris Hunt were born at Brattleboro, and Rudyard Kipling lived near there for a time. There are ski resorts in the vicinity. Pop. of town, 11,522 (1950); of village, 9,606 (1950).

Bratton (brat'ọn), **Henry de.** See **Bracton, Henry de.**

Bratton, John. b. at Winnsboro, S.C., March 7, 1831; d. there, Jan. 12, 1898. American Civil War soldier and politician. A Confederate brigadier general (1864 *et seq.*) in the Army of Northern Virginia, he was a member (1865) of the South Carolina constitutional convention. He was elected (1865) to the state senate, and was a member (1884–85) of Congress.

Brauchitsch (brou'ċhich), **Walther von.** [Full name, **Heinrich Alfred Hermann Walther von Brauchitsch.**] b. at Berlin, Oct. 4, 1881; d. at Hamburg, Oct. 18, 1948. German field marshal. At the beginning of World War I he was a captain in the German army; by 1931 he had attained the rank of major general. His rise to power thereafter was accelerated by his support of the National Socialist (Nazi) Party, and he acquired great influence with Adolf Hitler. He became military commander of the East Prussian area in 1933 and of the Leipzig area in 1937. In 1938, with the rank of colonel general, he became commander in chief of the German Army. In laying his plans for conquest, Hitler relied chiefly on the trio consisting of Brauchitsch, with Hermann Goering, for the air force, and Erich Raeder, chief of the German navy. Brauchitsch planned and directed the Nazi occupation of Austria and Czechoslovakia, the conquest of Poland, and the campaign which overran the Netherlands, Belgium, and France. At the peak of his influence with Hitler in June, 1941, he directed the initial attack upon the U.S.S.R., but in December of the same year, after the failure of the German campaign to capture Moscow, he was relieved of command by Hitler, and had no leading role throughout the later years of World War II. At the time of his death, he was awaiting trial by the Allied War Crimes Tribunal.

Brauer (brou'ėr), **Max.** b. at Altona, Germany, Sept. 3, 1887—. German public servant. A Social Democrat, he was Prussian state councillor in 1924. Forced to go into exile in 1933, he served as administrative expert to the Chinese government until 1936, when he came to the U.S.; he became a U.S. citizen, but re-assumed his German citizenship when he was elected (1946) first mayor of Hamburg after World War II.

Braun (broun), **August Emil.** b. at Gotha, Germany, April 19, 1809; d. at Rome, Sept. 12, 1856. German archaeologist and homeopathic physician.

Braun, Felix. b. at Vienna, 1885—. Austrian lyric poet and lyric prose writer, less successful in the dramatic field. He is known as one of the outstanding disciples of Hugo von Hofmannsthal.

Braun, Heinrich. b. at Budapest, Hungary, Nov. 23, 1854; d. at Berlin, Feb. 9, 1927. German politician, and journalist; husband (married 1896) of Lily Braun and father of Otto Braun (1897–1918). He was a cofounder and editor of *Neue Zeit,* a Social Democratic journal.

Braun, Heinrich. b. at Rawitsch, Germany, Jan. 1, 1862; d. at Überlingen am Bodensee, Germany, April 26, 1934. German surgeon. He was assistant to R. Volkmann and V. Bramann at Halle, and became a privatdocent (1894) and professor (1905) at Leipzig. He did important work on anesthesia, synthesized novocaine or procaine and used it clinically, added adrenalin, and introduced (1913) an operation consisting of ligation of the ileocolic vein to prevent complications in appendicitis. Author of *Über Infiltrationsanaesthesie und regionäre Anästhesie* (1898), *Über einige neue örtliche Anaesthetica* (*Stovain, Alypin, Novocain*) (1905), and *Die Lokalanaesthesie, ihre wissenschaftlichen Grundlagen und praktische Anwendung* (1905; Eng. trans., *Local Anesthesia: Its Scientific Basis and Practical Use,* 1914).

Braun, Johann Wilhelm Joseph. b. at Gronau, near Düren, Prussia, April 27, 1801; d. at Bonn, Prussia, Sept. 30, 1863. German Roman Catholic theologian, a professor at Bonn (1829). He was the author of *Die Lehre des sogenannten Hermesianismus* (1835), and one of the founders of the *Zeitschrift für Philosophie und Katholische Theologie.*

Braun, Karl Ferdinand. b. at Fulda, Germany, June 6, 1850; d. at New York, April 20, 1918. German physicist. He studied mathematics and the natural sciences at Marburg and Berlin, and after occupying chairs at various German universities became professor of physics and director of the Physical Institute at Strasbourg in 1895. He investigated the elasticity of matter and the relation between chemical energy and electricity, and made improvements in the use of cathode rays. In 1901 he published *Drahtlose Telegraphie durch Wasser und Luft* (Wireless Telegraphy through Water and Air), and in 1909, together with Guglielmo Marconi, was awarded the Nobel prize for physics.

Braun, Lily. [Maiden name, **von Kretschman.**] b. at Halberstadt, Germany, July 2, 1865; d. at Berlin, Aug. 9, 1916. German socialist and writer; wife of Heinrich Braun (1854–1927) and mother of Otto Braun (1897–1918). The daughter of a Prussian general, she grew up in a conservative home, but was attracted by the socialist movement. In 1896 she married the socialist Heinrich Braun. Many of her publications were about women and politics; they included *Die Frauenfrage* (1901), *Frauenarbeit und Hauswirtschaft* (1901), and *Die Politik und die Frauen* (1904). She also published *Im Schatten der Titanen,* a fictionalized biography of her grandmother, Jenny von Gustedt, an illegitimate daughter of Jérôme Bonaparte, who grew up in the Weimar of Goethe's time. This book was widely read, as was her later *Memoiren einer Sozialistin* (2 vols., 1910, 1911). This autobiographical novel is an excellent source of material on the development of the Social Democratic movement in Germany.

Braun, Otto. b. at Königsberg, January 28, 1874—. German statesman. A Social Democratic member of the Prussian diet (1913 *et seq.*), he was a member of the Reichstag from 1920 to 1933. He served as Prussian minister of agriculture (1918–21), and struggled to break the political power of the feudal estate owners. He was prime minister of Prussia (1920–32) until he was ousted by Franz von Papen's coup d'état. He fled to Switzerland in 1933; there he established (1945) the *Arbeitsgemeinschaft Demokratisches Deutschland* (Action Committee for a Democratic Germany). He continued to live in Switzerland after World War II.

Braun, Otto. b. at Berlin, June 27, 1897; killed in action at Marcelcave, France, April 29, 1918. German author; son of Heinrich Braun (1854–1927) and Lily Braun. His poems and essays, published as *Aus nachgelassenen Schriften eines Frühvollendeten* (1919), show great gifts and precocious maturity.

Braunau am Inn (brou'nou äm in'). Town in W central Austria, in the province of Upper Austria, in the Innviertel region, situated on the Bavarian frontier on the right bank of the Inn River, N of Salzburg and SW of Passau. It is a station on the railroad line from Linz to Munich. It has remains of medieval town walls, and numerous houses from the 16th and 17th centuries. In the Palm Park is the statue of Johann Palm, a Nuremberg bookseller shot by order of Napoleon I in 1806. The town was ceded to Austria by Bavaria in the year 1779 and except for a brief interval in the Napoleonic era remained Austrian thereafter. It was the birthplace (April 20, 1889) of Adolf Hitler. 11,559 (1951).

Braune (brou'nẹ), **Wilhelm.** b. at Grosshiemig, Germany, Feb. 20, 1850; d. 1926. Professor of Germanic philology at the University of Heidelberg. His *Althochdeutsches Lesebuch* (1874; ninth edition, 1928), *Gotische Grammatik* (1880; tenth edition, 1928), and *Althochdeutsche Grammatik* (1886; fourth edition, 1911) are standard handbooks in the field.

Brauner (brou'nėr), **Bohuslav.** b. at Prague, 1855; d. 1935. Czech inorganic chemist. He first realized and stated that the rare earths occupy a *zone* corresponding to a single element's *place* elsewhere in the periodic table (1902). His experimental work includes extensive accurate atomic-weight determinations, particularly of the rare earths. He served as a professor at Prague (1890–1925).

Braunfels (broun'fels), **Walter.** b. at Frankfurt on the Main, Germany, Dec. 19, 1882—. German composer and pianist. He headed (1925–33) the Hochschule für Musik at Cologne. His compositions include the operas *Die Vögel* (1920) and *Don Gil,* liturgical choral works, orchestral pieces, concertos, and art songs.

Braunsberg (brouns'berk). German name of **Braniewo.**

Braunschweig (broun'shvīk). Modern German name of **Brunswick,** Germany.

Brauronia (brô.rō'ni.ạ). In Greek antiquity, a festival held at the shrine of Artemis at Brauron, in Attica, at regular intervals of several years. At this festival, Attic girl-children performed a bear-imitation ceremony.

Brauwer (brou'wėr), **Adriaen.** See **Brouwer** or **Brauwer, Adriaen.**

Brava's Knight (brä'vạz). A name applied to Orlando Furioso, because he was the marquis of Brava, in Lodovico Ariosto's *Orlando Furioso.*

Brave New World. Novel (1932) by Aldous Huxley. In it Huxley seeks, through his portrayal of a nightmarish utopia, to depict the futility of scientific "progress." The scene is a scientist's utopia, a world of nonhuman perfection in which men and women live as much as possible like machines. If a specifically human state recurs in one of them he is made unconscious by a drug called soma until he has recovered a suitable equilibrium.

Bravo (brä'bō), **Nicolás.** b. at Chilpancingo, Mexico, c1787; d. there, April 22, 1854. Mexican general, twice (1824–27, 1846) vice-president and for a few days (1846) president of Mexico. He joined the revolutionist Morelos y Pavón in May, 1811, and kept up a determined resistance to the Spanish until he was captured in 1817. Released by the amnesty of 1820, he joined Augustín de Iturbide in 1821. But he subsequently declared against Iturbide's enthronement, was one of the leaders of the republicans who overthrew him, and a member of the provisional government of April, 1823. He became vice-president on April 1, 1824. Notwithstanding his office, he led a rebellion against the president, Guadalupe Victoria, in 1827, was defeated and captured (Jan. 6, 1828) at Tulancingo, and banished for several years. Under Antonio Lopéz de Santa Anna he was president of the council and twice (July, 1839, and October, 1842–March, 1843) acting president. In June, 1846, he became vice-president under Mariano Paredes y Arrillaga; the latter resigned (July 28, 1846) the power to him, but in the universal anarchy which prevailed Bravo was able to hold the office for only a few days.

Bravo or **Bravo del Norte** (del nôr′tā), **Río.** See **Rio Grande,** in North America.

Bravo (brä′vō), **The.** Novel by James Fenimore Cooper, published in 1831. Buckstone produced a melodrama in the 1830's with the same title, a dramatization of the novel. One of the novels Cooper wrote to prove the superiority of democracy to oligarchy, it has as a background Venice during the 15th century, when the Council of Ten ruled with supreme power.

Bravo de Saravia Sotomayor (brä′ʙō dā sä.rä.ʙē′ä sō″tō.mä.yōr′), **Melchor.** b. at Soria, Spain, c1505; d. there, c1580. Spanish lawyer and administrator. He went to Peru in 1547 as one of the judges of the Audience under Pedro de la Gasca, and later was dean of the Audience during the rebellion of Francisco Hernández Girón. From 1567 to 1574 he governed Chile as president of the Audience at Santiago.

Bravo-Murillo (brä′ʙō.mö.rē′lyō), **Juan.** b. at Frejenal de la Sierra, Badajoz, Spain, in June, 1803; d. at Madrid, Jan. 11, 1873. Spanish statesman and diplomat. He served as prime minister in the period 1851–52.

Brawe (brä′vẹ), **Joachim Wilhelm von.** b. at Weissenfels, Germany, Feb. 4, 1738; d. at Dresden, Germany, April 7, 1758. German dramatist; friend of Gotthold Ephraim Lessing. His untimely death cut short a dramatic career of promise. Lessing edited (1768) his two posthumous tragedies: *Der Freigeist,* which followed the lines of Lessing's *Miss Sarah Sampson,* and *Brutus.* The latter was one of the first original German plays to use blank verse.

Brawley (brô′li). City in S California, in Imperial County, SE of Los Angeles: one of the most important produce-shipping points of the Imperial Valley. This irrigated desert country produces practically all of the winter cantaloupes and two thirds of the early lettuce of the U.S. The land on which the city stands is 115 ft. below sea level. 11,922 (1950).

Brawley, Benjamin Griffith. b. at Columbia, S.C., April 22, 1882; d. at Washington, D.C., Feb. 1, 1939. American educator, writer, and Baptist clergyman. He taught English at Atlanta Baptist College (1902–10), Howard University (1910–12, 1931 *et seq.*), Morehouse College (1912–20), and Shaw University (1923–31). He served as president (1920–21) of the Association of Colleges for Negro Youth. His works include *A Short History of the American Negro* (1913), *The Negro in Literature and Art* (1918), *A Short History of the English Drama* (1921), *The Negro Genius* (1937), and *Negro Builders and Heroes* (1937).

Brawne (brôn), **Fanny.** See under **Keats, John.**

Braxton (braks′tọn), **Carter.** b. at Newington, Va., Sept. 10, 1736; d. at Richmond, Va., Oct. 10, 1797. American politician, one of the signers of the Declaration of Independence. A representative (1774, 1775, 1776) in Revolutionary conventions, he was a member (1775 *et seq.*) of the Virginia Committee of Safety, and was appointed (1776) to succeed Peyton Randolph in Congress.

Bray (brā). Parish in Berkshire, England, ab. 26 mi. W of London. A vicar of Bray, Simon Alleyn, is said to have been twice a Roman Catholic and twice a Protestant in the course of the reigns of Henry VIII, Edward VI, Mary, and Elizabeth, but always vicar of Bray: hence the modern application of the title to a turncoat.

Bray. Grazing district in N France, in the E part of the department of Seine-Inférieure, famous for butter and cheese.

Bray. [Irish, **Bri.**] Urban district, market town, and resort in Leinster province, Irish Republic, in County Wicklow, situated on the river Bray, ab. 12 mi. SE of Dublin. 12,071 (1951).

Bray, Anna Eliza. [Maiden name, **Kempe.**] b. at Newington, Surrey, England, Dec. 25, 1790; d. at London, Jan. 21, 1883. English novelist. She wrote *De Foix* (1826), *The Borders of the Tamar and the Tavy* (1836), *Trelawney of Trelawney* (1837), *Courtenay of Walreddon* (1844), and others.

Bray, Madeline. Young lady of singular beauty in Charles Dickens's *Nicholas Nickleby,* the slave of a profligate father. She becomes the wife of Nicholas Nickleby.

Bray, Sir **Reginald.** b. in the parish of St. John Bedwardine, near Worcester, England; d. 1503. English architect and politician. He was steward of the household of Sir Henry Stafford, and later a favorite of Henry VII, who appointed him privy councilor and chancellor of the duchy of Lancaster, and employed him in various other offices. He supervised the construction of, and probably designed, the chapel of Henry VII at Westminster; he also founded Saint George's Chapel at Windsor.

Bray, Thomas. b. at Marton, Shropshire, England, 1656; d. at London, Feb. 15, 1730. English clergyman and philanthropist. Selected (1699) by the bishop of London to advance the cause of the Anglican Church in Maryland, he organized a society for the propagation of gospel teaching in the British colonies.

Bray, Vicar of. See under **Bray,** England.

Brayley (brā′li), **Edward Wedlake.** b. at Lambeth (now part of London), 1773; d. 1854. English topographer and archaeologist who wrote his most extensive work, *Topographical History of the County of Surrey* (1841–48), between the ages of 68 and 76. He collaborated with John Britton (1771–1857) in publishing *Beauties of England and Wales* (1816), descriptions of the western, midland, and Welsh counties that cost 50,000 pounds to print. He was elected (1823) a fellow of the Society of Antiquaries and appointed librarian and secretary of the Russell Institution in 1825. He also published other topographical and archaeological works.

Brazeau (brạ.zō′), **Mount.** Mountain in the Rocky Mountains, in Alberta, Canada, situated in the S part of Jasper National Park. Elevation, ab. 12,250 ft.

Brazen (brā′zẹn), **Captain.** Rival recruiting officer to Captain Plume, an impudent, ignorant braggart, in George Farquhar's comedy *The Recruiting Officer.*

Brazen Age, The. Play by Thomas Heywood, printed in 1613, founded on Ovid's *Metamorphoses.*

Brazenhead the Great (brā′zẹn.hed). Historical novel by Maurice Hewlett, published in 1911. It deals with the rebellion (1450) led by Jack Cade.

Brazil (brạ.zil′). [Official Portuguese name, **Estados Unidos do Brasil,** meaning "United States of Brazil"; Portuguese and Spanish, **Brasil;** French, **Brésil;** German, **Brasilien.**] Republic in South America, fourth largest country in the world and the largest in South America, bounded on the NW by Colombia, on the N by Venezuela, British and French Guiana, and Surinam, on the E by the Atlantic Ocean, on the S by Uruguay, on the SW by Argentina and Paraguay, and on the W by Bolivia, Peru, and Colombia.

Population, Area, and Political Divisions. Brazil is divided for administrative purposes into 20 states, 5 federal territories, 1 federal district, and one unclassified area in dispute between the states of Minas Gerais and Espírito Santo. Capital, Rio de Janeiro; area, 3,286,043 sq. mi.; pop. 41,236,415 (1940), 52,645,479 (1950).

Terrain and Climate. The physiography of Brazil is divided into three principal regions: the plains of the Amazon basin, extending E from the Andes to the flood plain of the Amazon River, and the lowlands of the upper Paraguay River in SW Brazil; the Brazilian highlands, S of the Amazon, comprising the greatest part of Brazilian territory and geologically related to the Guiana highlands; and the mountains of SE Brazil. The country is drained by two river systems: the Amazon, the world's largest river (if the Mississippi and Missouri are not taken as a single river), with the Tapajós, Tocantins, Xingú, and Negro rivers as its principal tributaries; and the Paraná River, receiving the rivers of S Brazil. A river of numerous waterfalls, the latter is best known for the Guayra Falls near the NE border of Paraguay and the Iguassú Falls near the border of Argentina. The São

Francisco River, emptying into the Atlantic Ocean, is noted for the Paulo Affonso Falls, The SE coast of Brazil is dominated by two lagoons: the Lagoa dos Patos and the Lagoa Mirim. The tropical climate of Brazil has few extremes of temperature or precipitation. The heaviest rainfall occurs during the summer months, and the winter months are for the most part dry. However, the area of the upper Amazon lowlands, the coastal region N of Belém, the W part of the state of Paraná, and the highland area between Santos and São Paulo receive an average annual rainfall of 80 in. or more, and have a lush tropical forest vegetation.

Industry, Agriculture, and Trade. Brazil is primarily an agricultural country. Coffee, the principal agricultural and export crop, is grown chiefly in the highland districts of São Paulo, the leading agricultural state in the country. Rice, cotton, cacao, tobacco, and rice are also important exports. Sugar, the leading Brazilian export of the 16th century, and cotton are grown in the northeast. In the middle 19th century, Brazil had a monopoly of the world's supply of rubber. The *Hevea brasiliensis* (the principal source of latex) is indigenous to the Amazon region. The 19th-century opulence of the cities of Manaus and Belém resulted from the great rubber trade, which has since declined because of competition from Malayan and East Indian rubber. The state of Minas Gerais, the principal mining state of the country, has the largest known iron-ore reserves in the world. Gold, diamonds, manganese, chromium, molybdenum, nickel, tungsten, beryl, commercial quartz crystal, and zirconium are to be found in workable ore bodies. The manufacture of cotton textiles is the principal fabricating industry. Most of the factories are located in the states of Minas Gerais and São Paulo. There are also meat-packing plants, flour mills, paper mills, and petroleum refineries. The principal forest products exported are carnauba wax (used for recording disks), tung oil, brazil nuts, and caroa fiber, a jute substitute. Brazil plays an important strategic role in international aviation. The route from Natal, Brazil, to Dakar, Africa, is the shortest in transatlantic aviation. Because of Brazil's dependence upon foreign trade, the shipping industry has always played an important role in its economy. To serve the needs of this industry there are 138 natural coastal ports, of which 91 are situated at river mouths.

History. The coast of Brazil was partly charted by Alonso de Ojeda and Amerigo Vespucci some time between May, 1499, and June, 1500, but the first white man known to have landed was Vicente Yañez Pinzón, in January, 1500. Pedro Álvarez Cabral landed in Brazil in April, 1500, claimed the region for Portugal, and named it Tierra de Vera Cruz. As the coast was in the hemisphere which, by papal decree, had been assigned to Portugal, it was claimed and colonized by the Portuguese. It was the residence of the exiled Portuguese royal family in the Napoleonic period. Its independence was proclaimed in 1822 and Dom Pedro, son of the Portuguese king, became the first emperor. He was compelled to resign in 1831 in favor of his son, Dom Pedro II. Brazil was in the period 1865–70 allied with Argentina and Uruguay against the Paraguayan dictator López, who was defeated. Slavery was abolished in the years 1871–88. By the revolution of Nov. 15, 1889, the emperor was deposed and a provisional government under Fonseca was established. A national congress was summoned in 1890, which in 1891 proclaimed the constitution of the United States of Brazil. Fonseca, the first president, assumed the dictatorship in 1891, but was obliged to resign the same year, and was succeeded by Peixoto as president. Revolts have occurred, especially in Rio Grande do Sul and Mato Grosso, and in 1893 a serious rebellion of the fleet broke out under Mello. In 1915, the A.B.C. Treaty was signed with Argentina and Chile providing for the peaceful arbitration and settlement of disputes. In October, 1930, Getulio Vargas became president. He was reëlected in 1934, and in 1937 he proclaimed a new constitution which gave him dictatorial powers. In 1945, Major General Eurico Gaspar Dutra was selected president. Vargas was again elected in 1950, to serve until 1956.

Culture. The Brazilian people speak a modified form of Portuguese and have produced, particularly in recent times, a considerable and excellent body of literature. Education is under state control, and many of the states maintain their own universities. The seat of the federal university is in Rio de Janeiro. In addition, there are the Universities of Minas Gerais, São Paulo, Rio Grande do Sul, Rio de Janeiro, Pernambuco, Paraná, Pará, and Fortaleza. The Butanta Institute in São Paulo specializes in herpeto'ogy, and is well known for manufactures of serums for treatment of snakebite.

Brazil. City in W Indiana, county seat of Clay County: important for coal mining, and brick and tile manufacture. 8,434 (1950).

Brazil. [Also, the **Brazils.**] Mythical island which appeared on maps of the Atlantic as early as the 14th century, and long remained on them. It was placed at first apparently in the Azores, and also appeared as W of Ireland.

Brazilian Guiana (gē.ä'nạ). Occasional name for that portion of N Brazil which lies N of the Amazon and E of the Río Negro.

Brazilian Labor Party. Brazilian political party led by Getulio Vargas. Its program is in general radical.

Brazo Casiquiare (brä'sō kä.sē.kyä'rā). See **Casiquiare.**

Brazos (braz'ọs). River in Texas, formed by the junction of Salt Fork and Double Mountain Fork, which flows SE into the Gulf of Mexico ab. 40 mi. SW of Galveston. Length, ab. 850 mi.; navigable, in high water, 250 mi.

Brazos de Santiago (dē san.ti.ä'gō). [Also, **Brazos Santiago.**] Harbor in S Texas, situated on the Gulf of Mexico ab. 6 mi. N of the mouth of the Rio Grande.

Braz Pereira Gomes (bräs pę.rā'rạ gō'mẹs), **Wenceslau.** b. in Minas Gerais, Brazil, Feb. 26, 1868—. Brazilian industrialist, politician, and president (1914–18) of Brazil. He was secretary of the interior (1898–1902) and president (1908–10) of Minas Gerais, federal deputy and leader of the Minas Gerais delegation (1903–05), and vice-president (1910–14) of Brazil.

Brazza (brät'tsä). Italian name of **Brač.**

Brazza, Giacomo de. d. at Rome, March 1, 1888. Italian explorer; younger brother of Pierre Paul François Camille Savorgnan de Brazza. He explored, in 1885, the countries of the Umbete, Osete, Mboko, Okota, and Djambi tribes, in the French Congo.

Brazza (brät'tsä; French, brà.zà), Count **Pierre Paul François Camille Savorgnan de.** b. at Rome, 1852; d. at Fort Dakar (now Dakar), French West Africa, Sept. 15, 1905. Italian count, African explorer, and French officer; brother of Giacomo de Brazza. He went (1875) with another explorer, on a commercial exploration of the Ogowe River, in West Africa. His companion by the river, and Brazza overland, explored the whole Ogowe basin, discovered the Alima and Likuala rivers, and returned to Gabon in 1878. In 1879 Brazza was sent by the French government on a political expedition. He founded Franceville on the Upper Ogowe, opened roads between the coast and the Congo, secured the kingdom of Makoko to France, founded Brazzaville, met Henry Morton Stanley on the Congo, and explored the Lalli and Niadi rivers. In 1880 he made more explorations and political extension in the Ogowe basin and on the coast. In 1883 he was appointed commissioner (governor) of the French Congo (which later became French Equatorial Africa), and explored the Nkoni River. In 1891 he led an expedition up the Sanga River, thus opening the way for an expedition to Lake Chad. He established many government posts in the French Congo.

Brazzaville (braz'ạ.vil; French, brà.zà.vēl). Capital and largest city of French Equatorial Africa, on the Congo River, on the N side of Stanley Pool, across from Léopoldville. It is connected with Pointe Noire, its port on the W African coast, by a railroad ab. 318 mi. long. Because the Congo River is navigable for ab. 1,000 mi. above Brazzaville, the city has become an important river port. It was founded by Pierre Paul François Camille Savorgnan de Brazza, a French explorer who opened up much of the country and claimed it for France. Brazzaville is the administrative center for the Middle Congo territory. Pop. ab. 50,000.

Brea (brē'ạ). City in S California, in Orange County, SE of Los Angeles, in a petroleum-producing area. 3,208 (1950).

Breadalbane (bred.ôl'bạn). [Also, **Albany.**] Mountainous district in C Scotland, in Perthshire. It occupies an area ab. 30 mi. long by 30 mi. wide in the W portion of the county, in the vicinity of Loch Tay.

Breadalbane, 1st Earl of. Title of **Campbell, John** (1635–1716).

Bread and Cheese Folk. Name given to the insurgent party at Haarlem, Netherlands, in 1492, who held temporary possession of the city.

Breadwinner, The. Play (1932) by William Somerset Maugham. In it he attacked what he considered to be the spoiled arrogance of young people in the generation following World War I.

Bread-Winners, The. [Full title, **The Bread-Winners: A Social Study.**] Novel by John Hay, published anonymously in 1884.

Breakers and Granite. Volume (1921) of verse by John Gould Fletcher.

Breakfast in Bed. Novel by Sylvia Thompson, published in 1934.

Breakspear (brāk'spir), **Nicholas.** Original name of Pope **Adrian IV.**

Bréal (brā.àl), **Michel Jules Alfred.** b. at Landau, in Rhenish Bavaria, Germany, March 26, 1832; d. 1915. French philologist. Of French parentage, he was educated both in Germany and in France. At Berlin he studied Sanskrit, and upon becoming a resident of France, he took employment in the department of Oriental manuscripts at what is now the Bibliothèque Nationale. In 1864 he became professor of comparative grammar at the Collège de France. He was the author of *Dictionnaire étymologique latin* (1885) and *Essai de sémantique* (1897). The last-named of these books played a considerable part in awakening an interest in the scientific study of semantics.

Breasted (bres'tẹd), **James Henry.** b. at Rockford, Ill., Aug. 27, 1865; d. at New York, Dec. 2, 1935. American Orientalist and Egyptologist, professor at the University of Chicago from 1905 to 1933. He carried out his graduate studies at the Chicago Theological Seminary, Yale University, and the University of Berlin. He was elected to the Royal Academy of Berlin in 1907. Among his publications are *The Battle of Kadesh* (1903), *A History of Egypt* (1905), *Ancient Records of Egypt* (1906), *Monuments of Sudanese Nubia* (1908), *History of the Ancient Egyptians* (1908), *Temples of Lower Nubia* (1908), *Development of Religion and Thought in Ancient Egypt* (1912), *The Edwin Smith Surgical Papyrus* (2 vols., 1930), and *The Dawn of Conscience* (1933).

Brébeuf (brā.bėf), **Jean de.** b. at Bayeux, France, March 25, 1593; killed in the Huron country, Canada, March 16, 1649. French Jesuit missionary among the Huron Indians in Canada. In a fight between the Hurons and Iroquois, he fell into the hands of the latter and was put to death by them. He had translated the catechism into the Huron language. He was canonized in 1930.

Brèche-de-Roland (bresh.dẹ.ro.läṅ). Narrow gorge in SW France, in the department of Hautes-Pyrénées, on the Spanish border ab. 37 mi. S of Tarbes. The defile is traversed by a trail. According to legend, Roland made the gorge with a single stroke of his sword. Elevation, 9,199 ft.

Brechin (brē'kin). City, royal burgh, market town, and manufacturing center in E Scotland, in Angus, situated on the river South Esk, ab. 12 mi. N of Arbroath, ab. 489 mi. N of London by rail. The town became an important linen-weaving center after 1850 and now has linen factories. It has a cathedral (now the parish church), an ancient round tower, and a castle. 7,121 (est. 1948).

Brecht (brecht), **Arnold.** b. at Lübeck, Germany, Jan. 26, 1884—. German economist. He was a councilor (1921–27) in the ministry of the interior, and served (1927–33) in the finance ministry. He was also a consultant to the Reichsrat on the federal budget. Forced to leave Germany in 1933, he became a professor at the New School for Social Research at New York.

Brecht, Bertolt (or **Bert**). b. at Augsburg, Germany, Feb. 10, 1898—. German playwright and poet. Although he began to write after expressionism had largely spent itself in Germany, he shows certain of its characteristics throughout his work. *Trommeln in der Nacht* (1922), a drama of the chaos that greets the returning soldier, first made him known. Exiled in 1935, Brecht has continued abroad his outcry against tyranny in such publications as *Furcht und Elend des Dritten Reiches* (New York, 1945). In verse his work consists chiefly of ballads (*Hauspostille*, 1927).

Breck (brek), **George William.** b. at Washington, D.C., Sept. 1, 1863; d. at Flushing, N.Y., Nov. 22, 1920. American mural painter and decorator, who was director of the American Academy at Rome from 1905 to 1909. He studied at the Art Students League of New York, and the American Academy at Rome, and was the first winner of the Lazarus Scholarship of the Metropolitan Museum of Art. He was also awarded a silver medal at the St. Louis Exposition of 1904. His works include *Apotheosis of Pennsylvania* and *Education* (at the Watertown, N.Y., library), a copy of Raphael's *School of Athens* for the University of Virginia, and the mosaics, façade, and interior of the American Church at Rome.

Breck, James Lloyd. b. near Philadelphia, June 27, 1818; d. at Benicia, Calif., March 30, 1876. American Episcopal missionary, responsible for the founding of many church schools in the West. He founded (c1842) a religious settlement at Nashotah, Wis., and established educational centers at Crow Wing and Leech Lake in Minnesota, where he was active in converting Indians until the outbreak of the Civil War. He also helped found the Seabury Divinity School, the chief Episcopal seminary west of the Mississippi, at Faribault, Minn.

Breckenridge (brek'ẹn.rij). City in W Minnesota, county seat of Wilkin County, near the confluence of the Bois de Sioux and Otter Tail rivers which forms the Red River: trading and shipping point for a grain and dairy region. 3,623 (1950).

Breckenridge. City in C Texas, county seat of Stephens County, W of Dallas, in a region producing oil, natural gas, and farm produce. 6,610 (1950).

Breckenridge. Former variant spelling of the name now usually Breckinridge when applied to people in the U.S. (in the family that included John Breckinridge and John Cabell Breckinridge, the change was made in the 18th century and has been followed by most of their descendants). In the case of geographical names, however, the spelling Breckenridge still prevails.

Breckenridge, Hugh Henry. b. at Leesburg, Va., 1870; d. Nov. 4, 1937. American painter of portraits and landscapes. He was director of the Breckenridge Summer School of Art at Gloucester, Mass., and instructor at the Pennsylvania Academy of the Fine Arts, Philadelphia. He studied at Paris under Adolphe William Bouguereau, Gabriel Joseph Marie Augustin Ferrier, and Henri Lucien Doucet, and exhibited widely in the U.S., and in France and South America, winning many prizes for his work. He began to instruct at the Pennsylvania Academy in 1894. In 1913 he was made an associate of the National Academy of Design. Among his better-known works are *Still Life, Altar Cloth, A Thread of Scarlet*, portraits in the University of Pennsylvania, the city hall, and the American Philosophical Society at Philadelphia, in the University of Virginia, the state capitol at Harrisburg, Pa., and the state house at Hartford, Conn., and landscapes in the St. Louis (Mo.) Club, and elsewhere.

Breckenridge Hills. Suburb of St. Louis, in E Missouri, in St. Louis County. 4,063 (1950).

Breckinridge (brek'in.rij), **John.** b. in Augusta County, Va., Dec. 2, 1760; d. at Lexington, Ky., Dec. 14, 1806. American statesman; grandfather of John Cabell Breckinridge. He was admitted to the bar in 1785, became attorney general of Kentucky in 1795, and served in the state legislature in the period 1797–1800. He helped draft, in a meeting with Thomas Jefferson at Monticello in 1798, the Kentucky Resolutions, which were adopted on his motion by the Kentucky legislature, on Nov. 10, 1798. He was a U.S. senator from Kentucky in the period 1801–05, and was attorney general in Jefferson's cabinet from Aug. 7, 1805, until his death.

Breckinridge, John Cabell. b. near Lexington, Ky., Jan. 15, 1821; d. at Lexington, Ky., May 17, 1875. American statesman and general; grandson of John Breckinridge. He was a member of Congress (1851–55), vice-president of the U.S. (1857–61), candidate of the Southern Democrats for president in 1860, and U.S. senator from Kentucky (1861). Having joined the Confederate army, in which he was promoted to major general on Aug. 5, 1862, he commanded the reserve troops at Shiloh, April 6–7, 1862. He made an unsuccessful attack on Baton Rouge in August, 1862, and commanded the right wing of Braxton Bragg's army at Murfreesboro on Dec. 31, 1862. He was at Chickamauga (Sept. 19–20, 1863), and at Chattanooga (Nov. 23–25, 1863), defeated General Franz Sigel near Newmarket on May 15, 1864, and was with General Robert E. Lee at Cold Harbor on June 3, 1864. Defeated by General Philip Henry Sheridan in the Shenandoah Valley in September, 1864, he in turn defeated a Union force in East Tennessee on Nov. 12, 1864, and was in the battle near Nashville on Dec. 15, 1864. He served as Confederate secretary of war from January until April, 1865.

Breckinridge, Sophonisba Preston. b. at Lexington, Ky., 1866; d. July 30, 1948. American social worker, educator, and writer. She was a graduate of Wellesley College, a member of the Kentucky bar, and of the faculty of the University of Chicago, where she was successively instructor and professor of household administration, professor of social economy, and professor of public welfare administration. From 1908 to 1920 she was associated with the work of Hull House at Chicago. In addition to educational and sociological problems, she was actively interested in woman's suffrage and in the cause of peace, and served as a delegate to the Women's Peace Congress at The Hague (1915), to the Pan-American Child Congress at Lima, Peru (1930) and to the Pan-American Congress at Montevideo, Uruguay (1933). She served as secretary of the Immigrants' Protective League for some years, was vice-president of the National American Woman's Suffrage Association in 1911, and held the presidency at various times of the American Association of Schools of Social Work, of the Illinois Welfare Association, and of the Chicago Woman's City Club. She was the author of *Legal Tender, A Study in American Monetary History* (1901), *New Homes for Old* (1921), *Madeline McDowell Breckinridge, a Leader in the New South* (1921), *Family Welfare Work in a Metropolitan Community* (1924), *Public Welfare Administration* (1927), *The Family and the State* (1934), and *The Illinois Poor Law and Its Administration* (1939), and coauthor of *The Delinquent Child and the Home* (1912), *The Modern Household* (1912), and *Truancy* (1917).

Brecknock (brek'nok) or **Brecon** (brek'on). Municipal borough in S Wales, in Brecknockshire, situated at the confluence of the rivers Honddu and Usk, ab. 13 mi. N of Merthyr Tydfyl, ab. 181 mi. W of London by rail. It is the county seat of Brecknockshire. The ancient priory church of Saint John, now the cathedral of the diocese of Swansea and Brecknock, the public school of Christ College, some of the buildings of which date back to the 13th century, and the ruins of an 11th-century castle are here. Brecknock was the birthplace of Sarah Siddons. 6,466 (1951).

Brecknock Beacons. See **Brecon Beacons.**

Brecknockshire (brek'nok.shir). [Also: **Brecknock, Brecon, Breconshire.**] Inland county in S Wales. It is bounded on the N by Radnorshire, on the E by Herefordshire and Monmouthshire (England), on the S by Monmouthshire and Glamorganshire, and on the W by Carmarthenshire and Cardiganshire. The surface is mountainous, rising to 2,907 ft. in the Brecon Beacons (the highest point in South Wales). Less than half of the area is under cultivation, most of the farms being of small acreage. Extensive pastures for sheep are found in the mountains, however. Limestone is quarried in the W portion, and part of the South Wales coal field lies in the S portion of the county. Ironstone ore is also abundant. Brecknock is the county seat; area of administrative county, ab. 733 sq. mi.; pop. of administrative county, 56,484 (1951).

Brecksville (breks'vil). Village in N Ohio, in Cuyahoga County, near the Cuyahoga River, ab. 10 mi. S of Cleveland in a residential and farming region. 2,664 (1950).

Břeclav (ber.zhets'läf). [German, **Lundenburg.**] Town in Czechoslovakia, in S Moravia, situated on the Dyje River and on the Austrian border, between Mikulov and Hodonín. There is a castle formerly belonging to the house of Liechtenstein, a brewery, a sugar refinery, and lumber mills. 10,371 (1947).

Brecon (brek'on). See **Brecknock** and **Brecknockshire.**

Brecon Beacons. [Also, **Brecknock Beacons.**] Highest peaks in S Wales, in Brecknockshire, ab. 5 mi. S of Brecknock. Greatest elevation, 2,907 ft.

Breconshire (brek'on.shir). See **Brecknockshire.**

Breda (brā.dä'). City in S Netherlands, in the province of North Brabant, situated on the Merk River, ab. 15 mi. W of Tilburg: river port and railroad junction. It has metallurgical and enamelware industries, furniture, chocolate, and cigar manufactures, canneries, a sugar refinery, and a brewery; vegetables and strawberries are grown in the vicinity. There is a 15th-century Gothic church, and a 16th-century town hall; beautiful modern suburbs. Breda came under the house of Nassau in 1404. The Compromise of Breda, initiating the insurrection of the Netherlands nobility against Spain, was concluded here in 1566. The city was taken by Maurice of Nassau in 1590, by Spinola in 1625, and by Henry of Orange in 1637. The treaty of Breda, leaving New Amsterdam (New York) to the British, was concluded here on July 31, 1667. The French occupied Breda in 1793 and in 1795, and held it until 1813. Pop. 91,055 (est. 1951).

Breda, Compromise of. In the history of the Netherlands, a league between the Protestants and the Catholics, composed chiefly of the lesser nobility, organized by Philip Marnix of St. Aldegonde and others in 1566, for the purpose of opposing the Inquisition and protecting the political liberties of the country against the encroachments of Philip II of Spain. A deputation of 300 nobles, headed by Count Brederode, presented (April 5, 1566) to the duchess regent, Margaret of Parma, at Brussels, a petition which requested the abolition of the royal edicts pertaining to the Inquisition.

Breda, Declaration of. Manifesto to end the Dutch war by Charles II of England, issued from Breda, on April 4. 1660. By it he proclaimed a general amnesty to apply to his late opponents in English politics.

Breda, Treaty of. Treaty concluded at Breda on July 31, 1667, between England and the Netherlands, France, and Denmark. By it, New York and New Jersey were confirmed to England, Acadia to France, and Surinam to the Netherlands.

Bredbury and Romiley (bred'bėr.i; rom'i.li). [Locally called **Woodley.**] Urban district in W England, in Cheshire, ab. 2 mi. NE of Stockport, ab. 180 mi. NW of London by rail. 17,810 (1951).

Bredero (brā'de.rō), **Gerbrand Adriaanszoon.** b. at Amsterdam, 1585; d. there, 1618. Dutch dramatist. His work includes the tragicomedies *Rodderijk ende Alphonsus* (1611) and *Griane* (1612), and several comedies, among them *Het Moortje* (1615, after the *Eunuchus* of Terence), and *Spaansche Brabanter Jerolimo* (1618), the last considered his principal work.

Bredichin (bri.dyē'ḣin), **Fyodor Aleksandrovich.** b. at Nikolaev, Russia, Dec. 8, 1830; d. at St. Petersburg, May 14, 1904. Russian astronomer, director of the observatory of the University of Moscow (1873–90) and of that of Pulkovo (1890 *et seq.*). His principal work was his investigation of the forms of comets, in connection with his theory of meteors.

Bredig (brā'diċh), **Georg.** b. at Glogau, Germany, 1868; d. at New York, 1944. German physical chemist. He developed an electric atomization process for producing lyophobic colloids, and early pointed out the existence of amphoteric electrolytes. Moreover, he experimented on catalysis by colloids, and measured ionic velocities. He edited volumes 1 through 14 of the *Handbuch für angewandte Chemie,* and held professorships at Heidelberg (1901 *et seq.*), Zurich (1910), and Karlsruhe (1911–33), retirement being forced on him by the accession of the Nazi government in Germany. He fled to the Netherlands in 1939, and moved to the U.S. in 1940.

Bredow (brā'dō), **Gabriel Gottfried.** b. at Berlin, Dec. 14, 1773; d. at Breslau, Sept. 5, 1814. German historian, professor of history at Helmstedt (1804). He wrote *Merkwürdige Begebenheiten aus der allgemeinen Weltgeschichte* (1810), *Lehrbuch der Weltgeschichte* (1810), and others.

Bredow, Hans. b. at Schlawe, in Pomerania (then part of Germany), Nov. 26, 1879—. German radio pioneer. He founded (1911) a firm for making broadcasts to South America. In charge (1926–33) of radio communications under the ministry of postal service, he was dismissed from the post in 1933.

Breeches Bible, The. Name given to the Geneva Bible (New Testament, 1557; Old Testament, 1560) because of its rather quaint rendering of Genesis, iii. 7: "Then the eyes of them both were opened, and they knew that they were naked, and they sewed figtree leaves together and made themselves breeches." The Breeches Bible was the first Bible to have the now familiar numbering of the verses for each chapter.

Breed's Hill (brēdz). Eminence at Charlestown, Mass., connected with Bunker Hill, and fortified by Prescott on the occasion of the battle of June 17, 1775. The battle, which is better known as that of Bunker Hill, actually took place chiefly on Breed's Hill.

Breen (brēn), **Patrick.** b. in Ireland; d. at San Juan Bautista, Calif., Dec. 21, 1868. American pioneer, remembered for his diary of the ill-fated Donner party. He came to the U.S. in 1828, and in 1846 set out for California with a party of 81 under George and Jacob Donner. His record of the events which took place (Nov. 20, 1846–March 1, 1847) when the party was trapped by snow and lost 45 of its members is considered by many historians to be the most vivid existing account of the disaster.

Breese (brēz), **Kidder Randolph.** b. at Philadelphia, April 14, 1831; d. Sept. 13, 1881. American naval officer, with the Union navy in the Civil War. A midshipman (1847) under Admiral Farragut during the Mexican War, he accompanied Commodore Perry on his expeditions to Formosa (1852) and Paraguay (1858). As a fleet-captain under Admiral David Porter during the Civil War, he commanded the storming of Fort Fisher (Jan. 15, 1865).

Brefeld (brā'felt), **Oskar.** b. at Telgte, Westphalia, Germany, Aug. 19, 1839; d. Jan. 12, 1925. German botanist. He was noted for his studies in mycology and originated the use of gelatine cultures in botanical studies. Educated at the universities of Halle, Munich, and Würzburg, he served (1878–1907) as a professor at the universities of Eberswald, Münster, and Breslau.

Bregendahl (brā'gen.däl), **Marie.** b. at Fly, Denmark, Nov. 6, 1867; d. at Copenhagen, July 22, 1940. Danish writer; wife (1893–1900) of Jeppe Aakjaer. Descended from peasant folk, she devoted her writings to describing their lives as she knew them in her childhood, particularly in the novels comprising the cycle *Billeder af Sødalfolkenes Liv* (Pictures from the Lives of the Sødal People, 1914–23).

Bregenz (brā'gents). [Latin, **Brigantium, Brigantia.**] City in W Austria, the capital of Vorarlberg province, situated at the E end of Lake Constance at the influx of the Bregenzer Ache. It is the terminus of the Arlberg railroad and of the Bregenzer Wald railroad, and a commercial center. Its museums contain natural history collections, coins, and Roman antiquities. The territory of Bregenz came to Austria in 1451 and 1523. The city was conquered by the Swedes in 1646, and occupied by the Bavarians in the period 1805–14. After World War II it became part of the French zone of occupation in Austria. 20,318 (1951).

Bregenzer Wald (brā'gen.tsėr vält"). [English, **Bregenz Forest.**] Mountainous region in N Vorarlberg, Austria, in the Vorarlberg range of the Algäu Alps.

Bréguet (brā.ge), **Louis Charles.** b. at Paris, Jan. 2, 1880—. French industrialist and aeronautical engineer. He built and equipped (1909) the first helicopter able to go aloft perpendicularly while carrying a passenger. He later constructed a model with a superimposed pair of coaxial rotors turning in opposite directions. He became managing director of the Société Anonyme des Ateliers d'Aviation Louis Bréguet and of Maison Bréguet, a firm manufacturing electrical equipment.

Brehm (brām), **Alfred Edmund.** b. at Renthendorf, near Neustadt an der Orla, Germany, Feb. 2, 1829; d. there, Nov. 11, 1884. German naturalist and traveler; son of Christian Ludwig Brehm. He established (after 1867) the Berlin Aquarium (opened 1869). His works include *Reiseskizzen aus Nordostafrika* (1855), *Das Leben der Vögel* (1860–61), and *Tierleben* (1863–69).

Brehm, Bruno von. b. at Laibach (now Ljubljana, Yugoslavia), July 23, 1892—. Austrian art historian and novelist.

Brehm, Christian Ludwig. b. at Schönau, near Gotha, Germany, Jan. 24, 1787; d. at Renthendorf, near Neustadt an der Orla, Germany, June 23, 1864. German naturalist, author of works on ornithology; father of Alfred Edmund Brehm.

Breisach (brī'zäċh). [Also: **Brisach, Alt-Breisach;** Latin, **Mons Brisiacus.**] Town in S Germany, in the *Land* (state) of Baden, French Zone, formerly in the free state of Baden, situated on the Rhine River at the foot of the Kaiserstuhl, ab. 13 mi. W of Freiburg im Breisgau: wine trade and small industries. It is an old town; the *Stephansmünster* (Cathedral of Saint Stephen) is an impressive Gothic building. Much embattled between Germanic tribesmen and the Roman legions in the time of Julius Caesar, Breisach was fortified by the emperor Valentinian I in 369 A.D. It was a free imperial city in the 13th century, and came under Hapsburg rule in the 14th century. In the Thirty Years' War it was occupied by the Swedes under Duke Bernhard of Weimar on Dec. 19, 1638, after a long siege; it came under the rule of France in 1648, that of Austria in 1697; changed hands again during the War of the Spanish Succession, during the War of the Austrian Succession, and during the revolutionary wars at the end of the 18th century. It became part of Baden in 1805. Pop. 2,093 (1947).

Breisgau (brīs'gou). Old district in S Germany, corresponding practically to the later districts of Freiburg and Lörrach in S Baden: a possession of the house of Hapsburg from the later Middle Ages. By the treaty of Lunéville (1801) it was ceded to the Duke of Modena. In 1805 the greater part was ceded to Baden and a part to Württemberg, and Baden acquired all in 1810.

Breislak (brā'ēs.läk), **Scipione.** b. at Rome, 1748; d. at Milan, Feb. 15, 1826. Italian geologist. He was professor of natural philosophy and mathematics at Ragusa, and then at the Collegio Nazareno at Rome, and later was one of the consuls of the Roman Republic. His chief works are *Topografia fisica della Campania* (1798) and *Instituzioni geologiche* (1818).

Breitenfeld (brī'ten.felt). Village in E central Germany, in NW Saxony, ab. 4 mi. N of Leipzig. Its name has been given to two battles of the Thirty Years' War. On Sept. 17, 1631 a Swedish-Saxon army of 47,000 men under Gustavus Adolphus of Sweden utterly defeated the imperialist force (i.e., of the Holy Roman Empire) of 40,000 men under Count Tilly. On Nov. 2, 1642 the Swedes under Lennart Torstensson defeated the imperialists under the archduke Leopold William of Austria and Octavio Piccolomini, and captured Leipzig.

Breithaupt (brīt'houpt), **Joachim Justus.** b. at Nordheim, Hanover, Germany, 1658; d. at Klosterberg, near Magdeburg, Germany, March 16, 1732. German pietistic theologian. He became court preacher and consistorial councilor at Meiningen in 1685, pastor and professor of theology at Erfurt in 1687, and professor of theology at Halle in 1691.

Breithorn (brīt'hôrn). Mountain of the Valais Alps, in S Switzerland on the border of Italy, S of Zermatt. 13,685 ft.

Breitinger (brī'ting.ėr), **Johann Jakob.** b. at Zurich, Switzerland, March 1, 1701; d. there, Dec. 13, 1776. Swiss critic, writing in German. He was professor of Hebrew and Greek at the Zurich *Gymnasium* (advanced secondary school). With J. J. Dobmer he established the Zurich school of literary criticism, insisting on the emotional and imaginative needs of poetry and deprecating the dry rationalism of the Leipzig school headed by Johann Christoph Gottsched. Breitinger's *Critische Dichtkunst* (1740) did much to decide the issue in favor of the Zurich school. He was coeditor of the *Discourse der Mahlern,* and first editor of many Middle High German texts.

Breitkopf (brīt'kopf), **Johann Gottlob Immanuel.** b. at Leipzig, Germany, Nov. 23, 1719; d. Jan. 29, 1794. German printer, bookseller, and publisher at Leipzig; author of several monographs on typographical subjects and pioneer (from 1750) in the development of movable type for the printing of music scores.

Breitner (brīt'nėr), **George Hendrik.** b. at Rotterdam, 1857; d. 1923. Dutch landscape and figure painter whose work is exhibited at Paris and London, as well as in the Netherlands. He studied first in his native country and then at Paris. He received many awards during his lifetime both in France and in the Netherlands. *Japanese Girl, Return from Maneuvers, Wind and Rain, Nude Study,*

Eunuch, and *Canal at Amsterdam* are among his better-known works.

Brema (brā'mạ), **Marie.** [Original name, **Minny Fehrmann.**] b. at Liverpool, England, Feb. 28, 1856; d. at Manchester, England, March 22, 1925. English operatic contralto. She made her debut (1891) at Bremen, Germany. After her first appearance (1891) in England in the première of *Cavalleria Rusticana*, she took part (1894 *et seq.*) in the Bayreuth Festivals. A member (1894) of the Damrosch Opera Company on its American tour, she alternately sang (1895) Brangäne and Isolde in Richard Wagner's *Tristan und Isolde*, for the Metropolitan Opera Company of New York. She taught at the Manchester Royal College of Music.

Bremen (brem'ẹn, brā'mẹn). *Land* (state) in NW Germany, entirely surrounded by the *Land* of Lower Saxony. It consists chiefly of the city of Bremen, and is administered by the American Zone, although it is geographically within the British Zone. The population is predominantly Protestant (86 percent); the decrease in population between 1939 and 1946 was 13.8 percent. Area, 156 sq. mi.; pop. 485,514 (1946), 558,619 (1950).

Bremen. City in NW Germany, in the *Land* (state) of Bremen, American Zone, formerly the free state of Bremen, situated on the Weser River, ab. 46 mi. from its mouth, and ab. 59 mi. SW of Hamburg. Together with its ocean port, Bremerhaven, it is the second largest port city of Germany. Before World War II it was of particular importance in the cotton, wool, grain, rice, tobacco, and coffee trade, and was one of the principal ports of embarkation in Europe for overseas emigration; after the war the latter function was revived as most of the displaced persons who were moved out of Europe embarked here. Bremen is the seat of large steamship lines, inactivated by the war, such as the North German Lloyd and the Hansa Lloyd. It has a stock exchange and a cotton exchange, large port facilities and shipyards (Weser A. G. and Atlas Works), iron, cement, béton, and automobile works, numerous flour mills, woolen textile, metallurgical, leather, and tobacco manufactures, canneries, and breweries. Cultural institutions include technical and nautical institutes, a library, a theater, scholarly societies, an art museum, the Paula Modersohn-Becker Museum, the Focke Museum of arts and crafts, and natural history, ethnological, and commercial collections. Much of the port facilities and of the old city of Bremen were destroyed or gravely damaged by air raids in the period 1943–45; the Gothic and Renaissance building of the old *Rathaus* (town hall), erected in the period 1405–09, and the statue of Roland still stand. The cathedral, in Romanesque style, dates from the 11th century; the churches of Saint Martin and Saint Anschar and the Church of Our Lady date from the 13th and 14th centuries. Most of the old guild and craft houses are gone, and many of the newer public buildings, some of them architecturally remarkable, were hit also. The residential quarters of Bremen are characterized by the prevalence of one and two family houses with gardens. 444,549 (1950).

History. Bremen became a bishopric in 788, an archbishopric in 845, and was the center of the North European missionary enterprise of the medieval church. It became a member of the Hanseatic League in 1260; at the same time the town council gained independence from ecclesiastical rule. In the 15th century a large part of the territory on the lower Weser River was acquired. In 1522 Protestantism was introduced. Bremen was twice besieged by the forces of the Holy Roman Empire in the Thirty Years' War; with the loss of the lower Weser territories to Sweden in 1648, its commerce declined. It belonged to France in the period 1810–13, and became a sovereign member of the German Bund in 1815. The modern prosperity of the city started in the early 19th century with the acquisition of Bremerhaven. The North German Lloyd was founded in 1857. Bremen's trade received a blow at the end of World War I, but recovered quickly; recovery was likely to be slower after the much more severe blow received at the end of World War II. Bremen was occupied by Allied troops on April 27, 1945; it belonged at first to the British Zone of occupation, and was later transferred to the American Zone.

Bremen (brē'mẹn). Town in N Indiana, in Marshall County, ab. 15 mi. S of South Bend. 2,664 (1950).

Bremen (brem'ẹn, brā'mẹn), **Duchy of.** Former duchy of Germany, which lay between the lower Elbe and lower Weser rivers. It consisted largely of the archbishopric of Bremen and Verden, and later belonged to the province of Hanover, Prussia. It was acquired by Sweden in 1648, and by Hanover in 1719.

Bremer (brā'mėr), **Fredrika.** b. at Tuorla, near Åbo (now Turku), Finland, Aug. 17, 1801; d. at Årsta, near Stockholm, Sweden, Dec. 31, 1865. Swedish novelist and feminist. She was a prolific writer. Her first novel, *Teckningar ur Hvardagslifvet* (Sketches of Every-day Life, 1828), is a description of middle-class life in Sweden. It was followed by others in the same vein, notably *Familjen H.* (The H. Family), *Presidentens Döttrar* (The President's Daughters), *Grannarna* (The Neighbors), *Axel och Anna* (Axel and Anna), *Hemmet* (The Home), and *Nina*. She was the author, besides, of several books of travel, among them *Hemmen i nya Verlden* (Homes in the New World, 1853), which contains her impressions of America. Her later works, like *Hertha* and *Syskonlif*, embody her opinions on philanthropy, religion, and the rights of women. Several of her works appeared simultaneously in Swedish and English, and numerous others have been translated.

Bremer Beiträge (brā'mėr bī'trā"gẹ). German literary journal (1745–48) which was edited at Leipzig and printed at Bremen. The full title was *Neue Beiträge zum Vergnügen des Verstandes und Witzes.* Among the contributors were Johann Adolf Schlegel, his gifted brother Johann Elias Schlegel, Rabener, Zachariä, and Gellert. Its most famous contribution was the first three cantos of Klopstock's *Messias* in 1748.

Bremerhaven (brem'ėr.hā.vẹn; German, brā'mėr.hä.fẹn). [Also, **Bremerhafen.**] City in NW Germany, in the *Land* (state) of Bremen, American Zone, formerly in the free state of Bremen, situated on the lower Weser River, at the mouth of the Geeste River, opposite the town of Geestemünde, ab. 35 mi. N of Bremen. It is the ocean port for Bremen; has docks, shipyards, repair shops and warehouses, mostly belonging to the North German Lloyd steamship company. Bremerhaven is a center of the fishing industry; there are large facilities for the smoking and canning of fish, particularly herring and codfish; also metallurgical, tobacco, and other manufactures. Petroleum, grain, lumber, cotton, tobacco, and other products are imported. The city was founded (1827) after Bremen had acquired the site from Hanover. The old harbor was built in 1830, the new harbor in 1851; there were additions in 1876 and in the period 1908–09. City and harbor facilities suffered grave damage from bombing during World War II. 114,070 (1950).

Bremerton (brem'ėr.tọn). City in W Washington, in Kitsap County. It is the site of the Puget Sound navy yard. 27,678 (1950).

Bremond (brẹ.môṅ), **Henri.** b. at Aix, Bouches-du-Rhône, France, July 30, 1855; d. 1933. French literary critic and historian, a specialist in the relations between religion and literature. Author of *Histoire littéraire du sentiment religieux en France* (11 vols., 1916–33; unfinished), *De la poésie pure* (1926), and *Prière et poésie* (1926). He retired from the Society of Jesus in 1904 to devote his life to literary studies, and was elected to the French Academy in 1926.

Brendan (bren'dạn) or **Brenainn** (bren'in), Saint. [Also: **Brandan** or **Borondon.**] b. at Tralee, County Kerry, Ireland, 484; d. 577. Irish monk, a contemporary of Saint Brendan of Birr, and sometimes called "son of Finnloga" or Saint Brendan of Clonfert to distinguish him. After completing his studies at Tuam he set forth on the expedition known as the "Navigation of Saint Brendan." According to the legendary account of his travels, he set sail with others to seek the terrestrial paradise which was supposed to exist in an island of the Atlantic. Various miracles are related of the voyage, but they are always connected with the great island where the monks are said to have landed. The legend was current in the time of Christopher Columbus and long after, and many connected Saint Brendan's island with the newly discovered America. He is commemorated on May 16.

Brendan of Birr, Saint. [Also, Saint **Brenainn of Birr.**] b. at Birr, Ireland, c490; d. Nov. 28, 573. Irish monk. A disciple of Saint Finnian of Clonard, he was a friend of Saint Columba, to whom he is said to have recommended Hy as a place of exile. He founded the monastery of Birr c563. Saint Columba is represented to have seen at Brendan's death "heaven open and choirs of angels descending" to meet his soul. He is commemorated on Nov. 29.

Brendel (bren'dẹl), **Karl Franz.** b. at Stolberg, in the Harz, Germany, Nov. 26, 1811; d. at Leipzig, Germany, Nov. 25, 1868. German music critic. His works include *Geschichte der Musik in Italien, Frankreich und Deutschland* (1852) and *Musik der Gegenwart* (1854). He was editor (1845 *et seq.*) of the *Neue Zeitschrift*, and also published (1856 *et seq.*) a periodical supporting, in general, the musical theories of Richard Wagner and Franz Liszt.

Brendle (bren'dl). Novel by Marmaduke Pickthall, published in 1905.

Brenet (brẹ.ne), **Michel.** [Pseudonym of **Marie Bobillier.**] b. at Lunéville, France, April 12, 1858; d. at Paris, Nov. 4, 1918. French music historian and musicologist. She was the author of *Histoire de la symphonie à orchestre* (1882), *Notes sur l'histoire du luth en France* (1899), *Les Musiciens de la Sainte-Chapelle* (1910), and *La Musique militaire* (1917).

Brenets (brẹ.ne), **Lac des.** Small lake in the Jura, formed by the Doubs River in its upper course, near Le Locle, Switzerland.

Brengwin (breng'win). See **Brangwaine.**

Brenham (bren'ạm). City in C Texas, county seat of Washington County, E of Austin. A shipping point for an agricultural area, it also manufactures cotton, cottonseed oil, mops, brooms, and dairy products; seat of Blinn College. The city was established in 1844. Pop. 6,941 (1950).

Brennabor (bren'nä.bôr). Slavic name of **Brandenburg,** city.

Brennaburg (bren'nä.bu̇rk). See **Brandenburg,** city.

Brennan (bren'ạn), **Christopher John.** b. at Sydney, Australia, Nov. 1, 1870: d. there, Oct. 7, 1932. Australian poet, a scholar of various languages and literatures. Educated in Australia and Germany, he was a member (1895–1909) of the staff of the public library in New South Wales, and lecturer and associate professor of German and comparative literature (1908–25) at the University of Sydney. His most important volume of poetry was *Poems* (dated 1913, published 1914), which established his position as a major Australian literary figure.

Brennan, Frederick Hazlitt. b. at St. Louis, Sept. 23, 1901—. American journalist, playwright, and scenarist. He has been a staff member of the St. Louis *Post-Dispatch* and the *Saturday Evening Post*, and a scenarist (1928–30) at Hollywood, Calif. He is the author of *Battleship Gertie* (1935), *Stick-In-the-Mud* (1935), *The Wookey* (1941), *Magdalena* (1948), and other stage productions.

Brennan, Louis. b. 1852; d. at Montreux, Switzerland, 1932. Irish inventor who constructed a dirigible torpedo and a monorail railway system (1909). A resident (1861–80) of Melbourne, Australia, he was superintendent and consulting expert with the Government Brennan Torpedo Factory (1887–1907). He was associated, during World War I and until 1926, with government aircraft research.

Brenner (bren'ėr), **Victor David.** b. at Shaulyai, in Lithuania, June 12, 1871; d. at New York, April 5, 1924. American sculptor and medalist, who did many portrait medals for several major institutions. He was a pupil of Louis Oscar Roty, at Paris, and came to the U.S. in 1890. His work was exhibited and honored at Paris and Brussels and in the U.S., and was acquired by collections in France and the U.S. and at Munich and Vienna. His works include a bust of Charles Eliot Norton; medallions of William M. Evarts, C. P. Huntington, Amerigo Vespucci, John Paul Jones, and J. A. M. Whistler; a set of medals for the Metropolitan Museum of Art, New York; and the Schenley memorial fountain at Pittsburgh, Pa.

Brenner Pass. [Italian, **Brennero** (bren.nā'rō).] Mountain pass in S central Europe. the lowest pass over the main chain of the Alps, situated in the Tyrol on the Austrian-Italian frontier, ab. 19 mi. SE of Innsbruck. It has been used since Roman times, is traversed by a railway (since 1867), and is the main line of travel between Italy and Germany. Hitler and Mussolini met here for conferences before and during the early part of World War II. 4,470 ft.

Brenneville (bren.vēl'), **Battle of.** Battle fought on Aug. 20, 1119, in Normandy, in which Henry I of England defeated Louis VI of France.

Brennoralt, or The Discontented Colonel (bren.ôr'ạlt). Tragedy by Sir John Suckling, written in 1639, printed in 1646.

Brennus (bren'us). fl. c389 B.C. Roman name of the leader of the Gauls who pillaged Rome after defeating (c389 B.C.) Marcus Manlius Capitolinus. The Romans took refuge in the capitol, where the Gauls besieged them until a ransom of 1,000 pounds of gold was paid. A legend relates that the Romans charged the Gauls with using false weights, and that Brennus threw his sword into the scale and exclaimed "Vae victis" (that is, "Woe to the vanquished," conveying, although in reverse, approximately the same meaning as, in more modern times, "to the victor belong the spoils").

Brennus. fl. 279 B.C. Reputed name of a leader of the Gauls who invaded Greece in 279 B.C., overcoming the defenders at Thermopylae, but suffering defeat at Delphi. The legend represents Brennus as drinking himself to death on wine, either because his pain from many wounds was unendurable, or because the shame of defeat was intolerable.

Brent (brent), **Charles Henry.** b. at Newcastle, Ontario, Canada, April 9, 1862; d. at Lausanne, Switzerland, March 27, 1929. American Protestant Episcopal clergyman. At first a curate (1888–91) and assistant minister (1891–1901) at Boston, he was later bishop of the Philippine Islands (1901–18) and of western New York (1918–26), and was in charge (1926–28) of Protestant Episcopal churches in Europe. He served on a committee (1903–04) to investigate opium conditions in the East. During World War I he was chief (1917–18) of the chaplain service in France. He was the author of *With God in the World* (1899), *The Splendour of the Human Body* (1904), and *A Master Builder* (1916).

Brent, Margaret. b. in England, 1600; d. 1670 or 1671. American pioneer and feminist. She emigrated (1638) from England to St. Mary's, Md., where she obtained (1639) the first land grant to be held by a woman in Maryland. Having aided the governor, Leonard Calvert, in suppressing the Claiborne Rebellion (1646), she was appointed executrix of his estate (1647). She was also appointed attorney for George Calvert, 1st Baron Baltimore.

Brenta (bren'tä). [Latin, **Medoacus Major.**] River in NE Italy which rises in the S part of the Tyrol, and flows into the Gulf of Venice. Length, ab. 108 mi.

Brentano (bren.tä'nō), **Clemens.** b. at Ehrenbreitstein, Prussia, Sept. 8, 1778; d. at Aschaffenburg, Bavaria, July 28, 1842. German romantic poet and novelist; brother of Elizabeth (Bettina) von Arnim and grandson of Sophie Laroche. At Jena (1797–1800) he came to know the leading members of the Romantic Movement in Germany. His association (1805) at Heidelberg with Ludwig Joachim von Arnim resulted in a joint compilation of folksongs, *Des Knaben Wunderhorn* (1806–08), and the joint editing of *Einsiedlerzeitung*. Meanwhile he published the novel *Godwi* (1800–02). From his story *Geschichte vom braven Kasperl und schönen Annerl* (1817), the development of the village tale in German literature is dated. His fairy stories (*Gockel, Hinkel und Gackeleia; Rheinmärchen;* 1838) are still popular. His most voluminous collection of lyrics is found in *Die Erfindung des Rosenkranzes* (1853). His lyric drama *Die Gründung Prags* (1815) treats the theme later used by Franz Grillparzer in *Libussa*.

Brentano, Franz. b. at Marienberg, near Boppard, Germany, Jan. 16, 1838; d. at Zurich, Switzerland, March 17, 1917. German Aristotelian philosopher and psychologist; brother of Lujo Brentano. An opponent of the theories of Immanuel Kant, he is chiefly remembered for his work in the field of psychology. Originally a Roman Catholic priest, he left the church in 1873; he served (1872 *et seq.*) as a professor at Würzburg and Vienna universities. He was the author of *Psychologie vom empirischen Standpunkt* (1874), *Vom Ursprung sittlicher*

Erkenntnis (1889), *Aristoteles' Lehre vom Ursprung des menschlichen Geistes* (1911), and *Vom Dasein Gottes* (1929). His psychological theories influenced the Gestalt psychologists, and were used by Edmund Husserl in his development of the theory of phenomenology.

Brentano, Lujo (or **Ludwig**). b. at Aschaffenburg, Bavaria, Germany, Dec. 18, 1844; d. at Munich, Sept. 9, 1931. German political economist, one of the leaders of the social-political school of German economics; brother of Franz Brentano. He was a fighter for betterment of the workers' status (higher wages, shorter working hours, trade unions), and for the system of free trade. In 1927 he won the Nobel peace prize. He served as a professor (1872 *et seq.*) at Breslau, Strasbourg, Vienna, Leipzig, and Munich. His works include *Die Arbeitergilden der Gegenwart* (Labor Guilds of Today, 1871–72), *Über das Verhältnis von Arbeitslohn und Arbeitszeit zur Arbeitsleistung* (On the Relation of Wages and Working Hours to the Work Performed, 1876), *Die Anfänge des modernen Kapitalismus* (The Beginnings of Modern Capitalism, 1916), and *Mein Leben im Kampf um die soziale Entwicklung Deutschlands* (My Life in the Fight for the Social Development of Germany, 1931).

Brentford (brent'fọrd). Former urban district, now comprising three wards of Brentford and Chiswick municipal borough (*q.v.*), in SE England, in Middlesex, situated at the confluence of the rivers Brent and Thames, ab. 2 mi. S of Ealing, ab. 11 mi. W of Waterloo station, London. Brentford is a market town. Here Edmund Ironside defeated the Danes, in May 1016, and Prince Rupert defeated the Parliamentarians under Holles, on Nov. 12, 1642. Pop. 20,372 (1931).

Brentford and Chiswick (chiz'ik). Municipal borough in SE England, in Middlesex, ab. 11 mi. W of Waterloo station, London. It comprises the former urban districts of Brentford and Chiswick, amalgamated in 1927. Brentford market is a large wholesale fruit and vegetable market. There is abundant evidence here of Roman, early British, and prehistoric settlement. 59,354 (1951).

Brenthe (bren'thẹ). Ancient name of **Karitaina.**

Brenton (bren'tọn), **Edward Pelham.** b. 1774; d. 1839. English naval captain and writer. He was promoted to a captaincy in 1808. After serving against the Americans in the War of 1812, he became (1815) flag-captain to Benjamin Hallowell. He published *Naval History of Great Britain, 1783-1822* (1823), *The Bible and the Spade* (1837), *Life and Correspondence of John, Earl of St. Vincent* (1838), and pamphlets on mendicity, poor laws, and juvenile vagrancy and similar subjects.

Brentwood (brent'wu̇d). Urban district, market town, and residential center in SE England, in Essex, ab. 11 mi. SW of Chelmsford, ab. 18 mi. NE of Liverpool Street station, London: seat of a grammar school founded in the 16th century. The town is ab. 400 ft. above sea level, and its parks form part of the London "Green Belt Scheme." 29,898 (1951).

Brentwood. Town in W central Maryland, in Prince Georges County, ab. 5 mi. NE of Washington, D.C. 3,523 (1950).

Brentwood. City in E Missouri, in St. Louis County: residential community, a residential suburb of St. Louis. 7,504 (1950).

Brentwood. Unincorporated community in SE New York, in Suffolk County, on Long Island ab. 35 mi. E of New York City: residential suburb. 2,803 (1950).

Brentwood. Borough in SW Pennsylvania, in Allegheny County: residential suburb of Pittsburgh. 12,535 (1950).

Brera (brā'rä). [Full name, **Pinacoteca di Brera.**] The name given to the so-called Palace of Sciences and Arts at Milan. It contains a noted art gallery, the Institute of Fine Arts, and the Brera Library, founded in 1770, which contains more than 627,000 volumes.

Brereley (brir'li), **Roger.** [Also, **Brierley.**] b. at Marland, Lancashire, England, Aug. 4, 1586; d. at Burnley, Lancashire, England, June, 1637. English clergyman and poet, now remembered chiefly as the founder of a small religious group known as the Grindletonians, from the name of the town and chapel of which he was curate. The Grindletonians were linked to the religious community known as Familists, a sect of the 16th and 17th centuries which sought to attain sympathy and love, and paid little heed to formal doctrines. Brereley was the author of sermons (published at Edinburgh, 1670, and at London, 1677), and of a few poems included in the latter edition of the sermons.

Brereton (brer'tọn), **Lewis Hyde.** b. at Pittsburgh, Pa., in June, 1890—. American air-force officer who headed (1944–45) the combined airborne forces of the U.S. and Great Britain in Europe. He is a graduate (1911) of the U.S. Naval Academy, Annapolis, Md., but served as a naval officer on active duty for only three days (June 3–5, 1911); his great interest in military aviation persuaded him that he could be most useful in the army, which was then developing an aviation arm as part of the signal corps, and he was commissioned a second lieutenant in the army in August, 1911. In World War I he served as an air officer in Europe. Commissioned a major general (1941), he commanded the Far East Air Force in the Philippines (1941), the U.S. air forces in the Middle East (1943), and the 9th Air Force in Europe (1943). He is the author of *The Brereton Diaries* (1946).

Brereton (brir'tọn), Sir **William.** b. 1604; d. at Croydon, England, April 7, 1661. English soldier, notable as an officer in Oliver Cromwell's army. As commander in chief of the Parliamentary forces in Cheshire, he defeated (1643) Sir Thomas Aston at Nantwich, and later (1644) captured Liverpool and Shrewsbury.

Brer Rabbit (brėr rab'it). Name of the principal animal character in the *Uncle Remus* stories by Joel Chandler Harris, who uses cunning, trickery, and deception to win against the superior force and strength of Brer Fox, Brer Wolf, and other stronger animals. The rabbit as a symbol of trickery is common in African folk tales.

Brescia (brā'shä). Province in NW Italy, in the *compartimento* (region) of Lombardy. Capital, Brescia; area, ab. 1,800 sq. mi.; pop. 744,571 (1936), 824,000 (est. 1946).

Brescia. [Latin, **Brixia.**] City and commune in NW Italy, in the *compartimento* (region) of Lombardy, the capital of the province of Brescia, situated at the foot of the Alps between Verona and Milan. It is a manufacturing center producing textiles (linen, woolen, silk), metallurgical products (weapons, machines, automobiles), paper, and leatherware. It is also a cultural center, and has an academy of arts and sciences, an excellent library (Biblioteca Civica), a number of theaters, and a philharmonic society (it played an important role in the history of Italian music in the 15th and 16th centuries). It has numerous art treasures, and interesting churches and palaces. There are Roman remains, particularly a temple of Vespasian, which now serves as the Museo Antico. Brescia is the seat of a bishopric. The old cathedral is a circular church in Romanesque style, dating probably from the 9th century; the new cathedral was built in the 17th century. Other notable churches include Santa Maria dei Miracoli, San Cristo, San Francesco, and the Chiesa del Carmine. Paintings by Titian and Paolo Veronese are in the churches of SS. Nazaro e Celso and Sant' Afra. The medieval castle of the Visconti family is on a hill above the city; other palaces date from the Renaissance and baroque periods. Originally a Celtic town, Brescia became a flourishing Roman colony under Augustus, which was later devastated by the Goths and the Huns; it became the seat of a Lombard duchy and of a bishopric, and from the 11th century was one of the most powerful free cities of Lombardy, a supporter of the cause of the Guelphs. Ezzelino da Romano, the German emperor Henry VII, the kings of Naples and Bohemia, and the Visconti and Malatesta families fought for dominion over the city until it fell to Venice in 1428; in 1797 it became part of the (French) Cisalpine Republic, and in 1815 part of Austria. The citizens revolted unsuccessfully against Austria in 1848 and 1849. The city was incorporated into Italy in 1859. In World War II, Allied troops entered Brescia on April 28, 1945. Severe damage was sustained during the war by some of the finest old buildings, among them the churches of Sant' Afra, San Francesco, and Santa Maria dei Miracoli; the new cathedral was hit only superficially; some of the palaces were completely destroyed; in most cases, however, repairs have been completed or are being carried out. Pop. of commune, 123,332 (1936), 146,532 (1951); of city, 92,583 (1936).

Breshkovsky (bresh.kôf'ski), **Catherine.** [Russian, **Ekaterina Konstantinovna Breshko-Breshkovskaya** (bresh'ko.brish.kôf'skạ.yạ); called **Babushka** or **Ba-**

boushka (which means "Little Grandmother") and the **"Grandmother of the Russian Revolution."**] b. near Vitebsk, Byelorussia, Russia, 1844; d. Sept. 12, 1934. Russian social reformer and revolutionist. The daughter of a wealthy landowner, she began, while still a young girl, her efforts to ameliorate the lot of the Russian peasants, and they remained her chief concern throughout her life. She was married to a nobleman of liberal views, by whom she had a son, but in 1870 she left both son and husband in order to be utterly free to work for revolt against the czar and the existing order, and became associated with the followers of Bakunin. She was arrested in 1874 and imprisoned at St. Petersburg until 1878, when she was exiled to Siberia. There, under close watch by the police, she remained until 1896. Upon her release she at once resumed her revolutionary activities, and in 1900 avoided arrest only by flight to Switzerland. In 1904 she visited the U.S. where her denunciations of the Czarist regime won considerable sympathy. Upon the outbreak of the revolution of 1905 she returned to Russia, where she was again arrested in 1907, and in 1910 again sent to Siberia. After the overthrow of the czar, the Kerensky government released her in 1917, and the populace of Petrograd (which had been called St. Petersburg until 1914, and was to be renamed Leningrad in 1924) welcomed her with enthusiastic demonstrations of affection. However, with the Bolshevik regime which succeeded the Kerensky government she was not in harmony, and after a lecture tour in the U.S. in 1919, she went to Czechoslovakia, where she spent her remaining years. She was the author of *Russia and the World* and *A Message to the American People* (both 1919), as well as of miscellaneous writings which (as edited by Alice Stone Blackwell) were published at Boston (1917).

Breslau (bres'lou). German name of **Wrocław.**

Bressanone (brās.sä.nō'nā). [German, **Brixen.**] Town and commune in NE Italy, in the *compartimento* (region) of Trentino-Alto Adige, in the province of Bolzano, situated on the Isarco River, NE of Bolzano. It is a health resort and tourist center, architecturally interesting because of the mixture of German and Italian elements in its buildings which can be followed through various styles: the Convent of Novacella is in Romanesque style, the Chiostro is Gothic, the episcopal palace is in Renaissance, the cathedral in baroque style. There are a number of medieval churches and a diocesan museum with good art collections. The bishops of Bressanone acquired the surrounding counties in the 11th century and retained, through several centuries, sovereignty over a wide Alpine territory within the framework of the medieval German empire. Town and territory passed in 1803 to the Austrian Tyrol, in 1805 to Bavaria, in 1810 to French Illyria, in 1813 again to Austria, and in 1919 (after World War I) to Italy. Because of its strategic location, the town was strongly fortified during the period of Austrian domination. Buildings of interest to tourists were undamaged in World War II. Pop. of commune, 11,242 (1936); of town 6,520 (1936).

Bressant (bre.säṅ), **Jean Baptiste Prosper.** b. at Châlons-sur-Saône, France, Oct. 24, 1815; d. at Nemours, France, Jan. 22, 1886. French comedian.

Bresse (bres). Historical region and former county district in E France, lying E of the Saône River, and comprised in the modern department of Ain. Its chief city is Bourg-en-Bresse. Bresse formed part of the Burgundian kingdom, passed to the house of Savoy in 1272, was ceded by Savoy to France in 1601, and thereafter was part of the province of Burgundy.

Bresslau (bres'lou), **Harry.** b. at Dannenberg, Germany, March 22, 1848; d. at Heidelberg, Germany, Oct. 27, 1926. German historian and paleographer. He served as a professor (1877 *et seq.*) at the universities of Berlin and Strasbourg. He was also a director of the *Monumenta Germaniae historica*, the standard edition of old German texts. Author of *Geschichte der Monumenta Germaniae historica* (1921).

Bressler-Gianoli (bres'lėr.jä.nō'lē), Madame **Chlotilde** or **Clotilde.** b. at Geneva, June 3, 1875; d. there, May 12, 1912. Swiss mezzo-soprano opera singer. She appeared as Carmen at the Théâtre de la Monnaie, Brussels, in 1895, and in the same part at the Opéra Comique at Paris in 1900, and made her appearance at the Manhattan Opera House, New York, in 1906. She was successful also in Wagnerian opera, in Gluck's *Orphée*, in Massenet's *Werther*, and in others.

Bresson (bre.sôṅ), **Charles,** Comte. b. at Paris, 1798; d. at Naples, Nov. 2, 1847. French diplomat. He was first secretary of legation at London (c1829), chargé d'affaires at Berlin (1833), minister of foreign affairs (1834), and ambassador at Madrid (1841) and Naples (1847), where he committed suicide. He negotiated (1846) at Madrid the marriages of Queen Isabella and of her sister, both of whom married French royalty.

Bressoux (bre.sö). Town in E Belgium, in the province of Liége, NE of Liége, of which it is a suburb. 15,529 (1947).

Bressuire (bre.swēr). Town in W France, in the department of Deux-Sèvres, ab. 45 mi. S of Angers. It has large stockyards, equipped with machinery for the freezing of meat. It has been the scene of severe fighting in several wars. 6,071 (1946).

Brest (brest). City in NW France, in the department of Finistère, situated on the Rade de Brest (Roads of Brest), a bay on the W coast of Brittany, N of Quimper. It is the terminus of a transatlantic cable; has a commercial harbor of growing importance and a large naval station; it is also a tourist center. In former times it was an object of dispute between Great Britain and France; it was attacked by the English in 1513, developed by Richelieu, and fortified by Vauban. In 1694 the French defeated the British here; the British fleet defeated the French here in 1794. During World War I Brest was an American base; in World War II it served as a German submarine base until the Allied invasion of France. In the period 1943–44, it was heavily damaged by British and American bombs dropped during air attacks on various facilities of the port and city which were built, or being used, by the Germans. It has been known for the manufacture of textiles, chemicals, and shoes. 74,991 (1946).

Brest. [Also: **Brest-Litovsk** (brest.li.tôfsk'), **Brest-Litovski** (-li.tôf'ski); Polish, **Brześć nad Bugiem, Brześć Litewski.**] City in the U.S.S.R., in the Byelorussian Soviet Socialist Republic, situated on the Bug River at the Polish border. It is an important rail and road junction. Ceded to Russia at the end of the 18th century, Brest was returned to Poland between World Wars I and II, during both of which it was occupied by Germany, but passed to the U.S.S.R. in 1945 as a result of agreements reached at the Potsdam Conference. 50,000 (est. 1940).

Brest American Naval Memorial. Tall shaft situated on an old fortification wall erected by the U.S. government at Brest, France, in commemoration of the transatlantic convoying operations of the U.S. navy in World War I. Brest was the site of American naval headquarters in France and the chief port of debarkation for AEF troops carried on American naval transports.

Brest-Litovsk, Treaty of. Treaty of peace between Russia and the Central Powers in World War I. Two facts about it are particularly noteworthy: first, it was the only treaty signed in World War I by Germany as the victor over a major opponent, and second, the severity of the German demands (which were finally accepted) was greater than that of any previous treaty ever signed by a Russian government. Formal negotiations for the treaty commenced when the government of Russia, which had been taken over by the Bolshevik party and which had signed an armistice on Dec. 15, 1917, announced a peace conference between itself (represented chiefly by Leon Trotsky) and the Central Powers at Brest (Brest-Litovsk). At first the Russians were hopeful of obtaining some modification of the German demands, but these were finally accepted by Lenin when the German armies moved still further eastward, thus pointedly emphasizing the inability of the Russians to offer further resistance. The Central Powers signed a treaty with an independent Ukrainian republic on Feb. 9, 1918. On March 3, 1918, the Russian Soviet Socialist Republic signed a treaty which provided for Russian evacuation of Finland, Estonia, Livonia, Courland, and Poland, as well as the recognition of an independent Ukraine and cession of some territories to Turkey. Additional treaties imposing indemnities on Russia and granting Germany considerable commercial advantages were concluded in August, 1918. The Russians proclaimed the abrogation of the Treaty of Brest-Litovsk on Nov. 13, 1918.

Bretagne (brȩ.tány'). French name of **Brittany.**

Breteuil (brȩ.tėy'). Town in N France, in the department of Oise, ab. 18 mi. S of Amiens. Pop. ab. 2,500.

Breteuil, Gabrielle Émilie le Tonnelier de, Marquise **du Châtelet.** See **du Châtelet, Gabrielle Émilie le Tonnelier de Breteuil,** Marquise.

Brethren of Purity. Moslem secret association established (c983) at Basra (in what is now Iraq). Its aims were religious, philosophical, and political. The name is a literal translation of the Arabic phrase *Ikhwan al-safa,* and it is a little misleading in that the Arabic does not, strictly speaking, imply the notion of brotherhood. However, usage in the Western world so unanimously supports this name that the use of any other might well be considered by many readers an instance of gratuitous obscurantism (it is not purely an English-language problem; the tradition is supported also by the German *Die lautern Brüder* and the French *Les frères de la pureté*). Moreover, the association was in fact and of necessity a brotherhood, although some may feel that Brethren of Sincerity would be a desirable new translation. Another recent and very plausible hypothesis, advanced in 1923, suggests that the Arabic was originally meant as a translation of the Greek *philosophos,* and it is unquestionably true that the devotion to knowledge implied by this word was a characteristic of the Brethren of Purity. The philosophy of the association was an eclectic gnosticism, including Iranian, Christian, Hebraic, Syriac, Hindu, Arabic, and Greek elements. The group appears to have had some knowledge of Aristotle, but was more familiar with Pythagorean and Platonic doctrines. To reconcile Greek science with the Koran the members of the association were naturally driven to give mythical and mystical interpretations of both, but their belief in the purifying power of knowledge was a basic factor in their epistemology. They wrote a series of 52 treatises forming a sort of encyclopedia: 14 deal with mathematics and logic; 17 deal with the natural sciences, including psychology; 10 deal with metaphysics; and 11 deal with mysticism, astrology, and magic. The work includes a classification of science which is essentially the Aristotelian one, but which has some historical importance because it contains most of the characteristic features of the later Jewish classifications. Included within the treatises are explanations of such natural phenomena as tides, earthquakes, and eclipses, and also the hypothesis that sound is produced by vibrations of the air (which led the group to ask, but not answer, the question: how is it that simultaneous sounds do not mix in the air?).

Brétigny (brā.tē.nyē; Anglicized, bre.tēn'yȩ), **Treaty** or **Peace of.** Treaty concluded at Brétigny, near Chartres, France, on May 8, 1360, between England and France. By it, England, in the person of Edward III, renounced its claims to the French crown, and to the territories of Maine, Anjou, Normandy, and Touraine, and released John II of France. None of these could be called points wrested from Edward III by the strength of French arms (which were, indeed, still not recovered from their defeat four years before at Poitiers); with the exception of the release of John II (for which the French paid three million gold crowns), the treaty was virtually a confirmation of the status quo at the time of its signing, and this was enormously in favor of the English. The territorial claims which they renounced applied to territories of which they were not, at the moment, in possession, and Edward III was confirmed in his title to all the vast duchy of Aquitaine (or Guienne, as it was still then often called) without fealty to the French crown. At the same time, feudal obligations were terminated with respect to English possession of various subfiefs, including Gascony, Poitou, Ponthieu, Aunis, Saintonge, Angoumois, and Calais (most of which, of course, fell within the area of Aquitaine). The treaty had no lasting effect whatever: the Hundred Years War was resumed almost immediately, and within less than 15 years the French were able to regain virtually everything which had been lost to them by the Treaty of Brétigny.

Breton (bret'ọn). [Also, **Armorican.**] Dialect of Brittany, imported into Brittany in the 5th and 6th centuries by Celtic emigrants from southwest Britain. Philologists distinguish three periods: ancient (5th to 11th centuries A.D.), middle (11th to 17th centuries), and modern (17th century to the present). There is also a regional breakdown into four distinct subdialects, each associated with a different city of Brittany. Breton is a member of the Cymric group of Celtic dialects, of which the closely allied Welsh is the only other living member.

Breton (brȩ.tôṅ), **André.** b. 1896—. French poet, essayist, and critic, leader of the surrealist school. He joined the Dadaist group in 1919 and collaborated with Philippe Soupault to write the important *Les Champs Magnétiques* (1924) a Dadaist experiment in automatic writing. Having become a surrealist (1924), he wrote the group's manifesto and the poem *Poisson soluble* (Eng. trans., *The Soluble Fish*). In 1930 he joined the Communists, taking orthodox surrealism with him. Critics disagree violently about the value of his later poetic work, *Point du jour* (1934), *L'Amour fou* (1937), and *Fata Morgana* (1942). His essay, *Qu'est-ce que le Surréalisme?* (1934; Eng. trans., *What is Surrealism?*, 1936), established him and his school as international phenomena of considerable importance in the literary world.

Breton, Émile Adélard. b. at Courrières, France, March 8, 1831; d. Nov. 26, 1902. French landscape painter; brother and pupil of Jules Adolphe Breton. He left the army to pursue his studies in art, and was decorated with the cross of the Legion of Honor in 1878. His favorite subjects were landscapes in autumn and winter, and at twilight or sunset.

Breton, Jules Adolphe (Aimé Louis). b. May 1, 1827; d. July 5, 1906. French genre painter; brother and teacher of Émile Adélard Breton. He was a pupil of Michel Drolling, and devoted himself to the representation of incidents taken from the life of the peasantry. In 1861 he was decorated with the cross of, and in 1889 became a commander of, the Legion of Honor. Among his best-known paintings are *Le Retour des moissonneurs* (1853), *Les Glaneuses* (1855), *La Bénédiction de blés* (1857), and *La Fin de la journée* (1865). He wrote poems, and an autobiography entitled *Vie d'un artiste, art et nature* (1890).

Breton (bret'ọn), **Nicholas.** [Also: **Brittaine, Britton.**] b. at London, c1545; d. c1626. English poet and prose writer; a stepson of George Gascoigne (c1525–77). Breton was a member of the special cult at Oxford associated with the memory of Sir Philip Sidney and having the patronage of his sister, the Countess of Pembroke. In 1592, Breton published at Oxford two long allegories which he inscribed to the countess: *The Pilgrimage to Paradise* and *Joined with the Countess of Pembroke's Love.* He was the author also of the pastoral *The Passionate Shepheard* (1604), *The Honour of Valour* (1605), and *The Fantasticks* (1626).

Breton (brȩ.tôṅ), **Raymond.** b. at Auxerre, France, 1609; d. at Caen, France, 1679. French Dominican missionary. From 1635 to 1643 he was in the French West Indies, most of the time living among the Caribs. He published several works on their language and customs.

Bretón (brā.tōn'), **Tomás.** [Full name, **Tomás Bretón y Hernández** (ē er.nän'dāth).] b. at Salamanca, Spain, Dec. 29, 1850; d. at Madrid, Dec. 2, 1923. Spanish composer, notably of operettas. He was director (1903 *et seq.*) of the Madrid Conservatory. His compositions other than operettas include *La Verbena de la Paloma* and other zarzuelas, operas, choral works, the oratorio *El Apocalipsis,* and a violin concerto.

Bretón de los Herreros (dā lōs er.rā'rōs), **Manuel.** b. at Quel, Logroño, Spain, Dec. 19, 1796; d. at Madrid, Nov. 13, 1873. Spanish dramatic and satiric poet, said to have been the author of more than 350 works of various kinds. He was also director (1847 *et seq.*) of the national library at Madrid. Among his comedies are *Los dos Sobrinos, El Ingenuo, El Hombre gordo,* and *Todo es farsa en este mundo.*

Bretonne (brȩ.ton), **Raitif de la.** See under **Lorrain, Jean.**

Bretonneau (brȩ.to.nō), **Pierre.** b. at Tours, France, April 3, 1778; d. Feb. 18, 1862. French physician and surgeon. He accomplished (1825) the first successful tracheotomy, and in his essay *Des inflammations spéciales du tissu muqueux et en particulier de la diphthérie* (1826) he first used the word which is translated into English as diphtheria. The originality of Bretonneau's thought is most strikingly shown by the fact that in 1855 he announced a theory of the origin and communication of infectious diseases which anticipated to some extent the germ theory of Pasteur.

Bretons (bret'ọnz). Natives of Brittany. Breton is the Old French word for Briton. Celtic emigrants from southwestern Britain settled in Brittany in the 5th and 6th centuries.

Bretschneider (bret'shnī''dėr), **Karl Gottlieb.** b. at Gersdorf, Germany, Feb. 11, 1776; d. at Gotha, Germany, Jan. 22, 1848. German Protestant theologian, general superintendent at Gotha (1816).

Brett (bret). Family name of **Esher,** Viscounts of.

Brett, George Howard. b. at Cleveland, Ohio, Feb. 7, 1886—. American soldier who served (1942–46) as head of the Caribbean defense command and the Panama Canal department. A graduate (1909) of the Virginia Military Institute, he was appointed a major general (1941). He was deputy supreme commander (1942) of the southwest Pacific area, and commander in chief (1942) of Allied air forces in Australia. He retired in 1946 with the rank of lieutenant general.

Brett, William Howard. b. at Braceville, Ohio, July 1, 1846; d. Aug. 24, 1918. American librarian, noted for the reforms he espoused in the library methods of his day. After being employed (1874 *et seq.*) as a bookstore clerk at Cleveland, he was appointed (1884) librarian of the Cleveland Public Library, where he greatly expanded the facilities (it is today one of the outstanding public libraries of the country). He organized (1894) the Library School of Western Reserve University, and founded the *Cumulative Index.*

Bretten (bret'ẹn). Town in SW Germany, in the *Land* (state) of Württemberg-Baden, American Zone, situated on the Saalbach River, ab. 15 mi. E of Karlsruhe. It has livestock markets, and metallurgical, machine, plastics, and paperware industries. It was the birthplace of the Reformation leader Melanchthon. Bretten belonged formerly to the Palatinate; it was sacked by the French in 1689; became part of Baden in 1805. The population is mixed, but predominantly Protestant. 8,447 (1946).

Bretton (bret'ọn), **Henry de.** See **Bracton, Henry de.**

Bretton Woods Conference. Name usually applied to the conference of representatives of 44 nations held in July, 1944, at Bretton Woods, N.H. The most noteworthy achievement of the conference was probably its detailed outline of plans for the International Bank for Reconstruction and Development and for the International Monetary Fund. The chief designers of these international financial structures were John Maynard Keynes of Great Britain and Harry D. White of the U.S. The U.S.S.R. took part only as an observer and had not, by 1952, joined either the Bank or Fund.

Breuckelen (brė'kẹ.lẹn). Original Dutch name of **Brooklyn.**

Breuer (broi'ėr), **Josef.** b. at Vienna, Jan. 15, 1842; d. there, June 20, 1925. Austrian physician. He became (1875) privatdocent of internal medicine and assistant, at Vienna, to J. von Oppolzer. He described the nervous mechanism which controls respiration by impulses mediated through the pulmonary vagi (called the Hering-Breuer reflex) and with Sigmund Freud introduced the cathartic treatment (questioning under hypnosis) which Freud later developed as a technique of his method of psychoanalysis.

Breuer, Marcel Lajos. b. at Pécs, Hungary, May 21, 1902—. Hungarian architect and industrial designer, now resident in the U.S. He first became known for his functional furniture constructed of tubular steel and plywood. Educated in Hungary and at the Bauhaus at Weimar, Germany, where he studied under Walter Gropius, he was director (1925–28) of the Bauhaus after it had been moved to Dessau. He pursued (1928–31) an independent architectural practice at Berlin, traveled widely, and practiced architecture (1935–37) at London. After coming to the U.S., he was in partnership with Gropius at Cambridge, Mass., and served as associate professor (1937 *et seq.*) at the Graduate School of Design at Harvard University. Always interested in prefabricated low-cost housing, he designed an example of such a house for exhibit (1949) in the garden at the Museum of Modern Art, New York. Among his writings are *Art in Our Time* (1939), *The Modern House* (1940), and *Design of Modern Interiors* (1942).

Breuer, Peter. b. May 19, 1856; d. at Berlin, May 2, 1930. German sculptor. He is known for his monumental sculptures in a naturalistic neo-baroque style, as well as for his statuettes and carvings in the applied arts. His group composition *Spring* (1891) was awarded a first prize at the Chicago World's Columbian Exposition (1893).

Breughel (brė'gẹl). See **Brueghel.**

Breuil (brėy'), **Henri Édouard Prosper.** b. at Mortani, France, Feb. 28, 1877—. French archaeologist. He served as professor of prehistoric ethnology at the Institut du Paléontologie Humaine, at Paris. Author of *L'Evolution de l'art quaternaire* (Evolution of Quaternery Art, 1909), and *Les Cavernes de la région cantabrique* (The Caverns of the Cantabrian Region, 1912).

Breul (broil), **Karl Hermann.** b. 1860; d. 1932. Professor of Germanics at Cambridge University. He was author of *The Romantic Movement in German Literature* (1927) and editor of *A Goliard's Song-Book of the XIth Century* (1915) and other German texts, as also of the revisions (1906 *et seq.*) of the *New German Dictionary.*

Breval (brev'ạl), **John Durant.** [Pseudonym, **Joseph Gay.**] b. c1680; d. at Paris, in January, 1738. English writer. He wrote much under the name of Joseph Gay. He attacked Alexander Pope under this pseudonym, and was in return held up to ridicule in Pope's *Dunciad.*

Brevard (brẹ.värd'). Town in W North Carolina, county seat of Transylvania County: at one time important for the manufacture of high hats ("beavers"). It is a summer resort in the Blue Ridge, and the seat of Brevard College. It was named for Ephraim Brevard, a Revolutionary soldier. 3,908 (1950).

Brévent (brā.väṅ). [Also, **Bréven.**] Mountain peak in E France, a summit of the Alps of the Mont Blanc group, NW of Chamonix. 8,285 ft.

Breviarium Alaricanum (brē.vi.är'i.um ạ.lar.i.kā'num). [Also: **Breviarium Alarici** (ạ.lar'i.sī), **Lex Romana Wisigothorum** (or **Visigothorum**); English, **Breviary of Alaric.**] Code of Roman law, compiled by direction of Alaric II, king of the Visigoths, and promulgated by him in 506 at Ayre (later Aire, in Gascony) for the use primarily of the people subject to him in Spain and what is now the S part of France. The compilation is now generally recognized as having been the most important made by any non-Roman ruler and was the chief source of Roman law in Western Europe until the rise during the 12th century of the law school at Bologna.

Brevoort (brẹ.vōrt', -vôrt'), **James Renwick.** b. in Westchester County, N.Y., July 20, 1832; d. Dec. 15, 1918. American painter, chiefly of landscapes. Renwick's schooling in his art was for the most part in Europe, and he traveled extensively in England and on the Continent, filling his sketchbooks with studies for future use. His landscapes are faithful to nature and technically expert. Among his better-known works are *Lake at Como, Storm on an English Moor, Morning in Early Winter, Scene in Holland, Heidelberg Castle at Sunset,* and *New England Scene.*

Brewer (brö'ėr). City in C Maine, in Penobscot County, on the Penobscot River opposite Bangor: manufactures pulp and paper. 6,862 (1950).

Brewer, Antony. fl. 1655. English dramatic writer. He wrote *The Love-sick King* (1655), which was reprinted as *The Perjured Nun.* He is possibly better known, however, from the fact that *Lingua, or the Combat of the Five Senses* (1607), and *The Merry Devil of Edmonton* (1608), were formerly ascribed to him. *The Country Girl* (1647), signed *T.B.,* was also at one time erroneously identified as his.

Brewer, David Josiah. b. June 20, 1837; d. March 28, 1910. American jurist; nephew of Stephen Johnson Field. Graduated from Yale in 1856 and from the Albany Law School in 1858, he served as a justice of the supreme court of Kansas (1870–84) and as a judge of a federal circuit court (1884–89), before being appointed (1889) an associate justice of the U.S. Supreme Court. In 1897 he was president of the commission appointed by President Cleveland to arbitrate a British-Venezuelan boundary dispute, and was a member of the tribunal that finally determined the Venezuelan boundary (Paris, 1899). He wrote *The Pew to the Pulpit* (1897), *The Twentieth Century from Another Viewpoint* (1899), *American Citizenship* (1902), and *The United States a Christian Nation* (1905).

Brewer, Ebenezer Cobham. b. 1810; d. 1897. English clergyman, schoolmaster, and miscellaneous writer; brother of John Sherren Brewer (1809–79). Graduated from Cambridge (1835), he was ordained a priest in the following year. His best-known work is *Dictionary of Phrase and Fable* (1870).

Brewer, John Sherren. b. at Norwich, England, 1809; d. in Essex, England, 1879. English historical writer and scholar; brother of Ebenezer Cobham Brewer (1810–97). He was graduated from Queen's College, Oxford in 1832, and became an honorary fellow there in 1870. A lecturer in classical literature (1839) and professor of English language and literature and lecturer in modern history (1855–77) at King's College, London, he was commissioned (1856) to prepare a calendar of Henry VIII's state papers. He was also principal of the Working Men's College, at London. He edited Aristotle's *Ethics* (1836), the works of Roger Bacon and Giraldus Cambrensis, Fuller's *Church History*, and the *Student's Hume* (1878).

Brewer, Thomas Mayo. b. at Boston, Nov. 21, 1814; d. Jan. 23, 1880. American ornithologist, notable for his contributions in the field of oölogy (which is the branch of ornithology that deals with the study of birds' eggs). Among his works are an edition of Alexander Wilson's *American Ornithology* (1840) and his own *North American Oölogy* (1857). He was associated with Spencer F. Baird and Robert Ridgway in the compilation of *History of North American Birds* (1875).

Brewer, William Henry. b. at Poughkeepsie, N.Y., Sept. 14, 1828; d. at New Haven, Conn., Nov. 2, 1910. American scientist. He studied at Heidelberg, Munich, and Paris, and served as professor of chemistry at the University of California (1863–64), and of agriculture at the Sheffield Scientific School, Yale University (1864–1903). He was engaged on the California Geological Survey (1860–64), on the topographical survey of Connecticut, and on the scientific survey of the Philippine Islands (1903). He also visited the arctic regions, and was president (1894–1909) of the Arctic Club. He published *Botany of California* (1875), and others.

Brewster (brö'stėr), **Benjamin.** b. at New Haven, Conn., Nov. 25, 1860; d. Feb. 2, 1941. American Protestant Episcopal clergyman; brother of Chauncey Bunce Brewster. He was rector at South Orange, N.J. (1891–95) and Colorado Springs, Colo. (1895–1906), and dean (1906–09) of Saint Mark's Cathedral at Salt Lake City, Utah. In 1909 he was named missionary bishop of Western Colorado and in 1916 bishop of Maine.

Brewster, Benjamin Harris. b. in Salem County, N.J., Oct. 13, 1816; d. at Philadelphia, April 4, 1888. American jurist. He was graduated from Princeton in 1834 and admitted to the Philadelphia bar in 1838. In 1867 he was appointed attorney general of Pennsylvania, and was U.S. attorney general in the period 1881–85.

Brewster, Chauncey Bunce. b. at Windham, Conn., Sept. 5, 1848; d. at Hartford, Conn., April 9, 1941. American Protestant Episcopal clergyman; brother of Benjamin Brewster. Ordained in 1873, he was rector at Rye, N.Y. (1873–81), Detroit (1881–85), Baltimore (1885–88), and Brooklyn, N.Y. (1888–97). He served as coadjutor bishop (1897–99) and as bishop (1899–1928) of Connecticut, resigning in 1928. Author of *Key of Life—Good Friday Addresses* (1894), *Aspects of Revelation* (1901), and *The Kingdom of God and American Life* (1912).

Brewster, Sir **David.** b. at Jedburgh, Scotland, Dec. 11, 1781; d. at Allerby, Montrose, Scotland, Feb. 10, 1868. Scottish physicist, noted especially for his discoveries in connection with the polarization of light. He invented (1816) the kaleidoscope, perfected (1849–50) the stereoscope, and developed for use in lighthouses a system of refractive beaming of light (the so-called dioptric system) which was adopted by the British government. He wrote a *Treatise on Optics* (1831), *More Worlds than One* (1854), *Memoirs . . . of Sir Isaac Newton* (1855), and others. In 1838 he became principal of the united colleges of St. Salvator and St. Leonard in the university of St. Andrews.

Brewster, George Thomas. b. at Kingston, Mass., Feb. 24, 1862; d. March 6, 1943. American sculptor, teacher, and lecturer, founder (1886) of the modeling class at the Art Students League of New York. He was educated at the Massachusetts State Normal Art School and at the École des Beaux-Arts at Paris. He taught at the Rhode Island School of Design and at Cooper Union, and his work is in many public buildings in the U.S., including the Providence, R.I., state house, the National Academy of Design, the Hall of Fame, the library of New York University, and the Brooklyn Institute of Arts and Sciences. Among his best-known pieces are *Thomas R. Proctor*, *Robert E. Lee*, *Indiana*, *Hope*, *Defense of the Flag*, *Greek Drama*, *Alexander Hamilton*, and *Victory and Peace*.

Brewster, Owen. [Full name, **Ralph Owen Brewster.**] b. at Dexter, Me., Feb. 22, 1888—. American politician. He served in the Maine house of representatives (1917–19, 1921–23) and in the state senate (1923–25). He was governor of Maine (1925–29) for two terms before going to the U.S. House of Representatives (1935–41) and the U.S. Senate (1941 *et seq.*). Brewster's opposition to the New Deal and Fair Deal programs of Presidents F. D. Roosevelt and Harry Truman has often made him the storm center of antiadministration fights in Congress.

Brewster, William. b. at Scrooby, Nottinghamshire, England, 1567; d. at Plymouth, Mass., April 10, 1644. English pioneer in America, one of the founders of the Plymouth colony in New England. He entered Cambridge University in 1580, but appears to have withdrawn within a few months. He subsequently (1583) joined the household of William Davison (himself of some note in history as secretary to Queen Elizabeth), and went with him on a mission to the Netherlands in 1584 and again in the period 1585–86. In 1589, Brewster returned to Scrooby, his family's home, where he was bailiff and postmaster from 1590 to 1608, and where he became a leading member of the congregation which withdrew (or "separated") from the Church of England in 1606. In 1608, this group (now known as "Pilgrims") emigrated to the Netherlands, and settled (1609) at Leiden. Brewster, now an elder of the church, here engaged in the printing of various dissenting tracts and religious works which had a wide circulation in England. In 1617 he returned to England to discuss with various officials the possibility of Pilgrim colonization in the New World. In 1620, he was one of those who sailed to America on the *Mayflower*, serving as chief religious leader of the group. At Plymouth, he was at first the only elder of the church, and, although not ordained and thus unable to administer any sacraments, was for almost a decade the only religious leader the colony had. In 1627 he was one of the "Undertakers," the group which "undertook" (or obligated itself) to pay off the debt to the company which had financed the voyage and the Plymouth settlement.

Brewster, William. b. at Wakefield, Mass., July 5, 1851; d. July 11, 1919. American ornithologist. He was curator of birds in the Museum of Comparative Zoology of Harvard University from 1900. His works include *Descriptions of the First Plumage in Various North American Birds* (1878–79), *Bird Migration* (1886), and *Birds of the Cape Region of Lower California* (1902).

Brewster's Millions. Fantasy by George Barr McCutcheon, published in 1902, and dramatized (1906) by Winchell Smith.

Brewton (brö'tọn). City in S Alabama, county seat of Escambia County, ab. 64 mi. NE of Mobile. 5,146 (1950).

Brézé (brā.zā), Comtesse **de.** A title of **Diane de Poitiers.**

Březina (bėr.zhe'zē.nä), **Otokar.** [Pseudonym of **Václav Jebavý.**] b. at Počátky, in Bohemia, 1868; d. 1929. Czech poet, notable as a leader of the symbolist movement in the literature of his country.

Bri (brē). Irish name of **Bray.**

Brialmont (brē.ȧl.môṅ), **Henri Alexis.** b. May 25, 1821; d. at Brussels, June 21, 1903. Belgian general and writer on military affairs. His works include *Considérations politiques et militaires sur la Belgique* (1851–52), *Précis d'art militaire* (1851), and *Histoire du duc de Wellington* (1856–57).

Brialmont Bay. See **Hughes Bay.**

Briana (brī.ā'nạ). In Edmund Spenser's *The Faerie Queene*, the owner of a strong castle, who could not obtain the love of Crudor unless she made him a mantle of "beards of knights and locks of ladies." No one was allowed to pass her domain without paying this toll.

Brian Boroimhe, or The Maid of Erin (brī'ạn bō.rö'). Play (1811) by James Sheridan Knowles, adapted from an earlier work of the same name. ("Brian Boroimhe" is the

Irish king and national hero more usually found in American references as "Brian Boru.")

Brian Boru (brī'an bō.rö'). [Also: **Brian Boroimhe** or **Borumha.**] b. 926; killed at Clontarf, Ireland, on Good Friday, 1014. Irish king and one of the principal national heroes of Ireland. He became sovereign of Munster c978, and principal king of Ireland in 1002. Many times victorious over the Danes, he was murdered (either by a Dane, or by one of the Irish allies of the Danes) in his tent after his victory (April 23, 1014) at Clontarf, near Dublin, had ended for all time the possibility of Scandinavian dominance in Ireland.

Briançon (brē.äṅ.sôṅ). [Latin, **Brigantio, Brigantium.**] Town in SE France, in the department of Hautes-Alpes, situated on the Durance River near the junction of that river with the Guisane River at the foot of Mont Genèvre and the Croix-de-Toulouse, in the vicinity of the Italian frontier. It is a tourist center, noted for the mountain climbing available nearby, and for winter sports. It has old fortifications erected by Vauban, and is still a strongly fortified frontier post with a large garrison. The town was severely damaged during World War II. 6,671 (1946).

Briand (brē.äṅ), **Aristide.** b. at Nantes, France, March 28, 1862; d. at Paris, March 7, 1932. French statesman, eleven times premier of France. He played a leading role in French political life for three decades (1902–32). Trained as a lawyer, he early became a leader of the Socialist Party and editor in chief of the newspaper *La Lanterne.* He served (1902–19) in the Chamber of Deputies, first from St.-Étienne and later representing a constituency in Loire-Inférieure. He held the ministry of public instruction (1906), and served as minister of justice (1908–09), premier and minister of the interior (1909–11, 1913), minister of justice (1912–13), minister of justice (1914–15), premier and foreign minister (1915–17, 1921–22, 1929), and foreign minister (1925, 1926–29, 1929–32). Though initially an advocate (1894 *et seq.*) of the general strike as an effective weapon of labor against its employers, he later disavowed this and gradually broke with the socialist movement. In 1905 he successfully sponsored a moderate program for separating the French state and the Catholic Church; in 1906 he split with the Socialists on the issue of participation in the government; and in 1910 he defeated the railwaymen's strike by mobilization of the striking reservists and other equally decisive measures. During World War I, he backed the maintenance of an Anglo-French force in the Near East and the establishment of a joint Allied economic and military program. He sought, but did not achieve, the dethronement of Constantine I of Greece (Constantine's emphasis on Greek neutrality in World War I was opposed by the Allies, for obvious reasons; in 1917, through a combination of Allied and popular Greek pressure, he was compelled to relinquish his throne, but Briand had then already been forced to resign as French premier by Lyautey's withdrawal as his war minister). After the war, Briand, as premier and foreign minister, supported moderate policies in domestic and foreign affairs, reopened diplomatic relations with the Vatican, negotiated the Locarno accords (1925), and signed, with the U.S. secretary of state, Frank B. Kellogg, the Briand-Kellogg Pact (1928), renouncing war as an instrument of national policy. In 1926 he shared the Nobel peace prize with the German foreign minister, Gustav Stresemann.

Brian de Bois-Guilbert (brē.äṅ dẹ bwä.gēl.ber). See **Bois-Guilbert, Brian de.**

Briand-Kellogg Pact. [Official name, **Pact of Paris.**] Treaty signed (Aug. 27, 1928) at Paris by 15 nations and later endorsed by 48 other governments. The signatory powers agreed to renounce war as "an instrument of national policy" and to seek the settlement of disputes by pacific means. The treaty was the final and formal result of informal negotiations between James T. Shotwell of Columbia University and Foreign Minister Aristide Briand of France. The official U.S. representative to the treaty meeting was Frank B. Kellogg, then secretary of state. Nicholas Murray Butler, president of Columbia University, and Senator W. E. Borah were among its supporters in the U.S.

Brianza (brē.än'tsä). District in N Italy, in the *compartimento* (region) of Lombardy, between Lake Como and Lake Lecco. It is noted for its fertility.

Briar Creek. River in E Georgia, in Severn County, which joins the Savannah River, ab. 57 mi. SE of Augusta. Here, in March, 1778, the British under Augustine Prevort defeated the Americans under John Ashe.

Briar Creek, Battle of. Engagement (March, 1778) in the Revolutionary War, fought at Briar Creek, Severn County, Ga., between American Continentals and militia led by Colonel John Ashe and a British force under General Augustine Prevost. The Americans suffered a heavy defeat, and lost 150 killed to 19 for the British. By this defeat also, the Americans lost the approaches to the Carolinas, and thus permitted their control by the British, with a possible consequent lengthening of the war.

Briareus (brī.ār'ẹ.us). [Also, **Aegaeon.**] In Greek mythology, a monster with a hundred arms, a son of Uranus and Ge.

Briary-Bush, The. Novel by Floyd Dell, published in 1921 as a sequel to *Moon-Calf* (1920).

Brice (brīs), **Saint.** b. at Tours, France; d. there, Nov. 13, 444. French prelate, made bishop of Tours on the death of Saint Martin. He is commemorated on Nov. 13. On Saint Brice's day, 1002, there was a massacre of the Danes in England by order of Ethelred.

Brice, Calvin Stewart. b. at Denmark, Ohio, Sept. 17, 1845; d. at New York, Dec. 15, 1898. American politician. He was graduated from Miami University (at Oxford, Ohio) in 1863, and was admitted to the bar in 1866. He served with the Union army in the Civil War, was identified with railroad interests in the U.S. and China, was chairman of the Democratic campaign committee which conducted the national campaign in 1888, and was U.S. senator from Ohio in the period 1891–97.

Brice, Fanny. [Original surname, **Borach.**] b. at New York, Oct. 29, 1891; d. at Hollywood, Calif., May 29, 1951. American actress, best known as a comedienne. She played during the 1920's and 1930's in musical shows, the *Ziegfeld Follies,* and a number of motion pictures. In 1936 she began to portray on the radio the character of "Baby Snooks," an irrepressible little girl, which she played up to the time of her death.

Briceno (brē.sā'nō), **Ramon.** b. 1814; d. 1882. Chilean bibliophile and author. In 1840 he was chosen professor of philosophy and natural law at the Chilean University, and in 1864 was named director of the national library. He held various judicial offices. Besides books on law and philosophy, he published *Estadistica bibliografica de la literatura Chilena.* His private library was one of the largest in South America.

Brick (brik), **Jefferson.** In Charles Dickens's *Martin Chuzzlewit,* a correspondent for a New York journal. He is of excessively mild and youthful aspect, but bloodthirsty in the extreme in his political views.

Bricker (brik'ėr), **John William.** b. on a farm near Mount Sterling, Madison County, Ohio, Sept. 6, 1893—. American politician, unsuccessful Republican vice-presidential candidate in 1944. He was governor of Ohio for three terms, and in 1946 became a U.S. senator from Ohio. After serving in the Chaplain's Corps during World War I, he held public office almost uninterruptedly from 1920 to 1944. As governor of Ohio, he strongly advocated states' rights and won national attention by transforming a treasury deficit of 40 million dollars into a surplus of 90 million dollars within six years.

Bricks and Mortar. Novel by Helen Ashton, published in 1932.

Bricks without Straw. Novel by Albion W. Tourgée, published in 1880. Set against a North Carolina background, it deals with the status of the Negro during the Reconstruction era. Tourgée advocated the betterment of education, arguing that the federal government should allocate funds in proportion to the illiteracy of the various communities.

Bridal of Triermain (trī.ėr.mān'), **The.** Poem by Sir Walter Scott, published in 1813. It is the first experiment by a 19th-century poet with the King Arthur legend. In it Scott tells as an Arthurian story the tale of the Sleeping Beauty (and thus crosses different strains of folklore with the easy license usually associated with medieval, rather than modern, romancers).

Bridal Veil. Waterfall in the Yosemite valley (and in Yosemite National Park), California. The height of the main fall is 620 ft. and that of the cascades ab. 300 ft. The total fall (nearly vertical) is ab. 900 ft.

Bride (brīd), Saint. See **Brigid** (*cf Kildare*), Saint.

Bride of Abydos (ą.bī'dos), **The.** Poem by Byron, a Turkish tale, published in 1813. A melodrama adapted from the poem was produced c1819.

Bride of Genoa (jen'ǫ.ą). Romantic drama by Epes Sargent. It was first played at the Tremont Theatre, Boston, on February 13, 1837, with Josephine Clifton playing the leading role. It deals with the struggle between the patrician and plebeian orders at Genoa in 1393.

Bride of Lammermoor (lam'ėr.mör), **The.** Novel by Sir Walter Scott, published in 1819. Several plays have been written on the subject, notably one by J. W. Cole under the pseudonym John William Calcraft, also called *The Bride of Lammermoor.* The opera *Lucia di Lammermoor*, by Gaetano Donizetti, is also based on this novel. The titular heroine of the novel is Lucy Ashton. She is in love with, and loved by, the Master of Ravenswood, an impoverished laird who regards Lucy's father as the cause of his family's ruin. However, under the influence of Lucy's affection, his wrath softens; nevertheless, although Lucy's father consents to the match, her mother forbids it, ordering her daughter instead to marry the Laird of Bucklaw. Lucy's letter to Ravenswood, apprising him of the situation, is intercepted, so that he remains for too long ignorant of the circumstances, and returns to Lucy just as the wedding ceremony with Bucklaw is ended. Ravenswood immediately challenges Lucy's brother and husband to a duel for the next day; but before this event can take place, Lucy, on her wedding night, stabs her husband to death, and is found in a state of hopeless insanity.

Bride of the Mistletoe, The. Novel by James Lane Allen, published in 1909.

Bridewell (brīd'wel). London prison, or house of detention, most of which had been demolished by 1864. It was founded upon a favorite palace of Henry VIII, which stood at the mouth of the Fleet between Blackfriars and Whitefriars. There was a royal residence here as early as the reign of Henry III, if not that of John. Henry VIII is said to have rebuilt the palace, and he and Catherine of Aragon lived there when the cardinals convened to rule on their divorce in Blackfriars opposite. In 1553 Edward VI gave his father's palace of Bridewell to the city of London for a workhouse, and formulated a system of municipal charity. It later became a temporary prison or house of detention, with which use its name is especially familiar. In old views and maps it appears as a castellated building of some architectural pretensions. The name has become a generic term for a house of correction or jail.

Bridge (brij), **Ann.** English novelist and short-story writer. The name "Ann Bridge" is a pseudonym; the writer's actual identity (and such vital statistics as the date and place of her birth) remain a secret known only to a few. Her books include *Peking Picnic* (1932), *The Ginger Griffin* (1934), *Illyrian Spring* (1935), *Enchanter's Nightshade* (1937), *Four-Part Setting* (1939), *Frontier Passage* (1942), *Singing Waters* (1945), and *The Dark Moment* (1952).

Bridge, Frank. b. at Brighton, England, Feb. 26, 1879; d. 1941. English composer and conductor. He was leader of the New Symphony Orchestra at London. His works include string quartets in E Minor (1904) and G Minor (1905), a piano quintet (1905), string sextet, piano sonata, the tone poems *Isabella* (1907) and *Suite for Summer* (1914), and *Lament* (1915) for strings.

Bridge, Sir **John Frederick.** b. at Oldbury, England, Dec. 5, 1844; d. at London, March 18, 1924. English organist and composer; brother of Joseph Cox Bridge (1853–1929). He was professor (1872–75) of harmony at Manchester, organist (1869–75) at Manchester cathedral, and permanent deputy-organist (1875–82) and organist (1882–1918) of Westminster Abbey. He composed oratorios, cantatas, and shorter liturgical works, as well as motets, songs, and choral ballads.

Bridge, Joseph Cox. b. at Rochester, England, Aug. 16, 1853; d. 1929. English organist; brother of Sir John Frederick Bridge (1844–1924). Organist (1877–1925) at Chester Cathedral, he reëstablished (1879) the Chester Musical Festivals. He was also a professor (1908 *et seq.*) at Durham University and director (1925 *et seq.*) of the Trinity College of Music.

Bridge, The. Poem by Henry Wadsworth Longfellow, published in *The Belfry of Bruges and Other Poems* (1845).

Bridge, The. Volume of poems by Hart Crane, published in 1930. In this series of poems, theoretically bound together by the symbol of the Brooklyn Bridge, Crane attempted to achieve a synthesis, in verse, of the essential meaning of America. Despite the fact that the poems are only theoretically unified (and that *The Bridge*, as a whole, is now considered by most critics to have been for this reason a failure), the book contains passages of considerable magnificence, and remains one of the most ambitious attempts by a contemporary American poet to deal with the entirety of his country's culture.

Bridgend (brij.end'). Urban district and market town in S Wales, in Glamorganshire, situated on the river Ogmore, ab. 20 mi. W of Cardiff, ab. 165 mi. W of London by rail. It has the ruins of an ancient castle. The town is located on the South Wales coal field. 13,646 (1951).

Bridgenorth (brij'nôrth), **Alice.** Principal female character in Sir Walter Scott's *Peveril of the Peak.*

Bridge of San Luis Rey (san lö''is rā'; Spanish, sän lö.ēs' rā'), **The.** Novel by Thornton Wilder, published in 1927. A best seller, it was awarded a Pulitzer prize in 1928. The book cleverly packs the life stories of five unrelated persons within a pseudo-philosophical framework. All five people were killed when a bridge near Lima, Peru, collapsed in the year 1714. Their individual stories present a variety of human dilemmas with telling sympathy. The story is supposedly a compilation by the Franciscan friar, Brother Juniper, who is burned as a heretic for attempting to prove that the disaster was the work of divine providence.

Bridge of Sighs. Bridge in Venice which spans the Rio della Paglia, and connects the ducal palace with the Carceri, or prisons. The bridge dates from 1597; it is an elliptical arch, ab. 32 ft. above the water, enclosed at the sides and arched overhead. It contains two separate passages, through which prisoners were led for trial or judgment (and it was from their plaints at this circumstance that the bridge gained its name).

Bridge of Sighs. Poem by Thomas Hood, composed in 1844.

Bridgeport (brij'pōrt). [Former name, **Newfield.**] City in SW Connecticut, a county seat of Fairfield County, on an inlet of Long Island Sound. It is one of the chief manufacturing cities in the state, producing airplanes, typewriters, hardware, brake linings, electrical equipment, plastics, textiles, brassware, rubber goods, and pharmaceuticals. In the 19th century it was an important whaling port. It has a university. 158,709 (1950).

Bridgeport. [Former name, **Canton.**] Village in E Ohio, in Belmont County: residential community near Wheeling, W. Va. It was platted in 1806 and received its present name in 1836. Pop. 4,309 (1950).

Bridgeport. Borough in SE Pennsylvania, in Montgomery County, on the Schuylkill River, in a stone-quarrying area: manufactures of wool textiles, coke, and iron. 5,827 (1950).

Bridger (brij'ėr), **Fort.** Trading post on Black's Fork, Uinta County, Wyo., built (1843) by the scout and trapper James Bridger, and his associate, Louis Vasquez. It was important as a stopping place for emigrants going to California, Oregon, and Utah. Mormons took over the post in 1855, and in 1857 the U.S. army converted it into a military post. It was garrisoned by troops until 1890.

Bridger, James. [Called **"Jim" Bridger.**] b. at Richmond, Va., March 17, 1804; d. July 17, 1881. American scout and fur trader. The first white man to visit (1824) Great Salt Lake, Utah, he later guided Albert Sidney Johnston's troops in their Utah campaign (1857–58), an expedition (1859–60) to the Yellowstone, and an engineering party (1861). With his partner, Louis Vasquez, he built (1843) Fort Bridger on Black's Fork, in Wyoming.

Bridges (brij'ez), **Calvin Blackman.** b. at Schuyler Falls, N.Y., Jan. 11, 1889; d. Dec. 27, 1938. American geneticist. He did research (1915–19) under Carnegie Institution grants, and was associated with the Carnegie Institution from 1919. He was one of the original members of the group of geneticists whose work with *Drosophila*, the common fruit fly, was the source of some of the most important concepts and facts of modern genetics, including definite proof of the vital part played by chromosomes in conveying hereditary characteristics from one generation of living organisms to the next. Author of *The Mechanism of Mendelian Heredity* (1915), *Sex-linked Inheritance in Drosophila* (1916, with T. H. Morgan), and *Genetics of Drosophila* (1925).

Bridges, Harry. [Full name, **Alfred Bryant Renton Bridges.**] b. at Melbourne, Australia, in July or August, 1900—. American labor leader. He came (1920) to the U.S., and became (1945) a naturalized citizen. He worked (1922 *et seq.*) as a longshoreman at San Francisco, where he was a founder and president (1936 *et seq.*) of an independent longshoreman's union which was engaged in a violent shipping strike (1934) at San Francisco. Subsequently he was Pacific Coast director for the Congress of Industrial Organizations, but was ousted from this post after supporting (1948) Henry Wallace for the presidency. In 1950 he was sentenced to five years in prison on a charge of perjury, when a jury found that he had sworn falsely, at his naturalization proceedings, that he had never been a member of the Communist party. (However, he was freed from jail, under bail of 25 thousand dollars, pending his appeal, by a 2–1 decision of the 9th Federal Circuit Court of Appeals, at San Francisco, on Aug. 24, 1950. The majority decision of the court was that "a Bridges . . . jailed by arbitrary judicial action while he is prosecuting with diligence his good-faith appeal poses . . . a more serious menace to the nation and its institutions than does a Bridges enlarged on bail in accordance with the established rules of law . . .") Prior to this, on June 20, 1950, Bridges had lost his U.S. citizenship, and was declared by a U.S. court at San Francisco to be a "legal alien." He remained, while free on bail, active in the labor unions of the extreme left, and won his appeal in 1953.

Bridges, John Henry. b. at Old Newton, Suffolk, England, Oct. 11, 1832; d. at Tunbridge Wells, Kent, England, June 15, 1906. English positivist philosopher, physician, translator, and editor. Educated at the Rugby School, and at Wadham College, Oxford, where he received a medical degree in 1859, he was medical inspector (1870–98) for London, and lecturer (1870–1900) in philosophy at the London Positivist Society. He contributed many articles to the *Positivist Review*, and wrote the introductions to several sections and a large part of the biographical section in *New Calendar of Great Men* (1892). He also wrote *The Unity of Comte's Life and Doctrine—A Reply to J. S. Mill* (1866), *Five Discourses on Positive Religion* (1882), and *Life and Work of Roger Bacon* (1914); translated Auguste Comte's *General View of Positivism* (1865) and *System of Positive Polity* (1875); and edited (1897–1900) Roger Bacon's *Opus Majus*.

Bridges, Robert. [Full name, **Robert Seymour Bridges.**] b. at Walmer, England, Oct. 23, 1844; d. 1930. English poet and essayist, appointed poet laureate in 1913. Educated at Eton and Oxford, he subsequently traveled widely in Egypt, Syria, and Germany. He also served as a physician in various London hospitals until 1881, when he gave up the practice of medicine. His first book, *Poems by Robert Bridges*, was published in 1873. Further volumes of poetry appeared from time to time, and in 1929 was published *The Testament of Beauty*, his swan song and greatest poetical work. Bridges wrote several plays, as follows: *Prometheus the Firegiver* (1883), *Nero* (Parts I, 1885, and II, 1894), *The Feast of Bacchus, Palicio, The Return of Ulysses* (1890), *The Christian Captives, Achilles in Scyros, The Humours of the Court*, and *Demeter*. He was deeply interested in prosody, and in addition to his own unusual experiments in English versification, he wrote of the prosody of John Milton (1893; final revision, 1921) and John Keats. His publication, in 1918, of the poems of his friend Gerard Manley Hopkins first brought that poet before the general public. He wrote hymns, odes which were set to music, and edited the *Yattendon Hymnal*. He was greatly interested in the history of the English language and its present-day use, including its pronunciation and spelling. In 1913, with Logan Pearsall Smith, Walter Raleigh, and others, he founded the Society for Pure English, and wrote and contributed to many of the Society's tracts. He was much concerned with the physical appearance of his published writings. After 1887 most of his books were printed and published by the Oxford University Press. Later in life Bridges developed a phonetic spelling, and a phonetic alphabet which was cast in a face based on Blado italic. Before his death this alphabet contained 39 characters, and was later expanded to 54 by his widow.

Bridges, Robert. [Pseudonym, **Droch.**] b. at Shippensburg, Pa., July 13, 1858; d. Sept. 2, 1941. American author, editor, and critic. Graduated from Princeton in 1879, he was a reporter for the Rochester *Democrat and Chronicle* in 1880, assistant news-editor (1881–87) of the New York *Evening Post*, literary reviewer (1883–1900) for *Life*, and assistant editor (1887 *et seq.*) of *Scribner's Magazine*. He was the author of *Overheard in Arcady* (1894), *Suppressed Chapters and Other Bookishness* (1895), and *Bramble Brae* (1902), a volume of poems.

Bridges, Styles. [Full name, **Henry Styles Bridges.**] b. at West Pembroke, Me., Sept. 4, 1898—. American politician. After working as a county agent and extension specialist for the University of New Hampshire's agricultural program, he served (1922–24) as secretary of the New Hampshire Farm Bureau, and as a member (1930–35) of the public service commission. He became governor of New Hampshire in 1935, serving until 1937, when he took his seat in the U.S. Senate; he was reëlected to the Senate in 1942 and 1948.

Bridget (brij'ẹt), Saint. See also **Brigid** (*of Kildare*), Saint.

Bridget (*of Sweden*), Saint. [Also: **Birgida, Birgit, Birgitta, Brigit, Brigitta.**] b. at Finstad, in Upland, Sweden, c1303; d. at Rome, July 23, 1373. Swedish nun. She was related to the royal family of Sweden. On the death of her husband, Ulf Gudmarson, in 1344, she decided to found an order, and obtained the papal confirmation of the proposed rule (regula Sancti Salvatoris) from Urban V in 1367, the order being established in 1370. She endeavored to get the popes to return to Rome from Avignon, and was also the author of *Revelationes*, which were denounced by the French theologian, Jean de Gerson, but which were nevertheless confirmed by the Council of Basel. She was canonized on Oct. 7, 1391, by Pope Boniface I.

Bridget, Mrs. See **Credulous, Justice, and Mrs. Bridget.**

Bridgeton (brij'tọn). City in SW New Jersey, county seat of Cumberland County, on Cohansey Creek, ab. 36 mi. S of Philadelphia: canning center for fruits and vegetables; manufactures glass. 18,378 (1950).

Bridgetown (brij'toun). City in SW Barbados, British West Indies, on the Caribbean Sea: capital of Barbados; exports sugar and rum. Pop. ab. 14,000.

Bridgeville (brij'vil). Borough in SW Pennsylvania, in Allegheny County, on Chartiers Creek, near Pittsburgh: manufactures chemicals and metals. It was incorporated in 1901. Pop. 5,650 (1950).

Bridgewater (brij'wô''tėr, -wot''ėr). Town (in Massachusetts the equivalent of township in many other states) and unincorporated village in SE Massachusetts, in Plymouth County, ab. 26 mi. S of Boston: manufactures cotton textiles. Seat of a state teachers college. Pop. of town, 9,512 (1950); of village, 3,445 (1950).

Bridgewater. Town in Nova Scotia, Canada, situated on the S shore of the province at the head of the Lahave River estuary, ab. 68 mi. W of Halifax: lumbering center, rail junction and fishing port. 4,010 (1951).

Bridgewater, Dukes and Earls of. See under **Egerton.**

Bridgewater Canal. Canal in W and NW England, in Cheshire and Lancashire. It extends from Manchester to Runcorn, near Liverpool, roughly paralleling the route of the Manchester Ship Canal. The traffic consists of barges up to 80 tons (called in England, from their wide use on the waterways connecting with the Mersey River, at Liverpool, "Mersey flats"). Length, 40 mi.

Bridgewater House. The town residence of Francis Egerton, 1st Earl of Ellesmere, at London, built in the period 1847–49 on the site of the former Cleveland House.

Bridgewater Madonna, The. Small painting (1512) by Raphael, in the great 19th-century collection of Bridgewater House, London. The Child lies on the Virgin's knees and clutches her veil.

Bridgewater Treatises. Series of treatises written in compliance with the terms of the will of Francis Henry Egerton, 8th Earl of Bridgewater, who died in 1829. He left 8,000 pounds to be paid to the author of the best treatise on "The Goodness of God as manifested in the Creation." Those with whom the selection of the author was left decided to give the subject to eight persons for separate treatises. These were *The Adaptation of External Nature to the Moral and Intellectual Constitution of Man* (Thomas Chalmers, 1833), *Chemistry, Meteorology, and Digestion* (William Prout, 1834), *History, Habits, and Instincts of Animals* (Kirby, 1835), *Geology and Mineralogy* (Dean Buckland, 1836), *The Hand, as evincing Design* (Sir Charles Bell, 1833), *The Adaptation of External Nature to the Physical Condition of Man* (J. Kidd, M.D., 1833), *Astronomy and General Physics* (William Whewell, 1833), and *Animal and Vegetable Physiology* (P. M. Roget, M.D., 1834).

Bridgman (brij'mạn), **Elijah Coleman.** b. at Belchertown, Mass., April 22, 1801; d. in China, Nov. 2, 1861. American missionary in China, believed to have been the first American Protestant missionary in that country. Arrived (1830) at Canton, he was there associated (1834) with the Society for the Diffusion of Useful Knowledge. He was a founder (1838) of the Morrison Education Society and Medical Missionary Society in China, and was founder (1832) and editor (until 1847) of the *Chinese Repository*. He wrote *Chinese Chrestomathy* (1841), and published (1862) a translation of the Bible into Chinese.

Bridgman, Frederic Arthur. b. at Tuskegee, Ala., 1847; d. Jan. 13, 1927. American genre painter; a pupil of Jean Léon Gérôme. He was resident for most of his professional career at Paris. His subjects were chiefly Eastern.

Bridgman, Herbert Lawrence. b. at Amherst, Mass., May 30, 1844; d. at sea, Sept. 24, 1924. American newspaperman and explorer, now remembered chiefly for his association with the arctic expeditions of Robert E. Peary. He was business manager (1887 *et seq.*) of the Brooklyn *Standard Union*. In 1894 he accompanied Peary on the *Falcon* expedition, and in 1899 led the *Diana* expedition for the relief of Peary. A cape in NE Greenland was named after him by Peary. The first to be informed (Sept. 6, 1909) of Peary's discovery of the North Pole, he helped to discredit F. A. Cook's claims to previous discovery. He also scaled (1897) Mesa Encantada, in New Mexico, and traveled (1904) to the headwaters of the Nile.

Bridgman, Laura Dewey. b. at Hanover, N.H., Dec. 21, 1829; d. at South Boston, Mass., May 24, 1889. Blind deaf-mute, noted as the first to be educated by methods which were the 19th-century progenitors of the ones now used for those similarly handicapped. Having lost sight and hearing, and having been partially deprived of the senses of taste and smell by scarlet fever at two years of age, she was placed in the blind asylum at South Boston at the age of eight, where she was educated by means of a raised alphabet (in some ways resembling the Braille System) devised by the principal, Dr. S. G. Howe. She was later a teacher under Howe, at the Perkins Institution (now located at Watertown, Mass.).

Bridgman, Percy Williams. b. at Cambridge, Mass., April 21, 1882—. American physicist and teacher, awarded (1946) the Nobel prize in physics for his investigations of various phenomena related to extremely high pressures. He was graduated from Harvard University (B.A., 1904; M.A., 1905; Ph.D., 1908), and became (1910) an instructor in physics at Harvard, where he was appointed (1926) Hollis professor of mathematics and natural history. He served (1942) as president of the American Physical Society. His works include *Dimensional Analysis* (1922), *The Logic of Modern Physics* (1927), *The Physics of High Pressure* (1931), *The Nature of Physical Theory* (1936), and *The Nature of Thermodynamics* (1941).

Bridgnorth (brij'nôrth). [Also, **Bridgenorth.**] Municipal borough, market town, and manufacturing center in W England, in Shropshire, situated on a hill overlooking the river Severn, ab. 18 mi. SE of Shrewsbury, ab. 146 mi. NW of London by rail. It is noted for its carpet industry. Its castle was taken by Henry I in 1102, by Henry II in 1157, and by the Parliamentarians in 1646, at which time it was demolished, only a fragment now remaining. 6,244 (1951).

Bridgton (brij'tọn). Town (in Maine the equivalent of township in many other states) and unincorporated village in SW Maine, in Cumberland County. The center of a summer and winter resort area, it also manufactures woolens. Pop. of town, 2,950 (1950); of village, 1,866 (1950).

Bridgwater (brij'wô"tėr, -wot"ėr). [Also, **Bridgewater.**] Municipal borough, seaport, holiday resort, and tourist center in SW England, in Somersetshire, situated on the river Parret near its mouth, ab. 29 mi. SW of Bristol, ab. 151 mi. SW of London by rail: an important port for coastal traffic. The river is navigable to vessels of 200 tons as far as the town. It is the only place in Britain where Bath bricks, a coarse, unbaked brick used for polishing metals, is made. It was the birthplace of Robert Blake. Near it are Sedgemoor, to the E, and the Quantock Hills, to the W. The town was taken by the Royalists in 1643, and by the Parliamentarians in 1645. It declared for the Duke of Monmouth in his attempt (1685) to wrest the English throne from James II. Pop. 22,221 (1951).

Bridlington (brid'ling.tọn; locally, bėr'ling tọn). Municipal borough, market town, and seaside resort in NE England, in the East Riding of Yorkshire, situated on Bridlington Bay, ab. 23 mi. N of Hull, ab. 228 mi. N of London by rail. The borough includes the old town of Bridlington, 1 mi. inland. Bridlington Quay, on the coast, is the seaside resort. 24,767 (1951).

Bridoie (brē.dwȧ). [English equivalent, **Bridlegoose.**] In François Rabelais's *Gargantua and Pantagruel*, a naïve and placidly ignorant judge who decides cases by means of dice. This he considers the most natural method. The character is a trenchant satire on the judicial proceedings of the day.

Brid'oison (brē.dwȧ.zôṅ). In *Le Mariage de Figaro*, by Jean Augustin Caron de Beaumarchais, a pretentious judge, taken from the Bridoie of François Rabelais.

Bridport (brid'pōrt). Municipal borough and seaport in S England, in Dorsetshire, situated on the river Brit ab. 14 mi. NW of Dorchester, ab. 149 mi. SW of London by rail. 6,273 (1951).

Brie (brē). Historical territory in N France, situated E of Paris. It is a level region, noted for its grain and for dairy products, especially for its cheese. It was divided into the Brie Française (in Île-de-France), whose capital was Brie-Comte-Robert, and the Brie Champenoise (in Champagne). The latter was subdivided into Haute-Brie, capital Meaux; Basse-Brie, capital Provins; and Brie-Pouilleuse, capital Château-Thierry. It was a county under the successors of Charlemagne. Later it generally followed the fortunes of Champagne.

Brie, Théodore de. See **Bry** or **Brie, Théodore de.**

Brief History of the War with the Indians in New-England. Prose work (1676) by Increase Mather. In it he describes King Philip's War, which had just ended, as evidence of his contention that to be lax as a Christian was to perish.

Briefs (brēfs), **Götz.** b. at Eschweiler, Germany, Jan. 1, 1889—. German economist. He has served as a professor (1919 *et seq.*) at Freiburg and Berlin, and is the author of *Untersuchungen zur klassischen Nationalökonomie* (Studies in Classical Political Economics, 1915) and *Das moderne Proletariat* (The Modern Proletariat, 1926).

Brieg (brēg). See also **Brigue.**

Brieg (brēk). German name of **Brzeg.**

Brieger (brē'gėr), **Johann Friedrich Theodor.** b. at Greifswald, Germany, 1842; d. 1915. German Protestant theologian and historian. He served as professor of church history at the University of Marburg (1873 *et seq.*) and the University of Leipzig (1886 *et seq.*), and was editor of *Zeitschrift für Kirchengeschichte*. An authority on the history of the Reformation, he wrote *Quellen und Forschungen zur Geschichte der Reformation* (1884).

Brienne (brē.en) or **Brienne-le-Château** (brē.en.lẹ.shä-tō). Town in N central France, in the department of Aube, ab. 23 mi. NE of Troyes. It contained, until 1790, a military school which was attended (1779–84) by Napoleon I. Here, on Jan. 29, 1814, Napoleon defeated the Allies under Blücher. Pop. ab. 2,000.

Brienne, Étienne Charles de Lomenie de. See **Lomenie de Brienne, Étienne Charles.**

Brienz (brē.ents'). Town in W Switzerland, in the canton of Bern, situated at the NE extremity of the Lake of Brienz, in an area of rich pastures and orchards. It is well known for its wood-carving industry. 2,637 (1941).

Brienz, Lake of. Lake in the canton of Bern, Switzerland, E of the Lake of Thun. It is traversed by the Aare River. Length, 8¾ mi.; breadth, ab. 3 mi.

Brierfield (brī′ėr.fēld). Urban district in NW England, in Lancashire, ab. 2 mi. NE of Burnley, ab. 213 mi. NW of London by rail. 7,005 (1951).

Brierley (brī′ėr.li), **Benjamin.** [Pseudonym, **Ab'-o'-th'-Yate.**] b. at Failsworth, near Manchester, England, June 26, 1825; d. at Harpurhey, Manchester, England, Jan. 18, 1896. English weaver, poet, dramatist, and short-story writer in Lancashire dialect. The son of a weaver, he was himself a weaver from the age of six to 38. Beginning his literary career with articles and essays in the *Oddfellows' Magazine* and the *Manchester Spectator*, he became (1863) subeditor of the *Oldham Times*, and founded and edited (April, 1869–Dec., 1891) *Ben Brierley's Journal;* he also dramatized some of his short stories and acted in them. His main works are *A Day's Out* (1856), *The Layrock of Langleyside* (1856, story and play), *Marlocks of Merriton* (1867), *Cotters of Mossburn* (1871), *Home Memories* (1886, an autobiography), and *Spring Blossoms and Autumn Leaves* (1893, poetry).

Brierley, Emma. Young woman engaged to Joe Hindle, in *Lonesome-Like*, a one-act play of Lancashire life by Harold Brighouse.

Brierley (brir′li), **Roger.** See **Brereley, Roger.**

Brierley Hill (brī′ėr.li). [Also, **Brierly Hill.**] Urban district in C England, in Staffordshire near Birmingham, ab. 123 mi. NW of London by rail. Industries include iron and steel, glass, ceramics, metal construction, and food products. A large portion of the district is residential. 48,943 (1951).

Brierly (brī′ėr.li), **Bob.** Titular hero of the play *Ticket-of-Leave Man* by Tom Taylor.

Brieux (brē.ė), **Eugène.** b. at Paris, Jan. 19, 1858; d. at Nice, France, Dec. 7, 1932. French dramatist. He worked as journalist on the Paris periodicals *La Patrie*, *Le Figaro*, and *Le Gaulois*. His first play, *Bernard Palissy*, written in collaboration with Gaston Salandri, was produced in 1880. André Antoine produced his *Ménage d'artistes* at the Théâtre Libre in 1890. This was followed by *Blanchette* (1892), *Les Bienfaiteurs* (1896), *Les Trois filles de M. Dupont* (1897), *Les Avariés* (1901, produced in the U.S. as *Damaged Goods*), *Les Hannetons* (1906), *Simone* (1908), and others. His purpose was to depict social evils, with a view to their reform.

Briey (brē.ā). Small town and commune in NE France, in the department of Meurthe-et-Moselle, ab. 14 mi. NW of Metz. Although located in an industrial region, near the great iron-ore deposits, Briey is an agricultural market town, away from the railways which traverse the region. The nearby Basin of Briey is one of the greatest iron-ore deposits of the world, with reserves estimated at ab. 4 billion metric tons of ore assaying 38 percent iron. Pop. of commune, 2,909 (1946), of town, 2,539 (1946).

Briffault (brē′fō), **Robert Stephen.** b. at London, 1876; d. in England, 1948. English novelist, surgeon, and anthropologist. He practiced medicine (1894 *et seq.*) in New Zealand, and served as an army surgeon during World War I; thereafter he retired from his medical practice, and lived in France. His writings on anthropology include *The Making of Humanity* (1919), *The Mothers* (1927), *Sin and Sex* (1931), and *The Decline and Fall of the British Empire* (1938). Among his novels are *Europa* (1935), *Europa in Limbo* (1937), and *New Life of Mr. Martin* (1946).

Brig (brēg). German name of **Brigue.**

Briga (brē′gä) or **Briga-Tenda** (brē′gä.ten′dä). See also the entry **Brigue** and **Tende.**

Briga. Ancient name of **Burgos,** city.

Brigadore (brig′a̤.dōr). The horse of Sir Guyon in Edmund Spenser's *The Faerie Queene.*

Brigantes (bri.gan′tēz). Confederation of tribes of Britain which in the 1st century A.D. occupied the region north of the river Humber.

Brigantia (bri.gan′shi.a̤). In ancient geography, the kingdom of the Brigantes, in what is now N England and S Scotland. The peoples designated (c50 A.D.) by the Romans under this single name were actually a confederation, occupying the region bounded, roughly, on the N by a line from just above Solway Firth across Scotland to the Firth of Forth and on the S by a line from the mouth of the river Mersey across England to Flamborough Head, near Bridlington.

Brigantia. A Latin name of **Bregenz.**

Brigantinus Lacus (brig.a̤n.tī′nus lā′kus). Latin name of **Constance, Lake.**

Brigantio (bri.gan′shi.ō). A Latin name of **Briançon.**

Brigantium (bri.gan′shi.um). Latin name of **Bregenz,** of **Briançon,** and of the city of **La Coruña.**

Briggs (brigz), **Charles Augustus.** b. at New York, Jan. 15, 1841; d. there, June 8, 1913. American theologian. He studied at Union Theological Seminary, New York (1861–63) and at the University of Berlin (1866–69), became pastor of a Presbyterian church at Roselle, N.J., in 1870, and in 1874 became professor of Hebrew and cognate languages at Union Theological Seminary. In 1880 he joined the editorial staff of the *Presbyterian Review.* His works in this period include *Biblical Study* (1883), *American Presbyterianism* (1885), and *Messianic Prophecy* (1886). His views in Biblical criticism, together with certain doctrinal views, led (1892) to his trial by the leaders of his church for heresy, which resulted in his condemnation and suspension by the Presbyterian general assembly. He was ordained in the Episcopal Church in 1899. Among his later works are *Incarnation of the Lord* (1902), *Ethical Teaching of Jesus* (1904), *New Light on the Life of Jesus* (1904), and *The Papal Commission and the Pentateuch* (1906, with Baron Friedrich von Hügel).

Briggs, Charles Frederick. b. at Nantucket, Mass., Dec. 30, 1804; d. at Brooklyn, N.Y., June 20, 1877. American journalist and author. He edited Putnam's *Monthly Magazine*, and wrote the novels *Harry Franco; a Tale of the Great Panic* (1839) and *Trippings of Tom Pepper* (1847).

Briggs, Clare A. b. at Reedsburg, Wis., Aug. 5, 1875; d. at New York, Jan. 3, 1930. American cartoonist who created the comic strips *Mr. and Mrs.* and *Skinnay*, and whose newspaper work was widely syndicated in the U.S. He was educated at Nebraska University, and first worked as a newspaper artist for the St. Louis *Democrat.* Later he worked for the New York *Journal*, Chicago *American* and *Examiner*, and finally the New York *Herald Tribune* (1914 *et seq.*) Some of his more popular series of cartoons were *When a Feller Needs a Friend*, *Ain't It a Grand and Glorious Feeling*, *Somebody is Always Taking the Joy Out of Life*, and *There's at Least One in Every Office.* He also wrote the books *Golf* and *Oh Man*, and some of his characters were adapted for radio and motion pictures. The *Mr. and Mrs.* comic strip was carried on after his death, closely following the original style.

Briggs, Henry. b. near Halifax, England, in February, 1561; d. at Oxford, England, Jan. 26, 1630. English mathematician who devised the "common" system of logarithms. He was professor of geometry at Gresham College, London (1596–1620), and Savilian professor of astronomy at Oxford (1620–30). After the publication of John Napier's system of logarithms, Briggs set up the tables by which they could be based on the number ten. Author of *Arithmetica logarithmica* (1624) and *Trigonometria britannica* (1633).

Briggs, Le Baron Russell. b. at Salem, Mass., Dec. 11, 1855; d. at Milwaukee, Wis., April 24, 1934. American educator. A graduate (1875) of Harvard, he was dean of the college (1891–1902) and of the faculty (1902–25) at Harvard, and president (1903–25) of Radcliffe College. As professor of English (1890–1925) at Harvard, he numbered among his students many who later became well-known writers.

Briggs, Lyman James. b. in Michigan, 1874—. American physicist. He attended the Michigan Agricultural College, the University of Michigan, and the Johns Hopkins University, served as a physicist with the U.S. bureau of plant industry, and was chief of the division of mechanics and sound (1920–33) of the U.S. bureau of standards, of which he became director in 1933. He is the author of *The Centrifugal Method of Soil Analysis* (1904), *The Moisture Equivalent of Soils* (1907), and *Electroculture* (1926).

Brigham (brig′a̤m). [Also: **Brigham City;** former name, **Box Elder.**] City in N Utah, county seat of Box Elder County: trading center for a peach-producing area. Settled in 1851, it was renamed for Brigham Young. 6,790 (1950).

Brigham, Albert Perry. b. at Perry, N.Y., June 12, 1855; d. March 31, 1932. American geologist, geographer, and Baptist minister. Ordained in 1882, he was a pastor

(1882–91) in New York state. In 1892 he was appointed professor of geology at Colgate University. He was the author of *A Text-Book of Geology* (1900), *Geographic Influences in American History* (1903), *Students' Laboratory Manual of Physical Geography* (1904), *From Trail to Railway Through the Appalachians* (1907), *Commercial Geography* (1911), *Cape Cod and the Old Colony* (1920), and *Glacial Geology and Geographic Conditions of the Lower Mohawk Valley* (1929).

Brigham, Amariah. b. at New Marlboro, Mass., Dec. 26, 1798; d. Sept. 8, 1849. American physician, notable chiefly as an alienist. After teaching (1837) at the College of Physicians and Surgeons at New York, he superintended the Hartford, Conn., Retreat for the Insane (1840) and New York State Lunatic Asylum (1842 *et seq.*). He also founded (1844) the *American Journal of Insanity* (which was later named the *American Journal of Psychiatry*). His writings include *A Treatise on Epidemic Cholera* (1832) and *An Inquiry Concerning the Diseases and Functions of the Brain, the Spinal Cord and Nerves.* His observations on mental disturbances appeared in three volumes: *Remarks on the Influence of Mental Cultivation on Health* (1832), *Observations on the Influence of Religion on the Health of Mankind* (1835), and *Asylum Souvenir*, his last work.

Brigham, William Tufts. b. at Boston, May 24, 1841; d. at Honolulu, Jan. 29, 1926. American ethnologist and educator. He took a leading part in the development of a method of art study now widely used in public schools as well as introducing the Sargent method of anthropometry into American colleges. He was director (1888–1918) of the Bishop Museum of Ethnology at Honolulu. His works include *Cast Catalogue of Antique Sculpture, Guatemala, the Land of the Quetzal, Ancient Hawaiian Stone Implements, Old Hawaiian Carvings,* and *A Journey Around the World to Study Music* (1912).

Brighella (brē.gel'lä). In old Italian comedy, a type of character in the Bergamask dances.

Brighouse (brig'hous). Municipal borough and manufacturing town in N central England, in the West Riding of Yorkshire, ab. 5 mi. N of Huddersfield, ab. 190 mi. NW of London by rail. It is the chief seat of silk spinning in the country. Other manufactures include woolens, worsteds, cottons, chemicals, dyestuffs, carpets, and wire. It formerly manufactured wool cards, the stiff wire brushes used for combing wool. 30,587 (1951).

Brighouse, Harold. b. at Eccles, Lancashire, England, July 26, 1882—. English novelist and playwright. His plays include *Lonesome-Like* (1911), *Hobson's Choice* (1916), *Mary's John* (1924), and *London Front* (1941). He is the author of the novels *Fossie for Short* (1917), *The Marbeck Inn* (1920), and *The Wrong Shadow* (1923).

Bright (brīt), Sir **Charles Tilston.** b. at Wanstead, London, June 8, 1832; d. at Abbey Wood, Kent, England, May 3, 1888. English telegraph engineer, remembered mainly as the chief engineer of the first Atlantic Telegraphy Company, which laid (1858) the transatlantic cable between Ireland and Newfoundland. Previously, he had laid cables on land, and in the sea between Port Patrick and Donaghadee, Ireland. Between 1860 and 1870 he was chief and consulting engineer to the Magnetic Company; during this time, he also laid cables in the Mediterranean Sea (1861–73) and in the West Indies. From 1865 to 1868 he was a Liberal member of Parliament.

Bright, James Wilson. b. at Aaronsburg, Pa., Oct. 2, 1852; d. Nov. 29, 1926. American philologist, noted for his scientific researches into Old English literature. Trained (1883–84) in Germany, he served (1885–1925) on the faculty of the Johns Hopkins University. His writings include the widely used *Outlines of Anglo-Saxon Grammar* (1891), *Anglo-Saxon Reader*, and various translations into West-Saxon of parts of the Bible.

Bright, John. b. at Greenbank, near Rochdale, Lancashire, England, Nov. 16, 1811; d. there, March 27, 1889. English Liberal statesman and orator. He was one of the chief agitators for the Anti-Corn-Law League in the period 1838–46, having first entered Parliament in 1843. He opposed the Crimean War, and favored the North in the American Civil War. He served as president of the Board of Trade (1868–70), and chancellor of the duchy of Lancaster (1873–74 and 1880–82), and became lord rector of the University of Glasgow in 1883. Author of *Speeches on Parliamentary Reform* (1867), *Speeches on Questions of Public Policy* (1869), and *Speeches on Public Affairs* (1869).

Bright, Mynors. b. 1818; d. Feb. 23, 1883. English scholar, proctor and president of Magdalene College, Cambridge, and editor of Samuel Pepys's *Diary.* His edition (1875–79) of Pepys, which is based upon a complete redeciphering of the original manuscript, corrects many errors in the earlier editions and includes a large number of passages previously suppressed.

Bright, Richard. b. at Bristol, England, Sept. 28, 1789; d. at London, Dec. 16, 1858. English physician. In 1827 he published *Reports of Medical Cases*, in which he traced to its source in the kidneys the condition later named "Bright's disease." He was active at London.

Bright, Timothy. b. near Sheffield, England, c1551; d. at York, England, 1615. English physician, regarded as the inventor of modern shorthand. After studying (1579 *et seq.*) medicine at Cambridge and Paris, he served (1586–90), as physician to St. Bartholomew's Hospital, but left the medical profession to take holy orders. His treatise, *Characterie*, on the lost art of shorthand, he dedicated (1588) to Queen Elizabeth, who presented to him the rectory of Methley (1591), and of Berwick-in-Elmet (1594), both in Yorkshire. His *Treatise of Melancholie* (1586) is thought by many to have suggested to Robert Burton his *Anatomy of Melancholy.*

Bright, William. b. at Doncaster, Yorkshire, England, Dec. 14, 1824; d. at Oxford, England, March 6, 1901. English hymnist, professor, and religious historian. Educated at Rugby and at University College, Oxford (B.A., 1846; D.D., 1849), he was a fellow and tutor in theology (1847–68) at University College, occupying the same position (1851–58) at Trinity College, Scotland. From 1868 until his death, he was regius professor of ecclesiastical history and canon of Christ Church College, Oxford. He was the author of *A History of the Church; A.D. 313–451* (1860), *Chapters of Early English Church History* (1878), *The Roman See in the Early Church* (1896), *The Age of the Fathers* (1903), and other scholarly works, and is still remembered for his hymns, published in *Hymns and Other Poems* (1866).

Bright Eyes. [Also, **Susette La Flesche.**] b. on the Nebraska reservation, 1854; d. there, May 26, 1903. American Omaha Indian, and advocate of Indian rights. Active (1879) in arousing public sympathy for the Poncas tribe, she made a speaking tour of the eastern U.S. and, later, of Scotland. She edited *Ploughed Under, The Story of an Indian Chief* (1881).

Brighton (brī'tọn). Municipality in S central Victoria, Australia, ab. 6 mi. S of Melbourne. It is a residential suburb of Melbourne, and a seaside resort on the shore of Port Phillip Bay. 39,769 (1947).

Brighton. City in C Colorado, county seat of Adams County: center for the processing of sugar beets. 4,336 (1950).

Brighton. [Former name, **Brighthelmston** or **Brighthelmstone;** sometimes called **"London-by-the-Sea."**] County borough and seaside resort in SE England, in East Sussex, situated on the English Channel, ab. 51 mi. by rail S of London. It extends ab. 4 mi. along the shore and forms one continuous town with its W suburb, Hove. Brighton, now the leading seaside resort in Great Britain, was formerly a fishing village. It has manufactures of electrical equipment and formerly had railway shops, now closed. Among its chief features are the Royal Pavilion, founded (1784) by the Prince of Wales (later George IV), the Esplanade, New Pier, and the Aquarium. Brighton was developed as a seaside resort in the second half of the 18th century, after the railroad was built. 156,440 (1951).

Brighton. Former town in E Massachusetts, ab. 4 mi. W of Boston, since 1874 the 25th ward of Boston.

Brighton. Town in W New York, in Monroe County: residential suburb of Rochester; nurseries and small industries. 18,036 (1950).

Brighton. Former name of **Beaver Falls.**

Bright Shawl, The. Novel by Joseph Hergesheimer, published in 1922.

Bright Star. Sonnet (1819) by John Keats, often miscalled his "Last Sonnet."

Bright Star. Play (1935) by Philip Barry. In it a pair of inherently honest people are unable to solve the problems raised by the fact that the husband is so absorbed in the affairs of life outside of marriage that he is unable to give his wife the tender and thoughtful affection which their marriage requires.

Brightwen (brīt'wen), **Eliza.** [Maiden name, **Elder.**] b. in Banffshire, Scotland, Oct. 30, 1830; d. at Stanmore, near London, May 5, 1906. English naturalist and nature writer; niece of Alexander Elder, founder of the publishing house of Smith, Elder and Company. She was the author of several nature books, including *Wild Nature Won by Kindness* (1890), *More About Wild Nature* (1892), *Inmates of My House and Garden* (1895), *Glimpses Into Plant Life* (1898), *Rambles With Nature Students* (1899), *Quiet Hours With Nature* (1903), and *Last Hours With Nature* (1908). Her autobiography, *The Life and Thoughts of a Naturalist* (1909) was edited by Edmund Gosse.

Brigid (*of Kildare*) (brij'id), Saint. [Also: **Bridget, Brigit** (brij'it), or **Bride.**] b. at Faughart, near Dundalk, Ireland, 451 or 452; d. at Kildare, Ireland, Feb. 1, 525. A patron saint of Ireland. According to an ancient Irish account of her life, she was born at Fochart (now Faugher or Faughart), and was the daughter of a Leinster chieftain by his bondmaid. She is said to have obtained her freedom through the intervention of the King of Leinster, who was impressed by her piety, and became the founder of a convent, in the shadow of which the present town of Kildare sprang up. Following close on Saint Patrick, whom she met before his death, Brigid is regarded as a patron of Ireland.

Brigit (brij'it) or **Brigitta** (bri.git'tä). See **Bridget** (*of Sweden*), Saint.

Brigliadoro (brē.lyä.dō'rō). Name of Orlando's horse in Matteo Maria Boiardo's *Orlando Innamorato.*

Brignoles (brē.nyol). Town in SE France, in the department of Var, ab. 23 mi. NE of Toulon. It has a 15th-century church. Nearby is Mount Loube, which looks down upon a superb panorama of the Alps as far as the Italian frontier. 5,983 (1946).

Brignoli (brē.nyô'lē), **Pasquale.** b. in Italy, 1823; d. at New York, in October, 1884. Italian tenor singer. After singing with marked success in the principal cities of Europe, he came to New York in 1855, where he achieved his highest reputation.

Brig o'Balgownie (brig ō bal.gou'ni). See **Balgownie, Brig o'.**

Brigue (brēg). [Also: **Brieg;** German, **Brig.**] Town in S Switzerland, in the E part of the canton of Valais, situated on the Rhone River, at the N entry to the Simplon Pass and the tunnel of the Simplon Railway. 3,278.

Brigue and **Tende** (tänd). [Also: **Briga-Tenda, La Brigue** and **Tende;** Italian, **Briga** and **Tenda.**] Districts in SE France, in the E part of the department of Alpes-Maritimes, ab. 30 mi. NE of Nice. These areas, with a few other small frontier zones, were ceded by Italy to France in the Treaty of Paris in 1947. A plebiscite was conducted by the French administration in October, 1947, in which the majority voted for the annexation. The region is thinly populated and very mountainous, and contains a hydroelectric station. It is traversed by the principal road and railway from Turin to the French Riviera. Area, ab. 202 sq. mi.; pop. 4,274 (1936).

Brihaddevata (bri.hạd.dā'vạ.tä). Ancient Sanskrit work ascribed to Shaunaka. Its object is to specify the deity for each verse of the *Rig-Veda.* In so doing it supports its views with many legends.

Brihaspati (bri.hạs.pa'ti). In Vedic mythology, a god in whom the activity of the pious man toward the gods is personified. Brihaspati is the prayer, sacrificer, priest, and intercessor for men with the gods, and their protector against the wicked. He appears as the prototype of the priest, and is called the *purohita,* or "house priest," of the gods. The Brahma of the later triad is a development of this concept.

Brihatkatha (bri.hat'kạ.tä). In Sanskrit literature, the "Great Narration," a collection of tales by Gunadhya, stated by Somadeva to be the source of his *Kathasaritsagara.* The *Brihatkatha* is believed to go back to the 1st or 2nd century A.D., but no manuscript of it has yet been published. Important evidence of its character is afforded by the two works founded upon it, the *Brihatkathamanjari* and the *Kathasaritsagara.*

Brihatkathamanjari (bri.hat"kạ.tä.man'jạ.rē). In Sanskrit literature, the "Great Blossom-cluster of Tales," a collection of tales by Kshemendra Vyasadasa, based on the *Brihatkatha.* Its date is c1037 A.D. Part of it was given in text and translation by Sylvain Levi in the *Journal Asiatique.*

Brihatsamhita (bri.hạt.sam'hi.tä). In Sanskrit literature, the "Great Collection," an astrological work by Varaha Mihira, who is believed to have flourished about the beginning of the 6th century A.D.

Brihtnoth (bricht'nōth). d. 991. Ealdorman of the East Saxons; son-in-law of the ealdorman Ælfgar whom he succeeded c953. He made lavish grants to ecclesiastical foundations, especially to the monasteries of Ely and Ramsey, and fell in battle against the Northmen near Maldon in 991.

Brihtwald (bricht'wäld). b. c650; d. in January, 731. English ecclesiastic, archbishop of Canterbury (692 *et seq.*). He was of noble parentage, but neither the place nor the exact year of his birth is known. He was elevated to the see of Canterbury in 692. In 705 he presided over a council near the river Nidd, at which a compromise was effected between Wilfrith, the exiled archbishop of York, and the king of Northumbria.

Bril (brēl). See **Brill, Mathys,** and **Brill, Paul.**

Brill (bril), **Abraham Arden.** b. in Austria, Oct. 12, 1874; d. at New York, March 2, 1948. American psychiatrist who first translated many works of Sigmund Freud into English. He was chief (1911–12) of the psychiatric clinic at Columbia University, lecturer on abnormal psychology and psychoanalysis at New York University (1914–25), and lecturer on psychoanalysis and psychosexual sciences at Columbia (1929 *et seq.*). Among his books are *Psychoanalysis—Its Theories and Practical Application, Fundamental Conceptions of Psychoanalysis,* and *Lectures on Psychoanalysis and Psychiatry;* he also translated several works of Carl Gustav Jung.

Brill (brēl), **Mathys.** [Also, **Bril.**] b. at Antwerp, c1550; d. 1584. Flemish painter; brother of Paul Brill. As a young man Mathys Brill went to Rome, where his talent attracted the favorable notice of Pope Gregory XIII, who employed him in the embellishment of the Vatican. His work in fresco in that palace is particularly notable.

Brill (bril), **Nathan Edwin.** b. at New York, Jan. 13, 1859; d. Dec. 13, 1925. American physician, especially known for his work as a clinician. While an attending physician (1893–1923) at Mt. Sinai Hospital, New York, he investigated (1910 *et seq.*) and described a form of typhus now known as Brill's disease. He was active also in the study of various other diseases, chiefly those of the blood-forming organs.

Brill (brēl), **Paul.** [Also, **Bril.**] b. at Antwerp, 1554; d. at Rome, 1626. Flemish painter, noted especially for landscapes.

Brillat-Savarin (brē.yå.så.vå.raṅ), **Anthelme.** b. at Belley, Ain, France, April 1, 1755; d. at Paris, Feb. 2, 1826. French lawyer and authority on gastronomy. A political emigré (1793–95) during the latter part of the French Revolution, he traveled in Switzerland, the Netherlands, and the U.S. Author of *Physiologie du goût* (1825; Eng. trans., *Physiology of Taste,* 1925; rev. ed., 1948), and other works.

Brilon (brē'lōn). Town in W Germany, in the *Land* (state) of North Rhine-Westphalia, British Zone, formerly in the province of Westphalia, Prussia, SW of Paderborn. It trades in lumber and has sawmills and furniture factories; there are stone quarries. It is a health resort, and has a Gothic church dating from the 11th century. 10,381 (1950).

Brimming Cup, The. Novel by Dorothy Canfield Fisher, published in 1921.

Brincklé (bring'klę), **William Draper.** b. at St. Jones' Neck, Del., Feb. 9, 1798; d. at Groveville, N.J., Dec. 16, 1862. American pomologist and physician, noted for his systematic nomenclature of experimentally bred fruits. He practiced medicine (until 1859) at Wilmington, Del., and at Philadelphia. His researches in the field of horticulture centered on the origination of small fruits. He published his findings variously in *Horticulturist* and *Hoffy's North American Pomologist.*

Brinckman (bringk'män), Baron **Karl Gustav von.** [Also: **Brinkman;** pseudonym, **Selmar.**] b. at Brännkyrka, near Stockholm, Feb. 24, 1764; d. at Stockholm, c1847. Swedish diplomat and poet.

Brinckmann (bringk'män), **John.** b. at Rostock, Germany, July 3, 1814; d. at Güstrow, Germany, Sept. 20, 1870. German schoolteacher and Low German poet. His *Kaspar Ohm un ik* (1855) is his best-known work. His collected works appeared at Leipzig in 1903. Brinckmann was in the U.S. during the period 1839–42.

Brindaban (brin'dạ.bạn). Town in the N central part of the Union of India, in W Uttar Pradesh (United Provinces), ab. 30 mi. NW of Agra. It is a popular center of pilgrimage, though the Jumna River has shifted its course away from the bathing ghats. Although it contains many large and magnificent Hindu shrines, the town is of relatively recent origin, dating from the 16th century. There is a branch railway to Muttra. 20,718 (1941).

Brindisi (brēn'dē.zē). Province in SE Italy, in the *compartimento* (region) of Apulia. Capital, Brindisi; area, ab. 710 sq. mi.; pop. 254,062 (1936), 295,000 (est. 1947).

Brindisi. [Latin, **Brundisium, Brundusium.**] City and commune in SE Italy, in the *compartimento* (region) of Apulia, in the province of Lecce, situated on a land tongue between two bays of the Adriatic Sea, SE of Bari. It is the seat of an archbishopric and an important seaport, exporting wine, figs, and oil, and also a naval station and a port of call for various steamship lines connecting Italy and C Europe with Greece, the Near East, and India. The location is also favorable for air traffic. There is an archaeological museum, and a medieval castle built by the emperor Frederick II; the churches of Santa Maria del Casale, Santa Lucia, and San Benedetto are in Romanesque style; there are beautiful early medieval murals. A number of old palaces are also preserved. The ancient town, occupied by the Romans c266 B.C., became a Roman colony and a naval station in 244; it assumed great strategic importance as the terminus of the Appian Way and port of embarkation for Greece and the Levant (Sulla and Julius Caesar embarked here). In the early Middle Ages, Brindisi was occupied successively by Byzantine, Lombards, and Moslems; in 1071 it was conquered by the Normans under Robert Guiscard. After the downfall of the Hohenstaufen regime the town declined, to rise again only after the unification of Italy and the opening of the Suez Canal; it served as a naval base during World War I. Slight damage was suffered during World War II by some buildings of tourist interest, but repairs have been completed or are being carried out. Pop. of commune, 41,699 (1936); of city, 35,984 (1936).

Brindley (brind'li), **James.** b. 1716; d. 1772. English canal engineer. He is remembered chiefly for the building (1759) of a canal connecting the Worsley coal mines and Manchester, and more specifically for the building of an aqueduct by which this canal was carried over the river Irwell. This canal was the first one of great industrial importance in England and formed the beginning of the system of inland navigation which was essential to the progress of the Industrial Revolution in that country. After this Brindley built a total of ab. 365 mi. of canal which included the Bridgewater Canal, between Runcorn (near Liverpool) and Manchester, and the Grand Trunk (or Trent and Mersey) Canal. Also interested in mechanical engineering, he is notable for the improvements which he contributed to the steam engine originally designed by Thomas Newcomen. Brindley was entirely self-taught, and is said to have done all his designing in his head, without drawings, plans, or written calculations.

Brinig (brin'ig), **Myron.** b. at Minneapolis, Minn., Dec. 22, 1900—. American novelist. His works include *Madonna Without Child* (1929), *Singermann* (1929), *Wide Open Town* (1931), *Out of Life* (1934), *The Sisters* (1937), *Anne Minton's Life* (1939), *The Family Way* (1942), *The Gambler Takes a Wife* (1943), *You and I* (1945), and *Footsteps on the Stair* (1950).

Brink (bringk), **Bernhard (Egidius Conrad) ten** b. at Amsterdam, Jan. 12, 1841; d. at Strasbourg, Jan. 29, 1892. Dutch philologist, noted especially for his studies in English literature and language. He was professor of modern languages at Marburg (1870–73), and of English at Strasbourg (1873–92). His works include *Chaucer Studien* (Vol. I, 1870) and *Geschichte der Englischen Literatur* (1877–89).

Brink, Jan ten. b. at Appingedam, Netherlands, June 15, 1834; d. at Leiden, Netherlands, July 19, 1901. Dutch author, educator, and critic. In 1889 he was appointed professor of the history of Dutch literature at Leiden. Among his critical works are *Schets eener geschiedenis der Nederlandsche letterkunde* (1867–69), *Vondel bekroond* (1868), *Bulwer Lytton; biografie en kritiek* (1873), *Letterkundige schetsen* (1874–75), *Émile Zola* (1879), *Onze hedendaagsche letterkundigen* (1882–87; reprinted in 1902 as *Geschiedenis der Noord-Nederlandsche letteren in de XIX. eeuw*), *Causerien over moderne romans* (1884), and *De Roman in brieven 1740–1840* (1889). He was also the author of a number of novels.

Brinkley (bringk'li). City in E Arkansas, in Monroe County: shipping point for rice, cotton, and lumber. 4,173 (1950).

Brinkman (bringk'män), Baron **Karl Gustav von.** See **Brinckman,** Baron **Karl Gustav von.**

Brinley (brin'li), **Daniel Putnam.** b. at Newport, R.I., March 8, 1879—. American painter, stained-glass designer, and illustrator. He decorated the lobby of the New York *Daily News* building with a great terrestrial globe, decorated the Metropolitan Life Insurance Building at New York, and executed stained-glass windows for the Fordham Lutheran Church at New York. He studied at the Dwight School, the Art Students League of New York, and at Florence and Paris. His work, which also includes murals, landscapes, and maps, has been exhibited at Paris and in the U.S., and in 1930 he was made an associate of the National Academy of Design. Among his better-known works are *Story of Huckleberry Finn, The Hunter's Dream, Brooklyn, Past, Present, and Future,* decoration war maps in the Liberty Memorial, Kansas City, Mo., stained-glass windows for two churches, and illustrations for Gordon Brinley's *Away to Cape Breton* and *Away to the Gaspé.*

Brinton (brin'tọn), **Christian.** b. at West Chester, Pa., Sept. 17, 1870; d. July 14, 1942. American art critic and lecturer. He studied at Haverford College, the University of Heidelberg, and the École du Louvre, Paris. He was associate editor (1900–04) of *The Critic,* and was later an advisory editor of *Art in America.* His achievements brought him decorations from King Gustavus V of Sweden and King Albert I of Belgium. His works include *Modern Artists* (1908), *Masterpieces of American Painting* (1910, Berlin and New York), *La Peinture américaine* (1913), *Introduction to History of Russian Painting* (1916), and *The Face of Soviet Art* (1934). He was also the author of numerous catalogues for major exhibitions of paintings, and of articles for *L'Art et Les Artistes, Magazine of Art, Vanity Fair,* and other periodicals.

Brinton, Daniel Garrison. b. at Thornbury, Pa., May 13, 1837; d. at Atlantic City, N.J., July 31, 1899. American anthropologist and surgeon. After abandoning a medical practice, he was professor of ethnology and archaeology at the Philadelphia Academy of Natural Sciences, and of American archaeology and linguistics at the University of Pennsylvania. His works include *The Myths of the New World* (1868), *Aboriginal American Authors and their Productions* (1882–90), *Races and Peoples* (1890), *The American Race* (1891), *Religions of Primitive Peoples* (1897), and *Basis of Social Relations* (1902). He centered his research on American Indians, and was the first to attempt a systematization of Indian languages; he opposed the diffusion theory of common mythology.

Brinvilliers (brań.vē.lyā), **Marie Madeleine d'Aubray,** Marquise **de.** b. c1630; executed at Paris, July 16, 1676. French murderess. She married (1651) the Marquis de Brinvilliers, from whom she obtained a separation after he had squandered his fortune. She was instructed in the use of a subtle poison, sometimes thought to have been aqua tofana, by her lover, Jean Baptiste de Gaudin, Seigneur de Sainte Croix. (Whether or not the poison she used was actually aqua tofana has never been determined, partly at least because no one has ever finally determined exactly what the ingredients of aqua tofana were. We know that it was colorless and tasteless, and that it probably contained arsenic; we know also that it was manufactured, according to most accounts, by a Sicilian woman named Tofana during the middle years of the 17th century (and used by her to poison upwards of 600 people). It is therefore quite possible that the Marquise de Brinvilliers may have used it, or something very close to it, but final proof of this will probably never be available.) With this, or whatever other poison she may have used, she killed her father and other members of her family in order to obtain possession of the inheritance. The crimes were discovered in consequence of the accidental poisoning of Sainte Croix in 1672. Her trial, confession, and conviction touched off an extensive investigation into Parisian crimes by poison.

Brion (brē.ôṅ), Admiral **de.** See **Chabot, Philippe de.**

Brion (brē′on), **Friederike Elisabeth.** b. at Niederrödern, in Alsace, 1752; d. at Meissenheim, Germany, 1813. Goethe's sweetheart in his Strasbourg days (1770–71). She was the daughter of the pastor in the village of Sesenheim near Strasbourg. Goethe has immortalized her by some of his best lyrics and by his account of their love affair in *Dichtung und Wahrheit.*

Brión (brē.ōn′), **(Pedro) Luis.** b. on the Dutch island of Curaçao, c1783; d. there, Sept. 27, 1821. Admiral of the Colombian navy. He joined Simon Bolívar in 1812, and commanded the patriot fleet in the Venezuelan and Colombian revolutions; in 1815 and 1816 he furnished the vessels and arms with which Bolívar recommenced the war. He was president of the council (October, 1817) which condemned General Piar to death at Angostura.

Brioni (brē.ō′nē). Small island in NW Yugoslavia, off the coast of Istria, NW of the city of Pula, now in the federative unit of Croatia, formerly part of the Italian province of Venezia Giulia. It is a famous resort. 310 (1936).

Brioschi (brē.ōs′kē), **Francesco.** b. at Milan, Dec. 22, 1824; d. there, Dec. 13, 1897. Italian algebraist, known especially for his work on the solutions of the quintic and sextic equations. He took his doctorate at Pavia in 1845, and was a professor there from 1852 to 1861. He was in charge of the Milan Academy of Sciences from 1862 to his death, and from 1884 on he was president of the Accademia dei Lincei. He was the author of over 275 papers on mathematics. His *Opere matematiche* appeared in five volumes in the period 1901–09.

Briosco (brē.ōs′kō), **Andrea.** [Called **Il Riccio,** meaning "the curly-haired."] b. at Padua, Italy, c1470; d. 1532. Italian sculptor and architect. Although he was in his day noted as an architect (his most celebrated work in this field being the Church of Santa Giustina in his native city), he is now best remembered as a sculptor and especially for his masterly work in bronze. The Louvre at Paris contains several bronze reliefs of Briosco's, which originally adorned the marble tomb of Girolamo della Torre in the Church of San Fermo at Verona, but the richest collection of his work is to be seen in the Church of San Antonio, Padua, including the reliefs of *David Dancing Before the Ark,* and *Judith and Holofernes.*

Brioude (brē.öd). [Ancient name, **Brivas.**] Town in S central France, in the department of Haute-Loire. It has a beautiful location and is a tourist center. The church of Saint-Julien, dating from the 12th and 13th centuries, is one of the most remarkable examples of Romanesque architecture in the Auvergne. Brioude is a trade center. 5,623 (1946).

Brisach (brē′zäch). See **Breisach.**

Brisbane (briz′bạn, -bān). City in E Australia, a seaport and the capital of the state of Queensland, situated on the river Brisbane, ab. 25 mi. from Moreton Bay, and a short distance from the border of New South Wales: seat of Queensland University (established 1911). Exports include wool, cotton, gold, and hides. Until 1842 Brisbane was a penal colony; it became the capital in 1859. Both city and river were named for Sir Thomas Makdougall Brisbane. Pop., including suburbs, 402,172 (1947), 440,000 (est. 1950).

Brisbane (briz′bān), **Albert.** b. at Batavia, N.Y., Aug. 22, 1809; d. at Richmond, Va., May 1, 1890. American social reformer, a chief exponent in the U.S. of Fourierism; father of Arthur Brisbane. He was aroused (1830) by Charles Fourier's writings at Paris; returned (1834) to America, he lectured (1839) at Philadelphia and New York, and wrote on Fourierism for the New York *Tribune,* the *Chronicle, Plebeian,* and *Dial.* He edited (with Horace Greeley) the *Future* for a period of two months and (with Osborne Macdaniel) the *Phalanx* (1843–45). His books on Fourierism are *Social Destiny of Man; or, Association and Reorganization of Industry* (1840), *Association, or, A Concise Exposition of the Practical Part of Fourier's Social Science* (1843), and *General Introduction to the Social Sciences* (1876).

Brisbane, Arthur. b. at Buffalo, N.Y., Dec. 12, 1864; d. at New York, Dec. 25, 1936. American newspaper editor; son of Albert Brisbane. He served first as a reporter, later as London correspondent, for the New York *Sun;* was for a time editor of the *Evening Sun,* and subsequently managing editor of the New York *World;* and served (1897–1921) as editor of the New York *Evening Journal.* He became (1918) editor of the Chicago *Herald and Examiner,* and later became widely known for his commentary appearing in the Hearst papers. Among his works are *Mary Baker Eddy* (1908), *The Book of Today* (1923), and *Today and The Future Day* (1925).

Brisbane (briz′bạn, -bān), Sir **Thomas Makdougall.** b. at Brisbane House, Largs, Ayrshire, Scotland, July 23, 1773; d. there, Jan. 27, 1860. British general and astronomer, governor of New South Wales (1821–25). He served in Flanders (1793–95), in the West Indies (1795–98), in the Peninsular War (1812), and in Canada (1813). He founded an observatory in Australia, and there catalogued 7,385 stars; later, he founded another observatory in Scotland. The city of Brisbane, Australia, and the river which flows past it were named for him.

Briscoe v. Bank of Kentucky, 11 Peters 257 (1837), (bris′kō). U.S. Supreme Court decision, rendered in an opinion by Justice John McLean, sustaining the issue of state bills of credit by a bank established by the state of Kentucky. The decision turned upon the interpretation of a bill of credit. "To constitute a bill of credit within the Constitution," said Justice McLean, "it must be issued by a State, on the faith of a State, and be designed to circulate as money. It must be a paper which circulates on the credit of the State, and is so received and used in the ordinary business of life." McLean's opinion held that the Kentucky notes were held not to circulate on the faith of the state. In this it differed from Chief Justice John Marshall's opinion in Craig v. Missouri (1830), and considerably weakened Marshall's finding in that case. In the Briscoe case Justice Joseph Story vigorously dissented, asserting that, when the cause had been formerly argued, a majority of the justices were decidedly of the opinion that the act was unconstitutional and amounted to an authority to issue bills of credit. The case reflected the demand of western settlements for an expanded currency.

Briseis (bri.sē′is). In the *Iliad,* a name given to Hippodameia, a slave girl captured by Achilles and taken by Agamemnon, the cause of the quarrel between Achilles and Agamemnon.

Brisighella (brē.zē.gel′lä). Town and commune in N Italy, in the *compartimento* (region) of Emilia-Romagna, in the province of Ravenna, situated on the Lamone River, SW of Ravenna. It has a Venetian castle which was built in the 16th century on older foundations. There are small agricultural industries. Thermal springs are in the vicinity. Pop. of commune, 15,652 (1936); of town, 2,397 (1936).

Brisk (brisk), **Fastidious.** In Ben Jonson's comedy *Every Man Out of His Humour,* a pert, petulant, and lively fop. He is devoted to the life of the court, and overly fashionable.

Brissa (bris′sä). See **Aowin.**

Brissac (brē.sȧk), **Pierre de Cossé,** Duc **de.** b. at Paris, March 13, 1900— French industrialist, associated (1924–39) with the Schneider arms company. He became (1948) general manager of Le Matériel Électrique, SW of Paris, and has been a director of many mining and industrial firms.

Brisson (brē.sôṅ), **Henri.** [Full name, **Eugène Henri Brisson.**] b. at Bourges, France, July 31, 1835; d. at Paris, April 13, 1912. French political leader. He was throughout his political life an advocate of a firm anticlerical policy. As a deputy (1870–1912), he belonged to the radical group. He was premier (1885–86, 1898) and president of the Chamber of Deputies (1881–85, 1894–98, 1904–12).

Brisson, Mathurin Jacques. b. April 30, 1723; d. June 23, 1806. French physicist and ornithologist. He was appointed (1796) a professor at the Écoles Centrales at Paris.

Brissot (brē.sō), **Jacques Pierre.** [Surnamed **de Warville.**] b. at Quarville, near Chartres, France. Jan. 14, 1754; guillotined at Paris, Oct. 31, 1793. French revolutionary politician and writer, a leader of the Girondists, who at first called themselves Brissotins. He was editor (1789–93) of the journal *Patriote français*, and was a member of the Legislative Assembly and Convention. His record of a visit (1788) to the U.S. was published as *Nouveau voyage dans les États-Unis de l'Amérique Septentrionale* (3 vols., 1791). He was also the author of *Théorie des lois criminelles* (1781) and *Bibliothèque philosophique du législateur* (1782).

Bristed (bris'tẹd), **Charles Astor.** [Pseudonym, **Carl Benson.**] b. at New York, Oct. 6, 1820; d. at Washington, D.C., Jan. 14, 1874. American author; son of John Bristed. He wrote *Five Years in an English University* (1852) and *The Upper Ten Thousand of New York* (1852).

Bristed, John. b. in Dorsetshire, England, Oct. 17, 1778; d. at Bristol, R.I., Feb. 23, 1855. American clergyman and author; father of Charles Astor Bristed. He came to New York in 1806, and married (1820) a daughter of John Jacob Astor. From 1829 to 1843 he was a rector at Bristol, R.I. He wrote *Resources of the United States* (1818) and others.

Bristoe Campaign (bris'tō). In the American Civil War, a name often applied to the action (Oct. 9–22, 1863) taken by General George Meade after General Robert E. Lee's crossing of the Rapidan in the direction of Washington, D.C. Meade's disposition of his troops was calculated to protect the capital. At Bristoe Station, on Oct. 14, Meade's rear guard, commanded by Warren, beat back the Confederate corps under A. P. Hill, and Lee turned back.

Bristol (bris'tọl). City in W central Connecticut, in Hartford County, ab. 15 mi. SW of Hartford: known since the 18th century as a clock-making center. It has machine shops and foundries, and manufactures clocks, tableware, brass goods, tools, and ball bearings. 35,961 (1950).

Bristol. [Middle English, **Bristow.**] City, county, county borough, seaport, and industrial town in W England, in Gloucestershire, situated at the confluence of the rivers Frome and Avon, near Bristol Channel ab. 118 mi. W of London by rail. It is the largest seaport in this part of England; the Port of Bristol now consists of two parts, one at Bristol, the other at Portishead and Avonmouth. It has a large commerce, trading mostly with Canada, Central America, and the West Indies, and dealing mostly in imports of raw materials and foodstuffs; there are few exports. Avonmouth, ab. 6 mi. NW on the Bristol Channel, is the principal landing-point for foodstuffs, especially bananas from the West Indies and dairy produce from Ireland. Bristol has a long list of industries, including the processing of sugar, tobacco, chocolate, soap, chemicals, leather, and ale. It has ferrous and nonferrous metallurgical industries, automobile and aircraft factories, boot and shoe manufactures, and a clothing industry. Bristol was the headquarters of the British African-West Indian slave and sugar trade in the 17th century. Its history of manufactures began in the 13th century. Bristol Cathedral dates from the 14th century, with a rebuilt modern nave. It is small, and chiefly notable in that its aisles are of the same height as the nave (which thus has no clerestory) and for its superb Norman chapter house. Bristol was made a county in the reign of Edward III. It was taken by Prince Rupert for the Royalists in 1643, and by the Parliamentarians in 1645. It was the scene of great riots in 1831. A musical festival is held triennially here, lasting four days; the first one was held in 1873. The university (chartered 1909) was formed on the nucleus of University College (1876); the art museum was opened in 1905. The city was severely damaged by bombing in World War II. Pop. of county borough, 442,281 (1951).

Bristol. Borough in SE Pennsylvania, in Bucks County, on the Delaware River ab. 19 mi. NE of Philadelphia: manufactures include carpets, machinery, and wool textiles. It was settled in 1697. Pop. 12,710 (1950).

Bristol. Town (in Rhode Island the equivalent of township in many other states) and unincorporated village in E Rhode Island, county seat of Bristol County, on Narragansett Bay ab. 13 mi. SE of Providence. Manufactures include cotton textiles, knitting yarns, automobile upholstery fabrics, and rifles. There are boatyards and fisheries. The town was settled c1670 and incorporated in 1681. It was raided (1675) in the early part of King Philip's War and the British burned it in 1778. In 1938 the hurricane which struck the NE part of the U.S. did serious damage here. Early industries included shipbuilding, tanning, and grist milling. Pop. of town, 12,320 (1950); of village, 10,335 (1950).

Bristol. City in NE Tennessee, in Sullivan County. It has railroad yards, and manufactures including mine cars, pulp, paper, veneer, leather goods, furniture, and structural steel; it is also a shipping point for the agricultural products of East Tennessee. King College is here. Bristol was incorporated as a town in 1856. What is to all appearances one city is divided into two separate municipalities by the Tennessee-Virginia border (see also Bristol, Va.). 16,771 (1950).

Bristol. [Former name, **Goodson.**] City in SW Virginia, twin city of Bristol, Tenn.. geographically in Washington County but independent of the county government. Manufactures include iron, lumber, textiles, paper, and leather. It was chartered as a city in 1890. It is the seat of Sullins College and Virginia Intermont College. 15,594 (1950).

Bristol, 1st and 2nd Earls of. See **Digby, John,** and **Digby, George;** also **Hervey, George William,** and **Hervey, John** (1665—1751).

Bristol, Mark Lambert. b. at Glassboro, N.J., April 17, 1868; d. May 13, 1939. American naval officer. Graduated (1887) from the U.S. Naval Academy at Annapolis, he was promoted to ensign (1889), captain (1913), and rear admiral (1921). During the Spanish-American War (1898), he served on the battleship *Texas;* in World War I, he commanded the *North Carolina* (1917) and the *Oklahoma* (1918). He headed (1913–16) aeronautical developments for the navy, was U.S. high commissioner (1919–27) to Turkey, served as commander in chief (1927–29) of the Asiatic fleet, as a full admiral, and was chairman (1930–32) of the navy general board.

Bristol Avon (ā'vọn, av'ọn). See **Avon River,** W and SW England.

Bristol Channel. Arm of the Atlantic Ocean, lying between South Wales and Monmouthshire (England) on the N and SW England on the S. It extends from the estuary of the river Severn W to the SW points of England and of Wales. The tide rises to a greater height here than anywhere else on the English coast. Length, ab. 85 mi.; width, 5 to 43 mi.; depth, 30 to 240 ft.

Bristol Madrigal Society. Vocal ensemble established (1837) at Bristol, England, for the performance of madrigals. The members are all male; choirboys are used for the higher voices.

Bristol Merchant, The. See **Bristowe (Bristol) Merchant, The.**

Bristow (bris'tō). City in E Oklahoma, in Creek County, in a petroleum and natural gas region: formerly a trading post in Indian Territory. 5,400 (1950).

Bristow. Middle English name of **Bristol,** England.

Bristow, Benjamin Helm. b. at Elkton, Ky., June 20, 1832; d. at New York, June 22, 1896. American lawyer and politician, noted for activities during the Reconstruction period. Elected (1863) to the Kentucky senate, where he strongly supported Lincoln, he was appointed after the Civil War (May 4, 1866) U.S. attorney for the Kentucky district. As U.S. secretary of the treasury (July 3, 1874–June 17, 1876) under Ulysses S. Grant, his attacks on the Whisky Ring led to a scheme by its leaders which forced his resignation.

Bristow, George Frederick. b. at Brooklyn, N.Y., Dec. 19, 1825; d. at New York, Dec. 13, 1898. American composer and violinist. He became (1842) a violinist with the New York Philharmonic Society, of which he was conductor in the period 1851–62. His works include the opera *Rip Van Winkle* (produced 1850), six symphonies, two oratorios, and two string quartets.

Bristowe (Bristol) Merchant (bris'tō; bris'tọl), **The.** Play by John Ford and Thomas Dekker, licensed in 1624, probably an alteration of another play on the same theme by John Day.

Bristowe Tragedy, or the Death of Sir Charles Bawdin (bô'din), **The.** Poem by Thomas Chatterton, written in 1768 and printed in 1772.

Britain (brit'ạn). [Middle English, **Britaine** (bri.tā'nẹ), **Bretayne** (bre-).] English equivalent of the Latin **Britannia** (*q. v.*); also a shortened form of Great Britain.

Britain, Battle of. See under **World War II.**

Britain, Benjamin (or **Little**). Character in Charles Dickens's story *The Battle of Life*, at first a servant, and afterward landlord, of the Nutmeg Grater Inn. He is very small, and announces himself as knowing and caring for absolutely nothing.

Britain's Daughter. Play (1921) by Gordon Bottomley. It is considered one of his finest dramas.

Britain's Pastorals. Pastoral verse (2 vols., 1613–16) by William Browne. A third volume was left incomplete in manuscript form. Begun before he reached the age of 20, it is Browne's largest and most Spenserian work.

"Britain's Playground." See **Blackpool.**

Britain's Remembrancer. Narrative verse (1628) by George Wither. It is an eye-witness account of the London plague of 1625.

Britanni (bri.tan'ī). A Celtic people in the NW part of Gaul, first mentioned in this location by Sidonius Apollonius. According to Jordanes they were leagued with the Romans against the West Goths. Gregory of Tours makes them subject to the neighboring Franks. They were called by the Franks "Breton," by Latin writers after the 5th century "Britanni," and "Britones," and their land "Britannia Cismarina," modern French Bretagne, English Brittany. They were, in all probability, the descendants of the Dumnonii whose original home had been the SW part of Britannia, or Britain, whence they had been driven out by the Anglo-Saxons.

Britannia (bri.tan'i.ạ). In ancient geography (after the time of Caesar), the name of the island of Great Britain, and specifically of the S part of the island; in modern times, a poetical name of the United Kingdom of Great Britain and Northern Ireland. Under the Romans Britannia Prima, the first province, was the district S of the river Thames, the Saxon Wessex under Egbert; Flavia Caesariensis, between the river Severn and the sea, was the Mercian kingdom of Offa; Britannia Secunda, W of the Severn, comprised Wales and the Welsh Marches; Maxima Caesariensis, between the rivers Humber and Tyne, is the Northumbrian province of Deira; and Valentia, whose N boundary was between the Firth of Forth and the river Clyde, embraced the Lowlands of Scotland and Northumberland. See also **Britannicae Insulae.**

Britannia. Historical work (1586) by William Camden. Written originally in Latin, it was translated into English in 1610.

Britannia Illustrata (i.lus'trạ.tạ). Prose work (1707–08) by Johannes Kip. In it Kip describes, with an obvious element of national pride, the Restoration houses and gardens of 18th-century England.

Britannia Major. A Latin name of **Great Britain.**

Britannia Minor or **Britannia Cismarina** (sis.mar'i.nạ). Latin names of **Brittany.**

Britannia Prima (prī'mạ). See under **Britannia.**

Britannia Secunda (sẹ.kun'dạ). In ancient geography, a Roman province nearly corresponding to Wales. See also **Britannia.**

Britannia Tubular Bridge. Railway bridge across Menai Strait, in Wales, built by Robert Stephenson between 1846 and 1850. It consists of two parallel rectangular tunnels of wrought iron, supported by three piers between the two shore piers. The central tower is ab. 230 ft. high. The total length is ab. 1,840 ft.; that of each of the central spans, ab. 460 ft.

Britannicae Insulae (bri.tan'i.sē in'sụ̄.lē). In ancient geography (before the time of Caesar), the Latin name of the British islands Albion (Great Britain) and Ierne (Ireland). See also **Britannia.**

Britannicus (bri.tan'i.kus). [Original name, **Claudius Tiberius Germanicus.**] b. c41 A.D.; d. at Rome, 55 A.D. Roman noble; son of the emperor Claudius and Messalina. He was heir apparent to the throne until the intrigues of his stepmother, Agrippina, and her paramour, the freedman Pallas, secured from Claudius the precedence for Nero, Agrippina's son by a former marriage. He is thought to have been poisoned at a banquet by Nero, whose mother had sought to work upon the fears of her rebellious son by threatening to bring the claims of Britannicus before the soldiery.

Britanny (brit'ạ.ni). See **Brittany.**

British Academy for the Promotion of Historical, Philosophical, and Philological Studies. Association incorporated by royal charter, on Aug. 8, 1902. Its formation was due to a suggestion made at the assembling of the International Association of Academies at Wiesbaden, Germany, in 1899, and a consequent meeting of representative scholars at the British Museum in 1901.

British America. Name sometimes applied to that part of North America, with the exception of Alaska, which lies N of the U.S. It comprises the Dominion of Canada. In a wider sense the name includes also Bermuda, the British West Indies, British Honduras, British Guiana, and the Falkland Islands (although British title to the last is disputed by Argentina).

British Baluchistan (bạ.lö.chi.stän'). Former British chief commissionership in SW Asia, formed in 1887 out of districts in SE Afghanistan: now part of the state of Baluchistan, in Pakistan.

British Bechuanaland (bech.ö.ä'nạ.land). See under **Bechuanaland,** region.

British Cameroons (kam.ẹ.rönz'). See **Cameroons.**

British Columbia. Westernmost province of the Dominion of Canada, lying between the Yukon and the Northwest Territories on the N, Alberta on the E, the U.S. on the S, and Alaska and the Pacific Ocean on the W, and including Vancouver and Queen Charlotte islands. It has a lieutenant governor and a legislative assembly of 48 members elected for 5 years, and sends 18 members to the Dominion House of Commons and 6 members to the Senate. The E portion of the province consists of mountains which provide a considerable barrier to intercourse with the rest of Canada; the mountains are crossed by the Canadian Pacific and Canadian National railways and a through highway. Minerals and fruits and vegetables from the highland valleys are the main sources of revenue for the province although there is a considerable tourist trade, especially on Vancouver island. Vancouver, the largest city, is the chief port. Capital, Victoria; area, 366,255 sq. mi. (including 6,976 sq. mi. of open fresh water); pop. 1,165,210 (1951).

British Commonwealth of Nations. [Also, **British Empire.**] Collective term for the United Kingdom of Great Britain and Northern Ireland, with its dominions, colonies, dependencies, and the associated republic of India (Union of India). The British Commonwealth is made up of political units of all degrees of attachment to the crown, ranging from the autonomy of India (a republic since 1950) and the dominions, with only nominal allegiance to the crown, to the military governorships that still prevail in some of its smallest units. In Europe: Great Britain and Northern Ireland, the Channel Islands, Gibraltar, the Isle of Man, and Malta. In Asia: Aden colony and protectorate, the Bahrein islands, North Borneo, Brunei, Sarawak, Ceylon, Cyprus, Hong Kong, the Union of India, the Federation of Malaya, Singapore, and Pakistan. In Africa: the Anglo-Egyptian Sudan (a condominium), British West Africa (Nigeria and British Cameroons, Sierra Leone, Gambia, the Gold Coast, and British Togoland), British East Africa (Kenya, Uganda, Zanzibar and Pemba, and Tanganyika), Mauritius and dependencies, British South Africa (Nyasaland, Northern Rhodesia, Southern Rhodesia, Basutoland, Bechuanaland, and Swaziland), St. Helena, Ascension, and Tristan da Cunha islands, the Seychelles, British Somaliland, South-west Africa, and the Union of South Africa. In the Americas: the Bahamas, Barbados, Bermuda, British Guiana, British Honduras, Canada, the Falkland Islands (disputed with Argentina), Jamaica, the Leeward Islands. Trinidad and Tobago, and the Windward Islands. In Australasia and Oceania: the Commonwealth of Australia and dependencies (including Tasmania, Papua and New Guinea, Norfolk, Nauru, the Solomons, and other islands), Fiji, New Hebrides (a condominium), New Zealand and dependencies, the Gilbert and Ellic Islands, Tonga, Pitcairn Island, and Western Samoa. Area: in Europe, ab. 93,800 sq. mi.; in Asia, ab. 1,856,100 sq. mi.; in Africa, ab. 3,788,000 sq. mi.; in the Americas, ab. 3,965,900 sq. mi.; in Australasia and Oceania, ab. 3,287,900 sq. mi.; total area of the British Commonwealth, ab. 12,991,700 sq. mi. Total pop. ab. 566,480,000 (based upon 1946–48 censuses and estimates).

British Critic, The. Periodical published (1793–1826) in England. It was a leading conservative review of the day, edited by William Beloe and Robert Nares.

British East Africa. [Also, **East Africa.**] Term applied to the three British territories on the central E coast of Africa. Under the term are included Uganda protectorate, Kenya colony and Kenya protectorate, and Tanganyika territory (a former mandate of the League of Nations, but after World War II a trust territory of the United Nations). The term is often used to include Zanzibar protectorate (which includes Pemba), although the East Africa High Commission, which administers the government of Kenya, Uganda, and Tanganyika, does not have jurisdiction over Zanzibar and Pemba.

British East Africa Company, Imperial. British commercial company, developed from the British East Africa Association, and chartered in 1888. Its head was Sir William Mackinnon. The territory of the company (ab. 200,000 sq. mi.) lay within the newly acquired British "sphere of influence" of East Africa, NE of Lake Victoria. The company had extended its operations into Uganda, but in 1892 it decided to abandon that region, and in 1895 it surrendered its charter to the British government.

British East Africa Protectorate. Former name of **Kenya.**

British East India Company. See **East India Company.**

British Empire. See **British Commonwealth of Nations.**

British Guiana (gē.ä′nạ). British crown colony in N South America, bounded by the Atlantic on the N and NE, Surinam (Dutch Guiana) on the E, Brazil on the S, and Brazil and Venezuela on the W. The leading products are sugar, rice, bauxite, gold, and diamonds. There are three counties: Berbice, Demerara, and Essequibo (formerly separate colonies, consolidated in 1831). The region was first settled by the Dutch between 1616 and 1620, was acquired by the British in 1803, and was formally ceded to them in 1814. The boundary with Venezuela was determined by arbitration in 1899; that with Brazil, on July 12, 1904. Capital, Georgetown; area, ab. 83,000 sq. mi.; pop. 425,156 (est. 1950).

British Honduras (hon.dö′rạs). [Also: **Balize, Belize.**] Crown colony of Great Britain, lying between Yucatán on the N, the Caribbean Sea on the E, and Guatemala on the S and W. It exports lumber (chiefly mahogany and pine), bananas, chicle, and citrus products. It was settled by woodcutters from Jamaica early in the 17th century, and since 1862 has been a crown colony of Great Britain. Capital, Belize; area, 8,867 sq. mi.; pop. 66,892 (est. 1950).

British Legion. In 19th-century history, name applied to a body of British troops, commanded by George de Lacy Evans, which fought (1836) for Queen Isabella of Spain against the Carlists.

British Legion. In 20th-century history, name applied to an association of war veterans in Great Britain. It was founded shortly after the close of World War I, and is approximately comparable in its aims and qualifications for membership to the American Legion in the U.S.

"British Loan." Financial agreement between the U.S. and Great Britain, signed by representatives of both countries in December, 1945, and upheld by the U.S. Congress in May, 1946. It provided for a 3,750,000-dollar credit to Great Britain to be drawn as needed up to Dec. 31, 1951. It was intended to help Great Britain meet its balance-of-payments deficits and bolster its gold and dollar reserve, and to facilitate multilateral trade agreements. Within approximately a year's time British needs had made it necessary to draw the full amount of the loan, and British aid was thereafter integrated with aid to all of western Europe under the Marshall Plan.

British Museum. Museum and library in Great Russell Street, Bloomsbury, London, founded in 1753. It contains collections of antiquities, drawings, prints, and a library of more than five million volumes, over 57,000 manuscripts, and 85,000 charters and rolls. The growth of the museum after its original establishment was very rapid: Montague House was first employed in 1754 when room was needed for Sir Hans Sloane's library and collections, which were bought for the nominal price of 20,000 pounds, being part of the funds raised by a lottery. The collection was opened to the public on Jan. 15, 1759. The Harleian manuscripts, the royal library presented in 1757, and 65,000 volumes transferred by George IV, raised the library to a position of world importance. The new building, designed by Sir Robert Smirke and completed by his brother Sydney Smirke, was begun soon after the beginning of the 19th century. The main building, completed in 1847, is in the Classic style. In 1816 the Elgin marbles were bought for the sum of 35,000 pounds. The first great Egyptian acquisition consisted of the objects taken with the French army in 1801. In 1802 the Rosetta Stone was deposited in the Museum. Subsequently the collection of Sir Gardiner Wilkinson was added. The museum has an extensive collection of Egyptian papyri, and 2,700 Greek and Latin papyri. The Assyrian, Babylonian, coin, and Greek vase collections are considered the best in any contemporary museum. The natural history collections have been removed to the Museum of Natural History at South Kensington. Modern English publications are added free of expense by a privilege, shared with three universities, of receiving gratis a copy of every copyrighted book. The files of newspapers are housed in a special department at Colindale, London.

British Music Society. British musical organization, founded (1918) by Eaglefield Hull for the promotion of music in Great Britain. It was active until 1933.

British North Borneo (bôr′nẹ.ō). See **North Borneo.**

British Prison Ship, The. Poem by Philip Freneau, published in 1781.

British Somaliland (sọ.mä′li.land). [Official name, **Somaliland Protectorate.**] British protectorate in E Africa, along the Gulf of Aden. It is bounded on the NE by French Somaliland, on the W and S by Ethiopia, and on the E by the former Italian Somaliland. It became a British protectorate in 1887, although British influence had been dominant in the area before that. It was occupied by the Italians in 1940 but retaken by the British in 1941. Camels, sheep, and goats are raised, some millet is grown, and fishing along the coast is profitable; myrrh and frankincense are found in the E part. The protectorate is administered by a military governor who is the sole executive and legislative authority. Capital, Hargeisa; area, 67,836 sq. mi.; pop. estimates range between 350,000 and 700,000.

British South Africa Company. British commercial company chartered in 1889 for the exploitation of Matabeleland and the neighboring regions. It was headed by Cecil Rhodes. The company built Fort Salisbury (now Salisbury, the capital of Southern Rhodesia), and developed Mashonaland. Its territory was extended to include British Central Africa (north of the Zambesi River), with the exception of Nyasaland, in what later became Rhodesia. In 1893 a Matabele rising under Lobengula was suppressed by its forces.

British Virgin Islands. Group of islands in the Caribbean Sea, E of Puerto Rico: a presidency in the British colony of the Leeward Islands. The most important of the 36 islands and rocks comprising the group are Tortola, Virgin Gorda, and Anegada. Truck gardening, fishing, and the preparation of charcoal are the major industries. Capital, Road Town; area, 67 sq. mi.; pop. 5,547 (1949).

British West Indies. Group of islands in the Caribbean Sea, SE of the U.S.: British colonies. They include the Bahamas, Jamaica, the Caymans, the Turks Islands, the Caicos Islands, Trinidad, Tobago, Barbados, the Windward Islands, and the Leeward Islands. The chief products are sugar and bananas; some of the islands produce oil, asphalt, and coconuts. In 1951 a commission appointed by the British secretary of state for colonies recommended the establishment of a customs union which would link the principal West Indian colonies with British Guiana and British Honduras. Area, ab. 12,000 sq. mi.; pop. ab. 2,500,000.

British Women's Symphony Orchestra. Ensemble established in 1924, drawing its participants from among professional women musicians.

British Zone. See under **German Federal Republic.**

Brito (brē′tö), **(Raimundo de) Farias.** b. at São Benedito, Cesará, Brazil, July 24, 1862; d. at Rio de Janeiro, Jan. 16, 1917. Brazilian philosopher, regarded by many critics as the most important that Brazil has produced. He was a professor of logic. Among his works are *Finalidade do Mundo* (1895–99), *A filosofia como atividade permanente* *do espírito humano* (1895), *A filosofia moderna* (1905), *Evolução e relatividade* (1905), *A verdade como regra das ações* (1905), *A base física do espírito* (1912), and *O mundo interior* (1914).

Brito Freire (frā'rẹ), **Francisco de.** b. at Coruche, Alentejo, Portugal, c1620; d. at Lisbon, Nov. 8, 1692. Portuguese admiral, administrator, and historian. He was captain-general of Pernambuco from 1661 to 1664, and wrote *Nova Lusitania*, an incomplete history of the wars between the Dutch and Portuguese in Brazil.

Britomart (brit'ọ.märt). In Edmund Spenser's *The Faerie Queene*, a female knight personifying chastity.

Britomartis (brit.ọ.mär'tis). In Greek mythology, a Cretan divinity of hunters and fishermen. The legends concerning her are various. According to one, to escape from the pursuit of Minos she threw herself among the fishermen's nets in the sea, and was rescued and made a deity by Artemis.

Briton (brit'ọn), **The.** Historical tragedy (1722) by Ambrose Philips.

Britons (brit'ọnz). Natives of Great Britain, and especially the original Celtic inhabitants of this island.

Brittain (brit'ạn), **Marion Luther.** b. in Wilkes County, Ga., Nov. 11, 1866; d. at Atlanta, Ga., July 1, 1953. American educator. He was superintendent (1900–01) of the Fulton County schools, served as Georgia state commissioner (1910–11) and state superintendent (1911–22) of schools, and was president (1922 *et seq.*) of the Georgia School of Technology.

Brittain, Vera. b. at Newcastle-under-Lyme, Staffordshire, England, c1896—. English novelist, poet, and journalist. She served as a volunteer nurse (1915–19) at London, Malta, and France, and lectured in America (1934, 1937, 1940, 1946), the Netherlands (1936), Scandinavia (1945), and Germany (1947). Her works include *Verses of a V.A.D.* (1918), *Not Without Honour* (1924), *Testament of Youth* (1933), *Poems of the War and After* (1934), *A Testament of Friendship* (1940), *Seed of Chaos* (1944), *On Becoming a Writer* (1947), *Born 1925: A Novel of Youth* (1948), and *Valiant Pilgrim* (1950).

Brittaine (brit'ạn), **Nicholas.** See **Breton, Nicholas.**

Brittany (brit'ạ.ni). [Also: **Britanny**; French, **Bretagne**; Latin, **Britannia Minor, Britannia Cismarina.**] Peninsula, region, and former government of France, capital Rennes, part of the Roman Armorica, bounded by the English Channel on the N, by the regions or former provinces of Normandy, Maine, and Anjou on the E and Poitou on the S, and by the Atlantic Ocean on the SW and W. It is traversed by hills and low mountains (the Montagnes d'Arrée, Montagnes Noires, and others); the western part is called in French Basse-Bretagne ("low Brittany") and the eastern, Haute-Bretagne ("high Brittany"). It comprises the five modern departments of Finistère, Côtes-du-Nord, Morbihan, Ille-et-Vilaine, and Loire-Inférieure. The vernacular language is Breton. Brittany is noted for its megalithic monuments (dolmens, menhirs, and cromlechs). A large part of the people are sailors and fishermen. The region was inhabited by the Veneti and other Gallic tribes, and formed a part of Lugdunensis under the Romans. It received the name of Lesser or Little Britain or Brittany (Britannia Minor; also Britannia Cismarina) in allusion to the Greater Britain across the Channel, from which it received colonists (from Cornwall) driven out by the Anglo-Saxons, probably the ancestors of the people whom the Romans called Britanni. The Frankish kings failed to retain a permanent hold on the country. In the 9th century it became independent, and was ruled by counts and dukes. In the 12th century it passed by marriage to Geoffrey, son of Henry II of England. It became a fief of France in 1204, and soon after passed under the rule of the dukes of the Dreux family. It was united to France by the marriages of Anne (the heiress of Brittany), with Charles VIII of France in 1491 and with Louis XII in 1499. It was finally incorporated with France in 1532. During the French Revolution and later it was a center of royalist sentiment.

Britten (brit'ẹn), **Benjamin.** [Full name, **Edward Benjamin Britten.**] b. at Lowestoft, Suffolk, England, Nov. 22, 1913—. English composer, pianist, and conductor. His formal musical education was obtained mainly at the Royal College of Music, London. He has written much work expressly for radio presentation or as incidental music to plays and motion pictures. His musical language is based upon classical principles, but he has successfully employed modern and original idioms. Britten came to the U.S. in 1938 and remained until 1942. Among his better-known works are: *Sinfonietta* (for chamber orchestra, 1932), *Phantasy* (oboe quartet, 1932), *A Boy was Born* (choral variations, 1932–33), *Simple Symphony* (string orchestra, 1934), *Holiday Tales* (piano, 1934); *Suite* (violin and piano), *Friday Afternoons* (school songs), and *Soirées Musicales* (all 1935); *Our Hunting Fathers* (symphonic cycle, in collaboration with the poet W. H. Auden, 1936), *Variations on a Theme of Frank Bridge* (strings, 1937), *On This Island* (songs with piano, again with W. H. Auden, 1937), *Mont Juic* (orchestra, 1937), *Piano Concerto Number One in D major* (1938), *Ballad of Heroes* (tenor solo, chorus and orchestra, 1939), and *Kermesse Canadienne* (orchestra, 1939). In the year 1940 he composed *Diversions on a Theme* (piano and orchestra), *Les Illuminations* (voice and strings, using words by Rimbaud), *Paul Bunyan* (operetta, with W. H. Auden), *Sinfonia da Requiem* (orchestra), *Sonnets of Michelangelo* (tenor and piano), and *Introduction and Rondo alla burlesca* (two pianos). His more recent works include *Elegiac Mazurka* (2 pianos, 1941) and *Peter Grimes* (opera, commissioned by the Koussevitzky Foundation, 1945). *Let's Make an Opera* (1950) is an opera in which the audience participates.

Britting (brit'ing), **Georg.** b. near Regensburg, Germany, Feb. 17, 1892—. German lyric poet and story writer. He emerged from World War I seriously wounded and convinced that "anyone who has experienced four years of comradeship in the trenches cannot help but be both a nationalist and a socialist." His poems were collected in the volume *Der irdische Tag* (1935). He wrote but one full-length novel, *Lebenslauf eines dicken Mannes, der Hamlet hiess* (1932).

Brittle (brit'l), **Barnaby.** In Thomas Betterton's play *The Amorous Widow*, the husband of Mrs. Brittle. A character not unlike Molière's George Dandin, he was played by Charles Macklin at Covent Garden.

Brittle, Mrs. Character in Thomas Betterton's play *The Amorous Widow*. The part was chosen (1707) by Anne Bracegirdle and Anne Oldfield as a means of testing their relative popularity with the London public of the day. They played the part on alternate nights, and Anne Oldfield was better liked (whereupon Anne Bracegirdle is said to have retired in disgust from the stage).

Britton (brit'ọn). Early summary of English law written in French, probably in the 13th century. A manuscript is in existence. It was first printed in London c1530. Some critics at first thought it an abridgment of Henry de Bracton's work.

Britton, Colonel. The lover of Isabella in Susannah Centlivre's comedy *The Wonder, a Woman Keeps a Secret.* It is to keep the secret of Colonel Britton and Isabella that Violante nearly loses her own lover.

Britton, John. b. at Kingston-St.-Michael, Wiltshire, England, July 7, 1771; d. at London, Jan. 1, 1857. English antiquary. His works include *The Beauties of Wiltshire* (1801–25; written in collaboration), *Architectural Antiquities of Great Britain* (1805–26), and *Cathedral Antiquities of England* (1814–35).

Britton, Nathaniel Lord. b. at New Dorp, Staten Island, N.Y., Jan. 15, 1859; d. June 25, 1934. American botanist, director of the New York Botanical Garden from 1896. He was graduated from the Columbia School of Mines in 1879, and was professor of botany (1888–96) at Columbia University. Among his publications are *Illustrated Flora of the Northern United States and Canada* and *Manual of the Flora of the Northern United States and Canada.*

Britton, Nicholas. See **Breton, Nicholas.**

Britton, Thomas. [Called **"the Musical Small-Coal Man."**] b. at Rushden, England, c1643; d. at London, Sept. 27, 1714. English coal merchant, remembered for his organization and support (1678 *et seq.*) of regular concerts in a room over his London store. Among the performers were George Frederick Handel, John Christopher Pepusch, and Henry Symonds.

Britton's Bower of Delights. Anthology (1591, 1597), issued by Richard Jones under Nicholas Breton's name (in one of its various spellings). Breton disclaimed responsibility for it, except the long opening poem on Sir Philip Sidney's death entitled *Amoris Lachrimae*, and "one or two other toys."

Brivas (brī'vạs). Ancient name of **Brioude.**

Brive-la-Gaillarde (brēv.lȧ gȧ.yȧrd). [Also: **Brive, Brives-la-Gaillarde**; ancient name, **Briva Curretia** (brī'vạ kū̦.rē'shạ).] Town in S central France, in the department of Corrèze, situated on the Corrèze River, between Tulle and Périgueux; it is a station on the railroad line from Paris to Toulouse. It has trade in cattle, poultry, vegetables, and truffles. There are beautiful boulevards and a local-art museum. The Church of Saint Martin is an example of 12th-century Romanesque art, but has additions from later periods. 33,501 (1946).

Brix (briks). A German name of **Most,** Czechoslovakia.

Brixen (brik'sẹn). German name of **Bressanone.**

Brixham (brik'sạm). Urban district, seaport, and fishing town in SW England, in Devonshire, situated on the S shore of Tor Bay, an inlet of the English Channel, ab. 23 mi. S of Exeter, ab. 207 mi. SW of London by rail. It has engaged in fishing since c1850, and good trawling grounds are located offshore. William of Orange landed (1688) at Brixham on his way to assume the English throne. 8,761 (1951).

Brixia (brik'si.ạ). Ancient name of **Brescia.**

Brizeux (brē.zė), **Julien Auguste Pélage.** b. at Lorient, France, c1803; d. at Montpellier, France, in May, 1858. French idyllic poet, who wrote in Breton as well as in French. His works include *Marie*, *La Fleur d'or*, *Primel et Nola*, and the Breton anthology *Le Télen Arvor*.

Brno (bėr'nō). Administrative region or county in W central Czechoslovakia, in C Moravia, established by decree of Dec. 21, 1948, which came into effect in 1949. Capital, Brno; area, 2,876 sq. mi.; pop. 934,437 (1947).

Brno. [German, **Brünn.**] City in W central Czechoslovakia, in C Moravia: until 1949 the capital of Moravia, and thereafter of the administrative region or county of Brno. It is situated between the Svitava and Svarzava rivers, at the base of the high hill called the Špilberk, or in German, Spielberg. In the castle on the Špilberk, later a prison, many Italian and Polish revolutionaries against the Hapsburg regime were confined during the 19th century. On another hill is a Gothic cathedral of some interest both from the standpoint of architecture and from that of history. In the city are the Gothic Church of Saint Jacob and the baroque Church of Saint Thomas, the old and new town halls are likewise of architectural interest. There is a Moravian museum and a municipal theater. Masaryk University, an institute of technology, and other educational institutions are located here. The biologist Gregor Mendl lived at Brno as the abbot of the Augustinian monastery. Pop., inner city, 133,637; including suburbs, 273,127 (1947).

History. Brno was settled in the 11th and 12th centuries by Slovak, German, and Dutch settlers. It was unsuccessfully besieged by the Hussites in 1428, by the Swedes in 1645, and by the Prussians in 1742, and was occupied by Napoleon I in 1805 and by the Prussians in 1866. It fell to Czechoslovakia in 1918. Brno is one of the principal manufacturing cities in modern Czechoslovakia, being known abroad particularly for its woolen, linen, cotton, jute, and hosiery mills, machine, leather, chemical, paper, and food industries, in addition to wholesale establishments in the grain, vegetable, fruit, coal, and lumber trades. The Czechoslovak arms factory is situated in Brno. However, the major part of its industrial and residential quarters was destroyed in World War II, partly by air raids, partly as a result of heavy ground fighting between the German and Russian armies. The baroque building of the provincial administration of Moravia, formerly the Augustinian monastery, was severely damaged in the course of the fighting. Ethnically, the city was contested throughout the 19th and early 20th centuries, but is now purely Czech in character owing to the expulsion of the German inhabitants after 1945.

Broach (brōch). [Also: **Baroach, Bharoch**; ancient name, **Barygaza.**] Capital of Broach and Panch Mahals district, in the W part of the Union of India, in Bombay state, on the Narbada River ab. 30 mi. from its mouth. It is a port and trading center, manufactures textiles, and exports some cotton. It was stormed by the British in 1772 and 1803. Pop. 55,810 (1941).

Broach and Panch Mahals (pänch mạ.hälz'). District in the N part of Bombay state, Union of India, ab. 200 mi. N of the city of Bombay. Cotton, wheat, and tobacco are grown in the area and there is some mining of manganese. Capital, Broach; area, 3,198 sq. mi.; pop. 924,527 (1941).

Broad (brôd). River in North and South Carolina which rises in the Blue Ridge, uniting at Columbia with the Saluda River to form the Congaree River. Length, over 200 mi.

Broad, Charlie Dunbar. b. at London, Dec. 30, 1887—. English philosopher, a professor (1933 *et seq.*) at Cambridge. In 1935 he was named president of the Society for Psychical Research. Author of *Perception, Physics, and Reality* (1914), and other works.

Broadbent (brôd'bent), Sir **William Henry.** b. at Lindley, near Huddersfield, Yorkshire, England, Jan. 23, 1835; d. at London, July 10, 1907. English physician and writer on medical subjects. After studying medicine at Manchester and Paris, he served on the staff of several London hospitals, and in 1892 attended Edward VII's eldest son, the Duke of Clarence and Avondale, during his last illness. This led to his becoming, in that same year, physician to Edward himself (who was then still Prince of Wales), and in 1896, physician to Queen Victoria. After Edward's accession to the throne of England, as Edward VII, Broadbent continued to attend him, and also became physician to the succeeding Prince of Wales, who later became George V of England. Meanwhile, he conducted researches in various fields, especially in cancer and paralysis, and his theories concerning some of the aspects of hemipligia or partial paralysis were of considerable value to medical science. He was active in public health work, and became one of the leaders of the National Association for the Prevention of Consumption and of the British Congress on Tuberculosis. He received many academic honors, became a Fellow of the Royal Society, and was made a baronet. In addition to numerous papers contributed to scientific periodicals, he was the author of *The Pulse* (1890) and *The Heart* (1897).

Broad Bottom Ministry. In British history, a name given to the ministry of 1743–54, under Henry Pelham, which was formed by a temporary and remarkable coalition of the Whig and Tory parties. In it Pelham served as both prime minister and chancellor of the exchequer. The ministry was preserved in power not so much by a genuine reconciliation of the chief British political factions as by Pelham's cynical and skillful technique of systematized corruption.

Broadhaven or **Broad Haven** (brôd'hā″vẹn). Bay in Connacht province, Irish Republic, in County Mayo, lying between the Mullet Peninsula and the Irish mainland. Length, ab. 7 mi.; width at entrance, ab. 6 mi.

Broadhurst (brôd'hėrst), **George Howells.** b. June 3, 1866; d. at Santa Barbara, Calif., Jan. 31, 1952. English playwright. In 1882 he came to the U.S., where his outstanding stage successes were *The Man of the Hour* (1907) and *Bought and Paid For* (1913). He returned to England in 1926 and devoted himself to writing fiction.

Broadhurst, Henry. b. at Littlemore, Oxfordshire, England, April 13, 1840; d. at Cromer, Norfolk, England, Oct 11, 1911. English labor leader. A stonemason's son, he worked (1853–58) as a stonemason, and was spokesman (1872) for the London masons in their agitation at that time for increased pay. As a union leader, he encouraged the establishment of a central executive committee with powers of negotiation on behalf of the entire union membership. He was secretary (1873) of the Labour Representation League which supported workingmen candidates for Parliament, and secretary (1875) of a parliamentary committee of the trade union congress. He agitated for amendments to the Factory Acts, employer's liability, and workman's compensation. While a member of Parliament (1880–92, 1894–1906), he was undersecretary (1886) in the Home Department. An opponent of the demand for an eight-hour working day, Broadhurst lost interest in later union policy. He published his autobiography in 1901.

Broads (brôdz). [Also, **Broadland** (brôd'lạnd).] Name for a region in E England, in Norfolk W of Yarmouth (Norfolk Broads) and in Suffolk near Lowestuft (Suffolk Broads), which is lowlying and covered with many lakes, or "broads," formed by the rivers Bure, Waveney, and Yare.

Broadstairs and St. Peters (brôd'stãrz"; sānt pē'tėrz). Urban district and seaside resort in SE England, in Kent, situated on the Strait of Dover ab. 16 mi. NE of Canterbury, between Margate and Ramsgate, ab. 75 mi. SE of London by rail. 15,082 (1951).

Broadview (brôd'vū). Village in NE Illinois, in Cook County, W of Chicago: residential suburb. In the decade between the last two U.S. censuses its population more than tripled. 1,457 (1940); 5,196 (1950).

Broadway (brôd'wā). Street in New York City, famous for the many theaters located along or near its midtown section. Strictly speaking, it extends from Bowling Green N along the Hudson River to Albany. Within the city it crosses, diagonally, Fifth Avenue at 23rd Street (Madison Square), Sixth Avenue, or the Avenue of the Americas, at 34th Street (Herald Square and Greeley Square), and Seventh Avenue at 43rd Street (Times Square). From Central Park, at Eighth Avenue and 59th Street (Columbus Circle), its continuation to 155th Street follows mostly the old Bloomingdale Road. From 107th Street to 170th Street it is identical with West End (Eleventh) Avenue. Broadway in the Times Square area is often called the "Great White Way" because it is lined with brightly lighted amusement places and enormous illuminated signs. Although the word "Broadway" is still used figuratively to mean the legitimate stage in New York, most of the theaters are now on nearby side streets.

Broadway Journal. Literary periodical published (1845–46) at New York. Edgar Allan Poe became its sole proprietor a few months after its establishment.

Broadway Pageant, A. Poem (1860) by Walt Whitman. It was inspired by the arrival in the U.S. of the first Japanese delegation to visit the West, and Whitman hailed Liberty as marching with the Asiatic procession.

Broadwood (brôd'wůd), **Henry Fowler.** b. 1811; d. 1893. English piano manufacturer; grandson of John Broadwood.

Broadwood, Henry John Tschudi. d. 1911. English piano manufacturer, patentee of the barless grand piano. He was director (1901 *et seq.*) of John Broadwood and Sons, Limited.

Broadwood, James. b. 1772; d. 1851. English piano manufacturer. He joined (1795) his father, John Broadwood (1732–1812), as a partner in the firm of John Broadwood and Sons.

Broadwood, John. b. at Cockburnspath, Scotland, 1732; d. 1812. English piano maker.

Brobdingnag (brob'ding.nag) or **Brobdignag** (-dig-). A country described in Jonathan Swift's *Gulliver's Travels*, in which the inhabitants and all objects were of gigantic size.

Broca (bro.kȧ), **Paul.** b. at Ste.-Foy-la-Grande, Gironde, France, June 28, 1824; d. at Paris, July 9, 1880. French anthropologist, founder of the Anthropological Society of Paris (1859), of the School of Anthropology (1876), and of the French Association for the Advancement of the Sciences (1872). He became a member of the Senate in 1880. Among his works are *Instructions générales pour les recherches anthropologiques* (1865), *Mémoires sur les caractères physiques de l'homme préhistorique* (1869), *Mémoires d'anthropologie* (1871–83; 5th vol., edited by Pozzi, 1888), and *Instructions craniologiques et craniométriques* (1875). He was an authority on aphasia, and located the section of the brain in which speech originates.

Brocard (bro.kȧr). [Also: **Brochard, Burcardus.**] fl. at Avignon, c1332. French Dominican friar. His real name is not known, since it does not appear on any of the manuscripts of his work, in the reports concerning it, nor in a translation of it into French which was made in 1333. The name here given was applied to the translation made in 1455 by the canon of Lille, who assumed, incorrectly, that the work had been written by a Dominican of this name who had indeed lived during the 14th century. It has been suggested in recent years that a Dominican named Guillaume (or William) Adam may actually have been the author, but this still awaits final proof. The work in question is entitled *Directorium ad passagium faciendum ad Terram Sanctam.* It was dedicated to Philip IV of France and is a plan for a crusade (in fact, it was probably written at the instigation of Pope John XXII, who was trying to persuade the French king to lead a new crusade). The work contains two central ideas: to fight the Saracens and to compel the Greek Church to defer to Rome. It is divided into two parts: the first one deals with the reasons for a new crusade, various details concerning provisions, ships, men, and the like, and discusses possible routes to the East (it favors the land route through Hungary); the second part takes up the matter of the various peoples of the Near East, and discusses the various ways in which it may be possible to bribe or force them to help the French. For the modern reader, however, these points about the work are secondary to the information it provides about the world of its time, for Brocard did not write on a basis of the accounts of others: he had actually been to most of the places he mentions. In 1307 he was at Constantinople and various parts of the Greek peninsula, and he gives valuable information of the economic and commercial life of that area. He was in Persia after 1312, visited an island at the entrance to the Gulf of Aden, and went so far south of the equator that he considered the belief in the antipodes to be neither false nor frivolous. (His reasons for believing he had gone south of the equator are of particular interest: he observed that the length of the days and nights at the equator are equal at all times of the year, that the stars were in different positions south of the line, and that the north star was no longer visible.) He also concluded that the size of the inhabited part of the earth was larger than had been indicated in earlier works on geography.

Brocard, (Pierre Jean Baptiste) Henri. b. at Vignot, France, May 13, 1845; d. at Bar-le-Duc, France, Jan. 16, 1922. French mathematician and meteorologist, noted especially for his geometry of the triangle, including the "Brocard point" and the "Brocard circle." He was educated at the École Polytechnique and occupied numerous positions in government service, rising to the rank of lieutenant colonel in the territorial engineers. His works include *Analyse indéterminée du premier degré* (1896), *Notes de bibliographie des courbes géométriques* (1897), and *Courbes géométriques remarquables* (in collaboration, 1922).

Broch (broċh), **Hermann.** b. at Vienna, Nov. 1, 1886; d. at New Haven, Conn., May 30, 1951. Austrian novelist, dramatist, and literary critic, best known for his highly original novel, *Der Tod des Vergil* (1945; Eng. trans., *The Death of Vergil*, 1946). Other novels which merit mention are *Die Schlafwandler* (1931–32; Eng. trans., *The Sleepwalkers*, 1932) and *Die unbekannte Grösse* (1933; Eng. trans., *The Unknown Quantity*, 1935). He left Vienna in 1938, and became a resident of the U.S.

Brochard (bro.shȧr). See **Brocard.**

Brock (brok), **Charles Edmund.** b. at Holloway, England, Feb. 5, 1870; d. 1938. English genre and portrait painter, noted particularly for his book illustrations. Educated at the Higher Grade School, Cambridge, he subsequently exhibited at the Royal Academy and at the Royal Institute. The books he illustrated include editions of Charles Lamb's *Essays of Elia*, Charles Kingsley's *Westward Ho!*, and the *English Idylls* series, published by the firm of J. M. Dent.

Brock, Sir **Isaac.** [Called the **"Hero of Upper Canada."**] b. on the island of Guernsey, Oct. 6, 1769; killed at Queenston, Ontario, Canada, Oct. 13, 1812. British major general. In 1806 he was named chief military commander in British North America. For his capture of General William Hull and the entire American force at Detroit, on Aug. 16, 1812, he was knighted. He fell later in the War of 1812, in the battle of Queenston Heights, above Niagara Falls.

Brock, Sir **Thomas.** b. at Worcester, England, 1847; d. 1922. English sculptor. He was elected to the Royal Academy in 1891. In 1911 his memorial to Queen Victoria, in front of Buckingham Palace, London, was unveiled, and in consideration of this work he was knighted.

Brockdorff-Rantzau (brok'dôrf rän'tsou), Count **Ulrich von.** b. at Schleswig, Germany, May 29, 1869; d. at Berlin, Sept. 8, 1928. German diplomat and statesman. He served at first as an attaché at Brussels, later (1897) at St. Petersburg, and, from 1901 to 1905, at Vienna. In 1912 he went as minister to Copenhagen, where he succeeded in keeping Denmark neutral during World War I. He became state secretary of foreign affairs in 1919 and led the German delegation at Versailles, but refused to accept the theory of German war guilt and resigned (June,

1919). In 1922 he became German ambassador at Moscow where he sought to achieve a Russian-German understanding. He opposed the League of Nations and the Locarno Treaty.

Brocken (brok'ẹn; German, brok'ẹn) or **Blocksberg** (bloks'berk). [Latin, **Mons Bructerus.**] Chief summit of the Harz Mountains, and the highest mountain in N Germany, situated in the *Land* (state) of Saxony-Anhalt, between Blankenburg and Clausthal. It is the traditional meeting place of the witches on Walpurgis Night, and is famous for the optical phenomenon called the "specter of the Brocken." 3,747 ft.

Brockes (brok'ẹs), **Barthold Heinrich.** b. at Hamburg, Germany, Sept. 22, 1680; d. there, Jan. 16, 1747. German poet. He spent his youth in travel, and upon his return to Hamburg was made senator, and later was entrusted with many missions and public offices. While governor of the district of Ritzebüttel (1735–41) he wrote a description of the life and scenery of that region in *Landleben in Ritzebüttel.* His poetry is contained in *Irdisches Vergnügen in Gott* (published in yearly installments from 1721 to 1748). He translated Pope's *An Essay on Man* in 1740 and Thomson's *The Seasons* in 1745. His work *Der sterbende Jesus* (1712) was set to music as an oratorio by Handel.

Brockhaus (brok'hous), **Friedrich Arnold.** b. at Dortmund, Germany, May 4, 1772; d. at Leipzig, Germany, Aug. 20, 1823. German publisher of reference books. His firm, F. A. Brockhaus, was founded at Amsterdam in 1805 and transferred to Leipzig in 1817. In 1808 he purchased the rights to an encyclopedia (begun in 1796) and completed its publication in 1811 under the title of *Allgemeine deutsche Real-Encyclopädie für die gebildeten Stände.* The 17th edition of this work is *Der Grosse Brockhaus* in 20 volumes (1928–35). The firm also published yearbooks, periodicals, pocket editions, and the like. After Friedrich Arnold's death, his sons Friedrich (1800–65) and Heinrich (1804–77) continued and expanded the business. In 1831 they began publishing Ersch and Gruber's *Allgemeine Encyklopädie der Wissenschaften und Künste,* of which volumes 62 to 99 were edited (1856 *et seq.*) by their brother Hermann (1806–77), a noted Orientalist and professor of Indology at Leipzig. Friedrich retired in 1850. Heinrich was succeeded by his sons Eduard (1829–1914) and Rudolf (1838–98).

Brockhaus, Hermann. b. at Amsterdam, Jan. 28, 1806; d. at Leipzig, Germany, Jan. 5, 1877. German Orientalist; son of Friedrich Arnold Brockhaus. He was the editor of Ersch and Gruber's *Allgemeine Encyklopädie der Wissenschaften und Künste* after 1856, and also of various Persian and Sanskrit works. He was professor of Indology at Leipzig.

Brockhurst (brok'hėrst), **Gerald Leslie.** b. at Birmingham, England, 1890—. English painter and etcher, noted primarily for his portraits. In 1907 he studied at the Royal Academy Schools, where he subsequently won a number of medals. In 1913 he received the studentship given by the Royal Academy Council. Exhibitions of his work have been held at the most important art associations at London. In addition, he was a member of the committee for the British Artists' Exhibitions, and a member of the jury for the International Exhibition at Venice in 1928 and for the Carnegie International at Pittsburgh in 1939.

Brocklehurst (brok'l.hėrst), **Mount.** Dome-shaped mountain in Antarctica, lying ab. 15 mi. W by SW of Mount Smith, in the Prince Albert Mountains of Victoria Land, in ab. 76°08′ S., 160°55′ E. Elevation, ab. 4,300 ft.

Brockport (brok'pōrt). Village in W New York, in Monroe County, on the New York State Barge Canal, near Rochester: nurseries and canneries. It is the seat of a state teachers college. 4,748 (1950).

Brockton (brok'tọn). [Former name, **North Bridgewater.**] City in SE Massachusetts, in Plymouth County, ab. 20 mi. S of Boston: noted for its manufactures of shoes and shoemaking tools and supplies. William Cullen Bryant lived here for a time. 62,860 (1950).

Brockville (brok'vil). Town and port of entry in Ontario, Canada, situated on the St. Lawrence River: county seat of Leeds and Grenville counties. It was a military training station during World War II. 12,301 (1951).

Brockway (brok'wā). Borough in W Pennsylvania, in Jefferson County, in a potato-producing area: manufactures include macaroni, bottles, jars, and clay products. It was settled in 1822. Pop. 2,650 (1950).

Brockway, Howard A. b. at Brooklyn, N.Y., Nov. 22, 1870; d. at New York, Feb. 20, 1951. American pianist, composer, and teacher (1925–41) at the Juilliard School of Music. He wrote for orchestra, piano, cello, and voice, his best-known work being *Sylvan Suite* for orchestra (1903).

Brockway, Zebulon Reed. b. at Lyme, Conn., April 28, 1827; d. Oct. 21, 1920. American penologist, superintendent (1876–1900) of the New York State Reformatory at Elmira, and mayor (1906–07) of that city. He was appointed deputy superintendent of the Albany Penitentiary in 1851, superintendent of the Monroe County, N.Y., Penitentiary in 1854, and of the Detroit House of Correction in 1861. He wrote numerous papers on the subject of penology, and was largely responsible for the introduction of the policy (now virtually universal in the states of the U.S.) of imposing an indeterminate sentence, which could be looked upon almost as a period of cure or treatment rather than punishment, for youthful first offenders.

Brod (brôd). [Also: **Slavonski Brod;** German, **Slavonisch-Brod.**] Town in N Yugoslavia, in the federative unit of Croatia, in the former *banovina* (province) of Savska, situated on the Sava River opposite Bosanski Brod, between Belgrade and Zagreb. It is an important river port, railroad junction, and commercial center; has the largest railway repair and construction yards in Yugoslavia. It was not destroyed by the Germans in World War II. 15,176 (1948).

Brod, Bosanski. See **Bosanski Brod.**

Broderick (brō'dẹ.rik), **David Colbreth.** b. at Washington, D.C., Feb. 4, 1820; d. near San Francisco, Sept. 16, 1859. American politician, associated with the early years of the state of California. A member (1840 *et seq.*) of Tammany Hall at New York, he moved to California, where he was elected (1850) to the state senate, and became its president in 1851. He was elected (Jan. 10, 1857) to the U.S. Senate, but soon became acrimoniously involved with President James Buchanan, and subsequently made many enemies in his own state, over the issue of patronage. He was mortally wounded in a duel with the California chief justice, David S. Terry.

Broderip (brod'rip), **William John.** b. at Bristol, England, Nov. 21, 1789; d. at London, Feb. 27, 1859. English lawyer and naturalist, secretary of the Geological Society. He was the author of numerous scientific books and papers, including zoölogical articles in the *Penny Cyclopedia, English Cyclopaedia,* and *Proceedings and Transactions of the Zoölogical Society;* and *Zoölogical Recreations* (1847) and *Leaves from the Note Book of a Naturalist* (1852).

Brodeur (bro.dėr), **Louis Philippe.** b. at Beloeil, Quebec, Canada, Aug. 21, 1862; d. at Quebec, Canada, Jan. 1, 1924. French-Canadian statesman, remembered chiefly for introducing (1910) in the Canadian Parliament the bill which created the Canadian navy. A member of the Canadian Parliament (1891–1911), he was speaker of the House of Commons (1901), minister of inland revenue (1904), and minister of marine and fisheries (1906). He also served (1907 and 1911) as a Canadian representative at imperial conferences at London. He died shortly after his assumption of duties of the lieutenant governorship of Quebec.

Brodhead (brod'hed), **John Romeyn.** b. at Philadelphia, Jan. 2, 1814; d. at New York, May 6, 1873. American historian. He wrote *History of the State of New York* (2 vols., 1853, 1871).

Brodie (brō'di), Sir **Benjamin Collins.** b. at Winterslow, Wiltshire, England, June 9, 1783; d. at Broome Park, Surrey, England, Oct. 21, 1862. English surgeon at St. George's Hospital, London. His works include *Pathological and Surgical Observations on the Diseases of the Joints* (1818) and *Psychological Inquiries* (1854–62). His suggestions, in the former work, of more conservative treatment of diseases of the joints led to a reduction in the number of amputations performed.

Brodie, Sir **Benjamin Collins.** b. 1817; d. 1880. English chemist; son of Sir Benjamin Collins Brodie (1783–1862). He became professor of chemistry at Oxford in 1865. His researches were chiefly concerned with carbon and graphite, and the graphitic acid which he discovered is known as Brodie's acid.

Brodnica (brôd.nē'tsä). [German, **Strasburg** or **Strasburg-an-der-Drewenz.**] Town in N Poland, in the *województwo* (province) of Pomorze, situated on the Drwęca (German, Drewenz) River, NW of Warsaw. Prior to 1919 it belonged to the German province of West Prussia. It is an agricultural market town. The parish church, built in the 13th century, is in the brick-Gothic style. In nearby Golub are the ruins of a huge castle of the Teutonic Knights. 10,665 (1946).

Brodrick (brod'rik), **George Charles.** b. at Castle Rising, Norfolk, England, May 5, 1831; d. at Merton College, Oxford, England, Nov. 8, 1903. English author, college official, and historian. Educated at Eton and at Balliol College, Oxford (B.A., 1854; M.A., 1856), he was a fellow (1855) and warden (1881–1903) of Merton College, Oxford. He had been president (1854–55) of the Oxford Union, a debating society. He was called to the bar in 1859, and later served as a staff member (1860–72) of the London *Times*. Author of *Political Studies* (1879), *English Land and English Landlords* (1881), *History of Merton College* (1885), *History of Oxford University* (1886), and *Memories and Impressions* (1900).

Brodrick, William St. John Fremantle. [Title, 1st Earl of **Midleton.**] b. Dec. 14, 1856; d. Feb. 13, 1942. British Conservative statesman. Educated at Eton and at Balliol College, Oxford, he represented West Surrey (1880–85) and South-West Surrey (1885–1906) in the House of Commons. He was financial secretary to the War Office (1886–92), undersecretary of state for war (1895–98), undersecretary of state for foreign affairs (1898–1900), secretary of state for war (1900–03), and secretary of state for India (1903–December, 1905).

Brodsky (brod'ski; Russian, brôt'ski), **Adolf.** b. at Taganrog, Russia, March 21, 1851; d. 1929. Russian violinist. He was a member of the Hellmesberger Quartet at Vienna and, from 1868 to 1870, of the imperial opera orchestra there, and later (1875–79) was a professor at the conservatory of Moscow. From 1879 to 1881 he was conductor of the symphony orchestra at Kiev; he made concert tours in Austria, Germany, and England (1881–83), and was professor at the Leipzig Conservatory (1883–91). From 1891 to 1894 he was in the U.S. and Canada. In 1895 he was appointed a professor, and later principal, at the Manchester Royal College of Music in England.

Brody (brô'di). Town in the U.S.S.R., in the Ukrainian Soviet Socialist Republic, ab. 20 mi. E of Lvov: an important trading center. It was a free commercial city in the period 1779–1879. Formerly in Poland, it was taken by the Russians in World War I, and became part of the U.S.S.R. under the terms of the Berlin Conference (July 17, 1945). Pop. ab. 12,000.

Brodziński (brô.jēn'skē), **Kazimierz.** b. at Krolowka, near Bochnia, in Galicia, March 8, 1791; d. at Dresden, Germany, Oct. 10, 1835. Polish soldier, poet, and scholar, professor of aesthetics at the University of Warsaw. He served in the Russian campaign of 1812 and in the campaign of 1813, and was taken prisoner at the battle of Leipzig. His complete works were published in the period 1842–44.

Broekhuizen (brök'hoi.zẹn), **Jan van.** [Latinized, **Janus Broukhusius.**] b. at Amsterdam, Nov. 20, 1649; d. near Amsterdam, Dec. 15, 1707. Dutch poet and classical scholar. He edited works of Propertius (1702) and Tibullus (1707), and published Latin poems (*Carmina*, 1684).

Brofferio (brōf.fä'ryō), **Angelo.** b. at Castelnuovo, near Asti, Italy, Dec. 24, 1802; d. at Verbanella, near Lago Maggiore, Italy, May 26, 1866. Italian poet and publicist. His works include *Canzoni Piemontesi* (6th ed., 1858), dramas, a history of Piedmont (1849–52), and others.

Brofoss (brō'fôs), **Erik.** b. at Kongsberg, Norway, June 21, 1908—. Norwegian government official and cabinet member, minister of finance (1945 *et seq.*) in the Gerhardsen government. During World War II he served in the Norwegian government in exile at London, and was vice-president (1945) of the Economic Coördination Council.

Brogan (brō'gan), **Denis William.** b. in Scotland, Aug. 11, 1900—. British political scientist and author, especially noted in the U.S. for such studies of American culture as *The American Political System* (1933), *The American Character* (1944), *American Themes* (1949), and *Government of the People.* Educated at Glasgow, Oxford, and Harvard universities, he taught at the University of London and at the London School of Economics, and was professor of political science at Cambridge. His other books include *French Personalities and Problems* (1946), *The English People*, *The Free State*, and *The Price of Revolution* (1952).

Bröger (brė'gėr), **Karl.** b. at Nuremberg, Germany, March 10, 1886—. German poet and novelist. He belongs to the group known as *Arbeiterdichter*, laboring men who have turned to poetry to relieve their strong, repressed feelings, and who have done much to restore the sincerity and simplicity of the German lyric. Bröger published some verse before World War I (*Die singende Stadt*, 1912) but his most significant work is generally considered to have grown out of his war experience. *Kamerad, als wir marschiert* (1916) and *Soldaten der Erde* (1918) are such products, as well as the novel *Bunker 17* (1929; Eng. trans., *Pillbox 17*, 1930). Two other novels are *Der Guldenschuh* (1934) and *Nürnberg* (1935). *Der Held im Schatten* (1920) is an autobiographical novel.

Brögger (brėg'ėr), **Waldemar Christofer.** b. at Oslo, Norway, Nov. 10, 1851; d. 1940. Norwegian geologist and mineralogist. He served as a professor (1881 *et seq.*) at the universities of Stockholm and Oslo. Author of *Fridtjof Nansen* (1861–93; Eng. trans., 1896), *Die Eruptivgesteine des Oslogebietes* (1930–33), and *On Several Archäan Rocks from the South Coast of Norway* (1933).

Broghill (brog'hil), Baron. A title of **Boyle, Roger.**

Broglie (broy'), **Achille Charles Léonce Victor,** Duc **de.** b. at Paris, Nov. 28, 1785; d. there, Jan. 25, 1870. French statesman and peer of France; son of Victor Claude, Prince de Broglie. He was minister of the interior and of public worship and instruction (1830), and minister of foreign affairs (October, 1832–April, 1834, November, 1834–February, 1836). He married (1816) Albertine Ida Gustavine de Staël, daughter of Madame de Staël.

Broglie, Duchesse **de.** [Maiden name, **Albertine Ida Gustavine de Staël.**] b. at Paris, 1797; d. Sept. 22, 1838. French writer; daughter of Madame de Staël, and wife of Achille Charles Léonce Victor, Duc de Broglie. She wrote moral and religious essays, collected after her death under the title of *Fragments sur divers sujets de religion et de morale* (1840).

Broglie, François Marie, Duc **de.** b. at Paris, Jan. 11, 1671; d. at Broglie, France, May 22, 1745. French soldier, a marshal of France; son of Victor Maurice, Comte de Broglie. He fought under Louis XIV in several campaigns.

Broglie, Jacques Victor Albert, Duc **de.** b. 1821; d. Jan. 19, 1901. French statesman, publicist, and historian; son of Achille Charles Léonce Victor, Duc de Broglie. He was ambassador to London (1871), and premier of France (1873–74, 1877). His chief work is *L'Église et l'empire romain au IVe siècle* (1856–66).

Broglie, Louis Victor, Prince **de.** b. at Dieppe, France, Aug. 15, 1892—. French physicist; grandson of Jacques Victor Albert, Duc de Broglie, and brother of Maurice, Duc de Broglie. He studied at the Sorbonne, where he was later a lecturer, served in World War I, and was appointed (1933) professor of theoretical physics at the Henri Poincaré Institute, University of Paris. Best known for his investigations in the wave theory of matter, he was awarded (1929) the Nobel prize for physics and the Henri Poincaré medal. He is the author of more than 20 works, including *La Physique moderne et les quanta* (1937), *Matière et lumière* (1937), *Continue et discontinue* (1941), *Mécanique ondulatoire des corpuscles à spire* (1942), and *De la mécanique ondulatoire à la théorie du Noyan* (1943).

Broglie, Maurice, Duc **de.** b. at Paris, April 27, 1875—. French physicist; grandson of Jacques Victor Albert, Duc de Broglie, and brother of Louis Victor, Prince de Broglie. He was educated at the École Navale, served in the French navy, and became professor of atomic physics at the École des Hautes Études. He is noted for his investigations in x-rays, radioactive substances, and nuclear physics. His works include *Les Spectres des rayons X* (1918), and *Introduction à la physique des rayons X et gamma* (1928).

Broglie, Victor Claude, Prince **de.** b. at Paris, 1757; d. there, June 27, 1794. French politician; son of Victor François, Duc de Broglie. He was president of the Constituent Assembly in 1791, and afterward became adjutant general in the French army of the Rhine. Having refused to recognize the decree of Aug. 10, 1792, suspending Louis XVI and ordering the election of the National Convention, he was sent to the guillotine by the revolutionary tribunal.

Broglie, Victor François, Duc **de.** b. Oct. 19, 1718; d. at Münster, Germany, March 29, 1804. French soldier, a marshal of France; son of François Marie, Duc de Broglie. He fought in the Seven Years' War, at Hastenbeck and Rossbach, commanded at the battle of Bergen (1759), and was appointed minister of war by Louis XVI. At the outbreak of the French Revolution (1789) he was in command of the troops stationed at Paris for the maintenance of order, but their adoption of the cause of the French Revolution led him to emigrate (c1790). He commanded a body of emigrants in the campaign of 1792, organized a corps of emigrants for the English service in 1794, and on the dissolution of this corps joined the Russian service in 1797.

Broglie, Victor Maurice, Comte **de.** b. c1647; d. Aug. 4, 1727. French soldier, a marshal of France, distinguished in the wars of Louis XIV.

Brogni (brọ.nyē), **Jean Allarmet de.** b. at Brogni, in Savoy, 1342; d. at Rome, Feb. 16, 1426. French cardinal who endeavored to heal the papal schism between Rome and Avignon (the Great Schism). He was president of the Council of Constance (1415–17), and as such pronounced the sentence of the council upon John Huss.

Brohan (brọ.äṅ), **Augustine Suzanne.** [Stage name, **Suzanne.**] b. at Paris, Jan. 29, 1807; d. Aug. 17, 1887. French actress; mother of Émilie Madeleine Brohan and Joséphine Félicité Augustine Brohan. She made her first appearance on the stage as Dorine in Molière's *Tartuffe.* She was a *sociétaire* (actress of the permanent company) of the Comédie Française, and was an extremely graceful, adroit, and original actress; ill health compelled her to retire from the stage at the age of 35.

Brohan, Émilie Madeleine. [Stage name, **Madeleine.**] b. at Paris, Oct. 21, 1833; d. there, Feb. 25, 1900. French actress; the younger daughter of Augustine Suzanne Brohan. In 1854 she married Mario Uchard, from whom she was divorced in 1884. She was a beautiful and accomplished actress. She retired from the stage in 1886.

Brohan, Joséphine Félicité Augustine. [Stage name, **Augustine.**] b. Dec. 2, 1824; d. Feb. 16, 1893. French actress and dramatic writer; daughter of Augustine Suzanne Brohan. She was a remarkably versatile and brilliant actress. She succeeded Rachel at the Conservatoire, and retired in 1866.

Broke or **Brooke** (brůk), **Arthur.** d. 1563. English translator who wrote *The Tragicall Historye of Romeus and Iulieit* (1562), one of the first English versions of that famous tragedy of love. This is probably the version used by Shakespeare as the source for the plot of his *Romeo and Juliet.* Broke translated freely from the French version of Matteo Bandello's Italian version of the story, published in the *Histoires tragiques* (Paris, 1559). George Turberville's "On the Death of Maister Arthur Brooke, drownde in passing to New Haven," in his *Epitaphes and other Poems* (1567), describes Broke as a young man.

Broke, Sir **Philip Bowes Vere.** b. at Broke Hall, near Ipswich, England, Sept. 9, 1776; d. at London, Jan. 2, 1841. British rear admiral. He was educated at the Royal Naval Academy in Portsmouth Dockyard, became a commander in 1799, was made a captain in 1801, and was appointed to command the frigate *Shannon* in 1806. During the War of 1812, while cruising off Boston, he sent a challenge to James Lawrence, captain of the American frigate *Chesapeake,* to fight an engagement. The *Chesapeake,* which stood out to sea before the challenge could be delivered, was captured by Broke after an engagement of 15 minutes, on June 1, 1813.

Broken Arrow. City in NE Oklahoma, in Tulsa County, ab. 12 mi. SE of Tulsa, in a coal and oil producing region. 3,262 (1950).

Broken Bow. City in C Nebraska, county seat of Custer County. A shipping center for grain, hay, and livestock, it also manufactures brooms and cigars. 3,396 (1950).

Broken-Face Gargoyles. Poem in free verse by Carl Sandburg, published in the volume *Smoke and Steel* (1920).

Broken Heart, The. Tragedy by John Ford, acted at the Blackfriars Theatre, London, in 1629, printed in 1633.

Broken Hill. City in S Australia, in New South Wales, near the W border of the state, ab. 580 mi. NW of Sydney. It is the chief center of silver production in Australia; lead and zinc are also mined in the area. Its silver-lead deposits are the richest yet found in the world. The Broken Hill mines have been the greatest source of Australian industrial capital. The first mining stake was made in 1883, by Charles Rasp, and development has since been continuous. 27,059 (1947), 31,580 (est. 1950).

Broken Hill. Important mining center in Northern Rhodesia, S central Africa. It is situated on the main railway line, ab. 655 mi. N of Bulawayo in the C portion of the colony. Valuable deposits of lead and zinc were discovered here in 1903 and are still being worked. The town was named after Broken Hill, Australia, a similar lead and zinc mining town. Vanadium is also a product of the mines. The town is an administrative and commercial center for the surrounding region. Pop. (European), ab. 1,800.

Broken Hill Proprietary, Limited. Australian concern named for the "broken hill" in the Barrier Ranges of New South Wales discovered by Charles Sturt in 1844, which has given its name to the city of Broken Hill. In 1883 Charles Rasp found that the hill was rich in silver, lead, and zinc ore; this discovery led to extensive mining at "broken hill" and the floating (1885) of Broken Hill Proprietary, Limited, which continued mining and smelting ore until 1915. When the steel works at Newcastle, New South Wales, were opened (1915), and the concern transferred, its interests were expanded to steel production; gradually it ramified its holdings into all materials for steel and steel processing, and chemicals.

Broken Soil. Play (1903) by Padraic Colum. A pioneering example of realistic drama, it was later rewritten by Colum as *The Fiddler's House.*

Broker of Bogota (bọ̄.gọ̄'tạ), **The.** Drama by Robert Montgomery Bird. It was first produced at the Bowery Theatre, New York, on February 12, 1834, with Edwin Forrest in the leading role. It is considered by most critics to have been Bird's best play.

Brokmeyer (brok'mī.ėr), **Henry Conrad.** b. near Minden, Prussia, Aug. 12, 1828; d. July 26, 1906. American philosopher and politician, a proponent of German Idealism. He emigrated (1844), penniless, from Prussia to the U.S.; as a resident (1858 *et seq.*) of St. Louis, Mo., he was elected (1862) to the legislature, to the board of aldermen (1866), and to the state senate (1870). He initiated the "St. Louis Movement," based upon Hegelian doctrine. Author of *A Foggy Night at Newport* (1860) and various philosophical essays, and of a translation of Hegel's *Larger Logic,* which was never published.

Bromberg (brom'berk). German name of **Bydgoszcz.**

Brom Bones (brom bōnz). Ichabod Crane's energetic rival in "The Legend of Sleepy Hollow," a story by Washington Irving included in *The Sketch Book* (1820). His formal name in the tale is Brom Van Brunt.

Brome (brōm), **Alexander.** b. 1620; d. June 30, 1666. English attorney and royalist poet. He wrote *Songs and Poems* (1661; 2nd ed., enlarged, 1664) and a comedy, *The Cunning Lovers* (1654). He edited two volumes of Richard Brome's plays, but is not known to have been related to him.

Brome, Richard. d. c1652. English dramatist, in his early years the servant of Ben Jonson. Of his life and death little is known. Among his numerous plays are *The City Wit, or the Woman Wears the Breeches, The Northern Lass* (printed 1632), *The Sparagus Garden* (acted 1635, printed 1640), *The Antipodes* (acted 1638, printed 1640), and *A Jovial Crew, or the Merry Beggars* (acted 1641, printed 1652).

Bromfield (brom'fēld), **Louis.** b. at Mansfield, Ohio, Dec. 27, 1896—. American novelist, essayist, and farmer. Among his works are *The Green Bay Tree* (1924), *Possession* (1925), *Early Autumn: A Story of a Lady* (1926), *A Good Woman* (1927), *The Strange Case of Miss Annie Spragg* (1928), *Awake and Rehearse* (1929), *The Rains Came* (1937), *Night in Bombay* (1939), *Wild Is the River*

(1941), *Mrs. Parkington* (1943), *A Few Brass Tacks* (1946), *Colorado* (1947), and *Mr. Smith* (1951).

Bromia (brō′mi.a̤). In John Dryden's *Amphitryon*, the scolding, ill-tempered wife of Sosia, who is slave of Amppitryon.

Bromley (brum′li, brom′-). Municipal borough in SE England, in Kent, situated on the river Ravensbourne ab. 11 mi. SE of London by rail. It is a popular shopping center and an area of increasing residential development. Bromley is in the area of continuous urban development surrounding London, and is one of the largest towns in Kent. 64,178 (1951).

Bromley, Sir **Thomas.** b. in Staffordshire, England, 1530; d. 1587. English judge who officiated (1586) at the trial of Mary, Queen of Scots. Appointed (1579) lord chancellor, he was seated (1582) in the House of Lords.

Brompton (bromp′ton). Ward of Kensington metropolitan borough, in SW London, in the County of London. It lies between Kensington and Pimlico, S of Hyde Park. The Imperial Institute, Victoria and Albert Museum, Royal Albert Hall, the Royal Geographical Society, and Brompton Oratory are here. 12,560 (1931).

Brömsebro (brėm′se̤.brö). Village in SE Sweden, in the *län* (county) of Kalmar. Here, in August of 1645, a treaty was concluded between Sweden and Denmark, by which the latter renounced Jämtland, the island of Gotland, and other territories.

Bromsgrove (bromz′grōv). Urban district and market town in W central England, in Worcestershire, ab. 12 mi. SW of Birmingham, ab. 127 mi. NW of London by rail. It is located on the coal field known as the South Staffordshire, and has a railway-car works. 27,924 (1951).

Bron (brôṅ). Town in E central France, in the department of Rhône, situated near the left (E) bank of the Rhone River, ab. 2 mi. SE of Lyons, of which it is a suburb. It is part of a highly industrialized region, and has an airport. 12,597 (1946).

Bronck (brongk), **Jonas.** [Also: **Bronk, Brunk.**] d. c1643. American colonial pioneer. A Danish settler, he received (1639) a land patent from William Kieft, head of the New Netherlands colony, and settled the first farm above the Harlem River in lower Westchester, in the area now known as the Bronx (also named finally from him are the Bronx River and Bronxville).

Brøndsted (brėn′steᴛʜ), **Peter Oluf.** b. at Fruering, near Horsens, Jutland, Denmark, Nov. 17, 1780; d. at Copenhagen, June 26, 1842. Danish archaeologist, professor at the University of Copenhagen.

Brong (brong). See **Abron.**

Brongniart (brôṅ.nyȧr), **Adolphe Théodore.** b. at Paris, Jan. 14, 1801; d. there, Feb. 19, 1876. French botanist; son of Alexandre Brongniart. A professor at the Jardin des Plantes, Paris, he made important contributions to the classification of botanical fossils. He wrote *Essai d'une classification naturelle des champignons* (1825), *Histoire des végétaux fossiles* (1828), *Prodrome d'une histoire des végétaux fossiles* (1828), *Mémoire sur la structure et les fonctions des feuilles* (1871), and other works.

Brongniart, Alexandre. b. at Paris, Feb. 5, 1770; d. there, Oct. 7, 1847. French mineralogist, chemist, and geologist; father of Adolphe Théodore Brongniart. He became professor of natural history at the École Centrale de Quatre Nations in 1797, director of the porcelain factory at Sèvres in 1800, and professor of mineralogy at the Jardin des Plantes, Paris, in 1822. He wrote *Essai d'une classification naturelle des reptiles* (1805) in which he set up the classification of reptiles into four groups, and *Traité élémentaire de minéralogie* (1807),*Traité des arts céramiques* (1844–45), and other works.

Broniewski (brô.nyef′skē), **Władysław.** b. at Warsaw, Poland, 1898—. Polish poet and publicist. In the period between World Wars I and II he was the leading spokesman of the young radicals of his country. During World War II he was imprisoned by the Russians. He resides in Poland.

Bronsart von Schellendorf (bron′zärt fon shel′e̤n.dôrf), **Hans.** [Professional name, **Hans von Bronsart.**] b. at Berlin, Feb. 11, 1830; d. at Munich, Nov. 3, 1913. German pianist and composer. After studying with Franz Liszt, he was named intendant at the Hanover theater (1867) and at Weimar (1887). His compositions include chamber works, orchestral pieces, and a piano concerto.

Brønsted (brėn′steᴛʜ), **Johannes Nicolaus.** b. at Varde, Denmark, 1879—. Danish physical chemist. Brønsted and T. M. Lowry independently presented (1923) the important proton transfer theory of acids and bases. His other work includes a significant ionic reaction rate equation, a quantitative expression for acid catalysis, and (with Hevesy) a method for isotope separation by means of low pressure evaporation. He has served as a professor at Copenhagen.

Bronte (brōn′tā). Town and commune in SW Italy, on the island of Sicily, in the province of Catania, situated at the W base of Mount Etna, ab. 20 mi. NW of Catania. It is the center of a rich agricultural district. In 1799, King Ferdinand of Naples conceded some of the feudal territory of the district to Admiral Horatio Nelson. Pop. of commune, 17,918 (1936); of town, 17,673 (1936).

Brontë Family (bron′ta̤). English family, originally of Irish descent, which produced three of the most important English novelists of the 19th century: Charlotte Brontë, Emily Brontë, and Anne Brontë. Their father, Patrick Brontë (b. at Emdale, County Down, Ireland, 1777; d. at Haworth, England, 1861) was the son of Hugh Brunty, an Irish farmer. At 25 he entered St. John's College, Cambridge, signing himself Patrick Brontë, a spelling borrowed from the title recently bestowed on Horatio Nelson, Duke of Bronte (in Sicily). He took orders in 1806, and from Cambridge went to a curacy in Essex. Three years later he removed to Yorkshire as curate of Heartshead-cum-Clifton. On Dec. 29, 1812, he married, in Guiseley Church, Maria Branwell, of Penzance, Cornwall, who was at that time staying with an uncle and aunt, the John Fennells, governor and governess of Woodhouse Grove Wesleyan Academy. At Heartshead were born two daughters, Maria (1813–25) and Elizabeth (1815–25). In 1815 the Brontës exchanged the living of Heartshead for that of Thornton, where were born four more children: Charlotte (1816–55), Patrick Branwell (1817–48), Emily Jane (1818–48), and Anne (1820–49). Early in 1820 Patrick Brontë became perpetual curate of Haworth. The family had been but 18 months in their more commodious home when Mrs. Brontë died of cancer, and her sister, Elizabeth Branwell, thereupon came from Penzance to take charge of the household. When Maria was ten years old, she with Elizabeth, Charlotte, and Emily, were entered in the Clergy's Daughters' School at Cowan Bridge. It was there that Maria and Elizabeth contracted the tuberculosis which brought their death shortly thereafter. For the next six years the four remaining children were at home, Branwell having regular lessons with his father, and the three girls learning domestic arts from their aunt, at the same time picking up a strange assortment of knowledge from wide and varied reading. For their further amusement, they made up games or plays of imagination. Around their toys, particularly Branwell's wooden soldiers, they created a clearly defined country having its capital at the mouth of the Niger River, in Africa. Called originally Glasstown or Verdopolis, it developed in the course of years into a vast African empire known as Angria, and ruled by Arthur Wellesley, elder son of the Duke of Wellington. Its heroes not only performed great deeds, but, turning artists and authors, perpetuated them in diminutive booklets of supposed proportions to their authors, the wooden soldiers, executed in minute hand printing and illustrated with pen and ink drawings. The African game, now five years old, and having outgrown the wooden soldiers, was interrupted in January, 1835, when Charlotte departed for Miss Wooler's school at Roe Head. Emily and Anne seized this opportunity to set up a play of their own, centered in "Gondal, an island in the North Pacific," and "Gaaldine, a newly discovered island in the South Pacific." But when Charlotte returned after a year and a half, she rejoined Branwell in the old play, infusing into it new life and color drawn from her reading of Byron and Scott. A goodly number of play books by Charlotte and Branwell have survived, but none by Emily and Anne. Such creative writing absorbed and satisfied the girls, and, though Branwell kept pace with Charlotte in number of Angrian "books," he found himself hopelessly outdistanced by her genius in turning his crude inventions into literature. For compensation he sought the admiration of village lads and men who gathered for drink and conversation in the nearby Black Bull Inn. To break this association, it was decided in family council that he should enter the Royal Academy, and to help provide the necessary funds for his instruction, Charlotte accepted Miss Wooler's offer of a teaching position in her school. With her went Emily to enroll as a pupil. However, if Branwell went to London, he did not enter the Royal Academy, and Emily at Roe Head became so homesick that she was allowed to return home. After two years Charlotte herself broke in health. Since work away from home was virtually impossible for the girls, they hit upon the plan of a school of their own in the parsonage, and Aunt Elizabeth advanced the money for Charlotte and Emily to improve their French by a term in a Brussels school for girls. They were making rapid progress when the death of Miss Branwell called them home. The small legacy she left them relieved the immediate need for employment. Anne went back to her post as governess, Charlotte returned to Brussels, and Emily settled down at home to look after her father.

First Published Work. It was in 1846, when the three were together in the parsonage, that they ventured to publish at their own cost a joint volume of poems, using pseudonyms to fit their true initials: Currer Bell (for Charlotte), Ellis Bell (for Emily), and Acton Bell (for Anne). The book was a failure, only two copies being sold. Undeterred, the three sisters, still using their earlier pseudonyms, soon had a novel each making the round of publishing houses. Emily's *Wuthering Heights* and Anne's *Agnes Gray* found early acceptance by Thomas Cautley Newby, but Charlotte's *The Professor* came back so many times that she retired the manuscript and pushed hard to finish a second novel called *Jane Eyre.* When completed, this manuscript was sent directly to Smith, Elder and Company, who accepted it enthusiastically, and put it into immediate printing. It was a phenomenal success from the first, while *Wuthering Heights* and *Agnes Gray* were received but coolly. Yet Anne persisted in her writing, publishing *The Tenant of Wildfell Hall* the next year. In the meanwhile, Branwell, whose dissipations had gone from bad to worse, died in September, 1848. Emily, taking cold at his funeral, followed him in December. In the following May, Anne died at Scarborough, where Charlotte had taken her, hoping she would benefit by the sea air. Charlotte in loneliness and grief turned again to her interrupted novel, *Shirley.* It, too, was well received, and its use of local setting betrayed the identity of Currer Bell to the public. In 1853, she completed *Villette*, the last written and generally considered to be the best of her four novels. *The Professor* was published posthumously. In all her novels Charlotte adapted to realistic English and Belgian settings characters and incidents from her Angrian stories, and there is considerable evidence that Emily's *Wuthering Heights* has its origin in lost Gondal stories. Anne wrote from real life. In June, 1853, Charlotte married her father's curate, Arthur Bell Nicholls. On March 31, 1854, she died. Her father lived on in the parsonage, cared for by Arthur Nicholls, until his death in 1861. Though Patrick Brontë never attained literary recognition, a list of his publications casts some light on the genius of his children: *Cottage Poems* (1811), *The Rural Minstrel* (1813), *The Cottage in the Woods* (1815), and *The Maid of Killarney* (1818), as well as tracts and sermons to the number of five.

Brontes (bron'tēz). One of the Cyclopes.

Bronx (brongks). [Sometimes called the **"Borough of Universities"**; Indian name, **Keskeskeck.**] Northernmost borough of New York City, coextensive with Bronx County, bounded by Westchester County on the N and situated NE of the Harlem River. Included in the borough are several adjacent islands among which are City Island, Riker's Island, and Hart's Island. The only one of the city's five boroughs on the mainland, it includes a number of sections, such as Fordham, Riverdale, Woodlawn, Throg's Neck (on a cape of the same name jutting into Long Island Sound), Pelham Bay, and Orchard Beach. The Bronx is traversed by several important highways, the Boston Road (which becomes the Boston Post Road in Westchester), the Henry Hudson Parkway, and the Bronx River Parkway, also by the Bronx River. Although the Bronx is noted mainly for its residential area of many large apartment houses, industry also plays an important role in the borough. Boat building is important on City Island; coal, lumber, and railroad yards are situated along the Harlem River; the Bronx Terminal Market is a receiving point for the city's fruits and vegetables. The borough is linked with Manhattan by the Henry Hudson Bridge and the Triborough Bridge, and others, and with Queens by the Triborough Bridge and the Bronx-Whitestone Bridge. It is the seat of the University Heights campus of New York University (notable for its Hall of Fame), Fordham University, the Bronx center of Hunter College, Manhattan College, the College of Mount St. Vincent, and the New York State Maritime College. In the borough are the Yankee Stadium (home of the New York Yankees baseball team), Poe Cottage (in which Edgar Allan Poe completed *Annabel Lee* and *Ulalume* and in which his young wife died), Van Cortlandt Park, Crotona Park, Pelham Bay Park (in which is located Orchard Beach), Bronx Park (containing the New York Zoological Park, popularly known as the Bronx Zoo, and the New York Botanical Garden), and Potter's Field (the city cemetery, on Hart's Island). The borough's area was purchased (1639) by the Dutch West Indies Company, and the name is derived from that of Jonas Bronck who is believed to have settled (1641) the region. Anne Hutchinson settled here after fleeing religious persecution in Massachusetts. The Bronx was also the home of Gouverneur Morris and Lewis Morris. It became a part of New York City in 1898, a separate county in 1931. Although governed as part of New York City, like each of the five boroughs it has its own borough president for the administration of local affairs. Area, 41 sq. mi.; pop. 1,394,711 (1940), 1,451,277 (1950).

Bronx River. River in SE New York, rising ab. 4 mi. N of White Plains, and flowing S to the East River. It bisects the Bronx borough. Length, ab. 22 mi.

Bronxville (brongks'vil). Village in SE New York, in Westchester County, on the Bronx River: residential suburb of New York City. It is the seat of Sarah Lawrence College. 6,778 (1950).

Bronze Age. Term generally applied to a stage of civilization (not to a distinct period of time) during which copper and bronze implements completely displaced the stone tools and weapons of the Stone Age; the intermediate Chalcolithic Age, when both stone and copper implements were used, is often distinguished. The use of metal appears to have spread from the Near East (Asia Minor and Caucasia), probably beginning in the middle of the 4th millennium B.C., and to have reached Europe c2000 B.C.; in many parts of the world, the change from stone to metal did not occur until very recently, when metal tools and weapons were introduced by Europeans. The Bronze Age, relying as it must on specialization (metallurgy, chemistry, trade with nonmetalliferous areas, and the like), marked the beginnings of urban civilization; the cultures of Mesopotamia, Egypt, India, and others notable in the early historical period began to expand during this era. Many advances (agriculture, extensive domestication of plants and animals, permanent building, and others) mark the Bronze Age. The superiority of the metal edge to the stone edge gave place in turn to the superiority of the more permanent edge of iron, and the Bronze Age was superseded by the Iron Age.

Bronzino (brôn.dzē'nō), **Alessandro.** Name sometimes used for **Allori, Alessandro** (1535–1607), Florentine painter and student of Il Bronzino.

Bronzino, Il. [Original name, **Agnolo** (or **Angiolo**) **di Cosimo Allori.**] b. at Monticelli, near Florence, c1502; d. at Florence, Nov. 23, 1572. Italian painter of the mannerist school, best remembered for his portraits. A favorite of Cosimo I de' Medici, he executed many portraits of his patron and his patron's family. In all his portraits, the style produces even, stony figures, imbued with a feeling of elegance and nobility. A pupil of Jacopo da Pontormo, he was influenced also by the work of Michelangelo. One of his portraits of Cosimo is in the collection of the Metropolitan Museum of Art at New York, and one of Cosimo's wife, Eleanor of Toledo, is in the Uffizi, Florence.

Brooch of Vulcan, The. Name given to Geoffrey Chaucer's *Complaint of Mars.*

Brook (brůk), **Alexander.** b. at Brooklyn, N.Y., July 14, 1898—. American painter and lithographer, best known for his portraits. In much of his work the treatment of textures and choice of subjects are used for the expression of particular moods, often melancholy or nostalgic. Having begun to paint as a child, he studied (1915–19) at the Art Students League of New York, under Kenneth Hayes Miller and J. C. Johansen. He was the winner (1931) of a Guggenheim Fellowship, and of prizes from the Chicago Art Institute, the Pennsylvania Academy of the Fine Arts, and others. His *Georgia Jungle*, which took first prize at the 1939 Carnegie International Exhibition, is one of a series on Southern Negroes, akin in effect to the American "social protest" movement of the 1920's and 1930's. He has taught at the Art Students League and has written articles on contemporary painting. He is the former husband (1920–40) of the artist Peggy Bacon. His works include *Katharine Hepburn* (1938), *Biddle Playing the Flute*, *The Yellow Fan*, and others, and are included in the collections of the Metropolitan Museum of Art and the Whitney Museum of American Art, at New York, the Art Institute of Chicago, the Corcoran Gallery of Art, Washington, D.C., the Albright Art Gallery, Buffalo, the Gallery of Living Art, New York, the Brooklyn Museum, and others. See monographs by W. Murrell (1922) and E. A. Jewell (1931).

Brook, Master. Name assumed by Ford, in Shakespeare's *Merry Wives of Windsor*, for the purpose of fooling Falstaff, who is seeking an affair with Ford's wife. Falstaff, all unaware of Brook's true identity, boasts to him of progress in his pursuit of Mistress Ford.

Brooke (brůk), Sir **Alan Francis.** [Title, 1st Viscount **Alanbrooke.**] b. at Bagnères-de-Bigorre, Hautes-Pyrénées, France, July 23, 1883—. British field marshal. His military education began at the Royal Military Academy, Woolwich, and in 1902 he entered the British army as a member of the Royal Field Artillery. In 1906 he was sent to India, from which he returned early in World War I as an officer of an Indian contingent. During World War II he held the antiaircraft command in 1939, the Southern command (1939–40), and command of the British Second Corps on the Continent in the early summer of 1940. He was one of the last to be evacuated from the beach at Dunkerque. Subsequently in 1940, and for part of 1941, he was in command of the home forces, and in the latter year he became chief of the Imperial General Staff. In June, 1942, he accompanied Prime Minister Winston Churchill to the U.S. He was elevated to the peerage in 1945 as 1st Baron Alanbrooke, and again honored in 1946, when he was made 1st Viscount Alanbrooke.

Brooke, Arthur. See **Broke** or **Brooke, Arthur.**

Brooke, Sir **Basil Stanlake.** b. at Colebrooke, Ireland, June 9, 1888—. British politician in Northern Ireland. Educated at Winchester and Sandhurst, he served (1914–18) in the Dardanelles during World War I. A member (1929 *et seq.*) of Parliament, he was minister of agriculture (1933–41) and of commerce (1941–45). In 1943 he became also prime minister of Northern Ireland.

Brooke, Celia. In George Eliot's novel *Middlemarch*, the sister of Dorothea Brooke. She is a pretty, practical girl whose common sense protests against the somewhat ideal philanthropy of Dorothea.

Brooke, Sir **Charles Anthony Johnson.** [Title, 2nd Rajah of **Sarawak;** original surname, **Johnson.**] b. at Berrow, Somersetshire, England, June 3, 1829; d. at Cirencester, Gloucestershire, England, May 17, 1917. Second British rajah of Sarawak, Borneo; nephew of Sir James Brooke (1803–68). He assisted in the administration of the sultanate from 1852 to 1868, when he succeeded to the title. He brought to fruition many of his uncle's plans for the peaceful development of the state, partly by encouraging the settlement of immigrant Chinese farmers and craftsmen, and especially by further pacification of the more primitive Malay tribes. With a greatly increased production for export trade, Sarawak was placed by him in 1888 under the formal protection of the British government.

Brooke, Sir **Charles Vyner.** [Title, 3rd Rajah of **Sarawak.**] b. at London, in September, 1874—. Third British rajah of Sarawak, Borneo; son of Sir Charles Anthony Johnson Brooke (1829–1917). He succeeded to the title in 1917 and ceded the protectorate to the British Crown on July 1, 1946. During the greater part of his rule, Sarawak actually was administered in close association with the Malayan Union, like the Unfederated Malay States, thus insuring not only military protection but also a strong economic development, the introduction of modern social legislation, and expert administrative services.

Brooke, Dorothea. Heroine of George Eliot's novel *Middlemarch*. Her temperament leads her to seek expression in work which shall be of permanent benefit to others. From admiration, she mistakenly marries a dried-up pedant, Casaubon, who hinders instead of helps her; after his death she abandons her high but vague ideal and marries a man who satisfies the common yearning of humanity for sympathy and love. She thereupon sinks into a happy obscurity.

Brooke, Emma Frances. d. 1926. English novelist and Fabian Socialist. She studied at Cambridge University, and went to London in the early 1880's; attracted to socialism, she joined the Fabian Society. She was the author of *A Superfluous Woman* (1894), *Transition* (1895), *Life the Accuser* (1896), *The Confession of Stephen Whapshare* (1898), *The Engrafted Rose* (1900), *Sir Elyot of the Woods* (1907), and *The House of Robershaye* (1912), all novels, and *A Tabulation of the Factory Laws of European Countries In So Far as They Relate to . . . Women, Young Persons, and Children* (1898).

Brooke, Frances Moore. b. 1724; d. at Sleaford, Lincolnshire, England, Jan. 23 or 26, 1789. English novelist, poet, and dramatist. She was the wife of John Brooke, rector of Colney, Norfolk, and chaplain to the garrison at Quebec, where for a time they resided. Her works include *The History of Lady Julia Mandeville* (1763), *History of Emily Montagu* (1769), and *The Excursion* (1777).

Brooke, Henry. [Title, 8th Baron **Cobham.**] d. Jan. 24, 1619. English conspirator. He was tried and convicted (1603) with Sir Walter Raleigh and others on the charge of conspiring to place Arabella Stuart on the throne. He was led to the scaffold, but was reprieved and sent to the Tower of London, where he remained till 1619. It is said that he died in poverty at the house of his laundress.

Brooke, Henry. b. at Rantavan, County Cavan, Ireland, c1703; d. at Dublin, Oct. 10, 1783. Irish novelist, dramatist, and poet. He wrote *Universal Beauty* (a poem, 1735), *Gustavus Vasa* (a drama, 1739), and *The Fool of Quality* (a novel, 1766–68).

Brooke, Henry James. b. May 25, 1771; d. June 26, 1857. English mineralogist, remembered for his discovery of 13 new mineral species. Originally a businessman in the Spanish wool trade, South American mining companies, and the London Life Assurance Association, he became known also as a geologist, botanist, and collector of shells and minerals. The latter collection is now at Cambridge University. His collection of engravings is in the British Museum. Author of *Familiar Introduction to Crystallography* (1823), and many other contributions on this subject and on mineralogy.

Brooke, Sir **James.** [Title, 1st Rajah of **Sarawak.**] b. at Benares, India, April 29, 1803; d. at Burrator, Devonshire, England, June 11, 1868. First British rajah of Sarawak, Borneo. He entered the service of the East India Company in 1825, took part in the First Burmese War, and was wounded and forced to return to England. In 1830, on a voyage to China, he was impressed with the economic possibilities of eastern Borneo. Succeeding to a large estate in 1838, he offered his aid to Rajah Muda Hassim of Sarawak, uncle of the reigning sultan, then engaged in an expedition against revolting Dyak tribes. For this service he received (1841) the title of rajah, and freedom to develop the economic resources and reform the laws of the sultanate. He won further good will by succeeding in the suppression of piracy with the aid of a small British fleet. On his return to London in 1847, Brooke received the freedom of the city and was appointed governor of the small island of Labuan off the east coast of Borneo. In 1849 he conducted a military campaign against insurgent Dyaks in coöperation with neighboring rulers. In 1851 he had to go to London to defend himself against charges of corruption made in Parliament, which later were referred to a royal commission sitting in Singapore and proven false. However, Brooke lost the governorship of Labuan and again entered the service of the sultan of Sarawak, on whose behalf he was successful in driving off a strong force of Chinese pirates and in freeing the capital of their exactions. Although subsequently retired to his estate in England, he returned twice to Sarawak to help in the suppression of rebellions.

Brooke, John Mercer. b. at Tampa, Fla., Dec. 18, 1826; d. at Lexington, Va., Dec. 14, 1906. American physicist. He was graduated from the U.S. Naval Academy at Annapolis in 1847, but resigned from the navy in 1860. In 1861 he entered the Confederate service and became chief of the bureau of ordnance and hydrography. He invented a gun, named for him, and made the plans which were used in refitting the *Merrimac* (which was renamed the *Virginia*, but has continued to be called the *Merrimac* by virtually all historians). He was professor of physics at the Virginia Military Institute in the period 1865–99.

Brooke, John Rutter. b. at Pottsville, Pa., July 21, 1838; d. at Philadelphia, Sept. 5, 1926. American soldier, promoted major general in the regular army in 1897. He enlisted in the Union army in 1861 and attained the brevet rank of major general of volunteers in 1864. In April, 1898, during the Spanish-American War, he was placed in command of the troops in Chickamauga Park, and in July was sent to Puerto Rico, where he was head of the military commission, and governor general, until December, when he became governor general of Cuba. In 1900 he was placed in command of the department of the East. He retired in 1902.

Brooke, Rupert. [Full name, **Rupert Chawner Brooke.**] b. at Rugby, Warwickshire, England, Aug. 3, 1887; d. of blood poisoning in a hospital on the Greek island of Skyros, April 23, 1915. English poet, essayist, and soldier. Educated at Rugby School and at King's College, Cambridge, where he became a fellow, he traveled in Germany, Italy, America, Canada, and the South Seas (1913), and saw service (1914) in Belgium. He sailed for, but never reached, the Dardanelles. He was the author of *The Bastille* (1905, a prize poem), *Poems* (1911), *1914 and Other Poems* (1915), and *Lithuania* (1915, a one-act play), and also wrote *Puritanism in the Early English Drama* (1910, a prize essay), *John Webster and the Elizabethan Drama* (1916, his fellowship thesis), and *Letters from America* (1916). He is remembered for his sonnet *The Soldier*, and for the poems *Dust, The Hill, Heaven, The Busy Heart, Dining-Room Tea, The Old Vicarage, Grantchester*, and *The Great Lover*.

Brooke, Stopford. [Full name, **Stopford Augustus Brooke.**] b. at Letterkenny, County Donegal, Ireland, Nov. 14, 1832; d. at Ewhurst, Surrey, England, March 18, 1916. English clergyman, critic, biographer, and anthologist. Educated at Trinity College, Dublin, where he won several prizes for poetry, he was ordained in 1857, and held various church posts at London. He served (1863–64) at Berlin as chaplain to the British embassy, was chaplain to Queen Victoria from 1872 until 1880, when he left the Church of England to become a Unitarian, and was later an independent preacher. He lectured on English poets and poetry (1900–05) at London University College. Author of *Theology in the English Poets* (1874), dealing with William Cowper, Samuel Taylor Coleridge, William Wordsworth, and Robert Burns, he also wrote *A Primer of English Literature* (1876), *History of Early English Literature* (1894), *Tennyson: His Art and Relation to Modern Life* (1894), *The Poetry of Browning* (1902), *Ten Plays of Shakespeare* (1905), and *Studies in Poetry* (1907). Among his other works are *Life and Letters of the Late Frederick W. Robertson* (1865), *Riquet of the Tuft* (1880), a verse drama, and *Poems* (1888); he edited the anthology *A Treasury of Irish Poetry in the English Tongue* (1900).

Brookenham (brůk'ẹn.ham), **Nanda.** Heroine of *The Awkward Age* (1899), a novel by Henry James.

Brooke-Popham (brůk.pop'ạm), Sir **Henry Robert Moore.** See **Popham,** Sir **Henry Robert Moore Brooke-.**

Brookes (brůks), Sir **Norman Everard.** b. at Melbourne, Australia, 1877—. Australian tennis champion and businessman. A member (1914, 1919, 1920) of the Australasian (but in popular U.S. parlance, Australian) Davis Cup tennis team, he helped this group win (1914) the Davis Cup for Australasia. He later (1919) won the American national doubles championship with Gerald L. Patterson. During World War I he served in France, Egypt, and Mesopotamia. Chairman of the Australasian Paper and Pulp Company and of the North British Insurance Company, he was knighted in 1939.

Brook Farm. Farm at West Roxbury (now in Boston), Mass., the scene of an experiment in agriculture and education by the "Brook Farm Association," of which the chief founders (1841) were George Ripley, George W. Curtis, and Charles A. Dana. Fourierism was introduced in 1844, the "Brook Farm Phalanx" was incorporated in 1845, and the organization was dissolved in 1847. Among its publications were *The Dial* (1840–44) and *The Phalanx* (1843–45).

Brookfield (brůk'fēld). Village in NE Illinois, in Cook County near Chicago: residential community. 15,472 (1950).

Brookfield. City in NW Missouri, in Linn County, ab. 90 mi. E of St. Joseph. It is a shipping point for grain, livestock, and coal. 5,810 (1950).

Brookfield, William Henry. b. at Sheffield, England, 1809; d. 1874. English educator and clergyman who was a friend of Tennyson, Thackeray, and Arthur Hallam. He received an M.A. degree at Cambridge in 1836, and was named a curate at Southampton (1840) and of St. Luke's, Berwick Street, London (1841). In 1848 he was appointed inspector of schools and was also at one time chaplain in ordinary to Queen Victoria. He is believed to have been the original in real life of Frank Whitestock in Thackeray's *Curate's Walk*.

Brookhart (brůk'härt), **Smith W.** b. in Scotland County, Mo., Feb. 2, 1869; d. in Arizona, Nov. 15, 1944. American lawyer and politician, twice (1922–24, 1926–32) U.S. senator from Iowa. He served in the Spanish-American War and in World War I, and was a special trade adviser (1932–36) on Russia to the U.S. secretary of agriculture. He practiced law (1936 *et seq.*) at Washington.

Brookhaven (brůk.hā'vẹn). City in SW Mississippi, county seat of Lincoln County, ab. 52 mi. SW of Jackson; shipping point for dairy products. It is the seat of Whitworth College. 7,801 (1950).

Brookhaven. Town in SE New York, on Long Island, in Suffolk County: residential community. The Brookhaven National Laboratory for Nuclear Research, one of the U.S. government's most extensive establishments for research into various means of producing power through nuclear fission (atomic power), adjoins the town, 44,522 (1950).

Brookings (brůk'ingz). [Former name, **Ada.**] City in E South Dakota, county seat of Brookings County, in an agricultural area: seat of the South Dakota State College of Agriculture and Mechanic Arts. 7,764 (1950).

Brookings, Robert Somers. b. in Cecil County, Maryland, Jan. 22, 1850; d. Nov. 15, 1932. American merchant and philanthropist. He was a partner (1872–96) in the Cupples Company, a woodenware establishment at St. Louis, Mo., and thereafter retired from business. He was an organizer of the Institute for Government Research (1916), the Institute of Economics (1922), and the Robert Brookings Graduate School of Economics and Government (1924), all of which were incorporated in the late 1920's as the Brookings Institution, at Washington, D.C., for research in the social sciences. He endowed (1913–14) the buildings for the medical school of Washington University, at St. Louis, and was president (1897–1928) of the corporation (or governing body) for the university as a whole. Author of *Industrial Ownership* (1925), *Economic Democracy* (1929), and *A Suggested Evolution of Capitalism* (1932).

Brookings Institution. Institution at Washington, D.C., incorporated in 1928 as an amalgamation of the Institute of Economics (1922), the Institute for Government Research (1916), and the Robert Brookings Graduate School of Economics and Government (1924). It undertakes research projects in the social sciences, trains scholars, and provides research resources for U.S. and visiting foreign scholars.

Brook Kerith: A Syrian Story (brůk ker'ith), **The.** A life of Christ in the form of fiction, by George Moore, published in 1916. Adopting the rationalistic theory that Jesus did not die on the cross but was taken down by Joseph and secretly nursed back to health, the story rises to its climax when the fanatical missionary Paul comes face to face with the man whose resurrection and divinity he has proclaimed, while Jesus, thinking better of what he now considers to have been madness, wants only to live out his life in an atmosphere of personal charity and philosophic calm.

Brookline (brůk'līn). [Former name, **Muddy River.**] Town in E Massachusetts, in Norfolk County, ab. 3 mi. SW of Boston: residential suburb of Boston. It was the birthplace of Amy Lowell. 57,589 (1950).

Brooklyn (brůk'lin). Village in SW Illinois, in St. Clair County, on the Mississippi River near East St. Louis. 2,568 (1950).

Brooklyn. [Sometimes called the **"City of Homes and Churches"** or simply the **"City of Homes"**; original Dutch name, **Breuckelen,** meaning "Broken Land."] Borough comprising the SE and much of the E section of New York City, coextensive with Kings County, located in the SW part of Long Island, and SE of Manhattan, from which it is separated by the East River. The largest of New York City's five boroughs in population, it includes a number of sections, such as Brooklyn Heights, Borough Hall, Williamsburg, Greenpoint, Bushwick, Ridgewood, Red Hook, Bay Ridge, Bensonhurst, East New York, Coney Island (famous amusement resort and public bathing beach), Flatbush, Sheepshead Bay, Brownsville, and Canarsie. Although a considerable area is still devoted to residences, Brooklyn today has much industry, principally shipping, lumber yards, warehouses, breweries, petroleum refineries, sugar refineries, and factories which manufacture shoes and varied types of machinery and mechanical equipment. The Brooklyn Bridge, spanning the East River between lower Manhattan and Brooklyn, was the world's first (1884) sizable suspension bridge. The borough is now also connected to Manhattan by the Williamsburg Bridge and the Manhattan Bridge. The Brooklyn-Battery Tunnel (9,117 ft. long), begun in 1940 and opened in 1950, is the world's longest underwater tunnel; built at a cost of 80 million dollars, it has two double-lane traffic tubes. Educational institutions located in the borough include the Brooklyn Law School, Polytechnic Institute of Brooklyn, St. Joseph's College for Women, St. Francis College, St. John's University, Long Island University, Long Island College of Medicine, Pratt Institute, Brooklyn College, and the Brooklyn Institute of Arts and Sciences. The Brooklyn Academy of Music is a sizable concert hall. The borough is also the site of a U.S. navy yard, the Atlantic Basin, the New York State Barge Canal terminal, the New York port of embarkation and army supply base, Bush Terminal, the Erie Basin, Fort Hamilton, Fort Lafayette, Ebbets Field (home of the Brooklyn Dodgers baseball team), Prospect Park (a large and attractive recreation area), the Brooklyn Museum, the Brooklyn Botanical Garden (known for its Japanese cherry trees), Floyd Bennett Field (U.S. naval air base), and Kings County Hospital. Brooklyn was for many years the home of Walt Whitman, who worked on the staff of newspapers there, notably the Brooklyn *Daily Eagle.* Henry Ward Beecher served as the pastor of the Plymouth Church of the Pilgrims at Brooklyn, and from his pulpit in that church made his famous effort to dramatize the evils of slavery by putting a mulatto girl slave up for sale. The borough was first settled in 1636 and 1637 by the Dutch and Walloons; the settlement made in the heart of the present Borough Hall district was called Breuckelen, after a Dutch town. Brooklyn was the scene (Aug. 27, 1776) of the Battle of Long Island; incorporated as a city in 1834, it flourished, gradually absorbing nearby villages such as New Utrecht, Flatbush, Williamsburg, and Bushwick, all dating from the 17th century. By 1896 its limits were identical with those of Kings County. Brooklyn became part of New York City in 1898. Although governed as part of the city, like each of the five boroughs it has its own borough president for the administration of purely local affairs. Area, 71 sq. mi.; pop. 2,738,175 (1950).

Brooklyn. Village in NE Ohio, in Cuyahoga County: a southern suburb of Cleveland. In the decade between the last two U.S. censuses its population grew from 1,108 (1940) to 6,317 (1950).

Brooklyn, The Battle of. See **Battle of Brooklyn, The.**

Brooklyn Bridge. Suspension bridge over the East River, uniting the boroughs of Manhattan and Brooklyn in New York City. The preliminary work was begun in 1867, and the bridge was officially completed in 1884. The bridge crosses the river by a single span 1,595½ ft. long, and 135 ft. above high water in the middle, suspended from two massive granite piers on opposite sides. The piers measure 59 by 140 ft. at the water level, and 40 by 120 ft. at the summit, and are 277 ft. high. Beyond the piers, on both banks, the bridge is continued on an easy incline, partly suspended and partly of masonry arches and steel trusses, until the street level is reached. The total length is 6,016 ft. There are four main cables of steel wires, each 15¾ inches in diameter. The width of the bridge is 85 ft., which is subdivided into two driveways and two railway tracks. It was designed and constructed by J. A. Roebling and his son W. A. Roebling. Until the opening (1903) of the Williamsburg Bridge, it was the longest suspension bridge in the world. It is still considered a masterpiece of design in steel and stone, and many of the principles of its construction, particularly in the making and hanging of the cables, had a great influence on the subsequent planning and construction of suspension bridges throughout the world.

Brooklyn Center. Village in SE Minnesota, in Hennepin County, near the Mississippi River: a northwestern suburb of Minneapolis. In the decade between the last two U.S. censuses its population more than doubled. 1,870 (1940); 4,284 (1950).

Brooklyn Institute of Arts and Sciences. Organization founded c1823 (incorporated under its present title in 1890) for the purpose of establishing and maintaining museums and libraries of art and science and promoting instruction and study in the arts and sciences. The institute maintains the Brooklyn Museum, the Brooklyn Museum Art School, the Brooklyn Children's Museum, and the Brooklyn Botanic Garden. Its library contains ab. 45,000 volumes. The institute publishes the *Brooklyn Museum Quarterly,* the *Children's Museum News,* and a *Bulletin.*

Brooklyn Oratorio Society. Choral group organized (1893) at Brooklyn, N.Y., with Walter Henry Hall as conductor.

Brook Park. Village in NE Ohio, in Cuyahoga County, near the Rocky River: a southwestern suburb of Cleveland. In the decade between the last two U.S. censuses its population more than doubled. 1,122 (1940); 2,606 (1950).

Brooks (brůks), **Alfred Hulse.** b. at Ann Arbor, Mich., July 18, 1871; d. in Alaska, Nov. 22, 1924. American geologist. He was a field worker (1898–1902) for the U.S. Geological Survey in Alaska, and later (1902–24) in charge of its work there, except for time spent as chief geologist with the American Expeditionary Forces during World War I. He was the author of *Geography and Geology of Alaska* (1906), *Geologic Features of Alaskan Metalliferous Lodes* (1911), *The Future of Gold Placer Mining in Alaska* (1915), *Antimony Deposits in Alaska* (1916), and *The Future of Alaska's Mining* (1920).

Brooks, Charles Stephen. b. at Cleveland, Ohio, June 25, 1878; d. June 29, 1934. American prose writer and playwright. He was associated (1900 *et seq.*) with the Brooks Company, printers at Cleveland, Ohio, and was president of the Play House Foundation. His works include *Journey to Bagdad* (1915), *There's Pippins and Cheese to Come* (1917), *Chimney-Pot Papers* (1919), *Roundabout to Canterbury* (1926), *An Italian Winter* (1933), and the plays *Wappin' Wharf* (1921) and *A Window at the Inn* (1934).

Brooks, Charles Timothy. b. at Salem, Mass., June 20, 1813; d. at Newport, R.I., June 14, 1883. American Unitarian clergyman and author, noted chiefly as a translator from the German.

Brooks, Charles William Shirley. b. at London, April 29, 1816; d. there, Feb. 23, 1874. English novelist and journalist. He was a contributor to *Punch* after 1851, and its editor after 1870. His chief works are the play *The Creole, or Love's Fetters* (produced 1847), and the novels *Aspen Court* (1855), *The Gordian Knot* (1860), *The Silver Cord* (1861), and *Sooner or Later* (1868).

Brooks, Henry Harlow. b. at Medo, Minn., March 31, 1871; d. April 13, 1936. American physician. He taught (1898 *et seq.*) at New York University. On active service (1917 *et seq.*) with the Medical Corps during World War I, he was chief consultant (1918) in medicine for the American 1st Army and chief surgeon (1919) of the 2nd Army

Brooks, James Gordon. b. at Claverack, N.Y., Sept. 3, 1801; d. at Albany, N.Y., Feb. 20, 1841. American poet and journalist. He married Mary Elizabeth Aiken (pseudonym "Norna") in 1828, and with her published a volume of poems entitled *The Rivals of Este, and other Poems* (1829).

Brooks, John. b. at Medford, Mass., 1752; d. March 1, 1825. American politician and officer in the Revolutionary War. He led the successful assault on the entrenchments held by the Hessian troops in the battle of Saratoga. From 1817 to 1823 he was governor of Massachusetts.

Brooks, John Graham. b. at Acworth, N.H., July 19, 1846; d. Feb. 8, 1938. American sociologist. He studied at the universities of Berlin, Jena, and Freiburg, lectured at Harvard and the University of Chicago, and was employed as an expert by the U.S. Department of Labor (for the use of which agency, in 1893, he drafted a report on workingmen's insurance in Germany). From 1909 he was a lecturer at the University of California. He was president of the National Consumers' League, and the author of *The Social Unrest* (1903), *As Others See Us* (1908), and *An American Citizen* (1910).

Brooks, Maria Gowen. [Pseudonym, **María del Occidente.**] b. at Medford, Mass., c1794; d. at Matanzas, Cuba, Nov. 11, 1845. American poet, author of *Zophiël, or the Bride of Seven* (1833). She was also known as María del Occidente, a sobriquet first given her by Robert Southey, and later used by her as a pseudonym. Among her other works are *Judith, Esther, and Other Poems* (1820) and *Idomen* (1843).

Brooks, Noah. b. at Castine, Me., Oct. 24, 1830; d. at Pasadena, Calif., Aug. 16, 1903. American journalist and writer of biography, history, and boys' fiction. As a young man, he emigrated to California, where he became joint editor and publisher of the Marysville *Daily Appeal*, and a contributor to the *Overland Monthly* (in the latter capacity he came to know Bret Harte, who was at that time editor of the magazine). In 1862 he left California to become Washington correspondent for the Sacramento *Union*; he now also renewed an acquaintance with Abraham Lincoln, and accompanied the president on various official trips. Returning to California, he took over (1866) the managing editorship of *Alta California*, at San Francisco; in this post he accepted and published an article by the then unknown Henry George, who was at the time a compositor on the magazine. After his removal (1871) to New York, Brooks worked on the New York *Tribune* (1871–76), New York *Times* (1876–84), and the Newark *Daily Advertiser* (1884–92). He wrote for boys such books as *The Boy Emigrants* (1876) and *The Boy Settlers* (1891). His biographical and historical works included *Abraham Lincoln and the Downfall of American Slavery* (1894), *History of the United States* (1896), and *Abraham Lincoln; His Youth and Early Manhood* (1901).

Brooks, Phillips. b. at Boston, Dec. 13, 1835; d. there, Jan. 23, 1893. American Episcopal bishop, widely known in his day as a pulpit orator but now perhaps even better known for the fact that he wrote the Christmas hymn *O Little Town of Bethlehem*. Graduated from Harvard College in 1855, and from the Episcopal Seminary at Alexandria, Va., in 1859, he became rector of the Church of the Advent, Philadelphia (1859), of the Church of the Holy Trinity in the same city (1861), and of Trinity Church, Boston (1869). He was elected bishop of the Episcopal diocese of Massachusetts in 1891.

Brooks, Preston Smith. b. in Edgefield County, S.C., Aug. 6, 1819; d. at Washington, D.C., Jan. 27, 1857. American politician, notorious in his day and since for a violent assault on Charles Sumner in the Senate chamber at Washington, on May 22, 1856. A member of Congress from South Carolina (1853–57), he was angered by an attack on his uncle, Senator Andrew Pickens Butler, in a speech by Sumner, and Brooks thereupon subjected Sumner to a caning so severe that Sumner suffered from its effects for the rest of his life. The episode is now probably notable not so much for its violence (Brooks' rage was certainly not without provocation: Sumner's vitriolic tongue had already earned him a great number of enemies) as for the fact that it provides clear evidence of the rift then widening between the extremist elements in the politics of the North and the South. Brooks resigned from the House of Representatives immediately after the episode but was at once reëlected by his constituents in South Carolina.

Brooks, Richard Edwin. b. at Braintree, Mass., Oct. 28, 1865; d. at Boston, May 2, 1919. American sculptor and medalist. He studied at Boston and Paris, and exhibited and won several prizes at Paris and in the U.S., including medals from the Paris Exposition (1900), the Pan American Exposition, Buffalo, N.Y. (1901), and the Panama-Pacific Exposition, San Francisco (1915). He belonged to the National Institute of Arts and Letters and the National Sculptural Society, and is represented in the Metropolitan Museum of Art at New York, and elsewhere. Among his best-known works are figures for the state capitol at Hartford, Conn., and *Colonel Thomas Cass, John Hanson, Charles Carroll, The Bather*, and *Song of the Wave*.

Brooks, Van Wyck. b. at Plainfield, N.J., Feb. 16, 1886—. American literary critic and historian, essayist, and translator. A graduate (1908) of Harvard, he served as an editor of *The Freeman* (1920–24) and the *American Caravan* (1927 *et seq.*). Among his works are *The Wine of the Puritans* (1909), *The Malady of the Ideal* (1913), *John Addington Symonds* (1914), *America's Coming-of-Age* (1915), *The Ordeal of Mark Twain* (1920), *The Pilgrimage of Henry James* (1925), *The Life of Emerson* (1932), *The Flowering of New England: 1815-1865* (1936; awarded a Pulitzer prize, 1937), *New England Indian Summer: 1865-1915* (1940), *The World of Washington Irving* (1944), *The Times of Melville and Whitman* (1947), *The Confident Years: 1885–1915* (1952), and others, including translations of works by Romain Rolland, Henri Frédéric Amiel, and Georges Duhamel.

Brooks, William Keith. b. at Cleveland, Ohio, March 25, 1848; d. at Lake Roland, near Baltimore, Nov. 12, 1908. American biologist, professor of zoölogy at Johns Hopkins University. He was graduated from Williams College in 1870, and was an assistant in the Boston Society of Natural History in the period 1875–76. Among his published works are *Handbook of Invertebrate Zoology* (1882), *Heredity* (1884), *Lucifer: a Study in Morphology* (1881), *The Stomatopoda of H.M.S. Challenger* (1886), and *Foundations of Zoology* (1898).

Brooks, William Robert. b. at Maidstone, England, June 11, 1844; d. May 3, 1921. American astronomer who discovered 27 comets, the first of which he sighted in 1881. He was in charge (1888 *et seq.*) of the William Smith Observatory at Geneva, N.Y., and became (1900) professor of astronomy at Hobart College.

Brooks, William Thomas Harbaugh. b. at New Lisbon, Ohio, Jan. 28, 1821; d. at Huntsville, Ala., July 19, 1870. American soldier. He became a brigadier general of volunteers in the Union army in 1861, was commander (1863–64) of the department of the Monongahela, and led the 10th army corps at Swift's Creek, Drury's Bluff, Bermuda Hundred, Cold Harbor, and Petersburg.

Brooks-Baxter War. In U.S. history, name applied to the political dispute (1873–74) in Arkansas between the elected governor, Elisha Baxter, and his opponent, Joseph Brooks, a clergyman. The latter refused to recognize the election returns and with his adherents led a march on the state house and took possession of it. Although Brooks's claim was supported by the state supreme court, President Ulysses S. Grant decided that the matter rested with the state legislature, which, on May 11, 1874, validated Baxter's claim.

Brooks of Sheffield (shef'ēld). In Charles Dickens's *David Copperfield*, an imaginary person named by Mr. Murdstone when speaking of David Copperfield in his presence, and hence since used for some person spoken of whose name it is not convenient to mention.

Brooks Range. Large mountain area in N central Alaska, crossing the territory from W to E ab. 150 mi. S of the Arctic Ocean. The area consists of a group of very rugged mountain ranges, with the highest peaks in the C portion and in the NE, where Mount Michelson reaches 9,239 ft. elevation. Only a few small mining camps have been established, and most of the region is completely uninhabited, with a severe arctic climate, and glaciers and permanent snowfields in the mountains. Length, E to W, ab. 600 mi.; width, ab. 150 mi.

Brooks's (brůk'sẹz). Conservative club at London established in 1764 by the Duke of Roxborough, the Duke of Portland, and others. It was formerly a gaming-house kept by William Almack, which was afterward kept by "Brooks, a wine merchant and money-lender," for whom it was named.

Brookville (brůk'vil). Town in SE Indiana, county seat of Franklin County, on the Whitewater River, a tributary of the Ohio, ab. 65 mi. SE of Indianapolis. It is the marketing center for an agricultural region, and was the birthplace of Lew Wallace. 2,538 (1950).

Brookville. Borough in W Pennsylvania, county seat of Jefferson County, in a coal-mining, oil and gas producing, and agricultural area: railroad shops. It was settled in 1801 and platted in 1830. Pop. 4,274 (1950).

Brookwood American Cemetery (brůk'wůd). American military cemetery situated near the village of Brookwood, Surrey, England, ab. 25 mi. SW of London. The 468 American dead of World War I who rest there died in Great Britain or in adjoining waters. The cemetery also contains the graves of American soldiers and sailors who lost their lives in these areas during World War II.

Broom (bröm), **Big Loch** and **Little Loch.** Two sealochs in N Scotland, in the county of Ross and Cromarty. They form inlets of the Minch on the NW coast of Scotland. Length of Big Loch Broom, ab. 14 mi.; width at entrance, ab. 5 mi. Length of Little Loch Broom, ab. 9 mi.; width at entrance, ab. 2 mi.

Broom, Robert. b. in Scotland, Nov. 30, 1866; d. April 6, 1951. South African paleontologist, famous for his discoveries of remains of prehistoric Australopithecine types at Sterkfontein (1936) and Kromdraai (1938) and for his study of the significance for human evolution of these African fossils. Graduated (1895) from the medical school of Glasgow University, he was professor (1903–10) of zoölogy and geology at Victoria College, Stellenbosch, South Africa. His works include *Mammal-like Reptiles of South Africa* (1932) and *The South African Fossil Ape-Men* (with G. W. H. Schepers, 1946).

Broome (bröm), Sir **Frederick Napier.** b. in Canada, 1842; d. 1896. English colonial administrator. He served as colonial secretary of Natal (1875) and of Mauritius (1877). Following a lieutenant governorship of Mauritius (1880), he returned to the Pacific as governor of Western Australia (1882–90). He was also governor of Barbados (1890), and later of Trinidad.

Broome, William. b. at Haslington, Cheshire, England, in May, 1689; d. at Bath, England, Nov. 16, 1745. English poet and divine. He assisted, as an accomplished Greek scholar, in Alexander Pope's translation of Homer. Having remained silent in respect to the indictment of Pope's originality implied by John Henley, he was ridiculed in the *Dunciad.*

Brophy (brō'fi), **John.** b. at Liverpool, England, Dec. 6, 1899—. English novelist. Educated at Liverpool and Durham universities, he served in World War I. He was coeditor with Eric Partridge of *Songs and Slang of the British Soldier: 1914–1918* (1930). His first novel, *The Bitter End* (1928), was followed by *Fanfare* (1930), *Flesh and Blood* (1931), *Waterfront* (1934), *The World Went Mad* (1934), *The Ramparts of Virtue* (1936), *The Ridiculous Hat* (1939), *Gentleman of Stratford* (1939), *Green Glory* (1940), *Immortal Sergeant* (1942), *The Woman from Nowhere* (1946), *City of Departures* (1946), *Body and Soul* (1947), and *Sarah* (1948). He also wrote *The Human Face* (1945).

Brophy, Truman William. b. at Goodings Grove, Ill., April 12, 1848; d. Feb. 4, 1928. American oral surgeon who developed (1886) a surgical treatment for cleft palate. For many years dean of the Chicago College of Dental Surgery, he was the author of *Oral Surgery* (1915) and *Cleft Lip and Palate* (1923).

Brosch (brosh), **Moritz.** b. at Prague, April 7, 1829; d. at Venice, July 15, 1907. German historian and journalist. His works include *Papst Julius II und die Gründung des Kirchenstaats* (1878), *Geschichte des Kirchenstaats* (1880–82), *Lord Bolingbroke und die Whigs und Tories seiner Zeit* (1883), *Oliver Cromwell und die puritanische Revolution* (1886), and *Geschichte von England, 1603–1850* (1890–97).

Broseley (brōz'li). Ward of Wenlock municipal borough, and a civil parish, in W England, in Shropshire, situated on the river Severn ab. 13 mi. SE of Shrewsbury, ab. 155 mi. NW of London by rail. 3,216 (1931).

Brosse (bros), **Salomon de.** b. c1565; d. c1626. French architect. He became architect to Marie de Médicis in 1614, and his chief monument is the Luxembourg Palace, designed at her command, and erected between 1615 and 1624. He also designed and built a château at Versailles (for the use of Louis XIII when hunting) which became the core of the great palace later evolved for the pleasure and glory of Louis XIV. Other examples of Brosse's art are the portal of the Church of Saint Gervais, dating from 1616, and the Parliament House, now the Palace of Justice, at Rennes.

Brosses (bros), **Charles de.** [Also, **Debrosses.**] b. at Dijon, France, Feb. 17, 1709; d. at Paris, May 17, 1777. French scholar and man of letters. A friend of many of the leading French thinkers and scientists of the 18th century (including the naturalist Buffon), he was, like many of them, a contributor to the *Encyclopédie.* He wrote *Lettres sur Herculaneum* (1750) and *Lettres sur l'Italie.*

Brostrøm (brö'strėm), **Daniel.** [Also, **Dan Brostrøm.**] b. at Kristinehamn, Denmark, Feb. 1, 1870; d. in an accident, at Trønninge, Denmark, July 24, 1925. Swedish shipping magnate, naval minister (1914–17) during World War I. He established numerous Swedish shipping firms, including lines to eastern Asia, Mexico, and the Levant. He served (1906–11) in the Swedish *Riksdag* (parliament).

Brother, The. Play by James Shirley, licensed for public performance in 1626.

Brother Jonathan (jon'ạ.thạn). See also **Jonathan.**

Brother Jonathan. Prose work (1825) by John Neal. Intended primarily for foreign consumption, it was a study of American character, with emphasis upon the alleged vulgarity of New York, cupidity of New England, and ignorance of the Quakers.

Brothers (bruᴛʜ'érz), **Richard.** b. at Placentia, Newfoundland, Canada, Dec. 25, 1757; d. at London, Jan. 25, 1824. English religious enthusiast and prophet. At one time a naval officer (lieutenant), he was retired on half pay in 1783. He prophesied, among other things (and at different times), that the destruction of the world would take place in 1795, and that complete restoration of the Jews would take place in 1798, with himself as ruler at Jerusalem. As the self-announced heir of David, he also laid claim to various "lesser" thrones, including that of England. He was finally placed in confinement as a lunatic. He wrote *A Revealed Knowledge of the Prophecies and Times* (1794), and others.

Brothers, The. Political club of wits and statesmen established at London in 1713. Jonathan Swift was its treasurer. In 1714 it was merged in the Scriblerus Club.

Brothers, The. Tragedy by Edward Young, produced in 1752.

Brothers, The. Comedy by Richard Cumberland, produced in 1769. Like most of the fashionable comedies of the day, it has a complicated plot, a deep-dyed villain contrasting with a completely virtuous younger brother, a secret marriage, and a quarrelsome married couple.

Brothers, The. Novel by L. A. G. Strong, published in 1932, and issued in America under the title *Brothers.*

Brother Sam. Comedy by John Oxenford from a German play, altered by E. A. Sothern and J. B. Buckstone, produced in 1874. Brother Sam is the brother of Lord Dundreary, and the part was written for Sothern. The play is a kind of sequel to Tom Taylor's *Our American Cousin.*

Brothers' Society. [Chinese, **Ko Lao Hui**; sometimes called **Elder Brother Society.**] One of the largest and most powerful of China's secret societies. During the period (1644–1911) of Manchu rule it helped keep Chinese nationalist sentiment alive and after the establishment (1911) of the republic continued to play an important role in Chinese politics.

Brouckère (brö.ker), **Charles Marie Joseph Ghislain de.** b. at Bruges, Belgium, Jan. 18, 1796; d. April 20, 1860. Belgian politician; brother of Henri M. J. G. de Brouckère (1801–91). He was minister of war (1831–32).

Brouckère, Henri Marie Joseph Ghislain de. b. at Bruges, Belgium, 1801; d. at Brussels, Jan. 25, 1891. Belgian statesman; brother of Charles M. J. G. de Brouckère (1796–1860). He was premier and minister of foreign affairs (1852–55).

Brough (bruf), **John.** b. at Marietta, Ohio, Sept. 17, 1811; d. Aug. 29, 1865. American politician, lawyer, and journalist. After serving as clerk (1835–37) of the Ohio senate, he was auditor (1839–45) of the state, revising the account system. In 1844 he became editor and part owner of the Cincinnati *Enquirer*, and proceeded to make that newspaper one of the most influential Democratic publications in the West. In spite of the fact that he was a Democrat, his staunch support of the Union brought him Republican endorsement in the gubernatorial election of 1863, and he was governor of Ohio during most of the latter part (Jan. 11, 1864–Aug. 29, 1865) of the Civil War. In this post he coöperated wholeheartedly with Abraham Lincoln in the increasingly difficult matter of providing troops for the Union armies. He was also the president (1848–63) of various railroads.

Brough, Robert Barnabas. b. at London, April 10, 1828; d. at Manchester, England, June 26, 1860. English author of burlesques, humorous verse, novels, short stories, and essays. Among his many works are a novel, *Miss Brown* (1860), and *Which is Which?*, a romance (1860). With his brother, William Brough, and by himself, he wrote many burlesque plays; he adapted plays from the French, and translated the poetry of Victor Hugo and some of the prose works of Alphonse Karr.

Brougham (bröm, brö'ạm), **Henry Peter.** [Title, Baron **Brougham and Vaux** (vôks, vôz).] b. at Edinburgh, Sept. 19, 1778; d. at Cannes, France, May 7, 1868. British statesman, orator, jurist, and scientist. He was one of the founders of the *Edinburgh Review* in 1802. Having entered Parliament in 1810, he was counsel for Queen Caroline in the period 1820–21, and was lord chancellor of England in the period 1830–34.

Brougham, John. b. at Dublin, Ireland, May 9, 1810; d. at New York, June 7, 1880. American comic actor and playwright.

Broughton (brô'tọn), **Hugh.** b. at Owlbury, parish of Bishop's Castle, Shropshire, England, 1549; d. at London, Aug. 4, 1612. English divine and rabbinical scholar. He published a Scripture chronology and genealogy, entitled *A Concent of Scripture* (1588), and *Explication of the Article of Christ's Descent into Hell* (1599), in which he maintains that *hades* never means a place of torment, but the state of departed souls. He was satirized by Ben Jonson in *Volpone* (1605) and the *Alchemist* (1610). His works were edited (1662) by John Lightfoot.

Broughton, Rhoda. b. near Denbigh, North Wales, Nov. 29, 1840; d. at Headington Hill, near Oxford, England, June 5, 1920. English novelist of country life. She was educated by her father, Delves Broughton (d. 1863), a clergyman. Author of *Cometh Up as a Flower* (1867), *Not Wisely But Too Well* (1867), *Red as a Rose is She* (1870), *Good-bye, Sweetheart* (1872), *Nancy* (1873), *Joan* (1876), *Belinda* (1883), *Dr. Cupid* (1886), *Dear Faustina* (1897), *Foes-in-Law* (1900), *A Waif's Progress* (1905), *The Devil and the Deep Sea* (1910), *Between Two Stools* (1912), and many others.

Broughton, Thomas. b. at London, July 5, 1704; d. at Bedminster, England, Dec. 21, 1774. English divine and miscellaneous writer. He wrote the lives marked *T* in the original edition of the *Biographia Britannica*, was the author of *An Historical Dictionary of all Religions from the Creation of the World to the Present Time* (1742), and furnished the words to the musical drama *Hercules*, by George Frederick Handel.

Broukhusius (brök.hū'zi.us), **Janus.** Latinized name of **Broekhuizen, Jan van.**

Broun (brön), **Heywood.** [Full name, **Matthew Heywood Campbell Broun.**] b. at Brooklyn, N.Y., Dec. 7, 1888; d. Dec. 18, 1939. American journalist, notable variously as a sports writer, drama critic, and columnist. An alumnus of Harvard, he served (1908–09, 1910–12) on the New York *Morning Telegraph*, and as a baseball writer and drama critic (1912–21) on the New York *Tribune*. In 1921, he joined the staff of the New York *World*, and there started his column, *It Seems to Me*. Always a foe of social injustice, he achieved considerable renown for his outspoken support of Sacco and Vanzetti. He was one of the prime movers in the establishment of the American Newspaper Guild, of which he was also first president (1933–39). His books include *Pieces of Hate* (1922) and *Gandle Follows His Nose* (1926); with Margaret Leech he collaborated on a biography (1927) of Anthony Comstock, and with George Britt on a study of anti-Semitism, *Christians Only* (1931).

Brounoff (brö.nôf'), **Platon G.** b. at Elisavetgrad (now Kirovograd), Russia, in May, 1863; d. 1924. American composer and teacher. He came (1891) to the U.S., and established himself (1892) at New York as a lecturer and singer. He instructed opera classes at the Institute of Musical Art, and conducted the Russian Choral Society and the People's Male Chorus at New York. His compositions include the opera *Ramona*, on American Indian themes; the oratorio *The Glory of God; Xilona*, a musical drama; four symphonies, one of which is known as the *Palestine;* and works for piano, violin, voice, and orchestra.

Broussa (brö.sä'). See **Bursa.**

Broussais (brö.se), **François Joseph Victor.** b. at St.-Malo, France, Dec. 17, 1772; d. at Vitry-sur-Seine, France, Nov. 17, 1838. French physician and medical theorist. His lectures on the sympathetic reaction of organs of the body to ailments of other organs attracted wide attention in France and abroad. His theories in this field were set forth in his *Examen de la doctrine médicale généralement adoptée,* published in 1816, and were angrily condemned by practically the entire body of French physicians. But eventually his ideas won respect and approval, and in 1831 he was made professor of general pathology in the academy of medicine. His statue in the Val-de-Grâce hospital at Paris commemorates the high esteem in which he came to be held.

Brousse (brös), **Paul.** b. at Montpellier, France, Jan. 23, 1844; d. 1912. French political leader, known for his advocacy of an evolutionary theory of socialism. In his earlier life (c1871–79) he was close to Mikhail Bakunin. However, he subsequently abandoned Bakunin's anarchist views, and joined (1905) the unified Socialist Party of France, became (1905) president of the municipal council of Paris, and was a member (1906 *et seq.*) of the Chamber of Deputies.

Brousson (brö.sôṅ), **Claude.** b. at Nîmes, France, 1647; executed at Montpellier, France, Nov. 4, 1698. French Protestant theologian and jurist. Although he was put to death for what were ostensibly political offenses, it should be remembered that the politics of 17th-century France could not help but reflect the bitter warfare between Huguenots and Catholics which had troubled the country through much of the previous century. Brousson was executed at a time when outspoken support of the Protestant point of view could easily impinge upon the political world. He was the author of *L'État des réformés de France* (1684), *Lettres au clergé de France* (1685), and *Lettres aux Catholiques Romains* (1689).

Broussonnet (brö.so.ne), **Pierre Marie Auguste.** b. at Montpellier, France, Feb. 28, 1761; d. there, July 27, 1807. French physician and naturalist, best known as a botanist. He was reputedly the first to introduce merino sheep and Angora goats into France.

Brouwer or **Brauwer** (brou'ėr), **Adriaen.** b. at Oudenarde (now in Belgium), c1606; d. at Antwerp, in January, 1638. Flemish painter. His chief works were acquired by collections at Munich and Dresden. He studied in France, and died in the hospital at Antwerp. The subjects of Brouwer are often tavern scenes and pictures from peasant life. Next to Frans Hals (under whom he studied) he is sometimes considered to have been the greatest technician of his time.

Brouwer, Luitzen Egbertus Jan. b. at Overschie, Netherlands, Feb. 27, 1881—. Dutch mathematician. A contributor to analysis situs, the theory of functions, and the theory of finite continuous groups, he is best known as the chief proponent of the intuitionist view in the philosophy of mathematics. He took his doctorate at Amsterdam in 1907 and taught there from 1909. His books include *Intuitionisme en formalisme* (1912), *Begründung der Mengeniehre* (1918–19), and *Wiskunde, waarheid, werkelijkheid* (1919).

Broward (brou'ạrd), **Napoleon Bonaparte.** b. in Duval County, Fla., April 19, 1857; d. Oct. 1, 1910. American politician who, as governor of Florida, was responsible for actually starting the vast project of drainage of the Everglades. He was sheriff (1889–96) of Duval County, and representative (1900) in the state legislature. During his governorship (1905–09), he also encouraged school and legislative reforms. He commanded (1896 *et seq.*) his steamer *Three Friends* on several gun-running expeditions in aid of the Cuban revolutionists against Spain.

Browder (brou'dėr), **Earl (Russell).** b. at Wichita, Kan., May 20, 1891—. American politician. He was Communist Party candidate for president in 1936 and 1940, but was ousted from the Party in 1946. He became an active Socialist Party member at the age of 15. Refusing to register (1917) for selective service, he spent a three-year prison term studying Karl Marx and Friedrich Engels. He joined the Communist Party upon his release in 1919 and became its general secretary in 1929. Sentenced (1939) to four years' imprisonment for passport fraud, he obtained his release in 1942 after the U.S. and U.S.S.R. had become associated in the war against Germany. He formally dissolved (January, 1944) the American Communist Party as a political organization, even declaring himself for free enterprise in the U.S., although with some qualifications. This step and this point of view were accepted without question by virtually all American Communists at the time, but criticism began to make itself heard as World War II drew to a close. Shortly thereafter, the American Communist Party was officially reestablished (July, 1945) under William Z. Foster, and Browder was stripped of all authority in it. In 1946 he was formally expelled from the Communist Party. In the same year, he visited Moscow, and returned to the U.S. as an agent for Soviet publishing firms.

Browdie (brou'di), **John.** In Charles Dickens's *Nicholas Nickleby*, a big, good-natured Yorkshireman. He marries Matilda Price.

Brown (broun), **Aaron Venable.** b. in Brunswick County, Va., Aug. 15, 1795; d. March 8, 1859. American politician, notable for his improvements, as U.S. postmaster general (1857–59) under President James Buchanan, of mail service between the eastern seaboard and the West. Elected to the Tennessee Senate (1821) and to that state's lower house (1831), he also served (1839–45) in Congress, where he helped formulate the tariff bill of 1842. He was governor (1845 *et seq.*) of Tennessee, and ended his public career as Buchanan's postmaster general.

Brown, Addison. b. at West Newbury, Mass., Feb. 21, 1830; d. at New York, April 9, 1913. American jurist and botanist. Admitted (1855) to the New York bar, he was appointed (1881) district judge for the southern district of New York, and remained on the bench until 1901. He was one of the founders (c1891) of the New York Botanical Garden, and coauthor, with Nathaniel L. Britton, of *Illustrated Flora of the Northern United States, Canada and the British Possessions* (3 vols., 1896–98).

Brown, Alexander. b. at Ballymena, County Antrim, Ireland, Nov. 17, 1764; d. April 3, 1834. American merchant and banker, among the first millionaires in the U.S. He emigrated (1800) to Baltimore, Md. Beginning in business with the importation of Irish linens, he built the firm of Alexander Brown and Sons, a banking house recognized the world over and the oldest institution of its kind in the U.S. With one of his sons, George Brown (1787–1859), he was among the organizers of the Baltimore and Ohio Railroad.

Brown, Alexander. b. at Glenmore, Va., Sept. 5, 1843; d. Aug. 25, 1906. American historian, an authority on early Virginian history. He was the author of *New Views of Early Virginia History* (1886), *The Genesis of the United States* (1890), *The Cabells and Their Kin* (1895), *The First Republic in America* (1898), *The History of Our Earliest History* (1898), and *English Politics in Early Virginia History* (1901).

Brown, Alexander Ephraim. b. May 14, 1852; d. April 26, 1911. American engineer, inventor (1879) of the Brown hoisting and conveying machine. He explored (1872) the Yellowstone region for the U.S. Geological Survey, was chief engineer (1873–75) with the Massillon Iron Bridge Company, Massillon, Ohio, and was an engineer (1875–78) in the iron-ore region bordering on the Great Lakes. He also served as vice-president (until 1910) and president (1910 *et seq.*) of the Brown Hoisting Machinery Company, which manufactured his machine for handling ore at lake ports.

Brown, Alice. b. at Hampton Falls, N.H., Dec. 5, 1857; d. June 21, 1948. American author, especially of stories of New England life. Her works include *Meadow-Grass* (1895), *By Oak and Thorn* (1896), *Tiverton Tales* (1899), *King's End* (1901), *Margaret Warrender* (1901), *The Mannerings* (1903), *Judgment* (1903), *High Noon* (1904), *The Court of Love* (1906), *The Story of Thyrza* (1909), *John Winterbourne's Family* (1910), *The Prisoner* (1916), *Bromley Neighborhood* (1917), *The Wind Between the Worlds* (1920), *Old Crow* (1922), and *Dear Old Templeton* (1927). She was the author also of *Children of Earth* (1915), a play.

Brown, Arthur Judson. b. at Holliston, Mass., Dec. 3, 1856—. American Presbyterian clergyman. Ordained in 1883, he was secretary (1895–1929) of the Presbyterian Board of Foreign Missions. Author of *The New Era in the Philippines* (1903), *New Forces in Old China* (1904), *The Foreign Missionary* (1907), *The Chinese Revolution* (1912), *Japan in the World of Today* (1928), and other books.

Brown, Bartholomew. fl. in the first half of the 19th century. American music teacher and musicologist. He taught (1880 *et seq.*) at Boston, was an editor (1802) of the *Bridgewater Collection* of sacred music, and served as conductor (1832–38) of the Handel and Haydn Society.

Brown, Benjamin Gratz. b. at Lexington, Ky., May 28, 1826; d. at St. Louis, Mo., Dec. 13, 1885. American politician and journalist. He was a U.S. senator from Missouri (1863–67), governor of Missouri (1871–72), and unsuccessful candidate of the Democrats and Liberal Republicans for vice-president in 1872. An advocate of the Free-Soil movement, he was also instrumental in the founding of the Republican Party in Missouri.

Brown, Bolton. b. at Dresden, N.Y., Nov. 27, 1865; d. at Zena, N.Y., Sept. 15, 1936. American landscape painter, etcher, lithographer, author, and potter. He was one of the founders of the art colony at Woodstock, N.Y., and a close associate of George Bellows. He studied at Syracuse University, and organized and headed the art department of Stanford University. He also lectured at the National Academy of Design and the Art Institute of Chicago, and taught at Cornell University. His work, which was exhibited widely in the U.S. and in England, includes *The Bather*, *Monterey Fishing Village*, *Sifting Shadows*, *Farmhouse in Winter*, and lithographs in the British Museum, Brooklyn Museum, and New York Public Library.

Brown, "Capability." See **Brown, Lancelot.**

Brown, Carleton. b. at Oberlin, Ohio, July 15, 1869; d. June 25, 1941. American teacher and philologist. He was an instructor (1903–05) and associate (1905–07) in English at Harvard, professor (1910–17, 1921–27) of English and philology at Bryn Mawr College, professor (1917–21) of English at the University of Minnesota, and professor (1927–39) of English at New York University. He served also as secretary (1920–34) and president (1936) of the Modern Language Association of America. He compiled *A Register of Middle English Religious and Didactic Verse* (Part I, 1916; Part II, 1920), *Religious Lyrics of the XIVth Century* (1924), *English Lyrics of the XIIIth Century* (1932), and *Religious Lyrics of the XVth Century* (1939). He was the author of *A Study of the Miracle of Our Lady Told By Chaucer's Prioress* (1910).

Brown, Charles Armitage. b. 1786; d. in New Zealand, 1842. English man of letters; a close friend of John Keats. He conducted (c1805–10) his merchant brother's business at St. Petersburg; after the business collapsed (1810), he returned to England, ruined, and remained penniless until an inheritance enabled him to devote himself to literature. He traveled (1818) in Scotland with Keats (whom he had met before 1817), and, for two years, made him an intimate of his house at Hampstead, where he introduced him to Fanny Brawne. In Italy (1822–25), where he became intimate (1824) with Walter Savage

Landor, he lectured on Keats and Shakespeare. In 1841 he went to New Zealand for reasons of health. Richard Monckton Milnes, 1st Baron Houghton, in his biography of Keats, includes many of Brown's papers about the poet. Brown's most important work is *Shakespeare's Autobiographical Poems* (1838), a personal interpretation of the sonnets.

Brown, Charles Brockden. b. at Philadelphia, Jan. 17, 1771; d. Feb. 22, 1810. American novelist. Son of Quaker parents, he early imbibed liberal opinions. Ill and melancholy most of his short life, he wrote seven Gothic and sentimental novels, edited three magazines, prepared political pamphlets against Jefferson, and compiled a semiannual historical register. His fame rests on four novels. The best one, *Wieland* (1798), portrays a religious fanatic who murders his wife and children at the command, he thinks, of God; the Gothic motives include the death by spontaneous combustion of Wieland's father. The novel *Ormond* (1799) pictures a maiden resisting the advances of a schemer. *Arthur Mervyn* (1799–1800) describes a noble youth's entanglement with criminality during the yellow fever epidemic in 1793 at Philadelphia. *Edgar Huntly* (1800) concerns a sleepwalker who pursues an Indian murderer in a frontier community. Called "the father of the American novel," Brown was inspired by cultural nationalism and employed native characters and scenes effectively. His well-plotted stories are deficient in technique but are spine-chilling in incident.

Brown, Charles Reynolds. b. at Bethany, W.Va., Oct. 1, 1862; d. Nov. 28, 1950. American clergyman and educator. A graduate of the University of Iowa (1886) and Boston University (1889), he was pastor (1896–1911) of the First Congregational Church at Oakland, Calif., and dean (1911–28) of the Yale Divinity School. He was the author of *The Special Message of the Modern Pulpit* (1906), *The Art of Preaching* (1922), *Why I Believe in Religion* (1923), *They Were Giants* (1934), *Being Made Over* (1939), *Dreams Come True* (1944), and other books.

Brown, Elmer Ellsworth. b. at Kiantone, N.Y., Aug. 28, 1861; d. Nov. 3, 1934. American educator and author. A professor at the University of California (1893–1906), he was appointed U.S. commissioner of education in 1906; he became chancellor of New York University in 1911. He wrote *The Making of Our Middle Schools* (1903), *Origin of American State Universities* (1905), *Government by Influence* (1909), and others.

Brown, Ernest. b. at Torquay, England, Aug. 27, 1881—. British politician. A member (1923–45) of Parliament, he was secretary in the ministry of health (1931–32) and the mines department (1932–34), minister of labor (1935–40) and national service (1939–40), secretary (1940–41) for Scotland, minister (1941–43) of health, chancellor (1943–45) of the Duchy of Lancaster, and minister (May–July, 1945) of aircraft production.

Brown, Ernest William. b. at Hull, England, Nov. 29, 1866; d. July 23, 1938. American mathematician. After teaching (1891–1907) at Haverford College, he was named (1907) professor of mathematics at Yale University. He is known for his investigations into the motion of the moon.

Brown, Fay Cluff. b. at Washington Court House, Ohio, Nov. 23, 1881—. American physicist. A graduate of Indiana University (B.A., 1904), the University of Illinois (M.A., 1906) and of Princeton (Ph.D., 1908), he was a member (1909–19) of the physics department at the University of Iowa, and a staff member (1919–27) of the U.S. Bureau of Standards. After serving as curator (1937–40) of the physics department in the Museum of Science and Industry, at Chicago, he became (1940) a member of the faculty of the Massachusetts Institute of Technology.

Brown, Ford Madox. b. at Calais, France, April 16, 1821; d. at London, Oct. 6, 1893. English painter, associated with the Pre-Raphaelites; father of Oliver Madox Brown (1855–74). At Manchester, England, he executed a series of murals depicting great events in that city's history. His other works include *Wyclif* (1849), *King Lear* (1849), *Chaucer Reciting His Poetry at the Court of Edward II* (1851), and *Christ Washing Peter's Feet* (1852).

Brown, Fort. U.S. military post at Brownsville, Tex., set up (1846) by General Zachary Taylor during the Mexican War. It was named not for Jacob Jennings Brown, who had been general in chief of the U.S. army from 1821 to 1828, but for another officer of the same first and last name who served under Taylor, and who commanded the fort when Taylor was temporarily forced to abandon his positions in the Brownsville vicinity. In 1865, Union forces seized it from the Confederates, and it subsequently became a federal army post.

Brown, Francis. b. at Chester, N.H., Jan. 11, 1784; d. July 27, 1820. American educator and clergyman; father of Samuel Gilman Brown (1813–85). While a pastor (1810–15) at North Yarmouth, Me., he published two pamphlets (1815) on Calvinism. He was overseer (1810–14) and a trustee (1814–15) of Bowdoin College, and president (1815 *et seq.*) of Dartmouth College at the time of the Dartmouth College Case.

Brown, Francis. b. at Hanover, N.H., Dec. 26, 1849; d. at Bethel, Me., Oct. 15, 1916. American scholar, clergyman, and educator, president of Union Theological Seminary (1908 *et seq.*); grandson of Francis Brown (1784–1820). He was instructor in Biblical philology (1879–81) and associate professor (1881–90) at Union Theological Seminary. In 1890 he was appointed professor of Hebrew and cognate languages there. He was the author of *Assyriology, Its Use and Abuse* (1885) and *The Christian Point of View* (1902, with George William Knox and Arthur C. McGiffert). He compiled, with S. R. Driver and C. A. Briggs, *Hebrew and English Lexicon of the Old Testament* (1891–1906).

Brown, George. b. at Ballymena, County Antrim, Ireland, April 17, 1787; d. Aug. 26, 1859. American railroad promoter; son of Alexander Brown (1764–1834). An organizer and treasurer (1827–34) of the Baltimore and Ohio Railroad, he supervised with his father the actual construction (1828 *et seq.*) of the road; he suggested (1831–32) the building of the first eight-wheel passenger car. From 1834 to 1859 he was head of the banking house of Alexander Brown and Sons.

Brown, Sir George. b. 1790; d. 1865. English general. Appointed (1851) a lieutenant general, he commanded (1855) a division in the Crimea, and was commander in chief (1860–65) in Ireland. At the conclusion of the Crimean War, he was made a knight grand cross of the Legion of Honor.

Brown, George. b. at Edinburgh, Nov. 29, 1818; d. at Toronto, Canada, May 9, 1880. Canadian politician and journalist. He founded the Toronto *Globe* in 1844, entered the Dominion House of Commons in 1851, and became a senator in 1873. An advocate of Canadian confederation, he also promoted a national secular school system and parliamentary representation based on population.

Brown, George Douglas. [Pseudonym, **George Douglas.**] b. at Ochiltree, Ayrshire, Scotland, Jan. 26, 1869; d. at London, Aug. 28, 1902. Scottish novelist. He was educated at Glasgow University and at Balliol College, Oxford, winning scholarships, prizes, and medals at both. He went to London in 1895, where he wrote for the metropolitan newspapers and was a publisher's reader. Under his pseudonym he wrote *The House with the Green Shutters* (1901), a realistic study of Scottish life.

Brown, George Loring. b. Feb. 2, 1814; d. June 25, 1889. American painter, noted especially for landscapes.

Brown, Glenn. b. in Fauquier County, Va., Sept. 13, 1854; d. April 22, 1932. American architect. He studied at Washington and Lee University, and took the architectural course at the Massachusetts Institute of Technology. A practicing architect from 1878, he wrote on various subjects, including house sanitation, and edited (1899–1909) the *Proceedings* of the American Institute of Architects.

Brown, Goold. b. at Providence, R.I., March 7, 1791; d. at Lynn, Mass., March 31, 1857. American grammarian. For many years he conducted an academy at New York. He wrote *Institutes of English Grammar* (1823), *First Lines of English Grammar* (1823), *Grammar of English Grammars* (1850–51), and others.

Brown, Harry. [Full name, **Harry Peter McNab Brown, Jr.**] b. at Portland, Me., April 30, 1917—. American author. In World War II, he served as a private, and was on the staff of the U.S. army magazine, *Yank*. Among his works are *Artie Greengroin, PFC* (1945) and the play *A Sound of Hunting* (1945). His novel *A Walk in the Sun* (1944) was made into a motion picture. His poetry includes *The End of a Decade* (1940), *The Poem of Bunker Hill* (1941), and *The Violent* (1943).

Brown, Henry Billings. b. at South Lee, Mass., March 2, 1836; d. Sept. 4, 1913. American jurist. Graduated from Yale (1856), he was admitted to the Michigan bar in 1860. He was a U.S. judge for the eastern district of Michigan (1875–90), and an associate justice of the U.S. Supreme Court (1890–1906). His publications include *Admiralty Reports* (1876), and articles in legal magazines.

Brown, Henry Kirke. b. at Leyden, Mass., Feb. 24, 1814; d. at Newburgh, N.Y., July 10, 1886. American sculptor, now perhaps most widely known for his equestrian statue of George Washington in Union Square at New York. Apprenticed (1832) to Chester Harding at Boston, he studied painting until he went to Cincinnati in 1836; there he became interested in sculpture, and in 1842 he went to Italy for further study in this field. To the period in Italy belong *Boy and Dog* (New York Historical Society) and several classical busts, all in marble. He established (1846) a studio at New York, where he produced the bronze group *Indian and Panther*. He was elected (1851) to the National Academy of Design. After the unveiling (1856) of the Washington statue, he produced two other equestrian groups, one of Winfield Scott and one of Nathanael Greene, both at Washington, D.C.

Brown, Jacob Jennings. b. in Bucks County, Pa., May 9, 1775; d. at Washington, D.C., Feb. 24, 1828. American general. In 1813 he received an appointment as brigadier general in the regular army, having been previously in the militia. He was placed in command of the Army of the Niagara, with the rank of major general, in 1814; he won battles at Chippewa (July 5), Lundy's Lane (July 25) and Fort Erie (Sept. 17, 1814). In 1821 he became general in chief of the U.S. Army.

Brown, James. b. in Ireland, Feb. 4, 1791; d. Nov. 1, 1877. American financier; son of Alexander Brown (1764–1834). He established (1825) the New York branch of the banking house of Alexander Brown and Sons, under the name of Brown Brothers and Company, keeping the business intact through the financial crisis of the Civil War.

Brown, John. b. at Rothbury, Northumberland, England, Nov. 5, 1715; committed suicide, Sept. 23, 1766. English clergyman and writer. He was the author of *An Estimate of the Manners and Principles of the Times* (1757), and others.

Brown, John. b. at Carpow, Perthshire, Scotland, 1722; d. at Haddington, East Lothian, Scotland, June 19, 1787. Scottish Biblical scholar. His works include *A Dictionary of the Bible* (1769), *The Self-interpreting Bible* (1778), and *A Compendious History of the British Churches* (1784; new edition, 1823).

Brown, John. b. at Buncle, Berwickshire, Scotland, 1735; d. at London, Oct. 17, 1788. British physician, founder of the "Brunonian" system in medicine. He published *Observations on the Present System of Spasm as taught in the University of Edinburgh* (1789), which was directed against the school of doctors who attempted to cure by bloodletting, and *Elementa Medicinae* (1780), in which he projected a new theory of medicine. He divided diseases into two classes, sthenic and asthenic, the former resulting from excess, the latter from deficiency of exciting power, and contended that the great majority of diseases belonged to the latter class. He moved to London in 1786.

Brown, John. b. Jan. 27, 1736; d. Sept. 20, 1803. American patriot and merchant; brother of Nicholas Brown (1729–91). He was associated (until c1770) with his brother in the mercantile house of Nicholas Brown and Company at Providence, R.I. He led (1772) in the destruction of the British schooner *Gaspee;* during the Revolution, he supplied American forces with cannon made of metal from the blast furnace at Scituate, R.I., known as "Furnace Hope." In the period 1799–1801 he served in Congress.

Brown, John. b. at Haverhill, Mass., Oct. 19, 1744; d. near Stone Arabia, N.Y., Oct. 19, 1780. American Revolutionary soldier and lawyer. He served (1774) on two revolutionary committees at Pittsfield, Mass., and represented (1774–75) the town at the Provincial Congress. In 1775 he was sent to Canada for the Boston committee of correspondence. His exploits during the Revolutionary War included the capture (Oct. 19, 1775) of Fort Chambly.

Brown, John. [Called **"John Brown of Ossawatomie."**] b. at Torrington, Conn., May 9, 1800; executed at Charles Town, Va. (in what is now West Virginia), Dec. 2, 1859. Famous abolitionist. His grandfather, Captain John Brown, had died in the Revolution. As a child he was taken to Hudson, Ohio, in 1805. He married Dianthe Lusk in 1820, by whom he had seven children, and married Mary Day in 1833, by whom he had 13 children. He lived (1826–35) at New Richmond, Pa., where he engaged in tanning, and established the first post office and also a station of the Underground Railway. He was an expert tanner and taught his cousin (who was Ulysses S. Grant's father) the tanning business, and was also an expert in judging livestock and wool. It is said that he would refuse to sell leather until the last drop of moisture had been dried from it "lest he should sell his customers water and reap the gain." He spent the happiest fourth of his turbulent adult life in Pennsylvania. In 1839 he conceived the idea of becoming a liberator of the slaves. He had in the meantime moved back to Ohio in 1836, then successively to Massachusetts, to North Elba, N.Y., and in 1855 to Kansas, with his sons and son-in-law. He was extremely active in the antislavery movement in Kansas, where his son Frederick was killed (1856) at Ossawatomie in an antislavery skirmish. He conceived the scheme of freeing the slaves by furnishing them with arms with which to revolt against their masters and in 1859 went to Virginia where, on Oct. 16, he and 21 followers captured the U.S. arsenal at Harpers Ferry. The arsenal was recaptured from him on October 18 by troops under Colonel Robert E. Lee. Brown was wounded and his sons Watson and Oliver were killed. He was tried by the Commonwealth of Virginia and executed.

Brown, John. b. at Biggar, Lanarkshire, Scotland, in September, 1810; d. May 11, 1882. Scottish physician and author. His chief work is *Horae Subsecivae* (1858, 1861, 1882), containing "Our Dogs," and "Rab and his Friends"; the latter was first published in 1859. He also wrote *John Leech and Other Papers* (1882).

Brown, Sir **John.** b. at Sheffield, England, Dec. 6, 1816; d. in Kent, England, Dec. 27, 1896. English steel manufacturer, notable for his pioneering work in the manufacture of armor plate for war vessels. He was also the inventor (1848) of the conical steel spring buffer for railway cars, produced by rolling instead of hammering. In 1856 he coördinated his various manufacturing plants and there first successfully developed the Bessemer process of steel making. He served as mayor of Sheffield (1862 and 1863).

Brown, John Alexander. b. in Ireland, May 21, 1788; d. Dec. 31, 1872. American financier; son of Alexander Brown (1764–1834). He established (1818) at Philadelphia the first American branch of the banking house of Alexander Brown and Sons, which he headed until 1837.

Brown, John Carter. b. Aug. 28, 1797; d. June 10, 1874. American book collector, noted for his library of Americana; grandson of Nicholas Brown (1729–91). His collection of books, numbering over 7,000 volumes dealing with America before 1800, is now at Brown University.

Brown, John George. b. at Durham, England, Nov. 11, 1831; d. Feb. 8, 1913. American figure and genre painter. He studied at Newcastle, at Edinburgh, and, in 1853, at New York, where he was elected a national academician in 1863. He was noted for his characteristic pictures of street boys.

Brown, Joseph. b. in December, 1733; d. Dec. 3, 1785. American manufacturer, remembered chiefly for his interest in the sciences; brother of Nicholas Brown (1729–91). He entered the family firm of Nicholas Brown and Company and was put in charge of the blast furnace known as "Furnace Hope," at Scituate, R.I. He experimented variously in physics, architecture, and astronomy.

Brown, Joseph Rogers. b. at Warren, R.I., Jan. 26, 1810; d. in the Isles of Shoals, off the coast of New Hampshire, July 23, 1876. American inventor and manufacturer of precision instruments and machine tools, including the universal grinding machine. In association (1833–41) with his father, and in business for himself (1841–53), he devised calipers, protractors, and precision instruments of extreme accuracy. He incorporated (1868) his business with Lucian Sharpe under the firm name of Brown and Sharpe Manufacturing Company.

Brown, Lancelot. [Called **"Capability" Brown.**] b. at Harle-Kirk, Northumberland, England, 1715; d. Feb. 6, 1783. English landscape gardener. He was considered by Humphrey Repton the founder of the modern or English style of landscape gardening, superseding the geometric style which had been perfected at Versailles in the early 17th century. Although the true founder of the modern style is more often considered to have been William Kent, Brown had worked independently with the aim of bringing out the undulating lines of natural landscape. He also served (1770) as high sheriff of Huntingdonshire.

Brown, Martha. [Maiden name, **McClellan.**] b. at Baltimore, April 16, 1838; d. Aug. 31, 1916. American lecturer and organizer of temperance movements. She started (1870) the Temperance Cadet movement. A founder (1869) of the Prohibition Party, introducing the women's suffrage plank, she led (1881, 1882) the National Conference of Prohibition and Woman Suffrage Workers. She was also a founder (1874) of the National Woman's Christian Temperance Union, and the first woman editor (1868–78) of a secular publication, the weekly *Alliance.*

Brown, Moses. b. in September, 1738; d. Sept. 7, 1836. American manufacturer, noted for introducing cotton manufacture into Rhode Island; brother of Nicholas Brown (1729–91) and associated with him in Nicholas Brown and Company. He established (1789) the firm of Brown and Almy for carding and spinning cotton, copying the Englishman Arkwright's method. Having become (1774) a Quaker, he helped start the Rhode Island Abolition Society and was treasurer (1784) and patron of what is now the Moses Brown School at Providence.

Brown, Mr. Pseudonym of William Makepeace Thackeray, under which he wrote (1849) letters to a young man about town, in *Punch.*

Brown, Nicholas. b. at Providence, R.I., July 28, 1729; d. May 29, 1791. American merchant, head of Nicholas Brown and Company, international trading house at Providence, R.I. With his brothers he expanded the firm and established (c1765) the blast furnace known as "Furnace Hope," at Scituate, R.I. It was thus possible to manufacture cannon from the iron produced from ore-deposits at nearby Cranston, R.I., and for Brown thereby to supply Revolutionary troops with guns, as well as clothing. He was active (1767) in securing the location at Providence of Rhode Island College, now known as Brown University.

Brown, Nicholas. b. at Providence, R.I., April 4, 1769; d. Oct. 27, 1841. American merchant; son of Nicholas Brown (1729–91). He was a patron of Brown University (formerly Rhode Island College), to which he gave in the aggregate 100,000 dollars.

Brown, Oliver Madox. b. at Finchley, London, Jan. 20, 1855; d. there, Nov. 5, 1874. English painter, poet, and novelist; son of Ford Madox Brown (1821–93).

Brown, Olympia. b. at Prairie Ronde, Mich., Jan. 5, 1835; d. at Baltimore, Oct. 23, 1926. American minister and suffragist, the first woman in the U.S. to hold the ministry of a regularly constituted church. Upon ordination she was appointed (1863) to the Universalist Church and held pastorates at Weymouth, Mass. (1864) and Bridgeport, Conn. (1869), among others. She campaigned (1867) for the feminist cause in Kansas, was president (1887–1917) of the Wisconsin Woman's Suffrage Association; and wrote *Acquaintances, Old and New, Among Reformers* (1911) and *Democratic Ideals* (1917).

Brown, Rawdon Lubbock. b. 1803; d. 1883. English historian, chiefly known for his researches in Venetian archives. During his residence (1833–83) at Venice, he carried on investigations of reports sent home by early Venetian ambassadors at London, and recorded the results of his research in *Four Years at the Court of Henry VIII* (1854). His *Calendar of State Papers and Manuscripts Relating to English Affairs Existing in the Archives . . . of Venice . . .* is now generally considered a basic source for the study of English history from 1202 to 1558.

Brown, Robert. b. at Montrose, Scotland, Dec. 21, 1773; d. at London, June 10, 1858. British botanist. Although his work in botanical classification was of great value (the classification of the Gymnospermae, or plants which have a naked seed or seeds, not enclosed in ovaries, was due to him, and he was active for part of his life in matters of classification through his position as librarian of the Linnaean Society), he is now probably best known for his description (1827) of the phenomenon of physics now universally known as the Brownian movement, which is the rapid oscillatory movement observable in minute particles of matter suspended in a liquid. This motion is continuous and without relationship to movement imparted to the liquid from outside; moreover, not only do even the smallest particles thus far observed through microscopes display this action, they also move at a velocity that increases as their size diminishes. This has long been used as one of the proofs of the kinetic molecular theory of matter, which maintains that constantly moving molecules (the smallest physical unit possible without undergoing chemical change) are the basis of all matter. The phenomenon of the Brownian movement is therefore taken to be simply the result of particles in the liquid being struck by the moving molecules that make up the liquid, and hence, logically, the smaller the particle, the greater the velocity of motion imparted. Brown was also the naturalist of Matthew Flinders's Australian expedition (1801–05) and keeper of the botanical department of the British Museum after 1827. He published *Prodromus florae Novae Hollandiae et Insulae Van Diemen* (1810; supplement, 1830) and *General Remarks on the Botany of Terra Australis* (1814).

Brown, Roy. b. at Decatur, Ill., 1879—. American landscape painter and water colorist. He studied at the Art Students League of New York, and at Paris. His work has been extensively exhibited; he has won many awards, was made an academician of the National Academy of Design in 1926, is a member of the American Art Association at Paris and the National Arts Club, and was president of the American Water Color Society, at New York. Some of his better-known works are *The Landing, Pines and Poplars, Maine Ledges, On the Dunes, The Riverfront, Wilton Hills, Façades,* and *October, Trepied, France.*

Brown, Samuel Gilman. b. Jan. 4, 1813; d. at Utica, N.Y., Nov. 4, 1885. American educator and clergyman; son of Francis Brown (1784–1820). He served on the faculty (1840–67) of Dartmouth College, and was president (1867–81) of Hamilton College. He also wrote and lectured widely on theology, and edited *The Works of Rufus Choate, with a Memoir of His Life* (2 vols., 1862).

Brown, Samuel Robbins. b. at East Windsor, Conn., June 16, 1810; d. June 20, 1880. American educator and missionary. He taught in the U.S. at the New York Institute for the Deaf and Dumb, conducted (1848–51) a school at Rome, N.Y., and was one of the founders of Elmira College, at Elmira, N.Y. As a missionary (1839–47) in China, he established for the Morrison Educational Association a school at Macao (which school was later to be transferred to Hong Kong); during a sojourn (1859–79) in Japan, he taught at Kanagawa and Yokohama. He was chairman (1874–79) of a committee to translate the New Testament into Japanese. In 1847 he brought the first Chinese students to America. He was the author of articles and books on the Far East.

Brown, Sidney George. b. at Chicago, July 6, 1873; d. at Sidmouth, Devonshire, England, Aug. 7, 1948. English inventor of electrical devices. His inventions include a drum cable relay and magnetic shunt with which the first messages could be sent over long underwater cables, the single-point iridium microphonic relay (1908), the granular carbon microphone relay (1910) whose principal use is in radiotelegraphy, a gyroscopic compass (1914) for shipboard use, a like compass for air use, a gun directorial compass, a turning indicator (1929) for airplanes, and an airplane speed indicator (1930).

Brown, Solyman. b. at Litchfield, Conn., Nov. 17, 1790; d. at Dodge Center, Minn., Feb. 13, 1876. American dentist and clergyman, now probably remembered chiefly for his success in establishing dentistry in the U.S. as an organized profession. At one time Congregational minister (1813–17) in N Connecticut, he was subsequently both a classics instructor (1820–32), and a Swedenborgian minister (1822 *et seq.*). As a practicing dentist, he was an organizer of the Society of Surgeon Dentists of the City and State of New York (1834) and of the American Society of Dental Surgeons (1840), the latter being the first national association of dentists in the U.S. He was the author of *The Importance of Regulating the Teeth of Children* (1841), *Treatise on Mechanical Dentistry* (1843), and a curious work of didactic verse entitled *Dentologia* (1833).

Brown, Tarleton. b. in Barnwell District, S.C., 1754; d. 1846. American soldier in the Revolutionary War. He served throughout the Revolutionary War, obtaining the rank of captain, and wrote *Memoirs* pertaining to contemporary events in the Carolinas (privately printed, with notes by Charles J. Bushnell, 1862).

Brown, Thomas. [Called, **Tom Brown.**] b. at Shifnal, Shropshire, England, 1663; d. at London, June 16, 1704. English satirical poet and prose writer. A collected edition of his works was published in the period 1707–08. Perhaps the best-known of his many verses is the quatrain beginning *I Do Not Love Thee, Dr. Fell.*

Brown, Thomas. b. at Kilmabreck, Kirkcudbrightshire, Scotland, Jan. 9, 1778; d. at Brompton, near London, April 2, 1820. Scottish physician, philosopher, and poet; a colleague (1810 *et seq.*) of Dugald Stewart. He is chiefly notable from his support of David Hume's theory of causation. His works include *Poems* (1804), *Paradise of Coquettes* (1814), *The War-fiend* (1816), *An Inquiry into the Relation of Cause and Effect* (1818), *Agnes* (1818), *Emily* (1819), and *Lectures on the Physiology of the Human Mind* (1820).

Brown, Thomas Edward. b. at Douglas, on the Isle of Man, May 5, 1830; d. at Clifton, Gloucestershire, England, Oct. 30, 1897. English poet, curate, and schoolmaster. Educated at King William's College on the Isle of Man and at Christ Church, Oxford, he was elected (1854) a fellow of Oriel College, Oxford. He served as vice-principal (1855–61) of King William's College, headmaster (1861–63) of the Crypt School in Gloucester, master (1863–92) of Clifton College, and curate (1884–93) at St. Barnabas, Bristol. He was the author of *Betsey Lee* (1873), *Fo'c's'le Yarns* (1881), *The Doctor* (1887), *The Manx Witch* (1889), and *Old John* (1893), narrative and lyric poetry, much of it in Manx dialect; his *Collected Poems* and his *Letters* were published in 1900. Among his best-known poems are "Vespers," "Disguises," "An Autumn Trinket," "Juventa Perennis," and "The Schooner."

Brown, Thomas, the Younger. See **Brown the Younger, Thomas.**

Brown, Walter Folger. b. at Massillon, Ohio, May 31, 1869—. American businessman and politician. He served (1929–33) as U.S. postmaster general, and was president and chairman of the board of the Hudson and Manhattan Railroad Company.

Brown, William. b. in Ireland, 1777; d. near Buenos Aires, May 3, 1857. Admiral of the Argentine navy. He emigrated to America with his family when a child, and in 1812 settled at Buenos Aires. In the war with Brazil (1825–27), he did efficient service, but was finally defeated. In the Argentine civil war (1842–45) he commanded the fleet of Buenos Aires, blockading Montevideo.

Brown, Sir **William.** b. at Ballymena, County Antrim, Ireland, May 30, 1784; d. at Liverpool, England, 1864. British merchant and banker; son of Alexander Brown (1764–1834) and brother of George Brown (1787–1859). When he was 16 years of age he accompanied his father, an Irish linen-merchant, to the U.S., staying for a time at Baltimore, but in 1809 he went to England, settling at Liverpool and establishing there a branch of the family enterprise, which by that time was dealing extensively in cotton as well as linen, and presently developed into a general merchandising business, from which eventually it branched into banking. In the financial crisis of 1837 disaster was averted when the Bank of England offered a loan of two million pounds sterling, of which the Browns accepted only one million and repaid it within six months. Within a few years thereafter the firm of Brown, Shipley, and Company, as the Liverpool house was known, achieved an important position in the trade between Great Britain and the U.S. with the coöperation of the banking houses established by other members of the family at Baltimore, Philadelphia, and New York. In 1856 the activities of British consuls in the U.S., who were enlisting recruits for the British forces then engaged in the Crimean War, caused tension between the British and American governments, which William Brown was able to ease in the course of an interview with Lord Palmerston, the British prime minister. From 1846 to 1859 William Brown sat in the House of Commons as a member for South Lancashire. In 1860 he erected and endowed a public library and museum at the city of Liverpool. He was made a baronet in 1863.

Brown, William Adams. b. at New York, Dec. 29, 1865; d. there, Dec. 15, 1943. American Presbyterian clergyman and theologian. Ordained in 1893, he served as professor of theology (1898–1936) at Union Theological Seminary, was a member (1917–34) of the Yale Corporation, and led the American section at the Oxford World Conference on Faith and Order (1937). He was the author of *Church and State in Contemporary America* (1937), *The Case for Theology in the University* (1938), *A Teacher and His Times* (1940), and other works.

Brown, William Garrott. b. at Marion, Ala., April 24, 1868; d. at New Canaan, Conn., Oct. 19, 1913. American historian and essayist, a specialist in the history of the South. He lectured (1902) at Harvard, and was the author of *Andrew Jackson* (1900), *The Lower South in American History* (1902), *Stephen Arnold Douglas* (1902), *The Foe of Compromise and Other Essays* (1903), and *A Continental Congressman; Oliver Ellsworth* (1905).

Brown, William Henry. b. at Richmond, Va., Oct. 6, 1884; d. Nov. 9, 1939. American botanist. He served as plant physiologist (1911–23) and director (1924–33) of the Bureau of Science at Manila, P.I., and was associate professor (1915–18) and professor and head of the department (1919–24) of botany at the University of the Philippines. His works include *Vegetation of Philippine Mountains* (1919), *A Textbook of General Botany* (1925), *Laboratory Botany* (1925), and *The Plant Kingdom* (1935); he was editor in chief (1924–33) of the *Philippine Journal of Science.*

Brown, Zenith. [Maiden name, **Jones**; pseudonyms: **Leslie Ford, David Frome.**] b. at Smith River, Calif., 1898—. American writer of detective fiction. Under the pseudonym David Frome, she is the author of the Pinkerton books, including *Mr. Pinkerton Goes to Scotland Yard* (1934), *Mr. Pinkerton Finds a Body* (1934), *Mr. Pinkerton Grows a Beard* (1935), and *Mr. Pinkerton and Inspector Bull* (1939). Under the pseudonym Leslie Ford, she has written *The Sound of Footsteps* (1932), *Siren in the Night* (1942), and *All for the Love of a Lady* (1943), in which the chief characters are Mrs. Latham and Colonel Primrose.

Brown Bess. Popular name of the English regulation flintlock musket toward the end of the 18th century.

Browne (broun), **Charles Albert.** b. at North Adams, Mass., Aug. 12, 1870; d. at Washington, D.C., Feb. 3, 1947. American agricultural chemist, an authority on the chemistry, technology, and analysis of sugar. He was a research chemist (1902–06) at the Louisiana State Experimental Station at New Orleans, headed (1907–23) the New York Sugar Trade Laboratory, and served as chief of the bureau of chemistry (1923–27), assistant chief of chemical and technological research (1927–35), and supervisor of chemical research (1935–40) for the U.S. Department of Agriculture.

Browne, Charles Farrar. [Pseudonym, **Artemus Ward.**] b. at Waterford, Me., April 26, 1834; d. at Southampton, England, March 6, 1867. American humorist and lecturer, noted for his sketches in Down East (Maine) dialect. He contributed "Artemus Ward's Sayings" (1858 *et seq.*) to the Cleveland *Plain Dealer*, and was subsequently an editor of *Vanity Fair.* His chief work is *Artemus Ward: His Book* (1862). He also wrote *Artemus Ward: His Travels* (1865), and *Artemus Ward in London* (1867).

Browne, Francis Fisher. b. at South Halifax, Vt., Dec. 1, 1843; d. at Santa Barbara, Calif., May 11, 1913. American magazine editor, notable as the founder and first editor (1880–1913) of *The Dial.* He edited the *Lakeside Monthly* (c1869–75) at Chicago, and established *The Dial* as the leading literary monthly of the period. He was also editor of several anthologies of poetry and author of *The Everyday Life of Abraham Lincoln* (1886).

Browne, George. [Title, Count **de Browne.**] b. at Camas, Limerick, Ireland, June 15, 1698; d. at Riga, in

Latvia, Feb. 18, 1792. Irish adventurer. He entered the Russian service in 1730, and served with distinction in the Polish, French, and Turkish wars. He was captured by the Turks, and three times sold as a slave. On gaining his freedom he was made a major general and served under Peter Lacy in Finland, and in the Seven Years' War (as a lieutenant general). He was made a field marshal, and given the chief command in the Danish war, by Peter III.

Browne, George Elmer. b. at Gloucester, Mass., May 6, 1871; d. at Provincetown, Mass., July 13, 1946. American painter, water colorist, etcher, and lithographer. He studied at the school of the Boston Museum of Fine Arts, and at Paris, and exhibited in France and the U.S. He won many prizes, was made an academician of the National Academy of Design (1927) and a chevalier of the Legion of Honor (1936), and is represented at the Metropolitan Museum of Art at New York, the National Gallery at Washington, D.C., the Art Institute of Chicago, and other leading galleries and museums. His works include *The White Cloud, Edge of the Grove, The Wain Team, The Port of Douarnenez, Brittany, The Church, Montreuil, After the Rain, Moonrise in Holland, Bait Sellers of Cape Cod,* and *The Golden Hour.*

Browne, Gordon Frederick. b. at Banstead, England, 1859; d. 1932. English landscape painter and illustrator; son of Hablot Knight Browne. He studied at the South Kensington Art Schools and under Thomas Heatherley. In 1886 he began to exhibit at the principal galleries and associations at London. His principal work, however, consisted of illustrations for the works of Robert Louis Stevenson, Washington Irving, and Shakespeare.

Browne, Hablot Knight. [Pseudonym, **Phiz.**] b. at Kennington, Surrey, England, June 15, 1815; d. at West Brighton, England, July 8, 1882. English artist, noted especially as a caricaturist; father of Gordon Frederick Browne. He is best known for his illustrations of the novels of Charles Dickens, Charles Lever, and Harrison Ainsworth. In 1836 he began his association with Dickens, with the illustrations to *Pickwick Papers;* thereafter, he supplied pictures for the first book editions of many later works by Dickens.

Browne, Henriette. [Pseudonym of **Sophie de Bouteiller,** later Madame **de Saux.**] b. at Paris, 1829; d. 1901. French painter and etcher. Among her paintings are *Consolation* (1861), *Intérieur de harem à Constantinople* (1861), *Écolier israélite à Tanger* (1865), *Danseuses en Nubie* (1869), and *La Perruche* (1875).

Browne, Isaac Hawkins. b. at Burton-on-Trent, England, Jan. 21, 1705; d. at London, Feb. 14, 1760. English poet. His chief work was a Latin poem, *De animi immortalitate* (1754).

Browne, James. b. at Whitefield, Scotland; d. near Edinburgh, 1841. Scottish journalist and historian. After brief service as a minister of the Church of Scotland, he settled (c1827) at Edinburgh as a journalist. He was an editor of the *Scots Magazine* and the *Caledonian Mercury,* assistant editor of the seventh edition of the *Encyclopædia Britannica,* and author of *History of the Inquisition* (1817), *History of the Highlands* (1835), and other historical studies.

Browne, John Ross. b. in Ireland, Feb. 11, 1821; d. at Oakland, Calif., Dec. 8, 1875. American traveler and humorist. From 1868 to 1869 he was U.S. minister to China. He was the author of *Yusef, or the Journey of the Fragi: a Crusade in the East* (1853).

Browne, Junius Henri. b. at Seneca Falls, N.Y., Oct. 14, 1833; d. at New York, April 2, 1902. American journalist and man of letters. He was a correspondent for the New York *Tribune* during the Civil War.

Browne, Lewis. b. at London, June 24, 1897; d. at Santa Monica, Calif., Jan. 3, 1949. American rabbi and writer. After his arrival (1912) in the U.S., he served as a rabbi (1920–26) at Temple Israel, Waterbury, Conn., and at the Free Synagogue, Newark, N.J. In 1925 he organized Newark Labor College. After 1926 he engaged in writing and lecturing. His books include *This Believing World* (1926), *Why Are Jews Like That?* (1929), *Blessed Spinoza* (1932), *How Odd of God* (1934), and *Oh, Say, Can You See?* (1937); he edited *The World's Scriptures* (1946), and other compilations.

Browne, Count **Maximilian Ulysses von.** [Additional titles, Baron **de Camus** and **Mountany.**] b. at Basel, Switzerland, Oct. 23, 1705; d. at Prague, June 26, 1757. Austrian field marshal. He was a commander in the War of the Austrian Succession and the Seven Years' War, and was defeated by Frederick the Great at Lobositz (now Lovosice) in 1756, and at Prague in 1757.

Browne, Patrick. b. at Woodstock, County Mayo, Ireland, c1720; d. at Rushbrook, County Mayo, Ireland, Aug. 29, 1790. Irish physician and author. He was twice in the West Indies, residing several years in Jamaica. His *Civil and Natural History of Jamaica* was published in 1756 (2nd ed., 1769).

Browne, Porter Emerson. b. at Beverly, Mass., June 22, 1879; d. Sept. 20, 1934. American playwright and novelist. Among his works are the plays *A Fool There Was* (1906), *The Spendthrift* (1908), *A Girl of Today* (1915), and *The Bad Man* (1920), and the novels *A Fool There Was* (1908), *Peace at Any Price* (1916), *Scars and Stripes* (1917), and *Someone and Somebody* (1917).

Browne or **Brown, Robert.** b. at Tolethorp, Rutlandshire, England, c1550; d. at Northampton, England, c1633. English cleric, the founder of the Brownist sect, a 17th-century group of Puritan separatists which was the progenitor of the Independents or Congregationalists (and hence of the modern Protestant group of this name). He was educated at Cambridge, and subsequently preached at Cambridge and elsewhere. About 1580 he organized at Norwich a congregation of dissenters, who became known as Brownists and who, finding themselves persecuted by the ecclesiastical authorities, removed in a body under his leadership to Middleburg, Holland, in 1581. He left Holland in 1583, in consequence of dissension among his followers, submitted to the Church of England, became master of Stamford Grammar School in 1586, and in 1591 was made rector of a parish in Northamptonshire, where he remained until his death.

Browne, Sir **Thomas.** b. at London, Oct. 19, 1605; d. at Norwich, England, Oct. 19, 1682. English physician and author. He studied at Winchester and Oxford (at Broadgate Hall, now Pembroke College). Upon completion of his classical education, he spent several years in medical studies at Montpellier, Padua, and Leiden (where he was made a doctor of medicine c1633). His first book, *Religio Medici* (A Doctor's Religion), written in a Yorkshire village, was the product of the vacant period after his return to England and before he settled into active practice. In 1637 he established himself at Norwich, and spent the rest of his long life as a provincial doctor there. He was knighted in September, 1671. *Religio Medici* is the author's private journal in which he attempts to read his own mind; it was not printed in an authorized edition until 1643, although two unauthorized editions by Andrew Croke appeared in 1642. Written in a solemn and sonorous style, the book is a fusion of the author's mystical acceptance of Christianity and his half-credulous skepticism. Enormously popular, there were nine English editions before 1660, and five in Latin. Before Browne's death it had also been translated into Dutch, French, and German. Browne's longest work is the *Pseudodoxia Epidemica, or Enquiries into Very Many Received Tenets and Commonly Presumed Truths,* which appeared in a folio volume in 1646 and reached its sixth edition in 1672. The spread of subject matter in this work is enormous and the author utilizes not only the quasi-scientific data compiled by Aristotle, Pliny, and their learned followers, but also the impressively large amount of accurate observation that he had made himself in botany, natural history, and medicine. In this book, Browne confutes dozens of false ideas which some educated persons have even today not thought of questioning. The style is less conscious than *Religio Medici,* but it marks the author's growing taste for elaborately periodic sentences and for Latin words. Emphasis on style is more conspicuous in the two shorter works which followed: *Hydriotaphia, or Urn Burial* and *The Garden of Cyrus: or the Quincuncial Lozenge,* printed together in 1658. *Hydriotaphia,* in part a scientific report on 40 or 50 Roman funeral urns which had then recently been exhumed near Norwich, becomes a disquisition on burial customs in general. *Miscellany Tracts* and *Christian Morals* were published posthumously.

Browne, Thomas. d. on St. Vincent Island, Bahamas, Aug. 3, 1825. Loyalist commander in the American Revolution. Tarred and feathered (c1775) for his pro-British sentiments, he organized (1778) a raiding regiment. In 1780 he occupied Augusta, Ga.; forced to surrender (June 5, 1781) to Andrew Pickens and Henry Lee, he was later exchanged as a prisoner of war.

Browne, Thomas Alexander. [Pseudonym, **Rolf Boldrewood.**] b. at London, Aug. 6, 1826; d. at Melbourne, Australia, March 11, 1915. Australian novelist; son of one of the founders of Melbourne. He was educated at the University of Sydney, New South Wales. His experiences as a farmer, squatter, magistrate, and gold prospector gave him material for more than 30 novels of adventure and excitement. Under his pseudonym he wrote *Old Melbourne Memories* (1884), *Robbery Under Arms* (1888), *The Miner's Right* (1890), *A Colonial Reformer* (1890), *The Squatter's Dream* (1890), *A Sydney-Side Saxon* (1891), *Nevermore* (1892), *A Modern Buccaneer* (1894), *A Canvas Town Romance* (1898), *The Babes in the Bush* (1900), *In Bad Company* (1901), and *Ghost Camp* (1902).

Browne, William. b. at Tavistock, Devonshire, England, c1591; d. c1643. English poet. Among his works are *Britannia's Pastorals* (1613–16) and *Shepherd's Pipe* (1614, written in collaboration).

Browne, William George. b. at London, July 25, 1768; killed in northern Persia, 1813. English traveler in Africa and the Orient. He wrote *Travels in Africa, Egypt, and Syria* (1800).

Brownell (brou'nel, brou.nel'), **Henry Howard.** b. at Providence, R.I., Feb. 6, 1820; d. at East Hartford, Conn., Oct. 31, 1872. American poet. His works include *Poems* (1847), *Lyrics of a Day* (1864), and *War Lyrics and Other Poems* (1866).

Brownell, Herbert, Jr. b. at Peru, Neb., Feb. 20, 1904—. American politician, U.S. attorney general (1953 *et seq.*) under Eisenhower. A graduate (1927) of Yale Law School, he became a member of the New York bar that year. He was chairman of the Republican national committee (1944–46) and was campaign manager for the Dewey-Warren ticket in the national election of 1948.

Brownell, William Crary. b. at New York, Aug. 30, 1851; d. at Williamstown, Mass., July 22, 1928. American author, critic, and editor. After graduating from Amherst College he was on the staff of the New York *World* (1871–79) and of *The Nation* (1879–81), before going to Europe (1881–84). Upon his return to the U.S. he became associated with the Philadelphia *Press* in 1885, remaining with that publication until 1888, when he became literary and editorial adviser to the publishing firm of Charles Scribner's Sons, a post he held until his death. For many years he was acknowledged as one of the most authoritative American critics of letters and the arts in general, and as a writer he was much esteemed for his sagacious views and his urbane style. He was a member of the American Academy of Arts and Letters. He was the author of *Newport* (1886), *French Traits* (1889), *French Art* (1892), *Victorian Prose Masters* (1901), *American Prose Masters* (1909), *Criticism* (1914), *Standards* (1917), *The Genius of Style* (1924), and *Democratic Distinction in America* (1927). *French Traits* and *French Art* were influential in disseminating among Americans an appreciation of French painting, sculpture, and other arts. *Democratic Distinction in America* was an avowal of Brownell's confidence in the power of American society to prevail over what he considered to be anarchic and antisocial tendencies.

Brownfield (broun'fēld). Town in W Texas, county seat of Terry County, SW of Lubbock: processing center for cotton and feed; chemical plants and chicken hatcheries. It is a leading cattle feeding and shipping point. 6,161 (1950).

Brownhills (broun'hilz). Urban district in C England, in Staffordshire, ab. 5 mi. NE of Walsall, ab. 123 mi. NW of London by rail. 21,482 (1951).

Brownian movement. See under **Brown, Robert.**

Browning (broun'ing). Critical work (1903) by Gilbert Keith Chesterton.

Browning, Lady. Title of **Du Maurier, Daphne.**

Browning, Elizabeth Barrett. [Maiden name originally **Moulton,** subsequently **Barrett.**] b. at Coxhoe Hall, Durham, England, March 6, 1806; d. at Florence, Italy, June 30, 1861. English poet. She was the eldest daughter of Edward Moulton (who took the name of Barrett on succeeding to an estate); married (1846) Robert Browning, and resided in Italy, chiefly at Florence, during the remainder of her life. An accident at 15 made her a partial invalid for many years. She was the author of *Prometheus Bound* (translation, 1833), *The Seraphim, and Other Poems* (1838), *Poems* (1844), *Poems* (including *Sonnets from the Portuguese,* 1850), *Casa Guidi Windows* (1851), *Aurora Leigh* (1857), *Poems before Congress* (1860), and *Last Poems* (1862, edited by her husband). Her prose works consist of *The Greek Christian Poets* (1842, 1862) and several volumes of *Letters.* Her best-known work is probably *Sonnets from the Portuguese,* a series of love poems addressed to Robert Browning, which include the popular "How do I love thee? Let me count the ways" and "If thou must love me, let it be for naught."

Browning, John Moses. b. at Ogden, Utah, Jan. 21, 1855; d. at Herstal, Belgium, Nov. 26, 1926. American inventor of firearms; brother of Jonathan Edmund Browning (1859–1939). His father was a gunsmith, and John Moses Browning worked out his first invention in the line of firearms in the family shop while he was still in his early youth. In 1879 he took out his first patent, on an improved rifle, and this led to a long association with Winchester, Colt, and other firearms manufacturers. In 1884 he devised a repeating rifle, and later a magazine rifle, and meanwhile he became one of the world's foremost designers of improved rapid-fire weapons. The involvement of the U.S. in World War I led to the production of automatic rifles, machine guns, and aircraft machine guns of Browning design widely used on European battlefields. In World War II the U.S. air force depended largely on machine guns worked out and improved by John Moses Browning.

Browning, Jonathan Edmund. b. at Ogden, Utah, 1859; d. at New Haven, Conn., May 16, 1939. American gunmaker. With his brother John Moses Browning (1855–1926), he invented and built repeating rifles, automatic pistols, and machine guns, notably the machine gun adopted (1918) by the U.S. Army. Known as the craftsman of the family, he improved models invented by John Moses Browning. He developed (1939) an improved automatic rifle which was later (1940) patented. This weapon, known like its predecessor as the Browning Automatic Rifle (and often called the "BAR"), was widely used by the armed forces of the U.S. in World War II and later.

Browning, Mount. Mountain in Antarctica, at the N end of the mountain mass dominated by Mount Abbott, at the W side of Terra Nova Bay, in Victoria Land, in ab. 74°45′ S., 164°00′ E. Elevation, ab. 2,500 ft.

Browning, Orville Hickman. b. in Harrison County, Ky., Feb. 10, 1806; d. Aug. 10, 1881. American lawyer and politician. After settling (1831) in Illinois, he practiced law and was active as a Whig in local politics. He joined the Republican Party, helping to draft its platform in 1856, and in the period 1861–62 filled the unexpired term of Stephen A. Douglas in the U.S. Senate. His opposition to some of Lincoln's policies, particularly emancipation, helped return him to private life in 1862. For the remainder of the Civil War he was a lobbyist for war contractors. He was secretary of the interior (1866–69) during Andrew Johnson's administration, also serving as attorney general for a brief time. His legal practice (c1850 *et seq.*) became closely tied to Midwestern railroads, notably the Chicago, Burlington and Quincy, which he defended in one of the outstanding Granger cases of the day.

Browning, Oscar. b. at London, Jan. 17, 1837; d. at Rome, Oct. 6, 1923. English historian, biographer, and professor. Educated at Eton and at King's College, Cambridge, he was classical master (1860–75) at Eton, and professor of history and political science (1876–1909) at Cambridge; later he served as principal of the Cambridge University Training College for Teachers. A prolific writer in many fields, he was the author of *The Netherlands in the 16th Century* (1869), *The Thirty Years' War* (1870), *Modern England* (1879), *History of Educational Theories* (1881), *England and Napoleon in 1803* (1889), *History of*

England (4 vols., 1890), *Life of George Eliot* (1890), *Life of Peter the Great* (1890), *Dante: His Life and Works* (1891), *Wars of the 19th Century* (1899), *History of Europe: 1814–1843* (1901), *Guelphs and Ghibellines* (1903), *Napoleon: The First Phase* (1905), *The Fall of Napoleon* (1907), *History of the Modern World: 1815–1910* (1912), *General History of the World* (1913), *History of Medieval Italy: 586–1530* (1914), and *General History of Italy* (1915). He also wrote *Memories of Sixty Years at Eton, Cambridge, and Elsewhere* (1910) and *Memories of Later Years* (1923).

Browning, Robert. b. at Camberwell, London, May 7, 1812; d. in the Palazzo Rezzonico, at Venice, Dec. 12, 1889. English poet. The son of a clerk in the Bank of England, Browning was privately educated and published his first work of verse, *Pauline*, in 1833. Copies of this later became among the most valuable first editions in English poetry. In 1846 Browning married Elizabeth Barrett and they resided at Pisa and later in the Casa Guidi at Florence until her death in 1861. One son, Robert Wiedemann Barrett Browning, was born to them in 1849. After his wife's death, Browning left Florence and lived thereafter mainly at London and Venice. With *The Ring and the Book* (1868–69) he reached his climax of popularity, and secured finally the recognition which he had sought for 50 years. This work is based upon an old manuscript telling the story of a "Roman Murder Case" which Browning picked up in the Square of San Lorenzo at Florence for a sum approximating 14 cents in modern currency. This poem established him as one of the greatest of English poets; its sections entitled "Caponsacchi," "Pompilia," and "The Pope" are considered to contain some of the finest blank verse in the English language. Browning's other chief works are *Paracelsus* (1835), *Bells and Pomegranates* (1841–46; in eight parts, including *Pippa Passes, A Blot in the 'Scutcheon,* and *Luria*), *Christmas Eve and Easter Day* (1850), *Men and Women* (1855), *Dramatis Personae* (1864), *Aristophanes' Apology* (1875), *The Agamemnon of Aeschylus*, a translation (1877), *Dramatic Idyls* (1879–80), and *Asolando* (1889). Among his best-known separate poems and dramatic monologues are *De Gustibus, Saul, The Guardian Angel, My Last Duchess, The Pied Piper of Hamelin, A Grammarian's Funeral, An Epistle of Kharshish, Andrea del Sarto, Abt Vogler, Rabbi Ben Ezra, A Death in the Desert, Prospice,* and *An Epilogue to Asolando.*

Browning, Robert Wiedemann Barrett. b. 1849; d. 1912. English genre painter and sculptor; son of Robert Browning and Elizabeth Barrett Browning. He was educated at Antwerp. From 1878 to 1884 he exhibited at the Royal Academy; in 1883 he exhibited at Brussels and in 1885 at the Paris Salon; in 1889 he received a medal at the Paris Exposition. His sculptural works were commissioned by various institutions, among them Balliol College; his paintings were purchased by the Boston Museum of Fine Arts and the Metropolitan Museum of Art. One of his best-known sculptures is *The River Bed;* one of his most popular paintings is *The Meuse from Bouvigne* (Metropolitan).

Brownists (broun'ists). Followers of Robert Browne (c1550–c1633), a Puritan, who is regarded as the founder of the sect of Independents or Congregationalists.

Brown, Jones, and Robinson, The Adventures of. Series of illustrated articles by Richard Doyle, begun in *Punch* and completed for book publication in 1854. It is a satire on the manners of the middle-class Englishman abroad or on his travels. Anthony Trollope published in 1862 *The Struggles of Brown, Jones, and Robinson*, a story illustrated by John Everett Millais.

Brownlow (broun'lō), **Mr.** In Charles Dickens's novel *Oliver Twist*, a kind-hearted and benevolent old gentleman, the protector of Oliver Twist.

Brownlow, William Gannaway. [Called **"Parson Brownlow"** and the **"Fighting Parson."**] b. in Wythe County, Va., Aug. 29, 1805; d. at Knoxville, Tenn., April 29, 1877. American newspaper editor, politician, and one-time Methodist itinerant preacher, notable for his stubborn support of the Union in Confederate Tennessee. As editor (1849–61) of the Knoxville *Whig*, he openly opposed secession (although he did not reject slavery). The last Union journal in the South, his paper was suppressed (1861) by the Confederacy; arrested (Dec. 6, 1861) for treason, he was subsequently released and later (March 3, 1862) sent through the Union lines. He was elected governor of Tennessee (1865, 1867) and a U.S. senator (1869).

Brownrigg (broun'rig), **Elizabeth.** fl. in the middle of the 18th century. English murderess. She was hanged, and her skeleton was long preserved.

Brownrigg, Sir **Robert.** b. 1759; d. at Monmouth, England, 1833. English soldier. He became a colonel of the 9th regiment (1805) and a lieutenant general (1808), and served (1809) as quartermaster general in the Walcheren expedition. Appointed (1811) governor and commander in chief of the island of Ceylon, he conquered (1815) the kingdom of Kandy with a force of 3,000 men. He was created a baronet in 1816 and was made a full general in 1819.

Brownrigg Papers, The. Collection of essays and sketches by Douglas Jerrold, published in 1860.

Brownsburg (brounz'bėrg). Village in Quebec, Canada, situated on the West River, a few miles N of the Ottawa River, in the S part of the province. It is ab. 30 mi. NW of Montreal and ab. 75 mi. E of Ottawa. 3,238 (1951).

Brown-Séquard (broun.sā.kȧr, -kwȧr), **Charles Édouard.** b. at Port Louis, on the island of Mauritius, April 8, 1817; d. at Paris, April 1, 1894. French physician and physiologist. He studied at Paris, was placed in charge of a hospital for the paralyzed and epileptic at London in 1860, was professor of the physiology and pathology of the nervous system at Harvard University (1864–69), and was appointed to the chair of experimental physiology at the Collège de France in 1878. He published numerous works and papers on physiological subjects, notably on animal heat and internal secretions.

Brown Shirts. See under **S. A.**

Brownson (broun'sọn), **Orestes Augustus.** b. at Stockbridge, Vt., Sept. 16, 1803; d. at Detroit, April 17, 1876. American clergyman, editor, and author. He grew up on a small farm remote from cities, and his formal education was slight, but his inquiring mind and impulsive nature, his talent for writing and his readiness for controversy, pointed to a career far removed from pastoral serenity. His lifelong search for God and for the key to human brotherhood began when he joined the Presbyterian Church in 1822, only to leave it two years later in favor of the Universalist denomination, of which he became a minister in 1826. The condition of the working class in those days distressed him, and in 1828 he was one of the founders of the Workingmen's Party, but presently he concluded that amelioration of the workers' lot must come by moral rather than political means. He embraced the socialistic theories of Robert Dale Owen, and became a corresponding editor of the *Free Enquirer*, an Owenite paper published at New York. During this period he also edited the *Gospel Advocate*, a Universalist organ, but his radical trend alarmed the leaders of that church, and in 1832 he became a Unitarian minister. In 1836 he established a church of his own under the name of the Society for Christian Union and Progress. In 1838 he founded the *Boston Quarterly Review*, making it a kind of Democratic Party organ; but when, in his issue of July, 1840, he called for the suppression of Christianity and the abolition of inheritance and of the wage system, the Whigs made such use of this, calling it the real program of the Democratic Party, that President Van Buren is said to have blamed this issue of Brownson's paper for his failure to win reëlection. In 1842 the *Boston Quarterly Review* was merged with the *Democratic Review* of New York, but two years later the merger was dissolved with the publication of *Brownson's Quarterly Review* at Boston, and this periodical appeared regularly until 1865, and was briefly revived in the period 1873–75. At Boston, Brownson moved in the circles of the New England liberals and Transcendentalists, becoming a friend of the Alcotts, George Bancroft, Margaret Fuller, George Ripley, and Henry David Thoreau. There was therefore a great deal of natural astonishment when in 1844 Brownson entered the Roman Catholic Church. Through all his changes of creed, Brownson continued to use his pen and voice in behalf of the working class and in condemnation of all forms of special privilege. During the Civil War he strongly supported the Union cause. Brownson's first book, *New Views of Christianity, Society, and the Church* (1836) was followed by two novels, *Charles*

Elwood or the Infidel Converted (1840) and *The Spirit-Rapper* (1854), and by *The Mediatorial Life of Jesus* (1842), *The Convert: or, Leaves from my Experience*, which was his autobiography (1857), and *The American Republic: its Constitution, Tendencies and Destiny* (1865).

Brownson's Quarterly Review (broun'sǫnz). Journal founded by Orestes A. Brownson after his conversion to Catholicism, and published in the period 1844–75.

Brownsville (brounz'vil). Unincorporated community in NW Florida, in Escambia County. Under the urban definition established for use in the 1950 census, Brownsville was counted with adjoining areas. The last official separate enumeration was 2,979 (1940).

Brownsville. Borough in SW Pennsylvania, in Fayette County, on the Monongahela River: industrial community. Founded in 1785, it was combined with South Brownsville in 1933. Pop. 7,643 (1950).

Brownsville. City in W Tennessee, county seat of Haywood County: trading center for a cotton-farming area; sawmills. 4,711 (1950).

Brownsville. City in S Texas, county seat of Cameron County, S of Corpus Christi, on the Rio Grande ab. 23 mi. from its mouth. It is the largest city in the lower Rio Grande valley, a port of entry, resort center, seaport, and shipping point for oil, citrus fruits, and early vegetables. It is connected by highway and railway with Mexico. The town was founded (1848) by Charles Stillman near Fort Brown (formerly Fort Taylor). The fort was bombarded by the Mexicans in May, 1846, and in coming to its relief General Zachary Taylor fought the first and second engagements of the Mexican War, at Palo Alto and at Resaca de la Palma. During the Civil War Brownsville was one of the chief Confederate ports. The last battle of the Civil War was fought near here, at Palmito Hill, on May 12–13, 1865, almost five weeks after Robert E. Lee's surrender at Appomattox. Brownsville served (1865) as the headquarters of General Philip H. Sheridan during the period of strained relations with the Maximilian regime in Mexico. 36,066 (1950).

Brownsville or **Brown Town.** Former names of **La Grande.**

Brown the Younger, Thomas. Pseudonym of Thomas Moore, under which he wrote *Intercepted Letters, or the Twopenny Post Bag*, in 1813.

Brown University. [Original name, **Rhode Island College.**] Institution of learning situated at Providence, R.I. It is one of the oldest universities in the U.S., having been founded in 1764, at Warren, R.I., as Rhode Island College. It was moved to Providence within the first decade of its history and formally renamed Brown University in 1804. The name was changed in honor of Nicholas Brown, a wealthy merchant of Providence, who gave the institution an aggregate of 100,000 dollars. Affiliated historically with the Baptist denomination, the university has for generations accepted students of all denominations and from all parts of the world. It now includes Pembroke College (founded 1892) for women. Its library facilities, which are among the best possessed by any educational institution in the U.S., include the John Carter Brown Library (the nucleus of which was made available to the university by a grandson of Nicholas Brown, in honor of his father, John Carter Brown; its shelves house one of the nation's outstanding collections of volumes and manuscripts in the field of Americana). Brown also boasts the John Hay Library and a notable collection of materials relating to engineering in its various specialized fields.

Brownville (broun'vil). Town (in New York the equivalent of township in many other states) and village in N New York, in Jefferson County: manufactures paper. Pop. of town, 3,806 (1950); of village, 1,013 (1950).

Brown v. Maryland, 12 Wheaton 419 (1827). U.S. Supreme Court decision, in an opinion rendered by Chief Justice John Marshall, holding unconstitutional an act of the state of Maryland requiring importers to pay a license fee. The case is notable for Marshall's formulation of the "original package" doctrine in reference to the commerce clause of the Constitution. The court held that goods imported from abroad could not be subjected to license tax requirements by the state as long as they remained unsold or in the original packages.

Brownwood (broun'wůd). City in C Texas, county seat of Brown County, ab. 150 mi. SW of Dallas, in a natural-gas and petroleum region: shipping center for oil, pecans, wool, dairy products, mohair, cotton, poultry, and grain. It is the seat of Howard Payne College and Daniel Baker College. 20,181 (1950).

Bruay-en-Artois (brü.ā.äṅ.nȧr.twȧ). Town in N France, in the department of Pas-de-Calais, ab. 6 mi. S of Béthune. It is situated in the center of a coal-mining region, and has a number of industries. 31,705 (1946).

Bruay-sur-L'Escaut (brü.ā.sür.les.kō). Town in N France, in the department of Nord, situated on the Escaut River, N of Valenciennes. Its industries produce hosiery, plastic goods, and malt. 9,144 (1946).

Bruce (brös). [Original forms, **Braose, Breaux, Brus.**] Noted Scottish family. They were of Norman descent, and in ancient records the name often appears with the particle "de." The first member of the family to achieve historical note, Robert de Bruce I, accompanied William the Conqueror to England and received lands in Yorkshire. His son, also named Robert, was given the lordship of Annandale in Scotland by King David I of that country (1084–1153). The marriage of another Robert Bruce, Lord of Annandale, to Isabella, daughter of David, Earl of Huntington, a brother of William the Lion, was the source of the later claim of the family to the throne of Scotland. A great-grandson of this Robert and Isabella, became Robert I, king of Scotland (Robert the Bruce), in 1306, and successfully defended his title against the English. His brother Edward Bruce, at the invitation of the Irish, accepted the crown of that country, but after early successes against the English was defeated and slain in battle. Robert I's son reigned as David II, and from him the crown of Scotland passed to his nephew, known as Robert II, who was the first of the house of Stewart to occupy the Scottish throne.

Bruce, Alexander Hugh. See **Balfour of Burleigh,** 6th Baron.

Bruce, Archibald. b. at New York, in February, 1777; d. there, Feb. 22, 1818. American mineralogist, physician and professor, best known for his discovery of brucite (magnesium hydroxide) in the U.S. Graduated (1797) from Columbia College and awarded (1800) his M.D. at Edinburgh, he spent two years in mineralogical study abroad before establishing (1803) a medical practice at New York. After securing a charter for New York's College of Physicians and Surgeons, he served (c1807–11) on its faculty as the first American professor of materia medica and mineralogy. He established (1810) the *American Mineralogical Journal*, the first journal in the U.S. devoted entirely to science.

Bruce, Blanche K. b. at Farmville, Va., March 1, 1841; d. March 17, 1898. American Negro legislator and public official. After filling several local and state government posts in Mississippi, he served (1875–81) as U.S. senator from that state. After the fall of the Reconstruction governments, he was appointed register of the U.S. treasury under President James A. Garfield. From 1889 until his death he was recorder of deeds in the District of Columbia.

Bruce, Sir **David.** b. at Melbourne, Australia, May 29, 1855; d. Nov. 27, 1931. Australian physician, known chiefly for his investigations on such tropical diseases as sleeping sickness and Mediterranean (undulant) fever. Internationally known and frequently honored, he was president (1905) of the Physiological Section of the British Association, South Africa, president (1917–19) of the Royal Society of Tropical Medicine and Hygiene, chairman (1914–19) of the British War Office Pathological Committee and Committees for Study of Tetanus and Trench Fever.

Bruce, David. See **David II** (of *Scotland*).

Bruce, Edward. Killed near Dundalk, Ireland, Oct. 5, 1318. Scottish adventurer; younger brother of Robert I of Scotland (Robert the Bruce). He was crowned king of Ireland in 1315.

Bruce, Sir **Frederick William Adolphus.** b. in Fifeshire, Scotland, 1814; d. at Boston, 1867. British diplomat who held major posts on four continents; son of Thomas Bruce (1766–1841), the 7th Earl of Elgin. Attached to the mission of Alexander Baring, 1st Baron Ashburton, to Washington (1842), he was subsequently colonial secretary at Hong Kong (1844), lieutenant governor of Newfoundland (1846), chargé d'affaires in Bolivia (1848) and Uruguay (1851), consul general in Egypt (1853), and envoy to China (1858) and to Washington (1865). He served as umpire (1864) for the adjustment of claims of American citizens against the Colombian government.

Bruce, George. b. near Edinburgh, June 26, 1781; d. July 5, 1866. American printer and type founder, noted as coinventor of a type-casting machine which is still widely used. At the age of 15, he emigrated from Scotland to Philadelphia, and later (1806) joined his elder brother, David, in establishing a book-printing house at New York, introducing and improving (1812 *et seq.*) the English process of stereotyping. After 1822, when his partnership with David was dissolved, he devoted his life to type founding.

Bruce, Henry Austin. [Title, 1st Baron **Aberdare.**] b. April 16, 1815; d. Feb. 25, 1895. British politician. He was home secretary (1868–73), was raised to the peerage in 1873, and became lord president of the council in the same year.

Bruce, Herbert Alexander. b. at Blackstock, Durham County, Ontario, Canada, Sept. 28, 1868—. Canadian surgeon and politician. He served as consulting surgeon (1914–18) to the British forces in France, and was professor of surgery at the University of Toronto, lieutenant governor (1932–37) of Ontario, and a member (1940–46) of the Canadian House of Commons.

Bruce, James. b. at Kinnaird, Scotland, Dec. 14, 1730; d. there, April 27, 1794. Scottish traveler in Africa. He explored Syria, the Nile valley, and Ethiopia (1768–73), reaching the source of the Blue Nile. His *Travels to Discover the Sources of the Nile,* in five volumes, appeared in 1790.

Bruce, James. [Titles: 8th Earl of **Elgin,** 12th Earl of **Kincardine.**] b. July 20, 1811; d. at Dhurmsala, India, Nov. 20, 1863. British diplomat and statesman; son of Thomas Bruce (1766–1841). He was governor general of Canada (1846–54), special envoy to China and Japan (1857–59), postmaster general (1859–60), and governor general of India (1862–63).

Bruce, John Collingwood. b. at Newcastle, England, 1805; d. there, 1892. English antiquary, who served as secretary and vice-president of the Society of Antiquaries of Newcastle (1846). He was the proprietor (1834–63) of the Percy Street Academy at Newcastle, and was editor of various antiquarian works.

Bruce, Michael. b. at Kinneswood, Kinross-shire, Scotland, March 27, 1746; d. there, July 5 or 6, 1767. Scottish poet and schoolteacher. His *Poems* were published by John Logan in 1770.

Bruce, Philip Alexander. b. at Staunton Hill, Charlotte County, Va., March 7, 1856; d. at Charlottesville, Va., Aug. 16, 1933. American writer, noted for his studies of Virginia history. His works include *The Plantation Negro as a Freeman* (1888), *Economic History of Virginia in the 17th Century* (1895), *Short History of the United States* (1903), *History of the University of Virginia* (1920–21), *History of Colonial Virginia* (*1606–1764*) (1923), and *The Virginia Plutarch* (1929).

Bruce, Robert. b. at Scone, Perthshire, Scotland, Feb. 20, 1778; d. June 14, 1846. American Presbyterian clergyman and educator. After theological training in Scotland, he came (c1806) to the U.S., where he spent two years as a wandering preacher in Pennsylvania and the Carolinas before settling in what was then the frontier village of Pittsburgh. In 1808 he was ordained and became pastor of Pittsburgh's Church (now the First United Presbyterian), occupying this post until his death. He was also a founder and first principal of Western University of Pennsylvania (1819).

Bruce, Robert the. See **Robert I** (of *Scotland*).

Bruce, Stanley Melbourne. [Title, Viscount **Bruce of Melbourne.**] b. at Melbourne, Australia, April 15, 1883—. Australian political figure and British government official, prime minister (1923–29) of Australia. He was educated in Australia and at Cambridge (B.A., 1908), and was called to the English bar in 1907. He served in World War I at Gallipoli and in France with United Kingdom regiments; twice wounded, he was invalided out of the army in 1917. He served in the Commonwealth house of representatives (1918–29 and 1931–33), and was treasurer (1921–23), prime minister (1923–29), Australian high commissioner at London (1933–45), and representative (1933–36) of the Australia Council at the League of Nations. He was president of the Council in 1936, and attended the Imperial conferences of 1923, 1926, and 1937, the Ottawa Conference of 1932, and the World Economic Conference of 1933. He served as president of the Montreux Conference in 1936.

Bruce, The. [Also, **The Brus.**] Poem (c1375) by John Barbour, on the subject of King Robert I of Scotland. It relates in more than 13,000 lines the story of the guerrilla warfare between Robert and the English. Barbour intended the narrative to be taken as history and some critics believe that in many places authentic tradition has been embodied in the poem.

Bruce, Thomas. [Titles: 7th Earl of **Elgin,** 11th Earl of **Kincardine.**] b. July 20, 1766; d. at Paris, Nov. 14, 1841. British diplomat; father of James Bruce (1811–63) and Sir Frederick William Adolphus Bruce (1814–67). While envoy to Constantinople (1799–1802) he began the removal from Athens to England of the Elgin Marbles, purchased by the nation in 1816, and now in the British Museum.

Bruce, Victor Alexander. [Titles: 9th Earl of **Elgin,** 13th Earl of **Kincardine.**] b. near Montreal, Canada, May 16, 1849; d. Jan. 18, 1917. British Liberal statesman. He was educated at Eton and at Balliol College, Oxford. He was viceroy of India (1894–99), chairman of the war commission in 1902, chairman of the royal commission on the Scottish church crisis in 1904, and secretary of state for the colonies in the period 1905–08.

Bruce, William Cabell. b. at Staunton Hill, Charlotte County, Va., March 12, 1860; d. at Baltimore, May 9, 1946. American biographer and politician, notable for his Pulitzer prize-winning *Benjamin Franklin Self-Revealed* (1918) and as a one-term (1923–29) senator from Maryland. A Democrat, he twice bolted his party: once in the Harding administration on the question of the Teapot Dome affair, and again (1936) when he supported Alfred M. Landon.

Bruce, William Speirs. b. Aug. 1, 1867; d. Oct. 31, 1921. Scottish explorer. He took part in the Scottish Antarctic Expedition of 1892–93, the Jackson-Harmsworth Polar Expedition of 1896–97, and the Andrew Coats Expedition to Novaya Zemlya in 1898, and accompanied Albert I of Monaco (a European prince who acquired world fame as an oceanographer) to Spitsbergen in the period 1898–99. He headed (1902–04) the Scottish National Antarctic Expedition on board the *Scotia,* exploring the Atlantic Ocean to lat. 74°1′ S., and discovering Coats Land. In the period 1906–09 he explored Prince Charles Foreland, Spitsbergen. He published an account of his voyage in the *Scotia.*

Bruce I, Robert de. d. c1094. Norman adventurer, an adherent of William the Conqueror. He was the progenitor of the noted Scottish family which produced Robert I of Scotland (Robert the Bruce). See under **Bruce.**

Bruce VI, Robert de. [Called (from his rivalry with John de Baliol) **"the Competitor."**] b. 1210; d. at Lochmaben Castle, Scotland, 1295. Scottish noble, Lord of Annandale; grandfather of King Robert I of Scotland (Robert the Bruce). He was one of the 15 regents of Scotland during the minority of Alexander III, and the chief rival of John de Baliol for the Scottish throne in the competition at Norham (1291–92), where, as arbiter, Edward I of England decided in favor of Baliol.

Bruce VII, Robert de. b. 1253; d. 1304. Scottish noble; father of King Robert I of Scotland (Robert the Bruce). He is said to have accompanied Edward (afterward Edward I) in the Crusade of 1269, and to have married Marjory, countess of Carrick, thereby becoming, by Scottish courtesy, earl of Carrick. He was appointed constable of the castle of Carlisle by Edward I in 1295, and sided with the English when John de Baliol attempted to assert his independence of Edward I.

Bruch (brủch), **Max.** b. at Cologne, Germany, Jan. 6, 1838; d. at Friedenau, Berlin, Oct. 2, 1920. German composer. He was director (1880–83) of the Liverpool Philharmonic Society, and director (1883–90) of the Orchesterverein at Breslau. In 1892 he became director of composition in the Hochschule at Berlin. His works include the operetta *Scherz, List und Rache,* the opera *Lorelei,* and *Szenen aus der Frithjofssaga, Odysseus, Armineus, Lied von der Glocke,* and *Kol Nidre* (for cello).

Bruchsal (brůch'zäl). City in S Germany, in the *Land* (state) of Württemberg-Baden, American Zone, situated on the Saalbach River, ab. 11 mi. NE of Karlsruhe. It has cigar manufactures, and factories producing wooden crates and other lumber products, as well as various small industries, and a wine trade. It is renowned for its castle, once the summer residence of the prince-bishops of Speyer, erected in the period 1720–51 and considered one of the most beautiful baroque castles in Germany; the staircase (1731) by Balthasar Neumann and the Fürstensaal (Hall of the Princes, 1751) by Feichtmayr, are outstanding examples of 18th-century architecture and decoration. The castle was largely ruined in World War II. The town came under Speyer in 1056, under Baden in 1802. On June 2, 1849, the Baden revolutionaries were defeated here by Prussian troops. The population is predominantly Roman Catholic. 16,282 (1950).

Bruck (brůk). Former name of **Fürstenfeldbruck.**

Bruck, Baron **Karl Ludwig von.** b. at Elberfeld, Rhenish Prussia, Oct. 8, 1798; d. April 23, 1860. Austrian statesman. He was minister of commerce and public works (1848–51) and minister of finance (1855–60); abruptly dismissed, he committed suicide. He was one of the chief founders of the Austrian Lloyd at Trieste.

Bruck an der Leitha (än dėr lī'tä). [Also, **Bruck.**] Town in E Austria, in the province of Lower Austria, situated on the Leitha River, on the former border between Austria and Hungary, now between Lower Austria and Burgenland, SE of Vienna. It has a castle and a botanical garden, and is a station on the railroad line from Vienna to Budapest. 7,854 (1946).

Bruck an der Mur (mör'). [Also, **Bruck.**] Town in SE Austria, in the province of Styria, situated at the junction of the Mürz and Mur rivers, NW of Graz. It is a station on the railroad lines from Vienna to Graz and from Bruck to Leoben. It was long important as a center for the Styrian salt and iron trade, and has iron and paper industries. 14,709 (1951).

Brückenau (brük'ẹ.nou). Town in S Germany, in the *Land* (state) of Bavaria, American Zone, in the *Regierungsbezirk* (government district) of Lower Franconia, situated on the Sinn River, in the Rhön Mountains, N of Würzburg: lumber trade, paper and knitwear manufactures. Nearby is Bad Brückenau, a health resort with ferruginous thermal springs, which are visited by people suffering from rheumatism and gout. 5,615 (1946).

Brucker (brůk'ėr), **Johann Jakob.** b. Jan. 22, 1696; d. Nov. 26, 1770. German philosophical writer, rector of a school at Kaufbeuren, and later pastor at Augsburg. His chief work is *Historia critica philosophiae* (1742–44).

Bruckmann (brůk'män), **Hugo.** b. at Munich, Oct. 13, 1863—. German publisher. He assisted the Nazi movement in its early stages.

Brückner (brük'nėr), **Aleksander.** b. at Tarnapol, Poland, Jan. 29, 1856; d. at Warsaw, 1939. Polish scholar. He was professor of Slavic languages and cultures at the universities of Vienna and Berlin (1880–1939). Though he spent the greater part of his life abroad, he published almost all his works in Polish. His main topics were the history of culture, of the Polish language, of the Reformation and its influence upon Polish cultural development, and of Polish literature. Some of his works were also published in German; these include *Geschichte der polnischen Literatur* (History of Polish Literature, 1901) and *Geschichte der russischen Literatur* (History of Russian Literature, 1909).

Bruckner (brůk'nėr), **Anton.** b. at Ansfelden, Austria, Sept. 4, 1824; d. at Vienna, Oct. 11, 1896. Austrian organist, composer, and teacher. He was professor of harmony and counterpoint in the Vienna Conservatory. His most important works are nine symphonies (the last unfinished) which show the strong influence of Richard Wagner; he also composed masses, a Te Deum, and other church music.

Brückner (brük'nėr), **Eduard.** b. at Jena, Germany, July 29, 1862; d. at Vienna, May 20, 1927. German geographer. He was a professor (1888–1904) at Bern, subsequently served at the University of Halle, and became (1906) professor at Vienna. He conducted important studies in climatology and glaciology. His chief works are *Klimaschwankungen seit 1700* (1890) and *Die feste Erdrinde und ihre Formen* (1897).

Bruckner (brůk'nėr), **Ferdinand.** [Pseudonym of **Theodor Tagger.**] b. at Vienna, Aug. 26, 1891—. Austrian playwright, especially skilled in the use of psychological and historical themes.

Brucomagus (brö.kō.mā'gus). Ancient name of **Brumath.**

Bructeri (bruk'tẹ.rī). German tribe which appears to have occupied the territory about the upper Ems River and on both sides of the Lippe River. Strabo divides them into "greater" and "lesser." They contributed to the defeat of Varus in the Teutoburg Forest, and took part in the rising of Civilis. Their tribal name appears as late as the 8th century. They were ultimately merged with the Franks.

Bructerus (brůk.tir'us), **Mons.** Latin name of the **Brocken.**

Brudenell (bröd'nel), **James Thomas.** See **Cardigan,** 7th Earl of.

Brueghel (brė'gẹl), **Jan.** [Also: **Bruegel, Breughel;** called **"Blumen-Brueghel," "Sammt-Brueghel,"** and **"Fluweelen-Brueghel."**] b. at Brussels, 1568; d. at Antwerp, 1625. Flemish painter; son of Pieter Brueghel (c1525–69). The nickname "Fluweelen-Brueghel," meaning "Velvet Brueghel," arose from his fondness for painting people dressed in apparel of that material. First instructed in painting by his maternal grandmother, his early pictures were of flowers and fruit, but after visiting Cologne and Italy he painted mostly landscapes with figures, and it was by these that he was chiefly known in his lifetime. His great contemporary Rubens was impressed by his skill, and there are a number of paintings in existence in which the landscapes are by Jan Brueghel and the figures by Rubens. As a landscapist, indeed, he is by some critics considered to have been superior to his father, and he was not much the latter's inferior in the delineation of character, in liveliness and humor, and in skilled technique. He was received into the Guild of Painters at Antwerp in 1597.

Brueghel, Pieter. [Also: **Bruegel, Breughel;** called **"Boeren Brueghel,"** meaning "Peasant Brueghel"; surname **"the Droll"** and **"the Elder."**] b. at Brueghel (now usually spelled Breughel), near Breda, Netherlands, c1525; d. at Brussels, 1569. Flemish painter. The son of a peasant, he was instructed in painting by Pieter Couke, but he was more influenced by the paintings of Hieronymus Bosch. In 1551 he was received into the Antwerp Guild of Painters as a master painter, and soon after this went on a leisurely tour of France and Italy, apparently spending less time studying old masters than sketching in the wilder corners of the Alps. However, no amount of foreign travel, no acquaintance with foreign scenes and the works of foreign masters, could wean him from his lively interest in his own Flemish landscape, his own Flemish people and their manners and customs. He returned to his native land in 1553 and settled at Antwerp, and ten years later moved to Brussels, where he spent the rest of his life. His works did not lack lively appreciation during his lifetime, and at all times since his death he has been accounted one of the great artists, but it was not until the 20th century that he came into the fullness of his fame. Only when the western world had become largely democratic, had passed through periods of severe classicism and exaggerated romanticism, had accepted realism without limit in all the arts, and had become habituated by the work of the impressionists and post-impressionists, and not least by the work of the 19th-century Fleming, Van Gogh, to strong, frank color, could the paintings of Pieter Brueghel the Elder be valued at their full worth. His roystering scenes of peasants eating and drinking, dancing and courting, his landscapes that praise earth and sky for their own sake and not as backgrounds for romantic ruined castles, his sunlit harvest scenes, and his grim records of winter that can make a spectator shiver, have passed in reproduction into countless homes, making him today one of the most popular of all the great artists. At the same time, painters and connoisseurs do not tire of admiring the subtlety of his design, his extraordinary powers of observation, his firm drawing, and his singular facul y of combining great sweeping compositions with minute depictions of detail down to the very buttons on a garment, the petals of a flower, or the anatomy of an insect. Inevitably he painted also many pictures based on themes from Biblical and religious legend, but peopling them with portraits of the men and women he saw about him (with whom he sometimes mingled, disguised as a peasant, in order better to study them). Examples of Brueghel's work are treasured in many museums and galleries, including the Louvre, at Paris, the Brussels Museum, the Darmstadt Gallery, the Vienna Gallery, the Pinakothek, at Munich, the Madrid Gallery, and the Uffizi, at Florence. One of his most famous works, *The Harvesters*, is to be seen in the Metropolitan Museum of Art, at New York.

Brueghel, Pieter. [Also: **Bruegel** or **Breughel**; called **"Höllen Brueghel,"** meaning "Hell Brueghel"; surnamed **"the Younger."**] b. at Brussels, 1564; d. 1637. Flemish painter; son of Pieter Brueghel (c1525–69). His nickname derived from his addiction to weird, grim, and terrifying subjects. He studied with Gillis van Connixloo at Antwerp, and was registered as a master painter with the Antwerp Guild of Painters in 1585. His work was well esteemed, but is considered not to rank with his father's achievements. He is represented in many galleries and museums in Europe, and his *Gamblers Quarreling* is in the Metropolitan Museum of Art, at New York.

Bruere (brö.ăr'), **Robert Walter.** b. at St. Charles, Mo., Jan. 6, 1876—. American authority on industrial relations. He was graduated from Washington University, taught at the Rand School of Social Science, was director (1917–23) of the Bureau of Industrial Research at New York, and was associate editor (1923–28) of *The Survey*. He served as U.S. delegate to sessions of the International Labor Organization, and was chairman (1938–42) of the U.S. Maritime Labor Board. He is the author of *The Coming of Coal* (1922) and *The Man with a Thousand Partners* (1931).

Brues (bröz), **Charles Thomas.** b. at Wheeling, W.Va., June 20, 1879—. American entomologist. He was graduated from the University of Texas (B.S., 1901; M.S., 1902), was curator of invertebrate zoölogy (1905–09) at the Milwaukee Public Museum, and served as professor of entomology (1912–45) at Harvard; he was also editor (1909 *et seq.*) of *Psyche*, a journal of entomology. He is the author of *Insects and Human Welfare* (1920; 2nd ed., 1947) and *Insect Dietary* (1945).

Brües (brü'ęs), **Otto.** b. at Krefeld, Germany, May 1, 1897—. German writer. His stories take for their locale the region of Cologne. He wrote *Jupp Brand*, which deals with conditions on the Rhine after World War I, and *Der Walfisch vom Rhein*.

Bruff (bruf), **Nancy.** b. at Fairfield, Conn. American novelist and poet. She attended the Nightingale-Bamford School at New York and the Sorbonne, and married (1937) Thurston Clarke. Among her novels are *The Manatee* (1945), *Cider from Eden* (1947), and *The Beloved Woman* (1949). *My Talon in Your Heart* (1946) is a volume of poetry.

Brügel (brü'gęl), **Fritz.** b. at Vienna, Feb. 13, 1897—. Austrian lyric poet, one of the foremost in his field.

Bruges (brözh; French, brüzh). [Flemish, **Brugge**; German, **Brügge.**] City in NW Belgium, the capital of the province of West Flanders, situated ab. 55 mi. NW of Brussels and ab. 8 mi. from the North Sea, on a network of canals connecting it with Ghent, Sluis, Ostende, and Zeebrugge. It is the seat of a bishopric. The city has a port, agricultural and export trade, and manufactures lace, linen, cotton, and woolen goods. Extensive horticultural activities are carried on in the vicinity. 52,748 (1947).

Art and Architecture. Architecturally, Bruges is the best-preserved medieval city in Belgium. It is traversed by many small waterways, spanned by bridges, encircled by a canal, and surrounded by walls; it has numerous picturesque squares and streets. The Cathedral of Saint Sauveur is an early-Gothic brick structure of the 13th and 14th centuries; the Church of Notre Dame is in the same style. Bruges has a famous chime of bells on its great market hall (Cloth Hall). There is a Gothic town hall, and interesting guild halls, market halls, and patrician houses. The hospital of Saint John and various churches contain works by the Flemish masters (Memling and others).

History. Bruges became the residence of Baldwin II, Count of Flanders, in 1093. It was a member of the Hanseatic League, and a center of the cloth trade of Flanders and a leading market for the English wool trade which provided the raw material. Its prosperity was highest in the 13th and 14th centuries, when it was not only a port and a place of transit but also one of the chief financial centers of Europe. Beginning in the 15th century, however, the silting of the Zryn caused commercial activities to be diverted to Antwerp. Also, the city suffered in the religious wars; it was several times besieged in the 18th century. Its economic leadership was lost, and it became a museum piece of quiet charm and beauty. The city was occupied by the Germans in World Wars I and II.

Brugg (brůk). Town in N Switzerland, in the canton of Aargau, situated on the Aare River, W of Baden: headquarters of various technical branches of the Swiss army. It was called the "Prophets' Town" in the Reformation, having been the birthplace of many Protestant theologians. 4,778 (1941).

Brugge (brüg'ę). Flemish name of **Bruges.**

Brügge (brüg'ę). German name of **Bruges.**

Bruggen (brůċh'ęn), **Joachim Van.** b. 1881—. South African novelist, writing in Afrikaans. After some novels and short stories in a realistic-humoristic manner (among others, *Op Veld en Rande*, 1920), his writings turned to a sharp description of life among small farmers and poor whites in South Africa, such as *Die Burgemeester van Slaplaagte* (1922) and *Ampie* (3 vols., 1924, 1928, 1942). *Booia* (1931) was a story of Kaffir life. He described Oom Paul Krüger's time in *Kranskop* (1943).

Brugger (brůg'ėr), **Friedrich.** b. at Munich, Jan. 13, 1815; d. there, April 9, 1870. German sculptor.

Brugmann (brůk'män), **Karl.** [Full name, **Friedrich Karl Brugmann.**] b. at Wiesbaden, Germany, March 10, 1849; d. June 29, 1919. German philologist. He became professor of comparative philology at the University of Leipzig in 1882, whence he went to the University of Freiburg to take the chair of Sanskrit and comparative philology, but returned to Leipzig in 1887. Brugmann, by his fresh and progressive views of a science that many believed to have become too static, greatly influenced the development of philology in Germany and elsewhere. His *Nasalis Sonans in der Indogermanischen Grundsprache* (1876) caused some controversy, but his *Grundriss der vergleichenden Grammatik der Indogermanischen Sprachen*, which appeared in the period 1886–93, and was translated into English under the title *Outline of the Comparative Grammar of the Indo-Germanic Languages*, was at once accepted as an authoritative work. He was coauthor also of *Morphologische Untersuchungen*, of which the first five volumes were published between 1878 and 1890, and the sixth volume in 1910. Brugmann, who was knighted by the king of Saxony, was among the notable scholars from many lands who by invitation attended the jubilee of Princeton University in 1896, on which occasion he received from that university the honorary degree of LL.D.

Brugsch (brůksh), **Heinrich Karl.** b. at Berlin, Feb. 18, 1827; d. there, Sept. 9, 1894. German Egyptologist. Probably his best-known work is *Hieroglyphisch-demotisches Wörterbuch* (1867–82). He also wrote *Reiseberichte aus Ägypten* (1855), *Monuments de l'Égypte* (1857), *Recueil de monuments égyptiens* (1862–66), *Geschichte Ägyptens unter den Pharaonen* (1877), *Dictionnaire géographique de l'ancienne Égypte* (1879–80), and others.

Brühl (brül). Town in W Germany, in the *Land* (state) of North Rhine-Westphalia, British Zone, formerly in the Rhine Province, Prussia, ab. 8 mi. S of Cologne. It has lignite mines, iron foundries, chemical and metallurgical factories, dairies, and a sugar refinery. Brühl is renowned for its *Schloss* (castle) Augustusburg, built in the period 1725–70 as a summer residence of the archbishop of Cologne according to plans by G. C. Schlaun and François Cuvilliés; the magnificent staircase is by Balthasar Neumann. The castle, an outstanding example of German baroque and Rococo architecture, with its adjacent buildings and gardens, was damaged in World War II; the staircase is intact. 29,791 (1950).

Brühl, Gustav. b. in Rhenish Prussia, May 31, 1826; d. Feb. 16, 1903. American physician and writer. A student successively at Munich, Halle, and Berlin, he participated in the revolution of 1848 and, after extensive travels, settled at Cincinnati, where he established a medical practice and where he wrote *Die Kulturvölker Amerikas* (1876), *Poesien des Urwalds* (1871), and *Charlotte* (1883). He wrote numerous poems on American Indians. He also lectured on medicine at a medical college at Cincinnati.

Brühl, Count **Heinrich von.** b. at Weissenfels, Prussia, Aug. 13, 1700; d. at Dresden, Saxony, Oct. 28, 1763. Saxon politician under Augustus III. He became prime minister in 1746, and induced the elector Augustus III to take sides against Prussia in the Seven Years' War. His library of about 62,000 volumes became a sizable part of the Royal Library at Dresden.

Bruhns (bröns), **Karl Christian.** b. at Ploen, Holstein, Germany, Nov. 22, 1830; d. at Leipzig, Germany, July 25, 1881. German astronomer. He was professor of astronomy and director of the observatory at Leipzig, and was especially noted for his observations and for the discovery of several comets. He wrote *Die astronomische Strahlenbrechung in ihrer historischen Entwickelung* (1861) and others.

Bruin (brö'in). Bear in *Reynard the Fox.*

Bruin. In Samuel Foote's play *The Mayor of Garratt,* a rough, overbearing man. He is a contrast to the henpecked Jerry Sneak. Mrs. Bruin is roughly treated by him.

Bruis (brü.ē), **Pierre de.** See **Bruys** or **Bruis, Pierre de.**

Brulat (brü.lȧ), **Paul Augustine.** b. at St. Jean-de-Muzols, France, May 26, 1866; d. 1940. French novelist and historian. He was the author of a series of *Histoires populaires* on Jules Ferry (1907), Zola (1907), Gambetta (1909), General Hoche (1910), and General Galliéni (1917).

Brulé (brü.lā), **Étienne.** b. at Champigny, France, c1592; d. in Canada, 1632. French explorer and one-time companion of Samuel de Champlain, whom he served as interpreter and prospector after arriving (1608) in New France. At various times a French agent among the Algonquins and Hurons, he made extensive explorations of North America. It is thought by some scholars that he was the first white man to see any of the Great Lakes, and also that he was the first European to travel (1622–24) over four of these lakes. In 1629 he betrayed Champlain's cause, selling his services to the British, and was killed while living among the Hurons, whom he had offended by his disreputable behavior.

Brulgruddery (brul.grud'ėr.i), **Dennis.** In the younger George Colman's comedy *John Bull,* an eccentric, whimsical Irishman, the host of the Red Cow.

Brüll (brül), **Ignaz.** b. at Prossnitz, in Moravia, Nov. 7, 1846; d. at Vienna, Sept. 17, 1907. Austrian pianist and composer, notably of the opera *Das Goldene Kreuz.* His tours included performances at Vienna and London. Other works by him include operas, a symphony, piano and violin concertos, and a sonata for piano and violin.

Brumaire (brü.mer). Name adopted in 1793 by the National Convention of the first French Republic for the second month of the year. In the years 1, 2, 3, 5, 6, and 7 it began on Oct. 23, and ended on Nov. 20; in the years 4, 8, 9, 10, 11, 13, and 14 it began on Oct. 23, and ended on Nov. 21; and in the year 12 it began on Oct. 24, and ended on Nov. 22.

Brumaire, the 18th. In French history, Nov. 9, 1799, when the coup d'état by which the Directory was overthrown was commenced. It was completed on the 19th Brumaire.

Brumath (brö.mät'). [Also: **Brumpt;** ancient name, **Brucomagus.**] Town in NE France, in the department of Bas-Rhin (formerly Lower Alsace), situated on the Zorn River, ab. 11 mi. N of Strasbourg. It is a port on the Marne-Rhine Canal and a station on the railroad line from Paris to Strasbourg. 5,732 (1946).

Brumby (brum'bi), **Richard Trapier.** b. in Sumter District, S.C., Aug. 4, 1804; d. Oct. 6, 1875. American lawyer and professor. Graduated from South Carolina College (1824), he practiced law periodically until his appointment to the faculty of the University of Alabama, where he occupied (1834–49) the chair of chemistry, mineralogy, and geology. In 1849 he joined the faculty of South Carolina College, remaining there until 1855, when ill health forced him to retire.

Brumidi (brö.mē'dē), **Constantino.** b. at Rome, July 26, 1805; d. at Washington, D.C., Feb. 19, 1880. American fresco painter, best known for his symbolic and historical paintings in the U.S. Capitol.

Brummagem (brum'ą.jęm). See under **Birmingham,** England.

Brummell (brum'ęl), **George Bryan.** [Called **Beau Brummell.**] b. at London, June 7, 1778; d. at Caen, France, March 30, 1840. English gentleman famous as a leader in the fashionable society of the early 19th century at London. He was an intimate friend of the prince regent (later George IV), who is said to have wept when Brummell, who was admired in his dress not as a fop but for his studied moderation, disapproved of one of his coats. Losses at the gaming table forced him to retire to Calais in 1816. In 1830 he was appointed consul at Caen; was imprisoned for debt in 1835, and after 1837 sank into a condition of imbecility, if not actual insanity, and died in an asylum.

Brumoy (brü.mwȧ), **Pierre.** b. at Rouen, France, 1688; d. at Paris, 1742. French Jesuit, scholar, and humanist writer. He was editor of and a contributor to *Journal de Trévoux.* Author of volumes XI and XII of *History of the Gallican Church,* and of *Le Théâtre des Grecs* in three volumes.

Brumpt (brůmpt). See **Brumath.**

Brun (brön), Saint. See **Bruno I,** Saint.

Brunai (brö.nī') or **Bruni** (-nē'). See **Borneo.**

Brunanburh (brö'nän.börċh). [Also, **Brunanburg.**] Place, probably in Northumbria, England, where Athelstan defeated (937) Anlaf of Ireland and Constantine of Scotland. A triumphal poem describing the battle and in praise of King Athelstan and his brother, Edmund, is inserted in the *Anglo-Saxon Chronicle* (*Old English Annals*).

Brunck (breṅk), **Richard François Philippe.** b. at Strasbourg, in Alsace, Dec. 30, 1729; d. June 12, 1803. French classical scholar. He published *Analecta veterum poetarum Graecorum* (1772–76), and editions of Aristophanes, Vergil, Sophocles, Plautus, and others.

Brundage (brun'dạ̄j), **Mount.** [Also, **Mount Burr Brundage.**] Mountain in Antarctica, on the Joerg Plateau, in ab. 75°40′ S., 65°00′ W. It was discovered by the Ronne Antarctic Research Expedition (1947–48), under the leadership of Commander Finn Ronne, who named this feature for Burr Brundage, of the U.S. Department of State, who assisted in making arrangements for the expedition.

Brundidge (brun'dij). Town in SE Alabama, in Pike County, ab. 55 mi. SE of Montgomery, in an agricultural region. 2,605 (1950).

Brundisium (brun.dizh'i.um) or **Brundusium** (-dū'zhi-um). Latin name of **Brindisi,** city.

Brune (brün), **Guillaume Marie Anne.** b. at Brives-la-Gaillarde, Corrèze, France, March 13, 1763; killed at Avignon, France, Aug. 2, 1815. French soldier, marshal of France. He served (1796–97) with distinction in the army of Italy, and commanded (1798–1801) in Switzerland, Holland, the Vendée, and Italy.

Bruneau (brü.nō), **(Louis Charles Bonaventure) Alfred.** b. at Paris, March 3, 1857; d. 1934. French composer and music critic. His most important works are the operas *Le Rêve* (1891), *L'Attaque du moulin* (1893), *Messidor* (1897), *L'Enfant roi* (1905), and *Naïs Micoulin* (1907). He also composed songs, and published several volumes of critical writings.

Brunechildis (brö.nę.ċhil'dis). See **Brunhilde.**

Brunehaut (brün.ō). See **Brunhilde.**

Brunehilde (brön.ę.hil'dę). See **Brunhilde.**

Brunei (brö.nī'). Sultanate and British protectorate in the NW part of Borneo, divided into two parts and bounded on three sides by Sarawak, and bordering on the NW on the South China Sea: placed under British protection in 1888. It has considerable reserves of oil and large tracts of valuable timber. The principal products are crude oil, rubber, cutch (mangrove extract), jelutong, and sago. Capital, Brunei (pop. ab. 10,500); area, 2,226 sq. mi.; pop. 40,657 (1947).

Brunel (brö.nel'), **Isambard Kingdom.** b. at Portsmouth, England, April 9, 1806; d. at Westminster, London, Sept. 15, 1859. English civil engineer and naval architect; son of Sir Marc Isambard Brunel. He was civil engineer for the Great Western Railway, and designed the steamships *Great Western* (1838), *Great Britain* (1845), and *Great Eastern* (1858).

Brunel, Sir **Marc Isambard.** b. at Hacqueville, Eure, France, April 25, 1769; d. at London, Dec. 12, 1849. English civil engineer; father of Isambard Kingdom Brunel. He emigrated from France to the U.S. in 1793. There he designed and built the Bowery Theater, New York, and was appointed chief engineer of New York. He settled in England in 1799, where he completed machinery for making ships' blocks in 1806, and constructed the Thames tunnel (1825–43).

Brunelleschi (brö.nel.les'kē), **Filippo.** b. at Florence, 1377; d. there, April 16, 1446. Italian architect, an early leader of the Renaissance. He at first studied jewelry and goldsmiths' work, and later experimented with mechanics, constructing clocks and machines of all sorts. He also attempted sculpture. In 1401 he entered into competition with Lorenzo Ghiberti for the doors of the baptistery at Florence, Ghiberti's designs being adopted. He associated himself with Donatello, and c1403 the two made a visit to Rome. His study of the Roman monuments was most exhaustive, and when he returned to Florence he had reconstructed for himself the entire scheme of antique architecture. He built the dome of the cathedral at Florence, Santa Maria del Fiore, which was begun c1417. The vault was started in 1425 and finished in 1436. Between 1445 and 1461 the lantern was built after his designs. This, because of the size of the area to be spanned by the dome, was one of the most important structural problems of the 15th century, and Brunelleschi's solution was in its essentials both original and brilliant, borrowing from the ancient architecture of Rome little more than its system of decoration. Brunelleschi also built the church of San Lorenzo at Florence, the Badia at Fiesole, the cloister of Santa Croce, that of Santo Spirito (finished from his designs after his death), and the Pazzi Chapel, also the Ospedale degli Innocenti, and the Pitti Palace.

Brunello (brö.nel'lō). In Matteo Maria Boiardo's *Orlando Innamorato* and Lodovico Ariosto's *Orlando Furioso*, a thief. He was of humble birth, but was made king of Tingitana by Agramante for his services, and, after a life spent in theft and subtle knavery, was hanged.

Bruner (brö'nėr), **Lawrence.** b. at Catasaqua, Pa., March 2, 1856; d. at Berkeley, Calif., Jan. 30, 1937. American entomologist. He taught (1890 *et seq.*) entomology at the University of Nebraska, was an assistant (1880) on the U.S. Entomological Commission, served as a field agent (1897–98) in Argentina, and was entomologist (1888–90) at the Nebraska Agricultural Experiment Station.

Brunet (brü.ne), **Jacques Charles.** b. at Paris, Nov. 2, 1780; d. there, Nov. 16, 1867. French bibliographer. He published a supplement to the bibliographical dictionary of Duclos (1790), *Manuel du libraire et de l'amateur de livres* (1810; 5th ed., 1865), and *Recherches bibliographiques et critiques sur les éditions originales des cinq livres du roman satirique de Rabelais* (1852).

Brunetière (brün.tyer), **(Vincent-de-Paul Marie) Ferdinand.** b. at Toulon, France, July 19, 1849; d. at Paris, Dec. 9, 1906. French editor and critic, especially known for his application of Darwinian theory to literary criticism. He began his studies at the Lycée de Marseilles, and was graduated from the Lycée Louis-le-Grand at Paris. He joined (1875) the staff of the *Revue des Deux Mondes*, of which he was later editor in chief (1893–1906), and was appointed (1886) lecturer at the École Normale. A member (1887 *et seq.*) of the Legion of Honor, he was elected (1893) to the French Academy, and was professor of literature at the Sorbonne. His publications include *Études critiques sur la littérature française* (8 vols., 1880–1907), *Le Roman naturaliste* (1883), *Histoire et littérature* (1884–86), *Questions de critique* (1889), *Nouvelles questions de critique* (1890), *L'Évolution des genres dans l'histoire de la littérature*, and *L'Évolution de la poésie lyrique au dix-neuvième siècle*. The first two series of the *Études critiques* and *Le Roman naturaliste* were issued by the French Academy. In addition to these works, he edited a number of books for classroom use.

Brünhild (brün'hilt). [Also, **Brünnehilde.**] In the *Nibelungenlied*, a famous legendary queen of Island (Iceland), the wife of King Gunther, for whom she is won by Siegfried. She takes vengeance on Siegfried for the trick played on her by having him murdered. See also **Brynhild.**

Brunhilde (brön.hil'dę). [Also: **Brunehilde, Brunehaut, Brunechildis.**] d. 613 A.D. Frankish queen of Austrasia; daughter of Athanagild, king of the Visigoths, and wife (561 *et seq.*) of Sigebert, king of Austrasia. She incited her husband to make war on his brother Chilperic, king of Neustria, who had murdered his wife Galeswintha (Galsuinda), sister of Brunhilde, in order to marry his mistress Fredegund (Fredegonda). Sigebert was murdered in 575 by Fredegonda, and Brunhilde became regent for her minor son Childebert II. She was captured, after many reverses of fortune, at the age of 80, by Clotaire II, who caused her to be dragged to death by a wild horse.

Bruni (brö'nē), **Leonardo.** [Called **Leonardo Aretino.**] b. at Arezzo, Italy, 1369; d. at Florence, March 9, 1444. Italian man of letters; a pupil of Emmanuel Chrysoloras. He served as apostolic secretary, and was chancellor of Florence (1427–44). He wrote *Historiarum Florentinarum libri XII* (1415), *De bello italico adversus Gothos gesto* (1470), *Epistolae familiares*, and a novel, *De amore Guiscardi*.

Brünig (brü'nich). Mountain pass over the Alps, in Switzerland, connecting Lucerne with Meiringen. The highest point is ab. 3,295 ft. It is traversed (since 1883–89) by a railway.

Brüning (brü'ning), **Heinrich.** b. at Münster, Westphalia, Germany, April 26, 1885—. German statesman. He was executive secretary (1921–30) of the Deutscher Gewerkschaftsbund (German League of Trade Unions), a Centrist Party member (1924 *et seq.*) of the Reichstag, and an authority on the fiscal problems of the German republic during the 1920's and early 1930's. He became chancellor (March, 1930), dissolved the Reichstag (July 17, 1930), and ruled by emergency decree according to the Weimar Constitution. He attempted to surmount the international crisis by solving the German reparations problem and by seeking a disarmament convention; he was partially successful by reason of the Hoover moratorium (1931) on reparations payments. He brought about the reëlection of Paul von Hindenburg, but was compelled to resign after he had advocated breaking up some of the East Prussian estates. Opposed to the Centrist Party's support of the law (1933) giving Hitler emergency powers, he went into exile shortly before the purge of June, 1934. He became (1939) professor of government at the Littauer School, Harvard University. He is the author of monographs on civil service and fiscal problems.

Brunk (brungk), **Jonas.** See **Bronck, Jonas.**

Brunkeberg (brung'kę.bery'). Height in SE Sweden, N of Stockholm. Here, in October, 1471, the Swedes under Sten Stur defeated Christian I of Denmark.

Brünn (brün). German name of **Brno.**

Brunn (brün), **Heinrich von.** b. at Wörlitz, in Anhalt, Germany, Jan. 23, 1822; d. at Munich, July 23, 1894. German archaeologist, professor of archaeology at Munich. His works include *Geschichte der griechischen Künstler* (1853–59) and *I rilievi delle urne etrusche* (1870).

Brünnehilde (brün.ę.hil'dę). See **Brunhild.**

Brunnen (brün'ęn). Village in C Switzerland, in the canton of Schwyz, situated on Lake Lucerne SW of the city of Schwyz: a lake port and a station on the St. Gotthard Railway. In 1315 at a meeting here, the confederation of the three central cantons was renewed. 3,200 (est.).

Brunner (brun'ėr), **Arnold William.** b. at New York, Sept. 25, 1857; d. Feb. 12, 1925. American architect and city planner. Graduated (1879) from the Massachusetts Institute of Technology, he entered (c1898) independent architectural practice at New York, and won national repute with his prize-winning designs for New York's Mount Sinai Hospital, the Federal Building at Cleveland, and others. His city planning included the Capitol Park state office buildings and plaza at Harrisburg, Pa., the civic center at Cleveland, Ohio, and improvement of the waterfront area at Albany, N.Y. He was a member of the city planning commissions of Baltimore, Denver, and Rochester, and served on the National Council of Fine Arts.

Brunner (brün'ėr), **Conrad.** b. at Diessenhofen am Rhein, Switzerland, Aug. 31, 1859; d. at Zurich, Switzerland, June 8, 1927. Swiss surgeon. He was assistant to R. U. Krönlein, became (1890) privatdocent of surgery at the University of Zurich, and was chief surgeon (1896–1922) at the Thurgau Kanton Hospital at Münsterlingen. He is known for his investigations in the field of the disinfection of wounds, and is eminent for his work on surface and deep disinfection of wounds (1921). He wrote a history of battle injuries in *Die Verwundeten in den Kriegen der alten Eidgenossenschaft* (1903).

Brunner, Constantin. [Pseudonym of **Leo Wertheimer.**] b. at Altona, Denmark (later in Germany), Aug. 28, 1862; d. at The Hague, Netherlands, 1937. German philosopher, a follower of Spinoza's philosophy. He wrote *Die Lehre von den Geistigen und von Volke* (1908), *Der Judenhass und die Juden* (1919), and *Von den Pflichten der Juden und den Pflichten des Staates* (1930).

Brunner, Emil. b. 1889—. Swiss Protestant theologian, professor of theology at the University of Zurich, who in 1938–39 and in 1946 visited the U.S., where his lectures aroused much interest in theological circles. Brunner's tenets, in many respects closely resembling those of Karl Barth, are fundamentalist. In the Bible he sees the sole revelation to man of the mind and will of God, and in faith the sole means of salvation; man excluded from divine grace cannot win it by good works. Among the better-known books of Emil Brunner are *Die Mystic und das Wort, Das Gebot und die Ordnungen* (translated into English as *The Divine Imperative*), and *Wahrheit als Begegung* (translated as *The Divine-Human Encounter*).

Brunner, Johann Conrad. b. near Schaffhausen, Switzerland, Jan. 16, 1653; d. at Mannheim, Germany, Oct. 2, 1727. German anatomist, noted for researches on the pancreas and the duodenum.

Brunner, Sebastian. b. at Vienna, Dec. 10, 1814; d. at Währing, near Vienna, Nov. 26, 1893. Austrian man of letters and Roman Catholic theologian. He was the author of a satirical poem, *Der Nebeljungen Lied* (1845), directed against the Hegelians, and other poems, several tales, and *Clemens Maria Hofbauer und seine Zeit* (1858) and *Die Kunstgenossen der Klosterzelle* (1863).

Brunner, William Otto. b. at Wattwil, Switzerland, July 7, 1878—. Swiss astronomer. After 1926 he was director of the solar observatory at Zurich. He is one of those who have continued the sun-spot number determinations started during the 19th century by Rudolf Wolf.

Brunngraber (brůn'grä.bėr), **Rudolf.** b. at Vienna, Sept. 20, 1901—. Austrian novelist writing on social and utopian themes.

Brunnow (brůn'ō), Count **Philipp von.** b. at Dresden, Germany, Aug. 31, 1797; d. at Darmstadt, Germany, April 12, 1875. Russian diplomat. He was ambassador at London (1840–54, 1858–74), Frankfort on the Main (1855), and Berlin (1856).

Bruno (brö'nō), Saint. [Also: **Boniface;** sometimes written **Bruno-Boniface;** called the **"Apostle to the Prussians."**] b. at Querfurt, in Prussian Saxony, c970; killed at Braunsberg, in East Prussia, Feb. 14, 1009. A Camaldolese monk and bishop of the Slavs (Ruthenians).

Bruno, Saint. b. at Cologne, Germany, c1030; d. in Calabria, Italy, Oct. 6, 1101. Ecclesiastical writer, notable as the founder of the Carthusian Order. A member of a German noble family, he studied first at Cologne and then at the episcopal school of Reims, became a canon of Saint Cunibert's at Cologne, and was ordained a priest in 1055. For 20 years he was head of the episcopal school at Reims, and then chancellor of the diocese. In 1075 Bruno and the canons Raoul and Fulcius vowed to embrace the religious life, which Bruno thought of doing under the solitary Saint Robert, at Molesme, who later (1098) founded the Cistercian Order. Bruno retired in 1084 with some companions to a wild spot near Grenoble, leading thereafter an eremetical life. He was called (1090) to assist Pope Urban II, with whom he remained for several years, finally retiring with some followers to a solitary life in Calabria. The Calabrian establishment finally merged with the Cistercian Order; that of Grenoble was the nucleus of the Carthusians.

Bruno, Saint. b. at Solero, Italy, c1048; d. 1123. Bishop of Segni and ecclesiastical writer. He opposed the doctrine of Berengarius on the Eucharist, was counselor to four popes, and an opponent of lay investiture. Becoming a monk of Monte Cassino in 1102 he was elected (1107) abbot, but was later forced to resign his abbacy and return to his diocese by Pope Pascal II, whom Bruno, with other Italian bishops, censured for having yielded to Henry V on the matter of lay investiture. He was canonized in 1183 by Lucius III.

Bruno I, Saint. [Also: **Brun** (brön); called **"Bruno the Great."**] b. 925; d. at Reims, France, Oct. 11, 965. German ruler and churchman; brother of Otto I of Germany. He was made archbishop of Cologne and duke of Lorraine in 953.

Bruno, Giordano. b. at Nola, Italy, c1548; d. at Rome, Feb. 17, 1600. Italian philosopher. He entered the Dominican order at Naples in 1563, but left Italy in 1576 to avoid the consequences of his disbelief in the doctrines of transubstantiation and of the immaculate conception of Mary; he was at Geneva in 1577, and arrived at Paris in 1579. In 1583 he went to London, where some of his most important works were written, and where he remained for two years under the protection of the French ambassador. In the period 1586–88 he lectured at the University of Wittenberg, and subsequently visited other cities in Germany, France, and Switzerland, returning to Italy in 1592. He was arrested at Naples, on May 22, 1592, by order of the Inquisition, and was burned at the stake as a heretic in the Campo dei Fiori at Rome. His philosophy was based on a complete repudiation of all theories which seemed to him dogmatic (including even the Copernican system, although he supported its main tenets). Believing that absolute truth was an impossibility, different positions postulating different points of view, he reconciled this disparity in pantheism. His theory of the existence of monads profoundly influenced Gottfried Wilhelm von Leibnitz; his views also made a profound impression on the later romantics. His chief works are *Spaccio della bestia trionfante* (Expulsion of the Triumphant Beast, 1584), *Della causa, principio et uno* (1584), *Dell' infinito, universo emondi* (1584), and *De monade numero et figura* (1591).

Bruno (brü.nō), **Pierre Antoine Noël.** Full family name of **Daru, Pierre Antoine,** Comte.

Brunoy (brü.nwå). Town in N France, in the department of Seine-et-Oise, SE of Paris and N of Corbeil. It is an industrial town included in the metropolitan region of Paris. 8,149 (1946).

Brunsum (brun'sum). [Also, **Brunssum.**] Town in SE Netherlands, in the province of Limbourg, ab. 10 mi. NE of Maastricht. It has textile manufactures, and there are coal mines in the vicinity. 20,702 (est. 1951).

Brunswick (brunz'wik). City in SE Georgia, in Glynn County, ab. 72 mi. SW of Savannah, in a resort region: seaport; shrimp canneries, paper mills, and turpentine and resin plants. 17,954 (1950).

Brunswick. [German, **Braunschweig.**] Former state in C Germany, now divided between the *Länder* (states) of Lower Saxony in West Germany (British Zone), and Saxony-Anhalt, in East Germany (Russian Zone). Brunswick was the original possession of the princes of the house of Welfen, and since 1180 their principal state. The old capital at Wolfenbüttel was moved to the city of Brunswick in 1753. From 1807 to 1813 Brunswick was united with the Napoleonic kingdom of Westphalia. It joined the German Customs Union in 1844, Prussia in 1866, and became a member state of the German Reich in 1870. In 1945 it was abolished by division. Area, 1,418 sq. mi.; pop. 583,922 (1939); area of West German part, 1,182 sq. mi.; pop. 782,950 (1946).

Brunswick. [Old High German, **Brunswyk;** Modern German, **Braunschweig.**] City in NW central Germany, in the *Land* (state) of Lower Saxony, British Zone, formerly the capital of Brunswick state, situated on the Oker River, ab. 125 mi. W of Berlin. It is known for the production of sausages, cured meats, and canned products, and as the seat of the piano-building firm of Grotrian-Steinweg and the publishing house of Georg Westermann. There are metallurgical, machine, and shoe industries, manufactures of tin cans, and breweries; before World War II the Büssing Works, producing automobiles and trucks, were well known. 181,375 (1946).

Cultural Institutions. There is an institute of technology, a school of arts and crafts, and other educational institutions, archives, a library, and a theater. Brunswick has a number of museums, the most important of which is the *Landesmuseum* (state museum), with paintings by Flemish and Dutch masters, and prehistoric and medieval collections; the Haussman Dürer Museum contains prints and drawings; there is a municipal museum, a natural history museum, and several others.

Art and Architecture. The old part of the city had preserved its medieval character prior to World War II; most of the center of Brunswick, however, was destroyed (1943–45) by bombing, and numerous historic buildings were gravely damaged. The *Altstadtrathaus* (old city hall), a remarkable Gothic building of the 14th century, was burned out; most of the old houses surrounding it, some of them survivals from the Middle Ages, some, like the Gewandhaus, in the Renaissance and baroque styles, were burned also. The churches still stand, in spite of the damage done to them; four of them are Romanesque-Gothic basilica churches: the cathedral, built in 1193 by Henry the Lion and containing numerous art treasures, the 12th-century *Martinikirche* (Church of Saint Martin) and *Catherinenkirche* (Church of Saint Catherine), and the 13th-century *Magnikirche* (Church of Saint Magnus). Others include the *Andreaskirche* (Church of Saint Andrew), the *Petrikirche* (Church of Saint Peter), the Church of the Brethren, and the *Franziskanerkirche* (Church of the Franciscans). On the Burgplatz is the statue of the Bronze Lion, erected by Henry the Lion in 1166. The *Lustschloss* (villa) Richmond dates from the 18th century; the former ducal castle is a modern building.

History. The first settlement dates back to the 10th century; the city developed in the reign of Henry the Lion in the 12th century; it supported the house of Welf (Guelph). In 1247 a member of, and soon one of the leading cities in, the Hanseatic League, Brunswick was, however, frequently at loggerheads with the ruling princes, accepting Lutheranism in 1528 while the prince remained in the Catholic faith. It submitted to the Welfs in 1671; in 1753 Karl I, Duke of Brunswick-Wolfenbüttel transferred his residence here. From 1806 to 1813 Brunswick belonged to the Napoleonic kingdom of Westphalia. It suffered from communist disturbances between November, 1918 and April, 1919, when it was occupied by the troops of the Reichswehr. In World War II, the Americans entered the town on April 13, 1945.

Brunswick. Town (in Maine the equivalent of township in many other states) and unincorporated village in SW Maine, in Cumberland County, on the Androscoggin River, ab. 25 mi. NE of Portland: manufactures include paper, pulp, and textiles. It is the seat of Bowdoin College. The site was first settled in 1628. Harriet Beecher Stowe lived at Brunswick (where she wrote *Uncle Tom's Cabin*), as did Henry Wadsworth Longfellow, who was a professor at Bowdoin College. Pop. of town, 10,996 (1950); of village, 7,342 (1950).

Brunswick. Town in NW Maryland, in Frederick County, on the Potomac River near Virginia: railroad repair shops. 3,752 (1950).

Brunswick, Caroline of. See **Caroline of Brunswick.**

Brunswick, Duke **Friedrich Wilhelm of.** b. at Brunswick, Germany, Oct. 9, 1771; killed at Quatre-Bras, Belgium, June 16, 1815. German nobleman; fourth son of Karl Wilhelm Ferdinand, Duke of Brunswick. He reigned from 1813 to 1815. He commanded the "Black Brunswickers" (1809), and lived in England from 1809 to 1813.

Brunswick, Duke **Karl (Friedrich Augustus Wilhelm) of.** [Also, **Karl II** (of Brunswick).] b. at Brunswick, Germany, Oct. 30, 1804; d. at Geneva, Switzerland, Aug. 18, 1873. German nobleman; eldest son of Duke Friedrich Wilhelm of Brunswick. He was deposed from the government in 1830.

Brunswick, Duke **Karl Wilhelm Ferdinand of.** b. at Wolfenbüttel, Germany, Oct. 9, 1735; d. at Ottensen, near Altona, Germany, Nov. 10, 1806. German nobleman; son of Karl I, Duke of Brunswick-Wolfenbüttel. He reigned from 1780 to 1806. He commanded the Prussian and Austrian army which invaded France in 1792, and the Prussian army at the battle of Auerstädt, Oct. 14, 1806, where he was fatally wounded.

Brunswick-Lüneburg (brunz'wik.lü'nẹ.bürk), Line of. Branch of the house of Brunswick from which the reigning house of Great Britain is descended.

Brunswick-Wolfenbüttel (brunz'wik.vol'fẹn.büt.ẹl), Line of. Branch of the house of Brunswick from which the late reigning house of Brunswick was descended.

Brunswick-Wolfenbüttel, Duke of. Title of **Anton Ulrich.**

Brunton (brun'tọn), **David William.** b. at Ayr, Ontario, Canada, June 11, 1849; d. Dec. 20, 1927. American inventor and mining engineer. He is noted for his achievements in driving long tunnels, among them the Cowenhoven tunnel under Smuggler Mountain in Colorado, the Roosevelt tunnel at Cripple Creek, Colo., and the Moffat railroad tunnel in the Rockies. He received his training as a civil engineer at Toronto, and attended (1874–75) the University of Michigan. During the 1890's he acted as consulting engineer and technical adviser to the Anaconda copper interests, making important contributions to American mining practice. Among his inventions are the Brunton pocket-transit for engineers (1904), a mine pump, and improvements in ore processing.

Brunton, Louisa. b. c1785; d. 1860. English actress. She married William Craven, 1st Earl of Craven, in 1807, when she left the stage. She was remarkable for her beauty and for her success in the leading roles of various comedies of the day.

Brunton, Mary. [Maiden name, **Balfour.**] b. at Barra, in the Orkney Islands, Nov. 1, 1778; d. at Edinburgh, Dec. 19, 1818. English novelist. She wrote *Self Control* (1810) and *Discipline* (1814).

Brunton, Sir **Thomas Lauder.** b. at Hiltonshill, Roxburghshire, Scotland, March 14, 1844; d. 1916. Scottish physician. His medical education was begun at the University of Edinburgh and continued on the Continent. While associated as a lecturer on materia medica with Middlesex and St. Bartholomew's Hospitals, at London, he engaged in fruitful research on the action of various drugs and on problems of the circulation of the blood, and made important contributions to the treatment of cardiac ailments. He was knighted in 1900 and created a baronet in 1908. He was the author of *Text-book of Pharmacology* (1885), *Lectures on the Action of Medicines* (1897), *Collected Papers on Circulation and Respiration* (1906), *Collected Papers on Physical and Military Training* (1898–1915), and *Disorders of Assimilation, Digestion . . .* (1901).

Brunton, William. b. May 26, 1777; d. at Camborne, Cornwall, England, Oct. 5, 1851. Scottish engineer and inventor, remembered for his contributions to the development of steam navigation. He built several original engines used on the Humber and the Trent, and at Plymouth, fitted out (1824) the *Sir Francis Drake*, the first steamer that ever took a man-of-war in tow. His other inventions included the calciner (much used in copper mines, and in Cornish and Mexican silver works) and the fan regulator. His most novel and ingenious invention was a walking machine (1813), called the Steam Horse, which exploded two years after he built it.

Brus (brös), **The.** See **Bruce, The.**

Brusa or **Brussa** (brö.sä'). See **Bursa.**

Bruselas (brö.sä'läs). Spanish name of **Brussels.**

Brush (brush), **Charles Francis.** b. in Euclid Township, Cuyahoga County, Ohio, March 17, 1849; d. at Cleveland, Ohio, June 15, 1929. American electrician. He was the inventor of the Brush dynamoelectric machine and the Brush electric arc lamp, both of which were extensively introduced in the U.S. in 1876. He was the recipient of numerous medals and awards.

Brush, Edward Nathaniel. b. at Glenwood, N.Y., April 23, 1852; d. Jan. 10, 1933. American psychiatrist. He was superintendent (1891–1920) of the Sheppard and Enoch Pratt Hospital at Baltimore, professor (1899–1920) of psychiatry at the University of Maryland and the College of Physicians and Surgeons at Baltimore, and editor (1874–79) of the *Buffalo Medical Journal.* He was also associate editor (1878–84, 1897–1904) and editor (1904 *et seq.*) of the *American Journal of Psychiatry.*

Brush, George de Forest. b. at Shelbyville, Tenn., 1855; d. April 24, 1941. American painter. He was a student of the National Academy of Design at New York from 1871 to 1873, and, from 1874 to 1880, in the studio of Jean Léon Gérôme at Paris. His best-known works are paintings of American Indian subjects and portrait groups. He was elected to the National Academy in 1906. In 1939 he served in the Tennessee legislature.

Brush, George Jarvis. b. at Brooklyn, N.Y., Dec. 15, 1831; d. at New Haven, Conn., Feb. 6, 1912. American mineralogist, teacher, and administrator. Graduated from Yale, he pursued mineralogical studies abroad from 1853 to 1855, when he joined the faculty of Yale's Sheffield Scientific School as professor of metallurgy (later mineralogy). He was director (1872–98) and president (1900 *et seq.*), respectively, of the school and its board of trustees. His *Manual of Determinative Mineralogy* (1874), in revised form, is a standard work. A member of several scientific societies here and abroad, he contributed (1904) the Brush Collection of 15,000 mineral specimens to Sheffield Scientific School.

Brush, Katharine. [Maiden name, **Ingham.**] b. Aug. 15, 1902; d. June 10, 1952. American novelist and short-story writer. She was the author of *Glitter* (1926), *Little Sins* (1927), *Young Man of Manhattan* (1930), *Red-Headed Woman* (1931), *The Boy from Maine* (1942), *This Man and This Woman* (1944), and other novels. Her volumes of short stories include *Night Club* (1929) and *Other Women* (1932).

Brusilov (brö.sē'lọf), **Aleksey Alekseyevich.** b. Aug. 19, 1853; d. at Moscow, March 17, 1926. Russian general. He began his military career early in life, and as a cavalry officer in the Russo-Turkish War (1877–78) won commendation and advancement by his bravery and skill. At the outbreak of World War I he was given command of the Russian Eighth Army, and his victories in Galicia resulted in his being placed in command of all Russian forces in the south. After the abdication of Czar Nicholas II, the government headed by Prince Lvov put Brusilov in command of all Russian military forces, and he so continued for a time under the Kerensky government. In 1920 he led the Soviet forces in the brief invasion of Poland, but thereafter he does not appear to have served the Soviet regime in any active capacity.

Brusilov Offensive (*of 1916*). [Sometimes called the **"Great Brusilov Offensive."**] In World War I, a military operation (June-September, 1916) on the Eastern Front between four Russian armies under Aleksey Alekseyevich Brusilov and the opposing Austrian forces (which were reinforced toward the latter part of the operation by 15 German divisions). The offensive was originally planned to begin in the middle of June, so that it might coincide with Joffre's offensive at the Somme on the Western Front, but Brusilov yielded to pleas for an action that would (by diverting Austrian troops to the Eastern Front) lighten the pressure then being brought against the Italians in the Trentino. He therefore began his operation on June 4, some ten days before Joffre. His initial successes were considerable: the Austrians lost approximately half a million prisoners and the Russians advanced in some points as much as 75 mi. beyond their original lines. However, almost from the start, Brusilov was hampered by poor transport facilities (for example, the rail lines running north and south, which were essential to the shifting of troops back and forth along the front, were hopelessly inadequate for the task), and the offensive was finally stopped completely when the Germans threw in 15 divisions to bolster the Austrians. The Russian losses have been estimated at upwards of one million men.

Brusilov Offensive (*of 1917*). In World War I, a military operation (July 1–21, 1917) on the Eastern Front between some 200,000 Russians under Aleksey Alekseyevich Brusilov and the opposing Austrian and German forces. It was the last major offensive effort of the Russians in World War I, and took place after the fall of the czarist regime. Kerensky, who was then minister of war, hoped that it might have a stabilizing effect on both the Russian soldiers and the civilian population. Attacking on the lightly held Galician front, with the aim of capturing Lemberg (now Lvov), Brusilov sent his troops in waves against the Austrians and Germans, and had some initial successes against the former. However, there were a considerable number of German divisions either in the line or in reserve, and the resistance quickly stiffened. At the end of three weeks, still far short of Lemberg, Brusilov's forces had exhausted themselves and the offensive collapsed. Within a matter of days, a German counteroffensive threw the Russians into a disorganized retreat from which, as an effective fighting force in World War I, they never recovered.

Brussa (brös'sä). See **Aowin.**

Brussels (brus'ẹlz). [Flemish, **Brussel** (brüs'ẹl); French, **Bruxelles**; German, **Brüssel** (brüs'ẹl); Spanish, **Bruselas.**] City in C Belgium, the capital of Belgium and of the province of Brabant, situated on the Senne River, S of Antwerp. Pop. without suburbs, 184,838 (1947); with suburbs, 920,380 (1947), 960,740 (est. 1948).

Commerce and Industry. Through the canal of Charleroi Brussels is connected with the S Belgian coal-mining district, and through the canal of Willebroek with the Schelde River and the sea. The port, constructed in the period 1896–1906, has a large volume of both imports and exports. There are many industries, particularly in luxury goods such as lace, gloves, leather, woolen and cotton textiles, hosiery, carpets, pottery, and glassware; there are chemical and furniture manufactures, printing establishments, and breweries. Brussels is the center of Belgian banking operations and the seat of a stock exchange; it is a railroad junction and has a large airport.

Cultural Institutions. Brussels is the seat of a university, founded in 1788 and enlarged in 1834. It has an academy of science, an academy of arts, a music conservatory, vocational schools, a number of scientific societies, art collections, and museums. The Belgian Congo Museum, at Jervueren, and the royal castle, at Laeken, are in the vicinity; there are numerous parks.

Chief Buildings. The Cathedral of Saint Gudule, also called Saint Michael's Church, built in the period 1220–72, is considered one of the finest specimens of Gothic style. It contains a richly carved oak pulpit. The stained-glass windows, which date from the 13th, 14th, and 15th centuries, depict members of the houses of Burgundy and Hapsburg. The 14th-century Church of the Sablon contains a monument to the princely family of Thurn and Taxis. The Grande Place is one of the most interesting public squares in Europe. At the S side is the ornate *Hôtel de Ville* (city hall), built in the 15th century; opposite is the Maison du Roi, in rich Gothic style, in which the royal addresses were read to the States General of the Netherlands. The Palais de la Nation was built in the reign of the Austrian empress Maria Theresa (1779–83); it was assigned to the States General in the period 1817–30. A newer building is the Palais de Justice (1866–83). New and spacious avenues were built in the 20th century. There are a number of beautiful old palaces, mainly in the Renaissance style of the 15th, 16th, and 17th centuries.

History. The origin of the city of Brussels dates back to the period of the great migration when the original Gallo-Roman population, seeking refuge before the conquering Franks, established themselves on isolated spots among the marshes along the Senne River. Commerce and industry, particularly clothmaking, developed in the early Middle Ages; the trade between Ghent and Bruges on the one hand and Cologne on the other passed through here. Duke John II of Brabant granted a charter in 1312 which, together with the "Golden Bull" (1349), of Emperor Charles II established the constitution of the South Netherlands which remained in force until the 18th century. Brussels became the residence of the dukes of Brabant in 1383; in 1430 it passed into the possession of the dukes of Burgundy. The city reached its greatest splendor and prosperity under the Hapsburg rule, especially in the reigns of Charles II and Philip II; it was then considered one of the finest and largest cities of Europe. Philip II of Spain made it the capital of the Spanish Netherlands; it was the scene of the earliest rising against the Spanish rule in 1566; it was here that Egmont and Horn, the martyrs of Flemish freedom, were executed in 1568. The numerous wars between France, Spain, and Austria destroyed the prosperity of the city; it suffered severely from the bombardment by the French army under Villeroy in 1695. After the War of the Spanish Succession (Peace of Utrecht, 1713), it passed from the rule of Spain to that of the Austrian Hapsburgs; it slowly recovered toward the 18th century. It was the capital of the French department of the Dyle in the period 1794–1814, alternately with The Hague the capital of the Netherlands in the period 1815–30, and has been the capital of Belgium since 1831. The Belgian revolution started here on Aug. 25, 1830. Brussels was the seat of numerous international conferences in the 19th and 20th centuries. In World War I the German occupation extended from August, 1914 to November, 1918. In World War II Brussels fell to the Germans on May 17, 1940. The city suffered damage in both world wars. The increase in population since the middle of the 19th century has taken place in the suburbs, many of which have separate communal administrations.

Brussels Conference. Convention of representatives from Great Britain, France, Germany, Italy, Austria-Hungary, Belgium, and Russia, which met at Brussels in

September, 1876, and again in 1877. It decided to establish an International African Association to explore and civilize central Africa, and provided for branch national committees. There was an antislavery conference at Brussels in 1890.

Brussels Conference. Meeting (November, 1937) at Brussels, to consider the Sino-Japanese hostilities which then threatened world peace. Nineteen nations, among them the U.S., attended, although both Japan and Germany were absent. On Nov. 15, 1937, 15 of the participating nations issued a declaration censuring Japan by declaring the conflict a matter of concern to all signatories of the Nine-Power Treaty and the Briand-Kellogg Pact (Pact of Paris). On adjournment a report was issued urging that hostilities be suspended and that a settlement be sought by peaceful processes and through other powers.

Brussels Conference. Conference held (March, 1948) at Brussels, marking an important step in the official recognition of the need for closer union of Western European states. This meeting was the culminating one in a series which led to the Brussels Five-Power Treaty of March 17, 1948. With Great Britain, France, Belgium, the Netherlands, and Luxembourg as signatories, a 50-year defensive treaty was put into effect. Largely a military alliance, it obligated all adherent states to provide assistance in case one or more members were attacked.

Brussels Five-Power Treaty. Fifty-year treaty between Great Britain, France, Belgium, the Netherlands, and Luxembourg signed on March 17, 1948, as a basis for common military association and planning. Though also bringing closer economic and political coöperation through the consultative council of the five foreign ministers and periodic financial meetings, the most important immediate accomplishment of the treaty was to set up a permanent joint defense organization seated at Fontainbleau with Field Marshal Bernard Montgomery of the British Army as chairman. The agreement became a nucleus of the later and more inclusive Atlantic Pact.

Brussels Sugar Conference. Conference in December, 1930, of large sugar-producing countries which attempted to find measures to combat the depressed price of sugar and to avoid large sugar surpluses. Under the plan, which the conference adopted, a permanent sugar council was located at The Hague with power to fix export sugar quotas. The agreement was, however, seriously weakened in March, 1932, when Cuba (one of the world's chief sugar-producing countries) renounced the plan.

Brute (bröt), **Sir John.** In John Vanbrugh's comedy *The Provok'd Wife*, a drunken, roistering, rough fellow. He passes through every phase of riot and debauchery, and is unbearably insolent to his "provok'd wife," though too much of a coward to resent her consequent actions.

Bruté De Rémur (brü.tā dẹ rā.mür), **Simon William Gabriel.** [Sometimes shortened to **Simon Gabriel Bruté.**] b. at Rennes, France, March 20, 1779; d. June 26, 1839. Catholic missionary, educator, and bishop. Originally trained in medicine at Paris, he entered the Seminary of Saint Sulpice and, shortly after his ordination (1808), became a professor at the College of Rennes. Having come to America as a missionary priest, he served on the staffs of several Catholic educational institutions, and was appointed (1834) first bishop of Vincennes, Ind.

Bruttium (brut'i.um). [Also: **Bruthius** (brö'thi.us), **Bruttii** (brut'i.ī); **Bruttiorum Ager** (brut.i.ō'rum ā'jėr).] In ancient geography, the southernmost division of Italy, corresponding to the modern provinces of Reggio di Calabria, Cosenza, and Catanzaro, and approximately coextensive with the modern *compartimento* (region) of Calabria.

Brutus (brö'tus). Tragedy by Voltaire, produced at the Comédie Française on Dec. 11, 1730. Vittorio Alfieri wrote two tragedies, called respectively *Marcus Brutus* and *Junius Brutus*, both inspired by Voltaire (1783). Catherine Barnard also produced a tragedy, *Brutus*, at the Comédie Française, on Dec. 18, 1690.

Brutus, Decimus Junius. [Surnamed **Gallaecus.**] fl. 138 B.C. Roman consul and military leader. The surname Gallaecus derived from his conquest of the Gallaeci, a people of NW Spain. He also repulsed the forays of the Lusitanians into the Roman colonies in Spain. He was consul in 138 B.C. He is remembered not only as a soldier, but also as a patron of poets.

Brutus, Decimus Junius. [Surnamed **Albinus.**] Executed 43 B.C. Roman general, one of the assassins of Julius Caesar. He was put to death by order of Mark Antony, with whom he disputed the province of Cisalpine Gaul. At the time of his death, Brutus was consul designate. He is not to be confused with Marcus Junius Brutus, Caesar's chief assassin.

Brutus, Lucius Junius. fl. in the 6th century B.C. Roman consul in 509 B.C. According to unhistorical legend, he feigned idiocy (whence the name *Brutus*, stupid; probably an erroneous etymology) to avoid exciting the fear of his uncle Tarquin the Proud, who had put to death the elder brother of Brutus to possess himself of their wealth. Tarquin, alarmed at the prodigy of a serpent appearing in the royal palace, sent his sons Titus and Aruns to consult the oracle at Delphi. They took with them for amusement Brutus, who propitiated the priestess with a hollow staff filled with gold. When the oracle, in response to an inquiry of Titus and Aruns as to who should succeed to the throne, replied, "He who first kisses his mother," Brutus stumbled to the ground and kissed mother earth. After the outrage on Lucretia, Brutus threw off his pretence of idiocy, expelled the Tarquins, and established (c510 B.C.) the republic. While consul he condemned his own sons Titus and Tiberius to death for having conspired to restore Tarquin. He led (c507) an army against Tarquin, who was returning to Rome. Brutus and Aruns fell in the battle, pierced by each other's spears.

Brutus, Marcus Junius. [Adoptive name, **Quintus Caepio Brutus.**] b. c85 B.C.; d. near Philippi, Macedonia, 42 B.C. Roman politician and general, remembered as Caesar's chief assassin. Originally an adherent of Pompey, he went over to Caesar after the battle of Pharsalia in 48. He was governor of Cisalpine Gaul in 46, and *praetor urbanus* in 44. Induced by Cassius, he joined in the assassination of Caesar, on March 15, 44 B.C. He gathered troops in Macedonia, with which he joined Cassius in Asia Minor in 42, and defeated Octavianus in the first battle of Philippi in 42. Cassius was defeated by Antony and committed suicide, and Brutus defeated in a second battle 20 days later, and fell upon his sword. His (second) wife Portia, daughter of Cato Uticensis, on receiving news of his death, committed suicide by swallowing live coals.

Brutus; or, The Fall of Tarquin (tär'kwin). Tragedy in blank verse by John Howard Payne, produced and published at London in 1818. It was performed at New York in 1819.

Brüx (brüks). A German name of **Most,** Czechoslovakia.

Bruxelles (brük.sel, brü.sel). French name of **Brussels.**

Bruyas (brü.yä), **Jacques.** b. at Lyons, France, July 13, 1637; d. at Sault St. Louis, Canada, June 15, 1712. French Jesuit, notable as a missionary to the Iroquois. He went to Canada in 1666 and labored as a missionary for 46 years. He was superior of the mission in the period 1693–98, wrote a catechism in Iroquois, and prepared the oldest existing grammar in that language.

Bruyn (broin), **Barthel** (or **Bartholomäus).** b. at Cologne, Germany, c1493; d. 1555. German painter of the Cologne School. It is supposed that he studied with the Flemish painter known as the Master of the Death of the Virgin, and his early work has characteristics of the Flemish school, but his later paintings show strong Italian influences. His paintings of religious subjects in general lack the strength of his portraits, yet perhaps his greatest single achievement is a series of pictures decorating a shrine in the church at Xanten.

Bruyn, Cornelis de. b. at The Hague, Netherlands, 1652; d. at Utrecht, Netherlands, c1726. Dutch traveler and painter. He wrote and illustrated *Voyage au Levant* (1698) and *Voyage par la Moscovie, en Perse* (1711).

Bruys or **Bruis** (brü.ē), **Pierre de.** Burned at the stake at St.-Gilles, France, c1126. French religious reformer. His followers were called Petrobrusians.

Bry or **Brie** (brē), **Jean Théodore de.** b. at Liége, Belgium, 1561; d. at Frankfort on the Main, Germany, 1623. Flemish engraver; son of Théodore de Bry. Working with his father in the printing and engraving shop which the latter established at Frankfort on the Main, Jean Théodore de Bry had a hand in engraving the plates for the *Florilegium novem*, and after his father's death he completed the plates for *Collectiones peregrinationum in In-*

diam orientalem et occidentalem which Théodore de Bry initiated at the suggestion of Richard Hakluyt, and the plates for J. J. Broissard's *Romanae urbis topographia et antiquitates*. He also continued the series of engraved portraits known as *Icones virorum illustrium*. He originated and published in 1596 a series of engravings entitled *Emblematica secularia*.

Bry or **Brie, Théodore de.** b. at Liége, Belgium, 1528; d. at Frankfort on the Main, Germany, 1598. Flemish goldsmith, engraver, and painter. About 1570 he established a printing and engraving house at Frankfort on the Main, his two sons assisting him. They illustrated many books, but are best known for their great collection of works of travel, of which there are different editions in Latin and German. The first was entitled *Collectiones peregrinationum in Indiam orientalem et occidentalem* (Frankfort, 1590). The volumes are illustrated with many plates from de Bry's hand.

Bryan (brī'ạn). Manufacturing village in NW Ohio, county seat of Williams County. 6,365 (1950).

Bryan. City in C Texas, county seat of Brazos County, NE of Austin: marketing center for fruits, vegetables, poultry, livestock, and dairy products. It is the seat of Allen Academy; the Agricultural and Mechanical College of Texas is near Bryan. 18,102 (1950).

Bryan, Charles Page. b. at Chicago, Oct. 2, 1856; d. March 13, 1918. American diplomat. He was a member of the Colorado house of representatives in 1880, and of the Illinois house of representatives in the period 1888–97. Subsequently he served as minister to China (1897–98), to Brazil (1898–1902), to Switzerland (1902–03), to Portugal (1903–10), and to Belgium (1910–11), and as ambassador to Japan (1911–12).

Bryan, Charles Wayland. b. 1867; d. 1945. American politician; brother of William Jennings Bryan (1860–1925). He acted as secretary to his brother, was associated (1901–23) with *The Commoner* as publisher and associate editor, and served as governor of Nebraska (1923–25, 1931–35).

Bryan, Sir **Francis.** d. at Clonmel, Ireland, Feb. 2, 1550. English poet, soldier, and diplomat. He went on missions to Rome and France in the service of Henry VIII. Some of his poetry appeared in *Tottel's Miscellany*. A cousin of Anne Boleyn, he was given the nickname "the vicar of hell" because of his acquiescence to her execution.

Bryan, George. b. at Dublin, Ireland, Aug. 11, 1731; d. Jan. 27, 1791. American jurist and politician. To him is attributed the framing (c1779) of the legislative act calling for gradual abolition of slavery in Pennsylvania. He emigrated (1752) to Philadelphia, where he became prominent in the political faction organized by the Scotch-Irish Presbyterians. A conservative in the pre-Revolutionary period, he served (1764 *et seq.*) on the colonial judiciary and as a member of the assembly. He shared in the framing of the new Pennsylvania constitution and was elected to the state's supreme executive council, serving as its vice-president (1777–79) and briefly (1778) as president. In 1780 he was commissioned a judge of the state supreme court, holding this post until his death.

Bryan, Mary Edwards. b. near Tallahassee, Fla., May 17, 1842; d. June 15, 1913. American journalist and author. In addition to writing novels of a sensational type, which were popular in their time, she was associated with the editorial staffs of several magazines, including the *Sunny South* (later to be called *Uncle Remus' Magazine*), the *Half Hour Magazine*, and *The Golden Age*. She was one of the first writers to work for the Street and Smith magazine group.

Bryan, Thomas Barbour. b. at Alexandria, Va., Dec. 22, 1828; d. at Washington, D.C., Jan. 25, 1906. American lawyer and business promoter. Graduated (1849) from Harvard, he established a law practice at Cincinnati (1849) and at Chicago (1853), where he was also active as a real estate promoter. During the Civil War, he devoted his oratorical bent to recruiting for the Union armies. He served as commissioner (1875–78) of the District of Columbia, and was an originator and vice-president of the World's Columbian Exposition (1893) at Chicago.

Bryan, William Jennings. b. at Salem, Ill., March 19, 1860; d. at Dayton, Tenn., July 26, 1925. American political leader, editor, and popular lecturer, three times a nominee for the presidency of the U.S. Graduated (1881) from Illinois College, he studied (until 1883) at Union College of Law, Chicago. He practiced law (1883–87) at Jacksonville, Ill., before moving to Lincoln, Neb. Elected (1890, 1892) as Democratic representative from Nebraska, he emerged as one of the leading exponents of the Western free-silver movement. Editor in chief (c1894 *et seq.*) of the Omaha *World-Herald*, he was also active as a speaker on the Chautauqua circuit, remaining one of its most popular lecturers for 30 years. His famous "Cross of Gold" speech at the Democratic convention (1896) at Chicago won him his party's presidential nomination, and he gained nation-wide fame as the champion of the agrarian struggle against Eastern high finance groups. He lost the contest, and was again defeated in 1900 and 1908. In 1900 he ran on an anti-imperialist platform opposing the forcible conquest of the Philippines. He was the first presidential candidate to espouse this policy. From 1901 until 1913, when he entered Woodrow Wilson's cabinet as secretary of state, he edited the weekly *Commoner*. An advocate (1905 *et seq.*) of the settlement of international disputes by arbitration, he embodied this principle in 30 treaties (all of which but two were ratified by the Senate) while he was secretary of state. In 1915 he resigned his cabinet post in disagreement with what he regarded as the administration's violation of strict neutrality in writing a stern note to Germany in World War I. This resignation lessened his influence and power in his party. Just before his death, Bryan figured (1925) as one of the prosecuting attorneys and a state's witness against the teaching of Darwinian evolution in the famed Scopes trial held at Dayton, Tenn. Bryan was the chief advocate of two amendments to the U.S. Constitution: the direct election of U.S. senators, and a graduated income tax. He gave powerful support to the woman's suffrage and prohibition amendments to the Constitution.

Bryan, William Lowe. b. near Bloomington, Ind., Nov. 11, 1860—. American educator. A graduate of Indiana University (1886) and Clark University (1892), he was professor of philosophy (1885–1902) at Indiana University, and the university's president (1902–37). He is the author of *The Spirit of Indiana* (1917), *Paradise* (1927), *Wars of Families of Minds* (1940), and other books.

Bryan-Chamorro Treaty (brī'ạn.chä.môr'rō). Treaty signed (Aug. 5, 1914) between the U.S. and Nicaragua which granted to the U.S. the exclusive option of building an interoceanic canal through Nicaragua as well as a 99-year lease of the Great and Little Corn Islands, off the E coast of Nicaragua, and the right to establish a naval base on the Gulf of Fonseca. For these privileges, the U.S. was to pay Nicaragua three million dollars. Costa Rica and El Salvador protested the treaty on the grounds that Nicaragua had leased territory over which she did not have sole jurisdiction. However, Nicaragua refused to comply with the adverse decision of an international tribunal, and the treaty remained in effect.

Bryanites (brī'ạn.īts). [Also, **Bible Christians.**] Methodist body founded (1816) by a Cornish preacher, William O'Bryan.

Bryansk (bryänsk; Anglicized, bri.änsk'). City in the U.S.S.R., capital of an *oblast* (region) of the same name, in the Russian Soviet Federated Socialist Republic, ab. 225 mi. SW of Moscow by rail. Important locomotive works are located here, and its many other machine and metal factories make it one of the leading industrial cities of the U.S.S.R. Hemp growing is important in the surrounding area. 87,473 (1939).

Bryant (brī'ạnt), **Arthur Wynne Morgan.** b. at Dersingham, England, Feb. 18, 1899—. English historian and columnist. A lecturer (1925–26) at Oxford, he produced pageants at Cambridge, Oxford, Wisbech, and Greenwich. On the death of G. K. Chesterton, he took over (1936) the writing of the column "Our Note Book" in the *Illustrated London News*. He is the author of *King Charles II* (1931), *Samuel Pepys, the Man in the Making* (1933), *The National Character* (1934), *The American Ideal* (1936), *The Years of Endurance* (1942), *Years of Victory* (1944), and *The Age of Elegance* (1951).

Bryant, Gridley. b. at Scituate, Mass., Aug. 26, 1789; d. there, June 13, 1867. American civil engineer and inventor. Achieving success as an independent contractor soon after completion of his apprenticeship, he invented (1823) a portable derrick, and was supervising engineer

(1826) for the Quincy Railroad, one of the nation's earliest and probably the first to cover wooden rails with iron plates. Also the inventor of an eight-wheeled car and other railroad improvements, he failed to patent his innovations and died a poor man.

Bryant, Henry Grier. b. at Allegheny, Pa., Nov. 7, 1859; d. Dec. 7, 1932. American explorer. He rediscovered (1891) the Grand Falls of the Hamilton River, in Labrador. Second in command (1892) of the Peary relief expedition, he headed (1894) the Peary auxiliary expedition, and led (1897) an exploring expedition to Mount Saint Elias in Alaska.

Bryant, Jacob. b. at Plymouth, England, 1715; d. at Cypenham, near Windsor, England, Nov. 14, 1804. English antiquary. Among his works is *A New System or an Analysis of Ancient Mythology* (1774–76).

Bryant, John Howard. b. at Cummington, Mass., July 22, 1807; d. at Princeton, Ill., Jan. 14, 1902. American pioneer and minor poet; brother of William Cullen Bryant. Having settled (1831) as a squatter on land near Princeton, Ill., he became one of the community's leading citizens. Active in politics, and a friend of Abraham Lincoln, he aided fugitive Negroes on the "Underground Railway" and was a delegate to the Republican Party conventions in 1856 and 1860. Largely self-taught, he wrote *Poems* (1855) and *Life and Poems* (1894).

Bryant, Joseph Decatur. b. at East Troy, Wis., March 12, 1845; d. April 7, 1914. American surgeon and author, noted for his life-saving operation (1893) on President Grover Cleveland, a feat that was not divulged until 1917. He received (1868) an M.D. degree from the Bellevue Hospital Medical College at New York, and was visiting and consulting surgeon to Bellevue, St. Vincent's, and other New York hospitals. He was the friend and private surgeon of President Cleveland, wrote the *Manual of Operative Surgery* (2 vols., 1884), and served as New York State and City Commissioner of Health. He was senior editor of the *American Practice of Surgery* (8 vols., 1906–11).

Bryant, William Cullen. b. at Cummington, Mass., Nov. 3, 1794; d. at New York, June 12, 1878. American poet and editor, now generally considered to have been, in point of chronology, the first great poet in the history of U.S. literature. He grew up in the Berkshire Hills of western Massachusetts. His father was a physician, politician, and for some years a member (Federalist) of the state legislature. The father's politics are reflected in the son's first poem, *The Embargo: or Sketches of the Times, a Satire, by a Youth of Thirteen*, a bitter attack on Jefferson now interesting only as proof of Bryant's precocity. In 1810 Bryant entered Williams College, as a sophomore, but left after seven months when the financial burden became too great for his father to bear. In 1811 he began to study law, and was formally admitted to the bar in August, 1815; he had disliked his studies, but practiced with some success until 1825. *Thanatopsis* was first published in the *North American Review* for September, 1817; although the poem in its original version is not in its entirety that which we now know (Bryant revised it for his volume of poems issued in 1821), it was nevertheless so good that Richard Henry Dana, one of the editors of the *Review* at that time, at first refused to believe that it could have been written by an American. *Thanatopsis* was followed, in 1818, by *To A Waterfowl*, and in 1821 (as the Phi Beta Kappa Poem at Harvard) by *The Ages*. With five others, these were the poems included in the volume published by Bryant in 1821, and from that time on, although he still continued to practice law until 1825, he was recognized as a major figure in American letters.

Career as a Newspaper Editor. From 1825 to the end of his life Bryant may be said to have had two careers: he remained a poet, but became also one of the most influential of the American newspaper editors of the 19th century. His career as a journalist began in 1825, when he became an editor of the *New York Review* and *Athenaeum Magazine*, a publication which never managed to achieve any considerable success (despite various mergers and changes of title), and Bryant actually thought at one point of returning to law. However, Bryant was offered the assistant editorship of the New York *Evening Post;* he accepted it, and filled it until July, 1829, when he became editor in chief. The *Post*, which was one of the leading newspapers of the U.S., had been Federalist until 1828, but supported Jackson in that year, and thereafter, under Bryant (who had also abandoned his early Federalist sympathies), remained Democratic in its editorial policy. Bryant himself was attracted to Jackson because of their common opposition to legislative restrictions upon commerce, to the Bank of the United States (which represented to Bryant the private control of money), and to any tariff except for revenue. Bryant never held political office, but his political influence, through his editorials in the *Post*, was enormous. He was a combination of idealist and party man, who did not believe in third parties and even opposed the Free Soil Party, much as he objected to slavery, on the practical grounds that a party based upon only a single idea had no prospect of obtaining a majority in a presidential election. However, when opposition to slavery became associated with preservation of the Union in 1860, he supported Lincoln (whom he had met for the first time in 1832,. when Lincoln was an obscure young captain of militia). He swung the *Post* to a limited support of the Republican Party, but withdrew himself during his later years from public participation in politics. Almost at the close of his life he revealed his clear understanding of the major political events of U.S. history in his essay "A Retrospective Glance," the introduction to *A Popular History of the United States*, written with S. H. Gay, in 1878. He here emphasizes the significance of the crusade against slavery and the struggle for preservation of the Union (and, on a lesser level, touches on the evil effect of the Civil War in the growth of crime and fraud). It was Bryant's last appeal in print, to celebrate a record of victories for free speech, free men, and free soil, and to plead for free trade among nations.

Bryan Treaties. Name given to 19 treaties of conciliation negotiated (1913–14) by U.S. Secretary of State William Jennings Bryan. Known as "cooling-off" treaties, they provided for international commissions of five members to conciliate disputes when ordinary diplomatic methods should fail. The treaties were similar to another set of 19 treaties which Secretary of State Frank B. Kellogg obtained in the period 1928–30.

Bryaxis (brī.ak'sis). fl. 4th century B.C. Greek sculptor. He is best known as one of the four sculptors (the others being Scopas, Leochares, and Timotheus) who created the world's first mausoleum, the tomb of Mausolus, king of Caria, at Halicarnassus, which was completed c353 B.C. The contributions of the four artists to this work cannot be discriminated. It is believed almost with certainty that Bryaxis was the sculptor of an *Apollo* which stood in the grove of Daphne near Antioch, and other notable ancient works have been attributed to him. A tripod having a base with sculptured figures of horsemen, recovered at Athens in 1891, is shown by its signature to have been his work.

Bryce (brīs), **James.** [Title, Viscount **Bryce of Dechmont.**] b. at Belfast, Ireland, May 10, 1838; d. at Sidmouth, Devonshire, England, Jan. 22, 1922. English diplomat, statesman, historian, and professor. Educated at the universities of Glasgow, Oxford (Trinity College, B.A., 1862), and Heidelberg, he was elected a fellow (1862) of Oriel College, Oxford. He was called to the bar in 1867, and engaged in law practice until 1882, as well as being regius professor of civil law (1870–93) at Oxford. A Liberal member of Parliament (1880–1907), he became undersecretary of foreign affairs in 1886, chancellor of the duchy of Lancaster in 1892, president of the board of trade in 1894, and served as chief secretary for Ireland (1905–06). From 1907 to 1913 he was British ambassador to the U.S. Awarded the Order of Merit, in 1907, he was created a viscount in 1914. He was one of the founders of the League of Nations. Among his works are *Two Centuries of Irish History; 1691–1870* (1888), *Impressions of South Africa* (1897), *William Ewart Gladstone* (1898), *Studies in History and Jurisprudence* (1901), *Studies in Contemporary Biography* (1903), *Hindrances to Good Citizenship* (1909), *South American Observations and Impressions* (1912), *Essays and Addresses in War Time* (1918), *Modern Democracies* (1921), *International Relations* (1922), *The Study of American History* (1922), and *Memories of Travel* (1923). His best-known writings are *The Holy Roman Empire*

(1862, originally a prize essay) and *The American Commonwealth* (1888), considered a classic in its field.

Bryce, Lloyd Stephens. b. at Flushing, Long Island, N.Y., Sept. 20, 1851; d. there, April 2, 1917. American author, editor, and diplomat. Graduated (1874) from Christ Church College, Oxford, he was elected (1886) a Congressional representative from New York, and was editor (1889–96) of the *North American Review*. His first novel, *Paradise* (1887), was followed by three others. From 1911 to 1913 he served as U.S. minister to the Netherlands and Luxembourg; he was a delegate to the Opium Conference (1913).

Bryce Canyon National Park. Park in S Utah, ab. 215 mi. S of Salt Lake City. It was established in 1928 to preserve an area of brilliantly colored desert rocks, with a box canyon, and many fantastic rock forms sculptured by wind erosion. Area, ab. 56 sq. mi.

Brydges (brij'ez), **James.** [Title, 1st Duke of **Chandos.**] b. Jan. 6, 1673; d. Aug. 9, 1744. English nobleman. He served (1707–12) as paymaster-general of the forces abroad, and was created Viscount Wilton and Earl of Carnarvon (1714), and Marquis of Carnarvon and Duke of Chandos (1719). George Frederick Handel spent two years at his house, producing *Esther*, his first English oratorio, and writing 20 anthems for the chapel services there. Brydges was mentioned by Alexander Pope in *Characters of Men* (February, 1733).

Brydges, John. [Title, 1st Baron **Chandos of Sudeley.**] b. c1490; d. April 12, 1556. English soldier. He was a Catholic companion of Henry VIII at Calais (1532), at Boulogne (1533), and at the reception (1539) of Anne of Cleves. A supporter of Mary Tudor, at her accession he became lieutenant of the Tower of London, a post which he resigned in 1554. He aided (1553–54) in suppressing the Wyatt rebellion, having fired the Tower guns on the rebels. He had custody (March 18–May 19, 1554) of the princess Elizabeth, toward whom he was lenient, of Lady Jane Grey, from whom he requested a memorial prior to her execution (Feb. 12, 1554), and of Thomas Wyatt, whose execution he also arranged (1554).

Brydges, Sir **Samuel Egerton.** b. at Wooton House, Kent, England, Nov. 30, 1762; d. near Geneva, Switzerland, Sept. 8, 1837. English lawyer, miscellaneous writer, and genealogist, a member of Parliament from 1812 to 1818. He was the author of poems, novels, *Censura Literaria* (1805–09), *British Bibliographer* (1810–14), *Res Literariae* (1821–22), *Autobiography* (1834), and others.

Brymner (brim'nėr), **William.** b. at Greenock, Scotland, Dec. 14, 1855; d. June 18, 1925. Canadian painter, who served (1909–18) as president of the Royal Canadian Academy. He studied at Paris, and exhibited in the U.S. and Canada, winning awards at the Pan-American Exposition of 1901, and the St. Louis Exposition of 1904.

Brynhild (brin'hild). In the *Volsunga Saga*, one of the Valkyries; a daughter of Odin, by whom she was put into a fire-encircled sleep for her disobedience in giving victory to the wrong warrior. Sigurd passed through the flame and wakened her, and they became lovers. In the kingdom of the Nibelungs, Sigurd forgot Brynhild, married Gudrun, and, in Gunnar's guise, helped Gunnar, the king, win Brynhild for his wife. When Brynhild learned of the deception, she had Sigurd murdered and took her own life.

Bryn Mawr (brin mär'). Unincorporated community in SE Pennsylvania, in Delaware and Montgomery counties: residential community near Philadelphia and seat of Bryn Mawr College. Under the urban definition established for use in the 1950 census, Bryn Mawr was counted with adjoining communities; the last official separate enumeration was 4,777 (1940).

Brynmawr (brin.mour'). Urban district in S Wales, in Brecknockshire, ab. 3 mi. NE of Ebbw Vale, ab. 156 mi. W of London by rail. 6,524 (1951).

Bryskett (bris'kẹt), **Lodowick** or **Lewis.** b. c1545; d. c1612. English poet and translator; a friend of Sir Philip Sidney and Edmund Spenser. Educated at Cambridge (1559), he served as clerk of the council in Ireland (c1571), clerk of chancery (succeeded by Spenser, c1581), and in other Irish offices until 1600, and was reputedly the holder of large estates at Dublin, Cavan, and Cork. He accompanied Sidney on a continental tour (1572–75), and studied Greek under Spenser (1582). His poems include two elegies contributed to Spenser's *Astrophel* (1586; published with *Colin Clout*). His chief original work was a translation from Baptista Giraldo's philosophical treatise, which he entitled *A Discourse of Civil Life* (published in 1606, written 20 years earlier).

Bryson of Heraclea (brī'sọn; her.ạ.klē'ạ). fl. 5th century B.C. Greek mathematician, a member of the Pythagorean school. He went a step further than his contemporary Antiphon toward the quadrature of the circle by considering not simply inscribed polygons of an increasing number of sides, but also circumscribed polygons. He believed, erroneously, that the area of the circle was the arithmetical mean between the areas of inscribed and circumscribed polygons.

Brython (brith'on). Name applied to themselves by the Celts of southern Britain who successfully resisted the Teutonic invaders in the mountainous regions of the western coast, and whose language, or languages, Brythonic, was subsequently found in Wales, Cumbria, and parts of Devon and Cornwall. The name is sometimes used interchangeably with Cymry (Cumbri).

Brythonic (bri.thon'ik). Group of languages including Gaulish, Welsh, Cornish, and Breton (or Armorican), belonging to the Celtic subfamily of Indo-European languages.

Bryusov (bryö'sọf), **Valeri Yakovlevich.** b. at Moscow, 1873; d. there, Oct. 9, 1924. Russian poet, leader of the symbolist school. He was a prolific man of letters, producing stories, novels, plays, critical essays, and studies in metrics, in addition to numerous lyrics and translations of verse. In spite of his bourgeois background he joined the Communist Party after the Russian Revolution and tried to reorient his writing accordingly. An English translation of several of his stories makes up *The Republic of the Southern Cross* (1918). A few of his poems in an English rendering are included in Avrahm Yarmolinsky's *A Treasury of Russian Verse* (1949).

Brzeg (bzhek). [German, **Brieg.**] City in SW Poland, in the *województwo* (province) of Wrocław, formerly in Silesia, Germany, situated on the Odra (Oder) River, ab. 26 mi. SE of the city of Wrocław (Breslau). Before World War II it had livestock markets, textile and machine industries, and a sugar refinery. Buildings of interest include two 14th-century Gothic churches, rebuilt in the 18th century, the Jesuit Church (1735), the castle of the former dukes of Brzeg, built (1547–70) in the Renaissance style by Italian architects and partially destroyed by bombardment in 1741, and a 14th-century town hall. Brzeg received town privileges in 1250, and became the residence of duke Boleslav III in the 13th century. It remained under the rule of the Silesian dukes of the Piast family from 1290 to 1675, when it came under Austria. The city was bombarded and conquered by Frederick II of Prussia in 1741; its fortifications were razed by the French in 1806. During World War II it was the site of a concentration camp. The Russians took the city on Feb. 7, 1945. Pop. 31,419 (1939); 7,744 (1946).

Brześć nad Bugiem (bzheshch näd bö'gyem) or **Brześć Litewski** (lē.tef'skē). Polish names of **Brest,** U.S.S.R.

Brzeżany (bzhe.zhä'ni). Town in the U.S.S.R., in the Ukrainian Soviet Socialist Republic, ab. 49 mi. SE of Lvov: formerly in Poland. Pop. ab. 11,700.

Bua (bö'ä). See also **Čiovo.**

Bua. One of four subgroups of the Sudanic-speaking Bobo people of W Africa, inhabiting the N part of the Ivory Coast. They are also known as Bobo-fing, or "black Bobo." Their population is estimated at ab. 65,000 (by M. Delafosse, *Haut-Sénégal-Niger*, 1912).

Buachalla (bö'ạ.ċhạ.lạ), **Dómhnall ua.** Irish name of **Buckley, Donal.**

Buache (bü.åsh), **Philippe.** b. at Paris, Feb. 7, 1700; d. Jan. 27, 1773. French geographer, uncle of Jean Nicolas Buache de la Neuville. His works include *Considérations géographiques et physiques sur les nouvelles découvertes de la grande mer* (1753) and *Atlas physique* (1754).

Buache de la Neuville (dẹ lå nė.vēl), **Jean Nicolas.** b. at La Neuville-au-Pont, Marne, France, Feb. 15, 1741; d. at Paris, Nov. 21, 1825. French geographer; nephew of Philippe Buache. He wrote *Géographie élémentaire ancienne et moderne* (1769–72) and other works.

Bubastis (bū.bas'tis). [Also: **Bubastus** (-tus); modern name, **Tel Basta**; Egyptian, **Pa-Bast**; in the Old Testament, **Pi-Beseth.**] City of ancient Egypt, near the modern Zagazig, situated on the Pelusiac branch of the Nile. It was the holy city of the Egyptian goddess Bast, whose sacred animal was the cat.

Bubble (bub'l). In John Cooke's comedy *Greene's Tu Quoque* (published in 1614), a servant. He becomes rich and endeavors to deceive people into believing that he is a gentleman by using the affectations of society, particularly the phrase "tu quoque," which is ever in his mouth. The character was played by a favorite actor named Greene (hence the title of the play).

Buber (bö'bėr), **Martin.** b. at Vienna, Feb. 8, 1878—. Jewish philosopher and religious scholar. He studied at the Universities of Vienna, Leipzig, Berlin, and Zurich, was editor (1901) of the Vienna *Welt,* edited (1916–24) *Der Jude,* was professor of religion and ethics (1924–33) at the University of Frankfort on the Main, and became (1938) professor of social philosophy at the Hebrew University, Jerusalem. Known for his role in the Zionist movement, he supported the creation of a Jewish culture and pioneered in the revival of Hasidic lore and thought. Among his works are *Die Geschichte des Rabbi Nachman* (1906), *Die Legende des Baalschem* (1907), *Ekstatische Konfessionen* (1908), *Völker, Staaten und Zion* (1916), *Mein Weg zum Chassidismus* (1918), *Ich und Du* (1923), *Die Stunde und die Erkenntnis* (1936), and *Between Man and Man* (1947).

Bubona (bų̄.bō'nạ). In Roman mythology, a female divinity, protectress of cows and oxen.

Bubu de Montparnasse (bü.bü dẹ môṅ.pȧr.nȧs). Novel, or connected short stories (1901) by the French writer Charles Louis Philippe; also a play and a motion picture based on Philippe's pathetic treatment of the theme of cuckoldry.

Buçaco (bö.sä'kö). Portuguese name of **Bussaco.**

Bucaramanga (bö"kä.rä.mäng'gä). City in N central Colombia, capital of Santander department: center of a rich coffee and tobacco growing district, with allied industries. 104,179 (1951).

Bucareli y Ursúa (bö.kä.rā'lē ē ör.sö'ä), **Antonio María.** b. at Seville, Spain, Jan. 24, 1717; d. in Mexico, April 9, 1779. Spanish general and administrator. From 1760 to 1771 he was governor of Cuba, and from 1771 until his death viceroy of New Spain (Mexico).

Bucas Islands (bö.käs'). Three small islands of the Philippines, lying NE of Mindanao and SW of Siargao, and forming part of the E boundary of Surigao Strait. On the E coast of Bucas Grande is Socorro, a harbor safe in all weather. Area of the three islands, 53.4 sq. mi.; of Bucas Grande, 50 sq. mi.

Buccaneers. Name applied originally to a gang of adventurers and pirates which, in the 17th century, attained an almost national importance in the West Indies and on the coasts of South America. It had its nucleus in the English, French, and Dutch smugglers who carried on a clandestine trade with the Spanish island of Santo Domingo (now Hispaniola); they hunted the wild cattle there, drying the meat over fires. Gradually they formed regular settlements, not only on Santo Domingo, but on many of the smaller islands. As they became stronger they began to prey on Spanish commerce. In 1630 they seized the island of Tortuga and made it their headquarters. In 1655 they aided the English in the conquest of Jamaica, and this became another center; and in 1664 they settled the Bahamas. Under their leader Sir Henry Morgan, they ravaged the coasts of the Gulf of Mexico and the Caribbean Sea, and made expeditions inland; Portobelo was sacked; in 1671 Morgan crossed the isthmus and burned Panama, and from that year to 1685 the Buccaneers practically commanded the West Indian seas. Their immense spoils were divided equally, only the captain of a ship taking a larger share; French, Dutch, English, and Germans were banded together, their only bond being a common interest in spoils and a deep hatred of the Spaniards. In 1680 they again crossed the isthmus, seized some Spanish ships in the Pacific, and for several years raided the western coasts of Mexico, Peru, and Chile. After 1690 the war between France and England tended to separate the pirates of these two nations, and the impoverished coasts could no longer support their depredations. They gradually returned to the West Indies and Europe, and were drawn into the armies and navies of different powers.

Bucentaur (bū.sen'tôr). The state ship of the Venetian Republic, used in the annual ceremony of wedding the Adriatic, which was enjoined upon the Venetians by Pope Alexander III to commemorate the victory of the Venetians under Doge Sebastiano Ziani over the fleet of Frederick Barbarossa, in the 12th century. On Ascension day of each year a ring was dropped from the *Bucentaur* into the Adriatic, with the words "We espouse thee, Sea, in token of true and lasting dominion." The ceremony was attended by the entire diplomatic corps. The ship perhaps took her name from the figure of a bucentaur (head of a man and body of a bull) in her bows. Three of the name were built. The last was destroyed by the French in 1798.

Bucephalus (bų̄.sef'ạ.lus). Favorite horse of Alexander the Great which, after accompanying its master through his principal campaigns, died (326 B.C.) at the age of 30. Alexander buried the horse with great pomp on the banks of the Hydaspes River (now the Jhelum), in India, and built at the site the city of Bucephala, traces of which exist across the river from the modern town of Jhelum, in Pakistan.

Bucer (bū'sėr), **Martin.** [Also, **Butzer;** original surname, **Kuhhorn.**] b. at Schlettstadt (Sélestat), in Alsace, 1491; d. at Cambridge, England, Feb. 28, 1551. German theologian; a coadjutor of Martin Luther. He became chaplain to the elector palatine Frederick in 1520, and pastor at Landstuhl in 1522, married (1522) the former nun Elizabeth Pallas, and became (1524) pastor of Saint Aurelia's at Strasbourg. Refusing (1548) to sign the Augsburg Interim, he accepted, at the invitation of Thomas Cranmer, a professorate of theology at Cambridge in 1549. He is chiefly noted for his efforts to unite the different Protestant bodies, especially the Lutherans and Zwinglians, in which he was only partially successful.

Buch (böċh), Baron **Christian Leopold von.** b. at Stolpe, Prussia, April 26, 1774; d. at Berlin, March 4, 1853. German geologist and traveler. He made valuable studies of the relationship between volcanic action and the formation of the earth's surface. His works include *Geognostische Beobachtungen auf Reisen durch Deutschland und Italien* (1802–09), *Reise durch Norwegen und Lappland* (1810), and *Physikalische Beschreibung der Canarischen Inseln* (1825).

Buchan (buk'ạn, buċh'-). Region in E Scotland, now a part of Aberdeenshire, ab. 25 mi. N of the city of Aberdeen. It is a hilly farming region. Originally it was a part of the earldom of Mar and Buchan, one of the seven original Scottish earldoms. In the 13th century Buchan separated from Mar, and was made an earldom, extending from the Ythan river to the Deveron river. It was later incorporated into the kingdom of Scotland, though the title remains.

Buchan, 2nd Earl of. Title of **Comyn, Alexander.**

Buchan, 3rd Earl of. Title of **Comyn, John** (d. c1313).

Buchan, Alexander. b. at Kinnesswood, Kinross-shire, Scotland, April 11, 1829; d. at Edinburgh, May 13, 1907. Scottish meteorologist. He published numerous works and papers upon meteorological subjects, including *The Handy Book of Meteorology* (1867), *Introductory Text-book of Meteorology* (1871), *Atmospheric Circulation* (1889), and *Oceanic Circulation* (1895). As secretary (1860 *et seq.*) of the Scottish Meteorological Society, he assisted in the establishment of an observatory on Ben Nevis.

Buchan, David. b. 1780; d. c1839. English naval commander and arctic explorer. He explored the Exploits River, Newfoundland, in 1811, penetrating 160 miles into the interior, and commanded an arctic expedition in 1818, reaching Spitsbergen with the *Dorothea* and the *Trent.* He became high sheriff of Newfoundland, and was subsequently promoted to the rank of captain. He was lost with the ship *Upton Castle,* and his name was struck from the list of living captains in 1839.

Buchan, Elspeth. [Maiden name, **Simpson.**] b. near Banff, Scotland, 1738; d. near Dumfries, Scotland, 1791. Scottish religious enthusiast. She was the daughter of John Simpson, an innkeeper, and married Robert Buchan, a potter, from whom she separated. She moved to Glasgow in 1781, where she heard (1783) Hugh White, of the Relief Church at Irvine, preach, with the result that she moved to Irvine and converted White to the belief that she was the woman of Revelation xii, in whom the light of God was restored to men, and that he was the man-child she had brought forth. They with others of the "Buchanites" were banished from Irvine in 1784, and settled at New Cample, where they enjoyed community of goods and person. The sect became extinct in 1848.

Buchan, Sir **John.** [Title, 1st Baron **Tweedsmuir.**] b. at Perth, Scotland, Aug. 26, 1875; d. at Montreal, Canada, Feb. 11, 1940. Scottish government official, novelist, essayist, biographer, and historian. Educated at Glasgow University and at Brasenose College, Oxford, he was called to the bar in 1901. During World War I, he served (1915) in France as a war correspondent, was a member (1916–17) of the British headquarters staff in France, and served (1917 *et seq.*) with the British information department. After serving (1927–35) as a member of Parliament for the Scottish universities, he was governor-general of Canada (1935–40). He was the author of *John Burnet of Barns* (1898), *A Lodge in the Wilderness* (1906), *Prester John* (1910), *Salute to Adventurers* (1915), *The 39 Steps* (1915), *Greenmantle* (1916), *The Path of the King* (1921), *The Three Hostages* (1924), *The Blanket of the Dark* (1931), *The Gap in the Curtain* (1932), and many other adventure novels and tales, several of which have for their hero Richard Hannay. He wrote biographies of Sir Walter Raleigh (1911), Lord Minto (1924), Julius Caesar (1932), Sir Walter Scott (1932), and Oliver Cromwell (1934). Author also of histories of Brasenose College (1898), the battle of Jutland (1917), the battle of the Somme (1917), South African forces in France (1920), World War I (4 vols., 1921–22), the British Empire in World War I (1923), and others, of volumes of essays (1896, 1908, 1935), of *Poems—Scots and English* (1917), and of the autobiographical *Pilgrim's Way* (1940).

Buchan, Peter. b. at Peterhead, Aberdeenshire, Scotland, 1790; d. at London, Sept. 19, 1854. Scottish poet, printer, dramatist, and collector and publisher of ballads. He opened a printing office (1816) at Peterhead, having learned the technique of printing in ten days, and devised (1819) a press worked by foot to take the place of the hand press. He collected and published *Ancient Ballads and Songs of the North of Scotland* (2 vols., 1828), containing many ballads never before printed and new versions of previously published ones, and also compiled *Scottish Traditional Versions of Ancient Ballads* (1845), which was published by the Percy Society. At his death he left two volumes of unpublished ballad material, now housed in the British Museum. He was the author also of *The Recreation of Leisure Hours, being Songs and Verses in the Scottish Dialect* (1814), *Annals of Peterhead* (1819), *Treatise proving that Brutes have Souls and are Immortal* (1824), *The Peterhead Smugglers of the Last Century, or William and Annie* (1834, a three-act melodrama), *Account of the Chivalry of the Ancients* (1840), and other works, many of them printed on his own Peterhead press.

Buchanan (bū̦.kan′a̦n, bu-). City in S Lower Michigan, in Berrien County. 5,224 (1950).

Buchanan, Dugald. [Called the **"Cowper of the Highlands."**] b. at Ardoch, Balquhidder Parish, Perthshire, Scotland, 1716; d. at Rannoch, Perthshire, Scotland, July 2, 1768. Scottish Gaelic schoolmaster, preacher, hymnist, and religious poet. He taught school in his native parish, and was schoolmaster and preacher (1755 *et seq.*) at Kinloch Rannoch in Fortingale. He was the author of *Spiritual Hymns* (1767), Gaelic poems, of which "The Day of Judgment," "The Skull," "The Dream," and "The Winter" are considered among his best. His poetry has been translated into English by various authors.

Buchanan, Franklin. b. at Baltimore, Sept. 17, 1800; d. in Talbot County, Md., May 11, 1874. American naval officer, with the Confederate navy in the Civil War. He was one of the organizers (1845) of the Naval Academy at Annapolis, and was its first superintendent (1845–47). During the Mexican War, he commanded the sloop *Germantown.* As commander of the flagship of Matthew C. Perry's expedition to Japan, he was the first U.S. officer to set foot (1853) in that country. His handling of the *Merrimac* in its battle (1862) against a Union squadron in Hampton Roads brought a promotion to admiral. Commander of the Confederate naval forces in the battle of Mobile Bay (1864), he was taken prisoner after his defeat by Farragut.

Buchanan, George. b. at Killearn, Stirlingshire, Scotland, in February, 1506; d. at Edinburgh, Sept. 29, 1582. Scottish historian and scholar; tutor (1570) of James VI of Scotland. He taught at Bordeaux (1540–43), Paris (1544–47), and St. Andrews (1566–70). In 1571 he published *Detectio Mariae Reginae,* a violent attack on Mary, Queen of Scots, whom he held responsible for the murder of Darnley. Among his other works are *De jure regni apud Scotos* (1579), *Rerum Scoticarum historia* (1582), a version of the Psalms, translations of the *Medea* and *Alcestis,* and the dramas *Baptistes,* and *Jephthes.*

Buchanan, Sir **George Cunningham.** b. April 20, 1865; d. April 14, 1940. British civil engineer, who built ports, dockyards, and river works in many parts of the world. He reorganized the port of Basra in Mesopotamia during World War I.

Buchanan, James. b. near Mercersburg, Pa., April 23, 1791; d. near Lancaster, Pa., June 1, 1868. Fifteenth president of the U.S. Graduated (1809) from Dickinson College, he studied law and was admitted (1812) to the bar at Lancaster. In 1814 he became a member of the Pennsylvania house of representatives, and subsequently he served as a member of Congress (1821–31), minister to Russia (1831–33), U.S. senator (1833–45), and secretary of state (1845–49) under Polk. In 1853 he became minister to Great Britain, in which post he aided in the drafting (1854) of the Ostend Manifesto. He was chosen Democratic presidential candidate in 1856. As president (1857–61), he was caught in the sharp struggle between Northern and Southern interests. Placing his faith in strict construction and the mechanical application of law, he was by character unequal to the problems which rent the Union. When he left his office to Lincoln, the Civil War had all but actually begun. The *Works of Jas. Buchanan* (12 vols., 1908–11) were edited by J. B. Moore.

Buchanan, John. b. in Prince Georges County, Md., 1772; d. Nov. 6, 1844. American jurist. He studied law at Winchester, Va., and Hagerstown, Md., and served as a member (1797–99) of the lower house of the Maryland state legislature. In 1806 he was appointed associate justice of the Maryland court of appeals. He became (1824) the court's chief justice, holding this post until his death, except for a brief period (1837) spent in England as member of a commission to negotiate the sale of state-secured stocks.

Buchanan, Joseph. b. in Washington County, Va., Aug. 24, 1785; d. Sept. 29, 1829. American philosopher, educator, journalist, and inventor. He attended (1804 *et seq.*) Transylvania University at Lexington, Ky., joining (1809) its faculty as professor of the institutes of medicine. His lectures, the *Philosophy of Human Nature* (1812), have been termed a pioneer venture in American philosophical thought. He introduced the Pestalozzian system of education into Kentucky, and edited a number of Kentucky newspapers, including the Lexington *Reporter* and the Louisville *Focus* (1826 *et seq.*). His interest in inventions, which began with experiments in the "music of light" produced by varicolored glasses, also resulted in the design (1821–22) of a spiral boiler.

Buchanan, Joseph Ray. b. at Hannibal, Mo., Dec. 6, 1851; d. at Montclair, N.J., Sept. 13, 1924. American labor leader and journalist. Following his early career as a journalist and typesetter in Colorado, he became a prominent trade-unionist at Denver, and was active in several strikes. A member of the Typographical Union, he established the *Labor Enquirer,* heading this Denver journal from 1882 to 1887, when he moved to Chicago. He was subsequently labor editor of the American Press Association, and labor editor (1904–15) of the New York *Evening Journal.* A Socialist in principle, he was also an organizer of the Populist Party, serving on its national committee (1892, 1896, 1900). His autobiography was printed as *The Story of a Labor Agitator* (1903).

Buchanan, Joseph Rodes. b. at Frankfort, Ky., Dec. 11, 1814; d. at San Jose, Calif., Dec. 26, 1899. American writer and medical-spiritualist practitioner. He graduated (1842) from the medical school of the University of Louisville, where his interest in phrenology and cerebral physiology formed the basis of the two alleged sciences he later outlined: "psychometry" and "sarcognomy." He maintained that a knowledge of the relations between the body and the soul could, in application by the skilled psychometer, cure all diseases. A popular lecturer of the day, he disseminated his views on eclectic medicine in his magazine, *The Journal of Man;* his works include *Therapeutic Sarcognomy* (1884) and *Manual of Psychometry* (1885).

Buchanan, Robert Christie. b. at Baltimore, March 1, 1811; d. at Washington, D.C., Nov. 29, 1878. American soldier, with the Union army in the Civil War. Graduated (1830) from the U.S. Military Academy, he participated in the Black Hawk War (1832) and the campaign against the Seminole Indians (1837–38), and was brevetted a lieutenant colonel in the Mexican War. He served at the battles of Antietam and Second Bull Run in the Civil War, and later (1868) commanded the Department of Louisiana.

Buchanan, Robert Williams. b. at Caverswall, Staffordshire, England, Aug. 18, 1841; d. at Streatham, London, June 10, 1901. Scottish poet, dramatist, and novelist. Educated at the University of Glasgow, he went to London at the age of 19, and wrote for the *Athenaeum, All the Year Round,* and other journals. He coined the phrase "the fleshly school of poetry," which he used as the title of an article (in the *Contemporary Review,* 1871), attacking Swinburne, Rossetti, and the Pre-Raphaelite leaders. The controversy lasted for ten years (1866–76); he sued Swinburne, and won, but later dedicated one of his novels, *God and the Man* (1881), to Rossetti. He was the author of *Undertones* (1863), *London Poems* (1866), *North Coast* (1867), *White Rose and Red* (1873), *Balder the Beautiful* (1877), *Ballads of Life, Love, and Humor* (1882), and other books of poetry. His novels include *The Shadow of the Sword* (1876), *A Child of Nature* (1881), and *Father Anthony* (1898). *A Nine Days' Queen* (1880), *Lady Clare* (1883), *Storm-Beaten* (1883), *Alone in London* (1884; with his sister-in-law, Harriet Jay), *A Man's Shadow* (1889), *The Charlatan* (1894), and *The Strange Adventures of Miss Brown* (1895) are all plays. He also dramatized Henry Fielding's *Tom Jones* as *Sophia* (1886), and the same author's *Joseph Andrews* as *Joseph's Sweetheart* (1888).

Buchanan, Thomas. b. at Glasgow, Scotland, Dec. 24, 1744; d. at New York, Nov. 10, 1815. American merchant. He attended the University of Glasgow, and came to New York in 1763 where, with a relative, he established the commercial firm of W. and T. Buchanan. His house occupied a leading place among colonial traders; during the Revolutionary War he was a Loyalist, continuing active trade, and was vice-president (1780–83) of the chamber of commerce.

Buchanan, William Insco. b. in Miami County, Ohio, Sept. 10, 1852; d. Oct. 16, 1909. American diplomat and businessman. He settled (1882) at Sioux City, Iowa where his ability as an amusement-manager led to his service as Democratic member of his state's commission to the World's Columbian Exposition (1893) at Chicago. He was appointed envoy extraordinary and minister plenipotentiary to the Argentine Republic (1894), director-general of the Pan-American Exposition (1901) at Buffalo, N.Y., and a delegate to the Second International Conference of American States (1901) at Mexico City. The first U.S. emissary to Panama (1903–05), he subsequently served as the agent of the U.S. on other international bodies, particularly those concerned with Latin-American affairs.

Bucharest (bū.kạ.rest′, bö-). [Also: **Bukharest;** Rumanian, **București.**] Capital of Rumania, in the region of Muntenia, situated in a plain on the Dâmbovița River, ab. 50 mi. N of the Bulgarian border. Formerly the capital of Walachia, it was the residence of the Walachian rulers from the 14th century until 1861. It is a railroad junction and an important industrial and commercial center; manufactures textiles, chemicals, leather, metal, and mill products, foodstuffs, spirits, oil, iron, and machinery. It is the seat of a metropolitan primateship of the Greek Orthodox Church and of a Roman Catholic archbishopric. 1,041,807 (1948).

Chief Buildings. There are in Bucharest public gardens, a castle, government buildings, many churches, the oldest university in Rumania, the only school of technology in the country, and schools of music, art, agriculture, forestry, and military science. Other important buildings include the Metropolitan Church (1649), the monastery church of Radu voda (1572), the Bucur Church (15th century), and the cathedral, and museums of natural history and archaeology, a picture gallery, the central and university libraries, and the national theater.

History. Bucharest was the scene of treaties between Russia and Turkey (May 28, 1812), between Serbia and Bulgaria (March 3, 1886), between Rumania, Serbia, Greece, Montenegro, and Bulgaria (Aug. 10, 1913), and between Rumania and the Central Powers (May 7, 1918). On Dec. 6, 1916, it was surrendered without resistance to the troops of General Mackensen and was held by the Germans until 1918. In World War II after the abdication of King Carol it was the scene of serious disturbances; it was taken by the Germans in 1940.

Bucharest, Treaty of. Treaty concluded on May 28, 1812. It put an end to the war which had been carried on between Russia and Turkey since 1806, and established the Prut and lower Danube rivers as the boundary between the two countries.

Bucharest, Treaty of. Treaty formalizing the settlements that followed the Second Balkan War, except for those between Turkey and Bulgaria. This treaty, signed on Aug. 10, 1913, embodied these main features: the N part of Dobruja was awarded to Rumania; Serbia and Greece were permitted to retain almost all the parts of Macedonia which they had occupied (including Salonika for Greece); and the Bulgarian seaboard was confined to the area between the Mesta and Maritsa rivers, with only one port, that of Dede Agach (now Alexandroúpolis).

Bucharest, Treaty of. Treaty marking the conclusion of peace arrangements between the Central Powers and Rumania on May 7, 1918. This treaty awarded to Bulgaria the Dobruja and to Austria-Hungary the eastern reaches and passes in the Transylvanian mountains. Rumania received Bessarabia from Russia, but its only outlet on the Black Sea lay in the use of Constanța. Oil-well leases to Germany and agricultural agreements with the Central Powers brought Rumanian economy under the control of the Central Powers. The armistice of November, 1918, did away with this agreement.

Bücheler (bü′ċhẹ.lėr), **Franz.** b. June 3, 1837; d. at Bonn, Germany, May 8, 1908. German philologist, appointed (1870) professor of classical philology at Bonn. He is especially known for his critical work on the classics.

Buchenwald (bö′ċhẹn.vält). Village in C Germany, in the *Land* (state) of Thuringia, Russian Zone, near Weimar. It began to be used as a concentration camp for political and racial prisoners immediately after the Nazis came to power in 1933. Many Jews and political prisoners were put to death here by a variety of methods, and those dead were quickly replaced by new arrivals; the emaciated survivors were liberated by American troops on April 13, 1945. Among the prisoners was at one time the former French premier Léon Blum.

Bucher (bū′kėr; German, bü′ċhėr), **John Conrad.** b. at Neunkirch, Switzerland, June 10, 1730; d. at Annville, Pa., Aug. 15, 1780. American German-Reformed clergyman and soldier. He attended the University of Marburg before coming (c1755) to America. After serving as an ensign in the 1st Battalion of the Pennsylvania Regiment during the French and Indian Wars, he was ordained as a preacher in 1767, he led congregations at Carlisle, Middletown, and Hummelstown, Pa. As a frontier missionary, he was the first minister to preach in German beyond the Alleghenies.

Bücher (bü′ċhėr), **Karl.** b. at Kirberg, Germany, Feb. 16, 1847; d. at Leipzig, Germany, Nov. 13, 1930. German economist, one of the champions of the younger historical school of political economics in Germany, notable as founder of *Zeitungskunde* (Science of Journalism). He served as a professor (1882 *et seq.*) at Dorpat, Munich, Basel, Karlsruhe, and Leipzig, where he founded the Institut für Zeitungskunde. Author of *Die Entstehung der Volkswirtschaft* (The Origin of National Economy, 1893, 1912), *Arbeit und Rhythmus* (Work and Rhythm, 1896), and *Gemischte Aufsätze zur Zeitungskunde* (Miscellaneous Essays on the Science of Journalism, 1925).

Buchez (bü.shā), **Philippe Joseph Benjamin.** b. at Matagne-la-Petite, Namur, Belgium, March 31, 1796; d. at Rodez, Aveyron, France, Aug. 12, 1865. French man of letters and politician. He wrote *Introduction à la science de l'histoire* (1833), *Essai d'un traité complet de philosophie* (1839), and *Histoire de la formation de la nationalité française* (1859), and edited *Histoire parlementaire de la révolution française* (1833–38).

Buchholtz (bȯċh'holts), **Johannes.** b. at Odense, Denmark, Feb. 22, 1882; d. at Struer, Denmark, Aug. 5, 1940. Danish writer of novels, poems, plays, and short stories. He is best known for his first work, the novel *Egholms Gud* (Egholm's God, 1915), and for his prize-winning *Susanne* (1931).

Buchholz (bȯċh'holts). Town in E Germany, in the *Land* (state) of Saxony, Russian Zone, formerly in the free state of Saxony, situated in the Erzgebirge near the border of Czechoslovakia, ab. 18 mi. S of Chemnitz: an old mining town. Prior to World War II it produced chiefly knitwear, ribbons, paperware, and machinery. The Church of Saint Catherine (1504–21) is in the Gothic style. The population is predominantly Protestant. 8,067 (1946).

Buchhorn (bȯċh'hôrn). Former name of **Friedrichshafen.**

Buchlau Conference (bȯċh'lou). Meeting in September, 1908 (at Buchlau Castle, in Moravia, home of Count Leopold von Berchtold, the Austro-Hungarian ambassador to Russia), between the Austro-Hungarian foreign minister Alois Lexa, Count von Aehrenthal, and the Russian foreign minister Aleksandr Petrovich Izvolsky, to discuss Bosnia-Hercegovina and the Straits (i.e., the Bosporus and the Dardanelles). In the agreement announced on Sept. 16, Russia promised not to interfere with the Austro-Hungarian annexation of Bosnia-Hercegovina, and Austria-Hungary pledged a similar attitude in relation to the opening up of the Straits to Russian warships. An international conference to ratify these agreements and to make some changes in the Berlin Treaty of 1878 was also proposed. Neither France nor Great Britain was willing, however, to accept the terms of the arrangement so far as Russian use of the Straits was concerned. Austria-Hungary therefore went ahead with the annexation of Bosnia-Hercegovina (thus precipitating the Balkan Crisis of 1908) without being compelled to make any important concessions to the Russians.

Buchman (bu̇k'ma̤n), **Frank Nathan Daniel.** b. at Pennsburg, Pa., June 4, 1878—. American evangelist, leader of the Oxford Group and the movement for Moral Re-Armament (MRA). He was graduated (B.A., 1899; M.A., 1902; D.D., 1926) from Muhlenberg College and attended (1921–22) Westminster College at Cambridge University, founding (1921) during a visit to Oxford University the program of spiritual restoration known as the Oxford Group (or Buchmanism). Based on the motto "world-changing through life-changing," Buchmanism advocates character improvement as the first step toward an ideal society. It stresses honesty and selflessness. Under Buchman's leadership the movement was organized in more than 60 countries. In 1938, at a meeting held at London, he introduced a campaign for Moral Re-Armament, extending his principles of individual and social change. The MRA was active in the U.S. and Canada during World War II and conducted a 30-nation world assembly in Switzerland in 1946. His works include *Rising Tide* (1937) and *You Can Defend America* (1941).

Buchmann (bȯċh'män), **Theodor.** Original name of **Bibliander, Theodore.**

Büchner (büċh'nėr). German (Hessian) family that distinguished itself in science, philosophy, literature, and public affairs. It included three brothers, Georg, Ludwig, and Alexander, and a sister, Luise.

Büchner, Alexander. b. at Darmstadt, Germany, Oct. 25, 1827; d. March 7, 1904. German professor and man of letters. He became an instructor at Zurich, Switzerland, in 1852, went to France in 1857, and was a professor of foreign literatures at Caen from 1862. He wrote many critical works in German and French, such as *Geschichte der englischen Poesie* (1855), *Französische Literaturbilder* (1858), and *Les comédies de Shakespeare* (1864).

Buchner (bȯċh'nėr), **Eduard.** b. at Munich, May 20, 1860; d. in World War I, at Focşani, Rumania, Aug. 13, 1917. German chemist; brother of Hans Buchner. He became assistant in the chemical laboratory at Munich in 1890, lecturer at Kiel in 1893, professor extraordinary at Tübingen in 1896, and professor in the Agricultural College, Berlin, in 1898, in the University of Breslau in 1909, and the University of Würzburg in 1911. He made various investigations in organic chemistry, and in particular demonstrated (with his brother) that alcoholic fermentation is caused by an enzyme (zymase) in the yeast-cells. In 1907 he received the Nobel prize for chemistry. He published *Die Zymasegärung* (Zymase-fermentation, 1903, in joint authorship with others) and *Beziehungen der Chemie zur Landwirtschaft* (Relations of Chemistry to Agriculture, 1904).

Buchner (buk'nėr), **Edward Franklin.** b. at Paxton, Ill., Sept. 3, 1868; d. Sept. 22, 1929. American psychologist, professor of education and philosophy at the Johns Hopkins University from 1908. He had previously been professor of philosophy and education at the University of Alabama (1903–08). He published *A Study of Kant's Psychology* (1897), *The Educational Theory of Immanuel Kant* (1904), and others.

Büchner (büċh'nėr), **Georg.** b. at Goddelau, near Darmstadt, Germany, Oct. 17, 1813; d. at Zurich, Switzerland, Feb. 19, 1837. German man of letters. He studied medicine at Strasbourg (1831), then history and philosophy at Giessen (1833), where he became politically involved by his revolutionary pamphlet *Der hessische Landbote.* He fled to Strasbourg and then to Zurich, where he was an instructor at the university until he died a few months later. His dramatic talent is shown by his tragedy *Dantons Tod* (1835), as well as by the comedy *Leonce und Lena*, and the fragment *Woczeck.*

Buchner (bȯċh'nėr), **Hans.** b. at Munich, Dec. 16, 1850; d. there, April 5, 1902. German hygienist and bacteriologist; brother of Eduard Buchner. Professor of hygiene and director (1894) of the Hygienic Institute at Munich, he discovered (1889) that cells of a body which recovered from an infection became immune against a similar infection by the production of a defensive protein by the blood, which he termed alexin (now called complement). He described a method for staining anaerobic cultures and spores. Author of *Die Naegeli'sche Theorie der Infektionskrankheiten in ihren Beziehungen zur medizinischen Erfahrung* (1877), *Über die Disposition verschiedener Menschenrassen gegenüber den Infektionskrankheiten und über Akklimatisation* (1887), and *Über die bakterientötende Wirkung des zellenfreien Blutserums* (1889).

Büchner (büċh'nėr), **Ludwig.** [Full name, **Friedrich Karl Christian Ludwig Büchner.**] b. at Darmstadt, Germany, March 28, 1824; d. there, April 30, 1899. German physician and science writer. He studied medicine, settled at Darmstadt, then began teaching at Tübingen, where he aroused so much opposition with his book *Kraft und Stoff* (1855) that he withdrew and returned to practice at Darmstadt. He devoted himself to the popularization of scientific knowledge by numerous works, such as *Natur und Geist* (1876), *Der Mensch und seine Stellung in der Natur* (1889), and *Darwinismus und Sozialismus* (1894).

Büchner, Luise. b. at Darmstadt, Germany, June 12, 1821; d. there, Nov. 28, 1877. German writer, particularly on the subject of women and their training (*Die Frauen und ihr Beruf,* 1855; *Praktische Versuche zur Lösung der Frauenfrage,* 1870; *Über weibliche Berufsarten,* 1872). Together with Princess Alice she founded and directed the so-called Alice Association for advising and assisting women. She wrote stories (*Aus dem Leben,* 1861), a novel (*Das Schloss zu Wimmis,* 1864), and poems (*Frauenherz,* 2nd ed., 1866).

Buchon (bü.shôn), **Jean Alexandre.** b. at Menetou-Salon, Cher, France, May 21, 1791; d. at Paris, April 29, 1846. French historian. He edited *Collection des chroniques nationales françaises* (1824–29), and was the author of works on Greek history and other topics.

Buchtel (buk'tel), **Henry Augustus.** b. near Akron, Ohio, Sept. 30, 1847; d. Oct. 22, 1924. American Methodist Episcopal clergyman and educator. Ordained in 1872, he was a missionary (1873) in Bulgaria, and pastor (1873–99) in various churches. He served as chancellor (1900–21) of the University of Denver, and governor (1907–09) of Colorado.

Buchtel, John Richards. b. in Green Township (now part of Summit County), Ohio, Jan. 18, 1820; d. May 23, 1892. American businessman and philanthropist. He was a salesman (1854 *et seq.*) for Ball, Aultman and Company of Canton, Ohio, makers of farm equipment, and participated (1877) in developing the mineral resources of the Hocking Valley, managing the venture for a group of investors. A donor of Buchtel College (now the University of Akron), and president of its board of trustees (c1870 *et seq.*), he contributed to the institution gifts which eventually aggregated some half-million dollars.

Buck (buk), **Albert Henry.** b. Oct. 20, 1842; d. Nov. 16, 1922. American physician and medical historian. Graduated (1864) from Yale University, he received (1867) his M.D. degree from the College of Physicians and Surgeons of Columbia University. He studied ear diseases abroad, was associated (1872 *et seq.*) with the New York Eye and Ear Infirmary, and served as clinical professor of diseases of the ear (1888–1904) in the College of Physicians and Surgeons. A writer of numerous medical articles in his field, he also edited the American edition of H.W. Ziemssen's *Cyclopaedia of the Practice of Medicine* (15 vols., 1874–80) and coedited the *American Practice of Surgery* (8 vols., 1906–11). His leading contribution was the *Diagnosis and Treatment of Ear Diseases* (1880), long a handbook in the field. After 1910 he concentrated on medical history, publishing two works on the subject.

Buck, Carl Darling. b. at Orland, Me., Oct. 2, 1866—. American philologist. He received the degrees of A.B. (1886) and Ph.D. (1889) from Yale University, and was professor of Sanskrit and Indo-European comparative philology (1900–33) at the University of Chicago. His works include *Grammar of Oscan and Umbrian* (1904), *Introduction to the Study of the Greek Dialects* (1909), *Comparative Grammar of Greek and Latin* (1933), and *A Dictionary of Selected Indo-European Synonyms* (1950); coauthor, with W. Petersen, of *Reverse Index of Greek Nouns and Adjectives* (1945).

Buck, Daniel. b. at Hebron, Conn., Nov. 9, 1753; d. Aug. 16, 1816. American lawyer, legislator, and Revolutionary soldier. He was one of the first settlers (c1784) of Norwich, Vt., where he studied law and was the first lawyer to open an office in the town. As a delegate (1791) to the state convention for ratification of the Constitution, he was the leader of the antiratification forces. He was elected (1793) speaker of the state assembly, served (1795–97) in Congress, and held several offices in local government.

Buck, Dudley. b. at Hartford, Conn., March 10, 1839; d. at Orange, N.J., Oct. 6, 1909. American composer and organist. After attending Trinity College, he studied (1858–62) music abroad, and was appointed (1862) organist at the North Congregational Church at Hartford He was subsequently organist at Saint James's Episcopal Church, Chicago. In 1872 he became organist at Saint Paul's Church, Boston, and, shortly after, became organist of the Music Hall Association in the same city. The remainder of his professional career until his retirement (1903) was spent at Brooklyn, N.Y. A pioneer in American organ music, he was a concert organist of high ability, and composed sonatas, anthems, hymns, cantatas, and solos.

Buck, Eugene Edward. [Called **Gene Buck.**] b. at Detroit, 1885—. American librettist, song writer, and producer. He wrote (1912 *et seq.*) librettos for the *Ziegfield Follies* and *Frolics*, served (1914 *et seq.*) as president of the American Society of Composers, Authors and Publishers (ASCAP), and composed popular songs such as *Hello Frisco, Tulip Time, No Foolin'*, and *Maybe.*

Buck, Gurdon. b. May 4, 1807; d. March 6, 1877. American surgeon, noted for his contributions to plastic surgery and methods of treating fractures. He received (1830) his M.D. degree from the College of Physicians and Surgeons at New York. He studied abroad (1832 *et seq.*), and established his practice (1837) at New York, where he was connected (1852–62) with the New York Eye and Ear Infirmary. One of the leading surgeons of his time, he evolved the device of weights and pulleys, known as "Buck's extension," since used throughout the world for treating fractures.

Buck, Leffert Lefferts. b. at Canton, N.Y., Feb. 5, 1837; d. July 17, 1909. American bridge builder, noted as the designer of the Williamsburg Bridge in New York. He is remembered also for his replacement (1877 *et seq.*) of major portions of the Railway Suspension Bridge at Niagara Falls without interrupting traffic during alterations. After serving as an officer with the Union army in the Civil War, he received (1868) the degree of civil engineer from Rensselaer Polytechnic Institute. He engaged in bridge construction in South America, erecting the highest bridge of its day (Verrugas Viaduct, in Peru), and designed many railroad bridges in various parts of the U.S.

Buck, Pearl. [Maiden name, **Sydenstricker.**] b. at Hillsboro, W.Va., June 26, 1892—. American novelist and Nobel prize winner (1938). She was a teacher (1921–31) in the University of Nanking. For many years a resident of China, she has used that country and its natives as the subject matter for many of her books. She is the author of *East Wind—West Wind* (1930); of a trilogy, *The House of Earth*, including *The Good Earth* (1931; awarded Pulitzer prize, 1932), *Sons* (1932), and *A House Divided* (1935); and of *The Mother* (1934), *The Exile* (1936), *Fighting Angel* (1936), *The Patriot* (1939), *Other Gods* (1940), *Dragon Seed* (1942), *The Dragon Fish* (1944), *Pavilion of Women* (1946), *God's Men* (1951), and *The Hidden Flower* (1952).

Buck, Sir **Peter Henry.** See **Te Rangi Hiroa.**

Buck, Philo Melvin. b. at Corning, N.Y., May 15, 1846; d. Sept. 8, 1924. American Methodist missionary, notable for his service in India. A member of the Kansas Conference of the Methodist Episcopal Church, he volunteered for foreign mission duty and went to India in 1870. His chief contribution as a missionary was made as superintendent of the Meerut District (1893–1914), where he led a large mass movement toward Christianity. Of his many books the most important is *Christianity in Doctrine and in Experience* (1914), translated into numerous languages.

Buckalew (buk'a.lū), **Charles Rollin.** b. in Columbia County, Pa., Dec. 28, 1821; d. at Bloomsburg, Pa., May 19, 1899. American legislator, notable as an advocate of a nation-wide system of proportional representation. A Democratic state senator (1850–58) in Pennsylvania, and local party leader, he was elected (1863) a U.S. senator, serving for one term; he returned to Congress as a representative in the period 1887–91.

Bückeburg (bük'e.bůrk). Town in NW Germany, in the *Land* (state) of Lower Saxony, British Zone, situated on the Aue River in the Weser Mountains, ab. 20 mi. SW of Hanover: agricultural trade. It has a museum and library. The Lutheran Church, in the early baroque style, dates from 1613 and remained undamaged in World War II; Johann Gottfried von Herder was pastor here in the period 1770–75. The former residential castle, built in the 17th century, contains the Golden Hall and art collections. The castle remained intact after World War II, while the collection, which had been dispersed for safety in the neighborhood, had suffered some losses. The town was formerly the capital of the principality of Schaumburg-Lippe. 11,772 (1950).

Bucket (buk'et), **Mr. Inspector.** In Charles Dickens's *Bleak House*, a detective officer. A character of great affability, but sagacious and extraordinarily persevering in carrying out his duties, he is said to have been based on Inspector Field of the London police force, whom Dickens knew well.

"Buckeye State." Nickname of **Ohio.**

Buckhannon (buk"han'on). City in C West Virginia, county seat of Upshur County: seat of the West Virginia Wesleyan College. It was settled in 1770. Pop. 6,016 (1950).

Buckhaven and Methil (buk.hā'ven; meth'il). Police burgh and seaport in E Scotland, in Fifeshire, situated on the N bank of the Firth of Forth, ab. 11 mi. S of Cupar, ab. 428 mi. N of London by rail. It is a fishing and coal-exporting port. 20,291 (est. 1948).

Buckhead (buk'hed). Unincorporated community in NW Georgia, in Fulton County: a northern suburb of Atlanta. Pop. of census district, 26,794 (1950).

Buckhout (buk'hout), **Isaac Craig.** b. at Eastchester, N.Y., Nov. 7, 1830; d. at White Plains, N.Y., Sept. 27, 1874. American civil engineer, designer of the old Grand Central Depot in New York. Most of his work as a railroad engineer was performed as superintendent of the New York and Harlem Railroad.

Buckhurst (buk'hėrst), Baron. A title of **Sackville, Thomas.**

Buckie (buk'i). Police burgh and seaport in N Scotland, in Banffshire, situated on Moray Firth, ab. 6 mi. W of Cullen, ab. 596 mi. N of London by rail. It is a fishing port. The harbor has recently been extended. 8,322 (est. 1948).

Buckingham (buk'ing.am, -ham), 1st Duke of. [Title of **George Villiers.**] b. in Leicestershire, England, Aug. 28,

1592; assassinated at Portsmouth, England, Aug. 23,1628. English nobleman, close adviser to James I and Charles I, noted in English history for unstable and impulsive policies that led to continual trouble with Parliament, with France and Spain, and to various military and naval disasters. James I was early attracted to Villiers by the youth's good looks. Created (1616) Baron Villiers, he was appointed (1617) lord high admiral. Urged James to defend Frederick, elector Palatine; later reversed this policy and made overtures to Spain's Gondomar; involved in an unpleasantness over monopolies; defended Bacon; accused by Hugh Spencer of threatening Spencer in order to force him to uphold certain monopolies; but remained a close friend of the king; failed (1623) in his attempt to marry Charles to Maria of Spain; created (1623) Duke of Buckingham; urged James to make war on Spain, and was upheld by Parliament; to demonstrate to the world his power in the court, he ordered the impeachment of Middlesex; unable to prosecute the war because of lack of funds; an expedition (1625) under Mansfield to the Palatinate failed; alienated the French by his unseemly behavior at court; and another expedition (1625) to Cadiz under Sir Edward Cecil failed. Charged (1625) with neglect, the first time since the reign of the Lancasters that the House had held an officer responsible for his actions; but Charles raised him to higher honors. All Buckingham's schemes for carrying on the war against France and Spain failed, and Parliament drew up a final remonstrance, but Charles stood by his courtier. While attempting to negotiate with Charles Portsmouth over raising the siege of the Protestants on the island of Rochelle, he was assassinated (1628) by John Felton.

Buckingham, 2nd Duke of. [Title of **George Villiers.**] b. at London, Jan. 30, 1627; d. at Kirkby Moorside, Yorkshire, England, April 17, 1688. English politician, courtier, and writer; son of the 1st Duke of Buckingham. He was a privy councilor (1662–67), and organized the "Cabal" in 1670. His collected works were published in 1704.

Buckingham. Small municipal borough in S central England, in Buckinghamshire, situated on the river Ouse ab. 17 mi. NW of Aylesbury, ab. 61 mi. NW of London by rail: seat of the former dukes of Buckingham; once a very considerable town. 3,944 (1951).

Buckingham. Town in Quebec, Canada, situated a few miles inland from the N bank of the Ottawa River on the Lièvre River, ab. 21 mi. E of Ottawa. 6,129 (1951).

Buckingham, James Silk. b. at Flushing, near Falmouth, England, Aug. 25, 1786; d. at London, June 30, 1855. English traveler and man of letters. He wrote *Travels in Palestine* (1822), *Travels in Mesopotamia* (1827), *Travels in Assyria, Media, and Persia* (1829), and others.

Buckingham, Joseph Tinker. b. at Windham, Conn., Dec. 21, 1779; d. at Cambridge, Mass., April 11, 1861. American editor and legislator. Beginning in 1806, he edited several New England monthlies and weeklies; the major part of his career was spent as editor (1824–48) of the Boston *Daily Courier;* he resigned that post when he refused to support the Whig ticket. He was one of the most outspoken and independent editors of the time. His legislative career, lasting for 11 years, was spent as representative and senator in the Massachusetts legislature.

Buckingham, William Alfred. b. at Lebanon, Conn., May 23, 1804; d. at Norwich, Conn., Feb. 5, 1875. American governor and legislator. He served as mayor of Norwich, Conn. (1849–50, 1856–57), governor of Connecticut (1858–66), and U.S. senator from that state (1869–75), dying shortly before the expiration of his term. A capable "war governor," he was instrumental, in the Civil War, in furnishing 54,882 volunteers to the Union army without resorting to conscription.

Buckingham and Normanby (nôr′mạn.bi), 1st Duke of. A title of **Sheffield, John.**

Buckingham Palace. London residence of the British sovereign, situated at the W end of St. James's Park. It was settled by act of Parliament in 1775 upon Queen Charlotte, and was hence first known as the "queen's house." It was remodeled under George IV; the eastern façade, ballroom, and some other portions were added by Queen Victoria, who began to occupy it in 1837, since which time it has served as the official royal residence at London. The chief façade, which was added in 1847, is ab. 360 ft. long. The state apartments are magnificently adorned and furnished, the grand staircase, the throne room, and the state ballroom being especially notable. There is a collection of French buhl and other furniture, and the picture gallery contains a number of old and modern masterpieces. No permanent damage was sustained by the building during World War II.

Buckinghamshire (buk′ing.ạm.shir). [Also: **Buckingham, Bucks;** Old English, **Buccingahamscīr.**] Administrative county in S central England, lying inland between Northamptonshire on the N, Bedfordshire, Hertfordshire, and Middlesex on the E, Berkshire on the S, and Oxfordshire on the W. It is chiefly an agricultural county, raising wheat, beans, and other crops in the N portion, and having pastures to the S; it supplies dairy products and vegetables to the London markets. Industries include furniture manufacture at High Wycombe, and the quarrying of sands for glassmaking at Leighton-Buzzard; there are also some tanneries. The county seat is Aylesbury, the chief town Buckingham; area of administrative county, ab. 750 sq. mi.; pop. 386,164 (1951).

Bucking Island (buk′ing). A former name of **Ellis Island.**

Buck in the Snow, The. Volume of poems by Edna St. Vincent Millay, published in 1928. One of the sections, "Justice in Massachusetts," is a requiem for civilization inspired by Miss Millay's distress over the execution of Sacco and Vanzetti at Boston for a crime which many persons believed they had not committed.

Buckland (buk′lạnd), **Cyrus.** b. at East Hartford, Conn., Aug. 10, 1799; d. at Springfield, Mass., Feb. 26, 1891. American machinist and inventor, notable for work with firearms. Gaining his early experience as a practical mechanic, he joined (1828) the government armory at Springfield, Mass., rising in ten years from a patternmaker to proof-master and inspector of barrels; at his retirement (1857) he was inspector of arms and master machinist. He contributed much to devising the interchangeability of parts in firearms, improved the manufacture of gunstocks by his invention of tools and machines, and designed (1855) a rifling machine.

Buckland, Francis Trevelyan. b. at Oxford, England, Dec. 17, 1826; d. at London, Dec. 19, 1880. English naturalist, noted for researches in fish culture; son of William Buckland. He wrote *Curiosities of Natural History* (1857), *Natural History of British Fishes* (1881), and others.

Buckland, Ralph Pomeroy. b. at Ravenna, Ohio, Jan. 20, 1812; d. at Fremont, Ohio, May 27, 1892. American lawyer, soldier, and legislator. He attended Kenyon College, studied law, and was admitted to the bar in 1837, establishing his practice at Fremont. He left the Whig Party to join the Republicans, served in the state senate (1855 *et seq.*), and commanded the fourth brigade of Sherman's division in the Civil War. For a time he commanded the District of Memphis, and in 1866 was brevetted a major general of U.S. Volunteers. He served as a Congressional representative (1865–69), and was government director (1878–81) of the Union Pacific Railroad.

Buckland, William. b. at Axminster, Devonshire, England, March 12, 1784; d. at Clapham, London, Aug. 15, 1856. English geologist and clergyman, appointed dean of Westminster in 1845; father of Francis Trevelyan Buckland. His chief works are *Reliquiae Diluvianae* (1823) and the Bridgewater treatise *Geology and Mineralogy Considered with Reference to Natural Theology* (1836).

Bucklaw (buk′lô), **Laird of.** In Sir Walter Scott's *The Bride of Lammermoor*, Frank Hayston, the dissipated but good-natured suitor of Lucy Ashton. He was married to her by her mother's machinations, and was thus involved in the tragedy which ensued.

Buckle (buk′l), **George Earle.** b. at Tiverton-on-Avon, near Bath, England, June 10, 1854; d. at London, March 12, 1935. British editor and biographer. He was editor (1884–1912) of the London *Times*. He wrote volumes three to six (1914–20) of *Life of Disraeli*, a continuation of the two volumes published (1910–12) by W. F. Moneypenny and edited a three-volume collection of letters (1862–95), upon the authority of King George V, of Queen Victoria.

Buckle, Henry Thomas. b. at Lee, Kent, England, Nov. 24, 1821; d. at Damascus, Syria, May 29, 1862. English historian. His health in early youth was delicate, on which account he was educated at home, chiefly by his mother. In 1840, on the death of his father, a wealthy shipowner at London, he inherited an ample fortune which enabled him to devote himself wholly to literary pursuits. In 1857 he published the first volume of his *History of Civilization in England*. The appearance of this volume, which is characterized by vigor of style and boldness of thought, produced a sensation in Europe and America, and raised the author from obscurity to fame. The special doctrine which it sought to uphold was that climate, soil, food, and the aspects of nature are the determining factors in intellectual progress. A second volume, considered by some critics inferior in execution and interest, appeared in 1861.

Buckler (buk'lėr), **Thomas Hepburn.** b. near Baltimore, Jan. 4, 1812; d. April 20, 1901. American physician and medical writer. He received his M.D. (1835) from the University of Maryland; after study abroad, he became physician to the city and county almshouse at Baltimore. During the height of his private practice after 1850, he treated such notables as President James Buchanan and Chief Justice Roger Brooke Taney. Partly as a result of his Confederate sympathies during the Civil War, he removed (1866) his practice to Paris, where he remained until 1890.

Buckley (buk'li). Urban district in N Wales, in Flintshire, ab. 3 mi. E of Mold, ab. 190 mi. NW of London by rail. 7,699 (1951).

Buckley. Town in W Washington, in Pierce County, on the White River ab. 20 mi. SE of Tacoma, in a forest and farm region. A large hydroelectric power plant is nearby. In the decade between the last two U.S. censuses the town's population more than doubled. 1,170 (1940); 2,705 (1950).

Buckley, Donal. [Irish, **Dómhnall ua Buachalla.**] b. at Maynooth, Ireland, 1866—. Irish political administrator who held (1932–37) the post of governor general (or *seanascal*) of the Irish Free State. He was a member (1919–23) of the Dail Eireann.

Buckley, James Monroe. b. at Rahway, N.J., Dec. 16, 1836; d. Feb. 8, 1920. American clergyman, author, and editor. From 1859 to 1880 he filled pastorates of the Methodist Episcopal Church in New Hampshire, Michigan, Connecticut, and Brooklyn, N.Y. He was editor (1880–1912) of *The Christian Advocate* of New York. Among his publications are *Oats or Wild Oats* (1885), *Faith Healing, Christian Science, and Kindred Phenomena* (1892), *History of Methodism in the United States* (1896), and *The Fundamentals and Their Contrasts* (1906).

Buckley, Samuel Botsford. b. at Torrey, N.Y., May 9, 1809; d. at Austin, Tex., Feb. 18, 1883. American botanist and geologist. He was assistant geologist and naturalist (1860–61) for the Texas Geological Survey, and Texas state geologist (1866–67, 1874–77). For him were named Mount Buckley, on the North Carolina-Tennessee border, the plant genus *Buckleya* (a parasitic shrub), and *Citellus variegatus buckleyi*, a species of Texas ground squirrel.

Buckley, William. b. near Macclesfield, England, 1780; d. in Tasmania, 1856. Australian colonist and one-time British soldier. He was deported to Australia for plotting (1802) to shoot the duke of Kent. Having escaped (1803) from the Port Phillip penal colony, near Melbourne, he lived with one of the nearby aboriginal tribes for 32 years, during which time he saw no white man. After his pardon (1835), he was employed as an interpreter by the Port Phillip Company; in 1837 he settled in Tasmania.

Buckmaster (buk'màs"tėr), **Stanley Owen.** [Title, 1st Viscount **Buckmaster.**] b. 1861; d. at London, Dec. 5, 1934. English lawyer who served (1915–16) as lord chancellor. Educated at Christ Church College, Oxford, he entered (1906) Parliament as a Liberal member; in 1913 he was appointed solicitor general. He was chairman of the governing body of the Imperial College of Science and Technology.

Bucknell (buk.nel'), **William.** b. near Marcus Hook, Pa., April 1, 1811; d. March 5, 1890. American businessman and philanthropist, noted for his gifts to the University of Lewisburg (renamed Bucknell University in 1887), and to Baptist missions and churches. A real estate speculator in and around Philadelphia, he also held interests in railroads and coal and iron mines. During his lifetime he gave a million dollars to religious and educational institutions.

Buckner (buk'nėr), **Simon Bolivar.** b. near Munfordville, Ky., April 1, 1823; d. there, Jan. 8, 1914. American army officer, a Confederate general in the Civil War and governor (1887–91) of Kentucky; father of Simon Bolivar Buckner (1886–1945). Graduated (1844) from the U.S. Military Academy, he served in the Mexican War, and was professor of infantry tactics (1848–50) at West Point; in 1855 he resigned from the army to go into business. At the outbreak of the Civil War he supported Kentucky's neutrality doctrine, but joined the Confederate forces when his state abandoned neutrality (1861). Sent to Fort Donelson to relieve the Confederate garrison under attack from Ulysses S. Grant, he surrendered unconditionally (1862) after generals J.B. Floyd and G. J. Pillow escaped, leaving him in command. Taken prisoner, he was exchanged (1862), and promoted by the Confederacy to major general. He spent the greater part of the remaining war years with Braxton Bragg's army. He was editor (1868 *et seq.*) of the Louisville *Courier*, and governor (1887–91) of Kentucky; in 1896 he was vice-presidential candidate of the "sound money" Democrats who had bolted the party on the issue of free silver.

Buckner, Simon Bolivar. b. at Munfordville, Ky., July 18, 1886; d. on Okinawa, Ryukyu Islands, June 18, 1945. American army officer; son of Simon Bolivar Buckner (1823–1914). He was graduated (1908) from West Point, served in the aviation branch of the Signal Corps during World War I, was an instructor of infantry tactics (1919 *et seq.*) at West Point, where he served (1933–36) as commandant, and became a general officer when he was named (1939) chief of staff of the 6th Division. He was commanding general (1940–44) of the Alaska Defense Force, was promoted (1943) to the rank of lieutenant general, and was killed in action while serving as commander of the 10th American Army in World War II.

Bucks (buks). See **Buckinghamshire.**

Bucksport (buks'pōrt). Town (in Maine the equivalent of township in many other states) and unincorporated village in S Maine, in Hancock County on the Penobscot River: paper mills. Pop. of town, 3,120 (1950); of village, 2,094 (1950).

Buckstone (buk'stọn), **John Baldwin.** b. at Hoxton, London, Sept. 14, 1802; d. at Sydenham, London, Oct. 31, 1879. English comedian and dramatist. Among his plays are *Married Life* (1834), *Single Life* (1839), and *The Flowers of the Forest* (1847).

Buckstown (buks'toun). Former name of **Dunmore,** Pa.

Bucktails (buk'tālz). Name originally given to the members of the Tammany Society at New York City, but extended (c1817–26) in its application to members of that faction of the Democratic-Republican Party in the state which opposed De Witt Clinton.

Buck v. Bell, 274 U.S. 200 (1927). U.S. Supreme Court decision which upheld as a legitimate exercise of state police power a Virginia law sanctioning the sterilization of mental defectives housed in pubic institutions. Speaking for the court, Justice Oliver Wendell Holmes said: "It is better for all the world, if, instead of waiting to execute degenerate offspring for crime, or let them starve for their imbecility, society can prevent those who are manifestly unfit from continuing their kind. . . . Three generations of imbeciles are enough."

Bucky (bů'ē, buk'i), **Gustav.** b. at Leipzig, Germany, Sept. 3, 1880—. German specialist in roentgenology and physical therapy. He obtained his medical degree (1907) at Leipzig, was a practicing physician at Berlin (1910–23), chief of the x-ray department of the Municipal Children's Hospital and of the Virchow Hospital at Berlin, and came (1923) to the U.S., where he became clinical professor and attending physician at New York University, and director of the physiotherapy department of the Sea View Hospital, Richmond, Staten Island. He devised (1912) a leading improvement in roentgenography, Bucky's diaphragm (a moving grid of alternate strips of lead and wood to cut off secondary rays from the object, thus producing pictures with sharper contrast). He is the author of *Die Röntgenstrahlen und ihre Anwendung* (1918), *An-*

leitung zur Diathermiebehandlung (1921), *Problem of Deep Therapy* (1924), and *Grenzstrahltherapie* (1928).

Bucolic Comedies. Volume of poems by Edith Sitwell, published in 1923.

Bucolic Mouth of the Nile. In ancient geography, a name of one of the mouths of the Nile, in the middle of the Delta.

Bucovina (bö.kǫ.vē'nạ). [Also: **Bukovina**; German, **Bukowina.**] Region in NE Rumania and SW Ukrainian Soviet Socialist Republic: formerly a duchy and crownland of the Cisleithan division of Austria-Hungary, with its capital at Chernovtsy (Czernowitz). It was bounded by Galicia on the N, Moldavia on the E and S, and Transylvania, Hungary proper, and Galicia on the W, and occupied in great part by the Carpathian Mountains. The crownland sent 14 members to the Reichsrat and had a Diet of 31 members. The leading nationalities were Ruthenian and Rumanian, the leading religion the Greek (not united). Its early history is obscure. It was acquired from Turkey by Austria in 1775, and became a crownland in 1849.

Bucovina, South. See **South Bucovina.**

București (bö.kö.resht'). Rumanian name of **Bucharest.**

Bucyrus (bū.sī'rus). City in N central Ohio, county seat of Crawford County, on the Sandusky River ab. 56 mi. N of Columbus: manufactures include road-scrapers, rollers, plows, cranes, hoists, copper kettles, and burial vaults. Originally settled in 1819, it became county seat in 1930. Pop. 10,327 (1950).

Buczacz (bö'chäch). Town in the W part of the U.S.S.R., in the Ukrainian Soviet Socialist Republic, in what was formerly E Galicia, Poland. By a treaty concluded here in 1672, Poland ceded the Ukraine and Podolia to Turkey. Pop. ab. 11,000.

Bud (bud), **Miss Rosa.** [Called **Rosebud.**] In Charles Dickens's *The Mystery of Edwin Drood*, an extremely pretty young lady, an orphan under the guardianship of Mr. Grewgious. A close friendship between their respective fathers has led to her betrothal, at a very tender age, to Edwin, but the two decide in later years to break off an engagement which was not of their wishing and to be thereafter as "brother and sister" to each other. Drood disappears soon afterward and is presumed to have been murdered. Many readers consider that, if Dickens had lived to complete the story, Rosa would have married Mr. Tartar.

Budaeus (bū.dē'us). Latinized surname of **Budé, Guillaume.**

Budafok (bö'dô.fōk). Town in C Hungary, situated on the W bank of the Danube River, opposite the Csepel Sziget (island), S of Budapest. It is a station on the railroad line from Budapest to Szekesfehérvár. Large government-owned wine cellars are located here. Most of the laborers who live in the town work in Budapest. 24,072 (1948).

Budantzev (bö.dän'tsif), **Sergey Fyodorovich.** b. at Glebkovo, Ryazan, Russia, Dec. 8, 1896—. Russian novelist, short-story writer, and playwright.

Budapest (bö'dạ.pest; Hungarian, bö'dô.pesht). [Latin, **Aquincum.**] City in C Hungary, the capital of the Hungarian republic, situated on both banks of the Danube River between Vienna and Belgrade and consisting of Buda (German, Ofen) on the W and Pest on the E bank of the river. 1,058,288 (est. 1948).

General Description. Budapest, architecturally a 19th-century city, is distinguished among European capitals by its beautiful location, and was once renowned for the gaiety of its life. The business and entertainment districts are located on the E bank of the Danube and adjacent to them are residential and industrial suburbs, stretching over a wide distance on the level plain. There are beautiful parks and public buildings, among which the neo-Gothic parliament building is outstanding; broad boulevards lined with numerous retail stores and open-air coffee houses lend to the city in part a Viennese and in part a Parisian character. Here was formerly the center of the elegant life for which Budapest was long famous. The city has an opera house, a national theater, a number of smaller theaters, and important libraries and museums. The national museum houses valuable archives and archaeological, paleontological, mineralogical, and zoölogical collections. There are also museums of art, agriculture, and ethnography and a municipal museum. Budapest contains many educational institutions. The University of Budapest, founded in 1635, was brought to Pest in 1783; the academy of science and the institutes of technology, geology, veterinary medicine, music, and fine arts were founded in the 19th century. A number of important newspapers are published here. The city is also a health resort, having numerous calcareous, sulfur, and radioactive springs, and bathing establishments. It is the seat of a Roman Catholic archbishopric and of Catholic, Reformed, and Jewish theological seminaries. The section on the W bank of the Danube occupies a rocky elevation, the summit of which is almost entirely taken up by the numerous buildings of the former royal castle, most of them erected in the 18th and 19th centuries. Several bridges span the Danube between the two parts of the city.

Industry and Commerce. Budapest is the financial, commercial, and industrial center of Hungary. There are metallurgical, chemical, textile, and ceramics industries and numerous plants manufacturing flour, pastry, sausages, canned fruits and vegetables, liquors, and beer, all of them nationalized after World War II. There are grain and cattle markets and extensive harbor installations.

History. Budapest was originally a Roman military post. The various early medieval settlements were destroyed by the Tartars and attained new importance only shortly before the Turkish occupation in 1541. The city was retaken from the Turks by the imperial army under Charles of Lorraine in 1686, which year marks the start of its modern history. In the 18th century, Maria Theresa of Austria erected the new castle and Joseph II gave his support to the university. In the period 1848–49, Pest was the seat of the Hungarian revolutionary government; in 1867 it became the capital of Hungary under an agreement with the crown. Buda and Pest were united under one administration in 1873. After World War I Budapest became the capital of independent Hungary. It passed through a period of communist rule under Béla Kun which was ended when Rumanian troops occupied the city. It was a period of much violence by both left-wing and right-wing elements. During the latter part of World War II, Budapest suffered heavy damage as the scene of bitter fighting between the advancing Russian armies and the German and Hungarian defenders of the city. Many lives were lost, numerous public and private buildings destroyed, and the economic and cultural life totally disrupted. Budapest was one of the most devastated cities of Europe, and reconstruction proceeded slowly after the war. The character of the population changed considerably during the 19th and 20th centuries. Originally predominantly German, it assumed Magyar character only in the second half of the 19th century. About 60 percent of the population was Roman Catholic, 25 percent Jewish, and 15 percent Protestant (Reformed and Lutheran) prior to World War II. The Jewish population was reduced by the end of World War II to about one third of its former size by slaughter and deportation, while Catholic religious life received a blow after the war in the trial and incarceration by the dominantly Communist Hungarian government of Cardinal Mindszenty.

Budapest String Quartet. Chamber music ensemble founded (1921) at Budapest, noted for excellent interpretation. Its original members were Josef Roisman, violin, Alexander Schneider, violin, Boris Kroyt, viola, and Mischa Schneider, cello. It has made many international tours.

Budaun (bů.doun'). District of the Rohilkhand division, Uttar Pradesh (United Provinces), Union of India: wheat, rice, sugar, and barley. It was ceded to the British in 1801. Area, 1,987 sq. mi.; pop. 1,162,322 (1941).

Budd (bud), **Joseph Lancaster.** b. near Peekskill, N.Y., July 3, 1835; d. at Phoenix, Ariz., Dec. 20, 1904. American horticulturist, noted for his pioneer work in devising horticultural methods adapted to the American Northwest. A successful nurseryman, orchardist, and instructor in horticulture in Illinois and Iowa, he became secretary of the Iowa Horticultural Society, and was appointed (1876) professor of horticulture and forestry in the Iowa Agricultural College. After a journey to Russia (1882), he introduced into the Northwest hardier types of fruit trees now in general use in Dakota and Manitoba. He was coauthor of the *Manual of American Horticulture* (2 vols., 1902–03).

Budde (bùd'ẹ), **Emil Arnold.** b. at Geldern, Germany, July 28, 1842; d. at Feldafing, Germany, Aug. 15, 1921. German physicist. He was a correspondent for the Cologne *Zeitung* at Paris, Rome, and Constantinople, was a physicist for Siemens and Halske, and devised one of the earliest successful electric lamps utilizing a metal filament. Author of *Lehrbuch der Physik* (1879), *Mechanik der Punkte und Starren Systeme* (1890), and *Tensoren und Dyaden im dreidimensionalen Raum* (1914).

Budde, Karl Ferdinand Reinhard. b. at Bensberg, near Cologne, Germany, April 13, 1850; d. at Marburg, Germany, Jan. 29, 1935. German evangelical theologian, professor of Old Testament theology (1900 *et seq.*) at the University of Marburg. Among his works are *Die Biblische Urgeschichte untersucht* (1883), *Die Bücher Richter und Samuel* (1890), *Der Kanon des Alten Testaments* (1900), and *Das Alte Testament und die Ausgrabungen* (1903).

Buddeus (bù.dā'ùs), **Johann Franz.** [Original surname, **Budde.**] b. at Anklam, Germany, June 25, 1667; d. at Gotha, Germany, Nov. 19, 1729. German Lutheran divine and scholar. He wrote *Historia juris naturae* (1695), *Elementa philosophiae instrumentalis* (1703), *Historia ecclesiastica veteris testamenti* (1709), and others.

Buddha (bùd'ạ, bö'dạ). [Family name, **Gautama** or (in Pali) **Gotama**; hence also, **Gautama** (or **Gotama**) **Buddha**; called also at various times, **Siddhartha** (or **Siddharta**), **Sakyamuni, Tathagata.**] b. at Kapilavastu (in what is now the S part of Nepal, India), c563 B.C.; d. at Kusinagara (also in what is now Nepal), c483 B.C. Indian philosopher and religious leader, founder of Buddhism. The various facts relating to his life are now so heavily encrusted with legend that it is possible to ascertain only approximately even such points as the dates of his birth and death: he is generally assumed to have died when he was 80 years old, and from a 4th-century Pali chronicle of the Indian kings which gives 218 years as the period intervening between the time of his death and the year when Asoka mounted the throne (a known date in history), recent scholars are in fairly general agreement on 483 B.C., or thereabouts, as the year of his death. From this, if he lived to the age of 80, 563 B.C. may be inferred as the year of his birth. However, it should be remembered that these dates are, at best, only informed guesses, and that various other dates have been and will continue to be advanced (for example, the Buddhist scholars of Ceylon reckon 544 B.C. as the date of Buddha's death). In the matter of Buddha's names there is also some degree of confusion: the name "Buddha" means, in Sanskrit, the "Enlightened," and was acquired only after Buddha had attained enlightenment under the famous Bo Tree in the village of Buddh Gaya, about 7 mi. S of the city of Gaya, in what is now the NE part of the Union of India. Prior to this enlightenment he was, in the terminology of Buddhist philosophy, simply a Bodhisattva, or potential Buddha; in the fashion in which names are most commonly used in the West, he would have been called Prince Gautama (or Gotama), of the Sakya clan. He is also called Sakyamuni (which means "sage of the Sakyas"), Siddhartha or Siddharta (which means "he who has accomplished his purpose"), and Tathagata (which means "he who has arrived at the truth" or the "Perfect One"). His father was the ruler of the Sakyas, but in the sense in which the word "king" is now most generally used he was perhaps more of a great and wealthy landowner than a king. Buddha's early years were spent at his father's "court" in circumstances which were, for that age and place, opulent indeed, and was married at the age of 16. At the age of 29, in accordance with a prophecy which had been made at the time of his conception, he saw an old man, a sick man, and a corpse, and realized for the first time that age, illness, and death were a part of life. It was this realization which led him to forsake his family and wife, and to seek truth, and truth alone, as a recluse (according to most accounts, it was because of his knowledge of this prophecy, and his desire that it should not come to pass, that Buddha's father reared him in sheltered and luxurious circumstances). Some six (or seven) years later, under the Bo Tree (which is the pipal, or sacred fig tree, of India, and except for this particular tree, not spelled, of course, with capital letters) at Buddh Gaya, he attained the perfect enlightenment which made him "the Buddha." For 49 (or 28) days thereafter he underwent various temptations, the most important of which was perhaps whether selfishly to keep for himself the great knowledge he had attained, or to share it. However, love triumphed, and for the rest of his life he sought to open the path to enlightenment for as many people as he could reach by his preaching (for some 44 years he preached in the area of Benares and Bihar). He formed an order of monks, and subsequently of nuns, and won the adherence of Ananda (who may be called, in a sense, the Saint John of Buddhism). He is said to have died of an illness contracted by eating spoiled, or improperly prepared, pork, and actually to have passed away in the arms of his devoted follower Ananda.

Buddh Gaya (bùd' gä'yạ). Ancient center of Buddhism, now in ruins, near Gaya, in W central Bihar state, Union of India. The temple is a celebrated foundation in the Buddhist faith.

Buddhism (bùd'iz.ẹm, bö'diz-). One of the great religions of the world, originating in the philosophy and ethical system established by Buddha during the latter part of the 6th century B.C. Its followers today may be found chiefly in Japan, Korea, Indochina, Ceylon, Burma, Thailand, and (in the form of Lamaism) in Tibet. Some recent estimates have placed the total of the world's Buddhists at upwards of 500 million people, but because of the fact that Buddhism coexists in the Far East with various other religions (Shinto, in Japan, and Taoism and Confucianism, in China), which may also be subscribed to by people who are at the same time Buddhists, no absolutely reliable figure as to the total number of Buddhists is possible. In its origin it stemmed at least partly from Hinduism (according to most accounts, Buddha studied with two Brahmins in the years immediately preceding his attainment of enlightenment under the Bo Tree at Buddh Gaya, and there is a similarity in the concepts of Brahman (in Hinduism) and Nirvana (in Buddhism) which will catch the eye of anyone making a comparative study of the two religions). In a more fundamental sense, however, it may be viewed as a protest against, if not an actual repudiation of, Hinduism, particularly with reference to the doctrine of metempsychosis.

Buddhist System of Ethics. The basis of the morals of Buddha is the Four Great Verities: (1) Pain and sorrow exist; (2) the cause of these is our affections and passions and our sins; (3) pain and sorrow can cease by Nirvana; (4) points out the way to Nirvana, the means of deliverance. The way to Nirvana consists of eight parts: (1) Right faith, or orthodoxy; (2) right judgment, dispersing all uncertainty and doubt; (3) right language, or the study of perfect and unswerving truthfulness; (4) right purpose, or the choice of an upright purpose in all words and deeds; (5) right practice, or the pursuit of a religious life; (6) right obedience, or the following of all the precepts of the Buddhist law; (7) right memory; (8) right meditation. These Four Verities alone comprise the earliest teaching of Buddha; he taught them indeed to the last, but with important additions in his latter years. The Four Verities are followed by a body of moral precepts. The first are the Five Great Commandments binding upon all, namely, not to kill, not to steal, not to commit adultery, not to lie, not to get drunk. Next come five precepts, of less importance, binding upon professed disciples, namely, to abstain from unseasonable meals, from public spectacles (music, dancing, singing), from expensive dresses and personal ornaments and perfumes, from having a large or soft bed, and from receiving gold or silver. For those who embrace a religious life, twelve observances of the severest character are prescribed: (1) to wear only clothes made of rags cast away by others; (2) to wear only three garments, made by their own hands from these rags; (3) to wear over these rags only a yellow cloak; (4) to live only on the alms they have collected; (5) to eat only one meal daily; (6) to take no food after noon; (7) to live in forests and solitary places, entering towns only to obtain alms; (8) the only shelter is to be the shadow of trees; (9) to rest only sitting at the foot of a tree; (10) to sleep there, without lying down, but resting against the tree; (11) when once settled not to move the sitting-carpet about; (12) to meditate at night among the tombs in the cemeteries on the vanity of all things. The title given to those who follow these last precepts is Sramana, meaning "victors over self." On ordinary persons, who could not attain such a height of virtue, were enjoined the Six Ordinary Virtues: almsgiving or charity, purity, patience, courage, contemplation, and knowledge. These virtues are inculcated in their very fullest extent. An instance of Buddha's charity is given for imitation. He saw one day a tigress starved and unable to feed her cubs, whereon he offered his body to be devoured by them. Among a number of minor precepts are included the government of the tongue, in its widest sense, humility, modesty, love for and dutifulness to parents and relations. One of the most remarkable of Buddha's institutions is that of public confession, before the whole congregation, of faults and sins.

Sacred Literature. The sacred literature of Buddhism is found today, in its most complete form, in the so-called Pali canon (which is the basis of Buddhism in Ceylon, Thailand, and Burma) and in the writings (originally in Sanskrit) of the Mahayana canon (which, in translation and subsequent retranslation, provide a basis for the Buddhism of China, Japan, Korea, and the Lamaism of Tibet). The Pali canon consists of the *Tripitaka* (which means "Three Baskets," i.e., three collections or compilations), which is made up of (1) the *Vinaya*, covering various rules and points of discipline, (2) the *Sutta*, which are Buddha's actual discourses, and (3) the *Abhidhamma*, which deals with metaphysics. This canon is generally considered to be the more "primitive," which means merely that it is the older and simpler. The Mahayana canon has a vastly greater number of written works (indeed, it has so many that no Buddhist ever now thinks of reading them all, but confines himself to a selected few) and reflects a type of Buddhism which has come to be more concerned with a conception of divinity (the Pali canon treats Buddha as having been basically good and very noble, but nevertheless still a mortal being). The various branches of Buddhism which follow the Mahayana canon have also, in some cases, been readier to adapt local divinities and sub-deities to their concept of Buddhism. This has resulted in a flexibility and diversity which is usually lacking in the Buddhism of those following the Pali canon.

Budé (bü.dā), **Guillaume.** [Latinized, **Budaeus.**] b. at Paris, 1468; d. Aug. 23, 1540. French humanist scholar. He was a friend of Erasmus, and was elevated by Francis I to the post of royal librarian, in which capacity he established the library at Fontainebleau which is now usually considered to have been the progenitor of the Bibliothèque Nationale. He was also instrumental, through his influence on Francis I, in the founding of the Collège de France. He was a student of Roman law and of Roman coins, as well as one of the scholars responsible for the revival of Greek learning in Europe. He was aware of, and emphasized, the need for religious reform, but did not accept the Protestant Reformation as a proper accomplishment of this end. Among his works are *De asse et partibus eius* (1514) and *De transitu hellenismi ad christianum* (1534–35).

Budejowice (bö'dye.yô.vi.tse). See **České Budějovice.**

Budenny (bö.dyôn'i), **Semyon Mikhailovich.** b. in Russia, 1883—. Russian soldier, notable as a leader of cavalry and as a marshal of the Soviet Army. A Cossack, son of a farmer, he entered the Russian army at least as early as 1903, and fought in the Russo-Japanese War and World War I (in which he rose to the grade of sergeant). From the time of the overthrow of the czarist regime in 1917 he engaged vigorously and effectively in revolutionary propaganda aimed at his fellow soldiers, and with the assumption of power by the Bolshevik-dominated Soviets after the October Revolution, he organized a cavalry force which took an effective part, under his leadership, in defeating the counterrevolutionary forces of Denikin and Wrangel. In 1919 he joined the Bolshevik Party, and in 1939 was made a member of its Central Committee. During the years between the consolidation of Soviet power and the outbreak of World War II he participated in the organization of the Red Army, especially of the cavalry, and in recognition of his services was made a marshal in 1935, and vice-commissar of defense in 1940. Following the German attack on the U.S.S.R., he was in command of the Russian southern front between July and November, 1941, but was relieved of this command at his own request, and was put in charge of the training of recruits to the Red Army, taking no further known part in the strategic planning or prosecution of the war.

Budenz (bų.denz'), **Louis Francis.** b. at Indianapolis, Ind., July 17, 1891—. American editor and educator. Active in union activities (associate editor of *The Carpenter*, 1912–13; organizer and strike leader for the American Federation of Labor, 1927–34), he was publicity director for the American Civil Liberties Union (1920–21) and editor of *The Labor Age* (1921–31). From 1935 to 1937 he was labor editor for the *Daily Worker*, New York Communist Party organ; after three years (1937–40) as editor of the *Midwest Daily Record*, he returned to New York as president and managing editor of the *Daily Worker*. Budenz broke (1945) with the Communist Party, returned to the Roman Catholic Church, and taught as professor of economics at Notre Dame (1945–46) and Fordham (1946 *et seq.*). He thereafter devoted his energies to exposing the principles and methods of the Communists in the U.S., appearing often as a witness before Congressional committees investigating Communist activities and identifying those whom he remembered, as he alleged, from his former high position in the party councils, as Communists or workers for the Communist cause. Author of *This Is My Story* (1946) and *Men Without Faces: The Communist Conspiracy in the U.S.A.* (1950).

Bude-Stratton (būd"strat'ǫn). [Former name, **Stratton and Bude.**] Urban district in SW England, in Cornwall, situated on the N coast, ab. 229 mi. SW of London by rail. It is a golfing resort. 5,230 (1951).

Budge (buj), **Donald.** [Full name, **John Donald Budge.**] b. at Oakland, Calif., June 13, 1915—. American tennis player. In 1937 he was U.S. men's singles champion, and retained the title in 1938. In 1937 also he was chiefly credited with bringing the Davis Cup back to the U.S. after six years in France and four in England, and in 1938 he helped to keep it in this country.

Budge, Ernest Alfred Wallis. b. in Cornwall, England, July 27, 1857; d. Nov. 23, 1934. English archaeologist. He was keeper (1893–1924) of Assyrian and Egyptian antiquities at the British Museum. He conducted explorations at Nineveh (Mesopotamia), Aswan (Egypt), and Barkal (Sudan), and published a large number of works on Oriental subjects.

Budgell (buj'ẹl), **Eustace.** b. at St. Thomas, near Exeter, England, Aug. 19, 1686; committed suicide by drowning in the Thames, near London, May 4, 1737. English miscellaneous writer. He was called to the bar, but his association with his cousin Joseph Addison induced him to turn his attention to literature. He contributed 37 papers to the *Spectator* in Addison's style. He wrote many pamphlets of a political nature, and in 1733 started *The Bee*, a weekly periodical which ran for about two years. He filled a number of positions after the accession of George I, when Addison became secretary to the lord lieutenant of Ireland, being at various times chief secretary to the lords justices, deputy clerk of the council, accountant-general, and a member of the Irish House of Commons. He fell into money difficulties, and after a scandal, connected with the disappearance of some bonds belonging to the estate of Matthew Tindal, he took his own life. He left a natural daughter, Anne Eustace, who became an actress.

Budget and Accounting Act of 1921. Act of the U.S. Congress, passed under the administration of President Warren G. Harding, providing for the establishment of the Bureau of the Budget (headed by a director responsible to the president) and a General Accounting Office (headed by a controller general). A similar bill passed by Congress in 1919 had been vetoed by President Woodrow Wilson.

Budissin (bö'di.sin). Wendish name of **Bautzen.**

Budrio (bö'drē.ō). Town and commune in N Italy, in the *compartimento* (region) of Emilia-Romagna, in the province of Bologna, situated on the Idice River, NE of Bologna. The town has preserved its medieval walls and ramparts. Sugar beets and excellent hemp are grown in the vicinity; there are several small industries. During World War II the Church of San Lorenzo lost its campanile and choir, and the Church of Sant'Agata sustained several hits. Pop. of commune, 16,870 (1936); of town, 2,892 (1936).

Bűdszentmihály (büd'sent.mē'häy'). Town in NE Hungary, situated a short distance from the upper Tisza River S of Tiszalők, between Nyíregyháza and Polgár. 11,996 (1941).

Budweis (bůt'vīs). German name of **České Budějovice.**

Buëa (bö.ā'ą). Town in the British trust territory of Cameroons, situated near the Gulf of Guinea, on the SE slope of Cameroons Mountain: former capital of the German territory of Kamerun. Its port is Victoria.

Buecheler (bü'ċhę.lėr), **Franz.** b. at Rheinberg, Germany, June 3, 1837; d. at Bonn, Germany, May 3, 1908. German classical scholar. He served as a professor (1858 *et seq.*) at the universities of Freiburg, Greifswald, and Bonn. His works include *Grundriss der lateinischen Deklination* (Outline of Latin Declension, 1866) and *Philologische Kritik* (Philological Criticism, 1878).

Buehler (bū'lėr), **Huber Gray.** b. at Gettysburg, Pa., Dec. 3, 1864; d. June 20, 1924. American educator and administrator. He studied at Pennsylvania College (B.A., 1883; M.A., 1886), and at the Lutheran Theological Seminary (both at Gettysburg), where he was a professor and principal until joining (1892) the faculty of the newly established Hotchkiss School for boys at Lakeville, Conn. In 1904 he was appointed headmaster of Hotchkiss after having served as master of English and acting headmaster. His work in improving and enlarging the school won him the presidency (1914–15) of the Headmasters' Association.

Buel (bū'ęl), **Clarence Clough.** b. at Laona, Chautauqua County, N.Y., July 29, 1850; d. May 22, 1933. American editor. He was connected (1875–81) with the New York *Tribune*, and was associate editor (1881–1913) and advisory editor (until 1914) of the *Century Magazine*. With Robert Underwood Johnson, he edited *Battles and Leaders of the Civil War* (1887).

Buel, Jesse. b. at Coventry, Conn., Jan. 4, 1778; d. at Danbury, Conn., Oct. 6, 1839. American journalist and agriculturist. After publishing five weekly newspapers, the last of which was the Albany *Argus* (1813–21), he devoted his efforts to agricultural improvements on an 85-acre tract west of Albany. His achievements in applying scientific principles to farming brought him a national and international reputation; he also labored for the improvement of rural life. He was recording secretary (1822 *et seq.*) to the New York State Board of Agriculture, and a member (1823 *et seq.*) of the state assembly. He established (1834) the *Cultivator*, an early popular agricultural publication. His chief work was *The Farmer's Companion* (1839), which went into several editions.

Buell (bū'ęl), **Abel.** b. at Killingworth, Conn., Feb. 1, 1741 or 1742; d. at New Haven, Conn., March 10, 1822. American silversmith, type founder, and engraver. His first feat after serving his apprenticeship as a silversmith was to counterfeit Connecticut five-pound notes, for which he was imprisoned (1764); after his release, he invented a lapidary machine and turned his mind to type founding, designing (1769) what have been termed the first American types set in this country. He next (c1770) applied himself to the art of copper engraving, achieving some reputation as an early mapmaker. For the last 40 years of his life, in addition to practicing his regular crafts, he dabbled in many ventures. He ended his years in the New Haven Alms House.

Buell, Don Carlos. b. near Marietta, Ohio, March 23, 1818; d. at Rockport, Ky., Nov. 19, 1898. American general, with the Union Army in the Civil War. Graduated (1841) from West Point, he served in the Mexican War. Appointed (1861) a brigadier general of U.S. volunteers, he was placed in command of the Army of the Ohio. The presence of his forces restored the Union balance at Shiloh (1862), and beat back the Confederate attack. He was promoted to major general, but his failure to pursue Braxton Bragg after the indecisive battle of Perryville (1862) cost him his command and placed him under investigation by a military commission. He resigned (1864) his regular commission, and settled in Kentucky, where he engaged in mining.

Buell, Raymond Leslie. b. at Chicago, July 13, 1896; d. Feb. 20, 1946. American teacher and publicist, an expert on foreign affairs. He was graduated (B.A., 1918) from Occidental College and from Princeton (M.A., 1920; Ph.D., 1923), was instructor (1922–25) and assistant professor (1926–27) of government at Harvard, and served as research director (1927–33) of the Foreign Policy Association, of which he was president from 1933 to 1939. Among his works are *Contemporary French Politics* (1920), *The Washington Conference* (1922), *International Relations* (1925, 1929), *The Native Problem in Africa* (2 vols., 1928), *Poland: Key to Europe* (1939), and *Isolated America* (1940).

Buen (bwen). Town and commune in NW Spain, in the province of Pontevedra. 10,023 (1940).

Buena (bū'ną, bwā'-). Town in S New Jersey, in Atlantic County, ab. 30 mi. NW of Atlantic City. 2,640 (1950).

Buen Aire or **Buen Ayre** (bwen ī'rā). See **Bonaire.**

Buena Park (bwā'ną). Unincorporated community in S California, in Orange County, ab. 20 mi. SE of Los Angeles. 5,483 (1950).

Buenaventura (bwā"nä.ʙen.tö'rä). City on the W coast of Colombia, in Valle del Cauca department. The most important Pacific port of Colombia and third largest in the country, it is a railway terminus and shipping point for coffee, gold, and platinum. It has a tropical climate, with almost daily rain. 14,514 (1938).

Buena Vista (bwā'nä ʙēs'tä). Site in N Mexico, in Coahuila state, ab. 6 mi. S of Saltillo, where in the period of Feb. 22–23, 1847, 5,000 Americans under General Zachary Taylor defeated 15,000 Mexicans under Antonio López de Santa Anna. The American loss was 746; that of the Mexicans, ab. 2,000.

Buena Vista (bū'ną vis'tą). City in C Virginia, geographically in Rockbridge County, but politically independent of the county government. Manufactures include silk textiles, leather, bricks, paper, and saddles. It is the seat of Southern Seminary and Junior College. 5,214 (1950).

Bueno da Silva (bwā'nö dą sil'vą), **Bartholomeu.** [Called **Anhanguera.**] b. at São Paulo, Brazil, c1635; d. there, c1695. Brazilian explorer; father of Bartholomeu Bueno da Silva (1670–1740). In 1682, at the head of a party in search of Indian slaves and mines, he penetrated to Goiás, and probably beyond the Araguaia River, in the Brazilian interior, bringing back the first definite account of these regions.

Bueno da Silva, Bartholomeu. b. at São Paulo, Brazil, 1670; d. in Goiás, Brazil, Sept. 19, 1740. Brazilian explorer; son of Bartholomeu Bueno da Silva (c1635–c1695). He was with his father in the exploration of 1682, and in 1722 was sent by the governor of São Paulo to seek the same route. He was absent three years, and discovered the gold mines of Goiás. In 1728 he was made captain of the Goiás colony, which later became a state of Brazil.

Buenos Aires (bwā'nōs ī'rās; Anglicized, bwā'nǫs ī'rēz, ãr'ēz, bō'nǫs ãrz). [Also: **Colonies of the Plata, La Plata;** Spanish, **Colonias de la Plata.**] Spanish viceroyalty in SE South America, established in 1776 and continued until the revolution of 1810. It included Buenos Aires (colony), Tucumán, Cuyo (separated from Chile), the Banda Oriental (now Uruguay), Paraguay, and Charcas or Upper Peru (now Bolivia); in other words, all now included in the Argentine Republic, Uruguay, Paraguay, and Bolivia, with the former Pacific coast of Bolivia, later annexed to Chile. The capital was Buenos Aires.

Buenos Aires. Province in E Argentina, lying S of Córdoba, Santa Fe, and Entre Ríos provinces and the Plata River (Río de la Plata), W and N of the Atlantic Ocean, and E of the territories of La Pampa and Río Negro. The largest, wealthiest, and most populous province in Argentina, it is chiefly important for wheat growing and stock raising, although there has been much industrial development, notably in food processing. Capital, La Plata; area, 116,322 sq. mi.; pop. 4,272,337 (1947).

Buenos Aires. [Sometimes called **"B.A."**] Capital of Argentina, situated on the estuary of the Plata River (Río de la Plata): the largest city in South America, and Argentina's chief export center. Site of the largest meat-refrigerating plant in the world, its other industries include textiles, publishing and printing, and metals. First permanently settled (1580) by the Spanish, it established its independence of Spain in 1810 and was a focal point for the growth of the Argentine nation. Greater Buenos Aires comprises the following politically independent units: Federal District, Avellaneda, Lomas,

San Isidro, and San Fernando. Pop. of city, 2,982,580 (1947); with suburbs, 4,560,959 (1947).

Buenos Aires, Lake. Lake partly in SW Argentina, in Santa Cruz territory, and partly in SE Chile, forming part of the border between Argentina and Chile. Length, ab. 75 mi.

Buenos Aires Conference. Inter-American Conference for Peace held (1936) at Buenos Aires, as suggested by President Franklin D. Roosevelt to the president of Argentina. Roosevelt attended the conference and delivered the opening address, in which he proclaimed hemispheric solidarity in the event of aggression from abroad. His implicit invitation to a binding Pan-American agreement was not accepted, and the consulting powers instead adopted a pact reasserting the principle of nonintervention and confirming their allegiance to several international peace treaties then in existence.

Bufano (bö.fä'nō), **Beniamino (Benvenuto).** b. at San Fele, Italy, Oct. 14, 1898—. American sculptor, art commissioner of the city of San Francisco. He studied at the National Academy of Design, the Beaux-Arts Institute of Design, and the Art Students League of New York. His work has been exhibited widely in the U.S., at Paris, Rome, and Moscow, and in Germany; he won awards from the Whitney Museum of American Art (1917) and the Art Students League (1914–16) at New York. He is represented in the Metropolitan Museum of Art, New York, the Palace of the Legion of Honor, and the Museum of Art, San Francisco. The Peace Memorial and Sun Yat-sen statue at San Francisco are two of his major works.

Buff (búf), **Charlotte.** b. at Wetzlar, Germany, Jan. 11, 1753; d. at Hanover, Germany, Jan. 16, 1828. The original of Lotte in Goethe's *Die Leiden des jungen Werthers* (1774). Goethe met her while attending the Imperial Law Courts at Wetzlar in the summer of 1772. His passion for her was curbed by the fact that she was already engaged to his friend Johann Christoph Kestner, whom she married the following year. Goethe did not see her again until her visit to Weimar in 1816, an event which Thomas Mann has used as the basis for his *Lotte in Weimar* (1939; Eng. trans., *The Beloved Returns*, 1940).

Buffalo (buf'a.lō). [Called the **"Queen City of the Lakes."**] City in W New York, county seat of Erie County, on Lake Erie at the mouth of the Niagara River. A lake port, and trading and industrial center, it is the second largest city in the state. It is a leading flour-milling city and one of the chief railroad centers of the U.S.; manufactures include steel, carborundum, dyes and chemicals, wallboard, rubber, and motor vehicles. It is a principal lake port, important for the transshipment of grain, coal, and ores. It is the seat of a state teachers college, Canisius College, and the University of Buffalo. The Peace Bridge connects the city with Fort Erie, Canada. Buffalo was founded in 1801, and incorporated as a city in 1832. President McKinley was assassinated here on Sept. 6, 1901. Pop. 580,132 (1950).

Buffalo. City in N Wyoming, county seat of Johnson County, on Clear Creek in the E foothills of the Bighorn Mountains. It is a tourist resort and the trading center for a farming and livestock-raising region. In its early days it was the scene of what is known as the Johnson County War (1892), a violent conflict over grazing lands and water rights between homesteaders and cattlemen. 2,674 (1950).

"Buffalo Bill." See **Cody, William Frederick.**

Buffalo Hunters' War. In U.S. history, a name for the attacks carried out (1877) by Comanche Indians against buffalo hunters in the Texas Panhandle. The Indians, under the leadership of Black Horse, were themselves attacked in March, 1877, and even though the white hunters were driven back, the Comanches thereafter carried out no raids against them.

Buffalo National Park. Former park in E Alberta, ab. 115 mi. SE of Edmonton. It was established in 1908 as a reserve for the Dominion herd of bison. The animals were transferred to Elk Island National Park, and Buffalo National Park was abolished in 1947.

Buffalo Society of Natural Sciences. Organization founded in 1861 (incorporated 1863) for the purpose of promoting and studying the arts and sciences, establishing and operating collections, museums, and libraries, and disseminating popular knowledge. It maintains headquarters at the Buffalo Museum of Science, Buffalo, N.Y., which it administers, has a research library containing more than 17,000 volumes, and issues *Hobbies* (five times a year) and the *Scientific Bulletin* (irregularly).

Buffier (bü.fyā), **Claude.** b. in Poland, May 25, 1661; d. at Paris, May 17, 1737. French grammarian and philosopher.

Buffington (buf'ing.tọn), **Adelbert Rinaldo.** b. at Wheeling, W.Va., Nov. 22, 1837; d. at Madison, N.J., July 10, 1922. American army officer. He fought (1861–65) in the Civil War, was brevetted (1865) major, and served (1881–97) with the ordnance department. His improvements in small arms include a disappearing gun carriage which he invented with William Crozier.

Buffon (bü.fôṅ), **Georges Louis Leclerc, Comte de.** b. at Montbard, Côte-d'Or, France, Sept. 7, 1707; d. at Paris, April 16, 1788. French naturalist. He was the son of Leclerc de Buffon, a counselor of the parliament of Burgundy, from whom he inherited a sizable fortune. At about the age of 19 he traveled in Italy, and in 1740 published a translation into French of Isaac Newton's *Treatise on Fluxions.* He was elected a member of the Academy of Sciences at Paris in 1739, and in the same year was appointed director of the Jardin du Roi (the national botanical garden of France, now named Jardin des Plantes). His chief work is *Histoire naturelle, générale et particulière, avec la description du cabinet du roi*, the first three volumes of which were published in 1749. The first volume contained *La Théorie de la terre* and *Le Système sur la formation des planètes*; the second, *L'Histoire générale des animaux* and *L'Histoire particulière de l'homme;* the third, *Description du cabinet du roi* (by Daubenton) and a chapter on *Les Variétés de l'espèce humaine.* The next 12 volumes (1755–67) dealt with the history of quadrupeds. Subsequently he published in ten volumes *L'Histoire naturelle des oiseaux et des minéraux* (1771–86), besides seven volumes of *Suppléments* (1774–89). The most striking of these is the fifth volume, *Les Époques de la nature* (1779). Lacépède completed Buffon's work from his notes by publishing a volume, *Les Serpents*, in 1789. The credit for the six volumes on *Les Poissons et les cétacés* (1799–1804) belongs to Lacépède alone. When Buffon was admitted to the French Academy in 1753, he delivered as his inaugural address the famous *Discours sur le style.*

Buffone (bö.fō'nā), **Carlo.** In Ben Jonson's *Every Man Out of His Humour*, an impudent, gluttonous jester. He is identified by some critics with John Marston; others think he was meant for Thomas Dekker.

Buffum (buf'um), **Arnold.** b. at Smithfield, R.I., Dec. 13, 1782; d. at Perth Amboy, N.J., March 13, 1859. American Quaker and antislavery lecturer, one of the founders of the American Anti-Slavery Society at Philadelphia (1833). A hatter by trade, he was president (1832 *et seq.*) of the New England Anti-Slavery Society, and active as a lecturer as far west as Ohio and Indiana.

Buford (bū'fọrd). City in N Georgia, in Gwinnett County: tanneries and glue factories. 3,812 (1950).

Buford, Abraham. b. in Culpeper County, Va., July 31, 1749; d. near Georgetown, Ky., June 30, 1833. American Revolutionary soldier. He was commissioned a major (1776) in the 14th Virginia, and colonel (1778), taking command (1781) of the 3rd Virginia. The alleged deception of Buford by the British colonel Banaster Tarleton during a truce parley (1780) at the Waxhaws, N.C., led to the common expression "Tarleton's Quarter," signifying treachery and murder in cold blood. Buford's name was the countersign among the frontiersmen under Isaac Shelby, John Sevier, and William Campbell during the battle of King's Mountain (Oct. 7, 1780).

Buford, Abraham. b. in Woodford County, Ky., Jan. 18, 1820; d. at Danville, Ind., June 9, 1884. American Confederate soldier. Graduated (1841) from West Point, he served in the Mexican War, and was appointed (1862) a brigadier general in the Confederate army. In 1864 he joined a cavalry brigade under General Nathan Bedford Forrest's command, took part in many operations and raids, and was badly wounded. After the war he became a leading Kentucky turfman.

Buford, Jefferson. See under **Buford Expedition.**

Buford, John. b. in Woodford County, Ky., March 4, 1826; d. at Washington D.C., Dec. 16, 1863. American army officer; half brother of Napoleon Bonaparte Buford (1807–83). Graduated (1848) from West Point, he served on the Texas, New Mexico, Kansas, and Utah frontiers, bringing his regiment to Washington after the outbreak of the Civil War. In 1862 he was promoted to brigadier general, was wounded while covering John Pope's retreat during the Manassas campaign, and was appointed chief of cavalry of the Army of the Potomac, serving under George B. McClellan and A. E. Burnside at South Mountain, Antietam, and Fredericksburg. He commanded a division at the battle of Gettysburg (1863), where his cavalry took part in the first engagement that touched off the action. He was commissioned major general just before his death.

Buford, Napoleon Bonaparte. b. in Woodford County, Ky., Jan. 13, 1807; d. at Chicago, March 28, 1883. American soldier; half brother of John Buford (1826–63). He was graduated (1827) from West Point, where he was professor of natural and experimental philosophy (1834–35); he resigned from the army (1835) to go into business in Illinois. Commissioned a colonel (1861) of the 27th Illinois Volunteers, he participated in operations in Kentucky, Tennessee, and Mississippi. Promoted to brigadier general (1862), he commanded (1863–65) the District of East Arkansas. He emerged from war as a major general, and entered business and government service.

Buford Expedition. In U.S. history, the name applied to an emigrant force, numbering about 400, organized (1856) under the leadership of a proslavery leader named Jefferson Buford for the purpose of establishing proslavery settlements in Kansas. The members of the expedition played an important role in the Kansas Border War.

Bug (bög; Russian and Polish, bök). [Also, **Western Bug.**] River in E Poland, which rises in the Ukraine, U.S.S.R., and joins the Vistula ab. 17 mi. NW of Warsaw. It forms part of the boundary, as established in 1919 and again after World War II, between Poland and the U.S.S.R. Length, ab. 450 mi.

Bug. [Also: **Southern Bug;** ancient name, **Hypanis.**] River in the U.S.S.R., in the Ukrainian Soviet Socialist Republic; it joins the marshy estuary of the Dnieper ab. 30 mi. W of Kherson. Length, ab. 500 mi.; navigable from Voznesensk.

Buga (bö'gä). City in W Colombia, in Valle del Cauca department: trade center for cattle and rice. It dates from colonial times. 19,595 (1938).

Buga, Kazimieras. b. at Pažiegė, Dusetos, Lithuania, Nov. 6, 1879; d. at Königsberg, Dec. 1, 1924. Lithuanian linguist. Graduated (1911) from the University of St. Petersburg, where he also did postgraduate work, he was a professor at the University of Perm, Russia (1916–19), and at the University at Kaunas (1922–24).

Bugabo (bö.gä'bō). Subgroup of the Bantu-speaking Haya of NW Tanganyika, in E Africa.

Buganda (bū.gan'dạ). Native kingdom in Uganda protectorate, British East Africa, forming a separate province and divided into Mengo, Masaka, and Mubende districts. It occupies the N and NW shores and adjacent islands of Lake Victoria. Its chief city, Kampala, is also the commercial and cultural center of Uganda as a whole. The province is peopled by the Baganda, a Bantu people well advanced when the first British appeared in the 1870's, and possessing their own king and government. It occupies a special place in the Uganda protectorate and has a treaty with Great Britain which recognizes its independence subject only to the advice of the governor. Capital, Kampala; area, 17,293 sq. mi. (exclusive of open water); pop. (adult males) 274,000 (est. 1947).

Bugayev (bö.gä'yif), **Boris Nicolayevich.** See **Bely, Andrey.**

Bugeaud de la Piconnerie (bü.zhō dẹ lȧ pē.kon.rē), **Thomas Robert.** [Title, Duc **d'Isly.**] b. at Limoges, France, Oct. 15, 1784; d. at Paris, June 10, 1849. French colonial official, marshal of France, and military writer. He served (1836–47) in Africa, was governor of Algeria (1840), and won the victory of Isly, in Morocco, on Aug. 14, 1844.

Bugenhagen (bö'gẹn.hä.gẹn), **Johann.** [Called Doctor **Pomeranus,** or Doctor **Pommer.**] b. at Wolin, in Pomerania, June 24, 1485; d. at Wittenberg, Germany, April 20, 1558. German reformer, a coadjutor of Martin Luther. A preacher and professor (1525) of Biblical exegesis at Wittenberg, he was a chief figure in the establishment of the first Protestant congregations in N and C Germany, and in Denmark. He translated the Bible into Low German, and published *Interpretatio in librum Psalmorum* (1524) and other works.

Bugey (bü.zhā). Region and former district in E France, lying N and W of the Rhone River, and S of Franche-Comté; comprised in the modern department of Ain. It formed part of the old Burgundian kingdom, passed to Savoy in the period 1137–1344, was ceded by Savoy to France in 1601, and was made by France a part of the general government of Burgundy.

Bugge (bö'gẹ), **(Elseus) Sophus.** b. at Laurvig, Norway, Jan. 5, 1833; d. at Christiania, July 8, 1907. Norwegian philologist, professor of comparative philology (1866 *et seq.*) at Christiania (now Oslo). He is best known from his work on the *Eddas* and old Norse runes.

Bugge, Thomas. b. at Copenhagen, Oct. 12, 1740; d. June 15, 1815. Danish astronomer and geographer.

Buginese (bö.gi.nēz', -nēs') or **Bugis** (bö'giz). A Malayo-Polynesian-speaking Moslem people of SW Celebes, numbering 1,533,035 (1930). Excellent sailors and warriors, they at one time extended their conquests as far as the Malay Peninsula, where the ruling family of Selangor is of Buginese origin. Buginese colonies are found today throughout Indonesia, especially in Borneo, where they number 95,000.

Bug Jargal (bug jar'gạl; French, büg zhȧr.gȧl). Novel by Victor Hugo. Its subject is the revolt of the Santo Domingo (i.e., Haitian) Negroes. The principal character, after whom the book is named, is a Negro who is in love with a white woman.

Buhl (būl). City in S Idaho, in Twin Falls County, near the Snake River, ab. 100 mi. SE of Boise in a farming region. 2,870 (1950).

Buhl (böl), **Charles André.** See **Boulle** or **Boule, Charles André.**

Buhl, Vilhelm. b. at Fredericia, Denmark, Oct. 16, 1881—. Danish political leader and jurist, who headed the underground Resistance movement against the Germans during World War II. He headed (1942; May–November, 1945) coalition governments as premier during and immediately after World War II. He served (1924) as director of taxes in Copenhagen, was a judge (1928–37) on the Permanent Court of Arbitration, and was elected (1932) as a Social-Democratic deputy to the *Landsting* (senate), becoming (1939) a *Folketing* (house of commons) member. While serving as finance minister (1937–42), he carried through important tax reforms. He became (1947) minister of economic coördination. He was active in the trade union and coöperative movements, organized the Copenhagen municipal employees' union, was cofounder (1916) of the Copenhagen retail coöperative society, and was chairman of the Workers Coöperative Housing Association and of the Danish branch of the Inter-Parliamentary Union.

Buhle (bö'lẹ), **Johann Gottlieb.** b. at Brunswick, Germany, Sept. 29, 1763; d. there, Aug. 11, 1821. German historian of philosophy. He wrote *Lehrbuch der Geschichte der Philosophie* (1796–1804), *Geschichte der neueren Philosophie* (1800–05), and others.

Bühler (bü'lėr), **Hans Adolf.** b. in Germany, July 4, 1877—. German painter, etcher, and designer. He studied (1898) at Karlsruhe, in the Academy of Fine Arts, and then became a pupil of Thomas until 1908; then he traveled to Italy, where he studied and worked. Michelangelo, Matthias Grünewald, and the French impressionists all were strong influences on his work. A list of his paintings includes *Brunehilde in Isenland, To the Unknown God, The Niebelungs, Job, The Clan,* and *Pietà.*

Bühren (bü'rẹn), **Ernst Johann.** See **Biron, Ernst Johann.**

Bührer (bü'rėr), **Jakob.** b. at Zurich, Switzerland, Nov. 8, 1882—. Swiss dramatist and novelist writing in German. He produced *Marignano* (1918), *Ein neues Tellenspiel* (1923), and other thought-provoking plays. His dialect comedy *Das Volk der Hirten* (1918), considered one of the most hilarious satires on Swiss types and idiosyncrasies, ran for many years in the theaters of Switzerland.

Buhuşi (bö.hösh′). Town in NE Rumania, in the region of Moldavia, situated on the Bistriţa River, ab. 20 mi. NW of Bacău; agricultural markets and textile factories. 8,198 (1948).

Buil (bwēl), **Bernardo.** b. in Catalonia, Spain, c1450; d. at the Cuxa convent, 1520. Spanish Benedictine monk. In 1493 he was chosen with 11 other Benedictines to go with Christopher Columbus to Hispaniola (Columbus's second voyage to the Western Hemisphere). The Pope named him superior and apostolical vicar of the New World. His position gave him much influence in Hispaniola, where he acted as counselor; but he showed an unrelenting disposition toward the Indians, and joined the malcontents who opposed Columbus. In 1494 he returned to Spain to prefer charges against him, and he was long a most dangerous enemy of the admiral. He did not go again to America, but was made abbot of the Cuxa convent.

Builder of Bridges, The. Four-act play (1909) by Alfred Sutro.

Builders, The. Novel (1919) by Ellen Glasgow. It reflects its author's hope for a national leadership to arise from the "new South" of the U.S.

Building of the Ship, The. Ode by Henry Wadsworth Longfellow, published (1849) in *The Seaside and the Fireside.* Written in trochaic meter, it concludes with the famous line extolling the Union: "Thou, too, sail on, O Ship of State!" The narrative poem deals metaphorically with the building and launching of a sailing vessel.

Builsa (bö.ēl′sä). [Also: **Boulea, Bulse, Kandiaga.**] Sudanic-speaking people of W Africa, inhabiting the N part of the Northern Territories of the Gold Coast. Their language is related to those of the Mossi and Dagombe. They practice hoe agriculture, and their principal food is millet. They are non-Mohammedan.

Buisson (bwē.sôṅ), **Ferdinand Édouard.** b. at Paris, Dec. 20, 1841; d. at Thieuloy-St.-Antoine, Oise, France, Feb. 2, 1932. French educator and politician, winner (with Ludwig Quidde) of the Nobel peace prize (1927). He served as professor of pedagogy at the Sorbonne, director of elementary teaching, and as a radical socialist member (1902–24) of the Chamber of Deputies. A champion of the League of Nations, he was for 13 years president of the Ligue de Droit de l'Homme; he also played a major role in helping to establish a system of free compulsory secular education in France. Author of *Dictionnaire de pédagogie* (Dictionary of Pedagogy, 1882–93).

Buitenzorg (boi′tẹn.zôrċh). City on the island of Java, in the Republic of Indonesia, ab. 36 mi. S of Batavia. It contains the palace of the former governor general, and important botanical gardens. In the federation (1946–50) known as the United States of Indonesia, it was part of the *negara* (state) of Pasoendan (West Java). Pop. ab. 65,000.

Buja (bö′jä). [Also: **Babudja, Wabudja.**] Subgroup of the Bantu-speaking Shona of SE Africa.

Bujalance (bö.Hä.län′thā). Town in S Spain, in the province of Córdoba, ab. 25 mi. E of the city of Córdoba: small textile and pottery manufactures, flour mills, and agricultural trade. It has the ruins of a Moorish castle. 15,728 (1940).

Bujayah (bö′jä.yä). Arabic name of **Bougie.**

Bukaa (bůk′ä), **El.** See **Bika, El.**

Bukavu (bö.kä′vö). See **Costermansville,** town.

Bukhara (bö.Hä′rạ, -kä′rạ). [Also, **Bokhara.**] Former emirate in C Asia, under Russian influence, bounded by Asiatic Russia on the N, E, and W, Khiva on the NW, and Afghanistan on the S: now largely incorporated in the Bukhara *oblast* (region) of the Uzbek Soviet Socialist Republic of the U.S.S.R. It corresponded partly to the ancient Sogdiana, and formed part of the dominions of Genghis Khan and of Tamerlane. The region occupied in part the lower basin of the Zeravshan River, produced grain, hemp, cotton, rice, fruits, tobacco, and livestock, and had manufactures of silk, firearms, jewelry, and cutlery. Its capital was Bukhara. The government was a hereditary despotism, with a Russian resident. The population was composed of Tadzhiks, Uzbeks, and Turkomans. The prevailing religion was Mohammedanism. Bukhara was taken by the Uzbeks c1505. It was at war with Russia in the period 1865–68, and ceded Samarkand to Russia in 1868.

Bukhara. [Also, **Bokhara.**] City in the U.S.S.R., in the Uzbek Soviet Socialist Republic: formerly the capital of the emirate of Bukhara. The manufacture of leather and shoes and the needle and loom industries are important here. An important Moslem city from early times, it was surnamed "the Noble," and was renowned as an intellectual center of C Asia. It contains many mosques, and formerly had Mohammedan theological schools. 50,382 (1939).

Bukharest (bū.kạ.rest′, bö-). See **Bucharest.**

Bukhari (bů.ċhä′rē), **al-.** [Full name, **Abu Abdallah Mohammed ibn-Ismail al-Bukhari al-Jufi.**] b. at Bukhara, in C Asia (now in the Uzbek Soviet Socialist Republic of the U.S.S.R.), 810; d. in Samarkand (also now in the Uzbek Soviet Socialist Republic), 870. Moslem scholar and compiler of a Mohammedan holy book. By birth an Iranian, he traveled throughout the Moslem world gathering and noting down religious traditions and legends. From among some 600,000 such traditions (which he is said to have obtained from upwards of 1,000 individuals), he selected 7,275, which he arranged under a title now usually shortened to *al-Sahih* ("the Genuine"). This work stands second only to the Koran in the reverence accorded it by pious Mohammedans, and as an authoritative source of Mohammedan law.

Bukharin (bö.Hä′rin), **Nikolai Ivanovich.** b. at Moscow, Oct. 9, 1888; d. March 13, 1938. Russian communist leader and editor, a victim of the 1938 "purge." A revolutionist even in his boyhood, he led a strike of secondary school pupils at the time of the abortive Russian revolt in 1905, and his many arrests and prison sentences may have begun even earlier than that. In 1906 he joined the Bolshevik faction of the Russian Social-Democratic Party, and in 1912 could be considered one of its leaders, collaborating with Lenin in editing *Pravda,* the party organ, then published in Austria. In 1916 he went to New York, where he edited the Russian-language newspaper *Novy Mir* (New World). After the October Revolution in 1917 he held important rank in the Moscow Communist Party and in the soviet government of that city. He also became a member of the central committee of the party and of the Politburo. The Bolsheviks, themselves the furthest left of major existing political groups, also had their right and left wings, and Bukharin was the leader of the left. He was head (1926–29) of the Third International, and to all appearances securely entrenched as a leader of the communist movement in the Soviet Union and throughout the world, but in 1929 he was expelled from the party on charges of deviations from orthodox doctrine. In 1934 he was restored to party membership and even to a position of great influence as editor of the newspaper *Izvestia,* but in 1937 he was removed from this, and all other official and party posts, and arrested on charges of conspiring with some of his own followers, with followers of Leon Trotsky, and with agents of foreign governments, to overthrow the Bolshevik regime. One of 20 who were tried before the Soviet supreme court in March, 1938, he was found guilty and sentenced to death.

Bukhtarma (böH.tär.mä′). River in the U.S.S.R., in the Kazakh Soviet Socialist Republic, a tributary of the Irtysh, in S Siberia. Length, ab. 250 mi.

Bukidnon (bö.kid′non). Province of the Philippine Islands, occupying the N central portion of Mindanao island. It is bounded by Misamis Oriental on the N, Agusan and Davao on the E, Cotabato on the S, and Cotabato and Lanao on the W. The C portion of the province is occupied by the Bukidnon Highland, the highest part of which is 7,803 ft. The Tagloan River rises in the highlands and traverses the province on its way to Macajalar Bay; the Pulangi-Mindanao River rises in the highlands and flows S and W to Illana Bay. Capital, Maylaybalay; area, 3,173 sq. mi.; pop. 63,470 (1948).

Bukn Fjord (bůk′ạn). See **Bokn Fjord.**

Bukoba (bö.kō′bạ). Inland lake port in E Africa, in Tanganyika territory, British East Africa, situated on the W shore of Lake Victoria, S of the Uganda-Tanganyika border. It is the commercial center for the surrounding region. Coffee plantations are situated in and about the town. Traces of tin and gold have been found in the region. European pop. ab. 200.

Bukovina (bö.kọ.vē'nạ). See **Bucovina.**

Bukowina (bö.kō.vē'nä). German name of **Bucovina.**

Bulacan (bö.lä.kän'). Province of the Philippine Islands, in C Luzon. It is bounded by Nueva Ecija on the N, Tayabas on the E, Rizal province and Manila Bay on the S, and Pampanga on the W. The Rio Grande de la Pampanga flows through it from N to S. The E part of the province is mountainous; the W part is fertile, producing sugar cane and rice. The population is Tagalog. Capital, Malolos; area, 1,008 sq. mi.; pop. 411,382 (1948).

Bulak (bö.läk'). [Also, **Bulaq.**] Port of Cairo, Egypt, in NE Africa, on the Nile River. It formerly contained the National Museum now within the city of Cairo proper.

Bulama (bö.lä'mạ). See **Bolama.**

Bulandshahr (bö.lạnd.shär'). [Also, **Bolandshahr.**] District of the Meerut division, Uttar Pradesh (United Provinces), Union of India, just E of Delhi: wheat, cotton, rice, barley, and sugar. Area, 1,899 sq. mi.; pop. 1,317,223 (1941).

Bulawayo (bö.lạ.wä'yō). [Also, **Buluwayo.**] City in Southern Rhodesia, S central Africa, situated in Matakeleland province, in the SW part of the colony, ab. 299 mi. SW of Salisbury and ab. 674 mi. NE of Johannesburg. It is one of the two chief towns in the territory and possesses many exceptionally fine buildings and streets. It was founded in 1893, and became a city in 1943. Gold reefs and deposits of coal are located in the vicinity. The town is in the center of a large grazing area, and is also the main railway center in Southern Rhodesia and the headquarters of the Rhodesian railways. It is a major industrial and educational city, and is continually growing. It is the site of the former home of Cecil J. Rhodes. Pop., with suburbs, 61,693, including 59,819 Europeans (1946).

Bulem (bůl'ẹm). See **Bullom.**

Bülffinger (bül'fing.ėr), **Georg Bernhard.** See **Bilfinger, Georg Bernhard.**

Bulfinch (bůl'finch), **Charles.** b. at Boston, Aug. 8, 1763; d. there, April 4, 1844. American architect; father of Thomas Bulfinch. He was graduated (1781) from Harvard. Some of his chief works in New England are the Doric column (1789) on Beacon Hill, the old State House at Hartford, Conn., and the Boston State House (completed in 1800). Before his departure (1817) for Washington, D.C., to assume the post of architect of the Capitol, he designed many public buildings and residences in Massachusetts, where he was largely responsible for introduction of the styles of Christopher Wren and Robert Adam. At Washington, where he succeeded Latrobe, his chief work was on the western front of the Capitol.

Bulfinch, Thomas. b. at Newton, Mass., July 15, 1796; d. at Boston, May 27, 1867. American author, now remembered chiefly for his widely read Greek and Roman mythology, *The Age of Fable* (1855); son of Charles Bulfinch. He was graduated (1814) from Harvard. As a clerk (1837 *et seq.*) in the Merchants' Bank of Boston he devoted his leisure hours to literary study. Among his other works are *Hebrew Lyrical History* (1853), *The Age of Chivalry* (1858), *Legends of Charlemagne* (1863), and *Poetry of the Age of Fable* (1863).

Bulgakov (böl.gä'kọf), **Leo.** b. at Moscow, March 22, 1889; d. at Binghamton, N.Y., July 20, 1948. Russian actor and stage director. After studying under Constantin Stanislavsky, he made his debut at the Moscow Art Theatre as Aloysha in Maxim Gorki's *The Lower Depths,* and remained in the company until 1926, visiting New York with it in 1923. In 1926 he came to New York to produce *Turandot* at the Provincetown Playhouse. Remaining in the U.S., he appeared in *Gods of the Lightning* (1928), *Street Scene* (1930), *Hope for the Best* (1945), and many other plays. He also staged a number of plays, his most successful production being James Hagan's *One Sunday Afternoon* (1933). In 1934 he went to Hollywood to direct the film *White Lies,* and appeared in other motion pictures.

Bulgakov, Mikhail Afanasyevich. b. at Kiev, Russia, May 15, 1891; d. 1940. Russian novelist and playwright. His best-known work is *The White Guard,* a novel of the civil war in the Ukraine, in which the White protagonists are treated rather sympathetically, even before they embrace Bolshevism. The author turned the novel into a play, *The Days of the Turbins,* which proved a great success. At one time its performance in the Soviet Union was forbidden. An English translation of the play is included in Eugene Lyons' *Six Soviet Plays* (1934).

Bulganin (böl.gä'nyin), **Nikolai Aleksandrovich.** b. 1895—. Russian Communist politician and soldier. A textile worker, he joined the Communist Party in 1917 and served with the secret police (*Cheka*) throughout the revolutionary period. After 1922 he was an industrial executive and served in various political posts. As chairman of the Moscow soviet at the time of Germany's attack on Russia in 1941, he became prominent in the defense of that city and before the end of the war had risen to army general and deputy defense commissar. In 1944 he was the Russian representative to the Polish Committee of National Liberation and for his work in helping to establish a Communist regime in Poland he was made a member of the Politburo in 1946. In 1947 he succeeded Stalin as minister of the armed forces and became deputy premier. Bulganin, a member of the central committee of the Communist Party of the U.S.S.R. since 1939 and a member of the presidium of the Communist Party (which replaced the Politburo in 1952), was often mentioned as the principal candidate to succeed Stalin. On the formation (1953) of Malenkov's government after Stalin's death, he became minister of war.

Bulgar (bul'gär). A member of a Turkic people that migrated to Europe from Central Asia in the 6th century A.D., establishing their rule from the Volga to the Danube. Although the western Bulgars were soon absorbed by the Slavs, the eastern Bulgars maintained a khanate on the Volga until the 14th century. The Volga Bulgars adopted agriculture, built cities, and conducted a thriving trade with North Russia, Siberia, and the Arab world. Their khanate came under Mongol domination in the 13th century and was finally destroyed by Tamerlane. The modern Chuvash are descendants of the old Bulgars.

Bulgar. [Also, **Great Bulgar.**] Capital of the Volga Bulgars, near what is now Kazan, U.S.S.R. It contains several outstanding examples of Mohammedan architecture.

Bulgaria (bul.gãr'i.ạ). [Bulgarian: **Blgariya**; in full-**Narodna Republika Blgariya.**] Republic in SE Europe, occupying the E central and E portions of the Balkan peninsula. It is bounded by Rumania on the N, the Black Sea on the E, European Turkey and Greece on the S, and Yugoslavia on the W.

Population, Area, and Political Divisions. In 1949 Bulgaria was subdivided into 14 new provinces, with the city of Sofia a separate administrative unit. The principal cities, in order of population at the 1946 census, are Sofia, Plovdiv, Stalin (formerly Varna), Ruse, and Burgas. Sofia is the chief center of trade and cultural life. Capital, Sofia; area, 42,796 sq. mi.; pop. 7,022,206 (1946), 7,160,-000 (est. 1949).

Terrain and Climate. Bulgaria is largely a mountainous or hilly country, with relatively small areas of plains. It may be subdivided into at least five great natural regions: (1) The Danubian tableland, lying S of the Danube River. This is a broad dissected plain, with fertile loess soils, and is Bulgaria's chief agricultural region. In the E there is a hilly karst region extending to the Black Sea. To the S the valleys become deeper, the land becomes hilly, and there is a transition to (2) the Balkan Mountains. This is a high range of rounded mountains, traversed by more than 30 passes, and 2 railways. (3) To the south of the Balkans is the deep interior valley of the Maritsa River. This is a broad fertile basin, ab. 125 mi. long, the chief center of tobacco growing. (4) The Rhodope Mountains are high, massive mountains, with the peak elevation of 9,592 ft., the highest summit in Bulgaria. Lumbering and sheep-raising are the chief activities. (5) Western Bulgaria is a mountainous region along the border of Yugoslavia, with some fertile basins, notably the plains of Sofia and Kyustendil. Lignite coal is mined at Pernik. The climate of Bulgaria is of the humid continental type, with hot summers and cold winters in the lowlands. The mountain regions have cool summers and cold winters; snow may remain in the higher mountains until summer. Severe cold waves may be experienced in winter, and snow is on the ground for several months, except near the Black Sea coast.

Agriculture, Industry, and Trade. Bulgaria is primarily an agrarian nation, with 80 percent of the working population in agriculture, and only 8 percent employed in all manufacturing industries in 1934. There has been some development of industry in recent years, but the chief handicap is a lack of capital. About 45 percent of the land is arable; in addition, 29 percent is productive forest. The agricultural economy is essentially a peasant subsistence type, with small farms, and principal emphasis on cereal grains and sunflower seed. Wheat occupies about a third of the total crop land, and maize about a quarter. Other crops in order of area (1947) are barley, rye, oats, sunflower seed, grapes, tobacco, mixed grains, sugar beets, and potatoes. The grazing of sheep and goats is important in the mountainous regions; in 1947 there were 8,784,000 sheep and 1,069,000 goats in Bulgaria. The forests are principally hardwoods, of Central European varieties. Industries in Bulgaria, mostly associated with agriculture, include grain mills, sugar refineries, tanneries, rose-oil distilleries, and tobacco plants. Foreign trade is chiefly an exchange of agricultural products for imports of manufactured goods and machinery. Transportation is one of Bulgaria's problems. There are only ab. 2,200 mi. of railway, and 16,000 mi. of roads, chiefly unimproved. Only the lower Maritsa and the Danube are navigable. The Black Sea ports of Stalin (Varna) and Burgas, and the Danube port of Ruse are the chief maritime outlets for trade. Only three mineral products are important in the Bulgarian economy: lignite coal (4,250,000 tons in 1948), salt (120,000 tons), and cement (325,000 tons). These are primarily consumed by the domestic market.

History. In the 8th century B.C. the region which is now Bulgaria and surrounding areas were occupied by an Indo-Germanic people, the Thracians. The Greeks had established trading colonies on the Black Sea coast at Odessus and Mesembria. Alexander the Great incorporated the Thracians into his empire, but they later broke away, and were finally incorporated into the Roman Empire by the conquest of Moesia in 29 B.C. During the 5th to 7th centuries, Slavic tribes moved into the region. The Bulgars, an Asiatic people, advanced westward from their previous home on the Volga steppes, and occupied Bulgaria in 679 A.D. They fused with the earlier inhabitants, and adopted much of their culture. Christianity was introduced in the 9th century. In 1018 Bulgaria was conquered and annexed by the Byzantine Empire. In 1186 a second Bulgarian state was established by Ivan I with its capital at Trnovo. In 1393 the Turks under Bajazet I conquered Bulgaria and merged it completely into their empire, suppressing the church. Not until the latter part of the 18th century did Bulgarian nationalism reawaken. In 1875 a rebellion broke out, which led to the Russo-Turkish War. Bulgaria was made an independent principality in 1878 under Prince Alexander, and in 1885 annexed Eastern Rumelia. In 1908 Bulgaria declared itself a fully independent kingdom, with Ferdinand I as ruler. The country was victorious in the First Balkan War of 1912–13, and acquired a strip of the Aegean coast. However, in the Second Balkan War and in World War I it was on the side of the Central Powers, and lost S Dobrudja to Rumania and the Aegean coastal territories to Greece. This left Bulgaria a member of the "revisionist" group of European states. There were numerous political changes in the years 1920–35, leading finally to a personal control of the government by king Boris III. On March 1, 1941, Bulgaria formally joined the Axis powers, and in April, 1941, occupied parts of Yugoslavia and Greece after the Nazi conquest of these countries. In September, 1940, Rumania had ceded S Dobruja to Bulgaria under German pressure. Though an Axis satellite, Bulgaria never declared war on the U.S.S.R., because of popular pro-Russian sentiment. In 1944 the German defeats led to a crisis in Bulgaria, resulting in the formation of a pro-Allied government in September, 1944. The U.S.S.R. formally declared war on Bulgaria, however, and this resulted in an armistice and a Bulgarian declaration of war on Germany. The Soviet army under Marshal Tolbukhin occupied Bulgaria, and Bulgarian troops were ordered withdrawn from Yugoslavia and Greece. A Fatherland-Front government was formed under Georgiev, and was confirmed by a one-ticket election in 1945. In 1946 the monarchy was abolished by plebiscite, and young Simeon II, heir to the throne, went into exile. The Communist leader Dimitrov became prime minister. In September, 1947 the leader of the opposition, Nikolai Petkov, was executed, and full control of the government passed to the Communists, who proclaimed a new constitution, the nationalization of industries and mines, and a new plan for the development of agricultural collectives, power stations, and the like, on the Soviet pattern. Bulgaria has thus joined the bloc of Soviet satellite states of Eastern Europe.

Culture. About seven eighths of the population are Bulgarian-speaking, and 10 percent speak Turkish. Religious grouping is: Eastern Orthodox church, ab. 85 percent; Mohammedan, 11½ percent; Roman Catholic, 1 percent, and small groups of Jews, Armenian Christians, and Protestants.

Bulgaria, Great. [Also, **White Bulgaria.**] Former name of the region between the Kama and Volga rivers, now in the S U.S.S.R., which was occupied by the eastern Bulgars.

Bulgarian Horrors and the Question of the East, The. Prose work (1876) by William Ewart Gladstone, published in pamphlet form. It very eloquently fanned the indignation engendered at the time in England by the Turkish treatment of their subject Christian populations in the Balkans.

Bulgarin (böl.gä′rin), **Faddey Venediktovich.** b. in Lithuania, 1789; d. at Tartu, in Estonia, Sept. 13, 1859. Russian novelist, journalist, and general writer. His chief work is the novel *Ivan Vyzhigin* (1829), sometimes called "The Russian Gil Blas" and available since 1831 in an English translation. He was a cofounder (1825) of a political journal known (in English) as *The Northern Bee*, which he used as a medium for violent attacks on Pushkin, Gogol, and other Russian writers of the day whose distrust of, or actual opposition to, the political absolutism which he espoused seemed to him to be dangerous to the point of treason.

Bulgarus (bul′ga̤.rus). b. at Bologna, Italy, in the latter part of the 11th century; d. 1166. Italian jurist, the most renowned of the "Four Doctors" of the school of law at the University of Bologna. His chief work is a commentary, *De regulis juris*. The other three scholars of the group known as the "Four Doctors" were Martinus Gosia, Hugo, and Jacobus. They sometimes served almost as a committee to give legal advice to rulers of the day (as at the Diet of Roncaglia in 1158), but had very separate identities indeed on the faculty at Bologna; Hugo and Jacobus were less often involved in controversies than were Martinus and Bulgarus (who headed rival schools of juristic theory at Bologna: the former insisting that the law could and should be accommodated to the "equity of the purse," while the latter maintained the position that the exact letter of the law should be applied in all cases). The position taken by Bulgarus was the one that eventually won out at Bologna, and the one which therefore had the greatest influence upon Accursius, Azo, and other later jurists at Bologna.

Bulgary (bul′ga̤.ri) or **Bulgar the Great** (bul′gär). See **Bolgary.**

Bulge, Battle of the. See **Battle of the Bulge.**

Bulkeley (bulk′li), **Morgan Gardner.** b. at East Haddam, Conn., Dec. 26, 1837; d. Nov. 6, 1922. American insurance executive and politician. He served in the Civil War with the 13th New York Infantry. One of the founders during the early 1870's of the United States Bank at Hartford, Conn., he became its first president, and was the third president (1879 *et seq.*) of the Aetna Life Insurance Company, which became, under his management, one of the largest life insurance firms in the U.S. He was mayor of Hartford (1880–88), Republican governor of Connecticut (1888 *et seq.*), and a U.S. senator (1905–11). He was also interested in sports, and became president of baseball's National League at the time of its founding in 1876.

Bulkeley, Peter. b. at Odell, Bedfordshire, England, Jan. 31, 1582 or 1583; d. at Concord, Mass., March 9, 1689. American Puritan clergyman, notable as the founder of the town of Concord, Mass. He received (1608) his M.A. degree at St. John's College, Cambridge. His differences with the ruling ecclesiasts of the Church of England caused him to emigrate (c1634) to Massachusetts where, after a brief stay at Cambridge, he founded the town of Concord and became its first minister. He was prominent in the New England theocracy.

Bulkley (bulk'li). River in W central British Columbia, Canada. It rises in the high mountainous interior of the Coast Ranges, and flows NW to join the Skeena River at Hazelton. Its valley is used as a route to the coast by the main line of the Canadian National railroad, and by a transcontinental highway. Length, ab. 118 mi.

Bulkley, John Williams. b. at Fairfield, Conn., Nov. 3, 1802; d. June 19, 1888. American educator. He attended Hamilton College, and taught at Fairfield, Conn., Troy, N.Y., and Albany, N.Y. (1838 *et seq.*). In 1850, he moved to Williamsburg, N.Y., and when Williamsburg, Bushwick, and Brooklyn combined to form the single municipality of Brooklyn, he became Brooklyn's first superintendent of schools. He helped found (1845) a New York state teachers' association, the first of its kind in the U.S., and served as its first president; he also helped organize the National Teachers' Association (now the National Education Association), becoming its first secretary and fourth president.

Bulkley, Lucius Duncan. b. at New York, Jan. 12, 1845; d. July 20, 1928. American physician and medical writer, notable as an expert on skin diseases. Graduated (1866) from Yale, he received (1869) an M.D. degree from New York's College of Physicians and Surgeons, and studied dermatology abroad before settling at New York in 1872. He helped to establish the principles of postgraduate teaching which became the basis of the method used by the New York Post-Graduate Medical School and the New York Polyclinic. He founded (1882) the New York Skin and Cancer Hospital, was professor of dermatology in the Post-Graduate Medical School and Hospital, and was president (1897) of the American Academy of Medicine. He founded (1874) the *Archives of Dermatology*, editing it for eight years, and also founded a quarterly journal, *Cancer*, which urged the nonsurgical treatment of the disease. (The recommendations advanced in this journal, and in several independent volumes written by Bulkley on the same subject, were rejected by virtually all of his professional colleagues. Some authorities have suggested that his curiously unscientific and almost belligerent interest in cancer, which was first evidenced in print after his retirement as a dermatologist, stemmed from his opposition to surgery in general, and from a deep conviction that death had often narrowly passed him by in order that he might live to make some contribution even greater than had been possible for him as a dermatologist.)

Bull, A Young. Oil painting by Paul Potter, in the museum at The Hague, Netherlands. It is a large canvas, with strong light effects. The bull is under a tree in a group with a cow, a ram, a sheep, a lamb, and a herdsman, with more animals in the distant landscape.

Bull (bůl), **Charles Stedman.** b. at New York, 1846; d. there, April 17, 1911. American ophthalmologist. He was a house physician (1867–68) at Bellevue Hospital, assistant surgeon (1871–73) at Manhattan Eye and Ear Hospital, assistant surgeon (1871–76) and surgeon (1876 *et seq.*) at the New York Eye and Ear Infirmary, and professor (1898 *et seq.*) of ophthalmology at Cornell University Medical College.

Bull, Ephraim Wales. b. at Boston, March 4, 1806; d. Sept. 26, 1895. American horticulturist, originator of the famous Concord grape, produced at some time between 1849 and 1853. By trade a goldbeater until he established himself firmly as a horticulturist, he cultivated grapes at Boston, and later at Concord, where he evolved his noted contribution as one of the strains of the northern fox grape. Initially he made money from the Concord grape, but received no income from it after it was cultivated commercially. He served (1855–56) in the Massachusetts state legislature, and was a member (1856–58) of the Massachusetts State Board of Agriculture.

Bull, John. See also **John Bull.**

Bull, John. b. in Somersetshire, England, 1563; d. at Antwerp, March 12, 1628. English composer and organist. The song *God Save the King* was wrongly attributed to him. He became (1591) organist of the chapel royal, and was named (1596) professor of music at Gresham College. Having left England in 1613, he was organist (1617–28) of Antwerp Cathedral.

Bull, Olaf. b. at Oslo, Nov. 10, 1883; d. June 23, 1933. Norwegian poet, held by many to be the greatest in the 20th century. He is noted for his intricate melodic effects, his exquisite choice of words, and his sensitivity of feeling.

Bull, Ole Bornemann. b. at Bergen, Norway, Feb. 5, 1810; d. at Lysø, Norway, Aug. 17, 1880. Norwegian violinist and composer, noted for his brilliant technique. He made his debut at Paris in 1832, and made five appearances (1843–79) in the U.S. In 1850 he established a national theater at Bergen. He also projected, but did not succeed in establishing, a Norwegian colony in the U.S., and lost much of his fortune through the purchase of 100,000 acres which were to serve as a basis for the settlement. His compositions include two concertos and several sets of variations especially suited to his own instrumental style.

Bull, William. b. in South Carolina, 1683; d. March 21, 1755. American Colonial government official; father of William Bull (1710–91). A member of the Commons House, South Carolina (1706–19), he was appointed (1719) Lord Proprietor's Deputy. He served as a member (1721–37) of the Council under the new government, and was lieutenant governor (1738 *et seq.*). In 1733 he advised James Edward Oglethorpe on the location of his first settlement in Georgia.

Bull, William. b. at Ashley Hall, S.C., Sept. 24, 1710; d. at London, July 4, 1791. American Colonial governor; second son of William Bull (1683–1755). He studied medicine at Leiden, and was the first native-born American to receive an M.D. degree. He was a member of the Commons House, South Carolina (1736–49), and its speaker (1740–42; 1744–49). A member (1748–59) of the Council, becoming lieutenant governor in 1759, he was also, on five occasions between 1760 and 1775, governor for eight years. A Loyalist in the Revolution, he departed with the British troops in 1782.

Bull, William Tillinghast. b. at Newport, R.I., May 18, 1849; d. Feb. 22, 1909. American surgeon, said to have been the first in the U.S. wholly to specialize in surgery from the outset of his professional career. He was graduated (1869) from Harvard, and received an M.D. degree (1872) from the College of Physicians and Surgeons, at New York, in which city he set up his practice after additional study and clinical training in Europe. He was connected with the New York Dispensary (1875–77), the Chambers Street Hospital (1877–78), St. Luke's Hospital (1880–83), and with other New York hospitals, and was professor of surgery (1889–1904) at the College of Physicians and Surgeons. He specialized in surgery of the abdomen, contributing methods for treatment of gunshot wounds, and was one of the first American surgeons to perceive the value of and adopt systematic methods of antisepsis.

Bullant (bü.läṅ), **Jean.** b. probably at Écouen, France, c1515; d. Oct. 10, 1578. French architect. Of his early career nothing is known. After 1570 he became architect of the Tuileries, and erected the pavilion called by his name. In the same year he succeeded Francesco Primaticcio as head artist at Fontainebleau.

Bullard (bůl'ạrd), **Arthur.** [Pseudonym, **Albert Edwards.**] b. at St. Joseph, Mo., Dec. 8, 1879; d. Sept. 10, 1929. American journalist, government official, and writer. He was a foreign correspondent (1905–17, 1921 *et seq.*) for *Harper's Weekly*, *Collier's Weekly*, and *The Outlook;* he covered (1912–13) the Balkan War for *The Outlook* and wrote (1914–17) news reports on World War I. He was a special assistant (1919–20) and chief (1920–21) of the Russian Division in the U.S. State Department, and a member (1926–27) of the secretariat of the League of Nations. Editor (1921–24) of *Our World;* author of *Panama* (1911), *Comrade Yetta* (1913), *The Barbary Coast* (1913), *The Diplomacy of the Great War* (1915), *Mobilizing America* (1917), *The Stranger* (1920), and *Pacific Problems* (1921).

Bullard, Henry Adams. b. at Pepperell, Mass., Sept. 9, 1788; d. at New Orleans, April 17, 1851. American jurist and legislator. Graduated from Harvard (B.A., 1807; M.A., 1836), he was a soldier of fortune (1812–13) with the Mexican revolutionary forces operating against the Spanish in Texas, after which he opened a law office in Natchitoches, La. He was a state district judge on two occasions between 1822 and 1830, judge of the supreme court of Louisiana (1834–46), and professor of civil law (1847–50) in the University of Louisiana (now Tulane University). He served briefly (1850) in the state house of representatives, and was a member of the 31st U.S. Congress. First president of the Louisiana Historical Society, he may have been its founder (1836).

Bullard, Robert Lee. [Called **"Counterattack Bullard."**] b. at Youngsboro, Ala., Jan. 15, 1861; d. on Governors Island, N.Y., Sept. 11, 1947. American commander of the U.S. Second Army during World War I. He was graduated (1885) from the U.S. Military Academy, campaigned (1899–1901) against the Philippine insurrectionists, and participated (1915–16) in fighting on the Mexican border. Appointed (1917) a brigadier general with the 1st Division of the American Expeditionary Forces, he commanded (1918) the 2nd Division as a major general, and led the Second Army as a lieutenant general (October, 1918). He was known as "Counterattack Bullard" for his aggressive military tactics. After his retirement (1925) from the service, he was active in patriotic movements, and contributed articles on national and international affairs to newspapers, magazines, and military journals.

Bullard, William Hannum Grubb. [Sometimes called **"the Father of American Radio."**] b. at Media, Pa., Dec. 6, 1866; d. Nov. 24, 1927. American naval officer, a pioneer in the use of radio by the U.S. navy. He was commander (1916–18) of the battleship *Arkansas* in World War I, and head (1921–22) of the Yangtze patrol force, U.S. Asiatic Fleet. He headed (1908–12) the department of electrical engineering at the U.S. Naval Academy, superintended (1912–16) the naval radio service, and directed (1919–21) communications in the naval department. He aided (1919) in the formation of what is now the Radio Corporation of America. In 1927 he was chairman of the Federal Radio Commission. Author of *Naval Electricians' Test and Hand Book* (1904).

Bullcalf (bul'kaf). In Shakespeare's *Henry IV*, part II, a recruit.

Bulle (bül). [German, **Boll.**] Town in W Switzerland, in the canton of Fribourg: the chief place of the Gruyère, a famous cattle-breeding and cheese-making district. 4,644 (1941).

Bulle (bul'e), **Konstantin.** b. at Minden, Germany, March 30, 1844; d. 1905. German historian. He was the author of *Geschichte der neuesten Zeit 1815–1885* (History of the Most Recent Time, 1815–1885, 1886) and *Geschichte des zweiten Kaiserreichs und des Königsreichs Italien* (History of the Second Empire and the Kingdom of Italy, 1880).

Bullen (bul'en), **Arthur Henry.** b. at London, Feb. 9, 1857; d. at Stratford-on-Avon, England, Feb. 29, 1920. English literary critic, scholar, biographer, editor, and poet. Educated at the City of London School and at Worcester College, Oxford, he contributed many articles to the *Dictionary of National Biography*, and founded the "Muses' Library" and the Shakespeare Head Press at Stratford, from which he published his "Stratford Town Shakespeare" in ten volumes. He was the author of *Weeping Cross* (1921), and *Elizabethans* (1924), essays, and edited the works (1881) of John Day, *Old English Plays* (1882–84), *Poems of Michael Drayton* (1883), *Carols and Poems from the 15th Century* (1884), *Lyrics from Elizabethan Song Books* (1886), the works of Thomas Campion (1889), *Speculum Amantis: Love Poems of the 17th Century* (1902), and other works. His edition of Campion, considered a major contribution to literary scholarship, was a virtual rediscovery of the genius of that poet.

Bullen, Frank Thomas. b. at London, April 5, 1857; d. March 1, 1915. English author and lecturer. He led a roving life from 1866 to 1883, chiefly at sea, rising from seaman to the rank of chief mate, and was a junior clerk (1883–99) in the meteorological office. He wrote *The Cruise of the Cachalot* (1898), *Idylls of the Sea* (1899), *The Log of a Sea-waif* (1899), *Men of the Merchant Service* (1900), *With Christ at Sea* (1900), *Deep-sea Plunderings* (1902), *Creatures of the Sea* (1904), *Back to Sunny Seas* (1905), *Son of the Sea* (1907), *Our Heritage—the Sea* (1907), *Call of the Deep* (1908), *Young Nemesis* (1909), and others.

Buller (bul'ėr), **Charles.** b. at Calcutta, Aug. 6, 1806; d. at London, 1848. English Liberal politician; a pupil (1822–25) of Thomas Carlyle. Member of Parliament for West Looe (1830–31) and for Kiskeard (1832–48), he became (1838) secretary to the governor general of Canada. He served as judge advocate general under Lord John Russell (1846), but declined the privy councillorship. As chief poor law commissioner (1847), he carried through various short-bill reforms. He was the author of numerous pamphlets and articles.

Buller, Sir **Redvers Henry.** b. in Devonshire, England, 1839; d. June 2, 1908. British general. After serving in China (1860) and with the Red River Expedition (1870), he took part in the Ashanti war (1873–74), the Kaffir war (1878), the Zulu war (1879), the Boer action of 1881, the Egyptian war (1882), and the Sudan campaigns of 1884–85. He was undersecretary for Ireland (1886–87) and quartermaster general (1887–90). Appointed lieutenant general (1891) and general (1896), he was commander in chief (1899) in South Africa; his failure to relieve the siege of Ladysmith, during the Boer War, lost him his command; he retired in 1901.

Bullet (bü.le), **Pierre.** b. 1639; d. 1716. French architect; a pupil of François Blondel. He constructed, after the plans of his master, the Porte St.-Denis, and built on his own designs the Porte St.-Martin (1674). He also built the porch of the Church of Saint Thomas d'Aquin, and made the decorations of two chapels at St.-Germain-des-Prés.

Bullett (bul'et), **Gerald.** b. at London, Dec. 30, 1893—. English fiction writer, anthologist, and critic. His works include *The Baker's Cart* (1925), *Modern English Fiction* (1926), *Helen's Lovers* (1932), *Eden River* (1934), *Judgment in Suspense* (1946), and *George Eliot, Her Life and Books* (1947).

Bullialdus (bul.i.al'dus). Latinized surname of **Boulliau, Ismaël.**

Bullinger (bul'ing.ėr), **Heinrich.** b. at Bremgarten, Aargau, Switzerland, July 18, 1504; d. at Zurich, Switzerland, Sept. 17, 1575. Swiss reformer and historian, successor of Huldreich Zwingli at Zurich. He was a leader in the drawing up (1536) of the First Helvetic Confession. With John Calvin he drew up (1549) Consensus Tigurinus on the Lord's Supper. He also prepared (1566) the Confession of Basel or Second Helvetic Confession.

"Bullion State." Nickname of **Missouri.**

Bullitt (bul'it), **Alexander Scott.** b. at Dumfries, Va., 1762; d. April 13, 1816. American lieutenant governor and Kentucky pioneer, for whom Bullitt County in that state is named. After serving briefly (1783) in the Virginia House of Delegates, he moved to Kentucky, settling in Shelby County, and later in Jefferson County. He served as county lieutenant (1786) of Jefferson County, and was appointed (1787) a trustee of Louisville. He was a member (1788) of the convention for Kentucky statehood, and a member (1792) of the convention which drafted the state's first constitution. He served in the state senate, and was lieutenant governor from 1800 to c1804.

Bullitt, Henry Massie. b. in Shelby County, Ky., Feb. 28, 1817; d. at Louisville, Ky., Feb. 5, 1880. American physician and teacher. Graduated (1838) from the University of Pennsylvania, he was a professor (1846–48) at the St. Louis Medical College, and was appointed (1849) professor of materia medica at Transylvania University. In 1850 he founded the Kentucky School of Medicine at Louisville, and in 1868 founded the Louisville Medical College, with which he was associated until he died. Both of these institutions have since become part of the University of Louisville.

Bullitt, William Christian. b. at Philadelphia, Pa., Jan. 25, 1891—. American diplomat, journalist, businessman, and novelist. In 1919 he went to Russia with Lincoln Steffens on an assignment the results of which were so controversial that Bullitt barred himself from diplomacy for 14 years, charging a betrayal by David Lloyd George of England and Woodrow Wilson of the U.S. He emerged (1933) from diplomatic retirement as first U.S. ambassador to the U.S.S.R., under Franklin D. Roosevelt, but asked to be relieved four years later, reportedly disillusioned with the Communist regime; he served till 1941 as ambassador to France. His second wife, whom he married in 1923, was the widow of the noted American Communist John Reed. His novel, *It's Not Done*, satirized the Philadelphia society and journalism of the early 1920's.

"Bull Moose" Party. Nickname given to the Progressive Party (1912–16) led by Theodore Roosevelt. The figure of a bull moose was adopted as the party symbol during the campaign of 1912.

Bulloch (bůl'ǫk), **Archibald.** b. at Charleston, S.C., c1730; d. in February, 1777. American colonial government official. He was a member (1768–73) of the Commons House of Georgia. A Revolutionary patriot, he signed the first appeal (1774) for an assembly of colonial irreconcilables at Savannah. He served as president (1775–77) of the Provincial Congress, and upon the flight of the royal governor was appointed (1776) "President and Commander-in-chief of Georgia." In 1776 he led a party of militia and Indians against the British base on Tybee Island.

Bulloch, James Dunwody. b. near Savannah, Ga., June 25, 1823; d. Jan. 7, 1901. American naval officer and Confederate agent. Appointed (1839) a midshipman in the U.S. navy, he served in foreign waters and in the coast survey (1849–51). After duty in the mail service, he retired to enter private shipping; soon after the outbreak of the Civil War he was commissioned as foreign agent of the Confederate navy and assigned to buy or build naval craft in England. He supervised the fitting out of all of the Confederate cruisers except the *Georgia.* When the British ministry frowned upon these merchant-raider operations in 1863, he went to Paris. After the war he established a cotton firm at Liverpool. He was the author of *The Secret Service of the Confederate States in Europe* (2 vols., 1884).

Bullock (bůl'ǫk), **Charles Jesse.** b. at Boston, May 21, 1869; d. at Hingham, Mass., March 17, 1941. American economist. He served as instructor (1895–99) of economics at Cornell University, assistant professor (1899–1902) and professor (1902–03) at Williams College, and assistant professor (1903–08) and professor (1908–35) of economics at Harvard. He was the author of *The Finances of the United States 1775–89* (1895), *Introduction to the Study of Economics* (1900), *Essays on the Monetary History of the U.S.* (1900), *Finances of Massachusetts 1780–1905* (1907), *Economic Essays* (1936), and *Politics, Finance and Consequences* (1939).

Bullock, Rufus Brown. b. at Bethlehem, N.Y., March 28, 1834; d. April 27, 1907. American governor. An official of the Southern Express Company before the Civil War, he volunteered his services to the Confederacy in 1861, and was active in telegraph and railroad construction. After leaving the war as a lieutenant colonel, he became president of the Macon and Augusta Railroad in 1867, entering Georgia politics as a Republican member of the constitutional convention in 1868. A supporter of Reconstruction, he was governor (1868–71) of a Georgia administration which has been accused of misrule and corruption. Fleeing from the state, he was arrested and brought back for trial (1876), but was acquitted for lack of evidence. He later became president of the Atlanta Cotton Mills, and a director of the Union Pacific Railroad.

Bullock, William A. b. at Greenville, N.Y., 1813; d April 12, 1867. American inventor and manufacturer. He was the deviser of mechanical improvements for feeding, cutting, and printing paper which fundamentally affected press construction. After spending some years as a mechanic at Savannah and New York, he established (1849) a patent agency and shop in Philadelphia, where he also published a daily newspaper, *The Banner of the Union* (1849–53). As a publisher, he became interested in printing machinery; after 1859, he continued his designing and manufacturing at Pittsburgh, where he developed the Bullock Press (patented 1863). He died as a result of an accident that occurred while he was testing one of his installations.

Bullokar (bůl'ǫ.kär), **John.** b. c1581; d. c1641. English physician and lexicographer; probably a son of William Bullokar (fl. 1586). He published *An English Expositor* (1616) and a life of Christ (1618) in metrical verse. The second English dictionary to be published (having been preceded only by Robert Cawdrey's *A Table Alphabeticall,* in 1604), *An English Expositor* concentrates on "the hardest words used in our Language" and their foreign origins; it also includes obsolete terms, and labels many of its entries with their specialized usage. With the second revised edition (1663), the book became very popular.

Bullokar, William. fl. 1586. English educator and phonetist who translated (1585) *Aesop's Fables* from Latin; probably father of John Bullokar (c1581–c1641). Service in the army (1557) called him away from teaching (1550–57), but after an interim of study of law and agriculture, he returned (1573) to it. He advocated spelling reform (the addition of 14 letters to the alphabet) in a pamphlet (1575), and in a book (1580), and issued an English grammar, *Bref Grammar* (1586), which was called by Warton "the first grammar that ever waz, except ... *Grammar at Large.*"

Bullom (bůl'ǫm). [Also: **Ballam, Boullom, Bulem, Sherbro.**] Sudanic-speaking people of W Africa, inhabiting the coastal region of Sierra Leone, SE of Freetown. Their population is estimated at ab. 95,000 (by T. N. Goddard, *The Handbook of Sierra Leone,* 1925). They are divided into some 20 independent subgroups ruled by hereditary chiefs. Boys and girls are isolated from society for several years in secret initiation schools, known as *Poro* for boys and *Sande* for girls, in which they are trained for their future roles as adult men and women. The Bullom practice hoe agriculture, and their principal food is rice.

Bull Run (bůl' run'). Small river in E Virginia, which joins the Occoquan (a tributary of the Potomac) ab. 25 mi. SW of Washington, D.C. Near it occurred two battles in the American Civil War: **1.** The Confederates under the immediate command of General P. G. T. Beauregard (about 31,000) defeated the Union forces under General Irvin McDowell (about 28,000) on July 21, 1861. The Union loss was 2,952; that of the Confederates, 1,752. This was called by the Confederates the first battle of Manassas. McDowell's original strategy in this battle was to overwhelm Beauregard's numerically inferior force while General Robert Patterson conducted a holding action against the separate Confederate force under General J. E. Johnston. However, by July 20 part of Johnston's command had reached Beauregard, and on July 21 (after McDowell had broken through the Confederate left flank, only to be stopped by "Stonewall" Jackson, who received his epithet of "Stonewall" as a result of this action) the arrival of a brigade under E. Kirby Smith enabled the Confederates to launch a successful counterattack. The Union retreat quickly lost almost all semblance of order, and McDowell's troops, in utter panic, streamed all the way back to Washington, D.C. The battle had little permanent tactical importance; the Confederates, whose discipline was hardly better than that of McDowell's troops, failed to exploit their advantage, and the Union forces were thereby given time to reorganize. However, in the overall progress of the Civil War, the battle had a considerable significance: the Union leaders, and particularly Abraham Lincoln, realized from it the necessity of forging a Union army of a size and quality far beyond that which had originally been considered necessary by most people in the North; the people of the Confederacy, on the other hand, tended to view the victory as clear proof of their contention that the merchants and factory hands of the North could not stand up in battle to the men of the South, and, at least partly for this reason, failed to take the measures necessary to build at once an army which might have pursued such an opportunity as the one which had slipped through their hands at Bull Run. **2.** The Confederates under General Robert E. Lee (about 46,000) defeated Union troops under General John Pope (about 35,000) on Aug. 29–30, 1862. The Union loss was about 15,000; that of the Confederates, 8,400. This was called by the Confederates the second battle of Manassas; the battle of Aug. 29 is sometimes styled the battle of Groveton. The Union defeat in this battle stemmed at least partly from Pope's mistaken belief that he had forced Jackson's force, on the Union right, to begin a retreat; actually, Jackson was simply reorganizing his lines, and Longstreet (with all the rest of Lee's army) was in reserve to support him. Realizing that Pope was not aware of this, Lee waited until Jackson had repulsed the Union attack of Aug. 29, and then ordered Longstreet to advance with all the elements under his command. The result was a Union defeat and Confederate advance which was not finally stopped until Aug. 1, at a point far beyond the field of battle.

Bulls and Bears. Farce by Colley Cibber, produced in 1715.

Bull Shoals Dam. Fifth largest dam in the U.S., dedicated July 2, 1952, on the White River, near Norfolk, Ark. The dam, 2,256 ft. long and 283 ft. high, was completed in October, 1951, and is both a power source and a means of flood control.

Bully-les-Mines (bü.lē.lā.mēn). Town in N France, in the department of Pas-de-Calais, situated between Béthune and Arras. It is a coal-mining town and has chemical industries. 10,500 (1946).

Bulmer (bul′mėr), **Valentine.** In Sir Walter Scott's novel *St. Ronan's Well*, the titular Earl of Hetherington. He substitutes himself for his supposed bastard brother Francis Tyrrel, the real earl, in a clandestine marriage with Clara Mowbray, and later endeavors to rob Tyrrel of the proofs of the latter's right to his title.

Bulnes (böl′nās), **Manuel.** b. at Concepción, Chile, Dec. 25, 1799; d. at Santiago, Chile, Oct. 18, 1866. Chilean general; president (1841–51) of Chile. In 1831 he became a brigadier general, and in 1838 commanded 5,000 men sent against Andrés Santa Cruz in Peru. His victories destroyed the Peru-Bolivian confederation. He was elected president in 1841, and reëlected in 1846.

Bülow (bü′lō), Prince **Bernhard (Heinrich Martin) von.** b. at Klein-Flottbeck, Holstein, Germany, May 9, 1849; d. at Rome, Oct. 28, 1929. German statesman, chancellor of the empire (1900–09); uncle of Bernhard (Wilhelm) von Bülow. He entered the diplomatic service in 1873, was a secretary of the Berlin Congress in 1878, second and afterward first secretary of the embassy at Paris (1879–83), first secretary of the embassy at St. Petersburg (1883–88), minister at Bucharest (1888–93), and ambassador at Rome (1893–97). He then served as minister of state and secretary of state for foreign affairs (1897–1900), and was imperial chancellor and Prussian president of the council of ministers from October, 1900. In June, 1905, he was created a prince, after he had secured the retirement of Théophile Delcassé, foreign minister of France, whose policy, especially with regard to Morocco, had become offensive to Germany. His diplomacy resulted in the Conference at Algeciras. He attempted (1908) unsuccessfully to win England's friendship for Germany. Having resigned from the chancellorship in 1909, he was sent (1914) to Rome as a special ambassador, but was unable to keep Italy from entering World War I.

Bülow, Bernhard (Wilhelm) von. b. at Potsdam, Germany, June 19, 1885; d. 1936. German diplomat; nephew of Prince Bernhard (Heinrich Martin) von Bülow. He entered the foreign service, and held posts at Washington, Constantinople, and Athens. A member of the German peace delegations to Brest-Litovsk (1917) and to Versailles (1919), he became (1923) chief of the League of Nations section of the German foreign office, and later (1930) state secretary for foreign affairs; he kept the latter position during the early years of Hitler's regime, allegedly as a link with the "resistance."

Bülow, Baron **Friedrich Wilhelm von.** b. at Falkenberg, in Prussia, Feb. 16, 1755; d. at Königsberg, in East Prussia, Feb. 25, 1816. Prussian general in the Napoleonic wars. He defeated Nicolas Charles Oudinot at Luckau and Grossbeeren, and Michel Ney at Dennewitz in 1813. He also served with distinction at Leipzig (1813), at Laon and Montmartre (1814), and at Waterloo (1815). He was made count of Dennewitz in 1814.

Bülow, Baron **Hans Guido von.** b. at Dresden, Germany, Jan. 8, 1830; d. at Cairo, Egypt, Feb. 12, 1894. German pianist, conductor, and composer. He studied under Franz Liszt, whose daughter Cosima he married in 1857 (she subsequently left him, and married Richard Wagner). He abandoned his legal studies to take up music, and became a leading exponent of Wagnerian music, both as a conductor of the operas and by his piano arrangements of the scores. After his first concert tour (1853), he was named (1864) conductor of the royal opera and director of the conservatory at Munich. In his concert tours, which included one to the U.S. in the period 1875–76, he did much to popularize the music of Brahms. His official positions included that of royal court *Kapellmeister* (choir leader; 1878) at Hanover, conductor (1880–85) at the court of Meiningen, and director (1885 *et seq.*) at Berlin and Hamburg.

Bülow, Karl von. b. at Berlin, March 24, 1864; d. there, Aug. 31, 1921. German field marshal. Trained from his early youth for a military career, he received his first commission in 1864 and acquired his early experience in the war with Austria in 1866 and the Franco-Prussian War in 1870. At the outbreak of World War I he was one of the ranking German general officers, and as the leader of the Second Army he directed the successful invasion of Belgium in 1914. On Jan. 27, 1915, he was advanced to the rank of field marshal, but in June of that year he was retired, at his own request, from active service.

Bulse (böl′sę). See **Builsa.**

Bulstrode (bůl′strōd), Sir **Richard.** b. 1610; d. at St.-Germain, France, Oct. 3, 1711. English Royalist soldier, diplomat, poet, and historical writer, knighted (1675) by Charles II of England. He was the author of a poem (written and published while he was a student at Pembroke College, Cambridge) on the birth of the duke of York, and of the posthumously published *Original Letters Written to the Earl of Arlington* (1712, written in 1674), *Life of James II* (1712), *Essays* (1715), and *Memoirs and Reflections upon the Reign and Government of King Charles I and King Charles II . . . wherein the Character of the Royal Martyr and of Charles II are Vindicated from Fanatical Aspersions* (1721). After passing his 80th birthday he wrote 185 Latin poems, some of which are included in the *Letters*.

Bulthaupt (bůlt′houpt), **Heinrich.** b. at Bremen, Germany, Oct. 26, 1849; d. there, Aug. 20, 1905. German dramatist and critic. He was librarian of the city of Bremen from 1879. His dramas, such as *Saul* (1870), *Die Arbeiter* (1876), *Die Malteser* (1883), *Gerold Wendel* (1884), and *Viktoria* (1894), now evoke little interest, but his *Dramaturgie des Schauspiels* (1882–1901), an exposition of the art of Shakespeare and of the great German dramatists, is considered to have real merit.

Bulti (bul′ti) or **Bultistan** (bul.ti.stän′). See **Baltistan.**

Bultmann (bůlt′män), **Rudolf.** b. at Wiefelstede, Germany, Aug. 20, 1884—. German Protestant theologian. He became (1921) professor of New Testament theology at the University of Marburg. Known for his fundamental revisions in Biblical criticism, he is the author of *Der Stil der paulinischen Predigt und die kynisch-stoische Diatribe* (1910), *Die Geschichte der synoptischen Tradition* (1921), and *Offenbarung und Heilgeschehen* (1941).

Bulu (bö′lö). [French, **Boulou.**] Subgroup of the Bantu-speaking Pangwe in C Africa, inhabiting an area near the town of Ebolowa, S of Yaoundé, in SW Cameroun. Their population is estimated at ab. 96,000 (by I. Dugast, *Inventaire Ethnique du Sud-Cameroun*, 1949).

Buluwayo (bö.lö.wä′yō). See **Bulawayo.**

Bulwark, The. Novel by Theodore Dreiser, published posthumously in 1946. Solon Barnes, guided by a Quaker ethical code, finds the unrest of a materialist society reflected in his children. His profound faith is tested by a series of misfortunes, including the suicide of one child and the death of Solon's wife, but shortly before his own death Solon finds solace in a philosophy of love and acceptance.

Bulwer (bůl′wėr), **John.** fl. c1654. English physician. He wrote a treatise on dactylology, entitled *Chirologia, or the Naturall Language of the Hand* (1644), and *Philocophus, or the Deafe and Dumbe Man's Friend* (1648).

Bulwer, William Henry Lytton Earle. [Title: Baron **Dalling and Bulwer;** often known as Sir **Henry Bulwer.**] b. at London, Feb. 13, 1801; d. at Naples, May 23, 1872. English diplomat, politician, and writer; brother of Edward Bulwer-Lytton, 1st Baron Lytton. While serving (1837–38) at Constantinople, he concluded a commercial treaty between England and Turkey. He was minister to Spain (1843–48) and to the U.S. (1849–52), in which latter capacity he negotiated (1850) the Bulwer-Clayton Treaty. Subsequently he was minister to Tuscany (1852–55) and ambassador to Turkey (1858–65). He wrote *Historical Characters* (1867) and others.

Bulwer-Clayton Treaty (bůl′wėr.klā′tǫn). See **Clayton-Bulwer Treaty.**

Bulwer-Lytton (bůl′wėr.lit′ǫn), **Edward George Earle Lytton.** [Title, 1st Baron **Lytton of Knebworth.**] b. at London, May 25, 1803; d. at Torquay, England, Jan. 18, 1873. English novelist, poet, dramatist, politician, and orator. He graduated at Cambridge (B.A., 1823), served as member of Parliament (1831–41, 1852–66), was colonial secretary (1858–59), and was raised to the peerage in 1866. He wrote *Falkland* (1827), *Pelham, or the Adventures of a Gentleman* (1828), *The Disowned* (1829), *Devereux* (1829), *Paul Clifford* (1830), *Eugene Aram* (1832), *Godolphin* (1833), *England and the English* (1833), *Pilgrims of the Rhine* (1834), *The Last Days of Pompeii* (1834), *Rienzi* (1835), *The Student* and *The Crisis* (1835), *Ernest Maltravers* (1837), *Athens, its Rise and Fall* (1837), *Alice, or the Mysteries* (1838), *Leila* (1838), *Night and Morning* (1841), *Zanoni* (1842), *Last of the Barons* (1843), *Lucretia, or the Children of the Night* (1846), *Harold* (1848), *The Caxtons* (1850), *My Novel, or Varieties of English Life* (1853), *What will He do with it?* (1858), *A Strange Story* (1861), *Caxtoniana* (1863), *The Coming Race* (1871), *Kenelm Chillingly* (1873), *The Parisians* (1873), and *Pausanias,* an unfinished romance, edited by his son (1876). Among his poems are *Poems and Ballads of Schiller* (translation, 1844), *The New Timon* (1847), *King Arthur* (1849), *St. Stephens* (1860), *Lost Tales of Miletus* (1866), and a translation of Horace's *Odes* (1869). Among his dramas are *The Lady of Lyons* (1838), *Richelieu* (1839), *Money* (1840), *Cromwell* (1842), *Not so Bad as we Seem* (1852), and *The Rightful Heir* (1869).

Bulwer-Lytton, Edward Robert Lytton. See **Meredith, Owen.**

Bumble (bum′bl). In Charles Dickens's *Oliver Twist,* a fat and officious beadle. From his arrogant self-importance and magnifying of his parochial office the word "bumbledom" has come to have a place in the language.

Bumke (bům′kẹ), **Oswald Conrad Edward.** b. at Stolp, in Pomerania, Germany, Sept. 25, 1877; d. in February, 1950. German neurologist and psychiatrist. He was an assistant (1901) at the psychiatric clinic of the University of Freiburg, became (1904) privatdocent of psychiatry, and was named full professor at the universities of Rostock (1914), Breslau (1916), Leipzig (1921), and Munich (1924). He described (1904) a peculiar dilatation of the pupil following a psychic stimulus (Bumke's pupil).

Bumm (bům), **Ernst.** b. at Würzburg, Germany, April 15, 1858; d. at Munich, Jan. 2, 1925. German gynecologist and obstetrician. He became a privatdocent (1885) at the University of Würzburg, professor (1894) at the University of Basel, professor (1900) at Halle, and professor (1904) at Berlin, and succeeded (1910) R. M. von Olshausen as director of the clinic of gynecology and obstetrics at the University of Berlin, He cultivated the gonococcus in pure culture (1885), demonstrating the effects of latent gonorrhoea in women. Author of *Der Mikroorganismus der gonorrhoischen Schleimhauterkrankungen "Gonococcus Neisser"* (1885), *Zur Aetiologie der septischen Peritonitis* (1889), *Grundriss zum Studium der Geburtshilfe* (1902), and *Gefrierdurchschnitt durch den Körper einer in der Austreibungsperiode gestorbenen Gebärenden* (1907).

Bummers. In the American Civil War, a term applied to foraging members of General William Tecumseh Sherman's army during its march from Atlanta to the sea and northward through South and North Carolina.

Bumper (bum′pėr), **Sir Harry.** Character in Richard Brinsley Sheridan's *The School for Scandal.*

Bumppo (bum′pō), **Natty.** Hero of *The Pioneers* (1823), one of the books in the "Leatherstocking" series by James Fenimore Cooper. He typifies the resourceful, moral, and freedom-loving frontiersman of the American forest as visualized by the romantic school.

Bumpus (bum′pus), **Hermon Carey.** b. at Buckfield, Me., May 5, 1862; d. at Pasadena, Calif., June 21, 1943. American biologist, director (1902–11) of the American Museum of Natural History at New York. He was professor of biology at Olivet College, Michigan (1886–89), and at Brown University (successively assistant professor and associate professor of zoölogy and professor of comparative anatomy) in the period 1890–1901. He was assistant director of the marine biological laboratory at Woods Hole, Mass. (1893–95), director of the biological laboratory of the U.S. Fish Commission at Woods Hole (1898–1901), and curator of invertebrate zoölogy in the American Museum of Natural History (1901–02). He was appointed business manager of the University of Wisconsin in 1911, and served as president (1914–19) of Tufts College.

Bumstead (bum′sted), **Freeman Josiah.** b. at Boston, April 21, 1826; d. Nov. 28, 1879. American surgeon, perhaps the first native professional to limit himself entirely to specializing in the treatment of venereal disease. Graduated (1847) from Williams College, he received (1851) an M.D. degree from Harvard. He studied abroad on various occasions after 1849. After settling (c1852) at New York, he was surgeon (1857–62) to the New York Eye and Ear Infirmary, but after 1860 specialized in venereal diseases. He translated two foreign books on the subject, and in 1861 published his most significant work, *Pathology and Treatment of Venereal Diseases,* which went through several editions. His professorship (1867–71) in venereal diseases at the College of Physicians and Surgeons was perhaps the first faculty position of its kind in the U.S.

Bumstead, Henry Andrews. b. at Pekin, Ill., March 12, 1870; d. Dec. 31, 1920. American teacher and physicist, chiefly remembered for his investigations (1911 *et seq.*) of the properties of delta and alpha rays. Having received (1897) his doctorate in physics at Yale, he was appointed (1900) assistant professor in the Sheffield Scientific School, later becoming professor of physics in Yale College, and director of the Sloane laboratory. For some time he was editor of the American Physical Society. During World War I he performed scientific work for the U.S. government.

Bumstead, Horace. b. at Boston, Sept. 29, 1841; d. Oct. 14, 1919. American Congregational minister and educator, noted for his interest in Negro education. He graduated from Yale (1863), and from Andover Theological Seminary (1870). During the Civil War he served (1864–65) as a major with the 43rd Massachusetts Regiment of colored troops. Ordained a Congregational minister, he held a pulpit in Minneapolis before accepting (1875) an instructorship in natural science at Atlanta University, an institution for Negro youth, where he was professor of Latin (1880–96), acting president (1886–87), and president (1888–1907). He was for many years active in raising funds for the university.

Buna (bö′nạ). Village in SE New Guinea, E Papua Territory, on the NE coast, ab. 102 mi. NE of Port Moresby. It is in a swampy lowland jungle region, and has a mission. In July, 1942 Buna was occupied by Japanese forces, which advanced overland toward Port Moresby. After numerous battles, American and Australian forces advanced from the south to recapture Buna in December, 1942.

Buna-Sananada Campaign (bö′nạ.san.ạ.nan′dạ). Campaign in World War II, a joint Australian-U.S. effort (December, 1942–January, 1943) to gain control of SE New Guinea from the Japanese. Despite the sustained violence of the attack, Allied progress was slow, the Japanese having established strong defenses against the infantry and light tanks which were used against them.

The effort reached its climax on Jan. 23 with the taking of Sanananda (a town on the NE coast of Papua territory), and an important threat to Australia was thus eliminated.

Bunau-Varilla (bü.nō.vå.rē.yå), **Maurice.** b. 1856; d. at Paris, Aug. 1, 1944. French newspaper owner, publisher of the newspaper *Le Matin;* brother of Philippe Bunau-Varilla (1859–1940). After the fall of France (1940) he supported the Vichy regime.

Bunau-Varilla, Philippe (Jean). b. at Paris, July 25, 1859; d. there, May 18, 1940. French engineer, noted for his role in the controversy attendant on the construction of the Panama Canal; brother of Maurice Bunau-Varilla (1856–1944). He became (1884) an engineer on the Panama Canal project while it was under construction by Ferdinand Marie de Lesseps, later becoming its chief engineer; after the bankruptcy of the de Lesseps venture he organized (1894) a new company and advocated the utilization of the Panama route in hearings (1901) before the U.S. Isthmian Commission. After winning Theodore Roosevelt's support of the Panama route, he fomented revolution in Panama and served (1903) as minister to the U.S. for the new republic of Panama. He negotiated the Hay-Bunau-Varilla Treaty (1903), giving the U.S. control of the Panama Canal Zone. Subsequently he served as an engineer in West Africa and Rumania. He was wounded while on active duty in France during World War I.

Bunbury (bun'bėr.i), Sir **Henry Edward.** b. 1778; d. in Suffolk, England, 1860. English soldier and historian, 7th baronet (succeeded in 1820) of Mildenhall and Barton Hall, Suffolk. He served with the Coldstream Guards, was in Holland with the duke of York (1799), and distinguished himself at Maida (1806) as chief of staff during the Mediterranean campaign. While undersecretary of state for war (1809–16) and major general (1815), he conveyed to Napoleon I the sentence of deportation to St. Helena (1815). A member of Parliament for Suffolk (1830) and a pioneer of the volunteer movement (1859), he wrote military narratives, the most important of which is *The Late War with France* (1852).

Bunce (buns), **Francis Marvin.** b. at Hartford, Conn., Dec. 25, 1836; d. there, Oct. 19, 1901. American naval officer, appointed a rear admiral in 1898. In the same year he retired from active service. He was graduated from the U.S. Naval Academy in 1857, served in the Union navy in the Civil War, and commanded (1895–97) the North Atlantic squadron.

Bunce, John. Pirate in Sir Walter Scott's novel *The Pirate.*

Bunce, Oliver Bell. b. at New York, Feb. 8, 1828; d. there, May 15, 1890. American author, playwright, editor, and publisher. His first play, *The Morning of Life,* produced at New York in 1848, was followed by three others, after which he turned to publishing. Heading his own house for a few years after 1853, he was later associated with Harper and Brothers, ultimately becoming literary manager for D. Appleton and Company, a post he held until his death. He was editor of *Appleton's Journal,* wrote the play *Love in '76* (1857), edited such popular picture-books as *Picturesque America* (1872–74) and *Picturesque Europe* (1875–79), and was the author of several others, including *The Romance of the Revolution* (1852), *A Bachelor's Story* (1859), and *The Adventures of Timias Terrystone* (1885).

Bunce, William Gedney. b. at Hartford, Conn., Sept. 19, 1840; d. there, Nov. 5, 1916. American landscape painter. He served in the Civil War with the 1st Connecticut Cavalry, being invalided out after suffering a leg wound. He received his initial art education at the Cooper Union School at New York, studied with William Hart, and received additional schooling at Munich and Antwerp. The greater portion of his work as a landscapist was done at Venice, where he worked out a highly personal method of securing striking effects by the use of oil paints applied with his fingers and scraping knife. His color paintings are impressionistic and poetical in spirit. Among his canvases are *Morning View in Venice* and *Early Morning,* both in the Metropolitan Museum of Art, and *Sunset, San Giorgio, Venice,* in the National Gallery, Washington, D.C.

Bunch (bunch), **Barnaby.** In John Webster's play *The Weakest Goeth to the Wall,* a comic character, an English botcher, or mender of old clothes.

Bunch, Mother. In Thomas Dekker's *Satiro-mastix,* a derisive name given by Tucca to Mistress Miniver, an alewife. The name was used for the hypothetical author of various books of jests in 1604 and 1760, and for *Mother Bunch's Fairy Tales.*

Bunche (bunch), **Ralph Johnson.** b. at Detroit, Aug. 7, 1904—. American expert on problems of colonialism. He is widely known for his successful mediation on behalf of the United Nations of a truce in Palestine between the Arabs and Jews in 1948, following the assassination of Count Folke Bernadotte, the original United Nations mediator, whose assistant he had been. He was able to bring the long drawn-out negotiations to a conclusion in a manner which appeared to provide a firm basis for permanent settlement in Palestine. For this work, he was voted the 1950 Nobel peace prize. Bunche was educated at the University of California, where he received his B.A. in 1927, and at Harvard University, where he received his M.A. in government in 1928 and his Ph.D. in 1934. He also did work in anthropology and colonial policy at Northwestern University, the London School of Economics, and the University of Capetown, South Africa. He taught political science at Howard University, becoming head of the department of political science there in 1929. A Rosenwald fellowship enabled him to study (1931–32) in Africa, Europe, and England, and a postdoctoral fellowship from the Social Science Research Council permitted him to study (1936–38) in Europe, Africa, Malaya, and the Netherlands Indies. During World War II he served with the Office of Strategic Services (1941–44) and the U.S. State Department (1944–45) as an adviser on African and colonial matters. As assistant secretary of the U.S. delegation he attended (August-October, 1944) the Dumbarton Oaks meeting which laid the foundations of the United Nations organization. Later he served as an adviser to the U.S. delegation at the United Nations Conference on International Organization held at San Francisco. He became head of the trusteeship section of the United Nations secretariat in 1946. In 1949 he declined President Harry S. Truman's offer of an appointment as an assistant secretary of state.

Bundahish (bön'dä.hēsh). [Eng. trans., "*The Beginning of the Creation.*"] Pahlavi theological work, treating of cosmography, the government of the world, and eschatology, as understood by the Mazdayasnians.

Bundelkhand (bun'dẹl.kund). [Also: **Bundelcund, Bundelkhand Agency.**] Collection of states in Vindhya Pradesh, N central Union of India, formerly a division of the British Central India Agency including the states of Orcha, Panna, and Samthar. Wheat, cattle, millet, and maize are grown here.

Bundesrepublik Deutschland (bun'dẹs.rā.pö''blēk doich'länt). German name of the **German Federal Republic.**

Bundi (bön'dẹ). Former state of the Union of India, in the Rajputana, ab. 250 mi. S of the city of Delhi: since 1949 part of Rajasthan. Cattle, cotton, wheat, and millet are the chief products. The capital, Bundi, is one of the most beautiful and historically interesting cities in the Rajputana region. Area, 2,200 sq. mi.; pop. 249,374 (1941).

Bundy (bun'di), **Jonas Mills.** b. at Colebrook, N.H., April 17, 1835; d. at Paris, Sept. 8, 1891. American journalist and editor. Graduated (1853) from Beloit College, he served on the staffs of the Milwaukee *Daily Wisconsin* and the Milwaukee *Sentinel* before joining the Union army in the Civil War. Discharged a major, he went to New York, where he acted as drama, music, and literary critic on the *Evening Post,* and helped to found (c1868) the New York *Evening Mail.* He was editor in chief of this journal, continuing to hold that post after the paper became (c1881) the *Mail and Express* under the proprietorship of Cyrus W. Field. A Republican, he was active in civic reform movements.

Bungay (bung'gā), **Thomas.** [Called **Friar Bungay.**] fl. c1290. English Franciscan monk, who lectured at Oxford and Cambridge. He was popularly supposed to have been a magician, and figures as such in later literature. In Robert Greene's play *The honorable historie of Frier Bacon and Frier Bongay*, the character is based on that presented in an anecdotal pamphlet of the day which contains legends about Roger Bacon and Thomas Bungay; in both of these he appears as Bacon's assistant in necromancy. Edward Bulwer-Lytton introduces a character based on Bungay in his novel *The Last of the Barons*.

Bunge (böng'hā), **Alejandro.** b. 1880; d. at Buenos Aires, May 24, 1943. Argentine financier, economist, and engineer, at the time of his death a director of the Banco Nacional de Buenos Aires. He was the founder of the business publication *Revista de economía argentina*, and twice (1916–20, 1922–24) director of the census.

Bunge (bùng'e), **Alexander von.** b. at Tartu, in Estonia, Nov. 9, 1851—. Russian physician and zoölogist; brother of Gustav von Bunge. He participated in expeditions (1885–86) to the New Siberian Islands, and was the author of *Untersuchungen zur Entwicklungsgeschichte des Beckengürtels der Amphibien, Reptilien und Vögel* (1880).

Bunge, Gustav von. b. at Tartu, in Estonia, Jan. 19, 1844; d. at Basel, Switzerland, Nov. 5, 1920. German physiologist; brother of Alexander von Bunge (1851—). He was professor of physiological chemistry (1885 *et seq.*) at Basel, and wrote works on pathological and physiological chemistry.

Bunge de Gálvez (böng'hā dā gäl'bes), **Delfina.** b. at Buenos Aires. Argentine writer of prose and verse, a frequent contributor to *La Nación, El Pueblo*, and *El Hogar*. She was formerly director of the magazine *Ichthys*, and has collaborated in the publication of textbooks. Author of *Nuestra Señora de Lourdes* (1916), *Las Imágenes del infinito* (1922; winner of a municipal prize), *El tesoro del mundo* (1923; winner of a national prize), *Viaje abrededor de mi infancia* (1938), and others.

Bungen (bùng'en). Name of a street in Hamelin (now usually spelled, in geographical references, Hameln) down which the Pied Piper enticed the children with his music. By tradition, no music has since been played in this street.

Bungert (bùng'ėrt), **August.** b. at Mülheim, Germany, March 14, 1846; d. at Leutesdorf, Germany, Oct. 26 1915. German composer, notably of songs. A follower of Richard Wagner, he wrote and composed the operatic tetralogy *Die homerische Welt*, of which *Odysseus' Heimkehr* (produced 1896) was the most successful. He also composed the symphony *Zeppelins erste grosse Fahrt*.

Bunhill Fields (bun'hil). Burial ground for dissenters, situated near Finsbury Square, London, opened in 1665, closed in 1850, and thereafter a public garden. John Bunyan and Daniel Defoe were buried there.

Bunin (bö'nyin), **Ivan Alekseyevich.** b. at Voronezh, Russia, 1870—. Russian poet and novelist, since 1920 an intransigently anti-Soviet émigré in France. His reputation rests less on his fine Parnassian lyrics, examples of which may be found in Avrahm Yarmolinsky's *A Treasury of Russian Verse* (1949), than on his realistic short stories and novels, many of which are available in English, notably *The Gentleman from San Francisco*, which has been included in a number of anthologies. *The Well of Days* (1933) is a translation of the first part of his autobiographical novel, of which two parts have appeared. His fiction is predominantly retrospective and nostalgic. The only Russian author to have received (1933) a Nobel prize in literature, he has also translated many British and American works of verse into Russian, most notably Henry Wadsworth Longfellow's *Hiawatha*.

Buning (bü'ning), **J. W. F. Weremeus.** b. 1891—. Dutch poet and journalist. At first he wrote mystical and tenderly mournful poetry, such as *In Memoriam* (1921) and *Dood en Leven* (Death and Life, 1926). He turned to earthly life again with *Hemel en Aarde* (Heaven and Earth, 1926) and *Et in terra* (1933). Later, he published popular and often pathetic ballads such as *Mária Lécina* (1932) and *Negen Balladen* (Nine Ballads, 1935). Original and delightful descriptions of Holland were given in *Ik zie, ik zie wat jij niet ziet* (3 vols., 1937–39). He also wrote essays on dramatic art (1924). An ingenious cook, he published the two-volume *Honderd avonturen met een pollepel* (One Hundred Adventures With a Ladle). English translations of some of his work may be found in *Coming After*, by A. J. Barnouw.

Bu-nin-to (bö.nin.tō). A Japanese name of **Bonin Islands.**

Bunker Hill (bung'kėr). Elevation at Charlestown, in Boston, Mass., ab. 110 ft. in height. It gives name to the famous battle fought on June 17, 1775, chiefly at Breed's Hill (*q.v.*), Charlestown, between 2,500 British under William Howe and Robert Pigott, and 1,500 Americans under William Prescott, assisted by Israel Putnam and John Stark. The loss of the British was about 1,050; that of the Americans, about 450, including Joseph Warren.

Bunker Hill Monument. Monument on Breed's Hill, at Charlestown, Mass., dedicated June 17, 1843, the 68th anniversary of the famous Revolutionary battle. It is a quadrangular tapering tower of granite, 221 ft. high, built in the form of an obelisk, with an obtusely pyramidal apex.

Bunkie (bung'ki). Town in S Louisiana, in Avoyelles Parish: cotton products. 4,666 (1950).

Bunn (bun), **Richard.** Original name of **Bonelli, Richard.**

Bunner (bun'ėr), **Henry Cuyler.** b. at Oswego, N.Y., Aug. 3, 1855; d. at Nutley, N.J., May 11, 1896. American author and editor, best remembered as editor (1877–96) of the American comic weekly *Puck*. While the greater part of his career was devoted to this journal, he also contributed to other magazines, achieved a reputation as a composer of light verse, and wrote novels and short stories. He was among the first native American fiction writers to use the themes of urban life. Among his works are *The Poems of H. C. Bunner* (1896) and the volumes of fiction *The Midge* (1886), *The Story of a New York House* (1887), *Short Sixes: Stories to be Read While the Candle Burns* (1891), *The Runaway Browns* (1892), and *Made in France* (1893).

Bunner Sisters. Short novel (1916) by Edith Wharton. It is a story of two middle-class maiden ladies who keep a millinery shop in a mean street near Stuyvesant Square.

Bunsen (bun'sen; German, bùn'zen), Baron **Christian Karl Josias von.** [Sometimes called **Chevalier Bunsen.**] b. at Korbach, Waldeck, Germany, Aug. 25, 1791; d. at Bonn, Prussia, Germany, Nov. 28, 1860. German scholar and diplomat. He was secretary of legation, chargé d'affaires, and minister at Rome (1818–38), and minister to Switzerland (1839–41) and to England (1841–54). He wrote *Ägyptens Stelle in der Weltgeschichte* (1845), *Die Basiliken des christlichen Rom* (1843), *Ignatius von Antiochien und seine Zeit* (1847), *Hippolytus und seine Zeit* (1852–53, *Hippolytus and his Age*, 1851), *Die Zeichen der Zeit* (1855, *Signs of the Times*, 1855–56), *Gott in der Geschichte* (1857–58), *Vollständiges Bibelwerk für die Gemeinde* (1858–70), and *Die Verfassung der Kirche der Zukunft* (1845).

Bunsen, Robert Wilhelm. b. at Göttingen, Germany, March 31, 1811; d. at Heidelberg, Germany, Aug. 16, 1899. German chemist whose name is now probably best known from the Bunsen burner. This device, which is still widely used in laboratories throughout the world, consists essentially of an upright tube which is attached to a source of illuminating gas and which has an adjustable air-intake at its base. By regulating the air-intake it is possible to produce a flame which is smokeless, practically nonluminous, and of intense heat. Bunsen also developed the Bunsen pump, Bunsen battery, and various other devices. He was a professor of chemistry at Kassel, Marburg, Breslau, and Heidelberg. In association with G. R. Kirchhoff, by means of spectrum analysis through a spectroscope which they devised, he discovered the elements rubidium and cesium. He also engaged in investigations in the fields of photochemistry and electrochemistry, and in the physical and chemical properties of gases.

Bunthorne (bun'thôrn). In Gilbert and Sullivan's opera *Patience*, an extremely commonplace youth who adopts the most extravagantly esthetic and lackadaisical style. The character was intended to satirize Oscar Wilde and his followers.

Bunting (bun'ting). Name of the Pied Piper, in the legend of that name.

Bunting, Jabez. b. at Manchester, England, May 13, 1779; d. at London, June 16, 1858. English clergyman of the Wesleyan Church; grandfather of Sir Percy Bunting

(1836–1911). He was received into full connection with the ministry in 1803, became senior secretary of the Wesleyan Missionary Society in 1833, and was president of the Wesleyan Theological Institute in the period 1835–58. He established the principle of associating laymen with the clergy in the management of the Wesleyan Church.

Bunting, Sir **Percy.** [Full name, **Percy William Bunting.**] b. at Ratcliffe, near Manchester, England, Feb. 1, 1836; d. at London, July 22, 1911. English editor and social reformer; grandson of Jabez Bunting (1779–1858). Educated at Owens College, Manchester, and Pembroke College, Cambridge (B.A., 1859), he was called to the bar in 1862. He edited the *Contemporary Review* (1882–1911) and the *Methodist Times* (1902–07), and founded (1873) the Leys School (a Wesleyan public school at Cambridge), the National Vigilance Association (1883), the West London Mission (1887), and the National Free Church Council (1891). He was knighted in 1908.

Bunting v. Oregon, 243 U.S. 426 (1917). Decision of the U.S. Supreme Court upholding as a legitimate exercise of state police power an Oregon law regulating hours of labor for both men and women. The ruling was in contrast to the court's decision in *Lochner v. New York* (1905), which it overruled only by implication.

Buntline (bunt′lin, -līn), **Ned.** [Pseudonym of **Edward Zane Carroll Judson.**] b. at Stamford, N.Y., 1823; d. 1886. American frontiersman, agitator, and writer. Little is known of his boyhood (in fact, some doubt exists even as to the date and place of his birth, although most authorities now accept those data given above), but he did unquestionably spend some of his early years at sea. In 1845 he established the magazine *Ned Buntline's Own* at Nashville, Tenn., but he transferred the headquarters of this flamboyant journal to New York in 1846 when it became evident that a considerable body of Nashville citizens had come to find his presence in their city objectionable (a lynching party actually hanged him for a murder, but he was cut down before death took place). A fanatical (and perhaps opportunistic) nativist, he was a leader at New York of the attack against the English actor Macready which resulted in the fatal Astor Place riot in 1849, and for which he was sentenced at St. Louis during the 1850's to a year in prison. He was one of the founders of the Know-Nothing Party. Virtually no reliable information can be secured as to his activities during much of the Civil War, but it is known that he received a dishonorable discharge from the Union army in 1864. Returning thereafter to the West, he met William F. Cody, and is believed to have given him the sobriquet of "Buffalo Bill." He proceeded to make "Buffalo Bill" the hero of a series of dime novels and of a play entitled *The Scouts of the Plains* (1872), in the leading role of which Cody took the stage. Judson wrote several hundred dime novels and is counted among the originators of that form of popular literature in America.

Bunyan (bun′yan), **John.** b. at Elstow, near Bedford, England, baptized Nov. 30, 1628; d. at London, Aug. 31, 1688. English writer and preacher. The son of a tinker, he received a meager education. He adopted his father's trade, served as a soldier in the parliamentary army from 1644 to 1646, and married in 1648 or 1649. In 1653 he joined a nonconformist body at Bedford, settling there c1655. He was appointed a preacher by his coreligionists in 1657, and as such traveled throughout all the midland counties. He led the resistance of dissenters against the Stuart effort to compel uniformity of worship and religious opinion, braving a long imprisonment as "a common upholder of unlawful meetings and conventicles" rather than compromise his spiritual liberty. He was arrested in 1660 near Bedford, under the statutes against nonconformists, and, except for a brief interval in 1666, was detained in prison at Bedford until 1672, when those statutes were suspended by Charles II. He was licensed (May 9, 1672) to preach by the crown, and during the remainder of his life was pastor of the nonconformist congregation at Bedford. In 1675 he was again imprisoned for a few months, and during this imprisonment he wrote his celebrated allegory *The Pilgrim's Progress*, which appeared in 1678. This book, more widely read for over 200 years than any other except the Bible, is a picture of "the practick part of religion"; it emphasizes the inescapable responsibility of each individual soul and the futility of merely formal observances. It is also a call to those in danger of compliance with authority when persecution endangers their loyalty. It displays the moral earnestness of Puritanism at its best, without a bigoted exclusion of joy, and is remarkable for its sympathetic portrayal of a great variety of types of religious experience. An epic of man's dealings with man, as well as of the soul's search, through trials and tribulations, for individual salvation, it gave great impetus to contemporary and later religious movements in which simple and unlettered men and women could feel sure of their value in the sight of God. Its second part ("safe arrival at the desired country"), written later, appeared in 1684. Among his other published and unpublished writings, over 40 in number, are *Some Gospel Truths Opened* (1656), in which Bunyan takes his stand on the literal interpretation of the gospels, as against the mystical approach of the Quakers, *Grace Abounding to the Chief of Sinners* (1666), self-portrait of a distracted and divided soul, the battleground of scruples versus tastes, *The Holy City, or the New Jerusalem* (1666), *A Confession of my Faith, and a Reason of my Practice* (1671), *The Life and Death of Mr. Badman* (1680), and *The Holy War* (1682), called by Thomas Babington Macaulay "the greatest allegory in the language if Pilgrim's Progress had not been written." One poem from his pen is remembered, which extols the steadfastness, "come wind, come weather," of a valiant pilgrim.

Bunyan, Paul. In American folklore, a mythical hero of gargantuan proportions, conceived perhaps by lumberjacks of the American Northwest. By dragging his pick he scooped out the Grand Canyon. For epicurean giants, Bunyan had a hot-cake griddle greased by servants who skated upon it with sides of bacon attached to their feet. Bunyan's loggers once worked in such extreme weather that their profanities froze, thawing suddenly on the following Fourth of July. Of almost equal importance in the tales is Bunyan's Babe, the blue ox, an outsized creature measuring more than 42 axe handles. Harold W. Fenton's anthology *Legends of Paul Bunyan* (1947) gives a good sampling of the whole body of material.

Bunyoro (bun.yō′rō). [Also, **Unyoro.**] Region in British East Africa, situated just N of the equator, between Lake Victoria and Lake Albert: a former native kingdom, now a district of the Western Province of Uganda protectorate. Area (excluding open water), 4,847 sq. mi.; pop. (adult males) 29,000 (1947).

Bunzlau (bünts′lou). German name of **Bolesławiec.**

Buol-Schauenstein (böl′shou′ẹn.shtīn), Count **Karl Ferdinand von.** b. May 17, 1797; d. at Vienna, Oct. 28, 1865. Austrian statesman and diplomat. He was premier and minister of foreign affairs (1852–59).

Buonaccorso (bwô.näk.kōr′sō). See **Accorso, Buono.**

Buonafede (bwô.nä.fā′dā), **Appiano.** b. at Comacchio, Ferrara, Italy, Jan. 4, 1716; d. at Rome, Dec. 17, 1793. Italian historian of philosophy. He was professor of theology at Naples.

Buonaparte (bwô.nä.pär′tā). See **Bonaparte.**

Buonarrotti (bwô.när.rôt′tē), **Filippo Michele.** b. at Pisa, Italy, Dec. 11, 1761; d. at Paris, Sept. 15, 1837. Italian political agitator, implicated in the conspiracy (1796) of François Émile Babeuf to overthrow the French Directory.

Buoninsegna (bwô.nēn.sā′nyä), **Duccio di.** See **Duccio di Buoninsegna.**

Buononcini (bwô.nōn.chē′nē). See **Bononcini.**

Bura (bū′ra). In ancient geography, a city in Achaea, Greece, destroyed by an earthquake in 373 B.C. It joined (275 B.C.) the Achaean League.

Bura (bö′rä). [Also: **Boura, Kasonboura.**] One of the Sudanic-speaking Gurunsi peoples of W Africa, inhabiting the N part of the Northern Territories of the Gold Coast (they are not to be confused with the Bura of NE Nigeria). They practice hoe agriculture, and their principal food is millet. They are non-Mohammedan.

Burali-Forti (bö.rä′lē.fôr′tē), **Cesare.** b. at Arezzo, Italy, Aug. 13, 1861; d. Jan. 21, 1931. Italian mathematician, contributor to projective geometry and mathematical logic, whose name is attached to "Burali-Forti's paradox" discovered by him in 1897, in the theory of ordinal numbers. He received his doctorate at Pisa in

1884, and from 1903 he taught at the military academy at Turin. He wrote numerous papers and books, including *Gnomonica grafica* (1889), *Applicazioni della geometria descrittiva e proiettiva* (1890), *Teoria delle grandezze* (1893), *Logica matematica* (1894), *Metodo de Grassmann nella geometria proiettiva* (1896–1901), *Espaces courbes* (1924), and *Analisi vettoriale gen. trasformaz. lineari* (2 vols., 1929–30).

Burano (bö.rä'nō). Town in NE Italy, on an island in the Venetian lagoon, ab. 5 mi. NE of Venice, incorporated into the city of Venice. It has a cathedral and fisheries.

Burauen (bö.rä'wen). Town in the N central part of Leyte island and province, Philippine Islands. 8,233 (1948).

Burbage (bėr'bāj), **James.** d. 1597. English actor, and the first builder of a theater in England; father of Richard Burbage. He was originally a joiner. In the period 1576–77 he erected the first English building specially intended for plays. It was "between Finsbury Fields and the public road from Bishopsgate and Shoreditch," in what is now part of London. It was of wood, and was called "The Theatre." The material was removed to the Bankside in 1598 and was rebuilt as the Globe Theatre. The Curtain Theatre was put up near The Theatre soon after the latter was opened, and Burbage was instrumental in the conversion of a large house at Blackfriars into Blackfriars Theatre, probably in November, 1596.

Burbage, Richard. b. c1567; d. 1619. English actor; son of James Burbage. He made his fame at the Blackfriars and Globe theaters of which, with his brother and sister, he was proprietor, and played the leading parts in all the best plays produced at the time. Shakespeare was a member of the Lord Chamberlain's Company, playing at Blackfriars at the same time, and had some part in the profit of the house, as also a little later in the Globe; but Burbage apparently had the lion's share. There is no authentic account of any intimacy with Shakespeare till after 1594. Burbage seems to have been the original Hamlet, Lear, and Othello. He excelled in tragedy, and was held in the very highest esteem by authors and public; he was even sometimes introduced into plays in his own proper person. Many poems and tributes were written in his memory. Besides his fame as an actor he was known as a painter. In 1613, when the Globe Theatre burned down, he narrowly escaped with his life.

Burbank (bėr'bangk). City in S California, in Los Angeles County, N of Los Angeles: aircraft factories and motion-picture studios. Its air-terminal facilities service the entire Los Angeles area. 78,577 (1950).

Burbank, Luther. b. at Lancaster, Mass., March 7, 1849; d. at Santa Rosa, Calif., April 11, 1926. American naturalist and plant breeder, noted for originating and introducing 618 new varieties of flowers, fruits, edible grains, grasses, lumber and shade trees, forage plants, nuts, vegetables, and ornamental shrubs. He had little formal schooling, deriving his early knowledge of science from lectures at Lancaster Academy and from public library books. In 1873, he found his first new variety, the Burbank potato, in his vegetable garden. In 1875, he moved to Santa Rosa, Calif., where he established his experimental farms and where he worked until his death in 1926. He produced the famous giant Shasta and Alaska daisies, the fragrant calla, and the blue Shirley poppy. Among his new kinds of fruits were outstanding varieties of plums, apples, peaches, plumcots, quinces, and nectarines; and in addition to producing several varieties of potatoes, he grew new forms of artichokes, beans, chard, sweet corn, squashes, asparagus, rhubarb, and peas. The components of his genius in the field of hybridization were a unique facility of observation and perception, and a virtually unmatched knowledge of correlations in plant characters. From 1905 to 1910 he received annual grants of 10,000 dollars from the Carnegie Institution; from his experiments with thousands of kinds of plants he did not, as is popularly believed, make great amounts of money. Ardently devoted to his work, he was interested in making only enough money to provide for his simple personal needs. His great ambition was to make contributions which would benefit mankind. This ambition was realized because he developed new plants which are grown in many parts of the world. Some idea of the value of Burbank's work may be gained through the following excerpt from Bulletin No. 691, published by the University of California in March, 1945: "Plums were Burbank's most valuable contribution. Twenty of his varieties—18 percent of the total introduced—are still widely planted throughout the United States and other countries. Ten of the number are standard shipping varieties wherever Oriental plums are grown for marketing, as in California, South Africa, Argentina, and Australia. In California alone, they form the basis of a major industry. At present there is, in this state, a total of about 24,000 acres of Burbank varieties—upwards of 2,000,000 trees. Thousands of carloads of fruit are shipped annually; and the money returns run into the millions—not a bad showing for the industry of one man."

Burbon (bėr'bon). In Edmund Spenser's *The Faerie Queene*, a knight, representing Henry IV of France. He is assailed by a mob, but escapes and also rescues his mistress.

Burbridge (bėr'brij), **Stephen Gano.** b. in Scott County, Ky., Aug. 19, 1831; d. at Brooklyn, N.Y., Dec. 2, 1894. American soldier. Having attended Georgetown College and Kentucky Military Institute, he entered the Civil War as a colonel of the 26th Kentucky infantry. He took part in the battle of Shiloh and became (1862) a brigadier general, serving in the Vicksburg campaign. In 1864 he was given command of the District of Kentucky, where his military operations were creditable; however, his civil administration of this border state, and the harsh reprisals he instituted to curb guerrilla warfare, antagonized many Kentucky citizens. He was relieved (1865) of his command and, an outcast in his native state, made his home elsewhere after the war.

Burcardus (bėr.kär'dus). See **Brocard.**

Burch (bėrch), **Charles Sumner.** b. at Pinckney, Mich., June 30, 1855; d. at New York, Dec. 20, 1920. American Protestant Episcopal clergyman and publisher. After having been employed (1876–90) in the publishing trades at Chicago, he was editor (1897–1905) of the Grand Rapids (Mich.) *Evening Press.* He was named deacon (1895), priest (1905), and suffragan bishop (1911) of New York, and was appointed (1919) bishop of New York.

Burchard (bėr'chard), **Samuel Dickinson.** b. at Steuben, N.Y., Sept. 6, 1812; d. at Saratoga, N.Y., Sept. 25, 1891. American Presbyterian clergyman. Graduated (1836) from Centre College; he was pastor of New York's Thirteenth Street Presbyterian Church (1839–79) and Murray Hill Presbyterian Church (1880–85). He gained notoriety in the presidential campaign of 1884 by an alliterative expression used in a speech on Oct. 29, when, with a large company of clergymen, he made a call on James G. Blaine, the Republican candidate, at the Fifth Avenue Hotel. It occurs in the sentence "We are Republicans, and don't propose to leave our party and identify ourselves with the party whose antecedents have been rum, Romanism, and rebellion," and was made the most of in Roman Catholic circles by the Democratic managers. It is believed that these words cost Blaine the New York State vote.

Burchell (bėr'chel), **Mr.** In Oliver Goldsmith's novel *The Vicar of Wakefield,* the name under which Sir William Thornhill dispenses joys and sorrows as a being from another sphere.

Burchell, William John. b. c1782; d. 1863. English naturalist and explorer. From the quiet occupation of a schoolmaster at St. Helena (1805–10) he turned to an adventurous and fruitful career in South Africa, where for some five years (1811–15) he explored wilderness and desert as far as Bechuanaland, collecting more than 60,000 specimens of faunal, floral, and geological interest. In the years 1826–29 he engaged in similar exploration in Brazil. During these expeditions he also compiled much astronomical and meteorological data. Burchell's name appears in the standard scientific nomenclature of many species of animals and plants.

Burchfield (bėrch'fēld), **Charles Ephraim.** b. at Ashtabula Harbor, Ohio, April 9, 1893—. American romantic painter and water-colorist, one of the leading painters of the American scene. He was educated at the Cleveland School of Art, but for financial reasons was unable to devote himself fully to art until 1929. His first one-man show was held (1919) at New York; since then he has exhibited extensively in the U.S., and has won many prizes, including a Carnegie International award in 1937. Much of his life has been spent near Lake Erie, and his paintings of the life and scenes there typify the Midwest. There is, however, an undercurrent of irony behind the too-dignified façades of his houses, brought out in the mysteriously nostalgic quality of his work. He is represented in the Metropolitan Museum of Art, the Museum of Modern Art, and the Whitney Museum of American Art at New York, as well as in the Boston Museum of Fine Arts, the Detroit Institute of Arts, the Cleveland Museum, Brooklyn Museum, and other major museums. Some of his better-known works are *False Front, February Thaw, August Afternoon, November Evening, March Wind, Railroad Gauntry, Sun-Glare, September Elms, Over the Dam, The Black Barn, Factory Town,* and *Mining Village in Winter.*

Burckhard (bůrk'härt), **Max Eugen.** b. at Korneuburg, Austria, July 14, 1854; d. at Vienna, March 16, 1912. Austrian writer. He was also director of the famous Burgtheater, at Vienna.

Burckhardt (bůrk'härt), **Jakob.** b. at Basel, Switzerland, May 25, 1818; d. there, Aug. 8, 1897. Swiss art historian, one of the originators of the school of cultural history; a teacher of Friedrich Nietzsche, whom he influenced to a large extent. Originally a student of theology, he began (1839) to study history of art at Berlin and Bonn, one of his teachers being Leopold von Ranke. He served as editor (1844–45) of the *Basler Zeitung* and lived for a time (1846–47) at Rome, before becoming a professor (1855) at Zurich; from 1858 to 1893 he was a professor at the University of Basel, and there wrote most of his works. A precursor of the school of cyclical interpretation of history, he believed that contemporary culture was on the decline, to be swallowed up by the ever-increasing demands of the organized state. In his major work, *Die Kultur der Renaissance in Italien* (1860; Eng. trans., *The Civilization of the Renaissance in Italy*), he expounds a theory of conscious creativity, making the artifacts of the period interpret the spirit of the time. He had led up to this work with *Cicerone* (1855), an introduction to Italian art. He expanded his theories in *Geschichte der Renaissance in Italien* (2 vols., 1867, 1878), *Griechische Kulturgeschichte* (4 vols., 1898–1902), and *Weltgeschichtliche Betrachtungen* (1905; Eng. trans., *Force and Freedom: Reflections on History*, 1943). Although his theories have been criticized by later scholars who feel, with justification, that the epochal view of history can be misleading, Burckhardt is universally regarded as one of the major Swiss scholars. Among his disciples, directly or indirectly, are Henrich Wölfflin and Oswald Spengler.

Burckhardt, Johann Karl. b. at Leipzig, Germany, April 30, 1773; d. at Paris, June 22, 1825. German astronomer, resident in France. He was in charge of the observatory of the École Militaire at Paris (1807–25). He published a set of lunar tables in 1812.

Burckhardt, Johann Ludwig. b. at Lausanne, Switzerland, Nov. 24, 1784; d. at Cairo, Egypt, Oct. 15, 1817. Swiss traveler. He visited (1810–17) the Orient, Egypt, and Nubia, and wrote *Travels in Nubia* (1819), an account of his travels in Syria and the Holy Land (1822) and in Arabia (1829), *Notes on the Bedouins and Wahabys* (1830), *Arabic Proverbs* (1831), and others. His perfect command of Moslem customs and of Arabic allowed him to pose as an Arab, enabling him to penetrate into places where non-Arabs were ordinarily rejected.

Burdach (bör'dăċh), **Karl Friedrich.** b. at Leipzig, Germany, June 12, 1776; d. at Königsberg, Germany, July 16, 1847. German physiologist, a specialist on the structure and functions of the nervous system. He was professor of anatomy and physiology at Tartu (1811), and later at Königsberg (1814 *et seq.*). He wrote *Vom Bau und Leben des Gehirns und Rückenmarks* (1819–25), *Die Physiologie als Erfahrungswissenschaft* (1826–40), and others.

Burdach, Konrad. b. at Königsberg, in East Prussia, May 29, 1859—. German scholar. He was a professor at Halle (1887–1902) and at Berlin (1902 *et seq.*), and a member of the Academy of Sciences. His work was on the German language (*Die Einigung der neuhochdeutschen Sprache*, 1884; *Vom Mittelalter zur Neuzeit*, 1893) and medieval literature (*Über den Ursprung des mittelalterlichen Minnesangs*, 1919; *Reformation, Renaissance und Humanismus*, 3rd ed., 1920). He was an authority on Walther von der Vogelweide (*Reinmar der Alte und Walther von der Vogelweide*, 1880; *Walther von der Vogelweide*, 1900).

Burdegala (bėr.deg'ą.lą). See **Bordeaux.**

Burdekin (bėr'dę.kin). River in Queensland, Australia, which flows into Upstart Bay, an arm of the Pacific Ocean. Length, ab. 350 mi.

Burden (bėr'dẹn), **Henry.** b. at Dunblane, Stirlingshire, Scotland, April 22, 1791; d. at Troy, N.Y., Jan. 19, 1871. American inventor and ironmaster. He studied at the University of Edinburgh, and came to America in 1819. While working for an agricultural implement manufacturer at Albany, N.Y., he invented an improved plow and a cultivator supposedly the first to achieve practical use in the U.S. In 1822 he went to Troy, N.Y., and, as superintendent of the Troy Nail and Iron Factory, made it one of the largest iron plants in the country. His other inventions include a machine for making wrought-iron spikes (1825), altered in 1834 and 1836 to make the hook-headed spike used in track-laying; a machine for rolling puddled iron into cylindrical bars (1840); and the horseshoe machine (1835, with improvements in 1843, 1857, and 1862), which made almost all the horseshoes used by the Union armies during the Civil War.

Burdenko (bör.dyen'kǫ), **Nikolai Nilovich.** b. at Kamenka, Penzenskoy, Russia, 1878; d. in Russia, Nov. 11, 1946. Russian surgeon who laid the foundation for neurosurgery in Russia. He served (1904) as a volunteer medical worker in the Russo-Japanese War, was house surgeon and assistant professor (1906–12) of the clinic at Yuriev Derpt University, was appointed (1912) to the chair of operational and clinical surgery, became a professor at the University of Voronezh, and was professor of surgery and director of the Scientific Research Institute of Neurosurgery, chief surgeon of the Red Army, and president of the Scientific Medical Council of the People's Commissariat of Public Health. Author of *Characteristics of Surgical Work in the Military District* (1939), *Fundamentals of Roentgen Diagnosis* (with N. N. Altgauzen, 1940), *Principles of Modern Study of Gun Shot Wounds of Arteries* (1942), *Amputation as a Neurosurgical Operation* (1942), *Field Surgery in the U.S.S.R.* (1943), and *An Historic Phase in the Development of Soviet Medicine* (1944).

Burder (bėr'dėr), **George.** b. at London, June 5, 1752; d. there, May 29, 1832. English clergyman of the Independent denomination. He was the author of *Village Sermons* (1799–1812).

Burdett (bėr.det'), Sir **Francis.** b. Jan. 25, 1770; d. at London, Jan. 23, 1844. English politician, member of Parliament for Westminster in the period 1807–37; father of Angela Georgina Burdett-Coutts. He published (1810), in Cobbett's *Register*, a speech denying the right of the Commons to imprison delinquents, and, his arrest being ordered, barricaded his house, and was taken only after four days' resistance.

Burdett-Coutts (bėr.det'köts'), Baroness **Angela Georgina.** b. April 21, 1814; d. at London, Dec. 30, 1906. English philanthropist; daughter of Sir Francis Burdett. She married W. L. Ashmead-Bartlett, an American, in 1881. Coutts had been her mother's name. For her many charitable foundations, which included the endowment of schools and bishoprics, reform societies, and scholarships, she was raised (1871) to the peerage by Queen Victoria. Among her friends was Charles Dickens.

Burdette (bėr.det'), **Robert Jones.** b. at Greensboro, Pa., July 30, 1844; d. Nov. 19, 1914. American Baptist clergyman, humorist, and lecturer. He served with the 47th Illinois Regiment in the Civil War. He helped found (1871) the Peoria *Review*, was a staff-member (1874 *et seq.*) of the Burlington *Daily Hawkeye*, for which he wrote a humorous column, and after 1876 spent much time on the public lecture platform. His first lecture, "The Rise and Fall of the Moustache," was delivered some 5,000 times throughout the U.S. Among his friends were Mark Twain and Bill Nye. In 1888 he was licensed to preach; after a period devoted to pulpit lecture tours, he became (1903) first pastor of the Temple Baptist Church at Los Angeles.

Burdick (bėr′dik), **Francis Marion.** b. at De Ruyter, N.Y., Aug. 1, 1845; d. there, June 3, 1920. American legal writer and teacher, an originator of what is generally termed the "case system" of instruction in law schools. Graduated (1869) from Hamilton College, he received an LL.B. degree from that institution, and was admitted to the bar in 1872. He held (1882 *et seq.*) the Maynard Knox professorship of law and history at Hamilton, was one of the first professors appointed to the newly founded (1887) college of law at Cornell University, and served as Theodore Dwight professor of law (c1891–1916) in the Columbia University Law School. A prolific writer of articles and books dealing with law and jurisprudence, he is perhaps best known for *Cases on Torts* (1891), *The Law of Sales of Personal Property* (1897), and *The Law of Partnership* (1899).

Burdigala (bėr.dig′a.la). See **Bordeaux.**

Burdigalensis (bėr.dig a.len′sis). Latin name of **Bordelais.**

Burdur (bör.dör′). *Il* (province or vilayet) in SW Turkey, in the lake region N of Antalya: a hilly area with many lakes, at the W end of the Taurus Mountains. Capital, Burdur; area, 2,553 sq. mi.; pop. 136,359 (1950).

Burdwan (bur.dwän′). [Also: **Bardhwan, Bardwan.**] Division of West Bengal, Union of India: jute, rice, and sugar. Area, ab. 14,000 sq. mi.; pop. 10,298,369 (1941).

Burdwan. [Also, **Bardhwan, Bardwan.**] District of Burdwan division, Union of India. Area, 2,689 sq. mi.; pop. 1,890,732 (1941).

Burdwan. [Also, **Bardhwan, Bardwan.**] Chief town of Burdwan district, West Bengal, Union of India, ab. 56 mi. NW of Calcutta: rail junction and major trading center. 62,910 (1941).

Bure (būr). River in E England, in Norfolk. It rises ab. 10 mi. NW of Aylsham and flows SE past Aylsham and through the Broads to a confluence with the river Yare at Great Yarmouth. Length, 50 mi.; navigable to Aylsham.

Büren (bür′en). Town in W Switzerland, in the canton of Bern, SW of the city of Bern on the Aare River. It has an old church, a castle, and an institute for the deaf and dumb. 13,004 (1941).

Buresch (bö′resh), **Karl.** b. at Gross Enzersdorf, Austria, Oct. 12, 1878; d. 1936. Austrian statesman. He became (1920) a Christian Socialist member of parliament, and was named (1931) *Bundeskanzler* (chancellor of the Bund, after the plan of a German-Austrian customs union had failed. He was succeeded (1932) as chancellor by Engelbert Dollfuss.

Bureya Mountains (bù.rä′ya). [Russian, **Buryeiskii Khryebyet.**] Mountain range in the SE part of the U.S.S.R., in E Siberia N of the Amur River. The mountains begin in foothills near the Amur, and rise higher toward the north, reaching a peak elevation of ab. 7,270 ft. The chief mineral resources known are gold, iron ore, graphite, and coal. There is some lumbering. Length, ab. 400 mi.

Burford (bėr′fọrd). Civil parish and town in S central England, in Oxfordshire, ab. 16 mi. NW of Oxford. It has no direct rail connections for passengers, being reached by rail to Oxford, ab. 57 mi. NW of London, thence by autobus. Nearby, in 752, Cuthred, king of Wessex, defeated Ethelbald, king of Mercia. 907 (1931).

Burg (bůrk). City in C Germany, in the *Land* (state) of Saxony-Anhalt, Russian Zone, formerly in the province of Saxony, Prussia, situated on the Ihle River, ab. 14 mi. NE of Magdeburg. An industrial center, before World War II it had leather, shoe, and furniture manufactures, and machine shops. Many industries were initiated by Protestant refugees from France, Belgium, and the Palatinate in the 17th century. The *Nikolaikirche* (Church of Saint Nicholas) dates from the 12th century, the *Frauenkirche* (Church of Our Lady) from the 14th century; there is a museum of antiquities. The city came under Brandenburg in 1688. Pop. 27,088 (1946).

Bur Gandak (bör gun′duk). See **Gandak, Little.**

Burgas (bör.gäs′). [Also: **Burgaz**; French, **Bourgas.**] Department in E Bulgaria, bounded by the Black Sea on the E, European Turkey on the S, the department of Shumen on the N, and the departments of Stara Zagora and Pleven on the W. Capital, Burgas; area, 5,258 sq. mi.; pop. 629,593 (1946).

Burgas. [Also: **Burgaz**; French, **Bourgas.**] City in SE Bulgaria, capital of the department of Burgas, situated on the Gulf of Burgas, an arm of the Black Sea, ab. 58 mi. SW of Varna. A large seaport and terminus of the railroad to Sofia, it exports agricultural products, especially grain, butter, and wine; also iron. It has many churches and mosques. The population consists of Greeks, Turks, and Bulgarians. 36,230 (1934); 43,684 (1946).

Burgdorf (bůrk′dôrf). Town in NW Germany, in the *Land* (state) of Lower Saxony, British Zone, formerly in the province of Hanover, Prussia, situated on the Aue River, NE of Hanover. A center of market gardening and fruit culture, it has canneries, a sugar refinery, livestock markets, and cement works. 10,942 (1950).

Burgdorf. [French, **Berthoud.**] Town in W Switzerland, in the canton of Bern, situated on the Emme River, NE of the city of Bern. The educator Johann Heinrich Pestalozzi opened his school here in 1799. Pop. 10,197 (1941).

Bürgel (bür′gel), **Bruno.** b. at Berlin, 1875—. German author of science fiction and popular treatises on astronomy (*Aus fernen Welten*, 1920; *Du und das Weltall*, 1922; *Der Stern von Afrika*, 1920). His autobiography, *Vom Arbeiter zum Astronomen* (1919), traces his career from lowly beginnings to a position of responsibility in the field of adult education.

Burgen (bůr′gen). German name of **Borgo.**

Burgenland (bėr′gen.land; German, bůr′gen.länt). [Sometimes called **"the Burgenland,"** and **West Hungary.**] Province of Austria, a long and narrow strip bounded on the E by Hungary, on the W by Lower Austria and Styria, while it barely touches upon Slovakia on the N and upon Yugoslavia (Croatia) on the S. The N part, around the Lake of Neusiedl, is a fertile plain, the S part a continuation of the E Styrian hill country. The population is predominantly German and Roman Catholic, but there are small Croatian and Hungarian minorities. Agriculture is diversified, producing grains, potatoes, sugar, vegetables, fruit, and wine; cattle, horse, hog, and poultry raising is highly developed. Lignite is mined. There are sugar, canning, textile, and woodenware industries. Capital, Eisenstadt; area, 1,531 sq. mi.; pop. 275,911 (1951).

Burgenland Dispute. Dispute between Austria and Hungary in the period 1919–21 over a small slice of territory at the Austrian-Hungarian border with a largely German population. Awarded to Austria at the Paris Peace Conference, it was thereupon invaded by Hungarian "irregulars." An Italian mediation offer in August, 1921, brought about a plebiscite, which compelled the return to Austria of the largest share of the territory.

Bürger (bür′gėr), **Gottfried August.** b. at Molmserwende, near Harzgerode, Germany, Jan. 1, 1748; d. at Göttingen, Germany, 1794. German poet, the most important member of the so-called Göttinger Dichterbund, or "poetical brotherhood." His collected works, *Sämmtliche Schriften*, appeared in four volumes (Göttingen, 1796–98). He was an official at Altgleichen, later docent, and subsequently professor at the University of Göttingen. His life, largely because of his own indiscretions, was unhappy and at times even miserable. He was the author of numerous ballads, songs, and sonnets. Foremost among his poems is the ballad "Lenore," which originally appeared in the Göttingen *Musenalmanach* (1774), and which inaugurated a type of German narrative poetry based on folklore and folk songs. He also wrote the ballads *Das Lied vom braven Mann* (1776), *Der Kaiser und der Abt* (1785), and *Der wilde Jäger* (1786).

Burger (bür′gėr), **Konrad.** b. at Berlin, March 2, 1856; d. at Leipzig, Germany, April 12, 1912. German librarian (1893 *et seq.*) of the Börsenverein der deutschen Buchhändler. He is notable for work in the field of incunabula.

Burges (bėr′jez), **George.** b. in Bengal, India, c1786; d. at Ramsgate, England, 1864. English classical scholar.

Burgess (bėr′jes), **Albert Franklin.** b. at Rockland, Mass., Oct. 2, 1873; d. at Brattleboro, Vt., Feb. 23, 1953. American entomologist. He was chief inspector of nurseries and orchards (1902–07) for the Ohio state department of agriculture, and in 1907 was placed in charge of breeding experiments in the U.S. Bureau of Entomology. He also conducted experiments (1913–28) for devising methods to prevent the spread of gypsy moths. From 1933 to 1942 he was principal entomologist of the U.S. Bureau of Entomology and Plant Quarantine.

Burgess, Alexander. b. at Providence, R.I., Oct. 31, 1819; d. at Saint Albans, Vt., Oct. 8, 1901. American bishop of the Protestant Episcopal church. Graduated from Brown University (1838), and from the General Theological Seminary, New York (1841), he was ordained (1842) a deacon in the Episcopal ministry. He was elevated (1843) to the priesthood, and served as head (c1843 *et seq.*) of St. Mark's Church, Augusta, Me. After 16 years with churches at Portland, Me., and at Brooklyn, he became rector of Christ Church, Springfield, Mass. Active in diocesan affairs, he was elected and consecrated (1878) the first bishop of the diocese of Quincy (Ill.).

Burgess, Charles Frederick. b. at Oshkosh, Wis., Jan. 5, 1873; d. at Chicago, Feb. 13, 1945. American chemical engineer. He received a B.S. degree (1895) and was a professor (1900–13) at the University of Wisconsin. He is known for a number of inventions, including a process for electrolytic purification of iron, various iron alloys, and improvements in dry cells. Awarded (1932) the Perkin medal for distinguished services in the field of applied chemistry, he also received (1944) an honorary degree of Doctor of Engineering from the Illinois Institute of Technology.

Burgess, Edward. b. at West Sandwich, Mass., June 30, 1848; d. at Boston, July 12, 1891. American yacht designer and entomologist. Graduated (1871) from Harvard, he studied yacht building abroad. He was an instructor of entomology (c1879–c1882) in the Bussey Institution at Harvard, publishing several scientific contributions in this field. In 1883 he and a brother established themselves as yacht designers under the company name of Burgess Brothers, a firm that was dissolved when business failed to materialize. The *Puritan*, which Edward Burgess designed for a group of Boston yachtsmen, defeated the English cutter, *Genesta* in the contest for the America's Cup in 1885. He also designed the *Mayflower* (1886), which defeated the English *Galatea*, and the *Volunteer*, which outsailed the English *Thistle* in 1887. He designed a total of more than 200 vessels.

Burgess, (Frank) Gelett. b. at Boston, Jan. 30, 1866; d. at Carmel, Calif., Sept. 18, 1951. American humorist, novelist, and illustrator. He was graduated (B.S., 1887) from the Massachusetts Institute of Technology, was a railroad draftsman (1887–90), and served as an instructor in topographical drawing (1891–94) at the University of California. After a period as associate editor (1894–95) of *The Wave*, he was an editor (1895–97) of *The Lark*, a magazine associated with Les Jeunes, a San Francisco literary group. His well-known quatrain "The Purple Cow" made its first appearance in *The Lark*. His ink drawings have illustrated many of his own books and articles. His works include *Vivette* (1897), *Goops and How to Be Them* (1900), *Are You a Bromide?* (1907), *Burgess Unabridged* (1914), *Why Men Hate Women* (1927), *Look Eleven Years Younger* (1937), and *Ladies in Boxes* (1942). He is also known for having introduced into the English language the word "blurb," to mean the written material appearing on a book jacket to praise the book's contents (he originally defined the word as follows: "self-praise: to make a noise like a publisher"). The word "bromide," to mean a person who inevitably responds to a given situation with the same meaningless remark (and hence also the remark itself), was also originated by Burgess.

Burgess, George. b. at Providence, R.I., Oct. 31, 1809; d. aboard ship off the coast of Haiti, April 23, 1866. American bishop of the Protestant Episcopal Church. Graduated (1826) from Brown University, he studied theology abroad (1832–34). He was advanced to the priesthood in 1834, and in the same year became rector of Christ Church, Hartford, Conn.; he was elected and consecrated (1847) the first bishop of the diocese of Maine. He published several books, and numerous sermons and addresses.

Burgess, George Kimball. b. at Newton, Mass., Jan. 4, 1874; d. July 2, 1932. American physicist, noted for his work in metallurgy and pyrometry. He was associate physicist (1903–13), physicist and chief (1913–23) of the division of metallurgy, and director (1923 *et seq.*) of the Bureau of Standards at Washington. Author of *Recherches sur la constante de gravitation* (1901), *Experimental Physics—Freshman Course* (1902), and *The Measurement of High Temperatures* (1912, with H. Le Châtelier).

Burgess, John William. b. in Giles County, Tenn., Aug. 26, 1844; d. at Brookline, Mass., Jan. 13, 1931. American historian and educator. Graduated from Amherst College in 1867, he was professor of English and political economy at Knox College (1869–71), professor of history and political science at Amherst College (1873–76), and professor of political science and constitutional law at Columbia University from 1876. In 1890 he was named dean of the Columbia faculty of political science. He was also Roosevelt professor of American history and institutions at the University of Berlin (1906–07). His works include *Political Science and Comparative Constitutional Law* (1890), *Middle Period, 1817–1853* (1897), *The Civil War and the Constitution, 1859–1865* (1901), and *Reconstruction and the Constitution, 1866–1876* (1902).

Burgess, Neil. b. at Boston, June 29, c1851; d. Feb. 19, 1910. American comedian, noted as a stage impersonator of elderly women. His extravagant burlesques of feminine character began in Providence, R.I., when he was called upon to make an emergency appearance as Mrs. Barnaby Bibbs in *The Quiet Family*. Thereafter he appeared in feminine costume in such plays as *Vim, or, A Visit to Puffy Farm*, and *Bedott, or, A Hunt for a Husband*. His most popular part was as Abigail Prue, and his outstanding play *The County Fair*, first produced in 1888 and staged more than 5,000 times.

Burgess, Thomas. b. at Odiham, Hampshire, England, Nov. 18, 1756; d. at Salisbury, England, Feb. 19, 1837. English clergyman, bishop of St. David's and later of Salisbury. He wrote *Considerations on the Abolition of Slavery* (1788) and others.

Burgess, Thornton Waldo. b. at Sandwich, Mass., Jan. 14, 1874—. American writer, known for his nature and animal stories for children. He was editor until 1911 of *Good Housekeeping*, and thereafter published nature stories (1912 *et seq.*), at first in the New York *Globe*, and later through a syndicate. He inaugurated *The Mother West Wind Series* (1910), *Bedtime Story Books* (1913), *Green Meadow Series* (1918), and others, and wrote *Burgess Bird Book for Children* (1919), *Burgess Animal Book for Children* (1920), *Burgess Flower Book for Children* (1923), *Tales from the Story Teller's House* (1937), and other books.

Burgess Hill. Urban district in SE England, in East Sussex, ab. 42 mi. S of London by rail. 8,524 (1951).

Burgevine (bėr'gẹ.vīn), **Henry Andrea.** b. in North Carolina, 1836; d. in China, June 26, 1865. American adventurer. He served in the Crimean War, and appeared (c1860) on the China Coast, where he became an officer in a foreign unit setting out to recapture Sungkiang from the Taiping rebels. He later joined the insurgent forces, and was eventually delivered to the U.S. consul at Shanghai.

Burgh (bėrg), **Hubert de.** d. at Banstead, Surrey, England, May 12, 1243. English statesman. He was appointed chamberlain to the king c1201, in which year he was placed at the head of a body of knights to guard the Welsh marches. On the authority of Ralph of Coggeshall, who has been followed by Shakespeare (*King John*, iv. 1, 2.), he was castellan of Falaise when Arthur of Brittany was captured at Mirabel in 1202, was entrusted with the custody of the prince's person, and refused to obey an order of Arthur's uncle, King John of England, to put out the prince's eyes. He was a partisan of the king at Runnymede in 1215, in which year he first appears as justiciar, and is mentioned in the great charter as one of the magnates of the realm by whose advice it was granted. He became regent for Henry III in 1219, and remained his chief minister for the period 1228–32.

Burgh (bur'ọ), **James.** b. at Madderty, Perthshire, Scotland, 1714; d. Aug. 26, 1775. Scottish miscellaneous writer. He wrote *Britain's Remembrancer* (1745), *Dignity of Human Nature* (1754), and others.

Burghers (bėr'gėrz). Body of Presbyterians in Scotland, constituting one of the divisions of the early Secession Church. This church became divided in 1747 into the Associate Synod, or Burghers, and the General Associate Synod, or Anti-Burghers, on the lawfulness of accepting the oath then required to be taken by the burgesses in Edinburgh, Glasgow, and Perth.

Burghley (bėr′li), 1st Baron. Title of **Cecil, William.**

Burghley, 2nd Baron. A title of **Cecil, Thomas.**

Bürgi (bēr′gē), **Joost** (or **Jobst**). See **Byrgius, Justus.**

Burgin (bėr′jin), **George Brown.** b. 1856; d. in June, 1944. English novelist and writer of memoirs. He was the author of the novels *Gascoigne's Ghost* (1896), *Fortune's Footballs* (1897), *Tomalyn's Quest* (1897), *Shutters of Silence, the Romance of a Trappist* (1908), *Slaves of Allah* (1909), *The King of Four Corners* (1910), *The Girl Who Got Out* (1916), *The Throw-Back* (1918), *A Gentle Despot* (1919), *A Rubber Princess* (1919), *The Young Lobell* (1924), and *The Lord of Little Laughton, A Modern Romance* (1925). He also wrote the autobiographical *Memoirs of a Clubman* (1921), *Many Memories* (1922), *More Memoirs and Some Travels* (1922), and *Some More Memoirs* (1925).

Burgis (bėr′jis), **William.** fl. 1717–1731. American engraver of maps and views. Having come to New York from London c1718, he published *A South Prospect of ye Flourishing City of New York.* At Boston, together with William Price and Thomas Selby, he published *A South East View of the Great Town of Boston,* which is probably the first portrayal of a two-masted schooner in a view made in America. Both views were engraved at London by John Harris. Burgis is connected, as delineator, engraver, or publisher, with several other early views of American scenes.

Burgkmair (bu̇rk′mīr), **Hans.** b. at Augsburg, Germany, 1473; d. 1531. German painter and engraver; probably a pupil of Albrecht Dürer. Among his most noted works is a series of wood engravings portraying a triumphal procession of Maximilian I. After a trip to Italy, he was instrumental in introducing the Italian Renaissance style into Germany.

Bürglen (bür′gln̩). Village in E central Switzerland, in Uri canton, ab. 21 mi. SE of Lucerne. Noted as the legendary home of William Tell, the village is beautifully located on a small hill at the entrance to a valley. Elevation, 1,811 ft.; pop. 2,527 (1941).

Burgmüller (bu̇rk′mül″ėr), **Johann Friedrich (Franz).** b. at Regensburg, Germany, 1806; d. at Beaulieu, France, Feb. 13, 1874. French composer of salon music and instructional piano pieces.

Burgmüller, Norbert. b. at Düsseldorf, Germany, Feb. 8, 1810; d. at Aachen, Germany, May 7, 1836. German composer, a founder and conductor of the Lower Rhine festivals; brother of Johann Friedrich Burgmüller. His works include an overture and two symphonies.

Burgoa (bör.gō′ä), **Francisco de.** b. in Oaxaca, Mexico, c1605; d. 1681. Mexican Dominican missionary and author. He took the Dominican habit in 1620, was twic provincial, represented the order at Rome in 1656, acted for the Inquisition, and during his later years was guardian of Huaxolotitlan and other convents. His *Geográfica descripción . . . de esta Provincia de Predicadores de Antiquera,* a chronicle of his order in Oaxaca, is of great historical value. Like his other historical and biographical works, it is now very rare.

Burgon (bėr′gọn), **John William.** b. at Smyrna (now Izmir, Turkey), Aug. 21, 1813; d. at Chichester, England, Aug. 4, 1888. English Biblical scholar and dean of Chichester (1876). He transferred (1841) from London University to Oxford University, where he became a fellow (1846), master of arts (1848), vicar of St. Mary's (1864), and Gresham professor of divinity (1867).

Burgos (bör′gōs). Province in N Spain, bounded by Santander and Vizcaya on the N, Álava, Logroño, and Soria on the E, Segovia on the S, and Valladolid and Palencia on the W: a part of Old Castile. The surface is largely hilly or mountainous. Forestry and livestock raising prevail over agriculture. Capital, Burgos; area, 5,425 sq. mi.; pop. 402,828 (1950).

Burgos. [Ancient name, **Briga.**] City in N Spain, the capital of the province of Burgos, situated on the Arlanzón River, ab. 132 mi. N of Madrid: agricultural trade center; woolen, leather, paper, and chemical industries. 72,640 (1950).

Buildings and Monuments. Burgos is the residence of a cardinal-archbishop, and has clerical and teachers' seminaries, libraries, and a museum. The white limestone cathedral, built in the period of the 13th–15th centuries, is one of the finest examples of the flamboyant Gothic style in Spain; the architects were French and German. It contains numerous chapels and monuments of artistic and historical interest. The Carthusian convent of Miraflores dates from the 15th century. There are many beautiful churches; various famous monasteries and convents are in the vicinity, as well as palaces of the nobility. Burgos was the home of the Spanish national hero, the Cid; his bones rest in the cathedral.

History. Burgos was founded c880 as a fortress against the advancing Moslems. It was an important and prosperous city in the 11th, 12th, and 13th centuries when it was the capital of Old Castile and León, but sank into political insignificance after 1560 when Madrid was declared the only court. However, the commercial leadership of Castile remained with Burgos because of the privileges bestowed by the crown on its merchant guild, extending even to foreign trade. Burgos was the seat (July, 1936, *et seq.*) of Francisco Franco's government during the Spanish Civil War.

Burgos, Laws of. System of laws for the regulation of Indian labor in Spanish America, promulgated at Burgos, Spain, on Dec. 27, 1612. The Dominicans of Hispaniola had represented that the Indians were very badly treated; the colonists opposed the monks, and the junta appointed to consider the question framed these laws. They provided that the Indian laborers should have houses, ground for culture, and religious instruction, with a peso of gold annually to buy clothes; those in the mines were to work only five consecutive months, and to have official inspectors. The laws caused much dissatisfaction.

Burgoyne (bėr.goin′), **John.** b. 1722; d. at London, June 4, 1792. English lieutenant general and dramatist. He commanded the British army which invaded New York in 1777, was defeated at Stillwater, on Sept. 19 and Oct. 7, 1777, and surrendered with 5,791 troops to Horatio Gates at Saratoga, on Oct. 17, 1777. In 1782 he was made commander in chief in Ireland, and in 1787 was one of the managers of the impeachment of Warren Hastings. He wrote satires directed against the administration of the elder William Pitt (the greater part of *Westminster Guide, The Lord of the Manor* (1780, the libretto of a comic opera), *The Heiress* (1786, a comedy which was very successful), and others.

Burgoyne, Sir **John Fox.** b. July 24, 1782; d. at London, Oct. 7, 1871. English engineer; illegitimate son of John Burgoyne (1722–92). He was commanding engineer of the expedition to New Orleans (1814), chairman of the Board of Public Works in Ireland (1831–45), and inspector general of fortifications in England (1845–68). He was sent to Constantinople to report on the defense of Turkey in 1854, conducted the siege of Sevastopol in the period October, 1854–February, 1855, was created a baronet in 1856; was constable of the Tower of London (1865–71), and became a field marshal in 1868. Author of *Our Defensive Forces* (1868) and others.

Burgschmiet (bu̇rk′shmēt), **Jakob Daniel.** b. at Nuremberg, Bavaria, Oct. 11, 1796; d. there, March 7, 1858. German sculptor. His chief works include statues of Albrecht Dürer, Melanchthon (at Nuremberg), Beethoven (at Bonn), Charles IV (at Prague), and Martin Luther (at Möhra).

Burgstädt (bu̇rk′shtet). Town in E Germany, in the *Land* (state) of Saxony, Russian Zone, formerly in the free state of Saxony, NW of Chemnitz. The center of an industrial district, before World War II it had manufactures of knitwear, gloves, and rayon. The first cotton factory in Saxony was founded here in 1750, the first silk mill in 1787. It has a school for the textile trades and a local museum. The population is predominantly Protestant. 19,453 (1946).

Burg Stein (bu̇rk shtīn). See under **Baden,** Switzerland.

Burgundian (bėr.gun′di.ạn). One of the Burgundii or Burgundiones, a Germanic (Gothic) tribe which settled in Gaul and founded the kingdom of Burgundy in the 5th century.

Burgundian. Native or an inhabitant of Burgundy, successively a kingdom and a duchy of W Europe, varying greatly in extent. A part of it finally became the province of Burgundy in E France.

Burgundy (bėr′gun.di). [French, **Bourgogne;** German, **Burgund** (bu̇r.gunt′); Italian, **Borgogna;** Spanish, **Borgoña;** Medieval Latin, **Burgundia** (bėr.gun′di.ạ).] Geographical division in W Europe, whose limits and character have varied greatly. The principal significations of the name are: **1.** The kingdom of Burgundy (Latin, *regnum Burgundionum*), founded in 406 A.D., occupying the whole valley of the Saône and lower Rhone rivers from Dijon to the Mediterranean, and including also the W half of Switzerland. It was destroyed by the sons of Clovis in 534 A.D. **2.** The kingdom of Burgundy (Latin, *regnum Burgundiae*), mentioned occasionally under the Merovingian kings as a separate principality, confined within boundaries apparently somewhat narrower than those of the older kingdom last named. **3.** The kingdom of Provence or Burgundy (Latin, *regnum Provinciae seu Burgundiae*)—also, though less accurately, called the kingdom of Cis-Jurane Burgundy—was founded by Boso in 879 A.D., and included Provence, Dauphiné, the S part of Savoy, and the country between the Saône River and the Jura Mountains. **4.** The kingdom of Trans-Jurane Burgundy (Latin, *regnum Iurense*, *Burgundia Transiurensis*), founded by Rudolf I in 888 A.D., recognized in the same year by the Holy Roman emperor Arnulf, included the N part of Savoy, and all Switzerland between the Reuss River and the Jura Mountains. **5.** The kingdom of Burgundy or Arles (Latin, *regnum Burgundiae, regnum Arelatense*), formed by the union (937 A.D.) under Conrad the Pacific of the kingdoms described above as 3 and 4. On the death (1032) of the last independent king, Rudolf III, it came, partly by bequest, partly by conquest, into the hands of the Holy Roman emperor Conrad II (the Salic), and thenceforward formed a part of the empire. In the 13th century, France began to absorb it, bit by bit, and has now (since the annexation of Savoy in 1861) acquired all except the Swiss portion. **6.** The lesser duchy of Burgundy (Latin, *Burgundia Minor;* German, *Klein Burgund*) corresponded very nearly with what is now Switzerland W of the Reuss River, including the canton of Valais. It was Trans-Jurane Burgundy (4) minus the parts of Savoy which had belonged to that kingdom. It disappears from history after the extinction of the house of Zahringen in the 13th century. Legally it was part of the Holy Roman Empire until 1648, though practically independent long before that date. **7.** The free county or palatinate of Burgundy (French, Franche-Comté; German, *Freigrafschaft;* called also Upper Burgundy), to which the name of Cis-Jurane Burgundy originally and properly belonged, lay between the Saône River and the Jura Mountains. It formed a part of 3 and 5, and was therefore a fief of the Holy Roman Empire. The French dukes of Burgundy were invested with it in 1384. Its capital, the imperial city of Besançon, was given to Spain in 1651, and by the treaties of Nijmegen (1678–79) it was ceded to the crown of France. **8.** The landgraviate (German, *Landgrafschaft*) of Burgundy was in what is now W Switzerland, on both sides of the Aare River, between Thun and Solothurn. It was a part of the lesser duchy (6) and, like it, is hardly mentioned after the 13th century. **9.** The circle of Burgundy (German, *Kreis Burgund*), an administrative division of the Holy Roman Empire, was established by Charles V, in 1548, and included the free county of Burgundy (7) and the 17 provinces of the Netherlands, which Charles inherited from his grandmother Mary of Burgundy, daughter of Charles the Bold. **10.** The duchy of Burgundy (Lower Burgundy), a great French fief held by various Carolingian and Capetian princes, and ceded by John II (the Good) to his son, Philip the Bold. Its capital was Dijon. Flanders and the county of Burgundy were united to it in 1384. It was ruled by Philip the Bold (1363–1404), by John the Fearless (1404–19), by Philip the Good (1419–67), and by Charles the Bold (1467–77). Under the two latter it was greatly extended in Belgium and E and C France, and became one of the most powerful monarchies of Europe. On the death of Charles the Bold (1477) the duchy proper passed (1479) to France. The other possessions—Franche-Comté and the Low Countries—passed by the marriage of Mary of Burgundy (daughter and successor of Charles the Bold) to the house of Hapsburg. The duchy of Burgundy proper became a province and great government of France. It lay between Champagne on the N, Franche-Comté and Savoy on the E, Dauphiné and Lyonnais on the S, and Bourbonnais, Nivernais, and Orléanais on the W, and corresponded to the departments Côte-d'Or, Saône-et-Loire, Ain, and a part of Yonne. The region is famous for its wines.

Burgundy, Duke of. See **Charles the Bold.**

Burgundy, House of. Reigning house (1095–1383) of Portugal which referred its origin to Henri, grandson of Robert, first duke of Burgundy. Henri was appointed count of Portugal by Alfonso VI, king of León, Castile, and Galicia, in 1094, and was in 1112 succeeded by his son, Alfonso I, who established Portugal as an independent kingdom in 1139. The legitimate line of the house of Burgundy became extinct in 1383 with the death of Ferdinand I, and was succeeded in 1385 by an illegitimate branch, the house of Avis. An illegitimate branch of the latter house, the house of Braganza, acceded to the throne in 1640, and was followed in 1853 by the recent reigning house, the house of Braganza-Coburg.

Burhanpur (bur'hän.pör). City in the W central part of the Union of India, in W Madhya Pradesh state (formerly Central Provinces), on the Tapti River ab. 310 mi. by rail NE of Bombay. Founded c1400 A.D., the town was annexed by the Mogul emperor Akbar c1600, and was the capital of the Deccan province of the Mogul Empire. In 1860 it passed to British India. It is noted for silk embroidery work in gold and silver, wire industries, and cotton textiles. 53,987 (1941).

Burial of Sir John Moore. Poem (1816) by Charles Wolfe, and published in a collection of his works in 1825.

Burian (bö'rę.än), **E. F. N.** b. 1904—. Czech stage director.

Burian, Karel. [Also, **Carl Burrian.**] b. near Rakovnik, in Bohemia, Jan. 12, 1870; d. in September, 1924. Czech tenor singer. He first appeared at Revel (now Tallin, in Estonia) in 1892, later singing in all the principal German cities, and finally becoming a permanent member of the Dresden Court Opera. He was a member (1906 *et seq.*) of the Metropolitan Opera Company, New York, singing the leading tenor roles in the Richard Wagner operas, and created the role of Herod in Richard Strauss's *Salome.*

Burian, Vlasta. b. 1891—. Czech actor who became the greatest comedian of his day in his country. Taking over the Svanda Theatre at Prague and renaming it the Burian, he opened it in 1925, producing plays by Molière, George Bernard Shaw, and native writers.

Burián von Rajecz (bö'rę.än fon rä'yets), Count **Stephan.** b. at Stampfen, Austria, 1851; d. at Vienna, Oct. 20, 1922. Austro-Hungarian statesman. He was finance minister (1912–16), and, in addition, succeeded Count Leopold von Berchtold as foreign minister (1915–16). He supported a policy calling for the annexation of Poland, and worked for an early peace. After Ottokar Czernin's resignation (April, 1918) he was again foreign minister, and directed his efforts toward a negotiated peace. His efforts failed, and he withdrew from public life after the revolution of November, 1918.

Burias (bö'ryäs). Island in the Philippines, situated in the Sibuyan Sea between Masbate and Luzon: part of Masbate province. Area, 163.5 sq. mi.; pop. 4,573 (1939).

Buriat-Mongolia (bůr.yät'mong.gō'li.ą) or **Buriat-Mongol** (or **Buriat-Mongolian**) **Autonomous Soviet Socialist Republic** (-mong'gǫl, -mong.gō'li.ąn). See **Buryat-Mongol Autonomous Soviet Socialist Republic.**

Buridan (būr'i.dąn; French, bü.rē.däṅ), **Jean.** b. at Béthune, in Artois, France; d. after 1358. French nominalist philosopher. He studied under William of Occam, and lectured on philosophy at the University of Paris, of which he became rector. He was a noted logician, and is popularly but probably incorrectly regarded as the author of the sophism known as "Buridan's Ass," which was used by the schoolmen to demonstrate the inability of the will to act between two equally powerful motives. According to this sophism an ass placed between two equidistant and equally attractive bundles of hay would starve to death for want of a reason to determine its choice between the two bundles.

Buried Alive. Novel (1908) by Arnold Bennett. Bennett made a play out of it under the title of *The Great Adventure* (1913), from which the motion picture *Holy Matrimony* was made.

Buried Treasure, A. Novel (1931) by Elizabeth Madox Roberts.

Burin (bū′rin). Fishing town in Newfoundland, Canada, situated on the S shore of the Burin Peninsula, which forms the W side of Placentia Bay. 796 (1951).

Burjasot (bör.hä.sōt′). Town in E Spain, in the province of Valencia, situated near the Turia River, ab. 3 mi. NW of Valencia, of which it is a suburb. 11,235 (1940).

Burk (bėrk), **Frederic Lister.** b. at Blenheim, Ontario, Canada, Sept. 1, 1862; d. June 12, 1924. American educator, noted as a pioneer in the field of motivated individual instruction. Graduated (1883) from the University of California, he received an M.A. degree (1892) from Stanford University, and a Ph.D. degree (1898) from Clark University, where he studied under G. Stanley Hall. He was president (1899 *et seq.*) of the State Normal School at San Francisco, a member (1899–1911) of the California State Board of Education, and the author of several works on education.

Burk, John Daly. b. in Ireland, c1775; d. in a duel, at Petersburg, Va., April 11, 1808. American dramatist and historian. He came to America in 1796, settling at Boston, where he published the *Polar Star and Boston Daily Advertiser* for a brief time. After another unsuccessful newspaper venture at New York, he settled at Petersburg, where he was killed in a duel. His chief contribution as an early American playwright was his adaptation of patriotic themes to the stage. In *Bunker Hill, or the Death of General Warren* (1797), he was among the first to include an American battle scene in a theatrical production. Among his other plays were *Female Patriotism, or the Death of Joan d'Arc* (1798), and *The Death of General Montgomery in Storming the City of Quebec* (1797). He also wrote *A History of the Late War in Ireland* (1799) and *History of Virginia* (4 vols., 1804, 1805, 1816).

Burkburnett (bėrk.bėr.net′). City in C Texas, in Wichita County, NW of Dallas: shipping center for livestock and agricultural products; has petroleum refineries and gasoline plants. 4,555 (1950).

Burke (bėrk), **Aedanus.** b. at Galway, Ireland, 1743; d. March 30, 1802. American jurist and politician. He studied law (c1769) in Stafford County, Va., and in the Revolutionary War held a lieutenant's commission in a Continental regiment, resigning (1778) to become an associate judge in the state supreme court of South Carolina. As a representative (1781–82, 1784–89) in the state legislature, he supported amnesty for the Loyalists; as a member of the South Carolina convention, he opposed the ratification of the Federal Constitution. He was a member (1789–91) of Congress, and in 1799 became chancellor of the court of equity in South Carolina.

Burke, Billie. b. at Washington, D.C., Aug. 7, 1886—. American actress; wife (married 1914) of Florenz Ziegfeld. Having made her stage debut in *The School Girl in England*, she had a leading role in *My Wife* (1907), presented by John Drew's company. She starred in *Love Watches* (1908), *Suzanne* (1911), *Caesar's Wife* (1919), *Happy Husbands* (1929), *Vinegar Tree* (1931), *The Truth Game*, and other plays, and appeared in such films as *A Bill of Divorcement* (1932), *The Young in Heart* (1938), *Topper Takes a Trip* (1939), and *Eternally Yours* (1939).

Burke, Charles St. Thomas. b. March 27, 1822; d. at New York, Nov. 10, 1854. American actor and dramatist whose stage version of the Rip Van Winkle tale was later employed by his half-brother, the American actor Joseph Jefferson. Burke's brief theatrical career was spent largely at New York and Philadelphia, where he acted comedy roles.

Burke, Edmund. b. at Dublin, probably on Jan. 12, 1729; d. at Beaconsfield, England, July 9, 1797. British parliamentarian, orator, and writer. The son of an Irish attorney, who was a Protestant, and of a Catholic mother, he was brought up and remained a Protestant, and was graduated (1748) from Trinity College in his native city before going to London, where he began his law studies in 1750. In 1756 he published *A Vindication of Natural Society*, a subtle satire of its supposed thesis, and in the same year an *Inquiry into the Sublime and the Beautiful*, which, despite some thought-provoking passages, left no permanent imprint on aesthetic theory in England. In 1759 he began publication of the *Annual Register*, a summary of the events of the preceding year seen within the framework of large trends and movements. In 1765 he became private secretary to the marquis of Rockingham when the latter became prime minister. Rockingham thereafter remained his firm friend and contributed to his financial support. In 1765 also Burke entered the House of Commons as member for Wendover, and the first of the many memorable speeches which he was to make there dealt, significantly enough, with a question involving the American colonies. Firmly attached to the Whig interests, from this time forward he made many vehement attacks upon the Tories. In 1768 he was affluent enough to acquire a large estate at Beaconsfield, where he lived with dignity but not ostentation, a patron of letters and art. In 1774 he became a member of Parliament for Bristol upon the invitation of citizens of that city, who probably supported his stand for compromise with the rebellious Americans, which had been made evident by his famous speeches (*On American Taxation*, in 1774, and the even better known *On Conciliation With the Colonies*, in 1775), but in 1780 they withdrew their support because of Burke's advocacy of free trade for Ireland, and of removal of the political restrictions then still imposed on Catholics in England. He reëntered Parliament in 1781 for the constituency of Malton in Yorkshire, and, by his attacks on the conduct of the war in America (particularly the use of Indians against the colonists), had a main part in bringing about the fall of Lord North's ministry. In the Whig government of 1782, and the coalition government which succeeded it, he was paymaster to the British forces and privy councilor. At this time also he began to take an interest in the conduct of the East India Company, and brought about the impeachment of Warren Hastings, governor general of India, during whose long trial (1786–94) in Parliament he delivered what some have considered to be his most forceful orations. (The full period of Burke's concern with Hastings may be said to have extended from 1781, when a committee report was made on Hastings's activities in India, to 1795, when Hastings was acquitted. Burke not only made a formal opening speech in the trial, but also delivered a nine-day reply to the defense in 1794.) Burke strongly supported Wilberforce in urging (1788–89) an end to the slave trade. The outbreak (1789) of the French Revolution brought to the fore all his love of order, temperance, tradition, and respect for authority, and led to his several books dealing with that world-shaking event. In November, 1790, he published his *Reflections on the Revolution in France* (which is the title now most often used; however, the full original title provides an interesting clue to the extent of his domestic concern: *Reflections on the Revolution in France, and on the proceedings in certain societies in London relative to that event*). As an almost inevitable corollary of his opposition to the French Revolution, his name became a rallying point for the forces not only of counterrevolution but of conservatism in general, and hence, by extension, of opposition to parliamentary reform, which led to separation (1791) from Charles James Fox and the bulk of the Whigs in Parliament. However, the intensity of Burke's opposition to the French Revolution actually increased during the next few years, and reached its highest point in the period 1795–97, when he published his four *Letters on a Regicide Peace*. In 1794 he retired from Parliament, and formally withdrew from political life in 1795, with a pension from the government. Burke's orations are among the greatest in any language in respect to their substance and logic, and although he was scarcely an original thinker, he may almost be said to have epitomized the liberalism of the 18th century. Some have suggested that, being an Irishman, his reverence for rank and royalty surpassed that of his liberal English confreres; he spoke for justice, but he abhorred radicalism. As a writer, he must be ranked among the masters of all who have ever written in English, having perfect command of a style that could be at one time the perfection of gravity, again the instrument of sentimentality, and yet again the portrayer of violence and horror.

Burke, Edward Raymond. b. at Runningwater, S.D., Nov. 28, 1880—. American lawyer and legislator. He was graduated (1906) from Beloit College, received (1911) an LL.B. degree from Harvard, and was admitted to the Nebraska bar in 1911. He served (1917–19) with the U.S. army in World War I, resumed his law practice at Omaha, was a member (1933–35) of the U.S. House of Representatives, and served (1935–41) in the U.S. Senate. He was one of the sponsors of the Burke-Wadsworth Act of 1940, the first peacetime draft in U.S. history.

Burke, Fielding. Pseudonym of **Dargan, Olive.**

Burke, John. b. 1787; d. 1848. Irish genealogist; father of Sir John Bernard Burke. In 1826 he published the *Genealogical and Heraldic Dictionary of the Peerage and Baronetage of the United Kingdom*, the first comprehensive and systematic compilation in that field. Since 1847 this work has been published annually and is widely known as *Burke's Peerage*. In 1833 he began the publication of a similar reference book entitled *Burke's Landed Gentry*, dealing with the principal landholding families not included in the peerage or baronetage.

Burke, John. b. at Sigourney, Iowa, Feb. 25, 1859; d. at Rochester, Minn., May 14, 1937. American politician and lawyer. He was governor (1907–13) of North Dakota, treasurer (1913–21) of the U.S., and an associate justice (1925–37) and chief justice (1935 *et seq.*) of the supreme court of North Dakota.

Burke, Sir **John Bernard.** b. at London, Jan. 5, 1814; d. at Dublin, Dec. 12, 1892. English genealogist and Ulster king-at-arms. He was editor of *Burke's Peerage* (established by his father, John Burke, in 1826), and author of *History* (later *Dictionary*) *of the Landed Gentry* (1833–49), and others.

Burke, Kenneth (Duva). b. at Pittsburgh, Pa., May 5, 1897—. American writer on the philosophy and symbolism of literature. Educated at Ohio State and Columbia universities, he served as music critic of *The Dial* (1927–29) and *The Nation* (1934–36), and has been a contributor to many literary reviews. He is the author of *The White Oxen and Other Stories* (1924), *Counter-Statement* (1931), *Towards a Better Life, a Series of Declamations or Epistles* (1932), *Permanence and Change: an Anatomy of Purpose* (1935), *Attitudes Toward History* (1937), *Philosophy of Literary Form—Studies in Symbolic Action* (1941), and *A Grammar of Motives* (1945).

Burke, Martha Jane. See **Calamity Jane.**

Burke, Maurice Francis. b. in Ireland, May 5, 1845; d. at St. Joseph, Mo., March 17, 1923. American Roman Catholic clergyman. After serving as rector (1878–87) of St. Mary's at Joliet, Ill., he was named (1887) bishop of Cheyenne, Wyo. In 1893 he became bishop of St. Joseph, Mo.

Burke, Robert O'Hara. b. at St. Clerans, County Galway, Ireland, 1820; d. in Australia, June 28, 1861. Australian explorer. He was successively a captain in the Austrian army, a member of the Irish constabulary, and an inspector of police in Victoria, Australia, whither he emigrated in 1853. He traversed (1860–61) the Australian continent with W. J. Wills, but died of starvation on the return journey.

Burke, Stevenson. b. near Ogdensburg, N.Y., Nov. 26, 1826; d. April 24, 1904. American corporation lawyer and railroad promoter. He practiced law at Elyria, Ohio (1848–62), and was a common pleas judge (1861–69). After settling at Cleveland, he became prominent as general counsel for railroad companies; later he ventured into railway management, and was president (1880 *et seq.*) of the Cleveland and Mahoning Valley Railway Company. He was also active in mining and manufacturing, and helped found the Cleveland School of Art.

Burke, Thomas. b. in County Galway, Ireland, c1747; d. at Hillsboro, N.C., Dec. 2, 1783. American Revolutionary governor. Settling in North Carolina as a lawyer after practicing medicine in Virginia, he soon entered politics. He was a member of successive provincial congresses, and was elected (1776) to the Continental Congress, serving until 1778. As governor (1781–82) of North Carolina, he was an energetic war leader, and at one time was held hostage by the British and Tories, from whom he escaped to resume his official duties.

Burke, Thomas. b. in Clinton County, N.Y., Dec. 22, 1849; d. at New York, Dec. 4, 1925. American lawyer, jurist, and railway promoter. He studied law at the University of Michigan, and was admitted (1873) to the bar. In 1875 he settled at Seattle, Wash., where he served as probate judge (1876–80) and temporarily (1888–89) as chief justice of the supreme court of Washington territory. He acted as general counsel for the extension of the Great Northern Railroad and was an organizer of the Seattle and Walla Walla Railway, and the Seattle, Lake Shore and Eastern Railway.

Burke, Thomas. b. 1886; d. at London, Sept. 22, 1945. English writer of fiction and essays, who created the character of Quong Lee, Chinatown philosopher, in *Limehouse Nights* (1916). With this book and others he popularized the Limehouse district of London. His other works include the autobiographical novel *The Wind and the Rain* (1924), and *Flower of Life* (1929), *The English Inn* (1930), *The Real East End* (1932), *Night Pieces* (1935), and *Travel in England* (1943).

Burke, Thomas Martin Aloysius. b. in Ireland, Jan. 10, 1840; d. Jan. 20, 1915. American Roman Catholic clergyman. He was rector (1865–74) and pastor (1874–94) of St. Joseph's at Albany, N.Y., and was consecrated bishop of Albany in 1894.

Burke, Victor. b. 1882—. American bacteriologist. In 1921 he was appointed a professor and in 1925 became head of the department of bacteriology at Washington State College. He is the author of *Cyclogasteridae* (1930).

Burke, William. b. in the parish of Orrery, County Cork, Ireland, 1792; hanged Jan. 28, 1829. Irish criminal, a partner of William Hare, who was keeper of a lodging house at Edinburgh. His criminal deeds started with the accidental death of an old pensioner at the lodging house; the corpse was sold to Dr. Robert Knox, a surgeon, for the purpose of dissection, at the price of seven pounds, ten shillings. This high price led the partners to deliberate murder of obscure wayfarers. In several months, assisted by their wives, they murdered at least 15 persons, all sold at similar prices for dissection, until the suspicions of neighbors were aroused. Burke was prosecuted, while Hare turned Crown witness.

Burke Act. Act of the U.S. Congress passed in 1906 which strengthened the Dawes General Allotment Act of 1887 relating to the break-up of land on Indian reservations. In contrast to the Dawes Act, which provided for granting citizenship to Indians upon the issuance of trust patents, the Burke Act stipulated conferral of citizenship upon the termination of a 25-year probationary period set for the full validation of such trust patents.

Bürkel (bür'kel), **Heinrich.** b. at Pirmasens, Bavaria, Germany, May 29, 1802; d. at Munich, June 10, 1869. German painter of landscapes and genre scenes.

Burkitt (bėr'kit), **William.** b. at Hitcham, Suffolk, England, 1650; d. 1703. English divine and Biblical commentator. After taking (1672) an M.A. degree at Cambridge, he became a chaplain for a brief time. He was curate (1672) and later vicar of Milden, Suffolk, and vicar of Dedham, Essex (1692–1703). He wrote sermons, religious treatises, and commentaries on the New Testament.

Burlace (bėr'las), **Edmund.** See **Borlase, Edmund.**

Burlamaqui (bür.lȧ.mȧ.kē), **Jean Jacques.** b. at Geneva, Switzerland, July 24, 1694; d. there, April 3, 1748. Swiss jurist, professor of law at Geneva. He wrote *Principes du droit naturel* (1747) and *Principes du droit politique* (1751), both of which were influential in the social movements of the late 18th century.

Burleigh (bėr'li), 1st Baron. See **Cecil, William.**

Burleigh, Charles Calistus. b. at Plainfield, Conn., Nov. 3, 1810; d. at Northampton, Mass., June 13, 1878. American abolitionist, for a time a coworker of William Lloyd Garrison on the *Liberator;* brother of George Shepard Burleigh and William Henry Burleigh. Abandoning the career of lawyer for that of reformer, he became a lecturer for the Middlesex Anti-Slavery Society, was editor (c1838 *et seq.*) of the *Pennsylvania Freeman*, the publication of the Eastern Pennsylvania Anti-Slavery Society, and was active in the affairs of the American Anti-Slavery Society. He also worked for the causes of woman suffrage and temperance reform.

Burleigh, Edwin Chick. b. at Linneus, Me., Nov. 27, 1843; d. June 16, 1916. American newspaperman and politician. He was publisher (1887 *et seq.*) of the Kennebec (Me.) *Journal*, governor (1889–92) of Maine, a representative (1897–1911) to Congress, and a senator (1913–16) from Maine.

Burleigh, George Shepard. b. at Plainfield, Conn., March 26, 1821; d. at Providence, R.I., July 20, 1903. American poet and abolitionist; brother of Charles Calistus Burleigh and William Henry Burleigh. A writer of antislavery verse, he also was active as an abolitionist lecturer, and was editor (1846–47) of the *Charter Oak*, a Hartford antislavery paper. Among his works are *Elegiac Poem on the Death of Nathaniel Peabody Rogers* (1846) and *The Maniac and Other Poems* (1849).

Burleigh, Henry Thacker. b. at Erie, Pa., 1866; d. 1949. American composer and transcriber of Negro folk music. Organist and singer at several New York churches, he was awarded (1917) the Spingarn medal for achievement.

Burleigh, Lord. In Richard Brinsley Sheridan's *The Critic*, a character in Mr. Puff's play-within-a-play *The Spanish Armada*. He has not a word to say, but confines himself to the memorable nod by which, according to Mr. Puff, he expresses volumes.

Burleigh, William Henry. b. at Woodstock, Conn., Feb. 2, 1812; d. at Brooklyn, N.Y., March 18, 1871. American poet, journalist, and abolitionist; brother of Charles Calistus Burleigh and George Shepard Burleigh. He was early interested in reform movements, and was active in the causes of abolition, woman suffrage, and temperance reform. He lectured (1836 *et seq.*) for the American Anti-Slavery Society, was editor of the *Literary Journal* at Schenectady, N.Y., and the *Christian Witness* (later the *Temperance Banner*) at Pittsburgh, and edited the *Christian Freeman* (later the *Charter Oak*) at Hartford. From 1849 to 1855, when he became harbor master of the port of New York, he was an agent of the New York State Temperance Society. His *Poems* (1841) went through three editions in addition to the original one.

Burleson (bėr'lę.sǫn), **Albert Sidney.** b. at San Marcos, Tex., June 7, 1863; d. at Austin, Tex., Nov. 24, 1937. American lawyer, postmaster general in the period 1913–21. He was a Democratic member of Congress from Texas (1899–1913).

Burleson, Edward. b. in Buncombe County, N.C., Dec. 15, 1798; d. at Austin, Tex., Dec. 26, 1851. American soldier and Texas pioneer. After service in the Tennessee militia, he moved to Texas, where he became a military leader in frontier defense against the Indians. He led the Texans who defeated (1835) a Mexican force at San Antonio, and led a regiment under Houston in the campaign against Antonio López de Santa Anna. Elected (1836) to the first senate of the Texas Republic, he became its vice-president in 1841.

Burleson, Rufus Clarence. b. in Morgan County, Ala., Aug. 7, 1823; d. May 14, 1901. American Baptist clergyman and educator. After his ordination as a Baptist preacher, he was graduated (1847) from the Western Baptist Theological Seminary, at Covington, Ky. He was pastor (1848–51) of the Baptist church at Houston, Tex., and president (1851–61) of Baylor University. Active (1861 *et seq.*) in the establishment and development of Waco University, he was again president (1886–97) of Baylor University after its consolidation with Waco.

Burley (bėr'li). City in S Idaho, county seat of Cassia County, on the Snake River in an irrigated agricultural area: marketing center for potatoes, alfalfa, and sugar beets. 5.924 (1950).

Burley, Sir **Simon.** b. 1336; executed May 5, 1388. English soldier, and counselor to Richard II. He served (1350) in the fleet which destroyed the Spanish corsairs and in the Calais expedition (1355), and became (1380) tutor to Richard II when the latter was 14. He was convicted on the charge of having influenced Richard during his youth to form a corrupt court, impeached by Parliament, and beheaded on Tower Hill.

Burley, Walter. [Surnamed the **"Plain Doctor."**] b. c1274; d. c1345. English scholastic philosopher. He studied first at Oxford, then at Paris, where he became a pupil of Duns Scotus. He was appointed (c1327), almoner to the Princess Philippa of Hainaut, who became the queen (1328) of Edward III of England, and subsequently became tutor to her son Edward, the Black Prince. He wrote numerous philosophical treatises and commentaries on the classics, most of which have remained in manuscript. His printed works include *De vita et moribus philosophorum* (probably published at Cologne in 1467), and *Tractatus de meteria et forma* (Oxford, 1500).

Burlin (bėr'lin), **Natalie.** [Maiden name, **Curtis.**] b. at New York, April 26, 1875; d. at Paris, Oct. 23, 1921. American writer, noted for her researches in Indian and Negro music. She studied at the National Conservatory of Music, New York, and later on the Continent. She gave up her career as a pianist, having become interested in Indian music while visiting Arizona, and compiled *The Indians' Book* (1907), containing 200 songs representing 18 different tribes. She also published *Songs and Tales from the Dark Continent* (1920).

Burlingame (bėr'ling.gām). Residential city in C California, in San Mateo County, S of San Francisco. 19,886 (1950).

Burlingame, Anson. b. at New Berlin, N.Y., Nov. 14, 1820; d. at St. Petersburg, Feb. 23, 1870. American diplomat and politician; father of Edward Livermore Burlingame, and grandfather of Roger Burlingame. He was a representative to Congress from Massachusetts (1855–61), and ambassador to China (1861–67). As envoy extraordinary of China, he negotiated treaties with the U.S. (including the Burlingame Treaty, 1868), England, Denmark, Sweden, Holland, and Prussia. He is noted for his contribution to Chinese-American understanding and good will during a difficult period.

Burlingame, Edward Livermore. b. at Boston, May 30, 1848; d. Nov. 15, 1922. American editor; son of Anson Burlingame. He was the first editor (1886–1914) of *Scribner's Magazine.*

Burlingame, Roger. [Full name, **William Roger Burlingame.**] b. at New York, May 7, 1889—. American author and editor; grandson of Anson Burlingame. He was graduated (B.A., 1913) from Harvard, served as an officer in the American Expeditionary Forces in World War I, and was on the staff of Charles Scribner's Sons from 1914. In World War II he served with the Office of War Information and as a war correspondent in Europe. Author of *You Too* (1924), *Susan Shane* (1926), *Peace Veterans* (1932), *Three Bags Full* (1936), *March of The Iron Men* (1938), *Engines of Democracy* (1940), *Whittling Boy* (1941), *Of Making Many Books* (1946), and *Backgrounds of Power* (1949).

Burlingame Treaty. Articles appended (July 28, 1868) to the Reed Treaty of 1858 and signed at Washington, D.C., by representatives of the U.S. and China, among whom was Anson Burlingame, serving in the capacity of envoy extraordinary and minister plenipotentiary of the emperor of China. Among the provisions were the U.S. acknowledgment of Chinese territorial jurisdiction in China and the U.S. guarantee not to interfere in Chinese domestic affairs.

Burlington (bėr'ling.tǫn). City in SE Iowa, county seat of Des Moines County, on the Mississippi River. It is a railroad center, and manufactures munitions, furniture, baskets, trailers, motors, fertilizer, and other items. It was laid out in 1833, named for Burlington, Vt., incorporated in 1837, and made the temporary capital of Iowa Territory in 1838. In the 1850's it was a pork-packing center (called "the Porkopolis of Iowa") and a passage point for Western settlers, and in the 1870's an important river port and lumber milling and shipping point. 30,613 (1950).

Burlington. City in C New Jersey, in Burlington County, on the Delaware River, ab. 19 mi. NE of Philadelphia: metal products. Settled in 1677 by Quakers, it was made (1681) capital of the province then called West Jersey; after the union (1702) of East and West Jersey it was alternate capital with Perth Amboy. It was bombarded by the British in 1778. James Fenimore Cooper was born here. 12,051 (1950).

Burlington. [Former name, **Company Shops.**] City in N North Carolina, in Alamance County. It has textile and hosiery mills and is a distributing center for tobacco. It was renamed in 1887. Elon College is nearby. 24,560 (1950).

Burlington. Town in Ontario, Canada, situated at the W tip of Lake Ontario, ab. 3 mi. E of the city of Hamilton. It is an important road junction, and a residential suburb of Hamilton. 6,017 (1951).

Burlington. [Called the **"Queen City of Vermont."**] City in N Vermont, county seat of Chittenden County, on Lake Champlain. It is a port of entry and tourist center and the largest city in Vermont, with wood, textile, maple syrup, paper, and other manufactures; formerly an important lake port, now connected with the Hudson River by a canal built in 1823 and since enlarged. Settled in 1773, it is the seat of the University of Vermont and of Trinity College. It was the birthplace of John Dewey.

Ethan Allen lived on a farm just N of Burlington. 33,155 (1950).

Burlington. [Former name, **Foxville.**] City in SE Wisconsin, in Racine County: processing center for dairy products. It was settled in 1835 and named for Burlington, Vt. 4,780 (1950).

Burlington, 3rd Earl of. A title of **Boyle, Richard.**

Burlington Arcade. Covered pathway in London, between Piccadilly and Burlington Gardens, parallel with Old Bond Street. It has shops on each side for all kinds of small wares. The Gardens, now a park, once adjoined Burlington House, seat of the Earls of Burlington, built in the 17th century; Handel once stayed (1715) in a room of this house which at that time overlooked the gardens and the open country outside of London.

Burlington Fine Arts Club. London club established in 1866 by artists and art collectors. It had ab. 500 members, and was housed at 17 Savile Row.

Burlington Gardens and **Burlington House.** See under **Burlington Arcade.**

"Burlington Route." See **Chicago, Burlington and Quincy Railroad.**

Burliuk (bör.lyök'), **David.** b. at Kharkov, Russia, July 22, 1882—. Russian painter, writer, and lecturer on modern art. He studied in Russia, at Paris in the Academie Cormon, and at Munich, and came to the U.S. in 1922. He is a member of the Société Anonyme as well as of several societies in Russia and Japan, and his work is owned by many galleries in Russia, Japan, and the U.S. In 1945 he was awarded one of the prizes in the Pepsi-Cola Annual competition. *Lobster Ships* is one of his better-known works.

Burma (bėr'mą). [Official name, **Union of Burma;** also, **Burmah.**] Republic in SE Asia, on the Bay of Bengal E of India, which came into being on Jan. 4, 1948, as the result of a treaty signed on Oct. 17, 1947, when Great Britain gave up her protectorate powers over the area. It was formerly a kingdom, then a part of the British empire and a lieutenant-governorship. It was divided into Lower Burma (the former British Burma), Upper Burma, and the Shan States. The constitution promulgated in 1947 provided for division of the republic into three states: the Shan State (former Federated Shan States and Wa States), the Kachin State (former Myitkyina and Bhamo districts), and the Karenni State (former Kantarawaddy, Bawlake, and Kyebogyi). It is bounded by China on the N, China, Indochina, and Thailand on the E, the Bay of Bengal and Pakistan on the W, and Manipur and Assam on the NW. Its exports include rice, teak, lead, zinc, tin, and silver. Buddhism is the prevailing religion, the kingdom having been a Buddhist monarchy from the Middle Ages. Lower Burma was conquered by the British in the period 1824–26 and in 1852, and Upper Burma and the Shan States were annexed in 1886, in consequence of the misgovernment of the last king, Thebaw (dethroned in 1885). Capital, Rangoon; area, 261,757 sq. mi.; pop. 16,823,798 (1941), ab. 17 million (est. 1947).

Burman (bėr'mąn). Member of the predominant ethnic group in Burma. The Burmans number 9,627,196 (1931) and occupy the coastal plains and the central regions on either side of the Irrawaddy and lower Chindwin rivers as far N as Tagaung. They are Hinayana Buddhists.

Burman, Ben Lucien. b. at Covington, Ky., Dec. 12, 1895—. American journalist and novelist. A graduate (1920) of Harvard, he was, in World War II, a war correspondent (1941) with the Free French and the British Eighth Army. His novels include *Blow for a Landing* (1938), *Big River to Cross* (1940), and *Rooster Crows for a Day* (1945). His *Mississippi* (1929) was filmed (1931) as *Heaven on Earth,* and his *Steamboat Round the Bend* (1933) was filmed in 1935, starring Will Rogers.

Burma Road. Narrow road ab. 700 mi. long between the Burmese railhead, at Lashio, and Kunming, in Yunnan province, China. The air, or straight-line, distance between the two places is only 260 mi., but difficult terrain required tortuous curves on the road. In the years immediately after the Japanese occupation of the Chinese coast in 1938, the Burma Road became the chief Chinese supply line. Protected by General Claire Lee Chennault's "Flying Tigers," and with American aid, the road was improved so that it eventually carried ab. 12,000 tons of supplies a month. When the Japanese capture of Burma in 1942 forced its abandonment, it was replaced by an air ferry over the Himalayas, and the construction of the Ledo Road further west.

Burmeister (bör'mīs"tėr), **Hermann.** b. at Stralsund (then under Sweden, but Prussian after 1815), Jan. 15, 1807; d. at Buenos Aires, in May, 1892. Prussian naturalist. He was a professor at Berlin and subsequently at Halle, and represented the latter university in the National Assembly in 1848; subsequently he was a member of the first Prussian chamber. From 1850 to 1852 he traveled in Brazil, and in 1861 went to Buenos Aires, where he was director of the National Museum until his death. He published several well-known handbooks of zoölogy and entomology, besides *Übersicht der Tiere Brasiliens* (2 vols., 1854–56), and numerous scientific papers, especially on the Tertiary and Quaternary mammalia of Argentina.

Burmese (bėr.mēz', -mēs'). Language of the Burmans; a member of the Tibeto-Burman language family.

Burmese War. War (1824–26) resulting from the attempted expansion of Burma into British Indian territory. This led to the invasion of Burma by a British Indian army. The action concluded with the cession of Arakan and of the provinces of Mergui, Tavoy, and Ye to India, as well as relinquishment by Burma of all claims to Assam, and the imposition of a heavy indemnity.

Burmese War. War (1852) resulting from a British Indian invasion of Burma when demands on the Burmese government remained unsatisfied. It ended with the annexation to India of the province of Pegu.

Burmese War. War (1885–86) which followed the imposition by the Burmese government of a fine and trading restrictions upon the Bombay-Burma Trading Company, a British concern. It took the form of an extensive invasion of Burmese territory and ended with the dethronement and exile of King Thebaw, after which all of Burma became a British dependency and the kingdom ceased to exist.

Burmester (bör'mā"stėr), **Willy.** b. at Hamburg, Germany, March 16, 1869; d. there, Jan. 16, 1933. German violinist. After studying under Joseph Joachim, he turned (1885) to the virtuoso repertory, specializing in the music of Nicolò Paganini.

Burn (bėrn), **Richard.** b. at Winton, Westmorland, England, 1709; d. at Orton, Westmorland, England, Nov. 12, 1785. English legal writer and clergyman. He was the author of *The Justice of the Peace and Parish Officer* (1755), *A Digest of Militia Laws* (1760), *Ecclesiastical Law* (1760), *A History of the Poor Laws* (1764), *The History and Antiquities of the Counties of Westmorland and Cumberland* (1777), *A New Law Dictionary* (1792), and others.

Burnaby (bėr'ną.bi), **Frederick Gustavus.** b. 1842; d. at Abu Klea, Sudan, Jan. 17, 1885. English soldier and traveler. Sent at the end of 1874 to join Charles George Gordon in the Sudan as a correspondent of the London *Times,* he traveled up the Nile. In 1875 he made a 300-mile horseback journey across the Russian steppes in winter, and in 1876 made a five-month journey across Armenia and Asia Minor for the purpose of studying the Turks. He was killed by a spear wound while serving as a brigadier general during a Nile expedition to relieve Khartoum. His publications include *Ride to Rhiva* (1876), which was translated into several foreign languages, and *On Horseback through Asia Minor* (1876), which had seven editions.

Burnam (bėr'nąm), **John Miller.** b. at Irvine, Ky., April 9, 1864; d. at Pomona, Calif., Nov. 21, 1921. American teacher and scholar. Educated (B.A., 1884; Ph.D., 1886) at Yale, where he specialized in Sanskrit and Latin, he studied (1886–88) abroad, before serving as professor of Latin and French (1889–91) in Georgetown (Kentucky) College. He was assistant professor of Latin (1891–99) in the University of Missouri, and professor of Latin (1900 *et seq.*) in the College of Liberal Arts of the University of Cincinnati. A linguist and a scholar, he worked among manuscripts in many European libraries, and for some years was research professor of Latin and Romance paleography in the Graduate School of the University of Cincinnati. His chief work in his main field, paleography, is *Palaeographia Iberica* (3 parts, 1912–25).

Burnand (bėr.nand'), Sir **Francis Cowley.** b. Nov. 29, 1836; d. 1917. English editor, author, and playwright. He produced many plays, chiefly burlesques and comedies (among which are *Black-eyed Susan, Ixion,* and *The Colonel*), and wrote two light operas (*Contrabandista* and *The Chieftain*) in collaboration with Arthur Sullivan, with whom he also wrote *Cox and Box*, a musical version of John Maddison Morton's farce *Box and Cox*. He was a member (c1862 *et seq.*) of the editorial staff of *Punch* and one of its principal contributors, and was its editor in chief in the period 1880–1906. He also wrote *Mokeanna*, several series of *Happy Thoughts, New Light on Darkest Africa, Eccentric Guide to the Isle of Thanet*, and a volume of reminiscences (1904).

Burnap (bėr′nap), **George Washington.** b. in Merrimack town, N.H., Nov. 30, 1802; d. Sept. 8, 1859. American Unitarian clergyman and writer. Graduated (c1827) from the Harvard Divinity School, he assumed the pastorate of the First Independent Church at Baltimore, where he was ordained (1828). He remained at this post until his death. He was an energetic lecturer and prolific writer in the cause of conservative Unitarianism.

Burne-Jones (bėrn′jōnz′), Sir **Edward Coley.** b. at Birmingham, England, Aug. 28, 1833; d. at London, June 17, 1898. English Pre-Raphaelite painter. He was a student at Exeter College, Oxford, at the same time as William Morris and Algernon Charles Swinburne, the latter of whom dedicated to him his first volume of poems. He went to London in 1856, and became a pupil of Dante Gabriel Rossetti, whose manner he imitated for several years. He soon formed, however, a style of his own, reminiscent of that of Botticelli, and inclining more to idealism and abstract beauty than to realism, and became one of the chief exponents in England of the romantic school. From 1857 to 1858 he was associated with Rossetti, Morris, and others in painting the Arthurian legends at Oxford. In 1861 he was one of the originators of the house of Morris and Company, and he made many designs for stained-glass windows and other decorative work. He was an associate of the Royal Academy in the period 1885–93. In 1894 he was made a baronet. Among his best-known works are *King Cophetua and the Beggar Maid, The Golden Stairs,* and *The Depths of the Sea.*

Burnell (bėr.nel′), **Arthur Coke.** b. at St. Briavels, Gloucestershire, England, 1840; d. at West Stratton, Hampshire, England, Oct. 12, 1882. English Sanskrit scholar and authority on the languages and literature of India. He was educated at King's College, London. Having entered the Indian Civil Service in 1857, he lived in India (except for terms of leave) from 1860 to 1880. His most important work, *Classified Index to the Sanskrit MSS. in the Palace at Tanjore*, was printed for the Madras government in 1880. He also published *Handbook of South Indian Palaeography* (1874), *The Aindra School of Sanskrit Grammarians* (1875), and translations from the Sanskrit. *Hobson Jobson, being a Glossary of Anglo-Indian Colloquial Words and Phrases*, a work which he compiled with Sir Henry Yule, was published in 1886.

Burnes (bėrnz), Sir **Alexander.** b. at Montrose, Scotland, May 16, 1805; killed at Kabul, Afghanistan, Nov. 2, 1841. British geographer, and traveler in central Asia.

Burnet (bėr′nęt), **David Gouverneur.** b. at Newark, N.J., April 4, 1788; d. at Galveston, Tex., Dec. 5, 1870. Texas politician; son of William Burnet (1730–91). After a varied early career as a soldier of fortune, merchant, law student, and speculator, he settled (c1831) in Texas, soon becoming active in the political life of the region. He was a member of the Washington Convention (1836) which issued the Texas Declaration of Independence, and was elected by that body as the Texas Republic's president *ad interim*. He resigned from that post after many difficulties, but became vice-president in 1838, and served as the new state's first secretary of state (1846–47).

Burnet, Gilbert. b. at Edinburgh, Sept. 18, 1643; d. at London, March 17, 1715. British prelate, historian, and theologian; father of William Burnet (1688–1729). He accompanied William III from Holland to England in 1688 as his chaplain, and was made bishop of Salisbury in 1689. His chief works are *History of the Reformation of the Church of England* (1679, 1681, 1715), *Exposition of the Thirty-nine Articles* (1699), and *A History of My Own Times* (edited by his son, 1723, 1734).

Burnet, Jacob. b. at Newark, N.J., Feb. 22, 1770; d. May 10, 1853. American lawyer, jurist, and senator; son of William Burnet (1730–91). After graduating (1791) from Nassau Hall, he studied law, and settled (1796) at Cincinnati. He served in many posts in the territorial government, was a member of the state legislature (1812–16), and was the moving spirit behind the national Land Act of 1820 which averted financial disaster in the West. After serving (1821–28) as a justice of the Ohio supreme court, he became (1828) a U.S. senator. His *Notes on the Northwestern Territory* (1847) is a valuable historical source; he also figures prominently as one of the pioneers in the Old Northwest.

Burnet, John. b. at Edinburgh, Dec. 6, 1863; d. at St. Andrews, Scotland, May 26, 1928. Scottish scholar in the field of Greek philosophy. Educated at Oxford, he first taught Greek in his native city, and later at Harrow and at Merton College, Oxford, before becoming professor of Greek at St. Andrews. His *Early Greek Philosophy* (1892) was recognized as an important study of the Hellenic thinkers who preceded Socrates. He edited several of the works of Plato and of Aristotle. His *Greek Philosophy: Thales to Plato* (1914) argued that the doctrines attributed to Socrates in the early Platonic dialogues were really those of the older philosopher, while Plato's own views are to be found in the later dialogues.

Burnet, Thomas. b. at Croft, Yorkshire, England, c1635; d. at London, Sept. 27, 1715. English author. He became a fellow of Christ's College in 1657, and master of the Charterhouse School in 1685. He is noted chiefly as the author of *Telluris Theoria Sacra* (1681), remarkable for its vivid imagery and pure Latinity, in which he attempts to prove that the earth originally resembled an egg, that at the deluge the shell was crushed and the waters rushed out, that the fragments of the shell formed the mountains and that the equator was diverted from its original coincidence with the ecliptic.

Burnet, William. b. at The Hague, in March, 1688; d. Sept. 7, 1729. American colonial governor; son of Gilbert Burnet. He was provincial governor (1720–28) of New York and Jersey. His difficulties there with the colonial merchants over Indian policy led to his transfer (1728) to Massachusetts, where he was governor until his death.

Burnet, William. b. at Lyon's Farms, N.J., Dec. 2, 1730; d. Oct. 7, 1791. American physician and Revolutionary patriot; father of David Gouverneur Burnet and Jacob Burnet. Graduated (1749) from the College of New Jersey, he studied medicine at New York, subsequently establishing his practice there. In 1775 he was active on the committees of public safety for Newark and Essex County, and founded (1775) a military hospital at Newark. He was a member (1776–77, 1780) of the Continental Congress, which appointed him (1777) physician and surgeon general of the Eastern District. He was prominent in curbing Loyalist elements in eastern New Jersey.

Burnett (bėr.net′), **Charles Henry.** b. at Philadelphia, May 28, 1842; d. at Bryn Mawr, Pa., Jan. 30, 1902. American otologist, noted for his investigations in the physiology of the ear. Graduated (1864) from Yale, he received (1867) an M.D. degree from the University of Pennsylvania. After studying abroad, he became an ear specialist at Philadelphia, where he was associated with several hospitals, and was professor of otology in the Philadelphia Polyclinic. He was a contributor to the *American Textbook of Surgery* and the *American Year-Book of Medicine and Surgery*, served as president of the American Otological Society, and was author and editor of several medical books.

Burnett, Frances Eliza Hodgson. b. at Cheetham Hill, Manchester, England, Nov. 24, 1849; d. Oct. 29, 1924. American author, best remembered for her popular novel *Little Lord Fauntleroy* (1886). She came to America in 1865, and settled near Knoxville, Tenn., and in 1873 married Swan Moses Burnett, from whom she was divorced in 1898; in 1900 she married Stephen Townesend. She was the author of several plays, and of novels such as *Haworth's* (1879) and *Through One Administration* (1883), but it was as a writer of children's books, including *Sara Crewe* (1888), *Little Saint Elizabeth* (1890), and *The Secret Garden* (1911) that she preformed her most memorable work. Her other writings include *Louisiana* (1880), *A Lady of Quality* (1896), *The Shuttle* (1907), *The Cozy Lion* (1907), and *The White People* (1917). With William

Gillette, she wrote a play, *Esmeralda* (1881). Her autobiography is *The One I Knew Best of All* (1893).

Burnett, Henry Lawrence. b. at Youngstown, Ohio, Dec. 26, 1838; d. at New York, Jan. 4, 1916. American soldier and lawyer. He was graduated (1859) from the Ohio State National Law School, and served as an officer in the Union army. He took part in the conspiracy trials in Indiana and Illinois, the treason trial of L. P. Milligan, and the trial of Lincoln's assassins. He was a prominent lawyer at New York, where he settled c1872, and served (1898 *et seq.*) as federal district attorney for the southern district of New York.

Burnett, James. See **Monboddo,** Lord.

Burnett, Joseph. b. at Southborough, Mass., Nov. 11, 1820; d. Aug. 11, 1894. American manufacturer and civic benefactor. A manufacturing chemist, he was among the first to establish a perfumery and extract firm in the U.S., and after 1854 headed his own business, Joseph Burnett and Company. His chief work as a philanthropist was the financial backing (1865) of St. Mark's School at Southborough.

Burnett, Peter Hardeman. [Original surname, **Burnet.**] b. at Nashville, Tenn., Nov. 15, 1807; d. at San Francisco, May 17, 1895. American western pioneer, a member of the 1843 migration to Oregon. He was active in the territorial government, and in 1848 was appointed one of its supreme court justices. He joined the California gold rush, and was elected governor of California just before it was admitted to statehood (1850). Resigning in 1851, he practiced law, and in the period 1857–58 served in the state supreme court. He was the author of *Recollections and Opinions of an Old Pioneer* (1880).

Burnett, Swan Moses. b. at New Market, Tenn., March 16, 1847; d. Jan. 18, 1906. American physician; husband (1873–98) of the American writer Frances Eliza Hodgson Burnett. He was graduated (1870) from the Bellevue Hospital Medical College, New York. After practicing medicine (1870–75) at Knoxville, Tenn., he studied otology and ophthalmology at London and Paris, settling at Washington, D.C., after his return in 1876. He was associated (1878 *et seq.*) with the faculty of the medical school of Georgetown University, becoming a professor in his special field in 1889. He was connected with several Washington hospitals, and worked extensively among the Negro population of that city. He helped compile the *National Medical Dictionary* (1889), and was the author of several books in his field.

Burnett, Whit. b. at Salt Lake City, Utah, Aug. 14, 1899—. American journalist, editor, and author; husband (married 1930) of Martha Foley. He was Associated Press editor at Los Angeles (1919–20) and San Francisco (1921), and city editor (1927–28) of the Paris edition of the New York *Herald*. With his wife, he founded (1931) and edited (1931–41) at Vienna the magazine *Story* (transferred to New York in 1933), remaining its sole editor after 1941. In 1935 he became editor of the Story Press. He is the author of *The Maker of Signs* (1934) and *The Literary Life and the Hell With It* (1939), editor of *This Is My Best* (1942) and *The World's Best* (1950), and coeditor with his wife of *A Story Anthology* (1933) and other books.

Burnett, William Riley. b. at Springfield, Ohio, Nov. 25, 1899—. American novelist and motion-picture writer. His novels include *Little Caesar* (1929), *Iron Man* (1930), *The Giant Swing* (1932), *Dark Hazard* (1933), *The Dark Command* (1938), *High Sierra* (1940), *The Quick Brown Fox* (1942), *Romellee* (1946), and *Little Men, Big World* (1951). He collaborated on such films as *Little Caesar, Scarface, High Sierra, Wake Island,* and *This Gun for Hire.*

Burney (bėr′ni), **Charles.** b. at Shrewsbury, England, April 12, 1726; d. at Chelsea, London, April 12, 1814. English composer and historian of music; father of Charles Burney, Fanny Burney, James Burney, and Sarah Harriet Burney. He was a church organist (1749–60) at London and Norfolk, and served (1783–1814) as organist of Chelsea College. He wrote *General History of Music* (4 vols., 1776–89) and *Life and Letters of Metastasio* (3 vols., 1796).

Burney, Charles. b. at King's Lynn, Norfolk, England, Dec. 4, 1757; d. at Deptford, London, Dec. 28, 1817. English classical scholar; son of Charles Burney (1726–1814). He is noted chiefly as the collector of the Burney Library, which was purchased by Parliament for 13,500 pounds and deposited in the British Museum.

Burney, Fanny. [Married name, Madame **d'Arblay;** original name, **Frances Burney.**] b. at King's Lynn, Norfolk, England, June 13, 1752; d. at Bath, England, Jan. 6, 1840. English novelist; daughter of Charles Burney (1726–1814). Her first book, the epistolary novel in the manner of Richardson, *Evelina, or a Young Lady's Entrance into the World* (1778), which she published anonymously, was well received and drew praise from Samuel Johnson. When her authorship of it was revealed, she was welcomed into the leading literary sets of her day, and was given, through the intervention of friends, a post at the court of Queen Charlotte, which she held from 1786 to 1791. In 1793 she married General Alexandre d'Arblay, a political refugee from the French Revolution. Her detailed journals and letters are a valuable source of information on contemporary court life, as well as furnishing anecdotes about Dr. Johnson's circle. Her other works include *Cecilia, or Memoirs of an Heiress* (1782), *Edwy and Elvina* (a tragedy, acted March 21, 1795), *Camilla, or a Picture of Youth* (1796), *Love and Fashion* (a comedy, 1800), *The Wanderer* (1814), *Memoirs of Dr. Burney* (1832), and *Letters and Diaries* (5 vols., 1842; 2 vols., 1846).

Burney, James. b. 1750; d. Nov. 17, 1821. English naval officer and author; son of Charles Burney (1726–1814). He entered the navy in 1764, attained the rank of captain, and served in America and India. He was with James Cook on his third voyage, in the period 1776–79. After 1784 he retired on half pay and devoted himself to writing. His principal works are *A Chronological History of the Discoveries in the South Sea or Pacific Ocean* (5 vols. 4to, 1803–17), *History of the Buccaneers of America* (1816), and *A Chronological History of North Eastern Voyages of Discovery* (1816).

Burney, Sarah Harriet. b. c1770; d. at Cheltenham, Gloucestershire, England, Feb. 8, 1844. English novelist; daughter of Charles Burney (1726–1814), and sister of Fanny and James Burney. She was the author of *Clarentine* (1796; published anonymously), *Geraldine Fauconberg* (1808; 2nd ed., 1813), *Traits of Nature* (1812), *Tales of Fancy* (1815), and *Romance of Private Life* (1839), novels and short narratives.

Burnham (bėr′nạm), 1st Baron. [Title of **Edward Levy-Lawson;** original surname, **Levy.**] b. at London, Dec. 28, 1833; d. there, Jan. 9, 1916. English newspaper owner, fund raiser, and social reformer; son of Joseph Moses Levy (1812–88), who in 1855 made the *Daily Telegraph* the first London penny paper; the son added Lawson to his name in 1875. Educated at London University College, he was drama critic (1851–55) on his father's *Sunday Times*, of which he was later (1855 *et seq.*) editor. Active in raising funds for hospitals, widows and orphans of soldiers and sailors, and similar causes, he also promoted the scientific researches and explorations of Henry Morton Stanley in Africa, George Smith in Assyria, and Sir Harry Johnston in East Africa. He served as vice-president and president (1867, 1908–16) of the Newspaper Press Fund, and president (1892) of the Institute of Journalists. He was created a baronet in 1892 and became Baron Burnham in 1903.

Burnham, 1st Viscount. [Title of **Harry Lawson Webster Lawson.**] b. at London, Dec. 18, 1862; d. there, July 20, 1933. English editor and newspaper proprietor who succeeded (1903) his father, the 1st Baron Burnham, as director of conduct and policy of the London *Daily Telegraph*. The newspaper was later (December, 1927) sold to Sir William Berry, James Gower Berry, and Edward Iliffe. Burnham served (1885–92, 1893–95, 1905–06) as a Liberal member of Parliament, and later (1910–16) as a Unionist member of Parliament. A member of the committee which drafted the Representation of the People Act, known as the Reform Act of 1918, he also presided over committees making an award on new scales of payment ("Burnham" scales) to teachers in Great Britain. He was president (1921, 1922, 1926) of the International Labor Conference at Geneva, and president (1916–28) of the Empire Press Union. In 1929 he was appointed president of Birkbeck College, University of London.

Burnham. [Former names, **Freedom Forge, Logan.**] Borough in C Pennsylvania, in Mifflin County: manufactures include locomotive castings, wheels, axles, bar iron, and steel. Founded in 1795, it was renamed in 1911. Pop. 2,954 (1950).

Burnham, Clara Louise Root. b. at Newton, Mass., May 26, 1854; d. on Bailey Island, in Casco Bay, Me., June 20, 1927. American novelist.

Burnham, Daniel Hudson. b. at Henderson, N.Y., Sept. 4, 1846; d. at Heidelberg, Germany, June 1, 1912. American architect and city planner. As a member (1873–91) of the architectural firm of Burnham and Root, he helped rebuild Chicago after the fire of 1871; the Montauk Building in that city, supposedly the first structure to be called a "skyscraper," was a pioneer venture in large fireproof construction. He was chief of construction (1890 *et seq.*) of the World's Columbian Exposition at Chicago, emerging as the most prominent architect of his day in the U.S. As head (c1893 *et seq.*) of his own firm, he took part in designing many buildings in America's largest cities. He was an expert in municipal planning, serving (1901 *et seq.*) on the commission for the improvement of Washington, D.C., which laid the foundations of the city-planning movement in this country. For his work on this commission, as for similar tasks in improving the cities of Cleveland, San Francisco, and Chicago, and Manila and Baguio in the Philippines, he refused to accept payment. He was appointed (1910) chairman of the National Commission of Fine Arts. Among the buildings designed by him are the Masonic Temple at Chicago, the Union Station at Washington, and the Flatiron Building at New York.

Burnham, Frederick Russell. b. at Tivoli, Minn., May 11, 1861; d. at Santa Barbara, Calif., Sept. 1, 1947. American explorer. A scout for the British in their war against the Matabele natives in Rhodesia, he discovered treasure buried in ancient Rhodesian ruins. He was chief (1900–01) of scouts in the British army during the Boer War, engaged (1902) in surveys on the Volta River, West Africa, explored (1903–04) the Congo basin region, discovered (1908) remains of Maya civilization in Mexico, and collaborated with John Hays Hammond in diverting the Yaquí River, in Mexico, through canals into a 700-square-mile delta. Author of *Scouting on Two Continents*, *Taking Chances*, and books on African exploration.

Burnham, Sherburne Wesley. b. at Thetford, Vt., Dec. 12, 1838; d. March 11, 1921. American astronomer, noted as a discoverer and observer of double stars. He was observer at the Dearborn Observatory (1877–81, 1882–84) and the Washburn Observatory (1881–82), astronomer at the Lick Observatory (1888–92), and senior astronomer of the Yerkes Observatory (1897–1914). He compiled *A General Catalogue of Double Stars* (1906).

Burnham-on-Sea. [Also, **Burnham.**] Urban district in SW England, in Somersetshire, situated on the E shore of Bridgwater Bay ab. 8 mi. N of Bridgwater, ab. 146 mi. SW of London by rail. 9,136 (1951).

Burni (bör′nē). Malay name of **Borneo.**

Burning Babe, The. Poem by Robert Southwell. It is the best known of Southwell's religious lyrics, which were written in prison and published in the year of his execution (1595).

Burning Cactus, The. Volume of short stories by Stephen Spender, published in 1936.

Burning Spear, The. Novel by John Galsworthy, published in 1921 under the pseudonym A. R. P. M., and reissued under the author's name in 1923. John Lavender, a quixotic hero with a touch of madness, is the central character in this satirical novel.

Burnley (bėrn′li). County borough, coal-mining city, and manufacturing center in NW England, in Lancashire, situated on the river Burn and on the Leeds and Liverpool Canal, ab. 21 mi. N of Manchester, ab. 211 mi. NW of London by rail. It is located on the North Lancashire coal field. Burnley has a cotton-textile industry, specializing in fine-grade cloths for cotton prints; it also has rayon mills and iron foundries. 84,950 (1951).

Burnouf (bür.nöf), **Émile Louis.** b. at Valognes, Manche, France, Aug. 25, 1821; d. 1907. French philologist, distinguished as an archaeologist and Orientalist. He collaborated on the first Sanskrit-French dictionary (1863).

Burnouf, Eugène. b. at Paris, Aug. 12, 1801; d. there, May 28, 1852 French Orientalist; son of Jean Louis Burnouf. He was noted for his researches in the Zend language. His chief works are *Commentaire sur le Yaçna* (1833–35), *Introduction à l'histoire du Bouddhisme indien* (1845), and *Le Lotus de la bonne loi, traduit du Sanscrit* (1852).

Burnouf, Jean Louis. b. at Urville, Manche, France, Sept. 14, 1775; d. at Paris, May 8, 1844. French philologist; father of Eugène Burnouf. He wrote *Méthode pour étudier la langue grecque* (1814), *Méthode pour étudier la langue latine* (1840), and a translation (1827–33) of Tacitus.

Burns (bėrnz). City in C Oregon, county seat of Harney County: center of a livestock-raising area. Established at the end of the 19th century and named for Robert Burns, it has lumber mills and is the site of a Paiute Indian village. 3,093 (1950).

Burns, Anthony. b. in Stafford County, Va., May 31, 1834; d. at St. Catharines, Ontario, Canada, July 27, 1862. American fugitive slave, the last to be seized in Massachusetts under the Fugitive Slave Law of 1850. He escaped from slavery in 1853, and his arrest at Boston on May 24, 1854, caused great indignation and public disturbance. An attempt was made on May 26, 1854, to rescue him, but it failed, and he was adjudged to his owner and sent back. His freedom was bought in the following year, and he later studied at Oberlin College, subsequently becoming a Baptist minister at St. Catharines, in Ontario, Canada.

Burns, John. b. at London, in October, 1858; d. 1943. British labor leader and cabinet officer. He was an unsuccessful Socialist candidate for the western division of Nottingham in 1885, represented Battersea in the House of Commons from 1892, and was appointed president of the Local Government Board, with a seat in the cabinet, in December, 1905. He headed (1914) the Board of Trade.

Burns, Otway. b. in Onslow County, N.C., c1755; d. Oct. 25, 1850. American privateersman, shipbuilder, and legislator. He commanded the privateer *Snap-Dragon* during the War of 1812, doing great damage to British shipping from Greenland to Brazil. After the war he engaged in shipbuilding, and served (1821–35) in the North Carolina general assembly.

Burns, Robert. b. at Alloway, Ayrshire, Scotland, Jan. 25, 1759; d. at Dumfries, Scotland, July 21, 1796. Scottish poet. He was the son of a farmer and nurseryman, whose family name was variously spelled Burnes or Burness. Born to poverty, he grew up with little schooling but much hard work (so much, in fact, that before he reached his majority his health was impaired by it, and he had contracted a fondness for Scotch whisky which remained with him to the end of his life). During his minority the family moved more than once, always hoping, but in vain, that a different farm would bring better fortune; and in 1784 Robert and a brother rented Mossgiel, a farm of 118 acres near Mauchline. Mossgiel proved no better a way to wealth than the previous holdings, and in 1786 Robert made arrangements to take a clerical position in the British West Indies. In the hope of raising money for the expenses of this emigration, he published in that year, at Kilmarnock, a book entitled *Poems, Chiefly in the Scottish Dialect* which, although it is said to have netted him at that time only 20 pounds, changed his destiny, influenced the future development of the art of poetry, and gave him a place in the hearts of his countrymen as great as or greater than that of any of their kings or heroes. It was in connection with this publication that he shortened the family name to Burns. It is said that ploughboys and servant girls were eager to spend the hard-earned wages they needed for food and clothing to possess the book, while the gentry and the intellectuals of Edinburgh invited him to the capital, where as Sir Walter Scott wrote, he "was much caressed . . . but the efforts made for his relief were extremely trifling." He could dine with lords and ladies and charm a salon with his wit and natural dignity, but had to sleep in the cheapest lodgings. In 1787, however, two additional printings of his poems were published, bringing him some 500 pounds, whereupon he bought a farm at Ellisland and formally married (1788) Jean Armour, by whom he already had had children. (Burns's sexual activities were promiscuous as well as fruitful. Jean Armour bore him twins in 1786 and again in 1788; in the former year, Burns is said to have been involved simultaneously in affairs with Jean Armour, Elizabeth Patron, and Mary Campbell ("Highland Mary"). His decision to emigrate stemmed at least partly from the complications created by his intimacies with these lasses, and he apparently had decided to marry Mary Campbell and leave Scotland, when Mary died in childbirth.) In 1789 his Edinburgh friends secured for him a post as exciseman at Dumfries, at a salary of 70 pounds per annum, and it was here that a third edition of his poems was printed in 1793. Meanwhile, he contributed to Edinburgh and London magazines and newspapers, but his enthusiasm for the principles of the French Revolution cooled the friendship of his aristocratic patrons. He wrote or adapted some 200 songs for James Johnsor's *Scots Musical Museum,* and about 100 for George Thompson's *Select Collection of Original Scottish Airs.* In 1794 he became alarmed at the threat of a French invasion of Britain, and joined the Dumfriesshire Volunteers, who gave him a military funeral when, his constitution weakened by excesses, he died in what should have been his middle years. His lyrics are diverse in mood and method. His songs of wooing range from the tender in *Mary Morison* to archness in *Tam Glen,* to a jocose treatment of bashfulness in *Duncan Gray,* and to uproarious delight in the story of *Last May a Braw Wooer.* Absence, though not his common theme, is sweetly treated in *Of a' the Airts,* and the elegiac tone of *Banks o' Doon* and *Highland Mary* expresses beautifully the tragedy of lost love. *Tam o' Shanter* alone would prove that Burns had superlative gifts in poetic narrative, but in his songs he seldom relies on story for substance. In *Auld Rob Morris, Open the Door,* and *Tam Glen,* however, story is exquisitely implied. The lover at parting perhaps protests too much in *Ae Fond Kiss,* but in the fervidly hyperbolic *Red, Red Rose* we surely have authentic passion if ever words conveyed it. His more "public" songs, such as the reworked *Auld Lang Syne, Is there for Honest Poverty,* and above all the battle song of *Scots Wha Hae wi' Wallace Bled,* are in their respective modes supremely eloquent.

Burns, William John. b. at Baltimore, Oct. 19, 1861; d. April 14, 1932. American detective, noted as the founder and president of the William J. Burns International Detective Agency. He was director (1921–24) of the Bureau of Investigation in the U.S. Department of Justice.

Burns Baking Co. v. Bryan, 264 U.S. 504 (1924). Decision of the U.S. Supreme Court, holding as an unreasonable exercise of state police power a Nebraska law establishing a maximum weight for loaves of bread. The case is notable as an example of the volume and complexity of technical details which the court occasionally must investigate in order to reach a decision.

Burns Fugitive Slave Case. In U.S. history in the 1850's, a case involving the fugitive Negro slave Anthony Burns, who had been apprehended by federal authorities under the Fugitive Slave Act of 1850 and confined at Boston. In an unsuccessful attempt to rescue Burns, members of the local vigilance committee broke into the courthouse on May 26, 1854, and killed a federal marshal named Batchelder. Burns was ultimately returned to his Southern master, but his freedom was purchased by several Massachusetts citizens in 1855.

Burnside (bėrn'sīd), **Ambrose Everett.** b. at Liberty, Ind., May 23, 1824; d. at Bristol, R.I., Sept. 13, 1881. American general and politician. He graduated (1847) from the U.S. Military Academy at West Point and, after serving briefly in the Mexican War and on frontier and garrison duty, withdrew (1853) from the army to manufacture a breech-loading rifle of his own invention. He organized (April, 1861) and was colonel of the 1st Rhode Island regiment, and led a brigade in the first Battle of Bull Run. Promoted (Aug. 6, 1861) to brigadier general of volunteers, he was commissioned major general (March 18, 1862) after leading a force which captured the Confederate base on Roanoke Island. Commanding the 1st and 9th corps in the Antietam campaign, he succeeded General George B. McClellan as commander of the Army of the Potomac, a post which he had previously twice declined. He led this army in the battle of Fredericksburg (December, 1862), in which his forces suffered heavy casualties; following differences with his divisional commanders, he was relieved of his command at his own request. He was given (March, 1863) the command of the Department of the Ohio, and during his drive against Confederate sympathizers in that area ordered the arrest and trial of Clement Vallandigham on the charge of disloyalty to the Union. Assigned (January, 1864) to the command of the 9th corps, he led it in the battles of the Wilderness, Spottsylvania, and Cold Harbor, and in the operations before Petersburg. The latter action resulted in 4,000 Union casualties, for which Burnside was held responsible by a court of inquiry set up at the order of General George Gordon Meade. Burnside went on leave and later resigned his commission. He became a director (1864) of the Illinois Central Railroad Company, president (1865) of the Cincinnati and Martinsville Railroad Company, president (1866) of the Rhode Island Locomotive Works, and president (1867) of the Indianapolis and Vincennes Railroad Company and director of the Narragansett Steamship Company. He was governor (1866 *et seq.*) of Rhode Island and represented that state in the U.S. Senate from 1874 to 1881. His mutton-chop sidewhiskers were so luxuriant that his name is now applied to the type.

Burnside, William. b. at London, July 2, 1852; d. at West Wickham, England, Aug. 21, 1927. English mathematician noted for his contributions to differential equations, theory of groups, hydrodynamics, and elliptic and automorphic functions. He was educated at Cambridge, and taught there (1875) as well as at the Royal Naval College at Greenwich (1885 *et seq.*). His books include *Theory of Equations* (1881), *Theory of Groups of Finite Order* (1897), and *Theory of Probability* (1928).

Burns, Philip and Company, Limited (bėrnz; filp). Australian shipping and merchant firm, established 1883 by Sir James Burns (1846–1923) and Sir Robert Philp (1851–1922). It played a large role in the economic development of Queensland and the South Pacific Islands.

Burnt Chimney. Former name of **Forest City,** N.C.

Burntisland (bėrnt'ī'lạnd). Royal burgh, seaport, industrial center, and resort in E Scotland, in Fifeshire, situated on the N bank of the Firth of Forth, ab. 4 mi. SW of Kirkcaldy, ab. 413 mi. N of London by rail. Industries include aluminum refining and shipbuilding (especially of cargo craft). The port exports coal and imports bauxite (aluminum ore) from France. 5,874 (est. 1948).

Burpee (bėr'pē), **Washington Atlee.** b. at Sheffield, New Brunswick, Canada, April 5, 1858; d. Nov. 26, 1915. American seed merchant. He began (1876) in the seed business with two partners, and established (1878) by himself the firm of W. Atlee Burpee and Company, which developed into the largest U.S. mail-order house for seeds.

Burr (bėr), **Aaron.** b. at Fairfield, Conn., c1716; d. Sept. 24, 1757. American clergyman, president of the College of New Jersey (now Princeton University) from 1748 to 1757.

Burr, Aaron. b. at Newark, N.J., Feb. 6, 1756; d. at Port Richmond, on Staten Island, N.Y., Sept. 14, 1836. American political leader and officer in the Revolutionary War. He attended the College of New Jersey (now Princeton University) and graduated in 1772. When the Revolution broke out he joined the forces before Boston; he went with the army that attacked Quebec, and was promoted to major; he was later promoted to lieutenant colonel for his service in the defense of New York. He became an aide to General Israel Putnam, and distinguished himself at Valley Forge. He commanded a brigade at the Battle of Monmouth. He resigned in 1778, partly because of ill-health and partly because of dissatisfaction with the way the war was being conducted. Four years later he was admitted to the bar at Albany, and was married to Mrs. Prevost. He took up his practice at New York in 1783 and rose rapidly to the top of his profession. He advanced from legislator to senator, defeating General Philip John Schuyler, Alexander Hamilton's father-in-law, and thus beginning an enmity which was to be ended only by the death of Hamilton as a result of a duel between the two men at Weehawken, N.J., on July 11, 1804. Burr became a power in New York politics; indeed he became head of the Republican faction of the East. He and Thomas Jefferson formulated the platform of the Republicans for the campaign of 1800, and in the election they were tied in the Electoral College for the office of president. The choice was thrown into the House of Representatives, where, after 36 ballots, Jefferson was selected, and Burr became vice-president. Had Burr been so disposed he might at this time have made a deal with the Federalists, and thus have been made president, but he felt that the people wanted Jefferson and he yielded. He was, however, never forgiven for his rivalry by Jefferson, who pursued him with persecutions, both personal and political, for many years. Some historians consider that here lies a blot on the escutcheon of Jefferson: the malice and vengeance heaped on Burr personally, and on the Westerners who were ready to march with Burr to conquer the Spanish colonies lying to the south and southwest, in the year 1806. Burr and the Westerners were charged with treason, a charge, under the circumstances, as black and defenseless as any in our records. As vice-president Burr achieved great distinction as an impartial presiding officer, but the schism in the party led to Burr's being read out of it. He became a candidate for the office of governor of New York, only to meet defeat, chiefly through what many consider to have been the slanderous efforts of Hamilton which were an immediate cause of the duel. Burr, however, was not to be put down, and now entered upon what is known as the Conspiracy, the chief instigator of which was General James Wilkinson, an arch-villain of American history. He had been ordered to drive the Spaniards out of disputed territory along the Sabine River, and thus had the power to bring on war with Spain; the Westerners were ready to march; and Burr and Wilkinson were ready to lead them. This, therefore, was the Conspiracy: the conquest of the Southwest. At the moment it was a dream challenging the imagination. It was to come to realization when the Texans took over the region from the Sabine to the Rio Grande in 1836. But Wilkinson betrayed Burr, and Jefferson seized on the incident to destroy him. Burr was tried for treason at Richmond in 1807, amid a great turmoil led by Jefferson's partisans, but there was no evidence worth considering, and Burr and his confederates were acquitted. In 1808 Burr went abroad, still intent on his plan to conquer the Spanish colonies. He had earlier got in touch with the French and English governments, trying to get them to advance him money for the purpose of his conquest. And now again he sought either to bring England or France to aid him in his enterprise. Finally, realizing the futility of his plans, he tried to get back to America, but through the efforts of representatives of the U.S. government, he was held in Europe, often on the verge of starvation. In 1812 he succeeded in getting home, and resumed his law practice at New York, again reaching high standing in his profession. But his life was embittered, and the loss of his daughter Theodosia made even more empty that which was left of it. See *Memoirs of Aaron Burr* by Matthew L. Davis (2 vols., 1836–37), the *Aaron Burr Conspiracy* by Walter F. McCaleb (1903, 1934), and *Aaron Burr* by Nathan Schachner (1937).

Burr, Alfred Edmund. b. March 27, 1815; d. Jan. 8, 1900. American newspaper editor. He was publisher and editor (1841–1900) of the Hartford (Conn.) *Daily Times*, and served as representative (1853, 1866) in the Connecticut legislature.

Burr, Enoch Fitch. b. near Westport, Conn., Oct. 21, 1818; d. May 8, 1907. American clergyman and mathematician. He was a pastor (1850–1907) at Hamburg, Conn., and a lecturer (1868–74) at Amherst, Yale, and Williams. Author of *Results of Analytical Researches in the Neptunian Theory of Uranus* (1848), *Ecce Coelum, or Parish Astronomy* (1867), the collected lectures *Pater Mundi* (1870), *The Doctrine of Evolution* (1873), *Celestial Empires* (1885), *Universal Beliefs* (1887), and three volumes of sermons, *Ad Fidem* (1871), *Toward the Strait Gate* (1875), and *In the Vineyard* (1876), as well as poetry and fiction.

Burr, George Lincoln. b. at Oramel, N.Y., Jan. 30, 1857; d. June 27, 1938. American librarian and historian. Graduated (B.A., 1881) from Cornell University, where he later became librarian of the President White Library, he studied (1884–88) at Leipzig, Paris, and Zurich. He was named (1888) a member of the Cornell faculty, and served (1892–1922) there as professor of ancient and medieval history. He was an historical expert (1896–97) with the Venezuelan Boundary Commission. His special field of study, the history of superstition, was reflected in such works as *The Literature of Witchcraft* (1890), *The Fate of Dietrich Flade* (1891), and *Narratives of the Witchcraft Cases (1648-1706)* (1913).

Burr, Theodosia. b. at Albany, N.Y., June 21, 1783; d. at sea, in January, 1813. Daughter of Aaron Burr (1756–1836), remembered for her devoted support of her father. She was hostess (1797 *et seq.*) at Burr's Richmond Hill home, on Staten Island, N.Y. After her marriage (1801) to Joseph Alston, she acted as Burr's agent (1808–12) in America during his exile. She died during a voyage to rejoin her father.

Burr, William Hubert. b. at Waterford, Conn., July 14, 1851; d. Dec. 13, 1934. American engineer, professor of civil engineering at Columbia University from 1893. He was consulting engineer to several of the departments of the city of New York. In 1904 he was appointed a member of the Isthmian Canal Commission to construct the Panama Canal, and in 1905 was made a member of the international board of consulting engineers to determine the plan of the canal. He published a number of works on engineering.

Burra (bur'ạ). Municipality in S Australia, in the SE part of the state of South Australia, ab. 77 mi. N of Adelaide. It was foremrly noted for large-scale copper mining at nearby Kooringa, which ceased c1877. The principal activity of the region is sheep raising. 1,520 (1947).

Burra, Edward. b. at London, 1905—. English surrealist painter, noted primarily for his satires on contemporary life. He studied at the Chelsea Polytechnic school and the Royal College of Art; later he traveled widely in Europe and America. His work includes the scenery and costumes for many ballets. Among his principal paintings are *Two Important Personages* and *Bal des Pendus*.

Burr Brundage (bėr brun'dạj), **Mount.** See **Brundage, Mount.**

Burrell (bur'ẹl), **George Arthur.** b. at Cleveland, Ohio, Jan. 23, 1882—. American chemical engineer. Associated (1908–17) with the U.S. Bureau of Mines, he was head of research (1917–18) of the U.S. Chemical Warfare Service, and director of the government helium program. He modernized (1930–31) the natural gas industry for the Russian government, was president of the Burrell Technical Supply Company and the Burrell-Mase Engineering Company, invented a gas detector and a gas analysis apparatus, and designed and built natural gas refineries. Author of *Handbook of Gasoline* (1917), *Recovery of Gasoline from Natural Gas* (1925), *An American Engineer Looks at Russia* (1932), and other books.

Burriana (bör.ryä'nä). Town in NE Spain, in the province of Castellón, situated near the Gulf of Valencia, ab. 8 mi. S of Castellón de la Plana. It is the center of a rich agricultural district, and exports wine, olive oil, and citrus fruits. 18,473 (1940).

Burrill (bur'il), **Thomas Jonathan.** b. near Pittsfield, Mass., April 25, 1839; d. April 14, 1916. American botanist and horticulturist, a pioneer in the study of bacterial plant diseases. He was superintendent (1865–68) of schools at Urbana, Ill., vice-president and acting president (1891–94, 1902) of the University of Illinois, and the author (1870 *et seq.*) of over 80 articles on botanical, horticultural and pathological subjects. During an epidemic (1877) of pear "fire blight," he first suggested the possibility of bacterial causes.

Burrillville (bur'il.vil). Town in N Rhode Island, in Providence County, ab. 22 mi. NW of Providence, near Wallum Lake: woolen mills; summer resort. 8,774 (1950).

Burrington (bur'ing.tọn). Former name of **Manchester,** Iowa.

Burritt (bur'it), **Elihu.** [Called **"the Learned Blacksmith."**] b. at New Britain, Conn., Dec. 8, 1810; d. there, March 6, 1879. American reformer, whose manuscript journals bear testimony to his heroic stature as an example of self-education in the face of adversity. His eager search for knowledge led him, while working at the blacksmith's forge, to supplement long hours of manual labor with the study of all the European tongues and a few Asiatic languages in addition to other fields of learning. By the time he left (1837) New Britain for Worcester, Mass., his achievements as a linguist were so outstanding that he was offered a Harvard education by the governor of Massachusetts, Edward Everett. Declining this offer, Burritt took up lecturing, which he later abandoned to become an exponent of international peace, expounding (1844–51) his doctrines in the Worcester weekly, the *Christian Citizen.* His work during the Oregon crisis between the U.S. and Great Britain, when he also edited the *Advocate of Peace and Universal Brotherhood,* resulted in his coöperation with English advocates of peace, and his organization (1846) while in England of the League of Universal Brotherhood. He organized the Brussels Peace Congress (1848), subsequently initiating similar conclaves held at Paris, Frankfort on the Main, London, and other cities, and was instrumental in building the peace movement in the U.S. in conjunction with Continental organizations. Although his pacifism made him oppose the Civil War, he was appointed (1863) by Lincoln as U.S. consular agent at Birmingham. His later years were spent in farming, writing, and teaching at New Britain. Among his writings are *Sparks from the Anvil* (1846), *Thoughts of Things at Home and Abroad, with a Memoir by Mary Howitt* (1854), *Lectures and Speeches* (1866), *Walk from London to John O'Groat's* (1864), and *Ten Minute Talks* (1873). Excerpts from his 28-volume manuscript journal appear in *Elihu Burritt: a Memorial Volume containing a Sketch of His Life and Labors* (1879, compiled by Charles Northend).

Burrough (bur'ō). See **Borough, Stephen,** and **Borough, William.**

Burroughs (bur'ōz), **Edgar Rice.** b. at Chicago, Sept. 1, 1875; d. at Encino, Calif, March 19, 1950. American writer of adventure novels, best known as the author of the Tarzan series. He wrote a total of 59 adventure novels, of which 23 involved Tarzan and were translated into a total of 56 languages. At the time of his death 24 films had been made on the subject of Tarzan (and the existence at the time of his death of a considerable body of uncompleted Tarzan manuscript promised to provide a basis for a considerable number of additional films based on the same character). Among the best known of his works are *Tarzan of the Apes* (1914), *The Return of Tarzan* (1915), *The Beasts of Tarzan* (1916), *The Son of Tarzan* (1917), *Tarzan and the Ant Men* (1925), *Tarzan the Magnificent* (1939), and a series of fantasy novels dealing with Mars, beginning with *A Princess of Mars* (1920), and a series dealing with Venus, beginning with *Pirates of Venus* (1934). His Pellucidar novels, dealing with a world within the earth (*At the Earth's Core,* 1922; *Pellucidar,* 1923; and others), were also widely read.

Burroughs, George. b. c1650; d. at Salem, Mass., Aug. 19, 1692. American clergyman. He was graduated from Harvard College in 1670, and served as pastor at Falmouth, Me., and at Salem. He was accused of having bewitched a woman named Mary Wolcott, and was condemned on the evidence of confessed witches, who affirmed that he had attended witch meetings with them. He moved many to tears by his last words at his execution, but Cotton Mather, who was sitting on horseback in the crowd, reminded the people that Satan often assumes the appearance of an angel of light.

Burroughs, John. b. near Roxbury, N.Y., April 3, 1837; d. March 29, 1921. American essayist, noted for his writings on nature. He attended the Ashland Collegiate Institute (Greene County, N.Y.) and the Cooperstown Seminary and, after several years of teaching, published an essay (1860) in the *Atlantic Monthly,* followed by nature essays for the New York *Leader.* It was this form, the nature essay, that constituted Burroughs's outstanding contribution to American literature in the many articles and books he published during his lifetime. In 1863, he went to Washington, D.C., where he was employed in the currency bureau of the treasury department; during his residence at the national capital, he formed a close friendship with Walt Whitman, the record of which appears in *Notes on Walt Whitman as Poet and Person* (1867; 2nd ed., 1871). During his years with the currency bureau, which he left in 1873, he continued to publish nature essays. After departing for the Catskills country, he bought a farm near Esopus, N.Y., in the vicinity of which he built (1895) the isolated cabin, "Slabsides," where he did much of his work. Among his works are *Wake-Robin* (1871), *Winter Sunshine* (1875), *Birds and Poets* (1877), *Fresh Fields* (1885), *Far and Near* (1904), *Camping and Tramping with Roosevelt* (1907), *Leaf and Tendril* (1908), *Time and Change* (1912), *The Summit of the Years* (1913), *The Breath of Life* (1915), and *Under the Apple-Trees* (1916). See *John Burroughs Talks: His Reminiscences and Comments,* by Clifton Johnson (1922), and *The Life and Letters of John Burroughs,* by Clara Barrus (1925).

Burrowe (bur'ō). See **Borough, Stephen,** and **Borough, William.**

Burrow Head (bur'ō). Promontory in S Scotland, in Wigtownshire. It lies at the S extremity of the Machars, a peninsula between Wigtown Bay and Luce Bay. Elevation, 150 ft.

Burrows (bur'ōz), **Julius Caesar.** b. at Northeast, Pa., Jan. 9, 1837; d. Nov. 16, 1915. American lawyer and politician. He was prosecuting attorney (1865–67) for Kalamazoo County, Mich., and a U.S. congressman (1873–75, 1879–83, and 1885–95). As a U.S. senator (1895–1911), he served on the Committee on Privileges and Elections, the Committee on Finance, and the Monetary Commission.

Burrows, William. b. near Philadelphia, Oct. 6, 1785; d. near Portland, Me., Sept. 5, 1813. American naval officer. In command of the *Enterprise* he captured the British brig *Boxer,* near Portland, Me., on Sept. 5, 1813. Both commanders fell in the action.

Burrus or **Burrhus** (bur'us), **Sextus Afranius.** Killed c62 A.D. Roman officer. He was appointed sole pretorian prefect by Claudius in 52, and was, together with Seneca, entrusted with the education of Nero. By his influence with the pretorian guards he secured the undisputed succession of his pupil in 54. He is thought to have been put to death by poison, probably for having offended Nero.

Burrville (bėr'vil). Former name of **Clinton,** Tenn.

Burry Inlet (bur'i). Arm of Carmarthen Bay, in S Wales, lying between Carmarthenshire and Glamorganshire. It is the estuary of the river Loughor. Length, ab. 11 mi.; greatest width, ab. 4 mi.

Burry Port or **Burryport** (bur'i.pōrt). Urban district and seaport in S Wales, in Carmarthenshire, situated on Burry Inlet, ab. 3 mi. W of Llanelly, ab. 204 mi. W of London by rail. 5,927 (1951).

Bursa (bör.sä'). [Also, **Brusa, Brussa, Broussa.**] *Il* (province or vilayet) in NW Turkey, a rich farmland of rolling plains and hills. It is crossed by several important highways and one railway line. It served as headquarters for the first Ottoman empire and the city of Bursa was the first Ottoman capital. Capital, Bursa; area, 5,230 sq. mi.; pop. 541,987 (1950).

Bursa. [Also: **Brusa, Brussa, Broussa;** ancient name, **Prusa.**] City in NW Turkey, the capital of the *il* (province or vilayet) of Bursa, situated at the foot of Mount Olympus, ab. 50 mi. S of Istanbul: center of the Turkish silk industry. The region of rolling hills and plains also produces wheat, barley, oats, olives, grapes, and tobacco, which are exported from the city. A meter-gauge railway line and a fine highway connect it with its port, Mudanya. The city manufactures tapestry and carpets. There are noted hot springs in its vicinity. It was the capital of Bithynia in the 2nd and 1st centuries B.C., and for a time the capital of the Ottoman empire, after its capture (1326) by Orkhan. 100,007 (1950).

Burschenschaft (bůr'shen.shäft). In 19th-century German history, a patriotic organization of German students. The liberation of Germany from French domination with the defeat of Napoleon in 1813 inspired a vigorous movement among the German people for national unity and also for liberalized laws and political institutions. Among university students these aspirations led to the formation of the Burschenschaft at Jena, where it had the patronage of the grand duke of Saxe-Weimar, in 1815, and by 1818 it had spread throughout all Germany, causing alarm among the rulers of the petty German states and their supporters, whose obvious interest lay in German disunity and reaction. Within the Burschenschaft a secret group was formed, known as the *Schwarzen* (Blacks), one of whose members on March 23, 1819, assassinated August Friedrich Ferdinand von Kotzebue, reactionary playwright, diplomat, and Russian agent. This occurrence, as a climax to other disorders incident to the agitation for unity and liberalization, led to a conference of ministers of the principal German states at Carlsbad, which in August, 1819, issued the Carlsbad Decrees, one of which ordered the suppression of the Burschenschaft. That this particular decree was less than wholly successful would appear from the fact that the organization was against interdicted in

1833, and that it continued to have a remarkable vitality is evident from the further fact that in 1848 all ordinances against it were rescinded. From that time, however, it ceased to have any positive political character, and became a purely social fraternity.

Burslem (bėrz′lẹm). Parish in C England, in Staffordshire, situated on the Grand Trunk Canal, ab. 17 mi. N of Stafford, ab. 149 mi. NW of London by rail. It was amalgamated into Stoke-on-Trent county borough in 1910. Burslem is the chief town of the Potteries district, and contains the Wedgwood Institute. It was the birthplace of Josiah Wedgwood.

Burt (bėrt), **Edward.** d. at London, Feb. 4, 1755. Irish soldier, agent of General George Wade (1673–1748), whom he assisted (1724–28) in constructing military roads through the Highlands. He was the author of *Letters from a Gentleman in the North of Scotland to his Friend in London* (written 1725–26; published at London, 1754), a work frequently quoted by both Sir Walter Scott and Thomas Babington Macaulay; other editions appeared at London in 1757, 1759, 1815, and 1818, at Dublin in 1755, and at Edinburgh in 1818.

Burt, John. b. at Wales, N.Y., April 18, 1814; d. at Detroit, Aug. 16, 1886. American inventor, promoter of the Michigan iron region; son of William Austin Burt. As deputy surveyor (1841–51) with the U.S. Geological Survey in the northern peninsula of Michigan, he discovered (c1848) several iron deposits. He purchased large tracts of land in the region, developed the mining industry, founded the city of Marquette, and built railroads.

Burt, Katharine. [Maiden name, **Newlin.**] b. at Fishkill-on-Hudson, N.Y., Sept. 6, 1882—. American writer; wife (married 1913) of Maxwell Struthers Burt. She became (1938) fiction editor of the *Ladies' Home Journal.* Her books include *The Branding Iron* (1919), *"Q"* (1922), *Beggars All* (1933), and *Close Pursuit* (1947).

Burt, Mary Elizabeth. b. at Lake Geneva, Wis., June 11, 1850; d. at Coytesville, N.J., Oct. 17, 1918. American educator and editor of the Scribner School Reading Series. She taught (1870 *et seq.*) in normal, public, and private schools at River Falls, Wis., Chicago, and New York, and wrote *Browning's Women* (1887), *Literary Landmarks* (1889), and *The World's Literature* (1890). Among the books she edited are *Birds and Bees* (1888), *Poems Every Child Should Know* (1904), and *Prose Every Child Should Know* (1908).

Burt, Maxwell Struthers. b. at Baltimore, Oct. 18, 1882—. American writer; husband (married 1913) of Katharine Burt. A cattle rancher (1908 *et seq.*) in Wyoming, he was president (until 1937) of the Bar B.C. Ranch Company. Author of *In the High Hills* (1914), *John O'May and Other Stories* (1918), *Chance Encounters* (1921), *The Interpreter's House* (1924), *The Diary of a Dude Wrangler* (1924), *The Delectable Mountains* (1926), *Festival* (1931), *Escape from America* (1936), *Along These Streets* (1941), the books of verse *Songs and Portraits* (1921) and *War Songs* (1942), and other works.

Burt, Thomas. b. at Tynemouth, England, 1837; d. 1922. English trade unionist and politician. A miner, he joined the trade union movement, serving (1865–1918) as general secretary of the Northumberland Miners Mutual Confidence Association. He was a member of Parliament (1874–1918), and was active in liberal reforms including the Employers Liability Act (1880), as well as factory and workshop legislation. He served as secretary (1892–95) of the Board of Trade, and later (1906) as privy councillor.

Burt, William Austin. b. at Petersham, Mass., June 13, 1792; d. Aug. 18, 1858. American surveyor and inventor, discoverer (1844) of iron ore in the upper peninsula of Michigan; father of John Burt. He served as a surveyor (1831) of Macomb County, Mich., associate judge (1833) of the district court, and deputy surveyor (until c1855). His patents include the "Typographer" (1829), forerunner of the typewriter, the solar compass (1836), and the equatorial sextant (1856).

Burte (bůr′tẹ), **Hermann.** [Original surname, **Strübe.**] b. at Maulberg, Baden, Germany, Feb. 15, 1879—. German novelist, dramatist, and poet. In his youth he spent five years in England and France studying art, but abandoned this career for one of writing. He began with *Der kranke König* (1907), three one-act plays, and has returned to the drama from time to time to proclaim his belief in self-sacrifice for the state. In 1927 the Schiller prize was awarded him.

Burton (bėr′tọn), 1st Baron. Title of **Bass, Michael Arthur.**

Burton, Ernest De Witt. b. at Granville, Ohio, Feb. 4, 1856; d. May 26, 1925. American educator and theologian. He was a professor (1883–92) at the Newton, Mass., Theological Seminary, and served as head of the department of New Testament and Early Christian Literature (1892–1923) and president (1923–25) of the University of Chicago. He was editor of *Biblical World* and *American Journal of Theology,* and author of *Harmony of the Gospels* (1894).

Burton, Frederick Russell. b. at Jonesville, Mich., Feb. 23, 1861; d. at Lake Hopatcong, N.J., Sept. 30, 1909. American author and composer. He was graduated from Harvard University in 1882 with musical and other honors. He was especially interested in the music of the North American Indians, among whom he spent some time. The music of his cantata *Hiawatha* (1898) is based on Indian themes, and he collected and published others under the titles *Songs of the Ojibway Indians* (1903) and *An Indian Campfire* (1907). Among his literary works are a novel, *Redcloud of the Lakes* (1909), and *American Primitive Music* (1909).

Burton, Harold Hitz. b. at Jamaica Plain, Mass., June 22, 1888—. American politician and jurist. He served (1929) in the Ohio legislature and was Cleveland law director (1929–32). He was mayor of Cleveland (1935–40) and was elected to the Senate from Ohio in 1940, serving from 1941 to 1945, when he was appointed an associate justice of the U.S. Supreme Court by President Truman.

Burton, Lady **Isabel.** [Maiden name, **Arundell.**] b. 1831; d. 1896. English author and traveler, who wrote a biography of her author husband (whom she had married in 1861), Sir Richard Francis Burton (1821–90). She shared her husband's life of travel and literature, and after his death issued a memorial edition of his works and his biography. She also published *Inner Life of Syria* (1875) and *Arabia, Egypt, and India* (1879).

Burton, John Hill. b. at Aberdeen, Scotland, Aug. 22, 1809; d. at Morton House, near Edinburgh, Aug. 10, 1881. Scottish historian and jurist. His chief works are a life of David Hume (1846), *A History of Scotland from Agricola's Invasion to the Rebellion of 1745* (1853–70), and *A History of the Reign of Queen Anne* (1880).

Burton, Lewis William. b. at Cleveland, Ohio, Nov. 9, 1852; d. at Lexington, Ky., Oct. 17, 1940. American Protestant Episcopal clergyman. Ordained (1878) to the priesthood, he was rector (1877–96) at various churches, and bishop (1896–1928) of Lexington, Ky.

Burton, Marion Le Roy. b. at Brooklyn, Iowa, Aug. 30, 1874; d. Feb. 18, 1925. American theologian and educator, president of Smith College from 1910. He was subsequently named president of the University of Minnesota (1917) and of the University of Michigan (1920). He was ordained to the Congregational ministry in 1905, was assistant professor of systematic theology at Yale University (1907–08), and was pastor of the Church of the Pilgrims, Brooklyn, N.Y. (1908–09). He was the author of *The Problem of Evil* (1909).

Burton, Richard Eugene. b. at Hartford, Conn., March 14, 1861; d. April 8, 1940. American poet and educator. He was professor of English literature at the University of Minnesota (1898–1902), lecturer in English literature at the University of Chicago (1902–06), and professor of English literature at the University of Minnesota (1906–25). His works include *Dumb in June* (1895), *Memorial Day* (1897), *Literary Likings* (1898), *Lyrics of Brotherhood* (1899), *John Greenleaf Whittier* (1901), *Forces in Fiction* (1902), *Message and Melody* (1903), *Literary Leaders of America* (1904), *Rahab* (1906), *From the Book of Life* (1909), *Masters of the English Novel* (1909), *Midsummer Memory* (1910), *Poems of Earth's Meaning* (1917), and *Collected Poems* (1931).

Burton, Sir **Richard Francis.** b. at Barham House, Hertfordshire, England, March 19, 1821; d. at Trieste, Oct. 20, 1890. English explorer and Orientalist, author of travel books; husband (married 1861) of Lady Isabel Burton. After serving in the East Indian army he went in

1853 to Mecca. His *First Footsteps in Eastern Africa* (1856) described travels made in 1854, when, disguised as an Arab, he accompanied John Speke to Harar, in Ethiopia. In 1858 he was again in East Africa with Speke, and discovered Lake Tanganyika, while Speke discovered Lake Victoria. In 1861 he was in West Africa as British consul at Fernando Po, in Spanish Guinea; he ascended Cameroon Mountain, and spent three months at the court of Dahomey. To the end of his life he continued in the consular service: at Santos, Brazil (1865–69), at Damascus (1869–71), and at Trieste (1872–90), where he died. Of the more than 30 volumes published by him, the principal ones are *Personal Narrative of a Pilgrimage to El Medinah and Meccah* (1855), *Lake Regions of Central Africa* (1860), *A Mission to the King of Dahomey* (1864), *Explorations of the Highlands of Brazil* (1868), and a literal version of *The Arabian Nights' Entertainments*. His biography and a memorial edition of his works were published after his death by his wife.

Burton, Robert. [Pseudonym, **Democritus Junior.**] b. at Lindley, Leicestershire, England, Feb. 8, 1577; d. Jan. 25, 1640. English writer and clergyman. He entered the University of Oxford in 1593, became a student of Christ Church College in 1599, and became rector of Segrave, in Leicestershire, in 1630. He was the author of *The Anatomy of Melancholy* (1621). In this work, which is the quintessence of the spirit of the late Renaissance in England, he expounded, with some wit and with a wealth of learned quotations, the causes and symptoms of melancholy, and its cures. The work went through several revisions before Burton's death, and had a lasting influence on much later English writing.

Burton, Theodore Elijah. b. at Jefferson, Ohio, Dec. 20, 1851; d. Oct. 28, 1929. American politician, lawyer, and writer. He was a congressman (1889–91, 1895–1909, 1921–29) and a senator (1909–15), serving as a member of the National Monetary Commission (1908–12) and of the Foreign Debt Commission (1922–27). He was also president (1911–15, 1925 *et seq.*) of the American Peace Society. Among his works are *Financial Crises and Periods of Commercial and Industrial Depression* (1902), *Life of John Sherman* (1906), *Corporations and the State* (1911), and *The Constitution, Its Origin and Distinctive Features* (1923).

Burton, William Evans. b. at London, Sept. 24, 1804; d. at New York, Feb. 10, 1860. American comedian, theater manager, and writer. He came to America in 1834, and made his first professional appearance in September of that year at the Arch Street Theater at Philadelphia, in which city he lived for 14 years. In 1837 he started *The Gentleman's Magazine*. In 1848 he moved to New York. With others he organized the American Shakespearian Club in 1852.

Burton, William Meriam. b. at Cleveland, Ohio, Nov. 17, 1865—. American industrial chemist, noted for inventing a process of cracking petroleum. He was a graduate of Western Reserve University (B.A., 1886), and of the Johns Hopkins University (Ph.D., 1889). A member of the board of directors (1911 *et seq.*), he was also president (1918–27) of the Standard Oil Company of Indiana. He received the Willard Gibbs medal (1918) and the Perkins medal (1921) for his work in petroleum chemistry.

Burton-on-Trent or **Burton-upon-Trent** (bėr'tǫn.on. trent, -u.pon'-). County borough and market town in C England, in Staffordshire, situated on the river Trent and on the Trent and Mersey Canal, ab. 11 mi. SW of Derby, ab. 123 mi. NW of London by rail. It is noted for the brewing of pale ale and stout, begun in 1708. The water is permanently hard, and particularly suitable for brewing. It also has manufactures of boots and shoes. 49,169 (1951).

Burton-Opitz (bėr'tǫn.ō'pits), **Russell.** b. at Fort Wayne, Ind., Oct. 25, 1875—. American physician and physiologist. He received his M.D. from Rush Medical College in 1895, and after postgraduate study at Vienna and Breslau joined (1901) the staff of the department of physiology at Harvard University, where he remained until 1923. In the latter year he was appointed lecturer in physiology at Columbia University. He is accounted one of the foremost American authorities in his field, and he has also served as a consultant of several New York hospitals. He is the author of *Text Book of Physiology*, first published in 1920 and several times reissued.

Burtscheid (bůrt'shīt). Town in W Germany, in the *Land* (state) of North Rhine-Westphalia, British Zone, formerly in the Rhine Province, Prussia, situated immediately SE of Aachen, of which it is a suburb. It has cloth manufactures, dye works, and shoe, leather, and paperware factories. 10,699 (1946).

Buru (bö'rö). See **Boeroe.**

Burujird (bö.rö.jērd'). City in W Iran, in the *Ustan Shashum* (Sixth Province), ab. 70 mi. S of Hamadan, on the Trans-Iranian railway. It is located in a fertile mountain valley, and is an important trading and manufacturing town, producing felt, cotton textiles, and carpets. Elevation, ab. 5,800 ft.; pop. 45,715 (1947).

Burullus (bu.rul'us), **Lake.** [Also, **Lake Boorlos.**] Large lagoon in NE Africa, in the delta of the Nile River, near the Mediterranean Sea.

Burwell Papers (bėr'wel). Manuscript record, apparently contemporary, of Bacon's Rebellion, which was first published (1814) in the *Collections* of the Massachusetts Historical Society. The papers take their name from a Captain Nathaniel Burwell, among whose effects they were found, and are now deposited in the Virginia Historical Society. The manuscript is attributed to John Cotton or his wife, Ann Cotton, residents of Williamsburg in the latter part of the 17th century.

Bury (ber'i). County borough, coal-mining center, and manufacturing city in NW England, in Lancashire, situated on the river Irwell, ab. 10 mi. N of Manchester, with which it has canal connections, and ab. 193 mi. NW of London by rail. Its industries include cotton spinning (coarse yarns), cotton finishing, manufactures of woolens, paper, bleaching and dyeing machinery, and boots and shoes, especially women's cheaper-grade shoes. It is located on the Lancashire coal field. 58,829 (1951).

Bury (bü.rē), **Blaze de.** See **Blaze de Bury.**

Bury (bū'ri), Lady **Charlotte Susan Maria.** b. at London, Jan. 28, 1775; d. at Chelsea, London, March 31, 1861. English beauty, novelist, diarist, and poet; daughter of John Campbell, 5th Duke of Argyll; her second husband, Edward John Bury, a minister, died in 1832. She was lady-in-waiting to Princess (later Queen) Caroline, and the author of *Poems on Several Occasions, by a Lady* (1797), *Flirtation* (1828), *A Marriage in High Life* (1828), *Separation* (1830), *The Devoted* (1836), *Love* (1837), *The Divorced* (1837), *The Two Baronets* (1864), and *Diary Illustrative of the Times of George IV* (2 vols., 1838).

Bury, John Bagnell. b. at Monaghan, Ireland, Oct. 16, 1861; d. 1927. Irish philologist, classical scholar, and historian. He is remembered chiefly as a historian of ancient Greece and the Roman Empire, whose original contribution was a clear exposition of Roman public law and administration. He was regius professor of modern history at Cambridge (1902–27). Editor of Edward Gibbon's *Decline and Fall of the Roman Empire* and of the *Cambridge Ancient History*, author of *History of the Later Roman Empire from Arcadius to Irene* (1889), *History of Greece to the Death of Alexander the Great* (1900), *Constitution of the Later Roman Empire* (1909), *History of the Freedom of Thought* (1913), and *History of the Later Roman Empire, 395–565* (1922).

Bury (ber'i), **Richard de.** See **Aungerville, Richard.**

Buryat (bůr.yät'). Division of the Mongols living S and E of Lake Baikal in Siberia, and numbering ab. 200,000. The main distinctions between the Buryat and the Mongols proper have been cultural and historical. Living in the northern forests and plains, the Buryat took no important role in the Mongol conquests. Even in the 19th century shamanism contested the inroads of Lama Buddhism; hunting and herding were major occupations. No large tribal units have ever existed among the Buryat, who are grouped in patrilineal clans. They write the Mongol literary language but speak a variety of local dialects.

Buryat-Mongol Autonomous Soviet Socialist Republic (bůr.yät'mong'gǫl). [Also: **Buryat-Mongolia, Buriat-Mongolia** (-mong.gō'li.ạ), **Buriat-Mongol** (or **Buriat-Mongolian**) **Autonomous Soviet Socialist Republic.**] Autonomous republic in the U.S.S.R., in the Russian Soviet Federated Socialist Republic, located in Siberia, S and E of Lake Baikal. The area is covered with mountains and hills. There is considerable coal mining and some iron ore and tin. The rural population is mostly concerned with the raising of animals and cereal crops; there are livestock, fox, and poultry farms, and apiaries. Capital Ulan-Ude; area, 127,920 sq. mi.; pop. 542,170 (1939).

Buryeiskii Khryebyet (bör.yās′ki hrā′byit). Russian name of the **Bureya Mountains.**

Bury Fair (ber′i). Play by Thomas Shadwell, produced c1690. It is an imitation of Molière's *Les Précieuses Ridicules.*

Bury Saint Edmunds (ber′i sānt ed′mundz). [Also, **Bury St. Edmunds.**] Municipal borough and small manufacturing town in E England, in West Suffolk, situated on the river Lark ab. 28 mi. E of Cambridge, ab. 85 mi. NE of London by rail. It was formerly a small textile center, but now manufactures agricultural machinery and brewing equipment. It contains the ruins of a Benedictine abbey founded (c630) by Canute, the abbey gateway, Norman tower, and several churches. The grave of Mary Tudor is here. The Roman Villa Faustini was probably here. It was the capital of East Anglia, and has been the seat of several parliaments. According to tradition it was the scene of the martyrdom of Saint Edmund (Edmund the Martyr), a king of East Anglia who refused after a defeat by the Danes to renounce Christianity and was therefore beheaded by them in 870. During the first decade of the 10th century (c903, according to some accounts) his remains were placed in the Benedictine abbey which had been founded by Canute. 20,045 (1951).

Bury the Dead. One-act play by Irwin Shaw, produced and published in 1936. Six American soldiers refuse to be buried after falling on the battlefield of a war laid in the future and demand the fundamental enjoyments in life of which war had deprived them. Despite the exhortations of sweethearts, relatives, and commanders, the "corpses" adhere to their pacifist sentiments and influence the surviving troops to join them in their rebellion against war and militarism. The play became fairly popular with amateur and semiprofessional acting groups, but in 1950 Shaw withdrew all permissions for performances, fearing that the play's pacifism might be misinterpreted within the framework of contemporary politics.

Bus (büs), **César de.** b. at Cavaillon, Vaucluse, France, Feb. 3, 1544; d. at Avignon, France, April 15, 1607. French priest, founder of the "Congregation of the Christian Doctrine." He wrote *Instructions familières* (1666).

Busa (bö′sa). [Also, **Bussa.**] Town in W Africa, in the Northern Provinces, Nigeria, on the W bank of the Niger River. It was in the rapids at this point that the explorer Mungo Park and his party lost their lives in 1806 while on their way from Gorée to the mouth of the Niger.

Busaco (bö.sä′kö). See **Bussaco.**

Busançois (bü.zäṅ.swȧ), Comte **de.** A title of **Chabot, Philippe de.**

Busansi (bö.sän′sē). [Also, **Boussansi.**] One of the Sudanic-speaking Gurunsi peoples of W Africa, inhabiting the NE part of the Ivory Coast, N of the Gold Coast. Their population is estimated at more than 100,000 (by M. Delafosse, *Haute-Sénégal-Niger*, (1912). They practice hoe agriculture, and their principal food is millet. They are non-Mohammedan.

Busbeck or **Busbecq** or **Busbecque** (büz.bek′), **Augier Ghislain de.** b. at Comines, Flanders, 1522; d. near Rouen, France, Oct. 28, 1592. Flemish diplomat and scholar. He was ambassador of Ferdinand I at Constantinople.

Busby (buz′bi), **James.** b. at Edinburgh, Feb. 7, 1801; d. near London, July 15, 1871. British public servant. He went to Australia in 1824 and held a variety of public offices until 1831. He served as British resident governor in New Zealand from 1832 to 1839, and laid the foundations of British supremacy there. He was the principal draftsman of the treaty of Waitangi.

Busby, Richard. b., probably at Sutton, Lincolnshire, England, Sept. 22, 1606; d. April 6, 1695. English teacher. He was made headmaster of the Westminster School in 1638.

Busca (bös′kä). Town and commune in NW Italy, in the *compartimento* (region) of Piedmont, in the province of Cuneo, situated on the Maira River, ab. 9 mi. NW of Cuneo. It has silk mills and metallurgical industries. Part of its medieval fortifications have been preserved. Pop. of commune, 8,494 (1936); of town, 2,698 (1936).

Busch (bu̇sh). Former name of **Elk City.**

Busch, Germán. Killed, or committed suicide, Aug. 23, 1939. Bolivian politician, president of Bolivia from 1937 to 1939. He became provisional president in 1937, after leading army officers in deposing Colonel David Toro; he was elected constitutional president on May 27, 1938. The next year (on April 24, 1939), encountering opposition to his effort to nationalize natural resources, including mines, he proclaimed himself dictator. His manner of death, declared suicide by official inquest, was persistently rumored to have been assassination.

Busch, Julius Hermann Moritz. b. at Dresden, Germany, Feb. 13, 1821; d. Nov. 16, 1899. German journalist and publicist. He was in the U.S. in 1851 (*Wanderungen zwischen Hudson and Mississippi*, 1853). He edited *Die Grenzboten* (1865 *et seq.*) and *Der Hannoverische Kurier* (1873 *et seq.*). He was employed by Otto von Bismarck in the department of state. His works from this period include *Schleswig-Holsteinische Briefe* (1854), and *Graf Bismarck und seine Leute* (1878).

Busch, Wilhelm. b. at Wiedensahl, Germany, April 15, 1832; d. 1908. German artist and poet, notable for his combination of pithy, humorous verse with line drawings. He studied art at Düsseldorf, Antwerp, and Munich, but feeling little drawn to painting he created what are now called comic strips for *Fliegende Blätter.* His characters *Max und Moritz, Die fromme Helene, Hans Huckebein, Maler Klecksel,* and many others have become household words in Germany. His wit is based on a fundamental pessimism, and his rhymed aphorisms are often terse expressions of disillusion. By implication, Busch also expresses his disapproval of the bigoted bourgeoisie. He also wrote serious poetry which he published without illustrations (*Kritik des Herzens,* 1874).

Busch, Wilhelm. b. at Bonn, Germany, Feb. 18, 1861; d. at Marburg, Germany, Sept. 23, 1929. German historian. He served as a professor (1890 *et seq.*) at the universities of Leipzig, Freiburg, Tübingen, and Marburg, and was the author of *England unter den Tudors, Bd. 1: König Heinrich VII* (England under the Reign of the Tudors, vol. I, King Henry VII, 1892) and *Bismarck und Moltke, Politik und Heerführung* (Bismarck and Moltke, Politics and Strategy, 1916).

Büsching (büsh′ing), **Anton Friedrich.** b. at Stadthagen, in Schaumburg-Lippe, Germany, Sept. 27, 1724; d. at Berlin, May 28, 1793. German geographer. His chief work is *Neue Erdbeschreibung* (11 vols., 1754–92), which was in part translated into English as *A New System of Geography* (1762).

Buschmann (bu̇sh′män), **Johann Karl Eduard.** b. at Magdeburg, Germany, Feb. 14, 1805; d. at Berlin, April 21, 1880. Prussian philologist. He spent a year (1827–28) in Mexico, and on his return was associated with Wilhelm von Humboldt in philological work. After 1832 he was employed in the Berlin Royal Library, eventually becoming librarian. After the death of Wilhelm von Humboldt, Buschmann was engaged by Alexander von Humboldt, assisting him in the preparation of *Kosmos* and other works.

Busembaum (bö′zem.boum) or **Busenbaum** (-zen-), **Hermann.** b. at Notteln, Westphalia, 1600; d. at Münster, Westphalia, Jan. 31, 1668. German Jesuit theologian. He taught dogmatic and moral theology, was rector of the colleges of Hildesheim and Münster, and was the author of a famous work on moral theology, *Medulla theologiae moralis,* which went through 40 editions during his lifetime. He was accused, without adequate foundation, of teaching doctrine that was subversive of authority and of the security of kings.

Bush (bu̇sh), **Vannevar.** b. at Everett, Mass., March 11, 1890—. American electrical engineer and administrator. A graduate of Tufts College (1913) and Harvard (1916), he was professor of engineering (1923–32) in the Massachusetts Institute of Technology and dean of engineering as well as vice-president (1932–38) there. In 1939 he became president of the Carnegie Institute of Washington. In 1941 he was named director of the U.S. Office of Scientific Research and Development. He constructed a machine for solving differential equations. Coauthor, with

W. H. Timbie, of *Principles of Electrical Engineering* (1923); author of *Operational Circuit Analysis* (1929) and *Modern Arms and Free Men* (1950).

Bush-Brown (bu̇sh'broun), **Henry Kirke.** b. at Ogdensburg, N.Y., April 21, 1857; d. at Washington, D.C., Feb. 28, 1935. American sculptor, best known for his equestrian statues. He studied at the National Academy of Design, New York, at Paris, and in Italy. His work is in many public buildings and national shrines, as well as in the Metropolitan Museum of Art, New York, and the National Museum, Washington, D.C. He was a member of the National Arts Club. Some of his better-known works are *General G. G. Meade, General John Sedgwick, General John F. Reynolds, General Anthony Wayne, Justinian,* and *Mountaineer Soldier.*

Bushey (bu̇sh'i). Urban district in S central England, in Hertfordshire, ab. 21 mi. NW of Broad Street station, London. 14,801 (1951).

Bushido (bö.shē.dō). "The way of the warrior," a Japanese system of practical ethics which developed in the 18th century out of the code of morals and behavior of the *samurai* (warrior) class. Its concepts include the loyalty of the warrior to his feudal overlord, Confucian ideas of virtuous conduct in familial and social relations, and the virtues of mental and physical self-discipline as honored in Zen Buddhism.

Bushire (bö.shēr'). [Also: **Abushehr, Bushahr** (bö-shär').] Seaport in SW Iran, in Fars (now *Ustan Haftum* or Seventh Province), on the Persian Gulf. This was the base of the Persian navy under Nadir Shah from 1736 to 1747. It is an important commercial center, and a port of call for steamship lines to India. Pop. ab. 20,000.

Bushiri bin Salim (bö.shē'rē bin sä.lēm'). b. c1834; d. 1889. Mulatto Arab of E Africa, leader of the Arab war against the Germans in the period 1888–89. Bushiri owned a plantation at Pangani, in what is now Tanganyika Territory, when the Germans annexed that region. In May, 1889, he was defeated by a German force under Captain Hermann von Wissmann; in June he captured Mpwapwa, ab. 50 mi. E of Dodoma, and induced the Mafiti tribe to attack the Germans; in October he again lost a battle to the Germans, and fled to the mountains in the Nguru region. There he was captured by pro-German natives, and in December hanged by the Germans at Pangani.

Bushman Land (bu̇sh'mạn), **Great.** Region in S Africa, in the NW part of Cape of Good Hope province, Union of South Africa, SE of South-West Africa. It is inhabited chiefly by Bushmen.

Bushmen (bu̇sh'mẹn). [Dutch, **Bosjesmans.**] Khoisan-speaking people of S Africa, inhabiting the Kalahari desert region of S Angola, South-West Africa, Bechuanaland, and the Union of South Africa. They are divided into a number of local groups within each of which the same dialect is spoken. The southern Bushmen, which include the Cape Bushmen and other groups, have been most affected by European colonization, and are now represented only by scattered remnants. In the center are the Aikwe, Galikwe, Heichware, Kukwe, Namib, Tsaukwe, and 12 other groups. In the north are the Auen, Heikum, Jung, and O Kung. The Bushmen are called *San, Sanqua, Sunqua, Saunqua,* or *Sonqua* by the Hottentots, *Batwa* or *Abatwa* by the Zulu and Xosa, *Barwa* by the Suto, *Masarwa* by the Tswana, and *Ovatwa* by the Herero. There is no name in the Bushman language for all the Bushman groups. The Bushmen have hereditary chiefs only in the northern groups, and succession is matrilineal only among the northern Heikum and Kung. Generally, descent is bilateral, and there are no clans. The Bushmen live by hunting and gathering. They do no farming, and unlike the Hottentots, have no domestic animals and practice no metalworking. They resemble the Hottentots in language and in physical type, but they average three inches less in stature.

Bushnell (bu̇sh'nẹl). City in W Illinois, in McDonough County, in an agricultural and stock-farming region. 3,317 (1950).

Bushnell, David. b. at Saybrook, Conn., c1742; d. 1824. American inventor. He invented (1775) a man-propelled submarine boat, nicknamed "Bushnell's Turtle," a precursor of the modern submarine. During the Revolutionary War, he failed (1776–77) in an attempt to use his invention to destroy British ships. He served as a captain-lieutenant (1779–81) and captain (1781–83) in a company of sappers and miners.

Bushnell, Horace. b. at Bantam, Conn., April 14, 1802; d. at Hartford, Conn., Feb. 17, 1876. American Congregational minister and theologian, noted for his interpretation and enrichment of New England Calvinism. He graduated (1827) from Yale and, after teaching at Norwich, Conn., and working on the staff of the New York *Journal of Commerce,* studied law and taught at Yale College before entering the Yale Divinity School. He was ordained (1833) pastor of the North Church of Hartford, Conn., serving in that post until his resignation (1861) because of poor health. Having gone to California in 1856 to seek relief from the bronchial illness that was to burden him for the rest of his life, he became one of the chief founders of what is now the University of California. During his life he became embroiled in theological controversies springing from his opposition, based on his conception of mystical truth and his belief in the inviolate integrity of the spirit, to the inflexible orthodoxy of Calvinism. His writings include *The True Wealth and Weal of Nations* (1837), *Christian Nurture* (1847), *God in Christ* (1849), *Christ in Theology* (1851), *Sermons for the New Life* (1858), *Work and Play* (1864), *Christ and his Salvation* (1864), *The Vicarious Sacrifice* (1866), *Moral Uses of Dark Things* (1868), *Forgiveness and Law* (1874), and *Building Eras in Religion* (published posthumously, 1881). A uniform edition of his works was published in 1881. See *Life and Letters of Horace Bushnell,* by Mary Bushnell Cheney *et al.* (1880, 1903).

Bushy (bu̇sh'i), **Sir John.** In Shakespeare's *King Richard II,* a follower of the king.

Bushy Run, Battle of. In the French and Indian Wars, an engagement (Aug. 5–6, 1763) at Bushy Run, Pa., between a British force under Colonel Henry Bouquet and Indian attackers who were finally driven off. The British victory made possible the relief of Fort Pitt.

Busirane (bū'si.rān). In Edmund Spenser's *The Faerie Queene,* an enchanter, the symbol of illicit love. He imprisoned Amoret, keeping her in torment until she was released by Britomarte.

Busiris (bụ.sī'ris). See also **Abusir.**

Busiris. Mythical king of Egypt who, to insure the cessation of a famine, each year sacrificed to the gods one stranger who had set foot on his shores. Hercules was seized by him, and would have fallen a victim had he not broken his bonds and slain Busiris with his club. In *Paradise Lost* John Milton, who follows other writers, gives the name Busiris to the Pharaoh who was drowned in the Red Sea.

Busiris. Tragedy by Edward Young, author of *Night Thoughts.* It was produced in 1719 and has an Oriental background.

Busk (busk), **Hans.** b. May 11, 1816; d. at Westminster, London, March 11, 1882. English instigator of a volunteer preparedness movement. Graduated (1839) from Trinity College, Cambridge, he was the first advocate of lifeship stations. He also revitalized (1858) the Victoria Rifles, the only volunteer corps existing at that time. His writings include *The Rifleman's Manual* and *Tabular Arrangement of Company Drill.*

Busken Huet (bus'kẹn hü.et'), **Conrad.** b. 1826; d. 1886. Dutch essayist and clergyman, later a journalist. His *Land van Rembrand* (3 vols., 1882–84) remains unsurpassed as a cultural history of the Netherlands in the 16th and 17th centuries. His reviews in the monthly *De Gids* of Dutch and foreign literature were eminent evidence of a brilliant and sharply discriminating spirit. After 1868 they were collected in *Litterarische Fantasieën en Kritieken* (31 vols.). He was a close friend of Everhardus Johannes Potgieter.

Buskerud (bös'kẹ.rö). *Fylke* (county) in S Norway, bounded by the *fylker* (counties) of Hordaland, Telemark, Vestfold, Akershus, Opland, and Sogn og Fjordane. Capital, Drammen; area, 5,738 sq. mi.; pop. 149,948 (1946).

Busoni (bö.zō'nē), **Ferruccio Benvenuto.** b. at Empoli, Italy, April 1, 1866; d. at Berlin, July 27, 1924. Italian pianist and composer. He appeared first in Vienna at the age of nine, and at 17 was elected a member of the Philharmonic Academy of Bologna. He toured Europe as a pianist, taught at Helsingfors Conservatory in 1888, won the Rubinstein prize at Moscow in 1890, and became professor in the Moscow Conservatory. He went to Boston in 1891, gave successful concerts at Berlin in 1894, and succeeded Sauer at the Vienna Conservatory in 1908. His compositions include operas, string quartets, violin, piano, and orchestral pieces, songs, and ballet scenes; he also made piano transcriptions of many of Johann Sebastian Bach's organ works.

Busra (bus′rą). See **Basra.**

Busra (bus′rą). See **Bosra.**

Bussa (bö′są). See **Bargu** and **Busa.**

Bussaco (bö.sä′kö). [Also: **Busaco;** Portuguese, **Buçaco.**] Hamlet in W Portugal, ab. 17 mi. NE of Coimbra. Here, on Sept. 27, 1810, the British and Portuguese under the Duke of Wellington defeated the French under André Masséna, in the Peninsular War. The loss of the French was ab. 4,500; of the Allies, 1,300.

Bussahir (bus′są.hēr). See **Bashahr.**

Bussang (bü.säṅ). Village in NE France, in the department of Vosges, ab. 27 mi. SE of Épinal: noted for its mineral springs.

Busse (bus′ę), **Carl.** b. at Lindenstadt, Germany, Nov. 12, 1872; d. at Berlin, Dec. 3, 1918. German poet, novelist, and literary historian. He took a Ph.D. degree in German, wrote *Geschichte der deutschen Dichtung im 19. Jahrhundert* (1901), and put out anthologies of German verse (*Neuere deutsche Lyrik*, 1895; *Deutsche Kriegslieder*, 1915). Between 1892 and 1910 he produced several volumes of his own verse, but turned latterly to novels (*Der Schüler von Polajewo*, 1900; *Im polnischen Wind*, 1906; *Winkelglück*, 1918).

Busse, Hermann Eris. b. at Freiburg im Breisgau, in Baden, Germany, March 9, 1891—. German novelist who has taken the Black Forest region as the scene of most of his stories. With the exception of *Tulipan und die Frauen* (1927), he has dealt largely with peasant life and its problems in a changing world. This applies especially to the trilogy of novels entitled *Bauernadel* (1929–30). He is also the author of *Hans Fram oder das deutsche Gesicht* (1932), *Heiner und Barbara* (1936), and *Der Tauträger* (1938).

Bussey (bus′i), **Benjamin.** b. at Canton, Mass., March 1, 1757; d. at Roxbury, near Boston, Jan. 13, 1842. American merchant, founder of the "Bussey Institution," a college of agriculture and horticulture connected with Harvard University, opened near Boston in the period 1869–70.

Busson (bü.sôṅ), **Charles.** b. at Montoire, Loir-et-Cher, France, July 15, 1822; d. April 4, 1908. French painter. His works are chiefly landscapes.

Bussorah (bus′ǫ.rą). See **Basra.**

Bussum (bus′um). [Also, **Naarden-Bussum.**] Town in W Netherlands, in the province of North Holland, situated near the Zuider Sea, SE of Amsterdam. A garden city belonging to the metropolitan region of Amsterdam, it has flower and fruit culture, chemical and paper manufactures, and a chocolate factory (van Bensdorp). 34,870 (est. 1951).

Bussy (bü.sē), Comte **de.** [Title of **Roger de Rabutin;** called **Bussy-Rabutin** (bü.sē.rȧ.bü.taṅ).] b. at Épiry, in Nivernais, France, April 13, 1618; d. at Autun, France, April 9, 1693. French soldier and man of letters. He was the author of *Histoire amoureuse des Gaules* (1665), *Mémoires* (1696), and *Lettres* (1697).

Bussy D'Ambois (bü.sē′ däṅ.bwȧ′). Tragedy by George Chapman, published in 1607. The allusions in it to the knights of James I, and to Elizabeth as an "old queen," forbid a date earlier than 1603; and the statement in Act I, Scene 2, "'Tis Leap Year," which must apply to the date of production, appears to set the first presentation at 1604. Thomas D'Urfey produced a play, adapted from Chapman's, with this title in 1691. The principal character in Chapman's play is a self-confident and arrogant adventurer who possesses some genuine loftiness of character. The plot is based on an actual incident involving a man named Louis de Bussy-d'Amboise at the court of Henry III of France. In the play Bussy D'Ambois is killed by the machinations of Monsieur, the king's brother, because of jealousy over the wife of the count of Mountsurry.

Bussy D'Ambois, The Revenge of. Play by George Chapman, a sequel to *Bussy D'Ambois;* it was published in 1613. The hero of this drama is Clermont D'Ambois, Bussy's brother, who tries to avenge his brother's slaying with an honorable duel.

Bustamante (bös.tä.män′tā), **Anastasio.** b. at Jiquilpán, Michoacán, Mexico, July 27, 1780; d. at San Miguel Allende, Guanajuato, Mexico, Feb. 6, 1853. Mexican politican and soldier, acting president (1829–32) and president (1837–41) of Mexico. He entered the Spanish army in 1808, and served against the early revolutionists. Having joined Agustín de Iturbide in 1821, he commanded a division in the march on Mexico City, and was a member of the provisional junta. The fall (1823) of Iturbide forced him into retirement, but in 1828 he was elected vice-president under Vicente Guerrero, commanding the army. Shortly afterward he revolted against Guerrero, heading the Centralist Party, and after its success served as acting president (1829–32) of Mexico. Antonio López de Santa Anna declared war against him, and after a bloody war Bustamante was deposed (December, 1832), and banished. After Santa Anna was captured (1836) by the Texans, Bustamante was called back and elected (1837) president of Mexico. There was a brief war with France in 1838, and new disorders which broke out in 1839 forced Bustamante to give up the presidency (1841) to Santa Anna. He served in the army until 1848.

Bustamante, Antonio Sánchez de. [Full surname, **Sánchez de Bustamante y Sirvén.**] b. at Havana, Cuba, April 13, 1865; d. Aug. 24, 1951. Cuban authority on international law. Professor of international law (1884 *et seq.*), University of Havana; senator (1902–18); member (1895), Institute of International Law; delegate plenipotentiary (1907), second Hague Peace Conference; member, Permanent Arbitration Tribunal of The Hague; custodian of alien enemy property (1918); represented Cuba (1919) at the Paris Peace Conference; judge (1921 *et seq.*), World Court. President of Sixth Pan-American Conference (1928), Havana, which approved his *Project for a Code of International Private Law* (1926).

Bustamante, Carlos María. b. in Oaxaca, Mexico, Nov. 4, 1774; d. at Mexico City, Sept. 21, 1848. Mexican statesman, journalist, and historian. He commanded (1812) a regiment under José Maria Morelos y Pavón, was captured and imprisoned at Vera Cruz, but was released by Antonio López de Santa Anna, and marched (1821) with him to the capital. Thereafter he took an active part in political life, supporting Augustín de Iturbide's Plan of Iguala. His historical works are considered of great importance for the revolutionary and modern period; the best known is *Cuadro histórico de la revolución de la América mejicana.* He also founded *La Avispa de Chilpancingo*, a weekly newspaper.

Bustamante y Guerra (ē ger′rä), **José.** b. c1750; d. c1822. Spanish naval officer and administrator. He was captain-general of Guatemala (March, 1811–March, 1818).

Bustan (bös.tän′). Name, meaning "garden of fruit," of several Persian works, among which the *Bustan* (1257) of Saadi is the most famous.

Busto Arsizio (bös′tō är.sē′tsyō). Town and commune in NW Italy, in the *compartimento* (region) of Lombardy, in the province of Varese, ab. 19 mi. NW of Milan. It has numerous cotton-textile and silk mills. The Church of Santa Maria in Piazza was built in the 16th century, probably according to plans by Donato d'Agnolo Bramante. Pop. of commune, 42,995 (1936); of town, 38,000 (1936).

Busuanga (bö.swäng′gä). Largest island of the Calamian group, between Mindoro and Palawan in the Philippine Islands. It belongs to Palawan province. There is an anchorage at Bintuan, on the S coast. Area, ab. 342 sq. mi.; pop. 10,109 (1939).

Büsum (bü′zům). Town in NW Germany, in the *Land* (state) of Schleswig-Holstein, British Zone, formerly in the province of Schleswig-Holstein, Prussia, situated on the North Sea, in the Dithmarschen district, S of Husum. It is a seaside resort, and has fisheries and agricultural trade. 4,969 (1946).

Busy (biz′i), **Zeal-of-the-Land.** [Known as **Rabbi Busy.**] In Ben Jonson's play *Bartholomew Fair*, an unctuous, gormandizing Puritan, grossly ignorant and a scorner of culture.

Busy Bees of Deseret (dez.ẹr.et′). Term applied to the Mormons who settled (1848) in what later became Utah.

In the Book of Mormon, Deseret is the "land of the honeybee."

Busybody, The. Comedy by Susannah Centlivre, produced and printed in 1709. In this play the character of Marplot is first introduced. The plot is partly from Ben Jonson's *The Devil is an Ass.* A second part, called *Marplot, or the Second Part of the Busybody,* was produced by Susannah Centlivre in 1710. Henry Woodward altered it and called it *Marplot in Lisbon.*

Busy Body Papers. Series of 32 epistolary articles which appeared in Andrew Bradford's *American Weekly Mercury* during 1729.

Butcher (buch'ėr), **Samuel Henry.** b. at Dublin, April 16, 1850; d. at London, Dec. 29, 1910. Irish classical scholar and teacher, translator of Homer. Educated at Marlborough School and at Trinity College, Cambridge, of which he was a fellow, he taught at Eton, at Trinity, and at University College, Oxford (1875–82), and was professor of Greek (1882–1903) at Edinburgh. In 1904 he visited the U.S. and lectured at Harvard. A Unionist member of Parliament (1906–10) for Cambridge University, he was also president of the English Classical Association and of the British Academy of Letters. He was the author of *Demosthenes* (1881), *Some Aspects of the Greek Genius* (1891), *Aristotle's Theory of Poetry and Fine Art* (1895), *Greek Idealism in the Common Things of Life* (1901), and *Harvard Lectures on Greek Subjects* (1904), and editor of the *Orationes* of Demosthenes (1903, 1907). His name is most familiar to students and readers as translator (with Andrew Lang) of a prose translation (1879–1887, 1889) of Homer's *Odyssey.*

"Butcher, the." Epithet of **Clifford, John de;** also of **Calleja del Rey, Félix María.**

Butcher's Cleaver. See under **Wain, Charles's.**

Bute (būt). Island situated in the Firth of Clyde, S of Argyllshire and W of Ayrshire, in Buteshire. Its chief town, Rothesay, had the first cotton mill in Scotland, in 1779, and is the county seat of Buteshire. Length of island, ab. 16 mi.; width, ab. 4 mi.; area, ab. 48 sq. mi.; pop. ab. 12,000.

Bute, Earls and Marquises of. See under **Stuart.**

Bute, Fort. [Also called **Manchac Post.**] British military and trading post named for John Stuart, 3rd Earl of Bute, who was prime minister of England in the period 1762–63. The fort was built in 1763 at the confluence of the Mississippi River and the Iberville River (Bayou Manchac), in the area then known as West Florida. In 1779 it was seized by a Spanish force.

Bute, Kyles of. Narrow strait, forming an arm of the Firth of Clyde, in W Scotland, separating the island of Bute from the mainland of Argyllshire. The strait encircles the N half of the island. Length, ab. 16 mi.; width, ab. 1 to 3 mi.

Bute Inlet. Fjord in SW British Columbia, Canada, ab. 120 mi. NW of Vancouver. It extends deep into the Coast Mountains, and has mountain walls over a mile high. Length, ab. 50 mi.; width, ab. 2 mi.

Butenandt (bö'tẹ.nänt), **Adolf Friedrich Johannes.** b. at Wesermünde, Germany, 1903—. German bio-organic chemist. In 1939 he was offered the Nobel prize with Leopold Ruzicka, but declined. His important work on the steroid sex hormones includes isolation of the first crystalline male hormone, androsterone (1934); isolation of oestrone (independently, with Doisy); synthesis of testosterone (independently, with Ruzicka); and isolation, structural determination of, and synthesis of progesterone. He has served as professor at Danzig (1933 *et seq.*). the Kaiser Wilhelm Institute of Biochemistry at Berlin (1936 *et seq.*), and Tübingen (1945 *et seq.*).

Buteshire (būt'shir) or **Bute** (būt). Insular county in W Scotland, lying between Kilbrennay Sound on the W and the Firth of Clyde on the E. It comprises the islands of Bute, Arran, Inchmarnock, Great Cumbrae, Little Cumbrae, Holy Isle, and Pladda Island. The principal industries are agriculture and fishing. County seat, Rothesay; area, ab. 218 sq. mi.; pop. 19,285 (1951).

Buthrotum (bụ.thrō'tum). [Modern name, **Butrinto, Vutrinto.**] In ancient geography, a seaport in Epirus, now in Albania. It is said to have been founded by Helenus, son of Priam.

Butjadingen (böt'ya"ding.ẹn). **Commune** in NW Germany, in the *Land* (state) of Lower Saxony, British Zone, formerly in Oldenburg, situated between the lower Weser River and the Jade Busen, NW of Bremen. A rich agricultural district, protected from the sea by dikes, it grows grain and vegetables, raises cattle and horses. The population is of Frisian origin; the district came under Oldenburg in 1523. Pop. 10,953 (1946).

Butkhak (böt.käk'). [Also, **Boothauk.**] Pass in the mountains of Afghanistan, E of Kabul. Through it pass many caravans to Peshawar and other points in Pakistan.

Butler (but'lėr). City in W Missouri, county seat of Bates County: marketing point for livestock. 3,333 (1950).

Butler. Borough in N New Jersey, in Morris County: residential community. 4,050 (1950).

Butler. City in W Pennsylvania, county seat of Butler County, on Connoquenessing Creek, in a coal, natural-gas, petroleum, and limestone area. Manufactures include plate glass, refrigerators, railroad cars, oil-drilling machinery, automobile parts, and metal products. It was platted in 1803. Pop. 23,482 (1950).

Butler. Name of a noble English family, originally from Ireland. Its members are best known in history under their titles as dukes, earls, and marquises of **Ormonde.** Members of a cadet branch of the same family are best known under their titles as earls of **Ossory.**

Butler, Alban. b. at Appletree, Northamptonshire, England, 1710; d. at St.-Omer, France, May 15, 1773. English Roman Catholic hagiographer; uncle of Charles Butler. He wrote *Lives of the Fathers, Martyrs, and Other Principal Saints* (4 vols., 1756–59) and others.

Butler, Amos William. b. at Brookville, Ind., Oct. 1, 1860; d. Aug. 5, 1937. American sociologist, anthropologist, and zoölogist. He was the founder (1930) of the International Committee on Mental Hygiene at Washington, and one of the founders of the American Anthropological Association and the American Association of Mammalogists. He served as lecturer (1905) in economics at Purdue, secretary (1897–1923) of the Indiana Board of State Charities, and chairman of the executive board (1918–25) and president (1925–30) of the Indiana Society for Mental Hygiene. His works include *Birds of Indiana, Indiana—A Century of Progress,* and *The Deveolpment of Public Charities and Corrections.*

Butler, Andrew Pickens. b. near Edgefield, S.C., Nov. 18, 1796; d. there, May 25, 1857. American politician and lawyer, a follower of John C. Calhoun. Elected (1824) to the South Carolina legislature, he was appointed (1833) a circuit judge, and sat on the bench (1833–45) of the court of appeals. He was elected (1846, 1848, and 1854) to the U.S. Senate, where he was chairman (1849) of the Judiciary Committee. A verbal attack (May 19, 1856) on him by Senator Charles Sumner of Massachusetts led to a physical attack on Sumner by Preston Brooks, nephew of Butler and congressman from South Carolina.

Butler, Arthur John. b. at Putney, London, June 21, 1844; d. at Weybridge, Surrey, England, Feb. 26, 1910. English scholar and teacher, translator of Dante. Educated at Eton and at Trinity College, Cambridge, he was an examiner (1870–87) for the London Board of Education, a partner (1887–94) in the Rivington publishing house, and professor of Italian (1898–1910) at London University College. An enthusiastic mountain climber from his early boyhood, he was a member (1886 *et seq.*) of the Alpine Club and editor (1890–93) of the *Alpine Journal.* He was the author of *Dante: His Times and his Work* (1895) and *The Forerunners of Dante* (1910), and editor (1899–1910) of *Calendars of Foreign State Papers.* A translator also of many works from French and German, he is best known for his translations of Dante's *Purgatory* (1880), *Paradise* (1885), and *Hell* (1892).

Butler, Benjamin Franklin. b. at Kinderhook Landing, N.Y., Dec. 14, 1795; d. at Paris, Nov. 8, 1858. American politician and lawyer; father of William Allen Butler. Admitted to the bar in 1817, he was a law partner (1817–21) of Martin Van Buren at Albany, N.Y. Elected (1827) to the New York state legislature, he served there until 1833. While Van Buren was serving as vice-president, Butler became (1833) attorney general in Jackson's cabinet. He held this post for five years, at the same time continuing his law practice, and also served (October, 1836–March, 1837) as secretary of war, succeeding Lewis Cass. More interested in practicing law than in holding cabinet posts, he was U.S. attorney for the southern district of New York (1838–41, 1845–48). He also taught at the University of the City of New York (later called New York University). Originally a Jacksonian Democrat, he left the Democratic Party in 1854, over the question of the Kansas-Nebraska Act, and joined the newly formed Republican Party.

Butler, Benjamin Franklin. b. at Deerfield, N.H., Nov. 5, 1818; d. at Washington, D.C., Jan. 11, 1893. American soldier and politician, remembered for his military administration (1862) of New Orleans during the Civil War. He studied law at Lowell, Mass., where he was admitted to the bar (1840) and commenced a lifelong practice specializing in criminal cases. He was elected (1853) to the state house of representatives and (1859) to the state senate. At the outbreak of war, he became commanding officer of a Massachusetts infantry regiment which was stationed (May 13, 1861) at Baltimore when that border city was troubled by numerous violent outbreaks between the Southern and Northern sympathizers among its citizens. He was promoted to major general of volunteers (May 16, 1861), commanded Fortress Monroe, conducted the unsuccessful operation culminating in the battle of Big Bethel, and led the forces which invested the forts at Hatteras Inlet. In command of the land contingents which helped take New Orleans (May 1, 1862), he became head of the military government after the city's occupation by the federal forces. His regime, which lasted until his removal on Dec. 16, 1862, was marred by what some have considered excessive severity and widespread corruption. One of his orders specified that any woman displaying "insult or . . . contempt" for members of the Union forces should "be regarded and held liable to be treated as a woman of the town plying her avocation." (It was this order in particular which provided the basis for the wave of popular i dignation against Butler which immediately broke out in the South, and has continued to make itself felt in historical writings to the present day. However, at the time when it was issued, Butler's chief purpose was simply to maintain order, and in a city as filled with violently partisan civilians as New Orleans in 1862 this was no easy task. The order was made known throughout the world, however, and had the immediate international effect of worsening still further the already precarious relations between Great Britain (and France) and the North. It is interesting to note, in this connection, that when a protest reached him from the British government stressing the crude lack of chivalry in his order, Butler coolly pointed out that a substantially similar ruling then existed in the statutes of the city of London.) He was assigned (1863) to the command of the districts of Eastern Virginia and North Carolina, and was placed at the head of the Army of the James; in 1864 he served as commissioner for the exchange of prisoners, and in November of that year was sent to New York to maintain order during the election. Ulysses S. Grant ordered him to Lowell, Mass., in January, 1865. Now a Republican of the radical wing, he served in Congress (1867–75) as a powerful member of that faction, and in 1878 was again elected to Congress, on this occasion running as an independent Greenbacker. He was governor of Massachusetts (elected in 1882), and in 1884 was the presidential nominee of the Anti-Monopoly and National (Greenback) parties.

Butler, Camp. Reception and discharge point (1861–66) east of Springfield, Ill., used for the handling of Illinois volunteers in the Union forces during the Civil War. At one time (1862) it was used as a camp for Confederate prisoners.

Butler, Charles. b. at London, Aug. 14, 1750; d. there, June 2, 1832. English jurist, Roman Catholic historian, and miscellaneous writer; nephew of Alban Butler. He was the first Roman Catholic to be admitted (1791) to the English bar after 1688. His works include *Horae Biblicae* (1797–1807), *Horae juridicae subsecivae* (1804), and *Reminiscences* (1822–27).

Butler, Elizabeth Southerden Thompson, Lady. b. at Lausanne, Switzerland, 1844 (or 1851); d. 1933. English battle painter and writer, whose paintings are in many British collections and museums; wife of Sir William Francis Butler. She studied at Florence, at Rome, and in the South Kensington Art Schools at London. In 1873 she began to exhibit at the Royal Academy. Among her principal paintings are *Scotland Forever* (Leeds), *Roll Call*, and *The Army Resting* (Tate Gallery). Her literary works include *Letters from the Holy Land* (1903) and *An Autobiography* (1923).

Butler, Ellis Parker. b. at Muscatine, Iowa, Dec. 5, 1869; d. Sept. 13, 1937. American humorist. After working as a bill clerk, salesman, and store clerk, he moved (1897) to New York and first achieved success with *Pigs is Pigs* (1906), a still popular sketch. His other writings include *The Incubator Baby* (1906), *Confessions of a Daddy* (1907), *That Pup* (1908), *Water Goats* (1910), *Red Head* (1916), *In Pawn* (1921), *Jibby Jones* (1923), *Pigs, Pets and Pies* (1927), *Hunting the Wow* (1934), and a novel, *The Jack Knife Man* (1913).

Butler, George. b. at London, 1774; d. at Peterborough, England, 1853. English clergyman and headmaster of Harrow (1805–29); father of George Butler (1819–90).

Butler, George. b. 1819; d. 1890. English educator and canon of Winchester (1882 *et seq.*); son of George Butler (1774–1853) and husband of Josephine Elizabeth Butler. After attending Harrow and Cambridge, he took (1846) an M.A. degree at Oxford, where he served as an examiner (1850–52), curate (1854), and principal of Butler's Hall (1856–58). He was vice-principal of Cheltenham College (1857–65) and principal of Liverpool College (1866–82). He published sermons and other writings.

Butler, Sir **George Geoffrey Gilbert.** b. 1887; d. 1929. English political official and teacher; grandson of George Butler (1774–1853). A member (1915) of the news department of the British Foreign Office, he was director (1917–19) of the British Bureau of Information at New York. Later, having returned to England to serve as librarian and teacher of diplomatic history at Cambridge University, Butler was made a burgess (1923) of Cambridge University, and served (1927) on the royal commission on the government of Ceylon.

Butler, Harold Beresford. b. Oct. 6, 1883; d. March 26, 1951. English politician and diplomat. He was secretary to the British delegation (1910) to the International Conference on Aerial Navigation at Paris, to the foreign trade department (1916) of the Foreign Office, to the ministry of labor (1917–19), to the labor commission (1919) of the peace conference, and to the International Labor Conference (1919) at Washington. Deputy director (1920–32) and director (1932–38) of the International Labor Office, he was attached (1942–46) to the embassy at Washington.

Butler, Howard Crosby. b. at Croton Falls, N.Y., March 7, 1872; d. at Neuilly, France, in August, 1922. American archaeologist. He organized and conducted archaeological expeditions to Syria (1899–1900, 1904–05, and 1909), and in 1910 took charge of excavations at Sardis. His published works include *Scotland's Ruined Abbeys* (1900) and *The Story of Athens* (1902).

Butler, James. See also under **Ormonde.**

Butler, James. b. in Prince William County, Va.; d. at Cloud's Creek, S.C., 1781. American patriot in the Revolutionary War. He distinguished himself in the partisan warfare with the British, and was killed in the massacre at Cloud's Creek.

Butler, John. See also **Ormonde,** 6th Earl of.

Butler, John. b. at New London, Conn., 1728; d. at Niagara, Canada, in May, 1796. American Tory commander in the Revolutionary War; father of Walter N. Butler. He was made deputy superintendent of Indian affairs by the British at the beginning of the Revolutionary War, and led (1778) a force of 900 Indians and 200 loyalists against settlers in Pennsylvania's Wyoming Valley, destroying many homes and farms, and permitting Indian outrages which culminated in the so-called Wyoming Massacre. After the war his estates in the U.S. were confiscated. He had already fled to Canada, where he was rewarded by the British government with the office of Indian agent, 5,000 acres of land, and a salary and pension of 3,500 dollars a year.

Butler, Joseph. b. at Wantage, Berkshire, England, May 18, 1692; d. at Bath, England, June 16, 1752. English prelate and theologian, made bishop of Bristol in 1738, and of Durham in 1750. His most noted work is *Analogy of Religion, Natural and Revealed, to the Constitution and Course of Nature* (1736).

Butler, Josephine Elizabeth. [Maiden name, **Grey.**] b. at Glendale, Northumberland, England, April 13, 1828; d. at Wooler, Northumberland, England, Dec. 30, 1906. English social reformer; wife of George Butler (1819–90). A supporter of the movement for higher education of women, she also established (1866) at Liverpool homes for working girls and fallen women. She campaigned as a speaker and writer to secure (1886) the repeal of the Contagious Diseases Act in England, as well as reform of the law affecting white slave traffic in Europe. She was the author of numerous pamphlets and family memoirs, her best-known works including *Life of Pastor Oberlin* (1882), *Personal Reminiscences of a Great Crusade* (1896), and *Life of Saint Catherine of Siena* (1898).

Butler, Marion. b. in Sampson County, N.C., May 20, 1863; d. June 3, 1938. American politician. As a representative (1890) in the North Carolina legislature, he founded a state university for women and headed the successful attempt to save the state university at Chapel Hill. An organizer of the People's Party, he was chairman (1896–1904) of its national executive committee. During his term (1896–1901) in the U.S. Senate, he sponsored the law to establish the rural free delivery system, secured the first favorable report on the bill advocating the establishment of postal savings banks, worked toward the establishment of parcel post, and headed the attempt to secure funds for constructing the first submarine ship. A member (1894) of the National Farmers' Alliance and Industrial Union, he was an organizer of coöperative marketing associations for the cotton and tobacco industries.

Butler, Matthew Calbraith. b. at Greenville, S.C., March 8, 1836; d. at Washington, D.C., April 14, 1909. American politician and Confederate army officer.

Butler, Nicholas Murray. b. at Elizabeth, N.J., April 2, 1862; d. at New York, Dec. 7, 1947. American educator, president of Columbia University from 1902. He was graduated from Columbia University in 1882, organized and was president (1886–91) of the Teachers College at New York, incorporating it into Columbia, and became professor of philosophy and education, and Columbia's first dean of the faculty of philosophy in 1890. He was the unsuccessful candidate (1912) for the vice-presidency on the Republican ticket. He served as President (1925–45) of the Carnegie Endowment for International Peace and was cowinner (1931) of the Nobel peace prize. He founded the *Educational Review* (1891), and wrote and edited educational publications.

Butler, Pierce. b. in Dakota County, Minn., March 17, 1866; d. at Washington, D.C., Nov. 16, 1939. American jurist. After his admission (1888) to the bar, he practiced law (until 1923) at St. Paul, Minn. Named (1922) by President Warren G. Harding to the U.S. Supreme Court, he served as an associate justice (1923–39) until his death.

Butler, Sir **Piers** (or **Pierce**). See **Ossory,** 1st Earl of.

Butler, Reuben. In Sir Walter Scott's novel *The Heart of Midlothian*, a weak and sensitive minister of the Scottish Church, who marries Jeanie Deans.

Butler, Rhett. In *Gone with the Wind* (1936), a novel by Margaret Mitchell, a Civil War profiteer, ruthless but not self-centered, whose character is not unlike that of the heroine, Scarlett O'Hara. His love for her cannot outlast her passion for Ashley Wilkes; he leaves her after several years of marriage, on the death of their daughter; it is not until then that Scarlett realizes she really loves him. In the motion-picture version of the novel, Butler was played by Clark Gable.

Butler, Samuel. b. at Strensham, Worcestershire, England, in February, 1612; d. at London, Sept. 25, 1680. English poet of the Restoration period, now perhaps best known for his mock-heroic *Hudibras* (1663–78). After serving as an attendant (c1628) to Elizabeth, Countess of Kent, he was employed in the families of various gentlemen, including the Presbyterian Sir Samuel Luke. It is generally, but probably erroneously, thought that Luke served as the model for Hudibras. The poem itself, in heroic couplets, satirizes Puritanism; its hero is something of a quixotic knight, though his arguments with his attendant are more biting than the ones conducted by Cervantes's hero. The poem, which abounds in burlesque and travesty, was well received; since most of Butler's other writings were published posthumously, his contemporary reputation was based almost entirely on *Hudibras*.

Butler, Samuel. b. at Kenilworth, Warwickshire, England, Jan. 30, 1774; d. at Eccleshall Castle, Staffordshire, England, Dec. 4, 1839. English prelate and classical scholar; grandfather of Samuel Butler (1835–1902). He was bishop of Lichfield and Coventry.

Butler, Samuel. b. at Langar, Nottinghamshire, England, Dec. 4, 1835; d. at London, June 18, 1902. English novelist, satirist, Homeric scholar, and translator; grandson of Samuel Butler (1774–1839). Educated at Shrewsbury School and at St. John's College, Cambridge, he was a sheep-farmer (1860–64) in New Zealand. A man of many interests, scientific and artistic, Butler was a painter (some of his pictures being in the Royal Academy, the British Museum, and the Tate Gallery), wrote on topography and evolution, and composed musical pieces in various forms. He was the author of *The Humor of Homer* (1892) and *The Authoress of the Odyssey* (1897, expounding his firm conviction that the *Odyssey* was written by a woman). Other literary theories are presented in *Shakespeare's Sonnets Reconsidered* (1899) and *Essays on Life, Art, and Science* (1904). *Life and Habit* (1877), *Evolution: Old and New* (1879), *Unconscious Memory* (1880), and *Luck or Cunning?* (1886) are scientific works. He also wrote several theological studies and translated the *Iliad* (1898) and the *Odyssey* (1900) into prose. However, the works by which he is best remembered are the autobiographical novel *The Way of All Flesh* (1903), *Erewhon* (1872) a Utopian romance satirizing Darwinism and orthodox Christianity, and its sequel, *Erewhon Revisited* (1901).

Butler, Smedley Darlington. b. at West Chester, Pa., July 30, 1881; d. at Philadelphia, June 21, 1940. American marine-corps officer. Promoted to colonel (1919), brigadier general (1921), and major general (1929), he retired in 1931. He was decorated with the Congressional Medal of Honor in recognition of his part in the capture of Veracruz (1914) and of Fort Rivière, Haiti (1917). As a temporary brigadier general, he commanded (1918–19) Camp Pontanezen at Brest, France, for which he was awarded the Distinguished Service Medal.

Butler, Thomas. See **Ormonde,** 10th Earl of; see also **Ossory,** Earl of.

Butler, Walter. d. near Schorndorf, Württemberg, Germany, 1634. Irish adventurer. In the imperial service in the Thirty Years' War, he was an accomplice in the assassination of Wallenstein.

Butler, Walter N. b. near Johnstown, N.Y., c1752; killed Oct. 30, 1781. American loyalist soldier in the Revolutionary War; son of John Butler (1728–96).

Butler, William Allen. b. at Albany, N.Y., Feb. 20, 1825; d. at Yonkers, N.Y., Sept. 9, 1902. American lawyer and poet; son of Benjamin Franklin Butler (1795–1858). He was graduated (1843) from the University of the City of New York, studied law with his father, and took up the practice of law at New York. He was the author of *Nothing to Wear: an Episode in City Life* (1857), *Two Millions* (1858), *General Average* (1860), and other books of verse.

Butler, William Archer. b. at Annerville, near Clonmel, Ireland, c1814; d. July 5, 1848. Irish clergyman and philosophical and theological writer, professor of moral philosophy at the University of Dublin. His works include *Sermons* (1849), *Letters on the Development of Christian Doctrine* (1850), and *Lectures on the History of Ancient Philosophy* (1856).

Butler, Sir **William Francis.** b. at Suirville, Tipperary, Ireland, Oct. 31, 1838; d. at Bansha Castle, Tipperary, Ireland, June 7, 1910. British soldier, travel-writer, and biographer; husband of Elizabeth Southerden Thompson, Lady Butler. In the British army from 1858 to 1905, he saw service in the Red River Expedition (1870–71) and in the Ashanti War (1873–74), commanded (1898–99) the British forces in South Africa, and was commander (1899–1905) of the Western District in England. He was the author of *The Great Lone Land* (1872), *The Wild North Land* (1873, describing his experiences in Canada), *Akim-Foo: The History of a Failure* (1875), *Far Out: Rovings Retold* (1880), *The Light of the West, with Some Other Wayside Thoughts* (1909), *Autobiography* (1911), and of the military biographies *Charles George Gordon* (1889), *Sir Charles Napier* (1890), and *Sir George Pomeroy Colley* (1899).

Butler, William Orlando. b. in Jessamine County, Ky., April 19, 1791; d. at Carrollton, Ky., Aug. 6, 1880. American general and politician. A graduate (1812) of Transylvania University, he enrolled as a law student at Lexington, Ky., but at the outbreak of the War of 1812 interrupted his studies to volunteer in the army. He distinguished himself in several actions, including the battle of New Orleans (1814), but resigned from the army in 1817. Having settled at Carrollton to practice law, he soon became an outstanding member of the Democratic Party in Kentucky. He again interrupted his law career in 1846, this time in order to participate in the Mexican War. Under Winfield Scott, he took part in the capture of Mexico City, and was named to succeed Scott toward the end of the war. He had previously served in the county legislature (1817–18) and in Congress (1839 *et seq.*); in 1848 he was nominated for the vice-presidency on the unsuccessful ticket headed by Lewis Cass. Offered (1855) the governorship of Nebraska, he declined the office. In 1861 he took a firm stand against the continuation of slavery, and remained a Union Democrat throughout the Civil War.

Butler, Zebulon. b. at Ipswich, Mass., Jan. 23, 1731; d. at Wilkes-Barre, Pa., July 28, 1795. American pioneer, and colonial and Revolutionary soldier. He served as an officer in the French and Indian Wars, after which he led a group of Connecticut colonists to the Wyoming Valley, in Pennsylvania, where they settled (1769) along the Susquehanna River. During the armed disputes between Pennsylvania and Connecticut, he led Wyoming Valley colonists in military operations against Pennsylvania forces; as director of the Susquehanna Company, he also represented (1774–76) the Wyoming settlers in the Connecticut assembly. He became a colonel (1775) of the Connecticut militia, and was retired as a colonel of the Continental army at the end of the Revolutionary War. In 1778, while on leave in the Wyoming Valley, he commanded the ill-fated stand of the Continental forces at Forty Fort against the invading loyalist and Indian army.

But Not for Love. Novel by Beatrice Kean Seymour, published in 1930.

Buto (bū'tō). [Also: **Butos** (-tos); modern site, **Tell-el-Fara'in.**] In ancient geography, a city in N Egypt, in the Nile delta ab. 50 mi. E of Alexandria. Buto was the seat of a king in pre-dynastic times, who dominated the delta region. In addition it was an important religious center, with temples dedicated to the goddess Buto and to Horus, and a famous oracle. The site is marked today by mounds of debris.

Buto. In Egyptian mythology, the guardian goddess of Lower Egypt, counterpart of Nekhbet, guardian of Upper Egypt. One of Buto's epithets, translated, means "she who is great with magic." Buto was a serpent goddess, Nekhbet a vulture goddess. They were often depicted together.

Buton (bö'tôn). See **Boetoeng.**

Bütow (bü'tō). German name of **Bytów.**

Butrinto (bö.trēn'tō). Modern name of **Buthrotum.**

Bütschli (büch'lē), **Otto.** b. at Frankfort on the Main, Germany, May 3, 1848; d. at Heidelberg, Germany, Feb. 3, 1920. German naturalist, professor of zoölogy and paleontology (1878 *et seq.*) at the University of Heidelberg. His investigations related to the developmental history of invertebrates, and in later years especially to cell-division and the physicochemical aspects of the vital processes. Among his works are *Protozoen* (1880–89), *Untersuchungen über Strukturen* (1898), *Untersuchungen über die Mikrostruktur künstlicher und natürlicher Kieselsäuregallerten* (1900), and *Mechanismus und Vitalismus* (1901).

Butt (but), **Archibald Willingham.** b. at Augusta, Ga., Sept. 26, 1866; d. at sea, April 15, 1912. American army officer. He served as quartermaster in the Philippine Islands (1901–03), at Washington (1903–06), and in Havana (1906–08), with the rank of captain (1901–11); in 1911 he was promoted to major. He was personal aide to Theodore Roosevelt (1908–09) and William Howard Taft (1909 *et seq.*). He died (1912) in the sinking of the *Titanic*. His letters are published in *The Letters of Archie Butt* (1924; ed. by L. F. Abbott) and *Taft and Roosevelt; The Intimate Letters of Archie Butt, Military Aide* (2 vols., 1930).

Butt, Dame **Clara.** b. at Southwick, England, Feb. 1, 1873; d. at Oxford, England, Jan. 23, 1936. English contralto singer, especially of ballads and oratorios; wife (married 1900) of Kennerly Rumford, a baritone. Her first appearance (1892) was at the Albert Hall at London. At the Norwich Festival (1899), she sang Sir Edward Elgar's *Sea Pictures*, composed especially for her.

Butt, Isaac. b. at Glenfin, County Donegal, Ireland, Sept. 6, 1813; d. near Dundrum, County Dublin, Ireland, May 5, 1879. Irish lawyer and politician. He entered Parliament in 1852, and was leader (1871–77) of the Home Rule Party. He was the author of *History of Italy from the Abdication of Napoleon I* (1860) and others.

Butte (būt). City in W Montana, county seat of Silver Bow County, in the Rocky Mountains: largest copper and zinc mining area and largest city in the state; also mines silver, manganese, and other minerals. Its interests are controlled largely by the Anaconda Copper Mining Company. It is the seat of the Montana School of Mines. 33,251 (1950).

Butter (but'ėr), **Nathaniel.** d. Feb. 22, 1664. English printer and journalist. He issued, at London, pamphlets describing murders and plays (1605–39), weekly editions of foreign news-letters (1622–39), and half-yearly volumes of foreign news (1630–40). His newssheets were the forerunners of the modern newspaper. Ben Jonson ridiculed him under the name of Cymbal in his *Staple of News* (1625), and John Fletcher and James Shirley also referred to him in their works.

Butter and Egg Man, The. Play (1925) by George S. Kaufman.

Butterfield (but'ėr.fēld), **Daniel.** b. at Utica, N.Y., Oct. 31, 1831; d. at Cold Spring, N.Y., July 17, 1901. American soldier, a brevet major general in the U.S. army during the Civil War. He entered the Union army in 1861 as colonel of the 12th New York regiment of militia, was promoted to brigadier general of volunteers in the same year, and commanded a brigade during the Peninsular Campaign of the Army of the Potomac and a division in the second battle of Bull Run. He was brevetted a major general of volunteers in 1862, and commanded the 5th army corps at the battle of Fredericksburg. He served as chief of staff to Joseph Hooker at Chancellorsville and to George Gordon Meade at Gettysburg, and was again chief of staff to Hooker during the battle of Chattanooga. During Sherman's Georgia campaign he commanded a division of the 20th corps. He was U.S. subtreasurer at New York (1869–70).

Butterfield, John. b. at Berne, N.Y., Nov. 18, 1801; d. Nov. 14, 1869. American expressman and stagecoach proprietor who developed (1857 *et seq.*) the first great stagecoach line on the southern route from St. Louis to California. Beginning as a coach driver at Utica, N.Y., he became owner of many lines, and formed (1849) Butterfield, Wasson and Company which was consolidated (1850) with two other lines as the American Express Company. He was also interested in telegraph lines and railroads. In 1865 he was elected mayor of Utica.

Butterfield, Kenyon Leech. b. at Lapeer, Mich., June 11, 1868; d. Nov. 26, 1935. American educator. He served as president of Rhode Island College of Agriculture and Mechanic Arts (1903–06), Massachusetts Agricultural College (1906–24), and Michigan State College (1924–28).

Butterick (but'ėr.ik), **Ebenezer.** b. at Sterling, Mass., May 29, 1826; d. March 31, 1903. American inventor, noted for his part in devising the widely used paper patterns for garments; it is not known whether the original idea was his or that of his wife, Ellen. A shirtmaker and tailor at Sterling, he produced (together with his wife) in 1863 a marketable shirt pattern on which the pair had been experimenting since about 1859. The inexpensive and practical patterns were an immediate success, and to satisfy a growing demand for them, he moved (1863) to a larger plant at Fitchburg, and opened (1864) an office at New York. The shirt patterns gave way in popularity to patterns for children's clothes, which in turn were succeeded by the large-scale manufacture of patterns for women's garments. In 1867, J. W. Wilder, formerly an agent for Butterick, became associated with him and with A. W. Pollard as E. Butterick and Company, and in 1869 the plant was moved to Brooklyn. The firm was reorganized (1881) as the Butterick Publishing Company, Ltd., with

Wilder as president and Butterick as secretary, a post he held until his retirement in 1894. One of Wilder's innovations was the magazine *The Metropolitan* (1869; later known as the *Delineator*).

Buttermere (but'ėr.mir). Small lake in NW England, in Cumberland, situated ab. 6 mi. SW of Derwentwater, ab 10 mi. SW of Keswick, in the Lake District. Length, ab. 1 mi.; width, ab. ½ mi.; elevation, 329 ft.

Butternuts. See **Copperheads.**

Butter Point. Low cape in Antarctica, forming the S entrance point to New Harbor, in Victoria Land, in ab. 77°40′ S., 164°09′ E. It was discovered by the National Antarctic Expedition (1901–04), under the leadership of Captain Robert F. Scott, and was so named by the expedition because the Ferrar Glacier party left a tin of butter here, in anticipation of obtaining fres hseal meat at this point on the return journey.

Butter Point Piedmont or **Butter Point Piedmont Glacier.** See **Bowers Piedmont Glacier.**

Butterworth (but'ėr.wėrth), **Hezekiah.** b. at Warren, R.I., Dec. 22, 1839; d. there, Sept. 5, 1905. American editor and writer of children's books. He was an editor (1870 *et seq.*) of the *Youth's Companion.* Among his works are a series of *Zigzag Journeys, Poems for Christmas, Easter, and New Year, Songs of History, Story of the Hymns, South America, In the Boyhood of Lincoln,* and *The Patriot Schoolmaster.*

Buttington (but'ing.tọn). Ward of Welshpool municipal borough in N Wales, in Montgomeryshire, situated on the river Severn, ab. 8 mi. N of Montgomery, ab. 170 mi. NW of London by rail. Here, in 894, the English under the ealdorman Ethelred defeated the Danes. 1,233 (1931).

Büttisholz (büt'is.holts). Village in C Switzerland, in the canton of Lucerne, NW of the city of Lucerne. Here, in 1375, the Swiss peasants defeated and slew 3,000 English under Ingelram de Coucy; their bodies were buried in the *Engländerhübel* (Englishman's mound). 1,698 (1941).

Buttmann (büt'män), **Philipp Karl.** b. at Frankfort on the Main, Germany, Dec. 5, 1764; d. at Berlin, June 21, 1829. German philologist. His works include *Griechische Grammatik* (1792), *Schulgrammatik* (1816), and *Lexilogus* (1818).

Button (but'ọn), Sir **Thomas.** d. 1634. English navigator. He commanded an expedition (1612–13) to search for the Northwest Passage, on which he explored for the first time the coasts of Hudson Bay, and named Nelson River, New Wales, and Button's Bay.

Buttrick (but'rik), **George Arthur.** b. at Seaham Harbor, Northumberland, England, March 23, 1892—. American clergyman, known also as an author. Ordained in 1915, he was named (1927) pastor of the Madison Avenue Presbyterian Church, at New York. He is the author of *The Parables of Jesus* (1928), *Jesus Came Preaching* (1931), *Prayer* (1942), *Christ and Man's Dilemma* (1946), and other works.

Buttrick, Wallace. b. at Potsdam, N.Y., Oct. 23, 1853; d. at Baltimore, May 27, 1926. American Baptist minister and educator. He was pastor (1883–1902) of various churches at New Haven, Conn., St. Paul, Minn., and Albany, N.Y. He also served as secretary (1902–17), director (1917–23), and chairman (1923–26) of the General Education Board established by John D. Rockefeller.

Butts (buts), Sir **William.** b. in Norfolk, England; d. Nov. 22, 1545. English physician. He was educated at Cambridge, being granted a medical degree in 1518. He subsequently became physician in ordinary to Henry VIII. He appears as one of the characters in Shakespeare's *Henry VIII.*

Buttz (buts), **Henry Anson.** b. at Middle Smithfield, Pa., April 18, 1835; d. Oct. 6, 1920. American educator and clergyman. He is identified with Drew Theological Seminary, at Madison, N.J., where he functioned as adjunct professor of Greek and Hebrew (1868–70), professor of Greek and New Testament Exegesis (1871–1918), president of the faculty (1880–1912), and president emeritus (1912–20). He was the editor of *Epistle to the Romans in Greek* (1876), *The New Life Dawning* (1873) by B. H. Nadal, and *The Student's Commentary—The Book of Psalms* (1896) by James Strong.

Butulan Mountains (bö.tö'län). Range of mountains in the E part of Davao province, Mindanao, in the Philippine Islands. It extends from the southernmost point of the island N to Casilaran Bay, an arm of the Gulf of Davao. Highest peak, 5,345 ft.

Buturlin (bö.tör.lēn'), **Dmitry Petrovich.** b. at St. Petersburg, 1790; d. near St. Petersburg, Oct. 21, 1849. Russian military writer. His works include *Relation de la campagne en Italie 1799* (1810) and *Tableau de la campagne de 1813 en Allemagne* (1815).

But Yet a Woman. Novel by Arthur Sherburne Hardy, published in 1883.

Butz (buts), **Kaspar.** b. at Hagen, Germany, Oct. 23, 1825; d. at Des Moines, Iowa, Oct. 17, 1885. American writer. A refugee from Germany as a result of the uprisings of 1848, he helped found the Republican Party at Chicago and, in his *Deutsche Monatshefte,* supported Abraham Lincoln. His play *Florian Geyer* was performed at St. Louis. His poems extol the German empire of 1870.

Butzer (böt'sėr), **Martin.** See **Bucer, Martin.**

Buvelot (büv.lō'), **Abram Louis.** b. at Morges, Switzerland, March 3, 1814; d. at Melbourne, Australia, May 30, 1888. Australian painter. He is considered by many the best of the transitional group between those who largely failed to perceive the qualities of Australian light, color, and form and those who, aided by impressionism, finally mastered them.

Buxar or **Baxar** (buk.sär'). Town in the E part of the Union of India, in Bihar state, on the border of Uttar Pradesh (formerly the United Provinces), ab. 60 mi. NE of Benares. Here, on Oct. 23, 1764, a British force (7,000) under Hector Munro defeated the native army (40,000). The loss of the latter was over 6,000, and British control of Bengal was secured. Pop. ab. 14,000.

Buxhöwden (böks.hėv'dẹn), Count **Friedrich Wilhelm von.** b. at Magnusthal, in Livonia, Sept. 25, 1750; d. at Lohde, in Estonia, Sept. 4, 1811. Russian general, distinguished in the campaigns in Poland and Sweden. He commanded the Russian left wing at the battle of Austerlitz (1805).

Buxtehude (bůks.tẹ.hö'dẹ). Town in NW Germany, in the *Land* (state) of Lower Saxony, British Zone, formerly in the province of Hanover, Prussia, situated on the Este River, near the lower Elbe River, SW of Hamburg. A river port, it also has livestock markets, flour mills, canneries, cement works, and chemical factories. There is a local museum. First mentioned in 959, Buxtehude became a member of the Hanseatic League in 1369; it passed to Sweden in 1648, later to Hanover, and to Prussia in 1866. The *Petrikirche* (Church of Saint Peter) and the Heimat Museum suffered no damage during World War II. 13,677 (1950).

Buxtehude, Dietrich. b. at Helsingborg, Sweden, 1637; d. at Lübeck, Germany, May 9, 1707. German organist and composer, organist at Lübeck from 1668. He exerted a strong influence on Johann Sebastian Bach, who is said once to have journeyed 200 miles on foot to hear him play at his famous *Abendmusiken* (musical evenings) at Lübeck. His most important compositions were organ pieces and sacred cantatas.

Buxton (buks'tọn). Municipal borough and mountain resort in N central England, in Derbyshire, situated among the Derbyshire Hills, ab. 20 mi. SE of Manchester, ab. 165 mi. NW of London by rail. It is the highest town in England, being 1,000 ft. above sea level. Buxton has been famous for its mineral waters since Roman times. Among its notable structures is the "Crescent," a series of 18th-century houses, and the objects of interest in the vicinity are Poole's Hole (stalactite cave), Diamond Hill, and the cliff Chee Tor. 19,556 (1951).

Buxton, Charles. b. Nov. 18, 1823; d. Aug. 10, 1871. English politician and philanthropist; son of Sir Thomas Fowell Buxton (1786–1845). Graduated from Trinity College, Cambridge, in 1843, he became a partner in the brewery of Truman, Hanbury and Company, at London, in 1845. He was a member of Parliament for Newport, Isle of Wight (1857–59), for Maidstone (1859–65), and for East Surrey (1865–71). He edited *Memoirs of Sir Thomas Fowell Buxton* (1848), *Slavery and Freedom in the British West Indies* (1860), and others.

Buxton, Jedediah. b. at Elmton, Derbyshire, England, March 20, 1707; d. there, 1772. English mathematical prodigy. He was the son of a schoolmaster, but remained throughout life a farm laborer, because his mind was so occupied by mental calculations that he could not absorb a conventional education.

Buxton, Sydney Charles. [Title, 1st Earl **Buxton.**] b. 1853; d. 1934. British statesman; son of Charles Buxton (1823–71). After studying at Cambridge, he served as a member of the London school board (1876–82), and during his long career in public life was also a member of Parliament in 1883 and from 1886 to 1914. A member of the Liberal Party, he was under secretary of the colonial office from 1892 to 1895, and held cabinet rank as postmaster general (1905–10). Under Prime Minister Herbert Asquith he was president of the Board of Trade (1910–14), and in that position was an initiator of legislation establishing unemployment insurance and revising the statutes governing bankruptcy, copyright, and other matters. In 1914 he was created 1st Viscount of Newtimber, and appointed governor general of South Africa. Upon his retirement from that post in 1920 he was named 1st Earl Buxton. In addition to several books dealing with technical aspects of British government and politics, he was the author of *Mr. Gladstone as Chancellor of the Exchequer* and of *General Botha*, a biography of the Boer military leader who was later prime minister of the Union of South Africa.

Buxton, Sir Thomas Fowell. b. April 1, 1786; d. Feb. 19, 1845. English philanthropist; father of Charles Buxton, and grandfather of Sir Thomas Fowell Buxton (1837–1915). An advocate of the abolition of slavery, he was parliamentary leader of the antislavery party after 1824; he also worked toward prison reform. His memoirs were edited (1848) by his son.

Buxton, Sir Thomas Fowell. b. Jan. 26, 1837; d. at Cromer, England, Oct. 28, 1915. English administrator and reformer; grandson of Sir Thomas Fowell Buxton (1786–1845). He was a member of Parliament from 1858 to 1868. President (1899) of the British and Foreign Anti-Slavery Society, he was also a supporter of other missionary, social welfare, and forest conservation movements. He served as governor (1895–98) of South Australia.

Buxtorf or **Buxtorff** (büks′tôrf), **Johannes.** [Surnamed **"the Elder."**] b. at Kamen, Westphalia, Germany, Dec. 25, 1564; d. at Basel, Switzerland, Sept. 13, 1629. German Protestant theologian, noted as a Hebraist; father of Johannes Buxtorf (1599–1644). He was a professor at Basel (1591–1629). His chief works are *Manuale hebraicum et chaldaicum* (1602), *Lexicon hebraicum et chaldaicum* (1607), and *Biblia hebraica rabbinica* (1618–19).

Buxtorf or **Buxtorff, Johannes.** [Surnamed **"the Younger."**] b. at Basel, Switzerland, Aug. 13, 1599; d. there, Aug. 16, 1664. Swiss Hebraist; son of Johannes Buxtorf (1564–1629). He succeeded his father as a professor at the University of Basel.

Buyides (bö′yidz). [Also, **Bowides.**] Persian dynasty of the 10th and 11th centuries, overthrown c1055.

Buys-Ballot (bois′bä.lō′), **Christoph Heinrich Diedrich.** b. at Kloetinge, in the province of Zealand, Netherlands, Oct. 10, 1817; d. at Utrecht, Netherlands, Feb. 3, 1890. Dutch meteorologist, director of the meteorological institute at Utrecht (1854–87). He was the first to establish a system of storm signals in Europe, and is best known as the propounder of the meteorological law or rule named for him, which states a relation between the difference of the barometrical readings at any two stations and the direction of the winds relative to a line joining the two stations.

Buysse (boi′sẹ), **Cyriel.** b. 1859; d. 1932. Flemish novelist and naturalist. Influenced by Zola, he wrote *Sterkste* (The Right of the Strongest, 1893). Descriptions of good-natured Flemish character prevail in *Sursum Corda* (1894), *Leeuw van Vlaanderen* (Lion of Flanders, 1900), *De nachtelijke Aanrding* (Assault at Night, 1912), *'t Bolleken* (Little Dab, 1916), and *'t Ezelken* (Little Donkey, 1916). The horrors of the German invasion were portrayed in *Oorlogsvisioenen* (Visions of War, 1915). Of his plays *Het gezin van Paemel* (Paemel's Family) was most successful. English translations of some of his works may be found in *Harvest of the Lowlands*, by Jan Greshoff.

Buzău (bö.zu′ö). [Also: **Buzeu;** Hungarian, **Bodza.**] City in S Rumania, in the region of Muntenia, situated on the Buzău River, ab. 62 mi. NE of Bucharest: railroad junction; trade in wheat, salt, and lumber. There are oil refineries, mills, distilleries, and hosiery factories. It is the seat of an Orthodox bishopric. 43,365 (1948).

Buzfuz (buz′fuz), **Sergeant.** In Charles Dickens's *Pickwick Papers*, the pompous and brutal counsel for Mrs. Bardell in the Bardell-Pickwick breach-of-promise suit.

Buzzard (buz′ạrd), **Mr. Justice.** In Henry Fielding's *Amelia*, a character whose "ignorance of law is as great as his readiness to take a bribe."

Buzzards Bay. Inlet of the Atlantic Ocean lying SE of Massachusetts. It is separated from Vineyard Sound by the Elizabeth Islands, and connected to Cape Cod Bay by the Cape Cod Canal. Length, 30 mi.; width, 5 to 10 mi.

Bwa (bwä). [Also: **Ababua, Babwa.**] Bantu-speaking people of C Africa, inhabiting an area S of the Uele River in NE Belgian Congo, N of Stanleyville. Their population is estimated at ab. 200,000 (by J. Halkin, *Les Ababua*, 1911). They are divided into a number of subgroups, ruled by independent chiefs. They have patrilineal clans. The Bwa practice hoe agriculture, and their principal foods are cassava and bananas.

Bwake (bwä′kā). See **Bouaké.**

By (bī), **John.** b. 1781; d. 1836. British military engineer and founder of Ottawa, Canada. He planned and directed the construction of a canal which the Duke of Wellington had decided should be built for strategic reasons from Kingston on Lake Ontario to a point on the Ottawa River. At the northern or Ottawa River end of this waterway, which is known as the Rideau Canal, John By in 1826 established a settlement which was at first known as Bytown, and subsequently, under the name of Ottawa, became the capital of the Dominion of Canada.

Byala Slatina (byä′lä slä′tē.nä). See **Bela-Slatina.**

Byalik (byä′lik), **Chaim Nachman.** See **Bialik, Chaim Nachman.**

Byalistock (byä.li′stôk). See **Białystok.**

Byblis (bib′lis). See **Biblis.**

Byblos (bib′los). [Also: **Byblus** (-lus); modern name, **Jubayl,** also spelled **Djebeïl, Jebail, Jebeil, Jubeil;** in the Bible, **Gebal.**] In ancient geography, a city in Phoenicia, situated on a hill close to the Mediterranean Sea ab. 18 mi. N of what is now Beirut. It was one of the earliest of the Phoenician settlements, and second in importance only to Tyre and Sidon. Its inhabitants, the Gebalites, are mentioned as skillful in hewing stones (1 Kings, v. 18) and in shipbuilding (Ezek. xxvii. 9). The word "Bible" comes (through Greek *biblos*, book) from the ancient name of the city, which exported papyrus. It was the birthplace of Philo, the translator of Sanchuniathon; but it was most celebrated as the oldest seat of the cult of Adonis, to whom the city was sacred, and after whom the river it stood on was named. Gebal is mentioned as a kingdom paying tribute to Assyria in the annals of Tiglath-pileser II and Esarhaddon. It was taken by Alexander the Great. Later it became a Christian see. The modern village has only a few hundred inhabitants. The excavations carried on there by Renan unearthed numerous tombs and sarcophagi and the substructions of a large temple, perhaps that of Adonis.

By Blue Ontario's Shore. Poem by Walt Whitman, published as "Poem of Many in One" in the 1856 edition of *Leaves of Grass*, published again (1867) under the title "As I Sat Alone by Blue Ontario's Shore," and given its present title in 1881.

Bydgoszcz (bid′gôshch). [German, **Bromberg.**] City in NW central Poland, capital of the *województwo* (province) of Pomorze, situated on the Brda (Brahe) River near its junction with the Vistula River, ab. 67 mi. NE of Poznań. The Bydgoszcz Canal connects the Brda and Notec, and thereby the Warta and Vistula, rivers. The city is a railroad junction, and a center of the grain and lumber trade; it has wood, metallurgical, garment, leather, and textile industries, flour mills, distilleries, and breweries. The parish church, in the Gothic style, dates from 1502, the Church of the Jesuits, in the baroque style, from 1640. Founded in the 14th century, Bydgoszcz became an important commercial center in the 15th and 16th centuries, suffered severely in the wars with the Swedes in the 17th century, and was occupied by Prussia in 1772.

It was developed as a commercial center by Frederick the Great, who also settled German colonists in the vicinity; in the 19th century railroads, parks, and educational institutions contributed to the growth of the city. It was returned to Poland in 1919 and was resettled by Poles. In 1939 it was occupied by the Germans and held until 1945. The city suffered some damage during World War II; reconstruction was begun according to new plans for rebuilding the city. 156,108 (est. 1950).

Byelorussians (byel'ǫ.rush'ạnz). [Also: **Belorussians, White Russians.**] Population inhabiting the Baltic-Black Sea water divide, particularly the headwaters of the Dnieper, upper Neman, and upper and middle Dvina rivers, numbering 5,267,000 (1939) and now largely included in the Byelorussian Soviet Socialist Republic of the U.S.S.R. The main distinction between the Byelorussians and the Great Russians is linguistic; a Byelorussian literary language has existed, with some interruptions, since the 15th century. Since 1918 a modern Byelorussian literary language has been created on the basis of the modern dialects. Numerous spoken dialects also are found. Byelorussia has had no independent history, having always been under Polish, Lithuanian, or Russian rule.

Byelorussian Soviet Socialist Republic. [Also: **Byelorussia, Belorussia** (byel.ǫ.rush'ạ), **White Russia.**] Republic in the W part of the U.S.S.R., composed of what was formerly White Russia plus the part of Poland annexed to the U.S.S.R. after World War II. It borders on Poland on the W, the Ukrainian Soviet Socialist Republic on the S, Lithuania and Latvia on the N, and the Russian Soviet Federated Socialist Republic on the E. Capital, Minsk; area, 80,150 sq. mi.; pop. 10,400,000 (1939).

Byelukha (byi.lö'chä). See **Belukha.**

Bye Plot (bī). [Also, **Surprise Plot.**] Conspiracy in 1603 to seize the person of James I of England and extort certain religious concessions. Its members were Sir Griffin Markham, George Brooke, Thomas Grey, 15th Baron Grey of Wilton, and others.

Byerly (bī'ėr.li), **William Elwood.** b. at Philadelphia, Dec. 13, 1849; d. at Swarthmore, Pa., Dec. 20, 1935. American mathematician, professor of mathematics at Harvard University from 1881. He was assistant professor of mathematics at Cornell University (1873–76) and at Harvard (1876–81).

Byers (bī'ėrz), **Samuel Hawkins Marshall.** b. at Pulaski, Pa., July 23, 1838; d. May 24, 1933. American poet, soldier, and diplomat, author of the war song *Sherman's March to the Sea.* He fought (1861–65) with the Union Army during the Civil War, and served as consul at Zurich (1869–84), and consul general (1884 *et seq.*) to Italy and Switzerland. His works include *Complete Poems* (1914), *The Bells of Capistrano* (1917), *The Pony Express, and other Poems* (1925), and *In Arcady* (1929).

Byers, William Newton. b. in Madison County, Ohio, Feb. 22, 1831; d. 1903. American surveyor and publisher, after whom the mineral "byerite" is named. He served as a government surveyor (1851 *et seq.*) in Iowa, Oregon, Washington, and Nebraska, and moved 1858 to Colorado, where he founded (1859) and edited (1859–78) the *Rocky Mountain News.*

Byington (bī'ing.tǫn), **Cyrus.** b. at Stockbridge, Mass., March 11, 1793; d. at Belpré, Ohio, Dec. 31, 1868. American missionary to the Choctaw Indians. In charge (1820) of a party of over 20 under the American Board, he prepared a Choctaw grammar and dictionary which is still of use to philologists. He subsequently translated into Choctaw various books of the Bible, and prepared an almanac.

Byles (bīlz), Sir **John Barnard.** b. at Stowmarket, England, Jan. 11, 1801; d. at Uxbridge, England, Feb. 3, 1884. English jurist. He held (until 1858) a position as justice of the court of common pleas. He was the author of *A Practical Compendium of the Law of Bills of Exchange* (1829, a standard work that went through 14 editions), *A Discourse on the Present State of the Law of England* (1829), *Sophisms of Free Trade* (1849), and *Foundations of Religion in the Mind and Heart of Man* (1876).

Byles, Mather. b. at Boston, March 15, 1707; d. there, July 5, 1788. American Congregational clergyman and writer; nephew of Cotton Mather. Ordained in 1732, he was appointed pastor of the Hollis Street Congregational Church at Boston, which had only that year been established. He served there until 1777, throughout the British occupation of Boston during the Revolutionary War, during which his Loyalist sympathies so antagonized his congregation that he was unable to hold his pulpit after Boston had been evacuated by the British. He spent the rest of his life in retirement, writing poetry and sermons. His prose is distinguished by puns, unusual for theological writing of the day. He published *Poems on Several Occasions* (1744).

Byll (bēl), **Gabriel.** See **Biel, Gabriel.**

Byng (bing), **Andrew.** b. at Cambridge, England, 1574; d. in Norfolk, England, 1651. English scholar, one of the translators of the King James Version of the Bible (1605). He was elected (1608) regius professor of Hebrew at Cambridge, where he had been educated.

Byng, George. [Title, Viscount **Torrington.**] b. at Wrotham, Kent, England, 1663; d. Jan. 17, 1733. English admiral; father of John Byng. He distinguished himself at the battle of Malaga (1704), defended the coast against James Edward Stuart, the Old Pretender, in 1715, and destroyed the Spanish fleet in the victory off Cape Passero in 1718. He became first lord of the admiralty in 1727.

Byng, John. b. 1704; executed in Portsmouth harbor, England, March 14, 1757. British admiral; son of George Byng, Viscount Torrington. He was unsuccessful in an expedition during the Seven Years' War to relieve Minorca, which was invaded by a French expedition under the Duc de Richelieu (a grandnephew of Cardinal Richelieu) in 1756. Although his failure aroused a considerable degree of public ire, it was probably largely at the instance of the British ministry then in power (which was controlled by the Duke of Newcastle and his brother Henry Pelham), whose ineffectual war policy had rendered it unpopular, that he was tried by a court-martial, and found guilty of neglect of duty. He was shot in spite of the unanimous recommendation to mercy by the court, which deplored that the article of war under which he was condemned admitted of no mitigation of punishment, even if the crime were committed through a mere error of judgment.

Byng, Julian Hedworth George. [Title, 1st Viscount **Byng of Vimy.**] b. Sept. 11, 1862; d. 1935. British field marshal, dominion governor, and police official. He began his service with the British army as a hussar in India in 1883. He fought in the Boer War, commanded the British forces in Egypt in 1912, and during World War I first came under wide public notice for his skillful retreat at the Dardanelles in 1916. In April, 1917, he commanded the Canadian forces in the battle at Vimy Ridge, and in November of the same year he directed a surprise attack on the German lines near Cambrai, and by his effective use of tanks broke through the Hindenburg Line. In 1921 he was appointed governor general of Canada, which post he held into 1926. In that year he was created a viscount, and added "of Vimy" to his title in memory of the battle with which his name was most notably associated. In 1928 he accepted the position of commissioner of the London Metropolitan Police, which he held into 1931. The rank of field marshal was conferred upon him in 1932.

Bynkershoek (bing'kėrs.hök), **Cornelis van.** b. at Middleburg, Zeeland, Netherlands, 1673; d. 1743. Dutch jurist and authority on international law. In 1703 he became a member of the supreme court of Holland, Zeeland, and West Friesland, and from 1724 was president of that body. He published a number of scholarly studies of Roman and of Dutch law, but his more important achievements were in the field of international law, and his views on such matters as control of the high seas, neutrality, and private property rights during war continue to be cited. Among his books those best remembered are *De domine maris* (1703) and *Questiones juris* (1737).

Bynner (bin'ėr), **Witter.** b. at Brooklyn, N.Y., Aug. 10, 1881—. American poet, playwright, and translator. He was president (1920–22) of the Poetry Society of America. His books of poetry include *Grenstone Poems* (1917), *A Canticle of Praise* (1919), *The Beloved Stranger* (1919), *Caravan* (1925), *Eden Tree* (1931), *Against the Cold* (1940), and others. Under the pseudonym Emanuel Morgan he wrote a satirical parody of modern poetry, *Spectra* (1916, in collaboration with Arthur Davison Ficke). His plays include *Tiger* (1913), *Iphigenia in Tauris* (1919), and *Cake* (1926). Other works by him are *The Way of Life According to Laotzu* (1944) and *Take Away the Darkness* (1947). He translated *A Book of Love* (1923) from the French of Charles Vildrac and translated, with Kiang Kang-hu, *The Jade Mountain,* from Chinese poets of the T'ang dynasty.

Byörkö (byėrk'ė''), **Treaty of.** See **Björkö, Treaty of.**

Byr (bür), **Robert.** See **Bayer, Karl Robert Emmerich von.**

Byrd (bėrd), **Harry Flood.** b. at Martinsburg, W.Va., June 10, 1887—. American politician, publisher, and U.S. senator (1933 *et seq.*) from Virginia; brother of Richard Evelyn Byrd (1888—). He served (1926–30) as governor of Virginia. Publisher of the Winchester *Star* and Harrisonburg *Daily News.*

Byrd, Richard Evelyn. b. at Austin, Tex., Aug. 13, 1860; d. Oct. 23, 1925. American lawyer; father of Richard Evelyn Byrd (1888—). Admitted (1884) to the bar, he was commonwealth attorney (1884–1904) for Frederick County, Va., a delegate (1906–14) in the Virginia legislature, U.S. district attorney (1914–20) for the Western District of Virginia, and a special assistant (1920–21) to the U.S. attorney general.

Byrd, Richard Evelyn. b. at Winchester, Va., Oct. 25, 1888—. American naval officer and polar explorer; son of Richard Evelyn Byrd (1860–1925), and brother of Harry Flood Byrd. A graduate (1912) of the U.S. Naval Academy, he commanded (1918) the U.S. air forces in Canada. He was commander (1925) of the aviation unit in the Navy-MacMillan Polar Expedition, and flew (1926) with Floyd Bennett over the North Pole, returning to Kings Bay, Spitsbergen. In 1927 he flew with three companions from New York to France in 42 hours. In 1929 he flew over the South Pole. He discovered the Edsel Ford Mountains and Marie Byrd Land on the South Pole expeditions of 1928–30 and 1933–35 and was promoted (1930) to rear admiral. The Antarctic expedition of 1939–40 under his leadership discovered five mountain ranges, five islands, a peninsula, and 700 miles of coastline. During World War II, he served with Admiral King at Washington and Admiral Nimitz in the Pacific. In 1946 he headed a U.S. Navy Antarctic expedition. He is the author of *Skyward* (1928), *Little America* (1930), *Discovery* (1935), *Exploring with Byrd* (1927), and *Alone* (1928).

Byrd or **Byrde** or **Bird** (bėrd), **William.** b. c1538; d. July 4, 1623. English composer and organist; pupil and associate of Thomas Tallis. He was named (1563) organist at Lincoln Cathedral, and appointed (1569) joint organist of the Chapel Royal. With Tallis, he was granted (1575) a monopoly for publishing printed music in England. The first composer of English madrigals, he also wrote masses and other sacred works (he has been credited by some authorities with the composition of the well-known Anglican canon *Non nobis Domine*). Among his publications are *Psalmes, Sonets, and Songs* (1588), *Songs of Sundrie Natures* (1589), and *Gradualia* (1607).

Byrd, William. b. at London, 1652; d. Dec. 4, 1704. American colonial planter and merchant in Virginia, dealing in slaves, tobacco, and fur; father of William Byrd (1674–1744). A member (1677–82) of the Virginia house of burgesses, he entered (1683) the council of state and served (1703–04) as its president.

Byrd, William. b. in Virginia, March 28, 1674; d. Aug. 26, 1744. American colonial planter, public official and writer, son of William Byrd (1652–1704). He was educated in Holland and England, returning to Virginia in 1692, when he was elected to the Virginia house of burgesses. He left for England in 1697 to defend Sir Edmund Andros against alleged antagonism to the Anglican Church in Virginia, and in 1698 served as agent for the Virginia colony, returning there c1705. He was appointed receiver-general in 1706, entering the council of state in 1709, where he became involved in disputes with the king's governor over the powers of the wealthy Virginian planters, of which Byrd was a prime exemplar. His last years were spent on his paternal estate at Westover; he was (1728) one of the commissioners who placed the dividing line between North Carolina and Virginia. From his father, who died in 1704, he inherited one of the great plantations of Virginia. He wrote "The History of the Dividing Line," "A Journey to the Land of Eden," and "Progress to the Mines" (published as *The Westover Manuscripts,* 1841).

Byrgius (bėr'ji.us), **Justus.** [Latinized name of **Joost** (or **Jobst**) **Bürgi.**] b. at Lichtensteig, St. Gallen, Switzerland, Feb. 28, 1552; d. at Kassel, Germany, Jan. 31, 1632. Swiss inventor and mathematician. He published (1620) logarithmic tables and constructed a celestial globe, sector, and other devices.

Byrne (bėrn), **Donn.** See **Donn-Byrne, Brian Oswald.**

Byrne, James. b. at Springfield, Mass., Jan. 16, 1857; d. at New York, Nov. 4, 1942. American lawyer and educator. A graduate (1882) of Harvard Law School, he practiced (1883 *et seq.*) at New York. He was a Red Cross commissioner during World War I, a regent (1916–37) and chancellor (1933–37) of the University of the State of New York, and a member of the Harvard Corporation.

Byrnes (bėrnz), **James Francis.** b. at Charleston, S.C., May 2, 1879—. American jurist, politician, and U.S secretary of state (1945–47). Admitted to the bar in 1903, he was a U.S. congressman (1911–25) and senator (1931–41) from South Carolina. Appointed (1941) an associate justice of the U.S. Supreme Court, he resigned (1942) to become director of economic stabilization. He served (1943–45) as director of war mobilization. In November, 1950, he was elected governor of South Carolina. He is generally conceded to be one of the most astute of contemporary American political leaders, and has become a leader among conservative Southern Democrats. He is the author of a book of memoirs entitled *Speaking Frankly* (1947), in which he gives an account, among other things, of his difficulties as secretary of state in dealing with the U.S.S.R. and its associated states.

Byrns (bėrnz), **Joseph Wellington.** b. at Cedar Hill, Tenn., July 20, 1869; d. at Washington, D.C., June 4, 1936. American politician, speaker of the House of Representatives (1935–36). He received (1890) the degree of LL.B. from Vanderbilt University and established his practice at Nashville, Tenn. He served (1895–1900) as a Democratic member of the Tennessee legislature, and was elected its speaker in 1899. He became (1900) a state senator, and was elected (1908) to the House of Representatives, serving there uninterruptedly until his death. He was for many years chairman of the powerful committee on appropriations, was chosen (1933) Democratic Party floor leader and was elected speaker of the House on Jan. 3, 1935. Upon his death he was succeeded as speaker by William B. Bankhead.

Byrom (bī'rom), **John.** b. at Kersall Cell, Broughton, near Manchester, England, Feb. 29, 1692; d. Sept. 26, 1763. English poet. He studied at Trinity College, Cambridge, of which he became a fellow in 1714. He invented a system of shorthand which was published in 1767 under the title *The Universal English Shorthand.* A collective edition of his poems, among the most notable of which are "Colin to Phoebe," "Three Black Crows," and "Figg and Sutton," appeared at Manchester in 1773.

Byron (bī'ron). Essay (1830) by Thomas Babington Macaulay.

Byron, Augusta Ada. See **Lovelace,** Countess of.

Byron, George Gordon Noel. [Title, 6th Baron **Byron of Rochdale** (roch'dāl).] b. at London, Jan. 22, 1788; d. at Missolonghi, Greece, April 19, 1824. English poet. The poet's profligate father, Captain John Byron, died in France in 1791, and the boy was brought up by his widowed mother, Catherine. At Harrow (1801–05) and at Trinity College, Cambridge (1805–08), he divided his time between wide reading and the acquisition of irregular habits, and was notably successful in both pursuits. He left Cambridge with an M.A., and having come into his great-uncle's title and estates, including Newstead Abbey, in 1798, took (1809) his seat in the House of Lords, but only to depart shortly afterwards with J. C. Hobhouse on the Mediterranean tour which took him all the way from Spain to the Near East. His crippled foot, the result of an early infantile paralysis, hardly impeded his vigorous living; he explored the Albanian wilderness and even, fired by the legend of Leander, swam the Hellespont. More important, in these travels he picked up what was to be material for some of his finest poetry. He had been writing since his Cambridge days, when his *Hours of Idleness* (1807) had been pilloried by a reviewer in the *Edinburgh Review;* Byron had, in turn, blasted the *Review* with his *English Bards and Scotch Reviewers* (1809), which left no doubt of his competence or virulence as a satirist. Following his return (1811) from abroad he published *Childe Harold,* Cantos I and II (1812), *The Giaour* and *The Bride of Abydos* (both 1813), and *The Corsair* and *Lara* (both 1814). His social success, which had been brilliant during the first few months after his return to England, was seriously compromised when, in 1813, gossip was heard of his liaison with his half sister, Augusta Leigh, and was dissipated completely within the year after his marriage (Jan. 2, 1815) to Annabella Milbanke, when that affluent and attractive heiress bore Byron a daughter but failed to render their marriage tolerable to her mercurial husband. Papers of separation were filed and public opinion unhesitatingly assigned the blame to the poet, even though knowledge of the details was not available and did not become so until the publication of Lord Lovelace's heavily documented account, *Astarte,* in 1905. Ostracized, but noteworthily unrepentant and violently blaming the English public for his mistreatment, Byron quit England (1816) for good. He traveled up the Rhine, joined the Shelleys near the Lake of Geneva, figured in a liaison with Clare Clairmont (their daughter, Allegra, died at the age of five in a convent near Ravenna), and in November of 1816 arrived in Venice in the company of his friend Hobhouse. The tortured Italy of the *Risorgimento* was his home for the next six years, and the cause of liberty found him a stout, if somewhat erratic, friend. No less intense was his devotion to the last of his great loves, Teresa, Countess Guiccioli, separated (by papal decree) wife of an elderly husband who had made a private peace with the Austrian overlords and lived quietly in his palace in Ravenna while Teresa moved about Italy according to the political fortunes of her own family, the Gambas. Byron met her in 1819, when she was 17, and followed her from Venice to Ravenna, to Pisa, and on to Genoa. Much of the enthusiasm for Italy that runs through his later work is attributed by critics to her influence. In 1822 he was associated with Leigh Hunt in editing the short-lived *Liberal* but the collapse of the Carbonari movement left them without a cause. In the same year Shelley was drowned near Viareggio and the remaining members of his group, which for some months had included Byron, E. J. Trelawney, and Hunt, were herded (September, 1822) into Genoa by the Austrians. The time was ripe for the London Greek Committee to persuade Byron to transfer his fight for liberty from Italy to Greece. He outfitted a 120-ton brig, said a final farewell to his friends and Teresa, and with her brother and Trelawney sailed from Genoa in July, 1823. He got near enough the scene of action for his presence to encourage the Greek leaders, but his health had been failing for some time; he was stricken by fever at Missolonghi and died there in January, 1824. His body was given full military honors and taken back to England for burial at Hucknall Torkard Church, near Newstead.

Mature Works. Neither his amatory nor his political adventures could interrupt the flow of Byron's work. *Childe Harold,* Canto III, and *The Prisoner of Chillon* (both 1816) reflect the mood of his retreat from England after the early successes. *Manfred* (1817) and *Childe Harold,* Canto IV, reach the heights of Romantic exaltation. *Don Juan,* his satiric medley (begun 1818, published 1819–24 but never completed), is less stagily Romantic, certainly more adult, and at times self-critical; the mood changes from the pathos which had succeeded the heroics of the earlier, "strenuous," poems, to a sometimes pained but invariably open-eyed irony. Other poems of the period include *Beppo* (1818), *The Lament of Tasso* (1817), *The Prophecy of Dante* (1821), and *The Island* (1823). Less successful were the dramas, to which he devoted himself more and more as time went on: *Cain, Marino Faliero, Sardanapalus, The Two Foscari* (all 1821), *Werner* (1823), and *Heaven and Earth* (1824). He also had time to defend Pope and his school against the attacks of Bowles, and to answer an attack by Southey, in *The Vision of Judgment* (1822).

Reputation and Influence. In spite of Byron's great technical virtuosity, his manifest cleverness, and his astounding facility in rhyming, Anglo-Saxon critics have been less attracted to his work than to the serener poetry of Wordsworth and the admittedly richer writing of Keats. He has struck them as "shallow" in comparison, and they have at times doubted his sincerity. The scandals attached to him made him more often the subject of sermons than of critical encomiums, especially among the Victorians, and the turn of taste toward earlier poetry and especially toward the "School of Donne" has delayed a revival of interest in him in the 20th century. On the other hand, Continental readers have always esteemed him above his English contemporaries. Goethe admired *Manfred* and incorporated its hero in *Faust;* the Frenchman Lamartine attempted a final Canto of his own for *Childe Harold;* Musset imitated him extensively. In France generally, he is considered one of the fountainheads of Romanticism, and his poetry is frequently placed near, though perhaps not quite on a par with, the prose of Chateaubriand in this respect: *le byronisme* is an honored rubric in histories of French literature. His influence entered Spanish literature through poets like the Romantic Zorilla. The bibliography about him is extensive; important biographies include those by Galt (1830), Thomas Moore (1831), Mayne (1912), and Bellamy (1924); Trelawney's *Recollections* (1858) and Lord Ernle's collection of Byron's *Letters* (6 vols., 1898–1901) are essential material; and Harriet Beecher Stowe's *Lady Byron Vindicated* (1870) has special interest for American readers.

Byron, Harriet. In Samuel Richardson's epistolary novel *Sir Charles Grandison,* a supposed orphan, attached to Sir Charles Grandison, and the principal writer of the letters. It is between her (the nice English girl) and Lady Clementina della Porretta (beautiful and exotic, but also an Italian and a Catholic, and hence, to 18th-century English readers, although possibly exciting, hardly capable of being a good wife) that Sir Charles Grandison wavers in his affections, and thus provides Richardson with the theme of his novel.

Byron, John. [Title, 1st Baron **Byron of Rochdale.**] b. c1600; d. 1652. English Cavalier commander. He served (1640) against the Scots, and fought at Powick Bridge (Sept. 22, 1642), Newbury (1643), and Montgomery (1644). Under Charles I he held the post (1641–42) of lieutenant of the Tower of London, and was created Baron Byron of Rochdale in 1643. In 1646 he was involved in the surrender of Carnarvon Castle to the Parliamentary forces.

Byron, John. [Called **"Foul-weather Jack."**] b. Nov. 8, 1723; d. April 10, 1786. English naval officer; grandfather of George Gordon Noel Byron. He entered the navy when a boy, and in 1740 was a midshipman of the *Wager* in George Anson's squadron which was wrecked near Cape Horn. He wrote an account of the disaster, and it is believed that this narrative was used by his grandson as the basis of several episodes in *Don Juan.* From 1764 to 1766 he commanded two vessels in a voyage of exploration around the world; but beyond certain curious observations on the Indians of Patagonia and the discovery of some small islands in the Pacific, he accomplished little. He was governor of Newfoundland (1769–72), became a vice-admiral in 1778, and on July 6, 1779, had an engagement with the French fleet of Jean Baptiste Charles Henri d'Estaing off Grenada, West Indies, but was defeated.

Byron, Robert. b. 1905—. English scholar, traveler, and author. He traveled widely in Europe, Asia, and America, and lectured in the U.S. on Persian art (1935) and in Europe on English civilization (1937). He is the author of *Europe in the Looking Glass* (1927), *The Byzantine Achievement* (1929), *The Birth of Western Painting* (1930), *First Russia, then Tibet* (1933), *The Road to Oxiana* (1937), and other books.

Byron's Conspiracy and **Byron's Tragedy.** Two plays by George Chapman, produced in 1605 and printed in 1608. They may be regarded as one. They were reprinted during the author's lifetime, with revisions, in 1625. The plot of each is based upon actual events in the career of Charles de Gontaut, the Duc de Biron (whence, in Chapman's spelling, "Byron"). In real life, Biron was a French nobleman who achieved considerable success as commander of the armies of Henry IV of France, but whose ambition finally led him to plot against his king. For this he was beheaded in 1602. He is represented by Chapman as a self-confident braggart of "boundless vainglory."

Byrsa (bėr′sạ). See under ancient **Carthage.**

By Still Waters. Book of lyrical poems by George William Russell, published (1906) under his pseudonym "Æ."

Byström (bü′strėm), **Johan Niklas.** b. at Philipstad, Sweden, Dec. 18, 1873; d. at Rome, March 13, 1848. Swedish sculptor. Most of his adult life was spent in Italy, and his style was formed by study of classical and Renaissance masters. The heroic statues of the kings of Sweden, to be seen in Stockholm, constitute his best-known work, but his qualities are more manifest in his smaller compositions and sculptured portraits, especially of women and children.

Bystrzyca (bis.tshi′tsä). [German, **Habelschwerdt.**] Town in SW Poland, in the *województwo* (province) of Wrocław (German, Breslau), formerly in Silesia, Germany, situated on the Nysa (Neisse) River, ab. 58 mi. SW of the city of Wrocław: lumber trade and industry. The town belonged to Prussia from 1742 to 1945, and was acquired by Poland at the time of the Potsdam Conference (Berlin Conference) on July 17, 1945. Pop. 7,067 (1939); 9,564 (1946).

By the Ionian Sea. Travel book (1901) by George Gissing. It was inspired by his wanderings in Calabria, in S Italy, in 1897.

By the Waters of Babylon. Poems by Emma Lazarus published in *The Century* for March, 1887. Called by Miss Lazarus "little poems in prose," they deal with Jewish history.

Bytom (bi′tôm). [German, **Beuthen.**] City in SW Poland, in the *województwo* (province) of Śląsk (Silesia), formerly in Silesia, Germany, situated in the center of the Upper Silesian coal-mining district, NW of Kraków. There are numerous coal mines, as well as zinc, lead, and iron mines in the area; the city has iron and steel works, lumber mills, furniture factories, and breweries. There are art and natural science collections, and various educational institutions. Bytom was first mentioned as being under the control of a Polish ruler in 1254; like other Silesian principalities it fell to Austria in the 16th century, and to Prussia in the 18th century. Mining activities begun in the Middle Ages were resumed in the 18th century. During World War II a concentration camp was established here. Bytom was taken by the Russians in January, 1945, and was incorporated into Poland, under the terms of the Berlin Conference, in the same year. 101,084 (1939), 112,336 (est. 1950).

Bytów (bi′töf). [German, **Bütow.**] Town in NW Poland, in the *województwo* (province) of Szczecin, formerly in Pomerania, Germany, situated on the Bytów River, near the old German-Polish border, ab. 100 mi. E of Koszalin. Before World War II it had livestock markets, machine, textile, and lumber industries, and flour mills. It came under the Teutonic Order in 1329, Poland in 1466, Brandenburg in 1657, and the republic of Poland in 1945. Pop. 10,045 (1939); 3,810 (1946).

Bytown (bī′toun). Early name of **Ottawa,** Ontario, Canada.

Bywater (bī′wô″tėr, -wot″ėr), **Hector Charles.** b. at London, Oct. 21, 1884; d. Aug. 17, 1940. English journalist, author, and expert on naval affairs. From 1898 to 1914 he lived in Canada, in the U.S., and on the Continent. During World War I he was engaged in intelligence work. He was European naval correspondent (1921–30) for the Baltimore *Sun,* and held the same post (1923–28) for the London *Daily News* and *Observer.* He was the author of *Sea Power in the Pacific* (1921, a study of the American-Japanese naval problem), *Navies and Nations* (1927, a survey of naval development since World War I), *Cruisers in Battle* (1939), and many articles in *Nineteenth Century and After,* the *Engineer, Atlantic Monthly,* and *Round Table.* His volume, *The Great Pacific War—A History of the American-Japanese Campaign of 1931–33* (1925), a fictitious account, was published (1942) with an added subtitle, *A Prophecy Now Being Fulfilled,* and an introduction by Hanson W. Baldwin.

Bywater, Ingram. b. at London, in June, 1840; d. there, Dec. 17, 1914. English classical scholar and teacher, editor, and translator of Aristotle. He was educated at University College School and King's College School at London, and at Queen's College, Oxford, where he studied under Benjamin Jowett and was a friend of Algernon Charles Swinburne and Walter Pater, and was a fellow, Greek tutor (1863–84), and reader in Greek (1883–1908) at Exeter College. He was editor (1879–1914) of the *Journal of Philology,* to which he also contributed, and president (1883–1908) of the Oxford Aristotelian Society. He edited *Fragments of Heraclitus* (1877), *Works of Priscianus Lydus* (1886), Aristotle's *Nicomachean Ethics* (1890), and *Contributions to the Textual Criticism of the Ethics* (1892), wrote *The Erasmian Pronunciation of Greek and Its Precursors* (1908), and translated and edited with notes and commentary Aristotle's *Art of Poetry* (1909).

Bywood (bī′wůd). Unincorporated community in SE Pennsylvania, in Delaware County near Philadelphia. Under the urban definition established for use in the 1950 census, Bywood was counted with adjoining urban areas; the last official separate enumeration was 6,678 (1940).

Byzantine Empire (biz′ạn.tēn, -tīn, bi.zan′tin). [Also: **Eastern Empire, Eastern Roman Empire, Greek Empire, Lower Empire.**] Name usually given to the empire formally established in 330 A.D. when the Roman emperor Constantine I gave the name Constantinople to the city he had built on the site of the ancient Byzantium (now Istanbul) and established it as his capital. From the standpoint of geography Constantine's empire was coextensive (and indeed, in his eyes, identical) with the Roman Empire, but the disagreements between his successors led finally to an actual separation of East and West, the former comprising at first approximately half of the Roman Empire; from the standpoint of history after Sept. 4, 476, when the last ruler of the Roman Empire in the West was deposed, it was the sole remaining political unit which could, by its unbroken historical link to the earliest days of Roman conquest in the Mediterranean, claim to be the "Roman Empire." Between 951 and 1057 this empire reached the height of its power. Crete, Cyprus, Cilicia, and the N portion of Syria were recaptured from Islam, part of Armenia was conquered, a great Russian invasion was repulsed, the strong Bulgarian kingdom was overthrown, and Roman territory was once more extended to the Danube. Thereafter the empire waned in size and power, and in 1204 it fell an easy prey to the Venetians and their allies of the Fourth Crusade, who maintained it as a seat of empire, but oriented it toward the West in religion and culture (under their control, the Byzantine Empire became once again a Latin, or Western, Empire). The empire was thereafter maintained, often precariously, until the Ottoman Turks captured Constantinople in 1453 A.D., at which time the Byzantine Empire, as a continuation of the Roman Empire, came finally to an end. At its greatest extent it had included all or most of SE Europe, W Asia, N Africa, part of Italy, and various islands in the Mediterranean and Black Sea.

Chronology. The sequence of rulers and major events of the Byzantine Empire included: the formal naming of Constantinople in 330; final complete separation of the Byzantine and Western Roman empires on the death of Theodosius in 395; the reign of Justinian (527–565), who was one of the great Byzantine rulers; the reign of Heraclius (610–641), during which the Byzantine Empire became in its culture explicitly Greek, although the historical Roman link remained (perhaps the most striking instance of how the people of Constantinople blended their culture with their political history was their insistence on calling themselves, in Greek, *Romaioi,* meaning Romans); reign of Leo the Isaurian (717–741); the Macedonian dynasty (867–1057), including Basil I, Constantine VII, Nicephorus II, John I, Basil II, and others; the dynasty of the Comneni (1081–1185), including Alexius I in whose reign occurred the First Crusade, Manuel I, and others; fall of the empire under Alexius III, conquest of Constantinople, and division of the realm by the Venetians and their allies (1204), thus closing that part of Byzantine history which had started when the second Comnenus, Alexius I, had sought to use his Christian coreligionists in the West to parry the threat of Islam, and thus opened the door to Christian allies fully as hungry for power as the Moslems they opposed; period (1206–61) of Latin empire at Constantinople, with the Greek empire continuing a rump existence from a capital at Nicaea; reëstablishment (1261) of the Greek empire at Constantinople under the Palaeologus dynasty; overthrow of the empire under Constantine XI, and capture of Constantinople by the Ottoman Turks, in 1453.

Religion and Culture. The Orthodox Church was the dominant factor in the civilization of the Byzantine Empire. It provided a bond in Byzantine society stronger than any political tie; Justinian's ideal of "one state, one law, one church" commanded virtually universal support throughout a great part of Byzantine history. When the Arabs captured Egypt and Syria, the adherents of the heretical sects that had maintained themselves in those countries in defiance of the imperial authority were lost to the empire, and heresy rarely again became a serious question. The emperor at his accession was required to confess the Orthodox faith and to agree to support the decrees of the church councils as well as the rights and privileges of the church. The cleavage that came in 1054 between the Orthodox and Roman Catholic churches was the culmination of a long series of differences between them. One of the chief causes of division was the fact that, while the Western Church had adopted Latin for its ritual and literature, Greek had remained in use in the East. As the knowledge of Greek died out in Italy, and as the people of the Byzantine Empire came to despise Latin as a barbarous tongue, a linguistic barrier arose between the clergy of the Eastern and Western churches. Another cause of the cleavage was the decline of the Byzantine emperors' power in Italy, which enabled the popes to assume a position of independence impossible for the patriarchs of Constantinople. The coronation of Charlemagne as emperor by the pope in 800 was a further source of friction, for the rulers of the Byzantine Empire claimed the exclusive right to the imperial title. These, and other points of difference or irritation, resulted in a separation of the two churches which has continued to this day, despite several efforts to achieve reconciliation. Scientific studies in the Byzantine Empire awakened little interest and did not, in the main, progress beyond the bounds of Aristotle's presentation. In the field of literature, Byzantine achievements were greatest in controversial theological writing and in history, the latter including various series of world chronicles, of universal scope and designed for popular consumption. In the 10th century, particularly, Byzantine scholarship produced quantities of written materials, including encyclopedic compilations in the form of philological, grammatical, and etymological studies, commentaries, and dictionaries, which have preserved a great deal of classical learning that would otherwise have been lost.

Byzantine Historians. Collective term for the Greek historians of the Byzantine Empire. Among the most important were Zosimus, Procopius, Agathias, Anna Comnena, Joannes Cinnamus, and Nicetas Acominatus.

Byzantinus (biz.ạn.tī'nus), **Josephus.** See **Genesius, Josephus.**

Byzantium (bi.zan'shi.um, -ti-). [Greek, **Byzantion.**] In ancient geography, the Latin name of a Greek city built on the E part of the site of Constantinople (modern Istanbul), into which it was formally merged by the emperor Constantine I in 330 A.D. It was noted for its control of the corn trade and for fisheries. It was founded (7th century B.C.) by Megarians, and was recolonized (479 B.C.) after the battle of Plataea. Alcibiades conquered it in 408 B.C., and Lysander in 405 B.C. In 339 B.C. it was besieged by Philip of Macedon and relieved by Phocion, and again besieged (194–196 A.D.) and taken by Severus.

C

Caaba (kä'bạ). See **Kaaba.**

Caagua (kä.ä'gwä). See **Caingua.**

Caamaño (kä.ä.mä'nyō), **José María Plácido.** b. at Guayaquil, Ecuador, Oct. 5, 1838; d. at Seville, Spain, Dec. 31, 1901. Ecuadorian statesman, president of Ecuador (1884–88). In 1882 he was banished for conspiring against the dictator Ignacio de Veintemilla. From Peru he led an expedition (1883) against Guayaquil which was eventually successful. The downfall of Veintemilla followed. Caamaño was made president ad interim (Oct. 11, 1883), and was regularly elected president on Feb. 17, 1884, holding the office until June 30, 1888. He was minister to Washington (1889, 1890).

Caapucú (kä"ä.pö.kö'). City in SW Paraguay, in Paraguarí department. 7,500 (1940).

Caazapá (kä"ä.sä.pä'). Department in SE Paraguay. Capital, Caazapá; area, 4,166 sq. mi.; pop. 70,197 (est. 1945).

Caazapá. City in S Paraguay, capital of Caazapá department. 19,953 (est. 1945).

Cabaiguán (kä.bī.gwän'). City in C Cuba, in Las Villas province. 9,853 (1943).

Cabal (kạ.bal'). In English history, an influential group at the court of Charles II, consisting of Clifford (Thomas Clifford, 1st Baron Clifford of Chudleigh), Ashley (Anthony Ashley Cooper, 1st Baron Ashley and 1st Earl of Shaftesbury), Buckingham (George Villiers, 2nd Duke of Buckingham), Arlington (Henry Bennet, 1st Earl of Arlington), and Lauderdale (John Maitland, 1st Duke of Lauderdale), the initials of whose names happened to compose the word. Although the group as a whole never formally comprised a British ministry, one or more of its members belonged to every ministry that existed between 1667 and 1674, and there was no question at any time during this period as to the power of the members of the Cabal, whether in or out of the government. The members of the group were guilty, individually and collectively, of intrigues and cynical corruption remarkable even in a day when public office was viewed by many as simply a means to power and wealth, and never hesitated to act accordingly. By coincidence, the initialism "Cabal" happened to be identical in spelling with the word "cabal," derived indirectly from the word "cabala," "cabbala," or "kabbala," which was the name of a medieval system of theosophy based on a mystical interpretation of the Scriptures. "Cabala" had long been popularly associated with black magic and various secret rites, and the word "cabal" was therefore reinforced in its invidious connotations by the activities of the members of the Cabal. Since that time, in political usage, the term has been applied to many secret or conspiratorial cliques in both British and American history.

Cabala (kab'ạ.lạ, kạ.bä'-), **The.** Prose work (1926) by Thornton Wilder. It is a group of connected stories about drawing-room intrigues in Roman high society.

Caballero (kä.bä.lyā'rō), **Fernán.** [Pseudonym of **Cecilia Francisca Josefa de Arrom**; maiden name, **Cecilia Böhl von Faber.**] b. at Morges, Switzerland, 1796; d. at Seville, Spain, April 7, 1877. Spanish novelist. Author of *La Familia de Alvareda* and *La Gaviota*, she is considered one of the founders of the modern Spanish novel.

Caballero, Francisco Largo. See **Largo Caballero, Francisco.**

Caballero y de la Torre (kä.bä.yā'rō ē dā lä tôr'rā), **José Agustin.** b. at Havana, Cuba, in February, 1771; d. there, April 6, 1835. Cuban educator and noted pulpit orator. He studied at the Seminary of San Carlos and at Havana University, and was long the director of the former institution and a lecturer on philosophy.

Caballero y Góngora (kä.bä.lyā'rō ē gông'gō.rä), **Antonio.** fl. 1780–89. Spanish prelate who in 1780, as archbishop of Santa Fe (now Bogotá, Colombia; then capital of New Granada), made an attempt to conciliate the rebels in the south. He was appointed viceroy, and ruled New Granada from 1782 to 1789, uniting the religious, military, and civil powers.

Caballero y Lastres (kä.bä.yā'rō ē läs'trās), **Ernesto.** b. at Lima, Peru, Nov. 3, 1872—. Peruvian naval officer. He supervised the French construction (1909) of the submarines *Ferre* and *Palacios*, the first ones in a South American navy. He was founder of the naval center Revista de

Marina and of the Peruvian league for national defense, was appointed (1930) a rear admiral, and has served as naval attaché in the U.S., Italy, Greece, and Spain. He has also been Peruvian delegate to international conferences on hydrography, aviation, geodetics, and oceanography, and has written articles on naval and oceanographic subjects.

Cabanagem (kä.bą.nä'zhāṅ) or **Cabanos** (ką.bu'nös). Names given in Brazil to the rebels who, from 1833 to 1836, overran the Amazon valley. The abdication of Pedro I was followed by a rumor that the regency desired to turn Brazil over to Portugal. Certain liberal leaders in Pará took advantage of this report, called to their aid the ignorant Indian and mulatto population, murdered the president, and committed many atrocities. Matters went from bad to worse until the whole province was in a state of anarchy and Pará was abandoned by the whites. The rebellion was subdued by Francisco José Soares de Andrea in 1836.

Cabañas (kä.ʙä'nyäs). Department in N El Salvador, bordering on Honduras. Capital, Sensuntepeque; area, 316 sq. mi.; pop. 81,632 (est. 1942).

Cabañas. Town in S Spain, in the province of Huelva. 11,285 (1940).

Cabañas, Trinidad. b. in Honduras, c1802; d. Jan. 8, 1871. Central American general, president (1852–55) of Honduras. He was an officer with Francisco Morazán, and an upholder of Central American unity. In 1844 he aided in the defense of León, Nicaragua, against Francisco Malespín, and in 1845 he led the Salvadorian troops which attempted to overthrow Malespín. He was made president of Honduras on March 1, 1852. An attempt to interfere with the affairs of Guatemala led to his deposition (July, 1855) by Guatemalan troops aided by revolutionists of Honduras. He fled to Salvador and remained in exile several years.

Cabanel (kȧ.bȧ.nel), **Alexandre.** b. at Montpellier, France, Sept. 28, 1823; d. at Paris, Jan. 23, 1889. French historical, genre, and portrait painter, a pupil of François Édouard Picot. He won the grand prix de Rome in 1845, a medal of the second class in 1852, a medal of the first class in 1855, and medals of honor in 1865, 1867, and 1878. He became a member of the Institute of France in 1863, and was a professor at the École des Beaux-Arts.

Cabanis (kä.bä.nēs'). Historical novel (1832) relating to the times of Frederick the Great, by Wilhelm Häring (writing under the pseudonym Wilibald Alexis).

Cabanis (kȧ.bȧ.nēs), **Pierre Jean Georges.** b. at Cosnac, Charente-Maritime, France, June 5, 1757; d. near Meulan, Seine-et-Oise, France, May 5, 1808. French physician and philosopher, noted as one of the founders of the "Idéalogues" school. A professor at Paris, he was also active in politics, being a member of the Council of Five Hundred. He was the author of *Rapports du physique et du moral de l'homme* (1802). In this work he discussed systematically the relations of soul and body, with materialistic conclusions. He regarded the physical and the psychical as two aspects of one faculty, looked at from different points of view, and the soul not as a being, but as a faculty.

Cabarrús (kä.bär.rös'), **Francisco,** Conde **de.** b. at Bayonne, France, 1752; d. at Seville, Spain, April 27, 1810. Spanish financier, of French origin. He was minister of finance (1808–10) under Joseph Bonaparte.

Cabarrús, Jeanne Marie Ignace Thérésa de. See **Tallien, Thérésa.**

Cabatuan (kä.bä.tö'än). Town in the C part of Iloilo province, Panay, Philippine Islands. 2,580 (1948).

Cabbages and Kings. Collection of short stories by William Sydney Porter, published under the pseudonym O. Henry, in 1904. The book is held together by a single group of characters in a Central American town who reappear in various episodes (and is thus classifiable, from a purely technical standpoint, as a novel).

Cabeça de Vaca (kä.ʙā'thä dā ʙä'kä), **Álvar Núñez.** See **Cabeza de Vaca, Álvar Núñez.**

Cabeiri (ką.bī'rī). See **Cabiri.**

Cabel (kȧ.bel) or **Cabu** (kȧ.bü), Madame **Marie Josèphe.** [Maiden name, **Dreullette.**] b. at Liége, Belgium, Jan. 31, 1827; d. at Maisons-Lafitte, France, May 23, 1885. Belgian opera singer. Giacomo Meyerbeer wrote the part of Dinorah for her.

Cabell (kab'ẹl), **James Branch.** b. at Richmond, Va., April 14, 1879—. American novelist and essayist. Graduated (1898) from William and Mary College, he taught French and Greek there for a year. He was for a short time thereafter a staff member of the New York *Herald* (1899–1901) and the Richmond *News* (1901). Editor (1932–35) of the *American Spectator*, he had himself been, since 1902, a contributor to various magazines. He is best known for his elaborately contrived series of romantic novels (which he himself groups as "the Biography of Manuel"), the best known of which is *Jurgen* (1919). His other works include *The Eagle's Shadow* (1904), *The Line of Love* (1905), *Gallantry* (1907), *Chivalry* (1909), *The Cords of Vanity* (1909), *The Rivet in Grandfather's Neck* (1915), *The Certain Hour* (1916), *From the Hidden Way* (1916), *The Cream of the Jest* (1917), *Domnei* (1920), *Figures of Earth* (1921), *The High Place* (1923), *The Music From Behind the Moon* (1926), *The Silver Stallion* (1926), *Townsend of Lichfield* (1930), *These Restless Heads* (1932), *Smirt* (1934), *Ladies and Gentlemen* (1934), *Smith* (1935), *Preface to the Past* (1936), *Smire* (1937), *The King Was in His Counting House* (1938), *The First Gentleman of America* (1942), *There Were Two Pirates* (1946), *Let Me Lie* (1947), and *The Devil's Own Dear Son* (1949).

Cabellio (ką.bel'i.ō). Ancient name of **Cavaillon.**

Cabero Díaz (kä.ʙā'rō dē'äs), **Alberto.** b. at Santiago, Chile, March 20, 1874—. Chilean lawyer, politician, and diplomat. He was a national deputy (1915 *et seq.*) from Antofagasta, senator (1926 *et seq.*) and president (1932) of the senate, minister of lands and colonization (1937), minister of national defense (1938–39), and ambassador (1940–43) to the U.S.

Cabes (kä'bes). See **Gabès.**

Cabestaing (kä.bes.tāny') or **Cabestan** (kä.bes.tän'), **Guillaume de.** fl. toward the end of the 12th century. Provençal poet (or, according to some critics, from Roussillon, a small region in the S part of France, bordering on Spain). According to most accounts, he was killed, out of jealousy, by Raymond of Roussillon, who, not unjustly, suspected his wife of unseemly dalliance with the poet. Legend has it that Raymond thereupon caused his wife to eat, unwittingly, of Cabestaing's heart. When she learned what she had done she declared that her lips, which had tasted such noble food, should touch no other, and died of starvation. Seven of Cabestaing's poems have been preserved.

Cabet (kȧ.be), **Étienne.** b. at Dijon, France, Jan. 1, 1788; d. at St. Louis, Mo., Nov. 8, 1856. French socialist. A lawyer by profession, he was elected to the Chamber of Deputies in 1831, founded *Le Populaire* in 1833, and fled to England in 1834 in order to escape punishment on account of an article which he had published in that journal. There he met Robert Owen, whose social ideas greatly influenced him. He returned to France in consequence of the amnesty of 1839. He wrote *Histoire populaire de la révolution française de 1789 à 1830*, and the Utopian *Voyage en Icarie, roman philosophique et social* (1840). He established a communistic settlement, called Icarie, in Texas, in 1848, which was removed to Nauvoo, Ill., in 1850.

Cabeza del Buey (kä.ʙā'thä del bwā'). Town in W Spain, in the province of Badajoz, ab. 90 mi. E of the city of Badajoz: cattle trade; lead and iron mines. 11,762 (1940).

Cabeza de Vaca (dā ʙä'kä), **Álvar Núñez.** [Also, **Cabeça de Vaca.**] b. at Jerez de la Frontera, Spain, c1490; d. at Seville, Spain, c1557. Spanish soldier, explorer, and colonial administrator. He served in Italy and Navarre (1511–26) as well as in Spain. He was comptroller and royal treasurer (1527–28) with the expedition of Pánfilo de Narváez to Florida. He and three others were the only ones who escaped from shipwreck on a Texas island and from the savages who captured them. After living for years among the Indians, they reached the Spanish settlements in northern Mexico in April, 1536. Cabeza de Vaca returned to Spain in 1537, and in 1540 he was appointed governor of Paraguay. He sailed with 400 men, landed on the coast of southern Brazil, and marched overland to Asunción, the 1,000-mile journey occupying nearly a year (1541–42). In 1543 he explored the upper Paraguay River. On April 25, 1544, he was deposed and imprisoned by the colonists for alleged arbitrary acts. Sent to Spain the next year, he was tried by the Council of the Indies and sentenced to be banished to Oran, Africa; but he was subsequently recalled by the king, received a pension, and was made judge of the supreme court of Seville. His two works: *Naufragios, peregrinaciones y milagros*, describing his Florida adventures, and *Commentarios*, relating to his administration in Paraguay, were both written for his own justification; but, making allowances for this, they are of great historical value. There are modern editions in several languages.

Cabhân (koun), **An.** Irish name of County **Cavan.**

Cabicungan (kä.bē.köng.gän'). Volcano in Cagayan province, in the N part of Luzon, Philippine Islands. 4,326 ft.

Cabildo (kä.ʙēl'dō). Administrative body established (1769) by the Spanish for governing the province of Louisiana. It was in existence until 1803, when the province was transferred to French hands.

Cabillonum (kab.i.lō'num). Ancient name of **Chalon-sur-Saône.**

Cabimas (kä.ʙē'mäs). City in NW Venezuela, in Zulia state. 32,691 (1950).

Cabinda (ka.bin'dạ). See also **Binda.**

Cabinda. [Also, **Kabinda.**] Town and harbor in Angola, SW Africa, a few miles N of the Congo estuary. It has developed rapidly since 1885, and especially during the period of high tariff in the Belgian Congo. It has an airport, with service to Luanda and Pointe Noire. The native people are the Binda. The part of Angola lying N of the Congo is also known as Cabinda. Pop. of town ab. 1,500.

Cabira (ka.bī'rạ). An ancient name of **Sivas,** Turkey.

Cabiri (kạ.bī'rī). [Also: **Cabeiri, Kabeiri.**] In Greek mythology, certain beneficent deities of whom little is known. They were worshiped in parts of Greece and in the islands of Imbros, Lemnos, and Samothrace. They are possibly of Phrygian origin. Their rites were secret. The mysteries of the Cabiri of Samothrace were regarded as inferior only to the Eleusinian. Later they became associated with the Dioscuri and gave protection against mishaps, especially by sea.

Cable (kā'bl), **George Washington.** b. at New Orleans, La., Oct. 12, 1844; d. Jan. 31, 1925. American author, noted for his depiction of Creole life and his contribution to the development of the "local color" school in U.S. literature. He served in the Confederate army during the Civil War and began writing soon afterward. His first publications, in the New Orleans *Picayune*, resulted in the adoption of his weekly column as a regular daily feature, and in 1869 he joined the paper as a reporter. After a brief career on the staff of the *Picayune*, he became an accountant with a local firm of cotton factors. In his leisure time he devoted himself to self-education and to research in the history of old New Orleans, committing some of his imaginative reconstructions to paper. A writer for *Scribner's Monthly* "discovered" Cable; the result was the publication (1873) of his short story "Sieur George" in that magazine, followed by five others in the next three years. These were included in his first volume, *Old Creole Days* (1879), which established his reputation. He left the business world to devote himself to writing, publishing *The Grandissimes* (1880), *Madame Delphine* (1881), *The Creoles of Louisiana* (1884), *Dr. Sevier* (1885), *Bonaventure* (1888), and *Strange True Stories of Louisiana* (1889). In the meantime, he had become interested in causes of social reform, including prison administration and the condition of the Negro. The reception accorded to his *The Silent South* (1885) was a factor in his decision to move to Northampton, Mass., in 1885. He took up lecturing and was the founder of the Home-Culture Clubs (later the Northampton People's Institute). Among his books on social problems are *The Negro Question* (1888) and *The Southern Struggle for Pure Government* (1890). His later works of fiction include *John March, Southerner* (1894), *Strong Hearts* (1899), *The Cavalier* (1901), *Bylow Hill* (1902), *Kincaid's Battery* (1908), *The Flower of the Chapdelaines* (1918), and *Lovers of Louisiana* (1918). See *George W. Cable, his Life and Letters*, by Lucy L. Cable Bikle (1928).

Cabo (Spanish, kä'ʙō; Portuguese, kä'bö). Spanish and Portuguese word meaning "cape": see the specific element of the name.

Caboche (kȧ.bosh), **Simon.** fl. 1413. French insurgent. He was the leader of a group of Paris tradesmen, called Cabochiens, in the service of John the Fearless, Duke of Burgundy, during the civil war between the Armagnacs and the Burgundians. Caboche, whose real name was Simon, or Simonet, Lecoustellier, was called Caboche from his trade as a skinner.

Cabochiens (kȧ.bo.shyaṅ). Early 15th-century organization at Paris, made up chiefly of artisans and small tradesmen, which demanded certain reforms in the government. The principal leader was Simon Lecoustellier, called Caboche, from his trade as a skinner. Taking the side of John the Fearless of Burgundy in the civil war of 1411–13, they seized power at Paris and enacted the *ordonnance cabochienne*, a radical code for those times. However, the defeat of the Burgundians by the Armagnacs resulted in their speedy suppression.

Cabot (kab'ọt), **George.** b. at Salem, Mass., Jan. 16, 1752; d. April 18, 1823. American merchant and politician, an outstanding figure among the New England Federalists. He attended Harvard College, leaving in 1768 after taking part in a protest movement of students against the college's administration. As a disciplinary measure, he was sent to sea by his brothers; within two years he was skipper of a schooner; his business acumen was such that by c1777 he was able to give up the sea and to join his brothers' mercantile firm. He became (1784) director of the Massachusetts Bank, the first in the state, helped organize (1788) the Essex Bridge and Beverly cotton factory corporations and, after forming a partnership with a brother-in-law in 1785, reaped such handsome rewards that he was able to retire within a decade. As early as 1778 he had begun to take an interest in politics, identifying himself with an Essex County faction which later became the seed of the Federalist party. He was a state senator (1783), was a member of the Massachusetts ratifying convention (1788), and served (1791–96) as a U.S. senator, during which time he was close to Alexander Hamilton and acted as a director of the Bank of the United States, serving in the latter post until 1793. In 1803 he became president of the Boston branch of the Bank of the United States and a director of the Suffolk Insurance Company and president (c1809) of the Boston Marine Insurance Company. During New England's disaffection after the Embargo Act he was a moderate, and also contributed his stabilizing influence to the Hartford Convention (1814), of which he acted as president. See *Life and Letters of George Cabot*, by Henry Cabot Lodge (1877).

Cabot, John. [Italian, **Giovanni Caboto** (jō.vän'nē kä.bō'tō); Spanish, **Gaboto.**] b. probably at Genoa, Italy, 1450; d. 1498. Italian navigator in the English service on whose discoveries were based English claims in North America; father of Sebastian Cabot. He was probably a native of Genoa or its neighborhood, and in 1476 became a citizen of Venice after a residence there of 15 years. He subsequently removed (c1484) to Bristol, England. Believing that a northwest passage would shorten the route to India, he determined to undertake an expedition in search of such a passage, and in 1496 obtained from Henry VII of England a patent for the discovery, at his own expense, of unknown lands in the eastern, western, or northern seas. He set sail from Bristol in May, 1497, in company with his sons, and returned in the same year. The expedition resulted in the discovery of what is probably Cape Breton Island and Nova Scotia. In the spring of 1498 he made a second voyage, reaching Greenland and Baffin Island, and exploring the coast as far south as the 38th parallel.

Cabot, Richard Clarke. b. at Brookline, Mass., May 21, 1868; d. at Cambridge, Mass., May 8, 1939. American physician and writer on medicine and ethics. Graduated (B.A., 1889; M.D., 1892) from Harvard University, he was physician (1898–1908) to outpatients, assistant visiting physician (1908–12), and chief (1912–21) of the medical staff at Massachusetts General Hospital. He also served as instructor (1903–08) in medicine, assistant professor (1908–19), and professor (1919–33) of clinical medicine, and professor (1920–34) of social ethics at Harvard. He was the author of *Clinical Examination of the Blood* (1896), *Physical Diagnosis* (1901), *Social Service and the Art of Healing* (1909), *Differential Diagnosis* (1911–15), *What Men Live By* (1914), *Social Work* (1919), *Facts on the Heart* (1926), *The Meaning of Right and Wrong* (1933), and *Christianity and Sex* (1937).

Cabot, Sebastian. b. at Venice, Italy, c1476; d. 1557. Explorer; son of John Cabot. He accompanied his father on the voyage of 1497, when the shore of North America was discovered (his name appears with his father's in the petition to Henry VII), and it is probable that he was with him also on the voyage of 1498. In the period 1508–09, it is said, he went in search of a northwest passage, touching the coast of Labrador and possibly entering Hudson Bay. Invited by Charles V to Spain, he was made (1519) grand pilot of Castile but gave up the post to take command of four ships which left San Lucar on April 3, 1526, to sail to the Moluccas by the Strait of Magellan. Lacking provisions, he landed on the coast of Brazil, where he had some encounters with the Portuguese; thence he sailed southward, discovered the river Uruguay, and erected a fort there. He discovered and ascended the Paraná River, and explored the lower Paraguay to the present site of Asunción. Convinced of the importance of this region, and joined by Diego Garcia, he relinquished the voyage to the Moluccas and despatched a ship for reinforcements; meanwhile he established himself at the fort of Espírito Santo on the Paraná. Not receiving aid, he returned in 1530, leaving a garrison at Espírito Santo. Cabot was subsequently in the service of Spain until c1547, when he returned to England. He was interested (1553–56) in explorations in the Baltic, as a founder and (after 1555) life governor of the Merchant Adventurers, a company whose search for a north-east passage to the Orient opened the routes for trade with Russia. A map of the world published in 1544 is ascribed to him.

Cabot Strait. Sea passage separating Newfoundland from Cape Breton Island, Nova Scotia, and connecting the Gulf of St. Lawrence with the Atlantic Ocean.

Cabot Trail. See under **Cape Breton Highlands National Park.**

Cabourg (kȧ.bör). Seaside resort in N France, in the department of Calvados, situated on the English Channel ab. 14 mi. NE of Caen. Pop. ab. 2,000.

Cabo Verde (kä′bö vär′dẹ), **Ilhas do.** Portuguese name of **Cape Verde Islands.**

Cabra (kä′brä). Town in S Spain, in the province of Córdoba, situated in the Sierra de Cabra, ab. 35 mi. SE of Córdoba. It is an agricultural trade center and has cloth, felt, brick, and earthenware factories. There is a ruined Moorish castle, and a parish church which was originally a mosque. Cabra was delivered from the Moslems by Ferdinand III of Castile and León in 1244, recaptured by them in 1331, and finally reunited to Christian Spain a century later. 20,779 (1940).

Cabral (kạ.bräl′), **Pedro Alvares.** [Prenames sometimes abbreviated to **Pedralvarez** or **Pedralvez.**] b. c1460; d. c1526. Portuguese navigator. After Vasco da Gama returned (1499) from India, Cabral was put in command of a fleet destined to follow up his discoveries. Leaving Lisbon on March 9, 1500, he followed his instructions and kept far out in the Atlantic; by this means he discovered (April 22, 1500) the coast of Brazil. This was two months after Vicente Yañez Pinzón had discovered the northeast coast. Cabral took possession for Portugal of the new land, which he called Santa Cruz. Sending back a ship with the tidings, he continued his voyage on May 2. On May 6 he lost four ships in a storm; with the rest he reached Mozambique and finally Calicut, where he erected a fort; this was destroyed, and Cabral then made an alliance with the sovereign of Cochin. Loading his vessels with spices, he returned, losing only one ship on the way, and arrived at Lisbon on July 23, 1501. Nothing is known of his subsequent life.

Cabrera (kä.brā′rä). See also **Caprera.**

Cabrera. Small island, belonging to the Balearic Islands, in the Spanish province of Baleares, situated in the Mediterranean Sea, ab. 10 mi. S of Majorca: part of the commune of Palma. It has few inhabitants, macchia vegetation, and numerous small bays; the coastal waters abound in fish.

Cabrera, Luis. [Pseudonyms, **Lucas Ribera** and **Lic. Blas Urrea.**] b. at Zacatlán, Mexico, July 17, 1876— Mexican author and lawyer. He took an LL.B. degree in 1901, and was professor of civil law (1907–08) and director (1912) of the Escuela Nacional de Jurisprudencia, at Mexico City. He served as a national deputy (1912, 1917), minister of finance (1914–17, 1919–20) under Venustiano Carranza, and a member (1916–17) of the Mexican-American Mixed Claims Commission and other official commissions. In 1920 he retired from politics to practice law. He has been a contributor to Mexican newspapers, and is the author of *El Cantar de los cantares* (1919) and *Musa peregrina* (1929) under the pseudonym Lucas Ribera; of *Obras políticas* (1920) and *La Herencia de Carranza* (1920) under the pseudonym Lic. Blas Urrea; and of *El Balance de la revolución* (1931), *Los Problemas trascendentales de México* (1934), and *Veinte años después* (1937).

Cabrera, Manuel Estrada. See **Estrada Cabrera, Manuel.**

Cabrera, Ramón. [Title, Count of **Morella.**] b. at Tortosa, Catalonia, Spain, c1810; d. at Wentworth, near Haines, England, May 24, 1877. Spanish guerrilla chief. He was intended for the church and had received the minor orders, when in 1833 the civil war broke out between the supporters of Isabella II of Spain and the Carlists, the latter of whom he joined. He took Valencia in 1837, surprised Morella in 1839, was created count of Morella by Don Carlos in 1839, was driven across the French frontier in 1840, instigated an unsuccessful Carlist rebellion in the period 1848–49, and recognized Alfonso XII as king of Spain in 1875.

Cabrera Bobadilla Cerda y Mendoza (bō.BӒ.ᴛʜē′lyä ther′ᴛʜä ē men.dō′thä), **Luis Gerónimo Fernández de.** See **Chinchón,** Count of.

Cabrera y Bobadilla (ē bō.BӒ.ᴛʜē′lyä), **Diego López Pacheco.** See **López Pacheco Cabrera y Bobadilla, Diego.**

Cabrillo (kä.brē′lyō), **Juan Rodríguez.** [Portuguese, **João Rodrigues Cabrillo.**] b. in Portugal toward the end of the 15th century; d. on San Miguel Island, Calif., Jan. 3, 1543. Portuguese navigator in the service of Spain. He joined Pánfilo de Narváez's expedition (1520) to Mexico, and participated in Hernando Cortés's capture (1521) of Mexico City. In 1540 he sailed up the west coast of Mexico, and explored the coast of California in 1542 (including San Diego Bay and Santa Catalina Island); he also discovered the Santa Barbara Islands. On his death the command was taken by his chief pilot, who continued the exploration of the coast.

Cabrini (kä.brē′nē), Saint **Frances Xavier.** [Known as **"Mother Cabrini."**] b. at Sant'Angelo Lodigiano, Lombardy, Italy, July 15, 1850; d. at Chicago, Dec. 22, 1917. American Roman Catholic religious figure. She founded (c1874) the Institute of the Missionary Sisters of the Sacred Heart at Codogno, becoming (1877) its prioress and subsequently founding orphanages and schools elsewhere in Italy. She came (1889) to the U.S., where she established country orphanages, schools, and convents; she also founded similar institutions in South America, France, England, and Spain. She performed noteworthy services in founding hospitals, including the Columbus Hospital (1892) at New York and the Columbus Hospital at Chicago, and in 1909 became a naturalized U.S. citizen. Her charitable work, and the authentication of two miracles attributed to her, caused her to be pronounced venerable in 1933, and in 1938 she was beatified in ceremonies at the Vatican Basilica, thus becoming the first beata from the U.S. In 1946 she was canonized by Pope Pius XII, who in 1950 named her the patron saint of emigrants.

Cabu (kȧ.bü), **Marie Josèphe.** See **Cabel** or **Cabu, Marie Josèphe.**

Cabul (kä′bul, kạ.böl′). See **Kabul.**

Cabusto (kä.bös′tō), **Battle of.** Engagement (November, 1540) on the Black Warrior River in what is now Alabama between the local Indians (possibly Chickasaws) and the force under Hernando DeSoto. The Spanish defeated the Indians and then used Cabusto as a base for a march through the Tombigbee valley.

Cacafogo (kak.ạ.fō′gō). In John Fletcher's play *Rule a Wife and Have a Wife,* a cowardly, bullying, and rich usurer. He has been said to be a direct copy of Shakespeare's character Falstaff, but his lack of courage is the only resemblance.

Cacama (kä′kä.mä) or **Cacamatzin** (kä.kä.mä tsēn′) or **Caminatzin** (kä.mē.nä tsēn′) or **Cacumazin** (kä.kö mä-sēn′). d. 1520. Aztec Indian; nephew of Montezuma II. He became chief of Tezcuco in 1516. Montezuma sent him to Hernando Cortés in 1519, inviting the latter to Mexico. After Montezuma's seizure (1519) by Cortés, Cacama planned an armed resistance, but was arrested by emissaries of the monarch and brought captive to the Spaniards. He was killed on the *Noche Triste* (June 30–July 1, 1520, when the Spaniards were forced to fight their way out of the city).

Caçapava (kä.sa̤.pä′va̤), Baron of. Title of **Andrea, Francisco José Soares de.**

Caccamo (käk.kä′mō). Town and commune in SW Italy, on the island of Sicily, situated on the N coast of the island, ab. 23 mi. SE of Palermo. It has an old castle from the Norman period, and marble quarries. Pop. of commune, 8,897 (1936); of town, 6,408 (1936).

Caccini (kät.chē′nē), **Giulio.** [Called **Giulio Romano** (or **Romani**).] b. at Rome, c1550; d. at Florence, 1618. Italian singer and composer. He wrote, with Jacopo Peri, the musical drama *Dafne* (1594) and, with Ottavio Rinuccini, *Euridice* (1600). These early attempts to make music dramatic are considered the first examples of modern opera. He also composed a number of other works, among which is *Le Nuove musiche*, a collection of madrigals.

Cáceres (kä′thā.rās). Province in W Spain, bounded by Salamanca and Ávila on the N, Toledo on the E, Badajoz on the S, and Portugal on the W: part of the region of Estremadura. It comprises the middle part of the valley of the Tajo River and mountainous regions; the climate is dry and continental. Agriculture and livestock raising are the principal occupations. Capital, Cáceres; area, 7,705 sq. mi.; pop. 555,518 (1950).

Cáceres. [Ancient name, **Castra Caecilia.**] City in W Spain, the capital of the province of Cáceres, situated on the Cáceres River, ab. 150 mi. S of Madrid. Manufactures include cork and leather goods, cloth, and pottery; grain, wire, livestock, and wool are exported; phosphates are mined in the vicinity. The upper town, dominated by the Gothic Church of San Mateo, has medieval palaces, turrets, and massive walls, half Roman, half Arabic. The once famous monastery of the Jesuits is now a hospital. The city, of Roman origin, was held by the Moslems from 1142 to 1229. Pop. 39,392 (1940).

Cáceres (kä′sā.rās), **Andrés Avelino.** b. c1836; d. c1923. Peruvian general and statesman, twice president (1886–90, 1894–95) of Peru; father of Zoila Aurora Cáceres. He was a colonel and afterward general in the Chilean War (1879–83), and after the taking of Lima by Chile was second vice-president in the provisional government of Francisco García Calderón. Calderón having been seized by the Chileans, and the first vice-president driven into Bolivia, Cáceres became the constitutional chief of Peru. Rejecting the treaty of Ancón, he held out against the Chileans, and refused to acknowledge Manuel Iglesias, whom they had made president of Peru. Attempting to retake Lima (August, 1884), Cáceres was repulsed after a bloody street fight. Raising a larger force, he entered the city (Dec. 1, 1885), and persuaded Iglesias to refer the presidential question to a general election. This resulted in favor of Cáceres, who was inaugurated president of Peru (June 3, 1886). Succeeded by Remigio Morales Bermúdez (Aug. 10, 1890), General Cáceres soon after went to Europe as Peruvian minister (1890–94) to France and England. Reëlected president in 1894, he was deposed the following year by a coalition of the radical and antimilitaristic parties, which elected Nicolás de Piérola. Absent from Peru until 1903, he later served (1905–11) as minister to Italy.

Cáceres, Zoila Aurora. b. at Lima, Peru, 1877—. Peruvian writer and lecturer; daughter of Andrés Avelino Cáceres, one-time president of Peru. She completed her education at the Sorbonne, at Paris, and subsequently (1908) lectured there, as well as, in later years, at universities and learned institutions in Spain, at her native city, and in other places in South America. She became the leader of the Catholic women's movement in Peru. Among her books are *Mujeres de ayer y de hoy, España en la poesía del Perú, La Ciudad del sol, La Princesa Sumática, Mi vida con Gomes Carillo,* and *El Arte pictórico en el Perú.*

Cachan (kå.shän). Town in N France, in the department of Seine, situated S of Paris, between Arceuil and Bourg-la-Reine. A suburb of Paris, it has remnants of a Roman aqueduct. 15,156 (1946).

Cachar (kä.chär′). District in Assam, Union of India, ab. 350 mi. NE of Calcutta: jute, timber products, rice, and tea. Area, 3,769 sq. mi.; pop. 641,181 (1941).

Cache (kash). River in NE Arkansas, originating in extreme SE Missouri, and flowing generally S across the level flood plain to join the White River at Newport, Ark. Length, ab. 200 mi.

Cacheu (kä.shā′ö). [Also, **Cacheo.**] Town in W Africa, a seaport in Portuguese Guinea, situated near the coast toward the NW border of the country. Pop. ab. 650.

Cachibo (kä.shē′bō). See **Cashibo.**

Cachin (kå.shaṅ), **Marcel.** b. at Paimpol, Côtes-du-Nord, France, Sept. 20, 1869—. French Communist political leader, editor (1918 *et seq.*) of *L'Humanité.* After joining (1891) the socialist movement, he took charge (1905) of its propaganda. A member (1914–32) of the Chamber of Deputies, he was elected a senator in 1935, and served as a deputy to the Constituent Assemblies (1945–46) and the National Assembly (1946) under the Fourth Republic. A Socialist delegate to Moscow in 1919, he helped form the French Communist Party at the Tours Socialist congress (1920), and was active in the Communist International (1922 *et seq.*). He was repeatedly imprisoned while a deputy, once for opposition to the Ruhr occupation (1923), again for opposition to the Riff war (1927–28), and finally for opposing French participation in World War II.

Cachoeira (kä.shō.ā′ra̤). City in E Brazil, in the state of Bahia, on the Paraguassú River. 11,088 (1950).

Cachoeira. City in S Brazil, in the state of Rio Grande do Sul. 23,827 (1950).

Cachoeiro do Itapemirim (kä.shwā′rö dö ē.tä″pe̤.mē-rēṅ′). [Also, **Cachoeiro.**] City in E Brazil, in the state of Espírito Santo. 24,611 (1950).

Caciquismo (kä.sē.kēz′mō). Spanish term translatable into English as "Bossism." Derived from the Indian name for tribal chieftains, the term is applied in Spain to local political bosses who exercise broad powers over the population in areas under their control. Under the constitutional regime of 1876, the corruption of the central government was spread throughout the nation by these local *caciques*, usually rural property-owners or estate-supervisors who managed the votes of their workers and in return received even greater control by obtaining the appointment of sympathetic government officials and the patronage of the local judge.

Cackchiquel (käk.chē.kel′). See **Cakchiquel.**

Cacons (kå.kôṅ). See **Colliberts.**

Cacos (kä′kōs). [Eng. trans., "*Pickpockets.*"] Nickname given to a political party of Guatemala which originated in 1820. Its members favored complete separation from Spain, and a republican form of government with essential equality to all. This was the germ of the Servile Party of later years. Their opponents, called Bacos or Gazistas, were opposed to equality. Cacos was also the name of a political party in Haiti.

Cacumazin (kä.kö.mä.sēn′). See **Cacama.**

Cacus (kā′kus). In Roman mythology, a giant and son of Vulcan, living near the spot on which Rome was built. He stole from Hercules some of the cattle of Geryon, dragging them backward into his cave under the Aventine, so that their footprints would not show the direction in which they had gone; but Hercules found them by their lowing, and slew the thief.

Cadalso Vázquez (kä.ᴛʜäl′sō väth′keth), **José de.** b. at Cádiz, Spain, Oct. 8, 1741; d. at Gibraltar, Feb. 27, 1782. Spanish poet, killed at the siege of Gibraltar. His works include the tragedy *Sancho Garcia* (1771), the satire *Los Eruditos a la violeta* (1772), *Poesías* (1773), *Cartas marruecas* (1793), and *Noches lugubres* (1798).

Cada Mosto or **Ca Da Mosto** (kä.dä.mōs′tō), **Alvise** (or **Luigi**) **da.** b. at Venice, Italy, c1432; d. there, c1480. Italian navigator. In the service of Prince Henry of Portugal, he explored the coast of Africa as far as the Gambia from 1455 to 1456, discovering the Cape Verde Islands in the latter year. Author of *El Libro de la prima navigazione per oceano alle terre de' Nigri de la Bassa Etiopia* (1507).

Cadbury (kad′bėr.i), **Elizabeth Mary.** [Maiden name, **Taylor.**] b. at London, 1858; d. at Birmingham, England, Dec. 4, 1951. English social worker; wife of George Cadbury. She was a city councilor (1919–24) of King's

Norton Ward, president of the National Union of Women Workers, a member of numerous educational and social committees, and the author of publications on education, peace, housing, and social problems.

Cadbury, George. b. at Edgbaston, Birmingham, England, 1839; d. Oct. 24, 1922. English manufacturer and philanthropist, founder of the Bournville model village; husband of Elizabeth Mary Cadbury. He was co-owner of a cocoa and chocolate factory at Birmingham.

Caddee (kä.dā'). Name given to a church league (*Gotteshaus-Bund*) formed in the canton of Graubünden, Switzerland, in 1396, to oppose internal misgovernment.

Caddo (kad'ō). Loose confederacy of a number of North American Indian tribes, all speaking closely related languages of the Caddoan family, that formerly inhabited NW Louisiana and E Texas. Remnants of these tribes are now on the Quapaw reservation, in Oklahoma.

Caddoan (kad'ō.ạn). Culture of the protohistoric Indians of N Texas, SE Oklahoma, NW Louisiana, and SW Arkansas. These Indians practiced agriculture, had temple mounds, made elaborately engraved pottery vessels, and possessed the Southern Cult, some or all of which they may have obtained from Mesoamerica via the plains of C and S Texas. They are believed to have transmitted the custom of erecting temple mounds, in particular, to their Middle Mississippi neighbors to the north and east.

Caddoan. North American Indian language family formerly distributed in NW Louisiana, E Texas, S Oklahoma, and discontinously also in N Kansas and S Nebraska.

Cade (kād), **John.** [Called **Jack Cade.**] b. probably in Ireland; killed near Heathfield, Sussex, England, July 12, 1450. English rebel, the leader in Cade's Rebellion, a rising chiefly of Kentishmen, in May and June, 1450. The rebels defeated the royal forces at Sevenoaks on June 27, and entered London on July 2. On July 3, they killed Henry IV's lord chamberlain, James Fiennes, Baron of Saye and Sele, but within a few days their rebellion was suppressed. Cade is said to have been regarded by his cohorts as a cousin of the Duke of York. He is introduced by Shakespeare in the second part of *Henry VI* as a reckless, ferocious, and vulgarly important rebel.

Cadell (kad'ẹl), **Robert.** b. at Cockenzie, East Lothian, Scotland, Dec. 16, 1788; d. at Edinburgh, Jan. 20, 1849. Scottish publisher and bookseller. He was a partner of Archibald Constable from 1811 until the failure of the firm, and a business associate and friend of Sir Walter Scott. He became the publisher of Scott's works in 1826.

Cadenus (kạ.dē'nus). Name by which Jonathan Swift calls himself in his poem *Cadenus and Vanessa* (1726). The name is an anagram of *decanus* (dean), his official title.

Cadenus and Vanessa (vạ.nes'ạ). Poem by Jonathan Swift. Considered one of Swift's best poems, it was written in 1712 or 1713 to cure Esther Vanhomrigh of a passion for Swift, and appeared in 1726, three years after her death.

Cadereita (kä.ᴛʜā.rā'tä), Marquis of. Title of **Díaz de Armendaris, Lope.**

Cader Idris (kad'ėr id'ris). Mountain in N Wales, in Merionethshire, ab. 3 mi. SW of Dolgelley. It is noted for its extensive view. 2,927 ft.

Caderousse (kȧd.rös). Character in *The Count of Monte Cristo* (*Le Comte de Monte Cristo*), novel by the elder Alexandre Dumas.

Cadesia (kạ.dē'zhạ). [Also: **Kadesia, Kadisiya, Qadisiya.**] Place in S central Iraq, near Al Kufa. Here, in 637 A.D., the Saracens defeated the Persians (120,000).

Cade's Rebellion (kādz). See under **Cade, John.**

Cadijah (kä.dē'jạ). See **Kadijah.**

Cadillac (kad'i.lak). City in N Lower Michigan, near Lake Mitchell, county seat of Wexford County. A resort community, it also manufactures automobile tires, potato flour, and wood products. It was named for Antoine de la Mothe Cadillac. Annual outboard-motor races and a winter sports carnival are held here. 10,425 (1950).

Cadillac (kad'i.lak; French, kȧ.dē.yȧk), Sieur **Antoine de la Mothe.** b. in Gascony, France, c1656; d. there, Oct. 18, 1730. French soldier, explorer, and colonial official, notable as the founder of Detroit, Mich., and governor of the French colony of Louisiana. An officer in the French army, and having already lived (1683–89) in America, he secured (1694) from Frontenac command of the vital French post at Mackinac in the western regions. He returned (1699) to France, where he outlined his scheme for establishing a post on the Detroit River to safeguard the area's fur trade against the British. Setting out in 1701 as a lieutenant of the French king and the head of a company enjoying the trade monopoly, he led a band of colonists in the founding of Detroit. In 1704 he was arrested, partly as a result of having antagonized the Jesuits in New France, but was acquitted after a trial at Quebec. He was recalled from Detroit in 1711, and assigned to the governorship of Louisiana, where he arrived in 1713. He was recalled to France in 1716 after years of dissatisfaction and disappointment, and is supposed to have been imprisoned for a short time in the Bastille.

Cadillac Mountain. [Also, **Green Mountain.**] Culminating summit of Mount Desert, Maine, in the E part of the island, in Acadia National Park. 1,532 ft.

Cadiz (kad'iz). Village in E Ohio, county seat of Harrison County, in a region that produces oil, coal, and gas. Sheep and cattle are raised in the vicinity. It was the birthplace of Edwin M. Stanton and of Clark Gable. Laid out in 1803, it became county seat in 1830. Pop. 3,020 (1950).

Cadiz (kä'dēs). Town on the N coast of Negros Occidental province, Negros island, in the Philippines. 9,195 (1948).

Cádiz (kạ.diz', kā'diz; Spanish, kä'ᴛʜēth). Province in S Spain, bounded by Sevilla on the N, Málaga on the E, the Mediterranean Sea on the SE, the British territory of Gibraltar and the Strait of Gibraltar on the S, the Atlantic Ocean on the SW, and Huelva on the W: part of the region of Andalusia. The province comprises hilly regions to the E, fertile agricultural districts in the center, and swampy flatlands around the lower Guadalquivir River to the W. The summers are long and hot. This region was the gateway for the Arabic invasion of Spain. Capital, Cádiz; area, 2,827 sq. mi.; pop. 699,372 (1950).

Cádiz. [Phoenician, **Gadir**; ancient Greek, **Gadeira;** Latin, **Gades**; English, formerly, **Cales.**] City in SW Spain, the capital of the province of Cádiz, situated on a narrow neck of land on the Atlantic Ocean and the Bay of Cádiz, ab. 60 mi. SW of Seville: important commercial center and seaport. 99,910 (1950).

Commerce and Industry. The port of Cádiz, used by a number of steamship lines, exports canned fish, sea salt, cork, wine, citrus fruits, and olive oil; imports include coal, textiles, and machinery. Industry is confined to the canning of fish, tobacco manufacture, and various foodstuff industries. The shipyards and arsenals of La Caracca are located behind the shallow Bay of Puntales.

Chief Buildings. The city, surrounded on three sides by water, is protected by high walls and old fortifications; it has two cathedrals, the monastery of San Francisco, and a theater; most of the buildings are of the 16th, 17th, and 18th centuries. Cádiz is the seat of a bishopric, and of the medical faculty of the university of Seville; it has a clerical seminary, libraries, and a museum.

History. One of the oldest cities of Spain, Cádiz was founded (as Gadir) c1100 B.C. by the Phoenicians, serving in the exchange of Oriental merchandise for Spanish tin and silver. After the fall of the Phoenician capital at Tyre, Cádiz became one of the strongholds of the Carthaginian trade with Africa and England; after the fall of Carthage, it became (as Gades) a Roman town. In 711 A.D. it was conquered by the Arabs, in 1262 by Castile. Cádiz flourished in the period of discovery as one of the chief ports of embarkation for the West Indies; it held the monopoly of trade with the Spanish colonies in America from 1509 to 1778. It was sacked by the British under Robert Devereux, 2nd Earl of Essex, in 1596, and besieged by the French in the period 1810–12. During the Peninsular War, it was the seat of the Central Junta; here the Cortes adopted the Constitution of March 18, 1812. The revolution of 1820, aiming at the renewal of this constitution, started here. In the Spanish Civil War, Cádiz fell quickly into the hands of the Nationalists in 1936 and served as port of entry for reënforcements from Spanish Morocco.

Cadman (kad'mạn), **Charles Wakefield.** b. at Johnstown, Pa., Dec. 24, 1881; d. 1946. American composer, noted for his use, in operatic and other works, of American Indian melodies. He served as music critic (1908–10) on the Pittsburgh *Dispatch*, as organist in several churches at Pittsburgh, and as conductor of the Pittsburgh Male Chorus. The influence of his studies of the vocal and flute music of North American Indian tribes is evident in *Four Indian Songs* (1909), the operas *Shanewis* (1918), *The Land of the Misty Water*, and *The Garden of Death*, and the orchestral *Thunderbird Suite*. He was composer also of the operas *The Garden of Mystery* (1915), *A Witch of Salem* (1924), and *The Willow Tree* (1925); the cantata *The Vision of Sir Launfal* (1910); sequences for mixed voices *The Morning of the Year* and *The Sunset Trail*, and the song cycle *White Enchantment;* suites for orchestra, piano, and strings; and a large number of songs, one of the most popular of which is *From the Land of the Sky-blue Water*.

Cadman, Samuel Parkes. b. at Wellington, England, Dec. 18, 1864; d. at Plattsburg, N.Y., July 12, 1936. American Congregationalist clergyman and author. He was educated at Wesleyan College, Richmond, Surrey, England, and came to the U.S. in 1890. His pastorates were at the Metropolitan Temple (1895–1901) at New York and the Central Congregational Church (1901–36) at Brooklyn, N.Y. As president (1924–28) of the Federal Council of Churches of Christ in America, he was the first radio minister (1928 *et seq.*). His writings include *William Owen, A Biography* (1912), *Ambassadors of God* (1920), *Christianity and the State* (1924), *The Lure of London* (1925), *Imagination and Religion* (1926), *Every Day Questions and Answers* (1930), *The Parables of Jesus* (1931), and *The Pursuit of Happiness* (1935).

Cadmeia (kad.mē′ạ). In ancient times, the citadel or acropolis of Thebes in Boeotia, Greece, named from its mythical founder, the hero Cadmus. In modern times, two Frankish towers of some size remained standing on the summit of the low hill. The only remains of the ancient fortifications consist of a stretch of ruined Cyclopean wall on the north side, and fragments of more recent walls on the southeastern slope.

Cadmeians (kad.mē′ạnz). Graeco-Phoenicians (their name merely signifying "the Easterns") who in pre-Trojan times occupied the country which was afterwards called Boeotia. Their name may have been derived from the legendary figure of Cadmus, whose name means "man of the East."

Cadmus (kad′mus). In Greek legend, a son of Agenor, king of Phoenicia, and Telephassa. He was the reputed founder of Thebes in Boeotia, and the introducer of the letters of the Greek alphabet. The particular legendary episode for which he is now probably best known is that which has him sowing the teeth of a dragon, which he had killed, and from each of which there immediately grew a warrior, fully armed and accoutered. It was these men who were the ancestors of the people of Thebes. However, because the dragon had been sacred to Ares, the god of war, the descendants of Cadmus himself were involved by Ares, in punishment for Cadmus's deed, in various tragedies.

Cadmus, Paul. b. at New York, Dec. 17, 1904—. American realistic painter and etcher, whose satiric paintings of the American scene, especially of New York, have gained widespread attention. He was educated at the National Academy of Design and the Art Students League of New York, then spent two years (1931–33) in Europe. His work, which is characterized by minute rendering of detail and texture, has been widely exhibited in the U.S., Canada, and England; in 1933 his painting *The Fleet's In* was criticized by the U.S. Navy, creating, at the time, a considerable furor. The Museum of Modern Art, the Whitney Museum of American Art, and the Metropolitan Museum of Art, at New York, the Art Institute of Chicago, Cranbrook Academy, the Library of Congress, and other museums and galleries have collected his works, which include *Coney Island, Greenwich Village Cafeteria, Sailors and Floosies, Gilding the Acrobats,* and *Hinky Dinky Parley Voo.*

Cadmus of Miletus (mī.lē′tus). fl. probably in the middle of the 6th century B.C. Greek historian, the earliest historian of whom we have any definite information. He wrote a history, in four books, of Ionia in the early period, and of the founding of Miletus. He also speculated on the cause of the periodical floods of the Nile.

Cadogan (kạ.dug′ạn), **Charles.** [Title, 2nd Baron **Cadogan.**] b. 1691; d. Sept. 24, 1776. Irish military officer; brother of William Cadogan (1675–1726), and an ancestor of George Henry Cadogan (1840–1915). Having entered (1706) the army in the Coldstream Guards, he served in some of Marlborough's later campaigns and in 1715 fought in Scotland; he also sat in several parliaments.

Cadogan, George Henry. [Title, 5th Earl **Cadogan.**] b. at Durham, England, May 9, 1840; d. at London, March 6, 1915. English statesman; in a later generation of the same family as Charles Cadogan (1691–1776) and William Cadogan (1675–1726). He served as undersecretary (1875) of state for war, undersecretary (1878) for the colonies, lord privy seal (1886–92), and lord lieutenant (1895–1902) of Ireland.

Cadogan, William. [Title, 1st Earl **Cadogan.**] b. 1675; d. July 17, 1726. Irish diplomat and military officer; brother of Charles Cadogan (1691–1776), and an ancestor of George Henry Cadogan (1840–1915). While quartermaster general (1701–11) to Marlborough, he conducted the allied march into Bavaria, ending with the Blenheim victory (Aug. 13, 1704). He commanded the advance guard in operations leading up to the battle of Oudenarde (July 11, 1708). He was shot in the neck during the battle of Mons. When the duke of Ormonde became commander of the army, Cadogan lost (1712) his rank, and was an exile (1712 *et seq.*) in the Netherlands; before the death of Queen Anne, he returned to London where he was reinstated (1714) as a lieutenant general. He served as lieutenant of the ordnance (1714–18), and was appointed master of the king's robes. Sent as envoy extraordinary and minister plenipotentiary to the States General of Holland, he signed (Nov. 15, 1715) at The Hague the third barrier treaty between England, Holland, and Germany, recognizing the Hanoverian succession to the British crown. He put down a Scottish insurrection (1715–16) with a force of 6,000 Dutch troops, and was appointed (July 12, 1717) a general. At Vienna, he arranged (1720) the terms of the Spanish accession, known as the Quadruple Alliance. Upon the death of Marlborough, he was made (1722) commander in chief of the army and master-general of the ordnance.

Cadoor (kạ.dör′). See **Kadur.**

Cadore (kä.dôr), Duc **de.** See **Champagny.**

Cadorna (kä.dōr′nä), Count **Carlo.** b. 1809; d. 1891. Italian statesman and author; brother of Raffaele Cadorna. Becoming a member of the chamber of deputies of Sardinia in 1848, he was president of that body (1850–55), also serving as minister of education (1848–49). After proclamation of the kingdom of Italy, he was minister of the interior (1868), ambassador to London (1869), and president of the council of state (1875). He was the author of *La Politica di Cavour nelle relazioni fra la chiesa e lo stato* (1882) and of *Dell'espansione coloniale dell'Italia,* (1885).

Cadorna, Luigi. b. at Pallanza, Italy, Sept. 4, 1850; d. at Bordighera, Italy, Dec. 23, 1928. Italian soldier; son of Raffaele Cadorna. In his military career he advanced from second lieutenant of artillery (1868) to service (1896) on the general staff, to commander (1910) of the seventh army corps at Genoa, and to lieutenant general (1911). Appointed (1914) Italian chief of staff, he was commander in chief (1915–17) of the Italian armies during the period that saw the Italian defeat on the Isonzo, in Gorizia. Relieved (Nov. 8, 1917) of his command in favor of Armando Diaz, he was sent to Versailles on the Interallied Military Committee. He was for many years a senator, and was restored to high military rank in 1924, when Mussolini gave him the title of marshal. He was the author of *Il Generale Raffaele Cadorna nel Risorgimento Italiano* (1903) and *La Guerra alla Fronte Italiana,* (2 vols., 1921).

Cadorna, Raffaele. b. at Milan, Italy, 1815; d. at Turin, Italy, Feb. 6, 1897. Italian general; brother of Carlo Cadorna and father of Luigi Cadorna. He commanded the troops of Victor Emmanuel II in the occupation of the States of the Church in 1870, and occupied Civitavecchia (Sept. 16, 1870) and Rome (Sept. 20, 1870). He retired in 1877.

Cà d'Oro (kä′ dō′rō). [Also, **Casa d'Oro.**] Medieval palace at Venice, originally built in the 14th century and later restored. It was built in three stories, divided vertically into two divisions. The left-hand division has in the lowest story five open arches, the middle one round, and in the two upper ones Gothic foliated arcades set between larger arches. The right-hand division consists of ornamented paneling, also set between decorated arches. Above there was set a picturesque cresting in marble. Although many of its decorative details are Gothic, the building retains the strong Byzantine flavor of many Venetian structures of this and earlier periods, in plan, flatness of wall surfaces, and the façade of polychrome marble which was originally also gilded, whence the name ("house of gold").

Cadoudal (kȧ.dö.dȧl), **Georges.** b. near Auray, Morbihan, France, Jan. 1, 1771; guillotined at Paris, June 25, 1804. French Chouan partisan and royalist conspirator, leader of the rising of 1799 against the first French Republic. He was implicated with Charles Pichegru in 1803 in a conspiracy (supported by the English) against Napoleon. Cadoudal's motives in this were certainly not venal and, in his eyes, not even anti-French: he simply sought to restore the Bourbon dynasty to what he believed to be their rightful position as rulers of France. He was willing to take help from England, or anyone else, in accomplishing this end. However, the plot was discovered and Cadoudal, with the other chief conspirators, was executed.

Cadres sociaux de la mémoire (kȧdr so.syō dẹ lȧ māmwȧr), **Les.** Social psychological monograph (1925) by the French social psychologist Maurice Halbwachs (1877–1945). It challenges the proposition that memory is distinctly an individual phenomenon. The author held that memory is a social process, and that individual memories exist only as part of collective memories.

Cadrilater (kad.ri.lā'tėr). See under **Dobruja.**

Cadsand (kät.sänt'). [Also, **Kadzand.**] Village in SW Netherlands, in the province of Zeeland, situated at the mouth of the Schelde River, ab. 14 mi. NE of Bruges, Belgium. Here in 1337 the English defeated the Count of Flanders.

Cadurcum (kạ.dėr'kum). A Latin name of **Cahors.**

Cadwal (kad'wạl). In Shakespeare's *Cymbeline*, the name under which Arviragus (actually the son of Cymbeline himself) is raised from infancy. As Cadwal, Arviragus believes himself to be the son of Belarius.

Cadwalader (kad.wol'ạ.dėr). See also **Caedwalla.**

Cadwalader or **Cadwallader.** [Called **"The Blessed."**] d. c664. British king. He was the son of Caedwalla, king of Gwynedd (North Wales), whom he succeeded in 634.

Cadwalader or **Cadwallader.** d. 1172. Welsh prince. A son of Gruffydd, king of Gwynedd (North Wales), he was threatened by his brother Owain and fled to Ireland. Raising an army among the Danes of Ireland, he returned to Wales, but before hostilities could occur, became reconciled with Owain. However, this enraged the Danes, who seized Cadwaladr and put out his eyes. He made his way to England, where Henry II befriended him and in 1159 restored him to his lands.

Cadwalader, John. b. at Philadelphia, in January, 1742; d. Feb. 10, 1786. American Revolutionary soldier; son of Thomas Cadwalader (c1708–99). Appointed (Dec. 25, 1776) a brigadier general of the Pennsylvania militia, he fought at Princeton, Brandywine, Germantown, and in the Monmouth campaign. During the period (1777–78) of the Conway Cabal, his pro-Washington convictions led to the wounding of Conway in a duel which was followed by collapse of the entire scheme against George Washington.

Cadwalader, Thomas. b. c1708; d. at Trenton, N.J., Nov. 14, 1799. American surgeon; father of John Cadwalader (1742–86). He practiced medicine in Pennsylvania and New Jersey. With Benjamin Franklin, he was one of the founders (1731) of the Philadelphia Library. In 1751 he was elected a trustee of what is now the University of Pennsylvania. He was the author of *An Essay on the West-India Dry-Gripes*, published (1745) by Franklin.

Cadwallader (kad.wol'ạ.dėr). In Tobias Smollett's *Peregrine Pickle*, a misanthropic character.

Cadwallader. Character in Samuel Foote's play *The Author.* This play was stopped by the lord chamberlain at the request of a Mr. Aprice, a friend of Foote, who was imitated and ridiculed in this part, especially in a habit he had of sucking his wrist as he talked.

Cadwallader, Rev. Mr. In George Eliot's novel *Middlemarch,* the rector of the parish. He exasperates his wife, a clever, keen, epigrammatic woman, by his good temper.

Cadwallader Crabtree. See **Crabtree, Cadwallader.**

Cadwallon (kad.wol'ọn). See also **Caedwalla.**

Cadwallon. In Sir Walter Scott's novel *The Betrothed,* a minstrel of Gwenwyn. He disguises himself as Renault Vidal to prosecute a revenge, for which he is executed.

Cady (kā'di), **Hamilton Perkins.** b. at Camden, Kan., May 2, 1874; d. 1943. American chemist. From 1899 to 1905 he was assistant professor of chemistry at the University of Kansas, and from 1911 to 1940, professor and chairman of the chemistry department at that university. He was one of the world's foremost authorities on helium and other constituents of natural gas. Among his books are *A Laboratory Guide to the Study of Qualitative Analysis* (1901), *The Principles of Inorganic Chemistry* (1916), and *General Chemistry* (1916).

Cady, Josiah Cleveland. b. at Providence, R.I., 1837; d. April 17, 1919. American architect. He designed buildings for Yale and Wesleyan universities and Trinity and Williams colleges, and for the New York Skin and Cancer Hospital, the Bellevue Medical College, the Metropolitan Opera House, and the American Museum of Natural History (all at New York). He served as president of the New York Skin and Cancer Hospital, a governor of the Presbyterian Hospital, a trustee of Berea College, and vice-president of the New York City Mission.

Cadzow Oaks (kad'zō). See under **Hamilton,** Scotland.

Caecilia gens (sẹ.sil'i.ạ jenz). In ancient Rome, a plebeian clan or house whose family names under the republic were Bassus, Denter, Metellus, Niger, Pinna, and Rufus.

Caecilius (sẹ.sil'i.us, -sil'yus). [Surnamed **Calactinus** and, erroneously, **Callantianus;** original name, **Archagathus.**] fl. 1st century A.D. Hellenistic scholar of Calacte in Sicily (whence his surname), naturalized at Rome, where he took the name of his patron, one of the Metelli. He enjoyed a very high repute at Rome in the time of Cicero and Augustus, but his numerous works are now lost, with the exception of a few fragments.

Caecilius Statius (stā'shi.us, -shus). [Also, **Statius Caecilius.**] d. c168 B.C. Roman comic poet, a member by birth of the Celtic tribe of the Insubrians, brought as a prisoner to Rome c200 B.C. His comedies were adaptations of Attic originals. Fragments of them are extant (edited by Ribbeck, 1873).

Caecus (sē'kus). See **Claudius, Appius.**

Caedmon (kad'mọn). [Also, **Cedmon.**] fl. c670. English poet, the reputed author of metrical paraphrases of the Old Testament. He was the earliest Christian poet in the history of English letters. He became late in life an inmate of the monastery at Whitby, under the abbess Hild. According to the account given by Bede in the *Ecclesiastical History,* he was an unlearned man, especially lacking in poetical talent, until he was commanded in a dream to sing of "the beginning of created things." A nine-line poem, preserved in several manuscripts, is recognized as the first product of Caedmon's versification. The miraculous gift thus bestowed upon him was fostered by Hild, and he is thought to have produced metrical paraphrases of Genesis and other parts of the Bible, none of which are, however, extant. Certain versions of Biblical fragments, at one time attributed to Caedmon, have been proven to be of later date. He is generally regarded as a saint.

Caedwalla (kad.wol'ạ). [Also: **Cadwalader, Cadwallon.**] d. 634. British king of Gwynedd, which was probably coextensive with North Wales. He invaded Northumbria in 629, but was repulsed by Edwin near Morpeth. In 633, in alliance with Penda, king of the Mercians, he totally defeated the Northumbrians at Heathfield, near Doncaster, Edwin and his son Osfrid being among the slain. He was defeated by Oswald, the nephew of Edwin, at the battle of Hevenfelth, on the Deniseburn, and was killed during the flight of his forces from the field of battle.

Caelia (or **Coelia**) **gens** (sē'li.ạ jenz). In ancient Rome, a plebeian clan or house whose family names were Caldus and Rufus. The first member of this gens who obtained the consulship was C. Caelius Caldus, in 94 B.C.

Caelian Hill (sē′li.ạn). [Latin, **Caelius Mons.**] Southeastern hill of the group of Seven Hills of ancient Rome, adjoining the Palatine, and between the Aventine and the Esquiline. The Lateran lies on its widely extending eastern slope.

Caelica (sē′li.kạ). See **Coelica.**

Caelius (sē′li.us). [Full name, **Marcus Caelius Rufus.**] b. at Puteoli, Italy, May 2, 82 B.C.; d. 48 B.C. Roman politician, a friend and correspondent of Cicero. It is said that his education was supervised by Crassus and Cicero, and he was an especially close friend of the latter during the great orator's public career. He was also for a time intimate with Catiline, but according to Cicero was not involved in the latter's conspiracy, and in fact he exposed the part played by C. Antonius in that intrigue. In 56 B.C. his mistress Clodia charged him with an attempt on her life, but he was acquitted with the aid of Cicero, whose oration in his defense, *Pro Caelio*, is one of the latter's most famous efforts. A tribune in 52 and an aedile in 50 B.C., Caelius supported Julius Caesar against Pompey in 49. Caesar appointed him peregrine praetor (that is, judge of legal actions between persons not Roman citizens), but whether from a resentful feeling that this reward was insufficient to his services, or from impatience with what he considered the slow pace of Caesar's measures to cancel debts, Caelius joined in a foredoomed conspiracy against Caesar's rising power and in 48 B.C. was killed by soldiers whom he was attempting to win over to his rebellious plans.

Caelius Aurelianus (ô.rē.li.ā′nus). See **Aurelianus, Caelius.**

Caelius Mons (monz). Latin name of the **Caelian Hill.**

Caen (käṅ). City in NW France, the capital of the department of Calvados, situated on the Orne River, near the Normandy coast, with which it is connected by a canal, between Lisieux and Bayeux. Caen has important metallurgical industries, including blast furnaces, potteries of long-established standing, and other industries. The port specializes in the handling of coal and iron shipments. It was fiercely besieged in the first days of the Normandy invasion in the summer of 1944, and many of its ancient architectural treasures were laid in ruins. Among the buildings completely or largely destroyed are the Church of Saint Gilles, dating from the 11th, 12th, and 13th centuries; the spire of the Church of Saint Pierre, regarded as the most perfect Gothic spire in the region; the castle, only remains of the extensive fortifications begun by William the Conqueror; the Escoville and Than mansions, fine examples of French Renaissance architecture; the city hall, a baroque building from the 18th century, and many others. 51,445 (1946).

Caepio (sē′pi.ō), **Quintus Servilius.** fl. c100 B.C. Roman consul in 106 B.C. As proconsul in Gaul (105), he was defeated with Mallius by the Cimbri.

Caere (sē′rē). [Earlier name, **Agylla.**] In ancient geography, a city in Etruria, Italy, situated ab. 25 mi. NW of Rome. Its site is occupied by the modern village of Cerveteri, noted for Etruscan ruins.

Caer Glowe (kär′ glō′ẹ). Ancient British name of **Gloucester,** England.

Caer Gwent (kär gwent). Ancient British name of **Winchester,** England.

Caer-Gybi (kīr.gi′bi). Welsh name of **Holyhead.**

Caerleon (kär.lē′ọn). [Latin, **Isca** or **Isca Silurum.**] Urban district in W England, in Monmouthshire, situated on the river Usk, ab. 3 mi. NE of Newport. It was an important city in the Roman period, being the headquarters of the second Augustan Legion, and known for its theater, temples, and palaces; part of the massive walls remain. Caerleon has a museum containing many interesting Roman relics found in the vicinity. It is one of several places identified as the traditional seat (Camelot) of King Arthur's court. 4,711 (1951).

Caerleon or **Caerlleon** (kär.lē′ọn). Welsh name of **Chester,** England.

Caer Luel (kär lö′ẹl). See **Carlisle,** England.

Caermarthen (kär.mär′ᴛʜẹn). See **Carmarthen.**

Caermarthenshire (kär.mär′ᴛʜẹn.shir). See **Carmarthenshire.**

Caernarvon (kär.när′vọn). [Also, **Carnarvon.**] Municipal borough and seaport in N Wales, the county seat of Caernarvonshire, situated at the mouth of the river Seiont, on Menai Strait, ab. 9 mi. SW of Bangor, ab. 248 mi. NW of London by rail: exports slate. It is near the site of the Roman station Segontium, and contains Caernarvon Castle, one of the greatest of surviving medieval strongholds, founded by Edward I toward the end of the 13th century. Its battlemented towers are polygonal, each surmounted by a slender turret of similar form. The castle has been in part restored, and contains some public offices. It was in this castle, in 1301, that Edward I made his son (who had been born there in 1284 and was later to be Edward II of England) the "Prince of Wales." The act was a gesture of conciliation toward the Welsh, who were still restive under an English king (despite their defeat in 1282, and the formal establishment of English rule in 1284, great numbers of Welshmen were still convinced that they not only should, but presently would, expel the English invaders). It was because of this gesture, however, that the heir to the English throne has ever since been known as the Prince of Wales. In addition to Caernarvon Castle, some of the old town walls remain. The town holds a monthly fair. 9,255 (1951).

Caernarvon Bay. [Also, **Carnarvon Bay.**] Large bay in N Wales, forming an inlet of the Irish Sea, lying between Anglesey and Caernarvonshire. Width at entrance, ab. 34 mi.

Caernarvonshire (kär.när′vọn.shir). [Also: **Caernarvon, Carnarvonshire.**] Maritime county in N Wales. It is bounded on the N by Beaumaris Bay (an inlet of the Irish Sea) and by the Irish Sea itself, on the E by Denbighshire, on the S by Merionethshire and Cardigan Bay, and on the W by Caernarvon Bay and the Menai Strait, across which is the island and county of Anglesey. Its surface is mountainous, as it contains the Snowdon range, rising to 3,560 ft., the highest point in England and Wales. Caernarvonshire has the largest slate quarries in the world, and this product takes first place among its exports. Lead, zinc, and ochre are mined and granite is quarried. The county formerly also produced manganese ore, but this industry has declined. Caernarvon is the county seat; area of administrative county, ab. 569 sq. mi.; pop. of administrative county, 124,074 (1951).

Caerphilly (kär.fil′i). Urban district and market town in S Wales, in Glamorganshire, ab. 7 mi. N of Cardiff, ab. 145 mi. W of London by rail. It has the ruins of Caerphilly Castle, the largest and most remarkable Edwardian castle in Wales. The district, in a coal-mining region and well known for its cheeses, is developing rapidly. 35,194 (1951).

Caerularius or **Cerularius** (sir.ů.lăr′i.us, ser′-, -ų̇.lăr′-), **Michael.** fl. in the middle of the 11th century. Patriarch of Constantinople. By reviving and exacerbating certain disputes between the Greek and the Roman churches, concerning ritualistic questions and especially matters connected with the celebration of the Eucharist, he brought to a head the schism between Eastern Orthodox and Roman Catholic Christianity. He was excommunicated by Pope Leo IX in 1054, and in 1059 he was banished from Constantinople by the emperor Isaac I, and died in exile.

Caer Went (kär went). Ancient name of **Winchester,** England.

Caesalpinus (ses.al.pī′nus), **Andreas.** [Latinized name of **Andrea Cesalpino.**] b. at Arezzo, Italy, June 6, 1519; d. Feb. 23, 1603. Italian physician, physiologist, and botanist, personal physician to Pope Clement VIII. He was, as a scientist, in some respects far ahead of his time (it is known, for instance, that he understood the circulation of the blood). However, his most notable achievement, contained in his work *De Plantis*, was to outline the first truly systematic scheme of botanical classification, which Linnaeus later praised and found useful.

Caesar (sē′zạr). In ancient Rome, a patrician family of the Julian gens, of which the origin was fancifully traced to a legendary Julius, son of Aeneas. The first Caesar actually to be noted in the annals was Sextus Julius, who was a praetor in 208 B.C. Lucius Julius Caesar, consul in 90 B.C., had an important part in shaping Roman institutions by securing the enactment of the law granting Roman citizenship to such of the Italian allies as had not fought against Rome in the Social War or who had laid down their arms at once. Lucius Julius Caesar was killed in 87 B.C., during the civil war, and with him his brother Gaius Julius Caesar Strabo Vopisius, whom Cicero numbered among the Roman orators. A son of Lucius Julius Caesar, bearing the same name, served in Gaul under that other Gaius Julius Caesar (c100 B.C.–44 B.C.) who made the family name one of the most noted in history. This younger Lucius Julius Caesar accompanied his great relative in the campaign which secured for the latter mastery of the Roman world, and after his assassination, joined the avenging forces of Mark Antony, whose mother, Julia, was a sister of Lucius. He quarrelled with Antony, however, and was saved from proscription only by Julia's intervention.

Caesar, Don. In Hannah Cowley's *A Bold Stroke for a Husband*, the father of Olivia.

Caesar, Drusus. See **Drusus Caesar.**

Caesar, Gaius Julius. b. July 12, 100 B.C. (according to Theodor Mommsen, 102); killed at Rome, March 15, 44 B.C. Roman general, statesman, orator, and writer. He served at Mytilene in 80, was captured by pirates in 76, and was made quaestor in 68, curule edile in 65, pontifex maximus in 63, praetor in 62, and propraetor in Spain in 61. He formed the "first triumvirate" with Pompey and Crassus in 60; was consul in 59, and proconsul in Gaul and Illyricum in 58; defeated the Helvetii and Ariovistus in 58, and the Belgae in 57; invaded Britain in 55 and 54; crossed the Rhine in 55 and 53; defeated Vercingetorix in 52; and crossed the Rubicon and commenced the civil war in 49. He was dictator in 49, 48, 47, 46, 45; defeated Pompey at Pharsalia in 48; ended the Alexandrine war in 47; and defeated Pharnaces at Zela in 47, and the Pompeians at Thapsus in 46, and at Munda in 45. He reformed the calendar in 46. On Feb. 15, 44, he refused the crown. He was assassinated by Brutus, Cassius, and others in the senate-house on March 15, 44. The *Commentaries* (or Memoirs) of Caesar, the only one of his literary works extant, contain the history of the first seven years of the Gallic war, in seven books, and three books of a history of the civil war. The name *Caesar* was assumed by all male members of the Julian dynasty, and after them by the successive emperors, as inseparable from the imperial dignity. It thus became the source of the German *Kaiser* and the Russian *Tsar* or *Czar*. After the death of Hadrian the title *Caesar* was specifically assigned to those who were designated by the emperors as their successors and associated with them in the government.

Caesar, Sir **Julius.** b. at Tottenham, England, 1558; d. 1636. English jurist of Italian extraction. He was appointed master of the rolls in 1614.

Caesar and Cleopatra. Play by George Bernard Shaw included in the volume *Three Plays for Puritans* (1901). It is a vindication of the character of Julius Caesar against the aspersions of Shakespeare's Roman heroes, and a revelation of what Shaw takes to be the great man's genuine intellectual processes. Shaw's Caesar is witty, and he never glosses over his actions with large, loose phrases designed to justify them on moral grounds. His philosophy, of which Shaw approved, is to do what he likes.

Caesaraugusta (sē″zạr.ô.gus′tạ). Latin name of **Saragossa.**

Caesarea (sē.zạ.rē′ạ, ses.ạ-, sez.ạ-). [Also: **Caesarea Sebaste, Caesarea Palestinae, Caesarea Maritima.**] In ancient geography, a seaport in Palestine, situated on the Mediterranean Sea, near the modern village of Kaisariyeh (or Qisarya). It was erected by Herod I, in the first decennium B.C., on the site of the former Turris Stratonis ("Strato's," or "Straton's, Tower," a Greek settlement), on the line of the great road from Tyre to Egypt, between Jaffa and Dora, and named in honor of the Roman emperor (Caesar) Augustus. Herod adorned the city with many magnificent buildings. It became the residence of the Roman governors in Palestine, and was mostly inhabited by a foreign population hostile to the Jews. Here the Jewish war under the governor Gessius Florus broke out. Vespasian gave it the name of Colonia prima Flaviana. It is often mentioned in the New Testament (Acts, viii. 40, ix. 30, x. 1, xxi. 9, xxiv. 17, etc.). About 200 A.D. it became the residence of a bishop, and possessed a Christian school at which Origen taught. It was the birthplace of the church historian Eusebius (d. 342).

Caesarea. See under **Antioch,** Turkey.

Caesarea. Latin name of **Cherchel.**

Caesarea. Medieval Latin name of **Jersey.**

Caesarea Mazaca (maz′ạ.kạ). Ancient name of **Kayseri,** city.

Caesarea Philippi (fi.lip′ī, fil′i.pī). Ancient name of **Baniyas,** in SW Syria.

Caesar in Egypt. Tragedy by Colley Cibber, produced at the Drury Lane Theatre, London, on Dec. 9, 1724, and published in 1728. It was taken from Philip Massinger and John Fletcher's *The False One* and Pierre Corneille's *La Mort de Pompée.*

Caesarion (sẹ.zãr′i.ọn). b. 47 B.C.; d. 30 B.C. Egyptian ruler; son of Cleopatra and (probably) Julius Caesar. He was executed by order of Augustus. As Ptolemy XIV (or XVI) he was, with his mother, a nominal ruler of Egypt from c44 B.C. to the time of his death.

Caesarius of Arles (sẹ.zãr′i.us; ȧrl), Saint. b. at Cabillonum (now Chalon-sur-Saône, France), c470; d. at Arles, France, Aug. 27, 542 or 543. Christian monk, bishop, and theologian. A descendant of a patrician Roman family, he took monastic vows at Lérins in 489, and was made bishop of Arles in 502. In an area which had only recently been converted to Christianity and in which the disorders of those times were particularly acute, he was for 40 years a courageous pastor, evangelist, and theologian, and an able administrator and builder of the church. Alaric II exiled him on charges of conspiring to deliver Arles to the Burgundians, but soon restored him to his see. Later, on similar suspicions, Theodoric summoned him to Ravenna, where Caesarius by his learning and his evident probity won that monarch's respect and friendship. Caesarius, to whom Pope Symmachus had given the pallium as a sign of especial authority, at the same time naming him apostolic vicar of Gaul and Spain, originated and presided over several councils, including those of Agde (506), Arles (524), Carpentras (527), and Vaison and Orange (529). The last-named of these councils is noted for its condemnation of of Semi-Pelagianism. Caesarius founded a number of monasteries and nunneries and framed their rules, and his rule for nuns especially was long influential in the western church. His lasting fame arises chiefly from his sermons, which are the earliest compositions of their sort to have survived to modern times. Being replete with sidelights on the life and customs of those days, they are uncommonly valuable source material for historians, and the same is true of his *Statuta ecclesiae antiqua*, which is an abstract of even more ancient codifications of canonical law. Caesarius has been canonized, and his feast is celebrated on August 27.

Caesarius of Heisterbach (hī′stėr.bäċh). b. at or near Cologne, Germany, c1170; d. c1240. German Cistercian monk. Educated at Cologne, he mastered the Fathers of the Church and classical authors. In 1199 he entered the Cistercian monastery of Heisterbach, later becoming master of novices, and prior (1228). He wrote much on ascetical subjects, including the popular *Dialogue of Vision and Miracles,* which relates incredible legends. He is also known for his sermons.

Caesarodunum (sē″zạr.ọ.dū′num). Latin name of **Tours,** France.

Caesaromagus (sē.zạr.om′ạ.gus). An ancient name of **Beauvais.**

Caesars, City of the. Mythical South American city, reputed of great size and wealth, which report located near the E base of the Andes in the S part of Argentina. By some it was supposed to have been founded by a man named César who, c1530, left Sebastian Cabot's fort of Espírito Santo on the Paraná River, and never returned. Others connected it with the crew of a Spanish ship which was wrecked on the coast of Patagonia. In the 16th and 17th centuries many expeditions were made in search of it, and even to the end of the 18th century the legend was regarded by many as true.

Caesars, Era of. See **Spain, Era of.**

Caesena (sẹ.zē′nạ). Ancient name of **Cesena.**

Caetani (kä.ā.tä′nē), **Gelasio.** b. at Rome, March 7, 1877; d. there, Oct. 23, 1934. Italian engineer and onetime ambassador to Washington; son of Onorato Caetani.

As a member of the family branch holding the title of duke of Sermoneta, he edited and published the family archives.

Caetani, Leone. b. at Rome, Sept. 12, 1869—. Italian scholar, a student of Mohammedanism; son of Onorato Caetani. He wrote *Studii di storia orientale* (Studies in Oriental History, 1911, 1914), and *Chronographia islamica* (Islamic Chronography, 1912).

Caetani, Onorato. b. at Rome, Jan. 18, 1842; d. there, Sept. 25, 1917. Italian politician; father of Gelasio Caetani and Leone Caetani. Trained for the law, he held office as mayor of Rome, right-wing deputy (1871 *et seq.*), senator (1900 *et seq.*), and minister of foreign affairs (1896) under Antonio di Rudinì. He presided (1879–87) over the royal geographic society and wrote widely on African geography.

Caete (kä.ā'tā). South American Indian tribe, now extinct, which once inhabited the Brazilian coast between the Paraíba and São Francisco rivers. The language was a member of the Tupí-Guaraní stock.

Caf (käf). See **Kaf.**

Caffa (käf'fä). Italian name of **Feodosiya.**

Caffarelli (käf.fä.rel'lē). [Stage name of **Gaetano Majorano.**] b. at Bari, Italy, April 16, 1703; d. at Naples, Italy, Nov. 30, 1783. Italian singer, one of the leading male sopranos of his time.

Caffarelli (kȧ.fȧ.re.lē), **François Marie Auguste.** b. at Falga, Haute-Garonne, France, Oct. 7, 1766; d. at Leschelles, Aisne, France, Jan. 23, 1849. French general; brother of L. M. J. M. Caffarelli.

Caffarelli, Louis Marie Joseph Maximilien. b. at Falga, Haute-Garonne, France, Feb. 13, 1756; d. near Acre, Syria, April 27, 1799. French general; brother of François Marie Auguste Caffarelli. He was commander of the engineer corps in the Egyptian campaign of Napoleon.

Caffarelli (käf.fä.rel'lē), **Scipione.** See **Borghese, Scipione.**

Caffery (kaf'ėr.i), **Jefferson.** b. at Lafayette, La., Dec. 1, 1886—. American diplomat. A graduate of Tulane University and a lawyer, he began his diplomatic career as secretary of the U.S. legation at Caracas, Venezuela, in 1911. He held the same rank at Stockholm (1913–16), Tehran (1916–17), and Paris (1917–19), before becoming, in 1919, counselor to the U.S. embassy at Madrid, a rank which he subsequently also held at Tokyo and Berlin. In Japan he served as director of American relief following the disastrous earthquake of 1923. Advanced to ministerial rank, he represented the U.S. in Salvador (1926–28) and Colombia (1928–33). By appointment of President Franklin D. Roosevelt he became an assistant secretary of state in 1933, in which year he represented the U.S. at the Pan-American Conference at Montevideo. In 1934 he was named ambassador to Cuba, where he negotiated a reciprocal trade treaty. From December, 1944, to April, 1949, he was U.S. ambassador to France, and during that time served on the U.S. delegation to the peace conference at Paris (July-October, 1946). He represented the U.S. at the signing of peace treaties with Italy, Rumania, Bulgaria, and Hungary in 1947. In 1949 he became ambassador to Egypt.

Caffi (käf'fē), **Ippolito.** b. at Belluno, Italy, 1814; killed in the battle of Lissa, July 20, 1866. Italian painter.

Caffin (kaf'in), **Charles Henry.** b. at Sittingbourne, England, June 4, 1854; d. Jan. 15, 1918. American art critic. He was employed in the decorative arts and in teaching in England before coming to the U.S. in 1892 in connection with the decoration of the World's Columbian Exposition at Chicago. Beginning in 1897 he became a permanent resident of New York, and was art critic successively of several newspapers and of the magazines *Harper's Weekly* and *International Studio*. He published many books, and perhaps had a wider influence than any other art critic up to that time in America in fostering an appreciation of art. Best known among his works were his series on "How to Study" the various visual arts, and on the "Stories" of American, French, Dutch, and other national schools of painting. In *Art for Life's Sake* (1913) he summarized his esthetic views and his philosophy.

Caffraria (ka̤.frăr'i.a̤). See **Kaffraria.**

Caffristan (kaf.ri.stän'). See **Kafiristan.**

Cagaba (kä.gä'bä). [Also, **Kagaba.**] Indian tribe speaking a language of the Chibchan linguistic stock and occupying the mountains of Santa Marta in N Colombia. They number ab. 2,000 (1941) and have managed to keep their culture relatively intact, though modified by 400 years of European contact.

Cagayan (kä.gä.yän'; Anglicized, kä.gä'ya̤n). Province of the Philippine Islands, the northeasternmost of Luzon. It is bounded by the Pacific Ocean on the N and E, Isabela province on the S, and Mountain province on the W. The province is bordered on the E coast by the Sierra Madre Mountains, which are densely wooded. The fertile central plain of the Cagayan River, running from N to S, produces large quantities of tobacco. The native races are chiefly Cagayanes and Ilocanos. Capital, Tuguegarao; area, ab. 3,500 sq. mi.; pop. 311,088 (1948).

Cagayan. [Also, **Cagayan de Misamis** (dā mē.sä'mēs).] Town in the Philippine Islands, the capital of Misamis Oriental province on Mindanao, situated near the mouth of the Cagayan River, on Macajalar Bay, an indentation of the Mindanao Sea. 15,159 (1948).

Cagayan. Lake once thought to have existed in the NE part of Cagayan province, Luzon. It was shown on the maps of the U.S. Coast and Geodetic Survey of the Philippines in 1900, but since then it has been proven not to exist.

Cagayan Islands. [Also, **Cagayanes** (kä.gä.yä'nās).] Group of small islands lying between Negros and Palawan, and belonging to Palawan province, Philippine Islands. It consists of eight islands. The largest of the group is Cagayan.

Cagayan River. [Also, **Rio Grande de Cagayan.**] Largest river in Luzon, Philippine Islands. It rises in the southern mountains of Isabela province and flows first NE and then NW to Aparri on the N coast of Cagayan province. It has a drainage of ab. 10,000 sq. mi., and is the medium of transportation to the coast of all the products of both provinces. Length, ab. 220 mi. It is navigable by vessels of 3-ft. draft as far as Tuguegarao, the capital of Cagayan province, by native boats ab. 160 mi., and by rafts 40 mi. further.

Cagayan River. River in Misamis Oriental province, Mindanao, Philippine Islands, flowing N into Macajalar Bay. It rises in Bukidnon province.

Cagayan Sulu (sö'lö). [Also: **Cagayan de Sulu** (dā sö'lö), **Cagayan de Jolo** (dā hō.lō').] Island in the Sulu Sea, NE of the island of Borneo, with adjacent islands ceded by Spain to the U.S. by a treaty signed on Nov. 7, 1900. The islands are a part of Sulu province, Philippines.

Cagli (kä'lyē). Town and commune in C Italy, in the *compartimento* (region) of Marches, in the province of Pesaro e Urbino, situated in the Apennines at the confluence of the Bosso and Burano rivers, ab. 30 mi. S of Urbino. It is the seat of a bishopric, and has a silk mill. There are Roman remains, a cathedral, a library, and notable churches (Sant'Angelo, Santa Maria della Misericordia, San Domenico) and houses from the Renaissance period. In the Middle Ages the town fought on the side of the Ghibellines; in 1287, in the course of civil strife, it was burned down. It became part of the States of the Church in 1631, and of Italy in 1860. Pop. of commune, 12,658 (1936); of town, 3,869 (1936).

Cagliari (kä'lyä.rē). Province on the island of Sardinia, belonging to Italy, in the *compartimento* (region) of Sardinia. Capital, Cagliari; area, ab. 3,600 sq. mi.; pop. 507,201 (1936).

Cagliari. [Ancient name, **Caralis.**] City and commune in W Italy, on the island of Sardinia, the capital of the *compartimento* (region) of Sardinia and of the province of Cagliari, situated between two lagoons on the Gulf of Cagliari. Extraction of sea salt and fisheries are the two main industries; there are also flour mills, distilleries, ceramic and chemical, and other manufactures. The port trades with Africa, Spain, Sicily, and the mainland of Italy. Cagliari is the seat of a university, founded in 1596, and of an archbishopric; it has a Roman amphitheater, a medieval castle, a cathedral dating from the 14th century, and the Romanesque Church of SS. Cosmo e Damiano; there are archaeological, mineralogical, and other museums. Settled by Phoenicians, ruled by Carthaginians, and used as a port by the Romans, the town was conquered by the Vandals in 455 A.D., and was afterward successively under Byzantine, Saracen, Genoese, and Pisan domination until it fell to Aragon in 1328; in 1713 it was ceded to Austria, and in 1720 to Piedmont (Savoy). Pop. of commune, 141,573 (1951); of city, 78,632 (1936).

Cagliari, Paolo. See **Veronese, Paolo.**

Cagliostro (kä.lyôs'trō), Count **Alessandro di.** [Assumed name of **Giuseppe Balsamo.**] b. at Palermo, Sicily, June 2, 1743; d. at San Leone, Urbino, Italy, Aug. 26, 1795. Italian adventurer, notorious for his activities in Russia, Paris, the East, and elsewhere. Among other adventures he was involved in the "Diamond Necklace Affair" at Paris, and was imprisoned in the Bastille, but escaped. He visited England, and was there imprisoned in the Fleet. On emerging he went to Rome, where he was arrested and condemned to death, but his sentence was commuted to perpetual imprisonment in the fortress of San Leone, where he died.

Cagnat (kà.nyà), **René Louis Victor.** b. at Paris, Oct. 10, 1852—. French classical archaeologist. He served as a professor (1887 *et seq.*) at the Collège de France, and was the author of *Cours d'épigraphie latine* (Course on Latin Epigraphy, 1885).

Cagnes-sur-Mer (kàny'.sür.mer). Town in SE France, in the department of Alpes-Maritimes, situated near the Mediterranean Sea, between Nice and Antibes. It has an old upper town, overlooked by a 14th-century castle, and a new lower town stretching toward the sea. It is a health resort, and has golf courses; as a horticultural center it is second only to Antibes. The town suffered damage in World War II. 9,315 (1946).

Cagni (kä'nyē), **Umberto.** b. at Asti, Italy, Feb. 24, 1863; d. at Genoa, Italy, April 22, 1932. Italian arctic and African explorer. After joining (1881) the navy, he took part in Pisani's three-year voyage (1882–85) of exploration and in the Duke of the Abruzzi's world circumnavigation (1894–96). Second in command (1899) of the polar expedition organized by the Duke of the Abruzzi, he was a member (February–June, 1900) of the North Pole sledge party; with the duke he ascended Mount St. Elias in Alaska (1897) and Mount Ruwenzori in Africa (1906). He headed the Italian occupation troops in Tripoli (1911) and the Mediterranean naval forces (1919–22), and served (1923) as minister of state. He was in charge (1928) of the expedition to investigate the outcome of the Nobile North Pole flight.

Cagniard de la Tour (kà.nyàr dẹ là tör), **Charles.** b. at Paris, March 31, 1777; d. there, July 5, 1859. French physicist, engineer, and inventor. He was a tireless student and experimenter in the field of physics, and the originator of many inventions, of which the best known were a siren used in studying the vibrations of sounds, and a blowing machine known as a "cagniardelle." Most important of his achievements, perhaps, was his demonstration of the degrees of heat at which liquids under pressure were resolved into gases. He was made a baron in 1818.

Cagnola (kä.nyō'lä), **Luigi,** Marchese. b. at Milan, Italy, June 9, 1762; d. at Inverigo, Italy, Aug. 14, 1833. Italian architect. His chief works are two triumphal arches at Milan, the Arco della Pace and Porta di Marengo.

Cagots (kä.gōz'). See **Colliberts.**

Cagoulards (kà.gö.làr). [Eng. trans., *"The Hooded Men"*; also called **Le Comité Secret d'Action Révolutionnaire,** meaning "The Secret Committee for Revolutionary Action," or **CSAR.**] French fascist group, exposed in 1937. Numerous arms caches organized by them were discovered (September–November, 1937) by the police. The group was accused of plotting the overthrow of the French Third Republic. Among those of its leaders who were arrested were Eugène Deloncle, a banker, and E. Duseigneur, a general; Duke J. Pozzo di Borgo, also arrested for connection with the organization, was released in 1939. Seventy-one alleged members were scheduled (July, 1939) to be tried shortly before the outbreak of World War II.

Cagua (kä'gwä). [Also, **Caua.**] Volcanic peak in Cagayan province, NE Luzon, Philippine Islands. Elevation, ab. 3,800 ft.

Caguas (kä'gwäs). City in E central Puerto Rico, ab. 23 mi. by road S of San Juan. It is located on a fertile inland plain which produces sugar cane and tobacco. The city has several tobacco factories and a sugar *central.* 33,733 (1950 census, preliminary).

Cahaba (kạ.hô'bạ). [Also, **Cahawba.**] River in Alabama which joins the Alabama River ab. 8 mi. SW of Selma. Length, ab. 200 mi.

Cahan (kän), **Abraham.** b. at Vilna, in Lithuania, July 7, 1860; d. at New York, Aug. 31, 1951. American editor and author. He arrived (1882) in the U.S., and was a founder of the first Social Democratic party in this country. He was a founder and editor (1897 *et seq.*) of the *Jewish Daily Forward,* the largest Yiddish newspaper in the U.S., and was associated (1897–1902) also with various English-language journals. Author of *Yekl: A Tale of the New York Ghetto* (1899), *The Rise of David Levinsky* (1917), and an autobiography in Yiddish, *Blätter von Mein Leben* (5 vols., 1926–31).

Cahawba (kạ.hô'bạ). See **Cahaba.**

Cahen (kä.aṅ), **Samuel.** b. at Metz, in Lorraine, France, Aug. 4, 1796; d. at Paris, Jan. 8, 1862. French Hebraist, author of a translation of the Old Testament into French (1841–53).

Caherbarnagh (kär.vär'nạ). See under County **Cork.**

Cahill (kā'hil), **Marie.** b. at Brooklyn, N.Y., 1874; d. Aug. 23, 1933. American actress. Her debut was made in *Kathleen Mavourneen* and her career in musical comedies started with *A Tin Soldier;* her starring vehicles included *Nancy Brown* (1902–03), *Sally in our Alley* (1902), *Molly Moonshine* (1904), *Marrying Mary,* in which she created the title role (1906–07), *The Boys and Betty* (1908), and *Judy Forgot* (1911).

Cahill, Thaddeus. b. in Iowa, 1867; d. April 12, 1934. American inventor. A student (1884–85) at Oberlin Academy, he received the degrees of LL.B. (1892), LL.M. (1893), and D.C.L. (1900) from what is now George Washington University. He set up laboratories at Washington, D.C., then Holyoke, Mass. (1902), and New York (1911). His inventions include an electric typewriter; telharmony, a system of producing music electrically at distances by the use of a keyboard controlling alternating current; and devices for composing machines and wireless telephony. He pioneered in the telephonic transmission of music from a central sending station.

Cahita (kä.hē'tä). A Uto-Aztecan language spoken in NW Mexico.

Cahokia (kạ.hō'ki.ạ). Extensive Middle Mississippi site situated in Illinois ab. 6 mi. E of St. Louis, which was inhabited during the Temple Mound II period (c1300–1700 A.D.). Monk's Mound, the central structure of this site, is the largest of the temple mounds, measuring ab. 1,080 ft. long and 710 ft. wide at the base. The height is over 100 ft.

Cahokia. Village in SW Illinois, on the Mississippi flood plain ab. 5 mi. S of St. Louis, Mo. A French mission was established here in 1699, and an important fur-trading post grew up around the mission. Cahokia passed to the British in 1765, and was taken by American forces under George Rogers Clark in 1778. It experienced numerous river floods, and declined as nearby St. Louis grew in importance. 794 (1950).

Cahors (kà.ôr). [Latin, **Civitas Cadurcorum, Cadurcum, Divona.**] City in S France, the capital of the department of Lot, situated on a peninsula formed by the Lot River, N of Montauban. Founded by the Gauls, Cahors was subsequently ravaged by the Visigoths, the Franks, the Vandals, the Saracens, and the Normans. It was a British possession from the 14th century until the end of the Hundred Years' War. In the Middle Ages it was a banking center. Later, it was a stronghold of the Calvinists. Cahors is one of the oldest cities of S France, and has preserved architectural monuments from many epochs. The Cathedral of Saint Étienne dates from the 12th century, the Palace of Pope John XXII and the Church of Saint Barthélemy from the 14th century. The Pont Valentré is one of the best examples of a fortified bridge in France. There are a museum with Roman and medieval remains, and a theater. Cahors is famous for its pâté de foie gras. 15,345 (1946).

Cahuapana (kä.wä.pä'nạ). See **Maina.**

Cahuenga Capitulation (kä.weng'gä). Agreement (Jan. 13, 1847) signed by John C. Frémont and a representative of the Mexicans in California, concluding California's role in the Mexican War and there ending all resistance to the U.S.

Caiaphas (kā'a̤.fa̤s). Surname (possibly from Babylonian *qêpu*, meaning "watchman") of Joseph, Jewish high priest from 27 (or 18) to 36 A.D., noted in New Testament history; son-in-law of Annas. He presided at the council which condemned Jesus to death, and took part in the trial of Peter and John. Matt. xxvi. 57–68; Acts, iv. 6.

Caibarién (kī.bä.ryen'). City on the N coast of Cuba, in Las Villas province: exports sugar. 21,382 (1943).

Caicos Islands (kā'ko̤s). See **Turks and Caicos Islands.**

Caieta (kā.ē'ta̤). An ancient name of **Gaeta.**

Caillaux (kȧ.yō), **Joseph (Marie Auguste).** b. at Le Mans, France, March 30, 1863; d. there, Nov. 21, 1944. French politician, one-time premier (1911–12) convicted of pro-German activities during World War I. He was professor at the École des Sciences Politiques, served as minister of finance in the cabinet of Waldeck-Rousseau (1899–1902), and held office under Clemenceau in 1906 and under Monis in 1911. On the fall of the Monis ministry in June, he was placed as premier at the head of the new cabinet, but resigned in January, 1912. While he was finance minister (1913–14) in the Doumergue cabinet, his second wife, incensed at the publication in *Le Figaro* of love letters sent by Caillaux to her while she was still the wife of Leo Claretie, shot to death (1914) Gaston Calmette, editor of *Le Figaro*, who had accused Caillaux of official misconduct. Caillaux resigned from office and won the acquittal of his wife. A deputy from 1898, he held the post of finance minister (1899–1902, 1906–09, 1911–12, 1914, 1925–26, 1935), and introduced the income tax into France. While premier he negotiated a treaty with Germany giving to the latter a part of the French Congo in return for allowing France freedom of action in Morocco. During World War I he was sent to South America on a governmental mission; seen there in the company of German agents, he was tried (1920) on the charge of correspondence with the enemy on the basis of evidence found in a safe-deposit box registered at Florence under his wife's name. Sentenced to prison, banishment, and deprivation of civil rights, he was amnestied (1924), and was reëlected (1925) as a senator; his political influence declined rapidly thereafter. He published his memoirs in France during World War II.

Caillavet (kȧ.yȧ.ve), **Gaston Arman de.** b. at Paris, March 16, 1869; d. Jan. 14, 1915. French journalist and playwright, author (with Robert de Flers) of *Les Sentiers de la vertu* (1903), *L'Âne de Buridan* (1909), *L'Habit vert* (1912), and others. Son of Madame de Caillavet, the protectress of Anatole France, and from youth a frequenter of her famous literary salon, his work reflects the urbanity of his milieu in its combination of subtlety with hilarious satire.

Caille (käy'), **Nicolas Louis de la.** See **Lacaille, Nicolas Louis de.**

Caillet (kȧ.ye), **Guillaume.** See **Cale, Guillaume.**

Cailletet (kȧ.ye̤.te), **Louis Paul.** b. at Châtillon-sur-Seine, France, Sept. 21, 1832; d. Jan. 5, 1913. French physicist and industrialist, noted for his researches in the liquefaction of gases. He was an ironmaster at his father's works in his native town, where he also attended the school of mines. He is best known for liquefying (1877) oxygen and for his subsequent liquefaction of nitrogen and air; in recognition of his achievements, he was elected to the French Academy of Sciences (1884) and the Legion of Honor. He also made studies in aeronautics.

Cailliaud (kȧ.yō), **Frédéric.** b. at Nantes, France, June 9, 1787; d. there, May 1, 1869. French traveler in Egypt and Nubia.

Caillié or **Caillé** (kȧ.yā), **René.** b. at Mauzé, in Poitou, France, Sept. 19, 1799; d. at Paris, May 8, 1838. French traveler in central Africa. He reached Timbuktu in 1828, having disguised himself as a Moslem for safety. He was the first white man to return alive from this region.

Caimanera (kī.mä.nā'rä). [Also, **Caimamera** (-mā'rä).] Town in SE Cuba, in Oriente province on Guantánamo Bay, connected by rail with Guantánamo, of which it is the port. Pop. under 5,000 (1943).

Cain (kān). In the Old Testament, the eldest son of Adam and Eve, and the murderer of his brother Abel. For his sin, he was condemned to be a fugitive for the rest of his life. Gen. iv.

Cain. Biblical drama (1821) by Byron. It is a challenge to submissive orthodoxy and an assertion of man's right to exercise the powers of reason implanted in him.

Cain. Poetic drama (1904) by George Cabot Lodge.

Cain (kaṅ), **Georges Jules Auguste.** b. at Paris, April 16, 1856; d. 1919. French historical, genre, and portrait painter, water colorist, and illustrator; brother of Henri Cain. He is known for his illustrations for Honoré de Balzac's *La Cousine Bette*, and for *The Barber of Seville.* He was a pupil of Alexandre Cabanel at Paris, and later exhibited and won several prizes in France and the U.S. Among his best-known works are *Napoleon in 1802*, *Pajou Making the Bust of Mme. DuBarry*, *Marie Antoinette Going to the Scaffold*, and *At the Church.*

Cain, Henri. b. at Paris, Oct. 11, 1859; d. 1937. French historical painter, portraitist, and dramatist; brother of Georges Jules Auguste Cain. He studied with J. P. Laurens and Édouard Detaille; he won numerous prizes for his work at Paris, and was made an officer of the Legion of Honor in 1911. His principal paintings include *End of a Conspiracy under Louis XVIII*, *Street Singers*, *The Duke of Orleans*, and *The Arrest of the Count de Sombreuil.*

Cain (kān), **James Mallahan.** b. at Annapolis, Md., July 1, 1892—. American journalist, writer, and scenarist. He served in World War I, was a staff member for five years of the Baltimore *Sun*, and joined (1924) the New York *World* as an editorial writer. His novels and novelettes, dealing usually with violence and lawlessness, include *Serenade* (1937), *Love's Lovely Counterfeit* (1942), *Three of A Kind* (1943), *Past All Dishonor* (1946), *The Butterfly* (1947), and *The Moth* (1948); *The Postman Always Rings Twice* (1934) was dramatized (1936) and filmed (1946); *Mildred Pierce* (1941) and *Double Indemnity* were also made into motion pictures.

Cain, Richard Harvey. b. in Greenbrier County, Va., April 12, 1825; d. Jan. 18, 1887. American clergyman and politician, notable (1868 *et seq.*) as a leader of South Carolina's newly enfranchised Negro voters. Licensed (1844) as a preacher by the Methodist Episcopal Church, he transferred almost at once to the African Methodist Episcopal Church, in which he was ordained a deacon (1859) and an elder (1862); he was elected (1872, 1876) to Congress, after serving (1868) as a member of South Carolina's post-Civil War constitutional convention. He spent the last years of his life (1880 *et seq.*) as bishop of the Louisiana-Texas diocese and as president of Paul Quinn College.

Cain, a Mystery. Dramatic poem by Byron, published in 1821. It was written at Ravenna, Italy.

Caine (kān), Sir **Hall.** [Full name, **Thomas Henry Hall Caine.**] b. at Runcorn, Cheshire, England, 1853; d. Aug. 31, 1931. English novelist, best known for his descriptions of life on the Isle of Man; brother of William Ralph Hall Caine (1865–1939). Among his works are *Sonnets of Three Centuries* (1882), *The Shadow of a Crime* (1885), *The Deemster* (1887), *The Manxman* (1894), *The Christian* (1897), *The Eternal City* (1901), *Drink* (1907), *My Story* (1909), *The White Prophet* (1909), *The Woman Thou Gavest Me* (1913), and *Master of Man* (1921). *Recollections of Rossetti* (1882) is an account of Caine's friendship with Dante Gabriel Rossetti. *The Bondman* was dramatized in 1907, *Pete* (with Louis N. Parker) in 1908, *The Bishop's Son* in 1910, and *The Eternal Question* in 1910.

Caine, William Ralph Hall. b. 1865; d. Jan. 14, 1939. English journalist, editor, anthologist, and author of works on the Isle of Man; brother of Hall Caine (1853–1931). He was a writer for the Liverpool *Mercury*, and editor of the *Court Circular*, the *Family Churchman*, and *Household Words.* Author of *The Isle of Man* (1909), *The Kingdom of Man and the Isles* (1919), *The Story of Sodor and Man* (1925), and *Annals of the Magic Isle* (1926); editor of two anthologies, *Humorous Poems of the Century* (1890) and *Love Songs of England* (1893).

Caingang (kä.in.gäng'). [Also, **Kaingang.**] Collective term for a group of culturally related South American Indian tribes in the states of São Paulo, Paraná, Santa Catarina, and Rio Grande do Sul, Brazil (longitude 50° W., latitude 20°–30° S.). The languages of the Caingang groups are members of the Ge linguistic family.

Caingua (kä.in.gwä'). [Also, **Caagua.**] Collective term for several South American Indian tribes which have remained independent of mission stations and inhabit portions of the interior of SE Brazil; their languages belong to the Tupí-Guaraní linguistic stock.

Cainites (kān′īts). Gnostic sect of the 2nd century A.D., which reverenced Cain, Esau, Korah, and Judas Iscariot.

Cainozoic Era (kī.nǫ.zō′ik, kā-). Alternate form of **Cenozoic Era.** See table at end of Vol. III.

Ça ira (sȧ ē.rȧ). First popular song (c1789) to grow out of the French Revolution. The music was that of a contredanse which was extremely popular under the name *Carillon national*, composed by a drummer in the orchestra of the opera, and was a great favorite with Marie Antoinette. The words are thought to have been suggested by Lafayette to Ladré, a street singer; he remembered them from hearing Benjamin Franklin say at various stages of the American Revolution, when asked for news, "Ça ira, Ça ira." There are five verses with different refrains, the words becoming more ferocious as the Revolution progressed. The best-known refrain is:

Ah! ça ira, ça ira, ça ira!
Les aristocrates à la lanterne!

Caird (kãrd), **Alice Mona.** [Pseudonym, **G. Noel Hatton**; maiden name, **Hector.**] b. on the Isle of Wight, 1858; d. Feb. 4, 1932. English feminist and novelist. She is noted for what at the time were considered to be radical ideas on questions relating to sex, marriage, and morality. Under her pseudonym she wrote her earliest novels, *Whom Nature Leadeth* (1883) and *One That Wins* (1887). She was the author also of *The Wing of Azrael* (1889), *A Romance of the Moors* (1891), *The Daughters of Danaus* (1894), *Beyond the Pale* (1896), *The Pathway of the Gods* (1898), and *The Stones of Sacrifice* (1915). Her other works include *The Morality of Marriage and Other Essays* (1897), and *The Romantic Cities of Provence* (1906).

Caird, Edward. b. at Greenock, Scotland, March 22, 1835; d. at Oxford, England, Nov. 1, 1908. Scottish philosopher and professor; brother of John Caird (1820–98). He was educated at Glasgow and St. Andrews universities, and at Balliol College, Oxford, of which he was subsequently (1893–1907) master. From 1866 to 1893 he was professor of moral philosophy at Glasgow. His works include *The Philosophy of Kant* (1878), *Hegel* (1883), *The Social Philosophy and Religion of Comte* (1885), *Critical Account of the Philosophy of Kant* (1889), *Essays in Literature and Philosophy* (1892), *Evolution of Religion* (1893), and *Evolution of Theology in the Greek Philosophers* (1904).

Caird, John. b. at Greenock, Scotland, Dec. 15, 1820; d. at Oxford, England, July 30, 1898. Scottish philosopher, teacher, and theologian; brother of Edward Caird (1835–1908). Educated (1840–45) at Glasgow University, with which he was later associated as professor of theology and vice-chancellor (1862–73) and principal (1873–98), he also held parishes (1845–57) at Newton-on-Ayr, at Edinburgh, and in Perthshire. He was the author of *Introduction to the Philosophy of Religion* (1880), *Spinoza* (1888), *University Sermons* (1899), *University Addresses* (1899), and *The Fundamental Ideas of Christianity* (1900, originally delivered in the period 1895–96 as the Gifford Lectures). He was popular for his sermon *Religion in Common Life* (1857), which he had delivered (1855) with great success before Queen Victoria.

Caire (ker), **Le.** French name of **Cairo,** Egypt.

Cairnes (kãrnz), **John Elliott.** b. at Castle Bellingham, County Louth, Ireland, Dec. 26, 1823; d. near London, July 8, 1875. British political economist, a follower of the theories of utilitarianism as laid down by John Stuart Mill. In 1866 he was appointed professor of political economy at University College, London. In a work entitled *The Slave Power* (1862) he discussed the basic weaknesses in any society which derived a major portion of its productive effort from slavery, and thereby was enabled accurately to forecast the eventual downfall of the Confederacy. The significance of this work, which had a marked effect on a considerable body of influential English opinion, was very great indeed; it dealt a blow to the hopes of the Confederacy for British alliance, and persuaded many Englishmen that their best interests would be served finally by Northern victory. His other works include *Character and Logical Method of Political Economy* (1857), *Essays in Political Economy* (1873), *Political Essays* (1873), and *Some Leading Principles of Political Economy, Newly Expounded* (1874).

Cairngorm (kãrn′gôrm). [Also, **Cairn Gorm.**] Mountain in N central Scotland, situated on the Banffshire-Inverness-shire boundary, ab. 40 mi. E of Fort-Augustus. 4,084 ft.

Cairns (kãrnz). City in NE Australia, in NE Queensland, ab. 1,043 mi. by rail NW of Brisbane. It is the chief raw-sugar export port of Australia, and in addition exports other products of its hinterland, including beef and dairy products and some metals. The climate is tropical. 16,644 (1947).

Cairns, Hugh McCalmont. [Title, 1st Earl **Cairns.**] b. at Culdra, County Down, Ireland, in December, 1819; d. at Bournemouth, Hampshire, England, April 2, 1885. English statesman. He entered Parliament in 1852, and was lord chancellor (1868, 1874–80) in the Benjamin Disraeli administration.

Cairo (kī′rō). [Arabic, **al-Qahirah, El Kahirah**; French, **Le Caire.**] Capital of Egypt, in NE Africa, on the E bank of the Nile River a short distance above the division of the Nile into its two main branches: the largest and one of the most beautiful cities in Africa. Sometimes referred to as "the diamond stud on the handle of the fan of the Nile delta," it ranks high as one of the most important cities of the Middle East. It is the commercial and industrial center of Egypt, connected to Alexandria and Port Saïd by rail and highway. It has important transit trade, and is the starting point for tours to neighboring pyramids, the sites of Memphis and Heliopolis (in the vicinity), and the upper Nile River. Its chief suburb is Bulak. 2,100,486 (1947).

History. It was founded by the Fatimite caliphs c970, and made their capital. It was taken by the Turks in 1517, was held by the French (1798–1801), and was occupied by the British in 1882. It was the scene of the massacre of the Mamelukes in 1811.

Architecture. Cairo contains a number of noted mosques: The Mosque of Akbar is a square, picturesquely ornamented building surmounted by a pointed dome covered with arabesques. The square minaret over one angle rises in recessed stages, and the entrance porch is formed by a high trifoliate arch. The entire interior is colored in dark and light horizontal bands. The Mosque of El-Azhar was founded in 970, but for the most part rebuilt at various subsequent times. It has six minarets. It is remarkable as the chief existing Mohammedan university. The divisions of the interior surround a large central court encircled by pointed arcades. The sanctuary, used for instruction, consists of nine aisles formed by 380 columns of ancient and Christian origin. Several subordinate mosques or chapels are included in the main foundation. The Mosque of El-Gouri, one of the most picturesque monuments in the city, was built c1513. The Mosque of Sultan Hassan, ranking as one of the chief monuments of Mohammedan architecture, was completed in 1360. The exterior, built of stones taken from the Pyramids, consists of a massive wall ab. 113 ft. high, enclosing an area of irregular form, and surmounted by two lofty minarets and the pointed brick dome of the sultan's mausoleum. The top of the wall is corbeled out ab. 6 ft. in successive ranges of dentils, forming a cornice, and its face is diversified by panels, arches, and *ajimez* windows, all used sparingly. The great minaret is 280 ft. high. The interior court measures 105 by 117 ft., and contains two fountain pavilions. In the middle of each side of the court opens a magnificent pointed arch. That on the E, 90 ft. high and deep and 69 in span, is the largest. At the back of this recess are the *mimbar* (pulpit) and *mihrab* (place of direction of prayer), and from it opens the mausoleum. The entrance porch is a large archway covered in by corbeling out the sides for part of its rise, and then throwing a small pointed arch over the opening; its piers are ornamented with rich vertical bands and angle-columns, and with paneling. The Tomb-Mosque of Kait Bey, built c1470, is one of the finest pieces of architecture in Cairo. The so-called Tombs of the Caliphs, properly of the Circassian Mamelukes, a number of comparatively small mosque-tombs of the 15th century, are grouped together about the mosque-tomb of Kait Bey. They are important in Arabic architecture for their angularly pointed stone domes covered with geometric ornament in relief, with small windows in the low drum; for their windows, consisting of a group of two or three slender round-headed arches surmounted by one or three circular openings arranged pyramidally; and for the fine, massive pointed arches usual in the lowest story. Some of them show incrustations of the beautiful colored porcelain tiles for which the older Arabic monuments of Cairo are famous. The Tombs of the Mamelukes, an extensive group of mosque-tombs on the SE side of the city, belong to the period of the Baharite sultans, and though in ruins are architecturally notable for their fine masonry and beautiful fluted, or chevroned, pointed domes, and for their graceful polygonal minarets, which rise in recessed stages. The Mosque of Amru, the oldest mosque in Egypt (founded 643 A.D.) is a remarkable Mohammedan monument. The enclosure is 350 ft. square, with exterior walls of brick. The entrance is on the W; here a single range of arcades borders the central court, while on the N there are three ranges, on the S four, and on the E side, which is the sanctuary, six ranges. There are in all 229 columns. The arches are round or keel-shaped, and a few are pointed. The nilometer, a monument for measuring the rise of the Nile River, is on the island of Roda. The present nilometer dates from c860 A.D.; it is a chamber ab. 18 ft. square, originally domed, in each side of which there is a niche covered with a pointed arch, an important example of the early use of this form. In the middle stands a pillar divided into 17 cubits of ab. $21\frac{7}{16}$ inches.

Cairo (kā′rō, kār′ō). City in SW Georgia, county seat of Grady County: manufacturing center for tung oil and syrup; canning and shipping point for okra, peanuts, pecans, and pickles. 5,577 (1950).

Cairo. City in S Illinois, county seat of Alexander County, at the confluence of the Ohio and Mississippi rivers: the southernmost city in Illinois. Its principal industry is the processing of cottonseed. Several attempts at settlement were made (notably in 1702, 1817, and 1837) before Cairo, protected by levees and aided by the development of the railroad, became in the 1850's a permanent city and a flourishing river port. Its flood- and fever-beset aspect was bitterly portrayed by Charles Dickens (who had visited it in the 1840's) in his novel *Martin Chuzzlewit* as Eden, where settlers were lured by speculators and suffered intolerable hardships. It was nearly destroyed by an inundation in 1858. The Ohio is here crossed by a railway bridge of the Illinois Central. 12,123 (1950).

Cairo Conference (kī′rō). Discussions between President Franklin Delano Roosevelt, Prime Minister Winston Churchill, and Generalissimo Chiang Kai-shek from Nov. 22 to 26, 1943, prior to the Tehran Conference. The chief purpose of the meeting was to survey war and peace problems in the Far East. The Conference declared that Japan should lose all Pacific islands acquired since 1914, that territories, including Formosa, Manchuria, and the Pescadores, taken from China should be restored, and that Korea should have independence. Agreements were also made concerning Pacific fleet allocations and the opening of supply lines into China from India and Burma.

Cairoli (kī.rō′lē), **Benedetto.** b. at Pavia, Italy, Jan. 28, 1825; d. 1889. Italian patriot and statesman of the Risorgimento. From the revolutionary year of 1848 his life was given to the achievement of Italian unity and the rehabilitation of his country. He was a conspirator against Austrian rule, a refugee, and an officer under Garibaldi during the period of struggle, and after the victory he became a member of the Italian parliament and eventually prime minister of the Italian kingdom. In 1870 he was the Italian spokesman in negotiations with Bismarck, who promised assistance toward bringing under the crown of Victor Emmanuel those Italian states which still remained independent, if Cairoli and his group would keep the king from an alliance with the French Emperor Napoleon III. However, Cairoli, as parliamentary leader of his party, and later as premier, pursued a pro-French policy. French designs concerning Tunis caused alarm in Italy, but Cairoli accepted French reassurances, and believed, moreover, that Great Britain would forbid a further extension of French power in Africa. When his confidence proved mistaken, and France actually occupied Tunis in 1881, his ministry fell, and thereafter he had no influential part in Italian political affairs.

Caissa (kạ.is′ạ). Goddess of chess. The name is said to have originated with Sir William Jones (1746–94), the Orientalist.

Caithness (kāth′nes, kāth.nes′). [Also, **Caithness-shire.**] Maritime county in N Scotland, lying between the Atlantic Ocean and Pentland Firth on the N, the North Sea on the E and SE, and Sutherland on the S and W. The coastline is mostly cliffed on the N and E as far as Wick; southward along the E coast from Wick it is low and sandy. The surface is chiefly level, especially in the NE portion where there are wide-open stretches of land under cultivation and few trees. Crops raised are oats and potatoes, with the land being periodically put into pasture to provide a crop rotation. About one fourth of the total area of the county is under cultivation. County seat, Wick; area, ab. 686 sq. mi.; pop. 22,705 (1951).

Caius (kā′us). See also **Gaius.**

Caius or **Gaius** (gā′us). fl. in the first part of the 3rd century A.D. Christian controversialist. He is mentioned by Eusebius as having carried on a theological dispute with one Proclus, a member of the Montanist sect. In the course of this discussion Caius mentions the presence of memorial chapels to Saints Peter and Paul at Rome, which is considered valuable evidence in support of the belief that they died at that city.

Caius or **Gaius,** Saint. b. in Dalmatia; d. April 22, 296. Pope from 283 to 296.

Caius. In Shakespeare's *King Lear*, the assumed name of Kent.

Caius, Dr. In Shakespeare's *The Merry Wives of Windsor*, a French doctor.

Caius (kēz), **John.** [Original surname: **Kay, Kaye, Kees,** or **Key.**] b. at Norwich, England, Oct. 6, 1510; d. at London, July 29, 1573. English physician and scholar. After attending what was then called Gonville Hall, at the University of Cambridge, he studied in Italy, taking a medical degree at Padua. A physician (1547 *et seq.*) at London, he enlarged and reëndowed his old college at Cambridge, whence its renaming as Gonville and Caius College; he became (c1559) its master, a position he held until 1573. In his medical capacity, he attended three English rulers: Edward VI, Mary Tudor, and Elizabeth.

Caius Aurelius Valerius Diocletianus (kā′us ô.rē′li.us vạ.lir′i.us dī.ọ.klē.shi.ā′nus). See **Diocletian.**

Caius Cestius (ses′ti.us), **Pyramid of.** Massive sepulchral monument of brick and stone, at Rome, ab. 114 ft. high, encrusted with white marble. Each side of the base measures 90 ft. The small burial chamber is painted with white arabesques. The pyramid is of the time of Augustus.

Caius College (kēz). See **Gonville and Caius College.**

Caius Gracchus (kā′us grak′us). Tragedy by James Sheridan Knowles, produced in 1815 at Belfast. He afterward revised it, and the new version was produced by William Charles Macready at Covent Garden in 1823.

Caius Marius (mãr′i.us). Drama by Penn Smith. It was produced by Edwin Forrest at the Arch Street Theatre, Philadelphia, Jan. 12, 1831. Because of Forrest's policy forbidding the publication of any of the plays he controlled lest they should be acted by others, nothing has been preserved of *Caius Marius* but fragments found in newspapers or theatrical histories. In one of these Marius is shown in the decline of his great powers, boasting of his triumphs and trembling at the approach of Sylla. Smith's lines here show the effect on Marius, the plebeian soldier, of the patrician prestige of Sylla, which he could not ignore either in his triumph or in his despair. Most critics consider this to have been Smith's most important play with excellent dramatic construction, vigor of language, and harmony of versification.

Caius Range (kēz). See **Gonville and Caius Range.**

Caivano (kī.vä′nō). [Also, **Calvano.**] Town and commune in S Italy, in the *compartimento* (region) of Campania, in the province of Napoli, N of Naples: belongs to the metropolitan district of Naples. It has a castle dating from the 15th century. Hemp culture is important in the vicinity. Pop. of commune, 16,356 (1936); of town, 15,164 (1936).

Cajabamba (kä.Hä.Bäm′bä). City in C Ecuador, in Chimborazo province. 15,043 (est. 1944).

Cajamarca (kä.Hä.mär′kä). [Also, **Caxamarca.**] Department in NW Peru, bordering on Ecuador. It is almost wholly in the Andean Cordilleras. Capital, Cajamarca;

area, ab. 12,540 sq. mi.; pop. 568,118 (1940), 674,072 (est. 1950).

Cajamarca. [Also, **Caxamarca.**] City in W Peru, the capital of Cajamarca department. It was an ancient Indian settlement, which the Incas overran. Grain is raised and gold, silver, and copper are mined in the region. There are interesting hot springs nearby, falsely called "Inca baths." Atahualpa had his headquarters here during the war with Huáscar (1530–32); here he was seized by Francisco Pizarro on Nov. 16, 1532, and executed on Aug. 29, 1533. Elevation, over 9,000 ft.; pop. 15,553 (1940).

Cajander (kä'yän.der), **Aino Kaarlo.** b. at Nystad, Finland, April 4, 1879; d. at Helsinki, Finland, Jan. 21, 1943. Finnish political leader and scientist, who resigned (1939) as premier to permit a coalition government to wage (1939–40) war with the U.S.S.R. He was three times (1922, 1924, 1937–39) premier, having been previously vice-minister of agriculture (1922) and defense minister (1928–29). He was a liberal member (1929–33) of parliament. His scientific field was botany, which he taught from 1904, holding (1911–33) a professorship at the Skoubrug secondary school, where he also supervised (1918 *et seq.*) scientific research.

Cajetan (kaj'ę.tan), Cardinal. [Latinized, **Cajetanus;** original name, **Giacomo de Vio;** later called **Tommaso de Vio Gaetano.**] b. at Gaeta, Italy, Feb. 20, 1469; d. at Rome, Aug. 9, 1534. Italian Dominican, cardinal, and scholar, a papal legate at Augsburg in 1518. He summoned Martin Luther before his tribunal. He became bishop of Gaeta (the ancient name of which was Caieta, hence Cajetan) in 1519.

Cajetan of Thiene (tye'nā), Saint. [Italian, **Gaetano;** Latinized, **Cajetanus.**] b. at Vicenza, Italy, 1480; d. at Naples, Italy, 1547. Italian lawyer and religious reformer. At the age of 24 he became doctor of canon and civil law at Padua, and subsequently served Pope Julius II. On the death of Julius he withdrew from the papal court and is said to have founded an association of pious priests known as the Oratory of Divine Love. He was himself ordained priest in 1516. In 1523 he founded a new congregation, approved by Pope Clement VII in 1524, which later became known as the Theatines from one of its members, Cardinal Pietro Caraffa, bishop of Chieti (Latin, *Theate*). He was canonized in 1671.

Cajigal (kä.ʜē.gäl'), **Juan Manuel.** b. at Cádiz, Spain, 1757; d. at Guanabacoa, Cuba, Nov. 26, 1823. Spanish general. From 1799 he was stationed in Venezuela, where he acted (1810–16) against the revolutionists, and was acting captain-general from 1813. He was defeated by Simon Bolívar at Carabobo, on May 28, 1814, but contributed to the successes of the royalists in 1815. Recalled to Spain in 1816, he was made a lieutenant general. From August, 1819, to March, 1821, he was captain-general of Cuba during a period of great disorder.

Cajigal de la Vega (dā lä ʙā'gä), **Francisco Antonio.** [Title, Marquis of **Casa-Cajigal.**] b. at Santander, Spain, Feb. 5, 1695; d. there, April 30, 1777. Spanish general and administrator. He was military commandant of Caracas, governor of Santiago de Cuba (1738–54), and of Havana (1747–60). For his defense against Edward Vernon's English fleet (July 1, 1741) he was made a brigadier, and subsequently field marshal. For about six months in 1760 he was viceroy ad interim of Mexico.

Cajón Pass (ką.hōn'). Pass between the San Bernardino and San Gabriel mountains, in S California, a route from the Mojave Desert to southern California known to white emigrants by 1776. The earliest U.S. citizen to traverse it was Jedediah Smith, in November, 1826.

Cajori (kä.yō'rē), **Florian.** b. at St. Aignan, Graubünden, Switzerland, Feb. 28, 1859; d. at Berkeley, Calif., Aug. 14, 1930. American historian of science, notably physics and mathematics. By birth he was Swiss, but he emigrated to America at the age of 16. He received the Ph.D. degree at Tulane University in 1894, and later was awarded a number of honorary doctorates. He taught at Tulane University (1887–88), Colorado College (1889–1918), and the University of California (1918 *et seq.*). His most important books are *History of Mathematics* (1897, 1919), *History of Physics* (1899, 1924, 1929), and *History of Mathematical Notations* (2 vols., 1928–29).

Cajuns (kā'junz). Name for descendants, in Louisiana, of the French settlers deported by the British in 1755 from Acadia, now Nova Scotia. As a group, the Cajuns have retained a remarkable degree of homogeneity: they live chiefly in communities in the bayou region of S Louisiana and speak French, in a dialect form, as their first language.

Cakchiquel (käk.chē.kel'). [Also, **Cackchiquel.**] Division of the Maya Indians, closely related culturally to the Quiche, located in highland Guatemala.

Cakchiquel, Annals of the. See **Annals of the Cakchiquel.**

Cakes, Land of. A name sometimes given to Scotland, which is famous for its oatmeal cakes. From this, also, has come the term "Cake Day" for "Hogmanay," as the Scots call New Year's Eve.

Cakes and Ale. Novel by W. Somerset Maugham, published in 1930. A satirical account of the life of a noted English author, its central character has been variously identified as Thomas Hardy and Hugh Walpole.

Çakmak (chäk.mäk'), **Fevzi.** b. at Istanbul, Jan. 12, 1876; d. April 10, 1950. Turkish soldier. He entered the Turkish army as a lieutenant, became (1910) a corps chief of staff, was promoted (1915) to brigadier general, took part in the Dardenelles campaign, and commanded (1916) the 2nd Caucasian army against the Russians. He was named (1918) chief of the general staff, was minister of war (1920), and was promoted (1922) to marshal. Associated with Kemal Atatürk in the nationalist movement, he served (1924–44) as chief of staff of the Turkish army, and became (1946) a deputy in the Turkish national assembly.

Čakste (chäk'ste), **Jānis.** [Also, **Tschakste.**] b. in Latvia, Sept. 14, 1859; d. March 14, 1927. Latvian statesman. He was graduated (1886) from the University of Moscow law school and practiced law (1887–1915) at Jelgava, where he was president of the Latvian Society. As publisher and editor of the newspaper *Tehwija* (1888), he fought for the interests of the Latvian small farmers and against the privileges of the landed nobility. In 1906 he was elected to the Russian Duma, where he defended the rights of the Latvian farmers. Elected (1918) chairman of the Latvian peoples council, he kept this post until convocation of the Latvian constituent assembly. He was chief of the Latvian delegation to the peace conference at Paris (1919). On May 1, 1920, Čakste opened the constituent assembly and was elected chairman. Elected (1922) first president of the republic of Latvia, he held this post until his death.

Calabar (kal'ą.bär). Province of Nigeria, W Africa, between the Cross and Rio del Rey rivers, in the former British Oil Rivers Protectorate; now one of the Eastern Provinces.

Calabar. [Former name, **Old Calabar.**] Town in Nigeria, W Africa, in the Eastern Provinces, situated near the head of the estuary of the Cross River: the administrative center of Calabar province, and one of the chief ports in Nigeria. Although its climate is unhealthful, the district is important for palm oil, which is produced on the banks of the river. The town is also an educational center. The Cross River is navigable for some distance. Duketown is the native quarter. Pop. ab. 17,000.

Calabozo (kä.lä.ʙō'sō). [Also, **Calaboso.**] Village in N Venezuela, in Guárico state, on the Guárico River. Pop. under 5,000 (1941).

Calabrese (kä.lä.brā'zā), **Il.** [Original name, **Mattia Preti.**] b. at Tavernia, Calabria (or at Ravenna), Italy, 1613; d. on the island of Malta, 1699. Italian painter. He studied with Giovanni Lanfranco at Rome and with Guercino at Cento, and also at Parma, and visited France and Spain. He was particularly successful in the decoration of public buildings, his most noted accomplishment being the frescoes in the cathedral of Malta, for which Pope Urban VIII created him a cavalier of the Knights of Malta. Examples of his work in fresco also adorned the walls of the churches of Sant'Andrea delle Valle at Rome and San Pietro a Maiella at Naples. He had a predilection for violent and gloomy subjects; his saints are likely to be depicted at the moment of martyrdom, and scenes of death fascinated him. Appropriately, his works are largely sombre in coloration. He was a man of violent nature, and it was his rage at marks of favor shown to other painters which caused him to leave Italy and spend his last years on Malta. Examples of his work are to be found in the

Louvre at Paris, the Uffizi Palace at Florence, the Brera at Milan, the Doria Palace at Milan, the Modena Museum, and the Naples Museum.

Calabria (ka̧.lā′bri.a̧). Name given until about the time of the Norman conquest in the 11th century to the SE part of Italy (the heel): now in S Apulia.

Calabria. [Ancient name, **Bruttium.**] *Compartimento* (region) in S Italy, containing the provinces of Catanzara, Cosenza, and Reggio Calabria. It forms the toe of the Italian boot between the Tyrrhenian Sea and the Strait of Messina on the W, the Ionian Sea on the E, and Lucania on the N. It has a long, swampy coastline, and a rugged mountainous interior. It has stone quarries, forests, and pasture lands (where sheep, goats, mules, and donkeys are raised), and produces olives, figs, almonds, and citrus and other fruits. The region has large feudal estates and a poor peasantry; it was one of the centers of overseas emigration in the 19th and 20th centuries. Many cities were founded by the Greeks. After the downfall of the Roman Empire it was under Byzantine, Norman, and Hohenstaufen rule until it became part of the Kingdom of Naples and the Two Sicilies in the 11th century. It was incorporated into Italy in 1860. Area, 5,828 sq. mi.; pop. 2,035,600 (1951).

Calactinus (kal.a̧k.tī′nus). See **Caecilius.**

Calae (kā′lē). Ancient name of **Chelles.**

Calagua Islands (kä.lä′gwä). Group of small islands N of Caramines Norte province, Luzon, Philippine Islands. The two main islands are Tinaga and Guintinua. Total area of group, ab. 20 sq. mi.

Calagurris Nassica (kal.a̧.gur′is nas′i.ka̧) or **Calagurris.** Ancient name of **Calahorra.**

Calah (kā′la̧). In the Old Testament (Gen. x. 10, 12), one of the four cities founded by Assur, the legendary progenitor and chief deity of the Assyrians. It is the Assyrian city called in the inscriptions Kalhu or Kalakh, now represented by the ruins of Nimrud, ab. 20 mi. N of the ruins of Nineveh (Kuyunjik), situated on an irregular wedge of land formed by the Tigris and the Upper Zab rivers. According to the Assyrian monuments it was founded by Shalmaneser I c1300 B.C. His successors abandoned it for Nineveh. Assurnazirpal (884–860 B.C.) rebuilt it and erected a royal palace in it, known as the "northwest palace"; others were built by his successors.

Calahorra (kä.lä.ôr′rä). [Ancient name, **Calagurris Nassica** or **Calagurris.**] City in N Spain, in the province of Logroño, situated on the Cidaco River near its junction with the Ebro River, ab. 25 mi. SE of Logroño. It has wine and cattle trade, and is the seat of a bishopric. A Roman town in ancient times, it was taken by Pompey after four years of siege in the Sertorian War (76–73 B.C.). It was the birthplace of Quintilian. 13,199 (1940).

Calais (ka̧.lā′, kal′ā, kal′is; French, kȧ.le). City in N France, in the department of Pas-de-Calais, situated on the narrowest part of the Strait of Dover, between Dunkerque and Cap Gris Nez. The port of Calais, aided by the Canal of Calais, specializes in the import of timber, and is also utilized for passenger transfer from England to Paris and to all the countries of C Europe. Calais is a world center for the manufacture of lace. It is also a resort, with a fine bathing beach. It was formerly strongly fortified and had a number of historical monuments such as the Cathedral of Notre Dame, the old city hall, and the Porte de Guise, but much of the city was destroyed in World War II. In former times, Calais was much contested between the English and the French, and was under British rule from 1347 to 1558. Pop. 50,048 (1946).

Calais (kal′is). City in SE Maine, in Washington County, on the St. Croix River, at the Canada-Maine border: port of entry, connected with St. Stephen, New Brunswick, by an international bridge. Its chief industry is lumber. 4,589 (1950).

Calais (kȧ.le), **Pas de.** French name of **Dover, Strait of.**

Calais (kȧ.le′), **William of St.** See **Carilef, William de St.**

Calamatta (kä.lä.mät′tä), **Luigi.** b. at Civitavecchia, Italy, July 12, 1802; d. at Milan, Italy, March 8, 1869. French engraver.

Calame (kȧ.lȧm), **Alexandre.** b. at Vevey, Switzerland, May 28, 1810; d. at Menton, France, March 17, 1864. Swiss landscape painter, noted for representations of Alpine scenery and of the ruins of Paestum.

Calamian Islands (kä.lä.myän′). [Also, **Calamianes** (-myä′näs).] Group of islands in the Philippines between Palawan and Mindoro islands. They form part of Palawan province. The two most important islands are Busuanga and Culion, on the latter of which there is a famous leper colony. Area, 677 sq. mi.

Calamis (kal′a̧.mis). fl. 5th century B.C. Greek sculptor.

Calamities of Authors. Work by Isaac D'Israeli, published in 1812.

Calamity Jane. [Nickname of **Martha Jane Burke;** maiden name, **Canary.**] b. at or near Princeton, Mo., c1852; d. at Deadwood, S.D., Aug. 1, 1903. American western frontier character. Her childhood was spent at her birthplace until her parents took her, in 1864, to Virginia City, Mont., where they separated. Growing up in frontier mining camps, she had little respect for the codes and restraints that usually govern the conduct of a girl and a woman, but her courage, her skilled horsemanship, and the accuracy of her aim with a rifle or a revolver, as well as her generous nature, made her popular and celebrated. Her sobriquet is said to have derived from her repeated warning that for a man to offend her was to court calamity. Customarily she dressed like a man, and it is believed by many, though some commentators doubt it, that she served as a scout for Generals Custer and Miles. She went to Deadwood in the Black Hills of South Dakota with the gold rush that started in 1876, and is said to have been for several years a U.S. Post Office mail carrier operating out of that community. Poverty beset her later years, when she was in large measure dependent on charity.

Calamus. Series of 45 poems published in the second edition (1860) of *Leaves of Grass*, by Walt Whitman. The spiritual relationship binding man to man provides the mystic theme, while the calamus plant (or sweet flag) is used to symbolize mortality, friendship, and eternal life.

Calamy (kal′a̧.mi), **Edmund.** b. at London, in February, 1600; d. there, Oct. 29, 1666. English Presbyterian clergyman; grandfather of Edmund Calamy (1671–1732). He is best remembered as one of the five authors of *Smectymnuus*, the answer to Joseph Hall's view of the divine right of episcopacy. He withdrew (1636) as a lecturer at Bury St. Edmunds, in protest over certain rules on church ceremony, and allied himself with the Puritans. He was pastor of a church at London from 1639, was active in the Westminster Assembly, opposed the execution of Charles I, and was chaplain to Charles II. In 1662, he was ejected from preaching, under the Act of Uniformity.

Calamy, Edmund. b. at London, April 5, 1671; d. June 3, 1732. English Nonconformist clergyman; grandson of Edmund Calamy (1600–66). A writer of many sermons, he also compiled an account of the ministers ejected under the Act of Uniformity.

Calancha (kä.län′chä), **Antonio de la.** b. at Chuquisaca (now Sucre, Bolivia), 1584; d. at Lima, Peru, March 1, 1654. Peruvian Augustine monk. He was rector of the College of San Ildefonso at Lima, and held various offices. His *Cronica moralizada del Orden de San Agustín en el Perú* (Barcelona, 1638) gives much information on the history and ethnology of South America.

Calandrino (kä.län.drē′nō). Subject of a story in Giovanni Boccaccio's *Decameron*. He is very unfortunate and very amusing.

Calantha (ka̧.lan′tha̧). In John Ford's tragedy *The Broken Heart*, the daughter of Amyclas, the king of Laconia. She drops dead of a broken heart after an extraordinary scene in a ballroom during which, with apparent calm and while continuing her dance, she listens to the announcement of the deaths, one after another, of her father, lover, and brother.

Călăraşi (ku.lu.räsh′). [Also: **Kalarash, Kalarashi.**] Town in S Rumania, in the region of Muntenia, situated near the Danube River, ab. 10 mi. NE of Silistra. A river port and a marketing center for agricultural products, especially grain and cattle, it also has mills and fisheries. 24,448 (1948).

Calas (kȧ.läs), **Jean.** b. at Lacaparède, in Languedoc, France, March 19, 1698; broken on the wheel at Toulouse, France, March 9, 1762. French Protestant merchant at Toulouse, a victim of religious fanaticism. He was judicially murdered on the baseless charge of having put his eldest son (actually a suicide) to death to prevent him from becoming a Roman Catholic.

Calasanzio (kä.lä.sän′thyō), San **José.** [English, Saint **Joseph of Calasanza.**] b. at Calasanza, in Aragon, Spain, Sept. 11, 1556; d. at Rome, Aug. 28, 1648. Spanish priest and founder of the Piarists. He studied law at Mérida, and attended the universities of Valencia and Alcalá de Henares. Ordained in 1583, he became secretary to Bishop Figuera at Albarracin and Lérida, and later the vicar general for the district of Tremp. In 1592 he went to Rome, joined the Confraternity of Christian Doctrine, taught poor children, and finally founded the Clerks Regular of the Pious Schools (Piarists), becoming its first superior. He was canonized in 1767.

Calasiao (kä.lä.sē.ou′). Town in Pangasinan province, in W Luzon, Philippine Islands. 1,645 (1948).

Calasparra (kä.läs.pär′rä). Town in E Spain, in the province of Murcia, situated on the Mundo River, NW of Murcia: agricultural trade. 10,342 (1940).

Calatafimi (kä.lä.tä.fē′mē). [Arabic, **Kalat-al-fimi.**] Town and commune in SW Italy, on the island of Sicily, in the province of Trapani, between Palermo and Trapani, on the Icoldo River, ab. 32 mi. SW of Palermo. It is an agricultural trade center, and has a sugar refinery, biscuit manufactures, marble quarries, and sulfur springs. The ruins of the ancient Segesta are in the vicinity. Near here, on May 15, 1860, Giuseppe Garibaldi, with about 2,000 men, defeated 3,600 Neapolitans. The town was taken, on April 22, 838, by the Moslems, who gave it its name (Kalat-al-fimi). Pop. of commune 11,484 (1936); of town, 11,125 (1936).

Calatayud (kä.lä.tä.yöᴛʜ′). [Arabic, **Kalat Ayub.**] City in NE Spain, in the province of Zaragoza, situated on the Jalón River, ab. 45 mi. SW of Saragossa: agricultural trade; leather and silk manufactures. Hemp is grown in the vicinity. The Collegiate Church of Santa María was originally a mosque; the Church of Santo Sepulcro, built in 1141 and restored in 1613, was long the principal church of the Spanish Knights Templar. There is a Moorish castle. Founded by the Moslems in the 8th century, the city was conquered (1120) by Alfonso I of Aragon. The ancient Bilbilis, nearby, was the birthplace of Martial. 18,419 (1940).

Calatrava la Vieja (kä.lä.trä′ʙä lä ʙyā′ʜä). [Also: **Calatrava, Old Calatrava.**] Ruined city in New Castile, Spain, situated on the Guadiana River N of Ciudad Real. It was an important medieval fortress, and seat of the Calatrava Order of Knights, founded in the 12th century for the defense of the frontier against the Moslems (it became an order of merit in 1808).

Calau (kä′lou), **Abraham.** See **Calov, Abraham.**

Calavar: or, The Knight of the Conquest (kal′a̤.vär). Novel (1834) by Robert Montgomery Bird.

Calaveras Big Trees (kal.a̤.ver′a̤s). [Also, **Calaveras Grove.**] State park in E central California, containing the northernmost grove of the Californian big trees, reached from Stockton. It contains about 100 giant redwoods, among them the "Mother of the Forest," 315 ft. in height and 61 in girth. Area, 1,951 acres.

Calaynos (kä.lī′nōs). Tragedy by George Henry Boker. His first play, it was produced at London at the Sadler's Wells Theatre, May 10, 1849, without Boker's consent, by the actor Samuel Phelps. It was first played in the U.S. at the Walnut Street Theatre, Philadelphia, Jan. 20, 1851, with James E. Murdoch taking the part of Calaynos. The main theme of the tragedy is the complex racial friction between the Spaniards and Moors, and the consequent horror felt by the Spaniards for what they deem the "taint" of Moorish blood. Its importance rests not so much upon the plot as upon the creation of lofty standards of race and conduct, the atmosphere of inevitable tragedy, and the distinction of its blank verse.

Calaynos, the Moor. One of the oldest Spanish ballads, in which the French paladins appear associated with various fabulous Spanish heroes.

Calbayog (käl.bä′yôg). Town in Samar province, on the W coast of Samar island, E central Philippine Islands. 7,853 (1948).

Calbe (käl′be̤). [Also, **Kalbe.**] City in C Germany, in the *Land* (state) of Saxony-Anhalt, Russian Zone, formerly in the province of Saxony, Prussia, situated on the Saale River, ab. 18 mi. S of Magdeburg: railroad junction and the center of a market-gardening district. Before World War II it had manufactures of woolens and chemicals, and sugar refineries. Lignite mines are in the vicinity. 15,161 (1946).

Calcar or **Kalkar** (käl′kär) or **Kalcker** (käl′kėr), **Jan Stephen von.** [Also: **John de Calcar** (or **Kalcker**), **Jan Stevenszoon van Calcar** (or **Kalkar** or **Kalcker**), **Jan Stephanus van Calcker.**] b. at Calcar, in the duchy of Cleve, Rhenish Prussia, c1499; d. at Naples, Italy, c1546. Dutch painter, illustrator, and designer. He seems to have begun his professional training at Dordrecht in the Netherlands before going to Italy, which became the scene of his career. He became a disciple of Titian and also made a special study of the works of Raphael, and is noted for imitations of those masters which are almost indistinguishable from their authentic works. Calcar painted portraits and landscapes and made designs for woodcuts. He is thought to have drawn the portraits for Vasari's *Lives of Painters, Sculptors and Architects*, and is known to have illustrated the *De humanis corporis fabrica* of Andreas Vesalius.

Calcaria (kal.kãr′i.a̤). Latin name of **Tadcaster.**

Calcasieu (kal′ka̤.shö). River in W Louisiana which flows through Lake Calcasieu into the Gulf of Mexico. Length, ab. 200 mi.

Calceta (käl.sā′tä). City in W Ecuador, in Manabí province. 13,366 (est. 1944).

Calchaquí (käl.chä.kē′). Subgroup of the Diaguita group of Indian peoples who lived in NW Argentina. They became so well known for their fierce resistance to the Spanish that the name has sometimes been applied to the whole Diaguita group.

Calchas (kal′ka̤s). In Greek legend, the wisest soothsayer who accompanied the expedition against Troy. He was a son of Thestor of Mycenae or Megara. According to the oracle he must die when he met a soothsayer wiser than himself; this happened when he met Miopsus at Claros. He is introduced in Shakespeare's *Troilus and Cressida.*

Calcraft (kal′kráft), **John William.** Pseudonym of **Cole, John William.**

Calcutta (kal.kut′a̤). [Hindustani, **Kalikata**; original name, probably **Kalighat,** referring to a shrine of the goddess Kali in the vicinity.] Capital and seaport of West Bengal state, Union of India, on the Hooghly River, ab. 120 mi. above the Bay of Bengal: the chief commercial center of Asia, served by several railroads and by national and international air and steamship lines. Exports include opium, tea, jute, grain, lac, indigo, hides, iron, vegetable oils and oilseeds, tobacco, and cotton. Calcutta is the center of the jute-manufacturing industry; there are also flour and paper manufacturing plants, match factories, chemical works, rice mills, vegetable-oil mills, ironworks, and tanneries. The greater metropolitan area includes Howrah and Serampore on the W and Barrackpore and Dum-Dum, both of which have major airports, on the N. Among the principal objects of interest are Fort William, Government House, an arsenal, Calcutta University (established 1857), botanical gardens, the Victoria Memorial (national gallery for India), and a Sanskrit college. It is also the seat of the high court of West Bengal and of an Indian government mint. Pop., with suburbs, 2,108,891 (1941); 5,007,772 (est. 1949).

History. Calcutta was founded as an East India Company factory c1690, was fortified in 1696, and was originally called Fort William. It was attacked by Siraj-ud-daula in 1756, and was the scene of the tragedy of the Black Hole. It was retaken by Clive in 1757, and became the capital of British India in 1773. The seat of government was transferred to Delhi in 1912.

Caldani (käl.dä′nē), **Leopoldo Marco Antonio.** b. at Bologna, Italy, Nov. 21, 1725; d. at Padua, Italy, Dec. 24, 1813. Italian anatomist. His chief works are *Icones anatomicae* (1801–14) and *Explicatio iconum anatomicarum* (1802–14).

Caldara (käl.dä′rä), **Antonio.** b. at Venice, c1670; d. Dec. 28, 1736. Italian composer of operas and oratorios. A pupil of Giovanni Legrenzi, he was a cellist at Rome, Venice, and Madrid, before being appointed (1716) *Kapellmeister* (choir leader) at Vienna. He composed some 90 operas and more than 30 oratorios, as well as masses and sonatas.

Caldara, Polidoro. See **Caravaggio, Polidoro da.**

Caldas (käl'däs). Department in C Colombia. Capital, Manizales; area, 5,162 sq. mi.; pop. 1,100,400 (est. 1950).

Caldas, Francisco José de. b. at Popayán, Cauca, Colombia, 1771; executed at Bogotá, Colombia, Oct. 29, 1816. Colombian naturalist. He made important studies in botany and geography, traveling for some time with Alexander von Humboldt and Aimé Jacques Alexandre Bonpland. In 1805 he was made director of the observatory at Bogotá. When the revolution of 1810 broke out, he became chief of engineers in the patriot army, but was not actively engaged in the field. The Spaniards captured him in 1816, and he was shot.

Caldas Barbosa (käl'dạs bạr.bô'zạ), **Domingos.** See **Barbosa, Domingos Caldas.**

Caldas da Rainha (käl'dạsh dạ rī'nyạ). Town and *concelho* (commune) in W Portugal, in the province of Estremadura, in the district of Lisboa (Lisbon), situated near the Atlantic Ocean, N of the city of Lisbon. A health resort, it has hot sulfur springs and famous bathing establishments. It is an important center for majolica manufacture. The Church of Nossa Senhora do Pópulo was finished in 1500. Pop. of concelho, 35,628 (1940); of town, 10,714 (1940).

Caldas de Monchique (dē mōṅ.shē'kẹ). See under **Monchique,** Portugal.

Caldecott (kôl'dẹ.kọt), **Randolph.** b. at Chester, England, March 22, 1846; d. at St. Augustine, Fla., Feb. 12, 1886. English painter and illustrator. He was educated at King Henry VIII's School at Chester, and in 1872 went to London. In 1882 he became a member of the Royal Institute of Painters in Water Colours, exhibiting there, at the Royal Academy, and at the Grosvenor Gallery. His most characteristic and interesting work was done for children's books; he also illustrated Washington Irving's *Old Christmas* and *Bracebridge Hall.*

Caldeira Brant Pontes (käl.dā'rạ brunt pōn'tēs), **Felisberto** (or **Feliberto**). [Title, Marquês **de Barbacena.**] b. near Mariana, Minas Gerais, Brazil, Sept. 19, 1772; d. at Rio de Janeiro, June 13, 1841. Brazilian soldier and statesman. In 1823 he was a member of the constituent assembly, in 1826 was chosen senator, and in January, 1827, assumed command of the Brazilian army in Uruguay, but was defeated at the battle of Ituzaingó, on Feb. 20, 1827, and soon after relieved. In 1828 he accompanied the young Queen of Portugal, Maria II, to Europe, and defended her rights there with great decision and skill. From December, 1829, to October, 1830, he was prime minister.

Calder (kôl'dėr). See also **Cawdor.**

Calder. River in C and NW England, in Lancashire and the West Riding of Yorkshire. It rises S of Burnley and flows E and SE, joining the river Aire at Castleford, ab. 9 mi. SE of Leeds. Length ab. 40 mi.

Calder, Alexander. b. at Philadelphia, June 22, 1898—. American sculptor, painter, and illustrator, most noted for his abstract compositions and constructions, called "mobiles" and "stabiles"; son of Alexander Stirling Calder, and grandson of Alexander Milne Calder. He studied at the Stevens Institute of Technology, Hoboken, N.J., and at the Art Students League of New York, and in 1926 went to Paris. His first mobiles ("plastic forms in motion") were executed in 1931, and he first exhibited at Paris in 1932. Later, his works were shown at Moscow and in the U.S. The Museum of Modern Art and the Metropolitan Museum of Art at New York, the Museum of Western Art at Moscow, Smith College, and the Chicago Art Club own his works, among which are many mobiles and stabiles ("static abstract sculptures"). He has also illustrated books, including *The Fables of Aesop* (1931) and *Three Young Rats* (1944).

Calder, Alexander Milne. b. at Aberdeen, Scotland, Aug. 23, 1846; d. at Philadelphia, June 14, 1923. American sculptor who executed the colossal statue of William Penn and groups on the city hall tower, at Philadelphia: father of Alexander Stirling Calder, and grandfather of Alexander Calder. He studied at Edinburgh and in England, and in 1868 went to Philadelphia, where he studied at the Pennsylvania Academy of the Fine Arts under Thomas Eakins and J. A. Bailly. His sculpture is in the Pennsylvania Academy of the Fine Arts, Drexel Institute, and public buildings and parks at Philadelphia. Some of his works are *General George G. Meade,* memorials of *Chief Justice Sharswood* and *John MacArthur,* and three portrait busts in the Union League Club, Philadelphia.

Calder, Alexander Stirling. b. at Philadelphia, Jan. 11, 1870; d. at New York, Jan. 6, 1945. American sculptor who taught at the National Academy of Design and the Art Students League of New York; son of Alexander Milne Calder, and father of Alexander Calder. He studied at the Pennsylvania Academy of the Fine Arts, and at Paris, and exhibited his work widely in the U.S., winning many prizes. He executed commissions for the Panama-Pacific Exposition (for which he was acting chief of the department of sculpture), the U.S. post office at Washington, D.C., the state capitol at Jefferson City, Mo., Saint Mary's Church at Detroit, and many others. In 1937 he was a sculptor member of the Fine Arts Commission at New York; he was made an associate of the National Academy in 1906, and an academician in 1913. Some of his better-known works are the statues *Witherspoon, M. Whitman,* and *Davies;* the *Lea Memorial* at Laurel Hill Cemetery, Philadelphia; *Fountain of Energy, The Star,* the *Washington Group* on the Washington Arch at New York, *The Island,* the *Ericsson Memorial, Continental Post Rider,* and *William Penn* and *John James Audubon* for the Hall of Fame.

Calder, Sir **Robert.** b. at Elgin, Moray, Scotland, July 2, 1745; d. at Holt, Hampshire, England, Aug. 31, 1818. British admiral. He served with distinction as captain of the fleet at Cape St. Vincent in 1797. In the summer of 1805 Calder, then a vice-admiral, met a section of the French fleet under Villeneuve off Cape Finisterre. He captured two ships and was afterward credited with having destroyed Napoleon's hope of invading England.

Caldera (käl.dā'rä). Seaport in the province of Atacama, in NW Chile: distributing point for a mineral district. The town disputes with Tucacas, Venezuela, according to some sources, the claim of having been the point of departure for the first steam train run in South America. Pop. under 5,000 (1940).

Calderón (käl.dā.rōn'), Conde **de.** Title of **Calleja del Rey, Félix María.**

Calderón, Francisco García. b. at Arequipa, Peru, c1834; d. at Lima, Peru, Sept. 21, 1905. Peruvian lawyer and statesman. In 1867 he was elected to congress, and in 1868 became minister of the treasury. After the Chileans occupied (1881) Lima, and President Nicolás de Piérola had fled, the citizens elected Calderón provisional president of Peru, a choice which was afterward ratified by congress. He attempted to treat with the Chileans and to secure the interference of the U.S. To prevent this the Chileans seized him and sent him to Valparaíso, where he was confined until the close of the war. He returned to Lima in 1886, and was made president of the senate. He was influential in arranging the Grace Contract by which the finances of Peru were put on a better footing. He published a dictionary of Peruvian legislation, and served as rector of San Marcos University.

Calderon (kôl'dėr.ọn), **Philip Hermogenes.** b. at Poitiers, France, May 3, 1833; d. April 30, 1898. English painter, of Spanish descent. His works include *Broken Vows* and *The Renunciation.*

Calderón (käl.dā.rōn'), **Serafín Estébanez.** [Pseudonym, **El Solitario.**] b. at Málaga, Spain, 1779; d. Feb. 7, 1867. Spanish poet and novelist. He wrote the novel *Cristianos y Moriscos* (1838), *Las Poesias del Solitario* (1833), and *Escenas Andaluzas* (1847).

Calderón Bridge. [Spanish, **Puente de Calderón.**] Bridge in W central Mexico, ab. 27 mi. E of Guadalajara, where the royal road from Lagos crossed the upper Santiago (or Lerma) River. It was the site of a battle in the Mexican revolution on Jan. 17, 1811, when a royalist force of about 5,000 soldiers led by Calleja del Rey decisively defeated a mob of 93,000 insurgents under Hidalgo y Costilla. The victory was largely due to an accident by which the long grass was set on fire in front of Hidalgo's army, forcing it to retreat in confusion. This battle decided the failure of the first attempt to make Mexico independent.

Calderón de la Barca (dā lä bär'kä), **Frances Inglis.** b. in Scotland, c1810. Scottish writer; wife of a Spanish diplomat. She was the author of *Life in Mexico* (1843).

Calderón de la Barca, Pedro. b. at Madrid, Jan. 17, 1600; d. there, May 25, 1681. Spanish dramatist and poet. He was educated first by the Jesuits and then at Salamanca, being graduated from the latter university in 1619. He had at that time already some reputation as a dramatist. His extraordinary popularity continued until his death. He himself made a list of 111 plays and 70 (or 73) sacramental *autos* which forms the basis for a proper knowledge of his works. His *comedias de capa y espada* (comedies of the cloak and sword) are peculiarly characteristic, and about 30 of these can be enumerated. Among them are *La Dama duende* (The Fairy Lady), *Mejor está que estaba* (It is Better than it Was), *Peor está que estaba* (It is Worse than it Was), and *Astrologo fingido* (The Mock Astrologer); John Dryden used this last in his *An Evening's Love, or The Mock Astrologer*. Among his other plays are *El Mágico prodigioso* (The Wonder-working Magician), *La Devoción de la cruz* (The Devotion of the Cross), *El Principe constante* (The Constant Prince), *La Vida es sueño* (Life is a Dream), *El Mayor encanto amor* (No Magic like Love), and *Las Armas de la hermosura* (The Weapons of Beauty).

Calderón Guardia (gwär'ᴛʜyä), **Rafael Ángel.** b. at San José, Costa Rica, March 10, 1900—. Costa Rican physician, surgeon, and statesman, president (1940–44) of Costa Rica. He received his medical degree in 1928. A national deputy (1934–42), and vice-president (1935–37), and president (1938–39) of the Congreso Nacional, he was also vice-president and later president (1935–37) of the municipality of San José. Third alternate for president (1936–40) of the Costa Rican republic, he was president from 1940 to 1944. He was also a member of the board of directors of the Durán Sanitarium, and served on the faculty of the University of Costa Rica.

Calderon the Courtier. Historical novel based on events in Spanish history, by Edward Bulwer-Lytton, published in 1838.

Calder v. Bull, 3 Dallas 386 (1798). U.S. Supreme Court decision upholding the constitutionality of the Connecticut legislature's grant of a retrial in a civil case. The high court here gave its classic definition of an ex post facto law, holding that "ex post facto laws extend to criminal, and not to civil cases," and indicating what provisions in an act would be considered ex post facto in character.

Calderwood (kôl'dėr.wůd), **David.** b., probably at Dalkeith, Scotland, 1575; d. at Jedburgh, Scotland, Oct. 29, 1650. Scottish clergyman and church historian. His chief works are *The Altar of Damascus* (1621; also in Latin, 1623) and *History of the Kirk of Scotland* (1678).

Calderwood, Henry. b. at Peebles, Scotland, May 10, 1830; d. at Edinburgh, Nov. 19, 1897. Scottish philosophical writer. He served as professor of moral philosophy in the University of Edinburgh (1868–97).

Caldicott (kôl'di.kọt), **Alfred James.** b. 1842; d. 1897. English composer and conductor. He led (1885–89) the concerts at the Albert Hall at London, and was professor (1892 *et seq.*) at the Royal College of Music, and subsequently conductor (1893) at the London Comedy Theatre, and principal of the London College of Music. His compositions include the cantatas *The Widow of Nain* and *A Rhine Legend*, and operettas, glees, and part songs.

Caldiero (käl.dye'rō). Village in N Italy, in Veneto, ab. 8 mi. E of Verona. Here, on Nov. 12, 1796, the Austrians under Josef Alvinczy repulsed Napoleon I, and in the period of Oct. 29 to Nov. 12, 1805, the archduke Charles Louis of Austria and the French marshal André Masséna fought two engagements, the first of which was won by the Austrians, the second by the French.

Caldwell (kôld'wel, -wẹl; kold'-). City in SW Idaho, county seat of Canyon County. It is the seat of the College of Idaho. Agricultural products are processed and roses grown here. 10,487 (1950).

Caldwell. Borough in NE New Jersey, in Essex County, near Montclair. It was the birthplace of Grover Cleveland. 6,270 (1950).

Caldwell. Town in E New York, in Warren County, at the S end of Lake George, ab. 53 mi. N of Albany: summer resort. Forts George and William Henry were situated here in the 18th century. 1,621 (1950).

Caldwell, Erskine (Preston). b. at White Oak, Ga., Dec. 17, 1903—. American novelist and short-story writer; husband (1939–42) of Margaret Bourke-White, his second wife. He became editor (1940) of *American Folkways*, and a correspondent (1941) in Russia for *Life*, the New York newspaper *PM*, and the Columbia Broadcasting System. He is best known for his novels and stories treating the lives of poor Southern whites, in which their humor and misery are both portrayed with peculiar vividness. His works include *The Bastard* (1929), *Poor Fool* (1930), *American Earth* (1931), *God's Little Acre* (1933), *We Are the Living* (1933), *Journeyman* (1935), *Kneel to the Rising Sun* (1935), *Some American People* (1935), *All-Out on the Road to Smolensk* (1942), *Tragic Ground* (1944), *A House in the Uplands* (1946), *This Very Earth* (1948), *A Place Called Estherville* (1949), and *A Lamp for Nightfall* (1952). He wrote with Margaret Bourke-White *You Have Seen Their Faces* (1937), *North of the Danube* (1938), *Shooting the Russian War* (1942), and other books. His *Tobacco Road* (1932) in dramatization surpassed (1939) the record of New York performances set by *Abie's Irish Rose*. The autobiographical *Call It Experience* was published in 1951.

Caldwell, Joseph. b. at Lamington, N.J., April 21, 1773; d. at Chapel Hill, N.C., Jan. 27, 1835. American clergyman and educator. He became president of the University of North Carolina in 1804.

Caldwell, Otis William. b. at Lebanon, Ind., Dec. 18, 1869; d. July 5, 1947. American botanist and educator. A graduate (1898) of the University of Chicago, he was associate professor of botany (1907–13), and a professor and dean of University College (1913–17) at the University of Chicago. In 1917 he became professor of education at Teachers College, Columbia University, a post he held until 1935. Author of *Laboratory and Field Manual of Botany* (1901), *Introduction to Botany* (1914), *Then and Now in Education* (1923), and *Open Doors to Science* (1925); coauthor, with F. D. Curtis, of *Introduction to Science* (1929) and *Everday Science* (1943).

Caldwell, Taylor. [Full name, **Janet Taylor Caldwell.**] b. at Preswich, Manchester, England, Sept. 7, 1900—. American novelist. She came to the U.S. in 1907. Her works include *Dynasty of Death* (1938), *The Eagles Gather* (1940), *The Earth Is the Lord's* (1941), *The Strong City* (1942), *The Final Hour* (1944), *This Side of Innocence* (1946), *Melissa* (1948), *The Devil's Advocate* (1952), and other novels.

Cale (kål), **Guillaume.** [Also, **Caillet.**] d. 1358. French peasant who assumed the name of Jacques Bonhomme, and was leader of the Jacquerie in 1358.

Caleb (kā'lẹb). In the Old Testament, a Hebrew leader at the time of the conquest of Canaan. He was one of those who were sent as spies into the land of Canaan. Num. xiii. 6.

Caleb. Character in John Dryden's satire *Absalom and Achitophel*. He is intended for Lord Grey of Wark, one of the adherents of the Duke of Monmouth.

Caleb Balderstone (bôl'dėr.stōn). See **Balderstone, Caleb.**

Caleb Plummer (plum'ėr). See **Plummer, Caleb.**

Caleb Quotem (kwōt'ẹm). See **Quotem, Caleb.**

Caleb Williams, or Things as They Are. Novel by William Godwin, published in 1794. In it Godwin sharply contrasts the power possessed by the privileged and the helplessness of the lowly.

Caled (kä'led). See **Khalid.**

Caledonia (kal.ẹ.dō'ni.ạ). Roman name for the N part of the island of Britain, comprising all of present-day Scotland N of the Firth of Forth and the Firth of Clyde. Although the Romans made numerous expeditions against the tribes of Caledonia between the 1st and 3rd centuries A.D., the region was never subjugated. The name Caledonia is often used in literature to mean Scotland.

Caledonian Canal (kal.ẹ.dō'ni.ạn). Canal in N Scotland, in Inverness-shire. It connects the North Sea (via Moray Firth) with the Atlantic Ocean (via Loch Linnhe, the Sound of Mull, etc.). The canal, constructed in the period 1803–47, and opened in 1822, extends from Inverness, at its NE end, through Loch Ness, Loch Oich, and Loch Lochy to Corpach on Loch Eil, at its SW terminus. The depth of the navigable channel averages 18 ft.; it has 29 locks. The canal has never had extensive use. Distance from Inverness to Corpach, ab. 61 mi., of which ab. 22 mi. is canalized.

Calef (kā′lḙf), **Robert.** b. 1648; d. at Roxbury, Mass., April 13, 1719. American merchant, notable as an opponent of witchcraft persecutions. Although it is supposed that he was of English birth, nothing is known of him until 1688, by which time he was established as a cloth merchant at Boston. In 1693 he began privately to circulate a vigorous criticism and condemnation of the Salem witchcraft trials and of the theory of witchcraft behind them (though he conceded the existence of witches). In this connection he accused Cotton Mather of trying to whip up a witch-persecuting hysteria at Boston. Mather caused Calef to be arrested, but desisted from prosecuting the matter when the merchant offered a mollifying, though perhaps disingenuous, explanation of his allegations. Thereafter Calef arranged for the publication of his polemic in London, where it was printed in 1700 under the title *More Wonders of the Invisible World.* It was widely circulated in New England, and though some commentators consider it unfair, it is generally credited with a salutary influence in curbing witch hunts; although Increase Mather burned a copy of it in the Harvard Yard, Cotton Mather made no reply to it. A rumor that the book was in fact written by his son Robert has little support, as the latter would have been a child when the polemic was first circulated, and still a minor when it was published. In his later years the elder Robert Calef evidently enjoyed public esteem, as he is known to have held public office at Boston and Roxbury.

Calenberg (kä′lḙn.berk). See **Kalenberg.**

Calendar Stone. Stone disk nearly 13 ft. in diameter which was a prominent feature in the religious life of the Aztec Indians of pre-conquest Mexico. It is believed to have been carved in 1479; the surface is covered with complex low-relief sculpture which records Aztec cosmogony, the ritual calendar of 20 days, and other symbols of important elements of the Aztec religion. It is now in the National Museum at Mexico City.

Calenders, The Three. In *The Arabian Nights' Entertainments,* three princes disguised as calenders, or begging dervishes. They have but one eye each.

Calentes Aquae (kạ.len′tēz ak′wē). Latin name of **Chaudesaigues.**

Calepine (kal′ḙ.pēn), **Sir.** In Edmund Spenser's *The Faerie Queene,* a knight who saves a child from a bear by squeezing the latter to death.

Calepino (kä.lā.pē′nō), **Ambrogio.** b. at Calepio, near Bergamo, Italy, June 6, 1435; d. there, Nov. 30, 1511. Italian lexicographer. He compiled a Latin-Italian dictionary, originally entitled *Cornucopiae* (1502), which passed through many editions, and became, after successive enlargements, in 1590 a polyglot of 11 languages. Jacopo Facciolati reduced this number to seven in his edition (1718).

Cales (kā′lēz). Former English name of the city of **Cádiz,** Spain.

Caleti (kạ.lē′tī) or **Caletes** (-tēz) or **Caletae** (-tē). Ancient Belgic tribe dwelling in the vicinity of what is now Rouen, France. In the period 52–51 B.C. they united with the Bellovaci to oppose Caesar, and were subjugated by him in the same years.

Caletti-Bruni (kä.lāt′tē.brö′nē), **Pietro Francesco.** Original name of **Cavalli, Pietro Francesco.**

Calexico (kạ.lek′si.kō). City in S California, in Imperial County on the Mexican border, S by SE of Los Angeles. 6,433 (1950).

Calf of Man. Small island immediately off the SW extremity of the Isle of Man, in the Irish Sea W of N central England. The island is overrun by wild rabbits. The ruins of an ancient chapel are here, on the highest point (360 ft.). Length, ab. 2 mi.; width, ab. 1 mi.

Calgary (kal′gạ.ri). City in S Alberta, Canada, the second largest in the province and the tenth largest in the Dominion. It is on the main line of the Canadian Pacific Railway and is connected by road and rail with Edmonton, ab. 190 mi. to the N. The city is a prosperous and growing one near the Turner Valley oil field and some coal fields. It is also the center of a vast irrigation project, and the commercial and business center for S Alberta. Pop. of city, 129,060 (1951); with suburbs, 139,105 (1951).

Calhoun (kal.hön′). City in NW Georgia, county seat of Gordon County. Cotton sheeting and bedspreads are manufactured. In the vicinity there are poultry and dairy farms. 3,231 (1950).

Calhoun, John. b. at Boston, Oct. 14, 1806; d. at St. Joseph, Mo., Oct. 13, 1859. American lawyer and politician, accused of complicity in the allegedly packed election of Dec. 21, 1857, which thrust the proslavery Lecompton Constitution on Kansas. He was later (1858) falsely accused of taking the ballots to Missouri when a free-state legislature called for an investigation. Despite his service (1857) as president of the constitutional convention at Lecompton, documents published after his death indicate that he may have been, in fact, a sincere opponent of the proslave Southern scheme to make Kansas a slave state. Although a leading Douglas Democrat, he was a lifelong friend of Lincoln, who was at one time his deputy as surveyor of Sangamon County.

Calhoun, John Caldwell. b. in Abbeville County, S.C., March 18, 1782; d. March 31, 1850. American statesman and political philosopher, famed for his part in the Nullification Controversy (1828–32), his interpretation and defense of states' rights and his staunch expression of the Southern point of view in national affairs, particularly after 1833. He graduated (1804) from Yale, studied law at Litchfield, Conn., and Charleston, S.C., was admitted to the bar (1807), and commenced law practice at Abbeville, S.C. Beginning his political career as a Republican (he became a Democrat after the mid-1830's), he was elected (1808) to the South Carolina legislature and went to Congress in 1811; as acting chairman of the committee on foreign affairs, he became prominent as one of the "war hawks" who pressed for a declaration of war against Great Britain. He was appointed (1817) secretary of war under President James Monroe, and during his tenure improved the military administration and set up the offices of the surgeon-general, quartermaster-general, and commissary-general. Elected vice-president in 1824, he served in the administration of John Quincy Adams and during the first term of Andrew Jackson, resigning in 1832. The mounting antagonism between Jackson and Calhoun was brought to a head during the Nullification Controversy, which sprang originally from the tariff issue but later embraced the question of states' rights vs. federal rights. Calhoun wrote the "South Carolina Exposition" (together with his other writings, it appears in his *Works,* edited by R. K. Crallé (6 vols., 1851–55), in which he denied the constitutionality of protective tariffs and defended the power of a state to block the enforcement of an unconstitutional act within its own borders. The "Exposition" formed the foundation of the nullification doctrine, which Calhoun later expanded into a general assertion of state sovereignty, including the right of nullification and secession, as a check against encroachment by the national power. The Nullification Controversy was finally settled by a compromise, but from this time onward, particularly as the slavery issue loomed larger on the national horizon, Calhoun drew steadily away from nationalism and became the ardent spokesman of the Southern section, ultimately defending slavery as a social necessity and good. His ideas as a political philosopher appear in his "Disquisition on Government" and "Discourse on the Constitution and Government of the United States." In them he appeared as the champion of checks upon absolute authority, and in the latter work advocated a dual presidency to safeguard the interests of North and South. He was the moving spirit behind the Nashville Convention (1850). See the biography by William M. Meigs (2 vols., 1917).

Calhoun, William James. b. at Pittsburgh, Pa., Oct. 5, 1843; d. Sept. 19, 1916. American diplomat. He was admitted to the bar in 1875, and subsequently practiced law. He was a member of the U.S. Interstate Commerce Commission (1898–1900), special commissioner to Venezuela in 1905, and minister to China from December, 1909.

Cali (kä′lē). City in W Colombia, capital of Valle del Cauca department: commercial and mining center; founded in 1536. Elevation, ab. 3,000 ft.; pop. 243,463 (1951).

Caliana (kä.lyä′nä) or **Calianan** (-nạn). See under **Kaliana.**

Caliari (kä.lyä′rē), **Paolo.** See **Veronese, Paolo.**

Caliban (kal′i.ban). In Shakespeare's *The Tempest,* a deformed and repulsive slave. The son of the witch Sycorax, who ruled the island before Prospero's shipwreck on it, he becomes a reluctant captive to Prospero's magic powers. He grumbles at his lot, and wishes to break free, allying himself with Stephano and Trinculo for that purpose. After Prospero's rescue, Caliban is left the sole inhabitant of the island.

Caliban. Novel by W. L. George, published in 1920. It is a study of newspaper life.

Caliban. Pseudonym of **Bergerat, Auguste Émile.**

Caliban by the Yellow Sands. Play (1916) by Percy MacKaye. It was written for the Shakespeare tercentenary.

Caliban upon Setebos; or, Natural Theology in the Island (set′ę.bos). Poem by Robert Browning, published in *Dramatis Personae* (1864). The poem reflects Browning's keen interest in the Darwinian hypothesis, which was a new, very much publicized, and extremely controversial issue at that time. Although the link between Browning's Caliban and the Caliban of Shakespeare is clear enough, Browning's use of the character to epitomize human superstition, vindictiveness, and abject terror at the thought that certain natural phenomena (such as thunderstorms) are measures taken by Setebos (who is Caliban's god) to punish human impudence is far more complex than Shakespeare's. A clue to Browning's purpose in the poem may be obtained from the line taken from the Fiftieth Psalm which immediately follows the title: "Thou thoughtest that I was altogether such a one as thyself." In other words, Caliban (and by extension, man) cannot think of the Deity except as being a more powerful extension of himself, and Caliban attributes to Setebos, indeed, all the aches, pains, appetites, and irresponsibility which mark his own character. Caliban's musing, at the very beginning of the poem, as to the manner and fashion of the Creation makes this clear, and also establishes in a few lines what may be called the flavor and direction of the poem as a whole:

Setebos, Setebos, and Setebos!
'Thinketh, He dwelleth i' the cold o' the moon.
'Thinketh He made it, with the sun to match,
But not the stars; the stars came otherwise;
Only made clouds, winds, meteors, such as that:
Also this isle, what lives and grows thereon,
And snaky sea which rounds and ends the same.
'Thinketh, it came of being ill at ease:
He hated that He cannot change His cold,
Nor cure its ache.

Caliburn (kal′i.bėrn). See **Excalibur.**

Calicut (kal′i.kut). [Also: **Kolikod**; Hindustani, **Kolikodu.**] Seaport in the Malabar district, Madras state, SW Union of India, on the Indian Ocean, ab. 170 mi. SW of Bangalore. The port is practically closed during the southwest monsoon season. The harbor is very shallow and steamers anchor ab. 3 mi. from shore. Exports include copra, tea, rubber, pepper, and raw cotton. The name "calico" was derived from this city, from which printed cotton cloth was exported to England as early as the 17th century. It was the first Indian port visited by Vasco da Gama in 1498. It was destroyed by Tipu Sahib in 1789, and ceded to the British in 1792. Pop. 126,352 (1941).

Calidore (kal′i.dōr), **Sir.** A knight in Edmund Spenser's *The Faerie Queene*, the personification of courtesy. He is modeled upon Sir Philip Sidney.

Calife de Bagdad (kȧ.lēf dė bȧg.dȧd), **Le.** Opera by François Adrien Boieldieu, first produced in Paris on Sept. 16, 1800.

California (kal.i.fôrn′yą, -fôr′ni.ą). [Called the **"Golden State"**; sometimes also **"El Dorado."**] State of the W United States, bounded by Oregon on the N, Nevada and Arizona on the E, Mexico (Baja California, or Lower California) on the S, and the Pacific Ocean on the W: one of the Pacific States.

Population, Area, and Political Divisions. California is divided for administrative purposes into 58 counties. It sends 23 representatives to Congress and has 25 electoral votes. Capital, Sacramento; area, 156,803 sq. mi. (158,693 sq. mi., including water); pop. 10,586,223 (1950). Among the states it ranks second in area, and second (on the basis of the 1950 census) in population. The leading cities include Los Angeles, San Francisco, Oakland, San Diego, Long Beach, Sacramento, Berkeley, Pasadena, Richmond, San Jose, Glendale, Fresno, Burbank, and Stockton.

Terrain and Climate. California's physical features are extremely varied, ranging from fertile coastal plain and desert to lofty mountain peaks, from the lowest to the highest points in the continental U.S. Higher of the state's two large mountain ranges is the Sierra Nevada, stretching along the E boundary and containing in the S part Mount Whitney (14,495 ft.), the highest mountain in the state and the highest in the continental U.S. In the N part of the Sierra Nevada is Mount Shasta (14,162 ft.). Lassen Peak, the only active volcano in the U.S., and the 103,429-acre Lassen National Park (established 1916) are also in the Sierra Nevada, as are the 385,100-acre Sequoia National Park (established 1890), which contains famous groves of giant sequoia trees, and the 756,441-acre Yosemite National Park. Death Valley, 276 ft. below sea level and the lowest point in the U.S., is a national monument lying S of the Sierra Nevada. Stretching along the Pacific Coast of California are the lower Coast Ranges. Through a gap at San Francisco Bay the Sacramento and San Joaquin rivers flow to the sea, draining the great Central Valley, a fertile valley bounded by the Sierra Nevada on the E. Supplemental water for these irrigated valley lands is provided by the Central Valley reclamation project, consisting of Shasta and Friant Dams, and Keswick Dam (still under construction in 1950). These reservoirs and canals provide added flood control, electric power, and river navigation. The valley, some 400 mi. in length, produces much of the agricultural wealth of the state. The Mojave Desert lies S of Death Valley. Still further S is the Colorado Desert containing Imperial Valley, former desert land reclaimed by extensive irrigation. In the valley is Salton Sea, created (1905) by flood waters of the Colorado River overflowing into the depression formerly known as Salton Sink. The Colorado forms the state's SE border. The Sacramento, starting near Mount Shasta, flows into San Francisco Bay after being joined near its mouth by the San Joaquin. Lake Tahoe, near the Nevada border, is a well-known tourist resort. Among the bays and inlets along the coast is San Francisco Bay, which, with its extension San Pablo Bay, discharges into the Pacific by a strait known as the Golden Gate (ab. 2 mi. wide). At the S entrance to the bay is the city of San Francisco, and on the NE shore is Oakland. The Farallons, a small group of barren islands, lie off San Francisco ab. 35 mi. W of the Golden Gate. Monterey Bay lies to the S, while still further S are the Santa Barbara Islands and the popular tourist resort Santa Catalina Island. Mare Island in San Pablo Bay is the site of a U.S. Navy Yard.

Industry, Agriculture, and Trade. Although the state ranks high in agriculture, mining, and fishery, manufacturing is its most important industry. Major groups of industries, in the order of their importance, are: food products (including a large percentage of the nation's canned fruit, tuna, and sardines), transportation equipment (including aircraft and parts, automobile assembly, and shipbuilding), fabricated metal products, machinery, chemical products, lumber and wood products, petroleum refinery products, apparel, primary metal products (including steel), stone, clay, and glass products (including ceramics), and paper and paper products. One of the best known of California industries is motion-picture production. California agriculture provides a large share of the country's fruits and nuts, as well as a sizable amount of its vegetables. Wines, brandies, grains, cotton, and sugar beets are also important. Petroleum, natural gas, natural gasoline, gold, mercury, cement, and timber are among the valuable resources. Annual income in the state from manufacturing ranges as high as eight billion dollars; from agriculture, as high as two billion dollars; from mineral output, as high as one billion dollars.

History. Spanish explorers named California after an island described in the Spanish romance *Las Sergas de Esplandian* (1510) as being fabulously rich in gold and precious stones. Cabrillo first explored (1542–43) the coast. Sir Francis Drake also reached (1579) the coast. Spanish missionaries established themselves in the region in the 18th century, the first Franciscan mission being located (1769) at San Diego. California was a Mexican state from 1822; it was occupied (1846–47) by U.S. troops in the Mexican War, and ceded (1848) by Mexico to the U.S. The discovery of gold at Sutter's Mill, Coloma, in El Dorado County, on Jan. 24, 1848, set off the rush for gold which brought hundreds of thousands of persons (called "forty-niners") to the coast in search of gold, and created many new towns. California was admitted to the Union (as the 31st state) as a free state on Sept. 9, 1850, under the Compromise of 1850. The present constitution was framed 1878–79, effective 1880. Heavy Chinese immigration during the gold rush and subsequent large-scale importation of Chinese labor for mines and railroads aroused considerable anti-Chinese feeling in the 1870's and greatly influenced Congressional enactment (1882) of the Chinese Exclusion Act. An earthquake and fire caused severe damage at San Francisco in 1906. The state experienced in the 1930's a heavy influx of migrant farmers, called "Okies" because many came from Oklahoma, who had lost their land owing to drought and insect plagues. The Golden Gate International Exposition (1939) and the United Nations Conference on International Organization (1945, with 46 nations participating) were held at San Francisco.

Culture. California's sunny climate has drawn to the state thousands of residents from other parts of the U.S. and has also made it the mecca of thousands of tourists each year. Hollywood has long been a center of the motion-picture industry, with Beverly Hills and Bel Air famous as the homes of film stars. Radio and television programs are more recent developments. The state experienced considerable industrial development, particularly in aircraft, shipbuilding, and metal industries, during World War II, and a resultant leap in population as workers flowed into the state. Although large fruit and vegetable ranches are located in the valley area of the state, only about ten percent of the population are farm residents. San Francisco is one of the great cultural cities of the U.S., known as a journalistic and literary center where Mark Twain, Bret Harte, Joaquin Miller, Frank Norris, Jack London, Ambrose Bierce, Gertrude Atherton, and others worked. Carmel is an art colony, known particularly as the residence of the poet Robinson Jeffers. The state has fostered the development of an individual style of architecture, notably the "California ranch house," which has become popular throughout the U.S. since World War II. Among the state's institutions of higher learning are the state-supported University of California, with branches at Berkeley, Los Angeles, San Francisco, Santa Barbara, Davis, and Riverside; the University of Southern California, at Los Angeles; Stanford University, near Palo Alto; and Mills College, at Oakland. The state motto is *Eureka*, meaning "I Have Found It." The state flower is the golden (or California) poppy.

California. City in C Missouri, county seat of Moniteau County. Manufactures include paper and woolen textiles. 2,627 (1950).

California. Borough in SW Pennsylvania, in Washington County: seat of a state teachers college. 2,831 (1950).

California, Gulf of. Arm of the Pacific Ocean lying between the peninsula of Lower California on the W and the Mexican states of Sonora and Sinaloa on the E. It receives the river Colorado at its head. In maps and books of the 16th century it was called Sea of Cortés, in honor of Hernando Cortés, one of its first explorers. Length, ab. 700 mi.; breadth at the entrance, 150 mi.

California, Lower. See **Lower California.**

California, University of. Educational institution in California, the largest coeducational establishment in the world, supported by land grants and state funds. In 1869 the state of California took over the private College of California located at Oakland. The main campus was removed to Berkeley. It was later amalgamated with the University of California at Los Angeles, and it has grown by taking over or setting up colleges, schools, institutes, bureaus, and curriculums at San Francisco, Santa Barbara, and other California cities, affording instruction in fine and applied arts, agriculture, architecture, biology, business, chemistry, commerce, engineering, law, letters and science, medicine, public health, social sciences, and many other branches of knowledge. Embraced within the university are museums of anthropology, paleontology, and zoölogy; the Lick Observatory; the Scripps Institute of Oceanography; a very valuable collection of art; a university press; and libraries which are particularly rich in books dealing with English and European literatures and with Oriental, Jewish, and Spanish, as well as with Western American, history. Greatest of the University's treasures in this field is the Bancroft Library, the world's largest repository of historical records concerning Spanish America and the region now comprising the Western states of the U.S.

California Academy of Sciences. Organization founded in 1853 (incorporated 1871) for the promotion of science and scientific research, the advancement of public education, and the maintenance of a scientific library, public museum, and aquarium. It is situated at Golden Gate Park, San Francisco, and maintains the Steinhart Aquarium and a library of ab. 90,000 volumes covering the natural sciences. The academy publishes the *Academy News Letter* (monthly) and *Occasional Papers and Proceedings*.

California and Oregon Trail, The. Prose work (1849) by Francis Parkman. It is a narrative of Parkman's Western experiences and the excitement and veracity of his account has made it one of the classics of American travel literature.

California . . . A Study of American Character. Prose work (1886) by Josiah Royce.

California Battalion. Unit of some 400 volunteers serving with the U.S. forces against the Spanish in California during the Mexican War. It was originally established (July 5, 1846) by Captain John C. Frémont, and on July 23 was mustered into the U.S. service as the "Navy Battalion of Mounted Riflemen"; at that time it numbered 234 men. The battalion received (Jan. 13, 1847) the Cahuenga Capitulation ending all resistance by the Spanish Californians. The battalion was in active service until April, 1847, and its status as a part of the regular U.S. forces later figured in the court-martial of Frémont.

California Institute of Technology. Educational institution in California, a nonsectarian school for men, devoted to engineering and related studies, located at Pasadena. Founded in 1891 by Amos G. Throop under the name of Throop Polytechnic Institute, it was known as Throop College of Technology from 1913 to 1920, when the present name was adopted. For some years it granted degrees in a limited range of engineering branches only, but it now embraces a wider range of subjects, and is a fully accredited institution, with the standing of a university. Courses in the humanities are included and are obligatory. It has excellent facilities for research in engineering, industrial design, marine biology, astrophysics, and other sciences. The institute controls the Mount Palomar Observatory and has working arrangements with the observatory at Mount Wilson. In recent years only 160 applicants have been admitted annually, and the student body is held to about 600 undergraduates and 250 graduate students. Three members of the faculty of the California Institute of Technology have been recipients of Nobel prizes: Robert A. Millikan for physics (1923), Thomas Hunt Morgan for medicine (1933), and Carl D. Anderson for physics (1936).

California Joe. [Nickname of **Moses Embree Milner.**] b. at Stanford, Ky., 1829; d. 1876. American frontier character. He went to California with the gold-seekers in 1849, but before long moved into the Oregon country, and little is known of his life until the time of the Civil War, when he joined the Union army as a sharpshooter. After Appomattox he continued with the army in the West as a scout in the campaigns against the plains Indians, serving under Custer and Sheridan. In October, 1868, Custer made California Joe chief of scouts, but had to rescind the appointment within a matter of hours because the recipient of the honor celebrated by getting prodigiously drunk. Sheridan wrote of him that he was "an invaluable guide and Indian fighter whenever the clause of the statute prohibiting liquors in the Indian country happened to be in full force." In 1875 he guided an expedition which entered the Black Hills to explore for sources of minerals, and in the following year he was preparing to serve another exploratory party when he was murdered by a personal enemy. A man of great stature and strength, black-bearded, careless in dress, customarily riding a mule, California Joe had in his sober periods many excellent qualities, and all in all was one of the most notable characters of the wild and hazardous frontier in the decades of the last wars against the Indians.

California Trail. Name given to several trails leading to California, of which the earliest (across the Gulf of California and up the peninsula of Lower California) was in existence as early as 1769. Other trails followed the Platte River into the Salt Lake valley, or west from Zuni (now in New Mexico) to the Mohave country.

Caligula (ka.lig'ū.la). [Original name, **Gaius Caesar.**] b. at Antium, Italy, Aug. 31, 12 A.D.; killed at Rome, Jan. 24, 41. Roman ruler, the third emperor of Rome (37–41 A.D.); youngest son of Germanicus and Agrippina. He succeeded Tiberius, whose death he had caused or accelerated. The beginning of his reign was marked by great moderation, but, after he had undergone an illness, the rest of his life was marked by cruelty and licentiousness little short of madness. He is said to have exclaimed in a fit of vexation, "Would that the Roman people had only one head!" with the clear implication that this would considerably simplify their beheading. He is also reputed to have had himself worshiped as a god, and to have raised his horse to the consulship. He invaded Gaul in 40. He was assassinated by Cassius Chaerea, Cornelius Sabinus, and others.

Caligula. Tragedy by John Crowne, printed in 1698.

Calila and Dimna (ka.lē'la; dim'na). See **Kalilah and Dimnah.**

Călinescu (ku.lē.nes'kö), **Armand.** b. at Pitești, Rumania, 1893; assassinated at Bucharest, Rumania, Sept. 21, 1939. Rumanian political leader. He served as minister of the interior (1937–39) and prime minister (1939), and was assassinated by fascist Iron Guardists.

Calingapatam (ka.ling"ga.pa.täm'). [Also, **Kalingapatam.**] Small seaport in Ganjam district, Madras state, Union of India, ab. 200 mi. SW of Cuttack, at the mouth of the Vangsedhara River. It is visited chiefly by small coastal steamers.

Calino (kä.lē'nō). Italian name of **Kalymnos.**

Caliphate. Term used to describe the position held by the successors of Mohammed, the word "caliph" meaning "successor," "lieutenant," "vice-regent," or "deputy." At the peak of its power, the Caliphate wielded a degree of temporal and spiritual might which had no rival in Islam. Theoretically, each caliph was vested with absolute authority in all matters of state, both civil and religious, as long as he ruled in conformity with the law of the Koran and the traditions of Islam. The caliph had to be a male, an adult, sane, a free man, a learned divine, a powerful ruler, a just person, and one of the Koreish (the Arab tribe to which Mohammed himself belonged). The Shiites (the schismatics of Islam) also long demanded that he should be a descendant of Mohammed's family through Ali, who was the fourth caliph and Mohammed's nephew. The first five caliphs were Abu-Bakr, Omar I, Othman, Ali, and Hasan, Ali's son. The last-named caliph ruled only nominally, because actual power had already passed into the hands of Muawiyah, who was to be the first Ommiad caliph, as a result of Ali's assassination in 661. Nevertheless, he is included in all tables of the caliphs. Among the Shiites his brother, Husain, is also reckoned as a caliph, as successor (680) to Muawiyah. According to some authorities, only the first five listed above have actual right to the title of caliph, all others being merely amirs or governors. The power of the Caliphate passed in 661 to the Ommiads, who, 14 in number, reigned until 750 at Damascus. They were succeeded by the Abbassides, with 37 caliphs reigning from 750 to 1258 at Baghdad (and hence sometimes called the Caliphate of Baghdad). After their temporal power had been overthrown by the Mongols in 1258, descendants of the Abbassides resided for almost three centuries in Egypt, and asserted their claim to the spiritual power. In 1517 their claim to the Caliphate passed over through one descendant of the Abbassides to Selim I, the ninth of the Ottoman dynasty of Turkish sultans. In this line, the Caliphate thereafter remained in the hands of the rulers of Turkey, until it was formally abolished in 1924. The Caliphate was also claimed at various times in history by descendants of an Ommiad who managed to escape the slaughter of his family by the Abbassides in 750 and established the Arab emirate at Córdoba, Spain. This came to be known as the Caliphate of Córdoba, or the Western Caliphate. Still another claim to the Caliphate existed from the early 10th century to the latter part of the 12th century, in North Africa, among various descendants (Fatimites) of Fatima, Mohammed's daughter and Ali's wife.

Caliphate Movement. [Also, **Khilafat Movement.**] Agitation (1919–23) by Indian Moslems to secure more favorable peace terms for Turkey in the post-World War I settlement and to prevent any reduction of the temporal powers of the sultan of Turkey, who was the caliph, or supreme head, of the Moslem world. The agitation was endorsed by Gandhi, and Hindus and Moslems united to secure rectification of the peace terms for Turkey. The favorable terms ultimately granted to Turkey under the Treaty of Lausanne (1923) removed the political grounds of the movement.

Calipolis (ka.lip'ō.lis). In George Peele's play *The Battle of Alcazar*, the wife of Muly Mahamet. During a famine her husband presents her with a bit of meat, stolen from a lioness, on his bloody sword, with these words: "Feed then and faint not, fair Calipolis." Pistol ridicules this line in Shakespeare's *Henry IV*, Part II, Act II, scene 4.

Calippus (ka.lip'us). See **Callippus.**

Calista (ka.lis'ta). One of the principal characters in Philip Massinger's *The Guardian.*

Calista. In John Fletcher and Philip Massinger's play *The Lover's Progress*, the faithful wife of Cleander. Her struggle with her unfortunate passion for Lysander affords a powerful scene.

Calista. In Nicholas Rowe's *The Fair Penitent*, the titular heroine. She is the proud, fierce wife of a forgiving husband, Altamont, and loves "that haughty gallant, gay Lothario," who has seduced her. After the latter's death her sense of guilt induces her to kill herself, though Foran remarks that she was more angry at being found out than sorry for what had happened.

Calista. In Sir Walter Scott's novel *The Talisman*, the queen's woman. She is wily and intriguing.

Calisto and Meliboea (ka.lis'tō; mel.i.bē'a), **The Tragicomedy of.** Full name of **Celestina.**

Calixtines (ka.liks'tinz). [Also, **Utraquists.**] A sect of Hussites in Bohemia whose center was the University of Prague. They separated (c1420) from the more radical Taborites, a sect led by Jan Žižka, and published (1421) their confession, called the "Articles of Prague," the leading article of which was a demand to partake of the cup (*calix*) as well as of the bread in the Lord's Supper. The Articles were accepted in the main by the Roman Catholic Church at the Council of Basel (1433) and priests were permitted to administer the Eucharist in both kinds, i.e., with both bread and wine, in Bohemia and Moravia. As the Protestant Reformation gained strength in central Europe the Calixtine sect itself split, some of its members being absorbed by Catholicism and some by Protestantism.

Calixtus I (ka.liks'tus), Saint. [Also, **Callistus.**] Pope from 217 to 222. He modified the severe penitential discipline, and opposed the Montanism of Tertullian. He is commemorated on Oct. 14.

Calixtus II. [Also: **Callistus**; original name, **Guido of Burgundy.**] Pope from 1119 to 1124. He concluded the Concordat of Worms with Henry V in 1122, bringing the investiture controversy to an end.

Calixtus III. [Also, **Callistus.**] Antipope (1168–78), in opposition to Pope Alexander III.

Calixtus III. [Also: **Callistus**; original name, **Alfonso Borgia.**] b. in Spain, 1378; d. Aug. 6, 1458. Pope from 1455 to 1458. He attempted fruitlessly a crusade against the Turks, and also revised the trial of Joan of Arc.

Calkins (kô'kinz), **Gary Nathan.** b. at Valparaiso, Ind., Jan. 18, 1869; d. at Scarsdale, N.Y., Jan. 4, 1943. American zoölogist, a professor at Columbia University from 1904. He was biologist (1902–08) of the New York State Cancer Laboratory in the University of Buffalo. He published *The Protozoa* (1901), *Protozoology* (1908), and others.

Calkins, Mary Whiton. b. at Hartford, Conn., March 30, 1863; d. Feb. 26, 1930. American research professor of philosophy and psychology at Wellesley College, where she taught from 1891. She was the author of *Introduction to Psychology* (1901), *Der doppelte Standpunkt in der Psychologie* (1905), *The Persistent Problems of Philosophy* (1907), *A First Book in Psychology* (1910), and *The Good Man and the Good* (1918).

Calkins, Norman Allison. b. at Gainsville, N.Y., Sept. 9, 1822; d. Dec. 22, 1895. American educator, an early supporter of the Pestalozzian doctrine of object teaching. He was in charge (until 1895) of primary grades in the New York schools, and served as editor (1846 *et seq.*) of the *Student* (later *Student and Schoolmate*). Author of *Primary Object Lessons for a Graduated Course of Development* (1861), *Teaching Color* (1877), *Manual of Object-Teaching* (1882), *First Reading, from Blackboard to Books* (1883), and *How to Teach Phonetics* (1889).

Calkins, Phineas Wolcott. b. at Painted Post, N.Y., June 10, 1831; d. Dec. 31, 1924. American clergyman. A graduate (1856) of Yale, he studied at Union Theological Seminary (1859–60) and at the University of Halle, Germany (1860–62). Ordained (Oct. 22, 1862) in the Congregational ministry, he was associate pastor at Hartford, Conn. (1862–64), and pastor at Philadelphia (1864–66), Buffalo, N.Y. (1866–80), Newton, Mass. (1880–95), Kansas City, Mo. (1896–98), and Woburn, Mass. (1898–1907). He was the author of newspaper articles from his trips abroad for the New York *Observer* and Boston *Transcript*, and of *Keystones of Faith* (1888), *Essays* (1890), and *Parables for Our Times* (1901).

Calkins, Raymond. b. at Buffalo, N.Y., Aug. 10, 1869—. American Congregational clergyman and author. He attended the Harvard Divinity School, was ordained a Congregational minister in 1896, received the D.D. from Bowdoin College in 1907, held various pastorates in Massachusetts and Maine, and from 1912 to 1940 was pastor of the First Church at Cambridge, Mass. His works include *Substitutes for The Saloon* (1901), *The Christian Idea in The Modern World* (1918), *The Christian Church in The Modern World* (1925), *The Holy Spirit* (1930), *The Romance of the Ministry* (1944), and many others.

Call (kôl), **Richard Keith.** b. near Petersburg, Va., 1791; d. at Tallahassee, Fla., Sept. 14, 1862. American soldier and territorial governor of Florida (1836–39, 1841–44). He served with the militia under Andrew Jackson against the Creek Indians in 1813, distinguishing himself by resoluteness and bravery which brought him to Jackson's attention, and Jackson became his friend and his lifelong idol. In 1814 Call entered the regular army with a commission as first lieutenant of infantry, and fought under Jackson through the Pensacola and New Orleans campaigns. In 1818 he was advanced to a captaincy, but in 1822 he resigned from the army, studied law, set up as an attorney with his office at Pensacola, and became a member of the Florida legislative council. In 1823 he was brigadier general of the West Florida militia; he served as a territorial delegate (1823–25) to Congress, became receiver of the West Florida land office in the latter year, and in 1836 began his first term as territorial governor of Florida. He took personal command of the territorial military forces during the war against the Seminoles and is credited with the victories over the Indians in battles fought in the Wahoo Swamp and at Omithlacoochie. The Seminole campaign, however, was subjected to much criticism, and Joel R. Poinsett, secretary of war in President Van Buren's cabinet, removed him from the governorship in 1839. In his resentment Call turned to the Whig Party and campaigned for the Whig candidate, William Henry Harrison. Harrison, being elected, in 1841 reappointed Call to the governorship of Florida. He held this post until 1844 and, Florida having been admitted to the Union, he bid for election as first governor of the state, but was defeated. Having participated with Jackson in events which so greatly extended the boundaries of the U.S., Call had a strongly nationalistic view, and though he defended slavery, he regarded secession as treason. Nevertheless, when Florida joined the Confederacy, he offered his services, but died before the Civil War was far advanced. One of Call's other claims to remembrance is that the third railroad in the U.S. was the one which he projected and built between Tallahassee and St. Marks.

Callabee Creek (kal'ạ.bē), **Battle of.** Engagement (Jan. 27, 1814) in the War of 1812, fought in Macon County, Ala., between an American force and a band of Red Stock Indians. American losses in this region were so heavy that a withdrawal was made to the Chattahoochee River.

Callaghan (kal'ạ.han), **Daniel Judson.** b. 1890; killed at sea off Guadalcanal in November, 1942. American naval officer. A graduate (1911) of the U.S. Naval Academy, he served on convoy duty during World War I, and was appointed (1938) naval aide to President Franklin Delano Roosevelt. In 1941 he was assigned command of the cruiser *San Francisco*.

Callaghan, Morley Edward. b. at Toronto, Canada, 1903—. Canadian writer. He received (1925) a B.A. degree from the University of Toronto. Among his novels are *Strange Fugitives* (1928), *Native Argosy* (1929), *Broken Journey* (1932). *They Shall Inherit the Earth* (1935), *More Joy in Heaven* (1937), and *The Loved and the Lost* (1951). He also published the collection of short stories *Now That April's Here* (1936).

Callahan (kal'ạ.han), **James Morton.** b. at Bedford, Ind., Nov. 4, 1864—. American historian and teacher. He was graduated (B.A., 1894; M.A., 1895) from Indiana University and received his Ph.D. (1897) from the Johns Hopkins University, where he was a lecturer (1898–1902) on diplomatic history. In 1902 he became professor of history and political science at West Virginia University, subsequently serving as dean of the college of arts and sciences (1916–29) and as research professor (1929 *et seq.*). His special field of study, U.S. foreign relations, is reflected in such works as *Neutrality of the American Lakes* (1898), *American Relations in the Pacific and the Far East* (1901), *Confederate Diplomacy* (1901), *The American Expansion Policy* (1903), and *Evolution of Seward's Mexican Policy* (1909).

Callander (kal'ạn.dėr). Police burgh and market town in C Scotland, in Perthshire, situated on the river Teith, ab. 7 mi. NW of Doune, ab. 433 mi. N of London by rail. It is a tourist center, at the E end of a chain of lochs ending with Loch Lomond in the W. 1,619 (est. 1948).

Callantianus (kạ.lan.shi.ā'nus). See **Caecilius.**

Callao (kä.yä'ō). Constitutional province (with departmental status) in W Peru. Capital, Callao; area, 14 sq. mi.; pop. 84,438 (1940), 103,353 (est. 1950).

Callao. City in W Peru, capital of and coextensive with Callao province, ab. 6 mi. W of Lima on the Bay of Callao: the chief port of Peru; exports wool, guano, and bark. On Oct. 28, 1746, the city was swept away by a tidal wave, the result of the earthquake which destroyed Lima; 4,600 people perished, and a frigate and 19 other vessels were stranded. San Felipe Castle was completed c1755; it was the last point occupied by the Spaniards in South America, being finally taken on Jan. 19, 1826. The castle was important in all later Peruvian wars. Callao was bombarded by a Spanish fleet on May 2, 1866, and by the Chileans in 1880. Pop. 84,438 (1940), 87,587 (est. 1950).

Callaway (kal'ạ.wā), **Henry.** b. in England, Jan. 17, 1817; d. March 27, 1890. English missionary in Africa. He was a successful physician until 1854, when he went to South Africa to assist Bishop John William Colenso in his work among the Zulus. In 1858 he founded the Spring Vale mission station; in 1874 he became bishop of independent Kaffraria, and founded the settlement of Umtata. He is noted as a folklorist. His principal works are *Nursery Tales of the Zulus* and *The Religious System of the Amazulu* (1868–71).

Callcott (kôl'kọt), Sir **Augustus Wall.** b. at Kensington, London, Feb. 20, 1779; d. there, Nov. 25, 1844. English landscape painter; husband of Maria Callcott and brother of John Wall Callcott.

Callcott, John Wall. b. at Kensington, London, Nov. 20, 1766; d. at Bristol, England, May 15, 1821. English composer of vocal works such as glees and catches; brother of Sir Augustus Wall Callcott and father of William Hutchins Callcott. He was the author of *Musical Grammar* (1806).

Callcott, Maria. [Maiden name, **Dundas.**] b. at Papcastle, near Cockermouth, England, 1785; d. at Kensington, London, Nov. 21, 1842. English writer; wife of Sir Augustus Wall Callcott (1779–1844). She wrote *Little Arthur's History of England* (1835).

Callcott, William Hutchins. b. Sept. 28, 1807; d. Aug. 5, 1882. English composer and arranger; son of John Wall Callcott (1766–1821).

Calle (kȧl), **La.** See **La Calle.**

Calle-Calle (kä'yä.kä'yä). See **Valdivia River.**

Calleja del Rey (kä.lyā'ᴛʜä del rā'), **Félix María.** [Title, Conde **de Calderón**; called **"the Butcher."**] b. at Medina del Campo, Old Castile, Spain, 1750; d. at Cádiz,

Spain, c1820. Spanish general. In 1789 he was sent to Mexico, and in 1810 was a brigadier, commanding at San Luis Potosí. Soon after Miguel Hidalgo y Costilla revolted he marched against him, defeated him at Aculco, near Querétaro, on Nov. 7, and on Jan. 17, 1811, won a great victory over him at the bridge of Calderón, near Guadalajara. His measures for repressing the revolution were very cruel, scores of his prisoners being shot. Called to the capital, he was sent against José Maria Morelos y Pavón, whom he besieged in Cuautla from Feb. 17 to May 2, finally obtaining a barren victory, as Morelos and his army escaped. On Dec. 29, 1812, he was made military commandant of Mexico City, and from March 4, 1813, to Sept. 19, 1816, he was viceroy. He executed both Hidalgo and Morelos, and was imprisoned (1819) at Cádiz by his own soldiers.

Callernish (ką.lėr′nish). Region on the island of Lewis, Hebrides, Scotland. It is noted for its ancient stone circles.

Calles (kä′yās), **Plutarco Elías.** b. at Guaymas, Sonora, Mexico, Sept. 25, 1877; d. Oct. 19, 1945. Mexican political leader, president (1924–28) of Mexico. A teacher at Guaymas, he became a professor at the Colegio de la Moneda. He joined (1910) the revolutionary forces of Francisco Indalecio Madero, and became a general in 1914, and was provisional governor and military commander (1915) of Sonora, and its constitutional governor (c1918). He served as minister (1919–20) of industry, commerce, labor, war and navy under Venustiano Carranza, and, under Álvaro Obregón, as minister of the interior (1920 *et seq.*). He was elected president despite the bitter opposition of Adolfo de la Huerta. Subsequently he was minister of finance (1933–35). Exiled to California after a struggle (1935) for power with President Lázaro Cárdenas, he was reinstated (1942) in the Mexican army. During his presidency, progress was made in education, in the organization of labor, and in agrarian reform; the first highways were constructed, the Bank of Mexico was founded, and the public debt was amortized; but there was friction between government and church. Conflicts with foreign oil interests over their rights in Mexico were resolved by Calles and U.S. ambassador Dwight W. Morrow.

Calleva Atrebatum (ką.lē′vą ą.treb′ą.tum). Important Roman town in ancient Britain: the modern Silchester.

Callias (kal′i.ąs). fl. 5th century B.C. Athenian statesman. He is known to have fought in the Battle of Marathon (490 B.C.). A member of one of the oldest Attic families, he was in his time the wealthiest citizen of Athens. It seems certain that he undertook an embassy to Artaxerxes I of Persia c460 B.C. (though some historians date it as late as 449 B.C.) and secured that monarch's promise to refrain from attacks upon the Delian League and from sending Persian war vessels into Greek waters, in return for Athenian acceptance of Persian hegemony in Asia Minor; but many authorities doubt that there was ever a "Treaty of Callias" in the form of a written agreement of this sort, and the story that upon his return to Athens he was accused of treason and fined 50 talents is also open to doubt. The agreement, however formal or informal, was beneficial to the cities of the Delian League, for it freed them from Persian interference for several decades. The "Treaty of Callias" is sometimes referred to as as the "Peace of Callias," by confusion with a pact proposed many years later and in very different circumstances by another Callias, the grandson of the Callias here referred to.

Callias. d. c370 B.C. Athenian soldier and leading citizen; grandson of Callias (5th century B.C.). A wealthy man, he was ridiculed in some of the plays of Aristophanes for his profligacy and ostentation. In 392 B.C. he commanded the Athenian hoplites in the victory over Sparta at Corinth. His name is associated with the so-called Peace of Callias, which was a proposal put forward by him at a conference in Sparta (371 B.C.) which, however, was disrupted by a quarrel between Sparta and Thebes. Callias was a friend of Xenophon and of Plato.

Callias, Peace of. Peace concluded at Sparta in 371 B.C., between Athens and Sparta, including their allies, from which, however, Thebes was excluded. It took its name from Callias, one of the Athenian envoys, prominent in the conferences.

Callicrates (ką.lik′rą.tēz). fl. 5th century B.C. Athenian architect and sculptor. His great claim to fame is that he was the collaborator of Ictinus in designing the Parthenon on the Acropolis of Athens. He is also known to have designed the much-admired small marble temple of Athena Nike or Wingless Victory, on the Acropolis near the Propylaea, which was completed in 438 B.C.

Callières Bonnevue (kå.yer bon.vü), **Louis Hector de.** b. in France, c1639; d. at Quebec, Canada, May 26, 1703. French colonial politician. He was governor of Montreal (1684), and of Canada (1699).

Calligrammes (kå.lē.gråm). Collection of poems (1918) by the French poet Guillaume Apollinaire (1880–1918), considered a landmark of French modernist poetry. It introduced the eccentric typographical practices characteristic of much "advanced" poetry of the following decade.

Calligrapher, The. A surname of Theodosius II, ruler (401–450) of the Eastern Roman Empire. He is said to have received it by reason of his skill in illuminating manuscripts.

Callimachus (ką.lim′ą.kus). fl. toward the end of the 5th century B.C. Greek sculptor, credited with having originated the Corinthian column, and with having been first to use the running drill for imitating the deep folds of drapery in statues.

Callimachus. b. at Cyrene, in North Africa; d. c240 B.C. Greek critic, grammarian, and poet, chief librarian of the Alexandrian library. Best known as a poet, he also compiled the *Pinakes*, an annotated catalogue of books which can be regarded as a literary history. He is known to have produced some 800 works, few of which are extant, and to have been a potent influence on Roman poets including Ovid, Catullus, and others.

Callinicus (kal.i.nī′kus), **Seleucus.** See **Seleucus II.**

Callinicus of Heliopolis (hē.li.op′ǫ.lis). fl. in the 7th century A.D. Egyptian architect who is commonly held to have been the inventor of "Greek fire." This was a highly inflammable substance which had many of the qualities of the combination of materials that produce the "liquid" fire of the modern flamethrower. It was probably a mixture of quicklime, naptha, pitch, sulfur, and possibly saltpeter (although this last is still a moot question). However, whatever its ingredients, it could be used to spread fire even under water. It is said to have been employed, with great success, against the Saracen fleet which attacked Constantinople in 673.

Callinus (ką.lī′nus). fl. c730–670 B.C. Greek poet of Ephesus, probably the first known writer of elegiacs, the invention of which was anciently attributed to Archilochus. There is extant one long fragment, attributed to Callinus, which is a patriotic exhortation.

Calliope (ką.lī′ǫ.pē). In Greek mythology, the Muse of epic poetry and eloquence. She was the mother of Orpheus.

Calliope. An asteroid (No. 22) discovered by John Russell Hind at London, on Nov. 16, 1852.

Callipolis (ką.lip′ǫ.lis). Ancient name of **Gallipoli,** Italy, and of **Gelibolu,** Turkey.

Callippus or **Calippus** (ką.lip′us). b. at Cyzicus, Asia Minor; fl. in the 4th century B.C. Greek astronomer. He instituted the "Callippic" cycle of 76 years, formed by quadrupling the Metonic cycle (19 years) and subtracting one day.

Callirrhoë (ką.lir′ǫ.ē). In Greek legend, the wife of Alcmaeon. She persuaded her husband to procure for her the peplum and necklace of Harmonia, and thus caused his death, which was avenged by his sons.

Callirrhoë. Historic fountain at Athens, architecturally adorned and provided with conduits by Pisistratus; the use of its water was prescribed for ceremonial rites. From the earliest study of Athenian topography, this fountain has been identified with the copious spring flowing in the bed of the Ilissus, near the temple of Olympian Zeus. Wilhelm Dörpfeld, however, demonstrated the probability that this identification is incorrect, and that the fountain was in fact situated at the SW angle of the Areopagus, on the border of the Agora. Excavation has revealed a water conduit of the Pisistratid epoch ending at the site indicated, which accords with literary testimony.

Callisthenes (ką.lis′thę.nēz). b. at Olynthus, Macedonia, c360 B.C.; d. c328 B.C. Greek philosopher; a cousin and pupil of Aristotle, and a companion of Alexander the Great in Asia. He incurred Alexander's ill will by his criticism of Alexander's adoption of Oriental customs, and was probably put to death by Alexander's order.

Callisto (ka.lis'tō). In Greek mythology, an Arcadian huntress, a companion of Artemis, beloved of Zeus and transformed either by him or by Artemis into a she bear. In this form she was slain by Artemis in the chase. She was placed among the stars as the constellation Ursa Major.

Callistratus (ka.lis'tra.tus). fl. in the 4th century B.C. Athenian orator. He commanded with Chabrias and Timotheus the forces which were despatched to the assistance of Thebes against Sparta in 378, and executed a number of embassies. In 366 he delivered a speech on the loss of Oropus, which is said to have determined Demosthenes to devote himself to the study of oratory.

Callistratus. fl. about the middle of the 2nd century B.C. Greek grammarian. He was the author of commentaries on the major poets of Greece, which were held in considerable repute by the ancients, but which are now lost. He is said on doubtful authority to have been the first to acquaint the Samians with the alphabet of 24 letters.

Callistratus. fl. at the beginning of the 3rd century A.D. Roman jurist. He is said to have been a pupil of Papinian and to have been a member of the council of Alexander Severus. He is known chiefly on account of the numerous extracts from his works in the *Digest* of Justinian. None of his works is extant.

Callistus (ka.lis'tus). A variant name (considered by some to be the preferable name) for the popes who are ordinarily listed by English reference works under **Calixtus.**

Call of the Wild, The. Novel by Jack London, published in 1903. It was London's first successful book. Buck, the canine hero, is stolen from his California home and sent to the Klondike, where he asserts his leadership by displacing Spitz, his rival in the dog team. Among other achievements, Buck pulls from a dead stop a thousand-pound load, thereby winning a wager for his master, John Thornton. After the latter's murder, the dog's atavistic traits lead him to respond to the call of the wild.

Callosa de Segura (kä.lyō'sä dā sä.gö'rä). Town in E Spain, in the province of Alicante. 10,599 (1940).

Callot (ka.lō), **Jacques.** b. at Nancy, France, 1592; d. there, March 28, 1635. French engraver and etcher. After study in Italy, he returned to France and there executed many of his works. He is best known for battle scenes, and is highly regarded for his ability to portray harmoniously large groups of people in action.

Call's Grove. Former name of **Algona.**

Call to the Unconverted. [Called **"Baxter's Call."**] Religious work by Richard Baxter, published in 1657.

Callum Beg (kal'um beg). See **Beg, Callum.**

Calmar (käl'mär). See **Kalmar.**

Calmes (kalm), **Albert.** b. at Paris, 1881—. Luxembourg economist, historian, and teacher. Graduated (D.Sc., 1905) from the University of Zurich, he taught at St. Gallen, Switzerland, and at the University of Frankfort on the Main on the faculties of economic and social sciences. He was a member of the council of the International Chamber of Commerce until 1940, president (1944–46) of the commission for economic readjustment of Luxembourg, a member of the superior council of the Belgian-Luxembourg Economic Union, chief delegate of Luxembourg to the Dutch-Belgian-Luxembourg Customs Union Convention, and a member of the Luxembourg delegation to the second session of the first United Nations Assembly. He is also known as a director of several companies, and author of a history of contemporary Luxembourg.

Calmet (kal.me), Dom **Augustin.** b. at Mesnil-la-Horgne, near Toul, France, Feb. 26, 1672; d. at Paris, Oct. 25, 1757. French Benedictine scholar and Biblical critic. He was the author of numerous works, including *Commentaire sur tous les livres de l'Ancien et du Nouveau Testament* (1707–16), and *Dictionnaire historique, critique et chronologique de la Bible* (1722–28).

Calmette (kal.met'), **Cape.** Extremity of a rocky peninsula in Antarctica, which projects from the Fallières Coast for ab. 3 mi. to form the S shore of Calmette Bay, in ab. 68°05′ S., 67°12′ W. The name was chosen by Jean Charcot for Gaston Calmette, editor of *Le Figaro*, who furnished the expedition with a complete file of *Le Figaro* for the two years preceding the expedition. Elevation, ab. 1,500 ft.

Calmette (kal.met), **Albert Léon Charles.** b. 1863; d. 1933. French physician and bacteriologist; brother of Gaston Calmette. He began his medical practice as a physician in the French navy. In the course of this service, being stationed at Saigon in French Indochina, he found a serum against snakebite. In 1889 he went to Oporto, Portugal, to study bubonic plague. Back in Saigon, in 1891 he established a bacteriological institute, which he directed into 1893. After his return to France, he established the Pasteur Institute at Lille, and was its director until 1919. He was a codiscoverer of the important vaccine "B-C-G," used to inoculate infants against tuberculosis.

Calmette, Gaston. b. at Montpellier, France, July 30, 1858; assassinated at Paris, March 16, 1914. French newspaper editor; brother of A. L. C. Calmette. He was shot to death at his office by the wife of Joseph Caillaux, minister of finance, against whom he had launched a press attack (January–March, 1914) in the newspaper *Le Figaro*.

Calmette Bay (kal.met'). Bay in Antarctica, ab. 4 mi. wide at its entrance between Camp Point and Cape Calmette on the Fallières Coast, and extending E by SE for ab. 3 mi.; in ab. 68°03′ S., 67°10′ W.

Calmon (kal.môn), **Marc Antoine.** b. at Tamniès, Dordogne, France, March 3, 1815; d. at Paris, Oct. 13, 1890. French politician and political economist. He was chosen a life senator in 1875. He published *Histoire parlementaire des finances de la restauration* (1868–70).

Calmón du Pin e Almeida (käl.mōn' dü pan' ē äl-mā'da), **Miguel.** [Titles, Viscount (1849) and Marquis (1854) of **Abrantes.**] b. at Santo Amaro, Bahia, Brazil, Dec. 22, 1796; d. at Rio de Janeiro, Oct. 5, 1865. Brazilian statesman. He was a member of the constituent assembly (1822), several times a deputy, senator from 1840, minister in many governments, and premier in 1840 and 1843. From 1844 to 1847 he was special envoy in Europe.

Calm Sea and Prosperous Voyage Overture. [German title, **Meeresstille und glückliche Fahrt.**] Orchestral composition by Felix Mendelssohn, composed in 1828 and based on a poem by Goethe.

Calmucks (kal'muks). See **Kalmucks.**

Calne (kän). Municipal borough and market town in S England, in Wiltshire, ab. 100 mi. W of London by rail. 5,552 (1951).

Calneh (kal'ne). In the Old Testament, one of the four cities of Nimrod in Shinar, or Babylonia (Gen. x. 10), which as yet has not been identified. It is to be distinguished from Calneh of Amos, vi. 2, and the Calno of Isa. x. 9, which perhaps refer to one and the same city, identified by some with the Kullani mentioned in the Assyrian inscriptions as having been conquered in 738 B.C. by Tiglath-pileser III, and now represented by ruins ab. 6 mi. from Arpad.

Calno (kal'nō). See under **Calneh.**

Calo-Joannes (kal"o.jō.an'ēz). See **John II** (of the *Byzantine Empire*).

Calonne (ka.lon), **Charles Alexandre de.** b. at Douai, France, Jan. 20, 1734; d. at Paris, Oct. 30, 1802. French financial expert. After serving as intendant of Metz (1768 *et seq.*) and Lille (1774 *et seq.*), he was named (Nov. 3, 1783) to succeed Necker as controller of finances. At this period, the French treasury was near depletion; Calonne attempted to improve the country's financial position by a program of spending, in order to establish credit for further loans. Virtual bankruptcy, however, resulted. An assembly of "notables" was then called (1787) by the king to pass on Calonne's proposal to levy a uniform property tax, ignoring the privileges of the clergy and the nobility. The assembly rejected this plan summarily, and Calonne was dismissed (April 8, 1787) and sent into exile. Thereafter he resided in England until 1802, about a month before his death, at which time he was allowed to reënter France. While in England he wrote several books, among them *État de la France à present et à venir* (1790; Eng. trans., *Considerations on the Present and Future State of France,* 1791).

Calonne-Ricouart (kȧ.lon.rē.kwȧr). Town in N France, in the department of Pas-de-Calais, situated on the Clarence River, ab. 9 mi. W of Béthune. It is a coal-mining town. 9,715 (1946).

Calov (kä'lof), **Abraham.** [Original name, **Abraham Kalau** (or **Calau**); Latinized surname, **Calovius.**] b. at Mohrungen, Germany, April 16, 1612; d. at Wittenberg, Germany, Feb. 25, 1686. German Lutheran theologian and polemic writer. He taught at Wittenberg, and attacked the views expressed in Arianism, Calvinism, Pietism, and Socinianism. His chief work is *Systema locorum theologicorum* (1655–77).

Calpe (kal'pē). Ancient name of the rock of Gibraltar. It and Abyla, as the facing promontory on the coast of Africa was then called, constituted the Pillars of Hercules.

Calprenède (kȧl.prẹ.ned). See **La Calprenède.**

Calpurnia (kal.pėr'ni.ạ). fl. in the 1st century B.C. Daughter of L. Calpurnius Piso Caesoninus, and last wife of Julius Caesar, whom she married in 59 B.C. She appears in Shakespeare's tragedy *Julius Caesar.*

Calpurnia gens. In ancient Rome, a plebeian clan or house which claimed to be descended from Calpus, the third son of Numa. Its family names under the republic were Bestia, Bibulus, Flamma, and Piso. The first member of this gens who obtained the consulship was C. Calpurnius Piso (180 B.C.).

Calpurnius (kal.pėr'ni.us), **Siculus Titus.** fl. in the 1st century A.D. Latin pastoral poet who lived about the time of Nero. Seven eclogues, a panegyric (*De laude Pisonis*), and two fragments of bucolic poems are attributed to him. Four other eclogues formerly regarded as his are now referred to Nemesianus, a poet once thought to be identical with Calpurnius.

Caltagirone (käl''tä.jē.rō'nä). [Arabic, **Qalat al-Ghiran.**] City and commune in SW Italy, on the island of Sicily, in the province of Catania, picturesquely situated on two steep hills near the Caltagirone River, between Catania and Gela. There is a flourishing terra-cotta and ceramics (majolica) industry here, dating from the Moslem period; sulfur mines are in the vicinity. The territory of the commune is one of the largest in Sicily. The city has a medieval castle and is the seat of a bishopric. An ancient Siculian settlement, the town was conquered by the Moslems in the 11th century, occupied by the Genoese in 1030, by the Normans in 1090; it was destroyed by an earthquake in 1693. For centuries, it was under feudal rule, being held successively by the Chiaramonte, Modica, Moncada, and Alagona families. Considerable damage was suffered during World War II by some buildings of tourist interest, but repairs have been completed or are being carried out. Pop. of commune, 39,320 (1936); of city, 31,022 (1936).

Caltanissetta (käl''tä.nēs.sāt'tä). Province on the island of Sicily, SW Italy. Capital, Caltanissetta; area, ab. 800 sq. mi.; pop. 256,687 (1936).

Caltanissetta. City and commune in SW Italy, on the island of Sicily, the capital of the province of Caltanissetta, situated on a height in the center of the island, W of Catania. It is one of the principal centers of sulfur mining in Sicily and has also a flourishing trade in grain; seat of a bishopric and of a number of educational institutions, among them a technical institute and a mining school. The Cathedral of San Giacomo and the palace of the Moncada family are in baroque style. The cathedral as well as other buildings of tourist interest suffered considerable damage during World War II; the Norman Church of Santo Spirito has been in ruins for a long time. Remains from ancient times are nearby. In earlier centuries under the domination of Moslems, Normans, the house of Hohenstaufen, and the Aragonese (Spain), it was given to Matteo Moncada in 1407 and remained long under the feudal overlordship of the Moncada family. The population supported the rule of the Spanish family and of the royal house of Naples against the Piedmontese in 1718 and against the Sicilian insurrectionists in 1820. Giuseppe Garibaldi's free corps entered the city in 1860 and annexed it to Italy. Pop. of commune, 50,467 (1936); of city, 37,463 (1936).

Calton Hill (kôl'tọn). Hill in S Scotland, in Midlothian, in the NE quarter of the city of Edinburgh. The City Observatory is on its summit. 355 ft.

Caluire-et-Cuire (kȧ.lwēr.ā.kwēr). Town in S France, in the department of Rhône, situated on the Saône River, ab. 7 mi. N of Lyons. It has textile and machine industries; known for coal mines. It belongs to the metropolitan region of Lyons. 17,592 (1946).

Calumet (kal.ū̦.met', kal'ū̦.met). Village in the W upper peninsula of Michigan, in Houghton County, in a copper-mining region. 1,256 (1950).

Calumet City. City in NE Illinois, in Cook County, S of Chicago: industrial and residential community. 15,799 (1950).

Calumet Park. Village in NE Illinois, in Cook County: a southern suburb of Chicago. 2,500 (1950).

Calumet River. [Also, **Calumick River** (kal'ū̦.mik).] River in NW Indiana, and in Cook County, Ill. It flows through Gary, Hammond, and East Chicago, Ind., and empties into Lake Michigan in South Chicago.

Calvados (kȧl.vȧ.dos). Department in N France, bounded by the English Channel on the N, the department of Eure on the E, the department of Orne on the S, and the department of Manche on the W and S. It is part of the region of Normandy. The beaches of Calvados, between Ouistreham and Issigny-sur-Mer, were the scene of the World War II invasion of France (June 6, 1944) by the Allied armies. Calvados was the home of William the Conqueror. Livestock raising is more important than agriculture, the latter producing mainly apples. There are metallurgical, textile, and other industries; the pottery industry is very old. There are numerous resorts and fishing villages along the coast. Many of the villages and cities of the department, particularly Caen, were destroyed or severely damaged in the course of the fighting during World War II. Capital, Caen; area, 2,197 sq. mi.; pop. 400,026 (1946).

Calvaert or **Calvart** (käl'värt), **Denis.** [Called **Dionisio Fiammingo,** meaning "Denis the Fleming."] b. at Antwerp, 1540; d. at Bologna, Italy, March 17, 1619. Flemish painter belonging to the 17th-century Bolognese school. His best works are at Bologna.

Calvano (käl.vä'nō). See **Caivano.**

Calvary (kal'vạ.ri). Word occurring in the New Testament (Luke, xxiii. 33), adopting the *calvaria* by which the Vulgate translates the Greek *kranion,* which itself is the rendering of the Aramean *golgotha,* skull; it was not in its original sense a proper name. The popular name "Mount Calvary" is not warranted by any statement in the gospels as being that of the place of the Crucifixion. Traditionally, however, Christ was crucified at the place now known as Calvary, outside the ancient Jerusalem. Golgotha is also often written with a capital letter, used as a variant of Calvary, and thought of as a place.

Calvary. [German title, **Des Heilands letzte Stunden,** meaning "The Saviour's Last Hours."] Oratorio by Louis Spohr, first performed in 1835 and, under the English title, in 1839.

Calvé (kȧl.vā'), **Emma.** [Stage name of **Emma de Roquer.**] b. at Decazeville, Aveyron, France, c1858; d. 1942. French operatic soprano. She studied at Paris, and made her debut in opera at the Théâtre de la Monnaie, at Brussels, in 1882, as Marguerite in Charles François Gounod's *Faust.* She played at Paris in 1884, made a tour in Italy, returned to Paris, made a European tour (covering Russia, Italy, Belgium, England, and Spain), and was in America in the periods 1893–94, 1895–96, 1896–97, and 1899–1900, and in 1908. Among her popular roles in America were Carmen, and Santuzza in *Cavalleria Rusticana.*

Calverley (kal'vėr.li). In *The Yorkshire Tragedy,* once attributed to Shakespeare, a ruined gamester, brutally cruel to his wife and children. The story is based on that of a real person of that name.

Calverley, Charles Stuart. b. at Martley, Worcestershire, England, Dec. 22, 1831; d. at London, Feb. 17, 1884. English poet and parodist.

Calvert (kal'vėrt). City in E central Texas, in Robertson County, near the Brazos River, ab. 80 mi. NE of Austin, in a farming and livestock-raising region. 2,548 (1950).

Calvert, Cecilius. [Title, 2nd Baron **Baltimore.**] b. c1605; d. at London, Nov. 30, 1675. English colonist, the first proprietor of Maryland; son of George Calvert, and father of Charles Calvert. Having applied for a grant of land in northern Virginia, George Calvert died before the charter had passed the great seal, in consequence of which it was issued in the name of his heir Cecilius, on June 20, 1632. In November, 1633, Cecilius sent a group of colonists under his brother Leonard to the new domain, which was named Maryland by Charles I in honor of the English queen. Calvert married (c1623) Anne Arundel, whose name is borne by one of the counties of Maryland.

Calvert, Charles. [Title, 3rd Baron **Baltimore.**] b. Aug. 27, 1637; d. Feb. 21, 1715. American colonial administrator; son of Cecilius Calvert. Commissioned (Sept. 14, 1661) governor of Maryland, he became its proprietor on the death (Nov. 20, 1675) of his father.

Calvert, George. [Title, 1st Baron **Baltimore.**] b. at Kipling, Yorkshire, England, c1580; d. April 15, 1632. British colonizer, the founder of Maryland; father of Cecilius Calvert and Leonard Calvert. He entered Parliament in 1609, and became secretary of state in 1619, a post which he resigned in 1625, on declaring his conversion to the Roman Catholic faith. He was at his resignation raised to the Irish peerage as Baron Baltimore. While secretary of state he obtained from James I a grant of land, called the province of Avalon, in Newfoundland, where in 1621 he established the settlement of Ferryland. He paid two visits to the colony between 1627 and 1629, which convinced him of the unsuitability of the climate, whereupon he applied for a grant of land (the present Maryland) in northern Virginia, the charter of which, as he died before it had passed the great seal, was issued in the name of his son Cecilius in 1632.

Calvert, George Henry. b. at Baltimore, June 2, 1803; d. at Newport, R.I., May 24, 1889. American journalist and poet. He was the author of *Introduction to Social Science* (1856), *The Gentleman* (1863), *Arnold and André* (1864), a play, and several collections of verse.

Calvert, Leonard. b. 1606; d. June 9, 1647. American colonial governor; second son of George Calvert. In 1633, having been entrusted with authority by his brother Cecilius, 2nd Baron Baltimore, to act as governor of the province of Maryland under royal charter, he led some 300 colonists from England, landing (1634) at St. Clements (now Blackistone) Island, Maryland. He set up the seat of his power at St. Marys, in St. Marys County, and was subsequently granted wide powers in the administration of the colony, of which his brother Cecilius was proprietor. Under his rule, however, popular government in Maryland had its beginning when the right to initiate legislation was granted to the assembly.

Calverton (kal′vėr.tọn), **Victor Francis.** [Original name, **George Goetz.**] b. at Baltimore, June 25, 1900; d. Nov. 20, 1940. American writer, critic, and editor. Graduated (1921) from the Johns Hopkins University, he was the founder (1923) and editor of *The Modern Monthly: A Journal of Radical Opinion* (1923 *et seq.;* later called *The Modern Monthly*). Among his works are *The Newer Spirit* (1925), *Sex Expression in Literature* (1926), *The Bankruptcy of Marriage* (1928), *Three Strange Loves* (1929), *American Literature at the Crossroads* (1931), *For Revolution* (1932), *The Liberation of American Literature* (1932), *The Passing of the Gods* (1934), *The Awakening of America* (1939), and *Where Angels Dared to Tread* (1941).

Calves' Head Club. Club said to have been instituted in ridicule of the memory of Charles I. It is first noticed in a tract reprinted in the *Harleian Miscellany,* called "The Secret History of the Calves' Head Club," undertaking to show how this club met for some years (1693–97) on the anniversary of the king's death. An ax was reverenced, and a dish of calves' heads represented the king and his friends. It seems to have met in secret after the Restoration and until 1734, when some ill feeling was excited against it, and riots are said to have ensued. In 1735 it was suppressed.

Calvi (käl′vē). Town on the island of Corsica, in the French department of Corse, situated on the Gulf of Calvi, on the NW coast of the island, N of Ajaccio. It is a winter resort. It was formerly a fortified port and has preserved its medieval ramparts. 2,053 (1946).

Calvin (kal′vin), **John.** [Original name, **Jean Chauvin** (or **Cauvin** or **Caulvin**); German, **Johann Calvin;** Italian, **Giovanni Calvino;** Latinized, **Johannes Calvinus.**] b. at Noyon, in Picardy, France, July 10, 1509; d. at Geneva, Switzerland, May 27, 1564. Protestant reformer and theologian. He studied at Paris, Orléans, and Bourges. Having embraced the Reformation (c1528), he was driven (1533) from Paris, published (1536) *Institutes of the Christian Religion* at Basel, and went (1536) to Geneva. The extreme nature of the reforms which Calvin, with Guillaume Farel, attempted to carry out there, caused (1538) their banishment. Calvin returned to Geneva in 1541, however. He had a controversy with Bolsec in 1551, and with Servetus in 1553, causing Servetus to be burned at the stake. He founded the Academy of Geneva in 1559.

Calvisius (kal.vish′i.us, -vish′us), **Sethus.** [Original name, **Seth Kallwitz.**] b. at Gorsleben, Germany, Feb. 21, 1556; d. at Leipzig, Germany, Nov. 24, 1615. German composer and musicologist. He was appointed cantor at Schulpforte (1582) and at the Thomasschule (1594), and named music director at the Thomaskirche, all at Leipzig. His compositions, consisting mainly of church music, include hymns and motets. He was the author of various treatises on music, such as *Exercitationes musicae* (1600, 1611).

Calvo (käl′vō), **Baldassarre.** One of the principal characters in George Eliot's novel *Romola.*

Calvo, Carlos. b. at Buenos Aires, Feb. 26, 1824; d. at Paris, May 2, 1906. Argentine jurist and diplomat whose doctrine that "recovery of debts and the pursuit of private claims do not justify *de plano* the armed intervention of governments" was aimed at precisely this sort of action by European governments against various Latin-American nations. The Calvo Doctrine was subsequently given practical application in the similar, but narrower, Drago Doctrine. At various times minister for Paraguay and Argentina to Paris, London, Berlin, St. Petersburg, Vienna, and the Holy See, Calvo is today perhaps best known for his great work on international law entitled *Derecho internacional teorico y practico de Europa y America* (1868). His doctrine remains, however, as a so-called Calvo Clause in many Latin-American constitutions, to protect these nations against diplomatic action by aliens in connection with concession contracts.

Calvo, Mariano Enrique. b. at Sucre, Bolivia, c1795; d. at Cochabamba, Bolivia, 1842. Bolivian politician. He was vice-president of the confederation of Peru and Bolivia (1836–39). In 1840 he attempted a revolt and was imprisoned.

Calvo, Monte. See under **Gargano, Monte.**

Calvo Doctrine. Doctrine of international law formulated (c1885) by the Argentinian jurist Carlos Calvo (*q.v.*). It asserted that the employment of force or diplomatic means is unjustifiable in prosecuting indemnities or claims covering private or public debts or losses arising from civil war or other causes.

Calvo Sotelo (käl′vō sō.tā′lō), **José.** b. at Tuy, in Galicia, Spain, 1892; d. at Madrid, 1936. Spanish politician and leader of the political right. At the age of 25 he was elected a deputy to the Cortes and joined the Conservative party headed by Antonio Maura. In 1922 he was elected civil governor of Valencia, and subsequently advanced to the post of finance minister (1925–30) under Primo de Rivera. At the fall of the dictatorship he retired to Portugal, but returned in 1933 to lead the monarchical opposition to the Popular Front. In the years of conflict preceding the Spanish Civil War (1936–39) he succeeded Gil Robles as head of the CEDA (*Confederación Española de Derechos Autónomos*) which combined most of the Rightist parties. On July 12, 1936, Falangists shot down Lieutenant José del Castillo of the assault guards, and republican extremists seized Calvo Sotelo on the following day, killing him in reprisal. His assassination, which capped an era of politics by terror and precipitated military action by the opposing parties in Spain, was one of the factors leading to the Civil War.

Calvus (kal′vus), **Gaius Licinius Macer.** b. May 28, 82 B.C.; d. c47 B.C. Roman poet and forensic orator.

Calw (kälv). [Also, **Kalw.**] Town in S Germany, in the *Land* (state) of Württemberg-Hohenzollern, French Zone, formerly in the Black Forest *Kreis* (district) of Württemberg, situated on the Nagold River, ab. 23 mi. W of Stuttgart: leather and metallurgical industries; cotton and woolen textile manufactures. It is an old town; the *Rathaus* (town hall) dates from 1673. The district is rich in pine forests; the health resorts of Wildbad, Liebenzell, and Teinach are in the vicinity; also nearby are the ruins of the convent of Hirsau, founded in 830, destroyed by the French in 1692. The population is predominantly Protestant. 6,795 (1946).

Calydon (kal'i.dọn). In ancient geography, a city of Aetolia, in C Greece, situated near the river Evenus. It is the legendary scene of the hunt of the Calydonian boar.

Calydon. Great forest celebrated in the Arthurian romances. It was supposed to be in the north of England.

Calydonian Hunt (kal.i.dō'ni.ạn). In Greek legend, the chase of a savage boar which the goddess Artemis, in punishment for a neglect of sacrifice by Oeneus, king of Calydon in Aetolia, sent to ravage his country. The boar was pursued by Meleager and a band of heroes, and was slain by him. In some accounts Atalanta, who was beloved of Meleager, joined the hunt and inflicted the first wound.

Calymnos (kạ.lim'nos), **Calymna** (-nạ), or **Calymno** (-nō). See **Kalymnos.**

Calypso (kạ.lip'sō). In Homer's *Odyssey*, a nymph living in the island of Ogygia, who detained Ulysses for seven years. She promised him perpetual youth and immortality if he would remain with her.

Cam (kam). [Also, **Granta.**] River in E central England, in Cambridgeshire, rising near Ashwell and flowing NE past Cambridge to its confluence with the river Ouse, ab. 4 mi. S of Ely. The names Cam and Granta have both appeared in literature and on maps of the region. Length, ab. 40 mi.; navigable to Cambridge.

Cam (kouṅ), **Diogo.** See **Cão, Diogo.**

Camacho (kä.mä'chō). In one of the episodes in Cervante's *Don Quixote*, a rich but unfortunate man. He is cheated out of his bride, Quiteria, just as he has provided a great feast for his wedding; hence the phrase "Camacho's wedding" has been used to signify great but useless show and expenditure.

Camacho, Manuel Ávila. See **Ávila Camacho, Manuel.**

Camagüey (kä.mä.gwā'). [Former name, **Puerto Príncipe.**] Province in C Cuba between the provinces of Las Villas and Oriente. Capital, Camagüey; area, 10,172 sq. mi.; pop. 487,701 (1943).

Camagüey. [Former names: **Ciudad del Príncipe, Puerto Príncipe.**] City in C Cuba, capital of Camagüey province: distributing point for a cattle-raising and agricultural district. 80,509 (1943).

Camaiore (kä.mä.yō'rā). Town and commune in C Italy, in the *compartimento* (region) of Tuscany, in the province of Lucca, situated in the foothills of the Apuanian Alps (the westernmost range of the Apennines), NE of Viareggio. It is a large agricultural commune, and a resort, with a much-frequented bathing beach on the nearby Tyrrhenian Sea; there are textile industries. The Church of San Michele dates from the 11th century, the Collegiate Church from the 13th century, the triumphal arch from 1531. Some damage was suffered during World War II by buildings of tourist interest, but repairs have been completed or are being carried out. Pop. of commune, 22,291 (1936); of town, 2,588 (1936).

Camajuaní (kä"mä.hwä.nē'). City in N Cuba, in Las Villas province. 11,339 (1943).

Camanche (kạ.man'chẹ). See **Comanche.**

Câmara (ku'mạ.rạ), **Manoel Arruda da.** See **Arruda da Câmara, Manoel.**

Camaracus (kam.ạ.rā'kus) or **Camaracum** (-kum). Latin names of **Cambrai.**

Câmara de Lobos (ku'mạ.rạ dē lō'bōsh). Town and *concelho* (commune) in the Madeira Islands, belonging to Portugal, situated on the N coast of the island of Madeira, ab. 6 mi. W of Funchal. Madeira wines are produced in the vicinity. Pop. of concelho, 24,092 (1940); of town, 11,652 (1940).

Camarão (ku.mạ.rouṅ'), **Antonio Felippe.** [Original name, **Poty** (pō.tē'), meaning "Shrimp."] b. in Rio Grande do Norte, Brazil, c1580; d. there, 1648. Brazilian Indian, chief of the Potyguarés tribe; uncle of Diogo Pinheiro Camarão. His Indian name was translated into the Portuguese Camarão when he was baptized. He joined the Portuguese in the wars against the Dutch of Pernambuco, and made several destructive raids into the Dutch territory. His wife, Clara, who always accompanied him and fought by his side, is a favorite heroine of Brazilian history. On Aug. 23 and 24, 1636, Camarão and his Indians defeated a force of Dutch regulars.

Camarão, Diogo Pinheiro. fl. in the 17th century. Brazilian Indian; nephew of Antonio Felippe Camarão. He was one of the Indian allies of the Portuguese in their wars with the Dutch, and on the death of his uncle in 1648 succeeded him in command of the Potyguarés tribe.

Camargo (kȧ.mȧr.gō). [Full name, **Marie Anne Cupis de Camargo.**] b. April 15, 1710; d. April 20, 1770. French dancer.

Camargo (kä.mär'gō). Town in N Spain, in the province of Santander, situated near the Bay of Santander, SW of the town of Santander. Stone-age skulls have been discovered in the vicinity. 10,198 (1940).

Camargo, Diego Muñoz. b. at Tlaxcala, Mexico, c1523; date of death not recorded. Mexican historian, said to have been the son of a Spaniard by an Indian mother. In 1585 he finished an account of Mexican aboriginal history and customs, and of the Spanish conquest. It was first published, in a faulty French translation, in *Nouvelles annales des voyages* (1845).

Camargue (kȧ.mȧrg). See **La Camargue.**

Camarina (kam.ạ.rī'nạ). In ancient geography, a city on the S coast of Sicily, ab. 45 mi. SW of Syracuse. It was founded (599 B.C.) as a Syracusan colony; a Roman fleet was wrecked near here in 255 B.C.

Camarines Norte (kä.mä.rē'nās nôr'tā). Province of the Philippine Islands, occupying the N part of the SE peninsula of Luzon island. It is bounded on the N by the Philippine Sea of the Pacific Ocean, on the E by San Miguel Bay and Camarines Sur province, on the S by Camarines Sur, Ragay Gulf, and Tayabas province, and on the W by Lamon Bay. The province includes the Calagua Islands off its N coast. Capital, Daet; area, ab. 800 sq. mi.; pop. 98,324 (1939), 103,702 (1948).

Camarines Sur (sör). Province of the Philippine Islands in the C part of the SE peninsula of Luzon. It is bounded by Camarines Norte and the Pacific Ocean on the N, Catanduanes island (separated by Maqueda Channel), Lagonoy Gulf, and Albay on the E, Albay and Tayabas (separated by mountains) on the S, and Tayabas (partly separated by the Gulf of Ragay) on the W. The N coast is deeply indented by San Miguel Bay, a safe harbor in all weather. The province is traversed by mountains, of which several exceed 5,000 ft. in height. The volcanoes Iriga and Isarog are in the S part. Gold, iron, and coal are found Camarines is well watered, heavily forested with good timber, and productive of large quantities of rice. The chief river, the Bicol Sur, is navigable by small steamers as far as Naga, ab. 25 mi. from its mouth. The native population is chiefly Bicol. Capital, Naga; area, ab. 2,072 sq. mi.; pop. 385,695 (1939), 553,691 (1948).

Camars (kä'märs). An Etruscan name of **Chiusi.**

Camas (kam'ạs). [Called the **"City of Paper."**] City in SW Washington, in Clark County: manufactures pulp and paper. 4,725 (1950).

Camathias (kä.mä'tyäs), **Flurin.** b. at Laax, Switzerland, March 6, 1871; d. at Ilanz, Switzerland, Feb. 3, 1946. Swiss author writing in Romansh. He was a Catholic priest, and added *Historias dil munt S. Gieri* (1921) and other narrative works to Romansh literature.

Camau (kä.mou'), **Point.** [Also: **Point Ca-mau, Cambodia Point**; French, **Pointe de Camau** (or **Ca-mau**).] Headland in S Indochina, in Cochin-China (South Viet-Nam), projecting into the Gulf of Thailand and separating it from the South China Sea, ab. 180 mi. SW of Saigon.

Cambaceres (käm.bä.sā'rās), **Eugenio.** b. 1843; d. 1888. Argentine lawyer and politician, who shocked his literary countrymen by writing the first Spanish-American novel of the naturalistic type, *Potpourri: silbidos de un vago* (1882). His later works, *Música sentimental* (1884), *Sin rumbo* (1885), and *En la sangre* (1887), follow a similarly naturalistic pattern.

Cambacérès (käṅ.bȧ.sā.res), **Jean Jacques Régis,** Duc **de.** b. at Montpellier, France, Oct. 18, 1753; d. at Paris, March 8, 1824. French statesman and jurist. He became a member of the Convention of 1792 (at which the First French Republic was officially established), was president of the Committee of Public Safety in 1794 and of the Council of Five Hundred in 1796, served as minister of justice in 1799, was second consul in 1799, and was arch-chancellor of the empire in 1804. He was made duke of Parma in 1808. He published *Projet du code civil* (1796).

Camballo (kam.bal'ō). In Geoffrey Chaucer's "The Squire's Tale," in *The Canterbury Tales*, the second son of Cambuscan. He is introduced by Edmund Spenser, who calls him Cambell, in *The Faerie Queene*.

Cambaluc (kam'ba.luk). [Also: **Cambuluc; **Mongol, **Khambalu, Khan baligh,** or **Khanbalik;** Chinese, **Tatu.**] Name given by Marco Polo, in his account of his voyages, to the great city of Kublai Khan in China. It is his version of the Mongol name, which is variously transcribed in the Western alphabet. The old city, called by the Chinese Tatu, is represented today by the Tartar section of Peiping.

Cambay (kam.bā'). [Also: **Kambay;** Hindustani, **Khambhat.**] Former state of the Union of India, one of the Gujarat States since 1948 merged with Bombay state, situated ab. 50 mi. S of the city of Ahmedabad. The region produces cotton, wheat, and millet. Capital, Cambay· area, ab. 350 sq. mi.; pop. 96,592 (1941).

Cambay. [Also: **Kambay;** Hindustani, **Khambhat.**] City in the W part of the Union of India, capital of the former state of Cambay, now in Bombay state, situated at the head of the Gulf of Cambay. It is a trading center and rail terminal, and was an important seaport before the silting up of its harbor. It was the reputed Hindu capital of W India in the 5th century A.D. 31,877 (1941).

Cambay, Gulf of. [Also, **Gulf of Kambay.**] Inlet of the Arabian Sea on the W coast of the Union of India, ab. 150 mi. N of Bombay. Length, ab. 150 mi.

Cambell (kam'bel) or **Camballo** (kam.bal'ō). Character in Edmund Spenser's *The Faerie Queene*, taken from Geoffrey Chaucer's *Canterbury Tales*, where he appears as Camballo, a son of King Cambuscan.

Camberiacum (kam.be.rī'a.kum). Latin name of **Chambéry.**

Cambert (käṅ.ber), **Robert.** b. at Paris, c1628; d. at London, 1677. French composer of opera, whose *Pomone* (1671) is considered the first French opera. He was associated with the Abbé Pierre Perrin in the production of French opera for 32 years, after which, Perrin having lost his right to organize performances through the influence of Jean Baptiste Lully, Cambert went to England. Here he may have become "Master of the Music" to Charles II, but this is doubtful. *La Pastorale en musique ou l'Opéra D'Issy* (1659), also written with Perrin, was a musical comedy and was also the first French production of its kind.

Camberwell (kam'bėr.wel, -wel). Metropolitan borough in SE London, in the County of London, situated S of the river Thames. Camberwell is one of the larger boroughs in London. The South London Art Gallery here has been closed due to air raid damage suffered during World War II. The Central Library was totally destroyed in the same action. 179,729 (1951).

Cambiaso (käm.byä'zō), **Giovanni.** [Also, **Cambiasi** (käm.byä'zē).] b. near Genoa, Italy, 1495; d. at an advanced age, year unknown. Italian painter, especially in fresco; father of Luca Cambiaso (1527–85). He modeled his style on the works of earlier artists in the Doria Palace at Genoa. He was not the equal of his more famous son in ability or fame, but he is of some importance in the history of art as the originator of the technique of dividing the human figure into squares as an aid to foreshortening.

Cambiaso, Luca. [Also: **Cambiasi, Cangiagio;** known as **Lucchetto da Genova** and **Luchino.**] b. at Moneglia, near Genoa, Italy, 1527; d. in the Escorial, near Madrid, Spain, 1585. Italian painter and sculptor of the Genoese school. He began his art study with his father, Giovanni Cambiaso, and while he was but 15 years of age, worked with the latter on the decoration of a house at Genoa. He soon surpassed his father in accomplishment and fame. Visiting Rome and Florence, he fed his native inclination toward large and majestic composition by intensive study of the works of Raphael, Michelangelo, and others of the great painters and sculptors. His own early works tended to be perhaps too grandiose, but the paintings of his best period are marked by grace of design and superior loveliness of color. He often painted, with complete assurance, with a brush in each hand. In 1583, at the invitation of Philip II of Spain, he undertook to complete certain frescoes in the Escorial, and his *Assemblage of the Blessed,* on the ceiling of the choir in that palace, is one of his most remarkable works. For this he received 12,000 ducats, the greatest sum paid up to that time for a single work. He died while working in the Escorial; it is said that the cause of his death was his cumulative grief at being unable to obtain the permission of the church to marry his deceased wife's sister. Luca Cambiaso was esteemed also as a sculptor, and is known too for a very large number of drawings. Those of his paintings to be seen at Genoa are generally considered his best, and one of them, a *Pietà* in the Church of Santa Maria da Carignano, has an especial interest because it includes a self-portrait. Examples of his work are in the Uffizi at Florence, the Pinacoteca at Bologna, the Palazzo Doria at Genoa, the Brera at Milan, the Pinakothek at Munich, and the Berlin Gallery.

Cambina (kam.bī'na). A daughter of the fairy Agape in Edmund Spenser's *The Faerie Queene*. She has magic powers, and in the end marries Cambell.

Cambini (käm.bē'nē), **Giovanni Giuseppe.** b. at Leghorn, Italy, Feb. 13, 1746; d. at Bicêtre, France, 1825. Italian violinist and composer. He wrote many symphonies, quartets, and concertos.

Cambio (käm'byō), **Arnolfo di.** See **Arnolfo di Cambio.**

Cambó (käm.bō'), **Francisco de Asís.** b. 1876—. Spanish politician, banker, industrialist, and director of the principal electrical company of Spain. His earliest interests were drawn to the struggle for autonomy sought by Catalonia, and in 1900 he became cofounder of the *Lliga Regionalista.* Because of this activity, after an election victory in 1907, an attempt was made on his life. In 1912 he submitted the draft law of *Mancomunidad,* which gave the Catalan provinces the right to act together in political and administrative matters. He held various ministerial posts under Alfonso XIII, but lost the sympathy of Catalan leftists because of his conservative and orthodox leanings. In 1931 he became cofounder of a monarchist party but, due to his industrial interests, maintained a progressive influence in the government when it fell into the hands of reactionary agrarian interests. He failed to obtain a seat in the elections of 1932. Although residing (as of 1950) in Buenos Aires, he continued to maintain many business enterprises in Spain.

Cambodia (kam.bō'di.a). [Also: **Camboja** (kam.bō'ja); French, **Cambodge** (käṅ.boj); Malay, **Kamboja** (kämbō'jä).] Associated state of the French Union, in Indochina, SE Asia, bounded by Thailand on the W and NW, Laos on the N, Annam (Central Viet-Nam) on the E, Cochin-China (South Viet-Nam) on the SE, and the Gulf of Thailand on the SW. Until 1949, when France recognized it as an independent kingdom within the Union, the status of Cambodia was governed by the *modus vivendi* signed with France on Jan. 7, 1946. It has a council of ministers, with French advisers, and, according to its constitution of 1947, an elected legislative assembly; the latter was dissolved by the king in 1949. The surface is generally level, and it is traversed by the Mekong River. Natural resources include forests, phosphates, jet, and precious stones. The chief product is rice; other crops are rubber, tobacco, cotton, pepper, sugar, kapok, and maize. Silk and cotton weaving are carried on in the homes; fish salting and smoking, cattle raising, and pottery are other important industries. The chief seaports are Kep and Réam. It was formerly a kingdom of large extent, but became a protectorate under French rule in 1863. Capital, Pnompenh; area, 67,550 sq. mi.; pop. 3,748,328 (1948).

Cambodia Point. See **Camau, Point.**

Cambodia River. See **Mekong.**

Cambodunum (kam.bo.dū'num). Ancient name of **Kempten.**

Cambon (käṅ.bôṅ), **Joseph.** [Full name, **Pierre Joseph Cambon.**] b. at Montpellier, France, June 17, 1754; d. near Brussels, Feb. 15, 1820. French revolutionist, member of the Legislative Assembly in 1791, of the Convention in 1792, and of the Committee of Public Safety in 1793. He was a specialist in matters of public finance and took a prominent part in their management during the revolution. A bitter enemy of Robespierre, he was partly responsible, through his speeches, for the latter's fall. Through his support of the left-wing group known as the Mountain, or Montagnards, he had lost his position of influence by 1795 and retired from public life. On the Bourbon restoration (1815) he was banished as a regicide for having voted for the execution of Louis XVI.

Cambon, Jules Martin. b. at Paris, April 5, 1845; d. at Vevey, Switzerland, Sept. 19, 1935. French diplomat and government official; brother of Paul Cambon (1843–1924). He entered public service as a prefect at Constantine, Algeria (1878) and in Nord department (1879). As governor general of Algeria (1891–97), he maintained close relations with Cardinal Charles Martial Allemand-Lavigerie. He was ambassador (1897–1902) to Washington, where he acted as mediator in the peace negotiations between Spain and the U.S., and subsequently held the embassies to Madrid (1902–07) and Berlin (1907–14). He was secretary general (1915) under Foreign Minister Aristide Briand. Though a leading negotiator at the Versailles conference (1919), he did not exert any influence over Premier Georges Clémenceau. He was elected (1918) to the French Academy.

Cambon, Paul. [Full name, **Pierre Paul Cambon.**] b. at Paris, Jan. 20, 1843; d. there, May 29, 1924. French diplomat and government official; brother of Jules Martin Cambon (1845–1935). During his embassy (1898–1920) to London, France and Great Britain turned to a policy of friendship and then to alliance during World War I. He made his entry into government service as the chief aide of Jules Ferry, prefect of the Seine (Paris) in 1870; subsequently he was prefect (1872–73) of Aube department, of Doubs department (1876), and of Nord department (1877–82). Beginning a diplomatic career in 1882, he was resident general of France at Tunis, and served (1886) as ambassador to Madrid, to Constantinople (1890), and finally to London (1898–1920). He helped to abate Anglo-French hostility over the Fashoda incident, took part in the negotiations leading to the formation of the Entente Cordiale, and aided in establishing an Anglo-Russian understanding. In the crisis following the assassination (1914) of the archduke Francis Ferdinand at Sarajevo, he successfully urged British entry into World War I at the side of France. He was elected (1891) to the Academy of Moral and Political Sciences.

Cambon, Victor. b. at Lyons, France, 1852; d. at Paris, 1927. French economist and publicist.

Camboricum (kam.bor'i.kum) or **Camboritum** (-tum). Roman name of an ancient town which occupied the site of the modern Cambridge, England.

Camborne (kam'bôrn, -bėrn). Former urban district, now amalgamated with Redruth as Camborne-Redruth (*q.v.*), in SW England, in Cornwall, ab. 12 mi. SW of Truro, ab. 292 mi. SW of London by rail. It was formerly an important copper and tin mining center which has now greatly declined. Some of the British tin-mining companies now operating in Malaya and elsewhere in the Far East still have their headquarters here and at Redruth. 14,160 (1931).

Camborne-Redruth (kam'bôrn.red'röth, -bėrn-). Urban district and market town in SW England, in Cornwall, ab. 11 mi. SW of Truro, ab. 292 mi. SW of London by rail. It comprises the former urban districts of Camborne and Redruth, amalgamated in 1934. Both were formerly dependent upon tin and copper mining, but the industry has declined and virtually ceased because of foreign competition. Both are now market towns. 35,829 (1951).

Cambrai (kam.brā'; French, kän.brā). [Former spelling, **Cambray**; Flemish, **Kambryk**; Latin, **Cameracum,** later **Camaracus, Camaracum.**] City in N France, in the department of Nord, situated on the Schelde River between Douai and St.-Quentin. The city is known for its linen and cotton fabrics, particularly batiste and cambric, but also has sugar refineries and manufactures of candy, soap, leather goods, and sugar. Phosphates are found in the vicinity. The ancient fortifications were dismantled at the end of the 19th century. Cambrai was a much disputed place during the wars of Francis I, Henry II, and Louis XIV. During World War I, Cambrai was occupied by the Germans, and the front lines were near the city for a long time. A number of buildings were burned down by the Germans before their retreat. The E part of the city was again badly damaged during World War II, but the Cathedral of Notre Dame, the Church of Saint Géry, and the museum are still standing. 26,129 (1946).

Cambrai, Battle of. Last major battle of the great Allied offensive on the Western Front in 1917, during World War I. It saw the successful use of infantry, cavalry, and tanks to enable a sudden penetration almost to the city of Cambrai on the Schelde River SE of Arras. The battle began on Nov. 20 and the British maintained the offensive until Nov. 30, when a German counteroffensive lasting until Dec. 7 regained most of the lost ground. However, the battle was important in that it inflicted serious losses on the Germans and brought tanks into a place of foremost tactical importance.

Cambrai, League of. Alliance between Louis XII of France, the Holy Roman emperor Maximilian I, Ferdinand "the Catholic" of Spain, Pope Julius II, and others, formed at Cambrai on Dec. 10, 1508, the object of which was opposition to the power of Venice, with the plan of partitioning her territories. The League was not unsuccessful in realizing its aims, and disbanded in 1510.

Cambrai, Peace of. [Called the **"Ladies' Peace."**] Peace negotiated at Cambrai, Aug. 5, 1529, between Francis I of France and Charles V of the Holy Roman Empire. France abandoned Italy to the emperor, and relinquished her claim to suzerainty over Flanders and Artois; her title to the duchy of Burgundy was recognized. It was also called the "Ladies' Peace" (*La Paix des dames*) because the preliminaries were conducted by Louise, mother of Francis I, and Margaret, aunt of Charles V.

Cambria (kam'bri.ạ). An ancient name of **Wales.**

Cambrian Mountains. Mountain system occupying central Wales, consisting of numerous mountain blocks with deep valleys intervening. The peak elevation is 2,970 ft., or 3,560 ft., according to whether the Snowdon massif in Caernarvonshire, highest point in England and Wales, is considered part of this range. Length, N to S, ab. 100 mi.

Cambrian Period. The earliest part of the Paleozoic Era. See table at end of Vol. III.

Cambridge (kām'brij). [Middle English, **Cambrigge, Cambrig, Cantebrigge**; earlier, **Grantebrigge, Grauntebrigge**; Old English, **Grantabrycg, Grantanbrycg,** meaning "bridge of (the river) Granta"; Latin, **Cantabrigia.**] Municipal borough in E central England, the county seat of Cambridgeshire, situated on the river Cam ab. 56 mi. NE of London by rail. It is located in the Fens, a marshy district SW of the Wash. Flour milling is the chief industry. Cambridge is the seat of a famous university. It is probably on the site of an ancient British town and of the Roman Camboricum or Camboritum. It had a castle (now destroyed), founded by William the Conqueror; the round Church of the Holy Sepulchre dates from the Norman period. 81,463 (1951).

Cambridge. Town in SE Maryland, capital of Dorchester County, on the S bank of the Choptank River, ab. 36 mi. SE of Annapolis. It is a fishing and canning center, and has shipyards and lumber mills; manufactures include textiles, flour, and fertilizer. 10,351 (1950).

Cambridge. City in E Massachusetts, county seat (with Lowell) of Middlesex County, separated from Boston by the Charles River, and practically a suburb of Boston: seat of Harvard University, Massachusetts Institute of Technology, and Radcliffe College (since 1943 part of Harvard). It has in its manufacturing quarters (East Cambridge and Cambridgeport) factories producing galvanized iron, machinery, rubber, paper, soap, wire cable, and boilers. It has been the residence of such notable literary figures as Oliver Wendell Holmes, Henry Wadsworth Longfellow, and James Russell Lowell. It was founded by English colonists under Winthrop in 1630, and called at first New Towne; its name was changed (1636) to Cambridge after the founding of Harvard College, in honor of Cambridge, England, where some of the early colonists were graduated. It was occupied by the American army in the period 1775–76, and incorporated as a city in 1846. Pop. 120,740 (1950).

Cambridge. Village in E Minnesota, county seat of Isanti County, on the Rum River ab. 40 mi. N of Minneapolis, in a farming region. 2,978 (1950).

Cambridge. City in E Ohio, county seat of Guernsey County, ab. 55 mi. SW of Canton: center of a dairying and livestock-raising area; manufactures glass, pottery, and other items. It was settled in 1806 and named for Cambridge, Md. 14,739 (1950).

Cambridge, Duke of. Title of **Adolphus Frederick** (of *England*).

Cambridge, 2nd Duke of. See **George William Frederick Charles.**

Cambridge, Ada. [Married name, Mrs. **George Frederick Cross.**] b. at Norfolk, England, Nov. 21, 1844; d. at Melbourne, Australia, July 20, 1926. Australian novelist and poet. She lived in England until she married (1870) George Frederick Cross (d. 1917), a minister; subsequently she was a resident of various parts of Australia. Her works include *A Mere Chance* (1882), *A Marked Man* (1891), *The Three Miss Kings* (1891), *Not All in Vain* (1892), *A Marriage Ceremony* (1894), *Materfamilias* (1898), *Sisters* (1904), and other novels; the autobiographical *Thirty Years in Australia* (1903) and *The Retrospect* (1912); and *The Hand in the Dark* (1913), a volume of poetry.

Cambridge, Alexander Augustus Frederick William Alfred George. See **Athlone,** 1st Earl of (2nd creation).

Cambridge, Richard Owen. b. at London, Feb. 14, 1717; d. at Twickenham, England, Sept. 17, 1802. English poet, satirist, essayist, and historian. He is known as the author of *The Scribleriad* (1751), a mock-heroic poem in the style of Alexander Pope, verse satires in imitation of Horace, and *History of the War upon the Coast of Coromandel* (1761). He contributed 21 essays (Nos. 50–51, 54–56, 65, 70–72, 76, 99, 102, 104, 106–108, 116, 118–119, 123, and 206) to the *World* (1753–56), one of the many imitators of the *Tatler* and *Spectator*. He entertained Samuel Johnson, Sir Joshua Reynolds, Thomas Gray, William Pitt, and many others at Twickenham, and is mentioned frequently in James Boswell's writings.

Cambridge, University of. [Also, **Cambridge University.**] University at Cambridge, England. The town was a center of learning in the 12th century, and in 1231 Henry III issued writs for the regulation of Cambridge "clerks." It contains the following colleges: St. Peter's (Peterhouse), founded as a hospital in 1257, converted into a college by Hugh de Balsham (charter, 1284); Clare, by Richard Badew in 1326 as University Hall, refounded by the Countess of Clare in 1359; Pembroke, by the Countess of Pembroke in 1347; Gonville and Caius, by Gonville in 1348 and Caius in 1558; Trinity Hall, by Bateman in 1350; Corpus Christi, or Benet College, by Cambridge guilds in 1352; King's, by Henry VI in 1441; Queens', by Margaret of Anjou in 1448 and Elizabeth Woodville in 1465; St. Catherine's, by Woodlark in 1473; Jesus, by Alcock in 1496; Christ's, by William Bingham as a school in 1439, refounded by Margaret Beaufort, mother of Henry VII, in 1505; St. John's, founded as a hospital c1210, refounded in 1511 by Margaret Beaufort; Magdalene, established as a hostel for students in 1428, given to Lord Audley who founded it as a college in 1519; Trinity, by Henry VIII in 1546 on several earlier foundations; Emmanuel, by Mildmay in 1584; Sidney Sussex, by the will of the Countess of Sussex (d. 1589) in 1594; Downing, by Sir George Downing (d. 1749; charter in 1800); Ayerst Hall, founded in 1884, "to provide an economical education for theological students and others," closed 1896; Cavendish College, in 1873, by an association, for younger students, closed 1891; Selwyn College (a hostel), in 1882 in memory of George Augustus Selwyn. It has two women's colleges: Girton (established 1869) and Newnham (established 1875; originally founded, 1873, as a hall of residence). The university library contains some 1,500,000 volumes, more than 12,000 manuscripts, and 250,000 maps.

Cambridge Agreement. Agreement (Aug. 29, 1629) entered into and signed by leading Puritan members of the Massachusetts Bay Company, binding them to embark for America and take the charter with them. The legal transfer of the charter to New England meant that a business company would be transformed into a colony, thus affording the Puritans an opportunity to establish their Calvinistic state in the American wilderness. The purpose of the agreement was to secure the enterprise from interference by the government of England. Among the signers were John Winthrop and Richard Saltonstall.

Cambridge City. Town in E Indiana, in Wayne County ab. 50 mi. E of Indianapolis. 2,559 (1950).

Cambridge Histories. Three series of histories which reflect, in large part, an ambitious outline (which called for a pooling of efforts and talents by leading historians of the day) drawn up by Lord Acton. They are *The Cambridge Ancient History* (12 vols., 1923–39), *The Cambridge Medieval History* (8 vols., 1911–36), and *The Cambridge Modern History* (12 vols., 1902–11). Acton was actually able to start work only on the last-named series, and his death in 1902 occurred when only the first volume of that had appeared.

Cambridge History of American Literature, The. Four-volume survey of American literature, published in the period 1917–21. It was edited by John Erskine, Stuart P. Sherman, W. P. Trent, and Carl Van Doren, and contained articles by 64 contributors including Vernon L. Parrington and Paul Elmer More.

Cambridge History of English Literature. Survey history of English literature from its beginnings to the end of the 19th century, each section written by a notable expert scholar in that field, and edited by A. W. Ward and A. R. Waller. The work, published in 14 volumes from 1907 to 1927, now is published in 15 volumes, the separate indexes for each volume having been combined in a general index.

Cambridge Platform. Declaration of principles respecting church government and doctrine adopted by a synod, composed of representatives of the Congregational churches of New England, held at Cambridge, Mass., in August, 1648.

Cambridgeport (kām'brij.pōrt). Manufacturing district of the city of Cambridge, Mass., lying on the Charles River opposite Boston, ab. 1½ mi. W of the state house.

Cambridgeshire (kām'brij.shir). [Also: **Cambridge, Cambs** (written without a period).] Geographical county and an administrative county, in E central England, lying inland between Lincolnshire on the N, Norfolk and Suffolk on the E. Essex and Hertfordshire on the S, and Northamptonshire, Huntingdonshire, and Bedfordshire on the W. It is divided into Cambridgeshire proper and the Isle of Ely; Cambridgeshire forms part of the fen country which was largely reclaimed in the 17th and 18th centuries. It is chiefly an agricultural county, with most of its production concentrated in grains and fruit. Aside from agriculture, the chief industries are brewing and malting. County seat, Cambridge; area of administrative county, ab. 492 sq. mi.; pop. 166,863 (1951).

Cambridgeshire Fens. See **Ely, Isle of.**

Cambridge Thirty Years Ago. Essay (1854) by James Russell Lowell. It is a charming and nostalgic picture of the town worthies and of Harvard, teachers, students, and customs, varied by quotable judgments upon things in general and by a notable portrait of Washington Allston.

Cambridge University. See **Cambridge, University of.**

Cambronne (käṅ.brọn), Count **Pierre Jacques Étienne.** b. at St.-Sébastien, near Nantes, France, Dec. 26, 1770; d. at Nantes, Jan. 8, 1842. French general. He fought against the Vendeans, participated as colonel in the campaigns of 1812 and 1813, accompanied Napoleon to Elba, was made lieutenant general and admitted to the Chamber of Peers during the Hundred Days, and commanded a division of the Imperial Guard at the battle of Waterloo (1815). He is the reputed author of the expression "La garde meurt et ne se rend pas" ("The guard dies, but never surrenders"), incorrectly said to have been used by him at Waterloo when asked to surrender. Another version, now generally accepted as correct, has him replying with a single word, conveying approximately the same adamant refusal to surrender as the "Nuts!" of the American paratroop commander during the Battle of Bastogne in World War II.

Cambs. See **Cambridgeshire.**

Cambuluc (kam'bu.luk). See **Cambaluc.**

Cambuscan (kam.bus.kan', kam.bus'kạn). In Geoffrey Chaucer's "The Squire's Tale," in *The Canterbury Tales*, a Tartar king who had extraordinary magical possessions —a ring, a glass, a sword, and a brazen horse. He is the father of Canace, Camballo, and Algarsife. Chaucer left the story incomplete.

Cambuskenneth Abbey (kam.bus.ken′eth). Abbey situated near Stirling, Scotland. The battle of Stirling took place near here in 1297.

Cambuslang (kam′bus.lang). Parish town in S central Scotland, in NW Lanarkshire, ab. 5 mi. SE of Glasgow. It is an industrial suburb of Glasgow, with coal mining. 26,861 (1951 census, preliminary).

Cambyses (kam.bī′sēz). Tragedy (1671) by Elkanah Settle.

Cambyses I. [Old Persian, **Ka(m)bujiya** (käm.bö′jē-yä).] Persian king whose historical character is doubtful. In the genealogy of Xerxes, as given by Herodotus, both he and his son Cyrus are omitted, and Diodorus, where he gives this name, seems to mean the father of Cyrus the Great. On the other hand, a Cambyses is mentioned whose sister was the ancestress in the fourth degree of one of the seven conspirators. Possibly Cambyses I was one of the sons of Theïspes (on the cuneiform monuments Chishpaïsh), and grandson of Achaemenes.

Cambyses II (or **I**). fl. c600 B.C. Persian ruler; son and successor of Cyrus I, and father of Cyrus II, called "Cyrus the Great." According to Herodotus he was merely a Persian nobleman, but Xenophon states that he was king of the country, and his statement is confirmed by native records. In those chronologies which do not enter the historically dubious Cambyses covered by the entry immediately preceding this one, he is shown as Cambyses I.

Cambyses III (or **II**). d. c521 B.C. Persian ruler; son and successor of Cyrus the Great. He reigned from 529 to c521 B.C. He is depicted as despotic and tyrannical. He defeated Psammetichus III (called by the Greeks Psammenit), king of Egypt, in the battle of Pelusium (525 B.C.), and incorporated that country in the Persian empire. His expeditions against Ammon and Ethiopia were unfortunate. While he was devastating Egypt, an imposter assuming the name of his brother Bardiya (called by the Greeks Smerdis), who had been secretly assassinated at Cambyses's instigation, forced him to return to Persia, but he died on the way from a presumably self-inflicted wound.

Cambyses, King of Persia. Play by Thomas Preston, written as early as 1561.

Camden (kam′dẹn). City in S Arkansas, county seat of Ouachita County. It is a rail center and river port, on the Ouachita River; paper, munitions, and pottery are among its manufactures. 11,372 (1950).

Camden. Town (in Maine the equivalent of township in many other states) and unincorporated village in S Maine, in Knox County: resort community. Pop. of town, 3,670 (1950); of village, 3,270 (1950).

Camden. City in C New Jersey, county seat of Camden County, on the Delaware River opposite Philadelphia. The principal commercial and industrial city of S New Jersey, it is notable for its canning factories, shipyards, and manufactures of steel pens, radios, and phonographs. It was the home (1873–92) of Walt Whitman. 124,555 (1950).

Camden. City in N South Carolina, county seat of Kershaw County, near the Wateree River, ab. 32 mi. NE of Columbia. It is a tourist resort; manufactures include textiles, cottonseed oil, wood veneers, and iron and brass products. A number of training stables and racecourses are at Camden, which holds two annual horse shows. Here, on Aug. 16, 1780, the British under General Charles Cornwallis defeated American forces under General Horatio Gates; the loss of the Americans was ab. 2,000, including General Johann Kalb, Baron de Kalb. Near here, at Hobkirk's Hill, on April 25, 1781, another defeat by British forces was inflicted upon American troops. The town was burned (1865) by Sherman in the Civil War. It was the birthplace of Bernard M. Baruch. 6,986 (1950).

Camden, 1st Earl of. See **Pratt,** Sir **Charles.**

Camden, Second Battle of. See under **Hobkirk's Hill.**

Camden, William. b. at London, May 2, 1551; d. at Chislehurst, Kent, England, Nov. 9, 1623. English historian and antiquary, noted for his study of Elizabethan times, *Annales rerum Anglicarum et Hibernicarum regnante Elizabetha* (1615). He was an usher (1575–93) and headmaster (1593–97) of the Westminster School, London, leaving there to take up an appointment as Clarenceux king-of-arms. He spent many years on writing and revising *Britannia* (1st ed., 1586), a survey of the British islands; written in Latin, it was first translated into English in 1610. He also compiled a Greek grammar (1597), and published various editions of historical works. The Camden Society, founded in 1838 for the purpose of publishing historical documents, was named for him.

Camden Society. English historical society formed in 1838 for the publication of documents relating to English history. It was named for William Camden.

Camden Town. District in St. Pancras metropolitan borough, in NW London, in the County of London, situated E of Regent's Park, ab. 5 mi. NW of Broad Street station. It takes its name from Charles Pratt, 1st Earl of Camden, who acquired large property here by marriage.

Camel, Battle of the. Battle fought at Basra, in 656, in which the Moslem caliph Ali defeated the rebels Talha, Zobair, and Ayesha, wife of Mohammed (the latter being present on a camel).

Camelford (kam′ẹl.fọrd). Rural district and market town in SW England, in Cornwall, situated on the river Camel ab. 15 mi. W of Launceston. It includes the parish of Tintagel. It is one of the places identified as the Camelot of the Arthurian cycle, and a traditional scene of the final battle between Arthur and Modred. 7,577 (1951).

Camelon (kam′ẹ.lon). *Quoad sacra* (i.e., ecclesiastical) parish in Falkirk parliamentary burgh, in E central Scotland, in Stirlingshire, situated on the Firth of Forth. It is said to be the site of the battle that ended the career of the historical King Arthur, in 537.

Camelopardalis (kạ.mel.ọ̄.pär′dạ.lis, kam″ẹ.lọ̄-). The Camelopard or Giraffe, a northern constellation named by Hevelius. It is situated between Cepheus, Perseus, Ursa Major and Minor, and Draco. As given originally by Hevelius, the name was Camelopardalus.

Camelot (kam′ẹ.lot). Legendary spot in England or Wales where King Arthur was said to have had his palace and court, and where the Round Table was. Shakespeare alludes to it in *King Lear:*

> Goose, if I had you upon Sarum plain,
> I'd drive ye cackling home to Camelot.

This is supposed to be in allusion to the fact that great quantities of geese were bred on the moors at Queens Camel, Somersetshire. In Geoffrey of Monmouth, Camelot was, or was near, Winchester; other critics locate it in Monmouthshire, at Caerleon; still others identify it with Camelford, in Cornwall.

Camel's Hump. One of the chief peaks of the Green Mountains, Vermont. It is W of Montpelier. Elevation, ab. 4,088 ft.

Camenae (kạ.mē′nē). In Italian mythology, four prophetic divinities, identified by Roman poets with the Muses.

Camenz (kä′ments). See **Kamenz.**

Cameracum (kam.ėr.ā′kum). Latin name of **Cambrai.**

Cameran (kam.ėr.an′). See **Kamaran.**

Camerarius (kam.ėr.ãr′i.us; German, kä.mä.rä′rē.ůs), **Joachim.** [Original surname, **Liebhard.**] b. at Bamberg, Germany, April 12, 1500; d. at Leipzig, Germany, April 17, 1574. German scholar, author of a life of Melanchthon (1556) and editor of Melanchthon's letters (1569).

Camerarius, Rudolf Jakob. b. at Tübingen, Württemberg, Germany, Feb. 12, 1665; d. there, Sept. 11, 1721. German physician and botanist. His pioneer work on the reproductive functions in plants was published in *De sexu plantarum epistola* (1694).

Camerino (kä.mā.rē′nō). [Ancient name, **Camerinum.**] Town and commune in C Italy, in the *compartimento* (region) of Marches, in the province of Macerata, situated in the Apennines, SW of Ancona: seat of an archbishopric and of a free university (founded 1727). There are woolen, leather, and candy manufactures. The archiepiscopal palace and cathedral date from the 16th century; there are a number of other remarkable churches and palaces. A Roman town, it was conquered by the Goths and much contested afterwards; completely destroyed in 1259. Reconstructed by the Varano family, it was given by Pope Alexander VI to his nephew Giovanni Borgia; in 1545 it came under the States of the Church. It came to

Italy by plebiscite in 1860. Pop. of commune, 12,012 (1936); of town, 4,269 (1936).

Cameron (kam'ėr.on). City in NW Missouri, in Clinton and DeKalb counties: garment manufactures. 3,570 (1950).

Cameron. City in C Texas, county seat of Milam County, NE of Austin: agricultural center. 5,052 (1950).

Cameron, Andrew Carr. b. at Berwick-upon-Tweed, England, 1834; d. 1890. American labor leader and journalist. Upon coming to the U.S., he settled in Illinois and entered newspaper work. In 1864 he became editor of the *Workingman's Advocate*, which he developed into one of the leading labor papers in the U.S. It became the organ of the National Labor Union, of which Cameron was one of the founders in 1866. He served as president of labor union associations at Chicago and elsewhere in Illinois, and was a national leader of the movement for an eight-hour day. He believed that organized labor's best prospect of attaining its objectives lay in political action, and was influential in causing the National Labor Union to support the Greenback Party in the presidential election of 1872. However, the trend of opinion among the unions ran otherwise, toward economic measures and the use of the strike, and Cameron lost his position of leadership. In 1880 he became editor of the publication *Inland Printer*, and in 1888 acquired ownership of, and edited, *The Artist Printer*.

Cameron, Basil. b. at Reading, England, Aug. 18, 1885—. English orchestra conductor. The groups and series he has led include the Hastings Municipal Orchestra (1923–30), the Harrogate Municipal Orchestra (1924–30), Royal Philharmonic Society concerts (1928 *et seq.*) at London, the British Broadcasting Corporation symphony concerts at London, the San Francisco Symphony Orchestra (1930–32), and the Seattle Symphony Orchestra (1933–38).

Cameron, Sir **David Young.** b. at Glasgow, Scotland, June 28, 1865; d. Sept. 16, 1945. Scottish painter and etcher, noted primarily for his architectural subjects. He studied at the Academy at Glasgow and at Edinburgh. His success was immediate. He exhibited at Glasgow, Berlin, and Munich, and received medals at Antwerp (1893), Chicago (1893), Brussels (1895), Dresden (1897), Paris (1900), and Munich (1905). His paintings were purchased by the museums at Manchester, Liverpool, Dublin, Adelaide, and Budapest, among others. His principal series of etchings include *Views of Northern Italy* (1896), *Views of London* (1900), and *Views of Paris* (1909).

Cameron, Edgar Spier. b. at Ottawa, Ill., May 26, 1862; d. at Chicago, Nov. 5, 1944. American figure, landscape, and mural painter, and art critic. He is known for murals in public buildings including the Chicago city hall, the Genesee County court house at Flint, Mich., the public library at Riverside, Ill., and the First National Bank at Oklahoma City, Okla. He studied at the Chicago Academy of Design, the Art Students League of New York, and at Paris, and exhibited extensively in the U.S. and at Paris, winning prizes in both places. Among his better-known works are *Youth and Moonlight, Cabaret Breton, Dreamland, The Rain Dance,* and *Nocturne*.

Cameron, James Donald. b. at Middletown, Dauphin County, Pa., May 14, 1833; d. Aug. 30, 1918. American politician. He graduated from Princeton in 1852, was president of the Northern Central Railway Company of Pennsylvania (1863–74), and was secretary of war under President Ulysses S. Grant from May 22, 1876 to March 3, 1877. In the latter year he was elected a U.S. senator from Pennsylvania as a Republican, serving until 1897.

Cameron, John. b. at Glasgow, Scotland, c1579; d. at Montauban, France, 1625. Scottish theologian, an advocate of passive obedience to James II, which brought him such unpopularity that he left his post as principal of Glasgow University. He became professor of divinity at Saumur, and later at Montauban, in France, where he was esteemed for his learning. His followers in France were called Cameronites.

Cameron, Richard. b. at Falkland, Fifeshire, Scotland; killed near Aird's Moss, Ayrshire, Scotland, July 20, 1680. Scottish Presbyterian minister, a leader of the Covenanters. His followers, a sect of Scottish dissenters, were called Cameronians, later taking the name Reformed Presbyterians. A field preacher, he refused to submit to the authority of Charles II. A group of his followers were the nucleus of the Cameronian regiment of the British army.

Cameron, Simon. b. in Lancaster County, Pa., March 8, 1799; d. June 26, 1889. American politician and diplomat, secretary of war (1861–62) in Lincoln's cabinet, from which he was removed after his partisan administration caused dissatisfaction. He was editor (1821) of the Bucks County *Messenger* (Doylestown, Pa.), which became the *Democrat* before its dissolution at the end of 1821. For a brief time thereafter he was a partner in the Pennsylvania *Intelligencer* (Harrisburg, Pa.), later leaving for Washington, D.C., where he cultivated political connections and worked in the printing firm of Gales and Seaton. He purchased (c1824) the *Republican* at Harrisburg, became state printer and, a power in state politics, was appointed (1826) adjutant general of Pennsylvania. He became active in banking, railroad, and iron ventures, gradually expanding into other lines while maintaining his political activity. In 1838 he became commissioner for settling claims made by the Winnebago Indians; his employment of his own bank in the adjustment of these claims gave him notoriety and the nickname "the Great Winnebago Chief." In 1845 he went to the U.S. Senate to occupy the seat vacated by James Buchanan, and returned (1857) to the Senate as a Republican. A leader of the party machine in Pennsylvania, and a staunch advocate of the protective tariff, he figured as a presidential possibility at the Republican Convention of 1860. His managers traded the Pennsylvania vote, supporting Lincoln in return for a cabinet post for Cameron, who resigned from the Senate to head the War Department. His administration was corrupt and ineptly managed, and featured by political favoritism in the letting out of contracts. In January, 1862, Lincoln appointed him minister to Russia in order to avoid further embarrassment. Cameron served in that post for a brief period, and in 1863 was back in Pennsylvania making a bid for the U.S. Senate. He went to the Senate in 1867, and in 1877 resigned his seat after being assured that the Pennsylvania legislature would vote his son, James Donald Cameron, into his place. A shrewd dispenser of patronage, he was the epitome of the modern machine politician; he handed his state dynasty over to his son in 1877, and retired from political life.

Cameron, Verney Lovett. b. near Weymouth, Dorsetshire, England, July 1, 1844; d. in Bedfordshire, England, March 27, 1894. English explorer. As a naval officer who knew East Africa, he was chosen in 1872, by the Royal Geographical Society, to lead an expedition in relief of David Livingstone. In March, 1873, he started from Bagamoyo, on the E coast of Tanganyika Territory. In the Unyanyembe region, near Tabora, Tanganyika, he met the bearers of the body of Livingstone (who had died near Lake Bangweulu, in Northern Rhodesia) on their way to the coast, but proceeded to Lake Tanganyika. His two European assistants returned with the body and one of them (Dillon) died. Cameron explored the southern portion of Lake Tanganyika, discovered the Lukuga River, and made his way through the Belgian Congo and Angola to Benguela on the Atlantic coast of Angola, where he arrived on Nov. 28, 1875. He was the first explorer to cross Africa from east to west, and was honored with the order of Companion of the Bath, the gold medal of the Royal Geographical Society, and an honorary degree from Oxford University, and promoted to commander. His *Across Africa* appeared in 1877. In 1878 he made a railroad survey in Asia Minor and Persia, and in 1882 went to West Africa with Sir Richard Francis Burton.

Cameronians (kam.ẹ.rō'ni.ạnz). Followers of Richard Cameron in Scotland. They refused to accept the indulgence granted to the Presbyterian clergy in the persecuting times of Charles II, lest by so doing they should be understood to recognize his ecclesiastical authority. They were known at first as the Societies, but were afterward organized as the Reformed Presbyterian Church of Scotland, most of which in 1876 was merged in the Free Church.

Cameronians. Name given to the 26th regiment of British infantry, from its having been originally composed of some of the Cameronians who flocked to

Edinburgh during the revolution of 1688. Their nucleus consisted of the men who fought under Richard Cameron at Aird's Moss in 1680, when he was killed.

Cameronites (kam'e.ron.īts). Group of French Protestants, professing a modified Calvinism, led by John Cameron, a native of Glasgow, professor of theology at Saumur and Montauban. They were condemned by the Synod of Dort.

Cameron of Lochiel (loċh.ēl'), **Donald.** [Called **"the Gentle Lochiel."**] b. c1695; d. 1748. Scottish chieftain and soldier; grandson of Sir Ewen Cameron of Lochiel (1629–1719). In 1719 he became chief of the Clan Cameron. He arrived (Aug. 19, 1745) with 800 clansmen to support Prince Charles Edward, a move which rallied other support for the Pretender. He captured Edinburgh (Sept. 17, 1745), fought at Prestonpans, where the Camerons distinguished themselves, and was wounded while taking Falkirk. A leader at Culloden (April 16, 1746), he opposed the night attack, during which he was severely wounded. He escaped with Prince Charles Edward, arriving (Sept. 29, 1746) on the coast of Brittany.

Cameron of Lochiel, Sir **Ewen** (or **Evan** or **Euan**). b. 1629; d. in February, 1719. Scottish chieftain; grandfather of Donald Cameron of Lochiel (c1695–1748). He joined Glencairn in the north with 700 of his clan, fighting (1652) for Charles II against the forces of the Commonwealth; despite large bribes offered him, he refused to submit to General George Monck until June, 1658. Present at the time of Charles II's entrance (1660) into London, he was received at Court. He raised his clan to join (1690) John Graham, Viscount Dundee, under whom they fought at the battle of Killiecrankie, and sent the clan, under the command of his son, to fight in the rising of 1714. He is said to have killed (1680) with his own hands the last wolf in the Highlands.

Cameroon (kam.e.rön'). [French, **Cameroun;** German, **Kamerun.**] River in W Africa which empties into the Bight of Biafra, in Cameroun (or French Cameroons), near the border of Nigeria.

Cameroon Mountain. [Also, **Fako.**] Volcanic peak in W Africa, in the British trust territory of the Cameroons, at the S end of the mountain chain which separates the British and French territories. The slopes of the mountain are forested, and the area in the immediate vicinity is suitable for European settlement. The peak, one of the highest in West Africa, can be seen far out at sea. Buëa, the principal city and former administrative center of the British territory of Cameroons, is situated on its E slope. 13,353 ft.

Cameroons (kam.e.rönz'). [French, **Cameroun;** German, **Kamerun.**] Former German protectorate in W Africa, extending from the Bight of Biafra NE to Lake Chad. In 1920 it was split up and given as mandated territory to Great Britain and France, with France receiving the major portion (Cameroun); both mandates became United Nations trust territories in 1946, the British being administered under Nigeria.

Cameroons. [Also, **British Cameroons.**] Trust territory of Great Britain, formerly part of the German protectorate of Cameroons (Kamerun), situated on the E side of Nigeria, W Africa, stretching NE from the Bight of Biafra to Lake Chad. The boundary between the British and French territories runs along the crest of the high mountains which culminate near the coast in Cameroon Mountain. The N portion of the territory is administered with Bornu, Adamawa, and Benue provinces, Nigeria, and the S part under the Eastern Provinces of Nigeria. The entire country tends to be mountainous, and is for the most part undeveloped economically and culturally. Palm oil, timber, rubber, bananas, cocoa, and cotton are produced near the coast. Area, 34,081 sq. mi.; pop. 1,051,988 (est. 1950).

Cameroun (kȧm.rön). [Also: **Cameroons, French Cameroons.**] French trust territory in W Africa extending NE from the Bight of Biafra, between the British territory of Cameroons and French Equatorial Africa. It is the major portion of the former German territory of Cameroons (Kamerun); given to France in 1920 as a mandate, it later became a trusteeship under the United Nations. It is bounded on the W by the Atlantic Ocean, on the NW by British Cameroons and Nigeria, and on the N, E, and S by French Equatorial Africa. Most of the country is high tableland having some mountain masses; it is fertile and well-watered in the S, and could support a European population in some areas. The territory is administered separately from French Equatorial Africa by a high commissioner and an elected representative assembly with headquarters at Yaoundé. Douala, on the Cameroun estuary, is the chief port, and is connected by railroad with Yaoundé and other inland points. Capital, Yaoundé; area, 166,489 sq. mi.; pop. 3,009,185 (1950).

Camiguin (kä.mē.gēn'). Volcanic island of the Babuyan group, N of Luzon, Philippine Islands. It belongs to Cagayan province, and contains Camiguin volcano. Highest elevation, 2,742 ft.; area, 63 sq. mi.; pop. 585 (1939).

Camiguin. Fertile, mountainous island in Mindanao Sea, N of Mindanao, Philippine Islands. It belongs to Misamis Oriental province, and contains Hibok Hibok, an active volcano. Violent eruptions in 1948 and 1951 drove thousands of people from their homes; in the latter year none of the usual warning signs preceded the disaster and over 200 were killed. Highest elevation, 5,620 ft.; area, 96 sq. mi.; pop. 40,805 (1939).

Camiguin. Volcano on Camiguin island in the Babuyan group, Philippine Islands. A great eruption took place in 1871, activity continuing into 1875. New solfataras appeared in 1897 and 1902. Elevation, 2,742 ft.

Camiling (kä.mē.lēng'). Town in Tarlac province, in W central Luzon, Philippine Islands. 7,765 (1948).

Camilla (ka.mil'a). City in SW Georgia, county seat of Mitchell County. 3,745 (1950).

Camilla. In Greek legend, a virgin warrior queen of the Volscians. She figures in Vergil's *Aeneid* as being killed by the Trojans.

Camilla. In John Lyly's *Euphues*, a lady with whom Philautus falls in love.

Camilla. Opera by Owen McSwiney, translated from the Italian in 1706.

Camilla. [Full title, **Camilla, or a Picture of Youth.**] Novel by Fanny Burney, published in 1796.

Camille (kȧ.mēy'). In Pierre Corneille's tragedy *Horace*, sister of the three Horatii. She denounces Rome when she finds that her lover has been killed by one of her brothers, and the latter kills her for her lack of patriotism.

Camille (ka.mil'). Title given to the English version of the French play *La Dame aux camélias* by the younger Alexandre Dumas. The heroine Marguerite of the original is called Camille in this translation.

Camillo (ka.mil'ō). In John Webster's tragedy *The White Devil*, the husband of Vittoria Corombona.

Camillo. In Shakespeare's *The Winter's Tale*, a Sicilian noble. He saves Polixenes and induces Leontes to protect Florizel and Perdita.

Camillo. Character in John Dryden's play *The Assignation.*

Camillus (ka.mil'us). Town (in New York the equivalent of township in many other states) and village in W central New York, in Onondaga County, in a farming region: manufactures pocket knives. Pop. of town, 6,735 (1950); of village, 1,225 (1950).

Camillus. A pseudonym of Alexander Hamilton, used in his political writings. Fisher Ames, who wrote pamphlets supporting Hamilton's policies, also used the name.

Camillus, Marcus Furius. d. c365 B.C. Roman general. He was several times dictator, took Veii c396, and after the sack of Rome by Brennus (c390) defeated the Gauls.

Caminatzin (kä.mē.nä.tsēn'). See **Cacama.**

Caminha (ka.mē'nya), **Pedro Vaz de.** d. c1500. Portuguese who accompanied Pedro Alvares Cabral in 1500 as secretary of the proposed factory at Calicut. He wrote a letter, preserved at Lisbon, which is the oldest extant description of the discovery of Brazil. This was first published in 1790, and there are subsequent editions. Caminha probably perished in the massacre at Calicut, on Dec. 16, 1500.

Caminhos cruzados (ka.mē'nyös krö.zä'dös). Collective novel of cosmopolitan life, by the contemporary Brazilian writer Érico Veríssimo (1905—). It was published in 1935, and an English translation appeared in 1943.

Camisards (kam'i.zärdz). Name given to a group of French Protestants in the Cévennes who revolted (1702–10) against the persecution which followed the revocation (1685) of the Edict of Nantes. They were probably so called from the blouses worn in night raids by the peasants, who were the chief participants in the insurrection. Inspired by prophecies of the fall of Babylon (the Roman Catholic Church), the Camisards burned churches and drove away many priests. With their religious fervor and strong sense of injustice and their knowledge of their own country, which had few roads, they were able to hold out against the large forces sent against them. On the offer of certain concessions to the Protestants, one of their leaders, Jean Cavalier, who had been successful in many guerrilla raids, submitted in 1704, and many of the Camisards disbanded, but scattered revolt continued until 1710.

Camlan (kam′lạn), **Battle of.** Legendary battle variously said to have taken place in Cornwall or (by Malory) near Salisbury, in which both King Arthur and his nephew Modred fell in single combat. See also under **Camelon.**

Cammaerts (käm′ärts), **Émile (Léon).** b. at Brussels, March 16, 1878—. Belgian poet and writer in England. He was active in Belgium as a journalist and author until 1908, when he settled in England, where he became a professor at the London School of Economics and professor of Belgian studies and institutions at the University of London. He is the author of *Belgian Poems* (1915), *New Belgian Poems* (1917), *Messines and Other Poems* (1918), *The Childhood of Christ as Seen by the Primitive Masters* (1922), *The Treasure House of Belgium* (1924), *The Poetry of Nonsense* (1925), *Discoveries in England* (1930), *Albert of Belgium* (1935), *The Seven Virtues and G. K. Chesterton* (1937), *Upon This Rock* (1942), and *The Peace that Was Left* (1945). He has also written plays, including *Les Deux Bossus*, and has translated works by John Ruskin and G. K. Chesterton.

Cammin (kä.mēn′). German name of **Kamień Pomorski.**

Camões (kạ.moiǹsh′), **Luiz (Vaz) de.** [English, **Camoëns** (kam′ō.ẹnz, kạ.mō′ẹnz).] b. in Portugal, c1524; d. at Lisbon, June 10, 1580. Portuguese poet, the most celebrated in that language, author of the epic poem *Os Lusíadas* (The Portuguese, 1572; commonly called the *Lusiads*), on the discovery of the sea route to India by the Portuguese navigator Vasco da Gama. Camões came of a family of the minor nobility and was educated at Coimbra, which he is believed to have left for Lisbon in the early 1540's. For about two years he lived in Ceuta, Africa, where he served in the army and lost the sight of his right eye, probably in a battle. At Lisbon, he was imprisoned (1522) for having wounded one of the king's equerries in a street fracas. He was pardoned (1553) on the condition of his immediate embarkation for India. He arrived in Goa in September of the same year, and went to Macao a few years later. About 1560 he was back in Goa. He embarked there for Portugal in 1567, but was left in Mozambique. At last he landed at Lisbon at the end of 1569 or the beginning of 1570, after about 17 years of exile. His lyric production is of extreme literary value, his sonnets being thought by many to have been unsurpassed. The most reliable edition of his lyrics is considered to be *Lírica de Camões*, a scholarly work published at Coimbra in 1932 by José Maria Rodrigues and Afonso Lopes Vieira, which contains all the lyric poems actually written by Camões, omitting those that for centuries had been unduly attributed to him. He also wrote three comedies in verse: *El-Rei Seleuco*, *Anfitriões*, and *Filodemo*.

Camonica (kä.mô′nē.kä). [Also, **Val Camonica.**] Valley of the Oglio River in its upper course, in Lombardy, Italy, N of Lake Iseo.

Camorra (kạ.môr′ạ). Secret terroristic society that first became prominent (c1830) in the S part of Italy. Its ultimate origin is not known, although some have suggested a borrowing from Spain (from the Spanish word *camorra*, meaning "quarrel"). In Italy it had what might be considered a comparatively respectable origin as a mutual aid society of inmates and former inmates of the prisons of the Kingdom of the Two Sicilies, most of whom were political prisoners or otherwise victims of Bourbon tyranny. Its power spread, especially at Naples, as liberated prisoners perceived that in the chaotic conditions then prevailing in S Italy a living could most easily be made by thuggery, extortion, and the organization of what later came to be called rackets. Apprising each other by means of secret signs and signals of the approach of likely victims or, on the other hand, of the police, the *camorristi*, as the members were called, roamed the streets in bands. Smuggling was soon added to highway robbery as a major source of emolument, and merchants were easily induced to hire camorristi to afford, to their goods in transit and at their warehouses, protection which the police were impotent to give. The police, indeed, often sought the aid of the Camorra in the solution of crimes. The society evolved its own code and ranks of officers, and settled its problems before its own tribunals. First coming to public notice during the third decade of the 19th century, before long it had acquired such power as to be, in fact if not by law, the government of Naples. From 1848 to 1860 the Camorra supported the Italian movement for independence, and if it had been dissolved after this succeeded it might appear in history in a relatively favorable light. It continued, however, as a purely criminal organization, taking toll of prostitution, gambling, and other activities of the underworld, and buying immunity by bribing police, government officials, and even members of the clergy. In 1877 an attempt at suppression was made, without effect. In 1900, however, facts came out in the course of a lawsuit which caused the Italian government to set aside the municipal government of Naples and to institute a searching inquiry. In 1901 an Honest Government League was formed in the city, which began to bring the Camorra under control, and in 1911, following a murder traced to the society, 20 of its leaders (of whom the reputed chief was extradited from the U.S.) were tried, convicted, and heavily sentenced, and the organization fell apart.

Camotes Islands (kä.mō′tās). Group of islands lying between Cebu and Leyte, in the Philippines, and belonging to Cebu province. The largest is Pacijan, and the two other main islands are Ponson and Poro.

Camp (käǹ), **Maxime Du.** See **Du Camp, Maxime.**

Camp (kamp), **Walter Chauncey.** b. at New Britain, Conn., April 7, 1859; d. at New York, March 14, 1925. American developer of the game of football, which he modified into an approximation of its characteristically American form. Graduated (1880) from Yale, he attended the Yale Medical School; as a student he was active in all outdoor sports, particularly football. He was associated (1883 *et seq.*) with the New Haven Clock Company. After establishing his residence at New Haven in 1888, he became general athletic director and chief advisory football coach at Yale, where he achieved national prominence for his changes in the game of football and his emphasis on sportsmanship and physical fitness. Among his important modifications were the substitution of the "scrimmage" for the "scrum," the creation of the position of quarterback, and the scaling down of the number of players from 15 to 11. He began his annual "All-American" selections in 1889, and during World War I was active in leading government-sponsored physical fitness programs, during which he helped originate the "daily dozen" exercises. Among his books are: *Football: How to Coach a Team* (1886), *American Football* (1891), *Walter Camp's Book of College Sports* (1893), *The Substitute* (1908), and *Jack Hall at Yale* (1909).

Campa (käm′pạ). One of the Arawakan-speaking tribes comprising the Anti.

Campagna (käm.pä′nyä). Town and commune in S Italy, in the *compartimento* (region) of Campania, in the province of Salerno, ab. 19 mi. E of Salerno. It is the seat of a bishopric, has a castle and a cathedral, and manufactures ceramics and food products. Pop. of commune, 10,808 (1936); of town, 5,122 (1936).

Campagna di Roma (dē rō′mä). Large plain in C Italy, surrounding Rome, lying between the Mediterranean Sea and the Sabine and Alban mountains. It corresponds in great part to the ancient Latium. It is of volcanic formation, and has been for centuries noted for its malarial climate, though in antiquity it was covered with villas and towns and was brought to a high state of cultivation. It has been largely reclaimed.

Campagnola (käm.pä.nyō′lä), **Domenico.** b. at Padua, Italy, c1482; d. c1564. Italian painter and engraver. A pupil of Giulio Campagnola and of Titian, he painted chiefly at Padua, where he assisted Titian in the decoration of the Scuola del Santo. A master both in fresco and in oil, his skill is said to have caused Titian to regard him with jealousy. Examples of his work as a painter are to be seen also in the Scuola del Carmine and the Museo Civico at Padua, in the Pitti Palace at Florence, and at Venice and Vienna. He executed many engravings and woodcuts as well as numerous drawings, and there are collections of these in the Uffizi Palace at Florence and in the British Museum.

Campagnola, Giulio. b. at Padua, Italy, 1481 or 1482; d. c1514. Italian painter and engraver. His oil paintings, some of them miniatures, have a strikingly modern appearance, and some of his numerous and distinguished engravings display techniques not found in the works of other engravers until modern times. In addition to his own, he engraved designs by Giorgione, Bellini, and other Renaissance masters.

Campagnoli (käm.pä.nyō′lē), **Bartolomeo.** b. at Cento, Italy, Sept. 10, 1751; d. at Neustrelitz, Germany, Nov. 6, 1827. Italian violinist. After studying with Pietro Nardini, he became (1797) conductor of the Gewandhaus concerts at Leipzig. Among his compositions are many works for the violin, including studies still employed in teaching, as well as caprices for the viola.

Campaign, The. Poem by Joseph Addison celebrating the battle of Blenheim, published in 1704.

Campan (käṅ.päṅ). Town in SW France, in the department of Hautes-Pyrénées, situated on the Adour River ab. 18 mi. SE of Tarbes. It is noted for its picturesque scenery. 1,821 (1946).

Campan, Jeanne Louise Henriette. [Maiden name, **Genest.**] b. at Paris, Oct. 6, 1752; d. at Mantes, France, March 16, 1822. French educator. At 15 she became reader to the three daughters of Louis XV, and was for nearly 20 years first lady of the bedchamber to Marie Antoinette. She narrowly escaped during the storming of the Tuileries in 1792. After the fall of Robespierre, she opened a boarding school for young ladies at St.-Germain, and in 1806 was appointed by Napoleon superintendent of the school at Écouen for daughters, sisters, and nieces of officers of the Legion of Honor, a post which she held till the abolition of the school by the Bourbons. She wrote *Mémoires sur la vie privée de Marie Antoinette* (1823).

Campaña (käm.pä′nyä), **Pedro.** See **Kempener, Pieter de.**

Campanari (käm.pä.nä′rē), **Giuseppe.** b. at Venice, Italy, Nov. 17, c1855; d. at Milan, Italy, May 31, 1927. American operatic baritone and cellist. After serving as an instrumentalist (1884–93) with the Boston Symphony Orchestra, he made his debut (1893) as leading baritone of Gustav Hinrichs's Opera Company at New York, and sang in the American première of the opera *Pagliacci*. From 1895 to 1898 he was a member of the Metropolitan Opera Company at New York.

Campanella (käm.pä.nel′lä), **Tommaso.** [Original name, **Giovanni Domenico Campanella.**] b. at Stilo, Calabria, Italy, Sept. 5, 1568; d. at Paris, May 21, 1639. Italian Renaissance theologian, philosopher, poet, and patriot. As a youth of 13 years he wrote creditable prose and verse, and before he was 15 he entered the Dominican order, at that time taking the name Tommaso. His first published work, *Philosophia sensibus demonstrata*, was a defense of naturalistic philosophy. He was much employed by his order as a preacher in various Italian cities, but about 1596 he was summoned before the Holy Office of the Inquisition in Rome on charges of heresy, of which he was acquitted in 1597. In 1599 another accusation of heresy was made against him, coupled with charges of organizing a conspiracy against Spanish rule in southern Italy. While he was being tried before the ecclesiastical court, the civil authorities subjected him to torture. In January, 1603, he was sentenced to imprisonment for life, and was confined at Naples. It was not until 1626 that his release was secured by an appeal of Pope Urban VIII to Philip IV of Spain, and even then he was held prisoner by the Holy Office until 1629. Upon the discovery in 1634 of another Calabrian conspiracy against Spanish rule, led by an associate of Campanella, he fled to France, where he was befriended and pensioned by Louis XIII and Richelieu. Campanella was not surpassed by any man of his time in the extent of his learning and his lively interest in philosophy and science. He might typify the man of the Renaissance in his effort to reconcile scholastic theology and the scientific approach. One thing that got him into trouble was that in the course of this effort he vigorously rejected the Aristotelian logic. The heart of his theological thought is a concept of *being* as having three attributes, namely power, wisdom, and love, and of God as pure being. In some respects his theological-philosophical trend was like that of Giordano Bruno, with the marked difference that it did not lead him out of the Catholic Church. His most noted work, written while in prison, was *Civitas Solio* (known in Italian as *Citta del Sole*, and in English as *City of the Sun*), an account of a fancied communistic state; and it is notable that the first heresy charge against him included an accusation of favoring such a state. However, three popes had confidence in him, and most Catholic commentators consider that his fidelity to his church was beyond question. His other writings include treatises on philosophical and political subjects, letters, and poems. John Addington Symonds, translating Campanella's sonnets along with those of Michelangelo, called him "the audacious Titan of the modern age . . . a poet and philosopher militant, who stood alone making war on the authority of Aristotle in science, of Machiavelli in statecraft, and of Petrarch in art."

Campania (käm.pä′nyä; in ancient geography, kam.pā′ni.ạ). *Compartimento* (region) in S Italy, containing the provinces of Avellino, Benevento, Caserta, Napoli, and Salerno. It includes the W slopes of the Apennines S of Latium, reaching down to the shores of the Tyrrhenian Sea, and includes around the volcanic structure of Mount Vesuvius and the Bay of Naples some of the most fertile agricultural lands of Italy and its most celebrated scenery. Agriculture produces wine, olives, citrus fruits, and grain; the manufactures, largely foodstuff, construction, and shipbuilding industries, are concentrated at Naples. Ever since Roman times the region has contained numerous seaside resorts; the layout of a Roman town is preserved in the ruins of Pompeii. The ancient region lay between Latium on the NW, Samnium on the N and E, Lucania on the SE, and the Mediterranean Sea on the W. Its original inhabitants were probably of the Oscan or the Ausonian race; it was settled later by the Greeks, and submitted to Rome in 340 B.C. It contained the ancient cities of Cumae, Capua, Baiae, Puteoli, Herculanaeum, and Pompeii. Later it was occupied by Goths, Byzantines, and Normans. It belonged to the Hohenstaufen domain in S Italy and witnessed the life and death struggle between the Roman Pope and the German emperor. Both in the kingdom of the Two Sicilies and later in the kingdom of Naples it was, together with the other regions of S Italy including Sicily, under Spanish influence, which made for a markedly different development as compared with the regions farther to the N. It was incorporated into Italy in 1860. Densely populated, the region was one of the centers of overseas emigration in the 19th and 20th centuries. It was the scene of Allied landings in the latter part of World War II and witnessed severe fighting and widespread destruction. Area, 5,249 sq. mi.; pop. 3,696,632 (1936), 4,328,201 (1951).

Campanile of Giotto (käm.pä.nē′lä; jôt′tō). Bell tower at Florence, Italy, begun by Giotto in 1334, and continued by Andrea Pisano after Giotto's death, in 1337. It is square in plan, ab. 37½ feet to a side, and ab. 275½ feet high, and is divided by string-courses into five stories, the two lowest of which are practically solid; the two middle ones have each, on each face, two canopied and traceried windows; and the highest, about twice as high as any of those below, has one large beautifully decorated and traceried window in each face, and a bold cornice. The whole exterior of the tower is encrusted with colored marbles arranged in panels. The basement is surrounded by two ranges of reliefs, the lower in hexagonal, the upper in diamond-shaped panels, by Giotto, Andrea Pisano, and Luca della Robbia. The subjects include the Creation, the Arts and Sciences, the Cardinal Virtues, and the Works of Mercy. These reliefs are famous for their simple and effective presentation of their story. Above is a range of large statues in niches. This campanile is one of the finest examples of the Italian Gothic style.

Campanile of Saint Mark's. Square belltower at Venice, measuring ab. 42 feet to a side, and ab. 323 feet high to the angel at the apex of the pyramidal spire. It was begun c900, but the arcaded belfry, with the square die and pyramid above, dates only from the 16th century. The lower part was an almost unbroken façade of brickwork, and the belfry was surmounted by a superstructure. It collapsed on July 14, 1902, and was restored according to original plans in 1912. The foundations were strengthened, and the rebuilding of the tower was begun in 1905, and finished in 1912.

Campanini (käm.pä.nē′nē), **Cleofonte.** b. at Parma, Italy, Sept. 1, 1860; d. at Chicago, Dec. 19, 1919. Italian musical director; brother of Italo Campanini (1846–96). He first appeared as a conductor at Parma, in 1883, directing *Carmen.* In the same season he appeared at New York as second conductor at the Metropolitan Opera House, and, in 1888, at the Academy of Music. He was musical director (1906–10) at the Manhattan Opera House, New York (where he conducted the first American performances of Debussy's *Pelléas et Mélisande* and Charpentier's *Louise*), leading conductor at Covent Garden, London, and conductor and director (1910–19) of the Chicago Opera Company, of which he was also general manager (1913–19).

Campanini, Italo. b. at Parma, Italy, June 29, 1846; d. near Parma, Nov. 22, 1896. Italian tenor singer; brother of Cleofonte Campanini (1860–1919). He first attracted attention in 1871 at Bologna. In 1872 he first appeared in England, and was subsequently successful at St. Petersburg and Moscow, and in America.

Campaspe (kam.pas′pē). [Also: **Pancaste, Pacate.**] Favorite concubine of Alexander the Great. She is said to have been the model for the statue of Venus Anadyomene of Apelles.

Campaspe, Alexander and. Prose comedy by John Lyly, printed in 1584, and reprinted as *Campaspe* in that year and in 1591. The theme of the comedy is the renunciation of Alexander the Great, who resigns his claim to the Theban captive when he discovers that she loves Apelles.

Campbell (kam′bẹl, kam′ẹl). City in NE Ohio, in Mahoning County: steel mills. 12,882 (1950).

Campbell, Alexander. [Title, 2nd Earl of **Marchmont.**] b. 1675; d. at London, 1740. Scottish nobleman, who opposed (1733) Robert Walpole's excise scheme in the hope of overthrowing the government of Archibald Campbell, 3rd Duke of Argyll, in Scotland. The son of Sir Patrick Hume (1641–1724), he took the name of Campbell after his marriage (1697) to Margaret Campbell. As a member (1706) of the Scottish parliament, he worked for union with England, and, in 1715, opposed rebellion against the Hanoverian succession. He served as ambassador to Denmark (1715–21), and privy councillor (1726). For his opposition to Walpole, he was dismissed (1733), after 11 years in office, from the lord clerk registership of Scotland.

Campbell, Alexander. b. near Ballymena, County Antrim, Ireland, Sept. 12, 1788; d. at Bethany, W.Va., March 4, 1866. American clergyman, founder of the sect of the Disciples of Christ; son of Thomas Campbell (1763–1854). Having accepted the Independent religion while still in Ireland, Campbell originated (1809), together with his father, the Christian Association of Washington, in Pennsylvania. Out of this group, originally only a local congregation, grew the Disciples of Christ, as Campbell spread his theological views by outdoor preaching through the countryside. His acquired belief in adult baptism alienated some members of his sect, while at the same time he failed to make as many converts as he had hoped. For a few years he ran the Buffalo Seminary, at Bethany, and engaged in many theological debates, making a name for himself for these discussions. In the periodical *Christian Baptist,* which he founded in 1823, he further disseminated his views. After 1826, his group lost the support of the Baptists, and thus became established as an entirely separate organization. He published a translation of the Bible (1827) and a hymnal (1828) and continued preaching and lecturing for some 20 years. In 1830, having become interested in the Second Coming, Campbell replaced the *Christian Baptist* with the *Millennial Harbinger;* subsequently he founded (1840) Bethany College, and lived to see his opinions gain wider acceptance. He was the author of *The Christian System* (1839) and *Memoirs of Elder Thomas Campbell* (1861), among others.

Campbell, Archibald. [Title, 2nd Earl of **Argyll.**] Killed at Flodden, Northumberland, England, 1513. Scottish soldier; son of Colin Campbell, 1st Earl of Argyll. He became master of the royal household in 1494, and shared with Matthew Stewart, Earl of Lennox, the command of the right wing of the Scottish army at the battle of Flodden, on Sept. 9, 1513, in which engagement he was killed.

Campbell, Archibald. [Title, 4th Earl of **Argyll.**] d. 1558. Scottish soldier, a leading supporter of the Reformation; grandson of Archibald Campbell, 2nd Earl of Argyll. He commanded the right wing of the Scottish army at the battle of Pinkie in 1547, and in the following year rendered important service at the siege of Haddington. He embraced the Reformation, and was a warm supporter of Knox, whom he entertained at Castle Campbell in 1556.

Campbell, Archibald. [Title, 5th Earl of **Argyll.**] b. 1530; d. Sept. 12, 1573. Scottish soldier, a supporter of Mary, Queen of Scots; son of Archibald Campbell, 4th Earl of Argyll. He was originally one of the leaders of the Lords of the Congregation, but afterward became a partisan of Mary, Queen of Scots, was presumed to have been a party to the murder of Darnley and the marriage of Mary to Bothwell, and commanded the queen's forces at Langside, on May 13, 1568, where the lukewarmness of his support is said to have caused the defeat. He made his submission to the regent Lord James Stewart, Earl of Moray, in 1569, and in 1572 was appointed lord high chancellor.

Campbell, Archibald. [Titles: 8th Earl and 1st Marquis of **Argyll.**] b. 1607; beheaded at Edinburgh, May 27, 1661. Scottish nobleman. He sided with the Covenanters, became a marquis in 1641, and was defeated by Montrose in 1645. He sided with Charles II after the death of Charles I, but submitted later to Oliver Cromwell. At the Restoration he was executed for treason.

Campbell, Archibald. [Title, 9th Earl of **Argyll.**] b. c1629; beheaded at Edinburgh, June 30, 1685. Scottish nobleman; son of Archibald Campbell, 8th Earl of Argyll. He supported the Royalists and Charles II after the Restoration. Obliged, on a charge of treason, to leave Scotland at the end of the reign of Charles II, he returned in 1685, to take part in the Duke of Monmouth's rising, and was captured and executed for treason.

Campbell, Archibald. [Title, 1st Duke of **Argyll.**] d. 1703. Scottish nobleman and warrior, who with John Campbell, Earl of Breadalbane (1635–1716), and Sir John Dalrymple (1648–1707), led the massacre of the robber clan of Macdonalds at Glencoe (1692); son of Archibald Campbell, 9th Earl of Argyll. Failing to obtain the restoration of the title and estates (taken from his father) by supporting James II, he welcomed (1609) William of Orange to England, and was commissioner to offer the Scottish crown to William and Mary. He was Scottish privy councillor, regained (1689) his titles and estates, served as extraordinary lord of session (1694), and was created Duke of Argyll in 1701.

Campbell, Archibald. [Title, 3rd Duke of **Argyll.**] b. at Petersham, Surrey, England, in June, 1682; d. April 15, 1761. Scottish statesman; brother of John Campbell, 2nd Duke of Argyll. He was a firm supporter of Robert Walpole, by whom he was entrusted with the chief management of Scottish affairs. He was appointed lord keeper of the privy seal in 1721, and keeper of the great seal in 1733, which latter post he occupied until his death.

Campbell, Sir **Archibald.** b. 1769; d. Oct. 6, 1843. English army officer. He served (1788–99) in India where he was present at the siege (1792) of Seringapatam, and at the reduction of Cochin (1795) and of the Dutch factories in Ceylon (1796). Sent (1809) to accompany William Carr Beresford to Portugal, he remained there until 1820, and was appointed (1816) major general and commander at Lisbon. He arrived (May, 1824) with 11,500 men at Rangoon, to direct the Burmese War which ended after he stormed (Jan. 2, 1826) Melloon. Subsequently he served as governor of British Burma and civil commissioner to the courts of Burma and Siam (1826–29), lieutenant governor of New Brunswick, Canada (1831–37), and as lieutenant general (1838) and colonel (1840) of the 62nd regiment.

Campbell, Colin. [Title, 1st Earl of **Argyll.**] d. 1493. Scottish nobleman, created earl in 1475. In 1487 he was one of the conspirators against James III.

Campbell, Sir **Colin.** [Title, Baron **Clyde.**] b. at Glasgow, Oct. 20, 1792; d. at Chatham, England, Aug. 14, 1863. British field marshal. He served with distinction at

Chillianwala and Gujarat, in India, in 1849. In the Crimean War he participated in the battles of the Alma River and Balaklava, in 1854. Again in India, he was commander in chief in Bengal in 1857, rescued Sir Henry Havelock and James Outram at the siege of Lucknow in the Sepoy rebellion, and then relieved Cawnpore, and recaptured Lucknow in 1858. He was made a knight commander of the Order of the Bath in 1849, and was elevated to the peerage as Baron Clyde of Clydesdale in 1858.

Campbell, Douglas. b. at Cooperstown, N.Y., July 13, 1840; d. at Schenectady, N.Y., March 7, 1893. American lawyer and historical writer. He was educated at Union College, served as captain of the 121st New York Volunteers in the Civil War, and practiced law at New York until 1890. He wrote *The Puritan in Holland, England, and America, an Introduction to American History* (1892).

Campbell, Douglas Houghton. b. at Detroit, Dec. 16, 1859; d. at Palo Alto, Calif., Feb. 23, 1953. American botanist, an authority on mosses and ferns. He was professor of botany (1888–91) at the University of Indiana, and held a similar post (1891–1925) at Stanford University. His works include *Elements of Structural and Systematic Botany* (1890), *Lectures on Evolution of Plants* (1899), *Outline of Plant Geography* (1926), and *Evolution of the Land Plants* (1940).

Campbell, George. b. at Aberdeen, Scotland, Dec. 25, 1719; d. there, April 6, 1796. Scottish theologian and philosophical writer. He was ordained in 1748, became minister at Aberdeen in 1757, and in 1759 was appointed principal of Marischal College. His chief works are *Dissertation on Miracles* (1762), *Philosophy of Rhetoric* (1776), and *Translation of the Gospels* (1789).

Campbell, Sir **George.** b. in Scotland, 1824; d. at Cairo, Egypt, Feb. 18, 1892. British administrator in India. In 1842 he left Scotland for India, where he served (1843–51) in the provinces as a collector and magistrate. He wrote (1857) an official account of the Sepoy mutiny for the British government. Appointed (1862) judge of the high court of Bengal, he was placed in charge (1866) of a commission to report the causes of Bengal famine. He also served as chief commissioner (1867–68) of the Central Provinces, and as lieutenant governor (1871–74) of India. A student of ethnology, Campbell published *The Ethnology of India* (1865).

Campbell, George Douglas. [Title, 8th Duke of **Argyll.**] b. April 30, 1823; d. April 24, 1900. Scottish statesman and writer. He was lord privy seal (1853–55, 1859–66, 1880–81), postmaster-general (1855–58), and secretary for India (1868–74). His chief works include *The Reign of Law* (1866) and *Scotland as It Was and as It Is* (1887).

Campbell, George Washington. b. at Tongue, Scotland, Feb. 8, 1769; d. Feb. 17, 1848. American statesman. After graduation (1794) from Princeton, he studied law and entered (1803) the House of Representatives, where he served for three terms. He was elected (1811) to the Senate, and was appointed (1814) secretary of the treasury. After another term as senator (1815–18), he was appointed (1818) ambassador to Russia, from which position he resigned after two years.

Campbell, James. b. at Southwark (now part of Philadelphia), Pa., Sept. 1, 1812; d. Jan. 27, 1893. American lawyer and cabinet member under President Franklin Pierce. Admitted to the bar in 1833, he was a judge (1842–52) for the court of common pleas, and was appointed attorney general in 1852. As postmaster general (1853–57), he lowered foreign postage rates.

Campbell, James Dykes. b. 1838; d. 1895. Scottish merchant, and biographer of Samuel Taylor Coleridge. He entered (1854) a pottery business at Glasgow, and was a partner (1873–81) in the firm of Ireland, Fraser and Company, in Mauritius. His biography of Coleridge was prefixed to an 1893 edition of Coleridge's poetical works, but appeared in a separate volume the following year.

Campbell, John. [Title, 1st Earl of **Loudoun.**] b. 1598; d. at Edinburgh, Scotland, 1663. Scottish soldier and lord chancellor of Scotland (1641–60). He opposed the act (1633) empowering the king to prescribe churchmen's apparel, and, after its passage, continued to petition for "supplicants," and took an important role in organizing (1638) the National Covenant. Turning to less peaceful pursuits, he served in the Scottish insurrection (1639), and remonstrated (1640) to Charles I against English interference in the Scottish parliament; for his remonstrations and alleged treason, he was held in the Tower of London. He fought at Dunbar in 1650, after assisting in the coronation of Charles II. Although he fought (1653) for the king, and was steadfastly loyal to him, upon the Restoration he was deprived of the chancellorship and heavily fined (1662).

Campbell, John. [Title, 1st Earl of **Breadalbane.**] b. c1635; d. c1716. Scottish politician and warrior, who, with Archibald Campbell, 1st Duke of Argyll, and Sir John Dalrymple (1648–1707), massacred the clan of Macdonalds at Glencoe (1692). He joined the insurrection (1653) for Charles II, and was a member of Parliament for Argyllshire (1661). In a dispute for the earldom of Caithness, he killed (1680) the followers of George Sinclair, the male heir, but lost the peerage when the privy council decided (1681) against his claim to it; he obtained instead the earldom of Breadalbane. In 1685, he was privy councillor. After submitting (1689) to William III, he was employed (1690–91) to convince other Highland chieftains to do the same. He supported, lukewarmly, the Jacobite rebellion (1715), but withdrew after the battle of Sheriffmuir. The village of Broadalbin in northern New York derives its name from the family title.

Campbell, John. b. in Scotland, 1653; d. c1728. American editor who established the first successful newspaper in America. He emigrated (c1695) to Massachusetts, where he was postmaster (1702–18) at Boston. He printed and distributed (April 24, 1704–1722) the Boston *News-Letter*, a weekly half-sheet of foreign news.

Campbell, John. [Titles: 2nd Duke of **Argyll,** Duke of **Greenwich.**] b. 1678; d. 1743. Scottish general and statesman; son of Archibald Campbell, 1st Duke of Argyll. He took part in effecting the union of England and Scotland, served under Marlborough, and commanded at Sheriffmuir in 1715. He sided at different times with the Whigs and Tories. He was created duke of Greenwich in 1719.

Campbell, John. [Title, 4th Earl of **Loudoun.**] b. May 5, 1705; d. April 27, 1782. English general; great-grandson of John Campbell, 1st Earl of Loudon (1598–1663). Having entered (1727) the army, he was appointed (1741) governor of Stirling Castle, and named (March 20, 1756) commander in chief of British forces in America. There he lost Forts Oswego and Ontario to the French, and failed to carry out the invasion of Canada, having delayed at Halifax. Recalled, he was replaced by General Geoffrey Amherst, and was appointed (1762) second in command of the British troops sent to Portugal.

Campbell, John. [Title, 1st Baron **Campbell.**] b. near Cupar, Fifeshire, Scotland, Sept. 15, 1779; d. at London, June 23, 1861. British jurist, politician, and author. A member of Parliament (1839 *et seq.*), he interested himself in law reform. He also sat on the commission on the law of real property from 1828 to 1833. He became chief justice of the Queen's Bench in 1850, and was lord chancellor of England in the period 1859–61. He wrote *Lives of the Lord Chancellors* (1845–47) and *Lives of the Chief Justices* (1849–57).

Campbell, John Archibald. b. at Washington, Ga., June 24, 1811; d. March 12, 1889. American lawyer and jurist, assistant secretary of war for the Confederacy during the Civil War. Graduated (1825) from Franklin College (now the University of Georgia), he attended West Point, which he left to study law. He was admitted to the bar (1829) in Georgia, and soon thereafter moved to Alabama, living first at Montgomery and then at Mobile. He achieved rapid success in his law practice, and at 24 years of age declined an appointment as associate justice of the state supreme court. His most celebrated case during this period was as counsel for Myra Clark Gaines (*Gaines* vs. *Relf*). He was a member of the Alabama State legislature and a delegate to the Nashville Convention (1850). In 1853, President Franklin Pierce appointed him associate justice of the U.S. Supreme Court; many of his opinions were distinguished by their adherence to the States'-rights school of thought. He sided with the majority in the Dred Scott decision, although he drew Southern criticism for his support of an indictment against William Walker and other filibusterers when he sat as a circuit judge at New Orleans. A moderate, he enlisted his services in the cause of compromise; after the outbreak of the Civil War he resigned from the high court and served (October, 1862 *et seq.*) as Confederate secretary of war in charge of conscription. He was a member of the Confederate commission which conferred (1865) with Abraham Lincoln and William Henry Seward at Hampton Roads. Held a prisoner for four months after the end of the war, he resumed his law practice at New Orleans after his release from Fort Pulaski.

Campbell, John Charles. b. at La Porte, Ind., Sept. 14, 1867; d. May 2, 1919. American educator. After teaching and serving as principal of various academies and public schools in Alabama, Wisconsin, and Tennessee, he became (1901) president of Piedmont College in Georgia. In 1907–08 he traveled in Italy and Sicily, and in the latter year, upon his return to the U.S., was appointed director of the Southern Highlands division of the Russell Sage Foundation. From his experience in the South he conceived the idea of establishing folk schools for the mountain people of that region, very much like the folk high schools which have been successful in Denmark. After his death such an institution, named the John C. Campbell Folk School, was brought into being near Brasstown in the North Carolina mountains. He was the author of *The Southern Highlander and His Home* (1921).

Campbell, John Francis. [Called **Campbell of Islay** (ī'lā).] b. on the island of Islay, Scotland, Dec. 29, 1822; d. at Cannes, France, Feb. 17, 1885. Scottish meteorologist and Gaelic scholar. Educated at Eton and at the University of Edinburgh, he occupied minor positions in the British government service, in the course of which he invented a device for recording the degree of sunshine, which is widely used at meteorological stations in Great Britain. But his greater fame arises from the use he made of his leisure time in collecting examples of the folklore of the western Highlands as related by Gaelic-speaking natives, and translating them for the enjoyment of a wider audience. His *Popular Tales of the Western Highlands, Orally Collected, with a Translation*, was published in four volumes (1860–62). He also published *The Book of the Fenians*, a collection of Ossianic poems, in Gaelic, several editions of Gaelic texts, *Thermography* (1883), and other works.

Campbell, John George Edward Henry Douglas Sutherland. [Titles: 9th Duke of **Argyll,** Marquis of **Lorne.**] b. at London, Aug. 6, 1845; d. May 2, 1914. British statesman; eldest son of George Douglas Campbell, 8th Duke of Argyll. He married the Princess Louise, fourth daughter of Queen Victoria, in 1871. He represented (1868–78) Argyllshire in Parliament, and was governor general (1878–83) of Canada. From 1895 to 1900 he was Unionist member of Parliament for South Manchester.

Campbell, Levin H., Jr. b. at Washington, D.C., Nov. 23, 1886—. American army officer. Graduated (1909) from the U.S. Naval Academy, he transferred (1911) to the U.S. army, where he introduced (1923) techniques for the manufacture of gun carriages at the Rock Island arsenal. Chief (1942–45) of army ordnance, he was promoted (1945) to lieutenant general. He later became a vice-president of the International Harvester Company.

Campbell, Lewis. b. at Edinburgh, Scotland, Sept. 3, 1830; d. at Alassio, Italy, Oct. 25, 1908. Scottish teacher, translator of Sophocles and Aeschylus. Educated at Edinburgh Academy, Glasgow University, and at Trinity and Balliol colleges, Oxford, winning medals, prizes, and fellowships, he was professor of Greek (1863–92) and Gifford Lecturer (1894–95) at St. Andrews University. He edited Plato and Sophocles, finished Benjamin Jowett's translation of Plato's *Republic*, and translated the extant tragedies of Sophocles and Aeschylus into English verse (1883 and 1890; both published 1906, and many times reprinted, in the *World's Classics* series). He was the author of *Life of James Clerk Maxwell* (1882), *Guide to Greek Tragedy* (1891), *Life of Jowett* (1897), *Religion in Greek Literature* (1898; Gifford Lectures), and *Tragic Drama in Aeschylus, Sophocles, and Euripides* (1904).

Campbell, Sir **Malcolm.** b. at Chislehurst, Kent, England, March 11, 1885; d. at Reigate, Surrey, England, Jan. 1, 1949. English automobile racer and financier. He joined (1906) Lloyd's of London, and served (1914–19) in World War I, transferring (1916) to the Royal Flying Corps as a pilot. He began (1910) speed racing as a hobby, and established various speed records, notably at Daytona Beach, Fla. (for speedboats, 141.74 miles per hour), and at Bonneville Salt Flats, near Salt Lake City (for racing cars, 301.1292 miles per hour). He was the author of *Speed* (1931), *My Thirty Years of Speed* (1935), *The Romance of Motor-Racing* (1936), *The Roads and the Problem of their Safety* (1937), and *Drifting to War* (1937).

Campbell, Sir **Neil.** b. May 1, 1776; d. in Sierra Leone, West Africa, Aug. 14, 1827. British officer, commissioner at Elba (1814–15) during Napoleon's stay there.

Campbell, Mrs. **Patrick.** [Maiden name, **Beatrice Stella Tanner.**] b. at London, 1865; d. April 9, 1940. English actress. She made her debut in 1888, at Liverpool, and thereafter toured with Ben Greet's company; following her first appearance at London she was engaged by Sir Arthur Wing Pinero to play Paula, the title role in *The Second Mrs. Tanqueray.* Thereafter she became to some extent identified with the modern drama of ideas; she made a success as Rita in Henrik Ibsen's *Little Eyolf*, and as Magda in Hermann Sudermann's play of that name, and originated the part of Eliza in George Bernard Shaw's *Pygmalion*, which he had written expressly for her. She also appeared in a number of Shakespearian parts, including Rosalind in *As You Like It*, Ophelia in *Hamlet*, Lady Macbeth, and Juliet. With Sarah Bernhardt she appeared in an original version of Maurice Maeterlinck's *Pelléas et Mélisande*, which she also presented in an English version. Among her modern parts was also that of Anastasia Rakonitz in Gladys Bronwyn Stern's *The Matriarch.* She toured widely in England and Ireland, and appeared in the U.S.

Campbell, Reginald John. b. at London, 1867—. English clergyman. He entered Oxford intending to prepare for the Anglican priesthood, but while there joined the Congregational Church, of which he became an ordained minister in 1895. His power as a preacher led to a call to the pulpit of the City Temple, London, in 1903. In 1907 his book *The New Theology* attracted wide attention. But in 1915 he left the Congregational fold and was ordained a priest of the Church of England, in which subsequently he filled several important positions. In addition to *The New Theology* he is the author of *A Faith for Today* (1900), *Christianity and the Social Order* (1908), *The War and the Soul* (1916), *Problems of Life* (1919), *The Call of Christ* (1933), and *The Peace of God* (1936).

Campbell, Robert. In Scottish history, one of the names of the actual person now best known as the Rob Roy of Sir Walter Scott's novel. Rob's clan name was MacGregor (he was actually the chief of the clan), but the MacGregors had been proscribed as a Scottish clan by order of the British crown for their participation in various risings against the English, and Rob took his mother's clan name of Campbell.

Campbell, Robert. b. at Aughlane, County Tyrone, Ireland, in March, 1804; d. at St. Louis, Oct. 15, 1879. American fur trader. Coming to the U.S. c1824 he settled at St. Louis, but in search of better health joined an expedition to the Northwest, where he engaged in trapping. In a fight with Indians in 1832 he saved the life of W. L. Sublette, whose partner he became in the same year. They had one try at getting a share of the fur trade of the northwestern Missouri valley, which was in effect at that time a monopoly of John Jacob Astor's American Fur Company, but the results were not fortunate and thereafter they operated only in the mountain regions. In 1835 Campbell returned to St. Louis, where he engaged in many enterprises, especially after the firm of Sublette and Campbell was discontinued in 1842. He invested in real estate, engaged in dry-goods merchandising, built a hotel, and became president of two banks, meanwhile taking a hand in public affairs. President Millard Fillmore in 1851 appointed him to the commission which held an important meeting with the Indians at Fort Laramie, Wyo., and in 1869 he again served as a commissioner to the Indians at the request of President Ulysses S. Grant.

Campbell, Robert. b. at Glenlyon, Perthshire, Scotland, 1808; d. 1894. Canadian fur trader and explorer. He entered the service of the Hudson's Bay Company in 1832, and from 1834 to 1852 operated in the Mackenzie River country in NW Canada and along the Liard River. In 1842 or 1843 he crossed the mountains and discovered the

Pelly River, which at that time and again in 1850 he followed to the point where it unites with the Lewes River to form the Yukon River. Upon returning to England in 1853, he supervised the making of maps of the region he had explored.

Campbell, Roy. [Full name, **Ignatius Roy Dunnachie Campbell.**] b. at Durban, South Africa, Oct. 2, 1901—. South African poet. He served with Francisco Franco's forces during the Spanish Civil War, and with British forces during World War II. His poetry includes *The Flaming Terrapin* (1924), *The Wayzgoose* (1928), *Adamastor* (1930), *The Georgiad* (1931), *Flowering Reeds* (1933), *Mithraic Emblems* (1936), and *Flowering Rifle* (1936). He also published the autobiography *Broken Record* (1934).

Campbell, Thomas. b. Feb. 1, 1763; d. at Bethany, W.Va., Jan. 4, 1854. Irish religious leader; father of Alexander Campbell (1788–1866). Graduated from the University of Glasgow, he served as a minister of the Secession Church which had broken with Presbyterianism. In 1807 he sailed to America, where he became a founder, with his son, of the Church of the Disciples of Christ. He was an advocate of church unity and at first had been unsympathetic to the formation of a new denomination.

Campbell, Thomas. b. at Glasgow, Scotland, July 27, 1777; d. at Boulogne, France, June 15, 1844. British poet and critic. He was lord rector (1826–29) of the University of Glasgow. His works include *The Pleasures of Hope* (1799), *Gertrude of Wyoming* (1809), and *Specimens of the British Poets* (1819). Among his short lyrics are *Lochiel's Warning, Hohenlinden, Mariners of England,* and *Battle of the Baltic.* He was buried in Westminster Abbey.

Campbell, Lord **William.** d. Sept. 5, 1778. British administrator. He was colonial governor of South Carolina in the period 1775–76.

Campbell, William. b. at Gateshead, England, June 24, 1876; d. Dec. 16, 1936. American scientist. He was adjunct professor (1907–10), associate professor (1910–14), and professor (1914 *et seq.*) of metallurgy at Columbia University School of Mines. His studies relate chiefly to the microstructure and physical properties of metals and alloys.

Campbell, William Wallace. b. in Hancock County, Ohio, April 11, 1862; d. at San Francisco, June 14, 1938. American astonomer and educator. He was director of the Lick Observatory from 1901, having been employed there from 1891. He conducted eclipse expeditions to India in 1898, to Georgia in 1900, and to Spain in 1905. His works include *The Elements of Practical Astronomy* (1899), *Stellar Motions* (1913), and numerous technical papers. He received the Lalande prize of the Paris Academy in 1903, the gold medal of the Royal Astronomical Society, and the Draper gold medal of the National Academy of Sciences in 1906. His later eclipse expeditions took him to Russia (1914), the state of Washington (1918), and Australia (1922). He served as Silliman lecturer at Yale (1909–10), and as president (1923–30) of the University of California.

Campbell, William Wilfred. b. at Berlin (now Kitchener), Ontario, Canada, June 1, 1861; d. at Ottawa, Canada, Jan. 1, 1918. Canadian poet, novelist, dramatist, and bibliographer. A clergyman's son, he was educated in Canada at the Toronto High School and Wycliffe College, and in the U.S. at the Cambridge (Mass.) Divinity School. Ordained in 1885, he gave up the ministry in 1891 and entered the Canadian civil service, becoming bibliographer of the Dominion Archives at Ottawa. He wrote literary criticism for the Toronto *Globe*, and edited the *Oxford Book of Canadian Verse* (1906). His books of poetry include *Lake Lyrics* (1889), *The Dread Voyage* (1893), *Beyond the Hills of Dream* (1898), *Sagas of Vaster Britain* (1906), *Collected Verse* (1906), *Poetical Tragedies* (1908), and *War Lyrics* (1915). He also wrote *Ian of the Orcades* (1906) and *A Beautiful Rebel* (1909), novels, and *The Scotsman in Canada* (1911).

Campbell-Bannerman (kam′bel.ban′ėr.man), Sir **Henry.** b. Sept. 7, 1836; d. April 22, 1908. British statesman. He was the son of Sir James Campbell, but assumed the additional surname of Bannerman (under the will of his maternal uncle) in 1872. He was educated at Glasgow University and Trinity College, Cambridge, and was Liberal member of Parliament for Stirling Burghs from 1868. He was financial secretary to the war office (1871–74, 1880–82), secretary to the admiralty (1882–84), chief secretary for Ireland (1884–85), secretary of state for war (1886, 1892–95), leader of the Liberal Party in the House of Commons (1899 *et seq.*), and prime minister and first lord of the treasury (December, 1905–April, 1908). In 1895 he was knighted (Grand Cross of the Bath). He was popularly referred to as "CB."

Campbellford (kam′bel.ford, kam′el-). Town on the Trent River, SE Ontario, Canada, ab. 30 mi. E of Peterborough. An airfield is situated nearby. The area surrounding the town is popular as a summer resort. 3,235 (1951).

Campbell Glacier (kam′bel, kam′el). Glacier in Antarctica, of low gradient, flowing SW from the W slopes of Mount Melbourne. Width, ab. 2½ mi.

Campbell Island. Small unhabited island in the Southern Ocean, S of New Zealand, of which country it is a part. It was discovered by Captain Hazelburgh of the whaler *Perseverance*, and named by him for the business house in Sydney which he represented. Area, 44 sq. mi.

Campbellites (kam′bel.īts, kam′el.īts). [Also, **New Lights.**] Nickname of the Disciples of Christ, a denomination founded by Thomas Campbell and his son, Alexander Campbell.

Campbellites. Followers of the Reverend John McLeod Campbell, a minister of the Church of Scotland, who, when deposed (1831) for teaching the universality of the atonement, founded a separate congregation.

Campbell of Islay (ī′lā). See **Campbell, John Francis.**

Campbell's Station. Village in E Tennessee, situated ab. 12 mi. SW of Knoxville. Here, on Nov. 16, 1863, Union forces under Ambrose Everett Burnside repulsed the Confederates under James Longstreet.

Campbellsville (kam′belz.vil, kam′elz-). City in C Kentucky, county seat of Taylor County, ab. 65 mi. SW of Lexington. 3,477 (1950).

Campbellton (kam′bel.ton, kam′el-). Town in New Brunswick, Canada, situated near the S shore of the Bay of Chaleur on the Restigouche River. It is on the railway line from Quebec and on a main highway to C Canada. There are paper mills in the vicinity. 7,754 (1951).

Campbelltown (kam′bel.toun, kam′el-). Former name of **Bluff**, New Zealand.

Campbeltown. Royal burgh and seaport in W Scotland, in Argyllshire, situated on the Kintyre peninsula, ab. 12 mi. NE of its tip (the Mull of Kintyre). The town has no rail connections for passengers, being reached by steamer from Glasgow, ab. 401 mi. N of London by rail. Campbeltown has a whisky-distilling industry. There is a famous golf course ab. 5 mi. from the town. 7,079 (est. 1948).

Camp Charlotte, Treaty of. See **Charlotte, Treaty of Camp.**

Campe (käm′pe), **Joachim Heinrich.** b. at Deensen, in Brunswick, Germany, June 29, 1746; d. near Brunswick, Germany, Oct. 22, 1818. German lexicographer and writer of juveniles. He was a tutor at Berlin, instructing in the house of the Humboldt family. His works include *Robinson der jüngere* (1779), *Die Entdeckung von Amerika* (1781), and a German dictionary (1807–11).

Campeche (kam.pē′chē; Spanish, käm.pā′chā). State in SE Mexico, part of the Yucatán peninsula. Capital, Campeche; area, 19,672 sq. mi.; pop. 121,361 (1950).

Campeche. [Colonial name, **San Lazaro.**] City in SE Mexico, capital of Campeche state, on the Bay of Campeche. It is a seaport; exports include chicle, logwood, sisal, and cordage. It was an old Indian town, was discovered by Francisco Fernández de Córdoba in 1517, and was named by him San Lazaro. 23,277 (1940).

Campeche, Bay of. [Also: **Gulf of Campeche, Bay** (or **Gulf**) **of Campeachy**; Spanish, **Bahía** (or **Golfo**) **de Campeche.**] Arm of the Gulf of Mexico, off the SE cost of Mexico, on the W side of Yucatán.

Campeggio (käm.pād′jō), **Lorenzo.** b. at Bologna, Italy, 1472; d. at Rome, July 25, 1539. Italian cardinal, legate to England in 1519 and 1528, bishop of Salisbury and archbishop of Bologna. He presided at the Diet of Ratisbon. In 1528 he was associated with Thomas Wolsey in hearing the divorce suit of Henry VIII of England against Catherine of Aragon.

Campellensis (kam.pe.len′sis). Latinized surname of **Guillaume de Champeaux.**

Campendonk (käm′pe̤n.dǫngk), **Heinrich.** b. at Krefeld, Germany, Nov. 3, 1889—. German painter and engraver, who participated in the Exposition of Contemporary German Painters at Paris in 1929. He also exhibited at the Bibliothèque Nationale at Paris. *Conte,* a woodcut, is considered one of his best works. His paintings reflect the influence of Marc Chagall and Franz Marc.

Campenhout (käm′pe̤n.hout), **François van.** b. at Brussels, Feb. 5, 1779; d. there, April 24, 1848. Belgian musician. His fame rests chiefly on *La Brabançonne,* the Belgian national air, which he composed in 1830.

Campenon (käṅ.pe̤.nôṅ), **François Nicolas Vincent.** b. on the island of Guadeloupe, in the French West Indies, March 29, 1772; d. near Paris, Nov. 24, 1843. French poet and writer. He was the author of *Voyage de Grenoble à Chambéry* (1795; prose and verse), *L'Enfant prodigue* (1811), and others.

Camper (käm′pėr), **Pieter.** b. at Leiden, Netherlands, May 11, 1722; d. at The Hague, April 7, 1789. Dutch physician and anatomist, noted for researches in comparative anatomy. He taught at Amsterdam (1761–63) and Groningen (1763–73). He presented a theory of the measurability of human intelligence by physiognomic evidence in *Dissertation physique sur les différences réelles que présentent les traits du visage . . .* (1781).

Camperdown (kam′pėr.doun). [Dutch, **Kamperduin.**] Dune in W Netherlands, in the province of North Holland, near the village of Kamp (or Camp), NW of Alkmaar. On Oct. 11, 1797 a British fleet under Duncan defeated the Dutch in a naval battle in the North Sea near here.

Campero (käm.pā′rō), **Narciso.** b. at Tojo, Argentina, c1815; d. 1896. Bolivian soldier and politician, president of Bolivia (1880–84). In 1872 he was minister of war for a short time. When the war with Chile broke out (1879), he raised an army in southern Bolivia, but was unable to reach Tarapaca, Peru, before the Chileans conquered that province. After the fall of Hilarión Daza he was elected (April 9, 1880), president of Bolivia, took command of the allied Bolivian and Peruvian armies at Tacna, Peru, and was defeated at the battle of Tacna (May 26, 1880). His term ended on Aug. 1, 1884.

Camp Fire Girls. American organization for young girls. It was founded in 1911 and incorporated in 1912 by Dr. and Mrs. Luther Halsey Gulick, Mr. and Mrs. Ernest Thompson Seton, and others. Membership is open to girls from ten to 18 years of age, each of whom upon joining takes an Indian name. The council fire around which gatherings are symbolically held, and the garb worn on such occasions, derive from Indian lore. There are three grades of membership, those of Wood Gatherer, Fire Maker, and Torch Bearer. Camp Fire Girls are taught to love beauty, to render service, to enjoy work, to be worthy of trust, to cultivate good health, and to be happy. The activities include camping, outdoor sports, homemaking and housekeeping, and practice in handcrafts according to their respective talents. Membership approaches 300,000. There is a junior order of the Camp Fire Girls, called the Blue Birds, which enrolls girls of eight to ten years of age.

Camphausen (kämp′hou.ze̤n), **Ludolf.** b. at Hünshoven, near Aachen, Germany, Jan. 3, 1803; d. at Cologne, Germany, Dec. 3, 1890. German statesman; brother of Otto von Camphausen. He was president of the Prussian ministry in 1848.

Camphausen, Otto von. b. at Hünshoven, near Aachen, Germany, Oct. 21, 1812; d. May 18, 1896. German statesman; brother of Ludolf Camphausen. He was Prussian minister of finance (1869–78) and vice-president of the Prussian ministry (1873–78).

Camphausen, Wilhelm. b. at Düsseldorf, Prussia, Feb. 8, 1818; d. there, June 16, 1885. German historical and battle painter of the Düsseldorf school.

Camp Hill. Borough in S Pennsylvania, in Cumberland County: residential suburb of Harrisburg. It was founded in 1756. Pop. 5,934 (1950).

Camphuysen (kämp′hoi.ze̤n), **Dirk Rafelsz.** b. at Gorinchem (Gorkum), Netherlands, 1586; d. at Dokkum, Netherlands, July 9, 1627. Dutch poet, painter, and theologian; father of Govaert Camphuysen and uncle of Raphael Camphuysen. A preacher and follower of Arminius, he was relieved of his post (1619) for his unorthodox views.

Camphuysen, Govaert. b. at Gorinchen (Gorkum), Netherlands, 1624; d. at Amsterdam, Netherlands, 1674. Dutch painter; son of Dirk Rafelsz Camphuysen (1586–1627). Much of his work was done at Stockholm, where he was painter to the Swedish court, but he was not without honor in his own country, being made a citizen of Amsterdam in 1650. He was much under the influence of Paul Potter, and painted landscapes with animals in the manner of that popular master. Perhaps because many of his paintings have been attributed to Potter or to his own father, there are few extant works known with certainty to be his, but some pictures in the Rotterdam Museum, the Brussels Gallery, the Hermitage at Leningrad and the Dulwich Gallery are attributed to him.

Camphuysen, Raphael. b. 1598; d. 1657. Dutch painter; nephew of Dirk Rafelsz Camphuysen (1586–1627). He is by many experts thought to have been the actual painter of some works attributed to his uncle.

Campi (käm′pē), **Antonio.** b. at Cremona, Italy, c1530; d. 1591. Italian painter, architect, sculptor, and historian of Cremona, son of Galeazzo Campi (c1475–1536). His paintings, chiefly of religious subjects, show very strongly the influence of Correggio, and are well esteemed both for color and for design. He was among the artists who, by commission of Philip II of Spain, executed the decorations of the Escorial palace. A man of many parts, he was known also as an architect and a sculptor, and he wrote and illustrated with original engravings a chronicle of the city of Cremona. His *Birth of Christ* in the church of San Paolo, Milan, is characteristic of his best achievement.

Campi, Bernardino. b. at Cremona, Italy, 1522; d. at Reggio nell'Emilia, Italy, c1590. Italian painter; possibly a son of Galeazzo Campi. Bernardino was a pupil at Cremona of Giulio Campi and thus may have been a younger brother like Antonio and Vincenzo Campi, who were also students of Giulio; there is some evidence, however, that he was the son of one Pietro Campi, also a painter, who may or may not have been a relative of Galeazzo and his sons. Like the latter, he was an enthusiastic follower of Titian, among others, and so devotedly studied the Venetian master's work that he was able to add a figure to Titian's series of Caesars which could not be distinguished as to authorship from the others. He developed a mastery of his own, however, and was influential in his own right on Italian painting. His skillful treatment of figures, both as to composition and perspective, is a feature of the frescoes in the cupola of the Church of San Sigismondo at Cremona, considered his masterpiece. Also well known are a *Descent from the Cross* in the Brera Gallery at Milan and a *Mater Dolorosa* in the Louvre at Paris. He was the author of *Parere sopra la pittura* (c1580).

Campi, Galeazzo. b. at Cremona, Italy, c1475; d. 1536. Italian painter, father of Giulio Campi (c1500–1572), Antonio Campi (c1530–1591), and Vincenzo Campi (c1532–1591). He painted chiefly religious pictures, some of them in imitation of Boccaccino, whose pupil he was in his youth, and others reminiscent of Perugino.

Campi, Giulio. b. at Cremona, Italy, c1500; d. there, 1572. Italian painter, founder of a school of painting at Cremona. There his pupils included Bernardino Campi, who is therefore believed by some to have been one of Giulio's several painter-brothers, while other critics call him the son of one Pietro Campi. Giulio was a student of his father, Galeazzo Campi, of Giulio Romano, and of the works of Titian, Raphael, and Correggio. His best works are at Mantua and at Cremona, especially the frescoes in the Church of Santa Margherita, at the latter city, and his *Virgin and Child with Saints Celsus and Nazarus,* which he painted at 27 for the Church of Sant'Abbondio at Cremona.

Campi, Vincenzo. b. at Cremona, Italy, c1532; d. 1591. Italian painter, noted for portraits and still lifes, son of Galeazzo Campi (c1475–1536). His instruction in painting was chiefly at the hands of his brother Giulio, and he also worked with his brother Antonio, accompanying the latter to Spain where both were employed by Philip II in the decoration of the Escorial palace. He varied the family tradition of painting mostly religious pictures, however, and became best known for his portraits, still lifes, and genre compositions. His color has been more admired than his design. Examples of his work survive chiefly in his native Lombardy, at Cremona and in the Brera Gallery at Milan.

Campian (kam′pi.a̤n), **Thomas.** See **Campion, Thomas.**

Campi Bisenzio (käm′pē bē.zen′tsyō). Town and commune in C Italy, in the *compartimento* (region) of Tuscany, in the province of Firenze, situated on the Bisenzio River, W of Florence: agricultural center; manufactures straw hats, silk, food and chemical products. Pop. of commune, 15,537 (1936); of town, 5,790 (1936).

Campi Catalaunici (kam′pī kat.a̤.lô′ni.sī). Latin name of the **Catalaunian Fields.**

Campi Flegrei (käm′pē flā.gre′ē). Italian name of the **Phlegraean Fields** or **Plain.**

Campiglia Marittima (käm.pē′lyä mä.rēt′tē.mä). Town and commune in C Italy, in the *compartimento* (region) of Tuscany, in the province of Livorno, situated near the Mediterranean coast between Livorno and Piombino. It has chemical and metallurgical industries, and marble and other stone quarries. Lead, iron, quartz, and zinc mines are in the vicinity; there is also an airport. The town, dominated by a castle, has preserved its medieval character. Pop. of commune, 11,591 (1936); of town, 2,566 (1936).

Câmpina (kim′pē.nä). Town in S Rumania, in the region of Muntenia, ab. 60 mi. NW of Bucharest. It has agricultural markets and oil refineries. In November, 1940, it was damaged by an earthquake, and in World War II large parts of the town were destroyed by air raids. 16,963 (1948).

Campina Grande (ka̤m.pē′na̤ grun′de̤). City in NE Brazil, in the state of Paraíba. 73,835 (1950).

Campinas (ka̤m.pē′na̤s). City in SE Brazil, in the state of São Paulo: distribution center for coffee and sugar; the surrounding farming region also produces cotton, grain, and dairy products. 101,746 (1950).

Campinchi (käṅ.paṅ.kē), **César.** b. at Calcatoggio, on the island of Corsica, France, May 4, 1882; d. at Marseilles, France, Feb. 23, 1941. French political leader and criminal lawyer, minister of the navy during the final years of the Third French Republic. A noted trial lawyer in criminal cases, he entered (1932) the Chamber of Deputies as a Radical-Socialist, became minister of the navy in June, 1937, was named minister of justice in January, 1938, and again served as minister of the navy (March, 1938–June, 1940). The Vichy government brought treason charges against him, but he died before he could be brought to trial.

Campine (käṅ.pēn). Coal-mining region in E Belgium, in the provinces of Antwerp and Limburg.

Campion (kam′pi.o̤n), **Edmund.** b. at London, Jan. 25, 1540; executed at Tyburn (now Marble Arch, in Hyde Park, London), Dec. 1, 1581. English Jesuit and scholar, remembered as one of the leading Jesuit missionaries in England. Although already subject to Roman Catholic leanings, he became (c1568) a deacon in the Church of England after having attended Oxford University. Having fled to France, he joined the Catholic Church, and in 1573 became a member of the Jesuit order. When the missionary movement to England was initiated (1580), he was among the first group to go there; his preaching was marked by a large number of conversions, although carried on illegally and therefore necessarily clandestinely. He wrote and distributed *Decem rationes*, a pamphlet listing his objections to the Anglican Church, which was so influential that the government's efforts to apprehend him were increased. Taken captive on July 14, 1581, he was taken to London where a recantation was sought from him; in spite of inducements by Queen Elizabeth, and three rackings, he stood firm, and expounded his views brilliantly at Protestant councils. He was finally found guilty of conspiracy and sedition, and condemned to death. His life forms the subject of a monograph (1935) by Evelyn Waugh.

Campion, Thomas. [Also, **Campian.**] b. at London, Feb. 12, 1567; d. there, March 1, 1620. English poet, physician, musician, song-writer, critic, and writer of masques. He was the author of *Poemata* (1595, Latin verses), *A Booke of Ayres* (1601), *Observations on the Art of English Poesie* (1602), and *Two Bookes of Ayres* (c1613). His *Songs of Mourning*, occasioned by the death of Prince Henry, was published in 1612; between 1607 and 1617 he wrote several elaborate court masques. His *New Way of Making Foure Parts in Counterpoint* (1617) was an important work in musical theory. Among his best-known poems are *Cherry Ripe*, *Of Corinna's Singing*, *Come, Cheerful Day*, *Now Winter Nights Enlarge*, *When Thou Must Home*, and *Chance and Change*.

Campi Raudii (kam′pī rô′di.ī). Latin name of the **Raudian Fields.**

Campistron (käṅ.pēs.trôṅ), **Jean Galbert de.** b. at Toulouse, France, 1656; d. May 11, 1723. French dramatic poet and follower of Jean Baptiste Racine. He was the author of *Virginie* (1683), *Andronic* (1685), *Acis et Galatée* (1686; an opera), *Tiridate* (1691), and others.

Campli (käm′plē). Town and commune in C Italy, in the *compartimento* (region) of Abruzzi e Molise, in the province of Teramo, situated in the Apennines between Teramo and Ascoli. The Collegiate Church of Santa Maria in Platea dates from the 12th, the town hall from the 15th century. There are terra-cotta, linen, and cotton-textile manufactures. Pop. of commune, 11,109 (1936); of town, 1,212 (1936).

Campo (kam′pō), **El.** See **El Campo.**

Campo (käm′pō), **Estanislao del.** See **del Campo, Estanislao.**

Campoamor y Campoosorio (käm″pō.ä.mōr′ ē käm″pō.ō.sō′ryō), **Ramón de.** b. at Navia, in Asturias, Spain, 1817; d. at Madrid, 1901. Spanish poet, philosopher, and statesman. He studied medicine at Madrid, and entered politics as a moderate, serving in various lesser posts until he was appointed governor of Castellón de la Plana, then of Alicante, and finally of Valencia. As a member of the Cortes (senator and member of the state council in 1874) he moved right to become a conservative. He was a member of the Spanish Academy and had a reputation for his work in many fields of literature. First acclaimed as a lyric poet upon the publication of *Ternezas y flores* (1840), he won fame for his epic *Colón* in 16 cantos (1853, 1857), for verse plays such as *Dies Irae* (1873), and for humorous works. His outstanding writings in the political and philosophical fields are *Polémicas con la democrácia* (1862) and *La Filosofía de las leyes* (1846).

Campobasso (käm.pō.bäs′sō). Province in the *compartimento* (region) of Abruzzi e Molise, SE Italy. It was formerly called Molise. Part of it belongs now to the newly created province of Caserta in Campania. Capital, Campobasso; area, ab. 1,800 sq. mi.; pop. 399,095 (1936), ab. 410,000 (est. 1946).

Campobasso. Town and commune in C Italy, in the *compartimento* (region) of Abruzzi e Molise, the capital of the province of Campobasso and the chief place of the Molise district, situated in the Apennines, NE of Naples. It is one of the oldest centers of the cutlery industry in Italy; also manufactures soap and building materials, and is the center of an agricultural district. It has a large penal establishment, and a museum of Samnitic antiquities. During the Volturno campaign, in World War II, the American and British forces joined here in 1943. Some war damage was suffered by some buildings of tourist interest, but repairs have been completed or are being carried out. Pop. of commune, 29,573 (1936); of town, 20,090 (1936).

Campobasso, Nicolo. fl. c1477. Neapolitan military adventurer in the service of Charles the Bold.

Campobello (kam.po̤.bel′ō). Island at the mouth of Passamaquoddy Bay, Bay of Fundy, E Canada, forming part of Charlotte County, New Brunswick: summer resort. President Franklin D. Roosevelt made his summer home here.

Campobello Affair. Attempt (April 9–28, 1866) by members of the Fenian Brotherhood to capture in the name of Ireland the island of Campobello, New Brunswick. British and U. S. action put an end to the scheme.

Campobello di Licata (käm.pō.bel′lō dē lē.kä′tä). Town and commune in SW Italy, on the island of Sicily, in the province of Agrigento, situated near the Sasso River, ab. 21 mi. E of Agrigento. Large sulfur mines are in the vicinity; also stone quarries and sulfur springs. Pop. of commune, 11,732 (1936); of town, 11,401 (1936).

Campobello di Mazara (mä.tsä′rä). [Also, **Campobello di Mazzara** (mät.tsä′rä).] Town and commune in SW Italy, on the island of Sicily, in the province of Trapani, situated near Cape Granitola, on the S shore of the island, ab. 42 mi. SW of Palermo. Stone quarries are in the vicinity. Pop. of commune, 10,285 (1936); of town, 10,206 (1936).

Campo de Criptana (käm′pō dā krēp.tä′nä). Town and commune in C Spain, in the province of Ciudad Real, ab. 50 mi. NE of the city of Ciudad Real: agricultural trade. Pop. of commune, 15,427 (1940).

Campo di Sangue (dē säng′gwā). See under **Cannae.**

Campodunum (kam.pǫ.dū′num). Ancient name of **Kempten.**

Campo Formio (käm′pō fôr′myō). [Also, **Campoformido** (käm.pō.fôr′mē.dō).] Village in the province of Friuli, in NE Italy, ab. 6 mi. SW of Udine. Here, on Oct. 17, 1797, a treaty was concluded between France and Austria, by which Austria ceded the Belgian provinces, recognized the Cisalpine Republic, and received the greater part of the Venetian territories; France retained the Ionian Islands. By secret articles, France was to receive the left bank of the Rhine.

Campo Grande (kum′pö grun′dę). City in SW Brazil, in the state of Mato Grosso: railway and airline junction. 32,848 (1950).

Campomanes (käm.pō.mä′nās), Conde **de.** [Title of **Pedro Rodríguez.**] b. in Asturias, Spain, July 1, 1723; d. Feb. 3, 1802. Spanish statesman and political economist, president of the council in 1788. He wrote *Discurso sobre el fomento de la industria popular* (1774), and *Discurso sobre la educación popular* (1775).

Campos (kum′pös). Seaport in E Brazil, in the state of Rio de Janeiro, near the mouth of the Paraíba River: sugar products and tropical fruit. 63,384 (1950).

Campos (käm′pōs), **Arsenio Martínez de.** See **Martínez de Campos, Arsenio.**

Campos (kum′pös), **Humberto de.** [Full name, **Humberto de Campos Veras.**] b. at Muritiba, Maranhão, Brazil, Oct. 25, 1886; d. at Rio de Janeiro, Dec. 5, 1934. Brazilian short-story writer, humorist, critic, columnist, and poet. His books of poetry include *Poeira* (1911, 1917), and *Poesias completas* (1933). Among his prose writings are the books of short stories *Vale de Josafá* (1919), *Tonel de Diógenes* (1920), and *A serpente de bronze* (1921), and the books of sketches *Sombras que sofrem* (1934) and *Destinos* (1935). Among his works of criticism are *Carvalhos e roseiras* (1923) and *Crítica* (1933–36). He also wrote the autobiographical works *Memórias* (1933) and *Memórias inacabadas* (1935).

Campos, José Joaquim Carneiro de. See **Carneiro de Campos, José Joaquim.**

Campos (käm′pōs), **Martínez Arsenio.** See **Martínez de Campos, Arsenio.**

Campos, Rubén M. b. at Guanajuato, Mexico, April 25, 1876—. Mexican educator, folklorist, and author. He was a professor of Spanish literature and language at various Mexican colleges, and professor of Mexican folklore at the Museo Nacional. He also served (1898–1919, 1922 *et seq.*) in the ministry of public education, and was Mexican consul (1920–21) at Milan. He was a contributor to magazines, and author of *El Folklore y la música mexicana*, *El Folklore literaria de México*, *El Folklore musical de las ciudades*, *La Producción literaria de los Aztecas*, *Tradiciones y legendas mexicanas*, and *El Bar* (*la vida literaria de México*).

Campo Santo (käm′pō sän′tō). Name of a famous cemetery at Pisa, Italy (the phrase "campo santo" means "holy field" (or cemetery) in Italian, and is applied generally to all burial places in that country. However, as a proper name, the phrase is ordinarily taken by art historians as applying to the one here defined). The mausoleum that dominates it was begun in 1278 by Giovanni Pisano. A series of frescoes by Benozzo Gozzoli, and several paintings attributed to Francesco Traini were considered the most important works of art at the cemetery. Much of the Compo Santo was damaged by bombardment and fire in the period 1944–45, including the north wall, on which were the Gozzoli works; the majority of these were destroyed beyond hope of restoration. The Traini works, on the south wall, were also partly destroyed.

Campos de Vacaria (kum′pös dē vä.kạ.rē′ạ). Elevated open region in the N part of the state of Rio Grande do Sul, Brazil, inland from the mountains. It forms the S extremity of the Brazilian plateau.

Campos dos Goitacazes (dös goi.tạ.kä′zęs). Open region on the banks of the Paraíba River, NE of Rio de Janeiro, Brazil. The region was so called ("fields of the Goitacazes") from a variant spelling of the name of the Indians who formerly occupied it. The name passed to a city on the Paraíba, abbreviated to Campos.

Campos dos Parecis (pä.rę.sēs′). Open region in W Brazil, E of the Guaporé and Madeira rivers, forming a portion of the Brazilian plateau, ab. 3,000 ft. above sea level. It was so called from the name of the Indians who once inhabited most of it, and were formerly very powerful. The Campos dos Parecis were visited by the Portuguese as early as 1720, but the region is still very imperfectly known.

Campos Salles (sä′lęs), **Manuel Ferraz** (or **Manoel Ferrez**) **de.** b. at Campinas, São Paulo, Brazil, c1846; d. 1913. Brazilian statesman, president (1898 *et seq.*) of Brazil. He was governor (1896–98) of São Paulo. Before his installation as president of the republic, he went to Europe to secure a funding loan from the Rothschild banking firm. His administration made an attempt to balance the budget by raising taxes and curtailing expenses, and settled boundary disputes with France over French Guiana and with Britain over British Guiana.

Campra (käṅ.prȧ), **André.** b. at Aix, France, 1660; d. at Versailles, France, June 29, 1744. French composer, notably of operas and motets. He was director of music at Toulon (1679), Arles (1681), Toulouse (1683–94), and Notre-Dame de Paris (1694–1700), and was appointed (1722) director of the chapel royal. His operas include *L'Europe galante* (1697), *Le Carnaval de Venise* (1699), *Tancrède* (1702), and *Camille* (1717).

Campsie Fells (kamp′si felz). Portion of the Lennox Hills, in C Scotland, in Stirlingshire, ab. 13 mi. SW of Stirling. 1,896 ft.

Câmpulung (kim.pö.löng′). [Also: **Kimpolung** (-pō-), **Kimpulung.**] Town in S Rumania, in the region of Muntenia, ab. 81 mi. NW of Bucharest on the S slopes of the Transylvanian Alps: summer resort; leather manufactures. Settled by German colonists in the 12th century, it was an early cultural center. 18,174 (1948).

Câmpulungul Moldov (kim.pö.löng′göl mōl′dōv). [Also, **Câmpulung.**] Town in NE Rumania, in the region of South Bucovina, situated on the Moldova River, ab. 40 mi. SW of Siret: cattle markets; wood industry. 11,041 (1948).

Campus Martius (kam′pus mär′shus). [Italian, **Campo Marzio** (käm′pō mär′tsyō); Eng. trans., *"Field of Mars."*] Historic area in ancient Rome, lying between the Pincian, Quirinal, and Capitoline hills and the Tiber River. Throughout the early history of Rome this plain remained free of buildings, and was used for popular assemblies and military exercises. During the reign of Augustus it had become encroached upon from the S by the building up of the Flaminian Meadows, and from the E by public and other buildings on the Via Cata, corresponding closely to the later Corso. Under Augustus, however, a great extent of the plain still remained free, and served for chariot races and horse races, ballplaying, and other athletic sports; it was surrounded by the finest monuments of the city, and presented an imposing spectacle. It is now occupied by one of the most important quarters of modern Rome, including the Pantheon and the parliament buildings.

Cam-ranh Bay (käm.rän′). [Also, **Camranh** (or **Kamranh**) **Bay.**] Bay on the SE coast of Indochina, in Annam (Central Viet-Nam) ab. 250 mi. NE of Saigon: an arm of the South China Sea. Length, ab. 20 mi.; width, ab. 15 mi.

Camrose (kam′rōz). Town in Alberta, Canada, ab. 68 mi. SE of Edmonton, with which it is connected by road. It is a distributing center for the nearby grain-growing area. Coal is also found in the vicinity. 4,131 (1951).

Camuccini (kä.möt.chē′nē), **Vincenzo.** b. at Rome, c1773; d. 1844. Italian painter of historical subjects and of portraits. His inclination toward classical composition and academic style was confirmed by his early study of Raphael and Domenichino and later by his admiration for David, aroused when that Franch master came to Rome. His series of works depicting the history of Rome, beginning with the *Romulus and Remus* in Saint Luke's Academy at that city, and including such paintings as the *Death of Caesar* and the *Death of Virginia*, and the mosaic of *Saint Thomas* in Saint Peter's, made him the dominant figure of the academic classical school in Italy.

Camulodunum (kam″ụ̄.lọ̄.dū′num). Latin name of **Colchester,** England.

Camus (kȧ.mü), **Albert.** b. near Algiers, North Africa, 1913—. French journalist, novelist, dramatist, and essayist. He is the author of two philosophical essays, *Le Mythe de Sisyphe* (1942) and *L'Homme révolté* (1951); two novels, *L'Étranger* (1942; Eng. trans., *The Stranger,* 1946) and *La Peste* (1947; Eng. trans., *The Plague,* 1948); plays including *Caligula* (1944) and *Le Malentendu* (1945); and of various short essays. He was cofounder during World War II of the clandestine newspaper *Combat* and emerged after the liberation of France as the chief (and much read) editorial writer of that paper.

Camus, Armand Gaston. b. at Paris, April 2, 1740; d. Nov. 2, 1804. French revolutionary statesman and archivist. He was a deputy to the States-General of 1789, a member of the convention of 1792, and president of the Council of Five Hundred in 1796. A staunch republican, he was noted for his speeches before the States-General and later for his opposition to Napoleon I. Probably his most noteworthy contribution to history was the recording and classifying, as archivist, of the papers and verbal proceedings of the constituent assembly. He was the author of *Lettres sur la profession d'avocat* (1772–77) and *Code judiciare, ou Recueil des décrets de l'Assemblée nationale et constituante sur l'ordre judiciare* (1792).

Camus, Baron **de.** A title of **Browne,** Count **Maximilian Ulysses von.**

Cana (kā′nạ). In the New Testament, a village in Galilee, Palestine, the scene of two of Christ's miracles. It has been identified with Kefr-Kenna, and with Kana-el-Jelil (both near Nazareth). John, ii; iv. 46, etc.

Cana, Marriage at. See **Marriage at Cana.**

Canaã (ku.nạ.uṅ′). Novel of Brazil as a land of immigration, by the Brazilian writer José Pereira da Graça Aranha (1868–1931). It was published in 1902 and an English translation (*Canaan*) appeared in 1920.

Canaan (kā′nạn). In the Old Testament, the fourth son of Ham, eponymic of the non-Israelite inhabitants of the land of the same name (promised by God to Abraham). Gen. x.

Canaan. [Also: **Land of Canaan;** called the **"Land of Promise,"** or the **"Promised Land."**] In Old Testament geography, the name generally denoting the country W of the Jordan and the Dead Sea to the Mediterranean Sea. Originally it comprised only the strip of land, from 10 to 15 mi. in breadth and 150 in length, shut in between the Lebanon and the Mediterranean, and extending from the Bay of Antioch to the promontory of the Carmel, i.e., S Phoenicia. To this maritime plain of the Phoenicians and Philistines passages like Isa. xxiii. 11, Zeph. ii. 5 refer. Later the name was extended to the whole W Jordanic territory. Thus also in the Tel-el-Amarna tablets, which date back a century before the exodus, Kinakk, or Canaan, denotes the district between the cities of Philistia and the country N of Gebal (Byblos). The Egyptians named it the land of Keft, or the "palm," of which the Greek (Phoenix) is a translation. In Biblical history, this was the land promised by God to Abraham. Gen. xii.

Canaan. In Old Testament history, the non-Israelite inhabitants of what is now Palestine (more frequently in the plural, "the Canaanites"). The origin and affinities of the various tribes are still disputed.

Canaanites (kā′nạn.īts). See under **Canaan,** immediately preceding.

Canaan's Calamity. Versified work (1618) by Thomas Dekker. It is the story of the destruction of Jerusalem by Titus.

Canace (kan′ạ.sē). In Greek legend, a daughter of Aeolus, put to death on account of her illicit love for her brother. Chaucer refers to the story in the introduction to his "Man of Law's Tale" in the *Canterbury Tales.*

Canace. Daughter of Cambuscan in Geoffrey **Chaucer's** "The Squire's Tale" in the *Canterbury Tales.*

Canachus (kan′ạ.kus). fl. 6th century B.C. Greek sculptor, of Sicyon in Achaea. Little is known of his work except that he executed two famous statues of Apollo, one in bronze for the city of Miletus in Asia Minor, and one in cedar for Thebes. The former is represented on some of the coins of Miletus.

Canada (kan′ạ.dạ). [Full name, **Dominion of Canada.**] Confederation of provinces in British North America, bounded by the Arctic Ocean on the N, the Atlantic Ocean on the E, the U.S. on the S, and the Pacific Ocean and Alaska on the W: a member of the British Commonwealth of Nations. It comprises the provinces of Quebec, Ontario, New Brunswick, Nova Scotia, Prince Edward Island, Manitoba, British Columbia, Alberta, Saskatchewan, and (since April 1, 1949) Newfoundland and Labrador (the coast of Labrador is an electoral district within the provincial government of Newfoundland), and also the Northwest Territory and Yukon Territory (the SW corner of the Yukon); the Arctic Archipelago is part of the Northwest Territories. The chief physical features of Canada are the St. Lawrence valley, the Saskatchewan and Mackenzie river systems (with their numerous large lakes, Great Bear, Great Slave, Athabaska, Winnipeg, and others), Hudson Bay, the great plains, the "Height of Land," Labrador plateau, and the Rocky and Cascade mountains. Mount Logan, 26 mi. NE of Mount St. Elias, is said to have an elevation of 19,850 ft. The Canadian government consists of a governor general and Parliament (Senate and House of Commons). Chief exports are timber, cheese, wheat, coal, and cattle. Canada was explored by Cartier in 1534–35. It was permanently settled at Quebec in 1608 by the French, and called New France. It was ceded to Great Britain in 1763. The Americans attacked it unsuccessfully in the Revolution and in the War of 1812. There was an unsuccessful rebellion in 1837–38. The provinces reunited in 1841, and the confederation was formed in 1867. The Red River rebellion, under Louis Riel, took place in 1869–70, and the second Riel rebellion in 1885. In 1886 the Canadian Pacific Railway was opened, and remains today, under private ownership, one of the most extensive transportation systems in the world. In 1923 the Canadian Northern, the Grand Trunk and Grand Trunk Pacific, the Intercolonial, and several smaller railway lines were amalgamated into the government-owned Canadian National Railways, which then provided a second transcontinental line. With the opening of the railways the Canadian West grew rapidly and thousands of new immigrants were settled on the land. Canada fought on the side of the Allies in both World Wars and, besides sending overseas large divisions of troops, contributed much in the way of war materials and equipment for all the Allies. In the fall of 1948 a referendum was held in Newfoundland, before then a separate dominion, and a majority vote was registered for union with Canada. The oldest British colony, and Canada's nearest British neighbor, thus became a province of Canada on April 1, 1949. Capital, Ottawa; area 3,733,144 sq. mi. (total land area, 3,504,837 sq. mi.); pop. 14,009,429 (1951).

Canada, Lower. See under **Quebec,** province of Canada.

Cañada de Gómez (kä.nyä′ᴛʜä dā gō′mes). City in E Argentina, in Santa Fe province, ab. 220 mi. NW of Buenos Aires. 12,354 (1947).

Canadarago Lake (kan″ạ.dạ.rä′gō). [Also, **Schuyler Lake.**] Small lake in E central New York, in Otsego County, ab. 24 mi. SE of Utica. It has its outlet into the Susquehanna River.

Canadian (kạ.nā′di.ạn). Town in NW Texas, in the Panhandle, county seat of Hemphill County, on the Canadian River ab. 90 mi. NE of Amarillo. It is a railroad and marketing center for a cattle-raising and farming region. 2,700 (1950).

Canadian Arctic Islands. See **Arctic Archipelago.**

Canadian Mounted Police. See **Royal Canadian Mounted Police.**

Canadian National Railways. See under **Canada.**

Canadian Pacific Railway. See under **Canada.**

Canadian River. River in New Mexico, N Texas, and Oklahoma, which rises in Colfax County, N.M., flows generally E, and joins the Arkansas River ab. 25 mi. S of Tahlequah, in Muskogee County, Okla. Length, ab. 900 mi. Its chief affluent is the North Fork, in Oklahoma (length, ab. 600 mi.).

Canadian Rockies. See under **Rocky Mountains.**

Canadian Shield. See **Laurentian Shield.**

Canajoharie (kan"ą.jǫ.har'i). Town (in New York the equivalent of township in many other states) and village in E central New York, in Montgomery County: food processing and packing center. Settled c1730, it has important collections of historical material and of paintings. Pop. of town, 4,294 (1950); of village, 2,761 (1950).

Çanakkale (chä.näk.kä.le'). *Il* (province or vilayet) in NW Turkey, reaching across the Dardanelles from Asia to Europe: a rich farming land which produces crops of sugar beets, wheat, rye, olives, and figs, and on which many sheep and cattle are raised. It is the site of ancient Troy, and of other historical spots. Capital, Çanakkale; area, 3,490 sq. mi.; pop. 288,813 (1950).

Çanakkale. [Also: **Chanak, Chanakkale, Chanak Kalessi, Kale Sultanie** (or **Sultaniye**), **Khanak Kalessi.**] Town in NW Turkey, capital of the *il* (province or vilayet) of Çanakkale, on the Dardanelles, ab. 10 mi. NE of the site of ancient Troy. The ancient ruins of the city of Abydos are located nearby. The town is a local trading center served by two important roads. Wheat, olives, oats, grapes, barley, and tobacco are the most important crops in the area. Pop. ab. 20,000.

Çanakkale Boğazı (bō.ä.zı'). Turkish name of the **Dardanelles.**

Canal (kä.näl'), **Antonio.** See **Canaletto, Antonio.**

Canal Casiquiare (kä.sē.kyä'rā). See **Casiquiare.**

Canal Dover. Former name of **Dover,** Tuscarawas County, Ohio.

Canal du Midi (kȧ.nȧl dü mē.dē). See **Midi, Canal du.**

Canale (kä.nä'lā). **Antonio.** See **Canaletto, Antonio.**

Canalejas y Méndez (kä.nä.le'ʜäs ē men'deth), **José.** b. at El Ferrol, Spain, 1854; assassinated at Madrid, Nov. 19, 1912. Spanish statesman and outstanding liberal leader under Alfonso XIII. He studied law at Madrid and became in 1881 a member of the Cortes. From 1888 to 1902 he held various ministerial posts, most frequently justice and finance, and advocated the adoption of socialist doctrines by the liberal party. In December, 1901, he published a radical program for social action by the government in the review *Nuestro Tiempo.* In 1906 he became president of the council. His program of anticlericalism and his campaign against the latifundia which led to the suspension of diplomatic relations with the Vatican were energetically pushed when he served as premier in 1910–11. In 1912 he suppressed a railroad strike by military force and fell victim to an anarchist bomb on Nov. 19, 1912.

Canaletto (kä.nä.lāt'tō), **Antonio.** [Original name, **Antonio Canale** or **Canal.**] b. at Venice, Oct. 18, 1697; d. there, April 20, 1768. Italian painter, noted chiefly for his pictures of Venice. He was a pupil of his father, Rinaldo Canale, a scene painter. He lived for a time (1746–55) in England, after having studied at Rome. His architectural views of Venice are in the collections of many museums, including the Metropolitan Museum of Art at New York, the National Gallery of Art at Washington, D.C., and the National Gallery at London. He is not to be confused with his nephew Bernardo Bellotto or Belotto (c1720–80), a painter who is also sometimes called Canaletto.

Canalizo (kä.nä.lē'sō), **Valentín.** b. at Monterrey, Mexico, c1797; d. c1847. Mexican general in the war with the U.S. From December, 1843, to June, 1844, he was acting president during the absence of Antonio López de Santa Anna. Again made acting president in September, 1844, he was impeached for arbitrary proceedings, and banished in May, 1845. He was allowed to return, and served in the war (1846–47) with the U.S., commanding the cavalry at Cerro Gordo, on April 17, 1847, and the entire army in the subsequent retreat.

Canal Zone. [Also: **Isthmian Canal Zone, Panama Canal Zone;** Spanish, **Zona del Canal.**] Strip of territory 10 mi. wide, extending 5 mi. in each direction from the central line of the canal route across the Isthmus of Panama. It begins in the Caribbean Sea "three marine miles from mean low-water mark," and extends "to and across the Isthmus of Panama into the Pacific Ocean to a distance of three marine miles from mean low-water mark." The cities of Panama and Colón, with their harbors, are excluded from the territory. The use, occupation, and control of this zone were ceded in perpetuity by the Republic of Panama to the U.S. by a treaty ratified by the U.S. Senate on Feb. 23, 1904. Panama granted to the U.S. "the use, occupation, and control of all islands within the limits of the zone above described, and in addition thereto the group of small islands in the Bay of Panama named Perico, Naos, Culebra, and Flamingo." Land area, 362 sq. mi.; pop. 51,827 (1940).

Canandaigua (kan.ạn.dā'gwạ). City in W central New York, county seat of Ontario County, at the N end of Canandaigua Lake, ab. 25 mi. SE of Rochester, in a resort and farming region. Manufactures include chemical solvents, knitted goods, enameled ware, and corsets. 8,332 (1950).

Canandaigua Lake. Lake in W New York: one of the Finger Lakes. Length, 15 mi.

Cananea (kä.nä.nā'ä). City in NW Mexico, in Sonora state, near the U.S. border: center of cattle-raising and of copper, zinc, lead, and silver mining. 11,006 (1940).

Cananites (kā.nạ.nī'tēz), **Athenodorus.** See **Athenodorus Cananites.**

Cananore (kan'ạ.nōr). See **Cannanore.**

Cañar (kä.nyär'). Province in C Ecuador, in the Andes: Inca relics. Capital, Azogues; area, 1,034 sq. mi.; pop. 125.109 (est. 1944).

Cañar. City in C Ecuador, in Cañar province. 11,925 (est. 1944).

Canara (kä'nạ.rạ). See **Kanara.**

Canaria (kä.nä'ryä), **Gran.** See **Grand Canary.**

Cañaris (kä.nyä'rēs). [Also, **Cañares** (-rās).] Most powerful Indian tribe in S and W Ecuador until its incorporation into the Inca empire by means of a negotiated peace (c1450). During the conquest they sided with the Spanish. The language and the tribal organization of the Cañaris have been obliterated, and the Indians of this region now speak Quechua.

Canaris or **Kanaris** (kä.nä'rēs), **Constantine.** b. on the island of Psara, in the Aegean Islands, 1790; d. Sept. 15, 1877. Greek admiral and politician. He distinguished himself in the Greek war for independence (1821–25), notably by actions against the Turkish naval forces. He represented Psara in the Greek national convention in 1827, and was one of the revolutionaries who gained (1862) the Greek throne for George I; thereafter he was president (1864–65, 1877) of the cabinet. He also served several times as minister of marine.

Canarsee (kạ.När'si). [Also, **Canarsie.**] Indian tribe of North America, of the Algonquian linguistic family. Now extinct, they were found in colonial times in the region of what is now W Long Island. They have given their name (in the spelling Canarsie) to a section of Brooklyn.

Canarsie (kạ.när'si). Section of New York City, in the S part of the borough of Brooklyn.

Canary Islands (kạ.nãr'i). [Also: **Canaries;** Spanish, **Islas Canarias** (ēs'läs kä.nä'ryäs).] Group of Spanish islands in the Atlantic Ocean, W of the African territory of Río de Oro. The name (Latin, *Canaria insula,* meaning "dog island," i.e., Grand Canary) is derived from the bloodhounds formerly raised there. The islands form the two provinces of Las Palmas and Santa Cruz de Tenerife; they include Tenerife, Palma, Gomera, Hierro, Grand Canary, Fuerteventura, Lanzarote, and some smaller uninhabited islands. The surface is mountainous and largely volcanic, the climate oceanic and subtropical, dry and warm, with a brief rainy period during the winter months. This circumstance, together with the great natural beauty of the location, makes the Canary Islands a world-renowned tourist center, and a health resort frequented particularly by tuberculosis patients. The flora is a mixture of Mediterranean and African elements. The chief occupation is the raising of bananas, replacing the earlier culture of wine and sugar cane; crops also include early vegetables, particularly tomatoes and potatoes. Goats and mules are raised; the latter are exported. Native embroidery manufacture, once an important industry, is declining. Las Palmas and Santa Cruz rank among the busiest Atlantic ports; European steamship lines serving South American, West African, and South African ports all call there. The islands are likewise important stopovers for international airlines. Area, 2,807 sq. mi.; pop. 758,328 (est. 1948).

History and Culture. The islands, probably already known to the Phoenicians, were called the "Fortunate Islands" or "Happy Islands" (Latin, *Fortunatae Insulae*, literally, "Islands of the Blest") by the Romans. The group was rediscovered in 1341 by a band of Portuguese and Spanish sailors under Luis de la Cerda but little actual settlement took place. The islands became a Castilian fief in 1402, and were purchased by Ferdinand of Aragon in 1476. Bloody suppression of the Guanches, the tall, blond natives of the islands, was carried out in the years 1478–96. The population is now chiefly Spanish, with strains of the original Guanche people, and Semitic and African strains. The religion is predominantly Catholic. The increase in population is rapid, and there is considerable emigration.

Canastota (kan.ạ.stō′tạ). Village in C New York, in Madison County, in a farming region: onions are one of the principal crops. 4,458 (1950).

Canaveral (kạ.nav′ėr.ạl), **Cape.** Promontory in E Florida, ab. 60 mi. SE of Daytona Beach. It is a low sandy cape projecting into the Atlantic Ocean, and has a lighthouse 145 ft. high.

Canberra (kan′ber.ạ, -bėr.ạ). Capital of the Commonwealth of Australia, situated in the Australian Capital District in SE New South Wales. It is also the seat of University College, a military college, and Canberra Technical College, and of the proposed national university. Ab. 14,000 (1947).

Canberra Pact. Agreement between Australia and New Zealand signed at Canberra on Jan. 21, 1944, strengthening the close coöperation between the two British dominions, especially in matters of defense, migration, aviation, and Pacific dependencies.

Canby (kan′bi), **Edward Richard Sprigg.** b. in Kentucky, in August, 1817; killed at the "Lava Beds," in northern California, April 11, 1873. American general with the Union army in the Civil War. He served (1847–48) in the Mexican War, commanded (1861–62) the forces in New Mexico, and repelled the incursion into New Mexico of the Confederate general Hopkins Henry Sibley in February, 1862. In July, 1863, he commanded the U.S. troops at New York and its harbor during the draft riots (uprisings protesting against the conscription law of March 3, 1863, which allowed for the buying of military exemption). He succeeded Nathaniel Prentiss Banks as commander of the army in Louisiana and of the departments W of the Mississippi River in 1864, captured Mobile on April 12, 1865, and was promoted to brigadier general in the regular army on July 28, 1866, having previously obtained the rank of major general of volunteers. Sent on a peacemaking mission to Indians in California, he was treacherously killed by Modoc Indians during a conference with them.

Canby, Henry Seidel. b. at Wilmington, Del., Sept. 6, 1878—. American author and editor. He was graduated (Ph.B., 1899; Ph.D., 1905) from Yale, where he became (1900) a member of the English department and was made a lecturer with professorial rank in 1922. He has been assistant editor (1911–20) of the *Yale Review*, editor (1920–24) of the New York *Evening Post's* "Literary Review," and editor (1924–36) and chairman of the editorial board (1936 *et seq.*) of the *Saturday Review of Literature*. In 1926 he became chairman of the Book-of-the-Month Club board of judges. His works include *The Short Story* (1902), *The Short Story in English* (1909), *College Sons and College Fathers* (1915), *Education by Violence* (1919), *Everyday Americans* (1920), *Definitions* (1922), *Definitions* (2nd series, 1924), *American Estimates* (1929), *Classic Americans* (1931), *The Age of Confidence* (1934), *Alma Mater—The Gothic Age of the American College* (1936), *Thoreau* (1939), *Handbook of English Usage* (1942), *Walt Whitman, an American* (1943), and *American Memoir* (1947).

Cancale (käṅ.kȧl). Town in W France, in the department of Ille-et-Vilaine, situated on Mont-St.-Michel Bay, ab. 10 mi. NE of St.-Malo. It is famous for its picturesque situation, partly at the foot and partly on top of high cliffs, and has important oyster fisheries. Much of the town was damaged in World War II. 5,567 (1946).

Cancao (käng kä′ō). See **Hatien.**

Cancer (kan′sėr). Constellation and also a sign of the zodiac, represented by the form of a crab, and showing the limits of the sun's course northward in summer; hence, the sign of the summer solstice.

Cancha-Rayada (kän′chä.rä.yä′ᴛʜä). Plain just N of the city of Talca, Chile. On March 28, 1814, a division of the patriot army was defeated there, and on March 19, 1818, the army commanded by Generals San Martín and O'Higgins was defeated at the same place by a night attack of the Spanish troops under General Osorio. It derived its name from a race track for horses.

Cancionero musical (kän.thyō.nā′rō mö.sē.käl′). Collection (1890) of 459 Spanish songs of the 15th and 16th centuries.

Cancrin (kän.krēn′), Count **Georg.** [Russian surname, **Kankrin.**] b. at Hanau, Prussia, Dec. 8, 1774; d. at St. Petersburg, Sept. 22, 1845. Russian general of infantry, and politician. He served as minister of finance in the period 1823–44. Author of the romance *Dagovert, Geschichte aus dem jetzigen Freiheitskrieg* (1796), and of economic works.

Candace (kan′dạ sē). Hereditary appellation of the ancient Ethiopian queens of Meroë, in Upper Nubia (now part of Anglo-Egyptian Sudan), like the name *Pharaoh* applied to the older Egyptian kings; specifically: **1.** According to an old tradition, the Queen of Sheba who visited Solomon. **2.** A queen of Meroë who invaded Egypt in 22 B.C. and captured Elephantine, Syene (modern Aswan), and Philae. She was defeated by the Roman general Petronius, renewed the attack, and was again defeated by him. **3.** In Biblical history, the queen of Ethiopia whose high treasurer was converted to Christianity by Philip, in 30 A.D. Acts, viii. 27.

Candahar (kan′dạ.här). See **Kandahar.**

Candamo (kän.dä′mō), **Francisco Antonio de Bances.** b. in Spain, 1662; d. 1709. Spanish poet and dramatist. His *Poesias comicas* were published in 1772.

Candaules (kan.dô′lēz) or **Myrsilus** (mėr.sī′lus). fl. in the 8th or 7th century B.C. Last Heracleid king of Lydia. He was slain by Gyges, who succeeded him.

Candeish (kan′dēsh). See **Khandesh.**

Candia (kan′di.ạ). See also **Crete.**

Candia. [Also: **Heraklion, Herakleion, Iraklion, Megalokastron.**] City in S Greece, the capital of the department of Heraklion, situated on the N coast of the island of Crete near the site of ancient Cnossus. It is a seaport and traffic junction, the largest city of the island of Crete; before 1841 it was the capital of the island. It is the seat of a bishopric. Founded in the 9th century by the Saracens, it became in the 10th century part of the Byzantine Empire, was taken and fortified by the Venetians in the 13th century, and was captured from Venice by the Turks in 1669. In World War II it was seriously damaged in the German invasion of Crete, in May, 1941. Pop. 42,357 (1940).

Candiac (käṅ.dyȧk), **Jean Louis Philippe Élisabeth Montcalm de.** b. at Château de Candiac, Gard, France, Nov. 7, 1719; d. at Paris, Oct. 8, 1726. Younger brother of Louis Joseph de Montcalm. He was noted for his remarkable precocity, based upon an extraordinary memory.

Candida (kan′di.dạ). Play by George Bernard Shaw, included in *Plays: Pleasant and Unpleasant* (1898). It deals with the choice the titular heroine must make between her husband, James Morrell, who is a stern and ascetic clergyman, and Eugene Marchbanks, a young poet who adores her. While Marchbanks freely confesses his weakness of character, Candida discerns that her undemanding husband needs her more deeply, and makes her decision accordingly. Rejected, the poet departs, to learn to find strength in himself.

Candidate for Truth, A. Novel by John Davys Beresford, published in 1912, the second volume of the Jacob Stahl trilogy. Its companion volumes are *The Early History of Jacob Stahl* (1911) and *The Invisible Event* (1915).

Candide, ou L'Optimisme (käṅ.dēd ö lop.tē.mēsm; Anglicized, kan.dēd′). Philosophical novel by Voltaire, published in 1759, a satire on the optimism of Leibnitz and his followers. Its titular hero bears all the worst ills of life, including such catastrophes as the Lisbon earthquake of 1755, in naïve puzzlement while his tutor Pangloss assures him that Leibnitz is right, all is for the best. The book ends with the exhortation to the hero, and by implication to the reader, "Let us cultivate our garden," that is, apply common sense to everyday problems and stop worrying over the metaphysical problems we cannot solve.

Candie (käṅ.dē). A French name of **Crete.**

Candioti (kän.dyō'tē), **Alberto María.** b. at Rosario, Argentina, Dec. 29, 1889—. Argentine diplomat and writer. He served (1913–39) in various consular posts, and as minister to Yugoslavia, Greece, Colombia, and Ecuador, ambassador to Colombia (1939–41), Japan (1941), and Mexico (1942–46). His written works include *El Jardín del amor.*

Candish (kan'dish), **Thomas.** See **Cavendish, Thomas.**

Candlemas (kan'dl.mas). Roman Catholic and Anglican feast day in commemoration of the presentation of Christ in the Temple, and the purification of the Virgin Mary. It falls annually on February 2.

Candle of Vision, The. Autobiographical fragment (1918) by Æ (George W. Russell).

Candler (kan'dlėr), **Asa Griggs.** b. near Villa Rica, Ga., Dec. 30, 1851; d. March 12, 1929. American manufacturer and philanthropist, noted as the improver of the Coca-Cola formula, which formed the nucleus of his great soft-drink enterprise; brother of Warren Akin Candler. While studying medicine privately, he turned to pharmacy and in 1873 settled at Atlanta, Ga., where he subsequently organized his own wholesale drug firm. Purchasing the Coca-Cola formula in 1887, he added improvements and abandoned (c1890) the drug business to concentrate on the manufacture of Coca-Cola. He sold the firm in 1919 for 25 million dollars. His gifts to Emory University totalled seven million dollars, and he made substantial contributions to the Methodist Church.

Candler, Warren Akin. b. in Carroll County, Ga., Aug. 23, 1857; d. at Atlanta, Ga., Sept. 25, 1941. American Methodist Episcopal clergyman; brother of Asa Griggs Candler (1851–1929). Graduated (1875) from Emory College at Oxford, Ga., he was a pastor (1875–86) in the North Georgia Conference, and was consecrated (1898) a bishop of the Methodist Episcopal Church (of the South). He also served as president (1888–98) of Emory College and chancellor (1914–21) of Emory University. His works include *Christus Auctor* (1899), *High Living and High Lives* (1901), *The Christ and the Creed* (1927), *Easter Meditations* (1930), and *Young J. Allen, the Man Who Seeded China* (1931).

Candlewood Lake (kan'dl.wůd). Reservoir in W Connecticut, ab. 3 mi. N of Danbury, created in 1926 by a power dam on the Rocky River. It has developed as a resort region. Area, ab. 9 sq. mi.

Candlish (kan'dlish), **Robert Smith.** b. at Edinburgh, March 23, 1806; d. Oct. 19, 1873. Scottish Free Church leader. Licensed in the Presbyterian ministry in 1828, his exceptional power as a preacher led to his being called to the pulpit of the church of Saint George, one of the most important in Edinburgh, in 1834. In the movement which led to what is known in Scottish church history as the "Great Disruption of 1843," the issue being the appointment of ministers by the civil authority without regard to the wishes of the congregations, he was eloquent in protest against this procedure, was closely associated with Thomas Chalmers in setting up the Scottish Free Church, and after Chalmers's death was its most prominent leader. In 1862 he accepted the principalship of New College, Edinburgh, on condition that he should not have to function as a professor, which would have interfered with the performance of his duties as minister. Among his many writings are *Contributions toward the Exposition of the Book of Genesis* (1842), *The Atonement, Its Reality and Extent* (1845), *The Fatherhood of God* (1865), and *The Gospel of Forgiveness* (posthumously published, 1878);

Candolle (käṅ.dol), **Alphonse Louis Pierre Pyrame de.** b. at Paris, Oct. 27, 1806; d. at Geneva, Switzerland, April 4, 1893. Swiss botanist, professor at the Academy of Geneva; son of Augustin Pyrame de Candolle, and father of Anne Casimir Pyrame de Candolle. He continued his father's *Prodromus systematis naturalis regni vegetabilis*, assisted by his son, and was the author of *Géographie botanique raisonnée* (1855), *Origine des plantes cultivées* (1883), and others.

Candolle, Anne Casimir Pyrame de. b. at Geneva, Switzerland, Feb. 26, 1836; d. 1925. Swiss botanist; son of Alphonse Louis Pierre Pyrame de Candolle. With his father, he continued the publication of *Prodromus systematis naturalis regni vegetabilis.*

Candolle, Augustin Pyrame de. b. at Geneva, Switzerland, Feb. 4, 1778; d. there, Sept. 9, 1841. Swiss botanist, professor at the Academy of Montpellier (1810), and at Geneva (1816–41), and the principal founder of the natural system of botany; father of Alphonse Louis Pierre Pyrame de Candolle. His works include *Théorie élémentaire de la botanique* (1813), *Regni vegetabilis systema naturale* (1818–21), *Prodromus systematis naturalis regni vegetabilis* (1824 *et seq.*), and others.

Candon (kän.dōn'). Town in Ilocos Sur province, on the NW coast of Luzon, Philippine Islands. 3,305 (1948).

Candour (kan'dor), **Mrs.** Slanderous woman with an affectation of frank amiability, in Richard Brinsley Sheridan's comedy *The School for Scandal.* Her name has since been used to describe any such person.

Candy (kan'di). See **Kandy.**

Canea (ka.nē'a). [Also: **Chania**; modern Greek, **Khania.**] *Nomos* (department) in S Greece, situated on the island of Crete, on and near the N coast. Capital, Canea; area, 921 sq. mi.; pop. 126,632 (1940).

Canea. [Also: **Chania**; modern Greek, **Khania**; ancient Greek, **Cydonia.**] City and seaport on the N coast of Crete, in S Greece, the capital of the *nomos* (department) of Canea and of Crete, situated on the Bay of Canea. It is a commercial center, and the seat of an Orthodox and a Catholic bishopric. It was taken by the Turks c1645 and occupied in World War II by the Germans in May, 1941. Pop. 28,865 (1940).

Cane Grande della Scala (kä'nā grän'dā del'lä skä'lä). See **Scala, Cane Grande della.**

Canelo (kä.nā'lō), **Tierra de.** See **Cinnamon, Land of.**

Canelones (kä.nā.lō'nās). Department in S Uruguay, on the Atlantic coast. Capital, Canelones; area, 1,835 sq. mi.; pop. 202,872 (est. 1947).

Canelones. [Also: **Guadelupe, Villa de Canelones.**] City in S Uruguay, capital of Canelones department. Cattle and cereals are raised in the area. Pop. under 5,000.

Cane Ridge Revival. Religious revival gathering (August, 1801) near the Cane Ridge Meeting House in Bourbon County, Kentucky. Some estimates place the attendance at this camp meeting at 25,000. The Cane Ridge episode was the high point of the religious awakening which swept over the (then) western regions of the U.S. during the period 1797–1805.

Cañete (kä.nyā'tā), Marquis of. Title of **Hurtado de Mendoza, Andrés**; and of **Hurtado de Mendoza, Garcia.**

Caneva (kä.nā'vä), **Carlo.** b. at Udine, Italy, April 22, 1845; d. at Rome, Sept. 25, 1922. Italian soldier. After service (1866) in Bohemia with the Austrian army, he transferred (1867) to the Italian forces where, with the rank of colonel, he took part (1896) in the Eritrean campaigns. Named a major general (1898), lieutenant general (1902), and deputy chief of staff (1904), he headed (1911) the Italian forces in the Tripolitan war. He was appointed (1912) to the senate, and took no military part in World War I. His leadership (1917) of the inquiry commission into the Caporetto defeat forced Cadorna's relinquishing of the command.

Caney (kā'ni). City in SE Kansas, in Montgomery County. It became a boom town with the opening of nearby oil fields in the 1890's; oil is still produced in the region. 2,876 (1950).

Caney (kä.nā'), **El.** See **El Caney.**

Canfield (kan'fēld), **Dorothy.** See **Fisher, Dorothy Canfield.**

Canfield, Richard Albert. b. June 17, 1855; d. Dec. 11, 1914. American gambler, for whom a game of solitaire is named. As a youth he acquired a passion for gambling while clerking in summer resort hotels. His first gaming house, at Providence, R.I., did a lucrative business for several years before the authorities closed it and sent Canfield to prison for a brief term. Upon his release he moved to New York, where he eventually set up, in the mid-1880's, his famous gambling establishment at 5 East 44th Street, next door to one of the city's most noted restaurants. In the 1890's Canfield extended his operations to Saratoga Springs, N.Y., and for a time he also had an establishment at Newport, R.I., which was then the leading summer resort of America's most wealthy people. In 1902 William Travers Jerome, district attorney of New York County, led a spectacular raid which smashed down the doors of the 44th Street establishment. The reluctance of witnesses to testify caused the prosecution to drag on for two years until, special legislation having been passed to compel testimony, Canfield, to save wealthy patrons from embarrassment, ceased to contest the state's action, and was let off with a fine of one thousand dollars. In 1907 his Saratoga establishment was closed by the authorities, and eventually he retired from his chosen field and became a solitary and successful operator on the stock market (and also the owner of lucrative glass and bottle manufacturing works). Canfield was a man of natural and cultivated good taste, especially in matters of ceramics, furniture, and paintings, and his collection of paintings and drawings by James McNeill Whistler was in its day perhaps the most notable of any in that artist's native land.

Canga Argüelles (käng′gä är.gwā′lyās), **José.** b. in Asturias, Spain, 1770: d. 1843. Spanish statesman and writer on finance. He was minister of finance in the period 1820–21.

Cangas (käng′gäs). Town and commune in NW Spain, in the province of Pontevedra, situated on the Bay of Vigo, ab. 15 mi. SW of Pontevedra. It is a fishing port, and has sardine canneries, clothing factories, and cattle markets. 15,836 (1940).

Cangas de Narcea (dā nạr.thā′ä). [Also, **Cangas de Tineo** (tē.nā′ō).] Town and commune in NW Spain, in the province of Oviedo, situated on the Narcea River, SW of Oviedo. A coal and lead mining town and a center of the local cattle trade, it also has cloth and leather manufactures. 21,296 (1940).

Cange (kähzh), Sieur **Du.** See **Du Cange** or **Ducange,** Sieur.

Cangiagio (kän.jä′jō). See **Cambiaso, Luca.**

Can Grande (kän grän′dā). See **Scala, Cane Grande della.**

Can Grande's Castle. Volume (1918) of verse by Amy Lowell.

Canicatti (kä.nē.kät′tē). Town and commune in S Italy, on the island of Sicily, in the province of Agrigento, situated on a hill above the Naro River, E of Agrigento. It is a large commune, the center of a grain, wine, and olive producing district, and has sulfur mines, and small industries of metallurgical and food products and building materials. Pop. of commune, 29,680 (1936); of town, 28,275 (1936).

Canidia (ką.nid′i.ą). fl. in the 2nd half of the 1st century B.C. Neapolitan hetaera, loved by Horace. She deserted him, and he reviled her as a sorceress. Her real name is said by some authorities to have been Gratidia.

Canidius (ką.nid′i.us). Lieutenant general to Antony in Shakespeare's *Antony and Cleopatra.*

Canigou (kä.nē.gö). Mountain in S France, in the department of Pyrénées-Orientales. 9,135 ft.

Canillas (kä.nē′lyäs). Town and commune in C Spain, in the province of Madrid, NE of Madrid, of which it is a suburb. 20,924 (1940).

Canina (kä.nē′nä), **Luigi.** b. at Casale, Piedmont, Italy, Oct. 23, 1795; d. at Florence, Oct. 17, 1856. Italian archaeologist and architect. He wrote *L'Architettura antica* (9 vols., 1834–44) and *Storia e topografia di Roma antica* (6 vols., 1839–48).

Caninefates (ką.nin.ę.fā′tēz). [Also, **Canninefates.**] German tribe, first mentioned by Tacitus, on the North Sea, to the north of the Rhine delta, closely related to the Batavi, their neighbors on the south. The Caninefates were subjugated to the Romans by Tiberius, but took part in the rising of Civilis. With the Batavi they were originally a part of the Chatti. They were ultimately merged with the Salic Franks.

Canino (kä.nē′nō), Prince of. Title of **Bonaparte, Lucien.**

Canino and Musignano (mö.sē.nyä′nō), Prince of. Title of **Bonaparte, Charles Lucien Jules Laurent.**

Canisius (ką.nish′ụs; German, kä.nē′zē.ůs), Saint **Petrus.** [Original name, **Pieter De Hondt.**] b. at Nijmegen, Netherlands, May 8, 1524; d. at Fribourg, Switzerland, Dec. 21, 1597. Jesuit missionary and scholar; first provincial of the order in Germany (1556). He was the author of a famous catechism, and was declared (1925) a Doctor of the Church.

Canis Major (kā′nis mā′jọr). The Great Dog, a constellation SE of Orion, and containing Sirius, the brightest star in the sky.

Canis Minor (mī′nọr). The Little Dog, a small ancient constellation following Orion and S of Gemini. It contains the star Procyon, of the first magnitude.

Canisteo (kan.is.tē′ō). Town (in New York the equivalent of township in many other states) and village in S New York, in Steuben County: residential community near Hornell. Pop. of town, 3,568 (1950); of village, 2,625 (1950).

Canitz (kä′nits), **Friedrich Rudolf Ludwig von.** b. at Berlin, Nov. 27, 1654; d. there, Aug. 11, 1699. Prussian poet and diplomat. He was the author of elegies, satires, and odes, principally in imitation of earlier poems in French and Latin.

Çankiri (chäng.ki.ri′). [Also: **Chankiri**; Turkish, **Çankırı.**] *Il* (province or vilayet) in N central Turkey, near the W end of the Pontus Mountains, a mountainous area where subsistence crops and herding are the chief occupations. Woolen goods and opium are exported. Capital, Çankiri; area, 3,345 sq. mi.; pop. 218,289 (1950).

Canlaon (kän.lä.ōn′). [Also, **Malaspina.**] Volcano in the NW part of Negros Oriental province, Negros, Philippine Islands. It is a picturesque mountain, always steaming. A notable eruption took place in 1902. Elevation, 8,087 ft.

Canmore (kan′mōr). See **Malcolm III** (of *Scotland*).

Canna (kan′ą). [Also, **Canna Island.**] Small island in the Inner Hebrides, N Scotland, in Inverness-shire, lying ab. 9 mi. SW of the Isle of Skye and ab. 4 mi. NW of Rum Island. Length, ab. 5 mi.; width, ab. 1 mi.

Cannabich (kän′ä.bich), **Christian.** b. at Mannheim, Germany, 1731; d. at Frankfort on the Main, Germany, 1798. German conductor and composer. He led the court orchestras at Mannheim (1775–78) and at Munich (1778 *et seq.*). His compositions include orchestral, chamber, and stage works.

Cannae (kan′ē). In ancient geography, a town in Apulia, Italy, situated S of the river Aufidus. Near here (and N of the river), Hannibal with a Carthaginian force of ab. 50,000 men virtually annihilated (216 B.C.) the Roman army of ab. 80,000–90,000 under Varro and Aemilius Paulus. It was one of the greatest military disasters ever suffered by the ancient Romans, and the site is still called locally the "Field of Blood" (Italian, *Campo di Sangue*). The Battle of Cannae remains even to this day of interest to military historians from the fact that it provides (with the earlier victory at Lake Trasimeno) clear evidence of Hannibal's military genius (his use of cavalry at Cannae is still studied by professional soldiers). Carthaginian fortunes were at their peak after Cannae, but lack of support from Carthage made it impossible for Hannibal to press his advantage and led finally to the defeat (201 B.C.) of Carthage by Rome in the Second Punic War.

Cannan (kan′ąn), **Gilbert.** b. at Manchester, England, June 25, 1884—. English novelist, playwright, and critic. Educated at the University of Manchester and at Cambridge University, he was admitted to the bar in 1908, but never practiced. He served as drama critic (1909–10) on the London *Star*, and was a founder of the Manchester Repertory Theatre. His novels include *Peter Homunculus* (1909), *Devious Ways* (1910), *Little Brother* (1912), *Round the Corner* (1913), *Old Mole* (1914), *Mendel* (1916), *The Stucco House* (1918), *Mummery* (1918), *Pugs and Peacocks* (1920), *Sembal* (1922), and *The House of Prophecy* (1924). Among his plays are *Miles Dixon* (1910), *James and John* (1911), *Mary's Wedding* (1912), *The Perfect Widow* (1912), *Everybody's Husband* (1917), and *The Release of the Soul* (1920).

Cannanore (kan′ą.nōr). [Also: **Cananore, Kananur**; erroneously, **Cranganore.**] Port on the Malabar coast, in Madras state, Union of India, ab. 50 mi. NW of Calicut: coastal trade in coffee, spices, and tea. It was early held by the Portuguese, and later by the Dutch (16th-18th centuries); acquired by the British in 1791. It is the traditional scene of the labors of Saint Thomas. 34,236 (1941).

Cannery Row. Novel (1945) by John Steinbeck. It is a whimsically sentimental story of the people who live in the shabby waterfront section of a fishing port and canning town in California. Like Steinbeck's later novel *The Wayward Bus* (1947), it carefully avoids the harsh and bitter (but essentially honest) tone of moral indignation which marked *The Grapes of Wrath* (1939), and is generally considered to have added little, if anything, to the novelist's reputation.

Cannes (kan, kanz; French, kån). Town in SE France, in the department of Alpes-Maritimes, situated on the Mediterranean coast, between St.-Raphaël and Antibes, ab. 18 mi. SW of Nice. It is one of the most fashionable winter resorts on the French Riviera. The Promenade de la Croissette, along the bay, is lined by hotels, casinos, and bathing establishments. Many villas and beautiful gardens are spread across the slopes of the surrounding hills. There are a bathing beach, various old churches, and many interesting points which attract excursionists. The town is known for its manufacture of candied fruits, perfumes, and soaps. It exports oils, anchovies, and fruits. The port handles import and export shipments. Napoleon landed near here upon coming from Elba, on March 1, 1815. Pop. 45,548 (1946).

Cannet (kå.ne), **Le.** See **Le Cannet.**

Caninefates (ką.nin.ę.fā'tēz). See **Caninefates.**

Canning (kan'ing), **Charles John.** [Title, Earl **Canning.**] b. at Brompton, near London, Dec. 14, 1812; d. at London, June 17, 1862. English statesman; son of George Canning. He was postmaster general of Great Britain (1853–55), governor general of India (1855–58), and first viceroy of India (1858–62). He was elected (1836) to a seat in the House of Commons, but succeeded (1837) to his mother's peerage and took his seat in the House of Lords as Viscount Canning; he was made an earl in 1859. In 1841 he was named undersecretary of state for foreign affairs in the government under Robert Peel, a position he relinquished in 1846. It was during his service as governor general of India that the Sepoy Rebellion broke out, and his expert and lenient (some Englishmen thought it too lenient) policy toward the Indian natives after the uprising had been put down brought him the nickname "Clemency" Canning. Nevertheless, he held the highest British office in India at what was unquestionably one of the most difficult periods of British control, and when the administration in India passed in 1858 from the British East India Company to the crown he was appointed first viceroy of this new addition to the empire of Queen Victoria. Although under his rule the British administration of India was made to run more smoothly, he was censured in some quarters for a proclamation declaring forfeit the lands of the province of Oudh, while rebellion was active there. He retired from office in 1862, while controversy over this action still continued.

Canning, Effie. Pseudonym of **Carlton, Effie.**

Canning, Elizabeth. b. 1734; d. 1773. English servant girl whose mysterious experiences aroused great public interest and controversy in 18th-century London. On Jan. 1, 1753, while she was in service at London, she vanished and was gone four weeks. When she returned, dirty, dishevelled, and weak from hunger, she told a story of being abducted and held in close confinement. A gypsy woman arrested on the charge of having been one of her abductors was identified by Elizabeth and sentenced to hang. However, the woman secured a second trial, and during its course, the Canning girl was accused of perjury, and was ordered into exile in America. Many persons believed her story, and her guilt or innocence was long a matter of lively debate.

Canning, George. b. at London, April 11, 1770; d. at Chiswick, near London, Aug. 8, 1827. English Liberal statesman and orator; father of Charles John Canning, and cousin of Stratford Canning. He first entered Parliament in 1793, and served during his subsequent political career as secretary for foreign affairs (1807–09, 1822–27), president of the board of control for India (1816–20), and prime minister (1827). He attended Eton and Christ Church, Oxford, where he formed a debating club (and managed to achieve some renown for opposition to the aristocracy). However, in spite of this, after having come to London in 1792 he formed a friendship with the younger William Pitt, with whom he shared a horror of the results of the French Revolution. He made his maiden speech in Parliament in 1794, and soon became known as a brilliant orator. Under the aegis of Pitt, he held (1793–1801) several government posts, including the undersecretaryship for foreign affairs (1791 *et seq.*), in which he took an active part in the peace negotiations (1797) at Lille, France; during this period he also contributed to the *Anti-Jacobin*, an antiradical weekly. After Pitt's retirement (1801), Canning went through a period (1801–09) of alternate opposition and support of the government; but took at all times a great interest in the maintenance of an aggressive military policy toward Napoleon I (he was a firm supporter of the joint Anglo-Spanish campaigns in Spain under the Duke of Wellington now usually called the Peninsular War, and had a chief part in planning the naval operation which resulted (1807) in the capture of the Danish fleet at Copenhagen). From 1809 to 1822, he was comparatively inactive in major political affairs (at least partly because he could not stomach what he considered to be the unjustified attack of most leading figures in the British government on Queen Caroline), but in 1822, with his second appointment as secretary for foreign affairs, he entered on the period of his greatest influence, becoming one of the foremost statesmen of his time. His foreign policy was one of nonintervention in the liberal movements of the Continent in those years. The waning of any British inclination to support the reactionary policies of the Holy Alliance (Russia, Austria, and Prussia), despite the fact that Great Britain, through the Quadruple Alliance of 1814, was committed to a considerable interest in European affairs, is usually said to have reached a decisive point in Canning's protest at the Congress of Verona (1822) against the sending of a French army to put down a Spanish revolution. This protest had an enormously important significance on the course of American history through the fact that it, plus the recognition by Great Britain of South American independence of Spain, made very clear indeed to the powers of Europe that Great Britain (and hence the British navy) would not take part in enabling Spain, or anyone else, to regain lost overseas colonies. Most historians now consider that it was this which actually made the Monroe Doctrine possible. He was also well known for his advocacy of greater political and social freedom for Roman Catholics in England.

Canning, Sir Samuel. b. at Ogbourne St. Andrew, Fifeshire, Scotland, July 21, 1823; d. at Kensington, London, Sept. 24, 1908. Scottish railway engineer, and a pioneer in the manufacture and submersion of submarine cable, remembered as the builder (1844–49) of the Great Western and the Liverpool, Ormskirk and Preston railways. He laid (1855–56) the first submarine cable between Cape Breton Island and Newfoundland. He served as assistant (1857) to Sir Charles Bright in the construction and laying of the first transatlantic cable, and afterward engaged (until 1865) in the laying of cables in the Mediterranean. He devised a special grappling machine for the recovery of broken cable in the Atlantic, and was knighted (1866) for this service. He also laid a cable between Brest, France, and Duxbury, Mass., in 1869.

Canning, Sir Stratford. [Title, 1st Viscount **Stratford de Redcliffe.**] b. at London, Nov. 4, 1786; d. Aug. 14, 1880. English diplomat; cousin of George Canning. He was educated at Eton and Cambridge, and entered the diplomatic service in 1807. He became first secretary at Constantinople in 1808, was minister plenipotentiary at Constantinople in the period 1810–12, negotiated the treaty of Bucharest, between Russia and Turkey, in 1812, was minister to Switzerland in the period 1814–18, and sat in the Congress of Vienna (1815). In 1820 he became minister to the U.S., and in 1824 was sent on a preliminary mission to St. Petersburg, where he remained until 1825. He was ambassador at Constantinople from 1842 to 1858, with some interruptions. He was raised to the peerage in 1852. His essays and a memoir were published in 1881.

Canning Dam. Dam in SW Western Australia, in the Canning River ab. 26 mi. SE of Perth. It was completed in 1940, and creates a reservoir ab. 6 mi. long, which supplies Perth with water. It is connected by a pipe line to the Mundaring Weir water system of Western Australia.

Cannizzaro (kän.nēt.tsä'rō), **Stanislao.** b. at Palermo, Italy, July 13, 1826; d. at Rome, May 9, 1910. Italian chemist and statesman. In 1858 he clarified and established the atomic weight concept and Avogadro's hypothesis, by clearly distinguishing between atomic and molecular weight, applying Avogadro's hypothesis correctly to associated gases, and insisting on the consistency of atomic weights determined through Avogadro's hypothesis, Dulong and Petits' specific heat law, or crystalline isomorphism. Moreover, he established the Cannizzaro reaction (1881), based on his discovery that aromatic aldehyde in an alcoholic base yields equal molecules of alcohol and acid. He was appointed a professor at Alexandria (1851), Geneva (1855), Palermo (1861), and Rome (1871). A Sicilian revolutionist, he had fled to France in 1849. After his return to Italy, he became (1871) a member of the senate, and later served as its vice-president. In 1891 he was awarded the Copley medal.

Cannobio (kän.nō'byō). [Also, **Canobbio.**] Town and commune in NW Italy, in the *compartimento* (region) of Piedmont, in the province of Novara, situated on the W shore of Lago Maggiore. It is a summer resort, and has silk, chemical, and food manufactures. The Church of the Pietà, in baroque style, dates from 1571. Buildings of interest to tourists were undamaged in World War II. Pop. of commune, 3,517 (1936); of town, 1,597 (1936).

Cannock (kan'ǫk). Urban district and coal-mining town in C England, in Staffordshire, situated in the center of the Cannock Chase coal field (part of the South Staffordshire field), ab. 8 mi. NW of Walsall, ab. 132 mi. NW of London by rail. The coal mined is especially good for domestic purposes. 40,927 (1951).

Cannon (kan'ǫn), **Annie Jump.** b. at Dover, Del., Dec. 11, 1863; d. April 13, 1941. American astronomer. Graduated (1884) from Wellesley, she did graduate work at Radcliffe. She was assistant curator (1897–1911) and curator (1911–38) of astronomical photographs, and William Cranch Bond astronomer and curator (1938 *et seq.*) at the Harvard College Observatory. Her contributions to astronomy consist of the photographic discovery of about 300 variable stars, five novae (new stars), and a spectroscopic binary; the cataloguing of almost 300,000 stellar spectra, published in ten quarto volumes; and a bibliography of approximately 200,000 references to variable stars. She was the author of *Maxima and Minima of Variable Stars of Long Period* (1909).

Cannon, Cornelia James. b. at St. Paul, Minn., Nov. 17, 1876—. American author of books for boys and girls; wife of Walter Bradford Cannon. Most of her stories have for their setting the life of the Pueblo Indians of the American Southwest, and, apart from the liveliness of the narrative, are notable for their faithful depiction of that life. Among her best-known books are *The Pueblo Boy* (1926), *Red Dust* (1928), *The Pueblo Girl Heirs* (1930), *Lazaro in the Pueblos* (1931), and *The Fight for the Pueblo* (1934).

Cannon, George Quayle. b. at Liverpool, England, Jan. 11, 1827; d. April 12, 1901. American Mormon leader and publisher. He was converted to Mormonism in 1840 and emigrated with his family to Nauvoo, Ill., where he learned the printing trade. He moved in 1847 to the Salt Lake valley, where he began his career as editor and publisher. He was sent on several missions, chief of which were a period (1850 *et seq.*) in Hawaii, where he made many converts, and four years (1860 *et seq.*) in England, where he edited the *Millennial Star*. He went in 1855 to California, where he edited and published (1856–58) the *Western Standard*. Returning (1858) to Utah at the request of Brigham Young, he had charge for a time of the *Deseret News* (with which he was again associated in 1867 and 1877) and later (1866) began publication of the *Juvenile Instructor*, an illustrated monthly for young people, which was one of his chief interests for most of his life. Elected to Congress in 1872, he served for ten years, but was forced to retire by the enactment of the Edmunds Law (1882) which made polygamy a punishable offense (and under which law he was imprisoned for a time in 1888).

Cannon, Harriet Starr. b. at Charleston, S.C., May 7, 1823; d. at Peekskill, N.Y., April 5, 1896. American religious worker, founder (1865) and mother superior (1865–96) of the Episcopal Sisterhood of Saint Mary. In 1856 she was a candidate for the Sisterhood of the Holy Communion; as a full member (1857 *et seq.*), she worked at Saint Luke's Hospital, until she withdrew from the order, and took charge (1863) of the House of Mercy.

Cannon, Henry White. b. at Delhi, N.Y., Sept. 27, 1850; d. April 27, 1934. American banker; brother of James Graham Cannon (1858-1916). He was founder (1871) and acting president (1871–84) of the Lumberman's National Bank at Stillwater, Minn., comptroller (1884–86) of U.S. currency, and president (1886–1904), chairman of the board (1904–11), and director (1911 *et seq.*) of the Chase National Bank at New York.

Cannon, James Graham. b. at Delhi, N.Y., July 26, 1858; d. July 5, 1916. American banker, notable as a pioneer in the development of the clearing-house system and of credit analysis; brother of Henry White Cannon (1850–1934). He was vice-president (1890–1910) and president (1910–14) of the Fourth National Bank, at New York. Author of *Clearing-houses, Their History, Methods and Administration* (1908).

Cannon, James, Jr. b. at Salisbury, Md., Nov. 13, 1864; d. Sept. 6, 1944. American Methodist Episcopal bishop. Graduated from Randolph Macon (B.A., 1884), Princeton Theological Seminary (B.D., 1888), and Princeton University (M.A., 1889), he was admitted in 1888 to the Virginia Conference of the Methodist Episcopal Church (of the South). He later served as president (1894–1918) of Blackstone College for Girls, and as editor (1904–18) of the *Christian Advocate*. Elected a bishop in 1918, he supervised (1918 *et seq.*) missions in Mexico, Cuba, Africa, and Brazil. In 1930, he was accused (and acquitted) of clerical misbehavior. A member of the Anti-Saloon League of America, he joined (1902) its executive committee, and became chairman of its national legislative committee (1914) and administrative committee (1927); in 1919 he became chairman of the executive committee of the World League Against Alcoholism, and was also on the executive committee of the National Temperance Council. A leader of the Southern Democrats who opposed the anti-prohibition platform of Alfred E. Smith's campaign, he was also chairman (1928) of the anti-Smith committee of Virginia.

Cannon, Joseph Gurney. b. at New Garden, N.C., May 7, 1836; d. Nov. 12, 1926. American politician, remembered for his iron rule of the procedure governing the House of Representatives while serving (1903–11) as its speaker. He attended the Cincinnati Law School, commencing (1858) his law practice at Shelbyville, Ill., and later shifting it to Danville. A Republican, he was (1861–68) state's attorney for the 27th judicial district of Illinois, and a member (1873–91) of Congress, where he established a reputation for coarse speech and the support of reactionary legislation. He was (1883–89) a minority member of the House Committee on Rules. He returned to Congress in 1893, serving until 1913. He was elected speaker in 1903; until 1910, when by House resolution the membership of the Committee on Rules was enlarged and the speaker excluded from it, he exercised virtually dictatorial control over House procedure. His high-handed tactics led to the coining of the term "Cannonism," and ill-feeling against him in Congress was so widespread that a motion was made (1910) to declare the speaker's seat vacant. The move failed, and Cannon held the speakership until March 3, 1911. He was defeated for reëlection in 1912, but was again a member of Congress from 1915 to 1923. He served 46 years in the House, longer than any other in U.S. history.

Cannon, Walter Bradford. b. at Prairie du Chien, Wis., Oct. 19, 1871; d. at Franklin, N.H., Oct. 1, 1945. American physiologist, known for work in neurology and endocrinology; husband of Cornelia James Cannon. He was graduated (B.A., 1896; M.D., 1900) from Harvard, where he was a teacher from 1899 to 1942, becoming a professor in 1906. While serving in the U.S. Army Medical Corps during World War I, he explained problems of traumatic shock and helped develop a method of storing blood for reinjection. In 1931 he discovered sympathin, an adrenalinlike hormone. His physiological researches include investigations of the movements of the stomach and intestines, the effects of emotions on bodily processes, and the functioning of the autonomic nervous system. He was the author of *A Laboratory Course in Physiology* (1910), *Traumatic Shock* (1923), *The Wisdom of the Body* (1932), and other works.

Cannon, William Austin. b. at Washington, Mich., 1870—. American botanist. He was graduated (Ph.D.,

1902) from Columbia University, was a member (1906–24) of the department of botanical research of the Carnegie Institution at Washington, D.C., and in 1926 became lecturer in botany at Stanford University. Among his works are *Studies in Heredity* . . . (1909), *Conditions of Parasitism in Plants* (1910), *Vegetation of South Africa* (1924), and *Physiological Features of Roots* (1925).

Cannonism. In U.S. history, a term used to describe the methods of Congressional control employed by Joseph Gurney Cannon during his service as speaker of the House of Representatives. Through his appointment of the house committees and his membership on the all-important rules committee, he and his followers managed to control the process of legislation even against majority opposition. As a member of the "Standpat" faction of the Republican Party, Cannon was identified with the most conservative interests in the country and was the target of the progressives because of his blocking of social legislation. The progressive Republicans joined forces with the Democrats in March, 1910, and passed the Norris Resolution amending the rules and disqualifying the speaker from membership on the rules committee. The office of speaker was thus reduced to that of presiding officer.

Cannonsburg (kan'ọnz.bėrg). A former name of **Murfreesboro,** Tenn.

Cannstatt (kän'shtät). [Also, **Canstadt.**] Town in S Germany, in the *Land* (state) of Württemberg-Baden, American Zone, situated on the Neckar River NE of Stuttgart: a suburb of Stuttgart; has numerous manufactures and warm mineral springs. Pop. ab. 34,000.

Cano (kä'nō), **Alonso.** b. at Granada, Spain, in March, 1601; d. there, 1667. Spanish architect, painter, and sculptor. Appointed court painter by Philip IV of Spain, he became canon of Granada, and chief architect of the cathedral there. Its façade is considered one of his masterpieces. In architecture, he employed some classical forms in baroque adaptations; his sculpture was realistic, and his paintings are distinguished by a fluency of line. Many of his works were acquired by collections in Spain.

Cano, Diego. Spanish name of **Cão, Diogo.**

Cano, Juan Sebastián del. b. at Guetaria, Guipúzcoa, Spain, c1460; d. at sea, Aug. 4, 1526. Spanish navigator. After commanding a ship in the Mediterranean, he was made (1519) captain of the *Concepción*, one of the ships in the fleet of Magellan. After the death of Magellan, and the deposition of the officer who immediately replaced him, Cano assumed command of the fleet. He reached the Moluccas, loaded his two remaining ships with spices, and finally in one of them (the *Victoria*) arrived (Sept. 6, 1522) at Spain by way of the Cape of Good Hope, being thus the actual commander, upon completion of the voyage, of the first vessel to circumnavigate the globe. He was second in command of a later expedition which was originally intended to follow the same course. Leaving Spain on July 24, 1525, the group encountered severe storms off the South American coast and in the Pacific; sickness appeared in the vessels, the commander perished, and Cano again took control, but died less than a week later.

Cano or **Canus** (kā'nus), **Melchior.** b. at Tarrançon, Spain, Jan. 1, 1509; d. at Toledo, Spain, Sept. 30, 1560. Spanish Dominican theologian, a bitter antagonist of the Jesuits, and an influential counselor of Philip II. He was professor at Alcalá de Henares and Salamanca, bishop of the Canary Islands, and provincial of Castile.

Canoas (kạ.nō'ạs). City in S Brazil, in the state of Rio Grande do Sul. 19,471 (1950).

Canobbio (kä.nôb'byō). See **Cannobio.**

Canobus (kạ.nō'bus). See **Canopus.**

Canoe and the Saddle, The. Collection of travel sketches by Theodore Winthrop, published in 1863.

Canoeiros (ku.nö.ā'rös). Collective term or appellative given by the early Portuguese settlers in Brazil to any one of numerous Indian tribes living along rivers or spending much time in their canoes.

Canogyza (kan.ọ.ji'zạ). Classical name of **Kanauj.**

Cañón (kä.nyōn'). Spanish word for "canyon": for place names containing this word which are not listed immediately below, see the specific element of the name.

Canon (kä'nōn), **Hans.** [Also, **Johann von Straschiripka.**] b. at Vienna, March 13, 1829; d. there, Sept. 12, 1885. Austrian genre, historical, and portrait painter, a pupil of Waldmüller. From 1848 to 1855 he was a cavalry officer in the Austrian army. From 1860 to 1869 he lived at Karlsruhe, then at Stuttgart, before he finally settled at Vienna where he became a professor at the Academy.

Canonbury Tower (kan'ọn.bẹr.i). Building at London, formerly the resort and lodging place of many literary men.

Canon City (kan'yọn). City in C Colorado, county seat of Fremont County, ab. 37 mi. NW of Pueblo, on the Arkansas River, just E of the Royal Gorge, and at an elevation of 5,350 ft. It is a tourist resort, noted for its fine climate and mineral springs; seat of the state penitentiary. Copper, silver, iron, coal, fire clay, marble, and limestone are found in the vicinity. 6,345 (1950).

Canongate (kan'ọn.gāt). Principal thoroughfare in the Old Town of Edinburgh. The little burgh of the Canongate grew around the abbey of Holyrood, which is about a mile E of the castle, in the 12th century, soon after the founding of the abbey. The street runs from that point, bearing different names at various parts of its course. Sir Walter Scott laid the scene of his *Chronicles of the Canongate* there.

Canonicus (kạ.non'i.kus), b. c1565; d. June 4, 1647. Chief of the Narragansett Indians who, alarmed by the alliance of the colonists at Plymouth with his enemy Massasoit, sent (January, 1622) Governor Bradford a hostile message consisting of a bundle of arrows wrapped in a rattlesnake's skin. He did not follow up the threat implied in this message when Bradford promptly returned the rattlesnake's skin stuffed with powder and ball. He later gave to Roger Williams the land on which Providence was founded in 1636, and acknowledged the sovereignty of Britain in a treaty concluded on April 19, 1644.

Canonsburg (kan'ọnz.bėrg). Borough in SW Pennsylvania, in Washington County near Pittsburgh: coal mining; manufactures of tin plate, metals, chemicals, and pottery products. Settled c1773, it was platted in 1787. Pop. 12,072 (1950).

Canon's Yeoman's Tale, The. One of Geoffrey Chaucer's *Canterbury Tales*. It exposes the tricks of the alchemists. Elias Ashmole, in a work entitled *Theatrum Chemicum*, quotes the whole poem, with the prologue, under the impression, apparently, that Chaucer was an adept in the art, and wrote in its favor. The canon of the tale is a ragged alchemist who has no gold but what he gets by trickery, and he and his hungry yeoman join the Canterbury pilgrims to practice their thieving arts upon them.

Canopic Mouth of the Nile (kạ.nō'pik). In ancient geography, a branch of the Nile River, NE Africa, the westernmost of the important mouths.

Canopus (kạ.nō'pus). [Also, **Canobus.**] In ancient geography, a seaport of Egypt, ab. 15 mi. NE of Alexandria, on the Canopic Mouth of the Nile. It had considerable trade and wealth.

Canopus. Second brightest star in the sky. It is one magnitude brighter than Arcturus, and only half a magnitude fainter than Sirius; α Argus or α Carinae. It is situated in one of the steering paddles of Argo Navis, about 35 degrees S of Sirius and about the same distance E of Achernar. It is yellow, and is conspicuous in Florida during the winter.

Canosa di Puglia (kä.nō'sä dē pö'lyä). [Also: **Canosa**; Latin, **Canusium.**] City and commune in SE Italy, in the *compartimento* (region) of Apulia, in the province of Bari, situated near the Otranto River, W of Bari. It is the center of a rich district producing grain, wine, olives, and dairy products. There are important Roman remains. The cathedral, in Romanesque style, was consecrated in 1101; the altar shows Byzantine and Arabic influences. An important commercial and military center in ancient times, the city served as refuge for the Roman army after its disastrous defeat at Cannae (216 B.C.). Much contested during the Middle Ages, it changed hands often, as did the entire region; it suffered frequently from earthquakes. Until the middle of the 19th century it was plagued by brigandage. Except for the Roman bridge, which was blown up, all the monuments were undamaged in World War II. Pop. of commune, 29,735 (1936); of city, 28,725 (1936).

Canossa (kä.nôs'sä; Anglicized, kạ.nos'ạ). Village and ruined castle SW of Reggio nell' Emilia, Italy. It is celebrated as the scene of the penance of the emperor

Henry IV before Pope Gregory VII, in January, 1077, to rescind the excommunication imposed by the Pope as a result of Henry's having made lay appointments to several sees. It is said that Henry stood for three days in the snow outside the castle where Gregory was the guest of Matilda of Tuscany, before the Pope would grant absolution.

Canova (kä.nō'vä), **Antonio.** b. at Possagno, near Treviso, Italy, Nov. 1, 1757; d. at Venice, Oct. 13, 1822. Italian sculptor, an important figure in the classical revival. At 17 he executed his *Orpheus and Eurydice*, which brought him commissions for the groups *Apollo and Daphne* and *Daedalus and Icarus*. In 1779 he obtained a pension from the municipality of Venice, and went to Rome. His first work of importance at Rome was *Theseus and the Minotaur*. For the remainder of his life he was established at Rome, although he made various journeys in Europe, and was three times at Paris—twice to execute commissions for Napoleon I and his family, and once, after the battle of Waterloo, on a mission from the Pope to recover the works of art taken from Italy by the emperor. At this time he was called to London to pronounce upon the artistic importance of the Elgin Marbles. He was very successful in his profession, and organized a system of reproducing his models mechanically, which enabled him to produce a vast amount of work. Among his most celebrated productions are the *Perseus* of the Belvedere (made to replace the *Apollo Belvedere* while the latter was being shown at Paris), the two boxers *Kreugas and Damoxenus* (also in the Belvedere), the *Venus* which stood on the pedestal of the *Medici Venus* when the latter was taken to Paris, the *Cupid and Psyche* of the Louvre, *Paris* of the Glyptothek at Munich, *Hercules and Lichas* (formerly at Venice, then transferred to a special building at Rome), and the great group of *Theseus and the Centaur* which was suggested by a metope of the Parthenon (placed in a specially designed temple at Vienna). At the end of his life Canova projected the temple of Possagno, in which he combined the characteristics of the Pantheon and Parthenon, and modeled some of the metopes.

Canovai (kä.nō.vä'ē), **Stanislao.** b. at Florence, March 27, 1740; d. there, Nov. 17, 1811. Italian ecclesiastic, mathematician, and historian, professor of mathematics at Parma.

Cánovas del Castillo (kä'nō.ƀäs del käs.tē'lyō), **Antonio.** b. at Málaga, Spain, in February, 1828; assassinated at Santa Agueda, near Vitoria, Spain, Aug. 8, 1897. Spanish Conservative statesman. He was several times premier under Alfonso XII, having been an advocate of the restoration of the Bourbons, and was the author of several books, including the historical novel *La Campaña de Huesca* (1854).

Canrobert (käṅ.ro.ber), **François Certain.** b. at St.-Céré, Lot, France, June 27, 1809; d. at Paris, Jan. 28, 1895. French soldier, a marshal of France (1855 *et seq.*). He participated (Dec. 2, 1851) in the coup d'état which led to Louis Napoleon's becoming (1852) emperor of France as Napoleon III. He commanded (1854–55) the French forces in the Crimea, served at Magenta and Solferino in 1859, commanded the 6th army corps in 1870, and was taken prisoner at Metz on Oct. 27, 1870. He became a senator in 1876.

Canseco (kän.sā'kō), **Alfredo Benavides y Díez.** See **Benavides y Díez Canseco, Alfredo.**

Canseco, Víctor Andrés Belaúnde y Díez. See **Belaúnde, Víctor Andrés.**

Canso (kan'sō), **Cape.** Headland at the E extremity of Nova Scotia, Canada.

Canso, Strait of. [Also, **Gut of Canso.**] Sea passage which separates the mainland of Nova Scotia from Cape Breton Island, Canada. Greatest width, ab. 2½ mi.

Canstadt (kän'shtät). See **Cannstatt.**

Can Such Things Be? Collection of 24 stories by Ambrose Bierce, published in 1893. Like the collection entitled *In the Midst of Life* (originally published in 1891 as *Tales of Soldiers and Civilians*), it reveals Bierce's technical skill in manipulation of suspense to produce a surprise ending to a story, and also to induce shock in the reader's mind.

Cantaber Oceanus (kan'tạ.bėr ọ.sē'ạ.nus). A Latin name of **Biscay, Bay of.**

Cantabria (kan.tā'bri.ạ). In ancient geography, a country in Hispania Tarraconensis, corresponding nearly to the modern Spanish provinces of Oviedo, Santander, Vizcaya, and Guipúzcoa. The name was restricted later to the W portion. The Cantabri resisted Rome until 19 B.C.

Cantabrian Mountains (kan.tā'bri.ạn). [Spanish, **Cordillera Cantábrica.**] Range of mountains in N Spain, extending from the Pyrenees W to Cape Finisterre. Highest peaks, over 8,000 ft.

Cantabricus (kan.tā'bri.kus), **Sinus.** A Latin name of **Biscay, Bay of.**

Cantabrigia (kan.tạ.brij'i.ạ). Latin name of **Cambridge,** England.

Cantacuzene (kan.tạ.kū.zēn'), Princess. [Maiden name, **Julia Dent Grant.**] b. at Washington, D.C., 1876—. American author; wife (1899 *et seq.*) of Prince Cantacuzene, a Russian major general. Her works include *Revolutionary Days* (1919), *The Russian People* (1920), and *My Life Here and There* (1921).

Cantacuzene or **Cantacuzenus** (-zē'nus), **Joannes** (or **John**) **VI** or **V.** See **John VI** or **V** (of the *Byzantine Empire*).

Cantagallo (kun.tạ.gä'lö). Town in SE Brazil, in the state of Rio de Janeiro: railroad terminus. Pop. under 5,000 (1940).

Cantal (käṅ.tál). Department in S central France, bounded by the department of Puy-de-Dôme on the N, the department of Haute-Loire on the E, the department of Lozère on the SE, the department of Aveyron on the S, and the departments of Corrèze and Lot on the W. It represents the main part of the former Haute-Auvergne. The department went to the French crown under Louis XIII. The surface is mountainous, the climate severe, the population sparse and declining. Livestock raising is more widespread than agriculture, and cheese production, mainly of the Cantal and blue types, is important. Coal, wolframite, and peat are found, and there are many sources of mineral waters which are used for medical purposes. Capital, Aurillac; area, 2,229 sq. mi.; pop. 186,843 (1946).

Cantal, Plomb du. Culminating summit of the mountains of Cantal, S central France, ab. 19 mi. NE of Aurillac. Elevation, ab. 6,090 ft.

Cantarini (kän.tä.rē'nē), **Simone.** [Also: **da Pesaro;** called **Il Pesarese.**] b. at Oropezza, near Pesaro, Italy, 1612; d. 1648. Italian painter and etcher; pupil of Guido Reni. His works include a portrait of Reni, acquired by the museum at Bologna, *Transfiguration*, in the Brera Gallery at Milan, and *Magdalene*, at Pesaro.

Cantelupe or **Cantilupe** (kan'ti.löp), **William de.** [Title, 1st Baron **Cantelupe.**] d. at Reading, England, 1239. English nobleman, counselor to King John of England and a signer of the Magna Charta. He served as sheriff of four counties. Justiciar (1203) on the death of John, whom he had supported through the interdict and civil war, he sided (1216 *et seq.*) with Henry III of England during his reign. He was justice itinerant in Bedfordshire (1218), custodian of Kenilworth Castle, and founder of Studley Hospital.

Cantemir (kän.ti.mēr'), **Antioch.** [Also: **Kantemir.**] b. at Constantinople, Sept. 21, 1709; d. April 11, 1744. Russian poet, diplomat, and author; son of Demetrius Cantemir. He is known for his satires and translations into Russian.

Cantemir, Demetrius. [Also, **Kantemir.**] b. Oct. 26, 1673; d. Aug. 23, 1723. Moldavian historian; father of Antioch Cantemir. Appointed (1711) *hospodar* (governor) of Moldavia by Turkey, he formed (1710) a treaty with Peter the Great of Russia, according to which Moldavia was declared independent of Turkey and placed under the protection of Russia. Driven from Moldavia, he received in compensation extensive domains in the Ukraine from Peter the Great. He wrote (in Latin) a history of the Ottoman Empire, which has not been printed in the original, but has been published in several translations, one of them entitled *Growth and Decline of the Ottoman Empire.*

Canterac (kän.tā.räk'), **José.** b. in France, c1775; d. at Madrid, 1835. General in the Spanish army. In 1815 he was sent (being then a brigadier general) with Pablo Morillo to America. He went to Peru in 1818, fought several campaigns with José de La Serna y Hinojosa in

Charcas, and led the military cabal which deposed the viceroy Joaquín de la Pezuela at Lima and put La Serna in his place (Jan. 29, 1821). In 1824 he opposed the march of Bolívar, was defeated in the cavalry engagement of Junín (Aug. 6), and in the final battle of Ayacucho (Dec. 9, 1824) commanded the reserve. He was shot while trying to suppress a mutiny at Madrid.

Canterbury (kan′tėr.ber.i, -bėr.i), Viscounts. See under **Manners-Sutton.**

Canterbury. [Middle English, also, **Cauntirbyry;** Old English, **Cantwaraburh;** Latin, **Durovernum.**] City and county borough in SE England, in Kent, situated on the river Stour ab. 60 mi. SE of London by rail: principal archiepiscopal see of the Church of England. Part of Canterbury's importance is due to its position in the water gap of the river Stour through the North Downs. Canterbury is located on the edge of the East Kent coal field. It has little industry, but has a good commerce in malt, hops, and grain. Flowers and vegetables for the London market are grown in the neighborhood. During World War II, considerable numbers of military personnel were billeted in the city and vicinity. Canterbury's buildings of interest are the cathedral (where Thomas à Becket was murdered in 1170), Saint Martin's Church, Saint Dunstan's Church, remains of the castle, the monastery of Saint Augustine, and many old houses. Air-raid damage during World War II revealed some fine examples of Roman mosaic pavements. Canterbury is one of the oldest cities in the country; it is on the site of a British village, and was a Roman military station and a Kentish town. Augustine became the first archbishop here in 600.It was sacked by the Danes in 1011. 27,778 (1951).

Canterbury Churches. The cathedral was founded in the 11th century. The existing choir was built by William of Sens (France) after 1174, and the Perpendicular nave, transepts, and great central tower date from the 15th century. In plan the cathedral is long and narrow, with double transepts. The interior is light and impressive. The choir is raised several feet, and separated from the nave by a sculptured 15th-century screen. The columns, arcades, vaulting, and chevet are very similar in character to those of the cathedral of Sens, which supplied the model. Some of the glass of the deambulatory is of the 13th century. The portion of the choir behind the altar contains several fine altar-tombs of early archbishops, and the tombs of Henry IV and the Black Prince. At the extreme E end is a beautiful circular chapel called the Corona. The crypt is very large, and early Norman in style. The Perpendicular cloisters are ornate and picturesque. The dimensions of the cathedral are 514 by 71 ft.; the height of the nave-vaulting 80 ft., and of the central tower 235 ft. Saint Martin's is called the "Mother Church of England." The original foundation was no doubt pre-Saxon, and there are Roman bricks in the lower parts of the walls. The upper parts of the long, low, quaint, ivy-clad structure are much later.

Canterbury. Provincial district on the E side of South Island, New Zealand. It stretches along the coast behind the Canterbury Bight and is the center of the sheep-raising industry in the dominion. Chief town, Christchurch; area, 13,940 sq. mi.; pop. 280,024 (1951).

Canterbury Bight. Embayment of the Pacific Ocean, on the E coast of South Island, New Zealand. It is bounded on the N by the Banks Peninsula, and on the W by the plains of the Canterbury district, famous for sheep raising.

Canterbury Cathedral. See under **Canterbury,** England.

Canterbury College. Former college of Oxford University, England. It was founded by Simon Islip, archbishop of Canterbury, in 1361 or 1362. John Wycliffe was its second warden. It was disbanded in the reign of Henry VII, and the last remains of its buildings were demolished in 1775.

Canterbury Pilgrims, The. Opera by Charles Villiers Stanford, with a libretto by Gilbert à Becket, first performed at London, at the Drury Lane Theatre, in 1884.

Canterbury Pilgrims, The. Play (1903) by Percy MacKaye. A Chaucerian revival, it is a skillful adaptation of an old literary theme to modern dramatic presentation.

Canterbury Pilgrims, The. Opera by Reginald de Koven, with a libretto by Percy MacKaye, first performed at the New York Metropolitan Opera House on March 18, 1917.

Canterbury Tales, The. Work by Geoffrey Chaucer. At the Tabard Inn, Southwark, Chaucer joins some 29 pilgrims bound for the shrine of Saint Thomas à Becket at Canterbury. The Prologue describes the vividly individualized pilgrims, ranging from an eminent jurist and a worthy knight to a plowman and a dishonest miller. The Host of the Tabard, Harry Bailey, suggests that on the journey each pilgrim tell four stories, the best to be rewarded by a supper on their return. Chaucer did not live to complete the projected series of 120 tales (outdoing Boccaccio's *Decameron* by a score); most of the 22 tales are in heroic couplets, a few in stanzas, and two in prose. First the Knight recounts a romance of fighting, love, and pageantry, condensed from Boccaccio's *Il Teseida.* The Host next calls upon the Monk, but Robin the Miller, already drunk, insists on his turn. With brilliant characterization he vitalizes a clever fabliau plot of an old uxorious carpenter deceived by an Oxford undergraduate who in turn is tricked by a parish clerk. Osewold, the "sclendre colerik" Reeve, formerly a carpenter, takes personal offense and retaliates with a fabliau of a thieving miller deceived by two Cambridge students. Then Roger of Ware, the uncleanly London Cook, starts a story of low London life (unfinished). The Man of Law retells the tale of the long-suffering Constance from the Anglo-Norman *Chronicle* of Nicholas Trivet. After the Shipman's fabliau comes the Prioress's miracle of a boy's devotion to the Virgin Mary; then Chaucer attempts the doggerel rime of Sir Thopas, a romance so "drasty" that the Host makes him stop. Chaucer tries again with the long prose allegory of Melibeus and his wife Prudence, a humanitarian document against the evils of war and the perversion of justice, originally by Albertano of Brescia. The Monk is not allowed to finish his "tragedies" of the falls of the great; the Nun's Priest satirically retells the barnyard beast-epic of Chauntecleer and Pertelote. Alice of Bath, looking for a sixth husband, defends her marriages, tells how she has handled her husbands, and recounts the folk tale of an old hag who becomes a beautiful maiden when her husband promises obedience. After Friar Huberd and the Summoner have chastised each other with fabliaux, the Clerk of Oxenford retells Petrarch's story of patient Griselda, who submits to her husband's every whim. The disillusioned Merchant, two months wed, bitterly tells of old January deceived by his young wife May; then the gay Squire starts an Eastern romance (unfinished). The country gentleman, the Franklin, tells of a perfect marriage based on truth and generosity. The Physician retells the old Roman "geste" of Appius and Virginia. The Pardoner shows how he wins money by preaching on "the root of all evil" and by telling his impressive exemplum of how avarice brought death to three revellers. After the second Nun's legend of the martyred Saint Cecilia, the Canon's Yeoman exposes his master's alchemical deceptions; the Manciple retells Ovid's story of Phoebus and the Crow; and as the company nears Canterbury, the Parson gives his prose sermon on Penance and the Seven Deadly Sins. The 83 complete or fragmentary manuscripts of *The Canterbury Tales* have been critically edited by John M. Manly and Edith Rickert, *The Text of the Canterbury Tales* (8 vols., 1940). The text in **F. N. Robinson's** edition of Chaucer's complete works is based on one of the best manuscripts, the Ellesmere, which is in the Huntington Library at San Marino, Calif.

Cantia (kan′shạ, -shi.ạ) or **Cantium** (kan′shum, -shi.um). Latin name of **Kent,** England.

Canticles (kan′ti.klz). See **Song of Solomon.**

Cantigny (käṅ.tē.nyē; Anglicized, kan.tēn′yē), **Battle of.** World War I military engagement involving troops of the U.S. 1st Division, aided by French tanks, who assaulted and captured the German-held town of Cantigny, France, on May 28, 1918. It was the first occasion during the war on which American forces seized enemy-occupied territory under fire. The action demonstrated the combat qualities of the American Expeditionary Forces and had a considerable influence in the subsequent decision to establish a separate (First American) army under the direct command of General John J. Pershing.

Cantigny War Monument. American World War I monument standing in a public square in the town of Cantigny, ab. 54 mi. S of Paris and 25 mi. N of Amiens. It was erected to commemorate the assault made by the 1st Division which resulted in the American capture of the town on May 28, 1918. It was the first attack made by an American division in World War I.

Cantii (kan'shi.ī). A Celtic people, a branch of the Belgae, which inhabited the whole SE coast region of Britain between the river Thames and the English Channel, where they are located by Caesar.

Cantillon (kän.tē.yôṅ), **Pierre Joseph.** b. at Wavre, Belgium, 1788; d. at Brussels, July 13, 1869. Belgian soldier, who served in the French army under Napoleon I. He was tried and acquitted for an attempt on the life of Arthur Wellesley, 1st Duke of Wellington, in 1815.

Cantilo (kän.tē'lō), **José María.** b. at Buenos Aires, Aug. 23, 1877—. Argentine diplomat and writer, onetime Argentine minister (1938–40) for foreign affairs and worship. His written works include *Les Jardins de France*, *Los Desorbitados*, and *La Ganga*.

Cantilupe (kan'ti.löp), **William de.** See **Cantelupe** or **Cantilupe, William de.**

Cantinflas (kän.tēn'fläs). [Original name, **Mario Moreno.**] b. 1911—. Mexican motion picture actor, often called "Mexico's Charlie Chaplin." An idol of the patrons of motion pictures throughout the Spanish-speaking world, he is considered, by those acquainted with his work, a most talented artist and one of the world's great clowns.

Cantire or **Cantyre** (kan.tīr'). See **Kintyre.**

Cantium (kan'shum, -shi.um). In ancient geography, a part of Britain corresponding to the modern Kent.

Canton (kan.ton'). See also **Canton River.**

Canton. [Chinese, **Kwangchow, Kwang-chowfu, Shengcheng.**] Seaport in SE China, the capital of the province of Kwangtung, on the Canton (or Pearl) River: one of the principal commercial cities of the country; its leading exports include tea, silk, and sugar. It contains a large population in river craft. Its trade with Portugal began as early as 1517. It was sacked by the Tartars c1650. An English factory was built in 1680. Canton was one of the five treaty ports in 1842. In 1857 it was captured by the Anglo-French forces and held until 1861; it was a center of revolutionary activity in 1911. Pop. 960,712 (est. 1947).

Canton (kan'tọn). Town in N Connecticut, in Hartford County, NW of Hartford: at one time called Suffrage because of the hardships endured (1740) by early settlers. 3,613 (1950).

Canton. Town in NW Georgia, county seat of Cherokee County: cotton-textile mills. 2,716 (1950).

Canton. City in C Illinois, in Fulton County, ab. 86 mi. NE of Quincy: coal-mining center; manufactures agricultural implements. 11,927 (1950).

Canton. Town (in Massachusetts the equivalent of township in many other states) and unincorporated village in SE Massachusetts, in Norfolk County, SW of Boston: manufactures include rubber goods and textiles. Pop. of town, 7,465 (1950); of village, 4,739 (1950).

Canton. City in C Mississippi, county seat of Madison County, between the Big Black and Pearl rivers: formerly a plantation town; now an agricultural trade center. 7,048 (1950).

Canton. Town (in New York the equivalent of township in many other states) and village in N New York, county seat of St. Lawrence County: seat of St. Lawrence University, and the birthplace of Frederic Remington. Pop. of town, 7,652 (1950); of village, 4,379 (1950).

Canton. Town in W North Carolina, in Haywood County: manufactures pulp and paper. 4,906 (1950).

Canton. City in E Ohio, county seat of Stark County, on Nimishillen Creek ab. 50 mi. SE of Cleveland: notable as a processing center for alloy steel and for the manufacture of steel and aluminum products; home and burial place of William McKinley. It became county seat in 1809, and was incorporated as a town in 1822. Pop. 116,912 (1950).

Canton. City in SE South Dakota, county seat of Lincoln County, in an agricultural area. Its name was derived from the belief of early residents that the city was directly opposite Canton, China. 2,530 (1950).

Canton. Former name of **Bridgeport,** Ohio.

Canton, John. b. at Stroud, Gloucestershire, England, July 31, 1718; d. March 22, 1772. English physicist, noted for investigations in regard to electricity. He verified Benjamin Franklin's discovery of the identity of lightning and electricity, and produced a phosphorescent chemical that came to be known as Canton's phosphorus.

Canton, William. b. on Chu Shan island, in the East China Sea, Oct. 27, 1845; d. at Hendon, Middlesex, England, May 2, 1926. English poet, teacher, journalist, and historian. He was engaged in teaching and journalistic work at London (1867–76) and at Glasgow (1876–91). Among his books are *Through the Ages—the Legend of a Stone Axe* (1873), *A Lost Epic and Other Poems* (1887), *The Invisible Playmate* (1894), *W. V. Her Book* (1896), *A Child's Book of Saints* (1898), *In Memory of W. V.* (1901), and *The Story of Saint Elizabeth of Hungary* (1912). Some of his best-known short poems are *The Comrades*, *L'Alouette*, *The Lost Brother*, *The Story of the Rheinfrid* and *The Ancient Gods Pursuing*. His most ambitious work is *History of the British and Foreign Bible Society* (5 vols., 1903–10), an authority in its field.

Canton and Enderbury (en'dėr.ber.i, -bėr.i). Anglo-American condominium, comprising two islands of the Phoenix group, N of Samoa in the mid-Pacific. Until the days of the airplane the islands were of little value to Great Britain, which claimed them. With the development of the trans-Pacific air routes, the islands became of strategic value as stopping bases. In 1938 both the U.S. and Great Britain claimed the islands and settled them to substantiate their claims. On Aug. 10, 1938 it was agreed that for the next 50 years the islands were to be placed under joint American and British control. Pan-American Airways has an airport on Canton. Canton (also called Mary, or Swallow, Island): length, 8 mi.; width, 4 mi.; pop. 40 (1940); Enderbury: length, 3 mi.; width, ¾ mi.; pop. 4 (1940).

Cantoni (kän.tō'nē), **Carlo.** b. at Groppello Cairoli, Italy, in November, 1840; d. at Pavia, Italy, Sept. 11, 1906. Italian philosopher. He served (1878 *et seq.*) as a professor at the University of Pavia, and was the author of *Emanuele Kant* (1879–84) and *Corso elementare di filosofia* (1896).

Canton River (kan.ton'). [Also: **Pearl River;** Chinese, **Chu-Kiang.**] Name given to the lower part of the river Peh-Kiang, in S China, in the province of Kwangtung. Ab. 40 mi. below Canton it becomes the estuary Boca Tigris.

Canton Uprising. [Also, **Canton Commune.**] Communist-led uprising at Canton, China, on Dec. 11, 1927, against the Kuomintang, which at Chiang Kai-shek's direction had abandoned the policy of collaboration with Communists. The city was retaken on Dec. 13 by General Li Fu-lin, who carried out bloody reprisals against the insurrectionists.

Cantor (kan'tọr), **Eddie.** b. at New York, Jan. 31, 1893—. American comedian. He began his career in a Gus Edwards show, and has appeared in vaudeville, burlesque, musical comedies, motion pictures, and on television and the radio. He starred in such musical comedies as *Kid Boots* (1923–26) and *Whoopee* (1929–30), appeared in films after 1926, including *Kid Boots*, *Palmy Days*, *The Kid from Spain*, *The Thief of Bagdad*, and *Roman Scandals*, and starred on the radio after 1931, and on television after 1948.

Cantor (kän'tôr), **Georg (Ferdinand Louis Philippe).** b. at St. Petersburg, March 3, 1845; d. at Halle, Germany, Jan. 6, 1918. German mathematician, founder of *Mengenlehre*, the theory of infinite ensembles. He and J. W. R. Dedekind were among the first to give satisfactory definitions of real numbers, and the assumption of a one-to-one correspondence between these numbers and the points on a line is therefore known as the "Cantor-Dedekind axiom." He studied at Zurich, Göttingen, and Berlin, and taught at the University of Halle from 1869 until his death. His introduction into mathematics of a completed infinite involved him in bitter controversy, but his views are now generally accepted. His correspondence with Dedekind was published in 1937, and his *Gesammelte Abhandlungen mathematischen und philosophischen Inhalts* appeared in 1932.

Cantor, Moritz Benedikt. b. at Mannheim, Germany, Aug. 23, 1829; d. at Heidelberg, Germany, April 10, 1920. German mathematician and historian. He studied at Mannheim, Heidelberg, and Göttingen, and taught at Heidelberg. In 1860 he became interested in the history of mathematics, and ultimately was recognized as an outstanding authority in this field. He edited, and contributed numerous articles to journals and collections on the history of mathematics. His most important work was the *Vorlesungen über Geschichte der Mathematik* (4 vols., 1880–1904), a book which remained into the second half of the 20th century the foremost treatise on the subject.

Cantos. Collection of poetry (still unfinished) by Ezra Pound. It is generally conceded to represent that poet's most ambitious work (and is, in fact, in its scope one of the most ambitious works in the history of world literature. Pound's design was to equal or surpass in number the cantos of Dante's *Divine Comedy*.) The *Cantos* were begun in 1919, continued after Pound's arrival (1924) in Italy, and were thereafter published in sections as these were completed. By 1948 he had completed 84 of the *Cantos*. Opinions as to the quality of the poetry have varied, but it was (and is) generally agreed that it became more and more arcane as Pound continued to work on it. Moreover, any truly objective judgment as to the quality of Pound's work became increasingly difficult to obtain by reason of his outspoken support of Mussolini and of the Italian cause during World War II. (He was tried for treason, as a U.S. citizen, in 1946, and was adjudged insane.) On Feb. 19, 1949, he was given the Library of Congress's Bollingen Prize (considered by many the leading award for poetry in the U.S.) for the section of ten published as *Pisan Cantos*, which had been written in an Italian jail. The fitness of Pound's work for this award was immediately and vociferously disputed by many reputable critics, and there was also a considerable expression of dismay from elements of the general public (although much of this unquestionably stemmed primarily from a reaction against Pound's politics rather than his poetry; indeed, few Americans not deeply interested in poetry have ever read any considerable part of the *Cantos*). The successive installments of the *Cantos* reveal a general theme of the decay of civilization; this theme, and Pound's disjunctive method of dealing with it, greatly influenced T. S. Eliot's *The Waste Land* (1922) and, to some extent, Hart Crane's *The Bridge* (1930).

Cantù (kän.tö'). Town and commune in NW Italy, in the *compartimento* (region) of Lombardy, in the province of Como, between Milan and Como. The surrounding area is rich in mulberry trees; there are furniture and textile manufactures. It has interesting Lombardic architectural monuments, particularly in the nearby village of Galliano. The Romanesque basilica of San Vincenzo dates from 1007. Pop. of commune, 18,517 (1936); of town, 11,295 (1936).

Cantù, Cesare. b. at Brivio, Italy, Dec. 5, 1804; d. at Milan, Italy, March 11, 1895. Italian historian, novelist, and poet. His works include *Margherita Pusterla* (1838; a historical romance), *Storia universale* (35 vols., 1838–46), and *Storia degli Italiani* (1854).

Cantwell (kant'wel), **Dr.** Hypocrite in Isaac Bickerstaff's play *The Hypocrite*.

Cantwell, Robert (Emmett). b. at Little Falls (now Vader), Wash., Jan. 31, 1908—. American writer. He joined *Time* magazine as a staff member in 1935 and became an associate editor in 1938. His books include the proletarian novels *Laugh and Lie Down* (1931) and *The Land of Plenty* (1934), and the biography *Nathaniel Hawthorne: The American Years* (1948).

Canus (kā'nus), **Melchior.** See **Cano, Melchior.**

Canusium (ka̤.nū'zi.um). Latin name of **Canosa di Puglia.**

Canute (ka̤.nūt'). [Also: **Cnut, Knut;** called **"Canute the Great."**] b. c994; d. at Shaftesbury, England, Nov. 12, 1035. King of England, Denmark, and Norway; younger son of Sweyn, king of Denmark. He was baptized before 1013, receiving the baptismal name of Lambert. In 1013 he was with his father in the invasion of England, succeeding him in February, 1014 (by election of the Danish peers) as king of England, his brother Harold ascending the Danish throne. Defeated by Ethelred the Unready, who was recalled from Normandy by the English *witan* or national council, he returned to Denmark in the same year. In 1015 he again invaded England with a large force; he besieged (May, 1016) London, and defeated the English under Edmund Ironside (who had succeeded his father Ethelred) at Assandun. At a conference held on the isle of Olney in the river Severn, he divided the kingdom with Edmund, retaining the northern part of the kingdom and leaving Wessex to Edmund. After Edmund's death, he was chosen (1017) sole king of England. Putting aside his first wife, Aelfgifu, he married Emma, the widow of Ethelred, who bore him Harthacanute. He visited (1019–20) Denmark, made (1026–27) a pilgrimage to Rome, and conquered (1028) Norway. His early career was marked by great barbarity, but after the conquest of England was completed his reign was that of a statesman and patriot, and he became one of the wisest as well as mightiest rulers of his age.

Canute II (of *Denmark*). See **Hardicanute.**

Canute the Saint. [Also: **Cnut, Knut.**] d. in July, 1086. King and patron saint of Denmark. The third of 13 natural sons of Sweyn II, he was elected king of Denmark in 1080 upon the death of his brother Harold. A stern, resolute, and pious man, he waged war to Christianize the pagans of Courland and Livonia, built churches, invested bishops with princely rank, and suppressed heathen customs among the Danes. In 1085, while preparing to invade England as an ally of the Saxons in a rebellion against William the Conqueror, he was confronted by a revolt among some of his own subjects, arising partly from resentment against the methods of some of his tax collectors, and partly from dissatisfaction with his attack upon ancient ways. With one of his brothers and a small company of faithful followers he was surrounded by his enemies and slain in July, 1086. He was canonized in 1100, and during the Middle Ages became the patron saint of Denmark, his feast being celebrated on Jan. 19.

Canvey Island (kan'vi). Urban district in SE England, in Essex, situated on the river Thames, which encircles it. Access is by bridge from Benfleet. It is the nearest seaside resort to London. Canvey suffered severely in the 1953 North Sea floods. 11,255 (1951).

Canyon (kan'yo̤n). City in NW Texas, county seat of Randall County, in the Panhandle S of Amarillo: cattle markets; seat of West Texas State Teachers College. 4,364 (1950).

Canyon de Chelly National Monument (de̤ shā). See under **Chelly.**

Can You Forgive Her? Novel (1864) by Anthony Trollope.

Cão (kouṅ), **Diogo.** [Also: **Cam;** Spanish, **Diego Cano.**] fl. in the last part of the 15th century. Portuguese navigator. He explored (1482–84) the West African coast to the Congo River and beyond.

Cao-Daism (kou.dī'iz.e̤m). [Also, **Caodaism.**] Religious and ethical movement in Indochina which originated in 1919 on the small Annamese island of Phu-Quoc. With one of the most ancient mystic symbols (the eye surrounded by solar rays) as its emblem, it is a cult based on Buddhism with large accretions of Taoist and Christian (Catholic) beliefs and Confucian moral teachings. Although it makes use of the traditional modes of divination and worship and thus primarily appeals to simple folk, the movement also represents a serious attempt to reconcile Eastern and Western concepts and on the religious side expresses the nationalist trend among intellectuals. Under the leadership of an Annamese official, Le-Van-Trung, the movement was organized in 1926 and in 20 years is estimated to have grown from a few thousand to between one million and three million adherents, mostly in Cochin-China (South Viet-Nam). Even before it attained this size, the movement was proscribed by the colonial authorities as subversive. Upon the partial reoccupation of Indochina, the French government vigorously suppressed it in the area under its control. One of its "popes," Phan Oong Tac, was exiled to Madagascar in 1943 for collaboration with the Japanese but, on returning in 1947, proved pro-French and for a time served as governor of Saigon. With the cessation of war between the French and the native republican forces, the cult came to be recognized on both sides as a possible element of reconciliation. Its present headquarters are near Saigon.

Caonabo (kä.ō.nä.bō'). d. at sea, 1496. Carib cacique of Maguana, Hispaniola, who in 1493 massacred the Spaniards who had been left by Columbus at Fort Navidad; husband of Anacáona. In 1494 he headed the general league against the whites, which was opposed by Columbus at the battle of the Vega Real (April 25, 1495). He was captured and sent to Spain, but died on the voyage.

Caora (kä'ō.rä). River described by old travelers (as reported by Hakluyt), near which lived a people whose heads grew in their breasts below their shoulders.

Caorle (kä.ôr'lā). Town and commune in NE Italy, in the *compartimento* (region) of Veneto, in the province of Venezia, situated at the mouth of the Livenza River on the Adriatic Sea, between Venice and Trieste. It is a large agricultural commune; formerly isolated among lagoons and swamps, it is now surrounded by reclaimed land. The cathedral, in basilica style, dates from the 11th century. Pop. of commune, 10,077 (1936); of town, 2,100 (1936).

Cap (kȧp). French word for "cape": for place names containing this word which are not listed immediately below, see the specific element of the name.

Cap, Le. See **Cap-Haïtien.**

Capability Brown. Nickname given to Lancelot Brown, an English landscape-gardener (1715–73).

Capablanca (kä.pä.bläng'kä), **José Raoul.** [Full surname, **Capablanca y Granperra** (kä.pä.bläng'kä ē gräm.per'rä).] b. at Havana, Cuba, Nov. 19, 1888; d. at New York, March 7, 1942. Cuban chess master and world chess champion (1921–27). A child prodigy who learned to play chess at the age of four, he became the most eminently successful tournament player of his time, his extremely small percentage of losses in actual play earning him the sobriquet of "the chess machine." His principal international tournament successes were first prizes at San Sebastián, Spain (1911), London (1922), New York (1927), and Budapest (1929), and equal first at Nottingham (1936). In 1921 his defeat of Emanuel Lasker made him world champion; in 1927 he lost the title to Alekhine.

Capac-Urcu (kä'päk.ör'kö). See **Altar.**

Capac (or **Ccapac**) **Yupanqui** (yö.pän'kē). fl. in the second quarter of the 14th century. Fifth, or sixth, war chief of the Inca line of Peru.

Capanaparo (kä''pä.nä.pä'rō). River in W Venezuela flowing E to the Orinoco River.

Capannori (kä.pän'nō.rē). Commune in C Italy, in the *compartimento* (region) of Tuscany, in the province of Lucca, situated between Lucca and Montecatini, E of Lucca. It is a large agricultural commune. 41,033 (1936).

Capart (kȧ.pȧr), **Jean François.** b. at Brussels, 1877; d. 1947. Belgian Egyptologist. Graduated (LL.D., 1898) from the University of Brussels, he lectured at Liége in 1903, and became (1911) a curator of the Royal Museum of Art and History, and chief curator in 1923. Appointed (1923) director of the Queen Elizabeth Egyptology Foundation, he was also professor of the history of art and archaeology at the University of Brussels, and honorary professor (1928) at Liége. In the period 1924–25, and in 1931, he lectured on Egyptian art in the U.S. He was a member of the Royal Academy of Belgium, a corresponding fellow of the British Academy, and a corresponding member of the French Institute; author of many articles in French, German, and English scholarly journals.

Capa y Espada (kä'pä ē es.pä'ᴛʜä), **Comedias de.** [Eng. trans., *"Comedies of Cloak and Sword."*] Class of plays written by Calderón de la Barca and Lope de Vega. They were so called from the national dress of the chief personages, which was that of the upper class of Spanish society, excluding royal personages and the humbler classes.

Cap d'Antibes (kȧp dän.tēb). See under **Antibes.**

Cap de la Madeleine (dę lȧ mȧd.len). City in Quebec, Canada, situated at the E side of the mouth of the St. Maurice River, on the St. Lawrence River, ab. 79 mi. W of the city of Quebec. 18,667 (1951).

Capdenac-Gare (kȧp.dę.nȧk.gȧr). [Also, **Capdenac.**] Town in S France, in the department of Aveyron, situated on the Lot River, NW of Rodez. The upper town has remnants of medieval ramparts. It was an important place in the Middle Ages, and possibly the Roman Uxellodunum. 5,417 (1946).

Capdevila (käp.ᴛʜä.vē'lä), **Arturo.** b. at Córdoba, Argentina, March 14, 1889—. Argentine professor and former judge, whose writings include history, poetry, drama, and stories. Three times a winner of the national literary prize, he is the author of *La Fiesta del mundo* (1922), *Zinzali* (1927), *Del infinito amor* (1928), *Babel y el castellano* (1928), *Simbad* (1930), and *Cuando el vals y los lanceros* (1938).

Cape, the. Nickname of the Cape of Good Hope; also of Cape of Good Hope province, Union of South Africa, of Cape Cod, and others.

Cape Armitage Promontory (är'mi.tāj). See **Hut Point Peninsula.**

Cape Barren Island (bar'ęn). See under **Furneaux Islands.**

Cape Breton Highlands National Park (brit'ǫn, bret'ǫn). Section of the N part of Cape Breton Island, Nova Scotia, Canada, set aside as a national park in 1936. The Cabot Trail, a scenic highway, permits motorists to see most of the park. Area, 390 sq. mi.

Cape Breton Island. Island belonging to the province of Nova Scotia, Canada, from which it is separated by the Strait of Canso. It exports coal and iron. It was settled by the French and called Île Royale, and contained the fortress of Louisburg. It was ceded to Great Britain in 1763, and united with Nova Scotia in 1820. It is well known as a tourist playground and for the Scottish games that are held there annually. Chief town, Sydney; length, 110 mi.; area, 3,970 sq. mi.; pop. ab. 150,000.

Cape Castle. See **Cape Coast.**

Capece-Latro (kä.pā'chā.lä'trō), **Giuseppe.** b. at Naples, Italy, Sept. 23, 1744; d. Nov. 2, 1836. Neapolitan prelate, archbishop of Tarentum, and state minister (1806–15).

Cape Coast. [Also: **Cape Castle;** former name, **Cape Coast Castle.**] Former British fort and now a seaport in Gold Coast colony, W Africa. The fort was taken from the Portuguese by the English in 1664. The town is an educational center for the area. 23,346 (1948).

Cape Cod. [Sometimes called **the Cape.**] Sandy peninsula in SE Massachusetts, forming Barnstable County. It was discovered by Bartholomew Gosnold in 1602. The Cape Cod Canal (1914; length, 8 mi.) crosses its W part, between Buzzards Bay and Cape Cod Bay. Length, ab. 65 mi.; width, from 1 mi. to 20 mi. See also **Cod, Cape.**

Cape Cod. Descriptive work by Henry David Thoreau, published posthumously in 1865. The essays, based upon the author's personal observation of the Cape, include comment upon the inhabitants and the physical environment.

Cape Cod Bay. Bay lying between the Cape Cod peninsula on the E and S, and Plymouth County, Mass., on the W.

Cape Cod Folks. Local-color novel by Sarah Pratt McLean, published in 1881. She used an autobiographical method and slighted plot to the advantage of manners and folkways, which she described with an accuracy gained through her work as a substitute teacher in a one-room schoolhouse on Cape Cod. When certain natives of Cape Cod whom she had described sued the publisher on the ground of defamation of character, the book immediately gained a degree of popular success which might otherwise never have been possible.

Cape Colony. Former name of **Cape of Good Hope** province.

Cape Elizabeth (ę.liz'ą.bęth). Town in SW Maine, in Cumberland County, on Casco Bay: summer resort; lighthouses and a U.S. Coast Guard station. 3,816 (1950).

Cape Engaño (eng.gä'nyō), **Battle of.** Naval engagement (Oct. 25, 1944) in World War II, between carrier elements of Admiral W. F. Halsey's Third Fleet and a Japanese force in the Pacific Ocean off the Philippine Islands. The Japanese lost four carriers, a light cruiser, and a destroyer, as well as several damaged ships. The success permitted Admiral Halsey to aid in the Battle of Leyte Gulf, in which the remaining Japanese naval strength in the Pacific was almost destroyed.

Cape Esperance (es'pėr.ąns), **Battle of.** World War II battle (1942) in the South Pacific. About 200 miles off Guadalcanal, this brief but concentrated naval engagement during the night of Oct. 11–12, 1942 saw the virtual elimination of a Japanese naval task force which protected Japanese convoys to Guadalcanal. A cruiser and destroyer were sunk, a second cruiser was made useless, and a third severely damaged. The chief U.S. ships which took part were the cruisers *San Francisco* and *Salt Lake City* and the light cruisers *Boise* and *Helena* under Rear Admiral Norman Scott.

Cape Fear. River in North Carolina, formed by the union of the Deep and Haw rivers in Chatham County. It flows generally SE, and enters the Atlantic at Cape Fear by two channels separated by Smith's Island. The entrances to it were blockaded during the Civil War. Length, ab. 250 mi.; navigable to Fayetteville (120 mi.).

Capefigue (kap.fēg), **Jean Baptiste Honoré Raymond.** b. at Marseilles, 1802; d. at Paris, Dec. 23, 1872. French historian. His works include *Histoire de Philippe Auguste* (1829) and *Histoire de la restauration* (1831–33).

Cape Girardeau (kāp ji.rär'dō). City in SE Missouri, in Cape Girardeau County, on the Mississippi River, ab. 97 mi. SE of St. Louis: manufactures include shoes, lumber, cement, and electrical appliances. It is the seat of St. Vincent's College and Southeast Missouri State Teachers College. 21,578 (1950).

Cape Haytien (kāp hā'shẹn). See **Cap-Haïtien.**

Čapek (chä'pek), **Josef.** b. 1887; d. 1927. Czech dramatist and illustrator. He collaborated with his brother Karel Čapek (1890–1938) in the writing of one of the best known of the Čapek plays, namely *Že života hmyzu* (1921; Eng. trans., *The Insect Play,* 1923). He supplied illustrations for several of Karel Čapek's books.

Čapek, Karel. b. at Malé Svatoňovice, in Bohemia, 1890; d. 1938. Czech novelist, playwright, and essayist, the best-known literary figure in modern Czechoslovakia. His main themes explore philosophical, political, and moral problems, and are conceived in a cosmopolitan rather than national setting. His plays and novels are available in English translation, as are his famous *Conversations with Masaryk* (3 vols., 1928–35). Among his dramas are *R.U.R.* (1921; Eng. trans., 1923), *Že života hmyzu* (1921; Eng. trans., *The Insect Play,* 1923), *Věc Makropulos* (1922; Eng. trans., *The Makropulos Secret,* 1925), and *Bílá Nemoc* (1937; Eng. trans., *Power and Glory,* 1938). Of these, *R.U.R.*, a satire, is probably best known, and served to introduce the word "robot" (apparently from the Czech word *robotnik,* meaning "serf"), to describe a machine-made man or automaton, into the language. Among his novels are *Hodrubal* (1933; Eng. trans., 1943), *Povětroň* (1934; Eng. trans., *The Meteor,* 1935), and *Obyčejny Život* (1935; Eng. trans., *An Ordinary Life,* 1936).

Capel (kā'pẹl), **Arthur.** [Title, 1st Baron **Capel of Hadham.**] b. c1610; executed March 9, 1649. English Royalist, raised to the peerage on Aug. 6, 1641; father of Arthur Capel (1631–83). He served Charles I in various offices, military and civil, during the civil war and struggle with Parliament, and in 1649 was arrested and condemned to death.

Capel, Arthur. [Titles, Viscount **Malden,** Earl of **Essex.**] b. in January, 1631; d. July, 1683. English statesman; eldest son of Arthur Capel (c1610–49). He was appointed ambassador to Denmark in 1670, became lord lieutenant of Ireland in February, 1672 (recalled on April 28, 1677), and was made head of the treasury commission in 1679 (resigned on Nov. 19, 1679). He was arrested for complicity in the Rye House Plot and sent to the Tower of London, where he probably committed suicide.

Capella (ka.pel'a). A star, the fifth brightest in the sky. It is situated in the left shoulder of Auriga, in front of the Great Bear, nearly on a line with the two northernmost of the seven stars forming Charles's Wain; and it is easily recognized by the proximity of "the Kids," three stars of the fourth magnitude forming an isosceles triangle. The color of Capella is the same as that of the sun.

Capella, Martianus. See **Martianus Capella.**

Capelle (kä.pel'ẹ), **Eduard von.** b. at Celle, Germany, Oct. 10, 1855; d. at Wiesbaden, Germany, Feb. 23, 1931. German admiral. He helped draft von Tirpitz's bills for naval construction, and served as undersecretary of the German naval office (1914–15). Successor to von Tirpitz as secretary of state for naval affairs (serving from March, 1916 to October, 1918), he influenced the German government to begin unrestricted submarine campaigns (1917) against the Allies.

Capello (kä.pel'lō) or **Cappello** (käp.pel'lō), **Bianca.** b. at Venice, c1548; d. at the castle Poggio di Cajano, Italy, Oct. 11, 1587. Italian adventuress belonging to a noble Venetian family. She eloped with Pietro Buonaventuri in 1563. In 1578 she married Francisco de' Medici, grand duke of Tuscany, whose mistress she had previously been, and was recognized as grand duchess in 1579.

Capello, Luigi. b. April 14, 1859; d. June 25, 1941. Italian soldier. Appointed (1915) a lieutenant general, he headed (1916) the 6th army corps which won the Gorizia victory in World War I; as commander (1917) of the 2nd army he took part (August, 1917) in winning the victory at Bainsizza; when the 2nd army was involved in the Caporetto disaster he came into conflict with Cadorna on strategy and retired in 1918. Entering politics, he supported Fascism until the assassination (1924) of Matteotti drove him with Tito Zaniboni into opposition; his presumed involvement in Zaniboni's plot (Nov. 4, 1925) against Mussolini caused his arrest, trial (1927), and condemnation to 30 years' imprisonment; age and bad health won him his release (c1937) under government surveillance.

Cape May (kāp' mā'). City at the S extremity of New Jersey, in Cape May County, on the Atlantic Ocean: notable as a summer resort. 3,607 (1950).

Capen (kā'pẹn), **Elmer Hewitt.** b. at Stoughton, Mass., April 5, 1838; d. March 22, 1905. American educator and Universalist minister, president of Tufts College (1875–1905); father of Samuel Paul Capen. He was a trustee (1875 *et seq.*) of the Universalist General Convention, and a delegate (1888) to the Republican national convention. His works include *Occasional Addresses* (1902) and *The College and the Higher Life* (1905).

Capen, Samuel Paul. b. at Somerville, Mass., March 21, 1878—. American educator; son of Elmer Hewitt Capen. He has served as director (1919–22) of the American Council on Education, chancellor (1922 *et seq.*) of the University of Buffalo, and editor (1920–22) of the *Educational Record.*

Cape of Good Hope. See also **Good Hope, Cape of.**

Cape of Good Hope. [Official name, **Province of the Cape of Good Hope**; South African Dutch, **Kaapland**; sometimes called **Cape Province** or **the Cape**; former name, **Cape Colony.**] Province of the Union of South Africa, formerly a British colony. It is bounded by South-West Africa, Bechuanaland, Orange Free State, and Basutoland on the N, Natal on the E, and the Indian and South Atlantic oceans on the S and W. It is traversed by the Swartebergen, Roggeveldt, Nieuwveldt, Sneeuwberg, and other mountains. Its chief river is the Orange. It exports wool, ostrich feathers, hides, and diamonds; grazing is the leading industry. Capital, Capetown; area, 277,113 sq. mi.; pop. 4,053,848, including 870,795 Europeans (1946).

Culture. About 75 percent of the inhabitants are natives (Kaffir, Hottentot, Malay); the remainder are Europeans of English, Dutch, and French descent. The leading church is the Dutch Reformed, with Church of England, Wesleyan, and others also represented. English, South African Dutch, Kaffir, Hottentot, and Bushman are spoken.

History and Government. The Cape Colony contained eight provinces, but now is divided into 132 magisterial districts and 95 divisional councils. It had a governor appointed by the crown, and a parliament consisting of a legislative council and legislative assembly (abolished by the act of 1909). It was colonized by the Dutch in 1651, and received French immigration in 1687. The Dutch East India Company abandoned it in 1795, and it was occupied by the British. It was restored to the Dutch in 1802, but regained by the British in 1806. It suffered from various Kaffir wars and troubles with the Boers. It received a constitution in 1850, but had no responsible government until 1872. The colony was at war with the Zulus in 1879, and with the Boers of the Transvaal, 1880–81. In 1894 Pondoland was annexed. In 1909 a bill was passed providing for the union of the Transvaal, Cape Colony, Orange Free State, and Natal into a single nation with a centralized government, known as the Union of

South Africa. The Cape Colony was to be known as the Cape of Good Hope. Included in Cape of Good Hope province was the small area around Walvis Bay in South-West Africa. The province is represented in the union Parliament by 8 members in the Senate and 56 in the House of Assembly.

Cape of Storms. [Portuguese, **Cabo Tormentoso** (kä′bö tôr.män.tō′zö).] Name first given by the Portuguese navigator Dias, in 1486, to the Cape of Good Hope.

Caper (kā′pėr). A "high fantastical" character in Allingham's comedy *Who Wins, or The Widow's Choice.*

Cape River. See **Segovia,** river in Central America.

Capern (kā′pėrn), **Edward.** b. at Tiverton, Devonshire, England, Jan. 21, 1819; d. at Braunton, near Bideford, Devonshire, England, June 4, 1894. English poet, lace-factory worker, and postman. He began his literary career by contributing to the "Poet's Corner" of the *North Devon Journal;* his work soon became popular, and was praised by Walter Savage Landor, Charles Kingsley, Charles Dickens, and Tennyson. He was the author of *Poems by Edward Capern, Rural Postman of Bideford, Devon* (1856; later editions), *Ballads and Songs* (1858), *Devonshire Melodist* (1862), and *Wayside Warbles* (1865).

Capernaum (ka̤.pėr′na̤.um). In the New Testament, an important place on or near the W shore of the Sea of Galilee, about an hour distant from where the JordanRiver emptied into the sea. It was the scene of many incidents and acts in the life of Christ, and is sometimes called "his own city" (Mat. ix. 1). It had a Roman garrison (Mat. viii. 5 ff.). It has been identified by some archaeologists with the ruins of Tel (or Tell) Hum, by others with Khan Minyeh.

Caperton (kā′pėr.tọn), **William Banks.** b. at Spring Hill, Tenn., June 30, 1855; d. at Newport, R.I., Dec. 21, 1941. American naval officer. Graduated (1875) from the U.S. Naval Academy at Annapolis, he was promoted (1913) to rear admiral, and named (1914) commander of the Atlantic reserve fleet. He headed (1915–16) the intervention naval forces in Haiti, at Veracruz (1915), and at Santo Domingo (1916). In 1916 he was named commander in chief of the Pacific fleet, as full admiral. In 1919 he retired.

Cape Sable Island (sā′bl). Island in SE Canada, at the extreme S tip of Nova Scotia, ab. 45 mi. SE of Yarmouth. It was settled in the 17th century by Acadian French, and has fishing and lobstering as chief activities. There is also an important lighthouse.

Capet (kā′pe̤t, kap′e̤t; French, kȧ.pe). Surname of the kings of France, commencing with Hugh Capet, who ascended the throne in 987.

Capetian (ka̤.pē′sha̤n). [French, **Capétien** (kȧ.pā.syaṅ).] Royal family reigning over France as the 3rd dynasty, in the period 987–1328, beginning with Hugh Capet and ending with Charles IV. Collateral branches were the ducal house of Burgundy, and the houses of Anjou, Bourbon, and Valois.

Capetown or **Cape Town** (kāp′toun). City in S Africa, the capital of Cape of Good Hope province and the seat of the legislature of the Union of South Africa, situated on Table Bay at the foot of Table Mountain. It was founded by the Dutch in 1651. It ranks with the great cities of the world as one of the most scenic, and is the chief port and second city in the Union, of which it is the "mother city." It is connected by rail with most of the major towns and cities between it and Elisabethville, Belgian Congo. Its outstanding feature, the Table Mountain, rises behind the city and forms an imposing background for the metropolis, which with its suburbs covers 78 sq. mi. The University of Capetown is located in the suburb of Rondebosch. Pop., including suburbs, 470,911 (1946).

Cape Verde (vėrd). See **Verde, Cape.**

Cape Verde Islands. [Also: **Cape Verd Islands;** Portuguese, **Ilhas do Cabo Verde.**] Group of islands, belonging to Portugal, situated in the Atlantic ocean ab. 320 mi. W of Cape Verde and the important French naval station of Dakar on the W coast of Africa. The ten main islands are divided into two groups, the *Barlavento* (windward) group and the *Sotavento* (leeward) group. The first includes São Vicente, Santo Antão, São Nicolau, Santa Luzia, Sal, and Boa Vista; the latter includes São Tiago (or Santiago), Maio, Fogo, and Brava. São Vicente is the chief coaling station supplying navigation to South America. The islands are mountainous, have a rich vegetation, grow excellent coffee, and export also oranges, castor oil, mustard, tobacco, sugar, and hides; there are brandy distilleries. The population is Portuguese; racially, about one half consists of Negroes and mulattoes. The islands were discovered in 1443 and subsequently colonized. A Portuguese governor is the chief administrator. Capital, Praia (on São Tiago); area, 1,557 sq. mi.; pop. 147,097 (1950).

Cape York Peninsula (yôrk). Northeastern peninsula of Queensland, Australia, separating the Gulf of Carpentaria from the Coral Sea. Its northern extremity is Cape York.

Cap Français (kȧp fräṅ.sā). A former name of **Cap-Haïtien.**

Capgrave (kap′grāv), **John.** b. at Lynn, Norfolk, England, April 21, 1393; d. there, Aug. 12, 1464. English historian, provincial of the Augustinian order in England. He wrote *Chronicle of England,* from the creation to 1417 A.D., *Liber de Illustribus Henricis* (Book of the Illustrious Henrys), *A Guide to the Antiquities of Rome,* and other historical and theological works in Latin. He is best known for *Nova legenda Angliae,* the first English hagiology.

Caph (kaf). The third-magnitude, slightly variable and spectroscopically interesting star β Cassiopeiae. The Arabic name refers, however, to a different form of the constellation from that represented on our modern star-maps, which show the star as on the framework of the lady's chair.

Cap-Haïtien (kāp.hā′she̤n; French, kȧp ȧ.ē.syaṅ). [Also, **Cape Haytien;** called **Le Cap;** former names, **Guárico, Cap Français.**] City in N Haiti, on the Caribbean Sea: second most important in the country. It was bombarded by the British in 1865. Nearby is the "Citadel," built by Henri Christophe, King of Haiti (1811–20). Pop. 24,957 (1950).

Caphis (kā′fis). Servant of Timon's creditors, in Shakespeare's *Timon of Athens.*

Caphtor (kaf′tôr). In the Old Testament, the name of a country mentioned as the starting point in the migrations of the Philistines; thus they are also called Caphtorim (Deut. ii. 23, Jer. xlvii. 4, Amos, ix. 7); formerly identified with Cappadocia or Cyprus, but considered by most modern scholars as identical with Crete. This view is borne out by many passages in which the Philistines are called Cretans (Cherethites) (Ezek. xxv. 16, Zeph. ii. 5, 1 Sam. xxx. 14), and it is supported by ancient writers who connected the Philistines with the island of Crete. In Gen. x. 14 the Caphtorim are enumerated among the descendants of Egypt (Mizraim), and it is therefore assumed that a portion of the Philistines emigrated from Crete by way of Egypt to Palestine.

Capiatá (kä.pyä.tä′). City in SW Paraguay, in Central department. Pop. ab. 22,000.

Capistrano (kä.pēs.trä′nō), Saint **Giovanni di.** [English, **John of Capistrano** or **John Capistran** (ka̤.pis′tra̤n); Latinized, **Johannes Capistranus** (kap.is.trā′nus).] b. at Capistrano, in the Abruzzi, Italy, June 24, 1386; d. at Illock, in Slavonia, Oct. 23, 1456. Italian Franciscan. He distinguished himself by his preachings against the Hussites in Bohemia and Moravia, and in 1456 led an army of crusaders to the relief of Belgrade which was besieged by Mohammed II. He was the author of *Speculum conscientiae.*

Capistrano de Abreu (kä.pēs.tru′nö dē a̤.brā′ö), **João.** See **Abreu, João Capistrano de.**

Capitaine Fracasse (kȧ.pē.ten frȧ.kȧs), **Le.** Novel by Théophile Gautier. The title of the book is the stage name adopted by De Sigognac, the hero, on joining a company of strolling players.

Capital Federal (kä.pē.täl′ fā.ᴛʜā.räl′). [English, **Federal Capital** (or **District**).] Civil division of Argentina, the seat of the national government, equivalent in political stature to a province. Its area, ab. 77 sq. mi., is included entirely within the limits of greater Buenos Aires. 2,982,580 (1947).

Capital Gains Tax. In U.S. history: **1.** Provision of the Revenue Act of 1936, which covered current earnings. It revised the treatment of corporate capital gains and losses in calculating taxable income and placed considerable levies upon the gains realized in the sales of capital assets, providing a progressive scale based upon the period of ownership preceding transfer. A limit of 2000 dollars was placed on deductions from taxable income resulting from capital losses. **2.** Part of the Revenue Act of 1938, which revised the Revenue Act of 1936 and became law without President Franklin D. Roosevelt's signature. Passed in response to charges that the existing capital gains tax structure discouraged investment and the creation of new enterprises, it clarified the distinction between speculative and investment gains and offered better terms for offsetting net losses and for gains on long-term transfers.

"Capital of the Highlands." Nickname of **Inverness,** Scotland.

Capital y su Jurisdicción (kä.pē.täl' ē sö hö"rēz.dēk-syōn'). Civil division in SW Paraguay, consisting of the national capital, Asunción, and neighboring communities. Area, 244 sq. mi.; pop. 205,605 (1950).

Capitan (kä.pē.tän'; French, kȧ.pē.täṅ). [Eng. trans., "*Captain.*"] As a proper name, a character of ridiculous bravado, introduced conventionally in early Italian comedy, probably originating in the *Miles Gloriosus* of the Roman comedies of Plautus, and introduced in French comedy before the time of Molière. He came upon the stage only to bluster, and talked of murder and bloodshed, but submitted with great meekness to punishment. When Charles V entered Italy, a Spanish Capitan was introduced into comedy who dealt in Spanish bravado and got rid of the Italian Capitan; when the Spanish influence ceased in Italy, the Capitan was turned into Scaramouche, who was still a cowardly character; hence the name Scaramouche was given to a person who behaved in this manner.

Capitan (kap.i.tan'), **El.** See **El Capitan.**

Capitanata (kä"pē.tä.nä'tä). Northwestern part of the *compartimento* (region) of Apulia, SE Italy, about the same in extent as the province of Foggia.

Capitant (kȧ.pē.täṅ), **René.** b. at La Tronche, Isère, France, Aug. 19, 1901—. French political leader and educator, active supporter of Charles de Gaulle. Founder of the newspaper *Combat* (1941) and the movement of the same name (1943) while at Algiers, he was Free French minister of education (1943–45). He had previously been professor of public law at Strasbourg (1930–40) and Algiers (1941).

Capito (kap'i.tō; German, kä'pē.tō), **Wolfgang Fabricius.** [Original surname, **Köpfel.**] b. at Hagenau, in Alsace, 1478; d. at Strasbourg, in November, 1541. German divine, a coadjutor of Martin Luther. He became (1515) a preacher at Basel, and later moved (1519) to Mainz, where he became chancellor to Albert, elector and archbishop of Mainz. In 1523 he went to Strasbourg, where he became the local leader of the Reformation. He was the chief author of the *Confessio Tetrapolitana,* and devoted himself to the conciliation of the Lutherans and the Swiss reformers.

Capitol (kap'i.tọl). In ancient Roman history, that part of the Capitoline Hill which was occupied by the Temple of Jupiter Capitolinus.

Capitol. Name applied to the Piazza del Campidoglio on the Capitoline Hill, Rome, with the palaces which face it on three sides. The piazza is approached on the northwest by a wide, monumental flight of steps from the Piazza Araceli in front, opposite the Palace of the Senator, and flanked by the Palazzo dei Conservatori and the Capitoline Museum. This area, occupying the depression between the citadel and the site of the Temple of Jupiter Capitolinus, is the historic center of Rome. Here, according to tradition, Romulus founded his asylum, and the earliest public assemblies met. In the 11th century, it again became the municipal center, as the residence of the prefect and the seat of popular meetings; and here, in the old Palace of the Senator, Petrarch was crowned in 1341, and in 1347 Rienzi was established as tribune of the people. The present Palace of the Senator was founded at the end of the 14th century by Pope Boniface IX. The existing façade, with its Corinthian pilasters and double flight of steps, as well as those of the flanking palaces, is based on designs by Michelangelo. In the center of the Piazza del Campidoglio stands the noted ancient bronze equestrian statue of Marcus Aurelius, which originally stood in the Forum Romanum, then near the Lateran, and has occupied its present position since 1538.

Capitol. Seat of the Congress of the U.S. at Washington, D.C. The original building was begun in 1793, from plans submitted by William Thornton, modified by Etienne S. Hallet; before it could be entirely completed, it was burned (1814) by the British during the War of 1812. The present building was begun by B. H. Latrobe, and finished, in 1830, by Charles Bulfinch. Additions were made (1861–65) by Thomas U. Walter. It consists of a central cruciform building crowned by a great dome, and connected at each end by galleries with a large rectangular wing, one of which contains the Senate Chamber, and the other the Hall of Representatives. The style is Renaissance, based on English models, the dome being inspired by that of Saint Paul's, London. The elevation exhibits a single main story, with an attic, over a high rusticated basement. The great feature of the exterior is the porticos of the central building and of the two wings, with their fine flights of steps. These porticos comprise 148 Corinthian columns ab. 30 ft. high exclusive of their high square pedestals. The dome is ab. 287½ ft. high to the top of the statue above the lantern, and ab. 94 ft. in interior diameter; it is built of cast iron. It rises from a circular drum, and is encircled by a Corinthian colonnade supporting a gallery. Beneath the dome is a monumental hall called the Rotunda, adorned with works of art relating to American history. The total length of the Capitol, N and S, is ab. 751 ft.

Capitol Heights. Town in W central Maryland, in Prince Georges County near Washington, D.C. 2,729 (1950).

Capitoline Hill (kap'i.tọ.līn). One of the seven hills of ancient Rome, NW of the Palatine, on the left bank of the Tiber. It constituted the citadel of the city after the construction of the Servian wall. Its SW summit was the famed Tarpeian Rock; on its NE summit rose the temple of Jupiter Capitolinus. The modern Capitol stands between the two summits. From the Capitoline the Forum Romanum extends its long, narrow area toward the SE, skirting the N foot of the Palatine.

Capitoline Museum. One of the chief museums of antiquities of Rome. It was founded in 1471 by Pope Sixtus IV, who presented the papal collections to the Roman people, and designated the Capitol as the place where the art treasures of Rome should be preserved. The museum was greatly enriched by Popes Clement XII and Benedict XIV. The collections now occupy the palace on the left-hand side of the Piazza del Campidoglio, which was built in the 17th century from modified designs of Michelangelo. Among the most noted of the antiquities acquired by the Capitoline Museum are the colossal statu e of *Mars* in armor, the *Dying Gaul,* the *Satyr* of Praxiteles, the *Centaurs* by Aristeas and Papias, and the *Capitoline Venus* (after Praxiteles).

Capitolinus (kap"i.tō.lī'nus), **Julius.** fl. c300 A.D. Roman historian, one of the writers of the Augustan History.

Capitulation of Baylén (bī.lān'). See **Baylén, Capitulation of.**

Capiz (kä'pēs). Province of the Philippine Islands, in the N part of Panay island, with adjacent small islands, in the W central Philippines. It is bounded by the Sibuyan Sea on the N, Iloilo (separated by mountains) on the E and S, and Antique (separated by mountains) on the W. It is a mountainous and densely forested province, with numerous small rivers and with fertile valleys that yield large crops, notably of hemp, corn, sugar cane, and rice. The chief river is the Panay. Among the minerals found here are gold, iron, and coal. The native race is Visayan. Capital, Capiz; area, 1,710 sq. mi.; pop. 441,871 (1948).

Capiz. Town in the Philippine Islands, the capital of Capiz province, situated on the N coast of Panay island near the mouth of the Panay River: seaport. 11,673 (1948).

Capmany y Montpalau (käp.mä'nē ē mōnt.pä.lä'ō), **Antonio de.** b. at Barcelona, Spain, Nov. 24, 1742; d. at Cádiz, Spain, Nov. 14, 1813. Spanish antiquary, historian, philologist, and critic.

Capo (kä'pō). Italian word for "cape": for place names containing this word which was not listed immediately below, see the specific element of the name.

Capodistria (kap.ọ.dis'tri.ạ; Italian, kä.pō.dēs'trē.ä). [Ancient names, **Aegidia, Justinopolis.**] Town in the Free Territory of Trieste, situated on the Gulf of Trieste, S of the city of Trieste: seaport, with shipyards, salines, fisheries, and canneries. There are old Venetian fortifications, a cathedral, *Palazzo del Podestà* (town hall), theater, and library. In the early Middle Ages under the patriarchs of Aquileia, the town was under Venetian rule from 1278 to 1797; in the 19th century it belonged to Austria and from 1919 to 1945 to Italy. In 1947 it was incorporated into the Free Territory of Trieste. 11,995 (1936).

Capo d'Istria (kä'pō dēs'trē.ä) or **Capodistrias** (kä.pō-ᴛʜēs'trē.äs), **Augustin.** [Greek, **Kapodistrias.**] b. 1778; d. on the island of Corfu, in May, 1857. Greek politician; brother of Giovanni Anton Capo d'Istria. He was provisional president of Greece (1831–32).

Capo d'Istria or **Capodistrias,** Count **Giovanni Anton.** [Greek, **Kapodistrias.**] b. on the island of Corfu, Feb. 11, 1776; killed at Nauplia, Greece, Oct. 9, 1831. Greek politician, president of Greece; brother of Augustin Capo d'Istria. He entered the Russian service in 1809, represented Russia in the Congress of Vienna from 1814 to 1815, and was Russian secretary of foreign affairs until 1822. Having left the Russian service, he devoted himself to the cause of Greek independence, was elected president of Greece through the influence of the Russian party in 1827, and served from 1828 to 1831, when he was assassinated by the brothers Constantine and George Mavromichalis.

Capone (ka̤.pōn'), **Al.** [Legal name, **Alphonse** (or **Alfonso**) **Capone;** called **"Scarface Al."**] b. at Naples, Italy, Jan. 17, 1899; d. at Miami, Fla., Jan. 25, 1947. American gangster and racketeer. His sobriquet arose from a scar received in a gang fight. He grew up in a slum area of New York City and at an early age became involved in criminal activities (by the age of 19 he had already twice been under suspicion of connection with gang murders). In 1920 he became a resident of Chicago and an associate of the leading members of that city's underworld, having an interest in many "speakeasies" during the Prohibition years, and branching out into gambling, organized vice, and the form of racketeering that consists of forcing businessmen and labor unions to pay for "protection" under penalty of a variety of serious troubles if they refuse (in promoting the labor angle of his racket, Capone spoke eloquently of the need to protect the workers against Communism). The "Capone mob" was certainly involved in more than a few flagrant murders, but through the elaborate bribery made possible by its great profits (the Federal Bureau of Investigation estimated that they amounted to $105,000,000 in 1927 alone) it long found means of escaping serious police opposition or prosecution under the law. Eventually (in 1931) Capone was indicted by a Federal grand jury and tried for income tax evasion, found guilty, and sentenced to 11 years in prison. In 1939 he was released, in a condition of physical and mental breakdown from paresis which precluded any resumption of his law-defying career.

Caporetto (kap.o̤.ret'o̤; Italian, kä.pō.rāt'tō). [German, **Karfreit;** Serbo-Croatian, **Kobarid.**] Town in NW Yugoslavia, in Slovenia near the Italian border (prior to 1947 belonging to the province of Gorizia, region of Venezia Giulia, Italy), situated on the Isonzo River, ab. 21 mi. NE of Udine. It was the scene of a defeat (1917) of the Italian army under Cadorna in World War I. The Italians retreated before the Austrian and German forces under von Below toward the Piave River line. Pop. ab. 6,300.

Caporetto, Battle of. [Also, **12th Battle of the Isonzo.**] Italian military disaster in the fall of 1917, in World War I. The operation began with a surprise thrust against the Italian line by the freshly formed German-Austrian 14th Army, and threatened to engulf all of NE Italy. Beginning on Oct. 24, 1917, the Italian forces steadily withdrew until they reached the Piave River on November 7. Able to hold their lines on the Piave, they broke the offensive, but had suffered heavy losses in both men and morale. A direct result of the battle was the appointment of Armando Diaz as commander of Italian forces, and indirectly it hastened the formation of the Supreme Allied War Council.

Capote (ka̤.pō'tē), **Truman.** b. at New Orleans, La., Sept. 30, 1924—. American novelist. His work, which deals principally with distintegrating Southern society, includes *Other Voices, Other Rooms* (1948), *Tree of Night* (short stories, 1949), and *The Grass Harp* (1951).

Capots (kȧ.pō). See **Colliberts.**

Cappadocia (kap.a̤.dō'sha̤). In ancient geography, a country in the E part of Asia Minor, lying W of the Euphrates, N of Cilicia, and E of Lycaonia; in a wider sense, the territory in Asia Minor between the lower Halys (Kizil Irmak) and Euphrates rivers, and the Taurus mountains and Euxine Sea (Black Sea); an elevated tableland intersected by mountain chains. It constituted under the Persians two satrapies, afterward two independent monarchies; they were Cappadocia on the Pontus, later called Pontus; and Cappadocia near the Taurus, called Great Cappadocia, the later Cappadocia in a narrower sense. In 17 A.D. Cappadocia became a Roman province. It had then only four cities, Mazaca, near Mount Argaeus, the residence of the Cappadocian kings, later called Eusebia, and by the Romans Caesarea, the episcopal see of Saint Basil (modern Kayseri); Tyana; Garsaura, later called Archelais; and Ariaratheia. Of its other cities, Samosata (Samsat), Myssa, and Nazianzus, the birthplaces or seats of celebrated ecclesiastics, are noteworthy.

Cappel (käp'e̤l). See **Kappel.**

Cappella Annunziata dell'Arena (käp.pel'lä än.nön-syä'tä del.lä.rā'nä). Italian name of the **Arena Chapel.**

Cappello (käp.pel'lō), **Bianca.** See **Capello** or **Cappello, Bianca.**

Capper (kap'ėr), **Arthur.** b. at Garnett, Kan., July 14, 1865; d. at Topeka, Kan., Dec. 19, 1951. American editor, politician, and U.S. senator (1919–49) from Kansas. A staff member (1884 *et seq.*) of the Topeka *Daily Capital,* he became its publisher and proprietor in 1892, and subsequently became the publisher and proprietor of *Capper's Weekly,* the *Kansas Farmer, Household Magazine, Capper's Farmer,* the *Missouri Ruralist,* the *Ohio Farmer,* the Kansas City *Kansan,* and other rural magazines. He was also the owner of the Kansas City *Daily Kansan.* From 1915 to 1919 he served as governor of Kansas.

Capperonnier (kȧp.ro.nyā), **Claude.** b. at Montdidier, France, May 1, 1671; d. at Paris, July 24, 1744. French classical scholar. He wrote *Traité de l'ancienne prononciation de la langue grecque* (1703), and edited the works of Quintilian (1725).

Capper-Volstead Coöperative Act (kap'ėr.vol'sted). Act passed by the U.S. Congress in 1922 in an effort to relieve the plight of the U.S. farmer after World War I. It allowed the establishment of agricultural associations and voluntary coöperatives for the production, processing, handling, and marketing of farm output, and placed such organizations beyond the bounds of the Sherman Antitrust Law, and under the supervision of the Department of Agriculture.

Capponi (käp.pō'nē), **Gino,** Marchese. b. at Florence, Sept. 14, 1792; d. there, Feb. 3, 1876. Florentine historian, statesman, and scholar. He was prime minister of Tuscany in 1848, and became a senator in 1860. He wrote *Storia della repubblica di Firenze* (1875) and other works.

Capponi, Piero. b. c1447; d. Sept. 25, 1496. Florentine statesman and soldier. For years he served Lorenzo de' Medici in diplomatic affairs, but after Lorenzo's death in 1492 he opposed the policies of Lorenzo's son Piero which led to French intervention in Italian affairs, and, with Piero de' Medici's fall from power, became the head of the Florentine republic. After the capture of the city by Charles VIII of France in 1494, he manifested such skill and courage in negotiating with the conqueror as to win favorable conditions of peace. Two years later Capponi was mortally wounded in an attack on the castle of Soiana while leading the Florentine armed forces in a war with Pisa.

Capps (kaps), **Washington Lee.** b. at Portsmouth, Va., Jan. 31, 1864; d. at Washington, D.C., May 31, 1935. American naval officer. Graduated (1884) from the U.S. Naval Academy at Annapolis, he received (1888) the B.S. degree at the University of Glasgow. He served on special duty abroad (1886–89), and on Admiral Dewey's staff (1898–99), was chief (1903–10) of the navy construction bureau, as rear admiral, and became (1910) permanent chief constructor. President of the Navy Compensation Board (1917–35) and of the Naval War Claims Board (1925–35), he was also general manager (1917) of the Emergency Fleet Corporation. In 1928 he was named to the retired list.

Capra (kap′rạ), **Frank.** b. at Palermo, Sicily, May 18, 1897—. American motion-picture director, resident in the U.S. since 1903. As director for Columbia Studios at Hollywood, Calif., he was responsible for such films as *Power of the Press, Ladies of Leisure, It Happened One Night, Mr. Deeds Goes to Town, Lost Horizon, Mr. Smith Goes to Washington, You Can't Take It With You, Meet John Doe,* and *Arsenic and Old Lace*. He also directed the army orientation films, *Why We Fight*. For his productions, he has received three Motion Picture Academy awards.

Capraia (kä.prä′yä). [Also: **Capraja;** Latin, **Capraria** kạ.prãr′i.ạ), **Caprasia** (kạ.prā′zhạ).] Island in the Mediterranean Sea, situated NE of Corsica.

Caprara (kä.prä′rä), **Giovanni Battista.** b. at Bologna, Italy, May 29, 1733; d. at Paris, July 27, 1810. Italian cardinal and diplomat, bishop of Milan. He negotiated the concordat at Paris in 1801.

Caprarola (kä.prä.rō′lä). Town and commune in C Italy, in the *compartimento* (region) of Latium, in the province of Viterbo, situated ab. 31 mi. N of Rome. The Palazzo Farnese, built (1547–59) for Cardinal Alessandro Farnese, nephew of Pope Paul III, with terraces, courtyard, garden, and richly decorated interior, is a famous example of Renaissance architecture; it was undamaged in World War II. Pop. of commune, 5,768 (1936); of town, 5,461 (1936).

Capreae (kap′rē.ē). Latin name of **Capri.**

Caprera (kä.prā′rä). [Also, **Cabrera.**] Island N of the island of Sardinia, belonging to the Italian province of Sassari. It was the residence of Garibaldi from c1854 to 1882.

Capri (kä′prē). [Latin, **Capreae.**] Island off the coast of Campania, S Italy, belonging to the province of Napoli, situated ab. 19 mi. S of Naples. It is a favorite resort for tourists and artists because of the beauty of its rocky scenery and its caves, including the Blue Grotto; high cliffs on the E coast rise to 900 ft.; highest point, Monte Solaro (1,920 ft.). It includes the settlements of Capri and Anacapri, the latter commanding a wide view. The Roman emperors Augustus and Tiberius resided here. Area, 5 sq. mi.; pop. 7,984 (1936).

Capricorn (kap′ri.kôrn). [Also: **Capricorn Africa, Dominion of Capricorn.**] Proposed dominion of the British empire in Africa, to be formed by uniting Southern Rhodesia, Northern Rhodesia, and Nyasaland, and perhaps to be joined by Kenya, Tanganyika, and Uganda.

Capricornus (kap.ri.kôr′nus). Ancient zodiacal constellation between Sagittarius and Aquarius; also, one of the 12 signs of the zodiac, the winter solstice. It is represented on ancient monuments by the figure of a goat, or a figure having the fore part like a goat and the hind part like a fish.

Caprivi (kä.prē′vē), Count **Leo von.** [Full name, **Georg Leo von Caprivi de Caprara de Montecuccoli** (kä.prē′vē dā kä.prä′rä dā mōn.tā.kök′kō.lē).] b. at Charlottenburg, Germany, Feb. 24, 1831; d. at Skyren, Germany, Feb. 6, 1899. German statesman, chancellor of the empire (1890–94). He was educated at the Werdersche Gymnasium at Berlin, and entered (1849) the Kaiser-Franz-Grenadier regiment, becoming a second lieutenant in 1850. He entered the military academy and became a first lieutenant (1859) and captain (1861) on the general staff. He rose rapidly in rank; made chief of the admiralty in 1883, he accomplished important results in the reorganization of the German navy. For his efficiency in this service he was promoted (1888) by the emperor William II to be commanding general of the tenth army corps in Hanover, and later was made a general of infantry. On the fall of Bismarck (March 20, 1890), Caprivi succeeded him as imperial chancellor, president of the Prussian ministry, and imperial minister of foreign affairs. He secured (1890) Helgoland from England in exchange for German claims in Zanzibar and Witu, strengthened the colonial policy, renewed (in June, 1891) the Triple Alliance, abrogated the anti-socialist law, negotiated trade treaties with Austria, lowered the grain tariff against strong agrarian opposition, and introduced the two-year compulsory military training program in 1893.

Caprivi Zipfel or **Caprivizipfel** (kä.prē′vē tsip″fẹl). [Also: **Caprivi Concession, Caprivi's Finger, Caprivi Strip.**] Strip of land in the NE corner of South-West Africa, ab. 300 mi. long and 50 mi. wide, between Bechuanaland and Angola and reaching the W bank of the Zambezi River across from Northern Rhodesia. It was named after Count Leo von Caprivi, the German chancellor who obtained the cession of the strip by Great Britain in 1893 on the grounds that the then German colony of South-West Africa needed an outlet on the Zambezi. It was taken over (1939) for administrative purposes by the Union of South Africa.

Capron (kā′prọn), **Horace.** b. at Attleboro, Mass., Aug. 31, 1804; d. Feb. 22, 1885. American farm expert. Superintendent (1829) of the James Buchanan and Company cotton factory at Warren, Md., he managed (1836–52) a model cotton factory at Laurel, Md. He was U.S. commissioner of agriculture (1867–71), before serving as chief adviser (1871–75) on agriculture to the Japanese government.

Caproni (kä.prō′nē), **Gianni.** b. at Trent, Italy, July 3, 1886—. Italian aircraft manufacturer and aeronautical engineer. Trained as an electrical and civil engineer, he made his first flight in 1910 and subsequently (1912, 1913) set several aeronautical records. He built a type of bomber used in World War I, developed (1918–20) an eight-motor, 100-passenger plane, and produced bombers used in the Spanish Civil War and in World War II. He is the chairman of several companies, including Isotta Fraschini and Nazionale Aeronautica.

Capron Trail (kā′prọn). Florida east-to-west trail traced c1850, and named for Captain Erastus A. Capron, who was killed in the Mexican War. It linked Fort Capron to Fort Brooke at Tampa.

Capsa (kap′sạ). Ancient name of **Gafsa.**

Captain. English line-of-battle ship of 72 guns. She served in the Mediterranean squadron of Samuel Hood before Corsica in the period 1794–95, was the flagship of Horatio Nelson in 1796, served in the battle off Cape St. Vincent, on Feb. 14, 1797, and was burned on March 22, 1813.

Captain. One of the earliest English armored turret ships, launched on March 29, 1869. She had an all-round waterline belt ten and seven inches thick, low freeboard, and two turrets on the upper deck 120 ft. apart. Her tonnage was 4,272. She foundered off Cape Finisterre with 500 men, on Sept. 6, 1870.

Captain, The. Bragging, coarse ruffian in Thomas Middleton's play *The Phoenix*.

Captain, The. Play attributed to John Fletcher and another, produced c1613, and printed in the folio of 1646.

Captain Bottell (bot′ẹl). Novel by James Hanley, published in 1933.

Captain Brassbound's Conversion (bràs′boundz). Play by George Bernard Shaw, included in his volume *Three Plays for Puritans* (1900). It deals with the pirate Brassbound, a man hungry for vengeance, whose feelings are finally softened by the shrewd Lady Cicely Waynflete.

Captain Car (kär). Middle English ballad. It tells the story of a border feud.

Captain Craig (krāg). Narrative in blank verse by Edwin Arlington Robinson, title-piece of a collection published in 1902.

Captain Jinks of the Horse Marines (jinks). Farce by Clyde Fitch, in which Ethel Barrymore made her debut. The play was presented in 1901.

Captain Margaret (mär′gạ.rẹt). Historical novel by John Masefield, published in 1908. It is set in South Devon, Cornwall, and the Spanish Main in the period 1685–88.

Captain Morgan: or, the Conspiracy Unveiled (môr′gạn). Play (1827) by C. S. Talbot. It dealt with a contemporary event which had stirred thousands of people: in 1826, William Morgan, a bricklayer, then resident at Batavia, N.Y., threatened to publish a book revealing the secrets of the Masonic order. He was kidnaped by a number of armed men and never seen again (with resultant agitation leading to the formation of the Anti-Masonic party).

Captain of Company K, The. Novel (1891) by Joseph Kirkland. In it there are true details of the behavior of raw recruits under fire and of the reaction in Chicago to the outbreak of the Civil War.

Captain of the Gray-Horse Troop, The. Novel by Hamlin Garland, published in 1902. Previously serialized in the *Saturday Evening Post,* it was Garland's first really successful novel, and was later made into a motion picture. In it, as well as in many of his other works, he espoused the cause of the Indians against the ranchers who sought to acquire their reservations.

Captains Courageous. Novel (1897) by Rudyard Kipling. It is the story of the redemption of a spoiled child of the rich who, falling overboard from a liner, learns courage and self-sacrifice among the fishermen of Newfoundland. A motion picture has been made from the book.

Captain's Doll, The. Novelette by D. H. Lawrence, published under this title in America in 1923. It was issued in England as *The Ladybird.* It is the story of an Englishman, Captain Hepburn, his Austrian mistress, Countess von Rassentlow, who makes dolls for a living, and the captain's wife, who dies, thus clearing the way for the marriage of the captain and the countess.

Captain Singleton (sing'gl.tǫn). [Full title, **Adventures of Captain Singleton.**] Fictional narrative by Daniel Defoe, published in 1720. It tells of a journey across the African continent, and of a career of piracy ending with the hero's repentance. One of the best characters is Quaker William, the pious adviser of the pirates.

Captain Thomas Stukeley (stūk'li). Play (1605) sometimes attributed to Thomas Heywood.

Captives, The. Play (c1624) by Thomas Heywood. It was a modernization of a comedy of Plautus.

Captives, The. Novel by Hugh Walpole, published in 1920. It draws a picture of a religious community. The work won the James Tait Black memorial prize.

Captivity. See **Babylonian Captivity.**

Capua (kap'ū.ą). Ancient city in Campania, Italy, ab. 17 mi. N of Naples, famous for its wealth and luxury. It was founded by the Etruscans, was taken (423 B.C.) by the Samnites, and came (343 B.C.) under Roman rule. It opened (216 B.C.) its gates to Hannibal, whose army wintered there (216–215). In 211 B.C. it was retaken by the Romans, and severely punished. It afterward flourished until sacked (456 A.D.) by Genseric. It was destroyed (840) by the Saracens, and its inhabitants colonized modern Capua. Its site is occupied by the village of Santa Maria di Capua Vetere. It contains the ruins of a triumphal arch and of a Roman amphitheater which dates from the early empire. In the early Middle Ages it was fortified as a citadel, and has suffered from sieges. The amphitheater was an imposing monument, much resembling the Roman Colosseum, and nearly as large. The axes of the outer ellipse are 557 and 458 ft.; of the arena, 250 and 150 ft.

Capua (kap'ū.ą; Italian, kä'pwä). [Ancient name, **Casilinum.**] Town and commune in S Italy, in the *compartimento* (region) of Campania, in the province of Caserta, situated on the Volturno River, N of Naples, ab. 2 mi. N of the ancient Capua. Center of an agricultural district, it has an important dairy industry and manufactures agricultural machinery. There is a Roman bridge; more numerous Roman remains are found on the site of the ancient Capua. The cathedral and the churches of San Salvatore Maggiore, San Giovanni, and San Michele a Corte date from the 9th and 10th centuries. The cathedral was laid in ruins in World War II, while other buildings of tourist interest were slightly damaged. There is an archaeological museum. Originally an Etruscan and Oscan settlement, Capua developed into one of the richest Italian cities in ancient times. It became in 343 B.C. subject to Rome, allied itself to Carthage after the battle of Cannae (216), but was reoccupied by the Romans in 211 and was resettled under Julius Caesar. In 456 A.D. the town was destroyed by the Vandals under Genseric and after a brief period of Norman rule, again by the Moslems. The present Capua was erected by the Lombards in 856, and became (966) the seat of an archbishopric. It was frequently the scene of battles; in 1501 conquered by the French and in 1707 by the Austrians, it was in 1860 occupied by Garibaldi's free corps after a battle against the Neapolitan army. During World War II, heavy fighting occurred here in October, 1943. Pop. of commune, 14,183 (1936); of town, 10,128 (1936).

Capuana (kä.pwä'nä), **Luigi.** b. at Mineo, Sicily, May 27, 1839; d. at Catania, Sicily, Nov. 28, 1915. Italian novelist, short-story writer, playwright, poet, and critic. His career began with the publication of a dramatic poem, *Garibaldi* (1861), but upon becoming acquainted with the stories of Balzac he joined the ranks of the realists. His first published fiction was a short story, *Dottor Cymbalus,* and this was followed by another work in the same genre, *Delfina* (1872). A collection entitled *Profili di Donne* appeared in 1878, and in the following year he published *Giacinta,* his first novel (and the first realistic novel in Italian). *Giacinta* did not please the critics in its original form nor when Capuana adapted it as a play in 1890, but it and his further voluminous output of novels and stories did please a large part of the reading public. His art is seen at its best in the novels *Il Profumo* (1890) and *Il marchese di Roccaverdina* (1901), which latter was praised by Benedetto Croce, in his volume of short stories, *Paesane* (1894), and in his plays *Malia* and *Paraninfo,* the latter published posthumously. In his later years he discounted the importance of realism, insisting that in art form is all; but his importance in the history of literature, nevertheless, is that he was foremost in establishing *verismo* (realism) as one of the techniques of modern Italian letters.

Capuccino (kä.pöt.chē'nō), **Il.** See **Strozzi, Bernardo.**

Capuchin (kap'ų̄.chin), **The.** Play by Samuel Foote, produced in 1776. It was an alteration of *A Trip to Calais,* which had been stopped by the public censor. The character of Lady Kitty Crocodile in *A Trip to Calais* was offensive to the duchess of Kingston, and was eliminated in *The Capuchin.*

Capuchins. Roman Catholic order of mendicant Franciscan monks, founded (c1528) in Italy by Matteo di Bascio, and named from the long pointed capuche, or hood, which is the distinguishing mark of their dress. According to the statutes of the order, drawn up in 1529, the monks were to live by begging; they were not to use gold or silver or silk in the decoration of their altars, and the chalices were to be of pewter. The Capuchins are numerous in many countries, and have a number of monasteries in the U.S.

Capucius (ką.pū'shus). In Shakespeare's *Henry VIII,* an ambassador from Charles V.

Capulet (kap'ų̄.lẹt). In Shakespeare's *Romeo and Juliet,* a coarse, jovial old man with a passionate temper, the father of Juliet.

Capuletti ed i Montecchi (kä.pö.let'tē ed ē mōn.tek'kē), **I.** [Eng. trans., *"The Capulets and Montagues."*] Opera by Vincenzo Bellini, first produced at Venice in 1830. It is a musical version of *Romeo and Juliet.*

Capus (kȧ.pü), **Alfred.** b. at Aix, Bouches-du-Rhône, France, Nov. 25, 1858; d. at Neuilly, France, Nov. 1, 1922. French novelist, dramatist, and journalist, author of novels, including *Qui perd gagne* (1890), *Faux départ* (1891), *Robinson* (1910), and of such comedies as *La Bourse ou la vie* (1900) and *Les Maris de Léontine* (1903). His fiction and drama display the same gently cynical brilliance which attracted wide attention to his political editorials in the newspaper *Figaro.*

Caquetá (kä.kä.tä'). Commissary in S Colombia. Capital, Florencia; area, 39,764 sq. mi.; pop. 21,100 (est. 1950).

Caquetá. Name of the **Japurá** in Colombia.

Caquetios (kä.kä.tē'ōz). South American Indian tribe, once numerous but now reduced in size, that originally inhabited the E shores of Lake Maracaibo, Venezuela. The language was of the Arawakan stock.

Caqueux (kȧ.kė). See **Colliberts.**

Cara (kä'rä). See **Quito,** Indians.

Caraballos Occidentales (kä.rä.bä'yōs ŏk"sē.den.tä'lās). Mountain system of Luzon, Philippine Islands, extending for ab. 200 mi. from N to S, and separating the valley of the Cagayan River from the China Sea. The N part of the range, between Cagayan and Ilocos Norte provinces, is called the Cordillera Norte; the C part, separating Cagayan and the mid-part of Mountain Province, the Cordillera Central; the S part, connecting the Sierra Madre with the Cordillera Central, the Caraballos Sur or Cordillera Sur. The Cordillera Norte gradually increases in height from N to S to its culminating peak, Pagsan (7,261 ft.). In the Cordillera Central are peaks 6,000 to 6,500 ft. in height, and in the Caraballos Sur is Mount Data (7,364 ft.). Spurs trending in different directions separate branches of the Cagayan River, or form the boundary between provinces. These spurs contain some of the higher peaks of the system.

Caraballos Sur (sör). [Also, **Caraballo Sur.**] Range of mountains in Luzon, Philippine Islands, extending E and W between Nueva Vizcaya and Nueva Écija provinces and connecting the Sierra Madre system on the E with the Caraballos Occidentales on the W. It is the source region of the Rio Grande de la Pampanga.

Carabanchel Alto (kä″rä.bän.chel′ äl′tō). Town in C Spain, in the province of Madrid, SW of Madrid, of which it is a suburb. 10,682 (1940).

Carabanchel Bajo (bä′ho). Town in C Spain, in the province of Madrid, SW of Madrid, of which it is a suburb. 26,970 (1940).

Carabas (kar′ạ.bas), **Marquis of.** Master for whom Puss in Boots wins great wealth and a beautiful princess in Perrault's tale *Le Chat Botté* (now best known in English as *Puss in Boots*). The name has since been used allusively for a pretentious aristocrat who refuses to go along with his age. The Marquis of Carabas in Disraeli's *Vivian Grey* (1826) is intended to represent the Marquis of Clanricarde (Ulick John de Burgh, who had been made 1st marquis of Clanricarde, in a second creation, in 1825).

Carabaya (kä.rä.bä′yä). [Also, **Caravaya.**] Mountainous region in E Peru, in the department of Puno. Gold was discovered there about 1543, and for a century the mines of this region were famous. Its towns, especially Sandia, San Gaban, and San Juan del Oro, were important. In 1767 they were all destroyed by the Chuncho Indians, not a Spaniard being left E of the Andes. The region is now almost unknown, being frequented only by cinchona-collectors. Area, ab. 12,000 sq. mi.

Carabobo (kä.rä.bō′bō). State in N Venezuela, bordering on the Caribbean Sea. Capital, Valencia; area, 1,795 sq. mi.; pop. 243,159 (1950).

Carabobo. Plain S of Valencia, Venezuela, in the same valley. Here, on May 28, 1814, Simon Bolívar with ab. 5,000 men defeated the Spanish captain-general Juan Manuel Cajigal with ab. 6,000 men. On June 24, 1821, Bolívar won a second victory on the same plain over the Spanish army of Miguel de La Torre. This was the last Spanish force of consequence in Venezuela, and the victory secured the independence of NW South America.

Caraça (kạ.rä′sạ). See under **Espinhaço, Serra.**

Caracal (kä.rä.käl′). [Also, **Karakal.**] Town in S Rumania, in the province of Oltenia, ab. 85 mi. SW of Bucharest. It has agricultural markets, particularly for grain. 17,892 (1948).

Caracalla (kar.ạ.kal′ạ) or **Caracallus** (-kal′us). [Nickname of **Marcus Aurelius Antoninus;** original name, **Bassianus.**] b. at Lugdunum, Gaul (now Lyons, France), in April, 188 A.D.; d. near Edessa, in Mesopotamia, April 8, 217 A.D. Emperor of Rome; son of Septimius Severus. Having become joint emperor of Rome with his brother Geta in 211, he murdered the latter with many of his adherents, including the jurist Papinian, and made himself sole emperor in 212. He extended by the *Constitutio Antoniana* the full citizenship to all free inhabitants of the empire, in order to increase the produce of the succession duty of five percent, which Augustus had imposed on the property of citizens. He conducted successful campaigns against the Germans at the Rhine (213) and the Danube (214), and fought (216) victoriously at the Euphrates. An extravagant ruler, he built many public structures; among them the Baths of Caracalla at Rome. He was murdered on an expedition against the Parthians. His adoption of the long tunic with hood worn by the Gauls earned him his name of Caracalla (or Caracallus).

Caracalla, Baths of. See **Baths of Caracalla.**

Caracas (kä.rä′käs). Spanish colonial province in South America which embraced approximately the present states of Miranda, Barinas, and Carabobo, in Venezuela. The captain-generalcy of Venezuela, formed in 1751, was commonly called Caracas, from the capital, just as New Spain was called Mexico.

Caracas. City in N Venezuela, in the Distrito Federal, near the Caribbean Sea: the national capital. It is an important commercial center, and has a cathedral and university. Its seaport is La Guaira. Founded in 1567, Caracas was the birthplace of Simon Bolívar and a center of the revolution against Spain, independence being declared here in 1811. The Spanish forces retook the city after it had been all but destroyed by an earthquake the next year, took it again from Bolívar in 1813, and held it until Bolívar's victory at Carabobo in 1821. 269,030 (1941), 695,095 (1950).

Caracas. Collective term for a group of South American Indian tribes, now extinct, which inhabited the valleys around what is now the city of Caracas, Venezuela. Their languages were of the Cariban stock.

Caracci (kä.rät′chē). See **Carracci.**

Caraccioli (kä.rät′chō.lē), Saint **Francesco.** b. at Villa Santa Maria, in Abruzzo, Italy, Oct. 13, 1563; d. at Agnone, Italy, June 4, 1608. Cofounder of the Congregation of Minor Clerks Regular (Clerici Regulares Minores). Cured of leprosy at the age of 22, he vowed himself to an ecclesiastical life. Ordained a priest in 1587, he assisted Giovanni Agostino Adorno to found the new congregation, approved in 1588 by Pope Sixtus V, of which he became general in 1593. He was canonized in 1807.

Caracciolo (kä.rät′chō.lō) or **Caraccioli, Francesco.** b. at Naples, Italy, 1752; hanged near there, 1799. Neapolitan admiral. Commander of the navy of the Parthenopean Republic (1799), he was condemned to death by order of Nelson.

Caractacus (kạ.rak′tạ.kus) or **Caratacus** (-rat′ạ-). [Latinized name of **Caradoc.**] fl. c50 A.D. British king, son of Cunobelin (who gave his name, in its variant form of Cymbeline, to a tragedy by Shakespeare), king of the Trinobantes. His capital was Camulodunum (Colchester). He was chief of the Catuvellauni, and resisted the Romans (under Aulus Plautius, Ostorius Scapula, and, for a short time, the emperor Claudius) for about nine years. Finally defeated, he took refuge among the Brigantes, but was delivered by Cartismandua, their queen, to the Romans, and was sent to Rome. Claudius granted him his life and his family. Caradoc, son of the legendary Brythonic Bran, is sometimes identified with this Caractacus.

Caractacus. Tragedy by William Mason, published in 1759. It follows the British story of Caractacus, in its general outline, and is modeled strictly upon the classical Greek tragic form, thus combining two traditions. However, in an age which was becoming increasingly fond of sentimental comedy, it was able to achieve little popular success.

Caractacus. Tragedy by J. R. Planché, an alteration of John Fletcher's tragedy *Bonduca;* in which, as in this, a principal character is based on the historical Caractacus. It was produced in 1837.

Caraculiambo (kä″rä.kö.lē.äm′bō). In Miguel de Cervantes' *Don Quixote,* a giant whom Don Quixote proposes to conquer.

Caradoc (kạ.rad′ọk). See also **Caractacus.**

Caradoc. [Also: **Cradock, Craddocke.**] Knight of the Round Table, in the Arthurian cycle of romance. The story goes that one day a boy arrived at King Arthur's court with a mantle which could not be worn by an unchaste woman. Of all the ladies of the court only Caradoc's wife could wear it. The tale is told in "The Boy and the Mantle," ballad 29 of F. J. Child's *English and Scottish Popular Ballads.* There is a version also in Thomas Percy's *Reliques of Ancient English Poetry.*

Caradog (kạ.rad′ọg). [Called **Caradog of Llancarvan.**] d. c1247. Welsh historian. His continuation of the *History* of his friend Geoffrey of Monmouth, though the original text is lost, is included in later Welsh chronicles.

Carafa (kä.rä′fä), **Michele.** [Full name, **Michele Enrico Carafa di Colobrano.**] b. at Naples, Italy, Nov. 17, 1787; d. at Paris, July 26, 1872. Composer of more than 35 operas, including *Le Solitaire* (1822) and *Masaniello* (1827). He was an officer in the bodyguard of Murat (at that time king of Naples), and served under Napoleon in the Russian campaign (1812). Retiring from the French army after the collapse of the empire, he devoted himself to music; in 1837 he was elected to the Académie des Beaux-Arts. Among his other operas are *Gabriele* (1818) and *La Violette* (1828).

Caraffa (kä.räf′fä), **Giovanni Pietro.** Original name of Pope **Paul IV.**

Caragiali (kä.rä.jä′li), **Ion Luca.** [Also, **Caragiale** (-le).] b. at Ploeşti, Rumania, Jan. 29, 1852; d. at Berlin, June 22, 1912. Rumanian author, playwright, and theatrical manager. Born of a family of itinerant actors, he had no formal education, yet became a journalist at an early age, and subsequently the author of successful stage comedies and satirical stories, editor of the humorous weekly *Moftul Roman* (Rumanian Trifle), and director general of the national theater at Bucharest. Best known of his plays are *Noptea furtunosa* (The Stormy Night, 1880), *Scrissaren perduta* (The Lost Letter, 1885), and Năpasta (False Charge, 1889). Caragiali's satire was directed against those who were too hasty in wishing to change Rumanian ways and customs to conform to Western European standards. Nevertheless after he came into an inheritance which made him independent, he took up his residence at Berlin, where he spent his last years in leisurely enjoyment of the arts, especially music.

Carajá (kä.rą.zhä'). Collective term for several South American Indian tribes inhabiting the middle portions of the Araguaia River valley, Brazil. The Carajá language appears to comprise a stock unto itself with no probable relationships to the languages of neighboring tribes.

Caralis (kar'ą.lis). Ancient name of the city of **Cagliari.**

Caraman (kä.rä.män'). See **Karaman.**

Caramania (kar.ą.mā'ni.ą). See **Karamania.**

Caramurú (kä.rą.mö.rö'). [Full original title, **Caramurú: poema épico do descubrimento da Bahia.**] Epic poem in ten cantos by the Brazilian poet José de Santa Rita Durão (c1720–84) dealing with the discovery of southern Brazil (approximately coextensive with what later came to be called Bahia) by the Portuguese adventurer Diogo Alvares, whose Indian name was Caramurú. It was published at Lisbon in 1781; there was a French translation in 1829. It is noted especially for the excellence of its treatment of Brazil's natural beauty and of its Indian life.

Caramurú. Nickname given to a political party in Brazil which, after the abdication of the emperor Pedro I in 1831, sought to secure his restoration. The name, if not officially adopted by the party, nevertheless became their common designation, and is generally used by historians. After the death of the ex-emperor most of the members of the Caramurú party joined the conservatives.

Caramurú. Indian name of **Alvares, Diogo.**

Caran d'Ache (kå.räṅ dåsh). [Pseudonym of **Emmanuel Poiré.**] b. at Moscow, 1858; d. at Paris, Feb. 26, 1909. French illustrator and caricaturist. His pseudonym derives from the Russian word *karandash*, which means "pencil." He was the grandson of a soldier in Napoleon's army, and was educated at Moscow. Having moved to Paris, he was first an attaché in the ministry of war and afterward became an illustrator of popular journals. His fame rests largely on his caricatures which appeared in *Tout Paris, La Vie Parisienne, Chat Noir*, and others. *Album Caran d'Ache* and *Bric-à-brac* are among well-known collections of his work.

Caransebes (kä.rän.sā'besh). [Also, **Karansebes.**] Town in NW Rumania, in the region of Banat, situated on the Timişul River, ab. 58 mi. SW of Timişoara: railroad junction; manufactures leather and metal goods. It is the seat of an Orthodox bishopric and a theological academy. 10,106 (1948).

Carapeguá (kä"rä.pā.gwä'). City in SW Paraguay, in Paraguarí department. Pop. ab. 17,000.

Caratacus (ką.rat'ą.kus). See **Caractacus.**

Carathéodory (kä"rä.tā.ō.dō'rē), **Constantin.** b. at Berlin, Sept. 13, 1873—. German mathematician of Greek parentage, who has contributed especially to the theory of functions and the calculus of variations. He was educated at Berlin and Göttingen, and has taught at various universities, including Hanover, Göttingen, Bonn, Breslau, Berlin, Smyrna, Athens, and Munich. His works include *Vorlesungen über Reale Funktionen* (1918), *Variationsrechnung* (1935), *Geometrische Optik* (1937), and *Elementare Theorie des Spiegelteleskops* (1940).

Carathis (kar'ą.this). Mother of Vathek, titular hero of William Beckford's *Vathek* (1786). She was a renowned sorceress and helped her son, who wished to behold the wonders of the underworld, to sell his soul to the devil in return for this and other favors.

Carausius (ką.rô'shi.us, -zhi.us). [Full name, **Marcus Aurelius Valerius Carausius.**] d. 293 A.D. Roman insurgent. He was a Menapian by birth, and in his youth is said to have been a river pilot. In 286 he distinguished himself in the campaign of the emperor Maximian against the revolted Bagaudae in Gaul, and was at about this period entrusted with the enterprise of suppressing the Frankish and Saxon pirates who ravaged the coasts of Britain and Gaul. Suspected of acting in collusion with the pirates, he was ordered executed, whereupon he made himself master of Britain and part of Gaul, and assumed (c287) the imperial title of Augustus. He was recognized as a colleague in the government of the empire by the emperors Maximian and Diocletian c290. On appointment of Galerius and Constantius Chlorus as Caesars in 292, the latter undertook a campaign against Carausius, who was assassinated in the following year by his chief minister, Allectus.

Caravaca (kä.rä.ʙä'kä). City in E Spain, in the province of Murcia, situated on the Caravaca River, ab. 40 mi. NW of Murcia. It has paper, leather, and textile factories; there are copper and iron mines and marble quarries in the vicinity. Notable buildings include the medieval castle and the Chapel of Santa Cruz. An annual festival is held on May 3. Pop. 20,645 (1940).

Caravaggio (kä.rä.väd'jō). Town and commune in NW Italy, in the *compartimento* (region) of Lombardy, in the province of Bergamo, between Milan and Brescia, ab. 22 mi. E of Milan. It has manufactures of hats and knitwear and a sugar refinery. Notable buildings include the Romanesque Church of San Bernardino and the Church of the Madonna di Caravaggio to which pilgrimages are made. Caravaggio was the birthplace of the painter Michelangelo Amerighi da Caravaggio. Pop. of commune, 10,691 (1936); of town, 7,816 (1936).

Caravaggio, Giovanni Francesco Straparola da. See **Straparola, Giovanni Francesco.**

Caravaggio, Michelangelo Amerighi (or **Merighi**) **da.** b. at Caravaggio, near Bergamo, Italy, c1565; d. at Porte d'Ercole, Italy, c1609. Italian painter, founder and chief exponent of the naturalistic school at Rome, master of exaggerated chiaroscuro as later exemplified especially by the Spanish painter Jusèpe de Ribera. He killed a companion in a gambling brawl at Rome and fled to Naples, and from there went to Sicily and Malta. Among his famous religious works are *The Entombment of Christ*, now in the Vatican at Rome, a self-portrait in the collection of the Uffizi at Florence, *Death of the Virgin Mary* in the Louvre at Paris, and *The Supper At Emmaus* in the National Gallery at London.

Caravaggio, Polidoro da. [Original surname, **Caldara.**] b. at Caravaggio, near Bergamo, Italy, c1495; killed at Messina, Sicily, 1543. Italian painter; pupil of Raphael. Under his master he made certain well-known friezes in the Vatican, and other architectural decorations. His works are best known through engravings made of them; *Christ Bearing the Cross*, at Naples, is one of his surviving paintings.

Caravan. Collection (1925) of 50 short stories by John Galsworthy. The volume contains stories taken from five previously published collections: *A Sheaf* (1916), *Another Sheaf, Five Tales* (both 1919), *The Burning Spear* and *Captures* (both 1923). Some of the best-known stories in it are "The First and the Last," "A Stoic," "The Apple Tree," "The Juryman," "A Feud," "Timber," "Santa Lucia," and "A Stroke of Lightning."

Caravaya (kä.rä.ʙä'yä). See **Carabaya.**

Caravelas (kä.rą.vā'ląs). [Also, **Caravellas.**] Seaport in E Brazil, in the state of Bahia. Pop. under 5,000 (1940).

Caravellas (kä.rą.vā'ląs), Marquis of. Title of **Carneiro de Campos, José Joaquim.**

Caravellas, Visconde **de.** Title of **Alves Branco, Manoel.**

Carazo (kä.rä'sō). Department in SW Nicaragua, on the Pacific coast. Capital, Jinotepe; area, 367 sq. mi.; pop. 52,138 (1952).

Carbajal (kär.ʙä.ʜäl'), **Francisco.** See **Carvajal** or **Carbajal, Francisco.**

Carballedo (kär.ʙä.lyā'ᴛʜō). Town and commune in NW Spain, in the province of Lugo, SW of Lugo. 10,483 (1940).

Carballo (kär.ʙä'lyō). Town in NW Spain, in the province of La Coruña, situated on the Allones River, ab. 20 mi. SW of La Coruña. It is a trade center for a dairying and grain-producing district, chiefly noted for the hot sulfur springs of San Juan de Carballo which are in the vicinity. 18,159 (1940).

Carberry Hill (kär'ber"i, -bėr.i). Place near Musselburgh, Midlothian, Scotland. It was here that the Scottish nobles, in rebellion against the marriage of Mary, Queen of Scots, to Bothwell, dispersed (June 15, 1567) Bothwell's forces, and made Mary herself a prisoner (Bothwell escaped capture, but had to flee Scotland).

Carbia (kär′вyä). Town and commune in NW Spain, in the province of Pontevedra, S of La Coruña. 10,314 (1940).

Carbo (kär′bō), **Gnaeus Papirius.** b. c130 B.C.; d. 82 B.C. Roman plebeian leader, soldier, and consul. A member of one of the most prominent of the plebeian families, Carbo vigorously supported Marius and fought in the Marian forces against Sulla. In 85 B.C. he became consul with Cinna, and remained as sole consul after Cinna's murder. In 82 B.C. he checked Sulla near Clusium (modern chiusi), but suffered disastrous defeat at the hands of Metellus Pius, one of Sulla's lieutenants, near Faventia (Faenza). Carbo fled abroad but was taken by Pompey on the island of Pantelleria, and put to death.

Carbonari (kär.bō.nä′rē). Secret society formed in the kingdom of Naples during the reign of Murat (1808–15) by republicans and others dissatisfied with the French rule. They were originally refugees among the mountains of the Abruzzi provinces, and took their name from the mountain charcoal-burners. Their aim was to free their country from foreign domination. After having aided the Austrians in the expulsion of the French, the organization spread over all Italy as the champions of the National Liberal cause against the reactionary governments. At one time the Carbonari numbered several hundred thousand adherents. They were concerned in the various revolutions of the times until crushed by the Austrian power in Italy, and absorbed into the subsequent Risorgimento movement. They spread (c1820) into France, and played an important part in French politics until the revolution of 1830.

Carbonaro (kär.bō.nä′rō). See **Napoleon III.**

Carbondale (kär′bon.dāl). City in S Illinois, in Jackson County, ab. 50 mi. N of Cairo: railroad and coal-mining center. It is the seat of Southern Illinois University. 10,921 (1950).

Carbondale. City in NE Pennsylvania, in Lackawanna County, on the Lackawanna River ab. 15 mi. NE of Scranton: anthracite coal mining; manufactures of dresses and machinery. Coal has been mined here since 1814. 16,296 (1950).

Carbonear (kär.bō.nir′). Growing seaport on the island of Newfoundland, Canada, situated at the end of a branch railway line on the W shore of Conception Bay in the SW part of the island: commercial fishing. 3,351 (1951).

Carbonell y Rivero (kär.вō.nel′′ ē rē.вä′rō), **José Manuel.** b. at Alquizar, Cuba, July 3, 1880—. Cuban statesman and author. He joined Martí in the Cuban revolutionary movement, was a lieutenant in the Cuban War, and served as a general in the civil war (1906). He was also head of the board of education and superintendent of schools. A delegate (1910, 1928) to the fourth and sixth Pan-American conferences, he served as minister (1934–37) to Brazil and as ambassador (1937–45) to Mexico. Founder and first secretary (1902) of *El Ateneo de la Habana,* he was coeditor, with his brother Néstor Carbonell y Rivero (1883—), of *Letras* (1905–17). He began publication of the annals of the Academia Nacional de Artes y Letras, and was editor of *Evolución de la cultura cubana.* Author of *Arpas cubanas* (1904), *Mi libro de amor* (1922), *Patria* (1922), *Penachos y exhalaciones* (1923), and critical works on Cuban literature.

Carbonia (kär.bô′nyä). Town in W Italy, on the island of Sardinia, in the province of Cagliari, situated on the Gulf of Carloforte opposite the island of San Pietro, in the SW corner of the island, W of Cagliari. It is a newly constructed town for miners. Coal is mined in the nearby Iglesiente region; there are also lead and zinc mines. 10,362 (1936).

Carboniferous Period (kär.bon.if′ėr.us). Geological period in the Paleozoic Era during which grew the plants that formed the modern coal beds. See table at end of Vol. III.

Carbonnières (kår.bo.nyer), **Louis François Elizabeth,** Baron **Ramond de.** See **Ramond de Carbonnières, Louis François Elizabeth,** Baron.

Carbutt (kär′but), **John.** b. at Sheffield, England, Dec. 2, 1832; d. at Philadelphia, July 26, 1905. American photographer, resident in the U.S. from 1853. He served as official photographer for the Canadian Pacific Railway, and first president of the Photographic Association of America. He devised (c1879) the first gelatin dry plate in America, standardized (c1879) the size of lantern slides, and introduced the orthochromatic plate for color photography.

Carcagente (kär.kä.нen′tā). [Also, **Carcajente.**] Town in E Spain, in the province of Valencia, situated on the Júcar River, ab. 30 mi. SW of Valencia. It is in a rich district, with abundant rice harvests, and olive, palm, mulberry, and orange groves. Silk and linen are manufactured. There are remnants of Roman and Moorish structures. 17,846 (1940).

Cárcano (kär′kä.nō), **Miguel Ángel.** b. at Buenos Aires, July 18, 1889—. Argentine diplomat and writer on political science. Active in negotiating the Roca-Runciman Commercial Treaty with Great Britain in 1932, he was later (1935–38) minister cf agriculture. He also served as ambassador to France (1938–41) and to Great Britain (1941–45). His *Evolución histórica del régimen de la tierra pública 1810–1916* (1917) wcn Argentina's first national literary prize.

Carcar (kär′kär). Town in Cebu province, on the E coast of Cebu island, in the Philippine Islands. 5,334 (1948).

Carcaraña (kär.kä.rä′nyä). [Also, **Carcaraná.**] River in C Argentina, a tributary of the Paraná River.

Carcassonne (kår.kå.son). [Ancient name, **Carcaso.**] City in S France, the capital of the department of Aude, situated on the Aude River and the Canal du Midi. It consists of two parts, the Upper Town (*la cité*) and the Lower Town. The Upper Town, now practically abandoned for the more convenient site below, is in its entirety one of the most remarkable remaining monuments of the Middle Ages in the South of France. In plan it is square, about a mile in circuit, enclosed by two lines of walls with 54 towers, all of admirable masonry, and retaining in their approaches, their gates, and battlements, all the defensive devices evolved by medieval military engineers. Some of the inner walls and towers date from the Visigothic rule in the 5th century; the greater portion dates from the 12th century, and the remainder from the reign of Saint Louis. On one side rises a powerful castle or citadel. The church of Saint Nazaire has a Romanesque nave, and a beautiful choir with stained-glass windows from the 14th century. This fortress was restored by Napoleon III. Founded by the Romans, the town was an Albigensian stronghold in the Middle Ages. The Lower Town, founded (1247) by Saint Louis, has a number of old churches and monuments. Carcassonne's industry produces candied fruits as a specialty; there are also flour mills, hat manufactures, and chemical and metallurgical factories. 38,139 (1946).

Car-cay (kär.kī′). A name given to the northeasternmost ramification of the Sierra Madre, in Mexico, lying due W from Corralitos in Chihuahua. It is a rugged and wild chain, difficult of access.

Carchemish (kär′ke.mish, kär.kē′mish). In Biblical geography, the capital of the Hittites. It was formerly identified with a town called Circessium or Circesium by the Romans, a fortified place near where the Habor (modern Khabur) River empties into the Euphrates. Later excavations brought out its identity with the Gargamis of the Assyrian inscriptions (Egyptian, Guargamesha), situated on the right bank of the Euphrates near the modern Turkish-Syrian border NE of Aleppo. The city is mentioned in the annals of Tiglath-pileser I, in 1110 B.C. Shalmaneser II in 858, and Sargon in 717, subjected this capital of the Hittites, and placed an Assyrian governor in it. In 605 B.C. the battle between Nebuchadnezzar and Necho of Egypt (Jer. xlvi. 2, 2 Chron. xxxv. 20), in which Egypt was thoroughly defeated by Western Asia, took place under its walls.

Carchi (kär′chē). Province in N Ecuador. Capital, Tulcán; area, 1,383 sq. mi.; pop. 79,155 (est. 1944).

Carco (kår.kō), **Francis.** [Pseudonym of **François Alexandre Marie Carcopino-Tusoli.**] b. at Nouméa, New Caledonia, July 3, 1886—. French novelist and poet, specializing in studies of Parisian bohemianism. He is the author of *Jésus-la-Caille* (1914) and many other studies of the French uuderworld, including *L'Homme traqué* (1922; Eng. trans., *The Noose of Sin,* 1923, also *The Hounded Man,* 1924), which studies similar moral aberrations in a more normal social setting, and for the last of which he received the grand prize of the French Academy. As the son of a government functionary, he moved constantly from place to place, and received an erratic education. He became a poet at 14 and an admirer of Rimbaud, Verlaine, and other Bohemian poets. From this interest developed the special literary vocation to which he has devoted his life.

Card, The. Realistic novel (1911), one of the Five Towns group, by Arnold Bennett. It is entitled *Denry the Audacious* in the American edition, after the chief quality of its lucky hero, who finally becomes mayor.

Cardale (kär′dạl), **John Bate.** b. at London, Nov. 7, 1802; d. there, July 18, 1877. English lawyer, first apostle (1831) of the Catholic Apostolic Church, whose members were commonly known as Irvingites, after their founder, Edward Irving. Cardale's apostleship followed upon his wife's "speaking with tongues," the special gift of this sect. He was the author of numerous sermons and anonymous controversial religious tracts.

Cardamom Hills (kär′dạ.mọm). [Also, **Cardamon Hills** (-mọn).] Mountain range in the S part of the Union of India, in E Travancore and S Madras. The ranges are rugged and largely covered by rain forest. The peak elevation is Devar Malai, 6,307 ft. Length, ab. 120 mi.

Cardano (kär.dä′nō), **Geronimo** or **Girolamo.** [English, **Jerome Cardan** (kär′dạn).] b. at Pavia, Italy, Sept. 24, 1501; d. at Rome, Sept. 21, 1576. Italian physician, mathematician, philosopher, and astrologer. He graduated in medicine from the university at Padua, taught geometry at Milan, and medicine at Pavia and Bologna. His works include *De subtilitate rerum* (1551), *De varietate rerum* (1554), and the autobiographical *De propria vita* (c1575; Eng. trans., 1930). One of his more interesting achievements, in the opinion of many readers, is that he cast a horoscope of Jesus Christ.

Card Castle. Novel by the English novelist Alec Waugh, published in 1924.

Cardenal (kär.dā.näl′) or **Cardinal** (kär.dē.näl′), **Peire.** fl. in the 13th century. Provençal troubadour, noted for his anticlerical and social satire, especially through the medium of his *sirventés* (which are typical Provençal songs of religious and moral comment).

Cardenal y Fernández (kär.ᴛʜā.näl′, ē fer.nän′deth), **Salvador.** b. at Valencia, Spain, Sept. 1, 1852; d. at Barcelona, Spain, April 23, 1927. Spanish surgeon. He served as anatomical preparator in the faculty of medicine at Barcelona and was professor of surgical pathology at the University of Barcelona. He was the pioneer of antiseptic surgery in Spain and devoted special attention to the study of general and local anesthesia. His works include *De la osteomielitis en sus relaciones con la pioémia y la septicémia* (1877), *Guia práctico para la cura de las heridas y la aplicación del método antiséptico en cirugia* (1880), and *Manual práctico de cirugia antiséptica* (1887).

Cardenal y Pujals (kär.ᴛʜā.näl′ ē pö.ʜäls′), **León.** b. in Spain, 1878—. Spanish pathologist; son of Salvador Cardenal y Fernández (1852–1927). Professor of pathology and clinical surgery at the University of Madrid, he is known for his works on rejuvenation by the transplantation of glands. He is editor of the *Dicionario terminológico de ciencias médicas* (1927 *et seq.*) and *Enfermo resecado de estómago y reoperato* (1935).

Cárdenas (kär′ᴛʜā.näs). City in NW Cuba, in Matanzas province, ab. 25 mi. E of Matanzas: Cuba's fourth largest commercial city, exporting sugar and sisal. An engagement occurred here on May 11, 1898, between the Spanish shore batteries and gunboats and several U.S. vessels. 37,059 (1943).

Cárdenas, Bernardino de. b. at Chuquisaca (Sucre), Bolivia (then Peru), in the 17th century. Spanish Franciscan friar. He devoted his life to missionary work among the natives of the country. He wrote three books relating to the field of his endeavors (thus acquiring the title of "Historian of Peru"), the chief being *Manual y relación de las cosas del reyno del Peru*, published at Madrid in 1634.

Cárdenas, García López de. fl. 1540. Spanish nobleman who became one of Coronado's captains on the expedition of 1540 to New Mexico and beyond. With his party he was the first to see and describe the Grand Canyon of the Colorado, which he beheld about September, 1540. He reported the gorge as extremely deep, with a distance of three or four leagues from brink to brink.

Cárdenas, Lázaro. b. in Michoacán, Mexico, May 21, 1895—. Mexican revolutionary soldier and politician, president (1934–40) of Mexico. He joined (1913) the revolutionary forces fighting against Huerta, served under Calles and Obregón, became a brigadier general in 1924, and a general of division in 1928. Provisional governor (1920) and governor (1928–32) of Michoacán, he was president (1930) of the Partido Revolucionario Nacional, minister of the interior (1931), and minister of war and navy (1933). His presidential administration (1934–40), though marred by difficulties between the government and the Roman Catholic Church, was notable for inauguration of the Six-Year Plan, providing agrarian reform, distribution of land to peasants, coöperative farms, credit banks, nationalization of foreign-owned oil properties, and extension and secularization of education. Subsequently he was commander (1942) of all Mexican forces on the Pacific coast, and minister of defense (1942–45).

Cardenio (kär.dā′ni.ō; Spanish, kär.ᴛʜā′nyō). Intellectual madman, crazed by disappointed love, but with lucid intervals, who appears in Miguel de Cervantes's *Don Quixote*. His love is finally restored to him. He is introduced in the younger George Colman's *The Mountaineers*, where he is called Octavian, and also in Thomas D'Urfey's *The Comical History of Don Quixote* (1694 and 1696).

Cardenio, The History of. Play entered on the Stationers' Register in 1653 as by John Fletcher and Shakespeare. Late 17th-century entries in the Stationers' Register, however, are no guarantee for Shakespeare's coauthorship.

Cardiff (kär′dif). City, county borough, market town, and seaport, in SE Wales, county seat of Glamorganshire, situated at the confluence of the river Taff with the estuary of the river Severn, ab. 38 mi. W of Bristol (England), ab. 145 mi. W of London by rail. Cardiff is the capital of the principality of Wales. Here, forming a group in a state and civic center, are the Welsh National War Memorial, the National Museum of Wales, the main buildings of the University College of South Wales and Monmouthshire, and the Registry of the University of Wales. Cardiff Castle, built in 1080, is also here. The town is important in the iron, steel, and tin-plate industries. The largest blast-furnace in Britain was erected here in 1932. Much iron ore, pig iron, and steel bar-stock is now imported for the steel manufactures. Cardiff is important for the export of coal from the valleys of the rivers Taff and Rhymney. It is also a shipbuilding center. Cardiff was the place of imprisonment (1106–34) of Robert of Normandy. 243,637 (1951).

Cardiff Giant. Gigantic human figure (10½ ft. high, weighing 2,966 pounds) passed off on the public as a prehistoric man in a state of petrifaction: one of the most famous and elaborate hoaxes in 19th-century American history. It created great public excitement until the hoax was exposed. The figure had been carved of gypsum at Chicago for one George Hull, shipped to Cardiff, N.Y., buried there on the Newell farm, "discovered" (1869), and exhibited, to the gain of the hoaxers, until the fake was revealed.

Cardigan (kär′di.gạn), 7th Earl of. [Title of **James Thomas Brudenell.**] b. at Hambledon, Hampshire, England, Oct. 16, 1797; d. at Deene Park, Northamptonshire, England, March 28, 1868. English soldier, commander of the "Light Brigade" in the charge at Balaklava. He was a member of Parliament (1818–29) and entered (1824) the army, becoming a lieutenant colonel (December, 1830) by purchase. As cavalry commander, he led the charge of the Light Brigade in the battle of Balaklava (Oct. 25, 1854) during the Crimean War, being the first man to reach the Russian guns. In 1861 he was appointed lieutenant general.

Cardigan. [Welsh, **Aberteifi.**] Municipal borough, market town, and seaport in S Wales, in Cardiganshire, situated on the river Teifi, ab. 3 mi. from its mouth, ab. 22 mi. NW of Carmarthen, and ab. 261 mi. W of London by rail. Cardigan is the county seat of Cardiganshire, and has the ruins of a castle, built in 1090. Pop. 3,497 (1951).

Cardigan Bay. Arm of St. George's Channel, on the W coast of Wales. It measures ab. 66 mi. N and S, and ab. 45 mi. E and W.

Cardiganshire (kär′di.gạn.shir) or **Cardigan.** Maritime county in S Wales. It is bounded on the N by Merionethshire, on the E by Montgomeryshire, Radnorshire, and Brecknockshire, on the S by Carmarthenshire and Pembrokeshire, and on the W and NW by Cardigan Bay. The surface is generally mountainous, but lower in the western two-thirds which is mostly in permanent pasture where cattle and sheep are extensively raised. The principal crops are oats and barley. Formerly lead, copper, and zinc mining were important, but these have now declined; manufactures of gloves and woolens are now among the chief industries. Cardigan is the county seat; area of administrative county, ab. 692 sq. mi.; pop. of administrative county, 53,267 (1951).

Cardim (kär.dēn′), **Fernão.** b. at Vienna do Alvito, in Alentejo, Portugal, 1540; d. at Bahia (now Salvador), Brazil, Jan. 27, 1625. Portuguese Jesuit, provincial of Brazil (1604–08). He wrote a narrative of his travels, first published at Lisbon in 1847.

Cardinal, The. Tragedy by James Shirley, produced in 1641. It was doubtless independently suggested by the contemporary career of Richelieu in France, but suffers by resemblance to and comparison with the finer *Duchess of Malfi,* by John Webster. The ambitious Cardinal schemes to marry his nephew Columbo, a general, to the widowed Duchess Rosaura, and gains the consent of the king of Navarre, whose daughter-in-law she is. The Duchess, however, loves the young Count D'Alvarez, and during Columbo's absence gains the king's consent to this marriage also. However, on their wedding night Alvarez is murdered by the returned Columbo. A series of murders follows, ending with the poisoning of the Duchess by the Cardinal and the murder of the Cardinal himself. At the end of the play, as in *Hamlet,* almost all the main characters are dead. *The Cardinal* is considered Shirley's best play, and he himself thought it "the best of my flock."

Cardinal Peak. See under **Chelan Mountains.**

Cardis (kär′dis), **Treaty of.** [Also, **Treaty of Kardis.**] Treaty of peace concluded at Cardis, an estate on the borders of Livonia and Estonia, between Russia and Sweden, in 1661. Russia restored Tartu (Dorpat) and other places.

Cardonnel (kär.don′ẹl), **Adam de.** d. at Westminster, London, Feb. 22, 1719. English politician; secretary and friend of John Churchill, 1st Duke of Marlborough. He was expelled from the House of Commons on a charge of corruption on Feb. 19, 1712.

Cardonnel (kȧr.do.nel), **Louis Le.** See **Le Cardonnel, Louis.**

Cardozo (kär.dō′zō), **Benjamin Nathan.** b. at New York, May 24, 1870; d. at Port Chester, N.Y., July 19, 1938. American jurist. Admitted to the bar in 1891, he practiced law at New York through 1913, in which year he was elected to the state supreme court. In February, 1914, Governor Glynn appointed him an associate judge of the court of appeals of the state of New York; in 1917 he was elected to the same office, and in 1927 was elected chief justice of that court. When the resignation of Associate Justice Oliver Wendell Holmes from the U.S. Supreme Court made an appointment to that bench necessary in 1932, President Hoover, in nominating Judge Cardozo, gave effect to the overwhelming preference of the legal profession and of nonprofessional public opinion. The extraordinary and commanding eminence which Cardozo had attained arose not only from his record on the bench, but from the impact of his several books, in which the essentials of legal principles seen in the light of traditional American liberalism were set forth in the exceptionally felicitous phrasing of a born literary stylist. He was the author of *Jurisdiction of the New York Court of Appeals* (1909), *The Nature of the Judicial Process* (1921), *The Growth of the Law* (1924), *The Paradoxes of Legal Science* (1928), and *Law and Literature, and Other Essays* (1931).

Cardross (kär.dros′). Civil parish in C Scotland, in Dumbartonshire, situated on the Firth of Clyde, ab. 3 mi. NW of Dumbarton. Robert the Bruce died there. 11,106 (1931).

Cardross, Baron. A title of **Erskine, John.**

Carducci (kär.döt′chē), **Bartolommeo.** [Spanish, **Bartolomé Carducho** (kär.ᴛʜō′chō).] b. at Florence, 1560; d. at Madrid, 1608. Italian painter, sculptor, and architect in Spain. He began painting at Florence at an early age, but from 1585 to his death lived and worked in Spain in the service of Philip II and Philip III, employed mainly on the frescoes in the library of the Escorial palace. His most noted work, and generally esteemed his best, is a *Descent from the Cross* in the Church of San Felipe el Real. Because of his identification chiefly with Spain, he is often mentioned in the history of art by the Spanish form of his name.

Carducci, Giosuè. b. at Valdicastello, Tuscany, Italy, July 27, 1835; d. at Bologna, Italy, Feb. 16, 1907. Italian poet, awarded (1906) the Nobel prize for literature, and generally numbered among the leading Italian poets of all time. From 1860 he taught literature at Bologna, and was also known as a critic and patriot. He was leader of a new classical school which sought its vitality in the cultures of the ancient world itself rather than in any neoclassic formulas. In his nature poems he expresses a pantheism not unlike that of Victor Hugo. Especially characteristic of this poet are the three collections of his *Odi barbare* (1877, 1882, 1889) and *Rime e ritmi* (1891 *et seq.*). His collected works were issued (1889–1924) in 20 volumes. Among his single poems are *Inno a Satano, Il Bove,* and *La Chiesa di polenta.*

Carducci, Vincenzo. [Spanish, **Vicente Carducho** (kär.ᴛʜö′chō).] b. at Florence, c1568; d. at Madrid, c1638. Italian painter, patronized by Philip III and Philip IV of Spain. His chief works are in Spain.

Carduchis (kär.dö′chẹz). See **Kurds.**

Cardwell (kärd′wel, -wẹl), **Edward.** b. at Blackburn, Lancashire, England, 1787; d. at Oxford, England, May 23, 1861. English clergyman and church historian; uncle of Edward Cardwell (1813–86). He was appointed select preacher to the University of Oxford in 1823, Camden professor of ancient history in 1826, and principal of St. Alban Hall in 1831. He proposed to write a history of the Church of England of which *Documentary Annals of the Reformed Church of England from 1546 to 1716* was finished in 1839 and the *History of Conferences, etc., connected with the Revision of the Book of Common Prayer* in 1840.

Cardwell, Edward. [Title, Viscount **Cardwell.**] b. at Liverpool, England, July 24, 1813; d. at Torquay, England, Feb. 15, 1886. English statesman, nephew of Edward Cardwell (1787–1861). He was president of the Board of Trade (1852–55), secretary for Ireland (1859–61), chancellor of the duchy of Lancaster (1861–64), colonial secretary (1864–66), and secretary for war (1868–74). In the last post he introduced reforms in the army, including the abolition of commissions by purchase and the formation of an army reserve.

Carea (kạ.rē′ạ). An ancient name of **Chieri.**

Careful and Strict Enquiry into the Modern Prevailing Notions of that Freedom of Will, Which is Supposed to be Essential to Moral Agency, Vertue and Vice, Reward and Punishment, Praise and Blame. Full original title of the work by Jonathan Edwards now better known as **Freedom of Will.**

Carei (kä.rā′ē). [Also, **Careii Mare** (or **Mari**) (kä.rā′ē mä′rā, mä′rē); Hungarian, **Nagykároly;** German, **Grosskarol.**] Town in NW Rumania, in the region of Transylvania, ab. 52 mi. NE of Oradea: frontier town to Hungary, and agricultural center. There is a Piarist monastery. 15,425 (1948).

Careless (kãr′lẹs). The friend of Mellefont in William Congreve's *The Double Dealer* (1694), a gay gallant who makes love to Lady Pliant.

Careless. Suitor of Lady Dainty in Colley Cibber's *The Double Gallant.*

Careless. The friend of Charles Surface in Richard Brinsley Sheridan's *The School for Scandal.* It is he who says of the portrait of Sir Oliver in the auction scene: "An unforgiving eye, and a damned disinheriting countenance."

Careless, Colonel. Gay, light-hearted lover of Ruth in Sir Robert Howard's play *The Committee.* The play was slightly altered and produced by T. Knight as *The Honest Thieves.* The character of Careless is the same in both plays.

Careless, William. See **Carlos** or **Careless, William.**

Careless Good Fellow, The. Drinking song by John Oldham, English Juvenalian poet of the Restoration period. Scholars are inclined to believe, on the basis of this song, that a number of anonymous Restoration ballads may well be his work.

Careless Husband, The. Comedy by Colley Cibber, produced in 1704 and printed in 1705. In the last act a wife, through a casual act of kindness, shames the heart of a moderately shameless husband.

Careless Lovers, The. Restoration farce-comedy (1673) by Edward Ravenscroft. Like virtually all his work it is not original, being actually nothing more than an adaptation from Molière.

Carême (kȧ.rem), **Marie Antoine.** b. at Paris, June 8, 1783; d. there, Jan. 11, 1833. French cook. He worked for Talleyrand, the Russian court, the English court, and Baron Rothschild. He wrote *Le Pâtissier royal* (1815).

Carew (ka̦.rö′), **Bamfylde Moore.** b. at Bickley, near Tiverton, England, in July, 1693; d. c1770. English vagabond. He ran away from school, joined a band of gypsies, and was eventually chosen king or chief of the gypsies. Convicted of vagrancy, he was transported to Maryland, whence he escaped and returned to England. He is said to have accompanied Charles Edward Stuart to Carlisle and Derby.

Carew, George. [Titles: Baron **Carew of Clopton,** Earl of **Totnes.**] b. in England, May 29, 1555; d. at London, March 27, 1629. English soldier and statesman, created Baron Carew on June 4, 1605, and Earl of Totnes on Feb. 5, 1626. He served in Ireland from 1574, became sheriff of Carlow in 1583 and master of ordnance in Ireland in 1588, was appointed lieutenant general of ordnance in England in 1592, and played an influential part in Ireland (in various offices) from 1599 until 1603, especially during the rebellion of Hugh O'Neill, Earl of Tyrone. He left a valuable collection of letters and manuscripts relating to such affairs.

Carew, Richard. b. at East Antony, Cornwall, England, July 17, 1555; d. there, Nov. 6, 1620. English poet and antiquary. He was high sheriff of Cornwall (1586), a member of Parliament, and the author of *Survey of Cornwall* (1602) and others.

Carew, Thomas. b. c1595; d. probably at London, c1639. English poet. He studied (but was not graduated) at Oxford, and afterward led a wandering life, serving for a time as secretary to Sir Dudley Carleton, ambassador at Venice and Turin, and later about the court of Charles I. He wrote *Coelum Britannicum* (1634), a masque, and the love poem *The Rapture.* A disciple of Ben Jonson, he was one of the Cavalier Poets.

Carey (kãr′i). Village in NW Ohio, in Wyandot County trading and shipping center for an agricultural region. Celery and onions are principal crops. 3,260 (1950).

Carey, George Saville. [Pseudonym, **Paul Tell-Truth.**] b. 1743; d. at London, 1807. English poet; son of Henry Carey (d. 1743). He was a printer by trade, and for a time an actor. He wrote *The Inoculator,* a comedy (published 1766), *Liberty Chastized, or Patriotism in Chains* (1768), *Shakespeare's Jubilee, a Masque* (1769), *The Nut-Brown Maid* (1770), *The Old Women Weatherwise, an Interlude* (1770), and *Balnea, or History of all the Popular Watering-places of England* (1799).

Carey, Henry. [Title, 1st Baron **Hunsdon.**] b. c1524; d. in Somersetshire, England, 1596. English soldier and diplomat; son of Ann Boleyn's sister, first cousin to Queen Elizabeth, and father of Robert Carey. A member of Parliament (1547–55) for Buckingham, he received lands there from Edward VI (1549) and in Hertfordshire and Kent from Queen Elizabeth (1561). He was knighted in 1558, and created a peer in 1559. Carey served as envoy to France (1564). As governor of Berwick (1568–87), he helped break (1569–70) the northern rebellion. In 1583 he was appointed lord chamberlain, and was commissioner of treason trials from 1585 to 1595, serving as one of the commissioners for the trial (1586) of Mary, Queen of Scots. He was envoy to Scotland (1587) and France (1591), and commanded (1588) the preparations at Tilbury to resist the Spanish Armada.

Carey, Henry. b. near the end of the 17th century; d. (probably by his own hand) at London, Oct. 4, 1743. English poet and composer of musical farces; said to have been the illegitimate son of George Saville, Marquis of Halifax; father of George Saville Carey (1743–1807). He was the reputed author of *God Save the King,* and author of the ballad *Sally in our Alley.* He wrote *Namby-Pamby, The Contrivances* (acted 1715), *Hanging and Marriage,* a farce (1722), *Poems* (1727), *Chrononhotonthologos,* a burlesque (acted Feb. 22, 1734), and *A Musical Century, or a hundred English Ballads.*

Carey, Henry Charles. b. at Philadelphia, Dec. 15, 1793; d. Oct. 13, 1879. American publisher and economist; son of Mathew Carey; leader of the American nationalist school of political economy founded by his father. In 1817 he became a partner (and later head) in the Philadelphia publishing house of Carey, Lea and Carey, the American publisher for Sir Walter Scott, Thomas Carlyle, and Washington Irving. He became interested in political economy relatively late in life. After writing *Essay on the Rate of Wages* (1835), he retired from business to concentrate on economic writing. He also published *Principles of Political Economy* (3 vols., 1837–38, 1840; later translated into Italian and Swedish), *Commercial Associations in France and England* (1845), *Past, Present and Future* (1848), *Harmony of Interests: Manufacturing and Commercial* (1851), *Slave Trade, Domestic and Foreign* (1853), *Letters to the President* (1858), *The Principles of Social Science* (3 vols., 1858–59), and *Unity of Law* (1872). A free trader at the outset, he later championed the protective tariff, and in his insistence upon the coöperation of an expanding industry and agriculture reflected the forward drive of the America of his lifetime. He was a critic of theEnglish classical economists and of the socialist school of economic thought. Among his disciples in the U.S. were Robert Ellis Thompson, Stephen Colwell, and William Elder; abroad, his followers included Ferrara and Dühring.

Carey, James. b. at Dublin, 1845; assassinated July 29, 1883. Irish political assassin. He was a bricklayer and builder by trade, and a town councilor of Dublin (1882). He became one of the leaders of the Irish political group known as the Invincibles in 1881, and was an accomplice in the assassination of T. H. Burke and Lord Frederick Cavendish in Phoenix Park at Dublin. He was arrested on Jan. 13, 1883, and turned Queen's evidence. In order to escape the vengeance of the Invincibles he was secretly shipped for Africa on the *Kinfauns Castle,* on July 6, 1883, under the name of Power; but his plan of escape was discovered, and he was followed on board the ship by Patrick O'Donnell, who shot him before the vessel reached its destination.

Carey, James F. b. at Haverhill, Mass., Aug. 19, 1867—. American socialist. He learned the shoemaking trade, joined the International Boot- and Shoemakers' Union, and became prominent in labor affairs. He was the first socialist elected to political office in New England, and a national organizer of the Socialist Party. He was a member of the Massachusetts House of Representatives in the period 1898–1902.

Carey, Joseph Maull. b. at Milton, Del., Jan. 19, 1845; d. Feb. 5, 1924. American jurist and legislator, a developer of irrigation in the western U.S., and member of the U.S. Senate; father of Robert Davis Carey. He was a young man when he went west under appointment by President Grant to the post of U.S. attorney for the Territory of Wyoming, then newly set up. In 1871 he became an associate justice of the territorial supreme court, serving until 1876, when he retired to devote his attention to the cattle business. He was, however, marked for public life; in 1881 he was elected mayor of the city of Cheyenne, serving until 1885 when he became delegate of Wyoming Territory to the House of Representatives at Washington. In this character it was his privilege to introduce the bill which admitted Wyoming to statehood in 1890, and from that year through 1895 he served as one of his state's first two members of the Senate. An early and a staunch advocate of woman suffrage, he ably defended the provision in the constitution of Wyoming by which that state became the first to enfranchise women. As chairman of the Public Lands Committee, Carey succeeded in obtaining the passage of an act which came to be known by his name, authorizing the secretary of the interior to cede arid public lands to states which would cause such areas to be irrigated. He was one of the pioneers in the movement for the reclamation of arid lands by irrigation, and in collaboration with the Irish agriculturist Sir Horace Plunkett, he promoted the development of an extensive irrigated area at Wheatlands. Upon retiring from the Senate, he resumed his legal practice, but in 1910 entered public life again as governor of Wyoming, and in 1912 took a prominent part in the formation of the Progressive Party.

Carey, Mathew. b. at Dublin, Jan. 28, 1760; d. Sept. 16, 1839. American publisher and political economist, intellectual founder of the U.S. nationalist school of thought in economics; father of Henry Charles Carey. Migrating from Dublin to Paris, he met Benjamin Franklin, for whom he worked in the printing shop Franklin had established at Passy. He returned to Ireland, becoming editor of the *Freeman's Journal* at Dublin, and in 1783 became proprietor of the *Volunteer's Journal;* an exponent of Irish nationalism, he was arrested (1784) for expressing anti-British sentiments, and in the same year fled from impending trial by sailing for America. He settled at Philadelphia and, with the aid of a gift of money from Lafayette (which Carey repaid in 1824) set up the Pennsylvania *Herald* (1785 *et seq.*), became a partner (1786) in the management of the *Columbian Magazine*, and publisher of the *American Museum.* He abandoned the latter venture to establish a publishing and bookselling business. He was one of the founders (1796) of the first Sunday school society in the U.S., became (1802) a director of the Bank of Pennsylvania, and wrote *Olive Branch* (1814) in an attempt to reconcile the Federalist and Republican parties. A founder of the Hibernian Society, he wrote *Vindiciae Hibernicae* (1819), which combated the charge that the Irish had been responsible for the massacre of 1641. A charter member of the Philadelphia Society for the Promotion of National Industry, he wrote many books and pamphlets favoring the national protective tariff and internal improvements. Together with Alexander Hamilton, he ranks as the establisher of the nationalist viewpoint in U.S. economic thought.

Carey, Philip. Hero of W. Somerset Maugham's realistic novel *Of Human Bondage* (1915). Philip, a shy, sensitive youth afflicted with a clubfoot, studies accounting and art, gives up both for medicine, and finally, after many hardships, becomes a doctor. His love affair with Mildred Rogers, a London waitress, is one of the most memorable episodes in the book.

Carey, Robert. [Title, 1st Earl of **Monmouth.**] b. c1560; d. April 12, 1639. English soldier; son of Henry Carey (c1524–96). He fought (1587) in the Netherlands, taking part in the attempts to relieve Sluys, served (1588) as a gentleman volunteer fighting against the Spanish Armada, commanded a regiment (1591) in Essex's expedition to Normandy, and served (1593–1603) as deputy warden of the east and west marches of the Scottish border. He rode to Holyrood, starting on the morning of Elizabeth's death (Sept. 24, 1603) and arriving late on the 26th, to bring the news of the Queen's end to James II of Scotland who made him one of the gentlemen of the King's chamber.

Carey, Robert Davis. b. 1878; d. 1937. American politician, governor of Wyoming and U.S. senator; son of Joseph Maull Carey. Inheriting his father's inclination toward public life, he served as governor of Wyoming (1919–23) and became a senator from that state in 1930.

Carey, Rosa Nouchette. b. at London, 1840; d. there, July 19, 1909. English novelist, whose stories for girls attained wide popularity. Among them are *Nellie's Memories* (1868), *Wee Wifie* (1869), *Heriot's Choice* (1879), *Not Like Other Girls* (1884), *The Old, Old Story* (1894), *Herb of Grace* (1901), *The Household of Peter* (1905), and *The Angel of Forgiveness* (1907).

Carey, William. b. at Paulerspury, Northamptonshire, England, Aug. 17, 1761; d. at Serampore, India, June 9, 1834. English Orientalist, and Baptist missionary in British India from c1793. He was the author of grammars of Mahratta (1805), Sanskrit (1806), Panjabi (1812), and Telinga (1814), and dictionaries of Mahratta (1810), Bengali (1818), and others. He also taught Sanskrit at Fort William College, near Calcutta.

Carey Act. [Full name, **Carey Desert Land Grant Act.**] Act (Aug. 18, 1894) of the U.S. Congress establishing a limited degree of federal responsibility for the irrigation and reclamation of desert lands. The President was authorized to grant to each public-land state up to one million acres of the public desert lands within its boundaries. The land was to be sold to settlers in tracts of 160 acres or less to be reclaimed and cultivated. It was further stipulated that unless 20 acres in each tract were cultivated, the tract would revert to the public domain. The state profits from the land sales were to be used in financing reclamation, the reserves being held for reclamation of the state's other desert land.

Carfax (kär′faks). At Oxford, England, the junction of Cornmarket Street, Queen Street, St. Aldgate's, and High Street.

Cargill (kär′gil), **Donald.** b. at Rattray, Perthshire, Scotland, c1619; executed at Edinburgh, July 27, 1681. Scottish preacher and Covenanter, condemned to death for high treason. After having lost (1622) his position as a minister subsequent to his denunciation of Charles II's reign, he participated in the battle of Bothwell Bridge (1679), where he was wounded. The charge of treason was laid against him for having excommunicated (1680) the king.

Carhart (kär′härt), **Henry Smith.** b. at Coeymans, N.Y., March 27, 1844; d. Feb. 13, 1920. American physicist, noted for his researches in electric standard cells and primary batteries, resulting in the invention of the Carhart-Clark cell. Graduated (1869) from Wesleyan University in Connecticut, he served as professor (1872–86) of physics and chemistry at Northwestern University and professor (1886–1909) of physics at the University of Michigan. His works include *University Physics* (1894–96), *College Physics* (1910), and *Physics with Applications*, (1917) with H. N. Chute.

Carheil (kȧ.rey′), **Étienne de.** b. at Carentoir, France, 1633; d. at Quebec, Canada, July 27, 1726. French Jesuit, a missionary among the Hurons and Iroquois in Canada.

Caria (kãr′i.ạ). In ancient geography, a division of Asia Minor, lying between Lydia on the N, Phrygia and Lycia on the E, and the Aegean Sea on the S and W. The Maeander (modern Menderes), a noted river, flows through it. Its chief towns were Halicarnassus, Miletus, and Cnidus. The early inhabitants may have been Hamitic, and the Dorian and Ionian Greeks formed colonies on the coasts. Its princes became tributary to Persia.

Cariamanga (kä.ryä.mäng′gä). City in S Ecuador, in Loja province. 15,598 (est. 1944).

Cariappa (kä.rē.äp′ä), **K. M.** b. at Mercara, Coorg, India, 1900—. Indian military leader, commander in chief of the Indian army and chief of staff (1948 *et seq.*). He played a distinguished role in the Burma campaign during World War II and was the first Indian to command (1942) a battalion.

Carías Andino (kä.rē′äs än.dē′nō), **Tiburcio.** b. at Tegucigalpa, Honduras, March 15, 1876—. Honduran statesman, president (1933–49) of Honduras. He graduated (LL.B., 1898) from the Central University, took part in the Honduran revolutions of 1893, 1894, and 1903, and was given the title of general of brigade, later general, by the national congress. He was a member of the national congress, and became president (Feb. 1, 1933) of Honduras; his term was extended (April, 1936) to 1943, and again in 1941 to 1949.

Carib (kar′ib). Collective name for a large number of Indian tribes, speaking languages of the Cariban stock, and widely distributed in the tropical forests of South America, especially N of the Amazon River and in the Lesser Antilles. Although many details of Carib culture were identical with or similar to the Arawak, they were more often warlike and in many areas had displaced Arawak tribes, in some instances (as in the Lesser Antilles) only shortly before the Spanish conquest. Carib Indians were encountered by Columbus. The Carib tribes of the Antilles bitterly resisted the French and English colonists until late in the 18th century when a number of them who had become mixed with Negroes were defeated at St. Vincent and transported to the islands off the coast of Honduras, eventually becoming the present-day "Black Caribs" of Honduras and Nicaragua. Like the Arawak the Carib are nearly extinct in the Antilles but survive in considerable numbers on the mainland of South America. Many of the Carib tribes practiced a form of ceremonial cannibalism as an adjunct of their warfare; it is from this circumstance and from the native word *cariba* (people) that the word cannibal in various languages is derived. Galibi, a variant form of the name Carib, is used especially in reference to the Carib tribes of British, French, and Dutch Guiana.

Cariban (kar'i.ban). One of the major South American Indian linguistic stocks. Spoken by a large number of tribes, it is distributed mainly in the area N of the Amazon River in Brazil, in the Guianas and Venezuela, in several smaller areas in the upper Amazon valley in the forested lowlands of Colombia and Peru, and in the Lesser Antilles, with a few outposts in several of the Greater Antilles. The distribution suggests that the Carib-speaking tribes penetrated widely into the areas previously held by Arawakan-speaking groups and replaced the latter during the several centuries prior to the European conquest. Traditions and early records support this theory.

Caribana (kä.ri.bä'na). Name given on some maps of the 16th century to Guiana, or the region between the Amazon and the Orinoco, sometimes including a portion of Venezuela. The name was evidently derived from the Carib Indians, who inhabited these coasts.

Caribbean (kar.i.bē'an, ka.rib'ē.an). [Early name, **North Sea.**] Arm of the Atlantic lying between the Greater Antilles on the N, the Lesser Antilles on the E, South America on the S, and Yucatán and Central America on the W. It is connected with the Gulf of Mexico by the Yucatán Channel. The name North Sea was often used in the 16th century to distinguish the Caribbean from the Pacific (the South Sea). Greatest depth, 22,788 ft.; area, ab. 750,000 sq. mi.

Caribbean Commission. [Original full name, **Anglo-American Caribbean Commission.**] Established on March 9, 1942, by the U.S. and Great Britain, this body seeks to encourage and strengthen social and economic coöperation between the two countries in the Caribbean area. In December, 1945, France and the Netherlands were admitted to membership on the Commission.

Caribbee Islands (kar'i.bē). See under **Bermudas.**

Caribbees. See under **Antilles.**

Cariboo Mountains (kar'i.bö). Mountain area in E central British Columbia, Canada. There are numerous rugged ranges and glacial lakes in this region. The peak elevation is Mount Spranger (9,920 ft.). Length, ab. 200 mi.; greatest width, ab. 90 mi.

Caribou (kar'i.bö). Town (in Maine the equivalent of township in many other states) and unincorporated village in NE Maine, in Aroostook County on the Aroostook River. It is a winter resort, and the shipping center for the largest potato-producing county in the U.S. Pop. of town, 9,923 (1950); of village, 4,500 (1950).

Caribou Eskimo. Eskimo group inhabiting the Chesterfield Inlet area, to the W of Hudson Bay.

Caridorf (kar'i.dôrf). Romantic tragedy (1827) by Robert Montgomery Bird. It has been praised for its imaginative power, but *The Broker of Bogota* (1834), with its South American setting in the 18th century, and its heroic money-lender, Febro, is regarded as his best play.

Cariès (kå.ryes), **Jean.** See **Carriès, Jean.**

Carigara (kä.rē.gä'rä). Town in the Philippine Islands, in the N part of Leyte province and island, on Carigara Bay. 6,669 (1948).

Carigara Bay. Indentation of the Samar Sea on the N coast of Leyte, Philippine Islands. It is partly enclosed by Biliran island, and is connected to San Pedro Bay by Janabatas Channel.

Carignan (kå.rē.nyäṅ). Village in NE France, in the department of Ardennes, ab. 12 mi. SE of Sedan. The French were repulsed here by the Prussians, on Aug. 31, 1870.

Carignan, Princesse **de.** See **Mancini, Olympe.**

Carignan, Marie Thérèse Louise de Savoie-. See **Lamballe,** Princesse **de.**

Carignano (kä.rē.nyä'nō). Town and commune in NW Italy, in the *compartimento* (region) of Piedmont, in the province of Torino, situated on the Po River, ab. 11 mi. S of Turin. Center of a rich agricultural district, it has woolen and silk manufactures, lumber mills, and dairies. The town came under the rule of the house of Savoy in 1286. Buildings of interest to tourists were undamaged in World War II. Pop. of commune, 7,392 (1936); of town, 4,992 (1936).

Carignan-Salières Regiment (kå.rē.nyäṅ.så.lyer). Largest body of French troops sent to New France. This regiment, which had acquired an excellent record, numbered more than 1,000 men when it was assigned to safeguard the region around the lower St. Lawrence River from hostile Indians. Several years later when security had been established and the regiment's return to France was ordered, fully half of its personnel, being offered land grants, elected to remain in Canada.

Carilef (kar'i.lef), **William de St.** [Also, **William of St. Calais.**] d. Jan. 2, 1096. English ecclesiastic and statesman, made bishop of Durham by William the Conqueror in 1081. He was influential in ecclesiastical and civil affairs (especially as an antagonist of Lanfranc and Anselm) during the reigns of William I and William II, and took an important part in the building of the cathedral of Durham.

Carillo (kä.rē'yō) or **Carrillo** (kär-), **Braulio.** b. at Cartago, Costa Rica, 1800; killed at San Miguel, El Salvador, 1845. Costa Rican statesman. He was president of Costa Rica in the period 1835–37, and again from 1838 to April, 1842, when he was overthrown, and then banished by Francisco Morazán. He subsequently became a practicing lawyer in El Salvador.

Carillon (kå.rē.yôṅ), **Fort.** See under **Ticonderoga, N.Y.**

Carimata Islands (kä.rē.mä'tä). See **Karimata Islands.**

Carimata Strait. See **Karimata Strait.**

Carini (kä.rē'nē). Town and commune in S Italy, on the island of Sicily, in the province of Palermo, situated on the Gulf of Carini, W of Palermo. Pop. of commune, 14,762 (1936); of town, 13,782 (1936).

Carino (kä.rē'nō). In Giovanni Battista Guarini's play, *Il Pastor fido*, a courtier.

Carino. Father of Zenocia in John Fletcher and Philip Massinger's *The Custom of the Country.*

Carinola (ka.rē'nō.lä). Town and commune in S Italy, in the *compartimento* (region) of Campania, in the province of Caserta, NW of Caserta. It is a market town for the surrounding agricultural area. Pop. of commune, 11,536 (1936); of town, 827 (1936).

Carinthia (ka.rin'thi.a). [German, **Kärnten.**] Province in S Austria, bounded on the N and E by Salzburg and Styria, on the S by Yugoslavia (Slovenia) and Italy, and on the W by East Tirol. It falls into three parts, namely the S slope of the main Alpine range, the hilly, lake-studded region between the Drava and Gail rivers, and the N slope of the Karawanken mountains, on the Yugoslav border. The highest peak in Austria, the Grossglockner (12,460 ft.), is in the extreme NW corner of the province. The population is predominantly Roman Catholic and the majority is German-speaking, but S of the Drava and Gail rivers there is settled a considerable Slovenian minority. Water power and forests stimulate lumbering, paper, and chemical industries. Livestock raising prevails all over the province, agriculture only in the central part. The province is traversed by important railroads. Capital, Klagenfurt; area, 3,681 sq. mi.; pop. 474,180 (1951).

History. Carinthia belonged to the Roman province of Noricum. The Slovenes settled in the region around the year 600, first dominated by the Avars, then from the 8th century under Bavarian and Franconian sovereignty. In the same period the country was colonized and Christianized by Germans. In 976 it became an independent duchy; in 1335 it fell to the Hapsburgs. In the 15th and 16th centuries it suffered from Turkish raids. In the Napoleonic era, part of the country belonged to the Illyrian provinces of France. It became a *Kronland* (crownland) of Austria in 1849. After the conclusion of World War I, the people of Carinthia fought successfully against an attempted invasion and occupation by Yugoslavia. The Paris Peace Conference decided upon a plebiscite which took place on Oct. 10, 1920, and resulted in a majority of 58 percent in favor of remaining within Austria. However, the Mies valley, occupied by Yugoslavian troops, was ceded to Yugoslavia and the Kanal valley to Italy. After World War II, Yugoslavia again claimed southern Carinthia. The province is within the British zone of occupation in Austria.

Carinus (ka.rī'nus). d. near Margum, in Moesia, 285 A.D. Roman emperor (283–285); elder son of Carus. He was appointed governor of the western provinces, with the titles of Caesar and Imperator, on the departure of his father and his brother Numerianus in 282 on an expedition against the Persians, in the course of which Carus died (283), leaving the two brothers joint emperors. Numerianus died soon after, and the army of Asia proclaimed Diocletian emperor of the East. A decisive battle was fought in 285 on the Margus, in Moesia, in which Carinus was victorious. He was, however, killed in the moment of triumph by his own officers.

Cariri (kä.rē'rē). [Also, **Kiriri.**] Linguistic stock, now almost extinct, of a group of South American Indians of the Brazil-Bolivian border. Formerly it was thought that it belonged to the great Carib family, but this has not been proved.

Carisbrooke (kar'is.brůk, -iz-). Civil parish (transferred for administrative purposes to the borough of Newport in 1933) and village in S England, in the Isle of Wight, ab. 1 mi. SW of Newport. It is noted for its castle, now in ruins, to which Charles I fled and where he was confined (1647–48). 5,232 (1931).

Carisbrooke, Marquis of. A title of **Mountbatten, Alexander.**

Carisbrooke Castle. Ancient castle at Carisbrooke, on the Isle of Wight, England, the place of captivity (1647–48) of Charles I. It is of Saxon foundation; but of the remains the keep is Norman, most of the towers and main walls are of the 13th century, and the outworks and chief residential buildings were added or remodeled under Queen Elizabeth. The castle is now in ruins.

Carissimi (kä.rēs'sē.mē), **Giacomo.** b. at Marino, Italy, c1604; d. at Rome, Jan. 12, 1674. Italian operatic composer. He served as choir leader at Assisi (1624–28) and in the church of Saint Apollinaris at Rome (1628–74). He did much toward perfecting the recitative in the then new operatic form, and developed the sacred cantata. His disciples included Alessandro Scarlatti, Giovanni Maria Bononcini, Marc' Antonio Cesti, and Giovanni Battista Bassani. Among his oratorios, which helped to fix the form of such works, are *Jephte*, *Lucifer*, *Jonas*, *Histoire de Job*, and *Ezéchias*.

Caritat (kȧ.rē.tȧ), **Marie Jean Antoine Nicolas.** See **Condorcet,** Marquis **de.**

Carker (kär'kėr), **James.** Manager in the offices of Dombey and Son, in Charles Dickens's novel of that name. He is "sly of manner, sharp of tooth, soft of foot, watchful of eye, oily of tongue, cruel of heart, nice of habit." He induces Edith, the second wife of Dombey, to elope with him, to revenge herself on her husband. He is killed by a train while trying to escape from Dombey, having been balked in his designs by Edith.

Carl (kärl), Prince. [Full name, Prince **Oskar Carl Wilhelm,** Duke of **Vestrogothia.**] b. at Stockholm, Sweden, Feb. 27, 1861; d. there, Oct. 24, 1951. Member of the Swedish royal family and army officer; son of Oscar II.

Carl (of *Denmark*). Original name of **Haakon VII** (of *Norway*).

Carl, William Crane. b. at Bloomfield, N.J., March 2, 1865; d. at New York, Dec. 8, 1936. American organist. A student under Alexandre Guilmant at Paris, he was organist (1882–90) of the First Presbyterian Church at Newark, N.J., and organist (1892–1936) of the First Presbyterian Church at New York. He was the founder (1899) and director of the Guilmant Organ School at New York, author of *Several Songs and Organ Arrangements* (1892), and editor of several collections of organ music.

Carlee (kär'lẹ). See **Karli.**

Carlell (kär.lel'), **Lodowick.** b. 1602; d. 1675. English dramatist. He is the reputed author of *The Deserving Favourite*, a tragicomedy (1629), *Arviragus and Philicia*, a tragicomedy (1636), *The Passionate Lovers* (1638), *The Fool would be a Favourite, or the Discreet Lover* (1657), *Osmund, the Great Turk*, a tragedy (1657), *Heraclius, Emperor of the East* (1664), and *The Spartan Ladies* (lost).

Carlén (kär.lān'), **Emilie Smith Flygare.** b. at Strömstad, Sweden, Aug. 8, 1807; d. at Stockholm, Feb. 5, 1892. Swedish novelist; wife first of Axel Flygare (d. 1833), then of Johan Gabriel Carlén. Her works include *Valdemar Klein* (1838), *Gustav Lindorm* (1839), *Rosen pā Tistelön* (1842; Eng. trans., *The Rose of Thistle Island*, 1844), and others, especially novels of life in the islands off the Swedish coast. Her home was a meeting place of noted literary figures.

Carlén, Johan Gabriel. b. in Västergötland, Sweden, July 9, 1814; d. at Stockholm, July 6, 1875. Swedish poet and author; second husband of Emilie Smith Flygare Carlén. He wrote *Romanser ur Svenska Volklifvet* (Romances of Swedish Life, 1846) and others.

Carlentini (kär.len.tē'nē). Town and commune in SW Italy, on the island of Sicily, in the province of Siracusa, situated near the Ionian Sea, NW of Syracuse. It was named in honor of Charles V of the Holy Roman Empire. An agricultural market town, it was entirely rebuilt after the earthquake of 1693. Pop. of commune, 10,580 (1936); of town, 8,870 (1936).

Carlet de Chamblain de Marivaux (kȧr.le dẹ shäṅ.blaṅ dẹ mȧ.rē.vō), **Pierre.** See **Marivaux, Pierre Carlet de Chamblain de.**

Carleton (kärl'tọn), **George.** Hero and supposed author of Daniel Defoe's *Memoirs of Captain George Carleton*, published in 1728. Attempts have been made to identify Carleton as a real soldier or to establish Jonathan Swift as the author, and historians often cite the work as a source, but it is now known to be one of Defoe's historical romances.

Carleton, Sir **Guy.** [Title, 1st Baron **Dorchester.**] b. at Strabane, County Tyrone, Ireland, Sept. 3, 1724; d. at Stubbings, near Maidenhead, England, Nov. 10, 1808. English soldier and administrator, created Baron Dorchester on Aug. 21, 1786. He was appointed a lieutenant colonel on June 18, 1757, took part in the siege of Louisburg, was wounded (while holding the rank of colonel) at the capture of Quebec, and served at the siege of Belle-Île-en-Mer in 1761 and at the siege of Havana in 1762, Appointed lieutenant governor of Quebec on Sept. 24, 1766, he took command of the British troops in Canada. defended Quebec successfully against the American forces under Richard Montgomery and Benedict Arnold in the period of December, 1775–May,1776, captured Crown Point in October, 1776, and was made a lieutenant general in August, 1777, having been named (Jan. 10, 1777) governor of Quebec. He succeeded Sir Henry Clinton as commander in chief in America on Feb. 23, 1782, arriving at New York on May 5, and evacuating the city on Nov. 25, 1783. After serving again as governor of Quebec, from April 11, 1786, he resigned the governorship in 1796.

Carleton, Henry Guy. b. at Fort Union, N.M., June 21, 1856; d. at Atlantic City, N.J., Dec. 10, 1910. American playwright, best remembered for *The Gilded Fool* (1892), starring vehicle for Nat Goodwin. His *Butterflies* (1894) was an early success of John Drew and Maude Adams.

Carleton, Mark Alfred. b. at Jerusalem, Ohio, March 7, 1866; d. 1925. American plant pathologist and botanist, notable for introducing into the U.S. foreign grains, such as the Kubanka wheat from western Asia which established the durum wheat industry. A graduate (B.S., 1887; M.S., 1893) of Kansas State College of Agriculture and Applied Science, he served as expert on grains (1894 *et seq.*) with the U.S. Department of Agriculture. He was also an agricultural explorer (1898–99) in Russia and Siberia.

Carleton, Mary. b. c1642; d. 1673. English criminal, cheat, bigamist, thief, and actress. She called herself "the German Princess," a title to which she had no claim, and she actually appeared in a play of that name, written at her request, at the Duke's House, in Lincoln's Inn Fields, in 1664. She succeeded in convincing a trusting soul, a Mrs. King, that she had a fortune close to 80,000 pounds a year, and in April, 1663 she married John Carleton, Mrs. King's brother, without taking the trouble to divorce another husband, John Stedman. She was sent to prison (where Pepys, who had seen her on the stage, visited her), and was tried at the Old Bailey on June 4, 1663, but defended herself with such skill that she was acquitted. Her luck, however, did not hold out, and when she was charged with a series of thefts in December, 1672, she was found guilty. The sentence at that time for her crimes was death, and she was hanged on Jan. 22, 1673 at Tyburn. She was supposed to be the daughter of Henry van Wolway, Lord of Holmstein, or of the Duke of Oundenia, but she admitted just before her death that she was simply Mary Moders, the daughter of a Canterbury Cathedral chorister. She was the subject of many books, both during her life and after her execution, of which a typical example is *The Counterfeit Lady Unveiled. Being a Full Account of the Birth, Life, Most Remarkable Actions, and Untimely Death of that Famous Cheat, Mary Carleton, Known by the Name of the German Princess* (1673), by Francis Kirkman.

Carleton, Will. [Full name **William McKendree Carleton.**] b. in Michigan, Oct. 21, 1845; d. Dec. 18, 1912. American poet, journalist, and lecturer. He was the author of *Farm Ballads* (1873), *Farm Festivals* (1881), *City Ballads* (1885), *Songs of Two Centuries* (1902), *In Old School Days* (1907), and *Drifted In* (1908). He wrote the sentimental "Over the Hill to the Poor House," his most famous single poem.

Carleton, William. b. at Prillisk, County Tyrone, Ireland, March 4, 1794; d. at Dublin, Jan. 30, 1869. Irish novelist, a delineator of Irish character and life. He wrote *Traits and Stories of the Irish Peasantry* (1830–33), *Tales of Ireland* (1834), *Fardorougha the Miser* (1839), *Valentine McClutchy* (1845), and others.

Carleton Place. Town in E Ontario, Canada, at the N end of Lake Mississippi, ab. 36 mi. SW of Ottawa. 4,725 (1951).

Carli (kär′lē) or **Carli-Rubbi** (-röb′bē), Count **Giovanni Rinaldo.** b. at Capodistria, near Trieste, April 11, 1720; d. at Milan, Italy, Feb. 22, 1795. Italian political economist and antiquary. Among his chief works are *Delle origini e del commercio della moneta e dell'istituzione delle zecche d'Italia* (1754–60), *Lettere Americane* (1780–81), and *Delle antichità italiche* (1788–91).

Carlile (kär.līl′; kär′līl), **John Snyder.** b. at Winchester, Va., Dec. 16, 1817; d. at Clarksburg, W.Va., Oct. 24, 1878. American political leader whose Union sympathies led him to instigate the formation of the state of West Virginia. He served as a senator (1847–51), member (1850) of the constitutional convention, and congressman (1855–57, 1861). On May 22, 1861 he drafted an address to the people of western Virginia urging them to form a new state; subsequently he was a senator (1861–65) from West Virginia.

Carlile, Richard. b. in Devonshire, England, 1790; d. at London, 1843. English freethinker and reformer; follower of Thomas Paine. He sold (1817) prohibited papers and wrote and printed free-thought pamphlets. For publishing (1818) Paine's works, he was imprisoned (1819–26) at Dorchester; while there, he supervised the publication of *The Republican*, a journal. In 1830 he opened a hall at London to promote free speech. He was again (1830–33 and 1834–35) imprisoned for his refusal to pay church rates. He wrote many controversial papers and serials. Emperor Alexander of Russia thought it necessary to forbid the report of his trial (1819) from being brought into his territory.

Carling (kär′ling), **Walter.** Sentimental character in *Point Counterpoint* (1928), a novel by Aldous Huxley dealing satirically with social and intellectual life at London in the decade following World War I.

Carlingford Lough (kär′ling.fọrd loċh). Arm of the Irish Sea lying between Ulster and Leinster provinces, and between County Down (Northern Ireland) and County Louth (Eire). Length, ab. 11 mi.; width at entrance, ab. 3 mi.

Carlino (kär.lē′nō), **Carlo Antonio Bertinazzi.** b. at Turin, Italy, 1713; d. at Paris, Sept. 7, 1783. Italian pantomimist and improvisator.

Carlinville (kär′lin.vil). City in C Illinois, county seat of Macoupin County: center of a natural-gas area. 5,116 (1950).

Carlisle (kär.līl′, kär′līl). [Formerly also **Carlile, Carlyle, Carleil**; Middle English, **Carlile, Karlile**; British, **Caer Luel, Luel**; Latin, **Luguvallum, Luguvallium, Luguballia.**] City and county borough in NW England, the county seat of Cumberland, situated at the confluence of the rivers Caldew, Peteril, and Eden, ab. 60 mi. W of Newcastle, ab. 299 mi. NW of London by rail. Its industries include a biscuit factory, tin-box manufacture, cotton printing, and machinery manufacture. Carlisle is the junction of six important rail lines. It was one of the early centers of the cotton-spinning industry. The city contains a cathedral and castle, and near it (at Bowness) is the end of the Roman (Hadrian's) wall. The cathedral, as it now stands, is almost wholly of the 14th century. The Norman nave was burned in the 13th century, except the two bays nearest the transept, which have since constituted the entire nave. The fine choir is in the Decorated style, with a remarkably large and handsome east window (50 by 30 ft.) in Perpendicular style. The stalls date from the 15th century, with contemporaneous paintings on their backs. Carlisle was an important Roman town. It was destroyed by the Danes c875, and was rebuilt by William II. Robert the Bruce besieged it unsuccessfully in 1315, and it was the place of imprisonment of Mary, Queen of Scots, in 1568. It was besieged and taken by the Parliamentarians in 1645, and a century later (1745) by the Young Pretender. 67,894 (1951).

Carlisle. Borough in S Pennsylvania, county seat of Cumberland County, ab. 17 mi. SW of Harrisbur[illegible], near the Susquehanna River. Manufactures include [illegible] textiles, clothing, furniture, carpets, rugs, and rubber [illegible]. It is the seat of Dickinson College, the Dickins[illegible]ool of Law, and the U.S. Army Medical Field Se[illegible]hool. The Carlisle Indian School, which was closed [illegible] was famous for such football figures as "Jim" [illegible] and Glenn ("Pop") Warner. Platted in 1751, Ca[illegible]ured in the French and Indian Wars, in the Whis[illegible]lion (when it was Washington's headquarters), an[illegible]tion on the Underground Railroad. In the Civil [illegible]was bombarded (July 1, 1863) by the Confeder[illegible]812 (1950).

Carlisle, Countess of. Title of **Hay, Lucy.**

Carlisle, 1st Earl of. A title of **Hay, James.**

Carlisle, Earls of. See under members of the **[illegible]ward** family of English nobility.

Carlisle, John Griffin. b. in what is now Kenton County, Ky., Sept. 5, 1835; d. at New York, July 31, 1910. American statesman. His family came from near Culpeper in Virginia. In 1855 he went to Covington, Ky., to study law, supporting himself as a teacher in the public schools. He was admitted to the bar in 1858, and in 1866 entered the state senate of Kentucky. He served his term, and was reëlected, but resigned. In 1876 he was elected to the 45th Congress, and remained in the House of Representatives until his promotion to the Senate in 1890 as successor to Senator Beck. He was Speaker of the House in the period 1883–89. A sound-money man and a tariff reformer, he was secretary of the treasury (1893–97) under Cleveland.

Carlisle Indian School. Former school at Carlisle, Pa., for the instruction of American Indians in trades and agriculture. It was established (1879) by Captain R. H. Pratt, and was in existence until 1918.

Carlism (kär′liz.ẹm). In Spanish history, a royalist, absolutist, and clerical movement which originated in 1823 and subsequently adopted the cause of Don Carlos, brother of Ferdinand VII, against the succession of Isabella II, daughter of Ferdinand VII. Ferdinand repealed in 1829 the Salic law of succession, introduced by Philip V in 1713, in accordance with which females could inherit the throne only in case of the total extinction of the male line; and by a decree of March, 1830, established the old Castilian law, in accordance with which the daughters and granddaughters of the king take precedence over his brothers and nephews. Ferdinand died on Sept. 29, 1833, without male issue, and the throne descended to his minor daughter Isabella Maria II, under the regency of her mother Donna Maria Christina. Carlos, who was heir presumptive to the throne under the Salic law, refused to recognize the pragmatic sanction, and inaugurated, with the aid of the clericals or absolutists, a civil war which lasted from 1833 to 1840. He resigned his claim in 1845 to his son Don Carlos, Duke of Montemolín, who entered Spain with 3,000 men in 1860, but was defeated at Tortosa and made prisoner. His claim descended to his nephew Don Carlos (III), who, after several short-lived risings in his name, headed a formidable insurrection from 1873 to 1876. In the 20th century the Carlists changed their party name to *Tradicionalistas* (Traditionalists). They devoted themselves to a program of preservation of "ancient functions and privileges" and organized reactionary terrorist bands (*requetés*). They made common cause with the nationalists in the Spanish Civil War (1936–39), but being essentially predisposed toward reaction and nostalgia for the pre-industrial age, they differ considerably from the Falange. They are strongest in Navarre and the north of Spain, and were as late as 1950 rallied around the claims of Carlos Pio, who called himself Carlos "VIII."

Carlo Buffone (kär′lō böf.fō′nā). See **Buffone, Carlo.**

Carlo Magno (mä′nyō). Italian name of **Charlemagne.**

Carloman (kär′lọ.man; French, kȧr.lo.mäṅ). b. at Vienne, France, Aug. 17, 754. Mayor of the palace of the kingdom of Austrasia; son of Charles Martel. After the death of Charles Martel, real ruler of the Merovingian kingdom of the Franks, in 741, his sons Pepin the Short and Carloman shared the mayoralty of the palace, Carloman taking jurisdiction over Austrasia, the eastern Frankish domain. He extended his power in warfare and was a patron of the church. In 747 he retired to a monastery on Monte Soracte in Italy, later going to Monte Cassino, but died during a visit to France.

Carloman. b. 751; d. 771. Brother of Charlemagne and joint king of France. The brothers, of whom Carloman was the younger, came to power at the death of their father Pepin the Short. Differences between them concerning the conduct of military operations came to an end with Carloman's early death.

Carloman. d. at Öttingen, Sept. 22, 880. King of Bavaria, Carinthina, Pannonia, and Moravia (876–79) and of Italy (877–79); son of Louis the German and father of the Emperor Arnulf. He reigned as duke of Bavaria from 865 to 876, when upon the death of Louis the German, he came into the title of king of that country and of Carinthia, Pannonia, and Moravia. The emperor Louis II, dying in 875, had named Carloman heir of his Italian domain, and in 877 he was at Pavia crowned king of the Lombards. He was the unsuccessful rival of his uncle Charles the Bald, king of the West Franks, for the imperial crown, which however was later worn by his son Arnulf.

Carloman. d. Dec. 12, 884. King of France; son of Louis II. At the death of Louis II of France, his sons Louis III and Carloman, despite questions of their legitimacy, succeeded him as joint rulers in 879. After dealing with revolts in Provence and Burgundy, Carloman soundly beat the Normans, and repeated his victory after Louis III's death in 882. Carloman himself died while hunting.

Carlos (kär'lǫs, -lōs), Don. b. at Valladolid, Spain, July 8, 1545; d. at Madrid, July 24, 1568. Spanish prince; eldest son of Philip II of Spain and Maria of Portugal. He was engaged to be married to Elizabeth of Valois, before she married his father, Philip II. He received the homage of the estates of Castile as crown prince (Prince of the Asturias) in 1560. In 1567, angered by the appointment of the Duke of Alva to the governorship of the Netherlands, he struck at the duke with a poniard in the presence of the king. Having laid plans to escape from Spain, he was apprehended by his father on Jan. 18, 1568, and a commission was appointed to investigate his conduct. He died in prison a few months after, the manner of his death being involved in mystery to this day. Tragedies with Don Carlos as subject have been written by Thomas Otway (1676), Jean Galbert de Campistron (1683), Vittorio Alfieri (1783), Schiller (1787), André Chénier (1789), and others.

Carlos, Don. [Full name, **Carlos María Isidro de Borbón;** known in later life as the Count of **Molina.**] b. March 29, 1788; d. at Trieste, March 10, 1855. Pretender to the throne of Spain; second son of Charles IV, and brother of Ferdinand VII. He was in 1808 compelled by Napoleon to renounce, with his brother, the right to the Spanish succession, and was detained with his brother at Valençay till 1814. He became after the restoration heir presumptive to the throne, but was deprived of this position by the setting aside of the Salic law through the pragmatic sanction of March 29, 1830, and by the birth of Ferdinand VII's daughter, the infanta Maria Isabella, Oct. 10, 1830. On the death of Ferdinand, on Sept. 29, 1833, she was made queen as Isabella II. But Carlos was proclaimed king by the clerical party, and was recognized by the pretender Dom Miguel of Portugal. Resistance being made hopeless by the Quadruple Treaty, concluded at London on April 22, 1834, between Spain, Portugal, England, and France, for the purpose of expelling the two pretenders (Don Carlos and Dom Miguel) from the Iberian Peninsula, he embarked (June 1, 1834) for England. He returned to Spain, however, and appeared at the headquarters of the Carlist insurgents in Navarre, on July 10, 1834, but was forced by the capture of his army by troops under the legitimist general Baldomero Espartero to seek refuge across the French border on Sept. 14, 1839. He resigned his claims to his son Don Carlos on May 18, 1845, and assumed the title of Count of Molina.

Carlos, Don. [Full name, **Carlos Luis Fernando de Borbón;** title, Count of **Montemolín.**] b. at Madrid, Jan. 31, 1818; d. at Trieste, Jan. 13, 1861. Spanish pretender; eldest son of Don Carlos (1788–1855). After his father's renunciation of his claim (1845), he was the recognized Carlist pretender to the Spanish throne. He headed an unsuccessful rising in 1860.

Carlos, Don. [Full name, **Carlos María de los Dolores Juan Isidro José Francisco de Borbón;** title, Duke of **Madrid.**] b. at Laibach, Austria (now Ljubljana, Yugoslavia), March 30, 1848; d. at Varese, Italy, July 18, 1909. Pretender to the Spanish throne; nephew of Don Carlos (1818–61), and son of Don Juan, who abdicated in his favor on Oct. 3, 1868. His standard was raised by the Carlists in the north of Spain on April 21, 1872, and he himself entered Spain on July 15, 1873. The war against King Amadeus and then the republic was carried on with some measure of success, the Carlists holding parts of northern Spain, till after the fall of the republic and the proclamation (1874) of Alfonso XII as king of Spain. Tolosa, the last Carlist stronghold, fell in January, 1876. After the death (1885) of Alfonso XII, Don Carlos did not press his claims in the field. He left a son, Jaime Juan Carlos Alfonso Felipe, born in 1870.

Carlos (kär'lǫs, -lōs; French, kår.los). Principal character in Pierre Corneille's heroic comedy *Don Sanche d'Aragon.* He is really Don Sanche, the heir to the throne of Aragon.

Carlos (kär'lǫs, -lōs). Treacherous younger brother of Biron in Thomas Southerne's play *Isabella* (a reworking of the same author's *The Fatal Marriage*).

Carlos. Apathetic pedant in Colley Cibber's comedy *Love Makes a Man.* He is transformed by love into an enthusiastic and manly fellow.

Carlos I (of *Portugal*) (kär'lǫs, -lōs; Portuguese, kär'lösh). [English, **Charles I.**] b. at Lisbon, Sept. 28, 1863; assassinated there (with his older son), Feb. 1, 1908. King of Portugal (1889–1908); son of Louis I and Maria Pia, daughter of Victor Emmanuel II of Italy.

Carlos "VIII" (of *Spain*) (kär'lǫs, -lōs). Spanish Carlist pretender; nephew of Don Carlos (1848–1909), Duke of Madrid. His claim to the Spanish throne is denied by most Spanish monarchists and even Carlists, but has been supported officially by the Falange as part of the policy to keep the Spanish monarchist parties split.

Carlos, Don. See also **Don Carlos.**

Carlos (kär'lǫs, -lōs; French, kår.los), **Don.** Principal character in Pierre Corneille's heroic comedy *Don Sanche d'Aragon.* He is really Don Sanche, the heir to the throne.

Carlos (kär'lǫs, -lōs), **Don.** Extravagant and profligate husband of Victoria in Hannah Cowley's comedy *A Bold Stroke for a Husband.*

Carlos (kär'lǫs) or **Careless** (kãr'lęs), **William.** fl. 1645 *et seq.;* d. 1689. English soldier and courtier, an adherent of the Cavalier faction during and after the English Civil War. He participated (Sept. 3, 1651) in the battle of Worcester, after which he shared (Sept. 6 and 7, 1651) with Charles II his hiding place in the branches of a tree (thereafter called the "Royal Oak") at Boscobel, Shropshire (and is remembered for his bravery in emerging from his place of hiding in it to procure food for his monarch). He further distinguished himself in battle (Sept. 8, 1651), and escaped to France under an assumed name. He continued in Charles's service until the Restoration, after which both Charles and his brother, James II, rewarded Carlos with grants and bounties.

Carlota (of *Portugal*) (kär.lō'tä). [English, **Charlotte;** full name, **Joaquina Carlota de Borbón.**] b. at Madrid, April 25, 1775; d. near Lisbon, 1830. Queen of Portugal; daughter of Charles IV of Spain. She married (1790) John, heir to the throne of Portugal, afterward John VI. In 1807 she fled with the royal family of Portugal to Brazil, and remained there until 1821. She encouraged the intrigues of her favorite son Miguel (usually called Dom Miguel), who in 1828 usurped the crown.

Carlotta (kär.lot'ą). [Called, in some older works, **Charlotte;** Spanish, **Carlota;** full name, **Marie Charlotte Amélie Augustine Victoire Clémentine Léopoldine.**] b. at Laeken, near Brussels, June 7, 1840; d. in Belgium, Jan. 19, 1927. Empress of Mexico (1864–67). The only daughter of Leopold I of Belgium, and Louise, princess of Orléans, she married (July 27, 1857), Maximilian, archduke of Austria; when in 1864 he accepted the Mexican crown (offered to him by an assembly of prominent Mexicans, but under French pressure), she accompanied him to Mexico. In 1866 she was sent by Maximilian to Napoleon III and Pope Pius IX to secure assistance against the anti-royalist faction then seeking to overthrow Maximilian. Failing in her mission, and foreseeing the fall of her husband, she became hopelessly insane (1866), and was subsequently confined in a Belgian château, where she remained until her death, 60 years after the execution of her husband and the end of his empire.

Carlotta Colony. Community in Mexico, settled (1865 *et seq.*) by Confederate emigrants. It occupied a tract of 500,000 acres. For various reasons, among them inadequate funds and the antagonism of local inhabitants, the colony failed. It was one of several of its kind in Mexico.

Carlovingian (kär.lō.vin′ji.an). See **Carolingian.**

Carlovingian Cycle. See **Charlemagne** (or **Carlovingian) Cycle of Romances.**

Carlow (kär′lō). [Irish, **Ceatharlach, Catherlogh.**] Inland county in Leinster province, in the SE part of the Irish Republic. It is bounded on the N by Counties Kildare and Wicklow, on the E by Counties Wicklow and Wexford, on the SW and W by County Kilkenny, and on the NW by County Laoighis. The surface is flat or gently undulating, except in the SE portion, where it rises to Mount Leinster (2,610 ft.) on the boundary with County Wexford. County Carlow is an important dairy region, and sugar-beet cultivation is becoming increasingly important. Carlow is the county seat; area, ab. 346 sq. mi.; pop. 34,168 (1951).

Carlow. [Irish, **Ceatharlach, Catherlogh.**] Urban district in Leinster province, Irish Republic in County Carlow, situated at the confluence of the rivers Barrow and Burren, ab. 45 mi. SW of Dublin. It is the county seat of County Carlow. Carlow was taken by the Parliamentarians under Ireton in 1650, and was the scene of a defeat of an Irish uprising in 1798. Near the river are the ruins of a castle supposed to have been founded by Hugh de Lacy in the 12th century. 7,668 (1951).

Carlowitz (kär′lō.vits). German name of **Sremski Karlovci.**

Carlowitz, Peace (or **Treaty**) **of.** See **Karlowitz, Treaty of.**

Carl Rosa Opera Company (kärl rō′za), **The Royal.** Organization established (1875) in England by Carl Rosa. Devoted to presenting opera in English, the company has appeared both at London and in the provinces.

Carlsbad (kärlz′bad). Unincorporated community in S California, in San Diego County, on the Pacific Ocean ab. 30 mi. N of San Diego. It is a seaside resort; a state park with swimming and camping facilities is nearby. 4,383 (1950).

Carlsbad. City in SE New Mexico, county seat of Eddy County, on the Pecos River. It is the center of an important potash-producing field. Carlsbad Caverns National Park is nearby. The surrounding region also produces cattle, oil, and farm products. In the decade between the last two U.S. censuses the city's population more than doubled, 7,116 (1940), 17,975 (1950).

Carlsbad (kärlz′bad; German, kärls′bät). German name of **Karlovy Vary.**

Carlsbad Caverns National Park (kärlz′bad). Park in SE New Mexico, ab. 27 mi. by road SW of Carlsbad. The enormous limestone caverns were discovered in 1901, and have not yet been fully explored. Over 32 miles of caverns have been explored, of which the greatest, the "Big Room" is 4,000 ft. long, 625 ft. wide, and 300 ft. high. The region was made a national park in 1930. Area, 45,527 acres.

Carlscrona (kärls.krön′ä). See **Karlskrona.**

Carlsen (kärl′sen), **Emil.** b. at Copenhagen, Denmark, Oct. 19, 1853; d. Jan. 4, 1931. American painter. He studied architecture at the Royal Academy in his native city but does not appear to have practiced that art after coming to the U.S. in 1872.

Carlshamn (kärls′häm). See **Karlshamn.**

Carlson (kärl′son), **Anton Julius.** b. in Bohus *Län* (County), Sweden, Jan. 29, 1875—. American physiologist. He arrived in the U.S. in 1891 and received a B.S. (1898) from Augustana College, Ill., and a Ph.D. (1902) from Stanford University. He became assistant professor (1904) and professor (1909) of physiology at the University of Chicago. His written works include *Control of Hunger in Health and Disease* (1916), *The Machinery of the Body* (1937), and scientific papers on heart and circulation, the heart nerves, lymph formation, saliva secretion, the thyroids, the parathyroids, the pancreas, immune bodies, gastric secretion, metabolism, and the physiological effects on a living body of free fall through the air.

Carlson, Evans Fordyce. b. at Sydney, N.Y., Feb. 26, 1896; d. on Mount Hood, near Portland, Ore., May 27, 1947. American Marine Corps officer who organized (1942) the 2nd Marine Raider Battalion, a guerrilla unit composed of men who volunteered for the duty and known as "Carlson's Raiders" or the "Gung-Ho Battalion." As an enlisted man (1912–15) in the U.S. Army, he served in the Philippines and in Hawaii; as an officer (1916–19) he was in Mexico and France. Having joined (1922) the Marine Corps, he saw service in China (1927–29), in Nicaragua (1930–33), and in China and Japan (1933–36). In the period 1937 to 1939 he accompanied the Chinese 8th Route Army (under the Communist leader Mao Tse-tung) on guerrilla campaigns over much of the interior of China as a military observer. In 1939 he resigned from the Marine Corps, but was recommissioned in 1941. He organized his raiders for action in the Pacific area during World War II. He headed the group in an attack (August, 1942) on the Japanese on Little Makin Island and in raids on Guadalcanal. In 1943 he was an observer on Tarawa. Wounded (1944) on Saipan, he was appointed (1944) colonel, having previously held the rank of lieutenant colonel. In 1946 he was made brigadier general and retired from active service. Author of *Twin Stars of China* (1940) and *The Chinese Army* (1940).

Carlson, Fredrik Ferdinand. b. in Upland, Sweden, June 13, 1811; d. at Stockholm, March 18, 1887. Swedish historian and politician. He was minister of ecclesiastical affairs in the periods 1863–70 and 1875–78, professor of history at Uppsala University (1849–77), and author of *History of Sweden* (7 vols., 1855–85).

Carlson, John Fabian. b. in Sweden, 1875; d. at New York, March 20, 1945. American landscape painter, writer, and lecturer. He founded the John F. Carlson School of Landscape Painting, at Woodstock, N.Y., and was an instructor at the Art Students League landscape school. He was made an associate of the National Academy of Design in 1911, and an academician in 1925.

"Carlson's Raiders." [Also, **"Gung-Ho Battalion."**] Name popularly given to a specially trained force of U.S. Marines under Colonel Evans Fordyce Carlson in World War II, designed for outstandingly difficult amphibious forays. Among the most successful operations accomplished by these men in the Pacific was the invasion of Little Makin Island in 1942.

Carlsruhe (kärls′rö″e; Anglicized, kärlz′-). See **Karlsruhe.**

Carlstad (kärl′städ). See **Karlstad.**

Carlstadt (kärl′shtät). See also **Karlstadt.**

Carlstadt (kärl′stat). [Former name, **Tailor Town.**] Borough in NE New Jersey, in Bergen County. 5,591 (1950).

Carlton (kärl′ton). Urban district and manufacturing town in N central England, in Nottinghamshire, adjoining the NE portion of Nottingham, ab. 127 mi. N of London by rail. It has manufactures of hosiery and lace. 34,248 (1951).

Carlton, Effie. [Maiden name, **Crockett; pseudonym, Effie Canning.**] b. c1857; d. at Boston, Jan. 7, 1940. American actress who is generally believed to have composed and published the lullaby *Rock-a-Bye Baby* (copyright in 1887) under the pseudonym of Effie Canning. Having made her debut when 21 years of age on the New York stage, she subsequently starred in *Shiloh, The Private Secretary,* and *Oliver Twist,* before she retired in 1922.

Carlton Club. London club established in 1832. A political club, strictly Conservative, it was founded by the Duke of Wellington.

Carlton House. House formerly standing in what became Carlton House Terrace, London. It was built for Henry Boyle, Lord Carlton, in 1709, and in 1732 was occupied by the Prince of Wales, and afterward by the prince regent (who was later George IV). It was torn down in 1827 when Waterloo Place was built.

Carluke (kär'lök). Civil parish and mining town in S Scotland, in Lanarkshire, ab. 5 mi. NW of Lanark, ab. 381 mi. N of London by rail. 10,507 (1931).

Carlyle (kär.līl', kär'līl). See also **Carlisle.**

Carlyle. City in S Illinois, county seat of Clinton County: flour mills. 2,669 (1950).

Carlyle, Alexander. b. in Dumfriesshire, Scotland, Jan. 26, 1722; d. at Inveresk, near Edinburgh, Aug. 25, 1805. Scottish clergyman, minister at Inveresk, Midlothian, from 1748 until his death, and leader of the moderate section of the Church of Scotland. He wrote an autobiography (edited by John Hill Burton, 1860) as well as some political and other pamphlets. He was a man of genial character, and an intimate friend of Hume, Smollett, and other Scottish men of letters. In appearance he was so impressive that he was nicknamed "Jupiter Carlyle." His patronage of the theater was a cause of scandal in the Church of Scotland.

Carlyle, Jane Baillie. [Maiden name, **Welsh.**] b. at Haddington, Scotland, July 14, 1801; d. while driving in Hyde Park, London, April 21, 1866. English writer; the daughter of John Welsh, a surgeon of Haddington. She was noted for her wit and beauty. She married Thomas Carlyle at Templand on Oct. 17, 1826. Her letters and memoirs were first edited by J. A. Froude in 1883, and there have been several editions by various other scholars since.

Carlyle, John Aitken. b. at Ecclefechan, Dumfriesshire, Scotland, July 7, 1801; d. at Dumfries, Scotland, Dec. 15, 1879. Scottish physician; younger brother of Thomas Carlyle. From 1831 to 1843 he was traveling physician, first to the countess of Clare, and then to the duke of Buccleuch. In 1852 he married, and after the death (1854) of his wife resided at Edinburgh. He published a translation of Dante's *Inferno* (1849).

Carlyle, Joseph Dacre. b. at Carlisle, England, 1759; d. at Newcastle, England, April 12, 1804. English Orientalist. A graduate of Cambridge University, he became professor of Arabic in 1795, and chancellor of Carlisle in 1793. He published *Specimens of Arabic Poetry* (1796) and *Poems, suggested chiefly by scenes in Asia Minor, Syria, and Greece* (1805).

Carlyle, Thomas. [Called the **"Sage of Chelsea."**] b. at Ecclefechan, Dumfriesshire, Scotland, Dec. 4, 1795; d. at London, Feb. 4, 1881. Scottish essayist and historian; son of a stonemason. Educated at Annan Academy and the University of Edinburgh (which he entered in 1809); taught mathematics at Annan (1814–16) and at Kircaldy, under Edward Irving (1816–18); gave up teaching and went to Edinburgh to study law (1819), which was soon abandoned in disgust. Wrote articles for *New Edinburgh Review* and for Brewster's *Edinburgh Encyclopedia*, and did translating and tutoring, all with little financial success; became a victim of dyspepsia and despair. Began (1820) a study of German literature; wrote *Life of Schiller* (published in *London Magazine*, 1823–24; separately, 1825) and translated Goethe's *Wilhelm Meister* (*Apprenticeship*, 1824; *Travels*, 1827); so gained reputation and learned to know writings of his first hero, of whom he wrote "the sight of such a man was to me a Gospel of Gospels." In 1824–25 visited Paris and London, where he met Coleridge, Lamb, Hazlitt, and other literary men; married Jane Welsh (1826); moved to Edinburgh and was admitted by Jeffrey, at that time the editor, to the *Edinburgh Review* with a short essay on Richter. Left Edinburgh to live at Craigenputtock, a solitary farmstead in Dumfriesshire (1828–34), where he wrote essays on Burns, Voltaire, Diderot, Goethe, and other subjects; *Signs of the Times* (1829), *Characteristics* (1831). He wrote also at this time his first original book, *Sartor Resartus* ("The Tailor Retailored") which was published in *Frazer's Magazine* (1833–34), separately at Boston (1835), and at London (1838). This work combines spiritual autobiography in fictional form and speculation on life (mainly German transcendentalism), according to which all material things and all conventions, creeds, customs of mankind are thought of as *clothes*, i.e., symbols of an immaterial, eternal reality beyond the reach of sense perception. In 1834, still seeking "bread and work," Carlyle settled at Cheyne Row, Chelsea, London, which was to be his home till death. *The French Revolution* (1837) established his reputation. Delivered four series of lectures (1837–40), the last of which, *Heroes and Hero-Worship*, he published in 1841. In *Chartism* (1839), *Past and Present* (1843), *Latter-Day Pamphlets* (1850), he attacked materialistic tendencies, corruptions, and shams of society in the spirit of a modern Elijah calling down punishment upon a world gone mad after strange gods. History and biography occupied Carlyle for about 20 years: *Oliver Cromwell's Letters and Speeches* (1845), *Life of John Sterling* (1851); *History of Frederick the Great* (6 vols., 1858–65), journeying twice to Germany (1852, 1858) for research, and visiting all the battlefields of Frederick. Carlyle conceived of history as a record and an interpretation of the past for the guidance of mankind in the present and future, as much less a chain of events (though it was that) than a revelation, through great leaders, of the operation of eternal justice in human society. Many critics consider that no other historian surpasses him in vividness of portraiture. Elected lord rector of Edinburgh University (1865); received the Prussian Order of Merit (1874). After death of wife (1866) wrote *Reminiscences* (2 vols., 1881); his last work, *Early Kings of Norway* (1875), composed by dictation because of palsied right hand. Carlyle's *Letters* published at various times in ten volumes; complete works in *People's Edition* (37 vols., 1871–74) and in *Centenary Edition* (30 vols., 1896–99). See *Life of Carlyle*, by J. A. Froude (4 vols., 1882–84), and *Life of Carlyle*, by D. A. Wilson (6 vols., 1923–34).

Carmagnola (kär.mä.nyô'lä). Town and commune in NW Italy, in the *compartimento* (region) of Piedmont, in the province of Torino, situated on the Mella River, ab. 15 mi. S of Turin, between Turin and Cuneo. It is in a rich agricultural district, with mulberry orchards and an important hemp industry. There are factories producing woolen and cotton textiles, metallurgical and typographical articles, dairy products, and sugar. A fortified city, it was the scene of many conflicts during the medieval and Renaissance periods; it came under the rule of the house of Savoy in 1588. Francesco Bussone da Carmagnola, a military leader of Milan and then of Venice in the 15th century, was born here; the town gave its name to the Carmagnole, a dance and song originating during the French Revolution, and to the costume of the Jacobins, a jacket with metal buttons, a tricolored vest, and a red cap. Buildings of interest to tourists were undamaged in World War II. Pop. of commune, 12,737 (1936); of town, 3,982 (1936).

Carmagnola, Francesco Bussone da. [Original name, **Francesco Bussone**; title, Conte **di Castelnuovo.**] b. at Carmagnola, Italy, 1380; d. at Venice, May 5, 1432. Italian condottiere (professional captain of mercenary soldiers). In the service of the family of Visconti, dukes of Milan, he defeated the forces of Genoa, Parma, Piacenza, and other cities, and restored to the Visconti territories which they had lost. Dissatisfied with the treatment accorded him by the Milanese ducal house, he engaged to lead the Venetians against Milan in 1426. There appears, however, to have been a secret reconciliation between Carmagnola and the Visconti; the failure of his campaign caused the Venetians to accuse him of treachery, and after conviction by the Council of Ten of Venice, he was beheaded on May 5, 1432. The episode is the subject of a tragedy by Alessandro Manzoni, *Il Conte di Carmagnola* (1820).

Carmalt (kär'môlt), **William Henry.** b. at Friendsville, Pa., Aug. 3, 1836; d. July 17, 1929. American surgeon. He was professor of ophthalmology and otology (1879–81) and of the principles and practice of surgery (1881–1907) at Yale University.

Carman (kär'man), **Bliss.** [Full name, **William Bliss Carman.**] b. at Fredericton, New Brunswick, Canada, April 15, 1861; d. June 8, 1929. Canadian poet, essayist, and journalist, resident (1888 *et seq.*) in Connecticut and New York. He was a staff member of *Current Literature* and the *Atlantic Monthly*. His works include *Low Tide on Grand Pré* (1893), *St. Kavin* (1894), *A Sea Mark* (1895), *Behind the Arras* (1895), *Ballads of Lost Haven* (1896), *By the Aurelian Wall* (1897), *The Vengeance of Noel Brassard* (1899), *Christmas Eve at St. Kavin's* (1901), *Ode on the Coronation of King Edward* (1902), *From the Book of Myths* (1902), *The Kinship of Nature* (1903), *From the Green Book of the Bards* (1903), *Songs of the Sea Children* (1903), *Sappho* (1903), *The Friendship of Art* (1904), *The*

Word of St. Kavin's (1904), *Songs from a Northern Garden* (1904), *From the Book of Valentines* (1905), *Collected Poems* (1905), *The Poetry of Life* (1905), *The Making of Personality* (1908), *The Rough Riders* (1909), *April Airs* (1916), *Far Horizons* (1925), and *Wild Garden* (1929). With Richard Hovey he wrote *Songs from Vagabondia* (1894), *More Songs from Vagabondia* (1896), and *Last Songs from Vagabondia* (1901).

Carman, Harry James. b. at Greenfield, N.Y., Jan. 22, 1884—. American educator and historian. He began his career in education as a teacher (1903–05) in grade schools and as principal (1909–13) of the high school at Rhinebeck, N.Y., but with his appointment as an instructor in history and political science at his alma mater, the University of Syracuse, in 1914, he entered the special field in which he has gained authority and leadership. He became assistant professor of political science at Syracuse in 1917, but went to Columbia University, New York, with which he has since been associated, in 1918 as an instructor in history. He became assistant professor of the same subject in 1921, an associate professor in 1925, and professor in 1931. In 1939 he was named Moore professor of history at Columbia. He has also served as assistant dean, and since 1943 as dean, of Columbia College. He has been a member of the Board of Higher Education of New York City since 1938, and a trustee of the Institute of International Education since 1942. He is a member of, among other learned bodies, the American Historical Association, American Catholic Historical Association, Academy of Political Science, American Academy of Political and Social Science, and the New York Historical Society. In 1928 he was president of the History Teachers Association of the Middle States and Maryland, held the same office in the Agricultural Historical Society in 1941, and has headed the Adult Education Council of New York since 1940. He is the author of numerous articles in professional and learned periodicals and of *The Street Surface Railway Franchises of New York* (1919), *Social and Economic History of the United States* (1930–32), *American Husbandry* (1939), and *Jesse Buel, Agricultural Reformer* (1946), and coauthor of *Civilization in the West* (1919), *Record of Political Events* (1919), *A History of the United States* (1931), *Lincoln and the Patronage* (1946), and *A History of the American People* (2 vols., 1952; with Harold C. Syrett).

Carmana (kär.mā′nạ). Ancient name of **Kerman,** city.

Carmania (kär.mā′ni.ạ, -mān′yạ). Ancient name of **Kerman,** region.

Carmarthen (kär.mär′ᴛʜẹn, kạr-). [Also: **Caermarthen;** Latin, **Maridunum.**] Municipal borough and river port in S Wales, in Carmarthenshire, situated on the river Towy, ab. 9 mi. N of Carmarthen Bay, ab. 221 mi. W of London by rail. It is the county seat of Carmarthenshire and one of the oldest royal boroughs in Wales, having received its first royal charter from Edward II in 1313. Small vessels of up to 300 tons can navigate the river Towy as far as Carmarthen. The town has a ruined castle, and there is a carefully preserved oak tree in the main street about which there is a local legend that the welfare of the town is dependent upon it. 12,121 (1951).

Carmarthen, Marquis of. A title of **Osborne, Francis** (1751–99), and **Osborne,** Sir **Thomas.**

Carmarthen Bay. [Also **Caermarthen Bay.**] Large bay in S Wales, forming an inlet of Bristol Channel. It lies between Pembrokeshire, Carmarthenshire, and Glamorganshire. Width at entrance, ab. 18 mi.

Carmarthenshire (kär.mär′ᴛʜẹn.shir, kạr-). [Also: **Carmarthen, Caermarthen, Caermarthenshire.**] Maritime county in S Wales: largest of the Welsh counties. It is bounded on the N by Cardiganshire, on the E by Brecknockshire, on the SE by Glamorganshire, on the S by Carmarthen Bay and Burry Inlet (inlets of Bristol Channel), and on the W by Pembrokeshire. The surface is generally mountainous or upland (especially in the northern portion), and the county has much land in permanent pasture which is of rather poor quality. Manufacture of woolens (chiefly flannels) is concentrated in the valley of the river Teifi between Lampeter and Newcastle Emlyn on the northern boundary with Cardiganshire. Coal and iron ore are mined in the SE part. Other minerals mined to some extent are gold (at Caio, in the NE part), copper, silver, lead, marble, slate, and building stone. It is probable that the Romans mined gold here. The county has a tin-plate industry. Carmarthen is the county seat; area of administrative county, ab. 919 sq. mi.; pop. of administrative county, 171,742 (1951).

Carmath (kär′mät), **Hamdan ben-Ashath.** See **Karmat.**

Carmathians (kär.mā′thi.ạnz). See **Karmathians.**

Carmaux (kȧr.mō). Town in S France, in the department of Tarn, situated on the Cernon River, N of Albi. It is a coal-mining town and manufactures glass and lingerie. 11,136 (1946).

Carmel (kär′mẹl). Town (in New York the equivalent of township in many other states) and unincorporated village in SE New York, county seat of Putnam County, near Peekskill: residential and resort community. Pop. of town, 5,458 (1950); of village, 1,529(1950).

Carmel. In Old Testament geography, a city in the mountains of Judah (Josh. xv. 55). The modern ruins of Kurmul are situated ab. 7 mi. below Hebron, in a slightly SE direction.

Carmel, Mount. Mountain ridge in NW Palestine which branches off from the mountains of Samaria, and stretches in a long line to the NW toward the Mediterranean. It is said to have fallen within the lot of the tribe of Asher, and is frequently mentioned in the Old Testament. It was the scene of many of the deeds of the prophets Elijah and Elisha. The mountain is formed of hard gray limestone with nodules and veins of flint, abounds in caves, and is covered with a rich vegetation. The highest part of the mountain, its NW end, rises ab. 1,700 ft. above the sea. Its grottoes were the abodes of Christian hermits from the early times of Christianity. In 1207 they were organized into the order of Carmelites, and their monastery (built in the 19th century) is situated 480 ft. above the sea, where the mountain slopes down to a promontory in the direction of the sea.

Carmel-by-the-Sea (kär.mel′). [Also: **Carmel;** called locally the **"Village."**] City in W California, in Monterey County, on the Pacific Ocean, S by SE of San Francisco. Long a literary and art colony, it is sometimes characterized as the artistic Bohemia of the post-World War II period. It has been the home of Robinson Jeffers, Henry Miller, and others, and has an open-air theater and annual music festivals. 4,351 (1950).

Carmeliano (kär.me.lyä′nō), **Pietro.** [Also, **Peter Carmelianus.**] b. at Brescia, Italy; d. 1527. Italian humanist. He went to England sometime after 1470 and before 1480 and was Latin secretary and chaplain to Henry VII, and lute-player to Henry VIII, who gave him 40 pounds a year. He was prebendary of Saint Paul's (1517–26), of Saint Stephen's (1524), and of York from 1498 until his death. He wrote poems on the life of Saint Mary of Egypt, on the death of the king of Scots (James IV) at the battle of Flodden, on the engagement of Prince Charles of Castile to Mary, daughter of Henry VII, and on Richard III, praising him while he lived as a perfect king, and attacking him after his death as a tyrant and a murderer. Some of his poetry was translated into English by Alexander Barclay, under the title *The Mirrour of Good Maners,* and included (1570) in Barclay's *The Ship of Fools.*

Carmelites (kär′mẹ.līts). One of the four principal orders of mendicant friars of the Roman Catholic Church. Traditionally the order originated on Mount Carmel in Palestine under the leadership of the prophet Elias; actually (and the dispute about these dates and facts aroused so great a storm that an official silence was decreed on the controversy in 1698) it seems to have begun there, in the middle of the 12th century, as an eremitical grouping under Saint Berthold. During the 13th century, after the failure of the armies of the Crusaders in the East, the order moved its base to Cyprus (c1240) and spread thence throughout Europe to England and (in later centuries) to the New World, Persia, India, and China. Under Saint Simon Stock (fl. 1247–65) the change from eremitic to mendicant life occurred, including the change of habit from the mantle with black and white rays (from which the friars were known as *Fratres barrati* or *virgulati* or *de pica*) to one of pure white wool (from which came their English appellation of White Friars). The Carmelites were royal confessors to the Lancastrian line in England, but were suppressed under Henry VIII, never again reaching the height of popular appeal they had previously attained there. Under the Spanish Saint Teresa of Ávila and Saint

John of the Cross, the Carmelites again expanded in the 16th century, undergoing at the same time a split into two groups: the Calced (so-called because they wore shoes) or older group, and the Discalced (who wore sandals) or reform group, who tended to return to the more austere tradition. The latter was recognized (1593) as a separate order and is now the more prominent of the two orders. The Carmelite sisterhood began about 1450 when several orders of Beguines joined the Carmelite order (from their ranks came Saint Teresa). The present convent of the order on Mount Carmel was built in the period from 1827 to 1853, replacing an earlier building (built 1720) blown up (1821) by the Turks.

Carmelo (kär.mā′lō). City in SW Uruguay, in Colonia department, on the Vaca River: nearby historic ruins. Pop. ab. 12,000.

Carmelo (or **Carmel**) **Mission.** See **San Carlos Borromeo de Monterey, Mission of.**

Carmen (kär′mẹn; French, kȧr.men). Story by Prosper Mérimée, published in 1847. It was used as the basis of Georges Bizet's opera of the same name. Its titular heroine is a gypsy who works in a cigarette factory. A young soldier, José Navarro, falls in love with her although she is fickle; in order to gain and keep her love, José robs, smuggles, and kills. In final anguish, he stabs Carmen.

Carmen. Opera in four acts by Georges Bizet, with libretto by Meilhac and Halévy founded on Mérimée's story, first produced at the Opéra Comique, Paris, on March 3, 1875.

Carmen del Paraná (kär′men del pä.rä.nä′). [Also, **Carmen.**] City in SE Paraguay, in Itapúa department. Pop. ab. 13,000.

Carmen Seculare (kär′mẹn sek.ū̦.lãr′ē). Hymn composed by Horace on the occasion of the "Secular Games," in 17 B.C.

Carmen-Sylva (kär′men.sēl′vä). [Also: **Techirghiol, Techirghiol-Movila.**] Village in S Rumania, in the region of Dobruja, situated on the Black Sea, ab. 13 mi. S of Constanța: a popular seaside resort. 1,075 (1948).

Carmen Sylva (kär′mẹn sil′vạ). Pseudonym of **Elizabeth** (of *Rumania*).

Carmer (kär′mėr), **Carl** (**Lamson**). b. at Cortland, N.Y., Oct. 16, 1893—. American poet and prose writer, noted as a folklorist. He received a Ph.B. (1914) from Hamilton and an M.A. (1915) from Harvard, and served in World War I. He was a professor (1924–27) at the University of Alabama, and served as assistant editor of *Vanity Fair* (1928–29) and *Theatre Arts Monthly* (1929–33). His works include *Stars Fell on Alabama* (1934), *Listen for a Lonesome Drum* (1936), *Genesee Fever* (1941), *America Sings* (1942), *American Scriptures* (1946), *The Jesse James of the Java* (1946), and *Dark Trees to the Wind* (1950).

Carmi (kär′mī). City in SE Illinois, county seat of White County, on the Little Wabash River. It is a manufacturing and farm market center. 5,574 (1950).

Carmichael (kär′mī″kẹl). Unincorporated community in N central California, in Sacramento County. 4,499 (1950).

Carmichael (kär′mī″kẹl, kär.mī′kẹl), Sir **Thomas David Gibson.** [Title, Baron **Carmichael of Skirling.**] b. 1859; d. 1926. British colonial governor and art collector. A graduate of Cambridge, he was a member of Parliament from 1895 to 1900. He served as governor of Victoria, Australia (1908–11), of Madras (1911–12), and of Bengal (1912–17). A noted art connoisseur, he was a trustee of the National Gallery at London.

Carmignano (kär.mē.nyä′nō). Town and commune in C Italy, in the *compartimento* (region) of Tuscany, in the province of Firenze, NW of Florence. The villas of Artemino and Poggio a Caiano, originally of the Medici family of Florence, are in the vicinity. Pop. of commune, 12,536 (1936); of town, 815 (1936).

Carmina Burana (kär′mi.nạ bū.ran′ạ). Manuscript of some 300 medieval songs from the 12th and 13th centuries, composed by *goliards*, i.e., wandering students. Most of the songs are in Latin, some in German, and some in a mixture of the two. They are satirical, roisterous, amorous, seldom serious. The name *Burana* derives from the Abbey of Benediktbeuren where the manuscript was found.

Carmody (kär′mọ.di), **Eileen.** Character in Eugene O'Neill's realistic tragedy *The Straw* (1921). The setting of the play, like that of *The Magic Mountain* of Thomas Mann, is a tuberculosis sanitarium, such as O'Neill knew from personal experience. In this cheerless background, Eileen falls in love with, and is loved by, Stephen Murray, a fellow patient.

Carmody, John Michael. b. at Towanda, Pa., c1882—. American administrator and industrial engineer who served (1939 *et seq.*) as administrator of the Federal Works Administration. Vice-president (1923–26) in charge of industrial relations for the Davis Coal and Coke Company, he edited (1927–33) *Coal Age* and *Factory and Industrial Management* at New York. He served as chief engineer (1933–35) in the Civil Works Administration and Federal Emergency Relief Administration, was chairman (1933) of the Bituminous Coal Labor Board, and was a member (1935–36) of the National Labor Relations Board. He also served (1936–39) as administrator of the Rural Electrification Administration and was a member (1941–46) of the U.S. Maritime Commission.

Carmona (kär.mō′nä). [Ancient name, **Carmo.**] Town in SW Spain, in the province of Sevilla, ab. 20 mi. NE of Seville. It has markets for oil, wine, grain, and other agricultural products, and soap, cloth, and pottery factories. There are remnants of Roman structures including a necropolis, an amphitheater, and the remains of a temple. The parish church is a converted mosque. Carmona was an important Roman town in ancient times; later strongly fortified by the Moslems, it was recaptured from them in 1247 by Ferdinand III of Castile. 24,876 (1940).

Carmona (kär.mō′nạ), **Antônio Oscar de Fragoso.** b. at Lisbon, Portugal, Nov. 24, 1869; d. there, April 18, 1951. Portuguese army officer and politician, who was for nearly 25 years (elected 1928, 1935, 1942, 1949) president of Portugal. From 1925 to 1928 he was acting head of the government during a period of considerable political unrest, and suppressed (1927) actual revolt at Oporto and Lisbon.

Carmontelle or **Carmontel** (kȧr.môṅ.tel), **Louis.** [Pseudonym of **Louis Carrogis.**] b. at Paris, Aug. 25, 1717; d. there, Dec. 26, 1806. French dramatist, author of *Proverbes dramatiques* (1768 *et seq.*) and *Théâtre de campagne* (1775).

Carnac (kȧr.nȧk; Anglicized, kär′nak). [Medieval Latin, **Carnacus.**] Town in NW France, in the department of Morbihan, Brittany, situated on the Baie de Quiberon, ab. 18 mi. SE of Lorient. It is famous for its prehistoric monuments, such as menhirs, dolmens, and other granite blocks of great antiquity and also for its archaeological museum. There are a fine bathing beach and fisheries, both in Carnac and in nearby La Trinité-sur-Mer. 3,065 (1946).

Carnahan (kär′nạ.han), **Peachey.** One of the two heroes in Rudyard Kipling's short story "The Man Who Would Be King." He is the companion (originally the servant) of the other hero, Daniel Dravot, "the man who would be king" (the country is never precisely located, but is somewhere beyond the Khyber Pass). When it is discovered that he is not a god, as he has succeeded in making the natives believe, but an ordinary man, Daniel is killed. Peachey, who lives to tell the tale, is crucified but manages to make his way back to India, mentally broken if not actually insane, carrying the head of Dravot as evidence of his story. The story is included in *The Phantom Rickshaw* (1889).

Carnarvon (kär.när′vọn, kạr-). See also **Caernarvon.**

Carnarvon, 4th Earl of. Title of **Herbert, Henry Howard Molyneux.**

Carnarvon, Edward II of. See **Edward II** (of *England*).

Carnarvonshire (kär.när′vọn.shir, kạr-). See **Caernarvonshire.**

Carnatic (kär.nat′ik). [Also, **Karnatic.**] Name formerly given to a country on the E coast of British India. It was governed in the 18th century by the nawab at Arcot, who was vassal to the Nizam of Hyderabad. It passed under British administration c1801; the last nawab died in 1853.

Carnaval (kȧr.nȧ.vȧl). Set of 21 short piano pieces (Opus 9, 1837) by Robert Schumann.

Carnaval de Venise (dẹ vẹ.nēz). [Eng. trans., "*Carnival of Venice.*"] Group of burlesque variations by Paganini on a popular air heard in Venice; it became a favorite all over the world.

Carnaval de Venise. [Eng. trans., *"Carnival of Venice."*] Opera by Ambroise Thomas, first performed on Dec. 9, 1853. The overture contains the melody of the Paganini variations of the same name.

Carnavalet Museum (kȧr.nȧ.vȧ.le). Historical museum at Paris. The Hôtel Carnavalet was built in 1550, in the farms which then occupied the eastern portion of Paris, on designs by Jean Bullant and Pierre Lescot, architects, and with a façade by Jean Goujon, sculptor. It derived its name from one of its early tenants, the Dame de Kernevenoy, called "Carnavalet" at court. Madame de Sévigné lived here from 1677 to 1695. In 1866 it was bought by the city of Paris for a museum. Since 1872 collections and a library have been formed, devoted to material relating to the history of Paris and the French Revolution.

Carnbee (kärn'bā), Baron **Pieter Melvill van.** See **Melvill van Carnbee,** Baron **Pieter.**

Carné (kȧr.nā), **Louis Marcien,** Comte **de.** b. at Quimper, France, Feb. 17, 1804; d. there, Feb. 12, 1876. French publicist. He was the author of *Études sur l'histoire du gouvernement représentatif en France de 1789 à 1848* (1855).

Carneades (kär.nē'ą.dēz). b. at Cyrene, c213 B.C.; died c129 B.C. Greek skeptical philosopher and rhetorician, called the founder of the Third or New Academy. Holding a firm belief in the necessity for suspending judgment at all times, he advocated probability in its various degrees as the only truly practical basis for human action.

Carnegie (kär'nẹ.gi, kär.nā'gi, -neg'i). Borough in SW Pennsylvania, in Allegheny County, ab. 7 mi. SW of Pittsburgh: manufactures of iron, steel, bedding, and beer. Established (1894) by the merger of Chartiers and Mansfield, it was named for Andrew Carnegie. 12,105 (1950).

Carnegie, Andrew. b. at Dunfermline, Scotland, Nov. 25, 1835; d. at "Shadowbrook," Lenox, Mass., Aug. 11, 1919. American steel magnate, writer, and philanthropist who promoted the "Gospel of Wealth." His father's family had been handloom weavers for many generations; his mother was the daughter of a then well-known political and educational reformer, Thomas Morrison. In an environment where physical comforts were few but conversation plentiful and stimulating, he was reared to think of social causes and responsibilities. When he emigrated (1848) with his family to Allegheny, Pa., he became a bobbin boy in a local cotton factory. In spite of long working hours he developed his alert mind with the aid of a library furnished to working boys by Colonel James Anderson. Employed (c1849) as a messenger boy in the Pittsburgh telegraph office at two dollars and a half a week, he soon taught himself to be an operator. There he met Thomas A. Scott, superintendent of the Pittsburgh division of the Pennsylvania Railroad, who employed him in 1853 as his private secretary and personal telegrapher at 35 dollars a month. Young Carnegie saved his money, and his position gave him opportunities to start his fortune with some excellent investments. His good offices in introducing Woodruff sleeping cars on the Pennsylvania secured him an eighth interest in this ancestor of the later Pullman Company. When Scott became vice-president of the Pennsylvania Railroad in 1859 Carnegie succeeded him as superintendent of the Western division. During the Civil War he again served briefly as Scott's aide when the latter was called to Washington to become assistant secretary of war in charge of military transportation. While still with the railroad Carnegie invested in the booming U.S. iron industry, and in 1865 left to give his full attention to iron manufacture and other ventures such as the Keystone Bridge Company, and various oil and security transactions in which J. Edgar Thomson and Scott, both prominent in the Pennsylvania Railroad, often had an interest. During a visit to England, he became the friend of Sir Henry Bessemer and learned the workings of the Bessemer process for making steel; beginning in 1873 he sold most of his holdings outside of the iron industry and, in spite of the depression, invested his capital in a steel plant. He became principal owner of the Homestead Steel Works and other plants, and in 1889 established the Carnegie Steel Company. Over the three decades from 1873 to 1901, the vast properties in iron and steel mills, ores, coal, railroads, and steamship lines developed by Carnegie helped establish U.S. world supremacy in the making of steel. His genius for marketing, his willingness to reinvest profits in new machinery and methods, and his ability to surround himself with such capable men as Henry Clay Frick and Charles W. Schwab, made his the leading company, which by 1900 was producing one quarter of the steel in the U.S. Characteristic of his business acumen and foresight was the development of his steel-producing facilities during times of depression in the 1870's and 1890's. While Carnegie wrote articles on the subject of good labor relations, in the long and bloody Homestead strike (1892) his manager, Frick, broke the power of the Amalgamated Association of Iron and Steel Workers. In 1900, the Carnegie Company listed a record-making profit of 40 million dollars, but meanwhile Frick had joined J. Pierpont Morgan and others in the organization of a strong rival company. Rather than enter a great competitive battle at a time when he was ready to retire, Carnegie sold his holdings in January, 1901, to the Morgan group, for 225 million dollars in the 5 percent bonds of the new United States Steel Company. From this time on he devoted his time mainly to the advancement of education and world peace, living most of the time at his estate in northern Scotland. A cultured and widely read man who loved Shakespeare and quoted Robert Burns, he had a gift for making friendships with some of the foremost American and British statesmen, diplomats, and writers of the time, including John Morley, William E. Gladstone, James Bryce, Theodore Roosevelt, Herbert Spencer, Matthew Arnold, and Mark Twain. He was a contributor to such periodicals as the *Nineteenth Century* and the *North American Review.* His book *Triumphant Democracy* (1886, rev. ed. 1893) was a glowing testimonial to the superiority of American republican institutions, and a criticism of the British institution of royalty. His famous article "Wealth" appeared (June, 1889) in the *North American Review;* published in the British *Pall Mall Gazette* as "The Gospel of Wealth," it asserted Carnegie's conviction that rich men, out of duty to their own unique abilities, had a social responsibility to serve the common weal by the wise and unselfish use of their fortunes for worthy purposes. After his retirement, Carnegie translated his doctrine into action, donating sums totaling 350 million dollars, of which 288 million dollars went to the U.S. and 62 million dollars to the British Empire. Among his chief gifts were 125 million dollars to the Carnegie Corporation of New York, 60 million dollars to public library buildings, 29 million dollars to the Carnegie Foundation for the Advancement of Teaching, 22 million dollars each to the Carnegie Institute of Pittsburgh and the Carnegie Institution of Washington, and 10 million dollars to the Endowment for International Peace. Deeply interested in the cause of world peace, he was an exponent of international arbitration, and erected the Peace Palace at The Hague. At the age of 52 he married Louise Whitfield of New York who bore him one daughter, Margaret, and lived happily with him until his death. Among his writings are *An American Four-in-Hand in Britain* (1883), *Round the World* (1884), *Triumphant Democracy* (1886), *The Gospel of Wealth and Other Timely Essays* (1900), *The Empire of Business* (1902), *Life of James Watt* (1905), and *Problems of Today* (1908). See his autobiography, edited by John C. Van Dyke (1920) and *The Life of Andrew Carnegie,* by Burton J. Hendrick (2 vols., 1932).

Carnegie Corporation of New York. Organization founded by Andrew Carnegie in 1911 for the purpose of promoting "the advancement and diffusion of knowledge and understanding" among the people of the U.S. and the British Empire. It grants funds, from income only, for aiding technical schools, libraries, institutions of higher learning, useful publications, scientific research, and other agencies and activities. Its headquarters are at New York. Its original total endowment was 135 million dollars.

Carnegie Endowment for International Peace. Organization founded by Andrew Carnegie in 1910 whose endowment of 10 million dollars is devoted to encouraging education in the cause of world peace. It grants financial aid to international projects and publications expressing the ideals of international coöperation and peace. It maintains headquarters at Washington, D.C.

Carnegie Foundation for the Advancement of Teaching. Institution founded by Andrew Carnegie in 1905, and incorporated by act of Congress in 1906, for the purpose of advancing the profession of teaching by a system of retiring-allowances for teachers and officers in colleges, universities, and technical schools in the U.S., Canada, and Newfoundland, and of pensions for their widows. The original fund of 10 million dollars was increased by Carnegie in 1908 to 15 million dollars, to include also in its scope teachers and officers in State institutions. An additional endowment of 1,250,000 dollars was used for establishing the foundation's Division of Educational Inquiry in 1913. The distribution of allowances and pensions is based on the qualifications, not of individual teachers, but of institutions, and in the course of determining what institutions meet the requirements of the foundation interesting and valuable reports have been made both on the standards and methods of institutions and on the condition of higher education in general. Thus the foundation has become an educational agency of more than national influence. Its headquarters are at New York.

Carnegie Hero Fund Commission. Organization that administers a fund created by Andrew Carnegie in April, 1904, for the benefit of persons in the U.S., Canada, and Newfoundland who have suffered injury in heroic efforts to save human life, or, in case of their death, for the benefit of their dependent families. Medals also are awarded for heroic acts. The endowment, which is based on a trust fund of 5 million dollars, is placed in the hands of a commission of 21 persons, who adjudicate upon cases submitted to them.

Carnegie Institution of Washington. Institution founded at Washington, D.C., by Andrew Carnegie, in 1902. He stated that his purpose was to "found in the city of Washington an institution which, with the coöperation of institutions now or hereafter established, shall in the broadest and most liberal manner encourage investigation, research, and discovery, show the application of knowledge to the improvement of mankind, and provide such buildings, laboratories, books, and apparatus as may be needed." By an act of Congress, approved on April 28, 1904, the Institution was placed under the control of a board of 24 trustees. The trustees meet annually, and during the intervals between such meetings the affairs of the Institution are conducted by an executive committee, chosen by and from the board of trustees, acting through the president of the Institution as chief executive officer. Daniel C. Gilman was the first president of the Institution, holding office until his resignation took effect in December, 1904. Many projects in widely different fields of inquiry have been considered or are under consideration by the executive committee, and over 850 volumes of scientific importance have been published. The endowment is 35 million dollars.

Carneia (kär.nē′ạ). Ancient Spartan festival (observed also by some of the other Doric peoples), lasting 9 days in the month of Karneios (a sacred month, approximating the modern August), held in honor of Apollo Carneius, in his aspect of god of flocks and fertility (Carneius probably being a more ancient fertility god assimilated to Apollo by the Dorians).

Carneiro (kär.nā′rö), **Cecílio.** b. in Minas Gerais, Brazil, 1911—. Brazilian novelist and physician. He wrote the novels *Memórias de cinco* (1939) and *A fogueira* (1942, Eng. trans., 1944).

Carneiro de Campos (dẹ kum′pös), **José Joaquim.** [Title, Marquis of **Caravellas.**] b. at Bahia (now Salvador), Brazil, March 4, 1768; d. at Rio de Janeiro, Sept. 8, 1836. Brazilian statesman. He was one of three regents chosen in April, 1831, to govern during the minority of Pedro II.

Carneiro de Sousa Bandeira (dẹ sō′zạ bạn.dā′rạ), **Manuel.** See **Bandeira, Manuel (Carneiro de Sousa).**

Carneiro Leão (lē.ouṅ′), **Honorio Hermeto.** [Title (created 1854), Marquis of **Paraná.**] b. in Minas Gerais, Brazil, Jan. 11, 1801; d. at Rio de Janeiro, Sept. 3, 1856. Brazilian statesman. He was minister of justice (September, 1832–March, 1833), prime minister (Jan. 20, 1843–February, 1844), president successively of Rio de Janeiro and Pernambuco, envoy to the Platine States (the territory of which is now included in Argentina, Uruguay, and Paraguay), and again prime minister from Dec. 5, 1854, until his death.

Carney (kär′ni), **Robert Bostwick.** b. at Vallejo, Calif., March 26, 1895—. American naval officer. A graduate (1916) of the U.S. Naval Academy, he was promoted (1942) to vice-admiral. He served as chief of staff (1943–45) to Admiral William F. Halsey, and was named deputy chief (1948) and chief (1953) of naval operations.

Carni (kär′nī). In ancient history, a name given by some to an Alpine tribe (probably Celtic) inhabiting the mountainous region between Venetia and Noricum. It was conquered (115 B.C.) by the Roman Scaurus.

Carnic Alps (kär′nik alps). Division of the Alps in NE Italy and in S Austria.

Carnicer (kär.nē.ther′), **Ramón.** b. at Tarrega, Lérida, Spain, Oct. 24, 1789; d. at Madrid, March 17, 1855. Spanish composer of operas, songs, and church music. From 1827 to 1830 he was director of the Barcelona Opera, and later taught harmony (1830–54) at the Madrid Conservatory. His best-known operas are *El Colón* (1831) and *Cristoforo Colombo*. He was the composer also of *Dulce Patria*, the national anthem of Chile.

Carnifex Ferry (kär′ni.feks). Place near Gauley River, Nicholas County, W.Va. Here, on Sept. 10, 1861, a force of Union soldiers under Rosecrans repulsed the attack of a Confederate brigade under General John B. Floyd, who had, on August 26, driven away an Ohio regiment stationed there.

Carniola (kär.ni.ō′lạ.) [Serbo-Croatian, **Kranj**; German, **Krain.**] Territory in SE Europe, formerly a province of Austria, now near the central part of the federative unit of Slovenia in Yugoslavia. It is separated from the present Austrian frontier by narrow belts of land formerly belonging to the Austrian provinces of Carinthia and Styria and now comprising frontier districts of Slovenia. The population is ethnically Slovenian, and predominantly Catholic in religion; the former German minority emigrated to Germany. Carniola was a medieval duchy and was incorporated into the Hapsburg realm in 1282. It became an Austrian province in 1849, and was divided between Italy and Yugoslavia after World War I. In 1947, it was united again (within Yugoslavia) as part of Slovenia. Its surface is mountainous, traversed by the Julian and Carnic Alps, and the Sava valley lies in the north. It has mines of coal, quicksilver, iron, and manganese.

Carnium (kär′ni.um). Ancient name of **Kranj.**

Carnochan (kär′nọ.kạn), **John Murray.** b. at Savannah, Ga., July 4, 1817; d. at New York, Oct. 28, 1887. American surgeon, noted especially for the treatment of elephantiasis Arabum by ligature of the femoral artery, and for the successful removal of the entire lower jaw in one operation.

Carnot (kår.nō), **(Lazare) Hippolyte.** b. at St.-Omer, France, April 6, 1801; d. at Paris, March 16, 1888. French politician and publicist; son of L. N. M. Carnot and father of Sadi Carnot. He was minister of public instruction in 1848, after having expressed sympathy with the revolutionary radicals. He was a member (1864–69) of the Legislative Assembly, and became a life senator in 1875.

Carnot, Lazare Nicolas Marguerite. [Called **"the great Carnot."**] b. at Nolay, in Burgundy, France, May 13, 1753; d. at Magdeburg, Prussia, Aug. 3, 1823. French statesman, military strategist, and man of science; father of (Lazare) Hippolyte Carnot and N. L. S. Carnot. He was a deputy to the Legislative Assembly in 1791, to the Convention in 1792, and served with great distinction as war minister (1793–95), his successful labors winning him the popular title of "organizer of victory." He was a member of the Directory (1795–97), of the tribune (1802–07), governor of Antwerp (1814), and served (1815) as minister of the interior under Napoleon. He wrote *Sur la métaphysique du calcul infinitésimal* (1797) and *De la défense des places fortes* (1810).

Carnot, Maurus. b. at Samnaun, Switzerland, Jan. 26, 1865; d. at Disentis, Switzerland, Jan. 2, 1935. Swiss scholar and author writing in Romansh. He was a Benedictine monk at the monastery of Disentis, where he served the cause of Romansh literature by writing in this dialect and by translating Romansh literary monuments into German.

Carnot, Nicolas Léonard Sadi. b. at Paris, June 1, 1796; d. there, Aug. 24, 1832. French physicist; son of L. N. M. Carnot. His work, embodying theories in the field later known as thermodynamics, preceded that of, and was later developed by, Clausius, Kelvin, Joule, and others. The Carnot cycle (of engine thermal efficiency) and Carnot's principle (basis of the second law of thermodynamics) are both named for him. His most noted work is *Réflexions sur la puissance motrice du feu et les machines propres à développer cette puissance* (1824).

Carnot, Sadi. [Full name, **Marie François Sadi Carnot.**] b. at Limoges, France, Aug. 11, 1837; d. at Lyons, France, June 24, 1894. French politician, fourth president of the Third Republic; son of (Lazare) Hippolyte Carnot. Entering public service as a young man, he first came into prominence as an organizer of resistance against the Germans in the Franco-Prussian War, as a result of which he was made prefect of the department of Seine-Inférieure in 1871, and in the same year was elected to the National Assembly from the department of Côte-d'Or. He sat in the National Assembly until 1876, and was a member of the Chamber of Deputies from 1876 into 1880, when he became minister of finance, a post he held until 1886. In a period when financial jobbery was endemic in France, Carnot remained without reproach and above suspicion, and when a inmisterial crisis ensued in 1887, he was chosen fourth president of the Third Republic, and guided his country through several dangerous situations, including the Panama Canal scandal in 1892. After he had delivered an address at a public banquet at Lyons, on June 24, 1894, President Carnot was stabbed by an Italian anarchist, and expired the same day.

Carnsore Point (kärn'sōr). Promontory in Leinster province, in the SE part of the Irish Republic, in County Wexford. It lies at the SE extremity of a peninsula projecting into St. George's Channel.

Carnutes (kär.nū'tēz) or **Carnuti** (-tī) or **Carnutae** (-tē). Ancient tribe of central Gaul, living in the vicinity of what are now Orléans and Chartres, and involved (52–51 B.C.) in wars against Caesar. The Carnutes, who lived in an area distinguished for its forests, are considered the center of Druidic worship.

Carnutum (kär.nū'tum). An ancient name of **Chartres.**

Caro (kār'ō). Village in C lower Michigan on the Cass River, county seat of Tuscola County, and center of a beet-sugar, potato, and grain farming area: beet-sugar refining. 3,464 (1950).

Caro (kä'rō), **Annibale.** b. at Civita Nuova, Ancona, Italy, 1507; d. at Rome, c1566. Italian writer of the Renaissance. His services as a tutor and a private secretary to a leading family of Florence put him in the way of lucrative employment at Rome and later with the Farnese dynasty at Parma, where he served two successive dukes and two cardinals of that family. Caro was one of the fountainheads of Renaissance Italian, a master of precise and elegant prose and facile verse, the latter including collections entitled *Rime* and *Canzone.* He also wrote a comedy, *Gli Straccione,* but his most influential works were his translations of Vergil, Aristotle, Gregory Nazianzen, and Cyprian; and of all these, his version of the *Aeneid* is considered his masterwork.

Caro (ká.rō), **Elme Marie.** b. at Poitiers, France, March 4, 1826; d. at Paris, July 13, 1887. French philosopher. He was appointed professor at the Sorbonne in 1864, and was elected to the French Academy in 1874. He was a contributor to the *Revue de l'instruction publique.* Among his published works are *Le Mysticisme au xviiie siècle* (1852), *L'Idée de Dieu et ses nouveaux critiques* (1864), *La Philosophie de Goethe* (1866), *Le Matérialisme et la science* (1868), and *Mélanges et portraits* (1888).

Caro (kä'rō), **Heinrich.** b. at Posen, Germany, 1834; d. at Dresden, Germany, 1910. German organic and industrial chemist. He discovered several important dyes, such as methylene blue (1877), and dye precursors, such as acridine (with Graebe). As director of Badische Anilin und Soda-Fabrik (1868–89), he brought many important dyes into production, as alizarin, eosin, and methylene blue; he is considered to be one of the chief founders of modern German and British techniques for the manufacture of dyes from coal tar.

Caro, José Eusebio. b. at Ocaña, Colombia, 1817; d. of yellow fever on shipboard at Santa Marta, Colombia, 1853. Colombian poet, journalist, and statesman. Cofounder (1836) of the literary periodical *La Estrella nacional* and editor (1837) of the political journal *El Granadino,* he held (1841–49) several government posts but spent the last three years of his life in exile. His best poems reflect his ardent belief in political freedom for the individual. They include *En boca del ultimo Inca, La Libertad y el socialismo, Despedida de la patria,* and *El Hacha del proscrito.*

Caro or **Karo** (kä'rō), **Joseph ben Ephraim.** b. at Toledo, Spain, 1488; d. in Palestine, 1575. Talmudic authority and author of a compendium of Jewish laws and customs. In 1492 his parents were expelled from Spain, and as a child and young man he lived at Adrianople, Salonika, Constantinople, and other cities before finding a permanent home in Palestine c1535. He is considered to have been the greatest Talmudic scholar of the 16th century, his great authority resting on two of his books, namely, *Beth Joseph* (The House of Joseph), a commentary on the writings of another rabbinical scholar, and *Shulchan Aruch* (Arranged Tables), which is a methodical codification not only of Jewish law, but as well of the customs regulating Jewish life. *Shulchan Aruch* itself became the subject of numerous commentaries and aroused much opposition, but it still carries authority in the field of Jewish orthodox religious controversy.

Caro, Miguel Antonio. b. at Bogotá, Colombia, 1843; d. 1909. Colombian politician, poet, and author, president (1894–98) of Colombia. Editor of a conservative paper, he was in sympathy with the centralist constitution of 1886. He was vice-president of Colombia, becoming president upon the death of Rafael Nuñez. His works deal with philosophy, literature, politics, grammar, finance, and history. His best known poem is *A la estatua del Libertador,* and some of his works are collected in *Horas de amor.*

Caro, Nikodem. b. at Łódź (in what is now Poland), 1871; d. at Berlin-Dahlem, Germany, 1935. German industrial chemist. With Adolf Frank, he developed the cyanamide process, the first commercial nitrogen fixation method. Later, he organized the German cyanamide industry. He worked in his own laboratory (1897–1902) then owned and managed various cyanamide factories.

Carol I (of *Rumania*) (kar'ǫl). [Original full name, Prince **Karl Eitel Friedrich of Hohenzollern-Sigmaringen.**] b. at Sigmaringen, Germany, April 20, 1839; d. Oct. 10, 1914. Prince of Rumania (1866–81) and first king of Rumania (1881–1914). At the Congress of Berlin (1878), he obtained recognition of Rumania's full independence. His reign was noted for the development of parliamentary government and the consolidation of the Rumanian state; during this period, also, the development of the Rumanian oil fields was begun. He married (1869) Elizabeth of Wied.

Carol II (of *Rumania*). b. at Sinaia, Rumania, 1893; d. at Estoril, near Lisbon, Portugal, April 4, 1953. King of Rumania (1930–40). He ended, by divorce, a morganatic marriage with Zizi Labrino to marry (1921) Princess Helen of Greece, by whom he was the father of Michael of Rumania. Having formed an open liaison with Magda Lupescu, he renounced (1925) his right to the succession and went to live with her at Paris. Michael was therefore proclaimed king in 1927 when Ferdinand died; but Carol, who divorced Helen in 1928, returned to Rumania in 1930 and ousted his son from the throne. His ten-year reign was marked by intermittent struggles for power between Carol and the Iron Guard, a fascist organization. He at first encouraged the group, but suppressed it in 1938, in the same year attempting to set up a royal dictatorship. In 1940, however, he was forced to call back the Iron Guard. Torn between the demands made on Rumania by Russia and Germany, Carol declared (1940) himself on the side of the Axis powers. However, a revolt forced his abdication in the same year, and Michael was returned to the throne. Carol went abroad and became a resident in South and Central America, where he married (Brazil, 1947) Magda Lupescu.

Carolan (kar'ǫ.lan), **Turlogh.** See **O'Carolan, Turlogh.**

Carolina (kä.rō.lē'nä), **La.** See **La Carolina.**

Carolina Chansons (kar.ō.lī′na shan′sonz, shän.sôn′). Volume (1922) of regional poetry by Hervey Allen and Du Bose Heyward.

Carolina Maria (kä.rō.lē′nä mä.rē′ä). See **Maria Carolina.**

Carolina: or a Description of the Present State of that Country (kar.ō.lī′na). Prose pamphlet (1682) by Thomas Ash printed at London. It sings the praises of Carolina in the hope of enticing hopeful fortune hunters. Like much such material of the colonial period, it is perhaps now chiefly important to students of history rather than literature.

Carolina Wilhelmina Amelia Skeggs (skegz). See **Skeggs, Carolina Wilhelmina Amelia.**

Caroline (of *England*) (kar′ō.līn, -lin). See **Caroline of Anspach** and **Caroline of Brunswick.**

Caroline, Fort. Former settlement in NE Florida, ab. 10 mi. NE of Jacksonville, on the S bank of the St. John's River. It was first settled by French Huguenots in 1564, who were massacred by the Spaniards under Pedro Menendez de Avilés in 1565. Renamed San Mateo by the Spanish, it was occupied by them until 1568, when a group of French, aided by Indians, captured it and avenged the earlier massacre.

Caroline Islands (kar′ō.līn). [Also: **Carolines;** German, **Karolinen.**] Archipelago in the Pacific, N of New Guinea and E of the Philippines. The name includes usually the Palau Islands. The chief islands and island groups are Yap, Ponape, Truk, and Kusaie. Its inhabitants are Micronesians. When the islands were occupied by Spain in 1686, they were called the New Philippines. The dispute between Spain and Germany in 1885 regarding Yap was settled in favor of Spain. Purchased by Germany in 1899, the Carolines remained a German possession until 1919, when they were given to Japan, which had occupied them during World War I, as a mandate under the League of Nations. During World War II they were partly occupied by the Americans and have since been administered by them as a trust territory of the United Nations. Area, 510 sq. mi.; pop. 54,944 (1949).

Caroline Matilda (kar′ō.līn, -lin, ma.til′da). b. at London, July 22, 1751; d. at Celle, Germany, May 11, 1775. Queen of Denmark and Norway; wife of Christian VII of Denmark, youngest (posthumous) child of Frederick Louis, Prince of Wales, and sister of George III of England. She was married on Nov. 8, 1766. She became involved in an amour with Struensee, court physician (later created, through her influence, a count and raised to the most influential position in the state), and in various political complications. She was arrested with Struensee and others on the night of Jan. 16–17, 1772, divorced, and banished.

Caroline of Anspach (anz′pak, äns′päk). [Full name, **Wilhelmina Caroline of Brandenburg-Anspach.**] b. March 1, 1683; d. Nov. 20, 1737. Queen of Great Britain and Ireland; wife of George II and daughter of John Frederick, margrave of Brandenburg-Ansbach (Anglicized in his daughter's name to "Anspach"). She married George, then electoral prince of Hanover, on Sept. 2, 1705. She went to England on the accession (1714) of George I. She took an active part in politics, after her coronation in 1727, was a firm supporter of Robert Walpole, and several times acted as regent during the absence of the king. Her bitter hostility toward her eldest son, Frederick Louis, Prince of Wales, was notorious. As princess and as queen she was a patroness of learning; Pope and Chesterfield were members of her circle. She is introduced by Sir Walter Scott in *The Heart of Midlothian,* where Jeanie Deans has an interview with her at Richmond.

Caroline of Brunswick (brunz′wik). [Full name, **Amelia Elizabeth Caroline of Brunswick-Wolfenbüttel.**] b. May 17, 1768; d. Aug. 7, 1821. Queen of George IV of England; second daughter of Charles William Ferdinand, Duke of Brunswick, and Augusta, sister of George III of England. She married George, then prince of Wales, on April 8, 1795. Formally separated from the prince in 1796, she lived in retirement until 1813, and traveled abroad in the period 1813–20, her manner of living being much talked of. Returning to England on July 5, 1820, she was accused of adultery and tried before the House of Lords, in August, 1820. The trial was abandoned on Nov. 10, 1820, because of public disapproval. Her domestic troubles and trial played an important part in English politics. Throughout she had strong popular support. After her forcible exclusion from the coronation of her husband in Westminster Abbey (July 29, 1821), she died within a month.

Carolingia or **Karolingia** (kar.ō.lin′ji.a). Name sometimes given to the western kingdom of the Franks, the nucleus of the modern France.

Carolingian (kar.ō.lin′ji.an) or **Carlovingian** (kär.lō.vin′ji.an). [French, **Carlovingien;** German, **Karolinger.**] Royal house descended from Frankish lords in Austrasia in the 7th century. It furnished the second dynasty of French kings (751–987) following the Merovingian dynasty, a dynasty of German emperors and kings (752–911), and a dynasty of Italian sovereigns (774–961). The Carolingian house began with Pepin the Short and attained its highest point with his son Charlemagne.

Carolopolis (kar.ō.lop′ō.lis). A medieval name of **Charleville.**

Carolsfeld (kä′rols.felt), **Julius Schnorr von.** See **Schnorr von Karolsfeld** or **Carolsfeld, Julius.**

Carolus Magnus (kar′ō.lus mag′nus). Latin name of **Charlemagne.**

Caron or **Carron** (kä.rôn′), **Franciscus.** b. in the Netherlands, of French parents; d. 1674. Dutch navigator. He went to Japan in his youth, became a member of the Dutch Council of the Indies, was appointed director-general of the French commerce in India by Colbert in 1666, and was drowned near Lisbon in 1674 as he was returning to France from the East. He was the author of *Description of Japan* (1636).

Caron (kar′on), **Henry le.** Pseudonym of **Beach, Thomas Miller.**

Caron (ka.rôn), **Pierre Augustin.** See **Beaumarchais, Pierre Augustin Caron de.**

Caron, René Édouard. b. at what is now Ste. Anne de Beaupré, Quebec, Canada, 1800; d. Dec. 13, 1876. Canadian politician and jurist. He became judge of the Court of Queen's Bench in 1853, served as commissioner for codifying the laws of Lower Canada in 1857, and was appointed lieutenant governor of the province of Quebec in February, 1873, which post he retained until his death.

Carondelet (ka.ron.de.let′). Mississippi River steamboat, with iron armor and carrying 13 guns, used by the Union forces in the actions at Fort Henry, Fort Donelson, and Island Number Ten during the Civil War. It was constructed at St. Louis by James B. Eads.

Carondelet (kä.rōn.dā.let′; Anglicized, ka.ron.de.let′), **Francisco Luis Héctor,** Barón **de.** b. at Noyelles, Flanders, c1748; d. in Quito (now Ecuador), Aug. 10, 1807. Administrator of Spanish possessions in America. As governor (1791 *et seq.*) of Louisiana and West Florida, he built (1794) a canal (the Carondelet Canal) giving New Orleans an outlet to the Gulf, reformed the police, and built a fleet of gunboats on the Mississippi as part of his program to protect the interests of Spain against the expanding pressure of the new United States. As a result of his intrigues among the Indians and separatist Kentucky frontiersmen, U.S.-Spanish relations became strained. Subsequently he was governor general (1799–1807) of Quito.

Carondelet Canal. Canal (1794) covering a distance of a mile and a half from New Orleans to Bayou St. John, affording a water link between that city and Lake Pontchartrain. It was named for its sponsor, the Spanish governor Francisco Luis Héctor, Barón de Carondelet.

Caroní (kä.rō.nē′). River in SE Venezuela. It flows N to the Orinoco River. Length, ab. 400 mi.

Caronium (ka.rō′ni.um). Medieval name of **La Coruña,** city.

Caroor (ka.rōr′). See **Karur.**

Carossa (kä.ros′ä), **Hans.** b. at Tölz, Bavaria, Dec. 15, 1878—. German poet and prose writer. A physician, son and grandson of a physician, he has effectively coupled his medical practice and his writing. All his work is frankly autobiographical: *Eine Kindheit* (1922; *A Childhood,* 1930), *Verwandlungen einer Jugend* (1928; *Boyhood and Youth,* 1930). The doctor is frequently in the title role (*Doktor Bürgers Ende,* 1913; *Der Arzt Gion,* 1931, *Doctor Gion,* 1933). His *Rumänisches Tagebuch* (1924; *A*

Roumanian Diary, 1929), based on his experiences as an army surgeon, is his best-known and possibly his best work. Other works are *Führung und Geleit* (1933), *Geheimnisse des reiferen Lebens* (1936), *Gesammelte Gedichte* (1938), and *Das Jahr der schönen Täuschungen* (1941).

Carothers (ką.ruтн'ėrz), **Wallace Hume.** b. at Burlington, Iowa, April 27, 1896; d. April 29, 1937. American chemist, associated with the invention of synthetic nylon material, for which the patent was assigned (1937) to the du Pont Company. Graduated (1920) from Tarkio College in Missouri, he received (1924) his Ph.D. from the University of Illinois. After a period as an instructor (1918–28) at various universities, he served as a research chemist (1928 *et seq.*) with the du Pont Company at Wilmington, Del.

Caroto (kä.rō'tō) or **Carotto** (-rōt'-), **Giovanni Francesco.** b. at Verona, Italy, c1480; d. there, c1555. Italian painter of the Veronese school. Among his instructors in painting was Mantegna, whom in his earlier years he often imitated, according to Vasari. His later pictures show his acquaintance with and regard for the work of Leonardo da Vinci, Raphael, and others of the great masters of the high Renaissance, but also give evidence of a greater fascination with landscape as such than was common in that time. His work is to be seen today mostly at Verona, in the churches of San Girolamo, Sant'Eufemia, and San Fermo Maggiore, but there are also examples in the Uffizi Gallery and Pitti Palace, Florence, in the Louvre at Paris, and in the Städel at Frankfort on the Main.

Carouge (kȧ.rözh). Town in W Switzerland, in the canton of Genève, an industrial suburb of the city of Geneva. In 1786, it was made a provincial capital of Savoy by King Victor Amadeus II of Sardinia (who was Duke Victor Amadeus III of Savoy); it was joined to France in 1792, and to the canton of Genève in 1815. 7,972 (1941).

Carpaccio (kär.pät'chō), **Vittore.** b. in Istria, c1450; d. c1522. Venetian painter. Little is known of his life. He was a pupil of Gentile Bellini, whom he is reported to have accompanied to Constantinople, to which experience may be attributed his fondness for Oriental costumes in his pictures. The series of nine pictures from the life of Saint Ursula, in the Academy at Venice, is representative of his style. The series of nine pictures on the life of Saint George, which Ruskin praised, was painted (1502–08) by the order of the Hospice of Saint George.

Carpani (kär.pä'nē), **Giuseppe Antonio.** b. at Villalbese, Italy, Jan. 28, 1752; d. at Vienna, Jan. 22, 1825. Italian librettist and musical writer. He published *La Haydine* (a work on Haydn, 1812).

Carpathian Mountains (kär.pā'thi.ąn). [Also: **Carpathians**; Russian, Czech, and Polish, **Karpaty**; German, **Karpaten, Karpathen**; Hungarian, **Kárpátok**; Rumanian, **Carpații** (kär.pä'tsē.ē); Latin, **Carpates** (kär.pā'tēz).] Mountain system in central Europe. It extends from Bratislava in a semicircle, through E Czechoslovakia, S Poland, W Ukraine, and N Rumania. This natural boundary formerly separated Hungary and Transylvania on one side from Moravia, Silesia, Galicia, Bucovina, and Rumania on the other. Its chief divisions are the West Carpathians (or West Beskids), the Central Carpathians (containing the Tátra Mountains, of which the highest is Stalin Peak, also called Gerlsdorfer Spitze, 8,737 ft.), East Carpathians (East Beskids), and Transylvanian Alps or South Carpathians (highest peak, Negoi, 8,346 ft.). It is noted for mineral wealth.

Carpathian Sea. [Latin, **Carpathium Mare.**] An Ancient name for a small part of the Aegean Sea lying N of Karpathos, in the Dodecanese islands.

Carpathos (kär'pą.thos). See **Karpathos.**

Carpathus (kär'pą.thus). Latin name of **Karpathos.**

Carpeaux (kȧr.pō), **Jean Baptiste.** b. at Valenciennes, France, May 11, 1827; d. at the Castle of Becon, near Asnières, France, Oct. 11, 1875. French sculptor. He studied first at the École d'Architecture of Valenciennes, and later went to Paris where he remained until 1844. He was associated with H. M. A. Chapu and Charles Garnier, and was a pupil of François Rude and F. J. Duret.

Carpentaria (kär.pęn.tãr'i.ą), **Gulf of.** Gulf which indents the N coast of Australia, W of Cape York Peninsula, S of the island of New Guinea. It was named by the Dutch navigator Abel Tasman in 1644, possibly for Pieter Carpentier, a Dutch colonial administrator in the East Indies. Width, 300–400 mi.

Carpenter (kär'pen.tėr), **Charlotte Mary.** b. 1776; d. May 15, 1826. Wife of Sir Walter Scott. The daughter of Jean Charpentier, a French royalist of Lyons, she came to England soon after his death in the Revolution. Scott first saw her in the autumn of 1797, at a small watering-place, Gilsland, was attracted by her beauty, asked for an introduction, and fell in love with her at first sight. She married Scott on Dec. 24, 1797, and bore him two sons and two daughters.

Carpenter, Edward. b. at Brighton, England, Aug. 29, 1844; d. at Guilford, Surrey, England, June 28, 1929. English poet, essayist, mystic, and social reformer; disciple of Walt Whitman. For much of his life he made his living by lecturing on music and science and by selling the products of his small Sheffield farm. While traveling in India, he became interested in Indian systems of philosophy. In 1884 Carpenter made a journey to the U.S., where he visited and became attached to Whitman. His works of poetry include *Narcissus* (1873), *Moses, a Drama* (1875), *Towards Democracy* (1883–1905), and *Sketches from Life in Town and Country* (1908). *Religious Influence of Art* (1870), *Prisons, Police, and Punishment* (1905), *Days with Walt Whitman* (1906), *Intermediate Types among Primitive Folk* (1914), and *My Days and Dreams* (1916) are all autobiographical. *Towards Industrial Freedom* (1918) and *Pagan and Christian Creeds* (1920) are among his other prose works. His best contributions are considered to be *England's Ideal* (1887), *Civilization—Its Cause and Cure* (1889), *Love's Coming of Age* (1896), *The Intermediate Sex* (1908), and *The Healing of Nations* (1915).

Carpenter, Ford Ashman. b. at Chicago, March 25, 1868; d. in November, 1947. American meteorologist, aeronaut, and inventor. He served (1888–1919) with the U.S. Weather Service, and was manager (1919–41) of the department of meteorology and aeronautics of the Los Angeles Chamber of Commerce. He also served as meteorological adviser to various steamship companies and railway and air lines. He was long active as a balloon pilot and edited (1919–41) *Meteorology and Aeronautics.* He invented the anemometric scale, ventograph, and televentscope. His published works include *Roadbeds of the Air* and *Commercial Climatology.*

Carpenter, Francis Bicknell. b. at Homer, N.Y., 1830; d. at New York, 1900. American portrait painter. He began painting, under local instruction at Syracuse, N.Y., while still in his 'teens, and by 1850 had established a studio at New York where he had among his subjects and patrons many of the eminent Americans of his time, including Presidents Tyler, Fillmore, Pierce and Lincoln, and figures in the worlds of literature and journalism including James Russell Lowell, Horace Greeley, and George William Curtis. In 1852 he was named an associate of the National Academy of Design. His most noted work, a large composition entitled *The Emancipation Proclamation*, showing Lincoln and his cabinet, was exhibited in a number of cities before being hung in the House of Representatives at Washington, where it is still to be seen. In connection with this work, Carpenter spent much time in the White House, which was the basis of his book *Six Months in the White House with Abraham Lincoln.*

Carpenter, George Lyndon. b. at Newcastle, New South Wales, Australia, June 20, 1872; d. at Sydney, Australia, April 9, 1948. British Salvation Army officer. He entered the Salvation Army in 1892, and served for 18 years in Australia. After acting as literary secretary (1911–27) at International Headquarters, and then in South America and Canada as territorial commander, he was general (1939–46).

Carpenter, John Alden. b. near Chicago, Feb. 28, 1876; d. at Chicago, April 26, 1951. American composer. He studied under John Knowles Paine at Harvard, under Sir Edward Elgar, and at Chicago (1908–12) under Bernhard Ziehn. Carpenter's best-known compositions include the three ballets *Birthday of the Infanta* (1919), *Krazy-Kat* (1922), and *Skyscrapers* (1926), the suite *Adventures in a Perambulator* (1915), *Concertino* (1917), the tone poem *Sea Drift* (1933), and *The Anxious Bugler* (1943). He also composed many songs and works for chamber orchestra.

Carpenter, Lant. b. at Kidderminster, England, Sept. 2, 1780; drowned off the Italian coast (probably washed overboard), April 5, 1840. English Unitarian clergyman; father of Mary Carpenter and William Benjamin Carpenter. He was pastor at Exeter in the period 1805–17, and subsequently at Bristol. In addition to his ministry (in which he took a broad view, substituting, for example, infant dedication for baptism), he was master of a school, Harriet and James Martineau being among his pupils. He wrote *Introduction to the Geography of the New Testament* (1806), *Harmony, a synoptical arrangement of the Gospels* (1835), and others.

Carpenter, Mary. b. at Exeter, England, April 3, 1807; d. at Bristol, England, June 14, 1877. English philanthropist and writer; daughter of Lant Carpenter, and sister of William Benjamin Carpenter. She founded a girls' school at Bristol in 1829. She established (1852) a reformatory school at Bristol as a practical experiment in her theory of the treatment of juvenile offenders, and at various times founded societies and schools (so-called "ragged schools") for the poor. Four times (1866–67, 1868–69, 1869–70, 1875–76) she visited India to study the education of Indian women and to teach there. In 1873 she spoke on prison reform in the U.S. and Canada. She was author of *Reformatory Schools for the Children of the Perishing and Dangerous Classes, and for Juvenile Offenders* (1851) and *Juvenile Delinquents, their Condition and Treatment* (1852).

Carpenter, Matthew Hale. [Original name, **Merritt Hammond Carpenter.**] b. at Moretown, Vt., Dec. 22, 1824; d. at Washington, D.C., Feb. 24, 1881. American politician and lawyer, U.S. senator from Wisconsin (1869–75, 1879–81). He represented Tilden at the electoral commission's inquiry into the closely contested election of 1876, which Hayes won by one electoral vote (185 to 184).

Carpenter, Rhys. b. at Cotuit, Mass., Aug. 5, 1889—. American archaeologist. He attended (1912–13) the American School of Classical Studies at Athens and was graduated (Ph.D., 1916) from Columbia University. He became (1918) professor of classical archaeology at Bryn Mawr, and served as director (1927–32, 1946–48) of the American School of Classical Studies. He is the author of *Tragedy of Etarre* (1912), *The Esthetic Basis of Greek Art* (1921), *The Greeks in Spain* (1925), *The Humanistic Value of Archaeology* (1933), and *Folk Tale, Fiction and Saga in the Homeric Epics* (1946).

Carpenter, William Benjamin. b. at Exeter, England, Oct. 29, 1813; d. at London, Nov. 19, 1885. English naturalist; son of Lant Carpenter. After a period as apprentice to a physician, he studied medicine at University College, London, and at the Edinburgh Medical School, graduating from the latter institution. He subsequently became Fullerian professor of physiology at the Royal Institution (1844) and a Fellow at the Royal Society (1844), and served as professor of forensic medicine at University College, lecturer on geology at the British Museum, principal of University Hall (1851–59), and registrar of the University of London (1856–79). He took part as naturalist in several expeditions for deep-sea exploration: in the *Lightning* (1868), between the north of Ireland and the Faeroe Islands; in the *Porcupine* (1869–70); in the *Shearwater* (1871), between Great Britain and Portugal; and in the *Challenger* (1872–76). He published numerous papers on physiological and zoölogical topics, including *The Principles of General and Comparative Physiology* (1839; *Comparative Physiology* separately published, 1854), *A Popular Cyclopedia of Science* (1843), *The Microscope and its Revelations* (1856), *Introduction to the Study of the Foraminifera* (1862), and *The Principles of Mental Physiology* (1874).

Carpenter, William Henry. b. at Utica, N.Y., July 15, 1853; d. Nov. 25, 1936. American philologist. Educated at Cornell University, and in Germany at the universities of Leipzig and Freiburg (Ph.D., 1881), he served as instructor (1883–89) and assistant professor (1889–90) of German and Scandinavian languages, adjunct professor (1890–95) of Germanic languages and literatures, professor (1895–1926) of Germanic philology, and provost (1912–26) at Columbia University. He was the author of *Grundriss der Neuisländischen Grammatik* (1881).

Carpentier (kȧr.päṅ.tyā; Anglicized, kär.pe̩n.tir′), **Georges.** b. 1894—. French light heavyweight boxer. He won (1920) the championship in his class by winning over Battling Levinsky by a four-round knockout, but he was defeated (1922) by Battling Siki. He contended (July 2, 1921) for the heavyweight championship against Jack Dempsey at Jersey City, N.J., but was knocked out in the fourth round. This bout is notable as having been the first in history to attract over a million-dollar attendance and also as the first to have radio coverage.

Carpentras (kȧr.päṅ.trȧs). [Gaulish, **Carpentoracte.**] Town in SE France, in the department of Vaucluse, situated on the Auzon River, ab. 15 mi. NE of Avignon. It was the capital of the Comtat Venaissin, under papal sovereignty, until 1791. It has a number of old monuments, such as the Church of Saint-Siffrein, the Porte d'Orange, the palace of justice, a museum, and a library. Carpentras is in the center of a fruit-growing district, producing particularly almonds, olives, and apricots, and specializes in the manufacture of candied fruits, and of hard candies called *berlingots.* 14,222 (1946).

Carpi (kär′pē). Town and commune in N Italy, in the *compartimento* (region) of Emilia-Romagna, in the province of Modena, situated ab. 10 mi. N of Modena. Its cathedral was built after plans by Baldassare Peruzzi in 1520, and is interesting as based on Bramante's design for Saint Peter's. A fragment in the sanctuary, with some curious sculpture, belongs to the original cathedral of the 11th century. Center of a rich agricultural region, Carpi has a number of agricultural industries (flour mills, distilleries, breweries, dairies, and canning factories). The most important architectural monument is the Castello del Pio, of the 14th–16th centuries. The town became part of the duchy of Modena in 1525. Buildings of interest to tourists were undamaged in World War II. Pop. of commune 34,189 (1936); of town, 14,452 (1936).

Carpi. Village in Italy, in the province of Verona, situated on the Adige River, ab. 28 mi. SE of Verona. It was the scene of a victory of Prince Eugene of Savoy over the French marshal under Nicolas de Catinat in 1701.

Carpini (kär.pē′nē), **Giovanni de Piano.** b. near Perugia, Italy, c1182; d. Aug. 1, 1252. Italian Franciscan. A companion of Saint Francis of Assisi and a principal bearer of Francis's message to the people of Germany and Spain, he was sent by Pope Innocent IV as legate to the khan of Tartary after the Mongols had swept through Europe. The embassy (1245–47) was unsuccessful in achieving its aim of diplomatic rapprochement between East and West, but Carpini's memoir of the voyage (*Liber Tartarorum*, edited by d'Avezac; not published in full until 1838) is the principal European account of overland travel to the East before Marco Polo.

Carpinteria (kär″pin.te̩.rē′a̩). Unincorporated community in SW California, in Santa Barbara County, on the Pacific Ocean ab. 10 mi. E of Santa Barbara. It is a seaside resort; lemons are grown in the vicinity. In the decade between the last two U.S. censuses its population more than doubled. 1,389 (1940), 2,864 (1950).

Carpio (kär′pyō), **Bernardo del.** See **Bernardo del Carpio.**

Carpio, Duque de. Title of **Haro,** Don **Luis de.**

Carpio, Lope Félix de Vega. See **Vega, Lope de.**

Carpocrates (kär.pok′ra̩.tēz) or **Carpocras** (kär′pō̩.kra̩s). fl. in the 2nd century A.D. Alexandrian Gnostic philosopher. He was the founder of the sect known after him as Carpocratians.

Carpocratians (kär.pō̩.krā′sha̩nz). Name of a sect of Gnostics of the 2nd century A.D., followers of Carpocrates or Carpocras of Alexandria.

Carpzov (kärp′tsof), **Benedikt.** b. at Brandenburg, Germany, Oct. 22, 1565; d. at Wittenburg, Germany, Nov. 26, 1624. German jurist; father of Benedikt Carpzov (1595–1666).

Carpzov, Benedikt. b. at Wittenberg, Germany, May 27, 1595; d. at Leipzig, Germany, Aug. 30, 1666. German jurist; son of Benedikt Carpzov (1565–1624). He wrote *Practica nova rerum criminalium* (1635), *Definitiones forenses* (1638), and other works.

Carpzov, Johann Gottlob. b. at Dresden, Germany, Sept. 20, 1679; d. at Lübeck, Germany, April 7, 1767. German theologian.

Carr (kär), **Benjamin.** b. in England, 1769; d. at Philadelphia, May 24, 1831. American music publisher, composer and singer. He established the first music store at Philadelphia and published the compositions of many contemporary Americans, acting also as a founder (1820) of the Musical Fund Society. Most notable of his compositions is the opera *The Archers* (1796); he also composed religious music, piano pieces, and songs.

Carr, Emma Perry. b. at Holmesville, Ohio, July 28, 1880—. American chemist. Beginning the teaching of her chosen subject as an assistant at Mount Holyoke College in 1901, she was on the chemistry faculty of the University of Chicago (1904–05), at Mount Holyoke again (1905–08), then Mary E. Wooley fellow at the University of Chicago (1908–09) and Lowenthal fellow at the same institution (1909–10) before returning to Mount Holyoke to become associate professor of chemistry (1910–13) and professor and chairman of the chemistry department (1913–46). In 1919 and 1925 she did research work in Ireland and Switzerland; in 1930 and 1934 she pursued her advanced studies with the aid of grants from the National Research Council, and in 1935 and 1937 was the recipient of grants from the Rockefeller Foundation. She was a delegate to the International Union of Pure and Applied Chemistry at Bucharest, Rumania, in 1925, and her eminence among the leaders in her science was signalized by the conferring upon her in 1937 of the Garvan gold medal of the American Chemical Society.

Carr, Eugene Asa. b. at Concord, N.Y., March 20, 1830; d. at Washington, D.C., Dec. 2, 1910. American cavalry officer, remembered as an Indian fighter. During the Civil War he served with the Union army in the battles of Wilson's Creek and Pea Ridge, the Vicksburg campaign, and the capture of Mobile; he was awarded the Medal of Honor for gallantry at Pea Ridge. Later he fought Indians (1868–91) in Nebraska, Colorado, and New Mexico.

Carr, Gene. b. at New York, Jan. 7, 1881—. American comic-strip artist and illustrator, best known for his cartoon strips *Dooley, Step Brothers,* and *Lady Bountiful.* He became a member of the staff of the New York *World* in 1903, and later his work was syndicated by the McClure Newspaper Syndicate and King Features. His illustrations have appeared in *Redbook, Cosmopolitan, American, Liberty, Colliers* and the *Saturday Evening Post.* Other cartoon strips include *The Prodigal Son, Father, Metropolitan Movies, All the Comforts of Home, Flirting Flora,* and *The Jones Boys.*

Carr, Howard. b. at Manchester, England, Dec. 26, 1880—. English composer and conductor. Appointed (1910) musical assistant at Covent Garden, he became a staff member (1928) of the Sydney Conservatorium in Australia, where he taught harmony and counterpoint, and was also named conductor of the Philharmonic Society of Sydney. His compositions, mainly of a light nature, include such theatrical selections, songs, and orchestral and symphonic works as *The Jolly Roger, Three Heroes, The Jovial Huntsmen,* and *The Shrine in the Wood.*

Carr, Joseph Bradford. b. at Albany, N.Y., Aug. 16, 1828; d. at Troy, N.Y., Feb. 24, 1895. American army officer, with the Union army in the Civil War. As a brigadier general (1863), he led the troops at the center of the Union line in the battle of Gettysburg. He was appointed (1867) major general of militia. After the war he served as secretary of state (1879, 1881, 1883) of New York.

Carr or **Ker** (kär, kãr, kėr), **Robert.** [Titles: Viscount **Rochester,** Earl of **Somerset.**] d. in July, 1645. English politician of Scottish birth; created Viscount Rochester on March 25, 1611, and Earl of Somerset on Nov. 3, 1613. He went to England to attend James I, won the king's favor, and was given a seat in the House of Lords. He fell in love with the wife of the earl of Essex; she obtained a divorce from her husband, and the two were married in 1613. In the same year Sir Thomas Overbury, formerly a friend of Carr's, was found poisoned. After Carr had fallen out of favor with the king, he and his wife were accused (1615) of Overbury's murder. She confessed (1616), but Carr's guilt, although suspected, has never been finally established. In the trial, which was conducted by Francis Bacon, both were found guilty and condemned to death. Both were pardoned, however, after they had been held in the Tower of London until 1622.

Carr, Sir Robert. b. in Northumberland, England; d. at Bristol, England, June 1, 1667. British commissioner in New England in 1664. With Richard Nicolls he took over New Amsterdam from the Dutch in 1664, and named it New York.

Carrà (kär.rä'), **Carlo.** b. at Querquento, Italy, Feb. 11, 1881—. Italian painter. He was associated at first with the futurists (1909–15), and then with Giorgio di Chirico and the *pittura metafisica* (metaphysical painting) movement (1915 *et seq.*). He studied at the Brera Academy, Milan, and first exhibited in 1911 at Paris with the original futurist group.

Carra (kar'ą), **Lough.** Lake in Connacht province, Irish Republic, in County Mayo, ab. 2 mi. N of Ballinrobe. Length, ab. 7 mi.; greatest width, ab. 2 mi.

Carracci (kär.rät'chē), **Agostino.** [Also, **Caracci.**] b. at Bologna, Italy, Aug. 16, 1557; d. at Parma, Italy, March 22, 1602. Italian engraver and painter of the Bolognese school; brother of Annibale Carracci, and cousin of Lodovico Carracci.

Carracci, Annibale. [Also, **Caracci.**] b. at Bolognaf Italy, 1560; d. at Rome, July 15, 1609. Italian painter o, the Bolognese school; brother of Agostino Carracci, and cousin of Lodovico Carracci, whose pupil he was. In 1580 he went to Parma to study the works of Correggio; subsequently he was associated with Lodovico Carracci in conducting an academy at Bologna. In 1600 he went to Rome where he was engaged in decorating a ceiling in the Farnese palace. A classicist, he was influenced by the works of Raphael, and in turn influenced Italian 17th-century painting styles. His compositions were much admired by Nicolas Poussin. Among his works are the frescoes in the Farnese palace, a self-portrait at Florence, and *Baptism of Christ* at Bologna.

Carracci, Lodovico. [Also, **Caracci.**] b. at Bologna, Italy, 1555; d. there, Nov. 13, 1619. Italian painter, founder of the Bolognese eclectic school, noted as a teacher; cousin of Agostino Carracci and Annibale Carracci. Among the pupils of his school were Domenichino and Guido Reni. His chief works are at Bologna.

Carrae (kar'ē). Latin name of **Haran.**

Carrantuohill (kar.ąn.tö'il). [Also: **Carrantual, Carrantuel.**] Mountain in Munster province, Irish Republic, in County Kerry, ab. 11 mi. SW of Killarney. It is the summit of Macgillicuddy's Reeks and the highest mountain in Ireland. 3,414 ft.

Carranza (kär.rän'sä; Anglicized, ką.ran'zą), **Venustiano,** [Called the **"First Chief."**] b. at Cuátro Ciénegas. Coahuila, Mexico, May 22, 1859; murdered by forces of Álvaro Obregón, at Tlaxcalaltongo, Mexico, May 21, 1920. Mexican revolutionist and political leader, president (May 1, 1917–May 8, 1920) of Mexico. He studied law at Mexico City. In 1893 he led a rebellion against the governor of Coahuila. He was a senator in the period 1901–11, joined (1910) Francisco I. Madero in revolt against Porfirio Díaz, and was elected governor of Coahuila after the victory of the revolutionary forces. He led the Constitutionalists after Madero's assassination (1913) in a rebellion against Victoriano Huerta, being recognized as "first chief," despite his struggle for power with Francisco Villa and Zapata. He issued (Jan. 6, 1915) a decree providing for social reform, and his administration was recognized (1915) by the U.S., though Pershing's Mexican expedition (1916), provoked by Villa's raids into the U.S., incurred increased ill feeling between the U.S. and Mexico. Carranza served as provisional president until elected under a new constitution (Feb. 5, 1917). He kept Mexico neutral during World War I. During the next election (1920) he refused to support Obregón as his successor; Obregón revolted, and Carranza fled and was assassinated.

Carranza de Miranda (kär.rän'thä dā mē.rän'dä), **Bartolomé de.** [Original name, **Bartolomé de Carranza;** surnamed **de Miranda** from his birthplace.] b. at Miranda de Arga, in Navarre, 1503; d. at Rome, May 2, 1576. Spanish churchman, archbishop of Toledo, imprisoned by the Inquisition. Coming of a landed family, he entered the Dominican order at an early age and quickly acquired prominence as a theologian and a preacher. He was appointed a professor of theology at Valladolid and became a censor for the Inquisition. He was much favored and trusted by the emperor Charles V and the latter's son Philip, who upon his betrothal to Queen Mary of England, sent Carranza de Miranda to that country as his representative. He became confessor to the queen and during his sojourn in England was active in efforts to prevent the teaching of Protestant doctrines. Prior to this he had twice, upon nomination by Charles V, participated in the deliberations of the Council of Trent. After his return from England, he was against his wish made archbishop of Toledo in December, 1557. At about this time he published his *Commentario sobre el catequismo cristiano* (Commentary on the Christian Catechism), which together with allegations that he had imparted heretical views to the abdicated Charles V during the latter's last illness, caused his imprisonment by the Inquisition, on charges of heresy, in 1559. Philip II, many delegates to the Council of Trent, members of the Congregaton of the Index in Rome, and even Pope Pius IV tried in vain to hasten the Inquisition's proceedings. In 1567 Pope Pius V ordered the case transferred to Rome, where Carranza was lodged in a papal apartment, yet the proceedings dragged on until April, 1576, when he was acquitted of heresy but directed to abjure a number of theses which were considered tainted with Lutheranism. He was also to be restrained from resuming the duties of his archiepiscopal see for five years. This proviso proved unnecessary, as he died in the month following his vindication. He was interred with great honors.

Carrara (kär.rä′rä). City in C Italy, in the *compartimento* (region) of Tuscany and province of Massa e Carrara, part of the commune of Massa, situated near the Ligurian Sea, E of La Spezia. It is famous for the extensive marble quarries in the nearby Apuanian Alps, which produce a marble of high quality that has been known since ancient times; it is exported to many countries. The export is done partly by rail, partly through the seaport of Marina di Carrara, situated on the Tyrrhenian Sea. There are other stone quarries, chemical plants, and foodstuff industries. The Cathedral of Sant'Andrea is a Romanesque building dating from the 12th century; there are a number of other churches and palaces of architectural interest. The Fabricotti museum contains Roman and medieval antiquities. Buildings of interest to tourists were undamaged in World War II. 26,118 (1936).

Carrasco (kạ.ras′kō; Spanish, kär.räs′kō), **Samson.** [Spanish, **Sansón.**] Bachelor or licentiate in Miguel de Cervantes's *Don Quixote*, a specialist in practical jokes.

Carratalá (kär″rä.tä.lä′), **José.** b. at Alicante, Spain, Dec. 14, 1781; d. at Madrid, 1854. Spanish general. In 1815 he went with Pablo Morillo to Venezuela, and then to Peru, and fought (1819–24) against the revolutionists there, attaining the rank of field marshal. In 1833 he commanded the forces in Tarragona against the Carlists, and shortly after fought against them in Vizcaya. He was made captain-general of Estremadura (March, 1835), and subsequently held the same office in Valencia, Murcia, and Old Castile. In 1840 he was named senator and minister of war, and his rank was raised to lieutenant general.

Carré (kȧ.rā), **Michel.** b. at Paris, 1819; d. there, June 27, 1872. French dramatist and librettist for operas, vaudevilles, and comic operas. He collaborated with Jules Barbier after 1849 in such works as *Galatée* (1852), *Mignon* (1867), and *Paul et Virginie* (1877). Independently, he wrote the librettos for Gounod's *Faust* (1859) and *Roméo et Juliette* (1867).

Carrea (kạ.rē′ạ) or **Carreum** (kạ.rē′um). Ancient names of **Chieri.**

Carrel (kar′ẹl, kạ.rel′; French, kȧ.rel), **Alexis.** b. near Lyons, France, June 28, 1873; d. at Paris, Nov. 5, 1944. French surgeon and research biologist. He received his education at the University of Lyons, came to the U.S. in 1905, and from 1909 was an associate member of the Rockefeller Institute for Medical Research. His work was chiefly concerned with the transplantation of tissues and organs, and the life of tissues outside of the organism. With Henry D. Dakin he evolved the Carrel-Dakin method for treating wounds which was widely used in World War I. He was awarded the Nobel prize for research in medicine in 1912, and in 1930 was awarded the Nordhoff-Jung prize for cancer research. He was the author of *Man, the Unknown* (1935) and *The Culture of Organs* (with C. A. Lindbergh, 1938).

Carrel (kȧ.rel), **Nicolas Armand.** b. at Rouen, France, May 8, 1800; d. at St.-Mandé, near Paris, July 24, 1836. French journalist and republican leader. He was editor (c1830–36) of the *National* at Paris, and was mortally wounded in a duel on July 22, 1836.

Carreño (kär.rā′nyō). Town in NW Spain, in the province of Oviedo, situated on the Bay of Biscay, ab. 15 mi. N of Oviedo. It is a fishing port, with sardine-packing plants, and also has cattle markets. 10,009 (1940).

Carreño, Teresa. b. at Caracas, Venezuela, Dec. 22, 1853; d. at New York, June 12, 1917. Venezuelan pianist and composer. She studied under Louis M. Gottschalk and Anton Rubinstein, appeared at the Academy of Music, New York, at the age of nine, and gave concerts until 1875, when she appeared as a singer in opera. In 1889 she returned to the concert stage as a pianist, and subsequently toured extensively in Europe and America. She married Eugène d'Albert in 1892, and married Arturo Tagliapietra in 1902. Among her compositions are a string quartet, a Venezuelan festival hymn, and piano pieces.

Carreño de Miranda (dā mē.rän′dä), **Juan.** b. at Avilés, in Asturias, Spain, March 25, 1614; d. at Madrid, in September, 1685. Spanish painter, chiefly of portraits and religious compositions. He was appointed to succeed Velázquez as court painter.

Carrera (kär.rā′rä), **José Miguel de.** b. at Santiago, Chile, Oct. 15, 1785; executed at Mendoza, Argentina, Sept. 4, 1821. Chilean revolutionist and, briefly, president of Chile during the war with Spain. With his brothers, Juan José and Luis, he headed (1811) the revolt against the Spaniards which had already broken out, and, as commander of the army, assumed the presidency of Chile, holding it until he was deposed in favor of Bernardo O'Higgins in 1813. Though the rivals joined forces in 1814, they were defeated by the Spaniards at the battle of Rancagua (Oct. 2, 1814). Carrera fled to Buenos Aires, and in 1815 went to the U.S. He returned in 1816, but was forbidden to proceed to Chile. Driven in 1821 to take refuge among the Indians, he was betrayed by his own men and shot as a rebel. His brothers had met a similar fate more than three years before.

Carrera, Juan José. Shot as a rebel, March 18, 1818. Chilean revolutionist; brother of José Miguel de Carrera (1785–1821) and Luis Carrera (d. 1818). He joined his brothers in the revolution of 1811–13, was captured (1817) near Mendoza, Argentina, and was tried on political charges and executed.

Carrera, Luis. Shot as a rebel, March 18, 1818. Chilean revolutionist; brother of José Miguel de Carrera (1785–1821) and Juan José Carrera (d. 1818).

Carrera, Rafael. b. at Guatemala City, c1814; d. there, April 4, 1865. Guatemalan revolutionist of mixed white and Indian descent, president (1844–48, 1852–65) of Guatemala. He joined the revolt against the federal party of Central America in 1837, became commander of the Guatemalan insurgents, overthrew and banished Gálvez, declared Guatemala's independence in 1839, and began (1840) his quarter-century domination not only of his own country but to a considerable extent of the other Central American states. President (1844–48) of Guatemala, and in virtual control of Paredes' administration (1849–52), he was reëlected (1852), and in 1854 was made president for life.

Carrera Andrade (än.drä′ᴛʜā), **Jorge.** b. at Quito, Ecuador, Sept. 28, 1903—. Ecuadorean poet and diplomat. In his youth he studied literature at the University of Barcelona in Spain, and also lived for a time in France. From his early years he was interested in politics, was actively associated with radical movements, and was secretary-general of the Socialist Party of Ecuador in the period 1927–28. Later he entered his country's consular service, and has filled posts not only in South American countries but in Europe and Asia. He has never allowed his political orientation or his ideological preoccupations to dilute his allegiance, as a poet, to purely artistic ideals. His poems reflect his travels, being studded with the names of cities, rivers, and places he has seen. He celebrates the world of reality, seen imaginatively and described in poetically figurative terms. Carrera Andrade is considered by many to be the greatest writer yet to arise in Ecuador, and, indeed, one of the chief poets in the Spanish language in the 20th century. Among his books are *Estanque inefable* (Secret Country, 1922), *Boletines de mar y tierra* (Bulletins of Sea and Land,

1930), *El Tiempo manual* (Manual Time, 1935), *Rol de la manzana* (Directory of the Block, 1935), *La Hora de las ventanas illuminadas* (The Hour of Lighted Windows, 1937), and *Biografia para uso de los pájaros* (Biography for Use of the Birds, 1937).

Carrère (kȧ.rer), **Jean.** b. at Agen, France, 1867—. French journalist, poet, and critic. Of strongly conservative tendencies, he is known mainly for his violently anti-modern *Les Mauvais Maîtres* (1922). His works also include poetry, *Les Buccins d'or* (1911), *Onze sonnets de la grande épopée* (1918), and others, as well as a *Manuel des partis politiques en France* and a translation (with F. Fournier) of Bonfante's *History of Roman Law* (both 1928).

Carrère (ka.rãr'), **John Merven.** b. at Rio de Janeiro, Nov. 9, 1858; d. at New York, March 1, 1911. American architect, codesigner (with Thomas Hastings) of the Senate and House Office Buildings at Washington, D.C., and the New York Public Library. He graduated (1882) from the École de Beaux-Arts at Paris, and in 1883 joined the New York office of McKim, Mead and White, working alongside Thomas Hastings, with whom he later formed a partnership. Their first outstanding commissions were the Flagler Ponce de Leon Hotel (1887) and the Grace Methodist Church (1887), both at St. Augustine, Fla., where the firm of Carrère and Hastings designed other notable structures. Most of their works are situated in the eastern part of the U.S.; among them are the Richmond Borough Hall at New York (1903–07), the architectural work on the Manhattan Bridge, New York (1905), and the Carnegie Institution at Washington, D.C. (1906). The greatest work by the partnership, executed in their characteristic monumental style as applied to public buildings, were the Senate (1905) and House (1906) Office Buildings, the New York Public Library (planned in 1897, completed in 1911), and the New Theatre (later known as the Century Theatre), New York. Carrère served (1901) as chief architect and chairman of the board of architects in charge of decorations, grounds, and gardens for the Pan-American Exposition at Buffalo, N.Y., and was on the city-planning commissions of Grand Rapids, Mich. (1909), Hartford, Conn. (1911), and Cleveland, Ohio. He was one of the founders of the Society of Beaux Arts Architects and on two occasions was president of the New York chapter of the American Institute of Architects. He was the author of *City Improvement from the Artistic Standpoint* (1908), *Preliminary Report of the City Plan for Grand Rapids, Mich.*, in collaboration with Arnold Brunner (1909), and *Plan of the City of Hartford* (1912).

Carrey (kȧ.rā), **Jacques.** b. at Troyes, France, 1646; d. 1726. French painter; a pupil of Charles Le Brun. He made numerous journeys to the Orient, during one of which he executed a series of sketches from the Parthenon, then (November, 1674) in a good state of preservation. These drawings, preserved in the Bibliothèque Nationale at Paris, have been invaluable to students of Greek art. Carrey also assisted Le Brun in his great compositions.

Carrhae (kar'ē). Latin name of **Haran.**

Carriacou (kar"i.ạ.kö'). See under **Grenadines.**

Carrick (kar'ik). Former borough of SW Pennsylvania, in Allegheny County, now a part of the city of Pittsburgh.

Carrick. The southern district of Ayrshire, in S Scotland, S of the river Doon. The Prince of Wales also bears the title of the Earl of Carrick.

Carrickfergus (kar.ik.fėr'gus). Urban district, market town, and seaport in Ulster province, Northern Ireland, in County Antrim, situated on the N bank of Belfast Lough, ab. 10 mi. NE of Belfast. It is a center for the mining of rock salt, widely obtained in the vicinity; other industries include fisheries and cheese manufacture. William III landed here in 1690 on his way to defeat the forces of James II at the battle of the Boyne. The spot is marked by an inscribed stone in the harbor. Carrickfergus was captured by the French in 1760. The castle, a splendid Norman fortress, was built in 1178, and has been used at various times since as a barracks. The castle stands on a rock, with water on three sides. The entrance is by a gateway flanked by semicircular towers and defended by a portcullis and other medieval devices. The donjon is an enormous square tower of five stories. 6,308 (1947).

Carrickfergus Bay. See **Belfast Lough.**

Carrick-on-Shannon (kar'ik.on.shan'ọn). Town in NW Irish Republic, the county town and chief town of County Leitrim, on the upper Shannon River ab. 90 mi. by rail NW of Dublin. It is a market town with trade in grain and provisions. 8,833 (1946).

Carrick-on-Suir (kar'ik.on.shůr'). Urban district in S Irish Republic, in SE County Tipperary, ab. 14 mi. by rail NW of Waterford. It has an active export trade in butter and grain. The old castle, across the river Suir in County Waterford, dates from 1309. Pop. 4,761 (1951).

Carrick's Ford. Place on the Cheat River, in Tucker County, W.Va. Here, on July 14, 1861, a Union force under Morris defeated the Confederates under Garnett.

Carrie (kar'i), **Sister.** See **Sister Carrie.**

Carrier (kar'i.ẹr). North American Indian tribe, whose language is of the Athabaskan family, inhabiting the Fraser River area, British Columbia.

Carrier (kȧ.ryā), **Jean Baptiste.** b. at Yolet, near Aurillac, France, 1756; guillotined at Paris, Dec. 16, 1794. French revolutionist. He was deputy to the Convention in 1792, and became notorious for his cruelty in the revolutionary tribunal at Nantes (1793–94).

Carriera (kär.rye'rä), **Rosalba.** [Often called **Rosalba.**] b. at Venice, Oct. 7, 1675; d. there, April 15, 1757. Italian portrait and miniature painter. At the height of her vogue she was compared with Correggio. She is represented in collections at Venice, Padua, Florence, Copenhagen, and Leningrad, in the Louvre at Paris, and especially in the Dresden Gallery, where 143 examples of her work are to be seen.

Carrière (kȧ.ryer), **Eugène** (**Anatole**). b. at Gournay, France, Jan. 17, 1849; d. at Paris, March 27, 1906. French painter. He studied at the École des Beaux-Arts and under Cabanel.

Carrière (kä.rē.er'), **Moritz.** b. March 5, 1817; d. Jan. 19, 1895. German philosopher and writer on aesthetics. He was professor of philosophy at Giessen and Munich.

Carriès (kȧ.ryes), **Jean.** [Original surname, **Cariès.**] b. c1856; d. July 1, 1894. French sculptor. He first exhibited in the Salon of 1892; on the opening day receiving the cross of the Legion of Honor. He was the discoverer of a stoneware in which many of his best effects were produced.

Carrillo (kär.rē'yō), **Braulio.** See **Carillo, Braulio.**

Carrillo, Julián. b. in Mexico, 1875—. Mexican composer of operas, chamber works, choral music, and symphonies. In his compositions as well as in his writings, such as *Tratado sintédico de harmonia* (1913), he has advocated smaller than enharmonic intervals, inventing special instruments to facilitate the new technique. He served as head (1913–15) of the Conservatorio Nacional at Mexico City.

Carrillo de Mendoza y Pimentel (kär.rē'lyō dā mendō'thä ē pē.men.tel'), **Diego.** [Titles: Count of **Priego,** Marquis of **Gelves.**] b. c1560; d. after 1627. Spanish general and administrator. He was viceroy of New Spain (Mexico) from Sept. 21, 1621. In 1623 he had a quarrel with the archbishop on questions of jurisdiction; this resulted in the triumph of the archbishop, and the viceroy was deposed and imprisoned by the Audience (January, 1624). He returned to Spain in 1626.

Carrington (kar'ing.tọn), Lord. Title of **Primrose,** Sir **Archibald.**

Carrington, FitzRoy. b. at Surbiton, Surrey, England, Nov. 6, 1869—. American art critic, a connoisseur of etchings and engravings who became curator of prints at the Boston Museum of Fine Arts in 1913; brother of H. H. L. Carrington (1880—). He was educated in England, and at Dickinson College, Carlisle, Pa. He arrived in the U.S. in 1886 and has lectured on engravings at Harvard and directed children's art centers at Boston and New York. He wrote *Engravers and Etchers*, and compiled and edited *Prints and Their Makers, The Queen's Garland, The King's Lyrics*, and *The Pilgrim's Staff;* editor of *The Print Collector's Quarterly.*

Carrington, Henry Beebee. b. at Wallingford, Conn., March 2, 1824; d. Oct. 26, 1912. American historian and soldier. He practiced (1848–57) law at Columbus, Ohio, and served in the Union army as a brigadier general (1862–65). In 1865 he was president of a commission to try guerrillas at Louisville, Ky., and was assigned to Indian service in Nebraska. He was the author of *American Classics* (1849), *Russia Among the Nations* (1851), *Hints to Soldiers Taking the Field* (1862), *Battles of the American Revolution* (1876), *Crisis Thoughts* (1878), *Battle Maps and Charts of the American Revolution* (1881), *The Six Nations* (1892), and *Washington, the Soldier* (1898).

Carrington, Hereward Hubert Lavington. b. on the island of Jersey, Channel Islands, Oct. 17, 1880—. American psychologist; brother of FitzRoy Carrington (1869—). Arrived (1899) in the U.S., he received (1918) a Ph.D. at Oskaloosa, Iowa. Director of the American Psychic Institute, he was American delegate to the First International Psychical Congress (1921) at Copenhagen. Denmark. His works include *The Physical Phenomena of Spiritualism* (1907), *The Coming Science* (1908), *Death Deferred* (1912), *Side Show and Animal Tricks* (1913), *Psychical Phenomena and the War* (1918), *Modern Psychical Phenomena* (1919), *Magic for Everyone* (1927), *Houdini and Conan Doyle* (in collaboration with B. M. L. Ernst, 1932), and *Introduction to the Maniac* (1937).

Carrington, Richard Christopher. b. at Chelsea, London, May 26, 1826; d. at Churt, Surrey, England, Nov. 27, 1875. English astronomer. He was noted for his observations of the minor planets, fixed stars, and the sun, made chiefly at his private observatory near Reigate in Surrey.

Carrión (kär.ryōn'), **Gerónimo.** b. at Loja, Ecuador, in May, 1812; d. c1879. Ecuadorian politician, elected president of Ecuador on Aug. 4, 1865. In January, 1866, he joined with Chile and Peru in a defensive alliance against Spain. After being subjected to a vote of censure by the congress, he resigned in November, 1867.

Carrizo Springs (ka̩.rē'zō). City in S Texas, county seat of Dimmit County, ab. 100 mi. SW of San Antonio, in an irrigated agricultural region. 4,316 (1950).

Carrodus (kar'ǫ.dus), **John Tiplady.** b. at Keighley, Yorkshire, England, Jan. 20, 1836; d. at London, in July, 1895. English violinist. After making his debut (1849) at London, he became a member of the Covent Garden orchestra. His first performance (1863) as a soloist was with the Musical Society of London. He also played with the Philharmonic (of Great Britain).

Carrogis (kå.ro.zhē), **Louis.** See **Carmontelle** or **Carmontel, Louis.**

Carroll (kar'ǫl). City in W Iowa, county seat of Carroll County, on the Middle Raccoon River: manufactures of agricultural machinery. It was named for Charles Carroll, a signer of the Declaration of Independence. 6,231 (1950).

Carroll, Anna Ella. b. 1815; d. 1893. Adviser to President Lincoln and his cabinet during the American Civil War. A member of a Protestant branch of the noted Carroll family of Maryland, she feared Roman Catholic influence and was an active promoter of the Know-Nothing Party and its nativist program. Early in the Civil War she became a confidential adviser to President Lincoln, and it is claimed for her that she first proposed the strategy of the campaigns in the West which split the Confederacy and thus fatally weakened its military potential.

Carroll, Charles. [Called **"Charles Carroll of Carrollton."**] b. at Annapolis, Md., Sept. 19, 1737; d. Nov. 14, 1832. American Revolutionary leader and legislator, noted as the last to die of the signers of the Declaration of Independence. He was educated in Maryland under the tutelage of the Society of Jesus and took his advanced education abroad (1748–65) in French Flanders, and at Paris and London. Returning to Maryland at the age of 28, he inherited from his father the 10,000-acre Carrollton Manor; upon his arrival he began using the manorial designation in order to avoid confusion with his father and cousins, who bore the same name. As a Roman Catholic, he was legally debarred from participation in political life, but by sheer force of character he made himself accepted in political spheres. He took part in the nonimportation proceedings of 1774, and during the next year he was, in the order named, a member of the Annapolis Committee of Correspondence, of the first Maryland Convention, of the Provincial Committee of Correspondence, and of the Committee of Safety. With Benjamin Franklin and others, he served (1776) on the unsuccessful mission sent by the Continental Congress to Canada for the purpose of exploring the possibilities of union between Canada and the colonies. He was a delegate to the Maryland Convention of 1776, where he helped enact the resolution of separation from England, and as a delegate to the Continental Congress voted for and signed (Aug. 2, 1776) the Declaration of Independence. He served in the Congress until 1778 and was a member of the Board of War. He was a U.S. senator in the first Federal Congress, resigning in 1792. He served in the Maryland senate until 1800 and then retired to develop his estate numbering some 70–80,000 acres in three states. As a Federalist, he was not sympathetic to the declaration of war against England in 1812. He was active in the Chesapeake and Ohio Canal Company, and was a member of the first board of directors of the Baltimore and Ohio Railroad. At his death he was the richest citizen in the U.S.

Carroll, Daniel. b. July 22, 1730; d. at Rock Creek, Md., May 7, 1796. American patriot. Elected (1781) to the Continental Congress, he was one of those who signed (March 1, 1781) the Articles of Confederation. He was appointed (May 26, 1787) to the Constitutional Convention, was a representative from Maryland to the First Congress of the U.S., and was named (Jan. 22, 1791) by Washington one of three commissioners to survey the District of Columbia.

Carroll, Earl. b. at Pittsburgh, Pa., Sept. 16, 1893; killed in airplane crash near Mt. Carmel, Pa., June 17, 1948. American theatrical producer. Engaged in journalism and missionary work in the Far East as a young man, he served in the infantry and air force during World War I. With Enrico Caruso he composed *Dreams of Long Ago* and other songs, and wrote the lyrics and music for *So Long Letty*, *The Love Mill*, and *Canary Cottage*. His productions include *Lady of the Lamp*, *Daddy Dumplings*, and *Fioretta*. He built (1922) and rebuilt (1931) the Earl Carroll Theater, where he produced and collaborated on *Vanities* (1923 *et seq.*).

Carroll, Gladys Hasty. b. at Rochester, N.H., June 26, 1904—. American novelist. Graduated from Berwick Academy (1921) at South Berwick, Me., and from Bates College (1925) at Lewiston, Me., she engaged in graduate study in fine arts at the University of Chicago, Harvard, and Columbia. Her books include the narrative of Maine farm life *As The Earth Turns* (1933), *A Few Foolish Ones* (1935), and *Neighbor to the Sky* (1937).

Carroll, Howard. b. at Albany, N.Y., Sept. 17, 1854; d. Dec. 30, 1916. American journalist and playwright. A staff member (1874 *et seq.*) of the New York *Times*, he was president of the New York Times Association. He wrote *A Mississippi Incident*, and *Twelve Americans: Their Lives and Times* (1883); his comedy *The American Countess* (1884) ran for 200 performances at New York.

Carroll, James. b. at Woolwich, England, June 5, 1854; d. at Washington, D.C., Sept. 16, 1907. American physician, a surgeon in the U.S. army. He was a member of the Havana Yellow Fever Commission appointed in 1900, and in the conduct of the experiments submitted himself to inoculation, with a consequent severe attack of the fever. Although he recovered, his death, several years later, was sometimes regarded as an ultimate result of the disease. He was promoted to the grade of major-surgeon by a special act of Congress, on March 2, 1907.

Carroll, John. b. at Upper Marlboro, Md., Jan. 8, 1735; d. Dec. 3, 1815. American Roman Catholic clergyman, first Roman Catholic bishop in the U.S. and first archbishop of Baltimore; cousin of Charles Carroll. He was educated abroad, studying in French Flanders, where he became (1758) a teacher at St.-Omer. Taking the vows as a Jesuit, he was ordained (either in 1767 or 1769) and after the suppression of the Society of Jesus (1773) by Pope Clement XIV, went to England and then to Maryland. In 1776 he was a member, together with Benjamin Franklin and his cousin, Charles Carroll of Carrollton, of the mission sent by the Continental Congress to Canada to sound out the possibilities of union between Canada and the colonies. He was named a bishop (Nov. 14, 1789) and was consecrated on Aug. 15, 1790, presiding over his first synod in 1791. He was active in founding Catholic educational institutions in the U.S. and was prominent as an opponent of foreign influences in the Catholic Church in the U.S. He became (1808) archbishop of Baltimore, holding that post until his death.

Carroll, John. b. at Wichita, Kan., Aug. 14, 1892—. American painter, most noted for his female figures and portraits. After studying at the University of California, he became a pupil of Frank Duveneck at Cincinnati. In 1926 he was associated with the Woodstock, N.Y., art colony and a teacher at the Art Students League of New York. He was given his first one-man show in 1922. He traveled in Europe, making his second trip on a Guggenheim Fellowship (1927), and later served as head of the painting department of the Detroit Society of Arts and Crafts. His work hangs in the Whitney Museum, New York, the Honolulu Museum, the Pennsylvania Academy of the Fine Arts, the Los Angeles Museum of Art, the Detroit Institute, the Toledo Museum, and elsewhere. *White Lace* is one of his well-known paintings.

Carroll, Lewis. Pseudonym of **Dodgson, Charles Lutwidge.**

Carroll, Paul Vincent. b. at Dundalk, Ireland, July 10, 1900—. Irish playwright. A teacher (1921–37) in the state schools in Scotland, he was cofounder and director of the Glasgow Citizens' Theatre. His works include *Shadow and Substance* (1934), *The White Steed* (1939), *Plays for My Children* (1939), *The Wise Have Not Spoken* (1947), and *Plays for Young and Old* (1947). He also wrote the screen play for the film *Saints and Sinners* (c1950).

Carrollton (kar'ọl.tọn). City in NW Georgia, county seat of Carroll County: textile mills. Nearby is West Georgia Junior College. 7,753 (1950).

Carrollton. City in N Kentucky, county seat of Carroll County, near the Kentucky River. It was incorporated in 1794 as Fort William and later named for Charles Carroll (1737–1832). 3,226 (1950).

Carrollton. Former town in Louisiana, now a part of New Orleans.

Carrollton. City in NW Missouri, county seat of Carroll County, in a farming region near the Missouri River. 4,380 (1950).

Carrollton. Village in E Ohio, county seat of Carroll County. 2,658 (1950).

Carron (kar'ọn). Village in C Scotland, in Stirlingshire, near the river Carron, ab. 9 mi. SE of Stirling. It is noted for its ironworks, established in 1760: the first carronades (muzzle-loading naval guns) were cast here in 1779. Pop. of electoral division, 3,172 (1931).

Carron, Franciscus. See **Caron** or **Carron, Franciscus.**

Carron River. River in C Scotland, in Stirlingshire. It rises ab. 12 mi. SW of Stirling and flows east to the Firth of Forth at Grangemouth, ab. 11 mi. SE of Stirling. At one time it was the northern boundary of the Roman Empire. Length, ab. 20 mi,

Carrousel (kȧ.rö.zel), **Place du.** See **Place du Carrousel.**

Carrowmore (kar'ọ.mōr), **Lough.** Lake in Connacht province, Irish Republic, in County Mayo, ab. 16 mi. SW of Ballycastle. Length, ab. 4 mi.; greatest width, ab. 2 mi.

Carrum (kar'um). See under **Charmouth.**

Carruthers (kạ.ruᴛʜ'ėrz), **Robert.** b. at Dumfries, Scotland, Nov. 5, 1799; d. at Inverness, Scotland, May 26, 1878. Scottish journalist and man of letters, editor and proprietor of the *Inverness Courier*. He was the biographer and editor of Alexander Pope, and the compiler, with Robert Chambers, of *Chambers's Cyclopedia of English Literature,* and others.

Carryl (kar'il), **Guy Wetmore.** b. at New York, March 4, 1873; d. there, April 1, 1904. American humorist. He was graduated from Columbia University in 1895. Among his publications are *Fables for the Frivolous* (1898), *Mother Goose for Grown-ups* (1900), *Grimm Tales Made Gay* (1902), *The Lieutenant-Governor* (1903), *Zut, and Other Parisians* (1903), *The Transgression of Andrew Vane* (1904), *Far from the Maddening Girls* (1904), and *The Garden of Years* (1904).

Çarşamba (chär.shäm.bä'). [Also, **Charshembe.**] Town in N Turkey, in the *il* (province or vilayet) of Samsun, on the Yesil Irmak (river), ab. 20 mi. E of Samsun at the end of the N-S railway line across Turkey, in a fertile plain laid down by the river. Tobacco is the most important crop; there is no month here without rain and as a result the olives of the area yield little oil. Pop. ab. 7,000.

Carse of Falkirk (kärs; fôl'kėrk). See **Falkirk, Carse of.**

Carse of Forth (fōrth). See under **Perthshire.**

Carse of Gowrie (gou'ri). See **Gowrie, Carse of.**

Carshalton (kär.shôl'tọn, kạr-). Urban district in SE England, in Surrey, ab. 2 mi. E of Sutton, ab. 11 mi. SW of Victoria station, London. 62,804 (1951).

Carso (kär'sō). Italian name of the **Karst.**

Carson (kär'sọn), **Alexander.** b. near Stewartstown, County Tyrone, Ireland, 1776; d. at Belfast, Ireland, Aug. 24, 1844. Baptist theologian. He was of Scottish parentage and was for a time a Presbyterian minister, but separated from that church in 1804. Later he adopted Baptist views. He published numerous controversial writings.

Carson, Christopher. [Called **"Kit" Carson.**] b. in Madison County, Ky., Dec. 24, 1809; d. in Colorado, May 23, 1868. American trapper, guide, and Indian fighter and agent, an almost legendary figure in the pantheon of American Indian fighters and heroes of the West. In 1826 he ran away from his home at Franklin, Mo., to join an expedition to Santa Fe, returning in 1831 as a trapper and Indian fighter after adventures in the Southwest. From 1831 to 1839 he was active as a hunter supplying buffalo meat, and was a guide on John C. Frémont's three expeditions (1842, 1843–44, 1845). His achievements brought him a national reputation after Frémont published his report on the first journey. His feats in the Mexican War made him a hero, but his appointment by President Polk as a lieutenant was rejected by the Senate for political reasons. Although illiterate (and remaining so until his last years), he was appointed (1853) a U.S. Indian agent; when the Civil War began, he took part in raising the 1st New Mexican Volunteer Infantry, of which he became colonel on Sept. 20, 1861. He participated in the battle of Valverde (Feb. 21, 1862) and in operations against the Navajos, Mescalero Apaches, Kiowas, and Comanches. On March 13, 1865, he was promoted to brevet brigadier general of volunteers and assumed command (1866) of Fort Garland, Colo. He resigned (1867) from the service because of poor health, and in the following year moved with his family to Boggsville, Colo. The published account of his life which he dictated (1857–58) to Lieutenant Colonel De Witt C. Peters is, as Carson himself admitted, highly untrustworthy. It appeared as *The Life and Adventures of Kit Carson, the Nestor of the Rocky Mts.* (1858). See *Kit Carson Days*, by Edwin L. Sabin (1914).

Carson, Edward Henry. [Title, Baron **Carson of Duncairn.**] b. at Dublin, Feb. 9, 1854; d. Oct. 22, 1935. Irish lawyer and politician, a leader in anti-Home Rule agitation. In 1913 he set up a provisional government for Ulster, to take power if Home Rule were enacted. With the outbreak of World War I the Home Rule bill was hastily passed but suspended for the duration of hostilities, and Carson in 1915 entered the Asquith cabinet as attorney general, and took the portfolio of first lord of the admiralty in 1917; later that year he became a member without portfolio of the coalition wartime cabinet. In 1918 he declined the nomination of the University of Dublin and reëntered Parliament as member for a division of Belfast, but he agreed to the Lloyd George proposal of separate parliaments for Ulster and for southern Ireland, coördinated by an All-Ireland Council. The substantial success of the Irish insurrection killed this scheme and led to the treaty of 1921 establishing the Irish Free State, which Carson, *pro forma,* denounced. In that same year he accepted a baronetcy and thereafter was politically inactive.

Carson City. City in W Nevada, capital of Nevada and county seat of Ormsby County. There are gold and silver mines in the vicinity. The city, which is the smallest state capital in the country, was founded (1858) as a silver-mining center, was named for Kit Carson, and grew rapidly with the discovery (1859) of the Comstock Lode. A U.S. mint was here from 1867 to 1893. Farming and livestock raising as well as mining are now principal occupations in the region. Carson City was the site of the world heavyweight championship bout (1897) between Bob Fitzsimmons and Jim Corbett, with Fitzsimmons the winner. 3,082 (1950).

Carson Sink. Large dry basin in W central Nevada, ab. 60 mi. E of Reno. The Carson River flows into the basin, and formerly an extensive saline lake occupied a part of it. Now most of the river's flow is conserved by Lahontan Dam. and used for water supply and irrigation.

Carstares or **Carstairs** (kär′stärz), **William.** b. at Cathcart, near Glasgow, Scotland, Feb. 11, 1649; d. Dec. 28, 1715. Scottish Presbyterian divine. A political prisoner (1675–79) at Edinburgh, he was again (1682) arrested on a charge of having been one of the conspirators involved in the Rye House Plot. He was chaplain to William, prince of Orange, in 1686, served as royal chaplain in the period 1688–1715, was named principal of the University of Edinburgh in 1703, and was four times moderator of the assembly.

Carstens (kär′stęns), **Asmus Jacob.** b. at Sankt Jürgen, in Schleswig, 1754; d. at Rome, 1798. Danish historical painter, engraver, and designer. As a youth he was apprenticed to a wine merchant, but the sight of paintings, especially historical and heroic compositions, excited in him a determination to be an artist despite all difficulties. He secured instruction at Copenhagen, but was from the first a rebel against academic methods, and in consequence was largely self-taught. He joined the Copenhagen Academy, but left it in indignation at what he considered shabby treatment of another artist, although at the time he was under consideration for an Academy award which would have allowed him to live and study at Rome for several years with all expenses paid. Presently he went to Italy at his own expense, but from lack of means, was able to go only as far as Mantua. Thence he went to Germany, settling at Lübeck, where he prospered moderately as a portraitist, but one of his heroic compositions, *The Fallen Angel*, led to his appointment as a professor at the Berlin Academy of Art. There he attracted the favorable interest of the king of Prussia, who in 1792 afforded him the means to go at last to Rome. In that city, where his abilities won acclaim and popularity, he remained until his death. Carstens' paintings and drawings of scenes drawn from classic mythology and from the works of Dante, Ossian, and Shakespeare, had a deep influence upon the course of German art in the later years of his life and in the period immediately following.

Carstensz (kär′stęnz), **Mount.** [Dutch, **Carstensz Toppen** (kär′stęns tôp′ęn).] Mountain peaks in W central New Guinea, in C Netherlands New Guinea, the highest point on the island. The peaks are of limestone, and snow-covered. Elevation, ab. 16,503 ft.

Carswell (kärz′wel, -węl), **Catherine Roxburgh.** [Maiden name, **Macfarlane.**] b. at Glasgow, Scotland, March 27, 1879; d. 1946. Scottish novelist, biographer, and literary and dramatic critic; wife (married 1915) of Donald Carswell. Educated at Glasgow University and in Germany, where she studied music, she was dramatic and literary critic (1907–15) for the Glasgow *Herald*. Her works include the novels *Open the Door* (1920) and *The Camomile* (1922), and *Life of Robert Burns* (1930), *Savage Pilgrimage—A Narrative of D. H. Lawrence* (1932), *The Scots Week-End* (1936; with Donald Carswell), and *Tranquil Heart—A Portrait of Giovanni Boccaccio* (1937).

Carswell, Donald. b. at Glasgow, Scotland, 1882; d. in January, 1940. English newspaperman, lawyer, soldier, and author; husband (married 1915) of Catherine Roxburgh Carswell. Educated at Glasgow University (M.A., 1904), he was associated (1904–12) with the Glasgow *Herald* and was a staff member (1912–17) of the London *Times*. He was the author of *The Trial of Ronald Tree* (1925), *Brother Scots* (1927), and *The Trial of Guy Fawkes* (1934), and collaborated with his wife in writing *The Scots Week-End* (1936).

Cartagena (kär.tä.ʜä′nä; Anglicized, kär.tą.jē′ną). [Called **Ciudad Heróica,** meaning "Heroic City."] City in N Colombia, capital of Bolívar department, on a low island between the Caribbean Sea and the Bay of Cartagena: export center for sugar, cattle, hides, gold, platinum, and timber. Founded (1533) by a Spanish conquistador named Pedro de Heredia, it was long the principal port and stronghold of this part of Spanish America. Several times taken and sacked by various sea raiders (Sir Francis Drake in 1585, and the French in 1697), it was fortified in the 18th century at an expense of 59 million dollars, and in 1741 successfully resisted the attack of the English admiral Edward Vernon. It was the first New Granadan city to declare for independence, but in 1815 was recaptured by the Spaniards after a four months' siege in which nearly all the garrison and inhabitants perished: for this it received the title of the "Heroic City." 110,504 (1951).

Cartagena. [Formerly also, **Carthagena**; ancient name, **Carthago Nova.**] City in SE Spain, in the province of Murcia, situated on the Mediterranean Sea W of Cape Palos, ab. 30 mi. SE of Murcia. Located on a protected bay, it has a large commercial harbor and a naval station; there are docks, shipyards, construction and repair shops, a marine arsenal, and strong fortifications. Iron, lead, and silver ores are exported; coal, foodstuffs, and machinery are imported. There are smelting works, and metallurgical, textile, and glass industries. Cartagena is the seat of a bishopric; has a Gothic cathedral, a theater, nautical and technical schools, and a ruined castle. 120,208 (1950).

History. Cartagena was founded by the Carthaginian leader Hasdrubal in 225 B.C. as Carthago Nova; conquered by the Romans under Scipio in 210, it was made a Roman colony under Augustus. In 425 A.D. pillaged by the Vandals, the town fell in 534 to the Byzantines, and in 624 to the Visigoths; it was destroyed by the Arabs in 711. Much contested during the struggle for supremacy between Christians and Moslems, Cartagena flourished again only in the 16th to 18th centuries. It was occupied by the British during the War of the Spanish Succession, in 1706 and 1707. A republican uprising took place here in 1873 which was suppressed in 1874. Cartagena was a Loyalist naval base during the Spanish civil war of 1936–39.

Cartagena, Alfonso de. See **Alphonsus a Sancta Maria.**

Cartagena, Conde **de.** Title of **Morillo, Pablo.**

Cartagena, Pact of. Agreement concluded (May 16, 1907) by Great Britain, France, and Spain, framed so as to avert supposed German designs on the Balearic and Canary islands, The pact affirmed a *status quo* in the Mediterranean and on the Atlantic coasts of Europe and Africa.

Cartago (kär.tä′gō). Town in W Colombia, in Valle Del Cauca department: center for cocoa, coffee, tobacco, and cattle. 14,750 (1938).

Cartago. Province in C Costa Rica. Capital, Cartago; area, 1,121 sq. mi.; pop. 100,725 (1950).

Cartago. Capital of Cartago province, in C Costa Rica, Central America, situated 13 mi. SE of San José: center of a rich agricultural district. It has been frequently damaged by earthquakes, notably in 1823, 1841, and 1910. Founded in 1553, it was the ancient capital of the country. 12,944 (1950).

Cartas de Indias (kär′täs dā ēn′dyäs). Collection of letters from early Spanish explorers, published (1887) by the Spanish government at Madrid. Some of those from Columbus, Vespucci, and others are given in facsimile.

Carte (kärt), **Richard D'Oyly.** b. at London, May 3, 1844; d. there, April 3, 1901. English impresario of light opera, remembered chiefly in connection with Gilbert and Sullivan, whose works he commissioned and sponsored. He organized an agency to represent singers and actors, and produced light operas, such as *Giroflé-Girofla*. In 1875 he commissioned *Trial by Jury*, the first work by Gilbert and Sullivan. Subsequently he built the Savoy Theatre, at London, where additional operettas by this team were staged, from *Patience* (1881) to *The Grand Duke* (1896). In an unsuccessful attempt to begin English serious opera, he produced *Ivanhoe* (1891) by Sullivan. He also established touring companies which were continued after his death.

Carte, Thomas. b. at Clifton-upon-Dunsmore, Warwickshire, England, in April, 1686; d. near Abingdon, Berkshire, England, April 2, 1754. English scholar and historian. He was the author of *Life of James, Duke of Ormonde* (1736), an important history of England to 1654 (1747–55), and others. He was a strong Jacobite.

Cartel Combination. In German politics, the temporary union (c1887) in the Reichstag of the members of the German Conservative, National Liberal, and Imperialist parties.

"Cartel des Gauches" (kär.tel dā gōsh). [Eng. trans., "*Cartel of the Left.*"] Coalition of French political parties which governed France in the period 1924–25. Composed chiefly of Radical-Socialists, Republican-Socialists, and

Socialists, it defeated (1924) the conservative parties and compelled President Alexandre Millerand to resign office. It broke up after the fall (April 10, 1925) of the Herriot cabinet.

Carter (kär'tėr), **Elizabeth.** b. at Deal, England, Dec. 16, 1717; d. at London, Feb. 19, 1806. English poet and translator. She is best known for her friendship for Dr. Samuel Johnson which lasted for 50 years, and was also the friend of Horace Walpole and Edmund Burke. Her letters to Elizabeth Vesey, Elizabeth Montagu, and Catherine Talbot were collected and printed in seven volumes (1809–17). She translated Epictetus, contributed to the *Gentleman's Magazine*, and published collections of poetry.

Carter, Franklin. b. at Waterbury, Conn., Sept. 30, 1837; d. at Williamstown, Mass., Nov, 22, 1919. American educator. He was graduated from Williams College in 1862. From 1865 to 1868 he was professor of Latin and French at Williams, from 1868 to 1872 of Latin only. From 1872 to 1881 he was professor of German at Yale College. He was president of Williams College in the period 1881–1901.

Carter, Henry. Original name of **Leslie, Frank.**

Carter, Henry Alpheus Peirce. b. at Honolulu, Aug. 7, 1837; d. at New York, Nov. 1, 1891. Hawaiian statesman and merchant. An employee (1854) and partner (c1862) of C. Brewer and Company, the largest mercantile house at Honolulu, he developed plantations of the growing sugar industry. He negotiated (1876) and secured (1887) an extension of the treaty to put sugar on the free import list to the U.S. He was Hawaiian minister of the interior (1880–82) and minister to the U.S. (1883–91).

Carter, Henry Rose. b. in Carolina County, Va., Aug. 25, 1852; d. at Washington, D.C., Sept. 14, 1925. American epidemiologist, noted for his observations on yellow fever. As physician (1879 *et seq.*) with the Marine Hospital Service, he determined (1888) the incubation period for yellow fever and introduced accordingly a regulated quarantine period for naval personnel. A representative (1893, 1897–98) of the U.S. government during epidemics in the South, he was also organizer (1904) and director of quarantine service in Cuba.

Carter, Hodding. [Full name, **William Hodding Carter, Jr.**] b. at Hammond, La., Feb. 3, 1907—. American journalist, newspaper publisher, and novelist. He was graduated from Bowdoin College (B.A., 1927) and from the Columbia University Graduate School of Journalism (1928). He served (1929–32) as a newspaper reporter at New Orleans and in 1932 established the *Daily Courier* at Hammond. He was the founder (1936) of the *Delta Star* at Greenville, Miss., and in 1938 consolidated it with another local journal as the Delta *Democrat-Times*, of which he is the editor and publisher. He served (1940–45) in the U.S. army and in 1946 was awarded a Pulitzer prize for his editorials. He is the author of two novels, *The Winds of Fear* (1944) and *Flood Crest* (1945). Other works by him include *Civilian Defense of the United States* (with E. R. DuPuy; 1942), *Lower Mississippi* (1942), and *Southern Legacy* (1950).

Carter, Howard. b. at Swaffham, Norfolk, England, 1873; d. at London, March 2, 1939. English archaeologist and Egyptologist, noted for his discovery (1922) with G. E. S. M. Herbert, 5th Earl of Carnarvon, of the tomb of Tutankhamen. He worked on Egyptian archaeological surveys, assisted (1892) Flinders Petrie, was appointed by the Egyptian government inspector general of the antiquities department, and made important Egyptian excavations, including the discovery of the tombs of Hatshepsut and Amenhotep I. His works include three volumes on the tomb of Tutankhamen and *The Tomb of Hatshepsut*.

Carter, James Coolidge. b. at Lancaster, Mass., Oct. 14, 1827; d. at New York, Feb. 14, 1905. American lawyer. He was graduated from Harvard University in 1850, and from the Harvard Law School in 1853. In 1875 he was appointed by Governor Tilden a member of the commission to devise a form of municipal government for the cities of New York State, and in 1892 was appointed one of the counsel to represent the U.S. before the Bering Sea tribunal. He published *The Proposed Codification of our Common Law* (1884) and other works.

Carter, James Gordon. b. at Leominster, Mass., Sept. 7, 1795; d. at Chicago, July 21, 1849. American educator, a pioneer in the establishment of normal schools. As a teacher (1820 *et seq.*), he furthered the growth of common schools; as a writer of textbooks (c1830), he applied the inductive method of learning; as a congressman (1835–38), he secured aid for the American Institute of Instruction which he had helped to found (1830). He was editor of the *United States Gazette* (1824) and the *New York Review* (1826), and author of *Letters to the Hon. William Prescott on the Free Schools of New England, with Remarks on the Principles of Instruction* (1824) and *Essays upon Popular Education with an Outline of an Institution for the Education of Teachers* (1826).

Carter, John Ridgely. b. at Baltimore, Nov. 28, 1864; d. at New York, June 3, 1944. American financier and diplomat, at the time of his death senior partner of Morgan et Companie, Paris. In the U.S. diplomatic service from 1894 to 1911, he served at London and Constantinople. Offered a post as minister to Argentina in 1911, he declined because "rent for a suitable house would equal my salary." His subsequent association with J. P. Morgan and Company took him to Paris in 1914.

Carter, Mrs. **Leslie.** [Maiden name, **Caroline Louise Dudley.**] b. at Lexington, Ky., June 10, 1862; d. Nov. 13, 1937. American actress. She first appeared (1890) on the New York stage in *The Ugly Duckling;* her later vehicles include *The Heart of Maryland, Zaza, La Tosca,* and *The Second Mrs. Tanqueray*. In all of these she was under the management of David Belasco.

Carter, Nick. Pseudonym used by Frederick Van Rensselaer Dey (1861–1922) and others in writing the popular dime detective novels concerning the adventures of Nick Carter. In all, more than 1,000 titles were produced by Dey and by other writers, including Thomas Chalmers Harbaugh (1849–1924) and John Russell Coryell (1848–1924). Coryell is the reputed originator of the Nick Carter character. The first Nick Carter novel was published in 1890.

Carter, Samuel Powhatan. b. at Elizabethton, Tenn., Aug. 6, 1819; d. May 26, 1891. American naval and army officer. The only man who has ever been both a rear admiral in the navy and a major general in the army of the U.S., he entered the first-named of the services as a midshipman in 1840, and after sailing on several cruises was enrolled at the Naval Academy at Annapolis, from which he graduated in 1846. After further service afloat he was an assistant professor of mathematics (1850–53) at Annapolis, but was again assigned to active duty and was with a squadron in South American waters when the Civil War erupted in the U.S. A declaration which he wrote in support of the Union cause was widely circulated in Tennessee, and in July, 1861, the navy assigned him to duty at the war department so that he might organize Union volunteers in that state. In May, 1862, he was made a brigadier general of volunteers, and although he was not brevetted major general until 1865, in fact he commonly commanded forces larger than a brigade during the last three years of the war. He organized successful cavalry raids behind the Confederate front, defeating among others the much-feared Confederate cavalry leader Morgan. Mustered out of the army with honors in January, 1866, he returned to naval duty as commander of the steamer *Monocacy*. In 1870 he attained the rank of captain in the navy, in 1878 he was made a commodore, and in 1882 he was given the rank of rear admiral, retired.

Carter, William Samuel. b. at Austin, Tex., Aug. 11, 1859; d. at Baltimore, March 15, 1923. American railroad-union official. He was general secretary and treasurer (1904–09) and president (1909–22) of the Brotherhood of Locomotive Firemen and Enginemen, director (1918–20) of the division of labor of the U.S. Railway Administration in World War I, and editor (1894–1904) of the *Brotherhood of Locomotive Firemen and Enginemen's Magazine*.

Carteret (kär.tėr.et'). Borough in C New Jersey, in Middlesex County: electrolytic copper-refining center. 13,030 (1950).

Carteret (kär'tėr.ẹt), Sir **George.** b. at St.-Ouen, Jersey, Channel Islands, c1610; d. in January, 1680. English sailor and Royalist politician; a nephew of Sir Philip de Carteret. He became a captain in the navy in 1633, and comptroller of the navy in 1639. An active supporter of the Royalist cause during the English Civil War, he was appointed by Charles I lieutenant governor of Jersey (from which he expelled the Parliamentary governor) and vice-admiral (Dec. 13, 1644). It is interesting to note that Charles II also granted him "a certain island and adjacent islets in America in perpetual inheritance, to be called New Jersey," but the formal grant, from James Stuart, was dated 1664. He surrendered (Dec. 12, 1651) the island of Jersey and went to France, where he obtained a command in the French navy. Imprisoned in the Bastille from August to December, 1657, he returned to England at the Restoration, was treasurer of the navy in the period 1661–67, and was suspended from the House of Commons for mismanagement of the funds of the navy, on Dec. 10, 1669. He was one of the original proprietors of Carolina, and, with John Berkeley, 1st Baron Berkeley, was formally granted (1664) the land between the Hudson and Delaware rivers, named in his honor New Jersey.

Carteret, John. [Titles: 2nd Baron **Carteret of Hawnes,** Earl **Granville.**] b. April 22, 1690; d. at London, Jan. 22, 1763. English statesman; grandson of Sir George Carteret. He succeeded to the title of Baron Carteret on Sept. 22, 1695, and became Earl Granville on the death of his mother, on Oct. 18, 1744. A member (1711 *et seq.*) of the House of Lords, he was an adherent of the Hanoverian family, reversing the family loyalty to the Stuarts. In 1719 he was named ambassador to Sweden, and successfully mediated (1720) a dispute between Sweden, Prussia, and Hanover. After his return to England, he served (1721–24) under Robert Walpole as secretary of state for the southern province. In 1724 he was sent to Dublin as lord lieutenant of Ireland to succeed the duke of Grafton. While there, he managed to put down the disturbances caused by the granting to William Wood of a profitable patent for copper coins, which had been violently opposed by the Irish (perhaps most notably by Jonathan Swift, Carteret's friend, who voiced his views in the famous series of letters signed with the name Drapier). On Carteret's return (1730) to London, he was leader of the opposition in the House of Lords until the fall of Walpole's ministry in 1742. During this time he joined in the condemnation of Walpole for opposing war with Spain (on Feb. 13, 1741, he made a motion in the House of Lords that the king be requested to remove Walpole from his "presence and counsels forever"). On the outbreak of the War of the Spanish Succession he sided with Maria Theresa of Austria. Once more in favor with George II, he was named secretary of state for the northern province in 1742, a post which he held until 1744. During this time he negotiated an agreement between Maria Theresa and Frederick of Prussia.

Carteret, Lionel. Youthful hero of Henry Arthur Jones's problem play *Mrs. Dane's Defence* (1900). He wishes to marry Mrs. Dane, a woman with a past, but his foster father, a clever lawyer, forces her, under a merciless cross-examination, to confess to an old love affair on the Continent. Ruled by arguments that he cannot answer, the chivalrous Lionel gives up Mrs. Dane, and the audience is given to understand that he will marry a "nice" Scottish girl after he has recovered from the shock of losing his first love.

Carteret, Philip. b. on the island of Jersey, Channel Islands, 1639; d. 1682. American colonial official, first governor of New Jersey. In 1664 he was commissioned governor of New Jersey by his cousin, Sir George Carteret, and John Berkeley, 1st Baron Berkeley, to whom James Stuart, who was then still Duke of York, had granted the colony. He arrived (1665) at what is present-day Elizabethport, and immediately became involved in difficulties with New England settlers who were unwilling to accept his authority and were particularly hostile to paying the quit-rents demanded by the Lords Proprietors. He was faced by a rebellion, which failed, when he attempted to make the first collection of the quit-rents. He later became the governor of East Jersey; while in this post, he became embroiled with Sir Edmund Andros of New York in a controversy over customs jurisdiction, was arrested by an expedition from New York, and placed on trial. He was acquitted, and retired in 1682.

Carteret, Philip. d. at Southampton, England, July 21, 1796. English rear admiral and explorer in the Southern Hemisphere. He was lieutenant of the *Dolphin* in John Byron's expedition (1764–66), and commanded the *Swallow* in the expedition under Samuel Wallis to the Southern Hemisphere (1766–69), on which were discovered Pitcairn Island (July 2, 1767), Osnabruck (now called Mehetia), in the Society Islands, Gower Island, in the Solomons, Simpson's Island, Carteret's Island (or Kilinailau, actually a group of islets near Bougainville), Wallis Island, and others. His journal was published in Hawkesworth's *Voyages* (1773). According to some accounts it was Carteret's description of Pitcairn which led a group of the *Bounty* mutineers to settle there in 1790.

Carteret, Sir **Philip de.** b. on the island of Jersey, Channel Islands, in February, 1584; d. there, Aug. 23, 1643. English royalist. He was seigneur of St.-Ouen, Jersey, and of Sark, and lieutenant governor of Jersey, which he held for the king until his death.

Cartersville (kär′tėrz.vil). City in NW Georgia, county seat of Bartow County. Limestone quarries, barite mines, and the Etowah Indian mounds are in the vicinity. 7,270 (1950).

Carter v. Carter Coal Co., 298 U.S. 238 (1936). U.S. Supreme Court decision declaring unconstitutional the Bituminous Coal Act of 1935 (also known as the Guffey Act). Justice George Sutherland's opinion invalidated the labor sections of the act on the ground that they regulated industrial production only indirectly related to interstate commerce, and also voided the act's price-fixing provisions. The decision, one of the major judicial defeats suffered by the New Deal, is notable for its narrow definition of national powers.

Carterville (kär′tėr.vil). City in S Illinois, in Williamson County. 2,716 (1950).

Carthage (kär′thạj). [Latin, **Carthago;** Phoenician, **Karthadasht,** meaning "New Town."] Ancient city and state in N Africa, situated on the Mediterranean, a few mi. NE of modern Tunis, and not far from the ancient city of Utica. It was founded by Phoenicians about the middle of the 9th century B.C. (According to tradition, Dido founded the city, having bought as much land as could be circumscribed by a buffalo hide; this she cut in strips with which, laid end to end, she encircled a sizable piece of ground and on it built the citadel called Byrsa, from the Greek word "hide.") It was a great commercial and colonizing center as early as the 6th century B.C., and was one of the largest cities of antiquity. It had two harbors, a naval and a mercantile. Its first treaty with Rome was made in 509 B.C. It was defeated at Himera in Sicily in 480, but overthrew Selinus and other Sicilian cities c400. It was the rival of Syracuse under Dionysius, Agathocles, and others. At the height of its power it had possessions in Sicily, Corsica, Sardinia, N Africa, and Spain. Its wars with Rome have the following dates: First Punic War, 264–241; Second Punic War, 218–201; Third Punic War, 149–146. It was recolonized as a Roman city by Gaius Gracchus and successfully by Augustus c29 B.C., was taken by the Vandals in 439 A.D., and was retaken by Belisarius in 533. It was an important center of Latin Christianity. The Saracens destroyed it c697. At present some cisterns, broken arches of an aqueduct, the Roman Catholic monastery of Saint Louis, and a museum mark the site of the former rival of Rome.

Carthage. City in W Illinois, county seat of Hancock County. It was incorporated in 1837, and is the seat of Carthage College. The founder of the Mormon Church, Joseph Smith, was jailed here in 1844 and mobbed to death. 3,214 (1950).

Carthage. City in SW Missouri, county seat of Jasper County. It is a processing center for dairy products and for marble; manufactures include flour, clothing, auto parts, and shoes. A Confederate victory (1861) and a number of violent border clashes occurred here during the Civil War. 11,188 (1950).

Carthage. Village in N New York, in Jefferson County, on the Black River: paper mills. 4,420 (1950).

Carthage. City in E Texas, county seat of Panola County, ab. 18 mi. from the Louisiana border and ab. 150 mi. SE of Dallas, in an agricultural region; oil is also produced. In the decade between the last two U.S. censuses its population more than doubled. 2,178 (1940), 4,750 (1950).

Carthagena (kär.tä.ʜä′nä). See **Cartagena,** Spain.

Carthaginian Wars (kär.thạ.jin′i.ạn). See **Punic Wars.**

Carthago Nova (kär.thā'gō nō'vạ). Ancient name of **Cartagena,** Spain.

Carthusians (kär.thū'zhạns). Monastic order of the Roman Catholic Church, founded (1084) by Saint Bruno (of Cologne) at La Grande Chartreuse, in SE France. The rule of the order, originally written in 1130, was put into its present form in 1681. The monks live an extremely austere and contemplative life, meeting together only at public worship and at stated meals. They are tonsured and beardless. Their isolation, in cells built to be completely separate from each other, has evoked the style of building known in English as the charterhouse, a cloister surrounded by separate houses. No woman, except a ruling queen, is permitted within the Carthusian monastery. The order is noted for the liqueur, chartreuse, made by it in France from a secret formula, the sale of which now brings its principal revenue. A globe with a cross and seven stars around it is the badge of the order.

Cartier (kȧr.tyā), Sir **Georges Étienne.** b. at St. Antoine, Lower Canada (now Quebec province), Sept. 6, 1814; d. May 20, 1873. Canadian statesman and lawyer. After having been admitted (1835) to the bar, he participated in the rebellion of 1837, being forced as a result temporarily to flee the country. Returning from a period spent in the U.S., he was elected (1848) to Parliament. A prominent member (1854 *et seq.*) of the Liberal-Conservative Party, he served as provincial secretary (1855 *et seq.*) and attorney general for Lower Canada, before becoming (1858) joint prime minister with John Macdonald. One of the leading advocates of confederation, he was responsible for achieving that end for his province. He was also active in aiding in the construction of Canadian railways. After his premiership had come to an end (1862), he was minister of defense until 1872.

Cartier, Jacques. b. at St.-Malo, France, 1491; d. there, Sept. 1, 1557. French navigator. He made three voyages to Canada. In the first (1534) he explored the Gulf of St. Lawrence; in the second (1535) he sailed up the St. Lawrence to Montreal; and in the third (1541–42) he made an unsuccessful attempt at colonization in Canada.

Cartismandua (kär.tis.man'd̦ū.ạ). fl. 1st century A.D. Queen of the Brigantes in the time of the Roman emperor Claudius I. She favored the Romans, and was forced to seek an asylum in their camp.

Carton (kär'tọn), **Sydney.** In Charles Dickens's *A Tale of Two Cities*, a character whose real abilities and worth have been largely sacrificed to careless dissipation, but whose love for Lucy Manette leads him finally to an act of self-sacrifice which many readers consider to be among the noblest in English fiction: Carton substitutes himself for Charles Darnay, Lucy's husband, on the guillotine. (A remarkably close resemblance between the two men makes the substitution possible.) Carton's last thought as the blade of the guillotine drops has taken its place among the best-known lines in Dickens's works (and, indeed, in world literature): "It is a far, far better thing that I do than I have ever done: it is a far, far better rest that I go to than I have ever known."

Carton de Wiart (kȧr.tôṅ dẹ vyȧr), **Henri Victor Marie Ghislain,** Comte. b. at Brussels, Jan. 31, 1869; d. May 6, 1951. Belgian lawyer and statesman. He graduated (LL.D., 1890) from the University of Brussels, became a member of the Brussels bar, and was named president of the federation of Belgian lawyers. A leader of the Catholic Party, he held posts in several cabinets as minister of justice, minister of the interior, and minister of social welfare and hygiene. He was prime minister (1920–21), having become minister of state in 1919. He was a member of the Royal Academy of Belgium, an associate member of the Institute of France, and a writer on moral, legal, political, and historical subjects.

Cartoons of Raphael. Name given to a group of drawings executed in the period 1515–16, for Pope Leo X, to be reproduced in Flemish tapestry. They were long in Hampton Court Palace, and are now in the Victoria and Albert Museum, London. The cartoons, of which there were originally at least ten, are now seven in number: *Christ's Charge to Peter, Death of Ananias, Peter and John Healing the Cripple, Paul and Barnabas at Lystra, Elymas Struck Blind, Paul Preaching at Athens*, and *The Draught of Fishes*. In composition and vigor of drawing they are considered among Raphael's best works (despite the fact that some authorities believe they were actually done by students of Raphael from his designs).

Cartouche (kȧr.tösh). [Nickname of **Louis Dominique Bourguignon.**] b. at Paris, 1693; broken on the wheel at Châtelet, France, Nov. 28, 1721. Parisian robber. He was the son of a wine merchant, and was stolen by gypsies from whom he learned his craft. He established himself at Paris, and after a short period of service in the army, formed a famous band of robbers. His history was extremely popular, and has been the foundation of various plays and stories.

Cartwright (kärt'rīt), **Edmund.** b. at Marnham, Nottinghamshire, England, April 24, 1743; d. at Hastings, England, Oct. 30, 1823. English clergyman and mechanician, the reputed inventor of the power loom; brother of John Cartwright. Graduated from University College, Oxford, he became a fellow of Magdalen College in 1764, curate of Brampton, and rector of Goadby Marwood, Leicestershire, in 1799. In 1784, during a visit to Arkwright's cotton mills at Cromford, the idea of a weaving machine, according to the account given by him, occurred to him. His first patent was taken out on April 4, 1785, and this was followed by others, on improvements, on Oct. 30, 1786, and Aug. 18, 1787. He also patented (1789) a wool-carding machine, and (1797) a steam engine in which alcohol was used, and assisted Robert Fulton in his experiments with steamboats.

Cartwright, John. [Called the **"Father of Reform."**] b. at Marnham, Nottinghamshire, England, Sept. 17, 1740; d. at London, Sept. 23, 1824. English radical politician and publicist, an advocate of parliamentary reform and of the abolition of slavery; brother of Edmund Cartwright. He was the author of *A Letter to Edmund Burke, controverting the Principles of American Government laid down in his lately published Speech on American Taxation* (1775), and of other political pamphlets. He was fined (1820) for sedition.

Cartwright, Peter. b. in Amherst County, Va., Sept. 1, 1785; d. at Pleasant Plains, Ill., Sept. 25, 1872. American circuit preacher of the Methodist Episcopal Church.

Cartwright, Sir **Richard John.** b. at Kingston, Ontario, Canada, Dec. 4, 1835; d. there, Sept. 24, 1912. Canadian statesman. He began his public career as a member of the Assembly of United Canada in 1863. He was at first a Conservative, but differences over fiscal policy causing him to leave that party and to join the Liberals. He became a member of the House of Commons of the Dominion of Canada at its first session in 1867, and served as minister of finance from 1873 to 1878. The chief rival of Sir Wilfred Laurier for Liberal Party leadership in the 1880's, he accepted the cabinet post of minister of trade under Laurier in 1896, and on occasion functioned as acting premier. He became a member of the Dominion senate in 1904, and in that body supported the policy of reciprocity with the U.S. In his later years he recorded his long life of political activity and patriotic service in a book of reminiscences.

Cartwright, Thomas. b. in Hertfordshire, England, c1535; d. at Warwick, England, Dec. 27, 1603. English Puritan clergyman, controversialist, and scholar.

Cartwright, Thomas. b. at Northampton, England, Sept. 1, 1634; d. at Dublin, April 15, 1689. English prelate. He was prebendary of Wells and of Durham, dean of Ripon, and bishop of Chester (1686 *et seq.*).

Cartwright, William. b. at Northway, near Tewkesbury, England, c1611; d. at Oxford, England, Nov. 29, 1643. English clergyman and dramatist. He was the son of an innkeeper at Cirencester, a student at Christ Church, Oxford, a member of the Council of War in 1642, and a proctor of the university in 1643. He wrote *The Ordinary, The Royal Slave, a Tragi-Comedy, The Lady-Errant, a Tragi-Comedy*, and *The Siege, or Love's Convert.* His plays and poems were collected in 1651.

Carty (kär'ti), **John Joseph.** b. at Cambridge, Mass., April 14, 1861; d. Dec. 27, 1932. American electrical engineer, widely recognized for his inventions toward the improvement of the telephone. He was chief engineer (1889–1907) of the New York Telephone Company and chief engineer (1907–19) and vice-president (1919–30) of the American Telephone and Telegraph Company.

Caruarú (kä.rwạ.rö'). City in NE Brazil, in the state of Pernambuco. 44,595 (1950).

Carúpano (kä.rö′pä.nō). City in NE Venezuela, in Sucre state, on the Caribbean Sea: manufactures include fiber, soap, and rum. 30,684 (1950).

Carus (kä′rụs), **Carl Gustav.** b. at Leipzig, Germany, Jan. 3, 1789; d. at Dresden, Germany, July 28, 1869. German physiologist and psychologist. His works include *Lehrbuch der Zootomie* (1818), *Über den Blutkreislauf der Insekten* (1827), *Grundzüge der vergleichenden Anatomie und Physiologie* (1828), *Vorlesungen über Psychologie* (1831), and *Psyche* (1846).

Carus, Julius Viktor. b. at Leipzig, Germany, Aug. 25, 1823; d. there, March 10, 1903. German zoölogist. He was custodian of the Museum of Comparative Anatomy at Oxford (1849–51), professor of comparative anatomy at Leipzig (1853–1903), and Professor Wyville Thomson's substitute at Edinburgh (1873–74). His works include *Zur näheren Kenntnis des Generationswechsels* (1849), *System der tierischen Morphologie* (1853), and *Icones zootomicae* (1857). He also translated many of the writings of Charles Darwin.

Carus (kãr′us), **Marcus Aurelius.** b. in Illyria, c222; d. near Ctesiphon, Mesopotamia, 283. Emperor of Rome (282–283). He was prefect of the Praetorian Guard under Probus, and was elevated to the throne by the soldiers on the murder of Probus at Sirmium. He was killed (according to one account, by lightning) on an expedition against the Parthians, as he was about to push conquests across the Tigris.

Carus (kä′rụs), **Paul.** b. at Ilsenburg, Germany, July 18, 1852; d. Feb. 11, 1919. American philosophical writer, editor of the *Monist* and *The Open Court,* at Chicago. He was educated at the universities of Strasbourg and Tübingen. Among his publications are *Fundamental Problems, The Gospel of Buddha, Karma, The Idea of God, The History of the Devil, The Nature of the State, The Pleroma,* and *Truth on Trial.*

Carus (kãr′us), **Titus Lucretius.** See **Lucretius.**

Caruso (ką.rö′sō; Italian, kä.rö′zō), **Enrico.** b. at Naples, Italy, Feb. 25, 1873; d. there, Aug. 2, 1921. Italian dramatic tenor, noted for the outstanding power and control of his voice. He made his debut in a small theater near Naples, and was not brought into prominence until 1896, when he sang at the Fondo Theater at Naples. In 1898 he sang at Milan. In 1903 he began a series of engagements at New York, where, as a member of the Metropolitan Opera Company, he sang more than 30 roles, that brought him great popularity and world renown. Among his vehicles were *Rigoletto* and *Pagliacci.* He also made phonograph records of operatic excerpts and folk songs.

Caruthers (ką.ruᴛʜ′ėrz), **William Alexander.** b. in Virginia, c1800; d. at Marietta, Ga., Aug. 29, 1846. American novelist and physician. He was a student in 1819–20 at Washington College (now Washington and Lee University), but there is no record of his having pursued medical studies (although he was a successful physician in the 1840's at Savannah, being mentioned with respect in the press of that city). Much of his writing, published in magazines which have long since ceased publication, is lost to us, but his historical novels give him a place in American literature. They are *The Kentuckian in New York* (1834), an epistolary novel in which the story is told by letters between two Virginia students, *The Cavaliers of Virginia* (1837), in which Nathaniel Bacon, of Bacon's Rebellion, is the hero, and *The Knights of the Horseshoe: A Traditionary Tale of the Cocked Hat Gentry in the Old Dominion* (1845), dealing with the character and the career of Alexander Spotswood, English colonial governor in America.

Caruthersville (ką.ruᴛʜ′ėrz.vil). City in SE Missouri, county seat of Pemiscot County, on the Mississippi River. It is a shipping point for sand, gravel, cotton, and wood products. 8,614 (1950).

Carvajal or **Carbajal** (kär.ʙä.ʜäl′), **Francisco de.** b. at Arévalo, Spain, c1464; executed near Cusco, Peru, April 10, 1548. Spanish soldier in South America. In 1528 he went to Mexico, and in 1536 Cortés sent him with others to aid Francisco Pizarro in Peru. As field marshal under Vaca de Castro, he directed (1542) the battle of Chupas, where the younger Almagro was overthrown. He took an active part in the struggle of Gonzalo Pizarro against Pedro de la Gasca, was captured on April 9, 1548, and condemned to death.

Carvalho (kár.vȧ.yō), **Léon.** [Original surname, **Carvaille.**] b. at Port-Louis, France, 1825; d. at Paris, Dec. 29, 1897. French opera director; husband of Marie Caroline Félix Carvalho. He was during his early career a singer in the company of the Opéra Comique, at Paris, and was later (1856–68) director of the Théatre Lyrique. Appointed (1876) manager of the Opéra Comique, he was dismissed (1887) after the fire which razed it, but regained his position in 1891.

Carvalho, Marie Caroline Félix. [Maiden name, **Miolan.**] b. Dec. 31, 1827; d. July 10, 1895. French singer; wife of Léon Carvalho, whom she married in 1853. She first went to London in 1860, and sang with great success both there and at Paris.

Carvalho (kąr.vä′lyö), **Ronald de.** b. at Rio de Janeiro, May 16, 1893; d. there, Feb. 15, 1935. Brazilian poet, journalist, essayist, critic, and diplomat. His poetical works include *Luz gloriosa* (1912), *Poemas e sonetos* (1919), *Epigramas irônicos e sentimentais* (1922), and *Toda a América* (1926). Among his prose writings are *Pequena história da literatura brasileira* (1919), *Espelho de Ariel* (1922), *Estudos brasileiros* (1924–31), and *Rabelais e o riso do Renascimento* (1931).

Carvalho, Vicente (Augusto) de. b. at Santos, Brazil, April 5, 1866; d. there, April 22, 1924. Brazilian poet, considered one of the greatest of the Parnassian school. He was a lawyer and a judge, and held various posts in his native state of São Paulo. Author of *Ardentias* (1885), *Relicário* (1888), *Rosa, Rosa de Amor* (1902), *Poemas e canções* (1908), and *Páginas soltas* (1911).

Carvalho e Mello (ē mä′lö), **Sebastião José de.** See **Pombal,** Marquis **de.**

Carvalho Paes de Andrade (pīs dẹ ąn.drä′dẹ), **Manuel de.** b. c1795; d. at Rio de Janeiro, June 18, 1855. Brazilian politician. He was elected (December, 1823) temporary president of Pernambuco, and during the succeeding year headed a revolt against the emperor Pedro I, proclaiming (July 2, 1824) a republic with the name of Confederação do Equador. The revolt was put down in October, and Carvalho escaped to England. He returned to Brazil, and was a senator from 1835.

Carvell (kär′vẹl), **Nicholas.** d. 1566. English poet, reputed author of two poems in *The Mirror for Magistrates.*

Carver (kär′vėr), **George Washington.** b. near Carthage, Mo., c1864; d. at Tuskegee, Ala., Jan. 5, 1943. American chemist, botanist, and educator, world-renowned for his researches in the industrial uses of vegetable crops. As an infant, the son of Negro slaves, he was kidnaped with his mother and later brought back by his original master for a 300-dollar horse. Carver received a B.S. (1894) and M.S. (1896) in agriculture at the Iowa State College of Agricultural and Mechanical Arts. He joined the mechanics faculty there and was placed in charge of the greenhouse, centering his attention on bacterial laboratory work in systematic botany. From 1896 he was connected with the Tuskegee Institute, as teacher and director of agricultural research, on the invitation of Booker T. Washington, principal of the institute. Carver's constant aims were, first, to educate the Southern farmer in the possibility of diversifying his crops, and, second, to discover more widespread uses for these crops. With this as his goal, his experiments with the peanut, the soybean, and the sweet potato developed, in the course of 40 years, hundreds of new uses for these plants and their byproducts. From peanuts, he made axle grease, shampoo, a coffee substitute, and other products; his discoveries in the uses of soybean oil in paint-making promoted new developments in paint sprays. Many authorities believe that it was largely as a result of Carver's work that acreage in the South devoted to peanut cultivation quadrupled in the years 1899–1942. In addition to this work with plants, he experimented with clay and was able to extract several pigments from the local earths. After 1935 Carver was associated with the division of mycology and disease survey, Bureau of Plant Industry, U.S. Department of Agriculture. He established (1940) at Tuskegee the Carver Foundation for research with his life savings of 33 thousand dollars.

Carver, John. b. in England, c1576; d. at Plymouth, Mass., April 5, 1621. American colonist, one of the Pilgrim Fathers and first governor (1620–21) of the Plymouth colony. Despite a successful career as a merchant at London, he was led by his nonconformist religious convictions to emigrate (1609) to the Netherlands. At Leiden he joined (c1610) the Pilgrims, and contributed his fortune toward the support of that congregation. A member of the *Mayflower* contingent, he was elected (1620) first governor of the Plymouth colony and was the principal Pilgrim negotiator (1621) of the treaty between that colony and the Indian chief Massasoit.

Carver, Jonathan. b. at Weymouth, Mass., April 13, 1710; d. at London, Jan. 31, 1780. American soldier, traveler, and explorer of the region beyond the Mississippi River. To find a northern passage to the Pacific, he started from Boston in June, 1766, explored the shores of Lake Superior, and proceeded as far west as the sources of the St. Pierre River, returning in 1768. In 1769 he went to England. He published *Travels through the Interior Parts of North America* (1778), including an account of the manners, customs, and languages of the Indians, as well as *A Treatise on the Cultivation of the Tobacco-plant* (1779), and others.

Carver, Thomas Nixon. b. at Kirkville, Ia., March 25, 1865—. American political economist. He was professor of economics at Oberlin College (1894–1900) and assistant professor of political economy at Harvard University (1900–02), where he was made a professor in 1902. He published *The Distribution of Wealth* (1904), *Sociology and Social Progress* (1905), and articles on economic subjects in various periodicals.

Carvilius (kär.vil′i.us), **Spurius.** fl. 235 B.C. Roman freedman, noted as one of the first to open a public school at Rome (meaning here a school open to those members of the public who paid its fees rather than one supported by public funds). He is credited, by Plutarch and others, with having devised the letter G for the Roman alphabet. The need for this letter arose from the fact that C (which had long represented in the Roman alphabet the phonetic values of the K which had disappeared at an early date) could not fill the necessity which had developed by the time of Carvilius for some means of indicating those phonetic values which are perhaps most familiar to the bulk of modern readers as the "hard C" and the "hard G." Carvilius, by a slight modification of the sign for C, produced the G, and put it in place of the almost unnecessary and little used Z (which was only restored, together with Y, in the time of Cicero, and was then placed at the end of the alphabet). After Carvilius, such Latin words as the prename Caius came to be spelled Gaius, and the latter form is now that preferred by the majority of Latin scholars (although the form Caius may be found in some sources, particularly those based upon earlier English works). Curiously enough, however, the name spelled as Gaius by the Romans after Spurius retained the abbreviation "C."

Carville (kär′vil). Unincorporated village in SE Louisiana, ab. 23 mi. by road SE of Baton Rouge. Nearby is the National Leprosarium, the only leper colony in the U.S. 300 (1940).

Carvin (kȧr.vaṅ). City in N France, in the department of Pas-de-Calais, situated ab. 11 mi. SW of Lille. It is a coal-mining town and has a number of industries. 20,294 (1946).

Carwar (kär′wär). See **Karwar.**

Cary (kãr′i), **Alice.** b. at North College Hill, near Cincinnati, Ohio, April 26, 1820; d. at New York, Feb. 12, 1871. American author; sister of Phoebe Cary (1824–71). Her works include poems, novels, sketches of Western life, *Clovernook Papers* (1851–53), and *Clovernook Children* (1854).

Cary, Edward. b. at Albany, N.Y., June 5, 1840; d. May 23, 1917. American newspaper editor. As editor of the Brooklyn *Union*, his editorials earned him the position of editorial writer (1871–1917) on the New York *Times.*

Cary, Elisabeth Luther. b. at Brooklyn, N.Y., 1867; d. July 13, 1936. American literary and art critic. She was owner and editor (until 1908) of *The Scrip*, and served as art critic (1908 *et seq.*) for the New York *Times.* Her works include *Alfred Tennyson, His Homes, His Friends and His Work* (1898), *The Rossettis, Dante Gabriel and Christina* (1900), *William Morris* (1902), *Ralph Waldo Emerson, Poet and Thinker* (1904), and *The Art of William Blake* (1907).

Cary, Sir **Henry.** [Title, 1st Viscount **Falkland.**] d. in September, 1633. English statesman; father of Lucius Cary, 2nd Viscount Falkland. He was created Viscount Falkland in the Scottish peerage on Nov. 10, 1620. In 1622 he was sent as lord deputy to Ireland, a post which he held until 1629.

Cary, Henry Francis. b. at Gibraltar, Dec. 6, 1772; d. at London, Aug. 14, 1844. English poet and scholar, chiefly known as a translator of Dante.

Cary, Joyce. [Full name, **Arthur Joyce Lunel Cary.**] b. at Londonderry, Ireland, Dec. 7, 1888—. British novelist. Author of *Aissa Saved* (1930), *The African Witch* (1936), *Castle Corner* (1938), *Mister Johnson* (1939), a trilogy comprising *Herself Surprised* (1941), *To Be a Pilgrim* (1942), and *The Horse's Mouth* (1944), *The Moonlight* (1946), *A Fearful Joy* (1949), *Prisoner of Grace* (1952), and other novels. He has also written *Marching Soldier* (1945) and *The Drunken Sailor* (1947), poetry; and *Power in Men* (1937), *The Case for African Freedom* (1941), and other politico-philosophical works.

Cary, Lucius. See **Falkland,** 2nd Viscount.

Cary, Phoebe. b. at North College Hill, near Cincinnati, Ohio, Sept. 4, 1824; d. at Newport, R.I., July 31, 1871. American author; sister of Alice Cary (1820–71). She wrote *Poems and Parodies* (1854), *Poems of Faith, Hope, and Love* (1868), and others, and was the author of the hymn *One Sweetly Solemn Thought.*

Cary, Thomas. See under **Cary's Rebellion.**

Cary's Rebellion. In American colonial history, an uprising in North Carolina resulting from Thomas Cary's denial of the franchise to the Quakers. Cary, lieutenant governor of the colony, was officially removed from office at the instigation of the Quakers, but refused to leave it. After two years, Edward Hyde was despatched from England to serve as governor of North Carolina. Cary, despite his pledge of support to Hyde, led a revolt against the latter's authority. Hyde was defeated and returned to England on a charge of treason, but never stood trial.

Carystius (ką.ris′ti.us), **Diocles.** See **Diocles Carystius.**

Casa (kä′sä), **Giovanni della.** b. at Mugello, near Florence, June 28, 1503; d. at Rome, Nov. 14, 1556. Italian poet and ecclesiastic. He was clerk of the chamber to Pope Paul III, and charged with various diplomatic duties; author of *Galatea* (a poem on etiquette, 1558, 1752). His collected works were published in 1707.

Casa, José Iglesias de la. See **Iglesias de la Casa, José.**

Casabianca (kä.są.byäng′ką). Narrative poem (1829) by Felicia Dorothea Hemans (1793–1835), the work for which she is chiefly remembered. It tells the story of a brave ten-year-old boy, Giacomo Jocante Casabianca, the son of a French naval officer, Louis Casabianca (c1752–98), who stays with his father's ship, *L'Orient*, until it is blown up and he dies, with his father, in carrying out the command to watch the ship. The poem has the frequently quoted opening line "The boy stood on the burning deck."

Casabianca (kä.są.byäng′ką; French, kȧ.zȧ.byäṅ.kȧ), **Louis.** b. at Bastia, Corsica, c1752; killed off Abukir, Egypt, Aug. 1, 1798. French naval officer. In company with his son, Giacomo Jocante Casabianca, he perished with his ship *L'Orient* (rather than leave the burning vessel, as he might have done) at the battle of the Nile. This event is the subject of the poem *Casabianca* by Felicia Hemans.

Casablanca (kä.sä.bläng′kä; Anglicized, kas.ą.blang′ką). [Arabic: **Dar-el-Beida, Dar-al-Baida.**] Seaport in NW Africa, in French Morocco, situated about one-third of the way down the Atlantic coast of Morocco. Casablanca is the largest city and the commercial, industrial, and shipping hub of French Morocco. Eighty percent of the trade of the area passes through this port, which is the headquarters for many importers, exporters, and merchants. It is a relatively modern city possessing many fine buildings. It is connected by rail with Tangier, Algiers, Oran, Constantine, Tunis, and Marrakech. Pop. 505,000 including 107,000 Europeans (1946).

History. On July 30, 1907, the Moors murdered eight Europeans and the city was bombarded (Aug. 5) by French ships and captured by French troops. The conflict between France and Morocco continued until August,

1908. The forcible removal by French soldiers from the protection of the German consulate (Sept. 5, 1908) of deserters from the French Foreign Legion led to a dispute between France and Germany which, after mutual explanations, was referred by them to the Hague Tribunal for arbitration. The decision of the court was accepted by both countries, in May, 1909. Casablanca was one of the points attacked by Anglo-American forces during the invasion of Africa in 1942. Roosevelt and Churchill met here in 1943 to formulate the World War II policy of "unconditional surrender."

Casablanca Conference. Meeting (Jan. 14–24, 1943) between President Franklin D. Roosevelt, Prime Minister Winston Churchill, and Allied military leaders held at Casablanca, French Morocco, shortly after its capture in World War II. It was agreed that the war should be waged until the enemy surrendered unconditionally. Roosevelt asked that the conference be known as the "Unconditional Surrender Conference." Roosevelt's trip to Casablanca was his first Atlantic flight and also made him the first president ever to leave the U.S. in a time of actual hostilities.

Casa-Cajigal (kä′sä.kä.hē.gäl′), Marquis of. Title of **Cajigal de la Vega, Francisco Antonio.**

Casa de Contratación de las Indias (kä′sä dā kōn″trä.tä.syōn′ dā läs ēn′dyäs). Spanish name of the **Council of Seville.**

Casadesus (kȧ.sȧd.süs), **Robert Marcel.** b. at Paris, April 7, 1899—. French pianist. Coming of a musical family, he began his studies in childhood under the tutelage of a relative, but in his 13th year he entered the Paris Conservatory of Music, and promptly began to win prizes. Upon graduating from the Conservatory he began his career as a concert pianist in European cities, extended his field to North Africa and South America, and in 1935 faced an American audience for the first time as soloist with the New York Philharmonic Symphony Society, under the baton of Hans Lange. His success was sensational; the critics uniformly praised his warm and poetic manner, and Olin Downes called him "a superior artist and a distinguished musical mind." Toscanini was present on this occasion, and promptly arranged with Casadesus to play with the same orchestra, under Toscanini's direction, in the following year. Since then his recitals and appearances as soloist with leading American orchestras have been numerous, especially since 1940, when he became a permanent U.S. resident. Between 1934 and 1940 he was head of the piano department in the American School of Music at Fontainebleau, France.

Casa d'Oro (kä′sä dō′rō). See **Cà d'Oro.**

Casa Fuerte (fwer′tā), Marquis of. Title of **Acuña y Bejarano, Juan de.**

Casa Grande (kas′ą gran′dę). National monument on the S bank of the Gila River, in Arizona, ab. 80 mi. NW of Tucson. The name is taken from the Spanish words meaning "great house." The principal structure, a large pueblo-like building of adobe, was built by the Salado people in the 14th century and is accompanied by a number of compounds in the Hohokam style.

Casa Grande. Town in S Arizona, in Pinal County, ab. 45 mi. SE of Phoenix, near the Santa Cruz River. It was named for the Casa Grande pueblo, now a national monument, ab. 20 mi. NE, on the Gila River. The surrounding agricultural region is irrigated by water from the Coolidge Dam. In the decade between the last two U.S. censuses the town's population more than doubled. 1,545 (1940), 4,181 (1950).

Casa grande e senzala (kä′zą grun′dę ę sȧn.zä′lą). Sociological study in the development of Brazilian civilization, by the contemporary Brazilian writer Gilberto Freyre (b. 1900). It appeared in 1933 and an English version (*The Masters and the Slaves*) was published in 1946. It is considered one of the most important books for the interpretation of Brazil's social and economic structure.

Casa Guidi Windows (kä′sä gwē′dē). Poem by Elizabeth Barrett Browning, published in 1851. It is named from the Casa Guidi, a house in Florence where the author resided during the composition of the poem, which was inspired by Mrs. Browning's enthusiasm for Italian freedom.

Casal (kä.säl′), **Julián del.** b. 1863; d. 1893. Cuban poet. He was a close friend of Rubén Darío, the great Nicaraguan poet, and like him a pioneer of modernism (*modernismo*) in Latin-American letters, though less concerned with social and political issues. Although he chose his themes sometimes from life about him in Cuba, and again from classical history and mythology, Casal's preoccupation was with sensuous elegance, and his style was formed by French writers as diverse as Verlaine and Baudelaire on the one hand and Hérédia on the other. His fascination with what has been called the decadent movement in French literature was shown by his study of Joris Karl Huysmans. Casal's best-known books are *Hojas al viento* (1890), *Nieve* (1891), and *Bustos y rimas* (1893).

Casale Monferrato (kä.sä′lā mōn.fer.rä′tō). [Also: **Casale**; Latin, **Bodincomagus.**] City and commune in NE Italy, in the *compartimento* (region) of Piedmont, in the province of Alessandria, situated on the Po River, ab. 38 mi. E of Turin. It is famous for its wines, but is also a center of the fruit and cattle trade. Of chief importance are building materials, particularly calcium and cement, of which there is large-scale production. Other industries produce agricultural and viticultural machinery, liquors, and chemicals. There is a good library and numerous educational institutions, among them the Leardi technical institute. The city has interesting monuments, such as the 12th-century Basilica of Sant' Evasio, the 15th-century Church of San Domenico, the Palazzi Trevisio, Langosco, Testa-Fochi, Treville (1730), and others. The citadel, one of the strongest in Italy, was founded in 1590. Rebuilt in 730 A.D. by the Lombards, it was made the capital of a margraviate by Emperor Otto III; in 1246 it came under the rule of marquises of Monferrato, in 1559 that of Mantua. Later it was contested between France and Spain, and was incorporated into Piedmont (the house of Savoy) in 1703. Buildings of interests to tourists were undamaged in World War II. Pop. of commune, 37,098 (1936); of city, 25,485 (1936).

Casalmaggiore (kä.säl.mäd.jō′rā). Town and commune in N Italy, in the *compartimento* (region) of Lombardy, in the province of Cremona, situated on the Po River, ab. 22 mi. SE of Cremona. It has old fortifications and a castle. There is a sugar refinery and dairies; glass, ceramics (majolica), and jewelry (gold) are produced. In 1509, Federigo Gonzago conquered the town for Louis XII of France; afterward it was under the rule of Maximilian Sforza, Duke of Milan; it shared in later periods the fate of Milan. Casalmaggiore is famous in the history of printing; one of the earliest Hebrew prints, now at Columbia University, New York, was printed here in 1486; an edition of Tasso's *Gerusalemme Liberata* (*Jerusalem Delivered*) was published here c1581. Pop. of commune, 15,345 (1936); of town, 5,302 (1936).

Casalnuovo di Napoli (kä.säl″nwō′vō dē nä′pō.lē). Town and commune in S Italy, in the *compartimento* (region) of Campania, in the province of Napoli, N of Naples. It is an agricultural commune. Pop. of commune, 11,794 (1936); of town, 6,133 (1936).

Casals (kä.säls′), **Pablo.** b. at Vendrell, Spain, in December, 1876—. Spanish cellist, generally considered to be the foremost modern master of his instrument and noted also as an outstanding interpreter of the works of Johann Sebastian Bach. He became (1897) professor of cello at Barcelona University and founded (1920) the Pau Casals orchestra at Barcelona. He toured widely in Europe and the U.S. (1901, 1903–04, 1914–16). With the advent of Francisco Franco in Spain, Casals went into retirement in S France. After a three-year period of complete public inactivity, he organized and led (1950) at Prades, France, a festival commemorating the 200th year of Bach's death; with an outstanding international orchestra, all the members of which participated without financial remuneration, he directed the Brandenburg Concertos, and as soloist performed Bach's unaccompanied cello suites. His own compositions include works for orchestra, cello, violin, piano, and organ. Casals, a member of UNESCO's international music institute, quit that body in 1952 when Spain was admitted to UNESCO.

Casamance (kȧ.zȧ.mäns). [Also, **Casamanza** (kä.sä.män′zä).] River in Senegal, French West Africa, which flows into the Atlantic Ocean ab. 60 mi. S of the Gambia River.

Casano al Ionio (kä.sä′nō äl yô′nyō). See **Cassano all'Ionio.**

Casanova (kä.sä.nô′vä), **Francesco Giuseppe.** b. at London, 1727; d. at Vienna, c1802. Italian painter and engraver; brother of Giovanni Battista Casanova. His studies took him to Venice and to Dresden before he settled at Paris, where he lived, and exhibited his work at the Royal Academy, for some years, eventually however returning to Italy in 1783.

Casanova, Giovanni Battista. b. at Venice, c1722; d. 1795. Italian painter; brother of Francesco Giuseppe Casanova. He is known to have studied at Dresden, but after 1752 he lived and worked for some years at Rome. Eventually he returned to Dresden, becoming a professor at the academy in that capital in 1764, and later its director.

Casanova de Seingalt (kä.sä.nô′vä dẹ saṅ.gȧl′; Anglicized, kaz.ạ.nō′vạ, kas-), **Giovanni Giacomo** (or **Jacopo**). b. at Venice, April 2, 1725; d. at Dux, in Bohemia, June 4, 1798. Italian adventurer, notorious, through his own writings, as a libertine. His parents were actors, but they entrusted his education to others while they traveled. At the age of 16 Casanova entered a seminary at Venice; he was soon expelled for misconduct, served briefly as secretary to Cardinal Acquaviva, became a soldier in the Venetian service, and thereafter lived by his wits, turning his not inconsiderable abilities to any rewarding course that came to hand. He was a violinist in a theater orchestra, a preacher, a gambler, an alchemist, a thaumaturgist, and above all a rogue with a glib tongue whose attractiveness to women helped him alternately to positions of eminence and disgrace; he traveled through Europe, was imprisoned (1755) for magic and freemasonry at Venice, made a daring escape, and fled to Paris. There he used the story of his adventure to push himself forward and became, through the influence of Marie Antoinette, director of the state lottery; it was in this period that the adopted the style "Chevalier de Seingalt." His large fortune and his position of importance did not remain with him for long; Casanova's restless spirit soon caused him to travel again and in 1759 he left Paris, eventually passing through almost every European court from St. Petersburg to Madrid, from London to Rome. He became acquainted with Voltaire, Cagliostro, Catherine the Great, Madame Pompadour, Albrecht von Haller, and other notables, but in the long run he attained so dubious a reputation because of his immorality and charlatanism that his welcome was worn out. After 1774 he served as a police spy at Venice, but in 1782 had to leave the city when he angered a powerful Venetian personage by his writing. He settled (1785) as librarian at Count Waldstein's castle of Dux in Bohemia, where he spent the rest of his life. Casanova's latter years were spent in writing his *Mémoires écrits par lui-même* (published in 12 volumes, 1826–38, but as yet never printed in full), sensational, highly colored as to his personal adventures, but well written and an excellent source for the history and manners of the period.

Casarano (kä.sä.rä′nō). Town and commune in SE Italy, in the *compartimento* (region) of Apulia, in the province of Lecce, situated on the Salentine Peninsula, S of Lecce. It is an agricultural market town. Pop. of commune, 11,225 (1936); of town, 10,843 (1936).

Casas (kä′säs), **Bartolomé de Las.** See **Las Casas, Bartolomé de.**

Casati (kä.sä′tē), **Gaetano.** b. at Lesmo, Italy, 1838; d. at Como, Italy, March 7, 1902. Italian soldier and explorer in Africa. In 1879 the Italian Society for Commercial Exploration sent him to the basin of the Bahr-el-Ghazal, where he arrived in 1880. After exploring the country of the Nyam-Nyam and the Mombuttu, he joined Emin Pasha and Wilhelm Junker in 1883. In 1886 Kabrega, a king of the Nyoro (or Banyoro) to whom Emin had sent him on a mission, detained him in semi-captivity. Stanley's arrival, in 1889, set him free. His reports were published in *Bolletino della Società d'Esplorazione* (1883–88). His *Dieci Anni in Equatoria* appeared in 1891.

Casaubon (kạ.sô′bọn; French, kȧ.zō.bôṅ), **Florence Étienne Méric.** b. at Geneva, Switzerland, Aug. 14, 1599; d. at Oxford, England, July 14, 1671. French divine and classical scholar, resident in England after 1611; son of Isaac Casaubon. He published a large number of works, of which the most important is an edition of his father's *Ephemerides*.

Casaubon, Isaac. b. at Geneva, Switzerland, Feb. 18, 1559; d. at London, July 12, 1614. French classical scholar and Protestant theologian; father of Florence Étienne Méric Casaubon. He was professor of Greek at Geneva (1582–96) and of languages at Montpellier (1596–1600), librarian to Henry IV of France at Paris (1601–10), and from 1610 until his death a prebendary of Canterbury and a pensioner of James I of England. He published commentaries on Athenaeus, Theophrastus (with a Latin translation), and Suetonius, and *Ephemerides*, a journal of his studies.

Casaubon (kạ.sô′bọn), **Rev. Edward.** In George Eliot's *Middlemarch*, the husband of Dorothea Brooke. She marries him in the belief that his high and noble ideals will raise her into a broad and generous intellectual life, but finds him to be only a timid, self-absorbed pedant.

Casbin (käz.bēn′). See **Kazvin.**

Casca (kas′kạ), **Publius Servilius.** d. after 42 B.C. Roman politician, one of the assassins of Julius Caesar (44 B.C.), and the first of them to strike a blow.

Cascade Range (kas.kād′). Range of mountains in California, Oregon, Washington, and British Columbia, nearly parallel to the Pacific. According to the U.S. Geographic Board, this range is limited on the S by the gap S of Lassen Peak, in California, and extends northward into British Columbia. It is connected with the Sierra Nevada on the S, and contains many extinct volcanoes. Among its chief peaks are Mounts Pitt, Scott, Three Sisters, Jefferson, Hood, Baker, St. Helen's, and Rainier, the highest (14,408 ft.).

Cascate delle Marmore (käs.kä′tā del′lā mär′mō.rā). See **Marmore, Cascate delle.**

Cascina (kä.shē′nä). Town and commune in C Italy, in the *compartimento* (region) of Tuscany, in the province of Pisa, situated on the Arno River, E of Pisa. A vast agricultural commune, it has also cotton-textile and furniture manufactures. The Church of Santa Maria, in Pisan Romanesque style, dates from the 12th century. In 1364, the Florentines defeated the Pisans here; Michelangelo's sketches of the battle are famous. Pop. of commune, 27,941 (1936); of town, 2,136 (1936).

Casco (kas′kō), **Treaty of.** In American colonial history: **1.** Treaty concluded on April 12, 1678, ending the war between the Massachusetts Bay settlers and the Indians of the eastern region. It formally brought to a close King Philip's War (which for all practical purposes had ended in 1676), and provided for the mutual restoration of property and captives. **2.** Attempt made by Governor Joseph Dudley of Massachusetts Bay to preserve friendly relations with the Indians to the north of the colony. The meeting of the Indians with Dudley and his associates was held at Casco, Me., on June 20, 1703, but despite the avowals of friendship made by the Indians, they resumed their hostilities a short time thereafter.

Casco Bay. Bay on the SW coast of Maine, extending from Cape Elizabeth, near Portland, NE ab. 20 mi. It abounds in islands.

Case (kās), **Anna.** b. at Clinton, N.J., Oct. 29, 1889—. American soprano. She made her debut (1909) at New York as the Dutch boy in *Werther*, and was a member (1909–16) of the Metropolitan Opera Company. She is notable for her performances in the roles of Feodor in *Boris Godunov* (1912), Sophie in *Der Rosenkavalier* (1913), Mimi in *La Bohème*, and Micaëla in *Carmen*. As a recital singer (1916 *et seq.*) she toured in the U.S., Europe, and Canada. In 1931, at the time of her retirement, she married Clarence H. Mackay.

Case, Everett Needham. b. at North Plainfield, N.J., April 9, 1901—. American educator. He received B.A. degrees from Princeton (1922) and from Cambridge (1924). He was assistant dean (1939–42) of the Harvard Graduate School of Business Administration before becoming (1942) president of Colgate University.

Case, Leonard. b. at Cleveland, Ohio, June 27, 1820; d. Jan. 6, 1880. American philanthropist, founder of the Case School of Applied Science (since 1947 the Case Institute of Technology) at Cleveland, Ohio. While practicing law at Cleveland he and a group of friends established in his office a small natural-history museum which engaged much of his attention and indicated the interest in science which was a guiding force through much of his life. He signed (1877) the trust deed to found the Case School, which was opened in 1881.

Case Is Altered, The. Comedy of intrigue by Ben Jonson, acted as early as 1599, based on two plays by Plautus, *Aulularia* and *Captivi.* He developed their classic themes into a comedy of Italy in his own day.

Case Is Altered, The. Novel by William Plomer, published in 1932.

Casella (kä.sel'lä), **Alfredo.** b. at Turin, Italy, July 25, 1883; d. 1947. Italian pianist and composer, a champion of modern music in Italy. He entered (1896) the Paris Conservatoire, where he studied under Xavier Leroux, Fauré, and Diémer. He was known at Paris as a concert pianist and critic. In 1915 he became an instructor at the Conservatorio di Santa Cecilia at Rome, and in 1917 founded the Societá Nazionale di Musica, which was incorporated (1923) as the Italian section of the International Society for Contemporary Music. His compositions include the ballet *La Giara* (1924), the orchestral works *Elegia eroica* (1916), *Pagine di guerra* (1916), *Concerto romano* (1926), and the operatic fragment *La Donna Serpente* (1932). He is also the author of a dissertation on the development of the cadenza, *L'Evoluzione della musica a traverso la storia della cadenza perfetta* (1919), of the monograph *Igor Stravinski* (1923), *Il Pianoforte* (1937), and the autobiographical *21 + 26* (1932).

Casement (kās'mẹnt), **Roger David.** b. at Kingstown (now Dun Laoghaire), Ireland, Sept. 1, 1864; d. at London, Aug. 3, 1916. British consular agent and Irish patriot. Son of a colonel in the British army who had Irish nationalist sentiments, Roger Casement entered the British consular service in 1892. Sent to a consular post in the Belgian Congo in 1900, he exposed the inhuman treatment of the natives by the rubber companies, which shocked the world and led to official British representations to the Belgian government and an end to the worst abuses. As British consul general (1908–12) at Rio de Janeiro, he revealed equally cruel mistreatment of the natives gathering rubber for the Anglo-Peruvian Amazon Company in the Putumayo region. For this he was knighted by the British government. The following year, his health impaired by long service in the tropics, he retired. Returning to Ireland in 1913, he dedicated himself to the cause of his country's independence. At the outbreak of World War I, being in the U.S. raising funds for the Irish Volunteers, he resolved to act on the maxim that "England's difficulty is Ireland's opportunity," and in November, 1914, went to Germany as an emissary of revolutionary groups in Ireland and America. His effort to form an Irish Brigade among British prisoners of war of Irish birth failed, largely because he would not allow those who took the risk of such a step to accept pay from the Germans. He induced the Germans to send him to the Irish coast in a submarine, but after landing he was captured before he could communicate with the leaders at Dublin, and the Easter Week Rising took place a few days later. He was taken to London, tried for high treason, and hanged at Pentonville prison.

Case of George Dedlow (ded'lō), **The.** Short story by Silas Weir Mitchell. The autobiography of an army surgeon who loses both arms and legs in the Civil War, it was first published in the *Atlantic Monthly* in July, 1866, and served to introduce Mitchell to readers of fiction. That the medical and surgical details are absolutely authentic is due to the fact that Mitchell was a graduate of Jefferson Medical College, a practicing physician, a surgeon in the Union army, and the author of well over a hundred medical works, both long and short.

Case of the Roman Catholics of Ireland, The. Prose work (1760) by Henry Brooke, an Irishman, who is much better known for his famous sentimental novel *The Fool of Quality, or the History of Henry, Earl of Moreland.*

Case of the Seven Bishops. See **Seven Bishops, Case of the.**

Caseros (kä.sā'rōs). See **Monte-Caseros.**

Caserta (kä.zer'tä). Province in S Italy, in the *compartimento* (region) of Campania, formed out of parts of the provinces of Campobasso, Benevento, and Napoli. Capital, Caserta; area, ab. 2,000 sq. mi.; pop. ab. 561,000 (est. 1946).

Caserta. City and commune in S Italy, in the *compartimento* (region) of Campania, the capital of the province of Caserta, ab. 17 mi. N of Naples. It is the seat of a bishopric, and has soap and chemical factories. The city contains a royal castle, begun in 1752, built according to plans by Luigi Vanvitelli for Charles III of Spain (who, as Charles IV, was also king of the Two Sicilies, which included the S part of Italy). It is one of the largest rococo palaces of Europe, of enormous extent, gorgeously decorated, in the midst of wide gardens which are adorned with statues and fountains, and is called the "Versailles of Naples." The palace is now the seat of an aeronautical academy. A short distance NE of Caserta is Caserta Vecchia, now an almost deserted village, which was of great importance in the period of Lombard and Norman domination. The cathedral, consecrated in 1152, is in pure Apulian Romanesque style. Caserta was the headquarters of the Garibaldian campaigns against Naples in 1860; it was Field Marshal Alexander's headquarters during the latter part of the Italian campaign in World War II; the act of surrender of the German army in Italy and Yugoslavia was signed here on April 29, 1945. The palace suffered some damage during World War II, but was repairable. Pop. of commune, 49,462 (1936); of city, 24,623 (1936).

Cases (käz), **Emmanuel Augustin Dieudonné,** Comte **de Las.** See **Las Cases, Emmanuel Augustin Dieudonné,** Comte **de.**

Casey (kā'si). City in E Illinois, in Clark County: manufactures of shoes; formerly the center of an oil boom. 2,734 (1950).

Casey, Edward P. b. at Portland, Me., June 18, 1864; d. at New York, Jan. 2, 1940. American architect who designed many monuments at Washington, D.C., and was vice-president of the Beaux-Arts Society. He studied at Columbia University and at the École des Beaux-Arts, Paris, and was the architect chosen to complete the Congressional Library at Washington. He also designed the Grant Monument and the Memorial Continental Hall at Washington, a building for the American College at Beirut, Syria, and monuments on the battlefields of Antietam and Gettysburg.

Casey, Joseph. b. at Ringgold's Manor, Md., Dec. 17, 1814; d. Feb. 10, 1879. American jurist. He was elected (1848) to Congress, and was appointed in 1855 a commissioner to investigate and end the "Erie Railroad War." He served as reporter (1855–61) of the decisions of the supreme court of Pennsylvania, and published *Pennsylvania State Reports* (1856–61), known as "Casey's Reports." He was appointed (1861) by Lincoln a judge of the U.S. Court of Claims and was first chief justice (1863–70) of that body after its reorganization.

Casey, Richard Gardiner. b. at Brisbane, Australia, Aug. 29, 1890—. Australian diplomat and soldier. He served (1914–18) in France and Gallipoli during World War I, was liaison officer (1924–31) between the Australian government and the British government, and held posts in the Australian cabinet as assistant federal treasurer (1933–35), treasurer (1935–39), and minister of development (1937–39) and of supply (1939–40). During World War II he was Australian minister (1940–42) to the U.S. and British minister of state (1942–43) in the Middle East. From 1944 to 1946 he was governor of Bengal. In 1949 he became minister of supply and development, of works and housing, in the Menzies coalition cabinet.

Casey at the Bat. Mock-heroic poem by Ernest Lawrence Thayer, published (June 3, 1888) in the San Francisco *Examiner.*

Casgrain (käs.grañ), **Henri Raymond.** b. at Rivière Ouelle, Quebec, Canada, 1831; d. 1904. French Canadian priest and historian. Ordained to the priesthood in 1856, he was rector of the Quebec basilica from 1860 to 1873, but thereafter devoted himself to literature. In the history of his native province and the character of his own people he found material for a long succession of books. From the publication of *Légendes canadiennes* (1861) he had an assured audience. His *Pèlerinage au pays d'Evangeline* (1887) was honored by the French Academy.

Cashel (kash'ẹl). Urban district, ancient episcopal city, and ancient seat of the kings of Munster, in Munster province, Irish Republic, in County Tipperary (South

Riding), ab. 33 mi. SE of Limerick. Jonathan Swift (1667–1745) was a native of the town. The "rock of Cashel" is a limestone formation, ab. 300 ft. in height. On its summit are the ruins of a Gothic cathedral (12th century), castle, abbey, chapel, and round tower. 3,072 (1946).

Cashel Byron's Profession (kash'e̱l bī'ro̱nz). Novel by George Bernard Shaw. Considered the best of his five novels, it was written in 1882, published 1885–86, and dramatized by him in blank verse as *The Admirable Bashville* (1901). It is the story of Cashel Byron, a pugilist, who loves, and finally marries, the wealthy Lydia Carew. He gives up boxing, enters politics, is elected as a Conservative, and has a large family. In his preface, Shaw declares "I never think of Cashel Byron's Profession without a shudder at the narrowness of my escape from becoming a successful novelist at the age of twenty-six." In its original stage version, the prizefighter James J. ("Gentleman Jim") Corbett had a considerable success as the fighting hero.

Cashibo (kä.shē'bō). [Also: **Cachibo, Caxibo.**] South American tribe living in the forested lowlands of E Peru, in the area ab. latitude 9° S., longitude 75° W. The Cashibo language may be one of the Panoan stock.

Cashmere (kash'mir, kash.mir'). See **Kashmir.**

Casiguran (kä.sē.gö'rän). Town in Tayabas province, E Luzon, Philippine Islands, situated at the head of Casiguran Bay. 6,360 (1939).

Casiguran Bay. Deep bay on the E coast of Luzon, Philippine Islands, indenting Tayabas province: a safe harbor for large vessels in all weather. It is connected with Casiguran Sound by a narrow neck of water.

Casilda (kä.sēl'dä). City in E Argentina, in Santa Fe province, ab. 200 mi. NW of Buenos Aires. 11,023 (1947).

Casilear (kas'i.lir), **John W.** b. at New York, June 25, 1811; d. at Saratoga Springs, N.Y., Aug. 18, 1893. American painter and engraver. He began to study engraving at the age of 15, and in 1831 was an engraver of banknotes. In 1840 and 1857 he went to Europe to study painting. He was elected a member of the National Academy of Design in 1851.

Casilinum (kas.i.lī'num). Ancient name of **Capua.**

Casimir I (of *Poland*) (kas'i.mir, kaz'-). [Polish, **Kazimierz**; German, **Kasimir**; called **"Casimir the Monk," "Casimir the Peaceful,"** the **"Restorer of Poland."**] d. Nov. 28, 1058. King of Poland (1040–58); son of Mieszko II and Rixa, a German princess. On the death of his father (1034) his mother became regent, but was obliged to flee from an outbreak of national hatred, aroused by the favoritism which she displayed toward her countrymen. Casimir was recalled (1040) from Germany, where he was living in retirement devoted to religious exercises. He restored Christianity, which had been hotly persecuted during his absence, and added Masovia and Breslau to Poland.

Casimir II (of *Poland*). [Polish, **Kasimierz**; German, **Kasimir**; called **"Casimir the Just."**] b. 1138; d. May 4, 1194. King of Poland (1177–94). He organized the Polish senate, which consisted of bishops, palatines, and castellans, and introduced laws protecting the peasants against the nobles.

Casimir III (of *Poland*). [Polish, **Kasimierz**; German, **Kasimir**; called **"Casimir the Great."**] b. 1310; d. Nov. 8, 1370. King of Poland (1333–70). He promulgated (1347) a double code of laws for Great and Little Poland, projected (1364) the University of Kraców, and made conquests in Silesia, Russia, and Lithuania. He was benevolent toward the Jews, and helpful to the peasants.

Casimir IV (of *Poland*). [Polish, **Kasimierz**; German, **Kasimir.**] b. Nov. 29, 1427; d. at Grodno, Poland, June 7, 1492. King of Poland (1447–92). He carried on a war of 14 years against the Teutonic Knights, which was terminated (1466) by the peace of Toruń (Thorn), and which gave Poland possession of West Prussia, with suzerainty over East Prussia.

Casimir V (of *Poland*). See **John II** (of *Poland*).

Casimir, John II. See **John II** (of *Poland*).

Casimir-Périer (kå.zē.me̱r.pā.ryā), **Jean Paul Pierre.** b. at Paris, Nov. 8, 1847; d. there, March 11, 1907. French statesman; grandson of Casimir Pierre Périer (1777–1832). Elected president of the French republic on June 27, 1894, he resigned on Jan. 15, 1895.

Casinum (ka̤.sī'num). Latin name of **Cassino.**

Casiquiare (kä.sē.kyä'rä). [Also: **Cassiquiare, Cassiquiari**; Spanish, **Brazo** ("arm") **Casiquiare, Canal** ("channel") **Casiquiare.**] River in S Venezuela. It diverges from the Orinoco River ab. 20 mi. W of Esmeralda, and joins the Río Negro, thus connecting the Orinoco system with that of the Amazon. The current is from the Orinoco to the Negro. Length, ab. 240 mi.

Casiri (kä.sē'rē), **Michael.** b. at Tripoli (now in Lebanon), 1710; d. at Madrid, March 12, 1791. Spanish Orientalist. He became chief librarian of the Escorial in Spain in 1763. His chief work is *Bibliotheca arabico-hispana escurialensis* (1760–70).

Casius (kā'si.us). [Also: **Bargylus**; Latin, **Casius Mons.**] Ancient name of the mountainous region in Asia Minor S of Antioch.

Caskets (kås'ke̱ts). [Also, **Casquets.**] Group of dangerous rocks in the English Channel, ab. 8 mi. W of Alderney (the northernmost of the Channel Islands). Now marked by a lighthouse, they are the traditional scene of the shipwreck of Prince William in 1120.

Caskoden (kas.kō'de̱n), **Edwin.** Pseudonym of **Major, Charles.**

Cask of Amontillado (a̤.mon.ti.lä'dō), **The.** Tale by Edgar Allan Poe, published (1846) in *Godey's Lady's Book.*

Čáslav (chäs'läf). [German, **Czaslau, Tschaslau.**] Town in Czechoslovakia, in C Bohemia, situated ab. 44 mi. SE of Prague, E of Kutná Hora. The Hussite leader Žižka was interred here in the Church of Peter and Paul, but in 1623 his bones were removed and his grave destroyed by order of Emperor Ferdinand II. 8,773 (1947).

Caslon (kaz'lo̱n), **William.** b. at Cradley, Worcestershire, England, 1692; d. at Bethnal Green, London, Jan. 23, 1766. London type founder, famous for his skill as a designer and type cutter. His simple "old-style" type faces are still used extensively. He established an important business which was carried on in partnership with his son William, and after his death by the latter alone.

Casmurro (ka̤z.mör'rö), **Dom.** See **Dom Casmurro.**

Casorati (kä.sō.rä'tē), **Felice.** b. at Novara, Italy, Dec. 4, 1886—. Italian portrait painter, best known for his series of character studies of women. He studied art in his native country and exhibited at Venice in 1909. *The Heiress, Old Woman,* and *The Cousin* are among his better-known works.

Casoria (kä.sô'ryä). Commune in S Italy, in the *compartimento* (region) of Campania, in the province of Napoli, N of Naples. It is situated in the midst of formerly malaria-infested swampland, now reclaimed and a rich agricultural district. 20,241 (1936).

Caspar (kas'pa̤r). See also **Gaspar.**

Casper (kas'pėr). City in C Wyoming, county seat of Natrona County, on the North Platte River. The second largest city in the state, it is a trading, power, and supply center for a stock-raising, lumbering, and oil-producing area; it has a number of oil refineries. First settled as a fort on the Oregon Trail, it was incorporated in 1889. The early oil fields (among which was Teapot Dome) began producing in the 1890's, and new wells were still being drilled in the 1940's. 23,673 (1950).

Casper (käs'pėr), **Leopold.** b. at Berlin, May 31, 1859—. German urologist. He became privatdocent of neurology (1892) and professor (1904) at the University of Berlin, and later settled at New York. He devised an uretercystoscope, introduced a test for permeability of the kidney, and wrote a textbook on genito-urinary diseases, including functional sexual disorders in man (1906). His works include *Impotentia et sterilitas virilis* (1890), *Die diagnostische Bedeutung des Katheterismus der Ureteren* (1896), *Lehrbuch der Cystoskopie* (1898), *Über funktionelle Nierendiagnostik* (1900), and *Lehrbuch der Urologie* (1903); he was coeditor of *Monatsberichte über die Gesamtleistungen auf dem Gebiete der Krankheiten des Harn- und Sexualapparates* (1897–1900), *Monatsberichte für Urologie* (1901–07), *Functional Diagnosis of Kidney Disease with Especial Reference to Renal Surgery* (1903), and *Lehrbuch der urologischen Diagnostik* (1930).

Caspian Gates (kas'pi.a̤n). [Also: **Albanian Gates**; Latin, **Albaniae Pylae, Caspiae Portae** (or **Pylae**); **Caucasiae Portae.**] An old name of the defile of Derbent between the Caucasus and the Caspian Sea. It has long been a trade route.

Caspian Sea. [Also: in the Middle Ages, **Sea of Tabaristan**; Latin, **Mare Caspium, Mare Hyrcanium.**] Salt inland sea on the boundary between Europe and Asia, bounded by Russian territory on the W, N, and E, and by Iran on the S. It is the largest inland sea in the world. Its chief tributaries are the Volga, Ural, Kuma, Emba, Terek, Kura, Atrek, and Sefid. It has no outlet. There are steamship connections with the Trans-Caspian Railway. Length, 760 mi.; greatest width, ab. 270 mi.; area, 169,330 sq. mi.; elevation at surface, 85 ft. below sea level.

Casquets (kȧs′kẹts). See **Caskets.**

Cass (kas), **Lewis.** b. at Exeter, N.H., Oct. 9, 1782; d. June 17, 1866. American soldier, diplomat, and politician. He attended Exeter Academy, was a teacher (1799) at Wilmington, Del., and then migrated to the West. He set up a law practice (1802) at Marietta, Ohio, moved to Zanesville, and became (1806) a member of the state legislature, where his opposition to the Western plans of Aaron Burr drew the attention of Jefferson, who appointed Cass marshal for Ohio. He rendered notable service in the War of 1812 and was appointed (1813) governor of the Michigan Territory; holding the post until 1831, he performed his duties efficiently, and was responsible for improving relations with the Indian tribes in his area. He entered Jackson's cabinet as secretary of war, and upon leaving that post (1836) became minister to France. He became (1845) a member of the U.S. Senate from Michigan, and in 1848 was the Democratic nominee for the presidency. In 1857 he became secretary of state under Buchanan, resigning (Dec. 12, 1860) in opposition to the administration's refusal to reinforce the forts at Charleston, S.C. During the Civil War he was a supporter of the Union cause. He was the author of several articles on military, Western, and Indian themes, and wrote *France, its King, Court, and Government By an American* (1840).

Cassagnac (kȧ.sȧ.nyȧk). See **Granier de Cassagnac.**

Cassai (kạ.sī′). See **Kasai.**

Cassander (kạ.san′dėr). b. c354 B.C.; d. 297 B.C. King of Macedonia; son of Antipater. He waged war with Alexander's successors, especially Polyperchon, after 319, and received Macedonia and Greece after the battle of Ipsus, in 301. In 316 he had conquered and killed Alexander's mother Olympias and in 311 he murdered Roxana and her son; he married Thessalonica, a sister of Alexander.

Cassandra (kạ.san′drạ). See also **Kassandra.**

Cassandra. [Also, **Alexandra.**] In Greek legend, a Trojan princess; daughter of Priam and Hecuba. Apollo taught her the gift of prophecy, but when she refused his advances he cursed her by commanding that, though her divinations should always be true, they should never be believed. In vain did she thereafter warn her countrymen of various impending disasters, including the coming of the wooden horse. After the Trojan War she was made a slave by Agamemnon, and was later killed by Clytemnestra. Her character, with its tragic element of impotent wisdom, has been variously introduced into later literature.

Cassandra. Narrative poem (1595) dealing with Priam's unfortunate daughter, Cassandra, who had the gift of prophecy but was punished by never being believed. The author, Richard Barnfield, wrote an ode, "As it fell upon a day," and a sonnet, "If music and sweet poetry agree," of such high quality that they were long thought to be by Shakespeare.

Cassandra. Poem by Edwin Arlington Robinson, included in *The Man Against the Sky* (1916). It is a reproach to America for its gross materialism.

Cassandra Southwick (south′wik). Narrative poem by John Greenleaf Whittier. It deals with the persecution, in 1658, of Lawrence Southwick of Salem, and of his young daughter, Cassandra, who was fined for not attending church. Unable to pay the fine, she was ordered, with her brother, to be sold "to any of the English nation of Virginia or Barbadoes," but the sentence could not be carried out because no captain could be persuaded by threats or rewards to carry her to the West Indies. The poem is in 37 stanzas of four lines, and Cassandra is the speaker. The theme of rebellion against unjust power, in church or government, was one that appealed strongly to Whittier.

Cassandre (kȧ.säṅdr). Romance by Gautier de Costes de la Calprenède.

Cassandre, Adolphe Mouron. b. at Kharkov, Russia, 1901—. French poster artist. The field of poster art early attracted him; his first poster was published in 1922, and by 1923 he was famous in that field. His designs advertising furniture, sports, festivals, publications, wines, travel, and many other products and services, have had an appreciable effect upon the modern evolution of the graphic arts.

Cassandreia (kas.ạn.drī′ạ). See **Potidaea.**

Cassano all'Ionio (käs.sä′nō äl.lyô′nyō). [Also: **Cassano, Casano al Ionio.**] Town and commune in S Italy, in the *compartimento* (region) of Calabria, in the province of Cosenza, situated on the Ionio River, near the Gulf of Tarento, N of Cosenza. It is a market town for grain, wine, and oil. The 9th-century cathedral was rebuilt in 1491, 1651, and 1795. Nearby are sulfurous springs which have been known since ancient times. Pop. of commune, 11,428 (1936); of town, 7,689 (1936).

Cassano d'Adda (däd′dä). Town and commune in NW Italy, in the *compartimento* (region) of Lombardy, in the province of Milano, situated on the Adda River, ab. 15 mi. NE of Milan. The town has a large linen and hemp factory. The Ghibellines under Ezzelino da Romano were defeated here by the Guelphs in 1259. On Aug. 16, 1705, the French under Vendôme defeated the Austrians under Prince Eugene of Savoy; on April 27, 1799, the Austrians and Russians under Suvarov defeated the French under Moreau. Pop. of commune, 8,964 (1936); of town, 4,404 (1936).

Cassatt (kạ.sat′), **Alexander Johnston.** b. at Pittsburgh, Pa., Dec. 8, 1839; d. Dec. 28, 1906. American civil engineer, president (1899–1906) of the Pennsylvania Railroad system; brother of Mary Cassatt (1845–1926). After studying at Pittsburgh and in Europe, he graduated (1859) from Rensselaer Polytechnic Institute and entered civil engineering. He joined the Pennsylvania Railroad in 1861, and by 1870 was its general superintendent, pioneering in the use of the air brake. He became (1873) general manager of the Pennsylvania lines east of Pittsburgh and Erie, and in the following year was elected third vice-president in charge of transportation and traffic. He became (1880) first vice-president, and retired (1882) from active service. He was recalled (1899) as president of the railroad. Perhaps his greatest achievement during his years in this post was the organization of a "community of interest" among various competing railroads, enabling them to refuse the rebates that had long been demanded by large industrial combinations. He was also influential in arousing opinion to support the passage (1903) of the Elkins Anti-Rebate law. He conceived and initiated the construction of the Pennsylvania Terminal at New York.

Cassatt, Mary. b. at Allegheny City, Pa., May 22, 1845; d. at Mesnil-Théribus-dans-l'Oise, France, June 14, 1926. American artist, noted for her association with the French Impressionist school of painters, with whom she exhibited her work from 1879 to 1886; sister of Alexander Johnston Cassatt. She received her art education in Italy, Spain, and Holland, and after settling (1874) at Paris, became a friend and disciple of Degas, who invited her to display her work with the Impressionists. She gave her first independent show in 1893, and was among the women artists who were commissioned to decorate the Woman's Building at the Chicago Exposition. She was also noted as an etcher. Her paintings, which typically include mothers and babies as their subjects, are in many private collections and museums.

Casse (käs), **Pierre Emmanuel Albert,** Baron **du.** See **Du Casse, Pierre Emmanuel Albert,** Baron.

Cassel (käs′ẹl). See also **Kassel.**

Cassel (kȧ.sel). [Latin, **Castellum Morinorum.**] Town in N France, in the department of Nord, ab. 20 mi. S of Dunkerque. 2,429 (1946).

Cassel, Battle of. Victory gained (1071) at Cassel, France, by Robert the Friesian over Philip I of France.

Cassel, Battle of. Victory gained (1328) at Cassel, France, by Philip VI of France over the Flemings.

Cassel, Battle of. Victory gained (1677) at Cassel, France, by the French over William of Orange (later William III of England).

Cassel (kas′ẹl), Sir **Ernest Joseph.** b. at Cologne, Germany, March 3, 1852; d. Sept. 21, 1921. English philanthropist. He was educated in his native city, but emigrated to London, where he founded a successful banking establishment. He rendered important aid to industrial enterprise in Sweden, and contributed large sums for charitable purposes in England. He was knighted in 1899 for his services in connection with Egypt.

Cassel (käs′sẹl), **Gustav.** [Full name, **Karl Gustav Cassel.**] b. at Stockholm, Oct. 20, 1866; d. at Jönköping, Sweden, Jan. 15, 1945. Swedish economist, an authority on international monetary problems. He served (1904 *et seq.*) at the University of Stockholm. In 1928 he lectured in the U.S. Author of *The Nature and Necessity of Interest* (1903), *The World's Monetary Problems* (1921), *The Theory of Social Economy* (1918; Eng. trans., 1923), and *The Downfall of the Gold Standard* (1936).

Cassell (kas′ẹl), **John.** b. at Manchester, England, 1817; d. at Regent's Park, London, April 2, 1865. English temperance advocate, merchant, author, and publisher. He went to London in 1836 as a carpenter, began a tea and coffee business in 1847, and undertook the publishing of educational works in 1850 with *The Working Man's Friend and Family Instructor*. This was followed by *Cassell's Popular Educator* and *Cassell's Magazine* (1852), *Cassell's Family Paper* (1853), *The Freeholder*, supporting a free land movement, *The Pathway*, a religious journal, and *The Quiver* (1861). In addition to these periodicals, he also published, in book form or as serials, such works as *Don Quixote, Pilgrim's Progress, Robinson Crusoe*, and *Gulliver's Travels*, as well as dictionaries, histories, and other works, all designed for the education and improvement of working people. In 1859 he founded the publishing firm that was to become the famous London house of Cassell and Company.

Casse-Noisette (käs.nwȧ.zet). Original title in French of the **Nutcracker Suite.**

Cassia gens (kash′i.ạ jenz). In ancient Rome, a clan or house, originally patrician, afterward plebeian. Its family names under the republic were Longinus, Hemina, Parmensis, Ravilla, Sabaco, Varus, and Viscellinus.

Cassianos Bassos (kas.i.ā′nọs bas′ọs). fl. late 6th century A.D. Byzantine compiler of writings on husbandry His work was the basis of the compilation made (c950) by order of the emperor Constantine VII Porphyrogenitus

Cassianus (kas.i.ā′nus), **Johannes.** [Also: **Cassian** (kash′ạn); called **Johannes Massiliensis,** meaning "John of Massilia" (Marseilles), and **Johannes Eremita,** meaning "John the Eremite."] b. c360 A.D.; d. after 433. A recluse and Semi-Pelagian theologian. He founded the monastery of Saint Victor, near Marseilles, and was a diligent promoter of monasticism.

Cassian Way (kash′ạn). See **Via Cassia.**

Cassiar Mountains (kash′i.ạr). Mountains in W Canada, in S Yukon territory, located W of the Liard River and N of the Alaska Highway. They are a rugged wilderness mountain area, with forest in the lower valleys. Earlier maps show the Cassiar Mountains where the present-day Stikine Mountains are named. The latest maps officially issued show the Cassiar Mountains in Yukon territory. Peak elevation, ab. 8,500 ft.

Cassidy (kas′i.di), **Hopalong.** See under **Boyd, William.**

Cassilis Engagement (kạ.sil′is), **The.** Satirical play (1905) by St. John Hankin. It is considered his best play, and was one of his most popular, being successful at London, Liverpool, Manchester, and Glasgow. It was published with "The Return of the Prodigal," and "The Charity That Began at Home," under the cynical title *Three Plays with Happy Endings* (1907). All Hankin's work illustrates his conviction that drama should "represent life, not argue about it."

Cassin (kas′in), **John.** b. in Upper Providence township, Pa., Sept. 6, 1813; d. Jan. 10, 1869. American ornithologist. He arranged and identified the collection of Thomas B. Wilson containing ab. 26,000 specimen of birds and published papers based upon West African bird collections made by Du Chaillu. Contributor to *Narrative of the Expedition to the Southern Hemisphere*, Vol. II; author of *Illustrations of the Birds of California, Texas, Onrego, British and Russian America* (1856) and other works.

Cassin (kȧ.saṅ), **René.** b. at Bayonne, France, Oct. 5, 1887—. French political leader and government official, vice-president and permanent head (1944 *et seq.*) of the Conseil d'État, the highest administrative tribunal in France. He joined (1940) the Free French movement, was national commissioner for justice and education (1941–43) in the French national council, and served as a delegate (1946) to the United Nations General Assembly. He was an expert (1922–23) at the International Labor Organization and a French delegate (1924–38) to the League of Nations.

Cassini (kạ.sē′nē; French, kȧ.sē.nē), **Jacques.** b. at Paris, Feb. 18, 1677; d. at Thury, France, April 16, 1756. French astronomer; son of Jean Dominique Cassini and father of César François Cassini de Thury. He succeeded his father as director of the observatory at Paris in 1712. He is chiefly known for his work in relation to the determination of the figure of the earth.

Cassini, Jacques Dominique, Comte **de.** b. at Paris, June 30, 1748; d. at Thury, France, Oct. 18, 1845. French astronomer; son of César François Cassini de Thury. He succeeded his father as director of the observatory at Paris in 1784, and resigned in 1793. He completed (1793) his father's map of France.

Cassini, Jean Dominique. b. at Perinaldo, near Nice, France, June 8, 1625; d. at Paris, Sept. 14, 1712. French astronomer, director of the observatory at Paris; father of Jacques Cassini. He discovered four satellites of Saturn (1671, 1672, and two in 1684).

Cassini de Thury (dẹ tü.rē), **César François.** b. at Paris, June 17, 1714; d. Sept. 4, 1784. French astronomer; son of Jacques Cassini and father of Jacques Dominique, Comte de Cassini. He succeeded his father as director of the observatory at Paris in 1756. He undertook a topographical map of France, which was completed by his son.

Cassino (käs.sē′nō). [Former name, **San Germano;** Latin, **Casinum.**] Town and commune in C Italy, in the *compartimento* (region) of Latium in the province of Frosinone, situated in a well-cultivated district near the Rapido River, between Rome and Naples. Ruins from ancient times are found. The Church of Santa Teresa dates from the 8th century. On a hill above the town is the monastery of Monte Cassino, until 1870 called San Germano, founded by the Benedictine order and one of the most famous monasteries in Italy. In 1230, the peace was signed here between Emperor Frederick II and Pope Gregory IX; in 1815, the Neapolitans under Murat were defeated here by the Austrians. In World War II, it was a key position of the German army barring access to Rome and central Italy to the advancing Allied armies; the battle for the possession of the town started on Feb. 1, 1944, lasting until May 17, when the town was captured; most of the buildings including the monastery were laid in ruins. Reconstruction of the latter according to the old plans was begun after the war. Pop. of commune, 20,064 (1936); of town, 15,000 (est. 1947).

Cassio (kash′i.ō), **Michael.** Lieutenant of Othello in Shakespeare's tragedy *Othello*, A somewhat weak but honorable man, he becomes, by the devices of Iago, the object of Othello's jealousy.

Cassiodorus (kas″i.ọ.dō′rus), **Flavius Magnus Aurelius.** b. at Scyllaceum, in southern Italy, c490; d. at Viviers, in Calabria, c583. Italian statesman and historian. He was an administrative officer under Theodoric the Great and his successors, and became a monk at Viviers (c538). His state papers and works were published (1679) by Garet. He founded a monastery in which the monks occupied themselves with copying and translating original documents. He collected, under the title *Variae epistolae*, many contemporary state papers, and was the author also of a history of the Goths, only an abridgment of which is preserved.

Cassiopeia (kas″i.ọ.pē′ạ) or **Cassiepeia** (kas″i.ẹ-). In classical mythology, the wife of Cepheus, an Ethiopian king, and mother of Andromeda. She was transferred to the heavens as a constellation.

Cassiopeia or **Cassiepeia.** A circumpolar constellation, supposed to represent the wife of Cepheus seated in a chair and holding up both arms. It contains 30 stars brighter than the sixth magnitude, and is always found opposite the Great Bear on the other side of the pole-star In this constellation appeared in 1572 a temporary star brighter than Venus at its brightest.

Cassique of Accabee and Other Pieces (ka̧.sēk′; ak′-a̧.bē), **The.** Volume (1849) of poetry by William Gilmore Simms, "the American Scott." It contains an Indian narrative poem, some nature poetry, and other verse, much of which shows the influence of Byron and of William Cullen Bryant.

Cassique of Kiawah (kī′a̧.wa̧), **The.** Romance by William Gilmore Simms, published in 1859. It has as background Charleston of 1684.

Cassiquiare (kä.sē.kyä′rā) or **Cassiquiari** (-rē). See **Casiquiare.**

Cassirer (kä.sē′rėr), **Ernst.** b. at Breslau, Germany (now in Poland), July 28, 1874; d. at New York, April 13, 1945. German philosopher, one of the leaders of the so-called Marburg school of neo-Kantian philosophy. Interested in the study of knowledge and perception, he explored man's ability to formulate symbols and ideas. He served (1919 *et seq.*) as a professor at the universities of Hamburg, Oxford, Göteborg, Yale, and Columbia. Author of *Substanzbegriff und Funktionsbegriff* (1910; Eng. trans., 1923), *Freiheit und Form* (1916), *Kants Leben und Lehre* (1918), *Philosophie der symbolischen Formen* (1923 *et seq.*), *Sprache und Mythos* (1925; Eng. trans., 1946), *Goethe und die geschichtliche Welt* (1932), *Descartes* (1939), *Zur Logik der Kulturwissenschaften* (1942), *An Essay on Man* (1944), and *The Myth of the State* (1946). He edited (with others) Kant's works.

Cassiterides (kas.i.ter′i.dēz), In ancient geography, the "tin islands," generally identified with the Scilly Isles, off Cornwall, England, though by some thought to have been the islands near Vigo in Spain.

Cassius (kash′us, kash′i.us), **Dio** (or **Dion**). See **Dio** (or **Dion**) **Cassius.**

Cassius Dionysius (dī.o̧.nish′us). fl. c88 B.C. Greek writer on botany and materia medica. His works include a translation from Punic to Greek of the Carthaginian Mago's great treatise on agriculture (to which he added many Greek examples), a work on roots, and a reported illustrated pharmacopoeia.

Cassius Longinus (lon.jī′nus), **Gaius.** d. near Philippi, Macedonia, 42 B.C. Roman general and politician, involved in the assassination of Julius Caesar. He was distinguished in the Parthian war of the period 53–51. A participant in the battle of Pharsala, he was subsequently pardoned by Caesar. Nevertheless, in 44 B.C. he was one of the leading conspirators against Caesar. A commander in Syria and Asia (44–42), he was defeated by Antony at Philippi in 42 and killed himself.

Cassius Longinus, Quintus. d. 45 B.C. Roman politician. Although he was accused of corruption during his tenure of the quaestorship in Spain in 54 B.C., he became a tribune, and with his fellow in that office, Mark Antony, in 49 B.C. vetoed a decision of the senate to order Julius Caesar to relinquish command of his army. When the senate nevertheless persisted in its purpose, Cassius and Antony joined Caesar, who thereupon crossed the Rubicon and began the campaign which made him master of Rome. In 47 B.C. Cassius was given a command in Spain, and presently was faced with a rebellion which he was unable to handle, so that Caesar had to come to his rescue.

Cassius Parmensis (pär.men′sis), **Gaius.** b. at Parma, Italy (whence his surname); executed at Athens, by order of Augustus, c30 B.C. Roman poet, one of the conspirators against Julius Caesar.

Cassius Viscellinus (vis.ȩ.lī′nus), **Spurius.** d. c485 B.C. Roman reformer. There is little doubt that Spurius Cassius Viscellinus was a historic person, though so much legend has gathered about him as to give him an almost mythical character. He appears to have held the consulship several times, and is named as the negotiator, in 493 B.C., of treaties between Rome and the cities of Latium. Trouble between the Roman patricians and the lower orders had long been festering because of the continual arrogation of public lands by the patricians. Cassius, while consul in 486 B.C., proposed a redistribution of lands, but the patricians accused him of courting popular support with the object of becoming king, and brought about his death in the following year.

Cassivellaunus (kas″i.vȩ.lô′nus). fl. 54 B.C. British prince, ruler of the Catuvellauni (occupying, approximately, modern Hertfordshire, Buckinghamshire, and Berkshire). A local conqueror and leading opponent of the Romans, he was conquered by Caesar's forces in 54 B.C.

Casson (kȧ.sôn), **François Dollier de.** See **Dollier de Casson, François.**

Castagna (käs.tä′nyä), **Giambattista.** Original name of Pope **Urban VII.**

Castagnette (kȧs.tȧ.nyet), **Captain.** Novel by Ernest L'Epine (1862), the central character of which is remarkable for having an artificial stomach.

Castagno (käs.tä′nyō), **Andrea del.** b. near Florence, c1390 or (according to Vasari) 1423; d. of the plague at Florence, Aug. 19, 1457. Florentine painter. In 1454 he was called to Rome by Pope Nicholas V to take part in the decoration of the official rooms of the Vatican. He was an outstanding draftsman, and his work is characterized by a certain monumentality of style. One of his best-known frescoes is an equestrian portrait of Niccolò da Tolentino, in the cathedral of Florence.

Castaigne (käs.teny′), **André.** b. at Angoulême, France, 1861—. French painter and illustrator; a pupil of Gérôme at Paris. He won many prizes there and was made a member of the Legion of Honor in 1899. He was also active in the U.S. Two of his best-known works are *Alexander in the Temple at Memphis* and *Portrait of Pope Leo XIII.*

Castaldi (käs.täl′dē), **Pamfilo.** b. at Feltre, Italy, c1398; d. c1490. Italian printer and physician. He is supposed, probably erroneously, by some Italians to have been the inventor of printing.

Castalia (kas.tā′li.a̧, -tāl′ya̧). Ancient fountain on the slope of Mount Parnassus, Greece, sacred to the Muses and Apollo.

Castalion (kas.tāl′yo̧n), **Sébastien.** [Also: **Castellio, Castellion;** Latinized forms of **Châtillon** or **Châteillon.**] b. 1515; d. 1563. French Protestant theologian. He was associated for some years with Calvin, but parted with him on doctrinal matters. Castalion in 1551 published a Latin translation of the Bible, with a preface in which he took a stand for toleration in religion, and it is supposed that he was the author of a book dealing with the execution of Servetus, of a similar tenor. For some years he held a professorial chair in Greek literature at the University of Basel.

Castañeda de Naçera (käs.tä.nyā′ᴛʜä dā nä.thä′rä), **Pedro de.** fl. in the middle of the 16th century. Spanish soldier with Coronado on the expedition of 1540–42 into what is now New Mexico, Texas, and Kansas, and its chief historian. He was a painstaking and critical recorder, though he seems to have written without official order or sanction. His narrative is entitled *Relacion de la Jornada de Cibola conquesta por Pedro de Castañeda de Naçera. Donde se trata de todos aquellos poblados y ritos, y costumbres, la qual fue el Año de 1540.* A manuscript, which is frequently alluded to as the "original," is owned by the New York Public Library, but since it ends with the words: "finished copying Saturday the 26th of October 1596 in Seville," there must have been another earlier manuscript.

Castanheda (kȧsh.ta̧.nyā′da̧), **Fernão Lopes de.** b. at Santarém, Portugal, c1500; d. at Coimbra, Portugal, March 23, 1559. Portuguese historian. In 1528 he went with his father to India, where he resided for 20 years. His *História do descobrimento e conquista da Índia pelos Portugueses* appeared in parts from 1551 to 1561 (incomplete).

Castaños (käs.tä′nyōs), **Francisco Javier de.** [Title, Duke of **Bailén.**] b. April 22, 1756; d. at Madrid, Sept. 24, 1852. Spanish general in the Peninsular War. He defeated the French at Bailén (July, 1808), was defeated by them at Tudela (November, 1808), and served with distinction under Wellington at Vitoria (1813). He became the guardian of Queen Isabella in 1843.

Castara (kas.tãr′a̧). Collection of poems in praise of Lucy Herbert, issued anonymously by William Habington in 1634. He had married Lucy sometime between 1630 and 1633. A subsequent edition (1640) also included some religious poems.

Castaway, The. Lyric by William Cowper. It was written in 1799, the last year of his life, and was his last poem. The lyric is intensely personal and reflects the deep despair of which Cowper was a victim the greater part of his unhappy life. The basis of the poem derives from *A Voyage Round the World* (1748) by the English admiral George Anson (1697–1762), who actually went through the experience so vividly described in the lyric. Cowper, who felt that he was eternally damned, regarded himself as a "castaway" in the sense that he was forgotten by God.

Caste. Comedy (1867) by T. W. Robertson.

Casteggio (käs.ted′jō). Village in N Italy, in the *compartimento* (region) of Lombardy, in the province of Pavia, ab. 12 mi. S of Pavia. Near here were fought the two battles of Montebello (1800 and 1859).

Castelar y Ripoll (käs.tā.lär′ ē rē.pōly″), **Emilio.** b. at Cádiz, Spain, Sept. 8, 1832; d. at San Pedro de Pinatar, Murcia, Spain, May 25, 1899. Spanish statesman, orator, and author. He fled from Spain after the rising of 1866, returned and became a republican leader in 1868, and was minister of foreign affairs in 1873, and president of the executive (September, 1873–January, 1874). His works include *La Civilización en los cinco primeros siglos del cristianismo* (1865), *Cuestiones políticas* (1870), *Discursos parlamentarios* (1871), and *Historia del movimiento republicano* (1875).

Castelbuono (käs.tel″bwô′nō). Town and commune in SW Italy, on the island of Sicily, situated near the N shore of Sicily, between Palermo and Messina. It is an agricultural market town, and has a medieval castle. Pop. of commune, 11,155 (1936); of town, 11,131 (1936).

Castel del Monte (käs.tel′ del mōn′tā). Town in C Italy, in the *compartimento* (region) of Abruzzi e Molise, in the province of L'Aquila, ab. 19 mi. E of L'Aquila. It contains a hunting castle of Emperor Frederick II, built in the 13th century, one of the most splendid medieval monuments in Italy. In 1277, Charles of Anjou imprisoned here the sons and partisans of Manfred of Hohenstaufen. 2,714 (1936).

Castelfidardo (käs.tel.fē.där′dō). Village in C Italy, in the *compartimento* (region) of Marches, in the province of Ancona, ab. 10 mi. S of Ancona. Near here, on Sept. 18, 1860, the Italians under Enrico Cialdini defeated the papal troops under the French general Lamoricière.

Castelfiorentino (käs.tel″fyō.ren.tē′nō). Town and commune in C Italy, in the *compartimento* (region) of Tuscany, in the province of Firenze, situated on the Elsa River, SW of Florence. It is an agricultural commune, and there are chemical and metallurgical manufactures, distilleries, and cement works. The town suffered heavily during World War II. Pop. of commune, 13,056 (1936); of town, 5,287 (1936).

Castelforte (käs.tel″fôr′tā). Town and commune in C Italy, in the *compartimento* (region) of Latium, in the province of Littoria, situated near the mouth of the Gargliano River, between Rome and Naples. Nearby are sulfur and iodine thermal springs, which are visited by people suffering from nervous and rheumatic diseases. Pop. of commune, 10,750 (1936); of town, 2,461 (1936).

Castelfranco Emilia (käs.tel″fräng′kō ā.mē′lyä). [Also, **Castelfranco dell' Emilia** (del.lā.mē′lyä).] Town and commune in N Italy, in the *compartimento* (region) of Emilia-Romagna, in the province of Modena, between Modena and Bologna. The town has dairies, macaroni and sausage manufactures, and other agricultural industries, and is a marketing center for a district producing grain, wine, hemp, and sugar beets. Pop. of commune, 19,360 (1936); of town, 4,980 (1936).

Castelfranco Veneto (ve′nā.tō). Town and commune in NE Italy, in the *compartimento* (region) of Veneto, in the province of Treviso, situated on the Musone River between Venice and Trent. The town has cattle markets and important agricultural fairs, and manufactures railroad materials and furniture. Inside the complex of the medieval castle wall is the cathedral, erected in the 18th century; it contains murals by Paolo Veronese and a painting by Giorgione, whose home was here. The *Duomo* (cathedral), the castle, and the town walls were undamaged in World War II. Pop. of commune, 17,349 (1936); of town, 6,914 (1936).

Castelfuerte (käs.tel.fwer′tā), Marqués **de.** Title of **Armendariz, José de.**

Castel Gandolfo (käs.tel′ gän.dôl′fō). Town and commune in C Italy, in the *compartimento* (region) of Latium, in the province of Roma, situated on Lake Albano, SE of Rome. It is the summer residence of the Pope. The papal palace, supposed to be on the site of an ancient villa of Domitian, was mainly built under popes Urban VIII and Alexander VII; the final purchase was made by Pope Clement VIII in 1596. The church was built according to plans by Bernini, in 1661. Under the terms of the Lateran pact of 1929, the castle is considered pontifical property and as such enjoys the rights of exterritoriality. The town suffered damage during World War II, but the papal palace was undamaged. Pop. of commune, 2,955 (1936); of town, 1,862 (1936).

Castell (kàs′tel), **Edmund.** b. at East Hatley, Cambridgeshire, England, 1606; d. at Higham Gobion, Bedfordshire, England, 1685. English Orientalist, canon of Canterbury and professor of Arabic at Cambridge. His chief work is *Lexicon heptaglotton, Hebraicum, Chaldaicum, Syriacum, Samaritanum, Aethiopicum, Arabicum conjunctim et Persicum separatim* (1669).

Castellammare del Golfo (käs.tel.läm.mä′rā del gōl′fō). [Also, **Castellammare.**] Town and commune in SW Italy, on the island of Sicily, in the province of Trapani, situated on the Gulf of Castellammare, ab. 27 mi. SW of Palermo. It was in ancient times the seaport of Segesta. The port is now only of local importance. Pop. of commune, 18,032 (1936); of town, 16,830 (1936).

Castellammare di Stabia (dē stä′byä). [Also: **Castellammare**; ancient name, **Stabiae.**] City and commune in S Italy, in the *compartimento* (region) of Campania, in the province of Napoli, situated on the Bay of Naples, ab. 15 mi. SE of Naples, near the site of the ancient Stabiae. It is a seaport and a popular health resort, with numerous mineral springs. It has a number of agricultural industries (producing cheese, oil, canned fruits and vegetables, etc.); manufactures include railroad cars, cement, and paperware. The docks and naval construction yards, founded in 1783 by one of the Bourbon kings of Naples, are among the oldest in Italy. There is a medieval castle. Pop. of commune, 46,469 (1936); of city, 37,539 (1936).

Castellana (käs.tel.lä′nä). Town and commune in SE Italy, in the *compartimento* (region) of Apulia, in the province of Bari, SE of Bari: wine cellars and oil mills. Pop. of commune, 12,488 (1936); of town, 9,944 (1936).

Castellaneta (käs.tel.lä.nā′tä). Town and commune in SE Italy, in the *compartimento* (region) of Apulia, in the province of Taranto, NW of Taranto. It is almost entirely surrounded by a deep gorge. The cathedral dates from the 12th and 15th centuries. Pop. of commune, 10,424 (1936); of town, 8,993 (1936).

Castellani (käs.tel.lä′nē), **Aldo.** b. at Florence, Sept. 8, 1878—. Italian physician, an eminent specialist on tropical diseases. While studying with W. Kruse at Bonn, Germany, he discovered (1902) the so-called absorption reaction used in the diagnosis of bacterial diseases. He isolated new strains of fungi as causes of dermatoses and, under British auspices, contributed to the etiology of African sleeping sickness. He found (1903) the Trypanosoma gambiense (later called Trypanosoma castellani) in the blood of natives and in the spinal fluid of patients suffering from sleeping sickness. At the Ceylon medical school he discovered (1905) that Spirochaeta pertenue was the cause of frambesia, a common disease in Ceylon, and isolated (1906) the cause of spirochetal hemorrhagic bronchitis. He served as lecturer (1919) at the School of Tropical Medicine at London and as lecturer (1924–30) at Tulane University, New Orleans. In 1931 he founded the Tropical Institute at Rome. Author of *On the Discovery of a Species of Trypanosoma in the Cerebrospinal Fluid of Cases of Sleeping Sickness* (1903), *On the Presence of Spirochaetes in Two Cases of Ulcerated Parangi (Yaws, framboesia tropica)* (1905), *Observations on the Fungi Found in Tropical Bronchomycosis* (1912), *Note on Typhoid-paratyphoid Vaccination with Mixed Vaccines* (1914), *Note on the Internal Treatment of Yaws* (1915), *Fungi and Fungous Diseases* (1918), and *Climate and Acclimatization*

(1930); coauthor (with Albert John Chalmers) of *Manual of Tropical Medicine* (1910).

Castellanos (käs.tä.lyä′nōs), **Juan de.** b. at Seville, Spain, early in the 16th century; d. 1606. Spanish curate and poet. He passed most of his life at Tunja in New Granada (now in Colombia). He wrote *Elegías de varones ilustres de las Indias,* a versified account of the exploits of early Spanish conquerors in America. It has considerable poetical and historical value. (Part I, Madrid, 1589; reprinted with parts II and III in the *Biblioteca de Autores Españoles,* Madrid, 1847–50.)

Castell-dos-Rios (käs.tely′.dōs.rē′ōs), Marquis of. See **Oms de Santa Pau, Manuel.**

Castell-Florit (käs.tely′.flō.rēt′), Marquis of. Title of **Dulce y Garay, Domingo.**

Castelli (käs.tel′lē), **Antonino Paternò.** See **San Giuliano,** Marchese **di.**

Castelli (käs.tel′ē), **Ignaz Franz.** b. at Vienna, March 6, 1781; d. there, Feb. 5, 1862. Austrian dramatist, poet, and journalist.

Castello (käs.tel′lō), **Adrian de.** See **Adrian de Castello.**

Castello or **Castelli** (käs.tel′lē), **Bernardo.** b. near Genoa, Italy, 1557; d. 1629. Italian painter; father of Valerio Castello. A friend of Torquato Tasso, he executed designs for that author's *Gerusalemme Liberata* (*Jerusalem Delivered*).

Castello, Giovanni Battista. [Surnamed **Il Bergamasco.**] b. at Bergamo, Italy, c1500; d. at Madrid, c1569. Italian historical painter and architect. Called to Spain by Philip II, he worked at Madrid, where he participated in the erection of the Escorial.

Castello, Guido di. Original name of Pope **Celestine II.**

Castello, Lago di. An Italian name of **Albano, Lake.**

Castello or **Castelli, Valerio.** b. at Genoa, Italy, 1625; d. there, 1659. Italian painter, particularly of battle scenes; son of Bernardo Castello. His *The Rape of the Sabines* is in the Palazzo Brignole at Genoa.

Castell of Pleasure, The. Dream poem by William Neville. It was printed in 1518 by Hary Pepwell, and later by Wynkyn de Worde. A quarto copy is in the British Museum. The abstract characters are Desire and Beauty, to whom Desire makes passionate love in the Garden of Affection, and Pity and Disdain, who become involved in a lively quarrel.

Castellón (käs.tā.yōn′), **Francisco.** b. c1815; d. Sept. 2, 1855. Nicaraguan revolutionist. In 1853 he headed a revolt of the liberal party at León, was defeated, and fled to Honduras, but returned in June, 1854, assumed the title of "provisional director," and for a time restricted the government of President Chamorro to the city of Granada. It was by his invitation that William Walker came from the U.S. ostensibly to aid the liberals. In the midst of these struggles Castellón died of cholera.

Castellón de la Plana (käs.tā.lyōn′ dā lä plä′nä). [Also, **Castellón.**] Province in E Spain, bounded on the NW and N by Teruel and Tarragona, on the E by the Mediterranean Sea, and on the S by Valencia: part of the region of Valencia. The surface is mountainous, the climate Mediterranean in character. Wine and citrus fruits are produced; there are some industries. Capital, Castellón de la Plana; area, 2,579 sq. mi.; pop. 351,159 (1950).

Castellón de la Plana. City in NE Spain, the capital of the province of Castellón de la Plana, situated near the Mediterranean Sea, ab. 40 mi. NE of Valencia. A seaport, it exports agricultural products, particularly citrus fruits; there are paper, porcelain, woolen, silk, and hemp manufactures and fisheries. The city has a technical school, theater, museum, and library. It was recaptured from the Moors by James I of Aragon in 1233, and developed as a manufacturing center in the 19th century. 56,734 (1950).

Castellum Ante Nacum (kas.tel′um an′tẹ nā′kum). A Latin name of **Andernach.**

Castellum Menapiorum (men″ạ.pī.ō′rum). A Latin name of **Kassel.**

Castellum Morinorum (mōr.i.nō′rum). Latin name of **Cassel,** France.

Castelmassa (käs.tel″mäs′sä). Town and commune in NE Italy, in the *compartimento* (region) of Veneto, in the province of Rovigo. It consists of the former communities of Castelnovo Bariano and Massa Superiore. The commune is known for silkworm culture and the largest enterprise in Italy for the manufacture of glucose and starches. Pop. of commune, 10,475 (1936); of town, 1,396 (1936).

Castel Moron (kås.tel mô.rôṅ), **Henri François Xavier de Belsunce de.** See **Belsunce de Castel Moron, Henri François Xavier de.**

Castelnau (kås.tel.nō), **Édouard,** Vicomte **de Curières de.** [Full name, **Noël Marie Joseph Édouard,** Vicomte **de Curières de Castelnau.**] b. at Saint-Affrique, Aveyron, France, Dec. 24, 1851; d. at Montastruc-la-Conseillère, Haute-Garonne, France, March 19, 1944. French army officer, best known for his successful defense (1914) of Nancy, France, during World War I. He opposed the dominant French military doctrine of extreme offensive tactics. In 1915 he became chief of staff, and was an army commander in the period 1916–18. A member (1919–24) of the Chamber of Deputies, he was an active figure in Catholic and rightist politics, but finally withdrew from public life. During World War II he refused to support the Pétain government.

Castelnau, Francis, Comte **de.** b. at London, 1812; d. at Melbourne, Australia, Feb. 4, 1880. French traveler. He visited (1837–41) the Canadian lakes, the U.S., and Mexico. In 1843 he went to South America as chief of a government scientific expedition which explored central and western Brazil, Bolivia, Peru, and the Amazon. He returned to France in 1847, and was subsequently consul at Bahia, Cape of Good Hope, and Singapore, and consul general at Melbourne. He published *Expédition dans les parties centrales de l'Amérique du sud* (Paris, 6 vols., 1850–51; the last volume, on Bolivia, by his assistant, M. Weddell; an atlas and scientific supplements were published later).

Castelnau, Michel de. [Title, Sieur **de la Mauvissière.**] b. at Mauvissière, in Touraine, France, c1520; d. at Joinville, in Champagne, France, 1592. French diplomat. He was ambassador to England from 1574 to 1584 and the author of *Mémoires* (1621), covering the period 1559–70.

Castelnaudary (kås.tel.nō.då.rē). Town in S France, in the department of Aude, situated on the Canal du Midi W of Carcassonne. It is an important trading center for agricultural products, and is known for its cement works and flour mills. It figured in the Albigensian crusade in the 13th century, and was burned down by Edward the Black Prince in 1355. The Church of Saint-Michel dates from the 14th century. 8,073 (1946).

Castelnuovo (käs.tel″nwô′vō). Italian name of **Herceg-novi.**

Castelnuovo, Conte **di.** Title of **Carmagnola, Francesco Bussone da.**

Castelnuovo Berardenga (bā.rär.deng′gä). Town and commune in C Italy, in the *compartimento* (region) of Tuscany, in the province of Siena, E of Siena. It is known for its 14th-century castle; there are many castles and villas in the surrounding countryside. Pop. of commune, 10,358 (1936); of town, 1,132 (1936).

Castelo Branco (kạsh.tā′lö brung′kö). District in C Portugal, in the province of Beira Baixa. Capital, Castelo Branco; area, 2,588 sq. mi.; pop. 323,940 (1950).

Castelo Branco. Town and *concelho* (commune) in E central Portugal, in the province of Beira Baixa, the capital of the district of Castelo Branco, situated near the Spanish border, ab. 115 mi. NE of Lisbon: markets for wine, olive oil, and cork. The town is the seat of a bishopric, and has a cathedral and a ruined castle. The Carmona Dam is in the vicinity. Pop. of concelho, 58,700 (1940); of town, 12,763 (1940).

Castelo Branco, Camilo. b. at Lisbon, Portugal, March 16, 1825; committed suicide at San Miguel de Seide, Portugal, June 1, 1890. Portuguese novelist, poet, playwright, critic, historian, and vigorous polemist. The most prolific writer in Portugal, having published over 260 books during his lifetime, he wrote both romantic and realistic novels. His most popular novel was *Amor de perdição* (1862). Among his other well-known works are *Onde está a felicidade?* (1856), *Eusébio Macário* (1879), and *A brasileira de Prazins* (1882). His books reflect the mastery of an impressively rich vocabulary.

Castel San Giovanni (käs.tel′ sän jō.vän′nē). Town and commune in N Italy, in the *compartimento* (region) of Emilia-Romagna, in the province of Piacenza, situated on the Po River, W of Piacenza, in an agricultural district rich in grain, grapes, and cattle. There are numerous agricultural industries. Except for the organ of the parish church, no buildings of interest to tourists were damaged in World War II. Pop. of commune, 10,191 (1936); of town, 5,441 (1936).

Castel San Pietro dell'Emilia (käs.tel' säm pye'trō del.lā.mē'lyä). Town and commune in N Italy, in the *compartimento* (region) of Emilia-Romagna, in the province of Bologna, situated in the foothills of the Apennines, between Bologna and Imola: agricultural trade center. There are small oil wells in the vicinity. The churches of Santa Maria Maggiore and San Bartolommeo sustained slight damage in World War II. Pop. of commune, 15,263 (1936); of town, 4,135 (1936).

Castelsarrasin (kȧs.tel.sȧ.rȧ.zaṅ). Town in SW France, in the department of Tarn-et-Garonne, situated on the Canal Latéral and near the Garonne River, ab. 13 mi. W of Montauban. It has important cattle markets, flour mills, and a copper foundry and rolling mill. The Church of Saint Sauveur dates from the 13th century. 8,360 (1946).

Casteltermini (käs.tel''ter'mē.nē). Town and commune in S Italy, on the island of Sicily, in the province of Agrigento, situated in the interior of the island, N of Agrigento. It has agricultural markets; sulfur and salt mines are in the vicinity. 12,256 (1936).

Castelvetere (käs.tel''ve'tā.rā). Former name of **Caulonia.**

Castelvetrano (käs.tel.vā.trä'nō). Town and commune in S Italy, on the island of Sicily, in the province of Trapani, between Trapani and Agrigento. It is a railroad junction and an agricultural trade center, known particularly for Marsala wines, and has textile and furniture manufactures. There is a Romanesque cathedral and other medieval churches. The ruins of the ancient city of Selinus, now Selinunte, are nearby; eight Greek temples and other buildings have been excavated and partly restored. Buildings of interest to tourists were undamaged in World War II. Pop. of commune, 26,129 (1936); of town, 25,010 (1936).

Castiglione (käs.tē.lyō'nā), **Baldassare,** Conte. b. at Casantico, near Mantua, Italy, 1478; d. at Toledo, Spain, Feb. 7, 1529. Italian courtier, diplomat, and writer. As a youth he served at the ducal court of Milan, but when Duke Lodovico Sforza was taken captive by the French, he became attached to Guidobaldo Malatesta, duke of Urbino, who employed him in diplomatic business with Henry VII of England. Guidobaldo's successor, Francesco della Rovere, brought Castiglione to the favorable notice of Pope Clement VII, who sent him to Spain to arbitrate the contentions of the papacy and the emperor Charles V. Charles made much of him and he remained in Spain as a Spanish subject. When in 1527 the emperor's army led by the Constable Bourbon attacked Rome and made the Pope captive, Castiglione was suspected of having played a treacherous role, but it is considered equally likely that he was tricked by Charles. Castiglione wrote shrewd and graceful letters and distinguished poetry in Latin and Italian, but his most memorable work is *Il Cortegiano* (*The Courtier*), one of the great books of the Italian Renaissance, being the mirror of the ideal conduct of the nobility and knightly class who thronged the courts and served the royal and ducal sovereigns of that time.

Castiglione, Count **Carlo Ottavio.** b. at Milan, Italy, 1784; d. at Genoa, Italy, April 10, 1849. Italian philologist and antiquary. He was coeditor with Angelo Mai of the Gothic version of the Scriptures (1819–39).

Castiglione, Duc de. Title of **Augereau, Pierre François Charles.**

Castiglione, Giovanni Benedetto. [Called **Il Grechetto.**] b. at Genoa, Italy, 1616; d. at Mantua, Italy, 1670. Italian painter, particularly of animal life, and etcher. He served as court painter at Mantua. Among his works are several versions of Noah and the animals entering the Ark, some portraits, and many rural landscapes with animal figures.

Castiglione, Goffredo. Original name of Pope **Celestine IV.**

Castiglione del Lago (del lä'gō). Town and commune in C Italy, in the *compartimento* (region) of Umbria, in the province of Perugia, situated on the W shore of Lake Trasimeno, W of Perugia. It is an agricultural commune. The medieval castle and the Church of San Domenico were slightly damaged and the Church of the Magdalene was badly hit during World War II. Pop. of commune, 16,828 (1936); of town, 732 (1936).

Castiglione delle Stiviere (del'lā stē.vye'rā). Village in N Italy, in the *compartimento* (region) of Lombardy, in the province of Mantova, ab. 22 mi. NW of Mantua. Here, on Aug. 5, 1796, the French under Napoleon I defeated the Austrians under Wurmser; the French officer Pierre Augereau received afterward the title of Duc de Castiglione.

Castiglione Fiorentino (fyô.ren.tē'nō). [Also, **Castiglion Fiorentino** (käs.tē.lyōn').] Town and commune in C Italy, in the *compartimento* (region) of Tuscany, in the province of Arezzo, ab. 10 mi. S of Arezzo. Many of the buildings which had been preserved for centuries, including a number of medieval houses, were destroyed or heavily damaged in World War II. Most of the valuable religious paintings in the churches escaped with little or no damage, however. Pop. of commune, 14,830 (1936); of town, 3,076 (1936).

Castiglioni (käs.tē.lyō'nē), **Arturo.** b. at Trieste, April 10, 1874—. Italian physician and authority on the history of medicine. He took his medical degree (1896) at Vienna, studied at Paris and Rome, and was professor of medical history (1922–38) at the University of Padua, serving concurrently as chief of the health department of the Österreichische Lloyd (later called Lloyd Triestino). He became (1939) research associate and lecturer in the history of medicine at Yale University, where he was named a professor in 1943. In 1947 he returned to Italy. He is the author of *La Vita e l'opera di Santorio Santorio* (1920), *Ugo Benzi da Siena e il Trattato utilissimo* (1921), *Il Libro della pestilenza di Giovanni de Albertis da Capodistria* (1924), *Il Volto di Ippocrate, Istorie di medici e medicine di altri tempi* (1925), *Storia dell' Igiene* (1926), *Storia della Medicina* (1927; Eng. trans., *A History of Medicine*, 1941, 1947), *Italian Medicine* (1932), *Incantesimo e magia* (1934; Eng. trans., *Adventures of the Mind*, 1946), *The Renaissance of Medicine in Italy* (1934), and *L'Orto della sanità* (1935).

Castiglioni, Francesco Xaviero. Original name of Pope **Pius VIII.**

Castile (kas.tēl'). [Spanish, **Castilla** (käs.tē'lyä).] Region and old kingdom of Spain, in the N and C part of the peninsula, named from the number of its frontier castles. Castile proper comprised Old Castile, containing the modern provinces of Santander, Burgos, Palencia, Valladolid, Logroño, Segovia, Soria, and Ávila; and New Castile, S of Old Castile, containing the modern provinces of Madrid, Toledo, Guadalajara, Cuenca, and Ciudad Real. It fell under Moslem rule, was governed by counts under the supremacy of Asturias and León, and was annexed by Sancho of Navarre (1026–35), who gave Castile to his son Ferdinand I in 1033. León was united to Castile in 1037, separated in 1065, and reunited under Alfonso VI in 1072, who also annexed Galicia. Afterward Castile and León were separated, but were finally reunited under Ferdinand III in 1230, who conquered large parts of S Spain, Seville, Córdoba, and others from the Moslems. Other noted kings were Alfonso X and Pedro the Cruel. Isabella of Castile married Ferdinand of Aragon in 1469, and became queen of Castile in 1474. Ferdinand became king of Aragon in 1479, and thenceforth Castile and Aragon were united.

Castilho (kąsh.tē'lyö), **Antônio Feliciano de.** b. at Lisbon, Portugal, Jan. 28, 1800; d. there, June 18, 1875. Portuguese poet, critic, translator, and educator. He was one of the outstanding figures of romanticism in Portugal, although his early works were written under classic influence. Among his books of poems were *Cartas de Eco a Narciso*, bucolic poetry (1821), and *A noite do castelo* and *Ciumes do Bardo*, romantic poetry (both 1836). *Quadros históricos de Portugal* (1839) was his chief work in prose. He translated Vergil, Ovid, Anacreon, Molière, Shakespeare, and Goethe.

Castilian Days (kas.til'yạn). Travel book by John Hay, published in 1871. The 17 essays on Spanish civilization consider the influence of the Church since the Middle Ages and the superstitions, character, and traditions of the people.

Castilla (käs.tē'yä), **Ramón.** b. at Tarapacá, Peru (now part of Chile), c1797; d. near there, May 30, 1867. Peruvian general and statesman, president (1845–51, 1855–62) of Peru. He joined the patriots (1821) and fought under Antonio José de Sucre in the war against Spain; exiled in 1836, he returned and defeated Vivanco in the Peruvian civil war, and was president of Peru (1845–51). During this term railway and telegraph lines were built between Lima and Callao and the important nitrate industry was established. In 1854 he headed the insurgents in southern Peru against his successor Echenique, took the title of provisional president on June 1, 1854, decreed the emancipation of Negro slaves and the abolition of Indian tribute, defeated Echenique's army at La Palma, near Lima, on Jan. 5, 1855, and was regularly reëlected president for four years on July 14, 1855. He promulgated (1860) a new constitution and continued as president until 1862.

Castilla del Oro or **Castilia del Oro** (käs.tē'lyä del ō'rō). Name first applied by Columbus to the N coast of the Isthmus of Panama, which he visited in 1502. In 1508 it was officially made the name of a province, extending from Cape Gracias á Dios, now in Honduras, to the Gulf of Darien, the inland extent being unknown. Early maps often use the name Castilla del Oro for this latter region, embracing what is now N Colombia to the exclusion of the isthmus; and this mistake has been adopted by some modern authors, who distinguished the original Castilla del Oro as Castilla Nueva, or New Castile.

Castilla la Nueva (lä nwä'bä). Spanish name of **New Castile.**

Castillejo (käs.tē.lye'hō), **Cristóbal de.** b. at Ciudad Rodrigo, Spain, c1490; d. at Vienna, c1550. Spanish poet. For more than 30 years he was secretary to Don Ferdinand, brother of the emperor Charles V.

Castillejos (käs.tē.lye'hōs). Place in N Morocco. Near here, on Jan. 1, 1860, the Moors were defeated by General Juan Prim, who received as a reward the title of Marquis de los Castillejos.

Castillejos, Marquis **de los.** A title of **Prim, Juan.**

Castillero Reyes (käs.tē.yā'rō rā'yās), **Ernesto de Jesús.** b. at Ocú, Panama, June 28, 1889—. Panamanian educator and historian. He was secretary general (1922–27) of the inspectorate of education, secretary (1927–33) of the Instituto Nacional, and professor of history (1929–35) at the Colegio de Artes y Oficios, Escuela Normal de Institutoras, and Instituto Nacional, and served (1936–40) as superintendent of schools. Author of *Panamá, breve historia de la República* (1939), *La Universidad interamericana: Historia de sus antecedentes y fundación* (1943), and other books.

Castillo (käs.tē'lyō), **Antonio Cánovas del.** See **Cánovas del Castillo, Antonio.**

Castillo, Bernal Díaz del. See **Díaz del Castillo, Bernal.**

Castillo, Diego Enríquez de. b. at Segovia, Spain; fl. c1475. Spanish chronicler, author of *Annals of the Reign of Henry IV, 1454–74* (published 1787).

Castillo, Enrique Peñaranda. Full name of **Peñaranda, Enrique.**

Castillo (käs.tē'yō), **Ramón S.** b. at Catamarca, Argentina, Nov. 20, 1873; d. Oct. 12, 1944. Argentine politician. He was elevated from the vice-presidency to the post of acting president of Argentina on July 3, 1940, when President Roberto M. Ortiz was compelled by ill health to retire. From the formal resignation of Ortiz, on June 27, 1942, to June 4, 1943, when he was deposed by a military junta under Generals Rawson and Ramírez, Castillo was president of Argentina. His conservative sympathies and policy of "prudent neutrality" in World War II resulted in an administration characterized by discreet, if not actually timid, foreign relations, which were viewed by many as evidence that Castillo was insincere in his support of hemispheric defense.

Castillo de San Marcos National Monument (kas.tē'-yō dẹ san mär'kọs). [Former name (until 1942), **Fort Marion National Monument.**] National monument at St. Augustine, Fla. The masonry fort was begun by the Spaniards in 1672 and completed in 1756 to defend the town of St. Augustine. In 1763 it was taken by the English and held for 20 years. It passed to the U.S. in 1825 by cession. In 1924 it was made a nationa monument. Area, ab. 18½ acres.

Castillon (kȧs.tē.yôn). [Also, **Castillon-sur-Dordogne** (-sür.dôr.dony').] Village in SW France, in the department of Gironde, situated on the Dordogne River ab. 26 mi. E of Bordeaux. Here, in 1453, the French defeated the English under John Talbot (the last battle of the Hundred Years' War).

Castillo Nájera (käs.tē'yō nä'hā.rä), **Francisco.** b. at Durango, Mexico, Nov. 25, 1886—. Mexican physician and diplomat. He was graduated (M.D., 1903), from the National university of Mexico, was professor of urology (1919) and director (1920) of the Escuela Médico Militar, and was a member (1921–25) of the international commission for the campaign against yellow fever. He served as minister plenipotentiary to China (1922–24), Belgium (1927–30), the Netherlands (1930–32), and France (1933–35), Mexican delegate to the League of Nations and member of the Council, ambassador (1935–45) to the U.S., and minister of foreign affairs (1945 *et seq.*). He is the author of several medical books and *The Campaign Against Yellow Fever in Mexico* (1923), *L'Éducation au Méxique* (1929), *Un Siglo de poesía belga (1830–1930)* (1931), *Corridos de Durango* (1933), *El Gavilán* (song, 1934), and *Una Voz de México en el extranjero* (1936).

Castillos (käs.tē'yōs), **Los Tres.** Mountain cluster in N Chihuahua, Mexico, to which the Apache chief Victorio retreated in the fall of 1880, and where he and his band were exterminated by the Mexican troops under Colonel Terrazas.

Castine (kas.tēn'). [Early name, **Penobscot.**] Town in S Maine, in Hancock County, on Penobscot Bay, ab. 30 mi. S of Bangor: summer resort. It was the seat of a contest over the course of nearly two centuries for the control of the Castine peninsula: between the British and French (1631), the British and Flemish (1670), the French and Dutch (1675), and the British and Americans (1779). It was named for Baron Vincent de Castine or Castin. 793 (1950).

Castine (kȧs.tēn) or **Castin** (kȧs.taṅ), **Vincent,** Baron **de.** b. at Oléron, France, 1650; d. there, 1722. French soldier in the French and Indian Wars. He went to Canada in 1665, and established a trading house at Penobscot (now Castine, Me.) in 1687, where he married the daughter of the Penobscot chief. He captured Pemaquid at the head of 200 Indians in 1696. In 1706 he assisted in defending Port Royal, and was wounded there in 1707. His son, who succeeded him as commander of the Penobscots, was taken as a prisoner to Boston in 1721.

Casting Away of Mrs. Lecks and Mrs. Aleshine (leks; āl'shīn), **The.** Humorous novel by Frank R. Stockton, published in 1886. Two Pennsylvania widows are shipwrecked on a Pacific island while en route to Japan. Together with another tourist, Mr. Craig, an erudite missionary named Mr. Enderton, the latter's daughter Ruth, and three sailors, the women live in the best Robinson Crusoe tradition until Mr. Craig and Ruth have time enough to fall in love and marry. The company then adjourns to an inhabited isle.

Castle (kȧs'l), **Agnes.** [Maiden name, **Sweetman.**] b. in Queen's County (now County Laoighis), Ireland; d. at Genoa, Italy, April 30, 1922. English novelist; wife of Egerton Castle (1858–1920). She was coauthor, with her husband, of many romantic and sentimental novels, including *The Pride of Jennico* (1898; also a play), *The Bath Comedy* (1900; a great dramatic success as *Sweet Kitty Bellairs*), *The Secret Orchard* (1901; dramatized, 1901), *The Star Dreamer* (1903), *The Incomparable Bellairs* (1904), *Rose of the World* (1905), *French Nan* (1905), *If Youth But Knew* (1906), *My Merry Rockhurst* (1907), *Flower o' the Orange and Other Stories* (1908), *The Ways of Miss Barbara* (1914), *Forlorn Adventurers* (1915), *The Black Office and other Chapters of Romance* (1917), *Wolf Lure* (1917), *New Wine* (1919), and *Pamela Pounce* (1921). Before her collaboration with Castle, she wrote *My Little Lady Anne* (1896), and, after his death, *Kitty and Others* (1922).

Castle, Egerton. b. at London, March 12, 1858; d. 1920. English novelist, short-story writer, and dramatist; husband of Agnes Sweetman (d. 1922). He was the author of *Schools and Masters of Fence* (1884), *Consequences* (1891), *English Book-plates* (1892), *The Jerningham Letters* (1896), *Young April* (1899), and *Marshfield, the Observer* (1900). Books which he wrote with his wife include *The Pride of Jennico* (1898), *The Bath Comedy* (1900; dramatized as *Sweet Kitty Bellairs*), *The Secret Orchard* (1901; dramatized, 1901), *The Star Dreamer* (1903), *The Incomparable Bellairs* (1904), *Rose of the World* (1905), *French Nan* (1905),

The Heart of Lady Anne (1905), *If Youth But Knew* (1906), *My Merry Rockhurst* (1907), *Flower o' the Orange and Other Stories* (1908), *Panther's Cub* (1910) and *New Wine* (1919).

Castle, Vernon Blythe. [Original surname, **Blythe.**] b. at Norwich, England, May 2, 1887; d. at Fort Worth, Tex., Feb. 15, 1918. Dancer and flyer, noted as a member of the famous dancing team of which his wife, Irene, was the other partner, and as the originator of the Castle-walk, one-step, turkey-trot, and many other steps popular in their day. Arriving at New York in 1906, he appeared (1907) in Lew Fields's *The Girl Behind the Counter*, where his creation of a dance routine brought him into the public eye. He married (May 28, 1911) Irene Foote, and with her as his dancing partner went (c1912) to Paris, where their success in a café soon led to contracts for work in New York. The height of their fame and success came between 1913 and 1916; in the latter year Castle enlisted in the Royal Flying Corps, was commissioned a lieutenant, and served on the Western Front under Foch's command, receiving the Croix de Guerre for shooting down two German aircraft. Going (1918) to Fort Worth as a flying instructor, he was killed there in a collision with another plane.

Castle, William Ernest. b. at Alexandria, Ohio, Oct. 25, 1867—. American zoölogist and geneticist. He graduated (B.A., 1893; Ph.D., 1895) from Harvard, where he was subsequently zoölogy instructor (1897 *et seq.*) and professor (1908–36). In 1936 he became a research associate in genetics at the University of California. He is the author of *Heredity in Relation to Evolution and Animal Breeding* (1911), *Genetics and Eugenics* (1916), *Genetics of Domestic Rabbits* (1930), *Mammalian Genetics* (1940), and scientific papers on heredity and evolution.

Castlebar (kås'l.bär). Urban district and market town in Connacht province, Irish Republic, in County Mayo, situated on the river Castlebar, ab. 45 mi. SW of Sligo. Castlebar is the county seat of County Mayo. It is situated in an agricultural district devoted to the raising of oats, potatoes, and livestock. The town was taken by the French and Irish Aug. 27, 1798, in the battle called "the Race of Castlebar," in which Generals Lake and Hutchinson, with 2,000 Irish militia, a large body of yeomanry, and Lord Roden's fencibles, were routed, Aug. 26, 1798, by General Humbert, with about 1,000 Irish insurgents and 800 French troops, the latter of whom had landed at Killala, Aug. 17. Humbert took 14 guns and 200 prisoners. 5,158 (1951).

Castlebay (kås'l.bā). Small village in W Scotland, on the S coast of Barra island in the Outer Hebrides. It is a center for the summer herring fisheries, and has a ruined castle dating from the 12th century.

Castle Clinton (klin'tọn). A former name of **Castle Garden.**

Castle Dangerous. Tale by Sir Walter Scott, published in 1831. It was published together with *Count Robert of Paris* as the fourth series of *Tales of My Landlord* (1832).

Castle Dismal. Novel (1844) of crime and the supernatural by William Gilmore Simms.

Castle Douglas (dug'lạs). [Also: **Castle-Douglas, Castledouglas.**] Police burgh and market town in S Scotland, in Kirkcudbrightshire, ab. 9 mi. NE of Kirkcudbright, ab. 352 mi. N of London by rail. 3,327 (est. 1948).

Castleford (kås'l.fọrd). Urban district in N central England, in the West Riding of Yorkshire, situated on the river Aire, ab. 9 mi. SE of Leeds, ab. 189 mi. N of London by rail. 43,116 (1951).

Castlegar (kås'l.gär). Town in S British Columbia, Canada, at the junction of the Kootenay and Columbia rivers, on the main line of the Canadian Pacific Railway: sawmills. There is a settlement of Doukhobors here.

Castle Garden. [Also (1896–1941), the **Aquarium**; former names, **Castle Clinton, West Battery.**] Former circular building situated on the Battery, at New York. It was built between 1807 and 1811 and was first known as West Battery, later as Castle Clinton. In 1823 it was granted to the city. It was for some years used as an opera house (Jenny Lind first sang there), and civic receptions were held there. From 1855 until 1890 it was used as a place of reception for immigrants, but the immigrant station was transferred to the Barge Office, and thence to Ellis Island, and the building became the possession of the city, and was converted into an aquarium under the control of the N.Y. Zoölogical Society. The aquarium was closed in 1941 and the building itself was subsequently dismantled.

Castlemaine (kås'l.mān). Town in SE Australia, in the gold region of Victoria state, ab. 75 mi. NW of Melbourne. 5,808 (1947).

Castlemaine, Earl of. Title of **Palmer, Roger.**

Castlemaine, Lady. A title of **Villiers, Barbara.**

Castle of Indolence, The. Poem by James Thomson, published in 1748.

Castle of Labour, The. Allegorical poem translated from the French of Pierre Gringoire (c1475–c1538), by Alexander Barclay. Barclay used rime royal for his translation, a form which had been made familiar to English readers by Chaucer in his *Troilus and Criseyde*. The poem was printed in 1505 by Richard Pynson and in 1606 by Wynkyn de Worde. The French title of the work is *Le Château de Labour* (1499).

Castle of Otranto (ō.trän'tō), **The.** [Full title, **The Castle of Otranto, a Gothic Story.**] Romance by Horace Walpole, published in 1764. The book influenced the subsequent fashion for tales of terror and the supernatural.

Castle of Perseverance, The. Early example (c1405) of the English morality play, and the longest (it contains over 3,600 lines). It traces the spiritual history of man from birth to death and to final judgment. The characters who struggle for possession of man's soul are the Good Angel and the Bad Angel and the Virtues and Vices that accompany them. The three main themes of all moralities (the conflict between vice and virtue, the debate of the heavenly graces, and the coming of death) are present in this play. Along with two other examples, *Mankynde* and *Wisdom* (also called *Mind, Will and Understanding*), it is one of the "Macro Plays," so called after an owner of the original manuscript, Cox Macro (1683–1767), Cambridge antiquary and divine, and chaplain to George II.

Castle Peak. See under **Elk Mountains.**

Castle Pinckney National Monument (pingk'ni). Old fortification on a small island ab. 1 mi. SE of Charleston, S.C., guarding the inner harbor. A fort was built here in 1797, which was replaced by the present fort in 1810. It was made a national monument in 1924. Area, ab. 3½ acres.

Castle Rackrent (rak'rent). Novel by Maria Edgeworth, published in 1800.

Castlereagh (kås'l.rā), **Viscount.** See **Stewart, Robert** (1769–1822).

Castle Shannon (shan'ọn). Borough in SW Pennsylvania, in Allegheny County near Pittsburgh. 5,459 (1950).

Castles in Spain. Lyric poem (1877) of 15 six-line stanzas by Henry Wadsworth Longfellow. It is in "Flight the Fifth" of a group of poems called *Birds of Passage*, and is the third poem in the series. It shows Longfellow's love for the romance of old Spain.

Castle Spectre, The. Play by Matthew Gregory Lewis, produced in 1797.

Castle Thunder. Tobacco warehouse at Richmond, Va., employed by the Confederates during the Civil War for the imprisonment of political prisoners and others charged with treason. It was notorious for the brutal treatment meted out to its inmates.

Castleton (kås'l.tọn). Civil parish and village in C England, in Derbyshire, ab. 12 mi. W of Sheffield. It is situated in the Peak District. Castleton is the site of Peveril Castle, and the Peak Cavern is nearby. 620 (1931).

Castletown (kås'l.toun). Town and seaport on the Isle of Man, situated on Castletown Bay, ab. 9 mi. SW of Douglas. It was the former capital of the island, and contains Castle Rushen. 1,749 (1951).

Castlewood (kås'l.wůd), **Colonel Francis Esmond, Lord.** The second Lord Castlewood in William Makepeace Thackeray's novel *Henry Esmond*, the father of Beatrix and Francis. He is a drunken sensualist who ill-treats and insults his wife, spoils his children, gambles away his property, and is killed in a duel.

Castlewood, Lady. The mother of Beatrix Esmond, and wife of the second Lord Castlewood, in Thackeray's *Henry Esmond*. She afterward marries Henry Esmond.

Castor (kas'tọr). In Greek and Roman mythology, the twin brother of Pollux, noted for his skill in the management of horses. He is regarded as the son of Zeus and Leda, wife of Tyndareus, king of Sparta, or of Tyndareus and Leda. According to one version of the legend, Zeus assumed the form of a swan. Two eggs were produced by Leda from one of which came Castor and Clytemnestra, from the other Pollux and Helen. The Dioscuri (Castor and Pollux) were the heroes of many adventures, and were worshiped as divinities, particularly by Dorians and at Rome. They were placed in the heavens as a constellation.

Castor and Pollux (pol'uks). The two principal stars of the zodiacal constellation Gemini, the Twins. Castor, α Geminorum, 1.6 magnitude, is 4 degrees NW of Pollux; β Geminorum, the brighter star, has a magnitude of 1.2.

Castorland Company (kas'tọr.lạnd). Colonizing company formed (1792) at Paris for the purpose of settling in the U.S. French aristocrats and others who wanted to flee the revolutionary regime in France. It was originally called the Compagnie de New Yorck. The first colonists arrived in 1796 and were settled in Lewis County, N.Y., but by 1800 the community had failed.

Castra (kas'trạ). A Latin name of **Chester,** England.

Castra Abusina (ab.ụ̄.sī'nạ). Latin name of **Abensberg.**

Castra Albiensium (al.bi.en'si.um). Ancient name of **Castres.**

Castra Bonnensia (bọ.nen'si.ạ). A Latin name of **Bonn.**

Castra Caecilia (sẹ̄.sil'i.ạ). Ancient name of **Cáceres,** city.

Castracani (käs.trä.kä'nē), **Castruccio.** b. 1281; d. 1328. Italian nobleman; duke of Lucca. His early life is obscure, and was passed mostly in exile, but he returned to Lucca at least as early as 1316, when he was made lord for life of that city and its territories. He became the leader of the Ghibelline party in Tuscany, and was engaged constantly in war with Florence and other cities. Recognized as duke of Lucca by the emperor Louis IV in 1327, he died the following year.

Castra Regina (rẹ̄.jī'nạ). An ancient name of **Regensburg.**

Castrén (käs.trān'), **Matthias Alexander.** b. at Tervola, near Tornio, Finland, Dec. 2, 1813; d. at Helsingfors (now Helsinki), Finland, May 7, 1852. Finnish philologist and explorer in Lapland, N Russia, and Siberia. He published a Swedish translation of *Kalevala* (1841) as well as other works, and was one of the first to do research in Finno-Ugric and Samoyedic languages.

Castres (kästr). [Ancient name, **Castra Albiensium.**] City in S France, in the department of Tarn, situated on the Agout River, ab. 39 mi. E of Toulouse. It is an important center for the manufacture of textiles, particularly of woolen and cotton goods, knitwear, hosiery, felt hats, and shirts; it also has machine and furniture factories. The textiles of Castres were famous as early as the 14th century. The museum contains paintings by the Spanish painter Goya. Castres was an Albigensian stronghold and later a Huguenot stronghold, and was severely affected when the Edict of Nantes was rescinded. 30,781 (1946).

Castries (kȧs.trē', käs'trēs). [Also, **Port Castries.**] Town on the NW coast of Saint Lucia, British West Indies, the capital and chief port of the island. It has an excellent landlocked harbor, and exports sugar, cacao, coconut products, and fruits. It was ravaged by fires in 1948 and in 1951. 24,300 (1948).

Castriota (käs.trē.ō'tä), **George.** Original name of **Scanderbeg.**

Castro (käs'trō), **Alfonso y.** b. at Zamora, Spain, 1495; d. at Brussels, Feb. 11, 1558. Franciscan theologian and preacher. He preached at Bruges and Salamanca, represented the Spanish church at the first session of the Council of Trent, and was one of the chaplains of Charles V. He accompanied Philip II to England in 1554 as counselor and spiritual director, and opposed the extreme measures of the English Catholics, strenuously condemning the burning of heretics. In 1557 he was appointed archbishop of Santiago de Compostela. His most noted work is his treatise *Adversus omnes haereses* (Cologne, 1539).

Castro, Américo. b. at Rio de Janeiro, May 4, 1885—. Spanish philologist. He is the author of *Vida de Lope de Vega* (1919, with H. A. Reunert) and *El Pensamiento de Cervantes* (1925).

Castro, Cipriano. b. at Capacho, Venezuela, c1858; d. 1924. Venezuelan military leader and politician, president (1902–08) of Venezuela. He took up arms in 1886 against the López government, supported Palacio against the revolt of Crespo in 1892, and then, ceasing to be the leader of the liberal party, for about six years was engaged in farming near Cúcuta, Santander, Colombia. In May, 1899, he invaded Venezuela with 60 men, rapidly gathered an army, won victories at Las Pilas and elsewhere, entered Caracas (from which the president, General Ignacio Andrade, had fled), and declared himself supreme military leader. The constitutional assembly made him provisional president on March 30, 1901; on Feb. 20, 1902, he was elected president, and was reëlected (1905) for a term of six years. This position he resigned temporarily on April 9, 1906. When he left again (1908) on a plea of ill-health he was suspended from the presidency by congress and replaced by Vice-President Gómez, on the grounds of malfeasance and a dictatorial policy. This was in consequence of the fact that, unable to secure settlement of claims of their nationals in Venezuela for injuries and losses entailed in the civil wars, England, Germany, and Italy had blockaded Venezuelan ports (1902–07); the U.S. also had objected (1904–08) to his seizure of American property, and had suspended diplomatic relations. Castro's subsequent attempts to return to Venezuela were unsuccessful.

Castro, Cristóbal Vaca de. See **Vaca de Castro, Cristóbal.**

Castro (käsh'trö), **Eugênio de.** See **Castro e Almeida, Eugênio de.**

Castro (käs'trō; Portuguese, käsh'trö), **Inés de.** Killed at Coimbra, Portugal, 1355. Spanish noblewoman; favorite of Pedro, son of Alfonso IV of Portugal, who claimed to have married her after the death of his wife. She was murdered by order of Alfonso, to prevent the consequences of an unequal union. Her tragic story has been celebrated by novelists and poets, all of whom have idealized her character.

Castro (käsh'trö), **João de.** b. at Lisbon, Feb. 7, 1500; d. at Ormuz, Persia, June 6, 1548. Portuguese naval commander, governor in India in 1545.

Castro (käs'trō), **José María.** [Called **"Founder of the Republic."**] b. at San José, Costa Rica, Sept. 1, 1818; d. April 4, 1893. Costa Rican statesman, vice-president of Costa Rica in 1846, and president in the period 1847–49. He separated (1848) the republic from the Central American federation. He was again president from 1866 to November, 1868, when he was overthrown by Jesús Jiménez.

Castro, Juan José. b. at Buenos Aires, March 7, 1895—. Argentine composer and conductor. He conducted at the Colón ballet theater. His works include the ballet *Mêkhâno* and *Sinfonia Argentina.*

Castro, Lope Garcia de. fl. in the middle of the 16th century. Governor and captain-general of Peru (September, 1564–November, 1569).

Castro, Paolo de. [Latinized, **Paulus Castrensis.**] d. at Padua, Italy, c1441. Italian student of civil and canon law, professor successively at Florence, Bologna, Ferrara, and Padua.

Castro (kas'trō), **Thomas.** An assumed name of **Orton, Arthur.**

Castro Alves (käs'trö äl'vẹ̄s), **Antônio de.** See **Alves, (Antônio de) Castro.**

Castro Andrade y Portugal (käs'trō än.drä'dā ē pōr.tö-gäl'), **Pedro Fernández de.** See **Fernández de Castro Andrade y Portugal, Pedro.**

Castro del Río (käs'trō del rē'ō). Town in S Spain, in the province of Córdoba, situated on the Guadajoz River, ab. 20 mi. SE of Córdoba. A manufacturing center, it has woolen factories, saltworks, and stone quarries. 17,298 (1940).

Castrodunum (kas.trọ.dū'num). Latin name of **Châteaudun.**

Castro e Almeida (käsh'trö ē äl.mā'dạ), **Eugênio de.** b. at Coimbra, Portugal, March 4, 1869; d. there, Aug. 17, 1944. Portuguese poet, leader of the symbolist school which he introduced in Portugal with *Oaristos* (1890) and *Horas* (1891). Among his other well-known books are

Belkiss (1894), *Saudades do céu* (1899), *Constança* (1900), *O anel de Policrates* (1907), and *Últimos versos* (1938). Some of his poems have been widely translated in Europe.

Castrogiovanni (käs″trō.jō.vän′nē). Former name of **Enna,** city.

Castro Marim (käsh′trō mą.rēn′). Town and *concelho* (commune) in SE Portugal, in the province of Algarve, on the Guadiana River opposite the Spanish town of Ayamonte. The Castle of the Templars is a very famous medieval stronghold crowning a mighty rock. The middle fortress has a quadrangular court with massive walls and covered way, and a huge square keep. Pop. of concelho, 9,327 (1940); of town, 4,630 (1940).

Castrone (käs.trō′nā), Cavaliere **de.** A title of **Marchesi, Salvatore.**

Castrop-Rauxel (käs′trop.rouk′sẹl). [Also: **Castrop, Kastrop-Rauxel.**] Town in W Germany, in the *Land* (state) of North Rhine-Westphalia, British Zone, formerly in the province of Westphalia, Prussia, ab. 30 mi. SW of Münster. There are large coal mines in the vicinity, and the town has cement works, chemical, metallurgical, and machine industries, and a school of mining. The population is predominantly Roman Catholic. 69,960 (1950).

Castroreale (käs″trō.rā.ä′lā). Town and large commune in SW Italy, on the island of Sicily, in the province of Messina, ab. 22 mi. SW of Messina. The central place, of antique Siculian or Greek origin, was rebuilt in 1328; it has a castle dating from this period. Castroreale Bagni, a health resort, which is visited by people suffering from rheumatism, arthritis, gout, and other diseases, is nearby. Pop. of commune, 12,240 (1936); of town, 230 (1936).

Castro Urdiales (käs′trō ör.ᴛʜyä′lās). Town in N Spain, in the province of Santander, situated on the Bay of Biscay, ab. 30 mi. SE of Santander. A seaport, with sardine fisheries, it exports iron ore, sardines in oil, and wine. It was a Roman colony in ancient times, and has a ruined medieval castle. The town was destroyed by the French in 1813, but soon rebuilt; the nearby iron mines contributed to its prosperity in the 19th century. 11,963 (1940).

Castro Valley (kas′trō). Unincorporated community in C California, in Alameda County, near San Francisco. Under the new urban definition established for use in the 1950 census, Castro Valley was counted with adjoining urban areas; its last official separate enumeration was 4,145 (1940).

Castroviejo (käs.trō.vye′hō), **Ramón.** b. at Logroño, Spain, Aug. 24, 1904—. American ophthalmologist. Arrived (1928) in the U.S., he became (1931) a staff member of the Presbyterian Medical Center at New York, and was named head of the ophthalmology department in Lincoln Hospital at New York.

Castrovillari (käs.trō.vēl′lä.rē). Town and commune in S Italy, in the *compartimento* (region) of Calabria, in the province of Cosenza, situated on the Coscile River, N of Cosenza. It is an important agricultural market town, with small agricultural industries. Large-scale emigration between 1880 and 1920 arrested the growth of its population. Pop. of commune, 11,943 (1936); of town, 10,508 (1936).

Castroville (kas′trō.vil). Village in S central Texas, in Medina County, ab. 25 mi. by road W of San Antonio. It was founded in 1844 by a group of Alsatian and other W European immigrants, and is noted for its preservation of Old World customs and architecture. Elevation, 787 ft.; pop. 985 (1950).

Castro y Bellvís (käs′trō ē bel.ʙēs′), **Guillén de.** b. at Valencia, Spain, 1569; d. at Madrid, July 28, 1631. Spanish dramatist. His chief play is *Las Mocedades del Cid,* which was used by Pierre Corneille as a source for his *Le Cid.*

Castro y Figueroa Salazar (fē.gā.rō′ä sä.lä.sär′), **Pedro de.** [Titles: Duke of **La Conquista,** Marquis of **Gracia Real.**] Said to have been a native of Spanish America; d. at Mexico City, Aug. 22, 1741. Spanish soldier and administrator. From Aug. 17, 1740, until his death he was viceroy of Mexico.

Castro y Velasco (ʙā.läs′kō), **Acisclo** (or **Acislo**) **Antonio Palomino de.** See **Palomino de Castro y Velasco, Acisclo** (or **Acislo**) **Antonio.**

Castrum Arearum (kas′trum ãr.ẹ.ãr′um). Latin name of **Hyères.**

Castrum Cameracense (kam″ėr.ą.sen′sē). Latin name of **Le Cateau.**

Castrum Heraldi (hẹ.ral′dī). Medieval Latin name of **Châtellerault.**

Castrum Matisconense (mą.tis.kǫ.nen′sē). A Latin name of **Mâcon.**

Castrum Muglae (mū′glē). Ancient name of **Muggia.**

Castrum Theodorici (thē.ǫ.dō′ri.sī). Latin name of **Château-Thierry.**

Casuals of the Sea. Novel by William McFee, published in 1916.

Casuentus (kaz̧.ū.en′tus). Latin name of the **Basento.**

Caswell (kaz′wel), **Fort.** Fort on Oak Island, at the mouth of Cape Fear River, N.C., held by the Confederates till 1865.

Caswell, Richard. b. in Maryland, Aug. 3, 1729; d. in North Carolina, in November, 1789. American Revolutionary politician and soldier. He served as governor of North Carolina (1777–79 and 1784–87).

Cat (kat), **Christopher.** fl. 1703–33. English innkeeper. His tavern, "The Cat and Fiddle," was in Shire Lane near Temple Bar, London. He is noted as the entertainer of the Kit-Cat Club.

Catacocha (kä.tä.kō′chä). City in S Ecuador, in Loja province. 14,240 (est. 1944).

Catacombs of Rome. Catacombs at Rome lying for the most part within a circle of three miles from the modern walls. The length of the galleries is estimated at ab. 600 miles. The vast network of subterranean passages and chambers is now held to have been formed, chiefly between the 2nd and the 6th century, expressly for the burial of Christians. Many of the chambers were later used as chapels. The Catacombs are the source of many sculptures, paintings, and inscriptions of high importance in early Christian art and archaeology.

Catalan (kat′ą.lạn). Romance language spoken in Catalonia, Spain. More conservative in character than Castilian, it belongs to the eastern group of Ibero-Romance dialects. It is also spoken in the French department of Pyrénées-Orientales, at Alghero (Sardinia), and in the Balearic Islands.

Catalan Grand Company. Band of mercenaries, mostly Catalans and Aragonese, who, after the wars in Sicily, entered the service of the Byzantine Empire under the leadership of Roger de Flor. After his death (c1306) they waged war against the Greeks and became masters of Boeotia and Attica. Their power disappeared before the end of the 14th century.

Catalani (kä.tä.lä′nē), **Alfredo.** b. at Lucca, Italy, June 19, 1854; d. at Milan, Italy, Aug. 7, 1893. Italian operatic composer. He was a pupil at the conservatories of Paris and Milan. He first composed church music, writing a mass at the age of 14. His compositions include *Ero e Leandro* (a symphonic poem for orchestra) and the operas *La Falce* (1875), *Elda* (1880), *Dejanire* (1883), *Edmea* (1886), *Loreley* (1890), and *La Wally* (1892).

Catalani, Angelica. b. at Sinigaglia, Italy, May 10, 1780; d. at Paris, June 12, 1849. Italian singer. She made her first appearance (1795) at Venice.

Catalans (kat′ą.lạnz). Name given to natives and inhabitants of Catalonia, Spain.

Catalauni (kat.ą.lô′nī). [Also, **Catelauni.**] Ancient people of Belgica Secunda (a division of the Roman province of Belgica, in N Gaul). Their name survives in the modern Châlons-sur-Marne.

Catalaunian Fields (kat.ą.lô′ni.ąn). [Also: **Catalaunian Plains;** Latin, **Campi Catalaunici.**] Plain in N France, near Châlons-sur-Marne, famous for the victory (451 A.D.) of Aëtius and the Gothic king Theodoric I over Attila.

Catalaunum (kat.ą.lô′num). Ancient name of **Châlons-sur-Marne.**

Catalina (kat.ą.lī′nạ). Novel by W. Somerset Maugham, published in 1948. It is set in Spain during the Inquisition.

Catalina Island (kat.ą.lē′nạ). See **Santa Catalina Island.**

Catalogue of the Royal and Noble Authors of England, The. Prose work (2 vols., 1758) by Horace Walpole. It is a compilation of literary and antiquarian gossip, and was published by the author on his own private printing press (the Strawberry Hill Press).

Catalonia (kat.ą.lō'ni.ą). [Spanish, **Cataluña** (kä.tä.lö'nyä); ancient name, **Hispania Tarraconensis.**] Region and former autonomous province in NE Spain, comprising the present provinces of Lérida, Gerona, Barcelona, and Tarragona. Its surface is mountainous, and it is the leading agricultural and manufacturing district of Spain. The language is Catalan. It was overrun by the Alani, Goths, and (in the S part) by the Saracens. It formed part of the Spanish march of the empire of Charlemagne, and was united to Aragon in 1137. It has been the scene in modern history of various insurrections. In 1714 it was conquered after a long struggle by Philip V, and deprived of its constitution.

Cataluña (kä.tä.lö'nyä), **Esquerra de.** See **Esquerra de Cataluña.**

Catamarca (kä.tä.mär'kä). Province in NW Argentina, lying E of Chile, N of La Rioja, S of Salta, and W of Santiago del Estero. Much of its area is in the Andes. It contains iron, some gold, silver, and lead, but is primarily an agricultural province. Capital, Catamarca; area, 45,829 sq. mi.; pop. 147,213 (1947).

Catamarca. City in NW Argentina, capital of Catamarca province, ab. 620 mi. NW of Buenos Aires: shipping center for wine, figs, and other agricultural products. Pop. 31,067 (1947).

Catana (kat'ą.ną). A Latin name of **Catania,** city.

Catanduanes (kä.tän.dwä'näs). Hilly island of the Philippines, E of the S part of Luzon, from which it is separated by Maqueda Channel. It belongs to the province of Albay. Capital, Virac; area, 550 sq. mi.; pop. 112,121 (1948).

Catanduva (kä.tąn.dö'vą). City in S Brazil, in the state of São Paulo. 22,186 (1950).

Catania (kä.tä'nyä; Anglicized, ką.tā'ni.ą). Province in the *compartimento* (region) and island of Sicily, SW Italy. Capital, Catania; area, ab. 1,400 sq. mi.; pop. ab. 766,000 (est. 1946).

Catania. [Ancient Greek, **Katanae;** Latin, **Catana, Catina.**] City and commune in SW Italy, on the island of Sicily, the capital of the province of Catania, situated on the Gulf of Catania on the E coast of the island. At the foot of volcanic Mount Etna, the city, the second largest of Sicily, is built on a base of lava and its buildings consist mainly of lava. Frequently destroyed by volcanic eruptions and earthquakes (the latest in 1693), it was always rebuilt and speedily flourished again as a commercial and industrial center, seaport, and resort. The surrounding plain is very fertile and densely populated, and the city is a marketing center for citrus fruits, oil, wine, nuts, almonds, fruit, tomato paste, and canned foods; the industries produce foodstuffs, textiles, leather, furniture, musical instruments (guitars and mandolins); there are extensive fisheries, and a number of hotels and bathing establishments. Catania is the seat of a university (founded in 1444) and of an archbishopric. The civic museum contains art collections and a good library. There are some architectural remains from ancient Greek and Roman times; the city itself is very largely of the baroque style of the 17th century; its chief architect was G. B. Vaccarini. There are numerous churches (including the cathedral and the Convent of the Benedictines), palaces (including the town hall), and public fountains dating from that period. The largest organ in all Italy is in the Church of San Nicoló. Only the castle dates from the Middle Ages. Founded by Greeks from the island of Naxos, Catania was frequently contested in ancient times; it was in the hands of Syracuse, Athens, and the tyrant Dionysius, and became as one of the first cities of Sicily an ally of Rome. In the Middle Ages it suffered under the occupation of Normans, Saracens, and the house of Hohenstaufen; it recovered under the rule of the house of Aragon. It was destroyed by an eruption of Mount Etna in 1669 and again by earthquake in 1693; its modern history starts with that year. Considerable damage was suffered during World War II by some buildings of tourist interest, but repairs have been completed or are being carried out. Pop. of commune, 257,243 (1936), 300,298 (1951); of city, 252,612 (1936).

Catanzaro (kä.tän.dzä'rō). Province in the *compartimento* (region) of Calabria, S Italy. Capital, Catanzaro; area, ab. 2,000 sq. mi.; pop. 606,364 (1936), ab. 694,000 (est. 1946).

Catanzaro. City and commune in S Italy, in the *compartimento* (region) of Calabria, the capital of the province of Catanzaro, situated in a fortresslike position on a hill, near the Gulf of Squillace, SE of Cosenza. The city is the seat of a bishopric and a number of administrative offices and educational institutions, but has only small industries (silk, olive oil, dried fruits); the port of Catanzaro Marina is nearby. The medieval cathedral, gravely damaged by previous earthquakes, was reconstructed in the 18th century; the Church of San Domenico dates from the 15th century; there is a castle and a provincial museum. Of Byzantine origin, Catanzaro was famous until the 11th century for its highly developed silk industry, which was based on close contact with the Near East through Byzantine, Saracen, and Jewish merchants; in the course of the Middle Ages this position was lost to the French. Under Norman, Hohenstaufen, Angevin, and Spanish domination, the city shared the fate of the region. The *Consuetudini* (law statutes) of Catanzaro, long in use, were codified in 1519. The city was largely destroyed in the earthquake of 1783, was the scene of an unsuccessful revolt in 1820–21, and joined the kingdom of Italy in 1860. Some damage was suffered during World War II by buildings of tourist interest. Pop. of commune, 45,400 (1936), ab. 50,000 (est. 1946); of city, 27,907 (1936).

Catargiu (kä.tär.jö'), **Lascăr.** b. 1823; d. 1899. Rumanian statesman. After being defeated by Alexander John Cuza in a contest for leadership of the state when Moldavia and Walachia were combined to form the new Rumania, he became the leader of the Conservative Party. He was twice prime minister (1871–76, 1891–95), and in his later years, as a member of the senate, led the opposition to Brătianu's Liberal Party government.

Catari (kä.tä'rē), **Tomás.** fl. in the 18th century. Peruvian revolutionist, an Aymará Indian. He secretly aspired to the position of *corregidor* (ruler) of the district in which he lived, and in 1780 went to Buenos Aires to advance his interests, under the pretext of laying the grievances of the Indians before the Spanish viceroy. He received only promises of redress, but on returning home showed documents which he asserted gave him authority to depose or kill the existing corregidors. An Indian uprising followed, during which Tomás Catari himself was killed. But his widow and his two brothers, Nicolás and Dámaso, gathered a large body of Indians and moved upon Sucre (then Chuquisaca), where the royal Audience resided, and were with difficulty repulsed by the Spanish forces. The Cataris were afterward captured and executed, and the rising was ended in 1781.

Catarina Cornaro (kä.tä.rē'nä kôr.nä'rō). Opera by Gaetano Donizetti, first produced at Naples in 1844. This was his last opera.

Catarroja (kä.tär.rō'ʜä). Town in E Spain, in the province of Valencia, situated near the Albufera Lagoon, S of Valencia, in an agricultural region. 10,437 (1940).

Catasauqua (kat.ą.sô'kwą). Borough in E Pennsylvania, in Lehigh County, on the Lehigh River, ab. 3 mi. above Allentown. 4,923 (1950).

Catatumbo (kä.tä.töm'bō). River in N Colombia and W Venezuela, rising in the eastern Colombian Andes and flowing N and E to Lake Maracaibo. Length, ab. 200 mi.; navigable for ab. 120 mi. from its mouth.

Catawba (ką.tô'bą). Confederation of over a score of North American Indian tribes formerly inhabiting South Carolina and portions of North Carolina. They spoke a Siouan language.

Catawba. [Also, **Great Catawba.**] River in North and South Carolina, called the Wateree in the lower part of its course, which unites with the Congaree to form the Santee ab. 31 mi. SE of Columbia, S.C. Total length, ab. 300 mi.

Catbalogan (kät.bä.lō'gän). Town in the Philippine Islands, the capital of Samar province, situated on the W coast of Samar island, NE of Daram island: seaport. 10,757 (1948).

Catch Club. [Full name, **The Noblemen and Gentlemen's Catch Club.**] Group organized (1761) at London for promoting the performance and composition of catches, glees, and canons. Still active in the 20th century, the club has in the past numbered among its members George IV and William IV, as well as many well-known musicians and members of the English peerage.

Cateau (kȧ.tō), **Le.** See **Le Cateau.**

Cateau-Cambrésis (kȧ.tō.käṅ.brā.zē), **Le.** Former name of **Le Cateau.**

Cateau-Cambrésis, Treaty of. Treaty between France, England, and Spain, concluded April 2–3, 1559. By it England formally acknowledged the right of France to retain Calais, but the most important sections of the treaty were those involving points of dispute between France and Spain, and by these France lost Savoy and territory on the boundary with the Netherlands to Spain. The French also accepted Spanish dominance in Italy. However, with this treaty the conflict which had existed between France and Spain (with occasional anti-French intervention by England) for more than 50 years was settled.

Catel (kä.tel′), **Franz.** b. at Berlin, Feb. 22, 1778; d. at Rome, Dec. 19, 1856. German painter, known especially for landscapes.

Catelauni (kat.ẹ.lô′nī). See **Catalauni.**

Catena (kä.tā′nä), **Vincenzo di Biagio.** b. at Treviso, Italy, 1470; d. at Venice, 1531. Venetian painter who has been ranked by some with Giorgione and Titian. Examples of his work are to be seen in the Ducal Palace, the Academy, and the Church of Santa Maria Mater Domini at Venice, and in various European and English collections. His *Christ Giving the Keys to Saint Peter* hangs in the Gardner Museum, Boston, and the National Gallery of Art at Washington displays his *Christ and the Samaritan Woman,* as well as two portraits by his hand.

Caterham and Warlingham (kā′tėr.ạm; wôr′ling.ạm). Urban district and residential center in SE England, in Surrey, ab. 6 mi. SE of Croydon, ab. 18 mi. S of Victoria station, London. The town has expanded rapidly in recent years. 31,290 (1951).

Caterina de' Medici (kä.tā.rē′nä dā mā′dē.chē). See **Catherine de Médicis.**

Catesby (kāts′bi), **Mark.** b. c1679; d. at London, Dec. 23, 1749. English naturalist. In 1712 he made a voyage to Virginia, from which he returned in 1719 with a rich collection of plants. He made a second voyage to America in 1722, explored the lower part of South Carolina, lived some time among the Indians at Fort Moore on the Savannah River, made excursions into Georgia and Florida, and after a visit to the Bahama Islands returned to England in 1726. He published *The Natural History of Carolina, Florida, and the Bahama Islands* (1731–43), *Hortus Britanno-Americanus, or a Collection of 85 Curious Trees and Shrubs, the Production of North America adapted to the Climate and Soil of Great Britain* (1737), *On the Migration of Birds* (1747), and others.

Catesby, Robert. b. at Lapworth, England, 1573; d. at Ashby St. Legers, England, 1605. English Roman Catholic conspirator who was involved, with Thomas Fuller, the more famous Guy Fawkes, and others, in the Gunpowder Plot (1604–05). The scheme (which entailed blowing up the Houses of Parliament) was discovered (on the night of Nov. 4, 1605) before it could be carried out, and Guy Fawkes, on whom had devolved the task of the actual firing the powder, was apprehended as he entered the cellar of the Houses of Parliament. Catesby, along with other conspirators, attempted to flee from London, but was killed in flight. Earlier he had been suspected of and arrested (but obtained a pardon) for complicity in the rebellion (1601) of Robert Devereux, 2nd Earl of Essex, and had been named an accomplice in the Rye Plot (1603) against James I.

Catfish's Camp. Former name of **Washington, Pa.**

Cathari (ka′tä.rē). See **Albigenses.**

Catharine (kath′ạ.rin). See also **Catherine.**

Catharine Archipelago. See **Aleutian Islands.**

Catharine Arrowpoint (ar′ō.point). See **Arrowpoint, Catharine.**

Catharine Coldstream (kōld′strēm), **Lady.** See **Coldstream, Lady Catharine.**

Cathay (kạ.thā′). Literary designation for China used in Western literature since the time of Marco Polo. The word survives in Russian as *Kitai,* and derives from Chinese *Ch'i-tan* (or *Kitan* or *Khitan*), the name of a tribe which established authority over what is now Manchuria and Mongolia, and ruled N China for two centuries before 1125 A.D., hence the reference to China. See *History of Chinese Society: Liao 907–1125* by Karl A. Wittfogel and Feng Chia-sheng.

Cathay. Volume of poetry (1915) by Ezra Pound. It contains translations from the Chinese based on the notebooks of Ernest Francisco Fenollosa (1853–1908), an American Orientalist. As his literary executor, Pound edited and published three volumes of poetry from Fenollosa's manuscripts: *Certain Noble Plays of Japan,* and *Noh, or Accomplishment* (both 1916), and *Cathay.*

Cathcart (kath′kärt, -kạrt), **Charles.** [Title, 9th Baron **Cathcart.**] b. 1721; d. at London, 1776. English soldier and diplomat who served as ambassador extraordinary to Russia (1768–71); father of Sir William Schaw Cathcart (1755–1843). He commanded under the Duke of Cumberland (a son of George II) in Flanders, Scotland, and Holland, held the office of lord high commissioner (1755–63 and 1773–76) in the general assembly of Scotland, and was appointed a lieutenant general in 1760. He sat twice (1761, 1773) for Sir Joshua Reynolds, and is said to have befriended James Watt and Adam Smith.

Cathcart, Sir **George.** b. at London, May 12, 1794; killed at Inkerman, in the Crimea, Nov. 5, 1854. British general; third son of Sir William Schaw Cathcart (1755–1843). He served in the campaigns against Napoleon in the period 1813–15, being in all the important battles of this span of years in which British troops participated. Appointed (January, 1852) governor and commander in chief in South Africa, he ended the Kaffir War (1852–53). In 1854 he was sent as commander of the fourth division to the Crimea, with a dormant commission to supersede Lord Raglan (the English commander in chief in the Crimean War) in case of accident to the latter. He wrote *Commentaries* (1850) on the war in Russia and Germany in 1812 and 1813.

Cathcart, Sir **William Schaw.** [Title, 1st Viscount and Earl **Cathcart.**] b. at Petersham, England, Sept. 17, 1755; d. at Cartside, near Glasgow, Scotland, June 16, 1843. British general and diplomat, 10th Baron Cathcart in the Scottish peerage, created Viscount (Nov. 3, 1807) and Earl (July 16, 1814) Cathcart in the peerage of the United Kingdom; son of Charles Cathcart (1721–76) and father of Sir George Cathcart (1794–1854). He served in the Revolutionary War (1777–80), and at the bombardment of Copenhagen (1807). He was also ambassador to Russia (1814–21).

Cathedral, The. Poem by James Russell Lowell, title piece of a volume published in 1877. Considered among the best of Lowell's later poems, it varies from appreciation of the past and the faith that had built the cathedral at Chartres to the skepticism that was a result of Lowell's own reaction against the Calvinism of his ancestors.

Cathelineau (kȧt.lē.nō, kȧ.tẹ-), **Jacques.** b. at Pin-en-Mauges, Maine-et-Loire, France, Jan. 5, 1759; d. at St.-Florent, France, July 11, 1793. French royalist, leader of the Vendeans in 1793.

Cather (kaᴛʜ′ėr), **Willa (Sibert).** b. near Winchester, Va., Dec. 7, 1876 (although some evidence indicates 1875 or 1874); d. at New York, April 24, 1947. American writer. Taken in 1885 to a ranch near Red Cloud, Neb., she grew up among Bohemian and Scandinavian homesteaders. She received her B.A. (1895) at the University of Nebraska, and served as a staff member (1897–1901) of the Pittsburgh *Daily Leader,* head of the English department (1901–06) of Allegheny High School, Pittsburgh, and associate and managing editor (1906–12) of *McClure's Magazine.* Her books reflect deep regional feeling for the American West, and interest in music. Novels published between 1913 and 1918 celebrate heroism and humanism on the prairie frontier; those between 1922 and 1926 trace the decline of the pioneer tradition and the rise of provincial materialism; later novels of the Spanish Southwest and colonial Quebec relate the frontier in its best phase to more traditional societies. The favorite theme of her work is character in conflict with a narrow village world. A selective realist, she protested against overfurnished books of the Balzac-Dreiser school; her own fiction shows economy of detail, simplicity of style. She was awarded the Prix Fémina Américaine (1933) and the gold medal (1944) of the National Institute of Arts and Letters. Her novels include *Alexander's Bridge* (1912),

O Pioneers! (1913), *The Song of the Lark* (1915), *My Ántonia* (1918), *One of Ours*, winner of the Pulitzer prize (1922), *A Lost Lady* (1923), *The Professor's House* (1925), *My Mortal Enemy* (1926), *Death Comes for the Archbishop* (1927), *Shadows on the Rock* (1931), *Lucy Gayheart* (1935), and *Sapphira and the Slave Girl* (1940). Collections of short stories are *The Troll Garden* (1905), *Youth and the Bright Medusa* (1920), *Obscure Destinies* (1932), and *The Old Beauty and Others* (1948). *April Twilights* (1903) is a book of rather conventional poems. *Not Under Forty* (1936) and *Willa Cather on Writing* (1949) are volumes of essays.

Catherine (kath'ẹ.rin). [Full title, **Catherine. A Shabby Genteel Story.**] Novel (published 1839–40 in *Fraser's Magazine*, and in book form in 1840) by William Makepeace Thackeray. It tells the story of a vicious woman who murdered her husband in 1726 and was burned at Tyburn for her crime. The "Catherine" of the novel is drawn from Mrs. Catherine Hayes (1690–1726), who did in real life what Thackeray portrays in his pages. It was Thackeray's aim to ridicule the contemporary literary fashion of picturing criminals as heroes, as in the narratives of William Harrison Ainsworth and Edward Bulwer-Lytton. The novel first appeared under one of his many pen names, Ikey Solomons, Esq., Junior.

Catherine, Saint. See the entries under **Catherine of Alexandria, Catherine of Bologna, Catherine of Genoa, Catherine of Ricci, Catherine of Siena, Catherine of Sweden.**

Catherine (of *England*). See **Catherine of Aragon.**

Catherine I (of *Russia*). [Also, **Catharine.**] b. at Jakobstadt, Courland, Russia (now Jekabpils, Latvia), c1684; d. at St. Petersburg, May 17, 1727. Empress of Russia (1725–27). She married Peter the Great and was acknowledged as his wife in 1712, was crowned as his empress in 1724, and, after his death, reigned in the period 1725–27. She was of peasant origin, was brought up in the family of a Protestant minister at Marienburg (now Malbork, Poland), named Glück, married a Swedish dragoon, fell into the hands of the Russians at the capture of Marienburg, on Aug. 23, 1702, and eventually became the serf of Prince Aleksandr Danilovich Menshikov, in whose house she attracted the attention of Peter the Great, who made her his mistress in 1703. She rescued him, by bribing the Turkish grand vizier, in 1711, from a dangerous position on the Prut River, when with an army of 38,000 men he was surrounded by 200,000 Turks. During her reign she was led chiefly by the influence of Menshikov. She founded the Russian Academy of Sciences, and fitted out the naval exploring expedition under Vitus Bering.

Catherine II (of *Russia*). [Also: **Catharine;** called **"Catherine the Great."**] b. at Stettin, Prussia, May 2, 1729; d. Nov. 17, 1796. Empress of Russia (1762–96); daughter of a prince of the German house of Anhalt-Zerbst. In 1745 she married the Russian empress Elizabeth's nephew, who ascended the throne on Jan. 5, 1762, as Peter III. Peter was mysteriously murdered on July 17, 1762, probably by a group of nobles including Grigori Orlov, Catherine's lover, and presumably with the full knowledge and approval of Catherine, who was thereupon named empress in her own right. Orlov remained one of her advisers, as was also, beginning in 1771, the officer Potemkin. A shrewd and intelligent woman, with a considerable range of intellectual interests, Catherine read many of the works of Voltaire, Rousseau, and the other rationalist humanitarians of the 18th century, but any tendencies this may have given her toward social equality were offset by the practical need to favor, or at least placate, the Russian nobility. To some extent, she reorganized local government, but she granted no rights to the serfs. Her foreign policy, ambitious and openly imperialistic, aimed at continuing the expansionist policies of Peter the Great. By the partitions (1772, 1792, 1795) of Poland (with Prussia and Austria) she greatly extended the SW frontier of Russia. Two wars with Turkey gained further territory: the first one (1768–74) established Russia as the leading power in the Near East; the second (1782–92) ended with the treaty of Iaşi (Jassy) confirming Russian acquisition of the Crimea, which Catherine had annexed in 1783. Catherine was much admired by Voltaire, who said with reference to her, "Light now comes from the North." She carried on correspondences with Voltaire, Frederick the Great, and others, and also wrote memoirs, historical and pedagogic works, and comedies.

Catherine de Médicis (dẹ mā'dē.sēs). [Italian, **Caterina de' Medici.**] b. at Florence, 1519; d. at Blois, France, Jan. 5, 1589. Queen of France, regent during the minority (1560–63) of Charles IX. She was the daughter of Lorenzo de' Medici, Duke of Urbino. She married (1533) the Duke of Orléans (who ruled France, as Henry II, in the period 1547–59), by whom she became the mother of Francis II (1559–60), Charles IX (1560–74), and Henry III (1574–89). During her regency, by the policy of attempting to hold the balance of power between the Huguenots and the Catholic party of the Guises, in accordance with which she intrigued alternately with both parties, she precipitated in 1562 the so-called Wars of the Huguenots, which, with interruptions, devastated France until 1596. On the occasion of the marriage of her daughter Marguerite of Valois with Henry of Navarre, she prevailed upon Charles to give the order for the Massacre of Saint Bartholomew's Day (Aug. 24, 1572). She had till her death an important though sometimes concealed share in the intrigues and party contests which distracted France.

Catherine Glover (gluv'ėr). See **Glover, Catherine.**

Catherine Howard (hou'ạrd). See **Howard, Catherine.**

Catherine Morland (môr'lạnd). See **Morland, Catherine.**

Catherine of Alexandria, Saint. According to tradition, a Christian martyr of the 4th century, tortured on the wheel and beheaded at Alexandria by order of the emperor Maximian. According to some accounts the torture was prevented by a miracle. The wheel became her symbol. She is commemorated on Nov. 25.

Catherine of Aragon. b. at Alcalá de Henares, Spain, in December, 1485; d. at Kimbolton, Huntingdonshire, England, Jan. 7, 1536. Queen of England; daughter of Ferdinand and Isabella of Spain. She married Arthur, Prince of Wales, in 1501, and, after his death, married Henry VIII of England in 1509. By him she became the mother of Mary Tudor (who subsequently ascended the throne of England) in 1516. About 1526 Henry, who was by that time in love with Anne Boleyn and eager to have a male heir, began to take measures toward a divorce, primarily on the grounds that his union with Catherine was invalid, the relationship between them, through her earlier marriage with his brother, being considered incestuous by the Church. The fact was that through several circumstances papal approval of the marriage had never been actually expressed; but the divorce proceedings instituted by Henry through Wolsey were not given sanction at Rome. In 1534 the Pope finally pronounced in favor of Catherine, bidding Henry to consider her his queen; by that time, however, it was too late. In 1533, the marriage had been declared void by Cranmer, archbishop of Canterbury, and Catherine had been forced into retirement, all earlier attempts at persuading her to relinquish her position voluntarily having been in vain. Henry's inability to receive the Pope's sanction to his divorce and remarriage occasioned him to pronounce the Act of Supremacy (1534), declaring himself sole head of religious rules and ceremonies in his land; thus England joined the general movement of the Reformation, and established the independent Church of England.

Catherine of Bologna, Saint. b. at Bologna, Italy, Sept. 8, 1413; d. there, March 9, 1463. Italian saint, lady of honor to Margaret d'Este, and later superioress of the Poor Clares. She was canonized in 1492.

Catherine of Braganza (brạ.gan'zạ). b. at the castle of Villa Viçosa, in the province of Alentejo, Portugal, Nov. 25, 1638; d. in Portugal, Dec. 31, 1705. Wife of Charles II of England, whom she married on May 20, 1662; daughter of John IV of Portugal. She did not live with her husband who, however, protected her on the occasion of her being accused by Titus Oates of complicity in a plot against Charles's person. Her continued childlessness militated against her at the English court. After Charles's death she returned to Portugal.

Catherine of Genoa, Saint. [Original name, **Caterina Fieschi.**] b. at Genoa, Italy, 1447; d. there, Sept. 14, 1510. Italian widow, famous for her charitable deeds during a visitation of the plague, and for her extraordinary spirit of prayer. She was the author of a *Treatise on Purgatory*. She was canonized in 1737.

Catherine of Ricci (rēt′chē), Saint. b. at Florence, 1522; d. Feb. 2, 1589. Italian saint. She took the veil among the Dominican nuns at Prato, Tuscany, in 1535, was subprioress or prioress from the age of 25 until her death, and became known for her visions. She was canonized in 1746 and is commemorated on Feb. 13.

Catherine of Siena, Saint. b. at Siena, Italy, March 25, 1347; d. at Rome, April 29, 1380. Italian saint. She became a Dominican tertiary in 1365, and obtained so great a fame for sanctity that she was enabled to mediate a peace between the Florentines and Pope Urban VI in 1378. She was canonized in 1461, and is commemorated on April 30.

Catherine of Sweden, Saint. b. 1331; d. in Sweden, March 24, 1381. Swedish saint. She was the daughter of Saint Bridget, whom she succeeded as abbess of Vadstena.

Catherine of Valois (val′wä, vȧ.lwȧ). b. at Paris, Oct. 27, 1401; d. at Bermondsey (now part of London), England, 1437. Queen of England; daughter of Charles VI of France, and wife of Henry V of England, whom she married in 1420. After Henry's death she married Owen Tudor c1425. She bore Henry a son, who was later to rule as Henry VI.

Catherlogh (kär′loċh). An Irish name of **Carlow.**

Catherwood (kath′ėr.wůd), **Mary Hartwell.** b. at Luray, Ohio, Dec. 16, 1847; d. at Chicago, Dec. 26, 1902. American novelist. She was the author of *The Romance of Dollard* (1889), *The Story of Tonty* (1890), *The Lady of Fort St. John* (1891), and *Days of Jeanne D'Arc* (1897).

Cathleen ni Houlihan (kath.lēn′ ni hö′li.han). One-act prose play (1902) by William Butler Yeats. Considered by many to be the best of Yeats's serious plays, it is a dramatization of a story of 1798 (when the Irish, with French help, sought to achieve independence) and noteworthy for its symbolic Irish nationalism. A poor old woman appears to Michael Gillane and urges him off to the wars. Despite his plans to marry and his duties at home, Michael follows this personification of patriotism out of the village. Not until the end of the play does any one on the stage become aware that the old woman is the ancient queen of Ireland in disguise.

Catholic Apostolic Church. Official name of the **Irvingites.**

Catholic Majesty. A title of the kings of Spain, assumed at times after the Council of Toledo, and permanently after the time of Ferdinand the Catholic (1474–1516).

Catholicon Anglicum (kạ.thol′i.kon ang′gli.kum). English-Latin dictionary, compiled c1483. It was edited by Sidney J. H. Herrtage for the Early English Text Society in 1881. He believed it to have been compiled in the East Riding of Yorkshire. The name "Catholicon" had first been used for such a work in a Latin grammar and dictionary written by Giovanni dei Balbi, a Genoese monk, frequently called Jannensis; it was finished in 1286, and the first edition was printed by Gutenberg in 1460.

Catholic Party (of *Belgium*). Former name of the **Christian Social Party** (of *Belgium*).

Catholic People's Party (of *The Netherlands*). Dutch political party which supports the doctrines of the Catholic Church and regards religion, the family, and property as the foundations of the social order. It favors limited state control of economic life and reorganization of the kingdom on the basis of equality for the colonies, and also supports the United Nations, strong defense forces, and participation in the economic control of Germany.

Catholic University of America. Institution of higher learning founded at Washington, D.C., in 1884, although classes did not begin until 1889, in which year it was granted papal sanction by Pope Leo XIII. It consists of five major schools: law, philosophy, literature, science, and sacred science. Undergraduate students are admitted, but most of the departments are for graduate students only.

Catholic University of Dublin. Educational institution founded in 1854 by the bishops of Ireland. John Henry Newman, who was later (1879) to become Cardinal Newman, was its rector from 1854 to 1858, and while holding that office he delivered his lectures on *The Idea of a University*. Although the institution itself eventually failed, Newman's lectures achieved and have retained note as masterpieces of English prose.

Catholic War Veterans. National society established in 1935 which is composed of honorably discharged veterans of the Catholic faith who have served in the armed forces of the U.S. during time of war. It maintains headquarters at New York.

Cathos (kȧ.tos). Female character in Molière's *Les Précieuses Ridicules*, who assumes the name Aminte. She affects the fashionable sentimentality of *les précieuses*, and is finally taken in by a valet who adopts the same style with greater success.

Catiline (kat′i.līn). [Full name, **Lucius Sergius Catilina.**] b. c108 B.C.; killed at Faesulae (now Fiesole), Italy, 62 B.C. Roman politician and conspirator. He was of an old but impoverished patrician family. As a partisan of Sulla he rendered himself infamous by his complicity in the horrors of the proscription, destroying with his own hand his brother-in-law, Q. Caecilius. He was praetor in 68, and governor of Africa in 67. After an abortive attempt, in conjunction with P. Autronius, to murder the consuls elect for 65, with a view to seizing power, and after an unsuccessful candidacy in the consular elections of 64, he organized a widespread conspiracy against the republic, whose object is said to have been the cancellation of debts, the proscription of the wealthy, and the distribution among the conspirators of all offices of honor and emolument. It was defeated by the vigilance and eloquence of Cicero, who was then consul. The rebellion having broken out in Etruria, on Oct. 27, Cicero pronounced in the senate, on Nov. 8, his first oration against Catiline, which caused the latter to leave the city. On Nov. 9 Cicero delivered in the Forum his second Catilinian oration, in which he acquainted the people with the events in the senate and the departure of Catiline from Rome. On Dec. 3 documentary evidence of the conspiracy was obtained from an embassy of Allobroges, which had been tampered with by the Catilinarians; and in the evening Cicero delivered in the Forum his third oration, in which he acquainted the people with the events of the day and the seizure of the conspirators remaining at Rome. On Dec. 5 Cicero delivered in the senate his fourth oration, which was followed by the execution in prison of Lentulus, Cethegus, Statilius, and Galinius. Meanwhile Catiline had assumed command of the revolutionary force, which amounted to about two legions, but was overtaken by the army of the senate as he was attempting to escape into Gaul, and was defeated and slain in the battle which ensued.

Catiline's Conspiracies. Play by Stephen Gosson, written before 1579. It was acted, but not printed.

Catiline's Conspiracies. Tragedy (1598) by Robert Wilson and Henry Chettle, perhaps a revised version of Gosson's play.

Catiline's Conspiracy. Tragedy by Ben Jonson, produced in 1611. Catiline is made inhumanly ferocious in this play.

Catina (kat′i.nạ). A Latin name of **Catania,** city.

Catinat (kȧ.tē.nȧ), **Nicolas de.** b. 1637; d. 1712. Marshal of France. Of comparatively humble birth, the son of a minor official, his rise to the highest military rank sufficiently proves his possession of unusual natural military talent. During the War of the Grand Alliance against France (1689–97) he won notable victories, but during the War of the Spanish Succession his reverses at the hands of Prince Eugene of Savoy led to his removal from command.

Cat Island. Island in the Atlantic Ocean, SE of Miami, Fla.; part of the Bahamas. It was once believed to have been the first island visited by Columbus. Fishing and farming are the major enterprises. Area, 160 sq. mi.; pop. 3,870 (1943).

Catlettsburg (kat′lẹts.bėrg). City in NE Kentucky, county seat of Boyd County, near the confluence of the Big Sandy and Ohio rivers. Founded in 1808, it was formerly important as a trading center and river port. 4,750 (1950).

Catley (kat′li), **Ann.** b. near Tower Hill, London, 1745; d. near Brentford, England, Oct. 14, 1789. English singer. In 1762 she appeared at Vauxhall, London, and from this time her beauty and voice made her not only successful but well known. In 1784 she made her last appearance, having then become the wife of Major-General Francis

Lascelles. The ladies eagerly copied her dress, and to be "Catleyfied" was to be dressed becomingly.

Catlin (kat′lin), **George.** b. at Wilkes-Barre, Pa., June 26, 1796; d. at Jersey City, N.J., Dec. 23, 1872. American artist, and traveler among the North American Indians and in Europe. His chief written work is *Illustrations of the Manners, Customs, and Condition of the North American Indians* (1841). He painted more than 500 portraits of Indians from life, a unique and valuable collection, now in the U.S. National Museum at Washington, D.C. Many of his sketches of Indians are in the American Museum of Natural History at New York.

Catmandoo (kät.män.dö′). See **Katmandu.**

Cato (kā′tō). Tragedy by Joseph Addison, produced at the Drury Lane Theatre, London, in 1713, but probably written for the most part ten years before. At the time it was produced, its popularity was due to a political situation: the Whigs identified Cato with the Duke of Marlborough; the Tories identified Marlborough with Caesar, the would-be dictator. Hence, but for different reasons, both parties were loud in their praise of the play, while Addison protested his innocence of any political intention.

Cato, Dionysius. Reputed author of a famous collection of precepts. Nothing is known about him except that he is supposed to have gathered and arranged the morally edifying apothegms known as *Dionysii Catonis disticha de moribus ad filium*, much admired, and widely used in the schools, during the Middle Ages.

Cato, Marcus Porcius. [Called **"Cato the Elder"** and **"Cato the Censor"**; surnamed **Priscus.**] b. at Tusculum, Italy, 234 B.C.; d. 149 B.C. Roman statesman, general, and writer. He was quaestor under Scipio in 204, served as consul in 195, served in Spain in 194 and against Antiochus in 191, was censor in 184, and was ambassador to Carthage in 150. He sought to restore the integrity of morals and the simplicity of manners prevalent in the early days of the republic, his severity as a censor earning him the epithet "Censorius." The prosperity of Rome's old enemy Carthage led him to advocate a third Punic war, in his effort to incite to which he for years closed every speech in the senate with the words, "Ceterum censeo Carthaginem esse delendam" ("Furthermore, I am of the opinion that Carthage ought to be destroyed"). He wrote *De agri cultura*, also called *De re rustica* (edited by Keil, 1882) and *Origines* (extant in fragments).

Cato, Marcus Porcius. [Called **"Cato the Younger"**; surnamed **Uticensis,** meaning "of Utica."] b. at Rome, 95 B.C.; committed suicide at Utica, North Africa, 46 B.C. Roman patriot and Stoic philosopher; great-grandson of Marcus Porcius Cato (234–149 B.C.). He fought under Gellius Publicola against Spartacus in 72, served as military tribune in Macedonia in 67, and was questor in 65, tribune of the people in 62, and praetor in 54. He supported Cicero against the faction of Catiline, and sided with Pompey against Caesar on the outbreak of the civil war in 49. After the battle of Pharsalia he retired to Utica, where he put himself to death on receiving intelligence of the victory of Caesar at Thapsus. He had a reputation for scrupulous fairness and honor, and his death was considered noble and courageous.

Catoche (kä.tō′chā), **Cape.** Cape in E Mexico, the NE extremity of the Yucatán peninsula. It is a low-lying cape, and was first sighted by the Spaniards in 1517. It has a lighthouse.

Cato Major (kā′tō mā′jo̤r). See **De senectute.**

Catonsville (kā′to̤nz.vil). Unincorporated community in N Maryland, in Baltimore County: residential suburb of Baltimore. It is the seat of St. Charles College. Under the urban definition established for use in the 1950 census, Catonsville was counted with adjoining urban areas; its last official separate enumeration was 13,565 (1940).

Cato's Letters. Collection (4 vols., 1724) of essays by John Trenchard and Thomas Gordon. They originally appeared in *The London Journal*, founded by Trenchard and Gordon in 1719. They presented the Whig viewpoint, and demanded the punishment of the promoters of the South Sea Bubble. Trenchard attacked standing armies, and superstition. Gordon, who translated Tacitus and Sallust, is supposed to be the Silenus of Pope's *Dunciad*.

Cato Street Conspiracy (kā′tō). [Also, **Thistlewood Conspiracy.**] In British history, a conspiracy under the lead of Arthur Thistlewood, which aimed to assassinate Robert Stewart, Viscount Castlereagh, and other cabinet officers. The plot was discovered on Feb. 23, 1820, and came to nothing.

Catriona (ka̤.trē′o̤.na̤). Romantic novel (1893) by Robert Louis Stevenson. It deals with the adventures of David Balfour, who also appears in *Kidnapped*, and with his love for Catriona Drummond, the daughter of James More Drummond, a rascal and a renegade. After much misunderstanding, David and Catriona are happily married.

Catron (kā′tro̤n), **John.** b. c1786; d. May 30, 1865. American jurist. Elected (1824) to the Tennessee court of last resort (later known as the supreme court of errors and appeals), he was first chief justice (1831–34) of Tennessee. In 1837 he was appointed by Jackson associate justice of the U.S. Supreme Court.

Catroux (kȧ.trö), **Georges.** b. at Limoges, France, Jan. 29, 1877—. French army officer and diplomat, first ambassador of the fourth French Republic to the U.S.S.R. After service in the French colonies, he fought in France during World War I; wounded, he was captured and imprisoned together with Charles de Gaulle, at Magdeburg fortress. He was governor general of Indochina (August, 1939–May, 1940), joined General de Gaulle at London after the armistice (June, 1940), and was deprived by Vichy of his French nationality (December, 1940) and condemned to death *in absentia* (April, 1941). Having entered (June, 1941) Syria with the Allied forces, he was named (July, 1941) French high commissioner for Syria and Lebanon. He became (November, 1942) commander of the French North African forces, served as governor of Algeria (June–November, 1943), and was military commander in Lebanon (November, 1943), and minister for North Africa (September, 1944). He was ambassador to the U.S.S.R. from December, 1944 to February, 1948.

Cats (käts), **Jakob.** b. at Brouwershaven, Netherlands, 1577; d. 1660. Dutch poet. He studied at Leiden and Orléans, where he received a doctor's degree, and was subsequently an advocate at The Hague and at Middelburg. In 1636 he was made pensionary of Holland. He died on his estate near Scheveningen. "Father Cats," as he was effectionately called, was for generations a popular favorite. His *Houwelijck* (Fidelity) appeared in 1625, *Spieghel van den Ouden en Nieuwen Tijdt* (Mirror of the Old and New Time) in 1632, and *Trouringh* (Wedding Ring) in 1637.

Cat's Cradle. Novel (1925) by Maurice Baring.

Catskill (kat′skil). [Former name, **Catskill Landing.**] Village in E New York, county seat of Greene County, on the W bank of the Hudson River, ab. 30 mi. S of Albany. It is a summer resort, and manufactures knitted goods, bricks, and distilled beverages. The Rip Van Winkle Bridge crosses the Hudson here. 5,392 (1950).

Catskill Mountains. [Also: **Catskills;** formerly also **Katzbergs.**] Group of mountains in SE New York, W of the Hudson River, in Greene, Ulster, and Delaware counties, belonging to the Appalachian system. They are noted for picturesque scenery, and contain many popular summer resorts. Among the chief summits are Slide Mountain (the highest point, 4,204 ft.), Kaaterskill High Peak (Mount Lincoln), Overlook Mountain, and Hunter Mountain. Ashokan Reservoir (part of the New York city water system), the sources of the Delaware River, and a state forest of 232,423 acres are in the Catskills.

Catt (kat), **Carrie Chapman.** [Maiden name, **Lane.**] b. at Ripon, Wis., Jan. 9, 1859; d. at New Rochelle, N.Y., March 9, 1947. American pioneer in the woman suffrage movement; first married (1884) to Leo Chapman (d. 1886), she married (1890) George William Catt (d. 1905). Educated at Iowa State College, she was appointed high-school principal (1881) and superintendent of schools (1883) at Mason City, Iowa. In 1887 she delivered her first speech on woman suffrage at Marshalltown, Iowa. She served (1890–92) as state lecturer and organizer for the Iowa Woman Suffrage Association, was a staff member (1892–1947) and president (1900–04, 1915–47) of the National American Woman Suffrage Association, and was president (1904–23) of the International Woman Suffrage Alliance. A leader in the campaign for the adoption of the 19th amendment to the U.S. Constitution (ratified and established in 1920), she was also active in work for world peace and international organization.

Cattack (ką.tak'). See **Cuttack.**

Cattaro (kät'tä.rō). Italian name of **Kotor.**

Cattegat (kat'ę.gat). See **Kattegat.**

Cattell (ką.tel'), **James McKeen.** b. at Easton, Pa., May 25, 1860; d. Jan. 20, 1944. American psychologist, professor of psychology at Columbia University from 1891 to 1917. He was editor of the periodicals *Science* (1894 *et seq.*) and *Scientific Monthly* (1900 *et seq.*), and founder of *American Men of Science.*

Catterall Quartet (kat'ėr.ąl). Ensemble established (1910–11) at London, with Arthur Catterall and O'Malley, violins, Johan C. Hock, cello, and David Reggel, viola.

Cattermole (kat'ėr.mōl), **George.** b. at Dickleborough, Norfolk, England, Aug. 8, 1800; d. at Clapham, London, July 24, 1868. English painter, one of the earliest English water-colorists. He illustrated Sir Walter Scott's *Waverley Novels.* His subjects were chiefly medieval.

Catti (kat'ī). See **Chatti.**

Cattier (kȧ.tyā), **Félicien.** b. 1869; d. 1947. Belgian political scientist. He taught civil law and the law of the Belgian Congo at the University of Brussels. In 1935 he became head of the National Cancer Foundation, after the death of Émile Frangui. His books on the Congo Free State (État Indépendant du Congo), a severe indictment of maladministration, were influential in the reform movement which got under way after the Free State became the Belgian Congo. These works are *Droit et administration du Congo* (1898) and *Étude sur la situation de l'État Indépendant du Congo* (1906).

Cattle Raid of Cooley (kö'lę). See **Tain Bo Cuailgne.**

Catullus (ką.tul'us), **Gaius Valerius.** b. at Verona, Italy, c84 B.C.; d. c54 B.C. Roman poet. Particularly effective in simple short lyric poems, he is ranked by many with Sappho and Shelley. Coming to Rome he became acquainted with the most celebrated men of his day, including Julius Caesar (whom he attacked in his verses but to whom he later was reconciled), Cicero, Asinius Pollio, Cornelius Nepos, and Calvus. His love poems are addressed to Lesbia, whose real name, according to Apuleius, was Clodia, the beautiful and fascinating wife of Caecilius Metellus and the sister of the demagogue Clodius, Cicero's enemy. This identification is now generally accepted. The stormy love affair (which gave to some of the poems a bitterness not usually found in lyric verse) ended in unhappiness for Catullus. The extant poems number 113, and include lyrics, epigrams, elegies, and even a short epic of 408 lines about the marriage of Peleus and Thetis. They fall into three groups: short lyrics, four longer poems (including two wedding hymns and the epic), and a group of epigrams and elegies. The themes of some of his most famous and charming poems are the death of Lesbia's pet sparrow, the "thousand kisses," the dinner invitation, the homecoming to Sirmio, the love of Acme and Septimius, the marriage of Torquatus, the death of a brother. The Attis, in galloping galliambics, is a metrical tour de force of extraordinary effectiveness. Catullus greatly influenced Horace in his *Odes*, Vergil in the *Aeneid*, Ovid and the other elegists, and the epigrammatist Martial.

Catulus (kat'ų.lus), **Gaius Lutatius.** fl. 3rd century B.C. Roman general. He was chosen consul for the year 242 B.C. When he entered office the first Punic war had been waged since 264, and the senate, discouraged by numerous losses, had abandoned the war at sea. He obtained command of a fleet built by wealthy patriots at Rome, and in 241 gained the decisive victory at the Aegadian Islands which resulted in a favorable treaty of peace.

Catulus, Quintus Lutatius. b. c152 B.C.; d. 87 B.C. Roman general; father of Quintus Lutatius Catulus (d. 60 B.C.). He was consul with Marius in 102 B.C., and was associated with him in the victory over the Cimbri, at Vercellae, in 101 B.C. He joined Sulla in the civil war, and, having in consequence been proscribed by Marius, he is thought to have committed suicide in 87 B.C.

Catulus, Quintus Lutatius. d. 60 B.C. Roman politician; son of Quintus Lutatius Catulus (c152–87 B.C.). He was consul (78 B.C.) and censor (65 B.C.). He was a strong supporter of Cicero against the conspiracy of Catiline, in 63 B.C.

Caturiges (kat.ų.rī'jēz). Celtic-speaking tribe which in ancient times dwelt between the Cottian and Maritime Alps.

Catuvellauni (kat"ų.vę.lô'nī). Ancient British people which lived in the region of modern Herefordshire and Bedfordshire, west of the Trinobantes and Iceni. The Catuvellaunian state was a central kingdom formed, or greatly extended, by the conquests of Cassivellaunus. There are various forms of the name.

Caua (kä'wä). See **Cagua.**

Caub (koup). [Also, **Kaub.**] Town in the former province of Hesse-Nassau, Prussia, situated on the Rhine above Oberwesel. The passage of the Rhine was effected here by Blücher, on Jan. 1, 1814.

Cauca (kou'kä). Department in SW Colombia. It is very mountainous, being traversed by the Cordillera Occidental, with the Cordillera Central on its eastern frontier, and is rich in mines and forests. Capital, Popayán; area, 11,660 sq. mi.; pop. 454,200 (est. 1950).

Cauca River. River in W Colombia, between the central and western Cordilleras (Cordillera Central and Cordillera Occidental) of the Andes, flowing N to join the Magdalena River. Length, over 600 mi.

Caucasia (kô.kā'zhą). [Also, **Caucasus.**] Region in E Europe, a former general district of the Russian empire, lying N of Iran and Asiatic Turkey, E of the Black Sea, and W of the Caspian Sea. It comprised the northern Caucasus, including the governments or provinces of Stavropol, Kuban, and Terek; and Transcaucasia, including Dagestan, Kutais, Tiflis (Tbilisi), Baku, Elisavetpol, Kars, Batum, and Erivan. It is now divided between the Azerbaijan, Georgian, and Armenian Soviet Socialist Republics and the Russian Soviet Federated Socialist Republic of the U.S.S.R. Its chief cities are Tiflis (Tbilisi), Baku, and Erivan. The chief natural features of the region are the Caucasus Mountains and the rivers Kura, Rion, Kuban, and Terek.

Caucasiae Portae (kô.kā'zi.ē pôr'tē). See **Caspian Gates.**

Caucasians (kô.kā'zhąnz, -kazh'ąnz). In Blumenthal's ethnological system, now obsolete, the highest type of the human family, including nearly all Europeans, the Circassians, Armenians, Persians, Hindus, Jews, and others. He gave this name to the "race" because he regarded a skull he had obtained from the Caucasus as the standard of the human type.

Caucasian Wall. See under **Derbent.**

Caucasus (kô'ką.sus). See **Caucasia.**

Caucasus Indicus (in'di.kus). An ancient name of the **Hindu Kush.**

Caucasus Mountains. [Russian: **Kavkaz**; sometimes also **Bolshoi Kavkaz,** meaning in English "Great Caucasus."] Mountain system in the U.S.S.R., between the Black and Caspian seas, extending SE and NW, often taken as the conventional boundary between Europe and Asia. The chief summits are Elbrus (18,481 ft.) and Kazbek (16,541 ft.). There are numerous passes, some of them reaching an elevation of 10,000–11,000 ft. The glaciers rival those of the Alps, but lakes are almost entirely lacking. The mountains have been extremely important historically as a barrier to migrations. Length of the system, ab. 800 mi.; greatest width, ab. 120 mi.

Cauchy (kō.shē), **Augustin Louis.** b. at Paris, Aug. 21, 1789; d. at Sceaux, France, May 23, 1857. French mathematician and poet. He taught at Paris, and at Turin, Italy (1830–48) where he had gone as a political refugee. His works include *Sur la théorie des ondes* (1815), *Cours d'analyse* (1821), *Leçons sur le calcul différentiel* (1826), and *Sur l'application du calcul de résidus* (1827).

Caudebec-en-Caux (kōd.bek.äṅ.kō). [Also, **Caudebec.**] Town in NW France, in the department of Seine-Inférieure, situated on the Seine River, ab. 20 mi. NW of Rouen. The Church of Notre Dame, in flamboyant Gothic style, one of the finest medieval buildings in the region, and many other buildings in the town were badly damaged in World War II. 1,680 (1946).

Caudebec-lès-Elbeuf (kōd.bek.le.zel.bėf). Town in NW France, in the department of Seine-Inférieure, situated on the Seine River, adjacent to the town of Elbeuf, S of Rouen. Textiles are manufactured. A large part of the town, including the Church of Notre Dame (14th–

16th century), was destroyed in World War II. 8,562 (1946).

Caudéran (kō.dā.räṅ). City in SW France, in the department of Gironde, W of Bordeaux. It is a suburb of Bordeaux. 25,377 (1946).

Caudillo (kou.ᴛʜē'lyō; in Spanish America, kou.ᴛʜē'yō). Spanish term for a leader or head man of an armed troop. In imitation of the use of the titles *Duce* by Mussolini and *Führer* by Hitler, Francisco Franco used it to create for himself a title as dictator. Although doubtless best known as a proper name (i.e. "*the Caudillo*") among English-speaking people for the use thus made of it by Franco, it has wide usage also in the Spanish-speaking countries of America.

Caudine Forks (kô'dīn). [Latin, **Furculae Caudinae.**] Two passes in the mountains of ancient Samnium, Italy, leading to an enclosed valley, between Capua and Benevento. Here the Romans under the consuls Spurius Postumius Albinus and T. Veturius were forced (321 B.C.) to surrender to the Samnites under Pontius. The Romans were forced to swear to a treaty of peace, and to give 600 Roman *equites* (knights) as hostages, while the whole Roman army was sent under the yoke (thus symbolizing their collective submission). Infuriated by this last humiliation, which was one of the worst ever accepted by a Roman military force, the Roman senate refused to approve the treaty, and delivered the consuls to the Samnites, who refused to accept them.

Caudle's Curtain Lectures (kô'dlz), **Mrs.** Series of sketches by Douglas Jerrold, published (1845) in *Punch.* They take the form of discourses on domestic subjects inflicted by Mrs. Caudle upon Mr. Caudle after they had gone to bed and the curtains were drawn for the night.

Caudry (kō.drē). Town in N France, in the department of Nord, ab. 17 mi. SW of Valenciennes. It has manufactures of lace and embroidery. 12,163 (1946).

Cauer (kou'ėr), **Emil.** b. at Kreuznach, Germany, Aug. 6, 1867—. German sculptor; son of Karl Cauer (1828–85), under whom he studied. He worked at Rome for one year before settling (1888) at Berlin. Of his many monuments and fountains, the best known is the Bismarck Monument for which he (together with his brother Ludwig) won the first prize in a competition.

Cauer, Hugo. b. at Kreuznach, Germany, May 5, 1864; d. there, July 31, 1918. German sculptor; son of Karl Cauer (1828–85). He studied at Rome and with Begas at the Berlin Academy. He designed many war memorials and sepulchres; his bust of the singer Lilli Lehmann is a noteworthy example of his work in portraiture.

Cauer, Karl. b. 1828; d. 1885. German sculptor; brother of Robert Cauer (1831–93) and father of Emil Cauer (1867—), Hugo Cauer (1864–1918), and Ludwig Cauer (1866—).

Cauer, Ludwig. b. at Kreuznach, Germany, May 28, 1866—. German sculptor; son of Karl Cauer (1828–85), under whom he studied. He was also a pupil of Begas at Berlin, where he settled after trips to Rome and London. Among his works are the allegorical figures of Commerce and Industry at Begas' National Monument for Emperor Wilhelm I at Berlin, his portrait statue of Emperor Charles IV, also at Berlin, and the bronze portrait of Sir Thomas More at London.

Cauer, Minna. b. at Freyenstein, Germany, Nov. 1, 1841; d. at Berlin, Aug. 3, 1922. German feminist. She organized (1888) the women white-collar workers, and in 1889 established a league of progressive women's organizations. She wrote *Die Frau im 19. Jahrhundert* (1898).

Cauer, Robert. b. 1831; d. 1893. German sculptor; brother of Karl Cauer (1828–85) and father of Stanislaus Cauer (1867—).

Cauer, Stanislaus. b. at Kreuznach, Germany, Oct. 18, 1867—. German sculptor; son of Robert Cauer (1831–93). He received his early training in his father's studio at Rome. After working at Berlin (1905–07), he taught at the academy at Königsberg. His bust of Paul von Hindenburg is considered one of his best portraits; he is also known for his genre figures and monuments.

Caughnawaga (kog.nạ.wog'ạ, kä'nạ.wä"gạ). Village in S Quebec, Canada, on the S bank of the St. Lawrence river ab. 11 mi. by road SW of Montreal. It was founded in 1667 as a refuge for Iroquois Christians, and is still an Indian community, though governed by municipal laws since 1890.

Caulaincourt (kō.laṅ.kör), Marquis **Armand Augustin Louis de.** [Additional title, Duke of **Vicenza.**] b. at Caulaincourt, Somme, France, Dec. 9, 1772; d. at Paris, Feb. 19, 1827. French diplomat and general. He was ambassador to Russia (1807–11) and minister of foreign affairs (1813–14, 1815). His memoirs were published more than a century after his death.

Caulfeild (kôl'fēld), **James.** [Titles: 4th Viscount and 1st Earl of **Charlemont.**] b. at Dublin, Aug. 18, 1728; d. Aug. 4, 1799. Irish statesman.

Caulfield (kôl'fēld), **James.** b. Feb. 11, 1764; d. at St. Bartholomew's Hospital, London, April 22, 1826. English print-seller, especially noted as a collector of engraved portraits.

Cauliac (kō.lyȧk), **Guy de.** See **Chauliac, Guy de.**

Caulier (kō.lyā), **Madeleine.** d. July 24, 1712. French peasant girl noted for bravery during the siege of Lille. On Sept. 8, 1708, she carried an important order from the Duke of Burgundy to Marshal Boufflers, commander of the besieged army. She was permitted, as a reward, to enlist in a regiment of dragoons, and fell in the battle of Denain.

Caulonia (kou.lô'nyä). [Former name, **Castelvetere.**] Town and commune in S Italy, in the *compartimento* (region) of Calabria, in the province of Reggio di Calabria, situated on a rocky elevation near the Mediterranean Sea, E of the town of Reggio di Calabria. The town was founded by the Greeks (Achaeans) and dates back to the 7th century B.C. It has markets for citrus fruits. Pop. of commune, 12,004 (1936); of town, 4,827 (1936).

Cauls or **Caulx** (kō), **Salomon de.** See **Caus, Salomon de.**

Caulvin (kō.vaṅ), **Jean.** See **Calvin, John.**

Caumont (kō.môṅ), **Arcisse de.** b. at Bayeux, France, Aug. 28, 1802; d. at Caen, France, April 15, 1873. French archaeologist.

Cauquenes (kou.kā'nās). Capital of Maule province, in W Chile. 12,987 (1940).

Caura (kou'rä). River in C Venezuela flowing N to the Orinoco River. Length, ab. 150 mi.

Caus (kō), **Salomon de.** [Also: **Caux, Cauls,** or **Caulx.**] b. 1576; d. 1626. French physicist. While serving as engineer to the Elector Palatine he published his notable book *Les Raisons des forces mouvantes avec diverses machines* (1615), in which the physical facts concerning the power of steam were examined and explained, so that he may be considered to have pioneered in stating the theory of the steam engine.

Causeries du lundi (kōz.rē dü lėṅ.dē). [Eng. trans., "*Monday Talks.*"] Series of critical essays contributed by Charles Augustin Sainte-Beuve to current French periodicals and later collected and published (1851–62) in book form. They were followed by *Nouveaux lundis* (1863–72).

Caussade (kō.sȧd). Town in S France, in the department of Tarn-et-Garonne, situated on the Lère River ab. 13 mi. NE of Montauban. It is one of the centers of the woolen industry and the manufacture of straw hats in the department. In the 16th century it was a Protestant stronghold. 4,203 (1946).

Causses (kōs). Group of limestone plateaus in S France, in the department of Lozère and the vicinity, near the headwaters of the Tarn River.

Caussin de Perceval (kō.saṅ de per.sẹ.vȧl), **Armand Pierre.** b. at Paris, Jan. 13, 1795; d. there, Jan. 15, 1871. French Orientalist and historian, a traveler in Syria, and professor of Arabic at the College of France, son of J. J. A. Caussin de Perceval. He wrote *Essais sur l'histoire des Arabes* (1847).

Caussin de Perceval, Jean Jacques Antoine. b. at Montdidier, France, June 24, 1759; d. July 29, 1835. French Orientalist and historian; father of Armand Pierre Caussin de Perceval. His best-known works are translations from Greek and Arabic.

Cauterets (kō.tẹ.re). Town in SW France, in the department of Hautes-Pyrénées, situated in an alpine valley surrounded by high peaks, ab. 28 mi. SW of Tarbes. It is a tourist and winter-sports center, as well as a famous health resort. It has 22 hot sulfur springs considered useful in the treatment of asthma, rheumatism, arthritis, and other ailments. There are numerous bathing establishments, casinos, clubs, hotels, parks, and trails. 1,253 (1946).

Cautín (kou.tēn'). Province in S central Chile. Apples, cattle, grain, and lumber are produced. The region was formerly occupied by the Araucanian Indians. Capital, Temuco; area, 6,707 sq. mi.; pop. 297,284 (est. 1950).

Caution, Mrs. Character in William Wycherley's *The Gentleman Dancing-Master.*

Cautionary Towns. Name given to the four communities in the Netherlands (Brielle, Vlissingen or Flushing, Middelburg, and Rammekens) held in the period 1585–1616 by England as security for payment due.

Cautley (kôt'li), Sir **Proby Thomas.** b. at Stratford St. Mary's, Suffolk, England, 1802; d. at Sydenham (now part of London), Jan. 25, 1871. English colonel of engineers in India, and paleontologist. He was especially noted as the superintendent of construction of the Ganges canal, in the period 1843–54. As a geologist he explored the Siwalik range, making large collections of fossils which he presented to the British Museum. He published numerous papers on scientific (chiefly paleontological) topics.

Cauto (kou'tō). River in S Cuba, flowing W to the Gulf of Guacanayabo. Length, ab. 150 mi.

Cauvery (kô'vėr.i). [Also: **Cavery, Kaveri.**] River in the state of Madras, SE Union of India, flowing E into the Bay of Bengal through a delta. It is much used for irrigation. Length, ab. 475 mi.

Cauvin (kō.vaṅ), **Jean.** See **Calvin, John.**

Cauwelaert (kou'we̦.lärt), **Frans Van.** b. at Onze-lieve-Vrouwe Lombeek, Belgium, 1880—. Belgian lawyer, teacher, and public official. Educated at Louvain, Leipzig, and Munich, he served as professor of experimental psychology and pedagogy (1907–10) at Fribourg, Switzerland. He was elected (1910) to the chamber of representatives, called to the bar at Antwerp in 1913, was burgomaster of Antwerp (1921–32), served as minister of economic affairs (1933–34), and became (1939) president of the chamber of representatives. He was a delegate (1925–27) to the League of Nations, and a leader of the Flemish Catholic Party. Author of *Verhandelingen en Voordrachten* (2 vols., 1906–08) and *Vrig Belgie* (1918); contributor to reviews on political and economic topics.

Caux (kō). Territory in Normandy, France, comprised in the department of Seine-Inférieure, and situated N of the Seine, bordering the English Channel. Its chief town is Caudebec-en-Caux.

Caux, Salomon de. See **Caus, Salomon de.**

Cava de' Tirreni (kä'vä dā tēr.re'nē). [Also: **Cava dei Tirreni, La Cava.**] Town and commune in S Italy, in the *compartimento* (region) of Campania, in the province of Salerno, situated at the foot of the Lattari mountains, near the Gulf of Salerno, ab. 26 mi. SE of Naples. It has manufactures of cotton textiles, and of cords and twines for fisheries; owing to its mild climate and beauty of scenery, it is a popular resort. The Benedictine Abbey of Santa Trinità, founded in 1025, was famous in the Middle Ages as a chief proponent of the Cluniac principles of reform. It contains art and numismatic collections and a library with important historical archives; the present church is in the baroque style. It was slightly damaged in World War II. Pop. of commune, 33,051 (1936); of town, 12,124 (1936).

Cavaignac (kȧ.ve.nyȧk), **Éléonore Louis Godefroy.** b. at Paris, 1801; d. there, May 5, 1845. French journalist and republican politician; son of Jean Baptiste Cavaignac. He was prominent as a republican leader in the events of 1830, 1832, and 1834.

Cavaignac, Eugène. b. at Le Havre, France, 1876—. French historian; son of J. M. E. G. Cavaignac. He served (1903 *et seq.*) as a member of the École d'Athenes. Author of *Histoire financière d'Athenes* (Financial History of Athens, 1909) and *Histoire de l'antiquité* (History of Ancient Times, 1912 *et seq.*).

Cavaignac, Jacques Marie Eugène Godefroy. b. at Paris, May 21, 1853; d. at Château Ourne, near Flée, Sarthe, France, Sept. 25, 1905. French political leader and engineer; son of Louis Eugène Cavaignac and father of Eugène Cavaignac. He resigned (1899) as war minister during the Dreyfus affair, after having publicly taken a stand as one of the believers in Dreyfus's guilt. A deputy since 1892, he had earlier been minister of the navy (1892) and minister of war (1895–96, 1898–99).

Cavaignac, Jean Baptiste. b. at Gourdon, Lot, France, 1762; d. at Brussels, March 24, 1829. French revolutionist; father of E. L. G. Cavaignac and Louis Eugène Cavaignac. He was a deputy to the Convention of 1792, which officially declared the first French Republic.

Cavaignac, Louis Eugène. b. at Paris, Oct. 15, 1802; d. at Ournes, near Flée, Sarthe, France, Oct. 28, 1857. French general; son of Jean Baptiste Cavaignac and father of J. M. E. G. Cavaignac. He served (1832–48) in Algeria, where he was governor (1848), and, while minister of war, suppressed an insurrection at Paris as military dictator (June 23–26). He was chief of the executive (June–December, 1848), and was an unsuccessful candidate (December, 1848) for president.

Cavaillon (kȧ.vȧ.yôṅ). [Ancient name, **Cabellio.**] Town in S France, in the department of Vaucluse, situated on the Durance River, ab. 12 mi. SE of Avignon. The beautiful Cathedral of Saint Veran was consecrated by Pope Innocent IV in 1251; the triumphal arch is a Roman structure. Cavaillon is in the heart of a fruit-growing region; produces kitchenware and tin cans. 13,804 (1946).

Cavala or **Cavalla** (ka̦.val'a̦). See **Kavalla.**

Cavalcade. Play (1931) by Noel Coward. It traces the fortunes of an English family, the Marryots, from 1899 to 1930. Coward's aim is to glorify the English spirit during that period, which includes the last years of Victoria's reign, that of Edward VII, World War I, and the greater part of the reign of George V. The screen version duplicated the success of the stage play.

Cavalcanti (kä.va̦l.kun'tē̦), **Domingos Olímpio Braga.** See **Olímpio, Domingos.**

Cavalcanti (kä.väl.kän'tē), **Guido.** b. at Florence, c1259; d. there, in August, 1300. Florentine poet and philosopher; a friend of Dante. He wrote sonnets and ballads in the "dolce stil nuovo," a lyrical style of the late 13th century intended for the elegant expression of tender feeling.

Cavalcanti (kä.va̦l.kun'tē̦), **José Lins do Rêgo.** See **Rêgo, José Lins do.**

Cavalcaselle (kä"väl.kä.sel'lā), **Giovanni Battista.** b. at Legnago, near Verona, Italy, Jan. 22, 1820; d. at Rome, Oct. 31, 1897. Italian art critic and historian. In 1848 he became involved in the struggle for liberation from Austria and was imprisoned. Later he was banished and sought refuge in England. With Joseph Archer Crowe he published *The Early Flemish Painters* (1857), *History of Painting in Italy* (1864–71), *Titian: his Life and Times* (1877), and *Raphael: his Life and Works* (1882). He was appointed inspector of the Museo Nazionale at Florence in 1867, and later became general inspector of fine arts in Rome.

Cavalese (kä.vä.lā'sā). Town and commune in NE Italy, in the *compartimento* (region) of Trentino-Alto Adige, in the province of Trento, the chief place in the Fiemme valley, SE of Bolzano: lumber trade and summer resort. Pop. of commune, 2,736 (1936); of town, 2,124 (1936).

Cavalier (kȧ.vȧ.lyā), **Jean.** b. at Ribaute, near Anduze, Gard, France, c1681; d. at Chelsea, London, in May, 1740. French general, a leader (1702–04) of the Camisards in the Cévennes. After leading the insurgents for a period, he submitted to the king, although some of his followers continued their resistance. Subsequently he fought for Savoy and England.

Cavalieri (kä.vä.lye'rē), **Emilio de'.** [Also, **del Cavaliere.**] b. at Rome, c1550; d. there, March 11, 1602. Italian composer, member of the group of Florentine musicians and poets who launched the new form of dramatic music at the end of the 16th century. His most important work was *La Rappresentazione di anima e di corpo*, the first oratorio. He was one of the first to use solo voices with instrumental accompaniment, and the mode of notation called figured bass.

Cavalieri, Francesco Bonaventura. [Also, **Cavalleri** (kä.väl.lā'rē).] b. at Milan, Italy, 1598; d. at Bologna, Italy, Dec. 3, 1647. Italian mathematician, celebrated as the inventor of the geometrical method of indivisibles. His chief work is *Geometria indivisibilium continuorum nova quadam ratione promota.*

Cavalieri, Lina. See **Muratore, Lina.**

Cavalier Marino (kä.vä.lyer' mä.rē'nō), **il.** See **Marini** (or **Marino**), **Giovanni Battista.**

Cavalier Parliament. See **Pensioned** (or **Pension**) **Parliament.**

Cavaliers. Name given to the supporters of the Stuart kings of England, particularly under the reign of Charles I. Some of them came to the Virginia colony after 1647, but until recently their influence upon the life and culture of that area was highly exaggerated.

Cavaliers of Virginia: or, the Recluse of Jamestown, The. Historical romance (1837) by William Alexander Caruthers. Although this work is presented as a piece of fiction it gives a remarkably full and accurate account of Bacon's Rebellion, in 1676, against the tyrannical policies of Sir William Berkeley, governor of the Virginia colony, and the leader of that uprising, Nathaniel Bacon, is the hero of the story.

Cavall (ka.val'). King Arthur's dog.

Cavalleria Rusticana (kä.väl.lä.rē'ä rös.tē.kä'nä). [Eng. trans., "*Rustic Gallantry*."] Opera in one act by Pietro Mascagni, with a libretto by Monsasci and Targioni-Tarzetti, first played at Rome on May 18, 1890.

Cavallero (kä.väl.lā'rō), Count **Ugo.** b. at Casale Monferrato, Italy, Sept. 20, 1880; d. at Frascati, Italy, Sept. 12, 1943. Italian soldier and industrialist. He headed (1918) the Italian military delegation at Versailles and was promoted to general. In 1920 he retired but was recalled (1925) to the armed forces to serve as undersecretary for war (1925–28); having been created a senator (1926) and count (1928), he became commander in chief (1937) of East African troops; as general of the army (1940) he returned to Italy to replace Badoglio as chief of staff (1940–43). He was found (Sept. 12, 1943) shot to death at German headquarters at Frascati.

Cavalli (kä.väl'lē), **Pietro Francesco.** [Original surname, **Caletti-Bruni.**] b. at Crema, Italy, Feb. 14, 1602; d. at Venice, Jan. 14, 1676. Italian composer, organist, and choir leader of Saint Mark's, Venice; a pupil of Monteverdi. He began to compose operas in 1637, and continued to produce them for 32 years; among them are *Giasone* (1655), *Serse* (1660), and *Ercole amante* (1662). He is now considered to have been the inventor of the da capo, which was long attributed to Scarlatti.

Cavallini (kä.väl.lē'nē), **Pietro.** b. 1250; d. at Rome, 1330. Italian painter, mosaicist, and sculptor. Little is known concerning this artist who flourished in the very dawn of the Renaissance, beyond the fact that some of the frescoes in the Church of San Francesco at Assisi, and others in the Church of Santa Cecilia at Rome, were his work. Nevertheless he is of some importance in the history of Italian art by reason of his influence on Cimabue and Giotto.

Cavallo (kä.väl'lō), **del.** Nickname of **Leopardi, Alessandro.**

Cavalotti (kä.vä.lôt'tē), **Felice Carlo Emmanuele.** b. 1842; d. 1898. Italian patriot, politician, and dramatist. From his youth, when he fought under Garibaldi, he remained an ardent, turbulent, and uncompromising radical. He entered the Italian parliament in 1873, and for some years before his death he was the leader of the left in that body. The vigor of his attacks, in his speeches and his plays, on his conservative opponents, embroiled him in 33 duels. The 33rd was fatal.

Cavan (kav'an), 10th Earl of. [Title of **Frederic Rudolph Lambart.**] b. 1865; d. at London, Aug. 28, 1946. British soldier. He served in South Africa, and in World War I, commanding a guards division in France (1916), British forces in Italy (1918), and the 10th Italian army (1918). He was chief (1922–26) of the imperial general staff, and retired in 1926.

Cavan. [Irish, **An Cabhán.**] Inland county of Ulster province, in the Irish Republic. It is bounded on the N by County Fermanagh (Northern Ireland), on the NE and E by County Monaghan, on the SE by County Meath, on the S by Counties Longford and Westmeath, and on the SW and W by County Leitrim. The surface of most of the county is undulating except in the NW portion where it is mountainous. There are many lakes and bogs widely scattered over the county. The principal industry is agriculture, including the raising of dairy cattle. Cavan is the county seat; area, ab. 730 sq. mi.; pop. 66,412 (1951).

Cavan. Urban district in Ulster province, Irish Republic, county seat of County Cavan, ab. 24 mi. SW of Monaghan. 3,564 (1951).

Cavan, John. Character in Noel Coward's anti-war play *Post Mortem* (1931). John Cavan returns from his French grave 13 years after he is dead, and is unable to convince anybody, except his mother, that the war has been a terrible mistake.

Cavarzere (kä.vär'dzā.rā). Town and large commune in NE Italy, in the *compartimento* (region) of Veneto, in the province of Venezia, situated on the Adige River near its mouth, S of Venice. It is a marketing center for a district producing grain, vegetables, and sugar beets on improved former swampland. It belonged to Venice until the fall of the Venetian republic in 1797. Pop. of commune, 25,199 (1936); of town, 4,973 (1936).

Cava Zuccherina (kä'vä dzök.ke.rē'nä). Former name of **Iesolo.**

Cavazzola or **Cavazzuola** (kä.väd.dzō'lä). [Original name, **Paolo Morando.**] b. at Verona, Italy, 1486; d. there, 1522. Italian painter. He executed frescoes in several of the churches of his native city, and his designs for scenes from the Passion have been especially admired.

Cave (kāv), **Anne (Estella Sarah Penfold).** [Title, Countess **Cave of Richmond;** maiden name, **Mathews.**] d. Jan. 7, 1938. English author of travel books and memoirs. She was awarded the Medal of Queen Elizabeth of the Belgians. Her works include *Memories of Old Richmond* (1922), *Three Journeys* (1928), and *Odds and Ends of My Life* (1929).

Cave, Edward. b. at Newton, Warwickshire, England, Feb. 27, 1691; d. at London, Jan. 10, 1754. English printer and bookseller. In 1731 he started a printing office at London under the name of R. Newton, and founded the *Gentleman's Magazine* which he edited under the pseudonym of Sylvanus Urban, Gent. He began in 1732 the publication of regular reports of parliamentary debates, based on the memory of reporters who had listened to the speeches, and put in proper literary shape by William Guthrie and, after him, for several years by Samuel Johnson. This publication of these reports brought upon him the censure of Parliament.

Cave, William. b. at Pickwell, Leicestershire, England, 1637; d. at Windsor, England, July 4, 1713. English divine and patristic scholar.

Caveat or Warning for Common Cursitors, Vulgarly Called Vagabones, A. Prose work (1566) by Thomas Harman, a country gentleman living at Crayford, Kent. He examined thieves, tramps, beggars, and other undesirable characters, who came to his door to beg. The knowledge thus obtained he used in the work by which he is remembered. It was dedicated to his neighbor, Elizabeth, Countess of Shrewsbury, and contains 24 essays, on different underworld types, examples of underworld slang, and some realistic woodcuts.

Caveau (kȧ.vō). Parisian literary and social club, founded in 1729, dissolved in 1739, and refounded in 1806 and 1834; its name was taken from a tavern of the same name.

Cavedoni (kä.vä.dō'nē), **Celestino.** b. at Levizzano Rangone, near Modena, Italy, May 18, 1795; d. at Modena, Italy, Nov. 26, 1865. Italian archaeologist and numismatist.

Caveeshar (kä.vē.shär'), **Sardul Singh.** [Also, **Singh Sirdar Sardul Caveeshar.**] b. at Amritsar, Punjab, India, 1886—. Sikh leader, politician, and journalist, president (1932, 1933) of the Indian National Congress, and president (1940) of the All-India Forward Bloc. Founder of the *Sikh Review*, he was secretary (1920) of the All-India Sikh League, and president (1925) of the Punjab provincial conference. Author of *India's Fight for Freedom* (1931).

Cavelier (kȧ.vẹ.lyā), **Pierre Jules.** b. Aug. 30, 1814; d. Jan. 28, 1894. French sculptor. His chief works include *Penelope*, *Truth*, *Abélard*, and *Cornelia* (all at Paris).

Cavelier de Cuverville Island (dẹ kü.ver.vēl). See **Cuverville Island.**

Cavelier de la Salle (dẹ lȧ sȧl), **Robert.** See **La Salle, Robert Cavelier,** Sieur **de.**

Cavell (kav'ẹl), **Edith Louisa.** b. in Norfolk, England, 1865; executed in Belgium, Oct. 12, 1915. English nurse who was executed by German military authorities during World War I. She adopted nursing as a career at London, and served as first matron of the Berkendael Medical Institute at Brussels, which became (1914) a Red Cross hospital. She assisted over 100 British, French, and Belgian soldiers to escape over the Dutch border during the German occupation of Belgium. Arrested for her activities by the Germans, she admitted her assistance in these escapes, and was condemned to death by a court-martial. She was shot (Oct. 12, 1915) by a firing squad.

Cavender's House (kav'ẹn.dėrz). Narrative poem (1929) in blank verse by Edwin Arlington Robinson. The story is told by means of dialogue between Cavender and his dead wife, Laramie, whom he had killed 12 years before.

Cavendish (kav'ẹn.dish). Pseudonym of **Jones, Henry.**

Cavendish, Lord **Frederick Charles.** b. at Eastbourne, England, Nov. 30, 1836; d. at Dublin, May 6, 1882. English politician; brother of Spencer Compton Cavendish. He was private secretary to Lord Granville (1859–64), a member of Parliament (1865–82), private secretary to W. E. Gladstone (July, 1872–August, 1873), financial secretary of the treasury (1880–82), and successor (May, 1882) to W. G. Forester as chief secretary to the lord lieutenant of Ireland. He was assassinated by Irish revolutionists together with Thomas Henry Burke, an undersecretary, while they were walking in Phoenix Park, Dublin.

Cavendish, George. b. 1500; d. c1561. English biographer and constant attendant of Cardinal Wolsey; brother of Sir William Cavendish (c1505–57). He served as an usher (1526–30) to Wolsey, retiring to Glensford, in Suffolk, after the cardinal's death. His *Life of Cardinal Wolsey*, written in 1557, was withheld from publication during Elizabeth's reign and, as a result, only abridged or garbled versions were in circulation until the definitive edition of S. W. Singer in the early 19th century.

Cavendish, Georgiana. b. June 9, 1757; d. at London, March 30, 1806. English society woman, famous for her beauty, wit, and social influence.

Cavendish, Henry. b. at Nice, France, Oct. 10, 1731; d. at London, March 10, 1810. English chemist and physicist; great-grandson of William Cavendish (1640–1707) and a cousin of William Cavendish (1720–64). He studied at Cambridge in the period 1750–53, but did not take a degree. He discovered nitric acid, and was the first who, by inductive experiments, combined oxygen and hydrogen into water. He also anticipated several later discoveries concerning the nature of electricity. He published numerous scientific papers, including "Experiments on Air, by Henry Cavendish, Esq.," in the *Philosophical Transactions* of the Royal Society, of which he became a member in 1760.

Cavendish, Sir **John.** Killed at Bury Saint Edmunds, England, 1381. English jurist. Chief justice of the king's bench (1372–81), he was killed with Sir John of Cambridge, prior of Saint Edmunds abbey, by Jack Straw's peasantry. Earlier he had been judge of the assize (1370–72) and chancellor (1371) of Cambridge University.

Cavendish, Margaret. [Title, Duchess of **Newcastle.**] b. at St. John's, near Colchester, Essex, England, 1624; d. at London, Jan. 7, 1674. English court lady, dramatist, poet, and biographer of her husband. In 1643 she was maid of honor to Queen Henrietta Maria, with whom she went to Paris, where she met and married (as his second wife) William Cavendish, 1st Duke of Newcastle. She wrote *Philosophical Fancies*, *Philosophical and Physical Opinions*, *Grounds of Natural Philosophy*, *A True Relation of My Birth, Breeding, and Life*, *Sociable Letters*, and several plays and poems, but she is best remembered for her enthusiastic life of her husband, written while he was still living, *The Life of the Thrice Noble, High and Puissant Prince, William Cavendish, Duke, Marquis, and Earl of Newcastle, Earl of Ogle, Viscount Mansfield, and Baron of Bolsover, of Ogle, Bothal, and Hepple* . . . (1667; another edition came out in 1675, and a Latin translation, in 1668, all published at London). Charles Lamb praised her, but Samuel Pepys, who called her *Humorous Lovers* "a silly play," thought she was "a mad, conceited, ridiculous woman." She is buried in Westminster Abbey.

Cavendish, Spencer Compton. [Title, 8th Duke of **Devonshire**; earlier known as Marquis of **Hartington.**] b. July 23, 1833; d. at Cannes, France, March 24, 1908. English statesman; brother of Lord Frederick Charles Cavendish and uncle of V. C. W. Cavendish, 9th Duke of Devonshire. He was educated at Trinity College, Cambridge, and entered Parliament for North Lancashire in 1857. He held various offices in the Liberal ministries of his time, and from 1875 to 1880 was leader of his party in the House of Commons. The position of prime minister was offered to him by Queen Victoria in 1880, but was declined. After the secession of Liberals caused by W. E. Gladstone's Home Rule Bill in 1886, he was the recognized leader of the Liberal Unionist Party. He also served as lord president of the council (1895–1903).

Cavendish or **Candish, Thomas.** b. in the parish of Trimlay St. Martin, Suffolk, England, c1555; d. at sea in the South Atlantic, in June, 1592. English navigator and freebooter. In 1585 he commanded a ship in the fleet of Richard Grenville, sent by Raleigh to Virginia. On July 21, 1586, he sailed from Plymouth with three small vessels, the *Desire*, the *Content*, and the *Hugh Gallant* (which was sunk in the Pacific). He touched at Africa and Brazil, and passed the Strait of Magellan in January, 1587, ravaged the shores of Spanish South America and Mexico, taking many vessels, and on Nov. 14, 1587, captured a ship from the Philippines with an immense booty. He then crossed the Pacific, and returned by way of the Cape of Good Hope, reaching England on Sept. 10, 1588. This was the third circumnavigation of the world. Cavendish undertook a similar voyage in 1591 with five ships; but, after enduring great hardships, he was unable to pass the Strait of Magellan. His ships were scattered, and he died while attempting to return. Only a few of his crew ever reached England.

Cavendish, Victor Christian William. [Title, 9th Duke of **Devonshire**; known as Lord **Hartington.**] b. May 31, 1868; d. May 6, 1938. English politician; nephew of Spencer Compton Cavendish, 8th Duke of Devonshire. A member of Parliament, he was financial secretary to the treasury, civil lord of the admiralty (c1914), governor general of Canada (1916–21), secretary of state for the colonies (1922–24), and high steward of Cambridge.

Cavendish, Sir **William.** b. at Cavendish, Suffolk, England, c1505; d. Oct. 25, 1557. English politician; younger brother of George Cavendish (1500–c1561), and father of William Cavendish (d. 1626). He was treasurer of the royal chamber under Henry VIII, Edward VI, and Mary.

Cavendish, William. [Title, 1st Earl of **Devonshire.**] d. March 3, 1626. English courtier; second son of Sir William Cavendish (c1505–57) by his third wife (afterward Countess of Shrewsbury). He was created 1st Earl of Devonshire on Aug. 2, 1618.

Cavendish, William. [Title, Duke of **Newcastle.**] b. 1592; d. Dec. 25, 1676. English statesman and writer, created earl of Newcastle March 7, 1628, and duke of Newcastle March 16, 1665; grandson of Sir William Cavendish (c1505–57) and nephew of William Cavendish (d. 1626). He was governor (1638–41) of the Prince of Wales; rendered important military services to the Royalist cause during the English civil war, fought as a volunteer at Marston Moor, and left England in 1644, returning at the Restoration.

Cavendish, William. [Title, 1st Duke of **Devonshire.**] b. Jan. 25, 1640; d. at London, Aug. 18, 1707. English nobleman; great-grandson of William Cavendish (d. 1626). He was created 1st Duke of Devonshire and Marquis of Hartington on May 12, 1694. He erected (1687–1706) Chatsworth, the seat of the dukes of Devonshire.

Cavendish, William. [Title, 4th Duke of **Devonshire.**] b. 1720; d. Oct. 3, 1764. English statesman, lord lieutenant and governor general of Ireland in 1755 and prime minister from November, 1756 to May, 1757; great-grandson of William Cavendish (1640–1707) and a cousin of Henry Cavendish.

Cavendish Laboratory. Scientific institute of Cambridge University, England, founded in 1873, opened in 1876, and reconstituted in 1888.

Caventou (kȧ.väṅ.tö), **Joseph Bienaimé.** b. 1795; d. 1877. French chemist. For many years he pursued his researches at the École de Pharmacie at Paris, where he was a professor. In collaboration with P. J. Pelletier he achieved results of very great importance in the isolation of strychnine, brucine, and quinine.

Cave of Adullam (ạ.dul'ạm). See **Adullam, Cave of.**

Cave of Mammon (mam'ọn). See **Mammon, Cave of.**

Cave of the Guacharos (gwä′chä.rōs). See **Guacharos, Cave of the.**

Cave of the Winds. Recess behind Niagara Falls, between them and the wall of rock, often visited by tourists.

Cavery (kô′vėr.i). See **Cauvery.**

Caves du Vatican (kȧv dü vȧ.tē.käṅ), **Les.** Brief comic novel (1914; Eng. trans., *The Vatican Swindle, The Adventures of Lafcadio*), by the French writer André Gide (1869–1951), relating the vicissitudes of a group of French people whose lives have been disturbed by the rumor of the kidnaping of the Pope. This story is credited with being the best example of Gide's ironic vein.

Caviana (ką.vyu′ną). [Also, **Cavianna.**] Island in NE Brazil, at the mouth of the Amazon River, near the Atlantic Ocean. Length, 50 mi.

Caviedes (kä.byā′ᴛʜās), **Eloi Temístocles.** b. at Rancagua, Chile, 1849; d. ? Chilean journalist and author. Among his works are *Viva San Juan!*, a novel, and *Las Islas de Juan Fernández*, the result of a voyage made in 1883.

Caviglia (kä.vē′lyä), **Enrico.** b. at Finale Ligure, Italy, May 4, 1862; d. there, March 22, 1945. Italian general. He joined the army in 1883. In 1918 he distinguished himself at Caporetto as commanding officer of the 24th Army Corps and headed the 8th Army in the Vittorio-Veneto campaign. He became (1919) a senator and minister of war; with the rank of general, he headed (December, 1920) the troops which took Fiume from Gabriele D'Annunzio. He was appointed (1926) a marshal of Italy and decorated (1929) with the Collar of the Annunziata, making him an honorary cousin of the king. At the change (Sept. 8, 1943) of government, he assumed for part of the day command of Rome and negotiated with the Germans for surrender of the city; after this he retired to private life.

Cavite (kä.vē′tā). Province of the Philippine Islands, in the S central part of Luzon. It is bounded by Manila Bay on the N, Rizal province on the NE, Laguna de Bay and Laguna province on the E, Batangas (separated by the Tagaytay range and Sungay Mountain) on the S and SE, and Manila Bay on the NW. The N part of Cavite, watered by many rivers, is very fertile and produces rice, abacá, sugar cane, and coffee. Over 25 percent of the land is agricultural. The native race is Tagalog. Capital, Cavite; area, 464 sq. mi.; pop. 238,581 (1939), 262,550 (1948).

Cavite. Fortified city on the island of Luzon, in the Philippines, situated on Manila Bay ab. 10 mi. SW of the city of Manila: capital of Cavite province. Near it a Spanish fleet was defeated by a U.S. squadron under Dewey, on May 1, 1898. Pop. 35,016 (1948).

Cavo (kä′vō), **Monte.** [Also, **Monte** (or **Mount**) **Albano.**] Highest summit of the Alban Hills, situated ab. 15 mi. SE of Rome. On it are the ruins of the temple of Jupiter Latiaris. 3,145 ft.

Cavour (kä.vör′), **Camillo Benso,** Conte **di.** b. at Turin, Italy, Aug. 10, 1810; d. there, June 6, 1861. Italian statesman, a leading figure in the Italian Risorgimento movement. He entered the Sardinian parliament in 1848, was a member of Azeglio's cabinet (1850–52), and became prime minister of Sardinia in 1852. He joined the alliance of the western powers and Turkey against Russia in 1855 and in the same year sent a contingent of 15,000 Sardinian troops under La Marmora to the Crimea. In 1856 he represented Sardinia at the Congress of Paris; he formed an alliance with Napoleon III against Austria at Plombières in 1858, and carried on, with the assistance of the French, a successful war against Austria in 1859. In the same year he resigned the premiership, dissatisfied with the terms of peace imposed by Napoleon at Villafranca di Verona. He resumed the premiership in 1860, secretly supported the expedition of Garibaldi against Sicily in the same year, and achieved the unification of Italy, except Venice and the Patrimonium Petri (a division of the Papal States), under the scepter of Victor Emmanuel II in 1861.

Cawahib (ką.wä′hib). See **Parentintins.**

Cawdor (kô′dǫr). [Also, **Calder.**] Civil parish in N Scotland, in Nairnshire, ab. 5 mi. SW of Nairn. Cawdor Castle is the traditional scene of the murder (1040) of Duncan by Macbeth. 767 (1931).

Cawdor. Narrative poem by Robinson Jeffers, title piece of a volume published in 1928.

Cawdor, Thane of. In Shakespeare's *Macbeth*, a prosperous gentleman whose rank was promised to Macbeth by the witches. No sooner had the prophecy been made than Macbeth learned that Cawdor was to be executed by order of Duncan for treason. He died nobly: "nothing in his life became him like the leaving it." It has sometimes been said that his behavior corresponds in almost every circumstance with that of the unfortunate Earl of Essex beheaded by Queen Elizabeth. The Thane of Cawdor does not appear upon the stage at all, but Macbeth succeeds to his office.

Cawein (kā.wīn′), **Madison Julius.** b. at Louisville, Ky., March 23, 1865; d. Dec. 8, 1914. American poet. His verse, much of it about Kentucky nature themes or the supernatural, was published in *Blooms of the Berry* (1887), *The Triumph of Music* (1888), *Lyrics and Idyls* (1890), *Poems of Nature and Love* (1893), *Shapes and Shadows* (1898), *Kentucky Poems* (1902), *The Giant and the Star* (1909), *The Poet and Nature and the Morning Road* (1914), and *The Cup of Comus* (1915). His work was admired by William Dean Howells, Edmund Gosse, and Joyce Kilmer.

Cawnpore (kôn.pōr′). [Also, **Cawnpur.**] District in the Allahabad division, Uttar Pradesh (United Provinces), Union of India, S of the Ganges River: wheat, rice, sugar, and barley. Area, 2,384 sq. mi.; pop. 1,556,247 (1941).

Cawnpore. [Also: **Cawnpur, Kanpur.**] City in Uttar Pradesh (United Provinces), N central Union of India, on the S bank of the Ganges River, ab. 50 mi. SW of Lucknow. Industries include flour mills, vegetable-oil mills, bristle factories, and chemical works; of major importance are the leather, woolen, and cotton-textile plants. It was an important military station under the British government. Here, in the Sepoy mutiny (June and July, 1857), the British garrison and their families were massacred by the mutineers under Nana Sahib. 487,324 (1941).

Caxamarca (kä.hä.mär′kä). See **Cajamarca.**

Caxias (ką.shē′ąs). City in E Brazil, in the state of Rio de Janeiro. 24,050 (1940).

Caxias. City in S Brazil, in the state of Rio Grande do Sul. 32,158 (1950).

Caxias, Duke of. Title of **Lima e Silva, Luiz** (or **Luis**) **Alves de.**

Caxibo (kä.shē′bō). See **Cashibo.**

Caxton (kaks′tǫn), **Pisistratus.** Principal character in *The Caxtons*, a novel by Edward Bulwer-Lytton. Under this name he wrote *My Novel* (the sequel to *The Caxtons*) and other works.

Caxton, William. b. in Kent, England, c1422; d. at Westminster, London, 1491. First English printer. He was first apprenticed to a London mercer, Robert Large (Lord Mayor of London in the period 1439–40), and after his master's death (1441) went to Bruges, where he served out the remainder of his apprenticeship (1446), and then established himself as a mercer, becoming c1465 governor of the English Association of Merchant Adventurers in that city. In 1469 he began a translation from French which he called *The Recuyell of the Historyes of Troye* (completed in 1471 at Cologne), and to supply the great demand for copies of the book set himself to learn the art of printing. *The Recuyell*, the first printed English book, appeared in 1475, having been printed probably at the press of Colard Mansion at Bruges. In 1475 he completed and had printed (perhaps by Mansion) a translation of a French version of the *Ludus scacchorum* of J. de Cessolis, under the title *The Game and Playe of the Chesse;* this was the second printed English book. He left Bruges in 1476, and set up his press at Westminster (the exact site is uncertain), from that time until his death being constantly engaged in translating and printing with several assistants, among whom was Wynkyn de Worde, his successor.

Caxtons, The. Novel by Edward Bulwer-Lytton, first published anonymously in *Blackwood's Magazine* in 1848 and in book form in 1850.

Cayaguas (kä.yä′gwäs). See under **Grande de Loíza.**

Cayambe (kä.yäm′bā). City in N Ecuador, in Pichincha province. 11,855 (est. 1944).

Cayambe. Volcano in Ecuador, NE of Quito. 19,187 ft.

Cayapó (kä.yä.pō′). [Also, **Kayapó.**] South American Indian tribe, now extinct, which formerly inhabited the area between latitudes 15°–22° S. and longitudes 49°–55° W. in Brazil. The language was of the Ge family.

Cayarí (kä.yą.rē′). River in W Brazil. See the **Madeira River.**

Cayce (kās). Town in C South Carolina, in Lexington County, on the Congaree River ab. 4 mi. S of Columbia. 3,294 (1950).

Cayenne (kī.en′, kā.en′). City in N French Guiana, South America, on the island of Cayenne, at the mouth of the Cayenne River: capital and seaport. 11,704 (1946).

Cayenne. A former name of **French Guiana.**

Cayes (kā). [Also: **Aux Cayes, Les Cayes.**] City in SW Haiti, on the Caribbean Sea: seaport. 11,835 (1950).

Cayey (kä.yā′). Town in SE Puerto Rico, ab. 39 mi. by road S of San Juan, in a mountain valley. Sugar is the chief cash crop. Just NW of Cayey is a large settlement of the rural rehabilitation program of PRRA (Puerto Rico Reconstruction Administration). Elevation, 1,233 ft.; pop. 18,402 (1950).

Cayey, Sierra de. See **Sierra de Cayey.**

Cayla (ke.lȧ), Comtesse **du.** [Title of **Zoé Victoire Talon.**] b. at Boullay-Thierry, near Dreux, France, Aug. 5, 1785; d. at St.-Ouen, near Paris, March 19, 1852. Favorite of Louis XVIII of France. After his death (1824) she became a patroness of agriculture and industry.

Cayley (kā′li), **Arthur.** b. Aug. 16, 1821; d. Jan. 26, 1895. English mathematician; brother of Charles Bagot Cayley. He was graduated from Trinity College, Cambridge, in 1842, was called to the bar in 1849, and became Sadlerian professor of pure mathematics in the University of Cambridge in 1863.

Cayley, Charles Bagot. b. near St. Petersburg, July 9, 1823; d. at London, Dec. 6, 1883. English poet; brother of Arthur Cayley. He is known chiefly as a translator of Dante, and also translated Homer, Petrarch, and Aeschylus.

Caylus (ke.lüs). Town in S France, in the department of Tarn-et-Garonne, ab. 24 mi. NE of Montauban. Pop. ab. 800.

Caylus, Anne Claude Philippe de Tubières, Comte **de.** b. at Paris, Oct. 31, 1692; d. there, Sept. 5, 1765. French archaeologist; son of Marie Marguerite Le Valois de Villette de Murçay, Comtesse de Caylus. His works include *Receuil d'antiquités égyptiennes, étrusques, grecques, romaines, et gauloises* (7 vols., 1752–67).

Caylus, Marie Marguerite Le Valois de Villette de Murçay, Comtesse **de.** b. in Poitou, France, 1673; d. April 15, 1729. French court lady and author; mother of Anne Claude Philippe de Tubières, Comte de Caylus, and niece of Madame de Maintenon, under whose protection she was educated at the court of Louis XIV. She left a work, much admired for its contemporary portraits and beauty of style, which was edited (1770) by Voltaire under the title *Souvenirs de Madame de Caylus.*

Cayman Islands (kā′mąn, kī.män′). [Also, **Caymans.**] Group of islands in the Caribbean Sea, ab. 200 mi. NW of Jamaica. Comprised of Grand Cayman, Little Cayman, and Cayman Brac, they are a dependency of the British colony of Jamaica. Turtle fishing, shipbuilding, and ropemaking are the major industries. Capital, Georgetown; area, 93 sq. mi.; pop. 6,670 (1943).

Cayo Hueso (kī′ō wā′sō). Spanish name of **Key West,** island.

Cayor (kä′yôr). One of three kingdoms of the Sudanic-speaking Wolof people of W Africa.

Caÿster (ką.is′tėr). [Also, **Caystrus** (ką.is′trus); modern Turkish, **Bayındır.**] In ancient geography, a river in Lydia, Asia Minor, which flows into the Aegean Sea ab. 35 mi. S by SE of Smyrna (Izmir); now called the Bayindir or, sometimes, the Little Menderes. The ancient city of Ephesus was near its mouth. Length, over 100 mi.

Cayuga (kā.ū′gą, ką-, kī-). One of the original five North American Indian tribes of the League of the Iroquois, and the smallest thereof. It is now scattered among several reservations, of which one is in Ontario, Canada.

Cayuga Lake. Lake in W central New York: one of the Finger Lakes. Its outlet is through the Cayuga, Seneca, and Oswego rivers into Lake Ontario, and it is connected by canal with Seneca Lake. The chief city on it is Ithaca. Length, ab. 40 mi.; average width, 2 mi.

Cayuse War (kī.ūs′). War (1847–50) between white settlers in Oregon and the Cayuse Indians of NE Oregon. It was touched off by the Whitman massacre, and was fought by the whites for the avowed purpose of apprehending those responsible for the slaughter. The war was brought to a close after the surrender of five Indians who confessed to the deed.

Cazalès (kȧ.zȧ.les), **Jacques Antoine Marie de.** b. at Grenade, Haute-Garonne, France, Feb. 1, 1758; d. at Engalin, Gers, France, Nov. 24, 1805. French politician and orator. He was a royalist advocate in the meeting of the States General of 1789, from which the republicans seceded to form the National Assembly.

Cazalla de la Sierra (kä.thä′lyä dā lä syer′rä). Town in S Spain, in the province of Sevilla, situated on the southern slopes of the Sierra Morena, ab. 40 mi. NE of Seville. There are iron and lead mines in the vicinity; the town has wine markets and distilleries. 10,220 (1940).

Cazamian (kȧ.zȧ.myäṅ), **Louis.** b. at Saint-Denis, on the French island of Réunion, April 2, 1877—. French scholar and authority on English literature. Author (with Émile Legouis) of an important *Histoire de la littérature anglaise* (1925; Eng. trans., *A History of English Literature,* 1927).

Cazane Defile (kä.zän′). See **Kazan Defile.**

Cazaubon (kȧ.zō.bôṅ). See under **Barbotan.**

Cazembe (ką.zem′bę). See **Kazembe.**

Cazenovia (kaz.ę.nō′vi.ą). Town (in New York the equivalent of township in many other states) and village in C New York, in Madison County, on Cazenovia Lake. It is the seat of Cazenovia Seminary and Junior College. The village was settled in 1793. Pop. of town, 3,969 (1950); of village, 1,946 (1950).

Cazin (kȧ.zaṅ), **Jean Charles.** b. at Samer, Pas-de-Calais, France, May 25, 1841; d. at Lavandon, near Toulon, France, March 27, 1901. French painter. He studied with Lecoq de Boisbaudran, and afterward in England, where he also designed ceramics. Among his Biblical pictures are *La Fuite en Égypte* (1877) and *Le Voyage de Tobie* (1878). He was best known for his tranquil landscapes.

Cazotte (kȧ.zot), **Jacques.** b. at Dijon, France, Oct. 17, 1719; d. at Paris, Sept. 25, 1792. French man of letters. His works include *Olivier* (1763), *Le Diable amoureux* (1771), *Le Lord impromptu* (1772), and others. He was arrested by the revolutionary tribunal and guillotined.

Ccapac (kä′päk), **Huayna.** See **Huaina Capac.**

Ccapac, Manco. See **Manco Capac** (or **Ccapac**).

Ccapac, Mayta. See **Mayta Ccapac.**

Ccapac Yupanqui (yö.päng′kē). See **Capac** (or **Ccapac**) **Yupanqui.**

"CCC." See **Civilian Conservation Corps.**

C C Clique. In Chinese politics, the extreme right-wing faction established (1928) within the Kuomintang by the two Ch'en brothers, Ch'en Li-fu and Ch'en Kuo-fu, with a neo-Confucian program emphasizing one party, one leader, one doctrine. Their long control of key posts in the party and also in the Kuomintang-dominated government has been blamed by many critics in and out of the party for leading to the final collapse of the Kuomintang.

CCF. See **Co-operative Commonwealth Federation.**

Ceadda (chad′dä), Saint. See **Chad** or **Ceadda,** Saint.

Ceán-Bermúdez (thā.äm′ber.mö′ᴛʜeth), **Juan Agustín.** b. 1749; d. 1829. Spanish painter and art historian. His work as an artist is largely forgotten, but as a historian of Spanish art he remains authoritative. He wrote extensively on painting, architecture, and antiquities, his most enduring works being *Diccionario histórico de los mâs ilustres profesores de las bellas artes en España* (1800) and *Descripción artistica de la catedral de Sevilla* (1804).

Ceannanus (or **Ceanannus**) **Mór** (kan′ą.nus mōr). Irish name of **Kells.**

Ceann Sáile (kan soi′lę). Irish name of **Kinsale.**

Ceará (sä.ą.rä′). See also **Fortaleza.**

Ceará. State in E Brazil, bounded on the N by the Atlantic Ocean. Capital, Fortaleza; area, 59,168 sq. mi.; pop. 2,101,325 (1940), 2,735,702 (1950).

Céard (sā.ȧr), **Henri.** [Pseudonym (infrequently used), **Nicolas Kerlio.**] b. at Bercy, France, Nov. 18, 1851; d. at Paris, Aug. 16, 1924. French poet and playwright of the naturalist group. Author of *Les Résignés* (1889), *Tout pour l'honneur* (1890; based on Zola's *Le Capitaine Burle*), and other plays, as well as of poems like *Sonnets de Guerre* (1920).

Cease Firing. Novel by Mary Johnston, published in 1912.

Ceatharlach (kär′lạch). Irish name of **Carlow.**

Ceawlin (ke.ou′lin). d. 593. King of the West Saxons; son of Cynric whom he succeeded in 560. He took part in the battle of Beranbyrig (Barbury Hill, near Marlborough) in 556, fought and defeated the Kentish Jutes at Wimbledon in 568, and defeated three British kings at Deorham (probably Dereham, Gloucestershire) in 577. He was defeated in 583 by the Britons, and in 591 was driven from his throne by a popular revolt.

Ceballos (sä.bä′yōs), **Juan Bautista.** b. in Durango, Mexico, 1811; d. after 1854. Mexican jurist. He was a member of congress, and in 1852 was made president of the supreme court. On the resignation of Mariano Arista he was chosen president ad interim of Mexico, on Jan. 6, 1853, and was given extraordinary powers for three months, but resigned on Feb. 7.

Ceballos, Mariano Herencia. See **Herencia Ceballos, Mariano.**

Ceballos Cortés y Calderón (thā.bä′lyōs kôr.tās′ ē käl-dā.rōn′; American-Spanish, sā.bä′yōs), **Pedro de.** [Also, **Pedro de Zevallos Cortés y Calderón.**] b. at Cádiz, Spain, June 29, 1715; d. at Córdoba, Spain, Dec. 26, 1778. Spanish general. As governor (1756 *et seq.*) of Buenos Aires, he forced the surrender of the Portuguese fort at Colonia del Sacramento (now Colonia, Uruguay), taking 26 English vessels (Nov. 2, 1762). He returned to Spain in 1767, was appointed first viceroy of Buenos Aires in 1776, took Santa Catarina from the Portuguese (February, 1777), retook and destroyed Colonia del Sacramento, which had reverted to the Portuguese by the peace of 1763, and returned to Spain in 1778.

Cebalrai (se.bal′rä.ē). The fourth-magnitude star β Serpentis, in the head of the creature.

Cebenna Mons (sẹ.ben′ạ monz). Latin name of the **Cévennes.**

Cebes (sē′bēz). fl. at Thebes, Boeotia, in the 5th century B.C. Greek philosopher; a friend and pupil of Socrates. He is one of the interlocutors in Plato's *Phaedo.* Three works were ascribed to him, probably erroneously, one of which, *Tabula,* is a philosophical explanation of a table symbolically representing the dangers and vicissitudes of life.

Ceboruco (sä.bō.rö′kō). Volcano in Mexico, near the Pacific Ocean. Elevation, ab. 7,100 ft.

Cebrián y Agustín (thā.brē.än′ ē ä.gös.tēn′; American Spanish, sā.brē.än′), **Pedro de.** [Title, Count of **Fuenclara.**] fl. in the 18th century. Spanish administrator, a grandee of Spain. From Nov. 3, 1742, to July 9, 1746, he was viceroy of New Spain (Mexico), and subsequently was Spanish ambassador to Vienna.

Cebu (sä.bö′). [Also, **Zebu.**] Island in the Philippines, between Negros and Leyte islands. Length, 139 mi.; area, 1,695 sq. mi.; pop. 947,309 (1939).

Cebu. Province of the Philippine Islands, consisting of Cebu and adjacent islands lying between Negros and Leyte in the Visayan Sea. The native race is Visayan. The main island is long and narrow, and is traversed from NE to SW by the mountains of the Cordillera Central, which, though not exceeding 2,000 ft. in height, interfere with communication between the E and W parts of the island, as there are few passes. The rivers are unimportant. Cebu contains the largest coal deposits of the Philippines. Petroleum has been reported in connection with the coal beds. Gold and marble are found in the W part of the island. Capital, Cebu; area, 1,867 sq. mi.; pop. 1,068,078 (1939), 1,123,107 (1948).

Cebu. City in the Philippine Islands, the capital and chief port of Cebu province. It is situated on the E coast of Cebu island on Bohol Strait. The harbor is excellent. 167,503 (1948).

Ceccano (chāk.kä′nō). Town and commune in C Italy, in the *compartimento* (region) of Latium, in the province of Frosinone, situated on the Sacco River, between Rome and Cassino. The commune has a paper mill, stone quarries, and mineral springs which are visited by people suffering from skin diseases. The oldest part of the town is surrounded by medieval walls. Considerable damage was suffered during World War II by some buildings of tourist interest; the Church of Santa Maria al Fiume was virtually destroyed. Pop. of commune, 15,139 (1936); of town, 5,487 (1936).

Cecco d'Ascoli (chāk′kō däs′kō.lē). [Nickname of **Francesco degli Stabili.**] b. at Ascoli, Italy, c1257; d. 1327. Italian astrologer, mathematician, and poet, burned for heresy. While teaching astrology and mathematics at the University of Bologna and elsewhere, he also wrote poetry, and his chief achievement in this art proved his undoing: in the ambitiously comprehensive poetic allegory entitled *L'Acerba,* the severity of his criticism of Dante's *Divine Comedy* led to charges of heresy, for which he was burnt at the stake.

Cecere (chẹ.cher′ẹ), **Gaetano.** b. at New York, Nov. 26, 1894—. American sculptor and lecturer on sculpture. His training included study at the National Academy of Design and the Beaux-Arts Institute of Design at New York, and the American Academy in Rome, and his work has been chiefly monumental, though he has also designed medals, some of them for the U.S. army. He was the sculptor of several war memorials in this country and one at Oudenarde, Belgium. He is a member of the National Academy of Design and a fellow of the American Academy in Rome.

Čech (cheн), **Svatopluk.** b. at Ostředek, Bohemia, 1846; d. at Prague, 1908. Czech poet, novelist, and patriot. Son of the manager of a landed estate, he studied for the law and practiced briefly before devoting himself wholly to literature and journalism. Pan-Slavic enthusiasm possessed him from his youth, to which was added in later years an idealistic faith in a future of universal liberty and brotherhood. Epic poems were his principal medium, though in this form he tended to become rhetorical, and his more gracious qualities are better revealed in his lyrics, his idylls of rural life, and his versified fairy tales. His novels were generally in a satirical vein. He was very prolific, and easily the most popular Czech writer of his time, from the publication of *The Adamites* (1874), dealing with the radical wing of the 15th-century Hussites, to the *Songs of a Slave* (1897). In *Europa* (1878) and *Slavia* (1882), he dealt with the problems of conflicts between nations and between the communist demand for speedy change and the democratic ideal of gradual progress, favoring the latter concept.

Čechy (che′нi). Czech name of **Bohemia.**

Cecil (ses′il, sis′il), **David George Brownlow.** b. Feb. 9, 1905—. English track athlete who served (1943–45) as governor of Bermuda; son and heir of the 5th marquis of Exeter. Educated at Eton and Cambridge, he held eight British track championships, won (1928) the Olympic 400-meter hurdles at Amsterdam, and was captain (1932) of the British team competing in the Olympics at Los Angeles. He became president of the British Olympic Association and a member of the International Olympic Committee. A member (1931 *et seq.*) of Parliament, he was appointed (1942) controller of American supplies and repairs in the ministry of aircraft production.

Cecil, Lord **Edward Christian David.** b. April 9, 1902—. English literary critic, son of J. E. H. Gascoyne-Cecil and brother of Robert Arthur James Cecil (1893—). He is the author of *Life of Cowper* (1929), *Sir Walter Scott* (1933), *Early Victorian Novelists* (1934), *Jane Austen* (1935), *The Young Melbourne* (1939), and *Hardy, the Novelist* (1943).

Cecil, James Edward Hubert Gascoyne-. [Title, 4th Marquis of **Salisbury.**] b. 1861; d. 1947. English politician and Conservative Party leader; son of R. A. T. Gascoyne-Cecil, 3rd Marquis of Salisbury, and brother of Robert Cecil (1864—). Educated at Oxford, he sat for 18 years in the House of Commons before succeeding to the peerage and taking his seat in the House of Lords. He served early in his life in the Boer War, and was for a time undersecretary for foreign affairs. In 1903 he was named lord privy seal, a position he again held from 1924 to 1929. At the same time (1925–29), he was leader in the House of Lords. During World War I he was an opponent of a coalition government; subsequently he opposed constitutional reform for India.

Cecil, Robert. [Titles: 1st Earl of **Salisbury,** 1st Viscount **Cranborne.**] b. at Westminster, London, c1563; d. at Marlborough, England, May 24, 1612. English statesman, one of the leading government officials under James I of England; son of William Cecil, 1st Baron Burghley, and brother of Thomas Cecil, 2nd Baron Burghley. Educated privately, he also attended Cambridge University before entering (1584) Parliament. He was a member (1588) of Lord Derby's mission to the Netherlands for peace negotiations with Spain. Under Elizabeth he subsequently held posts as nominal (c1589 *et seq.*) and official (1596 *et seq.*) secretary of state and chancellor of the duchy of Lancaster (1597 *et seq.*). On his father's death he was preferred over Francis Bacon and Essex to head the government. After the fall of Essex he entered into secret negotiations with James IV of Scotland, paving the way for that ruler to take over the English throne as James I on the death of Elizabeth (1603). On James I's accession, Cecil continued in office, was created Viscount Cranborne in 1604, and became Earl of Salisbury in 1605. At the trial of Sir Walter Raleigh in 1603, Cecil took a leading part, showing himself opposed to undue harshness. When he was named (May 6, 1608) lord treasurer in addition to his other positions, Cecil virtually controlled the government. He hoped to create in England the center of a Protestant alliance of nations, and thus aimed at making England, for all practical purposes, a greater world power than either France or Spain. He imposed new duties in an effort to increase the national revenue, but in his effort to keep the treasury filled he did his part in destroying the unity that had existed under Elizabeth between the people and the throne. He built Hatfield House, the family seat of the earls of Salisbury.

Cecil, Robert. [Full name: **Edgar Algernon Robert Cecil**; title, 1st Viscount **Cecil of Chelwood.**] b. at London, Sept. 14, 1864—. English statesman, winner of the 1937 Nobel peace award; third son of R. A. T. Gascoyne-Cecil, 3rd Marquis of Salisbury, and brother of J. E. H. Gascoyne-Cecil. He studied at Oxford. A member (1906–23) of Parliament, he was named (1915) undersecretary for foreign affairs, served as minister (1916 *et seq.*) of blockade, and was assistant secretary (1918) of state for foreign affairs. He took part in drafting the covenant for the League of Nations. As lord privy seal (1923–24) and chancellor (1924–27) of the duchy of Lancaster, he was in both of Stanley Baldwin's cabinets until his resignation (1927) in protest over the cabinet's refusal to support the compromise agreement with America over the cruiser question. He became president of the League of Nations Union. Author of *A Way of Peace* (1918) and *A Real Peace* (1941).

Cecil, Robert Arthur James. [Titles: Viscount **Cranborne,** 1st Baron **Cecil of Essendon.**] b. Aug. 27, 1893—. English politician; son of J. E. H. Gascoyne-Cecil and brother of Lord Edward Christian David Cecil (1902—). Educated at Oxford, he was a member of Parliament (1929–41) for South Dorset, serving also as undersecretary of state for foreign affairs (1935–38), paymaster general (1940), secretary of state for dominion affairs (1940–42), secretary of state for colonies (1942), and lord privy seal (November, 1942 to 1943).

Cecil, Robert Arthur Talbot Gascoyne-. [Title, 3rd Marquis of **Salisbury.**] b. at Hatfield House, Hertfordshire, England, Feb. 3, 1830; d. there, Aug. 22, 1903. English Conservative statesman; second son of the 2nd marquis of Salisbury and father of J. E. H. Gascoyne-Cecil and Robert Cecil (1864—). Known at first as Lord Robert Cecil, and after his elder brother's death (June 14, 1865) by the courtesy title of Viscount Cranborne, he succeeded his father as marquis on April 12, 1868. He was educated at Eton and at Oxford (Christ Church College), graduating in 1850. He entered Parliament as member for Stamford in February, 1854, and took an active part in the discussion of public questions—notably in opposing the abolition of church rates in 1858, and in support of Benjamin Disraeli's reform bill in 1859. He held the office of secretary for India in Lord Derby's ministry from July, 1866, to March, 1867. In 1869 he was elected chancellor of the University of Oxford. In 1874 he entered the cabinet of Disraeli, again as secretary for India. On the reopening of the Eastern Question he was sent to Constantinople as the representative of England in a conference of the European powers, and on Lord Derby's resignation in April, 1878, he became foreign secretary. The same year he accompanied Disraeli to the Congress of Berlin. The death of Disraeli (April 19, 1881) made him leader of the Conservative Party, and he held office as prime minister in four administrations: June, 1885–February, 1886, August, 1886–August, 1892, July, 1895–November, 1900, and November, 1900–July, 1902. In the first, during the greater part of the second, and the third, he was foreign secretary as well as premier until November, 1900.

Cecil, Thomas. [Titles: 1st Earl of **Exeter,** 2nd Baron **Burghley.**] b. May 5, 1542; d. Feb. 7, 1623. English nobleman; eldest son of William Cecil, 1st Baron Burghley, by his first wife, and brother of Robert Cecil (c1563–1612). He was created first earl of Exeter on May 4, 1605.

Cecil, William. [Title, 1st Baron **Burghley** (or **Burleigh.**)] b. at Bourn, Lincolnshire, England, Sept. 13, 1520; d. at London, Aug. 4, 1598. English statesman who occupied a position of great power in the government of Elizabeth of England. From 1535 to 1541 he attended Cambridge University; subsequently he served under Edward Seymour, the protector, until named (1550) a secretary of state. He did not hold this office under Mary Tudor, but with the accession of Elizabeth he again held office. As Elizabeth's chief minister, he took the responsibility for the execution (1587) of Mary, Queen of Scots. He served (1558–72) as chief secretary of state, and in this position organized (1570) a vigilant group against potential papist plots. In 1572 he was made lord high treasurer, a position he held until his death.

Cecil Dreeme (ses'il drēm, sis'-). Novel by Theodore Winthrop, published in 1862.

Cecilia (sẹ.sil'yạ), Saint. d. at Rome, probably c230. Christian martyr. According to the legend, she was compelled, in spite of a vow of celibacy, to marry a young nobleman, Valerian. She succeeded in converting him to her views and also to Christianity, for which they suffered death. She has generally been considered the patron saint of music, particularly church music, and is represented in art as singing and playing on some musical instrument, or as listening to the music of an angel who has been drawn from heaven by her harmony. Dryden alludes to this in his *Ode for Saint Cecilia's Day*. Her story is also told by Chaucer in the "Second Nun's Tale," one of the *Canterbury Tales*. In the Roman and Anglican calendars her feast is celebrated on Nov. 22.

Cecilia, Saint. Painting by Raphael, acquired by the Accademia at Bologna, Italy. The figure of the saint, richly clad, occupies the middle of the picture; she listens entranced to the heavenly choir of angels above her, while discarded earthly musical instruments lie at her feet.

Cecilia, Saint. Painting by Peter Paul Rubens. The saint is playing on a harpsichord and singing, attended by four angels. As a model Rubens used his second wife, Hélène Fourment.

Cecilia, Story of Saint. Series of five frescoes (1616–17) by Domenichino, in San Luigi dei Francesi (French Church of Saint Louis), Rome. The subjects are the saint distributing her clothes among the poor, her contempt for idols, her martyrdom, her reception of the martyr's crown, and her assumption. These paintings are typical of Domenichino's early baroque style.

Cecilia, or Memoirs of an Heiress. Novel by Fanny Burney, published in 1782.

Cecina (che'chē.nä). Town and commune in C Italy, in the *compartimento* (region) of Tuscany, in the province of Livorno, situated near the mouth of the Cecina River, S of Leghorn, on former swampland improved during the 19th century. The nearby Marina di Cecina is a seaside resort. Pop. of commune, 10,527 (1936); of town, 5,570 (1936).

Cecropia (sẹ.krō'pi.ạ). Widow of the younger brother of King Basilius in Sir Philip Sidney's romance *Arcadia*.

Cecrops (sē'krops). In Greek mythology, founder and first king of Athens, the introducer of civilization into Greece. He was regarded as autochthonous, and as a being whose upper half was human and the lower half reptile. He was believed to have given the people their institutions of marriage, burial, and writing.

CEDA. [Full name, **Confederación de Derechos Autónomos,** meaning "Confederation for Autonomous Rights."] Combination of Spanish rightist parties led by Gil Robles during the years of the Spanish republic (1931–39). The confederation was built around the Catholic Acción Popular, and had as members the confederation of fathers of families, Catholic youth organizations, and others. During the Spanish Civil War (1936–39)

CEDA was joined to the Falange primarily through its youth organizations.

Cedar (sē′dạr). River in SE Minnesota and E Iowa, flowing SE to join the Iowa River ab. 27 mi. SE of Iowa City. Cedar Rapids is the chief city on the river. Length, ab. 330 mi.

Cedarburg (sē′dạr.bėrg). City in E Wisconsin, in Ozaukee County, on the Milwaukee River ab. 15 mi. N of Milwaukee. 2,810 (1950).

Cedar City. Town in SW Utah, in Iron County, in a coal, iron, and livestock area: shipping point for iron ore; seat of the Branch Agricultural College. It was settled in 1851. Bryce Canyon, Zion Canyon, Cedar Breaks, and Dixie National Forest are nearby. 6,106 (1950).

Cedar Creek. Stream in the Shenandoah Valley, Virginia, which joins the North Fork of the Shenandoah River ab. 4 mi. from Strasburg. Here, on Oct. 19, 1864, a Confederate force under Jubal A. Early surprised Union troops under Horatio G. Wright. Later in the day the Confederates were defeated by Philip H. Sheridan. The Union loss was ab. 5,995; that of the Confederates, ab. 4,200.

Cedar Falls. City in NE Iowa, in Black Hawk County, on the Cedar River, ab. 99 mi. W of Dubuque. Manufactures include rotary pumps, elevator equipment, seed-corn sorting machines and other farm machinery, brooms, and concrete mixers. It is the seat of Iowa State Teachers College. Settled in 1845 and platted in 1851, Cedar Falls was important as a flour and lumber milling center in the second half of the 19th century. It was the birthplace of Bess Streeter Aldrich, and the home of Ruth Suckow. 14,334 (1950).

Cedar Grove. Township in NE New Jersey, in Essex County, ab. 8 mi. N of Newark. It is a suburban community, with some small industries, and the Essex County mental asylum. 8,022 (1950).

Cedarhurst (sē′dạr.hėrst). Village in SE New York, in Nassau County, on Long Island: residential community. 6,051 (1950).

Cedar Keys. City in W Florida, in Levy County, on small islands in the Gulf of Mexico, ab. 3 mi. from the mainland. It has a trade in sponges, fish, turtles, and palmetto brushes. There are government bird sanctuaries and pre-Columbian Indian burial mounds on some of the islands. 900 (1950).

Cedar Lake. Unincorporated community in NW Indiana, in Lake County ab. 15 mi. SW of Gary. 3,907 (1950).

Cedar Mountain. Hill ab. 2 mi. W of Mitchell's Station, Culpeper County, Va. Here, on Aug. 9, 1862, the Confederates (20,000–25,000) under Thomas J. Jackson ("Stonewall" Jackson) defeated part of John Pope's army (ab. 7,500) under Nathaniel P. Banks. The loss of the Confederates was ab. 1,307; Union loss, ab. 1,400.

Cedar Rapids. City in E Iowa, county seat of Linn County, on the river Cedar. It is a railroad center and has meat-packing plants, cereal mills, and corn-processing plants, and manufactures of radio equipment, dairying and mining machinery, and other items. Coe College is here. Settled in 1838, the city was platted in 1841. It has a number of important museums, housing historical, zoological, ethnological, and art collections. 72,296 (1950).

Cedartown (sē′dạr.toun). City in NW Georgia, county seat of Polk County. Manufactures include textiles and tires. 9,470 (1950).

Cedd (ched) or **Cedda** (ched′ä), Saint. b. in Northumbria; d. Oct. 26, 664. English missionary saint, bishop of the East Saxons; brother of Saint Chad.

Cedmon (ked′mọn). See **Caedmon.**

Cedric of Rotherwood or **Cedric the Saxon** (sed′rik, sē′drik; roᴛʜ′ėr.wůd). Guardian of Rowena in Sir Walter Scott's novel *Ivanhoe.*

Cefalù (chā.fä.lö′). [Ancient name, **Cephaloedium.**] Town and commune in SW Italy, on the island of Sicily, in the province of Palermo, situated on the N coast of the island, ab. 35 mi. E of Palermo. The town has fisheries, and fruit and olive-oil markets. The oldest monument of Cefalù is the Temple of Diana, a sanctuary. The cathedral (1131–48), in Romanesque style, shows both Germanic and Oriental influences; there are notable gold-ground mosaics in the choir and apse. The civic museum contains valuable antiquities, and numismatic and other collections. The town, in ancient times an ally of the Carthaginians, was later conquered by Dionysius and Agathocles, in the early Middle Ages by the Arabs (858), and finally by the Normans. Buildings of interest to tourists were undamaged in World War II. Pop. of commune, 10,730 (1936); of town, 9,654 (1936).

Cegléd (tse′glād). [Also, **Czegléd.**] City in C Hungary, situated in the central Hungarian plain, between Budapest and Szolnok. It is the center of an intensively cultivated district in the northern Alföld, and has flour mills and fruit markets; poultry is shipped from here. 37,956 (1948).

Ceglie Messapico (che′lyā mās.sä′pē.kō). [Also, **Ceglie Messapica.**] Town and commune in SE Italy, in the *compartimento* (region) of Apulia, in the province of Brindisi, ab. 20 mi. W of Brindisi. It has flour mills and is a market center for the agricultural products of the district. Remains of a Greek settlement have been excavated. Pop. of commune, 20,764 (1936); of town, 17,077 (1936).

Cehegín (thā.ā.ʜēn′). Town in E Spain, in the province of Murcia, situated on the Arcos River, ab. 35 mi. NW of Murcia. It is a market center for wine, olive oil, and hemp; there are marble quarries in the vicinity. The Convent of San Francisco contains Roman inscriptions. 17,316 (1940).

Ceiba (sā′ʙä), **La.** See **La Ceiba.**

Ceiram (sā.ruṅ′). See **Ceram.**

Ceiriog (kī′ri.ôg). Pseudonym of **Hughes, John Ceiriog.**

Céladon (sā.lȧ.dôṅ). Lover of the beautiful Astrée in Honoré d'Urfé's romance *L'Astrée.* His is one of the stock names for a lover in the French drama.

Celadon (sel′ą.don). Sort of generic name in English pastoral poetry for a rustic lover, as Chloe is for the maid he loves.

Celadon. Witty, inconstant gallant in John Dryden's play *Secret Love, or The Maiden Queen.* He marries the flirt Florimel, with the understanding that they may each have their own way after marriage.

Celadon. Character in James Thomson's *The Seasons.*

Celaenae (se.lē′nē). Ancient name of **Dinar.**

Celaeno (se.lē′nō). In Greek mythology, one of the Harpies; also, a Pleiad, a daughter of Atlas and Pleione.

Celaeno. The sixth-magnitude star 16 Pleiadum, barely visible with the naked eye.

Čelakovský (che′lä.kôf.skē), **František Ladislav.** [Also, **Czelakowski.**] b. at Strakonice, Bohemia, March 7, 1799; d. at Prague, Aug. 5, 1852. Czech poet and philologist; father of Ladislav Čelakovský. He published *Centifolia* (1840), a collection of Slavic folk songs (1822–27), and other works.

Čelakovský, Ladislav. b. at Prague, 1834; d. there, 1902. Czech botanist; son of František Ladislav Čelakovský. He became (1860) custodian of the botanical department of the Bohemian Museum at Prague and served (1880 *et. seq.*) as professor of botany at Prague. He was the author of *Prodromus der Flora von Böhmen* (1867–81), *Die Gymnospermen* (1890), and *Das Reduktionsgesetz der Blüten* (1895).

Celano (chā.lä′nō). Town and commune in C Italy, in the *compartimento* (region) of Abruzzi e Molise, in the province of L'Aquila, situated in the reclaimed Conca Fucino district, S of L'Aquila: an agricultural market town. The most conspicuous monument is the 14th-century castle; the churches of San Giovanni Evangelista and San Giovanni Battista date from the 13th century. The Hohenstaufen emperor Frederick II was educated here under the tutelage of Count Pietro di Celano. Pietro's successor Tommaso rebelled and the town was subsequently destroyed by the emperor (1222), which in turn led to the rebellion of the entire region on the side of Pope Gregory IX. Buildings of interest to tourists were undamaged in World War II. Pop. of commune, 11,653 (1936); of town, 9,784 (1936).

Celano. Former lake. See **Fucino.**

Celaya (sä.lä′yä). City in C Mexico, in Guanajuato state: railway junction; distribution center for agricultural products. 22,766 (1940).

Celebes (sel′ę.bēz; Dutch, se.lā′bes). [Dutch also **Selébès.**] Third in size of the East India islands, situated E of Borneo: a former Dutch possession, now a province of the Republic of Indonesia (during the federation of 1946–50 it was part of the *negara* (state) of East Indonesia, in the United States of Indonesia). It is very irregular in shape, with four large peninsulas. The chief export is coffee; nickel and palm oil are also very important. Celebes was discovered by the Portuguese in the 16th century; they were expelled by the Dutch in 1660. Area, 72,986 sq. mi.; pop. 4,231,906 (1930).

Celebes. [Indonesian, **Sulawesi.**] Province of Indonesia, including the island of Celebes and nearby smaller islands. Area, ab. 73,180 sq. mi.; pop. 4,226,586 (1930), ab. 5 million (1951).

Celebes Sea. Arm of the Pacific Ocean, bounded on the S by the islands of Borneo and Celebes, on the W by Borneo, and on the N and NW by the Philippine Islands. It is connected with the Java Sea by Makassar Strait. Length, ab. 500 mi.; width, ab. 400 mi.

Celebrated Jumping Frog of Calaveras County (kal-ạ.ver′ạs), **The.** Sketch by Samuel Langhorne Clemens, written under the pseudonym Mark Twain and published in 1865. The story, adapted from an old folk tale, involves Dan'l Webster, Jim Smiley's jumping frog, which loses a race as a result of sabotage on the part of a stranger who loads his gullet with quail shot. The piece was originally published in the New York *Saturday Press.* It, together with other pieces, was published (1867) under the title *The Celebrated Jumping Frog of Calaveras County and Other Sketches* and was his first book. The story is described as taking place at Angels' Camp, near Sonora, Calif., where an annual jumping-frog match has been held since the 1920's to commemorate the event.

Celer (sē′lėr), **Quintus Caecilius Metellus.** See **Metellus Celer, Quintus Caecilius.**

Céleron de Blainville (sā.lẹ.rôṅ dẹ blaṅ.vēl), **Jean Baptiste.** b. at Montreal, Canada, 1693; d. 1759. French Canadian soldier. He commanded several of the important French strongholds in Canada, and in the period 1739–40 campaigned against the Chickasaw Indians as far south as what is now the state of Tennessee. In 1749 he led an expedition which staked the claim of France to the possession of the Ohio Valley, posting signs on trees warning English traders against trespass, and burying, at various points, metal tablets asserting French sovereignty.

Céleste (sā.lest), Madame **Céline.** b. at Paris, c1814; d. there, Feb. 12, 1882. French actress and dancer. She began her professional career, in the latter capacity, at the Bowery Theater, New York, in October, 1827, and afterward danced and acted chiefly at London, visiting America a second time in the period 1834–37.

Celestial Elegies. Group of sonnets (1598) by Thomas Rogers. They differ from the conventional sonnet sequences, as their title suggests, in dealing not with love but with funeral lamentations.

Celestial Empire. See **Chinese Empire.**

Celestial Omnibus, The. Short story of a bus that goes to Heaven, by Edward Morgan Forster. It is the third in a collection of six, not the first, although the volume (1911) is named after it. The other stories are "The Story of a Panic," "The Other Side of the Hedge," "Other Kingdom," "The Curate's Friend," and "The Road from Colonus."

Celestial Railroad, The. Allegorical tale by Nathaniel Hawthorne, originally published in 1843 and included in *Mosses from an Old Manse* (1846).

Celestina (thā.les.tē′nä). [Original full name, **The Tragicomedy of Calisto and Meliboea.**] Spanish prose drama in 21 acts, or parts. From its length and structure, it is apparent that it could never have been played on the stage, but its dramatic spirit and movement have left their mark on the national drama ever since. The first act, which is much the longest, is believed by some to have been written by Rodrigo Cota, of Toledo, c1480. The entire book is more commonly ascribed to Fernando de Rojas.

Celestine I (sel′ẹs.tīn, sẹ.les′tin, -tīn), Saint. [Also, **Coelestine.**] b. in Campania, Italy; fl. in the 5th century. Pope from 422 to 432. He sent legates to the Council of Ephesus, which in 431 condemned the heresy of Nestorius, and is said by some to have sent Saint Patrick to Ireland and Palladius to Scotland, although it is not clear that either of these missionaries came from Rome. He is commemorated on April 6.

Celestine II. fl. at the beginning of the 12th century. Antipope in 1124. In the dispute following the death (1124) of Callistus II the lawful pope elected was Honorius II.

Celestine II. [Also: **Coelestine**; original name, **Guido di Castello.**] b. at Città di Castello, Umbria, Italy; fl. in the 12th century. Pope from 1143 to 1144. He absolved Louis VII of France, who had been placed under interdict by his predecessor.

Celestine III. [Also: **Coelestine**; original name, **Giacinto Orsini.**] b. c1106; d. at Rome, Jan. 8, 1198. Pope from 1191 to 1198. He crowned Henry VI of Germany in 1191, and confirmed the Teutonic Order in 1192.

Celestine IV. [Also: **Coelestine**; original name, **Goffredo Castiglione.**] d. Nov. 10, 1241. Pope, elected Oct. 25, 1241. He reigned only 15 days.

Celestine V, Saint. [Also: **Coelestine**; original name, **Pietro di Murrhone.**] b. in Italy, c1215; d. at the castle Fumone, in the Campagna, Italy, May 19, 1296. Pope from July to December, 1294. He founded the order of the Celestines c1254, and was elected Pope, at the age of 80, in July, 1294. Being unfitted for this exalted station by his previous life as a hermit and consequent ignorance of the world, he abdicated on Dec. 13, 1294, and was imprisoned at Fumone by Boniface VIII, who feared that, if left at liberty, he might become the occasion of schism.

Cele-Syria (sē′lẹ.sir′i.ạ). Ancient name of **Bika, El.**

Celetrum (sẹ.lē′trum). Ancient name of **Kastoria.**

Celia (sēl′yạ). Character in Edmund Spenser's *The Faerie Queene;* mother of Faith, Hope, and Charity. She lived in the hospice called Holiness.

Celia. In Shakespeare's comedy *As You Like It,* the cousin and devoted friend of Rosalind, and daughter of the usurping Duke Frederick. She masquerades with Rosalind in the Forest of Arden, in the disguise of Aliena, a shepherdess. She falls in love with and marries Oliver, older brother to Orlando.

Celia. Wife of Corvino in Ben Jonson's *Volpone.*

Celia. Straightforward, affectionate English girl, with no squeamishness, in Beaumont and Fletcher's play *The Humorous Lieutenant,* made love to by both Antigonus and his son Demetrius. She disguises herself as Enanthe.

Celia. Very young girl in William Whitehead's *School for Lovers.* The part was written for Susannah Cibber, then nearly 50 years old.

Celia Brooke (brůk). See **Brooke, Celia.**

Celibates. Group (1895) of short stories by George Moore, dealing with more or less abnormal and neurotic people. The collection was later published as *In Single Strictness* (1922) and as *Celibate Lives* (1927).

Celica (sā.lē′kä). City in S Ecuador, in Loja province. 10,904 (est. 1944).

Célimène (sā.lē.men). Character in Molière's *Les Précieuses Ridicules.*

Célimène. Artificial, coquettish, but charming and sparkling lady in Molière's comedy *Le Misanthrope.* She makes Acaste and Clitandre both believe she loves them, but finally consents to marry the "misanthrope," Alceste, though declining to seclude herself from the world with him, whereupon he rejects her. Her name is sometimes applied proverbially to a coquette.

Celina (sẹ.lī′nạ). Village in W Ohio, county seat of Mercer County: summer resort; manufactures furniture. It was established in 1834. Pop. 5,703 (1950).

Céline (sā.lēn), **Louis-Ferdinand.** Pseudonym of **Destouches, Louis Fuch.**

Celje (tse′lye). [German, **Cilli**; Latin, **Claudia Celeia.**] City in NW Yugoslavia, in the federative unit of Slovenia, in the former *banovina* (province) of Dravska, situated on the Sarina River, E of Ljubljana and SW of Maribor. The Roman Claudia Celeja was founded by the emperor Claudius. There is a museum of Roman antiquities. The modern city is a summer resort, a station on the railroad line from Ljubljana to Maribor, and a commercial center for the lumber, leather, and grain trade. Corn, hops, fruit, and wine are produced in the vicinity; zinc is manufactured in nearby Storé. Celje was a center of the German population of the S part of the Austrian crownland of Styria prior to 1918, although the surrounding countryside had always been Slavic. Re-Germanization was attempted during World War II, but the German population has since disappeared. 7,602 (1931), 22,048 (1948).

Cellach (kel′ạċh), Saint. See Saint **Celsus** or **Cellach,** and Saint **Gall.**

Cellamare (chel.lä.mä′rā), Prince of. [Title of **Antonio Giudice**; additional title, Duke of **Giovenazza.**] b. at

Naples, Italy, 1657; d. at Seville, Spain, May 16, 1733. Spanish general and diplomat, ambassador to France (1715–18).

Celle (tsel'ẹ). City in NW Germany, in the *Land* (state) of Lower Saxony, British Zone, formerly in the province of Hanover, Prussia, situated on the Aller River, ab. 20 mi. NE of Hanover. It is known for its garment and knitwear manufactures, also for shoe, leather, rubber, and tobacco factories, canneries, and the production of musical instruments. Petroleum, potash, and salt are mined in the vicinity. Celle has a number of educational institutions, including agricultural schools. The old part of the city is well preserved and suffered little damage in World War II. The castle of the dukes of Brunswick-Lüneburg-Celle was erected in the period 1290–1380 and restored between 1670 and 1680; the *Rathaus* (city hall) is a Renaissance building of the 16th century; the town church, dating originally from 1300, was rebuilt in 1678; there are a number of houses built in the 16th and 17th centuries, and a local museum. The population is predominantly Protestant; the increase between 1939 and 1947, largely due to the influx of East German refugees, amounted to 46.7 percent. 52,281 (1947), 59,667 (1950).

Cellier (sel'yėr), **Alfred.** b. at Hackney, London, Dec. 1, 1844; d. at London, Dec. 28, 1891. English light-opera composer. He conducted the Belfast Philharmonic Society (1865–68), and at the Manchester Prince's Theatre (1871–75) and the London Opera Comique (1877–79). His works include *The Sultan of Mocha* (1874), *Dorothy* (1886), and *The Mountebanks* (1892), the latter with a libretto by W. S. Gilbert.

Celliers (sel'yėrz), **Jan F. E.** b. 1865; d. 1940. South African poet. He served as a librarian at Pretoria and as a professor at Stellenbosch University. He was one of the first to use Afrikaans as a literary vehicle. His first poetry, published in 1908, was *Die Vlakte en andere gedigte* (The Plain and Other Verses), with moving recollections of the Boer War. In 1909 he published *Die Revier* (The River), in 1910 *Unie-Kantate* (Cantata of the Union); this highly patriotic poetry had a great appeal, as did also *Die Saaier en ander nuwe gedigte* (The Sower and Other New Verses, 1918) and *En Jopie Fourie en ander nuwe gedigte* (1920). Love of nature and home life characterized *Die Lewenstuin* (Life's Garden, 1923) and *Liefdelewe* (Love's Life, 1924). *Die Groot Geheim* (The Deep Secret, 1924) consisted of allegorical poetry. His plays included *Liefde en Plig* (Love and Duty, 1909) and *Heldinne van die Oorlog* (Heroines of War, 1924).

Cellini (chel.lē'nē), **Benvenuto.** b. at Florence, Nov. 1, 1500; d. Feb. 14, 1571. Italian sculptor, goldsmith, and silversmith, now probably best known for his colorful and detailed autobiography. He studied with Michelangelo Bandinelli, father of the sculptor Bandinelli, and with Marcone the goldsmith. From 1516 to 1517 he worked at Pisa. In 1517 he returned to Florence, where he met Torregiano, who tried to secure him for his work in England. Benvenuto's loyalty to Michelangelo, however, prevented the engagement. From 1523 to 1540 he was at Rome under the patronage of Popes Clement VII and Paul III, occupied entirely with his work as goldsmith. In May, 1527, occurred the siege and sack of Rome by the troops of the Constable de Bourbon, in which Cellini assisted in the defense of the Castle of Sant'Angelo, and claimed to have killed Bourbon and wounded the Prince of Orange. At the instigation of Pier Luigi Farnese, illegitimate son of Pope Paul III, he was imprisoned in the Castle of Sant'Angelo in October, 1538. The account of his escape, in December, 1539, is one of the most sensational exploits told in his sensational autobiography. From 1540 to 1544 he lived in France at the court of Francis I. He had his atelier in the Petit Nesle. At this time his first attempts at sculpture were made, the chief being the *Nymph of Fontainebleau*, now in the collection of the Louvre. From 1544 to his death in 1571 he served Cosimo I and the Medici family at Florence. His well-known statue in bronze of *Perseus with the Head of Medusa* was made in this period for the Loggia dei Lanzi at Florence; perhaps the best-known example of his work in gold is a large saltcellar, made for Francis I. His autobiography, one of the most famous of Italian classics, circulated in manuscript until it was printed in 1730. It was translated into German by Goethe. The standard English translation is by J. A. Symonds.

Cellites (sel'īts). See **Lollards.**

Celmán (sel.män'), **Miguel Juárez.** See **Juárez Celmán, Miguel.**

Celsius (sel'si.us), **Anders.** b. at Uppsala, Sweden, Nov. 27, 1701; d. there, April 25, 1744. Swedish astronomer, remembered as the deviser (1742) of the Celsius, or centigrade, thermometer; nephew of Olaf Celsius (1670–1756). He served as professor of astronomy (1730–44) at Uppsala and became (1741) director of the Uppsala observatory, which he had helped found (1740). In 1733 he published a collection of observations, including some by himself, on the aurora borealis. He also participated (1736) in an expedition to the polar region for purposes of meridian measurement.

Celsius, Olaf. b. July 19, 1670; d. at Uppsala, Sweden, June 24, 1756. Swedish botanist; uncle of Anders Celsius (1701–44) and father of Olaf Celsius (1716–94). He was professor of theology and Oriental language at the University of Uppsala, and became famous as the result of his researches on the plants mentioned in the Scriptures. He was the instructor and patron of Linnaeus.

Celsius, Olaf. b. at Uppsala, Sweden, Dec. 15, 1716; d. at Lund, Sweden, Feb. 15, 1794. Swedish historian; son of Olaf Celsius (1670–1756). He became professor of history at the University of Uppsala in 1747, and bishop of Lund in 1777. He wrote a history of Gustavus I (1746–53) and a history of Eric XIV (1774). He was ennobled in 1756.

Celso (sel'sö), **Afonso.** [Full name, **Afonso Celso de Assís Figueiredo.**] b. at Ouro Preto, Brazil, March 31, 1860; d. at Rio de Janeiro, 1938. Brazilian historian, poet, essayist, and novelist. His books of poems include *Prelúdios* (1875), *Devaneios* (1877), and *Telas sonantes* (1879). Among his best-known prose writings are *Minha filha* (1893), *O imperador no exílio* (1893), *Oito anos de parlamento* (1898), and *Porque me ufano do meu país* (1901).

Celsus (sel'sus). fl. 2nd century A.D. Platonist philosopher. He was the author of a famous treatise against Christianity, *Alethes Logos*, sometimes translated as "True Discourse," the substance of which is preserved in the *Contra Celsum* by Origen.

Celsus or **Cellach** (kel'ạch), Saint. b. 1079; d. at Ardpatrick, Munster, Ireland, April 1, 1129. Irish ecclesiastic, archbishop of Armagh after 1104.

Celsus, Aulus Cornelius. fl. in the first half of the 1st century A.D. Roman writer, author of a comprehensive encyclopedia treating of farming, medicine, military art, oratory, jurisprudence, and philosophy. The medical part, the only one extant, is a fundamental source for the history of Alexandrian mẹdicine, surpassed only by the works of Hippocrates and Galen. Celsus's attitude was one of moderation between empiricism and methodism; theory and practice to him are equally indispensable.

Celt and Saxon (selt, sak'sọn). Fragment of a novel by George Meredith. It was published in 1910, a year after his death. The date of composition is unknown, but it seems to be an early work overlaid with later, highly mannered, revision. A conversation piece, it breaks off with no indication of the author's final intention as to the plot.

Celtes (tsel'tẹs), **Conrad.** [Original name, **Konrad Pickel.**] b. at Wipfeld, Germany, Feb. 1, 1459; d. at Vienna, Feb. 4, 1508. German poet and scholar, an outstanding humanist, diligent in spreading the new knowledge in his time. After the manner of wandering scholars he studied at many universities and taught at Erfurt, Rostock, Leipzig, and Vienna. Wherever he went he waged everlasting battle for humanism. He founded learned societies (*Sodalitates*) to this end, and was himself made head of the *Collegium poetarum* at Vienna by Maximilian (1502). He wrote a poetic (*Ars versificandi et carminum,* 1486), and his own poems (like all of his writings, in Latin) were considered the best of the time. He was crowned poet laureate by Frederick III, the first German ever to be thus honored. He gained lasting fame by discovering and publishing (1501) the writings of Hroswitha of Gandersheim.

Celtiberia (sel.ti.bir'i.ạ). In ancient geography, a region in Spain corresponding to the SW part of Aragon and the greater part of the provinces of Soria, Cuenca, and Burgos; in an extended application nearly identical with an early division set up by the Romans and called Hispania Citerior or Hispania Tarraconensis. The Celtiberi (Celtiberians) were thought to be a mixture of the indigenous Iberians and invading Celts from Gaul (whence their name). They offered a vigorous resistance to Rome, and were finally subdued after 72 B.C. Among their chief towns were Numantia (near modern Soria) and Segobriga (near modern Sagunto).

Celtica (sel'ti.ka). Central division of Transalpine Gaul, according to the threefold division of the Gauls by Julius Caesar (Gauls or Celts, Aquitanians, Belgians). It coincided with the Roman province of Lugdunensis, except that it extended SW to the Garonne River.

Celtic Galatia (sel'tik ga.lā'sha, kel'-). See under **Gaul.**

Celtic Twilight, The. Volume (1893) of stories and sketches by William Butler Yeats. Its subtitle, "Men and Women, Ghouls and Faeries," indicates that the material is based upon folklore and suggests the mystical strain of the Irish in their belief in the spirit world. The title of the work is also used, sometimes with a slight degree of irony, to mean the literary movement known as the Irish Renaissance, of which Yeats was a recognized leader.

Celts (selts, kelts). [Also, **Kelts.**] Name at first vaguely applied to a Western people, afterward the regular designation of the peoples which speak languages akin to those of Wales, Ireland, the Highlands of Scotland, and Brittany, and constitute a branch or principal division of the Indo-European language family. Formerly, these people occupied, partly or wholly, France, Spain, northern Italy, the western part of Germany, and the British islands. Of the remaining Celtic languages there are two chief divisions: the Goidelic, comprising the Highlands of Scotland, the Irish, and the Manx; and the Cymric, comprising Welsh, and Breton; the Cornish of Cornwall, related to the latter, is functionally extinct, but still survives as a literary language cultivated by some bilingual speakers of Cornish and English.

Cembalo (sem'ba.lō). Medieval name of **Balaklava.**

Cemetery of Père Lachaise (per là.shez). See **Père Lachaise, Cemetery of.**

Cemetery Ridge. Low ridge S of the town Gettysburg, Pa. Cemetery Hill, at the northern end of Cemetery Ridge, was the center of the Union line and the key to the Union position in the battle of Gettysburg (July 1–4, 1863). It was here that the Union 2nd Corps beat off Pickett's charge after its first lines had been taken.

Cempoala (sem.pō.ä'lä). [Also, **Zumpual.**] Ancient town of the Totonac Indians of Mexico, not far from the present site of Veracruz, and a little back from the coast. It is described as a city of 23,000 inhabitants, with many palaces and temples; but these accounts are probably exaggerated. In 1519 the Cempoalans gave Cortés a friendly reception, and some of their chiefs marched with him to Mexico. The inhabitants were removed to a mission village near Jalapa c1600, and the original site of Cempoala is now uncertain, though there is a village with the same name.

Cenabum (se.nā'bum). Ancient name of **Orléans.**

Cenchreae (seng'krē.ē). [Also, **Cenchrea** (-krē.a).] In ancient and Biblical geography, a port in S central Greece, on the Saronic Gulf ab. 7 mi. E of ancient Corinth. The port handled Corinthian trade to the east, and was connected with the city by a road. Acts, xviii. 18.

Cenci (chen'chē), **Beatrice.** b. at Rome, Feb. 12, 1577; executed there, Sept. 11, 1599. Italian noblewoman. Her father, Francesco Cenci, a dissipated and violent man, treated his family with such severity that his second wife, Lucrezia Petroni, his eldest son, Giacomo, the two younger sons, Bernardo and Paolo, and Beatrice procured his murder at the hands of Olimpio Calvetti, Beatrice's friend, and a hired murderer, Marzio, at the palace of Petrella in the kingdom of Naples, on Sept. 9, 1598. For this crime Lucrezia, Giacomo, and Beatrice were hanged at Rome, on Sept. 11, 1599, and Bernardo was condemned to the galleys for life, being, however, pardoned on March 20, 1606. Paolo died shortly after the murder. At the trial Beatrice's counsel, in order to justify the murder, accused Francesco, apparently without foundation, of having attempted incest with Beatrice, which has placed her in the light of a martyr. This, together with her tragic end and her patrician birth, has caused her life to become a favorite theme of poetry and art. She has been made the subject of a tragedy by Percy Bysshe Shelley, *The Cenci* (1819), a novel by Francesco Guerrazzi, *Beatrice Cenci* (1854), and, probably, of a painting by Guido Reni, in the Barberini palace at Rome.

Cencio Savelli (chen'chō sä.vel'lē). Original name of Pope **Honorius III.**

Cencius (sen'shi.us). See **Crescentius.**

Cendrars (säṅ.drår), **Blaise.** b. at Paris, Sept. 1, 1887—. French poet and fiction writer. Author of *Pâques* (1912), *Le Panama ou les adventures de mes sept oncles* (1918; Eng. trans., by John Dos Passos, *Panama*, 1931), as well as of numerous collections of travel notes and *L'Or. La Merveilleuse histoire du Général Johann-Auguste Suter* (1925), about the discovery of gold in California. He is considered a forerunner of Cocteau and other "modernists."

Cendrillon (säṅ.drē.yôṅ). Opera in four acts by Jules Massenet, with a libretto by Henry Cain, based on Charles Perrault's version of the Cinderella story, *Cendrillon* (1697). It was first performed at the Opéra-Comique, Paris, on May 24, 1899.

Cenerentola (chā.nā.rān'tō.lä). [German title, **Aschenbrödel.**] Opera by Ermanno Wolf-Ferrari (1876–1948), based on the Cinderella theme. It was first performed at Venice on Feb. 22, 1900; in 1902 it was performed at Bremen, Germany, under the title *Aschenbrödel.*

Cenerentola, La. [German title, **Aschenbrödel.**] Comic opera by Gioacchino Rossini, with a libretto by Giacomo Ferretti, first performed at Rome on Jan. 25, 1817. This is one of several adaptations to opera of the Cinderella story.

Ceneri (che'nā.rē) or **Cenere** (che'nā.rā), **Monte.** Mountain in Switzerland, SW of Bellinzona. It is penetrated by a railway tunnel. Elevation, ab. 2,064 ft.

Cenimagni (sen.i.mag'nī). British tribe located by Caesar in the E coast region of ancient Britain, N of the Thames.

Cenis (se.nē), **Mont.** [Italian, **Moncenisio, Monte Cenisio.**] Massif of the Graian Alps, crossed by an important mountain pass between France and Italy. The present Mont Cenis road was made (1803–10) by Napoleon I to connect the valley of the Isère River in France with Susa in Italy; it reaches the height of 6,835 ft. The Mont Cenis tunnel, on the Mont Cenis railway route between France and Italy, built in the period 1861–70, passes under the Col de Fréjus, ab. 14 mi. from the Mont Cenis pass. Its length is 7¾ mi. and it reaches the height of 4,245 ft.

Cennini (chen.nē'nē), **Cennino.** [Full name, **Cennino di Drea Cennini.**] b. at Colle di Val d'Elsa, near Siena, Italy, c1365; d. c1440. Italian painter and writer on art. Very few of his known or identifiable paintings remain, but he is remembered for his valuable work on the techniques of painting in the 14th century, *Trattato della Pittura.*

Cenomani (sen.o.mā'nī). Celtic people, a part of the army of Bellovesus, which with his sanction crossed (c400 B.C.) the Alps under a legendary leader, Etitovius, and settled north of the Po about Brescia and Verona, according to the detailed account of Livy. They were a branch of the Aulerci. Their original seat in Gaul, where they were called Aulerci Cenomani, was on the Sarthe River near what is now Le Mans. The Aulerci were included among the tribes constituting the Armorici.

Cenon (se.nôṅ). Town in SW France, in the department of Gironde, situated on the left bank of the Gironde River, NE of Bordeaux. It is an industrial suburb of Bordeaux. 10,051 (1946).

Cenozoic Era (sē.no.zō'ik, sen'o-). [Also: **Cainozoic, Kainozoic.**] Geologic era marked by the rise of modern life forms. See table at end of Vol. III.

Censorinus (sen.so.rī'nus). fl. c238. Roman scholar. Virtually nothing is known of him other than his authorship of the work, dated 238, *De Die Natale* (On the Day of Birth), which mirrors the thought of his time on astrology, astronomy, religion, philosophy, natural history and chronology. What makes this book of interest and of some importance today is the light it throws on ancient systems of reckoning time.

Centaurus (sen.tô'rus). Southern constellation, known from ancient times, situated between Argo and Scorpio, pictured to represent a centaur holding a Bacchic wand. Its brightest star, Alpha (α) Centauri, is third brightest in the sky. Its second star is about as bright as Betelgeuse, and is reckoned the eleventh in the heavens in order of brightness. The two stars are situated near each other on the parallel of 60° S., a little E of the Southern Cross. Centaurus has, besides, two stars of the second magnitude and seven of the third. Alpha Centauri and Proxima Centauri, a faint star within the constellation, are thought to be the closest (4.3 light years) stars to our solar system.

Centennial Exposition, International. World's Fair, Philadelphia, 1876, the most extensive and ambitious seen in the Western Hemisphere up to that time, was planned by a group of Philadelphians to commemorate the signing of the Declaration of Independence in that city in 1776, and to review the progress of the U.S. in the first century of national existence. In 1871 Congress authorized the project and appointed a commission, composed of representatives of the various states and territories, to plan the event. Congress also set up a financial authority to raise ten million dollars, much of which was provided by the city of Philadelphia, the state of Pennsylvania, and the federal government. Occupying 236 acres in Fairmount Park, the Exposition opened May 10, 1876, between which date and its close on November 10, it was visited by 9,910,966 persons. Twenty-six states and many of the 46 participating foreign countries erected buildings for their exhibits, which were dominated by the Main Building covering 20 acres and other huge structures including Machinery Hall, Agricultural Hall, and Memorial Hall. The Centennial Exposition was an event of considerable importance in the history of the U.S. in that for the first time it made evident to the American people themselves and to other countries the expansion of American industry and the technical importance of American inventions. It gave a great impetus to national pride and national confidence.

"Centennial State." Nickname of **Colorado.**

Center. City in E Texas, county seat of Shelby County, NE of Houston: processing and trading center for a lumber and cotton producing region; manufactures include brooms and mattresses. It was established in 1866, and so named because it was approximately in the center of the county. 4,323 (1950).

Center Line. [Also, **Centerline.**] City in S Lower Michigan, in Macomb County: residential suburb of Detroit. In the decade between the last two U.S. censuses its population more than doubled. 3,198 (1940), 7,659 (1950).

Centerville (sen'tėr.vil). [Former names: **Chaldea, Sentersville.**] City in S Iowa, county seat of Appanoose County, ab. 32 mi. SW of Ottumwa. Coal and gypsum mining are the principal industries. Platted in 1846, it was incorporated in 1855. Pop. 7,625 (1950).

Centerville. Borough in SW Pennsylvania, in Washington County, on the Monongahela River, in a mining and farming area. It was settled in 1766 and platted in 1821. Pop. 5,845 (1950).

Centerville. Former name of **Centralia,** Wash.

Centerville. A former name of **Etna,** Pa.

Centinel of the North-Western Territory. Weekly newspaper (Nov. 9, 1793–June, 1796) published at Cincinnati by William Maxwell. The first publication of its kind in the Northwest Territory, it was absorbed by *Freeman's Journal.*

Centla (sen'tlä). Ancient town in S Mexico, situated near the present town of Álvaro Obregón (formerly Frontera), in Tabasco: scene of the first victory of Cortés, 1519.

Centlivre (sent.liv'ėr, –lē'vėr), **Susannah.** b. c1667; d. at London, Dec. 1, 1723. English actress and dramatist. She is said to have been the daughter of a man named Freeman, of Lincolnshire, who removed to Ireland shortly before her birth. About 1706 she married Joseph Centlivre, chief cook to Queen Anne and George I. Among her 19 plays are *The Platonic Lady* (acted 1706), *The Busybody* (acted 1709), *The Wonder! A Woman Keeps a Secret* (1714), which furnished David Garrick with one of his best roles, *A Gotham Election* (published 1715; 2nd ed., 1737, entitled *Humours of Elections*), and *A Bold Stroke for a Wife* (acted 1718) in which one of the characters, Simon Pure, after being impersonated, arrives in the last act as "the real Simon Pure." This is the origin of the popular reference to Simon Pure as a standard of genuineness.

Cent Nouvelles Nouvelles (säṅ nö.vel nö.vel), **Les.** [Eng. trans., *"One Hundred New Tales."*] Collection of medieval French tales, first printed in folio, without date, from a manuscript of the year 1456. Authorship is attributed to Antoine de la Salle. The *Cent Nouvelles Nouvelles,* although in prose, bear much resemblance to the metrical, comic, or satiric medieval writings called fabliaux. Many of them are taken from the work of the Italian writers, but all of them are reworked in an original manner.

Cento (chen'tō). Town and commune in N Italy, in the *compartimento* (region) of Emilia-Romagna, in the province of Ferrara, situated near the Reno River, ab. 17 mi. N of Bologna. It has a medieval castle and a small art gallery. Pope Alexander VI conceded the town to the duchy of Ferrara in 1502. Buildings of interest to tourists were undamaged in World War II. Pop. of commune, 22,371 (1936); of town, 5,677 (1936).

Centoatl (sen.tō.ät'l). See **Cinteotl.**

Centones Homerici (sen.tō'nēz hō.mer'i.sī). Account in Homeric hexameter of the life of Christ, attributed to the 5th-century Byzantine empress Eudocia (who was baptized as a Christian shortly before her marriage in 421 to the emperor Theodosius II).

Cento novelle antiche (chen'tō nō.vel'lā än.tē'kā). [Eng. trans., *"One Hundred Old Tales."*] Collection of tales and anecdotes from ancient and medieval history, from Oriental and Greek mythology and legend, from the Bible, and from the popular tales of Italy, Provence, and Brittany, compiled in Italy about the end of the 13th century.

Centorbi (chen.tôr'bē). See **Centuripe.**

Central (sen.träl'), **Cordillera.** See **Cordillera Central.**

Central Africa Railway. Railway in S Africa, partly in Mozambique and partly in Nyasaland, built in 1915, and connecting Chindio, Mozambique, on the Zambezi River, with the Shiré Highlands railroad at Port Herald, Nyasaland. After the completion (1935) of a bridge across the lower Zambezi, the Central Africa railway was linked with Beira, Mozambique, on the Indian Ocean, and the latter port became the entrepôt for Nyasaland. Length of railway, 61 mi., of which 45 mi. are in Portuguese territory.

Central America. Name applied collectively to the six republics of Guatemala, Honduras, El Salvador, Nicaragua, Costa Rica, and Panama, and the crown colony of British Honduras.

Central American Arbitration Treaty. Treaty signed on Dec. 20, 1907, by the representatives of five Central American states (Guatemala, El Salvador, Honduras, Nicaragua, and Costa Rica) at a conference at Washington, D.C., by which all the states agreed to submit disputed matters to a court of arbitration, the judges, one from each of the five countries, to be appointed by the congress of each country, and its decisions to be binding on all parties.

Central American Confederation. See **Confederación Centro-Americana.**

Central American Court of Justice. Tribunal established (May 25, 1908) at Cartago, Costa Rica, by five Central American republics (Guatemala, El Salvador, Honduras, Nicaragua, and Costa Rica), in accordance with the Central American Arbitration Treaty signed (1907) by representatives of these countries at Washington, D.C. It was given jurisdiction over all cases which the signatory powers were unable to settle by a negotiated agreement. The court decided two suits brought (1916, 1917) by Costa Rica and El Salvador protesting the Bryan-Chamorro treaty between the U.S. and Nicaragua, but Nicaragua's refusal to abide by unfavorable decisions destroyed the tribunal's effectiveness. When the treaty decreeing its establishment expired (1918) and was not renewed, the court was dissolved.

Central City. [Former name, **Morehead's Horse Mill.**] City in W Kentucky, in Muhlenberg County. Coal mining is the principal industry. It was renamed in 1870. Pop. 4,110 (1950).

Central Europe. See **Mitteleuropa.**

Central Falls. [Former name, **Chocolate Mill.**] City in N Rhode Island, in Providence County, on the Blackstone River near Pawtucket: manufactures include electric light bulbs, laboratory glassware, and textiles. An old industrial center, it was incorporated in 1895 as a city. 23,550 (1950).

Central Highlands. See **Cordillera de Venezuela.**

Centralia (sen.trāl′yą). City in S Illinois, in Clinton and Marion counties, ab. 60 mi. SE of St. Louis. An important Illinois bituminous-coal mining center, it was the site of a major mine explosion, killing 111 men, on March 25, 1947. Oil has also been a principal product since the 1930's. Centralia is a railroad center and has a considerable trade in fruit, especially apples, peaches, strawberries, and pears. 13,863 (1950).

Centralia. [Former name, **Centerville;** called the **"Hub City."**] City in SW Washington, in Lewis County, near the confluence of the Chehalis and Skookumchuck rivers, ab. 24 mi. SW of Olympia, adjoining Chehalis. Manufactures include lumber products and food products. It is the seat of Centralia Junior College. 8,657 (1950).

Centralia. Former town in C Wisconsin, now part of **Wisconsin Rapids.**

Centralid (sen.tral′id). Name sometimes applied to a type of round-headed and relatively broad-faced North American Indian, formerly concentrated in the C part of the U.S. and typically associated with the Middle Mississippi pattern of culture.

Central India Agency. Former official name for a collection of native states in India which were under the control of Great Britain, situated between Rajputana and the United Provinces on the N, and the Central Provinces on the S. The chief states were Gwalior, Indore, Bhopal, and Rewa. The E part of the Agency was sometimes called the Central India states or Baghelkhand. Gwalior and Indore merged (1948) with the state, or union, of Madhya Bharat, and Rewa joined (1950) Vindhya Pradesh; the latter and Bhopal are "centrally administered areas" under the new constitution of India. The capital of the Agency was at Indore; area, 52,072 sq. mi.; pop. 7,511,694 (1941).

Central India States. [Also, **Baghelkhand.**] Group of states in C India, formerly a political unit as part of the Central India Agency; the most important state in this group was Rewa. They were merged in 1950 with Vindhya Pradesh. The capital was at Rewa.

Central Islip (ī′slip). Unincorporated residential community in SE New York, in Suffolk County on Long Island. 3,067 (1950).

Centralists (sen′trąl.ists). Political party in Mexico which began in 1823, was reorganized in 1837, and was prominent for many years thereafter. The Centralists favored a single centralized republican government, and were opposed by the Federalists, who desired autonomy of the states. The struggles for ascendancy of these two parties caused many of the civil wars which were waged in Mexico. At various times each of the parties, or branches of them, was known by other names. Antonio López de Santa Anna was long the leading spirit of the Centralists. Centralist and Federalist parties were prominent in the affairs of other Spanish-American countries, notably Argentina, Venezuela, and Central America, but were commonly distinguished by other names.

Central Java (jä′vą, jav′ą). [Indonesian, **Djawa-Tengah.**] Province of the Republic of Indonesia, on the island of Java. Area, ab. 14,435 sq. mi.; pop. 15,265,504 (1930), 15,168,786 (1951).

Central Massif. See **Massif Central.**

Central Overland, California and Pikes Peak Express. [Abbreviation, **C.O.C. and P.P.;** nickname, from the initials, **"Clean Out of Cash and Poor Pay."**] Stage line (1860–62) chartered by the Kansas legislature, operating the lines from Missouri to Denver and Salt Lake City. In May, 1860, it assumed the contract for bringing mail from Utah to California. It is best known for its inauguration of the Pony Express, a venture which contributed to the enterprise's financial decline and led its workers to pin upon it its derisive nickname. In 1862 the company's holdings were put up for public sale, after a financial scandal resulting in the indictment of its president, William H. Russell, and the secretary of war, John B. Floyd.

Central Park. Unincorporated community in SE New York, in Nassau County, on Long Island. Under the urban definition established for use in the 1950 census it was counted with adjoining urban areas; the last official separate enumeration was 2,590 (1940).

Central Park. Principal park in New York City, extending from 59th Street (here called Central Park South) to 110th Street, and from Fifth Avenue to Eighth Avenue (here called Central Park West). It was designed by Frederick Law Olmsted and Calvert Vaux, and contains besides numerous drives and recreational areas, the Mall (where concerts and dances are held), Cleopatra's Needle (the Obelisk), the Metropolitan Museum of Art, formal gardens, a reservoir, a zoo, a blockhouse (1812) near the site of Fort Clinton, a U.S. Weather Bureau station, and other spots of note. Length, 2½ mi.; area, 840 acres.

Central Plateau. See **Mexican Plateau.**

Central Powers. Term applied to those countries in World War I which fought against the Allied powers. The chief of these nations were Germany, Austria-Hungary, Turkey, Bulgaria, and Rumania.

Central Province. Province in S central Ceylon, in hilly to mountainous land. Farming is the principal occupation; the chief crops are millet, cacao, cinnamon, and tea. Capital, Kandy; area, 2,290 sq. mi.; pop. 1,135,290 (1946).

Central Provinces. [Official name (from 1950), **Madhya Pradesh;** former official name, **Central Provinces and Berar.**] Group of states in the Union of India, in the central part of the country, N of the state of Hyderabad. There is much manganese, some iron, and some coal mined here. The important crops are cotton, linseed, wheat, millet, and barley. It contains four divisions: Nagpur, Jubbulpone, Narbada, and Chhattisgarh. Berar became part of the administration of the Central Provinces in 1903. Capitals: Nagpur (winter), Pachmarhi (summer); total area, 98,574 sq. mi.; total pop., 16,813,584 (1941).

Central Route. Name often applied to the overland route used (especially 1848–68) by many emigrants traveling to California. Although there were many branches, the route generally followed led from the Missouri River NW along the Platte, through Wyoming (South Pass) and the region to the north of Great Salt Lake, along the Humboldt River, and through various passes in the Sierras.

Central Sumatra (sọ.mä′trą). Province of the Republic of Indonesia, in Sumatra.

Central Viet-Nam (vēt′näm′, vẹ.et′näm′). Official name since 1949 of **Annam.**

Centro (sen′trō), **El.** See **El Centro.**

Centum Cellae (sen′tum sel′ē). An ancient name of **Civitavecchia.**

Centuries of Magdeburg (mäg′dẹ.bėrg). See **Magdeburg, Centuries of.**

Centuripe (chen.tö′rē.pā). [Also: **Centorbi;** ancient name, **Centuripae.**] Town and commune in SW Italy, on the island of Sicily, in the province of Enna, ab. 20 mi. NW of Catania. It is an agricultural market center; sulfur mines are in the vicinity. The town, founded by the Greeks, flourished in the period of the late Roman Empire; a number of antiquities are preserved. It was destroyed by the emperor Frederick II in 1232. Some damage was suffered during World War II by the Church of the Immacolata, but it was not beyond repair. Pop. of commune, 10,802 (1936); of town, 9,255 (1936).

Century Association. New York club for men, incorporated in 1857 for the advancement of art and literature. Its house is at 7 West 43rd Street.

Century Dictionary of the English Language, The. Six-volume work (1889–91) edited by William Dwight Whitney, containing 450,000 entries and notable for its encyclopedic scope. *The Century Dictionary of Names* (1894, and subsequent eds.), edited by Benjamin E. Smith, was an outgrowth of *The Century Dictionary;* with the addition (1897) of another volume, an atlas, the general work known as *The Century Dictionary and Cyclopedia* (now in ten volumes) was brought to completion. In 1909 a two-volume supplement to the dictionary was published, and the entire work was reissued (1911) in 12 volumes. A two-volume abridgment, *The New Century Dictionary,* appeared in 1927.

Century Illustrated Monthly Magazine, The. American magazine published (1881–1930) at New York as a continuation of *Scribner's Monthly,* under the editorship of Richard Watson Gilder (1881–1909). In 1909 it became *The Century*, under the editorship (1909–13) of Robert Underwood Johnson (1853–1937). In 1930 it was consolidated with *The Forum*.

Century of Dishonor, A. Treatise (1881) by Helen Hunt Jackson, criticizing the U.S. government's treatment of the Indians.

"Century" White. Nickname of **White, John.**

Cenú (sä.nö'). Name given c1515 to a region on the northern coast of South America, about midway between Darien (in what is now Panama) and Cartagena (now in Colombia). Martin Fernández de Enciso, sent from Darien to conquer it (1515), tried to treat with the Indians, but afterward ravaged their country. A second expedition, sent soon after, was entirely destroyed by the natives.

Cenwalh (kān'wälċh). fl. c643–672. King of the West Saxons; son of Cynegils, whom he succeeded in 643.

Ceos (sē'os). Latin name of **Keos.**

Cepeda (thā.pā'ᴛʜä), **Diego.** b. at Tordesillas, Spain, c1495; d. at Valladolid, Spain, c1549. Spanish judge. He was *oidor* (magistrate) of the Canary Islands, and subsequently one of the royal audience which accompanied (1544) the viceroy Blasco Nuñez Vela to Peru. There he led the judges in their opposition to Vela, imprisoned him, joined Gonzalo Pizarro, and took part in the battle of Anaquito (just outside Quito, Ecuador), where the viceroy was killed (Jan. 18, 1546). Foreseeing Pizarro's defeat, he deserted him on the battlefield of Sacsahuaman (April 8, 1548), was sent to be tried in Spain, and, it is said, poisoned himself in prison.

Cephaloedium (sef.ạ.lē'di.um). Ancient name of **Cefalù.**

Cephalonia (sef.ạ.lō'ni.ạ). [Also: **Kefallinia, Kephallenia;** ancient name, **Cephallenia.**] One of the Ionian Islands, W of Greece, forming a department of Greece. It includes the provinces of Ithaka, Cranea, Pale, and Same. Its surface is mountainous. The island may be the one called by Homer Same or Samos. It became subject to Rome in 189 B.C., and later came under Byzantine, Venetian, and Turkish rule, and a British protectorate. Capital, Argostoli; area, ab. 300 sq. mi.; length, 30 mi.; pop. 47,311 (1951).

Cephalus (sef'ạ.lus). In ancient Greek mythology, the son of Deion, and the husband of Procris whom he accidentally slew while hunting. Eos, the goddess of the dawn, had a liaison with him and suggested that he test Procris's fidelity. He disguised himself and managed to seduce her. She fled, returned in disguise, seduced him, and presented him with a never-failing spear in token of their reconciliation. But her jealousy led her to spy on him as he hunted and when she made an involuntary movement on hearing him invoke the breeze to cool him (she thought he uttered a woman's name) he threw the spear and killed her.

Cephas (sē'fạs). See Saint **Peter.**

Cepheus (sē'fūs, -fẹ.us). In ancient Greek mythology, a king, usually of Ethiopia, son of Belus, husband of Cassiopeia, and father of Andromeda.

Cepheus. One of the northern constellations, recognized in ancient times, between Cassiopeia and Draco. It is figured to represent the Ethiopian king Cepheus wearing a tiara and having his arms somewhat extended. Its brightest stars are of the third magnitude. The Cepheid variables, a class of stars varying in brightness because of internal pulsation, are called after one of the stars in this constellation.

Cephisodotus (sef.i.sod'ọ.tus). fl. 4th century B.C. Name of two Greek sculptors, often confused with each other. One was a relative, possibly the father or a brother of Praxiteles, and something is known of his work from a copy, at Munich, of a statue of Pluto, or Wealth, as an infant in the arms of Irene, or Peace. The other Cephisodotus was a son of Praxiteles; it is known that he made portrait sculptures, but no examples of his work survive.

Cephissus (sẹ.fis'us). [Also: **Cephisus** (-fī'sus), **Kephisos.**] In ancient geography, a river in Attica, Greece, flowing through the plain of Eleusis into the Gulf of Eleusis.

Cephissus. [Also: **Cephisus, Kephisos.**] In ancient geography, a river in Attica, Greece, flowing through the plain of Athens into the Saronic Gulf.

Cephissus. [Also: **Cephisus, Kephisos.**] In ancient geography, a river in Phocis and Boeotia, Greece, flowing into Lake Copais (Topolias).

Ceracchi (chä.räk'kē), **Giuseppe.** b. in Corsica, c1760; executed at Paris, c1801. Italian sculptor. He was a conspirator against the life of Napoleon in 1800. He did portrait busts of George Washington, Benjamin Franklin, and Alexander Hamilton, a replica of the latter being in the Hall of Fame.

Ceram (sẹ.ram'; Dutch, sā'räm; Portuguese, sẹ.ruṅ'). [Also: **Ceiram, Séran, Serang, Zeram.**] Island in the Moluccas, East Indies, E of Celebes and W of New Guinea, in the Republic of Indonesia, formerly (under the federal government of 1946–50) in the *negara* (state) of East Indonesia. Its inhabitants are Malays and Alfuras. Abacá and coconut products are important here. Area, ab. 6,600 sq. mi.; pop. ab. 100,000.

Ceramicus (ser.ạ.mī'kus). Large area on the NW side of ancient Athens, Greece, so named from the early gathering in it of potters, attracted by the presence of water and excellent clay. It was divided into two parts, the Inner Ceramicus, within the walls, traversed by the Dromos Street from the Dipylon Gate, and including the Agora; and the Outer Ceramicus, continuing the first division outside of the walls. The Outer Ceramicus became a favorite place of burial for the Athenians, and here were interred those honored with a public funeral. The tombs were ranged beside and near the various roads which radiated from the Dipylon Gate. Little trace of them remains, except of the unique group upon and near the inception of the Sacred Way to Eleusis, a group which was preserved by being buried in 86 B.C. in the siege *agger* (earthwork) of Sulla, and contains historical and plastic memorials of very high value, among them the sculptured monument of Dexileos, who fell (393 B.C.) before Corinth, and tombs of Euphrosyne, Hegeso, Aristion, Demetria, and Pamphile.

Cerasus (ser'ạ.sus). See **Giresun,** town.

Ceraunian Mountains (sẹ.rô'ni.ạn). [Also, occasionally, **Acroceraunia or Acroceraunian Mountains.**] In ancient geography, a chain of mountains in NW Epirus, terminating in the promontory Acroceraunia.

Ceraunian Mountains. In ancient geography, a range of mountains in the E part of the Caucasus system, exact position undetermined.

Cerberus (sėr'bėr.us). In Greek mythology, the watchdog at the entrance to Hades, the infernal regions. Offspring of Typhon and Echidna, he was usually represented as having three heads, a serpent's tail, and a mane made of serpent's heads. Hercules, as one of his labors, brought Cerberus up from Hades. As one of their burial customs, the Greeks buried with the corpse a honey cake, with which the spirit was to quiet Cerberus so that it might pass the monster-dog on its way to Elysium; thence the expression "a sop to Cerberus."

Cercina (sėr.sī'nạ). Ancient name of the **Kerkennah Islands.**

Cercinitis (sėr.si.nī'tis). [Also: **Cercinites** (-tēz), **Kerkinitis, Limne Kerkinitis;** modern Greek, **Akhinos, Akhinou, Tachyno, Takhino, Takinos.**] In ancient geography, the lake or enlargement of the river Strymon (in Macedonia), near its mouth.

Cercops (sėr'kops). Ancient Greek Orphic poet. He is said to have been the author of a poem, *The Descent into Hades,* also attributed to Prodicus of Samos and others.

Cercops. fl. c6th century B.C. Greek poet of Miletus. To him a poem on the war of Aegimius, king of the Dorians, against the Lapithae is by some assigned; by others it is attributed to Hesiod.

Cerda (ther'ᴛʜä), **Juan de Leiva y de la.** See **Leiva y de la Cerda, Juan de.**

Cerda (ser'ᴛʜä), **Pedro Aguirre.** See **Aguirre Cerda, Pedro.**

Cerda (ther'ᴛʜä), **Tomás Antonio Manrique de la.** [Titles: Count of **Paredes,** Marquis of **La Laguna.**] b. c1620; d. 1688. Spanish administrator. He was a member of the royal council, and from 1680 to 1686 was viceroy of New Spain (Mexico). During his term the buccaneers sacked Veracruz in May, 1683, and committed other ravages.

Cerdagne (ser.dány'). [Spanish, **La Cerdaña.**] Medieval countship on both sides of the eastern Pyrenees. Part of it is now in the department of Pyrénées-Orientales in France, and part is in Spain. It followed in the later Middle Ages the fortunes of Catalonia, and then of Aragon. It was released from homage to France in 1258, was acquired by France in 1462, and was restored to Aragon in 1493. The part to the north of the Pyrenees was ceded to France in 1659.

Cerdagne, Count of. See **James I** and **James II** (of *Majorca*).

Cerda Sandoval Silva y Mendoza (ther′ᴛʜä sän.dō.ʙäl′ sēl′ʙä ē men.dō′thä), **Gaspar de la.** [Title (created in 1688), Count of **Galve.**] b. c1630; d. 1697. Spanish administrator. As viceroy of Mexico (November, 1688–July, 1695), he sent expeditions (1690–91) against the French of Santo Domingo and Louisiana. He returned to Spain in May, 1696.

Cerdeña (ther.ᴛʜā′nyä). Spanish name of **Sardinia.**

Cerdic (cher′dich, sėr′dik). d. c534. Saxon ealdorman who founded a settlement on the coast of Hampshire, England, in 495 A.D., assumed the title of King of the West Saxons in 519, and became ancestor of the English royal line. He defeated the Britons at Charford (in Hampshire) in 519, was himself defeated at Mount Badon (or Badbury, in Dorsetshire) in 520, and conquered the Isle of Wight in 530.

Cerdicsford (sėr′diks.fǫrd). Scene of the victory of Cerdic and Cynric over the Britons in 519: usually identified with Charford, in Hampshire, on the Lower Avon.

Cerdo (sėr′dō). b. in Syria; fl. c137 A.D. Gnostic teacher at Rome, founder of a sect named from him Cerdonians.

Cerdonians (sėr.dō′ni.ąnz). Name of a Gnostic sect of the 2nd century A.D., named after its founder Cerdo, a Syrian at Rome. They held that there were two first causes, one good (the unknown father of Jesus Christ) and one evil (the Creator revealed in the law and the prophets), and that one was not subject or inferior to the other.

Cerea (chā.rā′ä). Town and commune in NE Italy, in the *compartimento* (region) of Veneto, in the province of Verona, SE of Verona. The district produces rice, grain, and tobacco. Pop. of commune, 10,343 (1936); of town, 1,942 (1936).

Ceres (sir′ēz, sē′rēz). In ancient Italian mythology, the goddess of grain and harvest, later identified by the Romans with the Greek Demeter. Her cult was quite old; one of the *flamens* (15 priests, each assigned to one god and his cult observance) was the *flamen Cerealis.*

Ceres. Asteroid (No. 1) discovered by Giuseppe Piazzi at Palermo on Jan. 1, 1801, following calculations according to Bode's law that a planet or planetary body should be in the orbit in which Ceres was found.

Ceresio (chā.rā′zyō), **Lago.** An Italian name of **Lugano, Lake.**

Ceresole (chā.rā.zô′lā). [Also: **Ceresole Alba** (äl′bä); French, **Cérisoles.**] Village in N Italy, in the *compartimento* (region) of Piedmont, ab. 13 mi. NW of Alba. Here, on April 14, 1544, the French under the Duc d'Enghien defeated the forces of Spain and the Holy Roman Empire.

Céret (sā.re). Town in S France, in the department of Pyrénées-Orientales, situated on the Tech River, ab. 17 mi. SW of Perpignan. It is the center of a fruit-growing district, particularly known for its cherries, and has factories which manufacture corks for bottles, and wooden materials for pipes, whips, chairs, and sandals. It has remnants of medieval fortifications. 5,148 (1946).

Céria (sā.ryȧ), **Edmond.** b. at Évian-les-Bains, France, Jan. 26, 1884—. French landscape and figure painter who has painted many small nude studies as well as scenes of the Mediterranean coasts. His work has been exhibited at the Salon des Tuileries, Paris, and a *Still Life* (1926) was exhibited at the Luxembourg Museum, Paris.

Cerialis or **Cerealis** (sir.i.ā′lis), **Petillius.** fl. A.D. 70. Roman general. He was a close relative of Vespasian, and is known to have been in Britain in the year 61, when the IXth Legion was defeated by the Britons. In the civil commotions of 69 he supported Vespasian against Vitellius. In 70 the emperor put him in command of the forces which suppressed a rebellion of Germans and Gauls led by Civilis, and in the following year he was appointed governor of Britain, where he defeated the Brigantes.

Ceridwen (ke.rid′wen). [Also: **Cerridwen, Keridwen.**] In Brythonic mythology, a nature goddess. Traditionally she was the mother of Taliesin, for whom she prepared the magic caldron of inspiration.

Cerignola (chā.rē.nyô′lä). Town and commune in SE Italy, in the *compartimento* (region) of Apulia, in the province of Foggia, between Foggia and Bari. It is a market town for a rich agricultural district, known for its mushrooms. Here, on April 28, 1503, the Spanish army under Gonzalo de Córdoba defeated the French under Gaston de Foix, Duc de Nemours. Pop. of commune, 39,540 (1936); of town, 38,043 (1936).

Cerigo (che′rē.gō) or **Cerigotto** (che.rē.gôt′tō). See **Cythera.**

Cerimon (ser′i.mon). Physician of Ephesus who saves the life of Thaisa, in *Pericles, Prince of Tyre,* attributed to Shakespeare.

Cerinthians (sē.rin′thi.ąnz). Sect of early heretics, followers of Cerinthus. Flourishing probably in the 1st and 2nd centuries A.D., they held partly Gnostic views.

Cerinthus (sē.rin′thus). b. in Egypt; fl. probably in the latter part of the 1st century A.D. Gnostic teacher, founder of the heretical sect of the Cerinthians or Merinthians. His teachings are a mixture of Gnosticism, Judaism, Ebionitism, and Chiliasm. He distinguished between a Supreme Being who is beyond knowledge, and lesser orders of divinities and angels who created the world, and he considered Jesus to have been a man merely, who became the Christ momentarily when illuminated by the Supreme Being. It is traditional that the Fourth Gospel was written by Saint John to refute these Cerinthian teachings. For a time Cerinthus, who seems to have been a native of Egypt and a Jew, had a school and disciples, but nothing written by him has survived.

Cerisius Lacus (sē.rē′zhi.us lā′kus). Latin name of **Lugano, Lake.**

Cérisoles (sā.rē.zol). French name of **Ceresole.**

Cerletti (cher.let′tē), **Ugo.** b. at Conegliano, Veneto, Italy, Sept. 26, 1877—. Italian physician. He was the first, together with L. Bini (1938), to use the electric shock treatment in shock therapy (which has the advantage of simple application). He is the author of *La Glandola tiroide nei fanciulli delle scuole di Roma e dei paesi ad endemia gozzo-cretinica* (1906), *Il Problema antropometrico nel cretinismo endemico* (1906), *Recerche sperimentali sull'origine dei plasmatociti* (1907), and *Riassunto delle lezioni di clinica delle malattie nervose e mentali* (1946); coeditor of *Funzioni e disfunzioni tiroidee* (1923).

Cerna (ser′nä), **Vicente.** fl. 1865–71. Guatemalan general. He was elected president of Guatemala, assuming the office on May 24, 1865. Reëlected in 1869, he held the office until June 29, 1871, when he was overthrown by forces in which Justo Rufino Barrios was prominent, and was succeeded by the provisional (1871–73) president, Miguel García Granado.

Cernăuţi (cher.nạ.öts′, -ö′tsē). Rumanian name of **Chernovtsy.**

Cernay (ser.ne). [German, **Sennheim.**] Town in E France, in the department of Haut-Rhin (formerly Upper Alsace), situated on the Thur River, ab. 9 mi. NW of Mulhouse. An industrial town, it was completely destroyed in World War I, reconstructed afterward, and again badly damaged in World War II. 5,800 (1946).

Cerne (sėr′nē). In ancient geography, an island W of Africa, discovered and colonized by the Carthaginian Hanno: perhaps the modern Arguin.

Cernuschi (cher.nös′kē), **Enrico** or **Henri.** b. at Milan, Italy, 1821; d. at Menton, France, May 12, 1896. Italian financier and political economist, an advocate of bimetallism (a word he is, by some, credited with inventing). He played a conspicuous part in the insurrections at Milan in 1848, and at Rome in 1849, but in 1850 escaped to France, where he was afterward naturalized. He wrote *Mécanique de l'échange* (1865), *Illusions des sociétés coöpératives* (1866), *La Diplomatie monétaire* (1878), *Le Bimétallisme en Angleterre* (1879), *Le Bimétallisme à quinze et demi* (1881), *Le Grand procès de l'union latine* (1884), *Les Assignats métalliques* (1885), and others.

Cernuschi (ser.nös′chē), **Félix.** b. at Montevideo, Uruguay, May 17, 1907—. Argentine physicist. His graduate studies at Cambridge (1933–37), the Institut Henri Poincaré, Paris (1937), Princeton, and the Massachusetts Institute of Technology (1938) led to a professorship (1939) of theoretical physics and applied mathematics at the University of Tucumán, Argentina. He is the author of numerous works in the field of physics.

Cerny (sėr'ni), **Frederick.** Pseudonym of **Guthrie, Frederick.**

Cerqueira e Silva (ser.kā'rą ē sil'vą), **Ignacio Accioli de.** See **Accioli de Cerqueira e Silva, Ignacio.**

Cerralvo (ser.räl'bō), Marquis of. Title of **Pacheco y Osorio, Rodrigo de.**

Cerré (ser.rā), **Jean Gabriel.** b. at Montreal, 1734; d. 1805. Frontiersman and trader in the American Midwest. Well-educated, adventurous, and able, he established himself as a fur trader at Kaskaskia in Illinois as early as 1755, and his business flourished under French, British, and American regimes alike. He outfitted a great many of the pioneer hunters of the region west of the Mississippi, and seems to have maintained good relations with the Indians. After the outbreak of the Revolutionary War both the British and the Americans solicited his support. Eventually he threw in his lot with the American cause, and George Rogers Clark has recorded that Cerré's aid in money and provisions, during the campaign for the conquest of Illinois, was very substantial. After the end of the war he became a magistrate of the newly-organized territory, but even before this he had begun to contemplate moving his base of operations to Missouri (where in 1780 he had established a trading post which he called New Madrid), and presently he did remove to St. Louis, where his trading operations, his wealth, and his influence continued to grow. It is said that between his many employees and the numerous relatives who followed him to St. Louis, he became a kind of tribal chief to a large part of the population of that city, where he was regarded with affection and respect not only because of his wealth, but as a man of kindliness and courteous manners. One of his daughters, Marie Thérèse, became the wife of Auguste Chouteau.

Cerrito (sę.rē'tō), **El.** See **El Cerrito.**

Cerrito (cher.rē'tō), **Francesca.** See **St. Léon, Fanny.**

Cerro (ther'rō; in Spanish America, ser'rō). [Plural, **Cerros** (-rōs).] Spanish word for "mountain," "hill," or "peak": for Spanish names of mountains, see the specific element of the name.

Cerro de Pasco (ser'rō dā päs'kō). [Also, **Pasco.**] City in C Peru, capital of Pasco (formerly part of Junín) department. It owes its existence to the celebrated copper and silver mines of the vicinity, long among the most productive in the world, and still very rich. Elevation, 14,280 ft.; pop. 19,187 (1940).

Cerro Gordo (gôr'dō). Pass by the side of the Río del Plan, between Veracruz and Jalapa, in the state of Veracruz, Mexico, through which passes the principal road from the coast to Mexico by Jalapa. The pass was carried (April 18, 1847) by the American forces advancing from Veracruz towards Mexico City under General Winfield Scott, despite its occupation and fortification in depth by Santa Anna; Captain Robert E. Lee distinguished himself in this battle, his reconnaissance establishing the strategy for the engagement.

Cerro Largo (lär'gō). Department in NE Uruguay. Capital, Melo; area, 5,764 sq. mi.; pop. 99,123 (est. 1947).

Certaldo (cher.täl'dō). Town and commune in C Italy, in the *compartimento* (region) of Tuscany, in the province of Firenze, situated on the Elsa River, ab. 17 mi. SW of Florence. It has preserved its medieval character. The Palazzo del Vicario, an early medieval building, was reconstructed c1400. The Florentine painter Benozzo Gozzoli worked here. It was the place of birth and death of Boccaccio; the tombstone of the Boccaccio family is in the Church of San Michele e Jacopo. Certaldo, first mentioned under Emperor Frederick I (Frederick Barbarossa), came under Florentine jurisdiction in the 13th century. Only slight damage was suffered during World War II by some buildings of tourist interest. Pop. of commune, 12,094 (1936); of town, 5,290 (1936).

Certosa (cher.tō'zä). [Also, **Certosa di Pavia** (dē pä'vyä).] Former Carthusian monastery at Pavia, Italy, one of the largest and most splendid of its kind. The church, founded in 1396, contains the tomb of Gian Galeazzo Visconti.

Cervantes (sėr.van'tēz; Spanish, ther.bän'tās), **Miguel de.** [Full surname, **Cervantes Saavedra** (sä.ä.bā'ᴛʜrä).] b. at Alcalá de Henares, Spain, possibly on Oct. 9, 1547; d. at Madrid, April 23, 1616. Spanish novelist, poet, and dramatist. His lineage was good, but the family was poverty stricken. Except that for a time he went to school at Madrid (ab. 20 mi. from his birthplace), where he published some verses (1568), nothing is known of his youth or education. In 1569 he went to Rome as the chamberlain of Cardinal Acquaviva. For the next five years he served in the Spanish army, based in Italy. In the naval battle of Lepanto (1571) he received the "beautiful" wounds that crippled his left hand and arm. En route home in 1575 he was captured by pirates and held at Algiers for five years, where his tireless bravery is well documented. After a brief turn with the army in Portugal he settled down to writing; but a number of plays brought neither fame nor wealth, nor did the pastoral *La Galatea* (1585). In 1584 he married a farmer's daughter. They had no children, but his household for long included two sisters, an illegitimate daughter, and a niece. A position as a government collector, first of grain and then of taxes, took him to Seville in 1587. His work yielded valuable knowledge of Andalusians, respectable and criminal, but his bad bookkeeping put him in jail at least twice. For a while he sojourned at Valladolid, then ended his days at Madrid (1608–16), "old, a soldier and gentleman, but poor." He had a considerable acquaintance among the writers of his day but no great reputation. The popular success of the first part of *Don Quixote* (Madrid, 1605) was a great surprise to his publisher, and probably to Cervantes. However, he dallied over the second part, first publishing the *Novelas Exemplares* (Twelve Instructive or Moral Tales, 1613) and the long poem *Viaje del Parnaso* (Journey to Parnassus, 1614). Aroused by the appearance of the spurious sequel to *Don Quixote* in 1614, he hurried his own second part to completion in 1615. In the same year he brought out his *Ocho Comedias* (Eight Comedies). He died of dropsy on April 23, 1616, and was buried, no one knows where, by the Franciscans, of whose Tertiary Order he was a member. *Persiles y Sigismunda,* a long prose romance, appeared posthumously in 1617. Though the beautiful dedication to this work was written only four days before his death, the book may well be largely early work. To the end of his life he was full of plans for other writings. Considering his age, illness, and financial worries, the productivity of his declining years is phenomenal.

Cervera y Topete (ther.bā'rä ē tō.pā'tā), **Pascual.** [Titles: Count of **Jerez,** Marquis of **Santa Ana.**] b. in Cádiz province, Spain, Feb. 18, 1839; d. at Puerto Real, Spain, April 3, 1909. Spanish admiral. He was a student (1848–51) at the naval academy at San Fernando, and served in Morocco and in the Cuban rebellion (1868–73). He held the office of minister of marine in 1892. On the outbreak of the Spanish-American War he sailed from the Cape Verde Islands with four cruisers and three torpedo-boat destroyers (April 29, 1898), entered the harbor of Santiago de Cuba (May 19), and lost his entire fleet off that port (July 3) in an attempt to force his way through an American blockading squadron under Admirals Sampson and Schley.

Cerveteri (cher.ve'tā.rē). See under **Caere.**

Cervia (cher'vyä). Town and commune in N Italy, in the *compartimento* (region) of Emilia-Romagna, in the province of Ravenna, situated on the Adriatic Sea between Ravenna and Rimini. Pop. of commune, 12,319 (1936); of town, 2,920 (1936).

Cervin (ser.vaṅ), **Mont.** French name of the **Matterhorn.**

Cervini degli Spannochi (cher.vē'nē de'lyē spän.nô'kē), **Marcello.** Original name of Pope **Marcellus II.**

Cervino (cher.vē'nō), **Monte.** Italian name of the **Matterhorn.**

Cerynean Hind (ser.i.nē'ąn). A fabled creature in Greek mythology, referred to in the legend of Hercules. With golden horns and hoofs of brass, this creature, sacred to Artemis, was as fleet as the wind. Its capture was the third of the twelve labors imposed upon Hercules, and he accomplished this after a long pursuit by driving it into a deep drift of snow in a northern region.

Cesalpino (chā.zäl.pē'nō), **Andrea.** See **Caesalpinus, Andreas.**

Cesano Maderno (chā.zä'nō mä.der'nō). Town and commune in NW Italy, in the *compartimento* (region) of

Lombardy, in the province of Milano, N of Milan: rayon and furniture manufactures. Pop. of commune, 12,125 (1936); of town, 5,771 (1936).

César (sā'sär). River in N Colombia, flowing S to the Magdalena River.

César de Bazan (sā'sär dā bä.sän'), **Don.** See **Don César de Bazan.**

Cesare Borgia (chā'zä.rā bôr'jä). Play (1920) by Arthur Symons.

Cesari (chā'zä.rē), **Antonio.** b. at Verona, Italy, Jan. 16, 1760; d. at Ravenna, Italy, Oct. 1, 1828. Italian philologist. He was the author of a new edition of *Vocabolario della Crusca* (1806–09), *Bellezze di Dante* (1824–26), translations of Terence (1816), and of Cicero's *Epistles* (1826–31), and others.

Cesari, Giuseppe. [Title, Cavaliere **d'Arpino;** called **Il Giuseppino.**] b. at Rome, c1568; d. there, 1640. Italian painter of the mannerist school. Among his chief works are frescoes in the Capitol and the Church of Santa Maria Maggiore, at Rome.

Cesarini (chā.zä.rē'nē), Cardinal **Giuliano.** [Called Cardinal **Julian.**] b. at Rome, 1398; d. at Varna, Bulgaria, Nov. 10, 1444. Italian ecclesiastical diplomat. Created cardinal by Pope Martin V on conclusion of the Schism of the West, he was sent to Germany to examine into ecclesiastical conditions. He became president of the Council of Basel, and later went to Hungary as papal envoy (1443).

Cesàro (chā.zä'rō), **Ernesto.** b. at Naples, Italy, March 12, 1859; d. there, Sept. 12, 1906. Italian mathematician, professor at the University of Naples, and author of several hundred papers on arithmetic, geometry, spherical trigonometry, analysis, and crystallography. His books include *Introduzione alla teoria matematica della elasticità* (1894), *Lezioni dei geometria intrinsica* (1896), and *Elementi di calcolo infinitesimale* (2nd ed., 1905).

Cesarotti (chā.zä.rôt'tē), **Melchiorre.** b. at Padua, Italy, May 15, 1730; d. Nov. 4, 1808. Italian poet and miscellaneous writer. His works include a translation of Ossian (1763), *Saggio sulla filosofia delle lingue* (1785), and others.

Cesena (chā.ze'nä). [Ancient name, **Caesena.**] City and commune in N Italy, in the *compartimento* (region) of Emilia-Romagna, in the province of Forlì, situated on the Sari River, ab. 20 mi. S of Ravenna. It is the center of a rich agricultural district, producing wine, grain, vegetables, tobacco, hemp, and sugar beets; there is a sugar refinery. The city has a cathedral dating from the 14th century, containing sculptures of the school of Donatello. The famous library, founded by Domenico Novello Malatesta, contains valuable incunabula and manuscripts; the building dates from 1447–52. One of the oldest bishoprics of Italy, it became, after numerous contests between Goths, Byzantines, and Lombards, a free city in the early Middle Ages. It was ruled by the Malatesta family in the period 1385–1465, and later incorporated into the Papal States. Some damage was suffered during World War II by buildings of tourist interest, but repairs have been completed or are being carried out. Pop. of commune, 61,314 (1936); of city, 20,043 (1936).

Cesenatico (chā.ze.nä'tē.kō). Town and commune in N Italy, in the *compartimento* (region) of Emilia-Romagna, in the province of Forlì, situated on the Adriatic Sea between Ravenna and Rimini. It is a seaside resort, and has fisheries. Pop. of commune, 11,646 (1936); of town, 4,298 (1936).

Česká Kamenice (ches'kä kä'me.nē.tse). [German, **Böhmisch-Kamnitz.**] Town in Czechoslovakia, in N Bohemia, situated on the Kamenica River, E of Děčín. The town is one of the centers of glassmaking in Bohemia. 4,885 (1947).

Česká Lípa (ches'kä lē'pä). [German, **Böhmisch-Leipa.**] Town in Czechoslovakia, in N Bohemia, ab. 42 mi. N of Prague, between Děčín and Liberec. The town has cotton-printing, silk, shoe, piano, and sugar factories and a brewery. It is a center for the grain trade and the glass-making industry. There is an Augustinian monastery which was founded in 1626 by the Austrian general Wallenstein. 11,991 (1947).

Česká Skalice (ches'kä skä'lē.tse). [German, **Böhmisch-Skalitz.**] Town in Czechoslovakia, in NE Bohemia, situated on the Upa River between Josefov and Turnov, ab. 73 mi. NE of Prague. There are cotton and silk manufactures, sawmills, and a brewery. Here, on June 28, 1866, the Prussians under Karl Friedrich von Steinmetz defeated the Austrians under Archduke Leopold. 2,679 (1947).

České Budějovice (ches'ke bö'dye.yô.vē.tse). Region or county in SW Czechoslovakia, in the S part of the former province of Bohemia, formed by decree of Dec. 21, 1948, which came into effect in 1949. Capital, České Budejovice; area, 3,461 sq. mi.; pop. 493,730 (est. 1949).

České Budějovice. [Also: (formerly) **Budejowice;** German, **Budweis.**] City in Czechoslovakia, in S Bohemia, capital of the region or county of České Budějovice, situated on the upper Vltava (Moldau) River, S of Prague and N of the Austrian border: a station on the railroad line from Prague to Linz. It is an important industrial center, with breweries, food and furniture factories, the largest enamelware and the largest match factory in Czechoslovakia, and the Hardtmuth pencil factory, founded in 1790, one of the largest factories of its kind in the world (Koh-i-noor is its trademark). In the vicinity of the city are many small lakes where commercial fishing is carried on. České Budějovice was founded by King Ottocar II in the 13th century. From this time date the Convent and the Church of the Holy Virgin and the Gothic convent of the Dominicans. The inner town is fortified. It is the seat of a Roman Catholic bishopric. 38,194 (1947).

Československá Republika (ches'kô.slô'ven.skä re'pö-blē.kä). Official Czech name of **Czechoslovakia.**

Československo (ches'kô.slô'ven.skô). Czech name of **Czechoslovakia.**

Český Brod (ches'kē brôt). [German, **Böhmisch-Brod.**] Town in Czechoslovakia, in C Bohemia, ab. 20 mi. E of Prague, between Prague and Kolín. Near here the final battle (sometimes called the Battle of Lipan or Lipany) of the Hussite wars took place (May 30, 1434), in which the extremists, or Taborites, were defeated by the moderate Utraquists and their leader Procop was killed. 5,754 (1947).

Český Krumlov (ches'kē kröm'lôf). [Also: **Krumlov;** German, **Krumau.**] Town in Czechoslovakia, in S Bohemia, situated in a hilly and wooded region, on the upper Vltava (Moldau) River, ab. 14 mi. SW of České Budějovice. It has various industries, particularly paper and cellulose factories and graphite mining. Český Krumlov was formerly the center of the domain of the princes of Schwarzenberg; a large Schwarzenberg castle is in the town. The population, prior to 1945 predominantly German, is now entirely Czech. 11,724 (1947).

Český Les (ches'kē les'). A Czech name of the **Bohemian Forest.**

Český Těšín (ches'kē tye'shēn). [Also: **Těšín, Těšín Český;** German, **Teschen.**] Town in Czechoslovakia, in E Moravia-Silesia, situated on the Olša River opposite Cieszyn on the Polish border, E of Ostrava. It has textile industries. It includes Czech and Polish inhabitants and, prior to 1945, had also a German minority. In the Middle Ages, the town and the surrounding duchy of Teschen were under Polish and Bohemian overlords; in 1766 the entire region fell to Saxony, and in 1822 to Austria. The Peace of Teschen, in 1779, terminated the war of the Bavarian Succession. The western part of the region where Český Těšín is situated became Czechoslovakian in 1920, was occupied by Poland in 1938, but was returned in 1945 to Czechoslovakia. 12,076 (1947).

Çeşme (chesh.me'). [Also: **Cheshme, Chesme, Tchesme.**] Small port on the W coast of Turkey, opposite Chios and W of Izmir (Smyrna). Near it, in July, 1770, the Russian fleet under Aleksei Orlov, aided by Rear Admiral John Elphinstone and Sir Samuel (later Admiral) Greig, nearly annihilated the Turkish fleet. The Turkish vessels were burned during the night. Pop. ab. 4,000.

Cesnola (chez.nô'lä), **Luigi Palma di.** b. at Rivarolo, near Turin, Italy, June 29, 1832; d. at New York, Nov. 20, 1904. American archaeologist. He fought with both the Italian and the Union armies, winning with the latter the Congressional Medal of Honor (awarded 1897). Appointed U.S. consul (1865–77) at Cyprus, he undertook a series of excavations, which resulted in the discovery of a large number of antiquities, about which a controversy arose, especially about Cesnola's restorations. The collection was purchased in 1873 by the Metropolitan Museum of Art at New York, of which he was director from 1879 until his death. He was the author of *Cyprus: its Ancient Cities, Tombs, and Temples* (1877), and *The Metropolitan Museum of Art* (1882).

Ce Soir (sę swår). Paris evening newspaper, founded March 1, 1937. Although not an official organ of the Communist Party, it reflected the communist viewpoint; outlawed in 1938, it reappeared in 1944. Its circulation was about 500,000. It was issued under the direction of Louis Aragon.

Cespedes (chās′pe.dās), **Alba De.** See **De Cespedes, Alba.**

Céspedes (sās′pā.ᴛʜās), **Carlos Manuel de.** b. at Bayamo, Cuba, April 18, 1819; killed March 22, 1874. Cuban revolutionist; father of Carlos Manuel de Céspedes y Quesada (1871–1939). In 1868 he headed an armed revolt which spread until nearly the whole island, except the coast towns, had declared against the Spaniards. A congress of the revolutionists declared Cuba independent, and elected (1869) Céspedes president. Deposed in 1873, he was driven at last to the mountains, and was shot while resisting capture.

Céspedes (thās′pā.ᴛʜās), **Pablo de.** b. at Córdoba, Spain, 1538; d. there, July 26, 1608. Spanish painter, poet, sculptor, and architect, noted as a colorist. Fragments of his poem *Arte de la pintura* were published in 1649. Among his paintings is *Last Supper* in the Córdoba cathedral.

Céspedes y Quesada (sās′pā.ᴛʜās ē kā.sä′ᴛʜä), **Carlos Manuel de.** b. Aug. 12, 1871; d. March 28, 1939. Cuban lawyer and diplomat; son of Carlos Manuel de Céspedes (1819–74). He held diplomatic posts at Rome, Athens, and Buenos Aires, and was minister (1914–22) at Washington. Secretary of state under Machado, he became provisional president of Cuba upon the overthrow (August, 1933) of Machado, serving until the military coup (Sept. 5, 1933) which installed Grau San Martín and the student liberals.

Cesti (chās′tē), **Marc'Antonio.** b. at Arezzo, Italy, 1623; d. in Italy, 1669. Italian composer of operas. He was maestro di capella at Florence and vice-kapellmeister at Vienna. He adapted many cantatas for the dramatic stage, and composed the song *Intorno all' idol mio* and the opera *Il Pomo d'Oro* (1667).

Cetatea Albă (chā.tä′tyä äl′bą). Rumanian name of **Belgorod-Dnestrovski.**

Cetewayo (set.ẹ.wä′ō). [Also: **Cettiwayo, Cetywayo, Ketchwayo, Ketshwayo.**] d. 1884. Zulu king, elected at Ulundi (now in Natal) in 1873. In 1878 he rebelled against British suzerainty. In the war which followed, a British regiment was annihilated by the Zulus at Isandula, in 1879, but General Wolseley defeated and captured Cetewayo the same year. Until 1882 he was held captive in Cape Colony. Owing to the efforts of a party which had formed in his favor among friends of the Zulus in South Africa and in Great Britain, he was transferred to England, where he was lionized. England tried to reinstate him as king of the Zulus, but he had lost his prestige. Beset on all sides by hostile chiefs, he had to seek refuge in British territory. More captive than free, he was kept at Ekowe until his death in 1884.

Cethegus (sẹ.thē′gus), **Marcus Cornelius.** d. 196 B.C. Roman general. He was curule edile (213), praetor (211), censor (209), and consul (204). In the following year he commanded as proconsul in Cisalpine Gaul, where, with the aid of the praetor Quintilius Varus, he defeated the Carthaginian general Mago, brother of Hannibal.

Cetinje (tse′ti.nye). [Italian, **Cettigne, Cettigno.**] Town in SW Yugoslavia, in the federative unit of Montenegro, the principal town of the former *banovina* (province) of Zetska and capital of the former kingdom of Montenegro, situated SE of Kotor, with which it is connected by a winding mountain road. It contains the palace of the former king of Montenegro and various government buildings. 9,040 (1948).

Ceto (sē′tō). A goddess of the sea in Greek mythology. She is related to have been a daughter of Gaea and Pontus, the wife of Phorcus, and the mother of a number of the more unpleasant mythological characters, including the Gorgons and the dragon who aided the Hesperides in guarding the apples of Hera.

Cette (set). Former name of **Sète.**

Cettigne (chet′tē.nyā) or **Cettigno** (-nyō). Italian name of **Cetinje.**

Cettiwayo (set.i.wä′ō). See **Cetewayo.**

Cetus (sē′tus). Southern constellation, the Whale, W of Orion. It was anciently pictured as some kind of marine animal, possibly a seal.

Cetywayo (set.i.wä′ō). See **Cetewayo.**

Ceuta (sū′tą; Spanish, the′ö.tä). [Moorish, **Sebta.**] Fortified town belonging to Spain (part of Cádiz province), situated on the N coast of Spanish Morocco, opposite Gibraltar. It is a seaport and a military and penal station, and is built on Jebel Musa (the ancient Abyla, one of the Pillars of Hercules). It is connected by rail with Tetuán, the capital of Spanish Morocco, ab. 20 mi. to the S. It was taken by Belisarius in 534, by the West Goths in 618, by the Arabs c709, and from the Moors by Portugal in 1415. It passed to Spain in 1580. Pop. 59,936 (1950), predominantly Spanish.

Cevallos (sā.ʙä′yōs), **Pedro Fermin.** b. July 7, 1812; d. May 21, 1893. Ecuadorian historian. He was a lawyer, held high judicial posts, and was a senator in 1867. He wrote *Resúmen de la historia del Ecuador* and other works.

Cevedale (chā.vā.dä′lā), **Monte.** [German, **Fürkelen, Zufall.**] Mountain peak in the Ortler Alps, on the borders of Tyrol and Italy. 12,378 ft.

Cévennes (sā.ven). Region and former province of France, in the NE part of Languedoc.

Cévennes. [Also: **Les Cévennes;** Latin, **Cebenna Mons.**] Mountain chain in S France. The Cévennes proper extend from the Canal du Midi northward, including the mountains of Vivarais, or northern Cévennes, to the Canal du Centre (which connects the Loire and Saône rivers, in the department of Saône-et-Loire). They separate the basins of the Loire and Garonne rivers from those of the Rhone and Saône, and are continued northward by the mountains of Lyonnais and Charolais to the plateau of Langres. They are celebrated as a stronghold of the Protestants and Camisards. The highest peak is Mont Mézenc (ab. 5,750 ft.). Mont Pilat, in the northern Cévennes, is ab. 4,705 ft. high.

Ceylon (sẹ.lon′). [Official name, **Dominion of Ceylon;** ancient Greek, **Taprobane;** Sanskrit, **Tamraparni;** called by early travelers **Serendib.**] Island in the Indian Ocean, a self-governing dominion in the British Commonwealth of Nations, S of the Union of India, from which it is separated by the Gulf of Mannar and Palk Strait. It is mountainous in the S, and produces coffee, cinchona bark, tea, cinnamon, cacao, coconuts, rubber, and other crops. It is celebrated for precious stones. The chief towns are Colombo, Galle, Trincomalee, Moratuwa, Kandy, and Jaffna. The leading races are Singhalese, Kandyans, Tamils, Moormen, and Veddas. Buddhism is the principal religion. Ceylon is ruled by a governor general, a cabinet, and a parliament. In ancient times it was governed by different native dynasties. The Portuguese took possession of it in the 16th century. It was conquered by the Dutch c1658, and by the British in 1795–96, and was formally ceded to Great Britain in 1802. The last king of Kandy was deposed in 1815. The Ceylon Independence Act became effective on Feb. 4, 1948, the republic of Ceylon attaining dominion status. Capital, Colombo; area, 25,332 sq. mi.; pop. 6,657,339 (1946).

Ceyx (sē′iks). In ancient Greek mythology, husband of Alcyone, daughter of Aeolus. The pair were arrogant enough to style themselves Zeus and Hera, and were accordingly changed by Zeus into birds of their own names, respectively a diver and a kingfisher. Another myth dwelt on the tender love of the pair for each other. Ceyx was drowned at sea, and Alcyone found his body cast upon his native shore. The gods took pity on her grief, and changed the husband and wife into kingfishers (alcyones), whose affection for each other in the mating season was proverbial. Their story is introduced into Geoffrey Chaucer's *The Boke of the Duchess.*

Cézanne (sā.zàn), **Paul.** b. at Aix, France, Jan. 19, 1839; d. there, Oct. 22, 1906. French landscape, portrait, and still-life painter and water colorist. The only son of a wealthy banker, he was educated at the Collège Bourbon, Aix, where he received rudimentary instruction in drawing and painting and where his closest friend was Émile Zola. After a brief unfruitful attempt to study law he went to Paris in 1861, sketched for some months at the informal Atelier Suisse, and met Manet and the group of young rebels against "official" art who later formed the nucleus of the Impressionist school: Pissarro, Monet, Sisley, Renoir, and Guillaumin. For many years he shuttled between Paris and Provence, painting assiduously but without achieving public recognition. In 1886 three important events occurred: he married Hortense Fiquet, who had borne him a son in 1872; his father died, leaving him and his two sisters a substantial fortune; and his 40-year friendship with Zola ended abruptly, chiefly because of Cézanne's abnormally sensitive, suspicious, moody temperament. He spent his last seven years in virtual retirement at Aix, suffering from diabetes but painting diligently until a few days before he died.

Technique and Development. Cézanne's early work, influenced by Delacroix and Courbet, was somber and heavy, executed in a very thick medium, often with a palette knife; but after he began to paint out of doors with Pissarro at Auvers-sur-Oise in 1872 he lightened his palette and experimented with the Impressionist technique of tiny dots and strokes of intense color. At the Impressionist exhibitions of 1874 and 1877 his pictures were greeted by a storm of critical abuse. Dissatisfied with the Impressionists' preoccupation with superficial light effects, he soon developed his own system, highly characteristic of his mature work, of elongated parallel brushstrokes thinly laid on, which enabled him to achieve three-dimensional solidity and richness. By emphasizing geometrical constructions, by deliberately distorting forms to produce harmonious patterns, and above all by abandoning the literal imitation of nature in favor of a more subjective approach which he called painting his "sensations in the presence of nature," he paved the way for modern nonrepresentational painting, including Cubism and all subsequent schools of abstract design. Although he predicted that he would become "the primitive of a new art," his pictures were so rarely displayed prior to his last decade that his enormous influence was not apparent until after his death. His works included landscapes executed near Aix, in the environs of Paris, at L'Estaque near Marseilles, and at Lake Annecy; portraits of himself, his wife and family, Chocquet, Geffroy, Vollard, Gasquet, and many others; a few genre scenes of Card Players; numerous still lifes of fruit and flowers; and a long sequence of strange distorted Bathers. See *Cézanne*, by Paul Rosenberg (1936).

Cezimbra (sẹ.zēm′brạ). See **Sesimbra.**

CFTC. See **Confédération Française des Travailleurs Chrétiens.**

CGT. See **Confédération Générale du Travail.**

CGTU. See **Confédération Générale du Travail Unitaire.**

Chabanel (shȧ.bȧ.nel), Saint **Noël.** b. in France, Feb. 2, 1613; d. Dec. 8, 1649. Jesuit missionary to the American Indians. He entered the Jesuit novitiate at the age of 17 and served as a professor of rhetoric at several colleges in the vicinity of Toulouse before going to Canada in 1643 as a missionary to the Indians (he had studied Algonquian in preparation for his work). He was assigned to work toward the conversion of the Hurons, whose ways and habits so strongly repelled him that he feared he might weaken and flee from the field. To prevent this he took a solemn vow to persevere, and this he kept. The story of his murder by a hostile Huron is told in a Jesuit record of 1649–50. Chabanel was one of the group of Jesuit martyrs of North America canonized by Pope Pius XI on June 29, 1930.

Chabannes (shȧ.bȧn), **Antoine de.** [Title, Comte **de Dammartin.**] b. c1411; d. 1488. French general in the Hundred Years War. He took part in a revolt in 1440, but was pardoned by Charles VII, and was later president of the commission which pronounced a judgment of treasonable conduct against Jacques Coeur. In the conditions of extreme disorder prevailing in France during the latter part of the Hundred Years War he became the leader of a company of *écorcheurs* (bandits). These were suppressed in the late 1440's, and little is thereafter known of Antoine de Chabannes until after the accession of Louis XI in 1461, when he was imprisoned, escaped, joined the League of Public Weal, but was pardoned and served Louis XI as one of his most loyal soldiers to the time of that monarch's death.

Chabannes, Jacques de. b. c1400; d 1453. French general in the Hundred Years War; brother of Antoine de Chabannes. He fought under Joan of Arc for the right of Charles VII to the throne of France. Like his brother, he was the leader at one time of a band of *écorcheurs* (bandits), but after the restoration of order in the late 1440's he was pardoned. He served with valor and distinction in the operations which drove the English from Normandy.

Chabar (chä.bär′). See **Chahbar.**

Chabas (shȧ.bȧs), **Paul Émile (Joseph).** b. at Nantes, France, 1869; d. 1937. French painter of portraits and nudes, who was made a commander of the Legion of Honor in 1928, and president of the Artistes Français in 1921. He was a pupil of Bouguereau, Maignan, and Robert-Fleury, and exhibited for the first time in 1885 at the Salon des Artistes Français. Thereafter he exhibited in many cities of Europe, and in the U.S. Many honors were bestowed on him for such works as *September Morn* and *Portrait of Mme. P.C.* Other works include *Morning Calm, In the Blue Water,* and *Portrait of Mlle. Cormon.*

Chablais (shȧ.ble). Region and former province of Savoy, since 1860 the arrondissement of Thonon, department of Haute-Savoie, France.

Chablis (shȧ.blē; Anglicized, shab′li, sha.blē′). Village in N central France, in the department of Yonne, ab. 11 mi. E of Auxerre, noted for the wines produced in its vicinity.

Chabot (shȧ.bō), **François.** b. at St.-Geniez, Aveyron, France, 1759; guillotined at Paris, April 5, 1794. French revolutionist. Before the Revolution a Franciscan friar, Chabot became a member of the extreme left in the Legislative Assembly and, as a member of the Convention, an extremist regarding the royal family's execution. He became involved in a bribery scandal and was executed.

Chabot, Philippe de. [Titles: Seigneur **de Brion**; Comte **de Charny,** Comte **de Busançois**; called **"L'Amiral de Brion"** or **"Admiral de Brion."**] b. 1480; d. June 1, 1543. French general, admiral of France. He successfully defended Marseilles against the Imperialists in 1524, was made a prisoner at the battle of Pavia in 1525, and on his release was appointed admiral to succeed Bonnivet, who had been killed in the action. He was sent to Italy in 1529 to negotiate the ratification of the treaty of Cambrai by Charles V. In 1535 he had the command in the war against the Duke of Savoy, in the course of which he conquered parts of Savoy and Piedmont, but incurred censure for not having properly followed up his victories. He was in 1541 convicted of fraud against the national treasury, on charges preferred by the constable Montmorency, but was pardoned by the king. He is said to have been the first to suggest that Canada be colonized.

Chabot, Admiral of France. Tragedy by George Chapman and James Shirley, licensed in 1635 and printed in 1639.

Chabrias (kā′bri.ạs). fl. 388–357 B.C.; killed near Chios, 357 B.C. Athenian general. Being in 388 sent to the assistance of Evagoras of Cyprus against the Persians, he landed on the way in Aegina, and gained by an ambuscade a decisive victory over the Spartan general Gorgopas, who fell in battle. In 378, in a campaign against Agesilaus, he acquired great celebrity by the adoption of a new maneuver, which consisted in receiving the enemy's attack on one knee with spears presented and shields resting on the ground. In 376 he gained a decisive naval victory over the Lacedaemonians at Naxos. On the outbreak of the Social War, in 357, he was placed in command of the Athenian fleet, which coöperated with the army under Chares. He was killed at the siege of Chios in the same year.

Chabrier (shȧ.brē.ā), **Alexis Emmanuel.** b. at Ambert, Puy-de-dôme, France, Jan. 18, 1841; d. at Paris, Sept. 13, 1894. French composer, chiefly of operas. His most important works are *Gwendoline* (1886), *Le Roi malgré lui* (1887), and some orchestral pieces.

Chabrillan (shȧ.brē.yäṅ), **Céleste Vénard,** Comtesse **de Moreton de.** [Called **Mogador.**] b. at Paris, Dec. 27, 1824; d. there, Feb. 19, 1909. French actress and writer of novels and operettas. Author of *La Sapho* (1858), *Est-il fou* (1860), *Un Drame sur le Tage* (1885), and others.

Chac (chäk). In Maya religion, the god of rain; also conceived of as four deities (chacs) in one, each being associated with one of the cardinal directions and with a color. The chacs remain in modern semi-Christian Mayan belief as servants of Jesucristo, scattering rain and performing other duties.

Chacabuco (chä.kä.bö′kō). Pass in a transverse spur of the Andes, on the N side of the plain of Santiago, Chile. During the South American war for independence, General José de San Martín's army, which had marched over the Andes, found this pass strongly defended by the Spaniards. It was carried by a bayonet charge led by General Bernardo O'Higgins, Feb. 12, 1817, thus opening the way to Santiago for the patriots.

Chachapoyas (chä.chä.pō′yäs). Region of ancient Peru, nearly corresponding to the present department of Amazonas. The inhabitants were noted for their warlike spirit and intelligence; they were conquered by the Incas after a long war. Alonso de Alvarado was sent by Pizarro to reduce this district in 1535, and was made governor of it.

Chachapoyas. Province of Peru, in the department of Amazonas. Previous to 1832 it was much larger. Chachapoyas borders on the gorge of the upper Marañon River, and the surface is much broken. Capital, Chachapoyas; area, ab. 4,300 sq. mi.; pop. ab. 20,000.

Chachapoyas. [Former name, **Ciudad de la Frontera.**] City in N Peru, capital of Amazonas department, and of Chachapoyas province, and episcopal city of the diocese of Chachapoyas. It was founded in 1540 by Alonso de Alvarado. 5,494 (1940).

Chac Mool (chäk möl′). Name given to a type of sculpture, representing a reclining human figure of stone with the head turned to one side, approximately life-size. A dozen or more have been found at the Maya city of Chichén Itzá, usually in front of temple doorways. The name became attached to the type when Le Plongeon called such a statue after a supposed chief of the Mayas.

Chaco (chä′kō) or **Chaco Boreal** (bō.rā.äl′). See also **Región Occidental,** Paraguay.

Chaco. [Also: **Gran Chaco** (or **Chacu**), **El Chaco.**] Vast tract of land in South America, extending from W Paraguay to E Bolivia. It is a low plain, generally open, with a few isolated hills, and portions are flooded every year; the great rivers Pilcomayo and Bermejo pass through it to the Paraguay. The Chaco region is divided between Argentina, Paraguay, and Bolivia; the greater part is very imperfectly known, and inhabited only by savage tribes of Indians. Since 1870 considerable settlements have been made in the Argentine Chaco. In the 17th century the name Chaco included the plains as far N as C Bolivia. Area, ab. 100,000 sq. mi. The Chaco War (1932–35) between Bolivia and Paraguay, following an earlier clash (1928–29) between the two countries and next to the War of the Triple Alliance (1865–70) the costliest in South American history, resulted from claims of both countries to the territory, Bolivia's on historical grounds, Paraguay's on the practical grounds of colonization. A treaty, signed Oct. 10, 1938, awarded most of the territory to Paraguay, but gave landlocked Bolivia an outlet on the Paraguay River.

Chaco. [Also: **El Chaco**; official name (since January, 1952), **Presidente Perón Province.**] Province, and former territory, in N Argentina, lying S of the territory of Formosa, W of Paraguay, N of Santa Fe, and E of Salta. Except for quebracho and some other kinds of wood, it is of slight economic importance and has attracted comparatively few settlers. Argentina's highest temperatures are reached in the northern Chaco in January. Early in 1952 it officially achieved the status of a province. Capital, Resistencia; area, 38,041 sq. mi.; pop. 430,555 (1947).

Chaco Canyon. [Spanish, **Cañon de Chaco.**] Canyon in NW New Mexico, ab. 64 mi. S of Aztec, containing one of the greatest concentrations of Pueblo ruins and now administered by the National Park Service as Chaco Canyon National Monument (established 1907; area, 18,039 acres). Chaco Canyon was a major population center during the Great Pueblo period (1100–1300 A.D.). It is the type locality for the Chaco branch of Anasazi culture, characterized by unusually large pueblos built around a central court, great kivas, and the most elaborate masonry in the Southwest.

Chacón (chä.kōn′), **Lázaro.** b. 1873; d. 1931. Guatemalan army officer and politician, president (Dec. 5, 1926–Dec. 16, 1930) of Guatemala. During his term, a boundary agreement was reached with Honduras. His government, headed by Baudillo Palma during his illness, was overthrown by a coup d'état led by General Manuel Orellana.

Chacón y Calvo (ē käl′bō), **José María.** b. 1893—. Cuban lawyer, diplomat, and writer. He served as consulting lawyer (1915–18) to the secretariat of justice, and was secretary (1918–34) at the Cuban legation (1918–26) and the Cuban embassy (1926–34) at Madrid; in 1934 he was named director of the cultural department in the ministry of education. He is the author of *Las Orígenes de la poésia en Cuba* (1913), *Ensayos de literatura cubana* (1922), *Ensayos sentimentales* (1923), and *Cedulario cubano, las orígenes de la colonización* (1929); compiler of *Las Cien majores poésias cubanas* (1922).

Chacón y Castellón (käs.tā.yōn′), **Luis.** b. at Havana, Cuba, c1670; d. there, c1716. Cuban soldier. From 1699 until his death he was governor of the Morro Castle at Havana, and during this time he was three times ad interim captain-general of the island (December, 1702–May 13, 1706, July 8, 1707–Jan. 18, 1708, and Feb. 18, 1711–Feb. 4, 1713). In 1707 he led an expedition against the English colonies in Carolina.

Chaco War (chä′kō). See under **Chaco,** South America.

Chad (chad) or **Ceadda** (chad′dä), Saint. d. 672. English ecclesiastic; brother of Saint Cedd. A Northumbrian by birth, he was educated at Lindisfarne under Saint Aidan. He was made abbot of Lastingham in Deira (N Yorkshire) in 664, bishop of York (c665–669), and later (c670) of Mercia. He established the latter see at Lichfield.

Chad (chad). [French, **Tchad.**] One of the four territories making up French Equatorial Africa. It is the northernmost of these territories and is bounded on the N by Libya, on the E by the Anglo-Egyptian Sudan, on the S by the Ubangi-Shari territory and Cameroun, and on the W by the Niger territory of French West Africa. The area surrounding Lake Chad, in the SW corner of the territory, is marsh and the remainder of the territory is desert land. Capital, Fort-Lamy; area, 461,202 sq. mi.; pop. 2,241,501 (2,238,200 natives and 3,301 Europeans; 1950).

Chad, Lake. [French, **Tchad**; German, **Tschad.**] Lake in N central Africa at the junction of Chad territory of French Equatorial Africa with Nigeria and Niger territory of French West Africa. It has no outlet. The shore line of the lake is indefinite since it fluctuates in relation to the supply of the water and its rate of evaporation. Its chief tributary is the Shari River. It was explored in the 19th century by Gustav Nachtigal, Heinrich Barth, and others. Length, ab. 140 mi.; area, 6,500 sq. mi.

Chadband (chad′band), **Rev. Mr.** Fat and hypocritical minister, much given to platitudes, in Charles Dickens's *Bleak House.* He is "in the ministry," but is "attached to no particular denomination." He has "a general appearance of having a good deal of train-oil in his system."

Chadbourne (chad′bėrn), **Paul Ansel.** b. at North Berwick, Me., Oct. 21, 1823; d. at New York, Feb. 23, 1883. American college administrator and professor of natural history. He was the first president (1866) of the Massachusetts Agricultural College at Amherst, president of the University of Wisconsin (1867–70), president of Williams College (1872–81), succeeding Mark Hopkins, and again president of the Agricultural College in 1882. He wrote *Lectures on Natural Theology* (1867) and other works on science and education.

Chadderton (chad′ėr.tọn). Urban district in NW England, in Lancashire, situated on the river Irk, ab. 1 mi. W of Oldham. It has no direct rail connections for passengers, being reached by rail to Oldham, ab. 188 mi. NW of London. 31,114 (1951).

Chaddock (chad′ọk), **Charles Gilbert.** b. at Jonesville, Mich., Nov. 14, 1861; d. July 20, 1936. American neurologist. He received (1885) his M.D. degree from the University of Michigan, studied at Munich and Paris, and served as professor (1892 *et seq.*) of nervous diseases in the medical department of St. Louis University. He translated several works of Richard von Krafft-Ebing, and wrote *Outline of Psychiatry, Sexual Crimes,* and *Hamilton's System of Legal Medicine.*

Chaderton (chad'ėr.tọn), **Laurence.** b. at Lees Hall, Oldham, Lancashire, England, c1536; d. at Cambridge, England, Nov. 13, 1640. English Puritan divine. A graduate (1567) of Christ's College, Cambridge, he was first master of Emmanuel College (1584–1622). He also served on the Cambridge committee for drawing up the Authorized Version of the Bible.

Chad Newsome (nū'sọm). See **Newsome, Chad.**

Chadron (shad'rọn). City in NW Nebraska, county seat of Dawes County: seat of a state teachers college. It is a railroad and industrial center, with oil refineries, flour mills, and creameries. 4,687 (1950).

Chadwick (chad'wik), Sir **Edwin.** b. at Longsight, Manchester, England, Jan. 24, 1800; d. at Park Cottage, Surrey, England, July 6, 1890. English social reformer, disciple of the English philosopher, Jeremy Bentham, and often referred to as "the first bureaucrat" of modern England. Chadwick was a lawyer at London when he published two essays which attracted the interest and admiration of Bentham. These were "Life Assurance" (1828) in the *Westminster Review* and "Preventive Police" (1892) in the *London Review.* These two essays formed the basis of his "sanitary idea," the enforcement of which was his life work. Shortly after making the acquaintance of Bentham, Chadwick assisted the philosopher in completing the administrative code. At one time Bentham offered him a post as the systematic and permanent expounder of his philosophy; this Chadwick declined. He has since been regarded as Bentham's most distinguished disciple. Chadwick's work as an administrator was done mainly in government commissions. In 1832 he was appointed assistant commissioner of the Poor Law Commission, and on the basis of his hard work and ability to collect facts on the existing poor-law system and to suggest remedies for various evils, he was promoted (1833) to chief commissioner. In the same year he served also on the commission to investigate the working conditions of children employed in factories, and was author of its report, recommending the establishment of factory inspectors, thus putting in practice the Benthamite formula of investigation, report, central administration, and inspection. In the new poor-law commission Chadwick was named (1834) secretary, i.e., chief executive, but unfortunately he came into conflict with the commissioners. In 1838 he was a member of the commission to inquire into the establishment of a constabulary force. The report of this commission embodied his ideas expounded in "Preventive Police" to get at the removable antecedents of crime. Epidemic outbreaks led to the appointment of the first sanitary commission of 1839, in which Chadwick was active; his report became the textbook of sanitation throughout the country. About the same time he persuaded Lord Lyndhurst to introduce the new Registration Act, which provided for the registration of causes of disease as well as the number of deaths. During the 1840's, Chadwick was active in preparing the report (1843) on the training of pauper children, and served (1844) on the second sanitary commission. In 1846 the poor-law commission broke up because of a dispute over Chadwick's ideas of centralized administration. In the next year he served as commissioner to inquire into the health of London; his report recommended a separate system of drainage for the metropolis. In 1848 he was appointed a commissioner on the first board of health, on which he served until 1854, when this board was merged with the local government board, and Chadwick was retired with a pension of 1,000 pounds a year. During the Crimean War he served on the commission on troop sanitation. He also worked (1858) on sanitation for the Indian army, and advocated (1855) a system of competitive examinations for the civil service. His last public service (1871) was an inspection of the drainage system at Cawnpore. He was president of the economy section of the British Association, and of the section of public health in the Social Science Association. He also presided (1878) over the congress of the Sanitary Institute and was president of the Association of Sanitary Inspectors. His chief work was condensed by Sir Benjamin Ward Richardson as *The Health of Nations: A Review of the Works of Edwin Chadwick, with a Biographical Introduction* (1889).

Chadwick, French Ensor. b. at Morgantown, W.Va., Feb. 29, 1844; d. at New York, Jan. 27, 1919. American naval officer, promoted to rear admiral in 1903. Graduated from the U.S. Naval Academy in 1865, he was naval attaché at London (1882–89), chief intelligence officer (1892–93), and chief of the navy equipment bureau (1893–97). He served as captain of the cruiser *New York* and chief of staff to Admiral Sampson during the Spanish-American War (1898). From 1900 to 1903 he was president of the Naval War College; he commanded the South Atlantic squadron in 1904 and retired in 1906.

Chadwick, George Alexander. b. Oct. 10, 1840; d. in December, 1923. Irish clergyman of the Anglican Church, poet, and editor. Educated at Trinity College, Dublin, he took holy orders in 1863, was rector (1872–96) and dean (1886–96) of Armagh, Ireland, and served as bishop (1896–1915) of Derry (Londonderry) and Raphoe, in Ireland. He published *My Devotional Life* (1882), *Pilate's Gift and Other Sermons* (1899), *Poems, Chiefly Sacred* (1900), and *The Intellect and the Heart* (1905). In 1865 he edited, with a preface, the *Poems* of Edmund John Armstrong, and in 1904 he was one of the contributors to *The Gospels in Art.*

Chadwick, George Whitefield. b. at Lowell, Mass., Nov. 13, 1854; d. 1931. American composer. He studied at Boston and later at Leipzig and Munich. On his return to America he became an organist at Boston and teacher of composition and director (1867 *et seq.*) at the New England Conservatory. He composed three symphonies, six overtures, five string quartets, a pianoforte quintet, the lyric drama *Judith* (1900), choral works such as *Phoenix Expirans* (1891), and many songs, and wrote a treatise on harmony.

Chadwick, Henry. b. at Exeter, England, Oct. 5, 1824; d. April 20, 1908. American sports writer. He came to the U.S. in 1837, and reported (1856–86) cricket and baseball for the New York *Times*, the Brooklyn *Eagle*, and the New York *Clipper*. He helped organize and foster baseball, developing playing rules and the scoring system. He compiled (1869 *et seq.*) a yearly baseball handbook which developed into Spalding's *Official Baseball Guide* under his editorship (1881–1908).

Chadwick, Sir **James.** b. Oct. 20, 1891—. English physicist, Nobel prize winner (1935) for his discovery (1932) of the neutron. He studied at Manchester, Berlin, and Cambridge, was lecturer and assistant director (1923–35) of radioactive research at the Cavendish Laboratory of Cambridge University, and served as professor (1935 *et seq.*) of physics at the University of Liverpool. A leading scientist on the British atomic bomb project, he was also scientific adviser (1946 *et seq.*) to the United Nations Commission on Atomic Energy.

Chadwick, John White. b. at Marblehead, Mass., Oct. 19, 1840; d. at Brooklyn, N.Y., Dec. 11, 1904. American Unitarian minister, literary critic, and author. He was graduated from the Cambridge Divinity School in 1864, and was minister of the Second Unitarian Society of Brooklyn in the period 1864–1904. Among his works are *The Bible of To-day* (1878), *Faith of Reason* (1879), *The Man Jesus* (1881), *A Book of Poems* (1888), *Old and New Unitarian Belief* (1894), *A Life for Liberty* (1899), *Theodore Parker* (1900), and *William Ellery Channing* (1903).

Chadzidakis (chad.zid'ạ.kis), **George N.** See **Hatzidakis** or **Chadzidakis, George N.**

Chaereas and Callirrhoe (kē'rẹ.ạs; kạ.lir'ọ.ē). Early Greek romance by Chariton Aphrodisiensis, only a part of which is extant.

Chaeronea (ker.ọ.nē'ạ). [Also, **Chaeroneia** (-nī'ạ).] In ancient geography, a town in W Boeotia, Greece. It was the birthplace of Plutarch. Here Philip of Macedon defeated (338 B.C.) the Boeotians and Athenians; in 86 B.C. Sulla, with 30,000–40,000 men, defeated the army of Mithridates VI (ab. 110,000) under Archelaus.

Chaffee (chaf'ẹ). City in SE Missouri, in Scott County: marketing center for an agricultural region. 3,134 (1950).

Chaffee, Adna Romanza. b. at Orwell, Ohio, April 14, 1842; d. Nov. 1, 1914. American general; father of Adna Romanza Chaffee (1884–1941). He entered the army as a private on July 22, 1861, and served in the Civil and Spanish-American wars. He was assigned to the command of the U.S. forces for the relief of the U.S. legation at Peking, on June 24, 1900, and entered the city on Aug. 14. He was nominated a major general on Feb. 5, 1901, and retired as a lieutenant general in 1906.

Chaffee, Adna Romanza. b. at Junction City, Kan., Sept. 23, 1884; d. Aug. 22, 1941. American army officer; son of Adna Romanza Chaffee (1842–1914). Graduated (1906) from the U.S. Military Academy at West Point, he was named adjutant (1917) with the rank of major to the 81st Division at Camp Jackson, S.C. He fought in the St.-Mihiel and Meuse-Argonne offensives during World War I and served with the army of occupation. In 1938 he was appointed commander of the 7th Cavalry Brigade (mechanized) with the rank of brigadier general.

Chaffee, George. b. at Brockville, Ontario, Canada, Jan. 28, 1848; d. at Los Angeles, Calif., March 1, 1932. Canadian irrigation pioneer in Australia. Chaffee had three careers, one in Canada and two in California, with the Australian episode occurring between the latter two. In Canada Chaffee was a shipbuilder on the Great Lakes, in association with his father and independently; in California he was an irrigationist. At the instance of the Australian statesman Alfred Deakin, who had investigated his work in California, Chaffee went to Australia in 1886 and selected a location on the Murray River at the site of what is now Medura, Victoria, which was granted him after involved political negotiations. Although Chaffee succeeded in establishing irrigated production, he was ruined financially in the Victoria bank crisis of 1893 and its aftermath; in 1897 he left Australia permanently. He demonstrated that irrigation was practical, and the exploitation of the waters of the Murray, Australia's principal river, has been continued intensively. Upon his return to California, Chaffee resumed work as an irrigationist, but ended his active life as a banker. He retired in 1917.

Chaga (chä'gä). [Also: **Chagga, Dschagga, Jagga, Wachaga.**] Bantu-speaking people of N Tanganyika in E Africa, inhabiting the lower slopes of Mount Kilimanjaro. Their population is estimated at 125,000 (by C. Dundas, *Kilimanjaro and Its People*, 1924). They are divided into 28 independent warring states numbering from one to 20 thousand, and ruled by autocratic chiefs. The chaga have patrilineal clans and military age grades based on circumcision. They practice hoe agriculture and animal husbandry, with the cattle complex. Their principal food is the banana.

Chagall (shạ.gäl'), **Marc.** b. at Vitebsk, Russia, 1887—. Russian painter, engraver, and illustrator, connected with the surrealist movement, but quite independent of it because of the individuality of his style. He studied in Russia under Bakst and went to Paris in 1910. There he joined a cubist group; later, he went back to Russia to start an art school at Vitebsk, but was compelled to move to Moscow in 1920 and give up the school. There he did some stage decorations for the Leningrad Academic Jewish Theater. In 1922, he returned to Paris, and in 1941 he came to the U.S. His work is strongly influenced by the Jewish-Russian folk culture, is vividly colored, often humorous, and imbued with fantasy. He has had large exhibitions in both Europe and the U.S. Among his best-known works are *The Village and I, Paris through the Window, Dedicated to my Fiancée, The Wedding, Wedding Anniversary, The Graveyard, The Rabbi of Vitebsk*, many religious scenes, and illustrations for Gogol's *Dead Souls.*

Chagas (shä'gạs), **Carlos.** b. at Oliveira, Brazil, 1879; d. at Rio de Janeiro, Nov. 8, 1934. Brazilian biophysicist and bacteriologist, notable for his demonstration (1909) that the transmitting agent for a tropical fever (since known as "Chagas Disease") peculiar to certain sections of Brazil was of the genus *Triatoma.* He was director (1917–34) of the Oswaldo Cruz Institute at Rio de Janeiro.

Chagatai (chag.ạ.tī'). See **Jagatai.**

Chagos Archipelago (chä'gōs). [Also: **Chagos Islands, Oil Islands.**] Group of islands in the Indian Ocean, ab. 1,000 mi. SW of Colombo, Ceylon, belonging to Great Britain: a dependency of Mauritius. They export large quantities of coconut oil. Diego Garcia is the largest of the group.

Chagres (chä'grās; Anglicized, chä'grẹs, chag'-). Seaport in Panama, ab. 12 mi. SW of Colón. Pop. under 5,000 (1940).

Chagres River. River in C Panama, which flows from Gatun Lake W to the Caribbean Sea. The line of the Panama Canal follows the valley of the Chagres.

Chagrin (shạ.grin'). Former name of **Willoughby,** Ohio.

Chagrin Falls (shạ.grin', shụg'rin). Village in NE Ohio, in Cuyahoga County, on the Chagrin River: residential community. 3,085 (1950).

Chahar (chä'här'). Province of China, in the NE part of the autonomous region of Inner Mongolia, bordered on the NW and N by the Mongolian People's Republic, on the N by the province of Heilungkiang, on the E by the provinces of Liaoning and Jehol, on the S by the provinces of Hopei and Shansi, and on the W by the province of Suiyuan. The S tip of the province is crossed by the Great Wall of China and this is the only section suitable for farming; wheat and kaoliang are the chief crops. The rest of the province is covered by a portion of the Gobi desert, except where mountains are found along the N and E borders. Crossing the Gobi are a few caravan trails and scattered nomads with their herds. Capital, Changkiakow; area, 107,705 sq. mi.; pop. 2,034,000 (est. 1947).

Chaharlang (chä.här.läng'). See under **Bakhtiari.**

Chahbar (chä.bär'). [Also: **Chabar, Charbar, Chubar.**] Bay on the S coast of Iran, on the Gulf of Oman. Width, ab. 9 mi.; length, ab. 11 mi.

Chahbar. [Also: **Chabar, Charbar, Chubar.**] Port in SE Iran, in Kerman on the bay of Chahbar: a minor trading center.

Chahinkapa (chạ.hing'kạ.pạ). Former name of **Wahpeton,** N.D.

Chaikovski (chī.kôf'skē). See **Chaykovsky;** also **Tchaikovsky.**

Chaillé-Long (shà.yā'lông'), **Charles.** b. at Princess Anne, Somerset County, Md., July 2, 1842; d. March 24, 1917. American soldier, explorer, and diplomat. He served as a volunteer in the American Civil War, attaining the rank of captain; in 1869 he received an appointment as a lieutenant colonel in the Egyptian army. He was made chief of staff to General C. G. Gordon in 1874, and in the same year was employed on a diplomatic and geographical mission to Uganda and explored the upper Nile valley. He resigned his commission in the Egyptian service in 1877, and in 1887 was appointed U.S. consul general and secretary of legation in Korea. He wrote *Central Africa* (1876) and *The Three Prophets—Chinese Gordon, the Mahdi, and Arabi Pasha* (1884).

Chaillu (shà.yü), **Paul Belloni Du.** See **Du Chaillu, Paul Belloni.**

Chainbearer, The. Novel by James Fenimore Cooper, published in 1845.

Chains. Collection of short stories by Theodore Dreiser, published in 1927.

Chaise (shez), **François d'Aix de La.** See **Lachaise** or **La Chaise, François d'Aix de.**

Chaitanya (chī.tän'yạ). b. at Nadia, in Bengal, 1485; d. 1527. Indian religious leader, founder of a sect of Vaishnavas found in Bengal. His first principle was that all the faithful worshipers of Vishnu as Krishna were to be treated as equals. Caste was to be subordinated to faith in Krishna. "The mercy of God," said Chaitanya, "regards neither tribe nor family." While the Vedic hymns and *Brahmanas* rely on works (*karma*), and the *Upanishads* on abstract meditation and divine knowledge as the path to blessedness, Chaitanya found it in intense devotion, displayed by complete union of the spirit with Krishna. He disappeared mysteriously in 1527, at the age of 42. His followers came to regard him as Krishna incarnate, and his disciples Advaita and Nityananda as manifestations of portions of the same deity. These three leaders are therefore called the three great lords (*Prabhus*). They form the triad of this phase of Vaishnavism.

Chaka (chä'kä). See **Shaka.**

Chakri (chä'krē), **Chao P'ya.** See **Rama I.**

Chalamari (chä.lạ.mä'rē). Hindustani name of **Chilmari.**

Chalatenango (chä''lä.tā.näng'gō). Department in NW El Salvador, bordering on Honduras. Capital, Chalatenango; area, 1,292 sq. mi.; pop. 112,939 (est. 1942).

Chalcedon (kal'sẹ.don, -dọn; kal.sē'dọn). [Modern Turkish name, **Kadiköy.**] In ancient geography, a town in Bithynia, situated on the Bosporus opposite Byzantium. It was founded (c685 B.C.) by Megarian colonists. The fourth ecumenical council, at which Eutychianism was condemned, was held there in 451 A.D. It was convoked by the emperor Marcianus, and was attended by 630 bishops (mostly from the Orient), the legates of Pope Leo I, and the commissioners of the emperor. It assembled originally at Nicaea in September, 451, but was on account of its turbulence transferred to Chalcedon in order that the imperial court and senate might attend in person. It condemned (449) the so-called Robber Council (Eutychian Synod) of Ephesus and adopted an orthodox confession of faith.

Chalcenterus (kal.sen'tėr.us). Surname of **Didymus.**

Chalchihuitlicue (chäl"chē.wē.tlē'kwā). [Eng. trans., "*Our Lady of the Turquoise Skirt.*"] In Aztec mythology, a water goddess who presided over the fourth era of the world, which ended in a flood and was followed by the present era.

Chalcidice (kal.sid'i.sē). [Also: **Chalkidike** (kal.kid'i.kē), **Khalkidhiki, Khalkidike, Khalkidiki.**] In ancient geography, the chief peninsula of Macedonia, terminating in the three smaller peninsulas of Pallene, Sithonia, and Acte, projecting into the Aegean Sea. It was settled (ab. the 7th century B.C.) by Euboeans. Its chief town was Olynthus.

Chalcidice. [Also: **Chalkidike, Khalkidhiki, Khalkidike, Khalkidiki.**] *Nomos* (department) of N Greece, situated in Macedonia. Capital, Polygyros; area, ab. 1,250 sq. mi.; pop. 75,801 (1951).

Chalcidius (kal.sid'i.us). fl. in the 6th (or 4th) century A.D. Platonic philosopher, author of a Latin translation of, and commentary on, the first part of Plato's *Timaeus.*

Chalcis (kal'sis), [Also: **Chalkis** (kal'kis), **Egripo, Evripos, Negropont**; Greek, **Khalkis.**] City in C Greece, the capital of the *nomos* (department) of Euboea, situated on the W coast of the island of Euboea on the Evripos strait ab. 34 mi. N of Athens. It was the chief town in ancient Euboea, and sent out many colonial settlers; in Italy and Sicily the colonies of Chalcis exceeded in number those of any other state. It was subdued (506 B.C.) by Athens, and was an important trading and colonizing center. Aristotle died here in 322 B.C. 26,097 (1951).

Chalco (chäl'kō). Village in S Mexico, in México state, on the E side of Lake Chalco, ab. 20 mi. SE of Mexico City. Before the Spanish conquest, Chalco was one of the most important pueblos of the Mexican valley. Pop. under 5,000 (1940).

Chalcolithic Age (kal.kō̜.lith'ik). See under **Bronze Age.**

Chalcondyles (kal.kon'di.lēz) or **Chalcocondyles** (kal-kō̜.kon'di.lēz) or **Chalcondylas** (kal.kon'di.lạs), **Demetrius.** b. at Athens, c1424; d. at Milan, Italy, 1511. Greek grammarian, teacher of Greek at Perugia, Rome, and elsewhere in Italy, and at Florence; brother of Laonicus Chalcondyles. He wrote a Greek grammar entitled *Erotemata* (c1493), and edited the works of Homer (1488), Isocrates (1493), and Suidas (1499).

Chalcondyles or **Chalcocondyles** or **Chalcondylas, Laonicus** (or **Nicolas**). b. at Athens; d. c1464. Byzantine historian, ambassador of John VII Palaeologus to the sultan Murad II of Turkey during the siege of Constantinople in 1446. He wrote a history of the Byzantine Empire from c1297 to c1462 (edited by Bekker, 1843).

Chaldea (kal.dē'ạ). [Also, **Chaldaea**; in the Old Testament, **Kasdim**; Assyrian, **Kaldu, Kashdu.**] In Biblical geography, middle Babylonia, the tract S of the city of Babylon in the direction toward the Persian Gulf; other portions of the country included Akkad and Sumer. Later the name Kaldu (like "Land of Kasdim" in Jer. xxiv. 5, Ezek. xii. 13) was extended to the whole country of Babylonia, i.e., the territory bounded on the N by Assyria, on the S by the Syrian desert and the Persian Gulf, on the E by Elam, and on the W by Syria. The origin of the Chaldeans is uncertain, but some have supposed that they were a mixed people composed of Babylonians and Cosseans.

Chaldea. A former name of **Centerville,** Iowa.

Chaldeans. See under **Chaldea,** and under **Nestorians.**

Chaldean Tetrapolis (te.trap'ō̜.lis). See **Tetrapolis, Chaldean.**

Châlet (shä.le), **Le.** Comic opera in three acts by Adolphe Adam, with a libretto by Scribe, first performed at Paris on Sept. 25, 1834.

Châlette-sur-Loing (shä.let.sür.lwaṅ). Town in C France, in the department of Loiret, situated on the Loing River and the Canal de Briarre, N of Montargis, of which it is an industrial suburb. It has a rubber industry. 6,856 (1946).

Chaleur Bay (shạ.lör'). [French, **Baie de Chaleur.**] Inlet of the Gulf of St. Lawrence, lying between the Gaspé Peninsula, Quebec, on the N and New Brunswick on the S. Length, 90 mi.; greatest width, 20 mi.

Chalfont St. Giles (chal'fō̜nt sānt jīlz', chä'-). Village in S central England, ab. 20 mi. NW of London, noted as the site of Milton's cottage, where the poet lived in the years 1665–66 to escape the plague in London. Pop. ab. 3,000.

Chalgrin (shål.graṅ), **Jean François Thérèse.** b. 1739; d. 1811. French architect, designer of the Arc de Triomphe. As a winner of the Grand Prix de Rome he studied in that city, and after returning to France became architect to the brother of Louis XVI who was later to reign as Louis XVIII. He supervised the enlargement of the Collège de France and built or rebuilt some of the notable churches of Paris. After the French Revolution he was employed to adapt the Luxembourg palace for use as the official seat of the Directory. In 1806 Napoleon selected him to design a great arch to celebrate the victories of the French armies, and this work, the Arc de Triomphe de l'Étoile, is his principal monument.

Chalgrove (chal'grōv). Civil parish and village in S England, in Oxfordshire, ab. 7 mi. SE of Oxford. Here, on June 18, 1643, Prince Rupert defeated the Parliamentarians. John Hampden was mortally wounded. 388 (1931).

Chaliapin (shä.lyä'pin), **Feodor Ivanovich.** [Also, **Chaliapine.**] b. at Kazan, Russia, in February, 1873; d. 1938. Russian bass singer. He first appeared as a boy soprano in his native town, and in opera, at the age of 20, as Mephistopheles in Gounod's *Faust* at Tiflis. Thereafter he sang in most of the principal opera houses in Europe and America. He won much of his fame in Boito's *Mefistofele,* in Russian works like Rimsky-Korsakov's *Ivan the Terrible* and Moussorgsky's *Boris Godunov,* and in Massenet's *Don Quichotte.* He appeared at New York, where he sang with the Metropolitan Opera Company.

Chalkhill (chôk'hil), **John.** fl. 1600. English poet. He was the author of *Thealma and Clearchus, a Pastoral History in smooth and easie Verse,* not published until 1683. The work was brought out by Izaak Walton, who had known Chalkhill as a young man. That Chalkhill was an imaginary person, that his name was a pseudonym for Walton, or that Walton was the author, are theories no longer held. Chalkhill is also the author of two songs, "O, the Sweet Contentment" and "O, the Gallant Fisher's Life," included in the *Compleat Angler* (1653). George Saintsbury rescued Chalkhill's reputation from neglect by including him in his anthology (1905–06) of Caroline poets.

Chalkley (chôk'li), **Thomas.** b. at London, March 3, 1675; d. on the island of Tortola, West Indies, Sept. 4, 1741. Itinerant preacher of the Society of Friends. He visited the American colonies in 1698, 1700, and 1710, and a few years before his death established a residence near Philadelphia.

Chalk River (chôk). Atomic research center in SE Ontario, Canada, ab. 130 mi. NW of Ottawa. The project was constructed on a 10,000-acre site along the S bank of the Ottawa River, and began operation in 1945. A few miles to the west is the village of Deep River (pop. 2,043 in 1951), housing the research workers employed at the plant. Chalk River was the world's first uranium-heavy water reactor plant, and has two reactors. In addition a high-power atomic pile was later added. Research is concentrated on peacetime and medical uses of atomic energy, and isotopes are produced in quantity.

Chalkstone (chôk'stōn), **Lord.** Character in David Garrick's play *Lethe.* Garrick himself played the part.

Challcuchima (chäl.kö.chē'mä) or **Chalicuchima** (chä-lē.kö.chē'mä). Burned to death near Cusco, Peru, in November, 1533. Peruvian Indian, said to have been a native of Quito and uncle of Atahualpa. He was one of the latter's Inca generals in the war with Huáscar, and after Atahualpa had been imprisoned by the Spaniards, Challcuchima was induced to visit him at Cajamarca. He was seized, kept a captive during the subsequent march of the Spaniards, and finally burned alive on the charge that he was inciting an Indian insurrection.

Challemel-Lacour (shȧl.mel.lȧ.kör), **Paul Armand.** b. at Avranches, France, May 19, 1827; d. at Paris, Oct. 26, 1896. French publicist and politician. He was a deputy (1872), senator (1876), ambassador to England (1880–82), and minister of foreign affairs (1883). Reëlected to the senate in 1885, he became its president in 1893.

Challener (chal'ẹ.nėr), **Frederick Sproston.** b. at Whetstone, England, 1869—. Canadian painter. Arriving in Canada in 1883, he studied at the Ontario School of Art and with private tutors, and later continued his art education in England and Italy, and also painted in Egypt and Syria. He became an instructor at the Ontario College of Art, and much of his work has consisted in murals which adorn public buildings, theatres, and hotels in various cities of that province, and in Montreal. His paintings are also to be seen in the building of the parliament of Ontario, in Toronto, in the Provincial Art Gallery in that city, and in the National Gallery at Ottawa. He was elected a member of the Royal Canadian Academy in 1899.

Challenge. Novel by V. Sackville-West, published in 1923.

Challenger Deep. One of the deepest portions of the Pacific Ocean. It occurs between Guam and the Caroline Islands, and was discovered by the British ship *Challenger*, which obtained a sounding of 4,475 fathoms at this place.

Challenger Expedition. British scientific expedition (1872–76), under the direction of Charles Wyville Thomson, for the exploration of the deep sea, undertaken on board the British vessel *Challenger*. The expedition was undertaken at the suggestion of the Royal Society, which drew up a complete scheme of instructions. George Nares was in command (1872–74). The ship sailed for a year in the Atlantic, reached Capetown in October, 1873, and Kerguelen island, in the Indian Ocean, in January, 1874. She was the first steamship to cross the Antarctic Circle. The expedition made researches in the Pacific, reached Hong Kong, recrossed the ocean to Valparaíso, and, passing through the Strait of Magellan, reached the dockyard at Sheerness, Kent, in May, 1876. The *Challenger* report was published in 50 volumes (1880–95).

Challis (chal'is), **James.** b. at Braintree, Essex, England, Dec. 12, 1803; d. at Cambridge, England, Dec. 3, 1882. English astronomer and physicist, Plumian professor of astronomy (1836 *et seq.*) and director of the observatory (until 1861) at Cambridge University.

Challoner (chal'ọ.nėr), **Richard.** b. at Lewes, Sussex, England, Sept. 29, 1691; d. at London, Jan. 12, 1781. English Roman Catholic divine, made titular bishop of Debra in 1740, and vicar apostolic of London in 1758. He was educated at the English College at Douai, France, and was professor of philosophy there in the period 1713–20, and vice-president and professor of divinity from 1720 to 1730, returning to London in the latter year. He published a large number of polemical and theological works, including *The Rheims New Testament and the Douay Bible, with Annotations* (1749–50). His version of the Douay Bible is substantially that since used by English-speaking Catholics.

Chalmers (chä'mėrz), **Alexander.** b. at Aberdeen, Scotland, March 29, 1759; d. at London, Dec. 10, 1834. Scottish biographer, editor, and miscellaneous writer. He is best known as the editor of the *General Biographical Dictionary* (1812–14), based on the *New and General Biographical Dictionary* of Tooke, Nares, and Beloe.

Chalmers, George. b. at Fochabers, Elginshire, Scotland, 1742; d. at London, May 31, 1825. Scottish historian and antiquary. He was the author of *Caledonia* (1807–24), *Life of Mary Queen of Scots* (1818), and numerous other works.

Chalmers, James. b. at Arbroath, Forfarshire (now Angus), Scotland, Feb. 2, 1782; d. at Comley Bank, Dundee, Scotland, Aug. 26, 1853. Scottish bookseller and post-office reformer, remembered as the inventor of an adhesive postage stamp. As publisher of the *Dundee Chronicle*, he was active in the town council and served as treasurer for many local charities and philanthropic organizations. He began (1825) an effort to improve mail services by suggesting a uniform rate of postage. His adhesive stamp was exhibited at Dundee in 1834. Chalmers's claim to the inventorship of the adhesive stamp was established in a controversy which his son carried on with the son of Sir Rowland Hill.

Chalmers, Mount. Mountain in Antarctica, in the Conway Range, lying SW of Mulock Inlet, on the W side of the Ross Shelf Ice, in ab. 79°22′ S., 159°30′ E. It was discovered by the National Antarctic Expedition (1901–04), under the command of Captain Robert F. Scott. Elevation, ab. 7,860 ft.

Chalmers, Thomas. b. at East Anstruther, Fifeshire, Scotland, March 17, 1780; d. at Morningside, near Edinburgh, May 31, 1847. Scottish divine and author. He was a minister at Glasgow (1815–23), professor of moral philosophy at St. Andrews (1823–28) and of divinity at Edinburgh (1828–43), and leader in the secession of 1843 from the Church of Scotland. He wrote *Discourses on Astronomy* (1817), *Natural Theology* (1823), *Political Economy* (1832), *Institutes of Theology* (1847–49), and others, including a Bridgewater treatise.

Chalmers (chal'mėrz), **Thomas Hardie.** b. at New York, Oct. 20, 1884—. American operatic baritone and actor. After study at New York and at Florence, he made his operatic debut (1911) as Marcel in *La Bohème* at Fossombrone, Italy. He first appeared (1911) in the U.S. with an English company in *The Girl of the Golden West*, and subsequently sang with the Aborn, Century, Rabinoff-Boston, and Metropolitan (1915–27) opera companies.

Chaloner (chal'ọ.nėr), Sir **Thomas.** b. at London, 1521; d. there, Oct. 14, 1565. English statesman and writer; father of Sir Thomas Chaloner (1561–1615). He was ambassador to the court of the emperor Ferdinand (1559), later to Philip II at Brussels (1559–60), and to Spain (1561–64). He translated into English the homilies of Saint John Chrysostom (1544), Erasmus's *Praise of Folie* (1549), and others.

Chaloner, Sir Thomas. b. 1561; d. Nov. 17, 1615. English naturalist; son of Sir Thomas Chaloner (1521–65) and father of Thomas Chaloner (1595–1661). He wrote *A Short Discourse of the most rare Vertue of Nitre* (1584). He opened the first alum mines in England, at Belman Bank, Guisborough, Yorkshire, c1600.

Chaloner, Thomas. b. at Steeple Claydon, Buckinghamshire, 1595; d. at Middelburg, Zeeland, Netherlands, 1661. English regicide; third son of Sir Thomas Chaloner (1561–1615). He acted as one of the judges of Charles I, in 1648, and was prominent in Parliament until the Restoration, when he fled to the Low Countries.

Châlons-sur-Marne (shä.lôṅ.sür.mȧrn). [Ancient name, **Catalaunum.**] Town in NE France, the capital of the department of Marne, situated on the Marne River and the Marne Canal. Châlons-sur-Marne is one of the centers of the champagne wine trade and has a number of industries. The Cathedral of Saint Étienne dates from the 13th century. Other interesting monuments are the churches of Notre Dame, Saint Loup, Saint Alpin, Saint Jean, and the Hôtel de la Préfecture. Nearby, on the Catalaunian Fields, Attila and his Huns were defeated (451). The town was taken by the Russian, Prussian, and Austrian troops (1814 and 1815), by the Germans (1870 and again in 1914), and suffered damages in the latter stages of World Wars I and II. 31,120 (1946).

Chalon-sur-Saône (shȧ.lôṅ.sür.sōn). [Ancient name, **Cabillonum.**] City in E France, in the department of Saône-et-Loire, situated on the Saône River and the Canal du Centre. It is an important commercial and industrial center. Metallurgical and construction industries, as well as glassmaking and garment manufacture, are of importance. The city has a large sugar refinery. Châlon-sur-Saône was the seat of church councils in the Middle Ages. The Doyoimé tower, dating from the 15th century, was restored in 1926 by the American millionnaire Frank Jay Gould. The Cathedral of Saint Vincent, dating from the 12th–15th centuries, was damaged in World War II. 32,683 (1946).

Châlus (shä.lüs). [Also, **Chaluz.**] Village in W central France, in the department of Haute-Vienne, ab. 20 mi. SW of Limoges. Richard I of England was mortally wounded at the siege of its castle in 1199.

Chalybäus (ċhä.lē.bā'ůs), **Heinrich Moritz.** b. at Pfaffroda, Saxony, Germany, July 3, 1796; d. at Dresden, Germany, Sept. 22, 1862. German philosophical writer. He was named a professor at Kiel in 1839.

Chalybes (kal'i.bēz). In ancient history: **1.** A people in Pontus, near the Black Sea, noted as workers in iron. **2.** A people living near the headwaters of the Euphrates.

Cham (chäm). A matrilineal people of Indochina, the remnants of the once powerful kingdom of Champa. Now numbering less than 100,000, the Cham live in S Annam and in scattered communities in Cambodia, where they are mixed with Malays. They are mostly Moslems, although in some villages in Annam a much-corrupted Hinduism is still practiced. Their language has affinities with both Mon-Khmer and Malayo-Polynesian, and is closely related to the languages of the Rhadé, Jarai, and a number of other tribes in the mountains of Annam. These latter are sometimes termed Cham-speaking tribes.

Cham (kȧm). [Pseudonym of **Amédée,** Comte **de Noé.**] b. at Paris, Jan. 26, 1819; d. there, Sept. 5, 1879. French caricaturist, noted for his illustrations in *Charivari.*

Chamalières (shȧ.mȧ.lyer). Town in C France, in the department of Puy-de-Dôme, ab. 1 mi. W of Clermont-Ferrand. It is a suburb of Clermont-Ferrand; manufactures rubber garments and other products. 8,564 (1946).

Chamars (kä'märs). An Etruscan name of **Chiusi.**

Chamart´n de la Rosa (chä.mär.tēn' dā lä rō'sä). Town in C Spain, in the province of Madrid, NE of Madrid, of which it is a suburb. 64,485 (1940).

Chamavi (ką.mā'vī). German tribe, according to Tacitus originally in the Rhine region north of the Lippe, but later further eastward, adjoining the Bructeri. Julian, in the 4th century, found the Chamavi again on the lower Rhine, and drove them back from the western side to the territory afterward called Hamaland. The Chamavi took a leading part in the establishment of the confederation of the Franks and merged so completely that their own tribal identity became lost during the 4th century A.D.

Chamba (chum'bą). Former state of East Punjab, Union of India. Since 1948 part of Himachal Pradesh, ab. 150 mi. NE of Lahore: forest products, tea, and silk. Area, 3,127 sq. mi.; pop. 168,908 (1941).

Chambal (chum'bąl). River in the C part of the Union of India, which rises in the Vindhya Mountains and flows generally NE into the Jumna River below Etawah. Length, 650 mi.

Chambellan (sham'bẹ.lan), **René Paul.** b. at West Hoboken, N.J., 1893. American architectural sculptor. He studied at New York University (1912–14), at the Beaux Arts Institute of Design (1914–17), and at the École Julian in Paris (1918–19), meanwhile serving in the U.S. army (1917–19). Returning to the U.S. he became an instructor in sculpture at New York University. Examples of his work are to be seen in the Criminal Courts Building, Rockefeller Center, and other noted structures in New York; in buildings of Yale, Cornell, and Northwestern Universities, and Lafayette College; in war memorials, official buildings, and mausoleums in Louvain, Belgium, and in Chicago, Buffalo, Detroit, Worcester, Mass., Nashville, Tenn., and Richmond, Va.

Chambered Nautilus, The. Poem by Oliver Wendell Holmes, published in *The Autocrat of the Breakfast-Table* (1858) and in subsequent collections.

Chamberlain (chām'bėr.lin), **Alexander Francis.** b. at Kenninghall, England, Jan. 12, 1865; d. April 8, 1914. American anthropologist, professor of anthropology at Clark University, Worcester, Mass. He was graduated from the University of Toronto in 1886. His works include *The Child: a Study in the Evolution of Man* (1900) and *Poems* (1904). He was editor (1900–08) of the *Journal of American Folklore.*

Chamberlain, Sir **Austen.** [Full name, **Joseph Austen Chamberlain.**] b. 1863; d. March 16, 1937. English Liberal-Unionist statesman; eldest son of Joseph Chamberlain. He was educated at Rugby, and at Trinity College, Cambridge, sat for Worcestershire (East) in the House of Commons from 1892, and served as a civil lord of the admiralty (1895–1900), financial secretary to the treasury (1900–02), postmaster general (1902–03), and chancellor of the exchequer (from 1903 to December, 1905). Appointed (1915) secretary of state for India, he resigned (1917) as a consequence of the judicial investigation to which the government had subjected the report of the Mesopotamia Commission. Having joined (1918) the war cabinet, he became (1919) chancellor of the exchequer, a post in which he advocated higher taxes. As Conservative leader (1921–23) of the House of Commons and lord privy seal, he promoted the establishment of the Irish Free State. After handling (1925) the establishment of the Locarno Pact in his capacity as foreign secretary (1924–29), he was awarded (1925) the Nobel peace prize. In 1931 he was first lord of the admiralty. He facilitated (1926) the entry of Germany into the League of Nations, was a supporter (1927–28) of the Briand-Kellogg peace pact, and stood in opposition (1933) to the Four-Power Pact. Author of *Peace in Our Time* (1928).

Chamberlain, Basil Hall. b. at Southampton, England, Oct. 18, 1850; d. at Geneva, Switzerland, Feb. 15, 1935. English scholar of Japanese. He served as professor of Japanese and philology at the Imperial University of Tokyo. His works include *The Classical Poetry of the Japanese, Handbook of Colloquial Japanese, Japanese Poetry, Luchuan Grammar,* and *Practical Introduction to the Study of Japanese Writing.*

Chamberlain, Charles Joseph. b. at Sullivan, Ohio, Feb. 23, 1863; d. at Chicago, Jan. 5, 1943. American botanist. He received a B.A. (1888) from Oberlin and a Ph.D. (1897) from the University of Chicago, and taught (1897–1929) at Chicago, as professor from 1915. Known for his work on plant-cell structure, he obtained for the University of Chicago the largest collection of cycads in existence. He was the author of *The Living Cycads* (1919), *Gymnosperms: Structure and Evolution* (1935), and other works.

Chamberlain, Daniel Henry. b. at West Brookfield, Mass., June 23, 1835; d. near Charlottesville, Va., April 13, 1907. American lawyer, politician, and writer. He was graduated from Yale University in 1862, and from the Harvard Law School in 1863. In the last years of the Civil War he served in the Union army. He established himself as a cotton planter in South Carolina in 1866 and was attorney general of that state in the period 1868–72 and its governor from 1874 to 1877.

Chamberlain, George Agnew. b. at São Paulo, Brazil, March 15, 1879—. American novelist. He studied at Princeton University and served (1917–19) as U.S. consul general at Mexico City. Among his novels are *Home* (1914), *Through Stained Glass* (1915), *John Bogardus* (1916), *White Man* (1919), *Cobweb* (1921), *No Ugly Ducklings* (1927), *When Beggars Ride* (1930), *The Auction* (1932), *Two On Safari* (1934), *In Defense of Mrs. Maxon* (1938), *The Red House* (1945), and *Scudda-Hoo! Scudda-Hay!* (1946). He also published the play *Lost* (1926).

Chamberlain, George Earle. b. near Natchez, Miss., Jan. 1, 1854; d. July 9, 1928. American politician. Elected (1880) to the Oregon legislature, he was named (1884) district attorney of the third judicial district and appointed (1891) first attorney general of Oregon. Elected (1902, 1906) governor of Oregon, he was a U.S. senator from 1909 to 1920. As chairman (1913 *et seq.*) of the Senate committee on military affairs, he aided measures for the selective draft, food control, and the financing of World War I.

Chamberlain, Houston Stewart. b. at Southsea, a suburb of Portsmouth, England, Sept. 9, 1855; d. Jan. 9, 1927. Anglo-German writer, remembered chiefly for his statement of racist theories which was the source from which Alfred Rosenberg and the Nazi racial theorists obtained much of their material. The son of a British admiral, he was early drawn to the study of Germanic history, literature, philosophy, and music, and became an ardent Teutophile, especially after his marriage, his second, in 1878 to Eva, the daughter of Richard Wagner. From 1870 he lived in various German cities, finally settling, in 1908, at Bayreuth, the center of the Wagner cult. In 1916, during World War I, he became a German citizen. He was the author of studies of Kant and Goethe and of an important biography of Wagner. The work, however, by which he is best if not most happily remembered is *Die Grundlagen des neunzehnten Jahrhunderts* (1899), translated (1911) into English as *The Foundations of the Nineteenth Century,* of which the thesis is that everything good which has gone into the making of the modern world is a contribution of the German "race," which is defined in a way that takes in large segments of the Celtic and Slavic peoples. Chamberlain emphasized the thought that since Galilee derives its very name from the fact that it was settled by a non-Semitic people, the name meaning in Hebrew "circle (of the Gentiles)," Jesus of Nazareth should be considered an Aryan, not a Jew (Semite). Insinuated, rather than avowed, anti-Semitism deeply colors the book, which must be considered one of the most influential works of modern times, providing for Adolf Hitler and other Nazi ideologists arguments supporting their racial fanaticism.

Chamberlain, John. b. at St. Olave's, in Old Jewry, London, in January (baptized Jan. 15), 1553; d. there, in March (buried March 20), 1627. English scholar and letter writer. He was a student at Trinity College, Cambridge, but did not earn a degree. Left in easy circumstances by his father, he was able to devote his time to corresponding and to cultivating the friendship of distinguished people, at whose homes he stayed. He traveled in Ireland (1597) and visited Venice (1610). His letters cover the period between May 4, 1598 and Jan. 19, 1625; the originals are housed in the Public Record Office, and copies are deposited in the British Museum. They were published in 1848, 1861, and 1939.

Chamberlain, John Rensselaer. b. at New Haven, Conn., Oct. 28, 1903—. American editor and writer. He received a Ph.B. degree (1925) from Yale University, joined (1926) the staff of the New York *Times*, and served (1933–36) as its book columnist. Book editor (1936–38) of *Scribner's Magazine*, he was named (1939) to an equivalent position on *Harper's Magazine*. From 1936 to 1941 he was also editor of *Fortune* magazine, and from 1941 to 1944 was an associate professor at the Columbia University School of Journalism. He is the author of *Farewell to Reform* (1932) and *The American Stakes* (1940).

Chamberlain, Joseph. b. at London, July 8, 1836; d. at Birmingham, England, July 2, 1914. English statesman, after 1886 a leader of the Liberal Unionists; father of Austen Chamberlain and Neville Chamberlain. He was mayor of Birmingham (1873–76), was returned (as a Radical) to Parliament from Birmingham in 1876, and sat for Birmingham, West, from 1885. He served as president of the Board of Trade (1880–85), president of the Local Government Board (1886), and colonial secretary (1895–1903).

Chamberlain, Joshua Lawrence. b. at Brewer, Me., Sept. 8, 1828; d. Feb. 24, 1914. American soldier and educator. During the Civil War he rendered distinguished service with the Army of the Potomac (1862–65). Subsequently he was governor of Maine (1867–70) and president of Bowdoin College (1871–83).

Chamberlain, Neville. [Full name, **Arthur Neville Chamberlain.**] b. March 18, 1869; d. Nov. 9, 1940. English statesman, chiefly remembered for his attempt at conciliation of Germany in the late 1930's; son of Joseph Chamberlain. Destined to enter the family business, he spent several years on his father's sisal plantation in the Bahamas, then entered the plant at Birmingham. He entered politics in 1911 when he took his place on the Birmingham city council, but did not enter Parliament until 1918. There he rose rapidly, becoming chancellor of the exchequer (1923) and minister of health (1924). In 1931 he was again named chancellor of the exchequer, and in 1937, on the resignation of Stanley Baldwin, became prime minister. In this position he worked for two years to avert a general war, and to maintain the *status quo* in Europe. Early in 1938 he recognized Italy's acquisitions from her war in East Africa. When Germany perpetrated the *Anschluss* with Austria, Chamberlain restricted England's opposition to one of formal protest. When Hitler threatened to annex border regions in Czechoslovakia to Germany, he despatched Walter, Viscount Runciman to Prague, himself met with Hitler at Berchtesgaden and Godesberg, and, on September 29 and 30, 1938, brought about the Munich Pact among Great Britain, Germany, France, and Italy. Having received from Hitler, backed by Mussolini, a guarantee that he would make no further territorial demands if the Sudetenland were annexed to Germany without armed interference from France and England, these latter two countries yielded, and Chamberlain returned to London to proclaim that he had definitely secured "peace in our time." When Hitler violated the Munich agreement by the German occupation (March, 1939) of Prague, Chamberlain inaugurated a reversal in British foreign policy by a promise of aid to Poland in case of foreign aggression, which he implemented with the declaration of war against Germany on September 3, 1939. His earlier conciliatory policy had already lost him many supporters and, with the reversals in the Low Countries and the German victory in Norway, he was forced to resign (May 10, 1940) the prime ministership, which passed to Winston Churchill. Chamberlain served under Churchill as president of the council until ill health forced him to retire (October 3, 1940). He published *The Struggle for Peace* (1939), a collection of speeches in defense of his foreign policy. During the crisis of 1938, when the course of world history seemed to depend on England's decisions, Chamberlain's figure became a familiar one, and the rolled umbrella, without which he hardly ever appeared, came to be a symbol of appeasement. There was considerable animosity toward this policy, which was regarded by many as cowardly and negligent. It has been suggested, however, that Chamberlain had no choice, England's armaments not being developed enough in 1938 to allow that country to fight a war; it has also been said that Baldwin's policy, preceding Chamberlain's, made any other attitude impossible.

Chamberland (shäṅ.ber.läṅ), **Charles Édouard.** b. at Chilly-le-Vignoble, France, March 12, 1851; d. at Paris, May 2, 1908. French bacteriologist. He worked with Pasteur and Roux at the Pasteur Institute at Paris, where he served (1904–08) as an assistant director. With Pasteur and Joubert he discovered the bacillus of malignant edema (*vibrion septique*), the first detection of an anaerobic microörganism of a pathogenic character, and he devised the celebrated filter of unglazed porcelain (the "porcelain candle") through which liquid is forced under pressure, allowing only ultramicroscopic organisms to pass through. With Pasteur and Roux he used attenuated bacterial cultures for therapeutic purposes (1880) and demonstrated the presence of rabies virus in the blood (1884). He was the author of *Sur l'étiologie du charbon* (1880), *Le Charbon et la vaccination charbonneuse d'après les travaux récents de M. Pasteur* (1883), *Nouvelle communication sur le rage* (1884), and *Les Eaux d'alimentation dans l'hygiène et les maladies épidémiques. Description des divers modèles du filtre Chamberland système Pasteur; leur application aux eaux, vins, bières . . .* (1885).

Chamberlayne (chām′bėr.lān, -lin), **Edward.** b. at Odington, Gloucestershire, England, Dec. 13, 1616; d. at Chelsea, London, in May, 1703. English writer; father of John Chamberlayne. He was a graduate of Oxford (B.A., 1638; M.A., 1641), tutor of Henry Fitzroy (illegitimate son of Charles II) and Prince George of Denmark, and one of the founders of the Royal Society. He was the author of *Angliae notitiae, or the Present State of England* (1669, anonymous; the 21st ed., 1708, bears the title *Magnae Britanniae notitia*), a handbook of English society and politics, *England's Wants* (1667), and others.

Chamberlayne, John. b. 1666; d. 1723. English writer; younger son of Edward Chamberlayne. He continued his father's *Magnae Britanniae notitia* and translated Brandt's *History of the Reformation in the Low Countries.*

Chamberlayne, William. b. 1619; d. Jan. 11, 1689. English poet, physician, and Royalist soldier. He saw action at the second battle of Newbury, on Oct. 27, 1644. He was the author of *Love's Victory* (1658), a tragicomedy, *Pharonnida* (1659), his chief work, a heroic romance in 14,000 lines consisting of five books of five cantos each, and *England's Jubilee: A Poem on the Happy Return of His Sacred Majesty Charles II* (1660).

Chamberlen (chām′bėr.lẹn), **Hugh.** b. at London, c1630; d. after November, 1720. English physician, celebrated as the projector of a financial scheme designed "to make England rich and happy," based on the issue of a large quantity of bank notes on the security of landed property. In 1673 he was physician in ordinary to the king. He was the author of *Manuale medicum* (1685).

Chamberlin (chām′bėr.lin), **Rollin Thomas.** b. at Beloit, Wis., Oct. 20, 1881; d. 1948. American geologist; son of Thomas Chrowder Chamberlin (1843–1928). He was graduated (B.S., 1903; Ph.D., 1907) from the University of Chicago, where he became (1923) professor of geology. He was managing editor (1922–28) and editor (1928 *et seq.*) of the *Journal of Geology.*

Chamberlin, Thomas Chrowder. b. at Mattoon, Ill., Sept. 25, 1843; d. Nov. 15, 1928. American geologist, professor of geology and director of the Walker Museum in the University of Chicago from 1892; father of Rollin Thomas Chamberlin (1881–1948). He was professor of geology at Beloit College (1873–82), assistant state geologist (1873–76) and chief geologist (1876–82) of Wisconsin, president of the University of Wisconsin (1887–92), and geologist of the Peary relief expedition (1894). He published *Geology of Wisconsin* (1877–83), *General Treatise on Geology* (1904–06; with R. D. Salisbury), *The Tidal and other Problems* (1909; with F. R. Moulton and others), *The Origin of the Earth* (1916), and many scientific papers, and was founder and first editor (1893–1922) of the *Journal of Geology*. He advanced, with F. R. Moulton, the "planetesimal hypothesis," of the formation of the planetary system, which states that minute masses of material (planetesimals) were thrown off by the sun at some remote time through the combined force of eruptions on the sun and the attraction of a star which passed close to the sun; some of these, held at a distance by a balance between the withdrawing force and the sun's gravitational force, moved in orbits around the sun, the larger masses becoming planets by aggregation of the smaller.

Chamberlin, William Henry. b. at Brooklyn, N.Y., Feb. 17, 1897—. American journalist and author of books on international politics. He served as a correspondent for the *Christian Science Monitor* at Moscow (1922–34), in the Far East (1935–39), and in France (1939–40). His books include *Soviet Russia* (1930), *The Soviet Planned Economic Order* (1931), *Russia's Iron Age* (1934), *The Russian Revolution 1917–21* (3 vols., 1935), *Collectivism—A False Utopia* (1937), *Japan Over Asia* (1937), *America: Partner in World Rule* (1945), *The European Cockpit* (1947), and *America's Second Crusade* (1950).

Chamber Music. Volume of poetry by James Joyce, published in 1907. The poems are written in the manner of the Elizabethan poets.

Chamber of Commerce, International. See **International Chamber of Commerce.**

Chamber of Saint Edward. Original name of **Painted Chamber, The.**

Chambers (chām′bėrz), Sir **Edmund Kerchever.** b. in Berkshire, England, March 16, 1866—. English educator and literary scholar. Entering the service of the Board of Education in 1892, and for some years holding the post of an assistant secretary of that official body, he pursued those studies in English literature of earlier periods which resulted in a series of books considered important contributions to critical scholarship. These include *The Mediæval Stage* (1903), *The Elizabethan Stage* (1923), *Shakespeare: A Survey* (1925), *Arthur of Britain* (1927), *William Shakespeare* (1930), *The English Folk-Play* (1933), *Sir Henry Lee* (1936), *Samuel Taylor Coleridge* (1938), and *A Sheaf of Studies* (1942). He also prepared editions of Donne, Vaughan and other poets.

Chambers, Ephraim. b. at Kendal, England, c1680; d. at London, May 15, 1740. English writer, compiler of *Cyclopaedia, or Universal Dictionary of Arts and Sciences* (1728), the first of its kind in English. It was used by Diderot and his coworkers as a basis of the French *Encyclopédie*.

Chambers, Robert. b. at Peebles, Scotland, July 10, 1802; d. at St. Andrews, Scotland, March 17, 1871. Scottish publisher and author; brother of William Chambers (1800–83) and father of Robert Chambers (1832–88). He wrote *Illustrations of the Author of Waverley* (1822), *Traditions of Edinburgh* (1823), *Walks in Edinburgh* (1825), *History of the Rebellion of 1745* (1828), *Biographical Dictionary of Eminent Scotsmen* (1832–34), *Book of Days* (1862–64), and the anonymously published *Vestiges of the Natural History of Creation* (1844). The last-named work, the authorship of which was not discovered until 1884, was an exposition of a theory of evolutionary development, and quickly became famous through both the criticism and the praise which its heterodox views aroused. He was founder (1832) and joint editor of *Chambers's Journal*, and a member of the Edinburgh publishing firm of W. and R. Chambers.

Chambers, Robert. b. at Edinburgh, Scotland, in March, 1832; d. there, March 23, 1888. Scottish publisher and editor; son of Robert Chambers (1802–71). He joined (1853) the publishing firm of W. and R. Chambers founded by his father and his uncle, became (1874) editor of *Chambers's Journal*, and was head (1883 *et seq.*) of the publishing house. He prepared and planned the publication of *Chambers's Encyclopaedia* (1st ed., 1859–68). Author of several scattered essays and *A Few Rambling Remarks on Golf* (1862).

Chambers, Robert. b. at Erzurum, Turkey, Oct. 23, 1881—. American biologist who invented an instrument for the microdissection and injection of living tissues and cells. Born of Canadian parents, he was educated in Turkey, Canada, and Germany, receiving a Ph.D. degree (1908) from the University of Munich. He served as professor of microscopic anatomy (1923–28) at Cornell University Medical College and as research professor of biology (1928 *et seq.*) at New York University.

Chambers, Robert William. b. at Brooklyn, N.Y., May 26, 1865; d. at New York, Dec. 16, 1933. American novelist and artist. He studied art abroad, exhibited at the Paris Salon in 1889, and in 1891 went to New York, where he worked as an illustrator. In 1893 he turned to writing, producing chiefly romantic historical novels. His works include *The King in Yellow* (1895), *Lorraine* (1898), *The Cambric Mask* (1900), *The Conspirators* (1900), *Cardigan* (1901), *The Maid-at-Arms* (1902), *The Reckoning* (1905), *Iole* (1905), *The Tracer of Lost Persons* (1906), *The Fighting Chance* (1906), *The Younger Set* (1907), *The Firing Line* (1908), *The Special Messenger* (1909), *Police!!!* (1915), *The Restless Sex* (1918), *The Hi-Jackers* (1923), and *The Drums of Aulone* (1927).

Chambers, Whittaker. [Full name, **Jay David Whittaker Chambers.**] b. at Philadelphia, April 1, 1901—. American writer. For some 15 years after 1924 he was a member of the Communist Party, working as a member of the staffs of the publications *The Daily Worker* and *New Masses*, but in 1938 or 1939 he left the party, becoming an editor for *Time*. In 1948, Chambers, testifying before the House Committee on Un-American Activities, implicated, in Communist activities he admitted he had previously undertaken, Alger Hiss, an official of the State Department and president of the Carnegie Endowment for International Peace. Chambers's autobiography, *Witness*, was published in 1952.

Chambers, Sir **William.** b. at Stockholm, 1726; d. at London, March 8, 1796. British architect. He rebuilt Somerset House at London, in 1775. He wrote *A Treatise of Civil Architecture* (1759).

Chambers, William. b. at Peebles, Scotland, April 16, 1800; d. at Edinburgh, May 20, 1883. Scottish publisher and writer; brother of Robert Chambers (1802–71). He was one of the founders of the Edinburgh publishing firm of W. and R. Chambers, known for its cheap editions of educational books, and for *Chambers's Journal* (1832 *et seq.*) and *Chambers's Encyclopaedia* (1st ed., 1859–68). He wrote *Things as they are in America* (1854) and *History of Peebles* (1864).

Chambersburg (chām′bėrz.bėrg). Borough in S Pennsylvania, county seat of Franklin County, ab. 49 mi. SW of Harrisburg: seat of Wilson College. It was the site of John Brown's headquarters in the summer of 1859. The town was burned by the Confederates on July 30, 1864. The surrounding region produces fruit and building stone; there are textile mills. 17,212 (1950).

Chambers of Reunion. See **Reunion, Chambers of.**

Chambers v. Florida, 309 U.S. 227 (1940). Decision of the U.S. Supreme Court which protected the rights of Negroes impaired in violation of the 14th Amendment. The case is notable for Justice Hugo Black's denunciation of the torture methods which had been employed to secure confessions from Negroes subsequently convicted of a capital offense.

Chamber Theatre. See **Kamerny Teatr.**

Chambertin (shäṅ.ber.taṅ). Vineyard region in E France, in the department of Côte-d'Or, in the commune of Gevrey, ab. 8 mi. SW of Dijon. It gives its name to a noted red Burgundy wine.

Chambéry (shäṅ.bā.rē). [Italian, **Ciamberi**; Latin, **Camberiacum.**] City in SE France, the capital of the department of Savoie, between Geneva and Grenoble. Situated in the valley of the Leysse River, in a mountainous region, it is a tourist center of first rank. It is the former capital of the duchy of Savoy, and the site of the ancient ducal castle founded in 1232. It is the seat of an archbishop. A Savoyan historical and archaeological museum and the Benoit-Molin Museum (art exhibits) are situated here. Chambéry has machine, textile, and garment industries. The annual fair exhibits all the agricultural and industrial products of the region. Heavy damage was suffered by the city during World War II. 29,975 (1946).

Chambezi (cham.bē′zi). River in S central Africa, in NW Northern Rhodesia, rising in the highlands S of Lake Tanganyika and continuing (S and W of Lake Bangweulu) as the Luapula, the headwaters of the Congo River.

Chamblee (cham.blē′). City in NW Georgia, in De Kalb County, ab. 10 mi. N of Atlanta. Lawson General Hospital and a U.S. Navy air base are nearby. In the decade between the last two U.S. censuses the city's population more than tripled. 1,081 (1940), 3,445 (1950).

Chambly (sham′bli; French, shäṅ.blē). Group of villages in S Quebec, Canada, on the Richelieu River ab. 16 mi. by road E of Montreal. Fort Chambly was built here by the French in 1665 as a strategic defense point against the English colonies to the south. It was ceded to the English in 1763, and in 1775 was attacked and captured by the Americans. The British reoccupied it in 1776, and Burgoyne made it his main base. The modern villages are Chambly Bassin, 2,160 (1951) and Chambly Canton, 1,636 (1951).

Chambly, Fort. British post constructed (1775) on the site of a French fort, at the foot of the Richelieu River rapids. It was seized (Oct. 20, 1775) by the Americans during their invasion of Canada, and was retained by them until the spring of 1776, when, forced to retreat, they burned the fort. The site is now a Canadian national historic park.

Chambly Bassin (bȧ.saṅ). See under **Chambly.**

Chambly Canton (käṅ.tôṅ). See under **Chambly.**

Chambonnières (shäṅ.bo.nyer), **Jacques Champion de.** b. 1602; d. at Paris, c1672. French harpsichordist and composer. He is regarded, on the basis of his two books of *Pièces de clavecin* and his performances, as the originator of the French school of harpsichord music.

Chambord (shäṅ.bôr). Village in N central France, in the department of Loir-et-Cher, ab. 11 mi. E of Blois. It contains a famous château, built by Francis I, a large structure illustrating the application of Renaissance principles to a French medieval type. The most striking feature is the series of six huge cylindrical, cone-roofed towers, 60 ft. in diameter, with decorated dormer windows and high chimneys. The central tower contains a remarkable double spiral stair, so devised that two sets of persons may ascend and descend at the same time without meeting; this tower is surmounted by an openwork lantern. The château (now the property of the French government) contains 440 rooms, and the stables were made to accommodate 1,200 horses.

Chambord, Comte **de.** [Title of **Henri Charles Ferdinand Marie Dieudonné d'Artois;** title before 1830, Duc **de Bordeaux;** sometimes called **Henri V.**] b. at Paris, Sept. 29, 1820; d. at Frohsdorf, near Vienna, Aug. 24, 1883. French Legitimist prince. The son of Charles Ferdinand, Duc de Berry, and grandson of Charles X, he was styled Duc de Bordeaux before 1830, and is sometimes called "Henri V," having been proclaimed as such by the Legitimists in 1830. He was the Bourbon claimant to the French throne.

Chambre (shäṅbr), **Guy La.** See **La Chambre, Guy.**

Chambre Introuvable (aṅ.trö.vȧbl). Nickname given to the French Chamber of Deputies of the period 1815–16, noted for its reactionary measures.

Chambres Ardentes (shäṅ.brẹ zȧr.däṅt). Extraordinary French tribunals sometimes convened under the old monarchy (before 1789) for the trial of cases of malversation, and others.

Chambrun (shäṅ.brėṅ), **Charles,** Comte **de.** b. at Paris, Feb. 10, 1875; d. there, Nov. 6, 1952. French diplomat, ambassador to Rome (1933–36); uncle of René, Comte de Chambrun.

Chambrun, René, Comte **de.** b. at Paris, Aug. 23, 1906—. French lawyer and soldier; son-in-law of Pierre Laval and nephew of Charles, Comte de Chambrun (1875–1952). A member of the Paris and New York bars, he was a liaison officer with the British army in Belgium during World War II. After the fall of France, he was reported by Free French sources to have aided Laval in his pro-German activities.

Chambure (shäṅ.bür), **Auguste Lepelletier de.** b. at Vitteaux, in Burgundy, France, March 31, 1789; d. at Paris, July 12, 1832. French officer, called "Le Diable" for his audacious bravery.

Chameleon (kạ.mē′lẹ.ọn). Constellation described by Johann Bayer, situated beneath the feet of Centaurus.

Chamfort or **Champfort** (shäṅ.fôr), **Sébastien Roch Nicolas.** b. in Auvergne, France, c1741; d. at Paris, April 13, 1794. French writer. He was the author of *Éloge de Molière* (1769), the plays *Le marchand de Smyrne* (1770) and *Mustapha et Zéangir* (1776), and other works, including the posthumously published *Maximes et pensées* (1803), for which he is best known.

Chamier (sham′yėr), **Frederick.** b. at London, 1796; d. at Waltham Abbey, Essex, England, in October, 1870. English naval captain and historian, and novelist of the sea. He entered the Royal Navy in 1809, retired in 1827, and was made a captain in 1856, 23 years after his retirement. He was the author of *Life of a Sailor* (1832), *Ben Brace the Last of Nelson's Agamemnons* (1835), *The Saucy Arethusa* (1836), *Jack Adams* (1838), *Tom Bowling* (1841), and other novels of life at sea. Chamier also edited (1837) *Naval History of Great Britain from the Declaration of War by France in 1793 to the Accession of George IV* (1822–24), by William James, and extended the narrative to 1827. In Paris in 1848, he produced as a result *Review of the French Revolution* (1849), and his continental travels were recorded in *An Unsentimental Journey through France, Switzerland, and Italy* (1855).

Chaminade (shȧ.mē.nȧd), **Cécile Louise Stéphanie.** b. at Paris, c1861; d. 1944. French composer and pianist. She wrote many popular piano pieces and songs, several orchestral suites, *Les Amazones* (1888), which is a symphony with chorus, and chamber music. Her *Scarf Dance* for piano is especially well known, as is the ballet symphony *Callirhoë*, first performed at Marseilles (1888).

Chamisso (shä.mēs′ō), **Adelbert von.** [Original French name, **Louis Charles Adélaïde de Chamisso.**] b. at the castle of Boncourt, in Champagne, France, Jan. 30, 1781; d. at Berlin, Aug. 21, 1838. German poet, member of an old French family. In 1796 his parents, who had left France in 1790, went to Berlin, where he became a page of the queen. In 1798 he entered the Prussian army, from which he retired in 1808. Subsequently, while staying at Coppet, Switzerland, in the entourage of Madame de Staël, he took up botany. In 1815 he accompanied as naturalist an exploring expedition under Captain Otto Kotzebue (son of August Kotzebue) in a journey around the world. He was subsequently custodian of the botanical collections at Berlin. His most celebrated prose work *Peter Schlemihls wunderbare Geschichte*, the story of the man who sold his shadow, appeared in 1814. His poetry comprises popular songs, ballads, and romances including the long poems *Salas y Gomez*, *Matteo Falcone*, and *Die Retraite*. His lyrics *Frauenliebe und -leben* (1831) were later set to music by Robert Schumann. His collected works appeared first at Leipzig (1836) in six volumes, and went through six editions.

Cham of Literature, The Great. See **Johnson, Samuel.**

Chamonix (shȧ.mo.nē). [Also: **Chamouni, Chamouny** (-mö-).] Valley in E France, in the department of Haute-Savoie, at the foot of Mont Blanc, watered by the Arve River. It is a celebrated resort for tourists, and the starting point for excursions to Mont Blanc, the Mer de Glace glacier, Montanvert, Flégère, Martigny (across the Swiss border), and other points; its center is the village of Chamonix. It was explored by Richard Pococke in 1743. Length of valley, 12 mi.; elevation, 3,445 ft.

Chamont (cham′ọnt). Rough and extremely fiery young soldier of fortune, the brother of Monimia, the titular heroine of Thomas Otway's blank-verse tragedy *The Orphan* (1680).

Chamorro (chä.môr′rō), **Fruto.** b. in Guatemala, c1810; d. near Granada, Nicaragua, March 12, 1855. Nicaraguan statesman. From April, 1853, until his death he was president of Nicaragua. During a part of this time his rule was limited to Granada, where he was besieged by revolutionists under Francisco Castellón.

Chamorro Vargas (chä.môr′rō bär′gäs), **Emiliano.** b. at Acoyapa, Nicaragua, May 11, 1871—. Nicaraguan engineer, army officer, and statesman, president (1917–20; 1926) of Nicaragua. A graduate (1889) of the Instituto Nacional de Oriente, he served as commander in chief (1909–10) of the armies for the restoration of constitutional government and, in 1912, of the Nicaraguan army. He was twice (1913–16, 1921–23) minister to the U.S. He negotiated (1916) the Bryan-Chamorro Treaty by which the U.S. obtained an option on the route of the proposed canal between the Atlantic and Pacific oceans across Nicaragua. He became president a second time by a coup (October, 1925), unseated President Solórzano and Vice-president Sacasa, was named (1926) presidential "designate" by the senate, but was not given U.S. recognition. Mexican armed intervention in the Nicaraguan civil war occasioned a landing of U.S. Marines and the resignation (October, 1926) of Chamorro. He served as minister (1927) to Great Britain, France, and Italy, was a national senator (1928 *et seq.*), and became (1933) head of the conservative party.

Chamouchouane (shä.mö.shwän). See **Ashuapmuchuan.**

Champa (chäm′pa). Former city in Bihar, India, the present Bhagalpur or near it. It is said to have been founded by Champa, a descendant of Yayati; but was named rather from its abundant champa or champac trees (*Michelia Champaca*), whence it was also called *Malini*, meaning "garlanded," from its being surrounded with champac trees as with a garland (*mala*).

Champagne (sham.pān′; French, shäṅ.päny′). Region and former province of France, celebrated for its wines. It was bounded by Belgium on the N, Lorraine on the E, Franche-Comté on the SE, Burgundy on the S, and Orléanais, Île-de-France, and Picardy on the W. The chief city of the region is Troyes. It comprises the modern departments of Marne, Haute-Marne, Aube, Ardennes, parts of Aisne, Yonne, Seine-et-Marne, and Meuse. In the Middle Ages it was a countship and one of the great fiefs of France. During this period and until the taxes imposed by Philip IV of France (Philip the Fair) killed them off, the Champagne fairs were the great trading center of western Europe. Some of its counts were noted as poets. Its heiress, Jeanne de Navarre, married Philip IV in 1284. It was formally annexed to France in 1314, and incorporated with France in 1361.

Champagne, Count of. Additional title of **Henry I** (of *Navarre*).

Champagne, Count of. See **Eudes** (d. 1037).

Champagne, Battles of. Three lengthy but largely stalemated battles of World War I, in the area roughly between Reims and the Meuse River. The first (late December, 1914 to mid-March, 1915) was a general Allied offensive that met no real success. The second (Sept. 22–Nov. 6, 1915) was a pivotal move in the Joffre offensive, but again made small gains. The last (April, 1917), an attempted surprise by General Nivelle, was a drastic failure.

Champagne Castle. See under **Drakensberg.**

Champagne-Marne Defensive (sham.pān′märn′). World War I military operation in France, involving U.S. and French troops facing a German offensive in the Marne salient in the direction of Épernay and Reims. The last serious German offensive of the war, it was a heavily massed assault on a front of almost 50 miles. It was aimed at the encirclement and capture of Reims in order to improve German lines of supply and to divert British troops from the north. The Germans hoped through the offensive eventually to extend their lines to the Marne River and the city of Châlons-sur-Marne. The assault was launched on July 15, 1918, and was stemmed by the French 4th Army supported by the U.S. 3rd and 42nd divisions and elements of the 28th Division. The 38th Infantry Regiment along the Surmelin River valley distinguished itself by holding off for 14 hours determined attacks (July 15) by picked German troops, an action which earned for this 3rd Division unit the title of "Rock of the Marne." Only in the north were the Germans able to reach the Marne. The enemy offensive was completely halted in the period July 17–18.

Champagny (shäṅ.pä.nyē), **François Joseph Nompère de.** b. at Vienna, Sept. 10, 1804; d. May 4, 1882. French publicist; son of Jean Baptiste Nompère de Champagny, 1st Duc de Cadore. His chief work is a history of the Roman empire in ten volumes (1841–70), of which the four-volume *Les Césars* (1841–43) is the best known.

Champagny, Jean Baptiste Nompère de. [Title, 1st **Duc de Cadore.**] b. at Roanne, Loire, France, Aug. 4, 1756; d. at Paris, July 3, 1834. French politician and diplomat; father of François Joseph Nompère de Champagny and Louis Alix Nompère de Champagny. He was ambassador at Vienna (1801–04), minister of the interior (1804–07), and minister of foreign affairs (1807–11).

Champagny, Louis Alix Nompère de. [Title, 2nd **Duc de Cadore.**] b. Jan. 12, 1796; d. at Boulogne, France, Jan. 27, 1870. French politician; son of Jean Baptiste Nompère de Champagny, 1st Duc de Cadore. He was ambassador at Rome in 1861.

Champaign (sham.pān′). City in E Illinois, in Champaign County, ab. 43 mi. NE of Decatur: with Urbana, it shares the campus of the University of Illinois. Champaign has railroad shops, and is an industrial and marketing center for a farming region. 39,563 (1950).

Champaigne (shäṅ.peny′) or **Champagne** (-päny′), **Philippe de.** b. at Brussels, May 26, 1602; d. at Paris, Aug. 12, 1674. Painter of the Flemish school. He went to Paris in 1621, where he executed certain decorations on the Luxembourg, and later did many religious paintings for Queen Marie de Médicis (wife of Henry IV of France) and for Richelieu. His portrait of Richelieu and of his own daughter as a nun are in the Louvre at Paris. His best-known works are at Paris, Vincennes, and Vienna; but the New York Historical Society and the Boston Museum of Fine Arts have a few of his paintings.

Champaran (chum.pä.run′). District in the Tirhut division, Bihar state, Union of India: cattle, wheat, and millet. Area, 3,531 sq. mi.; pop. 2,397,569 (1941).

Champ d'Asile (shäṅ dä.zēl). Fortified colony along the Trinity River, in Texas, erected (1817) by a band of Napoleonic exiles under the leadership of generals Rigaud and Lallemand. It was rumored that the French group had designs on Mexico and were scheming to take Napoleon from St. Helena. Soon after the exiles completed their fortifications, the Spanish compelled them to leave. They went to Galveston Island and later settled in Louisiana.

Champ de Mai (me). See under **Champ de Mars.**

Champ-de-Mars (shäṅ.dẹ.märs). [Eng. trans., "*Field of Mars.*"] Large square in the Grenelle quarter of Paris, on the left bank of the Seine, formerly used for military exercises. It has been the scene of battles and historical episodes from the 9th century, and of festivals, pageants, and exhibitions, including that of 1889, at which time the Eiffel Tower was erected here. Here occurred, on July 14, 1790, the Fête de la Fédération, the occasion on which Louis XVI promised to support the new constitution. On July 17, 1791, an attempt at insurrection ("massacres du Champ-de-Mars") took place here, and on June 8, 1794, the Fête à l'Être Suprême was held in this square.

Champ de Mars. [Eng. trans., "*Field of March.*"] In early French institutional history, an annual political and military assembly, held in March. The time of meeting was changed to May in the 8th century, and thereafter the assembly was called "Champ de Mai."

Champeaux (shäṅ.pō), **Guillaume de.** See **Guillaume de Champeaux.**

Champetier de Ribes (shäṅ.pẹ.tyā dẹ rēb), **Auguste.** b. at Antony, Seine, France, July 30, 1882; d. at Paris, March 6, 1947. French political leader and lawyer, first president of the Council of the Republic, the upper house of the French parliament under the Fourth Republic. He was active in the Resistance movement during World War II, was arrested (1942) by the Germans, but escaped (1944). Principal French prosecuting attorney at the Nuremberg trials, he was elected president of the Council of the Republic in 1946 and again in 1947. A lawyer at the Paris bar for more than four decades, he entered (1924) the Chamber of Deputies, was minister of pensions (1930–32, 1938–39), and voted against the Pétain regime in July, 1940.

Champfleury (shäṅ.flė.rē). [Pseudonym of **Jules Fleury-Husson.**] b. at Laon, France, Sept. 10, 1821; d. at

Sèvres, France, Dec. 5, 1889. French novelist and miscellaneous writer. His works include *Chien-Callou* (1847), *Les Bourgeois de Molinchart* (1855), and *Histoire de la caricature* in six volumes (1865–80).

Champigny-sur-Marne (shäṅ.pē.nyē.sür.märn). [Also, **Champigny.**] Town in N France, in the department of Seine, situated on the Marne River, SE of Nogent-sur-Marne and E of Paris. It is a suburb of Paris. There are monuments commemorating the battles that took place here; Nov. 30 and Dec. 2, 1870, between the Germans and the French under General Auguste Ducrot in the defense of Paris. 30,239 (1946).

Champion (shäṅ.pyôṅ), **Étienne Marie Antoine.** See **Nansouty, Étienne Marie Antoine Champion, Comte de.**

Champion, The. Journal which first appeared in 1739, written and edited by Henry Fielding with the American poet and pamphleteer James Ralph. It was based on the model of the *Spectator* and *Tatler*, and combined literature and politics. Two volumes of the paper were republished in 1741. It ridiculed the Jacobite party.

Championnet (shäṅ.pyo.ne), **Jean Antoine Étienne.** b. at Valence, France, 1762; d. at Antibes, France, Jan. 9, 1800. General in the armies of the French Revolution. His military career began before the Revolution, but it was during that upheaval that he rose to general command. He won the commendation of Pichegru and of Hoche during campaigns in Germany and the Low Countries, and in 1798 was entrusted with command of the army of Rome, with the duty of saving the French-sponsored Roman Republic from Neapolitan, British, and Austrian attacks, which he did in the face of apparently overwhelming odds. Taking the offensive, he captured Naples and set up the Parthenopean Republic, but was relieved of his command when his stern rule led to popular disorders in that city. In the following year Napoleon put him at the head of the army of the Alps. This force was poorly organized and equipped, and in the ensuing campaign Championnet suffered successive defeats and eventually resigned.

Champion's Hill. Locality in Hinds County, Miss., W of Jackson. Here, on May 16, 1863, a Union force (32,000) under Grant, advancing on Vicksburg, defeated the Confederates (about 25,000) under General J. C. Pemberton. Loss of Union side, 2,457; of Confederates, 4,300. It is also called the battle of Baker's Creek.

Champions of Freedom, The. Only novel by Samuel Woodworth, published in 1816. It deals with the War of 1812, with action set in the Great Lakes region.

Champion v. Ames, 188 U.S. 321 (1903). [Also known as the **"Lottery Case."**] U.S. Supreme Court decision upholding a federal law of 1895 which suppressed interstate commerce in lottery tickets. It is notable as an initial move in the direction of invoking the commerce power for federal regulation in areas not susceptible of effective regulation under the police powers of the states.

Champlain (sham.plān'). Town (in New York the equivalent of township in many other states) and village in NE New York, in Clinton County, near the Canadian border: manufactures of bookbinding machines. Pop. of town, 5,118 (1950); of village, 1,505 (1950).

Champlain, Lake. Lake between Vermont and New York, extending from Whitehall, N.Y., to St. Johns, Canada. Its outlet is the Richelieu River (into the St. Lawrence), and it is connected with the Hudson by a canal. It was discovered by Samuel de Champlain in 1609. On Oct. 11, 1776, a British flotilla defeated the Americans under Arnold. In the battle of Plattsburg, Sept. 11, 1814, an American squadron consisting of 14 vessels of all classes, carrying 86 guns and ab. 850 men, under the command of Captain Thomas Macdonough, defeated a British force consisting of 16 vessels of all classes, carrying 95 guns and ab. 1,000 men, under the command of Captain George Downie, which supported an invasion of New York by Sir George Prevost. A precipitate retreat of the British land force followed the battle. Length, ab. 125 mi.; width in the northern part, 10 to 12 mi.; elevation, 96 ft.

Champlain (sham.plān'; French, shäṅ.plaṅ), **Samuel de.** b. at Brouage, on the Bay of Biscay, France, c1567; d. at Quebec, Dec. 25, 1635. French explorer and a founder of New France (Canada). After serving in both the army and navy under Henry of Navarre, he commanded (1599 *et seq.*) the *St. Julien* in its voyage, as part of a Spanish fleet, to New Spain. Upon his return he submitted a detailed report on the Spanish holdings to Henry IV, who granted him a patent of nobility and a pension, and induced him to set out on a voyage of exploration (1603), the first of several made by Champlain under the French flag. The initial voyage, which took him up the St. Lawrence River, was in the nature of a preliminary survey; in 1604, although anxious to penetrate the North American interior, he was compelled by Pierre de Guast, Sieur de Monts, the patron of the North American claims held by France, to found a colony south of the St. Lawrence. It was established on Douchet Island at the mouth of the St. Croix River in New Brunswick and moved (1605) to Port Royal in what is now Nova Scotia. Champlain made three exploratory voyages along the New England coast, and in 1608 secured royal permission to establish a colony on the St. Lawrence. The settlement, at Quebec, was the first permanent French colony in America. In 1609, accompanying a party of Algonquins and Hurons against the Iroquois to the south, he discovered Lake Champlain. In 1613 he set out on a voyage to find a northwest route to the Orient, going as far as Morrison or Allumette Island in the Ottawa River; in 1615 he became the first white man to survey Lake Huron (which he named), traced the St. Lawrence to its source, and penetrated what is now New York state. Following the voyage of 1615–16, he concentrated on developing the colony of New France, spent four years (1629–33) in England as a prisoner during the strife between France and England, and in 1633 returned as governor of New France. For his writings, see *The Works of Samuel de Champlain*, published (1922–27) by the Champlain Society.

Champlin (cham'plin), **James Tift.** b. at Colchester, Conn., June 9, 1811; d. at Portland, Me., March 15, 1882. American clergyman and teacher, president of Colby University at Waterville, Me., in the period 1857–72.

Champmeslé (shäṅ.me.lā), **Charles Chevillet de.** b. at Paris, 1645; d. there, April 22, 1701. French dramatic author and comedian; husband of Marie de Champmeslé. He was, by his own styling, "Sieur de Champmeslé."

Champmeslé, Marie de. [Maiden name, **Desmares.**] b. at Rouen, France, c1641; d. at Auteuil, France, May 15, 1698. French actress; wife of Charles de Champmeslé. She was closely associated with Racine, and created the parts of Hermione, Monimia, Phèdre, and Berenice in his plays.

Champney (champ'ni), **Benjamin.** b. at New Ipswich, N.H., Nov. 29, 1817; d. at Woburn, Mass., Dec. 14, 1907. American landscape painter. His parents being poor, he went to work in a mill, from which he could observe the operations in an adjacent engraving plant. He made the acquaintance of one of the engravers, whose instructions in drawing enabled him to secure employment in that craft. Subsequently he found means to study painting at Boston and to visit France and Italy. At Fontainebleau he painted from nature, and his canvases were several times exhibited at the Paris Salon. He executed a vast panoramic picture of the Rhine River and its surrounding scenes, which was exhibited at several American cities before being destroyed in the fire which razed the Crystal Palace at New York. He was a founder and one-time president of the Boston Art Club, but in his later years his time was divided between Woburn, Mass., and the White Mountains of New Hampshire. His work was much in the style of the Hudson River School, but he was among the first Americans to understand and welcome the innovations of the French Impressionists. Examples of Champney's art are to be seen in the Boston Art Club, the Woburn Museum, and the Woburn Public Library.

Champney, James Wells. b. at Boston, July 16, 1843; d. at New York, May 1, 1903. American painter and illustrator. He learned wood engraving at Boston, and in 1866 went to Paris and became a pupil of Édouard Frère. He also studied in the academy at Antwerp. In 1873 he toured the South with Edward S. King (1848–86), American journalist, and made some 500 drawings for King's *The Great South,* which ran serially in *Scribner's*

Monthly and was published (1875) in book form. He was professor of art at Smith College (1877–84).

Champneys (champ′niz), **Basil.** b. at Lichfield, England, 1842; d. 1935. English architect and writer on art, noted primarily for his school and church buildings; son of William Weldon Champneys. He studied at Cambridge University and with the architect John Prichard. Among the buildings which he designed are the Archaeological Museum and other buildings at Cambridge, Ryland's Library at Manchester, also buildings at Oxford University, at Harrow, and at London. His literary works include *A Quiet Corner of England* (1875), *Henry Merrit, Art Criticism and Romance* (1879), and *Coventry Patmore, Memoirs and Correspondence* (1900).

Champneys, William Weldon. b. at London, April 6, 1807; d. at Lichfield, England, Feb. 4, 1875. English clergyman and writer; father of Basil Champneys. A graduate of Oxford (Brasenose College), he was appointed dean of Lichfield in November, 1868.

Champoeg Convention (cham.pō′eg). Provisional government established (May 2, 1843) by Oregon colonists at a meeting at Champoeg in the Willamette Valley. It was intended to serve until the final settlement of the Anglo-American Oregon dispute, and was opposed by British colonists who regarded it as sympathetic to the American cause. This civil government was the only one of its kind in the Pacific Northwest until the Oregon territorial government was set up (1849) by the U.S. government.

Champollion (shäṅ.po.lyôṅ), **Jean François.** [Sometimes called **"Champollion le Jeune."**] b. at Figeac, Lot, France, Dec. 23, 1790; d. at Paris, March 4, 1832. French Egyptologist, considered the founder of that branch of study; brother of Jean Jacques Champollion-Figeac. With the use of the Rosetta Stone, he managed to decipher the Egyptian hieroglyphics, establishing the principles of interpretation still in use today. This discovery he made public in *Lettre à Monsieur Dacier* (1822), and further published *Précis du système hiéroglyphique des anciens Égyptiens* (1824). In 1831 a chair of Egyptology was created for him at the Collège de France. He was author also of *Grammaire égyptienne* (1836–41) and *Dictionnaire égyptien* (1841–43).

Champollion-Figeac (shäṅ.po.lyôṅ.fē.zhȧk), **Jean Jacques.** b. at Figeac, Lot, France, Oct. 5, 1778; d. at Fontainebleau, France, May 9, 1867. French archaeologist; brother of Jean François Champollion. He wrote *Antiquités de Grenoble* (1807), *Annales des Lagides* (1819), *Paléographie universelle* (1839–41), and *Le Palais de Fontainebleau* (1867).

Champs Élysées (shäṅ zā.lē.zā). [Eng. trans., *"Elysian Fields."*] Avenue, and the gardens surrounding it, at Paris, extending from the Place de la Concorde, 1¼ mi. to the Place d'Étoile, celebrated as a place of public resort. It was acquired by the crown in 1616, and ceded to the city in 1828.

Champvallon (shäṅ.vȧ.lôṅ), **François de Harlay de.** See **Harlay de Champvallon, François de.**

Chamson (shäṅ.sôṅ), **André.** b. at Nîmes, France, 1900—. French novelist, essayist, and geographer. He is the author of regionalist novels set in his native Cévennes mountains, including *Roux le bandit* (1925; Eng. trans., *Roux the Bandit,* 1929), *Les Hommes de la route* (1927; Eng. trans., *The Road,* 1929), and *Le Crime des justes* (1929; Eng. trans., *The Crime of the Just,* 1930). Later novels, *Héritage* (1932) and *La Galère* (1939), the latter an attack on corrupt politics, have broader implications. He has also written essays, including *L'Homme contre l'histoire* (1937). A leftist, he has been coeditor of the weekly *Vendredi* (1935–38), chief assistant in the cabinet of Daladier (1934), and curator of the Musée de Versailles under Léon Blum and the Popular Front.

Chamunda (chä.mön′dä). In Hindu mythology, an aspect of the goddess Durga, who in turn is an aspect of the goddess Devi: said to have been so named on account of her destruction of the two demons Chanda and Munda.

Chan (chan), **Charlie.** See **Charlie Chan.**

Chaná (chä.nä′). See **Chané.**

Chanak (chä.näk′) or **Chanakkale** (chä.näk.kä.le′) or **Chanak Kalessi** (kä.le.sē′). See **Çanakkale,** town.

Chanakya (chä′nä.kyạ). [Also: **Vishnugupta, Kautilya.**] Brahman, minister to Chandragupta. He took a leading part in the overthrow of the Nanda dynasty of Magadha, and the elevation of Chandragupta (known also by the Greek form of his name, Sandracottus) to their throne as first of the Maurya dynasty, c320 B.C. A work upon morals and politics called *Chanakyasutra* is ascribed to him. He is the chief character in the political drama *Mudrarakshasa.*

Chanca (chäng′kä), **Diego Álvarez.** fl. in the late 15th century. Spanish physician, native of Seville, who accompanied Columbus on his second voyage in 1493. He wrote a letter to the cathedral chapter of Seville, giving an account of what he saw; this is one of the main historical authorities for the voyage. Nothing is known of his previous or subsequent life.

Chancas (chäng′käs). Indian tribe of Peru which occupied the Andean valleys between the Apurímac and Mantaro rivers. They were a grave threat to Inca expansion and, at one time, very nearly succeeded in breaking the Inca power. They were finally defeated in the early 15th century.

Chance. Novel by Joseph Conrad, published in 1913. It deals with the effect of greed upon character.

Chance Acquaintance, A. Novel by William Dean Howells, published in 1873.

Chancellor (chȧn′sẹ.lọr), **Olive.** Character in *The Bostonians* (1886), novel by Henry James. She is intensely working for the cause of feminism, partly from sincere intellectual conviction, and partly from an inner need to forge relationships with others. She befriends Verena Tarrant, but cannot persuade the girl to embrace the same way of life.

Chancellor, Richard. d. Nov. 10, 1556. English navigator. He accompanied Roger Bodenham on a journey to Candia (Crete) and Chios in 1550. In 1553 he became captain of the *Edward Bonaventure* and pilot-general of the expedition which set out in that year under the command of Sir Hugh Willoughby in search of a northeast passage to India. Becoming separated from the other ships of the expedition in a gale off the Lofoten Islands, he pushed on alone into the White Sea and Arkhangelsk, whence he made his way overland to Moscow. He obtained valuable trade concessions from the Russian court in behalf of the English, which led to the organization of the Muscovy Company on his return to England in 1554. He made a second visit to Moscow in 1555, and was shipwrecked off Pitsligo, on the coast of Aberdeenshire, on the return voyage. A narrative of his first visit to Moscow, written by Clement Adams, was published in Hakluyt's *Navigations,* and is the first considerable account of the Russian people in the English language.

Chancellorsville (chȧn′sẹ.lọrz.vil). [Now called **Chancellor.**] Post office in Spotsylvania County, Va., ab. 55 mi. NW of Richmond. Here, May 2–4, 1863, the Confederates (ab. 65,000) under Lee defeated a Union force (ab. 132,000) under Hooker. Loss of the Union army, ab. 17,000; of the Confederates, ab. 12,000 (including "Stonewall" Jackson).

Chancery Lane (chȧn′sẹ.ri). Street at London, leading from Fleet Street to Holborn, and passing by the Record Office, Lincoln's Inn, and Cliffords Inn.

Chances, The. Comedy by John Fletcher. It was published in 1647, but had been played before 1625. The plot is from *La Señora Cornelia,* a novel by Miguel de Cervantes. George Villiers, 2nd Duke of Buckingham, produced an alteration of it in 1682, and David Garrick brought out a second alteration in 1773. In 1821 a musical drama founded on it, called *Don John, or the Two Violettas,* was produced.

Chanchan (chän′chän). [Also, **Chan Chan.**] Capital of the former Chimu Indian kingdom and once a city covering ab. 11 sq. mi., but now in ruins, near the modern Peruvian city of Trujillo. It was destroyed (c1400) by the Incas after a siege when the Chimu kingdom was defeated.

Chanda (chän′dạ). District in the Nagpur division of the Madhya Pradesh (Central Provinces), Union of India, SE of Nagpur: millet, linseed, and cotton. Capital, Chanda; area, 10,785 sq. mi.; pop. 873,284 (1941).

Chanda. Capital of the Chanda district, Union of India, near the Penganga River, ab. 90 mi. S of Nagpur: trading center and rail junction. Pop. ab. 30,000.

Chandaburi (chän″dạ.bu.rē′). See **Chantaburi.**

Chandernagor (chun″dėr.nạ.gôr′). [Also, **Chandarnagar** (chun.dėr.nug′ạr).] Former French town and settlement (*ville libre*) in West Bengal, Union of India, on the Hooghli River, ab. 20 mi. N of Calcutta. It was a possession of the French, under the jurisdiction of Pondichéry, was taken by the English in 1757 and 1793, and was ceded finally to France in 1816. As the result of a referendum (1949), it was ceded in May, 1950 to the Union of India, the formal treaty of cession being signed in February, 1951. Area, 3½ sq. mi.; pop.: settlement, 44,786 (1948); town, 38,284 (1941).

Chandi (chän′dē). [Also, **Tjandi.**] Malayan term designating a type of Hindu-Javanese stone temple, not a building erected to wall in a large room or rooms for cult purposes but an essentially solid structure, often in the shape of a modified stepped pyramid surrounded by open courtyards. It contains one or more cella rooms as openings within the architectural mass-cella as well as niches designed for statues of deities. Chandis were originally sepulchral monuments with ash-containing urns somewhere embedded in their structure, often erected in memory of a king or queen and dedicated to a deity. The buried personage was apparently thought of as an incarnation of this deity. Later the term embraced single monuments or groups of monuments built solely as an expression of veneration for a god or goddess. Everything about a Chandi, its location, orientation, shape, and structure, has symbolic significance, is an allegorical materialization of metaphysical concepts. The building of Chandis stopped with the advent of Islam in the 16th century; the earliest ruins (Dieng plateau) may stem from the 7th century A.D. Hindu-Javanese art consists largely of the abundant sculptural decoration of the Chandis, of the stone reliefs adorning their walls, portals, and surrounding galleries, of the figures and groups growing out of innumerable niches. The chief Chandis are Chandi Djago, Chandi Kalasan, Chandi Panataran, and Chandi Prambanan.

Chandi. [In some older sources, **Chanda.**] In Hindu mythology, the goddess Durga, or Devi, applied especially to her incarnation for the purpose of destroying the buffalo-headed demon Mahisha. This exploit, which is treated in a section of the *Markandeyapurana*, is particularly celebrated in Bengal at the Durgapuja, or festival held in honor of the goddess toward the close of the year (about October to November).

Chandi Djago (jä′gō). See **Djago, Chandi.**

Chandi Kalasan (kä.lä.sän′). See **Kalasan, Chandi.**

Chandi Panataran (pä.nä.tä.rän′). See **Panataran, Chandi.**

Chandipatha (chän.dē.pä′tạ). Poem of 700 verses, forming an episode of the *Markandeyapurana*. It celebrates Durga's victories over the Asuras, and is read daily in the temple of that goddess.

Chandi Prambanan (präm.bä.nän′). See **Prambanan, Chandi.**

Chandler (chån′dlėr). Town in S central Arizona, in Maricopa County ab. 15 mi. SE of Phoenix: tourist resort in a rich agricultural region supplied by Roosevelt Dam and others in the Salt River Valley irrigation system. In the decade between the last two U.S. censuses its population more than tripled. 1,239 (1940), 3,799 (1950).

Chandler. City in C Oklahoma, county seat of Lincoln County: important processing and shipping point for pecans. It was devastated by a cyclone in 1897. Pop. 2,724 (1950).

Chandler, Albert Benjamin. [Called **"Happy" Chandler.**] b. at Corydon, Ky., July 14, 1898—. American baseball commissioner. Beginning the practice of law at Versailles, Ky., in 1924, he also entered political life, and was elected to the state senate of Kentucky in 1929, to the lieutenant governorship in 1931, and to the gubernatorial office in 1935. In October of the latter year he resigned the governorship and was appointed to fill a vacancy in the Kentucky representation in the U.S. Senate. In November, 1940, he was elected to complete the remainder of that senatorial term, running to January, 1943, and in November, 1942, he won election to a full six-year term. In 1943 he was one of five senators selected by the Senate to inspect and report on battle-front conditions during World War II. In April, 1945, the magnates of organized baseball elected Chandler to the post of baseball commissioner, which he held until 1951.

Chandler, Charles Frederick. b. at Lancaster, Mass., Dec. 6, 1836; d. Aug. 25, 1925. American scientist, professor of chemistry in Columbia University (1877–1910). He was adjunct professor of chemistry and medical jurisprudence in Columbia's College of Physicians and Surgeons at New York in the period 1872–76, and professor there from 1876 to 1897. He was also president of, and professor of organic chemistry at, the New York College of Pharmacy, and was chemist and later president of the Metropolitan Board of Health in the period 1867–84. In 1920 he was awarded the Perkin medal by the Society of Chemical Industries. His work in sanitation (invention of the flush water-closet, control over adulteration of milk), advocacy of compulsory vaccination, measures towards reducing kerosene-lamp explosions, and work in industrial chemistry mark him as one of the leading servants of the public good of the period.

Chandler, Ellen Louise. See **Moulton, Louise Chandler.**

Chandler, Francis Ward. b. at Boston, Sept. 30, 1844; d. Sept. 8, 1926. American architect. He practiced his profession at Boston in the period 1874–88, and was professor of architecture at the Massachusetts Institute of Technology from 1888 and advisory architect to the mayor of Boston from 1896. He published *Construction Details* (1892), *Notes on Limes, Cements, Mortars, and Concretes* (1892), and others.

Chandler, Frank Wadleigh. b. at Brooklyn, N.Y., June 16, 1873; d. at Prouts Neck, Me., June 13, 1947. American professor and writer, chiefly known for his lectures and writings on English literature, comparative literature, and drama. He was a graduate of Brooklyn Polytechnic Institute (B.A., 1894) and of Columbia University (Ph.D., 1899). He taught (1899–1910) at Brooklyn Polytechnic Institute, served (1901–04) as lecturer on comparative literature at Columbia, and was appointed Ropes professor of comparative literature (1910) and dean (1913) of the College of Liberal Arts at the University of Cincinnati. His works include *Romances of Roguery, an Episode in the History of the Novel* (1899), *Aspects of Modern Drama* (1914), *The Contemporary Drama of France* (1920), and *Modern Continental Playwrights* (1931).

Chandler, Raymond Thornton. b. at Chicago, July 23, 1888—. American author of detective stories. Educated abroad, in 1909 he began contributing verse, articles, and reviews to London newspapers and magazines. During World War I he served with the Canadian forces and with the Royal Air Force. After the war, returning to the U.S., he spent some years in the oil business, and when he resumed his literary career in 1933 it was as a contributor of fiction to popular magazines, from which he went on to detective stories of book length, achieving a wide following. Among his better-known titles are *The Big Sleep* (1939), *Farewell, My Lovely* (1940), *The High Window* (1942), *The Lady in the Lake* (1943), *Red Wind* and *Spanish Blood* (1946), and *The Little Sister* (1949).

Chandler, Richard. b. at Elson, Hampshire, England, 1738; d. at Tilehurst, Berkshire, England, 1810. English classical scholar, antiquary, and traveler. Educated at Winchester and at Magdalen College, Oxford, where he was M.A. (1761), doctor of divinity (1773), and fellow (1770), he published *Elegiaca Graeca* (1759), fragments of the Greek lyrists, and *Marmora Oxoniensia* (1763), a description of the Arundel marbles. The latter work won him a commission from the Dilettanti Society to undertake exploration in Asia Minor and Greece. He published the results of his travels (1764–66) in *Ionian Antiquities* (1769), *Inscriptiones Antiquae* (1774), and *Travels* (1775–76). He also wrote *History of Ilium or Troy* (1802), and *The Life of W. Wayneflete, Bishop of Winchester* (1811), and collated manuscripts of Pindar (1787).

Chandler, Seth Carlo. b. at Boston, Sept. 17, 1846; d. at Wellesley, Mass., Dec. 31, 1913. American astronomer. He was a member of the U.S. Coast Survey (now U.S. Coast and Geodetic Survey, Department of Commerce) in the period 1864–70, and conducted private investigations in stellar astronomy from 1886. He edited the *Astronomical Journal* from 1896.

Chandler, William Eaton. b. at Concord, N.H., Dec. 28, 1835; d. there, Nov. 30, 1917. American politician, secretary of the navy (1882–85). He was graduated (1854) from the Harvard Law School; after serving as a court reporter, he entered politics as the controller of the Concord *Monitor and Statesman*. He was a member (1863–65) of the New Hampshire legislature, also serving as speaker of the assembly. He became (1865) solicitor and judge advocate general of the navy department, and served (1865–67) as assistant secretary of the treasury. After his return from Washington, he resumed his law practice and became prominent in Republican politics, serving as secretary of the Republican national committee for Grant's campaigns in 1868 and 1872. He played an outstanding part in the refusal to concede the election of Tilden (1876) and in the electoral contest that finally gave the presidency to Hayes. During his tenure as secretary of the navy under Arthur, he inaugurated the program of building steel vessels, then in an experimental stage in the U.S. He was (1887–1901) a member of the U.S. Senate, and in 1901 was appointed chairman of the Spanish Treaty Claims Commission by McKinley.

Chandler, Zachariah. b. at Bedford, N.H., Dec. 10, 1813; d. at Chicago, Nov. 1, 1879. American politician. He settled (1833) at Detroit, became the owner of a general store, and subsequently amassed a fortune through land speculation, banking, and commerce. He was mayor (1851–52) of Detroit, and was among those who signed the call for the Jackson, Mich., meeting (1854) which is said to have founded the Republican party. He became (1856) a member of the Republican national committee and served (1857–75) in the U.S. Senate, where he emerged as a Radical Republican; was a member of the Joint Committee on the Conduct of the War; and was chairman (1861–75) of the Committee on Commerce, where he used patronage to consolidate his political power. He was the boss of the Republican machine in Michigan, chairman of the Republican Congressional Committee during the campaigns of 1868 and 1876, and served (1875–77) as secretary of the interior under Grant. He was elected (1879) to the Senate to fill a vacant seat, and died in the same year.

Chandor (chän.dōr'). [Also, **Chandur** (-dör').] Fortified town in Bombay state, Union of India, in the Western Ghats at an elevation of ab. 4,000 ft. It was ceded to the British in 1818.

Chandos (chan'dos, shan'-), 1st Duke of. Title of **Brydges, James.**

Chandos, Sir **John.** d. at Mortemer, France, Jan. 1, 1370. English soldier. He served at the siege of Cambrai (1337) and at the battles of Crécy (1346) and Poitiers (1356); at the latter he saved the life of Edward, the Black Prince. Appointed regent and lieutenant of Edward III of England in France in 1360, and constable of Guienne in 1362, he commanded the English forces at the battle of Auray (Oct. 6, 1364), and, with John of Gaunt, led the English advance guard at the battle of Nájera (or Navarrete) on April 3, 1367. At Auray and Nájera, his opponent was Bertrand du Guesclin, constable of France, who was captured at both battles. In 1369 he was made seneschal of Poitiers. He died from the effects of a wound received (Dec. 31, 1369) in an engagement at Lussac, near Poitiers.

Chandos of Sudeley (söd'li), 1st Baron of. Title of **Brydges, John.**

Chandra (chun'dra̩). In Hindu mythology, the moon, either as the satellite or as a deity, the moon god; hence, any eminent or illustrious person (the moon being regarded as the most beautiful of heavenly bodies), as in Chandragupta or Ramachandra.

Chandragupta (chun.dra̩.gu̇p'ta̩). See **Sandrocottus** or **Sandrokottos.**

Chandrakanta (chun.dra̩.kän'ta̩). In Hindu mythology, a fabulous gem, the moonstone, formed from the congelation of the rays of the moon, and dissolving under the influence of its light.

Chandrasekhar (chun.dra̩.shā'ka̩r), **Subrahmanyan.** b. at Lahore, India (now in Pakistan), Oct. 19, 1910—. American astrophysicist, professor of theoretical astrophysics (1944 *et seq.*) at the University of Chicago. He received a Ph.D. (1933) from Cambridge University, England, and came to the U.S. in 1936. He was assistant professor (1938–41) and associate professor (1942–44) of theoretical astrophysics at Chicago and a visiting member (1941) of the Institute for Advanced Study, at Princeton, N.J. His works include *An Introduction to the Study of Stellar Structure* (1939), *Principles of Stellar Dynamics* (1942), and others.

Chané (chä.nā'). [Also, **Chaná.**] Group of Indian tribes, once large but now greatly reduced in numbers, inhabiting several areas in South America, in the W Chaco region, along the foothills of the Andes, between latitudes 18° and 23° S. Of peaceful bent, they were long held in state of vassalage by the neighboring Guaraní-speaking Chiriguano. Their language is of the Arawakan stock.

Chaney (chā'ni), **Lon.** b. at Colorado Springs, Colo., April 1, 1883; d. at Los Angeles, Calif., Aug. 26, 1930. American film actor. He specialized in roles calling for elaborate make-up to simulate ugliness and distortion of appearance, and appeared in a vast number of horror movies. He is perhaps best remembered for the part of Quasimodo, the misshapen hero of *The Hunchback of Notre Dame.* His other vehicles include *The Phantom of the Opera, Miracle Man, The Unholy Three, Thunder,* and *The Shock.*

Chang (chang), **Carson.** [Chinese, **Chang Chün-mai** (chäng' chün'mī').] b. at Paoshan, near Shanghai, China, 1886—. Chinese leader of a defunct minor political party; elder brother of the financier Chang Kia-ngau. He studied political science in Japan, Germany, and England. In 1931 he founded the Chinese National Socialist Party, which joined (1941) with what subsequently (1944) became the Democratic League, but later (1946) he opposed League coöperation with the Communists and permitted his group to join the Kuomintang-dominated government established in April, 1947.

Changan or **Ch'ang-an** (chäng'än'). See **Sian.**

Changarnier (shäṅ.gȧr.nyā), **Nicolas Anne Théodule.** b. at Autun, France, April 26, 1793; d. at Paris, Feb. 14, 1877. French general. He served (1830–48) in Algeria, became governor general there in 1848, was in command (1848–51) at Paris, was banished for his opposition to Napoleon III in 1852, and was with Bazaine at Metz in October, 1870. As a deputy (1871 *et seq.*), he fought the establishment of the Third Republic and supported the attempts to reconstitute the monarchy. He was elected a life senator in 1875.

Chang-Chau (chäng'jō'). See **Changchow;** also **Lungki.**

Chang Chih-chung (chäng' chė'chu̇ng'). b. at Chaohsien, Anhwei, China, Oct. 27, 1890—. Chinese veteran military officer educated in Germany, at one time close to Chiang Kai-shek and the Political Science Clique. He was governor of Hunan province (1937–38) and secretary-general (1939 *et seq.*) to Chiang. He was sent as a troubleshooter to Sinkiang, where he served (July, 1946–June, 1947) as governor. Sent (April, 1949) to Peiping as chairman of the Kuomintang Peace Mission to the Communists, he joined with them, helped swing the northwestern provinces to the Communists, and became (December, 1949) vice-chairman of the Northwest Regional Government of the People's Republic of China.

Chang Ching-hui (chäng' ching'hwā'). b. at Taian, near Mukden, China, 1871—. Chinese military leader and civilian bureaucrat who was a close colleague of the Manchurian warlord Chang Tso-lin. He graduated from a military academy in Manchuria and pursued a military career in Manchuria, Mongolia, and China. Joining the Japanese after their invasion in 1931, he became (1935) premier of the puppet state of Manchukuo, a post which he held until his capture by Soviet forces in 1945.

Changchow (chäng'jō'). See also **Lungki.**

Changchow. [Also: **Chang-chau, Wutsin.**] City in E China, in the province of Kiangsu, ab. 60 mi. SE of Nanking, on the Nanking-Shanghai railroad: important trading center in a silk-growing area. 79,196 (1935).

Chang Ch'ün (jäng' chün'). b. at Huayang, Szechwan, China, 1888—. Chinese leader of the Political Science Clique, who succeeded Huang Fu and was close to Chiang Kai-shek. After holding many military and police posts in Szechwan, Honan, Kwangtung, and elsewhere, he was elected (1929) to the Kuomintang Central Executive Committee. He served as foreign minister (1935–37), governor of Szechwan (1940–47), and head of the Kuomintang delegation to the Political Consultative Conference (1946). After serving (1947–48) as premier he resigned to become (1948) head of Chiang Kai-shek's headquarters in SW China, from which he fled (December, 1949) to Hong Kong and thence to Formosa.

Changchun (chäng'chůn'). [Also: **Hsinking, Kwanchengtze.**] City in NE China, the capital of the province of Kirin, Manchuria, and of the nine Northeastern Provinces comprising Manchuria, 70 mi. W of Kirin, just outside the Willow Wall. It is a major rail and road junction with a large railroad repair shop. Flour milling and the manufacture of cigarettes are important industries. 605,276 (est. 1946).

Change Alley. Alley in the Cornhill district of London, formerly Exchange Alley, leading into Lombard Street. It was the focal point of 18th-century financial transactions, when the Stock Exchange was conducted here at Jonathan's Coffee House. It was the center of action in the South Sea Bubble of 1720, by which many thousands were ruined. Another coffee house in this alley which played a leading role at the time of the South Sea Bubble was Garraway's, so called from Garway, its original proprietor. It was here that tea was first sold at London.

Changeling, The. Play by Thomas Middleton and William Rowley, acted as early as 1623.

Chang Han-fu (chäng' hän'fö'). b. in Kiangsu province, China, c1900—. Chinese Communist leader. During the anti-Japanese war (1937–45) he served as editor in chief of the Communist *Hsin Hua Jih-pao*. He later accompanied (1945) Tung Pi-wu to the U.S. for the United Nations organizing conference and, after serving (1949) as director of the Alien Affairs Bureau under Communist general Ch'en Yi, became (1949) third deputy foreign minister of the People's Republic of China.

Chang Hsi-jo (chäng' shē'jō'). b. at Yulin, Shensi, China, c1889—. Chinese liberal political science professor with wide influence among Chinese intellectuals. He was educated in England and America. After participating (1911) in the Chinese Revolution, he taught political science at Tsinghua University. After the Japanese invasion (1937) he fled to SW China, where he championed liberalism and criticized Chiang Kai-shek. In 1949 he was elected a member of the Central People's Government Council at Peiping.

Chang Hsüeh-liang (chäng' shwe'lyäng'). [Popularly known as the **"Young Marshal."**] b. at Haicheng, Liaoning, China, 1898—. Manchurian military leader who is best known for seizing (1936) Chiang Kai-shek at Sian; son of Chang Tso-lin. Driven (1931) from Manchuria by the Japanese, he was assigned by Chiang Kai-shek to combat the Chinese Communists, but seized (1936) Chiang Kai-shek in order to bring about national military resistance against the Japanese invasion. Convinced that the civil war would give way to united resistance, he released Chiang, was himself arrested by Chiang, and was confined, first at Nanking and later in Formosa.

Changkiakow (chäng'jyä'kō'). [Also: **Changchiakow, Kalgan, Wanchuan.**] City in N China, capital of the province of Chahar, Inner Mongolia, situated on the line of the Great Wall, ab. 120 mi. NW of Peiping. It has important transit trade, especially in tea. 144,829 (1935).

Chang Kia-ngau (chäng' jyä'ngou'). [Peking form, **Chang Chia-ao** (chyä'ou').] b. at Paoshan, near Shanghai, China, Oct. 21, 1888—. Chinese banker and financier, a prominent member of the Political Science Clique; younger brother of Carson Chang. After graduating from Keio University at Tokyo, he held (1917 *et seq.*) many high positions in private concerns and in the Bank of China, the Central Bank of China, the ministry of communications, and the ministry of finance under the Kuomintang.

Changkufeng (chäng'kö'feng'). [Russian, **Zaozernaya.**] Hill in the SE part of the U.S.S.R., in the extreme S part of the *Primorski Krai* (Maritime Territory), on the E bank of the Tumen River ab. 12 mi. above its mouth, near where the borders of Korea, Manchuria, and the U.S.S.R. meet. In July, 1938, Soviet troops built defenses here, which were attacked by Japanese forces from Manchukuo, and captured. The Soviets counterattacked, and fighting ceased on August 10, by an armistice. The hill remains within Soviet territory.

Chang Lan (chäng' län'). b. at Nanchung, Szechwan, China, 1875—. Chinese liberal leader. After helping overthrow (1911) the imperial regime, he held various posts in Szechwan, including governor (1920–21) of the province and president (1928–31) of Chengtu University. Appointed (1938) to the People's Political Council, he increasingly criticized Kuomintang policies, and shortly after the formation (1941) of the Federation of Chinese Democratic Parties became its chairman, continuing in this post when the Federation was renamed (1944) the Democratic League. In 1949 he was elected one of the six vice-chairmen of the Central People's Government Council in the Peiping government.

Chango (chäng'gō). [Also: **Chiango, Chaonco.**] Extinct Indian tribe of the N Chilean coast of which nothing much is known other than that its members were fishers and hunters of the sea lion. The term is now applied to the poorer peoples of this region who live by fishing and horticulture.

Changpai Shan (chäng'bī' shän'). [Also: **Changpai, Ch'ang-pai, Chang Pai Shan.**] Mountain range in SE Manchuria, China, just N of the Korean border. The mountains are high and rugged, and extensively forested. The peak elevation is ab. 8,992 ft. Length of range, ab. 85 mi.

Chang Po-ling (chäng' pō'ling'). b. at Tientsin, China, 1874; d. 1951. Chinese educator, associated with Chang Tso-lin and with Chiang Kai-shek. He founded (1920) Nankai University, which he built up from a lower school originally established (1904) by him. He has held several political posts, including vice-president (1938–45) of the People's Political Council and president (1948) of the Examination Yuan.

Changsha (chäng'shä'). City in SE China, the capital of the province of Hunan, on the Siang River ab. 550 mi. W by SW of Shanghai. It was a treaty port, opened to foreign commerce in 1903. The city is located opposite a sand bar in the river; the name means the city of the "long sand." There is much coal in the area but little of it is mined. 421,616 (est. 1947).

Archaeological Discoveries. Excavations there (1936–37) brought to light a series of tombs which yielded important materials for the study of Chou culture. Earliest were the deep shaft tombs of the late Chou period (770–256 B.C.). Sunk as much as 25 or 30 ft. below the surface, some had wooden chambers which had been well preserved because they lay below the water table; they contained painted wood sculpture of remarkable spirit and quality, the earliest known lacquers, and a considerable variety of jades, bronzes, and ceramics. The most important object associated with these early tombs is a piece of silk about two feet square on which is written with brush and ink an as yet undeciphered text of some 980 characters surrounded by a border of figures painted in colors. The curious representations of animal and human forms are in keeping with some of the other early Changsha materials and hint at the presence of certain non-Chinese elements in this cultural outpost of late Chou. The second group of tombs, large, vaulted structures of brick covered with tumuli some 15 ft. high, date from the Han and early Six dynasties, and yielded bronzes, ceramics, carved talc ornaments, and glass. The latest group consisted of shallow graves without structural features, they contained miscellaneous bronzes and ceramics from the 6th to the 14th centuries.

Changshu (chäng'shö'). City in E China, in the province of Kiangsu, ab. 40 mi. NW of Shanghai. A large trading city, it is important for cotton and silk products and has plants for making rice wine. 102,734 (est. 1935).

Changteh (chäng'du'). City in S central China, in N central Hunan province ab. 200 mi. SW of Hankow. The city is located at the foot of the Wuling Mountains on the N bank of the Yuan River where it emerges upon the plain. It has an active entrepôt commerce, as only flat-bottomed boats can navigate upstream, because of rapids. Rice, fruit, opium, tung oil, and vegetable tallow are produced in the region, and cotton goods are also exported. Salt, petroleum products, and varnish are imports. During World War II a Japanese attack on Changteh was decisively repulsed by Chinese armies, but the city was almost totally destroyed (December, 1943). 300,000 (est. 1947).

Chang Tso-lin (jäng' tsō'lin'). b. at Haicheng, Liaoning, China, 1873; assassinated en route to Mukden, China, 1928. Chinese warlord who controlled Manchuria from

1911 to 1928; father of Chang Hsüeh-liang. Starting as a bandit leader in Manchuria, he fought in the Russo-Japanese War (1904–05) on the side of Japan; then entered the Chinese imperial military service, rose in power, and took over Manchuria after the 1911 revolution. He bested rival warlords to control (1920–22 and 1924–28) Peiping, the capital of China, but was driven out by Nationalist troops and withdrew to Manchuria, where he was killed (1928) by the Japanese, who bombed his train.

Chania (ċhä.nyä′). See **Canea.**

Chankiang (chän′jyäng′). See **Kwangchowan.**

Chankiri (chäng.ki.ri′). See **Çankiri.**

Channel (chan′ẹl). Village in SW Newfoundland, on the S coast ab. 1 mi. S of the rail terminus at Port-aux-Basques. It is a fishing village. 1,309 (1945).

Channel Islands. [Also: **Norman Isles;** French, **Îles Anglo-Normandes, Îles Normandes.**] Group of islands in the English Channel, belonging to Great Britain, 7–30 mi. from the coast of Normandy, France, near the Bay of St.-Malo. They comprise Jersey, Guernsey, Alderney, Sark, and a number of islets, some of which are uninhabited. They are noted for their picturesque scenery and mild climate. Jersey, Guernsey, and Alderney are each noted for a particular breed of cattle. The chief industry is the growing of early fruits and vegetables for the British market. Both English and Norman-French are spoken, the latter being the official language. English is gradually replacing Norman-French as the language of the people, especially on Jersey and on Guernsey. The Channel Islands were occupied by the Germans (June, 1940–May, 1945) during World War II. They came under Norman rule early in the 10th century, and were Norman and English after 1066. They are the only part of Normandy to be retained by the English after 1204. They are ruled by lieutenant governors for the King of England in his capacity of Duke of Normandy. Jersey and Guernsey (with its dependencies) each have separate legislatures. Area, 75 sq. mi., pop. 93,205 (1931).

Channing (chan′ing), **Edward.** b. at Dorchester, Mass., June 15, 1856; d. at Cambridge, Mass., Jan. 7, 1931. American historian; son of the poet William Ellery Channing (1818–1901). He was graduated (B.A., 1878; Ph.D., 1880) from Harvard University, where he served as instructor (1883–87), assistant professor (1887–97), and professor (1897–1913) of history, and McLean professor (1913 *et seq.*) of ancient and modern history. His writings include *Town and County Government in the English Colonies of North America* (1884), *The Narragansett Planter* (1886), *The Navigation Laws* (1890), *The United States of America, 1765–1865* (1896), *First Lessons in United States History* (1903), and *History of the United States* in six volumes covering the years 1000–1865 published (1905–25) separately, for the last volume (*The War for Southern Independence*) of which he was awarded (1925) the Pulitzer prize.

Channing, Edward Tyrrell. b. at Newport, R.I., Dec. 12, 1790; d. at Cambridge, Mass., Feb. 8, 1856. American scholar; brother of the clergyman William Ellery Channing (1780–1842). He was one of the founders of the *North American Review* in 1815, and served (1819–51) as Boylston professor of rhetoric and oratory at Yale. Emerson, Holmes, Parkman, Motley, Lowell, and Edward Everett Hale were among his students.

Channing, Grace Ellery. [Also, **Channing-Stetson.**] b. at Providence, R.I., Dec. 27, 1862; d. April 4, 1937. American writer; daughter of William Francis Channing (1820–1901) and wife (1894 *et seq.*) of Charles Walter Stetson (d. 1911). She was the editor of *Dr. Channing's Note Book* and *War Letters of Edmond Genet* (1918), and author of *The Sister of a Saint* (1895), *The Fortune of a Day* (1900), and *Sea Drift* (1899), a volume of verse.

Channing, Walter. b. at Newport, R.I., April 15, 1786; d. July 27, 1876. American obstetrician, a pioneer in the use of ether in childbirth; brother of the clergyman William Ellery Channing. He was first professor (1815 *et seq.*) of obstetrics and medical jurisprudence and dean (1819–47) at the Harvard Medical School, took part (1832) in the founding of the Boston Lying-In Hospital, and was coeditor (1828) with John Ware of the Boston *Medical and Surgical Journal.* In 1847 he began to use ether in childbirth cases. His works include *Six Cases of Inhalation of Ether in Labor* (1847) and *Treatise on Etherization in Childbirth* (1848).

Channing, William Ellery. b. at Newport, R.I., April 7, 1780; d. at Bennington, Vt., Oct. 2, 1842. American Unitarian clergyman and writer, noted for his prominent role in the "Unitarian Controversy" in New England and for his influence upon the intellectual life of that region; brother of Edward Tyrrell Channing (1790–1856), father of William Francis Channing (1820–1901), and uncle of William Ellery Channing (1818–1901) and William Henry Channing (1810–84). Graduated (1798) from Harvard, he joined its staff in 1802 and in the following year was ordained and installed as minister of the Federal Street Church at Boston, holding that post until his death. When sharp differences arose (c1815) among the New England Congregationalists, he at first took an independent position, looking with reluctance upon the formation of a new sect, and then became the leader of the Unitarian party, defending it in a sermon (1819) which created a wide stir. He organized (1820) the Berry Street Conference of ministers from which grew (1825) the American Unitarian Association. His revolt against New England orthodoxy, as expressed in his noted sermon "The Moral Argument against Calvinism," placed him on the side of a liberal interpretation of Christian doctrine; its broad humanity and embrace of reason in faith affected writers such as Longfellow, Emerson, and Holmes. An anti-slavery man, he believed the question could be solved by moral reform rather than by forcible means. His writings include *American Literature* (1830), in which he called for a school of native writers freed from colonial ties, *Slavery* (1835), *The Abolitionist* (1836), *Open Letter to Henry Clay* (1837), and *Duty of the Free States* (1842).

Channing, William Ellery. b. Nov. 29, 1818; d. Dec. 23, 1901. American poet, journalist, and general writer; nephew of William Ellery Channing (1780–1842) and father of Edward Channing (1856–1931). He was the author of *Poems* (1843), *Poems, Second Series* (1847), *The Woodman and Other Poems* (1849), *The Wanderer* (1871), *Thoreau, The Poet-Naturalist* (1873; enlarged ed., 1902), *Eliot* (1885), and *John Brown and the Heroes of Harper's Ferry* (1886).

Channing, William Francis. b. at Boston, Feb. 22, 1820; d. March 19, 1901. American inventor; son of the clergyman William Ellery Channing (1780–1842) and father of Grace Ellery Channing (1862–1937). He patented (1857), with Moses G. Farmer, an electric fire-alarm system, patented (1865) a ship railway for the inter-oceanic transportation of ships, and invented (1877) a portable electromagnetic telegraph. Author of *Notes on the Medical Application of Electricity* (1849), "On the Municipal Electric Telegraph," in the *American Journal of Science and Arts* (1852), and "The American Fire Alarm Telegraph" in *Smithsonian Institution Annual Report* (1854).

Channing, William Henry. b. at Boston, May 25, 1810; d. at London, Dec. 23, 1884. American Unitarian minister and writer; nephew of the clergyman William Ellery Channing (1780–1842). He was graduated from Harvard College in 1829 and from the Cambridge Divinity School in 1833. In 1857 he succeeded James Martineau as minister of the Hope Street Unitarian Chapel at Liverpool, England. Returned to the U.S. in 1861, he filled a Unitarian pulpit at Washington, D.C., going again to England soon after the end of the Civil War. He was interested in the Brook Farm experiment, contributed to *The Harbinger*, and with Emerson and J. F. Clarke wrote *Memoirs of Margaret Fuller Ossoli* (1852). He also published a translation of Jouffroy's *Ethics* (1840), *Life of William Ellery Channing* (1848), and others.

Chanson de Roland (shäṅ.sôṅ dẹ ro.läṅ). [Eng. trans., *Song of Roland;* also **Chanson de Roncevaux,** meaning in English, "Song of Roncevaux."] French epic poem, or *chanson de geste*, ascribed to Théroulde or Turoldus, an unidentified Norman who probably lived in the 11th century. It was first published as a whole by M. P. Michel in 1837. The Oxford manuscript gives its earliest form. The text of this manuscript is probably that of the end of the 11th century; the date of the manuscript probably the middle of the 12th. It contains ab. 4,000 lines, and is the story of the death of Roland with the peers of Charlemagne at Roncevaux or Roncesvalles in the Pyrenees, and of Charlemagne's vengeance. The treason of Ganelon and his miserable death and the refusal of Roland to blow his horn to summon aid until his friend Oliver has been killed are the best-known of the incidents related in the poem.

Chanson du roi Dagobert (dü rwȧ dȧ.go.ber). See **Dagobert, Chanson du roi.**

Chantaburi (chän″tạ.bu.rē′). [Also: **Chandaburi, Chanthaburi, Chantabon** (chän.tạ.bōn′), **Chantabun** (chän.tạ.bön′).] City in Thailand (Siam), situated near the Gulf of Thailand, ab. 150 mi. SE of Bangkok. It is a small trading center with a port, and is served by one highway. Pop. ab. 5,000.

Chantada (chän.tä′ᴛʜä). Town in NW Spain, in the province of Lugo, ab. 30 mi. SW of Lugo. It is a market town for grain, flax, potatoes, and dairy produce, and has small industries. 15,127 (1940).

Chantal (shäṅ.tȧl), Saint. [Also: Saint **Jane Frances de Chantal**; original name, **Jeanne Françoise Frémiot,** Baronne **de Chantal.**] b. at Dijon, France, Jan. 28, 1572; d. at Moulins, France, Dec. 13, 1641. French religious, founder of the Order of the Visitation at Annecy in 1610.

Chantavoine (shäṅ.tȧ.vwȧn), **Henri.** b. at Montpellier, France, 1850; d. near Lyons, France, Aug. 15, 1918. French historian and poet. He served as a professor at Paris and Sèvres. Author of *Poèmes sincères* (Sincere Poetry, 1877), *Satires contemporaines* (Contemporary Satires, 1881), and *Les Principes de 1789* (Principles of 1789, 1908).

Chant du départ (shän dü dā.pȧr). [Eng. trans., *Song of Departure.*] French military song with words (1794) by Marie Joseph Chénier and music by Étienne Nicolas Méhul.

Chanteloup (shäṅ.tẹ.lö), Comte **de.** Title of **Chaptal, Jean Antoine.**

Chanti (chän′tē). See **Ostyak.**

Chanticleer (chan′ti.klir). Cock who is the hero of "The Nun's Priest's Tale" in Geoffrey Chaucer's *The Canterbury Tales.* The same name is also given to the cock in the medieval stories dealing with Reynard the Fox.

Chantilly (shäṅ.tē.yē; Anglicized, shan.til′i). Town in N France, in the department of Oise, ab. 23 mi. NE of Paris. It is noted for its lace manufactures, horse races, entertainments, and its castles. The small castle was built for Duke Anne de Montmorency (c1493–1567); Louis II, the "Great" Condé, had the gardens designed by Lenôtre; later additions are from the 18th century. The great castle, destroyed during the French Revolution, was rebuilt in the 19th century. Henri d'Orléans, Duc d'Aumale, combined various valuable collections and donated them (1886) to the Institut de France. They are now contained in the Musée de Condé and housed in the castle. The large forest of Chantilly lies S of the town. 6,002 (1946).

Chantilly (shan.til′i). Village in Fairfax County, Va., ab. 20 mi. W of Washington, D.C. It was the scene of a battle, Sept. 1, 1862, between the Confederates under "Stonewall" Jackson, and a part of Pope's army, retreating from the second battle of Bull Run, under Jesse Reno, Isaac I. Stevens, and Philip Kearny (the two latter were killed). Loss of the Union army, 1,300; of the Confederates, 800.

Chantre (shäṅtr), **Ernest.** b. at Lyons, France, Jan. 13, 1845; d. at Ecully, near Lyons, France, Nov. 24, 1924. French archaeologist who served as assistant director of the museum at Lyons and also as a professor at Lyons. He was the author of *Age du fer* (The Iron Age, 1880), and *Recherches anthropologiques dans le Caucase* (Anthropological Researches in the Caucasus, 1895–97).

Chantrey (chan′tri), Sir **Francis Legatt.** b. near Norton, Derbyshire, England, April 7, 1781; d. Nov. 25, 1841. English portrait sculptor and painter. He is known chiefly for his portrait sculpture, his sitters including many of the most distinguished men of his time. The greater part of his property was left to the Royal Academy to establish a fund for the purchase of the most meritorious work in sculpture and painting executed in Great Britain by artists of any nation.

Chanukah (ċhä′nu̇.kä). See **Hanukkah.**

Chanute (shạ.nöt′). City in SE Kansas, in Neosho County, on the Neosho River, ab. 42 mi. SW of Fort Scott: oil refineries, cement works, railway repair shops, and poultry hatcheries. Incorporated in 1872, it was named for Octave Chanute. 10,109 (1950).

Chanute, Octave. b. at Paris, Feb. 18, 1832; d. at Chicago, Nov. 23, 1910. American civil engineer and experimenter in aviation. He came to the U.S. in 1838, was engaged for many years in the construction of railroads, and was president of the American Society of Civil Engineers in the period 1891–92. In 1894 he published his *Progress in Flying Machines,* a study of the experiments hitherto made in aviation, and in 1896 instituted further experiments with various forms of gliding machine, and devised means of securing equilibrium by automatic movements of the machine. His design and his active encouragement and advice were acknowledged as being of aid in their work by the Wright brothers.

Chanzy (shäṅ.zē), **Antoine Eugène Alfred.** b. at Nouart, Ardennes, France, March 18, 1823; d. at Châlons-sur-Marne, France, Jan. 4, 1883. French general. He became commander of division in October, 1870, and of the 2d Army of the Loire in December, 1870. Distinguished in the battles near Orléans (December, 1870), he was defeated at Le Mans (Jan. 10–12, 1871). In 1873 he became governor general of Algeria. In 1879 Chanzy received a large number of votes for the French presidency but was defeated by Jules Grévy.

Chaoan (chou′än′). [Former names, **Chaochow** (chou′-jō′), **Chaochowfu** (chou′jō′fö′).] City in SE China, in the province of Kwangtung, ab. 20 mi. N of Swatow, on the Han River. It is a river port and important trading center, with plants for the processing of sugar and tobacco. The largest crop in the area is rice. 179,068 (est. 1935).

Chao-Nam (chou′näm′). Siamese name of **Orang Laut.**

Chaonco (chä.ông′kō). See **Chango.**

Chao Phraya (chou′ prä.yä′). See **Menam.**

Chao P'ya Chakri (chou′ pyä′ chä.krē′). See **Rama I.**

Chaos (kā′os). In Greek mythology, the original formless state of the universe; or, the deity presiding over it. Perhaps no other myth exhibits quite so much confusion and variety as are found in the concepts of Chaos. The one thing common to all versions was the idea of infinite space in which matter existed without form and in complete darkness; to some of the ancient poets, this was Chaos, and alone existed, but others said that Earth and Eros were coeval with Chaos. In some cosmogonies, the first of all things was Chronos (Time), from whom proceeded Chaos and Aether (Light, or the upper air). But in another formulation, Chaos was the deity presiding over the formless mass with his wife Nyx (Night). Their son Erebus (Darkness) slew or dethroned Chaos and married his mother; from this union came Aether and Hemera (Day), who with the aid of their son Eros (Love) created Pontus (the Sea) and Gaea (the Earth). But in other accounts, Gaea proceeded directly from Chaos, and was the mother of Eros as well as of Tartarus (the Nether World).

Chaos Islands (shä′os). See **Bird Islands.**

Chaoyang (chou′yäng′). City in SE China, in the province of Kwangtung, across the bay from Swatow: a port and trading center with important fisheries; manufactures of pewter ware and sugar. 127,714 (est. 1935).

Chapaevsk (chä.pä′yifsk). [Also: **Chapayevsk;** former name, **Ivashchenkovo.**] City in the U.S.S.R., in the Kuibyshev *oblast* (region) of the Russian Soviet Federated Socialist Republic, ab. 185 mi. NE of Sartov, on the Volga River. Machine construction and food industries are important here, and the city is the terminus of two oil pipe lines. 57,995 (1939).

Chapais (shȧ.pe), **Jean Charles.** b. 1811; d. 1885. Canadian statesman; father of Sir Thomas Chapais. Known as one of the "Fathers of Confederation," he sat in the Canadian legislative assembly (1851–67) and was appointed to the senate in 1868. He was commissioner of public works (1864–67), minister of agriculture (1867–69), and receiver-general (1869–73) in the first Dominion government.

Chapais, Sir Thomas. [Full name, Sir **Joseph Amable Thomas Chapais.**] b. at Saint Denis de la Bouteillerie, Quebec, Canada, 1858; d. 1946. Canadian public man and historian; son of Jean Charles Chapais (1811–85). He was editor of *Le Courier du Canada* (1884–1901), and entered political life by accepting appointment (1892) to the provincial legislative council, of which he served as speaker (1895) before becoming president (1896) of the executive council. In 1897 he turned from active participation in public affairs to take the chair of professor of history at Laval University, Quebec, but in 1919 he accepted appointment to the Canadian senate, and in 1930 he represented the Dominion in the Assembly of the League of Nations. The French government made him a chevalier of the Legion of Honor (1902) and he was knighted by the British government (1935). His historical biographies, *L'Intendant Talon* (1905) and *Montcalm* (1911), brought a new manner to the writing of French Canadian history, and prepared the way for the success of his four-volume *Cours d'histoire du Canada* (1919–23).

Chapala (chä.pä'lä), **Lake.** Lake in SW Mexico, chiefly in the state of Jalisco. Area, over 1,300 sq. mi.

Chapdelaine (shå.dẹ.len), **Maria.** See **Maria Chapdelaine.**

Chapeau de Paille (shå.pō dẹ påy'). [Eng. trans., "*Straw Hat.*"] Painting by Peter Paul Rubens, in the National Gallery, London. It is a half-length portrait of a young girl robed in black velvet and crimson, and wearing a broad-brimmed plumed hat which shades the face completely, yet without obscuring the vivid coloring.

Chapelain (shå.plañ), **Jean.** b. at Paris, Dec. 4, 1595; d. there, Feb. 22, 1674. French poet and littérateur. One of the first members of the French Academy, he was influential in determining its policies. He was the author of *La Pucelle* (1656), an epic about Joan of Arc.

Chapel Hill. Town in C North Carolina, in Orange County, ab. 25 mi. NW of Raleigh: seat of the University of North Carolina. In the decade between the last two U.S. censuses, its population more than doubled. 3,654 (1940), 9,177 (1950).

Chaperon Rouge (shåp.rôñ rözh), **Le.** French name of **Red Ridinghood, Little.**

Chapí (chä.pē'), **Ruperto.** [Full surname, **Chapí y Lorente** (ē lō.ren'tā).] b. at Villena, Spain, March 27, 1851; d. at Madrid, March 25, 1909. Spanish composer of light operas and of several serious operas, such as *Margarita la Tornera.* He also wrote chamber music, piano pieces, and symphonic works.

Chapin (chā'pin), **Chester William.** b. at Ludlow, Mass., Dec. 16, 1798; d. June 10, 1883. American railroad promoter. Coowner, with Horatio Sargeant, of the Brattleboro and Hartford stage line, he also became owner of steamship lines on the Connecticut River and Long Island Sound from Hartford and New Haven to New York, a stockholder in the Western Railroad (now part of the Boston and Albany), president (1850–54) of the Connecticut River Railroad, and president (1854–77) of the Boston and Albany Railroad. He was elected (1844) to the Massachusetts legislature, to the Massachusetts constitutional convention of 1853, and to Congress in 1874.

Chapin, James. [Full name, **James Ormsbee Chapin.**] b. at West Orange, N.J., July 9, 1887—. American landscape and portrait painter and lithographer, known for his portraits of the Marvin family and others, as well as for his scenes of American life. He was educated at the Cooper Union Art School, the Art Students League of New York, and the Royal Academy of Art at Antwerp, and has exhibited at the Museum of Modern Art and the Whitney Museum at New York, the Art Institute of Chicago, the Carnegie Institute, the Pennsylvania Academy of the Fine Arts, and elsewhere. He lived for many years on a farm in New Jersey with the Marvin family, whom he used as subjects for many paintings. Among his better-known works are *Motherhood, Portrait of Emmet Marvin, George Marvin and His Daughter, Hubbard Squash, Two Calves, Batter Up, Pretzelman, The Fox Hunter, Planting Potatoes, Grindstone,* and *Negro Girl.*

Chapin, Roy Dikeman. b. at Lansing, Mich., Feb. 23, 1880; d. Feb. 16, 1936. American industrialist and cabinet member. He attended (1899–1901) the University of Michigan, and began (1901) his career in the automobile industry. After working as general sales manager (1904–06) of the Olds Motor Works, he founded (1906) the E. R. Thomas-Detroit Company and served (1906–10) as treasurer and general manager of it and its successor, the Chalmers-Detroit Motor Company. From this post he went (1910) to the Hudson Motor Company as president (to 1923) and chairman of the board (1923–32). He served as secretary of commerce (1932–33) under President Hoover, returning to Hudson in 1933 as president.

"Chaplain Smith." See **Smith, Hezekiah.**

Chaplin (chap'lin), **Charles.** b. at Les Andelys, Eure, France, June 8, 1825; d. at Paris, Jan. 30, 1891. French painter and engraver, of English parentage, naturalized in France. He was a pupil of Michel Drolling.

Chaplin, Charles Spencer. b. at London, April 16, 1889—. American motion-picture actor, producer, and director, internationally famous for his role of the tramp character known as Charlie. His first stage appearance was made as a child, playing Billy in *The Painful Predicament of Sherlock Holmes;* in 1910 he arrived in the U.S. with Fred Karno's vaudeville act. He made his screen debut in 1914 with the Keystone Film Company, and during the next few years made such pictures as *Tillie's Punctured Romance, The Count, Easy Street,* and *The Cure.* He built (1918) his own Hollywood studios, First National Films, and later (1923) was one of the founders of United Artists. He produced and starred in *A Dog's Life, The Kid, The Gold Rush, The Circus, City Lights* (1931), *Modern Times* (1936), *The Great Dictator* (1940), *Monsieur Verdoux* (1947), *Limelight* (1952), and other films. Chaplin has injected social satire in all his films, especially through the adventures of his hero, the tramp. His appearance has included a tilted derby hat, a small mustache, baggy trousers, and large shoes; he carries a bamboo cane and has an awkward walk. Always acted in pantomime (Chaplin on the screen did not speak until *The Great Dictator,* a film in which he did not assume the tramp identity), the character is one of enormous tenderness and trust, with an irrepressible affection for all of mankind. This naïveté again and again leads him into incredibly dangerous situations, from all of which he emerges triumphant, rescued, as it were, by his own simple goodness. Chaplin's activities in the political arena, and his failure to become a U.S. citizen, exasperated a section of American opinion; in 1952, after he had left the U.S. for a journey abroad, steps were taken to bar his readmittance to the country.

Chaplin, Jeremiah. b. at Rowley, Mass., Jan. 2, 1776; d. at Hamilton, N.Y., May 7, 1841. American Baptist clergyman and educator. He was the first president of Waterville Literary (now Colby) College in Maine, in the period 1821–33.

Chapman (chap'mạn), **Frank Michler.** b. at Englewood, N.J., June 12, 1864; d. at New York, Nov. 15, 1945. American ornithologist. He was associate curator (1888–1908) of ornithology and mammalogy and curator (1908 *et seq.*) of ornithology in the American Museum of Natural History at New York, and editor and founder of *Bird-Lore* and associate editor of *The Auk.* He published *Handbook of Birds of Eastern North America* (1895), *Bird-Life* (1897), *Bird Studies with a Camera* (1900), *A Color Key to North American Birds* (1903), *The Economic Value of Birds to the State* (1903), *Warblers of North America* (1907), *Camps and Cruises of an Ornithologist* (1908), and others.

Chapman, George. b. near Hitchin, Hertfordshire, England, c1559; buried at London, in the parish of St. Giles-in-the-Fields, May 12, 1634. English poet and dramatist, chiefly celebrated for his translation of Homer. He is said to have studied at Oxford and afterward at Cambridge. He lived, according to report, in straitened circumstances, but was intimate with Ben Jonson, John Fletcher, and other prominent figures of the time. Among his dramatic works are *The Blind Beggar of Alexandria* (printed in 1598), *All Fools* (produced c1598, printed in 1605), *Eastward Ho!* with Jonson and John Marston (printed 1605) which, because of its satire on the Scottish nobility surrounding James I, caused the authors' imprisonment, *The Gentleman-Usher* (printed 1606), *Monsieur d'Olive* (printed 1606), *Bussy d'Ambois* (printed 1607), *The Revenge of Bussy d'Ambois* (printed 1613), *The Conspiracy and Tragedy of Charles, Duke of Byron* (1608), *May Day* (printed 1611), *The Widow's Tears* (printed 1612), *Caesar and Pompey* (printed 1631), and *The Tragedy of Chabot, Admiral of France* with James Shirley (printed 1639). He completed Marlowe's fragment of *Hero and Leander* in 1598. The first part of his translation of the *Iliad* was published in 1598; the whole was not issued before 1609 (entered on the Stationers' Register in 1611). The translation of the *Odyssey* was entered on the Stationers' Register in 1614. Finally, the *Iliad* and *Odyssey* were issued together with the date 1616 on Chapman's portrait prefixed. He translated also the Homeric hymns, Petrarch, Musaeus, Hesiod, and Juvenal.

Chapman, John. [Called **"Johnny Appleseed."**] b. in Leominster, Mass., Sept. 26, 1775; d. in Allen County, Ind., in March, 1845. American pioneer in the Northwest Territory, subject of many legends, and now a major folklore hero. In the last years of the 18th century he is said to have had a large nursery in Pennsylvania, where he sold saplings or apple seeds to migrants en route to the West, or gave them without charge to those who would not buy. He collected the residue of cider presses, sorted out the seeds, dried them, and did them up in bags. Some time between 1800 and 1806, acting as volunteer missionary for the Swedenborgian Church of New Jerusalem, he loaded two canoes with these bags of apple seed, and paddled down the Ohio and up the Muskingum River, planting orchards at what he judged to be suitable locations. Thereafter during 40 years he wandered through Ohio, Indiana, and Illinois, pruning these orchards, making further plantations, and pressing apple seeds upon all the frontier settlers. At night, by the light of candles or of logs in the fireplace, he read Swedenborg to all who would listen. He may never have gone about, as some stories imply, clad only in burlap bags with holes cut for head, arms, and legs, but it is evident that he neglected all niceties of dress. His eccentricities made him a marked character in the then frontier regions, and his eagerness to help in the planting and care of orchards made him everywhere welcome, the more so because it was known that during the War of 1812 he had saved the people of Mansfield, Ohio, from massacre at the hands of Indians, by a perilous night-long journey through the wilderness. "Johnny Appleseed" also scattered such medicinal herbs as catnip, rattlesnake weed, pennyroyal, and hoarhound throughout the region. The ragged, gentle, tramplike character of folk tradition is the subject of many works of literature, music, and art, including Vachel Lindsay's "In Praise of Johnny Appleseed" in the *Century Magazine* (1921). Monuments have been erected in his honor at Leominster and Springfield, Mass., Ashland, Dexter City, and Mansfield, Ohio, and Fort Wayne, Ind., and numerous other memorials exist.

Chapman, John. b. at Nottingham, England, 1822; d. at Paris, Nov. 25, 1894. English physician, publisher, editor, and medical and scientific writer. He studied medicine at Paris and London, and received his degree (1857) from St. Andrews. Owner and editor (1851 *et seq.*) of the *Westminster Review*, where George Eliot was his assistant editor for two years, he retired from publishing in 1860, and went to Paris in 1874, where he spent the remainder of his life. He was editor and publisher of *Chapman's Library for the People* (1851–54); author of *Human Nature* (1844), *Characteristics of Men of Genius* (1847), *The Bookselling System* (1852), and *Prostitution* (1870).

Chapman, John Gadsby. b. at Alexandria, Va., Dec. 8, 1808; d. at Brooklyn, N.Y., Nov. 28, 1889. American painter, etcher, and wood engraver. He was elected a national academician in 1836, and lived at Rome in the period 1848–90. Among his works is *The Baptism of Pocahontas*, in the rotunda of the Capitol at Washington, D.C. His text, *The American Drawing Book* (1847), is considered one of the best ever written.

Chapman, John Jay. b. at New York, March 2, 1862; d. at Poughkeepsie, N.Y., Nov. 3, 1933. American essayist, poet, and playwright. Graduated (1884) from Harvard, he was admitted (1888) to the bar and practiced until 1898. His works include *Emerson and Other Essays* (1898), *Causes and Consequences* (1898), *Practical Agitation* (1900), *Learning and Other Essays* (1911), *Neptune's Isle* (1912), *William Lloyd Garrison* (1913), *Memories and Milestones* (1915), *Greek Genius and Other Essays* (1915), *A Glance Toward Shakespeare* (1922), *Letters and Religion* (1923), and *Dante* (1927). He also wrote *Four Plays for Children* (1908) and the verse plays *The Maid's Forgiveness* (1908), *A Sausage from Bologna* (1909), and *Benedict Arnold* (1911), as well as a volume of verse, *Songs and Other Poems* (1919). *John Jay Chapman and His Letters* (1937) was edited by M. A. DeWolfe Howe.

Chapman, John Stanton Higham. [Pseudonym (with Mary Hamilton Ilsley Chapman), **Maristan Chapman.**] b. at London, May 21, 1891—. American novelist and aeronautical engineer, husband (married 1917) of Mary Hamilton Ilsley Chapman (b. at Chattanooga, Tenn., Sept. 10, 1895—). Before his arrival (1917) in the U.S. and naturalization (1926), he had served (1914–17) in the British Army Reserve Air Service, from which he transferred (1917) to the U.S. Signal Corps. He is the author, with his wife, of *Happy Mountain* (1928), *Homeplace* (1929), *Imperial Brother* (1931), *Timber Trail* (1933), *Eagle Cliff* (1934), *Rogues on Red Hill* (1937), *Green Garnet Mystery* (1945), *Mystery of Horseshoe Caves* (1947), and other novels.

Chapman, Nathaniel. b. at Summer Hill, Va., May 28, 1780; d. July 1, 1853. American physician. A pupil (1797) of Dr. Benjamin Rush, he received his M.D. (1801) from the University of Pennsylvania and settled (1804) at Philadelphia. On the staff (1810–50) of the Medical School of the University of Pennsylvania, he founded (1817) the Medical Institute of Philadelphia, the first postgraduate medical school in America. He served as editor (1820 *et seq.*) of the *Journal of Medical and Physical Sciences* (later known as the *American Journal of the Medical Sciences*) and was first president (1848) of the American Medical Association. Author of *Elements of Therapeutics and Materia Medica* (1817) and *A Compendium of Lectures on the Theory and Practice of Medicine* (1846).

Chapman, Oscar Littleton. b. at Omega, Va., Oct. 22, 1896—. American administrator, U.S. secretary of the interior (1949–53) under Truman. He served (1922–27) as a probation officer in the Denver juvenile court presided over by Judge Ben Lindsey. In May, 1933, he became assistant secretary of the interior and one of the "Little Cabinet" advisers of President Franklin Roosevelt. Chapman was entrusted with a number of special assignments by the administration, for example heading war bond drives, and in 1946 became undersecretary of the interior department. In 1949, after the resignation of Julius Krug, he became secretary of the interior.

Chapman, Sir **Sydney John.** b. at Wells, Norfolk, England, April 20, 1871—. English political economist. He served as professor (1901–17) of political economy at Owens College at Manchester, assistant secretary (1918–19) and permanent secretary (1920–27) of the board of trade, head economic adviser (1927–32) to the British government, member (1927–32) of the imperial shipping committee, and member (1932–39) of the import duties advisory committee. He is the author of *The Lancashire Cotton Industry* (1904), *The Cotton Industry and Trade* (1905), and *Outlines of Political Economy* (1911).

Chappe (shȧp), **Claude.** b. at Brûlon, France, 1763; d. at Paris, Jan. 23, 1805. French engineer. He was the coinventor of a system of telegraphy much used in France before the coming of the electric telegraph. The instrument used in this system consisted of movable arms affixed to a horizontal bar atop a vertical post; these arms were manipulated to represent words and letters according to an agreed code, and over a line of these machines spaced out but visible one from another, a message could be sent over hundreds of miles in a few minutes. During the French Revolution the Legislative Assembly approved of this system and appointed Claude Chappe to the post of ingénieur-télégraphe; but doubts cast on the originality of the invention preyed upon his mind and his death, it is believed, was by suicide.

Chappe d'Auteroche (dō.trosh), **Jean.** b. at Mauriac, Cantal, France, March 2, 1722; d. in California, Aug. 1, 1769. French astronomer. He observed the transit of Venus at Tobolsk in 1761 (described in *Voyage en Sibérie*, 1768), and went to California in 1769 to observe another transit (described in *Voyage de la Californie*, 1772), but died soon after his arrival.

Chappell (chap'ẹl), **William.** b. at London, Nov. 20, 1809; d. there, Aug. 20, 1888. English music publisher and historian. Successor (1834) to his father, Samuel Chappell (1776–1834) as head of Chappell and Company, Limited, a music-publishing firm, he was also a founder (1840) of the Musical Antiquarian Society. He was the author of *Popular Music of the Olden Time* (2 vols., 1855–59).

Chappell and Company, Limited. Music-publishing firm, acting also as concert agents and piano manufacturers, established (1812) at London.

Chapra (chu'prą). [Also, **Chupra.**] Capital of the district of Saran, Bihar state, Union of India, ab. 115 mi. NE of Benares, near the junction of the Gogra and Ganges rivers. It is an important trading center and road junction. 55,142 (1941).

Chaptal (shȧp.tȧl), **Jean Antoine.** [Title, Comte **de Chanteloup.**] b. at Nogaret, Lozère, France, June 5, 1756; d. at Paris, July 30, 1832. French chemist and politician. Professor of chemistry at Montpellier University, he developed many applications of the science to industry. He was minister of the interior (1800 *et seq.*). His works include *Le Perfectionnement des arts chimiques en France* (1800) and *Chimie appliquée aux arts* (1806).

Chapter Coffee House. Former London coffee house situated at the corner of Chapter-house Court, on the south side of Paternoster Row, noted in the 18th century as the resort of men of letters. It was famous for its punch, pamphlets, and good supply of newspapers. It was closed as a coffee house in 1854, and then altered to a tavern.

Chapu (shȧ.pü), **Henri Michel Antoine.** b. at Le Mée, Seine-et-Marne, France, Sept. 29, 1833; d. at Paris, April 20, 1891. French sculptor. He was a pupil of James Pradier, François Duret, and Léon Cogniet, and won the grand prix de Rome in sculpture in 1855. His works include the statue *Jeanne d'Arc Hearing Voices* (1870), the monument (*La Jeunesse*, 1876) to Henri Regnault in the École des Beaux-Arts, the tomb of Monsignor Dupanloup (1886), the monument to the Duchess of Orléans, and many important statues and busts. He won the medal of honor at the Paris Salon in 1875 and 1877, and was elected a member of the French Institute in 1880.

Chapultepec (chä.pöl.tā.pek'; Anglicized, chą.pöl'tę.pek). Rocky eminence ab. 3 mi. SW of Mexico City. About 1248, when it was surrounded by swamps, it was occupied by the Tenochcas (Aztecs), and subsequently an aqueduct from the hill furnished water to Tenochtitlan (Mexico City). It is said by some historians that the Aztec monarchs had a summer residence at Chapultepec, but this has been denied by recent investigators. Like all places strong in position and in natural resources, it was the site of some kind of worship. At the foot of the hill and in the park there are some interesting vestiges of rock-carvings, which date from the first decade of the 16th century. About 1785 the viceroy of Mexico, José Gálvez, began the erection of a palace on the Chapultepec hill. This was made in the form of a fort or castle, and was, in fact, intended for a stronghold as well as a summer residence. The building remained unfinished until after the revolution. Under the republic a portion was used for a military school, and the National Astronomical Observatory was erected on the hill. During the war with the U.S. the castle was stormed by U.S. forces under General Gideon Pillow and General J. A. Quitman, on Sept. 13, 1847. The emperor Maximilian made Chapultepec his principal palace, and it was occupied until the 1930's as a summer residence of the president, portions being reserved for the military school and observatory. The former palace is now a museum. The hill is surrounded by a beautiful park, a favorite resort of the residents of Mexico City.

Chapultepec, Act of. See **Act of Chapultepec.**

Chapultepec Conference. See **International Conference on Problems of War and Peace.**

Chapygin (chä.pē'gin), **Aleksey Pavlovich.** b. at Bolshoy Ugol, Olonetzk, Russia, 1870; d. at Leningrad, Oct. 21, 1937. Russian novelist and short-story writer. Of peasant birth and, before he turned to literature, a house painter by trade, he depicted the life of the peasants and workmen of his native north country. His best-known books are two historical novels laid in 17th-century Russia.

Chara (kā'rą). Properly, the name of the southern of the two dogs in the constellation of Canes Venatici (β Canum Venaticorum), but also used as the name of the fourth-magnitude star β Canum Venaticorum.

Character and Opinion in the United States. Essays by George Santayana, published in 1920. The author interprets the sources and development of the American mind and the traits of the national character.

Characteristics. Novel by S. Weir Mitchell, published in 1892. Its sequel is *Dr. North and His Friends* (1900). Both books are brilliantly conversational rather than narrative.

Charaes (chä.rä'äs). [Also: **Jaraes, Xaraes.**] Name given in maps of the 16th and 17th centuries to a great lake near the center of South America, represented as the source of the Paraguay River. The upper Paraguay is bordered by vast plains which are flooded every year, and are still sometimes known as the Charaes marshes or flood plains. Probably the story of the lake originated with them, but some suppose that it referred to one of the small lakes which communicate with the Paraguay on the western side. The Charaes marshes cover 80,000 sq. mi.

Charalois (chȧ.rȧ.lwä'). In Philip Massinger and Nathaniel Field's comedy *The Fatal Dowry* (c1618), the principal character, who goes to prison to release the body of his father who died in debt. He marries Rochfort's daughter, discovers her to be dishonest, and kills her when she is condemned by her father.

Charasiab (chä.rä.sē.äb'). [Also, **Charasia** (-ä').] Place in Afghanistan, ab. 10–12 mi. S of Kabul. Here, on Oct. 6, 1879, a British force defeated the Afghans.

Charbar (chä.bär'). See **Chahbar.**

Charcas (chär'käs). Aymará tribe of SW Bolivia, principally in the highlands of Chuquisaca.

Charcas. [Also: **Chuquisaca, Upper Peru** (Spanish, **Alto Perú**).] Portion of the old viceroyalty of Peru, nearly corresponding to the modern Bolivia.

Charcas. A former name of **Sucre,** Bolivia.

Charcot (shȧr.kō), **Jean Baptiste Étienne Auguste.** b. at Neuilly-sur-Seine, France, July 15, 1867; d. at sea, near Iceland, Sept. 16, 1936. French physician and explorer; son of Jean Martin Charcot. As leader of the French antarctic expedition of 1903–05 in the *Français*, he established the connection of Bismarck Strait with the sea E of Graham Land (later named Graham Coast), and mapped the W coast of what is now named Palmer Peninsula. He commanded (1908–10) a second expedition to the Antarctic, in the *Pourquois-Pas?*, the main objects of which were to make a collection of the fossils to which attention was drawn by Nordenskjöld, to explore the region S of Loubet Island (Adelaide Island), and, if possible, to reach the South Pole. He wrote accounts of his journeys in *Le Français au Pôle Sud* and *Le Voyage du Pourquoi-Pas?*.

Charcot, Jean Martin. b. at Paris, Nov. 29, 1825; d. Aug. 16, 1893. French physician; father of J. B. E. A. Charcot. A pioneer in psychopathology, he was particularly noted for his treatment of nervous and mental diseases and for his experiments in hypnotism and mental suggestion at the Salpêtrière, Paris, where he founded a clinic for nervous diseases in 1880. Both Alfred Binet and Sigmund Freud studied with him. His most important work is *Leçons sur les maladies du système nerveux* (1873; Eng. trans., 1877). His works, including studies of the diseases of old age, insanity, and hysteria, were collected in *Oeuvres complètes* (9 vols., 1886–90).

Charcot Bay (shär'kō). Reëntrant in Antarctica, lying on the N side of the Nordenskjöld Ice Tongue, on the coast of Victoria Land, in ab. 76°07′ S., 162°45′ E. It was discovered by the National Antarctic Expedition (1901–04), under the leadership of Captain Robert F. Scott, who named this bay for J. B. E. A. Charcot (1867–1936), French antarctic explorer.

Chard (chärd). Municipal borough and market town in SW England, in Somersetshire ab. 12 mi. E of Taunton, ab. 143 mi. SW of London by rail. It has manufactures of lace. 5,218 (1951).

Chardin (shȧr.dan̂), **Jean Baptiste Siméon.** b. at Paris, Nov. 2, 1699; d. there, Dec. 6, 1779. French painter, famous for his paintings of still life and interiors. He was admitted to the French Academy in 1728. He served as treasurer of the Academy and for many years as a curator of paintings at the Louvre. In his choice of subjects he resembled the genre painters of the Dutch and Flemish schools more than his French contemporaries. He developed a mastery of technique in both oil and pastel, distinguished by fine coloring and sensitive treatment of light and shadow, that was the despair of those who tried to imitate it.

Chardonne (shȧr.don), **Jacques.** [Pseudonym of **Jacques Boutelleau.**] b. at Barbezieux, France, 1884—. French novelist. Author of *L'Épithalame* (1921; Eng. trans., *Epithalamium*, 1923), *Eva* (1930; Eng. trans., *Eva, or the*

Interrupted Diary, 1930), *Claire* (1931), and the cyclical *Les Destinées sentimentales* (1934–35). After taking his law degree in 1910 he entered the publishing firm of Stock; he began writing during a five-year convalescence following the collapse of his health in 1915.

Chardonnet (shär.do.ne), Count (**Louis Marie**) **Hilaire Bernigaud.** b. at Besançon, France, 1839; d. 1924. French inventor, industrialist, and physiologist. He prepared (1878 *et seq.*) and put into production the first synthetic "silk" (actually a nitrocellulose thread).

Chardzhou (chär.jō'). [Also: **Chardzhov** (chär.jôf'); former name, **Chardzhoui, Chardzhuy** (chär.jö'i).] City in the U.S.S.R., in the Turkmen *oblast* (region) of the Russian Soviet Federated Socialist Republic, on the Amu Darya River, ab. 70 mi. SW of Bukhara. Textiles are very important here, with special emphasis on cotton. 54,739 (1939).

Charente (shȧ.räṅt). Department in W France, bounded by the departments of Deux-Sèvres and Vienne on the N, the department of Haute-Vienne on the E, the department of Dordogne on the E and S, and the department of Charente-Maritime on the S and W. It was formed chiefly from the former province of Angoumois. There are two distinct agricultural zones: the NE, where cereal production dominates, and the SW, where potatoes, fruits, and white wines are cultivated. The wines are basis for the distillery and liquor industry of the department, which is concentrated in Cognac and other places of world renown. The raising of cattle, horses, and sheep, and the dairy industry are also highly developed. Paper and metallurgical industries are centered at Angoulême, and there are minor industries of local importance. The famous castle of La Rochefoucauld is situated within the department. Capital, Angoulême; area, 2,294 sq. mi.; pop. 311,137 (1946).

Charente-Maritime (shȧ.räṅt.mȧ.rē.tēm). [Former name, **Charente-Inférieure.**] Department in W France, bounded by the departments of Vendée and Deux-Sèvres on the N, the departments of Charente and Dordogne on the E, the department of Gironde on the S, and the Gironde River and the Bay of Biscay on the W. It is nearly identical with the old provinces of Saintonge and Aunis. The region was occupied by the British in the early Middle Ages and later suffered from frequent political and religious strife. The siege of La Rochelle by Richelieu concluded this period. The region is flat and has a maritime climate with high precipitation. The soil is very fertile, and agricultural production is of great variety, with grains, wine, and vegetables predominating. Ample pasture land permits livestock-raising and supports an important dairy industry. There are stone quarries and coal mines, flour mills, distilleries, chemical plants, and construction industries. The department has a number of seaports. Capital, La Rochelle; area, 2,791 sq. mi.; pop. 416,187 (1946).

Charente River. River in W France which flows into the Bay of Biscay ab. 14 mi. S of La Rochelle. Length, over 200 mi.

Charenton-le-Pont (shȧ.räṅ.tôṅ.lẹ.pôṅ). Town in N France, in the department of Seine, situated on the Marne River near its junction with the Seine River, 1 mi. SE of Paris. It is a suburb of Paris. The town is known for manufactures of porcelain, boats, rubber articles, and pianos. 21,457 (1946).

Chares (kā'rēz, kãr'ēz). d. after 332 B.C. Athenian general. He was prominent in wars until 332, especially in the Social War when he became (357) an associate of Chabrias.

Chares. b. at Lindus, Rhodes; fl. c292–c280 B.C. Rhodian sculptor, noted as the creator of the Colossus of Rhodes; a pupil of Lysippus. He is considered the founder of the Rhodian school. The Colossus of Rhodes was made to commemorate the successful defense of that place against Demetrius I (Demetrius Poliorcetes) in 305 and 304 B.C. It required 12 years for its completion, and was probably finished before 280 B.C. Representing the Rhodian sun god, Helios, it was over 105 ft. high, and was considered one of the seven wonders of the Old World. Its cost is said to have been defrayed from the engines of war which Demetrius was obliged to abandon.

Charette de la Contrie (shȧ.ret dẹ lȧ kôṅ.trē), **François Athanase.** b. at Couffé, Loire-Inférieure, France, April 21, 1763; d. at Nantes, France, March 29, 1796. French insurgent, one of the leaders of the Vendeans against the French republic. He placed himself at the head of a force of insurgents in 1793, gained a number of victories (1793–94) over the republicans, and signed a treaty of peace (Feb. 15, 1795) which he soon violated. He suffered a decisive defeat at St.-Cyr on March 25, 1796, and, taken prisoner shortly after, was executed.

Charford (chär'fọrd). See under **Cerdicsford.**

Charge of the Light Brigade. Poem by Alfred Lord Tennyson, written in the same meter as Michael Drayton's *The Battle of Agincourt.* It commemorates the heroic charge at Balaklava during the Crimean War, and contains the well-known lines:

> Theirs not to reason why,
> Theirs but to do or die. . . .
> Into the jaws of death,
> Into the mouth of hell,
> Rode the six hundred.

Chari (shȧ.rē). See **Shari.**

Chariclea (kar.i.klē'ạ). Heroine of Heliodorus's novel *Theagenes and Chariclea* (also called *Aethiopica*).

Charing Cross (char'ing krôs'). Place at Westminster, London, S of Trafalgar Square at the junction of Whitehall Street and the Strand. Charing Cross railways terminal is located here. The space took its name from the circumstance that one of the crosses to the memory of Eleanor of Castile stood here. It was demolished (1647) by the Long Parliament. A copy was erected (1865) by the South Eastern Railway Company. In traveling N to join her husband (Edward I of England) in Scotland, Eleanor was seized with a fever at Hardeby, near Grantham in Lincolnshire, and died there on Nov. 29, 1290. Edward followed her corpse in person during a 13 days' progress from Grantham to Westminster Abbey, and wherever the royal bier rested, at the end of each stage, a memorial cross was erected. Thirteen of these monuments once existed; those of Northampton and Waltham still remain

"Charing Cross of the Highlands." See **Oban.**

Chariot Wheels. Novel by Sylvia Thompson, published in 1929.

Charis (kā'ris). In Greek mythology, the personification of grace and beauty; wife of Hephaestus. In later mythology the three Charites were daughters of Zeus, often depicted as attendants of Aphrodite. The Romans identified them with their Graces.

Charité-sur-Loire (shȧ.rē.tā.sür.lwȧr), **La.** See **La Charité-sur-Loire.**

Chariton (shar'i.tọn). [Former names, **Polk, Chariton Point.**] City in S Iowa, county seat of Lucas County, on the Chariton River. Manufactures include brooms, dairy products, ice cream, and candy; there are railroad shops. 5,320 (1950).

Chariton of Aphrodisias (kar'i.tọn; af.rọ.diz'i.ạs). [Also, **Chariton Aphrodisiensis** (-diz.i.en'sis).] fl. 4th century A.D. Greek author, probably under an assumed name, of the romance *Chaereas and Callirrhoë.*

Chariton River (shar'i.tọn). River in S Iowa and N Missouri, which joins the Missouri ab. 60 mi. NW of Jefferson City. Length, ab. 200 mi.

Charlatan (shȧr.lȧ.täṅ), **Le.** Novel by Honoré de Balzac, written in 1830.

Charlemagne (shär'lẹ.mān; French, shȧr.lẹ.mȧny'). [Also: **Charles I; Charles the Great;** German, **Karl der Grosse;** Italian, **Carlo Magno;** Latin, **Carolus Magnus.**] b. c742; d. Jan. 28, 814. King of the Franks and emperor of the Romans. He was the son of Pepin the Short, king of the Franks, on whose death in 768 he acceded to the throne conjointly with a brother, Carloman. He usurped the entire government on the death of the latter in 771. In 772 he began a war against the Saxons, the most notable events of which were the storming of Eresburg, the destruction of the Saxon idol Irminsul (Irmensäule), the May-field at Paderborn (777), and the submission of the Saxon leader Wittekind (785), and which resulted in 804 in the complete subjugation and Christianization of Saxony. In 773, at the instance of Pope Adrian I, he made war upon Desiderius, king of the Lombards, who had occupied the Pentapolis (the five cities of Rimini, Ancona, Fano, Pesaro, and Senigallia) and was threatening Rome. He captured the Lombard capital, Pavia, in 774, and the same year incorporated the kingdom of the Lombards with that of the Franks. In 778 he made an expedition against the Arabs in Spain, which terminated in the destruction of the Frankish rear guard under Roland at Roncevaux. He subdued Bavaria in 788, conquered the Avars (791–796), was crowned emperor at Saint Peter's, Dec. 25, 800, and in 808–810 defeated the Danes, whom he compelled to retire behind the Eider River. His kingdom, for the protection of which he erected in the border districts the so-called marks or margravates, extended at the close of his reign from the Ebro River in N Spain to the Raab in Austria, and from the Eider in what is now Schleswig-Holstein to the Garigliano, which is nearly 100 miles below Rome. He resided chiefly at Aix-la-Chapelle (Aachen), and by his patronage of letters attracted to his court the scholars Eginhard, Paul Warnefried, and Alcuin, the last-mentioned of whom wrote an account of his life entitled *Vita Caroli Magni*. He was buried at Aix-la-Chapelle.

Charlemagne. Tragedy in five acts by Louis Jean Népomucène Lemercier, first played at the Théâtre Français, Paris, on June 27, 1816.

Charlemagne (or **Carlovingian**) **Cycle of Romances.** Series of medieval romances, having Charlemagne or some one of his 12 peers or paladins as a center. The Frankish heroic ballads were reduced to writing by the order of Charlemagne, and from these similar ballads were written about himself and his warriors. These *chansons de geste* were arranged as cyclic poems in the 13th century, and may be divided into three groups: the *Geste of the King* (Charlemagne), the *Geste of Provence* (or of Garin de Montglane), and the *Geste of Doolin* (or *Doon*) *of Mayence*. These are all composed of many parts, but may be described, as a whole, as a legendary history of Charlemagne, his peers, and the wars they undertook.

Charlemont (chärl'mont), 1st Earl and 4th Viscount of. See **Caulfeild, James.**

Charlemont; or, The Pride of the Village. Novel by William Gilmore Simms, published in 1856. It is one of his series of Border Romances. With *Beauchampe* (1842), it forms the sequence known as the Kentucky Tragedy.

Charleroi (shår.lẹ.rwȧ). Town in S Belgium, in the province of Hainaut, situated on the Sambre River, ab. 31 mi. S of Brussels. At the center of a large coal-mining district, it has iron foundries, and metallurgical, chemical, glass, construction, and other industries. There is an industrial school (Université du Travail) and an archaeological museum. The town was fortified by the Spaniards in 1666 and named after King Charles II; conquered by the French Marshal Turenne in 1667, it was incorporated into France in 1668. The fortifications were strengthened by Vauban. Charleroi was returned to Spain in 1678 by the peace of Nijmegen; from 1794 to 1814 it was again under French rule. Fierce fighting took place here in August, 1914, in World War I. 25,894 (1947).

Charleroi (shär'lẹ.roi). Borough in SW Pennsylvania, in Washington County, ab. 22 mi. SE of Pittsburgh: coal mining; manufacturers of glass. It was platted in 1890. Pop. 9,872 (1950).

Charleroi (shår.lẹ.rwȧ), **Battle of Namur and.** See **Namur and Charleroi, Battle of.**

Charles (chärlz). See also **Carl, Carlo, Carlos, Carol, Karl.**

Charles. [Full German name, **Karl Theodor Maximilian August.**] b. at Munich, July 7, 1795; d. near Tegernsee, Bavaria, Aug. 16, 1875. Prince of Bavaria, and a Bavarian general, son of King Maximilian I. He was commander of the Bavarian contingent in 1866.

Charles. Wrestler in Shakespeare's *As You Like It.*

Charles (of *Anjou*). See **Charles I** and **Charles III** (of *Naples*).

Charles (of *England*), Prince. [Full name, **Charles Philip Arthur George**; title, Duke of **Cornwall.**] b. at Buckingham Palace, London, Nov. 14, 1948—. Crown prince of England, heir apparent (after 1952) to the English throne; son of Elizabeth II and Philip, Duke of Edinburgh.

Charles I. See also **Charlemagne.**

Charles I (of *England*). b. at Dunfermline, Scotland, Nov. 19, 1600; d. at London, Jan. 30, 1649. King of England; second son of James I of England. He became prince of Wales in 1616, and in 1623, accompanied by George Villiers, 1st Duke of Buckingham, presented in person an ineffectual suit at the court of Madrid for the hand of the infanta Maria. He acceded to the throne on the death of his father in 1625, and in the same year married the Catholic Henrietta Maria of France. He retained in office the Duke of Buckingham, his father's unpopular minister, in consequence of which he became involved in a dispute with Parliament amounting in substance to a question of sovereignty. He granted the Petition of Right, on June 7, 1628. On the assassination of the Duke of Buckingham in August, 1628, he made William Laud and Thomas Wentworth his chief advisers. He governed without Parliament from 1629 to 1640, meeting the expenses of government by forced loans, the taxation known as poundage and tonnage, ship-money, and other extraordinary means of revenue. His ecclesiastical policy, which looked, among other things, to the introduction of the Episcopal liturgy in Scotland, provoked the adoption by the Scots of the Solemn League and Covenant, on Feb. 28, 1638, and the outbreak of a civil war, which terminated without a battle in the pacification of Berwick, on June 18, 1639. The war having broken out anew in 1640, he was compelled to summon a parliament, which met on Nov. 3, 1640. This parliament, the so-called Long Parliament (in contrast to one Charles had called earlier in the same year and which had broken up after a short sitting, called the Short Parliament), impeached Laud and Wentworth (who had been created Earl of Strafford), and proceeded to the redress of grievances. The House of Commons having ordered the publication of the Grand Remonstrance, on Dec. 14, 1641, Charles replied by impeaching and attempting to arrest (Jan. 4, 1642) five of the Parliamentary leaders, failing in which he left London, on Jan. 10, 1642, the English Civil War being now in full action. He raised the royal standard at Nottingham on Aug. 22, 1642, suffered a decisive defeat at the hands of the Parliamentary forces under Fairfax at Naseby on June 14, 1645, delivered himself to the Scottish army at Newark on May 5, 1646, and was surrendered to Parliament on Jan. 30, 1647. Tried for treason by the so-called Rump Parliament, in the period Jan. 20–27, 1649, he was executed at Whitehall, London. The members of the court which judged his case came to be known as regicides.

Charles II (of *England*). b. at St. James's Palace, London, May 29, 1630; d. there, Feb. 6, 1685. King of England; son of Charles I of England. He was appointed to the command of the Royalist forces in the western counties of England in the Civil War, and after the decisive victory of the Parliamentary army at Naseby left England on March 2, 1646, living during his exile chiefly in France and the Netherlands. He was proclaimed king at Edinburgh on Feb. 5, 1649, arrived in the Firth of Cromarty on June 16, 1650, and was crowned at Scone on Jan. 1, 1651. Totally defeated by Oliver Cromwell at Worcester on Sept. 3, 1651, after an attempt to march into England, Charles escaped, after numerous adventures, to Fécamp, in Normandy, on Oct. 16, 1651. Owing to the influence of General Monck and the effect of Charles's Declaration of Breda, he was proclaimed king at Westminster on May 8, 1660, entered London on May 29, 1660, and was crowned on April 23, 1661. He married Catherine of Braganza on May 20, 1662. He assented at his restoration to the abolition of the feudal rights of knight service, wardship, and purveyance, in consideration of a yearly income to the crown of 1,200,000 pounds, and to an act of indemnity for all political offenses committed between Jan. 1, 1637, and June 24, 1660, from the operation of which act, however, the regicides (those responsible for the condemnation and execution of Charles I) were excluded. During his reign the Dutch wars continued, colonization in America and India flourished, and the Great Fire of London (1666) took place shortly after the great plague of London (1665). The power of Parliament increased during the period, and the Rye House Plot against Charles was foiled. Charles is remembered for his immoral and pleasure-loving life; of his various mistresses the best known is the actress Nell Gwynn.

Charles I (of *France*). See **Charles II** (of the *Holy Roman Empire*).

Charles II (of *France*). See **Charles III** (of the *Holy Roman Empire*).

Charles III (of *France*). [Called **Charles the Simple;** French, **Charles le Simple** (shárl lẹ saṅpl), or **le Sot**

(lę sō).] b. Sept. 17, 879; d. at Péronne, France, Oct. 7, 929. King of France; son of Louis II of France. He was crowned in 893 by his partisans among the nobles in opposition to Eudes, who had been elected king in 888 during Charles's minority. On the death of Eudes in 898 he became sole king. In 911 he ceded Normandy to Rollo, but subsequently acquired Lorraine. In 922 he was opposed by a group who supported Robert, brother of Eudes. Defeated at the battle of Soissons (923), Charles was imprisoned.

Charles IV (of *France*). [Called **Charles the Fair**; French, **Charles le Bel** (shårl lę bel).] b. 1294; d. at Vincennes, near Paris, 1328. King of France and (as Charles I) of Navarre, the last of the Capetian line; youngest son of Philip IV of France. He reigned from 1322 to 1328. His sister Isabella was married to Edward II of England, with whom Charles was at war over the duchy of Guienne. Isabella having been sent to France to negotiate the question, he aided her in planning the dethronement of Edward. Charles deepened the power of the king and, by a policy of taxation, duties, and debasing of the coinage, enriched the royal treasury.

Charles V (of *France*). [Called **Charles the Wise**; French, **Charles le Sage** (shårl lę såzh).] b. at Vincennes, near Paris, Jan. 21, 1337; d. there, Sept. 16, 1380. King of France; son of John II of France. He reigned from 1364 to 1380. He was lieutenant general or regent of France (1356–60) during the captivity of his father in England. In this time he faced the revolt (1358) of the Jacquerie, a French peasant group who were unsuccessful in their uprising. During his reign Charles, aided by Bertrand du Guesclin, made war against the free companies, which he managed to suppress, and against the English, France recovering all the territory that had been conquered by Edward III of England, except Calais and Bordeaux. He was a patron of learning, and founded the Royal Library of Paris.

Charles VI (of *France*). [Called **Charles the Well-Beloved**; French, **Charles le Bien-Aimé** (shårl lę byan̄ne.mā).] b. at Paris, Dec. 3, 1368; d. there, Oct. 21, 1422. King of France; son of Charles V of France. He reigned from 1380 to 1422. Being a minor at his accession, he was placed under a regency conducted by his uncles, the dukes of Anjou, Burgundy, and Berry. He defeated the Flemings under Philip van Artevelde at Rosebecque, on Nov. 27, 1382. In 1388 he assumed the government, but becoming subject to fits of insanity in 1392, he retired from active government. A dispute for power arose between the Duke of Burgundy and the Duke of Orléans, the king's brother whom Charles had chosen to advise him. The ascendancy was gained by the former, who died in 1404. His son Jean procured the murder of the Duke of Orléans (1407), which provoked civil war, the so-called war of the Burgundians and Armagnacs. Henry V of England invaded the country, and on Oct. 25, 1415, defeated the French at Agincourt. Supported by Queen Isabella, Charles's wife, the Burgundians concluded at Troyes a treaty (May 21, 1420) with Henry V, according to which he was to be king of France on the death of Charles.

Charles VII (of *France*). [Called **Charles the Victorious**; French, **Charles le Victorieux** (shårl lę vēk.to.ryė).] b. at Paris, Feb. 22, 1403; d. at Mehun-sur-Yèvre, near Bourges, France, July 22, 1461. King of France; son of Charles VI of France. He reigned from 1422 to 1461. At his accession he found a rival in Henry VI of England, who claimed the French throne by virtue of the Treaty of Troyes (1420) which had promised Henry V of England the French throne on the death of Charles VI of France. Charles's actual power at the time he ascended the throne was limited by the fact that the English were masters of the country north of the Loire River, including the capital, and in 1428 besieged Orléans. It was not until 1429, with the help of Joan of Arc who liberated Orléans, that Charles began to win France back from the English. He was crowned at Reims in 1429, and entered Paris in 1437. He effected a reconciliation between the Armagnac and Burgundian factions, and regained all of France except Calais from the English. Thereafter he ruled a relatively peaceful and prosperous country. In 1438 he recognized, by the Pragmatic sanction of Bourges, the rights of the Gallican Church, while limiting papal power in France. He was influenced in many of his decisions by Agnès Sorel

Charles VIII (of *France*). b. at Amboise, France, June 30, 1470; d. there, April 7, 1498. King of France; son of Louis XI of France. He reigned from 1483 to 1498 (under his sister Anne of Beaujeu's regency from 1483 to 1491, in which latter year he married Anne of Brittany). He invaded Italy in 1494 with a view to conquering Naples, which he entered in 1495. Ferdinand of Aragon, Maximilian I, and the Italian powers having united against him, he left the Duke of Montpensier with a strong force at Naples and returned to France with the remainder of his army, defeating on the way the numerically superior allies at Fornovo di Taro, on July 6, 1495. The French were soon after expelled from Naples by the Spaniards.

Charles IX (of *France*). b. at St.-Germain-en-Laye, near Paris, June 27, 1550; d. at Vincennes, near Paris, May 30, 1574. King of France (1560–74); the second son of Henry II of France. Being a minor at his accession, he was placed under the regency of his mother, Catherine de Médicis. He was declared of age in 1563, but the policy of the government continued to be dictated by his mother, under whose influence he consented to the Saint Bartholomew's Day Massacre, on Aug. 24, 1572.

Charles X (of *France*). [Called (before accession to throne) **Charles Philippe,** Comte **d'Artois.**] b. at Versailles, France, Oct. 9, 1757; d. at Görz, Austria (now Gorizia, Italy), Nov. 6, 1836. King of France; younger brother of Louis XVIII of France. He reigned from 1824 to 1830. He received at birth the name of Charles Philippe and the title of Comte d'Artois. He joined the royalist emigration of 1789 to escape the French Revolution. In 1795, having obtained ships and men from England, he commanded an expedition which was to land on the coast of Brittany and join the Vendean chief, Charette, but which resulted in failure through the cowardice of its leader, who did not venture to attempt a landing. On the restoration of the monarchy, he entered Paris with the allies in April, 1814, and on Sept. 16, 1824, succeeded his brother, Louis XVIII. His government, whose policy was dictated by the ecclesiastical party, became extremely unpopular. After the defeat of the ministries of Villèle and Martignac, the king formed an extreme royalist ministry under Jules Armand de Polignac on Aug. 8, 1829. The Chamber of Deputies voted (March, 1830) an address hostile to the ministers, who, appealing to the country, were defeated. Resolving on a coup d'état, the king and ministry issued on July 25, 1830, a body of ordinances which restricted the freedom of the press, established a new mode of election, and declared the recent elections illegal. As a consequence the so-called July revolution (July 27–29, 1830) broke out, in the course of which Charles lost the throne.

Charles I (of the *Holy Roman Empire*). See **Charlemagne.**

Charles II (of the *Holy Roman Empire*). [Called **Charles the Bald**; French, **Charles le Chauve** (shårl lę shōv); German, **Karl der Kahle.**] b. at Frankfort on the Main, Germany, June 13, 823; d. near Mont Cenis, in the Alps, Oct. 6, 877. King of France (as Charles I) and emperor of the Holy Roman Empire; younger son of Louis I. Louis died in 840, after dividing his empire among his sons Lothair, Louis, and Charles, the last of whom received all of France lying west of the Rhone River. Lothair having claimed the preëminence, his brothers united against him, defeated him at Fontenay on June 25, 841, and compelled him to accept the treaty of Verdun, concluded in August, 843. In 875, on the death of Louis II of Italy without issue, Charles invaded Italy, and after defeating the army of his brother Louis, the rightful heir of Louis II, was crowned emperor by Pope John VIII at Rome, on Dec. 25, 875. During his reign France was ravaged by the Normans, who sacked Bordeaux, Tours, Rouen, Orléans, and other cities, including some quarters of Paris.

Charles III (of the *Holy Roman Empire*). [Called **Charles the Fat**; French, **Charles le Gros** (shårl lę grō); German, **Karl der Dicke.**] b. 839; d. at Neidingen, Swabia, Jan. 13, 888. King of France (as Charles II) and emperor of the Holy Roman Empire; son of Louis the German. Louis died in 876, after dividing his kingdom among his sons Carloman, Louis, and Charles. His brothers dying without lawful issue, Charles inherited their portions. He was crowned emperor in 881, and in

885 became king of France, or more properly regent since the heir, Charles III, was a minor. In 886, he concluded a humiliating treaty with the Normans. He was deposed as emperor by Arnulf in 887.

Charles IV (of the *Holy Roman Empire*). [Called **Charles of Luxemburg.**] b. at Prague, May 14, 1316; d. there, Nov. 29, 1378. Emperor of the Holy Roman Empire; son of John of Luxemburg, king of Bohemia. He reigned from 1347 to 1378, and published (1356) the Golden Bull, an electoral code for the empire.

Charles V (of the *Holy Roman Empire*). b. at Ghent, Flanders, Feb. 24, 1500; d. at Yuste, near Placiencia, Estremadura, Spain, Sept. 21, 1558. Emperor of the Holy Roman Empire and king (as Charles I) of Spain; son of Philip, duke of Burgundy (later Philip I of Spain) and Joanna or Juana (Joanna the Mad), daughter of Ferdinand and Isabella of Spain, and grandson of the emperor Maximilian I and Mary of Burgundy. Charles was under the early influence of his aunt Margaret of Austria, who acted as regent for him in the Low Countries when he was a boy, and of Adrian Dedel, vice-chancellor of the University of Louvain, who was chosen as his tutor by Maximilian, who instilled into his pupil a deep devotion to the Roman Catholic Church (Dedel was later elected pope as Adrian VI). Charles became king of Spain on the death (1516) of his grandfather Ferdinand V, ruling Castile as regent for his insane mother, and as heir in his own right to Aragon, Navarre, Granada, the Spanish dominions in America, Naples, Sardinia, and Sicily. When Maximilian died in 1519, Charles inherited the Hapsburg lands, was elected the same year emperor of the Holy Roman Empire, and was crowned (1520) at Aachen (Aix-la-Chapelle).

Early Years of Reign. Charles immediately became embroiled in the religious struggle going on in Germany, presiding at a diet held at Worms in 1521, from which resulted the Edict of Worms, in which Charles declared his unswerving determination to stamp out the "heresy" of Luther's doctrines. Charles's seeming preoccupation with Germany, his Flemish birth and education, his ties to the German financiers resulting from his bribery of the seven electors to the imperial crown, and the high-handed methods he used in establishing his own followers in Spanish office combined to arouse feeling against him in Spain, climaxing (1520–21) in revolts in Castile, which were suppressed. War broke out (1521) in Italy over the rival claims of Charles and Francis I of France to Milan, Burgundy, Navarre, and Naples. In 1525 Francis was defeated and captured at Pavia and forced to sign (January, 1526) at Madrid a treaty giving Charles great concessions. This he repudiated immediately upon his release and, joining with Milan, Venice, Florence, and Pope Clement VII, reopened hostilities. The German forces of Charles marched down the Italian peninsula and into Rome, which was sacked in 1527. With the treaty of Cambrai (1529) with France, Charles became undisputed master of Italy and was crowned (1530) by the Pope at Bologna, the last Holy Roman emperor to have a papal coronation.

Wars with France and the Turks. Charles was now forced to attend to the inroads being made on Europe by the Turks under Suleiman I (Suleiman the Magnificent). In 1535 he took the Ottoman city of Tunis in Africa and sacked it. For the third time, a war against Francis I broke out (1536) over Francis's claims to Milan. Charles marched into Provence, and Francis entered Savoy and Piedmont, but the struggle came to an inconclusive halt by truce in 1538. Intermittently from that time Charles fought against Suleiman and Francis, who had allied himself with the Turkish ruler; in 1538, a league formed by Charles, the city of Venice, and the Pope was defeated; in 1541, Charles sent an expedition against Algiers, in Africa, which failed. Again in 1542 war began over claims to Milan by Charles and Francis; this ended in 1544 with the peace of Crespy, in which Francis agreed not to press claims to Milan and Naples, and Charles gave up his claims to Burgundy.

Troubles in Germany. In 1530 a diet was held at Augsburg under the emperor, who reiterated that he wanted the Protestant innovations ended. It was at this diet that Philip Melanchthon's Confession of Augsburg was first read. Later that year there was arranged, and in 1531 formally organized, the Schmalkaldic League (named for Schmalkalden, the city in Prussia where it was formed) of many of the Protestant rulers (rulers who "protested" against the emperor's edict at Augsburg) of the German states and a number of cities of the empire. But Charles was occupied with matters elsewhere and could not at the moment attempt to crush this expression of independence. By 1546 he was able to turn his attention to the German situation and, at the battle of Mühlberg (April 24, 1547), defeated and captured the elector of Saxony, John Frederick I, one of the leaders of the League. Charles in turn was attacked (1551) by Maurice of Saxony, formerly one of his allies in Germany, and by the convention of Passau (1552) recognized the Confession of Augsburg. On this basis the peace of Augsburg was concluded (Sept. 25, 1555) under which the states and cities acknowledging the Confession were to have the freedom of adopting the reformed religion.

End of Reign. At war again, beginning in 1551, with France, now under Henry II, Charles in 1555 decided to give up his several kingships. On Oct. 25, 1555, he resigned the throne of the Netherlands, being succeeded by his son Philip II; on Jan. 15, 1556, the crown of Spain too went to Philip, and the Hapsburg holdings in Germany and the imperial crown were resigned in favor of his brother Ferdinand I, to whom since the beginning of Charles's reign he had relinquished the sole sovereignty over these lands and who had inaugurated the Hapsburg rule in Bohemia and Hungary. Charles retired to a monastery at Yuste, Spain, where he lived until his death in 1558. His rule had extended over nearly 40 years, in which time he ruled over an area reaching from the Americas to eastern Europe. The Spanish conquests in Mexico and Peru by Cortes and Pizzaro brought tremendous wealth to the Spanish treasury. He and his contemporaries (Henry VIII of England, Francis I of France, Suleiman I of Turkey) form a constellation of kings that make the first half of the 16th century outstanding in political history. Several portraits of Charles V by Titian, painted at different periods in his life, may be seen at the Royal Museum, Madrid (one of these, an equestrian portrait, has been held by some to be the finest portrait ever painted).

Charles VI (of the *Holy Roman Empire*). b. Oct. 1, 1685; d. at Vienna, Oct. 20, 1740. Emperor of the Holy Roman Empire and king (as Charles III) of Hungary; son of Leopold I. He reigned from 1711 to 1740. He issued his pragmatic sanction regarding the succession in 1713, securing the throne of Austria for his daughter Maria Theresa. He was pretender to the throne of Spain (as Charles III), thus precipitating the War of the Spanish Succession, in which he was unsuccessful.

Charles VII (of the *Holy Roman Empire*). [Also: **Charles Albert**; German, **Karl Albrecht**; sometimes called **Charles of Bavaria.**] b. at Brussels, Aug. 6, 1697; d. at Munich, Jan. 20, 1745. Emperor of the Holy Roman Empire; son of Maximilian Emanuel, elector of Bavaria, whom he succeeded in 1726. A claimant of the Austrian inheritance, he participated in the War of the Austrian Succession, which broke out in 1740 as an attempt to take the throne from Maria Theresa, on whom it had devolved in accordance with Charles VI's pragmatic sanction of 1713. He was proclaimed king of Bohemia (1741) and was crowned emperor in 1742. He died during the war.

Charles I (of *Hungary*). [Called (before his accession to the throne) **Charles Robert of Anjou.**] b. 1288; d. 1342. King of Hungary (1308–42), crowned in 1310. He established the Angevin line in Hungary. Having married a daughter of Ladislas I of Poland, he secured the succession of that country for his son Louis I. He increased the privileges of towns and cities, reorganized the army, and encouraged trade.

Charles II (of *Hungary*). See **Charles III** (of *Naples*).

Charles III (of *Hungary*). See **Charles VI** (of the *Holy Roman Empire*).

Charles V (of *Lorraine*). [Also: **Charles IV, Charles Leopold.**] b. at Vienna, April 3, 1643; d. at Wels, Austria, April 18, 1690. Austrian general, titular duke of Lorraine. He distinguished himself at the relief of Vienna in 1683, and decisively defeated the Turks near

Mohács in 1687. Twice a candidate for the Polish throne, he was neither time chosen.

Charles I (of *Naples*). b. 1226; d. at Foggia, Italy, 1285. King of Naples and Sicily, and count of Anjou; brother of Louis IX of France. With the consent of the Pope he attacked Manfred, king of Naples, who was defeated and slain in the battle of Benevento (Feb. 26, 1266), and ascended his throne. He defeated and captured (Aug. 23, 1268) at Lake Fucino near Tagliacozzo, Conradin, who claimed Naples as the son and heir of Conrad IV. His rule was thus firmly established, but his tyranny and extortion provoked a rebellion in Sicily, known as the Sicilian Vespers, in 1282, which cost him that island.

Charles III (of *Naples*). [Called **Charles of Durazzo.**] b. 1345; d. at Buda, Hungary, 1386. King of Naples, king of Hungary (as Charles II), and count of Anjou. Instigated by Pope Urban VI, he attacked Joanna I, queen of Naples, whom he put to death, and whose throne he ascended in 1382. He had been adopted by her much earlier, but she later repudiated him for Louis I of Anjou. Charles defended his throne against attacks (1382–84) from Louis. He was chosen (1385) king of Hungary, but was killed at Buda in the following year.

Charles IV (of *Naples*). See **Charles III** (of *Spain*).

Charles I (of *Navarre*). See **Charles IV** (of *France*).

Charles II (of *Navarre*). [Called **Charles the Bad**; French, **Charles le Mauvais** (shärl lẹ mō.ve).] b. 1332; d. 1387. King of Navarre in the period 1349–87 and count of Évreux. His reign was marked by intrigues and territorial disputes, notably with John II of France, his father-in-law, who took Charles prisoner in 1356. Released (1357), Charles was active (1358) in suppressing the peasant revolt of the Jacquerie.

Charles IV (of *Navarre*). See **Charles of Viana.**

Charles I (of *Portugal*). See **Carlos I** (of *Portugal*).

Charles I (of *Spain*). See **Charles V** (of the *Holy Roman Empire*).

Charles II (of *Spain*). b. Nov. 6, 1661; d. Nov. 1, 1700. King of Spain; son of Philip IV of Spain. He reigned from 1665 to 1700. He was the last of the Hapsburg line in Spain, and, since he died without direct issue, his death was the signal for the outbreak of the War of the Spanish Succession (in which the Holy Roman emperor Charles VI sought unsuccessfully to attain the throne of Spain). During his minority he was under the regency of his mother, Mariana of Austria; she remained in power until succeeded by John of Austria.

Charles III (of *Spain*). Title assumed by **Charles VI** (of the *Holy Roman Empire*) as pretender to the Spanish throne. Charles's claim was the basis of the War of the Spanish Succession.

Charles III (of *Spain*). b. Jan. 20, 1716; d. at Madrid, Dec. 14, 1788. King of Spain; second son of Philip V of Spain. As Charles IV, he was king of Naples (1735–59); he was king of Spain from 1759 to 1788. He sided with France in the Seven Years' War (making the so-called Family Compact of 1761) and entered the Revolutionary War on the side of America. In 1767 he expelled the Jesuits from Spain and all its dependencies. During Charles's rule Spain prospered.

Charles IV (of *Spain*). b. at Naples, Nov. 12, 1748; d. in Italy, Jan. 19, 1819. King of Spain; son of Charles III of Spain, whom he succeeded in 1788. He was under the influence of his wife, María Louisa Theresa of Parma, and of Manuel de Godoy, whom he elevated (1792) to the post of prime minister. He participated in the French Napoleonic Wars, allied himself with France, and took part in the naval battle of Trafalgar against England. A revolution having been provoked through Godoy's incompetence and Charles having been forced to abdicate, Napoleon seized the opportunity to expel (1808) the house of Bourbon from Spain.

Charles I through **Charles VI** (of *Sweden*). Rulers of Sweden, of extremely doubtful historical authenticity and hence seldom if ever now listed in biographical lists of known rulers. However, the chronology of Swedish kings is traditionally taken to include them.

Charles VII (of *Sweden*). [Called in Swedish, **Karl Swerkerson.**] d. c1167. King of Sweden. He succeeded his father Swerker I as king of Gotland in 1155, and in 1161 assumed the government of Sweden also. The primacy of Uppsala was established (1164) in his reign. Although the first historical Swedish king of the name of Charles, he is commonly styled the seventh, in accordance with the Swedish chronicler Johan Magnus, who inserts six kings of that name before him.

Charles VIII (of *Sweden*). [Called in Swedish, **Karl Knutsson.**] b. c1409; d. 1470. King of Sweden, elected in 1448. He was occupied in almost continuous warfare against the Danes, by whom he was twice expelled from the government.

Charles IX (of *Sweden*). [Earlier title, Duke of **Södermanland.**] b. Oct. 4, 1550; d. at Nyköping, Sweden, Oct. 30, 1611. King of Sweden; youngest son of Gustavus I (Gustavus Vasa). He reigned from 1604 to 1611. As regent for Sigismund III of Poland, he restored Protestantism as the state religion. Having ousted Sigismund, Charles became king. In 1600 he began war with Poland, and in 1611 with Denmark.

Charles X (of *Sweden*). [Also, **Charles Gustavus.**] b. at Nyköping, Sweden, Nov. 8, 1622; d. at Göteborg, Sweden, Feb. 13, 1660. King of Sweden; a cousin of Queen Christina of Sweden. He reigned from 1654 to 1660. In 1656 he defeated the Poles near Warsaw. In 1658 he invaded Denmark (leading his armies across the frozen sea) and unsuccessfully besieged (1658–59) Copenhagen, but won back extensive lands in S Sweden and parts of Norway by the Treaty of Roskilde (1658).

Charles XI (of *Sweden*). b. Nov. 24, 1655; d. at Stockholm, April 5, 1697. King of Sweden; son of Charles X of Sweden. He reigned from 1660 to 1697. After the Treaty of St.-Germain (1679), by which Sweden acquired Pomerania, and the Peace of Lund (1679) with Denmark, Charles turned to the reorganization of internal affairs, being given (1682) what amounted to absolute power.

Charles XII (of *Sweden*). b. at Stockholm, June 27, 1682; killed at Fredrikshald (now Halden), Norway, Dec. 11, 1718. King of Sweden; son of Charles XI of Sweden. He reigned from 1697 to 1718. He invaded Denmark in 1700, defeated (Nov. 30, 1700) the Russians at Narva, and defeated (1701–06) the Saxons and Poles. He was himself defeated (July 8, 1709) by Peter the Great at Poltava and escaped (1709) into Turkey. In 1714 he returned to Sweden.

Charles XIII (of *Sweden and Norway*). b. Oct. 7, 1748; d. Feb. 5, 1818. King of Sweden (1809–18) and Norway (1814–18); second son of Adolphus Frederick. He took part in the revolution of 1772, was regent in the period 1792–96, and became king of Norway in 1814. He ruled under a new constitution which limited royal power.

Charles XIV (of *Sweden and Norway*). [Also, **Charles John**; original name, **Jean Baptiste Jules Bernadotte;** additional title, Prince of **Pontecorvo.**] b. at Pau, France, Jan. 26, 1763; d. at Stockholm, March 8, 1844. King of Sweden and Norway (1818–44). He was a French general in the period 1794–1809, served (1799) as French minister of war, became (1804) a marshal of France, and served (1805) with distinction at Austerlitz. In 1810 he was elected crown prince of Sweden and adopted by Charles XIII. In consequence he changed his allegiance and in 1813 commanded the "army of the North" against Napoleon. It is from him that the noble family of the Bernadottes, linked to subsequent rulers of both Sweden and Denmark, is descended.

Charles XV (of *Sweden and Norway*). b. at Stockholm, May 3, 1826; d. at Malmö, Sweden, Sept. 18, 1872. King of Sweden and Norway; son of Oscar I. He reigned from 1859 to 1872. He established a two-chamber legislature in his country.

Charles, Cape. Cape in E Virginia, on the N side of the entrance to Chesapeake Bay ab. 24 mi. NE of Norfolk, Va. It is a low, sandy point, with tidal marshes. The Cape Charles lighthouse is on Smith Island, ab. 3½ mi. E of the cape.

Charles, Elizabeth. [Maiden name, **Rundle.**] b. 1828; d. March 29, 1896. English novelist. Her works include *Chronicles of the Schönberg-Cotta Family* (1863), *Diary of Mrs. Kitty Trevylyan* (1864), *Draytons and Davenants* (1866), *Winifred Bertram* (1866), *Against the Stream* (1873), *Lapsed but not Lost* (1881), and *Our Seven Homes* (1897).

Charles, Enid. [Married name, **Hogben.**] b. in December, 1894—. English geneticist and sociologist; wife of Lancelot Hogben (1895—). Her works include *The Prac-*

tice of Birth Control (1932), *The Twilight of Parenthood* (1935), and numerous monographs and papers on comparative physiology, mathematical genetics, and vital statistics.

Charles (shȧrl), **Jacques Alexandre César.** b. at Beaugency, France, Nov. 12, 1746; d. at Paris, April 7, 1823. French physicist and pioneer in balloon flight. He conducted experiments to confirm Benjamin Franklin's discoveries concerning electricity and lightning, and won the approval of the American scientist. Subsequently, when Montgolfier's demonstration of a hot air balloon in 1783 caused the Académie des Sciences to sponsor a flight in a similar machine inflated by hydrogen, Jacques Charles was chosen to generate the gas, inflate the bag and make the ascent, which with one companion he did in that same year, achieving a height of 7,000 feet. In 1785 he was elected to the Académie. The principle of the expansion of gases by heat, which he discovered in 1787, is often referred to as "Charles's law."

Charles (chärlz), **Thomas.** b. at Longmoor, Carmarthenshire, Wales, Oct. 14, 1755; d. Oct. 5, 1814. Welsh nonconformist minister and religious educator. He studied at Oxford for the Church of England priesthood, was ordained, and served for a time as a curate in Somersetshire, but his inclination was toward a more evangelistic ministry, and in 1783 he left the Anglican communion, returned to Wales, and joined the Methodists. He traveled about a great deal, being in much demand as a preacher. He had a lively interest in the religious education of the young, and promoted several "circulating schools" to this end. He wrote religious tracts and books in Welsh, established a Welsh press, and advocated the use of spoken and written Gaelic in religious work in Scotland and Ireland. Thomas Charles is also credited with a leading part in framing the rules and regulations of the Welsh Methodist Church.

Charles, William. b. at Edinburgh, c1776; d. at Philadelphia, August 29, 1820. American engraver and caricaturist. From his native Scotland he went to London, where his earliest known caricatures appeared about 1803. In danger of prosecution on account of one of these satirical works (supposedly one entitled "A Fallen Pillar of the Kirk") he escaped to America, probably about 1805. He worked in New York for some years, attracting little attention until he began issuing a series of caricatures on subjects connected with the War of 1812. He may have moved to Philadelphia even earlier than 1816, but from that year to his death he is known to have been in business in that city as an engraver, publisher, bookseller, and stationer. His caricatures have vigor and humor, but the artistic quality of his etchings, aquatints, and other engravings is not considered very high, and in editions which he published of *Doctor Syntax in Search of the Picturesque* and of *The Vicar of Wakefield,* his imitations of Rowlandson's illustrations are notably inferior.

Charles Albert. See also **Charles VII** (of the *Holy Roman Empire*).

Charles Albert (of *Sardinia*). b. in October, 1798; d. at Oporto, Portugal, July 28, 1849. King of Sardinia (1831–49). He became regent in 1821, following the deposition of Victor Emmanuel I, ruling until Charles Felix assumed the crown. On the death of Charles Felix, Charles Albert became king. He joined the movement for Italian independence from Austria in 1848, was defeated by the Austrians at Custozza in the same year, and abdicated after his decisive defeat at Novara, on March 23, 1849.

Charles Augustus (of *Saxe-Weimar*). [German, **Karl August.**] b. Sept. 3, 1757; d. at Graditz, near Torgau, Prussia, June 14, 1828. Grand duke of Saxe-Weimar. His mother, Anna Amalia, served as regent for him from 1758 to 1775, when he succeeded to the dukedom. He belonged to the confederacy of the Rhine in the period 1806–13, and was created grand duke in 1815. He became friendly with Goethe in 1775, and made his court at Weimar the intellectual and literary center of Germany.

Charles Belmont (bel'mont). See **Belmont, Charles.**

Charles Borromeo (bōr.rō.mā'ō), Saint. See **Borromeo, Saint Carlo.**

Charlesbourg (shäl'bůrg). Town in Quebec, Canada, situated on the main highway ab. 5 mi. NW of the city of Quebec: residential suburb. 5,734 (1951).

Charles City. [Former name, **The Ford.**] City in N Iowa, county seat of Floyd County, on the Cedar River, ab. 110 mi. NE of Dubuque: manufactures tractors. It is the seat of an Iowa State College experiment station. Charles City was the home of Carrie Chapman Catt. It was settled in 1850, and renamed in 1869 for the son of the founder. 10,309 (1950).

Charles City Cross Roads. See **Frayser's Farm.**

Charles Coldstream (kōld'strēm), **Sir.** See **Coldstream, Sir Charles.**

Charles Courtly (kōrt'li). See **Courtly, Charles.**

Charles Darnay (där'nā). See **Darnay, Charles.**

Charles Edward. See **Stuart, Charles Edward Louis Philip Casimir.**

Charles Emmanuel I (of *Sardinia*). [Italian, **Carlo Emanuele.**] b. at Turin, Italy, April 27, 1701; d. Feb. 19, 1773. King of Sardinia (1730–73) and duke of Savoy (as Charles Emmanuel III). He defeated the Austrians at Guastalla in 1734.

Charles Emmanuel II (of *Sardinia*). [Italian, **Carlo Emanuele.**] b. May 24, 1751; d. at Rome, Oct. 6, 1819. King of Sardinia and duke of Savoy (as Charles Emmanuel IV). He ascended the throne on Oct. 16, 1796, and abdicated on June 4, 1802.

Charles Emmanuel I (of *Savoy*). [Surnamed **"the Great"**; Italian, **Carlo Emanuele.**] b. at Rivoli, Italy, Jan. 12, 1562; d. at Savigliano, Piedmont, Italy, July 26, 1630. Duke of Savoy (1580–1630). He acquired Saluzzo in 1601. He gave his allegiance alternately to France and Spain.

Charles Emmanuel III (of *Savoy*). See **Charles Emmanuel I** (of *Sardinia*).

Charles Emmanuel IV (of *Savoy*). See **Charles Emmanuel II** (of *Sardinia*).

Charles Fitz Marshall (fits mär'shąl). See **Jingle, Alfred.**

Charles I Frederick Alexander. [German, **Karl Friedrich Alexander.**] b. at Stuttgart, in Württemberg, March 6, 1823; d. Oct. 6, 1891. King of Württemberg. He succeeded his father (William I) in 1864. He sided with Austria against Prussia in 1866, and with Prussia in 1870–71. He joined the new German Empire in 1871.

Charles Garnier (gȧr.nyā), Saint. See **Garnier, Saint Charles.**

Charles Gayless (gā'lẹs). See **Gayless, Charles.**

Charles Gould (göld). See **Gould, Charles.**

Charles Grandison (gran'di.sọn), **Sir.** Novel by Samuel Richardson, published in 1753.

Charles Gustavus. See **Charles X** (of *Sweden*).

Charles Heath (hēth). See **Heath, Charles.**

Charles John. See **Charles XIV** (of *Sweden and Norway*).

Charles Louis (of *Austria*). [Additional title, Duke of **Teschen.**] b. at Florence, Sept. 5, 1771; d. April 30, 1847. Austrian archduke and general; third son of the emperor Leopold II. Distinguished as commander (1796, 1799) of the Rhine armies, he later defeated Masséna at Caldiero, Italy, in 1805 (having earlier in the same year suffered defeat from Masséna's forces), defeated Napoleon at Aspern, near Vienna (May, 1809), and was defeated by him at Wagram, Austria (July 5–6, 1809).

Charles Martel (mär.tel'). [German, **Karl Martell.**] b. c689; d. at Quierzy-sur-Oise, France, Oct. 22, 741. Duke of Austrasia; son of Pepin of Héristal and grandfather of Charlemagne. He became mayor of the palace, and defeated the Saracens between Poitiers and Tours in 732. In English, his name may be translated as "Charles the Hammer." Although never in title king himself, he established the Frankish kingdom and the Carolingian dynasty by allotting his lands, which he had extended during his time, to his two sons, Carloman and Pepin the Short.

Charles Mound. Hill in NW Illinois, ab. 12 mi. NE of Galena. It is the highest point in the state. Elevation, ab. 1,241 ft.

Charles of Bavaria (bą.vär'i.ą). See **Charles VII** (of the *Holy Roman Empire*).

Charles of Durazzo (dö.rät'tsō). See **Charles III** (of *Naples*).

Charles of Luxemburg (luk'sęm.bėrg). See **Charles IV** (of the *Holy Roman Empire*).

Charles of Valois. b. March 12, 1270; d. at Perray, France, Dec. 16, 1325. French prince and soldier; son of Philip III and father of Philip VI of France. By marriage to a daughter of the king of Naples, he became count of Anjou and Maine, but for politic reasons he renounced a claim to the throne of Aragon. After his first wife's death he married a daughter of Baldwin II, the last Latin emperor at Constantinople, and upon Baldwin's death he claimed the succession to the Byzantine Empire, but was unable to make his claim good. He tried without success to secure the crown of the Western Empire. He participated in many wars, among other things serving the Guelfs against the Ghibellines, for which reason Dante placed him among the sufferers in his Purgatory. Three years after his death his son became king of France as Philip VI, the first of the Valois kings.

Charles of Viana. [Also, **Charles IV** (of *Navarre*).] b. 1421; d. 1461. Spanish prince. From his mother and from his maternal grandfather, he inherited Navarre, but upon his mother's death, his father seized power there. Charles submitted, but when his father's second wife interfered in Navarrese affairs, civil war ensued, in the course of which Charles was imprisoned by his father. Released upon his promise not to claim his crown until his father's death, he nevertheless resorted to arms, was defeated, and took refuge with Alfonso V, king of Aragon, Naples, and Sicily. Following Alfonso's death in 1458, Charles of Viana's father became John II of Aragon, and offered his son the crown of Naples and Sicily, which the latter refused. Reconciled with his father in 1459, Charles returned to Navarre, but upon his proposing to marry a princess of Castille, he was again imprisoned by John. This led to a popular insurrection, and Charles was released, but died soon afterward. Charles of Viana was a poet and a scholar, who translated Aristotle's *Ethics* into Spanish, and wrote a chronicle of the kings of Navarre.

Charles Philippe, Comte **d'Artois.** See **Charles X** (of *France*).

Charles Primrose (prim'rōz). See **Primrose, Charles.**

Charles River. River in E Massachusetts, in Worcester, Middlesex, and Norfolk counties, which flows into Boston Harbor at Boston (separating it from Cambridge). Length, ab. 75 mi.

Charles River Bridge v. Warren Bridge, 11 Peters 420 (1837). U.S. Supreme Court decision upholding the validity of a Massachusetts act which chartered a corporation, the Warren Bridge Company, and gave it the power to build a toll bridge across the Charles River, from Charlestown to Boston. The bridge competed for traffic with another bridge, owned and managed by the Charles River Bridge Company, a corporation created by the state some 50 years before. The Warren Bridge was to be surrendered to the state as soon as the cost of construction should be recovered. The Charles River Bridge Company sued for an injunction on the ground that the construction of a competing bridge constituted an impairment of contract. The question before the court was whether the original grant should be so construed as to constitute an exclusive grant. The decision, Chief Justice Roger B. Taney's first constitutional opinion, was of utmost importance in establishing the principle that legislative grants are to be construed narrowly in favor of the state, and that any ambiguity in a grant must operate against the corporation and in favor of the public. One of the most momentous aspects of the decision was the court's disposal of the supposition that the federal courts were to interpret the Constitution and especially the contract clause (unless that clause had been plainly violated) so as to protect property from assaults by state legislation. This modified the significance of the court's decision in the Dartmouth College Case, and marked what some students of constitutional law have regarded as a retreat from the advanced position taken by the court under Chief Justice John Marshall.

Charles Robert of Anjou (an'jö). See **Charles I** (of *Hungary*).

Charles Strickland (strik'lạnd). See **Strickland, Charles.**

Charles Surface (sėr'fạs). See **Surface, Charles.**

Charles's Wain. See **Wain, Charles's.**

Charles the Bad. See **Charles II** (of *Navarre*).

Charles the Bald. See **Charles II** (of the *Holy Roman Empire*).

Charles the Bold. [French, **Charles le Téméraire** (shàrl lẹ tā.mā.rer); early title, Comte **de Charolais.**] b. at Dijon, France, Nov. 10, 1433; killed at Nancy, France, Jan. 5, 1477. Duke of Burgundy (1467–77); son of Philip the Good. He married Margaret, sister of Edward IV of England. An opponent of Louis XI of France, he joined in defeating him. He conquered Lorraine in 1475, but was defeated by the Swiss at Grandson (March 2, 1476), at Morat (June 22, 1476), and finally at Nancy (Jan. 5, 1477).

Charles the Fair. See **Charles IV** (of *France*).

Charles the Great. See **Charlemagne.**

Charles Théodore Henri Antoine Meinrad (shàrl tā.o-dôr äṅ.rē äṅ.twän men.rȧd). [Title, Count of **Flanders.**] b. Oct. 10, 1903—. Prince regent of Belgium. He was created regent on Sept. 20, 1944, by joint vote of the chambers of parliament, to serve in the absence of his brother, King Leopold III, at that time a prisoner of the Germans. The regency was confirmed at Salzburg by Leopold III after the latter's release by American troops. He paid an official visit to the Congo in 1947; in 1948, at the invitation of the president of the U.S. and the prime minister of Canada, he visited the U.S. and Canada, accompanied by the Belgian prime minister and the minister of economic coöperation.

Charles the Second; or, the Merry Monarch. Comedy by John Howard Payne, produced and published in 1824.

Charles the Simple. See **Charles III** (of *France*).

Charles the Victorious. See **Charles VII** (of *France*).

Charles the Well-Beloved. See **Charles VI** (of *France*).

Charles the Wise. See **Charles V** (of *France*).

Charleston (chärlz'tọn). City in E Illinois, county seat of Coles County, ab. 43 mi. W of Terre Haute, Ind.: seat of the Eastern Illinois State College. In the county fairgrounds are the site of the fourth Lincoln-Douglas debate (Sept. 8, 1858) and the grave of Lincoln's cousin, Dennis Hanks. 9,164 (1950).

Charleston. City in NW Mississippi, a county seat (with Sumner) of Tallahatchie County, ab. 120 mi. N of Jackson. 2,629 (1950).

Charleston. City in SE Missouri, county seat of Mississippi County: marketing point for cotton; manufactures of shoes. 5,501 (1950).

Charleston. [Former name, **Charles Town.**] City in S South Carolina, county seat of Charleston County, at the confluence of the Ashley and Cooper rivers: oldest and largest city in the state. It is a port of entry, a tourist resort noted for its fine old houses, churches, and gardens, and a marketing center for timber, fruit, vegetables, and seafood. Manufactures include fertilizer, cigars, asbestos, rubber, paint, oil, and cotton bagging. It is the seat of the College of Charleston, the Medical College of the State of South Carolina, and The Citadel (a military college for men). It has a large landlocked harbor (site of Forts Sumter and Moultrie and Castle Pinckney) and has important army and navy installations in and near its limits. Charleston was founded in 1680 at its present site, the original settlement having been at Albemarle Point, ab. 7 mi. distant, some 10 years earlier. A British attack on Sullivan's Island was repulsed by William Moultrie in 1776. The city was unsuccessfully attacked in 1779, and was besieged by Sir Henry Clinton and taken in May, 1780. Charleston was the center of the nullification movement of 1832–33. It was the place of meeting of the Democratic national convention of 1860. The first secession ordinance was passed (Dec. 20, 1860) here, and the bombardment (April 12, 1861) of Fort Sumter began the Civil War. The city was evacuated by Confederate forces on Feb. 17, 1865. It was considerably damaged by an earthquake on Aug. 31, 1886 and by the 1938 hurricane. 70,174 (1950).

Charleston. [Former names, **Clendenin's Settlement, Charles Town.**] City in W West Virginia, capital of West Virginia and of Kanawha County, on the Kanawha River, ab. 44 mi. from its mouth. It is a shipping center for coal and other products; manufactures include chemicals, glass, machinery, armor plate, projectiles, and gun-forgings. It was settled in 1788 around Fort Lee. The state capital was moved here from Wheeling in 1870, its selection being ratified by vote in 1885. It is the seat of Morris Harvey College and the Mason College of Music and Fine Arts. 73,501 (1950).

Charleston. A former name of **Lorain.**

Charlestown (chärlz′toun). Town in S Indiana, in Clark County, ab. 15 mi. N of Jeffersonville. Explosives are manufactured here. In the decade between the last two U.S. censuses its population grew from 939 (1940) to 4,785 (1950).

Charlestown. Former city, now the Charlestown district of Boston, separated from Boston by the Charles River. It contains the state prison, a U.S. navy yard, and Bunker Hill monument. It was settled in 1629, was burned by the British on June 17, 1775, and was incorporated with Boston in 1874.

Charles Town. Town in E West Virginia, county seat of Jefferson County, ab. 8 mi. SW of Harpers Ferry, and 53 mi. NW of Washington, D.C.: residential community. John Brown was executed here, on Dec. 2, 1859. Several buildings are preserved from the time of George Washington's brother, Charles Washington, for whom the town was named. 3,035 (1950).

Charles Town. Former name of **Charleston,** S.C., of **Charleston,** W.Va., and of **Wellsburg,** W.Va.

Charles University. [Also: **University of Prague;** Czech, **Karlová Universita.**] University founded by the Bohemian king and Holy Roman emperor Charles IV in 1348, the first institution of higher learning in Bohemia. Originally an international institution, it acquired its Czech character during the Hussite period (15th century) but was Germanized and fell entirely under Jesuit influence in the 17th and subsequent centuries. In 1882 it was divided into a Czech and German section and continued thus into the 20th century. It is located in various buildings throughout Prague, the Karolínum, Klementínum, and the library being of special artistic value. It is the largest university in modern Czechoslovakia.

Charlet (shȧr.le), **Nicolas Toussaint.** b. at Paris, 1792; d. there, 1845. French painter and lithographer. Although he painted genre subjects, street scenes, and rural episodes, of ingratiating quality, his canvases depicting military scenes, and his lithographs glorifying the wars of Napoleon, were what brought him fame. Altogether he executed more than 2,000 lithographs. Examples of his work can be seen in the Louvre at Paris.

Charleville (shȧr.lẹ.vēl). [Medieval names, **Arcae Remorum, Carolopolis.**] Town in NE France, in the department of Ardennes, situated on the Meuse River opposite the town of Mézière, with which it forms a single urban area. It is one of the centers of the metallurgical industry of the Meuse valley. Ferrous as well as nonferrous metals, machine tools, brushes, leather, and sugar are produced. The town was founded in 1606 and the *place ducale* still gives the architectural impression of the period of Louis XIII. Parts of the town suffered damage in World War II. 20,193 (1946).

Charlevoix (shär′lẹ.voi). City in N Lower Michigan, county seat of Charlevoix County, on Lake Michigan and Pine Lake, ab. 160 mi. N of Grand Rapids. It is a winter and summer resort, noted especially for fishing. 2,695 (1950).

Charlevoix (shär′lẹ.voi; French, shȧr.lẹ.vwȧ), **Pierre François Xavier de.** b. at St.-Quentin, France, Oct. 29, 1682; d. at La Flèche, France, Feb. 1, 1761. French Jesuit missionary and historian. In 1720 he visited the missions of Canada, where he traveled extensively. Descending the Mississippi in 1721, he went from Louisiana to Santo Domingo, returning to France in December, 1722. He subsequently traveled in Italy. His *Histoire de la Nouvelle France* contains the account of his voyages and a history of the Canadian and Louisiana missions. He also wrote historical works on Santo Domingo, Paraguay, and Japan.

Charley Bates (chär′li bāts). See **Bates, Charley.**

Charlie or **Charley.** Nickname formerly given (c1640) to any one of the night watchmen of London; from King Charles I, who somewhat improved the police system.

Charlie Chan (chan). Hero of detective novels by Earl Derr Biggers.

Charlier (shär.lyer′), **Carl Ludwig Wilhelm.** b. at Östersund, Sweden, April 1, 1862; d. Nov. 4, 1934. Swedish astronomer. He was professor and director of the Lund observatory from 1897 to 1927. His work was principally in stellar statistics, and the motions and distribution of the stars.

Charlieu (shȧr.lyė). Town in C France, in the department of Loire, ab. 41 mi. NW of Lyons. The town is built around the architecturally remarkable remains of a ruined abbey dating from the 11th century and built in Romanesque style. 4,976 (1946).

Charlot (shär′lō), **André Eugene Maurice.** b. at Paris, July 26, 1882—. English producer and theater manager. He was manager (1912–15) of the Alhambra Theatre at London and became a naturalized British subject in 1922. He has specialized in revues, such as *Kill That Fly* (1912), *Eightpence a Mile* (1913), *Charlot's Revues* (1924–25), *How d'You Do* (1933), *Wonder Bar* (1930), and *The Town Talks* (1936). *Charlot's Revues* have also been seen in the U.S. Their casts included Gertrude Lawrence and Beatrice Lillie.

Charlot, Jean. b. at Paris, 1898—. American painter, color lithographer, and illustrator, director of the Colorado Springs Fine Arts Center until June, 1949. He has worked in Europe, Mexico, and the U.S., and is considered one of the foremost exponents of the color lithograph, having executed landscapes, genre, and ballet scenes in this medium. In Mexico, he worked with Rivera and Orozco on several frescoes, and completed a fresco in the National Preparatory School at Mexico City, *The Combat of the Great Temple,* in 1922. Other works include *Woman Lifting Rebozo* and *Landscape, Milpa Alta* in the Museum of Modern Art, New York, and a *Mother and Child.*

Charlot (shȧr.lō), **Louis.** b. at Cussy-en-Morvan, France, April 26, 1878—. French neoimpressionist painter, a member of the Société Nationale des Beaux-Arts. He exhibited at the galleries of Georges Petit and Durand-Ruel in 1929, as well as at the Salon des Tuileries and the Salon d'Automne; his work is in permanent collections of the Tuileries and the Luxembourg Museum. A list of his better-known paintings includes *The Shepherd, The Drinker, Portrait of My Parents, View of Morvan,* and *Morvan in Spring.*

Charlotte (shär.lot′, shạr-). City in S lower Michigan, county seat of Eaton County: chief distributing point in Michigan for maple sugar. A child welfare unit of the Kellogg Foundation is here. 6,606 (1950).

Charlotte (shär′lọt). City in W North Carolina, county seat of Mecklenburg County: important tobacco and textile distributing center. Before the California gold rush of 1848, it was the center of a gold-mining region. It was the site of the "Mecklenburg Declaration of Independence," May 20, 1775, and was occupied by the British under Cornwallis, Sept. 26, 1780. It is the seat of Queens College and Johnson C. Smith University. 134,042 (1950).

Charlotte. In Isaac Bickerstaffe's *The Hypocrite,* a lively, giddy girl who finally marries Darnley, though she has been promised to Cantwell, the titular hero. In Molière's *Tartuffe,* on which the play is based, the equivalent character is called Marianne.

Charlotte. In Colley Cibber's comedy *The Refusal, or The Ladies' Philosophy,* the daughter of Sir Gilbert Wrangle and sister of Sophronia. She is courted by Frankly, with whom she is in love.

Charlotte. In Henry Fielding's *The Mock Doctor,* the daughter of Sir Jasper, who pretends to be dumb so as to avoid a marriage with Dapper. Her prototype in Molière's *Le Médecin Malgré Lui* is called Lucinde.

Charlotte (of *England*). See **Charlotte Sophia.**

Charlotte (of *Luxembourg*). b. at Schloss Berg, Luxembourg, Jan. 23, 1896—. Grand duchess of Luxembourg; married (Nov. 6, 1919) Prince Félix Marie Vincent of Bourbon-Parma; mother of six children. She succeeded to the duchy upon the abdication of her elder sister, the grand Duchess Marie Adélaïde, on Jan. 9, 1919. She resided at London during the German occupation of Luxembourg in World War II, returning after the duchy's liberation by the Allies, in April, 1945.

Charlotte (of *Mexico*). See **Carlotta** (of *Mexico*).

Charlotte (of *Portugal*). See **Carlota** (of *Portugal*).

Charlotte (of *Tonga*). [Native, **Salote.**] Queen of Tonga, the only remaining Polynesian kingdom. She succeeded her father, King George Tubou II, in 1918. Her husband, William Tungi, acted as premier until his death in 1941, when he was succeeded by Ata, a high chief. Since the establishment of a British protectorate in 1900, the British agent and consul has acted as adviser to the queen. In 1924 Queen Charlotte did much to heal a breach among

Protestant Christians in the kingdom by persuading most of the members of the Tongan Free Church to reunite with the Wesleyan Church. Of imposing physical presence, Queen Charlotte is a worthy example of Polynesian royalty. During her reign, serious crimes have been rare, and there was, at last report, no public debt.

Charlotte, Fort. Name bestowed (1763) by the British upon the French Fort Condé at Mobile (in what is now Alabama) when the British occupied that town at the conclusion of the French and Indian Wars. In 1780 the post was seized by the Spaniards, and in 1813 it was taken by an American force under General James Wilkinson. It was abandoned after 1819, when Florida came into the possession of the U.S.

Charlotte, Treaty of Camp. Treaty (October, 1774) between the British and the Shawnee Indians, concluding Lord Dunmore's War. It was signed on Pickaway plains, in Pickaway County, Ohio, with Chief Cornstalk acting as the Indian spokesman.

Charlotte Amalie (shär'lọt ạ.mäl'yẹ). [Former name, **St. Thomas.**] City in S St. Thomas island, U.S. Virgin Islands, on the Caribbean Sea: capital and chief port of the islands; naval center; shipping point for bay rum. 9,801 (1940).

Charlotte Augusta, Princess. b. at Carlton House, London, Jan. 7, 1796; d. at Claremont, Surrey, England, Nov. 5, 1817. Only daughter of George IV and Caroline of Brunswick; wife of Prince Leopold of Saxe-Coburg (later King of the Belgians), whom she married May 2, 1816.

Charlotte Elizabeth. See **Elizabeth Charlotte,** Duchess of **Orléans.**

Charlotte Elizabeth. Pseudonym of **Tonna, Charlotte Elizabeth.**

Charlotte Harbor. Inlet in SW Florida, a shallow arm of the Gulf of Mexico ab. 35 mi. long, and ab. 7 mi. wide in its wider portions. There are fisheries.

Charlottenburg (shär.lot'ẹn.bůrk). Town in NE Germany, in the Western Sector of Berlin, situated on the Spree River, W of Berlin: a suburb, incorporated into the municipality of Greater Berlin. 220,326 (1950).

Charlotte Sophia. b. 1744; d. at Kew, England, Nov. 17, 1818. Queen of England; niece of Frederick, Duke of Mecklenburg-Strelitz, and wife of George III of England. During her husband's attacks of mental illness, she was in charge of his household. For a time Fanny Burney served in her entourage.

Charlotte Strait. Sea passage separating the N end of Vancouver Island from the mainland of British Columbia. It connects Johnstone Strait on the S with Queen Charlotte Sound on the N.

Charlottesville (shär'lọts.vil). Independent city in C Virginia, formerly county seat of Albemarle County, on the Rivanna River near the Blue Ridge Mountains, ab. 65 mi. NW of Richmond. Manufactures include woolen and silk goods; apples, horses, and other farm products are raised in the vicinity. It is the seat of the University of Virginia. Monticello, residence of Thomas Jefferson, is nearby, as is Ash Lawn, residence of James Monroe. 25,969 (1950).

Charlotte Temple. [Full title, **Charlotte Temple: or, a Tale of Truth.**] Sentimental novel by Susanna Rowson, published in England in 1791 and in the U.S. in 1794. It has been many times republished. The heroine, an innocent 15-year-old school-girl, is induced to come to America by Montraville, a lieutenant in the British service, on his promise of marriage upon arrival. This promise is not fulfilled; he deserts her, and she dies after giving birth to a child. A grave marked by a tombstone bearing the name of "Charlotte Temple," erected by a sexton in the eighteenth century, lies in the graveyard of Old Trinity Church at New York. The author in her preface states that the tale is a true one, "yet I have substituted names and places according to my own fancy." The real name of Charlotte Temple is said to have been Stanley.

Charlottetown (shär'lọt.toun). Seaport and the capital of Prince Edward Island, Canada, situated on the S side of the island at the head of Hillsborough Bay. It is connected by road with other points on the island, and by steamship with Montreal and other cities. Settled in the 18th century, it was named for Charlotte Sophia of England. It is an important fishing port, and the seat of Prince of Wales College and St. Dunstan's University. 15,887 (1951).

Charlton (chärl'tọn). Town in S Massachusetts, in Worcester County: agricultural community. It is the site of a memorial to Dr. William Morton, who first perfected the use of ether as an anesthetic in dentistry. 3,136 (1950).

Charlton Kings. Urban district, in W England, in Gloucestershire, ab. 105 mi. NW of London by rail. It is a suburb of Cheltenham. 5,836 (1951).

Charlus (shår.lü, -lüs), **Baron.** Character recurrent in several parts of the novel *À la recherche du temps perdu* (1913–27; Eng. trans., *Remembrance of Things Past*), by the French writer Marcel Proust (1871–1922). His increasing depravity reflects one aspect of the decadence of the French nobility.

Charmes (shårm), **Francis.** [Full French name, **Marie Julien Joseph François Charmes.**] b. at Aurillac, France, April 21, 1848; d. at Paris, Jan. 4, 1916. French journalist. He was the author of *Études historiques et diplomatiques* (1893), *Les Questions actuelles de politique étrangère en Europe* (1907), and *L'Allemagne contre l'Europe* (1915).

Charmian (chär'mi.ạn). Cleopatra's favorite waiting-woman in Shakespeare's *Antony and Cleopatra.* She kills herself after Cleopatra's death.

Charmides (kär'mi.dēz). Dialogue of Plato, the narration by Socrates of a conversation on the subject of temperance (moderation or practical wisdom) between himself, Charmides (a beautiful youth renowned for his moderation), Critias, and Chaerephon, which took place at Athens at the Palaestra of Taureas, near the porch of the King Archon, immediately after the battle of Potidaea, from which Socrates had just returned. Charmides was an Athenian, son of Glaucon, cousin of Critias, and uncle of Plato.

Charmouth (chär'muth). Civil parish, village, and seaside resort in S England, in Dorsetshire, ab. 2 mi. NE of Lyme Regis. It has no direct rail connections for passengers, being reached by rail to Lyme Regis, ab. 152 mi. SW of London. Charmouth is situated at the mouth of the river Char. The town is usually identified with Carrum, the scene of a victory of the Danes over Egbert in 835. Ethelwulf was defeated near here by the Danes in 840 or 842. Pop. 719 (1931).

Charnay (shår.ne), **Claude Joseph Désiré.** b. at Fleury, France, May 2, 1828; d. at Paris, Oct. 24, 1915. French archaeologist. He was the author of *Cités et ruines américaines* (American Cities and Ruins, 1863), and *Les Anciennes Villes du nouveau monde* (The Ancient Cities of the New World, 1884).

Charnock (chär'nọk), **Job.** d. 1693. English colonizer, remembered as the founder of Calcutta. Charnock arrived in India between 1655 and 1656, and soon afterwards joined the East India Company and remained in its service until his death. He was one of the most praised and trusted of the company's court of directors. In 1690 he secured from Aurangzeb a grant of the tract of land on which Calcutta now stands.

Charnock or **Chernock** (chär'nọk), **Robert.** b. c1663; hanged at Tyburn Hill (at what is now Marble Arch, London), March 18, 1696. English Jacobite who plotted to assassinate William III. He became an M.A. (1686) and was made fellow of Magdalen College, Oxford, the same year, and its vice-president in 1688, by order of James II, after he had become a Roman Catholic and an agent of James. Shortly after expelling 14 demies (originally, endowed scholars with half the allowance of fellows), he was himself expelled (October, 1688). As an enthusiastic supporter of the Jacobite revolt, he planned with George Barclay to murder William III. He was caught, tried, and executed (1696).

Charnock, Stephen. b. at London, 1628; d. there, July 27, 1680. English nonconformist clergyman. A graduate of Emmanuel College, Cambridge, he was the author of *A Treatise on the Excellence and Attributes of God* and other works.

Charnwood (chärn'wůd), 1st Baron. [Title of **Godfrey Rathbone Benson.**] b. at Alresford, Hampshire, England, Nov. 6, 1864; d. at London, 1945. English politician and writer; brother of Sir Frank Robert Benson. Educated at Oxford, he served as a member of the House of Commons (1892–95) and the House of Lords (1928 *et* *seq.*). He was the author of biographies of Abraham Lincoln (1916) and Theodore Roosevelt (1928). His other books include *According to St. John* (1926) and the detective story *Tracks in the Snow* (1906, published again in 1927).

Charnwood Forest. Barren upland tract in C England, in NW Leicestershire, ab. 5 mi. SW of Loughborough.

Charny (shär′nē). Village on the right bank of the Chaudière River, Quebec, Canada, a few miles inland from where the river empties into the St. Lawrence, ab. 5 mi. upstream from the city of Quebec. 3,300 (1951).

Charny (shȧr.nē), Comte **de.** A title of **Chabot, Philippe de.**

Charolais (shȧ.ro.le). [Also, **Charollais.**] Region and former county of France, in the department of Saône-et-Loire. Its capital was Charolles.

Charolais, Comte de. See **Charles the Bold.**

Charolles (shȧ.rol). Town in E central France, in the department of Saône-et-Loire. It was the capital of the county of Charolais.

Charon (kãr′ǫn). In Greek mythology, the ferryman, a son of Erebus, who transported the souls of the dead (whose bodies had been buried) over the river Styx to the lower world. His fee was an obolus or other coin, and this was placed for him in the mouth of the dead at the time of burial.

Charon (kä′rōn). German journal devoted to lyric poetry, founded in 1904 by Otto zur Linde and Rudolf Pannwitz. It never attained a large circulation and did not survive World War I.

Charondas (ką.ron′dąs). b. at Catana, Sicily; fl. c500 B.C. Sicilian lawgiver who legislated for the cities of Chalcidian origin in Sicily and Italy.

Charon's Staircase. In classical Greek drama, a name given to a flight of steps leading from the center of the stage into the audience.

Charpentier (shȧr.päṅ.tyā), **Gustave.** b. at Dieuze, France, June 25, 1860—. French composer. He studied at the Conservatoire at Paris, where he was awarded (1887) the Prix de Rome. Among his most important works are a suite for orchestra, *Impressions d'Italie*, which was adapted (1913) for a ballet; the opera *Louise* (produced at the Opéra-Comique, Paris, in 1900, with great success), which has been considered one of the most noteworthy of modern French operas; and the cantata *La Vie du poète* (1892).

Charpentier, Marc Antoine. b. at Paris, c1634; d. Feb. 24, 1704. French composer. He was a student of Carissimi and music master (1684 *et seq.*) at Paris. His works include operas, songs, and much liturgical music.

Charra (kar′ą) or **Charran** (kar′an). See **Haran.**

Charras (shȧ.räs), **Jean Baptiste Adolphe.** b. at Pfalzburg, in Lorraine, Jan. 7, 1810; d. at Basel, Switzerland, Jan. 23, 1865. French military writer. His chief work is *Histoire de la campagne de 1815* (1857).

Charrière (shȧ.ryer), **Isabelle de.** [Pseudonym, **Abbé de la Tour;** maiden name, **Isabella van Tuyll.**] b. at Utrecht, Netherlands, 1740; d. near Neuchâtel, Switzerland, Dec. 27, 1805. Swiss author. Her chief works are *Lettres neuchâteloises* (1784) and *Caliste, ou lettres écrites de Lausanne* (1788).

Charron (shȧ.rôṅ), **Pierre.** b. at Paris, 1541; d. there, Nov. 16, 1603. French preacher, philosopher, and moralist. His works include *Traité des trois vérités* (1594) and *Traité de la sagesse* (1601).

Charrúa (chä.rö′ą). Collective term for a number of South American Indian tribes which once occupied nearly all of the present territory of Uruguay. Their languages, which are only imperfectly known, are usually regarded as comprising an independent family. As with other Indians of the pampas area, the Charrúa early adopted the horse after its introduction into South America, and many of the present-day Uruguayan Gauchos (cowboys celebrated for their horsemanship) are of Charrúa descent.

Charshembe (chär.shem.be′). See **Çarşamba.**

Charterhouse (chär′tėr.hous). Originally a Carthusian monastery, later a hospital, and then a school for boys, at London, founded in 1371 by Sir Walter Manny and the bishop of Northburgh. At the dissolution of the monasteries, the Charter House was given by Henry VIII to Sir Thomas Audley, and passed through various hands to Sir Thomas Sutton, who in 1611 endowed it as a charity under the name of the Hospital of King James. This foundation long existed as a hospital for the aged and a school for boys. The school was transferred to Godalming, Surrey, in 1872, and the premises were occupied by the school of the Merchant Taylors' Company.

Charteris (chär′tėr.is), Sir **Evan.** b. Jan. 29, 1864; d. at Jesmond Hill, Pangbourne, Berkshire, England, Nov. 16, 1940. English art connoisseur and writer. He served in World War I. Among the posts he filled were those of chairman of trustees (1928 *et seq.*) of the National Portrait Gallery, chairman (1934–40) of the Tate Gallery, and trustee (1932–39) of the National Gallery. His writings include *William Augustus, Duke of Cumberland* (1913), *John Sargent* (1927), and *The Life and Letters of Sir Edmund Gosse* (1931).

Charteris, Leslie. b. 1907—. English novelist, creator of "the Saint," a fictional criminal-detective who has also been featured in films, comic strips, and on the radio. He studied at Cambridge, and was a contributor to *Cosmopolitan, American*, and other magazines, as well as serving as a Hollywood scenarist. He is the author of *Meet the Tiger* (1928), *Follow the Saint* (1938), *The Saint Goes West* (1942), *The Saint Sees it Through* (1946), *Call for the Saint* (1948), and *Saint Errant* (1948).

Charter Oak. Tree celebrated in American history, which formerly stood at Hartford, Conn. According to tradition, when Governor Andros came to Hartford in 1687 to demand of the Assembly the surrender of the colonial charter, the debate in that body over the governor's demand was prolonged beyond daylight, when suddenly the lights were extinguished, and in the darkness a patriot, Captain Joseph Wadsworth, escaped with the charter and hid it in a hollow oak. There is, however, no contemporary record of this event. The Charter Oak was overthrown by a storm in 1856.

Charters Towers (chär′tėrz). Town in NE Australia, in N central Queensland, ab. 84 mi. by road SW of Townsville. Gold was discovered here in 1872, and the town became an important mining center, reaching peak production in 1905. Since then mining has declined in the region, and farming has become the chief activity, with production of beef cattle, dairy products, citrus fruit, tobacco, and timber. 7,561 (1947).

Chartier (shȧr.tyā), **Alain.** b. at Bayeux, France, c1385; d. c1430 or 1433. French poet and man of letters. He wrote *Le Quadrilogue invectif, L'Espérance, La Belle Dame sans mercy*, and numerous other works. His poetry consists mainly of allegorical love poems and moral verse.

Chartier, Émile. [Pseudonym, **Alain.**] b. at Mortagne, France, March 3, 1868; d. June 3, 1951. French author. His essays, *Propos d'Alain*, appeared successively in various newspapers and reviews from 1906 and finally became a much-read department of Gide's *Nouvelle Revue Française*. He is also the author of *Mars ou la guerre jugée* (1921), *Les Éléments de la doctrine radicale* (1925), and others.

Chartists (chär′tists). Body of political reformers (chiefly workingmen) that sprang up in England c1838 in protest against the Reform Bill of 1832 which had not given the vote to workingmen. The Chartists advocated as their leading principles universal manhood suffrage, the abolition of the property qualification for a seat in Parliament, annual election of parliaments, equal representation, payment of members of Parliament, and vote by ballot, all of which demands were set forth in the People's Charter, of which William Lovett was a coauthor. The members of the extreme section of the party, under Feargus O'Connor, which favored an appeal to arms or popular risings if the charter could not be obtained by legitimate means, were called "physical-force men," whereas the more conservative section was known as the "party of moral force." The Chartists disappeared as a party after 1849.

Charton (shȧr.tôṅ), **Édouard Thomas.** b. at Sens, Yonne, France, May 11, 1807; d. at Paris, Feb. 28, 1890. French politician and writer. He was elected to the Constituent Assembly in 1848, and to the National Assembly at Bordeaux and Versailles in 1871. In 1878 he became a senator. He founded the *Magasin Pittoresque* (1833), *L'Illustration* (1843), and *Le Tour du Monde* (1860). He was the author of *Les Voyageurs anciens et modernes* (1855–57), and others.

Chartran (shär.träṅ), **Théobald.** b. at Besançon, France, 1849; d. at Paris, July 16, 1907. French painter; a pupil of Cabanel. His works are chiefly portraits and religious subjects.

Chartres (shär'trẹ; French, shártr). [Ancient names, **Autricum, Carnutum.**] City in W France, the capital of the department of Eure-et-Loir, situated on the Eure River, ab. 48 mi. SW of Paris. The Cathedral of Notre Dame, built in the 12th and 13th centuries, is among the most famous churches of France. Towers, portals, sculptures, and stained-glass windows are equally remarkable. The interior gives an impression of unity and harmony found in few other places of worship. The churches of Saint-Pierre and Saint-André are also medieval monuments; there are many houses from the medieval and Renaissance periods. The municipal museum contains tapestries. The city is a station on the railroad line from Paris to Nantes and has various industries, as well as grain, horse, and cattle markets. Large airfields are located nearby. Chartres was damaged in World War II, but most of the old buildings are intact. 26,422 (1946).

Chartres, County of. Medieval county in N France, comprised in the government of Orléanais, and partly corresponding to the department of Eure-et-Loir. It was united to Champagne from 1125 to 1152, and was purchased by Saint Louis (Louis IX) in 1234. It was afterward a duchy and a royal appanage. The capital was at Chartres.

Chartres, Fort de. Fort built (1719–20) by the French near the site of Prairie du Rocher, Randolph County, Ill., which served as the seat of government in the Illinois country from 1719 to 1772. It was named for Louis, Duc de Chartres, the son of the regent of France, Philippe II, Duc d'Orléans, and during its history occupied several sites. The one built between 1753 and 1756, near the site of the original fort, had stone walls 490 ft. long. The fort came into the possession of the British in 1765 and, until 1772, when it was destroyed, was called Fort Cavendish.

Chartres, Robert d'Orléans, Duc **de.** [Full name: **Robert Philippe Louis Eugène Ferdinand d'Orléans,** Duc **de Chartres;** pseudonym, **Robert le Fort.**] b. at Paris, Nov. 9, 1840; d. at Château Saint-Firmin, near Chantilly, Oise, France, Dec. 5, 1910. French prince, head of the house of Bourbon-Orléans, claimant to the French throne; younger brother of Louis Philippe Albert d'Orléans, Comte de Paris, and grandson of Louis Philippe. Exiled in 1848, he served (1859) in the Italian army against Austria, and was a member (1861–62) of General McClellan's staff during the American Civil War. After the revolution of Sept. 4, 1870, he returned incognito to France, served under the pseudonym of Robert le Fort in General Chanzy's army, and in 1871, when the National Assembly revoked the law banishing the Orléans family, was appointed a major. He became a colonel in 1878, and was in command of the 12th Chasseurs, stationed at Rouen, when by the decree of Feb. 24, 1883, he was suspended from the active list; by the law of June 23, 1886, he was expelled from the army. He married (June 11, 1863) Françoise Marie Amélie of Orléans.

Chartreuse (shár.trėz), **La Grande.** Formerly the leading Carthusian monastery, situated ab. 13 mi. NE of Grenoble, in the department of Isère, France. It was founded by Saint Bruno c1084. It gives its name to the liqueur chartreuse, manufactured there until 1903.

Chartreuse de Parme (dẹ párm), **La.** [Eng. trans., *"The Charterhouse of Parma."*] Novel by Stendhal (pseudonym of Henri Beyle), published in 1839. The story is laid for the most part in Parma. Its hero, Fabrice del Dongo, after serving with Napoleon's armies, being involved in political intrigues, committing manslaughter, and suffering imprisonment, becomes a priest and, finally, enters a Carthusian monastery.

Charudes (kạ.rö'dēz). See **Harudes.**

Charwoman's Daughter, The. Novel by James Stephens, published in 1912. It was issued in the U.S. under the title *Mary, Mary.*

Charybdis (kạ.rib'dis). In Greek mythology, a sea monster which three times a day sucks in the sea and discharges it again in a terrible whirlpool; depicted as a maiden with the tail of a fish begirt with hideous dogs. Opposite her was the other monster Scylla. In later times they were located in the Straits of Messina, Scylla being identified with a projecting rock on the Italian side, Charybdis with a whirlpool facing it.

Charyllis (kạ.ril'is). In Edmund Spenser's *Colin Clout's Come Home Again*, a character intended for Lady Anne Compton, one of the six daughters of Sir John Spenser of Althorpe.

Chasdai ben Isaac ben Shaphrut (chäz.dī' ben ī'zạk ben shäp.röt'). fl. 915–970. Jewish statesman and physician in Córdoba, Spain, body physician and minister of finance under the caliphs Abd-er-Rahman III and Al-Hakim. He was appointed by them *Nasi* (prince, head) over the Jews in the caliphate. He was a generous promoter of literature, and translated the botanical work of Dioscorides from Latin into Arabic. His correspondence with Joseph, the Jewish king of the Khazar kingdom, near the Caspian Sea, is extant.

Chase (chās), **Camp.** Union military training camp west of Columbus, Ohio, which during the Civil War was also used as a prison camp for Confederates.

Chase, Frederick Lincoln. b. at Boulder, Colo., June 28, 1865; d. Nov. 8, 1933. American astronomer. He took his Ph.D. (1891) at Yale University and was assistant astronomer (1891–1911) and acting director (1910–13) of the Yale Observatory. His findings were published in *Triangulation of the Victoria Comparison Stars* (1897), *Parallax Investigations on 163 Stars, mainly of Large Proper Motion* (1906), *Parallax Investigations on 35 Selected Stars* (1910), *Parallax of 41 Southern Stars* (1912), and *Catalogue of Yale Parallax Results* (1912).

Chase, Harry Woodburn. b. at Groveland, Mass., April 11, 1883—. American educator. A graduate of Dartmouth College (B.A., 1904) and of Clark University (Ph.D., 1910), he served as professor of psychology (1910 *et seq.*) at the University of North Carolina, and was its president from 1919 to 1930. After a period (1930–33) as president of the University of Illinois, he became (1933) chancellor of New York University. He retired in 1951.

Chase, Mary Ellen. b. at Blue Hill, Me., Feb. 24, 1887—. American novelist, essayist, and teacher. Graduated from the University of Maine (B.A., 1909) and from the University of Minnesota (M.A., 1918; Ph.D., 1922), she served as assistant professor of English (1922–26) at the University of Minnesota and as associate professor (1926–29) and professor (1929 *et seq.*) of English at Smith College. She is the author of the books for children *The Girl from the Big Horn Country* (1916) and *Virginia of Elk Creek Valley* (1917). Among her novels are *Uplands* (1927), *Mary Peters* (1934), *Silas Crockett* (1935), *Dawn in Lyonesse* (1938), and *Windswept* (1941). Her other works include *The Art of Narration* (with F. K. Del Plaine, 1926), *Thomas Hardy from Serial to Novel* (1927), *Writing of Informal Essays* (1928), *This England* (1936), *A Goodly Fellowship* (1939), and *Jonathan Fisher, Maine Parson, 1768–1847* (1948).

Chase, Philander. b. at Cornish, N.H., Dec. 14, 1775; d. at Robin's Nest, Ill., Sept. 20, 1852. American missionary bishop of the Episcopal Church, one of the founders of Kenyon College (1824), in Ohio, and Jubilee College (1839), in Illinois (only the former of which now remains in existence). He was bishop of Ohio, bishop of Illinois, and (from 1843 to 1852) presiding bishop of the Episcopal Church.

Chase, Salmon Portland. b. at Cornish, N.H., Jan. 13, 1808; d. at New York, May 7, 1873. American jurist and statesman, secretary of the treasury in Lincoln's cabinet and chief justice of the U.S. Supreme Court; nephew of Philander Chase. Graduated (1826) from Dartmouth, he was admitted to the bar (1829), and established his practice at Cincinnati, where he compiled the *Statutes of Ohio* (3 vols., 1833–35) and for a time devoted himself to lecturing. He became prominent as an antislavery man, defending many escaped slaves apprehended under the fugitive-slave act. Active as a member of the Whig and Liberty parties, he went (1849) to the U.S. Senate as a Free Soiler from Ohio, but soon devoted himself to attempts to swing over the Democratic Party to the antislavery viewpoint. Failing in this, he joined the Republicans and was elected (1855) governor of Ohio; elected a Republican U.S. senator in 1860, he resigned to become secretary of the treasury (1861–64). During his tenure he did much to finance the Civil War expenditures of the Union government, strengthening its credit by devising the national banking system (1863). As a cabinet member, he participated in the making of policy, but his sympathies with the Radical Republicans led him to oppose Lincoln and Seward at various points. The dissension culminated in the resignation of both Chase and Seward, which Lincoln refused to countenance. For a time in 1864 Chase was put forward by Republicans who considered Lincoln too weak a president as the hope of the party in the approaching election. The call came in the "Pomeroy Circular," and added to the poor feeling between Lincoln and Chase which, upon the latter's resignation from the cabinet in 1864, was termed by the president as "mutual embarrassment in our official relations which it seems cannot be overcome or longer sustained consistently with the public service." After his departure from the cabinet Chase was again boomed as a Republican nominee by the Radicals; but he eventually supported Lincoln during the second campaign. As chief justice of the Supreme Court (1864 *et seq.*), the successor to Taney in that post, he presided at the inconclusive trial of Jefferson Davis in 1868, presided at the Senate's impeachment proceedings against President Johnson, and faced a series of complicated problems arising from the necessity to interpret many pieces of Reconstruction legislation, as in *Mississippi v. Johnson, Texas v. White, Georgia v. Stanton,* and *Ex parte Garland.* See *Account of the Private Life and Public Services of Salmon Portland Chase,* by Robert B. Warden (1874).

Chase, Samuel. b. in Somerset County, Md., April 17, 1741; d. June 19, 1811. American Revolutionary leader, signer of the Declaration of Independence, and justice of the U.S. Supreme Court, noted for his impeachment and trial (1804–05) instigated by Jefferson. He studied law at Annapolis, established his practice there in 1761, and served (1764–84) as a member of the Maryland assembly. He soon identified himself with "The Sons of Liberty," became (1774) a member of the Maryland committee of correspondence, and a delegate to the First Continental Congress; he was (1775) a member of the council of safety and of the Maryland convention. He served (1776), together with Benjamin Franklin and others, on the commission sent to Canada by the Continental Congress to explore the possibility of union between Canada and the colonies. He signed (Aug. 2, 1776) the Declaration of Independence and served on the Congress's Maryland delegation until 1778, sitting as a member of many committees. He moved to Baltimore in 1786 and became (1788) chief judge of the criminal court. He opposed the ratification of the Constitution, but emerged (c1794) as a Federalist. He was appointed (Jan. 26, 1796) to the high court by Washington and, in the performance of his duties, established a high standard. Among his more notable opinions are *Hylton v. United States, Ware v. Hylton, Calder v. Bull, Hollingsworth v. Virginia,* and *United States v. Worrall.* His impeachment and trial, with their complicated background, stemmed in part from his unfavorable remarks concerning the state of the republic under Jefferson's administration. Jefferson recommended impeachment, but the trial, conducted in 1805, ended in Chase's acquittal despite Jefferson's attempt to influence the Senate.

Chase, Stuart. b. at Somersworth, N.H., March 8, 1888—. American economist and writer. Graduated (B.S., 1910) from Harvard, he served as an investigator (1917–22) for the U.S. Federal Trade Commission, and was associated with Labor Bureau, Inc. (1922–39) and with the Tennessee Valley Authority (1940–41). He is the author of *A Honeymoon Experiment* (1916), *The Tragedy of Waste* (1925), *Men and Machines* (1929), *A New Deal* (1932), *The Economy of Abundance* (1934), *Rich Land, Poor Land* (1936), *The Tyranny of Words* (1938), *The New Western Front* (1939), *Tomorrow's Trade* (1945), *For This We Fought* (1946), *The Proper Study of Mankind* (1948), and other works; coauthor, with F. J. Schlink, of *Your Money's Worth* (1927).

Chase, William Merritt. b. at Williamsburg, Ind., Nov. 1, 1849; d. at New York, Oct. 25, 1916. American painter of portraits, still life, and landscapes. He was a pupil of the schools of the National Academy of Design at New York. In 1871 he went to St. Louis, where he had some success as a portrait painter, and in 1872 to Germany, where he studied under Karl von Piloty and others at Munich. He went from Munich to Venice, returning to New York in 1878. He taught at the Art Students League of New York for 18 years, and opened his own school in 1896. He was a member of the National Academy, was president of the Society of American Artists, and was the recipient of many honors at home and abroad.

Chase City. Town in S Virginia, in Mecklenburg County, ab. 80 mi. SW of Richmond: tobacco markets. 2,519 (1950).

Chasella (ką.sel′ą). A Latin name of **Kassel.**

Chasins (chā′sinz), **Abram.** b. at New York, Aug. 17, 1903—. American pianist and composer. He studied music under Hutcheson, Godowsky, Hofmann, and Rubin Goldmark; and taught (1926–35) piano at the Curtis Institute at Philadelphia. In 1935 he became active in broadcasting. His compositions include *Concerto in F Minor* and *The Parade;* he also transcribed for two pianos Johann Sebastian Bach's *Passacaglia* and the younger Johann Strauss's *Blue Danube.*

Chasles (shäl), **Michel.** b. at Épernon, Eure-et-Loir, France, Nov. 15, 1793; d. at Paris, Dec. 19, 1880. French geometrician, professor at the École Polytechnique, and later at the Sorbonne. He was the author of *Aperçu historique sur l'origine et le développement des méthodes en géométrie* (1837), *Traité de géométrie supérieure* (1852), *Traité des sections coniques* (1865), and *Rapport sur les progrès de la géométrie* (1870). He was the victim of a literary forgery (by Irene Lucas) in 1867, being persuaded of the genuineness of a large number of forged letters of Pascal, Dante, Shakespeare, and others. On those of Pascal he made a report to the French Academy.

Chasles, Victor Euphémion Philarète. b. at Mainvilliers, near Chartres, France, Oct. 8, 1798; d. at Venice, July 18, 1873. French literary critic, novelist, and general writer. His essays were collected in 11 volumes, under the title *Études de littérature comparée.*

Chassé (shä.sā′), Baron **David Hendrik.** b. at Thiel, Netherlands, March 18, 1765; d. at Breda, Neth rlands, May 2, 1849. Dutch general. He was distinguished in the French service in the Penninsular campaign, and in the Dutch service at Waterloo (1815), and at Antwerp (1830–32). From his predilection for attacking with the bayonet, he was nicknamed by the soldiers "General Bayonet."

Chassé, General. A pseudonym of **Dixon, Henry Hall.**

Chassebœuf (shås.bėf), **Constantin François de.** See **Volney, Constantin François de Chassebœuf,** Comte **de.**

Chasseforêt (shås.fo.re), **Dôme de.** See **Dôme de Chasseforêt.**

Chasseloup-Laubat (shås.lö.lō.bå), **François,** Marquis **de.** b. at St.-Sernin, Charente-Maritime, France, Aug. 18, 1754; d. at Paris, Oct. 10, 1833. French military engineer, distinguished in the campaigns between 1792 and 1812; father of Justin Prosper, Comte de Chasseloup-Laubat, and Justin Prudent, Marquis de Chasseloup-Laubat.

Chasseloup-Laubat, Justin (Napoléon Samuel) Prosper, Comte **de.** b. at Alessandria, Italy, March 29, 1805; d. at Versailles, France, in March, 1873. French politician; son of François, Marquis de Chasseloup-Laubat. He was minister of marine and colonies (1859–67).

Chasseloup-Laubat, Justin Prudent, Marquis **de.** b. at Paris, 1802; d. there, Dec. 17, 1863. French general and politician; son of François, Marquis de Chasseloup-Laubat.

Chassepot (shås.pō), **Antoine Alphonse.** b. May 4, 1833; d. Feb. 13, 1905. French mechanic. He was the inventor of the Chassepot rifle, adopted by the French army in 1866.

Chassériau (shå.sā.ryō), **Théodore.** b. in the West Indies, 1819; d. at Paris, 1856. French historical painter, portraitist, and etcher.

Chasta Costa (chas′tą kos′tą). North American Indian tribe formerly inhabiting the upper Rogue River valley, Oregon. The language was of the Athabaskan family.

Chasteau (shä.tō), **Marcelle.** See **Tinayre, Marcelle.**

Chaste Diana, The. Historical novel by Lily Adams Beck, published in 1923 under the pseudonym E. Barrington. It deals with the beautiful 18th-century actress Lavinia Fenton.

Chastel (shä.tel), **Jean.** See **Châtel, Jean.**

Chastelard (shas'tẹ.lärd). Tragedy by Algernon Charles Swinburne, published in 1865. It is based on the life of Pierre de Boscosel de Chastelard, a French poet who was executed at Edinburgh for his love of Mary, Queen of Scots.

Chastelard (shä.tẹ.lär), **Pierre de Boscosel de.** b. in Dauphiné, France, c1540; executed at the Tolbooth, Edinburgh, 1563. French poet at the court of Francis II of France and Mary, Queen of Scots; a descendant of Pierre de Terrail, Seigneur de Bayard. He was a page in the household of the constable Montmorency, and afterward in that of Marshal Damville. When Mary went to Scotland after the death of her husband, in 1561, Chastelard followed her in the train of Henride Damville, who escorted her. Violently in love with her, he went back to France, but returned in 1563. He was twice discovered in her bedchamber; she pardoned him the first offense, but for the second sacrificed him mercilessly to public opinion, and he was taken to the Tolbooth and hung.

Chasteler (shä.tẹ.lā'), **Jean Gabriel Joseph Albert,** Marquis **du.** b. at Malbais, near Mons, Belgium, Jan. 22, 1763; d. at Venice, May 7, 1825. Austrian general. He distinguished himself at Wattignies (1793), in Italy (1799), and in the Tyrol (1800, 1805, and 1809).

Chastellain or **Chastelain** (shä.tẹ.laṅ), **Georges.** b. near Aalst, Flanders, c1405; d. in February or March, 1475. Flemish chronicler and poet, author of *Chronique des ducs de Burgogne,* and others. His collected works were edited (1863–66) by Kervyn de Lettenhove.

Chastellux (shä.tẹ.lü), **François Jean,** Marquis **de.** b. at Paris, 1734; d. there, Oct. 28, 1788. French general and author. He served in the Seven Years' War and the American Revolution. His chief works are *De la félicité publique* (1772) and *Voyages dans l'Amérique Septentrionale* (1786).

Chaste Maid in Cheapside, A. Play by Thomas Middleton, thought to have been acted on Dec. 25, 1612 and printed in 1630.

Château (shä.tō). French word for "castle" or "fortress," also part of the names of many French towns. For the names of famous French castles, see under the distinguishing element.

Chateaubriand (shȧ.tō.brē.äṅ), **François René,** Vicomte **de.** b. at St.-Malo, France, Sept. 4, 1768; d. at Paris, July 4, 1848. French author and statesman. He entered the army in 1786, traveled in America (1791–92), served in the royalist army at Thionville in September, 1792, and subsequently emigrated to England, where in 1797 he published *Essai historique, politique, et moral sur les révolutions anciennes et modernes.* He returned to France in 1800, and, having been converted by the death of his mother to the Roman Catholic faith, published in 1802 a eulogy of Christianity, entitled *Le Génie du christianisme.* In 1803 he was appointed by Napoleon secretary of legation at Rome, and in the same year became minister to the republic of Valais, a post which he resigned on the execution of the Duke of Enghien in 1804. In 1814 he supported the Bourbons in a pamphlet entitled *De Buonaparte et des Bourbons.* He was created a peer of France in 1815, was ambassador at London in 1822, and was minister of foreign affairs (1823–24). Other works by him include *Atala* (1801), *René* (1802), *Les Martyrs* (1809), *Itinéraire de Paris à Jérusalem* (1811), *Les Natchez* (1826), *Les Adventures du dernier des Abencérages* (1826), and *Mémoires d'outre-tombe* (1849–50, an autobiography). Chateaubriand is considered one of the first and leading writers of the Romantic Movement, and his influence on subsequent French literature was considerable, especially through *Le Génie du christianisme. Atala* and *René,* both of which had originally been written as episodes in the religious work, gained immense success on their separate publication as novels. In *Atala* he tells the story of an American Indian girl who becomes converted to Christianity. In this, as in other works, he drew on his travels in America for romantic descriptions of nature; it is thought now that to some extent these were invented, his travels never having extended beyond Pittsburgh, although he gives accounts of further regions. *René,* also a work with a religious moral, has for its hero an introspective young man, considered to have been to some extent autobiographical, who became the prototype of the Romantic hero.

Châteaubriant (shä.tō.brē.äṅ). Town in W France, in the department of Loire-Inférieure, on the Chère River, ab. 35 mi. NE of Nantes. It has a castle composed of two parts: the old castle dating from the 11th, 12th, and 15th centuries, and the new castle built in Renaissance style under Francis I in the 16th century. 9,276 (1946).

Chateaubriant (shȧ.tō.brē.äṅ), **Alphonse de.** b. at Rennes, France, March 25, 1877—. French author of novels on provincial life. His works include *M. de Lourdines* (1911; Eng. trans., *The Keynote,* 1912), *La Brière* (1923; Eng. trans., *The Peat Cutters,* 1927), and *La Réponse du Seigneur* (1933). Born and raised in Brittany, a nobleman of marked reactionary principles, and author of a favorable account of a trip to Nazi Germany, *Gerbe des Forces* (1937), he has been *non grata* with the government of the Fourth Republic.

Châteaubriant (shä.tō.brē.äṅ), Comtesse **de.** [Title of **Françoise de Foix.**] b. c1490; d. at Châteaubriant, France, Oct. 16, 1537. Mistress of Francis I, king of France.

Château-Chinon (shä.tō.shē.nôṅ). Town in N central France, in the department of Nièvre, ab. 20 mi. NW of Autun. 2,477 (1946).

Châteaudun (shä.tō.dėṅ). [Latin, **Castrodunum.**] Town in W France, in the department of Eure-et-Loir, situated on the Loir River, ab. 30 mi. NW of Orléans. It contains a castle of the counts of Dunois, and a number of old churches and other medieval monuments. A large part of the town was severely damaged in World War II. 8,145 (1946).

Chateaugay (shat'ẹ.gē, -gā). [In Canada, **Châteauguay** (French, shä.tō.gā).] River in N New York, and in S Quebec, Canada, flowing from the Adirondacks N and NE to join the St. Lawrence ab. 15 mi. above Montreal. In October, 1813, an American force advancing on Montreal was routed and turned back by a small Canadian force along the Chateauguay ab. 10 mi. N of the border. Length, ab. 60 mi.

Chateaugay. A former name of **Conway,** N. H.

Chateaugay, Battle of. Engagement (Oct. 25–26, 1813) in the War of 1812, fought along the Chateaugay River in Canada, between some 800 British soldiers and several thousand American troops under General Wade Hampton. The action ended with Hampton's withdrawal to U.S. soil.

Château-Gontier (shä.tō.gôṅ.tyā). Town in NW France, in the department of Mayenne, situated on the Mayenne River, S of Laval. The collegiate church of Saint-Jean is a Romanesque building dating from the 11th and 12th centuries. 6,676 (1946).

Chtâeauguay (shä.tō.gā), Sieur **de.** See **Le Moyne, Antoine.**

Châteaulin (shä.tō.laṅ). Village in NW France, in the department of Finistère, ab 14 mi. N of Quimper, on the Aune River.

Châteaurenard-Provence (shä.tō.rẹ.när.pro.väṅs). [Also, **Châteaurenard.**] Town in SE France, in the department of Bouches-du-Rhône, situated near the Durance River, S of Avignon. It is a market town for the early vegetables which are grown in the region. 8,604 (1946).

Châteaurenault (shä.tō.rẹ.nō). Town in W central France, in the department of Indre-et-Loire, ab. 19 mi. NE of Tours. Pop. ab. 4,000.

Chateau-Renault or **Chateaurenault** or **Chateaurenaut** or **Chateauregnaud, François Louis Rousselet,** Marquis **de.** b. 1637; d. at Paris, Nov. 15, 1716. Vice admiral and marshal of France. He entered the army in 1658 but changed to the navy in 1661, and in the course of years rose to high rank in that service. In 1689 he was entrusted with the task of escorting James II and his army to Ireland. He was second in command of the French fleet when it defeated the English and the Dutch at Beachy Head in 1690. In 1701 he was named vice admiral of France, but in the following year a combined English and Dutch fleet overwhelmed him off the coast of Vigo, Spain. He was held not to have been at fault for this disaster, and in 1703 Louis XIV added to his honors the titles of marshal of France and lieutenant general of Brittany.

Châteauroux (shä.tō.rö). Town in C France, the capital of the department of Indre, situated on the Indre River, between Bourges and Limoges, a station on the railroad line from Paris to Toulouse. During the French Revolution it was called Indreville. It is a developing industrial town, with a number of metallurgical and machine industries; woolen, leather, and shoe manufactures; breweries, distilleries, and tobacco factories. Notable buildings are the Château Raoul, dating from the 15th century, old churches, a museum, and a library. 34,611 (1946).

Châteauroux, Duchesse **de.** [Title of **Marie Anne de Mailly;** additional title, Marquise **de la Tournelle.**] b. in October, 1717; d. at Paris, Dec. 8, 1744. Mistress of Louis XV of France, in the period 1742–44.

Château-Thierry (shä.tō.tye.rē; Anglicized, sha.tō′ti.ăr′i, -tē′ę.ri). [Latin, **Castrum Theodorici.**] Town in N France, in the department of Aisne, situated on the Marne River, ab. 50 mi. NE of Paris. It contains a ruined castle, with ramparts and towers dating from the 13th century. Napoleon I defeated (1814) Russian and Prussian forces here. In 1918 the Germans carried their spring offensive to Château-Thierry, causing severe damage. The town suffered again in World War II. 8,094 (1946).

Château-Thierry, Battle of. Military engagement (May 31–June 4, 1918) of World War I, in which troops of the American 2nd Division with French colonial reinforcements were able to hold their lines against a major German attack and consolidate a position for launching a counteroffensive. Celebrated in large part for the substantial role played by American troops, this encounter on the Marne River, 60 mi. from Paris, did much to halt the German summer offensive of 1918.

Châtel (shä.tel), **Ferdinand Toussaint François.** b. at Gannat, Allier, France, Jan. 9, 1795; d. at Paris, Feb. 13, 1857. French religious reformer. He wrote *Profession de foi de l'église catholique française* (1831) and other works.

Châtel, Jean. [Also, **Chastel.**] b. c1575; executed at Paris, Dec. 29, 1594. French fanatic who attempted to assassinate Henry IV of France, on Dec. 27, 1594.

Chatelain (shä.tę.laṅ), **Heli.** b. at Morat, Switzerland, 1859; d. at Lausanne, Switzerland, July 22, 1908. Swiss missionary and Africanist. He came to the U.S. in 1883, and went to Angola in 1884 as a missionary linguist. He became philologist of a U.S. scientific expedition to West Africa in 1889, and a U.S. commercial agent in 1891. He published *Grammatica do Kimbundu* (1889), *Grundzüge des Kimbundu* (1890), *Folk-Tales of Angola* (1894), and others. In 1897 he founded the Phil-African Mission, near the edge of the Angola highlands, for the industrial training of the natives under Christian influence.

Châtelain de Coucy et de la dame de Fayel (shä.tę.laṅ dę kö.sē ā dę là dàm dę fā.yel), **Histoire du.** French romance, of which the personages were real, written about the beginning of the 13th century. It was published in a modern version in 1829.

Châtelard (shä.tlàr), **Le.** See **Le Châtelard.**

Châtelet (shä.tę.le). Town in S Belgium, in the province of Hainaut, situated on the Sambre River, W of Namur. It has coal mines, stone quarries, and iron industries. 14,605 (1947).

Châtelet, Gabrielle Émilie le Tonnelier de Breteuil, Marquise **du.** See **du Châtelet, Gabrielle Émilie le Tonnelier de Breteuil,** Marquise.

Châtelet, Le Grand. Ancient fortress at Paris, situated on the right bank of the Seine, on the present Place du Châtelet, used for a prison and for courts of justice until 1802, when it was destroyed. Its origin is very obscure. It was at first simply a tower commanding the northern approach to the city. There was probably a wooden tower here as early as 885. The earliest mention is in a charter of Louis VII of France in 1147. The Châtelet was the city prison of Paris in the medieval and Renaissance periods, and was considered one of the most terrible prisons of the Old World. The prisoners were generally of the more or less helpless class of city malefactors, but occasionally persons of a better class were confined in it.

Châtelet, Le Petit. Ancient fortress at Paris, situated on the left bank of the Seine, near the Hôtel-Dieu, used for a prison. It was destroyed in 1782.

Châtelier (shä.tę.lyā), **Henry Louis Le.** See **Le Châtelier, Henry Louis.**

Châtelineau (shä.tlē.nō). Town in S Belgium, in the province of Hainaut, situated on the Sambre River opposite the town of Châtelet, W of Namur. An industrial town, it has blast furnaces and manufactures machinery. 18,230 (1947).

Châtellerault (shä.tel.rō). [Also: **Châtelherault;** medieval Latin, **Castrum Heraldi.**] Town in W central France, in the department of Vienne, situated on the Vienne River, ab. 19 mi. NE of Poitiers. It is an industrial town producing mainly cutlery and firearms, but also other ferrous and nonferrous products of the metallurgical industry, and textiles. The Church of Saint Jacques dates from the 11th–13th centuries. 22,809 (1946).

Chatellerault, Duke of. A title of **Hamilton, James** (c1515–1575).

Chatfield (chat′fēld), **Alfred Ernle Montacute.** [Title, 1st Baron **Chatfield.**] b. at Southsea, England, Sept. 27, 1873—. English naval officer. He joined the naval forces in 1886 and was promoted to captain (1909), rear admiral (1920), vice-admiral (1926), admiral (1930), and admiral of the fleet (1935). In World War I he served as flag-captain to Sir David Beatty on the *Lion* during the actions off Helgoland (1914), Dogger Bank (1915), and Jutland (1916). He was assistant chief (1920–22) and first sea lord and chief (1933–38) of the naval staff. During World War II he was minister (1939–40) for coördination of defense, and head (1940–46) of the civil defense honors committee.

Chatfield-Taylor (chat′fēld.tā′lọr), **Hobart C.** b. at Chicago, March 24, 1865; d. at Montecito, Calif., Jan. 16, 1945. American writer. Among his works are *With Edge-Tools* (1891), *An American Peeress* (1893), *The Vice of Fools* (1898), *The Idle Born* (1900), *Molière* (1906), *Goldoni* (1913), *Tawny Spain* (1927), *Charmed Circles* (1935), and other books.

Chatham (chat′ạm). Municipal borough and seaport in SE England, in Kent, situated on the river Medway adjoining Rochester on the W, ab. 33 mi. SE of London by rail. It is one of the chief military stations and naval arsenals in England. Its royal dockyard (founded by Queen Elizabeth) extends 3 mi. along the river Medway and contains extensive docks, wharves, mills, and also barracks for infantry, artillery, and engineers. It was attacked (1667) by the Dutch fleet under De Ruyter. 46,940 (1951).

Chatham. Seaport in New Brunswick, Canada, on the S bank of the Miramichi River near its mouth. The town is connected by motor road with Moncton and with Newcastle. It is a fishing and lumbering center. 5,223 (1951).

Chatham. [Former name, **Bonnel Town.**] Borough in N New Jersey, in Morris County: residential community. 7,391 (1950).

Chatham. County seat of Kent County, Ontario, Canada, situated on the Thames River, ab. 45 mi. NE of Detroit, and ab. 60 mi. W of London. It is marketing center for a rich farming area, and has several large factories. 21,218 (1951).

Chatham, 1st Earl of. Title of **Pitt, William** (1708–78).

Chatham Islands. Group of islands in the Pacific Ocean, ab. 480 mi. SE of Wellington, New Zealand, of which country they are a part. The chief islands are Chatham and Pitt. They were discovered (1791) by the English ship *Chatham.* Area, 372 sq. mi.; pop. 720 (1940).

Châtillon (shä.tē.yôṅ). Town in N France, in the department of Seine, situated SW of Paris and NW of Sceaux. It is a suburb of Paris. 11,673 (1946).

Chatillon (shä.tē.yôṅ′). In Shakespeare's *King John,* an ambassador from France.

Châtillon (shä.tē.yôṅ), **Charles de.** See **Blois, Charles de.**

Châtillon, Lake. See **Bourget, Lake.**

Châtillon-sur-Seine (shä.tē.yôṅ.sür.sen). Town in E France, in the department of Côte-d'Or, picturesquely situated on the upper Seine River, ab. 44 mi. NW of Dijon. It is overlooked by the ruins of a castle of the dukes of Burgundy and the Church of Saint-Vorles, which dates from the 10th century. The center of the town, with a number of medieval churches and houses, was almost entirely ruined in World War II. 4,240 (1946).

Châtillon-sur-Seine, Congress (or **Conference**) **of.** Unsuccessful conference of the allies (Feb. 5–March, 1814) for the negotiation of peace with France. The allies offered Napoleon, through his envoy, Caulaincourt, the possession of France with the boundaries of 1792. The negotiations came to nothing in consequence of the attitude of Napoleon, who, encouraged by his recent successes, considered that he could gain better terms.

Chat Moss (chat'môs''). Former peat bog (later reclaimed) in Lancashire, England, between Manchester and Liverpool. A railway was built (1828–30) across it by George Stephenson. Area, ab. 6,000 acres.

Chatou (shä.tö). Town in N France, in the department of Seine-et-Oise, situated on the Seine River, between Paris and St.-Germain-en-Laye, W of Paris. It has chemical and metallurgical industries; known as a summer resort. 12,811 (1946).

Chatrian (shȧ.trē.äṅ), **Louis Gratien Charles Alexandre.** See under **Erckmann-Chatrian.**

Chatsworth (chats'wėrth). Seat of the dukes of Devonshire, situated on the river Derwent ab. 3½ mi. NE of Bakewell, Derbyshire, England. Chatsworth House, the Renaissance-style palace, c500 ft. long, was begun in 1688. The interior is rich in painting and sculpture, and contains an extensive collection of drawings, some fine old and modern paintings, a *Venus* by Thorvaldsen, and Canova's *Napoleon, Madame Lētitia,* and *Endymion.* The formal gardens are also famous. They contain elaborate fountains and fine conservatories.

Chattahoochee (chat.ạ.hö'chē). [Former name, **River Junction.**] Town in NW Florida, in Gadsden County, near the confluence of the Flint and Chattahoochee rivers and the Georgia border, ab. 40 mi. NW of Tallahassee. 8,473 (1950).

Chattahoochee River. River in Georgia which forms part of its western boundary, and unites with the Flint to form the Apalachicola at the SW extremity of the state. Length, ab. 420 mi.; navigable to Columbus (over 200 mi.).

Chattanooga (chat.ạ.nö'gạ). [Former name, **Ross's Landing.**] City in SE Tennessee, county seat of Hamilton County, on the Tennessee River near the Georgia border: manufactures cement, brick and tile, furniture, iron and steel, hosiery, and knit goods. The gateway to the valley of East Tennessee, it is a major rail and river transportation center, and headquarters of the Tennessee Valley Authority. Lookout Mountain, Signal Mountain, Missionary Ridge, and the Chickamauga and Chattanooga National Military Park are nearby. Settled at the beginning of the 19th century as a Cherokee trading post, it attained importance as the salt-trading center of E Tennessee, N Georgia, and N Alabama. It was platted and renamed in 1838, probably for the Creek word *Chat-to-to-noog-gee* ("rock rising to a point"). One of the principal objectives of Union strategy during the Civil War, it was occupied by Union forces in September, 1863 (where they were besieged by the Confederates until Nov. 25), and served as the base for Sherman's Atlanta campaign. It is the seat of the University of Chattanooga and was the home of Adolph S. Ochs. 131,041 (1950).

Chattanooga, Battle of. [Also, **Chattanooga Campaign.**] In U.S. history, the name sometimes applied to a series of Civil War military engagements near Chattanooga in the period from August through most of November, 1863. In a more specific sense, the Battle of Chattanooga is taken to be the culminating encounter in this operation, including the fighting on Lookout Mountain (the Battle above the Clouds) in which Hooker's Union troops defeated the Confederates on Nov. 24, and the successful Union assault on the next day against Missionary Ridge. Bragg, the Confederate commander, was compelled by these Union successes to withdraw all the way to Georgia, and the Chattanooga area was never thereafter threatened by a Confederate force. The Union troops in the culminating phase of the battle numbered ab. 60,000 (and were under the overall command of Grant), while Bragg's effective forces totaled perhaps 50,000. Union losses, 5,616; of Confederates, 8,684 (6,142 prisoners).

Chatteris (chat'ėr.is). Urban district and market town in E England, in the Isle of Ely (administrative county of the geographical county of Cambridgeshire), ab. 81 mi. N of London by rail. 5,528 (1951).

Chatterji (chä'tėr.jē), Sir **Atul.** b. 1874—. Indian statesman and diplomat, high commissioner for India (1925–31) at London, and delegate to the League of Nations. A delegate to the international labor conferences at Washington (1919) and at Geneva (1921, 1924–33), he was also a representative in the League of Nations assembly, and president (1927) of the labor conference of the International Labor Office. He served in various responsible posts in the Indian government, in which he was a member of the imperial economic committee (1925–31), a member (1923 *et seq.*) of the viceroy's executive cabinet, and a member (1931–36) of the council of India. He is the joint author of *A Short History of India.*

Chatterton (chat'ėr.tọn), **Edward Keble.** b. at Sheffield, England, 1878; d. 1944. English soldier, journalist, and author of books on naval subjects. Educated at Sheffield and Oxford, he saw service in World War I. His works include *Sailing Ships* (1909), *Story of the British Navy* (1911), *Britain's Record: What She Has Done For the World* (1911), *Romance of Piracy* (1914), *Ship Models* (1923), *Whalers and Whaling* (1925), *Battles by Sea* (1925), *Chats on Naval Prints* (1926), *Brotherhood of the Sea* (1927), *Captain John Smith* (1927), *Daring Deeds of Sea Rovers . . . From the Phoenicians . . . down to the Present Day* (1929), *England's Greatest Statesman, a Life of William Pitt* (1930), *The Sea Raiders* (1931), *Danger Zone* (1934), *Dardanelles Dilemma* (1935), *Amazing Adventure: A Biography of Commander Geoffrey Herbert* (1935), *Leaders of the Royal Navy* (1940), *The Epic of Dunkirk* (1940), and *Fighting the U-Boats* (1942). He also wrote the novels *Sea Spy* (1937) and *Secret Ship* (1939).

Chatterton, Thomas. b. at Bristol, England, Nov. 20, 1752; committed suicide at London, Aug. 24, 1770. English poet, perhaps chiefly noted for his literary hoaxes (works written in a pseudo-medieval style and purporting to be the long-lost literary remains of a 15th-century monk). From his seventh year on, he became interested in the study of literary antiquities; his first pseudo-antique work was "Elinoure and Juga" (written 1764; published in the *Town and Country Magazine,* 1769), followed by a pseudo-archaic account (1768) of the opening (1248) of Bristol Bridge. He also fabricated pedigrees, claiming, as in the instance of his other literary frauds, to have discovered and be in possession of the original documents. His most famous hoax involved a number of poems which he represented as the work of Thomas Rowley, an imaginary 15th-century monk and poet. In 1769 he succeeded in temporarily deceiving Horace Walpole, to whom he sent a "transcript" of a prose work he attributed to Rowley, *The Ryse of Peyneteyne yn Englande, wroten by T. Rowleie, 1469, for Mastre Canynge.* Impressed, Walpole sent a letter of thanks to Chatterton, who responded with a number of "manuscript" poems which, upon being shown to Gray and Mason, were characterized by them as forgeries. The fraud was exposed by Thomas Tyrwhitt in 1777 and 1778, but the authenticity of the Rowley poems became the subject of a controversy which lasted for 80 years, until W. W. Skeat showed conclusively (in his 1871 edition of Chatterton) that there was no doubt that the archaic English of the Rowley works came from the hand of Chatterton. Chatterton, who left Bristol for London in 1770, also wrote squibs, political essays, letters after the style of Junius, and other works, including *Excelente Balade of Charitie.* After a brief period of literary success, he became impoverished and is thought to have been reduced to starvation. Locking himself in his garret, he ended his life by taking arsenic, at the age of 17. Among his other works are a satire, *Apostate Will* (1764), and *The Revenge* (1770), a burlesque opera. His literary hoaxes are distinguished by an undeniable poetic genius and lyric power.

Chatti or **Catti** (kat'ī). German tribe, a branch of the Suevi, first mentioned by Strabo. They originally occupied the Taunus region N of the Main River, but were assigned by Drusus to the old territory of the Sugambri further northward, back from the Rhine, in the region about the Fulda and the middle Weser rivers. They took part in the rising under Civilis, and were afterward, down into the 3rd century, in frequent conflict with the Romans. They were one of the most powerful of the German inland tribes. Two minor tribes of the Chatti, the Batavi and the Canninefates, were ultimately merged with the Salic Franks. Those left behind in the old territory became, finally, the Hessians, a name which first appears early in the 8th century.

Chattrpur (chut'ėr.pör). See **Chhatarpur.**

Chaucer (chô′sėr), **Geoffrey.** b. c1344; d. 1400. He was born around 1344 to the wealthy London vintner, John Chaucer, whose family had long been wholesale importers and merchants of wine, and collectors of the king's customs. Chaucer was early in a courtly environment, probably as a page; our first certain record, dated London, May, 1357, reveals him in the service of Elizabeth, Countess of Ulster and wife of Prince Lionel, son of King Edward III. At Christmas he was in her train at Hatfield, Yorkshire, where John of Gaunt, Lionel's younger brother, was visiting. In the same household records appears a lady-in-waiting, "Philippa, daughter of Pan'," probably the Philippa, daughter of Sir Paneto de Roet of Hainaut, who later served the queen and whom Chaucer married by 1366. In the winter of 1359–60 Chaucer was with the English army invading France, was taken prisoner near Reims, and was then ransomed. Late in 1360 he carried letters from Lionel to England. From 1361 through 1366 Lionel served as the king's lieutenant in Ireland, but his very full records do not mention Chaucer. Perhaps during this period Chaucer obtained legal training at the Inns of Court. There is a convincing tradition that he studied at the Inner Temple, which offered a liberal education sufficiently broad to prepare Chaucer for his later career at court and in business. In 1367 Chaucer was a yeoman in the King's Household (dilectus vallectus noster) with a pension of 20 marks for life, and the following year was listed as "esquire." In 1369 he was with an English army raiding in France, probably under John of Gaunt, by that time Duke of Lancaster. Later that year John's wife, the Duchess Blanche, died of the pestilence, and Chaucer wrote his first long poem, *The Book of the Duchess,* an elegy in the form of a conventional French love-vision, praising Blanche and consoling the bereaved duke. From 1368 on, Chaucer undertook seven or more diplomatic missions to the Continent, to arrange for commercial treaties, for a marriage for Prince Richard, for help in the French war, and on secret business. He was envoy in 1373 to Genoa and Florence, and in 1378 to Milan; and though he probably met neither Petrarch nor Boccaccio, he came to know their writings and those of Dante, and Italian influences appear in his next poems, such as *The House of Fame* and *The Parliament of Fowls.* From 1374 through 1384 he was actively controller of the customs on wool, skins, and hides, for the Port of London, and lived rent-free in the house over Aldgate in the city wall. He had many business affairs, and often appointed a deputy in the customs. In these years Philippa Chaucer was in the favor of John of Gaunt's second duchess, Constance; while Philippa's sister Katherine was governess of John's children, and his mistress until she became his third duchess in 1396. In 1377 the new king, Richard II, confirmed the annuities from Edward III to both Geoffrey and Philippa Chaucer; but no payment of Philippa's annuity is recorded after June, 1387, and she must have died within the year. In 1385 Chaucer had a permanent deputy in the customs, and became justice of the peace for Kent; in 1386 he became a member of Parliament for Kent, and his customs position officially terminated. Chaucer's move from London to the countryside (probably Greenwich) and his new activities apparently afforded him leisure to bring to completion two long narratives based on poems by Boccaccio, *Troilus and Criseyde* and the story of Palamon and Arcite (later *The Knight's Tale*). Soon he started *The Legend of Good Women* and also *The Canterbury Tales.* From 1389 to 1391 he was clerk of the king's works, in charge of building and repairs for the Tower of London, Westminster Palace, and eight other royal residences scattered from Surrey to Worcester. From 1391 until 1398 Chaucer was deputy forester of North Petherton Forest, Somersetshire, and probably lived chiefly in the Park House, where he may have composed most of *The Canterbury Tales.* In 1391 he composed *The Treatise on the Astrolabe* for his "little son Lewis." (Another son, Thomas Chaucer, became prominent in the next century.) In 1395–96 at London Chaucer seems to have been briefly in attendance upon Henry of Derby, son of John of Gaunt, who was later crowned Henry IV. As king, in 1399, he renewed the annuity to Chaucer and added another of 40 marks, and the poet leased a house in the garden of St. Mary's Chapel, Westminster Abbey. The traditional date of his death is Oct. 25, 1400, and he was buried in that part of the Abbey which has become the Poets' Corner. *The Complete Works of Geoffrey Chaucer* (Cambridge edition) was edited by F. N. Robinson in 1933. *The Book of the Duchess* (c1369) shows Chaucer's familiarity with Roman poetry (especially Ovid) and his intense preoccupation with courtly writings: the *Roman de la Rose* (of which he translated at least part), and poems by Deschamps, Froissart, and Machaut (poets whose lyrics and complaints he imitated). After 1373 come *The House of Fame, Anelida and Arcite,* and *The Parliament of Fowls,* with continued admiration of Roman poetry and courtly conventions, but with a new handling of detail and sensuous imagery learned from Dante and Boccaccio, and with a transition from French octosyllabics to the rime royal, which he invented. He translated the *De Consolatione Philosophiae* of Boethius, whose ideas are reflected in *Troilus and Criseyde* (c1385) and the story of Palamon and Arcite (later *The Knight's Tale*), poems retelling long romances by Boccaccio. The *Troilus* excels in characterization; *The Knight's Tale* and *The Legend of Good Women* show growth of narrative power, and mastery of the decasyllabic or heroic couplet, which he was the first to use in English. *The Canterbury Tales* (c1387–1400) reveal wider reading, freedom from earlier conventionalism, and greater control over materials. In his fullest maturity Chaucer exercised an unsurpassed combination of narrative skill, powerful characterization, mastery of cadence, vivid realism, poetic intensity, and rich humor.

Chaucer, Thomas. b. c1367; d. March 14, 1434. English statesman; thought to be the eldest son of Geoffrey Chaucer. He was chief butler of Richard II, constable of Wallingford Castle, steward of the honors of Wallingford and St. Valery and of the Chiltern Hundreds, successor of Geoffrey Chaucer as forester of North Petherton Park, Somersetshire, and a member of Parliament in the period 1400–31. He was chosen speaker of the House of Commons in 1407, 1410, 1411, and 1414. He was present at the battle of Agincourt (1415).

Chaucer's Dream. Name at one time given by some to *The Book of the Duchesse,* in which the poet relates his dream.

Chaucer's Dream. Title given to an independent poem, first printed by Thomas Speght in the 1597 edition of the works of Geoffrey Chaucer. Speght prefixed to it a note saying: "That which heretofore hath gone under the name of his Dreame, is the book of the Duchesse: on the death of Blanche, Duchesse of Lancaster." This poem is not, however, now assigned to Chaucer.

Chaucer Society. Society founded by F. J. Furnivall in 1868 for the purpose of furnishing to scholars material (manuscripts, early texts, and others) relating to Chaucer which was not accessible to the public, and of facilitating collation.

Chauci (kô′sī). German tribe, first mentioned by Strabo, in the region along the North Sea, on both sides of the Weser River from the Ems River to the Elbe River. Pliny divides them into "greater" and "lesser." They were brought by Drusus and Tiberius into subjection to the Romans. The name disappears early in the 5th century. In the 3rd century A.D. they became part of the confederation of the Franks, and thereafter gradually lost their tribal identity in history.

Chaudesaigues (shōd.zeg). [Latin, **Calentes Aquae.**] Small spa in S central France, in the department of Cantal. It is noted for its hot springs.

Chaudhuri (chou.dö′rē), **J. N.** b. 1908—. Indian military leader, chief (1948) of the general staff. Commander of the Indian forces which occupied (1948) Hyderabad, he became (1948) military governor of Hyderabad. A graduate of the military academy at Sandhurst, England, he was a staff officer of the famous 5th Indian division in World War II, and rose to the post of brigadier in charge of administration of the Malaya command.

Chaudière (shō.dyer′). River in Quebec, Canada, which joins the St. Lawrence River, ab. 7 mi. above the city of Quebec. Length, ab. 120 mi.

Chaudière Falls. Cataract in the Chaudière River, in Quebec, Canada, near its mouth. Height, ab. 100 ft.

Chaudière Falls. Cataract in the Ottawa River, in Ontario, Canada, in the city of Ottawa. Height, ab. 50 ft.

Chaudière Lake. Term sometimes applied to the expansion of the Ottawa River on which Ottawa, Canada, is situated.

Chauffeurs (shō.fėrz). [Also, **Garrotteurs.**] In French history, the name applied to a band of brigands, organized under the leadership of Johann Bückler, surnamed "Schinderhannes," which during the Reign of Terror infested the forests of Argères, near Chartres, and which was dispersed by the Consulate in 1803. The term derived from their practice of burning the feet of their victims to make them reveal their treasures. (Hence "Chauffeur," from the French verb *chauffer*, meaning "to heat." Their other name, "Garrotteurs," may be traced to their alternative practice of strangling or throttling (that is, "garroting") their victims.)

Chauliac (shō.lyȧk), **Guy de.** [Also: **Cauliac, Chaulieu**; in Italy, **Guido de Cauliaco.**] b. c1300; d. c1370. French surgeon, physician at Lyons and later at Avignon. He wrote a noted treatise on surgery, long used as an authority, *Chirurgia magna* (1363; printed in French, 1478). He left a description of the great plague of 1348.

Chaulieu (shō.lyė), **Guillaume Amfrye de.** b. at Fontenay, Eure, France, 1639; d. at Paris, June 27, 1720. French poet and ecclesiastic, a member of the libertine society of the Temple (and called the "Anacreon of the Temple"). He was the author of light verses of an occasional character. His work is closely associated with that of the Marquis de la Fare.

Chaumette (shō.met), **Pierre Gaspard.** b. at Nevers, France, May 24, 1763; guillotined at Paris, April 13, 1794. French revolutionist. He was appointed attorney of the commune of Paris in 1792. An opponent of the Girondists, he was a member of the Cordeliers and with them fought against the Girondists. When Robespierre began to persecute the followers of Hébert, the leader of the extreme faction of Cordeliers, Chaumette was included in the group and executed. One of the early adherents, with Hébert, of the cult of Reason, Chaumette was active on behalf of the abolition of corporal punishment in the schools, the suppression of obscene literature, and improvements in hospital care.

Chaumière Indienne (shō.myer aṅ.dyen), **La.** [Eng. trans., *"The Indian Cottage."*] Philosophical tale by Bernardin de Saint-Pierre, published in 1790.

Chaumonot (shō.mo.nō), **Pierre Joseph Marie.** b. near Châtillon-sur-Seine, France, 1611; d. at Lorette, near Quebec, Canada, Feb. 21, 1693. French Jesuit missionary among the Indians of Canada. He arrived at Quebec in 1639, and resided among the Hurons until they were dispersed by the Iroquois c1650. He left a grammar of the Huron language, which was published by the Literary and Historical Society of Quebec in 1835.

Chaumont (shō.môṅ). [Also, **Chaumont-en-Bassigny** (-äṅ.bȧ.sē.nyē).] Town in E France, capital of the department of Haute-Marne, situated between the Marne and Suize rivers, near the Marne-Saône Canal, SE of Troyes. It has paper and leather industries. The Church of Saint Jean Baptiste dates from the 13th–16th centuries. Chaumont was formerly the capital of Bassigny. A treaty was made here between the Allies, on March 9, 1814. In 1917 the Americans established their headquarters here. The town suffered damage in World War II. 16,851 (1946).

Chaumont, Treaty of. Offensive and defensive alliance against Napoleon I, concluded at Chaumont, France, between Austria, Great Britain, Prussia, and Russia, on March 9, 1814.

Chaun Bay (chä.ön'). [Russian, **Chaunskaya Guba** (chä.ön'skạ.yạ gö.bä').] Large bay in NE U.S.S.R., in N Chukchi national territory, an inlet of the East Siberian Sea. The west side of the bay is a lowland, with some sandstone ridges; its eastern shore is formed of rocky cliffs with many small bays. Length, ab. 100 mi.; greatest width, ab. 65 mi.

Chauncey (chôn'si, chän'-), **Isaac.** b. at Black Rock, Conn., Feb. 20, 1772; d. at Washington, D.C., Jan. 27, 1840. American naval officer. He served (1804–05) under commodores Preble and Rodgers in the war with Tripoli, became a captain in 1806, and was placed in command of the naval forces on the northern lakes (except Champlain) in 1812. He carried General Dearborn's army to York (what is now Toronto) in April, 1813, and in October defeated an English fleet of seven vessels, capturing five, on Lake Ontario.

Chauncy (chôn'si, chän'-), **Charles.** b. in Hertfordshire, England, 1592; d. c1672. American clergyman, the second president of Harvard College. He served as professor, first of Hebrew then of Greek, at the University of Cambridge, and became vicar of Ware, England, in 1627. He emigrated to New England in 1638, became (c1641) a pastor at Scituate, Mass., and was named president of Harvard College in 1654.

Chauny (shō.nē). Town in N France, in the department of Aisne, situated on the Oise River, S of St.-Quentin. It is an industrial town and has iron foundries, wire and glass works, and chemical factories. Destroyed in World War I, it was rebuilt, only to be damaged again in World War II. 9,330 (1946).

Chaussard (shō.sȧr), **Pierre Jean Baptiste.** [Pseudonym, **Publicola.**] b. at Paris, Oct. 8, 1766; d. there, Jan. 9, 1823. French poet and writer. He took an active part in the French Revolution, whose theories he advocated in the public prints under the pseudonym of Publicola.

Chaussée (shō.sā), **Pierre Claude Nivelle de La.** See **La Chaussée, Pierre Claude Nivelle de.**

Chausson (shō.sôṅ), **Ernest.** b. at Paris, Jan. 21, 1855; d. at Limay, France, June 10, 1899. French composer; a pupil and follower of César Franck. Among his most important works are the opera *Le Roi Arthus* (produced in 1903), a symphony, the symphonic poem *Viviane* (1888), chamber music, and songs.

Chautauqua (shạ.tô'kwạ). Town in SW New York, in Chautauqua County, on Chautauqua Lake: notable as the seat of the nationwide cultural Chautauqua Movement, initiated in 1874. Pop. 4,222 (1950).

Chautauqua Lake. Lake in W New York, ab. 8 mi. from Lake Erie. Its outlet, Conewango Creek, empties into the Allegheny River. Length, ab. 18 mi.; elevation, ab. 1,300 ft.

Chautauqua Literary and Scientific Circle. Association for the purpose of promoting home reading and study, founded in 1878 by John Heyl Vincent, a minister of the Methodist Episcopal Church. It was one of several lesser organizations that stemmed from the Chautauqua Movement, which Vincent had founded four years earlier.

Chautauqua Movement. Name applied to a popular adult education institution initiated in 1874 by John Heyl Vincent, a Methodist Episcopal minister, and Lewis Miller, an Ohio manufacturer, at Chautauqua Lake, N.Y. The institution, a major cultural influence in the years before World War I, expanded rapidly after 1878, drawing many thousands each year to its assembly grounds and schools of arts and sciences at Chautauqua. The original scheme was used as a model by numerous U.S. and Canadian communities which applied it on a smaller scale, and in 1899 the International Chautauqua Alliance was organized. The so-called traveling Chautauquas achieved a wide popularity in rural areas during the years 1900–15.

Chautemps (shō.täṅ), **Camille.** b. at Paris, Feb. 1, 1885—. French politician and lawyer, several times premier during the final decade of the third French Republic. A leader of the Radical-Socialist Party, he was a deputy for many years until his election (1934) as senator. After holding subordinate ministries, he formed a short-lived cabinet (February, 1930), was minister of the interior (October–November, 1933), and again served (November, 1933–January, 1934) as premier, until forced out of office as a result of the Stavisky scandal. He was minister of public works (January–June, 1936) and minister of state in the first Blum cabinet (June, 1936–June, 1937). Again premier (June, 1937–March, 1938), he resigned after the German annexation of Austria. He was subsequently vice-premier (April, 1938–June, 1940) in the Daladier and Reynaud cabinets. After the defeat of France, he supported the armistice signed by Pétain, was a member of the first Pétain cabinet, was sent by the Vichy government to the U.S. on a secret mission (November, 1940), continued to draw pay from Vichy until July, 1941, and thereafter offered support to various Free French movements but was refused membership. After the liberation of France, he was convicted *in absentia* of impairing French security and was deprived of his citizenship (March, 1947).

Chauveau (shō.vō), **Pierre Joseph Olivier.** b. at Quebec, Canada, May 30, 1820; d. there, April 4, 1890. Canadian politician and man of letters, premier of Quebec in the period 1867–73. He was the author of a novel, *Charles Guerin* (1853), and of other books.

Chauveau-Lagarde (shō.vō.là.gàrd), **Claude François.** b. at Chartres, France, Jan. 21, 1756; d. at Paris, Feb. 28, 1841. French lawyer. He is noted as the defender of Francisco Miranda, Marie Antoinette, Charlotte Corday, and Brissot de Warville before the Revolutionary Tribunal.

Chauvenet (shō.vẹ.nā′), **William.** b. at Milford, Pa., May 24, 1820; d. at St. Paul, Minn., Dec. 13, 1870. American mathematician. He was a professor at the U.S. Naval Academy at Annapolis, Md., in the period 1845–59 and later at Washington University, St. Louis, Mo.

Chauve-Souris (shōv.sö.rē). [Eng. trans., "*Bat.*"] Name of a Russian variety company founded and directed by Nikita Baliev (1877–1936), a low comedian, who started a private cabaret for actors and friends at Moscow in 1908 under the name of *Tutchaya Muish* ("Blind Bat"). The enterprise proved so successful that it was opened to the general public at once. Primarily given over to comedy, a typical Chauve-Souris performance originally consisted of a marionette act, music and songs sung by costumed performers, a short comedy or farce by Pushkin or Gogol, or occasionally some serious piece. The leading actors of the company were Tamara Daykharhanova, later the founder and director of a dramatic school at New York, and Baliev himself, who played host or "Conferencier" to the audience at every performance with a 15-minute comic monologue. Noted artists, such as Sergei Soudeikine and Nikolai Remisov, attended to the décor. In 1921 Baliev took the company on a world tour and reached New York in 1922 under the management of the impresario Morris Gest. The Chauve-Souris continued to tour Europe and America until Baliev's death in 1936.

Chauvin (shō.vaṅ), **Jean.** See **Calvin, John.**

Chauvin, Nicolas. b. at Rochefort, France; fl. in the 18th and early 19th century. French soldier of the Republic and the Empire. He was severely wounded and mutilated in the wars of Napoleon and received as reward for his services a saber of honor, a red ribbon, and a pension of 200 francs. His enthusiasm for the emperor was so demonstrative that it won for him the ridicule of his comrades and gave rise to the term "chauvinism." The word has come to denote blind and excessive nationalism.

Chaux-de-Fonds (shōd.fôṅ), **La.** See **La Chaux-de-Fonds.**

Chavannes (shà.vàn), **Édouard.** b. at Lyons, France, Oct. 5, 1865; d. at Paris, Jan. 29, 1918. French Orientalist. He served as a professor (1893 *et seq.*) at the Collège de France, and was the author of *Mission archéologique dans la Chine septentrionale* (Archaeological Mission in Northern China, 1909–15).

Chavannes, Pierre Puvis de. See **Puvis de Chavannes, Pierre.**

Chavante (shă.văn′tā). See **Shavante.**

Chaves (shä′vẹsh). [Latin, **Aquae Flaviae.**] Town and *concelho* (commune) in N Portugal, in the province of Tráz-os-Montes e Alto Douro, in the district of Vila Real, situated on the Tamega River near the Spanish border, NE of Oporto: agricultural trade center and health resort, with hot saline springs. There is a medieval castle; a Roman bridge, built in the reign of Emperor Trajan, spans the Tamega River. Pop. of concelho, 47,372 (1940); of town, 9,753 (1940).

Chaves (chä′bās), **Francisco de.** Assassinated at Lima, Peru, June 26, 1541. Spanish knight who went to America and was with Pizarro in the conquest of Peru (1532–33). He was one of those who protested against the death of Atahualpa. Subsequently he became one of Pizarro's most trusted captains, and was sent (c1539) to settle Conchucas. He was assassinated with Pizarro.

Chaves (shä′vẹsh), **Manoel de Silveira Pinto de Fonseca,** Marquis **de.** [Additional title, Count of **Amarante.**] b. at Vila Real, Portugal; d. at Lisbon, March 7, 1830. Portuguese general and absolutist politician (1823–28).

Chaves (chä′bās), **Nuflo de.** b. at Trujillo, in Estremadura, Spain, c1510; d. in the Chaco, in South America, 1568. Spanish soldier. He went with Cabeza de Vaca to Paraguay, marching overland (1541–42) from the Brazilian coast to Asunción. Having taken part in the deposition of Cabeza de Vaca, he was thereafter a leading and very turbulent force in the affairs of Paraguay.

Chávez (chä′bās), **Carlos.** b. 1899—. Mexican composer and conductor. Founder (1928) of the Mexican Symphony Orchestra, he became (1928) head of the Mexican National Conservatory of Music. He has been guest conductor in the U.S. with the Boston Symphony Orchestra (1936) and the New York Philharmonic (1937). His compositions include *Sinfonia India* (1936), *Sinfonia de Antigona*, and the ballet *H.P.*

Chávez Franco (fräng′kō), **Modesto.** b. at Guayaquil, Ecuador, 1872—. Ecuadorian politician, journalist, and historian. He began (1905) his career as an attorney, became (1925) director of the municipal library and museum of Guayaquil, was professor of languages, literature, and history (1902–03, 1905–12, 1932–33) at the Colegio Nacional Rocafuerte, at Guayaquil, served as minister of foreign affairs of the republic (1911–12), and was several times a national deputy and senator. Author of numerous newspaper and magazine articles and several books.

Chaville (shà.vēl). Town in N France, in the department of Seine-et-Oise, between Versailles and Sèvres. It belongs to the metropolitan region of Paris. 13,226 (1946).

Chavin (chä′vin). Earliest of the three pan-Peruvian Indian cultures, the other two being Tiahuanaco and Inca. Absolute dates are tentative; the beginning of this archaeological horizon has been put as late as 400 A.D. by some authorities, and before the birth of Christ by others. In terms of relative dating, revealed by archaeology, this is the oldest cultural horizon with agriculture based on maize. The cultivation of maize, ceramics, true loom-weaving, and metallurgy appear for the first time, while stone architecture, especially for temples, and art work become progressively more elaborate. It is evident that social and political organization and religious practices had become much more complex than those of hunting and gathering tribes.

Chaykovsky (chī.kôf′ski), **Nikolai Vasilyevich.** [Also, **Chaikovski.**] b. 1850; d. 1926. Russian agitator, leader of the Narodniki. The Narodnik (Populist) movement originated in a group which gathered around Chaykovsky at St. Petersburg. In the 1870's he went to the U.S. and attempted to establish an idealistic community in Kansas. After the failure of this experiment he settled at London c1880, returning to Russia during the insurrection of 1905. After the October Revolution of 1917 he assisted in Denikin's attempt to set up a counterrevolutionary government, and upon the defeat of Denikin, went again into exile. He remained to his death an uncompromising enemy of Bolshevism.

Chazar (ċhà.zär′). See **Khazar.**

Chazelles (shà.zel), **Jean Mathieu de.** b. at Lyons, France, July 24, 1657; d. at Paris, Jan. 16, 1710. French mathematician, astronomer, and cartographer. He was professor of hydrography at Marseilles.

Chazelles-sur-Lyon (shà.zel.sür.lyôṅ). Town in C France, in the department of Loire, situated on the Lyon River, N of St.-Étienne. It has manufactures of felt hats. 6,108 (1946).

Chazy (shă.zē′). Town in NE New York, in Clinton County, on the Little Chazy River, in an apple-growing area. 2,741 (1950).

Cheadle (chē′dl). Rural district, coal-mining town, and manufacturing center in C England, in Staffordshire, ab. 13 mi. NE of Stafford, ab. 157 mi. NW of London by rail. Its industries include quarrying of limestone and sandstone, agriculture, copper and brass manufacture, papermaking, and silk manufactures. The coal field on which its coal mining depended is now largely depleted. 32,839 (1951).

Cheadle and Gatley (gat′li). Urban district in W England, in Cheshire, ab. 5 mi. S of Manchester (of which it is a residential suburb), ab. 185 mi. NW of London by rail. 31,508 (1951).

Cheaha (chē′hô). Mountain in E Alabama, ab. 14 mi. S of Anniston. It is located in the 2,200-acre Cheaha State Park, and is the highest point in Alabama. 2,407 ft.

Cheapside (chēp′sīd). [Former name, **Chepe.**] Central east-and-west thoroughfare of the City of London, originally a large open common in the course of Watling Street (one of the great Roman roads of ancient Britain) where the markets and public assemblies were held. Different kinds of wares were sold separately, and the names were perpetuated in the streets which were built up where the old booths had stood. In the Middle Ages Chepe was the great street of the retail trade. It was built with the finest houses in the city, and well supplied with churches (the principal one being the original Saint Mary-le-Bow, burned in the Great Fire of 1666, and so called from its great vault or bow, on the S side). On the S side of the street also was the stone gallery from which royalty reviewed the tournaments which were held here. There were two crosses in Chepe; the principal one was one of the 12 erected by Edward I to mark the resting places of the coffin containing the body of his wife, Eleanor of Castile, in its progress from the place of her death in E England to the site of its burial at London. The highway ran through the S portion of the market place, and became known as Cheapside. Before the Great Fire of London in 1666 it was twice as wide as the present street, and was lined with houses five stories high, each story projecting over the one below, and with high gables. Many of the shops were destroyed and Saint Mary-le-Bow Church (the modern one, built by Christopher Wren after the Great Fire) was severely damaged in World War II. Cheapside is 59 ft. above tidewater.

Cheat (chēt). River in West Virginia which joins the Monongahela ab. 52 mi. S of Pittsburgh. Total length, ab. 150 mi.

Cheatham (chēt'ạm), **Benjamin Franklin.** b. at Nashville, Tenn., Oct. 20, 1820; d. there, Sept. 4, 1886. American Confederate major general in the Civil War. He served in the Mexican War, entered the Confederate army in 1861, and fought at Belmont, Shiloh, Chickamauga, Chattanooga, and elsewhere.

Cheatham, Kitty. [Full name, **Catharine Smiley Cheatham.**] b. at Nashville, Tenn., c1846; d. 1946. American soprano and author. She studied in the U.S., in France, and at the University of Berlin. Specializing in the literature and songs of childhood, she prepared with Walter Prichard Eaton an adaptation of E. T. A. Hoffman's *Fairy Tales*, and lectured in Russia, France, England, Germany, Scandinavia, and Iceland. Author of *Kitty Cheatham—Her Book*, *A Nursery Garland*, *Early Voyages of the Norsemen*, *The Discovery of America by Leif Ericson*, and *Children and the Bible;* she has also composed songs and anthems.

Cheats, The. Comedy by John Wilson, written in 1662. This play was temporarily suppressed, it is thought on account of its ridicule of some prominent nonconformist in the part of Scruple.

Cheats of Scapin (skä.paṅ'), **The.** Farce by Thomas Otway, acted in 1677. It was based on Molière's *Les Fourberies de Scapin.*

Cheb (ʜep). [German, **Eger.**] City in Czechoslovakia, in NW Bohemia, situated on the Ohře River W of Karlovy Vary, in the vicinity of the German (Bavarian) border. It is a station on the railroad line from Prague to Frankfort on the Main and to Paris, and also has railroad connections with Plzeň, Vienna, Nuremberg, and Plauen. There is an interesting municipal museum. The industries of Cheb produce textiles, agricultural machinery, ceramics, flour, and beer but have suffered some loss of skilled labor from the expulsion of the formerly predominantly German population, which was only partially replaced by Czech immigrants. The population declined from 31,546 (1930) to 14,533 (1947).

History. Cheb was originally a castle of the Bavarian margraves, was then acquired by Conrad III of Hohenstaufen, and became a free imperial town in 1167. Later it came into the possession of King Ottokar II of Bohemia. It was granted a special charter by King Rudolph of Hapsburg. It contains an imperial castle, built (1167–75) by Emperor Frederick I (Frederick Barbarossa), of the house of Hohenstaufen, on a rock above the river; it has been in ruins since 1742. The town hall was the scene of the assassination of Wallenstein, Austrian general during the Thirty Years' War, by the Irish officer Devereux, on Feb. 25, 1634.

Chebar (kē'bär). In ancient geography, a river mentioned in Ezek. i. 3 as being in the "land of the Chaldeans," on the banks of which the Jewish exiles lived. The river or canal is as yet not identified with any of the numerous canals of Babylonia mentioned in the cuneiform inscriptions. The view, held formerly, that it was the same as Habor (modern Khabur), a tributary of the Euphrates, is now, for philological and geographical reasons, generally abandoned.

Cheboksary (chi.bok.sä'ri). City in W central U.S.S.R., in N Chuvash Autonomous Soviet Socialist Republic, on the S bank of the Volga River ab. 179 mi. by river E of Gorki. It has grown rapidly in recent years as the capital of the Chuvash republic. There are chiefly light industries, including sugar refining, alcohol, flour milling, and leather industries. Founded in 1555, the city has an old monastery dating from 1566, and a cathedral built in 1657. Pop. 15,700 (1933).

Cheboygan (shē.boi'gạn). City in N Lower Michigan, on Lake Huron, county seat of Cheboygan County: shipping point for fish; manufactures include paper and snowplows. It is a flourishing summer tourist resort and a center for hunters and fishermen. 5,687 (1950).

Cheboygan River. River in N Michigan, flowing generally N to Lake Huron at Cheboygan, Mich. It was one of the chief lumbering rivers of Michigan in the late 19th century. Length, ab. 40 mi.

Chebyshev (chi.bi.shof'), **Pafnuti Lvovich.** [Also, **Tchebychef.**] b. at Okatovo, Russia, May 26, 1821; d. at St. Petersburg, Dec. 8, 1894. Russian mathematician, considered one of his country's greatest, noted particularly for his results on the theory of prime numbers. In 1832 his family moved to Moscow, where he attended the university and earned his doctorate in 1849. In 1847 he went to St. Petersburg, where he was a professor at the university for 35 years. He began a long series of publications in 1846 with a paper on probability. His works were published in two volumes in the period 1899–1907.

Chechen (che.chen'). Mountain people (and language) of the N Caucasus in the U.S.S.R. Their culture has been marked through most of its history by the practice of agriculture and herding, and a community based on patriarchal clans. They are predominantly Mohammedans, and have fiercely resisted the Russians, especially between 1785 and 1859. Estimated to number 392,600 in 1926, they have probably been decimated since the liquidation of their autonomous region by the U.S.S.R. for disloyalty (siding with Germany) during World War II.

Checotah (shę.kō'tạ, chę-). City in E Oklahoma, in McIntosh County, ab. 110 mi. E of Oklahoma City, in a farming and livestock-raising region. 2,638 (1950).

Cheddar (ched'ạr). Village in SW England, in NE Somersetshire, ab. 19 mi. by road SW of Bristol. Just NE of the village, in the Mendip Hills, are caverns, and the Cheddar Gorge, with cliffs 450 ft. high. Manufacture of the well-known Cheddar cheese began in this area in the 17th century. 2,154 (1931).

Cheddar Cliffs. Picturesque group of limestone cliffs, in SW England, in Somersetshire. They are in the Mendip Hills, near Wells and Cheddar. Height, 450 ft.

Chedorlaomer (ked"ọr.lā̤.ō'mėr). In the Old Testament, a king of Elam who (according to Gen. xiv.), in the time of Abraham, with his three tributary kings Amraphel of Shinar (Shumir of the inscriptions), Arioch of Ellasar (Larsa), and Tidal of Goyim, invaded Palestine and subdued the five kings of Siddim (in the vicinity of the Dead Sea). For 12 years they remained in subjection; in the 13th year they rebelled, whereupon Chedorlaomer came again with his three allies and defeated the five kings, pillaging the whole country and carrying away with him Lot, the nephew of Abraham. According to the inscriptions on the Assyrian monuments, Elamite kings conquered Babylonia and reigned over it during the period between 2300 and 2076 B.C. Among the Elamite kings mentioned are Kudur-Mabuk and Kudur-Nahundu. The first calls himself "conqueror of the Westland." Chedorlaomer, or as the name would have been read in the ancient Elamite language, Kudur-Lagamar, may be assigned to c2000 B.C. Lagamar is, as ascertained by the Assyrian inscriptions, the name of an Elamite deity, and Kudur probably means "servant."

Chédotel (shā.do.tel). fl. c1600. French navigator and explorer in Canada. Having been selected to guide an expedition to New France, he landed (1598) 50 men on Sable Island, whom on his return from an exploring expedition along the coast of Acadia he was compelled by stress of weather to abandon. He was sent to their rescue by the Parliament of Rouen in 1605, but recovered only 12 men, all that had survived.

Cheduba (che.dö'bą, ched'ū.bą). [Also, **Man-Aung.**] Island in the Bay of Bengal, W of Arakan, Burma, ab. 220 mi. NW of Rangoon. It was taken from the Burmese in 1824, and returned to them in 1948. Petroleum is produced here. Area, 220 sq. mi.; pop. ab. 30,000.

Cheeryble (chir'i.bl), **Frank.** Nephew of Charles and Edwin Cheeryble in Charles Dickens's novel *Nicholas Nickleby.* He marries Kate Nickleby.

Cheeryble Brothers. Twin brothers, merchants, named separately Charles and Edwin, in Charles Dickens's novel *Nicholas Nickleby.* They are liberal, simple-minded, and noble-hearted, and are friends and patrons of Nicholas Nickleby. The originals of these characters are said to have been the Grant brothers, cotton-spinners, near Manchester.

Cheever (chē'vėr), **Ezekiel.** b. at London, c1615; d. Aug. 21, 1708. American educator. One of the signers (June 4, 1639) of "the Plantation Covenant," he later represented (1646) the free burgesses at the General Court (the Massachusetts legislature). He served as master (1638) of the New Haven public school, developed (1650–61) the Ipswich free school, taught (1661–70) at Charleston, and was master (1670–1708) of the Boston Latin School. He wrote *Accidence, a Short Introduction to the Latin Tongue,* used in America until after 1838.

Cheevy (chē'vi), **Miniver.** See **Miniver Cheevy.**

Chefoo (chē'fö'). [Also: **Chi-fu, Yentai.**] Seaport in E China, in the province of Shantung. It is a distributing center of foreign manufactured goods, and exports straw braid, pulse, and silk. It was a treaty port and is an important rival of Tsingtao, but is without rail connections. 139,512 (est. 1934).

Cheggs (chegz), **Mr.** Market-gardener in Charles Dickens's *Old Curiosity Shop,* the successful rival of Dick Swiveller in the affections of Sophy Wackles.

Chehalis (chē.hā'lis). [Former name, **Saundersville.**] City in SE Washington, county seat of Lewis County, on the Chehalis River ab. 27 mi. SW of Olympia and adjoining Centralia. Manufactures include lumber products, condensed milk, bricks, tiles, and portable houses; shipping center for ferns and coal. 5,639 (1950).

Chehalis River. River in SW Washington, flowing generally NW and W to Grays Harbor at Aberdeen, Wash. It flows through a farming and lumbering region. Length, ab. 125 mi.

Cheharlang (che'här'läng'). See under **Bakhtiari.**

Cheiron (kī'ron). See **Chiron.**

Cheju (chā'jö'). [Full name, **Cheju-do** (-dō') (*do*-"island"); Japanese, **Saishu, Saishu-to, Shishu;** former name, **Quelpart, Quelpaerd.**] Island at the entrance of Korea Strait, situated ab. 60 mi. S of Korea. Formerly under Japanese rule, it was given to Korea in 1945. Area, ab. 700 sq. mi.; pop. ab. 150,000.

Cheke (chēk), Sir **John.** b. at Cambridge, England, June 16, 1514; d. at London, Sept. 13, 1557. English scholar of Greek, tutor to the Prince of Wales (later Edward VI of England). He studied at Cambridge (St. John's College), was professor of Greek there in the period 1540–51, was appointed tutor to Prince Edward in 1544, was knighted in 1552, and became a chamberlain of the exchequer in August, 1552, and a secretary of state in June, 1553. He was a zealous Protestant and partisan of Lady Jane Grey, and on Mary Tudor's accession was accused of treason and committed (July 27, 1553) to the Tower of London, but pardoned (Sept. 13, 1554) and permitted to travel abroad. In 1556 he was arrested near Antwerp, brought to England, and again thrown into the Tower, where he was induced to renounce his Protestant beliefs. He wrote numerous works in Latin and English.

Chekhov (che'ʜof; Anglicized, chek'of), **Anton Pavlovich.** [Also: **Chekov, Tchehov, Tchekhov.**] b. at Taganrog, Russia, Jan. 17, 1860; d. at Badenweiler, Germany, in July, 1904. Russian dramatist and short-story writer, considered one of the foremost and most influential of the Russian writers of the late 19th century. By profession a doctor, he seldom practiced medicine, devoting almost his entire career to writing. Ill health forced him to live (1897 *et seq.*) in the Crimea except for periods spent at other health resorts. While still at the university he began to contribute short humorous stories to the magazines. In 1886 he published his first collection of stories and came under the patronage of Suvorin, who encouraged him. Later he became a friend of Tolstoi and Gorki, and relinquished his membership in the Russian Academy in 1902 in protest against its barring of Gorki. A journey to a convict island (1890) resulted in a book discussing contemporary penal conditions; in 1888 he wrote his first play, *Ivanov;* otherwise his output consisted almost entirely of short stories until c1897, when he began to devote himself chiefly to writing for the theater. In 1896 his second play, known in English as *The Sea-Gull,* was produced at St. Petersburg, but was not a success; a revival (1898) of it, however, by Stanislavsky's Moscow Art Theatre proved immensely popular, and thereafter all of Chekhov's plays were performed by the same group. The plays have all been acclaimed since, and have been widely translated and performed. The remaining ones are *Uncle Vanya* (first performed in 1900), *The Three Sisters* (first performed in 1901), and *The Cherry Orchard* (first performed in 1904). Even more popular than the plays were the short stories, which have exerted a profound influence on subsequent writing in that medium, notably in England (on the work of Katherine Mansfield, for example). They take for their protagonists little people, peasants, or intellectuals, and deal chiefly with an isolated and superficially minor experience in their lives. They all succeed, however, in conveying the theme of the frustrations and difficulties with which the individual sensitive life is beset, and in many cases show the gradual breaking of the human spirit. Imbued as they are, however, with gentle humor and great sympathy, these stories cannot be called wholly pessimistic. The plays as well as the stories portray the corroding stagnation that pervaded some sections of Russian life in his day. Chekhov's works are available in English in the translations of Constance Garnett (*The Tales of Tchekhov,* 13 vols., 1916–22; *The Plays of Tchehov,* 2 vols., 1923), and other partial collections, and in numerous anthologies.

Chekhov, Michael. b. at St. Petersburg, Aug. 29, 1891—. Russian actor and director; nephew of Anton Pavlovich Chekhov. He became a member of the Moscow Art Theatre (1912) and later (1914) was one of the founders and the directors of the First Studio, later to be known as the Second Moscow Art Theatre. His most famous roles with this group were Hamlet, Malvolio, and Ivan in *The Inspector-General.* He joined Max Reinhardt's company in 1929, playing at Berlin and Vienna. In 1930 he was director of the Habima Theatre, and in the period 1931–32 he played in *Hamlet* and *Prince Ivan* at Paris. In 1932, he founded the Studio Theatre in Latvia, and in 1934 came to New York. In 1936, he established an acting studio theater in Devonshire, England. In 1938, he transferred his studio to Ridgefield, Conn., and brought some of his productions to New York. He closed his studio at the start of World War II, and after 1943 acted in Hollywood-made films.

Chekiang (che'kyang'; Chinese, ju'jyäng'). Maritime province in E China, lying between Kiangsu on the N, the East China Sea on the E, Fukien on the S, and Anhwei and Kiangsi on the W. Its seaport is Ninghsien. The chief foreign export is silk; tea, hemp, and cotton are also important. Capital, Hangchow; area, ab. 39,486 sq. mi.; pop. 21,776,000 (est. 1947).

Chelan (chē.lan', shē-), **Lake.** Lake in N central Washington, in Chelan County. It is ab. 50 mi. long and 1 to 2 mi. wide.

Chelan Mountains. [Also, **Chelan Range.**] Range in N central Washington, along the W shore of Lake Chelan, consisting of high, rugged, largely uninhabited mountains. The peak elevation is Cardinal Peak (8,595 ft.). Length, ab. 35 mi.

Chelard (shę.lår), **Hippolyte André Jean Baptiste.** b. at Paris, Feb. 1, 1789; d. at Weimar, Germany, Feb. 12, 1861. French composer. Among his works are the operas *Macbeth* (1827; text by Rouget de Lisle) and *Hermannsschlacht* (1835).

Cheliabinsk (chi.lyä'binsk). See **Chelyabinsk.**

Chéliff (shā.lēf'). [Also: **Oued Chéliff, Sheliff;** ancient name, **Chinalaph.**] River in NW Africa, the largest river in Algeria. It rises in the Atlas Mountains and flows into the Mediterranean Sea near Mostaganem. Length, between 350 and 400 mi.

Chelishev (chā'lyi.shif), **Pavel.** See **Tchelitchew, Pavel.**

Chelius (ċhā'lē.u̇s), **Maximilian Joseph von.** b. at Mannheim, Baden, Germany, Jan. 16, 1794; d. at Heidelberg, Baden, Germany, Aug. 17, 1876. German surgeon. He wrote *Handbuch der Chirurgie* (1822) and others.

Cheliuskin (chi.lyös'kin), **Cape.** See **Chelyuskin, Cape.**

Chellean Period (shel'ē.ạn). Stage of early Paleolithic development during which chipped stone implements were first used by man. It is the first period in which adaptation of the stone by altering its shape is clear; a Pre-Chellean stage is sometimes distinguished at the very beginnings of the Paleolithic Period, but there is controversy about the extent of the changes made in the rough stone. Chellean artifacts include borers, scrapers, and hand axes, all primitively and roughly done. The period apparently preceded the last glaciation.

Chelles (shel). [Ancient name, **Calae.**] Town in N France, in the department of Seine-et-Marne, situated on the Marne River, ab. 12 mi. E of Paris. An industrial town, it suffered damage during World War II. The name "Chellean" has been applied to a Stone Age culture as a result of the discovery of crude stone implements here. 14,378 (1946).

Chelles, Jean de. French architect and sculptor. He constructed (1257) the southern portal of the Cathedral of Notre Dame at Paris as it exists today.

Chelly (shā). Canyon in NE Arizona, ab. 100 mi. NW of Gallup, N.M., which contains some of the largest ruins of the Kayenta branch of Anasazi culture, including extensive cliff dwellings. It is now included in Canyon de Chelly National Monument (established 1931; area, 83,840 acres).

Chelm (ʜelm). [Russian, **Kholm.**] Town in E Poland, in the *województwo* (province) of Lublin, situated on a tributary of the Bug River, ab. 42 mi. E of Lublin: the center of a fertile agricultural district and a railroad junction. It has a Roman Catholic cathedral. In World War I, the Germans defeated the Russians here, Aug. 1–3, 1915. About half of the population was Jewish prior to World War II; it is now almost entirely Roman Catholic. 23,320 (1946).

Chelmiński (ʜel.mēn'skē), **Jan.** b. in Russian Poland, Jan. 27, 1851; d. at London, 1925. Polish painter. He received his professional training at the academy at Munich and under Franz Adam. In 1873 he began painting, independently, genre subjects taken from the common life of Poland. His work is widely distributed.

Chełmno (ʜelm'nô). [German, **Kulm, Culm.**] Town in N Poland, in the *województwo* (province) of Pomorze, situated on the Vistula River, ab. 70 mi. S of Danzig. It has agricultural and livestock markets, and before World War II had metallurgical and lumber industries. Medieval walls and fortifications are preserved. The parish church and the churches of the Benedictines, Dominicans, and Franciscans are brick-Gothic buildings of the 13th and 14th centuries; the town hall, erected (1567–97) after the designs of an Italian architect, is in the Renaissance style. Castle and town were founded in 1231 and 1233 by the Teutonic Order; the Law of Chełmno, codified in 1397, was widely adopted in the regions dominated by the Order. Chełmno was a member of the Hanseatic League. From 1245 to 1821 it was the seat of a bishopric. After the breakdown of the Teutonic Order Chełmno came to Poland; it belonged to Prussia from 1773 to 1807 and again from 1815 to 1919. In World War II, it was occupied by the Germans on Sept. 3, 1939, and was returned to Poland in 1945. Pop. 11,634 (1946).

Chelmsford (chems'fọrd), 2nd Baron. [Title of **Frederic Augustus Thesiger.**] b. May 31, 1827; d. April 9, 1905. English general; father of the 1st Viscount Chelmsford. He served as an aide-de-camp in the Crimean campaign, and as an adjutant general in the Abyssinian campaign of 1868. Adjutant general of the forces in India (1869–74), he became a major general in 1877, and had chief command of the British troops in the Zulu war of 1879 until relieved by Sir Garnet Wolseley. He gained a decisive victory over the Zulus under Cetewayo at Ulundi on July 4, 1879.

Chelmsford, 1st Viscount. [Title of **Frederick John Napier Thesiger.**] b. Aug. 12, 1868; d. at London, April 2, 1933. English politician; eldest son of the 2nd Baron Chelmsford. A graduate (M.A., 1892) of Oxford, he was governor of Queensland (1905–09) and New South Wales (1909–13). As viceroy (1916–21) of India, he established with Edwin S. Montagu a constitution for that country, which was, however, repudiated by Gandhi. He subsequently served as first lord of the admiralty (1924) in the Labour ministry and agent general (1926–28) in England for New South Wales.

Chelmsford (cheṃs'fọrd, chemz'-, chelmz'-). Municipal borough and market town in SE England, county seat of Essex, situated on the river Chelmer, ab. 30 mi. NE of London by rail. It is an important agricultural center, specializing in the production of milk for the London market. 37,888 (1951).

Chelmsford. Town in NE Massachusetts, in Middlesex County, ab. 23 mi. NW of Boston: manufactures include woolen textiles and iron. 9,407 (1950).

Chełmża (ʜelm'zhä). [German, **Kulmsee, Culmsee.**] Town in N Poland, in the *województwo* (province) of Pomorze, formerly in West Prussia, Germany, situated on the Chełmża Lake, ab. 12 mi. N of Torun. It has a Gothic cathedral church dating from 1251. Chełmża is marketing center for a fertile agricultural district, and has a sugar refinery. After World War II new chemical industries, especially the manufacture of ethyl alcohol, developed. 10,764 (1946).

Chelsea (chel'si). [Former spelling, **Chelsey;** Middle English, **Chelchith;** Old English, **Celchyth.**] Metropolitan borough in SW London, in the County of London, situated on the N bank of the river Thames, ab. 3 mi. SW of Saint Paul's. The borough has all types of residential development: large mansions, 17th-century houses, workmen's cottages, and large blocks of modern apartment houses. It has been the residence of many celebrated people, including Sir Thomas More, Elizabeth, Steele, Swift, the painters Turner and Whistler, Walpole, Dante Gabriel Rossetti, George Eliot, and Carlyle (who is sometimes called the "Sage of Chelsea"); Carlyle's house in Cheyne Row escaped bomb damage in World War II and is maintained as a museum. It contains the Chelsea Hospital for invalid soldiers, designed by Wren, built between 1682 and 1690, which sustained heavy war damage. Chelsea is the fourth smallest borough in London. 50,912 (1951).

Chelsea. City in E Massachusetts, in Suffolk County, ab. 3 mi. NE of Boston, separated from Charlestown by the Mystic River. Manufactures include rubber, shoes, clocks, and paper. It was settled as Winnisimmet in 1624, was separated from Boston in 1738, and was incorporated as a city in 1857. A fire in April, 1908 did extensive damage. A U.S. naval hospital is here. 38,912 (1950).

Chelsea. Manufacturing village in SE Lower Michigan, in Washtenaw County near Ann Arbor. 2,580 (1950).

Chelsea. [Also, **Chelsea Village.**] Part of New York City; a section, originally the farm of Clement C. Moore, lying on the W side of the city. Chelsea Square, lying between Ninth and Tenth avenues and 20th and 21st streets, still marks part of its site. The General Theological Seminary occupies the square.

"Chelsea, Sage of." See **Carlyle, Thomas.**

Chelsea Rooming House. Collection of poems by Horace Gregory, published in 1930.

Cheltenham (chelt'nạm, chel'tẹn.ạm). [Also, **Cheltenham Spa.**] Municipal borough in W England, in Gloucestershire, situated on the river Severn at the W end of the Cotswolds, ab. 109 mi. NW of London by rail. It is a famous inland spa, summer resort, and a pleasant residential town. Cheltenham is in a rich agricultural belt. During World War II, aircraft industries were set up in and around Cheltenham. The mineral springs for which it is now famous were discovered in 1714. Pop. 62,823 (1951).

Chelyabinsk (chi.lyä'binsk). [Also, **Cheliabinsk.**] *Oblast* (region) in the U.S.S.R., in the Russian Soviet Federated Socialist Republic, located in the S Ural Mountains. The area is dotted with numerous industrial cities and is very rich in lignite, iron ore, aluminum, nickel, and chromium. It is crossed by many railroad lines and has become one of the very important industrial centers of the U.S.S.R.

Capital, Chelyabinsk; area, 63,111 sq. mi.; pop. 2,802,949 (1939).

Chelyabinsk. [Also, **Cheliabinsk.**] City in the U.S.S.R., capital of the Chelyabinsk *oblast* (region) of the Russian Soviet Federated Socialist Republic, just E of the Urals. Machine construction and metal works, iron ore, lignite, textiles, and food processing as well as the manufacture of tractors and automobiles make it a leading industrial city. 273,127 (1939).

Chelyuskin (chi.lyös'kin), **Cape.** [Also: **Cape Cheliuskin, Cape Severo, Northeast Cape** (Russian, **Severovostochny**).] Northernmost cape on the continent of Asia, situated at the extremity of the Taimyr peninsula in Siberia, in the Krasnoyarsk *krai* (territory) of the Russian Soviet Federated Socialist Republic of the U.S.S.R. It was visited by Nordenskjöld in 1878.

Chemehuevi (chem.ẹ.hwā'vē). North American Indian tribe, now nearly extinct, formerly distributed through SE California and SW Nevada; the language was of the Uto-Aztecan family.

Chemillé (she.mē.yā). Town in W France, in the department of Maine-et-Loire, ab. 20 mi. SW of Angers. Pop. ab. 3,000.

Chemin des Dames (shẹ.man̈ dā dȧm). Road in NE France, ab. 6 mi. NW of Soissons, extending along the high ridge N of the Aisne River. A wagon road was built here in the 18th century, but the chief fame of the Chemin des Dames is a result of the great battles of World War I fought here. The German armies captured the ridge in September, 1914, were temporarily defeated by a French attack in 1917, but regained the strategic ridge, which they held until the final Allied offensive in October, 1918. Length, ab. 12 mi.

Chemineau (shẹ.mē.nō), **Le.** Lyric opera in four acts by Zavier Leroux, with a poetic libretto by Jean Richepin, first produced at Paris in 1907.

Chemnitz (kem'nits). City in E Germany, in the *Land* (state) of Saxony, Russian Zone, formerly in the free state of Saxony, situated on the Chemnitz River, ab. 45 mi. SE of Leipzig: the chief manufacturing city of Saxony, sometimes called the "Manchester of Saxony." Before World War II it specialized in the manufacture of knitwear, hosiery, carpets, rugs, and related products, and had also factories producing gloves, sewing thread, textile machinery, locomotives, automobiles, bicycles, metallurgical articles, and chemicals. Which ones of these industries are still operating is unknown. Chemnitz is a railroad junction with seven railroad stations. The city has numerous educational institutions, particularly vocational schools serving the textile and knitwear industries. There is a theater, an opera house, and a museum. The former castle was built between 1136 and 1539; the castle church, in Gothic style, dates mainly from the 16th century. 250,188 (1946).

History. Chemnitz came under the rule of the house of Wettin in 1308; it was famous in the Middle Ages for its cloth manufacture and linen fabrics. Cotton weaving was introduced in the 17th century; hosiery was produced in the surrounding villages. Cotton printing started in 1770, and cotton spinning and machine-weaving followed by the end of the 18th century, patterned on English precedents. The city grew rapidly in the 19th century; its workers were among the earliest adherents of the Social Democratic Party. It was frequently bombed during World War II and much damage was done; the decline of population between 1939 and 1946 amounted to 25.3 percent. In religion Chemnitz is predominantly Protestant.

Chemnitz, Bogislaw Philipp von. b. at Stettin, Germany, May 9, 1605; d. at Hallstad, Sweden, May 17, 1678. German historian, councilor and historiographer of Christina of Sweden, grandson of Martin Chemnitz. He wrote *De ratione status in imperio nostro Romano-Germanico* (1640) and *Der königliche schwedische in Deutschland geführte Krieg* (1648).

Chemnitz, Martin. [Also, **Kemnitz.**] b. at Treuenbrietzen, Brandenburg, Germany, Nov. 9, 1522; d. at Brunswick, Germany, April 8, 1586. German Lutheran theologian, superintendent at Brunswick (1567 *et seq.*); grandfather of Bogislaw Philipp von Chemnitz. He was one of the persons responsible for the Formula of Concord. He wrote *Theologiae Jesuitarum praecipua capita* (1562), *Examen concilii Tridentini* (1565–73), *Loci Theologici* (1591), and others.

Chemnitzer (ʜem.nē'tsėr), **Ivan Ivanovich.** [Also, **Khemnitser.**] b. at Arkhangelsk, Russia, Jan. 16, 1745; d. at Smyrna (now Izmir), Turkey, March 20, 1784. Russian fabulist. His fables were published in the period 1778–81 (ed. by Grot, 1873).

Chemosh (kē'mosh). In the Old Testament, the principal deity, or Baal, of the Moabites. In Judges, xi. 24. Chemosh also appears as the national god of Ammon. His worship was introduced in Judah under Solomon, but was abolished by Josiah (1 Kings, xi. 7; 2 Kings, xxiii. 13).

Chemulpo (che'möl'pô'). See **Inchon.**

Chemung (shẹ.mung'). River in S central New York, formed just W of Corning by the junction of the Tioga and Cohocton rivers, and flowing generally SE in a narrow valley to the Susquehanna River near Sayre, Pa. Length, ab. 45 mi.

Ch'en (chun), **Eugene.** [Original name, **Ch'en Yu-jen** (chun' yö'jun').] b. in Trinidad, West Indies, 1878; d. 1944. Chinese nationalist leader educated in England. He went (1912) to China, where he edited (1914–25) several strongly anti-British periodicals, and served as foreign minister of the Nationalist government at Canton (1926) and Wuhan (1927). He retired to Europe after the Kuomintang split (1927), and became (1934) foreign minister in the Foochow separatist government. Captured at Kowloon by the Japanese when Hong Kong fell (December, 1941), he refused to collaborate.

Ch'en, K. P. [Full name, **Ch'en Kuang-p'u** (chun' gwäng'pö').] b. at Chinkiang, Kiangsu, China, 1880—. Chinese banker and government official.

Chenab (chē.näb'). [Also: **Chinab**; ancient name, **Acesines.**] Central river of the Punjab, N Pakistan: one of the five rivers from which the name Punjab was derived. It rises in the mountains of Kashmir and flows SW, uniting with the Sutlej to form the Panjnad, an E affluent of the Indus. Length, ab. 700 mi.

Chenango (shẹ.nang'gō). River in C and S New York, a tributary of the Susquehanna, which it joins at Binghamton, N.Y. Length, ab. 100 mi.

Chenavard (shẹ.nȧ.vȧr), **Paul Joseph.** b. Dec. 9, 1808; d. April 12, 1895. French historical painter, a pupil of Delacroix and Ingrès. He executed a series of cartoons for decorations in the Pantheon at Paris.

Ch'en Ch'eng (chun' chung'). b. at Chingtien, Chekiang, China, 1897—. Chinese military leader close to Chiang Kai-shek and opposed to Ho Ying-ch'in. He won the regard of U.S. military men as commander of the Chinese Expeditionary Force fighting with the Americans in Yunnan. He served as war minister (1944–46), chief of staff (1946–48), governor (1948–49) of Formosa, where he trained additional troops for the Chinese civil war, and premier (from March, 1950).

Ch'en Chiung-ming (jyung'ming'). b. at Haifeng, Kwangtung, China, 1875; d. 1933. Chinese militarist. Having supported Sun Yat-sen in the 1911 revolution, he later turned against him and helped drive him from Canton (1922). He was himself defeated (1925), whereupon he retired to Dairen, Manchuria.

Chênedollé (shen.do.lā), **Charles Julien Lioult de.** b. at Vire, France, in 1769; d. in 1833. French romantic poet.

Chênée (she.nā). Town in E Belgium in the province of Liége, situated at the junction of the Vesdre and Ourthe rivers, SE of Liége, of which it is a suburb: coal mines, iron foundries, and glassworks. 10,352 (1947).

Chenery (chen'ėr.i), **Thomas.** b. on Barbados, British West Indies, 1826; d. 1884. English Orientalist and editor (1877–84) of the London *Times*. He received an M.A. from Cambridge in 1858. He served as Crimean War correspondent (1854–56) for the *Times* out of its Constantinople office, and was employed on its staff from 1877 until his death, as a leader writer, a reviewer, and a writer of original papers. Gifted in languages, he also served as professor of Arabic at Oxford (1868–77) and helped revise the Old Testament. He wrote on Arabic and Hebrew.

Chenevix (chen'ẹ.viks), **Richard.** b. in Ireland, 1774; d. April 5, 1830. English chemist, mineralogist, and man of letters. He was named a fellow of the Royal Society in 1801, and received the Copley medal in 1803. Besides numerous scientific papers, he wrote *Mantuan Revels* (a comedy), *Henry the Seventh* (a tragedy), and poems.

Cheney (chē'ni). City in E Washington, in Spokane County ab. 12 mi. SW of Spokane. It is a railroad junction point, and seat of a state teachers college. 2,797 (1950).

Cheney, Amy Marcy. See **Beach, Amy Marcy.**

Cheney, Charles Edward. b. at Canandaigua, N.Y., Feb. 12, 1836; d. Nov. 15, 1916. American Episcopal bishop. He was a graduate (1857) of Hobart College. During his rectorate (1860–1916) of Christ Church at Chicago he was tried (1869 *et seq.*) by an ecclesiastical court and found guilty of heresy; when he ignored this sentence, he was deposed for contumacy, but was reinstated in 1874 when a secular court ruled the canons' pronouncement null and void. In 1873 he organized with Bishop George David Cummins the Reformed Episcopal Church. He was consecrated (1873) missionary bishop of the Northwest and named (1878) bishop of the synod of Chicago. Author of *Sermons* (1880), *What Do Reformed Episcopalians Believe* (1888), and *A Neglected Power and Other Sermons* (1916).

Cheney, John. b. at South Manchester, Conn., Oct. 20, 1801; d. there, Aug. 20, 1885. American engraver and illustrator; brother of Seth Wells Cheney and Ward Cheney. He is known to have been employed as an engraver at Boston as early as 1826, and his first published work appeared in 1827. In 1830 he went to Europe for study, precariously supported by commissions from American publishers, and remained there several years, until he had to return with his brother Seth Wells Cheney, who had joined him at Paris but became ill from overwork. Discouraged by lack of appreciation, and made financially independent by the success of a family enterprise in the manufacture of silk, he abandoned his artistic career while still in his middle years. His engravings, including his illustrations for books, are considered to have been unequaled in their time in America, and unsurpassed by similar work in any country.

Cheney, John Vance. b. at Groveland, N.Y., Dec. 29, 1848; d. May 1, 1922. American poet and librarian. He studied law at Woodstock, Vt. (1871–74) and at Haverhill, Mass. (1874–75), and practiced at New York for a year. He was librarian of the Free Public Library at San Francisco (1887–94) and of the Newberry Library at Chicago (1894–1909). He published two volumes of essays, *The Golden Guess* (1892) and *That Dome in Air* (1895), and several volumes of poems, among them *Thistle-Drift* (1887), *Wood Blooms* (1888), *Lyrics* (1901), and *Poems* (1905).

Cheney, Oren Burbank. b. in New Hampshire, Dec. 10, 1816; d. Dec. 22, 1903. American Baptist clergyman and educator. A graduate (B.A., 1839; and M.A., 1842) of Dartmouth College, he was a pastor at West Lebanon and Augusta, Me., and was elected (1851) to the Maine legislature. He established (1857) and served as principal of the Maine State Seminary at Lewiston, Me., and as its president (until 1894) after its reincorporation (1863) as Bates College.

Cheney, Seth Wells. b. at South Manchester, Conn., Nov. 26, 1810; d. at Boston, Sept. 10, 1856. American crayon artist and engraver; brother of John Cheney (1801–85) and Ward Cheney (1813–76). In 1834 he went to Paris, where John Cheney was studying, but before long suffered a breakdown from overwork and had to be brought home. About that time Ward Cheney and two other brothers of John and Seth Wells Cheney were caught up in the speculative enthusiasm for the growing of mulberry trees which then swept the U.S., as a prerequisite for cultivating silkworms, and Seth Wells Cheney was sent abroad to buy trees. These speculative hopes were deflated in 1840, but fortunately the Cheneys had also established a silk mill which flourished and provided support for all. In 1841 Seth Wells Cheney opened a studio at Boston where he executed portraits mostly in black and white crayon. In 1843 he went abroad and studied at Rome until 1845, when he returned and again set up as a crayon portraitist, but his health languished, and in his later years he did little work. He was the first notable American "black and white" artist; as an engraver, though his output was small, he equaled and perhaps sometimes surpassed the very distinguished work of John Cheney.

Cheney, Sheldon Warren. b. at Berkeley, Calif., June 29, 1886—. American drama and art critic. He was graduated (1908) from the University of California. In 1916 he founded and until 1921 edited *Theatre Arts Magazine.* His works include *The New Movement in the Theatre* (1914), *Modern Art and the Theatre* (1921), *A Primer of Modern Art* (1923), *The Art Theatre* (1925), *Stage Decoration* (1927), *The Theatre: Three Thousand Years of Drama, Acting and Stagecraft* (1929), *Expressionism in Art* (1934), *Art and the Machine* (1936; with his wife), and *A World History of Art* (1937).

Cheney, Ward. b. at South Manchester, Conn., Feb. 23, 1813; d. March 22, 1876. American silk manufacturer; brother of John Cheney (1801–85) and Seth Wells Cheney (1810–56). With his brothers Frank and Rush Cheney, he operated (1836–41) a silkworm nursery. In 1838 he organized with Ralph, Rush, and Fred Cheney, and with Edward Arnold, the Mount Nebo Silk Manufacturing Company, and served as its president (1854–76) after its incorporation (1854) as Cheney Brothers Silk Manufacturing Company, at South Manchester, Conn.

Chengalpatt (cheng'gal.put). See **Chingleput.**

Chengchiatun (chung'jyä'dün'). See **Liaoyuan.**

Chenghsien (jung'shyen'). [Former name, **Chengchow** (jung'jō').] City in E China, in the province of Honan. It was on the Hwang Ho (Yellow River) from 1938 to 1947, when the river was put back in its old channel farther north. A trading center, it became more important when the Lung-Hai railroad crossed the Pieping-Hankow railroad there. 80,000 (1931).

Chengteh (chung'du'). [Also: **Jehol, Cheng-te.**] City in NE China, in the province of Jehol: capital of the province; cotton mills, gold, and silver. It contains a summer residence of the former Chinese emperor. 343,735 (est. 1947).

Chengtu (chung'dö'). [Also, **Chingtu.**] City in C China, the capital of the province of Szechwan, on the river Min-Kiang. It is of considerable importance as a trading center and for small manufactures, the center of one of the most heavily populated areas of China. 620,302 (est. 1948).

Chénier (shā.nyā), **André Marie de.** b. at Constantinople, Oct. 30, 1762; guillotined at Paris, July 25, 1794. French poet, considered by some the greatest writer in French classic verse since the days of Racine and Boileau; son of Louis de Chénier. He attended the Collège de Navarre in France, was in the army in 1782, traveled (1783–84) in Switzerland and Italy, lived (1784–87) at Paris, was secretary to the French embassy at London till 1790, and finally returned to literary occupations and studies at Paris. Only two poetical compositions of Chénier were published during his lifetime, these being *Le Jeu de paume à David peintre* (suggested by the painter J. L. David's *Serment du jeu de paume*, the painting of the Tennis Court Oath of June, 1789) and *Hymne aux soldats de Châteauvieux.* His pamphlet directed against the Jacobins *Avis au peuple français sur ses véritables ennemis,* brought him a medal of recognition from Stanislaus II, king of Poland. Chénier's plain words in political matters, notably in opposition to the excesses of the Reign of Terror, led to his inscription on the exile list, but he seems to have been of assistance to Malesherbes in preparing the defense of Louis XVI, and to the king himself in preparing the latter's appeal to the people. On March 7, 1794, he was accused of sheltering a political criminal, and was sent to prison. On the 7th Thermidor he was one of 24 guillotined on a charge of prison conspiracy. "La Jeune captive" was published on Jan. 9, 1795, in the *Décade philosophique,* with reprints in *L'Almanach des muses* and *Le Magasin encyclopédique.* "La Jeune Tarentine" came out in the *Mercure* of March 22, 1801. In a note to Châteaubriand's *Le Génie du christianisme* several passages were quoted from the *Élégies.* Other fragments were inserted by Fayolle in his *Mélanges littéraires* (1816). The first complete edition of Chénier's works was made by Latouche in 1819, the second by D. C. Robert, the third and fourth again by Latouche in 1833 and 1839 respectively. Becq de Fouquières published the first critical edition in 1862, and the second in 1872. An indifferent edition was given by Gabriel de Chénier in 1874. Becq de Fouquières pointed out its shortcomings in his *Documents nouveaux sur André Chénier* (1875). He also published in 1881 a revised and enlarged edition of Chénier's *Oeuvres en prose,* based on the version of Hugo and Lacroix in 1840, and finally gave the results of his latest research in his *Lettres critiques d'André Chénier* (1881).

Chénier, Louis de. b. at Montfort, France, c1723; d. at Paris, May 25, 1796. French historian; father of André Marie de Chénier and Marie Joseph de Chénier. He resided at Constantinople for many years, and was consul general there until 1764. His works include *Recherches historiques sur les Maures et l'histoire de l'empire de Maroc* (1787) and *Révolutions de l'empire Ottoman* (1789).

Chénier, Marie Joseph de. b. at Constantinople, Feb. 11, 1764; d. at Paris, Jan. 10, 1811. French poet and politician of the republic; son of Louis de Chénier. Despite his prominence as a member of the Convention and of the Council of Five Hundred, he was unable to save his brother André from the guillotine. He was the author of the words of the revolutionary song *Chant du départ*, and the tragedies *Charles IX* (1789), *Henri VIII* (1791), and others. His complete works were published in the period 1824–26.

Chénin (shā.naṅ), **Émile.** See **Moselly, Émile.**

Chenkiang (chen'kyang'). See **Chinkiang.**

Ch'en Kung-po (chun' kủng'pō'). b. at Canton, China, 1890; executed, 1946. Chinese poet, orator, and traitor who was the second most important Chinese figure (after Wang Ching-wei) in the Japanese-sponsored Nanking government. He received (1924) a B.A. from Columbia University. Renouncing earlier Communist ties, he became (1925) a leader of the Kuomintang left wing. After expulsion in 1929, he was reinstated in 1931 in the Kuomintang central executive committee, and served (1932–33) as minister of industries. In 1940 he became puppet mayor of Shanghai and in 1944 head of the Nanking government following Wang's death. He was executed (1946) by Chiang Kai-shek for treason.

Ch'en Kuo-fu (kwō'fö'). b. at Wuhsing, Chekiang, China, 1892; d. Aug. 25, 1951. Chinese Kuomintang leader; brother of Ch'en Li-fu. He supported (1913) Sun Yat-sen against Yuan Shih-kai, at which time he became acquainted with future leaders of the Kuomintang, especially Chiang Kai-shek. After 1918 he was a cotton merchant and stock exchange broker. In 1926 he became a member of the Kuomintang central executive committee. Together with his brother, Ch'en Li-fu, he organized (1928) the so-called CC Clique which subsequently dominated the Kuomintang ministry of organization and other key government organs.

Ch'en Li-fu (lē'fö'). b. at Wuhsing, Chekiang, China, 1899—. Chinese right-wing Kuomintang political boss close to Chiang Kai-shek; brother of Ch'en Kuo-fu. He received advanced technical education in the U.S. Together with his brother he set up (1928) the Special Service Organization, i.e., the much-feared secret police. In 1929 he became secretary-general of the Kuomintang central headquarters, and served as minister of education (1938–44) in the government and minister of organization (1944–48) in the Kuomintang. With others of the CC Clique (named after the two Ch'en brothers), he controlled several official banks and businesses. His book *Philosophy of Life* is available in English.

Chennault (shẹ.nôlt'), **Claire Lee.** b. at Commerce, Texas, Sept. 6, 1890—. American air-force officer. He joined (1917) the U.S. army air corps, during World War I. He remained an officer on active duty after the end of the war, and pioneered in the use (1926) of paratroops and parachute-landed supplies. He retired in 1937 from the army, and became air adviser to Chiang Kai-shek after the Japanese invasion (1937) of China. In 1941 he organized the "Flying Tigers," a volunteer air force mostly composed of U.S. personnel, which achieved fame for protecting the Burma Road against Japanese air attack (1941). After his appointment (1942) as brigadier general in charge of U.S. air forces in China, he was promoted (1943) to major general. He later commanded (1944–45) the 14th air force in China, and retired (1945). Author of *The Role of Defensive Pursuit* (1935) and the autobiography *Way of a Fighter* (1949).

Chenonceaux (shẹ.nôṅ.sō). Village in W central France, in the department of Indre-et-Loire, situated on the Cher River ab. 19 mi. SE of Tours. It is famous for the castle built under Francis I in a graceful Renaissance style, to which picturesqueness is added by the introduction of medieval round, cone-roofed towers. The beautiful chapel has fine glass, and the old furniture and ornament of the interior remain in great part. A unique feature is the bridge over the Cher, covered with a range of buildings, built by Philibert Delorme for Catherine de Médicis.

Chenoweth (chen'ọ.weth), **Alice.** Original name of **Gardener, Helen Hamilton.**

Chenstokhov (chin.sto.ʜôf'). Russian name of **Częstochowa.**

Ch'en Tu-hsiu (chun' dö'shyö'). b. at Hwaining, Anhwei, China, 1879; d. 1942. Chinese intellectual and political leader who helped initiate (1917) the so-called Chinese Literary Renaissance. He joined in founding (1921) the Chinese Communist Party, which he dominated (1921-27) until deposed (1927) by an opposition group led by Mao Tse-tung. Arrested (1933) at Shanghai by Kuomintang authorities, he was imprisoned but later (1937) pardoned and released.

Ch'en Yi (yē'). b. at Shaohsing, Chekiang, China, 1883; executed in June, 1950. Chinese military leader belonging to the Political Science Clique. He was first prominent in banking and military circles in Chekiang province in the period 1924–27. He helped suppress the rebellion (1933–34) in Fukien province and was rewarded with the post of governor of Fukien (1934–41). After his election (1935) to the Kuomintang central executive committee, he held a succession of high party posts. He was assigned (1945) by Chiang Kai-shek to take over Formosa from the Japanese, but was removed (April, 1947) following his massacre of Formosans in the preceding month. He plotted (1948) to go over to the Communists, but was arrested by Chiang, imprisoned in Formosa, and finally executed (June, 1950).

Ch'en Yi. b. near Chengtu, Szechwan, China, c1902—. Chinese Communist orator, strategist, and military leader famous for campaigns in E China. He studied in France, where he became a socialist. In 1923 he joined the Communist Party. He remained behind after the so-called Long March (1934–35) of the Communist armies under Chu Teh from Kiangsi in S China to Shensi and Shansi in N China to continue warfare in S China. In 1941 he became vice-commander of the New Fourth Army and in 1946 commander, after the death of Yeh T'ing. He led the armies which took (1949) Shanghai from the Kuomintang, and became mayor of the city.

Ch'en Yün (yün'). b. in Shantung, China, c1900—. Chinese Communist leader who has occupied several key economic posts. Joining the labor movement while working for the *Commercial Press* at Shanghai, he went on to head the organization department of the Communist Party. During the Japanese invasion (1937–45) he gained experience in business management by running a trading corporation at Yenan. After Japan's defeat (1945) he headed the economic administration in the Communist areas of Manchuria and became (1949) minister of heavy industry, chairman of the economic and financial committee, and one of the four vice-premiers of the State Administrative Council in the Peiping government.

Cheops (kē'ops). See **Khufu.**

Chepe (chēp). See **Cheapside.**

Chephren (kef'ren). See **Khafre.**

Chepman (chep'mạn), **Walter.** b. c1473; d. c1538. Scottish printer and merchant of Edinburgh. He established (c1507) the earliest Scottish press, paying Andrew Myllar, who had learned the trade at Rouen, to run the plant.

Chepping Wycombe (chip'ing wik'ọm). See **High Wycombe.**

Chepstow (chep'stō). Urban district, market town, and river port in W England, in Monmouthshire, situated on the river Wye, ab. 12 mi. S of Monmouth, ab. 142 mi. W of London by rail. It contains the ruins of Chepstow Castle on a cliff above the river Wye, a fortress of the 13th and 14th centuries, with high walls and massive cylindrical towers. There are four interior courts. 5,285 (1951).

Chequamegon Bay (shi.kwä'mẹ.gọn). Bay in N Wisconsin, an arm of Lake Superior. It was visited by Radisson in 1659, and in the period 1665–71 there was a French mission on the W side of the bay. It is one of the finest natural harbors on the Great Lakes, but is frozen for about 5 months in winter. Ashland, Wis. is the chief port. Length, ab. 11 mi.

Cher (sher). See also **Cher River.**

Cher. Departmant in C France. It is bounded by the department of Loiret on the N, the department of Nièvre on the E, the departments of Allier and Creuse on the S, and the departments of Indre and Loir-et-Cher on the W. It is formed from parts of the regions of Berry and Bourbonnais. The department is both agricultural and industrial in character. In Bourges and other places there are blast furnaces, iron foundries, steel mills, and machine, construction, and chemical industries. Shirtmaking is also an export industry. Bourges has important military establishments and vocational schools. A number of old churches in the department are national monuments. Capital, Bourges; area, 2,819 sq. mi.; pop. 286,070 (1946).

Cherasco (kä.räs′kō). [Ancient name, **Clarascum.**] Town and commune in NW Italy, in the *compartimento* (region) of Piedmont, in the province of Cuneo, situated near the junction of the Stura and Tanaro rivers, ab. 30 mi. S of Turin. There are stone quarries and a silk mill. The castle of the Visconti dates from the 14th century. The town was definitively joined to Savoy by the Treaty of Cambrai (1529). Buildings of interest to tourists were undamaged in World War II. Pop. of commune, 8,388 (1936); of town, 2,395 (1936).

Cherasco, Armistice of. Armistice concluded between Napoleon and Victor Amadeus III, Duke of Savoy (King Victor Amadeus II of Sardinia), on April 29, 1796. By the terms of the formal peace that followed (May 15, 1796) great concessions were made to France.

Cherasco, Treaty of. Treaty of peace, signed on April 6, 1631, which confirmed the treaty of Ratisbon (Regensburg), concluded (1630) between Cardinal Richelieu (acting for France) and Ferdinand II. The latter invested the Duke of Nevers with Mantua and Montferrat. Savoy received concessions. The treaty ended the so-called Mantuan War.

Chérau (shā.rō), **Gaston.** b. at Niort, France, 1874—. French novelist, author of light novels directed toward a popular audience. Among his best-known works are *La Maison de Patrice Perrier* (1924), *Le vent du destin* (1926), and *Apprends-moi à être amoureuse* (1929).

Cheraw (chē′rô). Town in NE South Carolina. in Chesterfield County, on the Pee Dee River ab. 85 mi. NE of Columbia. Established by Welsh settlers in the 1750's, it was a prominent river port in the next century. It is known for its wide streets, some with several rows of trees. 4,836 (1950).

Cherbourg (shãr′bụrg; French, sher.bör). Town in NW France, in the department of Manche, situated on the N shore of the Cotentin peninsula, between Cap Lévi and Cap de la Hague, facing the English Channel. It is an important commercial port and naval station, with a marine arsenal and extensive docks. It is the terminus of a number of transatlantic lines. Owing to its strategic position, it was in the past variously contested between England and France; its original major fortifications were built under Louis XIV by Vauban (late 17th century) but were largely dismantled shortly thereafter. During the Seven Years' War, in 1758, the English fleet raided the harbor and inflicted considerable damage. Under Napoleon I and Napoleon III new and very strong fortifications were built. In World War II, this major French seaport was one of the primary objectives in the Normandy landings of June, 1944. Air attacks and street-to-street fighting completely devastated the city including all the major harbor installations and facilities. Fighting within the city from June 22 to 27 was among the most difficult and bitterest of the war. Only after several months was the harbor again usable, while it took almost three years to bring the port back into full commercial use. 39,760 (1946).

Cherbuliez (sher.bü.lyā), **Antoine Élisée.** b. at Geneva, Switzerland, July 29, 1797; d. at Zurich, Switzerland, March 7, 1869. Swiss political economist; uncle of Victor Cherbuliez. He was the author of *L'Utilitaire* and other works.

Cherbuliez, (Charles) Victor. [Pseudonym, **G. Valbert.**] b. at Geneva, Switzerland, July 19, 1829; d. at Combs, near Melun, France, July 1, 1899. French novelist and critic; nephew of Antoine Élisée Cherbuliez. He began his career as a teacher, but resigned his professorship and traveled extensively in the East. On his return he published in the form of a novel the result of his studies in archaeology. The first edition was called *À propos d'un cheval* (1860), and the second *Un Cheval de Phidias* (1864). Two other works of a similar character, *Le Prince Vitale* (1864) and *Le Grand Œuvre* (1867), embody his views on the origin, transformation, and destiny of the world. In the *Revue des Deux Mondes* he first published a long series of novels later brought out in book form, including *Le Comte Kostia* (1863), *Paule Méré* (1864), *Le Roman d'une honnête femme* (1866), *Prosper Randoce* (1868), *L'Aventure de Ladislas Bolski* (1869), *La Revanche de Joseph Noirel* (1872), *Meta Holdenis* (1873), *Le Fiancé de Mlle. Saint-Maur* (1876), *Samuel Brohl et Cie* (1877), *L'Idée de Jean Têterol* (1878), *Amours fragiles* (1880), *Noirs et rouges* (1881), *La Ferme du Choquart* (1883), *Olivier Maugant* (1885), *La Bête* (1887), *La Vocation du Comte Ghislain* (1888), and *Une Gageure* (1890). Among his other productions were "L'Art et la nature" (*Revue des Deux Mondes*, 1891) and "Le Secret du précepteur" (*Revue des Deux Mondes*, 1892–93). Both over his own name and under the nom de plume of C. Valbert, Cherbuliez also contributed to the same review several papers on foreign politics and historical literature. These articles were collected in part and published as *L'Allemagne politique depuis la paix de Prague* (1870), *L'Espagne politique* (1874), *Hommes et choses d'Allemagne* (1877), *Hommes et choses du temps présent* (1883), and *Profils étrangers* (1889). His art criticisms in *Le Temps* give an account of the annual art exhibit at Paris, the Salon of 1872. They were published separately under the title *Études de littérature et d'art* (1873). Two novels of Cherbuliez were dramatized, *Samuel Brohl* (1879) and *L'Aventure de Ladislas Bolski* (1879), but as plays neither scored the success attained in the original form. Cherbuliez was a distant relative of J. J. Rousseau. He became a naturalized French citizen after 1870. He was elected to the French Academy, on Dec. 8, 1881.

Cherchefelle (shersh′fel). See under **Reigate,** England.

Cherchel (sher.shel′). [Also: **Cherchell, Shershel;** Latin, **Caesarea.**] Seaport and commune in the department of Algiers, Algeria, in NW Africa, on the Mediterranean Sea ab. 54 mi. SW of Algiers. The port is small and important only for coastal traffic. Pop. of commune, 12,225 (1946); of town, 6,799 (1946).

Cheremiss (che′re.mis). See **Mari.**

Cheremkhovo (chi.rim.нô′vọ). City in the U.S.S.R., in the Irkustk *oblast* (region) of the Russian Soviet Federated Socialist Republic, on the trans-Siberian railroad: coal-mining center. 65,907 (1939).

Cherepovets (chi.ri.po.vyets′). City in the W part of the U.S.S.R., in SW Vologda *oblast* (region), ab. 75 mi. W of the city of Vologda. Situated on the high N bank of the Sheksna River where it enters the Rybinsk Reservoir, the city has both rail and water transport; industries include sawmills, machinery, and food products. It was founded about the middle of the 15th century. Pop. ab. 25,000.

Chéret (shā.re), **Jules.** b. at Paris, 1836; d. 1932. French painter, lithographer, and draftsman, especially noted for his color lithographs and posters. He started his career by becoming a letterer for a lithography house, and taught himself to sketch and paint. In 1856 he went to England to study color lithography and returned to Paris in 1866; there he became highly successful as an illustrator. A gold medal was awarded him at the Exposition Universelle of 1900, and in the same year he became an officer of the Legion of Honor. Among his works are *The Opera Ball, Woman in Yellow,* and *The Song of Columbine.*

Chéri (shā.rē). Novel (1920) by the French novelist Colette (1873—), frequently cited by critics as an example of the author's ability to understand and create erratic but sympathetic characters. In a second volume, *La Fin de Chéri* (1926), she brings her hero to a pathetic end. These two novels in an English translation were included in a volume published in the U.S. in 1951.

Chéri, Rose. [Original name, **Rose Marie Cizos.**] b. at Étampes, France, Oct. 27, 1824; d. at Passy, near Paris, Sept. 22, 1861. French comedienne. She first appeared at the Gymnase at Paris on March 30, 1842, and afterwards several times in England. In 1846 the role of Clarissa Harlowe placed her in the first rank of her profession. In May, 1847, she married Lemoine Montigny, but continued to play under the name of Rose Chéri.

Cheribon (cher.i.bon′). [Also, **Sheribon.**] Seaport on the N coast of Java, in the Republic of Indonesia. Its main products are rubber and coconut products. Near here, at the resort town of Linggadjati, was drafted (November, 1946) the Linggadjati Agreement, between the Netherlands government and the Republic of Indonesia, which was signed at Batavia in March, 1947. Pop. 52,200 (1930).

Cheribon Agreement. See **Linggadjati Agreement.**

Cherif (chā.rēf′), **Cipriano Rivas.** b. 1891—. Spanish actor, stage director, and playwright. After studying with Gordon Craig in Italy and with the ultra-modernists at Paris, he acted in Pío Baroja's *Harlequin in the Pharmacy* (1926), directed a number of companies, and acted as adviser to the Margarita Zirgú repertory company at the Teatro Español. Subsequently, he founded (1933) the Dramatic Studio of the Teatro Español. Here he directed students in a number of unusual productions, including a dramatization of Andreyev's *The Seven Who Were Hanged.* This school grew into the Teatro-Escuela de Arte, which gave modernistic, simplified productions of many modernist plays including August Strindberg's *The Green Cockatoo* and Georg Kaiser's expressionist drama *Gas.*

Cherkassy (chir.kä′si). City in the U.S.S.R., in the Ukrainian Soviet Socialist Republic, on the Dnieper River. It is a food-processing and wheat-milling center. 51,693 (1939).

Cherkesov (chir.ke′sǫf), **Zemlya.** A Russian name of **Circassia.**

Cherkess (chir.kes′). See also **Circassians.**

Cherkess. Autonomous *oblast* (region) in SW European U.S.S.R., extending from the N slopes of the Caucasus Mountains to the Kuban valley. It was formed as a territory in 1926 and became an autonomous oblast of the Russian Soviet Federated Socialist Republic in 1928. About 40 percent of the land is cultivated; grazing and hay land covers ab. 36 percent and 13 percent is mountain forest. The population (mostly Circassians) is concentrated in the capital, Cherkessk, and in the lowland steppe. Area, ab. 1,280 sq. mi.; pop. 92,534 (1939).

Cherkessk (chir.kesk′). [Former names, **Batalpashinsk, Sulimov.**] City in the SW part of the U.S.S.R., capital of Cherkess autonomous *oblast* (region) of the Russian Soviet Federated Socialist Republic, on the Kuban River. Pop. ab. 29,000.

Cherle (ker′lā), **Johann Kaspar.** See **Kerll, Johann Kaspar.**

Chermayev (cher.mä′yẹf), **Serge.** b. in the Caucasus, Russia, Oct. 8, 1900—. Architect, city planner, and painter, designer of the British Broadcasting Corporation studio at London. Educated in England, he studied in Germany, France, and Switzerland. After working in England he came to the U.S., where he served (1942–46) as chairman of the department of design at Brooklyn College, and became (1947) head of the Institute of Design at Chicago.

Chernaya (chôr′nạ.yạ). [Also: **Chorgun, Tchernaya.**] Small river in the U.S.S.R., in the Crimean *oblast* (region) of the Russian Soviet Federated Socialist Republic, which flows westward into the Black Sea near Sevastopol. On its banks, Aug. 16, 1855, the allies (England, France, Sardinia) repelled an attack by the Russians, the battle marking a further step towards Cavour's aim of showing the Italian power, through the Sardinian (Piedmontese) troops. Length, ab. 40 mi.

Chernigov (chir.nyē′gǫf). [Also, **Tchernigoff.**] *Oblast* (region) in N Ukrainian Soviet Socialist Republic, U.S.S.R., adjoining the Byelorussian Soviet Socialist Republic and Bryansk oblast of the Russian Soviet Federated Socialist Republic on the N. It lies in the basin of the Dnieper River, which forms part of its W boundary. It was a powerful medieval state, and formed a government of pre-Revolutionary Russia. Its capital is Chernigov.

Chernigov. [Also, **Tchernigoff.**] City in the U.S.S.R., capital of Chernigov *oblast* (region) of the Ukrainian Soviet Socialist Republic, on the Desna River ab. 100 mi. N of Kiev by rail. It is a center for food processing and wheat milling, an important rail junction, and one of the oldest towns in Russia, founded probably in the early 10th century. 67,356 (1939).

Chernock (chär′nǫk), **Robert.** See **Charnock** or **Chernock, Robert.**

Chernoe More (chôr′nǫ.yẹ mô′ryẹ). Russian name of the **Black Sea.**

Chernov (chir.nôf′), **Viktor Mikhailovich.** b. 1876; d. April 15, 1952. Russian politician. He joined the revolutionary movement in Russia in 1893, founded the Russian Social Revolutionary Party, and became minister of agriculture in the government set up after the revolution of February, 1917. Following the October Revolution in which the Bolsheviks seized power, he joined the counterrevolutionary White Russian army, and was president of an All-Russian Constituent Assembly in 1918. Subsequently he joined the Constructive Socialist Party. For some years he edited the periodical *Revolutionary Russia.*

Chernovtsy (chir.nôf′tsi). [German, **Czernowitz;** Rumanian, **Cernăuţi.**] City in the U.S.S.R., in W Ukrainian Soviet Socialist Republic, on the Prut River: chief city in the region known as North Bucovina, which between World Wars I and II belonged to Rumania, and former capital of the Austro-Hungarian province of Bucovina. It is the seat of a university founded by Germans, and formerly had a large German population. 110,000 (est. 1940).

Chernyakhovsk (chir.nyä′ʜǫfsk). [German, **Insterburg.**] City in the U.S.S.R., in the Kaliningrad subdivision of the Russian Soviet Federated Socialist Republic, situated at the junction of the Angerapp and Inster rivers, ab. 53 mi. E of Kaliningrad. Before World War II it was in East Prussia. It was founded in the 14th century, and is a manufacturing and railroad center. Pop. ab. 49,000.

Chernyshevsky (cher.ni.shef′ski), **Nikolai Gavrilovich.** b. at Saratov, Russia, 1828; d. there, Oct. 29, 1889. Russian historical and political writer and novelist. In 1862 he was convicted of revolutionary activity and exiled to E Siberia. There he wrote *What Is To Be Done?* (1863; Eng. editions in 1886), a novel setting forth in utopian fashion his ideas of social revolution in politics and art, one of the best-known works of the young intellectual school of the period.

Cherokee (cher′ǫ.kē, cher.ǫ.kē′). North American Indian tribe formerly widely settled in the S Appalachian Mountains. During the early 19th century (especially 1835–38 when Georgia used military force to oust the tribe) the greater part of the Cherokee were moved to reservations in Indian Territory (now Oklahoma), but a section remained in W North Carolina. Their language was a member of the Iroquoian family.

Cherokee. City in NW Iowa, county seat of Cherokee County, on the Little Sioux River: commercial center for a farming region. 7,705 (1950).

Cherokee. City in NW Oklahoma, county seat of Alfalfa County: processing center for wheat, alfalfa, corn, and sorghum. 2,635 (1950).

Cherokee Nation v. Georgia, 5 Peters 1 (1831). U.S. Supreme Court decision holding that an Indian tribe is neither a foreign nation nor a state in the federal Union, and therefore not competent to appear as a party to an action in the federal courts. The case arose over the state of Georgia's action in enforcing its laws over the independent Cherokee government and its seizure of Cherokee lands. The opinion by Chief Justice John Marshall was notable for its definition of the legal relations of the Indians with the U.S. government.

Cherokee Strip. Area in the U.S. between the 36th and 37th parallels and the 96th and 100th meridians, embracing an area of ab. 12,000 sq. mi., and now part of the W section of the state of Oklahoma. In 1891 it was purchased by the U.S. from the Cherokee Nation for a little under 8,600,000 dollars.

Cherokee Trail. [Also called the **Trappers' Trail.**] Route in the U.S. leading from a point near Fort Gibson, near the confluence of the Arkansas and Grand rivers, up the Cimarron to Middle Cimarron, where it joined the Santa Fe Trail. It was surveyed and marked (1848) by a party of U.S. soldiers, although it had been used earlier by trappers bound for the Rocky Mountains. It was also used by the Cherokee and by many white emigrants who left the Arkansas area for the Pacific Coast.

Cherokee Wars. Series of attacks (1776–81) carried out by the Cherokee Indians upon the frontiers of Virginia, the Carolinas, and Georgia. The period was marked by intervals of peace broken by Indians disturbed over the loss of their lands to white settlers. In 1779 the Cherokee threw their support to the British and were defeated in the latter part of that year by a military expedition dispatched by North Carolina and Virginia. In April, 1781, a treaty of peace was concluded with the Cherokee and was observed by all of them with the exception of the recently formed Chickamauga tribe, who thereafter continued sporadic resistance.

Chéron (shā.rôṅ), **Henry.** b. at Lisieux, Calvados, France, May 11, 1867; d. there, April 14, 1936. French political leader and lawyer, whose resignation as minister of justice was forced (1934) by Marshal Henri Philippe Pétain following the riots occasioned by the Stavisky scandal (revelations of the large-scale sale of fraudulent bonds by the promoter Alexandre Stavisky caused a serious political upheaval in the period 1934–35 in France). He enjoyed a successful period (1922–24) as minister of agriculture and is credited with sponsoring (1926–28) the financial legislation of the Poincaré cabinet. He also held at various times the ministries of labor (1913) and finance (1928–30, 1932–33).

Cherrapunji (chu.rä.pön′jē, -pön.jē′). Village in NE Union of India, in S central Assam state, on the S slope of the Khasi Hills ab. 29 mi. NW of Sylhet. The moist summer monsoon from the Bay of Bengal here rises sharply over the hill range, resulting in one of the heaviest rainfalls in the world, an average of ab. 430 inches yearly. Elevation, ab. 4,309 ft.

Cher River (sher). River in C France, rising in the Massif Central, and flowing N and W to join the Loire River just W of Tours. The upper Cher flows rapidly in a deep gorge in the old mountains, emerging onto the plain at Montluçon. The river is navigable only to Saint-Aignan, but a canal parallels it upstream to Montluçon. Length, ab. 200 mi.

Cherry (cher′i). Daughter of the landlord Boniface in George Farquhar's play *The Beaux' Stratagem* (1707).

Cherryvale (cher′i.vāl). City in SE Kansas, in Montgomery County. It was founded in the 1870's as a railroad terminus. 2,952 (1950).

Cherry Valley Massacre. Attack (Nov. 11, 1778) during the American Revolution by Walter Butler's Rangers (who were aided by an Indian force under Joseph Brant) upon Cherry Valley, a frontier post in the upper Susquehanna valley, N.Y. Thirty settlers and 16 soldiers were slain and the fort laid waste by fire.

Cherryville (cher′i.vil). Town in W North Carolina, in Gaston County: cotton and other farm products. 3,492 (1950).

Chersiphron (kėr′si.fron). b. at Cnossus, Crete; fl. c576 B.C. Cretan architect, traditionally considered the designer of the first Artemision (temple of Artemis) at Ephesus. He was associated with his son Metagenes, and with Theodorus. The Artemision was 120 years in building, and was finished c456 B.C. It was later destroyed by fire, and rebuilt about the time of Alexander the Great by Dinocrates; this building, usually called the Temple of Diana of Ephesus, was one of the seven wonders of the ancient world.

Cherskogo Range (chir.skô′vǫ). [Also, **Cherski Range** (cher′ski).] Range of mountains in the U.S.S.R., in the Yakutsk Autonomous Soviet Socialist Republic of the Russian Soviet Federated Socialist Republic; discovered in 1926. The range runs NW to SE for 450 mi., and reaches a height of 9,843 ft.

Cherso (ker′sō). Italian name of **Cres.**

Chersonesus (kėr.sǫ.nē′sus). [Also, **Chersonese** (kėr′-sǫ.nēz, -nēs).] Ancient Greek word for peninsula, specifically applied to the following: **1.** Chersonesus Aurea, the modern Malay Peninsula. **2.** Chersonesus Cimbrica, the modern peninsula of Jutland, Denmark. **3.** Chersonesus Taurica or Scythica, the modern Crimea, U.S.S.R. **4.** Chersonesus Thracica, the modern Gallipoli Peninsula, between the Hellespont and the Gulf of Saros.

Chersonesus. [Also: **Cherson** (kėr′son), **Chersonesus Heracleotica** (hir″ą.klę.ot′i.ką); Russian, **Khersones.**] Ancient city situated on the SW tip of the Crimean Peninsula, near what is now Sevastopol, founded by the Ionians at the beginning of the 5th century B.C. Because of its situation, it soon became an important trading city-state. Alliance with the kingdom of Cimmerian Bosporus was followed by subjection to the Roman Empire. Later, Chersonesus formed a part of the Byzantine Empire, was taken by the Russian Prince Vladimir, went back to Byzantium, formed part of the domain of Trebizond and, subsequently, of the Turkish Empire, until the Russian conquest of Crimea. After the 15th century A.D. Chersonesus entered upon an era of gradual decay. It is archaeologically of interest, containing the remains of city walls and towers of the Byzantine era, foundations of some private dwellings, and foundations of basilicas, with mosaic floors and traces of frescoes. Many old Greek inscriptions were found here, and the necropolis contains numerous objects of the Greco-Roman and Byzantine periods. There were also found some traces of a neolithic culture.

Chertsey (chėrt′si). [Old English, **Certes ēg, Ceortes īg** (or **ēg**), meaning "Ceort's island."] Urban district and market town in SE England, in Surrey, situated on the river Thames, ab. 23 mi. SW of London. It is part of an almost continuous line of urban development along the Thames between London and Reading, but is included in the Green Belt scheme of wooded areas to be preserved surrounding London. It was the ancient capital of the South Saxons, and contains a Benedictine monastery founded in the 7th century. 31,029 (1951).

Chérubin (shā.rü.baṅ). Page in *Le Mariage de Figaro*, by Beaumarchais. Timid before the Countess Almaviva, he is extremely boastful with Suzanne. He also appears in the sequel, *La Mère coupable*, where he has overcome this weakness, and is proved to be the rival of Almaviva, the father of Almaviva's supposed son Léon, and the cause of the "guilty mother's" tears. In Mozart's opera *Le Nozze di Figaro* (*The Marriage of Figaro*), based on the earlier Beaumarchais work, he appears as Cherubino.

Chérubin de la Ronda (dę là rôṅ.dà), **Don.** Titular hero of Alain René Le Sage's novel *The Bachelor of Salamanca.*

Cherubini (kā.rö.bē′nē), **Maria Luigi Carlo Zenobio Salvatore.** b. at Florence, Sept. 14, 1760; d. at Paris, March 15, 1842. Italian composer, notably of operas. He studied under Sarti at Bologna, and finally established himself at Paris in 1788, where he became professor of composition (1816) and then director (1821) of the Paris conservatory of music. His works include the operas *Armida* (1782), *La Finta Principessa* (1785), *Ifigenia in Aulide* (1787), *Demophon* (1788), *Lodoiska* (1791), *Médée* (1797), *Les Deux Journées* (1800), *Faniska* (1806), and *Ali Baba* (originally *Koukourgi*, 1793; produced in 1833), as well as *Requiem in C* (1817) and *Requiem in D* (1836). He also wrote many motets, masses, string quartets, and one-act operas.

Cherubino (kā.rö.bē′nō). See under **Chérubin.**

Cherusci (ke.rus′ī). German tribe, in the time of Caesar dwelling about the middle Weser River in territory extending as far E as the Elbe River. They were subjugated to the Romans by Drusus Germanicus and Tiberius, but rose (9 A.D.) against Varus under the leadership of their own countryman, Arminius. In the time (c100 A.D.) of Tacitus they had sunk into comparative unimportance. The name disappears early in the 5th century. They are thought to have become ultimately a constituent part of the Saxons.

Chervin (sher.vaṅ), **Nicolas.** b. in Rhône, France, Oct. 6, 1783; d. at Bourbonne-les-Bains, Haute-Marne, France, 1843. French physician. He is noted for research concerned with yellow fever, on which he published several monographs. He also wrote *Recherches médico-philosophiques sur les causes de la polygamie dans les pays chauds* (1812; Eng. trans., *Medico-philosophical Researches on the Causes of Polygamy in the Warm Countries*).

Cherwell (chär′wel, -węl). Small river in C and S England, in Northamptonshire and Oxfordshire. It rises S of Daventry, flowing 30 mi. S to its confluence with the river Thames near Oxford.

Cherwell, 1st Baron. Title of **Lindemann, Frederick Alexander.**

Chesapeake (ches′ą.pēk). Town in W central West Virginia, in Kanawha County. 2,566 (1950).

Chesapeake. American frigate of 38 guns, built at Norfolk, Va., in 1799. On June 22, 1807, while under the command of Captain James Barron, the ship was stopped by the British *Leopard* and ordered to turn over alleged deserters. Barron, although not ready for action, refused; the *Leopard* opened fire and soon disabled the *Chesapeake.*

Four seamen, one a deserter and three Americans, were removed and the *Chesapeake* was forced to return to Hampton Roads. During the campaign of 1812 she cruised in South American waters. In May, 1813, she returned to Boston, and was placed under the command of Captain James Lawrence. The British frigate *Shannon*, 38 guns rating, commanded by Captain Philip Vere Broke, was at this time cruising off Boston harbor. Broke had brought his ship to a high state of efficiency. On June 1, 1813, the *Chesapeake* sailed out of Boston harbor, the *Shannon* being in sight in the offing. The battle occurred six leagues east of Boston light. Immediately after opening fire both ships fell aboard. Within ten minutes of the first shot, all American officers aboard were disabled and Captain Lawrence was mortally wounded. He was carried below exclaiming "Don't give up the ship!" Captain Broke boarded the *Chesapeake*, and at 6:05 P.M., 15 minutes after the first gun was fired, her flag was struck.

Chesapeake and Delaware Canal. Canal linking Chesapeake and Delaware bays, covering a distance of a little over 13½ mi. and built between 1825 and 1829. The U.S. government bought it (1919) and converted the waterway into a sea-level ship canal.

Chesapeake and Ohio Canal. [Nickname, **"the Old Ditch."**] Inland waterway projected as a link between Chesapeake Bay and the Ohio River. It was built (1828–50) up to Cumberland, Md., but never reached the Ohio. The construction was undertaken jointly by the U.S. government and the state governments of Virginia and Maryland. It went into receivership in 1889, long after it had become apparent that it could not compete with the Baltimore and Ohio Railroad, and in 1938 was sold to the U.S. government.

Chesapeake Bay. Inlet of the Atlantic Ocean, in Virginia and Maryland. It enters the Atlantic between Capes Charles and Henry. Its chief affluents are the Susquehanna, Patapsco, Potomac, York, Rappahannock, and James rivers. It was first explored by Captain John Smith in 1608. Length, ab. 200 mi.; breadth, 4 to 40 mi.

Chesapeake Capes, Battle of. Naval battle (Sept. 5–9, 1781) off the entrance to Chesapeake Bay between a French fleet (24 ships) under Count de Grasse and a British fleet (19 ships) under Thomas Graves carrying fresh troops for Cornwallis. The damage, including one ship sunk, sustained by the British fleet caused it to return to New York, and the French vessels, bearing siege guns for the assault on Yorktown, entered the capes. The action thereby contributed heavily to Cornwallis's defeat at Yorktown, which ended the fighting in the Revolutionary War.

Chesebrough (chēz'brō), **Caroline.** b. at Canandaigua, N.Y., March 30, 1825; d. at Piermont, N.Y., Feb. 16, 1873. American novelist. She was the author of *Dream-Land by Daylight* (1852), *Susan: The Fisherman's Daughter* (1855), and other novels for adults and children.

Cheselden (chez'ẹl.dẹn), **William.** b. at Somerby, Leicestershire, England, Oct. 19, 1688; d. at Bath, England, April 10, 1752. English surgeon, celebrated for his "lateral operation for the stone" (a method of removing kidney stones) and for operations upon the eye. In a day when lack of anesthetics made speed important in surgery, Cheselden could, according to report, remove a stone in 54 seconds. He wrote *The Anatomy of the Human Body* (1713), *Treatise on the High Operation for the Stone* (1723), and *Osteographia, or the Anatomy of the Bones* (1733). A short paper (*Phil. Trans.* XXXV. 447) upon the case of a 13-year-old boy, born blind, upon whom couching (an obsolete operation in which a cataract is turned down and away into the vitreous humor of the eye) was performed has been much quoted.

Chesham (chesh'ạm, ches'ạm). Urban district and market town in S central England, in Buckinghamshire, situated on the river Chess, ab. 25 mi. NW of London by rail. 11,428 (1951).

Cheshire (chesh'ir). Town (in Connecticut the equivalent of township in many other states) and unincorporated village in C Connecticut, in New Haven County, near the Mill River: seat of Cheshire Academy. Pop. of town. 6,295 (1950); of village, 1,826 (1950).

Cheshire (chesh'ir) or **Chester** (ches'tėr). Maritime county in W England. It is bounded on the N by the estuary of the river Mersey and Lancashire, on the NE by Yorkshire, on the E by Derbyshire, on the SE by Staffordshire, on the S by Shropshire and the detached portion of Flintshire, on the W by Flintshire and Denbighshire, and on the NW by Liverpool Bay and the estuary of the river Dee. The surface is generally level, most of the county being included within the Plain of Lancastria. The Wirral peninsula, flat and low-lying, is situated between the estuaries of the rivers Mersey and Dee, in the NW portion of the county. Cheshire is perhaps the most important dairying region in the British Isles, especially in the S part of the county. A famous local cheese is produced near Oswestry, and milk is supplied to the London markets. Cheese making is declining in favor of milk production. The cattle are shorthorns. Many pigs and some sheep are also raised. North Cheshire is mainly under crops, raising principally oats and potatoes. The county has long been important for its salt deposits (worked mainly at Middlewich, Nantwich, Northwich, and Sandbach), which have provided the basis for an important chemical industry. Other industries are silk, linen, and worsted manufactures, textile-machinery manufactures, flour milling, the repair and manufacture of railway rolling stock, and shipbuilding. There are several important seaports situated on the Mersey estuary, and Cheshire has a well-developed canal system. Cheshire was made a county palatine by William the Conqueror. The palatinate court was abolished in 1830. County seat, Chester; area of administrative county, ab. 973 sq. mi.; pop. of administrative county, 824,438 (1951).

Cheshme or **Chesme** (chesh.me'). See **Çeşme.**

Cheshskaya Bay (chesh'skạ.yạ). [Also: **Cheskaya Bay, Gulf of Tcheskaya.**] Gulf in the U.S.S.R., in the Arkhangelsk *oblast* (region) of the Russian Soviet Federated Socialist Republic: an arm of the Barents Sea. Length, ab. 100 mi.; width, ab. 50 mi.

Cheshunt (ches'unt). Urban district in E central England, in Hertfordshire, ab. 14 mi. N of Liverpool Street station, London. Cheshunt is a rapidly expanding village and is chiefly noted for its large acreages of fruits, vegetables, and flowers cultivated under glass. 23,016 (1951).

Chesil Bank (ches'il). Long bar in SW England, in Dorsetshire on the English Channel, connecting the Isle of Portland with the mainland near Abbotsbury. Length, ab. 10 mi.

Cheskaya Bay (ches'kạ.yạ). See **Cheshskaya Bay.**

Chesnay (she.nā), **Le.** See **Le Chesnay.**

Chesney (ches'ni, chez'ni), **Charles Cornwallis.** b. in Ireland, 1826; d. at Aldershot, England, 1876. English soldier and military critic; brother of Sir George Tomkyns Chesney and nephew of Francis Rawdon Chesney. As a sublieutenant of royal engineers, he served (1845–56) in Ireland and the colonies. As professor of military history at Sandhurst (c1856–68), he won recognition as the best military critic of his day. In 1868 he was made a lieutenant colonel. His chief works are *Campaigns in Virginia and Maryland* (1863), written while the Civil War was still in progress; *Waterloo Lectures* (1868), which credited the victory at the battle of Waterloo to Blücher rather than to Wellington and criticized sharply Napoleon's strategy; and *Essays in Military Biography* (1874). He was a member of the royal commission on military education.

Chesney, Francis Rawdon. b. at Annalong, County Down, Ireland, March 16, 1789; d. at Mourne, County Down, Ireland, Jan. 30, 1872. Irish general and engineer; uncle of Charles Cornwallis Chesney and Sir George Tomkyns Chesney. He examined the isthmus of Suez in 1830, and demonstrated the feasibility of a canal across it (his report serving later as the starting point of Ferdinand De Lesseps). He explored the valley of the Euphrates in 1831, and later (1835–36) established an overland route to India. In the next decade he was in command (1843–47) of the artillery at the station at Hong Kong, China. He published *Expedition for the Survey of the Rivers Euphrates and Tigris* (1850) and other works relating to his expeditions.

Chesney, Sir George Tomkyns. b. at Tiverton, Devonshire, England, April 30, 1830; d. at London, March 31, 1895. British general, engineer, and author; brother of Charles Cornwallis Chesney and nephew of Francis Rawdon Chesney. Having entered the army in 1848, he served during the Indian mutiny. He was president of the engineering college at Calcutta, the first president (1871–80) of the Royal Indian Civil Engineering College, Cooper's

Hill, Staines, near London, secretary (1880–86) to the military department of the Indian government, and military member (1886–91) of the governor's council. He was knighted in 1890, and was elected a Conservative member of Parliament for Oxford in 1892. In 1871 he published anonymously in *Blackwood's Magazine* "The Battle of Dorking, or Reminiscences of a Volunteer," an account of an imaginary German assault upon England which attracted much attention. He also published *Indian Polity* (1868), *The True Reformer* (1874), and *The Dilemma* (1876), all novels dealing with army affairs, and *The Lesters, or a Capitalist's Labor* (1893).

Chesnutt (ches'nut), **Charles Waddell.** b. at Cleveland, Ohio, June 20, 1858; d. Nov. 15, 1932. American Negro author. He grew up and was educated in North Carolina, where he became principal of a state normal school at Fayetteville. Subsequently he went to New York and engaged in journalism, but eventually returned to Cleveland, where, having studied the law, he was admitted to the bar in 1887. In 1889 he was revealed as a gifted writer of fiction with the publication of *The Conjure Woman;* this was followed by *The Wife of His Youth and Other Stories* (1899), *The House Behind the Cedars* (1900), *The Marrow of Tradition* (1901), and *The Colonel's Dream* (1905). He also wrote a *Life of Frederick Douglass*, published in 1899.

Chester (ches'tėr). See also **Cheshire,** England.

Chester. [Latin, **Deva, Devana Castra, Castra;** Welsh, **Caerleon, Caerlleon.**] City and county borough in W England, county seat of Cheshire, situated on the river Dee, ab. 15 mi. SE of Liverpool, ab. 179 mi. NW of London by rail. It is in the dairying region of Cheshire, and is an important railway center. The Ellesmere Canal connects it with the estuary of the river Mersey. Chester was a seaport in the Middle Ages, at one time overshadowing Liverpool, but silting up of the estuary of the river Dee, which began in the 14th century, has destroyed its maritime position. It contains many Roman antiquities, and is notably medieval in appearance, being famous for its "Rows," or galleries which front the first floors of the timbered Tudor buildings on the four main streets. They are now used for shops. It has a cathedral, built of red sandstone, which presents every variety of English medieval architecture, from the Norman to the last Perpendicular. It has recently been well restored. The exterior is marked by its fine ranges of windows and its square central tower. The interior is very effective, the various architectural styles grouping in such manner as to contrast agreeably. The nave has modern fan vaulting in oak. The south transept is as large as the choir, while the Norman north transept is very small. The choir dates from the 13th century; its 15-century stalls are elaborately canopied and pinnacled. The Lady Chapel is an excellent example of Early English style. The dimensions of the cathedral are 355 by 75 ft.; length of transepts, 200 ft.; height of vaulting, 78 ft. The cloister is in Perpendicular style, the rectangular chapter house and the refectory are Early English. Chester was an important Roman military station, was destroyed by Ethelfrith of Northumbria c613, and was rebuilt by Ethelflaed 300 years later. It surrendered to William the Conqueror in 1070. Chester was long besieged by the Parliamentarians, and was taken by them in 1646. It was the northern terminus of Watling Street, the old Roman road from the Strait of Dover which passed through London. Chester, under the Romans, later became known as the *Civitas Legionum* (or city of the legion). This was translated by the English to *Legeceaster*, of which Chester is a contraction. It is the only city in England that still possesses its walls (now used as a promenade) entire. 48,229 (1951).

Chester. City in S Illinois, county seat of Randolph County, on the Mississippi River: shipping center for products of nearby mines. 5,389 (1950).

Chester. Town (in New York the equivalent of township in many other states) and village in SE New York, in Orange County. Horses are raised here. It is the site of the grave of Hambletonian, one of the most famous of trotting horses. Pop. of town, 2,878 (1950); of village, 1,215 (1950).

Chester. [Former names, **Upland, Oplandt.**] City in SE Pennsylvania, in Delaware County, on the Delaware River, ab. 12 mi. SW of Philadelphia: port with shipyards, auto assembly plants, and oil refineries; manufactures include glass, steel, paper, and silk. It is the seat of Pennsylvania Military College and the Crozer Theological Seminary. Settled (c1644) by Swedes, it was occupied (1655) by the Dutch and taken (1664) by the English. It is one of the oldest settlements in the state. 66,039 (1950).

Chester. City in N South Carolina, county seat of Chester County, in a cotton and livestock producing area: textile manufactures. 6,893 (1950).

Chester. City in N West Virginia, in Hancock County: residential community: manufactures of pottery. Platted in 1896, it was incorporated in 1907. Pop. 3,758 (1950).

Chester, Earl of. Title of **Blundevill, Randulph de.**

Chester, Earl of. Title of **Hugh of Avranches.**

Chester, (palatine) Earl of. Title (palatine) of **Hugh of Cyveiliog** (or **Kevelioc**).

Chester, Earl of. Title of **Randulf de Gernons.**

Chester, Battle of. Battle in which Ethelfrith of Northumbria defeated (c613) the Cymry of Strathclyde under Brochmael, prince of Powys. As a result he annexed Chester and the surrounding district, thus doing much toward sundering the Cymry of Strathclyde from those of Wales. It is said that a thousand Cymric monks, who prayed on the field of battle for their countrymen, were killed by the order of Ethelfrith.

Chester, Colby Mitchell. b. at New London, Conn., Feb. 29, 1844; d. at Rye, N.Y., May 4, 1932. American naval officer, astronomer, and naval engineer. A graduate (1863) of the U.S. Naval Academy, he was an instructor there in the period 1874–77, and served as hydrographic inspector in the U.S. Coast (later U.S. Coast and Geodetic) Survey from 1880 to 1885. From 1902 to 1906 he was superintendent of the U.S. Naval Observatory. He directed the U.S. surveys in China and Korea in the period 1871–73. He served in the Civil War, was promoted to rear admiral in 1903, and retired in 1906. He visited Turkey on two government-authorized missions (1908, 1922) for the promotion of trade.

Chester, George Randolph. b. in Ohio, 1869; d. at New York, Feb. 26, 1924. American writer, best known for the "Get-Rich-Quick Wallingford" stories (1908 *et seq.*). He was Sunday editor (until 1908) of the Cincinnati *Enquirer* and a contributor (1905 *et seq.*) to the periodicals *Cosmopolitan, McClure's, Everybody's*, and *The Saturday Evening Post.* He was the author of plays, motion-picture scenarios, and *The Cash Intrigue* (1909), *The Making of Bobby Burnit* (1909), *Young Wallingford* (1910), *Five Thousand an Hour* (1912), *Wallingford and Blackie Daw* (1913), *Wallingford in His Prime* (1913), and others. In collaboration with his wife he wrote *The Ball of Fire* (1914), *Cordelia Blossom* (1914), *The Son of Wallingford* (1921), and *On the Lot and Off* (1924).

Chester, Joseph Lemuel. b. at Norwich, Conn., April 30, 1821; d. at London, May 26, 1882. American genealogist, resident in England after 1858. He engaged in various occupations (teacher, clerk, commissioner of deeds, journalist), and was aide-de-camp with the rank of colonel to the governor of Pennsylvania in the period 1855–58. His genealogical work was begun in England, and he came to be regarded as the foremost English-speaking genealogist of his day, hunting out the English connections of emigrants to New England. Among his compilations are *Matriculations at the University of Oxford* and *The Marriage, Baptismal, and Burial Registers of the Abbey of St. Peter, Westminster.*

Chester, Mr. [Later, **Sir John Chester.**] Polished but unprincipled character in Charles Dickens's *Barnaby Rudge.* In order to avoid an alliance which will add nothing to his prestige and wealth, he attempts, without success, to avert the match between his son Edward and the worthy (but poor) Emma Haredale. Dickens based the character of Mr. Chester on what he knew of Philip Dormer Stanhope (Lord Chesterfield).

Chesterfield (ches'tėr.fēld). Municipal borough and manufacturing town in C England, in Derbyshire, situated on the rivers Rother and Hipper, ab.11 mi. S of Sheffield, ab. 146 mi. N of London by rail. It has an iron industry. Chesterfield is noted for the spire (built in the 14th century) of lead-covered timber surmounting the parish church. The spire leans ab. 7 ft. out of the vertical. 68,540 (1951).

Chesterfield, 4th Earl of. Title of **Stanhope, Philip Dormer.**

Chesterfield, 5th Earl of. Title of **Stanhope, Philip.**

Chesterfield Canal. Canal in C England, in Derbyshire and Nottinghamshire. It extends from Chesterfield to the river Trent ab. 10 mi. NE of East Retford. Classified as a "narrow canal" (width under 14 ft.), it is limited to a maximum capacity of narrow boats (30 tons or less). It passes through two tunnels, the longer of which is over 8,500 ft. long. Length of canal, 46 mi.

Chesterfield Inlet. Arm of Hudson Bay in the district of Keewatin, Northwest Territories, Canada, on the W side of the bay just S of Southampton Island. Length, ab. 200 mi.; greatest breadth, ab. 25 mi.

Chesterfield Islands. Group of 11 coral islets in the Coral Sea midway between the French colony of New Caledonia of which they are a part, and Australia: valuable for their guano deposits. Area, 250 acres.

Chester-le-Street (ches'tėr.lę.strēt'). [Latin, **Condercum;** Early English, **Cuneceastre.**] Urban district and old fortress town in NE England, in Durham, ab. 6 mi. N of Durham, ab. 260 mi. N of London by rail. It was the seat in the 10th century of the bishops of Bernicia or Lindisfarne. 18,539 (1951).

Chester Plays, The. Collection of medieval mysteries (miracle plays) based on scriptural subjects, formerly presented by the guilds of Chester, England, at Whitsuntide. They were 25 in number, and were played during three days. Their authorship is sometimes ascribed to the 14th-century chronicler Ranulf Higden. A complete publication (1843) of them was edited for the Shakespeare Society by Thomas Wright.

Chesterton (ches'tėr.tǫn). Town in NW Indiana, in Porter County, near Gary and Lake Michigan. 3,175 (1950).

Chesterton, Ada Elizabeth. [Maiden name, **Jones.**] b. at London, 1888—. English newspaper writer, social worker, and dramatist; sister-in-law of G.K. Chesterton. She traveled in Russia, Poland, China, and Japan as a correspondent for the London *Daily Express.* Her works include *In Darkest London* (1926), *Women of the Underworld* (1930), *My Russian Venture* (1931), *Young China and New Japan* (1933), *What Price Youth* (1939), and *Salute the Soviet* (1942), works on social and international problems. In collaboration with Ralph Neale, she wrote the plays *The Man Who Was Thursday* (a dramatization of G.K. Chesterton's novel of the same name) and *The Love Game.* Interested in improving the living conditions of working girls and homeless women, she established homes (Cecil Houses) and a club (Cecil Residential Club for Working Girls) for their comfort and convenience.

Chesterton, G. K. [Full name, **Gilbert Keith Chesterton.**] b. at Campden Hill, London, May 29, 1874; d. at Beaconsfield, England. June 14, 1936. English poet, journalist, novelist, and critic. He was educated at St. Paul's School and at the Slade School of Art. For a time he worked for book-publishing houses, and then turned to journalism. His writing was stylistically brilliant and made a great point of paradox. Among his literary creations is the Roman Catholic priest-detective Father Brown, drawn after Chesterton's friend Father O'Connor. Received (July, 1922) into the Roman Catholic Church, he defended Catholicism in his subsequent writings. He was the author of *The Wild Knight and Other Poems* (1900), *Greybeards at Play* (1900), *Robert Browning* (1903), *G. F. Watts* (1904), *The Napoleon of Notting Hill* (1904), *Charles Dickens* (1906), *The Man Who Was Thursday* (1908), *All Things Considered* (1908), *Orthodoxy* (1909), *George Bernard Shaw* (1910), *What's Wrong with the World* (1910), *William Blake* (1910), *Alarms and Discursions* (1910), *Appreciations and Criticisms of the Works of Charles Dickens* (1911), *The Innocence of Father Brown* (1911), *A Short History of England* (1917), *St. Francis of Assisi* (1923), *The Everlasting Man* (1925), *The Secret of Father Brown* (1927), *William Cobbett* (1925), *The Resurrection of Rome* (1930), *Chaucer* (1932), *Autobiography* (1936), and *The Paradoxes of Mr. Pond* (1936).

Chestertown (ches'tėr.toun). Town in C Maryland, in Kent County, on the Chester River: a residential community, which retains much of its 18th-century appearance. Manufactures include clothing and fertilizer. It is the seat of Washington College, founded in 1782. Pop. 3,143 (1950).

Chesuncook Lake (chę.sun'kůk). Lake in N central Maine, ab. 37 mi. NE of Greenville. It is in a hilly wilderness region, and has some campsites. Elevation, ab. 900 ft.; length, ab. 23 mi.; width, from ½ to 4 mi.

Chetco (chet'kō). North American Indian tribe formerly inhabiting the valley of a river now named for them, in SW Oregon, which flows into the Pacific Ocean in Curry County. The language was of the Athabaskan family.

Chettle (chet'l), **Henry.** d. c1607. English dramatist and pamphleteer, son of a dyer of London, and a stationer by trade. He was the author or joint author of a large number of plays. *The Tragedy of Hoffman* (1602) is the only play now extant that is attributed to Chettle.

Chetumal (chā.tö.mäl'). City in SE Mexico, capital of Quintana Roo territory, on Chetumal Bay. Pop. under 5,000 (1940).

Chetwode (chet'wůd), Sir **Philip Walhouse.** b. 1869; d. July 6, 1950. English soldier, commander in chief (1930–35) of the British army in India. He participated (1892–93) in the Burma campaign, and served (1899–1902) in the Boer War. In World War I he commanded (1915–16) the 2nd Cavalry Division before being appointed (1916) head of the desert column and Egypt canal defenses; subsequently he commanded (1917) the army corps which captured Jerusalem. From 1928 to 1930 he was chief of the general staff in India. He was promoted to brigadier general (1914), major general (1916), lieutenant general (1919), general (1926), and field marshal (1933). During the Spanish Civil War, he was chairman of the British commission for the exchange of war prisoners.

Chetwood (chet'wůd), **William Rufus.** d. March 3, 1766. English dramatist, bookseller, and prompter at Drury Lane Theatre, London. He was the author of *General History of the Stage* (1749), several dramatic pieces, and others.

Chetwynd (chet'wind), **Mount.** Massif in Antarctica, in Victoria Land, capped by black rock rising to ab. 5,000 ft., lying ab. 3 mi. SW of Mount Gauss on the S side of the Mawson Glacier, in the Prince Albert Mountains, in ab. 76°23′ S., 162°13′ E. It was discovered and named by the National Antarctic Expedition (1901–04), under the leadership of Captain Robert F. Scott.

Cheval de fust (shę.vål dę füst), **Le.** See **Cléomadès, Adventures of.**

Chevalier (shę.val'yā, shev.ą.lir'), **Albert.** b. at Notting Hill, London, March 21, 1861; d. at London, July 11, 1923. English music-hall singer. Although he came to be, for millions throughout the world, the type and symbol of the London cockney, he was of French, Italian, and Welsh ancestry. His career on the stage began in 1877 and for some years he appeared in legitimate drama with the Kendals, the Bancrofts, and others, but in 1891 he became a music-hall singer and quickly won fame and affection. In the years following he gave more than 1,000 recitals in the Queen's Hall, London, toured Britain many times, and visited the U.S., everywhere captivating audiences with *Mrs. 'Enery 'Awkins, Knocked 'em in the Old Kent Road, My Old Dutch,* and others of the scores of songs of which he was composer and librettist in whole or in collaboration. To give a framework to his songs he wrote many short plays and sketches; he took the titular role in Sir James Barrie's *Pantaloon;* and he gave joint recitals with Yvette Guilbert.

Chevalier (shę.vå.lyā; Anglicized, shę.val'yā), **Maurice.** b. 1899—. French actor and singer famous for his witty and suggestive songs. After attaining popularity in French music-hall performances, he won success in American motion pictures (*The Merry Widow, The Beloved Vagabond,* and others). Chevalier retained enormous favor with the French public until the fall of France in World War II, when his reputation was clouded by suspicions of collaboration with the Germans. He has since regained much of his old popularity.

Chevalier, Michel. b. at Limoges, France, Jan. 13, 1806; d. at Montpellier, France, Nov. 28, 1879. French political economist, a proponent of free trade. His works include *Lettres sur l'Amérique du Nord* (1836), *Des intérêts matériels en France* (1838), *Cours d'économie politique* (1842–50),

Essais de politique industrielle (1843), *La Liberté aux États-Unis*, and several works on Mexico.

Chevalier, Sulpice Guillaume. See **Gavarni, Paul.**

Chevalier à l'Épée (shę.vȧ.lyā ȧ lā.pā), **Le.** Old French romance of the 12th century, at one time erroneously ascribed to Chrestien de Troyes.

Chevalier au Cygne (ō sēny'), **Le.** [Eng. trans., "*The Knight of the Swan.*"] Title of a group of *chansons*, the members of which bear separate headings, such as *Antioche, Les Chétifs, Les Enfances de Godefroy. Antioche*, the first of these, which describes the exploits of the Christian host, first in attacking and then in defending Antioch, is one of the finest of the *chansons*, and was probably written by an eye-witness.

Chevalier de Maison-Rouge (dę me.zôṅ.rözh), **Le.** [Eng. trans., "*The Knight of the Red House.*"] Historical novel by the elder Alexandre Dumas, published in 1846.

Chevalier de Ramsay (ram'zi). See **Ramsay, Andrew Michael.**

"Chevalier de St. George." See **Stuart, James Francis Edward.**

Chevalier d'Harmental (dȧr.mäṅ.tȧl), **Le.** Romance by the elder Alexandre Dumas, published in 1843.

Chevalier of Pensieri-Vani (shev.ạ.lir'; pen.si.er'i.vä'ni), **The.** Novel (1890) by Henry B. Fuller, written under the pseudonym Stanton Page.

Cheverel (shev'ę.rẹl), **Sir Christopher** and **Lady.** Two of the principal characters in George Eliot's novel *Mr. Gilfil's Love-Story.*

Cheverly (chev'ėr.li). Town in W central Maryland, in Prince Georges County, near Washington, D.C. In the decade between the last two U.S. censuses, its population more than tripled. 996 (1940), 3,318 (1950).

Cheverus (shę.vrüs; Anglicized, shev'ę.rus), **Jean Louis Anne Madeleine Lefebvre de.** b. at Mayenne, France, Jan. 28, 1768; d. at Bordeaux, France, July 19, 1836. French prelate, first Roman Catholic bishop of Boston, Mass. (1808 *et seq.*), archbishop of Bordeaux (1827 *et seq.*), and cardinal (1836).

Cheves (chiv'is), **Langdon.** b. at Rocky River, S.C., Sept. 17, 1776; d. at Columbia, S.C., June 26, 1857. American politician. He entered the House of Representatives in 1811, was its speaker in the period 1814–15, and was president of the Second Bank of the United States from 1819 to 1822.

Chevillard (shę.vē.yȧr), **Paul Alexandre Camille.** b. at Paris, Oct. 14, 1859; d. at Châtou, France, May 30, 1923. French composer and orchestra leader; son of Pierre Alexandre François Chevillard (1811–77). He succeeded (1899) his father-in-law, Charles Lamoureux, as conductor of the Concerts Lamoureux, and founded (1895) the Trio Chevillard-Hayot-Salmon. His compositions include *Étude chromatique, Fantaisie symphonique*, and *Le Chêne et le roseau*, a symphonic ballad.

Chevillard, Pierre Alexandre François. b. at Antwerp, Belgium, Jan. 15, 1811; d. at Paris, in December, 1877. French cellist; father of Paul Alexandre Camille Chevillard (1859–1923). Professor (1860 *et seq.*) at the Paris Conservatory, he established the Société des Derniers Quatuors de Beethoven, an early and influential chamber-work group.

Chevillet (shę.vē.ye), **Charles.** See **Champmeslé, Charles Chevillet de.**

Cheviot (shev'i.ọt, shiv'-). City in SW Ohio, in Hamilton County near Cincinnati. 9,944 (1950).

Cheviot Hills (chev'i.ọt, chē'vi.ọt). Mountain range in NE England and SE Scotland, in Northumberland, England, and Roxburghshire, Scotland. The surface is mostly regular and covered with rich pasture for the Cheviot breed of sheep. These hills are celebrated in history and romance. The highest peak is Cheviot Hill (2,676 ft.). Length, 35 mi.

Chevreul (shę.vrėl), **Michel Eugène.** b. at Angers, France, Aug. 31, 1786; d. at Paris, April 9, 1889. French chemist. He was chemist (1824–89) at the Gobelin tapestry factory, professor (1830–83) at the museum of natural history at Paris, and author of numerous scientific works. His researches on animal fats led to his discovery of stearin and olein.

Chevreuse (shę.vrėz), Duchesse **de.** [Title of **Marie de Rohan-Montbazon.**] b. in December, 1600; d. at Gagny, near Paris, Aug. 12, 1679. French political intriguer. She was the daughter of Hercule de Rohan, Duc de Montbazon, and was the wife first of Charles d'Albert, Duc de Luynes, and, after his death, of the Duc de Chevreuse. She was one of the most formidable enemies at court of Cardinal Richelieu, by whom she was, however, eventually forced to leave France. On the death of Louis XII she returned, but was coldly received by the queen regent, Anne of Austria. Having acted in concert with Cardinal de Retz against Mazarin, she was a second time sent into exile.

Chevrolet (shev.rọ.lā'), **Louis.** b. at La-Chaux-de-Fonds, Switzerland, 1879; d. at Detroit, Mich., June 6, 1941. American automobile racer, designer, and manufacturer. Arrived (c1900) in the U.S., he gained fame as an automobile racer after driving (1905) a measured mile in 52.8 seconds at Sheepshead Bay, N.Y., and establishing other records. He was associated with W. C. Durant in founding (1911) the Chevrolet Motor Company, later incorporated (1915) with General Motors. He built (c1914) the Frontenac racer and organized the Chevrolet Aircraft Company at Indianapolis.

Chevy Chase (chev'i chās). [Full title, **The Ballad of Chevy Chase.**] English ballad, probably from the 15th century, which recounts the incidents of the battle of Otterburn between the Scots and the English.

Chew (chö), **Benjamin.** b. at West River, Md., Nov. 29, 1722; d. Jan. 20, 1810. American jurist. His father was a judge, and at an early age he began to read law in the Philadelphia office of Andrew Hamilton. Going to London in 1741 to continue his studies, he returned following his father's death in 1743, and was admitted to the bar of the supreme court of Pennsylvania in 1746. For some years he practiced at Dover and New Castle, Del., but in 1754 he moved to Philadelphia, and in the following year became attorney general of the Province of Pennsylvania and a member of the provincial council. He was also designated register-general of the province. In 1774 he became chief justice of the supreme court of Pennsylvania. With the outbreak of the Revolutionary War some of his offices were abolished, but he remained register-general until March, 1777. Because of his lack of enthusiasm for the Declaration of Independence he was made a house prisoner and later for a time interned in a guarded area. After the war Washington befriended him and attended the wedding dinner of Peggy Chew at "Cliveden," the Chew mansion at Germantown, Pa., on May 23, 1787. In 1791 Chew became a judge and president of the high court of errors and appeals of the state of Pennsylvania, filling this office until the court was abolished in 1808. As lawyer and judge, Benjamin Chew's eminence rested not on oratorical powers but on an unusually comprehensive grasp of the common law and a faculty of close and precise reasoning.

Chew, Samuel Claggett. b. at Baltimore, 1888—. American teacher and author. He was graduated (Ph.D., 1913) from the Johns Hopkins University, and in 1920 became professor of English literature at Bryn Mawr. From 1943 to 1944 he was research associate at the Henry E. Huntington Library. Among his works are *Thomas Hardy* (1921), *Byron in England* (1924), *Swinburne* (1929), *The Crescent and the Rose* (1937), and *The Virtues Reconciled* (1947). He also contributed the section on 19th and 20th-century literature to *A Literary History of England* (1948), edited by Albert C. Baugh, and was the editor of the anthology *Fruit Among the Leaves* (1950).

Chewa (chā'wä). [Also: **Acawa, Achewa, Bachewa.**] Bantu-speaking people of SE Africa, inhabiting the E part of Northern Rhodesia and adjoining portions of Nyasaland. They are closely related to the Nyanja in language and culture.

Cheyenne (shī.en'). North American Indian tribe, formerly containing two branches: the northern Cheyenne in the area of the North Platte River, in SE Wyoming, and the southern Cheyenne in W Kansas. The tribal remnants are now scattered over several reservations in Wyoming and Oklahoma. The language is of the Algonquian family.

Cheyenne. City in SE Wyoming, capital of Wyoming and county seat of Laramie County: largest city in the state, at an elevation of more than 6,000 ft. It is a railroad and airline center, a marketing point for cattle, and has oil refineries, an aviation tool plant, window-sash factories, bakeries, and creameries. Fort Francis E. Warren is nearby. Cheyenne was settled in 1867, incorporated in the same year, and in 1868 was made county seat. 31,935 (1950).

Cheyenne River. River in E Wyoming and W central South Dakota, flowing generally NE to join the Missouri River ab. 34 mi. NW of Pierre, S.D. It flows in a canyon in its middle course, and traverses badlands. The river has been dammed near Hot Springs, S.D., by Angostura Dam. Length, ab. 525 mi.

Cheyne (chā′ni, chān), **George.** b. at Methlick, Aberdeenshire, Scotland, 1671; d. at Bath, England, April 13, 1743. English physician. He wrote *A New Theory of Fevers* (1702), *Observations on the Gout* (1720), *The English Malady, Hypochondria* (1733), and others. He began and carried on the practice of his profession at London.

Cheyne, Thomas Kelly. b. at London, Sept. 18, 1841; d. Feb. 16, 1915. English clergyman and Biblical critic, the proponent of a new kind of criticism in England. He was a member of the Old Testament revision company in 1884, was rector of Tendring, Essex, in the period 1880–85, and was Oriel professor of the interpretation of Scripture at Oxford, and canon of Rochester, from 1885 to 1908. In 1904 he was elected a member of the British Academy. Among the best known of his works are *The Prophecies of Isaiah* (1880–81), *The Book of Psalms* (a new translation, 1884–88, 1904), *Founders of Old Testament Criticism* (1893), *Introduction to the Book of Isaiah* (1895), *Isaiah* (critically revised text, and translation in *Sacred Books of the Old Testament*, 1898), *Jewish Religious Life after the Exile* (1898), *Critica Biblica* (1904), *Traditions and Beliefs of Ancient Israel* (1907), *Decline and Fall of the Kingdom of Judah* (1908), and *The Two Religions of Israel* (1910).

Cheyney (chā′ni), **Edward Potts.** b. at Wallingford, Pa., Jan. 17, 1861; d. at Chester, Pa., Feb. 1, 1947. American historian. Graduated (B.A., 1883) from the University of Pennsylvania, he taught European history (1884–1934; professor from 1897) and was curator (1934–40) of the Henry Charles Lea Library there. Author of *Social and Industrial History of England* (1901), *European Background of American History* (1904), *A History of England from the Defeat of the Armada to the Death of Elizabeth, Dawn of a New Era, 1250–1453*, and other works.

Chézy (shā.zē), **Antoine Léonard de.** b. at Neuilly, France, Jan. 15, 1773; d. at Paris, Aug. 31, 1832. French Orientalist; husband of Wilhelmine Christine de Chézy. He was the author of various translations from Persian and Sanskrit.

Chézy, Wilhelmine Christine (or **Helmine**) **de.** [Maiden name, **von Klencke.**] b. at Berlin, Jan. 26, 1783; d. near Geneva, Switzerland, 1856. German poet and novelist; wife of A. L. de Chézy, and daughter of Anna Luise Karsch.

Chézy, Wilhelm von. b. at Paris, March 21, 1806; d. at Vienna, March 14, 1865. German novelist and general writer; son of A. L. de Chézy.

Chhatarpur (chut′ąr.pör). [Also: **Chattrpur, Chutterpur.**] City in N central Union of India, in Vindhya Pradesh, ab. 115 mi. SW of Cawnpore: a trading center and important road junction; former capital of a state of the same name, one of the Central India states. Pop. ab. 10,000.

Chhattisgarh (chut′is.gär). [Also, **Chhatisgarh.**] Division of Madhya Pradesh (Central Provinces), Union of India, ab. 200 mi. E of Nagpur: rice, wheat, and forest products. Much of the soil is arid. Area, 21,240 sq. mi.; pop. 5,592,621 (1941).

Chhindwara (chin.dwä′rą). [Also, **Chindwara.**] District of the Nagpur division, Madhya Pradesh (Central Provinces), Union of India, N of Nagpur: coal and manganese. Chief town, Chhindwara; area, 4,630 sq. mi.; pop. 1,034,040 (1941).

Chhindwara. [Also, **Chindwara.**] Chief town of the district of Chhindwara, Nagpur division, Madhya Pradesh (Central Provinces), Union of India, ab. 70 mi. N of Nagpur: important trading center and road junction. Pop. ab. 17,000.

Chiabrera (kyä.bre′rä), **Gabriello.** b. at Savona, Italy, in June, 1552; d. there, Oct. 14, 1637. Italian lyric poet. He introduced forgotten metrical devices, and based some of his work on classical Greek verse.

Chiahsing (jyä′shing′). See **Kashing.**

Chiaja (kyä′yä). [Also: **La Chiaja**; full name, **Riviera di Chiaja.**] Fashionable drive in modern Naples, Italy.

Chia-ling (chyä′ling′). See **Kialing.**

Chia-mu-ssu (chyä′mö′sö′). See **Kiamusze.**

Chiana (kyä′nä). [Latin, **Clanis.**] River in Tuscany, Italy. It is conducted by engineering works partly into the Arno, partly into the Tiber.

Chiana Valley. [Italian, **Val** (or **Valle**) **di Chiana.**] Level and fruitful valley of the Chiana River, in Tuscany, Italy, near Chiusi.

Ch'iang (chyäng). Pastoral people of NE Tibet and W Szechwan province, China, who are mentioned in Chinese literature from very early times. They speak a Tibeto-Burman language.

Chiang Kai-shek (jyäng′ kī′shek′; Anglicized, chang′-). [Peking form, **Chiang Chieh-shih** (jye′shė′); formal name, **Chiang Chung-cheng** (jůng′jung′).] b. at Fenghwa, Chekiang, China, 1888—. Chinese ruler, leader of the Chinese Kuomintang, or Nationalist Party. From a merchant family which controlled the salt monopoly in Fenghwa, he studied military science at Paoting Academy (1906) and in Japan (1907–11). He first (1911) became a military officer, then (1920) an exchange broker, and, after visiting the U.S.S.R. (1923), principal of Whampoa Military Academy, at which Chou En-lai, a Communist, was chief of the political department. During the Northern Expedition he broke (1927) with the Communists, drove the Leftists from the Nationalist coalition, and became (1928) commander in chief of all Chinese military and naval forces and chairman of the national government at Nanking. He fought the Communists until his seizure (1936) by Chang Hsüeh-liang, coming on top of popular pressure for resistance, induced him to abandon civil war and join in a general resistance (1937–45) against Japanese invasion. He became (1943) president of the Kuomintang government. Initially partly successful after the revival (1945) of the civil war, he later suffered defeats and "retired" (1949) in favor of Li Tsung-jen, but resumed (1950) the presidency over the latter's objections. Many of his speeches, as well as his *China's Destiny* and *Chinese Economic Theory*, have been translated into English.

Chiang Kai-shek, Madame. [Maiden name, **Mei-ling Sung** (or **Mayling Soong**).] b. at Shanghai, China, 1892—. Chinese government official; youngest sister of Madame Sun Yat-sen, Madame H. H. Kung, and T. V. Soong. She received (1917) a B.A. degree from Wellesley. In 1927 she was married to Generalissimo Chiang Kai-shek. She held numerous posts in the Chinese government, but perhaps her most important task was acting as her husband's interpreter and confidante in dealings with Westerners. She visited America repeatedly, including 1948, when she sought further aid for the collapsing Kuomintang. Failing, she returned (1950) to Formosa.

Chiang Mai (chyäng′ mī′). [Also: **Chiengmai, Chieng Mai.**] City in NW Thailand (Siam). It is a trading center and a terminus of the railroad line to Burma. Much teakwood is cut in the area, and cotton, rice, and opium are raised. Pop. ab. 60,000.

Chiango (chyäng′gō). See **Chango.**

Chiang T'ing-fu (jyäng′ ting′fö′). Original name of **Tsiang, T. F.**

Chiangtu (jyäng′dö′). See **Kiangtu.**

Chianti Mountains (kyän′tē; Anglicized, ki.än′ti). [Italian, **Monti Chianti.**] Mountain group in Tuscany, Italy, near Siena. It gives name to celebrated wines.

Chiao-hsien (jyou′shyen′). See **Kiaohsien.**

Chiapas (chyä′päs). State in SE Mexico, bounded on the N by Tabasco, on the W by Veracruz and Oaxaca, on the SW and S by the Gulf of Tehuantepec, and on the E by Guatemala. Capital, Tuxtla Gutiérrez; area, 28,732 sq. mi.; pop. 903,200 (1950).

Chiapas, Sierra Madre de. See **Sierra Madre de Chiapas.**

Chiappe (shyȧp), **Jean.** b. at Ajaccio, Corsica, May 3, 1878; d. in an air battle over the Mediterranean, en route from Marseilles to Tunis, Nov. 27, 1940. French police official and politician, who as police prefect of Paris (1927–34) severely repressed Leftist political demonstrations. His election to the Chamber of Deputies from Corsica in 1936 was invalidated, but he later won a seat from Paris. He was made president of the Paris municipal council after the German invasion (1940). Traveling to Syria, of which he had been named French high commissioner, he died when his plane was machinegunned by a British fighter.

Chiaramonte Gulfi (kyä.rä.mōn'tā göl'fē). Town and commune in SW Italy, on the island of Sicily, in the province of Ragusa, N of the city of Ragusa. The town derives its name from the Chiaramonte family which formerly held it in feud. Pop. of commune, 11,143 (1936); of town, 7,365 (1936).

Chiaramonti (kyä.rä.mōn'tē), **Gregorio Luigi Barnaba.** Original name of Pope **Pius VII.**

Chiarelli (kyä.rel'lē), **Luigi.** b. at Trani, Italy, 1884—. Italian playwright. His name is linked to the movement in the Italian theater known as the *grotteschi*, which produces plays notable for their combination of satire on social conventions with a startling blend of comic and tragic incident. The basic principles of this school of the "grotesque" derive in large part from what is generally considered to be Chiarelli's best play, *La Maschera ed il volto* (1916), which was translated into English as *The Mask and the Face* (reprinted 1950), in which he treats with originality the old theme of a husband's jealousy. Others of his plays are *Vita intima* (1909), *Extra Dry* (1912), *La Scala di seta* (1917), *La Morte degli amanti* (1921), and *Jolly* (1928).

Chiari (kyä'rē). [Ancient name, **Clarium.**] Town and commune in NW Italy, in the *compartimento* (region) of Lombardy, in the province of Brescia, ab. 14 mi. W of Brescia: manufactures of knitwear and hosiery. Here, on Sept. 1, 1701, Prince Eugene of Savoy defeated the French and Spaniards under Villeroi. Pop. of commune, 13,880 (1936); of town, 7,097 (1936).

Chiarini (kyä.rē'nē), **Giuseppe.** b. at Arezzo, Italy, Aug. 17, 1833; d. 1908. Italian educator, poet, and critic. As a young man he joined the department of education, and from 1892 was superintendent of secondary education for all Italy. He contributed to and edited literary periodicals and was through most of his life a student of foreign literature, especially in German and English. In 1880 he published a translation of Heine's *Atta Troll.* At that time he was already the author of three books of lyrical poetry: *Poems* (1874), *In Memoriam* (1875), and *Lacrymae* (1879). Among Chiarini's services to Italian letters must be counted the assistance he gave Giosuè Carducci, and his encouragement of Gabriele D'Annunzio when the latter was a novice.

Chiarraighe (kir'ạch). Irish name of County **Kerry.**

Chiarugi (kyä.rö'jē), **Giulio.** b. at Siena, Italy, Jan. 28, 1859; d. at Florence, March 17, 1944. Italian anatomist and histologist. He became privatdocent (1886) and professor (1888) of normal anatomy at the University of Siena, and professor of anatomy (1891) at the University of Florence. He worked on the development of the central and peripheral nervous systems and on normal and pathological embryology. Author of *Contribuzioni allo studio dello sviluppo dei nervi encefalici nei mammiferi in confronto con altri vertebrati* (1874), *Delle omologie e dei rapporti reciproci della fossetta occipitale media e del lobo mediano del cervelletto nell'uomo e negli altri mammiferi* (1885), *La Forma del cervello umano e le variazioni correlative del cranio e della superficie cerebrale* (1886), *Lezioni elementari di anatomia generale* (1891–92), *Istituzioni di anatomia dell'uomo* (1904–12), and *Trattato di embriologia* (1932); founder of the *Archivio italiano di anatomia e di embriologia* and coeditor of the *Monitore zoologico italiano.*

Chiasso (kyäs'sō). Town in extreme S Switzerland, in the canton of Ticino, ab. 37 mi. by rail N of Milan, Italy. It is a border station, and has trade in wines, and a tobacco industry. 5,625 (1941).

Chiatura (chē.ạ.tö'rạ). [Former name, **Chiaturi** (-rē).] Mining town in SW U.S.S.R., in W central Georgian Soviet Socialist Republic, located in a mountain valley ab. 85 mi. E of Poti at the E end of the Black Sea. It is the greatest manganese-ore mining center in Caucasia, with reserves estimated at 100 to 150 million tons. Ore mining was begun in 1879 by a French company. In the period 1928–32, 3,867,000 tons of ore were mined, which made 2,079,000 tons of concentrate ore. The goal for 1933–37 was 3 million tons of concentrate. The ore is chiefly exported via the ports of Poti and Batum. 10,164 (1932).

Chiavari (kyä'vä.rē). Town and commune in NW Italy, in the *compartimento* (region) of Liguria, in the province of Genova, situated on the Riviera di Levante, between Genoa and Spezia. It is a seaside resort, and has beautiful homes and palaces. There are silk mills and furniture manufactures; horticulture in the district. It was under Genoese rule during the Middle Ages, and was fortified by the Genoese. The cathedral, the Basilica dei Fieschi, the Church of the Madonna delle Grazie, and the Palazzo dei Fieschi were undamaged in World War II. Pop. of commune, 17,520 (1936); of town, 14,042 (1936).

Chiavenna (kyä.ven'nä). [Latin, **Clavenna;** German, **Cläven, Clefen.**] Town and commune in NW Italy, in the *compartimento* (region) of Lombardy, in the province of Sondrio, on the Mera River at the entrance to a picturesque valley, N of Lake Como. Situated at the junction of the routes over the Splügen and Maloya passes near the Swiss border, it is a tourist center. Beer, cotton textiles, and wooden articles are produced. The town was under the Lombards, under the bishop of Como, belonged to Milan, and for a short period to the Swiss Confederation; later it was part of the Cisalpine Republic and after the Congress of Vienna (1815) went to Austria; it was incorporated into Italy in 1859. Pop. of commune, 5,379 (1936); of town, 3,803 (1936).

Chiba (chē.bä). City in SE Honshu, Japan, on Tokyo Bay ab. 25 mi. by rail E of Tokyo. It is a trade center, with some light industries, a bathing resort, and seat of a medical school. The temple of Chiba-dera is said to date from the 8th century, and an important daimyo was resident here from the 12th to the 16th century. 133,844 (1950).

Chibcha (chēb'chạ). One of the main groups of Indian tribes in the Andean region, concentrated in the upper drainage area of the Bogotá and Sogamoso rivers in the eastern cordillera of Colombia. This was the nucleus of Chibchan territory. The Chibchans are noteworthy in that they developed true states, of which that ruled by the Zipa was most important. There were perhaps a million Chibchans at the time of the Spanish conquest, with an economy based on agriculture. Maize and potatoes were the main crops. There was a little irrigation. Salt was an important item of trade. They were well known for their gold work with the use of an alloy of copper and gold (*tumbaga*). Power, in the larger states, seems to have fluctuated among individuals of the nobility, depending on the fortunes of civil war. Priests and chiefs came from the same class and their offices were hereditary in the matrilineal line. There was no stone architecture, houses and palaces being built of mud-daubed cane walls and thatched roofs. Archaeological data is so scanty that not much is known of their history. After an ineffective guerrilla warfare, they were completely conquered (1541) by the Spanish and their culture rapidly disappeared. Only a few small groups of Chibchans are left in Colombia today.

Chibchan (chēb'chạn). [Also: **Muysca, Muisca.**] Large linguistic stock to which a number of Indian languages belong, distributed through the Andean portion of Ecuador and Colombia, and continuously through Central America as far as Nicaragua and Honduras.

Chicacole (chik.ạ.kōl'). [Also, **Cicacole.**] Town in the district of Ganjam, Madras state, Union of India, on the Langulya River, ab. 200 mi. SW of Cuttack. It is a trading center. Pop. ab. 17,000.

Chicago (shi.kô'gō, -kä'-). [Called the **"Windy City."**] City in NE Illinois, county seat of Cook County, on the SW shore of Lake Michigan: the largest city in the state, and the second largest in the U.S. Its chief quarters are the North, South, and West Sides. Chicago has a vast commerce by many railroads and by the lake, and exports wheat, meat, and manufactured goods. There are manufactures of machinery, iron, steel, furniture, clothing, tobacco, liquors, agricultural implements, and leather. Among its largest industries are beef-packing and pork-packing, and printing and publishing. It is the seat of the University of Chicago, and of several theological seminaries and other institutions, and has important libraries and art collections. The site was visited by Marquette in

1673. Fort Dearborn was built in 1804, evacuated in 1812, and rebuilt in 1816. Chicago was incorporated as a city in 1837. Two thousand one hundred acres were burned, with a loss of about 200 million dollars, in the great fire of Oct. 8–10, 1871. Owing to its position it has been the meeting place of many national political conventions. The World's Columbian Exposition was held here from May 1 to Oct. 30, 1893, and the Century of Progress Exposition in 1933–34. Pop. 3,396,808 (1940), 3,620,962 (1950).

Chicago. Poem in free verse by Carl Sandburg, published in 1914 and included in his volume *Chicago Poems* (1916). It describes the tempo of the city, the Chicago that is "Hog Butcher, Tool Maker, Stacker of Wheat, Player with Railroads and Freight Handler to the Nation."

Chicago Academy of Sciences. Organization founded in 1856 (incorporated 1859) for the purpose of advancing and diffusing scientific knowledge by means of publication and the maintenance of a museum. The Matthew Laflin Memorial, the present museum building, was opened in 1894. The academy maintains a library of 2,000 volumes on the natural sciences and publishes the *Chicago Naturalist, Special Publications,* and a *Bulletin.*

Chicago and North Western Railway. [Called the **"North Western Line."**] Rail system in the U.S. organized in 1859 whose inception of its present form began in 1864, when it was merged with the Galena and Chicago Union, the first line constructed west of Chicago and Lake Michigan. In 1867, when it was extended to Council Bluffs, Iowa, it became the first railroad link with the Union Pacific. It subsequently absorbed many other lines, and in 1938 operated a total of 13,248 miles of trackage in nine states in the West and Middle West.

Chicago, Burlington and Quincy Railroad. [Also called the **"Burlington Route."**] Rail system of the U.S. Middle West, originating in the consolidation (1849–55) of four Illinois lines which subsequently had their terminal at Burlington, Iowa. The line received its present name in 1855, and thereafter reached west of the Mississippi. It occupied a key role in developing the economy of the prairie states. In 1939 it operated (as owned or leased trackage) a total of 8,948 miles.

Chicago Daily News. Newspaper founded in 1875 and purchased in 1931 by Colonel Frank Knox, who made it an organ for the Republican Party.

Chicago Drainage Canal. Former name of the **Chicago Sanitary and Ship Canal.**

Chicago Heights. City in NE Illinois, in Cook County: manufactures include steel, glass, and railroad equipment. It was incorporated in 1901. Pop. 24,551 (1950).

Chicago Institute of Design. See under **Bauhaus.**

Chicago Madrigal Club. Choral and composing group with 60 singers, established (1900) by D. A. Clippinger, conductor.

Chicago, Milwaukee and St. Paul Ry. Co. v. Minnesota, 134 U.S. 418 (1890). U.S. Supreme Court decision holding unconstitutional a Minnesota railway rate law of 1887 on the ground that it violated the due process clause of the 14th Amendment. Although the court's majority opinion was limited to procedural due process, its substantive implication placed under court review all rate schedules established by legislative authority. It effectively limited the doctrine of public interest.

Chicago, Milwaukee, St. Paul and Pacific Railroad. Railroad in the U.S. incorporated (1927) for the purpose of reorganizing the properties of the Chicago, Milwaukee and St. Paul Railway Company. It had its inception in the Milwaukee and Waukesha Railroad, chartered in 1847 as the first through service between the Twin Cities and Chicago. In 1938 it operated (as owned or leased trackage) a total of 10,954 miles.

Chicago Musical College. Music school established (1867) by the musicologist Florenz Ziegfeld (d. 1923), who headed it for nearly 50 years.

Chicago Natural History Museum. [Former name, **Field Columbian Museum.**] Museum situated at the N end of Jackson Park, Chicago, formed out of the art building of the World's Columbian Exposition of 1893 at the expense of Marshall Field. It contains collections in anthropology, ethnology, geology, and natural history. Among its publications are the *Chicago Natural History Museum Bulletin, Fieldiana,* and *General Guide.*

Chicago Orchestral Association. Corporation established in 1891 which embraced the trustees of the Chicago Symphony Orchestra.

Chicago River. River in NE Illinois, at Chicago, formerly flowing into Lake Michigan, but reversed since 1900 to divert water from the lake for the Chicago Drainage Canal (later named the Chicago Sanitary and Ship Canal). The diversion resulted in many court actions and decisions regulating the amount of flow permitted. Originally the easy portage between the south branch of the Chicago River and the Desplaines River furnished an easy route for the French fur-traders, and with an elevation of only ab. 630 ft. is one of the lowest divides between the Great Lakes and the Mississippi valley. Length, ab. 1 mi.

Chicago Road. Name given to the route leading from Chicago to Detroit which had been in use by the Indians long before La Salle traversed it in 1680, covering the approximate line now traced by U.S. Highway 112. It became known as the Chicago Road after c1830, and played an important role in the settlement of the Northwest.

Chicago, Rock Island and Pacific Railway Company. Railroad incorporated (1847) in Illinois as the Rock Island and La Salle Railroad Company, which became known (1851) as the Chicago and Rock Island Railroad. It was the first line to reach the Mississippi River. Successive mergers led to the incorporation (1880) in Illinois and Iowa of the present parent company. In 1938 the enterprise operated a total of 7,341 miles of trackage.

Chicago Sanitary and Ship Canal. [Former name, **Chicago Drainage Canal.**] Canal which extends from the west fork of the south branch of the Chicago River in Damen Avenue, Chicago, to Lockport, Ill., a distance of ab. 28 mi., and thence to Joliet, a further distance of 7 mi. It discharges the sewage of Chicago into the Illinois River, a branch of the Mississippi. Work was begun in 1892 and the canal was formally opened in 1900, having cost 33 million dollars. It is designed to be also used for shipping and is flushed by 300,000 cubic ft. of water (drawn from Lake Michigan) per minute. The flow reverses the direction of that of the Chicago River.

Chicago Sun-Times. See under **Chicago Times.**

Chicago Symphony Orchestra. Ensemble established by Theodore Thomas in 1891, making it the third oldest such group in the U.S.

Chicago Times. Paper founded in 1854 which supported the Democratic Party and was critical of Lincoln during the Civil War. Carter Harrison purchased the paper in 1891, and in 1895 it became the *Times-Herald.* It merged shortly after World War II with the Chicago *Sun,* and has been most recently known as the Chicago *Sun-Times.* Many of the "Mr. Dooley" sketches by Finley Peter Dunne appeared in its pages.

Chicago Treaty. Either of two treaties made at Chicago between the U.S. government and representatives of the Potawatomi and associated tribes: **1.** Treaty concluded in August, 1821, providing for the cession to the government of the SW area of Michigan. **2.** Treaty concluded in 1833, providing for the cession to the government of several million acres of land between the NE area of Illinois and the SE area of Wisconsin. The government pledged to establish the Indians in localities W of the Mississippi River.

Chicago Tribune. Newspaper founded in 1847 and converted into a Republican organ under the editorship (1855–99) of Joseph Medill. In the years after World War I it became known as one of the leading spokesmen for the "isolationist" viewpoint in U.S. foreign affairs.

Chicago World's Fair. **1.** World's Columbian Exposition (*q.v.*), held at Chicago May 1 to Oct. 30, 1893. **2.** Century of Progress International Exposition held at Chicago (1933–34) to mark the 100th anniversary of the founding of the village of Chicago. More than 39 million admissions were registered at the fair, whose modernistic lines influenced later architectural practice in the U.S.

Chicagua (shē.kä'gwä). See **Sigua.**

Chicaneau (shē.kà.nō). One of the principal characters in the comedy *Les Plaideurs,* by Jean Baptiste Racine. He is a tradesman with a mania for going to court, and is the type of the captious, litigious plaintiff, as his name (from *chicaner,* meaning to quibble, wrangle) implies.

Chichagof Island (chich'ą.gof). Island in SE Alaska, in the Alexander Archipelago, nearest point ab. 27 mi. SW of Juneau. It is a rugged mountainous island, with peaks up to 4,000 ft. elevation, and extensively forested. The island is ab. 65 mi. long, and very irregular in shape, being broken deeply by several inlets. There are several settlements, engaged in fish canning, gold mining, and lumbering.

Chichele or **Chicheley** (chich'ę.li), **Henry.** b. at Higham Ferrers, Northampton, England, c1362; d. at Canterbury, England, April 12, 1443. English prelate, appointed archbishop of Canterbury on Feb. 19, 1414. He was a graduate of Oxford, and founded All Souls' College at Oxford in 1437.

Chichén Itzá (chē.chān' ē.tsä'). Maya city and religious center in NE Yucatán, Mexico, ab. 18 mi. SW of Valladolid. Founded in the 6th century, it attained importance in the 11th, 12th, and 13th centuries under religious and political rulers who came from the central Mexican plateau area. The site comprises several square miles of scattered pyramid-temples, palaces, colonnades, plazas, and courts. These structures were of typical Mayan style in the earlier period and of Mexican style in later times. The latter are decorated with a number of feathered serpents, sculptured in stone, that are representations of Kukulkán, the patron deity of the city.

Chicherin (chē.che'rin), **Georgi Vasilyevich.** b. at Karaul, Tambov, Russia, 1872; d. 1936. Russian statesman. Coming from a landowning family, he entered the Russian diplomatic service in Czarist days, but as early as 1897 became involved in the revolutionary movement, and in 1904 divested himself of his landed property and resigned from government service. Because of illness he took no part in the attempted revolution of 1905, but during the next decade and more he had to live in exile, actively engaged in the plans and plots of the Russian Social-Democratic Party. Being in England at the time of the October Revolution in 1917, he was imprisoned by the British government, but in January, 1918, was released in exchange for Sir George Buchanan, former British ambassador to Russia, whom the Bolshevists had seized. He was appointed people's commissar for foreign affairs of the Soviet government, a post he held from 1918 to 1930. His most notable achievement was the Soviet-German treaty signed at the Genoa Conference in 1922.

Chichester (chich'ęs.tėr). [Old English, **Cissanceaster;** Latin, **Regnum, Cissae Castrum.**] Municipal borough and cathedral city in SE England, in West Sussex, situated ab. 15 mi. NE of Portsmouth, ab. 70 mi. SW of London by rail. It contains a noted cathedral, for the most part a Norman building of the 12th and 13th centuries, showing many details, as the paired lancets surmounted by quatrefoils of the central tower, which might have been transported bodily from Normandy. The tall, slender, spire awkwardly placed on this tower is later. The interior has double aisles and narrow nave, and very beautiful carved choir stalls. There are cloisters in Perpendicular style, and a late, detached bell tower. The dimensions are 410 by 91 ft.; width of transepts, 131 ft.; height of nave, 62 ft. The town was refounded by Cissa in the 6th century. 19,110 (1951).

Chichester, 2nd Earl of. Title of **Pelham, Thomas.**

Chichester, Arthur. [Title, Baron **Chichester of Belfast.**] b. at Rawleigh, near Barnstable, England, in May, 1563; d. Feb. 19, 1625. English soldier and statesman, elevated to the Irish peerage on Feb. 23, 1613. He was appointed governor of Carrickfergus and sergeant-major general of the English army in Ireland, and was lord deputy of Ireland from Feb. 3, 1605, to Nov. 29, 1614. After his recall he was appointed lord treasurer of Ireland.

Chichevache (chē'chę.väch; French, shēsh.vash). Fabulous beast which devoured patient and submissive wives. The fable, of Old French origin, became a favorite with Middle English writers, who made the beast a lean cow, and ascribed her leanness to the scarcity of her peculiar diet. They added another beast named Bicorne or Bycorne (literally, "two-horned"), who lived only on patient and submissive husbands, and was in consequence always fat. Lydgate wrote a poem called *Bycorne and Chichevache.*

Ch'i-chia P'ing (chē'jyä' ping'). Neolithic site in the Pan Shan area of the Tao River valley in S Kansu province, China. The name applies to a distinctive kind of finely made, buff-colored pottery, for the most part plain but having lavendar triangles painted on some pieces. First considered earliest of the Kansu wares, its position is no longer clear, and there is recent evidence that it may be of a period later than Yang-shao. The suggestion has also been made that it represents another culture complex intruding at this point into the Yang-shao area.

Chichibu (chē.chē.bö), Prince. [Full name, **Yasuhito Chichibu-no-miya.**] b. June 25, 1902; d. Jan. 4, 1953. Japanese prince; second son of Emperor Yoshihito, and brother of Emperor Hirohito.

Chichimec (chē.chē.mek'). Collective term for a number of Mexican Indian groups which fought with or established dynastic lineages among the Toltecs and others at various of their settlements prior to the rise of the Aztec nation; hence also "Chichimec Period" which, on the basis of archaeological evidence and *Annals of Cuauhtitlan,* extended from 950 to 1299 A.D.

Chick (chik), **Mrs. Louisa.** Mr. Dombey's sister in Charles Dickens's *Dombey and Son,* a weak and self-satisfied woman who urged the fading Mrs. Dombey to "make an effort."

Chickahominy (chik.ą.hom'i.ni). River in Virginia which joins the James River ab. 40 mi. SE of Richmond. Near it were fought the battles of Fair Oaks, Mechanicsville, Gaines's Mill, Savage's Station, and Frayser's Farm in 1862, and Cold Harbor, in 1864. Length, ab. 90 mi.

Chickamauga (chik.ą.mô'gą). Creek which joins the Tennessee River ab. 7 mi. above Chattanooga. Near it, on Sept. 19 and 20, 1863, the Confederates (about 50,000) under Bragg defeated the Union forces (55,000–60,000) under Rosecrans. The Union loss was 15,851; that of the Confederates, 17,804.

Chickamauga and Chattanooga National Military Park. National reservation in Georgia and Tennessee, containing the battlefield of Chickamauga and others. It was established in 1890 and dedicated in September, 1895. Area, 8,149 acres.

Chickasaw (chik'ą.sô). North American Indian tribe, formerly inhabiting W Tennessee, N Mississippi, and N Alabama. Remnants of the tribe are now on reservations in Oklahoma. They speak a Natchez-Muskogean language.

Chickasaw. Town in SW Alabama, in Mobile County, ab. 7 mi. N of Mobile, on a tributary of the Mobile River: residential community and fishing resort. 4,920 (1950).

Chickasaw Bluffs. Place near Vicksburg, Miss. Here, on Dec. 29, 1862, a Union force under Sherman was repulsed by the Confederates. The Union loss was 1,929; that of the Confederates, 207.

Chickasaw Center. Former name of **New Hampton,** Iowa.

Chickasaw Council House, Treaty of. Treaty concluded (Sept. 20, 1816) between the Chickasaw nation and the U.S. government, providing for regular annual payments by the U.S. to the Chickasaw nation and the cession by the Indians of land along the Tennessee River.

Chickasaw-Creek War. Indian war (Feb. 13–Oct. 28, 1793) between the Chickasaw and Creek tribes which involved, on both sides, more discussion and maneuvers for American support than it did fighting. It was finally concluded by the treaty of Nogales, reaffirming the alliance of the Indians with Spain.

Chickasaw-French War. War (1736–40) between the Chickasaw tribe and the French, precipitated by Bienville's decision to end the Chickasaw hostility impeding the French imperial scheme to link the St. Lawrence communities with the settlements on the Gulf of Mexico. The war, which consisted of two major military engagements, both of which were lost by the French, was terminated without any conclusive result.

Chickasaw Treaty. Agreement concluded (1783) at Nashborough (now Nashville), N.C., between the Chickasaw tribe and representatives of Virginia, providing for the surrender of the Chickasaw title to the tract between the Cumberland River and a point south of Nashborough. The Virginians failed in their attempt to gain title to western Kentucky, but the treaty gave to North Carolina a claim to territory uncontested by Indian title.

Chickasha (chik'ą.shā). City in C Oklahoma, county seat of Grady County, on the Washita River ab. 34 mi. S of El Reno: marketing and processing center for grain, cotton, and dairy products. It is the seat of the Oklahoma College for Women. The site of Chickasha was a stopping place on the Chisolm Trail. 15,842 (1950).

Chickenstalker (chik'ẹn.stô.kėr), **Mrs.** Old shopkeeper in Charles Dickens's story *The Chimes*.

Chickering (chik'ėr.ing), **Jonas.** b. at Mason Village, N.H., April 5, 1798; d. Dec. 8, 1853. American piano manufacturer. Employed (c1818) at Boston by John Osborne, piano maker, he later (1823) established with James Stewart a piano-manufacturing firm under the name of Stewart and Chickering, and entered (1830) into partnership with John Mackay, who financed the firm. He introduced (1837) the first iron frame in the grand piano, patented (1843) a new deflection of the strings, and invented (1845) the first practical method for overstringing grand pianos.

Chiclana de la Frontera (chē.klä'nä dā lä frōn.tā'rä). [Also, **Chiclana.**] Town in S Spain, in the province of Cádiz, situated on the Irio River, ab. 12 mi. SE of Cádiz: center of a fertile fruit and wine producing district and a summer resort for the merchants of Cádiz; hot sulfur springs. 17,047 (1940).

Chiclayo (chē.klä'yō). City in NW Peru, capital of Lambayeque department: cotton, rice, and sugar. It is the seat of the national college. 32,646 (1940).

Chico (chē'kō). Town in N California, in Butte County, NE of San Francisco: trading center for fruit and grain. It is the seat of Chico State College. 12,272 (1950).

Chico, El. See **Boabdil.**

Chicomecoatl (chē''kō.mā.kō.ät'l). Aztec goddess of crops and subsistence; the female counterpart of Cinteotl.

Chicopee (chik'ọ.pē). City in S Massachusetts, in Hampden County, at the junction of the Chicopee River with the Connecticut River, ab. 4 mi. N of Springfield. Manufactures include rubber and sporting goods. It was the birthplace of Edward Bellamy. The College of Our Lady of the Elms is here. 49,211 (1950).

Chicora (chē.kō'rä). In American colonial history, a section of the Spanish territory known as "La Florida," situated in what is now North and South Carolina. It was believed by the Spaniards to be occupied by Indians of grotesque form.

Chicoutimi (shi.kö'ti.mi). Capital of Chicoutimi County, Quebec, Canada, situated at the confluence of the Chicoutimi and Saguenay rivers, ab. 80 mi. from the mouth of the Saguenay: commercial center for the surrounding region. 23,216 (1951).

Chicoutimi River. River in S Quebec, Canada, rising in Laurentides Provincial Park N of Quebec city, and flowing generally N to join the Saguenay River at Chicoutimi, Quebec. The river rises on the mountain plateau at over 3,000 ft. elevation, and has numerous falls and rapids. Two great power dams have created Lake Kenogami reservoir, and have a capacity of 31,000 kw. Length, ab. 100 mi.

Chico Vecino (chē'kō vẹ.sē'nō). Unincorporated community in N California, in Butte County, NE of San Francisco. 3,967 (1950).

Chidambaram (chi.dum'bạ.rạm). Town in S Union of India, in SE Madras state, ab. 151 mi. by rail S of Madras. Its magnificent temples are considered the oldest in S India, and are good examples of Dravidian art. The principal temple is dedicated to Siva. Chidambaram was a capital of Chola from 907 to 1310 A.D. 26,212 (1941).

Chidley (chid'li), **Cape.** [Also, **Cape Chudleigh.**] Cape at the entrance of Hudson Strait, on the N coast of Labrador.

Chiem Lake (kēm). [German, **Chiemsee** (kēm'zā'').] Largest lake in Bavaria, S Germany, ab. 40 mi. SE of Munich, noted for its fish. Its outlet is the Alz River (into the Inn, thence to the Danube). Length, ab. 8 mi.

Chien (chyun). Chinese name of a Sung dynasty ceramic ware characterized by a coarse black stoneware body sometimes fired to deep brick red on exposed surfaces and covered with a thick, heavily ferruginous glaze usually dark in tone. Such terms as "hare's fur," "partridge feather," and "oil spot" are used to describe its general appearance. The ware occurs almost entirely in the form of tea bowls and has long been highly esteemed by the Japanese, who call it *temmoku*. The Chinese name derives from the second character in the name of the province of Fukien (Fu-chien) where it was made (near the village of Shuichi ab. 110 mi. NW of Foochow).

Chiengmai or **Chieng Mai** (chyeng'mī'). See **Chiang Mai.**

Chieri (kye'rē). [Ancient names, **Carea, Carrea, Carreum.**] Town and commune in NW Italy, in the *compartimento* (region) of Piedmont, in the province of Torino, situated in the Monferrato hills, ab. 8 mi. SE of Turin. It is one of the oldest industrial centers in the region, producing linen and cotton textiles, agricultural machinery, and vermouth; there are cattle, wine, and lumber markets. The cathedral, on the site of a very old Christian church, was rebuilt in its present form in the period 1405–36. There is an arch dedicated to one of the dukes of Savoy (1580). The town passed to Savoy in part in 1347, and totally in 1418. Buildings of interest to tourists were undamaged in World War II. Pop. of commune, 13,736 (1936); of town, 9,601 (1936).

Chiesa (kyā'zä), **Francesco.** b. at Sagno, Ticino, Switzerland, 1871—. Swiss poet, novelist, and short-story writer, writing in Italian. A teacher by profession, Chiesa has found time to write poems, novels, and short stories which appeal to a small but enthusiastic reading public made up mainly of people from his native city. In the collections of his best poems, *La Cattedrale* (1903) and *La Reggia* (1904), the meagerness of content is compensated for by the ease and simplicity of expression. Even in his prose works, Chiesa is still the poet, but in addition he injects a psychological analysis of the motives and drives in the lives of his characters. His best novels are *Tempo di Marzo* (1925) and *Villadorna* (1928) and his short stories are *Istorie e favole* (1913), *Racconti puerili* (1920), and *Scoperte nel mio mondo* (1934).

Chiesa, Giacomo della. Original name of Pope **Benedict XV.**

Chieti (kyā'tē). [Former name, **Abruzzo Citeriore.**] Province in SE Italy, in the *compartimento* (region) of Abruzzi e Molise. Capital, Chieti; area, ab. 1,100 sq. mi.; pop. 374,727 (1936), 400,000 (est. 1946).

Chieti. [Ancient names, **Teate, Teate Marrucinorum.**] City and commune in C Italy, in the *compartimento* (region) of Abruzzi e Molise, the capital of the province of Chieti, situated near the Pescara River and the Adriatic Sea, S of Ancona. It is the seat of a bishopric and of educational institutions. There are metallurgical and textile industries, and wine, grain, and silk markets. Some Roman antiquities have been preserved. The cathedral, in Romanesque style, has a campanile dating from 1335. There are other notable churches, of both the medieval and baroque periods. Founded by the Romans, the town was successively under Gothic, Lombard, Frankish, and Norman rule. The religious order of the Teatines, or Theatines, was founded here in the 16th century. Buildings of interest to tourists were undamaged in World War II. Pop. of commune, 30,266 (1936); of city, 17,565 (1936).

Chiffinch (chif'inch), **Master Thomas.** Drinking and intriguing minister to the pleasures of King Charles II, in Sir Walter Scott's novel *Peveril of the Peak*.

Chifley (chif'li), **Joseph Benedict.** b. at Bathurst, New South Wales, Australia, Sept. 22, 1885; d. June 13, 1951. Australian politician, prime minister (1945–49) of Australia. He became an engine-driver on the New South Wales railways, and in 1928 was sent to the federal house of representatives as a Labour member, serving until 1931; in 1940 he was reëlected. He was minister of defense (1931–32) and a member (1936) of the royal commission on monetary and banking systems. He became minister of postwar reconstruction in 1942. In 1945 he succeeded John Curtin as prime minister. He was defeated in the 1949 elections and was succeeded by R. G. Menzies.

Chi-fu (jė'fö'). See **Chefoo.**

Chigi (kē'jē), **Fabio.** Original name of Pope **Alexander VII.**

Chigirin (chē.gi.rēn'). Country town in SW U.S.S.R., in C Ukrainian Soviet Socialist Republic, ab. 37 mi. SE of Cherkassy. Founded as a fortress in 1589, it played a leading role in the liberation of the Ukrainians from the Turks, and c1694 it was the capital and chief center of the Cossacks. It was besieged several times by Turks, Kazakhs, and Poles. Sugar beets are grown in the region. 7,954 (1932).

Chignecto (shig.nek'tō). Isthmus in SE Canada, in E New Brunswick and NW Nova Scotia, joining the latter to the mainland. It is crossed by the main line of the Canadian National Railways, and by a highway. Width, ab. 15 mi. at narrowest point.

Chignecto Bay. Bay at the head of the Bay of Fundy, separating the provinces of New Brunswick and Nova Scotia, Canada. It is separated from Northumberland Strait by Chignecto isthmus.

Chigorin (chē.gô'rin), **Mikhail I.** [Also, **Tschigorin.**] b. in Russia, Nov. 12, 1850; d. there, Feb. 7, 1908. Russian chess master, founder of the "Russian School" in chess. He exerted a wide and lasting influence on the theory and development of his native country's most popular game, and is considered the leading Russian master of his period. He was a successful competitor in international tournaments and matches.

Chigwell (chig'wel). Urban district in SE England, in Essex, ab. 14 mi. NE of London by rail. 51,775 (1951).

Chihli (ji'lē', chē'lē'). [Also, **Chi-li.**] Former province of N China, lying between Mongolia on the N, the Po Hai (formerly the Gulf of Chihli) and Shantung on the E, Shantung and Honan on the S, and Shansi on the W. This area now includes parts of Hopeh, Jehol, and Chahar provinces. Chief cities, Peiping and Tientsin. Area, ab. 115,800 sq. mi.; pop. ab. 20,937,000 (1912).

Chihli, Gulf of. A former name of **Po Hai.**

Chihuahua (chē.wä'wä). State in N Mexico, lying between New Mexico and Texas on the N, Coahuila on the E, Durango on the S, and Sonora and Sinaloa on the W: traversed by the Sierra Madre, and rich in mineral wealth, notably silver. Capital, Chihuahua; area, 94,831 sq. mi.; pop. 841,077 (1950).

Chihuahua. City in NW Mexico, capital of Chihuahua state, in a zinc, silver, and lead mining district. It was founded in 1706, and is the seat of a cathedral. 56,805 (1940), 110,779 (1950).

Chihuahua Trail. In 16th-century America, a 1,500-mile route linking the base of Spanish colonization at Mexico City to Santa Fe at the north. Part of it is approximated by state highway 85 in New Mexico, and the trail as a whole covers the approximate route of a Mexican automobile highway.

Chihui-cahui (chē.wē.kä'wē). See **Chiricahua.**

Chikamatsu (chē.kä.mä.tsö), **Monzaemon.** b. c1653; d. 1724. Japanese playwright. He was an innovator, who brought a more romantic type of drama to the Japanese stage, and has sometimes been called by Western students a "Japanese Shakespeare."

Chikunda (chē.kön'dä). [Also: **Achikunda, Nyungwe, Wachikunda, Wafungwe.**] Subgroup of the Bantu-speaking Shona, of SE Africa, living S of the Zambesi River, in the N part of Southern Rhodesia and in W Mozambique.

Chilam Balam (chē.läm' bä.läm'). [Also, **Chilan Balam.**] Class of priests among the Maya Indians. The "Books of Chilam Balam" were written by these priests in the Maya language, but in Spanish script, and contain native chronicles of events both before and after the Spanish conquest. Originally there were probably many of these manuscripts, each pertaining to a different town, but only fragments of about a dozen have been preserved.

Chilcotin (chil.kō'tin). River in S central British Columbia, Canada, flowing generally SE to join the Fraser River ab. 170 mi. N of Vancouver. It rises in a wild, rugged mountain region, but there is some farming settlement in the middle Chilcotin valley. Length, ab. 146 mi.

Child (chīld), **Charles Manning.** b. at Ypsilanti, Mich., 1869—. American biologist. He was graduated (Ph.D., 1894) from the University of Leipzig, and until 1934 was professor of zoölogy at the University of Chicago. Subsequently he became lecturer in biology at Stanford University. Among his works are *Senescence and Rejuvenescence* (1915), *Individuality in Organisms* (1915), *Physiological Foundations of Behavior* (1924), and *Patterns and Problems of Development* (1941).

Child, Edwin Burrage. b. at Gouverneur, N.Y., May 29, 1868; d. at Dorset, Vt., March 10, 1937. American painter of landscapes, portraits, and murals, and illustrator, best known for his portraits of dignitaries in the fields of politics and education. He studied at Amherst College, and at the Art Students League of New York under John La Farge, with whom he later painted murals and worked on glass. He next did illustrations for magazines. After 1908 he concentrated on portraits and landscapes. His paintings have been widely exhibited and hang in many galleries and collections in the U.S. Among his better-known works are the portraits *John Dewey, Dwight Morrow, Thorsten Veblen, Wilbur Cross,* and *T. Coleman Du Pont.* His other paintings include *The Runaway, Sunset Clouds, Early September, End of Winter, After the Rain, Mountain Shadows,* and *The Old Covered Bridge.*

Child, Francis James. b. at Boston, Feb. 1, 1825; d. Sept. 11, 1896. American philologist. He was educated at Harvard College, and was professor of rhetoric and oratory there from 1851 to 1876, when he became professor of English literature. His best-known work is an edition of *English and Scottish Ballads,* which he first brought out in the period 1857–58 in 8 volumes, and which was followed by *English and Scottish Popular Ballads* (5 vols., 1883–98). He also published *Poetical Works of Edmund Spenser* (5 vols., 1855; a critical edition) and "Observations on the Language of Chaucer" (in *Memoirs of the American Academy of Arts and Sciences,* 1863).

Child, Frank Samuel. b. at Exeter, N.Y., March 20, 1854; d. May 4, 1922. American author and Congregational clergyman. After a pastorate (until 1881) at Greenwich, Conn., and a charge (1884–88) at New Preston, Conn., he was appointed to the First Church at Fairfield, Conn. Fairfield was the subject of some of his books, including *An Old New England Town* (1895). He was the author also of *The Colonial Parson of New England* (1896), *A Colonial Witch* (1897), *A Puritan Wooing* (1898), *The House with Sixty Closets* (1899), *An Unknown Patriot* (1899), *Fairfield, Ancient and Modern* (1909), *An Old New England Church* (1910), and *A Country Parish* (1911).

Child, Sir **John.** d. at Bombay, India, Feb. 4, 1690. English colonial official, for a period (1686–90) governor of all British East India Company possessions in India; brother of Sir Josiah Child (1630–99). Because he had carried out military campaigns aiming to gain territory for the East India Company, his removal from India was made a condition of the peace terms by the emperor of Delhi.

Child, Sir **Josiah.** b. at London, 1630; d. 1699. English merchant, economist, and writer on trade; brother of Sir John Child (d. 1690). He made a fortune as a naval-stores dealer at Portsmouth and became (1655) mayor of that city. As chairman of the East India Company, he sought to extend its political power.

Child, Lydia Maria. [Maiden name, **Francis.**] b. at Medford, Mass., Feb. 11, 1802; d. Oct. 20, 1880. American author and abolitionist. She began her literary career with *Hobomok* (1824) and *The Rebels, or, Boston before the Revolution* (1825), founded (1826) a magazine, *Juvenile Miscellany,* and conducted (1825–28) a private school at Watertown, Mass. She was married (1828) to David Lee Child, a lawyer of Boston, and with him embarked upon abolitionist activity. In support of that cause she wrote the influential *An Appeal in Favor of That Class of Americans Called Africans* (1833), which made her many enemies, cost her a reduced sale in her books, and forced her to discontinue (1834) her magazine. She edited (1841–49) the *National Anti-Slavery Standard* at New York, retiring with her husband in 1852 to a farm at Weyland, Mass., from which she continued her antislavery activity. Her pamphlet *Correspondence between Lydia Maria Child and Gov. Wise and Mrs. Mason of Virginia* (1860), arising from her appeal for permission to nurse John Brown after his wounding and capture at Harpers Ferry, sold 300,000 copies. Among her other writings were *The First Settlers of New England* (1829), *The Frugal Housewife* (1829), *The Mother's Book* (1831), *Philothea* (1836), *The Right Way the Safe Way* (1860), *The Freedman's Book* (1865), and *A Romance of the Republic* (1867). See her *Letters from New York* (2 vols., 1843, 1845) and *Letters of Lydia Maria Child* (1883).

Child, Richard Washburn. b. at Worcester, Mass., Aug. 5, 1881; d. at New York, Jan. 31, 1935. American diplomat and writer. A graduate (B.A., 1903; LL.B., 1906) of Harvard University, he was admitted to the bar in 1906. He served as ambassador extraordinary and plenipotentiary (1921–24) to Italy and chief U.S. representative (1922) at the Genoa and Lausanne conferences, and was founder of the Council of Foreign Relations. Editor (1919) of *Collier's Weekly;* author of *Jim Hands* (1910), *The Man in the Shadow* (1911), *The Blue Wall* (1912), *Potential Russia* (1916), *Bodbank* (1916), *Vanishing Men* (1919), *Velvet Black* (1920), *Fresh Waters* (1924), *A Diplomat Looks at Europe* (1925), *Writing on the Wall* (1928), and *Pitcher of Romance* (1930).

Childebert I (chil'dḙ.bėrt, kil'-; French, shēl.dḙ.ber; German, ċhēl'dḙ.bert). b. c495; d. 558. Frankish king; son of Clovis I, king of the Franks, whom he succeeded (as king of Paris) in 511. He inherited (524) part of the dominions of his brother Chlodomir of Orléans, and in conjunction with his brother Clothaire I of Soissons and his nephew Theudebert I of Austrasia conquered part of Burgundy in 534 and part of Provence in 536.

Childebert II. b. 570; d. 596. Son of Sigebert I of Austrasia by the West-Gothic princess Brunehilde. Having remained under the regency of his mother in the period 575–585, he attempted, on reaching his majority, to deprive the young son of Fredegunde of Neustria, Clothaire II, of his kingdom, but was himself utterly defeated by Fredegunde.

Childe Harold's Pilgrimage (chīld har'ǫldz). Poem by Byron, of which the first and second cantos were published in 1812, the third in 1816, and the fourth in 1818. The poem, written in Spenserian stanzas, takes its hero, a romantically melancholy young man, on travels through Portugal, Spain, the Ionian islands, Albania, Greece, Belgium, and the Alps. In the fourth canto the device of the hero is abandoned, and the poem is a straight description of Italian cities and their artistic and historic associations. Appealing to the popular taste of the day for descriptions of foreign places, the poem made Byron famous.

Childe Morrice (mor'is). See **Morrice, Gil (or Childe).**

Childeric I (chil'dḙ.rik, kil'-). [French, **Childéric** (shēl-dā.rēk); German, **Childerich** (ċhēl'dḙ.riċh).] d. 481. Frankish king; father of Clovis I. He ruled from c458. He sustained friendly relations with the Romans, who assisted him against the West Goths, the Alamanni, and the Saxons. His tomb was discovered at Tournai in 1653, and contained, among other things, his seal ring and a number of gold bees. The latter had presumably served to ornament his mantle, and suggested to Napoleon I the adoption of the bee as an imperial emblem.

Childermas Day (chil'dėr.mạs). [Also, **Feast of the Holy Innocents.**] Christian holy day celebrated on December 28 in commemoration of Herod's wholesale slaughter of male infants after the birth of Christ.

Childers (chil'dėrz), **Hugh Culling Eardley.** b. at London, June 25, 1827; d. Jan. 29, 1896. English politician. He was first lord of the admiralty in the period 1868–71, chancellor of the duchy of Lancaster from 1872 to 1873, secretary for war (1880–82), chancellor of the exchequer (1882–85), and home secretary (1886).

Childers, Robert Caesar. b. 1838; d. July 25, 1876. English Orientalist. He was the author of *Pali-English Dictionary* (1875) and others.

Childersburg (chil'dėrz.bėrg). Town in E central Alabama, in Talladega County, on the Coosa River ab. 30 mi. SE of Birmingham. Powder and newsprint are manufactured. In the decade between the last two U.S. censuses its population grew from 515 (1940) to 4,023 (1950).

Child Labor Amendment. Amendment to the U.S. Constitution which would grant Congress power "to limit, regulate, and prohibit the labor of persons under 18 years of age." Although Congress submitted this amendment to the states for ratification in June, 1924, by 1938 it had been ratified by only 28 of the 36 states necessary to secure its adoption. However, the Fair Labor Standards Act of 1938 gives the national government power to regulate and prohibit the employment of child labor engaged in interstate commerce.

Child Labor Cases. See **Hammer v. Dagenhart, 247 U.S. 251 (1918), Bailey v. Drexel Furniture Co., 259 U.S. 20 (1922), and U.S. v. Darby, 312 U.S. 100 (1941).**

Child of Lübeck (lü'bek). See **Heinecken, Christian Heinrich.**

Child of Nature, The. Play by Elizabeth Inchbald, produced at Covent Garden Theatre, London, on Nov. 28, 1788. It is based on a work by Madame de Genlis.

Child of the Sea. Name sometimes applied to the legendary Amadis of Gaul, who, being illegitimate, was set adrift upon the sea in his cradle by his mother.

Children (chil'drḙn), **John George.** b. at Tunbridge Wells, England, May 18, 1777; d. at Halstead Place, Kent, England, Jan. 1, 1852. English physicist and naturalist, best known for his experiments in electricity. He was a secretary of the Royal Society in the periods 1826–27 and 1830–37, and was librarian in the department of antiquities in the British Museum from 1816 to 1840.

Children in the Wood. Novel by Naomi Royde-Smith, published in 1928. Its American title is *In the Wood.*

Children in the Wood, The. [Also, **Babes in the Wood.**] Early English ballad, of unknown authorship, preserved in Ritson's, Percy's, and other collections. The ballad was entered in the Stationers' Register in 1595. In 1601 a play was published "of a young child murthered in a wood by two ruffins with the consent of his unkle."

Children of Adam. Section of *Leaves of Grass* by Walt Whitman, included in the 1860 edition as "Enfants d'Adam" and published under its present title in the edition of 1867.

Children of God. Novel by Vardis Fisher about the Mormon exodus and settlement in Utah, published in 1939.

Children of No Man's Land. Novel by G. B. Stern, published in 1919. It was issued under the American title *Debatable Ground* (1921).

Children of the Abbey, The. Story by Regina Maria Roche, published in 1798.

Children of the Don (don), **The.** Opera in three acts by Joseph Holbrooke, first performed at the London Opera House on June 12, 1912. The work is based on a Welsh legend.

Children of the Mist. Band of Highland outlaws in Sir Walter Scott's *Legend of Montrose.* There is also a painting with this title by Landseer.

Children of the Night, The. Collection of poems by Edwin Arlington Robinson, published in 1897.

Children of the Nile, The. Novel by Marmaduke Pickthall, published in 1908.

Children's Bureau. Federal unit established in 1912 under the U.S. Department of Labor which is charged with promoting the health and welfare of U.S. children. It provides grants-in-aid to states for advancing child and maternal health and exercises jurisdiction over national legislation pertaining to this field.

Children's Hour. Poem by Henry Wadsworth Longfellow, published in *Birds of Passage* (1860). It describes the delightful characters of the poet's daughters, Alice, Allegra, and Edith, who nightly invade his study.

Children's Hour, The. Play (1934) by Lillian Hellman.

Childress (chil'drḙs). City in NW Texas, in the Panhandle, county seat of Childress County, SE of Amarillo: railroad junction and distributing point for cattle, wheat, feed, and cotton. 7,619 (1950).

Childs (chīldz), **George William.** b. at Baltimore, May 12, 1829; d. at Philadelphia, Feb. 3, 1894. American publisher and philanthropist. He was the publisher (1864–94) of the Philadelphia *Public Ledger.*

Childs, Marquis William. b. at Clinton, Iowa, March 17, 1903—. American journalist and author. He was a reporter (1923, 1925–26) with the United Press, a staff member (1926–44) of the St. Louis *Post-Dispatch,* and in 1944 became a columnist with United Features Syndicate. Author of *Sweden—The Middle Way* (1936), *They Hate Roosevelt* (1936), *Washington Calling* (1937), *I Write from Washington* (1942), *The Cabin* (1944), and other books.

Childs, William. b. c1865; d. at Bernardsville, N.J., May 22, 1938. American restaurateur who founded (1889) with his brother a restaurant chain bearing their name and extending at the time of their deaths throughout the U.S. and Canada. He resigned from the company presidency in 1928 and relinquished control in 1929.

Child Study Association of America. Organization established in 1888 for the purpose of promoting the sound personality development of the child and the advancement of family and community relations. It maintains headquarters at New York, has a library of 6,000 volumes on child study, family guidance, and related fields, and publishes *Child Study* (quarterly).

Chile (chil'ẹ; Spanish, chē'lā). [Official Spanish name, **República de Chile**; sometimes called the **"Shoestring Republic"**; formerly also, **Chili.**] Republic in SW South America, bounded on the N by Peru, on the E by Bolivia and Argentina, and on the W by the Pacific Ocean.

Population, Area, and Political Divisions. Chile is divided for administrative purposes into 25 provinces. Capital, Santiago; area, 286,396 sq. mi.; pop. 5,866,189 (est. 1950).

Terrain and Climate. Aptly characterized as a "shoestring," Chile's length is ab. 2,600 mi. and average width 110 mi. It is bounded by the Andes on the E and the Pacific Ocean on the W. Physiographically, it is divided into three major regions: an arid region rich in minerals in the N, the central valley, and the humid forests and grazing regions of the S. Northern Chile, dominated by the Atacama Desert, is one of the most desolate and arid regions in the entire world. Its average annual rainfall has been computed at one tenth of an inch. However, in a given 20-year period, 14 years are likely to have absolutely no precipitation, and the remaining 6 years will have a total of 1.1 inches. Settlement in this area is therefore dependent upon the supply of water. Oases are very infrequent, and only one through-flowing stream, the Río Loa, crosses the desert. The central valley is ab. 600 mi. long and some 25 to 30 mi. wide. The most densely populated section of the country, it contains more than 80 percent of the total population. Much of the area has a climate not unlike that of the Mediterranean countries, where the greatest amount of rainfall occurs during the winter months and the summer months are dry. In the N part of the valley, irrigation is necessary during the summer months for the successful pursuit of agriculture. The S part of the valley has a rainy, cool climate similar to the coastal area of the states of Oregon and Washington. Southern Chile extends from Chiloé south. A heavily glaciated area, it is characterized by a fiorded coast and active volcanoes, and is a land of almost continual rainfall. Some portions receive more than 200 in. of rain per year, and in Tierra del Fuego, a zone of permanent snow begins at 2,300 ft. above sea level. Severe winds, abundant rain, and low temperatures combine to make this a virtually uninhabitable region with only one percent of the total population, although it constitutes ab. 33 percent of the total land area.

"Chilean Pereda" (pā.rā'ᴛʜä). See **Latorre, Mariano.**

Chile-Peruvian War. See **Pacific, War of the.**

Chi-li (jē'lē', chē'lē'). See **Chihli.**

Chilia (kē'li.ạ; Rumanian, kē.lē'ä). [Also: **Kilia**; Russian, **Kiliya.**] Northern mouth of the Danube, flowing into the Black Sea between SW U.S.S.R. and E Rumania. It forms part of the S boundary of Bessarabia.

Chilka Lake (chil'kạ). Lagoon on the E coast of the Union of India, in the state of Orissa, near the Bay of Bengal. Length, ab. 30 mi.; width, ab. 10 mi.

Chilkoot Pass (chil'köt). Pass in SE Alaska and NW British Columbia, Canada, ab. 17 mi. N of Skagway, Alaska. It is a steep, narrow, and dangerous pass, but was used in 1899 by many thousands of gold-rush miners on their way to the Klondike. In July, 1900, the railroad through White Pass was opened, and supplanted the Chilkoot trail. Elevation, ab. 3,500 ft.

Chillán (chē.yän'). Capital of Ñuble province, in C Chile: agricultural market center. It was the birthplace of Bernardo O'Higgins. It has been reconstructed since the 1939 earthquake, which killed 10,000 persons. 42,817 (1940).

Chillianwalla or **Chilianwalla** (chil''i.ạn.wä'lạ). Town in West Punjab, Pakistan, ab. 120 mi. NW of Lahore, near the Jhelum River. Here, in January, 1849, a battle occurred between the British army (ab. 15,000) under Lord Gough, and the Sikhs (ab. 23,000). It was technically a British victory. Loss of the British force, 2,400.

Chillicothe (chil.i.koth'ẹ). City in N central Illinois, in Peoria County, on the Illinois River ab. 12 mi. N of Peoria. 2,767 (1950).

Chillicothe. City in NW Missouri, county seat of Livingston County. In a stock-raising and coal-mining region, it manufactures farm machinery. It is the seat of Chillicothe Business College. 8,694 (1950).

Chillicothe. City in S Ohio, county seat of Ross County, on the Scioto River, ab. 45 mi. S of Columbus: agricultural markets; manufactures include shoes, canned foods, and paper. Settled in 1796, it was the first capital (1803–10) of Ohio. The Adena Indian burial mound and others are nearby. 20,133 (1950).

Chillicothe Junto. In U.S. political history, name given to a number of Jeffersonian Republican political leaders at Chillicothe, Ohio, who were instrumental in securing the admission (1803) of Ohio as a state, and dominated Ohio politics during succeeding years. Among the most prominent members of the group were Nathaniel Massie and Edward Tiffin.

Chillingham (chil'ing.ạm). Civil parish and village in NE England, in Northumberland, situated on the river Till, ab. 11 mi. NW of Alnwick. 108 (1931).

Chillingworth (chil'ing.wėrth), **Roger.** Injured and malicious husband of Hester Prynne in *The Scarlet Letter* (1850) by Nathaniel Hawthorne.

Chillingworth, William. b. at Oxford, England, in October, 1602; d. at Chichester, England, Jan. 30, 1644. English divine and controversialist. The most famous of his works is *The Religion of Protestants, a Safe Way to Salvation* (1637).

Chillip (chil'ip), **Mr.** Mild and gentle little doctor who attended Mrs. Copperfield, in Charles Dickens's *David Copperfield.*

Chilliwack (chil'i.wak). City in British Columbia, Canada, situated on the S bank of the Thompson River, ab. 60 mi. E of its mouth. It is connected by rail with Vancouver: center of a dairying and stock-raising district; some lumbering is carried on in the vicinity. 5,663 (1951).

Chillon (shē.yôṅ; Anglicized, shi.lon', shil'ọn). Castle in the canton of Vaud, Switzerland, at the E end of the Lake of Geneva. It covers an isolated rock on the edge of the lake, and is a very picturesque combination of semicircular and square towers and machicolated curtains grouped about a higher central tower. It is famous in literature and song (Byron), especially as the prison of Bonnivard (1530–36), a defender of Swiss liberties against the Duke of Savoy in the 16th century. The castle is of very early foundation, though, as it now stands, essentially of the 13th century. Some of the rooms preserve curious wooden ceilings, and the massive ribbed vaulting of the two-aisled dungeon crypt is impressive. It was taken by the Bernese in 1536, and was used for a state prison in the 18th century, and later as an arsenal.

Chilmari (chil.mä'rē). [Hindustani, **Chalamari.**] Village in the district of Rangpur, East Bengal, Pakistan, ab. 30 mi. SE of Rangpur, on the Brahmaputra River: seat of a religious and commercial festival.

Chiloé (chē.lō.ā'). [Full Spanish name, **Isla de Chiloé.**] Island in the Pacific Ocean, in S Chile, S of Valdivia; comprising part of Chiloé province. It was discovered by the Spaniards in 1558. Chief town, Ancud; length, ab. 120 mi.; greatest width, ab. 40 mi.

Chiloé. Province in S Chile, including the island of Chiloé. Capital, Ancud; area, 9,052 sq. mi.; pop. 94,187 (est. 1950).

Chilon (kī'lon) or **Chilo** (kī'lō). fl. in the first part of the 6th century B.C. Spartan, one of the Seven Sages of Greece. He was ephor eponymos at Sparta in 556 B.C. and is said to have died of joy caused by the victory of his son in boxing at the Olympic games.

Chilpancingo (chēl.pän.sēng'gō). [Full name, **Chilpancingo de los Bravos** (dā lōs brä'ʙōs); also called **Ciudad Bravos.**] City in SW Mexico, capital of Guerrero state. It is the site of ruins of an aboriginal culture more advanced than the Aztecs'. Its name honors three members of the Bravo family who fought in the war for independence. 8,834 (1940).

Chilperic I (chil'pėr.ik, kil'-). [French, **Chilpéric** (shēl-pā.rēk); German, **Chilperich** (ċhēl'pẹ.riċh).] d. 584. King of Neustria in the period 561–584. He murdered his second wife, the West-Gothic princess Galswintha, sister of Brunehilde of Austrasia, in order to marry his mistress Fredegunde, thereby bringing on a war with the husband of Brunehilde, his brother Sigebert I of Austrasia.

Chiltern Hills (chil'tėrn). Range of low chalk hills in S and SE England, extending NE from near the river

Thames, in Oxfordshire, across Buckinghamshire, the SE portion of Bedfordshire, Hertfordshire, and the NW portion of Essex, almost to the Essex-Suffolk border. The hills were formerly forested and infested with robbers and highwaymen. They reach their highest elevation (828 ft.) in Buckinghamshire. Length, ab. 50 mi.; average width, ab. 15 mi.

Chiltern Hundreds. The three hundreds of Stoke, Desborough, and Bodenham, in Buckinghamshire. The stewardship of the Chiltern Hundreds (originally an office charged with the suppression of the robbers who infested the Chiltern Hills) is a nominal office, conferred upon a member of Parliament who wishes to resign his seat, such resignation being impossible unless the member is disqualified by the acceptance of a place of honor and profit under the crown, or by some other cause. The place is the gift of the chancellor of the exchequer.

Chilwa (chil'wä). [Also, **Shirwa.**] Lake in E Africa, SE of Lake Nyasa and E of the Shiré River, on the border between Nyasaland and Mozambique. Length, ab. 40 mi.

Chimaera (ki.mir'ą, kī-). [Also, **Chimera.**] In Greek mythology, a fire-breathing monster of divine origin (according to Hesiod, a daughter of Typhaon and Echidna). It was often shown in art as having a goat's head in the middle of the back and a dragon's head at the end of the tail. It dwelt in Lycia, and was slain by Bellerophon.

Chimakum (chim'ą.kum). North American Indian tribe, now almost extinct, that formerly occupied the coast of Puget Sound, Washington, between Port Townsend and Port Ludlow. Together with Quileute, this language formed an independent family called Chimakuan.

Chimalpáin Quautlehuanitzín (chē.mäl.pīn' kwou.tle-wä.nē.tsēn'), **Juan Bautista de San Anton Muñon.** fl. in the late 16th century. Mexican Indian, a descendant of the chiefs of Amecameca. Educated by the Franciscans, he taught in their college of Santiago Tlatelolco. He wrote several works on ancient Aztec history, and is said to have written one on the Spanish conquest.

Chimalpopoca (chē.mäl.pō.pō'kä). fl. in the 15th century. Third ruler (1417–28, or 1410–22) of ancient Mexico; brother of his predecessor, Huitzilihuitl. He interfered in a quarrel of rival Tepanec chiefs, was seized by one of them, Maxtla, and committed suicide while in confinement.

Chimaltenango (chē.mäl.tā.näng'gō). Department in S Guatemala. Capital, Chimaltenango; area, 764 sq. mi.; pop. 120,718 (1950).

Chimaltenango. City in S Guatemala, capital of Chimaltenango department. 6,059 (1950).

Chimay (shē.mā). Town in SW Belgium, in the province of Hainaut, ab. 32 mi. SE of Mons. It was the place of Froissart's death. Pop. ab. 3,000.

Chimay, Princesse de. See **Tallien, Thérésa.**

Chimborazo (chēm.bō.rä'sō). Province in W Ecuador. Capital, Riobamba; area, 2,379 sq. mi.; pop. 276,685 (est. 1944).

Chimborazo. One of the highest mountains of the Andes, in Ecuador, SW of Quito. It was nearly ascended by Humboldt in 1802, and was ascended by Whymper in 1880. Elevation above sea level, 20,498 ft.; above the plain of Quito, ab. 12,000 ft.

Chimène (shē.men). Faithful daughter of Don Gomès in Pierre Corneille's tragedy *Le Cid*.

Chimera (ki.mir'ą, kī-). See **Chimaera.**

Chimes, The. Charles Dickens's Christmas story for 1844. It is one of his most sociological narratives: a bitter attack upon the political economy of Victorian England.

Chimkent (chēm.kent'). City in the U.S.S.R., in the Kazakh Soviet Socialist Republic, ab. 80 mi. N of Tashkent. Metallurgical industry is important here. It is a highway junction. 74,185 (1939).

Chimmesyan (chi.mā'si.ąn) or **Chimsian** (chim'syän'). See **Tsimshian.**

Chimu (chē'mö). [Also: **Chimo** (chē'mō), **Yunca.**] Indian kingdom that included some 10 or 12 river valleys of N coastal Peru from Lambayeque (just N of Chiclayo) to Paramonga (N of Lima), which was conquered by the Incas in the 15th century. On the basis of extensive irrigation projects, population increased and true cities were developed of which the largest, and the capital, was Chanchan, later destroyed by the Incas and used as a cemetery by them.

Ch'in (chin). Fourth Chinese dynasty, traditionally dated 221–207 B.C. The western state of Ch'in emerged victorious from the struggle for power among the feudatories of Eastern Chou; all China was united for the first time, and the boundaries were expanded by the Ch'in ruler Shih Huang Ti, who was the first to call himself "emperor." He ordered the burning of the *Classics* so that the feudal ideas of the past might not subvert his plans; and by uniting and improving the local border walls in the north, he built the Great Wall of China to prevent the inroads of the barbarian tribes. The name Ch'in is the probable origin of the modern word "China."

Chin (chin). The name given in Burma to the southern tribes of the Kuki-Chin people, living in Assam and Burma.

China (chī'nạ). [Official name, **Republic of China,** Chinese, **Chung-Hua Min-Kuo**; called by medieval geographers **Cathay.**] Republic in E Asia, S of the U.S.S.R. and the Mongolian People's Republic, and bordering on the Pacific Ocean. Greater China (including Manchuria, Formosa, and Inner Mongolia) is divided into 35 provinces: Shantung, Shansi, Shensi, Kansu, Honan, Anhwei, Kiangsu, Chekiang, Kiangsi, Hunan, Kweichow, Yunnan, Kwangsi, Kwangtung, Antung, Chahar, Chinghai, Formosa, Fukien, Heilungkiang, Hokiang, Hopei, Hsingan, Hupeh, Jehol, Kirin, Liaoning, Liaopei, Ninghsia, Nunkiang, Sikang, Sinkiang, Suiyuan, Sunkiang, and Szechwan. The surface, except in part in the NE, is largely mountainous, with many of the summits attaining an elevation of 10,000–11,000 ft. The chief rivers are the Peh-Kiang, Hwang Ho (Yellow River), Yangtze-Kiang, Min-Kiang, and Canton (or Pearl). The leading products are rice, tea, silk, cotton, sugar, pulse, cereals, tobacco, coal, iron, and copper. The chief exports include tea, silk, straw goods, and porcelain. The designation China is not used for the country by the Chinese themselves, but is said to be derived from the name of the dynasty, Ch'in, which unified the empire in the years 255–207 B.C. This was the period when China first became known to the West. The principal religions are Sinism, Buddhism, and Taoism: the philosophical system known as Confucianism is sometimes erroneously classed with them. Capital of the Nationalist government, officially, Nanking; its actual headquarters (since 1949) are on Formosa; capital of the Communist government, Peiping; area, excluding Tibet, 3,097,836 sq. mi.; pop. 463,493,000 (est. 1948).

History. The Chinese assign a fabulously early origin to their nation. Among the semi-mythical kings is Fu Hsi, who reigned c2800 B.C. according to tradition, and who invented the alphabet, the *pa kua* or eight trigrams (used in amulets and the like), and other elements of Chinese culture. From about the era of Confucius (in the 6th century B.C.) the dates become more trustworthy. In the 3rd century B.C. the Ch'in dynasty reigned and built the Great Wall. To it succeeded the Han dynasty when the empire was consolidated. Buddhism was introduced from India in the 1st century A.D. Soon afterwards, the empire became disorganized, but was again consolidated c600 under the Sui dynasty. There followed, while the T'ang dynasty ruled, a brilliant period, especially in literature, interrupted by Tartar attacks. Genghis Khan occupied the N portion of the empire in 1215, and the Mongol (Yüan) dynasty was fully established by Kublai Khan in 1280. The Ming dynasty followed in 1368. In the 16th century Portugal obtained a foothold at Macao (permanently after 1557). The recent (until 1912) Manchu dynasty of Ch'ing acceded in 1644. The empire attained a westward extension in the 18th century. The Opium War with Great Britain began in 1840, and ended in 1842 with the cession of Hong Kong and the opening of certain treaty ports: ports were opened to France and the U.S. in 1844. The Taiping rebellion broke out in 1850, and was suppressed in 1864. Meanwhile fighting against the English and French in 1856–58 and 1859–60 resulted in the victory of these European powers, and consequent concessions to them. China ceded the Amur country to Russia (treaty of Aigun, 1858). In 1881 she recovered Kuldja by treaty with Russia. War with France (1884–85) terminated in favor of the French. In 1894 disturbances in Korea, whither Chinese and Japanese troops were dispatched, led to the seizure of the Korean government by Japan and a war (declared July 31) between that country and China in which the latter was completely defeated on land and sea. A treaty of peace, which included the payment of a heavy indemnity by China, the cession of Formosa, the independence of Korea, and other concessions, was agreed on at Shimonoseki, Japan, on April 16, 1895. Toward the end of 1899 an uprising headed by the so-called Boxers (a group of violently nationalistic and xenophobic Chinese) against native Christians and foreigners began, which resulted, in June, 1900, in an attack upon the foreign legations at Peiping (Peking), and the murder of the Japanese secretary of legation and the German minister, Baron Klemens von Ketteler. The legations were besieged and cut off from communication with the outside world. Their relief was at once undertaken by their governments. The first expedition under Admiral Sir Edward Hobart Seymour (June 10–26) from Tientsin was unsuccessful, and a second one was organized. The Taku forts were taken June 17, Tientsin was recaptured July 14, and Peiping (Peking) was captured Aug. 14. Manchuria was occupied by Russia as a result of the Boxer uprising, but was restored to China, with the exception of the Liaotung Peninsula, by the treaty of Portsmouth (N.H.), Sept. 5, 1905, at the end of the Russo-Japanese War. By treaty (Dec. 22, 1905), China thereupon leased to Japan the Liaotung Peninsula and ceded the control of the railways as far as Chanchun, and the right to construct a railway from Antung to Mukden, and agreed to open 16 Manchurian ports and cities to foreign commerce. On Nov. 21, 1906, regulations were issued providing for a gradual decrease in the use, growth, and importation of opium. Provincial assemblies were inaugurated in October, 1909, and the first imperial senate met in October, 1910. A revolution in 1911–12 resulted in the abdication of the Manchu dynasty and the establishment (Feb. 12, 1912) of the Republic of China. In 1945, at the end of World War II, the Liaotung Peninsula was returned to China. Immediately after the end of international hostilities the Chinese Communist armies started their bid for power and control of the republic. By June, 1949, they had driven the existing government to the island of Formosa and had taken all of China as far S as Hangchow.

China, Great Wall of. See **Great Wall of China.**

Chinab (chē.näb'). See **Chenab.**

China Clipper. Seaplane which made (Nov. 22–29, 1935) the first trans-Pacific mail flight between San Francisco and Manila. It was piloted by Captain Edwin C. Musick and carried a crew of seven. In 1936 it initiated the first trans-Pacific passenger service to Manila.

Chinalaph (ki.nal'ạf). Ancient name of the **Chéliff.**

Chinam-pho (chē'näm'pō'). See **Chinnampo.**

Chinan (jē'nän'). See **Tsinan.**

Chinandega (chē.nän.dā'gä). Department in W Nicaragua, bordering on Honduras and the Pacific Ocean. Capital, Chinandega; area, 1,776 sq. mi.; pop. 82,970 (1950).

Chinandega. City in W Nicaragua, capital of Chinandega department, ab. 20 mi. NW of León: refinery center for a sugar district. 13,172 (1950).

Chinantla (chē.nän'tlä). Ancient name for the mountainous region in the N part of the present state of Oaxaca, Mexico, long occupied by the Chinantec Indians (this tribe aided Cortés in the Spanish conquest of Mexico).

China Sea. Part of W Pacific Ocean, bordering on China, Korea and the SE mainland of Asia, and separated from the Pacific by the Philippines, Formosa, the Ryukyu Islands, and S Japan. The Strait of Formosa divides the China Sea into two parts, the East China Sea (Chinese, Tung Hai) and the South China Sea (Chinese, Nan Hai). The East China Sea is a shallow continental sea with an average depth of ab. 617 ft.; to the NE of Formosa is a deep trench with a maximum depth of 7800 ft. The South China Sea is much deeper, excepting on the W margins in the shallow gulfs, and has its greatest depth of ab. 17,200 ft. W of Mindoro. It is a warm sea, lying in the tropics, with surface water temperatures of 83° F. in the S part, and ab. 77° F. in the N part. Sudden tropical storms and typhoons occur. The name "China Sea" is sometimes used for the South China Sea, and also for this plus the East China Sea and Yellow Sea.

"China's Sorrow." See under **Hwang Ho.**

Chincha Alta (chēn'chä äl'tä). Town in W Peru, in Ica department, near the Pacific coast: cotton, fruits, and allied industries. 12,768 (1940).

Chincha Islands (chin'chạ; Spanish, chēn'chä). Group of three islands in the Pacific Ocean, ab. 12 mi. from Pisco, Peru, belonging to Peru. The islands have at times had a population of several million sea birds, whose excrement formed the guano deposits collected and used commercially for fertilizer until the deposits were exhausted in 1874.

Chinchas (chēn'chạz). Ancient people of Peru who occupied the coastal valleys S of the Chimu kingdom, and S of the present site of Lima. They had attained a considerable degree of civilization before they were conquered by the Inca ruler Tupac Yupanqui, c1450, and incorporated into the Inca empire.

Chinchaycocha (chēn.chī.kō'chä). See **Junín Lake.**

Chinchay-suyu (chēn.chī.sö'yö) or **Chinchasuyu** (chēn-chä.sö'yö). Kechua term used to designate the regions north of Cusco, Peru, in general. It was not a circumscribed province, only a vague designation of regions visited by the Incas, and lying in the north.

Chinchero (chēn.chā'rō). Village in S Peru, in Cusco department, ab. 15 mi. N of the city of Cusco. The ruins there are possibly Incan. Pop. under 5,000 (1940).

Chincheu or **Chinchew** or **Chinchu** (jin'jō'). Former name of **Lungki** and of **Tsinkiang.**

Chinchiang (jin'jyäng'). See **Tsinkiang.**

Chinchón (chēn.chōn'), Conde **de.** [Title of **Luis Gerónimo Fernández de Cabrera Bobadilla Cerda y Mendoza.**] b. at Madrid, c1590; d. near that city, Oct. 28, 1647. Spanish nobleman, viceroy of Peru. This fourth holder of the title of Conde de Chinchón ruled the rich Andean colony in the name of the king of Spain from January, 1629, to December, 1639, and among other acts, sponsored explorations down the Amazon River. His wife contracted a fever which was relieved by a medicine made by the Indians from quina-quina bark, and it is widely believed that in this way the medicinal value of what has since been known as quinine was revealed to the world at large, but the story is disputed. Nevertheless, in classifying trees from which quinine is derived, Linnaeus gave them the name "Cinchona."

Chinchón, Condesa **de.** [Title of **Ana de Osorio.**] b. at Astorga, in Castile, Spain, 1576; d. at Cartagena, Colombia, in December, 1639. Spanish lady; daughter of the 8th Marquis of Astorga. She married Don Luis de Velasco, Marquis of Salinas, twice viceroy of Mexico and once of Peru; and, after his death (c1617), Don Luis Gerónimo de Cabrera, Conde de Chinchón, who was appointed viceroy of Peru in 1629. During her second residence at Lima she was attacked with a tertian ague, and was cured by some powdered Peruvian bark which had been sent to her physician by the *corregidor* (chief magistrate) of Loja, Don Juan López de Canizares. When the countess embarked for Spain she carried a quantity of the bark with her. She died on the voyage, but it was through her cure that the cinchona bark was first introduced into Europe.

Chinchou (jin'jō'). [Also: **Kinchau, Kinchow.**] City in NE China, in the province of Liaoning, S Manchuria, ab. 15 mi. NE of Dairen, situated near the isthmus which joins the Kwangtung peninsula to the mainland. It is a trading and fishing center, with asbestos mines and several canning factories. It was captured from the Russians by the Japanese in May, 1904, in the Russo-Japanese War. 155,435 (1947).

Chinchow (jin'jō'). Former name of **Chinhsien.**

Chincoteague (ching'kọ.tēg, shing'-). Town in E Virginia, in Accomack County, on an island off the Atlantic coast. It is a fishing port for oysters, crabs, clams, and fish. An annual roundup of Chincoteague ponies, a type peculiar to the region and believed to be descended from stray horses of the colonial period, is a tourist attraction here. 2,724 (1950).

Chinda (chēn.dä), Count **Sutemi.** b. at Hirosaki, Japan, 1856; d. at Tokyo, Jan. 16, 1929. Japanese diplomat, remembered chiefly for his services as peacemaker at the end of the Russo-Japanese War (1904–05). He was Japanese delegate to the Paris peace conference (1919) and adviser (1927–29) to Emperor Hirohito of Japan.

He also served as ambassador to Germany (1908–11), the U.S. (1911–16), and Great Britain (1916–20).

Chindwara (chin.dwä′ra). See **Chhindwara.**

Chindwin (chin′dwin). [In N Burma, **Tanai Hka.**] River in N Burma, rising in the Kumon Bum mountains ab. 27 mi. NW of Myitkyina, and flowing through the Hukawng valley, and thence generally S to join the Irrawaddy ab. 65 mi. SW of Mandalay. In the dry season (winter) it is navigable to Pantha, ab. 275 mi. above its mouth, and in the wet season to Homalin, ab. 410 mi. above its mouth. In a hilly and mountainous region, with few roads, the river is an important route. It flows through several gorges. Length, ab. 800 mi.

Chinese Eastern Railway (chī.nēz′, -nēs′). Rail system in E Asia. In 1896 the Russian government, desiring to shorten the mileage of the Trans-Siberian Railway between the Urals and Vladivostok, obtained by negotiation with China the right to build this line across N Manchuria. It was financed by the Russo-Chinese Bank; the president of the railway company was to be Chinese, and China was given the option of acquiring the road by purchase after 30 years; if this option was not taken up, it would become the property of China in 80 years. The line, comprising 1,078 miles of track including branches, running from Lupin to Suifenho, began operations in 1903, but by the terms of peace following the Russo-Japanese War (1904–05), the branch connecting Changchun and Port Arthur came under Japanese control, as part of the South Manchuria Railroad. At Suifenho the main line connects with the Ussuri Railway running E to Vladivostok and S from Harbin to Changchun. In 1935 the Japanese-sponsored regime in Manchuria, then known as Manchukuo, bought from the U.S.S.R. full control of the Chinese Eastern, which, however, as a result of World War II passed to the Kuomintang government of China. In 1945, by treaty between this government and the U.S.S.R., the Chinese Eastern and South Manchuria Railways were consolidated as the Chinese Changchun Railway, to be under joint Soviet-Chinese operation for 30 years and thereafter to revert to Chinese ownership. For a time the U.S.S.R. withdrew from administration of the railway because of difficulties in coöperation with the Chinese, but with the collapse of the Kuomintang power on the Chinese mainland, the Soviets took control, and in 1950 agreed by treaty with the Chinese People's Republic to restore Chinese co-administrative rights upon the conclusion of a treaty of peace with Japan, or in any event, not later than 1952.

Chinese Empire. [Chinese, **Tien Chao,** literally translated "Heavenly Dynasty," popularly translated **Celestial Empire.**] Former empire of Asia, bounded by Asiatic Russia on the N, the Pacific on the E, Tonkin and India on the S, and the Pamirs and Asiatic Russia on the W. It included China proper, or the 18 provinces, and its dependencies, Manchuria, Mongolia, Tibet, Eastern Turkistan (Kashgaria), and Dzungaria. A republican form of government was adopted Feb. 12, 1912, and the name changed to Republic of China (Chung-Hua Min-Kuo which means, approximately, middle glorious people's country).

Chinese Exclusion Acts. In U.S. history, name given collectively to various acts passed (1882–94) by the U.S. Congress restricting and ultimately excluding Chinese laborers from entering the U.S. The original agitation for the passage of the acts came from Pacific Coast workingmen led by Denis Kearney who feared the inroads of Chinese competition in the labor market. The acts were extended to Hawaii (1900) and the Philippines (1902) and were reinforced by the U.S. immigration laws of 1917 and 1924. They are part of the body of statutes generally referred to as the Oriental Exclusion Acts, the Japanese also being openly barred by the provisions of the 1924 Act. The Chinese Exclusion Acts were repealed by the U.S. Congress in 1943; an immigration quota was provided for the Chinese, and they were made eligible for citizenship.

Chinese Gordon (gôr′don). See **Gordon, Charles George.**

Chinese Morrison (mor′i.son). See **Morrison, George Ernest.**

Chinese National Socialist Party. Political party founded (1931) by Carson Chang with a following chiefly among conservative university professors who advocated a kind of state capitalism. Because it incorrectly suggested a Nazi party, the name was later (1946) changed to Democratic Socialist Party. The party affiliated with other minor parties to form (1941) the middle-of-the-road Federation of Democratic Parties, itself renamed (1944) the Democratic League. When Chang broke (1947) with the League, some of his followers stayed with it, and his party disappeared following the defeats suffered by the Kuomintang at the hands of the Chinese Communists.

Chinese Nightingale: A Song in Chinese Tapestries, The. Poem by Vachel Lindsay, included in the volume published in 1917 under the title *The Chinese Nightingale and Other Poems.*

Chinese Tartary (tär′ta.ri). Old name given vaguely to a vast region in the N and NW parts of what is now the Chinese republic, including Mongolia, Dzungaria, Kashgaria (Chinese or East Turkistan); sometimes restricted to Kashgaria.

Chinese Turkistan (tėr.ki.stan′, -stän′). See **Kashgaria;** see also under **Sinkiang.**

Ch'ing (ching). Chinese name taken by the Manchus for their dynasty when they conquered China in 1644. The Manchu period was one of increasing contact with Europe and America. Internal dissension over foreign relations contributed to the downfall of the dynasty and the success of the republican revolution of 1912.

Chingford (ching′ford). Municipal borough and residential center in SE England, in Essex, situated SW of Epping Forest, which bounds it on the N and E, ab. 11 mi. NE of Liverpool Street station, London. The borough includes many acres of forest land. 48,330 (1951).

Chinghai or **Ching-hai** (ching′hī′). See **Chinhai** (city) and **Tsinghai** (province).

Ching Hai (ching′ hī′). See **Tsing Hai.**

Chingleput (ching′gl.put). [Also, **Chengalpatt.**] District in Madras state, Union of India, just S of the city of Madras: rice, indigo, nuts, and millet. Chief town, Chingleput; area, 3,074 sq. mi.; pop. 1,823,955 (1941).

Chingleput. [Also, **Chengalpatt.**] Chief town of the district of Chingleput, Union of India, ab. 35 mi. SW of Madras, on the Palar River. It was taken by the French in 1751, by the English under Clive in 1752, and withstood a siege by Hyder Ali's forces in 1780–81. Pop. ab. 15,000.

Ch'ing-ming (ching′ming′). [Eng. trans., "*Pure Brightness.*"] Chinese spring festival, which usually falls on or near April 5. On this day it is customary to sweep the graves, offer sacrifices, and burn paper money, in memory of deceased ancestors. It is also observed by nation-wide planting of trees.

Chingolo (chēng.gō′lō). [Also: **Cingolo, Quingolo.**] One of the 13 independent kingdoms of the Bantu-speaking people of SW Africa, living in C Angola.

Chingtao (jing′dou′). See **Tsingtao.**

Ching-te Chen (jing′du′ jun′). Former name of **Fowliang.**

Chingtu (ching′dö′). See **Chengtu.**

Chingú (chēng.gö′). See **Xingú.**

Chinhai (chin′hī′). [Also: **Ching-hai, Chin-hae.**] Seaport in E China, in the province of Chekiang, ab. 12 mi. NE of Ninghsien. Pop. ab. 10,000.

Chin Hills (chin). Mountain region in W Burma, on the Assam border ab. 160 mi. W of Mandalay. The region consists of a series of rugged ranges, much dissected by deep valleys, and mostly jungle-covered. The hill tribes inhabiting the hills are a Tibeto-Burman people, and were long feared as plunderers; they now cultivate rice and maize. Length, ab. 200 mi.; peak elevation, ab. 9,009 ft.

Chinhsien (jin′shyen′). [Former name, **Chinchow.**] City in NE China, in the province of Liaoning, Manchuria, situated near the extreme NW coast of Liaotung Gulf, on the Eastern Chinese Railway: a trading and rail center; several coal mines in the area. Pop. ab. 140,000.

Chini (kē′nē) or **Chino** (-nō), **Eusebio Francisco.** See **Kino, Eusebio Francisco.**

Chinjiri (chēn.jē′rē). [Also, **Machinjiri.**] Bantu-speaking people of C Mozambique, in SE Africa, closely related to the Nyanja in language and culture.

Chinkiang (jin′jyäng′; Anglicized, chin.kyang′). [Also, **Chenkiang.**] City in E China, capital of the province of Kiangsu, situated at the junction of the Grand Canal with the Yangtze-Kiang. The Yangtze once emptied into the sea at this point but sedimentation has pushed the present-day mouth to the east. Chinkiang was a treaty port. 204,723 (1936).

Chin Ling Shan (chin' ling' shän'). See **Tsinling Shan.**

Chinnampo (chin.näm.pō). [Also: **Chinam-pho; Chinnamp'o.**] Port on the W coast of Korea, ab. 100 mi. NW of Seoul, in the province of Plyongan-namdo (Heian Nan or South Heian). There are iron and coal mines in the area. Rice, millet, and wheat are the chief crops. 61,457 (est. 1938).

Chinnereth (kin'ę.reth) or **Chinneroth** (-roth), **Sea of.** See **Galilee, Sea of.**

Chino (chē'nō). City in S California, in San Bernardino County, SE of Los Angeles: trading center for a citrus and beet-sugar area. 5,784 (1950).

Chinon (shē.nôn). Town in W France, in the department of Indre-et-Loire, situated on the Vienne River, ab. 26 mi. SW of Tours. The town preserves much of its medieval character and has numerous old churches and houses. It is overlooked by the ruins of an enormous castle dating from the 12th to 14th centuries. Chinon was the residence of Henry II (Plantagenet) of England, who died here; it went to the crown of France under Philip II of France. Joan of Arc was presented (1428) here to Charles VII. From 1631 to 1793 Chinon was in the possession of Cardinal Richelieu and his heirs. Rabelais was born near here. Some damage was caused during World War II. 6,069 (1946).

Chinookan (chi.nök'ạn). Collective term for a group of North American Indian tribes formerly inhabiting the region of the Columbia River from its mouth inland ab. 200 mi., in the area of the present states of Washington and Oregon. Most of the Chinook tribes are now extinct. Their languages probably formed an independent family.

"Chinook State" (chi.nök'). Occasional nickname of **Washington** state.

Chinsura (chin.sö'rạ). Town in West Bengal, Union of India, on the Hooghly River, ab. 24 mi. N of Calcutta: the seat of Hooghly College. It was settled by the Dutch in 1656, and ceded to the English in 1825 as part of a general trade of Indian-Sumatran possessions. It is now a joint municipality with Hooghly.

Chintamani (chin.tä'mạ.ni). In Indian folklore, the wishing gem, or "thought jewel," i.e., a jewel that possesses the magic power of securing that to which the possessor has directed his thoughts. The term is also an epithet of Brahma, who is said once to have possessed the gem.

Chintsun (jin'tsön'). Village in E central China, in Honan province, ab. 13 mi. E of Loyang: site of the tombs of the princes of the Han state of Late Chou times. The name is now used to describe the style of certain bronzes inlaid with gold and silver, jades, and other objects of a type said to have been found at this site in the early 1930's; these materials may be dated roughly 430–250 B.C.

Chinwangtao (chin'wäng'dou'). Seaport and former treaty port in NE China, in Hopeh province, on the Pohai ("Po gulf"), ab. 130 mi. NE of the city of Tientsin: one of the better ice-free ports of this area, serving as the winter port for Tientsin and Peiping when the port of Taku is frozen. It was first used for the export of coal from the N part of the province. 20,020 (1931).

Chioggia (kyôd'jä). City and commune in NE Italy, in the *compartimento* (region) of Veneto, in the province of Venezia, situated on the island of Chioggia, in the Gulf of Venice, ab. 15 mi. S of Venice. A picturesque maritime city, it has fisheries, fish markets, and fish exports; it is the largest fishing port of Italy; there are also shipyards. The nearby Sottomarina is a seaside resort and grows great quantities of vegetables. Chioggia is the seat of an archbishopric. The cathedral, on older foundations, was reconstructed in the period 1663–74; the Church of San Martino is a remarkable Romanesque building of 1392; the Church of San Domenico contains a painting by Carpaccio. There are other churches, palaces, and statues of interest. The struggle between Venice and Genoa for trade supremacy in the Mediterranean reached its climax in the war of Chioggia (1378–80). The Genoese seized the Venetian town, but their position was blockaded by Venetian forces and their fleet destroyed. The victory decided the ascendancy of Venice over Genoa thenceforth in the trade with the Near East. Buildings of interest to tourists were undamaged in World War II. Pop. of commune, 42,567 (1936); of city, 23,577 (1936).

Chios (kī'os). [Also: **Khios**; Italian, **Scio**; Turkish, **Saki-Adasi, Saki-Adassi.**] Greek island in the Aegean Sea, situated W of Asia Minor. The surface is hilly and rocky. The island has been noted in ancient and modern times for wine and fruit. The inhabitants are mostly Greeks. It was settled by Ionians, passed to Persian rule in the 6th century B.C., and was a member of the original Confederacy of Delos until 412 B.C. It was noted in the ancient world as a center of art and literature, particularly for its school of epic poets, and claim was made that it was the birthplace of Homer. Chios was part of the Macedonian, Roman, and other dominions in the area. The Genoese took the island in the 14th century; it was conquered by the Turks in 1566, and was lost by them to, and retaken from, the Florentines and Venetians during the 16th and 17th centuries. It was the scene of a terrible massacre of its inhabitants by the Turks in 1822, and was ravaged by earthquakes in 1881 and 1882. Chios forms a *nomos* (department) of Greece, of which it became a part in 1912. Capital, Chios; area, 355 sq. mi.; length, 30 mi.; pop. 66,549 (1951).

Chios. [Also: **Kastro, Khios**; Italian, **Scio.**] Chief town of the island of Chios, E Greece, the capital of the *nomos* (department) of Chios, situated on the E coast: wine, oranges, and resin of mastic (for the production of strong liquor). It is the seat of a bishopric and one of the places which claimed to be the birthplace of Homer. The city was nearly destroyed by earthquakes in 1881 and 1882. Pop. 26,879 (1940).

Chipeta (chē.pā'tä). [Also: **Achipeta, Cipeta, Maravi, Ravi.**] Bantu-speaking people of SE Africa, inhabiting S Nyasaland and W Mozambique. They are closely related to the Nyanja in language and culture.

Chipewyan (chip.ę.wī'ạn). [Formerly, **Fort Chipewyan.**] Trading post in NE Alberta, Canada, at the W end of Lake Athabaska, on the N shore at the outlet of the Slave River. The old Fort Chipewyan was established on the S shore of the lake, ab. 22 mi. E of the present settlement, in 1788, as a trading center for the Indians in the area. In 1804 a new post was established on the present location, which was taken over by the Hudson's Bay Company in 1821. It has long been one of Canada's major fur-trading posts. 654 (township, 1946).

Chipewyan. Group of North American Indian tribes formerly living in W Canada in the region of Lake Athabaska. They were of the Athabaskan linguistic stock.

Chipley (chip'li). Town in NW Florida, county seat of Washington County, ab. 110 mi. NE of Pensacola. 2,959 (1950).

Chippawa (chip'ạ.wä). [Also, **Chippewa.**] Manufacturing village in Welland County, Ontario, Canada, ab. 21 mi. NW of Buffalo. Here, on July 5, 1814, American troops (ab. 4,000) under the command of Winfield Scott defeated a British force (ab. 2,100) under General Phineas Riall. Loss of the Americans, 335; of the British, 503. Pop. 1,762 (1951).

Chippendale (chip'ẹn.dāl), **Thomas.** b. in Yorkshire, England, c1718; d. at London, 1779. English furniture maker. His business was carried on at London. His work is heavier in design than that of Sheraton and other later cabinetmakers. He added to the common style of the early 18th century several details adapted from French rococo (Louis Quinze), Gothic, and Chinese. His work nearly always is in dark mahogany, and in this material he designed and built chairs and tables, desks and bookcases, cabinets and settees, his designs, emphasizing carving to give a light effect to the heavy material and solid construction, being so good that his work was quickly imitated in England and the U.S., and his name given to the entire style. He published *Gentleman and Cabinet-Maker's Director* (1754), a catalogue of various pieces turned out by his workshop.

Chippenham (chip'ẹn.ạm). Municipal borough and market town in S England, in Wiltshire, situated on the river Avon ab. 12 mi. NE of Bath. It has trade in grain, butter, and cheese, and was formerly a clothing-manufacturing center. Railway-signal equipment is now made at Chippenham. 11,850 (1951).

Chippewa (chip'e.wä, -wā, -wa). See also **Ojibwa.**

Chippewa. [Also, **Ojibway.**] River of Wisconsin which joins the Mississippi ab. 64 mi. SE of St. Paul. Length, ab. 200 mi.

Chippewa Falls. City in W Wisconsin, county seat of Chippewa County on the Chippewa River: manufactures include shoes and woolen textiles; there are meat-packing and food-processing plants. It occupies the site of a former Indian village. 11,088 (1950).

Chipping Barnet (chip'ing bär'net). See **Barnet.**

Chipping Wycombe (chip'ing wik'om). See **High Wycombe.**

Chiputneticook Lakes (chip.ut.net'i.kůk). Chain of lakes in E Maine and SW New Brunswick, Canada, flowing into the St. Croix River. Elevation, Grand Lake, ab. 434 ft.; Spednik Lake, ab. 380 ft. Length of chain, ab. 30 miles.

Chiquimula (chē.kē.mö'lä). Department in SE Guatemala. Capital, Chiquimula; area, 917 sq. mi.; pop. 112,275 (1950).

Chiquimula. City in E Guatemala, capital of Chiquimula department, ab. 62 mi. NE of Guatemala City. 8,848 (1950).

Chiquinquirá (chē.kēng.kē.rä'). Town in C Colombia, in Boyacá department, ab. 85 mi. N of Bogotá; commercial center and trading point of an important cattle country. It is noted for nearby emerald mines, and for a shrine of the Virgin which has been visited by 80,000 pilgrims in one year. 6,998 (1938).

Chiquito (chē.kē'tō). Collective term for a number of South American Indian tribes inhabiting E Bolivia. The languages and dialects of these tribes comprise a distinct linguistic family unrelated to any of the neighboring groups.

Chiquitos (chē.kē'tōs), **Llanos de.** [Also, **Llanos de los Chiquitos.**] Extensive plain in E Bolivia, in Santa Cruz and Chuquisaca departments, extending from the mountains of Santa Cruz de la Sierra nearly to the Paraguay River. It is continuous with the Chaco on the S, consists of grasslands varied with woods or with scattered trees, has occasional isolated hills, and contains few inhabitants except Indians. Portions in the E are annually overflowed.

Chire (shē'rē). See **Shiré.**

Chiricahua (chir.i.kä'wa). [Also: **Chiricahui** (chir.i.kä'wē), **Chihui-cahui** (chē.wē.kä'wē), meaning "Turkey Mountain."] Mountain range in SE Arizona, S of the Southern Pacific Railroad, now a national monument (established 1924; area, 10,530 acres), set aside because of its unusual rock formations. During the wars with the Apaches, and earlier, the Chiricahua were the refuge and stronghold of some of the wildest bands.

Chirico (kē'rē.kō), **Andrea de.** See **Savinio, Alberto.**

Chirico, Giorgio de. b. at Volos, Thessaly, Greece, July 10, 1888—. Italian painter who was one of the innovators of the surrealist movement early in his career, later becoming head of the *pittura metafisica* movement. He was schooled in Italy and France, and first exhibited in the Paris Salon d'Automne of 1911. He continued to show his work uninterruptedly at Paris until 1925. The enigmatic and mysterious aspects of life fascinated him, and this is clearly reflected in his work. In his early work, he depicted long vistas of empty spaces, buildings distorted to give them remoteness, and figures constructed on mechanical principles. He abandoned surrealism, however, and took (c1950) a stand for purely representational art based on Rennaissance models. He was awarded a number of prizes and his paintings hang in important collections all over Europe and the U.S. A list of his better-known works includes *The Enigma of the Oracle, Horses by the Sea, The Gladiators, The Melancholy and Mystery of the Street, Dream Flowers, The Disquieting Muses, Metaphysical Interior,* and the settings for the ballet *La Giarra* (1924).

Chiriguano (chē.rē.gwä'nō). [Also: **Shiriguanos, Xiriguanos.**] South American Indian tribe, inhabiting the W Bolivian Chaco, between latitudes 18° and 22° S. The language is of the Tupí-Guaraní stock.

Chirikov (chē'ri.kof), **Yevgeni Nikolayevich.** b. at Kazan, Russia, Aug. 5, 1864; d. 1932. Russian playwright, novelist, and short-story writer. An émigré after the Russian Revolution, he wrote works representative of the unpretentious, reportorial naturalism that became established at the turn of the century. Many of his plays, and particularly *Jews* (translated into English in 1907 as *The Chosen People*), were great stage successes.

Chiriquí (chē.rē.kē'). Province in SW Panama, bordering on Costa Rica and the Pacific Ocean. Capital, David; area, 3,693 sq. mi.; pop. 137,422 (1950).

Chiriquí. [Full Spanish name, **Volcán de Chiriquí.**] Mountain in W Panama. Elevation, ab. 11,970 ft.

Chiriquí. American Indian culture known through extensive archaeological remains, and located in W Panama and S Costa Rica. Chiriqui sites consist mainly of deep graves containing a rich variety of ceramic forms, stone sculpture, and, especially, large quantities of gold objects. No clear connection has yet been established between this culture, which antedates the Spanish conquest, and the Indian tribes of the area in historic times.

Chiriquí Bay. [Spanish, **Laguna de Chiriquí.**] Bay on the NW coast of the isthmus of Panama, W of Colón.

Chirol (chir'ol), Sir **Valentine.** [Full name, **Ignatius Valentine Chirol.**] b. May 23, 1852; d. at London, Oct. 22, 1929. English journalist, author, and traveler. Educated in France and Germany, he graduated from the University of Paris. He served (1872–76) as a British foreign office clerk, later (1876–92) traveling in the Far and Near East. From 1892 to 1899 he was Berlin correspondent of the London *Times,* on which he served (1899–1912) as foreign editor. He was a member (1912–16) of the Indian Royal Commission, and was knighted in 1912. Author of *'Twixt Greek and Turk* (1881), *The Far Eastern Question* (1896), *The Middle Eastern Question* (1903), *Indian Unrest* (1910), and the two autobiographical volumes *Fifty Years in a Changing World* (1927) and *With Pen and Brush in Eastern Lands* (1929).

Chiron or **Cheiron** (kī'ron). In Greek mythology, a centaur; son of Kronos and one of the Oceanids. Chiron was the pupil of Apollo and Artemis, the friend and protector of Peleus, and the instructor of Achilles, Aesculapius, Hercules, Jason, and many other legendary Greek heroes. He was renowned for his wisdom and skill in medicine, hunting, music, and prophecy. Chiron lived on Mount Pelion. During Hercules's fight with the centaurs, one of the Hydra-poisoned arrows of the hero accidentally struck Chiron. Knowing that his immortality doomed him to unending pain from the venom, Chiron asked to die, giving his immortality to Prometheus. On his death he was placed by Zeus among the stars, where he may be seen as Sagittarius, the Archer.

Chiron. Son of Tamora, queen of the Goths, in *Titus Andronicus,* attributed to Shakespeare. He and his brother Demetrius are guilty of the vilest crimes, relying upon their royal descent to protect them; Titus kills both by cutting their throats.

Chirpan (chir.pän'). [Also: **Čirpan, Tchirpan.**] Town in SE Bulgaria, in the department of Stara Zagora, ab. 23 mi. SW of Stara Zagora: silkworm and rose culture. 13,231 (1946).

Chishima (chē.shē.mä). Japanese name of the **Kurile Islands.**

Chisholm (chiz'om). City in NW Minnesota, in St. Louis County, on Longyear Lake: mining and shipping point for the iron ore of the Mesabi range. 6,861 (1950).

Chisholm, Hugh. b. at London, Feb. 22, 1866; d. there, Sept. 29, 1924. English journalist and editor. Educated at Felsted and at Corpus Christi College, Oxford, from which he received his M.A. in 1888, he was called to the bar in 1892. He was assistant editor (1892–97) and editor (1897–99) of the *St. James's Gazette,* resigning in order to write for *The Standard.* In 1900 he became a staff member of the London *Times,* and was that paper's city and financial editor from 1913 to 1920. He was also coeditor of the tenth edition (1902), and editor of the 11th (1910–11) and 12th (1922) editions of the *Encyclopaedia Britannica.*

Chisholm Trail. In U.S. history, a cattle route running north from Texas, and through Oklahoma to Abilene, Kan. The precise line of the trail, as well as the origin of the name, are disputed to this day. Some authorities hold that it was named for Jesse Chisholm, supposedly a part Cherokee guide and trader. During the period c1867–71 the Chisholm Trail was the route most widely used by cattlemen who brought their herds to Abilene for shipment north and east, but the trail lost its prominence after the shift in the tide of western settlement caused the decline of Abilene as a shipping point for cattle brought up from Texas. In 1880, however, the Chisholm Trail again became a chief route for bringing cattle to Caldwell, Tex., but the subsequent construction of a rail network led to the abandonment of bringing Texas cattle northward on the hoof. One of the most famous of cowboy ballads is named for the Chisholm Trail, its refrain echoing the whoops of the cowboys as they herded their cattle.

Chisholm v. Georgia, 2 Dallas 419 (1793). Decision of the U.S. Supreme Court in a case arising out of the effort of the heirs of Alexander Chisholm, who were citizens of South Carolina and executors of the estate of an English creditor, to secure compensation from Georgia for property confiscated during the American Revolution. Article III, section 2, of the federal Constitution provided that the judicial power of the U.S. should extend to controversies between states and between a state and citizens of another state. The question at issue was whether a citizen could sue a state in the federal courts. The high court upheld the right of Chisholm's heirs to sue Georgia in the Supreme Court. Georgia refused to appear before the high court, denied the validity of the judgment, and threatened to punish by death any official who should attempt to execute the decree of the court. Other states joined in the protest. Shortly after the decision an amendment to the Constitution was introduced which deprived the federal courts of jurisdiction in cases against one of the states by citizens of another state. This, the Eleventh Amendment, was ratified on Jan. 8, 1798.

Chisimaio (kē.sē.mä'yō). Italian name of **Kismayu.**

Chişinău (kē.shē.nu'ö). Rumanian name of **Kishinev.**

Chislehurst (chiz'l.hėrst). Former urban district in SE England, in Kent, ab. 3 mi. E of Bromley, ab. 11 mi. SE of Charing Cross station, London. The town is a residential center. It was the home of Napoleon III from 1871 to 1873, and of the empress Eugénie until 1880. Elevation, ab. 300 ft.; pop. 9,876 (1931).

Chislehurst and Sidcup (sid'kup). Urban district in SE England, in Kent, ab. 11 mi. SE of Charing Cross station, London. It comprises the formerly separate Chislehurst and Sidcup urban districts. 83,837 (1951).

Chislev (kis'lef). See **Kislev.**

Chistopol (chis.tô'pǫl). City in W central U.S.S.R., in C Tatar Autonomous Soviet Socialist Republic, on the S bank of the Kama River ab. 65 mi. SE of Kazan. It is an important center for shipping lumber and grain of the surrounding region, and has sawmills, furniture industries, grain mills, and machinery industries. 32,000 (1939).

Chisum (chiz'um), **John Simpson.** b. in Hardeman County, Tenn., Aug. 15, 1824; d. at Eureka Springs, Ark., Dec. 23, 1884. Cattle magnate of the western American plains. The son of poor parents, taken to Texas in 1837, he had little schooling, and had to work from an early age. He became a builder and contractor in Lamar County, Texas, went into politics, and served as county clerk of that county for several years. From 1854 on, he engaged in the cattle business, first in partnership and later independently. About 1863 he shifted his operations to New Mexico, where in 1873 he established his home at South Springs. Indians and rustlers harassed the cattle drovers at that time, but Chisum prospered, and at one period owned close to 100,000 head of cattle, probably the largest herd in the U.S. and perhaps in the world. In 1878–79 disorders known locally as the Lincoln County War resulted from depredations on the Chisum and other herds. It has been maintained that no deaths were caused by Chisum or his employees, but he is known to have paid Billy the Kid (William Bonney) for services in protecting his property. In 1880, however, when lawlessness became rampant in Lincoln County, Chisum was instrumental in the election of Pat Garrett as sheriff, who killed Billy the Kid and restored the reign of law. Chisum, who was sometimes referred to in the press as "the cattle king of America," was regarded by those who knew him as an amiable, honest, public-spirited, and courageous man.

Chiswell's Mines (chiz'welz). Mines in what is now Wythe County, Va., named for their first operator, a certain John Chiswell, and taken over by the Virginia state government in 1776. In 1779–80 disaffected Tories plotted to seize the mines, but the plot was exposed and the Tories were subsequently executed by a mob under Colonel Lynch. It is believed by some that the treatment accorded by the patriots to the Tory plotters is the origin of the term "lynching."

Chiswick (chiz'ik). Civil parish and former urban district, now combined with Brentford as Brentford and Chiswick municipal borough, in SE England, in Middlesex, situated on the river Thames, ab. 9 mi. W of Waterloo station, London. It is a western suburb of London. 42,246 (1931).

Chiswick House. Former seat of the dukes of Devonshire, situated at Chiswick. Charles James Fox died here in 1806, and George Canning in 1827.

Chita (chē.tä'). [Also, **Tchita.**] *Oblast* (region) in the U.S.S.R., in the Russian Soviet Federated Socialist Republic, located in Siberia, E of Lake Baikal and N of the borders of China. The area is mountainous and hilly. Coal, iron ore, tin, and zinc are mined in modest amounts, and the area is covered with heavy forests. Both lines of the Trans-Siberian Railroad cross this oblast. Capital, Chita; area, 180,455 sq. mi.; pop. 1,159,478 (1939).

Chita. [Also, **Tchita.**] City in the U.S.S.R., capital of the Chita *oblast* (region) of the Russian Soviet Federated Socialist Republic. It is a rail junction on the Trans-Siberian Railroad and a meat-packing center. Coal mining, leather processing, and flour milling are also important. 102,555 (1939).

Chita (chē'tą). [Full title, **Chita: A Memory of Last Island.**] Tale by Lafcadio Hearn, published in 1889. The novelette tells, in florid style, of the devastation of an island in a storm and of a child lost in the tempest. The plot, though appealing, is of less interest than the descriptive parts of the story.

Chitaldroog (chit'ąl.drög). [Also: **Chitradurg, Chitteldrug.**] Capital of the district of Chitaldroog, in Mysore state, Union of India, ab. 140 mi. N. of the city of Mysore. It contains a remarkable rock fortress. It was besieged by Hyder Ali in 1776, and taken by him in 1779. Pop. ab. 10,000.

Chitata (chē.tä'tä). [Also: **Citata, Quitata.**] One of the 13 independent kingdoms of the Mbundu, a Bantu-speaking people of SW Africa, living in C Angola.

Chitimacha (shit.i.mash'ą). North American Indian tribe, now nearly extinct, formerly inhabiting the coastal area of Louisiana, W of the Mississippi River. The language formed an independent family belonging to the Tunican stock.

Chitradurg (chit'rą.dörg). See **Chitaldroog.**

Chitrakuta (chit.rą.kö'tą). [Also, **Chitrakut** (chit'rą.köt); Eng. trans., "*Bright Peak.*"] Hill and place of pilgrimage in Banda district, Uttar Pradesh (United Provinces), N central Union of India. It was the forest habitation of Rama and his half-brother and friend Lakshmana in their exile after leaving Ajodhya, and, as the holiest spot of the worshipers of Rama, was crowded with temples and shrines.

Chitral (chi.träl'). Small state in W Pakistan, in the North-West Frontier Province. Capital, Chitral; area, 4,000 sq. mi.; pop. 107,906 (est. 1947).

Chitral. Town in W Pakistan, capital of the state of Chitral, ab. 180 mi. W of the city of Gilgit, on the Kunar River: frontier town and trading center.

Chittagong (chit'ą.gong). Division in East Bengal, E Pakistan, on the E shore of the Bay of Bengal. Capital, Chittagong; area, 11,765 sq. mi.; pop. 8,477,809 (1941).

Chittagong. District of the Chittagong division, East Bengal, Pakistan, located just E of the Sundarbans. Capital, Chittagong; area, 2,563 sq. mi.; pop. 2,153,296 (1941).

Chittagong. [Also, **Islamabad.**] Town in E Pakistan, in East Bengal, seaport and chief town of the Chittagong district, on the Karnafuli River: terminal of a narrow-gauge railroad to the tea and jute districts. 143,264 (1951).

Chittagong Hill Tracts. District in the Chittagong division, East Bengal, Pakistan, E of the Chittagong district: forest products and tea. Area, 5,138 sq. mi.; pop. 247,053 (1941).

Chitteldrug (chit'ęl.drög). See **Chitaldroog.**

Chittenden (chit'ęn.dęn), **Hiram Martin.** b. at Yorkshire, Cattaraugus County, N.Y., Oct. 25, 1858; d. Oct. 9, 1917. American military engineer and historian. Graduated from the U.S. Military Academy at West

Point in 1884 with the rank of second lieutenant of engineers, he subsequently held the rank of lieutenant-colonel of volunteers and was chief engineer of an army corps in the Spanish-American War. For a time before and again after that war he was in charge of road construction in the Yellowstone National Park and was also engaged in other federal engineering operations, including flood control and irrigation. In connection with these employments he published several books including *The Yellowstone National Park: Historical and Descriptive* (1893), *Reservoir Systems in the Great Lakes* (1898), and *Flood Control* (1915). He was the author also of two historical works of considerable authority, *The American Fur Trade of the Far West* (1901) and *History of Steamboat Navigation on the Missouri River* (1903), and he collaborated in the writing of *Life, Letters and Travels of Father Pierre Jean de Smet* (1905). Retired from the army with the rank of brigadier general in 1910, he wrote *War or Peace* (1911) and *Letters to an Ultra-Pacifist* (1916), the latter becoming popular enough to call for several editions. As president of the port commission of Seattle, Wash. (1911–15), he had much to do with the development of that city as one of the great seaports of the Pacific.

Chittenden, Kate Sara. b. at Hamilton, Ontario, Canada, April 17, 1856; d. Sept. 16, 1949. American organist and music educator. She was organist and choir director (1879–1906) at the Calvary Baptist Church, New York, first woman lecturer (1892–1919) under the New York Board of Education, and head (1899–1930) of the piano department of Vassar College. She wrote part of *The Synthetic Method*. Her compositions are mainly technical selections for the piano and pieces for children.

Chittenden, Martin. b. at Salisbury, Conn., March 12, 1763; d. at Williston, Vt., Sept. 5, 1840. American politician; son of Thomas Chittenden. He was governor of Vermont in the period 1813–15.

Chittenden, Russell Henry. b. at New Haven, Conn., Feb. 18, 1856; d. Dec. 26, 1943. American chemist, professor of physiological chemistry (1882–1922) at Yale University, and director (1898–1922) of the Sheffield Scientific School (Yale). He was graduated from Yale in 1875. Among his important publications are *Studies in Physiological Chemistry* and *Physiological Economy in Nutrition.*

Chittenden, Thomas. b. at East Guilford, Conn., Jan. 6, 1730; d. at Williston, Vt., Aug. 25, 1797. American politician; father of Martin Chittenden. He held public office in Connecticut before he moved (1774) to Vermont. In 1777 he aided in writing the proclamation of Vermont as an independent state (both New York and New Hampshire claimed the territory) and battled for recognition of its independence by the national government until 1791, when the state was admitted to the Union. He was first governor of Vermont, serving from 1778 to 1789 and from 1790 to 1797.

Chittim (kit′im). See **Kittim.**

Chitty (chit′i), **Edward.** b. 1804; d. near London, Sept. 28, 1863. English legal reporter and publisher; son of Joseph Chitty (1776–1841). He was the author of *Equity Index* (1831), and coauthor of two reports of cases in bankruptcy (1833–37, 1840).

Chitty, Joseph. b. 1776; d. at London, Feb. 17, 1841. English legal writer and special pleader; father of Joseph Chitty (d. 1838) and Edward Chitty (1804–63). His works include *A Treatise on Bills of Exchange* (1799), *A Treatise on the Law of Nations* (1812), *A Treatise on Criminal Law* (1816), *A Treatise on Commercial Law* (1818), *Reports of Cases on Practice and Pleading, with Notes* (1820–23), *On Commercial Contracts* (1823), and *A Treatise on Medical Jurisprudence* (1834).

Chitty, Joseph. d. 1838. English jurist; son of Joseph Chitty (1776–1841). He was the author of legal works, best known of which is *Chitty on Contracts* (1841).

Chitty, Sir **Joseph William.** b. 1828; d. 1899. English jurist. Barrister (1856), bencher (1875), and treasurer (1895) of Lincoln's Inn, he was appointed Queen's Counsel (1874) and lord justice of appeal (1897), and nominated (1898) a judge under the Benefices Act.

Chiusa San Michele (kyö′zä sän mē.kā′lā). [Also, **Chiusa.**] Village ab. 11 mi. NE of Turin, Italy, formerly called the "Gates of Lombardy." It has a noted Benedictine abbey.

Chiusi (kyö′sē). [Latin, **Clusium;** Etruscan, **Camars, Chamars.**] Town and commune in C Italy, in the *compartimento* (region) of Tuscany, in the province of Siena, situated near the Chiana River, between Siena and Orvieto. It is the seat of a bishopric, and a railroad junction; trades in olive oil, wine, and grain. The cathedral, built in the 6th century, was reconstructed in the 19th century. The town, originally one of the 12 confederated ancient Etruscan cities, has a museum of Etruscan antiquities. Considerable damage was suffered during World War II by some buildings of tourist interest. Pop. of commune, 8,043 (1936); of town, 2,534 (1936).

Chivasso (kē.väs′sō). Town and commune in NW Italy, in the *compartimento* (region) of Piedmont, in the province of Torino, situated near the junction of the Orco and Po rivers, ab. 15 mi. NE of Turin. The town has flour mills, distilleries, metallurgical, hat, leather, and candy manufactures. One of the earliest printing presses of Piedmont was operated here in 1486. The cathedral, in Romanesque style, dates from 1415. Buildings of interest to tourists were undamaged in World War II. Pop. of commune, 11,590 (1936); of town, 6,002 (1936).

Chivers (chiv′ėrz), **Thomas Holley.** b. at Digby Manor, Wilkes County, Ga., Oct. 18, 1809; d. at Decatur, Ga., Dec. 18, 1858. American poet. He practiced medicine for a short time after getting his M.D., but soon abandoned it for literature. He was associated (1840–49) with Edgar Allan Poe, who accused Chivers of plagiarism, a charge to which Chivers replied with a counterblast. To substantiate his claim Chivers published several articles in 1853, under the pseudonym "Fiat Justitia." Both Poe and Chivers, experimenting in similar manner in poetry, seem to have borrowed elements from each other. He was the author of the poems *Isadore* and *The Lost Pleiad.* He published nine volumes of verse and *Search After Truth; or, A New Revelation of the Psycho-physiological Nature of Man* (1848).

Chivery (chiv′ėr.i), **John.** "The sentimental son of a turnkey" in Charles Dickens's *Little Dorrit.* He passed his time in composing heartbreaking epitaphs. He was very weak and small, but "great of soul, poetical, expansive, faithful," and in love with Little Dorrit.

Chivilcoy (chē.ʙēl.koi′). City in E Argentina, in Buenos Aires province, ab. 100 mi. SW of the city of Buenos Aires. 23,386 (1947).

Chivula (chē.vō′lä). [Also: **Civula, Quibula.**] One of the 13 independent kingdoms of the Mbundu, a Bantu-speaking people of SW Africa, living in C Angola.

Chiwere (chē′we.re). Division of the Siouan North American Indian language family embracing the Iowa, Oto, and Missouri tribes.

Chixoy (chē.ʜoi′). River in C Guatemala. It flows N to the Usumacinta River to form part of the border between Mexico and Guatemala.

Chiyaka (chē.yä′kä). [Also: **Ciyaka, Quiaca, Quiyaka.**] One of the 13 independent kingdoms of the Mbundu, a Bantu-speaking people of SW Africa, living in C Angola.

Chkalov (chkä′lof). [Former name, **Orenburg.**] *Oblast* (region) in the U.S.S.R., in the Russian Soviet Federated Socialist Republic, located at the S end of the Ural Mountains, on the border of the Kazakh Soviet Socialist Republic. Most of the area is a plain but it is crossed from N to S by a range of hills, the S extention of the Ural Mountains. There are several growing mining and manufacturing cities in the area. The chief minerals now being worked are aluminum and nickel. Grazing is a very important occupation. Capital, Chkalov; area, 47,778 sq. mi.; pop. 1,677,013 (1939).

Chkalov. [Former name, **Orenburg.**] City in the U.S.S.R., the capital of the Chkalov *oblast* (region) of the Russian Soviet Federated Socialist Republic: a road and rail junction, grain-producing center, and the location of several large chemical plants. 172,975 (1939).

Chkalov, Valeri Pavlovich. b. 1904; d. 1938. Russian flier. A test pilot who had been awarded (1935) the Order of Lenin, he piloted the ANT-25 on a nonstop flight (June 18–20, 1937) 5,400 miles from Moscow to Vancouver, Wash., flying over the White Sea, Barents Sea, Franz Josef Land, the North Pole, the Arctic Ocean, and Canada.

Chladni (kläd′nē), **Ernst Florens Friedrich.** b. at Wittenberg, Prussia, Nov. 30, 1756; d. at Breslau, Prussia, April 4, 1827. German physicist, noted for his discoveries in acoustics. His experiments with sand spread on vibrating surfaces led to the name "Chladni figures" being applied to the figures thus developed in the sand. He also invented the euphonium, a musical instrument of vibrating glass. His works include *Entdeckungen über die Theorie des Klanges* (1802), *Die Akustik* (1802), and *Über Feuermeteore* (1819).

Chlodowech (klō′dō.veċh). See **Clovis.**

Chlodvald (klōd′väld) or **Chlodoald** (klō′dō.ald), Saint. See Saint **Cloud.**

Chlodwig (klōt′vēċh). German form of **Clovis.**

Chloe (klō′ē). Country maiden in love with Daphnis, in the Greek pastoral romance *Daphnis and Chloe*, attributed to Longus, a 3rd-century Greek poet.

Chloe. Shepherdess in Sir Philip Sidney's *Arcadia*.

Chloe. Ambitious wife of an honest, commonplace citizen in Ben Jonson's comedy *The Poetaster*.

Chloe. [Also, **Cloe.**] Wanton shepherdess in John Fletcher's *The Faithful Shepherdess*, intended as a contrast to the chaste Clorin, the faithful shepherdess.

Chlopicki (hlô.pets′kē), **Józef.** b. in Galicia, March 24, 1771; d. at Kraków, Poland, Sept. 30, 1854. Polish general. He fought on the side of the French in the Napoleonic Wars, and joined the Russian service in 1815, but resigned in 1818. He acted as dictator from Dec. 5, 1830, to Jan. 23, 1831, in the revolution which broke out at Warsaw on Nov. 29, 1830. Having resigned in deference to the opposition aroused by his policy, which sought to attain the objects of the revolution by diplomacy rather than by war, he fought with distinction against the Russians until wounded in February, 1831.

Chloris (klō′ris). In Greek mythology, the goddess of flowers; wife of Zephyrus. She is identified with the Roman goddess Flora.

Chlothar (klō′tär). German form of **Clotaire.**

Chlothilde (klō.til′dẹ). German form of **Clotilda.**

Chlumberg (klům′berk), **Hans Bardach Edler von.** b. at Vienna, June 30, 1897; d. at Leipzig, Germany, Oct. 25, 1930. Austrian dramatist who was a severe, effective critic of the post-World War I society.

Chlumec (hlö′mets). [German, **Kulm.**] Village in Czechoslovakia, in N Bohemia, between Teplice and Podmokly, ab. 48 mi. NW of Prague. Here, on Aug. 29 and 30, 1813, the Russians and Prussians under Ostermann and Kleist defeated the French under Vandamme, who was compelled to surrender. 539 (1947).

Chmielnicki or **Khmelnitsky** (hmyel.nēts′kē), **Bogdan.** b. c1593; d. Aug. 25, 1657. Cossack hetman of Polish descent, leader of the Cossack revolt c1648. Turning to Russia for aid, he agreed to the uniting of the Ukraine to Russia.

Chmielowski (hmye.lôf′skē), **Piotr.** b. 1848; d. 1904. Polish scholar. His monographs on Polish literary figures (Mickiewicz, Kraszewski, Słowacki, and others), together with his history of Polish literature (6 vols., 1886) are considered to constitute the foundation of modern literary scholarship in Poland.

Choapa (chō.ä′pä). [Also, **Chuapa.**] River in C Chile which separates the provinces of Coquimbo and Aconcagua, flowing W into the Pacific Ocean ab. 100 mi. N of Valparaíso. Length, ab. 120 mi.

Choaspes (kọ.as′pēz). Ancient name of the **Karkheh.**

Choate (chōt), **Joseph Hodges.** b. at Salem, Mass., Jan. 24, 1832; d. May 14, 1917. American lawyer, diplomat, and political figure. Graduated (1852) from Harvard and (1854) from the Harvard Law School, and admitted to the bar (1855) in Massachusetts, he moved to New York in the same year, later joining the law firm of Butler, Evarts and Southmayd, in which he became a partner. During his legal career of more than 55 years, he was engaged in a wide variety of cases covering wills, libel, corporation proceedings, and admiralty, and appeared many times before the U.S. Supreme Court. He served (1890) on the commission for the revision of the judicial system of New York state, was the president of the American Bar Association, and achieved fame as an after-dinner speaker at the many clubs of which he was a member, including the Union League Club, the Century Association, and the Pilgrim Society. A Republican, he was active as a party speaker from 1856 to 1916. He became (1899) ambassador at the Court of St. James's, serving in that post for six years, and in 1907 served as head of the U.S. delegation to the second Hague Conference. He was a founder and a trustee (1869–1917) of the American Museum of Natural History, an incorporator and trustee of the Metropolitan Museum of Art, and vice-president of the Carnegie Endowment for International Peace. See *Life of Joseph Hodges Choate as Gathered Chiefly from His Letters*, by Edward S. Martin (2 vols., 1920).

Choate, Rufus. b. at Ipswich, Mass., Oct. 1, 1799; d. at Halifax, Nova Scotia, July 13, 1859. American lawyer, orator, and statesman. He was graduated as valedictorian of his class from Dartmouth in 1819, admitted to the bar in 1823, and elected a representative to Congress from Massachusetts in 1830; reëlected in 1832, he resigned in 1834. In the period 1841–45 he served as successor in the Senate to Daniel Webster, who had been appointed secretary of state by President Harrison. Choate twice declined appointment to the U.S. Supreme Court. Tall, black-eyed, olive-skinned, preternaturally homely, evangelically zealous on behalf of his clients, gifted with an exuberant vocabulary and a voice of organlike sonority, he lavished learning and eloquence upon juries and judges, winning even the most hopeless cases in a manner long since legendary. A Whig in politics, he defended the Compromise of 1850 as necessary to avoid civil war. He nominated Webster for President in 1852, refusing the nomination himself when the convention became deadlocked. Choate's *Discourse Commemorative of Daniel Webster*, one of the greatest elegiac orations in the English language, reflects his life-long study of classical oratory. In the judgment of many legal historians, Rufus Choate stands preëminent among the greatest of American advocates. See *Works of Rufus Choate* (2 vols., 1862), and *Rufus Choate, Wizard of the Law* (1928) by Claude M. Fuess.

Chocano (chō.kä′nō), **José Santos.** b. 1875; killed in Chile, 1934. Peruvian modernist poet, considered by some critics to have been the best of his school. At various times a revolutionary nationalist, he was in his verse also a defender of the Indian and an opponent of North American imperialism. His poems, several of which have been translated into English, include *La Epopeya del Pacífico*, *Blasón*, *Caupolicán*, *Cuathemoc*, *Ollantá*, *El Sueño del caimán*, and *Tres notas de nuestra alma indígena*.

Choceň (hô′tsen, -tseny′). [German, **Chotzen.**] Town in Czechoslovakia, in NE Bohemia, situated on the Orlice River between Pardubice and Litomyšl, a station on the railroad line from Prague to Brno. It has machine and cement factories, cotton and lumber mills. 6,789 (1947).

Chocim (hô′chēm). See **Khotin.**

Chocó (chō.kō′). Indian tribe inhabiting the Atrato River valley and W lowland of Colombia, between ab. latitudes 3° and 7° N. Some of the Chocó groups are now mixed with Negroes. The language is generally regarded as forming an independent family.

Chocó. In South American colonial history, a province of the Spanish viceroyalty of New Granada, in what is now Colombia, embracing the Atrato valley and the region westward to the Pacific.

Chocó. Department in W Colombia. Capital, Quibdó; area, 17,981 sq. mi.; pop. 112,400 (est. 1950).

Chocolate Mill. Former name of **Central Falls.**

Chocolatière (sho.ko.lȧ.tyer), **La Belle.** Portrait by Jean Étienne Liotard of Annette Beldauf, a servant in a Vienna café. She married the Prince of Dietrichstein. The picture was acquired by the Dresden gallery.

Chocorua (shọ.kor′ö.ạ). One of the principal outlying peaks of the White Mountains in New Hampshire, N of Lake Winnipesaukee. 3,475 ft.

Choctaw (chok′tô). North American Indian tribe, formerly quite large, chiefly in C and N Mississippi, and W Alabama. Remnants of the tribe are now on reservations in Oklahoma. They speak a Natchez-Muskogean language.

Choctaw Trading House, Treaty of. Agreement concluded (Oct. 24, 1816) at St. Stephens, Ala., between the U.S. government and the Choctaw tribe, providing for the sale to the U.S. of Choctaw lands.

Choctaw Trail. Term applied to any given one of several Indian routes leading through the Choctaw lands (W Alabama and S Mississippi). The chief trail was that linking the Mobile region to the Mississippi River; another was later merged with the Natchez Trace.

Choderlos de Laclos (sho.der.lō dę là.klō), **Pierre Ambroise François.** See **Laclos, Pierre Ambroise François Choderlos de.**

Chodowiecki (ċhō.dō.vyets′kē), **Daniel Nikolaus.** b. at Danzig, 1726; d. at Berlin, 1801. Polish-German painter and engraver. His career was made entirely in Germany, though on one occasion at least he revisited his native city, sketching as he traveled. As a youth he had to work as a shop-clerk, and for years could study art only in spare time. He began by decorating snuffboxes and went on to miniatures and oil paintings, and finally in 1758 turned to engraving and thereby found his way to fame and fortune. His painting *The Departure of Jean Calas* attracted much attention, but the etching he made from it led to such a vogue for his work among collectors, and to so many commissions from publishers for illustrations to books and almanacs, that he was hard put to it to meet the demands, and in fact his health was affected. His book illustrations include designs for the works of Shakespeare, Cervantes, Schiller, Sterne, and Goldsmith, and altogether he engraved more than 2,000 plates. He combined a distinguished sense of design with striking realism in the depiction of scenes, characters, and costumes of his times, and he is considered a revealing commentator on the morals and manners of that period. In 1764 he was received into the Academy of Painting at Berlin, and he became its vice-director in 1788 and its director in 1797.

Chodźko (Hôch′kô), **Aleksander.** b. July 11, 1804; d. Dec. 20, 1891. Polish poet, Orientalist, and Slavic scholar. His works include *Grammaire persane* (1852) and translations from the Persian and Old Slavic.

Chodźko, Leonard Jakób. b. at Oborek, near Vilna, Russia, Nov. 6, 1800; d. at Poitiers, France, March 12, 1871. Polish historian. He was the author of *La Pologne historique, littéraire* (1835–37) and others.

Choëphoroe (kǫ.ef′ǫ.rē), **The.** Tragedy by Aeschylus, so named because of the chorus bearing vessels with offerings to the tomb of Agamemnon (the name literally meaning bearers of a drink-offering, or libation bearers). In it Orestes returns to Argos to avenge the murder of his father Agamemnon, and slays his mother Clytemnestra and her lover Aegisthus. It forms the second part of the trilogy *Oresteia.*

Choerilus (kē′ri.lus). fl. in the 6th century B.C. Athenian tragic poet; a contemporary of Aeschylus.

Choerilus of Samos (sā′mos). fl. in the 5th century B.C. Samian poet; a younger contemporary of Herodotus. He is noted for having attempted what was then a novelty: the relation in epic form of the Persian wars.

Choi (ċhoi). See **Khoi.**

Choibalsan (choi′bäl.sän′). See **San Beise Urgo.**

Choibalsang (choi′bäl.säng′). b. in Dornot, Outer Mongolia (now Mongolian People's Republic), 1895—. Mongolian revolutionary leader who rose to the post of premier. He was cofounder (1920), with Sukhe Bator, of the Mongolian People's Revolutionary Party, and aided in the establishment (1921) of the revolutionary government. After serving (1922–24) in the army created by Sukhe Bator, he studied (1924–25) in Russia. He became commander in chief of the army (1925) and foreign minister (1929). Opposing the ultra-leftist policies of the early 1930's, he became (1937) vice-premier and later (1939) premier of the Mongolian People's Republic.

Choice, The. Four-act play (1919) by Alfred Sutro.

Choir Invisible, The. Romance by James Lane Allen, published as *John Gray* in 1893 and revised and renamed in 1897.

Choiseul (shwà.zėl), **César,** Duc **de.** [Additional title, Sieur **du Plessis-Praslin**; also called Marshal **du Plessis.**] b. at Paris, Feb. 12, 1598; d. there, Dec. 23, 1675. French general. He distinguished himself at the siege of La Rochelle (1628), served in Piedmont (1636–45), became marshal in 1645, and won a decisive victory over the Spaniards at Trancheron (1648). He commanded the royal forces in the war of the Fronde, and defeated Turenne at Rethel in 1650. He was created duke in 1663.

Choiseul or **Choiseul-Amboise** (shwà.zėl.äṅ.bwàz), **Étienne François,** Duc **de.** [Early title, Comte de **Stainville.**] b. June 28, 1719; d. at Paris, May 8, 1785. French statesman. He entered the army in his youth, and in 1759 attained the rank of lieutenant general. Through the influence of Madame de Pompadour, mistress of Louis XV of France, he was appointed ambassador to Rome in 1756. Some months after this appointment he succeeded the Abbé Bernis as ambassador to Vienna. In November, 1758, he was appointed minister and created Duc de Choiseul (having hitherto been known as Comte de Stainville). On his accession to office he continued the alliance of France with Maria Theresa of Austria in the Seven Years' War. He sought to prosecute hostilities against England with vigor in Europe, to the neglect of the proper defense of the colonies, a policy which resulted in the loss of Canada and Cape Breton Island to England, and of Louisiana to Spain, at the peace of Paris in 1763. He negotiated the Family Compact between the Bourbon sovereigns of France, Spain, and the Two Sicilies in 1761, and in 1764 aided in suppressing the Jesuits in France. He was dismissed from office in 1770 through the influence of the king's new mistress, Madame du Barry.

Choiseul-Gouffier (shwà.zėl.gö.fyā), Comte **de.** [Full name, **Marie Gabriel Florent Auguste de Choiseul-Gouffier.**] b. at Paris, Sept. 27, 1752; d. at Aachen, Germany, June 20, 1817. French diplomat and archaeologist. His chief work is *Voyage pittoresque de la Grèce* (1782; new ed., 1841).

Choisy (shwà.zē), **François Auguste.** b. at Vitry-le-François, France, 1841; d. 1909. French archaeologist, who served as chief engineer and professor of architecture at the École des ponts et chaussées. He was the author of *L'Art de bâtir chez les Romains* (The Roman Art of Building, 1873), and *Études épigraphiques sur l'architecture greque* (Epigraphic Studies of Greek Architecture, 1884).

Choisy, François Timoléon de. b. at Paris, Aug. 16, 1644; d. Oct. 2, 1724. French ecclesiastic and littérateur. His works include *Histoire de France sous les règnes de Saint Louis, de Philippe de Valois . . .* (1750), *Histoire de madame la comtesse des Barres* (1735), and *Mémoires pour servir à l'histoire de Louis XIV* (1727).

Choisy-le-Roi (shwà.zē.lę.rwà). Town in N France, in the department of Seine. Suburb of Paris, situated on the Seine River, ab. 7 mi. SE of the city. It is a river port. Rouget de Lisle died here. 27,333 (1946).

Chojnice (Hoi.nē′tse). [German, **Konitz.**] Town in N Poland, in the *województwo* (province) of Pomorze, situated near the former German border, ab. 64 mi. SW of Danzig: lumber trade; sawmills; machine factory. In 1454 the Teutonic Order defeated a Polish army here; it was the last victory of the Order. The town came under Prussian rule in 1772. In 1900 it was the scene of a ritual murder trial. It was incorporated into Poland in 1919. In World War II, it was occupied by the Germans on Sept. 3, 1939, and was returned to Poland in 1945. Pop. 12,444 (1946).

Chojnów (Hoi′nöf). [German, **Hainau, Haynau.**] Town in SW Poland, in the *województwo* (province) of Wrocław: sugar refinery; paper and leather manufactures. There is a castle dating from the 16th century. Here, on May 26, 1813, the Prussians defeated the French. The town belonged to Prussia from 1742 to 1945. The German population has emigrated since World War II. 11,114 (1939); 5,467 (1946).

Choke (chōk), **General Cyrus.** In Charles Dickens's *Martin Chuzzlewit,* an American, "one of the most remarkable men in the country," encountered by Martin Chuzzlewit.

Chokwe (chōk′wā). [Also: **Bachokwe, Bajok, Batshioko, Batshiokwe, Kioko, Kiokque, Koque, Tsokwe, Tutshokwe.**] Bantu-speaking people of C Africa, inhabiting NE Angola and SW Belgian Congo. A Southern Chokwe group inhabits the upper Kasai River, near Luau; a large central group lives between the Kasai and Cuilo rivers, W of Monana; and a small northern group occupies an area S and W of the Kasai River and E of the Loango River. Tradition states that the Chokwe were once a part of the Lunda. They have matrilineal descent. They practice hoe agriculture, and their principal crops are cassava, maize, and sorghum.

Chol (chōl). [Also: **Choles, Cholti.**] Tribe or division of the Maya Indians in Chiapas, Mexico.

Chol. Language in the Mayan linguistic stock.

Chola (chō′lạ). Ancient Tamil kingdom in S India, in the present area of Madras state. It was an independent kingdom as early as the 4th century B.C., but its period of great power dated from the 10th to the 14th centuries A.D. During this period it was supreme in S India, and extended its original area (a 300-mile strip along the coast from Nellore to Pudukottai) by the conquest of Ceylon (ab. 1000 A.D.) and parts of the Deccan. In 1310 A.D. Chola was overwhelmed by the Moslem invasion of South India under Malik Kafur. It never recovered its former importance. The chief capital was Tanjore.

Choleric Man, The. Play by Richard Cumberland, produced in 1774.

Cholet (sho.le). Town in W France, in the department of Maine-et-Loire, ab. 33 mi. SW of Angers. It is an industrial town, specializing in the manufacture of table linen, handkerchiefs, and cotton goods. It also ships to the Paris markets great quantities of fattened cattle, hogs, and sheep. The city suffered considerable damage in the Vendéaŋ wars, when it was taken and retaken several times by the royalist and republican armies. 26,086 (1946).

Chollup (chol′up), **Major Hannibal.** In Charles Dickens's *Martin Chuzzlewit*, an American, a worshiper of freedom, lynch-law and slavery.

Cholmondeley (chum′li), **George.** [Title, 2nd Earl of **Cholmondeley.**] d. May 7, 1733. English general and poet.

Cholmondeley, Mary. [Pseudonym, **Pax.**] b. at Hodnet, Shropshire, England; d. July 5, 1925. English novelist. Among her best-known works are *The Danvers Jewels* (1887; written under the pseudonym Pax), *Diana Tempest* (1893), *Red Pottage* (1899), *Prisoners* (1906), *The Lowest Rung* (1908), *Hand on the Latch* (1909), and *Under One Roof* (1918).

Cholon (chọ.lun′; French, sho.lôṅ). City in Indochina, in N central Cochin-China (South Viet-Nam), just SW of Saïgon: seaport. There are rice mills, sawmills, soap factories, fruit-packing plants, and cigarette factories here. 207,055 (est. 1940).

Cholula (chō.lö′lä). [Full name, **Cholula de Rivadabia** (dā rē.bä.ᴛʜä′byä); also, **San Pedro Cholula.**] Town in SE Mexico, in Puebla state: an Indian town, inhabited at the time of the Spanish conquest by an independent tribe of Nahuatl Indians. It lies ab. 60 mi. SE of Mexico City, ab. 15 mi. from the foot of the great volcano on the E, and, in a direct line, 5 or 6 mi. W of the city of Puebla de Zaragoza. The town of Cholula is surrounded by five villages, all except two of which are modern. Previous to the 16th century Cholula had a population of not over 25,000, and these were congregated in the central settlement. The average elevation of the district is 7,000 ft.; pop. 8,424 (1940).

Cholula. Archaeological site in W Puebla, Mexico, largely coextensive with the modern town of the same name. Its principal feature is an enormous truncated pyramid, made of sun-dried bricks, ab. 1,000 ft. square at the base and originally ab. 200 ft. high. The earlier, lower strata of the pyramid are associated with the Toltec, the later with the early Aztec culture. The site was occupied, and successively reconstructed throughout the period from c300 A.D. to the Spanish conquest, and the great pyramid now has a church on its summit.

Choluteca (chō.lö.tä′kä). Department in S Honduras, on the Nicaraguan border: coffee, livestock, and rubber. Capital, Choluteca; area, 1,662 sq. mi.; pop. 107,271 (1950).

Choluteca. Town in S Honduras, capital of Choluteca department: center for cattle, coffee, and minerals. It was founded in the 16th century. 22,139 (1950).

Chomedey (shom.dā), **Paul de.** See **Maisonneuve, Sieur de.**

Chomette (sho.met), **René.** See **Clair, René.**

Chomo-lungma (chō′mō.lüng′mä). Tibetan name of **Everest, Mount.**

Chomůtov (ʜō′mö.tôf). [German, **Komotau.**] City in Czechoslovakia, in NW Bohemia, situated on the S slope of the Krusnehory Mountains, between Most and Kadaň, ab. 52 mi. NW of Prague. The market place is surrounded by arcades. There is a 16th-century church and a municipal museum. The industries produce tubes, iron, paper, hats, beer, flour, and various food products. Lignite coal mines are in the vicinity. The town was founded in the 11th century and suffered considerable destruction during the Hussite wars and the Thirty Years' War. 26,697 (1947).

Chon (tsōn). See **Tehuelche.**

Chone (chō′nā). City in W Ecuador, in Manabí province. 21,834 (est. 1944).

Choniates (kō.ni.ā′tēz), **Nicetas.** See **Nicetas Acominatus.**

Chono (chō′nō). Indian tribe, now extinct, which inhabited the Chilean coastal islands from S of the island of Chiloé to ab. latitude 48° S. The Chono were closely related to the Alacaluf.

Chonos Archipelago (chō′nōs). [Spanish, **Archipiélago de los Chonos.**] Group of ab. 120 islands in the Pacific Ocean along the coast of S Chile, in the provinces of Aisén and Chonos.

Chontales (chōn.tä′lās). Department in S Nicaragua, E of Lake Nicaragua: noted for its mineral wealth. Area, 4,170 sq. mi.; pop. 50,411 (1950).

Chontals (chōn.tälz′). Division of the Maya Indians, located mainly in the state of Tabasco, Mexico.

Chontaquiro (chōn.tä.kē′rō). See under **Piro,** South American Indians.

Chonyi (chōn′yē). One of nine Bantu-speaking peoples of SE Kenya, in E Africa, known collectively as Nyika.

Chopi (chō′pē). [Also: **Batchopi, Tshopi, Tsopi, Vachopi.**] Bantu-speaking people of SE Africa, inhabiting S Mozambique, S of Inhambane Bay. Their population is estimated at ab. 175,000 (by H. P. Junod, "The VaChopi of Portuguese East Africa," in *The Bantu Tribes of South Africa,* edited by A. M. Duggan-Cronin, 1936). They are divided into three subgroups, the Chopi proper in the center, the Lenge in the S, and the Khoka in the N. They are completely surrounded by the Tonga of S Mozambique, who have strongly influenced their language and culture. They have patrilineal sibs. They practice hoe agriculture and cattle herding, with the cattle complex, and their principal food is maize.

Chopin (sho.paṅ), **Frédéric François.** b. at Zelazowa-Wola, near Warsaw, Poland, Feb. 22, 1810; d. at Paris, Oct. 17, 1849. Composer and pianist, noted for his piano works. His father was French, his mother a Pole. His earliest compositions included dances, mazurkas, and polonaises. His masters were a Bohemian, Zwyny, and Elsner, the director of the school of music at Warsaw. At 19 he was considered a finished virtuoso. He began at this age, with his two concertos and some smaller works, to give concerts at Vienna, Munich, and Paris. In the latter place he settled. About 1837 began a romantic connection with George Sand. In 1838 she took him to Majorca for his health, and nursed him there. She left him after a friendship of eight years, and he lived in retirement, giving lessons and composing. His works include two concertos for piano and orchestra, 27 études, 52 mazurkas, many preludes, nocturnes, rondos, and 16 Polish songs. His romantic, patriotic compositions enjoy wide popularity.

Chopin (shō′pan), **Kate O'Flaherty.** b. at St. Louis, Feb. 8, 1851; d. Aug. 22, 1904. American author, noted for tales dealing with the Creoles, the Cajuns, and the Negroes she came to know during her years in Louisiana.

Choptank (chop′tangk). River and estuary in E Maryland which flows into Chesapeake Bay ab. 25 mi. SE of Annapolis. Length, ab. 100 mi.; navigable for ab. 45 mi.

Choragic Monument of Lysicrates (lī.sik′rạ.tēz). See **Lysicrates, Choragic Monument of.**

Choral Symphony. Name applied to the ninth symphony (Opus 125) in D minor by Ludwig van Beethoven, first performed at the Vienna Kärnthnerthor Theater, on May 7, 1824. The fourth movement is a setting of Schiller's poem *An die Freude* (*Ode to Joy*) and incorporates a chorus and four solo voices.

Chorazin (kọ.rā′zin). In New Testament geography, a city in Palestine, situated near the NW shore of the Sea of Galilee, 2½ mi. N of Tel Hum.

Chorcaighe (kôr′kiċh). An Irish name of **Cork.**

Chorea Machabaeorum (kō′rę.ạ mak″ạ.bę.ō′rum). Latin name of the **Dance of Death.**

Chorgun (chôr′gun). See **Chernaya.**

Choris (ċhō′ris), **Ludwig.** b. at Ekaterinoslav (now Dnepropetrovsk), Russia, March 22, 1795; murdered near Jalapa, Mexico, March 22, 1828. Russian traveler and painter. He illustrated the works *Voyage pittoresque autour du monde* (1821–23) and *Vues et paysages des régions équinoxiales* (1826).

Chorizontes (kō.ri.zon′tēz). Name given to the separatists, a party among the older critics who maintained that the *Iliad* and *Odyssey* were by different authors and belonged to different ages.

Chorley (chôr′li). Municipal borough, coal-mining town, and manufacturing center in NW England, in Lancashire, ab. 8 mi. SE of Preston, ab. 202 mi. NW of London by rail. It has manufactures of fine cotton yarns. 32,636 (1951).

Chorley, Henry Fothergill. [Pseudonym, **Paul Bell.**] b. at Blackley Hurst, Lancashire, England, Dec. 15, 1808; d. at London, Feb. 16, 1872. English journalist, novelist, dramatist, and poet, music critic and reviewer for the London *Athenaeum.* His works include *Modern German Music* (1854) and *Thirty Years' Musical Recollections* (1862). He also wrote a number of unsuccessful novels, including *Roccabella* which was published under the pseudonym Paul Bell, and several dramas, among them *Old Love and New Fortune.*

Choromański (Hô.rô.män′skē), **Michał.** b. 1904—. Polish novelist and playwright. Author of the best-seller *Envy and Medicine* (1932; later translated into English), he was a leading exponent of the psychological novel in Poland between the wars. He has become a resident of Canada.

Choron (sho.rôn), **Alexandre Étienne.** b. at Caen, France, Oct. 21, 1772; d. at Paris, June 29, 1834. French musical writer, teacher, and composer. He wrote *Principes de composition des écoles d'Italie* (1808), *Dictionnaire des musiciens* (with F. J. M. Fayolle, 2 vols., 1810–11), *Méthode concertante de musique à plusieurs parties* (1817), *Méthode de plain-chant* (1818), and *Encyclopédie musicale* (6 vols., 1836–38).

Chorotega (chō.rǫ.tā′gą). Collective term for several Indian tribes which occupied areas along the Pacific coast of Nicaragua and Costa Rica at the time of the Spanish conquest. They are thought to have migrated to this area from C Mexico several centuries prior to the conquest; their languages, which are now extinct, show affiliation to the Otomian language family of C Mexico.

Chorrillos (chôr.rē′yōs). City in W Peru, in Lima department, on the Pacific coast ab. 10 mi. S of Lima: noted resort. Here the Peruvians under Iglesias and Cáceres were defeated by the Chileans on Jan. 13, 1881, Iglesias surrendering with 5,000 men. Pop. under 5,000 (1940).

Chorum (chō.röm′). See **Çorum.**

Chorzów (Hô′zhöf). City in SW Poland, in the *województwo* (province) of Śląsk (Silesia), ab. 5 mi. NW of Katowice. It was formed in 1934 through a fusion of the formerly independent communities of Chorzów, Królewska Huta (German, Königshütte), and Hajduki Nowi. It has numerous coal and iron-ore mines, blast furnaces, iron foundries, iron and steel works, steel construction works, leather and textile industries, and meat-packing establishments; it has one of the largest nitrogen fertilizer plants in Europe, erected by the Germans during World War I, taken over by the Poles after 1922, and later enlarged. There are also cement works and glass and pottery manufactures. Chorzów has a number of educational institutions. The city became part of Poland when the Upper Silesian coal-mining district was divided between Germany and Poland after the plebiscite of 1921. Pop. 110,675 (1946), 130,901 (est. 1950).

Chosen (chō.sen). Japanese name of **Korea.**

Choshi (chō.shē). City in SE Honshu, Japan, ab. 75 mi. by rail E of Tokyo. Located at the mouth of the Tone River, it is an important fishing center for fisheries of mackerel, tuna, bonito, and sardines. The chief industry of the city is the processing and shipping of fish, including canned, and dried and salted fish. 73,512 (1950).

Choson (chō.son). Korean name of **Korea.**

Chosroes (koz′rǭ.ēz). Greek form of **Khosru.**

Chota Nagpur (chō′tą näg′pör). [Also, **Chutia Nagpur.**] Former division of Bengal, India. In December, 1911, Chota Nagpur, Orissa, and Bihar were united into a lieutenant-governorship; Orissa became a separate province in 1936, and a state in 1948, and Chota Nagpur remained part of the province (now state) of Bihar.

Chota Nagpur Tributary States. [Also, **Chutia Nagpur Tributary States.**] Former name of certain Indian states. They are the seven tributary states of Chang Bakar, Koria, Sirguja, Udaipur, Jashpur (all transferred in 1905 to the Central Provinces, now Madhya Pradesh), Gangpur, and Bonai (later attached to Orissa), and the two feudatory states of Kharsawan and Saraikela (area, 602 sq. mi.; merged in 1948 with Bihar state).

Chotin (Ho.tyen′). See **Khotin.**

Chott Djerid (shot je.rēd′). See under **Beled el Jerid.**

Chotusice (Hô′tö.sē.tse). [German, **Chotusitz** (ċhō′tö-zits).] Village in Czechoslovakia, in C Bohemia, E of Kutná Hora and N of Čáslav, ab. 45 mi. E of Prague. Here, on May 17, 1742, the Prussians under Frederick the Great defeated the Austrians under Charles of Lorraine. 1,053 (1947).

Chotzen (ċhō′tsen). German name of **Choceň.**

Chotzinov (shot′si.nôf, -nof), **Samuel.** b. at Vitebsk, Russia, July 4, 1889—. American pianist and music critic. He emigrated to the U.S. at the age of six, and was educated at Columbia University. He served as accompanist for Heifetz, Alma Gluck, and Zimbalist on their concert tours. He succeeded Deems Taylor as music critic (1925–30) for the New York *World,* and in 1934 became critic for the New York *Post;* he has also been music lecturer at the Carnegie Foundation. He is the author of *Eroica,* a novelized life of Beethoven.

Chou (jō). Third Chinese dynasty and the longest; its traditional dates are from 1122 to 256 B.C., although it may have begun about a century later. The Chou tribe grew to dominate the Wei River valley, moved E to conquer Shang, and eventually controlled most of China N of the Yellow River. The capitals were near modern Sian (Changan), and the large territories were governed by a feudal system allotting local authority to relatives and friends of the ruling house. Internal jealousies and strife so weakened the royal power that it was victimized by neighboring barbarian tribes and by 771 B.C. was forced to flee eastward for safety and make its capital at Loyang. The period before this date is known as Western Chou and the later period as Eastern Chou. The continuing struggle for power among the states resulted in complete victory for Ch'in in 256 B.C. and the death of the last Chou ruler in 249. Chou religion included belief in a supreme god, in lesser nature gods and in the culture heroes of the race, the legendary founders of characteristic Chinese culture traits: agriculture, weaving, pottery making, hydraulic engineering, etc. These, added to the Shang beliefs in ancestor worship and divination, made up the native religion of the Chinese. Eastern Chou was the period of the philosophers Confucius, Mencius, Mo-tzu, Lao-tzu, Chuang-tzu, and the other molders of Chinese thought; the gradual compilation of their teachings and the commentaries thereon made up the *Classics* which have been the cornerstone of Chinese culture ever since. The material culture of Late Chou included the use of iron and the skillful inlay of gold and silver in bronze weapons and implements. The Chinese of this period were well advanced in astronomy, used the traction plow, and minted round coins; in warfare they used the crossbow and sword, and their cavalry was dressed in boots and trousers. They built extensive canals for irrigation and reservoirs for drought prevention. Series of border walls were built in the north as protection against nomadic incursions into the agricultural areas of the Yellow River plain.

Chouans (shö′ąnz; French, shwäñ). During the French Revolution, a name given to the royalist insurgents of Brittany. The name is sometimes thought to be derived from the appellation *chat-huant* (meaning "screechowl") given to their leader Jean Cottereau.

Chouans (shwäñ), **Les.** [Original title, **Le Dernier Chouan.**] Novel by Honoré de Balzac, published in 1829. It has been dramatized.

Chouart (shwȧr, shö.ȧr), **Médart.** See **Groseilliers, Sieur de.**

Chou En-lai (jō′ en′lī′). b. at Huaian, Kiangsu, China, 1896—. Chinese Communist leader, best known as a diplomat and publicist. He came from an official Mandarin family. While studying at Nankai University he was imprisoned (1919) for leading a demonstration against China's treatment in the Versailles peace treaty. He went to France (1920), where he helped organize the Chinese Communist Youth Party. Returning (1924) to China, he became secretary of the Whampoa Academy and chief of its political department under Chiang Kai-shek, participated (1927) in the Shanghai and Nanchang Uprising, and joined (1931) the Kiangsi Soviet, holding a succession of posts. He became (1937) liaison officer between the Kuomintang and Communist parties during the war, and served (1946) as chief Communist negotiator in the three-cornered Marshall negotiations with the Political Consultative Council. In 1949 he was elected premier and foreign minister of the People's Republic of China. He is the model for Kyo Gisors, the hero of *Man's Fate*, by André Malraux.

Choukoutien (jō'kō'tyen'). Village in NE China, in Hopeh province, ab. 30 mi. SW of Peiping. In a cave nearby were discovered the teeth, jaws, and skull caps of an early hominid since known as *Sinanthropus pekinensis*, or Peking Man. Remains of more than 40 individuals were found. The site has early Pleistocene characteristics, and the period of Peking Man's existence has been estimated very roughly at 300,000 to 500,000 years ago.

Choumen (shö'men). See **Shumen.**

Chou Shan (jō' shän'). See **Chu Shan.**

Chouteau (shö.tō'), **Auguste Pierre.** b. at St. Louis, Mo., May 9, 1786; d. Dec. 25, 1838. American fur trader and pioneer; son of Jean Pierre Chouteau (1758–1849) and brother of Pierre Chouteau (1789–1865). He accompanied (1807) Ensign Nathaniel Pryor's expedition to restore the Mandan chief, Big White, to his tribe, accompanied (1809) the expedition to the mouth of Knife River, and led (1815), with Jules de Mun, a trading and trapping expedition to the upper Arkansas River, where he was captured (1817). In 1823 he bought the trading house of Brand and Barbour near the junction of the Verdigris and Arkansas rivers.

Chouteau, Jean Pierre. b. at New Orleans, 1758; d. at what is now St. Louis, Mo., in July, 1849. American pioneer; father of Auguste Pierre Chouteau (1786–1838) and Pierre Chouteau (1789–1865). He was associated with his brother, René Auguste Chouteau, in the founding of St. Louis in 1764.

Chouteau, Pierre. b. at St. Louis, Mo., Jan. 19, 1789; d. there, Sept. 6, 1865. American fur trader; son of Jean Pierre Chouteau (1758–1849) and brother of Auguste Pierre Chouteau (1786–1838).

Chouteau, René Auguste. b. at New Orleans, 1749; d. at what is now St. Louis, Mo., Feb. 24, 1829. American pioneer, one of the founders of St. Louis. With his brother, Jean Pierre Chouteau, he joined in August, 1763, the expedition of Laclède to establish the fur trade in the region watered by the Missouri River and its tributaries, and was in command of a party which on Feb. 15, 1764, began the establishment of a trading post called St. Louis on the site of the present city of that name in Missouri.

Chowbent (chou'bent). See **Atherton.**

Chowchilla (chou.chil'ạ). City in C California, ab. 38 mi. NW of Fresno, in the San Joaquin valley. It is a local trade and processing center in an agricultural area producing cotton, dairy products, grain, and fruit. 3,893 (1950).

Choyo (chō.yō). See under **Shinto.**

Chrestien (krā.tyaṅ), **Florent.** b. at Orléans, France, 1541; d. at Vendôme, France, 1596. French satirist and composer of Latin verse. He was one of the authors of *Satyre Ménippée.*

Chrétien (or **Chrestien**) **de Troyes** (krā.tyaṅ dẹ trwà). fl. c1150–90. Most famous of the medieval French writers of metrical romances, and the first to relate original stories concerning King Arthur and the knights of the Round Table in a modern language. All that is known of his life is derived from the dedications of his works. He dedicated the third of his extant romances to Marie, Countess of Champagne, probably soon after her marriage in 1164; and the last of his works to Count Philip of Flanders probably about ten years before the latter went as a crusader to the Holy Land in 1191. Chrétien's works are (in chronological order): (1) translations of Ovid's *Ars Amatoria* and *Remedia Amoris* and of parts of the *Metamorphoses* (all now lost); (2) a story about Mark and Isolt (also lost, but probably a version of the Tristan romance); (3) *Erec et Enide* (the earliest Arthurian romance in French); (4) *Cligés* (an Arthurian romance which mingles Celtic and Byzantine themes); (5) *Lancelot, ou le Chevalier de la Charrette;* (6) *Guillaume d'Angleterre* (of uncertain date and attribution; not an Arthurian romance, but a romanticized saint's life); (7) *Yvain, ou le Chevalier au Lion* (his masterpiece from the point of view of composition and style); (8) *Perceval, ou le Conte du Graal* (the first appearance of the Holy Grail in literature; left unfinished by Chrétien, but continued by four other versifiers who wrote at intervals over a period of about 50 years, spinning the story out to a total of more than 60,000 lines). The *Erec et Enide* and the *Cligés* were written before 1164; the *Yvain* and the *Lancelot* after 1164, but before 1172; and the *Perceval* before 1191, probably about 1180–81. Chrétien wrote his *Perceval* earlier than Robert de Boron, who also composed an early verse romance on the subject of the Holy Grail (associating it for the first time with the vessel of the Last Supper and with the legend of Joseph of Arimathea), but there is no evidence of any connection between the two writers. The works of both Chrétien and Robert de Boron were, in the early years of the 13th century, used as the bases of voluminous romances in French prose, which also drew from other sources and which in turn served as the sources of inspiration for Malory, and through him for Tennyson and Swinburne. Through the direct influence of Chrétien on Wolfram von Eschenbach (whose *Parzival* was written about 1202), the *Conte du Graal* or Perceval story of Chrétien served as the ultimate source of Wagner's opera *Parsifal.*

Chriemhild (krēm'hild). See **Kriemhild.**

Chrisanthos (ḉhrē'sän.thôs), Archbishop. See **Chrysanthos** or **Chrisanthos,** Archbishop.

Chris Christopherson (kris' kris'tọ.fėr.sọn). See **Christopherson, Chris.**

Chrisman (kris'mạn). Unincorporated community in SW California, in Ventura County NW of Los Angeles. 4,211 (1950).

Chrisman, Arthur Bowie. b. near White Post, Va., July 16, 1889; d. near Clinton, Ark., in February, 1953. American writer awarded (1925) the John Newbery Medal for his collection of Chinese tales for children, *Shen of the Sea.* He was the author also of *The Wind That Wouldn't Blow* (1927) and other children's books.

Christ (krīst), **Jesus.** See **Jesus.**

Christ (krist), **Wilhelm von.** b. at Geisenheim, Germany, Feb. 8, 1831; d. at Munich, Feb. 8, 1906. German scholar in the field of Greek literature. During his long term as a professor at the University of Munich (1860–1902), he prepared new editions of Homer, Pindar, and Aristotle, and wrote two authoritative works in the field of Greek studies, *Metrik der Griechen und Römer* (1879) and *Geschichte der griechischen Literatur* (1888).

Christabel (kris'tạ.bel). Heroine of Samuel Taylor Coleridge's poem of that name, published in 1816. The gentle and pious daughter of Sir Leoline, she is induced by a powerful spell to bring into her father's castle the enchantress who calls herself the Lady Geraldine.

Christabel. Daughter of a king who secretly betrothed herself to Sir Cauline, in the old ballad concerning Sir Cauline. The king discovered the betrothal and Sir Cauline performed prodigies of valor to win her. He was at length killed while freeing her from a giant, and she "burste her gentle hearte in twayne."

Christadelphians (kris.tạ.del'fi.ạnz). Religious denomination. This sect was founded by John Thomas, who was born at London, England, in 1805, the son of an independent minister and himself a physician. Coming to the U.S. in 1832, before the year was out he joined the Disciples of Christ (Campbellites), but in 1834 began to rally followers who called themselves Christadelphians ("Brothers of Christ"), as a sign that they repudiated the name "Christian" because they said that it had become associated with all things anti-Christian. The Christadelphian creed is trinitarian, and calls for acceptance of the Scriptures as understood by Thomas and his followers. They expect the early Second Coming of Christ (the founder himself predicted that it would begin in the period 1866–68 and would be accomplished in 42 years) and believe that only those of their faith will arise from the dead and live eternally in bodily form. They regard themselves not as a new sect but as a revival of the Christian congregations of the 1st century. They observe uniform practices but have no central authority nor headquarters, and do not hold general assemblies. The denomination numbers only a very few thousand adherents.

Christ à la Paille (krēst à lȧ pȧy'). [Eng. trans., "*Christ of the Straw.*"] Painting by Peter Paul Rubens, acquired by the museum of Antwerp, Belgium. It represents the dead Christ lying on a stone bench covered with straw, supported by Joseph of Arimathea, with the Virgin, Saint John, and the Magdalen grieving. On the side panels are Saint John the Apostle and a Virgin and Child.

Christ Among the Doctors. Painting by Ingres, acquired by the collection of the Musée Municipal at Montauban, France.

Christ Bearing the Cross. Statue by Michelangelo, in the church of Santa Maria sopra Minerva, Rome.

Christchurch (krīst'chėrch, krīs'-). Municipal borough, seaport, and seaside resort in S England, in Southampton (administrative county of the geographical county of Hampshire), situated at the confluence of the rivers Avon and Stour, ab. 104 mi. SW of London by rail. The river Stour divides Bournemouth and Christchurch. It is a rapidly developing residential area and seaside resort. Christchurch has a notable priory church. 20,506 (1951).

Christchurch. City in New Zealand, situated on the S side of Pegasus Bay at the base of Banks Peninsula, in NE South Island. It is the chief town of Canterbury district, and the seat of Canterbury University College (a branch of the University of New Zealand) and a school for the deaf. Its harbor is Port Lyttelton. Pop., with suburbs, 174,221 (1951).

Christ Church. One of the largest colleges of Oxford University, England, founded in 1525 by Cardinal Wolsey as Cardinal College, remodeled as King Henry VIII's College in 1532, and refounded as Christ Church by Henry VIII in 1546. The gateway, in Perpendicular Gothic style, to the great quadrangle ("Tom Quad"), which is the largest in Oxford, opens beneath the Tom Tower, whose upper stage was built by Wren in 1682. On the south side of the quadrangle is the beautiful Perpendicular Gothic hall, ab. 115 by ab. 40 ft., and ab. 50 ft. high to the carved oak ceiling. It possesses many fine old and modern portraits.

Christchurch, Mount. Mountain in Antarctica, in the Queen Alexandra Range, rising on the S side of the Shackleton Inlet, on the W side of the Ross Shelf Ice, in ab. 82°34′ S., 163°10′ E. It was discovered by the National Antarctic Expedition (1901–04), under the command of Captain Robert F. Scott, who named this mountain for the city of Christchurch, New Zealand. Elevation, ab. 4,700 ft.

Christ Crucified between the Two Thieves. Fresco by Fra Angelico, in the Convent of San Marco, Florence. The mourning spectators include the most prominent figures of the church, and particularly of the order of Saint Dominic.

Christensen (kris'tẹn.sẹn), **Jens Christian.** [Also, **J. C. Christensen.**] b. at Paabøl, Denmark, Nov. 21, 1856; d. at He, Denmark, Dec. 19, 1930. Danish statesman who, as premier (1905–09), carried through extensive though moderate reforms in local suffrage, the church and school systems, taxes and tariffs, and the legal system. His cabinet faced a violent campaign when the minister of justice was arrested (1908) as a swindler. Charges were brought against Christensen, who was exonerated at a state trial (1910). He was concerned particularly with the farm population and its interests and demands. He taught (1886–1901) school in a village, served (1888–91) as a parish council member, was elected (1897) chairman of the Left Reform Party committee, served (1890–1924) in the *Folketing* (parliament), was minister (1901–05) for church and school affairs, exerting the dominant influence in the government, and became (1905) premier and minister of defense. He was elected (1908) chairman of the *Venstre* (Left, or Liberal) Party, was minister of defense (1908), served (1916–18) as minister without portfolio during World War I, and held (1920–22) the post of minister of church affairs. In 1924 he withdrew from political activity.

Christensen Peak. See **Lars Christensen Peak.**

Christian (kris'chạn). d. at Tusculum, Italy, Aug. 25, 1183. German prelate. Made archbishop of Mainz in September, 1165, he was a general of Frederick Barbarossa in Italy (1167–83).

Christian. Hero of John Bunyan's *Pilgrim's Progress.*

Christian I (of *Denmark*). b. 1426; d. at Copenhagen, May 21, 1481. King of Denmark, the founder of the house of Oldenburg in Denmark. He was a son of Theodoric, count of Oldenburg, and Hedwig, heiress of Schleswig and Holstein. Elected (1448) to succeed Christopher III, who had died the same year without issue, he was crowned king of Norway in 1450. He took possession of the government of Sweden in 1457, but was expelled (1470) from the country by Sten Sture. He was elected (1460) duke of Schleswig and Count of Holstein. He was the founder of the University of Copenhagen, on June 1, 1479.

Christian II (of *Denmark* and *Norway*). [Called **"Christian the Cruel."**] b. at Nyborg, Denmark, July 2, 1481; d. at Kallundborg, Denmark, Jan. 25, 1559. King of Denmark and Norway in the period 1513–23; son of John, whom he succeeded. He married (1515) Isabella, sister of the emperor Charles V. He conquered (1520) Sweden, but by his massacre of the Swedish nobility at Stockholm the same year provoked an uprising under Gustavus Vasa (who later ruled Sweden as Gustavus I), which resulted in the liberation of Sweden. He was deposed in 1523, and driven out of Denmark. He made a descent (1531) on Norway, but was captured (1532) and detained in prison until his death.

Christian III (of *Denmark* and *Norway*). b. 1503; d. at Kolding, Denmark, Jan. 1, 1559. King of Denmark and Norway in the period 1534–59. He introduced the Reformation into Denmark and Norway, destroyed the influence of the Hansa towns in his dominions, and reduced Norway to a province.

Christian IV (of *Denmark* and *Norway*). b. at Frederiksborg, Denmark, April 12, 1577; d. at Copenhagen, Feb. 28, 1648. King of Denmark and Norway in the period 1588–1648; son of Frederick II. He carried on a successful war against Sweden in the period 1611–13. As duke of Holstein he was invited (1625), in the Thirty Years' War, to take the lead in the rising of the Protestants in N Germany. He was defeated (August, 1626) by Tilly at Lutter am Barenberge, in Brunswick, and forced (May, 1629) to accept the peace of Lübeck. In a second war with Sweden, begun in 1643 and concluded in August, 1645, by the peace of Brömsebro, he lost the Norwegian districts of Jemtland and Herjeland, and the islands of Gotland and Ösel (now Saaremaa), and was forced to make other important concessions. He promoted commerce and enterprise, founded the Danish settlement at Tranquebar in the East Indies, founded the city of Christiania (now Oslo) on the site of an earlier burned-out city, and by his courage and magnanimity acquired in a high degree the favor of his subjects.

Christian V (of *Denmark* and *Norway*). b. April 15, 1646; d. at Copenhagen, Aug. 25, 1699. King of Denmark and Norway from 1670 to 1699; son of Frederick III. He carried on an unsuccessful war against Sweden in the period 1675–79, and published (1638) a code which bears his name.

Christian VI (of *Denmark* and *Norway*). b. Nov. 30, 1699; d. Aug. 6, 1746. King of Denmark and Norway in the period 1730–46; son of Frederick IV. He is said to have been completely under the influence of his wife, Sophie Magdalene of Brandenburg-Kulmbach, who engaged in magnificent building operations, including the palace of Kristiansborg.

Christian VII (of *Denmark* and *Norway*). b. at Copenhagen, Jan. 29, 1749; d. at Rendsburg, Holstein, March 13, 1808. King of Denmark and Norway in the period 1766–1808, and Duke of Schleswig-Holstein; son of Frederick V by Louisa, daughter of George II of England.

Christian VIII (of *Denmark*). [Also, temporarily, **Christian I** of Norway.] b. at Copenhagen, Sept. 18, 1786; d. there, Jan. 20, 1848. King of Denmark in the period 1839–48, and Duke of Schleswig-Holstein and Lauenburg; eldest son of Frederick, stepbrother of Christian VII. He was governor of Norway when the peace of Kiel (concluded on Jan. 14, 1814), which ceded Norway to Sweden, was repudiated (Jan. 28, 1814) by the Norwegians. He came forward as the champion of national independence, collected an army of some 12,000 men, convened (April 10) a diet at Eidswold, which adopted (May 17) a constitution, and was proclaimed (May 19, 1814) king of Norway under the title of Christian I. Unable, however, to maintain his position against the Swedes, supported by the allied powers, he concluded (Aug. 14) a truce at Moss, and relinquished (Oct. 10, 1814) the crown. He issued (July 8, 1846) a proclamation, in which he declared Schleswig and Holstein to be indissolubly united to Denmark.

Christian IX (of *Denmark*). b. near Schleswig, April 8, 1818; d. at Copenhagen, Jan. 29, 1906. King of Denmark in the period 1863–1906; fourth son of Frederick, duke of Schleswig-Holstein-Sonderburg-Glücksburg. He succeeded (Nov. 15, 1863) Frederick VII. He proclaimed himself sovereign of Schleswig and Holstein, the succession to which duchies was claimed by Prince Frederick of Sonderburg-Augustenburg, who was supported by the inhabitants, and on Nov. 18, 1863, he ratified a constitution incorporating Schleswig with Denmark. The Schleswig-Holstein dispute finally involved him in a war with Prussia and Austria, whose forces invaded Schleswig on Feb. 1, 1864, and after an obstinate resistance occupied Jutland. By the treaty of Oct. 30, 1864, Christian formally renounced all claims to Schleswig, Holstein, and Lauenburg. His children were Frederick VIII of Denmark (b. June 3, 1843); Alexandra, queen of England (b. Dec. 1, 1844); George I, king of Greece (b. Dec. 24, 1845); Dagmar, dowager empress of Russia (b. Nov. 26, 1847); Thyra, duchess of Cumberland (b. Sept. 29, 1853); and Prince Waldemar (b. Oct. 27, 1858).

Christian X (of *Denmark*). [Full name, **Carl Frederik Albert Alexander Vilhelm.**] b. at Charlottenlund, Denmark, Sept. 26, 1870; d. at Copenhagen, April 20, 1947. King of Denmark (1912–47); son of king Frederick VIII of Denmark and grandson of Christian IX. He married (1898) Duchess Alexandrine Augusta of Mecklenburg. During World War II he refused to surrender to the Germans, going into voluntary seclusion in preference; this gesture made him a national hero and symbol of resistance. In 1944 Iceland asserted its independence from the Danish crown which had held nominal sovereignty over that island since 1918. Christian was succeeded by his son, Frederick IX.

Christian, Edward. d. at Cambridge, England, March 29, 1823. English jurist; brother of Fletcher Christian. He was professor of laws at Downing College, Cambridge.

Christian, Fletcher. fl. in the last half of the 18th century. English seaman, master's mate and leader of the mutineers of the ship *Bounty;* younger brother of Edward Christian. After the ship reached Tahiti, what became of Christian is not known; according to Adams, the surviving mutineer found on Pitcairn Island, he was murdered by the Tahitians. It is possible that he escaped and returned to England. The founding of the colony on Pitcairn Island is variously attributed to Adams and Christian.

Christiana (kris.ti.an′ạ). Wife of Christian, and the chief female character in the second part of John Bunyan's *Pilgrim's Progress*. She also left the City of Destruction after Christian's flight.

"Christian Cicero." See **Lactantius Firmianus, Lucius Caelius** (or **Caecilius**).

Christian Commission, U.S. Organization founded (1861) at New York for the purpose of providing comforts to members of the Union forces. Supported chiefly by church bodies, it collected during the course of the Civil War over 2,500,000 dollars, as well as much clothing and other supplies.

Christian Democratic Union. German political party purporting to follow a program based on Christian ethics in politics and drawing its support from diverse groups, principally conservatives and Christian Socialists. Its principal leader is Konrad Adenauer.

Christian Disciple, The. Unitarian magazine (1813–69) published at Boston and New York. It became known as *The Christian Examiner* in 1823 and was published at New York beginning in 1866.

Christian Endeavor, Young People's Society of. Interdenominational and international organization embracing the youth of evangelical Protestant churches whose original unit was established in 1881, at the Williston Congregational Church, Portland, Me., by Francis E. Clark. Its 80,000 societies are active in more than 100 countries.

Christian Front. U.S. nativist and anti-Semitic organization whose following was confined largely to U.S. eastern urban areas and drew much of its strength from members of Father Charles E. Coughlin's National Union for Social Justice. It became active in the late 1930's and gradually disappeared after 1941.

"Christian General." See **Feng Yü-hsiang.**

Christian Hero, The. Work by Richard Steele, published in 1701.

Christian Historical Union (of *The Netherlands*). Dutch Protestant and conservative political party whose program is similar to that of the Anti-Revolutionary party.

Christian Hook. A former name of **Oceanside,** N.Y.

Christiania (kris.ti.an′i.ạ). Former name of **Oslo.**

Christian Mission. Original name of the **Salvation Army.**

Christian Observer, The. Periodical edited (1802–16) by Zachary Macaulay (1768–1838), father of Thomas Babington Macaulay. It was a chief organ of the English abolitionist movement and devoted itself to constant attacks on British participation in the slave-trade and on the continuing existence of slavery in some colonial areas within the British Empire or under British influence. Macaulay had gained a first-hand knowledge of this problem during his service (1793–99) as governor (under a private company) of Sierra Leone, on the W coast of Africa, which was then being settled in large part by liberated slaves under the sponsorship of antislavery elements in Great Britain.

Christian of Brunswick. b. Sept. 20, 1599; d. at Wolfenbüttel, Brunswick, Germany, June 16, 1626. Leader of Protestant armies in the Thirty Years' War. In accordance with an ancient feudal arrangement, he became titular bishop of Halberstadt in 1616; he was sometimes called "the Madman of Halberstadt," an epithet which recognized the impetuosity and courage that characterized him. He first took service in the Protestant cause under Prince Maurice of Orange, and later raised an army for the Elector Palatine Frederick V, but was dismissed by that monarch after being defeated by Tilly at Höchst in 1622. He returned to the wars as a leader of the forces of the United Provinces, and lost an arm at the battle of Fleurus; but he was evidently no match for Tilly, who in 1623 defeated him again at Stadtlohn. In 1625 he took the field again in the service of Christian IV of Denmark, but died in the following year without having accomplished anything of note.

Christian Philosopher, The. Essay by Cotton Mather, published in 1721.

Christiansand (kris.tyän.sän′). See **Kristiansand.**

Christiansburg (kris′chạnz.bėrg). Town in SW Virginia, county seat of Montgomery County, ab. 25 mi. SW of Roanoke: stockyards. 2,967 (1950).

Christian Science. System of religious teaching founded by Mary Baker Eddy, and viewed by its adherents as being, essentially, the reinstatement of primitive Christianity and its lost element of healing. The Bible (Authorized Version) and *Science and Health with Key to the Scriptures* by Mrs. Eddy are its only textbooks. The basic teaching of Christian Science is that God, Mind, Spirit, is "the divine Principle of all that really is" (*Science and Health*, page 275). Since God is infinite good, all His works, including man made in His image and likeness, are good also. Such apparent evils as sin, sickness, and death, according to Christian Science, are not creations of God, and, therefore, are no part of His kingdom. With an understanding of divine law, such conditions may be overcome, just as Christ Jesus overcame them. Because of this, Christian Scientists hold that living in accordance with the teachings of Jesus improves mental and moral welfare and insures physical well-being. As Christian Science is based on the word and works of Jesus, Christian Scientists recognize the lawful and scientific nature of what he did and regard his example as one to be followed in healing the sick and in overcoming sin. Thus, from the point of view of Christian Science, freedom from all human discordant conditions, including disease and sin, follows the scientific knowing of the truth about God and man, and the universal value of Christian Science is the availability of its spiritual resources under all circumstances. Jesus once said, "Every plant, which my heavenly Father hath not planted, shall be rooted up." In other words, nothing is real or enduring but that of which God is the author. This is the basis on which Christian Science healing is accomplished.

Christian Science. Prose work (1907) by Samuel Langhorne Clemens (Mark Twain). A lengthy attack on the system of religious teaching devised by Mary Baker Eddy, it is now regarded by most authorities as one of the great American writer's poorest efforts.

Christian Science Monitor, The. Daily newspaper, published at Boston, Mass., under the general guidance of The Christian Science Board of Directors of The First Church of Christ, Scientist. Its existence dates from Aug. 8, 1908, when Mary Baker Eddy, the discoverer and founder of Christian Science, told the trustees of The Christian Science Publishing Society, "It is my request that you start a daily newspaper at once, and that you call it The Christian Science Monitor." Unique in journalistic history, the *Monitor* has an important bearing on world progress and peace, and few newspapers in the world are better known, more widely read, or more often quoted. The success of the *Monitor* is due in large part to the efforts of those whose responsibility it is to follow the principles laid down when it was founded in 1908, "To injure no man, but to bless all mankind," a motto given to it by Mrs. Eddy. In appearance, the *Monitor* differs somewhat from most American newspapers. This is partially due to the elimination of continuing stories from page one to inside pages; also, it has more conservative headlines than most other papers. The *Monitor* has key U.S. bureaus at Washington, New York, Chicago, Los Angeles, and San Francisco. Overseas news is received from offices at London, Paris, Berlin, Beirut, Rome, Sydney, and Tokyo. There are special correspondents in South America and Canada. Constructiveness is the keynote in the paper's news coverage. Its editors believe that news of most consequence, when properly presented, can be more interesting than the sensational combative variety. The aim of the paper is to furnish an abundance of clean, constructive, informative, and entertaining news.

Christiansen (kris'tyän.sen), **Sigurd Wesley.** b. at Drammen, Norway, Nov. 17, 1891; d. Oct. 23, 1947. Norwegian author. He won an inter-Scandinavian prize with his novel *To Levende og en Død* (Two Living and One Dead, 1931).

Christian Social Party (of *Belgium*). [Former name, **Catholic Party.**] Belgian political party which supports the defense of Catholic interests, equal treatment of religious and public schools, social reform, and women's suffrage. In the realm of foreign policy, it is an exponent of freedom from alliances. In 1936 the Flemish and French-speaking branches united as the Catholic Bloc.

Christian Social Party (of *Luxembourg*). Luxembourg political party which supports the interests of the Catholic Church, the maintenance of existing legislation concerning schools, progressive labor legislation, and the protection of small business and agriculture.

Christians of Saint John. See **Mandaeans.**

Christianstad (kris.tyän'städ). See **Kristianstad.**

Christiansted (kris'chan.sted). [Also, **Bassin.**] City in N St. Croix, U.S. Virgin Islands, on the Caribbean Sea: exports sugar and rum. 4,495 (1940).

Christiansund (kris.tyän.sun'). See **Kristiansund.**

Christianville (kris'chan.vil). A former name of **Kingsport.**

Christian Year, The. Volume of sacred poems (1827) by the English poet John Keble, who was for many years a professor of poetry at Oxford, and was also a chief initiator of the Oxford (or Tractarian) Movement. Published anonymously, with the subtitle *Thoughts in Verse for the Sundays and Holy Days Throughout the Year*, it became immensely popular and has retained a considerable body of readers even to this day. Some of the best-known selections in the book are "Evening Hymn," "Sun of My Soul," "Thou Saviour Dear," and "The Voice that Breathed O'er Eden."

Christias (kris'ti.as). Epic poem on the life of Christ, written in Latin (1535) by Marco Girolamo Vida.

Christie (kris'ti), **Agatha.** [Full name, **Agatha Mary Clarissa Christie**; maiden name, **Miller.**] b. at Torquay, Devonshire, England, —. English author of detective fiction and creator of the highly successful character of the Belgian detective Hercule Poirot. Her very successful career was begun with *The Mysterious Affair at Styles* (1920), which she wrote to disprove her sister's belief that it was practically impossible to write a detective story in which the reader could not guess who committed the crime, *The Secret Adversary* (1922), *The Murder on the Links* (1923), *Poirot Investigates* and *The Man in the Brown Suit* (both 1924), *The Secret of Chimneys* (1925), *The Murder of Roger Ackroyd* (1926), which is regarded not only as one of her best works but as one of the best detective novels of the 20th century, *The Big Four* (1927), *The Mystery of the Blue Train* (1928), *The Seven Dials Mystery* (1929), *The Mysterious Mr. Quin* and *Murder at the Vicarage* (both 1930), *The Sittaford Mystery* (1931; American title, *Murder at Hazlemoore*), *Peril at End House* (1932), *The Thirteen Problems* (1933; American title, *The Tuesday Club Murders*), *Lord Edgeware Dies* (1933; American title, *Thirteen at Dinner*), *Murder in the Calais Coach* and *Murder in Three Acts* (both 1934), *Death in the Air* and *Boomerang Clue* (both 1935), *The ABC Murders* (1936), *Cards on the Table*, *Dead Man's Mirror*, *Death on the Nile*, *Poirot Loses a Client* (all 1937), *Appointment with Death* (1938), *The Regatta Mystery* and *Murder for Christmas* (both 1939), *Ten Little Niggers* (1940; American title, *And Then There Were None*), which was successful on both the stage and screen, *The Sad Cypress* (1940), *The Patriotic Murders*, *N or M*, and *Evil Under the Sun* (all 1941), *The Body in the Library* and *Murder in Retrospect* (both 1942), *Triple Threat* (1943), *Death Comes as the End* (1944), *Sparkling Cyanide* (1945), *The Hollow* (1946), and *They Came to Baghdad* (1951).

Christie, Alexander. b. at Edinburgh, 1807; d. May 5, 1860. Scottish painter, elected an associate of the Royal Scottish Academy in 1848.

Christie, Anna. See **Anna Christie.**

Christie, James. b. 1730; d. 1803. English auctioneer; father of James Christie (1773–1831) and grandfather of Sir William Henry Mahoney Christie (1845–1922). In 1766 he opened Christie's, a world-famous auction room at London which was carried on after his death by his son.

Christie, James. b. at London, 1773; d. 1831. English antiquarian, auctioneer, and author of works on Etruscan and Greek vases; son of James Christie (1730–1803).

Christie, Richard Copley. b. 1830; d. 1901. English scholar, educator, and bibliophile. He was professor of ancient and modern history (1854–66), political economy and commercial science (1855–66), and jurisprudence and law (1855–69) at Owens College, Manchester, to which he bequeathed a sizable library. A member of the council and university court of Victoria University (1880), he served as chancellor of the see of Manchester (1872–94) and chairman of the Chetham Society (1883–1901). He contributed to the *Dictionary of National Biography* and the *Encyclopaedia Britannica*. His publications include *Etienne Dolet, the Martyr of the Renaissance* (1880).

Christie, Sir **William Henry Mahoney.** b. at Woolwich, England, Oct. 1, 1845; d. at sea, Jan. 22, 1922. British astronomer; grandson of James Christie (1730–1803). In 1870 he was appointed chief assistant at the Royal Observatory, Greenwich, and in 1881 became astronomer royal, holding that post until 1910. During his administration the facilities at Greenwich were enlarged and improved, and more attention was given to photographic and spectroscopic techniques. Christie himself was especially a student of solar eclipses and sunspots. He was a member of numerous learned societies and his services were recognized by knighthood. He was the author of a *Manual of Elementary Astronomy* (1875).

Christie's. Auction-room at London. On December 5, 1766, James Christie (1730–1803) held his initial public auction on the site of the United Service Club in Pall Mall, London. The business was at first general, but the picture sales soon became the chief attraction. The "private view-day" was especially popular with the prominent people of the time. Christie was succeeded by his son James Christie (1773–1831), who in 1824 moved to 8 King Street; after his death the business was carried on by his two sons. The firm name of Christie, Manson, and Woods was adopted in 1859, but the establishment has remained generally known even to this day simply as "Christie's." Many of the world's leading private art collections, including some of the most famous paintings in the history of Western art, have "gone under the hammer" at Christie's.

Christina (of *Sweden*) (kris.tē′nạ). b. at Stockholm, Dec. 18, 1626; d. at Rome, April 19, 1689. Queen of Sweden; daughter of Gustavus II Adolphus, whom she succeeded in 1632 under a regency composed of the five chief officers of the crown, including Axel Oxenstierna. She assumed actual control of the government in 1644, terminated (1645) by the treaty of Brömsebro the war which had been waged against Denmark since 1643, and contrary to the advice of Oxenstierna hastened the conclusion of peace in Germany. She attracted to her court many scholars and thinkers, among them Descartes. Having secured (1649) the election of her cousin Charles X as her successor, she abdicated (1654) the throne, and shortly after embraced the Roman Catholic faith. She was involved in two attempts (1660, 1667) to regain the Swedish throne after Charles's death, but both were unsuccessful. She eventually settled at Rome, where she patronized men of letters and science, and collected a library which was purchased after her death by Pope Alexander VIII.

Christina, Fort. Fort built (1638) on the Delaware River by Peter Minuit and a party of Swedish settlers. (Minuit, a Dutchman perhaps best known for his purchase (1631) of Manhattan Island from the Indians, had accepted a commission to establish the colony for Sweden.) It served (1638–43, 1654–55) as the capital of New Sweden and was the nucleus of the first permanent settlement made by whites in the valley of the Delaware River. It was the predecessor of what is now Wilmington, Del.

Christina Alberta's Father. Novel (1925) by H. G. Wells, dealing with the theme (a favorite one with Wells, as it has been with many other 20th-century authors) of sexual conflict, and the unhappiness which this causes. In this book Wells presented views which were, for his time, both advanced and controversial, but which conveyed his idea as to possible methods of improving the relationship between men and women.

Christine (kris.tēn′), **Elizabeth** or **Elisabeth.** See **Elizabeth Christine.**

Christine de Pisan (krēs.tēn dẹ pē.zäṅ). b. at Venice, c1363; d. c1431. French writer, of Italian parentage (daughter of Thomas de Pisan, who was a councilor of the Venetian republic and also noted as an astrologer). She was educated at Paris, and spent virtually all of her adult life in France. She is of interest to modern historians of literature from the fact that she was one of the first European writers to secure a living from her writing (from the Roman era through to the early Renaissance writing was usually an avocation rather than a vocation, and was practiced by people whose actual support came usually from the Church or royal patronage; Christine de Pisan may thus be considered to have been, in some ways, a "modern writer," at least insofar as her profession was also her means of livelihood). Several of her works have been published in English, perhaps most notably *The Book of Fayettes of Armes and of Chivalry*, which was most recently issued in 1932 from an original English edition published by Caxton.

Christison (kris′ti.sọn), Sir **Robert.** b. July 18, 1797; d. Jan. 23, 1882. Scottish physician. He was professor of medical jurisprudence at Edinburgh from 1822 to 1832, and of materia medica and therapeutics from 1832 to 1877. He received a baronetcy in 1871.

Christ Jesus (krīst jē′zus). See **Jesus.**

Christmas (kris′mạs). Legal and religious holiday of the Western world, celebrated on December 25 to commemorate the birth of Christ. In Germanic countries, where the feast is of pagan origin, the ritual of the holiday includes the wide giving of presents. In the Romance countries it is primarily a day of religious services, and presents are distributed on Epiphany. Customs associated with the celebration of Christmas in English-speaking countries are the singing of Christmas carols, the decoration of the home with holly and yew, and the burning of the Yule log, among many others.

Christmas, Father. See **Father Christmas.**

Christmas Carol, A. [Full title, **A Christmas Carol in Prose; Being a Ghost Story of Christmas.**] Christmas story in prose (December, 1843), by Charles Dickens. It is regarded as one of the best, and is certainly one of the best known, examples of the "dream-and-reformation" type of story, familiar in English drama and poetry as well as fiction. Dickens states his aim in writing it in his short Preface: "I have endeavored," he says, "in this ghostly little book, to raise the Ghost of an Idea, which shall not put my readers out of humour with themselves, with each other, with the season, or with me. May it haunt their houses pleasantly, and no one wish to lay it!" The story is told in five staves (a term belonging to poetry rather than prose): I. Marley's Ghost, II. The First of the Three Spirits, III. The Second of the Three Spirits, IV. The Last of the Spirits, V. The End of It. The chief characters are Ebenezer Scrooge, his dead partner Jacob Marley, who appears as a ghost; Scrooge's happy (although poorly paid) clerk Bob Cratchit, his equally happy wife, and their son Tiny Tim, a pathetic little cripple. By means of a visit from Marley's ghost, and by visits from the Spirits of Christmas Past, Present, and Future, Scrooge is made to realize that he has never known the meaning of Christmas and that his will be a horrible end unless he changes his ways before it is too late. The dream visits take place on Christmas Eve, after Scrooge has returned from his office in a nasty, uncharitable mood, and he wakes up on Christmas morning, after a night of terror, a changed man, eager and anxious to observe Christmas as it should be observed, and with his heart full of friendliness for his fellows. The story is famous for its opening sentence, "Marley was dead, to begin with," and for the frequent cry of Tiny Tim, which closes it, "God bless us, every one!" Although less than a novel, it is something more than a short story, occupying, as it does, at least a hundred pages (more, in some editions). Dickens's classic has found equal popularity on the stage, on the screen, and on the air, and there are several phonographic recordings. The character of Scrooge has been interpreted by Alastair Sim, Eustace Wyatt, Basil Rathbone, Lionel Barrymore, and Ronald Colman.

Christmas Island. Small island in the Indian Ocean, ab. 233 mi. S of the western end of Java. In 1946, when Singapore became a separate British crown colony, Christmas Island was added to it. Length, 11 mi.; width, 4.5 mi.; area, ab. 60 sq. mi.; pop. 1,522 (est. 1951).

Christmas Island. Small island in the Pacific, ab. 1,300 mi. S of Honolulu. It is a British possession, administered as part of the Gilbert and Ellice Islands colony. Area, 60,000 acres; pop. 42 (1944).

Christmas Oratorio. Choral work by Johann Sebastian Bach, composed in 1734.

Christodulus (kris.tod′ū.lus), **Joasaph.** See **John VI** or **V** (of the *Byzantine Empire*).

Christoffel (kris.tof′ẹl), **Elwin Bruno.** b. at Montjoie (now Monschau, Germany), Nov. 10, 1829; d. at Strasbourg, March 15, 1900. German mathematician who is best known for the "Christoffel symbols" in tensor analysis. He was educated at Cologne and Berlin, and taught at Berlin (1859), Zurich (1862), and Strasbourg. He contributed many papers on differential equations, differential geometry, and theory of functions. His *Gesammelte mathematische Abhandlungen* appeared in two volumes in 1910.

Christ of the Andes. Name given to a famous statue symbolizing peace between Argentina and Chile. Following the settlement of a number of disputes between Argentina and Chile, and especially the conclusion in 1902 of a treaty defining the boundary between the two countries, money was raised by popular subscription for the erection at the summit of Uspallata Pass in the Andes, where the mountains are pierced by the Trans-Andean tunnel, of this statue of greater than twice life-size, cast from the bronze of ancient cannon, and standing on a pedestal hewn from the rock of the vicinity. In 1937 a tablet was affixed to the pedestal with an inscription in Spanish which reads, in translation, "Sooner shall these mountains crumble into dust than Argentines and Chileans break the peace sworn at the feet of Christ the Redeemer."

Christophe (krēs.tof), **Henri.** [Also: **Cristophe**; called **Henri I** (of Haiti).] b. Oct. 6, 1767; committed suicide at Port-au-Prince, Haiti, Oct. 8, 1820. Haitian Negro, king (1811–20) of Haiti. He took part in the anti-French revolution of 1791–93 and became the most trusted general of Toussaint L'Ouverture, serving (1802) against the French forces of Leclerc. He subsequently commanded (1803 *et seq.*) under Dessalines in the so-called black republic of northern Haiti, and succeeded him in 1806. In 1811 Christophe was proclaimed king of Haiti, and was formally crowned on June 2. His wars with Pétion's republic of the south, and rebellions caused by his tyranny, brought about a rebellion (1818) and, finally, his downfall (1820). Attacked by the rebels, he shot himself, according to legend, with a silver bullet.

Christophe, Jean. See **Jean Christophe.**

Christopher (kris'tọ.fėr), Saint. fl. c3rd century. Early Christian martyr. Virtually nothing is known about him except that somewhere in Asia Minor, perhaps in Syria, and probably in the 3rd century, there was a pious man who took or was given the name (in Latin) "Christophorus," meaning "Christ-Bearer," and that he was martyred for his faith. As early as the 6th century at least one church and one monastery are known to have been dedicated to him. The significance of his name is supposed at first to have been that he bore Christ in his heart, but from an early time the legend as we know it today began to take form. According to this account, Christopher was a man of giant stature and prodigious strength, who vowed to serve only the strongest master. He bound himself first to Satan and then to an earthly king, but found neither of them really strong; he was then persuaded by a hermit that God is the strongest master, and he was baptized and entered the service of God. He would not undertake to pray and fast, but offered to carry across a certain raging torrent all Christian pilgrims who came that way. One day he started carrying a child across the stream, but the child's weight increased at every step, so that the giant porter was barely able to reach the other bank. There the child revealed himself as Christ, and said "Marvel not, for with me thou hast borne the sins of all the world." Then, at the Christ-child's bidding, he struck his staff into the ground, where overnight it grew into a palm tree. News of this miracle caused many conversions, which enraged the ruler of that land, who thereupon caused Christopher to be seized, tortured, and beheaded. Saint Christopher, who usually appears in art bearing the Christ-child and the staff, has been adopted as patron by a number of cities and by various classes of artisans and workers, including mariners and ferrymen; in modern times he has become a patron of travelers in general, and medals with his image are frequently affixed to automobiles or carried by motorists, while his name has been given to a number of shrines and churches located on much-traveled highways.

Christopher or **Christophorus** (kris.tof'ọ.rus). fl. in the 10th century. Antipope from 903 to 904. He forcibly dethroned and imprisoned his predecessor, Leo V, and in turn was ejected by the lawful pope, Sergius III.

Christopher. City in S Illinois, in Franklin County. Coal is mined in the area. 3,545 (1950).

Christopher Blake. Drama (1947) by the American dramatist Moss Hart, which shows what his parents' divorce does to a young boy.

Christopher Cheverel (shev'ẹ.rẹl), **Sir.** See **Cheverel, Sir Christopher** and **Lady.**

Christopher Newman (nū'mạn). See **Newman, Christopher.**

Christopher Robin (rob'in). Small boy in A. A. Milne's *Winnie the Pooh* and *The House at Pooh Corner*, also the hero of various children's poems in Milne's *When We Were Very Young* and *Now We Are Six.* He is taken to represent the author's son, Christopher Milne, for whom these stories and poems were written.

Christopher Sly (slī). See **Sly, Christopher.**

Christopherson (kris'tọ.fėr.sọn), **Chris.** Father of the heroine in *Anna Christie* (1921), a play by Eugene O'Neill. A Swedish-American seaman, he is captain of a coal barge, but fears and hates "dat ole davil sea."

Christopulos (ċhrē.stô'pö.lôs), **Athanasios.** b. at Kastoria, in Macedonia, 1772; d. in Walachia, Jan. 29, 1847. Greek lyric poet. His lyrics were published at Paris (1833, 1841). He also made translations from classical Greek.

Christ's College. College of Cambridge University, England, founded in 1505 by Margaret Beaufort, Countess of Richmond. The Tudor arms remain over the gateway, but the buildings were renovated in the 18th century. The gardens are celebrated for their beauty.

Christ's Hospital. School, formerly in Newgate Street, London, known as the Blue Coat School from the ancient dress of the scholars, which is still retained. It was founded by Edward VI on the site of the monastery of Grey Friars, given by Henry VIII to the city near the end of his reign for the relief of the poor. The school was moved to Horsham, Sussex, in 1902. Charles Lamb and Samuel Taylor Coleridge attended this school.

Christ's Teares Over Jerusalem. Prose religious tract (1593) by the Elizabethan satirist Thomas Nashe. In it the author turns to Christ's prophecy of the fall of Jerusalem in order to drive home, by implying a parallel fate, the moral degradation evidenced by the sinful life led by many London citizens in his day.

Christ, the Anointed. See **Messiah.**

Christus (kris'tus), **Petrus.** [Also: **Cristus, Pieter Christophsen.**] b. at Baerle, a village in Brabant, c1400; d. at Bruges, in Flanders, 1473. Flemish painter. He is thought to have studied with the Van Eycks, and it was from them certainly that his style was derived. Little is known of his career until in 1444 he purchased citizenship at Bruges, and became a member of the Guild of Saint Luke. Among the few works attributed to him with certainty are a portrait of Edward Grimstone, now in the collection of the Earl of Verulam in England, a portrait of Marco Barberigo in the National Gallery, London, a *Pietà* in the Brussels Museum, a *Nativity* in the National Gallery of Art at Washington, and a *Deposition from the Cross*, in the Metropolitan Museum of Art, New York.

Christus, a Mystery. Dramatic poem by Henry Wadsworth Longfellow, published in three volumes in 1872. It includes *The Golden Legend* (1851), *The New England Tragedies* (1868), and *The Divine Tragedy* (1871).

Christy (kris'ti), **Edwin P.** b. at Philadelphia, May 21, 1815; d. 1862. Developer of the American minstrel show. Little is known of his life until 1842, when the troupe known as Christy's Minstrels began its enormously successful career with a performance at Buffalo, N.Y. Minstrel shows had been given before, but Christy's showmanship fixed the definite conventions of this form of entertainment: the semicircle or arc of musicians (white men in blackface) the interlocutor, the end men who acted as foils for his jokes, and the variety acts which broke what would have otherwise been the monotony of the songs and dialogue. Christy's Minstrels first braved the verdict of a New York City audience in 1846, and the verdict was highly favorable. For ten years thereafter the troupe, with Christy always acting as interlocutor, gave thousands of performances in American cities, and in a tour of England made the minstrel show a popular form of entertainment there. Stephen Collins Foster wrote and composed some of his songs for this troupe (and Christy was not above publishing some of them under his own name). By 1854 he was wealthy enough to retire, and the show was taken over by George N. Harrington, who assumed the name Christy. During his latter years Christy became subject to intermittent spells of insanity, in one of which he jumped from a window in New York, with fatal results.

Christy, Henry. b. at Kingston-on-Thames, England, July 26, 1810; d. at La Palisse, France, May 4, 1865. English ethnologist, noted especially for his exploration of the caves in the valley of the Vézère River, a tributary of the Dordogne, in S France. He began the preparation of a work containing the results of his investigations, which was completed, after his death, by Lartet and Rupert-Jones, under the title *Reliquiae Aquitanicae: being Contributions to the Archaeology and Palaeontology of Perigord and the adjacent Provinces of Southern France.*

Christy, Howard Chandler. b. in Ohio, Jan. 10, 1873; d. March 3, 1952. American illustrator, painter, and sculptor. His portraits hang in the White House, the State Department building, and the Post Office building, at Washington, D.C.; he also painted *The Signing of the Constitution*, for the Capitol building. He studied at the National Academy of Design and the Art Students League of New York, and the Chase School of Art. His illustrations have appeared in *Cosmopolitan* and many other publications (his style in the drawing of young women, in particular, is distinctive and has led to coining of the label "Christy girl"). In a more serious vein, he has painted portraits of Warren G. Harding, President and Mrs. Calvin Coolidge, Charles E. Hughes, Benito Mussolini, and John Nance Garner. He has also illustrated many books.

Christy Mahon (mą.hōn′). See **Mahon, Christy.**

Chrodegang (krō′dę.gang) or **Godegrand** (gō′dę.grand), Saint. d. at Metz, France, March 6, 766. Bishop of Metz. He was a native of Hasbania (Belgian Limburg), and was descended from a distinguished family among the Ripuarian Franks. He was appointed bishop of Metz by Pepin the Short in 742, conducted Pope Stephen II on a journey from Rome to Gaul in 753, and in 764 brought from Rome the relics which had been presented by the Pope to the churches and monasteries of Gaul. He was the author of the *Vita Canonica*, a rule for priests borrowed in part from that of Saint Benedict, and of which there are two versions: an older one intended for the cathedral of Metz, and a more recent one, intended for the church in general.

Chronica (kron′i.ką). Latin prose work by Ethelwerd, an Anglo-Latin chronicler who died toward the end of the 10th century. It is a history of the world from the beginning to 973, and is in four books. The work was first edited in 1596 by Sir Henry Savile, and was translated from Latin into English by Giles in his *Six Old English Chronicles.*

Chronicle of Paros (pãr′os, pā′ros). Greek historical inscription found on the island of Paros, and now preserved among the Arundel marbles in the Ashmolean Museum at Oxford. It extended originally from the mythical reign of Cecrops, king of Athens, taken as c1581 B.C., to the archonship of Diogenetus, 264 B.C.; but the end is now lost, and the surviving part extends only to c354 B.C. The chronicle embraces an outline of Greek history, with special attention to festivals, poetry, and music. Political and military events are less carefully recorded, many of importance being omitted entirely. A second, similar marble, of later date and covering a subsequent period (c365–c299 B.C.) is in a museum on Paros.

Chronicle of the Conquest of Granada, A. Semi-fictional historical work in prose (1829, revised 1850), by Washington Irving. Although he follows the facts of history and actually did considerable research in Spanish sources, Irving allows himself a certain romantic freedom by pretending that his authority is "from the manuscripts of Fray Antonio Agapida," both of which are fictitious (as was frequently the case with Irving's "authorities" when he wished to allow himself a degree of latitude in plot which could not otherwise be sustained).

Chronicle of the Kings of England from the Time of the Romans' Government unto the Death of King James. Principal work of Sir Richard Baker. It was published in 1643, and its popularity is attested by its many editions, a ninth appearing in 1696. It was continued by another author to the time of George I.

Chronicles. Two books of the Old Testament, supplementary to the books of Kings. They formed originally one book, the division into two having been made for convenience in the Septuagint, the translation of the Bible into Greek in the 3rd or 2nd century B.C. The name *Chronica* (Eng. trans., *Chronicles*), which is given in some copies of the Vulgate, appears to date from Jerome. In the Septuagint they are called Paralipomenon ("omitted things"), and in the Hebrew "Journals" or diaries. They probably consist of materials which may have been in part collected by Ezra, and were revised about the second half of the 4th century B.C. by another, probably a Levite.

Chronicles of England, Scotland, and Ireland, The. [Called **Holinshed's Chronicles.**] Prose historical work (published 1577, in two folio volumes, and a second edition in three volumes in 1587) by Raphael Holinshed, with the assistance of William Harrison, Richard Stanyhurst, Edward Campion and others. The tremendous literary importance of the work is due partly to the fact that Shakespeare drew much from it for his *Cymbeline, Richard II, Richard III*, and all his *Henry* (IV, V, VI, VIII) plays.

Chronicles of the Canongate (kan′on.gāt). Collection of stories by Sir Walter Scott. The first series, published in 1827, includes "The Highland Widow," "Two Drovers," and "The Surgeon's Daughter." The second series (*The Fair Maid of Perth*) was published in 1828. The tales are supposed to be narrated by Mr. Chrystal Croftangry, to whom they are told by Mrs. Baliol.

Chronicles of the House of Borgia. Prose historical work (1901) by a contributor to *The Yellow Book*, an English novelist, musician, and photographer with the cumbersome name of Frederick William Serafino Austin Lewis Mary Rolfe (who, it is not surprising to learn, preferred to be called "Baron Corvo"). The *Chronicles*, a remarkable combination of scholarship, fantasy, and tricks of style, is considered one of Rolfe's best works, although he is perhaps better remembered for his autobiographical romance *Hadrian the Seventh* (1904).

Chronicles of the Schönberg-Cotta Family (shėn′bėrk.kot′ą). Historical novel by Elizabeth Charles, published in 1863.

Chronique des Pasquier (kro.nēk dā pås.kyā), **La.** Cyclical novel (10 vols., 1933–41; Eng. trans., *The Pasquier Chronicles*, 1937 *et seq.*) by the French writer Georges Duhamel (1884—). The book is at once the story of a Parisian bourgeois family and an attempt to present a panorama of ordinary French life at the beginning of the 20th century.

Chrononhotonthologos (krō.non″hō.ton.thol′ǫ.gos). Burlesque by Henry Carey, "the most tragical tragedy ever yet tragedized," first performed in 1734. It was imitated to some degree from Henry Fielding's play *Tom Thumb*. Chrononhotonthologos is the King of Queerummania. His name is occasionally used as a nickname for any particularly bombastic and inflated talker.

Chrudim (ʜrö′dēm). Town in Czechoslovakia, in NE Bohemia, situated on the Chrudimka River, S of Pardubice. It has machine, shoe, malt, sugar, and liquor factories and is a center for the local horse trade. There is a parish church dating from the 13th century, a folklore museum, and a commercial academy. 13,217 (1947).

Chrypffs (kripfs), **Nikolas.** See **Nicholas of Cusa.**

Chrysalde (krē.zåld). Character in Molière's comedy *L'École des femmes.*

Chrysale (krē.zål). Good, stupid citizen of the middle class, the husband of Philaminte, in Molière's comedy *Les Femmes savantes.*

Chrysal, or the Adventures of a Guinea (kris′ąl). Novel by Charles Johnstone, published in 1760. Chrysal is an elementary spirit whose abode is in a piece of gold converted into a guinea. In that form the spirit passes from man to man, and takes accurate note of the different scenes of which it becomes a witness.

Chrysander (krü.zän′dėr), **Friedrich.** b. at Lübtheen, Germany, July 8, 1826; d. at Bergedorf, Germany, Sept. 3, 1901. German music historian and biographer. His chief work is his biography of Handel, unfinished, in three volumes (1858–67). From 1868 to 1871 and from 1875 to 1882 he was editor of the *Allgemeine Musikalische Zeitung*, and he founded the *Vierteljahrsschrift für Musikwissenschaft*. He was the founder of the German Händelgesellschaft (Handel Society) and edited its complete edition of Handel's works.

Chrysanthemum, Order of the. See **Order of the Chrysanthemum.**

Chrysanthos or **Chrisanthos** (ĉhrē′sän.thôs), Archbishop. [Original name, **Philippides.**] b. at Komotini, in Thrace, 1882; d. 1949. Greek divine. He studied (1897–1903) at Chalki Theological School, was archdeacon and assistant (1903–07) to the bishop of Trabzon (Trebizond), and studied at Leipzig (1907–08) and Lausanne (1908–11). He was archimandrite and archivist of the Constantinople patriarchate, and editor (1911–13) of the official publication *Church Truth*. From 1913 to 1938 he was metropolitan (bishop) of Trabzon. Representative of the Greek church at the conferences (1919–20) at Paris, London, and San Remo, on behalf of the Greek population of Turkey, he was officially condemned to death by the Turks (1922). From 1926 to 1938 he was also representative of the patriarchate at Athens. He was sent on various missions for the church to Albania (1926–27), Athos (1928), Belgrade, Bucharest and Warsaw (1929), and Syria (1931). Picked (1938) by Metaxas in preference to Damaskinos as archbishop of Athens, primate of all Greece, he was removed by the puppet government and replaced by Damaskinos in 1941. A member of the

Academy of Athens (1939–49), he was also an active worker (1940–41) in war relief.

Chrysaor (krī.sā'ôr, kris'ā.ôr). In classical mythology, a son of Poseidon and Medusa, and father (by Callirrhoe) of the three-headed Geryon and Echidna. He sprang forth from the head of Medusa when Perseus cut it off.

Chrysaor. The sword of Sir Artegall, in Edmund Spenser's *The Faerie Queene*. It represents justice.

Chryse (krī'sē). See **Comana.**

Chryseis (krī.sē'is). In Homeric legend, Astynome, the daughter of Chryses, seized as a slave by Agamemnon. When the king refused to give her up, Chryses prayed to Apollo for vengeance, and the god sent a plague upon the camp of the Greeks, which was not stayed until the maiden was taken back to her father by Odysseus.

Chryses (krī'sēz). In Homeric legend, a priest of Apollo at Comana (Chryse), in Asia Minor; father of Chryseis.

Chrysippus (krī.sip'us, kri-). b. at Soli, Cilicia, c280 B.C.; d. at Athens, c207 B.C. Greek Stoic philosopher; a disciple of Cleanthes, whom he succeeded as head of the Academy. He was considered, next to Zeno, who founded the Stoic school and who died in the early 3rd century B.C., the most eminent of the Stoic philosophers. He is said to have died from an immoderate fit of laughter on seeing an ass eating some figs destined for his (Chrysippus's) own supper. (One account, translated from K. O. Müller's *History of the Literature of Ancient Greece*, has it that the sight of the ass solemnly eating human food so delighted him that he cried "Give him a bumper of wine" to the old woman who was attending him, and thereupon sank, exhausted by his merriment, into death.)

Chrysler (krīs'lėr), **Walter Percy.** b. at Wamego, Kan., April 2, 1875; d. Aug. 18, 1940. American automobile manufacturer, founder and chairman of the Chrysler Corporation. Named assistant manager (1910) and manager (1911) of the American Locomotive Company at Pittsburgh, he was subsequently works manager (1912–16) and president and general manager (1916–19) of the Buick Motor Company, vice-president (1919–20) in charge of operations for the General Motors Company, and executive vice-president (1920–22) of the Willys-Overland Company.

Chrysler's Field, Battle of. Engagement (Nov. 10, 1813) in the War of 1812, fought in Canada, near Chrysler's farm on the north bank of the St. Lawrence River. The American force, under General James Wilkinson, was intent upon seizing Montreal, but a British attack from land and water caused severe losses among the Americans and compelled them to withdraw.

Chrysologus (kri.sol'ō.gus), Saint **Peter.** See Saint **Peter Chrysologus.**

Chrysoloras (kris.ō.lō'ras), **Manuel.** b. probably at Constantinople, c1355; d. at Konstanz, Germany, April 15, 1415. Greek scholar, teacher of Greek in Italy. Many distinguished scholars were his pupils. He wrote *Erotemata sive quaestiones*, one of the first Greek grammars used in Italy.

Chrysopolis (kri.sop'ō.lis). Ancient name of **Üsküdar.**

Chrysorrhoas (kri.sor'ō.as). Greek name of the **Barada.**

Chrysorrhoas. Surname of Saint **John Damascene.**

Chrysostom (kris'os.tom, kri.sos'tom) or **Chrysostomus** (kri.sos'tō.mus), **Dion.** See **Dion Chrysostomus.**

Chrysostom, Saint **John.** b. at Antioch, Syria, probably in 347 A.D.; d. near Comana, in Cappadocia, Sept. 4, 407. One of the fathers of the Greek Church. He was preacher and prelate at Antioch, was patriarch of Constantinople (398–404), and was exiled to Cappadocia from 404 to 407. His works were published in the edition called the "Benedictine" (13 vols. fol., 1718) and that of the Abbé Migne (13 vols., 1863). He is commemorated in the Greek Church on Jan. 27 and Nov. 13, in the Roman Church on Jan. 27.

Chrysostome (kris'os.tōm). Character in Miguel de Cervantes's *Don Quixote*, a learned man who died for love.

Chrzanów (hshä'nöf). Town in S Poland, in the *województwo* (province) of Kraków, ab. 27 mi. W of Kraków. There are coal and lead mines in the vicinity. The town has agricultural markets, locomotive works, brick kilns, tar-paper factories, and tanneries. Prior to 1919, it belonged to the Austrian crownland of Galicia. 12,121 (1946).

Chrzanowski (hshä.nôf'skē), **Adalbert.** b. near Kraków, Poland, 1788; d. at Paris, March 5, 1861. Polish general in the revolution of 1830–31. He was commander of the Sardinian army in the Novara campaign, in 1849.

Chrzciciel (hshchē'chel), **Jan.** Polish name of **Albertrandy, John Baptist.**

Ch'u (chö). Chinese state which in Late Chou times occupied a large part of the central Yangtze valley and the areas drained by the Huai and Han rivers. Two important cultural centers were Changsha and Shou Chou; both have been archaeologically important in recent years. Little is yet known of Ch'u history and culture; but there is enough material to suggest the possibility that it may have been a repository of Shang culture after the Chou conquest, as well as an area where Chinese culture came into contact with the barbarian cultures to the south and exchanged influences with them.

Chu (chö). [Also, **Tchu.**] River in the U.S.S.R., in C Asia; it rises in the Tien Shan Mountains in the Kirgiz Soviet Socialist Republic, near Lake Issyk Kul, and is lost in the sands of the Kazakh Soviet Socialist Republic. It was formerly a tributary of the Syr Darya. Length, ab. 600 mi.

Chuana (chwä'nä). See **Tswana.**

Chuanchow (chwän'jō') or **Chuanchowfu** (-jō'fö'). Former names of **Tsinkiang.**

Chuang-tze or **Chwang-tse** (jwäng'dzu'). Chinese mystic and philosopher, noted as an expounder of Taoism. Only a comparatively small portion of his writings survive, and even this probably contains matter which is erroneously attributed to him, but it seems evident that he was the greatest Taoist writer after Lao-tze and the most persuasive commentator on that master's thought. Chuang-tze was often quite blunt in his adverse comments on the utilitarian system of Confucius. One of his fancifully poetic illustrations of the essence of Taoism which has particularly charmed the Western mind is that in which he represents that he is uncertain whether he is Chuang-tze dreaming himself a butterfly, or a butterfly dreaming himself Chuang-tze.

Chuapa (chwä'pä). See **Choapa.**

Chubar (chu.bär'). See **Chahbar.**

Chubb (chub), **Thomas.** b. at East Harnham, near Salisbury, England, Sept. 29, 1679; d. at Salisbury, England, Feb. 8, 1746. English deist and religious writer.

Chubb Crater. Crater in N Canada, near Hudson Bay, believed originally to have been caused by a meteor and reported in 1951 to be the deepest depression of its kind in the world. Discovered in 1949, it was explored in August, 1951, by an expedition under the auspices of the National Geographic Society and the Royal Ontario (Canada) Museum. It is 1,350 ft. deep and contains a lake whose deepest point is 850 ft. The walls of the crater, which geologists believe to have been made from 3,000 to 15,000 years ago, are of granite.

Chubut (chö.BÖT'). Territory in S Argentina, lying S of the territory of Río Negro, N of the territory of Santa Cruz, W of the Atlantic Ocean, and E of Chile. Despite the existence of oil in the south, it remains of minor economic importance. It is perhaps chiefly noteworthy for its small Welsh communities, which date back to 1865 and remain today Welsh in customs and speech. Capital, Rawson; area, 65,669 sq. mi.; pop. 53,986 (1947).

Chubut River. River in S Argentina, flowing E to the Atlantic Ocean in Chubut territory.

Chu Chia-hua (chö' chyä'hwä'). b. at Wuhsing, Chekiang, China, 1893—. Chinese geologist and Kuomintang political leader, educated in Germany. He held a succession of educational and cultural positions including minister of education (1932, 1944–48), chairman of the Sino-German Cultural Association (1935), and acting president of the Academia Sinica (1942–49). His political posts include those of chief (1940–44) of the key Kuomintang ministry of organization, which he held as a rival of the Ch'en brothers, and vice-premier (1949) in Yen Hsi-shan's cabinet.

Chucuito (chö.kwē'tō). [Also: **Chucuyto, Chuquito** (chö.kē'tō).] Town in S Peru, in Puno department, on Lake Titicaca ab. 15 mi. SE of Puno. Under the Incas this was the most important town of the Collao, and ancient ruins still exist near it. Pop. under 5,000 (1940).

Chudleigh (chud′li). Civil parish and market town in SW England, in Devonshire, situated on the river Teign, ab. 8 mi. SW of Exeter, ab. 188 mi. SW of London by rail. 1,944 (1931).

Chudleigh, Cape. See **Chidley, Cape.**

Chudleigh, Elizabeth. Maiden name of **Pierrepont, Elizabeth.**

Chudskoe Ozero (chöt′skǫ.yę ô′zyi.rǫ). See **Peipus, Lake.**

Chuffey (chuf′i). Superannuated clerk who saves the life of old Anthony Chuzzlewit in Charles Dickens's *Martin Chuzzlewit.*

Chufut-Kale (chö.föt′kä.le′). [Russian, **Zhidovskii gorod** (*gorod* = "city").] Ruined city in SW U.S.S.R., in the S central part of the Crimean peninsula, ab. 2 mi. E of Bakhchisarai. The earliest known settlement was the nearby Tartar fortress of Kirkor, which dated back at least to the 11th century. The Karaites, a Jewish sect, were in Chufut-Kale at least as early as the 14th century, and in the 18th century they numbered 300 families, the largest such settlement in the Crimea. The town was built on cliffs at an elevation of ab. 790 ft., and had many cave dwellings, now deserted.

Chugach Mountains (chö′gak). Mountain range in S Alaska, extending from ab. 9 mi. E of Anchorage, eastward to the Canadian border. It is a high rugged range, composed of sedimentary and old volcanic rocks, with numerous glaciers and permanent snowfields. The peak (known) elevation is Mount Marcus Baker (ab. 13,250 ft.). Length, ab. 300 mi.; greatest width, ab. 90 mi.

Chukchi (chök′chē). [Also, **Luoravetlany.**] Population of the most northeasterly extension of Siberia, from Bering Strait W to the Kolyma River, and largely N of 64° N. The Chukchi, who number 12,000 (1936), are extensive reindeer herders, owning about half a million heads in 1934. A third of the Chukchi are settled coastal dwellers, who live largely on sea mammals. The Chukchi language is related to that of the Koryak and Kamchadal; a close historical connection between the Chukchi and the Indians of North America was suggested by Franz Boas.

Chukchi Peninsula. [Russian, **Chukotski Poluostrov** (chö.kôt′ski po.lö.ôs′trǫf).] Large peninsula in extreme NE U.S.S.R. between the Bering Sea and the Arctic Ocean, separated from Alaska by the Bering Strait. The area is largely mountainous or hilly, and is barren in appearance, lying entirely within the tundra zone. There are some minerals; coal is found near the N coast. About 12,000 nomadic Chukchis inhabit the area, and about 1,000 Eskimos live on the coast.

Chu-Kiang (jö′jyäng′). Chinese name of the **Canton River.**

Chukovsky (chö.kôf′ski), **Korney Ivanovich.** b. 1882—. Russian critic and writer of juveniles. An English translation of his *Crocodile,* a tale in verse for children, was published in 1931.

Chulalok (chu̇′lä′lôk′), **P'ra P'utt'a Yot.** See **Rama I.**

Chulalongkorn (chu̇.lä.lông.kôn′), **Maha.** See **Rama V.**

Chula Vista (chö′lạ vis′tạ). City in S California, in San Diego County, ab. 10 mi. SE of the center of San Diego. Flowers and bulbs are grown here commercially. In the decade between the last two U.S. censuses its population more than tripled. 5,138 (1940), 15,927 (1950).

Chulucanas (chö.lö.kä′näs). City in NW Peru, in Piura department. 12,622 (1940).

Chulym (chö.lim′). [Also, **Chulim.**] River in the U.S.S.R., in C Siberia; it rises within 6 mi. of the Yenisei River, N of Krasnoyarsk, and flows eastward to the Ob River, which it joins ab. 75 mi. N of Tomsk. Length, ab. 500 mi.

Chumashan (chö′mash.ạn). North American Indian tribe, now extinct, formerly inhabiting a portion of the S California coast and parts of the Santa Barbara Islands. The language formed an independent family.

Chumbaba (ku̇m.bä′bạ). See **Khumbaba.**

Chunar (chu.när′). [Also, **Chunarghur** (chu.när′gur).] Fortified town in the district of Mirzapur, Uttar Pradesh (United Provinces), Union of India, on the Ganges River, ab. 19 mi. SW of Benares. It was taken by the English in 1764. The treaty of Chumar between Hastings and the Nawab of Oudh was concluded in 1781. Pop. ab. 9,000.

Chuncho (chön′chō). See **Anti,** Indian tribes.

Chung-chia (ju̇ng′jyä′). A non-Chinese people living in the Chinese provinces of Kweichow and Yunnan. They have a phonetic writing resembling in part that of the Lolo.

Chung-ch'iu (ju̇ng′chö′). [Eng. trans., "*Mid-Autumn.*"] Popular festival in China, held on the 15th of the eighth moon (lunar calendar) when the moon is full. At this season presents are exchanged, and a round "moon cake" is eaten. This is one of three periods in the year when Chinese merchants settle their accounts.

Chung-Hua Min-Kuo (ju̇ng′hwä′ min′gwô′). Chinese name of **China.**

Chungking (chu̇ng′ching′; Anglicized, chung.king′). [Also, **Pahsien.**] City in S central China, in the province of Szechwan, at the junction of the Kialing River with the Yangtze-Kiang. It was the capital of China during World War II, and is important as the major city in the Szechwan basin for trading and small manufacturing. It is a special municipality in the Chinese administrative system, with an area of 116 sq. mi.; pop. 1,002,787 (1946).

Chupas (chö′päs). Elevated plain W of Guamanga (now Ayacucho), Peru, ab. midway between Cusco and Lima. Here the younger Almagro was finally beaten by the royalist forces under Vaca de Castro, on Sept. 16, 1542.

Chupra (chu′prạ). See **Chapra.**

Chuquicamata (chö.kē.kä.mä′tä). Mining town in N Chile, ab. 162 mi. by rail NE of Antofagasta, in the foothills of the Western Andes. The copper ore deposit here is the greatest known in the world, with reserves estimated at 700 million tons of ore. Production of copper at the smelter of the Chile Exploration Company in the period 1946–49 averaged ab. 225,000 tons yearly, ab. 8½ percent of the world copper production. Expansion to a capacity of 270,000 tons annually is under way. Because of its location in a desert, water and electric power must be brought in from a distance. About 8,000 men are employed. Elevation, ab. 8,838 ft.; pop. 19,202 (1940).

Chuquisaca (chö.kē.sä′kä). See also **Charcas.**

Chuquisaca. Department in SE Bolivia. Capital, Sucre; area, 19,643 sq. mi.; pop. 282,980 (1950).

Chuquisaca. Indian name of **Sucre,** Bolivia.

Chuquito (chö.kē′tō). See **Chucuito.**

Chur (kör). [French, **Coire**; Italian, **Coira**; Romansh, **Cuera**; Latin, **Curia Rhaetorum.**] Town in SE Switzerland, the capital of the canton of Graubünden, situated on the Plessur River, near the Rhine. In spite of the elevation (1,926 ft.) the climate is mild. The surrounding region has orchards and vineyards. Buildings of interest include a natural history museum, a Rhaetian museum, an episcopal palace, and a very old Gothic and Romanesque cathedral, in part dating back to the 4th century. The present building was begun in 1175 and consecrated in 1282. It was restored in the period 1921–26. Pop. 17,060 (1941).

Church (chėrch). Urban district in NW England, in Lancashire, situated on the Leeds and Liverpool Canal, ab. 1 mi. W of Accrington, ab. 212 mi. NW of London by rail. 5,199 (1951).

Church, Benjamin. b. at Duxbury, Mass., 1639; d. at Little Compton, R.I., Jan. 17, 1718. American soldier. He took part in King Philip's War, including the swamp fight with the Narragansetts on Dec. 19, 1675, and was in command of the party which hunted and killed King Philip on Aug. 12, 1676. Under his direction and from his notes his son Thomas compiled *Entertaining Passages relating to Philip's War* (1716).

Church, Francis Pharcellus. b. at Rochester, N.Y., Feb. 22, 1839; d. at New York, April 11, 1906. American editor. He was the cofounder (1863) with his brother William Conant Church (1836–1917) of the *Army and Navy Journal,* editor of *The Galaxy* and the *Internal Revenue Record,* and an editorial writer (1874 *et seq.*) on the New York *Sun.*

Church, Frederick Edwin. b. at Hartford, Conn., May 4, 1826; d. at New York, April 7, 1900. American landscape painter; a pupil of Thomas Cole. Among his best-known works are *Niagara Falls from the Canadian Shore* (1857: in the Corcoran Gallery, Washington), *The Heart of the Andes* (1859), and *Cotopaxi* (1862).

Church, Frederick Stuart. b. at Grand Rapids, Mich., 1842; d. Feb. 18, 1923. American painter, especially of animals and people. He worked in water colors as well as in oils.

Church, Sir Richard. b. in County Cork, Ireland, 1784; d. at Athens, Greece, March 30, 1873. British soldier, long a military commander and official in the Greek service. He served as an ensign in the Egyptian campaign of 1801, became a captain in the Corsican Rangers in 1806, was present at the battle of Maida and took part in the defense of Capri and (as assistant quartermaster general) in various actions in the Ionian Islands, and was appointed lieutenant colonel of a Greek infantry regiment in 1812. When the Greek revolution began, he joined the insurgents on March 7, 1827, and possessed great influence as a leader of the movement and as a military commander. He also took part in the revolution of 1843. In that year he was appointed a senator, and in 1854 general in the Greek army.

Church, Richard. b. at London, March 26, 1893—. English poet, novelist, and critic. His published verse includes *Flood of Life* (1917), *Hurricane* (1919), *Philip* (1923), *The Dream* (1927), *Twelve Noon* (1936), *The Solitary Man* (1941), and *The Lamp* (1946). Among his prose works are *Mary Shelley* (1928), *Oliver's Daughter* (1930), *The Prodigal Father* (1933), *The Porch* (1937), *The Stronghold* (1939), *Calling for a Spade* (1939), *Plato's Mistake* (1941), *The Sampler* (1942), and *Kent* (1948).

Church, Richard William. b. at Lisbon, Portugal, April 25, 1815; d. at Dover, England, Dec. 9, 1890. English clergyman and writer, dean of Saint Paul's in the period 1871–90. He lived at Florence (1818–28), was graduated from Oxford in 1836, was a fellow of Oriel College (1838–52), was ordained a priest in 1852, and received the living of Whatley in Somerset in the same year. While a student at Oxford, he became a friend of Newman. During his subsequent career, he was a leader in the High Church movement. He was select preacher at Oxford in 1868 and in the periods 1876–78 and 1881–82. He wrote *Anselm* (1843: enlarged, 1870), *Dante* (1850), *Spenser* (1879), *Bacon* (1884), *A History of the Oxford Movement* (1891), and others.

Church, Sanford Elias. b. at Milford, N.Y., April 18, 1815; d. at Albion, N.Y., May 14, 1880. American jurist and politician. He was lieutenant governor of New York (1851–54), and chief justice of the state court of appeals (1871–80).

Church, William Conant. b. at Rochester, N.Y., Aug. 11, 1836; d. May 23, 1917. American editor. He assisted (1855–60) his father in editing the New York *Chronicle*, was publisher (1860–61) of the New York *Sun*, and served as Washington correspondent (1861–62) for the New York *Times*. After serving in the Civil War, he founded (1863) with his brother, Francis Pharcellus Church (1839–1906), the *Army and Navy Journal*. In 1866 he established, again with his brother, *The Galaxy* (which was merged in 1878 with the *Atlantic Monthly*), publishing works by Charles Reade and Anthony Trollope and the early writings of Henry James and Mark Twain.

Churches of Christ. See **Disciples of Christ.**

Churches Quarrel Espoused, The. Polemical writing by John Wise, published in 1710.

Church History of Britain, The. Prose work (1655) by Thomas Fuller. A huge work, a folio volume of 1300 pages, it is a successful attempt to continue the work of the Anglo-Saxon Bede.

Churchill (chėrch'il). Port in the province of Manitoba, Canada, situated on the right bank of the mouth of the Churchill River where that river enters Hudson Bay. The port was built in 1926 to provide a short route for western Canadian grain going to Europe. It is connected by rail with The Pas in Manitoba and with points further S in Saskatchewan. It is 978 mi. by rail from Winnipeg. The site of Churchill was occupied from 1737 on by old Prince of Wales Fort, a station of the Hudson Bay Company and a base for many explorers setting out to open up the West. Since the completion of the port facilities the number of ships docking has never reached expected levels and the grain continues to come to Montreal and other eastern ports. 2,168 (1951).

Churchill, Arabella. b. 1648; d. 1730. English lady; eldest daughter of Sir Winston Churchill (c1620–88), and elder sister of John Churchill, 1st Duke of Marlborough. She was a mistress of James II while he was still Duke of York.

Churchill, Charles. b. in Vine Street, at Westminster, London, in February, 1731; d. of fever at Boulogne, France, Nov. 4, 1764. English satirical poet, clergyman, teacher, and friend of John Wilkes. He was educated (1739–48) at Westminster School, London, but did not go to Christ Church, Oxford, or to Trinity College, Cambridge, as most Westminster boys did. He became a clergyman in 1756, and held curacies in Somersetshire, at Rainham, in Essex, and at Westminster (1758–63), as his father (also Charles) had done before him. At 17, he made an unwise marriage with a Westminster girl, named Scot, from whom he separated in 1761. He made a poor living by opening a school at Rainham, or Westminster, and taught in a girls' school kept by a Mrs. Dennis. He loved John Wilkes, hated all enemies of Wilkes, and detested Alexander Pope. He was generous in many ways, was free with his money, when he had it, and helped those whose need was greater than his. He left an annuity of 60 pounds to his wife, and of 50 pounds to his mistress, but did not leave any property to cover the annuities. Johnson thought him "a shallow fellow," but Byron visited his grave before his last departure from England, and wrote a poem on the occasion. His works are *The Rosciad* (1761), in which he bitterly satirizes practically every leading actor of the day, with the exception of Mrs. Cibber, Mrs. Clive, Mrs. Pritchard, and Garrick, *The Apology: Addressed to the Critical Reviewers* (1761), in which he attacked Smollett and warned Garrick, whom he had praised in the *Rosciad*, to be careful, *The Ghost* (1763), ridiculing Johnson for his investigation of the Cock Lane Ghost mystery, *The Prophecy of Famine: a Scots Pastoral* (1763), a satire on Bute, *The Duellist* (1763), defending Wilkes, who was wounded in a duel with Samuel Martin, and attacking all who opposed Wilkes, *The Author* (1763), another attack on Smollett, *Gotham* (1764), a political philosophy in verse in three books, and *The Candidate* (1764), attacking Lord Sandwich, who is satirized as Jemmy Twitcher, a character in Gay's *Beggar's Opera*. A minor work, a verse epistle to his friend Robert Lloyd, entitled *Night* (1762), is an attack on the *Day* of John Armstrong. *Independence* (September, 1764) has a special interest in that it gives us a portrait of the author as he saw himself. In a short writing life, Churchill produced a considerable amount of material, but his reputation rests largely on *The Rosciad*, which ranks with Pope's *Dunciad* and Byron's *English Bards and Scotch Reviewers*, on *The Duellist*, which brought him 450 pounds, a large sum in his time, and on *Gotham*, which was enthusiastically praised by Cowper (born in the same year as Churchill), who remembered him, 17 years after his death, as "the great Churchill."

Churchill, Frank. Handsome, lively young man in the novel *Emma* by Jane Austen. Emma picks him out as a very suitable match for her protegée, the orphaned Harriet Smith, only to find that he is already secretly engaged to Jane Fairfax.

Churchill, John. See **Marlborough,** 1st Duke of.

Churchill, Randolph Henry Spencer. [Called Lord **Randolph Churchill.**] b. Feb. 13, 1849; d. at London, Jan. 24, 1895. English politician, son of the 7th Duke of Marlborough and father of Winston L. S. Churchill (1874—). He entered Parliament in 1874, serving as Conservative member for Woodstock from 1874 to 1885, when he was returned for South Paddington. He was reëlected for South Paddington in 1886 and in 1892, was secretary for India in Lord Salisbury's first ministry (June, 1885–January, 1886), and in Salisbury's second ministry was chancellor of the exchequer and leader of the House of Commons from July to December, 1886. He married Jennie Jerome of New York in 1874.

Churchill, William. b. at Brooklyn, N.Y., Oct. 5, 1859; d. June 9, 1920. American ethnologist and philologist. As U.S. consul general (1896–99) to Samoa, he studied Polynesian languages. While department editor (1902–15) on the New York *Sun*, he published *Polynesian Wanderings* (1910), *Beach-la-Mar* (1911), and *Easter Island, Rapanui Speech and the Peopling of Southeast Polynesia* (1912).

Churchill, Sir Winston. b. at Wooton Glanville, England, c1620; d. March 26, 1688. English Royalist; father of John Churchill, 1st Duke of Marlborough. After the Restoration, he was elected (1681) a member of Parliament from Plymouth, served at court as a minor official under Charles II and James II, was a member of Parliament for Lynn Regis during the reign of James II, and was elected (1664) a Fellow of the Royal Society.

Churchill, Winston. b. at St. Louis, Mo., Nov. 10, 1871; d. at Winter Park, Fla., March 12, 1947. American historical novelist, dramatist, and essayist. He was educated at Smith Academy, St. Louis, and at the U.S. Naval Academy, Annapolis, graduating with the class of 1894. Before he turned to novel writing, he was editor of the *Army and Navy Journal* and on the staff of the *Cosmopolitan Magazine*, a post he resigned when he married Mabel Hall, on Oct. 22, 1895. In the period 1903–05 he served in the New Hampshire legislature, having moved to Cornish, N.H., at the time of his marriage, and in 1912 he ran for governor as the candidate of the Progressive Party, receiving over 14,000 votes. His literary works are *The Celebrity* (1898), *Richard Carvel* (1899), a novel of the American Revolution, with John Paul Jones, George Fox, Horace Walpole, and other historical characters, *The Crisis* (1901), a Civil War novel with a Northern hero and a Southern heroine, and with Grant and Lincoln as characters, *The Crossing* (1904), the story of David Ritchie, a drummer boy in the Clark expedition, *Coniston* (1906), a political novel exposing the kind of political corruption that defeated the author when he was a candidate for governor, *Mr. Crewe's Career* (1908), a reform novel attacking graft and railroad corporations, *A Modern Chronicle* (1910), dealing with the question of divorce, *The Inside of the Cup* (1913), presenting the conflict between Christianity and capitalism, *A Far Country* (1915), the story of a lawyer's tragic love affair, and *The Dwelling-Place of Light* (1917), dealing with the emotional problems of love and marriage. In addition to his novels of American history and politics, Churchill wrote *A Traveler in War-Time*, impressions of France and England, and *The American Contribution and the Democratic Idea*, an essay (both 1918), *The Title Mart* (1905), *Dr. Jonathan* (1919), *The Crisis* (1927), plays, and *The Unchartered Way* and *The Psychology of the Gospel Doctrine* (both 1940), religious works.

Churchill, Sir **Winston.** [Full name: **Winston Leonard Spencer Churchill.**] b. at Blenheim Palace, Oxfordshire, England, Nov. 30, 1874—. English statesman, prime minister (1940–45) during World War II and again in 1951, journalist and author, originator or popularizer of slogans and phrases like "blood, toil, tears and sweat" and the "V for victory" finger gesture; a descendant of John Churchill, 1st Duke of Marlborough, and son of Randolph Henry Spencer Churchill and the American Jennie Jerome.

Early Years. Churchill was educated at Harrow and was a cavalry cadet at the Royal Military College at Sandhurst. He entered the army, took leave to fight on the side of the Spanish forces in Cuba in 1895, fought in India (1897) and in the Sudan (1898), where he was decorated for services at the battle of Khartoum. In 1899 he was sent to South Africa to cover the Boer War as correspondent for the London *Morning Post.* He was captured there by Louis Botha but escaped after a month's imprisonment and thereafter participated actively in the military campaigns. In 1900 he was elected a Conservative member of Parliament, then joined the Liberal Party and served (1905–08) as undersecretary for the colonies under Henry Campbell-Bannerman, promoting the establishment of self-government in the Transvaal and Orange River Colony in South Africa. He was a member of the Asquith cabinet as president of the board of trade (1908–10) and home secretary (1910–11). In 1911 he became first lord of the admiralty, to carry out Asquith's program of readying the fleet for possible international conflict. He drove forward the building program, established a naval war staff (thereby creating an upheaval in settled English naval customs) to coöperate with the war office on strategy.

World War I. When war came in 1914, the Royal Navy was so well prepared that it was able at once to confine the German fleet, except for submarines and a few raiders, to its own home ports (the Battle of Jutland was the only instance in World War I when a major German naval force ventured within reach of the Royal Navy, and although this battle can hardly be said to have resulted in a clear-cut British victory on the pattern of Trafalgar, it did serve to convince the German naval staff of the inadvisability of an all-out test of strength between the two fleets. For this reason, the bulk of the German surface navy was thereafter held close to the German coast, and was thus unable to play a decisive part in the war. It was this, among other factors, which led the Germans more and more into a reliance upon the submarine as their major weapon on the high seas.) It was under Churchill's ministry also that the Royal Air Force (originally the Royal Flying Corps) was established. He directed the naval campaign against Antwerp and espoused the Dardanelles (Gallipoli) campaign. When the latter failed dismally, Churchill resigned (1915) and was succeeded by Arthur James Balfour. In 1916 he was a lieutenant-colonel on active service in France, but resigned his commission to accept the post of minister of munitions in the Lloyd George cabinet. He was (1918–21) secretary of state for war and for air, during which time occurred the clash with Lloyd George over Churchill's use of British troops in an attempt to put down the new Bolshevist regime in Russia. When the opportunity came to appoint a new chancellor of the exchequer, Lloyd George appointed Sir Robert Horne instead of Churchill, who was expected to get the appointment. Churchill was secretary of state for the colonies in 1921–22. In 1924 he was elected to Parliament from Epping, which he represented until 1945. In the second Baldwin cabinet he was (1924–29) chancellor of the exchequer. From 1929 to 1939, he held no cabinet posts but increasingly made it clear that he expected another war to occur, and that he considered his country to be taking woefully few measures to prepare for it. He fought the Neville Chamberlain policy of appeasement of Germany, and, on the outbreak of war in September, 1939, he was given the post of first lord of the admiralty in response to a general desire to see Churchill in the cabinet.

World War II. After the complete failure of British arms in Norway, the Chamberlain government fell and on May 10, 1940, Churchill became prime minister. In his first speech following his appointment, he said he had nothing to offer but "blood, toil, tears and sweat" to the English. In August, 1941, he met at sea off Newfoundland with President Franklin Roosevelt and together they issued the statement of international policy known as the Atlantic Charter. This was followed by numerous conferences on strategy, war aims, conciliation, and planning with the heads of the countries fighting Germany and Japan: at Washington in 1942 and 1943 with Roosevelt; at Moscow in 1942 and 1944 with Stalin; at Casablanca, Morocco, in 1943, when Churchill and Roosevelt agreed that only the unconditional surrender of Germany would be acceptable as an end to the war; at Quebec, Canada, in 1943 and 1944; at Cairo in 1943 with Chiang Kai-shek and Roosevelt, and at Tehran, Iran, the following month with Stalin and Roosevelt; at Yalta in the Crimea in 1945 with Stalin and Roosevelt; at Potsdam, Berlin, Germany, in 1945 with Stalin and President Truman, Churchill himself being replaced during the conference by the new prime minister, Clement Attlee. Churchill had, after the German defeat, removed from the cabinet its Labour members and thus enabled a general election. In July, 1945, the Conservatives were defeated and Clement Attlee became prime minister.

Later Years. Churchill now became leader of the opposition in Parliament. In 1946, in a speech at Westminster College in Fulton, Mo., he denounced Russian aggrandizement and asked for strong ties to bind the U.S. and Great Britain closely, describing the borders of Russian-held territory as being an "iron curtain." In February, 1950, his Conservative Party came very close to beating the Labour Party in a general election, and in October, 1951, it succeeded in ousting the Labour Party, Churchill again becoming prime minister. He was a constant supporter of the idea of a federal union of Western European states as a preventive measure against further wars. Churchill has several times refused to be elevated to the peerage, but was made a Knight of the Garter in 1953. Among his books are *Life of Lord Randolph Churchill* (1906), *My African Journey* (1908), *Liberalism and the Social Problem* (1909), a four-volume history of World War I, *The World Crisis* (1923–29; abridged and revised in one volume, 1931), *My Early Life* (1930), *Marlborough, his Life and Times* (4 volumes, 1933–38), and a series on World War II, including *The Gathering Storm* (1948), *Their Finest Hour* (1949), *The Grand Alliance* (1950), and *The Hinge of Fate* (1950).

Churchill River. [Also: **Beaver, English, Missinipi, Missinnippi.**] River in Manitoba, Canada, which rises in N Saskatchewan, and flows through various lakes into Hudson Bay, in the extreme NE corner of Manitoba. Length, 1,000 mi.

Church Island. See **Antelope Island.**

Church Music Society. English musical organization founded (1906) at London for the purpose of selecting and facilitating performances of sacred works of music.

Church of Jesus Christ of Latter-Day Saints. See **Latter-Day Saints.**

Church of the Holy Sepulcher. See **Holy Sepulcher, Church of the.**

Church of the Madeleine (màd.len). See **Madeleine, Church of the.**

Church Point. Town in S Louisiana, in Acadia Parish, ab. 60 mi. W of Baton Rouge in a rice-producing region. 2,897 (1950).

Churchyard (chèrch'yärd), **Thomas.** b. at Shrewsbury, England, c1520; d. at London, April 4, 1604. English poet, page to Henry Howard, Earl of Surrey, vagrant, hanger-on at court, and soldier. Between 1560 and 1603 he wrote a considerable amount of prose and poetry, much of it of autobiographical interest and referring to current happenings. Some of his works are *The Worthines of Wales* (1587), a long historical poem, *Shore's Wife*, a tragedy (in the 1563 enlarged edition of *A Mirror for Magistrates*), the story of Cardinal Wolsey (in the 1587 edition of the same work) and a volume of prose and poetry, *Churchyard's Challenge* (1593). As a soldier he saw service in Scotland, France, Ireland, and the Low Countries, and he drew on his own military experience in *Wofull Warres in Flaunders* (1578) and *General Rehearsal* (1579). Specimens of his verse are to be found in volumes with such curious titles as *Churchyard's Chips, Churchyard's Chance, Churchyard's Charge*, and *Churchyard's Good Will*, and he is represented in the famous Elizabethan anthologies *Tottel's Miscellany*, the *Paradise of Dainty Devices*, and a *Gorgeous Gallery of Gallant Inventions.* In Spenser's *Colin Clout's Come Home Again*, Churchyard is Old Palemon "that sang so long until quite hoarse he grew." He wrote to the very end of his long life, which included the reigns of Henry VIII, Edward VI, Mary, Elizabeth, and James I, and in his last years he dedicated *The Wonders of the Ayre, the Trembling of the Earth, and the Warnings of the World Before the Judgement Day* (1602) to a new patron, Dr. (later Sir) Julius Caesar, expressing gratitude to him "for the little that I live upon and am likely to die withall." He was buried in Saint Margaret's Church at Westminster, London.

Churriguera (chör.rē.gā'rä), **José.** b. at Salamanca, Spain, 1650; d. 1725. Spanish sculptor and architectural innovator. He went to Madrid in 1688, and in the reign of Charles II of Spain became the royal architect. His own work is to be seen in the design of various Spanish churches and palaces, and in sculptured altars, tombs, and statues; but his considerable importance arises from the fact that he was able to put the impress of his taste, for good or ill, on Spanish ecclesiastical architecture to such an extent that the resulting type is known as Churrigueresque. It has been described as a combination of the baroque and the rococo. It made some startling innovations in matters of columns and capitals, and added all the grandiose, extravagant, and capricious ornamentation that a structure would bear. Churrigueresque is seen in full flower in the cathedral at Murcia, Spain, and it dominated the design of churches and missions in Mexico and California, where it can be seen to this day, though in some instances the lack of skilled artisans in Spanish America during the colonial period prevented it from achieving its richest effects.

Churubusco (chö.rö.bös'kō). Village in S Mexico, in the Distrito Federal, ab. 5 mi. S of Mexico City. During the Mexican War, on Aug. 20, 1847 (after the battle of Contreras), about 8,000 U.S. troops under Scott defeated there a force of 20,000–25,000 Mexicans under Santa Anna. An old convent in the village, garrisoned by about 800 Mexican troops under General Pedro María Anaya, was attacked by about 6,000 U.S. soldiers under Generals Twiggs, Smith, and Worth. The strong convent walls served as a fortress, and it was only carried after a severe battle, the ammunition of the defenders being exhausted. The losses were: U.S., 1,053; Mexico, ab. 7,000 (including the battle of Contreras).

Churwalden (kör'väl.dẹn). Town in SE Switzerland, in the canton of Graubünden: a health resort. 758 (1941).

Chu Shan (chö' shän'). [Also: **Chusan** (chö.sän'), **Chou Shan** (Chinese, jō' shän').] Largest island of the Chu Shan Archipelago, situated in the East China Sea. It belongs to the province of Chekiang, China.

Chu Shan Archipelago. [Also: **Chusan, Chou Shan.**] Group of islands E of China, belonging to the province of Chekiang. They are located in the East China Sea, just off the coast of Chekiang. Chu Shan is the largest of the group. Capital, Tinghai; pop. ab. 400,000.

Chusovaya (chö.so.vä'yạ). [Also, **Tchusovaya.**] River in the U.S.S.R., in the Molotov *oblast* (region) of the Russian Soviet Federated Socialist Republic. It rises in the Ural Mountains, flows NW, and joins the Kama River NE of Molotov. Length, 300–400 mi.

Chust (ċhüst). Czech name of **Khust.**

Chut (shüt), **de.** A pseudonym of **Mirabeau,** Comtesse **de.**

Chu Teh (jö' du'). b. at Ilung, Szechwan, China, 1886—. Chinese soldier, the foremost Communist military leader in his country. Starting as an old-style militarist in Yunnan under Ts'ai Ao, he broke with his past, accompanied some Chinese students to Germany, and there joined (1922) a branch of the Chinese Communist Party. Returned (1924) to China, he joined (1926–27) in the Northern Expedition and participated (1927) in the Nanchang Uprising and in establishing (1928) the precursor of the Kiangsi Soviet. Chiefly responsible for building up the Chinese Communist army, he led it on the Long March (1934–35), in the anti-Japanese war (1937–45), and in the civil war after 1945. He became (1949) deputy chairman of the military committee and one of the six vice-chairmen of the Central People's Government Council in the Peiping government.

Chutia Nagpur (chö'ti.ạ näg'pör). See **Chota Nagpur.**

Chutterpur (chut'ėr.pör). See **Chhatarpur.**

Chuuichupa (chö.wē.chö'pä). Occasional name of the region of the sources of the Yaqui River in the Sierra Madre, near the confines of Sonora and Chihuahua, Mexico.

Chuvash (chö.väsh'). Turkic people, numbering 1,368,000 (1939), and largely living in the Chuvash Autonomous Soviet Socialist Republic of the U.S.S.R., on the Upper Volga River. Descendants of the Volga Bulgars, they early adopted intensive agriculture and Christianity. Until recently, however, many pagan beliefs were still current.

Chuvash Autonomous Soviet Socialist Republic. [Also, **Chuvashia** (chö.väsh'i.ạ).] Republic in the U.S.S.R., in the Russian Soviet Federated Socialist Republic, centered ab. 375 mi. E of Moscow, in the Volga uplands. There are few minerals in the area; the chief crops are spring wheat, rye, flax, and sunflowers; the main occupations of the people are farming, lumbering, herding, and the working of leather goods. The republic was formed on April 21, 1925. Capital, Cheboksary; area, 6,909 sq. mi.; pop. 1,077,614 (1939).

Chuzenji (chö.zen.jē). Lake in C Honshu, Japan, ab. 7 mi. W of Nikko. It is beautifully located in the mountains, and has become a favorite summer resort for foreign diplomats. Elevation, ab. 4,170 ft.; area, ab. 4½ sq. mi.

Chuzzlewit (chuz'l.wit), **Anthony.** Shrewd and cunning father of Jonas, in Charles Dickens's *Martin Chuzzlewit.*

Chuzzlewit, Jonas. Unscrupulous, selfish, and overreaching fellow, the cousin of Martin and son of Anthony Chuzzlewit, in Charles Dickens's *Martin Chuzzlewit.* His slyness, selfish ignorance, and brutality finally culminate in murder.

Chuzzlewit, Martin. Young architect, the principal character in Charles Dickens's novel of that name. At first dissipated, he is reformed by dint of many hard knocks from fortune, especially in his dreary American adventures with Mark Tapley in search of wealth, and eventually becomes the heir of his rich grandfather. (The section of the book dealing with Martin's travels in the U.S., from his arrival at New York and subsequent emigration to a settlement on the frontier, clearly reveals Dickens's distaste for certain aspects of 19th-century American culture, and led at the time of its first publication to a tremendous amount of resentment among his readers in the U.S.)

Chuzzlewit, Martin. Grandfather of Martin Chuzzlewit, in Charles Dickens's novel of that name.

Chvostek (hvôs'tek), **Franz.** b. at Vienna, Oct. 3, 1864—. Austrian clinician, known for his studies on nervous diseases. He was assistant at Vienna to H. Bamberger, O. Kahler, and E. von Neusser at the internal clinic, and to Th. Meynert at the psychiatric clinic. He became privatdocent of internal medicine in 1894, professor in 1897, and full professor in 1909. In 1911 he was named director of the Third Medical Clinic at Vienna. The increased sensitivity of nerves in tetanus, described by him in 1891, is called Chvostek's sign. He wrote on bone lesions in parathyroid disease (1908), and on anemia of pancreatic origin (which bears his name). He is the author of *Über das Verhalten der sensiblen Nerven, der Höhrnerven und des Hautleitungswiderstandes bei Tetanie* (1889), *Zur Symptomatologie der Chlorose* (1893), *Über das Wesen der paroxysmalen Haemoglobinurie* (1894), *Gangraena cutis* (1905), *Beiträge zur Lehre von der Tetanie* (1907), *Myasthenia gravis und Epithelkörper* (1908), and *Morbus Basedowi und die Hyperthyreosen* (1917).

Chwana (chwä'nä). See **Tswana.**

Chyavana (chyä.vä'na). In the mythology of India, a *Rishi* (sage) who, when old, was made again a youth by the Asvins. This idea, all that is found in the *Rig-Veda*, is variously developed in stories of Chyavana in the *Satapatha Brahmana* and the *Mahabharata*, a motive of which is to explain how the Asvins came to share libations of soma.

Chyosyon (chyō.syėn). A Korean name of **Korea.**

Chypre (shepr). French name of **Cyprus.**

Cialdini (chäl.dē'nē), **Enrico.** [Title, Duke of **Gaeta.**] b. at Castelvetro, Modena, Italy, Aug. 10, 1811; d. at Leghorn, Italy, Sept. 8, 1892. Italian general, politician, and diplomat. He served with distinction in the campaigns of the period 1860–61, and was ambassador to France (1876–79, 1880–81).

Ciamberi (chäm'be.rē). Italian name of **Chambéry.**

Ciamician (chä.mē.chän'), **Giacomo Luigi.** b. at Trieste, 1857; d. at Bologna, Italy, 1922. Italian organic chemist. He carried out (1880–1905) an important investigation of pyrrole and its derivatives, and made (1900–15) numerous pioneer photochemical studies, with P. Silber. Professor at Padua (1887–89) and Bologna (1889–1922), he also served as a senator in the period 1910–22. He was awarded a royal prize by the Accademia dei Lincei.

Ciampi (chäm'pē), **Lorenzio Vincenzo.** b. at Piacenza, Italy, 1719; d. 1762. Italian operatic composer, remembered chiefly for his son *Tre giorni son che Nina.* He was active at London (1748 *et seq.*) conducting his operas, which include *Adriano in Siria, Didone,* and *Bertolde in Corte.*

Ciança (thyän'thä), **Andres de.** b. at Peñafiel, in the diocese of Palencia, Spain; fl. mid-16th century. Spanish lawyer. He went with Casca to Peru in 1546, was made a member of the Audience there, and was one of the judges who condemned Gonzalo Pizarro and Carvajal to death. From January, 1550, to September, 1551, he governed Peru as president of the Audience.

Ciano (chä'nō), Count **Costanzo.** b. at Leghorn, Italy, Aug. 30, 1876; d. at Ponte a Moriano, Italy, June 27, 1939. Italian statesman and naval hero; father of Galeazzo Ciano. He enlisted in the Italian navy (1896) as an ensign, and led (November, 1917) as admiral of the fleet the attack on the Austrian ships *Wien* and *Budapest,* forcing them to give up Cortellazzo; for this action he received the title of count. He retired after World War I. As an early Fascist he participated (1922) with Mussolini in the march on Rome; he was appointed a deputy (1921), undersecretary of state for the navy (1922), and minister of posts and communications (1924). In 1934 he headed the chamber of deputies, and became (1939) head of the chamber of Fasces and corporations.

Ciano, Count Galeazzo. [Full surname, **Ciano di Cortellazzo.**] b. at Leghorn, Italy, March 18, 1903; d. at Verona, Italy, Jan. 11, 1944. Italian statesman and Fascist leader; son of Costanzo Ciano. He took part (1922) in the march on Rome, and joined (1925) the Italian foreign service, in which he served (1925–30) at Rio de Janeiro, Peiping, and the Vatican City. In 1930 he became consul general at Shanghai and subsequently minister plenipotentiary to China. In 1930 he married Edda Mussolini, eldest daughter of the head of the Fascist Party. He served as chief (1933) of the Italian press office, undersecretary (1934) for press and propaganda, and minister (1935) for the same department. In the Ethiopian war (1935–36) he held high rank in the Italian air force, with responsibility particularly for the Italian strategic and tactical bombing efforts in that conflict. While serving (1936–43) as minister of foreign affairs, he developed an increasing antagonism toward the Germans (and toward Ribbentrop in particular); this reached a peak in 1940, and by 1942 he was also in conflict with Mussolini on matters of policy. Forced (Feb. 5, 1943) to leave the foreign office, he became ambassador to Vatican City. He was a member (1943) of the group which plotted to oust Mussolini. Interned (1944) in Germany, he was handed over to northern Italian Fascists who held a special treason trial at Verona and shot him. His diary was published in 1946 in Italy and appeared in the U.S. in translation.

Ciardi (chär'dē), **Guglielmo.** b. at Venice, Sept. 13, 1843; d. 1917. Venetian marine, landscape, and genre painter, especially noted for his seascapes. He studied art at Venice and Florence, later traveling to Germany. He won several awards, and his work has been exhibited in many European galleries. Among his better-known works are *Summer, Towards Evening, Morning at Venice, Fishing Boats, The Torrent,* and *In the Fields.*

Cibalae (sib'a.lē). [Also, **Cibalis** (-lis).] In ancient geography, a town in Pannonia, near what is now Osijek in Yugoslavia. Here Constantine defeated (314) Licinius.

Cibao (sē.bä'ō). See **Cordillera Central,** Hispaniola.

Cibber (sib'ėr) or **Cibert** (sib'ėrt), **Caius Gabriel.** b. at Flensborg, Holstein, 1630; d. at London, 1700. Danish sculptor, resident in England; father of Colley Cibber. Among his better-known works are the statues *Melancholy* and *Raving Madness.*

Cibber, Colley. b. at London, Nov. 6, 1671; d. there, Dec. 12, 1757. English comic actor, dramatist, theater manager, biographer, and a victim of Pope's malice who represents him as the King of Dullness in his *Dunciad.* He was the son of Caius Gabriel Cibber (or Cibert, 1630–1700), a sculptor who was born in Flensborg, Holstein, and he was the father of Theophilus Cibber, like himself an actor and a dramatist. He was educated in Lincolnshire, at the Grantham Free School, which goes back to Edward VI, but he did not attend either Cambridge or Oxford. He began his stage career about 1690, as a member of Betterton's company, and in 1691 he was acting minor roles in the London Theatre Royal. He was attacked, on grounds of immorality and indecency, by Jeremy Collier, in his famous *Short View,* and, on literary and artistic grounds, by Fielding. From 1711–32, he was, with Wilks and Doggett, one of the managers of London's famous Drury Lane Theatre. In 1730, he was made poet laureate, an appointment that was severely attacked by his fellow writers, Pope being only one of many who belittled him. Cibber was an inferior poet, probably one of the worst to hold the office, and he frankly admitted that the post was given to him as a reward for being a good Whig. He made his first stage success in 1692 as the Chaplain in Otway's tragedy *The Orphan,* and his last, on Feb. 15, 1745, as Pandulph in *Papal Tyranny in the Reign of King John,* a "wretched version" of Shakespeare's *King John.* As an actor he was at his best in eccentric parts, but he failed as a tragedian, being more than once hissed off the stage. Some of the roles associated with him are Don Manuel in his own *She Would and She Would Not* (1702), the title role in Crowne's *Sir Courtly Nice* (1703), Sir Fopling Flutter in *The Man of Mode* (1706) of Etherege, Ben in Congreve's *Love for Love* (1708), Gloster in his own version of *King Lear,* Iago in *Othello,* Sparkish in Wycherley's *Country Wife* (1708–09), Fondlewife in Congreve's *Old Bachelor,* Tinsel in Addison's

The Drummer (1716), Barnaby Brittle in *The Amorous Widow* of Betterton, Bayes in *The Rehearsal*, Shallow in Betterton's version of *Henry IV*, Jaques in *Love in a Forest*, an alteration of *As You Like It*, Dr. Wolf in his own play *The Nonjuror* (1717), Wolsey in *Henry VIII*, and Lord Richly in *The Modern Husband* of Fielding (1732). Perhaps his most successful role was that of Sir Novelty Fashion, newly created Lord Foppington, in Vanbrugh's *The Relapse, or Virtue in Danger* (1697), which was a sequel to Cibber's own *Love's Last Shift, or the Fool in Fashion* (1696). Some of the many plays he wrote, either original or adaptations of other works, English or Continental, are *Woman's Wit, or The Lady in Fashion* (1697), *Xerxes* (1699), a tragedy whose first performance, at Lincoln's Inn Fields, was its last, his version of *Richard III*, which still holds the stage today, *Love Makes the Man, or the Fop's Fortune* (a combination of two plays, *The Custom of the Country* and *The Elder Brother*, by Beaumont and Fletcher), *The Careless Husband* (1704), a comedy of intrigue, *Perolla and Izadora* (1705), a tragedy, *The Comical Lovers* (1707), combining two plays by Dryden, *The Rival Fools* (1709), altered from Beaumont and Fletcher, *Venus and Adonis* (1716), a masque, *Ximena, or the Heroick Daughter* (1718), a tragedy based partly on the *Cid;* also *The Refusal, or the Ladies' Philosophy* (1721), from *Les Femmes savantes* of Molière, *Caesar in Egypt* (1725) (based on *The False One* of Beaumont and Fletcher and a French play, *The Death of Pompey*, by Corneille), *The Provoked Husband* (1728), a completed version of Sir John Vanbrugh's unfinished comedy, *A Journey to London* (in which Cibber appeared as Sir Francis Wronghead, a country gentleman, who is called Headpiece in Vanbrugh's fragment), *The Rival Queans, with the Humours of Alexander the Great* (1729), a comical tragedy, *Love in a Riddle* (1729, 1719 being a printer's error), a pastoral that was met with hisses, an imitation of Gay's *Beggar's Opera*, and *Damon and Phillida* (1729), a ballad opera which was simply *Love in a Riddle* in a converted form and which was immediately successful and for a long time after.

Cibber, Susannah Maria. [Maiden name, **Arne.**] b. at London, in February, 1714; d. at Westminster, London, Jan. 30, 1766. English actress and singer; wife of Theophilus Cibber and sister of Thomas Arne. Her first appearance was at the Haymarket in 1732, in the opera *Amelia* by Lumpé, and her reputation was for several years chiefly founded upon her singing. Handel wrote leading parts for her in some of his oratorios. In 1736 she made her debut as a tragic actress in the part of Zarah, in Hill's version of Voltaire's *Zaïre*, and rapidly became famous.

Cibber, Theophilus. b. Nov. 26, 1703; perished in a shipwreck in the Irish Channel, in October, 1758. English actor and dramatist; son of Colley Cibber and husband of Susannah Maria Cibber. He wrote *The Lover* (1730), *Patie and Peggy, or the Fair Foundling* (1730), *The Harlot's Progress, or the Ridotto al Fresco* (1733), *The Auction* (1757), and others. He also published an alteration of *Henry VI*. His wife abandoned him a few years after their marriage; Cibber was said to be a man of unsavory reputation.

Cibert (sib'ėrt), **Caius Gabriel.** See **Cibber** or **Cibert, Caius Gabriel.**

Cibò (chē.bō'), **Giovanni Battista.** Original name of Pope **Innocent VIII.**

Cíbola (sē'bō.lä; Anglicized, sē'bọ.lạ). Spanish name (apparently first used c1539 by Fray Marcos de Niza) for the pueblos of the Zuñi region in E Arizona and W New Mexico, called by Coronado the Seven Cities of Cíbola. It is believed to be an adaptation of the Zuñi tribal name "Shiwi," or "Shiuona." This term is also used for the distinctive culture of the region during the Regressive Pueblo period (1300–1700 A.D.), of which glazed pottery is characteristic.

Cíbola, Seven Cities of. Name given by Coronado and his companions to the seven Zuñi towns in New Mexico during explorations in the period 1540–42 of what is now the American Southwest. It was believed at the time that the various Pueblo Indian groups such as the Zuñi possessed riches comparable to those which the Spaniards had found in the Aztec and Inca cities of Central and South America. As Coronado discovered, no such treasure existed, but it was the legend of Pueblo wealth which led to his expedition and its discoveries.

Ciboney (sē.bō.nā'). Name of an archaeological culture and of several extinct Indian groups in SW Haiti and W Cuba. The Ciboney were a nonagricultural population, of uncertain extent, in the Antilles, and preceded the Arawak and Carib movement into the Antilles. The language is unknown today.

Cibot (sē.bō), **François Barthélemy Michel Édouard.** b. at Paris, Feb. 11, 1799; d. there, Jan. 10, 1877. French painter, noted especially for historical subjects and landscapes.

Cibot, Pierre Martial. b. at Limoges, France, 1727; d. at Peiping, China, Aug. 8, 1780. French Jesuit missionary in China. He was the author of many dissertations and treatises, comprised in the *Mémoires concernant l'histoire des lettres, sciences et arts de la Chine.*

Cibrario (chē.brä'ryō), Conte **Giovanni Antonio Luigi.** b. at Turin, Italy, Feb. 23, 1802; d. at Salo, Brescia, Italy, Oct. 1, 1870. Italian jurist, historian, and politician, cabinet minister from 1852 to 1856. He wrote *Storia della monarchia di Savoia* (1840–47), *Della economia politica del Medio Evo* (1842), *Origini e progressi delle instituzioni della monarchia di Savoia* (1854–55), and others.

Cibyra (sib'i.rạ). [Called **Cibyra Magna** (mag'nạ).] In ancient geography, a town in Phrygia, Asia Minor, near the site of the Turkish village of Korzum, ab. 65 mi. NW of Antalya. It was surnamed "Magna" to distinguish it from a smaller town of the same name in Pamphylia. Its ruins comprise an odeum, 175 ft. in diameter, with 13 tiers of seats visible above ground. The front wall is noteworthy, and is practically complete; it has five arched doorways between two square ones. There are also an ancient theater of some size and considerable interest, and a stadium, in part excavated from a hillside. There are 21 tiers of seats in marble, which remain in place around the curved end. There was a monumental entrance, consisting of three lofty arches.

Cicacole (sik.ạ.kōl'). See **Chicacole.**

Cicely Homespun (hōm'spun). See **Homespun, Zekiel and Cicely.**

Cicero (sis'ẹ.rō). City in NE Illinois, in Cook County, adjoining Chicago on the W. Manufactures include building materials, telephone equipment, and iron products; there are over 100 industries. During the Prohibition era, it attained considerable notoriety from the fact that Al Capone made it the headquarters for a major portion of his organization in the Chicago area. 67,544 (1950).

Cicero, Marcus Tullius. [Formerly called **Tully.**] b. at Arpinum (now Arpino), Italy, Jan. 3, 106 B.C.; assassinated near Formiae (now Formia), Italy, Dec. 7, 43 B.C. Roman orator, philosopher, and statesman; brother of Quintus Tullius Cicero. He served in the Social War in 89, traveled in Greece and Asia in the period 79–77, and was quaestor in Sicily in 75. On behalf of the Sicilians, he accused (70) Verres, who had been propraetor in Sicily, of criminal extortions; his orations were so effective that Verres left Rome and was found guilty in his absence. Cicero was aedile in 69, served as praetor in 66, and as consul suppressed Catiline's conspiracy to kill the consuls in 63. Cicero was banished in 58 for his action in killing members of Catiline's group, living in Thessalonica, but was recalled by Pompey in 57. He was proconsul of Cilicia in the period 51–50, and joined Pompey against Caesar in 49. He lived at Brundisium from September, 48, to September, 47, having been pardoned and received by Caesar. After the slaying of Caesar in 44, Cicero pronounced the Philippics in 44 and 43 against Antony, whom he detested, for which he was proscribed by the Second Triumvirate (Octavian, Antony, Lepidus) and slain in 43. Of his orations 57 are extant (with fragments of 20 more), including *Against Verres* (*In Verrem;* six speeches, 70 B.C., five of which were never delivered), *Against Catiline* (*In Catilinam;* four speeches, 63 B.C.), *For Archias* (*Pro Archia;* 62 B.C.), *Against Piso* (*In Pisonem;* 55 B.C.), *For Milo* (*Pro Milone;* 52 B.C.), *For Marcellus* (*Pro Marcello;* 46 B.C.), and the *Philippics* (*Philippicae;* 14 speeches, 44–43 B.C.). His other works include books on rhetoric and oratory, *On the Republic* (*De republica;* 51 B.C.), *On Law* (*De legibus;* c52 B.C.), *On the Ends of Good and Evil* (*De finibus bonorum et* *malorum*), *Tusculan Disputations* (*Tusculanae disputationes*), *On the Nature of the Gods* (*De natura deorum*), *Cato major* (also known as *De senectute*, On Old Age), *On Divination* (*De divinatione*), *Laelius* (also known as *De amicitia*, On Friendship), and *On Duty* (*De officiis*). There are, besides, four collections of his letters. He also wrote poetry, including an epic on Marius. Cicero is known as a supreme master of Latin, and imitation of his work and emulation of his style have been the aim of Latin scholars since the Renaissance.

Cicero, Quintus Tullius. b. c102 B.C.; killed 43 B.C. Roman commander; younger brother of Marcus Tullius Cicero. He distinguished himself in Gaul in 54. He was condemned to death by the same proscription issued against his brother. He was the author of letters and an epistle to his brother.

Cicerone (chē.che.rō′nā). Work in the form of a guidebook by Jakob Burckhardt which contains a historic and descriptive account of the ancient and modern art of Italy. The first edition was published at Basel, Switzerland, in 1855 in seven small volumes.

Cicester (sis′ęs.tėr). See **Cirencester.**

Cicogna (chē.kō′nyä), **Emmanuele Antonio.** b. at Venice, Jan. 17, 1789; d. there, Feb. 22, 1868. Italian historian and archaeologist. He wrote *Delle inscrizioni Veneziane* (1824–53) and others.

Cicognani (chē.kō.nyä′nē), **Bruno.** b. at Florence, 1879—. Italian novelist and playwright. A Tuscan by birth and education, Cicognani has all the well-known merits of writers from that region: clarity, simplicity, and directness. He draws from his own wide experience as a lawyer for the delineation of his characters which for the most part are intellectually mediocre or morally weak types. Some critics acclaim his ability to penetrate the motives and drives of the human personality while others charge him with a too minute exposition of small details. Inherent in all his works is an attempt to correlate the physical and moral aspects of a person coupled with a deep feeling of sympathy and understanding for the weaknesses and tragedies of the human lot. His works include *La Velia* (1923), *Villa Beatrice* (1932), both novels, *Il Figurinaio* (1934, 1942), a series of sketches, and his dramatic fable which was presented in Italy by the Pirandello company, *Bellinda e il mostro* (1927). Cicognani is at his best in his novels or sketches.

Cicognara (chē.kō.nyä′rä), Count **Leopoldo.** b. at Ferrara, Italy, Nov. 17, 1767; d. at Venice, March 5, 1834. Italian antiquary and diplomat. He was the author of *Storia della scultura* (1813–18), and others. The library he collected in his travels through Italy is now in the Vatican library.

Cicuique (sē.kē.kā). See under **Pecos, N.M.**

Cid (thēᴛʜ), **Crónica del.** [Eng. trans., "*Chronicle of the Cid.*"] Name of one of the Spanish accounts of the Cid (date of writing unknown, but printed in 1512). It is the same in substance with the history of the Cid in the *Crónica general ó estovia de España* (General Chronicle of the History of Spain) composed and compiled (c1260) by King Alfonso X of Spain (Alfonso el Sabio).

Cid (sēd), **Le.** French tragedy by Pierre Corneille, first acted in 1637 (rather than, as it was long believed, 1636). It was a brilliant success, and is considered the chief stimulus for later French tragedy. His rivals' jealousy of Corneille's success aroused much heated criticism of the play during the "Cid quarrel," a literary controversy in which Corneille was severely criticized by Georges de Scudéry and other prominent men of letters for his deviation from classical form and for plagiarism.

Cid (sid), **Romances of the.** Name often applied to the group of dramatic works and chronicles, written usually in verse, by various known and unknown Spanish authors on the theme of the Cid. Among them is the old poetical Spanish chronicle, *Crónica Rimada de las Cosas de España*, nearly the whole of which is devoted to the story of the Cid. It is later than the *Song of the Cid*, and was first published (1846) by Michel in the *Jahrbücher der Literatur*, vol. CXV, at Vienna. Both these poems seem built up from older ballads.

Cid, Song of the. [Spanish, **Poema del Cid.**] Poem composed by an unknown author c1150. It consists of more than 3,000 lines, and is a bold and spirited exhibition of national peculiarities in the chivalrous times of Spain. It was printed first by Sanchez in the first volume of his *Poesías Castellanas Anteriores al Siglo XV* (Madrid, 1779–90).

Cid (sid; Spanish, thēᴛʜ), **the.** [Called **El Cid Campeador,** meaning "The Lord Champion"; original name, **Rodrigo** (or **Ruy**) **Díaz de Bivar**; Arabic, **Seyyid.**] b. at the castle of Bivar, near Burgos, Spain, c1040; d. at Valencia, Spain, July, 1099. Principal national hero of Spain, famous for his exploits in the wars with the Moors. He first achieved renown while fighting on the side of Sancho II of Castile in the battles against Sancho IV of Navarre; siding with Sancho also in the conflict with Alfonso VI (Alfonso el Bravo), he was exiled by the latter and became a soldier of fortune, serving often on the side of the Moors. He conquered Valencia in 1094 and ruled the city for the rest of his life. His death occurred as the result of a successful attack by the Moslem dynasty of the Almoravides. He had married Ximena, daughter of the count of Oviedo, and she attempted to carry on his rule. His glamorous life became a source of many legends almost at once and the 12th-century epic poems *Cantar de mio Cid* (*Song of the Cid*) and the *Crónica Rimada* (*Rhymed Chronicle of the Cid*) attribute to him deeds and actions of purely legendary origin. These works remained such great sources of literary and popular inspiration that they served as a basis not only for countless historical ballads, but for further Spanish poems, popular translations such as John Gibson Lockhart's "The Young Cid" in his *Ancient Spanish Ballads, Historical and Romantic* (1823), also for Corneille's tragedy *Le Cid* (1637) and an opera (1885) by Jules Massenet.

Cid (sid), **The.** Opera in four acts by Jules Massenet, with a libretto by Adolphe Philippe D'Ennery, Louis Gallet, and Edouard Blau, first performed at the Opéra at Paris, on Nov. 30, 1885.

Cid Campeador (thēᴛʜ käm″pā.ä.ᴛʜôr′), **Las Mocedades del.** Spanish tragedy on the theme of the Cid, by Guillén de Castro y Bellvís. It appeared c1618.

Cid Hamet Benengeli (sid hä.met′ ben.en.gā′lē; Spanish, thēᴛʜ ä.māt′ bā.nen.ʜā′lē). Imaginary chronicler from whom Miguel de Cervantes said he received his account of Don Quixote.

Ciechanów (che.ʜä′nöf). Town in C Poland, in the *województwo* (province) of Warszawa, situated on the Lidynia River, ab. 49 mi. NW of Warsaw: agricultural trade and small industries. In World War II the town was occupied by the Germans on Sept. 6, 1939. There is a ruined castle of the 14th century, formerly belonging to the dukes of Mazovia, in the vicinity. 11,831 (1946).

Ciechocinek (che.ʜō.chē′nek). Town in N Poland, in the *województwo* (province) of Pomorze, ab. 17 mi. SE of Torun. A summer and health resort, with saline springs, it has hotels, parks, and bathing establishments. 4,131 (1946).

Ciego de Ávila (syā′gō dā ä′ʙē.lä). City in C Cuba, in Camagüey province: railway junction in a large sugar-growing district. 23,802 (1943).

Ciénaga (syā′nä.gä). City in N Colombia, in Magdalena department, a port on the Ciénaga (lagoon or swamp) de Santa Marta: shipping point for bananas, cocoa, cotton, and tobacco. 22,783 (1938).

Cienfuegos (syen.fwā′gōs). City on the S coast of Cuba, in Las Villas province: Cuba's third most important commercial city, exporting sugar and other agricultural produce; site of Arnold Arboretum, where Harvard students train for tropical work. On May 11, 1898, during the Spanish-American War, a fight occurred here between American vessels and Spanish troops while men of the former were cutting cables. 52,910 (1943).

Cienfuegos (thyen.fwā′gōs), **Nicasio Álvarez de.** b. at Madrid, Dec. 14, 1764; d. at Orthez, France, July, 1809. Spanish poet and dramatist. His poems were published in 1798.

Cienfuegos y Jovellanos (thyen.fwā′gōs ē hō.ʙā.lyä′nōs; American Spanish, syen.fwā′gōs ē hō.ʙā.yä′nōs), **José.** b. at Gigon, in Asturias, Spain, 1768; d. at Madrid, 1825. Spanish general for whom the city of Cienfuegos, Cuba, is named. He was a cadet in 1777, served in the French wars, and from April, 1816, to the end of 1819 was captain-general of Cuba. In 1822 he was minister of war, and at the time of his death was councilor of war and lieutenant general, and director-general of artillery.

Cieplice Zdrój (che.plē'tse zdrö'i). [Also: **Cieplice**; German, **Warmbrunn.**] Town in SW Poland, in the *województwo* (province) of Wrocław, formerly in Silesia, Germany, situated on the Zacken River and at the foot of the Riesengebirge (Karkonosze), SW of Jelenia Góra. It is a health resort, with sulfurous, radioactive springs, which are visited by people suffering from gout, rheumatism, nervous and skin diseases, and has several bathing establishments, a park, theater, museum, castle, and library. It had formerly also glass and embroidery industries. The town came under Polish administration after the Potsdam Conference in 1945, and Polish immigrants have now largely replaced the former German population. 12,938 (1946).

Cierva (thyer'bä), **Juan de la.** b. c1896; d. at Croydon, England, Dec. 9, 1936. Spanish flier and aircraft designer. He originated and developed (1919 *et seq.*) the Autogiro, a gyroplane which he first flew in 1923. He lost his life in a flying accident at Croydon, near London, in 1936.

Cieszyn (che'shin). [German, **Teschen**; Czech, **Těšín.**] City in SW Poland, in the *województwo* (province) of Śląsk (Silesia), formerly in Austria, situated on the Olsa River, ab. 61 mi. SW of Kraków. It is on the Czechoslovakian border opposite the town of Český Těšín. It is an industrial center, with lumber mills, furniture, paperware, and food factories, and important textile mills; after World War II manufacture of electrical equipment for the railways was begun here. Notable buildings include the remains of an old castle formerly belonging to the Silesian Piast dukes, the Church of the Dominicans, and a local museum. The Silesian Piasts ruled here and in the neighboring Czech territory from 1290 to 1653. The peace of Cieszyn, concluded here in May, 1779, ended the War of the Bavarian Succession. Austrian headquarters were established here during World War I. The surrounding territory was divided between Poland and Czechoslovakia in 1920. Pop. 16,536 (1946).

Cieza (thyā'thä). Town in E Spain, in the province of Murcia, situated on the Segura River, ab. 25 mi. NW of Murcia. It is a manufacturing center, with sawmills, paper mills, flour mills, and distilleries. The town contains the remains of Roman and Moorish buildings which date, respectively, from the early years of the Christian era and from the Middle Ages. 23,499 (1940).

Cieza de León (thyā'thä dā lā.ōn'), **Pedro de.** b. at Llerena, Spain, c1518; d. at Seville, Spain, 1560. Spanish soldier, author of *Crónica del Perú.* From about 1534 to 1552 he was with the Spanish armies in America, serving in New Granada and Peru and traveling extensively. His *Crónica*, or history, of Peru was commenced in 1541, and consisted of four parts. The first part, a general description of the country, was published in 1553; the second part, with a portion of the third part, was published in the 19th century. Other portions are known in manuscript, but several books are lost. Cieza de León is considered one of the best early authorities on the early history of Peru and the customs of the Incas. He also wrote *Historia de la Nueva España* and others.

Cigarette-Maker's Romance, A. Novel (1890) by F. Marion Crawford. It is a story, laid in Germany, of the love for a Polish girl of a Russian nobleman forced by circumstances to work in a cigarette factory.

Cignani (chē.nyä'nē), Count **Carlo.** b. at Bologna, Italy, May 15, 1628; d. at Forlì, Italy, Sept. 6, 1719. Italian painter of the Bolognese school. A pupil of Francesco Albani and a fresco painter of the baroque style, he worked for 20 years on his *Assumption of the Virgin*, painted in the cupola of the cathedral at Forlì.

Cignaroli (chē.nyä.rō'lē), **Giovanni Bettino.** b. at Salo, near Verona, Italy, 1706; d. at Verona, Italy, Dec. 1, 1770. Italian painter of the Venetian school. In 1769 he became director of the academy (of which he had been a founder) at Verona.

Cigua (sē'gwä). See **Sigua.**

Ciguay (thē.gwī'). See **Higuay.**

Cihuacoatl (sē''wä.kō.ät'l). Title of the civil chieftain in the Aztec government of Tenochtitlán (Mexico) who had charge of intratribal affairs. He was one of the four elected officers of the tribe and the office was considered a stepping-stone to the office of "chief of men."

Cihuacoatl. [Also, **Tonantzin.**] In Aztec mythology and religion, a fertility goddess who ruled over childbirth and death. The name means "Snake Woman."

Ciléa (chē.lā'ä), **Francesco.** b. at Palmi, Calabria, Italy, July 29, 1866—. Italian composer. He has written mostly for the operatic stage, and his works include *Gina* (1889), *La Tilda* (1892), *L'Arlesiana* (1896), *Adrienne Lecouvreur* (1902), which has been sung in America, and *Gloria* (1907). He was director (1916 *et seq.*) of the Naples Conservatory. He has also written an orchestral suite, some piano pieces, a trio, and a sonata for cello and piano.

Cilicia (si.lish'ạ). In ancient geography, a province in SE Asia Minor, separated by the Taurus range from Lycaonia and Cappadocia on the N, and by the Amanus range from Syria on the E, and extending toward the sea. During the Syrian period many Greeks and Jews settled in Cilicia. It was repeatedly invaded by the Assyrian kings, and was successively under Persian, Macedonian, Syrian, and Roman dominion. The dreaded Cilician pirates were subdued (67 B.C.) by Pompey. It was later held by the Byzantine Empire and, after becoming an independent kingdom in the 11th century and aiding the rulers of the kingdom of Jerusalem, was absorbed by the Turks in the 15th century. The capital was Tarsus.

Cilician Gates (si.lish'ạn). [Also: **Beilan Pass, Syrian Gates**; modern Turkish, **Gülek Boğaz**; Latin, **Pylae Ciliciae.**] Pass between the Taurus mountains and the NE angle of the Mediterranean, ab. 25 mi. N of Tarsus, Turkey, leading from Cilicia to Syria. The pass has been in use for almost 3,000 years as a passageway through the Taurus.

Cill Áirne (kil oir'nẹ). Irish name of **Killarney.**

Cill Chainnigh (kil ċhen'iċh). Irish name of **Kilkenny.**

Cill Dara (kil dä'rạ). Irish name of **Kildare.**

Cilli (tsil'ē). German name of **Celje.**

Cill Mantán (kil mạn.tôn'). Irish name of **Wicklow.**

Cill Ruis (kil rö'ish). Irish name of **Kilrush.**

Cilombo-coñoma (si.lom'bō.kō.nyō'mä). See **Kakonda.**

Cima (chē'mä), **Giovanni Battista** or **Giambattista.** [Called **Cima da Conegliano.**] b. at Conegliano, Veneto, Italy, c1459; d. c1517. Italian painter of the Venetian school. He was probably a pupil of Giovanni Bellini, but later came under the influence of Giorgione. His works were mostly religious paintings with, characteristically, a loving depiction of landscape in the background. Surviving examples are his *David and Jonathan* and *Incredulity of Saint Thomas* in the National Gallery, London (another *Incredulity* being in the Academy at Venice), *Tobias With the Angels*, also at Venice, and *The Glorification of Saint Peter, Martyr*, at Milan. He is also represented in the Louvre at Paris, the Vienna Gallery, the Dresden Museum, the Pinakothek at Munich, and in churches of his native Conegliano.

Cimabue (chē.mä.bö'ä), **Giovanni.** [Original name, **Cenni di Pepo.**] b. at Florence, c1240; d. there, c1302. Noted Italian painter, sometimes called the "Father of Modern Painting." He is mentioned as a forerunner of Giotto by Dante, who thereby gives occasion to his own anonymous commentator, writing in 1334, to make some remarks upon Cimabue's fame and ambition, which remarks were later quoted by Giorgio Vasari. Cimabue practiced painting on wall-panels and mosaics. The works accredited to him by Vasari consist of: (*a*) Several large Madonnas on panels with gold grounds. The most celebrated is that in the chapel of the Rucellai family in Santa Maria Novella at Florence. There is another in the Louvre, and another in the Accademia delle Belle Arti at Florence. They are effective in their mild solemnity and simple color, which is lively and clear in the flesh-tints. (*b*) Frescoes in the Church of San Francesco d'Assisi, quite similar to the panels, but slighter and more decorative. (*c*) Mosaics in the apse of the cathedral of Pisa, the only work well authenticated as his by original documents, and probably his last. Cimabue is generally considered the first modern European painter because in his work for the first time the Byzantine forms take on what are now usually classified as a characteristically European expression. Dante's naming of him as Giotto's teacher probably gave rise to the story, related by Vasari but without any historical foundation, of Cimabue's coming upon the young Giotto drawing a sheep on a rock and, recognizing the boy's talent, taking him as a pupil.

Cima di Jazzi (chē′mä dē yät′tsē). See **Jazzi, Cima di.**

Cimarosa (chē.mä.rō′zä), **Domenico.** b. at Aversa, Italy, Dec. 17, 1749; d. at Venice, Jan. 11, 1801. Italian composer of operas. His chief opera is *Il Matrimonio segreto* (*The Secret Marriage*, 1792), composed during his service as *kapellmeister* (choir leader) at Vienna. Cimarosa also composed at St. Petersburg, where he had been invited by Catherine II, and at Naples, from which city he was exiled when he proclaimed his belief in republican principles. He also wrote cantatas, oratorios, and masses.

Cimarron (sim′ą.rōn, -ron). River rising in New Mexico, and flowing generally E across SE Colorado, SW Kansas, and W and N central Oklahoma, to join the Arkansas River ab. 16 mi. W of Tulsa, Okla. In its upper course, it flows in a canyon, and to the E, on the Great Plains, it has a wide sandy bed, nearly a mile wide in places, bordered by sand dunes. The volume of water flow varies greatly. Length, ab. 600 mi.

Cimarron. American novel (1930) by Edna Ferber, dealing with the Oklahoma land rush in 1889 and the adventures of Yancey Cravat. One of her most popular novels, it was equally successful on the screen with Irene Dunne.

Cimarron, Territory of. See under **Beaver,** Okla.

Cimarrones (sē.mär.rō′nās). Name given in the Spanish colonies of America to fugitive slaves; in particular, the bands of fugitive Negroes who collected on the isthmus of Panama about the middle of the 16th century. They numbered many hundred, built walled towns, attacked the Spanish settlements, robbed treasure trains, and made their name a terror in all parts of the isthmus. Under their chief or "king," Bayano, they resisted the forces of Pedro de Ursúa for two years, but were at length obliged to submit. They soon revolted. In 1572 they joined forces with the English adventurer Francis Drake, and for many years they aided the Buccaneers in their descents on the isthmus. Finally they became amalgamated with the Indian tribes.

Cimbri (sim′brī). Ancient people of central Europe, of uncertain local habitation and ethnographical position. They probably pushed into the Roman provinces in 113 B.C., and in company with the Teutons and Gauls engaged with and defeated Roman armies in southern Gaul and elsewhere (the most notable defeat being that at Arausio of Caepio and Mallius in 105 B.C.) until 101 B.C., when they were defeated and virtually exterminated by Marius on the Raudian fields in the Po Valley, N Italy. The peninsula now known as Jutland was named by ancient geographers the Chersonesus Cimbrica (peninsula of the Cimbri) after them.

Cimbrica (sim′bri.ką), **Chersonesus.** Ancient name of **Jutland.**

Cimetière marin (sēm.tyer mȧ.raṅ), **Le.** Poem (1920; Eng. trans., *The Graveyard By the Sea*, 1932) by the French poet Paul Valéry (1871–1945). Symbolic, highly intellectualized, obscure, and much commented upon by critics, it has been treated by students like Edmund Wilson as representing (with James Joyce's *Ulysses*, Marcel Proust's *À la recherche du temps perdu*, the poetry of Yeats, and the prose of Gertrude Stein), the central tendency of European literature in the first half of the 20th century.

Cimmeria (si.mir′i.ą). Country of the legendary Cimmerians of ancient Greek tales, fabled to be a place of perpetual darkness. They are mentioned in Homer. The Cimmerians of legend are not to be confused with the historical Cimmerians who lived near the Black Sea.

Cimmerian Bosporus (si.mir′i.ąn bos′pō.rus). [Also, **Bosporus Cimmerius.**] In ancient geography, the name of a kingdom in S Sarmatia and also of the strait (modern Kerch Strait) between the Black Sea and the Sea of Azov. The Crimean side was colonized (c600 B.C.) by a Greek expedition from Miletus which founded Panticapaeum there. It flourished until absorbed in the dominions of Mithridates VI of Pontus, and for some centuries afterward experienced alternating periods of hardship and prosperity. Close relations were early established with Athens, which sent oil, jewelry, and works of industrial art in return for Crimean wheat. The chief city was Panticapaeum, the modern Kerch, the center of the highly important archaeological discoveries which have been yielded by this region as well as by the territory around it. The first systematic excavations were made in 1816. After 1832 explorations were regularly conducted by the Russian imperial government, and their results, rich in Greek industrial antiquities, were placed in the Hermitage Museum at St. Petersburg. The architectural remains are scanty, perhaps the chief of them being the fine revetment, in quarry-faced ashlar with margin-draft, of the so-called Tumulus of the Czar at Kerch. The sculpture found, too, is scanty in quantity, late in date, and poor in style. The great archaeological wealth of the region lies in its abundant burial tumuli and catacombs. It was the practice of the ancient inhabitants to bury with their dead a large part of their possessions; hence the remarkable harvest of jewelry, vases, implements, and even textile fabrics and a pair of woman's leather boots, found in these graves. Little or nothing discovered is older than the 4th century B.C.; the finest specimens of jewelry and pottery are Athenian, and include some of the most beautiful work known in their classes. Many of the vases are decorated in brilliant polychrome; others have gilded ornament, and others bear figures in relief. Some of the tomb chambers bear interesting mural paintings.

Cimmerians (si.mir′i.ąnz, ki-). [Older variant names: **Gimir, Kimmerians.**] Early inhabitants of the N shore of the Black Sea, between the Danube and Don rivers. The Cimmerians were forced into Asia Minor by Scythian pressure during the 8th century B.C. Gradually moving west, they came into conflict with the Vannic kingdom (Urartu), the Assyrians, and the Phrygians. They disappeared from history after defeat by the Lydians in the 7th century B.C. These people are mentioned in Homer. Herodotus speaks of "Cimmerian cities," and says that the strait which unites the Azov Sea and the Black Sea was called the Cimmerian Bosporus. In the Old Testament they are mentioned by the name of Gomer. Gen. x. 2.

Cimon (sī′mǫn). d. at Citium, Cyprus, 449 B.C. Athenian commander; son of Miltiades. He defeated the Persians on sea and land near the Eurymedon c468 and reduced Thasos in 463. He was exceptionally powerful in Athenian politics in this period and held for a truce with Sparta to combat the Persians. But with the rising influence of Pericles and the failure of an Athenian expedition to aid Sparta in their struggle with the helots, he was ostracized (c461). He returned to Athens later and in 451 arranged a truce between Athens and Sparta. He died leading an Athenian force to Cyprus.

Cimon of Cleonae (klę̄.ō′nē). b. at Cleonae, in Chalcidice. Greek painter, famous in antiquity. He is mentioned in two epigrams of Simonides.

Cinaloa (sē.nä.lö′ä). See **Sinaloa.**

Cinamus (sin′ą.mus), **Joannes.** See **Cinnamus** or **Cinamus** or **Sinnamus, Joannes.**

Cincar-Marković (tsēn′kär mär′kô.vich), **Aleksandar.** b. 1889—. Yugoslav diplomat and political leader, minister of foreign affairs (1939–41) in the cabinet overthrown (1941) by General Dušan Simović.

Cincinnati (sin.si.nat′i, -nat′ą). [Called the **"Queen City"** and the **"Queen of the West"**; former name, **Losantiville.**] City in SW Ohio, county seat of Hamilton County, on the Ohio River: second largest city in Ohio and largest city in the Ohio Valley. Manufactures include clothing, plastics, playing cards, radios, shoes, and textbooks; it is one of the world's leading cities in the manufacture of soap and its chief producer of machine tools, and also has steelworks, breweries, and meat-packing plants. The site was settled in 1788 and named Cincinnati in 1790, in honor of the Revolutionary officers' Society of the Cincinnati; incorporated as a city in 1819. By 1825, it was an important shipping point on the Ohio River and the Miami and Erie Canal, and had shipyards. It is the seat of Xavier University, the Cincinnati Conservatory of Music, the University of Cincinnati, and Hebrew Union College. Greater Cincinnati includes the cities of Covington and Newport, both in Kentucky. 455,610 (1940), 503,998 (1950).

Cincinnati (sin.si.nat′i), **Society of the.** Association founded by the regular officers of the Continental army at the quarters of Baron Friedrich von Steuben on the Hudson River, in 1783, at the suggestion of General Henry Knox. Its name, derived from that of the Roman dictator Lucius Quinctius Cincinnatus, was adopted in allusion to the approaching change from military to civil pursuits.

Its chief stated immediate objects were to raise a fund for the relief of the widows and orphans of those who fell in the Revolutionary War, and to promote a closer political union between the states. Its members were to consist of the officers of the Continental army and of their eldest male descendants, in failure of which collateral descendants were to be eligible for membership. It was divided into state societies, including a branch society in France. It met with considerable opposition on account of its alleged aristocratic tendencies. Its first president was George Washington, who was succeeded by Alexander Hamilton and the Pinckneys. It is divided into 13 state societies. The branch society in France, which was organized under the most favorable auspices, was dispersed by the revolution of 1792.

Cincinnati Symphony Orchestra. Ensemble organized (1895) with Frank Van der Stucken as conductor. Disbanded in 1907, it was reorganized in 1909. Among its conductors have been Leopold Stokowski (1909–12), Eugene Ysaye (1918–22), Fritz Reiner (1922–31), and Eugene Goossens (1931–47).

Cincinnatus (sin.si.nā′tus, -nat′us), **Lucius Quinctius** or **Titus Quinctius.** b. c519 B.C.; fl. 1st half of the 5th century B.C. Roman legendary hero. He was consul suffectus in 460, and distinguished himself as an opponent of the plebeians in the struggle between them and the patricians in the period 462–454. In 458 a Roman army under Lucius Minucius having been surrounded by the Aequians in a defile of Mount Algidus, he was named dictator by the senate, whose deputies, dispatched to inform him of his appointment, found him digging in the field on his farm beyond the Tiber. He gained a complete victory over the Aequians, and laid down the dictatorship after the lapse of only 16 days, returning to his farm. In 439, at the age of 80, he was appointed dictator to oppose the traitor Spurius Melius, who was defeated and slain. The details of his story vary; the story of the first dictatorship is probably legendary embellishment on a factual basis; that of the second dictatorship is probably wholly false.

Cinco de Mayo (sēng′kō dā mä′yō), **Battle of the.** Name given by Mexicans to an action fought on May 5, 1862, before Puebla, in which the French under General Charles Latrille, Comte de Lorencez, were defeated by the Mexicans. This battle did not prevent the establishment of the empire under the archduke Maximilian two years later, but it was regarded as a great national triumph, and the anniversary is still celebrated.

Cinderella (sin.dạ.rel′ạ). Title and heroine of the most famous, and probably most widespread, of all folk tales Cinderella is the beautiful, mistreated little girl who serves as a household drudge to her ugly stepmother and two ugly stepsisters (whose jealousy of her beauty provides a very usual element of the story). According to the best-known version of the tale, the prince of the country falls in love with her at a ball which she attends dressed by her fairy godmother in magic finery which will vanish at midnight. Fleeing from the palace as the clock strikes midnight, she loses one tiny glass slipper, by means of which, as it would fit no one else, the prince finds and marries her. In some versions she is aided by a kindly animal or her own dead mother, instead of the fairy godmother, and her slipper is caught, as she runs from the palace (usually on the third night) by pitch spread, by order of the prince, on the staircase. The story is of very ancient, probably Eastern, origin; some 500 versions in Europe alone have been examined; and it is known and told from Alaska to Indonesia, South America, and South Africa. There is a 9th-century Chinese version. It was told in Egypt of Rhodopis and Psammetichus. In France, Perrault and Madame d'Aulnoy include it in their *Fairy Tales* as "Cendrillon" and "Finette Cendroi"; the brothers Grimm give it in their *Household Tales* as "Aschenbrödel" or "Aschenputtel." There has been some debate as to whether the famous slipper (in the French versions) was of *verre* (glass) or of *vair* (fur), but the detail is of no actual importance to the story and discussion has now been virtually abandoned. The basic human motif underlying the story is that of sudden and very great success, against odds, and the justification of the lowly, despised, and mistreated central character, with whom the hearer or reader identifies himself. This doubtless not only accounts for its popularity and tenacity throughout the world, but also for the fact that it has been used to provide a theme for countless ostensibly "new" stories and plays by professional writers in virtually every one of the world's literatures.

Cineas (sin′ẹ.ạs). d. probably in Sicily, c277 B.C. Thessalian politician in the service of Pyrrhus, king of Epirus. He was ambassador to Rome after the battle of Heraclea, in 280, in which Pyrrhus had defeated the Romans, but could not persuade the senate to accept his terms.

Cingoli (chēng′gō.lē). [Ancient name, **Cingulum.**] Town and commune in C Italy, in the *compartimento* (region) of Marches, in the province of Macerata, situated in the Apennines, SW of Ancona. It is the seat of a bishopric. There are a number of medieval churches, of which the most important is Sant' Esuperanzio (13th century). Cingoli was destroyed by the Goths and Lombards in the early Middle Ages, and incorporated into the Papal States in the 15th century. Pop. of commune, 15,496 (1936); of town, 1,751 (1936).

Cingolo (chēng′gō.lō). See **Chingolo.**

Cinisello Balsamo (chē.nē.zel′lō bäl′zä.mō). Town and commune in NW Italy, in the *compartimento* (region) of Lombardy, in the province of Milano, NE of Milan, of which it is a suburb. Pop. of commune, 11,859 (1936); of town, 6,438 (1936).

Cinna (sē.nà). [Full title: **Cinna ou la Clémence d'Auguste** (sē.nà ö là klā.mäṅs dō.güst).] Tragedy by Pierre Corneille, produced in 1640 or 1641. An anonymous tragedy called *Cinna's Conspiracy*, and attributed by Daniel Defoe to Colley Cibber, was taken from this and played (1713) at the Drury Lane Theatre, London.

Cinna (sin′ạ), **Gaius Helvius.** d. 44 B.C. Roman tribune and poet; a friend of Catullus. On the occasion of the funeral of Julius Caesar he was slain by the populace, who mistook him for Lucius Cornelius Cinna (fl. 44 B.C.).

Cinna, Lucius Cornelius. Slain in a mutiny at Brundisium, Italy, 84 B.C. Roman general and statesman, celebrated as a leader of the popular party and an opponent of Sulla; father of Lucius Cornelius Cinna (fl. 44 B.C.). He was consul with Octavius in 87, with Marius in 86, and with Carbo in the period 85–84. During his first consulship he took advantage of Sulla's absence from Rome to recall Marius and attempt to pass a voting bill in opposition to Sulla's partisans. Cinna was defeated in his attempt and was removed as consul. He raised a force, and besieged the city. A massacre of Sulla's supporters took place after Marius's return. Cinna's daughter Cornelia was Julius Caesar's first wife.

Cinna, Lucius Cornelius. fl. 44 B.C. Roman politician; son of Lucius Cornelius Cinna (d. 84 B.C.) and brother-in-law of Julius Caesar. He was praetor in 44 B.C. He sided with the conspirators against Caesar.

Cinnamon (sin′ạ.mọn), **Land of.** [Spanish, **Tierra de Canelo.**] Name given by the early Spanish conquerors of Peru to a region E of the Andes, in the forest-covered plains about the Napo River, where there were trees with aromatic bark. Gonzalo Pizarro led an expedition into it in 1541, and returned after two years of terrible suffering. Francisco de Orellana, leaving Pizarro's party there, discovered the Amazon and explored it. The first settlements were made in 1552.

Cinnamus or **Cinamus** or **Sinnamus** (sin′ạ.mus), **Joannes.** fl. in the 12th century. Byzantine historian, a notary of the emperor Manuel I Comnenus. He was the author of a history of the period from 1118 to 1176, covering the reign of Manuel I (to the end of the siege of Iconium) and that of his father John II.

Cinna Val Dritta (chēn′nä väl drēt′tä). See under **Baldo, Monte.**

Cino da Pistoia (chē′nō dä pēs.tō′yä). [Original name, **Guittoncino de'Sinibaldi.**] b. at Pistoia, Italy, c1270; d. there, c1336. Italian jurist and poet; friend of Dante and Petrarch. He was a teacher of law and author of a commentary on the Justinian Code and of several sensitive poems, praised by Dante.

Cinq-Mars (saṅk màrs). [Full title, **Cinq-Mars ou une Conjuration sous Louis XIII.**] Opera in four acts by Gounod, first produced at Paris on April 5, 1877.

Cinq-Mars, Marquis de. [Title of **Henri Coiffier de Ruzé.**] b. 1620; d. at Lyons, France, Sept. 12, 1642. French courtier. He was at the age of 18 introduced to the court by Cardinal Richelieu, and, gaining the favor of Louis XIII, rose quickly to the posts of grand master of the wardrobe and grand master of the horse. Richelieu having refused to countenance his claim to a seat in the royal council and his aspiration to the hand of Maria de Gonzaga, princess of Mantua, Cinq-Mars formed a conspiracy against the cardinal, in the course of which he entered into treasonable communication with Spain. With one of his fellow-conspirators, the youthful François de Thou, he was beheaded at Lyons. Alfred de Vigny based a novel on this historical incident, and Gounod made it the basis of an opera.

Cinq-Mars, ou une Conjuration sous Louis XIII (ö ün kôṅ.zhü.rȧ.syôṅ sö lwē trez). Historical novel by Alfred de Vigny, published in 1826, and founded on the life and conspiracy of the Marquis de Cinq-Mars.

Cinque Ports (singk). [Eng. trans., *"Five Ports."*] Collective name for the five English channel ports: Hastings, New Romney, Hythe, Dover, and Sandwich. Winchelsea and Rye were added later. They furnished the chief naval contingent until the time of Henry VII and in return received certain privileges. For all practical purposes, their special privileges have now been abolished, but they are still governed, technically, by a lord warden, who is admiral of the ports and governor of Dover Castle. Of them all, only Dover still remains a seaport (the English coast has moved far enough E and S to make the others now inland towns).

Cinteotl (sēn.tā.ōt′l). [Also, **Centoatl, Tzinteutl.**] In Aztec religion, the maize god, and male counterpart of Chicomecoatl, the maize goddess; in Aztec mythology, he was husband of Xochiquetzal, goddess of flowers.

Cinthio or **Cintio** (chēn′tsyō). See **Giraldi, Giovanni Battista.**

Cinti (saṅ.tē), Mademoiselle. Stage name of **Damoreau, Laure Cinthie.**

Cinto (chēn′tō), **Monte.** Peak in NW Corsica, ab. 33 mi. N of Ajaccio. It is the highest point on the island, in a rugged high-mountain region of many peaks. Elevation, ab. 8,880 ft.

Cintra (sēn′trä). See also **Sintra.**

Cintra, Convention of. Convention concluded on Aug. 30, 1808, between the French under General Junot and the English and Portuguese, during the Peninsular War. By its provisions the French evacuated Portugal, and were conveyed to France in English vessels.

CIO. See **Committee for Industrial Organization,** and **Congress of Industrial Organizations.**

Cione (chō′nā), **Andrea di.** See **Orcagna, Andrea.**

Ciotat (syo.tȧ), **La.** See **La Ciotat.**

Čiovo (chē′ô.vô). [Also: **Bua**; ancient names, **Bavo, Boae.**] Yugoslav island off the Dalmatian coast, opposite Trogir, just W of Split. It was a place of banishment under the Roman emperors.

Cipa (sē′pä). Variant spelling of **Zipa,** the title of the head of a once-powerful Indian state in Colombia.

Cipango (si.pang′gō). [Also: **Zipangu, Zumpango.**] Name, derived from Marco Polo's narrative, given to an island or islands E of Asia, supposed to be the modern Japan. Columbus imagined that the West Indies were outlying portions of it.

Cipeta (chē.pā′tä). See **Chipeta.**

Cipriani (chē.prē.ä′nē), **Amilcare.** b. at Anzio, Italy, 1844; d. at Paris, May 2, 1918. Italian communist revolutionary. As a Garibaldian revolutionary (1859–63) he was in touch with Mazzini and his group, and took part (1863) in the Athens republican uprising. His support (1870–71) of the Paris Commune caused his trial by the Versailles government which sentenced him (1871) to death, but commuted the punishment to imprisonment in New Caledonia, where he stayed eight years. After his return he took part in several revolts and was again imprisoned (1891) in Italy; during this time he was 11 times elected to the chamber of deputies, and finally seated in 1914; but his refusal to swear allegiance to the crown caused his removal (1915) from office. He lived at Paris except for his sojourns in Italy and during the period of the Greco-Turkish war (1897), in which he took an active part.

Cipriani, Giovanni Battista. b. at Florence, 1727; d. at Hammersmith, London, 1785. Italian painter, designer, and engraver, who found his career in England. He worked at first at Florence, but upon visiting Rome for further study (1750–53), he made the acquaintance of English architects and sculptors, at whose suggestion he went to London in 1755. Some of the mural decorations and historical paintings in Buckingham Palace are his work. He was one of the founders (1768) of the Royal Academy.

Cipro (chē′prō). Italian name of **Cyprus.**

Circars (sėr.kärz′), **Northern.** See **Northern Circars.**

Circassia (sėr.kash′ą). [Russian, **Zemlya Cherkesov,** meaning "Land of the Circassians."] Former region in the U.S.S.R., in the Caucasus, lying between the Kuban River on the N, the land of the Lesghians on the E, Mingrelia on the S, and the Black Sea on the W. It included Great and Little Kabarda, the countries of the Abkhazians and the Cherkess (Circassians). It was incorporated with Russia in 1829. The Circassians emigrated in large numbers c1864. The area is now divided between the Krasnodar *krai* (subdivision) and the Adygei and Cherkess autonomous *oblasts* (regions) of the Russian Soviet Federated Socialist Republic and the Georgian Soviet Socialist Republic in the U.S.S.R.

Circassians (sėr.kash′ąnz). [Also: **Adyge, Cherkess.**] People of the Caucasus region of SE Europe, living now in the region between the Caucasus Mountains, the Kuban River, and the Black Sea in the Russian Soviet Federated Socialist Republic (RSFSR), or in Turkey; their principal city is Maikop. Circassian society, based on a pastoral and agricultural culture, was divided into three classes (princes, nobles, and peasants), but in the councils of the tribe any freeman (prisoners of war were often bond servants or slaves) was entitled to speak and the rulers acted through delegated powers. The blood feud existed and the clan organization of the people permitted open warfare between family groups. Professedly Moslem since the 17th century, the Circassians observed a religion in which earlier Christian observances and a still earlier polytheism were apparent. Circassian women, noted for their beauty, were much in demand for harems. Following the cession of their territory by the Turks to the Russians in the treaty of Adrianople (1829), the Circassians offered severe resistance to Russian conquest and many of them fled to Turkey rather than submit to Russian rule.

Circassienne (sėr.kȧ.syen), **La.** Comic opera in three acts by Daniel Auber, with a libretto by Augustin Eugène Scribe, first performed at the Paris Opéra-Comique on Feb. 2, 1861.

Circe (sėr′sē). In Greek mythology, an enchantress, and magician, daughter of Helios, on the island of Aeaea. Circe was the aunt of Medea, with whom she shares the distinction of being one of the two great witches of Greek legend. Odysseus and his crew came in their wanderings to her home. She metamorphosed some of the hero's companions into swine. Odysseus resisted her magic but was induced to remain a year with her. Before she would let him depart she sent him to the lower world to consult the seer Tiresias about his voyage home.

Circe. An asteroid (No. 34) discovered by Jean Chacornac at Paris, April 6, 1855.

Circeii (sėr.sē′ī). In ancient geography, a town in Latium, Italy, situated near the sea, ab. 57 mi. SE of Rome. It belonged (340 B.C.) to the Latin League.

Circeo (chēr.che′ō), **Monte.** [Also: **Monte Circeio** or **Circello** (chēr.chel′lō); Latin, **Circeius Mons, Circaeum** (or **Circoeum**) **Promontorium.**] Promontory or isolated rock on the W coast of Italy, near Terracina. It was a frequented resort in ancient times. It has some antiquities of the Roman town Circeii, and abounds in grottoes.

Circleville (sėr′kl.vil). City in S Ohio, county seat of Pickaway County, on the Scioto River, ab. 26 mi. S of Columbus: manufactures of canned and pork products, and of strawpaper. It was settled in 1810 and incorporated in 1853; and occupies the site of an aboriginal mound-builders' fort (whence the name). 8,723 (1950).

Circuit Rider, The. Novel by Edward Eggleston, published in 1874, depicting realistically the rough, lawless life of the Ohio frontier in the early 19th century.

Circumcellions (sėr.kum.sel′yǫnz). Party, chiefly peasants, who joined the Donatists in N Africa, in the 4th and 5th centuries A.D.; so called because they wandered about in bands from place to place. They persistently courted death, wantonly insulting pagans, and challenging all they met to kill them, looking upon such a death as martyrdom. They supported themselves by plunder, and committed so many acts of violence, aggravated by their religious differences from the orthodox, that soldiers often had to be employed against them. They were not entirely extinct until about the close of the 5th century.

Circumlocution Office. Name by which Charles Dickens in *Little Dorrit* (1857) satirizes the red tape of the public-office system in England.

Circumstance. Novel by S. Weir Mitchell, published in 1901.

Circus Maximus (sėr′kus mak′si.mus). Great Roman circus which occupied the hollow between the Palatine and Aventine hills at Rome. According to tradition, the site was already used for athletic exhibitions and provided with wooden seats under the legendary Tarquinius Priscus (c600 B.C.). Under Caesar and Augustus it was for the first time largely built of stone, and splendidly adorned. The present obelisks of the Piazza del Popolo and of the Lateran ornamented its *spina* (wall within the arena). It was rebuilt by Nero, and again by Domitian and Trajan, and in its final form is said to have accommodated 385,000 spectators. The site is for the most part covered with modern structures, and the remains are scanty. Some of the vaulted substructures which upheld the seats survive, and there are considerable ruins about Santa Maria in Cosmedin of the *carceres*, or pens, from which the racers were started. The length of the arena was 2,200 ft.

Circus of Romulus (rom′ū.lus) or **Maxentius** (mak.sen′shus). Roman circus built at Rome in 311 A.D., considered to be the most perfect ancient circus surviving. It is 1,580 ft. long and 260 wide. The outer wall remains almost complete, and the central *spina* (the wall down the center of the arena), 892 ft. long, can be traced throughout. At the west end, between two towers, are the chief entrance and 12 pens (*carceres*) for competing chariots; the east end is semicircular.

Cirenaica (chē.re.nä′ē.kä). See modern **Cyrenaica.**

Cirencester (sis′i.tėr, sī′rẹn.ses.tėr). [Called **Cicester**; Latin, **Corinium, Durocornovium.**] Urban district and market town in W England, in Gloucestershire, situated on the rivers Churn and Thames (which is here only a small stream, having its origin on the outskirts of the town), ab. 16 mi. SE of Gloucester, ab. 95 mi. W of London by rail. It was formerly a textile center, and later concentrated particularly on the spinning of wool. Cirencester is situated on the old Roman cross-country route from Lincoln to Exeter and was an important town in ancient Britain. It has the remains of an abbey founded in 1117. Pop. 11,188 (1951).

Cirene (chē.rā′nā). See **Cyrene.**

Cirey (sē.rā). Château on the borders of Champagne and Lorraine, which Voltaire fitted up in 1734, and where he lived with the Marquise du Châtelet-Lomont until 1749 with occasional visits from her husband.

Ciriè (chē.rye′). Town and commune in NW Italy, in the *compartimento* (region) of Piedmont, in the province of Torino, situated on the Banna River, N of Turin. The town has woolen, cotton, and silk textile manufactures, paper and lumber industries, agricultural markets, and silkworm culture. The cathedral dates from the 13th and 14th centuries. Buildings of interest to tourists were undamaged in World War II. Pop. of commune, 10,210 (1936); of town, 6,131 (1936).

Čirpan (chir.pän′). See **Chirpan.**

Cirque de Gavarnie (sērk dẹ gå.vår.nē). See **Gavarnie, Cirque de.**

Cirquenizza (chēr.kwe′nēt.tsä). Italian name of **Crikvenica.**

Cirrha (sir′ạ). In ancient geography, the seaport of Crisa (with which it is often confused) in Phocis, Greece. It was destroyed (c575 B.C.) in the first Sacred War, on account of sacrilege in interfering with pilgrims to Delphi.

Cirta (sėr′tạ). Ancient name of **Constantine,** city.

Cisalpine Gaul (sis.al′pīn gôl, -al′pin). See **Gaul, Cisalpine.**

Cisalpine Republic. State formed by Napoleon I in N Italy in 1797, including the previously formed Cispadane and Transpadane republics, S and N of the Po River, with Milan for its capital, and comprising Bologna, Ferrara, Milan, Modena, and Romagna. It was abolished in 1799, restored in 1800, and in 1802 was reconstituted as the Italian Republic (which was itself ended within a few years).

Cisco (sis′kō). City in C Texas, in Eastland County, NW of Austin. 5,230 (1950).

Cis-Jurane Burgundy (sis.jūr′ān bėr′gun.di). See under **Burgundy, 3** and **7.**

Cisleithania (sis.lī.thā′ni.ạ). [Also, **Cisleithan Division** (sis.lī′thạn).] Name given popularly (not officially) to those crownlands of Austria-Hungary which were represented in the Austrian *Reichsrat* (parliament): so named from the Leitha River, part of the boundary between Austria and Hungary. It comprised Lower Austria, Upper Austria, Salzburg, Styria, Carinthia, Carniola, Küstenland, Tirol and Vorarlberg, Bohemia, Moravia, Silesia, Galicia, Bucovina, Dalmatia.

Cismon (chēz.mōn′), Count **Cesare Maria De Vecchi di Val.** See **De Vecchi di Val Cismon,** Count **Cesare Maria.**

Cisneros (thēs.nā′rōs, sēs-), Fray **Diego.** d. 1812. Spanish Hieronymite friar who went (c1785) to Lima, Peru, and resided there until his death. He had been confessor of the princess María Luisa Teresa (afterward queen of Spain), and her influence gave him the protection of the Spanish viceroys. While attending to the business of his order he opened a kind of bookstore, a small circle of advanced thinkers gathered about him, and after encountering great opposition they succeeded in introducing marked reforms in the universities and schools, and in giving greater liberty to the press. They constantly opposed the Inquisition. Fray Diego's library, bequeathed to the university, became the nucleus of the public library of Lima.

Cisneros, Francisco Jiménez (or **Jimenes** or **Ximenes**) **de.** See **Jiménez de Cisneros, Francisco.**

Cisneros y Latorre (ē lä.tôr′rā), **Baltazar Hidalgo de.** See **Hidalgo de Cisneros y Latorre, Baltazar.**

Cispadane Gaul (sis.pā′dān gôl, -pạ.dān′). See **Gaul, Cispadane.**

Cispadane Republic. Republic formed in 1796 by Napoleon I out of the dominions of Bologna, Ferrara, Modena, and Reggio, and modeled on that of France. In 1797 it was merged with the Transpadane Republic in the new Cisalpine Republic.

Cissae Castrum (sis′ē kas′trum). A Latin name of **Chichester.**

Cissey (sē.sā), **Ernest Louis Octave Courtot de.** b. at Paris, Dec. 23, 1810; d. there, June 15, 1882. French general and politician. He served with distinction in Algeria, in the Crimea, and in the Franco-Prussian War, and took part in the suppression (1871) of the Paris Commune. He was also minister of war (1871–73, 1874–76).

Cis-Sutlej States (sis.sut′lej). Name formerly given to a territorial division of British India, S of the Sutlej River. The states were later incorporated in the Punjab.

Cistercians (sis.tėr′shạnz). Monastic order in the Roman Catholic Church.

Cistercium (sis.tėr′shi.um). Ancient name of **Cîteaux.**

Cisterna di Latina (chēs.ter′nä dē lä.tē′nä). [Also: **Cisterna di Littoria** (lēt.tō′ryä), **Cisterna di Roma** (rō′mä).] Town and commune in C Italy, in the *compartimento* (region) of Latium, in the province of Latina (formerly Littoria), situated on the Via Appia between Velletri and Latina, NE of Anzio. Horses and cattle are raised in the vicinity. Pop. of commune, 12,471 (1936); of town, 6,149 (1936).

Cist Ficoroni (chēst fē.kō.rō′nē). See **Ficoroni Cist.**

Citata (chē.tä′tä). See **Chitata.**

Citation. American race horse who in 1948 won over 700,000 dollars in winning 19 of the 20 races in which he started, including the "triple crown" (Kentucky Derby, Preakness, and Belmont Stakes), the Empire Gold Cup, and the Jockey Club Gold Cup. Because of an injury, Citation did not run as a four-year-old in 1949, but after a bad year in 1950 he brought his winnings in 1951 to over a million dollars, thus establishing an all-time record. He was then retired to stud.

Cîteaux (sē.tō). [Ancient name, **Cistercium.**] Village in E France, in the department of Côte-d'Or, ab. 12 mi. S of Dijon. It is celebrated for its abbey, founded 1098, the headquarters formerly of the Cistercian order.

Cithaeron (si.thē′ron). [Also: **Elatea, Kithairon, Kythairon.**] In ancient geography, a range of mountains separating Boeotia from Megaris and Attica. It was celebrated in Greek myth and legend, and was sacred to Zeus and to Dionysus.

Citharista (sith.a.ris′ta). Ancient name of **La Ciotat.**

Citium (sish′i.um). Ancient name of **Larnaca**; see also under **Kittim.**

Citizen, The. Farce (1761) by Arthur Murphy.

"Citizen King." See **Louis Philippe.**

Citizen of the World, The. The signature of Oliver Goldsmith in *Letters from a Chinese Philosopher Residing in London to his Friends in the East,* published in 1762, and often used as the title of the work.

Citizens' Alliance. Name given to any of several organizations in Kansas, Nebraska, and Iowa, formed during the late 1880's by townspeople in sympathy with the Farmers' Alliances. They were later organized into the National Citizens' Alliance, and ultimately merged in the People's Party.

Citizens' Military Training Camps. [Called the **"CMTC."**] Units established in the U.S. in 1913 for military training of college students who paid their own way during the course of military instruction at summer camps. The units came to public notice in 1915 when, as the "Plattsburg idea," the camps became an important element in the U.S. preparedness movement on the eve of American participation in World War I. In 1920 the government undertook to pay expenses for trainees, and the units continued to be active until shortly before World War II.

Citlahuatzin (sēt.lä.wä.tsēn′). See **Cuitlahuatzin.**

Citlaltépetl (sē.tläl.tā′pet.l). See **Orizaba, Pico de.**

Citrine (si.trēn′), Sir **Walter McLennan.** [Title, 1st Baron **Citrine.**] b. at Liverpool, England, Aug. 22, 1887—. English trade-unionist. Associated (1914–23) with the Electrical Trades Union, he was chairman (1919) of the Wallasey Labour Party, and served as general secretary (1926 *et seq.*) of the Trades Union Congress, president (1928–46) of the International Federation of Trade Unions, member (1930–33) of the national economic advisory council, and armaments production adviser (1940) in America. He is the author of *The British Trade Union Movement* (1926), *Labour and the Community* (1928), *I Search for Truth in Russia* (1936), *My American Diary* (1941), *In Russia Now* (1942), and *British Trade Unions* (1942). He was elevated to the peerage in 1946.

Citroën (sē.tro.en), **André Gustave.** b. at Paris, Feb. 5, 1878; d. there, July 3, 1935. French industrialist, founder of one of the largest automobile manufacturing companies in France. A graduate engineer, he invented (1901) a transmission system, reorganized (1908) the Mors company, was assigned (1915) to develop mass production of sorely needed munitions, and built the huge plant which later became the center of his own automobile concern. After the armistice of World War I (1918) he began the production of cars by assembly-line methods. He lost control (1934) of his company shortly before his death. He sponsored scientific explorations in Africa and Central Asia.

Cittadella (chēt.tä.del′lä). Town and commune in NE Italy, in the *compartimento* (region) of Veneto, in the province of Padova, situated on the Brentalla River, ab. 16 mi. NW of Padua. There are agricultural markets, textile mills, and other manufactures; it is a railroad junction. Buildings of interest to tourists were undamaged in World War II. Pop. of commune, 12,966 (1936); of town, 5,588 (1936).

Città della Pieve (chēt.tä′ del.lä pye′vā). Town and commune in C Italy, in the *compartimento* (region) of Umbria, in the province of Perugia, SW of Perugia. A climatic health resort, it also trades in wine and olive oil, and is the seat of a bishopric. There are medieval walls; the cathedral, in Romanesque style, dates from the 12th and 13th centuries. Works of the painter Perugino, who was born here, are in various churches. Considerable damage was suffered during World War II by some buildings of tourist interest; however, the Church of Santa Maria della Mercede was unharmed. Pop. of commune, 9,374 (1936); of town, 2,457 (1936).

Città di Castello (dē käs.tel′lō). Town and commune in C Italy, in the *compartimento* (region) of Umbria, in the province of Perugia, situated at the S extremity of the Tributina Valley, on the Tiber River, ab. 26 mi. N of Perugia. The mineral springs of Bagni di Fontecchio are within the commune. The town is on the site of the ancient Tifernum Tiberinum, destroyed by Totila, the Ostrogoth, in the 6th century A.D. The cathedral is in the Renaissance style; there are numerous other churches and palaces, some of which date from the 16th–18th centuries, and old printing establishments (16th and 17th centuries). The town was of considerable cultural importance in the Renaissance period. The Porta Santa Maria Maggiore suffered damage during World War II, but was not beyond repair. Pop. of commune, 32,658 (1936); of town, 8,816 (1936).

Cittanova (chēt.tä.nô′vä). Town and commune in S Italy, in the *compartimento* (region) of Calabria, in the province of Reggio di Calabria, situated in the mountainous interior of the Calabrian peninsula, E of Palmi. It is an agricultural market town, commanding a wide view reaching to the Tyrrhenian Sea. Pop. of commune, 13,796 (1936); of town, 12,097 (1936).

Città Vecchia (chēt.tä′ vek′kyä) or **Città Notabile** (nō.tä′bē.lā). [Also, **Mdina.**] Town in the C part of Malta, ab. 6 mi. W of Valetta. It was formerly the capital.

City, the. See **London, City of.**

City Club. New York club for men, incorporated in 1892. Its object is to aid in securing permanent good government for the city of New York through the election and appointment of honest and able municipal officers and the establishment of a clear and stable system of city laws.

City Commission Plan. Type of city government, first adopted as a temporary device at Galveston, Tex., in 1901 after a hurricane disaster, in which all municipal powers are vested in an elected council whose members separately administer the various city agencies. The number of members on the council, which combines legislative, executive, and policy-making functions, is usually five or six. Although some 400 U.S. and Canadian cities adopted the scheme between 1908 and 1914, it has since been increasingly replaced by the commission-manager form of city government.

City Glee Club. Vocal group established (1853) at London, now consisting of ab. 150 members, many of whom are singers in the choirs of Westminster Abbey, the Chapel Royal, and Saint Paul's Cathedral.

City Heiress, The. Play by Aphra Behn, adapted from Middleton's *A Mad World, My Masters,* and produced in 1682.

City in the Sea, The. Poem by Edgar Allan Poe, included in the volume *Poems by Edgar A. Poe* (1831).

City Island. Small island in Long Island Sound, off the E coast of the Bronx in New York City: boatyards and shipbuilding. It is included in the borough of the Bronx. Area, 230 acres.

City Madam, The. Comedy attributed to Philip Massinger, licensed in 1632 and printed in 1658. A 19th-century version of the play was entitled *Riches.*

City Manager Plan. System of municipal government first instituted (1908) in Staunton, Va., and subsequently adopted by several hundred American cities in an effort to separate administration from politics. The voting population of the city elects the city council which in turn appoints the city manager. The manager serves as the chief administrative officer, transacts the city's business, appoints his subordinates, and prepares the city's budget. The mayor and the council retain the power to enact ordinances, make appropriations, and decide general policy.

City Match, The. Comedy by Jasper Mayne, produced in 1639.

City Nightcap, The. Play by Robert Davenport, licensed in 1624. It was adapted by Aphra Behn as *The Amorous Prince* in 1671, and itself is an adaptation of the plot of Robert Greene's novel *Philomela.*

"City of Brotherly Love." A nickname of **Philadelphia.**

City of Destruction. In John Bunyan's *Pilgrim's Progress,* the starting point of Christian in his journey.

City of Dreadful Night, The. Poem by James Thomson, published first in the *National Reformer* in 1874. It is a long and gloomy work expressive of deep melancholy. The title also belongs to a volume of stories by Rudyard Kipling, one of which gives its name to the book.

City of God, Of the. See **De civitate Dei.**

City of Hickory. A former name of **Hickory,** N.C.

City of London. See **London, City of.**

City of the Caesars. See **Caesars, City of the.**

City of the Plague. Poem by John Wilson, published in 1816, taking its theme and material from Daniel Defoe's *Journal of the Plague Year.*

City Point. Former village of E Virginia, now a part of the independent city of Hopewell. At the confluence of the James and Appomattox rivers, ab. 22 mi. SE of Richmond, it was a base of supplies and operations in the Civil War.

City Politiques (pol.i.tēks'). Comedy by John Crowne (1683) in which the Whigs are ridiculed, and Shaftesbury, Oates, and Sir William Jones are parodied, the last in the character of Bartoline. John Geneste dates the first printed edition as 1688.

City Ramble, The. Play, adapted from Beaumont and Fletcher's *The Knight of the Burning Pestle,* by Elkanah Settle.

City Wit, or the Woman Wears the Breeches, The. Comedy by Richard Brome, played c1632 and published in 1653.

Ciudad Bolívar (syö.ᴛʜäᴛʜ' bō.lē'bär). [Also: **Bolívar;** former name, **Angostura.**] City in E Venezuela, capital of Bolívar state, on the Orinoco River, ab. 240 mi. above its mouth: exports gold, diamonds, chicle, and tonka beans. 31,009 (1950).

Ciudad Bravos (brä'ʙōs). See **Chilpancingo.**

Ciudad Cura (kö'rä). See **Villa de Cura,** Venezuela.

Ciudad de la Frontera (dā lä frôn.tā'rä). Former name of **Chachapoyas,** city.

Ciudad de las Casas (dā läs kä'säs). See **San Cristóbal de las Casas.**

Ciudad de los Reyes (dā lōs rā'yās). Name given by Pizarro to the capital of Peru, founded by him in 1535. It was long the official appellation, but was gradually supplanted by the name Lima, and was seldom used after the 17th century.

Ciudad del Príncipe (del prēn'sē.pā). A former name of **Camagüey,** city.

Ciudad de México (or **Méjico**) (dā me'ʜē.kō). Spanish name of **Mexico City.**

Ciudadela (thyö.ᴛʜä.ᴛʜā'lä). Town in the Balearic Islands, in the Spanish province of Baleares, situated on the W coast of the island of Minorca, ab. 70 mi. NE of Palma. It has a small harbor, fisheries, and trade in olive oil and wine. The Gothic cathedral dates from the 14th century; there are a number of medieval palaces; caves in the vicinity. 10,716 (1940).

Ciudad Guzmán (syö.ᴛʜäᴛʜ' gös.män'). [Also: **Guzmán, Zapotlán el Grande.**] City in W Mexico, in Jalisco state. 22,170 (1940).

Ciudad Heróica (ā.rō'ē.kä). See **Cartagena,** Columbia

Ciudad Juárez (ʜwä'res). [Also: **Juárez;** former name, **El Paso del Norte.**] City in NW Mexico, in Chihuahua state, on the S bank of the Rio Grande, connected by a bridge with El Paso, Tex.: northern terminus of the Mexican Central Railroad. Founded (1659) as an Indian mission, until 1680 it was only an Indian village, and the only relay between Parral in S Chihuahua and Santa Fe, N.M. In 1680, when the Pueblo Indians of New Mexico drove the Spaniards from Santa Fe, the retreating colonists and a few soldiers halted here and established their camp. Thereafter it became the seat of the government for the province of New Mexico until 1693, and the base of operations against the hostile Pueblos. A Spanish town gradually arose, and the Indian settlements became merged in that place in the course of time. It remained attached to New Mexico until after the war between the U.S. and Mexico, when it was, after the conclusion of peace, included in the Mexican state of Chihuahua. During the latter part of the reign of Maximilian, Ciudad Juárez formed the headquarters of the national forces and of President Juárez. 128,782 (1950).

Ciudad Lerdo (ler'ᴛʜō). See **Lerdo.**

Ciudad Madero (mä.ᴛʜā'rō). City in E Mexico, in Tamaulipas state. 28,075 (1940).

Ciudad Mendoza (men.dō'sä). [Also, **Mendoza.**] City in E Mexico, in Veracruz state. 10,970 (1940).

Ciudad Obregón (ō.brā.gōn'). City in NW Mexico, in Sonora state. 12,497 (1940).

Ciudad Real (thyö.ᴛʜäᴛʜ' rā.äl'). Province in C Spain, bounded by Toledo and Cuenca on the N, Albacete on the E, Jaén and Córdoba on the W: corresponds to the ancient region of La Mancha. Most of the surface is a high plateau; the climate is dry and continental. Livestock raising prevails over agriculture; there are mercury and lead mines. Capital, Ciudad Real; area, 7,622 sq. mi.; pop. 581,836 (1950).

Ciudad Real. [Eng. trans., *"Royal City."*] City in C Spain, the capital of the province of Ciudad Real and the former capital of La Mancha, situated near the Guadiana River, ab. 100 mi. S of Madrid. It is a market place for grain, oil, potatoes, and other agricultural products, and has woolen and linen manufacture. There is a Gothic cathedral. The city was founded by Alfonso X of Castile and fortified against the Moors. During the Peninsular War, a Spanish force was defeated here on March 27, 1809, by the French. 32,931 (1940).

Ciudad Real. Former name of **San Cristóbal de las Casas.**

Ciudad Rodrigo (rōᴛʜ.rē'gō). City in W Spain, in the province of Salamanca, situated on the Agueda River, ab. 48 mi. SW of Salamanca. For many centuries an important frontier fortress, it has a Roman aqueduct and bridge. It is the seat of a bishopric; the 12th-century Gothic cathedral has additions built in 1538. During the Peninsular War, the city was taken by the French under Marshal Ney in 1810, and retaken in 1812 by the British under Viscount Wellington who, subsequently, received the title of Duke of Ciudad Rodrigo. 12,082 (1940).

Ciudad Trujillo (syö.ᴛʜäᴛʜ' trö.ʜē'yō). [Also: **Trujillo;** former name, **Santo Domingo.**] Capital of the Dominican Republic, in the SW part, in the Distrito de Santo Domingo, at the mouth of the Ozama River. It was founded by Bartholomew Columbus in 1496, and is the oldest European settlement, and was long the most important place, in the New World. It was sacked by Sir Francis Drake in 1586. Christopher Columbus is buried in the 16th-century cathedral. 181,533 (1950).

Ciudad Victoria (bēk.tō'ryä). [Also, **Victoria.**] City in E Mexico, capital of Tamaulipas state. 19,513 (1940).

Ciudad Vieja (bye'ʜä). Town in S central Guatemala, ab. 27 mi. by road SW of Guatemala City. It was founded in 1527 as Almolonga, and was the third capital of the Guatemalan captaincy-general. Only some ruins are left of this once flourishing town; the present-day settlement is a large agricultural community subsisting on maize and beans. 6,011 (1940).

Čiurlionis (chör.lyō'nis), **Nikalojus Konstantinas.** b. in Lithuania, Oct. 22, 1875; d. in a sanatorium near Warsaw, Poland, March 28, 1911. Lithuanian composer and painter. He was graduated from the Warsaw Conservatory of Music (1898) and from the Leipzig Conservatory (1902). Later he became interested in painting and studied at Warsaw. In 1907 he settled in Vilna, where he helped to organize the Lithuanian Art Society and its exhibits. From here he moved to St. Petersburg, where he was equally successful. Čiurlionis painted symbolic visions, frequently reaching into cosmic spheres, as in his series of pictures about the creation of the world and the zodiac. Being a musician, and feeling strongly an interrelationship between music and painting, he often gave musical titles to his paintings, as *Sonatas of Spring.* He is also known for his musical compositions, especially the two symphonic poems *Miške* (In the Forest) and *Jūra* (The Sea). Čiurlionis was very much interested in Lithuanian folk songs, harmonized many of them, and used their motifs in his compositions.

Civiale (sē.vyàl), **Jean.** b. at Thiézac, Cantal, France, July, 1792; d. at Paris, June 13, 1867. French surgeon, considered the discoverer of the operation of lithotrity. He wrote *De la lithotritie* (1827).

Cividale del Friuli (chē.vē.dä'lā del frē.ö'lē). [Ancient name, **Forum Julii.**] Town and commune in NE Italy, in the *compartimento* (region) of Friuli-Venezia Giulia, in the province of Udine, situated on the Natisone River near the Yugoslav border, E of Udine. Occupations include paper and textile manufactures, silkworm raising, and construction industries. The museum contains numerous Roman antiquities. The cathedral dates from the 15th century. The location of the town S of the Predil pass where Germanic, Slavic, and Latin influences converged, gave it considerable importance through the centuries. An important council of the church took place here in 796. The town was destroyed by the Hungarians in the 9th century; it was later under the patriarchate of Aquileia and then under the Republic of Venice. Buildings of interest to tourists were undamaged in World War II. Pop. of commune, 10,424 (1936); of town, 4,715 (1936).

Civil Aeronautics Act. [Also, the **Lea-McCarran Civil Aeronautics Act.**] Act passed (1938) by the U.S. Congress, creating a Civil Aeronautics Authority (now called the Civil Aeronautics Administration) composed of five members appointed by the president, who also has the power of appointment over the five-man safety board. The Civil Aeronautics Authority assumed over aviation the authority formerly vested in the Bureau of Commercial Aviation, the Interstate Commerce Commission, and the Post Office. It regulates civilian fliers and civilian air routes and facilities, approves air lines for the carrying of mail, designates and sets up new airways, sets forth safety regulations, and regulates rates and schedules for freight and passenger services.

Civil Aviation Organization, International. See **International Civil Aviation Organization.**

Civil Disobedience. Essay by Henry David Thoreau, published (1849) in Elizabeth Peabody's *Aesthetic Papers* under the title "Resistance to Civil Government." It is also known under the title "On the Duty of Civil Disobedience."

Civilian Conservation Corps. [Called the **"CCC."**] Federal organization set up by acts of Congress in 1933 and 1937 with the aim of furnishing employment to young jobless men. The workers recruited by the "CCC" lived in camps and in addition to maintenance received individual cash payments of 30 dollars a month for working on reforestation, public works, and other projects under government direction. More than two million persons served in the "CCC," which was dissolved in 1942.

Civilis (si.vī′lis), **Julius** (or **Claudius**). fl. 70 A.D. Batavian warrior, leader of the Batavian revolt against Rome in the period 69–70 A.D. The uprising, begun in Germany, spread to Gaul. Civilis was successful until defeated by Cerealis in 70.

Civilistas (sē.ʙē.lēs′täs). Name given in Peru to those who opposed the union of military and civil power in the chief magistrate and generally objected to the election of army officers to the presidency. After 1860 the Civilistas became a well-defined political party. They called their opponents Militaristas or Militares.

Civil Rights Act. U.S. statute (April 9, 1866) designed to protect the Negro freedmen from such discriminatory legislation as the Black Codes enacted by various Southern states. First passed on March 13, 1866, it was vetoed by President Andrew Johnson on March 27, but was passed over his veto. It is significant as the first federal law defining citizenship, and effectively conferred citizenship upon the Negroes, a step necessitated by the Dred Scott decision. Doubt as to the constitutionality of the measure induced Congress to enact most of its provisions into the 14th Amendment. Supplementary Civil Rights Acts (1870, 1871, 1875) are usually referred to as Force Acts.

Civil Rights Cases, 109 U.S. 3 (1883). U.S. Supreme Court decision which invalidated the Supplementary Civil Rights Act of 1875. The essence of the court's interpretation of the 14th Amendment held that discrimination against Negroes by private individuals was beyond the scope of federal legislation. The decision is a landmark in the history of the U.S. Reconstruction era.

Civil Service Reform. In U.S. history, a movement to remedy corruption and abuses involved in political appointment to federal civil service positions. It had its inception before the Civil War, with the national laws of 1853 and 1855. Effective reform, however, was instituted in 1883, when the Pendleton Act was passed by the U.S. Congress. Its provisions for limited classified civil service were strengthened by the Civil Service Rules and Orders of 1903 and the Classification Act of 1923, both of which extended the merit system. Civil service reform among the states was formally instituted by New York's Civil Service Act of 1883, the first of its kind in the U.S.

Civil War. [Also: the **War Between the States,** the **War for Southern Independence,** the **War of Secession,** the **War of the Rebellion.**] In U.S. history, name given to a war from 1861 to 1865, between the North (the Union: 23 states) and the South (the Confederacy: 11 states). Its chief causes were the antislavery agitation of the more radical groups in the newly formed Republican Party, the Abolitionists, and the congressmen representing these groups, and the development of the doctrine of state sovereignty. The former had been gaining ground since the Missouri Compromise of 1820, when Missouri had been admitted to the Union as a slave state, with the express provision made that in the remaining parts of the Louisiana Purchase north of 36°30′ slavery would not be permitted. Emphasizing the growing division of the U.S. into proslavery and antislavery factions were the Wilmot Proviso of 1846, a measure passed by the House of Representatives but failing in the Senate, providing that slavery would be excluded from any of the territory obtained from Mexico; the Omnibus Bill of 1850, also called the Compromise of 1850, in reality a series of bills which admitted California as a free state, provided for the admission of new states as free or slave as their own desires went, abolished the slave trade in the District of Columbia, established a more rigid fugitive-slave law, and which touched off a notable debate in the Senate in which Henry Clay, the sponsor of the compromise, opposed the proslavery, states' rights spokesman, John C. Calhoun, with the great orators in the Senate pleading the causes on both sides; and the trouble over the admission of Kansas and Nebraska as states, when the Missouri Compromise was thrown out and guerrilla warfare turned "bleeding Kansas" into a battleground of proslavery and antislavery groups. The doctrine of state sovereignty found expression in the Kentucky resolutions written (1798–99) by Thomas Jefferson, declaring that a state had the right to declare null within its own territory any act of Congress. It was emphasized by the growth of the nullification doctrine, especially in the teachings of John C. Calhoun.

Immediate Causes. The immediate occasion of the war was the election in 1860 of the Republican Abraham Lincoln to the presidency. The South felt that Lincoln stood for abolition, and in December, 1860, South Carolina announced its intention to secede from the federal union. Despite conferences and attempted conciliation and compromise, ten other Southern states (Mississippi, Florida, Alabama, Georgia, Louisiana, Texas, Arkansas, North Carolina, Virginia, and Tennessee) joined her within the next six months, uniting as the Confederate States of America (formed February, 1861). Jefferson Davis, who had been a U.S. senator from Mississippi, was chosen president of the new federation.

1861. On April 12, after demands had been made for its evacuation, Fort Sumter, in Charleston Harbor, S.C., was fired upon by Confederate batteries commanded by P. G. T. Beauregard, and it was surrendered (April 13) by Major Robert Anderson. President Lincoln called (April 15) for 75,000 volunteers, and declared (April 19) a blockade of Southern ports. On May 13, Great Britain recognized the Confederate States as belligerents, but not, as many in the South had hoped, as an independent state. (The Confederates counted on both British and French aid, in view of Southern cotton resources, but despite many incidents which might have led to such recognition, neither so acted during the early years of the war, and by the time that either Britain or Napoleon III of France might have helped, it became obvious that the North would win. France actually did attempt to set up an empire in Mexico in 1864, but this failed. Late in 1861, the British steamer *Trent* was stopped by the U.S. sloop *San Jacinto* and two Confederate commissioners, James M. Mason and John Slidell, on their way to England, were removed from the *Trent*. Since the U.S. had maintained, and had fought the War of 1812 over, freedom of the seas from such seizures, this act of Captain Charles Wilkes was repudiated when Britain protested and the two commissioners were released early in 1862.) At Lincoln's summons, Congress convened (July 4). The demand was for action, and Union forces moved to attack Beauregard's troops at Manassas Junction, Va., where, in the first battle of Bull Run (July 21), they were defeated, falling back on Washington. Union forces captured Forts Clark and Hatteras on August 28 and 29. In Missouri, a Confederate force defeated (Aug. 10) Union troops at Wilson's Creek, but by autumn Missouri, split into two warring camps, was safely in the hands of the Union. However, matters in the east were not going well for the Union, and on Nov. 1, George B. McClellan who had campaigned successfully in the western part of Virginia to save for the Union those sections desiring to remain loyal, succeeded Winfield Scott as commander of the Army of the Potomac.

1862. At Mill Springs, Ky., the Confederates were defeated (Jan. 19) by a force under George H. Thomas. Opening a campaign to split the Confederacy by gaining control of the Mississippi River, a Union force under Ulysses S. Grant attacked and captured (Feb. 6) Fort Henry on the Tennessee River and then, in a four-day battle, captured (Feb. 16) Fort Donelson on the Cumberland River. Driving southward up the Tennessee, Grant was attacked at Pittsburg Landing, Tenn., by a Confederate force under Albert S. Johnston, and in the battle of Shiloh (April 6–7), Johnston was killed and the Confederate troops forced back into Mississippi. On April 24 and 25, a naval force under David Farragut passed the forts of New Orleans and caused a Confederate withdrawal from the city, which was occupied (May 1) by Union troops under Benjamin F. Butler. Corinth, Miss., was evacuated (May 30) by the Confederates, and Memphis surrendered on June 6. Naval forces under Andrew Foote and troops under John Pope, after the reduction (April 7) of Island No. 10, on the Mississippi north of Memphis, secured the river as far south as Vicksburg. In the east, a Confederate ironclad ship, the *Virginia* (formerly the frigate *Merrimac*) appeared (March 8) in Hampton Roads and sank the *Congress* and the *Cumberland*, but the next day, faced by the *Monitor* in the first battle of ironclads in history, the vessel retired beyond reach of the *Monitor's* heavy shells. At New Berne, N.C., on March 14, Union forces under Ambrose Burnside defeated Confederate troops and took the town, to remain a continued threat to the Confederate capital of Richmond. In April, Union troops laid siege to Yorktown, Va., and early in May the city fell. At Williamsburg, on May 5, the first battle of the Peninsular Campaign was fought; McClellan, pushed into action against Richmond by orders from Washington, advanced up the peninsula between the James and York rivers. At Fair Oaks (Seven Pines), Va., less than ten miles from Richmond, McClellan's forces defeated (May 31–June 1) Confederates under Joseph E. Johnston, but McClellan felt that his position was exposed and shifted south to the James River. In a series of battles, the Seven Days' battles (June 25–July 1) at Mechanicsville, Oak Grove, Gaines's Mill, Frayser's Farm, and Malverne Hill, Robert E. Lee, since June 1 commander of the Confederate armies in Virginia, was defeated, but again McClellan cautiously retreated to the James. At Cedar Mountain, Confederate troops under T. J. ("Stonewall") Jackson, who was a chief cause of McClellan's vacillation by reason of his brilliant successes in the Shenandoah Valley, defeated (Aug. 9) a Union force under Nathaniel Banks. Three weeks later (Aug. 30) Jackson, under Lee's command, defeated John Pope (McClellan's successor as commander of the Union Army of the Potomac) in the second battle of Bull Run (or Second Manassas). Jackson defeated (Sept. 1) parts of Pope's army at Chantilly and crossed the Potomac on Sept. 4. At South Mountain (Boonsboro) on Sept. 14, and at Antietam (Sharpsburg), just north of Harpers Ferry, W.Va., on Sept. 17, Lee's forces clashed with the Union armies, but no decision was reached and Lee fell back across the Potomac on Sept. 18. Burnside was named commander of the Union forces on Nov. 7 and assaulted (Dec. 13) Lee's army at Fredericksburg but was driven off. In the west, battles were fought at Iuka, Miss. (Sept. 19), Perrysville, Ky. (Oct. 8), and Corinth, Miss. (Oct. 4), with the Union forces maintaining their grip on the Mississippi except for the stretch between Vicksburg, Miss., and Port Hudson, La. At Murfreesboro, Tenn., a great battle was fought (Dec. 31–Jan. 2) between Union troops under W. S. Rosecrans and Confederate forces under Braxton Bragg, Bragg finally leaving the field to the Union army.

1863. On Jan. 1, Lincoln issued the Emancipation Proclamation, freeing all slaves in the states then in rebellion against the United States, in an attempt to cause dissension in the South and to gain support in England and France. Burnside was replaced (Jan. 25) by Joseph Hooker as commander following Burnside's defeat at Fredericksburg. At Chancellorsville, Va., the Confederates defeated Union troops on May 1–4, but suffered the loss of Stonewall Jackson, killed by one of his own marksmen who mistook him for a Union officer. Lee now advanced into Pennsylvania. Union fortunes were at their low point; desertions were numerous and replacements were difficult to find. Attempts at a draft of manpower met with resistance, as for example at New York where riots occurred (July 13–16) resulting in great property damage and loss of life. On June 28, George Meade became Hooker's successor as commander of the Army of the Potomac. Meade confronted Lee at Gettysburg, Pa., where on July 1–3 the decisive battle of the war was fought. At first successful, Lee could not cope with the fresh Union troops that kept arriving at the scene and on July 4 he was in retreat. The "high water mark" of the Confederacy had been reached in the disastrous charge of Pickett's troops. On the same day, July 4, climaxing a campaign that saw battles at Grand Gulf (April 29–May 1), Raymond (May 12), Jackson (May 14), and Champion's Hill (May 16), Vicksburg fell to Grant and within the week Port Hudson too had fallen (July 8) to N. P. Banks. The Union now controlled the Mississippi, and Texas, Arkansas, and Louisiana were cut off from the eastern Confederacy. Union strategy now called for a drive to push the Confederates back in the east, and thus to flank them, while pressure from the north forced them out of Virginia into Georgia. Rosecrans, operating further east in Tennessee, took Chattanooga on Sept. 9, but Bragg made a stand (Sept. 19–20) and drove him back at Chickamauga, Ga. Grant's army from Vicksburg came up and in battles at Chattanooga on Nov. 23–25 forced the Confederate troops back into Georgia.

1864. Strong Confederate resistance was now confined to the east. Grant was placed in charge (March 9) of all Union armies. On May 3 he began his advance towards Richmond in the Wilderness campaign, fighting along the route from the Rapidan to the James. From May 3 to June 3 he fought at Spotsylvania Court House, the North Anna River, and Cold Harbor. On June 15 he was before Petersburg but he was unable to take the city and on the 18th he began a siege. Meanwhile, W. T. Sherman, who had been placed in charge of the western armies by Grant, advanced on Atlanta from Chattanooga, beginning May 5. Joseph E. Johnston, opposing him, avoided battle and was replaced by John B. Hood. Hood made his stand at Atlanta, where a battle was fought (July 22), but the city fell (Sept. 2). In August, Farragut had entered Mobile Bay and defeated the Confederate ships there, to take away the last Gulf port of the Confederacy. In a naval battle still earlier, the Union ship *Kearsarge* met and sank (June 19) the Confederate cruiser *Alabama*, which had been raiding shipping, off Cherbourg, France. At Winchester (Opequan Creek) on Sept. 19, Fisher's Hill on Sept. 22, and Cedar Creek on Oct. 19, Philip Sheridan defeated Jubal Early's forces and caused the withdrawal of the Confederates from the Shenandoah Valley. On Nov. 8, the national election was held, and Lincoln, who had given up hope of reëlection during the losses of the Wilderness campaign earlier in the year, won easily over the Democratic candidate, General McClellan. Sherman, on Nov. 16, began his march to the sea, in a campaign to cut the Confederacy in two. On Dec. 20 he was before Savannah, having destroyed and burned a swath across the state and destroyed its military potential. Savannah fell and Sherman turned northward. A diversionary attempt by the Confederate Hood was met by G. H. Thomas at Nashville, where Hood was defeated (Dec. 15–16).

1865. Fort Fisher, N.C., fell (Jan. 15), closing the port of Wilmington, N.C.; Columbia, S.C., was taken (Feb.

17); the Union naval arm forced Charleston, S.C., to surrender (Feb. 18). At Averysboro, N.C. (March 16), Bentonville, N.C. (March 19–21), and Five Forks, Va. (March 31–April 1), Union forces were victorious. The siege of Petersburg ended (April 2) with the evacuation of the city by the Confederate forces. Richmond was now defenseless and fell on April 3. Lee's position was hopeless; on April 9 he surrendered to Grant at Appomattox Court House, Va. Johnston surrendered (April 26) to Sherman, and Kirby Smith, commanding the last active Confederate force, surrendered at Shreveport, La., on May 26. The theater of war had been mainly in the Southern and border states. Enlistments in the Union army had been slightly less than 2,900,000, in the Confederate army ab. 1,300,000. Union losses amounted to almost 360,000; those of the Confederates to about 260,000. The cost of the war directly was some four and three-quarters billions of dollars, and was probably close to ten billions when property destruction, pensions, interest on loans and the like are considered.

Civil War, English. [Also, **The Great Rebellion.**] A civil war (1642–46) between adherents of Charles I of England and the party of Parliament. It found its roots in the dissatisfaction of certain classes (merchants, artisans, nobility) with the Stuart theory of an absolute monarch not answerable to his subjects for his acts. Charles found his chief support in the landed class and the peasantry and in the Anglican clergy. When Charles called Parliament into session (Nov. 30, 1640; it sat until March 16, 1660) he wanted money to pay his Scottish army. Instead of voting the disbursement, Parliament presented to him on Dec. 1, 1641, a Grand Remonstrance, stating the many grievances they held to his account. The king retaliated by ordering (Jan. 3, 1642) the arrest of five leaders of the House of Commons; when they hid from his personal search, he left London and thereafter rejected all Parliamentary proposals at compromise of his stand.

Military. The Royalists threw back (Oct. 23, 1642) the Parliamentarians at Edgehill, but Charles did not advance on London. Several lesser engagements occurred: capture of Reading (April 27, 1643) by the Parliamentarians under their commander, Robert Devereux, 3rd Earl of Essex; the fall of Bristol (Aug. 25) to the Royalists under Prince Rupert; the relief of Gloucester by Essex in September; the battle of Newbury (Sept. 20) between Charles and Essex; the battle of Nantwich (Jan. 25, 1644), where Sir Thomas Fairfax defeated the Royalists. On July 2, 1644, Oliver Cromwell, Thomas and Fernandino Fairfax, and Scots troops under Alexander Leslie met Prince Rupert at Marston Moor in Yorkshire. Cromwell's Ironsides (his own troops) saved the day and put the Royalists to flight. As a result of the battle York (July 16) and Newcastle (Oct. 16) were taken. On June 29, Parliamentary forces under Sir William Waller were defeated at Cropredy Bridge. Essex engaged in a campaign in Cornwall but met defeat and lost his army. Again at Newbury a battle was fought (Oct. 27), but the Parliamentary victory was inconclusive. In Scotland, James Graham, 5th Earl of Montrose, gained one victory after another over Scots adherents to the Parliamentary cause: at Tippermuir (Sept. 1), Inverlochy (Feb. 2, 1645), Auldcarn (May 1), Alford (July 2), and Kilsyth (Aug. 16). He took Aberdeen and Dundee and was appointed captain-general of Scotland by Charles. However, the decisive battle of the war was fought at Naseby in Northamptonshire on June 14, 1645, when Cromwell's cavalry turned the tide of battle and routed the Royalists. Soon after this, Montrose, on his way to support Charles, was met by Parliamentarians under David Leslie at Philiphaugh and defeated (Sept. 13). Royalist resistance now crumbled and at Stowe-on-the-Wold the last battle of the war was fought (March 26, 1646), Sir Jacob Astley being defeated and captured.

Political. Before hostilities broke out, Parliament had abolished some of the sore spots of English absolutism, including the Court of Star Chamber, which often had acted arbitrarily and without reference to its stated authority. Several offers of conciliation were fought by Charles; he refused to sign bills or recognize protests. On the other hand, he made attempts to reach a peaceful settlement, even signing the bill of attainder that resulted in the death of the Earl of Strafford, who had been his chief adviser. When Parliament submitted (June 2, 1642) a series of propositions limiting the king's military and political powers, he refused to have anything to do with it. Parliament thereafter placed the military power in the hands of a committee and appointed its own commander, Essex, to lead the army. In September, 1643, by signing the Solemn League and Covenant, it attracted to its cause the Scots, who had fought the episcopacy of England in favor of their own Presbyterianism. Charles surrendered (May 5, 1646) to the Scots, and was turned over (Jan. 30, 1647) to Parliament. Shrewdly he widened a breach between Parliament and the army, but his intransigence when it came to Parliamentary proposals and bills led Parliament to renounce their allegiance to him on Jan. 15, 1648. When the army resolved to try Charles, Parliament tried once more to make peace with the king, but the army, forcibly excluding (Dec. 6, 7, 1648) more than half the membership of Parliament through the action of Colonel Thomas Pride, made certain that Parliament would accede to the trial. Charles was tried (Jan. 20–27, 1649) and beheaded (Jan. 30). The Commonwealth, with its basic power in the army led by Cromwell, was established and ruled England from 1649 to 1660 (in its later stages, 1653–1659, being known as the Protectorate).

Civil Wars in France. Play (1598) by Dekker and Drayton.

Civil Works Administration. [Called the **"CWA."**] Federal agency established (1933) as a branch of the Federal Emergency Relief Administration to create temporary employment for four million people at prevailing wages until they could be transferred to the Public Works Administration or be otherwise employed. The projects undertaken by the "CWA" included local improvements, such as the maintenance of roads, the landscaping of public parks and school grounds, the repair and maintenance of public utilities, and erosion control. It was dissolved in the spring of 1934.

Civita Castellana (chē'vē.tä käs.tel.lä'nä). [Ancient name, **Falerii.**] Town and commune in C Italy, in the *compartimento* (region) of Latium, in the province of Viterbo, ab. 27 mi. N of Rome: on the site of the Etruscan town of Falerii, which belonged to the Etruscan Confederation and was destroyed (241 B.C.) by the Romans. The modern town produces quality ceramics, and has stone quarries. The medieval walls are preserved. Buildings of interest include the castle and cathedral (an old foundation, with additions of the 13th century); these were undamaged in World War II. Pop. of commune, 8,622 (1936); of town, 7,289 (1936).

Civita di Penne (dē pān'nä). See **Penne,** Italy.

Civita Lavinia (lä.vē'nyä). See under **Lanuvium.**

Civitali (chē.vē.tä'lē), **Matteo.** b. at Lucca, Italy, June 5, 1435; d. Oct. 12, 1501. Italian sculptor and architect of the early Renaissance. A barber by trade until about his 35th year, he found means to study sculpture and architecture. As to the latter, he is known to have engaged in bridge-building and to have built fortifications for his native city. His sculptures survive chiefly in the cathedral and other churches at Lucca, but there are examples of his work, marked by honest simplicity and strength, in the Uffizi Gallery, Florence, and the Metropolitan Museum at New York owns one of his painted terra-cotta pieces, *Angel of the Annunciation.*

Civitanova Marche (chē"vē.tä.nô'vä mär'kā). Town and commune in C Italy, in the *compartimento* (region) of Marches, in the province of Macerata, situated near the Adriatic Sea, E of Macerata. There are lumber mills and silk textile manufactures. Pop. of commune, 17,424 (1936); of town, 8,153 (1936).

Civitas Aurelia Aquensis (siv'i.tas ô.rēl'yạ ạ.kwen'sis). Latin name of **Baden-Baden,** Germany.

Civitas Cadurcorum (kad.ur.kō'rum). A Latin name of **Cahors.**

Civitas Eburovicum (ẹ.bū.rọ.vī'kum). Latin name of **Évreux.**

Civitas Legionum (lē.ji.ō'num). See under **Chester,** England.

Civitas Nemetum (nẹ.mē'tum). Ancient name of **Speyer.**

Civitas Redonum (rẹ.dō'num). An ancient name of **Rennes.**

Civitas Vangionum (van.ji.ō′num). Roman name of **Worms,** Germany.

Civitavecchia (chē″vē.tä.vek′kyä). [Also: **Civita Vecchia**; ancient name, **Centum Cellae,** later **Portus Trajani.**] City and commune in C Italy, in the *compartimento* (region) of Latium, in the province of Roma, situated on the Mediterranean Sea, NW of Rome. It is a popular seaside resort. The port, constructed in the time of the Roman emperor Trajan, now exports building materials, chemicals, hides, and cheeses; building materials, chemicals, and food products are manufactured; there are stone quarries in the vicinity. The port is dominated by a medieval castle; the jetty was started by Bramante and finished by Michelangelo; Bernini constructed the arsenal. The ancient town, an Etruscan and Roman port, was destroyed by the Saracens in 828 A.D. It became the port of the Papal States in the 15th century; Popes Julius II, Urban VIII, and Alexander VII engaged in extensive building activities here. Considerable damage was suffered during World War II by some buildings of tourist interest. Pop. of commune, 31,858 (1936); of city, 24,822 (1936).

Civitella del Tronto (chē.vē.tel′lä del trôn′tō). Town and commune in C Italy, in the *compartimento* (region) of Abruzzi e Molise, in the province of Teramo, situated on a rocky elevation above the Salinello River, ab. 8 mi. NW of Teramo. It is a climatic health resort, and has a medieval castle and fortifications. It was the last place in the kingdom of Naples to surrender to the Italians in 1861. Pop. of commune, 10,609 (1936); of town, 729 (1936).

Civula (chē.vö′lä). See **Chivula.**

Civaka (chē.yä′kä). See **Chiyaka.**

Cizos (sē.zō), **Rose Marie.** See **Chéri, Rose.**

Clackmannan (klak.man′ąn). Civil parish in C Scotland, county seat of Clackmannanshire, situated on the river Black Devon, near its confluence with the river Forth, ab. 2 mi. E of Alloa. The town is situated on the Central (or Lanarkshire) coal field. 2,585 (1931).

Clackmannanshire (klak.man′ąn.shir) or **Clackmannan.** Maritime county in C Scotland. It is bounded on the N by Perthshire, on the E by Kinross-shire and Fifeshire, on the S by the river Forth, and on the W by Stirlingshire. The surface slopes from the Ochil Hills in the N part to the river Forth. The county is largely agricultural in character. Though it is situated on the Central (or Lanarkshire) coal field, there is not much coal mining in the county. The lowlands are well cultivated. Clackmannanshire is the smallest county in area in Scotland. Clackmannan is the county seat; area, ab. 55 sq. mi.; pop. 37,528 (1951).

Clacton (klak′tǫn). [Also: **Clacton-on-Sea, Clacton-on-Sea and Southcliff.**] Urban district and seaside resort in SE England, in Essex, ab. 70 mi. NE of London by rail. It was formerly a fishing village, but since the building of the railroad has become an important seaside resort. 24,065 (1951).

Claes (kläz), **Balthazar.** Philosopher in Honoré de Balzac's novel *La Recherche de l'absolu.* He gives up his life to a search for the philosopher's stone, and is the victim of his devotion to science.

Claflin (klaf′lin), **Tennessee Celeste.** [Married names, **Bartels,** Lady **Cook.**] b. in Ohio, 1845; d. 1923. American spiritualist; sister of Victoria Claflin Woodhull (1838–1927). With her sister, she began giving spiritualist demonstrations in the Midwest; after extended stays at Cincinnati and Chicago, she accompanied her sister to New York in 1868, where they founded (1870) *Woodhull and Claflin's Weekly,* which in 1872 made the original revelations concerning Henry Ward Beecher and Mrs. Theodore Tilton. Although she married (before 1868) a John Bartels, she used her maiden name. With her sister, she went (1877) to England, where she married (1885) Francis Cook, later the Viscount de Montserrat, and died as Lady Cook.

Claflin, Victoria. See **Woodhull, Victoria Claflin.**

Claiborne (klā′bǫrn), **William.** [Also, **Clayborne.**] b. in Westmorland, England, c1587; d. in Virginia, c1677. American colonial politician. He emigrated to Virginia in 1621, and in 1625 became secretary of state for the colony. As the agent of Cloberry and Company of London, he established a trading post in Kent Island in 1631. The trading post became the nucleus of a flourishing settlement, which in 1632 sent a burgess to the general assembly of Virginia. It was later (1634) claimed by Leonard Calvert, governor of Maryland, as a part of that colony, and was long a subject of disputes resulting in some bloodshed. On the execution of Charles I of England, Maryland and Virginia proclaimed Charles II, whereupon Claiborne, at his own request, was in 1651 appointed by Parliament member of a commission to reduce those colonies. The commissioners reached Virginia at the head of an English expedition in March, 1652, overthrew the Cavalier government, and established a Roundhead government with Richard Bennet as governor and Claiborne as secretary of state. In 1658, however, the province was restored to Lord Baltimore by the commonwealth.

Claiborne, William Charles Coles. b. in Sussex County, Va., 1775; d. Nov. 23, 1817. American lawyer, legislator, and governor. He attended William and Mary College, studied law in Virginia, and established his practice in Sullivan County, Tenn., serving (1796) as a member of the state constitutional convention and becoming a judge of the new state's supreme court. He was (1797–1801) a member of Congress, and became (1801) governor of the Mississippi Territory, also acting as superintendent of Indian affairs. In 1803 he became governor of the Louisiana Territory, and later governor of the state of Louisiana. He was elected (1817) to the U.S. Senate, but died before he could take his seat.

Clair (kler), **René.** [Professional name of **René Chomette.**] b. 1898—. French journalist and motion-picture director and producer. He has been associated in France with such successes as the fantasy-comedy film *Le Million,* and in Hollywood with *The Ghost Goes West.*

Clairac (kle.ràk). Town in SW France, in the department of Lot-et-Garonne, situated on the Lot River ab. 56 mi. SE of Bordeaux. Pop. ab. 1,200.

Clairaut or **Clairault** (kle.rō), **Alexis Claude.** b. at Paris, May 13, 1713; d. there, May 17, 1765. French mathematician. He was famous for both the strength and the extraordinary precocity of his genius. At six years of age he is said to have understood L'Hôpital's treatise on infinitesimals, at 12 he read before the Academy of Sciences a paper on certain curves which he had discovered, and at 18 he became a member of the Academy. Among his best-known works is his analytical study of the problem of "the three bodies," and the application of its results to the study of the moon and of Halley's comet. He also wrote *Recherches sur les courbes à double courbure* (1731), *Théorie de la figure de la terre* (1743), *Théorie de la lune* (1752), and *Recherches sur les comètes des années 1531, 1607, 1682 et 1759* (1760).

Claire (klãr), **Ina.** [Original surname, **Fagan.**] b. at Washington, D.C., Oct. 15, 1892—. American actress; married (1919) James Whittaker (divorced); married (1929) John Gilbert (divorced 1931); married (1939) William Ross Wallace. She made her first appearance on stage in 1907 as a vaudeville entertainer, and subsequently appeared in *The Quaker Girl* (1911), *The Honeymoon Express* (1913), and *The Ziegfeld Follies* (1915–16), and appeared in England in *The Girl from Utah* (1913) and *The Belle of Bond Street* (1913). She was starred in such stage productions as *The Gold Diggers* (1919), *Bluebeard's Eighth Wife, The Awful Truth, Grounds for Divorce* (1924), *The Last of Mrs. Cheyney* (1925), *Our Betters* (1928), *Biography* (1932–34), *Once is Enough* (1938), *Ode to Liberty,* and *The Fatal Weakness.* Her motion-picture successes (1928–32) include *The Royal Family of Broadway, Rebound,* and *The Greeks Had a Word For It.*

Clairfayt (kler.fe′), Count **von.** See **Clerfayt** or **Clairfayt,** Count **von.**

Clairmont (klãr′mont, -mǫnt), **Clara Mary Jane.** [Called **Claire Clairmont.**] b. April 27, 1798; d. 1879. Stepdaughter of William Godwin and mother of Byron's daughter Allegra. From Godwin's house she accompanied (1814) Mary Godwin in the latter's elopement with the poet Shelley. Upon her return she resided with the Shelleys at London and afterwards went to Lynmouth, eventually returning to the Godwin home. She met Byron in 1816, having supposedly introduced herself to him with a view toward getting an acting engagement at the Drury Lane Theatre. She was then only 18. The summer of 1816 was passed by the Shelleys, Claire, and Byron together in Switzerland. Upon the birth of her daughter Allegra in

1817, Byron offered to bring up the child. After Byron's death she served in various European countries as a governess.

Clairmont (kler.môn'), **Paul Johann.** b. at Vienna, June 10, 1875; d. at St. Prex, Switzerland, Jan. 1, 1942. Austrian surgeon. He was assistant to A. von Eiselsberg at Königsberg and Vienna, became (1908) privatdocent of surgery at the University of Vienna and professor in 1912, and was called (1918) to the chair of surgery at the University of Zurich. He is known for his methods of gastric surgery and for his operation (1908) for recurrent dislocation of the shoulder. He showed (1904) that fluid in a closed segment of the small bowel is poisonous when injected into the vein of another animal. Author of *Die Bedeutung der Magenradiologie für die Chirurgie* (1911), *Die Bekämpfung des Blutverlustes durch Transfusion und Gefässfüllung* (1928), *Chirurgie der Mundhöhle und der Speicheldrüsen* (1930), *Chirurgie der Brustdrüse* (1930), *Chirurgie des Afters und Mastdarms* (1930), *Die Chirurgie der Tuberkulose* (1931), *Über das Zwölffingerdarmgeschwür* (1936), *Gutachten über die Chiropraktik* (1937), and *Allgemeine Gegenanzeigen bei nicht dringlichen chirurgischen Eingriffen* (1936); coeditor of *Fehler und Gefahren bei chirurgischen Operationen* (1923), *Diagnostische und therapeutische Irrtümer* (1925), *Klinik der bösartigen Geschwülste* (1925), and Scheff's *Handbuch der Zahnheilkunde* (1925).

Clairon (kle.rôn), Mademoiselle. [Original name, **Claire Josèphe Hippolyte Léris de la Tude.**] b. near Condé-sur-l'Escaut, Nord, France, 1723; d. at Paris, Jan. 18, 1803. French actress. Originally a comedienne, she turned to tragedy and enjoyed extraordinary popularity. She was especially noted for acting in Voltaire's plays. She died at an advanced age, poor and forgotten. Her *Mémoires* were published in 1799.

Clairton (klãr'tọn). City in SW Pennsylvania, in Allegheny County: manufactures glass, brick, steel, benzol, coal tar, fertilizer, and dyes. 19,652 (1950).

Clairvaux (kler.vō). Village in NE France, in the department of Aube, situated on the Aube River ab. 32 mi. SE of Troyes. It is celebrated for its Cistercian abbey, whose first abbot was Saint Bernard, 1115. The abbey buildings are now used for a prison.

Claisen (klī'zẹn), **Ludwig.** b. at Godesberg, Germany, 1851; d. there, 1930. German organic chemist. During the period 1887–89, he clarified a reaction earlier discovered by Geuther, the condensation of esters (in the presence of sodium ethylate) to B-diketones. This "Claisen condensation" became one of the most important of synthetic methods. He served as a professor at Aix-la-Chapelle (now Aachen, Germany), and Kiel (1897–1904). In 1907 he established a private laboratory at Godesberg.

Clajus (klä'yůs), **Johann.** See **Klaj, Johann.**

Clamart (klå.mår). Town in N France, in the department of Seine, situated SW of Paris, bordering on the Bois de Meudon. It is a suburb of Paris. 33,817 (1946).

Clamecy (klåm.sē). Town in C France, in the department of Nièvre, situated at the junction of the Beuvron and Yonne rivers, between Nevers and Auxerre-St.-Gervais. It is a center of the lumber industry and the lumber trade and has chemical manufactures and a large flour mill. There are various old churches and medieval buildings. 5,819 (1946).

Clam-Martinic (kläm'mär'tē.nēts), Count **Heinrich Jaroslaw von.** b. at Vienna, Jan. 1, 1863; d. 1932. Austro-Hungarian statesman. A friend of the Archduke Franz Ferdinand, he was minister of agriculture (1916), *Ministerpräsident* (prime minister) in the period 1916–17, and governor of Montenegro (1917).

Clancy Name (klan'si), **The.** One-act tragedy by Lennox Robinson, produced in 1908 and published in 1910. It is a study of Irish pride in the family name and honor.

Clandeboye (klan'dẹ.boi), Baron. See **Blackwood, Frederick Temple Hamilton-Temple.**

Clandestine Marriage, The. Play by Garrick and Colman, produced on Feb. 20, 1766. It was largely taken from an unprinted farce, *The False Concord* (1764), by James Townley.

Claneboye (klan'ẹ.boi), 1st Viscount. Title of **Hamilton, James** (1559–1643).

Clanis (klan'is). Latin name of the **Chiana.**

Clansman, The. Novel by Thomas Dixon, published in 1905. Laid against the background of the South during the Reconstruction period after the Civil War, it views the early Klu Klux Klan in a favorable light. The script for the motion picture *The Birth of a Nation* (1915) was written by Dixon, who based it on his novel.

Clanton (klan'tọn). Town in C Alabama, county seat of Chilton County, ab. 49 mi. S of Birmingham: cotton gins and sawmills. 4,640 (1950).

Clap (klap), **Thomas.** b. at Scituate, Mass., June 26, 1703; d. at New Haven, Conn., Jan. 7, 1767. American clergyman and educator. He was rector (corresponding to the office of president) of Yale College in the period 1740–66. Previously he had served as pastor at Windham, Conn. from 1726–1740.

Claparède (klå.på.red), **Jean Louis René Antoine Édouard.** b. at Geneva, Switzerland, April 24, 1832; d. at Siena, Italy, May 31, 1871. Swiss naturalist. He served as professor of comparative anatomy at Geneva. His works include papers on rhizopods, spiders, annelids, oligochaetes, and Infusoria.

Clapham (klap'ạm). Two wards of Wandsworth metropolitan borough, in SW London, in the County of London, situated on the S side of the river Thames, ab. 3 mi. SW of Victoria station, London. Its houses surround a common ab. 220 acres in extent, once a favorite location for fairs, which were abolished in 1873. Pop. 60,925 (1931).

Clapham, John Harold. b. 1873; d. 1946. English economist, author of the three-volume *An Economic History of Modern Britain* (1926–38). He was professor of economic history at Cambridge (1928–38), where he had been educated, and vice-provost of King's College, Cambridge (1933–46). His other works include *The Woollen and Worsted Industries* (1907) and *The Economic Development of France and Germany, 1815–1915* (1921).

Clapiers (klå.pyā), **Luc de.** See **Vauvenargues,** Marquis **de.**

Clapisson (klå.pē.sôn), **Antoine Louis.** b. at Naples, Italy, Sept. 15, 1808; d. at Paris, March 19, 1866. French composer of operas, songs, and romances. His works include the operas *La Promise* (1854), *La Fanchonnette* (1856), and *Madame Grégoire* (1861).

Clapp (klap), **Frederick Mortimer.** b. at New York, July 26, 1879—. American art connoisseur, poet, critic, lecturer, and writer, director of the Frick Collection at New York since 1936. He was educated at the College of the City of New York, Yale, the University of Lausanne, Switzerland, in Italy, and at Paris. He served as a lecturer at the University of California (1906–14), was head of the fine arts department at the University of Pittsburgh (1926–37), and became associated with the Frick Collection in 1931. Some of his books are *Les Dessins de Pontormo*, *Jacopo Carucci, His Life and Works*, *On the Overland and Other Poems*, *New York and Other Verses*, and *Said Before Sunset.*

Clapp, Sir **Harold Winthrop.** b. at Melbourne, Australia, May 7, 1875—. Australian electrical engineer, an authority on railway electrification. He studied at Melbourne, and was named (1898) superintendent of motive power for the Brisbane Tramway Company. In 1902 he joined the General Electric Company at Schenectady, N.Y., representing that firm in the building of New York City subways and tunnels, in construction on the New York Central and Pennsylvania railroads, and in the electrification (1908) of the California railroads. He was associated (1908–12) with the Southern Pacific Company at San Francisco. He has also served as chairman (1920–39) of the Railway Commissioners at Victoria, Australia, head (1939–42) of the Aircraft Production Commission of the Commonwealth of Australia, and commonwealth director-general of transport.

Clapperton (klap'ėr.tọn), **Hugh.** b. at Annan, Scotland, 1788; d. at Sokoto, Nigeria, April 13, 1827. Scottish traveler in Africa. He was a lieutenant in the navy when Oudney and Denham started, in 1822, on their exploration of the Sudan. He accompanied them, and returned with Denham in 1824. In the same year, as commander, he proceeded, with Lander and three other assistants, to the mouth of the Niger River, and explored its course up to Sokoto. The journal of this expedition was published in 1829.

Clara (klar'ạ). In Thomas Otway's *Cheats of Scapin*, a character corresponding to Hyacinthe in Molière's *Fourberies de Scapin*.

Clara. Girl in love with Ferdinand, in Richard Brinsley Sheridan's *The Duenna*.

Clara, Saint. See Saint **Clare** (or **Clara**) **of Assisi.**

Clara Barley (bär'li). See **Barley, Clara.**

Clarac (klå.råk), Comte **Charles Othon Frédéric Jean Baptiste de.** b. at Paris, June 16, 1777; d. 1847. French antiquary and artist. He was the author of *Musée de sculpture antique et moderne* (1826–55) and other works.

Clara Howard (hou'ạrd). Novel by Charles Brockden Brown, published in 1801.

Clarascum (klạ.ras'kum). Ancient name of **Cherasco.**

Clärchen (kler'ċhẹn). Simple cottage girl in Goethe's tragedy *Egmont*, in love with that hero. She takes poison when he dies.

Clare (klãr). [Irish, **An Clár.**] Maritime county in Munster province, in the Irish Republic. It is bounded on the N by Galway Bay and County Galway, on the E by Lough Derg and County Tipperary, on the S by County Limerick and the river Shannon (including the wide estuary known as the Mouth of the Shannon), and on the W by the Atlantic Ocean. The surface is varied, with many grassy moors and numerous flat-topped limestone hills. The county is predominantly agricultural, with potatoes being raised and dairy cattle being pastured on the lowlands, and sheep being pastured on the uplands. Ennis is the county seat; area, ab. 1,231 sq. mi.; pop. 81,350 (1951).

Clare, Saint. See Saint **Clare** (or **Clara**) **of Assisi.**

Clare, 1st Earl of. Title of **Fitzgibbon, John.**

Clare, 1st Earl of. Title of **Holles, John.**

Clare, Ada. [Pseudonym and stage name of **Jane McElhenney.**] b. at Charleston, S.C., 1836; d. at New York, March 4, 1874. American actress and writer.

Clare, Ada. Friend and charge of Esther Summerson in Charles Dickens's *Bleak House*. She marries Richard Carstone.

Clare, Elizabeth de. d. Nov. 4, 1360. Third daughter of Gilbert de Clare, 9th Earl of Clare. She was married three times: first to John de Burgh, son of the 2nd Earl of Ulster, and after his death to Theobald, Lord Verdon, and again to Robert Damory, Baron of Armoy. She was the founder (1359) of Clare College, Cambridge (which had originally been established as University Hall).

Clare, John. b. at Helpstone, near Peterborough, England, July 13, 1793; d. at Northampton, England, May 20, 1864. English nature poet, known as the "Northamptonshire Peasant Poet." The son of a laborer, he was a gardener, a shepherd, an unsuccessful farmer, and, frequently, a vagrant. He enlisted in the militia in 1812. He became insane in 1837 and died so, 27 years later. His works are *Poems Descriptive of Rural Life and Scenery* (1820), *The Village Minstrel* (1821), *The Shepherd's Calendar* (1827), and *The Rural Muse* (1835). His pathetic poem, *Written in Northampton County Asylum* ("I am! yet what I am who cares, or knows?") has been praised by many critics.

Clare, Lady Clare de. English heiress in Sir Walter Scott's poem *Marmion*, to obtain whose hand Marmion ruins her lover, Ralph de Wilton.

Clare, Richard de. [Title: 2nd Earl of **Pembroke and Strigul;** called **Richard Strongbow.**] d. 1176. English nobleman. In May, 1170, he went to Ireland with a strong force to aid Dermot, king of Leinster, who had been driven from his kingdom, and captured Waterford and Dublin. He married Eva, daughter of Dermot, and became governor of Ireland (after service with Henry II of England in Normandy) in 1173.

Clare, Richard de. [Titles: 8th Earl of **Clare,** 6th Earl of **Hertford,** and 7th Earl of **Gloucester.**] b. Aug. 4, 1222; d. near Canterbury, England, July 15, 1262. English nobleman. He joined Simon de Montfort's forces in the Barons' War against King Henry III of England.

Clare College. One of the 19 colleges of Cambridge University. The second oldest of the Cambridge colleges, it was founded in 1326, as University Hall, by Richard de Badew, then chancellor of the university, and was refounded in 1338 by Elizabeth de Clare, daughter of Gilbert de Clare, Earl of Gloucester and Hertford, and granddaughter of Edward I.

Clare Island. Small island in Connacht province, Irish Republic, in County Mayo. It lies off the W coast of Ireland, at the entrance of Clew Bay. Length, ab. 5 mi.; greatest width, ab. 3 mi.

Clarel: A Poem and Pilgrimage in the Holy Land (klãr'ẹl). Religious poem by Herman Melville, published in 1876 in two volumes.

Claremont (klãr'mont). City in S California, in Los Angeles County, NE of Los Angeles, in a citrus-growing area: seat of Claremont College, and of Pomona and Scripps colleges, which are associated with it. In the decade between the last two U.S. censuses its population more than doubled. 3,057 (1940), 6,327 (1950).

Claremont. Town in C New Hampshire, in Sullivan County, near the confluence of the Sugar and Connecticut rivers, ab. 45 mi. NW of Concord. It is a tourist center. Manufactures include paper, mining and mill machinery, and needles. It was named for Robert Clive's palace outside of London, in Surrey, England. 12,811 (1950).

Claremont. Palace at Esher, Surrey, England, ab. 14 mi. SW of London, built by Robert Clive in 1768. It was subsequently the residence of Prince Leopold of Saxe-Coburg (later king of the Belgians) and Princess Charlotte. It was put by Queen Victoria at the disposal of Louis Phillipe of France, in the period 1848–50; he died at Claremont.

Claremore (klãr'mōr). City in NE Oklahoma, county seat of Rogers County: noted for its mineral springs. It is the site of the Will Rogers Memorial, and is the seat of the Oklahoma Military Academy and a U.S. Indian hospital. Nearby is the site of an Osage-Cherokee battle (1817). 5,494 (1950).

Clarence (klar'ẹns), Duke of. [Title of **Lionel Plantagenet;** called **Lionel of Antwerp.**] b. at Antwerp, Belgium, 1338; d. 1368. Son of Edward III of England. He presided over the Irish Parliament when it enacted the Statute of Kilkenny which (not very effectively) prohibited any adoption of Irish manners and customs by the English in Ireland, and required the Irish within the Pale to conform to English law and custom. He was an ancestor of the Yorkist claimants to the throne of England in the War of the Roses.

Clarence, Duke of. [Title of **George Plantagenet.**] b. at Dublin, 1449; murdered in the Tower of London, Feb. 18, 1478. English prince; brother of Edward IV and Richard III of England. He married Isabel, daughter of Richard, Earl of Warwick, in 1469, and intrigued with Warwick in the period 1469–71. Thereafter he was reconciled to Edward, but came under suspicion of plotting against the king's life, whereupon he was imprisoned and the death sentence passed on him. According to legend, he was drowned in a butt of malmsey wine. He appears as a character in Shakespeare's *Richard III* and *Henry VI*.

Clarence and Avondale (av'ọn.dāl), Duke of. Title of **Albert Victor Christian Edward.**

Clarence Strait. Channel off NW North America, between Alaska and Prince of Wales Island. Length, ab. 100 mi.

Clarence Strait. Sea passage off NW Australia, connecting Van Diemen Gulf with the Timor Sea, between Melville Island and the mainland of Australia.

Clarendon (klar'ẹn.dọn). City in E Arkansas, county seat of Monroe County, on the Cache and White rivers: important for the manufacture of pearl buttons, obtained from mussels taken from the White River. Rice is raised nearby. 2,547 (1950).

Clarendon. City in NW Texas, county seat of Donley County, in the Panhandle ab. 50 mi. SE of Amarillo: marketing and shipping point for a cotton and cattle raising region. 2,577 (1950).

Clarendon. Hunting lodge near Salisbury, England, which gave its name to the Constitutions of Clarendon.

Clarendon, 1st Earl of. Title of **Hyde, Edward.**

Clarendon, 3rd Earl of. See **Cornbury, Edward Hyde,** Viscount.

Clarendon, 4th Earl of. A title of **Villiers, George William Frederick.**

Clarendon, Assize of. See **Assize of Clarendon.**

Clarendon, Constitutions of. Ordinances adopted at the Council of Clarendon (held at a hunting lodge of that name near Salisbury, England) in 1164, with a view to limiting the jurisdiction of the ecclesiastical courts. There were 16 ordinances in all, including decrees that a member of the clergy accused of a crime should be tried by a royal court (instead of an ecclesiastical one as had previously been the practice) and that papal excommunication of a noble should be subject to the king's approval. Established by Henry II of England, these ordinances were most unwillingly agreed to by Saint Thomas à Becket. He subsequently won the Pope's support in his opposition to them, and after Becket's death popular feeling ran so high in his favor that Henry was forced to modify his position with reference to them.

Clarendon, Council of. Council held in 1164. It was occasioned by the opposition of Thomas à Becket to the ecclesiastical policy of Henry II of England, and comprised the king, the archbishops of Canterbury and York, 11 bishops, 40 of the higher nobility, and numerous barons. It enacted the Constitutions of Clarendon.

Clarendon Code. Collective designation for several statutes enacted by the English Parliament in the period 1661–65. The purpose of these laws, which were passed by the "Cavalier Parliament" when Edward Hyde, 1st Earl of Clarendon, was lord chancellor for Charles II, was to strengthen the Anglican Church. The so-called Code embraced four statutes. The Corporation Act (1661) required municipal officials to take the sacrament according to the Anglican rite and to renounce the Presbyterian Solemn League and Covenant. By the Act of Uniformity (1662) all ministers in England and Wales were bound to use the Book of Common Prayer (more than 2,000 of them, who refused to do so, were deprived of their livings). By the Conventicle Act (1664), it was made a crime for five or more persons to come together for divine worship according to any other than the Anglican rite. Finally the Five-mile Act (1665) penalized any nonconforming clergyman or lay teacher who might be found within that distance of any place where he had previously officiated, or of any incorporated town. To what extent Clarendon approved of these several laws is not quite clear, but he did endeavor to enforce them. Charles II, to woo support among Dissenters and Catholics, tried to ameliorate the effects of the Code by Declarations of Indulgence in 1662 and later, but because of their importance as a deterrent of the growth of Whig influence, they remained in effect, though with modifications, for a considerable time.

Clarendon Press. Printing establishment at Oxford, England, in which the University of Oxford long had the preponderant influence, and which is now an adjunct of the Oxford University Press. It was founded partly with profits from the copyright of *History of the Rebellion*, by Edward Hyde, 1st Earl of Clarendon.

Clarens (klȧ.räṅ). Village in W Switzerland, in the canton of Vaud, situated on the Lake of Geneva, W of Montreux: a villa colony. It is the scene of Rousseau's *Nouvelle Héloïse*. The poet Byron lived here in 1816 (there is a commemorative tablet) and Paul Kruger, last president of the Transvaal, died here in exile in 1904. Population included in Montreux.

Clare (or **Clara**) **of Assisi** (klãr; klar'ạ; ạ.sē'zẹ), Saint. b. at Assisi, Italy, July 16, 1194; d. Aug. 11, 1253. Italian nun, cofounder of the Order of Poor Clares, or Poor Ladies (Clarissines; in France, called Les Clarisses). Daughter of Favorino Scifi, Count of Sasso-Rosso, she heard Saint Francis of Assisi preach in the Church of San Giorgio, and was inspired to follow his way of poverty. In 1212 she was clothed in the Franciscan habit and temporarily lived in the Benedictine convent until the Convent of San Damiano, of which she was first abbess, was prepared by Francis. Cardinal Ugolino, protector of the Franciscans, gave the Poor Clares a rule in 1219, but this was later revised and approved by him, as Pope Gregory IX, in 1228. The definitive rule of the order was approved in 1253. Clare was canonized in 1255.

Clarétie (klȧ.rā.tē), **Jules.** [Original name, **Arsène Arnaud Clarétie.**] b. at Limoges, France, Dec. 3, 1840; d. 1913. French novelist and journalist. He was in turn war correspondent and drama critic, and was appointed director of the Comédie Française on the death of Perrin. He was war correspondent of the *Rappel* and the *Opinion Nationale* in the period 1870–71, and wrote several books on the Franco-Prussian War. He became a member of the French Academy in 1889. His works include *Un Assassin* (1866; in a later edition entitled *Robert Burat*), *Monsieur le ministre* (1881), *Le Prince Silah* (1884), and *Puyjoli* (1890).

Clari (klȧ.rē). Opera by Halévy, first produced at Paris on Dec. 9, 1828.

Clari (klä'rē), **Giovanni Carlo Maria.** b. at Pisa, Italy, c1669; d. c1745. Italian composer. His chief work is a collection of vocal duets and trios (1720).

Claribel (klar'i.bel). In Edmund Spenser's *The Faerie Queene*, the chosen bride of Phaon. She is slandered by Philemon. Phaon slays her, and, finding how he has been deceived, poisons Philemon.

"Claribel." Pseudonym of **Barnard, Charlotte Alington.**

Claribel, Sir. In Edmund Spenser's *The Faerie Queene*, one of four knights who had a fray about the false Florimel. Britomart fights with them, and the combat is "stinted" by Prince Arthur.

Clarice (klar'is; French, klȧ.rēs; Italian, klä.rē'chā). Sister of Huon of Bordeaux in the early French and Italian romances. She marries Rinaldo.

Clariden Pass (klä.rē'dẹn). [Also, **Glariden Pass.**] Glacier pass in the Swiss Alps, leading from the Maderaner Valley to Stachelberg in the canton of Glarus. Elevation, ab. 9,800 ft.

Claridoro (klar.i.dō'rō). Rival of Felisbravo in Antonio de Mendoza's Spanish play *Querer por solo querer* (*To Love for Love's Sake*), translated by Sir Richard Fanshawe.

Clarin (klar'in) or **Clarinda** (klạ.rin'dạ). Trusted handmaid of Queen Radigund in Edmund Spenser's *The Faerie Queene*. She betrays her mistress, seeking to alienate her from Artegall.

Clarinda (klạ.rin'dạ). City in SW Iowa, county seat of Page County. It was a station on the Underground Railway in 1861. It was named for Clarinda Buck, a girl popular in the early life of the settlement. 5,086 (1950).

Clarinda. In Fletcher's *The Lover's Progress*, the adroit and unscrupulous waiting-woman of Calista.

Clarinda. Waiting-woman to Carniola in Philip Massinger's play *The Maid of Honor*.

Clarinda. In Thomas Shadwell's comedy *The Virtuoso*, a niece of the Virtuoso, in love with Longvil.

Clarinda. Principal female character in Susannah Centlivre's play *The Beau's Duel*, in love with Colonel Manly.

Clarinda. Niece of Sir Solomon Sadlife in Colley Cibber's comedy *The Double Gallant*. She "blows cold and hot" upon the passion of Clerimont.

Clarinda. Name used by **Maclehose, Agnes** (1759–1841), a Glasgow lady, in writing to Robert Burns (1759–96), who was "Sylvander."

Clarington (klar'ing.tọn), **Sir Arthur.** Profligate, heartless, and avaricious scoundrel in *The Witch of Edmonton* by Dekker, Ford, and others.

Clarion (klar'i.ọn). City in N Iowa, county seat of Wright County. It was incorporated in 1881, and named for Clarion, Pa. 3,150 (1950).

Clarion. Borough in W Pennsylvania, county seat of Clarion County, on the Clarion River, in an area producing natural gas, coal, and clay: manufactures include bottles and jars. It was platted in 1840. A state teachers college is here. 4,409 (1950).

Clarion River. See under **Allegheny River.**

Clarissa (klạ.ris'ạ). Wife of Gripe, a rich but stingy husband, and stepmother of Corinna, in Sir John Vanbrugh's comedy *The Confederacy*, first acted at the London Haymarket, Oct. 30, 1705. In the *dramatis personae* of the play, Clarissa, performed by the famous Mrs. Barry, is described as "an expensive luxurious woman, a great admirer of quality."

Clarissa Harlowe (här'lō). Epistolary novel (his second) by Samuel Richardson. It was published in 1747 (vols. 1–2) and 1748 (vols. 3–5). The story is told by means of 537 letters written by Clarissa, the heroine, to her "most intimate friend," Miss Howe, and by Robert Lovelace, Esq., to his "principal intimate and confidant," John Belford. The moral aim of the author was to show, as the title page indicates, "the Distresses that May Attend Misconduct both of Parents and Children in Relation to Marriage."

Clarisses (klȧ.rēs), **Les.** See under Saint **Clare** (or **Clara**) **of Assisi.**

Clarissines (klar'i.sēnz). See under Saint **Clare** (or **Clara) of Assisi.**

Clari, the Maid of Milan. Opera by Sir Henry Rowley Bishop, produced at London on May 8, 1823. In it *Home, Sweet Home* (words by John Howard Payne) was first introduced.

Clarium (klā'ri.um). Ancient name of **Chiari.**

Clark (klärk), **Abraham.** b. at Elizabethtown (now Elizabeth), N.J., Feb. 15, 1726; d. at Rahway, N.J., Sept. 15, 1794. American patriot, one of the signers of the Declaration of Independence. He served in the Continental Congress for several terms, beginning in 1776.

Clark, Allan. b. at Missoula, Mont., June 8, 1896; d. April 17, 1950. American sculptor.

Clark, Alvan. b. at Ashfield, Mass., March 8, 1804; d. at Cambridge, Mass., Aug. 19, 1887. American optician, famous as a manufacturer of telescopes (at Cambridge, Mass.); father of Alvan Graham Clark. He was originally an engraver and portrait painter. The firm of Alvan Clark and Sons, founded in 1846, made telescopes for the University of Mississippi (lens 18½ inches, finally purchased by the University of Chicago), the University of Virginia (26 inches), the U.S. Naval Observatory at Washington (26 inches), the national observatory at Pulkovo, Russia (30 inches), the Lick Observatory in California (36 inches), and others.

Clark, Alvan Graham. b. at Fall River, Mass., July 10, 1832; d. at Cambridge, Mass., June 9, 1897. American optician and astronomer; son of Alvan Clark. He became a member of the firm of Alvan Clark and Sons in 1852, and completed the telescope for the Lick Observatory in California (lens 36 inches). He made the 30-inch refractor for the Imperial Observatory at St. Petersburg, for which he was presented with a gold medal by the emperor, the 40-inch lens for the Yerkes Observatory of the University of Chicago (at Williams Bay, Wis.), and many others. He was also known as an astronomer, and made many discoveries of double stars, among them that of the companion of Sirius, for which he was awarded the Lalande gold medal by the French Academy.

Clark, Sir **Andrew.** b. Oct. 28, 1826; d. Nov. 6, 1893. Scottish physician. He resided at London.

Clark, Austin Hobart. b. at Wellesley, Mass., Dec. 17, 1880—. American biologist and zoölogist. He became (1908) a member of the staff of the Smithsonian Institution at Washington, D.C. He was graduated (B.A., 1903) from Harvard, and served as director of the American Association for the Advancement of Science press service. He is the author of *Animals of Land and Sea* (1925), *Nature Narratives* (2 vols.; 1929, 1931), *The New Evolution* (1930), and *The Butterflies of the District of Columbia and Vicinity* (1932).

Clark, Barrett Harper. b. at Toronto, Canada, Aug. 26, 1890; d. at Briarcliff Manor, N.Y., Aug. 5, 1953. American drama editor and critic. Educated at the University of Chicago and the University of Paris, he became (1936) executive director of the Dramatists Play Service, Inc., of New York, serving also on the editorial board of Samuel French and Company, play publishers, and as a member of the Authors' League of America. He edited *America's Lost Plays* (20 vols.) for the Princeton University Press, and was the author of the biography *Eugene O'Neill, The Man and His Plays*, and the critical works *European Theories of the Drama* and *A Study of the Modern Drama.*

Clark, Bennett Champ. b. at Bowling Green, Mo., Jan. 8, 1890—. American lawyer and politician; son of Champ Clark (1850–1921). He received a B.A. (1913) from the University of Missouri and an LL.B. (1914) from George Washington University, parliamentarian (1913–17) in the U.S. House of Representatives, practiced law (1919 *et seq.*) at St. Louis, before serving (1933–35, 1938–45) as a U.S. Senator from Missouri. In 1945 he was named an associate justice of the U.S. Court of Appeals. Author of *John Quincy Adams—Old Man Eloquent* (1932).

Clark, Champ. [Original name **James Beauchamp Clark.**] b. near Lawrenceburg, Ky., March 7, 1850; d. March 2, 1921. American politician, speaker (1911–19) of the House of Representatives; father of Bennett Champ Clark. Graduated (1873) from Bethany College, he was president (c1873–74) of Marshall College at Huntington, the first normal school in West Virginia, and in 1875 was graduated from the Cincinnati Law School. Moving (1876) to Louisiana, Mo., he became city attorney, edited the *Daily News*, and was owner and editor of the *Riverside Press*. He entered national political life as a Democratic presidential elector in 1880, the year of his removal to Bowling Green, Mo., where he also was city attorney. He served (1885–89) as Pike County prosecuting attorney, was a member (1889–91) of the Missouri legislature, and from 1893 until his death (with the exception of one term in 1895–97) was a Democratic member of Congress. He became Democratic minority leader in 1907, and led the House "revolt" against "Uncle Joe" Cannon. A noted orator, he was a member of the committees of Foreign Affairs and Ways and Means. He became speaker in 1911 and at the Baltimore Democratic convention (1912) led until the 14th ballot, losing to Woodrow Wilson when William Jennings Bryan switched his support. He served as minority leader from 1919 to 1921.

Clark, Charles Badger. b. at Albia, Iowa, Jan. 1, 1883—. American poet and short-story writer, especially interested in folklore material and in cowboy songs. His works are *Sun and Saddle Leather* (1915), *Grass Grown Trails* (1917), *Sky Lines and Wood Smoke* (1935), poetry, and *Spike* (1923), collected short stories. As a balladist he is best known for his *High Chin Bob*, or *Way Up High in the Mokiones*. Clark was educated at Dakota Wesleyan University, which made him an honorary Doctor of Letters, and he is poet laureate of South Dakota.

Clark, Charles Edgar. b. at Bradford, Vt., Aug. 10, 1843; d. Oct. 2, 1922. American naval officer, promoted rear admiral in 1902. Ordered, with his class at the U.S. Naval Academy, into active service in 1863, he took part in the battle of Mobile Bay and the bombardment of Fort Morgan, and rose to the rank of captain in 1896. At the outbreak of the Spanish-American War (1898) he was appointed to the command of the battleship *Oregon*, then at San Francisco, and with remarkable skill brought her to Key West, Fla., upward of 14,000 miles, in time to take a very important part in the battle of Santiago. He retired in 1905.

Clark, Charles Heber. b. at Berlin, Md., July 11, 1847; d. at Philadelphia, Aug. 10, 1915. American journalist, novelist, critic, and soldier in the Union army during the Civil War. He was a reporter for the Philadelphia *Inquirer*, wrote dramatic and music criticism for the *Evening Bulletin*, and was editorial writer for the *North American* and owner of the *Textile Record*. His most popular book, his first, was *Out of the Hurly Burly* (1874), humorous sketches of life in a small town. Other works are *Elbow Room* (1876), *Captain Bluitt* (1901), *In Happy Hollow* (1903), *The Quakeress* (1905), novels, and *The Fortunate Island* (1882) and *By the Bend in the River* (1914), collections of short stories. He frequently used "Max Adeler" as a pseudonym.

Clark, Colin Grant. b. at London, Nov. 2, 1905—. Australian statistician and economist. Educated at Oxford (M.A.) and Cambridge (M.A. in Sc.), he served (1930–31) as assistant secretary on the staff of the British government's economic advisory council, and as lecturer in statistics (1931–38) at Cambridge. He went to Australia in 1938 as director of the bureau of industry for the state of Queensland and adviser to the Queensland treasury. He is a prolific author of statistical studies, of which *Conditions of Economic Progress* (1940) is internationally known.

Clark, Fort. Frontier military post built (September, 1813) on the site of Peoria Ill., and named for George Rogers Clark. It was occupied by troops during part of the War of 1812 and in 1818 was completely laid waste by Indians.

Clark, Francis Edward. b. at Aylmer, Quebec, Canada, Sept. 12, 1851; d. May 26, 1927. American Congregational clergyman. As pastor of the Williston Church at Portland, Me., he organized (1881) the first group of the Young People's Society of Christian Endeavor. Having purchased (1886) and become editor of the *Golden Rule*, he changed its name in 1897 to *Christian Endeavor World*. He served as president (1887–1925) of the United Society of Christian Endeavor, and also as president from its inception (1895) of the World's Christian Endeavor

Union. His works include *The Children and the Church* (1882), *Our Journey Around the World* (1894), *World-Wide Endeavor* (1895), *In the Footsteps of St. Paul* (1917), *Our Italian Fellow Citizens* (1919), and *Memories of Many Men in Many Lands* (1922).

Clark, George Lindenberg. b. at Anderson, Ind., Sept. 6, 1892—. American chemist who established and directed the first industrial x-ray research laboratory. Graduated (B.A., 1914) from DePauw, he received M.S. (1914) and Ph.D. (1918) degrees from Chicago. He held posts as associate professor of chemistry (1919–21) at Vanderbilt and assistant professor of applied chemical research (1924–27) at the Massachusetts Institute of Technology, before becoming (1927) professor of chemistry at Illinois. Author of *Applied X-rays* (1927).

Clark, George Rogers. b. near Charlottesville, Va., Nov. 19, 1752; d. at Locust Grove, Ky., Feb. 13, 1818. American soldier, noted as the conqueror of the Old Northwest during the Revolutionary War; brother of William Clark (1770–1838). After making explorations along the Ohio River (1772 *et seq.*), he served as a captain in Lord Dunmore's War (1774), and became a surveyor for the Ohio Company. He soon became a leader in Kentucky, appealing to Governor Patrick Henry of Virginia for aid in protection against the Indians and the Transylvania scheme of Judge Richard Henderson. Clark's great achievement during the Revolution was in eliminating the British threat in the region west of the Alleghenies. Commissioned a major, he was promoted to lieutenant colonel and, leading a force of 175 men in a heroic six-day march through the wilderness, captured Kaskaskia (July 4, 1778). He later seized Cahokia and Vincennes and made plans to march upon Detroit, where the British Lieutenant Governor Henry Hamilton had organized Indian forces which had previously attacked (1776) the Kentucky forts at Harrodsburg, Boonesborough, and Logan's Fort. However, Hamilton set out (October, 1778) with a sizable expedition, determined to recover the Illinois posts, and seized the poorly guarded fort at Vincennes. Clark retrieved the situation by making another epic march with 170 men whom he led 180 miles to take Vincennes (Feb. 25, 1779). By this and subsequent efforts he effectively prevented the British and their Indian allies from breaking through the Illinois and Kentucky country to link up with the British forces in the South. His seizure (1786) of goods from Spanish traders in order to provide for the Vincennes garrison ultimately led to his falling into disfavor with the federal and Virginian governments, despite the fact that Virginia owed him almost 20,000 dollars in pay and for funds he had allocated to furnish equipment and supplies for his soldiers. Beginning in 1793, he was active in advancing a scheme, proposed by him to the French government, to conquer Louisiana in the name of France. He spent his last years in Kentucky. His manuscript *Memoir*, which he wrote in 1791, is valuable as a source on the history of the Old Northwest. A memorial bridge across the Wabash River at Vincennes was opened in 1932. See *George Rogers Clark* (1928), by J. A. James.

Clark, Georgia Neese. b. at Richland, Kan., Jan. 27, 1900—. American politician. After a career (1923 *et seq.*) as an actress with touring stock companies, she became (1935) assistant cashier in her father's bank, of which she became president (1937) after his death. Active in politics after 1930, she became a Democratic national committeewoman in 1936. On the death (1939) of W. A. Julian, who had been treasurer of the U.S. since 1933, she was appointed to the post by President Truman.

Clark, Hubert Lyman. b. at Amherst, Mass., 1870—. American zoölogist. Graduated (Ph.D., 1897) from the Johns Hopkins University, he was professor of biology (1899–1905) at Olivet College, and a staff member (1905 *et seq.*) of the museum of comparative zoölogy at Harvard. He has made scientific expeditions to Bermuda, Australia, and elsewhere.

Clark, Sir James. b. at Cullen, Banffshire, Scotland, Dec. 14, 1788; d. at Bagshot Park, England, June 29, 1870. Scottish physician. He was physician in ordinary to Queen Victoria of England from 1837. He wrote *The Influence of Climate in the Prevention and Cure of Chronic Diseases* (1829), *Treatise on Pulmonary Consumption* (1835), and others.

Clark, John Bates. b. at Providence, R.I., Jan. 26, 1847; d. at New York, March 21, 1938. American economist and educator; father of John Maurice Clark. After holding professorial chairs in political economy, political science, and history, at Carleton College, Smith College, and Amherst College, between 1877 and 1895, in the latter year he became professor of political economy at Columbia University, New York, and so continued until 1923. As an exponent of conservative economic theory, which, however, he examined critically, he had an extensive influence, which he exercised also as editor (1895–1911) of *Political Science Quarterly*. Of his books, the most admired were *The Philosophy of Wealth* (1899), *The Control of Trusts* (1901; 2nd edition, 1912), *The Problem of Monopoly* (1904), and *The Essentials of Economic Theory* (1907).

Clark, John Maurice. b. at Northampton, Mass., Nov. 30, 1884—. American economist and educator; son of John Bates Clark (1847–1938). Beginning in 1908 he taught economics and sociology at Colorado College, Amherst College, and the University of Chicago, before joining the staff of Columbia University at New York, where he has been a professor of economics since 1926. He has served on the National Resources Planning Board and other government bodies, and is a member of many American and foreign learned societies. His general concept of economics is less conservative than was his father's, and he has given especial study to the influence of sociological and psychological factors on economic trends, and the feasibility of economic and social planning. His principal works are *Social Control in Business* (1926), *Strategic Factors in Business Cycles* (1934), *Preface to Social Economics* (1937), *Alternative to Serfdom* (1948), and *Guide-Posts of Change* (1949).

Clark, Jonas Gilman. b. at Hubbardston, Mass., Feb. 1, 1815; d. May 23, 1900. American merchant and philanthropist. He manufactured carriages, owned a hardware store, shipped goods to California, and was a real estate investor. He is remembered as the founder (1887) and benefactor of Clark University at Worcester, Mass., which opened (1889) under the presidency of G. Stanley Hall.

Clark, Josiah Latimer. b. at Great Marlow, Buckinghamshire, England, 1822; d. 1898. English engineer, inventor, and electrical scientist. As a young man he engaged in bridge-building, and he invented a pneumatic tube carrier system and a specialized camera, but eventually his interests came to center upon electrical problems and techniques. He was chief engineer of the Electric and International Telegraph Company (1860–70). He devised a method of insulation which greatly improved the efficiency of submarine cables, and he assisted in laying the first telegraph cable under the South Atlantic, from French West Africa to Brazil. His name is particularly known in electrical circles in connection with his invention of the technically important "Clark cell." He was an active member of several companies engaged in manufacturing electrical equipment, in laying submarine cables, and in other branches of engineering.

Clark, Lewis Gaylord. b. at Otisco, N.Y., Oct. 5, 1808; d. at Piermont, N.Y., Nov. 3, 1873. American editor and author; twin brother of Willis Gaylord Clark. Under his editorship (1834–61), the *Knickerbocker Magazine* became the leading literary journal of its day. He edited the *Knickerbocker Sketch-Book* (1845), to which Washington Irving contributed, and he wrote *Knicknacks from an Editor's Table* (1852). He published the *Literary Remains* (1844) of his brother, and a *Life* (1854) of Daniel Webster.

Clark, Mark Wayne. b. at Madison Barracks, N.Y., May 1, 1896—. American army officer. A graduate (1917) of the U.S. Military Academy, he served as a battalion commander in World War I. Promoted (1942) to major general, in command of U.S. ground forces in Europe, he went to French North Africa in October, 1942, on a secret mission to plan the invasion. He arranged for protective custody of Admiral Darlan after the European landings (Nov. 9, 1942). Promoted (November, 1942) to lieutenant general, he commanded (January, 1943–November, 1944) the Fifth Army in North Africa and Italy, and commanded the 15th army group (1944–45). Promoted (1945) to general, he headed (1945–47) U.S. occupation troops in Austria. In 1947 he became commander of the Sixth Army, in the U.S. In 1951 he was nominated U.S. ambassador to the Vatican, but the nomination was withdrawn after a storm of protests (not against Clark, but against such a U.S. diplomatic relationship with the Vatican). He assumed command (1952) of the United Nations forces in Korea. Author of *Calculated Risk* (1950).

Clark, Tom Campbell. b. at Dallas, Tex., Sept. 23, 1899—. Associate justice of the Supreme Court of the U.S. Admitted to the Texas bar in 1922, he practiced law in association with his father and brother until 1927, when he became district attorney of Dallas County, and won the reputation of never losing a case during his several years in that office. Returning to private life he built up a lucrative practice with corporate clients, but in 1937 entered the service of the federal government as a special assistant to the attorney general, being successively in charge of various bureaus, and making an especial impression by the thoroughness of his preparation of antitrust suits. In 1942 he coöperated, on behalf of the Department of Justice, with the army in the relocation of Japanese aliens and Nisei in the Pacific Coast states, and in that year also he took charge of war fraud suits, an assignment which brought him into close touch with the Senate committee investigating the war program, and with the head of that committee, Senator and future President Harry S. Truman. Thus, although Tom Clark was little known to the public at large, his qualifications were known to President Truman when the latter nominated him for attorney general of the U.S. in 1945. In his name as attorney general, under a requirement of the law, was issued an extensive list of organizations, past and present, which were charged with having disloyal or subversive purposes or tendencies, and membership in which acted as a bar to governmental employment. By nomination of President Truman and confirmation of the Senate, Clark became an associate justice of the Supreme Court in August, 1949. Although some sources indicate that his prename is "Thomas," it is actually (and by Clark's own expressed wish will continue to be) simply "Tom."

Clark, Walter Appleton. b. at Worcester, Mass., 1876; d. at New York, Dec. 27, 1906. American artist and illustrator.

Clark, Walter Van Tilburg. b. at East Orland, Me., Aug. 3, 1909—. American novelist and short-story writer. He attended the University of Nevada and the University of Vermont and was a public-school teacher at Cazenovia, N.Y. His short stories have appeared in *Accent*, *Atlantic Monthly*, *Yale Review*, and other periodicals. His novels include *The Ox-Bow Incident* (1940), *The City of Trembling Leaves* (1945), and *The Track of the Cat* (1949).

Clark, William. b. in Caroline County, Va., Aug. 1, 1770; d. Sept. 1, 1838. American soldier, explorer, and governor, famed as one of the leaders of the Lewis and Clark expedition (1804–06) into the American West; brother of George Rogers Clark. Beginning in 1789, he participated in expeditions against the Indians in the Kentucky and Illinois country; commissioned (1792) a lieutenant of infantry, he served under General Anthony Wayne and took part in the Battle of the Fallen Timbers (1794). He resigned his military commission in 1796 and returned to his family home at "Mulberry Hill," near Louisville, Ky., inheriting the estate in 1799. When his friend Captain Meriwether Lewis invited him (1803) to take part in the continental exploration projected by Jefferson, Clark readily accepted and set out (May 14, 1804) with the party which ascended the Missouri River, went down the Columbia River, and reached the Pacific Ocean. The expedition, which returned to St. Louis on Sept. 23, 1806, set up a route to the Pacific and was an important chapter in the expansion of the American nation. Clark, like Lewis, kept a diary of the expedition, and in addition served as mapmaker and artist. He resigned again from the army in 1807, and in the same year was made brigadier general of militia for Louisiana (afterwards Missouri) Territory and superintendent of Indian affairs at St. Louis, where he established his residence. In 1813 he became governor of the Missouri Territory, and during the War of 1812 led expeditions against the Indians allied with Great Britain. He was afterwards active in the conduct of Indian affairs in the territory. He was surveyor general (1824–25) for Illinois, and in 1828 laid out Paducah, Ky. See *History of the Expedition under the Commands of Captains Lewis and Clark*, by Elliott Coues (4 vols., 1893). The journals (published 1814) of the expedition are deposited at the American Philosophical Society at Philadelphia.

Clark, William Andrews. b. in Fayette County, Pa., Jan. 8, 1839; d. March 2, 1925. American mining executive and politician. Having panned a quantity of gold (c1863) in Montana, he established a store at Virginia City and set up (1866) another one at Elk City, established (1870) with S. E. Larabie and R. W. Donnell a bank at Deer Lodge, bought (1872) the Original, Colusa, Mountain Chief, and Gambetta copper-mining claims at Butte, and built the first smelter at Butte. During his political struggle (1888–1900) with Marcus Daly, he was said to have offered (1899) bribes for votes to the Senate and was pronounced "not duly and legally elected," forcing his resignation. In 1901 he was again elected, and this time served his term, as a senator from Montana.

Clark, William Bullock. b. at Brattleboro, Vt., Dec. 15, 1860; d. at North Haven, Me., July 27, 1917. American geologist, professor and director of the geological laboratory at the Johns Hopkins University from 1894. He was graduated from Amherst College in 1884, studied abroad, and became an instructor (1887) and later associate professor (1892) at Johns Hopkins. State geologist (1896 *et seq.*) of Maryland and on the staff of the U.S. Geological Survey, he was also appointed (1900), by the governor of Maryland commissioner for that state in the rerunning of Mason and Dixon's line.

Clark, William George. b. in March, 1821; d. at York, Nov. 6, 1878. English scholar, editor, lecturer, poet, and travel writer. He was educated at the grammar school at Sedbergh, at Shrewsbury, and (1840–44) at Trinity College, Cambridge, of which he later became a fellow. He wrote poetry, essays, travel works, and delivered lectures (which were published) on *The Middle Ages* and the *Revival of Learning* (1872), but he is best known for his work in connection with the *Cambridge Shakespeare* (1863–66), and the *Globe Shakespeare* (1864). The Clark lectureship in English literature, at Trinity, named after him, was founded by funds he left the college.

Clark, William Tierney. b. at Bristol, England, Aug. 23, 1783; d. Sept. 22, 1852. English civil engineer. He was the builder of the Hammersmith suspension bridge (taken down in 1885), and of the suspension bridge over the Danube, uniting Pest and Buda (built in the period 1839–49).

Clark, Willis Gaylord. b. at Otisco, N.Y., Oct. 5, 1808; d. June 12, 1841, of consumption. American poet, journalist, lecturer, and champion of international copyright; twin brother of Lewis Gaylord Clark, who edited his *Literary Remains* (1844). Examples of his prose are to be found in the "Ollapodianna" department of the *Knickerbocker Magazine*, edited by his brother, and in the *Souvenir*, the *Token*, the *Keepsake*, and other American periodicals. *The Spirit of Life* (1833) and *The Past and Present* (1834), both read before college societies, are considered his best poems. Poe declared that there was "a deep abiding sense of religion" in every piece that Clark wrote, and called him "almost the first poet to render the poetry of religion attractive." Clark made his last appearance on a college platform on July 4, 1840, when he spoke before the Washington Society of Lafayette College on "The Characters of Lafayette and Washington."

Clark City. Former name of **Livingston,** Mont.

Clarke (klärk), **Adam.** b. at Moybeg, County Londonderry, Ireland, c1762; d. at London, Aug. 26, 1832. Irish Wesleyan clergyman and Biblical scholar. He wrote *Commentary on the Holy Bible* (1810–26), and other works. From 1808 to 1818 he was occupied in editing Rymer's *Foedera.*

Clarke, Sir **Alured.** b. c1745; d. at Llangollen, Wales, Sept. 16, 1832. English soldier, appointed field marshal on the accession of William IV of England. He served as a lieutenant colonel under Howe in New York in 1776, and succeeded John Burgoyne as master-general of the Hessian troops. Appointed lieutenant governor of Jamaica, he served there in the period 1782–90, and was stationed at Quebec from 1791 to 1793. He went to India in 1795, took part in the capture of Cape Colony in September of the same year, and succeeded Sir Robert Abercromby as commander in chief in India on May 17, 1798.

Clarke, Sir **Andrew.** b. at Southsea, England, July 27, 1824; d. March 29, 1902. English colonial official and construction engineer. An officer (1844 *et seq.*) in the Royal Engineers, he transferred (1848) to New Zealand, where he was sent on a mission to reconcile the Maori leaders. In 1854 he drafted a bill for a new constitution of the colony at Victoria. After serving (1856–57) as surveyor-general and commissioner of lands, he returned to England where he was director (1864–73) of navy engineering works. As governor (1873–75) of the Straits Settlements, he quelled piracy. He subsequently was director (1875–80) of public works in India and agent-general (1891–94, 1897–1902) for Victoria.

Clarke, Austin. b. 1896—. Irish novelist and poet. He was educated at Dublin University College, and won the 1932 prize for national poetry at the Tailtean Games. His works are *The Bright Temptation* (1932), *The Singing-Men at Cashel* (1936), novels; *The Vengeance of Fionn* (1917), *The Fires of Baal* (1920), *The Sword of the West* (1921), *The Cattledrive in Connaught* (1925), *Pilgrimage* (1929), *Night and Morning* (1938), poetry; and *The Flame* (1930) and *Sister Eucharia* (1939), poetic plays.

Clarke, Sir **Caspar Purdon.** b. at London, 1846; d. there, March 29, 1911. British archaeologist, director of the Metropolitan Museum of Art at New York from 1905 to 1910. He was connected with the South Kensington Museum, London, from 1862, becoming in 1883 keeper of the Indian collections, in 1892 keeper of the art collections, in 1893 assistant director, and in 1896 director. In 1878 he was made a chevalier of the Legion of Honor, in 1883 a companion of the Indian Empire, and a commander of the Victorian Order in 1905. He was knighted in 1902.

Clarke, Charles Cowden. b. at Enfield, near London, Dec. 15, 1787; d. at Genoa, Italy, March 13, 1877. English Shakespearian scholar, editor, lecturer, teacher, and friend of many great literary figures of the 19th century; husband of Mary Victoria Novello, whom he married on July 5, 1828. He began his remarkable lecturing career in 1834, with a lecture on Chaucer, at the Mechanics' Institute at Royston, and he ended it in 1856, with a lecture on Molière, at the Mechanics' Institute at Northampton. During those years, he lectured before thousands of people at London and throughout the provinces, on *Shakespeare, British Poets, Poets from Charles II to Queen Anne, Poetry by Prose Writers, Four Great European Novelists* (Boccaccio, Cervantes, Lesage, Richardson), *Schools of Painting in Italy, Ancient Ballads,* and *Sonnet Writers.* Many of these were later published. Other works were *Carmina Minima* (1859), poetry, and a series of essays on *The English Comic Poets* (1871, originally published in the *Gentleman's Magazine*). With his wife he wrote *The Shakespeare Key: Unlocking the Treasures of his Style, Elucidating the Peculiarities of his Construction, and Displaying the Beauties of his Expression* (1879), and *Recollections of Writers* (1878), the latter a work they were well qualified for, knowing, as they did, most of the leading authors and artists of their day. Clarke taught Keats his letters and introduced him to Vergil, Homer, and Spenser, and he was a friend of Leigh Hunt, Charles and Mary Lamb, Hazlitt, Dickens, Douglas Jerrold, Macready, and Mendelssohn.

Clarke, Donald Henderson. b. at South Hadley, Mass., Aug. 24, 1887—. American novelist. He attended Harvard and served on the staffs of the *World,* the *Times,* and the *American* at New York. Among his novels are *Louis Beretti* (1929), *Millie* (1930), *Impatient Virgin* (1931), *The Chastity of Gloria Boyd* (1932), *Housekeeper's Daughter* (1938), *A Lady Named Lou* (1941), and *Joe and Jennie* (1949).

Clarke, Edward Daniel. b. at Willingdon, Sussex, England, June 5, 1769; d. at London, March 9, 1822. English traveler and mineralogist, appointed professor of mineralogy at Cambridge in 1808, and librarian in 1817. His works include *Travels in Various Countries of Europe, Asia, and Africa* (1810–23), and numerous scientific papers. He made important collections of minerals (purchased by Cambridge University), manuscripts, and coins. He brought to England the so-called Ceres, a colossal statue (a cistophorus), found at Eleusis in 1676, and later located in the Fitzwilliam Museum.

Clarke, Frank Wigglesworth. b. at Boston, March 19, 1847; d. May 23, 1931. American chemist. Graduated (1867) from the Lawrence Scientific School of Harvard University, he was a professor (1874–83) at the University of Cincinnati before serving as chief chemist with the U.S. Geological Survey. He was the author of *Report on the Teaching of Chemistry and Physics in the United States* (1881), *Recalculation of Atomic Weights* (3rd ed., 1910), and *Treatise on the Dicta of Geochemistry,* as well as of bulletins of the Geological Survey.

Clarke, Helen Archibald. b. at Philadelphia, Nov. 13, 1860; d. Feb. 8, 1926. American editor and critic. She was the cofounder and editor (1888 *et seq.*) with Charlotte Endymion Porter of *Poet Lore,* "Devoted to Shakespeare, Browning, and the Comparative Study of Literature." With Miss Porter she also edited a two-volume edition of Browning's poems (1896), *The Ring and the Book* (1897), Browning's complete poetical works in 12 volumes (1898), a six-volume edition of Elizabeth Barrett Browning's works (1900), and a 12-volume Shakespeare (1912). She was the author of *Browning's Italy: a Study of Italian Life and Art in Browning* (1907), *Browning's England: A Study of English Influences in Browning* (1908), *A Child's Guide to Mythology* (1908), *Longfellow's Country* (1909), *Hawthorne's Country* (1910), *A Guide to Mythology for Young Readers* (1910), *Ancient Myths in Modern Poets* (1910), *The Poet's New England* (1911), *Browning and his Century* (1912), and *Balaustion's Euripides* (1915).

Clarke, Henri Jacques Guillaume. [Titles: Comte **d'Hunebourg,** Duc **de Feltre.**] b. at Landrecies, Nord, France, Oct. 17, 1765; d. at Neuviller, France, Oct. 28, 1818. French soldier, a marshal of France. He served as minister of war from 1815 to 1817.

Clarke, Henry Butler. b. in Staffordshire, England, Nov. 9, 1863; d. by suicide at St.-Jean-de-Luz, France, Sept. 10, 1904. English specialist in Spanish literature and civilization, and scholar of Arabic. Educated by tutors in Yorkshire, at St.-Jean-de-Luz, and at Wadham College, Oxford (B.A., 1888), he was a lecturer in Spanish (1890–92) at Oxford, and a fellow (1894 *et seq.*) of St. John's College. Author of *A Spanish Grammar* (1892), *History of Spanish Literature* (1893), *The Cid Campeador* (1897), and *Modern Spain: 1815–1898* (1906).

Clarke, Hyde. b. at London, Dec. 14, 1815; d. there, March 1, 1895. English philologist and engineer. His works include *A New and Comprehensive Dictionary of the English Language* (1853) and numerous philological and ethnological treatises.

Clarke, James Freeman. b. at Hanover, N.H., April 4, 1810; d. at Jamaica Plains, Mass., June 8, 1888. American Unitarian clergyman, religious author, editor, and reformer. He was educated at the famous Boston Latin School, at Harvard (graduating in 1829, with Oliver Wendell Holmes as a classmate), and at Harvard Divinity School (1833). He edited the *Western Messenger,* to the pages of which Emerson and Channing contributed. His works are *The Christian Doctrine of Forgiveness of Sin* (1852), *The Christian Doctrine of Prayer* (1854), *Ten Great Religions* (1871), *Common Sense in Religion* (1874), *Self-Culture* (1882), and many others of a similar nature. Perhaps more important than his books is the fact that he was an abolitionist and an advocate of woman suffrage.

Clarke, John. b. in England, Oct. 8, 1609; d. at Newport, R.I., April 20, 1676. English physician, one of the founders of Rhode Island. He was driven from Massachusetts in 1638, and was one of the purchasers of Aquidneck (Rhode Island) from the Indians. He served as pastor of the Baptist church founded by him in 1644 at Newport, R.I. He went to England in 1651 with Roger Williams, and there promoted a liberal charter for Rhode Island.

Clarke, John Hessin. b. at Lisbon, Ohio, Sept. 18, 1857; d. at San Diego, Calif., March 22, 1945. American jurist who served (1916–22) as associate justice of the U.S. Supreme Court. Graduated (B.A., 1877; M.A., 1880) from Western Reserve University, he practiced law in Ohio at Lisbon (1878–80), Youngstown (1880–97), and Cleveland (1897–1914). In 1916 he was appointed U.S. district judge for northern Ohio. He resigned from the U.S. Supreme Court in 1922 to serve (1922–28) as president of the League of Nations Non-Partisan Association of the U.S.

Clarke, John Mason. b. at Canandaigua, N.Y., April 15, 1857; d. May 29, 1925. American naturalist, director of the New York State Museum. He was graduated from Amherst College in 1877, studied at Göttingen, was professor of geology at the Rensselaer Polytechnic Institute at Troy, N.Y., from 1894, and became assistant state geologist in 1894, state paleontologist in 1898, and state geologist and paleontologist in 1904. He published numerous scientific books and monographs.

Clarke, John Sleeper. b. at Baltimore, Sept. 3, 1833; d. at Surbiton-on-Thames, England, Sept. 24, 1899. American comedian. He made his first appearance at Boston in 1851. He married Asia, daughter of Junius Booth, in 1859. In 1863, with Edwin Booth, he bought the Walnut Street Theater at Philadelphia. He undertook the next year the management of the Winter Garden Theater at New York with William Stuart and Edwin Booth; this he gave up in 1867. In 1866 they obtained the lease of the Boston Theater. In October of the following year he appeared at London, where, with brief interruptions, he remained. He became proprietor of the Charing Cross Theatre in 1872, afterward managing the Haymarket. His characterizations of Doctor Pangloss, Ollapod, Major Wellington de Boots, and Salem Scudder were particularly successful.

Clarke, Marcus Andrew Hislop. b. at London, April 24, 1846; d. at Melbourne, Australia, Aug. 2, 1881. Australian novelist and miscellaneous writer. He went (1863) to Australia, where he became a prolific free-lance writer of news stories, plays, pantomimes, light verse, and full-length novels. He is remembered for his novel *For the Term of His Natural Life*, a classic reconstruction of convict days in Tasmania, serialized in the period 1870–72, abbreviated, and slightly rewritten for book publication in 1874; the serial version was published as a book in 1929.

Clarke, Mary Anne. b. at London, 1776; d. at Boulogne, France, June 21, 1852. English woman of obscure origin; mistress of Frederick Augustus, Duke of York. She became notorious from the public scandals which grew out of her connection with the duke. She wrote *The Rival Princes* (dealing with the dukes of York and Kent). She was condemned to nine months' imprisonment for libel in 1813. After 1815 she lived at Paris.

Clarke, Mary Victoria Cowden-. [Maiden name, **Novello.**] b. at London, June 22, 1809; d. at Genoa, Italy, Jan. 12, 1898. English Shakespearian scholar and author; wife of Charles Cowden Clarke. She published *The Complete Concordance to Shakespeare* (1846), which was compiled during the assiduous labor of 16 years (it does not contain the words of the sonnets and poems), *The Girlhood of Shakespeare's Heroines* (1850), *The Iron Cousin*, a novel (1854), *Memorial Sonnets* (1888), and other works. She also collaborated with her husband on several works.

Clarke, McDonald. [Called **"the Mad Poet."**] b. at Bath, Me., June 18, 1798; d. at New York, March 5, 1842. American poet. A number of collections of his poems have been published, including *A Review of the Eve of Eternity, and other Poems* (1820), *The Elixir of Moonshine, by the Mad Poet* (1822), *The Gossip* (1825), *Poetic Sketches* (1826), *The Belles of Broadway* (1833), and *Poems* (1836).

Clarke, Rebecca Sophia. [Pseudonym, **Sophie May.**] b. at Norridgewock, Me., Feb. 22, 1833; d. there, Aug. 16, 1906. American novelist and writer of children's books. She was the author of six-volume sets of *Little Prudy Stories, Dotty Dimple Stories, Little Prudy's Flyaway Series* (1870–73), *Quinnebasset Series* (1871–91), *Flaxie Frizzle Stories* (1876–84), and *Little Prudy's Children Series* (1894–1901). For adults she wrote *Drone's Honey* (1887) and *Pauline Wyman* (1897).

Clarke, Richard W. Original name of **Deadwood Dick.**

Clarke, Samuel. b. at Norwich, England, Oct. 11, 1675; d. at London, May 17, 1729. English divine and metaphysical writer; son of an alderman of Norwich. He was a graduate of Cambridge (Caius College), and was successively rector of Drayton, near Norwich, of St. Bennet's at London (1706), and of St. James's at Westminster, London (1709). He was also one of the chaplains of Queen Anne. His metaphysical argument for the existence of God is especially famous, and he also holds a high place in the history of the science of ethics. He upheld the views of Newton against those of Leibnitz, and based his ethic on the principle of the "fitness of things." His most celebrated work is his series of Boyle Lectures (1704–05), published as *A Discourse concerning the Being and Attributes of God, the Obligations of Natural Religion, and the Truth and Certainty of the Christian Revelation, in answer to Mr. Hobbes, Spinoza, . . . and Other Deniers of Natural and Revealed Religion.*

Clarke, Thomas Shields. b. at Pittsburgh, Pa., April 25, 1860; d. at New York, Nov. 15, 1920. American sculptor and painter who was made an associate of the National Academy (1902), and was a member of the National Arts Club. He studied at Princeton, the École des Beaux-Arts, Paris, and at Rome and Florence. Some of his better-known works are the paintings *A Fool's Fool* (Pennsylvania Academy of the Fine Arts) and *Night Market in Morocco*. Among his sculptures are *Four Seasons* for the Supreme Court building at New York, *Alma Mater* for Princeton University, and a bronze group for the Golden Gate Park, San Francisco.

Clarke, Walter. b. at Newport, R.I., c1638; d. May 23, 1714. American colonial administrator. He was deputy (1667, 1670, 1672, and 1673), assistant (1673–75, 1699), and deputy-governor (1679–86, 1700–14), as well as governor (1676–77, 1686, and 1696–98) of Rhode Island. When Sir Edmund Andros suspended the charter in 1686, Clarke refused to surrender the document, and was one of two to sign (April 23, 1689) the declaration reëstablishing the charter.

Clarke, William Branwhite. b. at East Bergholt, Suffolk, England, June 2, 1798; d. near Sydney, New South Wales, Australia, June 17, 1878. English geologist. A Church of England clergyman with a curacy in Suffolk, he was also an enthusiastic and well-grounded geologist, and made many trips to the Continent in connection with his studies in this field. In 1839 he went to Australia in search of better health, accepted a church living there, and there remained for life. He seems to have been the first to discover gold, tin, and diamonds in Australia, and his studies of the coal fields in that island continent greatly forwarded their exploitation. He was a member of learned societies in Australia, and in Great Britain his achievements were recognized by his election as a Fellow of the Royal Society in 1876, and by the award to him of the Murchison Medal of the Geological Society of London in 1877. He was the author of *Researches in the Southern Goldfields of New South Wales* (1860).

Clarke-Whitfield (klärk'hwit'fēld), **John.** [Original name, **John Clarke.**] b. at Gloucester, England, Dec. 13, 1770; d. near Hereford, England, Feb. 22, 1836. English organist. In 1798 he became choirmaster of Saint Patrick's Cathedral at Dublin. Soon after he served as organist of Trinity and Saint John's Colleges, Cambridge. From 1820 to 1833 he was organist of Hereford cathedral. From 1821 he was professor of music at the University of Cambridge. He edited Handel's oratorios.

Clark Fork. [Also, **Clarke's** (or **Clarkes**) **Fork** (or **River**).] River in Montana, Idaho, and Washington, formed by the Bitterroot and Flathead rivers near Butte, Mont., and flowing into the Columbia River. It was named for Captain William Clark. Total length, including headstream, ab. 700 mi.

Clarksburg (klärks'bėrg). City in N West Virginia, county seat of Harrison County, on the W branch of the Monongahela River, ab. 58 mi. SE of Wheeling: trading center for a coal, petroleum, natural gas, and livestock area; manufactures include glass, pottery, beer, tinplate, cinder blocks, and carbon electrodes. It was the birthplace of Thomas Jonathan ("Stonewall") Jackson. 32,014 (1950).

Clarksdale (klärks'dāl). City in NW Mississippi, county seat of Coahoma County, on the Sunflower River: trading and processing point for cotton. 16,539 (1950).

Clark's Field. Novel by Robert Herrick, published in 1914. Adelle Clark inherits Clark's Field, and she and her dissipated husband recklessly squander the income derived from the valuable tract of land. Tom Clark, a workman on their estate, has a claim to the income; after his attempt to rescue Adelle's child from a fire, she concedes his joint right to the property and solicits his advice in her philanthropic activities.

Clarkson (klärk'sǫn), **Matthew.** b. Oct. 17, 1758; d. April 25, 1825. American Revolutionary soldier. He was a volunteer in the battle of Long Island. As aide-de-camp to Benedict Arnold, he took part in the battles of Fort Edward and Saratoga. He was a member (1789–90) of the New York assembly, U.S. marshal (1791–92), and state senator (1794, 1795).

Clarkson, Ralph. [Full name, **Ralph Elmer Clarkson.**] b. at Amesbury, Mass., Aug. 3, 1861; d. at Orlando, Fla., April 5, 1942. American painter and teacher who served as president of the Chicago Municipal Art Commission. He was educated at the Boston Museum of Fine Arts School, and at the Julian Academy, Paris. His work was exhibited in the U.S., and he was made an Associate of the National Academy of Design in 1910. He taught at the Art Institute of Chicago. A list of his works includes *A Daughter of Armenia, Studio Corner, Twilight Harmony,* and many portraits.

Clarkson, Thomas. b. at Wisbeach, Cambridgeshire, England, March 28, 1760; d. at Playford Hall, near Ipswich, England, Sept. 26, 1846. English abolitionist, occupied as a pamphleteer and agitator in the period 1786–94. He wrote *History of the Abolition of the Slave Trade* (1808), and other works.

Clarks Summit. Borough in NE Pennsylvania, in Lackawanna County, near Scranton: residential community. It was settled at the end of the 18th century. 2,940 (1950).

Clarkston (klärks'tǫn). [Former names: **Jawbone Flats, Vineland, Concord.**] City in SE Washington, the county seat of Asotin County, on the Snake River: processing and shipping center for meat, flour, feed, and boxes. 5,617 (1950).

Clarksville (klärks'vil). City in W Arkansas, county seat of Johnson County: center of a fruit-growing, coal-mining, and natural gas district. It is the seat of the College of the Ozarks. 4,343 (1950).

Clarksville. Town in S Indiana, in Clark County, on the Ohio River adjoining Jeffersonville and opposite Louisville, Ky. It was founded (c1784) by George Rogers Clark. In the decade between the last two U.S. censuses its population more than doubled. 2,386 (1940), 5,905 (1950).

Clarksville. City in NW Tennessee, in Montgomery County, on the N bank of the Cumberland River, near the mouth of the Red River, in a tobacco area: marketing center for fire-cured tobacco; seat of Austin Peay Normal School. It was settled in 1784 and named for George Rogers Clark. 16,246 (1950).

Clarksville. City in E Texas, county seat of Red River County, NE of Dallas: center for a cotton, lumber, livestock, and petroleum area. 4,353 (1950).

Classen (kläs'ęn), **Alexander.** b. at Aachen, Germany, 1843; d. there, 1934. German chemist. He did extensive and important work in analytical chemistry and particularly electrochemistry. His numerous and widely translated textbooks include *Grundriss der Analytischen Chemie* (1873 *et seq.*) and *Quantitative Analyse durch Elektrolyse* (1897 *et seq.*). He was a professor at Aachen from 1883 to 1921.

Classis (klas'is). In ancient geography, the harbor of Ravenna. Built up by Augustus, it served in Roman times as a port and arsenal.

Clau (klou), **Christopher.** See **Clavius, Christopher.**

Claude (klōd), **Georges.** b. 1870—. French industrial and physical chemist. His experiments on rare-gas discharge tubes (1910) led to the neon sign industry. His observations (with A. Hess, 1897 *et seq.*) of the high solubility of acetylene in acetone led to the present method of storing and supplying acetylene. In addition, he developed an important modification of the Haber process, known as the Claude process. He became director of a liquid-air company.

Claude, Jean. b. at La Sauvetat, near Agen, France, 1619; d. at The Hague, Netherlands, Jan. 13, 1687. French Protestant clergyman and controversialist. He was pastor of La Treyne, then at St.-Affrique, and later at Nîmes, where he was also professor of theology and in 1661 was prohibited from exercising his ecclesiastical functions. In 1662 he was appointed pastor and professor of theology at Montauban, but was suspended in 1666. He entered into controversies with Nicole, Arnauld, Bossuet, and others, concerning the maintenance of the Edict of Nantes. On the revocation of the Edict of Nantes he retired to the Netherlands. His chief work is *Défense de la réformation* (1673).

Claude (or **Claudin**) (klō.dañ), **Le Jeune.** See **Jeune Claude** (or **Claudin**), **Le.**

Claude d'Abbeville (dȧb.vēl). b. at Abbeville, France; d. at Rouen, France, 1616. French Capuchin. From 1612 to 1614 he was a missionary in the French colony of Maranhão, in Brazil. His *Histoire de la mission des pères Capucins en l'Isle de Maragnan* (Paris, 1614) is of great historical and ethnological value. It is now very rare. There is a more recent Portuguese translation (Maranhão, 1874).

Claude Frollo (fro.lō). See **Frollo, Claude.**

Claudel (klō.del), **Paul Louis Charles.** b. at Villeneuve-sur-Fère, France, Aug. 6, 1868—. French diplomat, poet, and dramatist, author of poems and plays which unite the French symbolist techniques and a material taken from traditional Catholicism. Son of a bourgeois functionary, descended from peasants, educated at the Lycée Louis-le-Grand at Paris, he was "reconverted" to Catholicism in 1886. In 1898 he entered the diplomatic service, served as consul successively in the U.S. (at Boston), China, Germany, and Italy, then as minister to Brazil, later as ambassador to Tokyo, then Washington, and still later Brussels. His poetry, largely on religious themes and written in versets which resemble the lines of the Psalms, is collected in *Connaissance de l'Est* (1900), *Cinq grandes odes* (1910), *Cette heure qui est entre le printemps et l'été* (1913 and reprinted, 1931, as *La Cantate à trois voix*), *Corona Benignitatis Anni Dei* (1914), and *La Messe là-bas* (1919). His works for the theater, which have brought his name before a wider audience than has his poetry, include *Tête d'or* (1889), *La Ville* (1890), *Le Repos du septième jour* (1901), *L'Annonce faite à Marie* (1910 in final form but written earlier as *La Jeune Fille Violaine*), and *Partage de Midi* (1906). In addition he has written numerous incidental essays and translated the *Orestaeia* of Aeschylus.

Claude Lorrain (klōd lo.rañ). [Original name, **Claude Gelée** or **Gellée.**] b. at Chamagne, in Lorraine, France, 1600; d. at Rome, Nov. 21, 1682. French painter, notably of landscapes. Taken in 1613 to Rome by a relative, he went on to Naples, and spent two years there. From 1619 to 1625 he lived at Rome, working as an apprentice and valet to Agostino Tassi, who was employed by the Cardinal di Montalto to decorate his palace. After this he returned to Lorraine by way of Venice and the Tyrol. At Nancy he found employment in decorating the Chapelle des Carmes for Duke Charles IV (sometimes known as Charles III), with figures and architectural ornaments, until the middle of the year 1627, when he returned to Rome to remain for the rest of his life. By 1634 Claude had become a celebrity at Rome, under papal patronage, and had painted many pictures. *Liber Veritatis,* a collection of 200 outline drawings of his paintings (later engraved and published) was begun c1634 and finished on March 25, 1675. Many of the drawings in this work are dated, and have affixed to them the name of the purchaser of the corresponding painting. The work was acquired by the collection of the Duke of Devonshire. Claude's landscapes exemplify the type of southern, classical painting. Peopled by mythological or Arcadian figures, woods and ruins are set side by side, united by an effect of diffused light. A contemporary of Poussin, Claude Lorrain differs from him in the feeling of serenity and quiet that he has imparted to his canvases. Claude's influence on the 18th century was considerable, extending to such figures as Goethe.

Claudet (klō.de), **Antoine François Jean.** b. at Lyons, France, Aug. 12, 1797; d. at London, Dec. 27, 1867. French photographer, resident at London after 1829. He was noted for his improvements and inventions in photographic apparatus and processes.

Claudia (klô'di.ạ). A common Roman female name.

Claudia Celeia (se.lē'yạ). Latin name of **Celje.**

Claudia gens. In ancient Rome, a plebeian and patrician clan or house. The patrician Claudii were of Sabine origin, and came to Rome c504 B.C. Their surnames were Caecus,

Caudex, Centho, Crassus, Pulcher, Regillensis, and Sabinus. The surnames of the plebeian Claudii were Asellus, Canina, Centumalus, Cicero, Flamen, and Marcellus.

Claudian (klô′di.an). [Full Latin name, **Claudius Claudianus.**] b. probably at Alexandria, Egypt; d. c408 A.D. Latin poet, known as the last great poet of the pagan classical world. He was the panegyrist of Stilicho, Theodosius, Honorius, and others. He also wrote epithalamia, idylls, epigrams, *De raptu Proserpinae* (an unfinished work on the rape of Proserpina), and others.

Claudia Quinta (klô′di.a kwin′ta). In Roman legend, a woman, probably the sister of Appius Claudius Pulcher. About 204 or 206 B.C., when the ship conveying the image of Cybele stuck fast in a shallow at the mouth of the Tiber and the soothsayers announced that only a chaste woman could move it, she cleared herself from an accusation of incontinency by stepping forward from among the matrons who went forth to receive the image, and towing the vessel to Rome. This story is one of numerous ancient legends in which the woman accused proves her chastity by coming victoriously through some such test, also often called the "act of truth."

Claudio (klô′di.ō). Young Florentine in love with Hero, in Shakespeare's *Much Ado about Nothing*. He falls too easily into belief in Hero's dishonor, but becomes convinced of her virtue and is finally married to her.

Claudio. Lover of Juliet in Shakespeare's *Measure for Measure.*

Claudius (klô′di.us). Servant of Brutus in Shakespeare's *Julius Caesar.*

Claudius. King of Denmark and uncle of Hamlet in Shakespeare's tragedy *Hamlet.*

Claudius (klō.dyüs). Pseudonym of **Petit, Eugène.**

Claudius I (klô′di.us). [Full name, **Tiberius Claudius Drusus Nero;** surnamed **Germanicus.**] b. at Lugdunum, in Gaul, Aug. 1, 10 B.C.; d. 54 A.D. Emperor of Rome in the period 41–54. He was the grandson of Tiberius Claudius Nero and Livia Drusilla, who afterward became the third wife of Augustus, and son of Drusus Germanicus (sometimes called Drusus Senior) and Antonia, the daughter of Mark Antony. He was excluded from public affairs by Caligula, his predecessor, although the empty honor of a consulship was bestowed on him in 37 by his nephew Caligula, on whose murder in 41 he was proclaimed emperor by the praetorian guards. Because Claudius was naturally of a mild and amiable disposition, his accession was signalized by acts of clemency and justice, which, however, under the influence of his third wife, Valeria Messalina, and his favorites, the freedmen Narcissus, Pallas, and others, were subsequently obscured by cruelty and bloodshed. He visited Britain in 43. In 49, after the execution of Messalina, who, during Claudius's absence at Ostia, had contracted a public marriage with Gaius Silius, he married his niece Agrippina the younger. She persuaded him to set aside his own son Britannicus, and to adopt her son by a former marriage, Lucius Domitius, as his successor. When he repented of this step soon after, he is thought to have been poisoned by Agrippina, and Lucius Domitius ascended the throne under the name of Nero. The Claudian aqueduct at Rome was built during his reign and named for him. Claudius was noted for his writing, but none of his works are extant.

Claudius II. [Full name, **Marcus Aurelius Claudius;** surnamed **Gothicus.**] b. in Dardania or Illyria, 214; d. at Sirmium, in Pannonia, 270 A.D. Emperor of Rome in the period 268–270. Previously he had served under Valerius and then under Gallienus, whom he succeeded as emperor. He defeated the Alamanni in northern Italy in 268, and decisively defeated the Goths near Naïssus (now in Niš), in Moesia (now part of Yugoslavia), in 269.

Claudius, Appius. [Surnamed **Crassus.**] fl. 471–450 B.C. Roman consul (471, 451 B.C.). In 451 he was a decemvir (one of ten magistrates) appointed to draw up a new code of laws. These decemvirs held virtually complete rulings powers during their time in office. In 450 the group was reconstituted, and Appius Claudius became its leading member, popular with patricians and plebeians alike, although his suggested legislation favoring plebeians roused considerable opposition. He remained in office until the group resigned in 449. Legend connects Claudius with Virginia, a young woman supposedly killed by her father. Virginius, to save her from being possessed by Appius Claudius, and advances this story as the cause for the public indignation that brought about the fall of the decemvirs. In fact, however, there may not be any connection at all.

Claudius, Appius. [Surnamed **Caecus,** meaning "the Blind."] d. after 280 B.C. Roman statesman. He was censor in the period 312–c308, and consul in 307 and 296. He commenced the Appian Way and completed the Appian aqueduct, the first at Rome. He abolished the limitation of the full right of citizenship to landed proprietors.

Claudius, Appius. [Surnamed **Pulcher.**] d. in Euboea, c48 B.C. Roman politician; brother of Clodius (Publius Clodius Pulcher). Before serving as governor in Sardinia he had been praetor in 57 B.C. He was consul in 54, proconsul in Cilicia from 53 to 51, and censor in 50. In 49 he was a follower of Pompey.

Claudius, Appius. [Surnamed **Sabinus Inregillensis** or **Regillensis.**] [Original name, **Attus** or **Attius Clausus.**] Roman consul. Coming from Regillum in the Sabine country to Rome c504 B.C., with others of the Claudian gens, of whom some were patricians and some plebeians, he seems to have gathered a number of gentes into a tribe which evidently was a force to be reckoned with, for he was admitted to the ranks of the patricians, at that time taking the name Appius Claudius, and was elected consul in 495 B.C. In that office he applied the laws concerning debts with a severity which caused the plebeians to take refuge on the sacred mount.

Claudius (klou′dē.us), **Hermann.** b. at Langenfelde, Germany, Oct. 24, 1878—. German lyric poet and novelist; great-grandson of Matthias Claudius (1740–1814), of whose verse he offered a new selection in *Das Buch Ehrfurcht* (1935). The two have much in common: interest in common people, love of simplicity, and faith in God. Hermann, who until 1934 was a schoolteacher, has put the cause of the laborer so well that he is usually classed with the workingman poets. Much of his verse is in Low German. His best-known collection is *Heimkehr* (1925).

Claudius, Matthias. b. at Reinfeld, in Holstein, Aug. 15, 1740; d. at Hamburg, Germany, Jan. 21, 1815. German poet. He studied at Jena, and settled afterward at Wandsbeck, near Altona, where, under the name of Asmus, he published a weekly periodical, *Der Wandsbecker Bote.* He was the author of numerous lyrics, some of which have become folk songs. A collection of his works with the title *Asmus omnia sua secum portans, oder Sämmtliche Werke des Wandsbecker Boten* appeared at Hamburg in the period 1775–1812.

Claudius (klô′di.us), **Publius.** [Surnamed **Pulcher.**] fl. in the 3rd century B.C. Roman consul; son of the consul Appius Claudius (surnamed Caecus). While consul in 249 B.C., he commanded the Roman fleet in the course of the First Punic War, and was disastrously defeated at Drepanum. It was believed that this disaster resulted from an impious act by Claudius. Just before the Roman and Carthaginian fleets clashed, the sacred chickens carried on the Roman ships are said to have refused to eat, which was an alarming omen. Claudius said that if they would not eat, "let them drink," and ordered them thrown overboard. For this and certain other acts he was accused of treason and heavily fined. It is thought that he died in 246 B.C. or earlier, probably a suicide.

Claudius of Turin (tū′rin, tū.rin′). d. 839. Bishop of Turin. He was a Spaniard by birth, was a pupil of Felix of Urgel, and was appointed bishop of Turin by Louis I of France (known as Louis le Débonnaire) in 820. He denied that the monastic vow possessed any peculiar merit, that Rome was the special seat of penitence and absolution, and that any special power of loosing and binding had been given to Peter, and rejected the worship of images and relics. He wrote *Apologeticum atque Rescriptum adversus Theutmirum Abbatem,* no copy of which is now known to exist.

Claudius-Petit (klō.dyüs.pe.tē), **Eugène.** See **Petit, Eugène.**

Claudius Ptolemaeus (klô′di.us tol.e.mē′us). Full Latin name of **Ptolemy.**

Claudius Tiberius Germanicus (tī.bir′i.us jėr.man′i-kus). Original name of **Britannicus.**

Claus (klous), **Émile.** b. at Vive-St.-Éloi (Sint-Elоois-Vijve), Belgium, Sept. 27, 1849; d. 1924. Flemish painter of landscapes, one of the leaders of the impressionist movement in Belgium. He was a pupil of Nicaise de Keyser, but his work often resembles that of Claude Monet and Camille Pisarro. His important works date from 1879 and after, and have been exhibited at most of the European capitals. A list of his paintings includes *Siesta, End of the Day, The Old Gardener*, and *Birds in the Wheat*, as well as a number of portraits.

Clausel or **Clauzel** (klō.zel), Count **Bertrand.** b. at Mirepoix, Ariège, France, Dec. 12, 1772; d. at Secourieu, near Toulouse, France, April 21, 1842. French soldier, a marshal of France. He served with distinction in the Napoleonic Wars, especially in Spain (1810–13), and joined Napoleon in the Hundred Days (March 20–June 28, 1815), Napoleon's attempt to regain power. When the coup failed, Clausel went into exile in the U.S., not returning to France until 1820. He was governor general (1835–37) of Algeria.

Clausen (klô'sen), Sir **George.** b. at London, 1852; d. Nov. 23, 1944. English landscape and figure painter and etcher, who was associated at one time with Holman Hunt and Walter Crane in a rebellion against the policy of the Royal Academy. He studied at the South Kensington Art schools and also at Paris under Adolphe Bouguereau. Later he forsook his independent position and even became director of the Royal Academy Schools and professor of painting there. His oils and watercolors are found in private collections and museums throughout Europe and the British Empire. Among his principal works are: *The Gleaners Returning* (Tate Gallery), *A Morning in June* (Johannesburg), and *The Boy and the Man* (Bradford Art Gallery). He was also the author of *Lectures on Painting* (1904).

Clausen (klou'sen), **Henrik Nikolai.** b. at Maribo, Denmark, April 22, 1793; d. at Copenhagen, March 28, 1877. Danish theologian. He was professor of theology at Copenhagen in the period 1822–76, and a state councilor from 1848 to 1851. His works include *Katholicismens og Protestantismens Kirkeforfatning Lære og Ritus* (Church Organization, Doctrine, and Ritual of Catholicism and Protestantism, 1825).

Clausenburg (klou'zen.bürk). German name of **Cluj.**

Clausentum (klô.sen'tum). Latin name of **Southampton,** England.

Clausewitz (klou'ze.vits), **Karl von.** b. at Burg, Prussia June 1, 1780; d. at Breslau, Nov. 16, 1831. Prussian officer and military writer. He entered the Prussian army in 1792, and from 1809 to 1812 worked under Scharnhorst on plans for the War of Liberation. After joining (1812) the Russian forces, he again served (1814 *et seq.*) in the Prussian army. In 1818 he was named to head the *Allgemeine Kriegsschule* (German War School). His posthumously published work *Vom Kriege* (*On War*), actually the first three volumes of *Hinterlassene Werke über Krieg und Kriegführung* (1832–37), is considered a masterpiece among works on military strategy. The theories expressed in it formed the basis of the science of war in the 19th and early 20th centuries. His other works include various studies of campaigns from 1796 to 1815 and those of famous military leaders, and a biography of Scharnhorst.

Clausius (klou'zē.ůs), **Rudolf Julius Emanuel.** b. at Köslin, Pomerania, Prussia, Jan. 2, 1822; d. at Bonn, Prussia, Aug. 24, 1888. German physicist. He became professor of physics at the University of Bonn in 1869, retaining that post until his death. He is known for his work in thermodynamics, especially for his formulation of the second law of thermodynamics (1850), which states that heat cannot pass of itself from a colder to a warmer body. He also introduced the concept of entropy and contributed to the kinetic theory of gases and the theory of electrolysis. He was author of *Die mechanische Wärmetheorie* (2nd ed., 1876–91), *Über das Wesen der Wärme* (1857), and *Die Potentialfunktion und das Potential* (1859).

Claussen (klou'sen), **Sophus Niels Christen.** b. at Helletoft, Denmark, Sept. 12, 1865; d. at Gentofte, Denmark, April 11, 1931. Danish lyric poet, noted as one of the leaders in the lyric renaissance of the 1890's. Though influenced by Heine, Baudelaire, and Mallarmé, he was a truly original poet, and is considered one of Denmark's most gifted artists.

Clauss-Szárvady (klous'sär'vô.dē), **Wilhelmine.** b. at Prague, Dec. 13, 1834; d. at Paris, Sept. 1, 1907. Czech pianist, noted for her interpretation of Bach and Beethoven.

Clausthal (klous'täl). [Also: **Klausthal;** former name, **Clausthal-Zellerfeld** (-tsel'ėr.felt).] Town in NW Germany, in the *Land* (state) of Lower Saxony, British Zone, formerly in the province of Hanover, Prussia, situated in the Harz Mountains, ab. 44 mi. SE of Hanover. It is a mining town, whose mining activities date back to the 12th century. In the 12th-14th, and later in the 16th-17th centuries, silver mining was the foremost enterprise; now lead, copper, and zinc are more important. There is a mining academy founded in 1775. Clausthal has some lumber mills and ceramics manufactures; it is also a climatic health resort and a center for winter sports. The market church, erected in 1642, is the largest wooden church structure in Germany. The population is predominantly Protestant. 16,851 (1950).

Cläven (klā'fen). A German name of **Chiavenna.**

Clavenna (kla.ven'a). Latin name of **Chiavenna.**

Claver (klä.ver'), Saint **Peter** or San **Pedro.** See Saint **Peter Claver.**

Claverack (klav'ėr.ak). Town in E New York, in Columbia County: residential suburb of Hudson. It was formerly the county seat. 4,406 (1950).

Claveret (klå.vre), **Jean.** b. at Orléans, France, 1590; d. 1666. French poet, chiefly notable as an adversary and would-be rival of Pierre Corneille. He wrote *Lettre contre le sieur Corneille, soi-disant auteur du Cid,* and others.

Claverhouse (klav'ėrz, klā'vėrz, klav'ėr.hous), **John Graham of.** See **Graham, John.**

Clavers (klav'ėrz), Mrs. **Mary.** See **Kirkland, Caroline Matilda.**

Clavière (klå.vyer), **Étienne.** b. at Geneva, Switzerland, Jan. 27, 1735; d. Dec. 8, 1793. French revolutionary politician and financier, who became minister of finance in 1792. He was the chief economic adviser of the Comte de Mirabeau early in the French Revolution. He was identified with the Girondins, and on their fall was accused and arrested. He committed suicide in prison the day before he was to face the Revolutionary tribunal.

Clavigo (klä.vē'gō). Tragedy by Goethe, published June 1, 1774, on the ruin of José Clavijo y Fajardo.

Clavijero or **Clavigero** (klä.ʙē.ʜā'rō), **Francisco Xavier** (or **Javier**) **Saverio.** b. at Veracruz, Mexico, 1731; d. at Bologna, Italy, 1787. Mexican Jesuit historian. He taught rhetoric and philosophy in the principal Jesuit colleges of Mexico, where he served as a missionary to the Indians, and after the expulsion of his order (1767) founded an academy at Bologna, Italy. His *Storia antica del Messico* (Cesena, 1780) includes the Aztec period of Mexican history and the Spanish conquest, and had an immediate and wide success. It was translated into various languages. His *Storia della California* was published after his death (Venice, 1789).

Clavijo (klä.ʙē'ʜō), **Don.** Accomplished cavalier in Cervantes's *Don Quixote,* who was metamorphosed into a crocodile and was disenchanted by Don Quixote.

Clavijo, Ruy González de. See **González de Clavijo, Ruy.**

Clavijo y Fajardo (ē fä.ʜär'ᴛʜō), **José.** b. in the Canary Islands, c1730; d. at Madrid, 1806. Spanish official (curator of the royal archives), journalist, and translator of Buffon. He is known chiefly for his quarrel (1764) with Beaumarchais on account of the latter's sister. He was forced to sign an acknowledgment of wrongdoing which cost him his honor and his official position. This incident was made the subject of Goethe's tragedy *Clavigo.*

Clavileño (klä.ʙē.lā'nyō), **El Alígero.** In Cervantes's *Don Quixote,* the wooden horse used by Don Quixote. It was managed by a wooden pin in its forehead. The magic horse is a folklore subject known throughout Europe and the Near East.

Clavius (klä'vē.ůs), **Christopher.** [Also, **Clau.**] b. at Bamberg, Bavaria, 1538; d. at Rome, Feb. 12, 1612. German astronomer and mathematician. He became a Jesuit in 1555, studied mathematics at Coimbra, Portugal, and taught at the Roman College until his death. He wrote a number of mathematical works, among them an exposition and defense of the Gregorian calendar reform.

Clawson (klô′sǫn). Village in S Lower Michigan, in Oakland County, near Detroit. 5,196 (1950).

Claxton (klaks′tǫn), **Kate.** [Maiden name, **Cone.**] b. at Somerville, N.J., 1848; d. at New York, May 5, 1924. American actress, identified with the role of the blind Louise in Adolphe d'Ennery's *The Two Orphans.* She made her debut (1869) at Chicago in *Andy Blake,* and later appeared in *Man and Wife, Fernande, Led Astray, The World Against Her,* and *Cruel London.*

Claxton, Philander Priestley. b. in Tennessee, 1862—. American educator. He was graduated (B.A., 1882; M.A., 1887) from the University of Tennessee, was U.S. commissioner of education (1911–21), and president (1930–46) of Austin Peay Normal School, Clarksville, Tenn. He was editor (1897–1901) of the *North Carolina Journal of Education* and a member of the Rockefeller Sanitary Commission.

Clay (klā), **Albert Tobias.** b. at Hanover, Pa., Dec. 4, 1866; d. Sept. 14, 1925. American Orientalist. After serving on the staff (1899–1910) of the department of Assyriology at the University of Pennsylvania, he was first professor (1910–25) of Assyriology at Yale. He was the author of *Business Documents of Murashu Sons of Nippur dated in the Reign of Artaxerxes I* (1898), *An Old Babylonian Version of the Gilgamesh Epic on the Basis of Recently Discovered Texts* (1902), *Amurru, the Home of the Northern Semites* (1909), *The Empire of the Amorites* (1919), *A Hebrew Deluge Story in Cuneiform* (1922), and *The Origin of Biblical Traditions* (1923).

Clay, Bertha M. English writer, whose real name was Charlotte Monica Braeme (1836–84), author of a long series of sensational romantic novels, many of them believed to have been written, under the name Bertha M. Clay, by Frederick Van Rensselaer Day (1861–1922), and Thomas Chalmers Harbaugh (1849–1924).

Clay, Cassius Marcellus. b. at Whitehall, Madison County, Ky., Oct. 19, 1810; d. there, July 22, 1903. American politician; son of Green Clay. He was an antislavery advocate, and founded (1845) at Lexington, Ky., *The True American,* an abolitionist journal, which, because of the active hostility in Lexington, he was forced to move to Cincinnati, Ohio. He served in the Mexican and Civil wars. Clay was U.S. minister to Russia in the periods 1861–62 and 1863–69.

Clay, Clement Claiborne. b. in Madison County, Ala., Dec. 13, 1816; d. near Huntsville, Ala., Jan. 3, 1882. American politician. He was U.S. senator from Alabama in the period 1854–61. On the outbreak of the Civil War he became a Confederate senator, and was sent (1864) to Canada by Jefferson Davis, there to attempt negotiations with Lincoln. After Lincoln's assassination he was suspected of having been implicated in secret plots, and was imprisoned, but was freed after a time.

Clay, Frederick or **Frédéric.** b. at Paris, Aug. 3, 1838; d. at Great Marlow, England, Nov. 24, 1889. English composer, notably of operettas. These include *The Pirate's Isle* (1859), *Ages Ago* (1869), *Princess Toto* (1875), the latter two with W. S. Gilbert collaborating, and *The Golden Ring* (1883). His other work includes the cantatas *The Knights of the Cross* (1866) and *Lalla Rookh* (1877), the latter containing his best-known song, *I'll Sing Thee Songs of Araby.*

Clay, Green. b. in Powhatan County, Va., Aug. 14, 1757; d. Oct. 31, 1826. American general; father of Cassius Marcellus Clay. He defended Fort Meigs against a British force in 1813.

Clay, Henry. b. in Hanover County, Va., April 12, 1777; d. at Washington, D.C., June 29, 1852. American statesman, noted as the proponent of the "American system" of internal improvements and protective tariffs, and for his efforts to preserve the Union by compromise. He studied law at Richmond, Va., where he was licensed to practice, and moved (1797) to Lexington, Ky., establishing himself as an outstanding criminal lawyer. He served (1803–06) in the state legislature, went to the U.S. Senate to fill a vacancy (1806–07), returned to the state legislature in 1807, serving as speaker, and remained there until 1809, when he again went to the U.S. Senate to fill an unexpired term. In 1810 he was elected to the U.S. House of Representatives and made speaker. An exponent of Western interests, he was one of the "war hawks" who led the U.S. into the War of 1812, and in 1814 was chosen to serve on the American commission which undertook negotiations with the British at Ghent. He returned to the House, again became speaker, succeeded in making effective (1821) the Missouri Compromise, and left Congress in 1821, but once again returned to Washington as a member of Congress and a candidate for the presidency. This eager ambition, never gratified, was to be frustrated time and again during his lifetime. He served in Congress (1823–25) and was again speaker. In 1824, when he failed in his first bid for the presidency, he struck the famous "bargain" which his enemies did not permit him to forget for many years after. Since no candidate had received an electoral majority, the House was called upon to exercise its constitutional duty to elect a president. Clay, who had received the Kentucky vote, was instructed by the Kentucky legislature to vote for Andrew Jackson, whom Clay had antagonized by his attack (1819) upon Jackson for invading Florida. Clay disobeyed the orders, voted for John Quincy Adams, and, upon his appointment (1825) as secretary of state under Adams, was accused by the Jackson faction of having received that post in reward for his maneuver. He supported Adams in the contest of 1828, and upon Jackson's victory returned to private life in 1829. He returned to the U.S. Senate in 1831, where he became an outspoken opponent of the administration, clashing bitterly with Jackson over the issue of rechartering the Second Bank of the United States. In 1832 he was again defeated for the presidency, and shortly thereafter performed an outstanding service in resolving the Nullification Controversy by submitting the bill which became the compromise tariff of 1833. He saw his desire for the Whig presidential nomination of 1840 come to nothing when the New York state political boss, Thurlow Weed, secured the nomination for William Henry Harrison at the party's Harrisburg convention. Clay resigned (1842) from the Senate and devoted his efforts to strengthening his position for the contest in 1844; he secured the Whig nomination, but lost the election to James K. Polk when Clay took what many regarded as an anti-expansionist stand on the question of Texas. His most memorable achievement, perhaps, came after his retur (1849) to the Senate, a weary and sick old man. He secured the passage of the Compromise of 1850 in his last attempt to save the Union from fatal division. By every American schoolchild he is remembered as "the Great Compromiser," and he stands, with Daniel Webster and John C. Calhoun, as a member of the great triumvirate of American statesmen who dominated the national legislature during the middle period of U.S. history. See the *Works of Henry Clay* (7 vols., 1896) and the classic biography by Carl Schurz (2 vols., 1887).

Clay, James. b. at London, 1805; d. at Brighton, England, 1873. English authority on the game of whist; father of Frederick Clay. He was author of "A Treatise on the Game of Whist by J. C.," affixed to Baldwin's *Laws of Short Whist* (1864). He was a member of Parliament from 1847 until 1873.

Clay, Lucius DuBignon. b. at Marietta, Ga., April 23, 1897—. American military engineer and general. After specializing in engineering at the West Point Military Academy and graduating therefrom in 1918, he rose through successive grades in the army while engaged in engineering works or holding administrative posts. He directed the construction of the Red River Dam in Texas (1938–40), administered the defense airport program of the Civil Aeronautics Administration (1940–41), was for a time deputy director of the Office of War Mobilization and Reconversion, and became deputy to General Eisenhower in the European theater of war in 1945. In 1946 he was named deputy chief of U.S. military government in Germany, and thereafter was commander of that government as well as of U.S. forces in Germany (1947–49). During these years, disputes with the Soviet occupation forces in Germany led to a virtual blockade of West Berlin, which was occupied by American, British, and French forces but was deep within the Russian Zone. This blockade was energetically countered by means of the "air-lift," that is to say the use of numerous American and other Western-power airplanes to fly essential supplies into West Berlin. General Clay's firm handling of affairs on the receiving end of the "air-lift" during this crisis caused great satisfaction in the U.S., and at his retirement from the army in 1949 he was given the rank of full general. Thereafter he engaged in private business and in public patriotic activities. His book *Decision in Germany* (1950) relates his experiences during the post-hostilities period including the months of the blockade.

Clayborne (klā′bọrn), **William.** See **Claiborne, William.**

Clay Center. City in NE Kansas, county seat of Clay County, on the Republican River: processing and shipping point for grain and dairy and poultry products. 4,528 (1950).

Clay Cross. Urban district in N central England, in Derbyshire, situated on the river Rother, ab. 4 mi. S of Chesterfield, ab. 142 mi. N of London by rail. 8,552 (1951).

Clayhanger (klā′hang″ėr). Novel (1910) by Arnold Bennett. It is the first of a series of three "Five Towns" or "Clayhanger" novels.

Claypole (klā′pōl), **Noah.** Mr. Sowerberry's apprentice, a charity boy and afterward a thief, a character in Charles Dickens's *Oliver Twist*. He marries Charlotte, Mrs. Sowerberry's servant.

Claypoole or **Claypole** (klā′pōl), **Elizabeth.** [Maiden name, **Cromwell.**] b. July 2, 1629; d. Aug. 6, 1658. Youngest daughter of Oliver Cromwell. She is said to have interceded with her father in behalf of many Royalist offenders. She was buried in Henry VII's chapel in Westminster Abbey, but after the Restoration her body was taken up and cast, with others, into a pit.

Clays (klä′ēs), **Paul Jean.** b. at Bruges, Belgium, Nov. 27, 1819; d. at Brussels, Feb. 9, 1900. Belgian marine painter, pupil of Théodore Gudin.

Clayton (klā′tọn). City in E Missouri, county seat of St. Louis County, near St. Louis: residential community. 16,035 (1950).

Clayton. Borough in SW New Jersey, in Gloucester County, ab. 20 mi. S of Camden. 3,023 (1950).

Clayton. Town in NE New Mexico, county seat of Union County: trading and shipping center for a cattle-raising area. 3,515 (1950).

Clayton. Town (in New York the equivalent of township in many other states) and village in N New York, in Jefferson County, on the St. Lawrence River near the Thousand Islands: summer resort; manufactures of snowplows. Pop. of town, 3,758 (1950); of village, 1,981 (1950).

Clayton, Henry De Lamar. b. in Barbour County, Ala., Feb. 10, 1857; d. at Montgomery, Ala., Dec. 21, 1929. American jurist and congressman, author of the Clayton Antitrust Act (1914). He graduated (1877) from the University of Alabama, received an LL.B. (1878) there, and later practiced law (1880–1914) at Eufaula, Ala. He was a representative (1897–1914) to the U.S. Congress, where he served as head (1911–14) of the Judiciary Committee, and was U.S. district judge (1914–29) for the C and N districts of Alabama.

Clayton, Henry Helm. b. at Murfreesboro, Tenn., March 12, 1861; d. at Norwood, Mass., in October, 1946. American meteorologist who developed (1918) a new method of weather forecasting based upon solar heat changes he had observed while working in Argentina. A staff member (1886–91, 1894–1909) of the Blue Hill Meteorological Observatory, he subsequently served as weather forecaster (1913–22) with the Oficina Meteorológica Argentina at Buenos Aires. He specialized in the relation of changes in the sun to weather developments. He was the author of *World Weather Records* (1927) and *Solar Relations to Weather* (1943).

Clayton, John. b. at Fulham, England, c1685; d. in Virginia, Dec. 15, 1773. American botanist. The genus Claytonia of succulent plants was named in his honor by Johann Friedrich Gronovius, for whom Clayton had collected plant specimens used in preparing Gronovius's *Flora Virginica*.

Clayton, John Middleton. b. at Dagsborough, Sussex County, Del., July 24, 1796; d. at Dover, Del., Nov. 9, 1856. American politician. He was a U.S. senator from Delaware in the periods 1829–36, 1845–49, and 1853–56. As Zachary Taylor's secretary of state (1849–50), he negotiated the Clayton-Bulwer treaty with Great Britain, in which the two countries agreed to respect the neutrality of the proposed canal across the Central American isthmus.

Clayton, Joshua. b. in Cecil County, Md., Dec. 20, 1774; d. at Bohemia Manor, Del., Aug. 11, 1798. American politician and physician. As colonel on the staff of George Washington, he served at the battle of Brandywine. Following terms (1785, 1787) in the Delaware House of Assembly, he was president (1789–92) and first governor (1792–96) of Delaware. In 1798 he was elected a U.S. senator.

Clayton, Powell. b. in Bethel County, Pa., Aug. 7, 1833; d. Aug. 25, 1914. American politician. In 1868 he was elected governor of Arkansas. Elected (1871) to the Senate, he served until 1877. He was also ambassador (1897–1905) to Mexico.

Clayton Antitrust Act. Act passed in 1914 amending the Sherman Antitrust Law to prohibit various corporate agreements and practices for which no provision had been made under the Sherman Law. It declared price discrimination illegal where such practice tended to establish monopoly; prohibited corporate devices (such as interlocking directorates) in restraint of trade; declared that federal antitrust laws could not be applied to labor and agricultural organizations pursuing their legitimate interests and activities; and forbade the use of injunctions or restraining orders in labor disputes unless they were required to prevent irreparable injury to property and property rights for which "there is no adequate remedy at law."

Clayton-Bulwer Treaty (klā′tọn.bu̇l′wėr). Treaty between Great Britain and the U.S., concluded at Washington, D.C., on April 19, and ratified on July 4, 1850. Both parties pledged themselves to respect the neutrality of the proposed ship canal across Central America. Great Britain was represented by its minister to Washington, Sir Henry Bulwer (William Henry Lytton Earle Bulwer, Baron Dalling and Bulwer), the U.S. by John M. Clayton, the secretary of state. The treaty was abrogated in 1901 by the Hay-Pauncefote Treaty, signed at Washington, D.C., on Nov. 18, and ratified by the U.S. Senate on Dec. 16, 1901.

Clayton Compromise. In U.S. political history, the name applied to the scheme (1848) for organizing the Oregon and Southwest territories. It was formulated by a Senate committee (consisting of Whig and Democratic members) headed by John Middleton Clayton. The plan provided for the exclusion of slavery from Oregon, forbade the territorial legislatures of California and New Mexico from taking any action with respect to slavery, and sanctioned the appeal of all cases involving slavery from the territorial judiciaries to the U.S. Supreme Court. Although it won an affirmative Senate vote, the measure was never submitted to a vote in the House of Representatives.

Clayton-le-Moors (klā′tọn.lẹ.mörz′, -mōrz′). Urban district in NW England, in Lancashire, ab. 6 mi. NE of Blackburn. It has no direct rail connections for passengers, being reached by rail to Blackburn, ab. 208 mi. NW of London. 6,823 (1951).

Clazomenae (klạ.zom′ẹ.nē). In ancient geography, an Ionian city in Asia Minor, situated ab. 20 mi. SW of Smyrna (Izmir), near what is now the village of Urla, Turkey. It was the birthplace of Anaxagoras.

Cléante (klā.äṅt). Son of Harpagon in Molière's *L'Avare* (The Miser). He is in love with Mariane, but his father wants to marry the girl. Cléante borrows money so that he may marry Mariane and discovers that his own father is the one fleecing him by the high rate of interest. At last, when it is discovered that Mariane is really an heiress, she and Cléante marry.

Cléante. Brother-in-law of Orgon, and brother of Elmire, in Molière's *Tartuffe*. He is as genuinely good as Tartuffe is hypocritical.

Cléante. Lover of Angélique in Molière's *Le Malade imaginaire*. Her father, Argan, insists that Angélique marry a doctor, so that he may have one in the family. But when Argan is convinced of the rascality of doctors and of the love Angélique has for him, he consents to her marriage to Cléante, if the latter will become a doctor. Argan himself becomes a doctor in a mock graduation and all ends happily.

Cleanthe (klę̄.an'thē). Sister of Siphax in John Fletcher's *The Mad Lover.*

Cleanthes (klę̄.an'thēz). b. at Assos, Asia Minor, c331 B.C.; d. at Athens, 232 B.C. Greek Stoic philosopher; a disciple of Zeno, whom he succeeded as head of the Stoic school.

Cleanthes. Son of Leonides in *The Old Law*, a play attributed to Philip Massinger, Thomas Middleton, and William Rowley. He is a model of filial piety and tenderness.

Cleanthes. Friend of Cleomenes, and captain of Ptolemy's guard, in John Dryden's tragedy *Cleomenes.*

Cleanthis (klę̄.an'this). Waiting-woman to Alcmena, and wife of Sosia, in Molière's *Amphitryon.*

Clear (klir), **Cape.** Headland in Munster province, Irish Republic, in County Cork, situated at the SW extremity of Clear Island (lying in the Atlantic Ocean), ab. 14 mi. SW of Skibbereen. It is the southernmost point of Ireland.

Clear, Claudius. Pseudonym of **Nicoll,** Sir **William Robertson.**

Clearchus (klę̄.är'kus). b. at Sparta; executed by Artaxerxes, 401 B.C. Lacedaemonian general. He fought at the battle of Cyzicus in 410 when the Spartan fleet was destroyed by Alcibiades. In 408 his tyrannous conduct as governor of Byzantium during the siege by the Athenians led to the surrender of the city by the inhabitants during his absence in Asia, whither he had gone to collect a force to raise the siege. In 406 he fought under Callicratidas at the naval battle of Arginusae, where the Spartans again were defeated, this time by Conon. After the Peloponnesian war he persuaded the *ephors* (magistrates) to send him as general to Thrace to protect the Greeks against the natives. Having proceeded thither in spite of an order for his recall which overtook him on the way, he was condemned to death. Defeated by a force sent against him, he fled to Cyrus the Younger, under whom he commanded a body of Greek mercenaries in the expedition against Artaxerxes II, in 401. After the battle of Cunaxa, in which Cyrus was killed, he was treacherously seized, with four other Grecian generals, by Tissaphernes at a conference, and sent to Artaxerxes, who ordered them to be put to death. The surviving Greeks chose new generals and accomplished the famous retreat known as the "Retreat of the Ten Thousand," the story of which is told in Xenophon's *Anabasis.*

Clearfield (klir'fēld). Borough in C Pennsylvania, county seat of Clearfield County, on the W branch of the Susquehanna River, ab. 90 mi NE of Pittsburgh: industrial and railroad center. It was platted in 1805. Pop. 9,357 (1950).

Clearfield. Town in N Utah, in Davis County, ab. 25 mi. N of Salt Lake City: site of an army ordnance depot. In the decade between the last two U.S. censuses its population rose from 1,053 (1940) to 4,723 (1950).

Clear Horizon. Novel by Dorothy M. Richardson, published in 1935. It is the 11th section of *Pilgrimage* (1915–38), a novel sequence in 12 parts employing the stream-of-consciousness technique.

Clear Island. Island in SW Irish Republic, in Munster province, County Cork, ab. 54 mi. SW of Cork. Cape Clear, on this island, is the southernmost part of Ireland, and has an important lighthouse. The chief occupations of the inhabitants are fishing and agriculture. Area, ab. 2½ sq. mi.; pop. ab. 700.

Clear Lake. Lake in N central California, ab. 80 mi. N of San Francisco. It is a large fresh-water lake surrounded by hills covered by oaks and vineyards. There are many summer resorts. Elevation, ab. 1,326 ft.; area, ab. 67 sq. mi.

Clear Lake. City in N Iowa, in Cerro Gordo County, on Clear Lake: summer resort. The lake (length, 6 mi.) is also the site of a state recreational area (area, 27 acres). 4,977 (1950).

Clearwater (klir'wô"tėr, -wot"ėr). City in W Florida, county seat of Pinellas County, on the Gulf of Mexico, W of Tampa: packing and shipping center for citrus fruits. It is a tourist resort, known for its gardens, and a fishing port. 15,581 (1950).

Clearwater. Lake in the province of Quebec, Canada, which drains into Richmond Gulf and thence into Hudson Bay. Elevation, 790 ft.; area, 410 sq. mi.

Clearwater River. River in N central Idaho, rising in several branches in the Bitterroot Range, and flowing generally NW and W to join the Snake River at Lewiston, Idaho. In the 1860's there was a gold rush in this region, but the principal activities now are stock raising and lumbering. Length, ab. 80 mi. (ab. 180 mi. to the headwaters).

Cleaveland (klēv'lạnd), **Moses.** b. at Canterbury, Conn., Jan. 29, 1754; d. Nov. 16, 1806. American pioneer who gave his name to Cleveland, Ohio. He served as a lieutenant (1777–81) with Washington's army, and later represented (1787–1806) Canterbury, Conn., in the state's general assembly. As a director of the Connecticut Land Company, he led (1796) the party to survey the land purchased (1795) in the Western Reserve. There he founded the principal settlement, subsequently named Cleaveland (and later Cleveland), at the mouth of the Cuyahoga River.

Cleaveland, Parker. b. at Byfield, Mass., Jan. 15, 1780; d. at Brunswick, Me., Oct. 15, 1858. American mineralogist. He was a professor at Bowdoin College (Maine) from 1805 to 1858. He wrote *Elementary Treatise on Mineralogy and Geology* (1816), the first book in the field written in the U.S.

Cleaver (klē'vėr), **Fanny.** [Called **"Jenny Wren."**] Deformed little dressmaker of dolls' clothes, in Charles Dickens's *Our Mutual Friend.* "My back's bad and my legs are queer," is her frequent excuse, and she always describes herself with dignity as "the person of the house."

Clebsch (klepsh), **Alfred.** [Full name, **Rudolf Friedrich Alfred Clebsch.**] b. at Königsberg, in East Prussia, Jan. 14, 1833; d. at Göttingen, Germany, Nov. 7, 1872. German mathematician noted especially for his work on binary algebraic forms and the application of Abelian functions to geometry. He received his doctorate at Königsberg in 1854, and taught at the universities of Giessen, Karlsruhe, and Göttingen. With Carl Gottfried Neumann he founded (1868) the journal *Mathematische Annalen.* His books include *Theorie der binären algebraischen Formen* (1872), *Vorlesungen über Geometrie* (2 vols., 1876–91), and *Theorie der Abelschen Funktionen* (1866). An account of his work is found in *Mathematische Annalen,* VII (1874).

Cleburne (klē'bėrn). City in C Texas, county seat of Johnson County, on West Buffalo Creek, ab. 45 mi. SW of Dallas. It is a shipping and trading center for livestock and dairy products. Manufactures include brooms, cottonseed oil, and other items; there are railroad shops. 12,905 (1950).

Cleburne, Patrick Ronayne. [Called **"the Stonewall of the West."**] b. near Cork, Ireland, March 17, 1828; d. at the battle of Franklin, Tenn., Nov. 30, 1864. American soldier, a general in the Confederate army in the Civil War. He served in the British army for three years, and came to America in 1849. He was admitted to the bar in Arkansas in 1855, and practiced law until the outbreak of the Civil War, when he enlisted as a private. He fought at Shiloh, Richmond, Chattanooga, Atlanta, and in Tennessee. He rose to be commander of a corps, and was distinguished for his courage and skill, which earned for him the title of "the Stonewall of the West" (in allusion to "Stonewall" Jackson).

Cleef (klāf), **Jan van.** b. at Venlo, Netherlands, 1646; d. at Ghent, Belgium, Dec. 18, 1716. Flemish painter.

Cleef, Joos van. See **Cleve** or **Cleef, Joos van.**

Cle Elum River (klē el'um). River in C Washington, flowing S to join the Yakima River in Kittitas County, Wash. Length, ab. 35 mi., including Cle Elum Lake (ab. 7 mi. long).

Cleethorpes (klē'thôrps). Municipal borough and seaside resort in E England, in Lincolnshire, in the Parts of Lindsey, situated at the mouth of the Humber estuary, ab. 2 mi. SE of Grimsby, ab. 158 mi. N of London by rail. 29,558 (1951).

Cleeve Cloud or **Cleeve Hill** (klēv). See under **Cotswold Hills.**

Clefen (klā'fẹn). A German name of **Chiavenna.**

Clegg (kleg), **Henry.** Jane Clegg's husband, in St. John Ervine's play of middle-class English life and character, *Jane Clegg* (1911). After being saved from a prison sentence by his wife, who is glad to get rid of him, he leaves home to live with his "fancy woman," Kitty, who is about to bear his child.

Cleinow (klī'nō), **Georg.** b. at Lublin (in territory then part of Russia), April 27, 1873; d. 1936. German journalist. A specialist in Russian affairs, he was editor of the national liberal periodical *Grenzboten* until 1923. He was the author of numerous books, among them *Die Zukunft Polens* (2 vols., 1908–14), *Deutsch-Russische Rechts- und Wirtschaftsverträge* (1926), and *Der Verlust der Ostmark* (1934).

Cleishbotham (klēsh'boᴛʜ.ạm), **Jedediah.** Assumed compiler of *Tales of My Landlord*, by Sir Walter Scott. Cleishbotham is a schoolmaster at Gandercleugh, and the stories are written by his assistant, one Peter Pattieson, who in turn has collected the tales from the landlord of the Wallace Inn, Gandercleugh.

Cleisthenes (klīs'thẹ.nēz) or **Clisthenes** (klis'-). fl. 580 B.C. Tyrant of Sicyon, a city in the Peloponnesus. He was leader of the Ionian part of the population, who turned upon the conquering Dorians and subjected and humiliated them. He forbade the recitation of Homeric poems praising Dorian heroes, and he attacked Argos, then a Dorian city. He supported the Amphictyonic League in defending Delphi in the first Sacred War, and destroyed Crisa and Cirrha. Valiant and able in war, he was reputed a wise and humane ruler.

Cleisthenes or **Clisthenes.** fl. in the 6th century B.C. Athenian politician; son of Megacles, grandson of Cleisthenes, tyrant of Sicyon, and the most prominent of the Alcmaeonidae, the noble family important in Athenian politics at that period. He developed in a democratic spirit the constitution of Solon (adopted 594 B.C.) by substituting ten new for four old tribes, with a view to breaking up the influence of the landowning aristocracy, the new tribes being composed not of contiguous *demes* (local administrative communities), but of demes scattered through the area and interspersed with those of other tribes. He was expelled in 507 by Isagoras, leader of the aristocratic party, aided by a Spartan army under Cleomenes, but was recalled in the same year by the populace, which compelled the Spartans to withdraw and sent Isagoras into exile. According to tradition, he established ostracism, the power of the sovereign popular assembly, the *ecclesia*, to decree, by means of a secret ballot, the banishment of any citizen who endangered the public liberty.

Cleitus (klī'tus). See **Clitus.**

Cleiveland (klēv'lạnd), **John.** See **Cleveland, John.**

Cleland (klē'lạnd), **John.** b. 1709; d. Jan. 23, 1789. English writer. He was the author of the notorious novel *Fanny Hill, or the Memoirs of a Woman of Pleasure* (1748–50) and of *Memoirs of a Coxcomb* (1751). He was consul at Smyrna, and in 1736 was in the service of the East India Company at Bombay. In the latter part of his life he wrote for the stage and also dabbled in philology.

Cleland, Robert Glass. b. at Shelbyville, Ky., Feb. 19, 1885—. American teacher and historian. He was graduated (B.A., 1907) from Occidental College and received his Ph.D. (1912) from Princeton. He served (1912–43) as professor of history and for a time as dean of the faculty at Occidental College, and was a research associate (1937–38) at the Huntington Library at San Marino, Calif., where he became (1943) a member of the permanent research staff. He is the author of *History of California, The American Period* (1922), *One Hundred Years of the Monroe Doctrine* (1923), *California Pathfinders* (1928), *The History of Occidental College, 1887–1937* (1937), *The Place Called Sespe* (1940), *The Cattle on a Thousand Hills* (1941), and *From Wilderness to Empire* (1944).

Cleland, William. b. at or near Douglas, Lanarkshire, Scotland, c1661; d. Aug. 26, 1689. Scottish Covenanter, soldier, and poet. He was educated at St. Andrews and Utrecht universities. He took part in the battles of Drumclog and Bothwell Bridge (both in 1679), and in the battle of Dunkeld. After receiving a fatal wound at Dunkeld, he is said to have attempted vainly to drag himself off the field so that his men, pitted against the Highland Jacobites, would not lose heart at seeing his dead body. *Hallo, My Fancy,* written during his student days in Scotland, and *A Mock Poem upon the Expedition of the Highland Host who Came to Destroy the Western Shires in Winter 1678,* a satire in the style of *Hudibras,* are considered among his best works. Cleland's collected poetry was not published until 1697.

Clélie (klā.lē). [English, **Clelia** (klē'li.ạ).] Romance by Mademoiselle de Scudéry, published in 1656, named after its heroine. The long novel, based on a theme from Roman history, is written in the precious, romantic style and introduces many of Mademoiselle de Scudéry's contemporaries, in fictional disguise, as characters.

Clemenceau (klem.ẹn.sō'; French, klā.mäṅ.sō), **Georges (Eugène Benjamin).** [Called **"Le Tigre,"** meaning "The Tiger," and, by French soldiers during World War I, **"Le Père la Victoire,"** meaning "Father Victory."] b. at Mouilleron-en-Pareds, Vendée, France, Sept. 28, 1841; d. at Paris, Nov. 24, 1929. French statesman who led France to victory in World War I and presided at the Versailles Peace Conference. He began his political activity while still a young medical student, engaging (1860–62) in opposition to the government of Napoleon III and spending two months in prison (1862). After receiving a diploma in medicine (1865) he traveled and taught in the U.S., where he married (1869) Mary Plummer of Springfield, Mass., before setting up a medical practice at Paris. On the proclamation of the Third Republic (September, 1870) he became mayor of the 18th arrondissement (Montmartre) and aided in the defense of Paris. Elected to the National Assembly (February, 1871) he opposed peace with the Germans and attempted without success to mediate between the Commune and the Versailles government. Again a deputy (1876–93) he headed the Left Wing republicans and became known as "The Tiger" because of his independence, his dueling, and his savage polemics. He helped to overthrow the Gambetta (1882), Ferry (1885), and Brisson (1886) cabinets and to force the resignation of President Jules Grévy (1887). He supported the appointment of Georges Boulanger as minister of war (1886) but opposed the Boulangist movement when the general sought dictatorial powers. In 1893 the electors repudiated him for suspected implication in the Panama scandal, in which the French company attempting to build a canal across Panama failed and ruined many French investors. An indefatigable journalist, he helped to organize *La Justice* (1880), *L'Aurore* (1897), *Le Bloc* (1900), and *L'Homme libre* (1913); his trenchant articles, supplementing those of Émile Zola and others, helped to force a revision of the decision in the Dreyfus case, causing a new trial to be held and eventually leading to the pardon of Dreyfus. Elected to the Senate (1902–20), he fought for the separation of church and state and became minister of the interior in the Sarrien cabinet (1906) and premier (1906–09). He used troops to quell strikes (1906) and agrarian disturbances (1908), strengthened the Franco-British accord, and urged firmer defense measures against Germany. His cabinet fell in 1909. In 1913 he voted against Raymond Poincaré's election as president of the republic. On the outbreak of World War I he headed the senate military commission and criticized all whom he considered guilty of laxity or inefficiency. In the darkest days of 1917 Poincaré called on him to form a cabinet (Nov. 16); he rallied French morale, launched a bold program to win the war, and brought two former cabinet members, Louis Malvy and Joseph Caillaux, to trial on charges of disloyalty and defeatism. He urged a unified command on the Western Front and firmly supported Ferdinand Foch as supreme commander of the Allied forces. Throughout the peace deliberations (January-June, 1919) he remained skeptical of the projected League of Nations and predicted the revival of German militarism. When his demand that the left bank of the Rhine remain under French control was overruled by Wilson and Lloyd George he compromised for an offer of Anglo-American guaranties to safeguard France; the guaranties were never ratified. After the signing of the Versailles Treaty (June 28, 1919) he lost public and parliamentary support. In January, 1920, he failed of election to the presidency of the republic against Paul Deschanel and retired from public life. He lectured in the U.S. (1922), proposed the cancellation of the French war debt to the U.S. (1926); and passed his last years in writing. His works include a dozen volumes of collected articles and sketches, his medical dissertation, *De la génération des éléments anatomiques* (1865), a novel, *Les Plus forts* (1898), a play, *Le Voile de bonheur* (1901), two biographical studies, *Démosthène* (1926) and *Claude Monet: les nymphéas* (1928), a philosophical testament, *Au soir de la pensée* (2 vols., 1927), and some final polemics on World

War I and its aftermath, *Grandeurs et misères d'une victoire* (1930).

Clemenceau, Mount. Peak in the Rocky Mountains, in British Columbia, Canada, named after Georges Clemenceau, premier of France during World War I. It is situated in the E central part of the province near the Alberta border. 12,001 ft.

Clémence d'Auguste (klā.mäṅs dō.güst), **La.** See **Cinna.**

Clemens (klem'ẹnz), **Jacob.** See **Clément, Jacques.**

Clemens, Samuel Langhorne. [Pseudonym, **Mark Twain.**] b. at Florida, Mo., Nov. 30, 1835; d. at Redding, Conn., April 21, 1910. American writer, humorist, and lecturer. He lived (1839–53) at Hannibal, Mo., a town on the Mississippi bank which has since become identified with his novels *The Adventures of Tom Sawyer* (1876) and *The Adventures of Huckleberry Finn* (1884), in which Twain drew upon some of his boyhood memories. Compelled to abandon his formal schooling after his father's death (1847), he became a printer's apprentice, and did some writing for a Hannibal newspaper under the management of his elder brother. He was a journeyman printer (1853–54), working at St. Louis, New York, Philadelphia, and Keokuk (Iowa). Becoming (1857) a river pilot's apprentice on the Mississippi, he became a licensed pilot in 1859 before he left (1861) for Nevada with Orion Clemens. His experiences on the river provided him with the subject matter for *Life on the Mississippi* (1883). In *Roughing It* (1872), he recorded his impressions of frontier life in Nevada, where he ventured into prospecting and was for brief periods secretary to his brother, and of travels to San Francisco and the Sandwich (Hawaiian) Islands. He adopted his pseudonym (in river pilot language, "mark twain" meant two fathoms deep) when he became (1862) a reporter at Virginia City, Nev. At this time he embarked on his literary career, developing the broad frontier humor which distinguished much of the first phase of his work. Receiving encouragement from the humorist Artemus Ward (Charles Farrar Browne), he left (1864) for California, where he resumed his work as a reporter and wrote (1865) a newspaper piece that later became the title story of his first book, *The Celebrated Jumping Frog of Calaveras County, and Other Sketches* (1867). The story brought him instant recognition throughout the country. He took to lecturing and, commissioned by a California journal to make a tour around the world, stopped off at New York and decided to go instead to the Mediterranean area. His account of the journey, published as *The Innocents Abroad; or, The New Pilgrim's Progress* (1869), established his American reputation and brought him financial rewards. He was married (1870) to Olivia Langdon of Elmira, N.Y., who, some critics have maintained, exercised an unfavorable influence over his subsequent literary work. He lived (1869–71) at Buffalo, N.Y., and from 1871 to 1888 resided at Hartford, Conn. Over these years he was active as a lecturer in the U.S. and Europe, and became involved in speculation, notably in publishing and in the manufacture of a typesetting machine, which led to heavy financial loss and (in 1894) to bankruptcy. In collaboration with Charles Dudley Warner, he wrote *The Gilded Age: A Tale of To-day* (1873), a satire on the life of the post-Civil War period. His comic strain flowered at its best in the Tom Sawyer and Huckleberry Finn books, in *A Tramp Abroad* (1880), *The Prince and the Pauper* (1882), and *A Connecticut Yankee in King Arthur's Court* (1889). Among his works in the decade before the turn of the century were: *The American Claimant* (1892), *Tom Sawyer, Detective* (1896), *The Tragedy of Pudd'nhead Wilson* (1894), and the *Personal Recollections of Joan of Arc* (1896). In 1894 he set off on a round-the-world lecture tour in order to redeem his debts, most of which he paid by 1898. His record of the journey, *Following the Equator* (1897), revealed a growing bitterness and disillusionment to which the death of his daughter, Susy, and his financial disasters probably contributed. The steadily lowering cloud of pessimism which darkened his mind was apparent in *The Man That Corrupted Hadleyburg* (1900), *What Is Man?* (printed privately, 1906; published 1917), and *The Mysterious Stranger* (1916), all written in 1898, in which he delivered mordant comments upon the hopelessness of human existence. He also wrote *Christian Science* (1907) and *Is Shakespeare Dead?* (1909), supporting the Baconian theory, and after 1906 devoted himself to the work published as *Mark Twain's Autobiography* (2 vols., 1924). Among his other works are *Extracts from Adam's Diary* (1904), *A Dog's Tale* (1904), *Editorial Wild Oats* (1905), *Eve's Diary* (1906), *The $30,000 Bequest* (1906), *A Horse's Tale* (1907), *Republican Letters* (1941), and *Washington in 1868* (1943). He received many honors during his lifetime, including an honorary M.A. (1888) from Yale, the degree of Doctor of Literature (1907) from Oxford, and the honorary degree of Doctor of Laws from the University of Missouri, when he visited his native state for the last time in 1902.

Clemens Alexandrinus (al"eg.zan.drī'nus). See **Clement of Alexandria.**

Clement I (klem'ẹnt), Saint. [Called **Clement of Rome;** Latin, **Clemens Romanus.**] fl. late 1st century A.D. Pope from 88 to 97; the third bishop of Rome after Saint Peter. Nothing is known with certainty concerning his personal history, except that he was a prominent presbyter of the Christian congregation at Rome immediately after the apostolical age. He is by some identified with the Clement mentioned by Paul in Phil. iv. 3 as his fellow laborer, by others with the consul Flavius Clemens who was put to death by Domitian on a charge of atheism. Tradition has reckoned him among the martyrs, but according to Eusebius and Jerome, he died a natural death in the third year of the reign of Trajan. Numerous writings, most of which are evidently spurious, have been attributed to him. The most celebrated among these are two *Epistles to the Corinthians,* only one of which is now generally considered to be genuine, but which were held in the greatest esteem by the early Christians. They disappeared from the Western Church after the 5th century, and were rediscovered in the *Codex Alexandrinus* (a present from Cyril Lucaris to Charles I) by Patricius Junius (Patrick Young), who published them at Oxford in 1633. Another manuscript was discovered by Philotheos Bryennios in the convent library of the patriarch of Jerusalem, and published in 1875.

Clement II. [Original name, **Suidger.**] b. in Saxony; d. at Pesaro, Italy, Oct. 9, 1047. Pope from 1046 to 1047. He was a repressor of simony. Clement II was elected after Benedict IX failed to appear at the Synod of Sutri and was therefore deposed.

Clement III. [Original name, **Guibert of Ravenna.**] b. at Parma, Italy; d. at Ravenna, Italy, 1100. Antipope from 1080 to 1099. An archbishop of Ravenna, he was elected to the papal chair through the influence of the emperor Henry IV, in 1080. After having been expelled from Rome, he made his submission to Paschal II in 1099.

Clement III. [Original name, **Paolo Scolari.**] b. at Rome; d. March 27, 1191. Pope from 1187 to 1191. He preached the Third Crusade against the Saracens, who under Saladin had retaken Jerusalem on Oct. 3, 1187.

Clement IV. [Earlier names: **Guy Foulques** or **Guido le Gros.**] b. at St.-Gilles, Gard, France; d. at Viterbo, Italy, Nov. 29, 1268. Pope from 1265 to 1268. He held a high position at the court of Louis IX, when the death of his wife led him to enter the church. He became bishop of Puy in 1256, archbishop of Narbonne in 1259, cardinal in 1261, and was on a journey to England as papal legate when he was unanimously elected Pope by the College of Cardinals. He favored Charles of Anjou (Charles I, king of Two Sicilies) in his conquest of Naples, which had been granted to Charles by the preceding pontiff, Urban IV.

Clement V. [Original name, **Bertrand d'Agoust** or **Bertrand de Got.**] b. at Villandraut, in Gascony, France, 1264; d. at Roquemaure, in Languedoc, France, April 20, 1314. Pope from 1305 to 1314. He was elected through the influence of Philip IV (known as Philip the Fair) of France, to please whom he removed the papal residence to Avignon in 1309, and dissolved the order of Templars in 1312.

Clement VI. [Original name, **Pierre Roger.**] b. at Maumont, France, 1291; d. at Avignon, France, Dec. 6, 1352. Pope from 1342 to 1352. He established the jubilee for every 50 years, and purchased Avignon in 1348 from Joanna I, queen of Naples. During his pontificate Cola di Rienzi attempted to reëstablish the republic at Rome.

Clement VII. [Original name, Count **Robert of Geneva.**] b. c1342; d. at Avignon, France, Sept. 16, 1394. Antipope elected in 1378 in opposition to Urban VI.

Clement VII. [Original name, **Giulio de' Medici.**] b. at Florence, 1478; d. at Rome, Sept. 25, 1534. Pope from 1523 to 1534. He was the illegitimate son of Giuliano de' Medici, and cousin of Pope Leo X. He entered into a league with France, Venice, and Milan against the emperor Charles V, and in 1527 Rome was stormed and sacked by the troops of the Constable de Bourbon (Duke Charles de Bourbon) and Clement was made prisoner. He was released and fled to Orvieto on Dec. 9, 1527, but concluded a peace with Charles in 1529, and crowned him emperor at Bologna in 1530. He forbade (1534) the divorce of Henry VIII of England from Catharine of Aragon. During Clement's reign, Lutheranism, with which he failed to cope adequately, first obtained a solid hold in Germany. Clement was a patron of the arts, Raphael, Cellini, and Michelangelo being among those he aided.

Clement VIII. [Earlier names: **Gil Sánchez Muñoz** or **Aegidius Muñoz.**] Antipope from 1424 to 1429. He resigned in 1429, thus terminating the great Western schism.

Clement VIII. [Original name, **Ippolito Aldobrandini.**] b. at Fano, Italy, in March, 1536; d. at Rome, March 5, 1605. Pope from 1592 to 1605. He absolved Henry IV (Henry of Navarre) of France in 1595 when he renounced Protestantism. He ordered a revised edition (the "Clementine") of the Vulgate Bible in 1592.

Clement IX. [Original name, **Giulio Rospigliosi.**] b. at Pistoia, Italy, Jan. 28, 1600; d. at Rome, Dec. 9, 1669. Pope from 1667 to 1669. He mediated in 1668 the peace of Aix-la-Chapelle (Aachen) between Louis XIV and Spain, and the "Pax Clementina," which brought the Jansenist controversy to a temporary conclusion.

Clement X. [Original name, **Emilio Altieri.**] b. at Rome, July 13, 1590; d. there, July 22, 1676. Pope from 1670 to 1676. He was 80 years old at his election, and was completely under the influence of his relative Cardinal Paluzzi. During his pontificate commenced the controversy with Louis XIV concerning the enjoyment, during vacancy, of episcopal revenues and benefices, and the right of appointment to such vacancies.

Clement XI. [Original name, **Giovanni Francesco Albani.**] b. at Urbino, Italy, July 23, 1649; d. at Rome, March 19, 1721. Pope from 1700 to 1721. He was at war (1708–09), with the emperor Joseph I, and published bulls directed against the Jansenists, *Vineam Domini* (1705) and *Unigenitus* (1713). He also strengthened the foreign missions of the Church and enlarged the Vatican library.

Clement XII. [Original name, **Lorenzo Corsini.**] b. at Florence, April 7, 1652; d. at Rome, Feb. 6, 1740. Pope from 1730 to 1740. He condemned the Freemasons in 1738 and opposed the Jansenists.

Clement XIII. [Original name, **Carlo della Torre Rezzonico.**] b. at Venice, March 7, 1693; d. at Rome, Feb. 2, 1769. Pope from 1758 to 1769. His pontificate was characterized by resistance to pressure from Jansenists and Regalists, as well as criticism from Voltaire and the Encyclopedists. He also defended the Society of Jesus (Jesuits) against these groups, and in their favor issued a bull on their expulsion from Portugal and France. In 1768 the French seized Avignon, and the Neapolitans Benevento, thus reducing the extent of the papal holdings.

Clement XIV. [Original name, **Giovanni Vincenzo Antonio Ganganelli.**] b. at Sant'Arcangelo di Romagna, near Rimini, Italy, Oct. 31, 1705; d. at Rome, Sept. 22, 1774. Pope from 1769 to 1774. As a result of pressure from the Bourbon courts of France and Spain as well as virtually all the other Roman Catholic rulers of Europe, who were themselves doubtless influenced to some extent by several of the most influential 18th-century rationalist philosophers, he suppressed the Society of Jesus (Jesuits) by the brief *Dominus ac Redemptor noster* (1773). He founded the Clementine Museum at the Vatican.

Clément (klā.mäṅ), **Edmond.** b. at Paris, March 28, 1867; d. at Nice, France, Feb. 23, 1928. French singer. After winning the first prize at the Paris Conservatory, he became a member of the company of the Opéra-Comique, Paris. He made his New York debut in 1909 with the Metropolitan Opera Company at the New Theater, singing the title part of Jules Massenet's *Werther*, and made a concert tour (1910–11) of America. He achieved his greatest success in such lyric tenor roles as Des Grieux in Massenet's *Manon*, and in Daniel Auber's *Fra Diavolo*.

Clément, Félix. b. at Paris, Jan. 13, 1822; d. in January, 1885. French musicologist and composer. He was director of music at the Sorbonne, Paris, and author of various theoretical works.

Clément, François. b. at Bèze, near Dijon, France, 1714; d. at Paris, March 29, 1793. French historian, a Benedictine of St.-Maur. He compiled from the plans of Maurice Dantine and the preliminary work of Charles Clémencet, both Benedictines also, the important chronological work *L'Art de vérifier les dates ou faits historiques . . . depuis la naissance de Jésus-Christ* (revised and improved edition, 1783–87).

Clément, Jacques. [Also: **Jacob Clemens;** called **Clemens non Papa,** meaning "Clement not Pope," to distinguish him from Pope Clement VII.] d. before 1558. Flemish composer, principally of sacred music. He was chief chapel master to Emperor Charles V. He is noted for his use of counterpoint and for his setting of certain psalms to popular tunes.

Clément, Jacques. b. at Sorbon, in the Ardennes, France, 1567; d. 1589. French monk and regicide. A member of the Dominican order and of the Catholic League (Holy League), he was inflamed to a fanatical pitch when King Henry III of France recognized the Protestant Henry of Navarre as legitimate heir to the throne. While King Henry and Henry of Navarre were besieging Paris, then held by the forces of the League, Clément gained access to the king and stabbed him to death. He was himself immediately killed by attendants of the king.

Clément, Jean Pierre. b. at Draguignan, Var, France, June 2, 1809; d. at Paris, Nov. 8, 1870. French political economist and historian, a member of the French Institute. His works include *Histoire de la vie et de l'administration de Colbert* (1846), *Le Gouvernement de Louis XIV* (1848), and *Jacques Cœur et Charles VII* (1853).

Clement (klem'ent), **Justice.** City magistrate in Ben Jonson's *Every Man in His Humour*.

Clement (klā'ment), **Knut Jungbohn.** b. in Amrum, Schleswig, Dec. 4, 1803; d. at Bergen, N.J., Oct. 7, 1873. Danish historian, resident in the U.S. after 1866. He wrote *Die nordgermanische Welt* (1840), *Die Lebens- und Leidensgeschichte der Friesen* (1845), and others.

Clement Cleveland (klem'ent klēv'land), **Captain.** See **Cleveland, Captain Clement.**

Clémentel (klā.mäṅ.tel), **Étienne.** b. at Riom, Puy-de-Dôme, France, March 29, 1862; d. at Prompsat, Puy-de-Dôme, France, in December, 1936. French political leader, organizer of joint Allied economic activity during World War I. As minister of national economy (1916–20), he sponsored the formation of the Inter-Allied Wheat Executive in 1916 and the Inter-Allied Maritime Transport Council a year later. A deputy (1900–20) and senator (1920–36), and a leader of the Radical-Socialist Party, he resigned (1925) as minister of finance during a disagreement with Édouard Herriot over the recurrent problem of inflation. He had previously been finance minister (1914) as well as minister of colonies (1905, 1906) and agriculture (1913). He was the founder and first president of the International Chamber of Commerce.

Clementi (klā.men'tē), **Muzio.** b. at Rome, Jan. 23, 1752; d. at Evesham, England, March 10, 1832. Italian pianist and composer, resident in England after c1766. He made tours on the European continent, and in Vienna was matched (1781) against the somewhat younger Mozart in a group of virtuoso tests, at the conclusion of which neither was considered the winner. His principal work is a series of technical piano studies, *Gradus ad Parnassum* (1817). He also composed sonatinas, symphonies, and overtures. Both his studies and his piano compositions show a realization of the differences between the piano and the harpsichord, and he is considered the founder of good piano technique.

Clementina (klem.ẹn.tē′nạ), **Lady.** Italian lady (Lady Clementina della Porretta) passionately in love with Sir Charles Grandison, in Samuel Richardson's novel *Sir Charles Grandison*. Sir Charles is engaged to her but a difference in religion has held off their marriage. He falls in love with Harriet Byron, an English girl. Clementina becomes deranged, but recovers and releases him from his promise since she will not marry a Protestant.

Clementine League (klem′ẹn.tīn). See **Cognac, Holy League of.**

Clementis (klā.men′tēs), **Vladimir.** b. at Tisovec, in Slovakia. Sept. 20, 1902; executed at Prague, Dec. 3, 1952. Czechoslovakian statesman. He was a member of the Czech parliament after 1935 and during World War II served with the Czech government-in-exile at London. After the war he was state secretary in the ministry of foreign affairs until 1948, when the death of Jan Masaryk left the post of foreign minister unoccupied. Clementis held the foreign portfolio until 1950, when he was forced out by the Communists, and in 1952, at the "purge" trial in which it was said that he was the only non-Jewish defendant, was found guilty of treason, espionage, and sabotage, and executed. Author of *T. G. Masaryk and Slovakia* (1937) and others.

Clement of Alexandria (klem′ẹnt). [Called also: **Clemens Alexandrinus;** full Latin name, **Titus Flavius Clemens.**] b. probably at Athens, c150 A.D.; d. in Palestine, c215 A.D. Greek theologian, a father of the primitive church. He was head of the cathechetical school at Alexandria, in the period c190–c203, Origen being his pupil and successor, and one of the most noted of the founders of the Alexandrian school of theology. His attempts to ally Greek pagan thought, which he knew thoroughly, with Christianity, and his efforts to use the arguments of heretic sects, such as the Gnostics, to strengthen Christianity mark him as a philosophic rather than an emotional believer in the truth of Christianity. Several of his works survive.

Clement of Rome. See Saint **Clement I.**

Clementon (klem′ẹn.tọn). Borough in SW New Jersey, in Camden County: manufactures of charcoal. 3,191 (1950).

Clements (klem′ẹnts), **Edith.** [Maiden name, **Schwartz.**] b. at Albany, N.Y.—. American botanist and illustrator; wife of Frederic Edward Clements. She was graduated (Ph.D., 1906) from the University of Nebraska, was instructor in botany (1909–13) at the University of Minnesota, and served as an investigator and illustrator (1918–41) for the Carnegie Institution at Washington, D.C. She is the author of *Relation of Leaf Structure to Physical Factors* (1905), *Flowers of Mountain and Plain* (1913), *Flower Pageant of the Midwest* (1939), and *Flowers of Prairie and Woodland* (1947).

Clements, Frederic Edward. b. at Lincoln, Neb., Sept. 16, 1874; d. July 26, 1945. American naturalist, professor of botany at the University of Minnesota from 1907; husband of Edith Clements. He taught at the University of Nebraska from 1894 to 1907. His studies relate especially to experimental evolution, alpine vegetation, and forest ecology. He was head (1917–41) of ecological research at the Carnegie Institution, Washington, D.C., and aided (1934 *et seq.*) on the U.S. soil conservation project.

Clement's Inn. Inn of court in London, W of the New Law Courts. The original structure has now long since disappeared. It was intended, at the time of its establishment, for the use of patients who came to take the waters of nearby St. Clement's Well, but Sir William Dugdale speaks of it as being in existence in the reign of Edward II as an inn of chancery. Shakespeare speaks of it as the home of Master Shallow in his youth. It was later rebuilt and became the home of the Fabian Society, the Playgoers' Club, and other societies. From it the famous London church of Saint Clement Danes derived its name.

Clemenza di Tito (klā.men′tsä dē tē′tō), **La.** [Eng. trans., "*The Clemency of Titus.*"] Opera in two acts by Wolfgang Amadeus Mozart, with a libretto by Caterino Mazzola, first performed at the Prague National Theater on Sept. 6, 1791. It was Mozart's last opera (Köchel catalogue number 621).

Clemmer (klem′ėr), **Mary.** [Married names: **Ames** and **Hudson.**] b. at Utica, N.Y., May 6, 1839; d. at Washington, D.C., Aug. 18, 1884. American writer and Washington correspondent of the New York *Independent*. She published novels, poems, sketches, and other works. After her divorce (1874) from Daniel Ames, she married Edmund Hudson in 1883.

Clemson (klem′sọn), **Thomas Green.** b. at Philadelphia, July 1, 1807; d. April 6, 1888. American mining engineer, founder of Clemson College in South Carolina through a provision in his will. He was a consulting mining engineer (1832–39) at Paris, Philadelphia, and Washington, chargé d'affaires (1844–51) in Belgium, and superintendent (1859–61) of agriculture and supervisor (1865) of mines and metal works of the Trans-Mississippi Department.

Clendening (klen.den′ing), **Logan.** b. at Kansas City, Mo., May 25, 1884; d. there, Jan. 31, 1945. American physician and author. He was graduated (M.D., 1907) from the University of Kansas, where he was instructor in internal medicine (1910–17), associate professor of medicine (1920–28), and professor of clinical medicine (1928 *et seq.*). He served in the Medical Corps of the U.S. army in World War I. His works include *Modern Methods of Treatment* (1924), *The Human Body* (1927), *The Care and Feeding of Adults* (1931), and *Behind the Doctor* (1933). Dr. Clendening became widely known through his syndicated newspaper column on medicine.

Clendenin's Settlement (klen.den′inz). Former name of **Charleston,** W.Va.

Clennam (klen′ạm), **Arthur.** In Charles Dickens's *Little Dorrit*, the adopted (although reputed to be the actual) son of Mrs. Clennam, employer of Amy Dorrit (called "Little Dorrit"). After a harsh childhood and 20 years in the Far East, Arthur returns home to a chilly welcome by the woman supposed to be his mother, and meets Amy in her house. A bond grows between the two and, after serving a sentence in prison for debts incurred by a failure in business, Arthur marries her.

Clennell (klen′ẹl), **Luke.** b. at Ulgham, near Morpeth, Northumberland, England, April 8, 1781; d. Feb. 9, 1840. English painter and wood engraver, an apprentice and pupil of Thomas Bewick.

Cleobis (klē′ọ.bis). See **Biton and Cleobis.**

Cleobulus (klē.ọ.bū′lus, klẹ.ob′ụ.lus). b. at Lindus, Rhodes; fl. in the 6th century B.C. One of the Seven Sages of Greece; tyrant of Lindus. The reputed author of various riddles, he is credited with having formulated the first literary riddle. His daughter Cleobuline shares his reputed skill in riddles, being credited with inventing the riddle on the year: "A father has 12 children, each has 30 daughters, white on one side, black on the other; all are immortal, yet they die."

Cleofas (klē′ọ.fạs), **Don.** High-spirited Spanish student in Alain René Le Sage's novel *Le Diable boiteux*. Asmodeus exhibits to him, in a very dramatic manner indeed, the fortunes of the inmates of the houses of Madrid by actually unroofing the houses so that he may look into them.

Cléomadès (klā.*o*.må.des), **Adventures of.** Early French poem (about the end of the 13th century), also known as *Le Cheval de fust* (The Wooden Horse), by Adenet (called le Roi). Its central incident is the introduction of a wooden horse, like that in *The Arabian Nights' Entertainments*, which transports its rider wherever he wishes to go. The poem, 20,000 lines long, enjoyed great popularity.

Cleombrotus I (klẹ.om′brọ.tus). Killed at Leuctra, 371 B.C. King of Sparta from 380 to 371. He waged war with the Thebans, and was defeated by them at Leuctra.

Cleomedes (klē.ọ.mē′dēz). fl. c150–200 B.C. Greek astronomer whose birthplace and residence are unknown. He wrote a treatise on astronomy and cosmography, entitled *The Circular Theory of the Heavenly Bodies*, in which he maintains that the earth is spherical, that the number of the fixed stars is infinite, and that the moon's rotation on its axis is performed in the same time as its synodical revolution about the earth. His treatise contains also the first notice of the theory of atmospherical refraction.

Cleomenes (klẹ.om′ẹ.nēz). Sicilian noble in Shakespeare's *The Winter's Tale*.

Cleomenes I. fl. c519–c491 B.C. King of Sparta from c519 to c491 B.C. He expelled Hippias from Athens in 510, and aided Isagoras in his attempt to oust Cleisthenes soon after. He deposed (491) his co-sovereign (Sparta had two kings ruling as colleagues) Demaratus, reportedly by bribing the Delphic oracle. He was one of Sparta's most able kings, but merciless; he is remembered for his killing of some 6,000 of the soldiers of Argos in battle.

Cleomenes III. d. c219 B.C. King of Sparta from c235 to c220 B.C. He abolished the ephorate (a magistracy controlling the kings) in 225, waged war with the Achaean League and Macedonia in the period 225–222, and was defeated at Sellasia c222.

Cleomenes, or The Spartan Hero. Play (1692) by John Dryden, modeled on the lines of French tragedy. Part of the fifth act is by Thomas Southerne. The story is taken from Plutarch's account of the life of Cleomenes III of Sparta.

Cleon (klē′on). Killed at Amphipolis, Macedon, 422 B.C. Athenian demagogue. He was the son of a tanner. Coming forward shortly after the death of Pericles as leader of the democratic party, he violently opposed Nicias, the head of the aristocratic party, who advocated peace with Sparta and the conclusion of the Peloponnesian War. He led a successful expedition against the Spartans at Pylos in 425, capturing a force on the island of Sphacteria and bringing them captive to Athens. Since he had promised to do so despite the Spartans' reputation for never being taken alive, his reputation swelled. Cleon was in 422 entrusted with the command of an expedition destined to act against Brasidas in Chalcidice. He was defeated by the latter at Amphipolis, and fell in the flight. He was satirized by Aristophanes, especially in the *Knights* (424) in which Aristophanes himself was forced to play Cleon, none of the players daring to take the role of the popular hero. Thucydides too, the historian of the Peloponnesian War, expressed a dislike for Cleon.

Cleon. In Shakespeare's *Pericles, Prince of Tyre,* the governor of Tarsus, burned to death to avenge the supposed murder of Marina.

Cléonte (klā.ônt). Lover of Lucille in Molière's comedy *Le Bourgeois gentilhomme.* Since Cléonte is not of noble birth, Jourdain, Lucille's father, refuses to countenance their marriage. Cléonte masquerades as the "Grand Turk," confers a nonsensical title on Jourdain, and obtains his consent.

Cleopas (klē′ō.pas). In the New Testament, one of the two disciples who were accompanied by the risen Jesus in their walk to Emmaus. Luke, xxiv.

Cleopatra (klē.ō.pā′tra, -pat′ra, -pä′tra). [In the chronology of Egyptian queens, **Cleopatra VII.**] b. at Alexandria, Egypt, 69 B.C.; d. there, 30 B.C. Last Macedonian queen of Egypt; daughter of Ptolemy XI (sometimes XIII), called Ptolemy Auletes. In accordance with Egyptian tradition, she was wife of and joint ruler with her brother Ptolemy XII (or XIV) from 51 to 49, when she was expelled by him. Her reinstatement in 48 by Caesar gave rise to war between Caesar and Ptolemy. The latter was defeated and killed, and his younger brother, Ptolemy XIII (or XV), was elevated to the throne in his stead and married to her. Cleopatra lived with Caesar at Rome from 46 to 44, and had by him a son, Ptolemy XIV (or XVI), usually known as Caesarion because of his father; the child was afterward put to death by Augustus. She returned to Egypt after the murder of Caesar, and in the civil war which ensued sided with the Triumvirate (Augustus, Antony, and Lepidus). Mark Antony having been appointed ruler of Asia and the East, she visited him at Tarsus, Cilicia, in 41, making a voyage of extraordinary splendor and magnificence up the Cydnus. She gained by her charms a complete ascendancy over him. On her account he divorced his wife Octavia, the sister of Augustus, in 32. Augustus declared war against her in 31. The fleet of Antony and Cleopatra was defeated in the same year at the battle of Actium, which was decided by the flight of Cleopatra's ships, Antony being forced to follow. After the death of Antony, who killed himself on hearing a false report of her death (according to some, a report deliberately spread by her in an attempt to win Augustus's favor by causing his death), she poisoned herself to avoid being exhibited at Rome at the triumph of Augustus, but not until she had made an attempt to charm Augustus as she had Caesar and Antony. According to the popular belief, she applied to her bosom an asp that had been secretly conveyed to her in a basket of figs. She had three children by Antony. Besides extraordinary charms of person, she possessed an active and cultivated mind, and is said to have been able to converse in seven languages. Her reputed personality and the events of the latter part of her reign, as described by Plutarch, form the basis of Shakespeare's *Antony and Cleopatra;* this play was later adapted by John Dryden as *All for Love.* Geroge Bernard Shaw's *Caesar and Cleopatra* tells the story (considerably modified by Shaw) of Julius Caesar and the young Cleopatra.

Cleopatra's Needles. Pair of Egyptian obelisks of red granite, made c1500 B.C., which were transported from Heliopolis to Alexandria in the 18th year (c14 B.C.) of Augustus. One of them was taken to London and set up on the Thames embankment in 1878, and the other was soon after brought to New York and erected in Central Park. The latter is ab. 67 ft. high to its sharp apex, and 7 ft. 7 in. in diameter at the base. It stands on a massive cube of granite, on which it is supported by four great bronze crabs, imitating the ancient originals. It is covered on all its faces with deeply incised hieroglyphs, which present the names of Thutmose III, Ramses II, and Seti II (16th–13th centuries B.C.). There is no known connection between these obelisks and Cleopatra.

Cleopatra's Night. Opera in two acts by Henry Hadley, with a libretto by Alice Leal Pollock based on one of Théophile Gautier's stories, first performed at the New York Metropolitan Opera House on Jan. 31, 1920.

Cléopâtre (klā.o.pätr). Queen in Pierre Corneille's tragedy *Rodogune.* A second Medea, she plots the death of her two sons in order to satisfy her ambition to reign. She succeeds, however, in killing only one of them.

Cléopâtre. Play by Victorien Sardou, with Émile Moreau. It was written for Sarah Bernhardt, and produced in 1890.

Cleophon (klē′ō.fon). d. c405 B.C. Athenian demagogue, said to have been of Thracian origin. He opposed the oligarchical party, and successfully used his influence to prevent peace with Sparta after the battles of Cyzicus (410), Arginusae (406), and Aegospotami (405). He was sentenced to death in 405 or 404 by the Athenian council.

Cleopolis (klē.op′ō.lis). Name given by Edmund Spenser in *The Faerie Queene* to the city of London.

Clerc (kler), **Jean Le.** See **Le Clerc, Jean.**

Clerc, Laurent. b. at La Balme, Isère, France, Dec. 26, 1785; d. at Hartford, Conn., July 18, 1869. French educator of the handicapped. A deaf-mute, he was one of the founders, with Thomas Hopkins Gallaudet, of a free school for the deaf and dumb at Hartford in 1817.

Clérel de Tocqueville (klā.rel de tok.vēl), **Alexis Charles Henri.** See **Tocqueville, Alexis Charles Henri Clérel de.**

Clerfayt (kler.fe′) or **Clairfayt,** Count **von.** [Title of **François Sébastien Charles Joseph de Croix.**] b. at Bruille, Hainaut, Low Countries, Oct. 14, 1733; d. at Vienna, July 19, 1798. Austrian general. He served with distinction in the Turkish war (1788–91), took part in actions against the French at Aldenhoven and Neerwinden (1793), and defeated Jean Baptiste Jourdan at Höchst (Oct. 11, 1795).

Clericis Laicos (kler′i.sis lā′i.kos). Name (actually the opening words) of a bull published by Pope Boniface VIII, on Feb. 25, 1296. It forbade the clergy to pay taxes on church property without the consent of the Holy See, and was intended to stop the continued use by Philip IV of France of a special tax originally meant for application to the campaigns against the Albigensian heresy. It was abrogated (1311) by Pope Clement V.

Clericus (kler′i.kus), **Johannes.** Latinized name of **Le Clerc, Jean.**

Clerimond (kler′i.mond). Sister of Ferragus the giant in the romance *Valentine and Orson,* a part of the Carolingian cycle of early French literature. She marries Valentine.

Clerimont (kler′i.mont). Gay friend of Sir Dauphine in Ben Jonson's *Epicoene, or the Silent Woman.*

Clerimont. Lover of Clarinda in Colley Cibber's comedy *The Double Gallant.* He assists Atall and Careless in their schemes.

Clerk (klärk), Sir **Dugald.** b. at Glasgow, Scotland, March 31, 1854; d. at Ewhurst, Surrey, England, Nov. 12, 1932. Scottish engineer and authority on internal-combustion engines. He invented (1877–81) the Clerk-cycle gas engine (an engine with a two-stroke cycle), and is known also for his researches on the properties and commercial possibilities of fuel in the gaseous state, gas lighting, and heating. During World War I he served as director of engineering research at the British Admiralty. He was the author of *The Gas Engine* (1886) and other works.

Clerk of Penicuik, Sir **John.** b. 1684; d. 1755. Scottish antiquary and patron of Allan Ramsay (1686–1758), Scottish poet. He was a member of the Scottish Parliament (1702–07) and a commissioner (1707) for the union with England. While judge of the court of exchequer in Scotland (1708–55), he collected antiquities and wrote antiquarian tracts.

Clerk of Eldin, **John.** b. at Penicuik, Scotland, Dec. 10, 1728; d. at Eldin, near Edinburgh, May 10, 1812. Scottish merchant of Edinburgh; son of Sir John Clerk of Penicuik. He was the author of *Essay on Naval Tactics* (1790; second and third parts, 1797) which gave rise to a heated controversy, due to the claim of the author, supported by others, that his plans (which were circulated privately before publication) had been adopted by Admiral George Rodney at Dominica, on April 12, 1782.

Clerke (klärk), **Agnes Mary.** b. in Ireland, Feb. 10, 1842; d. at London, Jan. 20, 1907. British astronomer. She made astronomical observations at the Royal Observatory, Cape of Good Hope, in 1888, won the Actonian prize in 1893, and in 1901 wrote the Hodgkins essay on low-temperature research at the Royal Institution. Her works include *The System of the Stars* (1890), *The Herschels and Modern Astronomy* (1895), *Astronomy* (1898; with A. Fowler and J. E. Gore), and *Problems in Astrophysics* (1903).

Clerke, Charles. b. 1741; d. in Kamchatka, Siberia, Aug. 22, 1779. British navigator. He served with Cook on all three of his voyages, and commanded the expedition after Cook's death in 1779.

Clerkenwell (klär′ken.wel, -wel). Former civil parish in E central London, in the County of London, in Finsbury metropolitan borough. It formerly bore an evil reputation. Clerkenwell Green was in the 17th century surrounded by fine mansions, and, among many other noted men, Izaak Walton lived there. Its name derives from the well beside which the clerks of London parish formerly enacted the old miracle plays.

Clerk-Maxwell (klärk′maks′wel, -wel), **James.** See **Maxwell, James Clerk.**

Clerk's Tale, The. Tale told by the Oxford student in Chaucer's *The Canterbury Tales*. It is founded upon Boccaccio's story of the patient Griselda, which the clerk states he read in Petrarch's version.

Clermont (kler.môn). Medieval county in France, in the government of Île-de-France. It was situated N of Paris. Capital, Clermont-de-l'Oise.

Clermont (kler′mont). Steamboat designed and used by Robert Fulton on his first trip (Aug. 17–22, 1807) from New York to Albany, in the beginning of steam navigation.

Clermont, Baron. A title of **Fortescue, Chichester Samuel.**

Clermont (kler.môn; Anglicized, kler′mont), **Council of.** Council convened (1095) by Pope Urban II at Clermont-Ferrand, France. It was attended by four archbishops, 225 bishops, and an immense number of lower clergy and laity. It proclaimed the first Crusade, forbade the investiture of bishops by the laity and the assumption of feudal obligations to laymen by the clergy, and excommunicated Philip I of France, who had repudiated his queen Bertha (daughter of Robert I, Count of Flanders, known as Robert the Frisian), and espoused Bertrada, the wife of Fulk of Anjou.

Clermont, Robert, Count of. See under **Bourbon.**

Clermont-de-l'Oise (kler.môn.de.lwäz). [Also: **Clermont, Clermont-en-Beauvaisis** (-tän.bō.ve.zē).] Town in N France, in the department of Oise, situated on the Brèche River, ab. 35 mi. N of Paris. The Hôtel de Ville, dating from 1328, rebuilt in the period 1874–87, and the Church of Saint-Samson, dating from the 14th century, are historical monuments. The medieval county of Clermont had its capital here. 5,331 (1946).

Clermont-Ferrand (-fe.rän). [Also: **Clermont;** Latin, **Augustonemetum.**] City in C France, the capital of the department of Puy-de-Dôme. The city, surrounded by mountains, is one of the centers of the European rubber industry but also has important metallurgical and construction industries and manufactures of precision instruments, chemicals, and linen. Candies, candied fruits, and fine chocolates are specialties. The cathedral, dating from the 13th–15th centuries and the Church of Notre-Dame-du-port, dating from the 12th century, are noteworthy. The quiet little town of Montferrand, which has preserved its Renaissance character, is nearby. Clermont-Ferrand was the birthplace of Gregory of Tours and of Blaise Pascal. The Council of Clermont was held here in 1095. Some damage was done in the city by air raids during World War II. 108,090 (1946).

Clermont-Ganneau (-gå.nō), **Charles.** b. at Paris, Feb. 19, 1846; d. there, Feb. 16, 1923. French Orientalist. He taught (1890 *et seq.*) at the Collège de France. While serving as a professional interpreter at Jerusalem (1868), he acquired for the Louvre parts of the famous so-called Mesha or Moabite stone, the only inscription recovered as yet from the kingdom of Moab. He was the author of *Recueil d'archéologie orientale* (Compendium of Oriental Archaeology, 1885–1924).

Clermont-l'Hérault (-lā.rō). [Also, **Clermont-de-Lodève** (-de.lo.dev).] Town in S France, in the department of Hérault, ab. 23 mi. W of Montpellier. It produces woolen cloth. 5,195 (1946).

Cléron (klā.rôn), **Gabriel Paul Othenin Bernard de.** See **Haussonville, Bernard,** Comte **d'.**

Cléry (klā.rē), **Jean Baptiste.** b. at Jardy, near Versailles, France, May 11, 1759; d. at Hietzing, near Vienna, May 27, 1809. Attendant of Louis XVI in his captivity (1792–93). He published (1798) a journal.

Clésinger (klā.zan.zhā), **Jean Baptiste Auguste.** b. at Besançon, France, Oct. 22, 1814; d. at Paris, Jan. 7, 1883. French sculptor. His works include *Girl Bitten by a Serpent* (1847) and *Cleopatra before Caesar* (1869).

Cletus (klē′tus). See **Anacletus,** Saint.

Cleuch (klöch), **Ben.** See under **Ochil Hills.**

Cleve (klā′ve). [Also: **Kleve;** Dutch, **Kleef;** English, **Cleves;** French, **Clèves.**] Ancient duchy of Germany, lying along the lower Rhine below Cologne. It was united with the county of Mark about 1400, and soon after raised to a duchy. Cleve, Jülich, and Berg were united in 1521. The extinction of the male line of the dukes of Cleve in 1609, and the outbreak of the Contest of the Jülich Succession, resulted in 1666 in the cession of Cleve, with Mark, to Brandenburg, which had taken them in 1614. In 1801 the part on the left bank of the Rhine, and in 1803 and 1805 the other portions, were ceded to France by Prussia. After the downfall of Napoleon, the duchy, with the exception of lands bordering on the Maas (Meuse) and some districts toward the north, was restored to Prussia, and became part of the *Kreis* (district or circle) of Düsseldorf.

Cleve. [Also: **Kleve;** Dutch, **Kleef;** English, **Cleves;** French, **Clèves.**] City in W Germany, in the *Land* (state) of North Rhine-Westphalia, British Zone, formerly in the Rhine Province, Prussia, situated on the Spoy Canal, near the lower Rhine River and the Dutch border, ab. 66 mi. W of Münster. It has dairies, oil and margarine factories, a sugar refinery, metallurgical, shoe, and furniture manufactures. There are ferruginous springs. The city, in which Dutch architecture prevails, was very heavily damaged in World War II; of the Gothic Stiftskirche only the chapel containing the tombs of the dukes of Cleve was saved; the Saalkirche, built in the 17th century, the residential castle, the Schwanenburg castle above the city, and other monuments were either entirely or nearly destroyed. The city was the seat of the counts of Cleve in the early Middle Ages; it came under the rule of the counts of Mark in 1368, who later became dukes of Cleve, Jülich, and Berg. Cleve fell to Brandenburg in 1614, to France in 1801, and back to Prussia in 1814. It was occupied by the Belgians from 1919 to 1925. It was the northern anchorage of the German Westwall (Siegfried Line) in World War II, and was occupied by Canadian troops on Feb. 12, 1945. The population is predominantly Roman Catholic. 23,154 (1946), 17,825 (1950).

Cleve (klā′ve̩) or **Cleef** (klāf), **Joos van.** [Original name, **Joos van der Beke**; identified with the **Master of the Death of Mary.**] d. 1540. Flemish painter. Active at Antwerp after 1511, he is known for his religious paintings as well as for his portraits. His portrait of Henry VIII is at Hampton Court. For many years art historians attributed a number of paintings, apparently by the same hand, to an unknown whom they called the Master of the Death of Mary because two paintings on that subject, of unknown authorship, were used as standards of comparison. Recent research has established Joos van Cleve as the painter of this group of works.

Cleve, Per Theodor. b. at Stockholm, Sweden, 1840; d. 1905. Swedish chemist. He experimented extensively on the chemistry of rare-earth compounds, chromium and platinum amine complexes, and isomers of the disubstituted naphthalenes. His rare-earth work included the demonstration that scandium is identical with Mendelejeff's eka boron. He is credited with the discovery of the elements holmium (which he named for Stockholm) and thulium (after Thule, ancient name for the far north). He was a professor at Uppsala, and was awarded the Davy Medal in 1894.

Clevedon (klēv′do̩n). Urban district and seaside resort in SW England, in Somersetshire, situated on the limestone headlands in the Severn Estuary ab. 15 mi. SW of Bristol, ab. 133 mi. W of London by rail. It was formerly a small seaport. 9,467 (1951).

Cleveland (klēv′la̩nd). Mountainous district in NE England, in the North Riding of Yorkshire. It is noted principally for its iron mining and its foundries. Iron ore found here is phosphoric and ab. 29 percent iron content. The reserves are estimated at 440 million tons; however, imported ores are now being used by the Cleveland foundries to an increasing extent. The district is ab. 28 mi. by 15 mi.

Cleveland. Town in NW Mississippi, a county seat (with Rosedale) of Bolivar County. It is the seat of Delta State Teachers College. 6,747 (1950).

Cleveland. [Sometimes called the **"Forest City."**] City in NE Ohio, county seat of Cuyahoga County, at the mouth of the Cuyahoga River on Lake Erie: largest city in Ohio and seventh largest in the U.S. Manufactures of iron and steel are among Cleveland's major industries; it is the second most important machine-tool manufacturing city in the U.S., and a large producer of clothing, rayon, salt, clay products, Diesel engines, storage batteries, refined petroleum, automobile and airplane parts, paints and varnishes, and electrical equipment. It is known for its well laid out streets, many shade trees, and beautiful suburbs. Educational institutions include Cleveland College, the John Huntington Polytechnic Institute, the Case School of Technology, Western Reserve University, Fenn College, John Carroll University, Ursuline College for Women, and the Cleveland School of Art. The plan of Cleveland was platted by Moses Cleaveland in 1796, and the name was originally spelled like his; it was incorporated as a city in 1836. Beginning with the first lake ships in the early 19th century, it began to receive traffic by canal, lake, and rail, and developed into one of the chief shipping and transportation centers of the Midwest. Marcus Hanna, John D. Rockefeller, Newton D. Baker, and the Van Sweringen brothers are among those who have lived at Cleveland. 878,336 (1940), 914,808 (1950).

Cleveland. City in SE Tennessee, county seat of Bradley County, ab. 26 mi. NE of Chattanooga: manufactures of hosiery and wood products. It was incorporated in 1838. Pop. 12,605 (1950).

Cleveland. City in E Texas, in Liberty County, in the San Jacinto valley ab. 40 mi. NE of Houston: lumber, oil, and farm products. In the decade between the last two U.S. censuses its population more than doubled. 1,783 (1940), 5,183 (1950).

Cleveland, Duchess of. A title of **Villiers, Barbara.**

Cleveland, Captain Clement. The pirate in Sir Walter Scott's novel *The Pirate*. He falls in love with Minna Troil but eventually is captured and parted from her.

Cleveland, Charles Dexter. b. at Salem, Mass., Dec. 3, 1802; d. at Philadelphia, Aug. 18, 1869. American author and educator. He published *Compendium of English Literature* (1850) and *Compendium of American Literature* (1858).

Cleveland, Frederick Albert. b. at Sterling, Ill., March 17, 1865; d. Jan. 26, 1946. American economist and educator. He studied for the bar but turned from a legal career to teach, first at the University of Chicago, later at the University of Pennsylvania and at New York University, serving (1903–05) as professor of finance at the last-named institution. He was director of the bureaus of municipal research of New York and of Philadelphia (1907–17), and as head of a commission (1910–13) appointed by President William Howard Taft to study efficiency in the federal government, he recommended a national budget. For a time he was financial adviser to the Chinese government, and from 1919 until his retirement in 1939 he taught citizenship at Boston University. Among his books on civic and economic matters are *Growth of Democracy in the United States* (1898), *Funds and Their Uses* (1902), *The Bank and the Treasury* (1905), and *Chapters on Municipal Administration and Accounting* (1909).

Cleveland, Grover. [Full name, **Stephen Grover Cleveland.**] b. at Caldwell, N.J., March 18, 1837; d. at Princeton, N.J., June 24, 1908. American statesman, twice (1885–89, 1893–97) president of the United States. He studied law at Buffalo, N.Y., was admitted to the bar in 1859, and was assistant district attorney (1863–66), of Erie County, in which Buffalo is located, but was defeated in a bid for election as district attorney in 1865. In 1871 he was elected sheriff of Erie County, holding office into 1874, and in 1881 became mayor of Buffalo. His campaign against corruption in the government of that city won him the Democratic Party nomination for the governorship of New York, to which he was elected in 1882. His support, as governor, of reform measures, alienated some of the machine politicians, but won him the Democratic nomination for president, and in the election of 1884 he became the first Democrat to win that office after 1856. In his first term as president he brought about limited civil service reform, curbed excessive pension legislation, and advocated lower tariffs on foreign commerce. In the election of 1888 he secured a popular majority but was defeated in the electoral college by Benjamin Harrison. In 1892, however, again running against Harrison, he was elected for the second time. The financial panic of 1893 confronted him, soon after his second inauguration, with grave problems. A large faction within his own party, and some Republicans, advocated the free coinage of silver as a panacea for the country's economic troubles, but President Cleveland secured the repeal, by a special session of Congress, of the purchasing clause of the so-called Sherman Silver Law. In 1894 a strike against the Pullman Parlor Car Company caused some violence at Chicago, and a member of Cleveland's cabinet induced him to send federal troops into Illinois over the protest of Governor Altgeld of that state. During both of his administrations Cleveland invoked the Monroe Doctrine to warn Great Britain against aggressive action against Venezuela over a disputed boundary with British Guiana. The nomination of William J. Bryan as Democratic candidate for president in 1896 was in effect a rebuke to President Cleveland's course in the matter of free coinage of silver and in the Pullman strike. After William McKinley succeeded him in the White House in 1897 he retired to Princeton, N.J., and took little part in public affairs. In 1904 he published *Presidential Problems*, a defense of his policies as chief magistrate of the nation.

Cleveland, John. [Also, **Cleiveland.**] b. at Loughborough, Leicestershire, England, in June, 1613; d. April 29, 1658. English poet, an active Royalist during the English Civil War, and a satirist of the Parliamentary party. He was graduated (B.A., 1631) from Christ's College, Cambridge, and was elected a fellow of St. John's College in 1634. He joined the Royalist army at Oxford, and was made judge-advocate, remaining with the garrison of Newark, in Nottinghamshire, until its surrender. In 1655 he was arrested and imprisoned at Yarmouth, but was soon released by order of Cromwell. One of the Cavalier poets, he wrote satires, including *Scots Apostasie, Hue and Cry after Sir John Presbyter, The Mixt Assembly*, and *Smectymnuus, or the Club Divine*. His poems were collected in 1661.

Cleveland, Mount. See under **Glacier National Park,** in Montana.

Cleveland Heights. [Former names: **Turkey Ridge, Heather Ridge.**] City in NE Ohio, in Cuyahoga County: residential suburb of Cleveland. It was established in 1905 and became a city in 1921. Pop. 59,141 (1950).

Cleveland Museum of Natural History. Museum at Cleveland, Ohio, incorporated in 1920, when it assumed the functions and holdings of the Kirtland Society of Natural Sciences and the Cleveland Academy of Sciences. It operates the Cleveland Zoo, and the Holden Arboretum at Kirtland, Ohio, ab. 30 mi. E of Cleveland. The museum publishes *The Explorer*, a quarterly, has a library of ab. 17,000 volumes and ab. 75,000 pamphlets on natural history, and features the ethnology of the Mound Builders and certain primitive African peoples.

Cleveland National Forest. Forest reserve in S California, formerly known as the San Jacinto and renamed in 1908 by President Theodore Roosevelt in honor of President Cleveland.

Clevenger (klev′ẹn.jėr), **Shobal Vail.** b. near Middletown, Ohio, 1812; d. at sea, Sept. 23, 1843. American sculptor; father of Shobal Vail Clevenger (1843–1920). He apprenticed himself to a stonecutter at Cincinnati and later studied and worked for a time in Italy. Among his works are portrait busts of Washington Allston, Daniel Webster, and Henry Clay.

Clevenger, Shobal Vail. b. at Florence, Italy, March 24, 1843; d. March 24, 1920. American psychiatrist; son of Shobal Vail Clevenger (1812–43). He was special pathologist (1883) at the Cook County Insane Asylum at Dunning, Ill., where he was the first to make brain autopsies. Later he lectured at the Chicago Art Institute, School of Pharmacy, and Law School, and was superintendent (1893) of the Illinois Eastern Hospital for the Insane at Kankakee, Ill. He was the author of *Comparative Physiology and Psychology* (1884), *Spinal Concussion* (1889), *Medical Jurisprudence of Insanity* (2 vols., 1898), *The Evolution of Man and His Mind* (1903), and *Therapeutics, Materia Medica and the Practice of Medicine* (1905).

Cleveringa (klā′vẹ.ring.ạ), **Rudolph Pabus.** b. at Appingendam, Netherlands, April 2, 1894—. Dutch teacher. He was graduated (LL.D., 1919) from the University of Leiden, where he later (1927) became professor of commercial and procedural law. He also served as editor of *Themis*. In 1945 he was appointed state counselor in special government service.

Cleves (klēvz). English name of **Cleve.**

Clèves (klev). French name of **Cleve.**

Clew Bay (klö). Small inlet of the Atlantic Ocean in Connacht province, Irish Republic, in County Mayo, ab. 12 mi. W of Castlebar. Length, ab. 15 mi.; width, ab. 8 mi.

Clews (klöz), **Henry.** b. in Staffordshire, England, Aug. 14, 1834; d. Jan. 31, 1923. American investment banker and stockbroker whose firm was by the end of the Civil War second only to Cooke and Company in handling of U.S. war bonds. He arrived (c1850) in the U.S. and organized (c1858) the firm of Stout, Clews and Mason. He wrote *Fifty Years of Wall Street* (1908) and other works.

Clichy (klē.shē). [Also: **Clichy-la-Garenne** (-là.gȧ.ren); ancient name, **Clippiacum.**] Town in N France, in the department of Seine, situated on the Seine River, 1 mi. N of the former fortifications of Paris. It is an industrial suburb of Paris and a river port. 53,029 (1946).

Clicquot (klē.kō), **François Henri.** [Also, **Cliquot.**] b. at Paris, 1728; d. there, 1790. French manufacturer of organs. He was responsible for constructing the organs at various Paris churches, including Notre-Dame, Saint Nicholas des Champs, and Saint Sulpice.

Clifden (klif′dẹn). Market town and seaport in Connacht province, Irish Republic, in County Galway, situated on an inlet of Ardbear Bay, ab. 43 mi. NW of Galway city. Clifden is situated in the Connemara district of County Galway, which is devoted to fishing and subsistence agriculture. It is a wireless telegraph station; commercial messages have been transmitted since 1907 between Clifden and Glace Bay, Nova Scotia. 1,019 (1936).

Cliff Dwellers. Collective term for the pre-Columbian Pueblo Indian tribes that built their towns at the bases of cliffs or under great overhanging shelves of rock in what is now N Mexico and the SW part of the U.S. They were a communal, agricultural people and developed the valleys below their dwellings. The remains of their kivas (religious ceremonial chambers) indicate that modern Pueblo rituals are similar to those of the Cliff Dwellers. The practice of cliff-dwelling was abandoned at about the time of the first contacts with the Spanish, and present Pueblo Indian towns are located in the open or on tablelands.

Cliff-Dwellers, The. Novel by Henry B. Fuller, published in 1893.

Clifford (klif′ọrd), Lady. [First married name, Mrs. **Henry de la Pasture;** maiden name, **Elizabeth Lydia Rosabelle Bonham.**] b. at Naples, Italy, 1866; d. 1945. English novelist and dramatist; daughter of Edward William Bonham; married (1887) Count Henry Philip Ducarel de la Pasture (d. 1908); married (1910) Sir Hugh Charles Clifford (1866–1941); mother of Elizabeth Monica Dashwood (1890–1943), known as E. M. Delafield. Among her novels are *The Little Squire* (1893; dramatized 1894), *A Toy Tragedy* (1894), *Deborah of Tod's* (1897; dramatized 1909), *Adam Grigson* (1899), *Catherine of Calais* (1901), *Cornelius* (1903), *Peter's Mother* (1905; dramatized 1906), *The Man from America* (1905), *The Lonely Lady of Grosvenor Square* (1907), *The Grey Knight* (1907), *Catherine's Child* (1909), *The Tyrant* (1909), *Master Christopher* (1911), *Erica* (1912), and *Michael Ferrys* (1913). She also wrote the plays *The Lonely Millionaires* (1906) and *Her Grace the Reformer* (1906).

Clifford, Sir Bede Edmund Hugh. b. 1890—. English colonial administrator. He has been secretary to the governor general of Australia (1919–20) and the governor general of South Africa (1921–24), imperial secretary in South Africa, and governor of the Bahamas (1932–37) and Mauritius (1937–42). He was governor (1942–46) of Trinidad and Tobago.

Clifford, George. [Title, 3rd Earl of **Cumberland.**] b. at Brougham Castle, Westmorland, England, Aug. 8, 1558; d. at London, Oct. 30, 1605. English naval commander. Both before and after he fought as commander of a ship against the Spanish Armada (1588), he fitted out and commanded a number of buccaneering expeditions against the Spaniards in South America, the largest of which consisted of 20 ships and was undertaken in 1598. This expedition plundered San Juan de Puerto Rico in June, but failed to intercept the annual Spanish treasure fleet, and returned to England in October, 1598.

Clifford, Henry. [Title, 5th Earl of **Cumberland.**] b. at Londesborough, England, Feb. 28, 1591; d. at York, England, Dec. 11, 1643. English nobleman and Royalist. He was granted a B.A. by Oxford in 1609 and was named a Knight of the Bath in 1610. He was an active supporter of Charles II of England in Scotland during the English civil war, though not distinguished as a soldier.

Clifford, Henry de. [Titles: 14th Baron **Clifford,** 10th Baron of **Westmorland,** 1st Baron **Vesci;** called the **"Shepherd Lord."**] b. c1455; d. 1523. English nobleman. Because his father, Sir John de Clifford, had been attainted (1461) by the Yorkists, Clifford lived disguised as a shepherd until his estates were restored (1485) by Henry VII of England. In 1513 he fought at Flodden Field. Episodes from his early life were later used by William Wordsworth in *Song at the Feast of Brougham Castle* and *The White Doe of Rylstone.*

Clifford, Henry de. [Titles: 1st Earl of **Cumberland,** 15th Baron **Clifford,** 11th Baron of **Westmorland,** 2nd Baron **Vesci.**] b. 1493; d. April 22, 1542. English soldier; son of Henry de Clifford (c1455–1523). As sheriff (1522) of Yorkshire, he was engaged (1522–26) in border warfare between England and Scotland. He was created (June 18, 1525) Earl of Cumberland and made a Knight of the Garter seven years later. He was also president of the council of the north. Remaining loyal to Henry VIII, he signed (1530) the letter requesting sanction of the king's divorce. In October, 1536, he held his castle of Skipton against rebel assault, although his defenses were weakened by desertion. He continued in service against the Scots.

Clifford, Sir Hugh. b. at London, March 5, 1866; d. Dec. 18, 1941. British colonial administrator and governor; husband of Lady Clifford. He was active in the suppression of the Pahang rebellion (1892), and later served (1894) as commissioner to the Cocos-Keeling Islands, colonial secretary (1903–07) at Trinidad and

Tobago, colonial secretary (1907–12) at Ceylon, governor (1912–19) of the Gold Coast, governor (1919–25) of Nigeria, governor (1925–27) of Ceylon, governor (1927–29) of the Straits Settlements, high commissioner for the Malay States, and British Agent for Borneo. He was the author of *Studies in Brown Humanity* (1898), *Further India* (1904), *The Downfall of the Gods* (1911), *Malayan Monochromes* (1913), *The Gold Coast Regiment in the East African Campaign* (1920), *A Prince of Malaya* (1926), *Some Reflections on the Ceylon Land Question* (1927), and *Bush-whacking and Other Asiatic Tales and Memories* (1929); joint author with Sir Frank Swettenham of *Dictionary of the Malay Language.*

Clifford, John. b. at Sawley, Derbyshire, England, Oct. 16, 1836; d. Nov. 20, 1923. English Baptist clergyman, named minister of the Westbourne Park Chapel, London, in 1877. He had previously been minister of the Praed Street Chapel, London, in the period 1858–77. He was also president of the London Baptist Association in 1879, of the Baptist Union in 1888 and 1899, of the National Council of Evangelical Churches in 1898, and of the Baptist World Alliance in the period 1905–11. He advocated and led the opposition to the Education Act of 1902 by a method which became known as "passive resistance." Among his publications are *The Fight for Education: Clericalism in British Politics* (1902) and *The Ultimate Problems of Christianity* (1906).

Clifford, John de. [Titles: 13th Baron **Clifford,** 9th Baron of **Westmorland;** called **"the Butcher."**] b. c1435; killed at Ferrybridge, in March, 1461. English soldier. While fighting for the Lancastrian Henry VI of England during the Wars of the Roses, he was called "the Butcher" because of his acts of cruelty which included cutting off (1460) the head of the dead Edmund, Duke of York, and presenting it crowned to Queen Margaret. During the battle of Wakefield (December, 1460) he killed the Earl of Rutland, son of the Duke of York, with his own hands. He was attainted (1461) by Parliament, when Edward IV of the house of York came to the throne. He was killed on the eve of the battle of Towton.

Clifford, Lucy. [Maiden name, **Lane.**] b. at Barbados, British West Indies; d. April 21, 1929. English novelist, dramatist, and writer of books for children; wife (married 1875) of William Kingdon Clifford. Her works of fiction include *Anyhow Stories* (1882), *Mrs. Keith's Crime* (1885), *Love Letters of a Worldly Woman* (1891), *A Woman Alone* (1891; produced as a play, 1914), *Aunt Anne* (1893), *A Flash of Summer* (1895), *A Long Duel* (1901), *Sir George's Objection* (1910), *The House in Marylebone* (1917), *Miss Fingal* (1919), and *Eve's Lover* (1927). She also wrote the plays *The Likeness of the Night* (1901), *The Searchlight* (1913), and *Two's Company* (1915).

Clifford, Nathan. b. at Rumney, N.H., Aug. 18, 1803; d. July 25, 1881. American jurist. Elected (1830) to the Maine assembly, he served subsequently as attorney general (1834) of Maine. In 1838 he was elected to Congress. He served (1846–48) as U.S. attorney general under President Polk, and was sent (c1848) on a diplomatic mission to Mexico in connection with the treaty ending the Mexican War. From 1858 to 1881 he was a U.S. Supreme Court justice. He headed the special electoral commission investigating the Hayes-Tilden election in 1877.

Clifford, Robert de. [Titles: 5th Baron **Clifford,** 1st Baron of **Westmorland.**] b. 1273; killed at the battle of Bannockburn, June 24, 1314. English soldier. In 1297 he was appointed justice of the forests beyond Trent, and in the same year was captain and warden of the Scottish marshes and the county of Cumberland and governor of Carlisle. He served on active duty against the Scots from 1296. In 1300 he participated in the fall of the fortress of Carlaverock which then came under his custody. In 1312 he besieged Piers Gaveston, Edward II's favorite, in Scarborough Castle and after Gaveston's death became one of the representatives of the baronial party. He was defeated with his 800 chosen soldiers by Sir Thomas Randolph during the siege of Stirling (1314).

Clifford, Rosamond. [Called **"the Fair Rosamond."**] d. c1176. Daughter of Walter de Clifford (son of Richard Fitz Ponce, ancestor of the great Clifford family), and mistress of Henry II of England. She appears to have been publicly acknowledged by Henry as his mistress c1175, after he had imprisoned his queen, Eleanor of Aquitaine, for her part in his sons' revolt against him. On her death Rosamond was interred in Godstow nunnery. It is said that Hugh, bishop of Lincoln, who visited Godstow in 1191, was offended at the sight of her richly adorned tomb in the middle of the church choir before the altar, and caused its removal, probably to the chapter house. According to a popular legend, which has no foundation in fact, Henry built a labyrinth or maze to conceal her from Queen Eleanor, who nevertheless discovered her and put her to death. Rosamond is commonly, though erroneously, stated to have been the mother of William Longsword and of Geoffrey, archbishop of York.

Clifford, Sir Thomas. Lover of Julia in James Sheridan Knowles's play *The Hunchback.*

Clifford, Thomas. [Title, 1st Baron **Clifford of Chudleigh.**] b. at Ugbrooke, near Exeter, England, Aug. 1, 1630; d. in September, 1673. English politician, created 1st Baron Clifford of Chudleigh on April 22, 1672. As a member of the Cabal (a group of advisers to Charles II of England) in the period from 1667 to 1673, he held several posts, including that of lord treasurer. But the passage of the Test Act (1673), which was aimed at removing Roman Catholics from the government, resulted in his resignation from office and, according to John Evelyn, to his suicide.

Clifford, William Kingdon. b. at Exeter, England, May 4, 1845; d. on the island of Madeira, March 3, 1879. English mathematician and philosophical writer; husband (married 1875) of Lucy Clifford. A graduate of Trinity College, Cambridge, he was a fellow of Trinity in the period 1868–71, and professor of applied mathematics at University College, London, from 1871. His works include *Lectures and Essays* (1879; ed. by F. Pollock and L. Stephen), *Mathematical Fragments* (1881), *Mathematical Papers* (1882; ed. by R. Tucker), and *Common Sense of the Exact Sciences* (1885; ed. and in part written by K. Pearson).

Clifford's Inn. One of the inns of chancery at London, named for Robert de Clifford (1273–1314), of the time of Edward II, whose town residence it originally was. It was first used as a law school in the 18th year of Edward III (1345). The building is N of Fleet Street, between Chancery Lane and Fetter Lane.

Cliffside Park (klif'sīd). Borough in NE New Jersey, in Bergen County: residential community, near the Palisades of the Hudson River. 17,116 (1950).

Clifton (klif'tọn). Town in SE Arizona, county seat of Greenlee County: center for copper mining and smelting operations in the district. It is also known for its hot saline springs. 3,466 (1950).

Clifton. Two wards (Clifton North and Clifton South) comprising a residential suburb of Bristol, in W England, in Gloucestershire, situated on the river Avon. There are many parks and gardens. Hot mineral springs, called the Hotwells, have been famous for 400 years. 17,115 (1931).

Clifton. City in NE New Jersey, in Passaic County: industrial suburb of Passaic. 64,511 (1950).

Clifton Forge. City in C Virginia, geographically in Alleghany County but independent of county administration, ab. 45 mi. NW of Lynchburg: railroad shops and iron foundries. 5,795 (1950).

Clifton Heights. Borough in SE Pennsylvania, in Delaware County near Philadelphia: manufactures of textiles. It was settled toward the end of the 18th century and was incorporated in 1885. Pop. 7,549 (1950).

Clifton Springs. Village in W New York, in Ontario County, ab. 29 mi. W of Auburn. It has mineral springs and is the seat of the Clifton Springs Sanitarium. 1,838 (1950).

Clim of the Clough (klim; kluf). [Also, **Clym of the Clough.**] Famous English outlaw and archer, celebrated especially in the English traditional ballad *Adam Bell, Clym of the Clough, and Willyam of Cloudeslee.* One of the best-known episodes in his legend is his rescue (with the aid of Adam Bell) of William of Cloudesley from the gallows. All three outlaws were eventually pardoned and favored by the king.

Clinch (klinch). River of SW Virginia and E Tennessee. It unites with the Holston to form the Tennessee River at Kingston, Tenn. Norris Dam, one of the units of the

Tennessee Valley Authority, forms Norris Lake from the Clinch and Powell rivers. Length, ab. 275 mi.

Clincher (klin′chėr). Character in George Farquhar's comedy *The Constant Couple*, also in *Sir Harry Wildair*, its sequel. He is a pert London apprentice turned beau, and affecting to have traveled widely.

Clinedinst (klīn′dinst), **Benjamin West.** b. at Woodstock, Va., 1860; d. at Pawling, N.Y., Sept. 12, 1931. American illustrator and genre and portrait painter, who executed portraits of many dignitaries. He studied under Cabanel and Bonnat at the École des Beaux-Arts, Paris, was made an academician of the National Academy in 1898, and won several prizes, including the Evans Prize, of the American Water Color Society (1900) and a silver medal at the Pan-American Exposition at Buffalo, in 1901. Some of his better-known works are the portraits *Theodore Roosevelt, Admiral Peary, General Curtis Lee,* and *General E. W. Nichols*, and illustrations for books by Nathaniel Hawthorne, R. L. Stevenson, Bret Harte, and Mark Twain.

Clingmans Dome (kling′mạnz). See under **Tennessee.**

Clinias (klin′i.ạs). Killed at the battle of Coronea, 447 B.C. Athenian commander; father of Alcibiades. He distinguished himself at Artemisium in 480 B.C.

Clinias. fl. c400 B.C. Pythagorean philosopher and friend of Plato; a native of Tarentum.

Clink (klingk). Prison which was situated at one end of Bankside, at Southwark, London. It belonged to the "Liberty of the Clink," a part of the manor of Southwark not included in the grant to the city of London and under the jurisdiction of the bishop of Winchester. The prison was for the delinquents of this manor. It was burned down in the Gordon riots of June, 1780. Its name is the origin of the slang word "clink," meaning prison.

Clinker (klingk′ėr), **Humphry.** Workhouse boy, in Tobias Smollett's *Humphry Clinker*. He is discovered to be a natural son of Mr. Bramble, into whose service he has entered as coach boy. Humphry is unjustly imprisoned but shortly released, and in the end marries Mrs. Winifred Jenkins, the Brambles' maid.

Clint (klint), **Alfred.** b. at London, March 22, 1807; d. there, March 22, 1883. English marine painter; son of George Clint.

Clint, George. b. at London, April 12, 1770; d. there, May 10, 1854. English portrait painter and engraver; father of Alfred Clint. He was elected an associate of the Royal Academy in 1821, an honor he resigned in 1836.

Clinton (klin′tọn). City in C Illinois, county seat of De Witt County, ab. 23 mi. S of Bloomington: railroad and trading center in a farming region. It was here, on July 27, 1858, in a debate with Stephen A. Douglas, that Lincoln made the remark that "you can fool all of the people part of the time and part of the people all of the time, but you cannot fool all of the people all of the time." 5,945 (1950).

Clinton. City in W Indiana, in Vermillion County, ab. 13 mi. N of Terre Haute. Manufactures include overalls and other items; coal mining is the principal industry. 6,462 (1950).

Clinton. [Former name, **New York.**] City in E Iowa, county seat of Clinton County, on the Mississippi River, ab. 29 mi. NE of Davenport: railroad center; manufactures include corn by-products and lumber products. It is the seat of Mount St. Claire Academy. Settled in 1835 and platted in 1838, it was renamed in 1855 for DeWitt Clinton, and incorporated in 1859. In the 1880's it was said to be the busiest lumbering center in the world. Clinton was the birthplace of Lillian Russell. 30,379 (1950).

Clinton. Town in C Massachusetts, in Worcester County, on the Nashua River, ab. 33 mi. W of Boston: formerly important for the production of carpets, it now makes metal products and cotton textiles. 12,287 (1950).

Clinton. City in W Missouri, county seat of Henry County: marketing center for butter, eggs, and cheese. 6,075 (1950).

Clinton. Village in C New York, in Oneida County, ab. 8 mi. SW of Utica, in a region formerly important for iron mining. It is the seat of Hamilton College. 1,630 (1950).

Clinton. Town in C North Carolina, county seat of Sampson County, in a huckleberry-producing area: manufactures of lumber products. It was founded in 1818. Pop. 4,414 (1950).

Clinton. City in W Oklahoma, in Custer County, near the Washita River: shipping center for a wheat-farming and cattle-raising area. 7,555 (1950).

Clinton. Town in NW South Carolina, in Laurens County. It is the seat of Presbyterian College. Manufactures include hosiery and fertilizer; cotton is raised in the surrounding region and processed here. The Thornwell Orphanage at Clinton is known as one of the first in the U.S. to use cottages for living quarters. 7,168 (1950).

Clinton. [Former name, **Burrville.**] Town in E Tennessee, county seat of Anderson County, in a farming area, near both Norris Dam and Oak Ridge. It was renamed (1809) for DeWitt Clinton. 3,712 (1950).

Clinton, Castle. A former name of **Castle Garden.**

Clinton, DeWitt. b. at Little Britain, N.Y., March 2, 1769; d. at Albany, N.Y., Feb. 11, 1828. American politician and civic benefactor, noted as the projector of the Erie Canal; nephew of George Clinton. Graduated (1786) from Columbia, he studied law, and was admitted to the bar, meanwhile developing an early active interest in politics. He acted as private secretary to his uncle, Governor George Clinton, and became secretary of the board of fortification and of the board of regents, holding these posts until 1795. He was elected (1797) to the state assembly and in 1798 went to the state senate; in 1801 he became a member of the council of appointment, which controlled official job distribution. He soon made use of his position to replace Federalists with Republicans. He went (1802) to the U.S. Senate to fill a vacancy, resigning in 1803 to become mayor of New York, serving in that post until 1815, with the exception of two terms in 1807–08 and 1810–11. While in office he also served as state senator (1806–11) and lieutenant governor (1811–13). His rule of the city was distinguished for its constructive work, but in the meantime he lost much of his political power because of differences with his party. In 1812 he was put forward as a presidential candidate by a group of Federalists, but lost the election to James Madison. He resumed his interest in a state canal linking the Great Lakes to the Hudson, having become a canal commissioner in 1810, and after publicizing the project saw it adopted (1816) by the state legislature. He became a member of the new canal commission and, elected governor in 1817, carried through the project until its completion (1825). He retired (Jan. 1, 1823) from the governorship, but returned to the office in 1824 as the candidate of the People's Party in opposition to his political enemies of the "Albany Regency" led by Martin Van Buren. He lost the state election in 1826, and retired from active politics. He was a founder of the New York Historical Society, becoming its president in 1817; he helped found (1816) the Literary and Philosophical Society, and was president of the American Academy of Art. He took a prominent part in introducing the Lancasterian schools in the U.S., and also aided the cause of popular education by his efforts in behalf of the Public School Society of New York. His deep interest in natural science is apparent in his *Introductory Discourse* (1814), and he discovered a new fish, the Salmo Otsego, and a native American wheat. See *Life of DeWitt Clinton*, by James Renwick (1840).

Clinton, Edward Fiennes de. [Titles: 9th Baron **Clinton and Saye,** 1st Earl of **Lincoln.**] b. 1512; d. Jan. 16, 1585. English naval officer. As a royal ward he was married c1530 to Elizabeth Blount, widow of Gilbert, Lord Talboys, and mistress of Henry VIII. He served in the naval expedition to Scotland in 1544, commanded the fleet sent to Scotland in 1547, was appointed governor of Boulogne, and became lord high admiral on May 14, 1550.

Clinton, Fort. Fort in the highlands of the Hudson River, S of West Point, N.Y., during the Revolutionary War.

Clinton, George. d. July 10, 1761. English admiral and colonial governor; second son of the 6th Earl of Lincoln and father of Sir Henry Clinton (c1738–95). He was governor of Newfoundland in the period 1732–41, and of New York from 1741 to 1751.

Clinton, George. b. at Little Britain, N.Y., July 26, 1739; d. April 20, 1812. American Revolutionary soldier, first governor of the state of New York, and twice vice-president of the U.S.; uncle of DeWitt Clinton. Studying law at New York, he set up his practice in Ulster County, N.Y., and was elected (1768) to the provincial assembly, where he served on the corresponding committee. He became a delegate to the Second Continental Congress and (1775) a brigadier general of militia, unsuccessful in fulfilling his mission to secure the defense of the Hudson River. He became (1777) a brigadier general of the Continental line and in 1777 was elected both governor and lieutenant governor, resigning from the latter post. This was the first of his seven terms as governor of New York State; declining the nomination in 1795 he served as vice-president of the U.S. (1805–12), dying while holding office. His most notable achievements were his services as war governor of New York during the Revolution.

Clinton, Sir **Henry.** b. in Newfoundland, c1738; d. at Gibraltar, Dec. 23, 1795. English general; son of George Clinton (d. 1761). He entered the British army in 1751, and arrived with Generals Howe and Burgoyne at Boston in May, 1775. He fought at the battle of Bunker Hill in June, 1775, participated in the battle of Long Island in August, 1776, and stormed Forts Clinton and Montgomery in October, 1777. In 1778 he succeeded Howe as commander in chief. He captured Charleston in May, 1780, and resigned his command to Sir Guy Carleton in 1782.

Clinton, Sir **Henry.** b. 1771; d. Dec. 11, 1829. English soldier; younger son of Sir Henry Clinton (c1738–95) and brother of William Henry Clinton (1769–1846). He served (1788–89) as a volunteer in the Brunswick corps acting with the Prussian army in Holland, was appointed (July 25, 1810) a major general, commanded (1811 *et seq.*) the 6th division under Wellington during the Peninsular War, commanded (1815) the 3rd division stationed on the right at Waterloo, and was made a lieutenant general on June 4, 1814.

Clinton, Henry Fynes. b. at Gamston, Nottinghamshire, England, Jan. 14, 1781; d. at Welwyn, England, Oct. 24, 1852. English classical scholar and chronologist. He was graduated from Oxford (Christ Church College) in 1803, and was a member of Parliament in the period 1806–26. He wrote *Fasti Hellenici* and *Fasti Romani*, standard works on the civil and literary chronology of Greece and of Rome and Constantinople. He also prepared an epitome of the chronology of Greece, and one of that of Rome (published posthumously).

Clinton, Henry Pelham Fiennes Pelham. [Title, 5th Duke of **Newcastle.**] b. May 22, 1811; d. Oct. 18, 1864. English politician. He was chief secretary for Ireland in 1846, colonial secretary (1852–54), secretary for war (1854–55), and again colonial secretary (1859–64).

Clinton, James. b. in Ulster County, N.Y., Aug. 9, 1733; d. at Little Britain, N.Y., Dec. 22, 1812. American general; son of Charles Clinton (1690–1773) and father of DeWitt Clinton (1796–1828). He defended Fort Clinton unsuccessfully in October, 1777, against Sir Henry Clinton, and took part in Sullivan's expedition against the Indians in 1779.

Clinton, Sir **William Henry.** b. 1769; d. Dec. 23, 1846. English general; elder son of Sir Henry Clinton (c1738–95) and brother of Sir Henry Clinton (1769–1846). Appointed (1801) to command a secret expedition, he later governed (1801–02) Madeira of which he had taken possession in 1801. In 1807 he was sent on a secret mission to Sweden. He was made a general on July 22, 1830.

Clintonville (klin′tọn.vil). [Former name, **Pigeon.**] City in E Wisconsin, in Waupaca County, at the confluence of Bear Creek and the Embarrass River: manufactures include trucks and cheeses. It was founded in 1855. Pop. 4,657 (1950).

Clio (klī′ō). In Greek mythology, the Muse, usually of history, sometimes of lyre-playing. She is most commonly represented in a sitting attitude, holding an open roll of papyrus.

Clio. Pseudonym of Addison, formed from his signatures "C.," "L.," "I.," and "O.," used at various times in *The Spectator;* perhaps the initials of Chelsea, London, Islington, and the "Office."

Clíodna (klē′nạ). In Old Irish mythology, the fair young daughter of a Druid, who was swept out of a curragh by a huge wave while asleep. The loud surge in Glandmore Bay in County Cork on the S shore of Ireland is still called Tonn Clíodna, or Clíodna's Wave, in commemoration of this story. In Munster folklore Clíodna survives today as one of three fairy queens still active on May Day Eve as a beguiler of handsome young men, and as protectress against disease, if invoked.

Clipperton (klip′ėr.tọn). Island in the E part of the Pacific Ocean, ab. 730 mi. SW of Manzanillo, Mexico. It is a low coral atoll, with one jagged rock pinnacle ab. 70 ft. high on the SE part of the island. It has been exploited for some guano, and turtles. Its sovereignty was long disputed, but it was finally awarded to France in 1931. Land area, ab. 0.6 sq. mi.; pop. ab. 30.

Clippiacum (kli.pī′ạ.kum). Ancient name of **Clichy.**

Cliquot (klē.kō), **François Henri.** See **Clicquot, François Henri.**

Clissa (klēs′sä). Italian name of **Klis.**

Clissold (klis′ọld), **Augustus.** b. near Stroud, Gloucestershire, England, c1797; d. at Tunbridge Wells, England, Oct. 30, 1882. English clergyman. Originally a member of the Church of England, he was identified after 1840 (when he withdrew from the ministry) with Swedenborgianism. He translated Swedenborg's *Principia rerum naturalium*, and published numerous works in support of his doctrines.

Clisson (klē.sôṅ). Town in W France, in the department of Loire-Inférieure, situated on the Sèvre River ab. 16 mi. SE of Nantes. It has a ruined castle. Pop. ab. 2,500.

Clisson, Olivier de. b. in Britanny, France, 1336; d. at Josselin, in Britanny, France, April 24, 1407. French soldier, a constable of France. He became companion in arms of Bertrand Du Guesclin in 1370, and constable in 1380, and commanded the vanguard at the battle of Roosebeke under Charles VI. He was eventually deprived of his honors, but left a reputation for great military ability.

Clisthenes (klis′thẹ.nēz). See **Cleisthenes.**

Clitandre (klē.täṅdr). [Full title, **Clitandre ou l'Innocence délivrée.**] Tragicomedy by Pierre Corneille, produced in 1630 or 1631.

Clitandre. In Molière's play *Le Misanthrope*, a delightful marquis, a lover of Célimène.

Clitandre. Lover of Angélique in Molière's comedy *George Dandin.*

Clitandre. Man of sense and spirit who makes fun of the "pédants" in Molière's *Les Femmes savantes*, and loves Henriette.

Clitandre. Lover of Lucinde in Molière's *L'Amour médecin.* He pretends to be a doctor to cure her.

Clitheroe (kliᴛʜ′ėr.ō). Municipal borough and market town in NW England, in Lancashire, situated on the river Ribble, ab. 28 mi. N of Manchester, ab. 218 mi. NW of London by rail. It has a cotton-textile industry. 12,057 (1951).

Clitomachus (klī.tom′ạ.kus). [Original name, **Hasdrubal.**] b. c186 B.C.; d. c110 B.C. Carthaginian philosopher. He settled at Athens before 146, and succeeded (c129) Carneades as leader of the New Academy.

Cliton (klē.tôṅ). Valet of Dorante in Pierre Corneille's *Le Menteur* and its sequel *La Suite du Menteur;* a witty, intelligent rascal.

Clitor (klī′tọr). In ancient geography, a city in Arcadia, Greece. It had several temples and, according to Ovid, a fountain, called the Clitorium, the water from which was said to destroy the desire for wine.

Clitunno (klē.tön′nō). [Also: **Clitumno;** Latin, **Clitumnus.**] River in Umbria, Italy, an affluent of the Tinia. It is celebrated (especially through the descriptions of the younger Pliny) for its sanctity and beauty. He mentions especially the existence of shrines to the river deity (Clitumnus) at its source.

Clitus (klī′tus). [Also: **Cleitus;** surnamed **Melas,** meaning the "Black."] d. at Maracanda, Sogdiana, c328 B.C. Macedonian general; a friend of Alexander, whose life he saved at Granicus in 334, and by whom he was slain during a quarrel at a banquet.

Clitus. In Shakespeare's *Julius Caesar*, a servant of Brutus.

Clive (klīv), **Caroline.** [Maiden name, **Meysey-Wigley.**] b. at London, June 24, 1801; d. at Whitfield, Herefordshire, England, July 13, 1873. English writer. She was the author of the novels *Paul Ferroll* (1855) and *Why*

Paul Ferroll Killed his Wife (1860), and also wrote *Poems by "V."* (1840, and other editions).

Clive, Catherine. [Called **Kitty Clive**; maiden name, **Raftor.**] b. 1711; d. at London, Dec. 6, 1785. English actress; the daughter of an Irish gentleman, William Raftor. After a childhood of obscurity and poverty she came to the notice of Colley Cibber, who was manager of Drury Lane Theatre, London. He gave her a position c1727, and by 1731 she had established a reputation as a comic actress. She retired from the stage on April 24, 1769. She was in Garrick's company from 1746. She early married George Clive, a barrister, but they separated by mutual consent. Her forte was rattling comedy and operatic farce, and she was especially known in Charles Coffey's *The Devil To Pay*. After her retirement from the stage she lived for many years in a house which Horace Walpole gave her, near Strawberry Hill. She wrote some small dramatic sketches, only one of which, *The Rehearsal, or Boys in Petticoats*, was printed (1753).

Clive, Robert. [Title, Baron **Clive of Plassey.**] b. at Styche, Shropshire, England, Sept. 29, 1725; d. at London, Nov. 22, 1774. British soldier and empire builder. The son of an impoverished country squire, he became in 1743 a minor employee of the East India Company at Madras. War having broken out between the British and the French in India, he applied for and obtained an ensign's commission in the company's armed forces in 1747, and in the following year served under Admiral Boscawen at the unsuccessful siege of Pondicherry. During a second war in India with the French (1751–54), he manifested his military abilities by capturing Arcot and defending it successfully against a greatly superior force of French and natives. He returned to England in 1753, but in 1755 was sent back to India with the rank of lieutenant governor of Fort St. David. In 1756 he commanded an expedition against Suráj ud Dowlah, nawab of Bengal, ostensibly to avenge the sufferings and deaths of English prisoners in the Black Hole of Calcutta. He defeated the nawab near that city, and after a short interval of peace, won a sweeping victory at Plassey, on June 23, 1757. Practicing the familiar strategy of playing one claimant to a throne against another, Clive had made an alliance with Mir Jaffier, whom he now made nawab of Bengal in place of Suráj ud Dowlah. Following the capture of Murshidabad, the capital city, Mir Jaffier conducted Clive through the treasury, inviting him to help himself, which Clive did to the value of 160,000 pounds sterling. Large sums were also distributed to other British soldiers and officials, and Clive subsequently defended his own course by saying that he marveled at his moderation. In 1758 he was appointed governor of Bengal, in 1759 he defeated the Dutch near Chinsura, and in 1760, his health impaired, he returned to England and was created Baron Clive of Plassey. In 1765, affairs in Bengal having fallen into disorder, he was again made governor of that province, but in 1767 he again resigned for reasons of health. Back in England, his official conduct was made the subject of a parliamentary inquiry, which resulted, in 1773, in his acquittal on the charges brought, and in commendation of his conduct. Nevertheless in the following year he died by his own hand. He had been instrumental in fastening British control on India, and as an administrator he was just and exceedingly able.

Cloaca Maxima (klō̍.ā'ka̤ mak'si.ma̤). Chief drain of ancient Rome, said to have been built by Tarquinius Priscus c600 B.C. Part of it is still in existence. The outlet on the Tiber River is an arch ab. 12 ft. high with three concentric tiers of massive voussoirs, fitted without cement.

Cloche (klosh), **James La.** See **La Cloche, James.**

Clockmaker; or, The Sayings and Doings of Slickville (slik'vil), **The.** Humorous sketches by Thomas Chandler Haliburton, the first series of which was published in 1837. Others appeared in 1838 and 1840. Sam Slick is a shrewd, hard-bargaining Yankee clockmaker who travels through Nova Scotia peddling his wares and delivering himself of salty and laconic folk sayings.

Clock Symphony. Name applied to the symphony No. 101 by Franz Joseph Haydn, composed at London in 1794. The andante movement incorporates a ticking motif which gave rise to the name.

Clodd (klod), **Edward.** b. at Margate, Kent, England, July 1, 1840; d. 1930. English banker and writer on science and folklore. He was a clerk (1862–72) and secretary (1872–1915) of the London Joint Stock Bank. Interested in folklore, religion, and science, he was the author of *The Childhood of the World* (1872), *Myths and Dreams* (1885), *Story of Creation* (1888), *Primitive Man* (1895), *Pioneers of Evolution* (1897), *Story of the Alphabet* (1900), *Animism, the Seed of Religion* (1905), and *Magic in Names* (1920). He also wrote lives (1900) of Grant Allen and T.H. Huxley. His *Memories* appeared in 1916.

Clodia (klō'di.a̤). fl. 1st century B.C. Roman woman of patrician family and reputedly of great beauty and unconventional morals; sister of Appius Claudius and of Publius Clodius (both surnamed Pulcher). Among her several lovers was Catullus, in whose poem she appears under the name of Lesbia. She was accused of murdering her husband Q. Caecilius Metellus Celer, and on her part she alleged that one of her lovers, M. Caelius Rufus, tried to murder her.

Clodian Way (klô'di.a̤n). See **Via Clodia.**

Clodion (klo.dyôṅ). [Original name, **Claude Michel.**] b. at Nancy, France, Dec. 20, 1738; d. March 29, 1814. French sculptor. Among his works are many figurines, in terra cotta and other materials, of children, fauns, and nymphs, both singly and in groups.

Clodius (klō'di.us), **Publius.** [Also: **Claudius**; surnamed **Pulcher.**] b. c93 B.C.; d. Jan. 20, 52 B.C. Roman adventurer, demagogue, and gangster; brother of Appius Claudius (also surnamed Pulcher) and of Clodia. He fought in the third Mithridatic War, and when his services were not as well rewarded as he wished, he instigated a revolt, beginning the career of violence which made him notorious. In 62 B.C., disguising himself as a woman, he got admitted to the house of Julius Caesar during the observance of the Bona Dea ceremonies which were for women only. This caused a great scandal; one result was that Caesar divorced his wife Pompeia, and another was that Cicero prosecuted Clodius, who won acquittal by bribery but became Cicero's relentless enemy. Clodius, a member of a patrician gens, arranged to be adopted by a plebeian so that he might qualify for the office of tribune, which offered the maximum opportunity for demagoguery. He was elected tribune in 58 B.C. and brought about the exile of Cicero and of Cato the Younger, causing Cicero's property, moreover, to be confiscated. Determined to dominate Rome, Clodius not only wooed public favor by demagogic means, but also organized gangs of strong-arm men to assault his enemies. Pompey and Milo organized a rival mob, and Rome was terrorized by the violent conflicts of these opposing forces until Clodius was killed by Milo's adherents. The disorders promoted by Clodius prepared the way for the civil war between Pompey and Caesar.

Clodpate (klod'pāt), **Justice.** Coarse rustic justice in Thomas Shadwell's comedy *Epsom Wells.*

Clodvald (klōd'väld) or **Clodoald** (klō'dō.äld), Saint. See Saint **Cloud.**

Cloe (klō'ē̤). A variant spelling of **Chloe,** found in some printings of the works of John Fletcher and other English poets of the 16th and 17th centuries.

Cloelia (klē'li.a̤). In Roman legend, a maiden of Rome, delivered as a hostage to Lars Porsena c508 B.C. She escaped by swimming across the Tiber and returned to Rome. The Romans in all honor returned her into the hands of Porsena. He, however, in token of her courage, released her along with her fellow hostages.

Cloelia gens. [Also, **Cluilia.**] In ancient Rome, a patrician clan or house of Alban origin, said to have derived its name from Cloelius, a companion of Aeneas. According to tradition, the last king of Alba was C. Cluilius or Cloelius, who led an army against Rome in the reign of Tullus Hostilius.

Cloete (klö'tē̤), **Stuart.** [Full name, **Edward Fairly Stuart Graham Cloete.**] b. at Paris, July 23, 1897—. South African novelist. A member (1914–25) of the British army, he was twice (1916, 1918) wounded in action during World War I. From 1925 to 1935 he engaged in farming in South Africa. In 1937 he visited the U.S. He is the author of *The Turning Wheels* (1937), *Watch for the Dawn* (1939), *The Hill of Doves* (1941), *Congo Song* (1943), and other novels.

Cloetta (klō.et'ä), **Max.** b. at Zurich, Switzerland, July 21, 1868; d. there, June 23, 1940. Swiss pharmacologist. He became privatdocent of pharmacology (1898) and full professor (1900) at the University of Zurich. He conducted studies in experimental pharmacology and introduced (1904) digalen. Author of *Über Digalen* (1904), *Die Vergiftungen durch Alkaloide und andere Pflanzenstoffe* (1927), and *Vergiftungen durch Schlafmittel* (1927); coeditor of *Lehrbuch der Toxikologie für Studium und Praxis* (1928).

Clofesho (klō'vẹs.hō). [Old English, **Clofes hō** (or **hoo**), meaning, apparently, "Clof's Point."] In early English history, the meeting place of several ecclesiastical councils in the 8th and 9th centuries: identical perhaps with a place called Cliffe, in Kent.

Clogher (kloċh'ėr). Rural district and village in Ulster province, Northern Ireland, in County Tyrone, situated on the river Blackwater, ab. 53 mi. SW of Belfast. It has a cathedral, and was formerly the seat of one of the earliest Irish bishoprics. 11,576 (1937).

Cloister and the Hearth, The. Historical novel by Charles Reade, published in 1861. The hero is the supposed father of Erasmus, and the scenes are laid mainly in Holland and Italy.

Cloisters, the. Museum of medieval art at New York City. The American sculptor George Grey Barnard acquired portions of early medieval French monasteries and caused them to be transported and reassembled at New York, with the hope that they would become a public museum (housing also his collection of several hundred examples of medieval painting, sculpture, and other objects of art). The consummation of his plan was threatened when the property on which he had reassembled the French structures was acquired as part of a public improvement which was backed by John D. Rockefeller, Jr., but the difficulty was resolved when Rockefeller purchased both the structures and Barnard's collection, and donated them to the Metropolitan Museum of Art. The Cloisters, which is thus a branch of the Metropolitan Museum, is an extensive modern building in Romanesque style, incorporating the several ancient cloisters which Barnard brought to New York. It stands on a hilltop in Fort Tryon Park, overlooking the Hudson River, near the highest point in Manhattan Island, and is visited by great numbers of persons annually.

Clonakilty (klon.ạ.kil'ti). Urban district in SW Irish Republic, in S County Cork ab. 33 mi. by rail SW of Cork city. It was chartered in 1613, and practically destroyed in an English-Irish battle in 1641. It is a market town and minor seaport, with some fishing, breweries, and grain and flour mills. 2,747 (1951).

Clonfert (klon'fėrt). Town and parish in Connacht province, Irish Republic, in County Galway, situated on the river Shannon and the Grand Canal, ab. 9 mi. SE of Ballinasloe. It was formerly the seat of one of the earliest Irish bishoprics. Pop. of electoral district, 449 (1936).

Clonmacnoise (klon.mạk.noiz'). Old religious center in C Irish Republic, in NW County Offaly, on the river Shannon ab. 9 mi. S of Athlone. The abbey was founded c548 A.D. and was subsequently made the seat of a bishopric, which it remained until 1568. The town was destroyed by the English in 1552. The ruins of church buildings and the ancient burial ground of the Irish kings are here. Pop. of parish, 1,899 (1926).

Clonmel (klon.mel'). [Irish, **Cluain Meala.**] Urban district and market town in Munster province, Irish Republic, county seat of County Tipperary (South Riding), situated on the river Suir, ab. 25 mi. NW of Waterford. It is noted as the birthplace of Laurence Sterne and Lady Blessington. 10,491 (1951).

Clontarf (klon.tärf'). Two wards (Clontarf East and Clontarf West) of Dublin, in Leinster province, Irish Republic, in County Dublin. They are situated in the NE quarter of the city. Here, on April 23, 1014, Brian Boru, king of Ireland, defeated the Danes and the rebels of Leinster. 26,154 (1936).

Clootie (klö'ti). Scottish and north of England euphemism for the devil, from "cloot," a dialect word for one half of a cleft hoof.

Cloots or **Clootz** (klōts), Baron **de.** [Title of **Jean Baptiste du Val-de-Grâce**; called **Anacharsis Cloots**; pseudonym, **Ali Gur-Ber.**] b. at Val-de-Grâce, near Cleve, Prussia, June 24, 1755; guillotined at Paris, March 24, 1794. French revolutionary enthusiast who assumed the title "Orator of the Human Race." He was a member of the Convention in 1792, and author of *La Certitude des preuves du mahométisme* (1780; published under the pseudonym Ali Gur-Ber), *L'Orateur du genre humain* (1791), and *La République universelle* (1792).

Clopinel (klo.pē.nel), **Jean.** See **Jean de Meung** (or **Meun**).

Cloppenburg (klop'ẹn.bůrk). Town in NW Germany, in the *Land* (state) of Lower Saxony, British Zone, formerly in the free state of Oldenburg, situated on the Soeste River, S of Oldenburg. It has metallurgical and leather industries, cement works, canneries, and farm markets specializing in honey. It belonged formerly to the bishopric of Münster, and became part of Oldenburg in 1803. The population is predominantly Roman Catholic. 13,822 (1950).

Clopton (klop'tọn), Sir **Hugh.** b. at Stratford-on-Avon, England; d. at London, Sept. 15, 1497. English mercer, notable as the lord mayor (1492) of London who built (c1483) at Stratford the house later famous as "New Place," bought (1597) by Shakespeare.

Cloquet (klō.kā'). City in E Minnesota, in Carlton County, on the St. Louis River, ab. 17 mi. SW of Duluth: manufactures of paper and wood products. It has been completely rebuilt since 1918, when forest fires destroyed the whole city. 7,685 (1950).

Cloridano (klō.rē.dä'nō). Friend of Medoro in Ariosto's *Orlando Furioso*. The two venture into the field of battle to find among the heaps of slain the body of their lord.

Clorinda (klō.rēn'dä). Amazonian leader in *Gerusalemme Liberata* (*Jerusalem Delivered*) of Torquato Tasso. She is of acknowledged prowess in the infidel army, and is loved by Tancred, but cares only for the glories of war. Tancred kills her unwittingly in a night attack, and gives her Christian baptism before she expires.

Cloris (klō'ris). Character in the farce *The Rehearsal* by George Villiers, 2nd Duke of Buckingham. She drowns herself because Prince Prettyman marries old Joan.

Close (klōs), **Upton.** See **Hall, Josef Washington.**

Closse (klos), **Raphael Lambert.** b. near Tours, France, c1620; d. at Montreal, Canada, Feb. 6, 1662. French soldier in the Indian wars in Canada. He came to Canada with Maisonneuve, governor of Montreal, in 1642, and became sergeant-major of the garrison and notary public. He was acting governor of Montreal during the absence of Maisonneuve in 1655, and was invested with the fief of St. Lambeth in 1658. He was killed in a skirmish with the Iroquois.

Closter (klos'tėr). Borough in NE New Jersey, in Bergen County: manufactures of textiles. 3,376 (1950).

Closterman (klō'stėr.mạn), **John.** [German, **Johann Klostermann.**] b. at Osnabrück, Hanover, Germany, 1656; d. at London, 1713. German portrait painter, resident in England after 1681.

Closter-Seven (klos'tėr.sev'ẹn), **Convention of.** See **Kloster-Zeven, Convention of.**

Clot (klō), **Antoine Barthélemy.** [Called **Clot Bey.**] b. at Grenoble, France, Nov. 7, 1793; d. at Marseilles, France, Aug. 28, 1868. French physician, chief physician (1822–49) to Mehemet Ali in Egypt. He wrote *De la peste observée en Égypte* (1840).

Clotaire I (klō.tãr'; French, klo.ter). [Also: **Lothar, Clothaire**; German, **Chlothar.**] d. 561. King of the Franks; fourth son of Clovis I. On the death of Clovis in 511, his empire was divided among his sons, Theodoric receiving Austrasia, Clodomir Orléans, Childebert Paris, and Clotaire Soissons. Clotaire succeeded, partly by violence, partly by inheritance, in reuniting the dominions of his father, over which he ruled in the period 558–561.

Clotaire II. [Also: **Lothar, Clothaire**; German, **Chlothar.**] b. 584; d. at Paris, 629. King of the Franks; son of Chilperic I, of Soissons, and Fredegonda. He was four months old on the death of his father in 584. The regency was conducted by his mother, who became involved in a protracted war with Brunehilde of Austrasia and Burgundy. The latter was, in 613, betrayed by the nobles of Burgundy into the hands of Clotaire, who put her to death and seized her dominions, thus reuniting under his sway the empire of Clovis.

Cloten (klō'tẹn). In Shakespeare's *Cymbeline*, the queen's son by a former husband. He is rejected by Imogen. In the earlier part of the play (written later) he is a foolish and malicious braggart; but in the fourth act, which belongs to an earlier version, he is not deficient in manliness.

Clotho (klō'thō). In Greek mythology, that one of the three Moirae or Fates who spins the thread of life.

Cloth of Gold, Field of the. See **Field of the Cloth of Gold.**

Clotilda (klō.til'dạ), Saint. [French, **Clotilde** (klo.tēld); German, **Chlothilde** (klō.til'dẹ).] b. probably at Lyons, France, c474; d. at Tours, France, June 3, 545. Queen of the Franks; daughter of Chilperic, king of the Burgundians. Her father, mother, and two brothers were murdered by her uncle Gundebald, joint king of the Burgundians, by whom she was educated in the Christian faith. She married (493) Clovis I, king of the Franks, whose conversion from paganism is said to have been accomplished chiefly through her instrumentality.

Clotilda. [French, **Clotilde;** German, **Chlothilde.**] d. 531. Daughter of Saint Clotilda. She married Amalaric, king of the Visigoths.

Clotilde (klo.tēld), **Sainte.** Church at Paris, in the Gothic style of the 14th century, begun in 1846. It has lofty pierced spires. The façade has three large sculptured doorways, and the interior is effective, and possesses good sculptures and paintings. The church measures ab. 330 by 105 ft., and ab. 85 ft. from vault to pavement.

Cloud (klö), Saint. [Also: **Clodvald, Chlodvald, Clodoald,** or **Chlodoald.**] fl. first half of the 6th century; d. 560. King of Orléans; youngest son of Clodomir, grandson of Clovis and Saint Clotilda. He became a monk.

Cloud Cuckoo Land. Novel by Naomi Mitchison, published in 1925.

Cloudesley or **Cloudeslie** or **Cloudeslee** (kloudz'li), **William** (or **Willyam**) **of.** See **William of Cloudesley** or **Cloudeslie.**

Cloud of Unknowing. Prose religious treatise of the Middle English period by an anonymous author who seems to have written it about 1350. His theme is the love of God and the knowledge of His presence through mysticism and spirituality. The work is intended for a serious young man of 24 who is contemplative by nature and who looks forward to a life of quiet devotion. The author attacks those who take their religion violently and show it by means of physical manifestation which he regards as hypocrisy. The "cloud" of the title, which stands between God and the Soul, is man's ignorance and God's incomprehensibility. The work has been issued in modern versions by Evelyn Underhill (1912), and Dom Justin McCann (1924). The suggestion that the *Cloud* is by Walter Hilton, a Nottinghamshire Augustinian (who died in 1396) does not seem to have met with general acceptance.

Cloud Peak. Mountain in N Wyoming, ab. 30 mi. SW of Sheridan, Wyo. It is a conical peak, standing out as the highest of the Big Horn Mountains. 13,165 ft.

Clouds, The. Comedy by Aristophanes. Strepsiades ("Turncoat") sends his spendthrift son Pheidippides to the phrontistery ("thinking-shop") of Socrates, who appears as a sophist, to be reformed by training in rhetoric. Pheidippides refuses to go; so Strepsiades goes himself, and finds Socrates swinging in a basket observing the sun and ether. Socrates summons the Clouds, his new deities, and undertakes to make a sophist of Strepsiades and free him from the religion of his fathers. Unfortunate results of his new knowledge show Strepsiades his error, and he abandons Socrates and sets the phrontistery on fire.

Clouet (klö.e), **François.** [Called **Janet** or **Jehannet.**] b. at Tours, France, c1516; d. c1572. French painter; son and pupil of Jean Clouet (c1485–c1541). He received letters of naturalization from Francis I of France in 1541 when he succeeded his father as painter to the king, and he held the same office under Henry II and Charles IX. Works attributed to him include a portrait of the dauphin Francis (1524), at Antwerp, a full-length portrait of Henry II (c1558), in the Louvre, and a portrait of Elizabeth of Austria (c1570), in the Louvre.

Clouet, Jean. [Called **Jehan, Jehannot, Jehannet.**] b. c1485; d. c1541. Portrait painter at the French court; father of François Clouet. Believed to have been a Fleming, he became attached to Francis I, king of France, as court painter and personal attendant in 1518 or even earlier. Great doubt prevails concerning the authenticity of everything attributed to this artist, including such admirable portraits as those of Francis I now in the Louvre at Paris, and of Charles de Cossé, in the Metropolitan Museum of Art, New York. Other supposed examples of his work exist in Antwerp and in the Bibliothèque Nationale, Paris, and if the attributions are correct, they prove him to have been a notable master of painting and drawing.

Clough (kluf), **Anne Jemima.** b. 1820; d. 1892. English educator, first principal of Newnham College, Cambridge; sister of Arthur Hugh Clough, English poet (1819–61). She founded a school at Liverpool in 1841, and moved it to Ambleside in 1852. From 1837 to 1870 she was secretary, and from 1873 to 1874 president, of the North of England council for the promotion of higher education for women. In 1871 she became head of the women's house at Cambridge, which later became Newnham College.

Clough, Arthur Hugh. b. at Liverpool, England, Jan. 1, 1819; d. at Florence, Italy, Nov. 13, 1861. English poet. He was educated at Rugby, where he came under the spell of its great master, Thomas Arnold, and at Balliol College, Oxford, where he formed his lifelong friendship with Arnold's son Matthew Arnold. He was made a fellow of Oriel College in 1841, but resigned in 1848 because of religious doubts. He was in America in 1852, writing and teaching, and when he returned to England he became an examiner in the Education Office, and acted as secretary to Florence Nightingale. In 1859 he went to Greece, Constantinople, the Pyrenees, and Italy, in a vain attempt to recover his shattered health. He died of paralysis in 1861, as his mother had done the year before. No one reads the long poems of Clough today, and only a few of his short ones are found in anthologies: *Qua Cursum Ventus* (a title taken from Vergil), *Qui Laborat, Orat* (He who labors, prays), and *Say Not the Struggle Naught Availeth* (a favorite of Winston Churchill and Franklin Delano Roosevelt). In his short life Clough made many friends: Carlyle, who called him "a diamond sifted out of the general rubbish heap," Thackeray, Emerson, Lowell, Charles Eliot Norton, and (the one who has done most for his memory) Arnold, who was inspired by Clough's death to write his great elegy *Thyrsis* (1867). It is interesting to note that Clough died in the same city, and in the same year, as another English poet, Elizabeth Barrett Browning.

Cloux (klö), **Olivier.** See **Aimard, Gustave.**

Clove and Orange. Inseparable pair of coxcombs in Ben Jonson's *Every Man Out of His Humour.*

Clovelly (klō.vel'i). Civil parish, village, and seaside resort in SW England, in Devonshire, situated on Barnstaple Bay, ab. 11 mi. SW of Bideford. It has no direct rail connections for passengers, being reached by rail to Bideford, ab. 221 mi. SW of London. It is noted for its picturesque appearance and the beauty of its environs. 529 (1931).

Clover (klō'vėr). Town in N South Carolina, in York County: textile manufactures. 3,276 (1950).

Clovio (klō'vyō), **Giorgio Giulio.** [Also, **Macedo.**] b. in Croatia (or possibly Macedonia), 1498; d. at Rome, 1578. Italian miniaturist. Well known among his works are a book of hours with 26 illuminations and 12 miniatures commemorating victories of Charles V (British Museum, London).

Clovis (klō'vis). City in S central California, in Fresno County, ab. 10 mi. by road NE of Fresno. It is a trade center in a rich farming area, shipping grapes and raisins. 2,766 (1950).

Clovis. City in E New Mexico, county seat of Curry County: railroad division point, and trading and shipping center for grains, and livestock. 17,318 (1950).

Clovis I (klō'vis; French, klo.vēs). [Also: **Chlodowech;** German, **Chlodwig.**] b. c466; d. at Paris, 511. Frankish king, the founder of the Merovingian line. He succeeded his father Childeric as king of the Salic Franks in 481. His defeat of Syagrius near Soissons in 486 expanded his territory to the Loire. In 493 he married the Christian princess Clotilda, and, having defeated the Alamanni in 496, was baptized by Remigius the same year, in fulfilment, it is traditionally said, of a vow made at this battle. He now had Roman support, and his followers were more united under common Christian motivation. He defeated the Burgundians in 500, and defeated the West Goths at Vouillé, near Poitiers, in 507. He established (c507) his court at Paris. After his death his lands were divided among his four sons.

Clovis II. [Also: **Chlodowech;** German, **Chlodwig.**] b. 632; d. c657. King of Neustria and Burgundy (638 *et seq.*); a descendant of Clovis I and second son of Dagobert.

Clowes (klouz, klöz), **Evelyn May.** See **Mordaunt, Elinor.**

Clowes (klouz), **John.** b. at Manchester, England, Oct. 31, 1743; d. at Leamington, England, May 29, 1831. English clergyman. A member of the Church of England, he was rector of Saint John's Church at Manchester, and an influential supporter of Swedenborgianism. He translated Swedenborg's treatise *On the Worship and Love of God* (1816).

Clowns' Houses. Collection of poems by Edith Sitwell, published in 1918.

Cloyne (kloin). Market town in Munster province, Irish Republic, in County Cork, ab. 15 mi. E of Cork city. It was formerly an episcopal see of which Bishop Berkeley was one of the incumbents. 684 (1936).

Cluain Meala (kloin ma'la̤). Irish name of **Clonmel.**

Cluett (klö'e̤t), **Ernest Harold.** b. at Troy, N.Y., July 13, 1874—. American shirt-manufacturer and legislator. He studied at Oxford, and graduated (1896) from Williams College. He has been treasurer (1900–16), vice-president (1916–27), director (1927–29), and chairman of the board of directors (1929–37) of Cluett, Peabody and Company. An unsuccessful Republican candidate (1934) for senator from New York, he was elected (1937) a congressman from New York.

Cluett, Robert. b. at Birmingham, England, June 14, 1846; d. Nov. 25, 1927. American shirt-manufacturer. A member (1866 *et seq.*) of the firm of George B. Cluett Brothers and Company at Troy, N.Y., he was vice-president (1901–02) and president (1902–07) of the firm after its incorporation (1901) as Cluett, Peabody and Company.

Cluett, Sanford Lockwood. b. at Troy, N.Y., June 6. 1874—. American shirt-manufacturer, noted as the inventor (1928) of a fabric preshrinking process called Sanforizing (and registered as a trademark under this name) Graduated (1898) from Rensselaer Polytechnic Institute he became (1919) director of engineering and research for Cluett, Peabody and Company, and has also been vice-president and member of the board of directors of the firm. In 1945 he was awarded the Edward Longstreth medal by the Franklin Institute for the development of his process of preshrinking.

Clugny (klü.nyē). Former spelling of **Cluny.**

Cluilia gens (klö.il'i.a̤ jenz). See **Cloelia gens.**

Cluj (klözh). [German, **Klausenburg, Clausenburg;** Hungarian, **Kolozsvár.**] City in NW Rumania, in the province of Transylvania, situated on the Little Someşu River, ab. 82 mi. SE of Oradea: industrial, cultural, and trade center. The main industries include factories producing leather, metals, textiles, ceramics, spirits, and tobacco, and canneries for fruits, vegetables, and meats. Among notable buildings are a Roman Catholic cathedral, the Gothic Church of Saint Michael (14-15th centuries), court of appeals, library, national theater, opera house, museums, agricultural academy, and two universities with large hospitals and laboratories. Cluj is the seat of three bishoprics, an Orthodox, a Catholic, and a Reformed. The town was founded in 1178 and taken by the Hungarians in 1848; in 1920 it became part of Rumania. 117,915 (1948).

Clumsy (klum'zi), **Sir Tunbelly.** Country gentleman in John Vanbrugh's play *The Relapse;* a coarse, unwieldy boor, the father of Miss Hoyden. The character is retained in Sheridan's *A Trip to Scarborough,* an adaptation of *The Relapse.*

Clunch (klunch). Husband of Old Madge in George Peele's *Old Wives' Tale.* He leads home three lost travelers, and she tells them a tale.

Clunia (klö'ni.a̤). Latin name of **Feldkirch.**

Cluny (klü.nē; Anglicized, klö'ni). [Former spelling, **Clugny.**] Town in E France, in the department of Saône-et-Loire, situated in the valley of the Grosne River, ab. 11 mi. NW of Mâcon. It is famous for the ruins of its Benedictine abbey which, founded in 910, became the focus, in the 11th and 12th centuries, for a rejuvenation of the medieval church and the intellectual center of Europe. Popes Gregory VIII, Urban II, and Pascal II were abbots of Cluny. The monks were expelled from the abbey in 1789, and of the formerly impressive buildings only the S transept, with a tower and two chapels, still stands. The town has other remains, dating from the 14th, 15th, and 16th centuries. Cluny is a resort; it produces pottery and lace. 4,257 (1946).

Cluny, Hôtel de. [Also, **Cluny Museum.**] Former palace of the abbots of Cluny, situated on the Boulevard St.-Michel, Paris. It was built in the 15th century on a part of the remains of Roman baths. Acquired in the 19th century by the art collector Alexandre Du Sommerard, it was used by him as a town house and as a place to keep his art treasures. In 1843 the property was purchased by the state and subsequently opened as a museum, the Du Sommerard collection forming the nucleus of the present aggregation of medieval and Renaissance objects of art.

Cluseret (klüz.re), **Gustave Paul.** b. June 13, 1823; d. at Toulon, France, Aug. 21, 1900. French army officer. He participated in the American Civil War, serving on George B. McClellan's staff in 1862, and becoming a brigadier general. In 1864 he edited the *New Nation* at New York. Having returned to France he was war minister (April 4–30, 1871) of the Paris Commune, and on its fall fled to England and Mexico. He was condemned to death by a military tribunal in 1872, but was amnestied and returned to Paris in 1884.

Cluses (klüz). Town in E France, in the department of Haute-Savoie, situated on the Arve River ab. 24 mi. SE of Geneva, Switzerland. Pop. ab. 2,400.

Clusium (klö'zi.um). Latin name of **Chiusi.**

Clute (klöt), **Willard Nelson.** b. at Painted Post, N.Y., 1869—. American botanist. He attended the University of Chicago, taught botany at several high schools in Illinois, was instructor in botany and director (1928–38) of the botanical garden at Butler University, and from 1938 to 1941 was director of the Holliday Park botanical garden. He founded and was editor of the *American Botanist* and the *Fern Bulletin.* Among his works are *A Flora of the Upper Susquehanna Valley* (1898), *The Fern Collector's Guide* (1902), and *American Plant Names* (1923).

Clutterbuck (klut'ėr.buk), **Captain Cuthbert.** Name which Sir Walter Scott assumed to publish *The Monastery, The Abbot,* and *The Fortunes of Nigel.* This, and various other pseudonyms adopted by Scott, were made necessary by the fact that the novelist was also a member of the Scottish bar and believed that the writing of fiction was too undignified an occupation for open acknowledgment by a scholar of the law. He therefore long disavowed the bulk of the work upon which his reputation now rests, and admitted only during his latter years that he had written it (although many people in English letters, including Jane Austen, had long since guessed the truth in the matter).

Clutton-Brock (klut'o̤n.brok'), **Arthur.** b. at Weybridge, Surrey, England, March 23, 1868; d. at Godalming, Surrey, England, Jan. 8, 1924. English editor, essayist, and art and literary critic. Educated at Eton and New College, Oxford, and called to the bar in 1895, he practiced law for several years. In 1904 he began writing with contributions to the *Times Literary Supplement* and as literary editor for the London *Speaker.* Subsequently he was art critic for the London papers *Tribune, Morning Post,* and *Times,* and a member (1909 *et seq.*) of the Fabian Society. The author of books on French and English cathedrals, he also wrote *Shelley—The Man and the Poet* (1909), *William Morris—His Work and Influence* (1914), *Thoughts on the War* (2 vols., 1914–15), *Studies in Christianity* (1918), *Essays on Art* (1918), *Essays on Books* (1920), *More Essays* (1921), and *The Necessity of Art* (1924).

Cluver (klö'vėr), **Philipp.** [Also: **Clüver** (klü'-); Latinized, **Cluverius.**] b. at Danzig, 1580; d. at Leiden, Netherlands, 1622. German geographer. He wrote *Introductio in universam geographiam* (1629), and other works.

Clwyd (klö'id). Small river in N Wales, in Denbighshire. It rises on the Denbighshire-Merionethshire boundary ab. 7 mi. SW of Ruthin and flows northward into the Irish Sea at Rhyl. Length, ab. 30 mi.

Clyde (klīd). Village in N Ohio, in Sandusky County: marketing center for cabbages, melons, strawberries, and cherries. It was settled in 1820. Clyde was the boyhood home of Sherwood Anderson, and is thought by some to be the town represented in his *Winesburg, Ohio*. 4,083 (1950).

Clyde, Baron. Title of **Campbell, Sir Colin** (1792–1863).

Clyde, Firth of. Lower estuary of the Clyde River, lying between C and S Scotland, between Argyllshire and Dunbartonshire on the N and Renfrewshire, Ayrshire, and Wigtownshire on the S and containing the insular county of Buteshire. It enters the Irish Sea between the Mull of Kintyre and Corsewall Point. The Firth has numerous inlets, the most important of which are Loch Long, Loch Striven, and the Kyles of Bute. Many seaside resorts and shipbuilding yards are situated along its banks. Greatest width, ab. 37 mi.

Clyde, William Pancoast. b. at Claymont, Del., Nov. 11, 1839; d. Nov. 18, 1923. American shipowner who organized and headed William P. Clyde and Company, subsequently named the Clyde Steamship Company.

Clydebank (klīd'bangk). Police burgh, seaport, and shipbuilding and industrial center in W central Scotland, in Dunbartonshire, situated on the N bank of the Clyde River, ab. 6 mi. NW of Glasgow, ab. 408 mi. N of London by rail. Its industries besides shipbuilding include sewing-machine manufactures, chemical manufactures, and whisky distilling. 44,625 (1951).

Clyde River. River in S Scotland. It rises in Lanarkshire, ab. 20 mi. SE of Lanark, and flows N to a point ab. 5 mi. E of Lanark, whence it flows generally NW by a rather devious course past Lanark, Hamilton, and Glasgow to the Firth of Clyde, ab. 3 mi. W of Greenock. It forms four waterfalls (known as the Falls of Clyde) near Lanark. Both banks of the estuary are highly industrialized, with many shipyards. The river is navigable to Glasgow. Length, ab. 91 mi.

Clymene (klim'ẹ.nē). In Greek mythology, a daughter of Oceanus and Tethys, beloved of Apollo, and mother of Atalanta. She was also the mother of Atlas, Prometheus, and Epimetheus by Iapetus.

Clymene. In Greek mythology, a nymph, and mother of Phaëthon, whose father was the sun god, Helios.

Clymene. Asteroid (No. 104) discovered by James Craig Watson, on Sept. 13, 1868.

Clymer (klī'mėr). Borough in W Pennsylvania, in Indiana County. 2,500 (1950).

Clymer, George. b. at Philadelphia, March 16, 1739; d. at Morrisville, Bucks County, Pa., Jan. 24, 1813. American politician. He was one of the signers of the Declaration of Independence, and a member of the Constitutional Convention in 1787. He also served in the Continental Congress in the periods 1776–78 and 1780–83.

Clymer, George E. b. in Bucks County, Pa., 1754; d. at London, Aug. 27, 1834. American inventor (c1818) of the "Columbian" printing press, involving the first really significant American contribution to printing processes.

Clym of the Clough (klim; kluf). See **Clim of the Clough.**

Clynes (klīnz), **John Robert.** b. at Oldham, England, March 27, 1869; d. at London, Oct. 23, 1949. English labor leader, secretary of state (1929–31) for home affairs. A member (1906–31, 1935–45) of Parliament, he served as food controller (1918–19), chairman (1921–22) of the Parliamentary Labour Party, and lord privy seal and deputy leader (1924) of the House of Commons in the first British Labour cabinet.

Clytemnestra or **Clytaemnestra** (klī.tẹm.nes'trạ, klit-ẹm-). In Greek legend, the daughter of Tyndareus and Leda, wife of Agamemnon, king of Argos, or Mycenae, and mother of Orestes, Electra, and Iphigenia. She took Aegisthus as paramour during the absence of her husband as leader of the expedition against Troy. The most common version of the legend is that she slew her husband in the bath on his return from Troy, partly to avoid the consequences of her adultery and partly from jealousy of Cassandra, daughter of Priam, whom at the taking of Troy Agamemnon had received as his prize, and by whom he had two sons. She and Aegisthus were in turn put to death by her son Orestes.

Clytie (klī'tē) or **Clytia** (klish'i.ạ). In Greek mythology, a water nymph so enamored of the sun god, Apollo, that every day she watched his course across the sky. The gods took pity on her unrequited love and metamorphosed her into a heliotrope, a flower whose face follows the course of the sun. Hence, the heliotrope has come to symbolize unwavering love.

"CMTC." See **Citizens' Military Training Camps.**

Cnaeus (or **Cneius**) **Pompeius Magnus** (nē'us pom-pē'us mag'nus). See **Pompey.**

Cnidus (nī'dus). Ancient city in Caria, Asia Minor, situated at the end of a narrow peninsula on the SW coast of what is now Turkey, between the islands of Rhodes and Kos. It was settled by the Lacedaemonians, and was a seat of worship of Aphrodite. The famous statue of Aphrodite (or Venus) by Praxiteles was here. On the site of Cnidus are, among other ruins, those of an ancient theater. The *cavea* is 400 ft. in diameter, with 36 tiers of seats divided by two precinctions, and survives almost perfect. There are considerable remains of the stage structure. Near here the Athenians under Conon defeated (394 B.C.) the Lacedaemonians.

Cnossus or **Knossos** (nos'us). [Also: **Cnosus, Gnossus, Gnosus.**] Ancient capital of Crete, near what is now Candia, celebrated in the myths of Zeus, Minos, Daedalus, Ariadne, Theseus, and others. Cnossus was the site of the famous Labyrinth which Daedalus built to imprison the Minotaur. The site, upon which is located a modern community known as Makro Teikho, was excavated (1900–08) by the English archaeologist Sir Arthur John Evans.

CNT. [Full name, **Confederación Nacional del Trabajo;** Eng. trans., *"National Confederation of Lab r."*] Spanish anarchist-syndicalist trade union founded (1910) in imitation of the French Confédération Général du Travail. It eventually joined together eight regional confederations. Spanish labor, particularly in the south and east, was impressed with the possibilities of direct action (strikes) for the achievement of social and economic as well as political change. The CNT advocated the use of the economic weapon of the strike to resist the political state based on exploitation. With two million members, including peasants, workers, and intellectuals, the CNT represented the largest anarchist movement in the international IWA (International Workingmen's Association). At the outbreak of the Spanish Civil War (1936–39) the CNT controlled the largest newspapers in Spain, *Solidaridad Obrera* (published at Barcelona), and *Castilla Libre* (published at Madrid). Dissident groups such as the FAI (Federación Anarchista Ibérica) and the Trentistas all joined with it to resist Franco. When Franco promulgated the Falangist labor charter of March 9, 1938, CNT and related labor organizations ceased legal function.

Cnut (knöt). See **Canute.**

Coachella (kō.ạ.chel'ạ). Town in S California, in Riverside County, in the Coachella Valley. 2,755 (1950).

Coachella Valley. Desert valley in SE California, NW of the Salton Sea. It is noted as the chief center of date growing in the U.S., and also produces grapefruit, cotton, and winter vegetables, using irrigation. Indio is the chief trade center of the valley, and Palm Springs is its best-known resort. Most of the lower end of the valley is below sea level. Length, ab. 48 mi.; greatest width, ab. 12 mi.

Coacoochee (kō.ạ.kö'chē). [Also, **Wild Cat.**] b. in Florida, c1810; d. at Alto, near Muzquiz, Coahuila, Mexico, in January, 1857. Seminole chief and Mexican army officer. He was the favorite son of King Philip, chief of the St. John's River Seminoles. He succeeded Osceola as the most active and daring Seminole war-leader, and attacked Fort Mellon, on Lake Monroe, on Feb. 8, 1837. He was himself a hostage under the Treaty of Fort Dade (March 6, 1837), but was a leader in carrying off the principal hostages on June 2, 1837. Seized at a conference at Fort Peyton, near St. Augustine, on Oct. 21, 1837, he was imprisoned in Fort Marion, at St. Augustine, but escaped (Nov. 29–30, 1837). A commander at the Battle of Okeechobee (Dec. 25, 1837), he operated on the St. John's River in the period 1837–41. Capture of his mother and daughter led to conferences in March,

1841, and he agreed to emigrate, but delayed, and was seized in early May, 1841, and shipped to New Orleans, but was soon sent back to Florida, where he assisted in obtaining the capture or surrender of various chiefs. He embarked for Indian Territory on Oct. 12, 1841, but refused to settle in Creek country. He headed the delegation to Washington (April–May, 1844) which resulted in Seminole local autonomy, was principal counselor to the head chief, Mikonopi, in 1845, and planned an alliance between the Texas tribes and the Seminoles against the Creeks (1846–48). Defeated for the head-chieftancy in early 1849, he left for Mexico with about 200 Indians and Negroes in October, 1849, and petitioned the Mexican authorities for land on July 24, 1850. Returning to Indian Territory for additional recruits in September, 1851, he had little success, and was likewise unsuccessful in bringing the Texas tribes under his command. He then returned to Coahuila, Mexico (where the Seminoles had been granted land as military colonists on Oct. 16, 1850), took the oath of fidelity to Mexico on Feb. 4, 1851, and was appointed a judge and commissioned a colonel. In the next year he visited Mexico City and obtained the grant of Nacimiento, near Muzquiz, on July 26, 1852. He was active and successful in warfare against wild Indians and Texas filibusters (1851–56), but given to intoxication. He died of smallpox.

Coahuila (kō.ä.wē′lä). [Also, **Coahuila de Zaragosa** (or **Saragoza**) (dā sä.rä.gō′sä).] State in N Mexico, lying between Texas on the N, Texas and Nuevo León on the E, San Luis Potosí, Zacatecas, and Durango on the S, and Chihuahua and Durango on the W. Capital, Saltillo; area, 58,067 sq. mi.; pop. 720,145 (1950).

Coahuiltecan (kō.ạ.wēl′tek.ạn). Extinct American Indian linguistic stock comprised of several languages once spoken among the Indians of the lower Rio Grande in Texas and the states of Coahuila, Nuevo León, and Tamaulipas, in NE Mexico.

Coalbrookdale (kōl′brůk.dāl). Ecclesiastical district and coal-mining village in W England, in Shropshire, situated on a part of the Forest of Wyre coal field known as the Coalbrookdale field, and on the river Severn, ab. 5 mi. S of Wellington, ab. 150 mi. NW of London by rail. Coke-smelted iron was first produced here (1709) by Abraham Darby, and until 1750 it was one of the only two places where this kind of iron was made.

Coaldale (kōl′dāl). Borough in E Pennsylvania, in Schuylkill County: coal mining. 5,318 (1950).

Coal Harbour. See **Cold Harbour.**

Coalinga (kō.ạ.ling′gạ). City in C California, in Fresno County, SE of San Francisco: supply point for the county's oil fields. 5,539 (1950).

Coalsmouth (kōlz′mouth). A former name of **St. Albans,** W.Va.

Coal Valley. Former name of **Montgomery,** W.Va.

Coalville (kōl′vil). Urban district and coal-mining town in C England, in Leicestershire, ab. 5 mi. SE of Ashby-de-la-Zouch, ab. 115 mi. N of London by rail. 25,739 (1951).

Coalville. A former name of **Ashley,** Pa.

Coamo (kō.ä′mō). City in S Puerto Rico, in the E part of Ponce department, on the Coamo River: thermal medicinal baths. 11,592 (1950).

Coan (kō′an), **Titus.** b. at Killingworth, Conn., Feb. 1, 1801; d. at Hilo, Hawaii, Dec. 1, 1882. American missionary in Hawaii (1835–82).

Coanaco (kō.ä.nä′kō) or **Coanacatzín** (kō.ä.nä.kä.tsēn′). b. c1495; d. after 1521. Aztec chief; son of Nezahualpilli, lord of Tezcuco, and brother of Cacama, who was seized by Cortés in 1520. Cortés put another brother, Cuicuitzcatl, in Cacama's place, but Coanaco claimed the chieftainship of Tezcuco, and after the *Noche Triste* ("Sad Night," i.e., that of June 30, 1520, when the Aztecs inflicted a disastrous defeat on the Spanish forces) he was upheld by the Mexican sovereigns. He seized and massacred a body of Spaniards who were passing through Tezcucan territory, but on the approach of Cortés (December, 1520), he fled to the city of Mexico, where he assisted in the defense. He was captured with Guatemotzin, on Aug. 13, 1521.

Coanza (kwän′zạ). See **Cuanza.**

Coarí (kō.ạ.rē′). [Also, **Coary.**] River of W Brazil which joins the Amazon from the S.

Coast and Geodetic Survey, U.S. [Former names, **Survey of the Coast, U.S. Coast Survey.**] Government bureau created (Feb. 10, 1807) by act of Congress at the suggestion of President Thomas Jefferson, for the purpose of gathering data to aid navigators along the E coast of the U.S. It was originally under the Treasury Department, but after the War of 1812 was temporarily under the jurisdiction of the Navy Department. The methods and organization advocated by the unit's first superintendent, Rudolph Hassler, were approved by Congress in 1843, and in June, 1878 the Survey received its present designation. In 1903 it was placed under the authority of the Department of Commerce and Labor (later the Department of Commerce). It maintains on a current basis charts on some 103,000 miles of coastline, and makes new surveys, conducts studies of tides and currents, and disseminates pertinent data to mariners and engineers, compiles and distributes magnetic information, determines inland geographical positions, furnishes seismological data, and compiles and issues aeronautical charts.

Coast Guard, U.S. Government unit established in 1915, when it replaced and absorbed the duties of the Revenue Cutter Service and the Life Saving Service. The Revenue Cutter Service (initially called the Revenue Marine) was created in 1790, at the suggestion of Alexander Hamilton, for aiding customs collectors; the Life Saving Service, established in 1871, took over all privately managed life-saving stations, and until 1878, when it was given the status of an independent bureau in the Treasury Department, was operated by the Revenue Cutter Service. The Coast Guard, consisting of some 35,000 officers and men, operates in peacetime under the Treasury Department, and in time of war becomes a part of the U.S. Navy, subject to the orders of the secretary of the navy. Among its peacetime duties are the enforcement of federal laws on the high seas and navigable inland waters of the U.S., the maintenance of the Bering Sea Patrol and the International Ice Patrol (North Atlantic), the removal of menaces and obstructions to navigation, the lending of aid to craft in distress, and the maintenance of lighthouses, buoys, radio stations, lightships, and other aids to safe navigation. It took part in all of the major invasions carried out by U.S. forces in World War II.

Coast Mountains. Mountain range of British Columbia, Canada, paralleling the Pacific coast from the Yukon border to the border of the U.S. The mountains extend to the coast in several places and reappear off the coast as numerous small islands. They do not range as high as the Rockies or the Selkirks. The two highest peaks are Mounts Waddington (13,260 ft.) and Tiedemann (12,000 ft.).

Coast Range or **Mountains.** See **Mar, Serra do.**

Coast Ranges. Series of mountain chains extending through most of the W part of California, NW Oregon, and W Washington, nearly parallel with the Pacific Ocean, and into Lower California and Canada. They include all mountains W of Puget Sound and the Willamette, Sacramento, and San Joaquin valleys, and SW of the Mohave Desert. The highest peak is Mount San Bernardino (10,630 ft.).

Coatbridge (kōt′brij). Municipal burgh and manufacturing town in S Scotland, in Lanarkshire, ab. 9 mi. E of Glasgow, ab. 394 mi. N of London by rail. Its leading industry is iron manufacture, now based mainly on imported iron ores. 47,538 (1951).

Coatepec (kō.ä.tā.pek′). City in SE Mexico, in Veracruz state. 11,459 (1940).

Coates (kōts), **Albert.** b. at St. Petersburg, April 23, 1882—. English conductor and composer. The son of an Englishman whose business took him to Russia, he entered (1902) the Leipzig Conservatory, studying under Nikisch. After conducting (1911) *Siegfried* on a guest appearance at St. Petersburg, he was invited to become principal conductor there for the next five years. When the revolution forced him to leave Russia, he went to London, where he was engaged by Beecham to conduct at Covent Garden the season that it reopened after World War I. In 1920 he went to the U.S. to conduct the New York Symphony Orchestra at the invitation of Walter Damrosch, and subsequently directed (1923–25) the Philharmonic Orchestra of Rochester, and appeared with the

Philharmonic Society of New York at the Lewisohn summer concerts. His compositions include the operas *Samuel Pepys* (1929) and *Pickwick* (1936), as well as the symphonic poem *The Eagle.*

Coates, Eric. b. at Hucknall, Nottinghamshire, England, Aug. 27, 1886—. English musician and composer. He studied under Georg Ellenberger, Ralph Horner, and Lionel Tertis, toured (1907) with the Hambourg String Quartet, and was appointed (1912) first viola in the Queen's Hall Orchestra at London. His compositions include *The Mill o' Dreams, The Green Hills o' Somerset, A Song Remembered,* and *Joyous Youth Suite.*

Coates, Florence. [Maiden name, **Earle.**] b. at Philadelphia, July 1, 1850; d. there, April 6, 1927. American lyric poet, author of *Mine and Thine* (1904), *Lyrics of Life* (1909), *The Unconquered Air and Other Poems* (1912), and *Pro Patria* (1917). Collected editions of her poetry appeared in 1898 and 1916.

Coates, George James. b. at Melbourne, Australia, 1869; d. 1930. British genre and portrait painter. He exhibited many times at the Paris Salon of the French Society of Decorative Arts and at the Royal Academy at London. The National Gallery at Melbourne has his *Motherhood* and *Portrait of Jean Grusset Richardot and His Son,* after Van Dyck.

Coates, John. b. at Girlington, England, June 29, 1865; d. at Norwood, England, Aug. 16, 1941. English tenor. He toured (c1895) America with the D'Oyly Carte company, created (1901) the role of Claudio in Stanford's *Much Ado About Nothing,* appeared in *Dream of Gerontius* (1902) and in *Apostles* (1903), and sang (1910, 1911) with the Beecham companies.

Coates, Joseph Gordon. b. at Matakohe, New Zealand, 1878; d. May 27, 1943. New Zealand statesman who served (1925–28) as prime minister of New Zealand. During World War I he was a member of the New Zealand forces in France. He served as New Zealand minister of justice (1919–20), postmaster general and minister of telegraphs (1919–25), minister of public works (1920–26), minister of railways (1923–28), minister of native affairs (1921–28), minister of external affairs (1928), minister of public works, employment, and transport in the coalition ministry (1931–33), and minister of finance, customs, and transport (1933–35). A member of the New Zealand war cabinet (1940–43), he was appointed (1941) minister of armed forces and war coördination. In 1935 he visited the U.S. to negotiate reciprocal trade agreements.

Coates, Robert M. [Full name, **Robert Myron Coates.**] b. at New Haven, Conn., April 6, 1897—. American novelist and short-story writer. He was graduated (B.A., 1919) from Yale, was a contributor to the expatriate "little magazines," including *Broom* and *transition,* and in 1930 published a historical study, *The Outlaw Years* (1930). Among his novels and collections of short stories are *The Eater of Darkness* (1929), *Yesterday's Burdens* (1933), *All the Year Round* (1943), *The Bitter Season* (1946), and *Wisteria Cottage* (1948).

Coatesville (kōts'vil). City in SE Pennsylvania, in Chester County, ab. 32 mi. W of Philadelphia, on the Brandywine River: manufactures of steel, textiles, and metal products. Armor plate for the *Monitor* was made at nearby Laurel Iron Works, now in ruins. 13,826 (1950).

Coaticook (kō.at'i.kůk). Town in Quebec, Canada, situated on the Coaticook River in the SE part of the province, ab. 10 mi. N of the Vermont border and ab. 18 mi. S of Sherbrooke. 6,341 (1951).

Coatlicue (kō.ät.lē'kwā). [Also, **Cohuatlicue.**] Aztec earth goddess and fertility goddess, and as such, associated with spring. She is also mother of the gods, and is worshiped especially as the mother of Huitzilopochtli (the Aztec war god). One statue represents her as having a head of twin serpents, a necklace of human hands and hearts, clawed hands and feet, and a skirt of intertwined snakes. For this reason she is called the "Lady of the Serpent Skirt."

Coats Land (kōts). Part of the Antarctic Continent W of Queen Maud Land which forms the E shore of the Wendell Sea. It was named in 1904 for two men who helped finance the *Scotia* Antarctic expedition.

Coatsworth (kōts'wėrth), **Elizabeth.** b. at Buffalo, N.Y., May 31, 1893—. American writer of books for children, known also as a poet; wife (1929 *et seq.*) of Henry Beston. In 1915 she graduated from Vassar College. She was awarded (1930) the annual John Newbery prize given for the outstanding children's book of the year, in this case *The Cat Who Went to Heaven.* Among her other children's books are *The Cat and the Captain* (1927), *Away Goes Sally* (1934), *Alice-All-by-Herself* (1937), and *Dancing Tom* (1938). Her poems have been published in the collections *Fox Footprints* (1923) and *Compass Rose* (1929). She also wrote the novel *Here I Stay* (1938) and the books on Maine life *Country Neighborhood* and *Maine Ways* (1947).

Coatzacoalcos (kō.ä″tsä.kō.äl'kōs). [Also: **Goazacoalco, Coaxacoalco** (kō.ä″ʜä.kō.äl'kō).] Ancient Indian name of a region in Mexico, in the N part of the isthmus of Tehuantepec, W of the Coatzacoalcos River, and now forming part of the state of Veracruz. It submitted to Sandoval in 1522, and in 1534 was made a province, corresponding nearly to the bishopric of Tlaxcala. The name as applied to this region soon fell into disuse.

Coatzacoalcos. [Former name, **Puerto México.**] City in SE Mexico, in Veracruz state, on the Coatzacoalcos River, near the Bay of Campeche: port of entry for the Isthmus of Tehuantepec. 11,740 (1940).

Coatzacoalcos River. [Also, **Goatzacoalcos.**] River in the Isthmus of Tehuantepec, SE Mexico, which flows N into the Gulf of Campeche. Length, ab. 150 mi.

Cob (kob), **Oliver.** Illiterate water-carrier in Ben Jonson's play *Every Man in His Humour.* Before water from the New River was brought into London the city was chiefly supplied from conduits, generally erected by rich citizens. Water was carried from these by men called "tankard-bearers," and sold. Cob was one of these, and gave a sort of notoriety to his class from his position in Jonson's play.

Cobalt (kō'bôlt). Mining town in E Ontario, Canada, ab. 340 mi. N of Toronto. It has become famous for its silver mines. It is situated in the clay belt; there is some good farming land in the region. 2,230 (1951).

Cobán (kō.ʙän'). City in C Guatemala, capital of Alta Verapaz department. 6,854 (1950).

Cobb (kob), **Fort.** U.S. military post erected (1859) on the Washita River, in Indian Territory. During part of the Civil War it was occupied by Confederate forces. It was again garrisoned by U.S. soldiers in 1868, and finally abandoned in 1869.

Cobb, Frank Irving. b. in Shawnee County, Kan., Aug. 6, 1869; d. Dec. 21, 1923. American journalist and newspaper editor, noted as chief editor of Joseph Pulitzer's New York *World.* He was raised in Michigan, where he became a reporter, served as city editor on the Grand Rapids *Herald,* and worked for the *Daily Eagle* in that city. He later joined the Detroit *Evening News* as a political correspondent and became its chief editorial writer in 1899; his editorials impressed Pulitzer, who brought him to New York in 1904 as his confidential adviser. Cobb was given control of the editorial page and after Pulitzer's death (1911) became editor in chief. His editorials, distinguished for their terseness, were often enlisted in the cause of reform in politics and business, and under Cobb's regime the *World* achieved a reputation as one of the leading crusading organs in the U.S.

Cobb, Howell. b. at Cherry Hill, Ga., Sept. 7, 1815; d. at New York, Oct. 9, 1868. American politician. He was member of Congress from Georgia in the periods 1843–51 and 1855–57 (acting as speaker in the years 1849–51), governor of Georgia (1851–53), and secretary of the treasury (1857–60). An advocate of secession for the state of Georgia, he served as president of the Confederate Congress (1861–62).

Cobb, Irvin S. [Full name, **Irvin Shrewsbury Cobb.**] b. at Paducah, Ky., June 23, 1876; d. at New York, March 10, 1944. American humorist and journalist. He served on the staffs of various magazines and newspapers, including the Louisville, Ky., *Evening Post* (1898–1901), for which he was a columnist as well as a correspondent, the Paducah *News Democrat* (1901–04), where he was managing editor, the New York *Evening Sun* (1904–05) and *World* (1905–11), the *Saturday Evening Post* (1911–22), and *Cosmopolitan* (1922–32). He became known as a humorist in his writings, but was also sought after as an after-dinner speaker, and in 1934 he began to act in motion pictures as well. His humorous books and short-story collections include *Back Home* (1912), *Cobb's Anatomy* (1912), *Old Judge Priest* (1915), *Speaking of Operations*—(1917), *The Life of the Party* (1919), *Jeff Poindexter* (1922), *Alias Ben Alibi* (1924), *Ladies and Gentlemen* (1927), *Judge Priest Turns Detective* (1936), *Azam: The Story of An Arabian Colt* (1937), and *Glory, Glory, Hallelujah!* (1941). He was the author, moreover, of the musical comedy *Funabashi* (1907), the musical sketch *Mr. Buoybody* (1908), and other plays. With Bayard Veiller he collaborated on the comedy *Back Home* (1915), and with Roi Megru on the drama *Under Sentence* (1916). He published an autobiography, *Exit Laughing* (1941), and was also the author of motion-picture scenarios.

Cobb, James. b. 1756; d. 1818. English playwright. He was the author of numerous comedies, operas, and other works.

Cobb, Sylvanus. b. at Norway, Me., July 17, 1798; d. at East Boston, Mass., Oct. 31, 1866. American Universalist clergyman and writer; father of Sylvanus Cobb, Jr. (1823–87). He became in 1838 editor of the *Christian Freeman*, which position he occupied upward of 20 years. He was the author of *The New Testament, with Explanatory Notes* (1864), and other works.

Cobb, Sylvanus, Jr. b. at Waterville, Me., June 5, 1823; d. at Hyde Park, Mass., July 20, 1887. American writer; son of Sylvanus Cobb (1798–1866). He wrote *The King's Talisman* (1851), *The Patriot Cruiser* (1859), and *Ben Hamed* (1864).

Cobb, Ty. [Full name, **Tyrus Raymond Cobb.**] b. at Narrows, Ga., Dec. 18, 1886—. American baseball player. He began his career in 1904, with a baseball club at Augusta, Ga. From 1905 to 1926 he played with Detroit in the American League, serving in the period 1921–26 as team manager. In 1926 he was sold to Philadelphia in the American League. During his career he held the league records in batting and base stealing.

Cobbe (kob), **Frances Power.** b. at Dublin, Ireland, Dec. 4, 1822; d. in Wales, April 5, 1904. British philanthropist, feminist, editor, and philosophical and religious writer. Largely self-educated, except for a brief period in a Brighton school, she traveled in Greece and Italy, meeting Mazzini, the Italian revolutionist, and becoming Italian correspondent for the London *Daily News*. She aided Mary Carpenter in the latter's work on behalf of neglected children, agitated in favor of votes and college degrees for women and against vivisection, wrote (1868–75) for the *Echo*, and edited the works (14 vols., 1863–71) of Theodore Parker. She was the author of *The Theory of Intuitive Morals* (1855; published anonymously), *Broken Lights* (1864), *Studies of Ethical and Social Subjects* (1865), *Dawning Lights* (1868), *The Final Cause of Women* (1869), *Darwinism in Morals* (1872), *Doomed to be Saved* (1874), *The Duties of Women* (1881), *The Scientific Spirit* (1888), and her *Autobiography* (2 vols., 1904).

Cobbett (kob'e̜t), **William.** [Pseudonym, **Peter Porcupine.**] b. at Farnham, Surrey, England, March 9, 1762; d. at Normandy Farm, near Guildford, England, June 18, 1835. English journalist, pamphleteer, and politician. After seeing military service in Nova Scotia, he began his journalistic career at Philadelphia, where he was three times sued for libel. Back in England in 1800, he began in 1802 to publish *Cobbett's Weekly Political Register*, which he edited until his death. He spent two years in prison (1810–12) and was fined 1,000 pounds for an article attacking flogging in the army. During the years 1817–19 he was again in America. He was elected a member of Parliament for Oldham in 1832, a vital year in English history. His works are *Observations on the Emigration of Dr. Joseph Priestley* (1794), an anonymous pamphlet, *A Bone to Gnaw for the Democrats*, *A Kick for a Bite*, and *A Little Plain English Addressed to the People of the United States* (all 1795), political pamphlets, *A New Year's Gift for the Democrats* (1796), *Grammar of the English Language* (1818), *A Journal of a Year's Residence in the United States* (1818–19), *History of the Protestant Reformation* (1824–27), *Advice to Young Men* (1829), and *Rural Rides* (1830), dealing with political and agricultural conditions in the English countryside. Cobbett did much of his writing under the name of "Peter Porcupine," which was appropriate enough in view of the invective in which he indulged. Students of style regard his English as clear, vigorous, and idiomatic.

Cobbler of Preston (pres'to̜n), **The.** Musical farce by Charles Johnson, founded on the adventures of Christopher Sly in Shakespeare's *Taming of the Shrew*. It was first acted in 1716, and altered and produced with music in 1817. Another version was produced by Christopher Bullock at about the same time.

Cobbold (kob'o̜ld), **Richard.** b. at Ipswich, Suffolk, England, 1797; d. Jan. 5, 1877. English novelist and divine; father of Thomas Spencer Cobbold (1828–86). His chief work is *History of Margaret Catchpole, a Suffolk Girl* (1845), a fictional life of an actual Margaret Catchpole (1773–1841), a servant girl and adventuress who twice escaped a death sentence and was transported to Australia, where she died, a respected woman, 40 years later. Cobbold told the story with her full knowledge and permission, omitting only (at her request) her married name. Other novels by him are *Freston Tower* (1850) and *Courtland* (1852).

Cobbold, Thomas Spencer. b. at Ipswich, England, 1828; d. at London, March 20, 1886. English naturalist, noted especially for his studies of worms parasitic on man and animals; son of Richard Cobbold (1797–1877). He was appointed lecturer on botany at Saint Mary's Hospital, London, in 1857, on zoölogy at the Middlesex Hospital in 1861, and on geology at the British Museum in 1868. In 1873 he became professor of botany, and later of helminthology, at the Royal Veterinary College.

Cobden (kob'de̜n), **Richard.** b. at Heyshott, near Midhurst, Sussex, England, June 3, 1804; d. at London, April 2, 1865. English statesman and publicist, especially noted as an advocate of free trade and of peace. He entered business as a salesman and in 1831 moved to Manchester to start, with partners, a calico-printing firm. In the boom period of the following years it flourished and he was soon able to indulge a strong bent for travel and for public affairs. He visited the U.S. in 1835 and 1859, traveled extensively in Europe, and spoke French fluently. From 1838 to 1846 he was the leading figure in the Anti-Corn Law League, which conducted a momentous campaign against protective duties for agriculture. Cobden was a member of Parliament most of the time from 1841 to his death, but declined party affiliation and opportunities to become a cabinet minister. In 1859–60 he negotiated a commercial treaty with France which seemed at the time to be an important step toward universal free trade. All his life Cobden was an "agitator" and reformer whose peculiar mark was persuasiveness, in Parliament, in pamphlets, and at public meetings. His faith in free trade and the power of education had a strong moralistic tinge and led him to strong advocacy of nonintervention in foreign affairs, peace by arbitration, and the freeing of colonies which could govern themselves. He was the most effective voice of the English middle class in the struggle against the monopoly of the old aristocracy and other vested interests, and did much to fix in English thought the principle that free enterprise would lead to universal prosperity and peace. He supported the cause of the North during the Civil War in the U.S. He failed, however, to carry his own Manchester with him in opposition to the Crimean War and died somewhat disillusioned with the selfishness and short-sightedness of the middle class. His *Political Writings* were published in 1867; his *Speeches on Questions of Public Policy* (ed. by Bright and Rogers) in 1870.

Cobden Club. Association for the promulgation of free-trade doctrines, founded at London in 1866.

Cobden-Sanderson (kob'de̜n.san'dėr.so̜n), **Thomas James.** b. 1840; d. 1922. English bookbinder. After a short stay with the binder Roger de Coverley, he opened a workshop, with his wife as assistant. The Doves bindery and press (Hammersmith, London), which he founded, were much influenced by William Morris and Walter Crane.

Cobet (kō.bet'), **Carel Gabriel.** b. at Paris, Nov. 28, 1813; d. at Leiden, Netherlands, Oct. 26, 1889. Dutch philologist, paleographer, and classical scholar. He was educated at The Hague *Gymnasium* (advanced secondary school) and at the University of Leiden, and was professor at Leiden from 1846 (emeritus from 1884). In 1856 he became joint editor of *Mnemosyne*, a philological review. He published *Variae lectiones* (1854), *Novae lectiones*

(1858), *Miscellanea critica* (1876), *Collectanea critica* (1878), and others.

Cóbh (kōv). [Also: **An Cób** (or **Cóf**); former name, **Queenstown.**] Urban district, market town, and seaport in Munster province, Irish Republic, in County Cork, situated on Great Island in Cork Harbour, ab. 9 mi. E of Cork city. It is the outlying seaport of Cork, and was formerly a port of call for transatlantic steamers. It is now primarily a passenger port, handling very little cargo traffic. Cóbh is the Irish word for "cove" (An means "the"); it was called Cove of Cork before the visit of Queen Victoria in 1849, after which the name was Queenstown until 1922. It is the headquarters of the Royal Cork Yacht Club, founded in 1720. In World War I it was a port of debarkation for American troops, and served as a repair and supply base for American and British war vessels engaged in convoy work from the U.S. and Canada. Because of Irish neutrality in World War II it played no part in that conflict. Pop. 5,713 (1951).

Cobham (kob'ąm), 8th Baron. Title of **Brooke, Henry.**

Cobham, Lord. See **Oldcastle,** Sir **John.**

Cobham, Eleanor. d. c1443. Second wife of Humphrey, Duke of Gloucester. She had dealings with Roger Bolingbroke, who professed the black art, and was tried for a conspiracy to kill the king by magic, that her husband might have the crown. She was imprisoned and sentenced to walk about the streets for three days bareheaded with a burning taper in her hand. She was afterward imprisoned in Chester Castle, Kenilworth, and the Isle of Man, and is said to have remained in Peel Castle till her death. She is referred to in Shakespeare's *Henry VI, Part II,* act 2, scene 3.

Cobi (kō'bē). See **Gobi.**

Cobija (kō.ʙē'hä). Capital of Pando department, in NW Bolivia. 1,726 (1950).

Cobija. [Also: **Gatico, Puerto Lamar.**] Seaport on the Pacific Ocean, in NW Chile: formerly capital of the Bolivian province of Atacama, but held by Chile since 1879. Pop. under 5,000 (1940).

Coblenz or **Coblentz** (kō'blents). See **Koblenz.**

Cobler of Aggawam (ag'ą.wąm), **The Simple.** See **Simple Cobler of Aggawam, The.**

Cobleskill (kob'l.skil). Village in C New York, in Schoharie County: manufactures of pancake flour and refrigerators. It is the seat of the Cobleskill Agricultural School. 3,208 (1950).

Cobourg (kō'bėrg). [Also, **Coburg.**] Lake port and the capital of Northumberland County, Ontario, Canada, situated on Lake Ontario, ab. 65 mi. E by NE of Toronto. It is connected by ferry with Rochester, N.Y., and by rail with most of the major cities to the E and W. Victoria College, formerly situated here, was removed to Toronto in 1890. Pop. 7,470 (1951).

Cobourg (ko.bör). French name of the duchy of **Coburg.**

Cobourg Peninsula (kō'bėrg). [Also, **Coburg Peninsula.**] Peninsula in the Northern Territory of Australia, W of the Gulf of Carpentaria and E of Melville Island. It partially encloses Van Diemen Gulf.

Cobre (kō'brā). [Also, **El Cobre.**] Town in SE Cuba, ab. 11 mi. by road W of Santiago de Cuba. It was founded in 1558 as a center for the nearby copper mines. On a hill just S of the town is the shrine of Nuestra Señora de la Caridad del Cobre, scene of an annual pilgrimage on Sept. 8. Pop. 1,990 (1941).

Coburg (kō'bėrg; German, kō'bůrk). [Also: **Koburg,** French, **Cobourg.**] Former duchy of Germany, later forming with Gotha the state of Saxe-Coburg-Gotha.

Coburg. [Also, **Koburg.**] City in S Germany, in the *Land* (state) of Bavaria, American Zone, in the *Regierungsbezirk* (government district) of Middle and Upper Franconia, situated on the Itz River, a tributary of the Main River, ab. 36 mi. NW of Bayreuth. It is a center of the basketry trade, and has manufactures of baskets, wicker furniture, toys, paperware, leatherware, chinaware, ceramics, metallurgical articles, textiles, and foodstuffs. Buildings of interest include the theater, library, museum of art and antiquities, local museum, and natural history museum, as well as several gates and Gothic churches, and a *Rathaus* (city hall), arsenal, and other monuments of the 16th and 17th centuries. The Ehrenberg Castle also dates from the 16th century. On a mountain above the city is the huge medieval castle of Coburg, which was rebuilt in the 19th century according to the original design. It served once as a refuge for Martin Luther. Coburg came under the rule of the house of Wettin in 1353, later that of the line of Saxe-Coburg-Gotha; it joined the free state of Bavaria in 1920. The population is predominantly Protestant; the increase in population between 1939 and 1946, largely due to the influx of Sudeten German refugees, was 41.6 percent. 42,390 (1946), 44,929 (1950).

Coburg Peninsula. See **Cobourg Peninsula.**

Coburn (kō'bėrn), **Charles Douville.** b. at Savannah, Ga., June 19, 1877—. American actor and theatrical producer; husband (married 1906) of Ivah Wills. In 1895 he became manager of a Savannah theater. Having made his stage debut in 1899, he played in stock companies until 1906, his first leading role being in *The Christian* (1903). In 1906 he and his wife organized the Coburn Players, a repertory company, and the two starred in its productions. He made his screen debut in 1937. On the stage he appeared in *Lysistrata* (1930–31), *The County Chairman* (1936), and other plays. He had roles in such films as *Rhapsody in Blue* and *The Parradine Case.*

Cobweb (kob'web). Fairy in Shakespeare's *A Midsummer Night's Dream.*

Cocagne (ko.kän'). See **Cockaigne.**

Cocama (kō.kä'mä). South American Indian tribe inhabiting portions of the area along the Ucayali and Huallaga rivers of E Peru. The language is a member of the Tupí-Guaraní stock.

Cocanada (kō.ką.nä'dą). Seaport in the Godavari district, Madras state, Union of India, on the Bay of Bengal, ab. 250 mi. E of Hyderabad. Large ships are forced to anchor 6 or 7 mi. from the shore because of a sand bar across the mouth of the harbor, which has to be constantly dredged to maintain a depth of 4 to 7 ft. The main exports are raw cotton, castor seeds, peanuts, and rice. 75,140 (1941).

Coccaio (kōk.kä'yō), **Merlino.** Pseudonym of **Folengo, Teofilo.**

Cocceians (kok.sē'ąnz). Followers of John Cocceius or Koch (1603–69), professor of theology at Leiden, the Netherlands, who founded the so-called Federal school of theology. He believed that the whole history of the Christian church to all time was prefigured in the Old Testament, and so opposed the Voëtians.

Cocceianus (kok.sē'ą.nus). See **Dio** (or **Dion**) **Cassius.**

Coccia (kōt'chä), **Carlo.** b. at Naples, Italy, April 14, 1782; d. at Novara, Italy, April 13, 1873. Italian composer of operas, cantatas, and masses. In 1820 he visited London, where he was an operatic conductor and also professor of composition at the Royal Academy, returning to Italy in 1828. He again visited England in 1835.

Coccium (kok'si.um). Latin name of **Wigan.**

Cochabamba (kō.chä.ʙäm'bä). Department in C Bolivia. Capital, Cochabamba; area, 23,327 sq. mi.; pop. 490,475 (1950).

Cochabamba. [Former name, **Oropeza.**] Second largest city in Bolivia, capital of Cochabamba department, in the C part of the country: agricultural and trading center; seat of a university. It was founded in 1574, and was prominent in the war of independence from Spain (1815 *et seq.*). 80,795 (1950).

Cochem (kō'ċhęm). See **Kochem.**

Cocherel (kosh.rel). Hamlet in NW France, in the department of Eure, ab. 12 mi. E of Évreux. Here in 1364 the French under Bertrand Du Guesclin defeated the forces of England and Navarre.

Cochet (ko.she; Anglicized, kō.shā'), **Henri.** b. at Lyons, France, 1901—. French tennis player. As an amateur, he won (1922) the world's hard-court championship and triumphed (1928) over Francis T. Hunter to become champion in the U.S. singles tournament. He played (1925–33) on the French Davis Cup team and, with Jean Borotra and others, he won (1927) and defended (1927–32) the cup. He became a professional in 1933.

Cochet, Jean Benoît Désiré. b. at Sanvic, near Le Havre, France, March 7, 1812; d. at Rouen, France, June 1, 1875. French archaeologist, best known for his explorations in Normandy.

Cochin (kō'chin'). Former state in S India, ab. 160 mi. NW of Cape Comorin: before 1947 a dependency of

Madras province, now part of the state of Travancove-Cochin, Union of India. It produces coconuts, rice, fruits, and rubber. Area, 1,361 sq. mi.; pop. 1,422,875 (1941).

Cochin. Seaport on the Malabar coast, SW Union of India, geographically within Travancore-Cochin state, but administered by Madras state. The most important port between Bombay and Colombo, it has a fine harbor and inland waterways connecting it with the hinterland. There are powerful tugs and modern suction dredges keeping the channel open at all times. The chief exports are coir, yarn, coir mats and matting, lemon-grass oil, cashew nuts, tea, coconut oil, and rubber. It was settled by the Portuguese in 1503, and was held by the Dutch from 1663 to 1796. Pop. 22,818 (1941).

Cochin (ko.shañ), **Augustin Denys Marie.** b. at Paris, 1876; killed at Hardécourt, France, 1916. French historian; son of Denys Cochin. He was the author of *Recueil des actes du gouvernement révolutionnaire* (Collection of the Acts of the Revolutionary Government, 1914; not completed) and *Les Sociétés de pensée et la révolution en Bretagne* (1926; posthumous).

Cochin, Charles Nicolas. b. at Paris, Feb. 22, 1715; d. there, April 29, 1790. French engraver and art critic. He wrote *Voyage d'Italie* (1758), and others.

Cochin, Denys. b. at Paris, Sept. 1, 1851; d. there, March 24, 1922. French conservative political leader and writer; son of P. S. A. Cochin and father of A. D. M. Cochin. He opposed the anticlerical policy of Premier Combes (1902–05) and was foreign undersecretary (1916–17) during World War I. He became (1911) a member of the French Academy.

Cochin, Pierre Suzanne Augustin. b. at Paris, Dec. 12, 1823; d. at Versailles, France, March 15, 1872. French publicist and economist; father of Denys Cochin.

Cochin China (kō'chin chī'nạ). [Also: **Cochinchina, Cochin-China, Lower Cochin China**; official name (since 1949), **South Viet-Nam**; French, **Cochinchine** (ko.shañ.shēn).] Province of Viet-Nam, in S Indochina, occupying the valley of the lower Mekong River. It is bounded by Cambodia on the NW and N, by Annam (Central Viet-Nam) on the NE, by the South China Sea on the E and S, and by the Gulf of Thailand on the W. River and coastal fishing are important. By far the most important crop is rice; others are sugar, tobacco, rubber, coffee, coconuts, oranges, and beans. Cochin China, formerly a French colony obtained from the king of Annam, was declared part of the republic of Viet-Nam in 1945, which was recognized in a provisional status by France in an agreement signed on March 6, 1946. An autonomous republic of Cochin China, also provisional, was set up on June 1, 1946. In 1949 Viet-Nam became a state in the French Union, and Cochin China was attached to it. Capital, Saigon; area, 26,476 sq. mi.; pop. 5,600,000 (est. 1943).

Cochin China, French. Name formerly used vaguely as nearly identical with the old Annamese empire, which occupied most of what became French Indochina, properly restricted to the eastern or maritime part, which became the French colony of Cochin China, later (1946) a republic within the Federation of Indochina, and in 1949 part of the state of Viet-Nam.

Cochin-Chinese or **Cochinchinese** (kō'chin.chī.nēz', -nēs'). Branch of the Vietnamese (predominantly Annamese) people of Indochina dwelling in Cochin China and distinguished by minor differences in customs, dress, and dialect.

Cochise (kō.chēs', kō.chē'sā). An archaeologically known North American Indian culture in SE Arizona and adjacent New Mexico, dated at about 1,300 to 500 B.C. It was probably contemporaneous with the Folsom culture, but the remains, especially stone grinding-tools, such as metates and hand stones, suggest a greater dependence on such vegetable foods as seeds and nuts, and therefore a type of culture from which later agricultural populations were in part derived.

Cochiti (kō.chē'tē). Pueblo Indian village ab. 27 mi. SW of Santa Fe, N.M. The language spoken at Cochiti belongs to the eastern branch of the Keresan family.

Cochituate (kọ.chit'ụ.āt), **Lake.** Small lake in Middlesex County, Mass., ab. 17 mi. W of Boston. It is one of the sources of Boston's water supply.

Cochlaeus (kok.lē'us; German, koċh.lā'ůs), **Johannes.** [Original name, **Johann Dobenek** (or **Dobneck**).] b. at Wendelstein, near Nuremberg, Germany, 1479; d. at Breslau, Jan. 11, 1552. German Roman Catholic humanist, theologian, and controversialist. He became secretary to the duke of Saxony in 1528, and canon at Breslau in 1539. He was associated at the diet of Augsburg (1530) with Eck, Faber, and Wimpina in the composition of the Refutation of the Augsburg Confession, and, on the death of Eck, was regarded as the leading opponent of the Reformation.

Cochran (kok'rạn). City in C Georgia, county seat of Bleckley County, ab. 35 mi. SE of Macon. It has textile mills and is the seat of Middle Georgia College. 3,357 (1950).

Cochran, Alexander Smith. b. at Yonkers, N.Y., Feb. 28, 1874; d. at Saranac Lake, N.Y., June 20, 1929. American carpet manufacturer and philanthropist, known as a yachtsman and bibliophile. As president (1902–10) of Alexander Smith and Sons Carpet Company, he inaugurated a system which gave his employees annual bonuses amounting to 10–30 percent of their pay. During World War I he served (1916 *et seq.*) as commander of his yacht *Warrior* in the British Navy. He donated large sums of money to hospitals, schools, and libraries, including Yale's Elizabethan Club, which contains his collection of 16th and 17th century English rare editions.

Cochran, Charles Blake. b. at Lindfield, Sussex, England, Sept. 25, 1872; d. Jan. 31, 1951. English theatrical producer. After making his acting debut (1891) at New York, he toured America for three years. He returned to London as personal representative of Richard Mansfield, and was manager (1926–38) of the Albert Hall. In 1924 he introduced the rodeo to England at Wembley. He also first promoted roller-skating in Germany, France, and Belgium, and presented Diaghileff's Russian Ballet and Pirandello's Italian Company at London.

Cochran, Jacqueline. [Married name, **Odlum.**] b. at Pensacola, Fla., c1912—. American businesswoman and airplane pilot, who headed the Women's Airforce Service Pilots during World War II; wife (married 1936) of Floyd Bostwick Odlum. In 1935 she established a cosmetics business. Having received (1932) a pilot's license, she was the only woman entrant in the London-Melbourne air race (1934), and the first woman entrant in the Bendix Trophy transcontinental race (1935). She established (1937) the women's national and international speed record, took first place in the Bendix Trophy transcontinental race (1938), was the first woman to pilot (1941) a bomber to England and the first woman civilian to receive (1945) the U.S. Distinguished Service Medal, and was also awarded (1947) the Harmon trophy for women for her war service.

Cochran, Margaret. See **Corbin, Margaret.**

Cochrane (kok'rạn). Capital of Cochrane County, N Ontario, Canada, situated in the middle of the clay belt, on the Abitibi River, ab. 474 mi. N of Toronto and 252 mi. N of North Bay. It is connected by road with most of the major centers of S Ontario, and is on the Ontario Northland Railroad from North Bay to Moosenee. 3,401 (1951).

Cochrane, Elizabeth. Maiden name of **Seaman, Elizabeth.**

Cochrane, John Dundas. b. 1780; d. at Valencia, Venezuela, Aug. 12, 1825. British traveler in Russia and Siberia in the period, 1820-23. He wrote *Narrative of a Pedestrian Journey through Russia and Siberian Tartary* (1824).

Cochrane, Thomas. [Title: 10th Earl of **Dundonald**; called Lord **Cochrane.**] b. at Annsfield, Lanarkshire, Scotland, Dec. 14, 1775; d. at Kensington, London, Oct. 31, 1860. Scottish noble and British naval commander. On May 6, 1801, in the *Speedy*, a small and poorly armed vessel with 54 men, he captured the Spanish frigate *El-gamo* of 600 tons and 319 men. He entered Parliament in 1806. On April 11, 1809, he attacked a French fleet in Aix roads, and destroyed four of the enemy's vessels. In February, 1814, Cochrane was accused of complicity in originating a fraudulent report of Napoleon's death for speculative purposes, and, though he claimed to be entirely innocent, was imprisoned for a year, fined, and expelled from the navy and from the House of Commons. His constituents stood by him, and at once returned him again to Parliament. Accepting an invitation to organize the infant navy of Chile, he reached Valparaíso in November, 1818. During the subsequent campaigns of the war of independence from Spain, with only one frigate and a few old vessels, he managed to neutralize the powerful Spanish squadron, took Valdivia in February, 1820, transported San Martín's army to Peru, blockaded Callao, performed the feat of cutting out a Spanish frigate from under the guns of the castle (Nov. 5, 1820), and contributed greatly to the capture of Lima. Owing to quarrels with San Martín and the Chilean authorities, he left their service, and from March, 1823 to 1825 commanded the Brazilian navy; during this time he recovered Bahia and Maranhão from the Portuguese. Accused of insubordination, he resigned. In 1827 and 1828 he commanded the Greek navy, but accomplished nothing. In 1832 he was virtually exonerated from the charges on which he had been imprisoned in 1814, and was restored to the Order of the Bath and to his rank in the British navy. He was appointed a vice-admiral on Nov. 23, 1841, admiral on March 21, 1851, and rear admiral of the United Kingdom on Oct. 23, 1854.

Cochut (ko.shü), **André.** b. at Paris, 1812; d. there, Jan. 18, 1890. French publicist.

Cock (kôk), **Hieronymus.** [Also, **Kock.**] b. at Antwerp, Belgium, 1510; d. there, 1570. Flemish painter, engraver, and publisher of prints. He studied at Rome, and while there is believed to have assisted Vasari in writing the lives of Dutch artists. He was received into the Guild of Saint Luke at Antwerp in 1545 as a painter, but not long thereafter he gave up painting and devoted himself to engraving and selling prints, being the first in his country to go into this business in a large way. He published numerous prints of good quality based on the works of Peter Brueghel, Hieronymus Bosch, and others.

Cock, The. Tavern in Fleet Street, London, opposite the Temple. Tennyson immortalized it in his *Will Waterproof's Lyrical Monologue.*

"Cockade State." Occasional nickname of **Maryland.**

Cockaigne (ko.kān'). [Also: **Cockayne, Cocagne.**] Name given to an imaginary country where idleness and luxury flourish and are encouraged. The name comes from Old French *pais de cocaigne,* meaning "land of cakes." In the land of Cockaigne the houses were built of cake, roast geese wandered slowly down the streets inviting passers-by to eat them, buttered cooked larks fell from the sky, and the rivers and fountains ran wine. The medieval concept of Cockaigne, which is identical with the German *Schlauraffenland* (meaning, roughly, "country of idlers") and which has influenced the American concept of the Big Rock Candy Mountain, was first recorded (c1305) in English in a manuscript which locates this fabulous land off the W coast of Spain. The idea was at first used purely with a motive of entertainment, but later assumed politico-satirical overtones. In 1598 Florio speaks of "*Cocagna,* as we say Lubberland." From that instance, the 17th century used the term Lubberland for the same concept. After the 17th century the idea of Cockaigne became less popular, and references to it in the 19th century became more and more literary. The term Cockaigne has also been applied derisively to London, as the abode of the cockneys, and also to Paris.

Cock and the Fox, The. Version of Geoffrey Chaucer's *The Nun's Priest's Tale,* by John Dryden.

Cockburn (kō'bėrn), Sir **Alexander James Edmund.** b. Dec. 24, 1802; d. at London, Nov. 21, 1880. British jurist of Scottish descent, lord chief justice of England. Graduated from Trinity Hall, Cambridge, where he became a fellow in 1829, he entered Parliament as a Liberal in 1847, was attorney general from 1851 to February, 1852, and again from December, 1852, to November, 1856, became chief justice of the Common Pleas in 1856, and was named lord chief justice of England on June 24, 1859. As the representative of the British government at the *Alabama* arbitration at Geneva, he dissented from the award, holding that in the case of the *Florida* and that of the *Shenandoah* the responsibility of his government had not been proved.

Cockburn, Alicia (or **Alison**). b. at Fairnalee, Selkirkshire, Scotland, c1710 or 1712; d. at Edinburgh, Nov. 22, 1794. Scottish lyric poet remembered for her ballad *The Flowers of the Forest* (1765), opening with the line, "I've seen the smiling of Fortune beguiling"; daughter of Robert Rutherford. She married Patrick Cockburn, advocate, in 1731 (who died in 1753), and had a son, a captain, who died in 1780. She knew Burns, who admired her lyric so much that he imitated it, and she was a friend of Hume. According to Scott, "in person and features, she somewhat resembled Queen Elizabeth . . she was proud of her auburn hair, which remained unbleached by time even when she was upwards of eighty years old." In her will, she left her emerald ring to Scott's mother.

Cockburn, Catherine. [Maiden name, **Trotter.**] b. at London, Aug. 16, 1679; d. May 11, 1749. English dramatist and philosophical writer; wife (married in 1708) of Patrick Cockburn, a clergyman. She wrote *Agnes de Castro* (acted 1696), *Fatal Friendship* (acted 1698), *Love at a Loss* (a comedy, 1700), and *Revolutions of Sweden* (acted 1706).

Cockburn, Sir **George.** b. at London, April 22, 1772; d. at Leamington, England, Aug. 19, 1853. English admiral. He served at the taking of Martinique in 1809, and assisted at the capture of Washington in 1814. Later he was on the ship which took Napoleon to St. Helena, where Cockburn stayed as governor from 1815 to 1816.

Cockburn, Henry Thomas. [Called Lord **Cockburn.**] b. probably at Edinburgh, Oct. 26, 1779; d. at Bonaly, near Edinburgh, April 26, 1854. Scottish jurist, appointed a judge of the Court of Session in 1834, and a lord of judiciary in 1837. His autobiography, *Memorials of his Time,* was published in 1856.

Cockcroft (kok'krôft), Sir **John Douglas.** b. at Todmorden, Yorkshire, England, May 27, 1897—. English physicist. A fellow of St. John's College, Cambridge (1928–46), he was Jacksonian professor of natural philosophy at Cambridge (1939–46), served as chief superintendent of the air defense research and development establishment (1941–44) and as director of the atomic energy division of the Canadian national research council (1944–46), and became (1946) director of the English atomic research establishment at Harwell, in Berkshire. He and E. T. S. Walton received the 1951 Nobel prize in physics for their researches (c1932) in the smashing of light atoms (lithium and others) by means of electrically speeded-up protons.

Cocke (kok), **John Hartwell.** b. in Surrey County, Va., Sept. 19, 1780; d. July 1, 1866. American planter and publicist. In the War of 1812 he guarded (1814–15) Richmond. A supporter of Bible, tract, and Sunday school societies, he was president (1836 *et seq.*) of the American Temperance Union, and violently opposed slavery and tobacco. He contributed to the founding, and served (1819–52) on the board of visitors, of the University of Virginia.

Cocker (kok'ėr), **Edward.** b. probably in Northamptonshire, England, 1631; d. 1675. English engraver and teacher of writing and arithmetic, and collector of manuscripts. He was the author of various works on calligraphy, arithmetic (*Tutor to Arithmetic,* 1664; *Complete Arithmetician,* before 1669; *Arithmetic,* ed. by John Hawkins, 1678), and others. It has sometimes been asserted that the long used *Arithmetic* is a forgery by Hawkins.

Cockeram (kok'ram), **Henry.** fl. about the middle of the 17th century. English scholar (of whose life virtually nothing is known), author of what is considered the first published dictionary of the English language. The book is entitled *The English Dictionarie, or a New Interpreter of Hard English Words* (c1623; 2nd ed., 1626; 12th ed., revised and enlarged by another editor, 1670). It had been preceded, however, by several books, notably Robert Cawdrey's *The Table Alphabeticall of Hard Words* (1604), which gave definitions and derivations of selected English words.

Cockerell (kok'ėr.el), **Charles Robert.** b. at London, April 28, 1788; d. there, Sept. 17, 1863. English architect. He became architect of the Bank of England in 1833, and was professor of architecture in the Royal Academy in the period 1840–57. He completed the Hanover Chapel in Regent Street in 1825, built the Taylor Buildings at Oxford (1841–42), and designed numerous other public and private buildings. His written works include *Ancient Sculptures in Lincoln Cathedral* (1848), *Iconography of the West Front of Wells Cathedral* (1851), and *A Descriptive Account of the Sculptures of the West Front of Wells Cathedral* (1862).

Cockerell, Theodore Dru Alison. b. at Norwood, England, Aug. 22, 1866; d. Jan. 26, 1948. American zoölogist. Coming to the U.S. in 1887, he lived in Colorado, studying botany and entomology, until 1891, when he became curator of a public museum at Kingston, Jamaica. Returning to the U.S. in 1893, he was entomologist of the New Mexico Agricultural Experiment Station until 1901. He next became curator of the Colorado College Museum (1903–04), and following this was associated with the Colorado State Preparatory School and with the University of Colorado, holding the chair of professor of zoölogy at the latter institution from 1912 on. He was the author of thousands of articles and notes in scientific publications on zoölogical and paleontological subjects.

Cockerill (kok'ėr.il), **William.** b. in Lancashire, England, 1759; d. near Aix-la-Chapelle (Aachen, Germany), 1832. English manufacturer of spinning and weaving machines at Liége, Belgium. Employed (1794) by Catherine II of Russia to make a machine, he was treated with disfavor by her successor. From Russia he went (1799) to Verviers, Belgium, to construct the locks of a public canal. His own inventions of spinning and other machinery were not appreciated, and so he moved (1807) to Liége, where he settled and established a successful machine-construction factory.

Cockermouth (kok'ėr.mouth, -muth). Urban district and market town in NW England, in Cumberland, situated at the confluence of the rivers Cocker and Derwent, ab. 25 mi. SW of Carlisle, ab. 312 mi. NW of London by rail. It is the agricultural market center for the surrounding district. The poet William Wordsworth was born here in a house which is still standing in the main street. 5,234 (1951).

Cock Lane Ghost. The ghost of a Mrs. Kent who appeared as a "luminous lady" and to whom knockings and other mysterious noises were attributed: exposed as an imposition perpetrated in 1762 in Cock Lane, Smithfield, London, by a man named Parsons and his 11-year-old daughter Elizabeth. Samuel Johnson, among others, visited the house, and took an interest in exposing the fraud. However, he was attacked for his supposed credulity by Charles Churchill in his long poem *The Ghost* (1763). Parsons was pilloried.

Cockledemoy (kok'l.dẹ.moi). Adroit and amusing trickster in John Marston's play *The Dutch Courtezan.*

Cockney School (kok'ni). Name derisively given by some English 19th-century critics to a set of writers including Hazlitt, Shelley, Keats, Leigh Hunt, and others. Leigh Hunt was considered the representative member of this coterie.

Cockpit, The. London theater which stood in a narrow court, called Pitt Place, formerly Cockpit Alley, running out of Drury Lane. It was erected c1615, but was pulled down by a mob in 1617. A second theater was built here, called the Phoenix. This in turn gave place to the Drury Lane Theatre.

Cockpit, The. Term formerly applied to the British Privy Council, which at one time had its place of assembly in Whitehall at a place near The Cockpit theater.

Cockran (kok'rạn), **William Bourke.** b. in Ireland, Feb. 28, 1854; d. March 1, 1923. American lawyer and politician. He came to the U.S. in 1871. Long identified with politics at New York, he was also a member (Democratic) of Congress in the periods 1887–89, 1891–95, 1904–09, and 1920–23.

Cockrell (kok'rẹl), **Francis Marion.** b. near Columbus, Johnson County, Mo., Oct. 1, 1834; d. Dec. 13, 1915. American Civil War general and U.S. senator. He began the practice of law at Warrensburg, Mo., in 1855, but early in the Civil War he enlisted in the Confederate forces, and rose from private to brigadier general in less than a year. Cockrell's Brigade was noted in the Southern armies for its discipline and its bravery, and Cockrell himself was five times wounded and three times taken prisoner. After the war he entered politics, and having in 1872 lost the Democratic nomination to the governorship of Missouri by a very narrow margin, he was in 1874 elected to the U.S. Senate, where he served until 1905, when President Theodore Roosevelt, a Republican, appointed him to the Interstate Commerce Commission. Cockrell had been refused a sixth nomination to the Senate as a result of a factional fight in his party, but the president said that while Missouri would lose his services, the country must not be deprived of them. At one time it appeared that Cockrell might have been Roosevelt's opponent in the election of 1904, his name having been proposed as the Democratic presidential nominee by such leaders as William J. Bryan and Champ Clark. His appointment to high office by a president of the opposite political faith reflected the high regard in which he had long been held by men of all parties for his integrity and intelligence. He sat with the Interstate Commerce Commission until 1910, when he was appointed U.S. commissioner to adjust the boundary between Texas and New Mexico.

Cocks (koks), **Mount.** Mountain peak in Antarctica, on the W side of the Ross Shelf Ice; in ab. 78°32′ S., 162°30′ E.

Cocktail Party, The. Play (1950) by T. S. Eliot. The theme, the broken marriage of Edward and Lavinia Chamberlayne, is symbolically treated so as to make it clear that modern society is broken and spiritually sick. The action of the play, in two acts and five scenes, takes place in the Chamberlayne's London flat, and in a consulting room in Harley Street. One of the leading characters, "An Unidentified Guest," turns out to be a psychiatrist who gets at the truth and tries to make his patients see it.

Cockton (kok'tọn), **Henry.** b. at London, Dec. 7, 1807; d. at Bury Saint Edmunds, Suffolk, England, June 26, 1853. English comic novelist. He was the author of *Valentine Vox the Ventriloquist* (1840), *Sylvester Sound the Somnambulist* (1843–44), *Lady Felicia* (1852), *Percy Effingham* (1852), and other novels illustrated by such artists as Cruikshank, Leech, and Thomas Onwhyn.

Cockwood (kok'wůd), **Lady.** In Etherege's comedy *She Would if She Could,* a female Tartuffe who hides a disgraceful intrigue under a great pretense of religious devotion.

Coclé (kō.klā'). Province in SW Panama. Capital, Penonomé; area, 1,470 sq. mi.; pop. 72,670 (1950).

Coclé. American Indian culture known through archaeological evidence, and located mainly in what is now the Coclé province of Panama. The sites consist of deep graves containing many skeletons, rich ceramics, and elaborate gold ornaments and ritual objects. The state of preservation strongly suggests that Coclé culture flourished shortly before the Spanish conquest, and may well be closely related to the culture of the Cuna and other tribes of Panama in historic times.

Cocles (kō'klēz), **Publius Horatius.** Roman legendary hero who with Spurius Lartius and Titus Herminius prevented the entire Etruscan army under Lars Porsena (c508 B.C.) from approaching the wooden Sublician bridge at Rome until it could be destroyed. Horatius then swam across the Tiber to the Roman shore. The story is the subject of one of Macaulay's *Lays of Ancient Rome.* The Greek historian Polybius states that Horatius, weakened by his wounds, was drowned in the Tiber.

Cocoa (kō'kō). City in C Florida, in Brevard County, on the Indian River, NW of Tampa: shipping center for citrus fruits. 4,245 (1950).

Cocoa-tree Club. London club which was the Tory Cocoa-tree Chocolate-house of Queen Anne's reign, at 64 St. James Street. It was converted into a gaming house and a club, probably before 1746, when the house was the headquarters of the Jacobite party, and the resort of the wits of the time. It still exists as a club.

Coco River (kō'kō). See **Segovia River,** Nicaragua.

Cocos Islands (kō'kōs). [Also, **Keeling Islands.**] Group of 20 small coral atolls in the Indian Ocean, 581 mi. SW of Java, and 1,161 mi. from Singapore. They became a British possession in 1857, were for a time administered by the government of Ceylon, became part (1903) of the Straits Settlements, and in 1946, when Singapore became a separate crown colony, were included in the new colony. Darwin found his perfect coral atoll here. Coconuts, copra, and coconut oil are produced. There is a cable station on one of the islands. 1,217 (est. 1951).

Cocospera (kō.kō.spā'rä). Peak in Sonora, Mexico, forming a part of one of the W ramifications of the Sierra Madre.

Cocteau (kok.tō), **Jean.** b. at Maisons-Lafitte, France, July 5, 1891—. French poet, novelist, playwright, film director, and miscellaneous writer, long the apostle to the general public of the various gospels of French modernism in the arts. He was born in easy circumstances and from youth was a disciple of Gide; his bohemianism is an acquired characteristic. His *Potomak* (written 1913; published 1919), a miscellany of prose, verse, and drawings, reflected an uneasy and somewhat tortured mind. His *Lettre à Jacques Maritain* (1926) records his attempt to find peace in Catholicism. His other work reveals less gravity. It includes ballets like *Le Bœuf sur le toit* (1920, score by Darius Milhaud) and *Les Mariés de la tour Eiffel* (1921, score by the "Group des six"); collections of poems, including *Poésie 1916–1923* (1924), *Mythologie* (1934), and *Allégories* (1941); novels such as *Les Enfants terribles* (1929; Eng. trans., *Enfants Terribles,* 1931); dramas like *La Machine infernale* (1934; Eng. trans., *The Infernal Machine,* 1936); and various essays in art theory and criticism. His originality has amused a larger public through such motion pictures as *Le Sang d'un poète.* Critics treat Cocteau alternately as charlatan and genius; he has repudiated neither attribute.

Cocx (koks), **Gonzales.** See **Coques** or **Cocx, Gonzales.**

Cocxie (kok'si), **Michiel.** See **Coxcie** or **Cocxie** or **Coxie, Michiel.**

Cocytus (kǫ.sī'tus). In Greek mythology, one of the five rivers surrounding Hades. Cocytus was the so-called Wailing River. The other four were: the Styx (Hateful), Acheron (Woeful), Pyriphlegethon (Fiery), and Lethe (Forgetful).

Cocytus. Ancient name of **Vuvos.**

Cod (kod), **Cape.** Terminating point of the Cape Cod peninsula.

Codazzi (kō.dät'tsē), **Agustin** (or **Agostino**). b. at Lugo, near Ferrara, Italy, 1792; d. in Colombia, 1859. Engineer and geographer in the N part of South America. He was the author of geographies of this region, including *Resumen de la geografia de Venezuela* (Paris, 1841).

Coddington (kod'ing.tǫn), **William.** b. in Lincolnshire, England, 1601; d. in Rhode Island, Nov. 1, 1678. English colonist in America. He was one of the founders of the colony of Rhode Island in 1638, and at various times (1640 *et seq.*) its governor. He came to Rhode Island after having joined in the protest against the persecution of Anne Hutchinson in Massachusetts.

Code, The. Dramatic narrative in blank verse by Robert Frost, published in his *North of Boston* (1914).

Codecido (or **Codesido**) (kō.ᴛʜā.sē'ᴛʜō), **Emilio Bello.** See **Bello Codecido** (or **Codesido**), **Emilio.**

Code Civil (kod sē.vēl). See **Code Napoléon.**

Code Frédéric (kod frā.dā.rēk). Name sometimes given to a codification of the laws of Prussia made by Frederick II (Frederick the Great) in 1751.

Code Napoléon (kod nȧ.po.lā.ôṅ). [Also: **Code Civil;** English, **Napoleonic Code.**] Compilation of the laws of France made under the auspices of Napoleon Bonaparte as first consul and emperor, and promulgated in the period 1804–10. It is founded on the civil law (the Roman law as it prevailed in many parts of Europe and as modified by local change and commentary), and has been largely copied in other countries where this tradition of law prevails. It was carried by Napoleon to parts of Germany, the Netherlands, and Italy, and through Spain it influenced the legal systems of Latin America. It is the basis of the legal systems of the state of Louisiana and the province of Quebec. In most countries and lesser political units of the English-speaking world (which may be taken broadly as comprising the U.S. and the British Commonwealth) except for Louisiana and Quebec (each of which may fairly claim to be, from the standpoint of both history and linguistics, descended from a predominantly French pattern of tradition, custom, and law) the legal system stems primarily from English common law, and has been influenced very slightly, if at all, by the Code Napoléon. To the average layman the most striking differences between the two legal systems would probably be found in the much greater emphasis placed by English common law on the right of trial by jury and on the role of a jury in determining guilt or innocence.

Code Noir (kod nwȧr). [Eng. trans., *"Black Code."*] Edict of Louis XIV of France in 1685, regulating the West Indian colonies and the condition and treatment of Negro slaves and freed Negroes.

Code of 1650. [Sometimes called **Ludlow's Code.**] Code of laws compiled for the colony of Connecticut by Roger Ludlow.

Codera (kō.ᴛʜā'rä), **Cape.** [Spanish, **Cabo Codera.**] Cape in N Venezuela on the Caribbean Sea.

Codex (kō'deks). Any one of three Maya or a number of Aztec native manuscripts written in pictographs and hieroglyphs, as the Dresden Codex or the Codex Nuttall. The Maya codices all antedate the Spanish conquest; the Aztec are both pre- and post-conquest.

Codex Alexandrinus (kō'deks al"eg.zan.drī'nus). Latin name of the **Alexandrian Codex.**

Codex Exoniensis (ek.sō.ni.en'sis). Latin name of **Exeter Book, The.**

Codigoro (kō.dē.gô'rō). Town and commune in N Italy, in the *compartimento* (region) of Emilia-Romagna, in the province of Ferrara, situated in the delta of the Po River, between the Po di Goro and the inlet of Comacchio, E of Ferrara. The land of the area has been reclaimed and is traversed by canals; the town has a sugar refinery, and paper and cellulose manufactures. Pop. of commune, 17,028 (1936); of town, 5,692 (1936).

Codlin (kod'lin), **Tom.** Cynical exhibitor of a Punch-and-Judy show, in Charles Dickens's *Old Curiosity Shop.* He is a partner in the show with "Short Trotters" Harris, who is a bright little person in contrast with Codlin's somberness.

Codogno (kō.dō'nyō). Town and commune in NW Italy, in the *compartimento* (region) of Lombardy, in the province of Milano, situated between the Adda and Po rivers, ab. 32 mi. SE of Milan. It is the chief market for Parmesan cheese, and has a number of dairy establishments and textile manufactures. Pop. of commune, 11,424 (1936); of town, 1,109 (1936).

Codomannus (kō.dō.man'us), **Darius.** See **Darius III** (of *Persia*).

Codreanu (kō.drā.ä'nö), **Corneliu.** [Full name, **Corneliu Zelea-Codreanu.**] b. at Iaşi, Rumania, c1899; shot at Bucharest, Nov. 30, 1938. Rumanian fascist leader, noted as founder and head of the Iron Guard organization. Implicated (1938) in plots against the government, he was shot by police, allegedly while trying to escape imprisonment.

Codrington (kod'ring.tǫn), **Christopher.** b. on the island of Barbados, 1668; d. April 7, 1710. English soldier. He served (1694–95) in Flanders under King William III of England, fighting with distinction in the battles of Huy and Namur (1695). He succeeded to his father's office of captain-general and commander in chief (1697) of the Leeward Islands.

Codrington, Sir **Edward.** b. April 27, 1770; d. at London, April 28, 1851. English admiral; father of Henry John Codrington and William John Codrington. He took part in the battle of Trafalgar, on Oct. 21, 1805, as commander of the *Orion,* was with Cochrane in Chesapeake Bay and at New Orleans in 1814, became vice-admiral in 1821, and admiral in 1837. He successfully commanded the allied fleet (composed of French, English, and Russian vessels) against the Turkish fleet off Navarino (Pylos) on Oct. 20, 1827.

Codrington, Sir **Henry John.** b. 1808; d. Aug. 4, 1877. English admiral; third son of Sir Edward Codrington. He took part, as commander of the *Talbot,* in the bombardment of Acre, on Nov. 4, 1840. He became a rear admiral in 1857, was admiral superintendent at Malta in the period 1858–63, and was appointed admiral in 1867 and admiral of the fleet in 1877.

Codrington, Sir **William John.** b. Nov. 26, 1804; d. at Heckfield, Hampshire, England, Aug. 4, 1884. English general; second son of Sir Edward Codrington. He served in the Crimean war, commanding a brigade at the battle of the Alma, and a division at Inkerman, and succeeded Sir James Simpson as commander in chief in the Crimea, on Nov. 11, 1855. He returned to England in 1856, and was appointed a lieutenant general and general in 1863.

Codroipo (kō.drô'ē.pō). Town and commune in NE Italy, in the *compartimento* (region) of Friuli-Venezia Giulia, in the province of Udine, situated near the Tagliamento River, between Udine and Treviso. In the vicinity is the grandiose villa of the last doge of the Republic of Venice. Napoleon I stayed here during the negotiations

(1797) leading to the peace of Campo Formio. Pop. of commune, 13,771 (1936); of town, 2,938 (1936).

Codrus (kod′rus). Last king of Athens. He reigned (according to tradition) c1068 B.C. The legend is that Doric invaders of Attica were assured by the Delphic oracle that success would come to that side whose king died. Codrus, having heard of this prophecy, disguised himself and in unrecognizable, humble garb began a quarrel with some Doric soldiers, taunting them until they killed him. This destroyed the premise by which the Dorians hoped to win, and Codrus thus saved his country by his own death. No one was considered worthy to succeed such a king. The archonship was established in Athens thenceforth, and Medon, son of Codrus, was appointed archon.

Cody (kō′di). Town in NW Wyoming, county seat of Park County, on the Shoshone River, near Shoshone National Forest: vacation resort. Platted in 1895, it was named for William F. Cody ("Buffalo Bill"). Buffalo Bill Day is celebrated annually on February 26, and many relics are to be seen in the Cody Museum, a copy of the ranchhouse where he lived ab. 6 mi. outside of the town. 3,872 (1950).

Cody, William Frederick. ["Called **"Buffalo Bill."**"] b. in Scott County, Iowa, Feb. 26, 1846; d. at Denver, Colo., Jan. 10, 1917. American plainsman and showman, famed for his popularly glorified achievements as a scout on the plains of the American West. As a boy, he ran messages by horse for a freighting company; in 1860, he became a rider for the Pony Express. He then served as a scout with the 9th Kansas Cavalry in Indian campaigns, and was a scout for the Union Army during the Civil War. In the years 1867–68 he won his nickname by virtue of his services as a supplier of buffalo meat to food contractors to the companies building the railroads. After service with the U.S. Army (c1868–72), during which time he became chief of scouts of the 5th Cavalry, he went on the stage, playing to large audiences in plays based on his exploits as a rifleman. He was influenced in taking this step by the promoter Ned Buntline (Edward Z. C. Judson), in whose play *The Scouts of the Plains* (1872) he first appeared on the stage. He returned to frontier service as chief of scouts of the 5th Cavalry in the Sioux War (1876), and then devoted himself to the stage. In 1883, he began his tours, which eventually took him all over the U.S. and to Europe, with Buffalo Bill's Wild West Show. At the same time he took up cattle ranching in Wyoming. Both of these interests occupied him for the rest of his life. His own accounts of his Western adventures are unreliable.

Coehoorn (kö′hōrn) or **Coehorn** or **Cohorn** (kō′hôrn), Baron **Menno van.** b. near Leeuwarden, Friesland, 1641; d. at The Hague, March 17, 1704. Dutch military engineer, called the Dutch Vauban, inventor (1674) of a small grenade-throwing mortar named the coehorn. He wrote *Nieuwe Vestingbouw* (New Fortification, 1685).

Coelebs in Search of a Wife (sē′lebz). Novel by Hannah More, published in 1809. It is a tract of social criticism, the episodes tied to the search of the hero for a wife having certain qualities. The name Coelebs was sometimes applied to any bachelor desirous of marrying.

Coelestine (sel′ẹs.tīn). Variant form of **Celestine,** sometimes used for the popes of that name.

Coelestius (sẹ.les′ṭi.us). fl. 412–417. Collaborator of Pelagius; a native of Ireland or Brittany. He was condemned as a heretic by a council at Carthage in 412, but was acquitted by Pope Zosimus in 417. He is said to have been ordained presbyter at Ephesus some time between 412 and 417.

Coele-Syria (sē′lē.sir′i.ạ). Ancient name of **Bika, El.**

Coelho (kwā′lyö), **Duarte de Albuquerque.** [Titles: Count of **Pernambuco,** Marquis of **Basto.**] b. at Lisbon, Portugal, Dec. 22, 1591; d. at Madrid, Sept. 24, 1658. Portuguese colonial administrator; eldest son of Jorge de Albuquerque Coelho. In 1627 he was made governor of Pernambuco, a position which he had, by feudal law, inherited from his father. He was driven out by the Dutch invasion of 1630, and in 1639 went to Spain, residing at Madrid, where he published his *Memorias diarias de la guerra del Brazil* in 1654.

Coelho, Gonçalo. fl. 1488–1506. Portuguese navigator who, in 1488, commanded a ship on the coast of Senegambia, Africa. It has been supposed that he had charge of the expedition of 1501 to explore the coast of Brazil, but of this there is no proof. It seems certain, however, that he commanded the six caravels which left Lisbon on June 10, 1503 to seek a route to the Moluccas around the southern end of Brazil, then supposed to be an island. One of his ships was wrecked; two others, one of them having Amerigo Vespucci for commander or pilot, separated from Coelho and returned to Lisbon in June, 1504. Coelho himself explored as far, at least, as Rio de Janeiro, and only returned in 1506. Nothing further is known of him.

Coelho, Joaquim Guilherme Gomes. See **Diniz, Júlio.**

Coelho, Jorge de Albuquerque. b. at Olinda, Pernambuco, Brazil, April 23, 1539; d. probably at Lisbon, Portugal, some time after 1596. Portuguese soldier; second son of Duarte Coelho Pereira and father of Duarte de Albuquerque Coelho. From 1560 to 1565 he was commander of the Portuguese forces in Pernambuco, under his brother, Duarte Coelho de Albuquerque. On the death of his brother (c1579) he inherited the captaincy (or governorship) of Pernambuco.

Coelho de Albuquerque (dẹ äl.bö.ker′kẹ), **Duarte.** b. at Olinda, Pernambuco, Brazil, 1537; d. at Fez, Morocco, c1579. Portuguese colonial administrator; eldest son of Duarte Coelho Pereira. He inherited the captaincy (or governorship) of Pernambuco in 1554, and governed it personally from 1560 to 1572. Returning to Portugal, he followed King Sebastian of Portugal to Africa, was taken prisoner by the Moors, and died in captivity.

Coelho Neto (ne′tö), **Henrique (Maximiano).** b. at Caxias, Maranhão, Brazil, Feb. 21, 1864; d. at Rio de Janeiro, Nov. 28, 1934. Brazilian novelist, playwright, journalist, short-story and sketch writer. He was a college professor of literature and the director of the Dramatic School of Rio de Janeiro city. His best-known novels include *A Capital Federal* (1893), *Inverno em flor* (1897), *A conquista* (1899), and *O rei negro* (1914). Among his other works are *Rapsódias* (1891), *Bilhetes postais* (1894), *Sertão* (1896), and many other books, including several volumes of plays.

Coelho Pereira (pẹ.rā′rạ), **Duarte.** b. c1485; d. at Olinda, Pernambuco, Brazil, Aug. 7, 1554. Portuguese soldier; father of Duarte Coelho de Albuquerque and Jorge de Albuquerque Coelho. He is said to have been the first to reach Cochin China, and was sent as an ambassador to Siam and China. In 1530 he was sent to the coast of Brazil, where he destroyed a French trading establishment. In April, 1534, the new captaincy of Pernambuco was granted to him and his heirs in perpetuity, and he speedily made it the most flourishing colony in Brazil, establishing the sugar-growing industry there. Olinda, his capital, was founded in 1535.

Coelia gens (sē′li.ạ). See **Caelia** or **Coelia gens.**

Coelica (sē′li.kạ). [Also, **Caelica.**] Collection of short poems of different lengths, by Fulke Greville, 1st Baron Brooke. It appeared in a folio volume containing plays and other poems in 1633. The latter are love poems or philosophical poems, for the most part written before 1590.

Coello (kō.ā′lyō), **Alonzo Sánchez.** b. at Benifayro, near Valencia, Spain, c1531; d. at Madrid, c1588. Spanish painter, especially noted for his portraits. He worked at the court of Philip II of Spain, succeeding his teacher Antonio Moro (Sir Anthony More).

Coello, Claudio. b. at Madrid, 1630; d. there, April 20, 1693. Spanish historical painter, court painter to Charles II of Spain. His best-known work is the large altarpiece on canvas in the Escorial, Madrid, in the Spanish baroque style.

Coen (kön), **Jan Pieterszoon.** b. at Hoorn, Netherlands, Jan. 8, 1587; d. at Batavia, Java, Sept. 20, 1629. Dutch official, governor general of the Dutch East Indies (1618–23 and 1627–29). He founded Batavia in 1619.

Coercive Acts. [Also called the **Restraining** or **Intolerable Acts.**] Four measures enacted (1774) by the British Parliament in retaliation for the Boston Tea Party (Dec. 16, 1773) and other disturbances by American colonists in Boston and other parts of Massachusetts. The measures were introduced by Frederick North (Lord North) as a means of pursuing a firm colonial policy adequate to the emergency. The Boston Port Act (March 31, 1774) was designed specifically as a punishment of Boston for the lawlessness of the Tea Party. It made the reopening of the Boston port conditional upon the payment of damages for losses sustained by the East India Company. The Massachusetts Government Act (May 20, 1774) stripped Massachusetts of its charter and reduced it to a crown colony. The Administration of Justice Act (May 20, 1774) was designed to provide for a more impartial administration of justice by transferring the capital trials of judges, soldiers, and revenue officers to England; it was directed not only toward the maintenance of order but to the more efficient administration of the customs laws. The Quartering Act assured the billeting of British troops in any Massachusetts town. Although the Quebec Act (June 22, 1774) is sometimes referred to as one of the Coercive Acts, it is not, properly speaking, one of them.

Coerne (kėrn), **Louis Adolphe.** b. at Newark, N.J., Feb. 27, 1870; d. at Boston, Sept. 11, 1922. American composer and teacher. He graduated (1893) with highest honors from the Royal Academy at Munich, was associate professor (1903–04) at Smith College, Northampton, Mass., received (1905) from Harvard the first Ph.D. in music from a U.S. university, was head (1910–15) of the music department of the University of Wisconsin, and served as professor (1915 *et seq.*) of music at Connecticut College for Women. Included among his more than 500 compositions are the operas *A Woman of Marblehead* (1897) and *The Maiden Queen*, the symphonic poem *Hiawatha*, *Mass in D Minor*, and *Zenobia*, the first opera by an American to be presented in Germany.

Coeroeni (kö.rö′nē). Dutch name of the **Courantyne** in its upper course.

Coesfeld (kōs′felt). [Also, **Koesfeld.**] Town in W Germany, in the *Land* (state) of North Rhine-Westphalia, British Zone, formerly in the province of Westphalia, Prussia, situated on the Berkel River, ab. 20 mi. W of Münster. It has metallurgical, machine, textile, and foodstuff industries, and agricultural markets. Notable buildings include churches of the 15th and 17th centuries. In the Middle Ages a member of the Hanseatic League, it came under Prussian rule in 1815. The population is predominantly Roman Catholic. During World War II the town suffered considerable damage. Of the old churches only the Lambertikirche survived. It was somewhat damaged, but the tower is intact. 14,579 (1950).

Cœur (kėr), **Jacques.** b. at Bourges, France, c1395; d. on the island of Chios, Nov. 25, 1456. French merchant and financier. Extensive trade with the Levant and other monopolies granted him brought him a great fortune. A favorite of Charles VII of France, he had charge (c1436 *et seq.*) of the coinage and financial affairs of the state and effected important reforms. His own money and agents were often used to support French interests, and one of the results of his policies was the eviction of the English from Normandy. He was imprisoned (c1451–c1455) on the false charge of having poisoned Agnès Sorel, the king's mistress, and his fortune was seized by the king. He escaped, entered the service of Pope Calixtus III, and was in charge of a fleet in the papal campaign against the Turks when he died.

Coeur d'Alene (kėr.dạ.lān′, kôr-). Tribe of North American Indians, and the name of their language, of Salishan linguistic stock. They now live, for the most part, on a reservation in N Idaho.

Coeur d'Alene. City in NW Idaho, county seat of Kootenai County, on Coeur d'Alene Lake ab. 30 mi. E of Spokane, Wash., in the largest silver-producing area in the U.S. It is important also for lead and zinc, lumber, and farm and dairy products. The Coeur d'Alene district produces more than 90 percent of Idaho's mineral output. 12,198 (1950).

Coeur d'Alene. Novel by Mary Hallock Foote, published in 1894. The story centers around the contest of union and non-union miners in Colorado.

Coeur d'Alene Lake. Lake in N Idaho, ab. 30 mi. E of Spokane, Wash., draining into the Spokane River. It is beautifully situated among the wooded mountains, and is a popular resort. Elevation, ab. 2,124 ft.; area, ab. 45 sq. mi.

Coeur d'Alene Strike. Violent labor dispute in the northern Idaho lead and silver mines which began on July 11, 1892, when a pitched battle was fought between union and non-union miners after the mine operators had secured an injunction against the union. Martial law was proclaimed and federal and state troops called in. Other strikes took place in 1893 and 1899, when federal troops again took charge.

Cœur-de-Lion (kėr′dẹ.lē′ǫn; French, kėr.dẹ.lyôṅ). See **Richard I** (of *England*).

Cœur innombrable (kėr ē.nôṅ.bràbl), **Le.** First collection (1901) of lyric poems by Anna Elisabeth de Brancovan, Comtesse de Noailles (1876–1933), considered by many critics the best example of her pathetic-lyric work.

Coeus (sē′us). In Greek mythology, one of the Titans, children of Uranus and Gaea. He became the husband of Phoebe and father of Leto and Asteria.

Coffee Club, the. See **Rota Club.**

Coffee-House Politician, The. Comedy by Henry Fielding, published in 1730.

Coffeyville (kôf′i.vil). City in SE Kansas, in Montgomery County, on the Verdigris River, ab. 75 mi. SW of Fort Scott: gasoline, lubricants, chemicals, flour, bricks, structural steel, tank cars, and machinery. The notorious desperadoes known as the Dalton boys conducted their famous raid here on Oct. 5, 1892, when two of the brothers were killed and one captured. 17,113 (1950).

Coffin (kôf′in, kof′in), **Charles Albert.** b. in Maine, Dec. 30, 1844; d. July 14, 1926. American businessman, first president (1892–1913) of the General Electric Company, notable for his part in the development of the Curtis steam turbine. He was subsequently (1913–22) chairman of General Electric's board of directors, organizer (1915) of the War Relief Clearing House, and a leader in the World War I activities of the Red Cross.

Coffin, Charles Carleton. b. at Boscawen, N.H., July 26, 1823; d. March 2, 1896. American journalist and author. He seems to have engaged briefly also in electrical engineering, at least to the extent of being associated with a brother-in-law in the installation, in 1852, of the first electric fire alarm system in Boston. By the following year, however, he had definitely turned to journalism, finding employment with the Boston *Atlas* and the Boston *Journal.* At the outbreak of the Civil War he was in Washington, and beginning with his report to the *Journal* on the first battle of Bull Run, he became one of the most eagerly read war correspondents in the North, his dispatches appearing under the pseudonym "Carleton." A man of impressive physical appearance, courageous and trustworthy, he was well liked by many of the Union commanders, especially Grant, who talked with him freely. In 1866 he covered the Austro-Prussian War (Seven Weeks' War), and after remaining in Europe into 1867, he returned home by way of India, China, Japan, and the Pacific. Meanwhile, in 1864, he had published the first of several books in which he capitalized on his Civil War experiences; this was *My Days and Nights on the Battlefield*, and its success led to publication of *Following the Flag* (1865) and *Four Years of Fighting* (1866; later reissued as *The Boys of '61*). His travels in Europe and Asia were recorded in *Our New Way Round the World* (1869), and a trip to the then still wild West was reported in *The Seat of Empire* (1870). In 1880 he published a life of Garfield, and in 1892 one of Lincoln. His two novels, *Winning His Way* (1866) and *Caleb Krinkle* (1875), are in the limbo of forgotten books, but some of his books for children have been reissued in recent years. His simple and vigorous style was well adapted to this type of literature, and such titles as *The Boys of '76* (1876), *The Story of Liberty* (1879), *Old Times in the Colonies* (1881), *Building the Nation* (1883), and *Daughters of the Revolution* (1895) were popular and profitable. Coffin appeared on the lecture platform more than 2,000 times, and was twice elected to the Massachusetts legislature.

Coffin, Henry Sloane. b. at New York, Jan. 5, 1877—. American Presbyterian clergyman and author. A graduate of Yale (B.A., 1897) and of Union Theological Seminary (B.D., 1900), he was ordained in 1900. He served as pastor of the Bedford Park Church (1900–05) and the Madison Avenue Church (1905–26), both at New York, and was president (1926–45) of Union Theological Seminary. He was named moderator of the Presbyterian Church in the U.S. in 1934. He is the author of *The Creed of Jesus* (1907), *Social Aspects of the Cross* (1911), *The Christian and the Church* (1912), *Portraits of Jesus*

Christ (1926), *The Meaning of the Cross* (1931), *Religion Yesterday and Today* (1940), *The Public Worship of God* (1946), and other books.

Coffin, Sir **Isaac.** b. at Boston, May 16, 1759; d. in England, July 23, 1839. British sailor, appointed vice-admiral in 1808, and admiral on June 4, 1814. He entered the navy in 1773, and became commander in 1781. In 1788, accused of signing a false muster, he was tried by court-martial, found guilty, and dismissed from the navy, but he was later reinstated.

Coffin, James Henry. b. in Massachusetts, Sept. 6, 1806; d. at Easton, Pa., Feb. 6, 1873. American mathematician and meteorologist, professor of mathematics and astronomy at Lafayette College, Easton, Pa. He wrote *Analytical Geometry* (1849), *Winds of the Northern Hemisphere* (1853), and other works.

Coffin, Levi. b. at New Garden, N.C., Oct. 28, 1789; d. Sept. 16, 1877. American abolitionist, active in the operations of the Underground Railroad. Despite his Southern birth, he was a descendant of the Coffins of Nantucket, and a Quaker. He had little education, yet from time to time he taught in country schools, and in 1821 he and a cousin opened a Sunday school for Negroes at New Garden which, however, before long, the planters of the region forbade their slaves to attend. In 1826 he moved to Newport (now Fountain City), Ind., a Quaker village, where he established a store and prospered. He let it be known that he would participate in the work of the so-called Underground Railroad, the system by which fugitives from Southern slave-masters were sent on to safety in Northern states or in Canada, and in fact he was so much to the fore in this work that he was sometimes called the "president" of the Underground Railroad.

Coffin, Long Tom. Sailor in *The Pilot* (1823), a novel by James Fenimore Cooper.

Coffin, Robert Peter Tristram. b. at Brunswick, Me., March 18, 1892—. American poet, essayist, novelist, biographer, professor, and 1936 Pulitzer prize winner in poetry for *Strange Holiness*. He was educated at Bowdoin College (where he later taught), at Princeton University, and at Oxford (where he was a Rhodes Scholar). He has written *Dew and Bronze* (1927), *Golden Falcon* (1929), *The Yoke of Thunder* (1932), *Ballads of Square-Toed Americans* (1932), containing some of his best verse, *Saltwater Farm* (1937), *Maine Ballads* (1938), and *There Will Be Bread and Love* (1942). His prose is represented by *Books of Crowns and Cottages* (1925), *An Attic Room* (1929), essays, *Laud: Storm Center of Stuart England* (1930), and *The Dukes of Buckingham* (1936), biography. In the field of fiction he has written *Lost Paradise* (1934), *Red Sky in the Morning* (1935), and *John Dawn* (1936), novels of the Maine Coast. *Kennebec: Cradle of Americans* (1937) is a regional history.

Coffman (kôf′mạn, kof′mạn), **Lotus Delta.** b. at Salem, Ind., Jan. 7, 1875; d. Sept. 22, 1938. American educator. He graduated (1906) from Indiana State University and received (1911) a Ph.D. degree from Columbia University. He was dean (1915–20) of the college of education and president (1920 *et seq.*) of the University of Minnesota. He wrote *Teacher Training Departments in Minnesota High Schools* (1920) and *The State University: Its Work and Problems* (1934).

Cofre de Perote (kō′frā dā pä.rō′tā). See **Perote, Cofre de.**

Cogălniceanu (kō″gul.nē.chä′nö), **Mihail.** See **Kogălniceanu Mihail.**

Coghetti (kō.get′tē), **Francesco.** b. at Bergamo, Italy, Oct. 4, 1804; d. at Rome, April 21, 1875. Italian painter. Among his best-known works are frescoes in the basilica at Savona.

Coghill (kog′hil), **George Ellett.** b. at Beaucoup, Ill., March 17, 1872; d. at Gainesville, Fla., July 23, 1941. American anatomist, distinguished for his original work on the development of behavior in relation to the maturation of the nervous system, summarized in his classic book *Anatomy and the Problem of Behavior* (1929). He taught zoölogy and anatomy at several colleges and universities and was managing editor (1927–33) of the *Journal of Comparative Neurology.* See *George Ellett Coghill* (1949), by C. Judson Herrick.

Coghlan (kog′lạn, kōg′lạn), Sir **Charles Patrick John.** b. in Cape Colony, South Africa, 1863; d. at Salisbury, Southern Rhodesia, 1927. British statesman; first premier of Southern Rhodesia. A lawyer, Coghlan was a representative (1908) for Bulawayo to the legislative council. He acquiesced (1908–09) in the decision that Southern Rhodesia should not join the South African union, opposed (1917) the union of Southern with Northern Rhodesia, and became (1923) premier of the first ministry of Southern Rhodesia.

Coghlan, Joseph Bullock. b. at Frankfort, Ky., Dec. 9, 1844; d. at New Rochelle, N.Y., Dec. 5, 1908. American naval officer. He was graduated from the U.S. Naval Academy in 1863. At the battle of Manila Bay (May 1, 1898) he commanded the cruiser *Raleigh.* He was, as rear admiral (1902), second in command of the North Atlantic fleet (1902–04), was appointed commandant of the navy yard at New York in 1904, and retired in December, 1906.

Coghlan, Rose. b. at Peterborough, England, c1851; d. at Harrison, N.Y., April 2, 1932. American actress. After a tour of the English provinces, she came (1872) to America to play with E. A. Sothern. She was leading lady (1880–89) of Wallack's Company, her successes including Countess Zicka in the première of *Diplomacy* (1878) and Stephanie in Herman Merivale and Charles Groves's *Forget Me Not* (1880). In 1902 she became an American citizen.

Coghlan, Sir **Timothy Augustine.** b. at Sydney, Australia, June 9, 1856; d. at London, April 30, 1926. Australian statistician, historian, and public servant. He served (1873–86) in the public works department of New South Wales, and was its first government statistician (1886–1905). He initiated (1887) the statistical survey *Wealth and Progress of New South Wales*, later titled *Official Year Book of New South Wales* and published to date. He also compiled *Statistical Account of the Seven Colonies of Australasia*, later displaced by official yearbooks of Australia and New Zealand. His chief historical work is considered to be *Labour and Industry in Australia, 1788–1901* (4 vols., London, 1918), covering the colonial period. From 1905 until his death, with brief intervals, he acted as agent-general for New South Wales at London. He was knighted in 1914.

Cogia Hassan Alhabbal or **al-Habbal** (kō′jạ has′ạn al.hab′ạl). [Eng. trans., "*Master Hassan the Ropemaker.*"] Titular hero of a story entitled "History of Cogia Hassan Alhabbal" in *The Arabian Nights' Entertainments*, based on the old motif that the hidden talent is less productive than the talent used. Two friends give Hassan gold, which he puts in his turban; a kite carries off the turban. Again they give him gold, which he hides in a jar of bran; his wife sells the jar. Next they give him a small coin, which he lends to a fisherman to buy twine to repair a net. The fisherman brings Hassan the first fish caught. The fish contains a rich jewel. With money from the sale of the jewel, Hassan buys factories and becomes rich. Later both the turban and the jar of bran are recovered with the original sums intact.

Cogia Houssam (hö′säm). Captain of the thieves in the story "Ali Baba and the Forty Thieves" in *The Arabian Nights' Entertainments.*

Cognac (ko.nyàk; Anglicized, kōn′yak). [Ancient names, **Condate, Compniacum,** medieval name, **Coniacus,** later **Coignac.**] Town in W France, in the department of Charente, situated on the Charente River, ab. 23 mi. W of Angoulême. It is known as the center of the distillery industry producing "cognacs." It is the birthplace of Francis I of France, was a Protestant stronghold under Henry III of France, and resisted successfully the troops of Louis II, Prince de Condé, during the wars of the Fronde. The church of Saint Léger shows a mixture of Romanesque and Gothic characteristics; seat also of the old castle of the dukes of Angoulême. 17,479 (1946).

Cognac, Holy League of. [Also, **Clementine League.**] League concluded on May 22, 1526, between Pope Clement VII, Francis I of France, and the cities of Milan and Venice, against the emperor Charles V. Henry VIII of England was in sympathy with the league.

Cognacq (ko.nyàk), **Ernest.** [Full name, **Théodore Ernest Cognacq.**] b. at St.-Martin-de-Ré, France, Oct. 2, 1839; d. at Paris, Feb. 21, 1928. French merchant and philanthropist, known particularly for organizing

(1870) the department store La Samaritaine at Paris; husband of Marie Louise Cognacq-Jay. He transferred (1914) ownership of the store to his employees and to charities, with his wife set up (1920) a foundation to aid large families, and bequeathed his art collection to the city of Paris.

Cognacq-Jay (ko.nyȧk.zhä), **Marie Louise.** [Also: **Marie Louise Cognacq**; maiden name, **Jay.**] b. at Samoëns, Haute-Savoie, France, July 1, 1838; d. at Paris, Dec. 26, 1925. French businesswoman and philanthropist; wife of Ernest Cognacq. She was his partner in his commercial and philanthropic endeavors.

Cogniard (ko.nyȧr), **Charles Théodore.** b. April 30, 1806; d. May 14, 1872. French theater director and writer of theatrical sketches in collaboration with his brother Jean Hippolyte Cogniard.

Cogniard, Jean Hippolyte. b. Nov. 20, 1807; d. Feb. 6, 1882. French theater director and writer of light theatrical pieces in collaboration with his brother Charles Théodore Cogniard.

Cogolludo (kō.gō.lyö′ᴛʜō), **Diego López de.** fl. in Yucatán c1650. Spanish Franciscan historian. His *Historia de Yucatán* (fol., Madrid, 1688) is a chief authority on the history of that country down to 1655. A second edition bears the title *Los Tres siglos de la dominación española en Yucatán* (2 vols., Campeche and Médria, 1842–45).

Cogswell (kogz′wel, -wẹl), **Joseph Green.** b. at Ipswich, Mass., Sept. 27, 1786; d. at Cambridge, Mass., Nov. 26, 1871. American librarian. He studied (1807–09) law at Harvard and practiced for a short time. From 1809 to 1811 he was in business in southern Europe. In 1817 he formed part of the early American contingent at Göttingen, where he was a fellow student of Edward Everett and George Ticknor, and where he became a friend of Goethe. He traveled in Europe from 1817 to 1820 and became interested in library work. In 1820 he accepted the post of librarian of the Harvard Library, teaching mineralogy and geology at the same time that he was reclassifying the library. He resigned (1823) to found, with George Bancroft, the Round Hill School at Northampton, Mass., modeled on the lines of the German *Gymnasium* (advanced secondary school). In 1834 the school closed. Cogswell edited (1839) and then owned (1839–42) the *New York Review*, a quarterly, but that too was forced to suspend. He became a friend of John Jacob Astor and helped him to buy books for the library Astor had projected at the time. After Astor's death (1848) Cogswell became superintendent of the library, added books to the collection, and planned the building to house them. Almost by himself and with his own money, he catalogued and printed the index to the collection, which forms the basis of the present collection of the New York Public Library. He retired in 1861, but until 1866 continued to work on a supplement to his original catalogue.

Cohan (kō.han′), **George M(ichael).** b. at Providence, R.I., July 4, 1878; d. at New York, Nov. 5, 1942. American actor, dramatist, theatrical manager and producer, and song writer. He made his first stage appearance at the age of 9 in *Daniel Boone* at Haverstraw, N.Y. With his parents and his first wife, Ethel Levy, all actors, he was one of "The Four Cohans." Some of the many plays he wrote (and in most of which he acted) are *The Wise Guy*, *The Governor's Son* (1901), *Running for Office* (1903), *Little Johnny Jones* (1904), *Forty-Five Minutes from Broadway* (1906), *George Washington, Jr.* (1906), *The Talk of New York* (1907), *Fifty Miles from Boston* (1907), *The Man Who Owns Broadway* (1908), *The Yankee Prince* (1909), *Get-Rich-Quick Wallingford* (1910), *The Little Millionaire* (1911), *Seven Keys to Baldpate* (1913), *The Tavern* (1920), and *The Song-and-Dance Man* (1923). In addition to his plays, the nature of which is revealed by their titles, he wrote several songs which were popular when he wrote them and which give evidence of retaining their popularity. *Over There* is still recognized as the best song that came out of World War I, and no one, Cohan included, was able to compose its equal for World War II. *Give My Regards to Broadway* (Remember me to Herald Square), *I'm a Yankee Doodle Dandy*, *You're a Grand Old Flag*, and *Mary's a Grand Old Name*, are only a few of the songs that have become a part of American life. Cohan was not a great actor or a singer, and he did not pretend to be, but he succeeded because of a remarkable stage personality that an audience could not resist. He spoke through his nose with a peculiar drawl, and walked and danced in a way that was all his own. He was intensely patriotic, was proud of having been born on July 4, and was fond of calling himself a son, or a nephew, of Uncle Sam. He used the American flag frequently in his plays, knowing that it was always good for applause, and declared that an actor should always wave an American flag when he was in doubt and didn't know what to do. He also referred to himself, and liked to be called by others, "just a song-and-dance man." As such he made a secure place for himself in the American theater. Apart from his own plays, in which the roles were tailored to suit him, he made his greatest success as the father in O'Neill's *Ah! Wilderness.* He wrote his autobiography in *Twenty Years on Broadway and the Years it Took to Get There*, and in 1941 he was awarded the Congressional Medal for building and maintaining national morale by his songs *Over There* and *You're a Grand Old Flag.* The incident appears in the film *Yankee Doodle Dandy*, in which Cohan meets and shakes hands with President Roosevelt, and in which James Cagney was nailed for a fine performance in the role of Cohan.

Cohasset (kō.has′ẹt). Town in E Massachusetts, in Norfolk County, on Massachusetts Bay, ab. 15 mi. SE of Boston: lobster-fishing port and summer resort. Minots Ledge lighthouse lies 1 mi. off the coast. 3,731 (1950).

Cohen (kō′ẹn), **Alfred Morton.** b. at Cincinnati, Oct. 19, 1859; d. there, March 9, 1949. American lawyer. He graduated (1880) from the Cincinnati Law School, and subsequently became known for his achievement in communal work. From 1925 to 1938 he was international president of B'nai B'rith and pioneered in the establishment of the B'nai B'rith Hillel Foundations.

Cohen, Benjamin Victor. b. at Muncie, Ind., Sept. 23, 1894—. American lawyer. A graduate of the University of Chicago (Ph.B., 1914; J.D., 1915) and of Harvard University (S.J.D., 1916), he was counsel to the American Zionists at the London and Paris peace conferences (1919–21). He was in private practice (1922–33) at Chicago and New York. He took part in drafting the Securities Act (1933), the Securities Exchange Act (1934), the Public Utility Holding Company Act (1935), and the Fair Labor Standards Act (1938). From 1942 to 1943 he assisted the Economic Stabilization Director, and in 1945 was named a counselor to the U.S. State Department. Beginning with the Bretton Woods and Dumbarton Oaks conferences in 1944, he has often been adviser to or member of U.S. delegations in international meetings, as to the United Nations general assemblies.

Cohen, Ernst Julius. b. at Amsterdam, Netherlands, 1869; killed by Germans in gas chamber at Auschwitz (Oświęcim), Poland, 1944. Dutch physical chemist and historian of chemistry. His extensive researches on allotropy (existence of the same element in several forms) helped demonstrate its universality rather than its uniqueness, and included elucidation of the polymorphism of tin, and the introduction of the concept of physical (as against chemical) purity. He also made numerous studies of chemists, particularly van't Hoff and others of the Utrecht school. He served as a professor (1902–39) at Utrecht.

Cohen, Hermann. b. at Coswig, Germany, July 4, 1842; d. at Berlin, April 4, 1918. German philosopher, founder of the so-called Marburg school of Neo-Kantianism. He served (1876 *et seq.*) as professor at the University of Marburg, and later lectured at the Lehranstalt für die Wissenschaft des Judentums at Berlin. He was the author of many works on Kant's philosophy, and of *System der Philosophie* (1902 *et seq.*), *Der Begriff der Religion im System der Philosophie* (1915), *Die Religion der Vernunft aus den Quellen des Judentums* (1919), and *Jüdische Schriften* (1924).

Cohen, I. Bernard. b. at Far Rockaway, N.Y., March 1, 1914—. American historian of science. He was librarian at Eliot House, Harvard (1937–42), and instructor in physics (1942–46), and instructor (1946–49) and assistant professor (1949 *et seq.*) in the history of science and general education at Harvard. He is the editor of *Isis.*

Cohen (ko.en), **Jules Émile David.** b. at Marseilles, France, Nov. 2, 1835; d. at Paris, in January, 1901. French composer. He was a professor at the Paris Conservatory and chorusmaster at the Paris Opéra. His compositions include such comic operas as *Maître Claude* (1861) and *José Maria* (1866), the serious opera *Les Bluets* (1867), symphonies, piano works, and religious music.

Cohen (kō'en), **Louis.** b. at Kiev, Russia, Dec. 16, 1876; d. Sept. 28, 1948. American electrical engineer. A graduate of the Armour Institute of Technology at Chicago (B.S.,1901), and of Columbia University (Ph.D., 1905), he was professor of electrical engineering (1916–29) at George Washington University. He is noted for having devised improvements in radio and cable telegraphy. He was the author of *Formulae and Tables for Calculation of Alternating Current Problems* (1913), *Heaviside's Electrical Circuit Theory* (1928), and many scientific articles.

Cohen, Morris Raphael. b. at Minsk, Russia, July 25, 1880; d. at Washington, D.C., Jan. 28, 1947. American philosopher and university professor. He came to the U.S. at the age of 12. He received a B.S. (1900) from the College of the City of New York and a Ph.D. (1906) from Harvard. After teaching mathematics (1902–12), he joined the department of philosophy at the College of the City of New York and was professor there (1912–38) and at the University of Chicago (1938–42). His work, especially his inquiries into the philosophy of law, is of great importance in the history of American philosophy. He was author of *Reason and Nature* (1931), *Law and the Social Order* (1933), *Preface to Logic* (1944), *The Faith of a Liberal* (1945), and *A Dreamer's Journey* (1949); and coauthor with Ernest Nagel of *An Introduction to Logic and the Scientific Method* (1934).

Cohen, Octavus Roy. b. at Charleston, S.C., June 26, 1891—. American novelist and short-story writer. Graduated (B.S., 1911) from Clemson College, he was admitted to the bar in 1913. After 1915 he turned to writing, and contributed (1918 *et seq.*) a series of humorous stories about Southern Negroes to the *Saturday Evening Post.* He is also known as an author of detective stories. Among his books are *The Crimson Alibi* (1919), *Polished Ebony* (1919), *Come Seven* (1920), *Jim Hanvey, Detective* (1923), *Black and Blue* (1926), *Detours* (1927), *Florian Slappey Goes Abroad* (1928), *Epic Peters, Pullman Porter* (1930), *The Townsend Murder Mystery* (1933), *Child of Evil* (1936), *Dangerous Lady* (1946), and *Don't Ever Love Me* (1947).

Cohen, Solomon Solis. [Also, **Solis-Cohen.**] b. at Philadelphia, Sept. 1, 1857; d. there, July 12, 1948. American physician. He was graduated (M.D., 1883) from the Jefferson Medical College, where he served (1902–27) as professor of clinical medicine. He was also professor of clinical medicine and therapeutics (1887–1902) at the Philadelphia Polyclinic and College for Graduates in Medicine, and physician (1887–1927) to the Jefferson, Jewish, and Philadelphia General hospitals. Active in the Zionist movement, he was a member (1920–40) of the council of the Jewish Agency for Palestine. He was the author of *Therapeutics of Tuberculosis* (1891) and *Essentials of Medical Diagnosis* (with A. A. Eshner, 1892–1900).

Cohens v. Virginia, 6 Wheaton 264 (1821). U.S. Supreme Court decision upholding the right to the high court to review the decision of a state court where the latter's finding was contrary to the federal Constitution or statutes. The case involved the conviction of several people by a Virginia court for selling lottery tickets in that state. The Cohens maintained that they had been deprived of their legal and constitutional rights, inasmuch as the lottery had been authorized by the U.S. Congress. Chief Justice John Marshall's opinion was a forceful assertion of national powers, and was construed by contemporaries as a reply to the adherents of states rights who had attacked the high court's decision in *Martin v. Hunter's Lessee* (1816).

Cohn (kōn), **Ferdinand Julius.** b. at Breslau, Jan. 24, 1828; d. there, June 25, 1898. German botanist, professor (1859 *et seq.*) of botany at Breslau. He is often considered the founder of the science of bacteriology, having been the first to treat bacteria as plants. He also worked with Robert Koch in the latter's published study concerning anthrax and inoculation against the disease. He was the author of *Untersuchungen über die Entwicklungsgeschichte der mikroskopischen Algen und Pilze* (1854) and *Die Pflanze* (1882).

Cohn, Oscar. b. at Guttentag (in territory then part of Germany), 1869; d. at Geneva, Switzerland, 1934. German politician. A Social Democratic member (1912–18) of the Reichstag, he became (1916) an Independent Social Democrat, was a member of the Weimar constitutional convention (1919–20), and served in the Prussian diet from 1919 to 1924. An active Zionist from 1925, he went into exile in 1933 when Hitler came to power.

Cohnheim (kōn'hīm), **Julius Friedrich.** b. at Demmin, Prussia, Germany, July 20, 1839; d. at Leipzig, Saxony, Germany, Aug. 14, 1884. German pathologist, noted especially for discoveries concerning pus corpuscles. He became professor of pathology and pathological anatomy at Kiel in 1868, at Breslau in 1872, and at Leipzig in 1878.

Cohoes (kō'hōz, kọ.hōz'). City in E New York, in Albany County, at the confluence of the Mohawk and Hudson rivers, ab. 8 mi. N of Albany. Manufactures include rayon, knitted goods, fire hydrants, paper boxes, wallpaper, and boats. 21,272 (1950).

Cohoes Falls. See under **Mohawk River.**

Cohorn (kō'hôrn), Baron **Menno van.** See **Coehoorn** or **Cohorn,** Baron **Menno van.**

Cohuatlicue (kō.wä.tlē'kwā). See **Coatlicue.**

Coi (koi). See under **Tonkin.**

Coiba (koi'bä). [Also, **Quibo.**] Island in the Pacific Ocean, SW of Panama. Length, ab. 20 mi.

Coignac (kwȧ.nyȧk). An early spelling of **Cognac.**

Coila (koi'lạ). Latinized name of **Kyle.**

Coimbatore (koim.bạ.tōr'). [Also, **Koimbatur.**] District in Madras state, Union of India, ab. 200 mi. N of Cape Comorin: tobacco, tea, fruit, coconuts, and millet. Capital, Coimbatore; area, 7,860 sq. mi.; pop. 2,809,648 (1941).

Coimbatore. [Also, **Koimbatur.**] Capital of Coimbatore district, Madras state, Union of India, on the Noyil River, ab. 85 mi. E of Calicut. 130,348 (1941).

Coimbra (kwēm'brạ). Brazilian frontier fort and settlement on the Paraguay River. It was founded in 1775, repulsed an attack of the Spaniards in 1801, and was taken by the Paraguayans in December, 1864, in the Paraguayan war.

Coimbra. District in C Portugal, in the province of Beira Litoral. Capital, Coimbra; area, 1,527 sq. mi.; pop. 433,891 (1950).

Coimbra. [Ancient name, **Conimbrica, Conimbriga;** Latin, **Endimium.**] City and *concelho* (commune) in C Portugal, in the province of Beira Litoral, the capital of the district of Coimbra, situated on the Mondego River ab. 108 mi. NE of Lisbon. It is a center for trade in wine and citrus fruit, and has textile and ceramics factories. Coimbra is the seat of a bishopric, and of a famous university which makes it the center of the scientific, literary, and artistic life of Portugal. Pop. of concelho, 85,702 (1940); of city, 28,282 (1940).

University; Chief Buildings. The university was founded in 1290 at Lisbon, brought to Coimbra in 1306, and, after an intervening period at Lisbon, again established here in 1537. It has a good library, chemical, astronomical, and botanical institutes, and a renowned botanical garden; the university buildings are largely in the Renaissance and baroque styles. The art museum contains interesting collections from the Roman, medieval, and Renaissance periods; there is also a museum of natural history; there are remnants of Roman structures in the city. The cathedral is the best preserved Romanesque monument in Portugal; the Church of Santa Cruz, likewise a Romanesque structure, was rebuilt in rich Manuelesque Gothic style in the 16th century; it contains the tombs of the kings Alfonso I (known as Affonso Henriques) and Sancho I. Other ecclesiastical and secular buildings, including the new cathedral, are in the Renaissance and baroque styles.

History. A Roman town in ancient times, it fell later into the hands of the Visigoths and the Arabs; it was retaken by the Christians in 1064, under the leadership of Ferdinand I of León and the Cid; from 1128 to 1260 it was capital of Portugal. Inés de Castro was murdered here in 1355. In 1834 it was the seat of the pretender to the Portuguese throne, Dom Miguel.

Coín (kō.ēn′). Town in S Spain, in the province of Málaga, ab. 20 mi. W of Málaga. It has soap, paper, and textile manufactures and agricultural markets; there are marble quarries in the vicinity. 17,348 (1940).

Coin's Financial School. Popular treatise written by W. H. ("Coin") Harvey which advocated the adoption by the U.S. government of a bimetallic standard providing for the coinage of silver at a 16-to-1 ratio. It was widely circulated after the panic of 1893 and was aimed at the agrarian and debtor classes who bore the larger burden of distress. It was composed in a folksy vein and was adorned with so many vividly phrased examples and names of famous personages that many readers thought the work an account of actual events.

Coira (koi′rä). Italian name of **Chur.**

Coire (kwår). French name of **Chur.**

Coit (koit), **Henry Leber.** b. at Peapack, N.J., March 16, 1854; d. March 12, 1917. American physician, a specialist in pediatrics. He instituted (c1890) a plan for obtaining germ-free milk for infants, which was put into effect (1893) at Fairfield, N.J., and originated (1890) the term "certified milk." From 1896 he aided the Newark Babies' Hospital. Author of *The Feeding of Infants* (1890), *The Care of the Baby* (1894), *Causation of Disease by Milk* (1894), *Clean Milk in its Economic and Medical Relations with Special Reference to Certified Milk* (1908), *The Public School as a Factor in Preventing Infant and Child Mortality* (1912), and *Certified Milk* (1912).

Coit, Stanton. b. at Columbus, Ohio, Aug. 11, 1857; d. at Birling Gap, near Eastbourne, England, Feb. 16, 1944. American leader in the ethical culture movement. A graduate (1879) of Amherst, he also attended Columbia, and received a Ph.D. (1885) from the University of Berlin. In 1886 he founded University Settlement (formerly Neighborhood Guild). Resident (1888 *et seq.*) at London, he founded (1928) the Foundation for Moral and Religious Leadership, was president of the West London Ethical Society, and was active in ethical culture work as a writer, minister, and organizer throughout England.

Cojedes (kō.ʜā′ᴛʜās). State in NW Venezuela. Capital, San Carlos; area, 5,714 sq. mi.; pop. 52,022 (1950).

Cojutepeque (kō.ʜö.tā.pā′kā). [Also, **Cojutepec** (kō-ʜö.tā.pek′).] City in C El Salvador, capital of Cuscatlán department, ab. 10 mi. NE of San Salvador: center of a rice, sugar, coffee, and indigo producing district. 10,005 (1950).

Cokayne (kō.kān′), Sir **Aston.** b. at Elvaston, Derbyshire, England, in December, 1608; d. at Derby, England, in February, 1684. English Royalist poet and dramatist; son of Thomas Cokayne (1587–1638). His works include the comedies *The Obstinate Lady* (1657) and *Trappolin Suppos'd a Prince* (1659), *Tragedy of Ovid* (1662), *Small Poems of Divers Sorts* (1658; reissued, 1652, 1659), and *Choice Poems of Several Sorts, with three new Plays* (1669).

Cokayne, Thomas. b. at Mapleton, Derbyshire, England, Jan. 21, 1587; d. at London, 1638. English lexicographer, author of an English-Greek lexicon (1658) containing derivations and definitions of "all the words in the New Testament"; father of Sir Aston Cokayne. He was educated at Oxford (Corpus Christi College), but did not take a degree. During the latter part of his life he lived at London.

Coke (kůk, kōk), Sir **Edward.** [Called Lord **Coke** (or **Cooke**).] b. at Mileham, Norfolk, England, Feb. 1, 1552; d. at Stoke Poges, England, Sept. 3, 1634. English jurist. He was speaker of the House of Commons (1592–93), attorney general (1593–94), chief justice of the Common Pleas (1606), and chief justice of the King's Bench (1613). He came into conflict with James I and Francis Bacon on matters touching the royal prerogative, and was removed from the bench on Nov. 15, 1616. Among the noted cases which he conducted as prosecutor are those of Essex and Southampton in 1601, of Sir Walter Raleigh in 1603 (in which he disgraced himself by the brutality of his language), and of the gunpowder plotters in 1605. In the later part of his life he rendered notable service, in Parliament, to the cause of English freedom, his last important speech being a direct attack on Buckingham. His chief works are his *Reports* (1600–15) and his *Institutes*, which consist of a reprint and translation of Littleton's *Tenures* with a commentary (popularly known as "Coke upon Littleton"); the text of various statutes from Magna Charta to the time of James I, with a commentary; a treatise on criminal law; and a treatise on the jurisdiction of the different law courts.

Coke, Thomas. b. at Brecknock, Wales, Sept. 9, 1747; d. at sea, May 2, 1814. British preacher and missionary, first bishop (1784) of the Methodist Episcopal Church in America. He was sent to America in 1784 by John Wesley as superintendent of his church, having renounced a ministry in the Church of England to join the nonconformists. He wrote *Commentary on the Holy Scriptures* (1807), *History of the West Indies* (1808), and others.

Coke, Thomas William. [Title, Earl of **Leicester of Holkham.**] b. May 4, 1752; d. at Longford Hall, Derbyshire, England, June 30, 1842. English nobleman and Whig politician. He was the son of Thomas Wenman, and assumed the name Coke on succeeding to the estate of his maternal uncle, Thomas Coke, Earl of Leicester. He is best known for his improvements in agriculture on his estates about Holkham, Norfolk, especially in the breeds of cattle, sheep, and pigs.

Cokes (kōks), **Bartholomew.** Foolish young squire in Ben Jonson's comedy *Bartholomew Fair.*

Col (kol). French word for "pass": for French names of mountain passes see the specific element of the name.

Colada (kō.lä′ᴛʜä). Second sword of the Cid.

Colar (kọ.lär′). See **Kolar.**

Colbaith or **Colbath** (kōl′bàth), **Jeremiah Jones.** Original name of **Wilson, Henry.**

Colban (kōl′bän), **Adolfine Marie.** [Maiden name, **Schmidt.**] b. Dec. 18, 1814; d. at Rome, March 27, 1884. Norwegian novelist. Her works include *Tre Noveller* (1873), *Tre nye Noveller* (1875), *Jeg lever* (1877), and *Cleopatra* (1880).

Colbeck Bay (kol′bek). Bay in Antarctica, in the S part of Robertson Bay, lying between the S end of Duke of York Island and the mainland of N Victoria Land, in ab. 71°38′ S., 170°07′ E. Width, ab. 1 mi.

Colberg (kol′berk). German name of **Kolobrzeg.**

Colbert (kol.ber), **Jean Baptiste.** b. at Reims, France, Aug. 29, 1619; d. at Paris, Sept. 6, 1683. French statesman; father of Jean Baptiste Colbert (1651–90). He was the son of a merchant of Reims, entered the service of Cardinal Mazarin, and in 1661, on the death of Mazarin, was appointed by Louis XIV minister of finance, a post which he held until his death, serving at the same time as minister of marine and of the interior. He introduced extensive fiscal reforms, as a result of which the income of the government was nearly trebled, and encouraged commerce and the industries by imposing a protective tariff, by the building of canals, and by the planting of colonies. He founded the Academy of Inscriptions (1663), the Academy of Sciences (1666), and other institutions for the promotion of art and science.

Colbert, Jean Baptiste. [Title, Marquis **de Seignelay.**] b. at Paris, 1651; d. Nov. 3, 1690. French official, minister of marine; son of Jean Baptiste Colbert (1619–83).

Colbert, Jean Baptiste. [Title, Marquis **de Torcy.**] b. 1665; d. 1746. French diplomat; nephew of Jean Baptiste Colbert (1619–83). He was the principal French representative in negotiating the several treaties (1713–14) which collectively constituted the Peace of Utrecht, bringing to an end the War of the Spanish Succession. It was a difficult assignment, in view of the defeat which France had sustained in that struggle.

Colbert Range (kol′bėrt). [Also: **Navy Range, U.S. Navy Range.**] Mountain range in Antarctica, lying in the C part of Alexander I Island, NW of Le May Range, in ab. 71°10′ S., 70°45′ W.

Colborne (kōl′bọrn), Sir **John.** [Title, 1st Baron **Seaton.**] b. at Lyndhurst, Hampshire, England, Feb. 16, 1778; d. at Torquay, Devonshire, England, April 17, 1863. English general. He entered the army in 1794, served under Wellington in Portugal, France, and Spain in the period 1809–14, and fought with distinction at the battle of Waterloo in 1815. In 1825 he was appointed lieutenant governor of Guernsey, and in 1830 he became lieutenant governor of Upper Canada, a post which he resigned on being promoted to lieutenant general in 1838. He returned to England in 1839, having in the meantime quelled the Canadian rebellion, and in the same year was raised to the peerage. He was promoted to general in 1854, was commander of the forces in Ireland in the period 1855–60, and was created a field marshal in 1860.

Colbrand (kōl′brand). [Also, **Coldbrand.**] Legendary Danish giant, slain by Guy of Warwick, as told in the 14th-century metrical romance *Guy of Warwick* and repeated in Michael Drayton's *Polyolbion.*

Colburn (kōl′bėrn), **Warren.** b. at Dedham, Mass., March 1, 1793; d. at Lowell, Mass., Sept. 13, 1833. American mathematician, best known as a writer on arithmetic.

Colburn, Zerah. b. at Cabot, Vt., Sept. 1, 1804; d. at Norwich, Vt., March 2, 1839. American teacher and minister, celebrated during his boyhood as an arithmetical prodigy.

Colburn, Zerah. b. at Saratoga Springs, N.Y., 1832; d. April 26, 1870. American mechanical engineer, founder (1866) of the journal *Engineering.*

Colby (kōl′bi). City in NW Kansas, county seat of Thomas County, on Prairie Dog Creek (a tributary of the Republican River) ab. 190 mi. NW of Hutchinson. Wheat is the principal product of the region. 3,859 (1950).

Colby, Bainbridge. b. at St. Louis, Dec. 22, 1869; d. at Bemus Point, N.J., April 11, 1950. American lawyer, notable as Woodrow Wilson's last secretary of state (1920–21). A Republican legislator in New York state, he bolted the party in 1912 to support Theodore Roosevelt and his Progressive Party, and became shortly thereafter a Wilsonian Democrat. He supported F. D. Roosevelt in 1932, but within a year had turned against him and by 1935 stated that the New Deal was aimed at "overturning . . . American institutions." Bitterly anti-Russian, he wrote the original U.S. note refusing recognition to the U.S.S.R. after World War I.

Colby, Frank Moore. b. at Washington, D.C., Feb. 10, 1865; d. March 3, 1925. American encyclopedist. He served as acting professor (1889–90) of history at Amherst College, lecturer at Columbia College, and was subsequently professor of economics at New York University. He was history and political science editor (1893–95) on *Johnson's Encyclopedia*, and served as editor (1898–1925) of the *International Year Book*, later called *New International Year Book*, and coeditor (1900–03) of the *New International Encyclopedia.* He was the author of *Outlines of General History* (1899) and of articles in *Harper's Weekly, Bookman, New Republic, Vanity Fair, North American Review,* and *Harper's Magazine.*

Colby, Gardner. b. at Bowdoinham, Me., Sept, 3, 1810; d. at Newton, Mass., April 2, 1879. American woolen manufacturer. He established Gardner Colby and Company, a firm of wholesale jobbers and importers, bought (1850) a half interest in the Maverick Mills at Dedham Mass., and was president (until 1878) of the Wisconsin Central Railroad. In honor of his contributions to the Waterville Literary College, it was renamed (1867) Colby College.

Colby, Myra. Maiden name of **Bradwell, Myra.**

Colchester (kōl′chęs.tėr, -ches″tėr). [Latin, **Camulodunum;** Old English, **Colneceaster.**] Municipal borough, market town, and industrial center in SE England, in Essex, situated on the river Colne ab. 22 mi. NE of Chelmsford, ab. 52 mi. NE of London by rail. It has long been famous for its oyster fishery. Other industries include printing and bookbinding, manufacture of clothing, and the manufacture of agricultural machinery and gasoline engines. Dairy cattle are kept in the vicinity of Colchester to supply milk to the London market. It was an important textile center in the Middle Ages, and was formerly a seaport, but became a market for agricultural produce when the silting of the estuary of the river Colne destroyed its maritime position. It contains many Roman antiquities, including Roman walls which remain almost entire. It has a castle and the ruins of Saint Botolph's Priory and of a Benedictine monastery. The castle is the most powerful Norman military structure in England. The dimensions of the keep are 168 by 126 ft., and its walls vary in thickness from 11 to 30 ft. In one portion of the walls appears Roman herringbone work in brick. The chapel is now a museum, containing one of the finest collections of Romano-British antiquities in N Europe. Camulodunum was the earliest Roman colony in Britain, and was destroyed by the Iceni, but rebuilt. Later it became a stronghold, and was taken by Fairfax in 1648. Camulodunum (called Camalodunum in the *Itinerary*), was the capital of the British princes after they had submitted to the Romans, and was the first Roman city in the island honored with the rank of a colonia. The Roman walls which have endured leave no doubt that Colchester is the site of the ancient Camulodunum. 57,436 (1951).

Colchester. Town in N Vermont, in Chittenden County, near Lake Champlain, ab. 6 mi. NE of Burlington. 3,897 (1950).

Colchester, 1st Baron. Title of **Abbot, Charles.**

Colchis (kol′kis). [Modern name, **Mingrelia.**] In ancient geography, a country in Asia, lying between the Caucasus on the N, Iberia on the E, Armenia on the S, Pontus on the SW, and the Euxine (Black Sea) on the W. In Greek legend it was the land of Medea, and the Golden Fleece, sought by Jason, hung in its sacred grove. Its inhabitants were famous for the manufacture of linen.

Colcord (kol′kǫrd), **Lincoln Ross.** b. at sea, off Cape Horn, Aug. 14, 1883—. American poet and writer of sea stories. Educated (1900–06) at the University of Maine, he was a civil engineer (1906–09) with the Bangor and Aroostook Railroad. From 1909 he devoted his entire time to writing. In the period 1919–20 he was associate editor of *The Nation.* His fiction includes *The Drifting Diamond* (1912) and *The Game of Life and Death* (1914). Among his volumes of verse are *Vision of War* (1915) and *An Instrument of the Gods* (1922). He collaborated with the author in translating O. E. Rolvaag's *Giants in the Earth* (1927), and with George Wasson in the writing of *Sailing Days on the Penobscot* (1932).

Colcur (kōl′kör). b. c1555; d. 1598. Araucanian Indian of Chile; grandson of the chief Caupolican. He was cacique of Angol, Chile, and one of the most determined foes of the Spaniards. In 1592 he was elected *toqui*, or war chief, of the nation. He was killed in an unsuccessful attack on Coya.

Coldbath Fields (kōld′bȧth). Part of Middlesex, England, from which the great Coldbath Fields prison took its name. The original house of correction here was built in the reign of James I. It was overcrowded and was closed in 1886.

Coldbrand (kōld′brand). See **Colbrand.**

Colden (kōl′dęn), **Cadwallader.** b. in Ireland, Feb. 7, 1688; d. on Long Island, N.Y., Sept. 28, 1776. American colonial official, Loyalist, scientist, and philosopher. Graduated (1705) from the University of Edinburgh, he studied medicine at London, and settled (1710) at Philadelphia, where he became active as a doctor and a businessman. Moving (1718) to New York, he became (1720) surveyor-general of the colony. He was appointed (1721) to the governor's council, and became (1761) the colony's lieutenant governor, holding these posts until his death. A mob burned him in effigy (1765) when he refused to take action on popular feeling against the Stamp Act, and in 1775 he withdrew to his estate. A man of wide and diversified interests, he turned his mind to the study of botany, history, mathematics, medicine, and philosophy; his correspondents included Samuel Johnson, Benjamin Franklin, Linnaeus, and Gronovius. Colden's *The History of the Five Indian Nations Depending on the Province of New York* (1727) still is considered a reliable source, despite its faults of composition. Independently, although he was not the first to do so, he invented the stereotyping process. He wrote on moral philosophy, and in the field of physics produced (as it was called in the revised edition of 1751), *The Principles of Action in Matter, the Gravitation of Bodies, and the Motion of the Planets explained from those Principles.* Published at London, it was preceded by editions at Leipzig and Hamburg. Two of his papers on botany were published by Linnaeus in his *Acta Societatis Regiae Scientiarum Upsaliensis.* His papers on medicine include studies of yellow fever and cancer.

Colden, Cadwallader David. b. near Flushing, L.I., N.Y., April 4, 1769; d. at Jersey City, N.J.; Feb. 7, 1834. American lawyer and politician; grandson of Cadwallader Colden (1688–1776).

Colden, Jane. b. March 27, 1724; d. March 10, 1766. American botanist; daughter of Cadwallader Colden (1688–1776). An adherent of the Linnaean method of plant classification, she was the first American woman to distinguish herself in botany.

Cold Harbor. Place in Hanover County, Va., ab. 9 mi. E by NE of Richmond, situated near the Chickahominy River. It was the scene of two battles during the Civil War: the first, fought June 27, 1862, is better known as the battle of Gaines's Mill; the second was fought June 3, 1864, and the Confederates (50,000–69,000) under Lee defeated the Union forces (150,000) under Grant. Losses (June 1–12): Union, 14,931; Confederate, 1,700.

Cold Harbor. Novel by Francis Brett Young, published in 1924. It is a modern example of the 18th-century novel of terror.

Cold Harbour. [Also, **Cole-Harbour**; corrupted, **Coal Harbour.**] Formerly a building in the parish of Allhallows the Less, near the Thames, London. Stow gives a long account of the various merchant princes and great men through whose hands it passed till it came to the Earl of Shrewsbury, who in 1553 changed its name to Shrewsbury House; the next earl "took it down, and in place thereof builded a number of small tenements, now letten out for great rents to people of all sorts." It was at this time a sanctuary for debtors, gamesters, and such; hence the phrase "To take sanctuary in Cold Harbour."

Coldingham (kōl'ding.ạm). Civil parish in S Scotland, in Berwickshire, ab. 3 mi. NW of Eyemouth. It has the remains of a famous priory, burned by the Danes c870. Pop. 2,398 (1931).

Coldstream (kōld'strēm). Police burgh in S Scotland, in Berwickshire, situated on the river Tweed, ab. 9 mi. SE of Duns, ab. 347 mi. N of London by rail. The Coldstream Guards were first enrolled here in the 17th century. 1,225 (est. 1948).

Coldstream, Lady Catharine. Scottish woman of quality in Samuel Foote's play *The Maid of Bath*. She is a shrewd old woman who tries her hand at matchmaking.

Coldstream, Sir Charles. Languid man of fashion in Mathew's farce *Used Up*.

Coldstream Guards. Regiment of British foot guards, first enrolled by General Monck at Coldstream, Scotland, in the period 1659–60.

Cold War. Popular name for the suppressed conflict existing between Russia and the West in the years almost immediately following World War II. It denotes the highly pitched tensions and hostility existing, without open war, as the East and West found themselves unable to reach agreement on any major world issues, such as atomic energy, Germany, Korea, Japan, Trieste, and similar matters.

Coldwater (kōld'wô"tėr, -wot"ėr). City in S Lower Michigan, county seat of Branch County. Manufactures of cement, furnaces, shoes, marine engines, and flour. Nearby lakes and rivers are popular with vacationers and fishermen. Coldwater is the seat of a state-sponsored "children's village." 8,594 (1950).

Coldwell (kōld'wẹl), **Major James.** b. in Devonshire, England, Dec. 2, 1888—. Canadian educator, political leader, and legislator. He went to western Canada in 1910, taught in small schools in Alberta and Saskatchewan, and from 1919 to 1934 was a high-school principal at Regina, capital of Saskatchewan. He was president of the Saskatchewan Teachers Alliance (1924–25), president of the Canadian Teachers Federation (1927–28), and secretary-treasurer of the last-named organization (1928–34). He entered political life in 1921 as a member of the board of aldermen of Regina, an office he filled until 1932. In 1925 he stood unsuccessfully for a seat in the Dominion Parliament as a candidate of the Progressive Party. When this party disintegrated, he joined the Independent Labor Party, was its president for Saskatchewan (1929–32), and subsequently became leader in that province of the Farmer-Labor Party. The Co-operative Commonwealth Federation was established in 1932; two years later Coldwell, as its candidate for local office in Saskatchewan, was defeated, but in 1935 he was elected to the Dominion House of Commons, and reëlected in 1940 and 1945. From the first he was Co-operative Commonwealth leader in Parliament, and became the national leader of the Federation in 1942. In 1945 he was a Canadian delegate to the United Nations Conference at San Francisco. In that year also he published *Left Turn, Canada*, an exposition of the program of the Co-operative Commonwealth Federation.

Cole (kōl), **Arthur Charles.** b. at Ann Arbor, Mich., April 22, 1886—. American historian and educator. He was an instructor at the University of Michigan (1907–08), a high-school teacher at Indianapolis (1908–09), a Harrison fellow at the University of Pennsylvania (1909–12), and taught at the University of Illinois (1912–20) before taking the chair of American history at Ohio State University (1920–30). He became professor of history at Western Reserve University in 1930, holding that post until 1944, when he accepted the professorship of history at Brooklyn College in the city of New York. He was associate editor (1928–34) of the *American Historical Review*, and is the author of many articles and of a number of books, including *The Era of the Civil War* (vol. III of the *Centennial History of Illinois*, 1919), *The Irrepressible Conflict* (1934), and *A Hundred Years of Mount Holyoke College* (1940).

Cole, Charles Woolsey. b. at Montclair, N.J., Feb. 8, 1906—. American historian and college president. He was an instructor in history at Columbia University (1929–35), associate professor (1935–37) and professor (1937–40) of economics at Amherst College, returning to Columbia as professor of history (1940–46), before being elected president of Amherst in 1946. During World War II he served in the Office of Price Administration and in other government departments. He is the author of *French Mercantilist Doctrines Before Colbert* (1931), *Colbert and a Century of French Mercantilism* (1939), and *French Mercantilism, 1683–1700* (1943), and coauthor of *Economic History of Europe* (1941) and *History of Europe Since 1500* (1949).

Cole, Sir **Galbraith Lowry.** b. 1772; d. Oct. 4, 1842. English cavalry officer. Appointed (Jan. 1, 1801) colonel in command of the 27th Inniskillings regiment, with which his family was associated, he assumed (1805) command at Malta and commanded (1809–14) a division during the Peninsular War, participating in the battles of Bussaco and La Albuera and the siege of Badajoz. In 1830 he was made a general.

Cole, G. D. H. [Full name, **George Douglas Howard Cole.**] b. at Cambridge, England, Sept. 25, 1889—. English economist, sociologist, professor, historian, biographer, and (with his wife, Margaret Isabel Cole) author of crime fiction. He was educated at St. Paul's School, London, and at Balliol College, Oxford (of which he is a B.A. 1912 and an M.A. 1915). He has taught philosophy at Durham University, and economics at London and Oxford universities. He is a Fabian Socialist and a member of the Labour Party. On Aug. 18, 1918, he married Margaret Isabel Postgate (b. 1893), who is also his literary partner. He is the author of *The World of Labour* (1913), *Labour in War Time* (1915), *Principles of Socialism* (1917), *Democracy in Industry* (1920), *Out of Work: A Study of Unemployment* (1923), *A Short History of the British Working-Class Movement* (1927), *A Guide to Modern Politics* (1934, with his wife), *What Marx Really Meant* (1934), *Europe, Russia, and the Future* (1941), *Fabian Socialism* (1943), and many other political, economic, and sociological studies. He has written lives of William Cobbett (1924, rev. 1925) and Robert Owen (1925, rev. 1930), and two volumes of poetry, *New Beginnings* (1914) and *The Crooked World* (1933). To a wider and more general reading public, Cole (with his wife) is not merely known but is popular as the author of *The Brooklyn Murders* (1923), *The Death of a Millionaire* (1925), *The Murder at Crome House* (1927), *The Man from the River*, *a Wilson Story* and *Superintendent Wilson's Holiday* (both 1928), *The Corpse in the Constable's Garden*, *Dead Man's Watch*, *The Great Southern Mystery* (the last called *The Walking Corpse* in the American ed.; all 1931), *Death of a Star* (1932), *End of an Ancient Mariner* (1933), *Death in the Quarry* and *Murder in Four Parts* (both 1934), *The Big Business Murder*, *Dr. Tancred Begins*, and *Scandal at School* (all 1935), *Disgrace to the College* and *The Missing Aunt* (both 1938), *Mrs. Warrender's Profession* and *Off With Her Head!* (both 1938), *Double Blackmail* and *Greek Tragedy* (both 1939), *Murder in the Munitions Works* (1940), *The Counterpoint Murder* (1941), *Knife in the Dark* and *Toper's End* (both 1942), *Death of a Bride* (1945), and many others.

Cole, George. b. at Portsmouth, England, 1810; d. at London, Sept. 7, 1883. English landscape painter; father of Vicat Cole.

Cole, George Watson. b. at Warren, Conn., Sept. 6, 1850; d. at Los Angeles, Oct. 10, 1939. American bibliographer and librarian, inventor of a system of measuring books by a size-card in accordance with American Library Association standards. Admitted (1876) to the bar, he practiced law in the period 1876–85. He was librarian of the Free Public Library (1891–95) at Jersey City, N.J., and of the Huntington Library and Art Gallery (1915–24), at San Marino, Calif. He published *Checklist of English Literature to 1640 in the Library of Henry E. Huntington* (1919), *Bibliography—A Forecast* (1920), *Elizabethan Americana* (1925), and *Bibliographical Pitfalls—Linked Books* (1926).

Cole, Sir **Henry.** [Pseudonym, **Felix Summerly.**] b. at Bath, England, July 15, 1808; d. at London, April 18, 1882. English official. He was a senior assistant keeper of the records in 1838, became secretary of the committee on penny postage in 1838, edited the *Journal of Design* (1849–52), was a member of the executive committee of the great exhibition of 1851, was the chief manager of the exhibitions of the period 1871–74, became secretary of the School of Design in 1851, and was secretary of the department of practical art from 1852 to 1873. He published, under the pseudonym Felix Summerly, *The Home Treasury* (1843–44), *Pleasure Excursions to Croydon* (1846), *Westminster Abbey* (1842), *Canterbury* (1843), *Hámpton Court* (1843), and others.

Cole, John William. [Pseudonym, **John William Calcraft.**] fl. in the second half of the 19th century. English miscellaneous writer. He was the author of *Russia and the Russians* (1854), *Life and Theatrical Times of Charles Kean* (1860), and *The Bride of Lammermoor*, a drama.

Cole, King. See **King Cole.**

Cole, Margaret Isabel. [Maiden name, **Postgate.**] b. at Cambridge, England, 1893—. English lecturer and writer; wife (married 1918) and literary partner of G. D. H. Cole, and sister of R. W. Postgate, with whom her husband also collaborated in his works on economics. Daughter of a Cambridge professor, she was educated at Rodean School and at the Cambridge college for women, Girton. She taught classical subjects at St. Paul's Girls' School, and has been a London University lecturer. From 1916 to 1925 she was an assistant secretary in the labor research department. Like her husband she is a Socialist and belongs to and has held office in Fabian groups. On her own, she is the author of pamphlets on labor subjects. As individuals or as a literary team, the Coles are considered the English equivalent of "S.S. Van Dine" (Willard Huntington Wright). Her works include *Margaret Postgate's Poems* (1918), *Twelve Studies in Soviet Russia* (1932), *Marriage Past and Present* (1938), and *Makers of the Labour Party* (1947). In collaboration with her husband she wrote the detective stories *The Brooklyn Murders* (1923), *A Lesson in Crime* (1933), *Last Will and Testament* (1936), *Greek Tragedy* (1939), and many others.

Cole, Mrs. Character played by Samuel Foote in his comedy *The Mirror*, a procuress whose pretended reformation was intended as a slur on the Methodists. Her reference to her friend Dr. Squintum gave very great offense, as he was at once identified with George Whitefield. She was based on a real person, a "Mother Douglass."

Cole, Rossetter Gleason. b. at Clyde, Mich., Feb. 5, 1866—. American musician, composer, and educator. Graduated (Ph.D., 1888) from the University of Michigan, where he studied under C. B. Cady, he was professor of music (1894–1901) at Grinnell College, Iowa, served on the staff (1907–09) of the University of Wisconsin, and was director of theory (1915 *et seq.*) and dean (1935 *et seq.*) at the Cosmopolitan School of Music, Chicago. His compositions include *Your Lad and My Lad* (1918), *The Rock of Liberty* (1920), and *The Maypole Lovers* (1928).

Cole, Thomas. b. at Bolton-le-Moors, Lancashire, England, Feb. 1, 1801; d. at Catskill, N.Y., Feb. 11, 1848. American landscape painter, known as an early member of the Hudson River School (a group of painters who specialized in romantic landscapes, including views of Niagara Falls as well as of scenic spots along the course of the Hudson).

Cole, Timothy. b. at London, April 6, 1852; d. May 17, 1937. American wood engraver. For *Scribner's Magazine* (later called *The Century Magazine*) he executed (1875 *et seq.*) many engravings of old and new art masterpieces, which were later published in book form. His most important work is *Old Italian Masters*, begun in 1883, published in 1892 (text by W. J. Stillman). His later works include *Old Dutch and Flemish Masters* (1895; text by John C. Van Dyke), *Old English Masters* (1902; notes by John C. Van Dyke and comments by the engraver), and *Old Spanish Masters* (1907; text by Charles H. Caffin).

Cole, Vicat. b. 1833; d. April 6, 1893. English landscape painter; son of George Cole.

Cole, William. b. at Little Abington, Cambridgeshire, England, Aug. 3, 1714; d. at Milton, near Cambridge, England, Dec. 16, 1782. English clergyman and antiquary, an authority on the antiquities of Cambridge and Cambridgeshire. His manuscripts are in the British Museum.

Colebrooke (kōl′brụk), **Henry Thomas.** b. at London, June 15, 1765; d. there, March 10, 1837. English Orientalist, celebrated as one of the first to study Sanskrit.

Cole-Harbour. See **Cold Harbour.**

Coleman (kōl′mạn). City in C Texas, county seat of Coleman County, NW of Austin, near the geographic center of the state, in a petroleum region. Nearby is the site of Camp Colorado, a pre-Civil War U.S. military post. 6,530 (1950).

Coleman, Charles. d. at London, 1664. English composer; father of Edward Coleman (d. 1669). In 1662 he was appointed composer to Charles II.

Coleman, Charles Caryl. b. at Buffalo, N.Y., 1840; d. Dec. 5, 1928. American painter. In 1859 he went to Europe to study art, but returned to serve three years in the Union army in the Civil War. From 1866 he lived and worked in Europe, his studio being on the island of Capri, Italy.

Coleman, D'Alton Corry. b. at Carleton Place, Ontario, Canada, July 9, 1879—. Canadian railway executive. He has been associated (1899 *et seq.*) with the Canadian Pacific Railway as vice-president (1934–42), president (1942 *et seq.*), and chairman (1943 *et seq.*).

Coleman, Edward. d. at Greenwich (now part of London), Aug. 29, 1669. English singing master and composer of songs; son of Charles Coleman (d. 1664). He wrote the music for Shirley's *Contention of Ajax and Achilles* (1653).

Coleman, Glenn O. b. at Springfield, Ohio, July 18, 1887; d. at Long Beach, Long Island, N.Y., May 8, 1932. American painter and lithographer. While a pupil of William M. Chase, Robert Henri, and Everett Shinn at the New York School of Art, he found the principal inspiration for his paintings and lithographs in the streets of New York and their denizens, and these remained his chief interest throughout his career. He had plenty of opportunity to study in this chosen field, for since he refused to paint prettily or go in for facile commercial art work, he was beset by poverty and accordingly lived most of his years in the shabbier sections of lower Manhattan. Late in life the gripping qualities of his sombre pictures, always skilfully composed and solidly executed, and often dramatic, brought him substantial recognition, and examples of his work are to be found in the Luxembourg Museum, Paris, the Metropolitan Museum of Art, New York, and museums in Brooklyn, Washington, and Newark.

Coleman, Lyman. b. at Middlefield, Mass., June 14, 1796; d. at Easton, Pa., March 16, 1882. American educator and theological writer. He was professor of Latin and Greek (1861–68) and of Latin (1868–82) at Lafayette College.

Coleman, William Tell. b. near Cynthiana, Ky., Feb. 29, 1824; d. at San Francisco, Nov. 22, 1893. American merchant, a pioneer in California. He started stores at Placerville and Sacramento and established (1850) with a partner a borax-manufacturing plant at San Francisco. In 1851 he served on the executive committee of the Committee of Vigilance, and was president, in 1856, of the second Committee of Vigilance.

Colenso (kō̤.len′zō), **John William.** b. at St. Austell, Cornwall, England, Jan. 24, 1814; d. at Durban, Natal, South Africa, June 20, 1883. English divine, appointed bishop of Natal in 1853. He was educated at Cambridge, and was a tutor at St. John's College in the period 1842–46. From that date until 1853 he was vicar of Forncett St. Mary in Norfolk. He published elementary treatises on arithmetic and algebra, volumes of sermons, works on the Zulu language, *Commentary on St. Paul's Epistle to the Romans* (1861), *The Pentateuch and Book of Joshua Critically Examined* (1862–79), and others. His writings on the Old Testament, in which he took what was considered very advanced critical ground, awakened great and bitter opposition; he was excommunicated by Bishop Gray, metropolitan of Capetown (a proceeding afterward declared to be null and void), and was subjected to attacks from many quarters.

Coleoni (kō.lā.ō′nē), **Bartolommeo.** See **Colleoni** or **Coleoni, Bartolommeo.**

Colepeper (kul′pep″ėr), **John.** [Title, 1st Baron **Colepeper of Thoresway.**] d. in England, June 11, 1660. English Royalist politician. He became a member of the Long Parliament in 1640, took part in the proceedings against Strafford, supported the episcopacy and opposed the Scottish demand for religious union, became a privy councilor and chancellor of the exchequer on Jan. 2, 1642, and was thenceforth an influential advisor of the king. He followed Charles to York, fought at the battle of Edgehill, became master of the rolls on Jan. 28, 1643, and accompanied the Prince of Wales (later Charles II) to France in 1646. He remained until his death a councilor and active supporter of the prince.

Colepeper, Lord **Thomas.** See **Culpeper** or **Colepeper,** Lord **Thomas.**

Colepepper (kul′pep″ėr), **Captain John.** [Also called **Peppercul.**] Bully and murderer in Sir Walter Scott's *The Fortunes of Nigel.*

Coler (kō′lẹr), **Alwin Gustav Edmund von.** b. at Gröningen, Netherlands, March 15, 1831; d. at Berlin, Aug. 26, 1901. Prussian military surgeon. He became (1889) *Generalstabsarzt* (surgeon-general) of the Prussian army, and improved the organization of the army medical department. He was coauthor (with O. von Schjerning) of *Über die Wirkung und die kriegschirurgische Bedeutung der neuen Handfeuerwaffen* (1894; translated into French), *Die transportable Lazarettbaracke* (1890), and *Friedenssanitätsordnung* (1891).

Coleraine (kōl.rān′). Municipal borough, seaport, and market town in Ulster province, Northern Ireland, in County Londonderry, situated on the river Bann, at the head of navigation, ab. 4 mi. from the sea, ab. 48 mi. NW of Belfast. The principal industry is whisky distilling. The town was formerly noted for its linen manufactures. Coleraine is situated in a district of mixed farming, and has exports of potatoes. It formerly had a cattle trade with Glasgow, Scotland, which trade is now practically extinct. Hugh Thompson, illustrator of Jane Austen's novels, lived here. 9,557 (1947).

Coleridge (kōl′rij), **Derwent.** b. at Keswick, England, Sept. 14, 1800; d. at Torquay, England, April 2, 1883. English clergyman and educator; son of Samuel Taylor Coleridge. He was master of the grammar school at Helston, Cornwall (1825–40), principal of St. Mark's College, Chelsea (1841–64), and rector of Hanwell (1864–80).

Coleridge, Hartley. [Full name, **David Hartley Coleridge.**] b. at Clevedon, Somersetshire, England, Sept. 17, 1796; d. at Rydal, Westmorland, England, Jan. 6, 1849. English poet, essayist, and editor; eldest son of Samuel Taylor Coleridge. He was educated at Ambleside, and at Merton College, Oxford. He tried teaching, in which he failed as he did in everything that he attempted. He had great possibilities but he did not know how to make the best of them. He wrote for the *London Magazine* and *Blackwood's,* and he published *Biographia Borealis* (1833), which came out three years later as *The Worthies of Yorkshire and Lancaster,* and edited the plays of Massinger and Ford in 1840. His *Poems* appeared in 1833, and his *Literary Remains* was edited in 1851 by his brother, Derwent. A few sonnets, *On Prayer, To Ho ner, To Shakespeare,* and the autobiographical *When I Review the Course that I Have Run,* have been praised by critics and lovers of poetry.

Coleridge, Henry Nelson. b. at Ottery St. Mary, Devonshire, England, Oct. 25, 1798; d. Jan. 26, 1843. English lawyer and man of letters; nephew of Samuel Taylor Coleridge and husband of Sara Coleridge. He became his uncle's literary executor, and edited several of his works, besides publishing his *Table Talk.*

Coleridge, Herbert. b. at Hampstead, London, Oct. 7, 1830; d. at London, April 23, 1861. English lawyer and philologist; son of Henry Nelson Coleridge, and grandson of Samuel Taylor Coleridge. He was one of the original promoters of the dictionary at first designed by the Philological Society to supply the deficiencies of Johnson's and Richardson's, which in the hands of later editors developed into the *New English Dictionary, on Historical Principles,* in process of publication from 1884, and completed in a revised edition in 1933.

Coleridge, John. b. 1719; d. 1781. English schoolmaster and clergyman; father of Samuel Taylor Coleridge. Vicar of Ottery St. Mary, Devonshire, he was also master of the grammar school there. He published *Biblical Tract* (1768) and *Latin Grammar* (1772).

Coleridge, Sir **John Duke.** [Title, 1st Baron **Coleridge.**] b. Dec. 3, 1820; d. June 14, 1894. English jurist; son of Sir John Taylor Coleridge. He became chief justice of the Court of Common Pleas in 1873, and lord chief justice of England in 1880.

Coleridge, Sir **John Taylor.** b. at Tiverton, Devonshire, England, 1790; d. at Ottery St. Mary, Devonshire, England, Feb. 11, 1876. English jurist; nephew of Samuel Taylor Coleridge. He was justice of the King's Bench in the period 1835–58, and edited Blackstone's *Commentaries* (1825).

Coleridge, Mary Elizabeth. b. at London, Sept. 23, 1861; d. at Harrogate, Yorkshire, England, Aug. 25, 1907. English poet, novelist, critic, biographer, and teacher; great-grandniece of Samuel Taylor Coleridge. Educated privately, she began writing and drawing at an early age; two of her literary favorites were Browning and Tolstoy. Influenced by the latter, she taught English literature to poor girls in her own home, and also taught (1895–1907) at the Working Women's College. She was the author of *Fancy's Following* (1896), *Fancy's Guerdon* (1897), *Last Poems* (1905), and *Poems Old and New* (1907), of the novels *The Seven Sleepers of Ephesus* (1893), *The King With Two Faces* (1897), *The Fiery Dawn* (1901), *The Shadow on the Wall* (1904), and *The Lady on the Drawing-Room Floor* (1906), and of *Holman Hunt* (1908), a biography.

Coleridge, Samuel Taylor. b. at Ottery St. Mary, Devonshire, England, Oct. 21, 1772; d. at Highgate, London, July 25, 1834. English poet, literary critic, lecturer, political journalist, philosopher, and theologian. After the death of his father, a poor clergyman with a large family, Coleridge received a presentation (1782) to the school Christ's Hospital, and from there passed to Jesus College, Cambridge (1791–93, 1794) by means of scholarships. He did not take his degree, but formed with Southey a plan called pantisocracy, of establishing a small communistic society in America. The plan fell through, because of lack of money. In 1795 Coleridge married Sarah Fricker, the sister of Southey's wife, and in 1796 published his first volume of poems. In the same year he began the publication of *The Watchman,* a liberal political periodical which failed after ten issues. After continued money troubles, he was considering entering the Unitarian ministry, but received in 1798 an annuity of 150 pounds from the brothers Josiah and Thomas Wedgwood, which permitted him to continue his literary life.

Peak of Poetic Power. During the year following June, 1797, Coleridge was stimulated by his companionship with Wordsworth to his greatest achievements in poetry, including *The Ancient Mariner, Kubla Khan,* and the first part of *Christabel.* After the joint publication by Wordsworth and Coleridge of *Lyrical Ballads* (1798), both poets went to Germany, where Coleridge learned the language and studied for some months at the University of Göttingen. After his return to England in 1799 he translated Schiller's *Wallenstein,* and wrote political leading articles for the antiministerial newspaper, *The Morning Post.* In 1800 he settled in the Lake District to be near Wordsworth again, but his health suffered in the damp climate, and he became a slave to opium, which he had used as a remedy. Though he wrote the second part of *Christabel* in 1800 and *Dejection* in 1802, he was henceforth to write little poetry. In 1804 he sailed for Malta in search of health and became acting secretary to the governor; but he returned in 1806 without improvement. He gave seven series of disorderly but brilliant lectures on Shakespeare and other literary subjects from 1808 to 1819, published another political and philosophical periodical called *The Friend* in 1809–10, and revised his tragedy *Osorio* (1797) for successful performance at Drury Lane in 1813, but he was often intellectually submerged by opium until in 1816 he became the guest of Mr. Gillman, a physician at Highgate, with whom he lived until his death in 1834. He was redeemed from his slavery to opium by Mr. Gillman, and published several religious or political works, but the collection of his poems in 1817 at the same time as his autobiography was the result of earlier labors. The autobiography *Biographia Literaria* contains his greatest literary criticism, chiefly concerned with Wordsworth.

Evaluation and Bibliography. Though his actual achievement in poetry was small in quantity, Coleridge was the intellectual center of the Romantic Movement, perhaps the greatest of English literary critics, influential in conservative politics and religion, and the first important spokesman of German idealistic metaphysics in England in the early 19th century. The standard edition of his poems is by E. H. Coleridge, and the standard biographies are by J. D. Campbell and E. K. Chambers. *The Road to Xanadu* by J. L. Lowes is the most influential criticism of his poetry. The *Cambridge Bibliography of English Literature* (vol. III) includes a conveniently accessible bibliography.

Coleridge, Sara. b. at Greta Hall, near Keswick, England, Dec. 22, 1802; d. at London, May 3, 1852. English writer; daughter of Samuel Taylor Coleridge and wife (married in 1829) of Henry Nelson Coleridge. She is best known as the editor, after her husband's death, of her father's writings, and for *Phantasmion* (1837), a fairy tale.

Coleridge-Taylor (kōl'rij.tā'lọr), **Samuel.** b. at London, Aug. 15, 1875; d. at Croydon, England, Sept. 1, 1912. English composer; son of an African Negro doctor and an English mother. His principal works are the three cantatas comprised in *Scenes from the Song of Hiawatha*, the oratorio *The Atonement*, songs, and piano pieces in which he reproduced certain characteristics of Negro music.

Colerus (kō.lā'rụs), **Egmont.** [Full name, **Egmont Colerus von Geldern.**] b. at Linz, Austria, May 12, 1888; d. at Vienna, April 8, 1939. Austrian novelist, whose books dealt with an astounding variety of themes.

Coles (kōlz), **Cowper Phipps.** b. 1819; lost at sea, Sept. 7, 1870. English naval officer who, in the Crimean war, served with distinction at Sevastopol in 1854. He gave much attention to the construction of turreted ships, and claimed to be the originator (a claim disproved in favor of Ericsson and others) of the monitor type of ironclad ships. He lost his life by the capsizing of the *Captain* (a ship of this class constructed under his own supervision) in a gale off Cape Finisterre, in which 523 persons were drowned.

Coles, Edward. b. in Albemarle County, Va., Dec. 15, 1786; d. at Philadelphia, July 7, 1868. American politician, governor of Illinois in the period 1823–26. He prevented, after a bitter and protracted struggle, the proslavery party from obtaining control of that state.

Coles, Elisha. b. at Wolverhampton, England, c1640; d. at Galway, Ireland, Dec. 20, 1680. English schoolteacher, stenographer, and lexicographer. He was the author of a work on shorthand (1674), *An English Dictionary explaining the difficult terms that are used in divinity* . . . (1676; and several subsequent editions), *A Dictionary, English-Latin and Latin-English* (1677, and several later editions), and others.

Colet (kol'ẹt), **John.** b. at London, c1467; d. there, Sept. 16, 1519. English theologian and classical scholar. He became dean of Saint Paul's in 1505, and refounded (1512) Saint Paul's School. He was the intimate friend of Erasmus and More, and one of the chief promoters of the "new learning" of the Renaissance and indirectly of the Reformation. Although not directly advocating the Reformation (he never relinquished his Catholicism), Colet promoted various reforms in clerical procedure. In 1514 he accompanied Erasmus on a pilgrimage to Canterbury. He preached (1515) at the installation of Wolsey as cardinal.

Colet (ko.le), **Louise.** [Maiden name, **Révoil.**] b. at Aix, France, Sept. 15, 1810; d. at Paris, March 8, 1876. French poet, novelist, and general writer. She was the mistress of Flaubert and of Victor Cousin. Her works include *Les Fleurs du midi* (1837), *Lui, roman contemporain* (1859), and *Les Dévotes du grand monde* (1873).

Colette (ko.let), Saint. b. at Corbie, France, Jan. 13, 1381; d. at Ghent, March 16, 1447. Flemish religious. She successively joined the Beguines, Benedictines, and Urbanist Poor Clares, and lived as a recluse. She was permitted by Pope Benedict XIII (Pedro de Luna) to enter the Poor Clares and was authorized by him to found new convents and promote reform of the order. She founded 17 convents during her lifetime, the nucleus of the Colettine Poor Clares. She was canonized in 1807.

Colette. [Pseudonym of **Sidonie Gabrielle Claudine Colette.**] b. at St.-Sauveur-en-Puisaye, France, Jan. 28, 1873—. French novelist. She is the author of the "Claudine series," *Claudine à l'école* (1900), *Claudine à Paris* (1901), and others (in collaboration with her first husband, Henri Gauthier-Villars, who used the pseudonym Willy); of *Dialogues des bêtes* (1904) and *Sept Dialogues des bêtes* (1905), and of other novels including *Chéri* (1920), *La Fin de Chéri* (1926), and *Gigi* (1945). After her divorce from Gauthier-Villars (1906) she appeared in music halls as dancer and mime, basing her *L'Envers du Music Hall* (1913) upon these experiences. She later married Henri de Jouvenel. Her work is praised for deep understanding of unfortunate human beings and for its warm love of nature.

Coley (kō'li), **William Bradley.** b. at Westport, Conn., Jan. 12, 1862; d. April 16, 1936. American surgeon. Graduated from Yale (1884) and the Harvard Medical School (1888), he set up in practice in 1888, and later became consulting physician at Memorial Hospital and surgeon in chief at the Hospital for the Ruptured and Crippled.

Colfax (kōl'faks). [Former name, **Belleville.**] City in SE Washington, county seat of Whitman County, on the Palouse River: marketing center for wheat. 3,057 (1950).

Colfax, Schuyler. b. at New York, March 23, 1823; d. at Mankato, Minn., Jan. 13, 1885. American politician, vice-president of the United States in Grant's first administration (1869–73). He was deputy auditor (1841 *et seq.*) at South Bend, Ind., assistant enrolling clerk of the state senate (1842–44), and served as correspondent of the *Indiana State Journal.* Active in politics as a Whig, he purchased (1845) an interest in the South Bend *Free Press* and converted it into one of the state's leading Whig publications under the name of the *St. Joseph Valley Register.* He transferred to the Republican Party after its founding; elected to Congress in 1855, he served in the House of Representatives until 1869, and was speaker from 1863 to 1869. He served (1869–73) as vice-president under Grant, but failed to secure renomination when Republican leaders lost confidence in Colfax after he had been eyed by the Liberal Republicans as a possible presidential candidate. His involvement in the Crédit Mobilier scandal, while it did not bring him Congressional censure, put an end to his political career.

Colgate (kōl'gāt), **James Boorman.** b. at New York, March 4, 1818; d. Feb. 7, 1904. American broker; son of William Colgate (1783–1857). He established (1852) with John B. Trevor the brokerage firm of Trevor and Colgate, later (1873) changed to James B. Colgate and Company, was the founder and president of the New York Gold Exchange, and was vice-president and director of the Bank of the State of New York. With other members of his family he endowed what is today Colgate University.

Colgate, Sidney Morse. b. at Orange, N.J., Sept. 11, 1862; d. Nov. 10, 1930. American soap manufacturer. He continued the soap business founded by his grandfather, William Colgate (1783–1857), served as chairman of the board of Colgate-Palmolive-Peet Company, and was head of the War Service Committee of the soap industry in World War I.

Colgate, William. b. at Hollingbourne, Kent, England, Jan. 25, 1783; d. at New York, March 25, 1857. American manufacturer of soaps and toilet preparations, and civic benefactor; father of James Boorman Colgate (1818–

1904). He was brought (1795) by his family to Baltimore, which he left (1804) to go to New York, where he worked for Slidell and Company, at that time the city's largest tallow-chandlers. In 1806 he founded his own firm, which for a time boasted one of the largest starch plants in the U.S. His chief efforts were devoted to the manufacture of soap, an industry in its infancy in the U.S. when Colgate entered the field. When Chevreul made public his findings (1841) concerning saponification, Colgate drew upon the discoveries, and gradually improved and widened his varieties of soaps. He moved (1847) his plant from New York to Jersey City, where the firm later began making toilet preparations. From the time he set up his own firm, Colgate annually set aside for civic benefactions ten percent of his business profits. He contributed to the support of the Hamilton Literary and Theological Seminary, Hamilton, N.Y., continuing his aid when it became (1846) Madison University. It has been since 1890 known as Colgate University. He helped found the first Bible Society in New York and was an organizer (1816) of the American Bible Society, later aiding in the organization of the American and Foreign Bible Society.

Colibri (ko.lē.brē), **Maman.** See **Maman Colibri.**

Coligny or **Coligni** (ko.lē.nyē), **Gaspard de.** b. at Châtillon-sur-Loing, France, Feb. 16, 1519; killed in the Saint Bartholomew's Day massacre, at Paris, Aug. 24, 1572. French general and Huguenot leader. He was presented at the court of Francis I by his uncle, the constable Anne de Montmorency in 1537, was knighted by Condé on the field of Ceresole (Cérisolles) in 1544, became admiral of France in 1552, and was taken prisoner of war by the Spaniards at St.-Quentin in 1557. On his return to France he openly embraced Calvinism, and not hesitating to use his official position where this could be of help, made several attempts to establish colonies in America as places of refuge for the Huguenots, including the expedition of Jean Ribault in 1562 and that of Laudonnière in 1564. Civil war having broken out in 1562, he was chosen second in command of the Huguenot forces. The murder of the Prince of Condé after the battle of Jarnac (1569) placed him at the head of the Huguenot party until superseded by Henry of Navarre, in whose name he fought the disastrous battle of Moncontour the same year. His victory over the Catholics at Arnay-le-Duc on June 27, 1570, however, resulted in the peace of St.-Germain, concluded on Aug. 8, 1570. On the occasion of the marriage of Henry of Navarre with Margaret of Valois, sister of Charles IX, he visited Paris, where, although treated with apparent cordiality by the king, he was detested by Catherine de Médicis and was murdered in his chamber in the presence of the Duke of Guise, falling as the first victim of the Saint Bartholomew's Day massacre.

Colima (kō.lē'mä). State in SW Mexico, lying between Jalisco on the N, Michoacán on the E and S, and the Pacific Ocean on the W. Capital, Colima; area, 2,010 sq. mi.; pop. 112,292 (1950).

Colima. City in SW Mexico, capital of Colima state: marketing center for a cattle-raising region. It is near the volcano Colima, whose latest eruption was in 1941. 22,601 (1940).

Colima. Volcano in SW Mexico, in the state of Jalisco, ab. 40 mi. NE of the city of Colima. It was in eruption in 1869, in 1881, and in 1941. Elevation, ab. 12,750 ft.

Colima. [Also, **Nevado de Colima.**] Snowy mountain in SW Mexico, on the boundary of Colima and Jalisco states, near the volcano Colima. Elevation, ab. 14,100 ft.

Colimas (kǫ.lē'mąz). Indian tribe of Chibchan linguistic stock, in Colombia, related to the Muzos.

Colin Clout (kō'lin klout'). See under **Colin Clout's Come Home Again.**

Colin Clout's Come Home Again. Poem by Edmund Spenser, written after visiting London (1589–91). Spenser took the name from Skelton's *Colyn Cloute*, and called himself Colin Clout in all his poems. Colin Clout is also a character in Gay's pastoral *The Shepherd's Week.*

Colines (ko.lēn), **Simon de.** d. 1546. French printer. His work was carried on at Paris, where he was the collaborator and successor of Henri Estienne the elder. It is thought that he was a type designer, though some of the faces he used are known to have been the creations of Geofroy Tory.

Colins or **Colin** or **Colyns** (ko.lan̈), **Alexander.** b. at Mechlin, Belgium, c1527; d. at Innsbruck, in the Tyrol, Aug. 17, 1612. Flemish sculptor. His best works are at Innsbruck (notably the mausoleum of Maximilian I). His works in wood and in ivory are also noted.

Coliseum (kol.i.sē'um). See also **Colosseum.**

Coliseum, The. Poem by Edgar Allan Poe, appearing in his uncompleted blank-verse tragedy, *Politian.*

Coll (kol). Island, in the Inner Hebrides, in W Scotland, in Argyllshire, lying ab. 9 mi. SW of Ardnamurchan Point. Length, ab. 13 mi.; greatest width, ab. 4 mi.

Colla (kō'yä). Subtribe of the South American Aymara Indians. In pre-Inca days they were one of the most powerful of Aymara tribes, occupying the region N of Lake Titicaca, in what is now S Peru and NE Bolivia. Their descendants comprise part of the population of this region today, and still speak a dialect of Aymara. The name has sometimes been used synonymously with Aymara.

Collamer (kol'ą.mėr), **Jacob.** b. at Troy, N.Y., Jan. 8, 1791; d. at Woodstock, Vt., Nov. 9, 1865. American politician. He was postmaster general (1849–50) and U.S. senator from Vermont (1855–65).

Collao (kō.yä'ō). Region in S Peru, embracing the Titicaca basin. The name is also extended to adjacent parts of Bolivia. The Collao consists of elevated plains and hilly lands, nowhere less than 12,000 ft. above the sea. It is limited on the E and W by two great chains of the Andean system, and N the Vilcañota cross-range separates it from the basin of Cusco. The greater part of the Peruvian department of Puno is included in the Collao.

Colla-suyu (kō.yä.sö'yö). [Eng. trans., *"Region of the Colla."*] Name given by the Incas to the southern quarter of their empire, embracing the highlands of Bolivia, and Peru S of Cusco.

Colle (kôl'lā). Italian word for "hills," which also appears as part of the names of certain towns in Italy; for Italian names of ranges of hills, see the specific element of the name.

Collé (ko.lā), **Charles.** b. at Paris, 1709; d. there, Nov. 3, 1783. French song writer and dramatist.

Colle (kôl'lā), **Raffaello** (or **Raffaellino**) **dal.** b. at or near San Sepolcro, Tuscany, Italy, c1490; d. c1540. Italian painter; a pupil of Raphael (whence his name Rafaellino).

Collector v. Day, 11 Wallace 113 (1871). U.S. Supreme Court decision declaring unconstitutional a federal income tax on the salary of an official of a state agency. The dissenting opinion of Justice Bradley expressed a view more widely held at present than at the time of its announcement. Bradley held that "the general government has the same power of taxing the income of officers of the state governments as it has of taxing that of its own officers. . . . No man ceases to be a citizen of the United States by being an officer under the state government. . . . How can we tell what the effect of this decision will be? I cannot but regard it as founded on a fallacy, and that it will lead to mischievous consequences."

Colle di Val d'Elsa (kôl'lā dē väl del'sä). [Also, **Colle.**] Town and commune in C Italy, in the *compartimento* (region) of Tuscany, in the province of Siena, situated on the Elsa River, NW of Siena. It has paper, glass, ceramics, and textile industries. The paper and woolen industries date back to the Middle Ages; there were also important printing establishments here in the 15th century. There are old walls and gates. Except for the Church of Sant'Agostino, which sustained a hit on the roof, buildings of interest to tourists were undamaged in World War II. Pop. of commune, 11,052 (1936); of town, 5,749 (1936).

Colleen Bawn, or, The Brides of Garry-Owen (kol'ēn bôn'; gar'i.ō'ęn), **The.** Play by Dion Boucicault, founded on Gerald Griffin's novel *The Collegians.* It was first performed on Sept. 10, 1860.

Collège de France (ko.lezh dę fräṅs). [Also, **Collège Royal** (rwå.yål).] Institution of learning founded at Paris by Francis I c1530. It was designed to promote the more advanced humanistic tendencies of the time, and to counteract the scholasticism of the university. It at first consisted of four chairs for instruction in Greek and Hebrew. Later were added medicine, mathematics, philosophy (in the reign of Henry II), eloquence, botany,

Arabic (Henry III), and Syriac (Louis XIII). In 1789 there were 18 chairs; in 1835 there were 24 chairs; later it was further expanded. The Collège de France was at first dependent upon the university for lecture rooms. In 1610 a new building was begun, which was completed in the 19th century. An independent institution, the Collège de France is directly under the jurisdiction of the French minister of education. Lectures may be attended by anyone free of charge; there are no examinations or certificates. Lecturers are called on nomination by the French Institute, and have in the past included Renan and Bergson.

College Farm. Former name of **Ames,** Iowa.

Collège Mazarin (ko.lezh må.zå.raṅ). College at Paris, founded by Mazarin, on March 6, 1661. He endowed it, and gave it his library of some 40,000 volumes. The building was erected on the site of the Tour de Nesle by the architect Le Vau, and was finished in 1672. In 1674 the new college was incorporated in the university. Its object was the gratuitous instruction and sustenance of 60 sons of gentlemen living in the four newly acquired provinces, Piguerol, Alsace, La Flandre, and Roussillon; hence its other name, Collège des Quatre Nations ("College of the Four Nations").

College Park. City in NW Georgia, in Clayton and Fulton counties, ab. 8 mi. S of Atlanta. It is the seat of the Georgia Military Academy. 14,535 (1950).

College Park. Village in W central Maryland, in Prince Georges County, ab. 8 mi. NE of Washington, D.C. It is a residential suburb of Washington, and seat of part of the University of Maryland (which also has branches at Baltimore). 11,170 (1950).

College Place. Town in S Washington, in Walla Walla County, on the Walla Walla River (a tributary of the Columbia). It is a southwestern suburb of Walla Walla and the seat of Walla Walla College. In the decade between the last two U.S. censuses its population more than doubled. 1,272 (1940), 3,174 (1950).

College Station. City in E central Texas, in Brazos County, ab. 85 mi. NE of Austin: seat of the Agricultural and Mechanical College of Texas. In the decade between the last two U.S. censuses its population more than tripled. 2,184 (1940), 7,925 (1950).

Collegians, The. Novel by Gerald Griffin, issued anonymously in 1829. In 1861 an edition was produced, illustrated by Phiz, and called *The Colleen Bawn; or, The Collegian's Wife.*

Collegiants (ko̩.lē'ji.a̩nts). Sect founded near Leiden, Netherlands, in 1619, the societies of which are called colleges. The sect spread rapidly in the Netherlands, and in Hanover, Germany.

Collegno (kôl.lā'nyō). Town and commune in NW Italy, in the *compartimento* (region) of Piedmont, in the province of Torino, situated on the Dora Riparia River, W of Turin. It is an industrial suburb of Turin, with flour and lumber mills, woolen and cotton textile manufactures, and distilleries. A large hospital for the insane is here. Buildings of interest to tourists were undamaged in World War II. Pop. of commune, 12,535 (1936); of town, 5,086 (1936).

Colleoni (kôl.lā.ō'nē) or **Coleoni** (kō.lā.ō'nē), **Bartolommeo.** b. at Solza, near Bergamo, Italy, 1400; d. Nov. 4, 1475. Italian mercenary commander, considered the foremost tactician and disciplinarian of the 15th century. He was of an ancient and noble family which exercised a minor sovereignty over the province of Bergamo. He served in his youth under the principal *condottieri,* or mercenary generals, of the time, and in wars between Milan and Venice followed his advantage by serving either side at discretion. The Visconti family of Milan cast him into prison, and the Council of Ten at Venice conspired for his assassination. In 1454 he finally became generalissimo of the land forces of Venice, and retained this post until his death. He was a patron of the arts. The most notable works which celebrate his greatness are the statue by Verrocchio and Leopardi at Venice, considered among the best equestrian statues in existence, the castle of Malpaga, near Bergamo, with its frescoes, and the Colleoni Chapel in the Alta Città at Bergamo, with the tombs of Bartolommeo and his daughter Medea. The statue by Verrocchio stands before the Church of Santi Giovanni e Paolo at Venice. It was cast in 1496, and is the second equestrian statue of the Italian Renaissance. It characterizes with striking naturalism the haughty and formidable mercenary soldier. The rich marble pedestal has Corinthian columns and entablature.

Collery (kol'ėr.i). [Also: **Colleries, Colleri.**] Ancient Dravidian tribe of S India, famous as thieves. Their distinctive missile weapon, resembling a boomerang, was called a collery stick.

Collerye (kol.rē), **Roger de.** See **Bontemps, Roger.**

Colles (kōlz), **Christopher.** b. in Ireland, 1738; d. at New York, Oct. 4, 1816. American engineer and inventor. After his arrival in America it is known that he lectured in 1772 on pneumatics and in 1773 on inland navigation. It was in 1774 that he drew up the first proposal to free New York City from dependence on wells for its water supply by constructing a system of reservoirs and pipes. This plan, later to be realized, was for the time being pushed aside by the events of the Revolution, in which he served (1775–77) as chief instructor of the Continental Army, prior to the arrival of Baron von Steuben, in the principles and use of artillery. He was one of the first Americans to experiment with the steam engine, and his design, which he lacked the means to carry out, was approved by the best scientific minds in America at that time. Colles had the quality of a scientific pioneer, foreseeing things that could and should be done, and which indeed came to pass, but without advantage to him. Thus he was the earliest advocate of a waterway to connect the Great Lakes and the Hudson River, a plan he set forth in careful detail in *Proposals for the Settlement of Western New York, and for the Improvement of Inland Navigation between Albany and Oswego* (1785). Neither this book nor his *Survey of the Roads of the United States* (1789), nor his *Geographical and Systematized Atlas* (1794), nor the small manufacturing and mercantile business he established in 1796, brought him any great prosperity, and during his last years he was employed first in the customs service, and finally as superintendent of the American Academy of Fine Arts, an honorable post which he held until his death.

Colles (kol'e̩s), **Henry Cope.** b. 1879; d. 1943. English musicologist. He was a graduate (1902) of Oxford, and became (1911) chief reviewer for the London *Times.* He edited the third (1927) and fourth (1940) editions of *Grove's Dictionary of Music and Musicians.* His books include *Brahms* (1908), *The Growth of Music* (1912–16), and the seventh volume of the *Oxford History of Music* (1934).

Colle Salvetti (kôl'lā säl.vāt'tē). Town and commune in C Italy, in the *compartimento* (region) of Tuscany, in the province of Livorno, E of Livorno. Pop. of commune, 10,027 (1936); of town, 1,456 (1936).

Collet (kol'e̩t), **John.** b. at London, c1725; d. at Chelsea, London, Aug. 6, 1780. English painter, chiefly of humorous scenes from low life.

Colleton (kol'e̩.to̩n), **James.** fl. late 17th century. American colonist, governor of South Carolina in the period 1686–90. He received with his appointment the dignity of landgrave and 48,000 acres of land. He attempted in vain to enforce the recognition of Locke's constitution by the colonial parliament. He was deposed and banished by the colonists on the proclamation of William and Mary in 1690.

Collett (kol'e̩t), **Camilla.** [Maiden name, **Wergeland.**] b. at Kristiansand, Norway, 1813; d. 1895. Norwegian feminist leader and novelist; sister of Henrik Wergeland. A woman of beauty and intelligence, she dedicated her literary talent to the promotion of the emancipation of women, who in the Norway of her youth had few educational facilities or opportunities for remunerative employment. She championed the cause of greater freedom and equality for women in a series of eloquent and moving novels. A personal friend of Henrik Ibsen, she deplored his acceptance of the contemporary code in his portrayal of women in his early books, and influenced him toward a more liberal view. There is a statue of Camilla Collett at Oslo, capital of Norway, evidencing her country's appreciation of her work for women's rights.

Colletta (kôl.lāt'tä), **Pietro.** b. at Naples, Italy, Jan. 23, 1775; d. at Florence, Nov. 11, 1833. Neapolitan general. He was made intendant of Calabria by Murat in 1808, obtained the rank of general in 1812, was one of the leaders of the constitutional party under the Bourbons, and on the outbreak of the revolution of 1820 was sent as viceroy to Sicily. He was named minister of war in February, 1821, but was banished through Austrian intervention and retired to Florence. He wrote *Storia del reame di Napoli 1734–1825* (1834).

Colley (kol'i), Sir **George Pomeroy.** b. 1835; killed Feb. 27, 1881. Irish major general in the English army. Appointed (1854) a lieutenant to serve in Cape Colony, South Africa, he was there employed to survey the Transkei country. In 1860 he served in China, participating in the capture of the Taku forts and the march on Peiping (Peking). In 1876 he was appointed military secretary to Lord Lytton in India, and subsequently was chief of staff to Wolseley in Zululand and the Transvaal until the murder of Sir Louis Cavagnari and the outbreak of the second Afghan war, when he was recalled to India. Named (1880) governor and commander in chief of Natal and high commissioner for South-eastern Africa, succeeding Sir Garnet Wolseley, Colley was shot by the Boers.

Colliberts (ko.lē.ber). [Also: **Cagots, Capots, Cacons, Caqueux, Gahets, Agotes.**] In France in the early 18th century, a name applied derogatorily to groups or individuals who had no fixed position in the social hierarchy. Various writers have disagreed as to their status, some considering them to have been serfs, others freemen. The consensus seems to be that they occupied an intermediary position between these two statuses. Formerly they existed in several parts of France; afterward they were chiefly found in Aunis and Poitou, where they lived in boats on the rivers, but now they are nearly extinct. They were so called from the medieval French feudal colliberts, who were freed serfs, yet still bound to certain services.

Collier (kol'yėr, kol'i.ėr), **Arthur.** b. at Langford Magna, Wiltshire, England, Oct. 12, 1680; d. there, 1732. English clergyman and metaphysical writer, rector of Langford after 1704. His chief work is *Clavis Universalis, or a New Inquiry into Truth, being a Demonstration of the Non-existence or Impossibility of an External World* (1713), in which he propounds a subjective idealism closely resembling that of Berkeley.

Collier, Constance. [Original surname, **Hardie.**] b. Jan. 22, 1878—. English actress; wife of Julian L'Estrange. Having made her debut in childhood as a fairy in *A Midsummer Night's Dream*, she first appeared (1893) at London in *Don Juan*. Later (1901–08) she was with Sir Beerbohm Tree's company at His Majesty's Theatre, London. She made her first appearance at New York in 1908 and has since played in the U.S. many times, notably in *Dinner at Eight* (1932–33). Among her other outstanding parts are Gertrude in *Hamlet* (opposite John Barrymore), Nancy in *Oliver Twist*, Mrs. Cheveley in *An Ideal Husband*, and the Duchess of Towers in *Peter Ibbetson*. She has also been seen in such motion pictures as *Stage Door* and *Shadow of a Doubt*.

Collier, Hiram Price. [Called **Price Collier.**] b. at Davenport, Iowa, May 25, 1860; d. on the island of Fyn, Denmark, Nov. 3, 1913. American writer, best known for his travel books. He served as a Unitarian minister (1882–91) and as European editor (1893–95) of the *Forum*. He was the author of *Mr. Picket Pin and His Friends* (London, 1894), *America and the Americans from the French Point of View* (1897), *A Parish for Two* (1903), *England and the English from an American Point of View* (1909), *The West in the East from an American Point of View* (1911), and *Germany and the Germans from an American Point of View* (1913).

Collier, Jeremy. b. at Stow-cum-Qui, Cambridgeshire, England, Sept. 23, 1650; d. at London, April 26, 1726. English nonjuring clergyman, noted as a controversialist. He was graduated from Cambridge in 1673, was rector (1679–85) of Ampton in Suffolk, and moved (1685) to London, where he was for some time lecturer at Grey's Inn. A political pamphlet, in which he maintained that the withdrawal of the king was not an abdication and that the throne was not vacant, caused his imprisonment for a short time in Newgate prison in 1688, and in 1692 he was again imprisoned for political reasons. In 1696, with two other nonjuring clergymen, he attended Sir John Friend and Sir William Parkyns (who were condemned to death as conspirators against the life of William III) to the scaffold and absolved them. Having concealed himself to avoid arrest, he was outlawed on July 2, 1696. He was consecrated (1713) a bishop. He wrote a large number of controversial pamphlets, *Historical, Geographical, Genealogical, and Poetical Dictionary* (1701–21), the learned *Ecclesiastical History of Great Britain . . . to the End of the Reign of Charles II* (1708–14), and the famous *Short View of the Immorality and Profaneness of the English Stage* (1698). The last work was a vigorous attack upon the coarseness of the contemporary theater, and produced a great impression. It brought from John Dryden a confession of fault and a declaration of repentance, won unwilling recognition from other dramatists, and initiated a reformation.

Collier, John. b. at London, 1850; d. there, April 12, 1934. English portrait painter, noted equally for his imaginary historical subjects and for his famous contemporary sitters. He studied with E. J. Poynters at London, with J. P. Laurens at Paris, and with Alma-Tadema. Beginning in 1874, he exhibited regularly at several London galleries; he also participated in the salons at Sydney, Australia. His paintings are owned by museums at London, Liverpool, Birmingham, Paris, Adelaide, and Sydney. Among his principal works are *The Priestess of Delphi, The Death of Cleopatra*, and portraits of Darwin and Thomas Huxley. He was also the author of *The Primer of Art* (1882), *A Manual of Oil Painting* (1886), and *The Art of Portrait Painting* (1905).

Collier, John. b. at Atlanta, Ga., May 4, 1884—. American sociologist, student of the American Indian, and author. Beginning as a social worker among immigrants in 1905, he served as civic secretary of the People's Institute of New York City (1909–19), meanwhile helping to establish, and serving as secretary of, the Board of Review of Motion Pictures (1910–14), while also directing the National Training School for Community Workers (1915–19). In 1919 he went to California, where he was director of community organizations for that state until some time in 1920, and director of social science training at the state teachers college at San Francisco (1921–22). His interest in Indian affairs had been growing, and he became executive secretary of the American Indian Defense Association (1923–33), and editor of *American Indian Life* (1926–33). The policy he fought for, designed to safeguard the rights and advance the progress of the Indians while fostering their tribal institutions and native culture, won the adherence of President Franklin D. Roosevelt, who in 1933 appointed John Collier as Commissioner of Indian Affairs, an office he held until after Roosevelt's death in 1945. In the latter year he became director of the National Indian Institute of the U.S.A., and at that time also accepted the presidency of the Institute of Ethnic Affairs, which reports on problems involving ethnic factors throughout the world, especially problems arising out of relations between colonial peoples and the colonizing powers. Since 1947 Collier has been professor of sociology at the College of the City of New York. His *Indians of the Americas* (1947) has been called the most perceptive and revealing of books on the progress of American Indians in recent years with emphasis on the ability of the tribal organization to meet the challenge of modern conditions. *Patterns and Ceremonials of the Indians of the Southwest* (1949) is also an authoritative and a highly interesting work. John Collier is highly regarded as a poet, the promise of his first book in that medium, *The Indwelling Splendor*, having been kept in his subsequent work.

Collier, John. b. at London, May 3, 1901—. English novelist, short-story writer, and poet. He was educated at home, and is not a university man. He began writing poetry in 1920, had a volume out in 1921, and won a prize for four of his poems in 1922. He has been poetry editor of *Time and Tide*, and he showed his scholarly interests by editing John Aubrey, the 17th-century biographer. His works are *His Monkey Wife, or Married to a Chimp* (1930), a satirical novel, *Tom's A-Cold* (1933; American title, *Full Circle*), a gloomy picture of England as it will be in 1995, a war-broken, shattered, primitive country; *Defy the Foul Fiend, or The Misadventures of a Heart* (1934), and *Gemini* (1931), poetry; and *No Traveler Returns* (1931), *Green Thoughts* (1932), *The Devil and All* (1934), and *Variations on a Theme* (1935), collections of short stories. He has been in the U.S. frequently, living in different parts of the country, and in Hollywood he met his wife, Shirley Lee Palmer, whom he married in 1936.

Collier, John Payne. b. at London, Jan. 11, 1789; d. at Maidenhead, England, Sept. 17, 1883. English journalist, lawyer, and Shakespearian critic. He was a reporter (1809–21) for the London *Times*, and parliamentary reporter, drama and literary critic, and editorial writer (1821–47) for the *Morning Chronicle*. In 1847 he was appointed secretary of the royal commission on the British Museum, and continued in that office until 1850, when he returned to Maidenhead. He published a new edition of Dodsley's *Old Plays* (1825–27), *History of English Dramatic Poetry and Annals of the Stage* (1831), two editions of Shakespeare (1842–44, 1875–78), *Shakespeare's Library* (1844), *A Booke of Roxburghe Ballads* (1847), *Extracts from the Registers of the Stationers' Company* (1848–49), *The Dramatic Works of Thomas Heywood* (1850–51), *The Works of Edmund Spenser* (1862), a *Biographical and Critical Account of the Rarest Books in the English Language* (1865), and *An Old Man's Diary—Forty Years Ago* (1871–72). His able and useful work on the older English literature is marred and brought under general suspicion by a series of literary frauds which he committed, of which the most notable is his use and defense of spurious annotations "by a seventeenth century hand" which he professed to have found on the margin of a copy of the second folio Shakespeare originally belonging to one "Thomas Perkins," and since known as the *Perkins Folio*.

Collier, Peter. b. at Chittenango, N.Y., Aug. 17, 1835; d. at Ann Arbor, Mich., June 29, 1886. American agricultural chemist. His lifelong interest in the employment of chemistry in agriculture began while he was a graduate student in chemistry at Yale University. In 1867 he became professor of chemistry, mineralogy, and metallurgy at the University of Vermont, also filling the chair of chemistry and toxicology in the medical school of that institution, and in 1871 he was made secretary of the Vermont state board of agriculture, mining, and manufacture. In 1877, however, he resigned his various posts in Vermont to become the chief chemist of the U.S. Department of Agriculture. The research work he conducted into the properties of sorghum and its availability as a source of sugar was that department's first notable achievement in that sort of investigation. He resigned from the Department of Agriculture in 1883, and in 1887 became director of the state agricultural experiment station at Geneva, N.Y., a position he filled until his last illness. He was a pioneer in demonstrating the practical use to agriculture of the results of scientific research.

Collier, Peter Fenelon. b. in County Carlow, Ireland, Dec. 12, 1849; d. April 24, 1909. American publisher; father of Robert Joseph Collier (1876–1918). He established a publishing house, issuing Catholic books sold on installment payments, and adding (1877) sets of the classics. In 1888 he founded the periodical *Once a Week*, replacing it in 1896 with *Collier's Weekly*.

Collier, Price. See **Collier, Hiram Price.**

Collier, Robert Joseph. b. at New York, June 17, 1876; d. Nov. 9, 1918. American publisher and editor; son of Peter Fenelon Collier (1849–1909). After the death of his father he headed (1909 *et seq.*) P. F. Collier's Sons, and edited *Collier's Weekly*. He was also the founder of the Lincoln Farm Association.

Collier, William. b. in November, 1866; d. at Beverly Hills, Calif., Jan. 13, 1944. American comedian and playwright. He was a member (1883–88) of the Daly Theatre Company, playing in *The Merry Wives of Windsor*, *The Taming of the Shrew*, and other Shakespearian revivals. His other roles were in *On the Quiet* (1901–02), *Personal* (1903), *The Dictator* (1905–06), *Caught in the Rain* (1906–07), *A Lucky Star* (1909), *Bunty Pulls the Strings* (1912–13), *The Wild Rose* (1926), and other plays. He was coauthor of and actor in *I'll be Hanged if I Do* (1910), *Take My Advice* (1911), and *Never Say Die* (1912), and appeared in such films as *The Bride Comes Home* (1936), *Say It in French* (1938), and *Invitation to Happiness* (1939). He wrote *Caught in the Rain* (1906) and *The Patriot* (1908).

Collier, William Miller. b. at Lodi, N.Y., Nov. 11, 1867—. American lawyer, educator, and diplomat. Graduated (B.A., 1889; M.A., 1892) from Hamilton College, he was admitted (1892) to the bar and practiced law (1892–1903) at Auburn, N.Y. He has been U.S. ambassador to Spain (1905–09) and Chile (1921–28), teacher of international law (1912–18) at New York Law School, and president (1918–21) of George Washington University. His works include *Collier on Bankruptcy* (1898), *The Trusts; What Can We Do with Them—What Can They Do for Us* (1900), *Collier on Civil Service Law* (1901), *At the Court of His Catholic Majesty* (1912), *The Influence of Lawyers in the Past and in the Future* (1921), and, with Don Guillermo Feliu Cruz, *La Primera Misión de los Estados Unidos en Chile* (1924).

Collier's. Weekly magazine founded by Peter F. Collier in 1888. It was known as *Once a Week* until 1896, when it was renamed *Collier's Weekly*. Its editors have included Norman Hapgood and Mark Sullivan. The magazine has supported woman suffrage, pure food laws, direct election of senators, and workmen's compensation benefits. It was one of the muckraking periodicals in the first decade of the 20th century, but since World War I has stressed popular fiction and articles, athletics, and cartoons.

Colline Gate (kol'in). Gate at the NE extremity of ancient Rome. Near here, in November, 82 B.C., Sulla defeated the Samnites under Pontius.

Collingdale (kol'ing.dāl). Borough in SE Pennsylvania, in Delaware County, near Philadelphia. 8,443 (1950).

Collings (kol'ingz), **Jesse.** b. at Littleham, Sussex, England, in December, 1831; d. at Birmingham, England, Nov. 20, 1920. English land and education reformer, remembered chiefly as the initiator of the slogan "three acres and a cow" in 1885, which was for many years the war-cry of land reformers. A close associate of Joseph Chamberlain, he aided in the latter's carrying out of municipal reforms at Birmingham, England. Founder (1883) of the Allotments Extension Association, he became (1888) its president. He also advocated free and nonsectarian elementary education.

Collingswood (kol'ingz.wůd). Borough in SW New Jersey, in Camden County: residential suburb of Camden. 15,800 (1950).

Collingwood (kol'ing.wůd). City in SE Australia, in Victoria state, a northeastern suburb of Melbourne. Its population (ab. 30,000) is officially counted as part of Greater Melbourne.

Collingwood. Lake port in Simcoe County, Ontario, Canada, situated on Georgian Bay, Lake Huron, ab. 72 mi. NW of Toronto, with which it is connected by road. 7,413 (1951).

Collingwood, Cuthbert. [Title, 1st Baron **Collingwood.**] b. at Newcastle, England, Sept. 26, 1750; d. at sea near Mahón, Balearic Islands, March 7, 1810. English admiral. He was appointed lieutenant for his services, with a party of seamen, at the battle of Bunker Hill, was promoted to commander (succeeding Nelson) in 1779, served with distinction in command of the *Excellent* in the battle off Cape St. Vincent on Feb. 14, 1797, and became rear admiral (1799) with a command in the Channel fleet and vice-admiral (1804). Second in command at the battle of Trafalgar, on Nelson's death in that action he succeeded to the chief command.

Collins (kol'inz), **Anthony.** b. at Heston or Isleworth, near London, June 21, 1676; d. at London, Dec. 13, 1729. English deist; a disciple and friend of John Locke. His *Discourse on Free Thinking* (1713) aroused much controversy. He also published *An Essay Concerning the Use of Reason* (1707), *Priestcraft in Perfection* (1709), *A Philosophical Enquiry Concerning Human Liberty* (1715), *A Discourse on the Grounds and Reasons of the Christian Religion* (1724), and others.

Collins, Charles Allston. b. at Hampstead, London, Jan. 25, 1828; d. at London, April 9, 1873. English painter of the Pre-Raphaelite school and writer; brother of Wilkie Collins. He married the younger daughter of Charles Dickens.

Collins, Dale. b. at Sydney, Australia, April 7, 1897—. Australian writer. His works of fiction include *Ordeal* (1924), *The Haven* (1925), *Vanity Under the Sun* (1928), *Idolaters* (1929), *The Fifth Victim* (1930), and *Richard Strange* (1931). He is the author also of the plays *Ordeal* (1924) and *Romantic Ladies* (1935) and of *Seatracks of* *the Speejacks, the Story of the first Motor-Boat Voyage Around the World* (1923).

Collins, Edward Trowbridge. b. at Millerton, N.Y., 1887; d. at Boston, March 25, 1951. American baseball player. He played with the Philadelphia Athletics (1906–14, 1927–30) and the Chicago White Sox (1914–26), before becoming (1933) manager of the Boston Red Sox in the American League. In 1939 he was elected to baseball's Hall of Fame.

Collins, Frank Shipley. b. at Boston, Feb. 6, 1848; d. at New Haven, Conn., May 25, 1920. American algologist, considered the foremost authority of his day on the algae of the New England coast. He revised the collections of algae of Harvard, the Missouri Botanical Garden, and the Boston Society of Natural History, and was the author of *The Green Algae of North America* (1909) and *Working Key to the Genera of North American Algae* (1918).

Collins, Sir **Godfrey P.** b. 1875; d. at Zurich, Switzerland, Oct. 13, 1936. British politician and army officer, who served (1932–36) as secretary of state for Scotland. From 1910 to 1936 he was a member of Parliament. He served in Egypt, Gallipoli, and Mesopotamia during World War I, with the rank of lieutenant colonel from 1916. He held (1924–26) the position of chief whip of the Liberal Party in the House of Commons, and led a financial reform movement in Parliament resulting in the appointment of a committee authorized to control national budgetary expenditures.

Collins, J. Lawton. [Full name, **Joseph Lawton Collins.**] b. at New Orleans, May 1, 1896—. American army officer. A graduate of West Point (1917), he served with the army of occupation in Germany after World War I, as an instructor at various army establishments, and as a staff officer. He was chief of staff of the Hawaiian department (1941–42) and commanded the 25th division (1942–44) in campaigns on Guadalcanal and New Guinea. He was in command of the 7th corps in England and France (1944–45). In 1945 he served as chief of staff of the army ground forces; he was in charge of public information at the War Department (1945–47), became vice-chief of staff of the army in 1947, and on Aug. 16, 1949, was appointed chief of staff of the U.S. army. In 1953 he was succeeded in the last-named post by General Ridgway.

Collins, John. b. at Bath, England, c1742; d. at Birmingham, England, May 2, 1808. English actor and poet.

Collins, John Churton. b. at Burton-on-the-Water, Gloucestershire, England, March 26, 1848; d. at Oulton Broad, Lowestoft, Suffolk, England, in September, 1908. English literary critic, essayist, biographer, and teacher. Educated at King Edward's School, Birmingham, and at Balliol College, Oxford, he wrote for the *Globe* and the *Quarterly*, was lecturer (1880–1907) in English for the London University Extension Society, and served as professor of English literature (1904–08) at the University of Birmingham. He edited *Plays and Poems of Cyril Tourneur* (1878), *Poems of Lord Herbert of Cherbury* (1881), *Plays and Poems of Robert Greene* (1899, 1905), Dryden's *Satires* (1901), and More's *Utopia* (1904). He was the author of *Sir Joshua Reynolds* (1874), *Bolingbroke and Voltaire in England* (1886), *Study of English Literature* (1891), *Dean Swift* (1893), *Essays and Studies* (1895), *Ephemera Critica* (1901), *Studies in Shakespeare* (1904), *Studies in Poetry and Criticism* (1905), *Memories* (1908), *Greek Influence* (1910), and *Posthumous Essays* (1912).

Collins, Joseph. b. at Brookfield, Conn., Sept. 22, 1866; d. June 11, 1950. American physician, neurologist, and writer. Graduated (M.D., 1888) from New York University, he was professor of neurology (1897–1909) at New York Post-Graduate Medical School. His works include *Diseases of the Brain* (1899), *Disease of the Nervous System* (1900), *The Faculty of Speech* (1900), *Pathology of Nervous Diseases* (1901), *Sleep and the Sleepless* (1912), *The Doctor Looks at Literature* (1923), *The Doctor Looks at Love and Life* (1926), and *The Doctor Looks at Life and Death* (1931).

Collins, Michael. b. near Clonakilty, County Cork, Ireland, 1890; d. near Bandon, County Cork, Ireland, Aug. 22, 1922. Irish patriot and statesman in the Sinn Fein movement. As a clerk (c1906–16) in England, he enlisted in the Irish Republican Brotherhood, a separatist group. On his return to Ireland in 1916, when he chose to fight for Irish freedom rather than to be drafted into the British army, he participated in the Easter Rebellion, fighting at the Dublin Post Office but escaping capture during the actual fighting. He was arrested soon after and jailed. After this he managed to avoid arrest in the general rounding up of the leaders of the movement by the British, and, as one of the few leaders at liberty, rose to high position in the Sinn Fein group. He was elected to Parliament in 1918 as a Sinn Fein member and was one of those who declared (January, 1919) the Irish Republic. He was chief of intelligence in the Irish Volunteers (later to become the Irish Republican Army) and minister of finance in the Irish Republic, which was headed by Eamon De Valera (who was in jail). Collins was instrumental in the escape of De Valera in February, 1918, and was in general the leading man of action of the independence movement during this period. A huge reward (10,000 pounds) was offered for him, but he continued to harass the British until their government in Ireland broke down, When a truce was declared in 1921, he and Arthur Griffith, vice-president of the Republic, headed a delegation to London to sign the compromise treaty setting up the Irish Free State. He supported the treaty vigorously and helped it through the Dáil (the parliament of the Irish Free State). But opposition from die-hard republicans brought on civil war. Griffith, head of the Free State after De Valera's resignation to combat the treaty, died suddenly (Aug. 12, 1922) and Collins found himself acting head of the Irish Free State. But, on August 22, he was ambushed by guerrillas while on his way to Cork and was shot to death.

Collins, Mortimer. b. at Plymouth, England, June 29, 1827; d. at Knowl Hill, Berkshire, England, July 28, 1876. English novelist and poet. Until 1856 he was mathematical master of Queen Elizabeth's College, on the island of Guernsey, and after 1862 was occupied with literary work at his residence at Knowl Hill. He published *Idyls and Rhymes* (1865), *Sweet Anne Page* (1868), *The Inn of Strange Meetings, and Other Poems* (1871), and *The Secret of Long Life* (1871).

Collins, Norman Richard. b. at Beaconsfield, Buckinghamshire, England, Oct. 3, 1907—. English writer. After serving as assistant literary editor (1929–33) on the *News-Chronicle* and deputy chairman (1934–41) of Victor Gollancz, Ltd., publishers, he was head of the light program (1946–47), until becoming (1947) head of television, for the British Broadcasting Corporation. He is the author of *The Facts of Fiction* (1932), *Penang Appointment* (1934), *The Three Friends* (1935), *Trinity Town* (1936), *Love in Our Time* (1938), *"I Shall Not Want"* (1940), *Anna* (1942), *London Belongs to Me* (1945), and *Black Ivory* (1947).

Collins, Tom. [Pseudonym of **Joseph Furphy.**] b. at Yarra Glen, Victoria, Australia, Sept. 26, 1843; d. at Claremont, Western Australia, Sept. 13, 1912. Australian novelist, author of the classic *Such is Life* (1903). At various times he worked as a threshing machine operator, farmer, road mender, owner and driver of bullock teams, and foundry hand. In 1884 he began writing for the press and by 1897 had produced *Such is Life*, which was published in 1903 and slowly won recognition as a major work. He was also the author of *Poems* (1916), *Rigby's Romance* (1921), and uncollected sketches.

Collins, Wilkie. [Full name, **William Wilkie Collins.**] b. at London, Jan. 8, 1824; d. there, Sept. 23, 1889. English novelist, recognized as a master of the involved plot. He knew how to construct a highly complicated plot, and, what is still more difficult, how to keep the mystery unrevealed until the last page. Among his best novels of this type are *The Dead Secret* (1857), *The Woman in White* (1860), *No Name* (1862), and *The Moonstone* (1868). His *Antonina* (1850), a historical novel, dealing with Rome in the 6th century, is considered an inferior work. *The Woman in White* uses the technique, now familiar, of having several characters tell the same story, each one dealing with those phases that he knows best. *The Moonstone*, the story of a huge diamond, is memorable for the character of Sergeant Cuff, first detective in English literature. Swinburne praised it highly, and T. S. Eliot regards it as "the first and the greatest of English detective novels." A master of intriguing titles, Collins also wrote *Mrs. Wray's Cash Box* (1852), *Hide and Seek* (1854), *After*

Dark (1856), *The Queen of Hearts* (1859), *Poor Miss Finch* (1872), *Miss or Mrs.?* (1873), *The Law and the Lady* (1875), *The Black Robe* (1881), *I Say No* (1884), *The Evil Genius* (1886), and *The Guilty River* (1886). On the basis of these stories and others, and on the ranking given to him by students of crime and mystery in fiction, Collins deserves his title, "the Father of the English detective novel."

Collins, William. b. at Chichester, Sussex, England, Dec. 25, 1721; d. there, June 12, 1759. English poet. The son of a hatter who was twice mayor of Chichester, he studied at Winchester and at Oxford, where he was graduated (B.A., 1743). About the year 1745 he went to London to follow literature as a profession. The later years of his life were obscured by insanity. He published *Persian Eclogues* (1742; republished as *Oriental Ecologues*, 1757), and *Odes* (1747). Among his best-known poems are *Ode to Simplicity, Ode to Evening, The Passions, On the Poetical Character, Dirge in Cymbeline* and *On the Popular Superstitions of the Highlands*.

Collins, William. b. at London, Sept. 8, 1788; d. there, Feb. 17, 1847. English landscape and figure painter; father of Wilkie Collins and of Charles Allston Collins.

Collins, William. Clergyman in Jane Austen's *Pride and Prejudice*. He is a conceited toady, overly impressed by rank and determined to marry at all costs.

Collinson (kol'in.sọn), **James.** b. at Mansfield, Nottinghamshire, England, c1825; d. in April, 1881. English painter, one of the original members of the Pre-Raphaelite Brotherhood, which he abandoned c1850. His work has been considered relatively unimportant.

Collinson, Peter. b. near Windermere, England, Jan. 14, 1694; d. in Essex, England, Aug. 11, 1768. English botanist and natural philosopher.

Collinson, Sir **Richard.** b. at Gateshead, England, 1811; d. at Ealing, England, Sept. 13, 1883. English admiral and arctic explorer. He commanded the expedition (1850–54) in search of Sir John Franklin and was cut off with the *Enterprise* in the arctic regions for three years, wintering at the S entrance to Prince of Wales Strait (1851–52), in Cambridge Bay, on the S coast of Victoria Island (1852–53), and in Camden Bay, on the N coast of Alaska (1853–54). His contribution to geographical knowledge was large and nearly included the discovery of the Northwest Passage, which was actually achieved by his subordinate McClure in the *Investigator*. He was knighted in 1875.

Collinsville (kol'inz.vil). City in S Illinois, in Madison and St. Clair counties, ab. 11 mi. NE of East St. Louis: coal-mining center; manufactures include chemicals and canned foods. 11,862 (1950).

Collioure (ko.lyör). Village in S France, in the department of Pyrénées-Orientales, situated on the Mediterranean Sea ab. 15 mi. SE of Perpignan. It has a castle and considerable trade in cork.

Collip (kol'ip), **James Bertram.** b. at Belleville, Ontario, Canada, Nov. 20, 1892—. Canadian biochemist, a specialist in the study of internal secretions. He has been professor of biochemistry at the University of Alberta (1922–28) and at McGill University (1928 *et seq.*), where he also became (1941) head of the Research Institute for Endocrinology.

Collishaw (kol'i.shô), **Raymond.** b. at Nanaimo, British Columbia, Canada, Nov. 22, 1893—. British military and naval aviator who served with the British air force during World Wars I and II. He served (1908–14) with the Royal Canadian navy, entered (1915) the Royal Naval Air Service, was a squadron commander (1916–18) in France credited with shooting down 60 enemy airplanes during World War I, and was awarded (August, 1918) the Distinguished Flying Cross. He commanded Royal Air Force units in S Russia (1919–20), Iraq (1921–23), the Sudan (1935–36), and Heliopolis (1936–39), and commanded British air squadrons in the Middle East with the rank of air commodore during World War II. In 1942 he was promoted to the rank of acting air-vice-marshal.

Collison (kol'i.sọn), **Wilson.** b. at Glouster, Ohio, Nov. 5, 1893; d. May 24, 1941. American playwright and novelist. He was coauthor with Avery Hopwood of *The Girl in the Limousine* (1919) and *Getting Gertie's Garter* (1921) and with Otto Harbach of *Up in Mabel's Room* (1919), and author of the plays *Desert Sands* (1924), *The Vagabond* (1927), and *Red Dust* (1927), among others. His novels include *The Murder in the Brownstone House* (1929), *Expensive Women* (1931), *Millstones* (1933), *Sexational Eve* (1933), and *Long Glittering Isle* (1936).

Collitz (kol'its; German, kol'its), **Hermann.** b. at Bleckede, Hanover, Germany, Feb. 4, 1855; d. May 13, 1935. American philologist. He came to the U.S. in 1886, and served as associate professor (1886–97) of German and professor (1897–1907) of comparative philology and German at Bryn Mawr College, and as professor (1907–27) of Germanic philology at the Johns Hopkins University. He was the author of *Die Verwandtschaftsverhältnisse der Griechischen Dialekte* (1885), *Die neueste Sprachforschung* (1886), and *Das schwache Praeteritum und seine Vorgeschichte* (1912).

Cölln (kėln), **Georg Friedrich Wilibald Ferdinand von.** b. at Örlinghausen, Lippe, Germany, 1766; d. at Berlin, May 31, 1820. German publicist. His works include *Vertraute Briefe* (1807–09) and *Neue Feuerbrände* (1807–08).

Collombet (ko.lôṅ.be), **François Zénon.** b. at Siéges, Jura, France, March 28, 1808; d. at Lyons, France, Oct. 16, 1853. French Roman Catholic historian and littérateur. He wrote *Histoire de St. Jérôme* (1844) and many other historical and critical works.

Collop Monday. In England, the day before Shrove Tuesday; named from the custom of eating collops (small slices or pieces) of salted meat and eggs on that day. The practice still survives in the provinces.

Colloquies. Prose work (1516; later editions 1519, 1522, 1536) in Latin by Erasmus, in which he bitterly and satirically attacks evil practices in the Catholic Church and improper conduct on the part of priests. In a single year, 24,000 copies were sold. In this work, according to the monks, "Erasmus laid the egg that Luther hatched."

Colloredo (kol.ō.rä'dō), **Rudolf von.** b. Nov. 2, 1585; d. Jan. 24, 1657. Austrian general in the Thirty Years' War. As field marshal of the imperial army he successfully defended Prague against the Swedes in 1648.

Colloredo-Mansfeld (-mäns'felt), Count **Hieronymus von.** b. at Wetzlar, Germany, March 30, 1775; d. at Vienna, July 23, 1822. Austrian general. He distinguished himself in the campaign of 1813.

Colloredo-Mels und Waldsee (-mels ůnt vält'zā''), Count **Joseph Maria von.** b. at Regensburg, Bavaria, Sept. 11, 1735; d. Nov. 26, 1818. Austrian general. He fought with distinction in the Seven Years' War, and was minister of state and conference, and director of the council of war (1805–09).

Collot d'Escury (ko.lō' des.kü.rē'), Baron **Cornelis Johannes.** b. at Palembang, Sumatra, Oct. 22, 1888—. Dutch industrialist and banker. Educated at commercial schools at Amsterdam and Cologne, he has been employed in banks at Berlin and London. He has been director of many corporations including the Incasso Bank of Amsterdam, Ned. Standaard Bank of Amsterdam, Kon. Holl. Lloyd (Royal Dutch Lloyd), and Heineken's Brewery, and president of the Nederlandsche Handel Maatschappij, N.V.

Collot d'Herbois (ko.lō der.bwä), **Jean Marie.** b. at Paris, 1750; d. at Cayenne, French Guiana, Jan. 8, 1796. French actor, remembered as a revolutionist. He was a deputy to the Convention in 1792, and a member of the Committee of Public Safety in 1793. In November, 1793, Robespierre sent him with Fouché as judge to Lyons, where he executed his commission with great cruelty. An unsuccessful attempt upon his life was made on May 23, 1794. Having become hostile to Robespierre, he joined the successful conspiracy against him (9 Thermidor), but was nevertheless expelled from the Convention (April, 1795) and transported. He published *Almanach du père Gérard* (1792).

Collyer (kol'yėr), **Joseph.** b. at London, Sept. 14, 1748; d. Dec. 24, 1827. English engraver, a member of the Royal Academy and engraver to Queen Charlotte.

Collyer, Robert. b. at Keighley, Yorkshire, England, Dec. 8, 1823; d. at New York, Nov. 30, 1912. American Unitarian minister. He was apprenticed to a blacksmith c1837, emigrated to the U.S. in 1850, where he followed the trade of a hammer-maker, joined the Unitarian Church in 1859; became a missionary to Chicago, where in 1860 he founded the Unity Church, and in 1879 became pastor of the Church of the Messiah at New York. He wrote *Nature and Life* (1866), *The Life that Now is* (1871), and others.

Colman (kōl′mạn, -môn), Saint. b. c605; d. 676. Irish Christian missionary among the English. Trained at Iona, the fountainhead of Irish evangelical missions to Britain and the Continent, he became the third abbot of Lindisfarne, an Irish foundation in the Saxon kingdom of Bernicia in N England, in 661. He was an ardent upholder of the Irish position in the controversy between the Irish church and Rome concerning the date of Easter and other matters, and when the synod of Whitby in 664 adopted the Roman view, Colman withdrew from Lindisfarne with other Irish clerics and with some 30 English followers. He continued in missionary activities for a time in northern Britain before returning to Iona, from which he departed to establish a monastery in 668 at Inisboffin, in what is now County Mayo in the west of Ireland. Thither English students resorted, but he thought it best to establish a separate abbey and school for them, and this in time became famous as "Mayo of the Saxons." Colman was a poet, and the author of a life of Saint Patrick.

Colman (kōl′mạn), **Benjamin.** b. at Boston, Oct. 19, 1673; d. Aug. 29, 1747. American clergyman, pastor (1699 *et seq.*) of the Brattle Street Church at Boston, which differed from strict Congregationalism in its adherence to the doctrines of the Westminster Confession. He was a fellow (1717–28), overseer, and benefactor of Harvard University, from which he had received degrees in 1692 and 1695.

Colman, George. [Called **Colman the Elder.**] b. at Florence, Italy, April 18, 1732; d. at Paddington, London, Aug. 14, 1794. English dramatist, essayist, poet, and manager of the Covent Garden and Haymarket theaters at London. He was educated at Westminster, and at Christ's Church, Oxford. His chief stage works are *Polly Honeycombe* (1760), a farce satirizing the sentimental novel, *The Jealous Wife* (1761), based partly on Fielding's *Tom Jones*, the success of which, as produced by Garrick, made him give up any thought he might have had of following the law, and *The Clandestine Marriage* (1766), suggested by Hogarth's caricatures. He also wrote one-act comedies and farces of a satirical nature. His poems and his periodical essays are of slight value. His prologues and epilogues, to his own plays and to those of his fellow-dramatists, are of some value as illustrations of his tastes and the standards of the time. Of greater importance is the fact that as manager of Covent Garden he produced Goldsmith's comedies, *The Good-Natured Man* and *She Stoops to Conquer*. He translated Terence, and edited the plays of Jonson and of Beaumont and Fletcher. He was a friend of Jonson, the Wartons, Garrick, Malone, and Walpole, and he was a member of The Club, in itself a high honor in his day. That he was willing to tamper with Shakespeare and to attempt to "improve" him, that he gave *Lear* a "happy ending," leaving the poor old king alive, simply shows that Colman was of his time, not ahead of it.

Colman, George. [Called **Colman the Younger.**] b. Oct. 21, 1762; d. at Brompton Square, London, Oct. 17, 1836. English dramatist, theater manager, censor of plays, song writer, and humorist. He was educated at Westminster, and at Christ's Church, Oxford (as was his father), and at King's College, in Aberdeen. From 1789 to 1820 he managed the London Haymarket theater, a post in which he succeeded the elder Colman, and in 1824 he was appointed examiner and censor of plays. As his own dramatic work was marked by vulgarity, it is interesting to note that he was exceedingly strict with the plays that came under his eye. His chief works are *Inkle and Yarico* (1787), a romantic comedy dealing with the situation Inkle, a London citizen, has to face when he must decide between Yarico, a lovely savage who has saved his life, and Narcissa, daughter of the wealthy governor of Barbados, and *The Iron Chest* (1796), a dramatization of Godwin's famous novel *Caleb Williams*. Two other comedies, *The Heir-at-Law* (1797) and *John Bull* (1803) are remembered mainly for two portraits that are important additions to the gallery of English characters, the pompous pedant Dr. Pangloss in the former, and rough-and-ready Job Thornberry, who stands for John Bull, in the latter. His humorous verse, *Broad Grins, My Nightgown and Slippers*, and *Poetical Vagaries*, is as good as work of that type usually is, and his *Random Records* (1830), although autobiographically interesting, is of no great value.

Colman, Norman Jay. b. near Richfield Springs, N.Y., May 16, 1827; d. Nov. 3, 1911. American agriculturist and publisher. He founded (1865) *Colman's Rural World.* Elected (1874) lieutenant governor of Missouri, he was a member (1865–1911) of the Missouri state board of agriculture. In 1885 he was appointed U.S. commissioner of agriculture, and in 1889 first secretary of agriculture.

Colman, Samuel. b. at Portland, Me., 1832; d. March 27, 1920. American landscape painter; a pupil of Asher B. Durand. He was the American Water Color Society's first president, and the author of *Nature's Harmonic Unity* (1913).

Colmar (kōl′mär; French kol.mȧr). [German, **Kolmar.**] City in NE France, the capital of the department of Haut-Rhin (formerly Upper Alsace), situated in the Alsatian plain on the Lauch River, a tributary of the Ill River, ab. 39 mi. SW of Strasbourg. It is connected with the Rhône-Rhine Canal. Colmar has preserved its medieval character. The Church of Saint-Martin dates from the 13th and 14th centuries. The Unterlinden Museum, formerly a Dominican convent, contains the famous altar of Isenheim, by Mathias Grünewald, and 16 Passion scenes by Martin Schongauer, masterpieces of medieval German art. The city has a number of industries, and is a center for excursions, particularly into the Munster valley and other parts of the Vosges Mountains. Colmar was incorporated into France in 1675 and changed hands several times between France and Germany, along with Alsace-Lorraine, before it became French again at the end of World War II. 46,124 (1946).

Cöln (kėln). German name of **Cologne.**

Colne (kōln, kōn). Municipal borough, market town, and textile-manufacturing center in NW England, in Lancashire, situated on a tributary of the river Calder, near the Leeds and Liverpool Canal, ab. 26 mi. N of Manchester, ab. 217 mi. NW of London by rail. It formerly had manufactures of woolens, but now specializes in the finer grades of cotton cloths. It also has factories producing dyed cotton thread, and a rayon industry. 20,674 (1951).

Colne Valley. Urban district, market town, and woolen and cotton manufacturing center in N central England, in the West Riding of Yorkshire, situated on the river Colne, ab. 5 mi. SW of Huddersfield, ab. 196 mi. N of London by rail. It comprises the former urban districts of Marsden, Scammonden, and Slaithwaite. There are mineral baths at Slaithwaite. Colne Valley imports Welsh wool to make heavy, low-priced woolens. 22,184 (1951).

Colney Hatch (kol′ni hach′). Village in SE England, in Middlesex, ab. 3 mi. SE of Barnet, ab. 6 mi. N of London, in which is the Colney Hatch Lunatic Asylum, founded in 1851.

Colôane (kō.lō′ạ.nẹ). See under **Macao.**

Colobrano (kō.lō.brä′nō), **Michele Enrico Carafa di.** Full name of **Carafa, Michele.**

Colocolo (kō.lō.kō′lō). b. c1490; killed in the battle of Quiapo, 1560 (according to some authorities, he died c1570). Araucanian chief of S Chile, celebrated in the *Araucana* of Ercilla. Probably Ercilla's verses gave him undue prominence.

Cologna Veneta (kô.lō′nyä ve′nä.tä). Town and commune in NE Italy, in the *compartimento* (region) of Veneto, in the province of Verona, ab. 20 mi. SE of Verona: silk industry. The town was destroyed by Attila, and rebuilt by Theodoric; it came under the rule of Venice in 1496. Pop. of commune, 10,700 (1936); of town, 2,776 (1936).

Cologne (kọ.lōn′). [German, **Köln, Cöln;** Latin, **Augusta Ubiorum, Colonia Agrippina.**] City in W Germany, in the *Land* (state) of North Rhine-Westphalia, British Zone, formerly in the Rhine Province, Prussia, situated on the W bank of the Rhine River, ab. 20 mi. SE of Düsseldorf. Located in the center of a fertile plain, easily accessible from all directions, and immediately adjacent to the Ruhr coal district, it is second only to Berlin as a hub of the German railroad system, a large river port, directly connected with the ports in the

Netherlands and on the North Sea, and a commercial and industrial center of the first order. 491,380 (1946), 594,941 (1950).

Industry and Trade. The industries of Cologne are of great variety. The metallurgical, machine, and electrotechnical industries are most important: industrial and mining equipment, tubes, motors, automobiles, railroad cars, tractors, bicycles, iceboxes, radios, precision instruments, and many similar articles are produced. Cologne is also the seat of the Rhenish Lignite Syndicate. Second in importance are the chemical industries: the output includes heavy chemicals, explosives, fertilizer, dyes, and pharmaceuticals (the great works of what was the I. G. Farben-Industrie at Leverkusen are in the vicinity), as well as cosmetics, such as the well-known original eau de cologne (Johann Maria Farina and "4711" brands). The textile industry, producing cotton, linen, and woolen materials, lace, lingerie, and other garments, ranks third. There are engineering firms, building construction works, shoe, leatherware, brush, asbestos, and paper factories, printing establishments, and finally, chocolate factories and sugar refineries. Market gardening and horticulture are prevalent on the outskirts. Cologne is even more important as a commercial center, not only for the industries of the city but also for those of the entire Rhenish-Westphalian agricultural district, as well as for the agricultural products of the Rhineland. Items marketed here include metals, machinery, motors, vehicles, tools and instruments, costume jewelry, chemical, pharmaceutical, and cosmetic articles, rubber and asbestos articles, oils and fats, textiles, paperware, glassware, chocolates and other candies, wine, liquors, tobacco, and cigarettes. Before World War II, a number of fairs and exhibitions served the purpose of bringing buyers and sellers together; some of them are being reestablished. Cologne was also, before the war, one of the most important civil aeronautics centers in Europe.

Culture and Architecture. Cologne has a municipal university, the Catholic Albertus Magnus Academy, various musical institutions, a number of commercial and vocational schools, archives and libraries, theaters, orchestras, and societies sponsoring the arts and sciences. The Wallraf-Richartz Museum contains art collections; the Schnütgen Museum and the Diocesan Museum house collections of sacred art. There are also collections of natural history, archaeology, and ethnology, a museum of hygiene, a museum of commerce and industry, and botanical and zoölogical gardens. Cologne is the seat of a Roman Catholic cardinal. Though a modern metropolis, Cologne until World War II had preserved the medieval character of the old city. The devastation caused by air raids and ground fighting was so complete that no part of the city and no monument of historical importance escaped. Many historical buildings were completely destroyed or drastically damaged, including the city hall (15th and 16th centuries), the Gürzenich (a medieval meeting house), the Spanish House, the Stapel House, and others; the Church of Sankt Maria im Kapitol, consecrated in 1049 by Pope Leo IX, the 12th-century churches of Saint Martin and Saint Ursula, the Church of the Apostles, the churches of the Assumption, Saint Kunibert, and Saint Severin; and all of the old gates with the exception of the Eigelstein Tor. The damage to the Church of Saint Gereon, a unique Romanesque building of very early date, rebuilt in the 13th century, is not total; the same is true of the churches of Saint Andrew, Saint George, and Saint Pantaleon. The *Dom* (Cathedral), the major example in Germany of the high Gothic style, on which construction was started in the 13th century, continued during the 14th century and until c1520, and finally completed in the period 1842–80, still stands but is gravely damaged. The cathedral archives, the Shrine of the Three Magi, and the altar paintings by Stephen Lochner, as well as the Shrine of Albertus Magnus from the Church of Saint Andrew, had been removed to safety.

History. Cologne was founded in 38 B.C. by the Roman commander Marcus Vipsanius Agrippa; one of the Latin names of the town was derived from the empress Agrippina, who was born here; urban privileges were bestowed in 50 A.D. The town was conquered by the Franks in the 4th century and made the residence of the Frankish kings. The archbishopric was founded by Charlemagne in 785; beginning with the archbishop Bruno (953–965), the archbishops were also territorial sovereigns and princes of the empire, imperial chancellors of Italy, and later prince-electors; many of them were among the most powerful figures of the medieval "Reich." As Cologne grew prosperous, the citizens and the ecclesiastical rulers were frequently at loggerheads, while within the city patrician families and craft guilds battled for supremacy. Cologne was one of the leading commercial cities of the time, dominating the trade routes from England and the Netherlands to upper as well as lower Germany; it was a member of the Hanseatic League. There were flourishing schools of painting, including the art of making stained-glass windows, of architecture, and of the goldsmith's craft. Leading Catholic scholars, such as Albertus Magnus and Duns Scotus, taught here; the mystic Master Eckart lived here. The university existed from 1388 to 1797, and was revived in 1919. The city declined after the Thirty Years' War; it was occupied by the French in 1794. From 1583 to 1761, the archbishops were of the Wittelsbach family; in 1815 Cologne was annexed to Prussia. The archbishopric was renewed in 1821; archbishop Johannes von Geissel (1846–64) was the first cardinal of Cologne. Cologne grew rapidly in the 19th century. The completion of the cathedral (1880) was considered an event of symbolic importance all over Germany. After World War I the fortifications were razed (1919), and the city was occupied by British troops until 1926. In World War II, Cologne suffered immense damage through air raids; it was first bombed on May 30, 1942, and was occupied by American troops on March 5, 1945. Chancellor Konrad Adenauer was formerly a mayor of Cologne. The population declined 39 percent between 1939 and 1947. However, reconstruction and resettlement have proceeded rapidly.

Cologne, Electorate of. Former archbishopric and electorate of the German empire. It extended mainly along the left bank of the Rhine, N and S of Cologne. It was made an archbishopric by Charlemagne in 785, acquired the duchy of Westphalia in 1180, was confirmed one of the seven electorates in 1356, and was secularized in 1801. In 1801 the portion on the left bank of the Rhine became French territory; that on the right bank passed in 1803 to Hesse-Darmstadt. The larger part was granted to Prussia in the period 1814–15.

Cologne, Three Kings of. In medieval Christian legend, the three Magi, or Wise Men of the East, who followed the star of Bethlehem from the East to lay gifts before the infant Jesus. Their names were Gaspar, or Caspar, Melchior, and Balthazar. They are so called (Three Kings of Cologne) because their bones are said to have been deposited by Barbarossa in Cologne Cathedral.

Coloma (kọ.lō′mạ). Unincorporated village in N central California, ab. 8 mi. NW of Placerville. Gold was discovered here at Sutter's mill in January, 1848, and the ensuing gold rush caused Coloma to grow into a boom town. Its population in 1860 was 888. There are a few houses and some old foundations remaining; the modern village is a rural center in a fruit-growing district. Pop. ab. 100.

Coloma (kō.lō′mä), **Luis.** b. in Spain, 1851; d. 1915. Spanish Jesuit priest. He wrote a number of short stories of a religious nature, but is known chiefly for his novel *Pequeñeces* (1891), a spectacular naturalistic work which satirizes the corruption of the aristocracy of Madrid.

Colomba (ko.lôṅ.bȧ). Story by Prosper Mérimée, published in 1830.

Colomb-Béchar (ko.lôṅ.bā.shȧr). [Also, **Colomb.**] Chief town in Aïn-Sefra territory, Algeria, in NW Africa, and headquarters of the military command there. It is ab. 430 mi. SW of Oran near the S terminus of the railroad from that city. It is an important jumping-off place for the trans-Saharan crossing and is on the Tanezrouft route from Aïn-Sefra to Gao in French Sudan. 51,811 (1948).

Colombe (ko.lôṅb) or **Colomb** or **Columb** (ko.lôṅ), **Michel.** b. at St.-Paul-de-Léon, in Britanny, France, c1430; d. 1512. French sculptor, considered one of the outstanding artists of the early French Renaissance.

Colombes (ko.lôṅb). Town in N France, in the department of Seine, situated within the bend of the Seine River, NW of Paris, opposite Argenteuil. It is a suburb of Paris. 61,046 (1946).

Colombey (ko.lôṅ.bā). [Also, **Colombey-Nouilly** (-nö-yē).] Place in NE France, in Lorraine ab. 4½ mi. E of Metz. Near it occurred the battle of Colombey-Nouilly, Aug. 14, 1870, in which the Germans under Steinmetz checked the French under Bazaine. The German loss was 4,906; that of the French, 3,608. It is also called the battle of Courcelles, and of Borny.

Colombia (kǫ.lum'bi.ą; Spanish, kō.lōm'byä). [Full Spanish name, **República de Colombia,** meaning "Republic of Colombia"; former Spanish name, **Estados Unidos de Colombia,** meaning "United States of Colombia."] Republic of South America, lying between Panama and the Caribbean Sea on the N, Venezuela and Brazil on the E, Peru and Ecuador on the S, and the Pacific Ocean on the W. It is traversed by the Andes, and is rich in agricultural and mineral products, among them gold, silver, and coffee. Its chief rivers are the Magdalena and the affluents of the Amazon and Orinoco. The prevailing language is Spanish, and the prevailing religion Roman Catholic. It is divided into 15 departments, 6 commissaries, and 3 intendencies. The government is republican, the executive power being vested in a president, and the legislative in a senate and chamber of representatives. The name was first given in 1811 to what is now Venezuela. It was proposed by General Francisco Miranda. It was afterward extended to the confederation of Venezuela, New Granada, and Quito, and was dropped when the union was dissolved. Later the old region of New Granada renewed the name. The Spanish power was established here in the first half of the 16th century, and independence was proclaimed in 1811. In 1819 this territory, with Venezuela and Ecuador, formed the Republic of Colombia, from which Venezuela and Ecuador withdrew in 1830. In 1831 the republic of New Granada was founded, in 1863 the name "United States of Colombia" was adopted, and in 1886 the present constitution was formed. Panama became independent of Colombia in 1903. Capital, Bogotá; area, 439,825 sq. mi.; pop. 11,259,700 (est. 1950).

Colombo (kǫ.lum'bō). Seaport and the capital of Ceylon, situated on the W coast, on the Indian Ocean: seat of the University of Ceylon (formed 1942 from Ceylon University College and Ceylon Medical College). It was fortified by the Portuguese in 1517, was taken from them by the Dutch in 1656, was ceded to the British in 1796, and became an important coaling station. The chief exports are rubber, tea, cacao, quinine, and coconuts. 362,000 (1946).

Colombo (kō.lōm'bō). Epic poem about the discovery of the New World, published in 1866 by the Brazilian romantic poet Araújo Pôrto-Alegre (1806–79). It is the longest poem ever written in Portuguese.

Colombo (kō.lōm'bō). Italian form of **Columbus.**

Colombo Plan (kǫ.lum'bō). Scheme for the economic development of S and SE Asia developed by members of the British Commonwealth in 1950 at conferences held at Colombo, Ceylon. Conceived as a countermeasure to the appeal of Communism to the peoples of Asia, the plan envisions the spending of nearly two thousand million pounds (about five and quarter billion dollars) in a six-year program of coöperative projects to raise living standards throughout the area in the Commonwealth and its allies. It was inaugurated July 1, 1951; participating were Great Britain, Canada, Australia, New Zealand, India, Pakistan, and Ceylon (later also Burma) of the Commonwealth nations, and Viet-Nam, Laos, and Cambodia.

Colón (kō.lōn'). River port in E Argentina, in Entre Ríos province, on the Uruguay River. 8,385 (1947).

Colón. City in W Cuba, in Matanzas province: a center of the sugar trade. 11,534 (1943).

Colón. Department in N Honduras. Rubber is the principal product. Capital, Trujillo; area, 10,282 sq. mi.; pop. 35,465 (1950).

Colón. Province in N Panama, E and W of the Canal Zone. Capital, Colón; area, 2,810 sq. mi.; pop. 89,643 (1950).

Colón. [Former name, **Aspinwall.**] City in N Panama: capital of Colón province and terminus of the Panama Railroad and also of the Panama Canal; connected with the city of Panama by the Boyd-Roosevelt (trans-Isthmian) Highway. It was founded in 1855 by W. H. Aspinwall and was burned by insurgents in 1885. Pop. 52,035 (1950).

Colón. Spanish form of **Columbus.**

Colón, Archipiélago de. See **Archipiélago de Colón.**

Colonel Bogey (bō'gi). In the folklore of sports, an imaginary competitor in the game of golf, whose score was never par, but always a good, average player's score, and hence a standard against which to compete. The term is now used also to signify the typical opponent in any game, whose score, though good, it is not impossible to equal. Colonel Bogey is so called from the golf term bogey, which is a preassigned score for each hole against which the players compete.

Colonel Chabert (ko.lo.nel shà.ber), **Le.** Story by Honoré de Balzac, written in 1832.

Colonel Jack (or **Jacque**), **History of.** Tale by Daniel Defoe, published in 1722. The hero is a pickpocket who winds up his checkered career as a virtuous Virginia planter.

Colonel Passy (ko.lo.nel pà.sē). Pseudonym of **Wavrin, André Charles de.**

Colonel Sellers (sel'ėrz). Play by Mark Twain (pseudonym of Samuel Langhorne Clemens) and William Dean Howells, written in 1883 and produced in 1886.

Colonel Stow (stō). Historical novel by Henry Christopher Bailey, published in 1908. Its setting is England during the period of the English Civil War (1642 *et seq.*).

Colonia (kō.lō'nyä). Department in S Uruguay, on the Río de la Plata opposite Argentina. Capital, Colonia; area, 2,194 sq. mi.; pop. 132,554 (est. 1947).

Colonia. [Full name, **Colonia del Sacramento** (del sä-krä.men'tō).] City in SW Uruguay, capital of Colonia department, on the Río de la Plata, opposite Buenos Aires. Pop. ab. 7,700.

Colonia Agrippina (kǫ.lō'ni.ą ag.ri.pī'ną). A Latin name of **Cologne.**

Colonia Augusta Gemella (ô.gus'tą jẹ.mel'ą). Latin name of **Martos,** Spain.

Colonia Faventia Julia Augusta Pia Barcino (fą.ven'-shą jöl'yą ô.gus'tą pī'ą bär.sī'nō). A Latin name of **Barcelona,** Spain.

Colonia Julia Augusta (jöl'yą ô.gus'tą). Latin name of **Parma,** Italy.

Colonia Julia Augusta Dertosa (dėr.tō'są). Latin name of **Tortosa,** Spain.

Colonia Julia Fanestris (fą.nes'tris). A Latin name of **Fano.**

Colonia Julia Felix Pisaurum (fē'liks pi.sô'rum). A Latin name of **Pesaro,** Italy.

Colonia Julia Romula (rom'ū̦.lą). Latin name of **Seville,** Spain.

Colonia Julia Senensis (sẹ.nen'sis). Latin name of **Siena,** Italy.

Colonial Dames of America. **1.** Patriotic society of women organized at New York, on May 23, 1890, and incorporated on April 23, 1891. Its object is to collect and preserve relics and traditions relating to the early history of the U.S. and to the Revolutionary War, and to educate the young in the history of their country by means of the celebration of events of national importance. **2.** Similar but distinct society, with branches in 36 states and a membership of over 5,500 women lineally descended from colonial ancestry. Its object is to preserve or restore manuscripts, traditions, relics, and buildings connected with the colonial period; to diffuse information concerning, and to create a popular interest in, the colonial period; and to stimulate, especially in the young, a spirit of true patriotism and a genuine love of country. The society was organized in April, 1891.

Colonial Heights. Town in E Virginia, in Chesterfield County near Petersburg. Robert E. Lee had his headquarters here (1864) at one time during the Civil War. 6,077 (1950).

Colonial National Historical Park. Park in SE Virginia, including Jamestown, the site of the first permanent English settlement in the U.S., and a long strip through Williamsburg, to Yorktown, famous as the site of the surrender of Cornwallis on Oct. 19, 1781. The park was established as a national monument in 1930, and as a historical park in 1936. Area, ab. 11 sq. mi.

Colonia Nemausensis (kǫ.lō'ni.ą nē.mô.sen'sis). A Latin name of **Nîmes.**

Colonia Neptunia (nep.tū′ni.ạ). A Latin name of **Taranto,** Italy.
Colonia Pacensis (pạ.sen′sis). A Latin name of **Badajoz,** Spain.
Colonia Placentia (plạ.sen′shi.ạ). Latin name of **Piacenza,** Italy.
Colonias de la Plata (kō.lō′nyäs dā lä plä′tä). Spanish name of the viceroyalty of **Buenos Aires.**
Colonias del Río de la Plata (del rē′ō dā lä plä′tä). Spanish name of the **Platine Provinces** or **Colonies.**
Colonia Vibia Augusta Perusia (kọ.lō′ni.ạ vib′i.ạ ô.gus′tạ pẹ.rö′zhạ). A Latin name of **Perugia,** Italy.
Colonies of the Plata (plä′tä). See **Buenos Aires,** viceroyalty.
Colonna (kô.lôn′nä), **Cape.** [Latin, **Sunium,** or **Sunium Promontorium.**] Promontory at the SE extremity of Attica, Greece.
Colonna (kō.lōn′nä), **Egidio.** See **Aegidius a Columnis.**
Colonna, Fabio. [Latinized name, **Fabius Columna.**] b. at Naples, Italy, 1567; d. there, c1650. Neapolitan scholar and botanist, author of various botanical works. He is considered the creator of genera as classifications in botany.
Colonna, Fabrizio. d. at Naples, Italy, 1520. Italian military leader, lord high constable of Naples; father of Vittoria Colonna.
Colonna, Fabrizio. [Title, Duke of **Paliano.**] b. at Rome, March 28, 1848; d. Aug. 8, 1923. Italian senator and military officer. He was elected (1882) to the chamber of deputies, and became (1889) a senator. He took part (1870) in the campaign of Porta Pia but retired (1880) from the army.
Colonna, Giovanni Paolo. b. at Bologna, Italy, 1637; d. Nov. 28, 1695. Italian composer of church music and of the opera *Amilcare* (1693).
Colonna, Marc Antonio. [Title, Duke of **Paliano.**] b. 1535; d. Aug. 1, 1584. Italian military commander. He led the papal contingent in 1571 at the battle of Lepanto, in which the allied Spanish, Venetian, and papal fleets under John of Austria gained a decisive victory over the Turks. He was viceroy of Sicily when he died.
Colonna, Oddone. Original name of Pope **Martin V.**
Colonna, Pompeo. d. 1532. Italian cardinal; nephew of Prospero Colonna. Chosen to represent his family in the Church, Pompeo did so reluctantly. He accumulated benefices, was created cardinal (1517) by Pope Leo X, and was vice-chancellor of Pope Clement VII. He sided with the emperor Charles V against the Pope.
Colonna, Prospero. b. 1452; d. 1523. Italian general. He commanded the united imperial and papal forces in Lombardy against Francis I of France (1521) and in conjunction with Georg von Freundsberg defeated Marshal Lautrec at La Bicocca (1522).
Colonna, Vittoria. b. at Marino, near Rome, 1490; d. at Rome, Feb. 25, 1547. Italian poet; daughter of Fabrizio Colonna, grand constable of Naples, by his marriage with Agnesina di Montefeltro, daughter of Federigo, Duke of Urbino. She was betrothed when four years old to a boy of the same age, the only son of the Marchese di Pescara. In their 19th year they were married at Ischia. Pescara died in November, 1525. His wife survived him by 22 years, spent partly at Ischia, in convents at Orvieto and Viterbo, and, finally, in semi-monastic seclusion at Rome. She was the center of a group of celebrated men of letters and artists, of whom the foremost was Michelangelo. Her poems consisted mainly of sonnets to the memory of her husband, or on sacred and moral subjects. Michelangelo preserved a large number of them and composed several madrigals and sonnets to her.
Colonne (ko.lon), **Édouard.** [Original name, **Judas Colonne.**] b. at Bordeaux, France, July 24, 1838; d. at Paris, March 28, 1910. French orchestra conductor. He founded (c1874) the Colonne Concerts (or Concerts du Châtelet) at Paris, and conducted them until his death. In these he brought out a very large number of musical works new to Paris, did much for the spread of Berlioz's fame, and introduced to Paris the music of Brahms, Wagner, and other contemporary composers.
Colonne de Juillet (ko.lon dẹ zhwē.ye). French name of the **Column of July.**
Colonne du Congrès (ko.lon dü kôn.gre). French name of the **Column of the Congress.**
Colonne Vendôme (väṅ.dōm). French name of the **Column of Vendôme.**
Colonsay (kol′ọn.zā). Island in the Inner Hebrides, in W Scotland, in Argyllshire, ab. 8 mi. W of the island of Jura, ab. 7 mi. N of the island of Islay. It is noted for its ecclesiastical antiquities. Length, ab. 8 mi.; width, ab. 3 mi.
Colonus (kọ.lō′nus). [Also: **White Hill of Colonus; Kolonos Hippios.**] Site ab. 1½ mi. NW of Athens, Greece, N of the Academy, on the banks of the Cephissus. It was the birthplace of Sophocles, and is immortalized by his description in the *Oedipus at Colonus.* Upon the hill now stand the tombs of two noted archaeologists, the German Hellenist Karl Otfried Müller and the French Orientalist Charles Lenormant.
Colony, the. See under **Lagos,** Nigeria.
Colony Club. Club for women, at New York, incorporated April 5, 1905, for social purposes.
Colony of Darien. See **Darien, Colony of.**
Colorado (kol.ọ.rad′ō, -rä′dō). [Called the **"Centennial State"**; also, the **"Silver State."**] State of the W central U.S., bounded by Wyoming and Nebraska on the N, Nebraska and Kansas on the E, Oklahoma and New Mexico on the S, and Utah on the W: one of the Mountain States.

Population, Area, and Political Divisions. Colorado is divided for administrative purposes into 63 counties. It sends four representatives to Congress and has six electoral votes. Capital, Denver; area, 103,967 sq. mi. (104,247 sq. mi., including water); pop. 1,123,296 (1940); 1,325,089 (1950), a gain of 18 percent from 1940. The state ranks seventh in area, and 34th (on the basis of the 1950 census) in population. Among the leading cities are Denver, Pueblo, Colorado Springs, Greeley, and Trinidad.

Terrain and Climate. The Continental Divide, the line of the Rocky Mountain peaks separating the waters flowing N or E from those flowing W, runs down the state, the Rockies themselves lying in the C and W parts. More than 50 peaks have an altitude of over 14,000 ft., among them the famous Pike's Peak (14,110 ft.), a popular tourist center noted for its magnificent view of the surrounding regions, and Mount Elbert (14,431 ft.), highest point in the state. Rocky Mountain National Park (405 sq. mi.), in the N and C part of the state and in the very heart of the Rockies, contains some of the most spectacular scenic views in the U.S., including Long's Peak (14,255 ft.), many deep gorges and canyons, and fishing lakes and streams. Mesa Verde National Park (50,275 acres), situated in the SW plateau section, contains the remains of prehistoric cliff dwellings. The largest river system is that of the Colorado, which rises in the N and flows SW into Utah; the Gunnison is among its numerous tributaries. The valleys of the Arkansas River (which rises in the C part of the state and flows E into Kansas) and of the South Platte (which flows NE to Nebraska from the C section) make up the state's richest agricultural area, largely as the result of extensive irrigation. The Rio Grande flows from the SW into N Mexico. The state has many forests, a good portion of which are protected by inclusion in state and national parks. The abundant wild life includes bear, elk, mountain lions, deer, and antelope. Extreme cold is always found in the mountains. The state experiences considerable heat in the summer, although its summer night temperatures are usually very low.

Industry, Agriculture, and Trade. Agriculture and mining are the leading industries. Much land has been reclaimed by irrigation, although some dry farming is carried on. Wheat, seed potatoes, sugar beets, barley, corn, and beans are important crops, and livestock raising and dairying are major occupations. The state ranks high in molybdenum, radium, and tungsten production, and also has valuable resources of coal, vanadium, uranium, gold, silver, zinc, lead, copper, helium, and petroleum. Lumbering, beet-sugar refining, and the manufacture of timber products, electrical machinery, explosives, and iron and steel products are major industrial activities. Annual income in the state from agriculture ranges as high as 526,133,000 dollars (1949); from mineral output, as high as 77 million dollars; from manufacturing, as high as 290.3 million (1947).

History. First explored by the Spanish, particularly in the latter half of the 18th century, Colorado formed part of the territory of the Louisiana Purchase (1803) and part of the country acquired (1848) from Mexico. The state was explored (1806) by Lieutenant Zebulon M. Pike, who discovered the peak named after him, later by Major S. J. Long, and by John C. Frémont (1842 *et seq.*). A temporary Mormon settlement was made (1846–47) at Pueblo. The discovery of gold in 1858 brought many immigrants in succeeding years and the subsequent establishment of mining camps and towns such as Central City, Leadville, Boulder, and Denver. Silver was discovered not long afterward. Colorado became a territory in 1861; it was admitted to the Union (as the 38th state) on Aug. 1, 1876, its constitution having been adopted that same year. Much of the state's history has centered about its mining camps and the allied milling and smelting works, with many strikes, lockouts, and labor incidents occurring in the early 1900's.

Culture. The most thickly settled of the Rocky Mountain states, Colorado has a more fully developed cultural life than some of its neighbors. Boulder, Aspen, and particularly Denver are cultural and intellectual centers. Colorado Springs is the seat of an art colony, and each year Central City's old opera house is the scene of a famous summer theater festival. Among the state's institutions of higher learning are the state-supported University of Colorado, at Boulder, and Colorado School of Mines, at Golden; Colorado College, at Colorado Springs; the University of Denver, at Denver. The state motto is *Nil Sine Numine*, meaning "Nothing Without Divine Will." The state flower is the columbine.

Colorado City. City in W Texas, county seat of Mitchell County, SE of Lubbock: shipping center for livestock; processing center for petroleum and cotton. 6,774 (1950).

Colorado Desert. Desert region in S California, lying in Imperial County and extending into Lower California.

Colorado of the West. See **Colorado River,** in Colorado.

Colorado Party (kō.lō.rä'ᴛʜō). [Also, **National Republican Party.**] Paraguayan political party, of diverse membership, but following a generally conservative program.

Colorado River. [Spanish, **Río Colorado.**] River in W Argentina which flows E into the Atlantic Ocean. Length, ab. 500 mi.

Colorado River (kol.ǫ.rad'ō, -rä'dō). [Also: **Eastern Colorado**; Spanish, **Río Colorado.**] River in Texas which flows into Matagorda Bay near Matagorda. Length, ab. 900 mi.; navigable, except in summer, to Austin.

Colorado River. [Also: **Colorado of the West**; Spanish, **Río Colorado.**] River formed in Grand County, Colo., and flowing through N and W Colorado, Utah, and Arizona, separating Arizona from Nevada and California, and emptying into the Gulf of California, in Lower California. It forms part of the boundary between the U.S. and Lower California, Mexico. It is famous for its canyons, of which the most celebrated, the Grand Canyon, situated in the middle course of the river, and explored by the Powell survey expedition in 1869, has walls from 4,000 to 6,500 ft. in height. The upper course, in Colorado, was called the Grand River until 1921, when it was changed by act of the U.S. Congress. Length, ab. 1,400 mi.

Colorados (kō.lō.rä'ᴛʜōs). Political party of Uruguay, opposed to the Blancos.

Colorado Springs (kol.ǫ.rad'ō, -rä'dō). City in C Colorado, capital of El Paso County, ab. 64 mi. S of Denver. It is a summer resort, near the foot of Pike's Peak, and serves as a smelting center for the Cripple Creek gold mines. It is the seat of Colorado College and of the Colorado Springs Fine Arts Center. 45,472 (1950).

Colossae (kǫ.los'ē). In ancient geography, a city in SW Phrygia, Asia Minor, situated on the Lycus. It was the seat of the early Christian church to which Paul wrote the *Epistle to the Colossians.*

Colosseum (kol.ǫ.sē'um). [Also, **Coliseum, Flavian Amphitheater.**] Amphitheater at Rome, just SE of the Forum. It was begun by Vespasian (T. Flavius Sabinus) in 72 A.D. and completed in 80 A.D. For 400 years it was the seat of gladiatorial shows, and was the traditional scene of the martyrdom of early Christians. The axes of this chief of amphitheaters are ab. 617 and 512 ft.; of the arena, ab. 282 and 177 ft. The exterior was ornamented with four tiers of engaged columns with their entablatures, the lowest three enclosing arches, and the highest walled up, with square windows in every second intercolumniation. The material of the interior is stone, of the inner passages and vaults largely brick and concrete. The marble seats accommodated between 40,000 and 50,000 people. The interior was faced with marble. In the substructions there is a most elaborate system of chambers, passages, dens, and drains. Despite the enormous mass of the existing ruin, it is estimated that a large part (perhaps as much as two thirds) has been carried away in the Middle Ages and later, as building material.

Colossians (kǫ.losh'ạnz). One of the Pauline Epistles. It was written by Saint Paul during his first imprisonment at Rome, and was addressed to the Christians of Laodicea as well as to those of Colossae, both cities being in Phrygia. The Apostle was prompted to write these congregations by reports that dangerous doctrines were being spread among them. There is the widest divergence of opinion among scholars concerning the nature of these heresies, but it seems most probable that they emphasized the importance of angels as an order of beings interposed between God and man, to an extent which called in doubt the doctrine of the divinity of Jesus, which would explain Paul's extended exposition of the concept of the mystical body of Christ.

Colossus of Rhodes (rōdz). Large bronze statue of the sun god Helios, which anciently stood adjacent to the harbor of Rhodes on the Greek island of that name. Known in ancient and medieval times as one of the Seven Wonders of the World, it was designed by Chares of Lindus, a city on Rhodes, and under his supervision erected between 292 and 280 B.C. It is reputed to have been 70 cubits high, or more than 100 ft., and is said to have been built from the abandoned bronze weapons and armor left by the soldiers of Demetrius I, king of Macedon, when they retired in defeat from their siege of Rhodes. It is a tradition that ships could sail between the colossal legs, which would have been possible especially if it rose above pedestals proportionate to its size. It is not known exactly at what point of the harbor it stood, for it did not stand much more than half a century; in 224 B.C. it was toppled by an earthquake. For many centuries great bronze fragments of the statue lay where they fell; eventually (8th century A.D.) they were sold to the Saracens.

Colot (ko.lō), **Laurent.** b. near Troyes, France; fl. c1550. French court surgeon in the reign (1547–59) of Henry II. He was noted as a lithotomist.

Coloured Dome, The. Novel by Francis Stuart, published in 1932.

Colquhoun (kǫ.hön'), **Archibald Ross.** b. at sea off the Cape of Good Hope, in March, 1848; d. Dec. 18, 1914. Scottish engineer, traveler, and writer. He held various official positions in India, Thailand (Siam), and Upper Burma, was the London *Times* correspondent in the Franco-Chinese war and the far East (1883–84), accompanied the pioneer expedition to South Africa in 1890, and upon the occupation of Mashonaland was made administrator. He retired in 1894. He traveled and explored extensively in many parts of the world. Author of *Across Chryse* (1883), *China in Transformation* (1898), *The "Overland" to China* (1900), *The Mastery of the Pacific* (1902), *Greater America* (1904), *The Africander Land* (1906), *From Dan to Beersheba* (1908), and others.

Colquhoun, Patrick. b. at Dumbarton, Scotland, March 14, 1745; d. at London, April 25, 1820. London police magistrate and writer on economic subjects. From c1760 to 1766 he lived in Virginia; he was lord provost of Glasgow in the period 1782–83, and from 1789 resided at London, where he became (1792) a police magistrate. He published *Treatise on the Police of the Metropolis* (1795), *Treatise on the Population, Wealth, Power, and Resources of the British Empire in every Quarter of the World* (1814), and other works treating especially of the condition and relief of the poor.

Colquitt (kol'kwit), **Alfred Holt.** b. in Walton County, Ga., April 20, 1824; d. March 26, 1894. American politician; son of Walter Terry Colquitt (1799–1855).

Colquitt, Walter Terry. b. in Halifax County, Va., Dec. 27, 1799; d. May 7, 1855. American statesman; father of Alfred Holt Colquitt (1824–94). Appointed (1826, 1829) to the Chattahoochee (Ga.) superior court circuit, he served (1834, 1837) two terms in the state senate. Twice elected (1838, 1842) to Congress, he was chosen U.S. senator at the beginning of second term. In 1848 he resigned from the Senate.

Colt (kōlt), **Samuel.** b. at Hartford, Conn., July 19, 1814; d. there, Jan. 10, 1862. American inventor. He patented his revolver in 1836, and developed (1848 *et seq.*) a noted factory of arms at Hartford, Conn. His revolvers were widely used in opening the American West.

Colter (kōl'tėr), **John.** b. near Staunton, Va., c1775; d. near Dundee, Mo., 1813. American frontiersman and guide. Enlisting in the Lewis and Clark expedition in 1803, his services were particularly commended by its leaders, and when during the return to civilization in 1806 he requested a discharge that he might join a party of trappers, it was readily granted. In the following year he guided the Manuel Lisa expedition to the Big Horn country, and at Lisa's request undertook a mission to the Crow Indians, which involved a journey alone and on foot, carrying a heavy pack as well as a gun and ammunition, over the Wind River and Teton mountains and into the Yellowstone area, which he was perhaps the first white man ever to see. In 1809 he guided a party sent by the St. Louis Missouri Fur Company to the region of the upper Missouri River. Having been severely wounded in a fight between the Blackfeet and the Crow Indians, and having on other occasions had narrow escapes, he decided in 1810 to retire to a farm near Dundee on the Missouri River, where he died in 1813.

Colton (kōl'ton). City in S California, in San Bernardino County, E of Los Angeles: industrial and railroad center. 14,465 (1950).

Colton, Charles Caleb. b. at Salisbury, England, c1780; d. at Fontainebleau, France, April 28, 1832. English clergyman and writer. He was a graduate of Cambridge (King's College), and rector of Kew and Petersham. He led an eccentric life, and committed suicide in preference to undergoing a surgical operation. He published *Lacon, or many things in a few words, addressed to those who think* (1820–22) and others.

Colton, Gardner Quincy. b. Feb. 7, 1814; d. at Rotterdam, Netherlands, Aug. 9, 1898. American anesthetist; brother of Walter Colton (1797–1851). During his study (1842) of medicine, he discovered the effects of nitrous oxide and gave public demonstrations. After Horace Wells, a dentist, had suggested (1844) the use of the gas as an anesthetic, Colton opened (c1863) at New York, with John Allen, the Colton Dental Association for the painless extraction of teeth.

Colton, Walter. b. at Rutland, Vt., May 9, 1797; d. at Philadelphia, Jan. 22, 1851. American clergyman and writer of voyages; brother of Gardner Quincy Colton. He founded *The Californian*, the first newspaper in California. Author of *Ship and Shore* (1835).

Colum (kol'um), **Mary.** [Maiden name, **Maguire.**] b. in Ireland—. Critic and short-story writer; wife of Padraic Colum (1881—), whom she married in 1912. She was graduated from the National University of Ireland, arrived (1914) in the U.S., and served as literary critic of the magazines *The Century* and *The Forum.* She is the author of *From These Roots* (1937) and *Life and the Dream* (1947).

Colum, Padraic. b. in County Longford, Ireland, Dec. 8, 1881—. Irish poet, novelist, dramatist, lecturer, anthologist, and author of juveniles. He was one of the founders, with James Stephens and Thomas MacDonagh, of the *Irish Review*, and, with Yeats and Lady Gregory, a founder of the famous Irish National Theatre (later known as the Abbey), where his first play, *Broken Soil* (1903), was produced. Other dramatic works are *The Land* (1905), *The Fiddler's House* (1907), *Thomas Muskerry* (1910), *Mogu the Wanderer* (1917), *The Miracle of the Corn* (1917), and *The Betrayal* (1920). As a poet he has written *Wild Earth* (1907), *Dramatic Legends* (1922), *Creatures* (1927), which shows his fondness for animals, *Poems* (1932), and *The Story of Lowry Maen* (1937). His works for young readers are *The Boy Who Knew What the Birds Said* (1918), *The Girl Who Sat by the Ashes* (1919), *The Children Who Followed the Piper* (1922), and others. *Castle Conquer* (1923) is a novel, and *The Big Tree of Bunlahy* (1933) and *The Frenzied Prince* (1943) are collected short stories. His *Anthology of Irish Poetry* (1921) is of value for students. He himself is represented in anthologies by *The Plower, An Old Woman of the Roads, Interior, A Drover, The Wild Ass, Polonius and the Ballad-Singers,* and *The Sea Bird to the Wave.* In 1912 he married Mary Maguire, critic and author; in 1914 he came (with his wife) to the U.S., where he has lived since.

Columb (ko.lôn), **Michel.** See **Colombe** or **Colomb** or **Columb, Michel.**

Columba (kǫ.lum'bą), Saint. [Irish: **Colum** (kol'um), meaning "Dove"; **Columcille,** meaning "Dove of the Church"; called the **"Apostle of Caledonia."**] b. at Gartan, Donegal, Ireland, Dec. 7, 521; d. at Iona, off the coast of what is now Scotland, June 9, 597. Irish missionary to the Picts and Scots, the founder of the monastery on the island of Iona (c565). He is one of the three patron saints of the Irish and related peoples in the N of Scotland, on the Isle of Man, and elsewhere (with Patrick and Brigid). His feast day is June 9.

Columba. The Dove: a small southern constellation preceding Canis Major. Medieval Christian astronomers identified it as Noah's Dove. It was first named in 1624 as *Columba Naochi.*

Columban (kǫ.lum'bąn) or **Columbanus** (kol.um.bā'nus), Saint. b. in Leinster, Ireland, c543; d. at Bobbio, Italy, Nov. 21, 615. Irish missionary in France, Switzerland, and Italy, noted for his scholarship. He founded the monastery of Luxeuil (Vosges) c590–595, and that of Bobbio in the Appenines (Italy), where he is buried. Both were important centers of learning. His feast days are Nov. 21 and (in Ireland) Nov. 24.

Columbia (kǫ.lum'bi.ą). City in S Mississippi, county seat of Marion County, on the Pearl River: manufactures of naval stores, canned vegetables, and wooden boxes. 6,124 (1950).

Columbia. City in C Missouri, county seat of Boone County, ab. 27 mi. NW of Jefferson City: seat of the University of Missouri, Stephens College, and Christian College. It is also a marketing point and distribution center for farm produce and has garment and shoe factories. 31,974 (1950).

Columbia. [Former name, **Wright's Ferry.**] Borough in SE Pennsylvania, in Lancaster County, on the Susquehanna River, ab. 24 mi. SE of Harrisburg: manufactures of tobacco, textiles, and metal products. It was settled in 1726 by John Wright, a Quaker missionary to the Indians. 11,993 (1950).

Columbia. City in C South Carolina, capital of South Carolina, and county seat of Richmond County, on the Congaree River. A textile-manufacturing center, it also produces cottonseed oil, mattresses, and fertilizer. It is the seat of the University of South Carolina, Allen University, and Benedict College. Fort Jackson, a U.S. army post, is nearby. Columbia became the state capital in 1790, and was burned (Feb. 17, 1865) about the time of its occupation by Union forces under General Sherman. 86,914 (1950).

Columbia. City in C Tennessee, county seat of Maury County, on the Duck River, ab. 42 mi. SW of Nashville: trading center for livestock and dairy products. It was the home of James K. Polk. 10,911 (1950).

Columbia. Poetical name and feminine personification of America or the U.S., taken from the name of Christopher Columbus.

Columbia. A former name of **Hillsboro,** Ore.

Columbia, Mount. Peak of the Rocky Mountains in the province of Alberta, Canada, situated in the S part of Jasper National Park near the border of British Columbia: the highest in Alberta. 12,294 ft.

Columbia City. City in NE Indiana, county seat of Whitley County: wool textile manufacturing and meat packing. It is a shipping point for agricultural products. 4,745 (1950).

Columbia Fur Company. Fur-trading enterprise in the U.S., organized c1822 and active, until its merger (1827) with the American Fur Company, in the lands of the Omaha and Sioux Indians. After 1827 it was known as the "Upper Missouri Outfit" and was active in the region north of the mouth of the Big Sioux River.

Columbia Heights. City in SE Minnesota, in Anoka County, on the Mississippi River, near Minneapolis: residential community. 8,175 (1950).

Columbiana (kǫ.lum.bi.an'ą). [Former name, **Dixonville.**] Village in NE Ohio, in Columbiana County:

manufactures of furniture and iron. Laid out in 1805, it was important for the production of agricultural machinery and carriages. It was the birthplace of Harvey S. Firestone. 3,369 (1950).

Columbian Lady's and Gentleman's Magazine. Monthly literary journal published (1844–49) at New York.

Columbian Magazine, The. One of the first successful American magazines, founded in 1786 by a group which included Matthew Carey and Francis Hopkinson. The magazine, emphasizing political, agricultural, and scientific subjects of interest to a young republic, included such contributors as Benjamin Rush, William Byrd, and Jeremy Belknap. When *The Columbian Magazine* ceased publication in 1792 it had inaugurated a new policy of accepting original contributions in place of reprinting uncopyrighted material.

Columbia River. [Early name, **Oregon River.**] River in W North America, the second in size on the Pacific coast. It rises in the Rocky Mountains in SE British Columbia, is joined by the Kootenay River near Trail, British Columbia, traverses Washington, flows between Washington and Oregon, and empties into the Pacific Ocean. Its chief tributaries in the U.S. are Clark Fork and the Snake River. Several large dams have been built on the Columbia, including Bonneville Dam and Grand Coulee Dam. It has very important salmon-fisheries. It was discovered in 1792 by Captain Robert Gray, and was explored (1804–05) by Lewis and Clark. Total length, ab. 1,200 mi.; length in Canada, 459 mi.

Columbia University. Educational institution at New York. With funds raised by public lotteries, and with a charter granted by George II of England, King's College was established in 1754 on a site provided by Trinity Church in what is now the downtown section of the borough of Manhattan. The first president was Samuel Johnson, a clergyman. He was succeeded by Myles Cooper, during whose incumbency operation of the college became impossible because of the conflicts of opinions and passions incident to the Revolutionary War. King's College, in fact, ceased to exist; Columbia College took its place when classes were resumed in 1784, under the direction of the Regents of the University of the State of New York. In 1787 authority was transferred to a board of trustees, who elected William Samuel Johnson, a layman and son of Samuel Johnson, as president. Criticism being directed at the predominance of Anglicans among the first trustees, provision was made in the charter for ministers of various Protestant denominations in the city to be represented on the board; in later years Roman Catholics and at least one Jewish rabbi have served as trustees. Because of this interdenominational character, Columbia has never had a theological faculty; but by a provision of the original deed of land from Trinity Church, religious services in the chapel must conform to the Episcopalian liturgy. The expanding college was moved to a site on Madison Avenue between 49th and 50th streets in 1857; in 1892 a large tract north of 116th Street on Morningside Heights was purchased, and as new buildings were completed, classes were moved to this ampler campus, which was dominated by an impressive library, the gift of the institutions's president at that time, Seth Low. During his administration also the increased diversification of the curricula of the college and its associated schools led to reorganization under the name of Columbia University, which during more than four decades (1902–45) under the presidency of Nicholas Murray Butler, became one of the largest universities in the world. In 1948 the presidency of Columbia was accepted by Dwight D. Eisenhower. In addition to Columbia College, the principal affiliates of the university (some of them having originated independently at different times from as early as 1767, often passing through various reorganizations with changes of name) are the School of Medicine, with which are affiliated the Schools of Dental and Oral Surgery, Public Health, and Nursing; the School of Law; the School of Engineering, which absorbed the former Schools of Mines and of Chemistry; the School of Architecture; the Graduate School of Journalism; the Graduate School of Business; the School of Library Service; the School of International Affairs; the School of General Studies, which alone has many thousands of students studying a wide variety of subjects with or without an academic degree in view; the School of Dramatic Arts; the School of Painting and Sculpture; the Faculties of Political Science, of Philosophy, and of Pure Science; the Russian Institute and the East Asian Institute; and Barnard College for women, Teachers' College, and the College of Pharmacy, which are independent corporations but fully integrated into the university. It is stated that in 1950 the number of full-time students at Columbia University was more than 22,100, served by a full-time faculty of nearly 3,200.

Columbine (kol'um.bīn). Traditional stock character in old Italian comedy, the *commedia dell'arte.* She is generally, but not always, the daughter of Pantaloon, and is usually the mistress, sometimes the wife, of Harlequin, whose power of being invisible to mortal eyes she shares. Historically, she goes back to the saucy waiting women of Plautus's comedies, and she anticipates the gay soubrette type. From Italian comedy she goes into French comedy and comic opera, and then into English pantomime. The name derives from the Latin *columbinus,* Italian *columbina,* meaning dovelike, and is used affectionately as a pet name.

Columbretes (kō.lōm.brā'tās). Group of small volcanic rocks in the Mediterranean Sea, E of Spain.

Columbula (kǫ.lum'bū.lą). See **Dyveke.**

Columbus (kǫ.lum'bus). City in W Georgia, county seat of Muscogee County, on the Chattahoochee River. It has manufactures of cotton textiles, iron, and steel, and is a shipping point for pecans, livestock, and dairy products. Fort Benning, largest infantry post in the U.S., is nearby. 79,611 (1950).

Columbus. City in C Indiana, county seat of Bartholomew County, in a farming area: manufactures include automobile accessories, radios, Diesel engines, and leather goods. 18,370 (1950).

Columbus. City in SE Kansas, county seat of Cherokee County. Coal, lead, and zinc are produced in the area. 3,490 (1950).

Columbus. City in SW Kentucky, in Hickman County, situated near the Mississippi River ab. 16 mi. S of Cairo, Ill. A nearby state park marks the site of a strategic point of the Confederates in 1861–62, and also the former site of Columbus, which was moved after the flood of 1927. Pop. 482 (1950).

Columbus. City in NW Mississippi, county seat of Lowndes County, on the Tombigbee and Luxapalila rivers. It is the seat of the Mississippi State College for Women, and a marketing and processing point for cotton, lumber, grass seed, honey, livestock, and other products of the region. 17,172 (1950).

Columbus. City in E Nebraska, county seat of Platte County, on the Loup River, ab. 55 mi. NW of Lincoln: headquarters for a public power development project on the Loup River; marketing center for livestock. 8,884 (1950).

Columbus. City in C Ohio, capital of the state and of Franklin County, at the confluence of the Olentangy and Scioto rivers, close to the geographic center of the state. Manufactures include iron, steel, machinery, and paper, and there are meat-packing plants; it is the nation's largest producer of mining machinery. Columbus, which was made state capital in 1816, is the seat of the Battelle Memorial Institute, Capital University, Franklin University, Saint Mary of the Springs College, Ohio State University, and others. Fort Hayes is also here. 375,901 (1950).

Columbus. Town in SE Texas, county seat of Colorado County, on the Colorado River ab. 65 mi. W of Houston. It is a marketing center for farm produce, and has gravel pits. 2,878 (1950).

Columbus. City in S Wisconsin, in Columbia County, in an agricultural area: canning center for peas. It was settled in 1839. Pop. 3,250 (1950).

Columbus. Dramatic monologue (1844, published 1848) by James Russell Lowell. It shows the influence of Tennyson's *Ulysses,* which came out in 1842.

Columbus. Poem (1896) by Joaquin Miller, in his volume *Songs of the Soul* (1896). It is considered one of his best works. The words "Sail on! sail on! and on!" are used as a chorus at the end of each stanza (there are 5) as Columbus' answer to his mate's question, as the "grand lesson" he gave the world, and as the lesson of the poem.

Columbus, Bartholomew. [Spanish, **Bartolomeo Colón.**] b. probably at Genoa, Italy, c1445; d. at Santo Domingo, on the island of Hispaniola, in May, 1515. Brother of Christopher Columbus. He was with Bartolomeu Diaz on the West African coast (1486–87), and went to England in 1488 in a vain attempt to interest Henry VII in his brother's project. He returned to Spain in 1493, after the admiral had sailed on his second voyage, but followed him, in command of a supply fleet, to the settlement of Isabella. The admiral made him *adelantado* (governor), and from 1496 to 1498 he governed the island during his brother's absence, founding the city of Santo Domingo in 1496. He subdued an Indian revolt, marched to Xaraguá in 1497, and in 1498 had the first trouble with the rebel Francisco Roldan. In 1500 Francisco de Bobadilla, the royal commissioner sent to restore order, sent him a prisoner to Spain, where he was released with the admiral. He was with his brother on the fourth voyage (1502–04) and was the leader where active work was required. In the struggle to subdue a new rebellion at Jamaica, he was wounded. After the admiral's death he seems to have been at Rome, and in 1509 he accompanied his brother and nephew, both Diego Columbus, to Hispaniola, where he held important and lucrative offices.

Columbus, Christopher. [Italian, **Cristoforo Colombo**; Spanish, **Cristóbal Colón**; Latin, **Christophorus Columbus.**] b. probably at or near Genoa, Italy, c1446; d. at Valladolid, Spain, May 20 or 21, 1506. The most famous discoverer of America. There has been much dispute concerning the place of his nativity and even his nationality, but it is generally accepted that he was the son of Genoese wool combers. He received a fairly good education, and certainly, like a true Genoese, took to the sea at an early age. In 1473 or thereabouts he was in Portugal, where he married and had a son, Diego; he also lived for a time on the island of Porto Santo, near Madeira. It is probable that he sailed with some of the Portuguese expeditions to the African coast; he is known to have visited Ireland, and there is some doubtful testimony that he voyaged as far as Iceland. Being among those who understood that the earth is round, he had already formed the conviction that Asia might be reached by sailing westward, and he tried to get the backing of the king of Portugal for an expedition in that direction. Failing in this, he went to Spain (c1484) and offered the enterprise to its monarchs, Ferdinand and Isabella, but the advisers whom they deputed to examine the project reported adversely. Columbus sent his brother Bartholomew to England in 1488 in a vain effort to interest Henry VII. Oppressed by poverty, he was about to go to France when he obtained a personal interview with the Spanish royal couple at Granada, but the rewards he demanded in case of success of the projected voyage were so excessive that they declined to aid. Columbus was about to leave Granada when some of his friends induced the queen to reconsider; and on April 17, 1492, Ferdinand and Isabella agreed over their signatures that Columbus should be admiral in all regions which he might discover, and viceroy in all countries which he might acquire for Spain, with full powers and a generous share of the revenues, and that these honors and powers should pass to his heirs. Partly with royal aid, partly with the help of the Pinzóns, merchants of Palos, three small ships were fitted out: the *Santa María*, the *Niña*, and the *Pinta*, with the first named as flagship. With crews totaling either 90 or 120 men (accounts differ), the little vessels left Palos on August 3. After touching at the Canaries they continued westward into the unknown, and on Oct. 12, 1492, came to a small island called by its natives Guanahani, but christened by Columbus San Salvador; it was one of the islands now called the Bahamas, but exactly which one is not known with certainty (some believe it to have been Watling Island). After landing and claiming the island for Spain, he sailed on, discovering and claiming other islands, obtaining small quantities of gold and other products. He coasted the northern side of Cuba and of Hispaniola, and at a point on the shore of the latter island, which he called Española, the *Santa María* was wrecked. At this point he built a fort which he called La Navidad and, leaving 40 men there, he returned to Spain in the *Niña*. After pausing to visit the king of Portugal he reached Palos on March 15, 1493, was summoned to the Spanish court, where he was received with great honor, confirmed in his privileges, and given ample means for a new expedition. On Sept. 25, 1493, he sailed from Palos again with 17 vessels and 1,500 men. On November 3 he discovered the island of Dominica, and thereafter touched at several of the Caribbees before making his way to La Navidad, where he found that his colony had been wiped out by the Indians. On a new site he founded Isabella, the first European town in the New World, and continued his explorations. Ill conduct by the Spaniards turned the original friendliness of the Indians into hostility; there were many bloody clashes, and Columbus proposed to enslave all hostile natives. The Spanish colonists also were restive under Columbus' rule, and conveyed their complaints to Spain, from which a commission was sent to investigate the state of affairs in Española. Columbus sailed to Spain, leaving his brothers in charge, and was well received by the king and queen, who dismissed the charges against him. He sailed westward again in 1498, and for the first time came to the mainland of South America, making a landfall near the mouth of the Orinoco. When he came to Española he found that a new town, Santo Domingo, had been founded by Bartholomew in his absence and was in the hands of rebels with whom he had to make humiliating terms. When word of these troubles reached Spain, Francisco de Bobadilla was sent to Española as royal commissioner, and presently the great admiral and his brothers were sent to Spain in chains. Arriving there in October, 1500, they were promptly released, but Columbus could not obtain a reinstatement of his dignities. He did obtain four caravels in which he sailed westward again, intent on circumnavigating the globe. In 1502 he sailed down the coast of Central America from Honduras to Panama, vainly seeking a westward passage. Defeated, he turned eastward, and at Jamaica his ships, worm-eaten, became unnavigable. By means of a canoe his plight was after awhile made known in Española, but not until June, 1504, were he and his men rescued. Once more the weary admiral returned to Spain (Nov. 7, 1504), but before the year was out Isabella died, his petitions for reinstatement were ineffective, and he passed his remaining days in poverty and neglect. Columbus was of course acquainted with the legends of Saint Brendan's Isle and of Hy-Brasil, and with other Irish accounts of a land beyond the western ocean, and similar legends were probably current in other countries, though there was by no means so extensive a knowledge of pre-Columbian transatlantic voyages then as modern scholarship has developed. His great merit was that having a scientific mind at the moment of history when the scientific approach became both possible and imperative, and having indomitable courage as well, he established once and for all the existence of lands westward across the Atlantic from Europe. But the Admiral of the Ocean Sea died believing that he had reached India, quite unaware that he had opened a New World to the peoples of Europe.

Columbus, Diego. [Italian, **Giacomo Colombo**; by Latin writers called **Jacobus.**] b. probably at Genoa, Italy, c1450; date and place of death unknown. Brother of Christopher Columbus, who accompanied him in the second voyage (1493) and was at times left in command at the settlement of Isabella or at Santo Domingo, on the island of Hispaniola. He was sent to Spain with his brothers in 1500, and about that time became a priest. In 1509 he accompanied his nephew Diego Columbus to Santo Domingo, and probably died soon after.

Columbus, Diego. [Spanish, **Diego Colón.**] b. probably at Lisbon, Portugal, c1476; d. at Montalvan, near Toledo, Spain, Feb. 23, 1526. Son of Christopher Columbus. In 1492 Queen Isabella made him a page at the Spanish court, where he remained until after his father's death. He was confirmed in 1509 as admiral of the Indies and governor of Hispaniola, but without the title of viceroy. He arrived at Santo Domingo on July 10, 1509, but the conflicting claims of jurisdiction, and dissatisfaction with his rule, soon made the position an uneasy one. Diego Velásquez, whom he sent to conquer Cuba in 1511, virtually threw off his authority, the establishment of a royal audience at Santo Domingo restricted his power, and though, in a visit to Spain, he obtained new favors (1520), he was finally called back by the Council of the Indies in 1523 to answer charges against him. His wife was left in charge of the government, but Diego followed the court, vainly seeking redress, until his death.

Columbus, Ferdinand. [Spanish, **Ferdinando Colón.**] b. at Córdoba, Spain, Aug. 15, 1488; d. at Seville, Spain, July 12, 1539. Illegitimate son of Christopher Columbus and Doña Beatrix Henríquez, a lady of Córdoba. He was made a page to Queen Isabella of Spain in 1498, was with his father on the fourth voyage (1502–04), and by the admiral's will received an ample income, afterward increased by royal grants. He amassed a library of over 20,000 volumes, which passed by will to the cathedral chapter of Seville, where it was known as the "Columbina"; only about 4,000 volumes remain. A history of the Indies by him is lost, as is the Spanish original of his biography of his father, which was used by Las Casas.

Columbus, Luis. [Spanish, **Colón**; titles: Duke of **Veragua,** Marquis of **Jamaica.**] Son of Diego Columbus and grandson of Christopher Columbus. In 1536 he gave up all claims to the title of viceroy of Hispaniola (inherited by the grant to his grandfather by Ferdinand and Isabella), receiving in return the island of Jamaica in fief, a large pension, lands in Veragua (in what is now Panama), and the titles of Duke of Veragua and Marquis of Jamaica. He was captain-general of Hispaniola from 1540 to 1541. In 1559 he was imprisoned for having three wives, and in 1565 banished to Oran. His descendants were the dukes of Veragua.

Columbus Day. American legal holiday, observed in 34 states and Puerto Rico, commemorating the anniversary of the discovery of America by Christopher Columbus on Oct. 12, 1492. The date is observed also in various Italian and Spanish localities, and in several Latin-American countries.

Columcille (kol.um.kil'ẹ). See Saint **Columba.**

Columella (kol.ū.mel'ạ), **Lucius Junius Moderatus.** b. at Cádiz, Spain; fl. in the 1st century A.D. Roman writer on agriculture. He wrote *De re rustica*, in 12 books (edited by Schneider in *Scriptores rei rusticae*, 1794), and an earlier work on the same subject, of which one book, *De arboribus*, is extant.

Columna (kō.lum'nạ), **Fabius.** Latinized name of **Colonna, Fabio.**

Column of July. [French, **Colonne de Juillet.**] Monument at Paris, erected (1840) on the site of the Bastille, in honor of the citizens killed in the attacks on the royal government in 1830. It is a Corinthian column of bronze, ab. 13 ft. in diameter, rising from a square base and marble substructure, and capped by a gilded statue of the winged Genius of Liberty. Its total height is ab. 154 ft.

Column of Marcus Aurelius (mär'kus ô.rēl'yus). [Also, **Antonine Column.**] Monument in the Piazza Colonna, Rome, erected in 174 A.D., in honor of the campaigns against the Marcomanni. It reproduces the type of the Column of Trajan, and consists of a Roman Doric column of marble raised on a square pedestal, the total height, without the statue of Saint Paul of Sixtus V, being ab. 123 ft. The shaft is sculptured in a spiral of 20 turns, with reliefs of the wars it commemorates.

Column of the Congress. [French, **Colonne du Congrès.**] Monument erected at Brussels, Belgium, in commemoration of the Belgian constitutional congress of 1831. It is a Roman Doric column ab. 147 ft. high, on the summit of which stands a statue of Leopold I. Reliefs on the pedestal represent the Belgian provinces. At the angles stand four female figures in bronze, personifying types of liberty.

Column of Trajan (trā'jạn). Monument at Rome, dedicated in 114 A.D. in honor of the emperor. It is a Roman Doric column of marble, on a square basement, the total height, exclusive of the present statue of Saint Peter, added later, being ab. 127½ ft. The base bears reliefs of warlike trophies and an inscription; the entire shaft is occupied by vigorous and lifelike reliefs ascending in a spiral, representing Trajan's campaigns. The reliefs contain ab. 2,500 human figures, besides those of animals and inanimate objects.

Column of Vendôme (väṅ.dōm'). [French, **Colonne Vendôme.**] Monument in the Place Vendôme, Paris. It is a Roman Doric column of masonry encased in bronze, in design imitating the Column of Trajan at Rome, and was erected by Napoleon I in honor of his victories over the Russians and Austrians in 1805. The shaft is encircled with reliefs referring to the campaigns in question, ascending in a spiral, the height of the figures being ab. 3 ft. The column is surmounted by a figure of the emperor. Its height is ab. 142 ft. and its diameter ab. 13 ft. It was overthrown by the Commune of Paris in 1871, but was restored in 1875.

Columns of Saint Mark and Saint Theodore. Two columns at Venice, situated at the end of the Piazzetta toward the Grand Canal. The massive plain cylindrical shafts are of granite, the western pink, the eastern gray, resting on spreading, stepped bases. The capitals are ascribed to a Lombard architect. The figure of Saint Theodore, with his crocodile, was erected on the western column in 1329. The eastern column bears the famous winged lion of Saint Mark, in bronze, with eyes inlaid in precious stones. The existing lion is of the 15th century.

Colusa (kō.lö'sạ). City in N central California, county seat of Colusa County, on the Sacramento River ab. 55 mi. NW of Sacramento. 3,031 (1950).

Colville (kōl'vil). City in NE Washington, county seat of Stevens County, on the Colville River, a tributary of the Columbia, ab. 65 mi. N of Spokane. In its early history a fur-traders' post and a gold-rush town, it is now a popular resort of hunters and fishermen. 3,033 (1950).

Colvin (kol'vin), Sir **Auckland.** b. at Calcutta, India, March 8, 1838; d. at Surbiton, England, March 24, 1908. English administrator in India and Egypt; son of John Russell Colvin (1807–57). He served (1858–78) in the Indian civil service, was English comptroller (1880 *et seq.*) of Egyptian finance, and was financial adviser to the khedive. He was satirized by Kipling in "The Rupaiyat of Omar Kal'vin" (from *Departmental Ditties*) for his unpopular tax measures as a financial member (1883–87) of the viceroy's council in India. From 1887 to 1892 he was lieutenant governor of the North-West Provinces. He was the author of a biography of his father (1895), and of *Makings of Modern Egypt* (1906).

Colvin, John Russell. b. at Calcutta, India, May, 1807; d. at Agra, India, Sept. 9, 1857. English colonial official; father of Sir Auckland Colvin (1838–1908). He was British East India Company lieutenant governor (1853–57) of the North-Western Provinces of Bengal at the outbreak (1857) of the Sepoy Mutiny. Although surprised and outnumbered by the mutineers, he managed to protect the European residents of Agra. He was known as an efficient and able administrator.

Colvin, Sir **Sidney.** b. at Norwood, England, June 18, 1845; d. at Kensington, London, May 11, 1927. English art and literary critic, professor, biographer, editor, and friend of Robert Louis Stevenson. He was educated at Trinity College, Cambridge, of which he was made a fellow in 1868. From 1873 to 1885 he was Slade professor of fine arts at Cambridge, and director of the Cambridge Fitzwilliam Museum from 1876 to 1884. From 1884 to 1912 he was keeper of prints and drawings at the British Museum. He was knighted on Jan. 1, 1911. His works are *Children in Italian and English Design* (1872), *A Florentine Picture Chronicle* (1898), and *Drawings by Old Oxford Masters* (1902–08). For the well-known *English Men of Letters Series*, he wrote lives of Landor (1881) and Keats (1887). He also edited *Selections from Landor* (1882), and wrote *John Keats: His Life and Poetry* (1917), a much more ambitious work than the slight life written 30 years earlier. Colvin knew Stevenson from 1873 until the latter died in 1894. He edited his letters in 1899 and again in 1911, and he published Stevenson's letters to him from Samoa, the *Vailima Letters*, in 1895. During the years 1894–97 he brought out the famous *Edinburgh Edition* of Stevenson's works, in 27 volumes. A student and critic of both art and literature, Colvin tended to be conservative in the former and liberal in the latter.

Colwell (kol'wel), **Stephen.** b. in Brooke County, W.Va., March 25, 1800; d. at Philadelphia, Jan. 15, 1871. American merchant, economist, and general writer. He wrote *Ways and Means of Payment* (1859) and others.

Colwyn Bay (kol'win). Municipal borough and seaside resort in N Wales, in Denbighshire, situated on the Irish Sea, ab. 6 mi. W of Abergele, ab. 220 mi. NW of London by rail. 22,276 (1951).

Colyn Clout (kol'in klout; kō'lin). Poem (c1520) by John Skelton, a satire against the clergy of his time.

Colyns (ko.laṅ). See **Colins, Alexander.**

Coma Berenices (kō'mą ber.ę.nī'sēz). Small constellation of the Northern Hemisphere, situated N of Virgo and between Boötes and Leo. It is an ancient constellation, having been first mentioned in the 3rd century B.C., although it is not listed as one of the 48 asterisms of the Alexandrian astronomer Ptolemy. Its legend is that Berenice, wife of the emperor Ptolemy III, in keeping with a vow, hung her hair in the temple of the war god. It disappeared from the temple but reappeared in the sky, as this tiny, beautiful constellation.

Comacchio (kō.mäk'kyō). Town and commune in N Italy, in the *compartimento* (region) of Emilia-Romagna, in the province of Ferrara, situated on 13 islands and a land tongue between the Adriatic Sea and the inlet of Comacchio, ab. 29 mi. SE of Ferrara. It has large-scale fisheries. The cathedral is in the baroque style. In ancient times successively an Etruscan, a Gallic, and a Roman town, it became the seat of a bishopric in the 5th century; it passed under the rule of the Goths and the Lombards, suffered at the hands of the Genoese and Venetians, and fell to the Papal States in 1598. Land reclamation has been in process in the vicinity during recent decades. Pop. of commune, 13,894 (1936); of town, 9,141 (1936).

Comagena (kom.ą.jē'ną). Latin name of **Tulln,** Austria.

Comalapa (kō.mä.lä'pä). City in S Guatemala, in Chimaltenango department. 7,458 (1950).

Çomali (sō.mä'lē). See **Somali.**

Coman (kō'mąn), **Mount.** [Also, **Mount Dana Coman.**] Mountain in Antarctica, lying ab. 50 mi. W of Mount Tricorn behind the Richard Black Coast, in ab. 74°02′ S., 65°4′ W. Elevation, ab. 12,000 ft.

Comana (kǫ.mā'ną). [Also, **Chryse.**] In ancient geography, a city in Cappadocia, Asia Minor, situated on the river Sarus. It was noted for its great temple to Ma, the Cappadocian mother goddess, with its elaborate festivals and great retinue of temple prostitutes and attendants, said to have numbered in the thousands.

Comana. In ancient geography, a city in Pontus, Asia Minor, situated ab. lat. 40°20′ N., long. 36°50′ E. It was perhaps a colony of the Cappadocian city of the same name and it was sacred to the same goddess, Ma.

Comanche (kǫ.man'chę). [Also, **Camanche.**] North American Indian tribe which once ranged widely in the Southern Plains, but in later periods was centered mainly in C Texas. They were warlike, nomadic, and of distinct Plains culture, but practiced only a modified version of the sun dance for which the Plains Indians were famous. Their language belongs to the Shoshonean group of the Uto-Aztecan family, and became the trade language in the regions they dominated in the 18th century. Some 1,600 or more of them now survive in Oklahoma in association with the Kiowa.

Comanche. Town in C Texas, county seat of Comanche County, NW of Austin: processing center for pecans, peanuts, and cheese. 3,840 (1950).

Comanians (kǫ.mā'ni.ąnz) or **Comans** (kō'mąnz). See **Cumans.**

Comayagua (kō.mä.yä'gwä). Department in W Honduras: rubber. Capital, Comayagua; area, 2,014 sq. mi.; pop. 68,171 (1950).

Comayagua. [Colonial name, **Nueva Valladolid.**] City in W Honduras, capital of Comayagua department, on the Humaya River: capital of Honduras until 1880. In colonial times it had 18,000 inhabitants, but it was burned in 1827, and has never fully recovered. 13,081 (1950).

Comayagüela (kō.mä.yä.gwā'lä). Town in S central Honduras, ab. 1 mi. SW of Tegucigalpa, separated from it by the Choluteca River. It was united with the larger city in 1898 to form the Distrito Central of Honduras, but retains its own name. It has a large market, and a notable modern school of arts and crafts. Pop. included with Tegucigalpa.

Combaconum (kom.bą.kō'num). See **Kumbakonam.**

Combat (kôn.bà). Paris daily newspaper, founded (1940) in World War II as an illegal Resistance paper. It was socialist and liberal in its political attitude. It was published and circulated openly after the liberation (1944) of France.

Combe (kōm, kōm), **Andrew.** b. at Edinburgh, Oct. 27, 1797; d. there, Aug. 9, 1847. Scottish physician and writer on physiology and phrenology. He founded (1823), with his brother George Combe and others, the *Phrenological Magazine,* of which he remained proprietor until 1837.

Combe, George. b. at Edinburgh, Oct. 21, 1788; d. at Moor Park, Farnham, England, Aug. 14, 1858. Scottish phrenologist; brother of Andrew Combe. His chief work is considered to be *An Essay on the Constitution of Man* (1828). He was associated with his brother and others in the founding (1823) of the *Phrenological Magazine.*

Combe, William. b. at Bristol, England, 1741; d. at Lambeth, London, June 19, 1823. English writer, creator of "Dr. Syntax." Educated at Eton and Oxford (where, however, he did not take a degree), he entered the law; thereafter he led for some time the life of an adventurer, being successively a soldier, a waiter, a lieutenant, and a cook, and for the last 43 years of his life resided within the rules of the King's Bench debtors' prison. He published a large number of works, including *The Diaboliad, a poem dedicated to the worst man* (*Simon, Lord Irnham*) *in His Majesty's Dominions* (1776), *The Devil upon Two Sticks in England* (1790), *The Tour of Dr. Syntax in Search of the Picturesque* (a poem first published in the *Poetical Magazine,* and republished in 1812), *The Second Tour of Dr. Syntax in Search of Consolation* (1820), and *The Third Tour of Dr. Syntax in Search of a Wife* (1821). Thomas Rowlandson illustrated the "Dr. Syntax" books, and Combe also wrote the text for Rowlandson's *Dance of Death* (1815–16) and *Dance of Life* (1816).

Combermere (kum'bėr.mir), Viscount. Title of **Cotton,** Sir **Stapleton.**

Comberton (kom'bėr.tǫn), **John de.** See **Northampton, John de.**

Combes (kônb), **Émile.** [Full name, **Justin Louis Émile Combes.**] b. at Roquecourbes, Tarn, France, Sept. 6, 1835; d. at Pons, Charente-Maritime, France, May 25, 1921. French political leader whose premiership (1902–05) was marked by steps to separate church and state. A leader in the Radical-Socialist Party, he entered the senate in 1885, became (June 7, 1902) premier, and enforced the 1901 law barring teaching by religious congregations. He was a minister without portfolio (1915–16) during World War I.

Combin (kôn.baṅ), **Grand.** See **Grand Combin.**

Combined Chiefs of Staff. Staff organization established (January, 1942) during World War II at Washington, D.C., by Great Britain and the U.S. in order to secure a coördinated war effort, especially in the matter of logistics. The members of the group included the top military leaders of both nations.

Combined Maze, The. Novel by May Sinclair, published in 1913.

Combined Production and Resources Board. Established in June, 1942, by the U.S., Great Britain, and Canada, this group sought to combine and relate the production programs of the three nations so as to assume maximum use and economy of all productive resources for war. Working with the Combined Chiefs of Staff, this working group also attempted to adjust production patterns and goals to changing military requirements.

Combined Raw Materials Board. Joint board established (January, 1942) during World War II by Great Britain and the U.S. in order to coördinate the development, utilization, and purchase of raw material resources necessary for the war. It reviewed periodically the supply and requirements position of the United Nations and served as a clearing house for requests from other allies for strategic raw materials.

Combined Shipping Adjustment Board. One of the joint committees which sought to coördinate the economic war efforts of the major Allies in World War II, this Board with U.S. and British membership worked on the pooling of shipping resources. Created on January 26, 1942, the Board's work unified the shipping schedules and policies of Great Britain and the U.S. in all major respects.

Côme (kōm). French name of the city of **Como.**

Côme, Lac de. French name of **Como, Lake.**

Comechingón (kō.mä.chēng.gōn'). Tribe of South American Indians which formerly occupied the highland areas of what are now Córdoba and San Luis provinces in NW Argentina. They had a simplified Andean culture with maize agriculture and llama herding. The Comechingón language cannot be classified with any certainty, since it is scarcely known.

Comedias de Capa y Espada (kō.mā′ᴛʜyäs dā kä′pä ē es.pä′ᴛʜä). See **Capa y Espada, Comedias de.**

Comédie Française (ko.mā.dē fräṅ.sez), **La.** [Also, **Théâtre Français.**] Official name of the French national theater. For all practical purposes, the Comédie Française may be said to have had its beginning in the Théâtre de l'Hôtel Bourgogne, established in 1552 and made *théâtre royal* (1588) under Henry III. It was followed (1600) by the Théâtre du Marais. A few years afterward the company of Molière was established in the great hall of the Hôtel Bourbon. In 1660 the Hôtel Bourbon was torn down, and in 1661 Molière was transferred to the theater of the Palais Royal. In 1673 Molière died, and his company was officially disbanded, but most of its members went to the Théâtre Guénégaud, where they continued to think of themselves (and to be thought of) as "the company of Molière." In 1680 there were thus three companies at Paris, that of the Hôtel Bourgogne, that of the Marais, and the company of Molière in the Théâtre Guénégaud; they were amalgamated (Oct. 21, 1680), and the Comédie Française organized by *lettre de cachet* of Louis XIV as "L'Hôtel des Comédiens du Roi entretenus par Sa Majesté." In the next several decades the Comédie Française moved frequently. In 1689 it had its home in the Rue des Fossés, St.-Germain-des-Prés; it was here and in this year that it first actually took the title of Comédie Française. In 1770 it removed to the Tuileries, and in 1782 the company played in what is now the Odéon. It was suppressed during the French Revolution, in 1793, and reconstituted by Napoleon, when he was first consul, and established in an official building of its own.

Comédie Humaine (ko.mā.dē ü.men), **La.** Collection of Honoré de Balzac's novels, arranged and connected with extensive classification by himself to form what he called a "complete society," the same persons and their relatives appearing and reappearing. "Each novel is in fact a page of the great work, which would be incomplete without it." It is a picture of the manners and morals of his own time. Among the well-known novels contained in the group are *Eugénie Grandet* (1833), *Le Père Goriot* (1835), *Le Cousin Pons* (1847), and *La Cousine Bette* (1847).

Comedy of Errors, The. Play by Shakespeare, first acted at Gray's Inn, in London, on Dec. 28, 1594. It is known certainly to have been one of the playwright's earliest works (most modern scholars believe 1592 or 1593 to be the years which may most probably be assigned to it, although neither 1591 nor 1594 can definitely be ruled out); some older reference works have suggested that its title was at one time simply *Errors.* Its plot was derived in great part from the *Menaechmi* of Plautus, with modifications that may be traced to the more serious *Amphitryon,* by the same playwright. The suggestion that Shakespeare's chief source was actually *The Historie of Error,* acted by the boys of Saint Paul's chapel on Jan. 1, 1577, is now discounted by virtually all scholars of Shakespeare; the derivation from Plautus seems not only likely beyond reasonable doubt, but also casts an interesting light on the actual meaning of Ben Jonson's much-quoted statement that his friend Shakespeare had "small Latin and less Greek." In view of the fact that no English translation of the *Menaechmi* is known to have been published before 1594 (and of the *Amphitryon* for about 100 years after that), it would appear that Shakespeare must have worked from Latin sources available at the time (indeed, there is much internal evidence that Shakespeare was influenced by Latin turns of phrase, although his use of the Latin was at no point close to translation). Other evidence, particularly from the stage directions, suggests that Shakespeare may very possibly have worked from Plautus in the original Greek. Clearly, therefore, the legend of Shakespeare's "classical illiteracy" is dealt a grievous blow by the circumstances relating to this play alone, and it should (in defense of Jonson) be pointed out that what was actually meant was that Shakespeare had far surpassed his great predecessors of classical times; in other words, in an age when much drama consisted simply of literal translation from Latin and Greek, Shakespeare alone had achieved really great heights of originality in his reworking of many of the age-old themes of comedy and tragedy. In the specific case of *The Comedy of Errors,* the general structure of the plot holds closely to that of Plautus's broadly farcical *Menaechmi* (it hinges on the extraordinary series of mistakes arising from the exact likeness between twin brothers, both named Antipholus, and the corresponding likeness between their twin servants, who are both named Dromio), but the play as a whole is given a quality of dignity and romantic depth by Shakespeare which Plautus's version completely lacked.

Comely Bank (kum′li). Row of two-storied houses in the NW part of Edinburgh. Carlyle lived there for a time, in the cottage numbered 21.

Comenius (kọ.mē′ni.us), **John Amos.** [Original surname, **Komenský.**] b. at Nivnice, or perhaps at Uherský Brod, in Moravia, March 28, 1592; d. at Amsterdam, Holland, Nov. 4, 1670. Czech theologian and scholar, noted particularly for his pioneering in educational reforms and in ecumenical endeavor. After preliminary studies in native schools, he matriculated at the Herborn *Gymnasium* (advanced secondary school), in Nassau, and at the University of Heidelberg. Upon his return to Moravia, and a few years after his ordination, he became in 1618 pastor of the Unity of Brethren congregation at Fulnek. But when this town was destroyed soon after the outbreak of the Thirty Years' War, he sought refuge in Bohemia. It was during this period of persecution that he wrote his celebrated *Labyrinth of the World.* But after the imperial edict of 1627 ordered all Protestant pastors to leave the country, he left never to return. He settled at Leszno in Poland, where he became co-rector of the local Gymnasium. Even prior to that he wrote the Czech version of what later became *Didactica magna,* upon which, and several other pedagogical works, his fame rests. As an educational reformer he was invited (1641) to England, and thence to Sweden where, under the auspices of Chancellor Axel Oxenstjerna, he engaged in the reform of that country's educational system. In 1648 he was elected bishop of the Unity of Brethren, but was engaged (1650–55) in the reform of the Hungarian school system and taught at Sáros-Patak. He returned to Leszno in 1655, only to be driven out the next year when that city was completely destroyed by the Poles in the Swedish-Polish War. He lost all his unpublished writings along with his other belongings. Having accepted the invitation to settle at Amsterdam, he removed to that city, where he resided for the rest of his life. He published some 90 works, although many other works were either lost (in the Leszno fire) or left incomplete. Among the most important of his works are *Labyrinth of the World, A Patterne of Universall Knowledge, Janua linquarum reserata, Via lucis, Orbis sensualis pictus, Didactica magna, Lux in tenebris,* and *Unum necessarium.* His educational labors have earned him the title of "the father of modern educational theory and practice," but he likewise pioneered in "pansophic knowledge," a project comprising a world scientific research center with uniform textbooks to be used in all schools throughout the civilized world, and, finally, he labored throughout his life in behalf of church unity, thus becoming a pioneer in ecumenicity.

Comeragh Mountains (kūm′rạ). Range of mountains in Munster province, Irish Republic, in County Waterford, extending ab. 13 mi. from NW to SE. The summit is Knockanaffrin (2,478 ft.).

Comersee (kō′mėr.zā). German name of **Como, Lake.**

Comfort (kum′fọrt), **George Fisk.** b. at Berkshire, N.Y., Sept. 20, 1833; d. at Syracuse, N.Y., 1910. American educator and teacher of aesthetics. Graduated (1857) from Wesleyan University, Middletown, Conn., he was lecturer (1868–72) on Christian art and archaeology at Drew Theological Seminary. In 1872 he was appointed professor at Syracuse University, where he taught modern languages, aesthetics, and the history of fine arts, and where he founded (1873) and headed (1873–93) the College of Fine Arts (by which Syracuse was enabled for the first time to bestow a degree in fine arts). He was also the organizer (1896) and director of the Syracuse Museum of Fine Arts, founder (1869) and secretary (1869–76) of the American Philological Association, and an organizer (1869–72) of the Metropolitan Museum of Art at New York.

Comfort, William Wistar. b. at Germantown, Pa., May 27, 1874—. American educator and philologist, who served (1917–40) as president of Haverford College. He received the B.A. degree from Haverford (1894) and from Harvard (1895), was awarded (1902) a Ph.D. from Harvard, served on the Haverford faculty until 1909, and was professor of Romance languages and literature (1909–17) at Cornell. He is the author of *Just Among Friends: The Quaker Way of Life* (1941).

Comfort, Will Levington. b. at Kalamazoo, Mich., Jan. 17, 1878; d. at Los Angeles, Nov. 2, 1932. American journalist and novelist. He served as a war correspondent in the Philippines and China (1899) for the Detroit *Journal* newspaper syndicate, and in Russia and Japan (1904) for the Pittsburgh *Dispatch* newspaper syndicate. Among his books are *Routledge Rides Alone* (1910), *Fate Knocks at the Door* (1912), *Midstream* (1914), *Lot and Company* (1915), *Child and Country* (1916), *The Hive* (1918), *This Man's World* (1921), *The Public Square* (1923), *Somewhere South in Sonora* (1925), *Samadhi* (1927), and *Apache* (1931).

Comical Gallant, or the Amours of Sir John Falstaff, The. Adaptation of Shakespeare's *The Merry Wives of Windsor* by John Dennis, played in 1702.

Comical Lovers, or Marriage à la Mode, The. Comedy by Colley Cibber, produced and printed in 1707. It is made from the comic scenes of John Dryden's *Secret Love* and *Marriage à la Mode*.

Comical Revenge, or Love in a Tub, The. Comedy by Sir George Etherege, produced in 1664. It was published in the same year.

Comines (ko.mēn). [Also, **Commines.**] Town in N France, in the department of Nord, situated on the Lys River and the Belgian border, ab. 10 mi. N of Lille. It has cotton manufactures (sewing cotton and ribbons). The *Hôtel de Ville* (town hall) dates from the 15th and 16th centuries. 6,964 (1946).

Comines or **Commines** or **Commynes** or **Comynes** (ko.mēn), **Philippe de.** [Title, Sieur **d'Argenton.**] b. c1447; d. at Argenton, Deux-Sèvres, France, c1511. French statesman and historian. He entered the service of Charles the Bold of Burgundy, and then (1472) went over to Louis XI of France, in whose household he rose to the dignity of confidant and counselor. In 1486 he was arrested for political reasons and imprisoned for over two years. At the command of Charles VIII he was arrested again later on, and exiled for ten years. After serving his time, he returned to court.

Cominform (kom'in.fôrm). [Also, **Fourth International.**] Organization officially designated as an "information bureau," but actually a reëstablishment of the Comintern. It was organized at a secret meeting at Warsaw, Poland, Sept. 21–28, 1947, attended by representatives from the Communist parties of the U.S.S.R., Poland, Bulgaria, Czechoslovakia, France, Italy, Hungary, Rumania, and Yugoslavia. Official announcement of the formation of the new organization was made at Moscow, on Oct. 5, 1947. Its actual purpose appeared to be an attempt to offer greater cohesion to the Communist parties of Europe and to offer a counterbalance to the European Recovery Program.

Comintern (kom'in.tėrn). [Also: **Communist International, Third International.**] Organization founded (March, 1919) by the leaders of the Russian Communist Party to "accelerate the development of events toward world revolution," and after the successful revolution to become the directorate of working-class action. By propaganda and political action it was to unify the efforts and allegiances of working-class parties throughout the world. In May, 1943, this International came to an end by degree from Moscow. While never able to play a major role in such vital countries as Great Britain, the U.S., and France, it did play a part in Communist uprisings in Hungary, Germany, the Baltic countries, and China. The name is a shortened form of Communist International.

Comiskey (ko̤.mis'ki), **Charles Albert.** [Called **"the Old Roman."**] b. at Chicago, Aug. 15, 1858; d. at Eagle River, Wis., Oct. 26, 1931. American baseball player and executive. He joined a Milwaukee team at the age of 17, and later played with the St. Louis Browns and served as their manager and captain (1883–90), was manager (1892–95) of a Cincinnati team, and was owner and president (1900–31) of the Chicago team in the American League from the date of its organization.

Comiso (kô'mē.zō). Town and commune in SW Italy, on the island of Sicily, in the province of Ragusa, W of the city of Ragusa. Situated in a fertile plain, producing abundant harvests of wine, grain, olives, and other agricultural commodities, the town is a trade center for the district. Stone quarries are in the vicinity. There are manufactures of building materials and food products. Pop. of commune, 23,496 (1936); of town, 21,914 (1936).

Comisso (kō.mēs'sō), **Giovanni.** b. at Treviso, Italy, 1895—. Italian novelist and journalist. He took part in D'Annunzio's Fiume adventure, which is the subject of his *Al vento dell'Adriatico* (1928). His *Gente di mare* (1929) is an account of his experiences as a deck hand on a sailing vessel plying the Adriatic coast.

Comitán (kō.mē.tän'). [Full name, **Comitán de Domínguez** (dā dō.mēng'ges); also, **Comitlán** (kō.mē.tlän').] Town in SE Mexico, in Chiapas state, near the Guatemalan border. 8,683 (1940).

Comité Secret d'Action Révolutionnaire (ko.mē.tā se̤.kre dȧk.syôṅ rā.vo.lü.syo.ner), **Le.** See **Cagoulards.**

Comitium (ko̤.mish'um, -mish'i.um). Paved area in ancient Rome, between the NE side of the Forum Romanum and the Curia, where the Comitia Curiata, or assembly of the patricians, met, and where the most important legal cases were tried. On the Comitium stood the original *rostra*, or official speakers' platform, and close to it was the *graecostasis*, the platform provided for foreign envoys.

Commagene (kom.a̤.jē'nē). In ancient geography, a district in N Syria, between the Euphrates on the E and Cilicia on the W. It was at one time tributary to the Assyrian empire, and was an independent kingdom from 65 B.C.–17 A.D. It is called Kummuh in the Assyrian cuneiform inscriptions.

Commager (kom'a̤.jėr), **Henry Steele.** b. at Pittsburgh, Pa., Oct. 25, 1902—. American historian and teacher. He was graduated (Ph.D., 1928) from the University of Chicago, was full professor of history (1931–38) at New York University, and in 1939 became professor of American history at Columbia University, where he has lectured on social, constitutional, and intellectual history. In 1947–48 he was William Pitt Professor of American History at Cambridge University. Author of *Theodore Parker* (1936), *Majority Rule and Minority Rights* (1943), and *The American Mind* (1950); editor of *Documents of American History* (1934, and later eds.), *America in Perspective* (1947), and *A St. Nicholas Anthology* (1948). With Samuel Eliot Morison, he wrote *The Growth of the American Republic* (3rd ed., 1942); with E. C. Barker wrote *Our Nation* (1941); and with Allan Nevins wrote *America: The Story of a Free People* (1942) and edited *The Heritage of America* (2nd ed., 1950).

Command. Novel by William McFee, published in 1922.

Commander Islands. See **Komandorski Islands.**

Commandos. In World War II, a specially trained force of British troops, originally under the direction of Sir Roger Keyes and Lord Louis Montbatten. Numbering several brigades, it was intended to serve as a shock force in probing German defenses, especially on the Continent. Trained for man-to-man fighting and difficult landing and patrol operations, the Commandos were notable in World War II for their part in the raid on St.-Nazaire in 1942, the Dieppe raid in August, 1942, and various missions in the North African campaign. The Rangers may be said to have been their equivalent in the U.S. forces.

Commedia (kôm.mā'dyä). Original title of Dante's **Divina Commedia.**

Commemoration Ode. See **Recited at the Commemoration of the Living and Dead Soldiers of Harvard University.**

Commendation of Our Lady. Ballade once attributed to Chaucer, but erroneously. It is not written in ballade form. Tyrwhitt believed there was evidence that Lydgate might have written it.

Commentry (ko.mäṅ.trē). Town in C France, in the department of Allier, situated SE of Montluçon. It is the center of a coal-mining region, and has an important iron and steel foundry (Usine de Commentry). 8,827 (1946).

Commer (kom′ėr), **Franz.** b. at Cologne, Germany, Jan. 23, 1813; d. Aug. 17, 1887. German musicologist and composer. A founder (1844) of the Berlin Tonkünstlerverein, he was also influential in the founding (1868) of the Gesellschaft für Musikforschung. He edited antique musical works, and composed chiefly religious works.

Commerce. City in N Georgia, in Jackson County. 3,351 (1950).

Commerce. City in E Texas, in Hunt County, NE of Dallas: processing and shipping center for cotton and cottonseed oil; railroad shops. It is the seat of East Texas State Teachers College. 5,889 (1950).

Commerce. Former name of **Nauvoo.**

Commerce, U.S. Department of. Executive department of the national government established by act of the U.S. Congress (Feb. 14, 1903) as the Department of Commerce and Labor, whose separate status dates from an act passed on March 4, 1913. It was created for the purpose of fostering, promoting, and developing the foreign and domestic commerce, the mining, manufacturing, shipping, and fishery industries, and the transportation facilities of the U.S. It is under the direction of the secretary of commerce, who enjoys cabinet status. Among the bureaus or other units under the department are the Coast and Geodetic Survey, the Bureau of Domestic and Foreign Commerce, the Civil Aeronautics Administration, the Weather Bureau, the Bureau of the Census, the National Bureau of Standards, the Patent Office, the Reconstruction Finance Corporation, and the Inland Waterways Corporation.

Commercial Committee. [Also called the **Committee of Commerce.**] In American history, a standing committee of the Continental Congress, established (Sept. 19, 1775) as the "Secret Committee" for the purpose of buying stores of powder. The scope of its functions was gradually extended, and it finally became the chief arm of the Continental Congress for negotiating purchases in Europe of arms and supplies for the Revolutionary forces. It became known (July 5, 1777) as the Committee of Commerce, but was more frequently called the Commercial Committee. The greater number of its functions were assumed (1781) by Robert Morris in his capacity as superintendent of finance.

Commercy (ko.mer.sē). Town in NE France, in the department of Meuse, situated on the Meuse River and the Canal de l'Est, ab. 20 mi. E of Bar-le-Duc. It is a commercial and industrial center, containing mainly metallurgical, machine, and lumber industries. Madeleine cakes are a specialty. Voltaire was once a guest at the 18th-century château. 6,224 (1946).

Commerson (ko.mer.sôṅ), **Philibert.** b. at Châtillon-les-Dombes, France, 1727; d. on the island of Mauritius, 1773. French naturalist. He studied medicine at Montpellier, taking his degree in 1755, became a collector of plants and traveled through Europe in search of specimens, wrote a description of the fishes of the Mediterranean at the request of Linnaeus, and in 1767 set out with Bougainville on his expedition around the world. During this voyage he made many drawings and collected many specimens of plants and animals. At Mauritius he remained for special researches, visiting Réunion and Madagascar, but died at Mauritius before he could publish the results of his investigations.

Commines (ko.mēn). See **Comines.**

Commines, Philippe de. See **Comines** or **Commines** or **Commynes** or **Comynes, Philippe de.**

Commissary, The. Comedy by Samuel Foote, produced in 1765.

Commission of Inquiry for European Union. European body which sought (1930–31) to achieve closer coöperation between the countries of Europe. Largely through the efforts of Aristide Briand, it was recognized (1930) by the Assembly of the League of Nations as a League commission. It gave special study to such matters as harvest surpluses, international mortgage credit, preference extension, and unemployment. The commission lapsed because of the bilateral German-Austrian Customs Union of 1931 and the political eclipse of Briand.

Commission on Pakistan and India, United Nations. See **United Nations Commission on Pakistan and India.**

Commission to the Five Civilized Tribes. See **Dawes Commission.**

Committee, The. Comedy by Sir Robert Howard, printed in 1665. John Evelyn saw it played in 1662. It was revised by T. Knight and produced as *The Honest Thieves* in 1797.

Committee for Industrial Organization. [Called the **CIO.**] Labor unit established within the American Federation of Labor by trade-union leaders who favored industrial unionism as opposed to the traditional craft union policy of the AFL. The contest between the two groups culminated at the AFL convention of 1935, following which the CIO was established. It became independent after defying an AFL order to dissolve, and in 1938 was formally organized as the Congress of Industrial Organizations.

Committee of Commerce. See **Commercial Committee.**

Committee of Sixteen. See **Organization for European Economic Coöperation.**

Committee of the States. In American history, a committee authorized under the Articles of Confederation to act during recesses of Congress under such powers as at least nine states of the Confederation should from time to time vest in it. The committee was in operation only once (June–August, 1784). Each state had one delegate on the committee.

Committee of the Whole. Term in legislative procedure applied to all members of a chamber sitting as a committee for the consideration of a specific bill. The procedure affords greater flexibility and speed for disposing of a measure, and is employed in the U.S. House of Representatives (but not in the Senate) and in numerous state legislatures. In the House of Representatives, however, there are, properly speaking, two such committees: the Committee of the Whole House on the State of the Union (which disposes of public bills) and the Committee of the Whole House (which handles private bills).

Committee of Thirteen. In U.S. political history, a select committee (1850) of the U.S. Senate established for the purpose of considering and reporting upon the slavery compromise resolutions submitteed by Senators Henry Clay and John Bell. The committee was headed by Clay and consisted of seven Whigs and six Democrats. The provisions of its report (May 8, 1850) later emerged as the substance of the Compromise of 1850.

Committee of Thirteen. In U.S. history, a committee of the U.S. Senate established on Dec. 18, 1860, for the purpose of considering the conciliatory measures advanced on the eve of the Civil War by Senator John J. Crittenden of Kentucky. The resolution for its creation was submitted by Senator Lazarus W. Powell of Kentucky, and its function was similar to that handled by the unwieldy Committee of Thirty-three of the House. Among its members were Stephen A. Douglas, William H. Seward, Robert M. T. Hunter, Robert Toombs, Jefferson Davis, and Benjamin F. Wade. The committee's deliberations (ending on Dec. 28, 1860) produced no compromise between Southern radicals and Northern opponents of slavery extension, and the committee reported its inability to reach an agreement.

Committee of Thirty-three. In U.S. history, a committee of the U.S. House of Representatives, established (Dec. 6, 1860) by resolution of Alexander R. Boteler of Virginia for the purpose of considering the compromise proposals advanced by Senator John J. Crittenden of Kentucky. Its function was similar to that undertaken by the Senate Committee of Thirteen, and, like the body in the upper house, it failed to reach any agreement between Southern extremists and Northern opponents of slavery extension. The committee's defeat (Dec. 22, 1860) of the Crittenden compromise brought the nation one step closer to the outbreak of the Civil War.

Committee on Public Information. Committee established (April 14, 1917) by the executive order of President Woodrow Wilson. George Creel, a newspaper editor, was placed in charge of the organization which, under his direction, issued and distributed throughout the world nearly

75 million pamphlets in many languages, as a means of publicizing American aims in World War I. Posters, photographs, motion pictures, magazines, and newspapers represented the same cause to the American public. Orators ("Four Minute Men") were active throughout the country to encourage bond purchase and fuller participation in the war effort.

Committee on the Conduct of the War. In U.S. history, a joint committee of the U.S. Congress established (Dec. 20, 1861) for the purpose of investigating the Union government's prosecution of the Civil War. It inquired into military affairs (including investigations of army commanders), expenditures, and contracts. The committee was dominated by the Radical Republicans, and among its members were such stalwart Radicals as Zachariah Chandler and George Julian. Long before its existence was brought to a close (June, 1865), the committee had given abundant evidence of its sharp differences with the administration. An effort to establish a similar committee during World War I was checked by President Woodrow Wilson.

Committees of Correspondence. In the period immediately preceding the military phase of the American Revolution, committees of local, county, and colony-wide scope established to facilitate the efforts of the patriot party. They performed important services in forming and marshaling public opinion during the critical period leading up to the outbreak of armed conflict. The first committees, set up under the guiding spirit of Samuel Adams, were established in Massachusetts in November, 1772.

Committees of Safety. Extralegal bodies established on a wide scale in the American colonies during the course of the American Revolution for the purpose of preserving order, carrying out the functions of government after the breakdown of British administration in the colonies, seizing Loyalists, and aiding the Continental forces. Even before the Second Continental Congress recommended (July 18, 1775) the creation of these committees, many such bodies had already been in existence for as much as a year. Although some states later replaced the committees with official bodies, others gladly countenanced the valuable work performed by these unofficial agencies. They served as models for the committees of safety established under the French Revolution.

Committee to Defend America by Aiding the Allies. Organization established in May, 1940, which opposed the position of the U.S. "isolationists" and advocated official aid "short of war" to Great Britain, and, subsequently, to the U.S.S.R. during the war against the Axis Powers. It was headed by William Allen White during the greater part of its existence. The committee, which operated locally and nationally, was dissolved shortly after the U.S. entry into World War II.

Commodianus (ko̩.mō.di.ā'nus). fl. (probably) middle of 3rd century. Christian poet. Two poems by him are extant: *Instructiones LXXX adversus gentium deos* and *Carmen Apologeticum,* a defense of Christianity. Some scholars have considered that he may have lived later than the 3rd century, placing him even as late as the 5th century.

Commodities Exchange Act. Act of the U.S. Congress passed in 1936, and in effect amending the Grain Futures Act of 1922, providing for the elimination of impediments to interstate commerce originating in trading manipulation and heavy speculation on agricultural commodity exchanges. The act established a Commodity Exchange Authority (later placed under the Department of Agriculture) governing exchange trading in commodities including grains and dairy products.

Commodore Hawser Trunnion (trun'yo̩n). See **Trunnion, Commodore Hawser.**

Commodus (kom'o̩.dus), **Lucius Aelius Aurelius.** b. at Lanuvium, Italy, Aug. 31, 161 A.D.; killed at Rome, Dec. 31, 192. Emperor of Rome in the period 180–192; son of Marcus Aurelius, whom he succeeded. He bought peace of the Germans at the price of a tribute, and, entrusting the direction of the government to favorites (Perennis, Cleander, Laetus, and Eclectus), abandoned himself to dissipation and cruelty. He put to death his wife Crispina and nearly all the public men who had risen to eminence under his father, is said to have appeared as a gladiator in the amphitheater more than 700 times against defenseless opponents, and to have claimed divine honors, appearing in public as Hercules and demanding to be worshiped as such. He was strangled by the athlete Narcissus, who was introduced into his sleeping apartment by conspirators, chief of whom was the emperor's mistress, Marcia.

Common (kom'o̩n), **Dol.** In Ben Jonson's comedy *The Alchemist,* the mistress of Subtle.

Common Ground. Quarterly (1940 *et seq.*) published by the Common Council for American Unity. It is devoted to the improvement of intergroup understanding and stresses the bond provided by a common cultural heritage.

Common Order, Book of. See **Book of Common Order.**

Common Prayer, Book of. See **Book of Common Prayer.**

Commons, House of. See **House of Commons.**

Commons (kom'o̩nz), **John Rogers.** b. at Hollandsburg, Ohio, Oct. 13, 1862; d. May 11, 1945. American political economist, professor at the University of Wisconsin from 1904. In 1892 he became professor of sociology at Oberlin College, subsequently holding similar positions at Indiana and Syracuse universities. In 1901 he acted as expert for the Industrial Commission, and in 1904 became director of the American Bureau of Industrial Research. In 1917 he headed the American Economic Association. His published works include *Social Reform and the Church, Proportional Representation, Trade Unionism and Labor Problems,* and *Races and Immigrants in America.*

Common Sense. Pamphlet by Thomas Paine, published at Philadelphia, on Jan. 1, 1776. It advocated entire separation from England; its arguments crystallized the prevailing current of feeling, and swept waverers along with it. The tract's call for American independence helped shape the colonial mind for the reception of the Declaration of Independence.

Common Sense. American monthly review (1932–46) devoted to the discussion of social, political, and economic questions from the liberal point of view. Among its contributors were Louis Adamic, John Dos Passos, Max Eastman, Upton Sinclair, and Norman Thomas.

Commonweal, The. Weekly publication (1924 *et seq.*) in the U.S., devoted primarily to expressing the lay Roman Catholic point of view in political and cultural affairs.

Commonwealth of Australia. Official name of **Australia.**

Commonwealth of England. Designation applied officially to the form of government existing in England from the abolition of the monarchy in February, 1649, after the execution of Charles I, until the establishment of the Protectorate under Cromwell in December, 1653, but often loosely used of the whole interval from the death of Charles I to the restoration of Charles II in May, 1660. During the former period, or that of the real Commonwealth, the government was vested in a council of state, composed of members of the House of Commons, and the House of Lords was abolished. Care should be taken that the superficial similarity in the terms does not lead to confusion between the 17th-century Commonwealth of England and the 20th-century British Commonwealth of Nations: there is no connection between the two whatever.

Commonwealth of Nations, British. See **British Commonwealth of Nations.**

Commonwealth of Oceana (ō.sē.ā'na̩, ō.shē̩.an'a̩), **The.** See **Oceana, The Commonwealth of.**

Commonwealth v. Hunt, Massachusetts Reports, 4 Metcalf 45 (1842). Decision of the Supreme Judicial Court of Massachusetts, rendered in an opinion by Chief Justice Lemuel Shaw, holding legal a combination of workingmen for the purpose of regulating the terms of employment and raising wages. By the common law which obtained in most American states, such action had previously been construed as conspiracy. Justice Shaw's pronouncements on the doctrine of conspiracy marked a turning point in American labor history. The case involved the Boston Journeymen Bootmakers Society.

Commune of Paris. Government of the city of Paris, France, as established by law and custom, with authority resting in a council. Historically, the term Commune of Paris refers specifically to the regimes in that city during the French Revolution beginning in 1789, and following the Franco-Prussian War of 1870–71. In the first of these instances, radicals, personally ambitious intriguers, and probably also a number of concealed monarchist counterrevolutionists, secured ascendancy in the Paris Commune, which became one of the chief instruments for disrupting and rendering powerless the National Convention, and which tried to extend its power over all of France. Danton, Marat, Hébert, and other extremists dominated the Commune, but the center of revolutionary power passed to the Committee of Public Safety and the Revolutionary Tribunal, dominated by Robespierre. In the second instance, following the collapse of the French imperial armies in 1870, Paris resisted the German besiegers until Jan. 28, 1871. On that same day Adolphe Thiers, provisional head of the French government, signed with Bismarck a peace agreement of a character so humiliating to France that the Parisian people rose against it and refused to disarm. The armies of the Thiers regime began a second siege of Paris on April 6, succeeded in entering the city on May 21, and put an end to organized resistance on May 28. During the weeks of this siege the Commune was dominated by radicals who attempted socialistic innovations, and there were excesses directed against aristocracy, property, and religion, but the majority of the Communards were neither socialists nor communists. However, following the defeat of the Commune, more than 17,000 Communards, including women and children, were put to death, mainly by firing-squads, the executions being carried out before audiences of appreciative aristocrats and bourgeoisie.

Communism (kom′ū̦.niz.e̦m). Political philosophy, based on Marxian socialism, and developed most fully by the Third or Communist International, especially as the controlling philosophy of government in Russia after 1917. The basic Communist tenet is that of the dictatorship of the proletariat, the control of government by the workers. That achieved, Communism sees the establishment of a socialism in which the means of production are controlled by the government and in which every man works to his best ability, since he is working for the good of all, and receives according to his needs; the end will be a classless society, all being workers to the same end, and in which finally the actual machinery of government and the state will disappear. The establishment of a Communist government in Russia following World War I led to a modification of the basic plan (theoretically a temporary expedient), whereby the ideal of worldwide Communism was surrendered for the immediate goal of establishing Communism in at least one country. The ideological base was similarly shifted from the proletariat as a whole (considered as insufficiently educated in socialism's ultimate aims) to the indoctrinated group of party members; from these strict adherence to doctrine was demanded, and members who deviated from the official "line" were either purged from the party or tried as enemies of the state. Through the Comintern, and later the Cominform, Communist parties, organized in every part of the world, were subjected to similar discipline, the aim of all Communists (especially after the victory of the Stalinist faction over the Trotskyist within the U.S.S.R.) being primarily to protect the socialist revolution in Russia and secondarily to promote the growth of socialism in their own countries.

Communist International. See **Comintern.**

Communist Party, U.S.A. Political organization established in 1919 and formally designated (1929) as the Communist Party of the United States of America. Its affiliation to the Comintern (Third International) with headquarters at Moscow was terminated in 1940 and the party was formally dissolved in 1944, when the Communist Political Association replaced it. The Association was in turn dissolved in 1945 and the party resumed its earlier designation.

Commutation Bill. In U.S. history, a resolution adopted (March 22, 1783) by the Continental Congress providing for the commutation of the half-pay pledged to officers of the Continental forces upon being mustered out. The officers were granted a single payment equivalent to a full payment for five years of service.

Commynes (ko̦.mēn), **Philippe de.** See **Comines** or **Commines** or **Commynes** or **Comynes, Philippe de.**

Comnena (kom.nē′na̦), **Anna.** See **Anna Comnena.**

Comnenus (kom.nē′nus). [Also: **Komnenos, the Comneni** (-nī).] Byzantine family, probably of Italian origin, which acquired historical importance in the 10th century, and from which descended six emperors of the Byzantine Empire in the period from 1057 to 1185, all the emperors of Trebizond (Trabzon), and many statesmen, generals, and authors. Among its notable members were Alexius I, Alexius II, Andronicus I, Isaac I, John II, Manuel I, and Anna Comnena.

Como (kō′mō). Province in NW Italy, in the *compartimento* (region) of Lombardy. Capital, Como; area, ab. 800 sq. mi.; pop. 501,725 (1936), 527,000 (est. 1946).

Como. [French, **Côme**; Latin, **Comum.**] City and commune in NW Italy, in the *compartimento* (region) of Lombardy, the capital of the province of Como, picturesquely situated at the S extremity of Lake Como, ab. 25 mi. NW of Milan. It is an industrial city, having manufactures of silk textiles, musical instruments, machinery (particularly for the silk industry), and food products; it is also a tourist center. Como has been the seat of a bishopric since the 11th century, and has numerous educational institutions, including a civic museum, containing archaeological and art collections, the communal library and historical archives, historical and archaeological societies, a national institute for the silk industry, and the Volta Museum. The cathedral, one of the finest in N Italy, begun in 1396 in Gothic style, was finished in Renaissance style in the 16th century. Other churches, such as Sant'Abbondio, San Fidele, and San Giacomo, in Romanesque style, show German architectural influence. There are medieval towers and palaces. An important commercial city under the Romans, Como was a partisan of the Ghibellines and of Emperor Frederick I (Barbarossa) in the 12th century; it belonged to Milan after 1451. The elder and the younger Pliny were born here in the 1st century A.D.; in the 19th century it was the birthplace of the physicist Alessandro Volta. Pop. of commune, 56,304 (1936); of city, 42,482 (1936).

Como, Lake. [Also: **Lake of Como**; Italian, **Lago di Como**; French, **Lac de Côme**; German, **Comersee**; Latin, **Lacus Larius.**] Lake in N Italy, near the Swiss border. It is traversed by the Adda River, and is famous for its scenery. It is surrounded by mountains, and its shores are bordered with villas. At Bellaggio it is divided into Lake Como (proper) and Lake Lecco. Length, ab. 30 mi.; greatest width, 2½ mi.; depth, 1,330 ft.

Comodoliacum (kom″o̦.do̦.lī′a̦.kum). Ancient name of **St.-Junien.**

Comodoro Rivadavia (kō.mō.ᴛʜō′rō rē.ʙä.ᴛʜä′ʙyä). City in S Argentina, in Chubut territory, ab. 900 mi. SW of Buenos Aires. Pop. ab. 22,000.

Comonfort (kō.mōn.fôrt′), **Ignacio.** b. at Puebla, Mexico, March 12, 1812; killed near Guanajuato, Mexico, Nov. 13, 1863. Mexican soldier and statesman, president (1857–58) of Mexico. He joined (April, 1854) Juan Álvarez in the revolution of Ayutla deposing Santa Anna, was secretary of war under Álvarez in October, 1855, and on the retirement of that leader became acting president. Under the constitution of February, 1857, he was elected constitutional president, assuming office on Dec. 1, 1857. As acting president he crushed a series of revolts led by the church and conservative parties. Soon after his regular election he tacitly encouraged the project of a dictatorship. Deposed after hard fighting, he fled to the U.S. in 1858. He returned c1862, took a prominent part against the French invasion, and was killed by irregular troops or bandits.

Comorin (kom′o̦.rin), **Cape.** [Also, **Cape Cormorin.**] Cape in the Union of India, the S extremity of peninsular India.

Comoro (kom′o̦.rō), **Great.** See **Grande-Comore.**

Comoro Islands. [Also: **Comores** (ko̦.mōrz′); French, **Archipel des Comores, Îles Comores.**] Group of small islands off SE Africa in the Mozambique Channel NW of Madagascar. The chief islands are Grande-Comore, Anjouan, Mohéli, and Mayotte. All the islands were placed under French protection in 1886; in 1912 they became a French colony and were made a dependency of Madagascar; in 1946 they became an autonomous territory under the partial supervision of the high commissioner at Tananarive. Area, 650 sq. mi.; pop. 158,000 (1946), 168,890 (est. 1950).

Compactata of Prague (kom.pak.tä′tą; präg). See **Prague, Compactata of.**

Compagnia della Calza (kōm.pä.nyē′ä del.lä käl′tsä). Society which existed in Italy during the 15th and 16th centuries, for the production of public and private entertainments, as games, feasts, and theatrical representations. In the course of time this society became divided into different fraternities, as the Compagnia dei Floridi, Sempiterni, and others, each of which was governed by particular laws and officers, and the members of each of which were distinguished by a certain garb or costume.

Compagnie de L'Occident (kôṅ.pá.nyē dẹ lok.sē.däṅ). [Eng. trans., "*Western Company.*"] Enterprise formed (1717) by John Law for the purpose of carrying out the development of the resources of French Louisiana. In 1719 it was combined with the French East India Company and received the designation Compagnie des Indes. Because of its association with Law's gross speculation (the so-called Mississippi Bubble), it is perhaps best known as the Mississippi Company.

Compagnie des Quinze (kôṅ.pá.nyē dā kaṅz). [Eng. trans., "*Company of the Fifteen.*"] Acting group headed by Michel St. Denis, nephew of Jacques Copeau, famous for carrying on Copeau's principles after the closing of the Théâtre du Vieux Colombier in 1924. When Copeau retired to his country home in 1924, several actors went along with him to study under him and to act under his supervision. Michel St. Denis became their leader and they gave their first performance at Basel, Switzerland, in 1926. In 1929 at Lyons, André Obey saw the group perform and joined them as a playwright. In April, 1931, taking over the Vieux Colombier playhouse, the group performed Obey's *Noah* and *The Rape of Lucrece.* They followed these productions with performances of other plays by this author, and added to their repertoire such plays as Jean Giono's *Lanceurs de Graines*, Henri Gheon's *Violante*, and Armand Salacrou's *La Vie en Rose.* In 1946, Michel St. Denis became general director of the Old Vic Theatre at London.

Compans (kôṅ.päṅ), **Henri Ternaux-.** See **Ternaux-Compans, Henri.**

Company (kum′pą.ni), **John.** See **John Company.**

Company of the Fifteen. See **Compagnie des Quinze.**

Companys (kōm.pä′nēs), **Luís.** b. 1873; executed at Barcelona, Spain, 1940. Spanish politician, leader of the Catalan *Esquerra* (Leftist party) and for 25 years prominent in the republican movement for Catalan autonomy. Frequently imprisoned during the monarchy, he was a member (1932–33) of the republican Cortes, served as minister of marine in the Azaña cabinet, and was prime minister of the Catalan federal government (*Generalitat*) from January to September, 1934. Arrested in 1934, he was later released and served as president of the Catalan state (1936–38). In April, 1938, the autonomous Catalan state was abolished and in 1940 Companys was tried and executed by the Franco government.

Company Shops. Former name of **Burlington, N.C.**

Compass (kum′pąs). Soldier and scholar in Ben Jonson's comedy *The Magnetic Lady*, "a Scholar Mathematic . . . one well read in Men and Manners." He, by playing one character against another, reconciles the various humors they represent, and he marries Placentia, the heiress.

Compass Berg (kum′pąs bėrg). See **Sneeuwberg.**

Compayré (kôṅ.pe.rā), **Jules Gabriel.** b. at Albi, France, Jan. 2, 1843; d. at Paris, Feb. 24, 1913. French educator, notable in the field of child psychology. He served as professor at Pau, Poitiers, and Toulouse. He was the author of *L'Évolution intellectuelle et morale de l'enfant* (Intellectual and Moral Evolution of the Child, 1893).

Compendium (kǫm.pen′di.um). Ancient name of **Compiègne.**

Compensation. Essay by Ralph Waldo Emerson, published in his *Essays, First Series* (1841). His poem of the same title was also published in 1841.

Compère (kôṅ.per), **Loyset.** d. at St.-Quentin, France, Aug. 16, 1518. French composer noted for his contrapuntal music. He was chorister and chancellor of the cathedral at St.-Quentin.

Compeyson (kom′pi.sǫn). Convict and hardened criminal in Charles Dickens's *Great Expectations.* He is a scoundrel whom Magwitch describes as having "no more heart than a iron file." He is finally killed in a struggle with Magwitch.

Compiègne (kôṅ.pyeny′). [Ancient name, **Compendium.**] Town in N France, in the department of Oise, situated on the Oise River, near its junction with the Aisne River, and near the forest of Compiègne, ab. 45 mi. NE of Paris. Compiègne is known for its spacious avenues, its quiet residential quarters, and its royal castle (built in the 18th century, in the reign of Louis XV, and, after neglect during the Revolution, restored by Napoleon I). The castle contains a museum. The churches of Saint Jacques and Saint Antoine date from the 13th century. Behind the castle is the park which blends into the forest of Compiègne, an extended excursion ground. The town has manufactures of muslin, rope, and hosiery. Sports and arts events frequently take place at Compiègne. The town was noted in Roman and Carolingian times. Joan of Arc was taken prisoner here by the Burgundians in 1430. In 1914 Compiègne was occupied by the Germans; from 1917 to 1918 it was the site of the French headquarters; in 1918 it was damaged in heavy fighting; the World War I armistice was signed (1918) nearby, as was the World War II armistice (1940) between Germany and France. The region around the river and the center of the town were heavily damaged again in World War II. 18,218 (1946).

Compiègne Armistice (1918). Armistice concluding hostilities in World War I. It was signed in a railroad car on Nov. 11, 1918, in the forest of Compiègne, near the town of the same name, in France. It obligated the Germans to accord with 35 specific clauses. The most important of these required the rapid German evacuation of France, Belgium, Alsace-Lorraine, and Luxembourg, and then of all land W of the Rhine; nullification of the treaties of Brest-Litovsk and Bucharest, with removal of all German troops from Russia, Austria-Hungary, and the Balkans; the immediate repatriation of all Allied prisoners of war without reciprocity; the surrender of most of the German navy, including all submarines, and 150,000 railway cars, large numbers of trucks, and war matériel of various kinds. The evacuated territory W of the Rhine, with bridgeheads at Cologne, Koblenz, and Mainz, was to come under Allied occupation as speedily as possible, and the Allied blockade of Germany remained in effect.

Compiègne Armistice (1940). Armistice (effective June 25, 1940) between Germany and France in World War II. It was signed (June 22, 1940) at the site of the Compiègne Armistice of 1918, which ended World War I, and the actual signing took place in the same railway car. Of its 24 articles the most important provided for the German occupation of over one half of France, including all important industrial sectors, the Atlantic ports, and Paris; virtually complete French demilitarization; cessation of all war manufacture in unoccupied France; release of all German prisoners of war; surrender of most of the French fleet, with a German pledge not to use it in actual warfare; and French payment of the costs of German occupation. The armistice was considered provisional until the actual conclusion of peace and could be renounced by Germany whenever it deemed France delinquent in the performance of its obligations.

Complaint of a Lover's Life. See **Lover's Life, Complaint of a.**

Complaint of Creseide (kres′id), **The.** See **Cressid** or **Creseide, Testament of.**

Complaint of Mars. Poem by Geoffrey Chaucer, written probably c1379. It is full of astronomical allusions, and contains the story of "the broche" which Vulcan wrought at Thebes. It is supposed to be sung on Saint Valentine's day by a bird. A *Complaint of Venus* is sometimes appended to it, but is much later, of a totally different character, and is a translation from the French of Sir Otes de Granson.

Complaint of Philomene (fil.ǫ.mē′nē), **The.** Poem by George Gascoigne, begun in 1562, but not completed until 1576.

Complaint of Venus, The. Poem by Geoffrey Chaucer, translated by him late in life from the French of Granson. It is made up of three independent ballades. The title was given by the copyists as a counterpart to the *Complaint of Mars*, to which it is sometimes appended.

Complaints. [Full title, **Complaints, containing Sundry Small Poems of the World's Vanity.**] Volume of poems by Edmund Spenser, published in 1591. It contains, among others, "Muiopotmos" and "Mother Hubberd's Tale."

Complaint to His Empty Purse. Poem by Geoffrey Chaucer, sometimes attributed to Thomas Hoccleve. It is believed that it was written sometime before 1399, but that in that year Chaucer appended a dedicatory postscript and sent the poem to Henry IV, on that monarch's accession to the English throne. Chaucer is known to have received an annuity from the king within a very short time after his taking the throne. It was printed before the 1532 edition.

Complaint Unto Pity. Poem by Geoffrey Chaucer, printed before 1532, and perhaps written c1367.

Compleat Angler, The. [Full original title, **The Compleat Angler, or the Contemplative Man's Recreation.**] Work by Izaak Walton, published in 1653. It is a treatise on the art of fishing, and attempts to prove that sport's superiority over hunting and fowling.

Complutum (kom.plö'tum). Latin name of **Alcalá de Henares.**

Compniacum (komp.nī'ą.kum). An ancient name of **Cognac.**

Compostela (kōm.pōs.tā'lä), **Diego Evelino de.** b. at Santiago (Santiago de Compostela), Spain, 1635; d. at Havana, Cuba, Aug. 27, 1704. Spanish prelate. He taught theology in the University of Valladolid, and was vicar of various parishes in Spain. In 1685 he was named bishop of Cuba and Florida, a position which he held until his death.

Compostela (kōm.pōs.tā'lä) or **Compostella** (-tā'lyä), **Santiago de.** See **Santiago,** Spain.

Compromise of 1850. [Also referred to as the **Omnibus Bill.**] Series of compromise measures passed by the Congress of the U.S. when it became evident that, as a result of the war with Mexico, much territory would be added to the national domain, and the slave states called for the westward extension of the line of the Missouri Compromise (1820–21). Debate on this and related issues began in the summer of 1846, and when application was made for admission of California to the Union as a free state, a decision could no longer be deferred. Henry Clay (for the last time in his career) took the lead in arranging a national compromise, the principal features of which originated with Stephen A. Douglas. An omnibus bill, reported to the Senate in May, 1850, was subsequently broken down into separate measures which were passed in September of that year. These enactments included the admission of California as a free state, the organization of New Mexico and Utah as territories on terms leaving it to their peoples whether to sanction or to bar slavery when at a future time they should become states, the abolition of the slave trade in the District of Columbia, and a more drastic fugitive slave law. Support of these measures cost Daniel Webster his popularity in the North. He, Clay, Douglas, and others hoped that the Compromise would quiet the controversy over slavery and avert danger of a disruption of the Union, but the fugitive slave law led to the ascendancy of the Abolitionists in the North and caused the slavery issue to become truly an "irrepressible conflict."

Compromise of Breda (brā.dä'). See **Breda, Compromise of.**

Compton (komp'tǫn). City in S California, in Los Angeles County: industrial suburb of Los Angeles. In the decade between the last two U.S. censuses its population more than doubled. 16,198 (1940), 47,991 (1950).

Compton, Arthur Holly. b. at Wooster, Ohio, Sept. 10, 1892—. American physicist who discovered the wave length change of scattered x-rays (known as the Compton effect), for which he shared (1927) the Nobel prize for physics with C. T. R. Wilson; brother of Karl Taylor Compton (1887—). A graduate of Wooster College (B.S., 1913) and of Princeton (Ph.D., 1916), he also studied (1919–20) at Cambridge University. He served as professor of physics and department head (1920–23) at Washington University, and professor of physics (1923–45) as well as head of the department and dean of physical sciences (1940–45) at the University of Chicago. In 1945 he was named chancellor of Washington University. He is known for the discovery of the total reflection of x-rays and the electrical nature of cosmic rays, for collaboration in the polarization of x-rays and the production of x-ray spectra from ruled gratings, and for work on the first atomic chain reaction. His works include *X-rays and Electrons* (1926), *The Freedom of Man* (1935), and *Human Meaning of Science* (1940).

Compton, Henry. b. at Compton Wynyates, Warwickshire, England, 1632; d. at Fulham (now part of London), July 7, 1713. English prelate, bishop of London; youngest son of Spencer Compton (1601–43). He studied at Queen's College, Oxford, and at Cambridge, was installed canon of Christ Church in 1669, became bishop of Oxford in 1674 and bishop of London in 1675, and was charged with the education of Mary and Anne, daughters of James, Duke of York (later James II). After the accession of James, he was tried before Lord Chancellor Jeffreys, as head of the high court of ecclesiastical commission, for disobeying the king (in refusing to suspend John Sharp, dean of Norwich), and suspended from the exercise of his episcopal functions; but he was reinstated in 1688. He was a vigorous opponent of Catholicism and an influential supporter of William III.

Compton, Karl Taylor. b. at Wooster, Ohio, Sept. 14, 1887—. American physicist and president (1930–49) of the Massachusetts Institute of Technology; brother of Arthur Holly Compton (1892—). A graduate of Wooster College (Ph.B., 1908) and of Princeton (Ph.D., 1912), he was assistant professor of physics (1915–19), professor (1919–30), and head of the department of physics (1929–30) at Princeton. In 1946 he was named chairman of the evaluation board on the atomic bomb test. He is known for experiments in photoelectricity, ionization, and other fields.

Compton, Spencer. [Title, 2nd Earl of **Northampton.**] b. in May, 1601; killed in the battle of Hopton Heath, England, March 19, 1643. English soldier; father of Henry Compton (1632–1713). A partisan of Charles I in his struggle with Parliament, he served actively in the king's army, commanding the Royalist forces at Hopton Heath, where he was slain.

Compton, Spencer. [Title, Earl of **Wilmington.**] b. c1673; d. July 2, 1743. English politician, created Viscount Pevensey and Earl of Wilmington in 1730. He was chosen speaker of the House of Commons on March 17, 1715, and reëlected on Oct. 9, 1722. In February, 1742, he was appointed first lord of the treasury.

Compton, Virginia. [Maiden name, **Bateman.**] b. Jan. 1, 1853; d. at London, May 4, 1940. English actress; mother of the novelist Compton Mackenzie. In 1865 she began her stage career in England. She played leading parts in a touring comedy company, opened a repertory theater at Nottingham, England, and was the founder of the Theatre Girls' Club, a home for needy chorus girls.

Compton, Sir **William.** b. 1625; d. at London, Oct. 18, 1663. English soldier and supporter of Charles I during the English Civil War. Lieutenant governor of Banbury during its 13-week siege (1644), he was also the leader (1648) of the Royalist forces in the Kentish expedition, at Greenwich, and during the siege of Colchester.

Comstock (kum'stok, kom'-), **Ada Louise.** b. at Moorhead, Minn., Dec. 11, 1876—. American educator; wife of Wallace Notestein. Graduated (B.L., 1897) from Smith College, she served (1912–23) as its dean before being president (1923–43) of Radcliffe College. In 1929 she served on the Wickersham Commission.

Comstock, Anna. [Maiden name, **Botsford.**] b. at Otto, N.Y., Sept. 1, 1854; d. at Ithaca, N.Y., Aug. 24, 1930. American naturalist, teacher, and wood engraver; wife (1878 *et seq.*) of John Henry Comstock. Graduated (1878) from Cornell University, she studied art at Cooper Union at New York. She was assistant professor (1913–20) and professor (1920–22) of nature study at Cornell, and editor (1917–23) of the *Nature Study Review.* Her writings include *Ways of the Six-Footed* (1903), *Handbook of Nature Study* (1911), *The Pet Book* (1914), and *Bird, Animal, Tree and Plant Notebooks* (1914).

Comstock, Anthony. b. at New Canaan, Conn., March 7, 1844; d. Sept. 21, 1915. American reformer, noted for his crusading operations as secretary of the Society for the Suppression of Vice, and as the moving spirit behind the organization (1876) of the Boston Watch and Ward Society. After serving with the Union Army in the Civil War, and working intermittently as a clerk in Connecticut and Tennessee, during which time he displayed his bent for moral crusading, in 1873 he took up reforming as a profession. Already, in 1871, he had enlisted his services in the cause of the Y.M.C.A. and aided in the founding of a committee for the suppression of vice. In 1873 he was instrumental in securing the passage of a postal law prohibiting the use of the mails for transmitting obscene matter. He was made a special agent of the Post Office Department and was secretary (1873 *et seq.*) of the Society for the Suppression of Vice; he spent his busy years tracking down and helping to bring to justice a wide variety of shady practitioners, including patent-medicine venders, abortionists, gamblers, and professional nudists. Perhaps his most noted efforts were undertaken against publishers of obscene literature, although Comstock, in his puritanical zeal, was wont to confuse freethinking and such plays as G. B. Shaw's *Mrs. Warren's Profession* with indecent works. A man single-minded and ruthless in his own way, he credited himself with having caused 15 suicides among the victims of his battles against vice. The term "comstockery," coined by G. B. Shaw, has found its way into the language, indicating an inability to distinguish between genuine art and obscene works. His two books are *Frauds Exposed* (1880) and *Traps for the Young* (1883). For both sides of his character, see *Anthony Comstock, Fighter*, by Charles G. Trumbull (1913) and *Anthony Comstock, Roundsman of the Lord*, by Heywood Broun and Margaret Leech (1927).

Comstock, Daniel Frost. b. at Newport, R.I., Aug. 14, 1883—. American physicist and inventor. During World War I he was instrumental in developing devices for the detection of enemy submarines, and during World War II he directed important research in connection with war projects. He is best known as a principal inventor of the technicolor process in the field of motion pictures, but he has also to his credit important achievements in electricity and in theoretical physics.

Comstock, Elizabeth L. b. at Maidenhead, Berkshire, England, Oct. 30, 1815; d. Aug. 3, 1891. American Quaker minister and humanitarian. Educated in England, where she also taught, she came (1854) as a widow to Belleville, Ontario, Canada, where she took up her ministry in the Society of Friends. She was married (1858) to John T. Comstock, with whom she moved in the same year to Rollin, Mich., where she was soon acknowledged a leader in the pioneer Quaker community at that settlement. She became devoted to the abolitionist cause, helping slaves on the Underground Railroad, and gradually became known in the West as a supporter of many causes, including temperance, peace, prison reform, and women's rights. During the Civil War she aided in the organization of relief work carried out by the Society of Friends, and visited many hospitals and prison camps. In 1864, during a visit with President Lincoln, she conducted a Quaker service at the White House. She was active in relief work during the mass migration of Negroes into Kansas (1879–80), and after 1885 lived at Union Springs, N.Y.

Comstock, George Cary. b. at Madison, Wis., Feb. 12, 1855; d. May 11, 1934. American astronomer. He was professor in the University of Wisconsin from 1887, and director of the Washburn Observatory from 1889. He published *Text-book of Astronomy* (1900) and *Field Astronomy for Engineers* (1902), and edited a number of volumes of the publications of the Washburn Observatory.

Comstock, Henry Tompkins Paige. b. at Trenton, Ontario, Canada, 1820; d. near Bozeman, Mont., Sept. 27, 1870. American prospector, active (1856–62) in Nevada. He staked claims on the ground where the so-called Comstock Lode (at what is now Virginia City, Nev.) was found, but sold his holdings for small sums and never profited otherwise from the fabulously rich mining property which bore his name.

Comstock, John Henry. b. near Janesville, Wis., Feb. 24, 1849; d. at Ithaca, N.Y., March 20, 1931. American entomologist; husband (1878 *et seq.*) of Anna Comstock. After graduation (1874) from Cornell, he studied (1874–75) at Yale and attended (1888–89) the University of Leipzig, Germany. He was instructor (1875–77), assistant professor (1877–78), and professor (1882–1914) of entomology and invertebrate zoölogy at Cornell, and served as U.S. entomologist (1879–81) at Washington. Author of *Introduction to Entomology* (1888), *Insect Life* (1897), *The Spider Book* (1912), *The Wings of Insects* (1918), and, with his wife, *How to Know the Butterflies* (1904).

Comstock Lode. Celebrated gold and silver mines at Virginia City, Nev., which yielded (1859–79) well over 500 million dollars in valuable ores. The lode was named for Henry Tompkins Paige Comstock (1820–70), who held a claim to the lode but sold his holdings before they were exploited. The profits made from the Comstock Lode accounted for much of San Francisco's economic growth during this period.

Comtat Venaissin (kôṅ.tȧ vẹ.ne.saṅ) and **Comtat d'Avignon** (dȧ.vē.nyôṅ). Two medieval counties of S France, lying between Dauphiné on the N, Provence on the E, the Durance on the S, and the Rhône on the W. They were ceded to the popes in the 13th century by Philip III, and were united to France in 1791. They correspond nearly to the department of Vaucluse.

Comte (kôṅt), **Auguste.** [Full name, **Isidore Auguste Marie François Xavier Comte.**] b. at Montpellier, France, Jan. 19, 1798; d. at Paris, Sept. 5, 1857. French philosopher, founder of positivism. About 1818 he became a friend and disciple of Saint-Simon, whose doctrines he expounded in a work entitled *Système de politique positive* (1822). This friendship terminated in a complete estrangement in 1824, but the trend of Comte's philosophical thought can be traced to this early association. Comte, who originated the term "sociology," proposed social reforms which would promote harmony and the well-being of individuals and nations. He developed his thought further in *Cours de philosophie positive* (1830–42), *Catéchisme positiviste* (1852), *Le Système de politique positive*, and *Synthèse subjective* (1856). Comte was a tutor at the École Polytechnique from 1832 to 1851.

Comte de Boursoufle (kôṅt dẹ bör.söfl), **Le.** Comedy by Voltaire, first produced as *Quand est-ce qu'on me marie?* It was privately performed for the first time under that title at the Château de Cirey in 1734, and again in 1747 at the Château d'Anet. It was produced (1862) at the Odéon, Paris, as *Le Comte de Boursoufle* as a posthumous play of Voltaire. It was really made from the broader parts of John Vanbrugh's *Relapse*. The hero, the Comte de Boursoufle, is a Gallicized Lord Foppington.

Comte de Monte Cristo (kôṅt dẹ môṅ.tā krēs.tō), **Le.** [English, **The Count of Monte Cristo.**] Novel by the elder Alexandre Dumas, first published in the period 1844–45. It takes its title from the assumed name of its hero, whose original name is Edmond Dantès. He has been unjustly imprisoned in the Château d'If by his enemies Fernand, Villefort, and Danglars. His position looks hopeless but, as the book opens, he perpetrates a daring escape by feigning death and letting himself be lowered into the sea. One of his fellow prisoners has told Dantès about a fabulous treasure buried on the island of Monte Cristo. Dantès finds and possesses himself of all this wealth and then, under his assumed and somewhat mysterious identity, proceeds to hunt down his enemies and reward his well-wishers.

Comte Ory (kôṅt *o*.rē), **Le.** Opera in two acts by Rossini, with libretto by Scribe and Delestre-Poirson, produced in French at Paris, on Aug. 20, 1828, and at London in Italian (Feb. 28, 1829) and in French (June 20, 1849). Both words and music were adaptations of works by the same authors written some years before.

Comtesse de Rudolstadt (kôṅ.tes dẹ rü.dol.stȧt), **La.** Novel by George Sand, published in 1844, a sequel to *Consuelo.*

Comtesse d'Escarbagnas (kôṅ.tes des.kȧr.bȧ.nyȧs), **La.** Comedy by Molière, first played (1691) for the king at St.-Germain. The next year it was performed at Paris on Feb. 2. It is a study of French provincial manners in the late 17th century.

Comum (kō'mum). Latin name of **Como, city.**

Comus (kō'mus). In late Roman mythology, the god of mirth and drunken revelry, represented as a white-clad winged youth carrying a torch.

Comus. Masque by John Milton, presented at Ludlow Castle, on Sept. 29, 1634, before the Earl of Bridgewater. It was first printed in 1637, and was included in Milton's works in 1645. Milton is said to be indebted to John Fletcher's *Faithful Shepherdess* for the lyrical portions, and for its central situation to George Peele's *Old Wives' Tale*. The elder George Colman produced an alteration of it at Covent Garden in 1773.

Comyn (kum'in), **Alexander.** [Title, 2nd Earl of **Buchan.**] d. 1289. Constable of Scotland; father of John Comyn (d. c1313).

Comyn, John. [Called **"the Black."**] d. c1300. Scottish noble, lord of Badenoch, and claimant to the Scottish throne; father of John Comyn (d. 1306). He laid claim to the Scottish throne after the death of Margaret (the Maid of Norway), but subsequently submitted to Edward I and advanced the successful claim of John de Baliol, his brother-in-law.

Comyn, John. [Called **"the Red."**] d. 1306. Scottish noble and claimant to the throne; son of John Comyn (d. c1300). He was murdered by Robert I (Robert the Bruce). With John de Baliol he resisted Edward I.

Comyn, John. [Title, 3rd Earl of **Buchan.**] b. in Scotland; d. in England, c1313. Scottish soldier; son of Alexander Comyn (d. 1289). He lost his estates as a result of his support of Edward I against Robert I (Robert the Bruce) of Scotland. His support of Edward ended with his alliance (1299–1306) with Robert. The murder (1306) of his cousin, John Comyn, by Robert caused him again to take up Edward's cause, despite his wife's crowning of Bruce as Robert I in 1306. Defeated (1308) by Robert at Inverury, he fled to England.

Comynes (ko.mēn), **Philippe de.** See **Comines** or **Commines** or **Commynes** or **Comynes Philippe de.**

Conachar (kon'ą.ċhär). Son of the chief of Clan Quhele in Sir Walter Scott's *The Fair Maid of Perth*. After becoming the chief himself, he realized that he was a coward, and killed himself in despair.

Conaire Mor (kon'ę.ri môr). High king of Ireland, said by the Old Irish chroniclers to have ruled c113–43 B.C.: hero of *The Destruction of Da Derga's Hostel*, one of the most famous epic stories in Old Irish literature. Conaire met his tragic death fighting off a raid of pirates on Ireland, the tragedy of the story lying in the fact that he was tricked by the *sidhe* (the supernaturals of Ireland) into breaking in one night all nine of the magical injunctions which had been placed upon him, and to break which meant death for him. Sir Samuel Ferguson's long poem *Conary* is based on this story.

Conakry (kon'ą.kri). [Also, **Konakri.**] Capital of French Guinea, French West Africa, on a peninsula forming the E side of the estuary of the Konkouré River. It is the terminus of the railway line to Kankan in the interior. The port has excellent wharf accommodations. 32,200 (1945).

Conant (kō'nạnt), **Charles Arthur.** b. at Winchester, Mass., July 2, 1861; d. at Havana, Cuba, July 5, 1915. American economic adviser. Financial correspondent (1889–1901) on the New York *Journal of Commerce* and the Springfield *Republican*, he was a delegate (1896) to the Gold Democratic Convention. In 1901 he was appointed by McKinley to investigate the monetary system of the Philippines. He was treasurer, subsequently (1902–06), of the Morton Trust Company at New York. In 1903 he went to Mexico as adviser in changing to a gold monetary system, and was a member (1903) of the Commission on International Exchange. Official delegate (1910, 1912) to the International Conference on Bills of Exchange at The Hague, Netherlands, he also assisted (1911–12) Nicaragua in currency reform and aided (c1915) Cuba in a similar enterprise. His journalistic career was begun on the Boston *Post*. Author of *A History of Modern Banks of Issue* (1896), *The United States in the Orient* (1900), *The Nature of the Economic Problem* (1900), *Wall Street and the Country* (1904), *Principles of Money and Banking* (2 vols., 1905), *Banking System of Mexico* (1910), and *National Bank of Belgium* (1910).

Conant, Hannah O'Brien. [Maiden name, **Chaplin.**] b. at Danvers, Mass., Sept. 5, 1809; d. at Brooklyn, N.Y., Feb. 18, 1865. American writer; wife of Thomas Jefferson Conant. Her chief work is *History of the English Bible* (1856).

Conant, James Bryant. b. at Dorchester, Mass., March 26, 1893—. American chemist, educator, and president (1933 *et seq.*) of Harvard University. A graduate (B.A., 1913; Ph.D., 1916) of Harvard, he became a member of the chemistry department there in 1916, served (1918) in World War I as a major in the Chemical Warfare Service, and returned to Harvard to become (1927) professor of chemistry. In World War II, he was chairman (1941–46) of the National Defense Research Committee, advising the government on scientific matters, most notably the atomic bomb. In 1946 he was appointed to the committee established to advise the Atomic Energy Commission, and in 1951 to the advisory committee to the director of defense mobilization. His administration at Harvard has reflected his firm opposition to too narrow specialization in education. In 1950 he became chairman of the Carnegie Foundation for the Advancement of Teaching. He became (1953) U.S. high commissioner for Germany. He is the author of *Organic Chemistry* (1928), *The Chemistry of Organic Compounds* (1933), *Our Fighting Faith* (1942), *General Education in a Free Society* (1945), *On Understanding Science* (1947), *Education in a Divided World* (1948), *Growth of the Experimental Sciences* (1949), and *Science and Common Sense* (1951).

Conant, Roger. b. at East Budleigh, England, c1592; d. Nov. 19, 1679. English colonist in America. Arrived (1623) in Massachusetts, he settled (1624) at Nantasket. In 1625 he was governor of the colony established by the Dorchester Company on Cape Ann. He moved to Naumkeag in 1626 and there served as governor until superseded (1628) by John Endicott.

Conant, Thomas Jefferson. b. at Brandon, Vt., Dec. 13, 1802; d. at Brooklyn, N.Y., April 30, 1891. American Baptist clergyman and Biblical critic; husband of Hannah O'Brien Conant. He translated Gesenius's Hebrew grammar (1839), and published annotated versions of the books of Job (1857), Matthew (1860), and Genesis (1868, 1873), and *New Testament, Common Version revised* (1871), *Historical Books of the Old Testament* (1884), and others.

Conary (kon'ą.ri). See under **Conaire Mor.**

Conaty (kon'ą.ti), **Thomas James.** b. in Ireland, Aug. 1, 1847; d. Sept. 18, 1915. American Roman Catholic prelate, bishop of Monterey and Los Angeles, Calif., from 1903. He was ordained to the priesthood in 1872, was pastor of the Church of the Sacred Heart at Worcester, Mass. (1880–97), and in 1896 was appointed rector of the Catholic University at Washington. He was consecrated titular bishop of Samos in 1901. In 1892 he helped to establish the Catholic summer school at Plattsburg, N.Y., of which he was president until 1896.

Concan (kōng'kạn). See **Konkan.**

Concarneau (kôṅ.kår.nō). Town in W France, in the department of Finistère, situated on the Atlantic coast (Baie de la Forêt) ab. 12 mi. SE of Quimper. It is a port for the sardine and tuna fishery and has fish and vegetable canning establishments and a fine bathing beach. 10,519 (1946).

Concepción (kōn.sep.syōn'). Province in C Chile. The principal product is wheat. Capital, Concepción; area, 2,201 sq. mi.; pop. 380,172 (est. 1950).

Concepción. Capital of Concepción province, in C Chile, on the Bío Bío River near its mouth on the Pacific. It is a rail center and port for coal and about half the country's grain and livestock. Founded 1541, it has been subject to destructive earthquakes, notably one in 1939 after which practically the whole city had to be rebuilt. 85,813 (1940).

Concepción. Department in C Paraguay. Capital, Concepción; area, 10,339 sq. mi.; pop. 44,304 (est. 1945).

Concepción. [Also, **Villa Concepción.**] City in C Paraguay, capital of Concepción department, on the Paraguay River. It is a marketing center for cattle and maté and has cotton gins and flour mills. 16,487 (est. 1945).

Concepción de la Vega (dā lä ʙā'gä). See **La Vega,** city.

Concepción del Río Cuarto (del rē'ō kwär'tō). Full name of **Río Cuarto,** Argentina.

Concepción del Uruguay (del ö.rö.gwī'). [Former name, **Arroyo de China.**] City in E Argentina, in Entre Ríos province, ab. 150 mi. N of Buenos Aires: rail center and river port for meat and agricultural products. 31,498 (1947).

Conception Bay. Inlet of the Atlantic Ocean deeply indenting the Avalon Peninsula of SE Newfoundland. It is separated from Trinity Bay to the N by a long peninsula of land.

Conception of God, The. Philosophic work (1897) by Josiah Royce.

Conceptistas (kōn.thep.tēs′täs). School of 17th-century Spanish writers whose works, in both prose and verse, were characterized by an extensive use of puns and metaphors. Many of the members were mystics. Among the leading figures in it were Alonso de Ledesma Buitrago (whose poem *Conceptos Espirituales*, in 1600, is considered to have been one of the first works of the school) and the satirical writer Francisco Gómez de Quevedo y Villegas.

Concha (kōn′chä), **José Gutiérrez de la.** See **Gutiérrez de la Concha, José.**

Concha, Manuel de la. [Title, Marqués de **Duero.**] b. at Córdoba, Argentina, April 25, 1808; killed at the battle of Muro, Spain, June 28, 1874. Spanish general; brother of José Gutiérrez de la Concha.

Conchagua (kōn.chä′gwä), **Gulf** or **Bay of.** Former name of **Fonseca, Gulf of.**

Conchita (kông.kē′tä). Opera in four acts by Riccardo Zandonai, with a libretto by Maurizio Vaucaire and Carlo Zangarini, first performed at Milan on Oct. 14, 1911. The text is taken from Pierre Louÿs' *La Femme et le pantin.*

Conchobar (kon.kō′bär). In the Ulster, or Ultonian, cycle of Old Irish epics and romances, king of Ulster about the beginning of the Christian era. His surname was macNessa, meaning son of Nessa. At the birth of a certain girl-child, Deirdre, the Druids prophesied that she would bring ruin to Ireland. For this reason Conchobar had her brought up in solitude and confinement, but planned to marry her when she was grown. However, she met and fell in love with Naoise, eldest of the three sons of Usnach, who, with his two brothers, escaped with her to Scotland. Conchobar lured them back to Ireland with false promises, and killed the three sons of Usnach. Conchobar was also the uncle and guardian of the hero Cuchulain. In Christian legend, Conchobar is said to have died the same day Christ was crucified, in a fit of rage and protest at the news.

Conchos (kōn′chōs). [Also, **Conchas** (-chäs).] River in NE Mexico, in Chihuahua state. It empties into the Rio Grande from the S. The name was given to the river on account of the many shells found on its shores. The now extinct tribe of Conchos Indians afterward derived its name from the stream.

Conciergerie (kôn.syerzh.rē), **La.** Old prison of the Palais de Justice at Paris. When the palace, which was originally fortified, was inhabited by the kings of France, the part of the building containing the home of the concierge of the palace received this name. Distinguished personages occupied this office, which, in 1348, was called the "concierge-bailli" (it existed till the Revolution, and was one of great responsibility). Among other things, the concierge had charge of all royal prisoners. The Conciergerie became widely known during the Reign of Terror. Three hundred and twenty-eight prisoners were put to death there in one week. The cell occupied by Marie Antoinette was destroyed by the Communards in 1871, but the prison continued to exist.

Concini (kōn.chē′nē), **Concino.** Original name of **Ancre, Marquis d'.**

Concio (kōn′chō), **Giacomo** (or **Jacopo**). See **Aconcio** or **Aconzio, Giacomo** (or **Jacopo**).

Conclusions of the Astrolabe, The. See **Astrolabe, The Treatise on the.**

Concone (kông.kō′nā), **Giuseppe.** b. at Turin, Italy, 1810; d. there, in June, 1861. Italian teacher of singing, remembered for his books of solfeggi. He lived (1832 *et seq.*) at Paris until the revolution of 1848 forced him to return to Turin, where he became organist at the chapel royal.

Concord (kong′kọrd). Town in W central California, in Contra Costa County, in the Walnut Creek valley ab. 25 NE of San Francisco. Farm products and oil are produced in the area. In the decade between the last two U.S. censuses its population rose from 1,373 (1940) to 6,953 (1950).

Concord. Town (in Massachusetts the equivalent of township in many other states) and unincorporated village in E Massachusetts, in Middlesex County, on the Concord River ab. 17 mi. NW of Boston. It is known in the history of literature as the home of Ralph Waldo Emerson, Nathaniel Hawthorne, Henry David Thoreau, and other men of letters, often called the Concord Group. The bridge over Concord River was the scene, April 19, 1775, of an engagement between British troops and Concord minutemen in the Revolutionary War. Concord was the center of the Transcendentalist movement in the 1830's, and later the seat of the so-called Concord school of philosophy led by Bronson Alcott. Pop. of town, 8,623 (1950); of village, 2,299 (1950).

Concord. City in C New Hampshire, capital of New Hampshire and county seat of Merrimack County, on the Merrimack River. It is a railway center; industries include quarrying of granite, printing and publishing, and silverware manufacture. From 1733 to 1765 it was called Rumford. It became a city in 1853. Nearby is St. Paul's School. Franklin Pierce had his law office and home at Concord, and the site of the birthplace of Mary Baker Eddy (1821–1910) is near here. 27,988 (1950).

Concord (kon′kôrd). City in W North Carolina, county seat of Cabarrus County, ab. 18 mi. NE of Charlotte: manufactures include cotton textiles, cottonseed oil, lumber, flour, hosiery, and mattresses. It is the seat of Barber-Scotia College. 16,486 (1950).

Concord. A former name of **Clarkston.**

Concord (kong′kọrd), **Battle of.** One of the opening skirmishes of the American Revolutionary War. A body of 800 British soldiers under Lieutenant-Colonel Smith and Major Pitcairn, detailed to destroy military stores at Concord, Mass., met there, on April 19, 1775, after a slight engagement at Lexington, an armed force of some 450 provincial troops under Major John Buttrick. After a brisk fusillade, in which several on both sides were killed and wounded, the British retreated toward Boston by way of Lexington, being harassed by the provincials on the road till the retreat became a rout.

Concordancia (kōng.kôr.ᴛʜän′syä). Alliance of moderate and extreme conservatives in the Argentine government which resulted in the election (September, 1937) of Roberto M. Ortiz and Ramón S. Castillo as president and vice-president, respectively.

Concordat of 1801. Agreement concluded on July 15, 1801, between Napoleon Bonaparte (then first consul) and Pope Pius VII. It reëstablished the Roman Catholic Church in France, and granted to the government the right of appointing archbishops and bishops, who were to be confirmed by the Pope. It went into operation on April 8, 1802, and was abrogated by the passage of the Briand bill, on Dec. 6, 1905, except in Alsace and Lorraine, where it continued operative.

Concordat of 1855. Agreement concluded at Vienna, on Aug. 18, 1855, between Franz Joseph of Austria and Pope Pius IX. It gave the clergy control of public instruction, and placed cases of the canon law, especially marriage affairs, under the jurisdiction of ecclesiastical courts. It was abrogated in July, 1870.

Concordat of Francis I. Convention concluded in 1516 between Francis I of France and Pope Leo X. It replaced the pragmatic sanction of Bourges, a modification of the reformatory decrees of the Council of Basel, which had been adopted at the Assembly of Bourges in 1438, but which had never been recognized by the Pope. It reestablished the *annates* (a fee on a bishopric payable to the Pope), referred the *causae majores* to Rome, and gave to the king the right of nominating bishops, subject to papal confirmation.

Concordat of Worms (wėrmz; German, vôrms). Convention concluded in 1122 between the emperor Henry V and Pope Calixtus II. The main point at issue between the emperors and the popes, the matter of the election of bishops and abbots, was settled in favor of the spiritual power, the concordat providing that the investiture should be conferred not with the ring and staff, but with the scepter. It was provided that the election should take place in the presence of the emperor or his representatives, that investiture by the emperor should precede consecration, and that ecclesiastics holding secular benefices should perform feudal services. This instrument put an end to the contest regarding investiture between the emperor and the Pope, and became a fundamental ordinance of the Holy Roman Empire.

Concorde (kôn.kord), **Place de la.** See **Place de la Concorde.**

Concord Group (kong'kord). Term applied to a loosely associated number of writers and other intellectuals who at one time or another lived at Concord, Mass., during the period familiarly known as "the flowering of New England." Among them were Ralph Waldo Emerson, Henry David Thoreau, William Ellery Channing, Amos Bronson Alcott, and Nathaniel Hawthorne.

Concordia (kōng.kôr'ᴛʜyä). City in E Argentina, in Entre Ríos province, ab. 220 mi. N of Buenos Aires: shipping center for preserved meat, grain, maté, quebracho, and leather. 52,213 (1947).

Concordia (kon.kôr'di.ạ). City in N Kansas, county seat of Cloud County, on the Republican River: flour mills and creameries. 7,175 (1950).

Concordia. In Roman mythology, the goddess of harmony and peace. There were several temples to her at Rome, the one on the Capitoline Hill dating from 367 B.C. She is represented as a buxom matron with an olive branch in her right hand, the cornucopia in her left.

Concordia Española del Perú (kōng.kôr'ᴛʜyä es.pä-nyō'lä del pā.rö'), Marqués **de la.** Title of **Abascal y Sousa, José Fernando.**

Concordia sulla Secchia (kông.kôr'dyä söl.lä sāk'kyä). Town and commune in N Italy, in the *compartimento* (region) of Emilia-Romagna, in the province of Modena, situated on the Secchia River, N of Modena. Pop. of commune, 11,143 (1936); of town, 1,341 (1936).

Concord River (kong'kord). River in NE Massachusetts, formed at Concord, Mass., by the junction of the Sudbury and Assabet rivers, and flowing generally N to join the Merrimack River at Lowell, Mass. Length, ab. 16 mi.

Concord Village. Former name of **Acton,** Mass.

Condamine (kôn.dà.mēn). See **La Condamine.**

Condamine, Charles Marie de La. See **La Condamine, Charles Marie de.**

Condate (kon.dā'tē). An ancient name of **Cognac,** of **Cosne,** and of **Rennes,** all in France.

Condé (kôn.dā), **Anne Geneviève de Bourbon-.** See **Longueville,** Duchesse **de.**

Condé, Prince **de.** [Title of **Louis I de Bourbon.**] b. at Vendôme, France, May 7, 1530; d. March 13, 1569. French general, first Prince de Condé; younger brother of Antoine de Bourbon, king of Navarre. He was one of the leaders in the conspiracy of Amboise, the object of which was to remove Francis II from the influence of the Guises. At the accession of Charles IX he was appointed governor of Picardy by Catherine de Médicis. On the massacre of the Huguenots at Vassy by the duke of Guise in 1562, he placed himself at the head of a Huguenot army, with the result that he was, after some preliminary successes, captured at the battle of Dreux, being, however, liberated in 1563 by the treaty of Amboise. He was captured at the battle of Jarnac, when, after having surrendered his sword, he was treacherously shot by a Catholic officer.

Condé, Prince **de.** [Title of **Henri I de Bourbon.**] b. at Ferté-sous-Jouarre, France, Dec. 7, 1552; poisoned at St.-Jean-d'Angély, France, March 5, 1588. French Protestant leader; son of the first Prince de Condé (1530–69).

Condé, Prince **de.** [Title of **Henri II de Bourbon.**] b. at St.-Jean-d'Angély, France, Sept. 1, 1588; d. at Paris, in December, 1646. Son of Henri I de Bourbon, Prince de Condé, and father of Louis II of Bourbon, Prince de Condé ("the Great Condé"). He headed a revolt against the regency during the minority of Louis XIII, in consequence of which he was imprisoned for three years at Vincennes. He subsequently became a partisan of Richelieu.

Condé, Prince **de.** [Title of **Louis II de Bourbon;** called **the Great Condé.**] b. at Paris, Sept. 8, 1621; d. at Fontainebleau, France, Dec. 11, 1686. French general, called during the lifetime of his father (Henry II de Bourbon, Prince de Condé) the Duc d'Enghien. In the Thirty Years' War he defeated the Spaniards at Rocroi on May 19, 1643, the forces of the Holy Roman Empire at Nördlingen on Aug. 3, 1645, and the Spaniards at Lens on Aug. 20, 1648. In the war of the Fronde he was at first loyal to the regency, but subsequently joined the Fronde. He defeated the army of the court at Bléneau on April 7, 1652, obtained in the same year the chief command of the Spanish army in the war against France, was condemned as a traitor by the Parliament of Paris, but was pardoned and restored to his dignities by the treaty of the Pyrenees in 1659. He conquered Franche-Comté in 1668, fought a drawn battle with the Prince of Orange at Seneffe in 1674, and succeeded Turenne as commander of the army of the Rhine in 1675.

Condé, Prince **de.** [Title of **Henri Jules de Bourbon.**] b. at Paris, July 29, 1643; d. there, April 1, 1709. French soldier; only son of Louis II de Bourbon, Prince de Condé ("the Great Condé"). He served with distinction at the siege of Tournai in 1667, and in 1674 participated in the battle of Seneffe, on which occasion he is said to have saved his father's life.

Condé, Prince **de.** [Title of **Louis Joseph de Bourbon.**] b. at Paris, Aug. 9, 1736; d. at Paris, May 13, 1818. French general; son of Louis Henri, Duc de Bourbon. He entered the army at the beginning of the Seven Years' War, became lieutenant general in 1758, an l won a victory at Johannisberg, Germany, in 1762. During the popular agitation which preceded the French Revolution he strenuously opposed all measures designed to limit the privileges of the nobility and the clergy. He emigrated in 1789, and organized a corps of emigrants, with which he joined the Austrian army in 1792. After the peace of Campo Formio (1797), he served with his corps in the Russian army until the withdrawal of Paul I from the coalition against France in 1800, when he reëntered the Austrian service. Compelled by the peace of Lunéville to disband his corps, he retired to England, whence he returned to France on the restoration in 1814. Author of *Essai sur la vie du grand Condé* (1806).

Condé, Prince **de.** [Title of **Louis Henri Joseph de Bourbon.**] b. 1756; d. Aug. 27, 1830. French emigré; son of Louis Joseph de Bourbon, Prince de Condé (1736–1818). At the time of the French Revolution he accompanied his father in flight from France, and was an officer of the emigré army which sought to undo the Revolution. Years later, during the Hundred Days (March 20–June 28, 1815) following Napoleon's return from Elba, he led an abortive insurrection in the Vendée. On Aug. 27, 1830, he was found dead by hanging, supposedly a suicide. He was the last prince of Condé.

Condé, Princesse **de.** [Title of **Louise Adélaïde de Bourbon.**] b. at Chantilly, France, Oct. 5, 1757; d. at Paris, March 10, 1824. Daughter of Louis Joseph de Bourbon, Prince de Condé (1736–1818). She became abbess of Remiremont in 1786, emigrated at the beginning of the French Revolution, and in 1815 returned to Paris, where she subsequently founded the religious order of "l'adoration perpetuelle."

Condé, Fort. Name given (1720 *et seq.*) to the second Fort Louis de la Mobile built (1711) by the French at the site of what is now Mobile, Ala. In 1763 it came into the possession of the British, who designated it Fort Charlotte.

Conde (kōn'dā), **José Antonio.** b. at Paraleja, Cuenca, Spain, c1765; d. at Madrid, Oct. 20, 1820. Spanish Orientalist and historian. He studied at the University of Alcalá de Henares, and obtained a subordinate position in the royal library. Having in 1808 identified himself with the French party, he was soon after promoted to librarian in chief by Joseph Bonaparte. He was exiled on the departure of the French, but returned in 1818 or 1819. His best-known work is *Historia de la dominación de los Árabes en España* (1820–21).

Conde Alarcos (kōn'dā ä.lär'kōs). Old Spanish ballad of unknown authorship, recounting the pseudohistorical deeds of Count Alarcos. Sir John Bowring and John Gibson Lockhart both translated it into English, and Disraeli wrote (1839) a tragedy with this subject and title.

Condell or **Cundell** (kun'dẹl), **Henry.** d. at Fulham, England, in December, 1627. English actor, and one of the two editors of the first folio edition of Shakespeare's plays. He was a member of the Lord Chamberlain's Company of players, to which Shakespeare and Burbage also belonged, and became a partner with the Burbages in the Globe Theatre in 1599. He is mentioned in Shakespeare's will.

Condell, Henry. b. 1757; d. at Battersea, London, June 24, 1824. English violinist and composer. He wrote overtures, glees, incidental music for plays, and set various musical farces. His glee *Loud Blowe the Wynds* took the prize at the Catch Club in 1811.

Conder (kon′dėr), **Claude Reignier.** b. at Cheltenham, Gloucestershire, England, Dec. 29, 1848; d. there, Feb. 16, 1910. English army officer, noted chiefly for services (1872–78) in charge of a survey of 4,700 sq. mi. of W Palestine, resulting in discovery of the sites of many previously unidentified places whose names are mentioned in the Bible; grandson of Josiah Conder. This work has been compared in its significance with the translation of the Bible into the vulgar tongue. He was also a scholar of prehistoric, Syrian, Hittite, and Altaic cultures, and the author of *Tent Work in Palestine* (1878), *Judas Maccabaeus and the Jewish War of Independence* (1879), *Handbook to the Bible* (1879), *Syrian Stone Lore* (1886), *The Canaanites* (1887), *Altaic Hieroglyphs and Hittite Inscriptions* (1887), *The Latin Kingdom of Jerusalem* (1897), *The Hittite and Their Language* (1898), and *The Rise of Man* (1908).

Conder, Josiah. b. at London, Sept. 17, 1789; d. there, Dec. 27, 1855. English bookseller and writer; grandfather of Claude Reignier Conder (1848–1910). He edited *The Modern Traveller* (1825–29).

Condercum (kon.dėr′kum). Latin name of **Chester-le-Street.**

Condé-sur-l'Escaut (kôṅ.dā.sür.les.kō). [Also, **Condé.**] Town in N France, in the department of Nord, situated at the junction of the Hayne and Escaut (Schelde) rivers and the canal from Condé to Mons, ab. 8 mi. N of Valenciennes. It is the center of a coal-mining region and has rayon manufactures. The castle of the princes of Condé was begun in 1410. The town was subject to many sieges in former centuries, and suffered damage in World War II. 7,114 (1946).

Condé-sur-Noireau (kôṅ.dā.sür.nwȧ.rō). Town in NW France, in the department of Calvados, situated at the junction of the Noireau and Drouance rivers, ab. 25 mi. SW of Caen. It has been known for its weaving and spinning of cotton. The town was almost entirely destroyed in World War II. 4,800 (1946).

Conde-suyu (kon′dẹ.sō′yö). See **Cuntisuyu.**

Condillac (kôṅ.dē.yȧk), **Étienne Bonnot de.** b. at Grenoble, France, Sept. 30, 1715; d. near Beaugency, France, Aug. 3, 1780. French philosopher, a leading advocate of sensationalism. His works include *Essai sur l'origine des connaissances humaines* (1746), *Traité des systèmes* (1749), *Traité des sensations* (1754), *Cours d'études* (1769), *Le Commerce et le gouvernement* (1776), *La Logique* (1781), and *Langue des calculs* (1798).

Condition humaine (kôṅ.dē.syôṅ ü.men), **La.** Novel (1933; Eng. trans., *Man's Fate*, 1934) by the French writer André Malraux (1899—). The action is set in Shanghai during the Communist uprising of 1927. Central figures are the Communist organizers who, after the International has reached a compromise with Chiang Kai-shek's Nationalists, are left to face execution by the latter's troops. It has been called the first "purely tragic" novel.

Condivicnum (kon.di.vik′num). An ancient name of **Nantes.**

Condolmieri (kōn.dōl.mye′rē), **Gabriele.** Original name of Pope **Eugenius IV.**

Condom (kôṅ.dôṅ). Town in SW France, in the department of Gers, situated on the Baise River, SW of Auch. It is a trade center for the agricultural products of the region, particularly for the distilleries of Armagnac. The Cathedral of Saint Pierre is a Gothic building dating from the 16th century. 6,725 (1946).

Condon (kon′dọn), **Edward Uhler.** b. at Alamogordo, N.M., March 2, 1902—. American physicist. Graduated (B.A., 1924; Ph.D., 1926) from the University of California, he has been associate professor of physics (1930–37) at Princeton, associate director (1937–45) of the Westinghouse research laboratories, and director (1945–51) of the National Bureau of Standards. He is the author, with P. M. Morse, of *Quantum Mechanics* (1929), and, with G. H. Shortley, of *Theory of Atomic Spectra* (1935).

Condorcet (kôṅ.dôr.se), Marquis **de.** [Title of **Marie Jean Antoine Nicolas Caritat.**] b. at Ribemont, in Picardy, France, Sept. 17, 1743; d. at Bourg-la-Reine, near Paris, April 7, 1794. French social philosopher and revolutionist. Of aristocratic lineage, Condorcet was brought up in the conservative, religious atmosphere of France under the Old Regime. Nevertheless he became an enthusiastic champion of the radical political, social, and religious ideas of Voltaire, Turgot, and Rousseau. Condorcet was the one outstanding *philosophe* who lived to become active in the French Revolution. He was elected in 1791 to the Legislative Assembly, and in 1792 to the National Convention. Though an independent he sided with the Girondists in favoring a democratic republic. During the Reign of Terror he was proscribed, along with the Girondists, as being opposed to the terroristic methods of the Jacobins. His arrest was ordered, but he cheated the guillotine by dying in prison, probably a suicide.

Contributions as Social Philosopher. Condorcet wrote many books and pamphlets, of which the most famous is *Esquisse d'un tableau historique des progrès de l'esprit humain.* His views were typical of the radical thought of 18th-century France. He was an anticlerical in religion, a constitutionalist in politics, a physiocrat in economics, and a pacifist and anti-imperialist in international relations. What gives him special distinction is that he anticipated the democratic liberalism of the 20th century. Condorcet advocated not only manhood suffrage but also woman suffrage. He favored equal rights of men and women, civil marriage, and birth control. Opposed to the Roman Catholic Church, he favored separation of church and state. He advocated social security legislation in the interest of the poor. In his report on education to the Legislative Assembly he recommended the establishment of a system of public elementary education on a coeducational basis, and urged that it be compulsory, free, and secular. These schools were to stress the teaching of the natural and social sciences. In the field of sociology the *Esquisse* has an important place. It is an outline of human progress from primitive times to the French Revolution, wherein the modern idea of progress toward "perfectibility" was, for the first time, clearly stated and developed. The book is typical of the altruism and the optimism of 18th-century thought. It roused great interest, and led Malthus to reply in his famous *Essay on the Principle of Population.* See *Condorcet and the Rise of Liberalism in France* (1934), by J. Salwyn Schapiro.

Conduct of Life, The. Essays by Ralph Waldo Emerson, published in 1860.

Conduitt (kun′dit), **John.** b. at London, 1688; d. there, May 23, 1737. English financier and economist, the successor of Sir Isaac Newton as master of the mint (1727); Newton's nephew by marriage.

Condulmer (kon′dul.mėr), **Gabriel.** See Pope **Eugenius IV.**

Cone (kōn), **Helen Gray.** b. at New York, March 8, 1859; d. Jan. 31, 1934. American poet, professor of English (1899–1926) at Hunter College. She was the author of *Oberon and Puck: Verses Grave and Gay* (1885), *The Ride to the Lady, and other Poems* (1891), *Soldiers of the Light* (1910), and *A Chant of Love for England, and Other Poems* (1915).

Cone, Hutchinson Ingham. b. at Brooklyn, N.Y., April 26, 1871; d. Feb. 12, 1941. American naval officer. Graduated (1894) from the U.S. Naval Academy at Annapolis, he served (May 1, 1898) on the *Baltimore* during the battle of Manila Bay in the Spanish-American War, was fleet engineer (1908–09) for the Atlantic fleet on its round-the-world voyage, and was named (1909) rear admiral and chief engineer of the Bureau of Steam Engineering. In World War I he headed (1917–18) the U.S. naval aviation forces in service abroad, and was injured (1918) in the sinking of the *Leinster* by a German submarine in the Irish Sea. Retired from the navy in 1922, he served (to 1925) as vice-president and general manager of the U.S. Shipping Board, later as its commissioner (1928).

Cone, Spencer Houghton. b. at Princeton, N.J., April 30, 1785; d. Aug. 28, 1855. American Baptist clergyman. After careers as an actor (1805–12) and as a journalist (1812–14), he was converted (1814) to Baptism. He was pastor (1816–23) of the Baptist Church at Alexandria, associated (1823–41) with the Oliver Street Church at New York, and pastor (1841–55) of the First Baptist Church at New York. He served as president (1832–41) of the Baptist General Convention, founder and president

(1837–50) of the American and Foreign Bible Society, and president (1850 *et seq.*) of the American Bible Union.

Conecte or **Connecte** (ko.nekt), **Thomas.** b. at Rennes, France, in the latter part of 14th century; burned at Rome, 1433. French Carmelite monk, famous as a preacher of moral reforms among the clergy and laity. He was put to death on a charge of heresy.

Conecuh (kǫ.nā'ku). See under **Escambia.**

Conegliano (kō.nā.lyä'nō). Town and commune in NE Italy, in the *compartimento* (region) of Veneto, in the province of Treviso, situated in the foothills of the Alps, N of Treviso. The district has good harvests in grain and many mulberry trees. Cattle and horses are raised and excellent white and red wines are produced; there are silk and cotton textile mills and furniture industries. There is a school of viticulture. The old walls of the town are preserved; there are a number of medieval and Renaissance palaces and churches, among them the Montalban Palace. The cathedral contains a painting by Giovanni Battista Cima (Cima da Conegliano), who was born here. Formerly under Hungarian, Austrian, and Venetian rule, in World War I the town was occupied by the Austrian army in the period 1917–18. Except for the Church of San Martino, buildings of interest to tourists were undamaged in World War II. Pop. of commune, 15,434 (1936); of town, 7,544 (1936).

Conegliano, Cima da. See **Cima, Giovanni Battista** or **Giambattista.**

Conegliano, Duc de. Title of **Moncey, Bon Adrien Jeannot de.**

Conemaugh (kon'ę.mô). River in SW Pennsylvania, formed at Johnstown, Pa., by the confluence of Stony Creek and the Little Conemaugh River, and flowing generally NW to join Loyalhanna Creek, forming the Kiskiminetas River. On May 31, 1889, an earth dam across South Fork, a tributary of the Little Conemaugh, broke, and a devastating flood swept down the valley with a crest ab. 40 ft. high, causing a loss of ab. 2,235 lives, and tremendous property damage, particularly at Johnstown. Length, ab. 51 mi.

Conendiú Cataract (kō.nen.dyö'). See **Guayra Falls.**

Conestoga (kon.ęs.tō'gą). North American Indian tribe, now extinct, formerly inhabiting the region of the lower Susquehanna River and upper Chesapeake Bay in Pennsylvania. The last surviving members of the tribe were exterminated by the whites, in the Conestoga Massacre, in 1763. The language was of the Iroquoian family.

Conestoga Massacre. Mass murder (December, 1763) of some 20 Conestoga Indians (the last members of this particular tribe) in Lancaster County, Pa., carried out by the vigilante group known as the "Paxton Boys." The massacre was touched off by resentment against raids made by other Indians of the vicinity.

Conestoga Wagon. Large canvas-topped vehicle of sturdy construction, drawn by four to six horses, the driver usually riding the left wheel horse. They were used as early as c1750 but more frequently after the American Revolution, when they were employed by emigrants bound for the trans-Allegheny regions. The type originated in colonial America, among the Pennsylvania Dutch, and was the predecessor of the "prairie schooner" used in settling the U.S. West after c1820. Among the characteristic marks of the Conestoga Wagon are its broad wheels, its high ends, and its color scheme (upper portions painted red, the lower ones painted blue).

Conewango (kon.ę.wong'gō). Creek in W New York and Pennsylvania. It is the outlet of Chautauqua Lake, and joins the Allegheny River at Warren, Pa.

Coney Island (kō''ni ī'lạnd). [Old Dutch name, **Konynen Eyland,** meaning "Rabbit Island."] Popular amusement resort in New York City, in the borough of Brooklyn, and located off the S coast of Long Island. Formerly an island 5 mi. in length, it has been linked with the rest of Brooklyn by the natural filling in of Coney Island Creek. It is probably the most famous and popular summer amusement resort in the U.S., and has a 2-mi. boardwalk, a public beach, two amusement parks, and numerous restaurants. On a hot summer day it is visited by an estimated 1,500,000 persons. It was named (1682), by Dutch settlers of the region, for the many rabbits then found on it. It began its history as a summer resort in 1814 when the first bathhouse and pavilion were erected.

Confederação do Equador (kōṅ.fā''dę.rą.souṅ' dö ē.kwą-dōr'). [Eng. trans., "*League of the Equator.*"] Name given to a political league formed at Pernambuco (now Recife), Brazil, in 1824, with the object of throwing off allegiance to the emperor and establishing a republic. The revolt was proclaimed by Manuel de Carvalho Paes de Andrade and his associates on July 2, 1824. The provinces (now states) of Rio Grande do Norte, Ceará, and Paraíba adhered to it, and Carvalho was made acting president. The revolutionists were conquered after some fighting in October, 1824.

Confederación Centro-Americana (kōn.fā''ᴛʜā.rä.syōn' sen''trō.ä.mä.rē.kä'nä). [English, **Central American Confederation**; often called the **"Pacto de Chinandega."**] Political league formed at Chinandega, Nicaragua, on July 27, 1842, by the delegates of Nicaragua, Honduras, and El Salvador. It was the result of an attempt to reunite the states of the Central American Republic, which had lately been dissolved. The scheme was to form a confederation of the states, with an executive officer called a supreme delegate, assisted by a delegate from each state. The plan was rejected by Guatemala; and though the confederacy installed a government, it was so little regarded by the states that it never had any political effect. After a year or two it was discontinued.

Confederación de Derechos Autónomos (kōn.fā''ᴛʜā-rä.thyōn' dā dā.rā'chōs ou.tō'nō.mōs). See **CEDA.**

Confederación Nacional del Trabajo (kōn.fā''ᴛʜā.rä-thyōn' nä.thyō.näl' del trä.ʙä'ʜō). See **CNT.**

Confederacy. Term commonly used to designate the Confederate States of America, the government established by 11 Southern states which announced their secession from the United States of America following the election of Abraham Lincoln to the presidency. South Carolina took the lead on Dec. 20, 1860, and was followed by Mississippi on Jan. 9, Florida on Jan. 10, Alabama on Jan. 11, Georgia on Jan. 19, Louisiana on Jan. 26, Texas on Feb. 1, Virginia on April 17, Tennessee on May 6, Arkansas on May 7, and North Carolina on May 20, all in 1861. Representatives of the first six seceding states met at Montgomery, Ala., on Feb. 4, 1861, on Feb. 8 adopted a provisional constitution and on Feb. 18 inaugurated Jefferson Davis and Alexander H. Stephens as, respectively, provisional president and vice-president. A permanent constitution was adopted on March 11, in the main following that of the U.S., but with some innovations, including special provisions for states' rights and the protection of slavery. On July 20, 1861, the capital was removed to Richmond, Va.; on Nov. 6, Davis and Stephens were confirmed in the presidency and vice-presidency, and were inaugurated for six-year terms on Feb. 22, 1862. A decision that the seceding states should take possession of U.S. property within their borders led to the bombardment and occupation of Fort Sumter in the harbor of Charleston, S.C., April 12–14, 1861. Less than four years later, on March 18, 1865, the Congress of the Confederacy adjourned for the last time. The Confederate capital, Richmond, was occupied by Union forces on April 3, and on April 9 General Lee, commanding the principal Confederate army, surrendered to General Grant. The Confederacy was from the first weaker than the North in manpower and industrial and financial resources. Moreover, despite considerable efforts to maintain trade with Europe, its commerce was slowly strangled by the Union navy. The 11 seceding states were readmitted to the Union at different times during the period 1866–70.

Confederacy, The. Comedy by Sir John Vanbrugh, produced on Oct. 30, 1705. It is a play of contrivance and intrigue, and is said to be adapted from Dancourt's *Modish Citizens* (*Bourgeois à la mode*).

Confederacy of Delos (dē'los). See **Delian League.**

Confederate Army. [Official title, **Army of the Confederate States of America.**] Regular armed force established (March 6, 1861) by act of the Confederate provisional congress. Relatively small, and hardly fashioned as an army by the outbreak of the American Civil War, it was soon relegated to secondary status by the organization of the volunteer forces or provisional army. Subsequent acts gave the Confederate president authority to accept, over a 12-month period, 100,000 volunteers and state troops. With the enactment (April, 1862) of the first conscription act, however, recruits were for the most part taken directly into the provisional force. The chief administrative units of the Confederate army were the military departments; at the head of each one was a commander who was responsible solely to the president and the war department. The absence of a unified command was a grave defect in the Confederate military machine, and it was not until the last year of the war that a military officer was chosen as commander in chief (Robert E. Lee being named to the post on Feb. 6, 1865). Perhaps the chief difficulties faced by the Confederate army were inadequate military supplies and transportation; the effectiveness of the force was also reduced by disease and desertion (the rate of desertion among the Confederate troops was aproximately equal to that prevailing among the Union forces, about 10 percent of the total number on the rolls). The highest rank in the Confederate forces was that of general, dating from its creation on May 16, 1861; among those who held this rank were Robert E. Lee, Joseph E. Johnston, and Pierre G. T. Beauregard. Accurate figures on the total number of enlistments are wholly lacking, although estimates have ranged as high as 1,500,000. Enrollments probably numbered about 900,000, although it is highly improbable that this number represented the total effective force at any given time. The number of Confederate troops who died in the war is estimated at 258,000.

Confederate Flag. [Commonly called the **"Stars and Bars."**] Official standard of the Confederacy (Confederate States of America). Properly speaking, the "Stars and Bars," the most familiar Confederate flag, was only one of three flags authorized by the Confederate congress, and was the first described by that body (March 4, 1861). The second one was officially described on May 1, 1863, and the third on March 4, 1865. The battle standard of the Confederacy was a white-bordered Greek cross of blue set against a red field, with a white star for each state.

Confederate Navy. Organized naval force of the Confederacy (Confederate States of America), established (Feb. 21, 1861) by act of the Confederate congress. The office of the secretary of the Confederate navy was occupied throughout the Civil War by Stephen Russell Mallory (1813–73), who was instrumental in securing the services of John Mercer Brooke, designer of the ironclad *Merrimack*. In addition to being credited with introducing the ironclad craft into naval warfare, the Confederate navy also anticipated modern naval weapons in improving the torpedo and using a rudimentary form of the submarine (the "David" semi-submarine). While the Confederacy was able to draw upon an adequate supply of naval personnel, it was hampered by a severe shortage of craft and of navy yards. The Confederate navy operated inland water vessels, privateers, and commissioned cruisers preying upon the foreign commerce of the U.S. government.

Confederate States of America. See **Confederacy.**

Confederation, Articles of. First instrument of government of the U.S. After the Declaration of Independence had formalized the decision of the 13 colonies to sever their link to Great Britain, it was realized that though they were associated for common action in the Continental Congress, a closer and more formal union was needed. Accordingly, articles of Confederation were drafted and, by decision of Congress on November 15, 1777, were submitted to the several states, all of which between that time and March 1, 1781, ratified them. The Articles provided for a perpetual union under the name of the United States of America. The government thus instituted was without an executive authority or a judiciary, consisting simply of a unicameral Congress, in which each state, though it might send from two to seven delegates, had one vote. The government had power to declare war and peace, to make treaties with foreign powers, to direct the land and naval forces of the nation in time of war, to make requisitions upon the separate states for their share of funds necessary for national expenses, to regulate the value of the coinage, to control the postal service, and to perform other functions; but as it had no power to enforce its laws upon the states, it was from the very outset unable adequately to cope with the problems arising from the rapid evolution of the new nation. This evident inadequacy led to the convocation of the Federal Constitutional Convention in 1787; and following the ratification of the new Constitution by nine states, the Articles of Confederation, as of March 4, 1789, ceased to have force and effect.

Confederation, Fort. Military post on the Tombigbee River in Alabama, erected (1794) by the Spanish, abandoned by them in 1797, and subsequently rebuilt and garrisoned by U.S. forces. It was not occupied after 1803.

Confédération Française des Travailleurs Chrétiens (kôṅ.fā.dā.rà.syôṅ fräṅ.sez dā trà.và.yėr krā.tyaṅ). [Eng. trans., *"French Confederation of Christian Workers"*; called **CFTC.**] French trade-union organization, founded at Paris, Nov. 1–2, 1919. Advocating protection of labor interests through the moral and social principles of Christianity, it was chiefly Catholic in membership and leadership. Its opposition to the Confédération Générale du Travail (CGT) was marked (1936–37) by a dispute over the right to represent trade-union interests under the Popular Front regime. It claimed a membership of about one million. It was dissolved (1940) by the Vichy government, and resumed legal activity after the liberation (1944) of France. Its leaders included Gaston Teissier, president, and Maurice Bouladoux, secretary-general. Its organ was the daily newspaper *Le Syndicalisme*.

Confédération Générale de l'Agriculture (zhā.nā.ràl dẹ là.grē.kül.tür). [Eng. trans., *"General Confederation of Farmers."*] French agrarian league, formed (Oct. 20–21, 1944) at Paris by representatives of the leading French farm credit and coöperative organization, the general farmer's union, and the union of farm laborers. It replaced the Corporation Paysanne ("Peasant Corporation") created (1940) by the Vichy government following dissolution of various pre-war farm organizations. Its president (1946 *et seq.*) was Martial Brousse.

Confédération Générale des Cadres (dā kàdr). [Eng. trans., *"General Confederation of Cadres."*] Organization of French employees engaged in technical, supervisory, and other leading positions in industry and government, formed on Oct. 15, 1944. It replaced various organized groups of engineers and technicians which existed before World War II. It also included traveling salesmen, public servants, and others. Its membership was estimated at about 200,000.

Confédération Générale du Travail (dü trà.vày'). [Eng. trans., *"General Confederation of Labor"*; called **CGT.**] French trade-union federation, founded (Sept. 25, 1895) at Limoges, France. At first including only the craft unions, it was joined (1902) by the *bourses du travail* (municipal labor exchanges). Syndicalist leadership and principles prevailed (1902–14) until World War I, when a majority of the organization supported the French war effort. In 1918 division of the organization into autonomous sections of craft unions and bourses du travail was brought to an end. Conflict between moderate and revolutionary elements led to the withdrawal of the latter group, which formed (1922) the Confédération Générale du Travail Unitaire. The two groups reunited (March, 1936) during the period of the Popular Front. The organization was dissolved (Nov. 9, 1940) by René Belin, a former CGT secretary who had become minister of labor in the Vichy cabinet. It was re-formed secretly, was legalized (July 27, 1944) during the liberation of France, and was split again when moderate elements withdrew to form the Confédération Générale du Travail-Force Ouvrière. It was a member (1945 *et seq.*) of the World Federation of Trade Unions. Its leaders included Léon Jouhaux (until his withdrawal to form the Force Ouvrière), and Benoît Frachon (1936 *et seq.*).

Confédération Générale du Travail-Force Ouvrière (-fôrs ö.vrē.er). [Eng. trans., *"General Confederation of Labor-Worker's Strength"*; also known as **Force Ouvrière.**] French trade-union federation, formed (Dec. 19–20, 1947) by withdrawal of conservative and Socialist trade unionists from the Confédération Générale du Travail (CGT) following a struggle with Communist leaders over strike policy. In 1948 it had about one-and-a-half million members. Its principal leaders were Léon Jouhaux, president, and Robert Bothereau, secretary-general.

Confédération Générale du Travail Unitaire (ü.nē.ter). [Eng. trans., *"Unitary General Confederation of Labor"*; called **CGTU.**] French trade-union federation, formed

(1922) by Communist-led revolutionary elements which withdrew from the Confédération Générale du Travail (CGT) after several years of struggle with moderate forces. A member of the Red International of Labor Unions, it merged with the CGT in 1936.

Confédération Nationale du Travail (nȧ.syo.nȧl dü trȧ.vȧy'). [Eng. trans., *"National Confederation of Labor."*] French trade-union federation, formed (May 4, 1946) by anarchist elements hostile to the Confédération Générale du Travail (CGT). In 1948 it had about 2,000 members.

Confederation of Free Trade Unions, International. See **International Confederation of Free Trade Unions.**

Confederation of the Rhine. League formed by the majority of the German states, under the protectorate of Napoleon I, in July, 1806. It comprised Bavaria, Württemberg, Saxony, Westphalia, Baden, Hesse-Darmstadt, and all the other minor German sovereignties excepting Brunswick and Electoral Hesse. The member states of the Confederation renounced allegiance to the Holy Roman Empire, and in the same year the ruler of Austria gave up the title of Holy Roman Emperor. After the defeat of Napoleon in Russia (1812–13), members of the Confederation turned against him, and the Confederation dissolved.

Conference Convention. [Also called: **Peace Convention** (or **Conference**), **Border Slave State Convention.**] In U.S. history, the gathering (Feb. 4–27, 1861) at Washington, D.C., of delegates from 21 states for the purpose of attaining a political formula for satisfying Southern interests and preserving the Union. Held on the eve of the Civil War, the Conference Convention, called at the invitation of the Virginia legislature, was conducted in secret at Willard's Hotel under the leadership of ex-President John Tyler. The Virginia legislature had proposed that the convention open with a consideration of the Crittenden Compromise. Successive compromises weakened broad agreement and only succeeded in sharpening differences, and the complicated proposals (representing a modification of the Crittenden Compromise) did not reach Congress until a few days before the end of the legislative session. This was the final attempt to conciliate differences over the slavery question in the territories.

Confession d'un enfant du siècle (kôṅ.fe.syôṅ dėn-näṅ.fäṅ dü syekl), **La.** [Eng. trans., *"The Confession of a Child of the Century."*] Prose work by Alfred de Musset, published in 1836. In it he says he endeavors to show how he suffered for three years from the malady of the age (doubt, disillusion, skepticism, and debauchery) and to point out to others a way of escape.

Confession of Basel (bä'zel). See **Basel, Confession of.**

Confessions (kôṅ.fe.syôṅ), **Les.** Autobiographical work by Jean Jacques Rousseau. It is in 12 volumes, six of which were written at Wootton, England (1766–67), and six in Dauphiné and at Trye, France (1768–70). It was his intention that they should not be published until 1800, as the persons alluded to in them were living; but those in charge of the manuscript published the first six volumes in 1781–82. In 1788 a new edition appeared, containing the whole.

Confessions—A Study in Pathology. Autobiographical work by Arthur Symons, published in 1930. It includes frank descriptions of his attacks of amnesia and insanity.

Confessions of an English Opium-Eater. Partly autobiographical work by Thomas De Quincey, published in 1821.

Confessions of Saint Augustine (ô'gus.tēn, ô.gus'tin), **The.** Memoirs of Saint Augustine, written by himself. They are divided into 13 books; the first 10 treat of the bad actions of his life, of his conversion, of the love of pleasure, of glory, and of science. The last three are an interpretation of the beginning of the book of Genesis.

Confessions of Ursula Trent (ėr'su.la trent'), **The.** Novel by W. L. George, published in 1921.

Confessor, the. See **Edward** (c1004–1066); see also Saints **Maximus** and **Theophanes.**

Confidence-Man: His Masquerade, The. Unfinished novel by Herman Melville, published in 1857.

Confines (kon'fīnz), **Audience of the.** [Spanish, **Audiencia de los Confines**; also called the **Audience of Guatemala.**] Supreme Spanish court of Central America. It was established in 1542, and held its first sitting at Gracias á Dios in 1545; the seat was changed to Guatemala in 1549, transferred to Panama in 1564, and returned in 1570 to Guatemala, where it remained until the revolution. Its jurisdiction at first embraced Chiapas, Yucatán, all of Central America, and the isthmus; at the end of the 16th century the isthmal portion was transferred to the new audience of Panama. The Audience of the Confines frequently appointed temporary governors.

Confinium Militare (kon.fin'i.um mil.i.tār'ē). Latin name of **Militärgrenze.**

Confins Man (kōn'fēnz). Name given to a human skeleton found, in association with the fossil bones of extinct animal forms, evidently Pleistocene, in a cave in the Lagoa Santa region of E Brazil. It is regarded by some archaeologists as representative of the early Indian population in this portion of the South American continent.

Confiscation Acts. Acts passed (1861–64) during the Civil War by both the Union and Confederate governments providing for the confiscation of private property among certain classes of hostile military and civilian populations. Virtually all of the possessions seized by Union forces under the Captured and Abandoned Property Acts (March 12, 1863, and July 2, 1864) consisted of stores of cotton.

Conflans (kôṅ.fläṅ). See also under **Albertville,** France.

Conflans, Treaty of. Treaty concluded in October, 1465, at the village of Conflans-l'Archevêque, France, between Louis XI of France and the dukes of Bourbon, Brittany, and Burgundy, according to which Normandy was ceded to the Duke of Berry, and the "War of the Public Good" ended. It was confirmed by the treaty of Péronne, 1468.

Conflans-l'Archevêque (kôṅ.fläṅ.lȧrsh.vek). Village in N France, situated 3 mi. SE of Paris. Here, in 1465, Louis XI signed what is known as the Treaty of Conflans, making certain concessions to the leaders of the "League of the Public Good."

Conflans-Ste.-Honorine (kôṅ.fläṅ.saṅ.to.no.rēn). Town in N France, in the department of Seine-et-Oise, situated at the junction of the Seine and Oise rivers, S of Pontoise. It has metallurgical and other industries. The Church of Saint Maclou dates from the 12th century, with later additions. A large part of the town was destroyed in World War II. 10,775 (1946).

Confluentes (kon.flö.en'tēz). Ancient name of **Koblenz.**

Confucianism (kon.fū'shan.iz.em). Body of concepts and precepts long and widely diffused throughout China, based on classical writings of great antiquity. K'ung Fu-tse (Confucius) was the sagest and most influential editor of these classics and expounder of their philosophy. Confucianism claims no origin in divine revelation, but, from the contemplation of man and of human society as they are, derives ethical, social, and political principles which are studied in the light of common sense, tolerance, and courtesy. The man who lives in accordance with these principles carries out the will of God, and by the observance of customs that accord with natural duties and natural rights, including respect for the rights of others, contributes to the achievement of social harmony. Himself an interpreter of ancient wisdom, Confucius has had many interpreters, most notably Mencius (372–289 B.C.) and Chu Hsi (1130–1200 A.D.). Some theological content was given Confucianism in the 2nd century B.C. through the concept of a God superior to all earthly power. At a time corresponding to the earliest Christian epoch, Confucius himself began to be an object of veneration as a saint, to whom many shrines have been erected.

Confucius (kon.fū'shus). [Latinized form of Chinese **K'ung Fu-tse;** also, **K'ung Ch'iu.**] b. in the principality of Lu (now included in Shantung province), China, 550 or 551 B.C.; d. 478 B.C. Celebrated Chinese philosopher. He was descended from an illustrious but impoverished family, and in his youth was successively keeper of stores and superintendent of parks and herds to the chief of the district in which he lived. In his twenty-second year he became a teacher, and in his fifty-second was made chief magistrate of the city of Chung-tu. He was subsequently appointed minister of crime by the Marquis of Lu, but in his fifty-sixth year retired from office in consequence of the intrigues of a neighboring prince. After 13 years of travel he returned in 483 to Lu, where he spent the rest of his life in completing his literary undertakings and in teaching. Apart from his maxims, which were recorded by his disciples, he wrote *Ch'un-chiu* (Spring and Autumn) and the *Four Books*.

Congaree (kong.ga.rē'). River in South Carolina, formed by the junction of the Broad and Saluda rivers at Columbia. It unites with the Wateree to form the Santee. Length, ab. 55 mi.

Conger (kong'gėr), **Edwin Hurd.** b. in Knox County, Ill., March 7, 1843; d. at Pasadena, Calif., May 18, 1907. American politician and diplomat. He was a Republican member of Congress (1885–91), and minister to Brazil (1891–93), and was again appointed minister to Brazil in 1897, but was transferred to China in 1898. He was at Peiping (Peking) during the siege of the legations, and conducted the negotiations on the part of the U.S. after the capture of the city by the allies.

Congleton (kong'gl.ton). Municipal borough, market town, and silk-manufacturing center in W England, in Cheshire, situated on the river Dane, ab. 9 mi. SW of Macclesfield, ab. 21 mi. S of Manchester, and ab. 157 mi. NW of London by rail. It is a part of the principal silk-manufacturing region in England, a satellite of Macclesfield, with which it is connected by canal. 15,492 (1951).

Congleton, 1st Baron. Title of **Parnell, Henry Brooke.**

Congo (kong'gō). See also **São Salvador,** Angola.

Congo. [Also: **Kongo;** Portuguese, **Zaire;** called by Stanley the **Livingstone.**] River in C Africa, one of the longest in the world. It rises as the Chambezi and Luapula rivers in the highlands separating the basins of Lakes Tanganyika and Nyasa, rounds Lake Bangweulu on the S, flows northward through Lake Mweru, and receives the Lukuga as an affluent from Lake Tanganyika. The united stream, now known as the Lualaba, flows northward to Stanley Falls, beyond the equator; from the equator to the sea, over its main course, it is called the Congo. It discharges into the Atlantic Ocean ab. 240 mi. SW of Stanley Pool. It is navigable by ocean-going vessels from its mouth to Matadi (ab. 100 mi.), and by river steamers from Stanley Pool to Stanley Falls. These two navigable sections are connected by a railroad. The Congo is second in volume to the Amazon and is, among African rivers, next to the Nile in length. Its chief tributaries are the Aruwimi, Ubangi, and Kasai rivers. It was explored by V. L. Cameron, Livingstone, Stanley, and others, in the 19th century. Length, ab. 2,900 mi.

Congo, Belgian. See **Belgian Congo.**

Congo: A Study of the Negro Race, The. Poem by Vachel Lindsay, title piece of a volume published in 1914. It attempts to delineate the spirit of the Negro people by the use of African rhythms.

Congregationalists. Religious body in the U.S., tracing its roots to the Separatist Puritans who arrived at Plymouth (1620) in the *Mayflower*. The Cambridge Platform (1648) was a formal expression of its church policy. After 1640, when the Puritan influx into the New England colonies increased, Congregationalism enjoyed a steady growth and played an important role in the social and cultural development of New England and, subsequently, other regions of the U.S., notably the Ohio country. Social and theological differences brought about the shift of many Congregationalist bodies to Presbyterianism before and after the American Revolution; in 1819–20 a New England group under the leadership of William Ellery Channing reacted against what it conceived to be a narrow and barren Calvinism and broke away under the banner of Unitarianism. Congregationalists established many outstanding colleges, including Harvard, Yale, Amherst, Williams, and Oberlin, and were responsible for carrying on extensive foreign missionary work. The American Congregational Union, the church's first nationwide body, was organized in 1852. In 1947 the body, officially known as the Congregational Christian Union, claimed 1,173,626 members.

Congregation de Propaganda Fide (dā prō.pä.gän'dä fē'dā), **Sacred.** Agency of the Roman Catholic Church, organized in 1622, whose authority governs the Church in all missionary countries. Next to the Pope, the officials of the Propaganda comprise the Church's highest court of appeal. Its jurisdiction extended to the Church in the U.S. until 1908.

Congressional Record. U.S. government publication (1873 *et seq.*) containing an account of the daily proceedings of the Senate and the House of Representatives, including a record of formal discussion, informal remarks, and extended remarks. It is not, however, the official account of the sessions of Congress; this is comprised by the Journal of Congress. The predecessors of *The Congressional Record* were the privately compiled and printed *Annals of Congress* (1789–1824), *Register of Debates* (1824–37), and *Congressional Globe* (1834–73).

Congress of Industrial Organizations. [Called the **CIO.**] Industrial labor organization established at Pittsburgh, Pa., in November, 1938, whose forerunner was the Committee for Industrial Organization. The latter was founded after the craft-union policy of the American Federation of Labor dominated the AFL convention of 1935. When the CIO defied an AFL order (1936) to dissolve and cease its promotion of dual unionism, the CIO became independent and was formally organized in 1938 to carry out its aim of unionizing mass-production workers. By 1947 the CIO claimed more than six million workers as members. Its chief strength lies in the steel, textile, and auto industries. Its first president was John L. Lewis, who was succeeded by Philip Murray.

Congress of the United States. Legislative branch of the U.S. national government, prescribed and defined by the Constitution (Article I) as consisting of two houses, the Senate and House of Representatives. It is one of the three equal and coördinate branches of the government. See **Representatives, House of, and Senate.**

Congress Party. Indian political party pursuing a nationalist program in line with the principles of the All-India Congresses of colonial India.

Congress Working Committee. Executive authority of the Indian National Congress (Party) organization, consisting of the president of the Congress and 14 members of the All-India Congress Committee, which has disciplinary powers of control over all the committees and members of the organization. The members are nominated by the newly elected president.

Congreve (kon'grēv, kong'-), **Richard.** b. at Leamington, England, Sept. 4, 1818; d. at Hampstead, London, July 5, 1899. English essayist and philosophical writer.

Congreve, William. b. at Bardsey, near Leeds, England, 1670 (baptized Feb. 10); d. at London, Jan. 19, 1729. English dramatist, one of the greatest writers of comedy. Soon after his birth his parents removed to Ireland, where his father became commander of the garrison at Youghal and also agent of the earl of Cork. He was educated at a school in Killkenny (where Swift was one of his schoolfellows) and at Trinity College, Dublin. After a brief period devoted to the study of law, he applied himself chiefly to literature until about 1700, but after this year wrote little or nothing. He filled several unimportant offices, including that of commissioner for licensing hackney coaches (from July, 1695, to October, 1707), that of commissioner of wine licenses (from December, 1705, to December, 1714), and that of secretary for Jamaica (from 1714). His plays include *The Old Bachelor* (acted in January, 1693), *The Double Dealer* (November, 1693), *Love for Love* (April, 1695), *The Mourning Bride* (1697), and *The Way of the World* (1700). Besides his plays he wrote a novel (his first literary work) entitled *Incognita, or Love and Duty reconciled,* a reply to Jeremy Collier's attack upon him in his work on the immorality of the stage, called *Amendments of Mr. Collier's False and Imperfect Citations,* and a few prologues and unimportant operas. The first collected edition of his works was published by him in 1710. He is celebrated especially for the brilliancy of his style and the wit and vigor of his dialogues.

Congreve, Sir **William.** b. at Woolwich (now part of London), May 20, 1772; d. at Toulouse, France, May 16, 1828. English engineer, best known as the inventor of the Congreve rocket. He was appointed, in April, 1814, comptroller of the royal laboratory at Woolwich, in which office he succeeded his father. He published a number of works on economical and technological topics.

Conibo (kō.nē'bō). South American Indian tribe living in the forested lowlands of E Peru, in the area ab. latitude 9° S., longitude 75° W. The language is a member of the Panoan stock.

Coningham (kun'ing.am), Sir **Arthur.** b. at Brisbane, Australia, Jan. 19, 1895—. British air officer. He studied at Wellington and Victoria colleges in New Zealand, served (1914–16) in Samoa and Egypt with the New Zealand troops, and was commissioned (1916) into the Royal Flying Corps, serving (1919 *et seq.*) as an officer in the Royal Air Force. In World War II he was air vice-marshal heading (1940–42) the R.A.F. in the Libyan offensives and in Tunisia (1943), and commanded the Allied First Tactical Air Force in the Mediterranean (1943–44) and the Second Tactical Force in Western Europe (1944–45). From 1945 he was commander in chief of the R.A.F.'s Flying Training Command.

Coningsby (kon'ingz.bi). Political novel by Benjamin Disraeli, published in 1844.

Conington (kon'ing.ton), **John.** b. at Boston, England, Aug. 10, 1825; d. there, Oct. 23, 1869. English classical scholar, a graduate of Oxford, where he became, in 1854, professor of the Latin language and literature. He published an edition and translation of the *Agamemnon* of Aeschylus (1848), an edition of the *Choephori* of Aeschylus (1857), a translation in verse of the *Odes of Horace* (1863), a translation in ballad meter of Vergil's *Aeneid* (1866), an edition of Vergil, and others.

Coninxloo (kō'ningks.lō), **Gillis** (or **Cornelis**) **van.** [Also: **Coninxlo, Conixlo, Koninksloo.**] b. at Antwerp, 1544; d. there, 1607 or 1609. Flemish painter, especially of landscapes. He studied in France and Italy, and after his return to Flanders engaged chiefly in painting landscapes, to which figures were often added by another artist. His work was held in high regard for its excellent color and spirited technique, and many of his paintings were made the subjects of engravings. Excellent examples of his work are extant in the Hermitage at Leningrad, the Liechtenstein Gallery at Vienna, and other collections.

Conisbrough (kon'is.bru). [Also **Conisborough** (kon'is.bur.ō).] Urban district in N central England, in the West Riding of Yorkshire, situated on the river Don, ab. 5 mi. SW of Doncaster, ab. 161 mi. N of London by rail. 16,412 (1951).

Coniston (kon'is.ton). Novel by Winston Churchill, published in 1906. Jethro Bass loses his sweetheart, Cynthia, because of his corrupt political deals. Later in life, however, he takes Cynthia's orphan daughter into his home and sacrifices a political interest in order to promote her happiness.

Coniston Old Man. Mountain in NW England, in Lancashire. It is situated in the English Lake District, in the mountain range known as the Coniston Fells, W of Coniston Water. Elevation, ab. 2,633 ft.

Coniston Water. [Also, **Lake Coniston.**] Lake in NW England, in Lancashire. It lies in the English Lake District, 143 ft. above sea level, ab. 6 mi. SW of Ambleside. Length, ab. 6 mi.; width, ½ mi.

Conjeeveram (kon.jē'vėr.am). [Tamil, **Kanchipuram.**] City in S Union of India, in E central Madras state ab. 57 mi. by rail SW of Madras. It is one of the oldest towns in India, having been important before the 5th century B.C. It was the capital of the Pallava empire from early in the Christian era until its conquest by Chola c1000 A.D. It was captured by Clive in 1752, passing to the British. Numerous temples survive, some from the Pallava empire. The chief industry is silk and cotton textiles, with the production of saris. 74,635 (1941).

Conklin (kongk'lin), **Edwin Grant.** b. at Waldo, Ohio, Nov. 24, 1863; d. at Princeton, N.J., Nov. 20, 1952. American biologist and author. He served as professor of biology at Ohio Wesleyan (1891–94) and Princeton (1908–33) universities and as professor of zoölogy at Northwestern University (1894–96) and the University of Pennsylvania (1896–1908). His works include *Heredity and Environment*, *Mechanism of Evolution*, *Freedom and Responsibility*, *What Is Man?*, and *Man, Real and Ideal.*

Conkling (kongk'ling), **Grace Walcott.** [Maiden name, **Hazard.**] b. at New York, c1878—. American poet. She received the B.L. degree (1899) from Smith College, and served as a member (1914 *et seq.*) of its English department. She is the author of *Afternoons of April* (1915), *Wilderness Songs* (1920), *Ship's Log and Other Poems* (1924), *Flying Fish—a Book of Songs and Sonnets* (1926), *Witch and Other Poems* (1929), and other books of verse.

Conkling, Roscoe. b. at Albany, N.Y., Oct. 30, 1829; d. April 18, 1888. American politician. He attended the Mount Washington Collegiate Institute at New York, studied law at Utica, N.Y., was admitted to the bar (1850), and became district attorney of Albany. He became (1858) mayor of Utica, was elected (1858) to Congress, remaining in the House of Representatives until 1867, with the exception of the term of 1863–65. At first a Whig and then a Republican, he became prominent as a Radical Republican during the Civil War years and the Reconstruction period. He became U.S. Senator from New York in 1873, serving until his resignation in 1881. Conkling's close affiliations with Grant aided his political position in New York, where he had built an organization based on patronage. Clashing with President Hayes on the issue of politics in the civil service, he refused to lend his support to Hayes in the Republican convention of 1880, and only half-heartedly supported Garfield, with whom he later became embroiled in the dispute over the New York patronage. After his retirement from political activity, he took up his law practice at New York.

Conlaoch (kon'lā, -lē). In Old Irish legend, the son of Cuchulain.

Conn (kon). Shaughraun in Dion Boucicault's play *The Shaughraun:* a gay, careless good-for-nothing.

Conn, Lough. Lake in Connacht province, Irish Republic, in County Mayo, ab. 4 mi. SW of Ballina. It is connected with the smaller Lough Cullin by a narrow passage at its S end. Elevation, 41 ft.; length, ab. 9 mi.; greatest width, ab. 4 mi.

Connacht (kon'ôt, kon'acht). [Also: **Connaught;** Irish, **Connachta** (kon'ach.ta).] Westernmost of the four great historic provincial divisions of Ireland, now included wholly within the Irish Republic. It is bounded on the N and W by the Atlantic Ocean, on the NE by Ulster province, on the E by Leinster province, and on the S by Munster province and Galway Bay. Connacht comprises the five counties of Galway, Leitrim, Mayo, Roscommon, and Sligo. It ceased to be a kingdom and was divided into counties c1580. Area, ab. 6,611 sq. mi.; pop. 471,978 (1951).

Connah's Quay (kon'az kē'). Urban district in N Wales, in Flintshire, situated on the estuary of the river Dee, ab. 4 mi. SE of Flint, ab. 188 mi. NW of London by rail. 7,365 (1951).

Connally (kon'a.li), **Tom.** [Full name, **Thomas Terry Connally.**] b. in McLennan County, Texas, Aug. 19, 1877—. American political leader. He sat in the state legislature of Texas (1901–04), was prosecuting attorney of Falls County in that state (1906–10), and went to Washington as a member of the House of Representatives in 1917, continuing to sit in that body until 1929, when he became a U.S. senator During the second administration of Woodrow Wilson, while a member of the House, Connally voted for American entrance into World War I and later advocated American membership in the League of Nations and in the World Court, but opposed application of the Wilsonian doctrine of self-determination for small nations. During the ensuing years he was a delegate to meetings of the Interparliamentary Union and other important international events, such as the Inter-American Conference at Rio de Janeiro in 1947. By seniority he was chairman of the Senate Committee on Foreign Relations (1941–47), and after the Democratic Party victory in 1948 resumed that post in 1949. He was vice-chairman of the U.S. delegation to the San Francisco Conference of 1945 which drafted the Charter of the United Nations, and was U.S. delegate to the United Nations General Assembly (1945–47). Senator Connally supported the foreign policies of Presidents Franklin D. Roosevelt and Harry S. Truman, but vigorously fought many of their domestic policies, including civil rights legislation. He was active in preventing the enactment of Federal legislation against lynching and against the poll tax, and in opposition to laws desired by organized labor. As chairman of the Senate Committee on Foreign Relations he guided through the Senate the legislation authorizing the first appropriation of 5,580,000,000 dollars to implement the Marshall Plan.

Connaught (kon'ôt). See also **Connacht.**

Connaught, Arthur Wettin, Prince of. [Family name changed (1917) to **Windsor.**] b. 1883; d. 1938. Member of the royal family of Great Britain; son of the 1st Duke of

Connaught (1850–1942). He was governor general of South Africa from 1920 to 1923.

Connaught, Arthur William Patrick Albert Wettin, Duke of. [Family name changed (1917) to **Windsor.**] b. in Buckingham Palace, London, May 1, 1850; d. 1942. Member of the royal family of Great Britain. This son of Queen Victoria and her consort Prince Albert was educated for a military career, and served with British forces in Egypt and India in the 1880's, as commander in England (1890–98), and as commander in chief in Ireland (1900) and in the Mediterranean (1907–09). He was governor general of Canada (1911–16). His titles, Duke of Connaught and Strathearn, and Earl of Essex, were conferred in 1874.

Conndae (kun'dā). Irish word meaning "county": for geographical entries of this kind see under the distinguishing element.

Conneau (ko.nō), **Jean.** [Also known as **André Beaumont.**] b. at Lodère, Hérault, France, Feb. 8, 1880—. French naval officer and aviator. Under the name of André Beaumont he won several early long-distance cross-country airplane races in Europe. Of these the most notable were a flight from Paris to Rome (910 mi.), which he made on May 28–31, 1911; a European circuit (Paris, Utrecht, London, Paris; 948¾ mi.), which he covered in 58 hours, 36 minutes from June 18 to July 7, 1911; and a British circuit (Brooklands, Edinburgh, Glasgow, Brooklands; 1,010 mi.) on July 22–26, 1911.

Conneaut (kon'ẹ.ôt). City in NE Ohio, in Ashtabula County, on Lake Erie: important lake port and shipping point for coal and iron ore. It was settled in the last decade of the 18th century. 10,230 (1950).

Connecticut (ko̦.net'i.kut). [Called the **"Nutmeg State"**; also the **"Constitution State,"** the **"Land of Steady Habits,"** and, formerly, the **"Freestone State."**] State in the NE U.S. and one of the 13 original states of the American Union, bounded by Massachusetts on the N, Rhode Island on the E, Long Island Sound on the S, and New York on the W: southernmost of the New England States.

Population, Area, and Political Divisions. Connecticut is divided into eight counties. It sends six representatives to Congress and has eight electoral votes. Many of its towns (which are the equivalent of townships in many other states) still adhere to the old New England custom of the open town meeting. Capital, Hartford; area, 4,899 sq. mi. (5,009 sq. mi., including water); pop. 2,007,280 (1950), an increase of 17.4 percent over the 1940 figure. The state ranks 46th in area and 28th (on the basis of the 1950 census) in population. Among the leading cities are Hartford, New Haven, Bridgeport, Waterbury, and New Britain.

Terrain and Climate. Connecticut consists of the fertile Connecticut River valley bordered by hilly uplands on the W and E. The Connecticut River crosses the C part of the state from N to S, discharging near Saybrook into Long Island Sound. The Farmington River is its chief tributary in the state. The Housatonic in the W empties into the Sound at Stratford and the Thames in the E discharges into the Sound near New London. Bear Mountain (2,355 ft.) in the NW corner of the state is its highest point. Forests cover about half of the state. The climate is moderate.

Industry, Agriculture, and Trade. Connecticut is primarily an industrial state devoted to such manufactures as firearms, machine tools, silverware, typewriters, textiles, footwear, hats, clocks, sewing machines, and airplane motors. In agriculture dairying is of top importance, followed by poultry raising and the production of a high grade of tobacco. Hartford, the financial and commercial center of the state, is the site of a multi-million-dollar insurance industry, thousands being employed in the home offices there of many leading insurance companies of the U.S. Gravel, sand, stone, sheet mica, lime, and clay products are found in Connecticut. The annual income in the state from agriculture ranges as high as 131 million dollars; from mineral output, as high as four million dollars; from manufacturing, in excess of two billion dollars.

History. Earliest European settlers in Connecticut were the Dutch, who made (1633) the first settlement there on the site of what is now the city of Hartford. English colonists from Massachusetts settled (1633–36) in the Connecticut valley at Wethersfield, Windsor, and Hartford, and eventually the Dutch were driven out. Separate English colonies were founded at Saybrook between 1635 and 1639, and at New Haven in 1638. In 1638 those Puritan groups which had settled along the Connecticut River adopted the Fundamental Orders, the first American constitution based on autonomous government (hence the name "Constitution State" sometimes applied to it). Charles II granted a charter to the Connecticut and New Haven colonies in 1662, and their union was completed soon after, with the Pacific Ocean as the colony's W boundary. As part of the Dominion of New England it was administered by the British governor Sir Edmund Andros, who attempted to take the colony's charter in order to dissolve its government; according to tradition residents hid the charter in a large oak tree, later known as "Charter Oak," at Hartford. Connecticut sent many soldiers to Washington's army during the American Revolution and in the Civil War actively supported the Union. It was reorganized as a state (1776) with the charter of 1662 as its constitution. In the period 1782–86 it relinquished its western lands with the exception of the Western Reserve in Ohio, which it gave up in full to Ohio in 1800. The Hartford Convention met (1814–15) at Hartford. The present state constitution was adopted in 1818. During World War II the state's industries contributed heavily to defense production. The state has been called the "Land of Steady Habits" because of the stringency of the so-called Blue Laws, which enjoined a rigid code of morals on its inhabitants. It has also been called the "Nutmeg State," because of the alleged early custom of its merchants of manufacturing nutmegs out of wood. Its sandstone quarries were a source of the material for "brownstone" houses (hence "Freestone State").

Culture. Connecticut today, like much of New England, has a heterogeneous population including Poles, Italians, Jews, Negroes, and Armenians, descendants of the colonial settlers forming a minority. Its urban population in 1950 comprised 77.6 percent of the total. Hartford and New Haven are leading cultural centers. A summer art colony flourishes at Lyme, and many New York residents have summer homes throughout the state. Connecticut is known for its educational facilities, being the location of many private preparatory schools. Among the best-known of its colleges and universities are Yale University, at New Haven; Wesleyan University, at Middletown; Trinity College, at Hartford; Connecticut College, at New London; the state-supported University of Connecticut at Storrs with branches at Hartford, New Haven, and Waterbury. The state motto is *Qui Transtulit Sustinet*, meaning "He Who Transplanted Still Sustains." The state flower is the mountain laurel.

Connecticut, Fundamental Orders of. Preamble and 11 orders (Jan. 14, 1639), notable as the first written constitution that created a government. The document established a government for the three "River Towns" of Hartford, Windsor, and Wethersfield, and was drawn up by the freemen of those towns. Its provisions are incorporated in the present state constitution of Connecticut.

Connecticut Academy of Arts and Sciences. Organization established in 1799 for the purpose of cultivating the arts and sciences. It maintains headquarters at Yale University and publishes *Memoirs* and *Transactions.*

Connecticut General Life Insurance Co. v. Johnson, 303 U.S. 77 (1938). U.S. Supreme Court decision invalidating a California law which levied taxes on insurance premiums paid in Connecticut by foreign insurance firms operating in California. The court's opinion was based on the ground that the California statute violated the due process clause of the Fourteenth Amendment. The case is notable for the dissent of Justice Hugo Black, who declared: "I do not believe the word 'persons' in the Fourteenth Amendment includes corporations. Neither the history nor the language of the Fourteenth Amendment justifies the belief that corporations are included within its protection."

Connecticut Lakes. Four lakes in extreme N New Hampshire, the source of the Connecticut River. The surroundings are largely forested hills and mountains.

First Connecticut Lake has some farms on the W shore, and is a resort. Elevation, ab. 1,631 ft.; area, ab. 4 sq. mi. Second Connecticut Lake is at 1,871 ft. elevation; area, ab. 2 sq. mi. Third Connecticut Lake is just S of the Canadian border. Elevation, ab. 2,191 ft.; area, ab. ½ sq. mi. Fourth Connecticut Lake is a small tarn on the W slope above Third Lake. Elevation, ab. 2,600 ft.

Connecticut River. River of New England, which rises in N New Hampshire, in the Connecticut Lakes, separates Vermont from New Hampshire, flows through Massachusetts and Connecticut, and empties into Long Island Sound at Saybrook. Among the chief places on it are Northampton, Holyoke, Springfield, Hartford, and Middletown. Length, ab. 345 mi.; navigable for small vessels to Windsor, Conn.

Connecticut Wits. [Also, **Hartford Wits.**] Group of writers who, in the last years of the 18th century and the first two decades of the 19th, essayed to create an American literature, especially poetry, inspired by pride in the new nation, its independence, its potentialities, and its ideals as seen by Federalists, and in the Calvinist tradition. Their center was Hartford, but most members of the group were instructors or students in Yale College at New Haven. They gloried in American institutions and opposed the principles of the French Revolution. Inevitably their literary standards and techniques closely followed English models. Their works are seldom read today except by students, but they played a role in the development of American patriotism and they gave future writers confidence in the concept of an American literature, even though it did not take the direction to which they pointed. The principal figures among the Connecticut Wits were Timothy Dwight, Theodore Dwight, Joel Barlow, John Trumbull, David Humphreys, Lemuel Hopkins, Richard Alsop, Elihu H. Smith, and Mason F. Cogswell. Among the ambitious productions of the collaborative efforts of the group were *The Anarchiad*, *The Echo*, and *The Political Greenhouse*.

Connecticut Yankee in King Arthur's Court, A. Fantasy by Samuel Langhorne Clemens under the pseudonym Mark Twain, published in 1889. The hero, a mechanic in Hartford, loses consciousness from a blow on the head and awakes to find himself in Camelot in the year 528. He avoids execution by serving as minister to King Arthur and under the guise of a magician utilizes his knowledge of 19th-century science to predict an eclipse. His attempts at social improvement in the interest of the peasants are bitterly opposed by the ruling circles. Returning from a brief excursion to France, he finds England in the midst of civil war. He proclaims a republic, but after warding off an attack in a cave succumbs to a sleep induced by Merlin which takes him back into the 19th century.

Connellsville (kon′e̥lz.vil). City in SW Pennsylvania, in Fayette County, near the confluence of the Monongahela and Youghiogheny rivers, ab. 58 mi. SE of Pittsburgh. Manufactures include metal products, silk textiles, glass, trousers, paper boxes, and beer; the city has railroad shops, and was formerly noted for its output of coke. Settled c1770, it was incorporated in 1806 and chartered in 1911 as a city. 13,293 (1950).

Connelly (kon′e̥.li), **Marc.** [Full name, **Marcus Cook Connelly.**] b. at McKeesport, Pa., Dec. 13, 1890—. American playwright. His collaborations with George S. Kaufman include *The Deep Tangled Wildwood* (1913), *Dulcy* (1921), a dramatization of *Merton of the Movies* (1922), *To the Ladies* (1923), and *Beggar on Horseback* (1924). He is the author with Frank Ball Elser of *The Farmer Takes a Wife* (1934), and sole author of *The Wisdom Tooth* (1926), *The Mole on Lincoln's Cheek* (1941), and other plays. His *The Green Pastures* (1930), based on Roark Bradford's *Old Man Adam an' His Chillun*, won a Pulitzer prize, and his story *Coroner's Inquest* won an O. Henry Memorial award, both in 1930.

Connely (kon′e̥.li), **Willard.** b. at Atlantic City, N.J., 1888—. American educator and author. He was graduated from Dartmouth (B.S., 1911) and Harvard (M.A., 1921), served on the staffs of *Harper's Weekly*, *McClure's Magazine*, and the International Film Service, and was director (1930–46) of the American University Union at London. He served in the U.S. navy during World War I and in World War II lectured to British troops on America's role in the world conflict. His works include *Brawny Wycherley* (1930), *Sir Richard Steele* (1934), *The True Chesterfield* (1939), and *Young George Farquhar* (1949).

Connemara (kon.e̥.mä′ra̧, -mar′a̧). Westernmost district of County Galway, in Connacht province, Irish Republic. It comprises the W third of County Galway and the SW corner of County Mayo. The district is noted for wildly picturesque scenery of bog-fringed, shallow lakes, and barren mountains rising from the lowlands. Most of the sparse settlement is found along the rugged coast, where the principal activity is fishing and subsistence farming. Many sheep are pastured on the uplands.

"Connemara, Princess of." See **Martin, Mary Letitia.**

Conner (kon′ėr), **David.** b. at Harrisburg, Pa., 1792; d. at Philadelphia, March 20, 1856. American naval commander. He served in the War of 1812 and in the Mexican War.

Conners (kon′ėrz), **William James.** b. at Buffalo, N.Y., Jan. 3, 1857; d. Oct. 5, 1929. American shipowner and newspaper publisher. He was proprietor of the Buffalo *Enquirer* (1895 *et seq.*) and *Courier* (1897 *et seq.*), and founded (1919) and served as chairman of the board of the Great Lakes Transit Corporation. In 1918 he acquired and began the drainage of 7,000 acres of the Florida Everglades, where he constructed (1924) the 51-mile Conners Highway. He endowed (1925) a fund of one million dollars as the Conners Foundation for the relief of the poor at Buffalo.

Conners, William James. b. at Buffalo, N.Y., Sept. 22, 1895; d. Feb. 3, 1951. American newspaper publisher; son of William James Conners. He published (1919 *et seq.*) the Buffalo *Courier*, later the *Courier-Express* (1926).

Connersville (kon′ėrz.vil). City in E Indiana, county seat of Fayette County. Its manufactures include toys, auto bodies, refrigerators, and furniture. 15,550 (1950).

Connoisseur (kon.i.sėr′), **The.** Periodical begun on Jan. 31, 1754, by George Colman the elder and Bonnell Thornton, and continued weekly for three years. In this periodical in 1756 appeared the first publications of William Cowper. His first paper was on "Keeping a Secret."

Connolly (kon′o̥.li), **Cyril.** [Full name, **Cyril Vernon Connolly.**] b. at Coventry, England, Sept. 10, 1903—. English author and editor. He is both a novelist and a critic, and as the editor of *Horizon*, a literary magazine which he established in 1939 (and which ceased publication in 1951), he held the door open to writers of various schools and tendencies, and exerted considerable influence in the field of criticism. He was literary editor (1942–43) of the London *Observer* and his writings have appeared with frequency in the *New Statesman and Nation* since 1927. His works are *The Rock Pool* (1935), a novel dealing with expatriate artists on the Riviera, *Enemies of Promise* (1938), a volume of literary essays, with some biographical material, *The Unquiet Grave* (1945), essays, for which the author used the name of Aeneas's pilot, Palinurus, and *The Condemned Playground* (1946), a volume of parodies and satires, many of them written at an earlier period. As an editor he has published an anthology of short stories that originally appeared in his own *Horizon*, and he has translated *Put Out the Light* and *The Silence of the Sea*, by Jean Bruller (Vercors), from the French.

Connolly, James. b. in Ulster, Ireland, 1870; d. 1916. Irish socialist.

Connolly, James Brendan. b. at South Boston, Mass., c1868—. American journalist and writer. A champion at first modern Olympics (1896); served in Spanish-American War with 9th Massachusetts Infantry; fought at siege of Santiago (1898); served (1907–08) in U.S. navy; correspondent for *Scribner's Magazine* in Europe (1901) and *Harper's Magazine* in Arctic Ocean (1902); war correspondent for *Collier's* in Mexico (1914) and in European waters (1917–18). Author of *Out of Gloucester* (1902), *The Seiners* (1904), *An Olympic Victor* (1908), *Open Water* (1910), *Wide Courses* (1911), *The U-Boat Hunters* (1918), *Tide Rips* (1922), *Gloucestermen* (1930), *Life and Voyages of Amasa Delano* (1943), *Sea-Borne: Thirty Years Avoyaging* (1944).

Connolly, Walter. b. at Cincinnati, Ohio, April 8, 1887; d. at Hollywood, Calif., May 28, 1940. American actor. He made his debut (1908) in *Classmates* at Norfolk, Va., toured (1911–14) with the Sothern-Marlowe Shakespearian company, and after 1916 played in various theaters at New York, at Philadelphia, and elsewhere, beginning his film career in 1932 in *The Bitter Tea of General Yen.* He starred in such plays as *Come Out of the Kitchen, The Woman of Bronze,* and *Applesauce,* and appeared in *Lady for a Day, Nothing Sacred, Four's a Crowd, It Happened One Night, The Great Victor Herbert,* and other films.

Connor (kon'ọr) or **O'Connor** (ọ.kon'ọr), **Bernard.** b. in County Kerry, Ireland, c1666; d. at London, October, 1698. Irish physician and historian. He was the author of *Dissertationes medico-physicae* (1695), *Evangelium medici . . .* (1697; written to prove that the miracles of Christ and his apostles can be explained on natural grounds), a *History of Poland* (1698), and others. He received his technical education in France, was appointed physician to King John Sobieski, lectured on contemporary medical discoveries at Oxford, and acquired a high reputation as a practitioner.

Connor, Ralph. Pseudonym of **Gordon, Charles William.**

Connubio (kōn.nö'byō). In Sardinian politics, the union of the left-center faction (under Rattazzi), in the chamber, with the right-center (under Cavour), c1852.

Conolly (kon'ọl.i), **John.** b. at Market Rasen, Lincolnshire, England, May 27, 1794; d. at Hanwell, near London, March 5, 1866. English physician. He was professor of the practice of medicine in University College, London (1828–30), and director of the insane asylum at Hanwell (1839–44), where he introduced the principle of nonrestraint (i.e., the abandonment of restraint by strait jackets and the like) in the care of the patients. His humanitarian labors were widely influential.

Conon (kō'non). d., probably in Cyprus, after 392 B.C. Athenian commander. He served in the Peloponnesian war, defeated the Spartan fleet off Cnidus in 394 B.C., and restored the fortifications of Athens and the Piraeus in 393 B.C.

Conon. fl. 3rd century B.C. Greek geometer and astronomer. A native or at least in early life a resident of Samos, and a friend of Archimedes, he traveled widely through the Greek world before settling at Alexandria. He was a student of solar eclipses and of the constellations, and in the history of mathematics is noted for his studies of conic intersections.

Conon. d. Sept. 21, 687. Pope from 686 to 687. A venerable man of simple character, he was elected by agreement of all factions after the death of Pope John V.

Conquered, The. Novel by Naomi Mitchison, published in 1923.

Conqueror, The. Novel by Gertrude Atherton, published in 1902, presenting a fictionalized biography of Alexander Hamilton with comment on his contemporaries.

Conqueror Worm, The. Poem (1843) by Edgar Allan Poe. It contains 40 lines, and its rhyme scheme is *ababcbcb.*

Conquest (kong'kwest), **Mrs.** Character in Colley Cibber's comedy *Love's Last Stake.*

Conquistador (kon.kwis'tạ.dôr; Spanish, kōng.kēs.tä-ᴛʜōr'). Narrative poem by Archibald MacLeish, published in 1932 and awarded a Pulitzer prize the following year. The work concerns Hernando Cortés' expedition to Mexico and is an imaginative treatment of the account by Bernal Díaz.

Conrad (kon'rad). [Title, Marquis of **Montferrat;** sometimes called Marquis of **Tyre and Montferrat.**] d. at Tyre, April 28, 1192. Crusader. He successfully defended (1187) Tyre against Saladin, married (1190) Isabella, a younger daughter of Amalric I of Jerusalem, and at the time of his death at the hand of an assassin had just been elected king of Jerusalem.

Conrad I. [German, **Konrad.**] d. Dec. 23, 918. King of the Germans from 911 to 918. On the extinction of the Carolingian house in Germany with the death of Louis the Child in 911, the election fell upon Conrad, then Duke of Franconia. During his reign the country was invaded by the Danes, Slavs, and Magyars, and he was constantly at war with his own subjects in a vain endeavor to enforce the recognition of his sovereignty, especially from Henry, Duke of Saxony, son of Otto the Illustrious.

Conrad II. [Called **"Conrad the Salian."**] b. c990; d. at Utrecht, June 4, 1039. King of the Germans from 1024 to 1039, and Holy Roman emperor; founder of the Franconian or Salian dynasty. He marched into Italy in 1026, brought the rebellious cities of Pavia and Ravenna to submission, and was crowned emperor at Rome (1027). He put down a rebellion of his stepson Ernst, Duke of Swabia (1025–30), made an inroad into Hungary (1030), regained Lusatia from the Poles (1031), and made himself master of Burgundy (i.e., the kingdom of Arles; 1033–34). He marched into Italy a second time in 1036, but was compelled by the successful opposition of Milan to acknowledge by the constitution of May 28, 1037, the hereditary character of all Italian fiefs, whether held immediately of the crown or not.

Conrad III. b. 1093; d. at Bamberg, Germany, Feb. 15, 1152. King of the Germans from 1138 to 1152, founder of the Hohenstaufen dynasty. He was elected in an irregular manner by the party opposed to the house of Saxony; the election gave rise to a war with the rival candidate, Henry the Proud, Duke of Saxony and Bavaria. The war was continued after Henry's death (1139) by his brother Welf VI, whence arose the party names of the Ghibellines (Italian alteration of the name of the Hohenstaufen castle Waiblingen), and the Welfs or Guelphs. Conrad defeated Welf at Weinsberg in 1140, and took part (1147–49) in the second Crusade.

Conrad IV. b. at Andria, Italy, April 25 or 27, 1228; d. at Lavello, Italy, May 21, 1254. King of the Germans; second son of Frederick II, whom he succeeded in 1250. The imperial crown was contested by William, Count of Holland, who maintained himself by the aid of the Guelphs. In 1251 Conrad undertook an expedition into Italy to enforce his rights of succession to the crown of the Two Sicilies. He is said to have died of poison, leaving his infant son Conradin as the last heir of his line. The throne was occupied as regent by Conrad's illegitimate brother Manfred.

Conrad V. See **Conradin.**

Conrad, Charles Magill. b. at Winchester, Va., Dec. 24, 1804; d. Feb. 11, 1878. American politician. He was elected (1842) senator from Louisiana, and served as U.S. congressman (1849–50), and secretary of war (1850–53). In 1861 he was a delegate to the provisional Confederate congress, and he sat as representative (1862–64) in the first and second Confederate congresses.

Conrad, Frank. b. at Pittsburgh, Pa., May 4, 1874; d. Dec. 11, 1941. American electrical engineer, known for various inventions and for his work on short-wave and frequency-modulation broadcasting. He was a general engineer (1914 *et seq.*) and assistant chief engineer (1921 *et seq.*) for the Westinghouse Electrical and Manufacturing Company at Pittsburgh, experimented (1919) with making broadcasts from phonograph records, and took part in organizing KDKA, the radio station at Pittsburgh where originated (1920) the first public broadcast. His contributions include a round-watt-hour electric meter, electric clocks, and devices for automobile ignition; he was awarded the Edison medal (1931) and the John Scott medal (1933).

Conrad (kon'rät), **Georg.** [Pseudonym of Prince **George of Prussia.**] b. at Düsseldorf, Germany, Feb. 12, 1826; d. at Berlin, May 2, 1902. German prince, a dilettante in the drama. He wrote *Sappho* (1887) and *Katharina von Medici* (1884). His memoirs (*Vergilbte Blätter,* 1872) are, however, today considered more interesting than his dramatic works.

Conrad, Johannes. b. at Gut Borkau, Germany, Feb. 28, 1839; d. at Halle, Germany, April 25, 1915. German economist, notable in the field of agrarian policy and agrarian statistics. He served as professor (1872 *et seq.*) at the University of Halle, and was the author of *Grundriss zum Studium der politischen Ökonomie* (Textbook for the study of Political Economics, 1896–1904). He edited (1870 *et seq.*) *Jahrbücher für Nationalökonomie und Statistik* (Yearbooks for Political Economics and Statistics).

Conrad (kon'rad), **Joseph.** [Original name, **Józef Teodor Konrad Nałęcz Korzeniowski.**] b. at Berdyczew, Poland (then under Russian rule), Dec. 3, 1857; d. near Canterbury, England, Aug. 3, 1924. English novelist of Polish birth and family, and strong patriotic and nationalist heritage. At the age of five he accompanied his father and mother into political exile in Russia. Left an orphan in 1869, he was educated under tutors and at high school at Kraków, and left Poland for France in 1874. At Marseilles (1874–78) he became involved in the Carlist cause in Spain, helping smuggle arms by sea to the Carlists. He made his first sea voyage on French merchant ships to Martinique (1875) and the West Indies (1876–77). Joining an English ship in 1878, he then first landed in England, joined the English merchant service, and sailed, chiefly on English ships, to all parts of the world (1878–94), rising from third mate (1880), to first mate (1883) and master (1886); he was naturalized a British subject in 1886. He made a journey up the Congo River for Belgian interests in 1890, and left the sea unwillingly in 1894. His first novel, *Almayer's Folly*, was published in 1895. Married (1896) to Jessie George, he was the father of two sons, Borys (b. 1898) and John Alexander (b. 1906). He revisited Poland in the summer of 1914 with his family, and was aided in returning to England after the outbreak of World War I by the American ambassador at Vienna, Frederic C. Penfield. He visited naval stations in the North Sea for the British Admiralty in 1916, and made a triumphal visit to the U.S. in the spring of 1923. He died suddenly on Aug. 3, 1924, and is buried at Canterbury.

Written Works. Conrad's novels and tales are marked by strong originality of style and treatment; by richly realized settings in the Orient and the tropics, on the high seas, or in European cities and countries; by probing moral and psychological analysis; by themes of honor, moral alienation, guilt, expiation, and heroism; and by a remarkable distinction of form. They include *Almayer's Folly* (1895), *An Outcast of the Islands* (1896), *The Nigger of the "Narcissus"* (1897), *Lord Jim* (1900), *The Inheritors* and *Romance* (1901, 1903; these two written in collaboration with Ford Madox Hueffer, later called Ford Madox Ford), *Typhoon* (1902), *Nostromo* (1904), *The Secret Agent* (1907), *Under Western Eyes* (1911), *Chance* (1914), *Victory* (1915), *The Shadow-Line* (1917), *The Arrow of Gold* (1919), *The Rescue* (1920), *The Rover* (1923), *Suspense* (1925, unfinished). Books of shorter tales: *Tales of Unrest* (1899), *Youth* (1902), *Typhoon* (1903), *A Set of Six* (1908), *'Twixt Land and Sea* (1912), *Within the Tides* (1915), *Tales of Hearsay* (1925). Books of reminiscence: *The Mirror of the Sea* (1906), *A Personal Record* (1912). Books of literary and personal essays: *Notes on Life and Letters* (1921), *Last Essays* (1926). He dramatized *The Secret Agent* in 1922 and *Victory* was dramatized by others in 1919. See *Life and Letters*, ed. by G. Jean-Aubry (1927).

Conrad (kon'rät), **Karl Emanuel.** b. at Berlin, March 30, 1810; d. at Cologne, July 12, 1873. German architectural painter and aquarellist. His chief work is the *Cathedral of Cologne*, in the Vatican.

Conrad, Michael Georg. b. at Gnodstadt, Bavaria, April 5, 1846; d. at Munich, Dec. 20, 1927. German critic and novelist who played an important part in the introduction of naturalism into Germany. Having broadened his horizon by living in Italy and France for more than a decade, he came home in 1882 proclaiming the virtues of his friend Zola. The journal which he founded at Munich, *Die Gesellschaft* (1885–1902), numbered among its contributors not only the firebrands of the new movement but almost every prominent writer of the time. After the manner of Zola he planned a cycle of novels exploring Munich life, but only three of the ten (*Was die Isar rauscht*, 1887; *Die klugen Jungfrauen*, 1889; *Die Beichte des Narren*, 1890) ever materialized, and these did not live up to expectations. His critical writings, such as *Madame Lutetia* (1883) and particularly *Von Emile Zola bis Gerhart Hauptmann* (1902), are today considered to have been his most important writings.

Conrad (kon'rad), **Robert Taylor.** b. at Philadelphia, June 10, 1810; d. there, June 27, 1858. American jurist and dramatist. He published the tragedy *Aylmere* in 1852.

Conrad, Timothy Abbott. b. in New Jersey, 1803; d. at Trenton, N.J., Aug. 8, 1877. American paleontologist, on the New York Geological Survey (1838–41). His works include *Fossil Shells of the Tertiary Formations of North America* (1832), and *Paleontology of the State of New York* (1838–40).

Conrade (kon'rad). Follower of Don John in Shakespeare's *Much Ado about Nothing;* the bastard brother of Don Pedro.

Conradi (kon.rä'dē), **August.** b. at Berlin, June 27, 1821; d. there, May 26, 1873. German composer and conductor. He directed orchestras at Stettin, Berlin, Düsseldorf, and Cologne; his works include operas, such as *Rübezahl* (1847) and *Musa, der letzte Maurenfürst* (1855), symphonies, overtures, and chamber works.

Conradi, Hermann. b. at Jessnitz, Germany, June 12, 1862; d. at Würzburg, Germany, March 8, 1890. German poet and novelist, one of the most outspoken of the early naturalists. His death in the midst of a trial brought against him, Conrad Alberti, and Wilhelm Arent for indecent writing lent his name the aura of martyrdom. In the opinion of most modern critics, neither his poems (*Lieder eines Sünders*, 1887), his stories (*Brutalitäten*, 1886), nor the novel (*Adam Mensch*, 1889) for which he was tried, may be said to have achieved enduring stature.

Conradin (kon'ra̤.dēn; German, kon'rä.dēn). [Also: **Conrad V**; called **"Conrad the Younger."**] b. near Landshut, Germany, March 25, 1252; beheaded at Naples, Italy, Oct. 29, 1268. Duke of Swabia, son of Conrad IV of Germany, and last of the house of Hohenstaufen. In 1268 he failed in an attempt to recover the kingdom of the Two Sicilies from the usurper Charles of Anjou, was captured at Tagliacozzo, and was executed.

Conrad in Quest of His Youth (kon'rad). Novel (1903) by Leonard Merrick. Considered his best work, it tells the love story of the hero Conrad, who wanted to be 19 again, and how he found his second youth in Rosalind.

Conradi Peak (kon.rad'i). Isolated peak in Antarctica, almost snow-covered, lying ab. 28 mi. S by SE of Cape Batterbee, in Enderby Land; in ab. 66°14′ S., 54°22′ E. Elevation, ab. 3,300 ft.

Conrad of Würzburg (kon'rad; German, kon'rät; vürts'bürk). See **Konrad von Würzburg.**

"Conrad the Younger" (kon'rad). See **Conradin.**

Conrad von Hötzendorf (kon'rät fon hėt'se̤n.dôrf), Count **Franz.** b. at Vienna, Nov. 11, 1852; d. at Mergentheim, Germany, Aug. 26, 1925. Austro-Hungarian general. A friend of the Archduke Franz Ferdinand, he became chief of staff in 1906. He reorganized the army in line with his belief that a preventive war was necessary. During World War I he defended Austria against Russian and Italian attacks and fought alongside the Germans in Serbia and Rumania. Emperor Charles dismissed him from his position as chief of staff in 1917 and transferred him to the Italian front. After the collapse Conrad withdrew from public life to write his memoirs, *Aus meiner Dienstzeit 1906–18* (1921–25).

Conrady (kon.rä'dē), **August.** b. at Wiesbaden, Germany, April 28, 1864; d. at Leipzig, Germany, June 4, 1925. German Orientalist, notable in the field of Indo-Chinese languages. He served as professor (1897 *et seq.*) at the University of Leipzig, and was the author of *Indischer Einfluss in China im 4. Jahrhundert v. Chr.* (Indian Influence in China in the 4th century B.C., 1906), *Geschichte Chinas* (History of China, 1910), and others.

Conrart (kôn.rår), **Valentin.** b. at Paris, 1603; d. Sept. 23, 1675. French man of letters, one of the founders of the French Academy, of which he was secretary from 1634 to 1675.

Conried (kon'rēd), **Heinrich.** b. at Bielitz, in Silesia, Sept. 13, 1855; d. at Meran (Morano), in the Tyrol, April 27, 1909. Austro-American actor, stage director, and impresario. He began his career at the Burgtheater, Vienna, as an actor, and afterward played in many German cities. He then came to New York, becoming stage-director of the Germania Theater in 1878 (where he also acted character parts), of the Thalia Theater in 1881, later of the Casino, and of the Irving Place Theater in 1892. He was appointed director of the Metropolitan Opera House in 1903, where he produced *Parsifal* during his first season and *Salome* in 1907, retiring on May 1, 1908. He assisted in planning the New Theater. He received honorary decorations from the rulers of Germany, Austria, Belgium, and Italy.

Conring (kon'ring), **Hermann.** b. at Norden, in East Friesland, Germany, Nov. 9, 1606; d. at Helmstedt, Brunswick, Germany, Dec. 12, 1681. German physician, scholar, writer on jurisprudence, and miscellaneous author. He became professor of natural philosophy at Helmstedt (1632), of medicine (1636), and later of politics. In 1660 he became privy councilor of the duke of Brunswick.

He was (1658) private physician of Charles X Gustavus of Sweden. He wrote *De origine juris Germanici* (1643), *Exercitationes de republica Germanica* (1675), and others.

Conroe (kon′rō). City in E Texas, county seat of Montgomery County, N of Houston: shipping center for lumber, livestock, poultry, and vegetables. 7,298 (1950).

Conroy (kon′roi), **Gabriel.** See **Gabriel Conroy.**

Consalvi (kōn.säl′vē), **Ercole.** b. at Rome, June 8, 1757; d. there, Jan. 24, 1824. Roman cardinal and statesman. He was secretary of state to Pope Pius VII during the periods 1800–06 and 1814–23, and concluded a concordat with Napoleon in 1801.

Conscience (kôṅ.syäṅs′), **Hendrik.** b. at Antwerp, Dec. 3, 1812; d. at Brussels, Sept. 10, 1883. Flemish novelist. He was first a teacher, then entered the army as a volunteer. In 1845 he became professor at the University of Ghent, and in 1868 custodian of the Wiertz Museum at Brussels. In 1837 appeared his first novel (the first, also, in modern Flemish), *In't Wonderjaer 1566* (In the Year of Marvels 1566). It was followed, the same year, by *Phantazy,* a volume of short stories, and in 1838 by the novel *De leeuw van Vlaanderen* (The Lion of Flanders). In 1841 he was made secretary of the Academy of Arts at Antwerp, which position he held until 1854. In 1857 he became a civil official at Courtrai. His most celebrated works are stories of Flemish life. Among them are *Hoe men schilder wordt* (How One becomes a Painter, 1843), *De arme edelman* (The Poor Nobleman, 1851), *Het geluk van ryk te zyn* (The Good Fortune to be Rich, 1855), *De burgemeester van Luik* (The Burgomaster of Liége), *De junge Dokter* (The Young Doctor), and *Benjamin van Vlaanderen* (1880).

Conscience Whigs. Faction of the Whig party in Massachusetts opposed to the Cotton Whigs on the slavery question during the pre-Civil War period.

Conscious Lovers, The. Comedy by Steele, produced in 1722. It was taken from Terence's *Andria.* In this play Steele attempted to free the stage from its indecencies.

Conseil National de la Résistance (kôṅ.sey′ nȧ.syo.nȧl dę lȧ rā.zēs.täṅs). [Eng. trans., "*National Council of the Resistance.*"] Central body of the French movement of opposition to the German occupation forces and the Vichy regime during World War II. It was formed (May 15, 1943) by representatives of Resistance movements, political parties, and trade-union federations. Its first president was Jean Moulin, known by the Resistance name of "Max," who was delegated to the group by the de Gaulle regime at London. After Moulin's arrest and execution by the Gestapo, it was headed by Georges Bidault and then by Louis Saillant. It issued a broad program of economic, political, and social reform.

Conseil National du Patronat Français (kôṅ.sey′ nȧ.syo.nȧl dü pȧ.tro.nȧ fräṅ.sā). [Eng. trans., "*National Council of French Employers.*"] French employers' federation, formed (1945) to replace the Confédération Générale du Patronat Français ("General Confederation of French Employers"), which represented French employers from 1936 until its dissolution (November, 1940) by the Vichy government. The preceding employers' group was the Confédération Générale de la Production Française ("General Confederation of French Producers"). Its principal leaders were Pierre Fournier and Georges Villiers.

Conselheiro Lafaiete (kōṅ.sę.lyā′rö lä.fą.yā′tę). City in S Brazil, in the state of Minas Gerais. 18,415 (1950).

Consensus Genevensis (kǫn.sen′sus jen.ę.ven′sis). Confession of faith, drawn up by Calvin, which was dedicated (Jan. 1, 1552) by the pastors of Geneva to the syndics and council of the city. It was occasioned by Calvin's dispute with Bolsec, who denied the doctrine of reprobation, and was designed to unite the Swiss churches on the subject of predestination, but failed to acquire symbolical authority outside Geneva.

Consensus Tigurinus (kǫn.sen′sus tig.ū̦.rī′nus). Confession of faith drawn up in 1549 at Zurich (Latin, Tigurium) by Calvin, in concert with Bullinger and the pastors of Zurich, for the purpose of uniting the Swiss churches on the doctrine of the Lord's Supper. It was published in 1551, and was adopted by all the Reformed cantons of Switzerland except Berne.

Conservation Movement. Term applied to the organized demand for the preservation and protection of natural resources including land, mineral deposits, forests, and water power. The U.S. conservation movement arose during the period of industrial expansion after the Civil War, and the term was later used to describe generally the measures adopted by the U.S. government to develop the national park system and forest and game preserves, the construction of power sites such as Hoover Dam, the planning of regional power systems such as the Tennessee Valley Authority (TVA), and the control of crude oil production. The major conservation activities of the U.S. government are under the direction of the Departments of Agriculture and the Interior.

Conservative Club, The. London political club established in 1840.

Conservative Party. Political party in Great Britain. In 1824 George Canning first used the term Conservative as a variant of Tory, and in 1830 an article by J. W. Croker in the *Quarterly Review* brought the new name into general use. The addition of about half a million new voters to the rolls following the Reform Act of 1832 made the continuance of old-time Toryism impossible, and in 1834 Peel took the lead in wooing the new voters of the mercantile and manufacturing classes. Clubs and groups using the names "Constitutional" and "Conservative" were formed in many places, and in 1867 the National Union of Conservative and Constitutional Associations was formed. In 1841 the Conservatives were called on to form a government, which with Peel as prime minister held office until 1846, when a split occurred over the issue of repeal of the Corn Laws; this measure was passed at Peel's insistence, but it alienated the protectionists among the Conservatives, chief among whom was Benjamin Disraeli, and led to the downfall of the Peel government. Between 1846 and 1874 the Conservatives were out of power except for three short periods, and during that time most of the "Peelites" became affiliated with the Liberals, successors to the Tories' old opponents, the Whigs. Returned to office in 1874 with Disraeli as prime minister, and with a program of ameliorative social reform at home and imperialism abroad, the Conservatives ruled until 1880 when the Liberals came to power under William Ewart Gladstone. A split in the Liberal ranks over the issue of Home Rule for Ireland brought the Conservatives (who from that time were also commonly known as Unionists) into control once more, and from 1885 to 1905 their ascendancy was interrupted only twice, when they gave way to Liberal cabinets in 1886 and 1892–95. A demand for tariff reform raised within the party by Joseph Chamberlain resulted in a split leading to defeat in 1905. The Liberal regime which began at that time continued into World War I, when a coalition government was formed. By 1922 there was a Conservative majority in the House of Commons, the coalition was broken, and the Conservative Party again assumed responsibility, the prime minister's portfolio being taken by A. Bonar Law, who in the following year resigned and was succeeded by Stanley Baldwin. Conservative rule was briefly broken by a Labour victory in 1924, and in 1929 the Labour Party again formed a cabinet which, however, in the face of the great economic crisis of that time, became in 1931 a coalition government, which was in fact dominated by the Conservatives, and in 1935 Stanley Baldwin again became prime minister, to be succeeded in 1937 by Neville Chamberlain. In May, 1940, a coalition government was again formed under the premiership of Winston Churchill, who after some years in Liberal cabinets had again become a Conservative. The war won, Churchill eliminated the Labour members of the cabinet, but in a general election in 1945 Labour captured the House of Commons with a large majority. A general election in February, 1950, increased Conservative strength while still leaving the party in opposition, but in October, 1951, with the aid of a majority of members and former members of the disintegrating Liberal Party, the Conservatives, though trailing Labour in the popular vote, won a slim majority in the House of Commons, and once more organized a government with Winston Churchill at its head.

Conservative Party. In the several dominions of the British Commonwealth, name of a political party. The Conservative parties, though they follow programs approximately parallel in opposing too rapid or radical change, are not necessarily connected.

Conservatoire National de Musique et d'Art Dramatique (kôṅ.ser.vȧ.twȧr nȧ.syo.nȧl dẹ mü.zēk ā dȧr drȧ.mȧ.tēk). French music school founded (1795) at Paris under the name Conservatoire de Musique, incorporating a library of scores and a museum of instruments.

Consett (kon'sẹt). Urban district and manufacturing town in NE England, in Durham, situated on the river Derwent, ab. 12 mi. SW of Newcastle, ab. 277 mi. N of London by rail. It has an important iron and steel industry, now dependent upon imported ores. 39,456 (1951).

Conshohocken (kon.shọ̄.hok'ẹn). Borough in SE Pennsylvania, in Montgomery County, on the Schuylkill River ab. 13 mi. NW of Philadelphia: manufactures include tires, iron, steel, boilers, and textiles. It was incorporated in 1850. Pop. 10,922 (1950).

Considérant (kôṅ.sē.dā.räṅ), **Victor Prosper.** b. Oct. 12, 1808; d. Dec. 27, 1893. French socialist; a disciple of Fourier. He was accused of high treason in 1849, and fled to Belgium; from there he went to Texas, where (after returning once to Brussels) he sought to establish a socialistic society near San Antonio. He returned to France in 1869. Author of *La Destinée sociale* (1834–38).

Consolato del Mare (kōn.sō.lä'tō del mä'rā). [Eng. trans., "*Consulate of the Sea.*"] Code of maritime law, supposed to be a compilation of the law and trading customs of various Italian cities, such as Venice, Genoa, Pisa, and Amalfi, together with those of the cities with which they traded, including Barcelona, Marseilles, and others. Its precise date is unknown, but a Spanish edition of it was published at Barcelona at the end of the 13th or the beginning of the 14th century. It has formed the basis of many subsequent complications of maritime law.

Conspiracy and Tragedy of Charles Duke of Byron, The. Melodramatic tragedy (1608) in two parts, each in five acts, by George Chapman. The "Byron" of the title was Charles de Gontaut, Duke of Biron (1562–1602), a brave French soldier, known as "the Thunderbolt of France." The two plays deal with his plots against his king, and his punishment.

Conspiracy of Pontiac (pon'ti.ak), **The.** Historical work by Francis Parkman, published in 1851.

Constable (kun'stạ.bl, kon'-), **Archibald.** b. at Carnbee, Fifeshire, Scotland, Feb. 24, 1774; d. at Edinburgh, July 21, 1827. Scottish publisher, founder of the *Edinburgh Review* (1802), and publisher of most of the works of Sir Walter Scott from 1805 until he became bankrupt in 1826. The failure of Constable and Company with that of James Ballantyne and Company, printers, involved Scott in a loss of 120,000 pounds. He edited the *Chronicle of Fife, being the Diary of John Lamont of Newton from 1649 to 1672* (1810), and wrote a *Memoir of George Heriot.*

Constable, Henry. b. at Newark, Nottinghamshire, England, 1562; d. at Liége, Belgium, Oct. 9, 1613. English poet. He was graduated at Cambridge (St. John's College) in 1580, became a Roman Catholic, and for the greater part of his later life resided at Paris, occupied with political affairs and especially with schemes for promoting the interests of Catholicism. In 1603 he went to London, and was for a short time confined in the Tower. He published in 1592 a collection of 23 sonnets entitled *Diana: the Praises of his Mistress in certaine sweete Sonnets by H. C.*

Constable, John. b. at East Bergholt, Suffolk, England, June 11, 1776; d. at London, March 30, 1837. English landscape painter. His father was a miller. In 1799 he became a student at the Royal Academy, in 1802 exhibited his first picture, in 1819 became an associate of the Royal Academy, and in 1829 became a Royal Academician. He was thoroughly English: no foreign master influenced him, and rustic life furnished his inspiration and material. He obtained little recognition in his own country during his lifetime, but was highly appreciated in France, where his work produced a notable effect.

Constable, Sir **Marmaduke.** b. c1455; d. Nov. 20, 1518. English soldier; father of Sir Marmaduke Constable (c1480–1545), and a relative of Sir William Constable (d. 1655). He fought in France with Edward IV (1475) and with Henry VII (1492), the latter campaign ending with the treaty of Étaples at which Constable was among those receiving the French delegates, and in 1513 accompanied the earl of Surrey at the battle of Flodden, where he commanded the left wing.

Constable, Sir **Marmaduke.** b. c1480; d. 1545. English soldier; son of Sir Marmaduke Constable (c1455–1518), and a relative of Sir William Constable (d. 1655). He served (1513) under his father at the battle of Flodden, and was knighted (Sept. 9, 1513) after the battle as Sir Marmaduke Constable of Everingham.

Constable, Sir **William.** d. at London, June 15, 1655. English soldier with the Parliamentary army in the English Civil War. He was a guard (1648) over Charles I during his imprisonment at Carisbrook, was later one of Charles's judges and a signer of his death warrant, and served in the council of state under Cromwell. After the Restoration his estates were confiscated and his body removed from Westminster Abbey.

Constance (kon'stạns). See also **Konstanz.**

Constance. b. 1152; d. 1198. Wife of Emperor Henry VI of the Holy Roman Empire. Her nephew William II of Sicily named her as his heir to the throne of that kingdom, but the Sicilian nobles gave the crown to the illegitimate Tancred of Lecce. Henry VI, claiming Sicily by virtue of his marriage to Constance, tried in vain to unseat Tancred, and after the latter's death in 1194, Henry did rule Sicily until his own death in 1197, when Constance secured the Pope's recognition of their infant son (later the Emperor Frederick II) as king of Sicily, and until her own death in the following year, Constance exercised power as regent.

Constance. In Chaucer's *Man of Law's Tale*, the unjustly accused daughter of the Roman emperor. She is cleared and married to King Alla.

Constance. In Shakespeare's *King John*, the mother of Arthur, duke of Bretagne.

Constance. The "Northern Lass," in Richard Brome's play of that name.

Constance. Daughter of Nonesuch, in love with Loveby, in Dryden's play *The Wild Gallant.*

Constance. Daughter of the provost, in G. W. Lovell's play *The Provost of Bruges.* She goes mad and dies when proved to be legally a serf.

Constance. Daughter of Fondlove in J. Sheridan Knowles's comedy *The Love Chase.* Her love affair with Wildrake is not unlike that of Benedick and Beatrice.

Constance, Council of. Important council of the Roman Catholic Church, held at Konstanz (Constance), Germany, from 1414 to 1418. Its objects were the healing of the papal schism, the suppression of the Bohemian heresy, and the reformation of the church. It condemned Hus to death in 1415, and Jerome of Prague in 1416, and elected (1417) Martin V as Pope.

Constance (or **Custance**), **Dame Christian.** Rich and beautiful widow in Nicholas Udall's play *Ralph Roister Doister.*

Constance, Lake. [Also: **Lake of Constance**; German, **Boden See, Bodensee**; Latin, **Brigantinus Lacus.**] Lake lying between Switzerland, Germany (Baden, Württemberg, and Bavaria), and Austria (Vorarlberg). The NW narrowed arm is frequently known as the Überlingersee; the W arm is called the Untersee or Zellersee. It is traversed by the Rhine. Length, ab. 46 mi.; greatest breadth, 6–8 mi.; area, 208 sq. mi.; elevation, 1,306 ft.; depth, ab. 825 ft.

Constance, Treaty of. Treaty of peace concluded at Konstanz (Constance), Germany, between Frederick I (Frederick Barbarossa) of the Holy Roman Empire and the Lombard League in 1183, at the expiration of the truce established after the defeat of the emperor at Legnano, near Milan, in 1176. Frederick renounced all the regalian rights which he claimed in the cities of the League, including those of levying war, erecting fortifications, and administering civil and criminal justice. The cities acknowledged the overlordship of the emperor, which carried with it the obligation to furnish the customary tributes of provision during his residence in Italy, to suffer the chief magistrates in every city to receive the investiture of office from an imperial legate, and to accept in every city an imperial judge of appeal in civil cases.

Constance Baines (bānz). See under **Baines.**

Constance de Beverley (dẹ bev'ėr.li). See **Beverley, Constance de.**

Constance Neville (nev'il). See **Neville, Constance.**

Constancio (kōn.stun'syō), **Francisco Solano.** b. at Lisbon, Portugal, 1777; d. at Paris, Dec. 21, 1846. Portuguese physician and author. He traveled extensively in Europe and North America, was diplomatic agent of Portugal at Paris (1820), and was minister to Washington (1822–29). Subsequently he resided at Paris. Constancio's works are now little esteemed. His best-known are his *Novo diccionario critico e etymologico da lingua Portugueza* (1836, 1844) and *Historia do Brasil* (2 vols., 1839).

Constans (kon'stanz). Grandfather of King Arthur, celebrated in the Arthurian romances.

Constans I. [Full name, **Flavius Julius Constans.**] b. c320; d. near Illiberis (now Elne), in Gaul, 350. Roman emperor, youngest of the three sons of Constantine the Great and Fausta. He received, in the division of the empire in 337, Italy, Africa, and western Illyricum. In 340, having successfully resisted the invasion of his brother Constantine, who fell in battle, he made himself master of the whole West. In 350 Magnentius usurped the throne, and Constans was slain by his emissaries.

Constans II. [Full name, **Flavius Heraclius Constans.**] b. Nov. 7, 630; killed at Syracuse, July 15, 668. Byzantine emperor (641–668); son of Constantine III. In his reign the Saracens conquered Rhodes, and the Lombards most of the Byzantine dominions in N Italy. He favored the Monothelites, and, in order to put an end to the controversy between them and the orthodox, issued an edict which forbade all religious discussion.

Constans (kôṅ.stäṅ), **Ernest.** [Full name, **Jean Antoine Ernest Constans.**] b. at Béziers, Hérault, France, May 3, 1833; d. at Paris, April 7, 1913. French political leader and diplomat. As minister of the interior (1880–81, 1889–92), he enforced laws against religious congregations and fought the Boulangist movement. He served as ambassador to China (1886), as governor general of China (1886–88), and as ambassador (1898–1907) to Turkey.

Constant (kon'stant). The lover of Lady Brute in Vanbrugh's comedy *The Provoked Wife.*

Constant (kōṅ.stunt'), **Benjamin.** Popular name of **Magalhães, Benjamin Constant Botelho de.**

Constant, (Jean Joseph) Benjamin. b. at Paris, June 10, 1845; d. May 26, 1902. French painter, known for his portraits and for Oriental scenes of considerable dramatic content, based on a sojourn in Morocco. He studied under Cabanel at the École des Beaux-Arts, and in 1869 exhibited his first picture, *Hamlet et le roi*, at the Paris Salon. Other paintings include *Trop tard* (1870), *Samson et Delilah* (1872), *Bouchersmaures à Tanger* (1873), *Carrefour à Tanger* (1874), *Mohamed II, le 29 Mai, 1453* (1878), *Favorite de l'émir* (1879), *La Vengeance du chérif* (1885), and *Victrix* (1890).

Constant, Paul Henri Benjamin Belluat, Baron de **Constant de Rebecque d'Estournelles de.** See **Estournelles de Constant, Paul Henri Benjamin Belluat,** Baron **de Constant de Rebecque d'.**

Constanța (kōn.stän'tsä). [Also: **Constantsa, Constantza;** Turkish, **Küstendje, Küstenja;** ancient names, **Constantiana, Tomi, Tomis.**] City in S Rumania, in the province of Dobruja, situated on the Black Sea, ab. 135 mi. E of Bucharest. It is next to Odessa the biggest port on the Black Sea, has large oil refineries, and is a terminus of the only oil pipe line on the Balkan Peninsula. Shipbuilding, leather processing, and chemical industries are also important. Constanța is the seat of an Orthodox bishopric, and of a naval academy and a university of commerce. It was under Turkish rule from 1413 to 1878. In World War II, on Aug. 29, 1944, the city was occupied by the Russians. 78,586 (1948).

Constant de Rebecque (kôṅ.stäṅ dẹ rẹ.bek), **Henri Benjamin.** b. at Lausanne, Switzerland, Oct. 25, 1767; d. at Paris, Dec. 8, 1830. French novelist, political orator, and politician. He settled in 1795 at Paris as the protégé of Madame de Staël, and was a member (1799–1802) of the Tribunate. Banished by Napoleon, he returned in 1814, but accepted office under Napoleon during the Hundred Days, with the result that on the return of the Bourbons he was again compelled to go into exile, whence he returned in 1816. He was a member (1819–30) of the Chamber of Deputies. His chief works are *Cours de politique constitutionnelle* (1818–20) and *De la religion considérée dans sa source, sa forme et son développement* (1823–25). His novel *Adolphe* (1816) is considered a masterpiece in the psychological tradition.

Constantina (kōn.stän.tē'nä). Town in S Spain, in the province of Sevilla, ab. 40 mi. NE of Seville: silver and lead mines, wine markets, and distilleries. There are remnants of Roman structures in the town, which was founded by the Roman emperor Constantine. 14,546 (1904).

Constantine (kon'stạn.tīn, -tēn). See also **Konstantin.**

Constantine. [Full name, **Flavius Claudius Constantinus.**] d. at Ravenna, Italy, 410 or 411. Coemperor of the Western Roman Empire. A common soldier possessing ability and ambition, he was proclaimed emperor by the legionaries in Britain in 407, and brought under his control Britain, Gaul, and (through his son Constans) Spain. The Western emperor, Honorius, having put Stilicho to death, feared to prolong the struggle against Constantine, and accepted him as coemperor. Constantine proceeded to Italy at the head of a large army, but the revolt of Gerontius, who proclaimed Maximus emperor (409), recalled him to Gaul, where Gerontius besieged him at Arles. Gerontius's forces fled at the approach of Honorius's legions led by Constantius (later Emperor Constantius III), who proceeded to defeat Constantine. The latter surrendered under a promise that his life would be spared, but he was taken to Ravenna and beheaded.

Constantine. b. in Syria; d. at Rome, April 9, 715. Pope from 708 to 715. Because of difficulties with the emperor Justinian II over the decrees of the Quinisext or Trullan Council (692), which the emperor supported, Constantine journeyed to Constantinople, where an agreement was reached between them. Under the emperor Philippicus, Constantine opposed imperial sanction of Monothelism, but saw orthodoxy restored when Anastasius gained the throne.

Constantine. b. at Nepi, Italy; fl. 8th century. Antipope from 767 to 768, a layman forcibly intruded into the chair of Peter in June or July, 767, by Toto of Nepi and a band of Tuscans, upon the death of Saint Paul I, who died June 28, 767. He was deposed in the spring of 768 in favor of Stephen IV.

Constantine (kon'stạn.tēn; French, kôṅ.stäṅ.tēn). Easternmost department of Algeria, in NW Africa, lying between the Mediterranean Sea on the N, Tunisia on the E, and Algiers department on the W. It has the largest population of the three Algerian departments. Capital, Constantine; area, 33,707 sq. mi.; pop. 3,102,396 (1948).

Constantine. [Ancient name, **Cirta.**] Capital of the department of Constantine, Algeria, in NW Africa, situated on a high plateau ab. 40 mi. S of the Mediterranean Sea. The seaport for its foreign trade is Philippeville, the third largest city of Algeria. Constantine is the cultural and commercial center of Constantine department; it is a great trading center, especially for grain. Cirta was an ancient city of Numidia, noted as a fortress. Destroyed in the 4th century, it was rebuilt and renamed by the Roman emperor Constantine I, was later part of the Turkish empire, and was captured by the French in 1837. The name is also applied to an *arrondissement* (administrative division), a commune, and a military division. Pop. of city, 118,774 (1948).

Constantine (kon'stạn.tīn, -tēn). Original name of Saint **Cyril.**

Constantine I. [Called **Constantine the Great;** full Latin name, **Flavius Valerius Aurelius Constantinus.**] b. at Naissus (modern Niš), in Upper Moesia (in what is now Yugoslavia), in February, 274 A.D.; d. at Nicomedia (modern Izmit), in Bithynia (in what is now Turkey), May 22, 337. Roman emperor. He was the eldest son of the emperor Constantius I (Constantius Chlorus) by his first wife Helena, and was appointed Caesar (subordinate emperor) at the death of his father in 306. About 308 he was recognized as Augustus (emperor) by the emperor Maximian, whose daughter Fausta he married (his first wife having died). In 310 he put to death Maximian, who was implicated in a plot to excite a rebellion among his subjects. He defeated in 312, near Rome, the emperor Maxentius, who was killed as he fled from the field of battle. Before this battle, according to tradition, the sign of a cross appeared in the heavens, with the inscription *In hoc signo vinces* (meaning, approximately, "under this sign be victorious"), which induced him to adopt the labarum (a purple banner hanging vertically from a horizontal crosspiece on a pike or spear, and bearing the monogram "XP," the initials in Greek of Jesus Christ) as his standard. In 323 he became sole emperor by a decisive victory at Chrysopolis (modern Üsküdar, in Turkey) over his colleague Licinius, who subsequently surrendered and was treacherously murdered (324). He caused Christianity to be recognized by the state, convened the Council of Nicaea in 325, and in 330 announced Constantinople (modern Istanbul) as the capital of the Roman Empire. In 324 he put to death his eldest son, Crispus, for high treason. According to tradition, Crispus was the victim of an intrigue on the part of his stepmother, Fausta, who was suffocated in a bath as soon as Constantine discovered the innocence of Crispus. That these two killings did occur on his orders is now accepted as fact by virtually every authority in the field, but Constantine's actual motivation is less easy to determine. His fits of rage were violent to the point of being uncontrollable, and his rule was absolute within his court and throughout his realm; the most plausible explanation of the "executions" is perhaps therefore simply quick temper abetted by unquestioned authority rather than any devious scheme to eliminate two people whose existence he no longer desired. Constantine was, on the whole, one of the most able rulers in the history of the ancient world. Unlike the petty despots and upstart generals who had so often in the generations just before him briefly held the title of "Augustus," he was a brilliant administrator and military leader who aimed at nothing less than the reestablishment of a strong, unified, and prosperous Roman empire from Britain to the East. The famous story of the cross that appeared in the sky before the battle against Maxentius in 312 has obscured, to some extent, Constantine's own probable attitude toward Christianity. Unquestionably he was influenced by it, but it is equally unquestionably a moot question as to whether this influence was (until the very end of his life) chiefly religious or the adaptation of what was clearly an important force in the world to serve the immediate, and very practical, end of consolidating the imperial power. He convened the Synod of Arles in 314 and the first Council of Nicaea in 325, and specifically dedicated his own imperial city of Constantinople (at the time of its naming, in 330) to Mary, the mother of Jesus; nevertheless, he was not himself actually baptized as a Christian until the time of his death, in 337, and he long encouraged a degree of paganism within his own court. Another fact about Constantine which may lead to some confusion on the part of the modern reader is that, although he may surely be said to have founded what most historians call the Byzantine Empire, he is himself generally and properly referred to as a Roman emperor. This confusion will be eliminated if the reader will recall that at the time of Constantine it was an accepted fact that the Roman Empire could (and usually did) have two emperors, who were theoretically supposed to rule jointly. This concept of joint rule was accepted by Constantine and by the people throughout the Empire (the fact that from the death of Licinius in 324 Constantine was the only emperor was taken by Constantine himself to be an exceptional circumstance, even though he had brought it about); paralleling (and, in a curious way, actually supporting) this concept of joint rule was the concept of the Roman Empire as being an essentially indivisible political unit (in other words, regardless of the number of emperors, there could be only one Empire). The result of this was that Constantine thought of himself as being the ruler of the Roman Empire in its fullest sense, and not simply of its eastern portion. This concept persisted long after Constantine's death, and it is from it that the later emperors at Constantinople (after the division of the Empire into Eastern and Western portions) traced their claim to be recognized as the only rightful "Roman" emperors (which led to the seeming paradox of Byzantine emperors stubbornly insisting on the title of "Roman emperor").

Constantine II. [Full Latin name, **Flavius Claudius Constantinus.**] b. at Arles, in Gaul (now France), in February, 317; killed near Aquileia, Italy, 340. Emperor of Rome; second son of Constantine I (Constantine the Great). He received, in the division of the empire in 337 between the three sons of Constantine I, Gaul, Britain, Spain, and part of Africa. Being dissatisfied with his share, he invaded the dominions of his brother Constans, but was defeated and killed at Aquileia in 340.

Constantine III. b. c612; d. (probably by poison) 641. Byzantine emperor. He accomplished little, and died (very possibly at the instigation of his half brother and fellow occupant of the imperial throne) in the year of his accession.

Constantine IV. [Full name, **Flavius Constantinus;** called **Constantine Pogonatus** (pō.gǫ.nā'tus), meaning "Constantine the Bearded."] d. 685. Byzantine emperor (668–685); son of Constans II. He repulsed (by means of the Greek fire which had recently been invented) the Saracens before Constantinople (672–679), and assembled (680) at Constantinople the sixth general council which condemned the Monothelites and restored peace to the church.

Constantine V. [Called **Constantine Copronymus** (kop.ron'i.mus).] b. at Constantinople, 719; d. off Thrace, Sept. 14, 775. Byzantine emperor (741–775); son of Leo III. He defeated (743) Artavasdes, who had usurped the government, and assembled (754) a council which condemned the worship of images.

Constantine VI. [Full name, **Flavius Constantinus.**] b. 771; killed at Constantinople, c797. Byzantine emperor (780–797), the last of the Isaurian emperors. He was the son of Leo IV, whom he succeeded under the regency of his mother Irene. During his reign a council held (787) at Nicaea restored the worship of images. He was put to death by order of his mother, who usurped the government.

Constantine VII. [Called **Constantine Porphyrogenitus** (pôr"fi.rǭ.jen'i.tus), meaning "Constantine Born to the Purple."] b. 905; poisoned Nov. 15, 959. Byzantine emperor; son of Leo VI, whom he succeeded in 912. The government was usurped in 919 by Romanus Lecapenus, who administered it, Constantine being nominally his colleague, until 944, when he was deposed by his own son, and Constantine became sole ruler. He was noted for his humanity and for his success in war, chiefly against the Arabs in Syria. He was poisoned by his son and successor, Romanus II. He was a liberal patron of learning, and himself holds a high rank in literature as the author of a treatise on the government and one on the *themes* (provinces) of the empire (*De administrando imperio* and *De thematibus*), and other works.

Constantine VIII. b. c960; d. 1028. Byzantine emperor. The son of the emperor Romanus II, he ruled jointly with his brother Basil II from 976 to 1025 and then alone, after his brother's death, from 1025 to 1028.

Constantine IX. [Called **Constantine Monomachus,** meaning "Constantine who fights alone."] b. c1000; d. 1055. Byzantine emperor. He was a soldier who married (1042) the empress Zoë and ruled jointly with her and her sister Theodora from 1042 to 1050. After Zoë's death, he and Theodora ruled together from 1050 to 1055, in which year he died. He was a lover of luxury who ignored the threats to the empire and disbanded a large part of his army, losing Italy completely and suffering attacks in Thrace and Macedonia. During his reign the Seljuk Turks made their appearance in Armenia.

Constantine X. [Also, **Constantine X Ducas.**] b. c1007; d. 1067. Byzantine emperor. He had been a capable administrator, but after he was chosen emperor to succeed Isaac I Comnenus he proved to be a weak emperor and was unable to stem the tide of invasions. Concentrating on the center of the empire rather than on defending its frontiers, he lost Armenia to the Seljuk Turks in 1064, Belgrade to the Magyars, and parts of Thrace and Macedonia to Turks from the Black Sea region (1065).

Constantine XI. [Also, **Constantine XI Palaeologus** (pā.lẹ.ol'ǭ.gus).] b. 1394; d. May 29, 1453. Byzantine emperor (1448–53), the last emperor of Constantinople. He was killed at the taking of the city by Mohammed II.

Constantine XIII. See **Constantine XI,** immediately preceding. In some of the older chronologies Constantine XI is erroneously carried as Constantine XIII.

Constantine I (of *Greece*). b. at Athens, Greece, 1868; d. at Palermo, Italy, 1922. King of the Hellenes (1913–17 and 1920–22); son of George I. Created Duke of

Sparta as a baby, he studied at the Greek military academy (1882–86) and in Germany at the Berlin war academy and at the Universities of Leipzig and Heidelberg (1886–89). Commissioned as a colonel in 1886, he served briefly in the German army. He married Sophia, sister of William II of Germany, in 1889, and was appointed a major general in the same year. He commanded the Thessalian army in the war with Turkey in 1897 and was blamed by many for the Greek defeat. Despite this he was commander in chief of Greek land forces in the period 1902–09 and during the Balkan War of 1912–13, his success in which restored him to popularity. He favored neutrality in World War I, quarreling with Venizelos on this and other matters, and left Greece after Venizelos' Salonica coup (1917), settling in Switzerland. He was restored to the throne in 1920 after Alexander's death, though bitterly opposed by the French and the British for his pro-German record in World War I. Although he went to the front during the war against Turkey in Asia Minor, he did not take command. After the disaster there, he abdicated (1922) in favor of his son George II and retired to Palermo.

Constantine I (of *Scotland*). d. 879. King of Scotland (north of the Forth and Clyde), reigning at Scone after 863.

Constantine II (of *Scotland*). d. 952. King of Scotland (north of the Forth and Clyde) from 900 to 943, when he resigned the throne to Malcolm, grandson of Constantine I.

Constantine Nikolayevich (nē.ko.lä'yi.vich). b. at St. Petersburg, Sept. 21, 1827; d. Jan. 24, 1892. Russian grand duke. He was a brother of Czar Alexander II, who made him commander of the Russian fleet in the Baltic (1854–55) and governor of Poland (1862–63). Approving the liberal tendencies of the Czar, he was nevertheless unable to forestall the insurrection of 1863. In 1865 he became president of the imperial council, but after the accession of Alexander III he came under suspicion of conspiring against that monarch, and thereafter was out of favor at the imperial court.

Constantine the African. [Latin, **Constantinus Africanus** (kon.stạn.tī'nus af.ri.kā'nus).] b. c1020; d. c1087. Translator of Arabic books into Latin. It is generally thought that he was a native of Carthage, but some scholars believe that he was born at Salerno, where there were in his day a good many speakers of Arabic and of Greek. Certainly he lived for a time at Salerno, and also at Carthage or elsewhere in North Africa, before taking the vows of a Benedictine and retiring to Monte Cassino, where most of his life was spent, and where he had the assistance of others in translating Arabic texts into Latin (for it is supposed that he was not much of a Latinist). The works he translated were mainly writings, in Arabic, of Jewish scholars in North Africa, dealing with Aristotelian and other philosophies, and with Greek medicine. The medical treatises at once aroused great interest, and many copies were made and circulated, eventually becoming known throughout Europe and exerting great influence during the Middle Ages and until the 17th century.

Constantine the Great. See **Constantine I.**

Constantinople (kon"stan.ti.nō'pl). [Ancient name, **Byzantium**; modern name (since 1930), **Istanbul,** Turkish, **İstanbul.**] Former capital of the Roman Empire, of the Byzantine (or Eastern Roman) Empire, and of the Ottoman (or Turkish) Empire, situated in what is now European Turkey, on the Bosporus, the Golden Horn, and the Sea of Marmara. In 330 A.D. Constantine I (Constantine the Great) named it and made it his capital of the Roman Empire. It was repeatedly besieged by the Saracens, and was taken by the Latins in 1203 and 1204, by Michael Palaeologus in 1261, and by the Turks on May 29, 1453.

Constantinople, Conference of. Conference of the six great powers (France, Great Britain, Austria-Hungary, Germany, Spain, Russia) and Turkey for the purpose of preventing war between Turkey and Russia, which latter was championing the cause of the Christian insurgents against Turkish rule in the Balkan peninsula. The conference was formally opened Dec. 23, 1876, after a preliminary conference between the great powers (Dec. 11–21). The powers demanded of the Porte (the Turkish government) administrative autonomy under Christian governors for Bosnia, Hercegovina, and Bulgaria, and proposed the establishment of an international commission with power to enforce by arms the decisions of the conference. These demands were rejected by the Turks on Jan. 18, 1877, whereupon the conference dissolved, on Jan. 20.

Constantinople, Councils of. Name of various ecumenical councils held at Constantinople: **1.** The First Council of Constantinople, or the second ecumenical council, convened here by the emperor Theodosius in 381 A.D. Its chief object was the settlement of the Arian difficulties. **2.** The Second Council of Constantinople, or the fifth ecumenical council, convened by Justinian in 553. Its object was the condemnation of the "three chapters." **3.** The Third Council of Constantinople, or the sixth ecumenical council, held in the years 680–681. Its object was the condemnation of the Monothelites. The Apostolic Constitutions were approved. **4.** The Fourth Council of Constantinople, or the eighth ecumenical council, held in 869. Its object was the condemnation of Photius.

Constantinople, Treaty of. One of the treaties ending the Balkan War of 1913 ("Second Balkan War"). An agreement between Bulgaria and Turkey, signed on Sept. 29, 1913, it favored the Turks by returning to them the city of Adrianople (Edirne) and a boundary running along the Maritsa River.

Constantin-Weyer (kôn.stän.tan.vā.yer), **Maurice.** b. at Bourbonne-les-Bains, France, 1881—. French novelist and translator of Shakespeare, known especially for his novel about Canada (where he resided c1902), *Un homme se penche sur son passé* (1929). His other works, aside from translations, include *Manitoba* (1925) and *La Bourrasque* (1926).

Constantiola (kon"stan.ti.ō'lạ). Ancient name of **Oltenița.**

Constantius I (kọn.stan'shus, -shi.us). [Full name, **Flavius Valerius Constantius**; surnamed **Chlorus,** meaning "the Pale."] b. probably 250 A.D.; d. at York, England, July 25, 306. Emperor of Rome; father of Constantine I (Constantine the Great). On March 1, 293, the joint emperors Diocletian and Maximian associated with themselves Constantius Chlorus and Galerius as junior partners under the title of Caesars. Gaul, Spain, and Britain were allotted to the former, who was required to repudiate his wife Helena and marry Theodora, the daughter of Maximian. After the abdication of Diocletian and Maximian in 305, he ruled as Augustus (joint emperor) with Galerius until his death in Britain while on an expedition against the Picts.

Constantius II. [Full name, **Flavius Julius Constantius.**] b. at Sirmium, in Pannonia, Aug. 6, 317; d. at Mopsocrene, in Cilicia, Nov. 3, 361. Roman emperor; third son of Constantine I (Constantine the Great), the second son by his second wife, Fausta. The will of Constantine I divided the empire among his three sons Constantine, Constantius, and Constans under the title of Augusti (joint emperors), and his nephews Dalmatius and Hannibalianus under the titles of Caesar and Nobilissimus, respectively. On the death of Constantine in 337 Constantius ordered, or permitted, the murder of Dalmatius and Hannibalianus, and the empire was redivided between himself and his brothers. Constantine received Gaul, Spain, Britain, and part of Africa; Constantius Thrace, Macedonia, Greece, the Asiatic provinces, and Egypt; and Constans Italy, western Illyricum, and the rest of Africa. In 340 Constans repelled an invasion of Constantine, who fell in battle, and made himself master of the West; but was himself deposed and slain in 350 by the usurper Magnentius. Constantius made war in 351 on the latter, whom he defeated at Mursa (modern Osijek), on the Drava River, in 351, and in Gaul in 353, after which he was master of the whole empire. He appointed his cousin Julian to be Caesar and commander in Gaul 355, and visited Rome 357. He favored the Arians, and banished the orthodox bishops. He died while marching to attack Julian, who had been proclaimed emperor by his soldiers.

Constantius III. d. in September, 421. Roman emperor. After the emperor Honorius had put his great general, Stilicho, to death, this Illyrian soldier became the ablest defender of the Western Empire. At Arles in 410 or 411 he scattered the army of the rebellious Gerontius, who had proclaimed Maximus as emperor, and defeated and captured Constantine, whom Honorius had, in fear, made coemperor. Already practically ruler of the West, Constantius wished to marry Honorius' sister Galla Placidia, but she was given in marriage to the Visigoth king Ataulf. Constantius drove Ataulf into Spain and harassed him there until his assassination (which Constantius does not seem to have brought about), and in 417 he married Galla Placidia. An astute statesman, Constantius was principally responsible for establishing local self-government in Gaul (418), and for settling the Visigoths in Aquitaine (419). In 421 Honorius conferred the title of Augustus on Constantius, making him coemperor of the West, but he died within a few months after attaining this distinction. He was the father of Valentinian (419–455), who as Valentinian III was emperor of the West (425–455).

Constant Maid, The. Play by Shirley, printed in 1640, reprinted in 1667 with the second title *Love will find out the Way.*

Constant Wife, The. Comedy of marital infidelity, in three acts, by W. Somerset Maugham. It was published in 1926, produced in 1927, and has been revived several times since.

Constanza (kon.stan′zạ). Gay and sportive girl, in Thomas Middleton's *Spanish Gipsy,* who follows her father into exile disguised as a gipsy under the name Pretiosa.

Constellation. Vessel of the U.S. navy. She was built in 1798, and under command of Commodore Truxton in 1799 captured the French *Insurgente.*

Constitution. [Called **"Old Ironsides."**] American frigate of 1,576 tons and 44 guns rating (actual armament 32 long 24-pounders and 20 32-pounder carronades), built at Boston in 1797. The *United States* and *President* were sister ships of the same rating. Her first commander was Captain Isaac Hull. At the declaration of war on June 18, 1812, the *Constitution* was at Annapolis. On July 17 she fell in with a British squadron composed of the *Shannon* (38 guns), *Africa* (64), *Aeolus* (32), *Belvidera* (36), and *Guerrière* (38), commanded by Commodore Philip Vere Broke. Her escape from this fleet, in a chase which lasted three days in an almost dead calm, is considered one of the greatest feats of seamanship of the war. On Aug. 19, 1812, she fought the *Guerrière.* The battle lasted from 5 to 7 P.M., when the *Guerrière* surrendered and was burned. The *Constitution* returned to Boston; Captain Hull resigned, and was succeeded by Captain Bainbridge of the *Constellation.* She sailed from Boston Oct. 26, 1812, and on Dec. 29 fell in with the frigate *Java* (38 guns), Captain Lambert, off the coast of Brazil. The battle lasted from 2 to 5 P.M., when the *Java* surrendered. On Feb. 20, 1815, she fought and captured the *Cyane* and *Levant* (20 and 18 guns). In September, 1830, it was proposed by the secretary of the navy to dismantle the ship and sell her. This excited public indignation, which found expression in the poem *Old Ironsides,* by Oliver Wendell Holmes, Sept. 15, 1830. She was afterward used as a school ship, later for a receiving ship at Portsmouth, N.H., and in 1897 was taken to Boston.

Constitution, Fort. See under **Constitution Island.**

Constitutional Club. London political club established in 1883.

Constitutional Convention of 1787. [Also called the **Federal Convention.**] In U.S. history, the body of delegates from the several states which framed the Constitution of the United States, sitting at Philadelphia from May 25 to Sept. 17, 1787. The convention was called in accordance with the recommendation of the Annapolis Convention of 1786 which, however, had designated as the major objective of the Philadelphia Convention the revision of the Articles of Confederation. The proceedings of the convention were held in secret.

Constitutional Courant (ku.rant′), **The.** Newspaper published Sept. 21, 1765 by James Parker in denunciation of the Stamp Act.

Constitutional History of England. [Full title, **The Constitutional History of England from the Accession of Henry VII to the Death of George II.**] Prose work (1827) by Henry Hallam. One of his three great works, it still holds its place as a standard reference in its field. It was continued (1861–63) by Sir Thomas May, in his *Constitutional History of England Since the Accession of George III.*

Constitutional History of England in its Origin and Development, The. Prose work in three volumes (1873, 1875, 1878), by William Stubbs. The period it covers is from the beginning of English history down to 1485.

Constitutional Union Party. Name adopted by the remnant of the Whig Party of the South in the U.S. presidential election of 1860. Delegates from 20 states met at Baltimore, May 9, 1860, and nominated John Bell for president and Edward Everett for vice-president. A platform was adopted which sought to evade the slavery question by declaring for "the Constitution of the country, the union of the States, and the enforcement of the laws." Its candidate received 588,879 votes.

Constitution Hill. Elevation near Buckingham Palace, London. Three attempts upon the life of Queen Victoria were made (1840, 1842, and 1849) here.

Constitution Island. Island in S New York, on the E side of the Hudson River ab. 10 mi. N of Peekskill, N.Y., and just across the river from West Point. The ruins of old Fort Constitution from the Revolutionary War are here; during this war a huge iron chain ab. 1,700 ft. long was stretched across the Hudson to block British ships from ascending the river. The main line of the New York Central Railroad now crosses the island.

Constitution of Athens. Work by Aristotle. Discovered in 1891 at the British Museum among papyrus rolls from Egypt, in the form of a manuscript probably written between 95 and 100 A.D., this is now conceded to be a copy of an authentic work by Aristotle. It is the almost complete text of a treatise on the history and character of the government of Athens.

Constitution of the United States. [Also, **Federal Constitution.**] Fundamental or organic law of the U.S. It was framed by the Constitutional Convention which met at Philadelphia, May 25, 1787, and adjourned Sept. 17, 1787, and it went into effect March 4, 1789, having been ratified by 11 of the 13 states (the others, North Carolina and Rhode Island, ratified it Nov. 21, 1789, and May 29, 1790, respectively). It consists of a Preamble, seven Articles, and 21 Amendments. Article I establishes a Congress consisting of a Senate and a House of Representatives and sets forth the qualifications for membership and duties in both houses. Article II vests the executive power in a President, states the method of his selection (by an electoral college rather than by direct vote), and states his duties. Article III puts the judicial power in a Supreme Court and minor courts and establishes their jurisdiction. Article IV relates to the states, their interrelationship, and their relationship to the Federal government. Article V sets forth the method of amending the Constitution. Article VI states the nature of the Constitution (it continues the union of the Confederation, becomes the supreme law of the land, is the organ to which federal officers take their oath). Article VII sets the manner of ratification of the Constitution. The first ten amendments (also, strictly speaking, called Articles) came into effect Dec. 15, 1791 and restrict the powers of the Federal government. Often called, collectively, the Bill of Rights, these ten amendments reserve certain rights to the people and the states. Amendment I bars Congress from making laws concerning religious establishment or restricting worship, abridging freedom of the press or of speech, or the right of the people to assemble or to petition the government. Amendment II states that the people's right to bear arms may not be infringed. Amendment III denies the privilege of quartering troops in private houses, except under legal sanction. Unreasonable search of persons and their houses, without warrant, is forbidden by Amendment IV. Amendment V sets forth the necessity of grand jury indictment in charges of crime, denies double jeopardy for the same crime, and states that no person may "be deprived of life, liberty, or property, without due process of law." A speedy, open, and fair trial for accused persons is maintained by Amendment VI. Trial by jury is established in Amendment VII. Excessive bail, fines, or punishments are forbidden under Amendment VIII. By Amendment IX, the people are not denied those rights not specifically delegated in the Constitution, and by Amendment X the powers not given to the U.S. nor prohibited the states are reserved to the states or the people. Amendment XI (in effect Jan. 8, 1798) restricts the judicial power of the U.S. Amendment XII (in effect Sept. 25, 1804) sets forth the manner of the election of the president and vice-president by separate ballot, instead of the previous method of first and second choices for president. Amendment XIII (in effect Dec. 18, 1865) abolishes slavery in the U.S. Amendment XIV (in effect July 28, 1868) reëstablishes, after the Civil War, the status of citizens and their rights, of their representation, and of the national debt. Amendment XV (in effect March 30, 1870) denies that a person may be barred from citizenship rights "on account of race, color, or previous condition of servitude." Amendment XVI (in effect Feb. 25, 1913) establishes the Congressional right to levy an income tax. Amendment XVII (in effect May 31, 1913) fixes popular, rather than legislatural, election for senators. Amendment XVIII (in effect Jan. 29, 1919) prohibits the sale or manufacture of intoxicating liquors in the U.S. (this was repealed by Amendment XXI). Amendment XIX (in effect Aug. 26, 1920) establishes women's suffrage. Amendment XX (in effect Feb. 6, 1933) eliminates the "lame duck" session of Congress (a session in which members who had been refused reëlection by their constituencies still voted) and provides for the succession to the presidency in case the president-elect shall have died. Amendment XXI (in effect Dec. 5, 1933) repeals the 18th Amendment. Tenure of office of the president is limited to a maximum of two full terms (plus a possible two years or less if he succeeds as vice-president) by Amendment XXII (Feb. 26, 1951).

Constitutions, Apostolic. See **Apostolic Constitutions.**

"Constitution State." Occasional nickname of **Connecticut.**

Consuelo (kon.sö.ā'lō; French, kôn.swā.lō). Novel by George Sand, published in 1842.

Consulate. In French history, the government which existed from Nov. 9, 1799 to May 18, 1804. Napoleon was First Consul, and his associates were Cambacérès and Lebrun.

Consus (kon'sus). In Roman mythology, a god, commonly called the god of good counsel, but having also certain very ancient agricultural and chthonian aspects. In his agricultural aspect of guardian of grain, the goddess Ops was his consort. His two festivals occurred in August and December. His underground altar in the Circus Maximus probably led the Romans to associate horses and horse racing with his festivals.

Contarina (kōn.tä.rē'nä). Town and commune in NE Italy, in the *compartimento* (region) of Veneto, in the province of Rovigo, situated in the delta of the Po River, W of Rovigo: fishing and silkworm raising. Pop. of commune, 10,444 (1936); of town, 4,500 (1936).

Contarini (kōn.tä.rē'nē), **Andrea.** b. c1300; d. 1382. Doge of Venice (1368–82), during whose reign occurred the War of Chioggia between Venice and Genoa. He is famed in history for the example of patriotism he gave by melting down his gold and silver plate and pledging his estate to raise funds for the prosecution of the war.

Contarini, Gasparo. b. at Venice, Oct. 16, 1483; d. at Bologna, Italy, Aug. 24, 1542. Italian cardinal (1535 *et seq.*), bishop of Bologna, and diplomat. He was papal legate at the Diet of Ratisbon (Regensburg), where he endeavored to effect a reconciliation between the Protestants and Catholics.

Contarini, Giovanni. b. at Venice, 1549; d. there, 1605. Venetian painter. He went to Vienna in 1580, where he practiced portrait painting.

Contarini Fleming (kon.tạ.rē'nē flem'ing). Psychological romance by Benjamin Disraeli, published in 1832.

Conte (kont), **John Le.** See **Le Conte, John.**

Conte, Joseph Le. See **Le Conte, Joseph.**

Conte de la Charette, or Lancelot (kônt dẹ là shà.ret; läṅs.lō), **Le.** Arthurian poem by Chrétien de Troyes. It was written during the 12th century at the order of the countess of Champagne, daughter of Louis VII and Eleanor of Aquitaine. It introduces Lancelot of the Lake, and is the first to make Lancelot the lover of Arthur's wife and queen, Guinevere.

Conte du Graal, or **Perceval** (kônt dü gräl; pers.vål), **Le.** Arthurian poem by Chrétien de Troyes. It was written during the 12th century for Philip, Count of Flanders, who acted (1180–82) as guardian to the young king, Philip Augustus. It is the earliest form in which we have the story of the Holy Grail. It was left unfinished by Chrétien, who wrote some 10,000 lines, and was completed by three writers, Gaucher (or Gautier), who added 20,000 more, Mennessier (or Manessier), who did his work c1220, and Gerbert de Montreuil, who told his readers that Chrétien died before he could finish his romance. In its final form, with all the additions, the poem is over 63,000 lines.

Contemplative Quarry, The. Volume of poetry by Anna Wickham, published in 1920.

Contemporary Music, International Society for. See **International Society for Contemporary Music.**

Contentment. Poem in *The Autocrat of the Breakfast-Table* (1858), by Oliver Wendell Holmes.

Contes d'Hoffman (kônt dof.män), **Les.** [English title, **The Tales of Hoffman.**] Opera in three acts by Jacques Offenbach, with a libretto by Jules Barbier, first produced at the Opéra-Comique at Paris on Feb. 10, 1881. Founded on the fantastic tales of E. T. A. Hoffman, the opera (which also includes a prologue and epilogue) relates three tragic love experiences as told by the writer. The barcarole from this work is very popular.

Contes Drolatiques (kônt dro.là.tēk). [Eng. trans., *"Droll Tales."*] Collection of stories by Honoré de Balzac, written in the manner and orthography of the 16th century. They are extremely broad, in the style of Rabelais, being "written for the diversion of the Pantagruelists and no others." They came out in three parts, in 1832, 1833, and 1837.

Contest of Wartburg (värt'burk). See **Wartburg, Contest of.**

Conti (kōn'tē), **Augusto.** b. at San Piero alle Fonti, near San Miniato, Italy, Dec. 6, 1822; d. at Florence, Italy, March 6, 1905. Italian philosopher who taught at the University of Pisa and the Instituto Superiore at Florence. He was the author of *Evidenza, amore e fede* (1858), *Storia della filosofia* (1864), *Il Bello nel Vero* (1872), *Il Buono nel Vero* (1873), and *L'Armonia delle cose* (1878).

Conti (kôṅ.tē; Italian, kōn'tē), Prince **de.** [Title of **Armand de Bourbon.**] b. at Paris, Oct. 11, 1629; d. at Pézénas, France, Feb. 21, 1666. Founder of the house of Conti; younger brother of the Prince de Condé (Louis II de Bourbon), called the "Great Condé." The princely title of Conti had been founded during the previous century, but it is from this nobleman that the line may be said to have had its continuous existence. He took part in the wars of the Fronde, at first with the "old Fronde" against his brother, and later with the "young Fronde" in company with his brother, with whom he was arrested in 1650. He was finally reconciled to the court, and married a niece of Cardinal Mazarin. In the Spanish war (1654) he captured Villafranca and Puigcerdá, and in 1657 commanded unsuccessfully in Italy.

Conti, Prince **de.** [Title of **François Louis de Bourbon.**] b. at Paris, April 30, 1664; d. Feb. 22, 1709. French general; son of the Prince de Conti (Armand de Bourbon, 1629–66).

Conti, Prince **de.** [Title of **Louis François de Bourbon.**] b. 1717; d. 1776. French nobleman; grandson of the Prince de Conti (François Louis de Bourbon, 1664–1709). During the War of the Austrian Succession he saw active service during the period 1741–47. As commander of the French forces in Piedmont in 1774 he was credited with a notable victory at Cuneo (Coni), and subsequently proved an able general in campaigns in Germany and in Flanders, but a clash of ambitions between him and Marshal Saxe led to his resignation in 1747. He had the support of Louis XV in an unsuccessful bid for the throne of Poland, but (not being in the good graces of Madame de Pompadour) presently lost favor with Louis, whom he further offended by his opposition to the edicts of Maupeou and the policies of Turgot. He was a man of taste and culture, a writer, and a friend of Jean Jacques Rousseau.

Conti, Prince **de.** [Title of **Louis François Joseph de Bourbon.**] b. 1734; d. 1814. French nobleman and soldier; son of the Prince de Conti (Louis François de Bourbon, 1717–76). He fought in the Seven Years War, and is remembered as the only prince of the blood who approved of the policies of Maupeou. As the storm of the French Revolution darkened, he joined in the protest of the princes (1789) and went into exile, but returned in 1790. In 1793 he was arrested, and though freed in 1795 by the National Convention, he was banished from France and his estates were forfeited. He refrained from involvement in plans to restore the French monarchy, living the rest of his life quietly at Barcelona. At his death the house of Conti became extinct.

Conti (kōn′tē), **Gioacchino.** Original name of **Gizziello.**

Conti, Giovanni Lotario de'. Original name of Pope **Innocent III.**

Conti, Gregorio. Original name of the antipope **Victor IV.**

Conti, Michelangelo dei. Original name of Pope **Innocent XIII.**

Conti, Niccolò de'. fl. 15th century. Venetian nobleman and traveler. It is supposed to have been about 1419 when he set out on a journey that was to take him to regions few, if any, Europeans had seen up to that time. He visited Damascus, Baghdad, adjacent regions of Arabia, and Persia, went on by sea to India, and even reached Sumatra and Java, before returning by way of Indo-China, Burma, the Red Sea, Mecca, and Egypt to his native city, where he arrived in 1444. It had been necessary for him in the course of his journeying through infidel regions to renounce Christianity, and as penance for this sin it is said that Pope Eugenius IV required him to tell the story of his wanderings and explorations to Poggio Bracciolini, the pontiff's secretary, who wrote them down. Belatedly they were published (1723) as part of Bracciolini's *Historiae de varietate fortunae*, of which an English translation was issued in 1857.

Con-Ticci or **Con-Ticsi** (kōn.tēk′sē). [Also, **Kon-Tiki.**] Name sometimes applied to Viracocha, supreme deity and creator of the Incas. In its variant spelling of Kon-Tiki it was taken as the name of the book by Thor Heyerdahl, recounting the story of the expedition which crossed on a raft from the coast of South America to the islands of the South Pacific in an effort to sustain Heyerdahl's contention that the ethnic groups of the Pacific islands could be traced to origins in South America.

Continental Celtic (sel′tik). See **Gaulish.**

Continental Congress. Legislature set up (1774) by the 13 English colonies in America and continued (until 1789) by the 13 original states during and immediately after the Revolutionary War. Public demand, made manifest especially by the Sons of Liberty and the Committees of Correspondence, led to the convening of the first Continental Congress, comprising representatives of all the colonies excepting Georgia, on Sept. 5, 1774. It sat in Philadelphia until Oct. 26 of that year, framed petitions to the king, rejected Joseph Galloway's proposals for reconciliation with Great Britain, and set up the Continental Association to bar importation and discourage use of British commodities. The second Continental Congress, in which (as in all future sessions) all of the colonies or states were represented, met at Philadelphia on May 10, 1775, and adjourned on Dec. 12, 1776. It established the Continental Army, rejected Lord North's conciliatory plan, sent Silas Deane on a diplomatic mission to France, took measures to keep American ports open to trade despite the British edicts closing them, adopted a resolution, on July 2, 1776, declaring that "these united colonies are, and of a right ought to be, free and independent states," and on July 4 issued the Declaration of Independence to justify its action to the world. The third session of the Congress met at Baltimore on Dec. 20, 1776, and lasted until the Articles of Confederation went into effect on March 1, 1781; in 1777 it moved to Philadelphia but because of British occupation of that city it had to hold some of its sessions that year and in 1778 at Lancaster and at York, Pa. After its return to Philadelphia in 1778, the Congress continued to meet in that city. During the years when the states were loosely united under the Articles of Confederation, the legislative body continued to be known as the Continental Congress. Until the adoption of the Constitution of the United States there was no national executive branch, and the Continental Congress at all times was harassed by refusals of various states to implement its enactments, by quarrels with the army, and by the difficulty of raising money. It did, however, manage to guide the country to a successful vindication of its independence, and after the war it succeeded in arbitrating the rival claims of various states to identical Western lands, to the advantage of the united nation.

Continental Divide. [Also, **Great Divide.**] Elevated ridge in the Rocky Mountain region of the U.S. which separates the streams tributary to the Pacific Ocean from those tributary to the Atlantic. In a more extended sense, it is taken to include the high ridges of the Canadian Rockies and the ranges of NW Canada, from which rivers flow W to the Pacific and E or N to Hudson Bay or the Arctic, and the southward continuation through Mexico and Central America to and including the Andes.

Continental Guinea (gin′i). See **Río Muni.**

Continental System. Plan (1806–12) by which Napoleon I waged economic warfare against Great Britain. Insisting that the British violated international law, as it prevailed among civilized nations, by treating individuals of enemy countries as belligerents even though they did not bear arms, and by confiscation of merchantmen and of private property and by treatment of merchant mariners as prisoners of war, Napoleon, by the successive decrees of Berlin (1806), Warsaw and Milan (1807), and Fontainebleau (1810), undertook to forbid all trade with Great Britain by France, her allies, and all neutral countries. The British Isles were declared to be in a state of blockade. The British retaliated by Orders in Council which in effect declared a blockade of all of the European Continent and still further extended the policy of search and seizure at sea. For a time it almost seemed as if each of the antagonists was seeking to outdo the other in arrogance, neither side taking into account that other nations would ultimately refuse to see their commerce ruined. Napoleon's hopes were doomed by the rapid rise of extensive smuggling in every Continental country, and by continued British domination of the sea. The refusal of Denmark to obey the British orders led to the bombardment of Copenhagen and the destruction of the Danish fleet; the refusal of the Czar to obey Napoleon's decrees led to the latter's disastrous invasion of Russia. American commerce was much harassed by both sides, which caused a brief period of hostilities with France, while the British search and seizure tactics were a chief contributing cause of the War of 1812. The downfall of Napoleon brought the operation of the Continental System to an end.

Continents. See **Encratites.**

Contractus (kọn.trak′tus), **Hermannus.** See **Hermann.**

Contrast, The. Social comedy by Royall Tyler, produced at New York on April 16, 1787. It was published in 1790. The theme involves the contrast of sincerity (as represented by Maria and Colonel Manly) and affectation (as exemplified by the wealthy Billy Dimple, Letitia, and Charlotte). A minor character is Jonathan, Manly's servant. The play was the first comedy and the second professionally produced play by a native American.

Contrat Social (kôṅ.trȧ sọ.syȧl). [Eng. trans., "*Social Contract.*"] Political work on the origins and structure of government, by Jean Jacques Rousseau, published in 1762. The influence of this book on the literature and life of the period was remarkable. Its theories were at the foundation of Jacobin politics.

Contreras (kōn.trā′räs). Village in S Mexico, in the Distrito Federal, ab. 8 mi. SW of Mexico City. Here, Aug. 19–20, 1847, the Americans under Scott defeated the Mexicans. Pop. under 5,000 (1940).

Contreras, Eleázar López. See **López Contreras, Eleázar.**

Contreras, Rodrigo de. b. at Segovia, Spain, c1495; d., probably in Peru, after 1557. Spanish cavalier who married the daughter of Pedrarias (Pedro Arias de Ávila), and in 1531 was appointed governor of Nicaragua. He sent an expedition which explored Lake Nicaragua and its outlet, and reached Nombre de Dios, on the N coast of Panama, by that route. There the men were seized by the governor, Robles, who tried to appropriate the region discovered, but was driven out. Subsequently Contreras got into disputes with the bishop and with the Audience of the Confines. Charges were made against him, and his *encomiendas* were confiscated (1549). After vainly seeking redress in Spain, he went to Peru.

Contrexéville (kôṅ.treg.zä.vēl). Small spa in NE France, in the department of Vosges, ab. 26 mi. W of Épinal. Pop. ab. 1,000.

Contucci da Monte Sansovino (kōn.töt′chē dä mōn′tä sän.sō.vē′nō), **Andrea.** See **Sansovino, Andrea.**

Convention and Statute of Tangier (tan.jir′). Two-part convention signed on Dec. 18, 1923, by Great Britain, France, and Spain. Part one, regarding the organization of the Statute of Tangier Zone, made the zone permanently neutral and placed it under an international legislative assembly of 26 members. Part two related to the port of Tangier. On May 14, 1924, this was modified to include ratification by the Western powers and the U.S., and further revisions were made in 1928. During World War II Tangier was occupied by Spanish troops.

Convention for the Suppression of Slavery, International. See **International Convention for the Suppression of Slavery.**

Conversano (kōn.ver.sä′nō). Town and commune in SE Italy, in the *compartimento* (region) of Apulia, in the province of Bari, situated near the Adriatic Sea, SE of Bari. It is a center for the production of cherries, which are widely exported. The medieval castle, formerly belonging to the counts of Almaviva di Aragona, is a national monument. The Romanesque cathedral dates from the 13th century, the bell tower of the Abbey of San Benedetto from the 16th century. Pop. of commune, 15,903 (1936); of town, 13,234 (1936).

Conversations. Prose work by William Drummond of Hawthornden, in which he gives an account of a visit Ben Jonson paid him in 1618. It is valuable to students of the period for the personal picture it gives of Jonson and because it records his opinions on various literary subjects. In a small way it does for the Elizabethan Jonson what Boswell did for the 18th-century Johnson. The work, left in manuscript form, was not published until 1832. Recent editions are those of R. F. Patterson (1923) and Percy Simpson (1925).

Converse (kon′vėrs), **Charles Crozat.** [Pseudonym, **Karl Redan.**] b. at Warren, Mass., Oct. 7, 1832; d. at Highwood, N.J., Oct. 18, 1918. American composer. He studied (1855–59) at the Leipzig Conservatory under Richter and Hauptmann, and also practiced law at Erie, Pa. His compositions include *Fest-Ouvertüre* (1870), *God for Us* (1887), and *What a Friend We Have in Jesus.*

Converse, Florence. b. at New Orleans, April 30, 1871—. American writer. She was graduated (B.S., 1893; M.A., 1903) from Wellesley, and served on the staffs of *The Churchman* and *The Atlantic Monthly.* Her works include *Diana Victrix* (1897), *Long Will* (1903), *The House of Prayer* (1908), *The Story of Wellesley* (1915), *Garments of Praise* (1921), *Collected Poems* (1937), and *Wellesley College, a Chronicle of the Years, 1875–1938* (1939).

Converse, Frederick Shepherd. b. at Newton, Mass., Jan. 5, 1871; d. 1940. American composer. He was instructor of harmony (1899–1901) at the New England Conservatory of Music, instructor of music (1902–05) and assistant professor of music (1903–07) at Harvard University, and vice-president of the Boston Opera Company. Among his works are *Sonata in A*, the symphonic poems *Festival of Pan, Endymion's Narrative,* and *The Mystic Trumpeter*, the oratorio *Job*, the operas *The Pipe of Desire* and *The Sacrifice*, a string quartet in A minor, *Serenade* for male voices and orchestra, a motet for male voices, *Laudate Dominum*, and songs and piano pieces.

Conway (kon′wā). City in C Arkansas, county seat of Faulkner County. It is the seat of Arkansas State Teachers College and Hendrix College. 8,610 (1950).

Conway. [Former names, **Conway Corner, Chateaugay, Shagigee.**] Town in C New Hampshire, in Carroll County, on the Saco and Swift rivers ab. 56 mi. NE of Concord. It is a summer and winter resort and manufactures wood products. 4,109 (1950).

Conway. [Former names, **Kingston, Conwayborough.**] Town in E South Carolina, county seat of Horry County, on the Waccamaw River. It is a center for lumbering, shipping of logs and turpentine, vegetable and tobacco raising, and also for hunting and fishing. 6,073 (1950).

Conway. [Also, **Aberconway.**] Municipal borough, market town, and seaport in N Wales, in Caernarvonshire, situated at the mouth of the river Conway, ab. 3 mi. S of Llandudno, ab. 225 mi. NW of London by rail. It is noted for its wall and castle, a highly picturesque fortress with an admirable group of eight cylindrical towers, built in 1284 by Edward I. The towers were originally surmounted by cylindrical turrets, four of which survive. The banqueting hall was a fine room 130 ft. long. Queen Eleanor's oratory possesses a graceful oriel window. Conway is one of the few places in Wales where the curfew is still rung. 10,237 (1951).

Conway, Frederick Bartlett. b. at Clifton, England, Feb. 10, 1819; d. at Manchester, Mass., Sept. 7, 1874. English actor. He first appeared (1850) on the American stage in Sheridan's *The School for Scandal* as Charles Surface. In 1852 he married Sarah Crocker, a sister of Mrs. D. P. Bowers, at that time leading lady of the New York stage. The Conways took over (1864) the Park Theatre (afterwards known as Conway's Theatre) in Brooklyn, N.Y., which became one of that city's popular amusement places.

Conway, Henry Seymour. b. 1721; d. at London, Oct. 12, 1795. English soldier and Whig politician; cousin of Horace Walpole. He early entered the army, was a member of Parliament 1741–84, and took part in the battle of Fontenoy as aide-de-camp to the Duke of Cumberland, and in the battle of Culloden. He became secretary to the lord lieutenant of Ireland (Lord Hartington) in 1754; was promoted to major general in 1756; commanded the unsuccessful expedition against Rochefort in 1757; became secretary of state under Rockingham in 1765; moved for the repeal of the Stamp Act in February, 1766; retained his office under the elder William Pitt (the Earl of Chatham); resigned in January, 1768, and was appointed field marshal on Oct. 12, 1793. He was a vigorous opponent of the policy of the British government toward the American colonies.

Conway, Moncure Daniel. b. in Stafford County, Va., March 17, 1832; d. at Paris, Nov. 15, 1907. American clergyman and writer. At first a Methodist minister, he subsequently became a Unitarian, and was for a time pastor of a Unitarian church at Washington, D.C. He was minister of the South Place Religious Society at London from 1863 to 1884. Author of *The Rejected Stone* (1861), *Testimonies concerning Slavery* (1864), *The Earthward Pilgrimage* (1870), *Christianity* (1876), *Idols and Ideals* (1877), *Demonology and Devil-Lore* (1878), *Thomas Carlyle* (1881), and others.

Conway, Thomas. [Called **"Count de Conway."**] b. in Ireland, Feb. 27, 1735; d. c1800. American general in the Revolutionary War, noted for his supposed role in the so-called Conway Cabal, an alleged conspiracy to remove George Washington as commander in chief of the Continental Army. A colonel in the French army, he came (1777) to America and was appointed brigadier general in the Continental Army. He participated in the battles of Brandywine and Germantown; when Washington registered his opposition to Conway's recommended promotion to major general, Conway resigned. The Continental Congress rejected his resignation, appointed him major general, and made him inspector general (1777). Following this demonstration by his friends in the Congress, Conway did actually engage with Gates and others in a correspondence attacking Washington. Meanwhile, the defeats sustained by Washington in mid-1777 encouraged certain members of Congress to press for Washington's removal in favor of General Horatio Gates. Washington learned of the sentiment against him and informed both Gates and the Congress of what Conway was supposed (incorrectly, as it turned out) to have written to Gates. Thereafter, Conway's military standing was considerably diminished, and he resigned his commission in 1778. Continuing his attacks upon Washington, he became involved in a duel (July 4, 1778) with General Cadwalader. He was badly wounded; almost at the point of death, he wrote (July 23, 1778) a full apology to Washington. Recovering, he returned to France, served in Flanders and India, and in 1787 was appointed governor general of the French possessions in India. He returned to France in 1793, but fled the country as a Royalist émigré. See *Secret History of the American Revolution* (1941), by Carl Van Doren.

Conway Cabal. In U.S. history, an alleged conspiracy (1777) to displace George Washington as commander in chief during the Revolutionary War. Washington's defeats at the Brandywine on September 11 and at Germantown on October 4 were followed by Horatio Gates's important victory at Saratoga on Oct. 17, 1777, and there was some sentiment in the army and in Congress for giving Gates the supreme command. At this time it became known that Thomas Conway, who still smarted under Washington's refusal to sanction his promotion to major general, had written to Gates, strongly criticizing Washington. James Wilkinson, then an officer on Gates's staff, communicated what he alleged to be a phrase from this letter to William Alexander (called Lord Stirling), who passed it on to Washington. It later transpired that Conway's letter contained no such passage, and thus the belief that there was a cabal against Washington, and that it was headed by Conway, seems to have resulted from one of the earliest of Wilkinson's lifelong series of intrigues. However, that Gates would have been happy to displace Washington seems certain, and that there were some who favored such a change is no secret. Conway was one of them, and happened to put his sentiments in writing. There is, however, no evidence of an actual organized conspiracy, and if such there was, no ground for supposing that Conway was its leader. It has been suggested that the currency of the term "Conway Cabal" is chiefly due to the charm of alliteration.

Conway of Allington, 1st Baron. [Title of Sir **William Martin Conway.**] b. at Rochester, England, April 12, 1856; d. April 19, 1937. English traveler, art critic, and geographer. He was professor of art in University College, Liverpool (1885–88) and Slade professor of fine arts in the University of Cambridge (1901–04). He traveled in the Himalayas, the Andes, Tierra del Fuego, Spitsbergen, and elsewhere. Among his publications are *Woodcutters of the Netherlands in the Fifteenth Century* (1884), *Early Flemish Artists* (1886), *The Bolivian Andes* (1901), *Early Tuscan Artists* (1902), *Aconcagua and Tierra del Fuego* (1902), *Great Masters* (1904), *The Alps* (1904), and *No Man's Land: a History of Spitzbergen* (1906).

Conway Range. Mountain range in Antarctica, lying on the W side of the Ross Shelf Ice, in ab. 79°18′ S., 159°20′ E.

Conway River. Small river in N Wales. It has its source in a lake of the same name, in Caernarvonshire, ab. 7 mi. S of Bettws-y-Coed. The river flows north, forming the Caernarvonshire-Denbighshire boundary, reaching the sea at Beaumaris Bay. It is noted for its scenery, having a waterfall with a drop of 50 ft. Length, ab. 30 mi.; the lower 10 mi. are navigable.

Conwell (kon′wel, -wel), **Russell Herman.** b. at South Worthington, Mass., Feb. 15, 1843; d. Dec. 6, 1925. American Baptist clergyman and educator. Admitted (1865) to the bar, he practiced law at Minneapolis and at Boston, and served as pastor (1881 *et seq.*) of the Grace Baptist Church at Philadelphia, out of the night school of which Temple University developed with Conwell as its first president. He delivered his lecture *Acres of Diamonds* more than 6,000 times, devoting the profits to the education of over 10,000 young men. Included among his publications are *Lessons in Travel* (1870) and *Why Lincoln Laughed* (1922).

Conybeare (kon′i.bir, kun′-), **John.** b. at Pinhoe, near Exeter, England, Jan. 31, 1692; d. at Bath, England, July 31, 1755. English divine, bishop of Bristol. He wrote a noted polemical work, *A Defence of Revealed Religion* (1732), directed against Tindal.

Conybeare, John Josias. b. at London, June, 1779; d. at Blackheath, near London, June 10, 1824. English divine, scholar, and scientific writer; grandson of John Conybeare. He was a graduate of Oxford, where he became professor of Anglo-Saxon in 1807, and professor of poetry in 1812. He was also vicar of Batheaston in Somersetshire. His works include papers on chemistry and geology, and *Illustrations of Anglo-Saxon Poetry,* edited after his death by his brother William.

Conybeare, William Daniel. b. at London, June 7, 1787; d. at Itchenstoke, near Portsmouth, England, Aug. 12, 1857. English geologist and divine; grandson of John Conybeare and younger brother of J. J. Conybeare. He was appointed dean of Llandaff in 1844. He published an important book on the geology of England and Wales (with William Phillips), as well as notable papers on various geological and paleontological topics, and edited his brother's work on Anglo-Saxon poetry.

Conyers (kon′yėrz), Sir **William.** See under **Robin of Redesdale.**

Conyngton (kon′ing.ton), **Richard.** d. 1330. English schoolman, a graduate of Oxford, chosen in 1310 provincial of the Franciscan order in England. His best-known work is a commentary on the *Sentences* of Peter the Lombard.

Conze (kon′tse), **Alexander Christian Leopold.** b. at Hanover, Germany, Dec. 10, 1831; d. at Berlin, July 19, 1914. German archaeologist, appointed (1887) professor at the University of Berlin. Among his works are *Melische Tongefässe* (1862), *Reise auf der Insel Lesbos* (1865), *Die attischen Grab-reliefs* (1893–1900; with Michaelis and others), and *Archäologische Untersuchungen auf Samothrake* (1875–80; with Hauser and Niemann).

Coo (kô′ō). Italian name of **Kos.**

Cooch Behar (köch bē.här′). [Also, **Kuch Behar.**] Former native state in the Union of India, ab. 80 mi. SE of Darjeeling: since January, 1950, part of the state of West Bengal. Its chief products are sugar, tobacco, tea, and rubber. Area, 1,318 sq. mi.; pop. 639,898 (1941).

Cook (kůk), **Albert Stanburrough.** b. at Montville, N.J., March 6, 1853; d. Sept. 1, 1927. American philologist, professor of the English language and literature at Yale University from 1889. He was graduated at Rutgers College in 1872, studied in Germany at Göttingen, Leipzig, and Jena, was associate in English at the Johns Hopkins University (1879–91), and was professor of English at the University of California (1882–89). His publications include a translation of Sievers's *Old English Grammar* (1885), and various treatises and monographs upon philological and literary topics. He was general editor of the *Yale Studies in English.*

Cook, Arthur Bernard. b. 1868—. English archaeologist and classicist. He studied at Cambridge University, where he later was reader in classical archaeology (1908–31) and professor (1931–34); in the interval he was professor of Greek (1892–1907) at Bedford College, London. He was general editor (1928 *et seq.*) of Methuen's *Handbooks of Archaeology,* and author of *The Metaphysical Basis of Plato's Ethics* (1895), *Zeus, A Study in Ancient Religion* (3 vols., 1914, 1925, 1940), and *The Rise and Progress of Classical Archaeology* (1931).

Cook, Arthur James. b. in Somersetshire, England, 1885; d. Nov. 2, 1931. Leader of British miners in the 1920's, particularly in connection with the General Strike of 1926. He was the author of a famous miners' pamphlet, *The Miners' Next Step* (1912), which was regarded as a revolutionary document. He was a member of the Executive Committee, Miners' Federation of Great Britain (1918), and served on three government coal commissions; he was also a member of the executive committee of the Labor Party. In 1931, he was general secretary of the Miners' Federation of Great Britain, and a member of the General Council of the Trades Union Congress.

Cook, Charles. b. at London, May 31, 1787; d. at Lausanne, Switzerland, Feb. 21, 1858. English clergyman, one of the founders of Methodism in France and Switzerland.

Cook, Charles Henry. [Pseudonym, **John Bickerdyke.**] b. at London, in July, 1858; d. Jan. 17, 1933. English novelist, journalist, and writer on sports. Among his works are *An Irish Midsummer Night's Dream* (1885), *The Curiosities of Ale and Beer* (1886; with J. M. Dixon), *The Book of the All Round Angler* (1889), *Sea Fishing* (1895), *Wild Sports in Ireland* (1897), *Practical Letters to Young Sea Fishers* (1898), and others.

Cook, Clarence Chatham. b. at Dorchester, Mass., Sept. 8, 1828; d. at Fishkill Landing (now part of Beacon), N.Y., June 2, 1900. American journalist and writer on art. He also wrote *The Central Park* (1868), the text of a heliotype reproduction of Dürer's *Life of the Virgin* (1874), and *The House Beautiful* (1878), and edited, with notes, the translation of Lübke's *History of Art* (7th German ed., 1878).

Cook, Edward Dutton. b. at London, Jan. 30, 1829; d. there, Sept. 11, 1883. English novelist and critic. He was drama critic for the *Pall Mall Gazette* and the *World,* and contributor to the first two volumes of the *Dictionary Of National Biography*. He published *Paul Foster's Daughter* (1861), *The Trials of the Tredgolds* (1864), and various other novels and works on the stage.

Cook, Eliza. b. at London, c1818; d. at Thornton Hill, Wimbledon, Surrey, England, Sept. 23, 1889. English poet. She wrote for various English periodicals, and in 1840 published *Melaia and other Poems*. In 1849 she began to publish *Eliza Cook's Journal*, which appeared until 1854. Among her books are *Jottings from my Journal* (1860) and *New Echoes* (1864); among her single poems are *The Old Arm-Chair*, *O why does the white man follow my path?*, *The Old Farm Gate*, and *Old Songs*.

Cook, Flavius Josephus. Original name of **Cook, Joseph.**

Cook, Frederick Albert. b. at Callicoon Depot, N.Y., June 10, 1865; d. Aug. 5, 1940. American physician and explorer. He was surgeon of the Peary arctic expedition (1891–92), and of the Belgian antarctic expedition (1897–99). In 1903 and 1906 he led expeditions for the exploration of Mount McKinley, announcing its ascent in September, 1906. In the summer of 1907 he started in an attempt to reach the North Pole. He returned in 1909 and announced that he had reached the Pole with two Eskimos on April 21, 1908, a statement which was not given credit by scientists because of lack of evidence. Cook maintained his fight for recognition of his priority of accomplishment over Peary's (Peary is generally recognized as having been first to reach the North Pole, on April 6, 1909) and had many supporters in his claim.

Cook, George Cram. b. at Davenport, Iowa, Oct. 7, 1873; d. in Greece, Jan. 14, 1924. American theater director and novelist; husband of Susan Glaspell. He was educated at the University of Iowa, Harvard, and the University of Heidelberg. He established (with his wife) and directed the Provincetown Players at Provincetown, Mass., and founded (1915) the influential Playwrights' Theater at New York. After 1921 he lived in Greece. He was the author of *Roderick Taliaferro, a Story of Maximilian's Empire* (1903), *The Chasm* (1911), and *The Athenian Women* (1926), and, with Susan Glaspell, of the play *Suppressed Desires* (1914).

Cook, James. b. at Marton, Yorkshire, Oct. 27, 1728; killed in Hawaii, Feb. 14, 1779. English navigator, son of a Yorkshire farm-laborer. He entered the navy as an able seaman in 1755, was appointed master of the *Mercury* in 1759, and sailed for America, where he was occupied in surveying the channel of the St. Lawrence River, and became marine surveyor of the coast of Newfoundland and Labrador in 1763. In May, 1768, he was appointed lieutenant and placed in command of the *Endeavor*, which carried a party of scientists to Tahiti to observe the transit of Venus. During this voyage, which lasted from Aug. 25, 1768, to June 12, 1771, New Zealand was explored, and the east coast of Australia. Cook was raised to the rank of commander in August, 1771, and on July 13, 1772, started with two ships, the *Resolution* (which he commanded) and the *Adventure*, on another voyage of exploration in the Pacific, which lasted (for the *Resolution*) until July 29, 1775, and during which an attempt was made to discover the reported great southern continent, and New Caledonia was discovered. On Aug. 9, 1775, he became captain, and on July 12, 1776, began his last voyage with the *Resolution* (which he again commanded), and the *Discovery* under Captain Charles Clerke. The object of the expedition was to discover a passage from the Pacific round the north of America. During his northward voyage the Sandwich Islands (Hawaiian Islands) were rediscovered (1778), and shortly after his return to them (January, 1779) he was murdered by the natives.

Cook, Joseph. [Original name, **Flavius Josephus Cook.**] b. at Ticonderoga, N.Y., Jan. 26, 1838; d. June 24, 1901. American lecturer. A theologian whose popular lectures in America and abroad concentrated on the reconciliation of science and religion, he was often accused of charlatanism. He was a graduate of Harvard (1865) and of Andover Theological Seminary (1868). His lectures at Tremont Hall, Boston, continued for almost 20 years, drawing crowds on Monday noon to hear Cook expound on science and philosophy. Among his published works were *Biology* (1877), *Transcendentalism* (1877), *Orthodoxy* (1877), *Conscience* (1878), *Heredity* (1878), *Marriage* (1878), *Labor* (1879), *Socialism* (1880), *Orient* (1886), and *Current Religious Perils* (1888), all collections of his lectures.

Cook, Sir Joseph. b. at Silverdale, Staffordshire, England, in December, 1860; d. at Sydney, Australia, July 30, 1947. Australian political leader, prime minister of Australia. He went to Australia (New South Wales) in 1886, and went to work as a coal miner. He became a trade-union official, and entered (1891) politics as a member of the legislative assembly of New South Wales, where he continued until 1901. He held cabinet posts as postmaster general (1894–98) and minister of mines and agriculture (1898–99), and was sent to the federal house of representatives from 1901 to 1921, becoming leader of the opposition in 1909, and serving as minister of defense (1909–10), prime minister (1913–14), minister of the navy (1917–20), and treasurer (1920–21). He was a member of the Australian delegation to Versailles, and was Australian high commissioner at London (1921–27). He was knighted in 1918.

Cook, Melville Thurston. b. at Coffeen, Ill., 1869—. American botanist. He was graduated from De Pauw and Stanford universities, and from 1911 to 1923 was plant pathologist at the New Jersey agricultural experiment station, state plant pathologist of New Jersey, and professor of plant pathology at Rutgers. He served (1923–40) as plant pathologist at the Rio Piedras insular experiment station in Puerto Rico, and in 1944 became visiting professor of botany at Louisiana State University. Among his works are *Diseases of Tropical Plants* (1912), *Applied Economic Botany* (1919), and *Viruses and Virus Diseases of Plants* (1947).

Cook, Mount. [Also, **Aorangi.**] Highest peak in New Zealand, situated on the W side of South Island. It was first ascended in 1882. Elevation, 12,349 ft.

Cook, Orator Fuller. b. at Clyde, N.Y., May 28, 1867; d. 1949. American botanist. He taught biology at the University of Syracuse, N.Y., in 1890 and 1891, but in the latter year went to Liberia as an agent of the New York Colonization Society, staying in that African country until 1897 and teaching the natural sciences at Liberia College, of which he was president in the years 1896–97. In 1898 he became assistant curator of the U.S. National Museum, and from 1900 devoted his studies particularly to tropical agriculture, under the auspices of the U.S. Department of Agriculture, going to Peru in this connection in 1922. Later he was associated with an expedition sent out by the Carnegie Institute to study the culture of the Maya Indians. After 1904 he held a professorial chair in botany at George Washington University, Washington, D.C. He originated important improvements in cotton cultivation, and wrote extensively on tropical agriculture, on botany and zoölogy, and on problems and aspects of evolution.

Cook, Robert Johnson. b. near Cookstown, Pa., March 21, 1849; d. Dec. 3, 1922. American rowing-crew coach and business manager (1882–97) of the Philadelphia *Press*. A graduate (1876) of Yale and coach (1876–97) of 13 Yale crews, he was the originator of the "Bob Cook stroke."

Cook, Stanley Arthur. b. at King's Lynn, Norfolk, England, April 12, 1873—. English Orientalist and Biblical scholar. He studied at Cambridge University and served on the editorial staff (1896–1903) of the *Encyclopaedia Biblica*, as editorial adviser to the eleventh edition of the *Encyclopaedia Britannica* on Old Testament and Semitic topics, and as editor (1902–32) for the Palestine Exploration Fund. He has been a college lecturer in Hebrew (1904–32) and comparative religion (1912–20), and professor (1932–38) of Hebrew at Cambridge. He is the author of *Glossary of Aramaic Inscriptions* (1898), *Religion of Ancient Palestine* (1908), *Ethical Monotheism* (1932), *The Old Testament: a Reinterpretation* (1936), *The "Truth" of the Bible* (1938), and *The Rebirth of Christianity* (1943), and joint editor of the *Cambridge Ancient History*.

Cook, Thomas. b. at Melbourne, Derbyshire, England, Nov. 22, 1808; d. at Walton-on-Thames, Surrey, England, July 18, 1892. English founder of a famous tourist agency. Originally a missionary traveler, he covered (1829) 2,692 miles, of which 2,106 miles were by foot. As a temperance worker he founded (1840) the *Children's*

Temperance Magazine, the first English publication of the kind. His work in arranging for a temperance meeting at Loughborough in 1841 first gave him the idea of organizing excursions. Between 1842 and 1844 Cook made several excursions for the temperance group.By 1845 he felt secure enough in this new business to devote to it his entire energy. His method was to obtain discounts from the railway companies and to supply travelers with information and guides. After successful tours were conducted between England and Scotland, he contemplated (1850) foreign tours. Trips were accordingly planned to Europe, the U.S., and the Bible lands of the East. The first around-the-world tour was planned in 1872.

Cooke (kůk), **Elisha.** b. Sept. 16, 1637; d. Oct. 31, 1715. American colonial political leader; father of Elisha Cooke (1678–1737). A Boston physician, he was deputy (1681–84) and speaker (1682–84) in the General Court, where he opposed the establishment of the royal prerogative, and was elected (1684) assistant (member of the governor's council) for his refusal to yield the old charter. He was one of the leaders (1689) in overthrowing Joseph Dudley, who had been appointed president of New England, and Sir Edmund Andros, governor of New England, and in reëstablishing the separate existence of the colony. From 1690 to 1692 he served as colony agent at London, opposing the acceptance of a new charter under William III (which was issued anyway and accepted by the other agents). Increase Mather, empowered to draw up the list of officers under the new charter, omitted Cooke's name, but he was elected to the Council and seated in 1694. He was influential in 1701 in ending Increase Mather's efforts to set up a new charter for Harvard (of which Cooke was an alumnus, having graduated in 1657) and in forcing Mather's resignation as president of Harvard. He served (until 1702) on the superior court. When Dudley was appointed royal governor, he removed Cooke from the superior court and refused for 13 years to recognize his repeated election to a Council seat. Finally Cooke won his fight and was seated (1715) but died soon after.

Cooke, Elisha. b. at Boston, Dec. 20, 1678; d. Aug. 24, 1737. American colonial politician; son of Elisha Cooke (1637–1715). He was elected (1715) representative from Boston, and chosen (1717, 1724–26, 1728) to the Council.

Cooke, George Frederick. b. at Westminster (now part of London), April 17, 1756; d. at New York, Sept. 26, 1811. English actor. He first appeared on the stage in 1776 at Brentford. His principal parts were Shakespeare's Richard III, Iago, and Shylock, Massinger's Sir Giles Overreach, and Macklin's Sir Archy McSarcasm and Sir Pertinax McSycophant.

Cooke, Henry. d. at Hampton, near London, July 13, 1672. English choirmaster and composer of anthems. Under his guidance the choir of the royal chapel was expanded and strengthened.

Cooke, James Francis. b. at Bay City, Mich., Nov. 14, 1875—. American composer and musicologist. As a teacher of piano technique, he has composed many works for that instrument as well as pieces for voice. He has served as editor (1907 *et seq.*) of *Etude*, and is the author of *Standard History of Music* (1910), *Musical Travelogues* (1934), *How To Memorize Music* (1947), and other works.

Cooke, Jay. b. at what is now Sandusky, Ohio, Aug. 10, 1821; d. Feb. 16, 1905. American banker and financier, noted for his part in marketing Union bonds during the Civil War and for his role in precipitating the panic of 1873. Beginning as a clerk in the West, he settled (1839) at Philadelphia, where he was employed in the banking firm of E. W. Clark and Company. In 1861 he formed Jay Cooke and Company, in which he was a partner; until its demise in 1873, this banking firm was one of the leading houses in the U.S. Through his brother, Henry David Cooke, who knew U.S. Secretary of the Treasury Salmon P. Chase, Cooke was introduced to Chase, and the latter increasingly relied upon the advice of the banker. After the battle of Bull Run (July, 1861), Cooke raised two million dollars for the federal government and, together with Chase, secured an advance of 50 million dollars from the New York bankers. Cooke opened a Philadelphia agency, and later one at Washington, for the sale of government bonds, and in 1862 was appointed by Chase as a treasury agent to dispose of bonds which the government had found difficulty in selling. By 1864 the entire issue of 500 million dollars had been sold. Again, in 1865, he was appointed an agent by the new secretary of the treasury, William P. Fessenden, and within six months had sold 600 million dollars in government bonds. Beginning in 1866, he expanded his operations, setting up a branch at New York and in 1870 one at London. For a time he was active in the promotion of the Central Pacific Railroad, but was forced to suspend his operations (Sept. 18, 1873) and close his banking house, thereby initiating the panic of that year. See *Jay Cooke, Financier of the Civil War*, by Ellis P. Oberholtzer (2 vols., 1907).

Cooke, John Esten. b. at Winchester, Va., Nov. 3, 1830; d. in Clarke County, Va., Sept. 27, 1886. American novelist; brother of Philip Pendleton Cooke. He wrote stories of Virginia life, among which are *Leather Stocking and Silk* (1854), *The Virginia Comedians* (1854), *Henry St. John, Gentleman* (1859), *Surry of Eagle's Nest* (1866), *Fairfax* (1868), *Virginia Bohemians* (1879), *Virginia: a History of the People* (1883), and *My Lady Pokahontas* (1885). He also wrote the life of Stonewall Jackson (1863) and of General R. E. Lee (1871), besides a number of stories, sketches, and verses.

Cooke, Josiah Parsons. b. at Boston, Oct. 12, 1827; d. at Newport, R.I., Sept. 3, 1894. American chemist, professor of chemistry at Harvard from 1850. He published *Elements of Chemical Physics* (1860), *First Principles of Chemical Philosophy* (1868), *The New Chemistry* (1872; revised 1884), *Chemical and Physical Researches* (1881), and others.

Cooke, Mordecai Cubitt. b. at Horning, Norfolk, England, 1825; d. 1912. English botanist. He was associated with the Royal Indian Museum from 1860 to 1880, and thereafter with the Royal Botanical Gardens, at Kew, near London. Learned in the whole field of botany, he was an authority especially on fungi. The Royal Horticultural Society gave him its medal of honor, and the Linnaean Society did the same. He was a very prolific writer, some of his better-known works being a *Manual of Botanic Terms* (1862), a *Handbook of British Fungi* (1874), *British Fresh-Water Algae* (1882), and *British Desmids* (1887).

Cooke, Philip Pendleton. b. at Martinsburg (now in W.Va.), Va., Oct. 26, 1816; d. Jan. 20, 1850. American poet and novelist, best known for the lyric *Florence Vane* (1840); brother of John Esten Cooke. He contributed (1835–50) to the *Southern Literary Messenger* stories including "The Gregories of Hackwood," "The Two Country Houses," "John Carper the Hunter of Lost River," "The Crime of Andrew Blair," "Erisicthon," and the unfinished "The Chevalier Merlin" (all of which were published 1848–49). He was also the author of *Froissart Ballads and Other Poems* (c1847).

Cooke, Rose Terry. b. at West Hartford, Conn., Feb. 17, 1827; d. at Pittsfield, Mass., July 18, 1892. American author. Among her works are *Poems by Rose Terry* (1860), *Somebody's Neighbors* (1881), *Steadfast*, a novel (1889), and *Poems by Rose Terry Cooke* (1888). Her most characteristic short stories were those of New England rural life, as in *Huckleberries Gathered from New England Hills* (1891).

Cooke, Thomas. b. at Braintree, Essex, England, Dec. 16, 1703; d. at Lambeth (now part of London), Dec. 20, 1756. English writer, best known as the author of a translation of Hesiod (from which he obtained the nickname of "Hesiod Cooke"). He also published translations of Terence and other Latin and Greek authors, a poem entitled *The Battle of the Poets* (which, with some criticisms of Pope's Greek, brought down upon him the wrath of that poet, who ridiculed him in the *Dunciad*), and various dramatic works. He succeeded Nicholas Amhurst in the editorship of *The Craftsman*.

Cooke, Thomas Simpson. b. at Dublin, 1782; d. at London, Feb. 26, 1848. Irish composer and singer. He was the principal tenor at the Drury Lane Theatre, and took entire charge of the music there in 1821. Among the many works he composed or adapted, "Love's Ritornella," a song from *The Brigand*, is his best-known composition.

Cooke, Sir **William Fothergill.** b. at Ealing, Middlesex, England, 1806; d. June 25, 1879. English electrician, the associate of Wheatstone from 1837 to 1843 in perfecting the electric telegraph.

Cookeville (kůk'vil). Town in C Tennessee, county seat of Putnam County: trading center for a farming region; manufactures of shirts and shoes. It is the seat of the Tennessee Polytechnic Institute. 6,924 (1950).

Cook Islands (kůk). [Also, **Hervey Islands.**] Archipelago in the South Pacific, ab. 1,800 mi. NE of New Zealand, between the Friendly and Society island groups. The group, consisting of six principal islands, was discovered by Captain James Cook in 1773, annexed by Great Britain in 1888, and administered by a British resident commissioner paid by New Zealand until 1901, when it was officially annexed by the Dominion of New Zealand. Since then it has been governed by a resident commissioner stationed at Raratonga. The natives have been converted to Christianity since 1823. The chief islands are Raratonga, Atiu, Aitutaki, and Mangaia. Area, ab. 99 sq. mi.; pop. 14,650 (est. 1949).

Cooks Peak (kůks). Prominent peak in SW New Mexico, in Grant County N of Deming. Elevation, ab. 8,300 ft.

Cook's Tale, The. One of Chaucer's *Canterbury Tales*. It is an unfinished poem, and a spurious ending was added to it in the folio of 1687.

Cook Strait. Sea passage in New Zealand, separating the North Island from the South Island. It was discovered by Captain James Cook in 1769. Greatest width, ab. 80 mi.

Cookworthy (kůk'wėr"ᴛʜi), **William.** b. at Kingsbridge, Devonshire, England, 1705; d. Oct. 16, 1780. English potter, remembered chiefly for his discovery that Cornish clay could be used for the manufacture of porcelain, and for his service in bringing a knowledge of chemistry to bear on pottery making, by showing the nature and property of materials with which potters worked. Originally a wholesale druggist at Plymouth, he retired (1781) to become active in the work of the Society of Friends. He learned (1745) of the European porcelain called Dresden china, and discovered on Tregonning Hill the Cornish china clay, soon afterwards noticing that the granite of the same district resembled the *petunze*. His experiments with it led him to discover (1755–58) the right clay and stone at Carlagges, St. Stephen's parish, near St. Austell Plymouth. For this discovery he obtained a patent (1768) for the exclusive right to use Cornish clay and stone.

Cool as a Cucumber. Farce by William Blanchard Jerrold, first played in 1851.

Coolbrith (köl'brith), **Ina Donna.** b. near Springfield, Ill., March 10, 1842; d. at Berkeley, Calif., Feb. 29, 1928. American lyric poet. She worked (1868 *et seq.*) with Bret Harte on the *Overland Monthly*, was a librarian (1873–1906) at Oakland and San Francisco, and was crowned (1915) poet laureate of California. Her works include *A Perfect Day and Other Poems* (1881), *The Singer of the Sea* (1894), and *Songs from the Golden Gate* (1895).

Coolen (kō'lẹn), **Albert.** b. 1897—. Dutch novelist. Very simply, but with great depth and delicate psychological insight, Coolen tells of men in poverty and distress, living mostly on the Brabant moor. His novels include *Kinderen van ons Volk* (Children of our People, 1928), *Het donkere licht* (The Dark Light, 1929), *Peelwerkers* (Workers in the Peelmoor, 1930), *De goede moordenaar* (The Good Murderer, 1931), *De schoone Voleinding* (The Fair Completion, 1932), *Dorp aan de Rivier* (Village on the River, 1935), and *Herberg in 't Misverstand* (Misunderstanding Inn, 1938). His plays include *De vier Jaargetijden* (The Four Seasons, 1934), and *De Vreemdeling* (The Stranger, 1935).

Cooley (kö'li), **Charles Horton.** b. at Ann Arbor, Mich., Aug. 17, 1864; d. 1929. American sociologist. He was educated at the University of Michigan in his native city, and from 1892 until his death, a period of 37 years, was associated with that institution, first as an instructor in political economy, but from 1894 as a pioneer in the new field of sociology. In 1907 he was made full professor of that subject. He was president of the American Sociological Society in 1918. Certain of his formulations continue to be considered basic to sociological science, particularly his views concerning the reciprocal influence of the individual upon society and of society upon the individual. His books *Human Nature and the Social Order* (1902), *Social Organization* (1909), *Social Process* (1918), and *Sociological Theory and Social Research* (1930) remain important in the canon of literature on the science of sociology.

Cooley, Thomas McIntyre. b. at Attica, N.Y., Jan. 6, 1824; d. Sept. 12, 1898. American jurist. He was admitted to the bar in 1846, and became professor of law at the University of Michigan in 1859. In 1864 he was elected justice of the supreme court of the state to fill a vacancy; he served as chief justice (1868–69), and was reëlected for a full term of eight years in 1869. He retired from the bench in 1885. In 1881 he became professor of constitutional and administrative law at the University of Michigan, and subsequently became professor of American history, lecturer on constitutional law, and dean of the School of Political Science. He was chairman (1887–91) of the U.S. Interstate Commerce Commission. His chief works are *A Treatise on the Constitutional Limitations which rest upon the Legislative Power of the States of the American Union* (1868), *A Treatise on the Law of Taxation* (1876), *A Treatise upon Wrongs and their Remedies* (Volume I, 1878), and *The General Principles of Constitutional Law in the United States* (1880).

Cooley, William Desborough. d. at London, March 1, 1883. English geographer, author of various works on the history of geographical discovery, especially in Africa, and of a manual of physical geography.

Cooley v. Board of Wardens, 12, Howard 299 (1851). [Also called the **Pilot Case.**] U.S. Supreme Court decision, upholding a pilotage act of the state of Pennsylvania, notable for its formulation of a doctrine concerning the commerce clause of the Constitution which helped clarify its subsequent application. The opinion of Justice Curtis held that those subjects of the power to regulate commerce which "are in their nature national, or admit only of one uniform system, or plan of regulation, may justly be said to be of such a nature as to require exclusive legislation by Congress," but "where the subject upon which Congress can act under its commercial power is local in its nature or sphere of operation, . . . the State can act until Congress interferes and supersedes its authority. . . . The absence of any law of Congress on the subject is equivalent to its declaration that commerce in that matter shall be free."

Coolidge (kö'lij). Town in S Arizona, in Pinal County, near the Gila River and the Casa Grande National Monument. 4,306 (1950).

Coolidge, Archibald Cary. b. at Boston, March 6, 1866; d. Jan. 14, 1928. American historian and diplomat; brother of Julian Lowell Coolidge. He served as acting secretary (1890–91) of the U.S. legation at St. Petersburg, private secretary (1892) to the U.S. minister to France, and secretary (1893) of the American legation at Vienna. On the history staff (1893 *et seq.*) of Harvard University, he served as director (1910–28) of the University Library and played a considerable part in establishing the Widener Memorial Library. He was first editor in chief (1922–27) of *Foreign Affairs*, and the author of *The United States as a World Power* (1908), *Origins of the Triple Alliance* (1917), and *Ten Years of War and Peace* (1927).

Coolidge, Calvin. [Full name, **John Calvin Coolidge.**] b. at Plymouth Notch, Windsor County, Vt., July 4, 1872; d. at Northampton, Mass., Jan. 5, 1933. American statesman, 30th President of the United States (1923–29). Graduated (1895) from Amherst College, he studied law and was admitted (1897) to the bar, beginning law practice (1898) at Northampton, Mass. He entered politics as a Republican, serving as councilman (1899), city solicitor (1900–01), and clerk of courts (1903), member of the General Court of Massachusetts (1907–08), mayor (1910–11) of Northampton, state senator (1912–15), and president (1914–15) of the state senate. He was lieutenant governor (1916–18) and governor (1919–20) of Massachusetts, where he achieved national prominence for his stand during the Boston Police Strike (1919), declaring "There is no right to strike against the public safety by anybody, anywhere, any time." A candidate for the Republican nomination for the presidency (1920), he was nominated for the vice-presidency on the ticket with Warren G. Harding; during his term (1921–25) as vice-president, President Harding died (Aug. 2, 1923), and he succeeded to the presidency. The oath of office was administered (Aug. 3, 1923) at 2:47 in the morning by his father, a notary and justice of the peace, at Plymouth, Vt.

He was nominated and elected president (1924) in his own right by the largest plurality ever given to a Republican; toward the end of this term he made the famous statement (Aug. 2, 1927) "I do not choose to run for President in nineteen twenty-eight." He retired from public life (March 4, 1929), returned to Northampton, and devoted himself to writing, publishing his *Autobiography* (1929) and various syndicated articles. He is buried in a hillside cemetery near his childhood home at Plymouth Vt.

Coolidge, Charles Allerton. b. at Boston, Nov. 30, 1858; d. at Locust Valley, N.Y., April 1, 1936. American architect.

Coolidge, Dane. b. at Natick, Mass., March 24, 1873; d. Aug. 8, 1940. American naturalist and novelist. He was graduated (1898) from Stanford. His works include many novels dealing with life in the American West, such as *Hidden Water* (1910), *The Desert Trail* (1915), *The Fighting Fool* (1918), *Silver and Gold* (1918), *The Fighting Danites* (1925), *Gun Smoke* (1927), *Silver Hat* (1934), *Rawhide Johnny* (1936), *Ranger Two-Rifles* (1937), and *Hell's Hip Pocket* (1938).

Coolidge, Julian Lowell. b. at Brookline, Mass., Sept. 28, 1873—. American mathematician who is noted particularly for his work on modern geometry and the history of mathematics; brother of Archibald Cary Coolidge. He received degrees from Harvard (B.A., 1895), Oxford (B.Sc., 1897), and Bonn (Ph.D., 1904), and he taught at Harvard from 1899, becoming professor of mathematics in 1918. He was a major in the American army (1917–19) in World War I, and he has filled various offices in learned societies. His works include *The Elements of Non-Euclidean Geometry* (1909), *A Treatise on the Circle and the Sphere* (1916), *The Geometry of the Complex Domain* (1924), *An Introduction to Mathematical Probability* (1925), *A Treatise on Algebraic Plane Curves* (1931), *A History of Geometrical Methods* (1940), *A History of the Conic Sections and the Quadric Surfaces* (1945), and *The Mathematics of Great Amateurs* (1949).

Coolidge, Susan. Pseudonym of **Woolsey, Sarah Chauncy.**

Coolidge, Thomas Jefferson. b. at Boston, Aug. 26, 1831; d. Nov. 17, 1920. American manufacturer and diplomat. He was U.S. minister to France (1892–93), and was appointed (1898) a member of the joint high commission to adjust disputes between the U.S. and Canada.

Coolidge, William Augustus Brevoort. b. at New York, 1850; d. 1926. American clergyman, historian, and Alpinist. He went to England, where he was educated at Oxford and ordained to the Anglican priesthood in 1883. He became a fellow of Magdalen College, Oxford, where he tutored in modern history, but from 1885 he lived mostly in Switzerland (remaining, however, an American citizen). He was a student of Swiss history, but his great passion was mountain climbing. He is known to have made more than 1,700 Alpine ascents, attaining the summits of most of the highest peaks. He was editor of the *Alpine Journal* (1880–89), and the author of *The Alps in Nature and History* (1908).

Coolidge, William David. b. at Hudson, Mass., Oct. 23, 1873—. American physical chemist, notable for his invention and applications of ductile tungsten and the Coolidge tube for production of x-rays. He received a B.S. (1896) from the Massachusetts Institute of Technology and a Ph.D. (1899) from University of Leipzig, and has been associated with the General Electric Company, at Schenectady, N.Y., as researcher in physicochemistry (1905–07), assistant director of the research laboratory (1908–28), associate director (1928–32), director (1932–40), vice-president and research director (1940–44), and consultant (1944 *et seq.*).

Coolidge Dam. Dam in S central Arizona, ab. 115 mi. by road E of Phoenix. It impounds the Gila River, forming San Carlos Reservoir, and providing power and water for irrigation of ab. 157 sq. mi., chiefly in the Casa Grande valley. The dam was dedicated in 1930. Height, ab. 259 ft. above bedrock.

Cool Tombs. Poem in free verse by Carl Sandburg, written in 1915 and included in the volume *Cornhuskers* (1918).

Coolus (kō.lüs), **Romain.** [Pseudonym of **René Weill.**] b. at Rennes, France, May 25, 1868—. French comic playwright. He is the author of *Les Amants de Sazy* (1901), *L'Éternel Masculin* (1921), and *La Fifille à sa mémère* (1926). A "complete" edition of his works was published in 1924.

Coomaraswamy (kụ.mä′rạ.swä′mi), **Ananda Kentish.** b. at Colombo, Ceylon, Aug. 22, 1877; d. at Needham, Mass., Sept. 9, 1947. Indian art expert, writer, and lecturer on the arts and philosophy of India, who served (1917–47) as research fellow in Indian, Iranian, and Mohammedan art at the Boston Museum of Fine Arts. Educated at Wycliff College and the University of London (D.Sc., 1904), he was appointed (1906) director of the mineralogical surveys of Ceylon. He was a prominent leader in the movement of Rabindranath Tagore to foster national education in India. His books on art, Buddhism, and the art and literature of India include *Indian Drawings* (2 vols., 1910–12), *Buddha and the Gospel of Buddhism* (1916), *The Dance of Siva* (1918), *The Mirror of Gesture* (1931), *A New Approach to the Vedas* (1933), *The Transformation of Nature in Art* (1934), *Elements of Buddhist Iconography* (1935), *Is Art a Superstition or a Way of Life?* (1937), and *Am I My Brother's Keeper?* (1947).

Coomptah (kụmp′tạ) or **Coomtah** (kụm′-). See **Kumta.**

Coon River. See **Raccoon River,** in Iowa.

Cooper (kö′pėr, kụp′ėr), **Alexander.** d. 1660. English painter, especially of miniatures; brother of Samuel Cooper (1609–72). He painted both large pictures in oil, and miniatures, but it is generally considered that he was not the equal, as an artist, of his brother Samuel. Dissatisfied with the patronage he secured in England, he went abroad, lingering for awhile in Flanders and then going to Sweden, where he became court painter to Queen Christina, a post which he held for many years, and in which his art was largely employed in the execution of miniatures.

Cooper, Alfred Duff. b. 1890—. English statesman and diplomat; husband of Lady Diana Duff Cooper. Graduated from Oxford, he served (1914–19) in World War I. A Conservative member of Parliament (1924–29, 1931 *et seq.*), he served in the war office (1928–29, 1931–34) and in the treasury (1934–35), and was secretary of state for war (1935–37), first lord of the admiralty (1937–38), minister of information (1940–41), chancellor of the duchy of Lancaster (1941–43), representative (1943–44) to the French Committee of National Liberation, and ambassador (1944–47) to France. He is the author of *Talleyrand* (1932), the two-volume *Haig* (1935, 1936), *The Second World War* (1939), and *David* (1943).

Cooper, Anthony Ashley. See **Shaftesbury,** Earls of.

Cooper, Sir **Astley Paston.** b. 1768; d. 1841. English anatomist and surgeon. Educated at London, Edinburgh, and Paris, he was surgeon at Gray's Hospital, London, and professor of comparative anatomy at the Royal College of Surgeons before his appointment, in 1828, as surgeon to George IV, who knighted him for his services. His lectures on anatomy were widely attended, and his operations for hernia and arterial tumors aroused great interest among surgeons.

Cooper, Charles Henry. b. at Great Marlow, Buckinghamshire, England, March 20, 1808; d. March 21, 1866. English biographer and antiquary, a lawyer by profession, resident at Cambridge. His chief work is *Athenae Cantabrigienses* (1858–61), consisting of biographies of noted persons who were educated at, or otherwise associated with, Cambridge University.

Cooper, Courtney Ryley. b. at Kansas City, Mo., Oct. 31, 1886; d. Sept. 29, 1940. American novelist and screenplay writer. He ran away (1901) from home, and was variously engaged as circus clown, newsboy, trucker, glove salesman, actor, monologist, vaudeville dancer, and circus manager. He worked as a special writer (1910–13) for various newspapers, and as press agent (1914–15) for Colonel W. F. ("Buffalo Bill") Cody. His writings include the books *The Cross Cut* (1921), *Under the Big Top* (1923), *High Country* (1926), *Challenge of the Bush* (1929), *Poor Man's Gold* (1935), and *The Pioneers* (1937), the photoplays *Weary River*, *Wild Cargo*, and *The Plainsman*, and also magazine articles and reports of the work of the Federal Bureau of Investigation.

Cooper, Lady **Diana Duff.** [Maiden name, **Manners.**] b. 1892—. English actress; granddaughter of John James Robert Manners, 7th Duke of Rutland, and wife of Alfred

Duff Cooper. She appeared on stage in the U.S. as the Madonna in Max Reinhardt's production of *The Miracle*.

Cooper, Edith Emma. [Pseudonym (with Katherine Harris Bradley), **Michael Field.**] b. at Kenilworth, Warwickshire, England, Jan. 12, 1862; d. at Richmond, Surrey, England, Dec. 13, 1913. English lyric and dramatic poet; niece of Katherine Harris Bradley (1848–1914).

Cooper, Edward. b. at New York, Oct. 26, 1824; d. there, Feb. 25, 1905. American iron and steel manufacturer and politician; son of Peter Cooper (1791–1883). He formed Cooper, Hewitt and Company with Abram S. Hewitt, and was the inventor of the regenerative hot-blast stove for blast furnaces and the Durham double bell and hopper, neither of them patented. In 1871 he instigated examination of William Marcy ("Boss") Tweed's accounts, and in 1879 was elected mayor of New York.

Cooper, Henry Ernest. b. at New Albany, Ind., Aug. 28, 1857; d. at Long Beach, Calif., May 14, 1929. American statesman in Hawaii. He was a member (1891–93) of the annexation party in Hawaii and one of the organizers of the revolution to establish a republic; after his appointment (1895) as minister of foreign affairs, he served variously (1895–1903) as acting president of the republic, acting governor and secretary of the territory, and treasurer *ad interim*. He was the first secretary (1900–03) after the establishment of the Territory of Hawaii, first chairman (1907–14) of the board of the College of Hawaii, and first judge (1910–14) of the circuit court at Oahu.

Cooper, Hugh Lincoln. b. at Sheldon, Minn., April 28, 1865; d. June 24, 1937. American hydraulic engineer. Beginning as a bridge engineer (1883–91), he was superintendent (1890–91) of the Chicago Bridge and Iron Company. He then applied himself (1891 *et seq.*) to hydraulic engineering in relation to electric power development, and was responsible for a number of large hydroelectric projects, including the plant of the Mississippi River Power Company, at Keokuk, Iowa, the plants at Niagara Falls for the Toronto Power Company, the Pennsylvania Water and Power Company at Holtwood, Pa., the water-power project at Muscle Shoals, Ala., and the water-power and navigation project on the Dnieper River in the Ukraine, Russia.

Cooper, James Fenimore. b. at Burlington, N.J., Sept. 15, 1789; d. at Cooperstown, N.Y., Sept. 14, 1851. American novelist, best remembered for his "Leather-Stocking Tales," a group of novels including *The Last of the Mohicans* (1826) and *The Deerslayer* (1841), notable for their narrative power and romantic depiction of life in the American wilderness. His father, William Cooper, settled and developed Cooperstown, N.Y., the scene of many of the son's novels. He spent three years at Yale, from which he was expelled (c1805) for high-spirited pranks. In 1806 he shipped out from New York, going to England and the Strait of Gibraltar; after his return (1807) he was commissioned a midshipman, and served on the Great Lakes and on the Atlantic. In 1811, the year of his marriage to Susan Augusta De Lancey, he resigned from the navy. They lived at Mamaroneck, N.Y., until 1814, and, after residing at Scarsdale, N.Y., moved to New York City in 1822. In 1826 he moved with his family to Paris, where he served nominally as U.S. consul at Lyons. He made trips to England, Switzerland, Italy, and Germany before returning to New York in 1833, and in 1834 established his residence at Otsego Hall, Cooperstown. His first novel, *Precaution* (1820), attracted little attention, but his next book, *The Spy* (1821), won instant success in the U.S. and Europe. He followed this with *The Pioneers* (1823), the first of what became the "Leather-Stocking Tales," *The Pilot* (1823), *Lionel Lincoln* (1825), *The Last of the Mohicans* (1826), and *The Prairie* (1827). In addition to *Notions of the Americans* (1828) and *Letter of J. Fenimore Cooper to General Lafayette* (1831), in both of which he praised American republican institutions, he published *The Red Rover* (1827), *The Wept of Wish-ton-Wish* (1829), *The Water-Witch* (1830), and three novels based on European themes, *The Bravo* (1831), *The Heidenmauer* (1832), and *The Headsman* (1833). Returning to the U.S. in 1833, he was disappointed in failing to find the image of conservative republican simplicity he had cherished during his years abroad. His idealization of American life developed into a sharply critical view of his people for what he felt was their failure to live up to their democratic principles. His first writings, upon his return, attacked the problem directly in satire and thinly disguised fiction. *A Letter to his Countrymen* (1834) was followed by *The Monikins* (1835), *The American Democrat* (1838), *Homeward Bound* (1838), and *Home as Found* (1838). He also wrote *Sketches of Switzerland* (1836), *Gleanings in Europe* (1837), *Gleanings in Europe: England* (1837), and *Gleanings in Europe: Italy* (1838). The counterattacks on Cooper brought a decrease in the sales of his books and involved him in libel suits against Whig newspapers in New York. Meanwhile, he devoted himself to *The History of the Navy of the United States of America* (1839), and returned to the "Leather-Stocking Tales" with *The Pathfinder* (1840) and *The Deerslayer* (1841), producing what some regard as his best achievement. His later writings are *Mercedes of Castile* (1840), *The Two Admirals* (1842), *The Wing-and-Wing* (1842), *Ned Myers* (1843), *Wyandotte* (1843), *Le Mouchoir* (1843), *Afloat and Ashore* (1844), *Miles Wallingford* (1844), *Lives of Distinguished American Naval Officers* (1846), and the "Littlepage Manuscripts" trilogy, consisting of *Satanstoe* (1845), *The Chainbearer* (1845), and *The Redskins* (1846). Here, in the thorough study of the changes in New York society through four generations from the time of the Indian wars to his own day, Cooper came very near to achieving his ambition to understand the civilization which was being shaped by American facts and opinions. But he also proved that he could still write an exciting historical romance of his country's past. His last novels, *The Crater* (1848), *Jack Tier* (1848), *The Sea Lions* (1848), and *The Ways of the Hour* (1850) show slight loss of narrative power and a deepening concern for the institutions of democracy. Still remembered chiefly for the "Leather-Stocking" series, where action and suspense are at their best, he is coming more and more to be valued as the first real chronicler of the underlying forces which shaped our country in the early days.

Cooper, John. b. at Bath, England, before 1810; d. at Tunbridge Wells, England, July 13, 1870. English actor. He appeared at Bath in 1811, making his London debut in the same year, and after some years in the provinces was a favorite with London audiences in the period 1820–58.

Cooper, Lane. b. at New Brunswick, N.J., 1875—. American teacher. He was graduated from Yale (M.A., 1898) and the University of Leipzig (Ph.D., 1901), and until 1941 was professor of English language and literature at Cornell. He has published *Theories of Style* (1907), *The Function of the Leader in Scholarship* (1911), *Louis Agassiz as a Teacher* (1917; rev. ed., 1945), *The Greek Genius and Its Influence* (1917), *Experiments in Education* (1943), and many others.

Cooper, Merian C. b. at Jacksonville, Fla., Oct. 24, 1893—. American writer and motion-picture producer. He served in World Wars I and II. He is the author of *Grass* (1925), and produced in collaboration with Ernest B. Schoedsack the adventure films *Grass, Chang, Four Feathers,* and *King Kong;* he also coproduced *Last Days of Pompeii.* From 1935 to 1936 he was head of Pioneer Pictures, and thereafter became copresident with John Ford of Argosy productions.

Cooper, Peter. b. at New York, Feb. 12, 1791; d. April 4, 1883. American inventor, manufacturer, and philanthropist, builder of the first American steam locomotive and founder of Cooper Union, at New York. After a successful career as a manufacturer of glue and isinglass at New York, he turned to his next important venture, the Canton Iron Works at Baltimore, which he established (1828) with two partners. It was here that he built the first American steam locomotive, popularly known as the "Teakettle" and "Tom Thumb," which made its run on the Baltimore and Ohio Railroad. He sold the ironworks in 1836 and amassed a number of properties in the years that followed. Among his holdings were foundries at Ringwood, N.J., and Durham, Pa., iron mines in northern New Jersey, a wire factory at Trenton, N.J., and a rolling mill at New York. His Trenton establishment turned out (1854) the first structural iron for fireproof buildings. Among his inventions were a washing machine, and a machine for using the tide as a source of power. He was president of the New York, Newfoundland and London Telegraph Company and of the North American Telegraph Company. In 1870 he was awarded the Bessemer Gold Medal by the Iron and Steel Institute of Great Britain. He was a member of the board of aldermen of New York, and in 1876 was the presidential candidate of the Greenback Party. His contribution to popular education was made through his founding (1857–59) of Cooper Union at New York. See *Peter Cooper*, by R. W. Raymond (1901).

Cooper, Samuel. b. at London, 1609; d. there, May 5, 1672. English miniaturist, called by Walpole "Vandyck in little"; brother of Alexander Cooper (d. 1660). He was a pupil of his uncle John Hoskins.

Cooper, Susan Fenimore. b. April 17, 1813; d. Dec. 31, 1894. American writer; daughter of James Fenimore Cooper. She was the author of *Rural Hours* (1850) and *William West Skiles: A Sketch of Missionary Life* (1890).

Cooper, Thomas. b. at Westminster, England, Oct. 22, 1759; d. May 11, 1839. American publicist, educator, and scientist. He attended Oxford, studied medicine at London and Manchester, and devoted himself to philosophy, chemistry, and political agitation. His differences with English conservatives contributed to his departure (1794) for America, where he settled at Northumberland, Pa., there serving as a lawyer and physician and subsequently entering into his pamphleteering activities as a supporter of the Jeffersonians. He was convicted, sentenced, and fined (1800) under the Sedition Act, but he displayed more conservative tendencies as a state judge (1804–11), from which post he was removed, however, by the governor of Pennsylvania at the instigation of the legislature. He was also (1801–04) commissioner in Luzerne County, Pa. He became (1811) professor of chemistry in Carlisle (now Dickinson) College, occupying the chair until 1815, and was professor of applied chemistry and mineralogy (1815–19) in the University of Pennsylvania. In 1820 he became professor of chemistry in South Carolina College (now the University of South Carolina), was chosen president soon thereafter, and remained in that post until 1834. He helped found the state's first school of medicine and first insane asylum, and became embroiled in political controversies and in clashes with the clergy on the issue between science and theology. After his retirement he spent much of his time editing the *Statutes at Large of South Carolina* (5 vols., 1836–39). Among his outstanding political pamphlets are *Political Essays* (1799), *Consolidation* (1824), and *On the Constitution* (1826). Also a teacher of political economy, he wrote *Lectures on the Elements of Political Economy* (1826). In the scientific field, he edited the *Emporium of Arts and Sciences* (1813–14) and wrote the *Discourse on the Connexion between Chemistry and Medicine* (1818). See *The Public Life of Thomas Cooper 1783–1839*, by Dumas Malone (1926).

Cooper, Thomas. b. at Leicester, England, March 20, 1805; d. at Lincoln, England, July 15, 1892. English Chartist agitator, poet, and author. Self-taught in Hebrew, Greek, Latin, and French, he became a schoolmaster and, later, a Methodist preacher. He led the Leicester Chartists in 1841, and was imprisoned for two years on a charge of sedition. He was the author of the poem *The Purgatory of Suicides* (1845), a collection of tales, *Wise Saws and Modern Instances* (1845), two novels, *Alderman Ralph* (1853) and *The Family Feud* (1854), and the autobiographical *Thoughts at Fourscore* (1885).

Cooper, Thomas Sidney. b. at Canterbury, England, Sept. 26, 1803; d. there, Feb. 7, 1902. English painter, chiefly of animals and landscapes.

Cooper, Thomas Thornville. b. at Bishopwearmouth, England, Sept. 13, 1839; d. at Bamo, Burma, April 24, 1878. English traveler in Australia, India, Burma, China, and Tibet, and author of books relating his experiences. He was murdered by a Sepoy of his guard.

Co-operative Commonwealth Federation. [Called the **CCF.**] Canadian political party. Colloquially known as the CCF, this party arose from the search for common political ground between representatives of farmer-labor, socialist, and other groups in the western Canadian provinces, and was formally launched at Calgary, Alberta, in August, 1932. A party convention held at Regina, Saskatchewan, in 1933 issued the so-called Regina Manifesto, setting forth the CCF program, which calls for the socialization of finance, public ownership of utilities, assistance to agriculture, old age, illness, and unemployment insurance, encouragement of the coöperative movement, and other policies and measures calculated to transform a competitive to a coöperative social-economic order. The first national leader of the party was J. S. Woodsworth, who after his death was succeeded by M. J. Coldwell. In 1944 the CCF won a majority in the provincial legislature of Saskatchewan, setting up a government with T. C. Douglas as prime minister, and renewed its domination of that province in the elections of 1948. In that year also the CCF became the official opposition party in the legislature of Ontario, and it also holds seats in other provincial legislatures, as well as in the Canadian House of Commons.

Cooper River (kö'pėr, kůp'ėr). River in South Carolina, uniting with the Ashley at Charleston to form Charleston harbor. Length, ab. 40 mi.

Cooper's Cave. See under **Glens Falls.**

Cooper's Hill. Poem by Sir John Denham, first published in 1642, and published in its final form in 1665. Pope, who imitated Denham, also wrote in praise of *Cooper's Hill* in his poem *Windsor Forest.*

Cooperstown (kö'pėrz.toun, kůp'ėrz-). Village in C New York, county seat of Otsego County, on Otsego Lake, ab. 62 mi. W of Albany: residential and resort community. Its Doubleday Field is notable as the site of the first baseball game (1839). The National Baseball Museum and baseball's Hall of Fame are situated here. Its Farmers' Museum is operated by the New York State Historical Association, and features objects of folk life, especially of the 1780–1850 period. Cooperstown was the home of James Fenimore Cooper, whose father founded the village. 2,727 (1950).

Cooper Union (kö'pėr, kůp'ėr). Coeducational institution at New York founded by Peter Cooper and opened in 1859. It provides instruction in the arts, sciences, and engineering, and has a library, museum, public reading rooms, art galleries, free lectures, and evening courses.

Coorg (kůrg). [Also, **Kurg.**] State in SW Union of India, ab. 65 mi. W of the city of Mysore. Coffee, rubber, tea, rice, and teakwood are the chief products. It was formerly a chief-commissionership of British India, under the administration of the governor general of India. It was annexed by Great Britain in 1834. Capital, Mercara; area, 1,593 sq. mi.; pop. 229,255 (1951).

Coornhert (kōrn'hert), **Dirck Volckertszoon.** b. at Amsterdam, Netherlands, 1522; d. at Gouda, Netherlands, 1590. Dutch author and poet. After 1540 he lived at Haarlem as an engraver and etcher, and became there notary (1561) and secretary to the city (1562). Against religious freedom, the great question of the day, he wrote a vast number of tracts and pamphlets, many of which have, besides, a political character.

Coos (kös). [Also, **Kus.**] Group of four small North American Indian tribes formerly inhabiting the Coos Bay area of Oregon. Their languages formed an independent family.

Coosa (kö'sa̤). River in Georgia and Alabama, formed by the junction of the Oostenaula and Etowah at Rome, Ga. It unites with the Tallapoosa to form the Alabama ab. 8 mi. N of Montgomery, Ala. Length, ab. 290 mi.

Coos Bay (kös). [Former name (until 1944), **Marshfield.**] City in SW Oregon, in Coos County, on the flat W shore of Coos Bay, an inlet of the Pacific Ocean, ab. 95 mi. N of the Oregon-California state line. The place was settled in 1853, and lumbering and shipbuilding (wood) industries started early. In 1908 a channel was dredged through the shallow bay, and a port was established. During World War I, the city experienced a boom, as a result of demand for lumber, and the Southern Pacific Railroad built a branch line here. Lumbering and lumber products (chiefly fir and cedar) are still large industries; there is also fish canning, and trade with surrounding farming areas. 6,223 (1950).

Coote (köt), Sir **Eyre.** b. at Ash Hill, County Limerick, Ireland, 1726; d. at Madras, India, April 26, 1783. British general, distinguished for his services in India. He went to India in 1754, was present at the capture of Calcutta in 1756, and (as a captain) at the battle of Plassey, and was appointed lieutenant colonel in January, 1759. In this year he took command of the troops in the Madras Presidency, defeated the French under Lally at Wandewash on Jan. 22, 1760, and captured Pondichéry in January, 1761, putting an end to the French power in India. From 1762 till 1769 he resided in England, returning to India in the latter year as commander in chief of the Madras Presidency, an office which he resigned in 1770, again returning to England. He was appointed commander in chief in India in April, and promoted lieutenant general in August, 1777. In March, 1779, he assumed command at Calcutta, and on July 1, 1781, at Porto Novo, with a force consisting of 2,000 Europeans and 6,000 Sepoys, defeated Haidar Ali with an army of 40,000 men.

Coote, Sir Eyre. b. 1762; d. c1824. British soldier; nephew of Sir Eyre Coote (1726–83). He served as ensign in the battle of Brooklyn and in other campaigns of the Revolutionary War until the surrender of Yorktown. He became major general and commander of Dover in 1798, led an expedition to cut the sluices at Ostend, and was captured by the French, in 1798, served in the battle of Bergen in 1799, and in the Egyptian campaign in 1800, and was appointed lieutenant general, and lieutenant governor and commander in chief of the island of Jamaica in 1805. He was dismissed from the army on a charge of indecent conduct.

Coote, Richard. [Title, 1st Earl of **Bellamont.**] b. 1636; d. at New York, March 5, 1701. English official, created 1st Earl of Bellamont, in the peerage of Ireland, Nov. 2, 1689. He was appointed colonial governor of New England in 1695, with a special mission to suppress piracy. He, with others, fitted out the *Adventure* for Captain Kidd, who was given special powers to arrest pirates. Kidd's own piratical acts led Bellamont to arrest him at Boston, where he had come under a promise of safety, and send him to England for trial.

Coowescoowe (kö″wẹs.kö.wē′). American Indian name of **Ross, John.**

Copacabana (kō″pä.kä.ʙä′nä). Peninsula in the S part of Lake Titicaca, crossed by the boundary line between Peru and Bolivia. It is trapezoidal in form, high and rocky, and joined to the mainland by a very narrow isthmus. Its area may be 50 sq. mi. Copacabana was an outpost of the Incas, and contains ruins mostly obliterated on the surface. It has been known in modern times for its chapel with a supposed miraculous painting of the Virgin, visited yearly by thousands of pilgrims.

Copala (kō.pä′lä). See under **Nueva Vizcaya.**

Copán (kō.pän′). See also **Santa Rosa de Copán.**

Copán. Department in W Honduras, on the Guatemalan border: coffee and rubber. Capital, Santa Rosa de Copán; area, 1,216 sq. mi.; pop. 95,880 (1950).

Copán. Early Maya city, near what is now Santa Rosa de Copán, in NW Honduras, which flourished during the 8th and early 9th centuries A.D. and was then abandoned. The ruins occur in nearly a score of groups, the largest of which covers ab. 75 acres, and consist of temples, courts, plazas, terraces, pyramids, and a famous hieroglyphic stairway which contains the longest Maya hieroglyphic inscription yet discovered. Copán was evidently a center of learning, especially in the earlier period of Maya history, and it is from deciphering the inscriptions here sculptured in stone that archaeologists have learned much concerning Maya knowledge of astronomy and calendar formulation.

Cope (kōp), **Edward Drinker.** b. at Philadelphia, July 28, 1840; d. there, April 12, 1897. American biologist and paleontologist, professor of geology in the University of Pennsylvania. He was professor of natural sciences in Haverford College (1864–67), and subsequently became paleontologist to the U.S. Geological Survey. He discovered a very large number of species of extinct and recent vertebrata. His works include *Synopsis of the Extinct Cetacea of the United States* (1867–68), *Systematic Arrangement of the Extinct Batrachia, Reptilia, and Aves of North America* (1869–70), *Relation of Man to Tertiary Mammalia* (1875), *Origin of the Fittest*, and others, besides numerous elaborate memoirs on the extinct vertebrates of North America, principally of the Cretaceous and Tertiary deposits.

Cope, Walter. b. at Philadelphia, Oct. 30, 1860; d. there, Nov. 3, 1902. American architect. In 1885 he formed a partnership with John Stewardson, who was succeeded at his death by his brother Emlen L. Stewardson. They erected buildings for Bryn Mawr College, the University of Pennsylvania, and Princeton University, and also numerous churches and private residences.

Copeau (ko.pō), **Jacques.** b. at Paris, Feb. 4, 1879; d. at Beaune, France, Oct. 20, 1949. French actor, manager, stage director, drama critic, and playwright who became a leader of modern theatrical style on the French stage. He turned to the theater after selling paintings in a gallery devoted to modern art. He wrote drama criticism for *L'Hermitage* (1904–06), for the *Grande Revue* (1907–10), and for other periodicals, and also founded (with Gide and others) and edited *La Nouvelle Revue Française* (1909–14). In 1911, he made an adaptation of *Brothers Karamazov* and staged it successfully at the Théâtre des Arts, and in 1913, in association with Charles Dullin and Louis Jouvet, he established his famous Théâtre du Vieux Colombier in Paris with a group of talented actors he had trained in the country. At this repertory theater, which produced works written in many periods (Shakespeare, Molière, Musset, Becque, and Claudel), he developed a new, antinaturalist style of production on a permanent architectural stage, with steps leading down into the auditorium, and with little more than suggestive screens for localizing the different scenes of a play. In this manner, he achieved a simplified realism and tasteful imaginativeness which stressed the spirit and meaning of a play, rather than the external elements of the setting. Paying special attention to acting art, he made his company the best acting group in Europe next to Stanislavski's Moscow Art Theatre. Between 1917 and 1919, his actors performed in French at New York under the sponsorship of Otto Kahn, and forged a cultural link between the wartime allies. When Copeau brought his players back to Paris in 1920, he introduced new plays by Jules Romains, André Gide, Charles Vildrac, and others to the postwar public. In October, 1920, he also established a famous school for the study of the dramatic arts at Paris, and he continued to train actors there after the collapse of the *Théâtre du Vieux Colombier* for lack of funds (1924). Copeau was made one of the four stage directors of the *Comédie Française* in 1936 and became chief director in 1940, retaining this position until the fall of Paris, in World War II. Copeau also appeared as an actor in French films. He returned to New York in 1926 to stage his version of *Brothers Karamazov* for the Theatre Guild in a production that included Alfred Lunt, Lynn Fontanne, and Edward G. Robinson in the cast.

Copeland (kōp′lạnd), **Charles Townsend.** b. at Calais, Me., April 27, 1860; d. July 24, 1952. American teacher. He was graduated (1882) from Harvard, where he was lecturer on English literature (1893–1910), assistant professor (1910–17) and associate professor (1917–25) of English, and held (1925–28) the Boylston chair of rhetoric and oratory. He exerted a considerable influence over an entire generation of Harvard writers in their formative period; among them were John Dos Passos, Malcolm Cowley, John Reed, and Robert Hillyer. He edited *The Copeland Reader* (1926).

Copeland, Edwin Bingham. b. at Monroe, Wis., Sept. 30, 1873—. American botanist, dean of the College of Agriculture of the University of the Philippines from 1909. He was botanist to the Philippine government (1903–08), and superintendent of the School of Agriculture in the Philippine Islands (1908–09). Later he was curator (1928–32) of the University of California herbarium. He published *Philippine Agriculture* (1908), *Cocoanut Cultivation* (1910), and others.

Copeland, Ralph. b. Sept. 3, 1837; d. Oct. 27, 1905. British astronomer, professor in the University of Edinburgh and astronomer royal to Scotland.

Copeland, Royal Samuel. b. at Dexter, Mich., Nov. 7, 1868; d. June 17, 1938. American physician and legislator. He received (1889) his M.D. degree from the University of Michigan, and served there as assistant (1889–90) to the professor of ophthalmology and professor (1895–1908) of ophthalmology. He then went to New York as dean (1908–18) and professor at Flower Hospital Medical College, and served as New York commissioner (1918–23) of health and president of the Board of Health. As senator (1923–38) from New York he advocated the pure food and drugs legislation. Author of *The Health Book* (1924) and *Dr. Copeland's Home Medical Book* (1935).

Copeland Park. Unincorporated community in SE Virginia, in Elizabeth City County, near Langley Field and Norfolk. 7,115 (1950).

Copello (kō.pā'yō), **Santiago Luis.** b. at San Isidro, Argentina, Jan. 7, 1880—. Argentine prelate, Roman Catholic primate (since 1936) of Argentina. He was appointed (1927) vicar-general of the Argentine army, and was archbishop of Buenos Aires (1932 *et seq.*) and cardinal (1935 *et seq.*).

Copena (kō.pē'na). American Indian burial mound culture of N Alabama, closely related to the Hopewell and late Adena cultures further north. It is dated at about 900–1300 A.D.

Copenhagen (kō.pen.hā'gen). [Danish, **København.**] *Amt* (county) of Denmark, in E Zealand, bounded by the amts of Præstø, Sorø, Holbæk, and Frederiksborg and the Øresund. Capital, Roskilde; area, 453 sq. mi.; pop. 429,242 (1945).

Copenhagen. [Danish, **København**; German, **Kopenhagen;** French, **Copenhague** (ko.pe.nàg); medieval name, **Havn** or **Hafnia.**] Capital of Denmark, situated on the island of Zealand (Sjælland) and the adjoining island of Amager, on the W shore of the Øresund (the Sound), opposite the Swedish city of Malmö. Pop. 927,404, with suburbs 1,078,892 (1945); 974,901 (1950).

Industry and Trade. It has a large harbor, with good facilities, and is the center of shipping activities, oceanic and coastwise, of Denmark, and of connecting links of the Danish and Swedish railroad systems; there is also an international airport, as well as various harbor basins, shipyards, and a naval arsenal. Copenhagen is the center of the Danish transit, export, and import trade, agricultural products being the principal exports, Great Britain and Germany the chief trade links. There is a stock exchange and a number of banking institutions. Outstanding among industries are machinery, gloves, and textiles; there are also famous porcelain manufactures, as well as sugar refineries, distilleries, breweries (Carlsberg), other food industries, and fish markets.

Cultural Institutions. Copenhagen is the seat of the central administration of Denmark, of a Lutheran bishopric, and of a university, founded in 1479. Educational resources include an institute of technology, institutes of geology, biology, and meteorology, schools of veterinary and dental medicine, commerce, and agriculture, a music conservatory, botanical and zoölogical gardens, and royal, municipal, and university libraries with more than two million volumes and valuable manuscripts. The concert hall and the Tivoli amusement gardens, one of the most famous parks in Europe, were blown up during the German occupation in World War II. Copenhagen museums house numerous collections. They include a museum of art, a museum of applied art, the national museum (containing antiquities, coins and medals, and ethnographic, prehistoric, and historical collections), the Thorvaldsen Museum (in memory of the sculptor), the Nye Carlsberg Glyptothek (with paintings and sculptures), a museum of arms, a museum of mineralogy, and a museum of musical history.

Architecture and Surroundings. Architecturally, Copenhagen is dominated by the classicistic Renaissance style which came in vogue during the reign of Christian IV (1588–1648); it has been variously altered, but not basically changed, during the baroque and later periods. Most of the churches (Holy Cross, Saint Peter's, Reformation, Saviour, Trinity, Holmens Church) date from the 15th–18th centuries; others, such as the Frederick's (or Marble) Church, Church of Our Lady, Castle Church, and Peace Church, were built in the early or late 19th century; most of them have beautiful steeples. The castles Rosenborg, Charlottenborg, Christiansborg (now the seat of parliament), Frederiksborg, and Amalienborg, and a number of smaller palaces are all of the 17th and 18th centuries; the town hall, built in the period 1894–1903, presents the old style in a modern interpretation. In the vicinity of Copenhagen are beautiful seaside resorts. Near Hillerod is Frederiksborg Castle, erected (1602–20) for Christian IV by Dutch architects and rebuilt in the 19th century; it is the largest Renaissance castle in Denmark, and contains the museum of national history.

History. In the early Middle Ages a small village, called Havn or Hafnia, Copenhagen received town privileges in 1254 and became a royal residence in 1445. It was variously attacked by Hanseatic fleets and in 1658–59 by the Swedes. An unsuccessful attempt was made to defend it against the British under Nelson in 1801, and it was again bombarded by the British navy in 1807. It was fortified in the 19th century. In World War II, the city was occupied on April 9, 1940, by the Germans, who encountered much passive and active opposition during the war: ships were blown up in the harbor on Aug. 29, 1943; on Oct. 1, 1943, those Danish Jews whom the Germans had not deported were concealed by the population and subsequently shipped across the Øresund to Sweden; in July, 1944, a general strike was carried on which ended with German concessions; sabotage was frequent. Some buildings were destroyed but the city escaped serious damage.

Copenhagen, Battle of. Victory gained near Copenhagen by the British fleet under Nelson over the Danish fleet, on April 2, 1801.

Copernicus (kō.pėr'ni.kus), **Nicolaus.** [Latin form of Polish **Mikołaj Kopernik.**] b. at Toruń, Poland, Feb. 19, 1473; d. at Frombork, Poland, May 24, 1543. Founder of modern astronomy. He entered the University of Kraków in 1491, studied law at Bologna (1495–1500), was appointed canon of the chapter of Frombork (Frauenburg) in 1497, lectured on astronomy at Rome in 1500, studied medicine at Padua (c1501), and became *doctor decretorum* at Ferrara in 1503. The rest of his life was spent chiefly at Frombork in the performance of his duties as canon and in the practice of medicine. He published in 1543 an exposition of his system of astronomy, which has since received the name of the Copernican, in a treatise entitled *De orbium coelestium revolutionibus.*

Copertino (kō.per.tē'nō). [Also, **Coppertino.**] Town and commune in SE Italy, in the *compartimento* (region) of Apulia, in the province of Lecce, situated in the center of the Salentina peninsula, SW of Lecce. The castle, built in 1540 for Alfonso Castriota, Prince of Albania and Count of Copertino, is in the baroque style; there are various baroque churches. Pop. of commune, 12,787 (1936); of town, 11,889 (1936).

Cophen (kō'fen). Ancient name of the **Kabul River.**

Cophetua (kō.fet'ū.a). Titular hero of an English ballad, *Cophetua and the Beggar Maid,* a legendary African king who wooed and married Penelophon, a beggar maid. The ballad is preserved in Percy's *Reliques.* Cophetua is alluded to by Shakespeare (who calls the girl Zenelophon) and by Ben Jonson. Tennyson also wrote a short poem on the subject entitled *The Beggar Maid.*

Copiapó (kō.pyä.pō'). Capital of Atacama province in N Chile: center of a mining region. 15,693 (1940).

Copiapó. [Also: **Azufre;** Spanish, **Cerro Copiapó, Cerro del Azufre, Volcán Copiapó.**] Volcanic mountain in N Chile. 19,947 ft.

Copland (kōp'land), **Aaron.** b. at New York, Nov. 14, 1900—. American composer. He studied under Wittgenstein, Wolfsohn, Adler, and R. Goldmark, twice received (1925 and 1926) a Guggenheim fellowship, and won the RCA Victor Company award in 1930. His compositions include *Hear Ye, Hear Ye* (1934, a ballet), *A Dance Symphony* (1925), *What Do We Plant?* (1936, a work for chorus), *The Second Hurricane* (1937, a play-opera); *El Salon Mexico* (1936, for orchestra), and the ballets *Billy the Kid* (1938) and *Appalachian Spring* (1944).

Copland, Douglas Berry. b. at Timaru, New Zealand, Feb. 24, 1894—. Australian economist and educator. He studied at the University of New Zealand, became professor of economics and dean of the faculty of commerce at the University of Melbourne in 1924, and subsequently became editor of the *Economic Record.* He served as chairman of the committee of economists that reported to the Commonwealth Loan Council in 1931 on Australian economy; from this report grew the premier's plan of recovery. Later he served as commonwealth prices commissioner, Australian minister to China, and vice-chancellor of the Australian National University. His publications include *Australia in the World Crisis 1929–1933* (1934) and *The Road to High Employment* (1945); he has also edited valuable collections of documents concerned with economic issues.

Copland, Robert. fl. 1508–47. English printer, publisher, poet, and translator. He may have worked for Caxton, and he undoubtedly was employed by Wynkyn de Worde, both of whom he calls "my mayster." The first book carrying his name as printer is *The Boke of Justices of Peas* (1515). Of his own works, the best known are two poems, *The Hye Way to the Spyttel Hous* (c1536) and *Jyl of Breyntford's Testament*, derived from a popular tale.

Coplay (kop'li). Borough in E Pennsylvania, in Lehigh County, near Allentown. 2,994 (1950).

Copleston (kop'l.ston), **Edward.** b. at Offwell, Devonshire, England, Feb. 2, 1776; d. near Chepstow, England, Oct. 14, 1849. English prelate and author, appointed professor of poetry at Oxford in 1802, and bishop of Llandaff and dean of Saint Paul's in 1828. He wrote *Praelectiones* (1813), *Enquiry into the Doctrines of Necessity and Predestination* (1821), and others.

Copley (kop'li), Sir **Godfrey.** d. at London, 1709. English baronet, donator of a fund of 100 pounds "in trust for the Royal Society of London for improving natural knowledge." The first award was made in 1731, the second in 1734. In 1736 the bequest was converted into a gold medal (the Copley Medal) to be awarded annually.

Copley, John Singleton. b. probably at Boston, 1738; d. at London, Sept. 9, 1815. American painter, noted as one of the leading portraitists in late colonial New England, and for his work, particularly in the genre of the historical painting, in England after 1775. His development as a painter during his early life remains obscure, but it is known that he was painting as early as his 14th year, and was a professional before reaching the age of 21. In 1766 his exhibition of his canvas *The Boy with the Squirrel* in England won Copley, then at Boston, election as a Fellow of the Society of Artists of Great Britain. It was at this time that he struck up his connection with the painter Benjamin West, whose advice from England was later to influence Copley in his departure from America. His flourishing years in New England came in the 1770's, when Copley received numerous commissions to paint the dignitaries of Boston and other places in New England. He also painted portraits (1771–72) at New York, but virtually all of his work was performed at his Boston studio. Of a Loyalist family, he left (1774) Boston for England, France, and Italy before settling (1775) at London. Resuming activity as a portrait painter, he later embarked upon historical and Biblical pieces, establishing his reputation with *The Death of Lord Chatham*. Others in this genre included *Hagar and Ishmael in the Wilderness, The Siege of Gibraltar, The Red Cross Knight, The Resurrection, Abraham Offering up Isaac*, and *The Arrest of Five Members of the Commons by Charles the First*. He was elected (1783) a full member of the Royal Academy. Among his portraits of New Englanders who visited London were those of John Adams and John Quincy Adams. After 1800 he fell upon increasingly hard times and in his last years was much enfeebled. See *The Life and Works of John Singleton Copley*, by Frank W. Bayley (1915).

Copley, John Singleton. [Title, Baron **Lyndhurst.**] b. at Boston, May 21, 1772; d. in England, Oct. 12, 1863. English jurist and statesman, created Baron Lyndhurst in 1827; son of John Singleton Copley (1738–1815). He was graduated at Cambridge University (Trinity College), became a "traveling fellow" of the university, and visited the U.S. in 1795–96. He rose rapidly at the bar, entered Parliament in 1818, became solicitor-general in June, 1819, was attorney general from 1824 to 1826, and was three times lord chancellor (1827–30, 1834, and 1841–45).

Copley Medal. See under **Copley,** Sir **Godfrey.**

Coppage v. Kansas, 236 U.S. 1 (1915) (kop'āj). U.S. Supreme Court decision holding unconstitutional a Kansas state law prohibiting "yellow dog" labor contracts. The court, referring to the precedent in *Adair v. United States (1908)*, held that the Kansas statute violated the due process clause of the Fourteenth Amendment and stressed the right to buy and sell labor as an essential part of the freedom of contract.

Coppard (kop'ärd), **A. E.** [Full name, **Alfred Edgar Coppard.**] b. at Folkestone, England, Jan. 4, 1878—. English short-story writer and poet. Among his collections of verse are *Hips and Haws* (1922), *Pelagea and Other Poems* (1926), *Collected Poems* (1928), and *Cherry Ripe* (1935); he is the author also of the volumes of stories *Adam and Eve and Pinch Me* (1921), *The Black Dog* (1923), *Fishmonger's Fiddle* (1925), *The Field of Mustard* (1926), *Pink Furniture* (1930), *Easter Day* (1931), *Rummy* (1932), *Tapster's Tapestry* (1938), *You Never Know, Do You?* (1939), and *Dark-eyed Lady* (1947).

Copparo (kōp.pä'rō). Town and commune in N Italy, in the *compartimento* (region) of Emilia-Romagna, situated S of the Po di Goro River, and E of Ferrara. The commune produces rich harvests of cereals and fruits. Pop. of commune, 23,777 (1936); of town, 4,618 (1936).

Coppée (ko.pā), **François Édouard Joachim.** b. at Paris, Jan. 12, 1842; d. there, May 23, 1908. French writer. He made his reputation first as a poet. He was made (1878) archivist of the Comédie Française, elected (1884) to the French Academy, and appointed (1888) an officer of the Legion of Honor. He published a number of volumes of poems, prose, sketches, and romances. Among his plays are *Le Passant* (1869), *Fais ce que dois* (1871), *Le Luthier de Crémone* (1877), *La Guerre de cent ans* (with M. d'Artois, 1878), *Madame de Maintenon* (1881), *Les Jacobites* (1885), and *Pour la couronne* (1895). Other works include an autobiographical romance, *Toute une jeunesse* (1890), *Le Coupable* (1897), *La Bonne Souffrance* (1898), *Dans la prière et dans la lutte* (1901), and *Contes pour les jours de fête* (1903).

Coppée (ko.pā'), **Henry.** b. Oct. 13, 1821; d. March 21, 1895. American educator and author. He was assistant professor of geography, history, and ethics at West Point (1850–55), professor of English literature in the University of Pennsylvania (1855–66), and president of Lehigh University (1866–75), in 1875 exchanging the latter position for the chair of history. He was made a regent of the Smithsonian Institution in 1874, and published *Elements of Logic* (1857), *Elements of Rhetoric* (1859), *Lectures on English Literature* (1872), and *History of the Conquest of Spain by the Arab-Moors* (1881), besides various works on military drill, and others.

Copper (kop'ėr). [Also, **Atna.**] River in Alaska which flows into the Pacific W of Mount St. Elias.

Copper Cliff. Mining town in northern Ontario, Canada, a few miles E of Sudbury: site of a smelter which processes the ores from the mines nearby. Nickel and copper are produced in large quantities. 3,974 (1951).

Copperfield (kop'ėr.fēld), **David.** See **David Copperfield.**

Copperheads (kop'ėr.hedz). [Also called **Butternuts, Peace Democrats.**] Name applied during the Civil War to Northern Democrats who by various means opposed Lincoln's war policy. The first use of the term is said to have been its appearance (July 20, 1861) in the New York *Tribune*. The chief Copperhead organization was the Knights of the Golden Circle (later known as the Order of American Knights and the Sons of Liberty), and the most prominent Copperhead leader was Clement L. Vallandigham. The so-called Northwestern Confederacy plot (1864) was undertaken by extreme opponents of the Union government, some of whom were tried and convicted of treason by military commissions. In the main, the Copperheads called for a restoration of the Union on the basis of negotiation, but some of their activities in the midst of armed conflict were generally construed as treasonable and posed constitutional issues that were not met squarely until after the close of the war. Copperhead policy dominated the national Democratic convention and platform of 1864.

Coppermine (kop'ėr.mīn). River in the Mackenzie District of the Northwest Territories, Canada, which flows into Coronation Inlet, an inlet of the Arctic Ocean. Length, 525 mi.

Coppet (ko.pe). Village in W Switzerland, in the canton of Vaud, situated on the Lake of Geneva, N of the city of Geneva. It was the residence of Necker, finance minister to Louis XVI of France, and his daughter, Mme. de Staël, who are buried here. 494 (1941).

Co-prosperity Sphere. Name given to the geographical framework of the Japanese imperial dream of the 1930's and early 1940's, envisaging Japanese hegemony over the entire area of E Asia, Indonesia, and Melanesia. This area was regarded by the Japanese leaders as capable of economic self-sufficiency. Early in 1942 the Japanese came close to realizing their hopes for political dominion when, in addition to large parts of China, they overran Indochina, the Dutch East Indies, Malaya, and many of the Pacific islands. Before the conquered peoples they then held the prospect of a share in the expected prosperity of an Asia dominated by Japan.

Coptic (kop′tik). Language of the Copts, descended from the ancient Egyptian (of the Hamitic family of languages), and used in Egypt until within the last three centuries, but now superseded as a living language by Arabic. The two chief dialects are the Memphitic and Thebaic. It is still the liturgical language of the Coptic (Egyptian Monophysite) Church, but the lections are read in Arabic as well as Coptic.

Coptos (kop′tos). [Modern site, **Quft** (also transliterated **Keft, Kobt, Qift,** etc.).] Ancient city in Egypt near the E bank of the Nile ab. 25 mi. NE of Luxor. The city was located where the Nile approaches nearest to the Red Sea, and from early times it was a terminus of desert routes to the E. In the 22nd century B.C. Coptos was eclipsed by the rise of Thebes, but in Roman times it was of great importance, being connected with the Nile by a canal ab. 2 mi. long. Granite, porphyry, and precious stones were obtained in the hinterland, and shipped out by river. There was regular trade with Arabia and India, and a Roman garrison to police the desert roads. In 292 A.D. the city participated in a rebellion, and was destroyed by the emperor Diocletian. It was later rebuilt and remained important until the Turkish conquest of Egypt in the 16th century A.D. Pop. of Quft, ab. 2,500 (1947).

Copts (kopts). Native Egyptians; the Egyptian Christians, especially those of the sect of Monophysites. The Copts are descendants of the ancient Egyptians, and formerly spoke the Coptic language. After the Council of Chalcedon (451 A.D.) the majority of Egyptian Christians separated from the Orthodox Church, and have ever since had their own succession of patriarchs. Their number is now very small. The Abyssinian or Ethiopic Church is a part of the Coptic communion, and its *abuna* (priest) or *metran* is always chosen and consecrated by the Coptic patriarch.

Coq (kok), **Albert August von Le.** See **Le Coq, Albert August von.**

Coq d'or (kok dôr), **Le.** Opera in three acts by Rimsky-Korsakov, first performed at Zimin's Theater at Moscow on Sept. 24, 1909. The libretto is taken from Pushkin's fairy tale about King Dodon, who is given a golden cockerel to administer his affairs but who must pay for him by relinquishing the queen of his dreams.

Coquard (ko.kår), **Arthur.** b. at Paris, May 26, 1846; d. at Noirmontier, France, Aug. 20, 1910. French composer of operas and dramatic interludes; author of *De la musique en France depuis Rameau.*

Coquelin (kok.laṅ), **Benoît Constant.** [Called **Coquelin Aîné.**] b. 1841; d. at Paris, Jan. 27, 1909. French romantic actor; brother of E. A. H. Coquelin and father of Jean Coquelin. Making his debut at the Comédie Française in 1860, he won success the next year with his *Figaro.* In 1864, Coquelin became a sociétaire of the Comédie Française, and thereafter created the leading roles in 44 new plays. In 1886, he resigned because of a dispute over his right to make provincial tours and toured Europe and America, but three years later rejoined the company. In 1892, he left the Comédie Française for good, and founded his own company and toured Europe. He became manager of the Porte-Saint-Martin Theatre in 1897, and here performed *Cyrano de Bergerac,* becoming world-famous in this role. In 1900 he toured America with Sarah Bernhardt. He was rehearsing for the première of Rostand's *Chantecler* when he died. He was also the author of a series of valuable essays on acting (1880, 1882).

Coquelin, Ernest Alexandre Honoré. [Called **Coquelin Cadet.**] b. at Boulogne-sur-Mer, France, May 16, 1848; d. at Suresnes, France, Feb. 8, 1909. French actor; brother of Benoît Constant Coquelin. He made his debut at the Odéon, but in 1868 joined his brother at the Comédie Française, and was made a sociétaire of that organization in 1879. He played nearly all the comic parts in the older plays, and in contemporary comedy such parts as Fréderic in *L'Ami Fritz* and Ulrich in *Le Sphinx.* He wrote, under the name of Pirouette as well as his own, various monologues and books on the subject of monologues, such as *Le Monologue moderne* (1881), *La Vie humoristique* (1883), and *Pirouette* (1888).

Coquelin, Jean. b. Dec. 1, 1865—. French actor; son of Benoît Constant Coquelin (1841–1909). He played with his father in *Cyrano de Bergerac,* taking the role of Ragueneau.

Coquerel (kok.rel), **Athanase Josué.** b. at Amsterdam, Netherlands, June 16, 1820; d. at Fismes, Marne, France, July 24, 1875. French Protestant clergyman, and theological and historical writer; son of Athanase Laurent Charles Coquerel (1795–1868). He wrote *Jean Calas et sa famille* (1858) and *Libres études* (1867).

Coquerel, Athanase Laurent Charles. b. at Paris, Aug. 25, 1795; d. there, Jan. 10, 1868. French Protestant clergyman (in Jersey, Amsterdam, Leiden, Utrecht, and Paris) and theological writer; father of Athanase Josué Coquerel and brother of Charles Augustin Coquerel. He was a member (1848–49) of the Constituent and Legislative assemblies. He wrote *Biographie sacrée* (1825–26), *Orthodoxie moderne* (1842), and *Christologie* (1858).

Coquerel, Charles Augustin. b. at Paris, April 17, 1797; d. there, Feb. 1, 1851. French theological writer; brother of Athanase Laurent Charles Coquerel (1795–1868). He was the author of *L'Histoire des églises du désert* (1841).

Coques or **Cocx** (koks), **Gonzales.** b. at Antwerp, 1614; d. there, April 18, 1684. Flemish portrait painter, noted for his family groups.

Coquette. Novel in the form of letters written by Hannah Webster Foster, published anonymously in 1797. The book relates the story of Elizabeth Whitman: her seduction, elopement, and death during childbirth. It is also well known as a play.

Coquette. Novel by Frank Swinnerton, published in 1921. The central character is Sally Minto.

Coquilhatville (ko.kē.yȧ.vēl). Town in C Africa, in the Belgian Congo, the capital of Equator province, situated at the junction of the Ruki and Congo rivers. It is connected with Tondo, on Lake Tumba, by road, and is the commercial center for the area. 414 European pop. (1946).

Coquilhatville. Former name of **Equator** province, Belgian Congo.

Coquillart (ko.kē.yår), **Guillaume.** b. in Champagne, France; d. c1490. French poet. He was the author of *Les Droits nouveaux,* in octosyllabic verse, and other poems. His complete works were published in 1847.

Coquille (kō.kēl′). City in SW Oregon, county seat of Coos County, on the Coquille River, in a dairying region. It was formerly a river port. 3,523 (1950).

Coquillett (kok.i.let′), **Daniel William.** b. near Woodstock, Ill., Jan. 23, 1856; d. July 8, 1911. American entomologist, a specialist in dipterology. Employed (c1880–82) by Cyrus Thomas, state entomologist of Illinois, he was later appointed (1885) field agent of the Division of Entomology of the U.S. Department of Agriculture, and served as custodian (1896–1911) of the Diptera in the U.S. National Museum at Washington. He was responsible for acclimatizing (1887) the first shipment of the ladybird beetle which proved of great value in destroying the cottony cushion scale on the citrus crop of California.

Coquimbo (kō.kēm′bō). Province in N Chile, lying between Atacama province on the N, Argentina on the E, Aconcagua province on the S, and the Pacific Ocean on the W: chief product, copper. Capital, La Serena; area, 15,401 sq. mi.; pop. 249,375 (est. 1950).

Coquimbo. Seaport and rail center in NW Chile, in Coquimbo province: minerals, agricultural produce, wine. Winter quarters for the Chilean navy are situated here. 18,863 (1940).

Cora (kō′rạ). See also **Kore.**

Cora. In Richard Brinsley Sheridan's *Pizarro,* the wife of Alonzo, the commander of Ataliba's troops.

Corabia (kō.rä′byä). Town in S Rumania, in the province of Oltenia, situated on the Danube River, ab. 95 mi. SW of Bucharest: river port; grain markets. 10,772 (1948).

Coral (kôr′ạl, kor′ạl). Former name of **Osage,** Iowa.

Coral Gables. City in S Florida, in Dade County, part of Greater Miami. It is a winter tourist resort and the seat of the University of Miami, of Riddle Inter-American College, and of the Fairchild Tropical Garden (83 acres), which has tropical plants and trees collected from many parts of the world by David G. Fairchild. In the decade between the last two U.S. censuses the population of Coral Gables more than doubled. 8,294 (1940), 19,837 (1950).

Coral Sea. That part of the Pacific Ocean extending from Australia to the New Hebrides, Solomon Islands, and the island of New Guinea.

Coral Sea, Battle of the. Japanese-U.S. naval-air engagement (May 7-8, 1942) in the Pacific Ocean, in World War II. The operation, which compelled the Japanese force to turn back from its objective in New Caledonia and New Guinea, saved the Allied supply lines to and from Australia. It involved a U.S. carrier force (including the *Yorktown*) under Admiral Fletcher which had, a few days earlier, destroyed a dozen Japanese supply vessels off Guadalcanal, and which then joined a similar force (including the *Lexington*) under Admiral Fitch. The battle was joined when American planes caught and sank the Japanese carrier *Ryukaku* before that vessel could get its fighter planes off the deck. Before the battle ended serious damage had been inflicted on two more Japanese carriers, and several other Japanese vessels had been sunk. The Americans lost the *Lexington*, a destroyer, and a tanker. The offensive during the entire engagement rested with planes; the surface vessels were at no time close enough to exchange fire from their guns.

Coram (kō'ram), **Thomas.** b. at Lyme Regis, England, c1668; d. at London, March 29, 1751. English philanthropist. He established the Foundling Hospital at London in 1740.

Corambis (kō.ram'bis). Name of Polonius in the first quarto *Hamlet* (1603). In the German play (*Fratricide Punished*) supposed to be the groundwork of the 1603 quarto, it is spelled Corambus.

Coraopolis (kō.rą.op'ō.lis). Borough in SW Pennsylvania, in Allegheny County, on the Ohio River, ab. 10 mi. NW of Pittsburgh: manufactures of glass and metal products. It was incorporated in 1886. Pop. 10,498 (1950).

Corato (kō.rä'tō). Town and city in SE Italy, in the *compartimento* (region) of Apulia, in the province of Bari, W of Bari. It is one of the largest centers in Apulia for the production of olive oil, and also has manufactures of alcohol and of cream of tartar, and wine cellars. The Church of Santa Maria Maggiore dates from the 13th century. Pop. of commune, 44,661 (1936); of city, 43,907 (1936).

Coray (kô.rà.ē), **Adamantios.** b. at Smyrna (Izmir), Turkey, April 7, 1748; d. at Paris, April 6, 1833. Greek scholar. He endeavored to bring about the political regeneration of Greece by means of education, and with this object in view published excellent editions of the Greek authors, which have been collected in the *Bibliothèque hellénique* (1805-26).

Corazón (kō.rä.sōn'). Mountain in the Andes of Ecuador, SW of Quito, so named from its supposed resemblance to a heart in outline. 15,871 ft.

Corbach (kôr'bäch). See **Korbach.**

Corbeil (kôr.bey'). [Ancient name, **Corbolium.**] Town in N France, in the department of Seine-et-Oise, situated at the junction of the Essonne and Seine rivers, ab. 17 mi. S of Paris. It is a river port and has potato-starch factories and flour mills. The Grands Moulins de Corbeil is one of the largest mills in France. 10,072 (1946).

Corbet (kôr'bet), **Richard.** b. at Elwell, Surrey, England, 1582; d. at Norwich, England, July 28, 1635. English prelate and poet, elected bishop of Oxford in 1624, and transferred to the see of Norwich in 1632. He was an intimate friend of Ben Jonson, and was noted for his convivial habits. The first collected edition of his poems was published in 1647; some of them were published separately in 1648, under the title *Poetica Stromata.*

Corbett (kôr'bet), **Boston.** b. at London, 1832; d. ?. American soldier, alleged slayer of John Wilkes Booth, the assassin of Abraham Lincoln. He came to the U.S., and took the name of "Boston" from the city in which he was baptized. He enlisted in the 12th Regiment of New York State militia, and later was a sergeant in the 16th New York Cavalry. He reputedly fired upon Booth at the time of his capture (April 26, 1865), and killed him. Corbett afterward became insane and was confined in an asylum in Kansas. He escaped from the asylum, on May 26, 1888, and was not heard from after that month.

Corbett, Gail Sherman. [Maiden name, **Sherman.**] d. at New York, Aug. 27, 1952. American sculptor who did many memorials in the U.S.; wife of Harvey Wiley Corbett. She studied at the Art Students League of New York and at the École des Beaux-Arts, Paris, and was a member of the National Sculpture Society. Her more important works include the *Hamilton S. White Memorial* and *Kirkpatrick Memorial Fountain*, at Syracuse, N.Y., bronze doors in the Springfield, Mass., municipal group, *Portrait of Washington* at George Washington Masonic Memorial, Alexandria, Va., and the *Leeds Memorial* at Tarrytown, N.Y.

Corbett, Harvey Wiley. b. at San Francisco, 1873—. American architect; husband of Gail Sherman Corbett. He was one of the designers of Radio City, Rockefeller Center, New York, of the Bushnell Memorial Hall at Hartford, Conn., and of many other large edifices. He studied at the University of California and at the École des Beaux-Arts, Paris. An academician of the National Academy of Design, he has also lectured on architecture at Columbia University and was architectural member of the Fine Arts Commission of New York State. Some of the more important buildings he designed are the Bush Terminal Building, Roerich Museum, new criminal courts building, and Metropolitan Life Insurance Company Building, all at New York; the Maryland Institute; and the Springfield, Mass., municipal group.

Corbett, James J. [Called **Gentleman Jim Corbett.**] b. at San Francisco, Sept. 1, 1866; d. at Queens, N.Y., Feb. 18, 1933. American pugilist, first heavyweight to win (1892) the championship of the world under the Marquis of Queensberry rules. He entered the professional ring at 18 and became famous after defeating (June 5, 1889) Joe Choynski; defeated Jake Kilrain (Feb. 18, 1890); fought Peter Jackson to a 61-round draw (May 21, 1891); won world's championship by knockout in round 21 of John L. Sullivan (Sept. 7, 1892); defended title against Charlie Mitchell, Peter Courtney, and others; lost championship to Bob Fitzsimmons in 14th round (March 17, 1897); failed (1900, 1903) to regain title from James J. Jeffries. He retired in 1903 and later appeared on the stage and radio, and in motion pictures. He was considered by many to have been the first scientific boxer. Author of an autobiography entitled *The Roar of the Crowd* (1925).

Corbett, Sir **Julian Stafford.** b. at Imber Court, Wiltshire, England, Nov. 12, 1854; d. at Stopham, Sussex, England, Sept. 21, 1922. English writer on naval strategy and naval historian. He served as lecturer in history at the Royal Naval College (1902), Ford lecturer at Oxford (1903), and Creighton lecturer at King's College, London (1921). His works include *The Fall of Asgard* (a novel, 1886), *Drake and the Tudor Navy* (1898), *The Successors of Drake* (1900), *England in the Mediterranean, 1603-1714* (1904), *England in the Seven Years' War* (1907), *The Campaign of Trafalgar* (1910), *Some Principles of Maritime Strategy* (1911), *Maritime Operations in the Russo-Japanese War* (1915), and *Naval Operations* (3 vols., 1921-23).

Corbie (kôr.bē). Town in N France, in the department of Somme, situated on the Somme River ab. 10 mi. E of Amiens. Pop. ab. 5,000.

Corbin (kôr'bin). City in SE Kentucky, in Knox and Whitley counties. Coal mining is the principal industry. 7,744 (1950).

Corbin, John. b. at Chicago, May 2, 1870—. American writer, critic, and theatrical producer. Graduated from Harvard (B.A., 1892; M.A., 1893), he was a staff member (1900-02) of the *Encyclopaedia Britannica*, drama critic on the New York *Times* (1902, 1917-19) and New York *Sun* (1905-07), and an editorial writer (1919-26) on the New York *Times*. In 1916 he produced, with Louis Calvert, Shakespeare's *The Tempest*. He is the author of *The Elizabethan Hamlet* (1895), *An American at Oxford* (1902), *The First Loves of Perilla* (1903), *The Cave Man* (1907), *The Return of the Middle Class* (1922), *The Unknown Washington* (1930), *Two Frontiers of Freedom* (1940), and other books.

Corbin, Margaret. [Maiden name, **Cochran.**] b. in Franklin County, Pa., Nov. 12, 1751; d. Jan. 16, 1800. American Revolutionary heroine. She followed her husband into the First Company of Pennsylvania Artillery;

when he was killed (Nov. 16, 1776) at the battle of Fort Washington she took his place and served his gun until she was seriously wounded.

Corbino (kôr.bē′nō), **Jon.** b. in Sicily, 1905—. American painter and sculptor, best known for his dramatic pictures of people and horses, often linked in spirit with those of Rubens and the 19th-century French romanticists. Brought up (1913 *et seq.*) on New York's East Side, he supported himself during and after study at the Art Students League of New York and the Pennsylvania Academy of the Fine Arts (1923) by working as a soda clerk, farm hand, and riding-academy attendant. His teachers were George Luks and Frank V. DuMond; later he became a teacher at the Art Students League. He has been the recipient of Guggenheim Fellowships (1936–37, 1947–48) and of awards from the Art Institute of Chicago (1937, 1944), the National Academy of Design (1938, 1944, 1945; member 1940), the Pennsylvania Academy (1938), the National Institute of Arts and Letters (1941), the Salmagundi Club (1945), and others. Well known among his paintings is *Flood Refugees* (1938); he is represented in the Pennsylvania Academy, Addison Gallery of American Art, Toledo Museum of Art, and others.

Corbould (kôr′bōld), **Henry.** b. at London, Aug. 11, 1787; d. at Robertsbridge, Sussex, England, Dec. 9, 1844. English landscape and miniature painter and book illustrator; son of Richard Corbould.

Corbould, Richard. b. at London, April 18, 1757; d. there, July 26, 1831. English painter and book illustrator; father of Henry Corbould.

Corbulo (kôr′bụ.lō), **Gnaeus Domitius.** d. 67 A.D. Roman soldier and administrator. As legate under Claudius he governed Lower Germany, and caused a canal to be dug between the Rhine and the Meuse, which is still in service. Given command of Roman forces in the East, he waged successful campaigns against the Parthians and Armenians; but Nero, succeeding Claudius as emperor, seems to have suspected Corbulo of conspiracy, and recalling him in 67 A.D., compelled him to take his own life.

Corbusier (kor.bü.zyā), **Le.** See **Le Corbusier.**

Cor Caroli (kôr kar′ọ.lī). A yellowish star of the third magnitude, below and behind the tail of the Great Bear, designated by Flamsteed as 12 Canum Venaticorum, but treated as a constellation on the globe of Senex (London, 1740), and by some other English astronomers.

Corcoran (kôr′kọ.rạn). City in S central California, in Kings County, ab. 45 mi. SE of Fresno in the San Joaquin valley. Cotton is raised in the vicinity. 3,150 (1950).

Corcoran, Thomas Gardiner. b. at Pawtucket, R.I., Dec. 29, 1900—. American lawyer and close associate of President Franklin D. Roosevelt. He received a B.A. from Brown University and an LL.B. (1925) from Harvard, and was an associate (1927–32) of Cotton and Franklin, law firm at New York. He served under the Roosevelt administration as special assistant (1932–35) to the U.S. attorney general, special counsel (1932, 1934–41) to the Reconstruction Finance Corporation, and assistant (1933) to the U.S. secretary of the treasury. With Benjamin V. Cohen, he assisted congressional committees in the drafting of the Securities Act (1933), Securities Exchange Act (1934), Public Utility Holding Company Act (1935), and other legislation.

Corcoran, William Wilson. b. in the District of Columbia, Dec. 27, 1798; d. Feb. 24, 1888. American financier and philanthropist. He organized (1847) the banking firm of Corcoran and Riggs, and founded (1872) the Corcoran Gallery of Art, to which he donated his own art collection.

Corcoran Gallery of Art. Art gallery at Washington, D.C., formally established (1872) and endowed by William Wilson Corcoran. It was earlier (1869) conveyed to a board of trustees for the benefit of the public, and contains collections of sculpture, rugs and tapestries, ceramics, and paintings and a school of art. The collection of American art is particularly well known.

Cordara (kôr.dä′rä), **Giulio Cesare.** b. at Alessandria, Italy, Dec. 17, 1704; d. there, May 6, 1785. Italian poet, and historiographer of the Jesuits.

Cordatus (kôr.dā′tus). Character in Ben Jonson's comedy *Every Man Out of His Humour*, who with Mitis performs the part of a critic with explanation and comment, always present on the scene, but standing aside.

Corday (kôr.dā), **Charlotte.** [Full name, **Marie Anne Charlotte Corday d'Armont** or **d'Armans** (kôr.dā dàr.mäṅ).] b. at St.-Saturnin, in Normandy, France, July 27, 1768; d. at Paris, July 17, 1793. French heroine. She was of noble birth, was educated in a convent at Caen, and, influenced by the writings of the rationalist philosophers, especially Voltaire and the Abbé Raynal, embraced the principles of the French Revolution. Filled with horror at the excesses of the Reign of Terror, she went to Paris on July 1, 1793, and on July 13, 1793, having gained admission to the chamber of Marat, stabbed him to death while he was in his bath. She was tried by the Revolutionary tribunal, and was sent to the guillotine.

Cordele (kôr.dēl′). City in S Georgia, county seat of Crisp County, ab. 65 mi. SW of Macon. It is in a peanut and cotton growing region, and has machine shops, cottonseed-oil factories, peanut-shelling plants, steel mills, lumber mills, and cotton gins. 9,462 (1950).

Cordelia (kôr.dēl′yạ). Youngest daughter of Lear in Shakespeare's tragedy *King Lear*. She offends him by the seeming coolness of her protestations of love for him, and he disinherits her. When, however, he is ill-treated, maddened, and turned out by his elder daughters, to whom he has given everything, she comes with an army to dethrone them, but is taken captive, and is killed in prison. Lear in a last outburst kills the slave who hanged her and dies upon her body.

Cordeliers (kôr.dẹ.lyā). Political club during the French Revolution. The actual name of this group, established in 1790, was (in English translation) "The Society of the Friends of the Rights of Man and of the Citizen," but the cumbersomeness of this title led to the club being popularly called by the name of its first headquarters, a former monastery of the Cordeliers or Franciscan Observantists. The principal purpose of the organization as stated in its charter was to bring to public attention and to denounce all offenses against the "Rights of Man" and all abuses of power by public bodies or officials. It was a kind of political watch and ward society, and its badge, an open eye, symbolized alertness in the public interest. This alertness soon took on the nature of suspiciousness, and the club's leaders, largely middle-class demagogues who played upon the miseries and the passions of the masses, used it to promote agitations and disorders and to assail all public figures whom they disliked, especially the moderately revolutionary Girondists. The Cordeliers, in fact, got beyond the control of their original leaders Danton and Desmoulins, and were dominated by Marat until his assassination, and later by Hébert. Infiltrating the army and the various sections of Paris, bullying the commune, and even threatening the Jacobins, the Cordeliers were high among the dominant forces of the Revolution until Robespierre turned upon Hébert and caused his execution in March, 1794, after which the club went out of existence.

Cordell (kôr.del′). City in W Oklahoma, county seat of Washita County: center of an agricultural area, and distributing and processing point for cotton, grain, and flour. 2,920 (1950).

Corder (kôr′dėr), **Frederick.** b. at London, Jan. 26, 1852; d. there, Aug. 21, 1932. English musician, conductor, and educator. He studied at the Royal Academy of Music and under Hiller at Cologne, and was professor of composition at the Royal Academy of Music, where he became (1889) curator. He included among his pupils Bax, Holbrooke, and Bantock. He and his wife made the first English translations of Wagner's *Die Meistersinger* and *Parsifal*. The opera *Nordissa* is one of his representative works.

Corder, Paul Walford. b. at London, 1879; d. Dec. 14, 1942. English musician and composer; son of Frederick Corder (1852–1932). He was professor of harmony and composition (1907 *et seq.*) at the Royal Academy of Music, London, where he had previously studied. His compositions include the musical drama *Dross*, *A Song of Battle*, and *Heroic Elegy*.

Cordes (kôrd). Small town in S France, in the department of Tarn, ab. 15 mi. NW of Albi. It has interesting medieval ramparts and buildings. Pop. ab. 1,000.

Cordier (kôr.dyā), **Marguerite Jeanne.** See **Staal-Delaunay,** Baronne **de.**

Cordière (kôr.dyer), **La Belle.** Epithet of **Labé, Louise.**

Cordillera Central (kôr.ᴛʜē.yä'rä sen.träl'). See also under **Caraballos Occidentales.**

Cordillera Central. [Also, **Cordillera del Quindió.**] Mountain range of the Andes in C Colombia. The highest of all the mountain ranges in Colombia, it extends for a distance of more than 500 mi.

Cordillera Central. [Also, **Cibao.**] Mountain range in the C part of the island of Hispaniola, West Indies, extending from Haiti to the Dominican Republic. Monte Tina, 10,300 ft. high, is the highest peak in the West Indies. At the time of the conquest it was included in the province of Maguana, governed by Caonabo. The Indians told Columbus that gold was found there, and he supposed it to be the Cipango (Japan) of Marco Polo. Ojeda entered this region in March, 1494, and a considerable amount of gold was obtained there.

Cordillera Central. Mountain range in Puerto Rico, part of the same chain as the Cordillera Central of Hispaniola. Elevation of highest peak, 4,500 ft.

Cordillera de San Blas (dā säm bläs'). See **San Blas, Cordillera de.**

Cordillera de Venezuela (dā bā.nā.swā'lä). [Also, **Central Highlands.**] Mountainous region of N Venezuela, bordering the Caribbean Sea, comprised of two ranges. Some peaks attain an elevation of 9,000 ft.

Cordillera Norte (nôr'tā). See under **Caraballos Occidentales.**

Cordillera Occidental (ôk"sē.ᴛʜen.täl'). [English, **Western Cordillera.**] Western range of the Andes in W Colombia. Its mountain peaks attain an elevation of over 12,000 ft.

Cordillera Oriental (ō.ryen.täl'). [English, **Eastern Cordillera.**] Mountain range of the Andes in C Bolivia. The urban communities of Cochabamba, Sucre, and Tarija are located here.

Cordillera Oriental. [English, **Eastern Cordillera.**] Eastern mountain range of the Andes, in C Colombia, E of Bogotá.

Cordilleras (kôr.dil'ẹ.rạz; Spanish, kôr.ᴛʜē.yä'räs). Name applied to various portions of the central mountain systems of America, as the Cordilleras of Mexico, of Central America, of the U.S. (Rocky Mountains), and of South America (Andes). It was first given to the ranges of the Andes (*las Cordilleras de los Andes*, "the chains of the Andes"), then to the continuation of these ranges into Mexico and further north. For convenience, it is now generally agreed among physical geographers to call the complex of ranges embraced between and including the Rocky Mountains and the Sierra Nevada, and their extension N into British Columbia (chiefly the Coast Ranges), the Cordilleras; those ranges occupying a similar continental position in South America are usually called simply the Andes. The entire western mountain side of the continent of North America is called the Cordilleran region. In its broadest part it has a development of a thousand miles E and W, and embraces, besides the Rocky Mountains and the Sierra Nevada, a large number of subordinate mountain chains, some of which are little, if at all, inferior to such chains as the Pyrenees in length and elevation.

Cordillera Sur (kôr.ᴛʜē.yä'rä sör). See under **Caraballos Occidentales.**

Córdoba (kôr'ᴛʜō.bä; Anglicized, kôr'dọ.bạ). Province in C Argentina, lying S of Santiago del Estero, W of Santa Fe, E of La Rioja, San Luis, and Catamarca, and N of the provinces of Buenos Aires and La Pampa (Eva Perón Province). Second in area only to Buenos Aires province, it is important for its stock raising, grain, and other agricultural products. Its climate and accessibility to Buenos Aires have made it a popular vacation area. Capital, Córdoba; area, 64,894 sq. mi.; pop. 1,497,987 (1947).

Córdoba. [Also, **Cordova** (kôr'ᴛʜō.bä; Anglicized, kôr'dọ.vạ).] City in C Argentina, capital of Córdoba province, ab. 410 mi. NW of Buenos Aires: manufacturing and export center for agricultural products; seat of a university. 369,886 (1947).

Córdoba. Town in SW Mexico, in Veracruz state, ab. 55 mi. W of the city of Veracruz: coffee. 17,865 (1940).

Córdoba. [Also, **Cordova.**] Province in S Spain, bounded by Ciudad Real on the N, Jaén on the E, Granada and Málaga on the S, Sevilla on the SW, and Badajoz on the NW: part of the region of Andalusia. The province comprises part of the valley of the Guadalquivir River; the climate is warm and mild; grain, wine, and sugar beets are grown. There are numerous reminders of the former Moslem culture of the region. Capital, Córdoba; area, 5,300 sq. mi.; pop. 826,570 (1950).

Córdoba. [Also: **Cordova**; Punic, **Karta-tuba**; Latin, **Corduba** (kôr'dụ.bạ), **Patricia.**] City in S Spain, the capital of the province of Córdoba, situated on the Guadalquivir River, ab. 73 mi. NE of Seville: manufacturing and trade center, noted for its Moorish cathedral; from 756 to 1031 capital of the Western Caliphate and center of Moslem culture in Spain. 164,415 (1950).

Commerce and Industry. Córdoba produces gold and silver filigree articles, and also has breweries, distilleries, and manufactures of silk textiles. The formerly famous crafts of silk embroidery and fine leather work have declined. It has agricultural markets, and ships copper from nearby mines.

Chief Buildings. Córdoba is the seat of a bishopric, and has a provincial museum, large libraries, and technical and art institutes. The old town, with narrow, winding streets, houses and palaces which are outwardly plain but open up into beautiful interior courtyards, the 16-arch bridge across the Guadalquivir, and the Alcazar, still bears architectural witness to its flowering under the Moorish rule; the most remarkable building is the cathedral, called "La Mesquita," the former central mosque of the Western Caliphate. Originally founded by Abd-er-Rahman I (756–788) on the site of a Roman temple and a Visigothic church, it was enlarged under subsequent caliphs in the 9th and 10th centuries until it was the largest sacred building of Islam, after the Kaaba at Mecca. It has beautiful columns, arcades, doors, and mosaics.

History. Founded by the Carthaginians, Córdoba was occupied by the Romans under Marcus Marcellus in 152 B.C.; after the battle of Munda in 45 B.C., the town was punished by Caesar for having supported the sons of Pompey; under Augustus it became the capital of the province of Baetica. It was conquered by the Visigoths in 571 and destroyed by the Moslems in 711. Made the capital of an independent caliphate under Abd-er-Rahman I in 756, it saw days of splendor under the rule of the Ommayad dynasty as a seat of learning and of the arts. The city was recaptured from the Moslems by Ferdinand III of Castile in 1236; it declined rapidly. It was sacked by the French in 1808. In the Spanish Civil War it was captured by Franco's Nationalist troops in 1936. Córdoba is known as the birthplace of the Roman rhetorician Marcus Annaeus Seneca, the philosopher Lucius Seneca, the poet Lucan, the Arab philosopher Averroës, and the Jewish philosopher Maimonides.

Córdoba or **Córdova, Francisco Hernández** (or **Fernández**) **de.** d. at Santo Espíritu, Cuba, in May or June, 1517. Spanish soldier and explorer. He went to Cuba with Velásquez in 1511, acquired wealth there, and in February, 1517, commanded an expedition of three vessels with 110 men, fitted out as a private speculation. Sailing westward, he discovered Yucatán, followed the coast around to beyond Campeche, and noticed many signs of a higher civilization than had before been found in America. On this expedition Córdoba was severely wounded in a fight with the Indians. He crossed over to Florida, thence returned to Cuba, and died of his wounds shortly after.

Córdoba or **Córdova, Francisco Hernández** (or **Fernández**) **de.** b. c1475; d. at León, Nicaragua, in March, 1526. Spanish soldier and explorer. In 1514 he went to the Isthmus of Panama with Pedrarias (Pedro Arias de Ávila), and in 1524 was sent by him to take possession of Nicaragua in defiance of the rights of the discoverer, Gil Gonzalez de Ávila. Córdoba founded Granada, León, and other towns, explored Lake Nicaragua, and found its outlet. He changed his allegiance from Pedrarias to Cortés, and was beheaded by Pedrarias for his defection.

Córdoba, Hernández Gonzalo de. See **Gonzalo de Córdoba, Hernández.**

Córdoba, Jorge. b. at La Paz, Bolivia, 1822; killed there, Oct. 23, 1861. Bolivian revolutionist. He was an ignorant soldier who acquired some importance by his marriage with the daughter of President Belzú. The revolutionists who drove out Belzú in 1855 proclaimed Córdoba in his place, and he held the position until 1857, when he was deposed by another outbreak. His rule was humane, but he showed little energy. He was shot during the disorders of 1861.

Córdoba, José María. b. c1797; killed Oct. 17, 1829. Colombian soldier. He joined the guerilla forces at the beginning of the war for independence, winning victories over the Spanish, and was made a colonel (1819) at the battle of Boyacá. He served under Sucre, and was appointed a general of division after his participation in the battle of Ayacucho. Under Bolívar he was made head of the war department (1828) of Colombia, but he revolted against Bolívar and was killed with many of his followers.

Córdoba, Sierras de. See **Sierras de Córdoba.**

Córdova (kôr'ᴛʜō.bä). For Spanish names not found under this spelling, see also under **Córdoba.**

Cordova (kôr'dō.vạ). Town in N central Alabama, in Walker County ab. 30 mi. NW of Birmingham: industrial center. In the decade between the last two U.S. censuses its population more than doubled. 1,565 (1940), 3,156 (1950).

Cordova (kôr.dō'vạ). Town in S Alaska, on Prince William Sound ab. 175 mi. SE of Anchorage. It developed as an important copper-shipping port after the opening of the Copper River and Northwestern Railway in 1911; since the closing down of the mines and railroad in 1938 it has depended upon locally available resources of fish, clams, crabs, and spruce and hemlock timber, for the canning, fish freezing, and lumber industries. 1,141 (1950).

Córdova (kôr'ᴛʜō.bä), **Pedro de.** b. 1483; d. at what is now Ciudad Trujillo, Hispaniola, June 28, 1525. Spanish Dominican, vicar of the first colony of his order in Hispaniola in 1510. He and his companions preached against Indian slavery in 1511, and in 1512 Córdova went to Spain to meet the junta which was employed in framing new laws with relation to the services of the Indians. In 1513 he sent a missionary colony to the coast of Venezuela, and when the missionaries were killed in 1515, Córdova went himself to establish another colony. He was a friend of Las Casas.

Córdova y Figueroa (kôr'ᴛʜō.bä ē fē.gä.rō'ä), **Pedro de.** b. at Concepción, Chile, 1692; d. there, probably after 1770. Chilean historian. He was a soldier, served in Araucania, and was alcalde of Concepción (c1740). His *Historia de Chile* includes the conquest and settlement to 1717, and was the most complete history of the country up to its date. The manuscript was preserved at Madrid, and it was first published from a copy in the *Coleccion de historiadores de Chile.*

Coreal (ko.rā.ål), **Francisco.** Name appended to the *Voyage aux Indes Occidentales,* published (1727) at Paris. The author claimed to have been born at Cartagena in 1648, and to have traveled over nearly all of Spanish and Portuguese America. The work is generally believed to be fictitious.

Corelli (kō.rel'lē), **Arcangelo.** b. at Fusignano, Italy, Feb. 12, 1653; d. at Rome, Jan. 10, 1713. Italian violinist and composer, noted as an early founder of the modern art of violin playing. He had many pupils of distinction who transmitted the traditions of his style. He composed sonatas for several instruments that are still regarded as classic.

Corelli (kọ.rel'i), **Marie.** [Pseudonym of **Mary Mackay.**] b. in England, 1864; d. 1924. British novelist. Of Italian and Scottish parentage, she was adopted in her infancy by Charles Mackay, the poet. She wrote *A Romance of Two Worlds* (1886), *Thelma* (1887), *Ardath* (1889), *Barabbas* (1893), *The Mighty Atom* (1896), *The Master Christian* (1900), *Temporal Power* (1902), *God's Good Man* (1904), *The Treasure of Heaven* (1906), *Holy Orders* (1908), *The Devil's Motor* (1910), *The Young Diana* (1917), and *The Secret Power* (1921).

Corey (kō'ri), **Paul (Frederick).** b. in Shelby County, Iowa, July 8, 1903—. American novelist. His works include *The Road Returns* (1940), *County Seat* (1941), and *Acres of Antaeus* (1946). He is also the author of works for children including *The Red Tractor* (1944), *Five Acre Hill* (1946), *Shad Haul* (1947), and *Corn Gold Farm* (1948).

Corey, William Ellis. b. at Braddock, Pa., May 4, 1866; d. May 11, 1934. American steel executive. Employed (1882–87) in the chemical laboratory of the Edgar Thompson Steel Works, he was later associated (1887–1901) in various capacities with the Homestead Steel Works and served as president of the Carnegie Steel Company (1901–03) and of the U.S. Steel Corporation (1903–11).

Corfe Castle (kôrf). Civil parish and town in S England, in Dorsetshire, situated on the Isle of Purbeck, ab. 18 mi. E of Dorchester, ab. 126 mi. SW of London by rail. The castle is now in ruins. It was the scene of the murder in 978 of Edward the Martyr. 1,409 (1931).

Corfinium (kôr.fin'i.um). In ancient geography, a town in C Italy, near the modern Sulmona. It was the capital of the Peligni, and of the confederates in the Social War (90–88 B.C.).

Corfu (kôr.fö', kôr'fū). [Also: **Kerkyra;** ancient name, **Corcyra.**] *Nomos* (department) in W Greece, coextensive with the island of Corfu (one of the Ionian islands), and including the provinces of Corfu and Paxos. It is mountainous, and exports mainly olives and wine. Capital, Corfu; area, 288 sq. mi.; length, 40 mi.; greatest breadth, 20 mi.; pop. 105,226 (1951).

Corfu. [Also: **Kerkyra;** ancient name, **Corcyra.**] City in E Greece, the capital of the *nomos* (department) of Corfu, situated on the E coast of the island of Corfu. It has steam communication with Mediterranean ports, and is a lively seaport and the seat of a Greek and a Roman Catholic bishopric. The beautiful castle called the "Achilleion" was built for the Empress Elisabeth of Austria in 1890 and acquired by William II of Germany in 1910; now it is in the possession of the Greek government. Corfu was colonized by Corinth in 734 B.C. It defeated Corinth, in the first recorded naval battle, in 665 B.C., was an ally of Athens in the Peloponnesian War, was conquered by Rome in 229 B.C., and came under Venetian rule in 1386. The island formed part of the Ionian Republic from 1815 to 1864. The city was defended by the Venetians against the Turks in 1716. On July 20, 1917, the "Pact of Corfu" was concluded here, by which was established the union of the states of Serbia, Croatia, and Slovenia. The city was bombed by the Italians between Aug. 31 and Sept. 27, 1923, in what is known as the Corfu Incident. In World War II it was occupied by the Germans in April, 1941, and retaken by the British and the Greeks on Oct. 6, 1944. Pop. 30,706 (1951).

Corfu Incident. Greek-Italian dispute precipitated by the murder (Aug. 27, 1923) on Greek soil of members of an Italian delegation attending a conference of ambassadors to fix the Greek-Albanian border. Italy thereupon submitted a 24-hour ultimatum of eight points, chief of which was an indemnity of 50 million lire. When the Greek government refused three of the points, including the indemnity, an Italian naval bombardment and occupation of the island of Corfu took place, with 15 people killed and 35 wounded. Greece appealed to the League of Nations Council, which referred suggested terms to the conference of ambassadors. The eventual settlement, which gave Italy the indemnity in return for evacuation, left the authority of the League Council in some question.

Cor Hydrae (kôr hī'drē). Star of the second magnitude, in the southern constellation Hydra.

Cori (kō'rē). [Ancient name, **Cora.**] Town and commune in C Italy, in the *compartimento* (region) of Latium, in the province of Latina (formerly Littoria), situated ab. 30 mi. SE of Rome. It contains many Roman antiquities, such as columns, walls, and a temple of Hercules, and also many medieval buildings. Considerable damage was suffered during World War II by the churches of Santa Maria della Pietà, Sant'Oliva, and San Salvatore; San Pietro was destroyed except for its campanile. Pop. of commune, 9,289 (1936); of town, 7,191 (1936).

Cori (kôr'i), **Carl Ferdinand.** b. at Prague, Dec. 5, 1896—. American pharmacologist, biochemist, and Nobel prize winner (whose professional career and honors have both been shared with his wife). Carl Ferdinand Cori and Gerty Theresa Radnitz were married in the year (1920) when they both graduated from the German University at Prague. In 1922 they emigrated to the U.S., where both were naturalized in 1928. Together they became associated with Washington University at St. Louis in 1931, Carl Ferdinand Cori being professor of pharmacology and biochemistry there from that year to 1942, professor of biochemistry until 1946, and chairman of the department of biochemistry after that year. Gerty Theresa Cori was a research associate in pharmacology until 1943, a research professor in biochemistry from then until 1946, and since 1947 a professor of biochemistry. Their eminence among the world's biochemists, and their specific contributions to the study of enzymes and of problems of metabolism, were recognized in 1947 when they shared with Bernardo Alberto Houssay the Nobel prize in physiology and medicine.

Cori, Gerty Theresa. [Maiden name, **Radnitz.**] b. at Prague, Aug. 15, 1896—. American pharmacologist, biochemist, and Nobel prize winner. See under **Cori, Carl Ferdinand.**

Coria del Río (kō'ryä del rē'ō). Town in S Spain, in the province of Sevilla, situated on the right bank of the Guadalquivir River, ab. 10 mi. S of Seville: river port. 11,038 (1940).

Coricancha (kō.rē.kän'chä). [Also, **Curicancha.**] Great temple at Cusco, Peru, capital of the Incas, known as the Court of Gold since so much gold went into the decoration of the interiors of its six major buildings. It was looted and destroyed by Pizarro and his followers at the time of the Spanish conquest.

Corigliano Calabro (kō.rē.lyä'nō kä'lä.brō). [Also, **Corigliano.**] Town and commune in S Italy, in the *compartimento* (region) of Calabria, in the province of Cosenza, situated on the S shore of the Gulf of Taranto, NE of Cosenza. There are a number of small food industries, sawmills, and manufactures of wagons. The town is of Byzantine origin; the castle dates from the 13th century. Pop. of commune, 16,285 (1936); of town, 12,698 (1936).

Corin (kō'rin). Shepherd in Shakespeare's comedy *As You Like It.*

Corinna (kǭ.rin'ạ). b. at Tanagra, Boeotia, Greece; fl. in the first part of the 5th century B.C. Greek lyric poet, sometimes called a Theban from her long residence at Thebes. She was a contemporary and instructor of Pindar, from whom she is said to have won the prize five times at the public games. A few fragments of her poems have been preserved.

Corinna's Going A-Maying. Pastoral poem (1648) of 70 lines by Robert Herrick. It was first published in *Hesperides,* his volume of secular poetry. A poem that is independent of time or place, it still maintains its popularity, and is to be found in numerous anthologies.

Corinne ou l'Italie (ko.rēn ö lē.tȧ.lē). [Eng. trans., "*Corinne or Italy.*"] Novel by Madame de Staël, published in 1807.

Corinth (kôr'inth, kor'-). [Also: **Gortho;** Greek, **Korinthos;** Latin, **Corinthia** (kǭ.rin'thi.ạ), **Corinthus** (-thus).] City in S Greece, in the *nomos* (department) of Argolis and Corinthia, on the Peloponnesus, situated near the Isthmus and Gulf of Corinth. It was originally called Ephyre, and was noted in ancient times as a center of commerce, literature, and art. It is now a railroad junction for the lines to Athens, Patras, and Argos. It is the seat of a bishopric. Corinth was founded c1350 B.C., was conquered by the Dorians in the 11th century, colonized Corcyra (Corfu) and Syracuse in 734, and prospered under the tyrant Periander c600. It sided with Sparta in the Peloponnesian War against Athens, and later (395–387) engaged in the "Corinthian war" against Sparta. It was defeated by Sparta in 394, and was held by the Macedonians until 243, when it joined the Achaean League, of which it was the capital. In 146 it was captured, sacked, and burned by the Romans, under Mummius; it was rebuilt by Julius Caesar in 46 B.C. In modern times it has been taken and retaken by Turks and Venetians, was destroyed by an earthquake in 1858, and was rebuilt on a site 3 mi. distant (New Corinth). In 1928 a new earthquake occurred. Corinth has been part of Greece since 1822. It was occupied in World War II by the Germans in April, 1941, and liberated by the British on Oct. 10, 1944. Pop. 17,699 (1951).

Corinth. City in NE Mississippi, county seat of Alcorn County, ab. 90 mi. SE of Memphis, Tenn. It is a railroad center. Manufactures include dairy products, hosiery, and garments. It was the site of a Civil War battle (Oct. 3–4, 1862), when a victory over Confederate forces was won by Rosecrans. 9,785 (1950).

Corinth. Village in E New York, in Saratoga County, on the Hudson River: clothing factories and paper mills. 3,161 (1950).

Corinth. A former name of **Syracuse,** N.Y.

Corinth, Gulf of. [Also: **Gulf of Lepanto;** Latin, **Corinthiacus Sinus** (kôr.in.thī'ạ.kus sī'nus, kor-).] Arm of the Mediterranean Sea, with which it is connected by the Gulf of Patras. It separates central Greece from the Peloponnesus.

Corinth, Isthmus of. Isthmus which connects the Peloponnesus with central Greece. It is now pierced by a canal. Width, 4–8 mi.

Corinth (kō.rint'), **Lovis** or **Louis.** b. at Tapaiu, East Prussia, July 7, 1858; d. in the Netherlands, 1925. German genre and portrait painter, water colorist, and illustrator, whose work is considered an important link between the impressionist and expressionist movements in German painting. He studied at the academy at Königsberg and then in the studio of W. Bouguereau, at Paris. He did many portraits; Gerhart Hauptmann was among his sitters.

Corinthe (ko.rant), **Le Siège de.** See **Siège de Corinthe, Le.**

Corinthia (kǭ.rin'thi.ạ). [Also: **Corinth;** Greek, **Korinthos.**] In ancient geography, a division of Greece, lying between the Gulf of Corinth on the N, Megaris on the NE, the Saronic Gulf on the E, Argolis on the S, and Argolis and Sicyonia on the W.

Corinthians (kǭ.rin'thi.ạnz), **First** and **Second Epistles to the.** Epistles of Paul, of which the first was composed of Ephesus in the spring of 57, and the second at some place in Macedonia in the summer or autumn of the same year.

Corinto (kō.rēn'tō). Seaport in NW Nicaragua, in Chinandega department, on the Pacific coast ab. 87 mi. by rail NW of Managua. It is the principal port of Nicaragua, and exports over three fourths of its total commerce, as it is the only maritime rail outlet. 5,257 (1945).

Coriolanus (kō''ri.ǭ.lā'nus, kôr''i-, kor''i-; kǭ.rī.ō.lan'us). [Surname of **Gnaeus** (or **Cnaeus**) or **Gaius** (or **Caius**) **Marcius.**] fl. in the first half of the 5th century B.C. Roman legendary hero, represented as the champion of the patricians, and afterward as leader of the Volscians against Rome. He was the conqueror of the Volscian city of Corioli (whence his surname).

Coriolanus. Tragedy by Shakespeare, produced c1608, and founded on North's *Plutarch.* It was printed in the 1623 folio. In the play the mother of Caius (Cnaeus) Marcius Coriolanus is Volumnia, not Veturia, and his wife is Virgila, not Volumnia as in the original. John Dennis produced a play in 1705 founded on *Coriolanus,* which he called *The Invader of his Country, or the Fatal Resentment.*

Coriolanus. Tragedy by James Thomson, left in manuscript by him, brought upon the stage by Sir George Littleton. It was published in 1748 or 1749.

Coriolanus Overture. Overture (Opus 62) by Ludwig van Beethoven, composed in 1807 and published in 1808, based upon a play by Heinrich Joseph von Collin produced at Vienna in 1802.

Corioli (kǭ.rī'ǭ.lī). In ancient geography, a city in Latium, Italy. Gaius Marcius conquered it in c493 B.C., and took from it his name Coriolanus. Its exact site is unknown, but is probably not far from Ariccia.

Corisca (kǭ.ris'kạ). In Guarini's *Pastor Fido,* a woman ruined by town life, contrasted with the Arcadian maidens.

Corisco (kǭ.ris'kō). Small group of islands located in the Bay of Corisco near the coast of Río Muni, W Africa. They include Corisco island and Great and Little Elabey, and form part of the Spanish colony of Spanish Guinea. Corisco island itself is 5½ sq. mi. in area.

Coritavi (kō.ri.tā'vī) or **Coritani** (kō.ri.tā'nī). Ancient British tribe which occupied territory that included the modern Lincolnshire and Leicestershire.

Coriza (kō.rēt'sä). Italian name of **Korçë.**

Cork (kôrk). [Irish, **Chorcaighe, Corcaigh.**] Maritime county in Munster province, Irish Republic, the southernmost and largest county in Ireland. It is bounded on the N by County Limerick, on the E by Counties Tipperary and Waterford, on the S by the Atlantic Ocean, and on the W by County Kerry. The coastline is extensive and much indented, providing numerous harbors. The surface is a generally rolling plain, rising to uplands and mountains in the west and southwest. Caherbarnagh (2,239 ft.) on the border with County Kerry, is the highest elevation. A variety of minerals are found, including copper, lead, coal, iron, and limestone, all of which are worked to some extent; abundant deposits of manganese are said to exist. The county is chiefly important as the center of the greatest dairying region of Ireland. Oats, barley, wheat, potatoes and other root crops, and fruits and berries are the crops raised here. Cork is the county seat and the commercial and industrial center; area, ab. 2,881 sq. mi.; pop. 341,229 (1951).

Cork. [Irish, **Chorcaighe, Corcaigh.**] City and county borough, seaport, and important manufacturing center in Munster province, Irish Republic, county seat of County Cork, situated on the river Lee at the head of Cork Harbour, ab. 138 mi. SW of Dublin. Its lower port is Cóbh. Cork is the second largest city in the Irish Republic, and the second-ranking seaport. Industries include automobile and farm-tractor manufactures, brewing and distilling, chemical manufactures, tanning, flour milling, and meat preserving (especially bacon curing). In addition, Cork has small manufactures of tweeds and some shipbuilding. The port can be reached by ocean-going vessels at high tide. It imports mainly coal, maize, wheat, and general cargo, and exports butter, livestock, provisions, and leather. Cork is the seat of University (formerly Queen's) College. The world-famous Shandon steeple and bells are in the city. The town was founded c600 A.D. on an island in the river Lee, was fortified by the Danes, and was surrendered by its king to Henry II in 1172. It was besieged and taken by Cromwell in 1649, and by John Churchill, 1st Duke of Marlborough, in 1690. Pop. 74,577 (1951).

Corkery (kôr′kėr.i), **Daniel.** b. at Cork, Ireland, 1878—. Irish playwright, critic, and fiction writer. His works include the plays *The Labour Leader, The Yellow Bittern, The Onus of Ownership,* and *Fohnam the Sculptor;* the novel *The Threshold of Quiet; A Munster Twilight* and *The Hounds of Banba,* short stories; literary criticism in *Staud of Irish Literature, The Hidden Ireland,* and *Synge ndy Anglo-Irish Literature* (1931).

Corleone (kôr.lā.ō′nā). [Arabic, **Qurlyun.**] Town and commune in SW Italy, on the island of Sicily, in the province of Palermo, situated in mountainous surroundings near the Belice Sinistro River, ab. 21 mi. S of Palermo. It is an agricultural trade center, known especially for its cattle markets. The origin and name of the town date back to the occupation of Sicily by the Saracens. Pop. of commune, 15,089 (1936); of town, 14,197 (1936).

Cor Leonis (kôr lē.ō′nis). Another name for Regulus, a star of the first magnitude in the constellation Leo.

Corliss (kôr′lis), **George Henry.** b. at Easton, N.Y., July 2, 1817; d. at Providence, R.I., Feb. 21, 1888. American inventor and manufacturer, noted as a designer of steam engines. He first patented improvements in engines in 1849.

Cormac (kôr′mak). b. 836; d. 908. King of Cashel, Ireland, who reigned from 900 to 908. He perished in a battle in the latter year. A glossary of Irish words is attributed to him.

Cormac Mac Art (kôr′mak mak ärt′). d. 260. King of Ireland (218–254).

Cormeilles-en-Parisis (kôr.mey′.zäṅ.pá.rē.zē). [Also, **Cormeilles.**] Town in N France, in the department of Seine-et-Oise, situated on the northern bend of the Seine River, NW of Argenteuil. It is an industrial and residential community. 8,460 (1946).

Cormenin (kôr.mẹ.naṅ), Vicomte **de.** [Title of **Louis Marie de la Haye.**] b. at Paris, Jan. 6, 1788; d. there, May 6, 1868. French jurist and political writer. He was the author of numerous books and pamphlets, including *Questions de droit administratif* (1822) and *Études sur les orateurs parlementaires* (1838).

Cormon (kôr.môṅ). [Pseudonym of **Fernand Anne Piestre.**] b. at Paris, Dec. 22, 1845; d. March 20, 1924. French historical painter and portraitist, who became a success early in life and became professor at the École des Beaux-Arts and a member of the Institute at Paris. He was a pupil of Cabanel and Fromentin at Paris, and of Portaels at Brussels. He first exhibited in the Paris Salon of 1868, and by 1873 his reputation was firmly established. Some of his better-known works are *Cain, Battle of Essling, Head of a Woman, Death of Mohammed, Jesus Resuscitating the Daughter of Jaire,* portraits of Mme. Recamier and Charlotte Corday, and decorations for the Petit Palais.

Cormontaigne (kôr.môn.teny′), **Louis de.** b. 1695; d. in Lorraine, Oct. 20, 1752. French military engineer. His works were published between 1806 and 1809.

Cornaro (kôr.nä′rō), **Caterina.** b. at Venice, Italy, 1454; d. there, July 5, 1510. Queen of Cyprus. She married in 1472 James of Lusignan, king of Cyprus, on whose death in 1473 she succeeded to the throne. She abdicated in favor of the Republic of Venice in 1489.

Cornaro, Luigi or **Ludovico.** b. c1467; d. 1566. Medieval dietary reformer. This Venetian nobleman, having suffered a number of serious sicknesses, lost all faith in the physicians and the medicines of his time, and regained his health by adopting measures based on his own observation of his condition, particularly measures of temperance in eating. When he was 82 years old he wrote *Discorsi della vita sobria,* which was published in 1558.

Corn Belt. Name given to a large region in E central U.S., in which corn (maize) is the dominant crop in the economy. It extends from W central Ohio, W through Indiana, Illinois, Iowa, N Missouri, SW Minnesota, to E and C Nebraska, N Kansas, and SE South Dakota. The region produces approximately half of all corn grown in the U.S.; of this more than three quarters is fed to livestock. In addition, soybeans and winter wheat are important as rotation and cash crops, and other small grains, especially oats, are grown for stock feed. Cattle and hogs are fattened and marketed; large numbers of other meat animals and poultry are produced, and the general standard of living is one of the highest to be found in any agricultural economy in the entire world. The Corn Belt supplies most of the meat consumed in the entire northeastern U.S., and large amounts of other products.

Cornbury (kôrn′bėr.i, -ber″i), **Edward Hyde,** Viscount. [Also, 3rd Earl of **Clarendon.**] b. 1661; d. at London, April 1, 1723. English politician. He was governor of New York (1702–08).

Corneille (kôr.ney′), **Pierre.** b. at Rouen, France, June 6, 1606; d. at Paris, Oct. 1, 1684. French dramatist. He is the earliest playwright of his country whose works are still produced at Paris and read by the general public. He graduated from the Jesuit College at Rouen, studied law, was admitted to the bar, but did not practice. From 1629 to 1650, however, he earned about 1,200 francs annually as a magistrate. In 1647 he was elected to the French Academy and in 1662 he moved to Paris, where he lived until his death. He began his dramatic career with a comedy, *Mélite,* produced in 1630 by the great actor Montdory at the Théâtre du Marais in Paris. Then followed at the same theater *Clitandre* (tragicomedy, produced in 1630 or 1631), *La Veuve* (comedy, 1631 or 1632), *La Galerie du Palais* (comedy, 1632), *La Suivante* (comedy, 1632 or 1633), and *La Place Royale* (comedy, 1633). The six plays won for their author recognition as the outstanding contemporary French writer of comedies. Corneille, however, now turned to tragedy, the genre which was to give him lasting fame. He produced *Médée* (tragedy, 1634 or 1635), then returned to comedy with *L'Illusion comique* (1635 or 1636), followed by his four masterpieces: *Le Cid* (tragedy, January, 1637), a struggle between love and duty; *Horace* (tragedy, 1640), a test of patriotism; *Cinna* (tragedy, 1640 or 1641), in praise of clemency; and *Polyeucte* (tragedy, 1641 or 1642), concerning the power of Christianity in early times. In these four are first found the dramatic traits for which the author is famous: strong characters, inner struggles between two passions, conflicts of wills, and eloquent expressions of lofty sentiments. With the success of *Polyeucte* Corneille found himself acknowledged as his country's greatest writer of tragedies, an honor which he held until he was forced to share it with Racine after the appearance of the latter's *Andromaque* (1667). From 1642 to 1651 he produced a variety of plays: *Pompée* (tragedy, 1642 or 1643); *Le Menteur* (comedy, 1643), his most popular comedy; *La Suite du Menteur* (comedy, 1644 or 1645); *Rodogune* (tragedy, 1644 or 1645), a favorite with Corneille, probably because it was nearly all his own invention; *Théodore* (tragedy, 1645), a religious play and a failure; *Héraclius* (tragedy, 1646 or 1647); *Don Sanche d'Aragon* (heroic comedy, 1649); *Andromède* (tragedy, 1650), a spectacular machine play; *Nicomède* (tragedy, 1650 or 1651), a remarkable play depicting the resistance of the East to the growing power of Rome; and *Pertharite* (tragedy, 1651), a failure. Corneille now retired from the stage and devoted himself to his *Imitation de Jésus-Christ*, a financial success. In 1659, however, he returned triumphantly with *Œdipe* (tragedy), followed by *La Toison d'or* (tragedy, 1660), a machine play written for the marriage of Louis XIV; *Sertorious* (tragedy, 1662); *Sophonisbe* (tragedy, 1663), a rewriting of Mairet's play of the same name; and *Othon* (tragedy, 1664). *Agésilas* (tragedy, 1666) was a failure, but *Attila* (tragedy, 1667) a great success. *Tite et Bérénice* (heroic comedy) was bought and produced by Molière in 1670. After producing two more plays, *Pulchérie* (tragedy, 1672) and *Suréna* (tragedy, 1674), both failures, Corneille devoted himself to the revision of his works for the 1682 edition and died two years after its publication. A striking trait of Corneille's tragedies is his rejection of love as a theme and his choice of such passions as magnanimity, patriotism, vengeance, ambition, and religious zeal. Guided by these emotions, the characters make sacrifices which arouse in the spectator a feeling of awe or wonder. Racine, on the other hand, preferred love as the subject of tragedy, and his principal characters approach more closely Aristotle's ideal of arousing pity and fear.

Corneille, Thomas. b. at Rouen, France, Aug. 20, 1625; d. at Les Andelys, France, Dec. 8, 1709. French dramatist and miscellaneous writer; younger brother of Pierre Corneille. His plays (which number over 40) include *Ariane* (1672), *Le Festin de pierre* (1673), and *Le Comte d'Essex* (1678).

Cornejo (kôr.ne'hō), **Mariano Harlan.** b. 1870—. Peruvian jurist, government official, and writer; notable as author of the Peruvian constitution and criminal code adopted in 1920. He was president (1919) of the constituent assembly, professor at Lima University, and served (1920–31) as minister to France. He is the author of *The Organisation of Peace* (1928), *General Sociology* (1930), *Balance of Continents*, and *Le Déséquilibre constructif*.

Cornelia (kôr.nēl'ya). fl. 2nd century B.C. Roman matron, daughter of the elder Scipio Africanus, wife of Tiberius Sempronius Gracchus, and mother of the Gracchi, the tribunes Tiberius and Caius Gracchus. She was celebrated for her accomplishments and virtues as a mother. After the death of her husband, she refused to marry again but devoted her life to her children. The story is told of her answering the boasts of another Roman matron about her jewels with the simple "These are my jewels," and pointing to her children.

Cornelia Blimber (blim'ėr). See **Blimber, Cornelia.**

Cornelia gens. Celebrated patrician and plebeian clan or house in ancient Rome. The patrician family names previous to the empire were Arvina, Blasio, Cethegus, Cinna, Cossus, Dolabella, Lentulus, Maluginensis, Mannula, Merenda, Merula, Rufinus, Scapula, Scipio, Sisenna, and Sulia. The plebeian family names were Balbus and Gallus.

Cornelian Laws (kôr.nēl'yan). [Latin, **Leges Corneliae.**] Body of laws introduced at Rome by the dictator L. Cornelius Sulla c80 B.C., with a view to restoring the aristocratic form of government, whose power had been weakened by the democratic legislation of the Gracchi and of Marius.

Cornelius (kôr.nēl'yus). In the Bible, a Roman centurion, stationed at Caesarea, whom Peter, in consequence of a special revelation, received into the communion of the Christian church directly by baptism, without circumcision (Acts, x.).

Cornelius, Saint. b. at Rome; d. at Centum Cellae (now Civitavecchia), near Rome, in June, 253. Pope from 251 to 253, successor of Fabianus. The Novatians having refused to recognize his election, and having chosen their leader Novatianus in his stead, Cornelius convened a council at Rome in 251, which confirmed his election. He was banished by the emperor Gallus to Centum Cellae, where he suffered martyrdom.

Cornelius. Friend of Faustus in Christopher Marlowe's play *Dr. Faustus*.

Cornelius. Courtier in Shakespeare's tragedy *Hamlet*. He and Voltimand are sent on an embassy to Norway by Claudius.

Cornelius. Physician in Shakespeare's play *Cymbeline*. He recognizes the queen's evil designs and gives her, not the poison she intends to use, but a sleep drug, and thus saves Imogen's life.

Cornelius (kôr.nā'lē.ůs), **Hans.** b. at Munich, Germany, Sept. 27, 1863—. German philosopher who served (1903 *et seq.*) as professor at the universities of Munich and Frankfort on the Main. He was the author of *Elementargesetze der bildenden Kunst* (1908), *Grundlagen der Erkenntnistheorie Transzendentale Systematik* (1916), and *Kommentar zu Kants Kritik der reinen Vernunft* (1926).

Cornelius, Karl Adolf. b. at Würzburg, Bavaria, March 12, 1819; d. at Munich, Feb. 10, 1903. German historian; nephew of Peter von Cornelius and brother of Peter Cornelius. He became professor of history at the University of Bonn in 1854, and at the University of Munich in 1856. His works include *Geschichte des münsterischen Aufruhrs der Wiedertäufer* (1855–60), *Kurfürst Moritz von Sachsen gegenüber der Fürstenverschwörung im Jahre 1550–51* (1867), and others.

Cornelius, Peter. b. at Mainz, Germany, Dec. 24, 1824; d. there, Oct. 26, 1874. German composer and poet; nephew of Peter von Cornelius and brother of Karl Adolf Cornelius. He was a follower of Liszt at Weimar, and a champion of Wagner, whose cause he upheld in numerous critical writings. He composed the opera *Der Barbier von Bagdad* (the failure of which in 1858 through factious opposition was the cause of Liszt's leaving Weimar), *Der Cid* (1865), *Gunlöd* (uncompleted), and many songs. He also published an autobiography (1874).

Cornelius, Peter von. b. at Düsseldorf, Germany, Sept. 23, 1783; d. at Berlin, March 6, 1867. German painter, leader of the new school of German art. He worked (1811–19) at Rome, and in the latter year left to take charge of the academy at Düsseldorf. From 1825 to 1841 he labored chiefly at Munich, and after 1841 at Berlin. His chief works are frescoes in the Glyptothek and Ludwigskirche at Munich, and cartoons for the Campo Santo in Berlin.

Cornell (kôr.nel'), **Alonzo B.** b. at Ithaca, N.Y., Jan. 22, 1832; d. there, Oct. 15, 1904. American business executive and politician; son of Ezra Cornell. He was organizer and cashier (1864–66) of the first national bank at Ithaca, N.Y. He was later director (1868–98), vice-president (1870–76), and acting president (1875) of the Western Union Company. Following appointments as surveyor of customs (1869) and naval officer in the New York customs house (1877), he was elected (1879) governor of New York, after his removal, along with Chester A. Arthur, the collector, from his customs-house post by President Hayes. His political life came to an end when he refused support to his patron, Roscoe Conkling, in the latter's 1881 fight with Garfield.

Cornell, Ezra. b. at Westchester Landing, N.Y., Jan. 11, 1807; d. at Ithaca, N.Y., Dec. 9, 1874. American telegraph promoter and civic benefactor, noted as the founder of Cornell University at Ithaca, N.Y. He worked as a laborer and mechanic before settling (1828) at Ithaca, where he became the general manager of a plaster and flouring mill. He was connected with Samuel F. B. Morse in the development of the magnetic telegraph, helping to build the Washington-Baltimore line and working out a system of insulation for the wires. He gradually became a leader in the field, helping to found the Magnetic Telegraph Company, which built (1845) the New York-Philadelphia line. He built other lines in New York, Vermont, and Quebec, and in 1847 organized the Erie and Michigan Telegraph Company, which connected Buffalo, Chicago, Cleveland, Detroit, and Milwaukee. He finally helped consolidate (1855) the many systems which had originated and became a director of the Western Union Telegraph Company, in which he was one of the largest stockholders. He devoted a large part of his fortune to civic benefactions, building (1863) a free public library at Ithaca, but his greatest achievement was his coöperation with Andrew D. White to found Cornell University, which opened in 1868. He was (1861 *et seq.*) a member of the New York legislature and became (1862) president of the state agricultural society. See *"True and*

Firm": Biography of Ezra Cornell, written anonymously by his son, Alonzo B. Cornell (1884).

Cornell, Katharine. b. at Berlin, Feb. 16, 1898—. American actress; wife (married 1921) of Guthrie McClintic (1893—). She was born of American parents abroad, and made her debut (1917) with the Washington Square Players at New York. She has starred in such plays as *A Bill of Divorcement, Casanova, The Green Hat, The Age of Innocence, The Barretts of Wimpole Street* (1931), *Alien Corn* (1933), *Romeo and Juliet* (1934), *Saint Joan* (1936), *The Wingless Victory* (1937), *Candida* (1937, 1946), a European production of *The Barretts of Wimpole Street* (1944–45) for troops abroad, *Antigone* (1946), and *The Constant Wife* (1951).

Cornell University. Nonsectarian, coeducational institution of higher learning, chartered in 1865 and opened in 1868, sustained by land grant and state aid and by private endowment, and named for its founder, Ezra Cornell (1807–74). The main campus is situated on the shore of Lake Cayuga at Ithaca, N.Y. The university comprises colleges of arts and sciences, architecture, engineering and medicine, and schools of law, business administration, nursing, industrial and labor relations, home economics, and veterinary medicine, and the New York State College of Agriculture is also an important affiliate of the university. The Cornell Medical College and School of Nursing are situated at New York City, in close association with New York Hospital. The College of Agriculture gives short courses and extension courses, and maintains an experiment station at Geneva, N.Y. At Ithaca there are an archaeological museum, a veterinary museum, an institute for paleontological research, an arboretum, and a herbarium; a U.S. weather bureau is also maintained there. At Ithaca also is located the university press. An aeronautical laboratory at Buffalo is another of the university's affiliates. In 1946 a five-year curriculum was established, specializing in atomic physics and electronics, and under contract with the U.S. government Cornell, with other institutions, conducts nuclear research at the Brookhaven National Laboratories on Long Island.

Cornelys (kôr.nā'lis), **Theresa.** b. at Venice, 1723; d. in the Fleet Prison, London, Aug. 19, 1797. Manager of public balls, concerts, and masquerades in Carlisle House, in Soho Square, London. At one time she had the direction of all the theaters in the Austrian Netherlands. She dropped into obscurity after a notorious life, and under the name of Mrs. Smith sold ass's milk at Knightsbridge for some time before her death.

Corner Brook. Seaport and the second largest town in Newfoundland, situated on the S shore of the Bay of Islands, on the W coast of the province. It is the center of Canada's pulp and paper industry and possesses one of the largest paper mills in the world. It is on the railroad to St. John's. Pop., including Corner Brook West, a suburb, 10,276 (1951).

Corneto Tarquinia (kôr.nā'tō tär.kwē'nyä). Former name of **Tarquinia,** Italy.

Cornford (kôrn'fǫrd), **Frances Crofts.** [Maiden name, **Darwin.**] b. at Cambridge, England, 1886—. English poet; granddaughter of Charles Darwin and daughter of Sir Francis Darwin. She is the author of *Poems* (1910), *Spring Morning* (1915), *Autumn Midnight* (1923), *Different Days* (1928), and *Mountains and Molehills* (1935). Some of her best-known poems are *Country Bedroom, The Watch, A Wasted Day, The Old Nurse, The Hills, Autumn Morning at Cambridge, The Unbeseechable,* and the triolet *To a Fat Lady Seen from the Train.*

Cornhill (kôrn'hil). One of the principal London streets, once a corn market.

Cornhill Magazine, The. Monthly periodical (founded 1860). It was first edited by Thackeray, but he soon resigned, as the nature of the work did not appeal to him. However, his last novels, *The Adventures of Philip, Lovel the Widower,* and the unfinished *Denis Duval,* first appeared in its pages, as did *Cousin Phillis* and *Wives and Daughters,* by Mrs. Gaskell. Others who contributed were Ruskin, Matthew Arnold, and Trollope. Among those who followed Thackeray as editor are Sir Leslie Stephen (from 1871 to 1882), James Payn (1883–96), John St. Loe Strachey, and Reginald John Smith. The name of the magazine derived from its place of publication, "our storehouse being in Cornhill," as Thackeray told his readers in the first issue.

Cornhuskers (kôrn'hus"kėrz). Collection of poems by Carl Sandburg, published in 1918. It included "Cool Tombs" and "Grass."

"Cornhusker State." Nickname of **Nebraska.**

Corniani (kôr.nyä'nē), Count **Giovanni Battista.** b. at Orzi-Nuovi, near Brescia, Italy, Feb. 28, 1742; d. there, Nov. 7, 1813. Italian literary historian and poet. His chief work is *I Secoli della letteratura italiana* (1804–13).

Corniche (kôr.nēsh), **La.** [Italian, **Cornice**; Eng. trans., *"The Cornice."*] Celebrated coast road along the Riviera of France and Italy from Nice to Genoa.

Cornimont (kôr.nē.môṅ). Town in E France, in the department of Vosges, situated on the W slope of the Vosges Mountains, ab. 22 mi. SE of Épinal. It is a tourist center and has textile manufactures. 4,705 (1946).

Corning (kôr'ning). City in N California, in Tehama County, in the Sacramento valley NW of Sacramento. Olives are grown in the area. 2,537 (1950).

Corning. City in S New York, in Steuben County, on the Chemung River, ab. 13 mi. W of Elmira: known for its manufacture of glass, particularly laboratory glassware. The Mount Palomar Observatory telescope mirror, the largest single piece (200 inches) of glass made up to that time (1934), was cast here. 17,684 (1950).

Corning, James Leonard. b. at Stamford, Conn., Aug. 26, 1855; d. at Morristown, N.J., Aug. 24, 1923. American neurologist, noted for his discovery (1885) of spinal anaesthesia. He demonstrated that the action of stimulants and sedatives may be heightened if the subject is exposed to air under pressure, and was the first to inject liquid paraffin into the body tissues. He was the author of *Carotid Compression* (1882), *Brain Rest* (1883), *A Treatise on Headache and Neuralgia* (1888), and *Pain in Its Neuro-Pathological and Neuro-Therapeutic Relations* (1894).

Corn Islands. Two islands in the W Caribbean Sea, ab. 36 mi. E of Puente de Perlas on the E coast of Nicaragua. Belonging to Nicaragua, they were leased for 99 years to the U.S. for the sum of three million dollars by the terms of the Bryan-Chamorro treaty of 1916, as a site for defenses for the proposed Nicaragua canal. Great Corn Island has a peak elevation of ab. 370 ft., and is inhabited by ab. 1,300 persons, mostly colored. There is a naval station here. Area, Great Corn, ab. 3½ sq. mi.; Little Corn, ab. 0.8 sq. mi.

Corn King and the Spring Queen, The. Novel by Naomi Mitchison, published in 1931.

Corn-Law Rhymer. See **Elliott, Ebenezer.**

Corn Laws. In English history, a series of laws, extending from 1436 to 1842, regulating the domestic and foreign grain trade of England. Until the repeal of the Corn Laws, the grain trade, both export and import, was the subject of elaborate and varying legislation, which consisted in levying protective or prohibitory duties, or in imposing restrictive conditions, or in granting government bounties for the encouragement of exportation. The passage of the Corn Law of 1815, enacted in an attempt to counteract the post-Napoleonic depression era, caused riots and led to widespread demands for reform. After a prolonged agitation, led by such men as Richard Cobden and John Bright, for the repeal of the Corn Laws by the Anti-Corn Law League (organized in 1839 as a consolidation of several such associations), Parliament in 1846, under the ministry of Sir Robert Peel, passed an act for a large immediate reduction of the duty on imported grain, and providing for a merely nominal duty after 1849, which was subsequently entirely removed.

Corn of Wheat, A. Novel by E. H. Young, published in 1910.

Cornouaille (kôr.nö.ȧy'). Region and medieval county of Brittany, France, in the vicinity of Quimper.

Cornplanter. [Iroquois, **Garganwahgah**; also known as **John O'Bail.**] b. c1740; d. Feb. 18, 1836. Chief of the Seneca Indians. Although his father was a white trader whose name is variously given as O'Bail and O'Bell, he was raised among the Seneca tribe of the Iroquois, seems to have become one of their chiefs, and certainly exercised great influence among them. During the Revolutionary War he sided with the British and led war parties against the patriots, especially harassing General Sullivan's columns during the Wyoming valley campaign in Pennsylvania. After the war he promoted friendship with the whites, and was one of the principal Iroquois signers of the Treaty of Fort Stanwix, by which the Six Nations ceded much territory. As a result, Cornplanter was much blamed in his tribe, and his life was threatened. In 1790, however, he was sent to Philadelphia to present complaints of the Indians to President Washington. He was given a grant of land on the Allegheny River, in Warren County, Pa., where he lived to an advanced age.

Cornu (kôr.nü), **Marie Alfred.** b. 1841; d. 1902. French physicist. He was professor of experimental physics (1867–1902) at the École Polytechnique at Paris and lectured at Cambridge University. He is noted for his studies in optics, the velocity of light, acoustics, and astronomy.

Cornu, Sébastien Melchior. b. at Lyons, France, 1804; d. at Longpont, Seine-et-Oise, France, in October, 1870. French painter, a pupil of Ingres.

Cornutus (kôr.nū'tus), **Lucius Annaeus.** b. at Leptis Magna, in Libya; d. after 68 A.D. Roman Stoic philosopher, and commentator on Aristotle. He was the friend and mentor of Persius.

Cornwall (kôrn'wôl, -wạl). [Middle English, **Cornwale** (kôrn.wä'lẹ), **Cornwayle** (-wā'lẹ); Old English, **Cornwealas** (kôrn.wa'läs); ancient name, **Belerium.**] Maritime county in SW England, lying between Devonshire on the E and the Atlantic on the N, W, and S. The administrative county excludes the Isles of Scilly (included in the geographical county). Its chief industries are mining of china clay (near St. Austell) and fishing (principally for pilchards and mackerel). Agriculture is important, with special emphasis on cattle raising and the market gardening of early potatoes, fruit, flowers, and other vegetables to supply the city markets. Several nonferrous minerals are found in Cornwall, and the tin and copper mines were formerly important, but most have closed down because of foreign competition. Cornwall contains many antiquities. It was conquered from the Britons by the West Saxons in the period from the 8th to the 10th century, and was made a duchy and appanage of the princes of Wales in 1337. In early times it was called West Wales. The ancient name Belerium is said to have been applied first by Posidonius, and also to have been derived from that of a Cornish giant, Bellerus. Truro is the county seat; area, ab. 1,350 sq. mi.; pop. 345,612 (1951).

Cornwall. Town (in New York the equivalent of township in many other states) in SE New York, in Orange County, on the Hudson River N of West Point: residential community. It includes the village of Cornwall (or Cornwall-on-Hudson). Pop. of town, 6,154 (1950); of village, 2,211 (1950).

Cornwall. Capital of Stormont County, and a port of entry, in Ontario, Canada, situated on the St. Lawrence River, opposite the New York boundary, ab. 52 mi. W of Montreal, on the main highway between that city and Toronto. 16,899 (1951).

Cornwall. 1st Duke of. Title of **Edward,** the Black Prince (1330–76).

Cornwall, Duke of. Title of **Charles** (of *England*), Prince.

Cornwall, Earl of. Title of **Gaveston, Piers.**

Cornwall, Earl of. Title of **Richard** (1209–72).

Cornwall, Barry. Pseudonym of **Procter, Bryan Waller.**

Cornwall, Duke of. Husband of Regan in Shakespeare's tragedy *King Lear;* a "gloomy, laconic, and powerful" man, inflexible in his decisions. He puts out Gloucester's eyes.

Cornwallis (kôrn.wol'is), **Caroline Frances.** b. 1786; d. at Lidwells, Kent, England, Jan. 8, 1858. English writer. Her father (William Cornwallis) was rector of Wittersham and Elham in Kent. She wrote *Philosophical Theories and Philosophical Experience, by a Pariah* (1842) and other works in the series entitled *Small Books on Great Subjects.* Her *Letters* were published in 1864.

Cornwallis, Charles. [Titles, 1st Marquis and 2nd Earl **Cornwallis.**] b. at London, Dec. 31, 1738; d. at Ghazipur, India, Oct. 5, 1805. English soldier and statesman, created Marquis Cornwallis on Aug. 15, 1792. He entered the army in 1756, and took part (1758–62) in the battles of Minden, Vellinghausen, Wilhelmstadt, and others in Germany in the Seven Years' War. He was elected member of Parliament in January, 1760, and entered the House of Lords in June, 1763, where he acted with the Whigs in opposing the taxes causing trouble in America; later he was (1766–69) chief justice in eyre south of the Trent. In 1775 he was promoted to major general, and in February, 1776, was sent with seven regiments to reinforce the English army in America. He joined Sir William Howe at Halifax, and served under him in the campaign on Long Island and about New York. In September, 1777, he aided Howe in defeating John Sullivan at the battle of Brandywine and in occupying Philadelphia, and in April, 1778, was promoted to lieutenant general and appointed second in command to Sir Henry Clinton, then commander in chief in America. At Camden, on Aug. 16, 1780, he defeated General Gates; he won, against General Greene, the battle of Guilford Court House, on March 15, 1781. Caught by the unexpected force of the Continental troops, he surrendered to Washington at Yorktown, on October 19, 1781. He was appointed governor general of India and commander in chief in February, 1786, and set about reforming the Indian administration. He waged successful war with Tippu Sahib in 1791–92, and then resigned his offices in 1793 and returned to England. In 1795 he was appointed master-general of the ordnance, with a seat in the cabinet. He was viceroy and commander in chief in Ireland from May, 1798, till his resignation in February, 1801, suppressing the rebellion of the former year and aiding the Act of Union of 1800, by which Ireland was joined to England. The treaty of Amiens, by which Napoleon was able to consolidate his position on the Continent and which brought peace for just about a year, was negotiated by Cornwallis in 1802.

Cornwell (kôrn'wel, -wẹl), **Dean.** b. at Louisville, Ky., March 5, 1892—. American artist, noted for his book illustrations and magazine covers and for murals in public buildings. He studied with Harvey Dunn and Charles S. Chapman, exhibiting later in many cities in the U.S., and winning many prizes for his water colors and illustrations. He is an associate of the National Academy of Design, and a life member of the National Arts Club. Among his better-known works are murals in the Los Angeles Public Library, the Lincoln Memorial at Redlands, Calif., the Detroit Athletic Club, the post office at Chapel Hill, N.C., and the Davidson County courthouse at Nashville, Tenn. He illustrated *Torrent, Kindred of the Dust, Valley of Silent Men, The Desert Healer, Find the Woman,* and stories by Rafael Sabatini. He has taught at the Art Students League of New York, and has done illustrations and covers for national magazines.

Coro (kō'rō). [Also, **Santa Ana** (or **Aña) de Coro.**] City in NW Venezuela, capital of Falcón state, near the Bay of Coro: export center for goat skins, coffee, and hardwoods. It was founded in 1527, and until 1578 was the capital of the province of Venezuela. 28,307 (1950).

Coroado (kō.rō ä'dō). [Also, **Purí-Coroado.**] Appellative given by the early Portuguese settlers to several Indian tribes in Brazil, in reference to their crownlike tonsures and feather-ornamented coiffures.

Coromandel Coast (kor.ọ.man'dẹl). Name applied to that part of the E seaboard of the Indian peninsula, bordering on the Bay of Bengal, S of the delta of the Godavari River. Length, ab. 500 mi.; width, ab. 75 mi.

Corombona (kō.rom.bō'nạ), **Vittoria.** "White devil" in John Webster's tragedy of that name. Having fascinated the Duke of Brachiano, she renounces everything for pleasure. At her instigation he procures the deaths of her husband and the duchess. She is brought before the tribunal and arraigned for these murders; her guilt is not proved, but she is confined in a house of convertites (penitent prostitutes) from which Brachiano secretly takes her and marries her. He is shortly poisoned and then strangled by the emissaries of the Great Duke (Francesco de' Medici), and she is stabbed by her brother Flamineo in revenge for Brachiano's failure to advance him, he having instigated his sister to her course of conduct to that end. The trial scene is one of great power. The play is based, rather inaccurately as to detail, on a real occurrence in 16th-century Italy.

Corona (kọ.rō′nạ). [Former name, **South Riverside.**] City in S California, in Riverside County, ab. 13 mi. SW of Riverside, in a citrus-growing district producing oranges and lemons. The city packs and ships citrus fruits and their products, and dairy products, and manufactures clay products. There is a large U.S. Naval Hospital at Norco, ab. 3 mi. N of Corona. The place was first settled in the 1890's. 10,223 (1950).

Corona Australis (kọ.rō′nạ ôs.trā′lis). [Also, **The Southern Crown.**] A southern constellation, S of Sagittarius. It was recognized by the ancients and represented by a garland about the knee of Sagittarius.

Corona Borealis (bō.rẹ.al′is, -ā′lis). [Also, **The Northern Crown.**] A northern constellation, between Hercules and Boötes. Its brightest star is Gemma, magnitude 2.3. It was recognized by the ancients and represented as a garland with two streamers.

Coronado (kor.ọ.nä′dō). City in S California, in San Diego County, on San Diego Bay across from San Diego. It is a residential and resort community. 12,700 (1950).

Coronado (kō.rō.nä′ᴛʜō), **Carolina.** b. at Almendralejo, Badajoz, Spain, 1823; d. 1909. Spanish poet and novelist. She married (c1840) Horatio J. Perry, an American.

Coronado (kor.ọ.nä′dō; Spanish, kō.rō.nä′ᴛʜō), **Francisco Vásquez de.** b. at Salamanca, Spain, 1510; d. at Mexico City, 1554. Spanish explorer of the American Southwest and governor in New Spain. Arriving in Mexico (1535) as an aide of the viceroy, Antonio de Mendoza, he became governor of Nueva Galicia (now parts of W Mexico) in 1538 and, following the return of Fray Marcos de Niza from an expedition to New Mexico with stories of the wealth of the Seven Cities of Cíbola, was given command of an exploration party to continue the quest begun by de Niza. Leading a large force consisting of more than 1,000 Spaniards and Indians, he started out (Feb. 25, 1540) for the north, tracing his way through Culiacán and reaching (July, 1540) the Zuñi pueblos. One of his confederates went to Lower California and some others, one of whom discovered the Grand Canyon, to the Colorado River. Proceeding to the Rio Grande, Coronado went in search (1541) of a country to the northeast called Gran Quivira. He crossed the Pecos River, traversed northern Texas and Oklahoma, finally reaching the supposed Quivira in eastern Kansas. What he thought would be a great city proved disappointing; it was, probably, a settlement of Wichita Indians. After his return to Nueva Galicia, he was removed (1544) from the governorship for his abuse of the natives, and subsequently became an official in the Mexico City administration.

Coronado, Juan Vásquez de. b. at Salamanca, Spain, c1525; drowned at sea, in October, 1565. Spanish administrator. He went to Guatemala in 1550, was made *alcalde* (mayor) of San Salvador and Honduras and, later, of Nicaragua, and in 1562 was appointed to the same office in Costa Rica. He explored the whole country, and founded Cartago in 1563. In 1564 he went to Spain, where, in recognition of his work, he was named hereditary captain-general of Costa Rica. He was shipwrecked and drowned while returning.

Coronados (kor.ọ.nä′dōz). See **Patangoros.**

Coronation, The. Play, licensed (1635) as by James Shirley, and claimed by him as his own in a list of his plays published by him in 1652. On the title page of its first edition, printed in 1640, it was attributed to John Fletcher, and is included in the earlier editions of Beaumont and Fletcher's works. There is no reason for supposing that Fletcher had any hand in it.

Coronation Gulf. Inlet of the Arctic Ocean, in the Northwest Territories, Canada, S of Victoria Island and W of Kent Peninsula. It is connected with the Beaufort Sea to the W by Dolphin and Union Strait.

Coronea (kor.ọ.nē′ạ). In ancient geography, a small town in Boeotia, Greece, situated W of Lake Copais. It was famous for two battles, in one of which (447 B.C.) the Boeotians defeated the Athenians, and in the other (394 B.C.) the Spartans under Agesilaus defeated the Thebans and other allied Greeks.

Coronel (kō.rō.nel′). Seaport on the W coast of Chile, in Concepción province, in the C part of the country: chief product, coal. It was the scene of a World War I naval victory (Nov. 1, 1914) by von Spee's five-ship German squadron over four British ships under Cradock; two British ships were sunk. 14,799 (1940).

Coronel, Jorge Icaza. See **Icaza** or **Icaza Coronel, Jorge.**

Coronel Bogado (kō.rō.nel′ bō.gä′ᴛʜō). City in SE Paraguay, in Itapúa department. 11,159 (est. 1945).

Coronelli (kō.rō.nel′lē), **Marco Vincenzo.** b. at Ravenna, Italy, Aug. 10, 1650; d. at Venice, Dec. 9, 1718. Italian ecclesiastic and geographer, cosmographer (1685 *et seq.*) of the Venetian republic, professor of geography at Venice, and general (1702 *et seq.*) of the Minorite order. He published a large number of maps and geographical works, and founded the Accademia degli Argonauti, the first geographical society.

Coronel Oviedo (kō.rō.nel′ ō.ʙyä′ᴛʜō). City in S Paraguay, capital of Caaguazú department. 33,098 (est. 1945).

Coronis (kọ.rō′nis). In ancient Greek mythology, mother of Aesculapius by Apollo. She was false to the god and Apollo's ubiquitous messenger, the raven, told him. Apollo in anger cursed the raven and turned its feathers, until then white, black, but he (or Artemis) killed Coronis and saved the unborn Aesculapius from the funeral pyre.

Corot (ko.rō; Anglicized, kọ.rō′), **Jean Baptiste Camille.** b. at Paris, July 28, 1796; d. there, Feb. 22, 1875. French painter. Although the immense popularity of Corot's shimmering trees and sunsets dwindled after his death, in part probably because so many poor reproductions of them were circulated, critics have in recent years been finding great strength in the earlier paintings, especially of architectural subjects, which Corot made in Italy, and in his portraits. He first exhibited at the Salon of 1827 (*Vue prise à Narni* and *La Campagne de Rome*). Among the pictures that gained the greatest popularity are *Vue d'Italie* (1834), *Souvenir des environs de Florence* (1839), *La Danse des nymphes* (1851), *Le Christ au Jardin des Oliviers* (1849), *Soleil couchant dans le Tyrol* (1850), *Matin and Soirée* (1855), *Soleil couchant* (1857), *Dante et Virgil* (1850), *Orphée*, *Le Repos* (1861), *La Solitude* (1866), *Pastorale* (1873), *Biblis*, and *Plaisirs du soir* (1875).

Corporation of Trinity House. See **Trinity House, Corporation of.**

Corpus Christi (kôr′pus kris′ti). City in S Texas, county seat of Nueces County, on Corpus Christi Bay: a leading Southern center in the manufacture of soda ash and caustic soda. Lime, one of the essential ingredients, is obtained from shells dredged from Nueces Bay. It is also an important shipping port for Gulf Coast oil, and a year-round resort especially popular with fishermen and duck hunters. It is believed that Jean Lafitte, the pirate, used the city's site as a hideout (c1817–21). The present city was founded (c1839) by Col. Henry L. Kinney, and called Kinney's Trading Post. The present name was adopted c1848. It served as a leading U.S. wool and cattle market in the late 19th century (1875–85). The U.S. naval air base here was a major training center in World War II. 108,287 (1950).

Corpus Christi, Feast of. Roman Catholic feast day in honor of the Holy Eucharist, celebrated on the first Thursday after Trinity Sunday. Originating in France in the 13th century, Corpus Christi was made a general festival by a bull of Pope Urban IV in 1264, Thomas Aquinas writing the office. By the 15th century it had become the most colorful of all feasts, its procession full of pageantry and followed by performances of miracle plays.

Corpus Christi College. College of Cambridge University. It was founded in 1352 by two religious societies, the Guild of Corpus Christi and the Guild of the Blessed Virgin Mary. It is the college of Sir Nicholas Bacon, father of the famous Francis (who was a Trinity man), Marlowe, Richard Cavendish, translator of Euclid, John Fletcher, the dramatist, Richard Boyle, 1st Earl of Cork, Archbishop Tenison, Samuel Wesley, father of John and Charles, General Braddock, who was killed trying to drive the French out of America, Stephen Hales, Richard Gough, who translated Camden's *Britannia*, and Peter Sandiford, Gresham professor of astronomy. Its library contains manuscripts of Matthew Paris' *History* and Chaucer's *Troilus and Criseyde*.

Corpus Christi College. College of Oxford University, England, founded in 1516 by Richard Fox, bishop of Winchester. Its statutes were issued in 1517.

Corpus Christi Day. Festival in the Anglican religious calendar, from the Roman Catholic Feast of Corpus Christi. It is held on the Thursday after Trinity Sunday. It is still in the English calendar. Religious plays were formerly performed in the streets by crafts or trade companies on Corpus Christi Day in England and also on the Continent. Lope de Vega raised them to a high level in Spain. A Corpus Christi guild was formed (1408) at York to celebrate the day with a procession, but this had nothing to do with the performance of the plays.

Corpus Juris Civilis (kôr′pus jö′ris si.vī′lis). Roman legal code instigated by Justinian I and executed by a commission whose leading member was Tribonian. The monumental work consisted of several parts: an abridgment in 12 books of former imperial codes from the time of Hadrian, called the "Codex Iustinianus" (529; revised, 534; only the revision has survived); the "Digesta" or "Pandectae" (533), quotations in 50 books from previous sources with regard to applicability; a new manual or textbook in four books in the manner of Gaius, called the "Institutiones"; and the 160 "Novellae" or new laws of Justinian (565). The *Corpus Juris* remained the chief source on Roman law and influenced later legislation, especially the Code Napoléon and the laws of 19th-century Europe derived from this code, most of which still are in force.

Corradini (kōr.rä.dē′nē), **Enrico.** b. at Sanminiatello, in Tuscany, Italy, 1865; d. 1931. Italian political writer, novelist, playwright, and journalist.

Corral (kôr.räl′), **Poinciano.** b. in Costa Rica, c1810; executed at Granada, Nicaragua, Nov. 8, 1855. Central American general. He defeated Castellon early in 1855, and the famous American filibuster, William Walker, in June of that year. In October he gave his adherence to Walker and Patricio Rivas, the provisional president, and was made minister of war; but he was detected in a correspondence with the leaders of the opposition, accused by Walker, tried, and shot.

Corrario (kôr.rä′ryō) or **Correr** (kor′ėr), **Angelo.** Original name of Pope **Gregory XII.**

Correa da Serra (kōr.rā′ą dą ser′rą), **José Francisco.** b. at Serpa, Portugal, June 6, 1750; d. at Caldas da Rainha, Portugal, Sept. 11, 1823. Portuguese naturalist, historian, and politician. He served as embassy secretary (1797–1802) in London and as minister (1816–20) to Washington. He edited the first three volumes of the *Collecção de livros inéditos da história Portugueza* (1790–1816).

Corrêa de Sá e Benevides (kōr.rā′ą dē sä′ ē bā.nę.vē′dęs), **Salvador.** See **Sá e Benevides, Salvador Corrêa de.**

Corrêa Garção (gąr.souṅ′), **Pedro António.** See **Garção, Pedro António Corrêa.**

Correggio (kǫ.rej′i.ō, -rej′ō; Italian, kôr.red′jō). Town and commune in N Italy, in the *compartimento* (region) of Emilia-Romagna, in the province of Reggio-Emilia, NE of Reggio. The commune has a flourishing dairy industry. In the town are a school of music and a school of design; it contains a number of palaces and churches built in the 15th and 16th centuries. The painter Antonio Allegri da Correggio, outstanding among the painters of the Italian baroque style, was born here. Buildings of interest to tourists were undamaged in World War II. Pop. of commune, 19,046 (1936); of town, 3,856 (1936).

Correggio, Antonio Allegri da. b. at Correggio, Italy, 1494; d. there, March 5, 1534. Italian painter of the Lombard school.

Correggio, Claudio da. See **Merulo, Claudio.**

Corregidor (kǫ.reg′i.dôr; Spanish, kôr.re.hē.ᴛʜōr′). Small rocky island guarding the entrance to Manila Bay, on the W coast of Luzon, Philippine Islands. It is heavily fortified and effectively blocks the entrance to Manila Bay and the port of Manila. It was the last bit of territory held (1942) by the Americans during the battle for the Philippines in World War II and it was from here that General MacArthur and President Quezon set out for Australia. Pop. 36 (1948).

Corregidor, Battle of. Battle (1941–42) for the island of Corregidor, in the Philippine Islands, in World War II. A fortress protecting the peninsula of Bataan, Corregidor became the scene of the final defensive effort of the U.S. and Philippine forces against the Japanese invasion of the Philippines in 1941. Even after the fall of Bataan in April, 1942, resistance on Corregidor continued for over a month. Finally, after incessant air and artillery bombardment and a landing on May 5th on the North Point of Corregidor by the Japanese, the troops of General Jonathan Wainwright had to surrender.

Correia (kōr.rā′ą), **Raimundo (da Mota de Azevedo).** b. aboard the ship *São Luís*, off the coast of the state of Maranhão, Brazil, May 13, 1860; d. at Paris, in September, 1911. Brazilian poet, by some considered one of the three greatest Brazilian Parnassians. He was also a lawyer, professor, public prosecutor, judge, and diplomat. He wrote *Primeiros sonhos* (1879), *Sinfonias* (1883), *Versos e versões* (1887), *Aleluias* (1891), and *Poesias* (1898).

Corrèze (ko.rez). Department in S central France, bounded by the departments of Haute-Vienne and Creuse on the N, the departments of Puy-de-Dôme and Cantal on the E, the departments of Lot on the S, and the department of Dordogne on the W. It formed part of the former province of Limousin and some neighboring territories. Agriculture produces chiefly grains, but livestock raising is more important. The milk production supports the cheese-making industry, especially of the Roquefort type, at Aveyron. There are various manufactures, such as those of the metallurgical industry of Tulle. The population is declining. Capital, Tulle; area, 2,272 sq. mi.; pop. 254,601 (1946).

Corrib (kor′ib), **Lough.** Lake in Connacht province, Irish Republic, lying mostly in County Galway, but also partly in County Mayo. It is the second largest lake in Ireland (next to Lough Neagh). Lough Corrib is fed from Lough Mask, and drains through the river Corrib to Galway Bay at Galway city. Area, ab. 68 sq. mi.; length, ab. 27 mi.; greatest width, ab. 7 mi.

Corrichie (kǫ.rich′i). Moor situated W of Aberdeen, Scotland. It was the scene of a victory of James Stuart, Earl of Moray, over George Gordon, 4th Earl of Huntly, in 1562 during the struggle over the return to Scotland of Mary, Queen of Scots.

Corrientes (kôr.ryen′tās). Province in NE Argentina, lying S of Paraguay, W of Brazil and Uruguay, N of Entre Ríos province, and E of Santa Fe province. Although it has some river shipyards and other industrial enterprises, its chief importance is agricultural. Capital, Corrientes; area, 33,544 sq. mi.; pop. 525,463 (1947).

Corrientes. City in E Argentina, capital of Corrientes province, on the Paraná River ab. 495 mi. N by NW of Buenos Aires: river port and rail center for beef and other agricultural products. 56,544 (1947).

Corrientes, Cape. [Spanish, **Cabo Corrientes.**] Cape on the W coast of Mexico, in Jalisco state.

Corriere della Sera (kôr.rē.ā′rā del.lä sā′rä). Italian newspaper, founded (1876) at Milan and long administered by the brothers Crespi.

Corrievrekin (kor.i.vrek′ąn). [Also: **Corrievreckan, Corryvreckan, Coryvreckan.**] Narrow strait and whirlpool in the Inner Hebrides, in W Scotland, in Argyllshire, lying between the islands of Jura and Scarba. Width, ab. 1 mi.

Corrigan (kor′i.gąn), **Michael Augustine.** b. at Newark, N.J., Aug. 13, 1839; d. at New York, May 5, 1902. Roman Catholic prelate, archbishop (1885–1902) of New York. He was president (1868–76) of Seton Hall College, South Orange, N.J., bishop of Newark (1873–80), and, as titular archbishop of Petra, coadjutor (1880–85) to the archbishop of New York.

Corril (kor′il), **Daniel.** b. 1777; d. at Madras, India, Feb. 5, 1837. English missionary in India, appointed archdeacon of Calcutta in 1823, and first bishop of Madras in 1835. He went to India as an army chaplain in 1806, and from the first added the labors of a missionary to his official duties. He founded several missions.

Corrodi (kô.rō′dē), **August.** b. at Zurich, Switzerland, 1826; d. there, 1885. Swiss artist and author writing in German. He wrote and illustrated a number of books for children, such as *Die Stadtkinder im Walde* (1856), *Geschichtenbuch für Kinder* (1865), and *Deutsches Kindertheater* (1874–79). His translations of poems by Robert Burns helped to introduce that Scottish lyricist to readers in Switzerland.

Corrupt Practices Act. Laws passed (1890 *et seq.*) by the individual states of the U.S. and (1910 *et seq.*) by the federal government to correct abuses in election practices. Although the laws varied greatly from state to state, in general they all made bribery illegal, strengthened the registration and voting regulations, and provided for some measure of control over campaign funds. The amount of money to be contributed or spent in a campaign was limited, as were the sources of the funds and the purposes for which they could be used. Publicity of campaign receipts and disbursements was also required.

Corry (kor′i). City in NW Pennsylvania, in Erie County, ab. 28 mi. SE of Erie, in a petroleum area: manufactures of leather, furniture, aircraft, and metal products. Founded in 1861, it was chartered as a city in 1866. 7,911 (1950).

Corry, Montagu William Lowry. [Title, Baron **Rowton.**] b. at London, Oct. 8, 1838; d. there, Nov. 9, 1903. English politician and philanthropist. A Cambridge graduate (1860), he was private secretary (1866–81) to Benjamin Disraeli, who left his correspondence and papers to Corry. He is noted for instituting a chain of club-hotels known as Rowton Houses where food and lodgings are provided at low rates for poor men.

Corsair, The. Poem in three cantos by Byron, published in 1814. It relates the adventures of the pirate Conrad, especially at the court of Sultan Seyd. *Lara* (1814) continues the story. Both poems are supposedly based on Jean Lafitte's career.

Corsairs. As a proper name, the group of sea robbers, chiefly from the Barbary coast, who infested the Mediterranean for many centuries. In the form "corsairs" it has come to be a general word for "pirates."

Cor Scorpionis (kôr skôr.pi.ō′nis). Another name for Antares, a star of the first magnitude in the zodiacal constellation Scorpio.

Corse (kôrs). Department of France, coextensive with the island of Corsica. Capital, Ajaccio; area, 3,367 sq. mi.; pop. 267,873 (1946).

Corse, John Murray. b. at Pittsburgh, Pa., April 27, 1835; d. at Winchester, Mass., April 27, 1893. American soldier. He entered West Point in 1853, but left before graduating, and studied law. At the outbreak of the Civil War he entered the Union army as a major of volunteers. He commanded a division at Memphis; was commissioned brigadier general in 1863; served in the Chattanooga campaign and participated in the battles of Chickamauga and Missionary Ridge; held out (Oct. 5, 1864) at Allatoona, Ga., against a largely superior force of the enemy; was made brevet major general in 1864; and commanded a division in Sherman's march to the sea. He was (1867–69) collector of internal revenue at Chicago, and was subsequently postmaster of Boston.

Cor Serpentis (kôr sėr.pen′tis). The second magnitude star α Serpentis, more often called Unukalhai.

Corsica (kôr′si.kạ). [French, **Corse;** Greek, **Cyrnos.**] Island and department of France, situated in the Mediterranean Sea, N of the Italian island of Sardinia, from which it is separated by the Strait of Bonifacio, and SE of Marseilles. It has a largely mountainous surface and Mediterranean climate and vegetation. The highest summit is Monte Cinto. The agriculture produces grain, vegetables, mulberries, wines, and various fruits, particularly olives, lemons, and oranges. Goats, horses, donkeys, mules, sheep, and forest products are raised; marble, porphyry, and antimony are mined. Fisheries are located along the coasts. Industries are small and mainly agricultural in nature, although some silk is produced. The countryside is picturesque, with numerous, attractive small towns. The population speaks an Italian dialect, but is ethnologically a mixture of numerous Mediterranean peoples, such as Phoenicians, Tyrrhenians, Etruscans, Carthaginians, and Romans. It was acquired by the Romans at the end of the first Punic War; the decline of the Roman Empire, invasions of Vandals, Goths, Franks, Arabs, and Saracens disrupted the island, which finally fell under the oppressive protectorate of the Republic of Genoa. Insurrections were frequent, banditry common. The island was ceded to France in 1768 (one year before Napoleon Bonaparte was born). After another insurrection, final inclusion in France occurred in 1796. Originally divided into two departments, Corse, as the department is called, became a single French department in 1811. Capital, Ajaccio; area, 3,367 sq. mi.; pop. 267,873 (1946).

"Corsican (kôr′si.kạn), **the."** See **Napoleon. I.**

Corsicana (kôr.si.kan′ạ). City in C Texas, county seat of Navarro County, ab. 50 mi. SE of Dallas; manufactures of cotton textiles, cottonseed products, and agricultural and petroleum machinery. The first commercial oil well in Texas was drilled here in 1894; the city was also the site of the first manufacture of the rotary drilling rig. 19,211 (1950).

Corsican Brothers, The. Translation by Dion Boucicault of a popular French play, *Les Frères corses.* The plot turns on the mysterious sympathy between Louis and Fabian dei Franchi, who are twin brothers.

Corsini (kôr.sē′nē), **Lorenzo.** Original name of Pope **Clement XII.**

Corso (kōr′sō). One of the principal streets of Rome. It extends for nearly a mile from the Piazza del Popolo, and is the chief scene of the annual carnival.

Corson (kôr′sọn), **Hiram.** b. at Philadelphia, Nov. 6, 1828; d. at Ithaca, N.Y., June 15, 1911. American scholar, author, and educator, professor at Cornell University (1870 *et seq.*; emeritus, 1903). He was connected with the library of the Smithsonian Institution (1849–56). He lectured (1859–65) on English literature at Philadelphia and was professor at Girard College (1865–66) and at St. John's College, Annapolis (1866–70). Among his works are *Hand-book of Anglo-Saxon and Early English* (1871), *An Introduction to the Study of Robert Browning's Poetry* (1886), *An Introduction to the Study of Shakespeare* (1889), *A Primer of English Verse* (1892), *The Aims of Literary Study* (1894), *The Voice and Spiritual Education* (1896), and *An Introduction to the Prose and Poetical Works of John Milton* (1899).

Corson, Juliet. b. at Roxbury, Mass., Feb. 14, 1842; d. at New York, June 18, 1897. American teacher of cooking. She opened (1876) a cooking school at New York and was the first to demonstrate (1880) cooking in a high school. She was the author of *Fifteen Cent Dinners for Workingmen's Families* (1877), *Cooking Manual* (1877), and *Family Living on $500 a Year* (1887).

Corssen (kôr′sẹn), **Wilhelm Paul.** b. at Bremen, Germany, Jan. 20, 1820; d. at Lichterfelde, near Berlin, June 18, 1875. German philologist. His works include *Über Aussprache, Vokalismus, und Betonung der lateinischen Sprache* (1858–59), *Kritische Beiträge zur lateinischen Formenlehre* (1863), and others.

Cort (kôrt), **Cornelis.** b. at Hoorn, Netherlands, after 1530; d. at Rome, 1578. Dutch engraver. He worked (c1565) at Venice for Titian, doing copperplates, went to Bologna, and then to Rome, where he established (c1571) a school whose exponent was Agostino Carracci. His works include noted engravings after Titian, Raphael, and other masters.

Cort, Henry. [Called **"the Father of the Iron Trade."**] b. at Lancaster, England, 1740; d. 1800. English ironmaster, the inventor (c1784) of the process of puddling, and of the "puddle-rolls" used to draw out the puddled ball of iron into bars.

Corte (kôr′tā). Town on the French island of Corsica, in the department of Corse, situated in the mountainous interior of the island, between Ajaccio and Bastia, ab. 35 mi. NE of Ajaccio. It was the headquarters of Pasquale Paoli's revolutionary government prior to the French occupation in 1769. Pop. 5,310 (1946).

Cortegiano (kôr.tā.jä′nō), **Il.** [English, **The Courtier;** full Italian title, **Il Libro del Cortegiano.**] Famous Italian book of manners, written by Baldassare Castiglione. It was translated (c1554; not printed until 1561) into English by Sir Thomas Hoby.

Cortelyou (kôr′tẹl.yö), **George Bruce.** b. at New York, July 26, 1862; d. Oct. 23, 1940. American cabinet officer. After acting as President Cleveland's stenographer from 1895, he was assistant secretary (1898–1900) and secretary (1900–03) to Presidents McKinley and Roosevelt, and was first secretary (1903–04) of the Department of Commerce and Labor. He was elected chairman of the Republican national committee in June, 1904, was postmaster general (1905–07) of the U.S., and secretary of the treasury (1907–09). He headed (1909–35) the N.Y. Consolidated Gas Company.

Cortenuova (kôr.tā.nwô′vä). Village in the province of Bergamo, Italy, ab. 32 mi. E of Milan. Here, in 1237, the emperor Frederick II defeated the Lombards. Pop. less than 1,500.

Corte-Real (kōr″tẹ.rē.äl′), **Gaspar.** [Also: **Cortereal, Corterreal.**] b. c1450; d. c1501. Portuguese navigator. He explored Labrador and Newfoundland in 1500, and in 1501 undertook a second voyage to the same regions, in the course of which he died.

Cortés (kôr.tās′). Department in W Honduras. Livestock and rubber are the chief products. Capital, San Pedro Sula; area, 1,569 sq. mi.; pop. 125,728 (1950).

Cortes (kōr′tẹsh). Former parliament of Portugal. It consisted of an upper house of hereditary and nominated princes, peers, and bishops, and a lower house elected by the people. The constitution of 1911 substituted two elected chambers.

Cortes (kôr′tās). National assembly or legislature of Spain, consisting of a senate and chamber of deputies. The senate was formerly composed of not over 360 members, one half princes of the blood, grandees, and certain ex-officio and nominated members, and one half elected. The chamber of deputies was formerly composed of members in the proportion of one for every 50,000 inhabitants, elected for five years. Under the law of July, 1942, the Franco regime reorganized the Cortes. It had, in 1949, 438 members.

Cortés or **Cortez** (kôr.tez′), **Hernando** or **Fernando.** [Title, Marquis of the **Valley of Oaxaca** (Marqués **del Valle**).] b. at Medellín, Estremadura, Spain, 1485; d. at Castillejo de la Cuesta, an estate near Seville, Spain, Dec. 2, 1547. Spanish soldier, the conqueror of Mexico. In 1504 he went to Española (the island of Hispaniola or Santo Domingo), and in 1511, as an officer in Diego Velásquez's expedition, to Cuba, where he acquired Malinche (baptized Marina), an Indian slave girl who became his mistress and his most intelligent and trustworthy aide. In 1518 Velásquez gave him command of 12 vessels and 508 soldiers, destined to follow up Juan de Grijalva's discoveries. Suspecting disloyalty, Velásquez wished to recall him at the last moment, but Cortés evaded him and finally left Cuba on Feb. 18, 1519. Rounding Yucatán, he came into conflict with the Indians of Tabasco, landed at San Juan de Ulúa and founded Veracruz in April, and, having scrapped his ships, in August began his march to Tenochtitlán, or Mexico City, notwithstanding the remonstrances of the messengers of Montezuma, the chief or "emperor" of that city. Montezuma did not directly resist him, but in September Cortés had to fight several severe battles with the independent Tlascalans, who eventually joined him with a large force. In October, at Cholula, he massacred a great number of natives as a punishment for a real or supposed conspiracy, and on Nov. 8 marched over the lake causeways into Tenochtitlán, Montezuma coming out to meet him. The Spaniards were hospitably lodged, and received rich presents; but on the rumor of an uprising Cortés seized and held Montezuma as a hostage. Velásquez having sent Panfilo de Narváez in pursuit of Cortés, the latter left 150 men under Pedro de Alvarado, to hold the city, made a rapid march, defeated and captured (May 28, 1520) Narváez at Cempoala, and enlisted most of his men. On his return he found the Spaniards closely besieged by the Mexicans, who had at last risen in arms. Cortés and his men were allowed to march in, but the fight was at once resumed. The captive Montezuma was killed, either by his own people or by the Spaniards; and on the night of June 30 (known thereafter as the *Noche Triste*, or "Sad Night") the Spaniards tried to leave the city secretly. They were discovered, and lost half their force and most of the treasure they had collected, in a fierce battle on one of the causeways; still hotly pursued, they fought another great battle at Otumba on July 7, finally escaping into Tlaxcala. Here Cortés reorganized his army, receiving many Indian allies, and, aided by ships which he built on the lakes, began the siege of Tenochtitlán in May, 1521. Under Guatemotzin the city was desperately defended, and most of it was leveled with the ground before it was taken; Guatemotzin was captured on Aug. 13, 1521. After this success, Cortés was empowered by the emperor to conquer all of New Spain, and in 1523 he was made governor. Mexico City was rebuilt. Expeditions were sent in various directions, and navigation to the Pacific commenced. To settle disorders in Honduras, Cortés marched (October, 1524–April, 1526) overland to that region, enduring terrible sufferings. During this long absence his enemies gained power; he was deposed (July, 1526) from the governorship, and in 1528 went to Spain to seek redress. Charles V received him with high honor: he was made marquis of the Valley of Oaxaca (Mexico) and military captain-general of New Spain, but was not restored to the governorship. Marina having died, he married the Count of Aguilar's daughter, a lady of noble birth (who bore his son Martín), and in 1530 returned to Mexico, where he lived in great splendor on the vast estates granted to him. But the machinations of his enemies continued; he discovered (1536) Lower California but his explorations (1533–39) of the west coast were greatly hampered, and in 1540 he again went to Spain to seek relief. In 1541 he was with the emperor in the Algerine campaign, and was shipwrecked. Charles refused or put off his demands, and, despairing of redress, Cortés was about to go back to Mexico, when he died. His honors, by failure of the direct line with his great-grandson, passed to the dukes of Terranova and Monteleone in Sicily; his Mexican estates were several times sequestrated, but portions were finally regained by the heirs.

Cortés (kôr.tās′), **José Domingo.** b. in Chile, c1830; d. 1884. Chilean author. He was long a journalist, subsequently attaché at Brussels, and finally government director of libraries in Bolivia. Among his numerous biographical and historical works are the *Diccionario biográfico americano, Poetas americanos, Historia de Bolivia,* and *Estadística bibliográfica de Bolivia.*

Cortés, Juan Francisco María de la Salud Donoso. See **Donoso Cortés, Juan Francisco María de la Salud.**

Cortés, Martín. [Title by inheritance, Marqués **del Valle.**] b. in Mexico, 1532; d. in Spain, Aug. 13, 1589. Son of Hernando Cortés. He went to Spain in 1540, was liberally educated, followed the court of Philip II to Flanders and England, and served with distinction in the army. He inherited the title of Marqués del Valle, and most of his father's Mexican estates were restored to him. In 1562 he went to Mexico, where he lived in great splendor until July, 1566, when he was accused of conspiring with the brothers Avila to make himself king. He was sent to Spain, but was exonerated after several years. His illegitimate brother, of the same name, was involved in the accusation and horribly tortured.

Cortés Castro (kôr.tās′ käs′trō), **León.** b. at Alajuela, Costa Rica, Dec. 8, 1882; d. at Santa Ana, Costa Rica, March 3, 1946. Costa Rican statesman, vice-president and president (1936–40) of Costa Rica. He was deputy and sometime secretary of the Congreso Nacional, minister to Guatemala, minister of public education, twice minister of public development, and administrator of the Ferrocarril Pacífico.

Cortez (kôr.tez′). Town in SE Colorado, county seat of Montezuma County, ab. 40 mi. W of Durango. Sheep and cattle are raised in the region. Nearby are Mesa Verde National Park and Yucca House National Monument. 2,680 (1950).

Cortiço (kōr.tē′sö), **O.** See **O Cortiço.**

Cortina d'Ampezzo (kôr.tē′nä däm.pet′tsō). [Also: **Cortina, Ampezzo.**] Market town and commune in NE Italy, in the *compartimento* (region) of Veneto, in the province of Belluno, the chief place in the Ampezzo Valley, in the Italian Tyrol, N of Belluno. It is a tourist center in the Dolomites section of the eastern Alps. The parish church was undamaged in World War II. Pop. of commune, 5,381 (1936); of town, 1,552 (1936).

Cortissoz (kôr.tē′sǫz), **Ellen Mackay.** [Maiden name, **Hutchinson.**] b. at New York; d. Aug. 13, 1933. American editor and poet; wife of Royal Cortissoz (1869–1948). She was an art editor of the New York *Herald-Tribune,* and edited with E. C. Stedman the 11-volume *Library of American Literature* (1889–90). She wrote *Songs and Lyrics* (1881).

Cortissoz, Royal. b. at Brooklyn, N.Y., 1869; d. Oct. 18, 1948. American art critic and writer, art editor of the New York *Herald-Tribune* from 1891; husband of Ellen Mackay Cortissoz. He was educated at Wesleyan University and Bowdoin College, and became literary editor of the *Herald-Tribune*, as well as its art editor. He was a member of the American Academy of Arts and Letters, a trustee of the American Academy at Rome, and a chevalier of the Order of Leopold. He was the author of *Augustus St. Gaudens* (1907), *John La Farge* (1911), *Art and Common Sense* (1913), *Life of Whitelaw Reid* (1921), *American Artists* (1923), *Personalities in Art* (1925), and *The Painter's Craft* (1930); he also edited *The Autobiography of Benvenuto Cellini*, Cervantes's *Don Quixote*, and Whitelaw Reid's *American and English Studies*.

Cortland (kôrt′lạnd). City in C New York, county seat of Cortland County, ab. 32 mi. S of Syracuse. Manufactures include wire cloth, truck parts, corsets, and lingerie. 18,152 (1950).

Cortona (kôr.tō′nä). Town and commune in C Italy, in the *compartimento* (region) of Tuscany, in the province of Arezzo, situated above the Mucellia River, ab. 50 mi. SE of Florence. It contains important Etruscan and Roman antiquities, many of them in the Museum of the Accademia Etrusca; there are also ancient walls and a temple. It was one of the 12 great Etruscan cities. Medieval and Renaissance buildings are also notable; they include a number of Romanesque churches, the town hall, palaces, and the cathedral, which was entirely rebuilt in the 14th and 15th centuries; some of the churches contain beautiful paintings. The painters Luca Signorelli and Pietro Berrettini (known as Pietro da Cortona) were born here. The tomb of Santa Margherita is in the Omonima church. Family strife characterizes Cortona's medieval history, when it was partly under Sienese, partly under Florentine influence. Some damage was suffered during World War II by buildings of tourist interest, but repairs have been completed or are being carried out. Pop. of commune, 31,518 (1936); of town, 3,736 (1936).

Cortona, Pietro da. [Original name, **Pietro Berrettini.**] b. at Cortona, Italy, 1596; d. 1669. Italian painter and architect. He was a master both of fresco and of oil painting. In the former medium his most impressive achievement was the decoration of the ceiling of the grand salon of the Barberini Palace at Rome, depicting the history of the Barberini family in allegorical guise, and scarcely less celebrated were his frescoes in the Pitti Palace at Florence. He was patronized by Popes Urban VIII and Alexander VII, and during his long residence at Rome executed architectural designs for a number of churches. Examples of his work in oils are *The Battle of Arbela* in the Louvre at Paris, and a *Nativity* in the Prado at Madrid.

Cortot (kôr.tō), **Alfred (Denis).** b. at Nyon, Switzerland, Sept. 26, 1877—. French pianist and conductor. He studied at the Paris Conservatory, conducted (1902) the first performance of *Götterdämmerung* at Paris, and founded (1905) a trio with Jacques Thibaud and Pablo Casals. He was appointed (1917) professor of piano at the Paris Conservatory, and was a founder (1919) of the École Normale de Musique, of which he became director. He has published two volumes of musical essays, and piano transcriptions of orchestral works by Gabriel Fauré.

Corubal (kō.rö.bäl′). [Also, **Rio Grande.**] River in Portuguese Guinea, W Africa, which flows into the Atlantic Ocean near the middle of the seacoast of the colony. Length, ab. 300 mi.

Coruche (kö.rö′shẹ). Town and *concelho* (commune) in C Portugal, in the province of Ribatejo, in the district of Santarém, situated on the Sorrata River, SE of Santarém: agricultural trade center. Pop. of concelho, 23,269 (1940); of town, 12,395 (1940).

Çoruh (chō.rö′). [Also, **Artvin.**] *Il* (province or vilayet) in NE Turkey, on the S slopes of the Pontus Mountains close to the border of the U.S.S.R. Woolen goods, opium, and subsistence crops are the chief products. Capital, Rize (also called Çoruh); area, 3,408 sq. mi.; pop. 174,511 (1950).

Çorum (chō.röm′). [Also, **Chorum.**] *Il* (province or vilayet) in N central Turkey, near the W end of the Pontus Mountains, a very hilly area cut by several river valleys. Four important highways and caravan trails cross this area. Capital, Çorum; area, 4,339 sq. mi.; pop. 342,290 (1950).

Çorum. [Also, **Chorum.**] City in N central Turkey, capital of the *il* (province or vilayet) of Çorum, ab. 120 mi. NE of Ankara, located in a small mountain basin at an elevation of ab. 2,600 ft. The region is noted for fruit growing, and the town has carpet-weaving and tanning industries. It is connected by road with Samsun on the N coast. 20,307 (1945).

Corumbá (kō.röm.bä′). Chief commercial city in the state of Mato Grosso, in SW Brazil, a river port on the Paraguay River near the Bolivian border: cattle products and ipecac. 19,211 (1950).

Coruña (kō.rö′nyä), **La.** See **La Coruña.**

Coruña, Count of **La.** Title of **Mendoza, Lorenzo Suarez de.**

Corvallis (kôr.val′is). [Former name, **Marysville.**] City in W Oregon, county seat of Benton County, on the Willamette River in a lumbering, dairying, and fruit-producing area: fruit and vegetable canneries, creameries, hatcheries, flour mills, and a sawmill. It is the seat of Oregon State Agricultural College. Settled in 1845, it was platted and made county seat in 1851, and renamed in 1853. Pop. 16,207 (1950).

Corvino (kôr.vē′nō). Merchant, the husband of Celia, in Ben Jonson's comedy *Volpone:* a mixture "of wittol, fool, and knave." Out of pure covetousness he falls into Mosca's plot to give his wife up to Volpone.

Corvinus (kôr.vē′nu̇s), **Jakob.** Pseudonym of **Raabe, Wilhelm.**

Corvinus (kôr.vī′nus), **Marcus Valerius Messala** (or **Messalla**). See **Messala** (or **Messalla**) **Corvinus, Marcus Valerius.**

Corvinus, Matthias. See **Matthias Corvinus.**

Corvin-Wiersbitzki (kôr′vin.vērs.bit′skē), **Otto Julius Bernhard.** b. at Gumbinnen, Germany, Oct. 12, 1812; d. at Wiesbaden, Germany, March 2, 1886. German politician, journalist, and miscellaneous writer. He published *Illustrirte Weltgeschichte* (1844–51) and other works.

Corvisart des Marets (kôr.vē.zàr dā mà.re), **Jean Nicolas,** Baron. b. at Drécourt, Ardennes, France, Feb. 15, 1755; d. at Courbevoie, near Paris, Sept. 18, 1821. French physician. He established the method of percussion in diagnosis of chest disease. He was the author of *Essai sur les maladies du coeur* (1808).

Corvo (kôr′vō), **Baron.** Name used by Frederick William (Serafino Austin Lewis Mary) Rolfe (1860–1913), English novelist, short-story writer, historian, and contributor to the *Yellow Book*.

Corvus (kôr′vus). A southern constellation, the Raven or Crow, S of Virgo. A constellation anciently recognized, it presents a characteristic quadrilateral configuration of four stars of the second and third magnitude.

Corvus, Valerius. See **Valerius, Marcus.**

Corwin (kôr′win), **Edward Samuel.** b. near Plymouth, Mich., Jan. 19, 1878—. American educator and author, noted as an authority on American political institutions. He was graduated from the University of Michigan (Ph.B., 1900) and the University of Pennsylvania (Ph.D., 1905), was among the original group of preceptors (1905) brought to Princeton by Woodrow Wilson, and served at Princeton as professor of politics (1911–18) and as McCormick professor of jurisprudence (1918–46). He was president (1931) of the American Political Association. Among his numerous works are *The Doctrine of Judicial Review* (1914), *The President's Control of Foreign Relations* (1917), *John Marshall and the Constitution* (1919), *The Constitution and What It Means Today* (1920; 10th ed., 1948), *The Twilight of the Supreme Court* (1934; 4th ed., 1937), *The President: Office and Powers* (1940; 3rd ed., 1948), and *Liberty Against Government* (1948).

Corwin, Norman. b. at Boston, May 3, 1910—. American writer, director, and producer of radio plays. He was awarded first prize by the 10th Radio Education Institution for his *Words Without Music* programs in 1938. Other productions which he wrote and directed include *They Fly Through the Air* (1938), *Seems Radio Is Here to Stay* (1939), *Columbia Presents Corwin* (1944), and *One World Flight* (1947). His fantasies, including *The Plot To Overthrow Christmas* and *My Client Curley*, and his political dramatizations, like *The Name Nobody Could Pronounce* and *On a Note of Triumph*, made him perhaps the most prominent radio writer of the 1940's. His publications include *The Plot to Overthrow Christmas* (1940), *Untitled and Other Plays* (1944), and others.

Corwin, Thomas. b. in Bourbon County, Ky., July 29, 1794; d. at Washington, D.C., Dec. 18, 1865. American statesman and orator. He entered Congress in 1831. He was governor of Ohio (1840–42), U.S. senator from Ohio (1845–50), secretary of the treasury (1850–53) under Fillmore, member of Congress (1859–61), and U.S. minister to Mexico (1861–64).

Cory (kō′ri), **Charles Barney.** [Pseudonym, **Owen Nox.**] b. at Boston, Jan. 31, 1857; d. July 29, 1921. American ornithologist. He was on the staff (1906 *et seq.*) of the Field Museum at Chicago. He was the author of *Birds of the Bahama Islands* (1880), *Beautiful and Curious Birds of the World* (1880–83), *The Birds of Haiti and San Domingo* (1885), *The Birds of the West Indies* (1889), *Birds of Illinois and Wisconsin* (1909), and the first two volumes of *Birds of the Americas* (1918–19).

Cory, William Johnson. [Original name, **William Johnson.**] b. Jan. 9, 1823; d. June 11, 1892. English educator and poet. In 1872, when he retired as assistant master at Eton after 26 years, he assumed the name of Cory. He wrote *Ionica* (1858; enlarged ed., 1891), *Lucretilis* (1871), *Iophon* (1873), and *Guide to Modern History from 1815 to 1835* (1882). His lyrics are in the polished style of later Greek poetry. *Extracts from the Letters and Journals of William Cory* (1897, ed. by F. W. Cornish) was published after his death.

Coryate or **Coryat** (kôr′yạt, -i.ạt), **Thomas.** b. at Odcombe, Somersetshire, England, c1577; d. at Surat, India, in December, 1617. English traveler. After a period at court as a jester, he made a journey through France, Savoy, Italy, Switzerland, and other countries of the Continent in 1608, an account of which was published in 1611 under the title *Coryat's Crudities, hastily gobled up in Five Months Travells in France, Savoy, Italy, Rhetia, Helvetia, High Germania and the Netherlands.* He is credited, as the result of seeing them used in Italy, with the introduction of forks into England. In 1612 he started on a tour of the East, and visited Palestine, Persia, and India, in which last-named country he fell a victim to disease.

Corybantes (kor.i.ban′tēz). Priests of the Great Mother goddess in Phrygia, whose worship they celebrated by orgiastic dances. From the identification of Rhea with the Asiatic Great Mother, they are often equated with the Curetes, Rhea's satellite deities, since the priests were themselves representatives of these minor fertility gods.

Corydon (kor′i.dọn). Shepherd in Vergil's seventh eclogue, and in the *Idyls* of Theocritus; hence, a conventional name in pastoral poetry for a shepherd or a rustic swain.

Corydon. Shepherd in Spenser's *Faerie Queene*, in love with Pastorella.

Corydon. Shepherd in Spenser's *Colin Clout's Come Home Again.*

Corydon. Shoemaker of Constantinople, in Scott's *Count Robert of Paris.*

Coryell (kôr.yel′), **John Russell.** See under **Carter, Nick.**

Corymbaeus (kor.im.bē′us). Pseudonym of **Brathwaite, Richard.**

Cosa (kō′sä), **Juan de la.** b. c1460; d. near Cartagena, in what is now Colombia, 1510. Spanish navigator, one of the most skillful of his time. He was with Columbus as master or pilot of the *Santa María*, the flagship, in the voyage of 1492 and during the exploration (1498) of Cuba, and he made at least five voyages to the northern coast of South America: with Alonso de Ojeda (May, 1499–June, 1500); with Bastidas (October, 1500–September, 1502); in command of successful expeditions in search of gold and treasure, 1504 to 1506, and 1507 to 1508; and finally with Ojeda in 1509, when he was killed by the Indians. Of Cosa's charts two or three are extant. His map of the New World, made in 1500, is the oldest known. It is now the property of the Spanish government.

Cosegüina (kō.sā.gwē′nä). [Also: **Cosigüina**; Spanish, **Volcán Coseguina.**] Volcano at the extreme W of Nicaragua, situated on a peninsula between the Gulf of Fonseca and the Pacific. It is notable for one of the most violent eruptions ever recorded. This began on Jan. 20, 1835, and lasted nearly four days; the cloud of ashes darkened the country for a distance of from 50 to 100 mi. from the crater; near the base ashes lay several feet thick, and were carried by the wind to Jamaica, Oaxaca in Mexico, and Bogotá in Colombia. The explosions are said to have been heard in Mexico City. 3,830 ft.

Coseley (kōz′li). Urban district in C England, in Staffordshire, ab. 3 mi. SE of Wolverhampton, ab. 123 mi. NW of London by rail. 34,414 (1951).

Cosenza (kō.zen′tsä). Province in S Italy, in the region of Calabria. Capital, Cosenza; area, ab. 2,600 sq. mi.; pop. 587,025 (1936), 669,000 (est. 1946).

Cosenza. [Ancient name, **Cosentia** (kọ.sen′shi.ạ) or **Consentia.**] City and commune in S Italy, in the *compartimento* (region) of Calabria, the capital of the province of Cosenza, situated near the confluence of the Busento and Crati rivers and separated from the Mediterranean Sea by the Costiera Mountains. It is the center of a fertile agricultural district; silkworm culture is a principal occupation, and there are lumber, leather, and woolen industries. Cosenza is the seat of an archbishopric, an agricultural school, and the Accademia Cosentina, the latter founded in the 16th century; there is also a museum. The cathedral, built in the 12th century, contains the tombs of Louis III, Duke of Anjou, and Isabella of Aragon (d. 1271), wife of Philip III of France, and daughter of James I of Aragon. Other churches date mostly from the 16th century; there is a medieval castle. Alaric I, king of the Ostrogoths, died and was buried here in 410, it is said in the bed of the Busento River. Cosenza flourished under Norman and Hohenstaufen rule, and declined under the Spaniards. A center of the revolutionary movement during the 19th century, it became part of Italy in 1860. The city has suffered frequently from earthquakes. Some damage was sustained during World War II by buildings of tourist interest, but repairs have been completed or are being carried out. Pop. of commune, 40,032 (1936); of city, 30,038 (1936).

Cosette (kō.zet′). In Victor Hugo's *Les Misérables*, the daughter of Fantine, adopted by Jean Valjean. Her name is given to the second part of the story.

Cosgrave (koz′grāv), **William Thomas.** b. at Dublin, 1880—. Irish statesman of the Sinn Fein and member (1917 *et seq.*) of the Dáil Éireann, the lower house of the legislature, from its inception in the Irish Free State. He was a member (1909–22) of the Dublin Corporation and chairman (1916–22) of its finance committee. He held the posts of minister (1917–21) for local government and president (1922) of the Dáil Éireann as well as chairman of the provisional government. Cosgrave was minister for finance (1922–23) and defense (1924), and president (1922–32) of the executive council of the Irish Free State, after which he led the opposition to De Valera's government.

Coshocton (kọ.shok′tọn). City in E Ohio, county seat of Coshocton County, near the confluence of the Tuscarawas and Walhonding rivers, ab. 23 mi. N of Zanesville; manufactures include metal, leather, and ceramic products and advertising novelties. It was the birthplace of William Green, the labor leader. 11,675 (1950).

Così Fan Tutte (kō.sē′ fän′ töt′tā). [Eng. trans., *"Thus Do They All,"* or, more freely, *"Women Are All Like That"*; full title, **Così Fan Tutte, ossia la scuola degli amanti.**] Opéra bouffe in two acts by Wolfgang Amadeus Mozart, with a libretto by Lorenzo da Ponte, first performed at the Burgtheater at Vienna on Jan. 26, 1790. Two young officers, Ferrando and Guglielmo, betting on the fidelity of their fiancées, disguise themselves to pay court to Fiordiligi and Dorabella, only to find them quite as fickle as the cynical Don Alfonso had predicted. But in the end the young men reveal themselves and in reconciliation join in the final *Fortunato l'uom.*

Cosimo (kô′zē.mō), **Piero di.** See **Piero di Cosimo.**

Cosimo de' Migliorati (dā mē.lyō.rä′tē). Original name of Pope **Innocent VII.**

Cosin (kuz′in), **John.** b. at Norwich, England, Nov. 30, 1594; d. at London, Jan. 15, 1672. English divine and writer. He was appointed master of Peterhouse, Cambridge, in 1635, vice-chancellor of Cambridge University in 1639, dean of Peterborough in 1640, and bishop of Durham in 1660. He was a churchman of the school of Laud, a believer in ritualism and decoration, and an active Royalist during the English Civil War; in 1644 he was obliged to retire to Paris, where he became chaplain to the household of Queen Henrietta Maria. After the Restoration he returned to England, and rose to a position of great influence in the church.

Cosmas (koz′mas). [Called **Cosmas Indicopleustes,** meaning "Cosmas the Indian Voyager."] fl. in the 6th century A.D. Egyptian monk and traveler in India, author of a work on geography and theology, *Topographia Christiana.*

Cosmas and **Damian** (dā′mi.an), Saints. d. c287. Two martyrs, who were brothers, famous in the Eastern Church. They are commemorated daily in the canon of the Roman Catholic mass. They worked as physicians and missionaries, and were martyred in Cilicia under Diocletian. A basilica was built in their honor at Constantinople by Justinian, and two buildings were combined at Rome by Pope Felix III (who is sometimes called Felix IV because of the antipope Felix II). Their feast day is September 27, and they are the patrons of doctors and druggists.

Cosmati (kōz.mä′tē). Family or school of sculptors in Rome who originated the scheme of decorated architecture called "Cosmatesque" about the middle of the 12th century. It flourished for more than 150 years. The beauty of the work depends mainly upon the skillful combination of mosaics, disks, and porphyry, and many-colored marbles found among the ruins of Rome. The principal members of the family were Lorenzo (fl. 12th century), Jacopo (fl. 1205–10), Cosimo (fl. 1210–35), Luca (fl. 1231–35), Jacopo (fl. 1231–93), Adeodato (fl. 1294), and Giovanni (fl. 1296–1303). Examples of their work are the *Duomo* (cathedral) of Civita Castellana, the cloisters of San Paolo, and the portico and pulpit of San Lorenzo.

Cosmo and Damian (koz′mō, dā′mi.an), **Order of Saints.** See **Order of Saints Cosmo and Damian.**

Cosmopolitan. Monthly magazine founded at Rochester, N.Y., in 1886. Since its inception it has been aimed at the American family audience. Contributors have included Mark Twain, Henry James, H. G. Wells, and Arthur Conan Doyle. The publication was purchased (1925) by William Randolph Hearst and combined with *Hearst's International Magazine.*

Cosne (kōn). [Also, **Cosne-sur-Loire** (kōn.sür.lwår); ancient name, **Condate.**] Town in C France, in the department of Nièvre, situated on the Loire River, ab. 31 mi. NW of Nevers. It manufactures bolts, nuts, files, and similar metal products. The Church of Saint Aignan has Romanesque sections; the Church of Saint Jacques dates from the 15th century. The town suffered damage in World War II. 7,913 (1946).

Cossa (kôs′sä), **Baltasare.** Original name of Antipope **John XXIII.**

Cossa, Francesco. [Also, **Francesco del Cossa.**] b. c1435; d. c1477. Italian painter, a founder of the Bolognese school. In the earlier years of his career he worked at Ferrara, where examples of his art in fresco adorned the Schifanoia Palace and other structures, but he is accounted one of the founders of the school of Bologna, where his later years were spent. In addition to religious paintings such as the *Madonna Enthroned* (at Bologna), the *Madonna and Child with Angels* (in the National Gallery of Art, Washington), and the altar piece of scenes from the life of Saint Vincent Ferrer (in the National Gallery, London), he executed a number of notable portraits.

Cossa, Luigi. b. at Milan, Italy, May 27, 1831; d. at Pavia, Italy, May 10, 1896. Italian political economist, professor at Pavia from 1858.

Cossa, Pietro. b. at Rome, 1830; d. 1881. Italian playwright. Having been involved in the unsuccessful fight for a Roman republic in 1849, he went into exile to South America, but soon returned to Italy, where after years of writing with small rewards, he suddenly became successful and renowned with the production in 1870 of a tragedy in verse on the subject of Nero. From that time on until his death he produced a poetic drama annually, and with uniform success. These works for the most part had classic themes, but his last play, produced in 1880, *I Napolitani nel 1799,* was of more modern inspiration.

Cossacks (kos′aks). [Eng. trans. (from Tartar), "*Freemen.*"] Originally, restless souls and escaped serfs who formed fortified villages on the unsettled Ukrainian frontier (Zaporozhye Cossacks) in the 15th and 16th centuries. They lived largely by fishing, saltmaking, and banditry, under elected leaders (*hetmans*). They developed an increasing reputation as mercenary soldiers, and became a special military caste of the Czarist regime, subject to lifelong service in return for which lands and other privileges were granted. Though they provided infantry as well as cavalry, the Cossacks' reputation is as daring horsemen. The number of Cossack legions increased steadily as the government formed new colonies to protect the empire's expanding frontiers. In the early 16th century, the Don, Ural, Siberian, and Terek Cossacks were in existence. The Volga (later, Astrakhan) Cossacks were formed in 1733, the Orenburg in 1755, the Black Sea (later, Kuban) in 1783, the Transbaikal in the period 1820–51, the Amur (in the Far East) in 1858, the Semirechye (in Central Asia) in 1867, and the Ussuri (in the Far East) in 1889. In 1910 the total Cossack population numbered four million, of whom more than half were Don and Kuban Cossacks. During the revolution and civil war in Russia, the Cossacks opposed the new regime, suffered heavy losses, and their historic organizations were subsequently broken up.

Cossacks, The. Novel by Leo Tolstoy, published in 1852. It was translated into English in 1878.

Cossé (ko.sā), **Charles de.** [Title, Comte **de Brissac.**] b. in Anjou, France, c1505; d. at Paris, Dec. 31, 1563. Marshal of France. He was present at the siege of Naples in 1528, served (1544–46) against the English and Imperialists in Champagne and Flanders, became grand master of the artillery in 1547, and marshal of France in 1550.

Cosseans (ko.sē′anz). See **Kassites.**

Cossimbazar (kos″im.ba.zär′). [Also, **Kasimbazar.**] Ruined town in West Bengal, Union of India, S of Murshidabad: formerly a flourishing commercial center.

Cossit's Corners (kos′its). A former name of **Syracuse,** N.Y.

Cossmann (kos′män), **Paul Nikolaus.** b. at Baden-Baden, Germany, April 6, 1869—. German journalist. A conservative, he founded and edited *Süddeutsche Monatshefte.* He wrote *Hans Pfitzner* (1904).

Cossura (ko.sö′ra) or **Cossyra** (ko.sī′ra). Ancient names of the island of **Pantelleria.**

Cossutius (ko.sö′shus). Roman architect who, under Antiochus IV Epiphanes (175 to 164 B.C.), built a large part of the temple of Zeus Olympius at Athens, begun in the time of Pisistratus (6th century B.C.) and finished in that of Hadrian (2nd century A.D.).

Costa (kôs′ta), **Alfonso Augusto da.** b. at Ceia, Beira, Portugal, 1871—. Portuguese statesman, politician, and orator. He was active (1910) in the revolutionary movement which preceded the establishment of the Portuguese republic and was minister of justice in the government which followed.

Costa, Cláudio Manuel da. b. at Ribeirão do Carmo (now Mariana), Minas Gerais, Brazil, June 6, 1729; d. in prison at Vila Rica (now Ouro Preto), Brazil, July 4, 1789. Brazilian poet. He studied law at Coimbra, Portugal, was a lawyer at Vila Rica, took part in the intellectual Minas conspiracy of 1789, and was arrested for that. Found dead in prison, he is generally believed to have committed suicide. Among his principal works are a volume of poetry entitled *Obras* (1768) and the epic poem "Vila Rica," written in 1773 but not published until 1813, in *O Patriota,* a magazine.

Costa (kôs′tä), **Lorenzo.** b. at Ferrara, Italy, 1460; d. 1535. Italian painter. His earliest work was done at Ferrara, and included frescoes in the Schifanoia Palace, but in 1480 he went to Bologna, where his chief patrons were the Bentivoglios, for whom he painted his impressive *Madonna and Child with the Bentivoglio Family.* There also he executed, for the Church of San Petronio, the noted *Madonna and Child with SS. Sebastian, James, Jerome, and George,* and other religious pictures, as well as scenes from classical history. The Bentivoglios were exiled from Bologna in 1509, and thereafter Costa lived and worked at Mantua. His *Court of Isabella d'Este* is in the Louvre at Paris, his *Adoration of the Magi* in the Brera at Milan, and his *Madonna and Child Enthroned* in the National Gallery, London.

Costa (kos'tạ), Sir **Michael Andrew Agnus.** b. at Naples, Italy, Feb. 4, 1808; d. at Hove, England, April 29, 1884. English composer of operas, oratorios, and ballets, and musical director. He wrote the oratorios *Eli* (1855) and *Naaman* (1864). The greater part of his life was spent in England as conductor at London, Birmingham, and Leeds.

Costa Cabral (kôs'tạ kạ.bräl'), **Antônio Bernardo da.** [Title, Conde **de Thomar.**] b. at Fornos de Algodres, Beira, Portugal, May 9, 1803; d. Sept. 1, 1889. Portuguese statesman. He was minister of justice and ecclesiastical affairs (1839–42), and of the interior (1842–46). In the latter year he was overthrown by a popular uprising against his tyranny and misgovernment. He was prime minister again from 1849 to 1851.

Costa Carvalho (kôs'tạ kạr.vä'lyö), **José da.** [Titles, Baron, Viscount, and Marquis of **Monte Alegre.**] b. at Penha, Brazil, Feb. 7, 1796; d. at Rio de Janeiro, Sept. 18, 1860. Brazilian statesman. He was a member of the constituent assembly in 1822, and deputy in several successive parliaments. At first an ardent liberal, he went over to the conservatives in 1838. He was senator from 1839, and organized the conservative cabinet of 1848.

Costain (kos'tān), **Thomas Bertram.** b. at Brantford, Ontario, Canada, May 8, 1885—. American editor and novelist. He was editor (1908–10) of the *Daily Mercury* at Guelph, Ontario, editor (1910–20) of *Maclean's Magazine* at Toronto, served (1920–34) as associate editor of the *Saturday Evening Post*, and in 1939 became advisory editor to Doubleday, Doran and Company. He is a naturalized U.S. citizen. His historical novels include *For My Great Folly* (1942), *Joshua* (written with Rogers MacVeagh; 1943), *Ride With Me* (1943), *The Black Rose* (1945), *The Moneyman* (1947), *The Silver Chalice* (1952); he is author of *The Conquerors* (1949) and *The Magnificent Century* (1951), first two panels in a 12-volume history under the general title *The Pageant of England.*

Costa Mesa (kos'tạ mā'sạ). Unincorporated community in S California, in Orange County, near the Pacific coast ab. 30 mi. SE of the center of Los Angeles. In the decade between the last two U.S. censuses its population more than tripled. 3,579 (1940), 11,844 (1950).

Costanoan (kos.tạ.nō'ạn). North American Indian language family, embracing a number of villages, formerly found in the coastal area of S California. The languages and the tribes speaking them are now extinct.

Costard (kos'tạrd). Character in Shakespeare's *Love's Labour's Lost*, a clownish peasant who tries to be a learned wit. Into his mouth Shakespeare puts such manifest idiocies as the word "honorificabilitudinitatibus" or has him speak of the "contempts" of a letter.

Costa Rica (kos'tạ rē'kạ). [Eng. trans., "*Rich Coast.*"] Republic in Central America, bounded by Nicaragua on the N, the Caribbean Sea and Panama on the E and SE, and the Pacific Ocean on the W and SW.

Population, Area, Political Divisions, Major Cities. The country is divided into seven provinces for administrative purposes. Chief cities: San José, Alajuela, Cartago, Heredia, Puntarenas, Liberia, and Limón. Capital, San José; area, 15,682 sq. mi.; pop. 800,875 (1950).

Terrain and Climate. It is comprised of a mountainous area extending NW to SE, with four volcanic cones dominating the C part of the country. The areas bordering the Caribbean Sea and Pacific Ocean are lowland plains. The principal rivers are the Reventazón, which flows E to the Caribbean, and the San Juan. Altitude determines the three different climates prevalent in Costa Rica. From sea level to an elevation of ab. 2,000 ft., the climate is hot; from 2,000 to ab. 5,500 ft., temperate; from 5,500 to 11,200 ft. (the highest elevation in the country), the climate is cool.

Industry, Agriculture, and Trade. Costa Rica is principally an agricultural country, producing coffee, abacá, balsa, bananas, and cacao for export markets. Potatoes, rice, beans, corn, tobacco, and sugar are raised for domestic consumption. The chief industries are processing plants for the export agricultural commodities. Secondary industries produce such consumer goods as textiles, clothing, leather, soap, edible oils, shoes, furniture, glass products, pottery, pharmaceuticals, and brooms.

History. Costa Rica is supposed to have been discovered by Columbus in 1502 on his last voyage. An unsuccessful attempt to colonize it was made in 1509. The first settlement was made in 1523, and the remainder of the country was conquered in the period 1526–65. Independence was declared in 1821. Costa Rica joined the Mexican empire (1821–23), and then formed part of the federal republic of Central America from 1824 to 1839. It was reconstituted as an independent republic in 1848. It has a republican form of government with a unicameral congress composed of 45 members elected by universal suffrage. The executive power is vested in the president assisted by a nine-member cabinet; there is no vice-president. The national language is Spanish, with English taught in the public schools. The national university is at San José, and the national school of agriculture is at San Pedro.

Costa y Martínez (kōs'tä ē mär.tē'neth), **Joaquín.** b. at Monzón, Spain, 1846; d. at Graus, Spain, 1911. Spanish jurist, sociologist, and politician. Active in the Spanish republican movement at the time of the Spanish-American War, he retired from politics after that conflict only to reappear once more in the opposition movement against the conservative government of Maura y Montaner. His fundamental work, *Colectivismo Agrario en España* (Madrid, 1898) and *Estudios jurídicos y políticos* (Madrid, 1884), has been compared to that of the Englishman Cobbett. He was also a student of Spanish tradition and folklore.

Coste (kost), **Dieudonné.** b. 1896—. French aviator. With Maurice Bellonte, he made the first westbound nonstop flight from Paris to New York (Sept. 2–3, 1930) in 37 hours and 18½ minutes, co-piloting the *Question Mark*, a Bréguet-Hispano craft. Coste, with Joseph Le Brix, made the first east-west nonstop flight in October, 1927, flying from Paris to Buenos Aires via Senegal and Natal. In 1929, he and Bellonte flew nonstop from Paris to Manchuria, 4,911 miles.

Coste-Floret (kost.flo.re), **Paul.** b. at Montpellier, France, April 9, 1911—. French political leader and lawyer, one of the chief authors of the constitution of the Fourth Republic. A professor of criminal law at Algiers, he was an organizer of the French resistance in North Africa, served (1943–45) in the Free French government, and was elected (1946) to the second Constituent Assembly, in which he was chief reporter on the new constitution. A leader of the Mouvement Républicain Populaire (MRP), he was war minister (January–November, 1947), minister for overseas France (November, 1947), and minister of information (1952).

Costello (kos.tel'ō), **Dudley.** b. in Sussex, England, 1803; d. at London, Sept. 30, 1865. British soldier, novelist, and journalist; brother of Louisa Stuart Costello. He wrote *A Tour through the Valley of the Meuse, with the Legends of the Walloon Country and the Ardennes* (1845), and *Piedmont and Italy, from the Alps to the Tiber* (1859–61). He served as ensign in the West Indies, retiring on half pay in 1828; later he was foreign correspondent of the London *Morning Herald* and *Daily News.*

Costello, Louisa Stuart. b. in Ireland, 1799; d. at Boulogne, France, April 24, 1870. British writer and miniature painter; sister of Dudley Costello. She wrote *Songs of a Stranger* (1825), *A Summer among the Bocages and Vines* (1840), *Gabrielle, or Pictures of a Reign* (1843), and *The Rose Garden of Persia* (1845).

Coster or **Koster** (kos'tėr), **Laurens Janszoon.** [Original name, **Laurens Janszoon;** surnamed **Coster** or **Koster,** meaning "the Sexton."] Citizen of Haarlem, Netherlands, who, according to Hadrianus Junius in his *Batavia* (1588), invented the art of printing with movable types (c1440). The claims of Coster (whose identity is uncertain) to the discovery have been maintained with great confidence by the Dutch and in other quarters, but may be invalid.

Costermansville (kos'tėr.mạnz.vil). [Also, **Bukavu.**] Town in the Belgian Congo in C Africa, the capital of Kivu province, on the S shore of Lake Kivu, on the border of the trust territory of Ruanda-Urundi. It is the chief commercial center of the Kivu region, which is rich in agricultural and mineral products. The area is also noted for its scenery. European pop. 896 (1946).

Costermansville. Former name of **Kivu** province, Belgian Congo.

Costes de La Calprenède (kost dẹ lȧ kȧl.prẹ.ned), **Gautier de.** See **La Calprenède, Gautier de Costes de.**

Costigan (kos′ti.gạn), **Captain.** In Thackeray's *Pendennis*, a rakish, shabby-genteel old ex-army officer.

Costigan, Emily or **Milly.** In Thackeray's novel *Pendennis*, the daughter of Captain Costigan, a commonplace but beautiful and industrious actress in the provincial theater, with whom Arthur Pendennis falls in love. She is 26, he 18. Her stage name is Fotheringay.

Costigan, John Edward. b. at Providence, R.I., Feb. 29, 1888—. Self-taught American painter, etcher, and water-colorist. He became an associate of the National Academy of Design in 1926, and an academician in 1928. His work has been exhibited many times, and he has won many prizes from such institutions as the National Academy of Design, Art Institute of Chicago, Salamagundi Club, National Arts Club, and the American Water Color Society. His work is represented in the Metropolitan Museum and Whitney Museum at New York, the Brooklyn Museum, the Art Institute of Chicago, the Phillips Memorial Gallery and the Library of Congress at Washington, the Rhode Island School of Design, the National Arts Club at New York, and elsewhere. *Landscape with Figures* is one of his better-known works.

Cosway (koz′wā), **Richard.** b. at Tiverton, Devonshire, England, 1740; d. at London, July 4, 1821. English artist, especially noted as a miniature painter. He resided during the greater part of his life at London, where he was very successful in the practice of his art, gaining especially the patronage of people of fashion.

Coswig (kos′viċh). [Also, **Koswig.**] Town in C Germany, in the *Land* (state) of Saxony-Anhalt, Russian Zone, formerly in Anhalt, situated on the Elbe River, ab. 39 mi. N of Leipzig. Before World War II it had paper mills, chemical and ceramics factories, and manufactures of matches. The church dates from the 12th century, the castle from the 14th century, and the town hall from the 15th century; there is a local museum. 14,591 (1946).

Coswig. Town in E Germany, in the *Land* (state) of Saxony, Russian Zone, formerly in the free state of Saxony, NW of Dresden. Before World War II it had chemical, leather, and wallpaper manufactures. 11,705 (1946).

Cosyra (kọ.sī′rạ). An ancient name of the island of **Pantelleria.**

Cot (kō), **Pierre.** b. at Grenoble, France, Nov. 20, 1895—. French political leader and educator, a controversial figure in modern French political life. After a brief career as a professor of public law and as a lawyer, he served (1928–40) as a Radical-Socialist deputy. He was air minister (October, 1933–February, 1934; June, 1936–January, 1938) and minister of commerce (January–April, 1938). As a Popular Front air minister (1936–38), he opposed the policy of nonintervention in the Spanish civil war and supported the nationalization of the aircraft industry. After the fall of France, he escaped (June, 1940) to London, taught (1941–43) at Yale University, was a member (November, 1943) of the Consultative Assembly at Algiers, and was elected (1946) to the National Assembly as an independent deputy. Scheduled to make a lecture tour with Henry A. Wallace, he was refused admission (April, 1949) to the U.S.

Cotabanama (kō″tä.bä.nä′mä) or **Cotubanama** (kō″tö-). Hanged at what was then Santo Domingo (now Ciudad Trujillo), Hispaniola, 1504. Indian cacique of Higuay, the eastern province of the island of Hispaniola in the time of Columbus. He rose against the Spaniards in 1502, and again in 1504. Finally defeated, he took refuge in a cave in the island of Saona, was discovered, taken to Santo Domingo, and hanged.

Cotabato (kō.tä.bä′tō). [Also, **Cottabato.**] Province of the Philippine Islands, on Mindanao island; formerly, a comandancia of SW Mindanao. It is bounded by Bukidnon and Lanao provinces on the N, Davao (separated by a mountain range) on the E, the Celebes Sea on the S and SE, and Illana Bay on the W. The S coast is deeply indented by Sarangani Bay, near the head of which is Mount Matutum. Mountains follow the SW coast. The largest river, the Rio Grande de Mindanao, flows circuitously through the province S to Lake Liguasan, thence NW to Illana Bay. The district is fertile but not developed. It is inhabited chiefly by Moros. Capital, Cotabato; area, 9,620 sq. mi.; pop. 298,935 (1939), 439,669 (1948).

Cotabato. [Also, **Cottabato.**] Town in the SE Philippine Islands, the capital of Cotabato province, Mindanao island, situated near the coast of Illana Bay, on the delta of the Rio Grande de Mindanao. 8,909 (1948).

Cota de Maguaque (kō′tä dā mä.gwä′kä), **Rodrigo.** b. at Toledo, Spain; fl. in the 15th century. Spanish poet. He was the reputed author of the first act of the romantic drama *Celestina* (1480), of the satire *Coplas de Mingo Revulgo*, and of a *Diálogo entre el Amor y un Caballero viejo.*

Côte-d'Azur (kōt.dȧ.zür). See under **Riviera.**

Côte-d'Or (kōt.dôr). Department in E France, bounded by the department of Aube on the N, the department of Haute-Marne on the NE, the departments of Haute-Saône and Jura on the E, the department of Saône-et-Loire on the S, and the departments of Yonne and Nièvre on the W. It is part of the region of Burgundy which long resisted unification under the crown of France. Numerous medieval remains still exist. The climate is mild. The department is famous for its production of red and white wines of the Burgundy type, but grains, livestock raising, and dairying are also of importance. Food and chemical products are exported; other industries are of minor importance. Capital, Dijon; area, 3,391 sq. mi.; pop. 335,602 (1946).

Cotelier (ko.tẹ.lyā), **Jean Baptiste.** b. at Nîmes, France, 1629; d. at Paris, Aug. 12, 1686. French Hellenist. He was professor of Greek (1676–86) at the Royal College of Paris. He was the author of *Monumenta Ecclesia Graecae* (1677–86).

Cotentin (ko.täṅ.taṅ). Peninsular region and medieval county in Normandy, France, forming the larger part of the department of Manche. Its capital was Coutances. It was settled by the Normans and annexed to Normandy apparently in the reign of the second duke of Normandy.

Cotentin, Anne Hilarion de. See **Tourville,** Comte **de.**

Cotes (kōts), **Everard.** b. 1862; d. 1944. English author, editor, and journalist; husband (married 1891) of Sara Jeannette Duncan Cotes. He was educated at Clifton College, and at Paris and Oxford, and served on the staff (1884–98) of the Indian Museum. He edited (1895–97) the *Indian Daily News*, and was a member (1922–39) of the London staff of the *Christian Science Monitor*, and managing director (1910–19) of the Eastern News Agency. In 1919–20, as Reuter's agent, he accompanied the Prince of Wales (later Edward VIII) on his travels in Canada, the U.S., Australasia, and the West Indies. His works include *Signs and Portents in the Far East* (1907), *Down Under with the Prince* (1921), *Indian Forest Zoology*, and others.

Cotes, Roger. b. at Burbage, Leicestershire, England, July 10, 1682; d. at Cambridge, England, June 5, 1716. English mathematician. He was a graduate of Cambridge (Trinity College), and Plumian professor (1706) of astronomy at that university. He was a friend of Newton, and aided him in preparing the second edition of the *Principia*, which appeared in 1713, for which he also wrote the preface. Their correspondence was published in 1850. He published only one scientific treatise, *Logometria* (1713), during his life, but his papers were edited by Robert Smith and published in 1722 and 1738.

Cotes, Sara Jeanette. [Maiden name, **Duncan.**] b. at Brantford, Ontario, 1862; d. July 22, 1922. British journalist and novelist; wife (married 1891) of Everard Cotes. Her first volume, *A Social Departure* (1890), included lẹtters written from Japan and the East to the Montreal *Star*, of which she had been correspondent. She also wrote *An American Girl in London* (1891), *His Honour and a Lady* (1896), *Those Delightful Americans* (1902), *The Pool in the Desert* (1903), *The Imperialist* (1904), *Set in Authority* (1906), *Cousin Cinderella* (1908), *The Burnt Offering* (1909), and others.

Côtes-du-Nord (kōt.dü.nôr). Department in NW France, bounded by the English Channel on the N, the department of Ille-et-Vilaine on the E, the department of Morbihan on the S, and the department of Finistère on the W. It is part of the region of Brittany. It has a humid, maritime climate and a number of small fishing ports. Druidic monuments of great antiquity still stand. It is a predominantly agricultural department, with grain, potato, and vegetable production prevailing. Pig and poultry raising are carried on and there are important fisheries. French naval personnel is largely recruited from here. The local industries manufacture canned foods, leatherware, furniture, and other products. Capital, St.-Brieuc; area, 2,786 sq. mi.; pop. 526,955 (1946).

Cotgrave (kot′grāv), **Randle.** b. in Cheshire, England; d. c1634. English lexicographer. He was the author of a French-English dictionary, still important in the study of English and French philology, first published in 1611 (2nd ed., 1632, with an English-French dictionary by Robert Sherwood; other eds., revised and enlarged by James Howell, in 1650, 1660, and 1673). He studied at Cambridge (St. John's College), and later became secretary to William Cecil, Lord Burghley.

Cotin (ko.taṅ), **Charles.** b. at Paris, 1604; d. there, in January, 1682. French preacher and author. He was councillor and almoner to the king, and became a member of the French Academy on May 3, 1655. Having incurred the enmity of Boileau by criticizing with great asperity, at the Hôtel de Rambouillet, some of his early productions, he was exposed to ridicule by the latter and by Molière, who satirized him in *Les Femmes savantes* under the character of Trissotin. He was the author of *Poésies chrétiennes* (1657).

Cotman (kot′mạn), **John Sell.** b. at Norwich, England, May 16, 1782; d. at London, July 24, 1842. English landscape painter and etcher, best known for his architectural drawings. He published *Specimens of Norman and Gothic Architecture in the County of Norfolk* (1817; 50 plates), *A Series of Etchings illustrative of the Architectural Antiquities of Norfolk* (1818; 60 plates), and others. He also executed the plates for Dawson Turner's *Architectural Antiquities of Normandy* (1822). His water colors and oil paintings hang in several museums.

Cotonou (kō.tō.nö′). [Also, **Kotonu.**] Chief port in Dahomey, French West Africa, on the Bight of Benin, a few miles W of Porto-Novo, capital of the colony. It is connected with Porto-Novo by rail, and with the interior of the colony by a rail line ab. 257 mi. in length. 15,155 (1943).

Cotopaxi (kō.tō.pak′si; Spanish, kō.tō.pä′hē). [Former name, **León.**] Province in NW Ecuador: grains, potatoes, beans, and some precious metals. It is inhabited largely by Indians. Capital, Latacunga; area, 1,781 sq. mi.; pop. 202,385 (est. 1944).

Cotopaxi. Volcano in the Andes of Ecuador, situated ab. 45 mi. SE of Quito, Ecuador. It is the highest active volcano known, and was first ascended by Wilhelm Reiss in 1872, and later by A. Stübel in 1873, Edward Whymper in 1880, and others. Noted eruptions occurred in 1533, 1698, 1738, 1744, 1746, 1766, 1768, 1803, 1855, 1877, and later. Elevation, ab. 19,500 ft.

Cotswold Hills (kots′wōld, -wọld). [Also: **Cotswolds, Cotteswolds, Coteswold Hills.**] Range of hills in W England, in Gloucestershire, extending approximately SW and NE. The district is famous for its breed of sheep. Its highest point is Cleeve Cloud, or Cleeve Hill (1,031 ft.), near Cheltenham. Length, ab. 54 mi.

Cotsworth (kots′wėrth), **Moses Bruines.** b. in Yorkshire, England, c1860; d. at Vancouver, British Columbia, Canada, June 4, 1943. English calendar reformer. He proposed a calendar based on 13 months of 28 days each with a new month (Sol) situated between June and July and with the odd day, the yearday, added to December or June. He originated (c1922) and directed the International Fixed Calendar League, supported by George Eastman and by numerous other American and Canadian businessmen.

Cotta (kot′ä), **Bernhard von.** b. at Klein-Zillbach, Germany, Oct. 24, 1808; d. at Freiberg, Saxony, Germany, Sept. 14, 1879. German geologist, professor at the school of mines at Freiberg (1842–74); son of Heinrich von Cotta. His works include *Geognostische Wanderungen* (1836–38), *Geologie der Gegenwart* (1866), *Der Altai* (1871), and others.

Cotta, Heinrich von. b. 1763; d. 1844. German forestry expert; father of Bernhard von Cotta. Founder of a school of forestry near Eisenach, and for many years director of the similar school at Tharandt, he was a noted innovator in arboriculture and forest management.

Cotta, Johann Friedrich. b. at Tübingen, Württemberg, Germany, May 12, 1701; d. there, Dec. 31, 1779. German theologian, professor of theology and history at Tübingen (1739–79). His chief work is *Entwurf einer ausführlichen Kirchenhistorie des Neuen Testaments* (1768–73).

Cotta, Johann Friedrich. [Title, Baron **Cotta von Cottendorf.**] b. at Stuttgart, Württemberg, Germany, April 27, 1764; d. there, Dec. 29, 1832. German publisher, financier, and civic leader. After graduating from the University of Tübingen and making a prolonged sojourn at Paris, he took over (1787) the management of the family firm, J. G. Cotta'scher Verlag, from his brother, Christoph Friedrich (1730–1807), who had been responsible for its removal from Tübingen to Stuttgart. The family was of noble Italian descent and had settled during the Reformation in Thuringia. The firm had passed from father to son through three generations of Johann Georg Cottas of whom the eldest (1631–92) may be considered its founder by virtue of his having married in 1659 the widow of the Tübingen bookseller Philipp Braun. Johann Friedrich, a great friend of Schiller's, undertook to publish the *Allgemeine Zeitung* in 1794 (it first appeared in 1798) and wanted Schiller to be its editor. For reasons of health, Schiller declined. However, Schiller's famous *Horen* (1795 *et seq.*) was organized for him by Cotta. Cotta became in the course of time the publisher of various writers of the era of German classicism including not only Schiller and Goethe but also Fichte and others. In 1799 Cotta was sent to Paris as the representative of the Württemberg estates. The German booksellers sent him as their spokesman to the Congress of Vienna. He was a member of his country's diet. He was interested in and practiced progressive farming. He was among the first landholders in Württemberg to abolish serfdom on his estates. In 1824 he tried out a steam-driven printing press and in 1825 and 1826 he operated steamboats on Lake Constance and the Rhine. His son, Johann Georg (1796–1863), expanded the firm's activities by the purchase of other houses (Göschen and Voegel) and the establishment of Bible branches at Stuttgart and Munich. These extensions were abandoned by the next generation, and when Karl von Cotta (Johann Georg's younger son) died in 1888, the firm was purchased by Adolf and Paul Kröner. In 1899 it became a corporation.

Cottabato (kō.tä.bä′tō). See **Cotabato.**

Cottage Grove. City in W Oregon, in Lane County, on the Coast Fork of the Willamette River, in a lumbering, livestock-raising, dairying, and fruit-producing area. 3,536 (1950).

Cottage Hills. Unincorporated residential community in SW Illinois, in Madison County near East St. Louis. 3,357 (1950).

Cottbus (kot′bůs). [Also, **Kottbus.**] City in NE Germany, in the *Land* (state) of Brandenburg, Russian Zone, formerly in the province of Brandenburg, Prussia, situated on the Spree River and near the new Polish border, ab. 68 mi. SE of Berlin: a railroad junction; has livestock markets. Before World War II it was a center of the woolen and cloth industries; there were also metallurgical industries and a chocolate factory. Cottbus has vocational schools for the textile industry, for agriculture, and for commerce. It is a center for excursions in the nearby Spreewald. There are few old buildings. The city came under the electorate of Brandenburg in 1445, and became part of Saxony in 1807 and of Prussia in 1813. In World War II, it was occupied by the Russians on April 24, 1945. The population is predominantly Protestant. 49,131 (1946).

Cotte (kot), **Robert de.** b. 1656; d. 1735. French architect. Versatile and industrious, in his long career he left a considerable impress on French architecture. In the ecclesiastical field he is credited with the design of bishops' palaces at Strasbourg and Verdun, and had a part in the design of the Church of Saint Roch and of the high altar of the Church of Notre Dame in Paris. In association with Jules Hardouin Mansart he created the Grand Trianon at Versailles, and completed the chapel of the chateau there. He was Mansart's successor as royal architect to Louis XV. He executed other public works, and in addition designed some of the most beautiful private residences of that time in Paris.

Cottenham (kot′ẹn.ạm), 1st Earl of. Title of **Pepys,** Sir **Charles Christopher.**

Cottereau (kot.rō), **Jean.** [Called **Jean Chouan.**] b. at St.-Berthevin, Mayenne, France, Oct. 30, 1757; killed near Laval, France, July 29, 1794. Leader (1793–94) of the insurgent royalists (Chouans) in Brittany and the neighboring regions.

Cotter's Saturday Night. Poem by Robert Burns, first published in a volume of poems in 1786.

Cottet (ko.te), **Charles.** b. at Puy, France, 1863; d. at Paris, 1925. French landscape, marine, religious, and genre painter, whose Oriental scenes won him popular acclaim. He studied in France under Puvis de Chavannes and Alfred Philippe Roll, and he first came into prominence as a painter of scenes on the coast of Brittany. A triptych, *Au pays de la mer*, appeared in the Salon of 1898 and is now in the Luxembourg Museum. His pictures in general represent the somber aspects of the lands by the sea and the pathos and sorrows of the people. His work hangs in many important collections in Europe, the U.S., and North Africa. Among his more important paintings are *Rays of the Sun, Women of Brittany, Fishing Boats, Port of Camaret, Dead Child*, and *Pardon of St. Anne.*

Cottin (ko.tañ), **Marie.** [Called **Sophie;** maiden name, **Risteau.**] b. March 22, 1770; d. at Paris, Aug. 25, 1807. French novelist. Her best-known work is *Élisabeth, ou les exilés de Sibérie* (1806).

Cottle (kot'l), **Amos Simon.** b. in Gloucestershire, England, c1768; d. at London, Sept. 28, 1800. English writer; elder brother of Joseph Cottle (1770–1853). He published *Icelandic Poetry, or the Edda of Saemund translated into English Verse* (1797), and several original poems.

Cottle, Joseph. b. 1770; d. at Bristol, June 7, 1853. English bookseller and poet; brother of Amos Simon Cottle. He was a friend of Coleridge, Southey, and Wordsworth, and the publisher of several of their works, including the *Lyrical Ballads* (1798) of Wordsworth and Coleridge. His poetry, *Malvern Hills* (1798), *John the Baptist* (1801), *Alfred* (1801), *The Fall of Cambria* (1809), and *Messiah* (1815), which was of inferior quality, is now known chiefly as an object of Byron's sarcasm. He also wrote *Early Recollections, chiefly relating to Samuel Taylor Coleridge* (1837).

Cotton (ko.tôn), **Aimé Auguste.** b. at Bourg, Ain, France, Oct. 9, 1869—. French physicist. Educated at the École Normale Supérieure, Paris, he was professor of physics at the University of Toulouse (1895–1900), at the École Normale Supérieure (1900–20), and at the Sorbonne (1920–41), where he was also director of the physics research laboratory until his arrest by the Germans during World War II. He served (1938) as president of the French Academy of Sciences. In collaboration with Mouton he constructed an apparatus for studying ultramicroscopic objects. He is the author of *Le Dichroisme circulaire et la dispersion rotatoire anomale des liquides actifs colorés* (1896), *Le Phénomène de Zeeman* (1900; setting forth his studies of the Zeeman effect, which is concerned with the splitting of lines in the spectrum as the result of magnetism), *Les Ultra-microscopes et les objets ultra-microscopiques* (1906), and *Symétrie des critaux et symétrie moléculaire* (1914).

Cotton (kot'on), **Bartholomew de.** d. c1298. English historian, a monk of Norwich. He was the author of the *Historia Anglicana* in three books, of which the first is taken literally from Geoffrey of Monmouth, the second (taken in part from Henry of Huntingdon) comprises the history of England from 449 to 1298, while the third is an abstract and continuation of the *De gestis pontificum* of William of Malmesbury.

Cotton, Charles. b. at Beresford, Staffordshire, England, April 28, 1630; d. at Westminster (now part of London), in February, 1687. English poet, best known as the translator of Montaigne's *Essays* (1685). He published anonymously *The Scarronides, or: The First Book of Virgil Travestie* (1664; reprinted with the fourth book in 1670), a translation of Corneille's *Horace* (1671), *A Voyage to Ireland in Burlesque*, a poem (1670), translations of Gerard's *Life of the Duke of Espernon* (1670) and of the *Commentaries of De Montluc, Marshal of France* (1674), a second part (on fly-fishing) to the fifth edition of Izaak Walton's *Compleat Angler* (1676), and other works. A collection of his poems was published in 1689. His poetry was much admired by Lamb, Wordsworth, and Coleridge.

Cotton, George Edward Lynch. b. at Chester, England, Oct. 29, 1813; drowned at Kushtea, India, Oct. 6, 1866. English educator and prelate, bishop of Calcutta (1858–66). He was (1837–52) assistant master at Rugby under Thomas Arnold, and as such figures in Thomas Hughes's *Tom Brown's School-days.*

Cotton, John. [Sometimes called the **"Patriarch of New England."**] b. at Derby, England, Dec. 4, 1584; d. at Boston, Mass., Dec. 23, 1652. Puritan clergyman; grandfather of Cotton Mather. He served (1612–33) as pastor at Boston, Lincolnshire, England, and, when called to the question for his nonconformity, resigned and came to America with members of his congregation. They settled at Boston (so named from their old home) in 1633. Cotton drew up, at the request of the General Court, an abstract of the laws of Moses, entitled *Moses, his Judicials*, which he handed to the court in October, 1636; and he is said to have introduced in New England the practice of keeping the Sabbath from Saturday evening to that of Sunday. He is principally responsible for the exiles of Anne Hutchinson and Roger Williams, with whom he clashed in upholding his belief in the primary place of religion and its ministers in all aspects of community life while at the same time holding with the supremacy of the magistrates.

Cotton, Sir **John.** b. 1679; d. 1731. English baronet who transferred (1700) the Cottonian Library to the nation. He succeeded his grandfather as 4th baronet. He was the great-grandson of Sir Robert Bruce Cotton (1571–1631), original compiler of the library.

Cotton, Nathaniel. b. at London, 1705; d. at St. Albans, Hertfordshire, England, Aug. 2, 1788. English poet and physician. He studied (1729) medicine in the Netherlands under Hermann Boerhaave, and practiced his profession and operated (1740–88) a lunatic asylum at St. Albans in which the poet William Cowper was a patient from 1763 to 1765. Cotton was the author of the anonymously published *Visions in Verse for the Entertainment and Instruction of Younger Minds* (1751), moral essays, sermons, and a medical paper, *Observations on a Particular Kind of Scarlet Fever* (1749). His *Various Pieces in Prose and Verse* (2 vols., 1791) was edited by his son, Nathaniel. Among his poems are "To a Child of Five Years Old," "The Fireside," and "Content," "Slander," and "Pleasure," from the *Visions.*

Cotton, Sir **Robert Bruce.** b. at Denton, Huntingtonshire, England, Jan. 22, 1571; d. May 6, 1631. English antiquary, a graduate of Cambridge (Jesus College) in 1585, famous as the founder of the Cottonian Library, now in the British Museum. He was an ardent collector of manuscripts in many languages, coins and antiquities of all kinds, and his library was consulted and his aid obtained by Francis Bacon, Ben Jonson, John Speed, William Camden, and many other men of learning of that day. His collection of original documents became so great as to be regarded as a source of danger to the government, and after he had fallen into disfavor at court, on political grounds, an opportunity was found of placing his library under seal (1629), and he never regained possession of it. His son, Sir Thomas Cotton, succeeded in obtaining it, and it remained in the family (though open to the use of scholars and, in 1700, of the public) until 1707, when it was purchased by the nation. It was kept at various places, suffering considerable damage by fire, Oct. 23, 1731, until the founding of the British Museum (1753), when it was transferred to that institution. Cotton was knighted in 1603, and created a baronet in 1611.

Cotton, Sir **Stapleton.** [Title, Viscount **Combermere.**] b. in Denbighshire, Wales, in November, 1773; d. at Clifton, England, Feb. 21, 1865. British general, distinguished in India, and in the Peninsular War, especially at Salamanca (1812). He was governor of Barbados, and commander in chief of the Leeward Islands (1817–20), commander in chief in Ireland (1822–25), and commander in chief in India (1825–30). He captured Bharatpur in 1826.

Cotton, Sir **Thomas.** b. 1594; d. at Connington, England, May 13, 1662. English antiquary; son of Sir Robert Bruce Cotton. He regained, after great effort, possession of his father's library, which had been sealed (1629) by order of Charles I, and allowed scholars free access to the library, to which he added.

Cotton, William Henry. b. at Newport, R.I., July 22, 1880—. American portrait and mural painter and illustrator, who has decorated many New York theaters and is also well known as a caricaturist. He studied at the Cowles Art School, Boston, and the Julian Academy, Paris, exhibiting later in many galleries in the U.S. He was made an associate of the National Academy of Design in 1916, and is a life member of the National Arts Club. He has won prizes at Philadelphia, New York, Dallas, and Boston. He has painted murals for the Capitol, Selwyn, and Apollo theaters at New York, the Hotel Gibson at Cincinnati, Ohio, and at Easton's Beach, Newport, R.I. He has also done illustrations for many magazines.

Cotton Belt. Term applied to the region of the U.S., in the South and the Southwest, which produces the national cotton crop. It had its inception (c1795), soon after the invention of the cotton gin, in South Carolina and Georgia, and on the eve of the Civil War embraced some 400,000 sq. mi.; afterward its center of gravity moved steadily toward the Southwest, with well over half the cotton crop being produced in states west of the Mississippi. Before the Civil War the area east of the Mississippi included virtually all of the cotton kingdom, and was characterized by slavery and plantation economy. The present Cotton Belt is worked to a large degree by sharecroppers and tenant farmers.

Cotton Boll, The. Ode by Henry Timrod, published in his volume *Poems* (1873).

"Cotton Ed Smith." See **Smith, Ellison DuRant.**

Cottrell (kot'rẹl), **Frederick Gardner.** b. at Oakland, Calif., Jan. 10, 1877; d. at Berkeley, Calif., Nov. 16, 1948. American physical chemist who invented the Cottrell process to remove dust and suspended particles from gases by an electrostatic apparatus called the Cottrell Precipitator. He received a B.S. (1896) from the University of California and a Ph.D. (1902) from the University of Leipzig. He was associated (1911–20) with the U.S. Bureau of Mines, was director (1922–27) of the Fixed Nitrogen Laboratory in the U.S. Department of Agriculture, was president (1935–38) of Research Associates, Inc., and was consulting chemist (1940–43) with the Bureau of Plants and Industry.

Cotubanama (kō"tö.bä.nä'mä). See **Cotabanama** or **Cotubanama.**

Cotulla (kọ.tul'ạ). City in S Texas, county seat of La Salle County, NW of Corpus Christi. Cattle, farm products, and oil are produced in the area. 4,418 (1950).

Coty (ko.tē; Anglicized, kō'ti), **François.** [Original surname, **Spoturno.**] b. at Ajaccio, Corsica, 1874; d. at Louveciennes, Seine-et-Oise, France, July 25, 1934. French perfume manufacturer and newspaper publisher. He controlled the famous Paris newspaper, *Le Figaro*, for a decade (1922–32). He also founded (1928) the newspaper *L'Ami du Peuple*, which sold at the low price of ten centimes and rapidly developed a huge circulation. He advocated a vigorously nationalist and pro-fascist policy, especially through the organization La Solidarité Française, which he founded. His election (1923) to the Senate from Corsica was invalidated, but he subsequently won a seat from the Seine district. He lost ownership of *Le Figaro* shortly before his death.

Cotys (kō'tis). Any of several kings of Thrace, especially one who reigned between 382 and 358 B.C., an enemy of the Athenians.

Cotys (kō'tis) or **Cotytto** (kọ.tit'ō). In ancient Greek mythology, a Thracian goddess, resembling the Phrygian Cybele. Her festival, the Cotyttia, was riotous and, later, licentious.

Coubertin (kö.ber.tañ), **Pierre.** b. at Paris, Jan. 1, 1862; d. at Geneva, Switzerland, Sept. 1, 1937. French educator and sportsman. He brought about the revival of the Olympic games, modeled after those of ancient Greece, and founded (1894) and directed (until 1925) the international Olympic committee.

Couch (köch), **Richard Quiller.** b. at Polperro, Cornwall, England, March 14, 1816; d. at Penzance, Cornwall, England, May 8, 1863. English naturalist; uncle of Sir Arthur Quiller-Couch.

Coucy (kö.sē), Châtelain **de.** fl. 12th century. Chevalier and French poet, said to have perished (c1200) in a battle with the Saracens. He is the hero of a popular legend to the effect that when dying he ordered his heart to be sent to his mistress, the Lady of Fayel, whose husband intercepted it and forced her to eat it. She made a vow never to eat again, and died of starvation.

Coucy-le-Château (kö.sē.lẹ.shä.tō). [Also, **Coucy-le-Château-Auffrique** (-ō.frēk).] Village in N France, in the department of Aisne, ab. 15 mi. SW of Laon. It is noted for the ruins of its feudal castle.

Coudekerque-Branche (köd.kerk.bräñsh). Town in N France, in the department of Nord, situated between the canals of Bergues and Bourbourg, SE of Dunkerque. It is an industrial suburb of Dunkerque, known for textile manufactures. A large part of the town was destroyed in World War II. 12,506 (1946).

Coudersport (kou'dėrz.pōrt). Borough in N Pennsylvania, county seat of Potter County, on the Allegheny River: resort community; manufactures include leather, hosiery, and surgical appliances. 3,210 (1950).

Coudert (kö.där'), **Amalia.** [Maiden name, **Küssner.**] b. at Terre Haute, Ind., March 26, 1876; d. at Teritet, Montreaux, Switzerland, in June, 1932. American painter of miniatures, noted for her portraits of European royalty. She studied at New York, then went to London, where she maintained a studio (1896–99). She had (1900 *et seq.*) a studio at New York. She did portraits of King Edward VII and other members of the English nobility. Among the subjects of her later paintings were Cecil Rhodes, the Czar and Czarina of Russia, and the Grand Duchesses Vladimir and Ellen.

Coudert, Frederic René. b. at New York, March 1, 1832; d. Dec. 20, 1903. American lawyer. He was commissioner (1883–84) of public schools at New York, and government director (1884–87) and government receiver (1892–98) of the Union Pacific Railroad. After serving as a member (1880) of the international conference at Berne, and as U.S. counsel (1893–95) in the Bering Sea fur-seal arbitration, he was appointed (1896) to the commission to investigate the Venezuelan boundary dispute.

Coué (kwā; Anglicized, kö'i), **Émile.** b. at Troyes, France, Feb. 26, 1857; d. at Nancy, France, July 2, 1926. French originator of the psychotherapeutic system called Couéism. Until past middle life he was an obscure pharmacist at Troyes, but soon after the turn of the century he began a study of hypnotism and of the therapeutic efficacy of autosuggestion, and in 1910 set up a clinic at Nancy for the practice of his system. His famous formula, "Day by day, in every way, I am getting better and better," which his patients were instructed frequently to repeat, attracted wide attention, and Coué visited England and the U.S., where his lectures were well attended, though his claim to having effected cures of organic illnesses was regarded skeptically by the medical profession. His teachings are summed up in his book *Self-Mastery Through Conscious Autosuggestion.*

Couëron or **Coüeron** (kwä.rôñ). Town in W France, in the department of Seine Inférieure, situated on the estuary of the Loire River, W of Nantes. It has a lead foundry and other metallurgical industries. 8,886 (1946).

Coues (kouz), **Elliott.** b. at Portsmouth, N.H., Sept. 9, 1842; d. at Baltimore, Dec. 25, 1899. American ornithologist and biologist. His works include *Key to North American Birds* (1st ed., 1872), *Field Ornithology* (1874), and part of the *Check-List of North American Birds* (1882). He contributed (1889–91), the definitions of biological (zoölogical) terms to *The Century Dictionary*, and edited the journals of Lewis and Clark on their travels, adding extended notes (1893).

Coughlin (kog'lin), **Charles Edward.** b. in Ontario, Canada, 1891—. American Roman Catholic priest. He was ordained to the Roman Catholic priesthood in 1916 and, coming to the U.S., was in 1926 made pastor of the Shrine of the Little Flower, at Royal Oak, Mich. He resorted to the radio to disseminate his social and political ideas, and during the 1930's his broadcasts influenced vast numbers of listeners, so that at times he decisively influenced national policy and legislation through the medium of many thousands of telegrams and letters which his followers sent to Congress at his request. He supported President Franklin D. Roosevelt during the latter's first term, but turned vigorously critical in 1936. When, however, he promoted a new political party, its candidate for the presidency made a poor showing. During the early years of World War II, his radio addresses and the contents and policy of his magazine, *Social Justice*, were considered by many to be demagogic, tinged with fascistic ideology, and actually sometimes to verge on disloyalty. Eventually *Social Justice* was barred from the mails under the espionage law and ceased publication in 1942, while Coughlin's ecclesiastical superiors, in deference to the government's views and taking account also of allegations that he had amassed a fortune by deals in silver, directed the discontinuance of his radio broadcasts.

Couillet (kö.ye). Town in S Belgium, in the province of Hainaut, situated SE of Charleroi. It is an industrial community, with coal mines, blast furnaces, iron foundries, and chemical, glass, and mirror (plate glass) manufactures. 12,931 (1947).

Coulevain (köl.vaṅ), **Augustine Favre de.** [Pseudonym, **Pierre de Coulevain.**] b. in the Pays de Gex, France, 1838; d. at Lausanne, Switzerland, 1913. French novelist. She was the author of *Noblesse américaine* (1898), *Ève victorieuse* (1901), *Sur la branche* (1904), *L'Île inconnue* (1906), and others. Her work, of minor consequence in France, was translated and much read in Spain.

Coulin (kö'lin). Giant in Spenser's *Faerie Queene*. He was killed when, after jumping across a pit, he slipped back and fell.

Coulmiers (köl.myā). Village in N central France, in the department of Loiret, ab. 13 mi. NW of Orléans. Here, on Nov. 9, 1870, during the Franco-Prussian War, the French (80,000) defeated the first Bavarian army corps (16,000). The loss of the French was 1,500; that of the Bavarians ab. 1,300.

Coulomb (kö.lôṅ), **Charles Augustin de.** b. at Angoulême, France, June 14, 1736; d. at Paris, Aug. 23, 1806. French physicist, noted for experiments on friction and researches in electricity and magnetism. He invented a torsion balance with which he investigated to prove that the electrical charge of a substance is on its surface. He formulated Coulomb's law of the forces existing between charged bodies. The coulomb, a unit of electrical quantity, is named for him.

Coulommiers (kö.lo.myā). Town in N France, in the department of Seine-et-Marne, situated on the Grand Morin River, ab. 33 mi. E of Paris. It is in the heart of a dairy region particularly known for the manufacture of Brie cheeses, and has metallurgical industries. The town has medieval churches and houses, old ramparts, and a castle. In the 16th century it was occupied by the English, in 1814 by the Russians, and in 1870 and 1914 by the Germans. It escaped damage in World War II. 7,660 (1946).

Coulsdon and Purley (kōlz'dọn; pėr'li). Urban district in SE England, in Surrey, ab. 5 mi. S of Croydon, ab. 15 mi. S of Victoria station, London. It is included in the London "Green Belt Scheme." 63,770 (1951).

Coulter (kōl'tėr), **Ellis Merton.** b. near Hickory, N.C., July 20, 1890—. American historian and educator. After serving as a high-school superintendent at Glen Alpine in his native state (1913–14), he taught history and political science at the University of Wisconsin and at Marietta College in Ohio before becoming associate professor of history at the University of Georgia in 1919, and full professor in 1923. He has also lectured extensively at other universities and colleges. His books have established him as one of the leading modern historians of the Civil War and Reconstruction periods in the South, among them *College Life in the Old South* (1928), *John Jacobus Flournoy, Champion of the Common Man in the Antebellum South* (1943), *Georgia: A Short History* (1947), *The South During Reconstruction* (1947), and *The Confederate States of America* (1950). He is the author also of numerous articles and brochures.

Coulter, Ernest Kent. b. in Ohio, Nov. 14, 1871; d. May 1, 1952. American lawyer, founder (1904) of the Big Brother Movement. A graduate (1893) of Ohio State, he received an LL.B. (1904) from New York Law School. He practiced at New York, where he was an organizer (1902–12) of New York children's court, and general manager and assistant (1914–36) to the president of the New York Society for the Prevention of Cruelty to Children. He served (1917–19) in World War I, as major and lieutenant colonel in France, and was commissioned colonel (1920). He wrote *The Children in Shadow* and *The History of Child Protection.*

Coulter, John Merle. b. at Ningpo, China, Nov. 20, 1851; d. Dec. 23, 1928. American naturalist, professor (1896–1925) of botany in the University of Chicago. He was graduated (1870) at Hanover College, Indiana, and was professor (1874–79) of natural sciences there. He was professor (1879–91) of biology at Wabash College, and later (1891–93) was president of, and professor of botany in, the University of Indiana. He served (1893–96) as president of Lake Forest University. He edited the *Botanical Gazette* from 1875. His works include *A Manual of Rocky Mountain Botany* (1885), *A Manual of Texan Botany* (1891), *Morphology of Gymnosperms* (1901; with C. J. Chamberlain), and *Morphology of Angiosperms* (1903; with C. J. Chamberlain). He edited the 6th edition (1890) of Gray's *Manual of Botany.*

Coulton (kōl'tọn), **George Gordon.** b. at King's Lynn, England, Oct. 15, 1858—. English historian, noted expert on medieval history. He studied at Cambridge and Heidelberg, was lecturer (1910 *et seq.*) in history at Cambridge, and professor (1919 *et seq.*) at St. John's College. His works include *St. Francis to Dante* (1906), *Five Centuries of Religion* (1923), *The Medieval Village* (1925), *Art and the Reformation* (1928), *Life in the Middle Ages* (4 vols., 1928–29), and *Medieval Thought* (1939).

Council Bluffs. [Former names, **Miller's Hollow, Kanesville.**] City in SW Iowa, county seat of Pottawattamie County, on the Missouri River: twin city of Omaha, Neb. It is the eastern terminus of the Union Pacific Railroad, a junction point for a number of other lines, and a distribution center for grain. Grapes and roses are also raised in large quantities. It was settled in 1837. Pop. 45,429 (1950).

Council Grove. City in E Kansas, county seat of Morris County, on the Neosho River: center of a cattle-raising and farming area. It was an important point on the Santa Fe Trail. 2,722 (1950).

Councilman (koun'sil.mạn), **William Thomas.** b. at Pikesville, Md., Jan. 1, 1854; d. at York Village, Me., May 26, 1933. American pathologist, professor in Harvard University from 1891. He was associate professor (1886–91) of pathology in the Johns Hopkins University. As a member (1916) of the Hamilton Rice expedition to the headwaters of the Amazon, he investigated tropical diseases.

Council of Ancients. In French history, name given to the upper chamber of the French legislature (*Corps Législatif*) under the constitution of 1795, consisting of 250 members, each at least 40 years old.

Council of Blood. [Also: **Council of Troubles, Court of Blood.**] In the history of the Netherlands, a court established by the Duke of Alva to suppress the popular agitation against the religious and political tyranny of Philip II of Spain. It held its first session on Sept. 20, 1567, and put to death 1,800 persons in less than three months, the counts of Egmont and of Hoorn being among its victims (1568).

Council of Clermont (kler'mont). See **Clermont, Council of.**

Council of Ephesus (ef'ẹ.sus). See **Ephesus, Council of** (449 A.D.).

Council of Ferrara-Florence (fe.rä'rạ.flor'ẹns). See **Ferrara-Florence, Council of.**

Council of Five Hundred. In French history, during the government of the Directory (1795–99), an assembly of 500 members, forming the second branch of the legislative body, the first branch being the Council of Ancients. It was overthrown by Napoleon on Nov. 10, 1799.

Council of Foreign Ministers. Council established at the Potsdam (Berlin) meeting of Great Britain, the U.S., and the U.S.S.R. in July, 1945, as a means for the preparation of peace settlements with the former Axis nations and for the discussion of such other problems as the member governments might refer to it. It was to consist of the foreign ministers of the U.S., Great Britain, the U.S.S.R., France, and China. As of 1952, however, China had taken no part in its meetings, which drafted peace treaties for Italy, Finland, Rumania, and Hungary and, after 1947, vainly considered settlements for Germany and Austria. Its first meeting was held at London in September, 1945.

Council of Frankfort (frank'fọrt). See **Frankfort, Council of.**

Council of Jerusalem (jẹ.rö'sạ.lẹm). See **Jerusalem, Council of.**

Council of National Defense. U.S. agency established (Aug. 29, 1916) by act of Congress and organized (March, 1917) before America's entry into World War I. It was designed to coördinate the country's industries and resources, its functions later being delegated to the War Industries Board and the other wartime agencies. The Council consisted of six cabinet members and seven civilian experts serving without pay.

Council of Pisa (pē'zạ). See **Pisa, Council of.**

Council of Salamanca (sal.ạ.mang'kạ). [Also, **Junta of Salamanca.**] Meeting held at Salamanca, Spain, apparently in the winter of 1486–87, to consider the projects of Columbus. King Ferdinand had referred them to Hernando de Talavera, the queen's confessor, to be laid by him before a gathering of scholars. The opinions of the majority were against Columbus. Probably the importance of this Council has been overestimated.

Council of Seville (sẹ.vil'). [Spanish, **Consejo de Sevilla;** also, **Casa de Contratación de las Indias.**] Office established at Seville, Spain, in 1503 for the regulation of commerce with the Indies.

Council of Siena (si.en'ạ). See **Siena, Council of.**

Council of State. In France, an advisory body existing from early times, but developed especially under Philip IV (1285–1314) and his sons. It was often modified, particularly in 1497 and in 1630 under Richelieu, and played an important part during the First Empire. Its chief duties under the several French republics was to give advice upon various administrative matters and legislative measures.

Council of State Governments. Organization founded in 1925 for the purpose of serving as a clearing house for information and research relating to the states of the American Union. It maintains headquarters at Chicago and issues *Legislative Session Sheet* (weekly), *State Government* (monthly), and *Proceedings: Governors' Conference* (annually).

Council of Ten. In the ancient republic of Venice, a secret tribunal instituted in 1310 and continuing to the overthrow of the republic in 1797. It was composed at first of 10 and later of 17 members, and exercised unlimited power in the supervision of internal and external affairs, often with great rigor and oppressiveness. It had its own secret police and inquisitors, and its sessions were secret and judgment final.

Council of the Indies (in'dēz). Body created in 1511, by King Ferdinand V of Castile, for the regulation of Spanish colonial affairs. Its powers were confirmed and enlarged by Charles V and his successors until they covered every branch of administration.

Council of Troubles. See **Council of Blood.**

Council of Whitby (whit'bi). See **Whitby, Council of.**

Counter, the. Name anciently given to two prisons under the rule of the sheriffs of London, one in the Poultry and one in Wood Street. There was another in Southwark which had the same name. This name was formerly a frequent subject of jokes and puns. Baret, in the *Alvearie* (1573), speaks of one who had been imprisoned as singing "his counter-tenor," and there are various similar allusions in the works of 17th-century dramatists.

Countess Kathleen, The. Poetic tragedy (1892) written by William Butler Yeats for the Irish Literary (which was later to become the famous Abbey) Theatre. The action takes place "in Ireland in old times." Suffering from hunger, the people of the village sell their souls for food to the evil spirits. Kathleen uses her wealth to help them, until the spirits rob her. Unable to stand the misery of her people, she sells her own soul in order to relieve them, well knowing that her act will mean the loss of her own salvation. She is forgiven at the end of the play because her motive was a humane one. The play created a disturbance when it was first produced, and police had to restrain members of the audience who thought that it was an insult to the country and to religion to show an Irishwoman bargaining with the devil and not being punished for it.

Countess of Pembroke's Arcadia, The. See **Arcadia.**

Count Julian (jöl'yạn). Tragedy by Walter Savage Landor, published in 1812. The subject is the story of Roderick, last of the Goths, also treated in Walter Scott's *Roderick.*

Count Julian. Romance by William Gilmore Simms, published in 1845. It is the sequel to *Pelayo* (1838).

Count of Monte Cristo (mon'tẹ kris'tō), **The.** See **Comte de Monte Cristo, Le.**

Count Robert of Paris. Novel by Sir Walter Scott, published in 1831, the 25th of the Waverley novels, in the fourth series of *Tales of My Landlord.* The scene is laid in the 11th century, during the first Crusade, when Godfrey of Bouillon was before Constantinople at the head of the Crusaders. Count Robert was a French Crusader, one of the most famous and reckless of the period.

Country Girl, The. Comedy attributed to Antony Brewer, produced in 1647. John Leanerd reprinted it in 1677, under the title of *Country Innocence,* as his own.

Country Girl, The. Alteration of William Wycherley's comedy *The Country Wife* by David Garrick, who produced it in 1766.

Country House, The. Comedy by Sir John Vanbrugh, produced in 1703. It was translated from the French of Florent Carton Dancourt.

Country House, The. Novel by John Galsworthy, published in 1907. It is a study of country life and customs and a severe condemnation of the complacent attitude towards life.

Country Lasses, or The Custom of the Manor. Play by Charles Johnson, produced in 1715. It was partly taken from John Fletcher and Philip Massinger's *Custom of the Country,* and Thomas Middleton's *A Mad World, My Masters.* John Philip Kemble used it in his *Farm House* (1789), and William Kenrick in *The Lady of the Manor.*

Country of the Blind, The. Collection of short stories by H. G. Wells, published in 1911.

Country of the Pointed Firs, The. Volume of local-color sketches by Sarah Orne Jewett, published in 1896. The book describes life in an isolated village in Maine. Narrated by a boarder at Mrs. Todd's home, the sketches depict the simple life of the fisher folk and the natural beauty of the setting.

Country Party. In English history, a political party, in the reign of Charles II, which opposed the court and sympathized with the nonconformists. It developed into the Petitioners, and later was absorbed into the Whig Party.

Country Party. Australian political party representing the interests of the farmers. It has acted in collaboration with the Liberal Party in opposition to the Labour Party.

Country Wife, The. Comedy by William Wycherley, produced in 1673. It was taken from Molière's *L'École des maris* and *L'École des femmes.*

Country Wit, The. Comedy by John Crowne, produced in 1675. The plot was partly from Molière's *Le Sicilien.*

Counts (kounts), **George Sylvester.** b. near Baldwin City, Kan., Dec. 9, 1889—. American educator. He received a B.A. (1911) from Baker University and a Ph.D. (1916) from Chicago. He was professor of secondary education (1924–26) at Yale, and professor of education at the University of Chicago (1926–27) and at Columbia (1927 *et seq.*). He was director (1942 *et seq.*) of Columbia's foundations of education division. He is the author of *Arithmetic Tests and Studies in the Psychology of Arithmetic* (1917), *The Selective Character of American Secondary Education* (1922), *The Senior High School Curriculum* (1926), *The American Road to Culture* (1930), *The Social Foundations of Education* (1934), *The Education of Free Men* (1941), *Education and the Promise of America* (1945), and other works.

County of London (lun'dọn). See **London, County of.**

Coupar-Angus or **Coupar Angus** (kö'pėr.ang'gus). Police burgh and market town in C Scotland, in Perthshire, situated near the river Isla, ab. 12 mi. NW of Dundee, ab. 457 mi. N of London by rail. It became an important linen-weaving center after 1850. The town has the ruins of an abbey founded in 1164 on the site of an old Roman camp. 2,223 (est. 1948).

Couper (kö'pėr), **William.** b. at Norfolk, Va., 1853; d. 1942. American sculptor. He began his art study at

Cooper Union, at New York, but went abroad in 1874, studying first at Munich and then going to Florence in the following year to become the pupil of Thomas Ball and to marry the latter's daughter. He remained in Italy until 1897, when he established his studio at New York. He executed many portrait busts, those of Henry Wadsworth Longfellow and President William McKinley being typical, and his ideal sculptures, both in the round and in bas-relief, were much admired.

Couperin (köp.rañ), **Armand Louis.** b. at Paris, Feb. 25, c1725; d. there, Feb. 2, 1789. French composer and organist at the Church of Saint Gervais, Paris (1748 *et seq.*) and to the king (1770 *et seq.*); son of Nicolas Couperin (1680–1748) and father of Gervais François Couperin (1759–1826). His works consist mainly of chamber music.

Couperin, Charles. b. 1638; d. at Paris, 1679. French organist at the Church of Saint Gervais, Paris; father of François Couperin (1668–1733) and brother of François (c1631–c1701) and Louis Couperin.

Couperin, François. [Called **"Sieur de Crouilly."**] b. c1631; d. at Paris, c1701. French composer and instrumentalist; brother of Charles and Louis Couperin, father of Nicolas Couperin, and uncle of François Couperin (1668–1733).

Couperin, François. b. at Paris, Nov. 10, 1668; d. there, Sept. 12, 1733. French organist and harpsichord player, and the first great composer for the harpsichord exclusively; son of Charles Couperin. He wrote many suites and pieces for the harpsichord, and these, as well as his method of playing the instrument, expounded in his book on the subject, had a strong influence on Bach and on the subsequent development of the art. Couperin was organist (1698–1733) at the Church of Saint Gervais, Paris.

Couperin, Gervais François. b. at Paris, May 12, 1759; d. there, in July, 1826. French organist; son of Armand Louis Couperin (1727–89). Like his father, he was organist at the Church of Saint Gervais, Paris.

Couperin, Louis. b. c1626; d. at Paris, Aug. 29, 1661. French organist (c1650 *et seq.*) at the Church of Saint Gervais, Paris, and composer of works for harpsichord, organ, violin, and viol; brother of Charles Couperin and François Couperin (c1631–c1701), and uncle of François Couperin (1668–1733).

Couperin, Nicolas. b. at Paris, Dec. 20, 1680; d. there, July 25, 1748. French organist (1733 *et seq.*) at the Church of Saint Gervais, Paris; son of François Couperin (c1631–c1701) and father of Armand Louis Couperin.

Couperus (kö.pā′rus), **Louis.** b. at The Hague, Netherlands, June 10, 1863; d. near Arnhem, Netherlands, July 16, 1923. Dutch novelist, a subtle delineator of psychic overrefinement and decay. These qualities are expressed in *Eline Vere* (1889; trans. into English), also *Noodlot* (Eng. trans., *Footsteps of Fate*, 1890), *Extaze* (Eng. trans., *Ecstasy*, 1892), *De Stille Kracht* (Eng. trans., *The Hidden Force*, 1900), *Langs lijnen van geleidelijkheid* (1900; Eng. trans., *The Law Inevitable*, also *Inevitable*), and the four *Boeken der kleine zielen* (1901–03; Eng. trans., *Small Souls*, *The Later Life*, *The Twilight of Souls*, and *Dr. Adriaan*). Couperus came to full development in his historical novels, descriptions of decay in the classical world; these included *Dionyzos* (1904), *Babel* (1901; trans. into English), *De Berg van Licht* (The Mountain of Light, 1906), *Antiek tourisme* (1911; Eng. trans., *The Tour*), *Herakles* (1913), *De Komedianten* (1917; Eng. trans., *The Comedians*), *Xerxes* (1919; Eng. trans., *Arrogance, the Conquests of Xerxes*), and *Iskander* (1920). Apart from these was the ironical novel *Het zwevende schaakbord* (The Flitting Chessboard, 1923). Other works by Couperus translated into English are *Majesteit* (Majesty, 1893), *Psyche* (1898), *Van oude menschen, de dingen, die voorbijgaan* (Old People and the Things that Pass, 1906), *Oostwaarts* (Eastward, 1924), and *Nippon* (1925). The richness of his language is difficult to translate.

Coupler (kup′lėr), **Mrs.** A matchmaker or go-between in Sir John Vanbrugh's play *The Relapse*, and in Richard Brinsley Sheridan's adaptation of it, *A Trip to Scarborough.*

Courant (kö′ränt), **Richard.** b. at Lublinitz, Germany, Jan. 8, 1888—. Mathematician noted especially for his work in the theory of functions, the calculus of variations, and mathematical physics. He studied at Breslau and Zurich, took his doctorate at Göttingen in 1910, and taught at Göttingen (1912–18, 1921–33), Münster (1919–20), Cambridge (1933–34), and New York University (1934 *et seq.*). His works include *Methoden der mathematischen Physik* (with D. Hilbert; 2 vols., 1924–27), *Vorlesungen über Differential- und Integralrechnung* (2 vols., 1927–29), and *Supersonic Flow and Shock Waves* (with K. O. Friedrichs, 1948).

Courantyne (kō′ran.tīn). [Also: **Corantyn, Corentyn, Corentyne**; Dutch names: (upper course), **Coeroeni**; (lower course), **Corantijn.**] River of South America which separates British Guiana and Surinam (Dutch Guiana). It flows into the Atlantic Ocean. Length, ab. 300 mi.; navigable 150 mi.

Courbet (kör.be), **Gustave.** b. at Ornans, Doubs, France, June 10, 1819; d. at La Tour de Peilz, Vaud, Switzerland, Dec. 31, 1877. French painter, chief of the realists who turned the trend of French painting away from mid-19th-century neoclassicism and romanticism. He studied theology at Besançon, but abandoned it for the study of art, which he pursued at Paris under Karl von Steuben and others and then through his own study of earlier masters. He was especially influenced by the Flemish and Venetian masters. Courbet's democratic tendencies led him to turn down Napoleon III's offer of the cross of the Legion of Honor. He became a member of the Commune of Paris in 1871, and directed the destruction of the column in the Place Vendôme. On the fall of the Commune he was imprisoned, and later was condemned to pay the cost of reërecting the column. He escaped to Switzerland in 1873. *After Dinner at Ornans*, *Funeral at Ornans*, *The Stonebreakers*, and *The Painter's Studio* are among his best-known paintings.

Courbevoie (kör.bẹ.vwȧ). Town in N France in the department of Seine, situated on the Seine River, 1 mi. NW of the former fortifications of Paris. An industrial suburb of Paris, it suffered damage in World War II. 55,080 (1946).

Courcelles (kör.sel). Town in S Belgium, in the province of Hainaut, NW of Charleroi. It is an industrial community, with coal mines, iron foundries, and glassworks; manufactures of mirrors (plate glass) is a specialty. 16,287 (1947).

Courcelles. [Also, **Courcelles-sur-Nied** (-sür.nyā).] Village in NE France, in Lorraine, situated near Metz. The battle fought near here on Aug. 14, 1870 is better known as the battle of Colombey.

Courier (kö.ryā), **Paul Louis.** b. at Paris, Jan. 4, 1772; murdered near Véretz, Indre-et-Loire, France, Aug. 18, 1825. French Hellenist and political writer. He studied at the artillery school at Châlons, and served in the army (1792–1809). In 1809 he went to Italy and in 1812 returned to France and lived upon his estate at Véretz. He edited the *Daphnis and Chloe* of Longus in 1810, and published *Le Pamphlet des Pamphlets* (1824). His collected works were published in 1834.

Courland (kör′lạnd). [Also, **Kurland.**] Former district of Russia, the southernmost of the Baltic provinces, bounded by the Gulf of Riga and Livonia (separated by the Dvina River) on the N, Vitebsk (separated by the Dvina) on the E, Kovno on the S, and the Baltic Sea on the W. The region is now chiefly in Latvia, with a small part in Lithuania. Its surface is mostly level, and abounds in lakes, but in parts is hilly. Three fourths of the inhabitants were Letts, but the land proprietors were mainly German. The prevailing religion was Protestant. Courland came under the control of the Teutonic Order in the middle of the 13th century, became a hereditary duchy and fief of Poland in 1561 or 1562, and passed to Russia in 1795. The capital was Jelgava.

Courmayeur (kör.mȧ.yėr). [Also: **Cormajeur**; Italian, **Cormaggiore, Cormajore.**] Village in NW Italy, in the *compartimento* (region) of Valle d'Aosta, formerly part of Piedmont, in the province of Aosta, situated near the foot of Mont Blanc. It is a tourist center. 1,264 (1936).

Cournos (kör′nọs), **John.** b. at Kiev, Russia, March 6, 1881—. American author. He arrived (1891) at Philadelphia and has lived in the U.S. except for a period (1922–30) spent in England. He has translated novels from the Russian, has edited anthologies, and is the author of original novels including *The Mask* (1919), *The Wall* (1921), *Babel* (1922), *The New Candide* (1924), *Miranda*

Masters (1926), and *Wandering Women* (1930). He edited the *Treasury of Russian Life and Humor* (1943).

Cournot (kör.nō), **Antoine Augustin.** b. 1801; d. 1877. French mathematician and economist, noted as a student of the mathematics of probability, and as a pioneer in developing applications of mathematics to problems of economics, a work for which he was well qualified by a sound knowledge of both sciences. His *Researches into the Mathematical Principles of the Theory of Wealth* (1838) is a book still studied and respected, as is his last work, *Revue sommaire des doctrines économiques* (1877).

Courrières (kö.ryer). Town in N France, in the department of Pas-de-Calais, situated on the canal of Lens and La Souchez, E of Béthune. It is a coal-mining town, remembered for the accident which took place here, March 10, 1906, killing more than 1,000 miners. The town suffered severe damage during World War II. 5,053 (1946).

Cours (kör). Town in E France, in the department of Rhône, ab. 33 mi. NW of Lyons. It manufactures cotton cloth and other textiles. 5,194 (1946).

Course of Time, The. Religious poem by Robert Pollok, published in 1827.

Court (kōrt). [Full name, **Alexander Court.**] In Shakespeare's *Henry V*, a soldier in the king's army.

Court (kör), **Antoine.** b. at Villeneuve-de-Berg, in Vivarais, France, May 17, 1696; d. at Lausanne, Switzerland, June 14, 1760. French Protestant clergyman, the chief restorer of the Reformed Church in France; father of Antoine Court de Gébelin. Because of his activity in organizing the scattered elements of the Calvinist groups, a reward was offered for his capture. Court fled to Lausanne, where he founded (c1730) and directed until his death a training seminary for Calvinist ministers.

Courtall (kōrt'ôl). Rake in Hannah Cowley's comedy *The Belle's Stratagem.* At a masquerade, he costumes himself like Lady Frances Touchwood's husband, tries to seduce her, and is foiled by Saville.

Court and City. Comedy adapted from Richard Steele's *Tender Husband* and Frances Sheridan's *Discovery*, produced by Richard Brinsley Peake.

Courtauld (kôr'tōld; French, kör.tō), **Augustine.** b. 1686; d. 1751. French founder of a Huguenot family in England, which by the early 19th century became owner of one of the largest silk manufactures and which is now one of the leading producers of rayons. Augustine himself, however, was a goldsmith, who resided at Chelsea. He died leaving a lucrative trade, being worth about 2,000 pounds.

Court Beggar, The. Play by Richard Brome, produced in 1632, printed in 1653.

Court de Gébelin (kör dẹ zhā.blaṅ), **Antoine.** b. at Nîmes, France, 1725; d. at Paris, May 10, 1784. French scholar; son of Antoine Court. He was one of the collaborators in the pro-American periodical *Affaires de l'Angleterre et de l'Amérique* (1776 *et seq.*). His works include *Le Monde primitif analysé et comparé avec le monde moderne* (1775–84), *Lettre sur le magnétisme animal* (1783), and *Histoire naturelle de la parole, ou grammaire universelle.*

Courteline (kör.tẹ.lēn), **Georges.** [Pseudonym of **Georges Moineaux;** sometimes called the **"Mark Twain of France."**] b. at Tours, France, June 25, 1861; d. at Paris, June 25, 1929. French humorist and playwright, specialist in a sort of gaily pessimistic satire reminiscent of Molière. He was the author of *Les Gaîtés de l'escadron* (1886), *Boubouroche* (1893), and others. At least part of his success lay in his ability to revivify the traditional themes of French comedy, especially the satire of women. After his military service and a brief period in the civil service, he devoted his entire life to the theater. He was awarded a prize by the French Academy (1926), was elected to the Goncourt Academy (1926), and was made a commander of the Legion of Honor.

Courtenay (kôrt'ni, kōrt'ni), **Edward.** [Title, **Earl of Devonshire.**] b. c1526; d. at Padua, Italy, in September, 1556. English nobleman; son of Henry Courtenay, Marquis of Exeter and Earl of Devonshire. He was committed to the Tower of London with his father in 1538, attainted in 1539, and released and restored in blood in 1553. Later he became an aspirant for the hand of Queen Mary, and on her choosing Philip II of Spain turned his attention to the Princess Elizabeth. He was suspected of complicity in Thomas Wyatt's rebellion, and was again sent to the Tower (1554), but was released on parole and exiled.

Courtenay, Henry. [Titles: Marquis of **Exeter,** Earl of **Devonshire.**] b. c1496; beheaded on Tower Hill, London, Dec. 9, 1538. English nobleman. He was (1520) a member of the privy council, upheld Henry VIII in his divorce proceedings against Catherine of Aragon, and was one of those who tried (1536) Anne Boleyn. He had some correspondence with Reginald Pole, who was attempting to arouse Continental forces to unseat Henry VIII and, because he was of royal blood, was accused of aspiring to the throne. He was arrested on a charge of treason in November, 1538, tried, condemned, and executed.

Courtenay, William. b. at Exeter, England, c1342; d. at Maidstone, Kent, England, July 31, 1396. English prelate, archbishop of Canterbury (1381–96). He studied at Oxford and became chancellor of the university in 1367. He became bishop of Hereford in 1370, and of London in 1375. He was an opponent of Lollardism and the prosecutor of Wycliffe.

Courthope (kôrt'ōp), **William John.** b. at South Malling, near Lewes, England, July 17, 1842; d. at Sussex, near Whiligh, England, April 10, 1917. English poet, historian of poetry, critic, editor, and biographer. He was educated at Harrow, and at Corpus Christi College and New College, Oxford. He won the Newdigate prize for poetry in 1864, and the Chancellor's Prize for English prose in 1868, with an essay on *The Genius of Spenser.* From 1895 to 1900 he was professor of poetry at Oxford, delivering a series of lectures published (1901) as *Life in Poetry, Law in Taste.* He wrote a life (1882) of Addison for the *English Men of Letters* series, and edited five (of the ten) volumes of the standard Elwin-Courthope edition of Pope's *Works.* As a poet he wrote *Ludibria Lunae* (1869), an allegorical and political satire, *The Paradise of Birds* (1870), especially attractive to young readers, *The Country Town and Other Poems* (1920), the "town" being his native Lewes, *The Hop Garden* (1905), suggestive of passages in Vergil, and other verse contributed to the *National Review* and *Blackwood's Magazine.* His chief work, the one by which he is remembered, is *The History of English Poetry*, in six volumes (1895–1910). A worthy example of English scholarship, it completes a work planned by Pope, contemplated by Gray, and begun, but not finished, by Thomas Warton. It begins with Chaucer (although there are chapters on poets and poetry before him) and ends with Scott.

Courths-Mahler (kůrts'mä'lėr), **Hedwig.** b. at Nebra, Germany, Feb. 18, 1867; d. at Tegernsee, Germany, Nov. 27, 1950. German novelist. Her numerous works of light fiction have enjoyed great popularity in Germany. She was the author of *Untreu* (1907), *Liselottes Heirat* (1911), and many others.

Courtin', The. Verse narrative in dialect by James Russell Lowell, appearing in the second series of *The Biglow Papers* (1867).

Courtly (kōrt'li, kôrt'li), **Charles.** In Dion Boucicault's comedy *London Assurance*, a fashionable young man about town. He is the son of Sir Harcourt Courtly, who persists in believing him a studious, retiring boy. Charles succeeds in securing the heart and hand of Grace Harkaway, the heiress, who has been promised to his father.

Courtly, Sir Harcourt. In Dion Boucicault's comedy *London Assurance*, an elderly fop devoted to fashion, and betrothed to a young heiress, Grace Harkaway, who finally rejects him and marries his son Charles.

Courtly, Sir James. In Susannah Centlivre's comedy *The Basset-Table*, a gay, airy, witty, and inconstant gentleman, devoted to gaming.

Courtney (kôrt'ni, kōrt'ni), **Charles Edward.** b. at Union Springs, N.Y., Nov. 13, 1849; d. July 17, 1920. American single sculler, both amateur (1868–77) and professional (1877–85). He was head crew coach (1885–1916) at Cornell University.

Courtney, Sir **Christopher Lloyd.** b. June 27, 1890—. English air officer. He served (1914–18) in the Royal Naval Air Service during World War I, was a member (1925–28) of the directing staff at the Royal Air Force Staff College, acted as chief staff officer (1931–33) of the Iraq Command, and directed (1933–34) training at the Air Ministry. He became director of operations and intelligence and deputy chief (1935–36) of air staff, and headed (1937–38) British air forces in Iraq. He was air marshal in command of the R.A.F.'s reserve command (1939–40), and a member (1940–45) of the Air Council for Supply and Organization.

Courtney, Leonard Henry. [Title, 1st Baron **Courtney of Penwith.**] b. at Penzance, Cornwall, July 6, 1832; d. May 11, 1918. English politician and author. He was professor (1872–75) of political economy in University College, London, Liberal member of the House of Commons for Liskeard, Cornwall (1876–85), and Liberal-Unionist member for the Bodmin division of Cornwall (1885–1900). He was undersecretary of state for the home department (1880–81), and for the colonies (1881–82), financial secretary to the treasury (1882–84), and chairman of committees and deputy speaker (1886–92). He wrote *The Working Constitution of the United Kingdom and its Outgrowths* (1901). He was created Baron Courtney of Penwith in 1906. He was a crusader for proportional representation, and an opponent of the Boer War and a seeker for peace in World War I.

Courtney, William Leonard. b. at Poona, India, Jan. 5, 1850; d. at London, Nov. 1, 1928. English journalist and author, editor (1894 *et seq.*) of the *Fortnightly Review.* He was (1872–90) a fellow at Oxford, then acted (1890–1924) as literary editor and drama critic for the London *Daily Telegraph.* Among his publications are *Studies in Philosophy* (1882), *Constructive Ethics* (1886), *Life of J. S. Mill* (1889), *The Development of Maeterlinck* (1904), *The Feminine Note in Fiction* (1905), and *The Literary Man's Bible* (1907).

Court of Blood. See **Council of Blood.**

Court of Commerce, U.S. Tribunal established by act of the U.S. Congress (June 18, 1910) for the purpose of handling the increasing flow of litigation in civil suits brought under the Elkins Act, the Interstate Commerce Act, and similar federal legislation. It was composed of five judges serving five-year terms. The impeachment, conviction, and removal (1913) of Judge Robert W. Archbald, one of its members, brought to a head the demand for the court's dissolution, and the body was abolished by Congress on Oct. 22, 1913. It was thought that some of the court's decisions had indicated strong sympathy for railroad interests.

Court of Lions. Celebrated court in the Alhambra, at Granada, Spain. Its many arches, supported by marble columns, surround a basin into which 12 figured lions pour the fountain of water.

Court of Love, The. Poem of 1,400 lines attributed to Chaucer by Stowe, and inserted in the 1561 edition, but believed to be of later origin. The poem is an allegory, written in rhyme royal.

Courtois (kör.twȧ), **Bernard.** b. 1777; d. 1838. French chemist. In 1811 he made the important discovery of the element iodine, and extracted it from the ash of seaweed.

Courtois, Gustave Claude Étienne. b. at Pusey, Haute-Saône, France, March 18, 1852; d. 1923. French painter, especially of portraits; a pupil of Gérôme. He obtained the second grand prix de Rome in 1877, and a gold medal and the decoration of the Legion of Honor at the exposition of 1889.

Courtois, Jacques. [Italian, **Jacopo Cortese;** called **le Bourguignon,** Italian, **Il Borgognone.**] b. at St.-Hippolyte, Doubs, France, 1621; d. at Rome, Nov. 14, 1676. French painter. He did battle scenes, especially of cavalry engagements, that are considered the best, by some, of the genre in his time. In 1655 he became a lay brother of the Jesuit order, and thereafter painted sacred subjects.

Court Party. In English history, a political party in the reign of Charles II, which supported the policy of the court. Its successor was the party of the Abhorrers, and later the Tories.

Courtrai (kör.trā). [Also: **Courtray;** Flemish, **Kortrijk, Kortryk;** ancient name, **Cortoriacum.**] Town in NW Belgium, in the province of West Flanders, situated on the Lys River, ab. 15 mi. NE of Lille. It has important linen, woolen, and cotton textile industries, and lace manufactures. Buildings of interest include a museum, an art academy, and a number of old churches. The Church of Our Lady dates from the 13th century, the Church of Saint Martin from the 14th–15th centuries, and the Church of Saint Michael from the 17th century; there is a belfry and a Gothic town hall of the 16th century. In the early Middle Ages, the town was destroyed by the Normans, but was rebuilt by Count Baldwin III of Flanders in the 10th century. Here, on July 11, 1302, the burghers of Ypres and Bruges defeated the French knights in the "Battle of the Spurs," so called because more than 700 pairs of spurs were afterwards taken from the bodies of French knights slain in the field. About half of the town's buildings were damaged by bombings during World War II. 39,813 (1947).

Court Secret, The. Play by James Shirley, printed in 1653, not acted till after the Restoration.

Courtship of Miles Standish (mīlz stan′dish), **The.** Poem by Henry Wadsworth Longfellow, published in 1858. Miles Standish, military chief of Plymouth, feels that he is too blunt-spoken to succeed in wooing Priscilla, so he asks his friend John Alden to speak to her for him. The girl, recognizing John's own love for her despite his loyal pressing of Standish's suit, asks: "Why don't you speak for yourself, John?" Standish is supposedly killed on an expedition against the Indians and John and Priscilla plan to marry. Standish turns up alive, shows that he is not angry, and the marriage proceeds.

Court Theatre. Theater in Sloane Square, London. It was opened in January, 1871, for the performance of lighter dramas. The building, which was originally erected in 1818 as a chapel, replaced an older theater.

Courvoisier (kör.vwȧ.zyā), **Louis Félix.** b. at Basel, Switzerland, Nov. 10, 1843; d. there, April 8, 1918. French surgeon. He was a military surgeon during the Franco-Prussian War. He became (1880) Privatdocent of surgery at the University of Basel and professor in 1888, and then succeeded Socin as full professor. He is known for his methods of surgery of the gall bladder and for his laws for determining malignant disease of the pancreas and the gall bladder. He also devised a method of operation to relieve pyloric obstruction, described a sign of a chronically obstructed gall bladder (Courvoisier's gall bladder), and devised (1883) a posterior gastroenterostomy to relieve pyloric obstruction. He was the author of *Die häusliche Krankenpflege* (1874), *Die Neurome* (1886), and *Kasuistisch-statistische Beiträge zur Pathologie und Chirurgie der Gallenwege* (1890).

Couse (kous), **Eanger Irving.** b. at Saginaw, Mich., 1866; d. 1936. American painter, especially of the American Indian. After studying for a time at the National Academy of Design at New York, he went to Paris and became a pupil of Bouguereau. Returning to the U.S., he established his studio at Taos, N.M., and concentrated largely on the depiction of the American Indian and scenes from Indian life. He was chosen a member of the National Academy of Design in 1911. His paintings are widely distributed in art galleries throughout the U.S.

Cousin (kö.zaṅ), **Jean.** b. at Soucy, near Sens, France, c1500; d. at Sens, France, c1590. French painter, engraver, and sculptor, noted especially for his paintings on glass and his miniatures.

Cousin, Jean. [Called **Jean the Younger.**] b. at Sens, France, c1522; d. 1594. French painter and writer on art; son of Jean Cousin (c1500–c1590). Although he was a noted portraitist, his most important achievements were, like those of his father, in the art of stained glass, and the work of the two men in this field has often been confused. The glass painting in the church of Saint Gervais at Paris is generally attributed to Jean the Younger, and it is known that he was the artist of the windows of the castle of Fleurigny at Sens. He was also the author of *Livre de Perspective* (1560), and of *Livre de Pourtraicture* (1571).

Cousin, Victor. b. at Paris, Nov. 28, 1792; d. at Cannes, France, Jan. 13, 1867. French philosopher and statesman. He began lecturing at the Sorbonne in 1815, traveled in Germany in 1817 and 1818, and was deprived (1820) of his position at the Sorbonne for political reasons. He traveled again in Germany in 1824, and was arrested at Dresden and imprisoned for a short time at Berlin. He regained (1828) his position at the Sorbonne, and became a member of the Council of Public Instruction in 1830, and minister of public instruction in 1840. As a philosopher he was at first a follower of the Scottish psychological school, but later under German influences developed a kind of eclecticism. His works include *Fragments philosophiques* (1826–28), *Cours d'histoire de la* *philosophie* (1827–40), *Cours d'histoire de la philosophie morale au XVIIIe siècle* (1840–41), *Cours d'histoire de la philosophie moderne* (1841), *Des pensées de Pascal* (1842), *Madame de Longueville* (1853), *Du vrai, du beau, et du bien* (1854), and *Histoire générale de la philosophie* (1864).

Cousine Bette (kö.zēn bet), **La.** Novel by Honoré de Balzac, published in 1846, and by some considered his best work.

Cousin-Montauban (kö.zaṅ.môṅ.tō.bäṅ), **Charles Guillaume Marie Apollinaire Antoine.** See **Palikao, Charles Guillaume Marie Apollinaire Antoine Cousin-Montauban,** Comte **de.**

Cousin Pons (kö.zaṅ pôṅs), **Le.** Novel by Honoré de Balzac, published in 1847.

Cousins (kuz'inz), **Samuel.** b. at Exeter, England, May 9, 1801; d. at London, May 7, 1887. English mezzotint engraver. He is best known for his copper engravings of Sir Thomas Lawrence's paintings. Among the other artists whose works were reinterpreted by Cousins were Joshua Reynolds and John Millais.

Coussemaker (kös.må.ker), **Charles Edmond Henri de.** b. at Bailleul, Nord, France, April 19, 1805; d. at Bourbourg, France, in January, 1876. French magistrate, and writer on the history of music. His works include *Histoire de l'harmonie au moyen âge* (1852), *Chants populaires des Flamands de France* (1856), and *L'Art harmonique au XIIe et XIIIe siècles* (1865).

Coustou (kös.tö), **Guillaume.** b. at Lyons, France, April 25, 1677; d. at Paris, Feb. 20, 1746. French sculptor, younger brother of Nicolas Coustou, and father of Guillaume Costou (1716–77). His most famous work is the group of Horses of Marly in the Champs-Elysées at Paris. Among his other works are the allegorical figures of the Ocean and the Mediterranean at Marly, the colossal statue of the Rhône at Lyons, those of Bacchus, Minerva, Hercules, and Pallas, and a great number of bas-reliefs.

Coustou, Guillaume. [Called **Guillaume the Younger** or **Guillaume II.**] b. at Paris, 1716; d. there, July 13, 1777. French sculptor; son of Guillaume Coustou (1677–1746). His statues of Venus and Mars, of heroic size, executed on the commission of the king of Prussia, and his monument to the dauphin and dauphiness of France, erected in the cathedral at Sens, were greatly admired. The Emperor Joseph II, during a visit to Paris, conferred on him the order of Saint Michael.

Coustou, Nicolas. b. at Lyons, France, Jan. 9, 1658; d. at Paris, May 1, 1733. French sculptor; brother of Guillaume Coustou (1677–1746). He learned the rudiments of his art from his father, a woodcarver, and at 18 entered the atelier of Antoine Coysevox, his uncle, then president of the Academy of Painting and Sculpture at Paris. Among his works are a Descent from the Cross, at Notre Dame, the colossal allegorical figures of the Seine and Marne, in the Tuileries Gardens, and many statues in the Tuileries and Versailles. He became a member of the French Academy in 1693.

Coutances (kö.täṅs). [Latin, **Constantia.**] Town in NW France, in the department of Manche, beautifully situated on top of a hill, ab. 40 mi. S of Cherbourg. The town suffered much in World War II when heavy fighting occurred here in the course of the Normandy invasion. The Cathedral of Notre Dame, one of the most beautiful religious buildings of the region, dating mainly from the 13th century, and the Church of Saint Pierre were severely damaged. Coutances is a center for trade in grain, cattle, and other agricultural products. 5,479 (1946).

Couthon (kö.tôṅ), **Georges.** b. at Orcet, near Clermont, France, c1755; guillotined at Paris, July 28, 1794. French revolutionist. He was deputy to the Legislative Assembly in 1791, and to the Convention in 1792. Couthon became an extreme Jacobin, though at the beginning of the revolution he was a constitutional monarchist. He directed the capture of Lyons when the counterrevolutionaries controlled the city but failed to mete out sufficiently drastic punishment and was relieved (Oct. 29, 1793) by Collot d'Herbois. He was president of the Convention and one of the Triumvirate with Robespierre and Saint-Just. The three were executed at the same time.

Coutinho (kō.tē'nyö), **José Joaquim da Cunha Azevedo.** See **Azevedo Coutinho, José Joaquim da Cunha.**

Couto (kō'tö), **(Rui) Ribeiro.** b. at Santos, Brazil, March 12, 1898—. Brazilian poet, novelist, short-story writer, journalist, lawyer, and diplomat. His books of poetry include *O jardim das confidências* (1921), *Poemetos de ternura e de melancolia* (1924), and *Um homem na multidão* (1926). Among his other works are the novels *Cabocla* (1931) and *Prima Belinha* (1940), the books of short stories *Baianinha e outras mulheres* (1927) and *Clube das esposas enganadas* (1933), and the volumes of sketches *A cidade do vício e da graça* (1924), *Conversa inocente* (1935), and *Chão de França* (1935).

Coutras (kö.trå). Town in SW France, in the department of Gironde, on the Dronne River ab. 25 mi. E of Bordeaux. Here, on Oct. 20, 1587, a victory was gained by Henry IV of France (Henry of Navarre) over the Holy League (of French anti-Protestant Roman Catholics). The town once contained a noted castle, now destroyed.

Coutts (köts), **Thomas.** b. at Edinburgh, Sept. 7, 1735; d. at London, Feb. 24, 1822. English banker, the founder, with his brother James, of the London banking house of Coutts and Company. His third daughter, Sophia, married Sir Francis Burdett.

Couture (kö.tür), **Thomas.** b. at Senlis, France, Dec. 21, 1815; d. near Paris, March 30, 1879. French painter, a pupil of Antoine Gros and Paul Delaroche and teacher of Édouard Manet and Puvis de Chavannes. He won the second grand prix de Rome in 1837. He first exhibited in the Salon in 1840 (*Jeune Venétien après une orgie*). Among his works are *L'Enfant prodigue, Une Veuve, Le Retour des champs* (1843), *Le Trouvère* (1844), *Joconde* (1847), and *Les Romains de la décadence* (1847).

Couturier (kö.tü.ryā), **Paul Vaillant-.** See **Vaillant-Couturier, Paul.**

Couvray (kö.vrā), **Jean Baptiste Louvet de.** See **Louvet de Couvray, Jean Baptiste.**

Couvreur (kö.vrėr), **Adrienne.** Original name of **Lecouvreur, Adrienne.**

Couzens (kuz'ẹnz), **James.** b. at Chatham, Ontario, Canada, Aug. 26, 1872; d. Oct. 22, 1936. American automobile manufacturer and politician. He came to the U.S. in his youth, and was associated (1903 *et seq.*) with Henry Ford in the manufacture of motor cars. Couzens had accumulated a fortune when he sold (1919) his interests to the Fords. He was mayor (1919–22) of Detroit, and senator (1922–36) from Michigan.

Covadonga (kō.bä.ᴛʜông'gä). Locality in N Spain, in E Oviedo province ab. 104 mi. by rail W of Santander. In 718 A.D. Don Pelayo with his small force of 300 men was besieged here by the Moors. They were hiding in caves and hurling stones and logs down on the great forces, when a sudden storm caused the river to flood the narrow valley, sweeping the Moorish army to its destruction. The independence of Asturias was saved, and the event was looked upon as a miracle, with the result that the shrine of Santa María de Covadonga was built here. There are several hotels to accommodate pilgrims and tourists.

Covarrubias (kō.vạ.rö'bi.ạs), **Miguel.** b. at Mexico City, 1902—. American painter, illustrator, and author. He arrived at New York in 1923, and won prompt acceptance with his caricatures and his studies of New York night life and metropolitan personalities, which have appeared in leading magazines. A versatile artist, with a keen eye, an original approach, a flair for large and simple design, and a competent technique, he has executed paintings, lithographs, and stage designs. In the 1930's and 1940's he traveled abroad, studying primitive societies and their cultures, among other regions in the island of Bali and in southern Mexico. Among the fruits of these travels were the books *Island of Bali* (1937) and *Mexico South* (1946), written and illustrated by the artist.

Covenanters. In Scottish history, name of the group which, in the 16th and 17th centuries, banded together in solemn covenants to defend and support Presbyterianism. The first of these religious covenants was that of 1557, by which certain Scottish adherents of the Reformation united to promote the evangelical movement. The fear of a revival of Roman Catholicism led to a second covenant in 1581. In 1638 the efforts of Archbishop Laud, supported by King Charles I, to impose an episcopal organization and the Book of Common Prayer on the Church of Scotland, was met by the National Covenant, which denounced all ecclesiastical measures inconsistent with the principles of the Reformation, demanding that such proposals be submitted to an uncoerced Parliament and Assembly. In November of that year the General Assembly declared against the episcopal and for the presbyterian system in Scotland. Charles thought to exact obedience by force, but faced by a determined army of Covenanters, agreed to abide by the decisions of the General Assembly. Again the Assembly, and the Scottish Parliament as well, declared for the presbyterian system, and in addition decreed certain limitations on royal authority, and in 1640 a Scottish army advanced into England with the purpose of compelling the king's compliance. This made it necessary for Charles to summon the English Parliament which is known in history as the Long Parliament and which was to become the source of Charles's downfall. In the ensuing English Civil War the Scots joined forces with the English Parliament when the latter accepted the Solemn League and Covenant, which called for changes in English church government in the direction of stricter Protestant concepts. Charles in May, 1646, surrendered to the Scottish army which, when he continued to reject the Solemn League and Covenant, turned him over to the English Parliamentary army. Following the ascendancy of the Independents in the English army and Parliament, war broke out between the Scots and the English, the former being defeated by Cromwell at Preston in 1648, and after the beheading of Charles I, the Scots espoused the cause of Charles II upon his acceptance of the Solemn League and Covenant. But, defeated by Cromwell in 1651, Charles II had to flee Britain, and when in 1660 he was finally restored to his father's throne, he agreed to the restoration of episcopacy and the suppression of Presbyterianism, measures which were only effectuated after many Presbyterians had been put to death. There followed nearly three decades of sanguinary struggle in Scotland, marked by new covenants and by determined rebellions which were ruthlessly suppressed, until peace was gradually restored in the aftermath of the English Revolution of 1688.

Cove Neck. See under **Oyster Bay,** N.Y.

Covent Garden (kuv′ẹnt). Space in London, between the Strand and Longacre, which as early as 1222 was the convent garden belonging to the monks of Saint Peter, Westminster. It was originally called Frère Pye Garden. During the period of dissolution when church properties were being taken by the crown it was granted with neighboring properties, by Edward VI, to the protector Edward Seymour, Duke of Somerset. After his attainder in 1552 it went to John Russell, 1st Earl of Bedford. The square was laid out for Francis Russell, 4th Earl of Bedford, and partly built (c1631) by Inigo Jones, whose church, Saint Paul's, Covent Garden, still remains, although rebuilt. The holdings of the Bedfords in this neighborhood were enormous. At one time Covent Garden's coffee houses and taverns were the fashionable lounging places for the authors, wits, and noted men of the kingdom. Dryden, Otway, Steele, Fielding, Peg Woffington, Kitty Clive, Samuel Foote, Barton Booth, David Garrick, and others were among its frequenters. It is now chiefly known as the site of Covent Garden Market, where fruits, flowers, and vegetables have been sold since the 17th century.

Covent Garden Journal. Biweekly periodical first issued in January, 1752, by Henry Fielding, under the name of "Sir Alexander Drawcansir, Knight, Censor of Great Britain." It was discontinued before the end of the year.

Covent Garden Market. Vegetable, fruit, and flower market held in Covent Garden, London. The space began to be used for this purpose during the 17th century by the venders from the villages nearby.

Covent Garden Theatre. [Also, **Covent Garden Opera House.**] Theater in Bow Street, Covent Garden, London, built by John Rich, the famous harlequin of Lincoln's Inn Fields Theatre, in 1731. It was opened, under the dormant patent granted by Charles II to Sir William Davenant, with Congreve's comedy *The Way of the World*, on Dec. 7, 1732. There was no first appearance at this house of any importance until that of Peg Woffington in *The Recruiting Officer*, on Nov. 8, 1740. In 1746 Garrick played here. During Rich's management pantomime reigned supreme. Rich died in 1761, leaving the theater to his son-in-law John Beard, the vocalist. In 1767 it was sold to George Colman the elder, Harris, Rutherford, and Powell for 60,000 pounds. On March 15, 1773, Goldsmith's play *She Stoops to Conquer* was brought out here. In 1774 Harris undertook the management alone. In 1803 John Kemble bought a one-sixth share in the patent-right from Harris for 22,000 pounds, and became manager. In September, 1808, the house was burned. Eight months later it was rebuilt, according to the design of Robert Smirke the architect, in imitation of the Parthenon (the pediment by John Flaxman), at a cost of 300,000 pounds. John Philip Kemble was still manager. On account of the great expense of the undertaking Kemble raised the price of admission and built an extra row of boxes. This brought about the famous O.P. (old price) riots, which lasted 61 days and resulted in a general reduction. On June 29, 1817, John Kemble was followed as manager by Charles Kemble. In 1822 the theater was thrown into chancery. In 1847, after a number of managers had tried to succeed with it, it commenced a new career as The Royal Italian Opera House, but on March 4, 1856, it was burned down. It was rebuilt and the present house opened May 15, 1858.

Coventry (kuv′ẹn.tri, kov′-). City, county borough, and manufacturing town in C England, in Warwickshire, situated on the river Sherbourne, ab. 17 mi. SE of Birmingham, ab. 94 mi. NW of London by rail. Its manufactures include automobiles, motorcycles, aircraft, radio apparatus and electrical equipment, heavy machinery, woolens, and rayons. It was formerly noted for its woolens ("Coventry true blues"). Coventry also has a bronze industry. The cathedral and much of the town was destroyed by air raids in World War II, especially in the huge raids of mid-November, 1940. Its chief buildings are the churches of Saint Michael, the Trinity, and Saint John, Christchurch, and St. Mary's Guildhall. According to legend it obtained its municipal rights from Earl Leofric of Mercia about 1044 by the ride of his wife, Lady Godiva, through the town naked. 258,211 (1951).

Coventry. Town in C Rhode Island, in Kent County, on the Pawtuxet River, ab. 14 mi. SW of Providence: textiles. 9,869 (1950).

Coventry, Countess of. Title of **Gunning, Maria.**

Coventry, Sir **John.** d. 1682. English Royalist during the English Civil War; nephew of Sir William Coventry. His nose was slit (1670) by Sir Thomas Sandys and others, as a result of his allusion, during a House of Commons debate on a tax for playhouses, to the relations of Charles II with Nell Gwyn and Moll Davies. He had earlier (1661) been made a Knight of the Bath for his loyalty to Charles during the Interregnum.

Coventry, Thomas. [Title, 1st Baron **Coventry.**] b. in Worcestershire, England, 1578; d. at London, 1640. English judge, remembered as the mediator (1629) between Charles I and the Parliamentary leaders. He became (1603) a member of the Inner Temple, and subsequently recorder of London (1616), solicitor general (1617), attorney general (1621), and lord keeper (1625). As judge (1634) of the Court of Star Chamber, he moderated its tyrannical actions.

Coventry, Sir **William.** b. c1628; d. at Somerhill, England, June 23, 1686. English Royalist, politician, and soldier. He fought with the Royalist army in the English Civil War. He was secretary (1660) to the Duke of York (later King James II), and was appointed (1662) commissioner of the navy and became a close friend of Samuel Pepys. He was (1665–68) a member of the Privy Council. His speeches in the House of Commons were largely responsible for the resignation (1667) of Edward Hyde, Earl of Clarendon. He was forced to leave the Privy Council (1668) as a result of his challenge of the Duke of Buckingham, George Villiers, who was about to caricature him on the stage.

Coventry Canal. Canal in C England, in Warwickshire. It extends N past Nuneaton to the vicinity of Tamworth. The canal rises 96 ft. through a series of 14 locks. Most of the traffic is comprised of coal and coke. Length, ab. 33 mi.

Coventry Plays. Series of 42 religious plays acted at Coventry, England, from an early date until about 1591. The first mention of them is in 1416. Some of these plays were written in 1468, but the title is thought to be of later date.

Coverdale (kuv′ėr.dāl), **Miles.** b. in the North Riding of Yorkshire, England, 1488; d. in February, 1568. First translator of the whole Bible into English. He studied at Cambridge, was ordained priest in 1514 at Norwich, and joined the Austin friars at Cambridge, where he was influenced by Robert Barnes, the prior, who was burned as a Lutheran heretic in 1540. About 1526 he assumed the habit of a secular priest, and, leaving the convent, devoted himself to evangelical preaching. In 1531 he took his degree as bachelor of canon law at Cambridge. He was probably on the Continent the greater part of the time from then until 1535. In this year his translation of the Bible from Dutch and Latin into English appeared at Zurich with a dedication to Henry VIII. This translation was based on William Tyndale's translations of the Old and New Testaments, the Vulgate, and Luther's German translation, among others. In 1538 he was sent by Thomas Cromwell to Paris to superintend a new English edition of the Bible. This was known as the "Great Bible." A second "Great Bible," known as "Cranmer's Bible" (1540), was also edited by him. He returned from Paris in 1539, but in 1540, on the execution of Cromwell, he was obliged to leave England. Shortly afterward he married Elizabeth Macheson. This repudiation of the celibacy of the priesthood identified him with the Reformers. He lived at Tübingen for a short time, and was made doctor of divinity. From 1543 to 1547 he lived at Bergzabern (Deux-Ponts, now Zweibrücken) in the Palatinate, Germany, as Lutheran minister and schoolmaster. In 1548 he returned to England, and was appointed chaplain to the king (Edward VI) through Cranmer's influence. In 1551 he was appointed bishop of Exeter, but was deprived of this office in 1553 when Mary I came to the throne, and went again to Bergzabern. It has been said that he assisted in preparing the Geneva Bible. In 1559 he again came to England, where Elizabeth now was queen. In 1563 he received from Cambridge the degree of doctor of divinity, and obtained the living of Saint Magnus, near London Bridge. In 1566 he resigned this office on account of his objection to the enforced strict observance of the liturgy. He continued preaching, however, and was listened to by great numbers of people.

Coverdale, Miles. Relater of events in *The Blithedale Romance* (1852) by Nathaniel Hawthorne. Coverdale's character has many points of intellectual affinity with that of Hawthorne himself.

Covered Wagon, The. Historical romance (1922) of pioneer life in the American West, by Emerson Hough. The story, which deals with the settlement and development of the West, was successful both as a book and as a motion picture.

Coverley (kuv′ėr.li), **Sir Roger de.** Chief character in the club that supposedly wrote *The Spectator;* an English country gentleman. He was sketched by Steele and developed by Addison. The name is taken from that of a country dance, similar to the American Virginia reel, which, according to Addison's fiction, was invented by Sir Roger's great-grandfather.

Covielle (ko.vyel). Valet of Cléonte in Molière's comedy *Le Bourgeois Gentilhomme.* His subtle inventions win the hand of Lucille for his master and that of Nicole the cook for himself.

Coviello (kō.vyel′lō). Conventional clown in old Italian comedy.

Covilhã (kö.vē.lyäṅ′). [Also, **Covilhão** (-lyouṅ′).] Town and *concelho* (commune) in C Portugal, in the province of Beira Baixa, in the district of Castelo Branco, situated in the Serra Estrella mountains, N of Castelo Branco. A center of the Portuguese textile industry, it manufactures woolen and cotton cloth, and has dye works. There are alkaline thermal springs in the vicinity. Pop. of concelho, 60,608 (1940); of town, 19,044 (1940).

Covilhão (kö.vē.lyouṅ′), **Pedro de.** [Also, **Covilham** or **Covilhã.**] b. at Covilhã, Portugal, c1450; d. in Ethiopia, c1540. Portuguese navigator. He was sent by John II of Portugal to Asia, in 1487, in search of the legendary Prester John. Having visited the principal towns of Ethiopia and Malabar and sent home a report of his journey, he presented himself in 1490 at the court of the prince of Ethiopia, who treated him with great kindness, but forced him to remain in the country. His report is said to have been of use to Vasco da Gama in his discovery of the route to India round the Cape of Good Hope.

Coville (kō′vil), **Frederick Vernon.** b. at Preston, N.Y., March 23, 1867; d. Jan. 9, 1937. American naturalist, assistant botanist of the U.S. Department of Agriculture and curator of the National Herbarium from 1893. In 1902 he procured the establishment, by the Carnegie Institution, of the Desert Botanical Laboratory, located at Tucson, Ariz. He published *Botany of the Death Valley Expedition* (1893) and various scientific papers.

Covina (kō.vē′na). City in S California, in Los Angeles County, E of Los Angeles in the San Gabriel Valley, in a citrus-growing region. 3,956 (1950).

Covington (kuv′ing.tǫn). City in N Georgia, county seat of Newton County: marketing and manufacturing center for cotton. 5,192 (1950).

Covington. City in N Kentucky, county seat of Kenton County, on the Ohio River, at the mouth of the Licking River, opposite Cincinnati, Ohio: second largest city in the state. Its industries produce beer, alcohol, yeast, razor-wrapping machinery, x-ray equipment, bricks, tile, rope, and tobacco products. 64,452 (1950).

Covington. Town in SE Louisiana, parish seat of St. Tammany Parish: year-round resort. 5,113 (1950).

Covington. Town in W Tennessee, county seat of Tipton County: shipping point for cotton. 4,379 (1950).

Covington. Town in C Virginia, county seat of Alleghany County, on the Jackson River: paper mills. 5,860 (1950).

Cowansville (kou′ąnz.vil). Town in Quebec, Canada, situated on the Yamaska River, in the SE part of the province, ab. 49 mi. SE of Montreal and ab. 15 mi. N of the Vermont border. 4,431 (1951).

Coward (kou′ąrd), **Noel.** b. at Teddington, England, Dec. 16, 1899—. English playwright, actor, and composer. He first appeared on the stage in 1910. His stage works include the plays *I'll Leave It to You, The Vortex* (1923), *Easy Virtue* (1925), *Fallen Angels* (1925), *Hay Fever* (1925), *The Queen Was in the Parlour* (1927), *The Marquise* (1927), *Sirocco* (1927), *Private Lives* (1930), *Cavalcade* (1931, made into a successful motion picture in 1932), *Design for Living* (1933), *Conversation Piece* (1934), *Point Valaine* (1934), *Operette* (1938), *Blithe Spirit* (1941), and *Peace in Our Time* (1947); the one-act group of plays *To-Night at Eight-Thirty* (1935); the revues *This Year of Grace* (1928), *On with the Dance, Words and Music* (1932), and *Sigh No More* (1945); the operettas *Bitter Sweet* (1929) and *Pacific 1860* (1946); the motion pictures *The Scoundrel* (1933), *In Which We Serve* (1942), and *This Happy Breed* (1945). He has published his autobiography, *Present Indicative* (1937) as well as *Collected Sketches and Lyrics* (1931), *To Step Aside* (1939), and *Middle East Diary* (1945). Coward's virtuosity of style, his sophistication, and his laconic wit have exerted some influence on other playwrights.

Cowdenbeath (kou′dęn.bēth). Police burgh and coal-mining center in E Scotland, in Fifeshire, ab. 7 mi. W of Kirkcaldy, ab. 416 mi. N of London by rail. 13,638 (est. 1948).

Cowdry (kou′dri), **Edmund Vincent.** b. at Macleod, Alberta, Canada, July 18, 1888—. American anatomist and biologist. He taught anatomy at the University of Chicago (1909–13), at the Johns Hopkins University (1913–17), and at the Peking Union Medical College in China (1917–21). From 1921 to 1928 he was an associate member of the Rockefeller Institute, and in the latter year became professor of cytology at Washington University, St. Louis, so continuing until 1941, when he took the chair of anatomy at the same institution. He has traveled widely in connection with scientific expeditions and as a lecturer, and has been active in many scientific bodies. He edited works on cytology and biology, and is the author of *Textbook of Histology* (1934) and *Microscopic Technique* (1943).

Cowell (kou′ęl), **Edward Byles.** b. Jan. 23, 1826; d. Feb. 9, 1903. English Sanskrit scholar. He was appointed professor at the Presidency College, Calcutta, in 1864, and Sanskrit professor at Cambridge, England, in 1867, the first to hold the position.

Cowell, John. b. at Ernsborough, Devonshire, England, 1554; d. at Cambridge, England, Oct. 11, 1611. English jurist. He was regius professor of civil law at Cambridge from 1594 to 1610, master of Trinity Hall in 1598, and vice-chancellor of the university in 1603 and 1604. He was the author of a legal dictionary entitled *The Interpreter, a booke containing the signification of words . . . mentioned in the lawwriters or statutes . . .* (1607). Certain passages in the book offended both the Commons and the king; the author was summoned before the council in 1610, and his dictionary was burned by the common hangman.

Cowell, Joseph Leathley. [Original name, **Hawkins Witchett.**] b. near Torquay, England, Aug. 7, 1792; d. near London, Nov. 13, 1863. English actor. He painted portraits, and was a clever and popular actor, particularly in the U.S., where he played (1821–44 and later) especially as Crack in *The Turnpike Gate.* He published an amusing autobiography in 1844. His daughter Sydney Frances (Mrs. H. L. Bateman) was the mother of Kate Bateman, the American actress.

Cowen (kou'ẹn), Sir **Frederic Hymen.** b. at Kingston, Jamaica, Jan. 29, 1852; d. at London, Oct. 6, 1935. English composer and conductor. From 1863 to 1868 he frequently appeared as a pianist. He conducted the London Philharmonic Society (1888–92, 1900–07), the concerts of the Melbourne Exposition in 1888, and the Hallé Orchestra (1896–99). His compositions include orchestral works (his *Scandinavian Symphony,* 1880, bringing him into general notice), concertos, operas, songs, and choral and chamber music. He was knighted in 1911.

Cowen, Joseph. b. at Blaydon, Durham, England, July 9, 1831; d. at Newcastle, Northumberland, England, Feb. 18, 1900. English editor, statesman, and social reformer. He was a contributor to the Newcastle *Daily Chronicle,* of which he was later owner and editor, and founder of the monthly *Northern Tribune.* He served (1873–86) as Liberal member of Parliament for Newcastle. Interested in the revolutionary philosophies of 1848, he aided Polish, Hungarian, and Russian revolutionists and their programs, supported the English Chartist movement, and preceded Gladstone as an advocate of home rule for Ireland.

Cowes (kouz). [Former name, **West Cowes.**] Urban district, seaport, and seaside resort in S England, in the Isle of Wight (an administrative county of the geographical county of Hampshire), situated on the river Medina, at its influx to the Solent, ab. 10 mi. SW of Portsmouth. It was amalgamated with East Cowes in 1933. West Cowes Castle is the headquarters of the Royal Yacht Squadron. 17,154 (1951).

Cowgate (kou'gāt), **the.** Noted and once fashionable street in the Old Town of Edinburgh. The suburb, situated on the southern side of the city in a valley, through which the street runs, was first enclosed within the walls in 1513.

Cowl (koul), **Jane.** [Original surname, **Cowles** (koulz).] b. at Boston, Dec. 14, 1884; d. at Santa Monica, Calif., June 22, 1950. American actress. She made (1903) her Broadway stage debut in *Sweet Kitty Bellaire,* and later scored outstanding successes in *Romeo and Juliet, Antony and Cleopatra, First Lady,* and *Old Acquaintance.* Miss Cowl also starred in such productions as *The Road to Rome, Within the Law, Common Clay, Lilac Time, Smilin' Through, Paola and Francesca, Rain from Heaven,* and *Camille.* She took a prominent part in New York Stage Door Canteen activities during World War II.

Cowles (kōlz), **Alfred Hutchinson.** b. at Cleveland, Ohio, Dec. 8, 1858; d. Aug. 13, 1929. American metallurgist, pioneer in electric smelting. He was co-organizer (1885) with his brother, and president (1895 *et seq.*), of the Electric Smelting and Aluminum Company, and president also of the Pecos Copper Company (1902–21) and the Cowles Detergent Company (1923 *et seq.*). He was awarded (1886) the Elliot Cresson and John Scott Legacy medals.

Cowles, Henry Chandler. b. at Kensington, Conn., Feb. 27, 1869; d. Sept. 12, 1939. American botanist. He was graduated (1893) from Oberlin College, and granted (1898) the Ph.D. degree from the University of Chicago, where he taught (1902–34) botany, becoming professor in 1915 and serving as chairman (1925–34) of the department of botany. He was a special field assistant (1895) for the U.S. Geological Survey. He wrote *Vegetation of Sand Dunes of Lake Michigan* (1899), *Plant Societies of Chicago* (1901), *Textbook of Plant Ecology* (1911), and *Plant Societies of Chicago and Vicinity* (1913), and was editor (1925–34) of the *Botanical Gazette.*

Cowley (kou'li), **Abraham.** b. at London, 1618; d. at Chertsey, Surrey, England, July 28, 1667. English metaphysical poet and essayist. The son of a stationer, he studied at Westminster and at Cambridge (B.A., 1639; M.A., 1642), and retired to Oxford (St. John's College) in 1644. He identified himself with the Royalists, and followed the queen, Henrietta Maria, to France in 1646. He carried messages from the exiles back to the British Isles several times, and coded the letters from the queen to Charles I. He remained in the service of the exiled court until 1656, when he returned to England, and finally settled (1665) at Chertsey. He was buried in Westminster Abbey. He was the author of *Poetical Blossoms* (1633) published while he was still at school, *Love's Riddle* (1638), a pastoral play, *The Mistress* (1647), and *Miscellanies* (1656). The last includes "Davideis," an unfinished epic poem in four books on the Biblical subject of David, his "Pindarique Odes," and several elegies. The first collected edition of his works appeared in 1668.

Cowley, Hannah. [Pseudonym, **Anna Matilda;** maiden name, **Parkhouse.**] b. at Tiverton, Devonshire, England, 1743; d. there, March 11, 1809. English poet and dramatist, daughter of a bookseller of Tiverton, and wife of a captain in the service of the East India Company. She was the author of *The Runaway* (acted February, 1776), *The Belle's Stratagem* (acted February, 1780), and *A Bold Stroke for a Husband* (acted February, 1783). Under the pseudonym "Anna Matilda," which has become a synonym for sentimentality, she carried on a poetical correspondence in the *World* with Robert Merry, who adopted the signature "Della Crusca."

Cowley, Malcolm. b. at Belsano, Pa., Aug. 24, 1898—. American writer, critic, editor, and translator. He was literary editor (1929–44) of *The New Republic.* He is the author of the collection of verse *Blue Juniata* (1929), the autobiographical *Exile's Return* (1934), and *The Dry Season* (1941); coeditor of *Books That Changed Our Minds* (1939); editor of *The Portable Faulkner* (1946), *The Portable Hawthorne* (1948), and *The Complete Whitman* (1948). His translations from the French include Paul Valéry's *Variety* (1926) and André Gide's *Imaginary Interviews* (1944).

Cowley and Iffley (if'li). Ward of the city of Oxford, in S central England, in Oxfordshire, situated on the river Thames, in the SE portion of Oxford. Iffley is noted for its church, which is of small size, but in many ways remarkable for the interesting moldings and other details of its early Norman architecture. It has a massive square central tower, also of Norman date. Cowley and Iffley has grown rapidly with the development of automobile manufacture at Cowley. 12,174 (1931).

Cowpens (kou'pẹnz, kup'ẹnz). Town in NW South Carolina, in Spartanburg County, ab. 8 mi. NE of Spartanburg, formerly important for cattle raising. Here, on Jan. 17, 1781, the Americans (ab. 1,000) under Daniel Morgan defeated 1,100 British under Tarleton. The loss of Americans, killed or wounded, was 72; that of the British, 800–900, 600 of them prisoners. 1,879 (1950).

Cowper (kö'per, kou'pėr), **Edward.** b. 1790; d. at Kensington, London, Oct. 17, 1852. English inventor of various important improvements in printing processes, including the system of inking-rollers and (with Augustus Applegath) the four-cylinder newspaper press. He became professor of mechanics at King's College, London.

Cowper, Francis Thomas de Grey. [Title, 7th Earl **Cowper.**] b. at London, June 11, 1834; d. at Panshanger, Hertfordshire, England, July 19, 1905. English nobleman and lord lieutenant of Ireland. A graduate (1855) of Oxford, Cowper was a pioneer in the voluntary army movement. After being appointed (1880) lord lieutenant of Ireland under Gladstone, he urged renewal of the Coercion Act. He arrested Parnell and suppressed (1880) the Land League. Cowper resigned (1882) and left Dublin two days before the Phoenix Park murders of the chief secretary for Ireland and the undersecretary. He opposed (1886) Gladstone's Home Rule Bill. He served as president (1886–87) of the royal commission on the workings of the Irish land acts of 1881 and 1885.

Cowper, Frank Cadogan. b. at Wicken Rectory, Northamptonshire, England, Oct. 16, 1877—. English painter, noted for his portraits and his romantic subjects from history and literature. He studied at the Cranleigh School and at the Royal Academy Schools, where he won the second Armitage prize. Later he exhibited regularly at the Royal Academy and elsewhere in England. His principal works include *The Devil Disguised as a Troubador*, *Lucretia Borgia* (in the Tate Gallery), and a fresco in the Houses of Parliament.

Cowper, William. [Title, 1st Earl **Cowper.**] b. c1665; d. Oct. 10, 1723. English statesman and jurist. He entered Parliament in 1695, became lord keeper and privy councilor in 1705, served on the commission which drew up the Act of Union (with Scotland) in 1706, and became the first lord chancellor of Great Britain on May 4, 1707. He presided at the trial of Dr. Sacheverell in 1710, resigned his office in September, 1710, was reappointed in September, 1714, and again resigned in 1718. He was a member of the Royal Society.

Cowper or **Cooper** (kö′pėr, kůp′ėr), **William.** b. in Sussex, England, 1666; d. March 8, 1709. English surgeon and anatomist at London, remembered chiefly for his study of the muscles and for his discovery of what are known as Cowper's glands. Cowper's originality was brought out by a controversy with a Dutch surgeon, Bidlo, who claimed that Cowper merely copied from his works. Cowper wrote *Myotomia Reformata; or a New Administration of the Muscles of the Humane Bodies . . .* (1694) and *The Anatomy of Humane Bodies . . .* (1698); his paper on Cowper's glands was published in 1702. Other papers reveal that his knowledge in pathology and comparative anatomy was equally respectable.

Cowper, William. b. at Great Berkhamstead Rectory, Hertfordshire, England, Nov. 26, 1731; d. at Dereham, Norfolk, England, April 25, 1800. English poet. Motherless at six, he entered Westminster School, London, at an early age, receiving there an excellent classical education. Later he studied law and entered the Middle Temple. He was called to the bar in June, 1754. A few years later, when a contemplated marriage with his cousin Theodora was forbidden by her father, Cowper returned to the law, verse writing, and the Nonsense Club in London. His funds eked out by his remuneration as a commissioner of bankrupts (1759), Cowper struggled against loneliness, insecurity, and religious doubt until 1763. It was at that time that anxiety over a public examination designed to secure him a clerical post in the House of Lords precipitated the first violent attack of that recurrent emotional insanity which was at last to destroy him. Taken to Dr. Nathaniel Cotton's asylum at St. Albans in December, 1763, Cowper finally recovered and experienced religious conversion. In June, 1765, he went to Huntingdon, shortly entering the household of Morley Unwin. After Unwin's death (1767), Cowper removed with the family to Olney, where he collaborated with John Newton, a Calvinist preacher, in producing the *Olney Hymns* (1779). The strain of religious duties, aggravated, perhaps, by a convention-impelled betrothal to the widowed Mary Unwin, induced another acute depression in January, 1773. In February of that year Cowper experienced the dream of God's explicit reprobation, which was to be thereafter a lurking obsession in his mind. Upon recovering he renounced marriage but shared the home of Mary Unwin until her death in 1796. Although Cowper attributed the fancied abandonment to his failure to commit suicide, a supposed divine command, biographers have equated the fatal dream with a belief in predestination, implicitly and explicitly rejected in various letters and poems. Far from doctrinaire, Cowper discounted scriptural "circumstantials" and considered metaphysics "a serious trifle." Notwithstanding depressions, the poet spent many fruitful years at Olney and (after 1786) at Weston, producing volumes of letters, translations from French, Italian, Latin, and Greek (Homer in 1791), and much felicitous verse inspired by the "slow-winding" Ouse region. The satires (*Poems*, 1782), were surpassed by *Tirocinium*, *John Gilpin*, and especially *The Task* (1785), which reflects the poet's patriotism, social concern, and fervid joy in nature. Lord David Cecil and other distinguished biographers have related the story of Cowper. According to John C. Bailey, who edited some letters and the *Poems* (1905), "to read him is to feel one's self in the presence of one of the most delightful of human beings."

Cowperwood (kö′pėr.wůd, kou′-), **Frank.** Philadelphia financier who is the central character of *The Financier* (1912; rev. ed., 1927), *The Titan* (1914), and *The Stoic* (1947), novels by Theodore Dreiser.

Cox (koks), **David.** b. near Birmingham, England, April 29, 1783; d. at Harborne Heath, near Birmingham, June 7, 1859. Noted English landscape painter, son of a Birmingham blacksmith. Among his best-known pictures are *Washing Day* (1843), *The Vale of Clwyd* (1846), *Peace and War* (1846), *Going to the Hay-field*, *The Challenge* (1853), and *The Summit of the Mountain* (1853).

Cox, Sir **George William.** b. at Benares, India, Jan. 10, 1827; d. at Walmer, Kent, England, Feb. 9, 1902. English historian, clergyman, and mythologist. Son of a captain in the service of the East India Company, he was educated at Rugby and at Trinity College, Oxford (B.A. and M.A., 1859). Ordained in 1850, he was in South Africa (1853–54) with Bishop John William Colenso, whose biography he wrote in 1888. He served as literary consultant (1861–85) for Longmans, Green and Company, London publishers, and rector (1881–87) of Scrayingham, Yorkshire. Although elected (1886) bishop of Natal to succeed Colenso, he never held the office. He was the author of *Poems Legendary and Historical* (1850), *Tales from Greek Mythology* and *The Great Persian War* (both 1861), *Manual of Mythology* (1867), *Latin and Teutonic Christendom* and *Mythology of the Aryan Nations* (both 1870), *History of Greece* and *The Crusades* (both 1874), *Greeks and Persians* and *The Athenian Empire* (both 1876), *Introduction to the Science of Comparative Mythology* (1881), and *Lives of Greek Statesmen* (1886); editor of *Dictionary of Science, Literature, and Art* (3 vols., 1865–67).

Cox, Jacob Dolson. b. at Montreal, Canada, Oct. 27, 1828; d. at Magnolia, Mass., Aug. 8, 1900. American Civil War general and politician. He served in West Virginia in 1861 and 1862, at Antietam in 1862, and in Georgia and Tennessee in 1864. He was governor of Ohio (1866–68), and secretary of the interior (1869–70).

Cox, James Middleton. b. at Jacksonburg, Ohio, March 31, 1870—. American newspaper publisher and politician who was Democratic candidate (1920) for president. He worked as a correspondent for the Cincinnati *Enquirer*, and in 1898 bought the Dayton *Daily News*. Thereafter he acquired the Springfield (Ohio) *Press-Republic* (1903) and Springfield (Ohio) *Sun* (1928), established (1923) the Miami *Daily News*, and bought (1939) the Atlanta *Journal*. He served as U.S. congressman (1909–13) from Ohio, governor (1913–15, 1917–21) of Ohio, and vice-chairman of the American delegation to the World Monetary and Economic Conference (1933) at London.

Cox, Kenyon. b. at Warren, Ohio, Oct. 27, 1856; d. March 17, 1919. American painter; son of Jacob D. Cox and husband of Louise Howland King Cox. He studied three years at the McMicken Art School at Cincinnati. In 1876 he went to the Philadelphia Academy of the Fine Arts and in 1877 to Paris, where he studied first under Carolus Duran, and later under Cabanel and Gérôme, in the École des Beaux-Arts, where he remained about three years. In 1883 he established himself at New York.

Cox, Louise Howland King. b. at San Francisco, 1865; d. 1945. American painter; wife of Kenyon Cox (1856–1919). She studied at the National Academy of Design, New York, and at the Art Students League of New York, and was long active as a painter, especially of portraits, her pictures of children being particularly admired. She is represented by the painting *May Flowers* in the National Gallery of Art at Washington.

Cox, Palmer. b. at Granby, Canada, April 28, 1840; d. there, July 24, 1924. Canadian illustrator and author of juveniles, remembered for the "Brownie" books. His work was written and published in the U.S. He was a contributor (1880 *et seq.*) to the *St. Nicholas Magazine*, and author and illustrator of *Squibs of California or Every-day Life Illustrated* (1875), *Hans Von Pelter's Trip to Gotham* (1876), *How Columbus Found America* (1877), *The Brownies, Their Book* (1887), *Another Brownie Book* (1890), *The Palmer Cox Brownie Primer* (1906), *Brownie Clown in Brownie Town* (1907), *The Brownies' Latest Adventures* (1910), and *The Brownies Many More Nights* (1913).

Cox, Sir **Percy Zachariah.** b. in November, 1864; d. at Melchbourne, Bedfordshire, England, Feb. 20, 1937.

English soldier and administrator. He served as consul and political agent at Muscat, Arabia (1899–1904), chief political officer (1914–18) of Indian Expeditionary Force "D," acting British minister (1918–20) to Persia, and high commissioner (1920–23) for Mesopotamia. In 1923 he was appointed British plenipotentiary for negotiations with Turkey and in 1924 was Indian representative at the Geneva conference on the control of the international arms traffic.

Cox, Richard. b. at Whaddon, Buckinghamshire, England, 1500; d. July 22, 1581. English prelate, appointed bishop of Ely in 1559. He was translator of the Acts of the Apostles and of Paul's Epistle to the Romans for the "Bishops' Bible."

Cox, Samuel Hanson. b. at Rahway, N.J., Aug. 25, 1793; d. at Bronxville, N.Y., Oct. 2, 1880. American Presbyterian clergyman. He was ordained in 1817, became pastor of the Spring Street Church at New York in 1821 and of the Laight Street Church in 1825, and was named professor of pastoral theology at Auburn in 1834. In 1837 he became pastor of the First Presbyterian Church at Brooklyn, N.Y. He was professor of ecclesiastical history for many years in the Union Theological Seminary. In 1852 he retired from active service in the church, but frequently preached and lectured. He favored the antislavery movement, though not its extreme measures, and took a strong conservative position with regard to the Southern question. He was considered a fine and powerful orator.

Cox, Samuel Sullivan. b. at Zanesville, Ohio, Sept. 30, 1824; d. at New York, Sept. 10, 1889. American politician and diplomat. He became editor of the Columbus (Ohio) *Statesman* in 1853, and gained the sobriquet of "Sunset" Cox by an extremely rhetorical description of a sunset which he printed in that journal. He was a Democratic member of Congress from Ohio (1857–65) and from New York City (1869–73 and 1875–85), was U.S. minister to Turkey (1885–86), was, on his return to New York, elected to Congress to fill a vacancy, and was reëlected in 1888. Author of *A Buckeye Abroad* (1852), *Eight Years in Congress* (1865), *Three Decades of Federal Legislation* (1886), and others.

Cox and Box. Operetta in one act by Arthur Sullivan, with a libretto by F. C. Burnand, first publicly performed at the London Adelphi Theatre, May 11, 1867.

Coxcie or **Cocxie** or **Coxie** (kok'sē), **Michiel.** b. at Mechlin (Mechelen or Malines), in the Low Countries (now in Belgium), 1499; d. there, March 5, 1592. Flemish painter. His best-known work is a copy of the *Adoration of the Lamb* by the brothers Van Eyck.

Coxcomb, The. Play attributed to Beaumont, Fletcher, and Rowley, produced in 1612 and published in 1647.

Coxe (koks), **Arthur Cleveland.** b. at Mendham, N.J., May 10, 1818; d. July 20, 1896. American clergyman of the Protestant Episcopal Church. He became assistant bishop of western New York in 1863 and bishop in 1865. He was the author of *Saul, a Mystery, and Other Poems* (1845), *Hallowe'en, a Romaunt, with Lays Meditative and Devotional* (1869), *The Ladye Chace* (1878), *Institutes of Christian History* (1887), and others.

Coxe, Henry Octavius. b. at Bucklebury, Berkshire, England, Sept. 20, 1811; d. July 8, 1881. English paleographer and chief librarian of the Bodleian Library. He was granted an M.A. at Oxford (1836), and joined the manuscript department of the British Museum (1833), which he left to become an assistant librarian at the Bodleian (1838), where he served as chief librarian from 1860 to 1881. In 1857 he made a tour of the Levant to search monastic libraries for manuscripts. He was the editor of *Forms of Bidding Prayer* (1840), *Rogeri de Wendover Chronica sive Flores Historiarum* (1841–44), *Poema quod dicitur Vox Clamantis, auctore Joanne Gower* (1850), and of catalogues of the Bodleian and Oxford college libraries.

Coxe, Tench. b. at Philadelphia, May 22, 1755; d. there, July 16, 1824. American political economist. He wrote *View of the United States* (1794), and others.

Coxe, William. b. at London, March 7, 1747; d. at Bemerton, Wiltshire, England, June 8, 1828. English clergyman, historian, and biographer. He was appointed rector of Bemerton in 1788, of Stourton in 1800, and of Fovant, Wiltshire, in 1811, and archdeacon of Wiltshire in 1804. He wrote *A History of the House of Austria* (1807), *Memoirs of Sir Robert Walpole* (1798), and others.

Coxey (kok'si), **Jacob Sechler.** b. at Selinsgrove, Pa., April 16, 1854; d. at Massillon, Ohio, May 18, 1951. American politician and businessman, known as the leader (1894) of "Coxey's Army," a group of unemployed workers which marched on Washington to demand federal aid. Coxey hoped to compel printing of 500 million dollars in paper money to give his followers work, but he was arrested and his movement (which had dwindled to 336 men) soon dispersed. In 1931 he was elected mayor of Massillon, Ohio, and endeavored once again to solve an unemployment problem through cheap money, but was prevented by state law from issuing special bonds and in 1934 was defeated in the primaries.

Coxey's Army. Group of jobless persons under the leadership of "General" Jacob S. Coxey, of Massillon, Ohio, which marched on Washington, D.C., to present a "living petition" of the unemployed to Congress on May 1, 1894. The petition was designed to stimulate public and legislative interest in Coxey's scheme for public works to aid the unemployed during the economic depression initiated by the panic of 1893. Although the marchers personally led by Coxey numbered only some 500 and had dwindled to 336 by the time the "army" reached Washington, other "Coxeyites" from throughout the U.S. made attempts to descend upon the national capital en masse.

Coxsackie (kůk.säk'i). Village in E New York, in Greene County, on the W bank of the Hudson River: manufactures of bricks. 2,722 (1950).

Coxwell (koks'wel), **Henry Tracey.** b. at Wouldham, Kent, England, March 2, 1819; d. Jan. 5, 1900. The son of a naval officer, he made his first ascent in 1844, and became a professional balloonist in 1848. In 1862, with James Glaisher and others, he reached a height of about seven miles during an ascension in which his companions were rendered insensible. Unable to use his hands because of frost-bite, he opened the valve of the gas-filled bag with his teeth, and made a safe descent. During his career he gathered data of great use to meteorologists. In the Franco-Prussian War he was a military balloonist with the German forces, and he advocated more use of balloons in warfare. He was the author of *My Life and Balloon Experiences* (1887–89).

Coyle (koil), **Kathleen.** d. March 25, 1952. Irish novelist. Her books include *Piccadilly* (1923), *Liv* (1929), *There Is a Door* (1931), *The Skeleton* (1933), *Immortal Ease*, and *Flock of Birds* (1939), and the autobiography *The Magical Realm* (1943).

Coyne (koin), **Joseph Stirling.** b. at Birr, King's County (now County Offaly), Ireland, 1803; d. at London, July 18, 1868. Irish humorist and playwright, author of a number of successful farces and other works.

Coyoacán (kō"yō.ä.kän'). City in S Mexico, in the Distrito Federal. 23,724 (1940).

"Coyote State." Occasional nickname of **South Dakota.**

Coypel (kwà.pel), **Antoine.** b. at Paris, April 11, 1661; d. there, Jan. 1, 1722. French painter; son of Noël Coypel and father of Charles Antoine Coypel.

Coypel, Charles Antoine. b. at Paris, June 11, 1694; d. June 14, 1752. French painter; son of Antoine Coypel.

Coypel, Noël. b. at Paris, Dec. 25, 1628; d. there, Dec. 21, 1707. French painter, an imitator of Poussin; father of Antoine Coypel. His best-known work is the *Martyrdom of Saint James*, in Notre Dame, Paris.

Coypel, Noël Nicolas. b. at Paris, Nov. 18, 1692; d. there, Dec. 14, 1734. French painter; stepbrother of Antoine Coypel.

Coysevox (kwàz.voks), **Antoine.** b. at Lyons, France, Sept. 29, 1640; d. at Paris, Oct. 10, 1720. French sculptor of Spanish origin. He went to Paris and entered the atelier of Lerambert, the celebrated sculptor, painter, and poet. He copied many ancient statues in marble, among them the *Venus di Medici* and the *Castor and Pollux.* In 1667 he was called to Strasbourg to execute the decorations of the palace of the Cardinal Prince de Fürstenberg. He returned to Paris in 1671, where he enjoyed the personal friendship of Louis XIV, who gave him large commissions at Versailles, then in process of construction. In 1687 he made the statue of Louis XIV at the Hôtel de

Ville; also an equestrian statue of the king for the city of Rennes in Britanny. In 1701 he made the two winged horses for the entrance to the Tuileries gardens. Among his works are portrait statues (Condé at Chantilly, the Dauphine Adelaide of Savoie as Diane Chasseresse, the kneeling statue of Louis XIV at Notre Dame), the tomb of Mazarin in the Église des Quatre Nations, and the monument to Colbert at Saint Eustache.

Cozad (kō̜.zad′). City in S central Nebraska, in Dawson County on the Platte River. It is a shipping point for hay and has alfalfa-processing mills. 2,910 (1950).

Cozeners (kuz′e̜n.ėrz), **The.** Comedy by Samuel Foote, produced in 1774.

Cozens (kuz′e̜nz), **Alexander.** d. 1786. English artist and writer on art; father of John Robert Cozens. A son of Czar Peter the Great of Russia by an English mother, he studied in Italy but eventually resided permanently in England. He painted and sketched, but much of his graphic work was in the nature of book illustrations, and his interest seems to have been mainly in teaching and in writing. He was the author of *The Shape, Skeleton and Foliage of Trees* (1771), and of *The Principles of Beauty, Relative to the Human Head* (1778).

Cozens, John Robert. b. at London, c1752; d. c1799. English water-colorist; son of Alexander Cozens. John Robert Cozens' water colors were much in advance of their time by virtue of a technique which in some of its effects anticipated impressionism, and they continue to be regarded with admiration and respect. The great colorist J. M. W. Turner said that he learned more from this artist's picture of *Hannibal Crossing the Alps* than from any other work whatsoever. The British Museum and the Victoria and Albert Museum are now the chief repositories of examples of his art.

Cozumel (kō.sö.mel′). Island in the Caribbean Sea, ab. 9 mi. off the NE coast of the Yucatán peninsula. It is low and flat, and bordered by reefs. When discovered by Grijalva (1518) and visited by Cortés (1519), it was inhabited by Maya Indians, and remains of their temples and houses still exist. Length, ab. 24 mi.; width, ab. 7 mi.; pop. ab. 2,000.

Cozzens (kuz′e̜nz), **Frederick Swartwout.** [Pen name, **Richard Haywarde.**] b. at New York, March 11, 1818; d. at Brooklyn, N.Y., Dec. 23, 1869. American writer. He was for many years a wine merchant at New York, and published in connection with his business a trade paper called *The Wine Press.* He wrote the *Sparrowgrass Papers* (1856).

Cozzens, James Gould. b. at Chicago, Aug. 19, 1903—. American novelist. He was educated (1922–24) at Harvard. His works include *Confusion* (1924), *Michael Scarlett* (1925), *Cockpit* (1928), *The Son of Perdition* (1929), *S.S. San Pedro* (1931), *The Last Adam* (1933), *Castaway* (1934), *Men and Brethren* (1936), *Ask Me Tomorrow* (1940), *The Just and the Unjust* (1942), and *Guard of Honor* (1948; awarded a Pulitzer prize).

Crab (krab). Dog of Launce in Shakespeare's *Two Gentlemen of Verona.*

Crab. Crusty guardian of the fortune of Buck in Samuel Foote's comedy *The Englishman Returned from Paris.*

Crabb (krab), **George.** b. at Palgrave, Suffolk, England, Dec. 8, 1778; d. at Hammersmith (now part of London), Dec. 4, 1851. English lawyer and legal and miscellaneous writer, best known as the author of *Dictionary of English Synonymes* (1816).

Crabbe (krab), **George.** b. at Aldeburgh, Suffolk, England, Dec. 24, 1754; d. at Trowbridge, Wiltshire, England, Feb. 3, 1832. English poet; father of George Crabbe (1785–1857). After having failed as a surgeon in his native town, he went (1780) to London, where, through the patronage of Burke, he was rescued from extreme poverty and enabled to publish *The Library* and other works, which gave him an established position in literature. He was for a number of years chaplain to the duke of Rutland, and in 1789 became rector of Muston and Allington. His chief works are *The Library* (1781), *The Village* (1783), *The Newspaper* (1785), *The Parish Register* (1807), and *Tales of the Hall* (1819). His biography was published (1834) by his son.

Crabbe, George. b. Nov. 16, 1785; d. at Bredfield, Suffolk, England, Sept. 16, 1857. English clergyman; son of George Crabbe (1754–1832). He received a B.A. at Cambridge (1807) and became vicar of Bredfield (1834). He published a life of his father in 1834, and was also the author of a book on natural theology.

Crabbed Youth and Age. Play by Lennox Robinson, produced in 1922 and published in 1924.

Crabeth (krä′bet), **Dirk.** b. at Gouda, Netherlands; d. c1601. Dutch painter on glass; brother of Wouter Crabeth.

Crabeth, Wouter. b. at Gouda, Netherlands; d. c1581. Dutch painter on glass; brother of Dirk Crabeth.

Crabshaw (krab′shô), **Timothy.** In Tobias Smollett's *Sir Launcelot Greaves,* a whipper-in, plowman, and carter, selected as a squire by Sir Launcelot when on his knight-errant expedition. He rode a vicious cart horse named Gilbert.

Crabtree (krab′trē). Mischief-maker in Richard Brinsley Sheridan's comedy *The School for Scandal.*

Crabtree, Cadwallader. Cynical deaf old man, a friend of Peregrine Pickle, in Tobias Smollett's novel *Peregrine Pickle.*

Crabtree, Lotta. [Known as **Lotta.**] b. at New York, Nov. 7, 1847; d. Sept. 25, 1924. American actress. She made her first appearance on the stage at the age of six, and ten years later made her debut at New York at Niblo's Garden. Her best-known role was that of the Marchioness in a dramatization of *The Old Curiosity Shop;* she also appeared in *Firefly, Topsy, Musette, Bob, Nitouche, The Little Detective,* and others. She retired from the stage in 1894.

Craddock (krad′o̜k), **Charles Egbert.** Pseudonym of **Murfree, Mary Noailles.**

Cradle of Liberty. See **Faneuil Hall.**

Cradle of the Deep, Rocked in the. See **Rocked in the Cradle of the Deep.**

Cradock or **Craddocke** (krad′o̜k). See **Caradoc.**

Craft of Lovers, The. Poem attributed to Chaucer by Stowe, but now generally conceded to have been the work of another writer, who is as yet unidentified.

Crafton (kraf′to̜n). Borough in SW Pennsylvania, in Allegheny County, on Chartiers Creek. It is a residential suburb of Pittsburgh and has manufactures of stoves. Founded in 1873, it occupies the site of a former Indian village. 8,066 (1950).

Crafts (kråfts), **James Mason.** b. at Boston, March 8, 1839; d. June 20, 1917. American chemist, professor of organic chemistry in the Massachusetts Institute of Technology (1892–97), and president of that institution (1897–1900).

Crafts, Samuel Chandler. b. at Woodstock, Vt., Oct. 6, 1768; d. at Craftsbury, Vt., Nov. 19, 1853. American politician, governor of Vermont from 1828 to 1831.

Crafts, William. b. at Charleston, S.C., Jan. 24, 1787; d. at Lebanon Springs, N.Y., Sept. 23, 1826. American lawyer and poet.

Craig (krāg). Town in NW Colorado, county seat of Moffat County, on the Yampa River (a tributary of the Green River) ab. 150 mi. NW of Denver, in a cattle-ranching, dry-farming, and oil-producing area. 3,080 (1950).

Craig, Charles Franklin. b. at Danbury, Conn., July 4, 1872—. American bacteriologist and army officer. He received his M.D. (1894) from Yale, and was commissioned (1903) a 1st lieutenant in the U.S. Army. He served as associate professor of bacteriology (1910–11) at George Washington University, was promoted (1918) to colonel, was professor of bacteriology and parasitology (1920–22) at the Army Medical School, Washington, D.C., commandant and director of clinical pathology and preventive medicine (1926–30) there, and professor of tropical medicine (1931–38) at Tulane. He is the author of *The Aestivo-Autumnal Malarial Fevers* (1901), *The Parasitic Amoebae of Man* (1911), *The Wassermann Test* (1918), *Amebiasis and Amebic Dysentery* (1935), *The Laboratory Diagnosis of Protozoan Diseases* (1941), and *The Etiology, Diagnosis and Treatment of Amebiasis* (1944).

Craig, Edward Gordon. b. Jan. 16, 1872—. English stage designer, producer, and actor; son of Ellen Terry (1847–1928). He was founder of *The Mask* (1908), a theater arts journal, and of the School for the Art of the Theatre (1913) at Florence. His productions with his own sets include Alfred de Musset's *On ne badine pas avec l'Amour, Dido and Aeneas* (1900), *The Masque of Love*

(1901), Handel's opera *Acis and Galatea* (1902), *Bethlehem* (1903) by Housman, Ibsen's *Vikings* (1903) and *Rosmersholm* (1906), the latter at Florence with Eleanora Duse, *Much Ado About Nothing* (1903), and *Hamlet* (1912) at Moscow. He is the author of *The Art of the Theatre* (1905), *On the Art of the Theatre* (1911), *Toward a New Theatre* (1913), *Scene* (1923), and *Ellen Terry and Her Secret Self* (1931).

Craig, James. See **Craigavon,** 1st Viscount.

Craig, Sir **James Henry.** b. at Gibraltar, 1748; d. at London, Jan. 12, 1812. British general and colonial governor. Joining the British army in 1763, he was in America at the time of the Revolutionary War, was wounded at Bunker Hill, and participated in the capture of Ticonderoga and in Burgoyne's campaign which ended at Saratoga. He served with the British forces in the Netherlands (1794) and was one of the commanders in the seizure of Dutch territories in South Africa, becoming governor of the Cape of Good Hope colony (1795–97). For his services in India (1797–1802) he was made a lieutenant general, and was subsequently (1805–06) in command of British forces in Italy and Sicily. His appointment (1807) as captain-general and governor general of Canada was a prelude to events which contributed to the lasting tension between the French and the British in that colony. Disdainful of popular government and unfriendly to the French Canadians, he dismissed the Assembly of Lower Canada (1809) and suppressed the French-language newspaper *Canadien.* These actions so strengthened anti-British sentiment among the French Canadians that Craig was removed in 1811. Shortly before his death he was promoted to the rank of general.

Craig, John. b. c1512; d. 1600. Scottish reformer, a friend and successor of Knox. He at first refused to publish the banns between Mary, Queen of Scots, and Bothwell, but finally consented.

Craig, Malin. b. at St. Joseph, Mo., Aug. 5, 1875; d. at Washington, D.C., July 25, 1945. American army officer. He was graduated (1898) from West Point, served in the Spanish-American War and with the China Relief Expedition, was graduated (1905) from the Army Staff College and from the Army War College in 1910, and served (1917–19) in France during World War I. In 1919 he was named director of the General Staff College. He became a brigadier general in 1921, a major general in 1924, and a general in 1935, was commander (1928–30) of the Panama Canal Department, and served (1935–39) as chief of staff of the U.S. army. He retired in 1939, but was recalled to duty in 1943.

Craig, Sir **Thomas.** b. 1538; d. at Edinburgh, Feb. 26, 1608. Scottish jurist and Latin poet. He was the author of a treatise on feudal law, *Jus feudale* (1603), still a standard authority in Scotland.

Craigavon (krāg.av'on), 1st Viscount. [Title of **James Craig.**] b. at Craigavon, County Down, Ireland, Jan. 8, 1871; d. near Belfast, Ireland, Nov. 24, 1940. Irish statesman who served (1921–40) as the first prime minister of Northern Ireland. He served in the British army in South Africa during the Boer War (1900–02). As a member (1906–21) of Parliament at London from County Down, he was treasurer of the royal household (1916–18), parliamentary secretary to the ministry of pensions (1919–20), and parliamentary and financial secretary to the admiralty (1920–21). He organized the Ulster Division of the British army during World War I. He was president of the Ulster Unionist Council and member (1921 *et seq.*) of the House of Commons of Northern Ireland. He was created baronet in 1918 and viscount in 1927. During his political career, he strongly opposed Irish independence movements.

Craigengelt (krā.gen.gelt'), **Captain.** Adventurer in Sir Walter Scott's novel *The Bride of Lammermoor.* He is the friend of Frank Hayston, and the enemy of the Master of Ravenswood.

Craigenputtock (krā.gen.put'ok). Farm ab. 15 mi. from Dumfries, Scotland, which for some years was the home of Thomas Carlyle. It belonged to Mrs. Carlyle before her marriage, and in May, 1828, they first went there to live, leaving it and returning from time to time. Here much of Carlyle's most brilliant work was done.

Craigie (krā'gi), **Pearl Mary Teresa.** [Pseudonym, **John Oliver Hobbes**; maiden name, **Richards.**] b. at Chelsea, Mass., Nov. 3, 1867; d. at London, Aug. 13, 1906. Anglo-American novelist and dramatist. She added the names Mary and Teresa to her own in 1892, when she entered the Roman Catholic Church. She was resident (1868 *et seq.*) in England, studying in private schools and at London University College. She wrote the novels *Some Emotions and a Moral* (1891), *The Sinner's Comedy* (1892), *A Study in Temptations* and *A Bundle of Life* (both 1893), *The Gods, Some Mortals, and Lord Wickenham* (1895), *The Herb-Moon* (1896), *School for Saints* (1897), *Robert Orange* (1900), *The Serious Wooing* (1901), *Love and the Soul Hunters* (1902), *The Vineyard* (1904), *The Flute of Pan* (1905), *The Dream and the Business* (1906), and *Saints in Society* (1907); the plays, *Journeys End in Lovers Meeting* (1894), *The Ambassador* (1898), *Osbern and Ursyne* and *A Repentance* (both 1899), *The Wisdom of the Wise* (1900), and *The Bishop's Move* (1902); and an account of her travels in India, in *Imperial India—Letters from the East* (1903).

Craigie, Sir **Robert Leslie.** b. at Southsea, Hampshire, England, Dec. 6, 1883—. English diplomat. He was second secretary (1916) at Berne, acting high commissioner (1920) at Sofia, and first secretary (1920) and chargé d'affaires (1921–23) at Washington. He served as assistant undersecretary of state (1934–37), and was British ambassador (1937–41) to Japan until the entry of that country into World War II.

Craigie, Sir **William.** [Full name, **William Alexander Craigie.**] b. at Dundee, Scotland, Aug. 13, 1867—. Scottish lexicographer, professor, and author. He was educated at the University of St. Andrews (M.A., 1888), Oxford University (B.A., 1893, and Honorary M.A., 1902). He holds doctorates in literature, law, and philosophy from St. Andrews (1907), Calcutta (1921), Oxford and Cambridge (both 1928), the universities of Michigan and Wisconsin (1929, 1932), and the University of Iceland (1946). He taught Latin at St. Andrews (1893–97), Scandinavian language and literature at Oxford (1905–16), and Anglo-Saxon (1916–25) and English (1925–36) at the University of Chicago, being made professor emeritus in the latter year. His works include *Icelandic Sagas* (1913), *The Pronunciation of English* (1917), *Easy Readings in Anglo-Saxon* (1923), *The Poetry of Iceland* (1925), and *The Study of American English* (1927). For various learned journals he has written papers on his three main interests, Scottish, Gaelic, and Scandinavian life, literature, and history. As a lexicographer, he has done his great work as coeditor (with Sir James Murray and Henry Bradley) of the *New English Dictionary* (1897–1933), as editor of *A Dictionary of the Older Scottish Tongue* (1931), and as coeditor (with James R. Hulbert) of *A Dictionary of American English on Historical Principles* (4 vols.; 1938, 1940, 1942, 1944). From 1917–25 he was a fellow of Oriel College, Oxford. He is a member of the British Academy, the London Philological Society, the Icelandic Society of Letters, and many other scholarly groups.

Craig's Wife. Play by George Kelly, produced in 1925 and awarded a Pulitzer prize in 1926. Harriet Craig, whose attention is centered upon the trappings of her home, finds herself living in a void when her husband, relatives, and servants recognize her coldness and leave her. Their desertion is precipitated by an analogous situation in which a neighbor murders his wife and then commits suicide.

Craig v. Missouri, 4 Peters 410 (1830). U.S. Supreme Court decision which invalidated and declared unconstitutional a Missouri law providing for the issue of certificates in various denominations which would be receivable in payment of taxes and could be loaned to citizens of the state. The law was held invalid on the ground that it contravened the explicit prohibition in the Constitution against the emission of bills of credit by a state. "To 'emit bills of credit,' " said Chief Justice John Marshall, "conveys to the mind the idea of issuing paper intended to circulate through the community for its ordinary purposes, as money, which paper is redeemable at a future day." The decision in the Craig case was considerably weakened, if not repudiated, by the majority finding in *Briscoe v. Bank of Kentucky* (*1837*).

Craik (krāk), **Dinah Maria.** [Also, **Dinah Maria Mulock.**] b. at Stoke-on-Trent, Staffordshire, England, 1826; d. at Shortlands, Kent, England, Oct. 12, 1887.

English novelist and poet. She was the author of *The Ogilvies* (1849), *The Head of the Family* (1851), *Agatha's Husband* (1853), *John Halifax, Gentleman* (1857), *A Life for a Life* (1859), *A Noble Life* (1866), *A Brave Lady* (1870), *Hannah* (1871), and other novels. She published a volume of poems in 1859 and *Thirty Years' Poems* in 1881, besides many children's books and fairy tales.

Craik, George Lillie. b. at Kennoway, Fifeshire, Scotland, in 1798; d. at Belfast, Ireland, June 25, 1866. Scottish historian and general writer, appointed professor of English literature and history at Queen's College, Belfast, in 1849. He was the author of *Compendious History of English Literature and of the English Language* (1861), and others.

Craik, Georgiana Marian. [Mrs. **A. W. May.**] b. at London, in April, 1831; d. at St. Leonards, Sussex, England, Nov. 1, 1895. English novelist; daughter of George Lillie Craik (1798–1866). Her works include *Riverstone* (1857), *Lost and Won* (1859), *Winifred's Wooing* (1862), *Mildred* (1868), *Sylvia's Choice* (1874), *Hilary's Love-Story* (1880), *Godfrey Helstone* (1884), and *Patience Holt* (1891).

Craik, Sir **Henry.** b. at Glasgow, Scotland, Oct. 18, 1846; d. at London, March 17, 1927. Scottish biographer, historian, and educator.

Craik, James. b. in Scotland, 1730; d. in Fairfax County, Va., Feb. 6, 1814. American physician. He accompanied Washington in the expedition against the French and Indians in 1754, served as physician under Braddock in 1755, entered the medical service of the Continental army in 1775, and served (1781–83) as its chief medical officer. He became the family physician of Washington, whom he attended in his last illness. On his authority rests the anecdote of the Indian chief who, at the time of Braddock's disastrous defeat, discharged his rifle 15 times at Washington without effect (and who years after made a long journey to see the man whom he therefore supposed must certainly enjoy a charmed existence).

Crail (krāl). Royal burgh, seaport, and popular seaside resort in E Scotland, in Fifeshire, situated at the mouth of the Firth of Forth on the North Sea, ab. 9 mi. SE of St. Andrews, ab. 447 mi. N of London by rail. It has the ruins of a priory college, and an old castle which was a royal residence in medieval times. 1,135 (est. 1948).

Crailsheim (krīls'hīm). Town in S Germany, in the *Land* (state) of Württemberg-Baden, American Zone, formerly in the state of Württemberg, situated on the Jagst River, ab. 48 mi. NE of Stuttgart. It has grain, lumber, leather, and cattle markets, machine and chemical industries, and manufactures leather goods and costume jewelry. The Church of Our Lady and the Church of Saint John date from the 14th century; there is a Gothic town hall. The population is predominantly Protestant. The town became part of Württemberg in 1810. Pop. 10,133 (1950).

Craiova (krä.yō'vä). [Also: **Crajova, Krajova, Krayova.**] City in S Rumania, the capital of the province of Oltenia, situated on the Jiu River, ab. 110 mi. W of Bucharest. It is a railroad junction and grain-marketing center, and manufactures textiles, leather, ceramics, canned goods, and mill products. It has a cathedral, university, military academy, theater, and museums. Here, in World War I, the Rumanian army suffered its worst defeat. 84,574 (1948).

Cram (kram), **Ralph Adams.** b. at Hampton Falls, N.H., Dec. 16, 1863; d. 1942. American architect and author. He practiced architecture (1889 *et seq.*), from 1892 as a member of the firm of Cram, Goodhue and Ferguson (later Cram and Ferguson) of Boston and New York, which designed (1903 *et seq.*) important additions to the U.S. Military Academy at West Point. In 1911 he succeeded Christopher Grant La Farge as consulting architect of the Cathedral of Saint John the Divine at New York. He designed numerous other churches as well as school and college buildings, and served as professor of architecture at the Massachusetts Institute of Technology from 1914 to 1922. He wrote *Church Building* (1901), *The Ruined Abbeys of Great Britain* (1906), *Impressions of Japanese Architecture and the Allied Arts* (1906), *The Gothic Quest* (1907), *Excalibur* (1909), *The Substance of Gothic* (1916), *The Nemesis of Mediocrity* (1918), *The Great Thousand Years* (1918), *The Sins of the Fathers* (1919), *Gold, Frankincense and Myrrh* (1919), *My Life in Architecture* (1936), and *The End of Democracy* (1937).

Cramer (krā'mėr; German, krä'mėr), **Franz** (or **François**). b. 1772; d. Aug. 1, 1848. Violinist, named (1827) master of the king's musicians at London. He was a son of Wilhelm Cramer (1745–99).

Cramer, Gabriel. b. at Geneva, Switzerland, July 31, 1704; d. at Bagnoles, France, Jan. 4, 1752. Swiss mathematician, noted for his discovery, independently of the earlier work by Leibnitz, of the methods of determinants and for his work on the theory of curves. He is remembered for "Cramer's rule" in the solution of linear equations by means of determinants and for "Cramer's paradox" in the number of intersections of algebraic plane curves. His *Introduction à l'analyse des lignes courbes algébriques* (1750) was for half a century a standard work on the theory of algebraic curves.

Cramer, Johann Andreas. b. at Jöhstadt, Saxony, Germany, Jan. 27, 1723; d. at Kiel, Holstein, Germany, June 12, 1788. German religious poet and pulpit orator. His collected poems were published in the period 1782–83, and in a posthumous edition in 1791.

Cramer, Johann Baptist. b. at Mannheim, Germany, Feb. 24, 1771; d. at London, April 16, 1858. Composer and pianist; son of Wilhelm Cramer (1745–1799). He was the author of studies for the piano, and founder (1824) of the London music publishing firm of J. B. Cramer and Company, in partnership with T. Frederick Beale and Robert Addison.

Cramer, Wilhelm. b. at Mannheim, Germany, 1745; d. at London, Oct. 5, 1799. German violinist, resident in London after 1772; father of Johann Baptist Cramer and Franz Cramer.

Cramerton (krā'mėr.tǫn). Unincorporated community in W North Carolina, in Gaston County: textile manufactures. 3,211 (1950).

Cramp (kramp), **Charles Henry.** b. May 9, 1828; d. June 6, 1913. American naval architect; son of William Cramp (1807–79). He was employed (1846 *et seq.*) in his father's shipyards, and president (1879 *et seq.*) of the firm after its incorporation (1872) as the William Cramp and Son's Ship and Engine Building Company, which constructed the steamships *St. Louis, St. Paul, Kroonland,* and *Finland*, and the warships *Maine, New York, Indiana, Massachusetts, Colorado,* and *Pennsylvania.*

Cramp, William. b. at Philadelphia, Sept. 22, 1807; d. at Atlantic City, N.J., July 6, 1879. American shipbuilder; father of Charles Henry Cramp. He founded (c1830) the William Cramp Shipbuilding Company, later changed (1872) to the William Cramp and Son's Ship and Engine Building Company. He built (1862) the *New Ironsides* for use in the Civil War.

Crampel (krän.pel), **Paul.** b. in France, 1863; d. in April, 1891. French explorer, chiefly in Africa. He began his African career in 1886 under Brazza (the Italian-born French explorer whose expeditions largely contributed to the establishment of the French colonial empire in C Africa). He made a successful journey (1888–89) from Madiville, on the Ogowe River, through the Fang country to Corisco Bay. In 1890 the Comité de l'Afrique Française sent him to Lake Chad to determine a route by which it would be possible to connect the French Sahara with the French Congo. At the head of 30 Senegalese soldiers and 250 carriers, and assisted by three Europeans, he left Stanley Pool on Aug. 15, 1890. From Bangui, the last European post on the Ubangi River, he marched northward as far as El Kuti. Here he was abandoned by most of his carriers, and while attempting to force his way to the north, fell a victim to the fanaticism of the Moslem tribesmen of the region. Of his white companions, one died, one was killed, and only one, Nébout, escaped to the coast.

Crampton (kramp'tǫn), **Henry Edward.** b. at New York, Jan. 5, 1875—. American zoölogist, a professor at Barnard College from 1904. He was instructor in embryology in the marine biological laboratory at Woods Hole, Mass., from 1895 to 1903, and had charge of the embryological work in the biological laboratory at Cold Spring Harbor from 1904 to 1906. In 1909 he was named curator of invertebrate zoölogy in the American Museum of Natural History at New York.

Crampton, Thomas Russell. b. at Broadstairs, Kent, England, Aug. 6, 1816; d. at Westminster, London,

March 19, 1888. English engineer, remembered for his design of the Crampton locomotive and for laying (1851) the first practical submarine cable between Dover and Calais. As a locomotive designer, he prepared (c1844) drawings for the first locomotive for the Great Western Railway under the direction of Sir Daniel Gooch, and improved (1842–44) details of earlier locomotives. He patented (1843) the Crampton locomotive, which is distinguished by a long boiler, outside cylinders set in the middle of the engine's length, and large driving wheels placed to the rear of the firebox.

Crampton's Gap. Pass in the South Mountain, Maryland.

Cranach (krä'näċh), **Lucas.** [Also: **Kranach, Kronach.**] b. at Kronach, near Bamberg, Germany, 1472; d. at Weimar, Germany, Oct. 16, 1553. German painter and engraver; father of Lucas Cranach (1515–86). He became in 1504 court painter to the elector Frederick the Wise, of Saxony. He was elected burgomaster of Wittenberg in 1537 and in 1540. His best-known works are altarpieces in Weimar, Wittenberg, and elsewhere.

Cranach, Lucas. [Called **Lucas Cranach the younger.**] b. at Wittenberg, Germany, Oct. 4, 1515; d. at Weimar, Germany, Jan. 25, 1586. German painter; son of Lucas Cranach (1472–1553).

Cranbrook (kran'brůk). Town in the SE corner of British Columbia, Canada, on the main line of the Canadian Pacific Railway, ab. 61 mi. W of Fernie: an important lumber center, with several large sawmills. 3,621 (1951).

Cranbrook. Rural district and market town in SE England, in Kent, situated on the river Crane, ab. 45 mi. SE of London by rail. It is located in an agricultural district. 13,788 (1951).

Cranbrook, 1st Earl of. Title of **Gathorne-Hardy, Gathorne.**

Cranbrook Institute of Science. Organization founded in 1930 for the purpose of promoting scientific research and education and maintaining a museum of natural history. It is situated at Bloomfield Hills, Mich., has a library of more than 6,000 volumes on natural science, and issues a *Bulletin* (irregularly) and *News Letter* (monthly).

Cranch (kranch), **Christopher Pearse.** b. at Alexandria, Va., March 8, 1813; d. at Cambridge, Mass., Jan. 20, 1892. American landscape painter, poet, and translator; son of William Cranch. He first entered the ministry, but retired from it in 1842 to devote himself to art. Among his more noted pictures are *October Afternoon* (1867), *Venice* (1870), and *Venetian Fishing-boats* (1871). He published *Poems* (1844), *The Bird and the Bell . . .* (1875), *Ariel and Caliban* (1887), and other books of poetry, and prose tales for children, which he illustrated.

Cranch, William. b. at Weymouth, Mass., July 17, 1769; d. at Washington, D.C., Sept. 1, 1855. American jurist; father of Christopher Pearse Cranch. He was chief justice of the circuit court for the District of Columbia from 1805 to 1855.

Crandall (kran'dal), **Prudence.** b. at Hopkinton, R.I., Sept. 3, 1803; d. at Elk Falls, Kan., Jan. 28, 1889. American teacher and reformer. She started (1831) a school for girls at Canterbury, Conn.; having subsequently decided to keep a school for Negroes only, she became involved in lawsuits and public controversy; the final verdict against her was handed down (1834) by the Connecticut supreme court.

Crane (krān), **Bruce.** [Full name, **Robert Bruce Crane.**] b. at New York, 1857; d. Oct. 29, 1937. American painter; a pupil of Alexander Helwig Wyant. He exhibited first at the National Academy of Design, New York, in 1879 and was elected an academician of that institution in 1902. He was a member of the American Water Color Society and was also a member of the Society of American Artists. His specialty was American landscape.

Crane, Charles Richard. b. at Chicago, Aug. 7, 1858; d. Feb. 15, 1939. American industrialist and diplomat. He was associated with the Crane Company, manufacturers of valves and fittings at Chicago, becoming first vice-president in 1894 and serving (1912–14) as president of the firm. He served as a member (1917) of the president's special diplomatic commission to Russia, U.S. commissioner (1919) on mandates in Turkey, and U.S. minister (1920–21) to China, and was active in the development of the Marine Biological Laboratory at Woods Hole, Mass.

Crane, Frank. b. at Urbana, Ill., May 12, 1861; d. at Nice, France, Nov. 5, 1928. American clergyman and essayist. He was a minister (1882–1909) in Methodist and Congregational churches, and turned in 1909 to newspaper writing. His syndicated essays were reprinted in *Four Minute Essays* (10 vols., 1919), *The Crane Classics* (10 vols., 1920), and *Everyday Wisdom* (1927); author also of *The Religion of Tomorrow* (1899), *Vision* (1906), *The Song of the Infinite* (1909), *War and World Government* (1915), *Why I Am a Christian* (1924), and *The Ten Commandments* (1928).

Crane, Hart. [Full name, **Harold Hart Crane.**] b. at Garrettsville, Ohio, July 21, 1899; committed suicide, April 27, 1932. American poet, best known for his long poem *The Bridge* (1930), in which the Brooklyn Bridge serves as a symbol of America. He was an advertising copywriter (1916–25) at New York, was awarded (1930) the Helen Waire Levinson prize awarded by *Poetry—A Magazine of Verse,* and received (1931–32) a Guggenheim Fellowship for creative writing abroad. His other works include *White Buildings* (1926) and the posthumously published *Collected Poems* (1933).

Crane, Ichabod. Country schoolmaster in "The Legend of Sleepy Hollow" by Washington Irving, included in *The Sketch Book* (1820). He is an excruciatingly awkward schoolmaster who loves Katrina Van Tassel, and is frightened out of the countryside by his adventure with his rival, who is disguised as the Headless Horseman.

Crane, Nathalia. [Full name, **Nathalia Clara Ruth Abarbanel Crane.**] b. at New York, Aug. 11, 1913—. American poet and novelist. Educated at the University of Madrid and at Barnard College, Columbia (1931–35), she became a faculty member of Pratt Institute, Brooklyn, N.Y. She drew wide notice when she wrote for publication at the age of nine. Her works include *The Janitor's Boy* (1924), *Lava Lane* (1925), *The Singing Crow* (1926), *Pocahontas* (1930), *Swear by the Night* (1936), *The Death of Poetry* (1941), and other books of verse, and the novels *The Sunken Garden* (1926) and *The Alien from Heaven* (1929).

Crane, Stephen. b. at Newark, N.J., Nov. 1, 1871; d. at Badenweiler, in the Black Forest, Germany, June 5, 1900. American novelist, short-story writer, poet, and war correspondent. He was educated (1887–90) at the Hudson River Institute, a military school at Claverack, N.Y., and attended Lafayette College and Syracuse University, graduating from neither. He worked for two New York papers, the *Herald* and the *Tribune*, and was a war correspondent for the *Journal* and the *World* during the Greco-Turkish and Spanish-American wars. His work falls into three categories: novels, short stories, and poetry. The first group is represented by *Maggie, A Girl of the Streets* (1892), a naturalistic story, of which less than a hundred copies sold, and *The Red Badge of Courage* (1895), a realistic story of the Civil War which was recently (1951) made into a film. Examples of Crane's mastery of the short story are seen in *The Little Regiment and Other Episodes of the Civil War* (1887; called *Pictures of the War* in the 1916 English edition), six stories; *The Open Boat and Other Tales of Adventure* (1898), eight stories, the title one being "the finest short story in English" in the opinion of W.D. Howells; and *The Monster* (1899), seven stories. His poetry is contained in two volumes, *The Black Riders* (1895) and *War Is Kind* (1899), both having the secondary title *and Other Lines.*

Crane, Walter. b. at Liverpool, England, August 15, 1845; d. at Horsham, England, 1915. English painter, illustrator, and artisan who was associated first with the Pre-Raphaelites and later with the arts and crafts movement of William Morris. He was a pupil of W. J. Linton. In 1862 his first painting, *The Lady of Shalot,* was accepted by the Royal Academy; thereafter he exhibited frequently at London. Among his principal works are: *Plato's Garden, Diana and the Shepherd,* and *Bridge of Life.* He is equally well known for his illustrations for such children's books as *Beauty and the Beast, Cinderella,* and *Goody Two Shoes.*

Crane, William Henry. b. at Leicester, Mass., April 30, 1845; d. at Hollywood, Calif., March 7, 1928. American comedian, best known for his impersonation of eccentric

American characters. He played leading parts in *The Henrietta, The Senator, On Probation, For Money, The American Minister, Brother John, A Fool of Fortune, A Virginia Courtship, David Harum,* and others. For many years he played in conjunction with Stuart Robson.

Crane, Winthrop Murray. b. at Dalton, Mass., April 23, 1853; d. Oct. 2, 1920. American paper manufacturer and politician, three times (1900, 1901, 1902) governor of Massachusetts and subsequently (1904–13) a U.S. senator from that state. He secured (1876) the first contract for manufacture of the silk-thread paper thereafter used in U.S. banknotes. Later said by President Taft to have been the Senate's "most influential member," he spent the last year of his life in a vain struggle to get the Republican national convention of 1920 to support U.S. entry into the League of Nations.

Cranfield (kran′fēld), **Lionel.** [Title, Earl of **Middlesex.**] b. 1575; d. Aug. 6, 1645. English merchant and government official. He was successful as a merchant adventurer and mercer and, appearing before the privy council for his company, attracted the favorable attention of James I and of the 1st Duke of Buckingham. He was appointed surveyor general of customs (1613), master of the great wardrobe (1618), master of the court of wards and chief commissioner of the navy (1619); became (1620) privy councillor; attacked (1621) Bacon's policies on patents and monopolies; was charged (1624) by Coke with making personal gain from the court of wards, was tried and found guilty, and sent to Tower; released (1624) and pardoned (1625).

Cranford (kran′fǫrd). Story (1853) of English village life in the second quarter of the 19th century, by Elizabeth Cleghorn Gaskell.

Cranmer (kran′mėr), **Thomas.** b. at Aslacton, Nottinghamshire, England, July 2, 1489; burned at the stake, March 21, 1556. English ecclesiastic and reformer, one of the most notable of the archbishops of Canterbury. He is remembered as one of the engineers of Henry VIII's divorce from Catherine of Aragon, as a leading figure in the movement for moderation within the then newly founded Anglican Church, and a staunch advocate of royal supremacy in ecclesiastical affairs. Born of an old Lincolnshire family, Cranmer went through a rigorous education, physical and mental, at an early age. As a public examiner in theology (1529) at Cambridge, he met with Henry VIII's advisers on the king's proceedings against Catherine. Largely through Cranmer's efforts, the divorce question was submitted to a disputation at the English universities, which gave Henry a favorable verdict. He served on diplomatic missions on the Continent (1530–33), but was recalled in 1533 and made archbishop of Canterbury. As such, Cranmer made possible Henry's divorce from Catherine and marriage with Ann Boleyn. Indeed, he succeeded in gaining so much of Henry's confidence that the king used to refer accusations against Cranmer back to the archbishop himself, and was selected (1540) by the Privy Council to inform Henry of the infidelity of the king's fifth wife, Catherine Howard. Cranmer was the English ecclesiastic who most strongly proclaimed independence from Rome, but had little to do with the dissolution of the monasteries. Upon the death of Henry (1547) Cranmer receded into the background of politics. In the convocation of that year he obtained a vote in favor of the marriage of the clergy. During the reign of Edward VI (1547–53), Cranmer supported many of the measures in reforming the Church and doctrine. As the young sovereign was about to die, he was persuaded to approve of the royal will which sought to modify the royal succession. After the collapse of the movement to enthrone Lady Jane Grey and the accession of Mary, Cranmer was one of the first to be investigated for his past actions. Charged with treason because of his aid to Lady Jane Grey, Cranmer pleaded guilty and was sentenced to death but pardoned. In the next year (1554) he was examined by Sir John Williams for heresy. Although his defense of himself won the admiration of his examiners, his case was transferred to a papal court. Maintaining his belief in judicial independence from papal authority, Cranmer refused to plead and was therefore condemned for heresy. He was degraded in 1556. Then followed a series of seven recantations by which he repudiated one after another of his past works as archbishop. In one of these he even acknowledged his submission to the Pope (using, not without a degree of casuistry, the justification that, both king and queen now being Roman Catholic, his belief in royal supremacy in ecclesiastical matters left him no choice but to accept their position, which, obviously, entailed a reversal of his actual former position). Two days before his execution it was arranged that he should make a final recantation in which he would declare his belief in every article of the Catholic faith and confess by repudiating his writings, particularly those against the sacrament of the altar. On the day of execution Cranmer made use of his final opportunity to confess his sin in having signed the previous recantations, and offered to have that hand of his which made the signature to be first burned. During his life Cranmer was married twice, before clerical marriage was allowed. It is said that during that time he used to carry his second wife about in a chest, perforated with air holes to let her breathe; and on one occasion, she and the chest were removed by an unknowing porter and deposited wrong side up, and thereupon she was compelled to disclose her situation by a scream. Of Cranmer's writings, the principal ones include *A Book on Henry VIII's Divorce, against marriage with a Brother's Widow; Preface to the Bible* (1540); *A Short Instruction into Christian Religion* (commonly called his *Catechism*); *Answer to the Devonshire Rebels; A Defense of the True and Catholic Doctrine of the Sacrament* (1550); *A Confutation of Unwritten Verities.*

Cranmer-Byng (kran′mėr.bing′), **L.** [Full name, **Launcelot Alfred Cranmer-Byng.**] b. Nov. 23, 1872; d. 1945. English editor, author, lecturer, translator, and specialist on Chinese poetry. Educated at Wellington College and at Trinity College, Cambridge, he became a justice of the peace and county alderman for Essex. Some of his works are *A Feast of Lanterns* (1916), *Salma* (1923), *Vision of Asia* (1932), *A Lute of Jade* (1934), selections from Chinese classical poets, *Odes of Confucius, The Rose Garden of Sa'di,* and *To-morrow's Star;* as editor of the *Wisdom of the East* series, he played an important part in introducing Chinese literature to Western readers.

Crannon (kran′ǫn) or **Cranon** (krā′nǫn). [Also, **Ephyra.**] In ancient geography, a city in Thessaly, Greece, ab. 10 mi. SW of Larissa; its exact site is not known. Here, in 322 B.C., Antipater defeated the confederated Greeks.

Cranston (kran′stǫn). City in C Rhode Island, in Providence County, on the Pawtuxet River. Manufactures include cotton textiles, textile machinery, brass and copper tubing, fire extinguishers, and beer. In the colonial period it was known for its iron foundries. 55,060 (1950).

Cranston, John. b. 1625; d. March 12, 1680. Governor of Rhode Island from 1678 to 1680; father of Samuel Cranston.

Cranston, Samuel. b. in August, 1659; d. April 26, 1727. Governor of Rhode Island from 1698 to 1727; son of John Cranston.

Cranstoun (kranz′tǫn), **Henry.** Character in Sir Walter Scott's poem *The Lay of the Last Minstrel.* He assumes the character of William of Deloraine in the trial by combat, and winning, reconciles the Lady of Banksome, his hereditary foe, to his marriage with her daughter Margaret.

Crantor (kran′tôr). b. at Soli, in Cilicia; fl. c325 B.C. Philosopher of the Old Academy, the first commentator on Plato. He wrote a treatise, *On Grief,* from which Cicero borrowed extensively in his *Tusculan Disputations.*

Cranworth (kran′wėrth), Baron. Title of **Rolfe, Robert Monsey.**

Cranz (kränts), **David.** [Also, **Krantz.**] b. 1723; d. at Gnadenfrei, in Silesia, June 6, 1777. German Moravian historian. He became secretary to Count Zinzendorf in 1747, was afterward sent on a mission to Greenland, whence he returned 1762, and in 1766 was appointed pastor at Rixdorf, near Berlin. He wrote *Historie von Grönland* (1765) and *Alte und neue Brüder-Historie oder Kurze Geschichte der evangelischen Brüder-Unität* (1771).

Craon (krän). Village in the department of Mayenne, France, ab. 18 mi. SW of Laval.

Craonne (krän). Village in the department of Aisne, France, ab. 13 mi. SE of Laon. Here, on March 7, 1814, Napoleon checked the allied army under Blücher and Wintzingerode.

Crapaud (krȧ.pō′), **Jean.** [Also, **Johnny Crapaud.**] In a use which is historically vulgar, and to some extent offensive, a nickname for a Frenchman.

Crapsey (krap′si), **Adelaide.** b. Sept. 9, 1878; d. Oct. 8, 1914. American poet; daughter of Algernon Sidney Crapsey (1847–1927). She was teacher (1903–05) of history and literature at Kempner Hall, Kenosha, Wis., instructor (1907–08) in literature and history at Miss Lowe's Preparatory School, Stamford, Conn., and instructor (1911–13) of poetics at Smith College. Her book *Verse* (1915) is a collection of poems, many of them cinquains, a technical device of her own invention.

Crapsey, Algernon Sidney. b. at Fairmount, Ohio, June 28, 1847; d. Dec. 31, 1927. American Episcopal clergyman and author; father of Adelaide Crapsey. As rector (1879–1906) of St. Andrew's Church at Rochester, N.Y., he was convicted (1906) of heresy and deposed. He was a delegate (1907) to the International Peace Conference at The Hague, Netherlands. His works include *Meditations on the Five Joyful Mysteries* (1888), *Sarah Thorne* (1900), *The Greater Love* (1902), *Religion and Politics* (1905), *The Rebirth of Religion* (1907), *The Rise of the Working Class* (1914), *International Republicanism* (1918), *The Ways of the Gods* (1920), *Lewis Henry Morgan* (1923), and *The Last of the Heretics* (1924).

Crashaw (krash′ô), **Richard.** b. at London, c1613; d. at Loretto, Italy, before Aug. 25, 1649. English secular and religious poet. He was the only child of the Puritan poet and clergyman William Crashaw (1572–1626), and of a mother whose name has not come down to us. He was educated at Charterhouse, the school of Addison, Steele, and Thackeray, and at Pembroke College, Cambridge, transferring in 1636 to Peterhouse, of which he was a fellow from 1637 to 1643, and from which he was expelled for religious reasons. Always unsympathetic to Puritanism, he became a Catholic in 1644. Between 1646 and 1649 he was at Paris (where his friend Abraham Cowley introduced him to Henrietta Maria, wife of England's Charles I) and at Rome. In 1649 he was appointed sub-canon of the Basilica Church of Our Lady of Loretto, but he died shortly after reaching Loretto (where he is buried), probably as a result of fever caused by traveling in the summer heat. There seems to be no evidence for the suggestion that he was poisoned. Crashaw wrote Greek and Latin poetry, as well as English, and was familiar with the classical languages, and Spanish and Italian. His chief works are *Steps to the Temple*, religious verse which, as the title suggests, was inspired by *The Temple* of George Herbert, and *The Delights of the Muses*, secular poetry, both published in one volume in 1646 (as Herrick did with his *Hesperides* and *Noble Numbers*, in 1648). Some of his best poems, contained in anthologies, are *In the Holy Nativity*, which was good enough to inspire Milton, *The Flaming Heart*, a hymn to Saint Teresa, *Description of a Religious House*, *Song of Divine Love*, *An Epitaph upon Husband and Wife Which Died and were Buried Together*, and the still popular *Wishes to his Supposed Mistress.* Less well known, but typical of a kind of poetry common in his day, are his poems on the birth of Princess Elizabeth (1635), Princess Anne (1637), and Prince Charles (1640). He is the subject of Cowley's poem *On the Death of Mr. Crashaw.* Faults have been found in his poetry, and critics have attacked them, but he influenced Milton, Pope, Coleridge, and Shelley.

Crashaw, William. b. at Handsworth, near Sheffield, Yorkshire, England, 1572; d. 1626. Puritan scholar, preacher, and poet; father, by his first wife, of Richard Crashaw (c1613–49). Educated at St. John's College, Cambridge, he held (1594) the bishop of Ely's fellowship, to which he was nominated by Queen Elizabeth, received his divinity degree in 1603, and subsequently held various church posts. He was the author of *Romish Forgeries and Falsifications* (1606), *The Complaint, or Dialogue betwixt the Soule and the Bodie of a Damned Man* (1616), poetry, *Milke for Babes or a North Countrie Catechisme* (1618), sermons, and other religious works in Latin and English.

Crassus (kras′us), **Lucius Licinius.** b. 140 B.C.; d. 91 B.C. Roman orator and statesman. He was consul in 95 and censor in 92. He is one of the chief speakers in Cicero's *De Oratore*.

Crassus, Marcus Licinius. [Surnamed **Dives,** meaning "the Rich."] b. probably c114 B.C.; d. 53 B.C. Roman general and statesman. He served under Sulla in the civil war with Marius, and profited by the liberality of his chief, and by the opportunities which the war offered for speculations in confiscated property, to amass a colossal fortune, which he utilized to further his political ambition. He suppressed the slaves' insurrection under Spartacus in 71, was elected consul with Pompey in 70, was censor in 65, formed with Caesar and Pompey the first triumvirate in 60, was elected consul with Pompey in 55, obtained (for five years) the province of Syria in 54, and in 53 undertook an expedition against the Parthians, in the course of which he suffered a terrible defeat at Carrhae (modern Haran) in Mesopotamia (now in Turkey). He was treacherously killed in an interview with a Persian satrap.

Cratchit (krach′it), **Bob.** Scrooge's poor clerk in Charles Dickens's *Christmas Carol;* a cheerful, unselfish fellow, the father of Tim Cratchit ("Tiny Tim").

Cratchit, Tim. [Known as **"Tiny Tim."**] Little cripple in Charles Dickens's *Christmas Carol.*

Crater (krā′tėr). An ancient southern constellation, S of Leo and Virgo. It is supposed to represent a vase with two handles and a base.

Crater, The. Novel by James Fenimore Cooper, published in 1848.

Crater Lake. Small lake in SW Oregon, in the crater of an extinct volcano in the midst of the Cascade Mountains. It is remarkable for its wall of perpendicular rock (1,000–2,000 ft. high) and the brilliant blue of the water, which reaches a depth of nearly 2,000 ft. With the adjoining district it is included in the Crater Lake National Park.

Crater Lake National Park. Park in SW Oregon ab. 62 mi. by road N of Klamath Falls, Ore. The chief feature of the park is the beautiful lake, occupying a large crater rimmed by sheer walls of colored rock, which reach a peak ab. 2,000 ft. above the lake on the SE edge. In the lake is a jagged rocky island, Wizard Island, rising ab. 780 ft. above the lake. The remarkable crater is thought to have been formed by the collapse of the old volcanic cone of Mount Mazama. Crater Lake was discovered in 1853 by prospectors, and remained rather inaccessible until the development of modern roads. In 1902 the area was made a national park. The natural forest of yellow pine, hemlock, and Douglas fir has been preserved. Area of park, ab. 250 sq. mi.; of lake, ab. 21 sq. mi.; elevation of lake, ab. 6,160 ft.; greatest depth, ab. 1,980 ft.

Craters of the Moon National Monument. Volcanic area in S central Idaho, on the Snake River plain ab. 103 mi. by road NW of Pocatello. The area contains numerous volcanic rock formations of fantastic shape, craters, and cinder cones. At least three different periods of eruption and lava flow are recorded by the rocks, the most recent activity having taken place several hundred years ago. The rough and jagged appearance of the landscape caused the region to be named "Craters of the Moon." It was made a national monument in 1924. Area, ab. 74 sq. mi.

Craterus (krat′ėr.us). Killed in Cappadocia, 321 B.C. Macedonian general. He served with distinction under Alexander the Great, and was co-ruler with Antipater in the government of Macedonia, Greece, etc. (323–321).

Crates (krā′tēz). fl. c440 B.C. Athenian comic poet. He was said to have first been an actor in the plays of Cratinus.

Crates. b. in Thebes; fl. c320 B.C. Greek Cynic philosopher, a disciple of Diogenes.

Crates. fl. c270 B.C. Athenian, the pupil and successor of Polemo in the Academy. The friendship of the two was famous in antiquity, and they were said to have been buried in the same tomb.

Crates. b. at Mallus, in Cilicia; fl. c150 B.C. Greek grammarian, founder of the Pergamene school of grammar. His chief work is a commentary on Homer, of which a few fragments remain.

Cratinus (krą.tī′nus). b. c520 B.C.; d. 423 B.C. Athenian comic poet. He exhibited 21 plays, and was victor nine times, triumphing once over Aristophanes. He was called by Mahaffy "the real originator—the Aeschylus—of political comedy." The titles and many fragments of his plays have survived.

Cratippus (krą.tip′us). fl. c400 B.C. Greek historian, the continuator of the history of Thucydides.

Cratippus. fl. c45 B.C. Peripatetic philosopher of Mytilene. He was the friend and instructor of Cicero, who accounted him one of the first philosophers of the Peripatetic school. He accompanied Pompey in his flight after the battle of Pharsalia, and endeavored to comfort and rouse him by engaging him in philosophical discourse. He opened a school at Athens c48 B.C., which was attended by many eminent Romans, including Brutus during his stay at Athens, after the murder of Caesar. He is thought to have written a work on divination.

Crato (krä'tö). City in NE Brazil, in the state of Ceará. 16,030 (1950).

Cratylus (krat'i.lus). Greek philosopher, an elder contemporary of Plato. He was a disciple of Heracleitus. Plato introduces him as the principal speaker in one of his dialogues (the *Cratylus*).

Crau (krō). See **Kru.**

Craufurd or **Crauford** (krô'fėrd), **Quintin.** [Also, **Crawford.**] b. at Kilwinnock, Ayrshire, Scotland, Sept. 22, 1743; d. at Paris, Nov. 23, 1819. Scottish historian, essayist, and civil servant. He was in the service of the East India Company from early youth until 1780, and subsequently spent the greater part of his life at Paris. There he enjoyed the complete confidence of Marie Antoinette and other members of the French royal family, whom he helped to escape from Paris, following the revolution of 1789. He was the author of *Secret History of the King of France, and his Escape from Paris in June, 1791* (first published in 1885), and also wrote works on the Hindus, French literature and history, and Greek culture, and essays on Swift, Marie Antoinette, Mary, Queen of Scots, Madame de Montespan, and others.

Craufurd, Robert. b. May 5, 1764; d. at Ciudad Rodrigo, Spain, Jan. 24, 1812. Noted English general. He served in India from 1790 to 1792, on the Continent with the Austrians until 1797, with Suvarov in Switzerland in 1799, in South America in 1807, and in the siege of Ciudad Rodrigo during the Peninsular campaign.

Crauk (krōk, krouk), **Gustave Adolphe Désiré.** b. at Valenciennes, France, 1827; d. there, 1905. French portrait and monumental sculptor. His statue of Admiral Coligny, and his statue and also his portrait bust of Marshal MacMahon, at Paris, are well known. A museum devoted to his works is maintained in his native city.

Cravant (krȧ.väṅ). [Also, **Crévant.**] Village in the department of Yonne, France, ab. 10 mi. SE of Auxerre. Here, in 1423, the allied English and Burgundians under the Earl of Salisbury defeated the allied French and Scotch.

Craven (krā'vẹn). Hilly district near the headwaters of the rivers Aire and Wharfe, in N central England, in the West Riding of Yorkshire, near Skipton. It is a dairying region, and some sheep are also raised. Formerly it had a worsted-spinning industry.

Craven, Alfred. b. at Bound Brook, N.J., Sept. 16, 1846; d. Sept. 30, 1926. American civil engineer. A graduate (1867) of the U.S. Naval Academy at Annapolis, Md., he was engaged (1871–84) in geological survey and irrigation work in California and in mining engineering in California and Nevada. He moved to New York and served as division engineer (1884–95) of the new Croton Aqueduct and headed (1895–1900) the construction of the Jerome Park Reservoir. In 1900 he was named division engineer (1900) of the Rapid Transit Commission and constructed a section of the subway, serving thereafter as departmental engineer (1907–10) for the Public Service Commission of subway construction, acting chief engineer and chief engineer (1910–16) in charge of the dual system of subway construction, and consulting engineer (1916 *et seq.*) of the Transit Construction Company.

Craven, Avery Odelle. b. in Randolph County, N.C., Aug. 12, 1886—. American historian and teacher. He was graduated from Simpson College (B.A., 1908) and the University of Chicago (Ph.D., 1923), and studied under Frederick Jackson Turner at Harvard. In 1929 he became professor of American history at the University of Chicago. He is the author of *Soil Exhaustion in Virginia and Maryland* (1925), *Edwin Ruffin, Southerner* (1931), *The Repressible Conflict* (1939), *Democracy in American Life* (1941), and *The Coming of the Civil War* (1942).

Craven, Frank. b. at Boston, 1880; d. at Beverly Hills, Calif., Sept. 1, 1945. American actor and playwright. He played in repertory at 16 years of age, and later starred in *The Silver King*, *Artie* (1907), *Bought and Paid For* (1910), *Two Many Cooks*, *This Way Out*, *New Brooms*, *Our Town* (1938), and other plays; his film appearances include *Dangerous Blondes*, *Jack London*, and *Our Town.* He was the author of *Two Many Cooks*, *The First Year*, *Spite Corner*, and other plays.

Craven, Thomas. b. at Salina, Kan., Jan. 6, 1889—. American author and art critic who has written many popular books on art. He was educated at Kansas Wesleyan University, and began his career as a newspaper reporter. He taught at the University of Puerto Rico from 1913 to 1914, and since then has written and lectured on art. Some of his better-known books are *Men of Art* (1931), *Modern Art* (1934), *A Treasury of Art Masterpieces* (1939), and *A Treasury of American Prints* (1939).

Craven, Sir **William.** b. at Burnsall, Yorkshire, England, c1548; d. at London, 1618. Lord mayor of London (1610); father of William Craven (1606–97). He obtained (1569) the freedom of the Merchant Taylors' Company, and was later (1593) made its warden. He was the founder of a grammar school at Burnsall (1602), and served as president of Christ's Hospital (1611–18).

Craven, William. [Title, Earl of **Craven.**] b. at London, 1606; d. at Pinley, England, April 9, 1697. English soldier; son of Sir William Craven (c1548–1618). He served under the prince of Orange (1623 *et seq.*), and was knighted (1627) on his return to England by Charles I. In 1631 he led English troops under Gustavus Adolphus on behalf of Frederick V against Ferdinand II. He was captured at the battle of Limgea in 1637 but ransomed himself in 1639. For his financial aid to Charles I during the English Civil War he was punished (1651) by loss of his estates. He also served Elizabeth of Bohemia, the daughter of Frederick V, and supplied her with money and a home in England. He was a member of the privy council in 1666 and in 1681.

Crawford (krô'fọrd), Earls of. Title of various members of the Scottish family whose notable members are defined under **Lindsay.**

Crawford, Edmund Thornton. b. at Cowden, near Dalkeith, Scotland, 1806; d. at Lasswade, Scotland, Sept. 27, 1885. Scottish painter of landscapes and marines.

Crawford, Francis Marion. b. at Lucca, Italy, Aug. 2, 1854; d. at Sorrento, Italy, April 9, 1909. American novelist; son of Thomas Crawford (1814–1857). He studied at Cambridge, England, and later at Heidelberg and Rome. In 1879 he went to India, where he edited the Allahabad *Indian Herald.* He returned to America in 1880, and after that lived chiefly in Italy. His many romantic and historical novels include *Mr. Isaacs* (1882), *Dr. Claudius* (1883), *To Leeward* (1884), *A Roman Singer* (1884), *An American Politician* (1884), *Zoroaster* (1885), *A Tale of a Lonely Parish* (1886), *Saracinesca* (1887), *Marzio's Crucifix* (1887), *Paul Patoff* (1887), *With the Immortals* (1888), *Greifenstein* (1889), *A Cigarette-Maker's Romance* (1890), *The Witch of Prague* (1891), *Khaled* (1891), *The Three Fates* (1892), *The Ralstons* (1895), *Casa Braccio* (1895), *Via Crucis* (1898), *Marietta* (1901), *The Heart of Rome* (1903), *Soprano* (1905), *Arethusa* (1907), *The White Sister* (1909), *Stradella* (1909), and *Wandering Ghosts* (1911).

Crawford, Isabella Valancy. b. at Dublin, Dec. 25, 1850; d. at Toronto, Canada, Feb. 12, 1887. Canadian poet. She wrote *Malcolm's Katie*, a long pastoral poem describing Paisley, in Upper Canada, and *Old Spookses' Pass*, both of which were published in one volume in 1884. She has been praised for her pictures of cowboy life in western Canada.

Crawford, Mrs. **Louisa.** [Maiden name, **Macartney.**] b. 1790; d. 1858. Author of the words of the Irish song *Kathleen Mavourneen*, the music for which was written by Frederick Nicholls Crouch (1808–96), English musician and composer. Authorship of the song has been attributed to a Mrs. Julia Crawford, a Mrs. Annie Crawford, and Lady Dufferin (1806–67).

Crawford, Mary. Maiden name of **Fraser, Mary.**

Crawford, Mary Caroline. b. at Boston, May 5, 1874; d. there, Nov. 15, 1932. American author, especially of popular historical works. Her books include *The Romance of Old New England Rooftrees* (1902), *The Romance of Old*

New England Churches (1903), *The College Girl of America* (1904), *Among Old New England Inns* (1907), *St. Botolph's Town* (1908), *Goethe and His Women Friends* (1911), *Social Life in Old New England* (1914), *In the Days of the Pilgrim Fathers* (1920), and *Famous Families of Massachusetts* (1930).

Crawford, Nathaniel Macon. b. near Lexington, Ga., March 22, 1811; d. near Atlanta, Ga., Oct. 27, 1871. American Baptist clergyman and educator.

Crawford, Nelson Antrim. b. at Miller, S.D., May 4, 1888—. American editor and author. He has served as director of information (1925–28) of the U.S. Department of Agriculture, and editor in chief (1928 *et seq.*) of *Household Magazine*. He is the author of the collection of verse *The Carrying of the Ghost* (1923), of the works of fiction *A Man of Learning* (1928) and *Unhappy Wind* (1930), and also of *We Liberals* (1936) and *Your Child Faces War* (1937); he won the Kansas poetry prize in 1920 and the Betty Earle lyric prize in 1923.

Crawford, Thomas. b. at New York, March 29, 1814; d. at London, Oct. 10, 1857. American sculptor; father of Francis Marion Crawford. He was a pupil of the Danish sculptor Thorvaldsen, and did most of his work at Rome. His works include the statue *Armed Liberty* on the Capitol dome and bronze doors for the Senate building, at Washington; *Beethoven*, a bust of Josiah Quincy, and *Orpheus*, at Boston; the Washington monument at Richmond, Va., and others.

Crawford, William Harris. b. in Amherst County, Va., Feb. 24, 1772; d. at Ellerton, Ga., Sept. 15, 1834. American statesman. He was U.S. senator from Georgia (1807–13), minister to France (1813–15), secretary of war (1815–16), secretary of the treasury (1816–25), and candidate for the presidency in 1824.

Crawford Notch. [Also, **the Notch.**] Deep, narrow valley in the White Mountains, in N New Hampshire, SW of Mount Washington, between Mount Webster and Mount Willey.

Crawfordsville (krô′fọrdz.vil). City in W Indiana, county seat of Montgomery County, ab. 44 mi. NW of Indianapolis: seat of Wabash College. The study where Lew Wallace, author of *Ben Hur*, did his writing is maintained as a museum. 12,851 (1950).

Crawfurd (krô′fėrd), **John.** b. on the island of Islay, Scotland, Aug. 13, 1783; d. at London, May 11, 1868. Scottish Orientalist and ethnologist, much of whose life was spent as a British army doctor in India. Sent by the British government on a mission to Thailand (Siam) in 1822 to negotiate a commercial treaty, he wrote one of the first detailed English accounts of that land and its people. Appointed administrator of Singapore (1823); collected and published valuable information on the Malay Archipelago.

Crawley (krô′li). Name of a well-known family in Thackeray's novel *Vanity Fair*. Sir Pitt Crawley, the head of the family, is a rich but sordid old man, fond of low society; to his house Becky Sharp goes as governess. She makes herself so attractive that he offers to marry her, and she is thereby forced to acknowledge her secret marriage with Rawdon Crawley, his youngest son. The latter is a blackleg and a gambler, but is fond of his wife and has a certain honor of his own. His brother, Mr. Pitt Crawley, is a prig with "hay-colored whiskers and straw-colored hair. . . . He was called Miss Crawley at Eton, where his younger brother Rawdon used to lick him violently." The second Lady Crawley, a pale and apathetic woman, is a contrast to her sister-in-law, the little, eager, active, black-eyed Mrs. Bute Crawley. The Reverend Bute Crawley is a "tall, stately, jolly, shovel-hatted man," a horse-racing parson whose wife writes his sermons for him. Miss Crawley, the sister of Sir Pitt and the Reverend Bute, is a kind and yet undeniably selfish, worldly and yet often generous old woman, "who had a balance at her banker's which would have made her beloved anywhere."

Crayer (krī′ėr), **Gaspar de.** b. at Antwerp, Nov. 18, 1584; d. at Ghent, Jan. 27, 1669. Flemish painter. Among his best-known works are *Saint Catharine*, at Ghent, and Madonnas at Munich and Vienna.

Crayford (krā′fọrd). Urban district in SE England, in Kent, ab. 15 mi. SE of London by rail. It is a highly developed residential area of suburban London, and also has some industrial development. Crayford was on the route of Watling Street, from the Strait of Dover through London to Chester, one of the great roads built by the Romans in ancient Britain. The town is usually identified with Creccanford, where Hengist defeated (c457) the Britons. 27,951 (1951).

Crayon Miscellany, The. Three volumes (1835) of prose by "Geoffrey Crayon," which was one of the pseudonyms of Washington Irving. The volumes are *A Tour on the Prairies*, describing a tour Irving made in October and November, 1832, in the American West, *Legends of the Conquest of Spain*, and *Abbotsford and Newstead Abbey.*

Crazy Castle. Nickname of Skelton Castle, the house in Yorkshire of John Hall Stevenson, who wrote a series of broad stories which he called *Crazy Tales.* Stevenson was a kinsman of Laurence Sterne, and is now generally recognized as having been the original in real life of the character Eugenius in *Tristram Shandy.*

Crazy Horse. [Indian name, **Tashunca-Uitco.**] b. c1849; d. Sept. 5, 1877. American Indian chief of the Oglala tribe of the Sioux. When he disregarded the order of the U.S. War Department that all roving tribes must return to their reservations by Jan. 1, 1876, his village near the mouth of the Little Powder River was destroyed (March 17, 1876) by a force of U.S. cavalry under Colonel J. J. Reynolds. He thereafter took a leading part in the Sioux uprising against U.S. authority which reached its high point in the annihilation (June 25, 1876) of Custer's command. He surrendered (May 6, 1877) and was killed (Sept. 5, 1877) in a scuffle while resisting confinement.

Creak (krēk), **Mount.** Sharp peak in Antarctica, lying N of the Fry Glacier, in the Prince Albert Mountains of Victoria Land, in ab. 76°34′ S., 162°05′ E. Elevation, ab. 5,200 ft.

Creakle (krē′kl), **Mr.** In Charles Dickens's *David Copperfield*, the principal of the school at Salem House where David Copperfield was sent; a man of fiery temper who could speak only in a whisper.

Cream of the Jest, The. Novel (1917) by James Branch Cabell.

Creasy (krē′si), Sir **Edward Shepherd.** b. at Bexley, Kent, England, Sept. 12, 1812; d. at London, Jan. 27, 1878. English historian. His works include *Fifteen Decisive Battles of the World* (1852), *Rise and Progress of the English Constitution* (1856), *History of the Ottoman Turks* (1856), and others.

Creation, The. Poem by Sir Richard Blackmore, published in 1712.

Creation, The. [German title, **Die Schöpfung.**] Oratorio by Franz Joseph Haydn, produced at Vienna on April 2, 1798.

Crébillon (krā.bē.yôṅ), **Claude Prosper Jolyot de.** b. at Paris, Feb. 14, 1707; d. there, April 12, 1777. French novelist; son of Prosper Jolyot de Crébillon (1674–1742).

Crébillon, Prosper Jolyot de. [Original name, **Prosper Jolyot,** Sieur de **Crais-Billon.**] b. at Dijon, France, Jan. 13, 1674; d. at Paris, June 17, 1762. French tragic poet. He was appointed censor in 1735, and received a place in the Royal Library in 1745. In 1731 he became a member of the French Academy. His plays include *Atrée et Thyeste* (1707), *Électre* (1709), *Rhadamiste et Zénobie* (1711), *Xerxès* (1714), *Sémiramis* (1717), *Pyrrhus* (1726), *Catilina* (1748), and *Le Triumvirat* (1754). Another play, *Cromwell*, was not completed.

Creccanford (krek′ạn.fọrd). See under **Crayford.**

Crécy (krā.sē). [Full name, **Crécy-en-Ponthieu** (-äṅ-pôṅ.tyė); English, **Cressy.**] Village in N France, in the department of Somme, ab. 30 mi. NW of Amiens. Here, on Aug. 26, 1346, the English under Edward III (ab. 30,000–40,000) defeated the French army under Philip VI (ab. 70,000). The loss of the French was ab. 30,000.

Credi (krā′dē), **Lorenzo di.** b. at Florence, Italy, 1459; d. there, Jan. 12, 1537. Florentine painter. He was originally a goldsmith, but turned to painting, which he studied under Andrea del Verrocchio. One of his most noted paintings is a *Nativity*, in the academy at Florence.

Crédit Mobilier (kred′it mọ.bēl′yėr; French, krā.dē mo-bē.lyā). In French history, a banking corporation formed in 1852, under the name of the Société Générale du Crédit Mobilier, with a capital of 60 million francs, for the placing of loans, handling the stocks of various other companies, and the transaction of a general banking business. It engaged in very extensive transactions, buying, selling, and loaning in such a manner as to bring into one organized whole all the stocks and credit of France, and was apparently in a most prosperous condition until it proposed to issue bonds to the amount of 240 million francs. This amount of paper currency frightened financiers, and the government forbade its issue. From this time the company rapidly declined, and closed its affairs in 1867, with great loss to all but its proprietors.

Crédit Mobilier. In U.S. history, a corporation chartered in Pennsylvania in 1863 with a capital of two and a half million dollars. In 1867, after passing into new hands, and increasing in stock to three and three quarters million dollars, it became a new company for the building of the Union Pacific Railroad. For a few years it paid large dividends, and its stock rose in value. However, in a trial in Pennsylvania in 1872 as to the ownership of some stock, it was shown that certain congressmen secretly possessed stock, and both houses of the Congress that met in December of that year appointed committees of investigation. The Senate committee recommended the expulsion of one member, but the Senate did nothing. The House committee recommended the expulsion of two of its members, but the House, instead, passed resolutions of censure.

Crediton (kred'i.tọn). Urban district and market town in SW England, in Devonshire, situated on the river Creedy near its confluence with the river Exe ab. 8 mi. NW of Exeter, ab. 179 mi. SW of London by rail. It was formerly a serge-manufacturing center. Crediton was the birthplace of Saint Boniface. 3,992 (1951).

Credner (krād'nėr), **Karl Hermann.** b. at Gotha, Germany, Oct. 1, 1841; d. 1913. German geologist, appointed (1870) professor at Leipzig. He traveled (1864–68) in North America. Among his scientific publications the most notable are those relating to glacial problems.

Credulous (kreḑ'ū.lus), **Justice** and **Mrs. Bridget.** Ignorant, good-natured pair in Richard Brinsley Sheridan's farce *St. Patrick's Day.* They are fooled by the scheming lieutenant who marries their daughter Lauretta. Mrs. Bridget is a kind of Mrs. Malaprop.

Cree (krē). Collective term for a number of North American Indian tribes inhabiting a large area in C Canada from W Quebec to E Saskatchewan. The languages are of the Algonquian family.

Creech (krēch), **Thomas.** b. at Blandford, Dorsetshire, England, 1659; committed suicide, in June, 1700. English writer, translator of *Lucretius* (1682) and other classical authors.

Creech, William. [Pseudonym, **Theophrastus.**] b. at Newbattle, Midlothian, Scotland, April 21, 1745; d. at Edinburgh, Jan. 14, 1815. Scottish essayist and letter writer, publisher of Burns. Educated at Edinburgh University, he went into business with a Scottish printer, Alexander Kincaid, becoming after Kincaid's retirement (1773) the head of the firm, which is noted as the first publisher of the works of Beattie, Blair, Cullen and Gregory, Dugald Stewart, Mackenzie, and of Burns, with whom he later quarreled. Creech was lord provost of Edinburgh (October, 1811–October, 1813), and a fellow of the Royal Society and the Antiquarian Society. He is the subject of Burns's *Burlesque Lament for the Absence of William Creech, Publisher* (1787). His essays, contributed under his pseudonym to the Edinburgh *Courant,* were published (1791, 1815) as *Fugitive Pieces.*

Creek (krēk). North American Indian tribe of more than a score of villages, formerly distributed over a large area of C Georgia and Alabama, but since the early 19th century chiefly settled in Oklahoma. The language is of the Muskogean family.

Creek Confederacy. Collective name for a number of villages of the Creek tribe of North American Indians. The confederacy represented, for its time, a formidable military obstacle to white expansion in the SE region of the U.S., reaching its high point (in a military sense) with the Creek War of 1814–15. In this conflict U.S. troops under Andrew Jackson were opposed by the Creeks under Tecumseh. In its original inception, however, the Creek Confederacy came into being primarily as a means of attaining security against attacks by other Indian tribes to the north of the Creek villages; opposition to white expansion did not become important until the late 18th century.

Creel (krēl), **George.** b. in Lafayette County, Missouri, Dec. 1, 1876—. American editor, publicity director, and author. He served as editor of the Kansas City *Independent* (1899–1909), Denver *Post* (1909–10), and *Rocky Mountain News* (1911–13), chairman (1917–19) of the Committee on Public Information, and chairman (1935) of the national advisory board of the Works Progress Administration, and was appointed (1939) U.S. commissioner of the Golden Gate Exposition at San Francisco. His works include *Quatrains of Christ* (1907), *Wilson and the Issues* (1916), *Ireland's Fight for Freedom* (1919), *The People Next Door* (1926), *Tom Paine—Liberty Bell* (1931), and *War Criminals and Punishment* (1944).

Creelman (krēl'mạn), **James.** b. at Montreal, Canada, Nov. 12, 1859; d. Feb. 12, 1915. American journalist and author. He was editor (1892–93) of the New York *Evening Telegram,* for 16 years in the service of the New York *Herald* as editor and correspondent, war correspondent for various American papers during the Sino-Japanese War, the Greco-Turkish War, the Spanish-American War, and the Philippine insurrection of 1899, on the editorial staff of the New York *World* (1899–1906), and associate editor (1906–10) of *Pearson's Magazine.* He was a member of the New York City Board of Education and was appointed president of the Civil Service Commission of New York in 1911. His works include *On the Great Highway* (1901), *Eagle Blood* (1902), *Why We Love Lincoln* (1909), and *Diaz, Master of Mexico* (1910).

Creevey (krē'vi), **Thomas.** b. at Liverpool, England, in March, 1768; d. at London, in February, 1838. English diarist and lawyer. He was on friendly terms with Fox, Sheridan, Grey, and other leading Whigs, and in 1806 was made secretary of the board of control in the "All-the-Talents" Fox-Grenville ministry. For 36 years he kept a diary and various papers that he sent to and received from important political and public characters of his day. This material, much of which was destroyed, is the basis of the *Creevey Papers,* and was not published until 1903, when it was edited by Sir Herbert Maxwell. It is of value for the picture it gives, from the Whig viewpoint, of life and conditions in the late Georgian era.

Creighton (krā'tọn), **Edward.** b. Aug. 31, 1820; d. Nov. 5, 1874. American pioneer in telegraph development. He was associated with his brother, John Andrew Creighton, and with Hiram Sibley in extending (1860–61) telegraph lines to the Pacific coast.

Creighton, James Edwin. b. at Pictou, Nova Scotia, 1861; d. Oct. 8, 1924. American philosopher, leading exponent of idealism in the U.S. He served as instructor (1889–92), associate professor (1892–95), and Sage professor (1895–1924) of logic and metaphysics and as dean of the graduate school (1914 *et seq.*) and faculty representative on the board of trustees (1922) of Cornell University, at Ithaca, N.Y. He was coeditor (1893–1902), with Jacob Gould Schurman, and editor in chief (1902–24) of the *Philosophical Review,* American editor (1896–1924) of *Kant-Studien,* and one of the founders and first president (1902–03) of the American Philosophical Association; author of *An Introductory Logic* (1898) and *Studies in Speculative Philosophy* (1925).

Creighton, John Andrew. [Called **"Count Creighton."**] b. in Licking County, Ohio, Oct. 15, 1831; d. Feb. 7, 1907. American philanthropist; brother of Edward Creighton (1820–74). He was associated (1860–61) with his brother in the extension of telegraph lines to the Pacific coast, and was a benefactor of Creighton University, at Omaha, Neb., which was endowed by his brother's widow.

Creighton (krī'tọn), **Mandell.** b. at Carlisle, Cumberland, England, July 5, 1843; d. at Fulham Palace, London, Jan. 14, 1901. English biographer, bishop, historian, and teacher. Educated at Durham grammar school and at Merton College, Oxford, of which he was a fellow, he was also a fellow of Emmanuel College, Cambridge, and first Dixie professor (1884) of ecclesiastical history at Cambridge. He was founder and first editor (1886–91) of the *English Historical Review.* He served as canon of Worcester and Windsor, bishop of Peterborough, and bishop (1897 *et seq.*) of London. Among his works are *Roman History* (1875), *The Age of Elizabeth* and *Simon de Montfort* (both 1876), *History of England* (1879), *History of the Papacy During the Reformation* (5 vols., 1882–

94), *Cardinal Wolsey* (1888), *The Early Renaissance in England* and *Persecution and Tolerance* (both 1895), *Queen Elizabeth* and *The English National Character* (both 1896), *History of the Papacy from the Great Schism to the Sack of Rome* (6 vols., 1897), many sermons, lectures, and essays, and biographical articles in the *Dictionary of National Biography*. His wife edited his *Historical Lectures and Addresses* (1903) and published his *Life and Letters* (2 vols., 1904).

Creil (krey'). Town in N France, in the department of Oise, situated on the Oise River, ab. 30 mi. N of Paris. It is an industrial center, having stone quarries, construction works, and metallurgical and machine tool factories. World War II damage was heavy. 10,024 (1946).

Creizenach (krī'zẹ.naċh), **Wilhelm.** b. at Frankfort on the Main, Germany, June 4, 1851; d. at Dresden, Germany, May 15, 1919. German historian of literature, professor at Kraków (1883–1913). He wrote a five-volume *Geschichte des neueren Dramas* (1894 *et seq.*). His lesser works include *Versuch einer Geschichte des Volksschauspiels vom Doctor Faust* (1878).

Crelle (krel'ẹ), **August Leopold.** b. at Eichwerder, Prussia, March 11, 1780; d. at Berlin, Oct. 6, 1855. German mathematician and engineer.

Crema (krā'mä). Town and commune in NW Italy, in the *compartimento* (region) of Lombardy, in the province of Cremona, situated on the Marzano canal and the Serio River, ab. 24 mi. SE of Milan. The town has textile and metallurgical industries, hat manufactures, and dairies; the surrounding district produces rice, grain, and cattle. Crema is the seat of a bishopric. The cathedral, in Lombard Gothic style, dates from the period 1284–1341; the Church of Santa Maria della Croce (c1500) is a notable Renaissance building. Conquered by the emperor Frederick I (Frederick Barbarossa) in 1160, the town was later under the rule of Milan (1338–1453) and of Venice (1453–1797), and in the first half of the 19th century belonged to Austria. Pop. of commune, 25,163 (1936); of town, 13,912 (1936).

Crémazie (krā.mȧ.zē), **(Joseph) Octave.** b. at Quebec, Canada, April 16, 1827; d. 1879. Canadian poet and scholar. He was educated at Quebec Seminary, and with his brothers established a bookshop that became a celebrated literary center. He contributed verse to the *Journal de Québec* and to *Les Soirées Canadiennes*, a magazine that grew out of the society he helped to found. In 1862 he left Canada for France, where he ended his days in poverty, under the name of Jules Fontaines. His works are *Promenade des trois morts*, a melancholy poem, *Chant du vieux soldat canadien* (1855), an intensely patriotic poem which gained him recognition as the official poet of Canada, and a prose journal, *Siège de Paris*, an eye-witness account of the siege of 1870.

Cremer (krā'mėr), **Herbert.** b. at Penang, Malaya, Dec. 22, 1873—. Dutch industrialist, with interests in shipping and in railroads and plantations in the East Indies. He was a member of the firm of Cremer and Heeren (1898–1916), dealers in tobacco, and later head (1916 *et seq.*) of the Deli Company and the Rimboen Tobacco Company.

Cremer, Max. b. at Ürdingen, near Düsseldorf, Germany, March 11, 1865; d. at Munich, Germany, May 22, 1935. German physiologist. He became (1893) Privatdocent of physiology at the University of Munich, where he was named (1901) professor, became (1909) professor at the Academy of Cologne, and in 1911 was appointed full professor of physiology and director of the Physiological Institute of the Veterinary School at Berlin. He was the author of *Phlorhizin* (1924), *Ursache der elektrischen Erscheinungen* (1928), and *Erregungsgesetze der Nerven* (1929).

Cremer (krē'mėr), Sir **William Randal.** b. at Fareham, Wiltshire, England, March 18, 1838; d. at London, July 22, 1908. English pacifist, winner of the Nobel peace prize in 1903. A trade unionist, he helped organize (1860) the Carpenters' and Joiners' Union and was secretary (1865–66) of the British section of the International Workingmen's Association, but resigned from the latter post in protest against the revolutionary program advocated by the organization's Continental representatives. As secretary (1871–1908) of the Workingmen's Peace Association, he traveled in Europe and America advocating international arbitration. He was twice (1885–95, 1900–08) member of Parliament and was editor (1889) of the *Arbitrator*, a monthly peace journal.

Cremera (krem'ẹ.rạ). In ancient geography, a small river in Etruria which joins the Tiber a few miles N of Rome. It is the traditional scene of the defeat of the Fabii in c477 B.C.

Crémieux (krā.myė), **Benjamin.** b. at Paris, Dec. 1, 1888; d. in a concentration camp, 1944. French literary critic and novelist. Author of *Le Premier de la classe* (1921), *Vingtième siècle* (1925), *Inquiétude et Réconstruction* (1931), and of various short studies, particularly of Italian literature, he was highly reputed as an interpreter of the moods of his contemporary intellectuals.

Crémieux, Isaac Moïse. [Known as **Adolphe Crémieux.**] b. at Nîmes, France, April 30, 1796; d. at Passy, Paris, Feb. 10, 1880. French jurist and politician. He was minister of justice (1848, 1870–71), and was appointed life senator in 1875.

Cremona (krẹ.mō'nạ; Italian, krā.mō'nä). Province in NW Italy, in the *compartimento* (region) of Lombardy. Capital, Cremona; area, ab. 700 sq. mi.; pop. 369,483 (1936), 374,000 (est. 1946).

Cremona. City and commune in NW Italy, in the *compartimento* (region) of Lombardy, the capital of the province of Cremona, on the Po River, ab. 50 mi. SE of Milan. It is an important commercial and industrial center. Situated in a cattle and hog raising district, it produces sausages and dairy products and also other foodstuffs, such as mustard and candies (torrone). In the Middle Ages it was famous for its terra-cotta manufactures and between the 16th and 18th centuries for several families of makers of musical instruments, including the Amati, Stradivari, and Guarneri. In addition to violins, pianos are manufactured today. Cremona's most important industry is silk; agricultural machinery and hats are also made. The oldest among the city's art treasures is the Romanesque basilica church of San Michele (12th century). Founded by the Gauls, Cremona became a Roman colony in 218 B.C., but was destroyed in 69 B.C. in the struggle between Vitellius and Vespasian. It followed the Ghibelline cause in the Middle Ages, but had to submit to Milan in 1334; in the 18th and 19th centuries it was under Austrian domination. Buildings of interest to tourists were undamaged in World War II. Pop. of commune, 64,019 (1936); of city, 51,963 (1936).

Cremona (krā.mō'nä), **Luigi.** b. at Pavia, Italy, Dec. 7, 1830; d. at Rome, June 10, 1903. Italian geometer, member of numerous academies in Italy and elsewhere, best known for his work on the so-called Cremona transformations. He graduated from the University of Pavia, and taught at various universities, including Bologna (1860) and Milan (1866). He also exerted a strong influence on mathematical education in Italy on the secondary school level. His books include *Introduzione ad una teoria geometrica delle curve piane* (1862) and *Elementi di geometria proietiva* (1872). His *Opere matematiche* appeared in three volumes (1914–17), published under the auspices of the Accademia dei Lincei.

Cremorne Gardens (krem'ọrn). Former place of amusement at London, situated near Battersea Bridge N of the Thames. It was closed in 1877.

Creon (krē'on). In Greek legend, a king of Thebes, contemporary with Oedipus.

Creon. In Greek legend, a king of Corinth, father of Creusa, or Glauce, the intended wife of Jason.

Crépy (krā.pē). [Also: **Crépy-en-Laonnois** (-äṅ.lȧ.nwȧ), **Crespy.**] Village in N France, in the department of Aisne, ab. 6 mi. NW of Laon. Here was signed, on Sept. 18, 1544, a treaty of peace between Francis I of France and the emperor Charles V. The former renounced claims to Lombardy, Naples, and the suzerainty of Flanders and Artois; the latter renounced claims to Burgundy.

Crerar (krē'rär, krir'är), **Henry Duncan Graham.** b. April 28, 1888—. Canadian army officer. He studied at the Royal Military College at Kingston, served (1914–18) in World War I, and was general staff officer (1929–35) in the department of national defense, director (1935–38) of military operations and intelligence, chief (1940–41) of the Canadian general staff, commander of the Canadian Corps (1942–44) in the Mediterranean and of the First Canadian Army (1944–45). He was promoted to general in 1944 and retired in 1945.

Crerar, John. b. at New York, March 8, 1827; d. at Chicago, Oct. 19, 1889. American financier and philanthropist. He was a manufacturer (1859 *et seq.*) of railroad supplies and contractors' materials at Chicago, and one of the incorporators (1867) of the Pullman Palace Car Company (later the Pullman Company). He gave financial aid toward St. Gaudens' statue of Lincoln and endowed the John Crerar Library at Chicago.

Crerar, Thomas Alexander. b. at Molesworth, Ontario, Canada, Oct. 17, 1876—. Canadian statesman. Farm-bred, he became a farmer and later a grain-elevator operator. He took a leading part in organizing the United Grain Growers, Ltd., which under his direction as president (1907–29) became one of the most successful of farmers' coöperative ventures in the Canadian West. In 1917, being at that time a Liberal in politics, he entered the coalition cabinet headed by the Conservative Robert Borden, as minister of agriculture, but resigned in 1919 because he could not support Borden's high tariff proposals. He became the leader (1920–21) of the National Progressive Party, and its leader in the Dominion House of Commons. In 1922 he retired from public life, only to return as minister of railways and canals (1929–30) in the Liberal Mackenzie King cabinet. Later he served, again under Mackenzie King, as minister of mines (1935–45). In 1945 he became a member of the Senate of Canada.

Cres (tsres). [Italian, **Cherso.**] Island in NW Yugoslavia, in the federative unit of Croatia, in the Adriatic Sea off the coast of Istria, S of Rijeka (Fiume). 7,570 (1936).

"Crescent City." Nickname of **New Orleans.**

Crescentini (krā.shen.tē′nē), **Girolamo.** b. at Urbania, near Urbino, Italy, Feb. 2, 1766; d. at Naples, Italy, April 24, 1846. Italian mezzo-soprano singer and composer, professor (1816 *et seq.*) at the Royal College of Music at Naples.

Crescentius (kre̤.sen′shus, -shi.us) or **Cencius** (sen′shi.us), **Johannes.** [Surnamed **"the Younger."**] d. 998. Leader of the popular faction at Rome. Having obtained the dignity of consul in 980, he usurped the government, and announced his intention of restoring the ancient republic. He opposed Pope Gregory V, who was elected through the influence of the emperor Otto III, and, supported by the Byzantine court, put forward John XVI as antipope. He was defeated by Otto at Sant' Angelo (April 29, 998) and put to death. According to the legend, Crescentius was revenged by his widow Stephania or Theodora, who, having succeeded in gaining the confidence and love of the emperor, put him to death by poison.

Crescent Moon. Novel by Francis Brett Young, published in 1918. It is based on the author's experience as a Royal Army Medical Corps officer in Africa during World War I.

Crescenzi (krā.shen′tsē), **Pietro.** b. at Bologna, Italy, 1230; d. there, c1307. Italian writer on agriculture, author of *Opus ruralium commodorum* (1471), one of the first of printed books, and others.

Crescimbeni (krā.shēm.bā′nē), **Giovanni Maria.** b. at Macerata, Italy, Oct. 9, 1663; d. March 8, 1728. Italian poet and literary historian, one of the founders (1690) of the Academy of Arcadians. He was the author of *L'Istoria della volgar poesia* (1698), and others.

Cresco (kres′kō). City in NE Iowa, county seat of Howard County: shipping point for dairy products, livestock, poultry, and eggs. 3,638 (1950).

Cresilas (kres′i.la̤s). b. at Cydonia, Crete; fl. c450 B.C. Greek sculptor. His career was made at Athens, where he was a contemporary of Phidias, and where he executed a portrait statue of Pericles. Copies exist of a figure of a wounded Amazon, which Cresilas carved for a competition held at Ephesus.

Crespi (krās′pē), **Giovanni Battista.** [Called **il Cerano** (from his birthplace).] b. at Cerano, Piedmont, Italy, 1557; d. at Milan, Italy, 1633. Italian painter. His best works are at Milan, where he was director (1629 *et seq.*) of work on the cathedral.

Crespi, Giuseppe Maria. [Surnamed **Lo Spagnuolo,** meaning "the Spaniard."] b. at Bologna, Italy, 1665; d. there, July 16, 1747. Italian painter. He did much of his work at Venice.

Crespi, Juan. b. 1721; d. 1782. Spanish Franciscan, notable as missionary and explorer in California. He came to America in 1749, and after serving in various missions in California he accompanied the expedition of Portolá (1769), which, exploring along the coast northward from Monterey and San Diego, discovered San Francisco Bay. He was chaplain to the exploratory expedition headed by Juan Pérez (1774), which had as its aim the assertion of Spanish suzerainty N to the 60th parallel. Crespi's diaries provide historically valuable information concerning the Pérez mission. From 1770 he was at the head of the Mission San Carlos Borromeo, now within the limits of Carmel-by-the-Sea, Calif.

Crespo (krās′pö), **Antônio Cândido Gonçalves.** b. at Rio de Janeiro, March 11, 1846; d. at Lisbon, Portugal, June 11, 1883. Brazilian-born poet who lived and wrote in Portugal, where he has been rated by many critics as the most typical representative of the Parnassian school of poetry. His books of poems were *Miniaturas* (1870) and *Nocturnos* (1882). He was also a journalist. In collaboration with his wife, Maria Amália Vaz de Carvalho, he wrote *Contos para os nossos filhos* (1882), a collection of tales officially adopted in Portugal as a school textbook.

Crespo (kres′pō), **Joaquín.** b. in Miranda, Venezuela, c1845; killed April 17, 1898. Venezuelan politician. He succeeded Guzmán Blanco as president (being elected as his candidate), and served from Feb. 20, 1884, to Feb. 20, 1886. In 1892 he headed a revolt against Palacio, occupied Caracas (Oct. 7, 1892), and soon after was elected president. A new constitution was adopted in June, 1893, and under it Crespo was inaugurated president for four years, on March 14, 1894. Friction with England as to the border of British Guiana brought U.S. intervention (1895) under the Monroe Doctrine. Crespo was killed during suppression of a revolt against his successor, Ignacio Andrade.

Cresques (kres′ke̤s), **Abraham.** See **Abraham Cresques.**

Cressent (kre.säṅ), **Charles.** b. at Amiens, France, Dec. 16, 1685; d. at Paris, Jan. 10, 1768. French cabinetmaker and sculptor, a master of the Regence style. His grandfather and father were cabinetmakers and sculptors. At first his interest was mainly in sculpture and bronze craft, but after studying with Boulle, cabinetmaker to Louis XIV, he was appointed to a similar post with Phillipe II, Duc d'Orléans, regent for Louis XV. In this position he strongly influenced the development of the Regence style and was one of its greater artists. Among those partial to ornate furniture, Cressent's creations are most highly regarded, with their elegant lines, rich veneers and inlays, and beautifully modeled gilt bronze ornamentation. The opulent female figures which typically are placed at the corners of his tables are especially admired.

Cressey (kres′i), **George Babcock.** b. at Tiffin, Ohio, Dec. 15, 1896—. American geographer and geologist. While assistant professor at the University of Shanghai (1923–29), he worked in the field in Mongolia, Tibet, and the Chinese interior. He was professor and chairman of the department of geology and geography at Syracuse (1931–45) and chairman of the geography department (1945 *et seq.*). He has done field work also in Asiatic U.S.S.R. (1923, 1937, 1944) and has served as a delegate to several scientific congresses and as consultant in geography to China, the U.S.S.R., and the U.S. Author of *Indiana Sand Dunes and Shore Lines of Lake Michigan Basin* (1928), *China's Geographical Foundations* (1934), *Asia's Lands and Peoples* (1944), *The Basis of Soviet Strength* (1945), and numerous articles on Asiatic geography.

Cressid (kres′id) or **Cressida** (kres′i.da̤). Mythical daughter of the Trojan priest Calchas, whose supposed infidelities have made her name a byword for female faithlessness. The story of Cressid is believed to have originated with Benoît de Sainte-Maure, a 12th-century trouvère, who called his character Briseida (she was thus identified with Homer's Briseis). Guido delle Colonne later reproduced the story in a popular Latin work, the *Historia Trojana.* The story was later taken up by Boccacio, Chaucer, and Shakespeare. A modern version may be found in Christopher Morley's *The Trojan Horse* (1937). Shakespeare's *Troilus and Cressida* is probably the best-known version of the tale.

Cressid or **Creseide** (kres′id), **Testament of,** and its continuation **The Complaint of Creseide.** Poems by Robert Henryson, attributed by Stowe (1561) to Chaucer.

Cressier (kre.syā), Baron **Frédéric Gonzague Reynold de.** See **Reynold de Cressier,** Baron **Frédéric Gonzague.**

Cressingham (kres′ing.ạm), **Lady.** In Thomas Middleton's play *Anything for a Quiet Life,* a whimsical and attractive woman whose caprices are accounted for by her desire to reconcile her husband and stepson and to benefit them both.

Cresskill (kres′kil). Borough in NE New Jersey, in Bergen County, near Paterson and the Hudson River, and opposite Yonkers, N.Y. 3,534 (1950).

Cresson (kres′ọn). Borough in S Pennsylvania, in Cambria County near Altoona: railroad shops. 2,569 (1950).

Cresswell (kres′wel, -wẹl), Sir **Cresswell.** b. at Newcastle, England, 1794; d. at London, July 29, 1863. English jurist, first judge of the English divorce court (1858).

Cressy (kres′i), **Hugh Paulinus Serenus.** b. at Thorpe-Salvin, Yorkshire, England, c1605; d. at East Grinstead, Sussex, England, Aug. 10, 1674. English Benedictine monk and theologian. As a young man he took Anglican orders and served as chaplain to various noblemen. Travel with one of his patrons in Roman Catholic countries resulted in his conversion to that Church, in 1646, and he was received into the Benedictine order at Douai, France. He was befriended by Queen Henrietta Maria of England, and later was chaplain to Catherine of Braganza, queen consort of Charles II. In his *Exomologesis* (1647) he justified his change of religion. He edited a number of theological works, and was himself a prolific writer, among his books being *Roman Catholic Doctrines No Novelties,* and *Church History of Brittany or England,* a work marked by an objectivity unusual in such works at that time.

Crest (krest). Town in SE France, in the department of Drôme, situated on the Drôme River, ab. 15 mi. SE of Valence. The medieval tower dating from the 12th century is one of the largest buildings of this sort in France. The town has manufactures of paper, silk, and woolens. 5,359 (1946).

Crestline (krest′līn). [Former spelling, **Crest Line.**] Village in C Ohio, in Crawford County: manufactures of road-making machinery, furnaces, stoves, and women's clothing; railroad shops. 4,614 (1950).

Creston (kres′tọn). City in S Iowa, county seat of Union County, in a bluegrass region: railroad yards and machine shops. 8,317 (1950).

Crestview (krest′vū). Town in NW Florida, county seat of Okaloosa County, ab. 45 mi. NE of Pensacola. Pecans and blueberries are raised in the area. In the decade between the last two U.S. censuses its population more than doubled. 2,252 (1940), 5,003 (1950).

Creswell (kres′wel, -wẹl), **John Angel James.** b. at Port Deposit, Md., Nov. 18, 1828; d. at Elkton, Md., Dec. 23, 1891. American politician and cabinet member. He was a member (1861–62) of the Maryland house of delegates, assistant adjutant general (1863), representative in Congress (1863–65), and U.S. senator (1865 *et seq.*). As postmaster general (1869–74), he lowered the rate of postage to foreign countries, speeded up delivery abroad, introduced one-cent post cards, and placed limits on the franking system.

Creswick (krez′ik, kres′wik), **Thomas.** b. at Sheffield, England, Feb. 5, 1811; d. at Bayswater, London, Dec. 28, 1869. English landscape painter. His subjects were chiefly English rural scenery.

Cret (krā), **Paul Philippe.** b. at Lyons, France, Oct. 23, 1876; d. 1945. American architect. He studied architecture at Lyons and at the École des Beaux-Arts, Paris, and was professor of design (1903 *et seq.*) at the University of Pennsylvania. He was the recipient of several prizes and medals, and was the architect of the Pan-American Union building at Washington, D.C., the Washington memorial arch at Valley Forge, the Folger Shakespeare Library and the Federal Reserve Building at Washington, and others.

Cretaceous Period (krẹ.tā′shus). Geologic age in the second half of the Mesozoic Era. See table at end of Vol. III.

Crete (krēt). [Also: **Candia;** Greek, **Kriti, Krete;** French, **Crète, Candie;** Italian and Latin, **Creta;** Old Turkish, **Kirid, Kirit.**] Island in the Mediterranean Sea, situated SE of Greece and SW of Asia Minor. It is a district of Greece and includes the *nomoi* (departments) of Canea, Heraklion, Lassithion, and Rethymni. Its surface is mostly mountainous, and it produces wheat, fruit, wool, olives, and wine. The chief towns are Canea and Candia. Its inhabitants are mainly of Greek descent. Crete was connected with legends of Zeus and Minos, and was celebrated in antiquity for its culture, out of which was developed one of the earliest codes of law. It was subdued by the Romans under Metellus in 67 B.C., conquered by the Saracens in 823, and later was a part of the Byzantine Empire. It was ceded to Venice in 1204. Its conquest by the Turks was completed in 1669. Its people took part, unsuccessfully, in the Greek war of independence during the early 19th century. The government was administered by Egypt from 1830 to 1840. In 1896–97 an effort was made by a part of the population, aided by Greek troops, to free the island from Turkish rule and annex it to Greece. This was opposed by the great powers, who established a blockade of the island, and, as a result of defeat in the Greco-Turkish War, the Greeks were obliged to withdraw. Beginning in December, 1898, it was administered by a high commissioner representing France, Great Britain, Italy, and Russia. On Aug. 14, 1906, the right of the King of the Hellenes to propose the high commissioner was recognized by these powers, and the constitution of February, 1907, provided for an assembly of 65 deputies, elected in the proportion of one for every 5,000 inhabitants. In May, 1908, the powers decided gradually to withdraw their troops from the island. In 1910 the preliminary union with Greece was proclaimed, and on Nov. 14, 1913, annexation was made final. This was verified in the Peace of London (May 30, 1913) and the Peace of Athens (Nov. 14, 1913) between Greece and Turkey. In World War II Crete was captured by the Germans on May 29–30, 1941, and held by them until 1944. Area, 3,235 sq. mi.; greatest width, 35 mi.; length, 160 mi.; pop. 442,339 (1940).

Crete. [Former name, **Blue River City.**] City in SE Nebraska, in Saline County: processing center for flour and dairy products. It is the seat of Doane College. 3,692 (1950).

Crete Campaign. Military operation (May 20–30, 1941) in the Mediterranean Sea, in World War II. It involved the German occupation of the island of Crete, which was one of the key German objectives in the invasion of the Balkans, and is noteworthy in military history as being the first major successful airborne invasion of a territory defended by large land and sea forces. The British defenders under General Sir Bernard Freyberg killed many paratroopers and sank several German convoys, but lacked sufficient antiaircraft artillery to stop heavy bombers and torpedo planes or the waves of gliders which brought 35,000 troops. About half of the 27,000 British garrison was saved in evacuation; 17,000 German casualties were incurred.

Créteil (krā.tey′). Town in N France, in the department of Seine, situated on the Marne River, E of Alfortville and SE of Paris. It is a suburb of Paris. 11,008 (1946).

Creticus (krē′ti.kus), **Metellus.** See **Metellus, Quintus Caecilius** (d. c56 B.C.).

Crétin (krā.taṅ), **Guillaume.** fl. late 15th and early 16th centuries. French poet who lived in the reigns of Charles VIII, Louis XII, and Francis I. The extreme reverence in which he was held by his contemporaries caused Rabelais to ridicule him.

Creus (krē′us). In Greek mythology, one of the Titans, and the father of Pallas, Astraeus, and Perses, children of Eurybia.

Creusa (krẹ.ö′sạ). In Homeric legend, the daughter of Priam, and wife of Aeneas.

Creusa. [Also, **Glauce.**] In Greek legend, daughter of Creon, king of Corinth. Jason the Argonaut, tiring of his wife Medea, fell in love with Creusa and planned to marry her. Medea sent Creusa as a wedding gown a magic robe which, when she put it on, burned her flesh and caused her to die in terrible convulsions.

Creusa. In Greek legend, a daughter of Erechtheus, king of Athens. She was seduced by Apollo, and tried to kill Ion, the son she bore the god, but did not succeed. Subsequently she married Xuthus, by whom she became the mother of Achaeus.

Creuse (krėz). Department in C France, bounded by the departments of Indre and Cher on the N, the departments of Allier and Puy-de-Dôme on the E, the department of Corrèze on the S, and the department of Haute-Vienne on the W. It was formed from the former province of Haute-Marche and small portions of Limousin, Bourbonnais, Poitou, and Berry. The department is mountainous, the agriculture fairly undeveloped, and the population declining. There are stone quarries, coal mines, and potteries. Leather manufacture is important; the manufacture of tapestry has been world-renowned since the 18th century. Capital, Guéret; area, 2,163 sq. mi.; pop. 188,669 (1946).

Creuse River. River in C France which joins the Vienne.

Creusot (krė.zō), **Le.** See **Le Creusot.**

Creutz (kroits), Count **Gustaf Philip.** b. in Finland, 1731; d. Oct. 30, 1785. Swedish politician and poet. He was appointed (1763) ambassador to Madrid, and three years later was transferred to Paris, where he became intimate with Franklin, with whom he concluded (April 3, 1783) a treaty of commerce between Sweden and the U.S. His poetical works included the idyll *Atis odr Camilla* and the pastoral poem *Daphne.*

Creuzer (kroi'tsėr), **Georg Friedrich.** b. at Marburg, Prussia, Germany, March 10, 1771; d. at Heidelberg, Baden, Germany, Feb. 16, 1858. German philologist and archaeologist, appointed professor of philology at Marburg in 1802, and at Heidelberg in 1807. He founded the Philological Seminary at Heidelberg in 1807. His chief work is *Symbolik und Mythologie der alten Völker, besonders der Griechen* (1810–12).

Creuznach (kroits'näċh). See **Kreuznach.**

Crevalcore (krā.väl.kô'rā). Town and commune in N Italy, in the *compartimento* (region) of Emilia-Romagna, in the province of Bologna, NW of Bologna, in a fertile agricultural district on improved swampland. Pop. of commune, 13,563 (1936); of town, 2,209 (1936).

Crevaux (krẹ.vō), **Jules Nicolas.** b. at Lorquin, in Lorraine, France, April 1, 1847; d. in the Chaco, Bolivia, April 24, 1882. French surgeon and traveler. In 1876, being stationed in French Guiana, he began explorations in the interior, twice crossing to the Amazon; later he explored the Japurá branch of the Amazon, and traveled on the Orinoco. In 1881 he left Buenos Aires with a number of companions, having planned an extended trip through the center of South America, but while ascending the Pilcomayo River all the company but two were killed by the Indians. The results of his explorations were published in the *Tour du monde*, and in the proceedings of various scientific societies.

Crevecoeur or **Creve Coeur** (krēv'kör'). Village in N Illinois, in Tazewell County, near Peoria. 5,499 (1950).

Crèvecœur (krev.kėr), **Fort.** See under **Illinois.**

Crève-Coeur (krev.kėr), **Le.** Poems (1941) written during World War II by the French novelist and poet Louis Aragon (1897—) on the twin themes of his love of country and love of his wife, Elsa Triolet. Critics admire them for a depth of tragic feeling previously unattained by Aragon in his cubist, dadaist, and surrealist periods.

Crèvecoeur (krev.kėr), **Michel Guillaume Jean de.** [Pseudonym, **J. Hector St. John.**] b. at Caen, France, 1731; d. near Paris, 1813. French statesman and agriculturist. He emigrated to America in 1754, and settled on a farm near New York. During the Revolutionary War, in 1780, as he was about to sail for Europe, he was arrested at New York by the British (who then held the city) on the suspicion of being a spy, and was detained several months. Returning from Europe in 1783, he was for many years French consul at New York, and enjoyed the friendship of Washington and Franklin. He wrote *Letters from an American Farmer* (1782) and *Voyage dans la haute Pensylvanie et dans l'état de New-York* (3 vols., 1801). A collection of his letters appeared, in 1925, in the volume *Sketches of Eighteenth Century America.*

Crèvecoeur, Philippe de. d. at La Bresle, near Lyons, France, 1494. French general. He commanded the French at the battle of Guinegate (1479), in which he was defeated by Maximilian of Austria with a large force of Flemings; became marshal of France in 1492.

Crévier (krā.vyā), **Jean Baptiste Louis.** b. at Paris, 1693; d. there, Dec. 1, 1765. French historian and man of letters. He continued Rollin's *Histoire romaine* and wrote *Histoire des empereurs jusqu'à Constantin* (1750–56) and *Rhétorique française* (1765).

Crevillente (krā.ʙē.lyen'tā). Town in E Spain, in the province of Alicante, situated in a mountainous region ab. 20 mi. SW of Alicante: center of an irrigated district producing citrus fruits and melons; cloth and esparto fabrics are manufactured. 11,403 (1940).

Crew (krö), **Henry.** b. at Richmond, Ohio, June 4, 1859—. American physicist, and researcher in spectroscopy. Graduated from Princeton University (B.A., 1882) and from the Johns Hopkins University (Ph.D., 1887), he was professor of physics (1892–1930) at Northwestern University. He is the author of *Principles of Mechanics* (1908), *General Physics* (1908), *Rise of Modern Physics* (1928), and other works.

Crewe (krö). Municipal borough, railway junction, and manufacturing town in W England, in Cheshire, ab. 31 mi. SE of Liverpool, ab. 158 mi. NW of London by rail. Crewe is an important railway junction, and has large railway repair shops. Other industries are steel works and the manufacture of aircraft engines. 52,415 (1951).

Crewe-Milnes (krö'milz'), **Robert Offley Ashburton.** [Title, 1st Marquis of **Crewe.**] b. at London, Jan. 12, 1858; d. at Leatherhead, Surrey, England, June 20, 1945. English public servant. He was secretary of state for the colonies (1908–10) and for India (1910–12), and lord privy seal (1912–16). Prior to this, he was lord lieutenant of Ireland (1892–95) and lord president of the council (1905–08). He was created earl of Crewe in 1895 and marquis of Crewe in 1911. In 1922 he was appointed British ambassador to France.

Crewe's Career (kröz), **Mr.** See **Mr. Crewe's Career.**

Crewler (krö'lėr). Name of a family in Charles Dickens's *David Copperfield.* Horace Crewler is a poor clergyman with a large family, and a wife who has lost the use of her legs; when anything annoys her or excites her it goes "to her legs directly." Sophy, the fourth daughter, is an unselfish girl who finally marries Tommy Traddles.

Crews (kröz), **Laura Hope.** b. at San Francisco, 1880; d. at New York, Nov. 13, 1942. American actress, noted for her comedy roles. She made her stage debut at four years of age in *Bootle's Baby;* later she supported Eleanor Robson in *Merely Mary Ann* and Henry Miller in *Zira* and *Joseph Entangled*, and played Polly Jordan in *The Great Divide* (1906). Her other appearances include *Peter Ibbetson* (1917), *Ariadne* (1925), *Hay Fever* (1925), and *Save Me the Waltz* (1938); she also played important parts in motion pictures including *Charming Sinners, Gone with the Wind*, and *Camille.*

Cribb (krib), **Tom.** [Called **"the Black Diamond."**] b. at Hanham, Gloucestershire, England, July 8, 1781; d. at Woolwich, England, May 11, 1848. English champion pugilist, by occupation a coal porter.

Cricca (krik'ạ). In Thomas Tomkis's comedy *Albumazar* (1615), the honest servant of Pandolfo.

Crichton (krī'tọn), **James.** [Called **"the Admirable Crichton."**] b. in Scotland, Aug. 19, 1560; killed at Mantua, Italy, July 3, c1582. Scottish scholar and adventurer, celebrated for his extraordinary accomplishments and attainments in the languages, sciences, and arts. At the age of 17 he started upon his travels on the Continent. He was then the reputed master of 12 languages. He enlisted (c1577) in the French army, but in 1579 he resigned and went to Italy. Here many debates both public and private were arranged for him, in all of which he was victorious except with Mazzoni. He wrote Latin odes and verses with ease, and his skill as a swordsman was highly lauded. In 1581 he disputed with the professors of the university at Padua on their interpretation of Aristotle. A misadventure led to his being denounced as a charlatan, whereupon he challenged the university, offering to confute their Aristotelian interpretations and to expose their errors in mathematics. The disputation lasted four days, and Crichton was completely successful. He won his first laurels in Mantua by killing in a duel a famous swordsman. His death took place there in a midnight street attack. Crichton is said to have recognized the leader of the brawlers as his pupil, the son of the duke of Mantua, and having drawn his sword upon him to have offered it to him by the handle; whereupon the prince seized it and stabbed him to the heart.

Crichton, The. London artistic, scientific, and literary club, established in 1872.

Crichton, The Admirable. See **Admirable Crichton, The.**

Crichton-Browne (krī′tọn.broun′), **Harold William Alexander Francis.** b. 1866; d. in Shropshire, England, Oct. 1, 1937. English soldier, explorer, and writer; son of Sir James Crichton-Browne (1840–1938). Educated at Cambridge, he joined (1888) Joseph Thomson's expedition to the Atlas Mountains in Morocco, was a member of the Bechuanaland border police for four years, and served (1900–02) in the Boer War. He later commanded (1911–18) the King's Own Scottish Borders, being promoted in 1918 to colonel. He was the author of *The Heart of Atlas, Two African Cities, Across the Veldt to Buluwayo,* and other books.

Crichton-Browne, Sir **James.** b. 1840; d. at Dumfries, Scotland, Jan. 31, 1938. British physician, chiefly known as specialist in mental and nervous diseases; father of H. W. A. F. Crichton-Browne. Educated at Trinity College, Edinburgh University, and the University of Paris, he served (1875–1922) as the lord chancellor's visitor in lunacy. His works include a defense (1928) of Robert Burns, *What the Doctor Thought* (1930), and *The Doctor's After-Thoughts* (1932).

Crichton-Stuart (krī′tọn.stū′ạrt), **John Patrick.** See **Stuart, John Patrick Crichton-.**

Cricket on the Hearth, The. Christmas book by Charles Dickens, published in 1845. The singing match between a teakettle and a cricket on a carrier's hearthstone, in which the latter comes out ahead, gives its name to the book: "To have a cricket on the hearth is the luckiest thing in the world."

Cricket on the Hearth, The. [German title, **Das Heimchen am Herd.**] Opera in three acts by Karl Goldmark, with a libretto by M. Willner based on the Christmas story by Charles Dickens, first performed at Vienna on March 21, 1896.

Crieff (krēf). Police burgh and market town in C Scotland, in Perthshire, situated on the river Earn, ab. 15 mi. W of Perth, ab. 443 mi. N of London by rail. 5,662 (est. 1948).

Crikvenica (tsrēk.ve′nē.tsä). [Italian, **Cirquenizza.**] Town in NW Yugoslavia, in the federative unit of Croatia, in the former *banovina* (province) of Savska, situated near the estuary of the Dubracina River on the Croatian coast of the Adriatic Sea. It is a major mineral-spring and beach resort. 4,792 (1931).

Crile (krīl), **George Washington.** b. at Chile, Ohio, Nov. 11, 1864; d. at Cleveland, Ohio, Jan. 7, 1943. American surgeon, notable for his development of the nerve-block system of anesthesia and credited with performing the first successful direct blood transfusion (1905). He received a B.A. (1884) from Ohio Northern and an M.D. (1887) from Western Reserve (then Wooster) University, and studied at Vienna (1893), London (1895), and Paris (1897). He was professor intermittently (1893–1924) at Western Reserve and visiting surgeon (1911–24) at Lakeside Hospital, Cleveland, served as brigade surgeon in the Spanish-American War and as a hospital director in France during World War I. He was a founder (1921) and director of the Cleveland Clinic Foundation, and surgeon (1924 *et seq.*) at the Cleveland Clinic Hospital. He is remembered also as a pioneer in the use of adrenalin and for his theory that thought is a product of electricity generated by matter. Author of *Surgical Shock* (1897), *Origin and Nature of the Emotions* (1915), *A Mechanistic View of War and Peace* (1915), *A Bipolar Theory of Living Processes* (1925), *The Phenomena of Life* (1936), and other works.

Crillon (krē.yôṅ), **Louis des Balbes de Berton de.** [Called **"L'Homme sans peur,"** meaning "the Man without Fear."] b. at Murs, in Provence, France, 1541; d. at Avignon, France, Dec. 2, 1615. French general. He fought against the Huguenots in the French civil wars, taking part in the battles of Rouen, Dreux, St.-Denis, Jarnac, Moncontour, and St.-Jean d'Angély, served as a Knight of Malta under Don John of Austria at Lepanto in 1571, and held a high command in the army of Henry III during the war of the League (1580–89). After the death of Henry III he entered the service of Henry IV, under whom he fought at the battle of Ivry in 1590, and from whom he received the title "le brave des braves" (meaning "the bravest of the brave").

Crillon, Louis des Balbes de Berton de. [Title, **Duc de Mahon.**] b. 1718; d. at Madrid, 1796. French general. He served (1745) with distinction at Fontenoy (Belgium) and also in the Seven Years' War. Later he passed into the Spanish service, conquered Minorca in 1782, and was made captain of the Spanish armies and duke of Mahon. His *Mémoires* were published in 1791.

Crimea (krī.mē′ạ). [Russian, **Krym, Krim**; French, **Crimée**; ancient names, **Chersonesus Scythica, Chersonesus Taurica.**] Peninsula in S U.S.S.R., nearly surrounded by the Black Sea and the Sea of Azov, coextensive with the Crimea *oblast* (region) of the Russian Soviet Federated Socialist Republic. In the northern portion its surface is a plain, but S of the Salgir River it is mountainous. Its inhabitants are principally Russians and Tartars; the ancient inhabitants were the Cimmerians, afterward called Taurians. The Crimea was the seat of the kingdom known as the Cimmerian Bosporus, and was frequently overrun in the Middle Ages. It became a dependency of Turkey in 1475, was annexed to Russia in 1783, and in the years 1853–56 was the scene of the Crimean War.

Crimea. [Russian, **Krym, Krim.**] *Oblast* (region) in S U.S.S.R., in the Russian Soviet Federated Socialist Republic. Capital, Simferopol; area, 9,936 sq. mi.; pop. 1,126,842 (1939).

Crimea Conference. See **Yalta Conference.**

Crime and Punishment. Novel by Feodor Dostoevski, published in 1866.

Crimean War (krī.mē′ạn). War waged from 1853 to 1856 between Russia and the allied forces of Turkey, France, Great Britain, and Sardinia. It arose through the demand on the part of Russia for a protectorate over the Greek subjects of the sultan of Turkey. Among its leading events were the battle of Sinope (1853), Russian occupation of the Danubian principalities of Moldavia and Walachia (1854), battle of the Alma River (Sept. 20, 1854), beginning of the siege of Sevastopol (October, 1854), battle of Balaklava (Oct. 25), battle of Inkerman (Nov. 5), attacks on Sevastopol (June, 1855), battle of the Chernaya River (Aug. 16), storming of the Malakhov fortress (Sept. 8), fall of Sevastopol (Sept. 11), and the capture of Kars, Turkey, by the Russians (Nov. 28, 1855). The war was ended, and its issues decided, by the treaty of Paris on March 30, 1856.

Crime do padre Amaro (krē′mẹ dö pä′drẹ ạ.mä′rö), **O.** Work of fiction which marked the introduction of the realistic novel in Portugal, by Eca de Queiroz (1843–1900). It was first published (1875) in the periodical *Revista Universal* and appeared in book form the following year.

"Crime of '73." Epithet applied to the U.S. Coinage Act of Feb. 12, 1873, which provided for the demonetization of silver. The term originated (c1876) after the increase in U.S. silver production due to discoveries of new deposits of silver ore in the West; the larger output of silver, combined with the sharply reduced use of silver by the government, caused the price of silver to fall. The leaders of the movement for the free coinage of silver claimed that the "crime of '73" was part of an Anglo-American conspiracy organized by financial interests supporting the gold standard. Although it is highly doubtful that such a plot existed, its fancied reality was an article of faith among many Americans during the period 1876–96, when the free coinage controversy was at its height.

Crimes Against Humanity, Four-Power Agreement on. See **Four-Power Agreement on Crimes Against Humanity.**

Criminal Code, The. Play of prison life (1929) by Martin Flavin, American novelist and dramatist. A study of the psychology of prisoners, its origin was a visit the author made to the San Quentin prison near San Francisco.

Crimisus (kri.mī′sus). [Also, **Crimissus** (kri.mis′us).] In ancient geography, a river in W Sicily, probably near Segesta. Here Timoleon with 11,000 men defeated (339 B.C.) 70,000 Carthaginians.

Crimmitschau (krim'it.shou). [Also: **Crimmitzschau, Krimmitschau.**] Town in E Germany, in the *Land* (state) of Saxony, Russian Zone, formerly in the free state of Saxony, situated on the Pleisse River, ab. 36 mi. S of Leipzig: the center of an industrial district. Before World War II it had cotton spinning and weaving mills, and manufactures of hosiery, knitwear, paperware, and machinery. There is a local museum and a vocational school. The Church of Laurentius dates from the 11th century. The population is predominantly Protestant. 30,504 (1946).

Crinan Canal (krī'nạn). Canal in W Scotland, in Argyllshire. It crosses the head of the Kintyre peninsula and connects Loch Fyne with the Sound of Jura. It was built in the period 1793–1801. Length, ab. 9 mi.

Cripple Creek (krip'l krēk). City in C Colorado, capital of Teller County, ab. 30 mi. SW of Colorado Springs, at the base of Pike's Peak: formerly important for gold mining. 853 (1950).

Cripplegate (krip'l.gāt). [Also, **Crepel-gate.**] Originally, one of the gates of London, and in modern times the name of a section of London. The gate was the fourth from the western end of the wall of the City of London. The original gate was probably built by King Alfred when he restored the walls in 886 A.D. Stow says that in 1010, when the body of Edmund the Martyr, king of the East Angles, was borne through this gate, many lame persons who were congregated there to beg rose upright and were cured by the miraculous influence of the body. The chambers connected to and under the gate were later a prison for debtors and common trespassers. It was rebuilt in 1244 and in 1491, and in the 15th year of the reign of Charles II it was repaired and an opening for pedestrians was made. The rooms over the gate were used by the city water-bailiff. Cripplegate was pulled down in 1760.

Cripple of Fenchurch (fen'chėrch). See **Fenchurch, Cripple of.**

Cripps (krips), **Charles Alfred.** [Title, 1st Baron **Parmoor.**] b. Oct. 3, 1852; d. at Henley-on-Thames, Buckinghamshire, England, June 30, 1941. English lawyer and politician. He was appointed (1890) queen's counsel, and served (1895–1914) as a Conservative member of Parliament. In 1900 he was made chancellor and vicar general of the archdiocese of York, later serving (1902–24) as vicar general of Canterbury. After World War I he became a member of the Labour Party and served (1924, 1929–31) as lord president of the council in the two Labour governments of the 1920's. In international affairs, he was a representative on the League of Nations council, a delegate to the League Assembly, and an author of the protocol to the League Covenant providing for arbitration of international disputes. He supported the Briand-Kellogg Pact (1928) and the London naval limitation treaty (1930).

Cripps, Sir Stafford. [Full name, Sir **Richard Stafford Cripps.**] b. at London, April 24, 1889; d. at Zurich, April 21, 1952. English statesman; son of C. A. Cripps (1852–1941). He studied at London's University College, and developed a tremendously remunerative practice (1913 *et seq.*) as a barrister-at-law. He was king's counsel (1927) and solicitor general (1930–31). As a Labour member (1931 *et seq.*) of Parliament, he championed (1936) the policy of greater or lesser affiliation with parties further to the left than Labour. He was executive officer (1937) of the Labour Party. Ambassador (1940–42) to Russia; appointed (February, 1942) lord privy seal and leader of the House of Commons; special envoy (March–April, 1942) to India; minister (1942–45) of aircraft production; president (1945–47) of the board of trade; chancellor (1947–50) of the exchequer. Cripps was generally conceded to be one of the most brilliant of contemporary English political thinkers, although this brilliance never displayed itself in the platform virtuosity of such other contemporary figures as Churchill, Bevan, or even Hartley Shawcross. The Spartan austerity of Cripps's own personal life, plus the fact of his forthright espousal of socialism, has given him a somewhat curious position in the minds of many people not intimately acquainted with the politics of his country: as a lawyer he can hardly be said to have been a "poor man's advocate" (his skill brought him fees that rank with the largest ever earned by an English barrister); as a public servant, perhaps most notably in his last two posts as president of the board of trade and as chancellor of the exchequer, he was one of the key factors in the great effort made after the end of World War II to stabilize the British economy by increasing production for export and limiting domestic consumption of many commodities to a level actually below that of the war years. In 1951 the Fabian Society, foundation of English socialism, named him president.

Criş (krēsh). Rumanian name of the **Kőrös.**

Crisa (krī'sạ). [Also, **Crissa.**] In ancient geography, a city in Phocis, Greece, situated SW of Delphi. It was styled "the divine" by Homer. It is often confused with its port, Cirrha.

Crişana-Maramureş or **Crişana and Maramureş** (krē.shä'nä; mä.rä.mö'resh). Region in NW Rumania, bounded by the U.S.S.R. in the N, Hungary in the W, and Banat in the S and Transylvania in the E; formerly a province. 1,391,672 (1948).

Crisfield (kris'fēld). City in SE Maryland, in Somerset County, on Tangier Sound: fishing and canning center for oysters and crabs. Fruits and vegetables are also canned here, boats are repaired, and there are manufactures of packing cases, clothing, and fishermen's supplies. 3,688 (1950).

Crisis, The. Historical novel by the American novelist Winston Churchill, published in 1901. It is set against a background of the Civil War era. The plot concerns the estrangement of Stephen Brice, a lawyer from the North, and Virginia Carvel, a loyal Southern belle. After many complications, they are reunited when their love proves stronger than their political sympathies.

Crisis, The. Magazine now published under the auspices of the National Association for the Advancement of Colored People. It was originally edited (1910–34) by W. E. B. Du Bois. It is aimed, as is the organization which sponsors it, at improving the social, political, and economic status of Negroes in the U.S.

Crisis, The American. Series of pamphlets by Thomas Paine, published between 1776 and 1783. The first pamphlet, issued (Dec. 19, 1776) at a time when the success of the American Revolution was in doubt, included the famous exhortation beginning "These are the times that try men's souls." Paine's challenging words were influential in lifting the spirit of the American cause.

Crisis, The Impending. See **Impending Crisis, The.**

Crisp (krisp), **Arthur.** b. at Hamilton, Ontario, Canada, April 26, 1881—. American painter, known for his mural decorations in many public buildings, including Rockefeller Center, the Roxy Theater, Bellevue Hospital, and the Belasco Theater at New York and the houses of Parliament at Ottawa. He studied at the Art Students League of New York and later taught there as well as at Cooper Union, the Beaux-Arts School of Design, and the National Academy of Design. He was made an academician of the National Academy, and a member of the National Arts Club. His work has been exhibited in North America and has won a number of prizes. Among his better-known works are the panels *Hamlet, Taming of the Shrew,* and *As You Like It* in the Belasco Theater, the painting *Garden Party,* and decorations for many schools, hotels, and offices.

Crisp, Charles Frederick. b. at Sheffield, England, Jan. 29, 1845; d. at Atlanta, Ga., Oct. 23, 1896. American politician. He served as a lieutenant in the Confederate army in the Civil War; was admitted to the bar in 1866; was appointed solicitor-general of the southwestern judicial district in 1872; was reappointed for a term of four years in 1873; was appointed judge of the Superior Court of the same district in 1877; was elected by the general assembly to the same office in 1878; was reëlected judge for a term of four years in 1880; resigned in 1882; was a Democratic representative from Georgia from the 48th through the 53rd Congress; and was speaker of the House in the Fifty-second and Fifty-third Congresses.

Crisparkle (kris'pär.kl), **Septimus.** Clergyman and "true Christian gentleman" in Charles Dickens's *The Mystery of Edwin Drood.* A minor canon of Cloisterham Cathedral, it is said of him that he has traveled "upon the chief Pagan high-roads, but [has been] since promoted by a patron (grateful for a well-taught son) to his present Christian beat."

Crispi (krēs′pē), **Francesco.** b. at Ribera, Sicily, Oct. 4, 1819; d. at Palermo, Sicily, Aug. 11, 1901. Italian statesman. He studied law, and in 1846 settled at Naples. He served as a major under Garibaldi at Calatafimi in 1860, was returned by Palermo to the first Italian Parliament in 1861, became president of the Chamber of Deputies in 1876, and was minister of the interior (1877–78) and prime minister (1887–91, 1893–96).

Crispin (kris′pin; French, krēs.paṅ). Impudent, boasting, and witty valet, a ready assistant in the love-affairs of his master; a conventional character in French comedy, introduced (c1654) apparently by Poirson from Italian comedy.

Crispin (kris′pin), **Gilbert.** d. c1117. English scholar and prelate, abbot of Westminster. Two of his works have survived, *Vita Herluini*, the chief authority for the early history of Bec, and *Disputatio Judaei cum Christiano*, a dialogue between a Jew and the author.

Crispin and **Crispinian** (kris.pin′i.ạn), Saints. d. Oct. 25, 285 or 286. Two martyrs of the early Church, believed (although not positively known) to have been brothers. According to legend, they were members of a noble Roman family, and fled to what is now Soissons, France, where they endeavored to spread the Christian faith and supported themselves by mending and making shoes. They were beheaded during the reign of Diocletian at the order of the co-emperor, Maximianus Herculius. They are the patron saints of shoemakers, tanners, and saddlers.

Crispinella (kris.pi.nel′ạ). In John Marston's play *The Dutch Courtezan*, a sparkling, lively girl, the opposite of her sister Beatrice.

Crispino e la Comare (krēs.pē′nō ā lä kō.mä′rā). [Eng. trans., *"The Shoemaker and the Fairy Godmother."*] Comic opera in three acts by Luigi Ricci, first produced at Venice in 1850. Federico Ricci assisted his brother in its composition. The words are by Piave.

Crispin Rival de son Maître (krēs.paṅ rē.vål dẹ sôṅ metr). Comedy by Alain René le Sage, produced in 1707.

Crispinus (kris.pī′nus). In Ben Jonson's *Poetaster*, a bad poet who gives the play its title. He is intended for Marston, with whom Jonson had a quarrel at the time.

Crispus (kris′pus), **Flavius Julius.** d. 326 A.D. Eldest son of Constantine I (Constantine the Great) and Minervina. He was made Caesar in 317, and consul in 318. He distinguished himself in a campaign against the Franks and in the war against Licinius, over whom he gained a great naval victory in the Hellespont in 323. He was put to death by his father on a charge of high treason.

Crispus, Gaius (or **Caius**) **Sallustius.** See **Sallust.**

Criss Kringle (kris kring′gẹl). See **Kriss Kringle.**

Cristinos (krēs.tē′nōs). In Spanish history, name given to the partisans of Donna Maria Christina, regent for her daughter Isabella Maria II from 1833 to 1840. They were thus, of course, the bitter enemies of the Carlists. Ferdinand VII, who married Christina in 1829, repealed the Salic law of succession, introduced by Philip V in 1713, in accordance with which females could inherit the throne only in case of the total extinction of the male line. By a decree of March, 1830, he invoked the old Castilian law in accordance with which the daughters and granddaughters of the king take precedence over his brothers and nephews. This pragmatic sanction was not recognized by the king's brother, Don Carlos, who, supported by the Carlists (comprised in large part of the clericals or absolutists), began a civil war on the death of Ferdinand, in 1833. Although this particular period of conflict came to an end in 1839, with the defeat of the Carlists, the issue continued to be a troublesome one in Spanish politics until 1873, when the last of the Carlist claimants able to attract any considerable body of public support was finally defeated.

Cristobal (kris.tō′bạl). [Spanish, **Cristóbal** (krēs.tō′ʙäl).] Town in NW Canal Zone, at the Atlantic end of the Panama Canal ab. 1 mi. S of Colón, Panama. The town has a large port and cold-storage plant, serving the Canal Zone, and shops of the Panama railroad. 414 (1950).

Cristóbal (krēs.tō′ʙäl). Baptismal name of **Paullu.**

Cristóbal Colón (krēs.tō′ʙäl kō.lōn′). [Eng. trans., *"Christopher Columbus."*] Spanish armored cruiser in the Spanish-American War, bought from the Italian government, of 6,840 tons displacement and a trial speed of 20 knots. In the battle of Santiago, July 3, 1898, under Captain Emilio Díaz Moreu, it was the last Spanish ship to surrender, being forced ashore by the *Brooklyn* and the *Oregon* at Rio Tarquino.

Cristofori (krē.stô′fō.rē), **Bartolommeo.** b. at Padua, Italy, May 4, 1665; d. at Florence, Jan. 27, 1731. Italian instrument maker, credited with inventing the piano. His improvement (c1711–20) of the hammer mechanism is generally regarded as the advance which enabled the development of the modern piano.

Cristus (kris′tus), **Petrus.** See **Christus, Petrus.**

Crites (krī′tēz). Man of "straight judgment and a strong mind," in Jonson's play *Cynthia's Revels*. He is supposed to have been designed by Jonson as a picture of himself.

Critias (krish′i.ạs, krit′i.ạs). Athenian orator and politician, a pupil of Socrates, and one of the 30 tyrants (404 B.C.), noted for his dissolute life, rapacity, and cruelty. He perished in the battle of Munychia (the citadel of Piraeus). Plato introduces him in a dialogue (a fragment) which bears his name.

Critic, The. Farce by Richard Brinsley Sheridan, produced on Oct. 30, 1779. It is an imitation of Buckingham's *Rehearsal.*

Critic, The. Weekly literary magazine and review published (1881–1906) by Jeannette and Joseph Gilder. Contributors included Julia Ward Howe, Walt Whitman, and James Lane Allen.

Critical Fable, A. Humorous critical verse by Amy Lowell, published anonymously in 1922.

Críticon (krē′tē.kōn). Allegory by the Spanish cleric and writer Baltasar Gracián. His outstanding work, it was published in three parts, between 1650 and 1653.

Critique de l'École des Femmes (krē.tēk dẹ lā.kol dā fåm). See **École des Femmes, Critique de l'.**

Critique of Pure Reason. [German, **Kritik der reinen Vernunft.**] Philosophical work by Kant, published in 1781. A second and revised edition appeared in 1787: the later editions are reprints of this. The changes introduced in the second edition have been the occasion of much discussion among German philosophers, many maintaining that they show an essential alteration of Kant's doctrines. Kant himself, however, declared that they were made solely to secure greater clearness.

Critius (krish′i.us, krit′-) and **Nesiotes** (nes.i.ō′tēz, nē-shi-). fl. 5th century B.C. Greek sculptors. Critius is thought to have been a pupil of Antenor, creator of the famous statues of Harmodius and Aristogiton, which were carried off from Athens by Xerxes and later recovered. Meanwhile Critius and Nesiotes executed new figures to replace those taken away by the Persian. Two sculptures still to be seen at Naples have been identified as copies of these works. Very little is known about Nesiotes, but Critius had a school of sculpture at Athens.

Crito (krī′tō). fl. c400 B.C. Athenian, a friend and follower of Socrates. He is a prominent character in the dialogue by Plato named for him.

Critolaus (krit.ọ.lā′us). d. 146 B.C. Achaean demagogue, last strategus of the Achaean League, defeated by Quintus Caecilius Metellus at Scarphea, near Thermopylae, in 146.

Critolaus. fl. 2nd century B.C. Greek Peripatetic philosopher. He was sent to Rome as an ambassador c140 B.C.

Crittenden (krit′ẹn.dẹn), **Eugene Casson.** b. at Oswayo, Pa., Dec. 19, 1880—. American physicist. Since 1909 he has been associated with the National Bureau of Standards, as a physicist (1909–21), in charge of the division of electricity (1921–46), and as assistant director (1933–46). In 1946 he became associate director of the bureau. He has been especially concerned with electrical problems and studies of light. On several occasions he has represented the U.S. on the International Commission on Illumination. He was recipient of the medal of the Illuminating Engineering Society in 1946.

Crittenden, George Bibb. b. at Russellville, Ky., March 20, 1812; d. at Danville, Ky., Nov. 27, 1880. American major general in the Civil War; son of J. J. Crittenden. He served throughout the Mexican War. At the outbreak of the Civil War he joined the Confederate service with the rank of brigadier general, and was shortly promoted major general. He was placed in command of SE Kentucky and a part of E Tennessee in November, 1861. He was defeated at Mill Springs on Jan. 19, 1862.

Crittenden, John Jordan. b. in Woodford County, Ky., Sept. 10, 1787; d. near Frankfort, Ky., July 26, 1863.

American politician; father of George B. Crittenden and Thomas L. Crittenden. He graduated at William and Mary College in 1807, and was subsequently admitted to the bar. He served in the War of 1812; was a member of the Kentucky house of representatives in 1816, U.S. senator from Kentucky (1817–19, 1835–41), attorney general under Harrison and Tyler (March 5–Sept. 13, 1841), again U.S. senator (1842–48), governor of Kentucky (1848–50), attorney general under Fillmore (1850–53), U.S. senator (1855–61), and a Unionist member of Congress (1861–63).

Crittenden, Thomas Leonidas. b. at Russellville, Ky., May 15, 1819; d. at Annandale, Staten Island, N.Y., Oct. 23, 1893. American Civil War general; son of J. J. Crittenden. He served in the Mexican War and became a brigadier general of volunteers in the Union army (Oct. 27, 1861). He commanded a division at the battle of Shiloh (April 6 and 7, 1862), was promoted major-general (July 17, 1862), commanded a corps at the battles of Stone River (Dec. 31, 1862–Jan. 3, 1863) and Chickamauga (Sept. 19–20, 1863), and was brevetted brigadier general on March 2, 1867.

Crittenden, Thomas Theodore. b. near Shelbyville, Ky., Jan. 1, 1832; d. at Kansas City, Mo., May 29, 1909. American politician; nephew of J. J. Crittenden. He served in the Civil War as lieutenant colonel of the 7th regiment of the Missouri state militia. He was twice elected (1872, 1876) to Congress, elected (1880) governor of Missouri, and served as consul general (1893–97) in Mexico.

Crittenden Compromise. Measure urged (1860–61) in the Senate by John Jordan Crittenden of Kentucky, providing for the prohibition of slavery in U.S. territory north of the line 36°30′, and for the enforcement of the fugitive slave laws. Designed to allay sectional friction between the North and South, it was never adopted.

Crittenton (krit′ẹn.tọn), **Charles Nelson.** b. at Henderson, N.Y., Feb. 20, 1833; d. at San Francisco, Nov. 16, 1909. American philanthropist. He founded (1861) the Charles N. Crittenton Company, a drug firm. Upon the death (1882) of his daughter, he organized a mission in her name at New York, and later expanded it into a series of missions incorporated (1895) as the National Florence Crittenton Mission, which he served (until 1909) as president.

Crivelli (krē.vel′lē), **Carlo.** b. at Venice, c1430; d. after 1493. Venetian painter. He worked chiefly in the cities of the Marches, and finally settled at Ascoli. In 1490 he was knighted by Prince Ferdinand of Capua. Among his paintings are a *Madonna with Saints*, in the Brera at Milan, an *Annunciation*, in the National Gallery at London, a *Magdalen*, in the Berlin Museum, and a *Pietà*, in the Vatican.

Crivelli, Uberto. Original name of Pope **Urban III.**

Crna Gora (tsėr′nä gō′rä). Serbo-Croatian name of **Montenegro.**

Croaghpatrick or **Croagh Patrick** (krō′pat′rik). Mountain in Connacht province, Irish Republic, in County Mayo, ab. 6 mi. SW of Westport. It is noted in the story of Saint Patrick. Elevation, ab. 2,510 ft.

Croaker (krō′kėr), **Mr.** and **Mrs.** Strongly contrasted pair in Oliver Goldsmith's *The Good-Natured Man*. He is gifted in saying sadly the most cutting things; she is both merry and spiteful.

Croaker Papers. Group of satirical poems by Fitz-Greene Halleck and Joseph Rodman Drake, published in 1819. The work satirized various facets of the contemporary American scene. A complete edition was issued in 1860.

Croatan (krō.ạ.tan′). Tribe of Indians who formerly lived in the coastal region of North Carolina, and who supposedly killed some and absorbed others of an early English settlement. In 1587 English settlers led by John White, appointed governor by Sir Walter Raleigh, landed on Roanoke Island. White went back to England and was not able to return to Roanoke until 1591, when he found no trace of the 140 men, women, and children he had left there. Carved on a tree was the word CROATOAN, which has generally been thought to indicate that the settlers had joined the Croatan Indians. Some years later Indians told the Jamestown settlers that the Roanoke colony had in fact accepted an invitation of the Croatans and had lived among them peacefully until the Indian medicine-men had incited the chief, Powhatan, against them, whereupon most of them were killed, and the few survivors removed to another region. Like the Shawnees in Florida and the Mandans in the Middle West, the Croatan Indians are reported to have shown some physical characteristics indicating an infusion of white blood, and certain evidences of apparent early white influence in their agriculture and housing. These reports lend credence to the supposition that the Roanoke colonists did join the Croatans and that intermarriages occurred before the alleged massacre. There is a Croatan Sound off the North Carolina Coast, and in recent years the name has become much used in that part of the country.

Croatia (krō.ā′shạ). [Serbo-Croatian, **Hrvatska;** French, **Croatie** (kro.à.sē); German, **Kroatien;** Hungarian, **Horvátország;** Italian, **Croazia.**] Federative unit of the Federal People's Republic of Yugoslavia, established in 1945, comprising the former *banovina* (province) of Savska, the larger (western) part of the former banovina of Primorska, and the southern part (the peninsula of Istria except Trieste) of the former Italian *compartimento* (region) of Venezia Giulia. It is bounded on the NW by Slovenia, on the N by Hungary, on the E by Serbia, on the S by Bosnia-Hercegovina, on the W by the Free Territory of Trieste and by the Adriatic Sea, and includes a long and narrow strip along the Adriatic coast (the region known as Dalmatia), bounded on the E by Bosnia-Hercegovina. The S part of Dalmatia, around Dubrovnik, is separated from the main part of Croatia by a narrow strip of Bosnian territory around the Neretva River. There are many islands along the Adriatic coast. In the C and E parts the country is hilly; there are fertile plains along the Drava, Sava, and Danube rivers. Towards the west, particularly near the Adriatic coast, the country is rocky and eroded. This is also true in those parts of Istria and Dalmatia which are now included in the federative unit of Croatia. The climate is Continental in Croatia proper but has a Mediterranean character along the coast. The inhabitants are mainly occupied with agriculture, growing chiefly cereals and fruits, and the raising of livestock, particularly cattle and pigs. However, Croatia has a number of light industries. In Dalmatia and Istria are located the largest bauxite mines of Europe; here, too, fishing, shipbuilding, and other maritime occupations, as well as the cultivation of grapes and olives, are carried on. The majority of the population is Roman Catholic, speaking the Croatian dialect. In antiquity, most of what is now Croatia belonged to the Roman province of Pannonia. It was overrun by the East Goths, reconquered by the Byzantines under the emperor Justinian, was again overrun by the Avars, and finally was settled by the Croats in the 7th century. Hungary fought its way to sovereignty over Croatia in 1102, but granted autonomous political institutions. The Hapsburgs ruled Croatia from 1527 although their rule was frequently contested by the Turks. During the period of widespread and acute political unrest in Europe, in 1848, the Croats sought separation from Hungary; nevertheless, they remained under the suzerainty of Austria-Hungary until the second decade of the 20th century. Under the kingdom of Yugoslavia, after World War I, many Croats were opposed to the central regime at Belgrade and some of their leaders were imprisoned. (For centuries there has been a degree of bitterness between the Croats and the Serbs, who constitute two of the three major ethnic groups of Yugoslavia. Many Croats insisted during the 1920's and 1930's that the Yugoslavian monarchy was actually a continuation, in spirit and in fact, of the Serbian kingdom that preceded it, and that they were being treated, for all practical purposes, as a subject people of a Serbian monarchy. Partly because of the resentment engendered by this situation, a considerable separatist movement developed among the Croats, who also provided the core of such terrorist organizations as the Ustashi. It is believed, however, that the present government of Yugoslavia has made considerable progress toward the reconciliation of the Croats, Serbs, and Slovenes within the framework of the present federal form of government.) During World War II Croatia was ruled, nominally, by an Axis puppet, and the country was formally affiliated with the Axis powers. However, many Croatian peasants fought with the partisans against the Axis occupation forces. Capital, Zagreb; area, 51,325 sq. mi.; pop. 3,756,807 (1948).

Croats (krō′ats). [Also, **Khorvat.**] Slavic peoples inhabiting Croatia, western Bosnia, and Istria in Central Europe. They have most recently been estimated to number 2,500,000 to 3,000,000, as an ethnic group. Almost identical in language with the Serbs, they have been under prolonged Austrian, rather than Turkish, influence. They are largely Roman Catholics, while the Serbs are mostly Greek Orthodox.

Croce (krō′chā), **Benedetto.** b. at Pescasseroli, L'Aquila, Italy, Feb. 25, 1866; d. at Naples, Nov. 20, 1952. Italian philosopher, historian, and editor. Most authorities agree in attributing to him a truly encyclopedic mind, and in pointing out that, in America, the full meaning and extent of his philosophical, literary, and political activity has never been adequately investigated. Specifically, Croce was considered a first-rate scholar of esthetics and was famous for his resistance to Fascism, but he left his mark also in the fields of Marxism, of history (especially the history of Italy, of the southern provinces of Italy, of the relations between Spain and Italy, and of Europe in the 19th century), of logic, of political economy, and of ethics. He was the author of several volumes of literary essays on Italian, European, Latin, and Greek authors and of two important works on Shakespeare and Goethe (he is considered to have been especially successful in his rendition into Italian of the poems of the latter). For 27 years he was editor in chief of a famous bimonthly magazine, *La Critica*, and he was the editor of collections of Italian classics and of standard philosophical works. Generally considered a liberal, he was as pro-German in 1914 as he was anti-German in 1940, and his liberal party now would be considered by many American or English liberals as conservative. The reader may question his theories and not always agree with him, but will at least always know where he stands; he thinks a problem through to the end and has a gift for clear expression. And if he is generally recognizable as a disciple of German idealism, his philosophical system has undergone countless modifications, and can be considered to be even now in a fluid state. The first few years of his intellectual life were spent in painstaking research in the archives of Naples, where he made interesting and at times significant discoveries (for example, the real origin of the Pulcinella mask). From there, he moved to more serious problems, such as a consideration of whether history is a science or an art. With the publication in 1902 of his *Esthetics* he attained fame. But it should always be kept in mind that his theory of esthetics is but one aspect of his philosophical edifice and should be considered only as a part of his general system. It is inseparable from his logic, his economics (or politics), and his ethics. In esthetics he maintains that art is intuition, or expression, and that this first step of human consciousness found its spiritual fulfillment in logic. For him art is knowledge of the individual, and logic, which follows, is knowledge of the universal. With this as a premise, he developed a great number of theories which refer to problems of the criticism and the history of art. Running parallel to his concept of esthetics and logic is the relation existing between his economics and ethics. The former follows the law of expediency and aims at particular designs, whereas ethics is directed at universal ends. The most important aspect of this concept of the human spirit, envisioned as a cycle in which one activity is a preparation for the next, is in its practical application, in the light which it throws on actual problems of human history. Croce always held that thought should be accompanied by actual participation in life. In his last few years his thought led him to an identification of history and philosophy, and he thus approached the current of thought which is known from Meinecke in Germany as historicism. Because of the very active part he took in politics (not always with success from the practical standpoint), his love for his country and for Naples (to which he bequeathed his house and his famous and magnificent library as a Foundation for Historical Studies), the bitter controversies he was engaged in, the variety of his scholarly pursuits, his unchallenged intellectual supremacy in Italy, he towers as one of the most important intellectual figures of the past 50 years not only of Italy but of the entire Western world. His books are too numerous to list, but a few will indicate the breadth of his intellectual interests: *Materialismo storico ed economia marxista* (1900; Eng. trans., *Historical Materialism and the Economics of Marx*, 1914), *Filosofia della pratica: economia ed etica* (1908; Eng. trans., *Philosophy of the Practical: Economics and Ethics*, 1913), *Frammenti di etica* (1922; Eng. trans., *The Conduct of Life*, 1924), *L'Intuizione pura e il carattere lirico dell'arte* (1908), *La Filosofia di Vico* (1911; Eng. trans., *The Philosophy of Vico*, 1913), *Ciò che è vivo e ciò che è morto della filosofia di Hegel* (1907; Eng. trans., *What Is Living and What Is Dead of the Philosophy of Hegel*, 1915), *Ariosto, Shakespeare e Corneille* (1920; Eng. trans., *Ariosto, Shakespeare and Corneille*, 1920), *La Letteratura della nuova Italia* (4 vols., 1914–15; vol. 5, 1939; vol. 6, 1940), *Storia d'Italia dal 1871 al 1915* (1927; Eng. trans., *A History of Italy 1871–1915*, 1929), *Storia d'Europa nel secolo decimonono* (1932; Eng. trans., *History of Europe in the Nineteenth Century*, 1933).

Crociato in Egitto (krō.chä′tō ēn ā.jēt′tō). Opera in two acts by Meyerbeer, with a libretto by Rossi, first performed at La Fenice theater, Venice, in 1824.

Crocker (krok′ėr), **Charles.** b. at Troy, N.Y., Sept. 16, 1822; d. at Monterey, Calif., Aug. 14, 1888. American railroad executive. He aided (1863–69) in the construction of the Central Pacific Railroad, and was elected (1871) president of the Southern Pacific Railroad of California. In 1884 he consolidated the Central Pacific and Southern Pacific railroads.

Crocker, Francis Bacon. b. at New York, July 4, 1861; d. July 9, 1921. American electrical engineer and educator, professor of electrical engineering in Columbia University from 1893. He was the author of works on the management of dynamos, electric lighting, and others, and developed (1917), with Peter Cooper Hewitt, the first airworthy helicopter in America.

Crocker, William. b. at Medina, Ohio, Jan. 27, 1876; d. at Athens, Ohio, Feb. 11, 1950. American botanist, known for his work on delayed germination of seeds, plant hormones, tropisms, and the effect of noxious gases on plants. Graduated from Illinois (B.A., 1902) and from Chicago (Ph.D., 1906), he taught plant physiology (1909–21) at Chicago, and was director (1921–49) of the Boyce Thompson Institute for Plant Research at Yonkers, N.Y. He also served as president (1937–46) of the Yonkers board of education. He was the author of *Twenty Years Research on Plants* (1947), and of many scientific articles.

Crockett (krok′ęt). Unincorporated community in C California, in Contra Costa County, near San Francisco: sugar refining. It was settled in 1867 and platted in 1877. Under the new urban definition established for use in the 1950 census, Crockett was counted with adjoining urban areas; the last official enumeration was 4,105 (1940).

Crockett. City in E Texas, county seat of Houston County, N of Houston: marketing center for pecans. The town was founded in the 1830's and named for David Crockett. Davy Crockett National Forest is nearby. 5,932 (1950).

Crockett, David. [Called **"Davy" Crockett.**] b. at Limestone, Tenn., Aug. 17, 1786; killed at the Alamo, San Antonio, Tex., March 6, 1836. American pioneer, hunter, and politician. He was a member of Congress from Tennessee (1827–31, 1833–35) and served in the war for Texan independence. He published his autobiography in 1834. He was a fine shot and an eccentric humorist, and the story is told of his having treed a coon which, when it recognized Crockett, called out to him: "Don't shoot, colonel; I'll come down, as I know I'm a gone coon." This story was originally told of a Captain Scott who was a famous shot. Some authorities have also suggested that the phrase originated in the fact that "in the American war" (that is, the Revolutionary War) a spy dressed in raccoon-skins took refuge in a tree and addressed an English rifleman in the same words.

Crockett, Samuel Rutherford. b. at Little Duchrae, near New Galloway, Scotland, Sept. 24, 1860; d. April 21, 1914. Scottish minister and novelist. He was educated at Edinburgh University and at the New Theological College, Edinburgh, and was minister of the Free Church at Penicuik, Midlothian, from 1886 until he resigned his charge (1895) to devote himself to authorship. His first book was published as *Dulce Cor: the Poems of Ford*

Bereton. His principal works are *The Stickit Minister* (1893), *The Raiders* (1894), *The Lilac Sunbonnet* (1894), *Mad Sir Uchtred of the Hills* (1894), *Play-Actress* (1894), *The Men of the Moss-Hags* (1895), *Bog-Myrtle and Peat* (1895), *The Gray Man* (1896), *Sweetheart Travellers* (1896), *Cleg Kelly* (1896), *A Galloway Herd* (1896), *Lad's Love* (1897), *Joan of the Sword Hand* (1900), *The Dark of the Moon* (1902), *An Adventurer in Spain* (1903), *Strong Mac* (1904), *Maid Margaret* (1905), *Cherry Ribband* (1905), *Deep Moat Grange* (1908), and *The Men of the Mountain* (1909).

Crockford's (krok'fọrdz). Gaming clubhouse at London, famous in the first half of the 19th century. It was built by William Crockford, originally a fishmonger, in 1827. He is said to have made a large fortune by gambling. He died May 24, 1844, but the house was reopened in 1849 for the Military, Naval, and Country Service Club. It was closed again in 1851. It was for several years a dining house, "The Wellington," and later became the Devonshire Club.

Crock of Gold, The. Novel by James Stephens, published in 1912. It won the 1913 Polignac prize.

Crocodile (krok'ọ.dīl), **Lady Kitty.** In Samuel Foote's *Trip to Calais*, a hypocritical, intriguing woman of quality, intended to satirize the notorious Duchess of Kingston, whose trial for bigamy was just coming on. The influence of the duchess was sufficient to stop the production of the play.

Croesus (krē'sus). fl. 6th century B.C. King of Lydia; son of Alyattes, whom he succeeded in 560 B.C. He subjugated the Ionian, Aeolian, and other neighboring peoples, and at the close of his reign ruled over the region extending from the N and W coasts of Asia Minor to the Halys River (modern Kizil Irmak) on the E and the Taurus Mountains on the S. According to Herodotus, he was visited at the height of his power by Solon, to whom he exhibited his innumerable treasures, and who, when pressed to acknowledge him as the happiest of mortals, answered, "Account no man happy before his death." Deceived by a response of the oracle at Delphi to the effect that, if he marched against the Persians, he would overthrow a great empire, he made war in 546 upon Cyrus, by whom he was defeated in the same year near Sardis and taken prisoner. He was, according to Herodotus, doomed to be burned alive, but as he stood upon the pyre he recalled the words of Solon, and exclaimed "Solon! Solon! Solon!" Desired by Cyrus to state upon whom he was calling, he related the story of Solon, which moved Cyrus to countermand the order for his execution, and to bestow upon him distinguished marks of favor.

Croft (krôft), **Herbert.** b. at Great Thame, Oxfordshire, England, Oct. 18, 1603; d. at Hereford, England, May 18, 1691. English clergyman, bishop of Hereford. He was originally intended for the Roman Catholic priesthood, but eventually took holy orders in the Church of England, having obtained the degree of B.D. at Oxford in 1636. He became chaplain to Charles I c1640, canon of Windsor in 1641, and dean of Hereford in 1644. He was deprived of his preferments during the English Civil War (which were restored to him on the accession of Charles II), became bishop of Hereford in 1662, and was dean of the Chapel Royal from 1668 to 1670. His chief work is *The Naked Truth, or the True State of the Primitive Church* (1675).

Croft, Sir **Herbert.** b. at Dunster Park, Berkshire, England, Nov. 1, 1751; d. at Paris, April 26, 1816. English author and lexicographer, known for his life of the English poet Edward Young, published in Johnson's *Lives of the Poets*. Educated at Oxford, he took holy orders (1785) and began collecting material for a new edition of Johnson's *Dictionary*, which failed, however, to gain enough subscribers and was abandoned in 1793. He was imprisoned for debt in 1795; later he visited Hamburg, Germany, returning to England in 1800, and went to France in 1802, where he spent the remainder of his life. In addition to his life of Young, written in imitation of Johnson, he was the author of *Love and Madness* (1780), *The Abbey of Kilkhampton* (1780), *Sunday Evenings* (1784), *The Will of King Alfred* (1788), *Horace éclairci par la ponctuation* (1810), and *Commentaires sur les meilleurs ouvrages de la langue française* (1815).

Croft or **Crofts** (krôfts), **William.** b. at Nether Ettington, Warwickshire, England, 1678; d. at Bath, England, Aug. 14, 1727. English composer of sacred music. His collection of anthems *Musica Sacra* was published in 1724.

Croftangry (krôf'tang.gri), **Chrystal.** Imaginary author of Sir Walter Scott's *Chronicles of the Canongate*. He gives his autobiography in some of the introductory chapters.

Croft-Cooke (krôft'kůk'), **Rupert.** b. at Edenbridge, Kent, England, June 20, 1904—. English poet, playwright, and novelist. He is the author of the plays *Banquo's Chair* (1930), *Tap Three Times* (1931), and *Deliberate Accident* (1934), the volume of poetry entitled *Some Poems* (1929), and of *Night Out* (1932), *Shoulder the Sky* (1934), *Crusade* (1936), *Same Way Home* (1939), *Glorious* (1940), *Octopus* (1946), and *Ladies Gay* (1946).

Crofts (krôfts), **Ernest.** b. at Leeds, England, Sept. 15, 1847; d. at London, March 19, 1911. English painter of historical and military scenes. He studied at London and at Düsseldorf, Germany. Among his pictures are *Napoleon at Ligny, Cromwell at Marston Moor, Marlborough after Ramillies, Napoleon Leaving Moscow, Wellington's March to Waterloo, The Funeral of Charles I, The Morning of the Battle of Waterloo, Oliver Cromwell at the Assault of Basing House*, and the fresco *Queen Elizabeth opening the First Royal Exchange*, at the Royal Exchange, London.

Crofts, Freeman Wills. b. at Dublin, 1879—. Irish civil engineer and detective-story writer. He created the fictional character of Inspector French, who appears as the central figure in such detective novels as *Inspector French's Greatest Case, Inspector French and the Cheyne Mystery*, and *Golden Ashes*. Among his other stories are *The Box Office Murders* and *Fatal Venture*.

Crofts, James. See **Monmouth,** Duke of.

Croghan (krō'gan), **George.** b. near Louisville, Ky., Nov. 15, 1791; d. at New Orleans, Jan. 8, 1849. American officer, distinguished at the defense of Forts Meigs and Stephenson in 1813.

Croia (krô'yä). Italian name of **Krujë.**

Crois de Bois (krwä dẹ bwä), **Les.** Novel (1919; Eng. trans., *Wooden Crosses*, 1921) of life in the French army of World War I, by the French novelist Roland Dorgelès (1886—).

Croiset (krwä.ze), **Marie Joseph Alfred.** b. at Paris, 1845; d. 1923. French Hellenist. He served as professor (1885 *et seq.*) and member of the Academy of Inscriptions and Belles-Lettres, and also as dean of the Faculté des Lettres at Paris. He wrote *La Poésie de Pindare et les loix de lyrisme grec* (Pindar's Poetry and the Rules of Greek Lyricism, 1880) and, with his brother Maurice Croiset, *Histoire de la littérature grecque* (History of Greek Literature, 1887).

Croiset, Maurice. b. at Paris, 1846; d. 1935. French Hellenic scholar; brother of Marie Joseph Alfred Croiset. He served as professor (1876 *et seq.*) at the Faculté des Lettres at Montpellier and the Collège de France. He wrote *Essai sur la vie et sur les œuvres de Lucien* (Essay on the Life and the Works of Lucian, 1882) and, with his brother, *Histoire de la littérature grecque* (History of Greek Literature, 1887).

Croissant-Rust (krwä.säṅ'rüst'), **Anna.** b. at Dürkheim, Germany, Dec. 10, 1860—. German short-story writer, novelist, and playwright, the only woman among the early German naturalists.

Croisset (krwä.se), **Francis de.** [Original name, **Francis Wiener.**] b. at Brussels, Belgium, 1877; d. 1937. French playwright, author of many light comedies frequently deplored for their alleged immorality. His work includes *Le Bonheur, Mesdames* (1905), *Le Cœur disposé* (1912), and *L'Épervier* (1913). His extensive knowledge of stagecraft made him a collaborator much sought by such well-known figures as Robert de Flers, with whom (after the death of de Flers's partner Caillavet) he did *Le Retour* (1920), *Les Vignes du Seigneur* (1923), and other plays.

Croix (krwä). Town in N France, in the department of Nord, situated on the Roubaix Canal, between Lille and Roubaix. It has metallurgical, textile, and dye industries, and breweries. 17,417 (1946).

Croix, Carlos Francisco de. [Title, Marqués **de Croix.**] b. at Lille, in Flanders, 1699; d. at Valencia, Spain, 1786. Spanish general and administrator. He served with distinction in the army, and was commandant at Ceuta, in

Morocco, and at Puerto de Santa María, Spain, captain-general of Galicia, Spain, and viceroy of New Spain (Mexico) from August, 1766, to September, 1771. His administration was able and prosperous. In 1770 he was advanced to the rank of captain-general in the army. After his return from Mexico, he was made viceroy of Valencia, an office which he held until his death.

Croix, Teodoro de. b. at Lille, in Flanders, c1730; d. at Madrid, April 8, 1791. Spanish soldier; nephew of Carlos Francisco de Croix. From 1766 to 1771 he served in Mexico under his uncle as commandant of the interior provinces and of Sonora, and his jurisdiction later extended (1776–83) over what now comprises the states of California (U.S.), Sonora (Mexico), New Mexico (U.S.), Texas (U.S.), and Sinaloa (Mexico). From April, 1784, to March, 1790, he was viceroy of Peru, and was known as an upright, kind-hearted, and religious ruler. He instituted various reforms in the laws affecting the Indians.

Croix de Feu (krwä dę fė), **Les.** [Eng. trans., *"The Crosses of Fire"*; also: **Parti Social Français, Progrès Social Français.**] French political movement, founded (c1919–20) by François de la Rocque. Originally designating itself an organization for French war veterans, it was soon extended to include others; advocated opposition to French republican institutions by violent street demonstrations and other means; was ordered disbanded (June 18, 1936) as "semimilitary" in character after it had come under vigorous attack as a fascist organization; and was reconstituted (July 11, 1936) as the Parti Social Français ("French Social Party") under its leaders, de la Rocque, Jean Ybarnégaray, and Charles Vallin, who were sentenced (December, 1937) for reconstitution of a banned league. After the formation (June, 1940) of the Vichy regime, it was redesignated as Progrès Social Français ("French Social Progress"), supported Pétain but came into conflict with Pierre Laval, and was again ordered dissolved (1945). Its supporters, some of whom had joined Resistance movements, transferred their backing to various right-wing parties.

Croizette (krwä.zet). [Original name, **Sophie Alexandrine Croisette.**] b. March 19, 1847; d. March 19, 1901. French actress. She was admitted to the Conservatoire in 1867, and made her debut in 1869. In 1873 she was made an associate of the Comédie Française, of which she was the jeune première. In 1881 she retired from the stage, and in 1885 married an American banker named Stern.

Croke (kruk) or **Crocus** (krō'kus), **Richard.** b. at London, probably in 1489; d. there, in August, 1558. English scholar and diplomat. He took the degree of B.A. at Cambridge in 1510; studied Greek under Grocyn at Oxford, and under Hieronymus Aleander at Paris (c1513); lectured on Greek at Louvain, Cologne (c1515), and Leipzig (1515–17); began to lecture on Greek at Cambridge in 1518; was ordained priest in 1519; was fellow of St. John's College in 1523; was sent in 1529 by Cranmer to Italy to collect the opinion of Italian canonists in reference to the king's divorce; became rector of Long Buckby, Northamptonshire, in 1531; and was subdean of King's College, Oxford, 1532–45. His most notable publications are an edition of Ausonius (1515) and a translation of the fourth book of Theodore Gaza's Greek grammar (1516).

Croker (krō'kėr), **John Wilson.** b. in County Galway, Ireland, Dec. 20, 1780; d. at Hampton, near London, Aug. 10, 1857. British politician and general writer. He was a leading contributor to the *Quarterly Review* after 1809, and editor of Boswell's *Life of Johnson* (1831).

Croker, Richard. b. at Blackrock, Ireland, Nov. 23, 1841; d. April 29, 1922. American politician. He was brought to the U.S. as a child and was educated in the New York public schools. He was an alderman of New York (1868–70, 1883), coroner (1873–76), fire commissioner (1883), and city chamberlain (1889–90). He was the recognized leader ("boss") of Tammany Hall for many years.

Croker, Thomas Crofton. b. at Cork, Ireland, Jan. 15, 1798; d. at London, Aug. 8, 1854. Irish antiquary. He wrote *Researches in the South of Ireland* (1824), *The Fairy Legends and Traditions of the South of Ireland* (1825), *The Adventures of Barney Mahoney* (1852), and others.

Croll (krōl), **James.** b. at Little Whitefield, Perthshire, Scotland, Jan. 2, 1821; d. near Perth, Scotland, Dec. 15, 1890. Scottish physical geologist. He was connected with the geological survey of Scotland from 1867 to 1880. His most important work is *Climate and Time* (1875).

Croly (krō'li), **David Goodman.** b. at New York, Nov. 3, 1829; d. there, April 29, 1889. American journalist; husband (married 1857) of Jane Cunningham Croly and father of Herbert Croly. He wrote a *History of Reconstruction* (1868) and a *Primer of Positivism* (1876).

Croly, George. b. at Dublin, Aug. 17, 1780; d. at London, Nov. 24, 1860. Irish clergyman, poet, and novelist. His chief novel is *Salathiel* (1829); he also wrote the poem *Paris in 1815* (1817), the tragedy *Catiline* (1822), *Marston*, a romance (1846), and *Life and Times of George IV* (1830).

Croly, Herbert (David). b. at New York, Jan. 23, 1869; d. at Santa Barbara, Calif., May 17, 1930. American editor and writer; son of David Goodman Croly and Jane Cunningham Croly. He was editor (1900–06) and on the staff until 1913 of the *Architectural Record;* founder (1914) and editor (1914–30) of the *New Republic.* His works inlude *The Promise of American Life* (1909), *Marcus Alonzo Hanna—His Life and Work* (1912), *Progressive Democracy* (1914), and *Willard Straight* (1924).

Croly, Jane Cunningham. [Pseudonym, **Jennie June.**] b. at Market Harborough, Leicestershire, England, Dec. 19, 1829; d. at New York, Dec. 23, 1901. American writer, known for her efforts for the advancement of women; wife (married 1857) of David Goodman Croly and mother of Herbert Croly. She called together the Woman's Congress at New York in 1856. In 1868 she founded Sorosis, a woman's organization, and was its president from 1868 to 1870 and from 1876 to 1886. She was the author of *The History of the Woman's Club Movement in America* (1898).

Cro-Magnon (krō.mag'nǫn; French, krō.mȧ.nyôṅ). Cave near Les Eyzies, Dordogne, France, in which were found, in 1868, prehistoric remains consisting of portions of several skeletons. They are taken as representing a type of man which inhabited SW Europe near the close of the Pleistocene period. Cro-Magnon man was the closest type to modern man of any of the prehistoric types. He approximated six feet in height, his forehead was high, his chin prominent; his cranial measurements were larger, than those of modern *homo sapiens;* his facial angle was orthognathous. Remains of bone and flint tools and weapons, shell and ivory ornaments, and polychrome cave art bespeak an advanced culture.

Cromarty (krom'ạr.ti) or **Cromartyshire** (krom'ạr.ti.shir). Former county in N Scotland, now united with the former county of Ross-shire as Ross and Cromarty.

Cromarty. Parliamentary burgh and seaport in N Scotland, in the county of Ross and Cromarty, situated at the entrance to Cromarty Firth, ab. 16 mi. NE of Dingwall. It has no direct rail connections for passengers, being reached by rail to Dingwall, ab. 577 mi. N of London, thence by bus. 795 (est. 1948).

Cromarty Firth. Inlet of the North Sea, in N Scotland, in the county of Ross and Cromarty, lying immediately N of the Black Isle. It is connected with Moray Firth ab. 2 mi. E of Cromarty. The entrance here is less than 1 mi. wide. Cromarty Firth provides a good harbor. Length, 18 mi.; greatest width, ab. 5 mi.

Crome (krōm), **John.** [Called **"Old Crome."**] b. at Norwich, England, Dec. 22, 1768; d. there, April 22, 1821. English landscape painter; father of John Bernay Crome. He was the son of a poor weaver, and began life as a doctor's assistant and as apprentice to a coach-and-sign painter. He early began to study painting directly from nature in the environs of his native town, later found an opportunity to study drawing, and obtained entrance to a neighboring collection of paintings, where he found some good Flemish pictures. In 1803 he created the Norwich Society of Arts. At the annual exhibitions of this society he exhibited many of his works, rarely sending them to the Royal Academy at London. His pupils and associates, among whom were James Stark and John Sell Cotman, acquired distinction, and formed with him the so-called school of Norwich.

Crome, John Bernay. [Called **"Young Crome."**] b. at Norwich, England, 1794; d. at Yarmouth, England, 1842. English landscape painter; son of John Crome (1768–1821). From his youth he was educated to be a painter, and throughout his career he imitated his father's style so closely as to lead to some confusion between their works. It is, however, generally considered that most of "Young Crome's" paintings are in artistic quality considerably below those of "Old Crome."

Crome Yellow. Novel by Aldous Huxley, published in 1921. The characters include Priscilla and Henry Wimbush, who own a country house from which the novel derives its name; Denis, a poet in love with Henry's niece Anne; Jenny Mullion, a deaf old maid; and Gombauld, an artist who paints Anne and makes love to her.

Crommelynck (kro.mẹ.laṅk), **Fernand.** b. at Brussels, Belgium, c1888—. Belgian dramatist. Trained for the stage at an early age, he wrote and staged before World War I three plays which revealed his skill in creating morbid atmosphere and character. *Le Cocu magnifique*, produced (1921) at Paris, made him famous; the study of a lover's jealousy, it was translated into many languages. His *Tripes d'or*, a social satire (1930), was translated into Russian and produced successfully at Moscow.

Crompton (krump'tọn). Urban district in NW England, in Lancashire, ab. 3 mi. N of Oldham, ab. 193 mi. NW of London. 12,558 (1951).

Crompton (krump'tọn, kromp'-), **George.** b. at Holcombe, England, March 23, 1829; d. Dec. 29, 1886. American textile manufacturer; son of William Crompton (1806–91). He established (c1851) with M. A. Furbush the manufacture at Worcester, Mass., of the weaving loom invented (1837) by his father, and took out in 1854 the first of many patents on the improvement of the loom.

Crompton, Henry. b. at Liverpool, England, Aug. 27, 1836; d. at Surrey, England, March 15, 1904. English positivist philosopher, social reformer, and author of sociological works. He was educated at Trinity College, Cambridge, graduating in 1858, and was a clerk of assize (1858–1901) on the Chester and North Wales circuit. His chief interests were the positivist philosophy of August Comte, which he adopted in 1859, social questions, and the trade-union movement. He was the author of *Letters on Social and Political Subjects* (1870), *Industrial Conciliation* (1876), and *Our Criminal Justice* (1905).

Crompton, Richmal. Pseudonym of **Lamburn, Richmal Crompton.**

Crompton, Samuel. b. at Firwood, near Bolton, England, Dec. 3, 1753; d. at Hall-in-the-Wood, near Bolton, June 26, 1827. English mechanic, inventor of the spinning-mule in 1779.

Crompton, William. b. at Preston, England, Sept. 10, 1806; d. at Windsor, Conn., May 1, 1891. English textile worker; father of George Crompton (1829–86). He came to the U.S. in 1836. In 1837 he invented at Taunton, Mass., a refinement of the weaving loom allowing for the first successful weaving of a pattern by power methods.

Cromwell (krom'wel, -wẹl). Town in C Connecticut, in Middlesex County, on the Connecticut River, in a farming and flower-growing region: manufactures of iron toys. Shipbuilding was important in the early 19th century. 4,286 (1950).

Cromwell (krom'wel, -wẹl, krum'-). Drama by Victor Hugo, published in 1827. This was his first dramatic venture, and was not intended to be acted.

Cromwell, Henry. b. at Huntingdon, England, Jan. 20, 1628; d. at Soham, Cambridgeshire, England, March 23, 1674. Younger son of Oliver Cromwell. He was lord deputy in Ireland (1655–57) and lord lieutenant (1657–59).

Cromwell, Oliver. b. at Huntingdon, England, April 25, 1599; d. at Whitehall, London, Sept. 3, 1658. English revolutionary leader and Lord Protector of the Realm. Not a great deal is known of the early years of this son of a landed proprietor and grazier, who first appeared in public life as a member of Parliament in 1628. From the first he was active among the Puritans, rising slowly to some prominence by virtue of effective work on committees, and by force of sound sense and determination of character rather than by oratory or other more brilliant qualities. As civil war between the forces of Charles I of England and the adherents of Parliament became inevitable, Cromwell was among the first to organize a regiment, which gave a good account of itself in a number of engagements, including those at Edgehill (1642) and Marston Moor (1644), and under his firm leadership won the designation of Ironsides. When the tension between Parliament, which was at that time effectively under Presbyterian control, and the army, dominated by Puritans and Independents, reached a point of danger, Cromwell proposed the reorganization which resulted in the New Model Army, of which (as a result of considerable intrigue, it is supposed) he shared command with Sir Thomas Fairfax. The victories over Charles I at Naseby and over the Scotch at Preston made the army the dominant force in England. Cromwell disavowed responsibility for "Pride's Purge," which eliminated the Presbyterian Parliamentary leadership, but he unquestionably approved of the action, which opened the way for the trial of the king. Cromwell, having sided with the army in its controversy with Parliament over proposals to disband it in part without guarantees of payment of arrears, and having at the same time restrained the extremists among the soldiery, was already the dominant figure in England. The army having seized Charles, Cromwell, who for a long while had apparently sincerely hoped for a compromise, negotiated with the monarch, proposing lenient terms in most respects, but insisting upon religious freedom in the sense that neither an episcopal nor a presbyterian order should be established. Charles's rejection of these terms sealed his fate, and at his trial, Cromwell was foremost in demanding his death. After the execution of the king, Cromwell led an army to Ireland, acting toward the Royalists and the Irish people so ruthlessly, as in the massacres at Drogheda and Wexford, that to this day "the curse of Cromwell" is the most terrible recollection of English rule among the Irish people. With the Irish helpless, he carried out the most extensive expropriation of Irish lands ever attempted, in the first place as an easy way to pay his soldiers, and with the purpose moreover of ensuring English domination once for all. In 1650 he defeated the Royalist Scots and turned back the first attempt of Charles II to recover the throne. The victorious Parliamentary revolutionaries were long involved in controversies and difficulties in fixing the form of the new government, and in 1653 a monarchy in all but name was established with the naming of Cromwell first as Captain-General, then as Lord Protector. He was offered the title of king on this occasion and subsequently, but refused it. One parliament after another proving intractable, Cromwell dismissed them and eventually ruled as a virtual dictator. He suppressed the Levellers, the real revolutionists, with great severity. A good administrator himself, he brought about efficiency in the government, but never won much popular affection, and could not unify the nation. In foreign affairs his policy was directed to the aggrandizement of his country, but, although ruthless on occasion, it was wavering and not, in the long view very effective. After his death his son Richard was not long able to rule effectively, and the Cromwellian generals themselves arranged for the restoration of the Stuart heir to the throne, whereupon the remains of Oliver Cromwell were dug up, beheaded, drawn and quartered, and displayed in public ignominy.

Cromwell, Richard. b. at Huntingdon, England, Oct. 4, 1626; d. at Cheshunt, near London, July 12, 1712. Son of Oliver Cromwell, whom he succeeded as Lord Protector in September, 1658. He resigned in May, 1659.

Cromwell, The Life and Death of Thomas, Lord. Anonymous play, printed in 1613, at one time attributed to Shakespeare. It was entered on the Stationers' Register in 1602.

Cromwell, Thomas. [Title, Earl of **Essex.**] b. probably c1485; d. at London, July 28, 1540. English statesman. The son of a blacksmith, he served in his youth in the French army in Italy, and after his return to England became a lawyer. He was appointed collector of the revenues of the see of York by Wolsey in 1514, became a member of Parliament in 1523, was appointed privy councilor by Henry VIII in 1531, and was made chancellor of the exchequer in 1533. In 1535 he was appointed vicar-general of the king to carry into effect the Act of Supremacy, in which capacity he began in 1536 the suppression of the monasteries and the confiscation of their property. He became lord privy seal in 1536 and lord high chamberlain of England in 1539, and was created Earl of Essex in 1540. In 1539 he negotiated the marriage of Henry VIII with Anne of Cleves, which took place in January, 1540. Having fallen under the king's displeasure, partly on account of his advocacy of this marriage, he was attainted by Parliament and beheaded on the charge of treason.

Cromwell Surveying the Body of Charles I in its Coffin. Painting by Paul Delaroche, in the museum at Nîmes, France.

Cronaca (krō'nä.kä), **Il.** See **Pollaiuolo, Simone.**

Cronholm (krön'hôlm), **Abraham Peter.** b. at Landskrona, Sweden, Oct. 22, 1809; d. at Stockholm, May 27, 1879. Swedish historian. His chief work (published 1857–72, in several volumes) deals with the history of Sweden under Gustavus II (Gustavus Adolphus), whose reign (1611–32) was, from the standpoint of military successes, the most brilliant in Swedish history.

Cronin (krō'nin), **A. J.** [Full name, **Archibald Joseph Cronin.**] b. at Cardross, Scotland, July 19, 1896—. British novelist and physician. Graduated from Glasgow University, he served as a surgeon sublieutenant in World War I, and was engaged in general practice in South Wales (1921–24) and at London (1926–30), giving up medicine in the latter year to devote himself to writing. He is the author of the novels *Hatter's Castle* (1931), *Three Loves* (1932), *Grand Canary* (1933), *The Stars Look Down* (1935), *The Citadel* (1937), *The Keys of the Kingdom* (1941), *The Green Years* (1944), *Shannon's Way* (1948), and *The Spanish Gardener* (1950), of the play *Jupiter Laughs* (1940) and of the autobiographical *Adventures in Two Worlds* (1952), the two worlds being medicine and literature.

Cronje (krōn'yę), **Piet Arnoldus.** b. 1835; d. Feb. 4, 1911. Boer general, noted for his resistance to the British under Lord Methuen (who was marching to the relief of Kimberley) at the Modder River (Nov. 28, 1899), and his crushing defeat of that general at Magersfontein (December 11). On the approach of Lord Roberts, in 1900, he retreated toward Bloemfontein, but was overtaken at Paardeberg and forced to surrender (February 27). In the earlier war against England, in 1881, he distinguished himself at Majuba Hill, and in 1896 dispersed the raiders led by Jameson into the Transvaal.

Cronstedt (krön'stet), Baron **Axel Fredrik.** b. 1722; d. 1765. Swedish mineralogist and chemist. He made the discovery, in 1751, of nickel, occurring in an impure state in niccolite. He was a pioneer in the use of the blowpipe in the study of minerals, and in assigning them to categories on the basis of their chemical composition. His name is perpetuated in the mineral cronstedtite, and he is remembered as the author of *An Essay Towards a System of Mineralogy* (1758).

Cronus (krō'nus) or **Cronos** (-nos). In Greek mythology, a Titan, son of Uranus and Ge. At the instigation of his mother, he emasculated his father for having thrown the Cyclopes (who were likewise the children of Uranus and Ge) into Tartarus. He thereupon usurped the government of the world, which had hitherto belonged to his father, but was in turn dethroned by Zeus. He was the husband of Rhea, by whom he became the father of Hestia, Demeter, Hera, Hades, Poseidon, and Zeus. He was identified with Saturnus by the Romans.

Croo (krö). See **Kru.**

Crook (kruk), **George.** b. near Dayton, Ohio, Sept. 23, 1829; d. at Chicago, March 21, 1890. American soldier, in the Union army in the Civil War, and Indian fighter. He graduated at West Point in 1852, and entered the regular army, in which he attained the rank of major general (April 6, 1888). On Sept. 13, 1861, he was appointed to a colonelcy in the volunteer service, in which he rose to the brevet rank of major general (July 18, 1864); he was mustered out on Jan. 15, 1866. He commanded the national forces in West Virginia in July and August, 1864, was in the engagements at Snicker's Ferry (July 19) and Kernstown (July 24), coöperated with General Sheridan in the Shenandoah valley from August to December of the same year, was in the battles at Berryville, Opequan, Fisher's Hill, Strasburg, and Cedar Creek, and commanded the cavalry of the Army of the Potomac (March 26–April 9, 1865). After the war he did duty among the hostile Indians in Idaho and Arizona. After the massacre of General Custer's command he pursued the Sioux to Slim Buttes, in the Dakota Territory, where he defeated them. In 1886 he conducted the campaign against the Apaches under Geronimo, whom he brought to a stand near San Bernardino, Mexico, but resigned his command before the conclusion of hostilities.

Crook and Willington (wil'ing.tǫn). Urban district in NE England, in Durham, ab. 5 mi. NW of Bishop-Auckland, ab. 251 mi. N of London by rail. It comprises the formerly separate urban districts of Crook and Willington. 27,606 (1951).

Crooked Island. Island in the Atlantic Ocean, N of Guantánamo, Cuba; part of the Bahamas. Fishing and vegetable gardening are the major industries. Area, 76 sq. mi.; pop. 1,078 (1943).

Crookes (kruks), Sir **William.** b. at London, June 17, 1832; d. April 4, 1919. English chemist and physicist. He discovered thallium in 1861, and invented the radiometer in 1874. He founded the *Chemical News* in 1859, edited the *Quarterly Journal of Science* from 1864, and published *Select Methods of Chemical Analysis* (1880), and others. He was knighted in June, 1897. He was an authority on sanitation and published a number of works on the subject, and was noted for his researches into the properties of radiant matter. In 1903 he invented the spinthariscope. He was known also for his investigation of psychic phenomena.

Crooks (kruks), **George Richard.** b. at Philadelphia, Feb. 3, 1822; d. at Madison, N.J., Feb. 20, 1897. American journalist and Methodist clergyman. He collaborated in the publication (1858) of a *Latin-English Lexicon.*

Crooks, Richard. [Full name, **Alexander Richard Crooks.**] b. at Trenton, N.J., June 26, 1900—. American operatic tenor. He made his debut (1927) as Cavaradossi in *Tosca* at the Hamburg Opera, and after 1933 sang with the Metropolitan Opera Company, making his debut there as Des Grieux in *Manon.*

Crookston (kruks'tǫn). City in NW Minnesota, county seat of Polk County, on the Red Lake River: trading center for the chief wheat-raising county of the state; manufactures include flour, flax, fiber, refined honey, and dairy products. It is the seat of an agricultural school and experiment station of the University of Minnesota. 7,352 (1950).

Crooksville (kruks'vil). Village in SE Ohio, in Perry County near Zanesville: manufactures ceramics. 2,960 (1950).

Croppies (krop'iz). Name given to the republican party in Ireland in 1798, who wore their hair cropped in imitation of the French revolutionists. The name was applied earlier, in 1642, to the Parliamentary soldiers during the English Civil War.

Crop Protection Institute. Organization founded (1920) at the behest of the National Research Council for the purpose of promoting the efficient control of injurious insects, plant diseases, and toxic substances affecting plant life and products, and the support of research and diffusion of knowledge in these fields. It maintains headquarters at Washington, D.C., and issues a *Circular* and *Crop Protection Digest.*

Cropredy Bridge (krop'red.i). Locality near Banbury, England, the scene of a Royalist defeat of the Parliamentarians under Waller, June 29, 1644.

Cropsey (krop'si), **Jasper Francis.** b. Feb. 18, 1823; d. June 22, 1900. American landscape painter, a pupil of Edward Maury. He was admitted as a member of the National Academy of Design in 1851.

Croquemitaine (krok.mē.ten). French legendary monster, with which nurses have traditionally sought to frighten naughty children. L'Épine in 1863 published *Légende de Croquemitaine*, a romance relating to the adventures of a certain Mitaine, a goddaughter of Charlemagne.

Croquis (krô.kē'), **Alfred.** Pseudonym of **Maclise, Daniel.**

Crosby (kroz'bi). [Called locally **Great Crosby.**] Municipal borough and residential town in NW England, in Lancashire, situated near the mouth of the river Mersey, ab. 5 mi. NW of Liverpool, ab. 200 mi. NW of London by rail. 58,362 (1951).

Crosby. Village in C Minnesota, in Crow Wing County: in the Cuyuna iron region (part of the great Mesabi range). Pulpwood is also an important industry. 2,777 (1950).

Crosby, Bing. [Full name, **Harry Lillis Crosby.**] b. at Tacoma, Wash., May 2, 1904—. American singer and motion-picture actor. After singing with dance bands for several years, developing his particular style and acquiring a following, in 1931 he entered both the radio and the motion-picture fields, in which he has prospered and won extensive international popularity. Many of his songs, such as *The Last Roundup* and *White Christmas*, caught the fancy of a large section of the public. Among the successful films in which he has starred are *Pennies from Heaven, The Bells of St. Mary's,* and *The Emperor Waltz.*

Crosby, Ernest Howard. b. at New York, Nov. 4, 1856; d. Jan. 3, 1907. American writer and social reformer; son of Howard Crosby (1826–91). He was graduated from Columbia Law School in 1878, practiced law (1878–89) at New York, and was appointed judge of the international court at Alexandria, Egypt, in 1889. He resigned in 1894 and returned to New York, where he devoted himself to social reform. He wrote *Plain Talk in Psalm and Parable* (1899), *Captain Jenks, Hero* (1902), *Swords and Plowshares* (1902), *Tolstoi and His Message* (1903), *Broadcast* (1905), *Tolstoi as a Schoolmaster* (1905), *Garrison, the Non-resistant* (1905), and *Labor and Neighbor* (1908).

Crosby, Fanny. [Full name, **Frances Jane Crosby.**] b. at Southeast, N.Y., March 24, 1820; d. at Bridgeport, Conn., Feb. 12, 1915. American hymn writer and poet. She became blind at the age of six weeks, and entered (c1835) the Institute for the Blind at New York, where she afterward taught English and history (1847–58) until her marriage (1858) to Alexander Van Alstyne, a blind organist. The best known of her hymns, of which she wrote (1864 *et seq.*) about 6,000, are *Safe in the Arms of Jesus, Jesus Keep Me Near the Cross, Pass Me Not, O Gentle Saviour, Jesus is Calling,* and *Jesus the Water of Life Will Give.* Her books include *The Blind Girl, and Other Poems* (1844), *Monterey, and Other Poems* (1849), *A Wreath of Columbia's Flowers* (1858), *Bells at Evening, and Other Poems* (1898), and *Memories of Eighty Years* (1906).

Crosby, Howard. b. at New York, Feb. 27, 1826; d. there, March 29, 1891. American Presbyterian clergyman; father of Ernest Howard Crosby (1856–1907). He was graduated at the University of New York in 1844, became professor of Greek there c1851, and was professor of Greek at Rutgers College, New Brunswick, N.J., from 1859 to 1863. From 1863 until his death he was pastor of the Fourth Avenue Presbyterian Church at New York. He was also chancellor of the University of New York (1870–81), a member of the American committee for the revision of the New Testament, and one of the chief instruments in effecting the organization (1877) of the Society for the Prevention of Crime, of which he became president.

Crosby, Percy Leo. b. at Brooklyn, N.Y., Dec. 8, 1891—. American cartoonist, artist, exhibitor, and pamphleteer, probably best known as the creator of Skippy. He was educated at local schools, and studied art at the Pratt Institute, Brooklyn, and the Art Students League of New York. He has shown his paintings in the National Academy of Design, the Anderson and Seligman Galleries, the Philadelphia Academy of the Fine Arts, and the Corcoran Gallery of Art at Washington, D.C. In 1932 he won the Olympic silver medal for drawing at the international art competition held at Los Angeles. In the years 1934–35 he exhibited at London, Rome, and Paris, and examples of his work were purchased by the British Museum and the Luxembourg Museum at Paris. He saw service in World War I. His works are *That Rooky of the 13th Squad* (1919), *Between Shots* (1919, cartoons of war life), *Skippy* (1925, humorous drawings of a character he created in 1923), *Skippy and Other Humor* (1929), *Skippy* (1929, a novel), *Dear Sookey* (1929), *A Cartoonist's Philosophy* (1931), *Patriotism* and *Skippy Rambles* (both 1932), *Always Belittlin'* and *Sport Drawings* (both 1933), *Three Cheers for the Red, Red, and Red!* (1936), *Essay on Roosevelt's Second Inaugural Address* (1937), and *Would Communism Work Out in America?* (1938).

Crosby Hall. [Also, **Crosby Place.**] Ancient house in Bishopsgate Street, London. The site was leased from Alice Ashfield, prioress of St. Helen's, in 1466 by Sir John Crosby, a grocer and lord mayor. He built the beautiful Gothic palace. The mansion covered a large part of what later became Crosby Place or Square. Richard of Gloucester lived here at the death of Edward IV, and here held his levees before his usurpation of the crown. It was afterward bought by Sir Thomas More, who wrote here the *Utopia* and the *Life of Richard III.* Crosby Hall was the central feature of Shakespeare's London. Shakespeare himself had a residence in the neighborhood.

Croskey (kros′ki), **John Welsh.** b. at Philadelphia, Jan. 26, 1858—. American ophthalmologist. He received his M.D. (1889) from the Medico-Chirurgical College at Philadelphia, and was professor of ophthalmology, laryngology, and otology (1902–05) at Temple University. He was the author of *Dictionary of Ophthalmic Terms* (1907) and other works.

Crosland (kroz′lạnd), **Camilla Toulmin.** b. at London, June 9, 1812; d. at Dulwich, London, Feb. 16, 1895. English poet and writer.

Crosley (kroz′li), **Powel.** b. at Cincinnati, Ohio, Sept. 18, 1886—. American manufacturer and business executive. President of the Crosley Corporation, manufacturers of radios, washing machines, refrigerators, and other products, he sold (1945) his holdings to the Aviation Corporation. He was a director of Transcontinental and Western Air, Inc. In 1947 he began the marketing of a low-priced midget automobile.

Crosman (kroz′mạn), **Henrietta.** b. at Wheeling, W.Va., Sept. 2, 1870; d. at Pelham Manor, N.Y., Oct. 31, 1944. American actress; wife (married 1897) of Maurice Campbell. She played in Daniel Frohman's Lyceum company and as leading woman with Charles Frohman's Comedians (1892–94), and starred in *Gloriana, Mistress Nell, The Sword of the King, One of Our Girls, The Real Thing,* and other plays. She was acclaimed in *As You Like It* (1902) as the best Rosalind of her day. From 1932 to 1936 she was under contract to Fox Films at Hollywood.

Cross (krôs), **Charles Frederick.** b. at Brentford, Middlesex, England, 1855; d. at Hove, Sussex, England, April 15, 1935. English industrial chemist, discoverer (1895) with Edward J. Bevan of viscose, used in the manufacture of artificial silk. He collaborated on improvements of spinning methods and on development of the Topham spinning box; he also developed a technique for manufacture of woodpulp paper by researches, again with Bevan, on cellulose. He was the author of *Cellulose, Researches in Cellulose,* and other works.

Cross, Hardy. b. in Mansemond County, Va., Feb. 10, 1885—. American civil engineer and teacher. He was graduated from the Massachusetts Institute of Technology (B.S. in C.E., 1908) and Harvard University (M.C.E., 1911), and was assistant professor of civil engineering (1921–37) at the University of Illinois and professor of civil engineering (1937 *et seq.*) at Yale. He is the author of *Continuous Frames of Reinforced Concrete.*

Cross, Richard Assheton. [Title, 1st Viscount **Cross.**] b. at Red Scar, Lancashire, England, May 30, 1823; d. 1914. English politician. He served as home secretary (1874–80, 1885–86), secretary of state for India (1886–92), and lord privy seal (1895–1900). He was raised to the peerage as Viscount Cross in 1886.

Cross, Roy. b. at Ellis, Kan., 1884—. American chemist.

Cross, Whitman. [Full name, **Charles Whitman Cross.**] b. at Amherst, Mass., Sept. 1, 1854; d. at Washington, D.C., April 20, 1949. American scientist, a geologist with the U.S. Geological Survey from 1880 to 1925. The mineral crossite is named for him. He published many geological and mineralogical papers and, with Pirsson, Iddings, and Washington, *Quantitative Classification of Igneous Rocks* (1903).

Cross, Wilbur Lucius. b. at Mansfield, Conn., April 10, 1862; d. at New Haven, Conn., Oct. 5, 1948. American educator, literary historian, and politician. Graduated from Yale (B.A., 1885; Ph.D., 1889), he was a member from 1894 of the Yale English department, as professor from 1902, editor of the *Yale Review* (1911–40), and dean (1916–30) of the Yale Graduate School. He served four terms, from 1931 to 1939, as governor of Connecticut. He was the author of *Development of the English Novel* (1899), *Life and Times of Laurence Sterne* (1909), *History of Henry Fielding* (1918), *Modern English Novel* (1929), *Four Contemporary Novelists* (1930), *Connecticut Yankee, an Autobiography* (1943), and other works;

editor of *Macbeth* (1900), *Sentimental Journey* (1926), and other English classics.

Crosse (krôs), **Andrew.** b. at Broomfield, Somersetshire, England, June 17, 1784; d. there, July 6, 1855. English electrician, noted for his experiments in electro-crystallization.

Crossett (kros'e̤t). Town in S Arkansas, in Ashley County: lumber and lumber products. 4,619 (1950).

Crossing, The. Historical novel by Winston Churchill, published in 1904. The hero, David Ritchie, heads a band of Kentucky settlers who accompany George Rogers Clark on his expedition. The work depicts the difficulties of the pioneers during the campaign in the wilderness.

Crossing Brooklyn Ferry. Poem by Walt Whitman, included as "Sun-Down Poem" in the 1856 edition of *Leaves of Grass* and published under its present title in 1860.

Crossing the Bar. Religious poem by Alfred Tennyson. It was written in October, 1889, when the poet was suffering fits of depression, and was first published, in the same year, as the last poem in the volume *Demeter and Other Poems.* It has since always been published at the end of every volume of his works in accordance with his frequently repeated request. It was composed at the suggestion of a nurse Emma Durham, who nursed him during his illness of 1888–89 and said to him, "instead of giving way to depression, you ought to write a hymn."

Cross Keys (krôs kēz). Place in Rockingham County, Va., ab. 20 mi. NE of Staunton. Here, on June 8, 1862, a battle took place between Jackson's army (ab. 8,000) under Ewell and a Union force (ab. 18,000) under Frémont. The Union loss was 625; that of the Confederates, 287.

Crossley (krôs'li), **Ada.** b. at Tarraville, Australia, March 3, 1874; d. at London, Oct. 17, 1929. Australian contralto. She studied at Melbourne, Australia, under Fanny Simonson and Zelmann, and made her first appearance (1892) with the Melbourne Philharmonic Society. She made her London debut (1895) at Queen's Hall, sang before Queen Victoria, and toured in the U.S. and South Africa. She was known for her oratorio and ballad singing.

Cross of Gold Speech. Speech delivered (July 9, 1896) by William Jennings Bryan, as delegate from Nebraska, at the Democratic national convention at Chicago. Bryan's attack on the single gold standard concluded with the peroration: "You shall not press down upon the brow of labor this crown of thorns—You shall not crucify mankind upon a cross of gold!" He was acclaimed the Democratic presidential candidate on a platform demanding the free and unlimited coinage of silver at a 16-to-1 ratio.

Cross Roads. A former name of **Woodruff,** S.C.

Cross-Roads, The. Play of Irish middle-class life by Lennox Robinson, published in 1909.

Croswell (kroz'wel), **Edwin.** b. at Catskill, N.Y., May 29, 1797; d. at Princeton, N.J., June 13, 1871. American journalist and politician; nephew of Harry Croswell. He was editor of the Albany *Argus* (1823–54), and was (with Martin Van Buren) a member of the "Albany Regency," the name popularly applied to the group of New York politicians that was able to achieve a degree of power within the state seldom equaled before or since.

Croswell, Harry. b. at West Hartford, Conn., June 16, 1778; d. at New Haven, Conn., March 13, 1858. American Federalist, journalist, and clergyman; uncle of Edwin Croswell.

Crotch (kroch), **William.** b. at Norwich, England, July 5, 1775; d. at Taunton, England, Dec. 29, 1847. English composer. He was organist of St. John's College, Oxford, and professor of music in the university; he later served (1822 *et seq.*) as principal of the Royal Academy of Music.

Crotchet Castle (kroch'e̤t). Novel by Thomas Love Peacock, published in 1831.

Crothers (kruᴛʜ'ėrz), **Rachel.** b. at Bloomington, Ill., Dec. 12, 1878—. American playwright. She was a graduate (1892) of Illinois State Normal University. Her works include *The Three of Us, The Coming of Mrs. Patrick, Myself Bettina, A Man's World, The Heart of Paddy-Whack, Once Upon a Time, Nice People, Everyday, A Lady's Virtue, Let Us Be Gay, When Ladies Meet,* and *Susan and God.*

Crothers, Samuel McChord. b. at Oswego, Ill., June 7, 1857; d. at Cambridge, Mass., Nov. 9, 1927. American clergyman and author. Originally a Presbyterian, he entered the Unitarian ministry in 1882, and was pastor of the First Church at Cambridge, Mass., from 1894. He wrote *Miss Muffet's Christmas Party* (1901), *The Gentle Reader* (1903), *The Understanding Heart* (1903), *The Pardoner's Wallet* (1905), *The Endless Life* (1905), *Oliver Wendell Holmes and his Fellow Boarders* (1909), *Book of Friendship* (1910), *Humanly Speaking* (1912), and others.

Croton (krō'to̤n) or **Crotona** (krō.tō'na̤). See also **Crotone.**

Croton. River in SE New York which joins the Hudson ab. 32 mi. N of New York City, which it supplies, by means of a series of dams and lakes, with water through the Croton Aqueduct (the old one was opened for use in 1842; the new, and chief, one was completed in 1891).

Croton Aqueduct. Aqueduct in SE New York, extending from the Croton River and reservoir to New York City. It was the first large water-supply project of New York City, and was built in 1837–42, to carry ab. 72 million gallons of water daily to the city.

Crotone (krō.tō'nā). [Former name, **Cotrone;** ancient names, **Crotona, Croton.**] Town and commune in S Italy, in the *compartimento* (region) of Calabria, in the province of Catanzaro, situated on the Ionian Sea N of Catanzaro. It has chemical and zinc industries and improved port facilities and is a market place for the agricultural products of the Marchesata district. A castle now stands on the site of the ancient acropolis; there is also a cathedral and a civic museum containing Greek relics. A Greek colony, one of the most important cities of Magna Graecia, it was noted in ancient times for its devotion to athletics and as the seat of the Pythagorean school. There is a Greek temple of Hera Lakinia at the extremity of the nearby promontory on the Ionian Sea. This famous shrine has been greatly damaged by vandalism and earthquakes, but its platform of masonry and the results of excavations have supplied data for a partial restoration. It was of the 5th century B.C., Doric, hexastyle, with 14 columns on the flanks, and an interior range of four columns before the pronaos. The Crotonians destroyed the rival town of Sybaris in 510 B.C. but were defeated by the Locrians at the Sagras River in 480 B.C.; later the city submitted to Syracuse; it was occupied by the Romans in 277 B.C. Hannibal embarked here on his return to Africa in 203. The Romans founded a colony here in 194 B.C. Under various rulers during the Middle Ages, the town regained some of its importance only in the 20th century. Slight damage was suffered during World War II by some buildings of tourist interest. Pop. of commune, 21,466 (1936); of town, 19,163 (1936).

Croton-on-Hudson (krō'to̤n; hud'so̤n). Village in SE New York, in Westchester County, on the Hudson River: residential community. It was the home of Edna St. Vincent Millay and Stuart Chase. 4,837 (1950).

Crotus Rubianus (krō'tus rö.bi.ā'nus). [Original name, **Johann Jäger.**] b. near Arnstadt, Germany, c1480; d. after 1539. German humanist and sometime friend of Luther. He taught school at Fulda (1510–15), visited Italy (1517–20), and espoused the Reformation, but then deserted it to become a canon at Halle in 1531. He is remembered chiefly for having written most of the letters in the famous satire *Epistolae obscurorum virorum* (1515).

Crouch (krouch), **Frederick Nicholls.** b. at London, July 31, 1808; d. at Portland, Me., Aug. 18, 1896. English musician, the composer of the music for the ballad *Kathleen Mavourneen.* He came to the U.S. in 1849.

"Crouchback" (krouch'bak). Nickname of **Lancaster, Edmund.**

"Crouchback." Nickname of **Richard III** (of *England*).

Crousaz (krö.zà), **Jean Pierre de.** b. at Lausanne, Switzerland, April 13, 1663; d. March 22, 1748. Swiss philosopher and mathematician. His chief work is a treatise on logic (1712; several later editions). He was a voluminous writer whose works did not achieve high rank.

Crouse (krous), **Russel.** b. at Findlay, Ohio, Feb. 20, 1893—. American journalist, playwright, and scenarist. He was a staff member (1911–16) of the Kansas City *Star* and a columnist (1925–31) on the New York *Evening Post.* His works include *Mr. Currier and Mr. Ives* (1930), *It*

Seems Like Yesterday (1931), *Murder Won't Out* (1932), *The American Keepsake* (1932), and other plays. He was librettist for the musical comedy *The Gang's All Here* (1931), coauthor, with Howard Lindsay, of *Arsenic and Old Lace*, of the dramatization of Clarence Day's *Life With Father*, and of the musical comedy *Call Me Madam* (1950), and scenarist for motion pictures such as *Mountain Music* and *The Great Victor Herbert*.

Crow (krō). Tribe of North American Indians formerly occupying the region of the Yellowstone. Their culture was typical Plains hunting culture. Their language belonged to the Missouri group of the Siouan family of languages.

Crow, Carl. [Full name, **Herbert Carl Crow.**] b. at Highland, Mo., Sept. 26, 1883—. American journalist and Sinologist. He was a member (1906–11) of the editorial staff of the Fort Worth *Star-Telegram*, was associate city editor (1911–13) of the *China Press* at Shanghai, and owned and operated (1919–37) an advertising agency at Shanghai, where he also established the Shanghai *Post*. His works include *America and the Philippines* (1914), *Japan and America* (1916), *Four Hundred Million Customers* (1937), *I Speak for the Chinese* (1938), *Master Kung* (1938), and *China Takes Her Place* (1944).

Crow, Jim. See **Jim Crow.**

Crow, Martha. [Maiden name, **Foote.**] b. at Sackets Harbor, N.Y., 1854; d. Jan. 1, 1924. American writer and teacher of English literature (1876 *et seq.*). A graduate of Syracuse University (Ph.B., 1876; Ph.D., 1885), she served as assistant professor (1892–1900) at the University of Chicago, and assistant professor and dean of women (1900–05) at Northwestern University. She was the author of *Elizabethan Sonnet-Cycles* (4 vols., 1896), *The World Above* (1905), *Elizabeth Barrett Browning* (1908), *Harriet Beecher Stowe, a Biography* (1913), *The American Country Girl* (1915), *LaFayette* (1916), and *Christ in the Poetry of Today* (1917).

Crowder (krou'dėr), **Enoch Herbert.** b. at Edinburg, Grundy County, Mo., April 11, 1859; d. at Washington, D.C., May 7, 1932. American army officer and diplomat, first American ambassador (1923–27) to Cuba. He was graduated (1881) from the U.S. Military Academy at West Point and received (1886) the LL.B. degree from the University of Missouri. He served as judge advocate (1901–11) and judge advocate general (1911–23), being promoted to brigadier general in 1911 and major general in 1917. As provost marshal general (1917–19), he drafted the Selective Service Act. He retired from the army in 1923.

Crowdero (krou.dir'ō). Character in Butler's *Hudibras*; a fiddler, and the leader of the mob.

Crowe (krō), **Captain.** Whimsical, impatient merchant captain in Tobias Smollett's *Sir Launcelot Greaves*. He insists upon being a knight errant with the latter.

Crowe, Catherine. [Maiden name, **Stevens.**] b. at Borough Green, Kent, England, c1800; d. in 1876. English writer, principally known by her writings on the supernatural. She was the author of *Night Side of Nature* (1848) and *Spiritualism and the Age We Live In* (1859), and also wrote the novels *Susan Hopley* (1841) and *Lily Dawson* (1847).

Crowe, Eyre Evans. b. at Redbridge, Southampton, England, March 20, 1799; d. at London, Feb. 25, 1868. English journalist, historian, and novelist; father of Sir Joseph Archer Crowe. He was the author of *History of France* (5 vols., 1858–68).

Crowe, Sir **Joseph Archer.** b. at London, Oct. 20, 1825; d. at Gamburg-on-the-Tauber, Baden, Germany, Sept. 6, 1896. English diplomat and connoisseur and historian of art; son of Eyre Evans Crowe. In 1847 he met Giovanni Battista Cavalcaselle, with whom he collaborated on *Early Flemish Painters* (1857) and other works on the history of art still considered among the best in their field.

Crowe, William. b. at Midgeham, Berkshire, England, 1745; d. at Bath, England, Feb. 9, 1829. English clergyman and poet. He was considered eccentric, but a popular preacher. He wrote *Lewesdon Hill* (1788), *A Treatise on English Versification* (1827), and published several volumes of sermons and orations, and others.

Crowell (krō'ẹl), **Grace.** [Maiden name, **Noll.**] b. at Inland, Iowa, Oct. 31, 1877—. American poet. She was poet laureate (1935–37) of Texas. Her works include *White Fire* (1925), *Songs for Courage* (1930), *Flame in the Wind* (1930), *Bright Destiny* (1936), *This Golden Summit* (1937), *Facing the Stars* (1941), and *Songs for Comfort* (1947).

Crowell, John Franklin. b. at York, Pa., Nov. 1, 1857; d. Aug. 6, 1931. American economist. Graduated (1883) from Yale University and from Columbia University (Ph.D., 1887), he was president (1887–94) of Trinity College in North Carolina and head (1895–97) of the department of economics and sociology at Smith College. He later served as an editor (1906–15) of the *Wall Street Journal* and as director (1919–21) of the World Market Institute of New York. His works include *Internal Commerce of the United States* (1902), *Trusts and Competition* (1915), and *Revised Work of Wall Street* (1920).

Crowell, Luther Childs. b. at West Dennis, Mass., Sept. 7, 1840; d. there, Sept. 16, 1903. American inventor. He was employed (1879–1903) by the R. Hoe and Company printing-press firm. In 1867 he took out a patent on a machine for the manufacture of paper bags; he also invented (1872) the modern square-bottomed paper bag and devised (1873) a sheet delivery and folding mechanism for newspaper printing presses.

Crowland (krō'lạnd). [Also, **Croyland.**] Parish, market town, and former rural district in E England, in Lincolnshire, in the Parts of Holland, situated on the river Welland ab. 8 mi. NE of Peterborough. It contains the ruins of a famous abbey founded by Ethelbald of Mercia in the 8th century. 2,809 (1931).

Crowley (krou'li). City in S Louisiana, parish seat of Acadia Parish, ab. 137 mi. NW of New Orleans. Its principal industries are the growing and milling of rice, and it is the seat of a rice experiment station operated by the U.S. Department of Agriculture and Louisiana State University. 12,784 (1950).

Crowley, Patrick Edward. b. at Cattaraugus, N.Y., 1864—. American railroad executive who served (1924–31) as president of New York Central Lines. He joined the New York Central in 1889 as a dispatcher.

Crowley (krō'li), **Robert.** [Also: **Crole, Croleus.**] b. in Gloucestershire, England, c1518; d. at London, June 18, 1588. English author, printer, and divine. He was educated at Oxford, embraced the doctrines of the Reformation, and set up (c1549) a printing press at Ely Rents, in Holborn (now part of London), which he conducted for three years. He was archdeacon of Hereford (1559–67) and vicar of Saint Lawrence Jewry, London (1576–78). His typographical fame rests chiefly on three impressions which he made in 1550 of the *Vision of Piers Plowman*. His most notable works are *An Informacion and Peticion agaynst the Oppressours of the Pore Commons of this Realme* (1548), *The Voyce of the Laste Trumpet* (1549), *The Way to Wealth* (1550), *One and Thyrtye Epigrammes* (1550), and *Pleasure and Payne, Heaven and Hell: Remember these Foure, and all shall be Well* (1551).

Crown, Oration on the. [Latin, **De Corona.**] Oration of Demosthenes, delivered in 330 B.C. Ctesiphon had proposed that Demosthenes should be publicly crowned with a golden crown, as a reward for public services rendered after the battle of Chaeronea, and for this was indicted by Aeschines as the proposer of an illegal act. In the oration Demosthenes defended his own acts and character, and attacked Aeschines, who was defeated.

Crowne (kroun), **John.** b. c1640; d. c1703. British dramatist. Among other plays he wrote *The Country Wit* (1675), *City Politiques* (played c1683), *Sir Courtly Nice, or It Cannot Be* (1685), and *The Married Beau* (1694).

Crowninshield (kroun'in.shēld), **Francis Welch.** [Better known as **Frank Crowninshield**; pseudonym, **Arthur Loring Bruce.**] b. at Paris, June 24, 1872; d. at New York, Dec. 28, 1947. American editor and author, born in France of American parents. He was publisher of *The Bookman* (1895–1900) and *Metropolitan Magazine* (1900–02), assistant editor (1903–07) of *Munsey's Magazine*, art editor (1910–13) of *Century Magazine*, editor (1914–35) of *Vanity Fair*, and editorial adviser to Condé Nast Publications. He wrote *Manners for the Metropolis* (1908) and *The Bridge Fiend* (1909) and translated (1926) Brillat-Savarin's *The Physiology of Taste*.

Crowninshield, Frederic. b. at Boston, Nov. 27, 1845; d. Sept. 13, 1918. American painter. He was graduated from Harvard University in 1866 and studied art for several years in Europe. From 1879 to 1885 he was instructor in drawing and painting at the school of the Boston Museum of Fine Arts. In 1885 he established a studio at New York and devoted himself to general artistic work, including glass and mural painting. He was director of the American Academy in Rome from 1909 to 1911. He published several volumes of poems and a manual of *Mural Painting* (1887).

Crown of Wild Olive, The. Series of four lectures (given in 1866) by John Ruskin. The lectures were *War* (delivered before the Royal Military Academy), *The Future of England* (before the Royal Artillery Institute), *Work* (before a labor club, or workingmen's institute), and *Traffic* (at the Bradford Town Hall), by which he meant commercial activity in buying and selling. The "crown" he had in mind was the one awarded as a prize to the victor in the ancient Greek Olympic Games, and Ruskin's idea is that one should work for the sake of the work itself, for the spiritual satisfaction it affords, and not for material reward in the shape of a prize or medal.

Crown Point. City in NW Indiana, county seat of Lake County, near Lake Michigan: residential community. 5,839 (1950).

Crown Point. Town in NE New York, in Essex County, on Lake Champlain ab. 90 mi. N of Albany: tourist resort. It was strongly fortified in the 18th century, was abandoned by the French in 1759, and was taken from the British by the Americans under Seth Warner in May, 1775. Pop. 1,707 (1950).

Crown Point. Unincorporated community in SW Ohio, in Montgomery County near Dayton. Under the new urban definition established for use in the 1950 census it was counted with adjoining urban areas. The last official enumeration was 2,635 (1940).

Crowsnest Pass (krōz'nest). Pass in the Canadian Rocky Mountains through which the southern line of the Canadian Pacific Railway passes. It is on the boundary between the provinces of Alberta and British Columbia near the U.S. border. Elevation, ab. 4,460 ft.

Crowther (krou'ᴛʜėr), **Samuel Adjai.** b. in Yoruba, Nigeria; d. 1891. First Negro bishop of the Church of England. He was carried off and sold into slavery in 1821. With many others he was freed by a British man-of-war in 1822, and landed at Sierra Leone, where he attended school and soon distinguished himself. His higher education he received in England. He accompanied the first and second Niger expeditions, and published an account of the latter. In 1864 he was ordained Bishop of the Niger, and proved himself worthy of the office. His books in and on the languages of the Niger region give him a prominent place among African linguists.

Croy (kroi), **Kate.** Character in *The Wings of the Dove* (1902), novel by Henry James.

Croydon (kroi'dǫn). County borough, market town, and southern suburb of London, in SE England, in Surrey, ab. 11 mi. S of Victoria station, London: seat of one of Great Britain's major airports. It is one of the largest towns in the south of England and is included in the Metropolitan Police District. Croydon is within the area of continuous urban development surrounding London. It shares some of the functions of a county seat (of Surrey) with Guildford and Kingston-upon-Thames. It has a ruined palace of the archbishops of Canterbury, used by them from the Norman Conquest until 1757. 249,592 (1951).

Croyland (kroi'lą̣nd). See **Crowland.**

Croysado (kroi.sä'dō), **the Great.** In Butler's *Hudibras*, a character intended for Lord Fairfax.

Crozet Islands (krō.zet'). [Also, **Krozet Islands.**] Group of small uninhabited islands in the Indian Ocean, ab. 1,400 mi. SE of Cape Ste.-Marie, Madagascar. Possession Island is the largest of the group. They were discovered (1772) by Marion de Fresne and named for one of the officers in his crew.

Crozier (krō'zhėr), **William.** b. at Carrollton, Ohio, Feb. 19, 1855; d. at Washington, D.C., Nov. 10, 1942. American soldier, inventor of a wire-wound rifled cannon and, with General Buffington, of a disappearing gun carriage. He was graduated from West Point in 1876, fought against the Indians in the West, and served as major and inspector general of U.S. volunteers in 1898, in the Spanish-American War. He was sent as a delegate to the peace conference at The Hague in 1899. He also served in the suppression of the Philippine insurrection, as chief ordnance officer, under General Chaffee, in the Peking relief expedition in 1900, and was appointed brigadier general and chief of ordnance in the U.S. army in 1901. From 1917 to 1918 he was a member of the War Council; he retired from the army in 1919.

Crozon (kro.zôṅ). Town in NW France, in the department of Finistère, situated on a peninsula between the harbors of Brest and Douarnenez, S of the town of Brest. It is the chief place on the peninsula. 7,712 (1946).

Cruchaga Tocornal (krö.chä'gä tō.kōr.näl'), **Miguel.** b. at Santiago, Chile, May 4, 1869; d. May 3, 1949. Chilean diplomat. He was professor of international law (1900–06) at the University of Chile, minister of finance (1903), and minister of the interior (1905–06). He also served as envoy extraordinary and minister plenipotentiary to Argentina, Uruguay, and Paraguay (1907–13) and to Germany and Holland (1913–20), ambassador to Brazil (1923–25) and to the U.S. (1926–27, 1931–32). He returned to Santiago as minister of foreign affairs in 1932, serving until 1937, when he became a senator; he was for a time president of the senate.

Crucifixion, The. Of the many paintings of this subject the following are among the best known: **1.** A large painting by Lucas Cranach in the Stadtkirche at Weimar, Germany. It contains portraits of the artist and of Luther and Melanchthon on the right, and on the left Christ overcomes Satan in the form of a Protean monster. **2.** A small painting by Albrecht Dürer (1506), in the museum at Dresden. **3.** A painting by Andrea Mantegna, in the Louvre at Paris. Christ is between the two thieves; on the left Saint John and the holy women wait in grief, and on the right a body of soldiers cast lots for the garment. This picture is part of the predella of an altarpiece for the Church of San Zeno at Verona; two other parts are in the museum at Tours. **4.** A painting by Anthony Van Dyck, in Saint Michael's at Ghent, Belgium. A mounted soldier holds out the sponge to Christ with his spear; Saint John and the Marys are grouped below, and angels appear above. **5.** A painting called "Le coup de lance," by Rubens, in the museum at Antwerp, Belgium. The time is evening; the three crosses stand side by side on Mount Calvary. Christ is already dead, and a mounted soldier is piercing his side with a spear. The three Marys and Saint John are grouped at the foot of the cross. This has been said to be the most carefully finished painting executed by Rubens. **6.** A fresco by Perugino, in the chapter house of Santa Maria Maddalena dei Pazzi, Florence. It is divided into three parts by architectural framework. In the central part, beneath the crucified Christ, are the two Marys; on the right are Saints John and Bernard; on the left is an impressive figure of the Virgin, with Saint Benedict. **7.** A painting by Tintoretto, in the Scuola di San Rocco at Venice. It is considered by some to be this painter's masterpiece.

Cruciger (krö'si.jėr; German, krö'tsē.gėr), **Kaspar.** [Also: **Creutziger, Creutzinger.**] b. at Leipzig, Germany, Jan. 1, 1504; d. at Wittenberg, Germany, Nov. 16, 1548. German Protestant theologian, a coworker with Luther in the translation of the Bible. He became (1528) a preacher at Wittenberg, and professor of philosophy (later of theology) at the university.

Cruden (krö'dęn), **Alexander.** b. at Aberdeen, Scotland, May 31, 1701; d. at London, Nov. 1, 1770. London bookseller, author of a famous *Concordance of the Holy Scriptures* (1737). An eccentric, he believed himself to have been specially appointed by God to correct the morals of the British nation, and accordingly assumed the title of "Alexander the Corrector" (probably suggested to him by his work as corrector of the press).

Crudor (krö'dôr), **Sir.** In Edmund Spenser's *Faerie Queene*, a knight who insists that Briana shall supply him with enough hair, consisting of ladies' curls and knights' beards, to purfle his cloak before he will marry her. Sir Calidore overthrows him, and Briana's raid on the passers-by is stopped.

Cruel Brother, The. Tragedy by Sir William D'Avenant, printed in 1630.

Cruel Gift, The. Tragedy by Susannah Centlivre, produced in 1716.

Crüger (krü'gėr), **Johann.** b. at Gross-Breese, Prussia, April 9, 1598; d. Feb. 23, 1662. German organist and church composer, remembered chiefly for his hymns, such as *Nun danket Alle Gott* and *Jesu meine Freude.* He was appointed (1622) organist at the Church of Saint Nicholas at Berlin.

Cruikshank (krůk′shank), **George.** b. at London, Sept. 27, 1792; d. Feb. 1, 1878. English artist, best known as a caricaturist. He was the son of a caricaturist, and his brother, Robert Cruikshank, was also a caricaturist. He began his career as an illustrator of children's books, and his satirical genius first found expression in *The Scourge,* a periodical published between 1811 and 1816. At this time his caricatures were in the style of Gillray, but c1819 he began to illustrate books and developed a style that was uniquely his own. Among the most noted of his caricatures were those of Napoleon, the impostures of Joanna Southcott, the Corn Laws, and the domestic infelicities (and alleged infidelities) of the Prince Regent (later to be George IV) and his wife. In 1827 William Hone issued a collection of Cruikshank's caricatures in connection with the latter scandal, which he called *Facetiae and Miscellanies.* Some of Cruikshank's best illustrations were for Sir Walter Scott and for a translation of German fairy tales. In 1823 he issued his designs for Chamisso's *Peter Schlemihl.* His arrangement with Dickens began with *Sketches by Boz* in 1836. He designed also for Richard Bentley (1837–43) and Harrison Ainsworth (1836–44). *The Bottle* (8 plates, 1847) and *The Drunkard's Children* (8 plates, 1848) were the first products of his satirical crusade against drunkenness. He continued to produce etchings and other works in rapid and brilliant succession until his eighty-third year; three years after this he died. He wrote various pamphlets and squibs and started several magazines of his own, and in his later years undertook to paint in oils. His most celebrated effort in this line is a large picture called *The Worship of Bacchus, or the Drinking Customs of Society* (1862), in the National Gallery at London.

Cruikshank, (Isaac) Robert. b. at London, Sept. 27, 1789; d. March 13, 1856. English caricaturist and miniature painter; elder brother of George Cruikshank.

Cruikshank, William Cumberland. b. at Edinburgh, 1745; d. at London, June 27, 1800. Scottish anatomist. He wrote *Anatomy of the Absorbent Vessels* (1786), and others.

Cruillas (krö.ē′lyäs), Marquis of. Title of **Monserrat, Joaquin de.**

Cruls (kröls), **Gastão (Luís).** b. at Rio de Janeiro, 1888—. Brazilian novelist, short-story writer, folklorist, and physician. His books of short stories include *Coivara, Ao embalo da rêde,* and *História puxa história.* Among his best-known novels are *A Amazônia misteriosa* (Eng. trans., 1944), *Vertigem,* and *A Criação e o Criador.*

Crumbling Idols. Volume of critical essays (1894) by Hamlin Garland, in which the author presents his philosophy of what he calls "veritism," a combination of realism (*verity*) and individualism. He suggests that one must be both a realist, dealing with things as they are, and an idealist, dealing with things as they ought to be. The work, regarded as an example of Garland's first, or early, period, characterized by realism, shows the influence of William Dean Howells.

Crummell (krum′ẹl), **Alexander.** b. at New York, 1819; d. Sept. 9, 1898. American minister, educator, and author. He studied for the church at the Boston Episcopal Seminary, and was ordained in 1844. Finding it difficult to continue his studies in America, he went to England, and was graduated from Queen's College, Cambridge, in 1853. For the next 20 years he was in Liberia as a missionary, and he was president of Liberia College. Returning to America in 1873, he founded Saint Luke's Church at Washington, D.C., serving as its pastor until a year before his death.

Crummer (krum′ėr), **Mount.** Brownish granite mountain in Antarctica, lying on the coast of Victoria Land, in ab. 75°05′ S., 162°40′ E. Elevation, ab. 3,000 ft.

Crummles (krum′lz), **Vincent.** In Charles Dickens's *Nicholas Nickleby,* an eccentric actor and manager associated with a cheap theatrical company. He is the father of two boys and a girl, also in the profession; the last is the "Infant Phenomenon."

Crump (krump), **Edward Hull.** b. near Holly Springs, Miss., 1876—. American politician, public official, and businessman. Becoming at an early age a resident of Memphis, Tenn., he entered public life as a member of the board of public works of that city in 1905, and four years later became mayor, an office which, being twice reëlected, he held until 1916. From that year to 1924 he was county trustee. Widening his field, he was elected to the Federal House of Representatives in 1930 and in 1932, but returning to the municipal arena, he again became mayor of Memphis (1939–41). Long before this he had become widely known as "Boss" Crump, the master of a political machine reputedly among the most efficient and tightly controlled in American political history, not only dominating Memphis, but deciding elections throughout the state. He became a member of the Democratic state committee in 1926, and later, Democratic national committeeman from Tennessee. In 1948 his power was challenged when his candidates for governor of the state and for U.S. senator were rejected at the polls. However, Crump-backed candidates swept the 1951 Memphis elections, and his opposition to Governor Gordon Browning in 1952 was held responsible for Browning's defeat in the primary elections.

Cruncher (krun′chėr), **Jerry.** Character in Charles Dickens's *Tale of Two Cities,* a man of all work at Tellson's banking house, who spent his nights as a "resurrection man" (a euphemism of the day for a man who dug up freshly buried corpses for sale to medical schools).

Crupp (krup), **Mrs.** In Charles Dickens's *David Copperfield,* David's landlady. She is afflicted with "spazzums."

Cruppi (krü.pē), **Jean.** b. at Toulouse, France, May 22, 1855; d. at Fontainebleau, France, Oct. 16, 1933. French political leader and lawyer, sent on various foreign confidential missions during World War I. His most important visit was to Czar Nicholas II in 1915. He was a Radical deputy (1898–1920) and senator (1920–24), was three times a cabinet minister, and was for a time president of the Radical-Socialist group in the Chamber of Deputies.

Crusade in Europe. Prose work (1948) by Dwight D. Eisenhower. A war chronicle, it is an example (and has been universally praised as an exceedingly fine one) of "living history," written by a man who takes part in and makes the history which he records. From the historical point of view the work is considered by some to be as important as the *Commentaries* of another great general, Julius Caesar. It was a selection of the Book-of-the-Month Club, which printed 750,000 copies, in addition to the 150,000 copies published in the first printing. A special English edition was issued and it has been translated into at least nine languages.

Crusades. In medieval history, a number of expeditions undertaken by the Christians of Europe for the recovery of the Holy Land from the Mohammedans. The crusading spirit was aroused throughout Europe in 1095 by the preaching of the monk Peter the Hermit, who with Walter the Penniless set out in 1096 with an immense rabble, which was for the most part destroyed on the way. The first Crusade (1096–99), properly so called, under Godfrey of Bouillon, resulted in the capture of Jerusalem and the establishment of a Christian kingdom in Palestine. The second (1147–49), preached by Saint Bernard, was unsuccessful. The third (1189–92), led by the princes Frederick Barbarossa of Germany, Richard the Lion-hearted of England, and Philip Augustus of France, failed to recover Jerusalem, which the Moslems had taken in 1187. The fourth (1202–04) ended in the establishment of a Latin empire at Constantinople, under Count Baldwin of Flanders. The fifth (1228–29), under the emperor Frederick II, the sixth (1248–50), under Saint Louis (Louis IX of France), and the seventh and last (1270–72), also under Saint Louis, were all unsuccessful. There were other expeditions called crusades including, in 1212, "the children's crusade," in which many thousands perished by shipwreck or were enslaved.

Crusca (krus′kạ), **Della.** Pseudonym of **Merry, Robert.**

Crusé (krö.sā′), **Christian Frederic.** b. at Philadelphia, 1794; d. at New York, Oct. 5, 1865. American Episcopalian clergyman and scholar. He translated Eusebius's *Ecclesiastical History* (1833).

Crusenstolpe (krö′sẹn.stôl.pẹ), **Magnus Jakob.** b. at Jönköping, Sweden, March 11, 1795; d. at Stockholm, Jan. 18, 1865. Swedish publicist, historical writer, and novelist. His works include the historical novel *Morianen* (1840–44), and others.

Crusius (krö′zē.ůs), **Christian August.** b. at Leuna, near Merseburg, Germany, Jan. 10, 1715; d. at Leipzig, Germany, Oct. 18, 1775. German philosopher and theologian, professor of theology at Leipzig. He was noted as an opponent of the Wolfian school.

Crusoe (krö′sō), **Robinson.** See **Robinson Crusoe.**

Crustumerium (krus.tū.mē′ri.um). In ancient geography, a city of the Sabines in Latium, Italy, situated a few miles NE of Rome.

Cruveilhier (krü.ve.yā), **Jean.** b. at Limoges, France, Feb. 9, 1791; d. at Jussac, Haute-Vienne, France, March 6, 1874. French physician and anatomist. His chief work is *Anatomie pathologique du corps humain* (1828–42).

Cruvelli (krö.vel′ē), **Johanne Sophie Charlotte.** [Original surname, **Crüwell.**] b. at Bielefeld, Germany, March 12, 1826; d. at Monte Carlo, Monaco, Nov. 6, 1907. German singer. She was successful at Vienna, and later at Paris and London. In 1854 she appeared at the Paris Grand Opera in Verdi's *Sicilian Vespers,* which was written for her.

Crux (kruks). The Southern Cross, the most celebrated constellation of the southern heavens. It was introduced as a constellation by Royer in 1679, but was often spoken of as a cross before; there even seems to be an obscure allusion to it in Dante. It is situated S of the western part of Centaurus, E of the keel of Argo Navis. It is a small constellation of four chief stars arranged in the form of a cross. Its brightest star, the southernmost, is of the first magnitude; the eastern, half a magnitude fainter; the northern, of the second magnitude; and the western, of the third magnitude and faint. The constellation owes its striking effect to its compression: for it subtends only 6 degrees from N to S, and still less from E to W. It looks more like a kite than a cross. All four stars are white except the northernmost, which is of a clear orange color. It contains a fifth star of the fourth magnitude, which is red.

Cruz (krös), **Eddy Dias da.** Original name of **Rebêlo, Marques.**

Cruz, José María de la. b. at Concepción, Chile, April 21, 1801; d. near there, Nov. 23, 1875. Chilean general. As a boy he was a cadet in the revolutionary army, serving in most of the campaigns. He rapidly rose in rank, becoming general of division in 1839, was twice minister of war and marine, was chief of staff in the Peruvian campaign of 1838, and held various other important positions. In 1851 he was the liberal candidate for president, but was unsuccessful. He then headed a revolt in the southern provinces, but was finally defeated on Dec. 8, 1851. He was pardoned, and thereafter lived in retirement on his estate.

Cruz, Juana Inés de la. [Called the **"Tenth Muse"** and the **"Mexican Nun."**] b. at Mexico City, Nov. 12, 1651; d. there, April 17, 1695. Mexican poet, a nun of the Convent of San Géronimo.

Cruz (kröth), San **Juan de la.** Spanish name of Saint **John of the Cross.**

Cruz (krös), **Oswaldo.** b. at São Luiz do Parahitinga, Brazil, Aug. 5, 1872; d. at Petrópolis, Brazil, 1917. Brazilian physician and bacteriologist, notable for his successful campaign against yellow fever in Rio de Janeiro and for establishing an efficient public hygiene service under the Brazilian government. Through a carefully planned drive against the mosquito which bears the disease, he began (1900) the mosquito-control program which has made Rio de Janeiro one of the healthiest tropical cities of the world. That city's Oswaldo Cruz Institute for the study of experimental pathology is named for him.

Cruz (kröth), **Ramón de la.** [Full name, **Ramón Francisco de la Cruz Cano y Olmedilla.**] b. at Madrid, 1731; d. after 1791. Spanish dramatist. His chief works are farces.

Cruz Alta (kröz äl′tą). City in S Brazil, in the state of Rio Grande do Sul. 19,824 (1950).

Cruz del Eje (krös del e′Hā). City in C Argentina, in Córdoba province, ab. 470 mi. NW of Buenos Aires. 15,563 (1947).

Cruzeiro (krö.zā′rö). City in SE Brazil, in the state of São Paulo. 14,498 (1950).

Cruz e Sousa (kröz ē sō′zą), **João da.** See **Sousa, João da Cruz e.**

Cruz y Goyeneche (krös′ ē gō.yā.nā′chā), **Luis de la.** b. at Concepción, Chile, Aug. 25, 1768; d. Oct. 14, 1828. Chilean general. During the colonial period he held important civil offices, and in 1806 made, at his own expense, an exploration of the Andes. His report of this journey was published in the Angelis collection at Buenos Aires in 1825. He was one of the leaders of the revolution of 1810, and commanded a division of the patriot army, but was captured and imprisoned until released by the victories of 1817. Subsequently he was commandant at Talca and, during the absence of O'Higgins, acting president of Chile, took part in the Peruvian campaign and received the title of grand marshal from Peru, was a member of the constituent congress of Chile in 1826, and was minister of marine at the time of his death.

Cryfts (krifts), **Nikolas.** See **Nicholas of Cusa.**

Cry of the Children, The. Poem by Elizabeth Barrett Browning.

Crystal (kris′tąl). Residential village in E Minnesota, in Hennepin County: a northwestern suburb of Minneapolis. In the decade between the last two U.S. censuses its population more than doubled. 2,373 (1940), 5,713 (1950).

Crystal City. City in E Missouri, in Jefferson County, in an area of high-grade silica sand: center for glass manufactures. 3,499 (1950).

Crystal City. City in S Texas, in Zavala County, NW of Corpus Christi: spinach-shipping center for the winter-garden agricultural area. The town square contains a statue of Popeye, erected in 1937 in honor of the comic-strip character whose appetite for spinach helped broaden the market for the vegetable. 7,198 (1950).

Crystal Lake. City in N Illinois, in McHenry County: summer resort. 4,832 (1950).

Crystal Palace. Name of two exhibition buildings put up in the mid-19th century, notable as early examples of large metal-and-glass structures: **1.** Building of iron and glass, erected in Hyde Park, London, for the great exhibition of 1851, reërected (1852–53) at Sydenham (now part of London), and there opened in 1854. It was designed by Sir Joseph Paxton, and was used for popular concerts and other entertainments, as well as for a permanent exhibition of the art and culture of various nations. The nave was 1,608 ft. long, the central transept 390 by 120 ft., and 175 ft. high, and the south transept 312 ft. long. A corresponding north transept was burned in 1866. After World War I it housed the Imperial War Museum. The structure was swept by fire, and utterly destroyed, on Nov. 30, 1936. **2.** In 1853 a similar but much smaller building called the Crystal Palace was erected for the World's Fair at New York, on Sixth Avenue between 40th and 42nd streets. It was also destroyed by fire, in 1856. The ground is now the site of Bryant Park.

Crystal Springs. Town in SW Mississippi, in Copiah County: shipping center for tomatoes. 3,676 (1950).

Csepel (che′pel). [Also, **Szepel.**] City in C Hungary, situated on the E bank of the Danube River, at the N edge of the Csepel Island (*Sziget*), S of Budapest. It is an industrial center, with a number of factories, an oil refinery, and an airport. 45,225 (1948).

Csepel Island. [Hungarian, **Csepel Sziget.**] Large, low-lying island formed between two branches of the Danube River, ab. 2 mi. S of Budapest, and extending S ab. 30 mi. The N end of the island has the large industrial port of Csepel, with numerous large factories and a petroleum refinery. Budapest municipal airport is located here. The remainder of the island is a fertile agricultural region, with several large villages, and is noted for fruit and wine production. Until the 16th century, Csepel Island was the summer resort and hunting ground of the Hungarian kings. Area, ab. 99 sq. mi.

Csokonai (chō′kō.nô.ē), **Vitéz Mihály.** b. at Debrecen, Hungary, Nov. 17, 1773; d. there, Jan. 28, 1805. Hungarian poet. His works include *Magyar-Musa* (1797), *Anacreontic Poems* (1803), *Dorottya,* a mock-heroic poem (1804), and comedies.

Csokor (chō′kōr), **Franz Theodor.** b. at Vienna, Sept. 6, 1885—. Austrian writer who has produced expressionistic dramas; he is also known as a writer of ballads.

Csoma (chō′mô), **Sándor Kőrösi.** See **Kőrösi Csoma, Sándor.**

Csoma de Kőrös (chō′mô dā kė′rėsh), **Alexander.** See **Kőrösi Csoma, Sándor.**

Csongrád (chōng′gräd). City in S central Hungary, situated at the junction of the Kőrös and Tisza rivers, between Szentes and Kiskunfélegyháza. It is a river port and has flour mills. 24,674 (1948).

Ctesias (tē′zi.ạs). b. at Cnidus, Caria, Asia Minor; d. after 398 B.C. Greek historian, a physician at the court of Artaxerxes Mnemon. He wrote a history of Persia (as *Persika*) in 24 books, fragments of which are extant, and a treatise on India (as *Indika*), parts of which also survive. There are meager abridgments of both works by Photius.

Ctesibius (tẹ.sib′i.us). b. at Alexandria; fl. probably c250 B.C. Alexandrian physicist noted for his mechanical inventions. He is said to have invented a clepsydra, a hydraulic organ, and other mechanical contrivances, and to have first applied the expansive force of air as a motive power.

Ctesiphon (tes′i.fon; tē′si-). fl. in the 4th century B.C. Athenian who proposed that Demosthenes should be honored with a crown, and for this was prosecuted by Aeschines and defended by Demosthenes in his *Oration on the Crown.*

Ctesiphon. Locality in C Iraq, site of an ancient city of Mesopotamia, situated on the Tigris opposite Seleucia, ab. 20 mi. SE of Baghdad. It was one of the chief cities of the Parthian and later Persian kingdoms. Its site is now occupied by ruins, including part of a great Sassanid palace. This spot is also known as the farthest point of advance in the British Mesopotamian campaign of 1915, in World War I, which was launched with the hope of reaching Baghdad. At Ctesiphon the Turkish resistance stiffened. The British were overwhelmingly defeated with a loss of almost a quarter of their men and repulsed to Kut-al-Imara, ab. 80 mi. farther south, where they were forced into siege.

Cuadrado (kwä.drä′dō). Peak in the W part of Pampanga province, SW Luzon, Philippine Islands. 4,376 ft.

Cuanza (kwän′zạ). [Also: **Coanza, Kuanza, Kwanza.**] River in W Africa, in Angola; it flows into the Atlantic Ocean S of the port of Luanda. Length, ab. 600 mi.

Cuaray (kwä.rī′). See **Quarai.**

Cuarto (kwär′tō). River in C Argentina, in its lower tributary course called the Caracana; a tributary of the Paraná River.

Cuauhtemoc (kwou.tā′môk). See **Guatemotzin** or **Guatemoc.**

Cuba (kū′bạ; Spanish, kö′bä). [Called the **"Pearl (or Queen) of the Antilles"** and **"Key of the Gulf"**; former names, **Juana** (or **Juanna**), and **Fernandina.**] Republic and largest island in the Caribbean Sea, SE of the U.S. and the Gulf of Mexico. It is separated from Florida on the N by the Strait of Florida, from Haiti on the E by the Windward Passage, and from Yucatán on the W by the Channel of Yucatán. It has three widely separated mountain ranges, the Sierra de los Organos in the NW, W of Havana, the Trinidad Mountains in the W central part, on the coast near Cienfuegos, and the Sierra Maestra in the SE, E and W of Guantánamo.

Population, Area, Major Cities. Cuba is divided into six provinces for administrative purposes. Major cities, Havana, Marianao, Santiago de Cuba, Camagüey, Santa Clara, Cienfuegos, Matanzas, and Guantánamo. Capital, Havana; length, 785 mi.; width, 25 mi. to 125 mi.; area, 44,217 sq. mi.; pop. 5,195,000 (est. 1948).

Industry, Agriculture, and Trade. Cuba is the leading sugar-producing country in the world, and is also noted for the production of leaf tobacco used for cigar filler. Chromium, copper, and iron ore are mined, and the island derives considerable income from the tourist trade.

History. From its discovery until 1898 it belonged to Spain, forming with its dependencies a captaincy-general, and sending, after 1878, deputies to the Spanish Cortes. It was discovered by Columbus in October, 1492 (and named by him Juana), and was conquered by the Spaniards in 1511. The name was officially changed to Fernandina c1508 in honor of Ferdinand V of Castile, but the name Cuba soon came into general use. It was held by the English from 1762 to 1763, was the object of various filibustering expeditions from 1849, and was the scene of rebellions in 1868–78 and 1895–98. Slavery was abolished in 1880. In 1898 it was freed from Spanish domination by the act of the U.S. It remained a protectorate of the U.S. from 1898 to 1934. In accordance with the requirements of the U.S. Congress, Cuba undertook (June 12, 1901) to make no treaty with any foreign power endangering its independence, to contract no debts for which current revenue would not suffice, to concede to the U.S. government a right of intervention, and also to grant to it the use of naval stations; on May 20, 1902, it was proclaimed a republic and the control of the island was formally transferred to the new Cuban government. An insurrection led the U.S. again to assume temporary control of Cuban affairs from September, 1906, to January, 1909. The U.S. Marines reëntered in 1917, and were withdrawn for the final time in 1922.

Cuba (kū′bạ). Town (in New York the equivalent of township in many other states) and village in S New York, in Alleghany County, near Olean: summer resort and farm trade center. Cheese is made here. Pop. of town, 2,784 (1950); of village, 1,783 (1950).

Cuba (kö′ʙä; Anglicized, kū′bạ). Shortened form (locally) of **Santiago de Cuba.**

Cuba (kö′bä), **La.** See **La Cuba.**

Cubanacán (kö″bä.nä.kän′). Name given in the old accounts to a region, or possibly a village, in the interior of Cuba, so called by the Lucayan Indians who were with Columbus when he discovered the island. From the similarity of sounds, Columbus, supposing himself to be on the coast of Asia, imagined that this must be the city of Kublai Khan, the great Tartar sovereign spoken of by Marco Polo.

Cubango (kö.bang′gō). [Also: **Kubango, Tonke.**] River in SW Africa, in Angola; it flows S and E to join the Okovanggo River and thus into Lake Ngami.

Cuban Treaty (kū′bạn). Cuban-American reciprocity treaty ratified in 1903 which served as the basis of commercial relations between the two countries until 1934, when it was replaced by the Hull trade agreement. It effected mutual reductions in tariff schedules.

Cubillo (kö.ʙē′lyō), **Álvaro de Aragón.** b. in Granada, Spain, toward the end of the 16th century. Spanish dramatic poet. He was a voluminous writer and successful dramatist.

Cub of the Panther, A Mountain Legend, The. Romance by William Gilmore Simms, published in 1869. It is one of his series of Border Romances.

Cuchulain (kö.ċhö′lin). [Also: **Cuculain, Cuchullin, Cu Chullin, Cu Cullin**; original name, **Setanta.**] d. c2 A.D. Irish warrior of pagan times, hero of legendary exploits, sometimes called "the Achilles of the Gael." Scholars now generally agree that he was a historical person, about whose history the poets wove ancient legends, some perhaps going back to the first home of the Gael in Scythia, with later scribes during many centuries adding ever more marvels. Ostensibly of mortal paternity, Cuchulain (as Setanta) is represented to have been in fact the son of Lugh, the sun god. From childhood he was fabulously brave, skilled, and warlike. Having as a mere child killed a ferocious hound which attacked him, and noted the grief of the hound's owner, Culain, he voluntarily assumed the role of watchdog until one as good as his victim could be found, and thereafter he was known as Cuchulain, meaning "the Hound of Culain." To complete his training in arms he became a pupil of the woman warrior Scathach on the island named for her, now called Skye. When another militant female, Aoife, attacked Scathach, Cuchulain overcame her and made love to her, and when leaving the isle, instructed Aoife to send their son, Conlaoch, to Ireland when he came of age to bear arms, under a vow to let no man stop him or compel him to give his name. Years later Conlaoch came to Ireland and slew so many warriors that at last Cuchulain confronted and killed him, learning his identity too late. One version of the legend represents them as killing each other; a variant has Cuchulain in his grief fighting with the sea and sinking exhausted into it. In the most widely known version, however, Cuchulain, while still a stripling, single-handed retards the invading army of Queen Maeve until the Red Branch warriors of Ulster wake from a spell put upon them for a cruelty they committed, as told in the epic of the Tain Bo Cuailgne, in which the most poignant episode is the duel between Cuchulain and his dearest friend, Ferdiad. Some years later, the men of Ulster being again entranced, Medb marshals an army expressly to kill Cuchulain (who as a son of the sun god is immune from the spell) and with the aid of magicians who create an illusory host with which he fights to exhaustion, accomplishes her purpose. Sorely wounded, Cuchulain binds himself to a pillar-stone and dies standing and facing the enemy. His widow Emer, to whom he had returned after being seduced by Fand, the wife of the sea god Mananaan, throws herself into his grave and dies.

Cuckfield (kuk′fēld). Urban district and market town in SE England, in East Sussex, ab. 14 mi. N of Brighton. 16,481 (1951).

Cuckoo and the Nightingale, The. Poem which appeared in the printed editions of Chaucer of the 16th century. When first printed it had following it a ballade with an envoy. There is nothing to indicate that they are by the same person. Tyrwhitt, who considered the poem Chaucer's, could not accept the ballade. The weight of evidence is against Chaucer's authorship of the poem. In the Bodleian manuscript it is called *The Boke of Cupide God of Love;* another manuscript is headed *Liber Cupidinis.* It is based on a popular superstition that he will be happy in love during the year who hears the nightingale before he hears the cuckoo.

Cuckoo Song. See **Sumer is icumen in.**

Cuculain or **Cu Cullin** (kö.kö′lin). See **Cuchulain.**

Cúcuta (kö′kö.tä). [Also, **San José de Cúcuta.**] City in NE Colombia, capital of Norte de Santander department, near the frontier of Venezuela: commercial center for an oil and coffee region. 73,437 (1951).

Cudahy (kud′ạ.hi). Unincorporated community in S California, in Los Angeles County. Under the new urban definition established for use in the 1950 census it was counted along with adjoining urban areas. The last official enumeration was 4,761 (1940).

Cudahy. City in SE Wisconsin, in Milwaukee County near Milwaukee. It has meat-packing plants, a box factory, tannery, vinegar distillery, and shoe factory, and also manufactures of bottle-washing and pasteurizing machinery. It was founded in 1893 and incorporated in 1907. Pop. 12,182 (1950).

Cudahy, Michael. b. at Callan, Ireland, Dec. 7, 1841; d. Nov. 27, 1910. American meat packer, an originator (1870–80) of summer refrigeration for meat. He came to the U.S. as a child. He was superintendent (1869 *et seq.*) of the packing house and a partner (1875–90) of Plankinton and Armour, and founded (1887) with Philip D. Armour and with his brother, the Armour-Cudahy Packing Company at South Omaha, Neb., which became (1890) the Cudahy Packing Company and of which he was thereafter (1890–1910) president.

Cuddalore (kud.ạ.lōr′). [Also: **Gudalur, Kudalur.**] Seaport in Madras state, Union of India, on the Bay of Bengal, at the mouth of the Punnaiyar River. Steamers anchor about a mile off shore and there are wharves situated on the W bank of the Uppanar backwater. The export trade consists chiefly of peanuts, colored piece goods, grain, and pulse. Boiled betel nuts are imported. The city was taken by the French in 1758, by the English in 1760, and retaken by the French in 1782; the scene of a repulse of the English in 1783, it was finally acquired by the English in 1785. Pop. 60,632 (1941).

Cuddapah (kud′ạ.pạ). [Also, **Kadapa.**] District in Madras state, Union of India, ab. 150 mi. NW of the city of Madras: millet, indigo, cotton, and wheat; some gold mining. Area, 5,923 sq. mi.; pop. 1,056,506 (1941).

Cuddy (kud′i). Shepherd with whom Colin Clout conducts his arguments in Spenser's *Shepherd's Calendar.*

Cuddy. Shepherd in love with Buxoma in John Gay's *The Shepherd's Week.*

Cudillero (kö.ᴛʜē.lyā′rō). Town in NW Spain, in the province of Oviedo, situated on the Bay of Biscay ab. 22 mi. NW of Oviedo. There are manganese mines in the vicinity. 10,630 (1940).

Cudjo's Cave (kuj′ōz). Antislavery novel by John Townsend Trowbridge, published in 1864. Penn Hapgood, a Quaker teacher in Tennessee, is exiled for his unpopular abolitionist tendencies. With Cudjo and Pomp, runaway slaves, he inhabits a cave, a haven for Union sympathizers.

Cudworth (kud′wėrth). Urban district in N central England, in the West Riding of Yorkshire, ab. 4 mi. NE of Barnsley, ab. 177 mi. N of London by rail. It contains the hamlets of High Cudworth and Low Cudworth. 8,757 (1951).

Cudworth, Ralph. b. at Aller, Somersetshire, England, 1617; d. at Cambridge, England, June 26, 1688. English philosopher and divine. He became in 1645 regius professor of Hebrew at Cambridge, a position which he retained until his death. His chief works are *True Intellectual System of the Universe* (1678) and *Treatise concerning Eternal and Immutable Morality* (1731).

Cuenca (kweng′kä). [Also, **Santa Ana de Cuenca.**] City in S Ecuador, capital of Azuay province: Ecuador's third most important city. Its industries produce cinchona, gold, hats, hides, and sugar. It has a cathedral. 52,519 (est. 1944).

Cuenca. Province in C Spain, bounded by Guadalajara on the N, Teruel on the NE, Valencia on the E, Albacete and Ciudad Real on the S, and Toledo and Madrid on the W: part of the region of New Castile. A large part of the province forms a high plateau; the climate is arid and continental. Livestock raising and forestry prevail over agriculture. Capital, Cuenca; area, 6,588 sq. mi.; pop. 343,383 (1950).

Cuenca. City in C Spain, the capital of the province of Cuenca, situated on the Júcar River, ab. 90 mi. SE of Madrid. Manufactures include pottery, paper, and leather goods; it was formerly famous for woolen and silver crafts. Buildings of interest include a number of old churches and convents and a celebrated Gothic cathedral of the 13th century. It is the seat of a bishopric. Once a Moorish fortress, Cuenca was reconquered by Alfonso VIII of Castile in 1177. It was held by the Loyalists until the end of the Spanish Civil War (1936–39). 24,702 (1940).

Cuernavaca (kwer.nä.ʙä′kä). City in S Mexico, capital of Morelos state, ab. 47 mi. S of Mexico City. It was an ancient Indian town, was captured by Cortés before the siege of Mexico, and became his favorite residence. The emperor Maximilian had a country seat here. The Palace of Cortés is noted for its epic murals by Diego Rivera. 14,336 (1940).

Cuero (kwãr′ō). City in S Texas, county seat of De Witt County, on Arroyo del Cuero Creek, N of Corpus Christi: shipping center for cotton and turkeys. 7,498 (1950).

Cuesmes (kwem). Town in S Belgium, in the province of Hainaut, SW of Mons. It is an industrial community, with coal mines, blast furnaces, and railroad repair shops. 10,540 (1947).

Cueva (kwā′ʙä), **Juan de la.** b. at Seville, Spain, c1550; d. c1608. Spanish poet. His works include *Primera parte de las comedias y tragedias* (1583–88), *La Conquista de la Bética* (1603), and *Ejemplar poético* (1605).

Cueva Henríquez Árias de Saavedra (kwā′ʙä en.rē′keth ä′ryäs dā sä.ä.ʙä′ᴛʜrä), **Baltazar de la.** [Titles: Count of **Castellar,** Marquis of **Malagon.**] b. at Madrid, 1626; d. there, April 3, 1686. Spanish nobleman; a younger son of the seventh Duke of Albuquerque. His titles came to him by marriage. He held various important posts, was ambassador to Germany, councilor of state and afterward of the Indies, and from August, 1674, to July, 1678, viceroy of Peru, Chile, and Tierra Firme (a division of N South America including the Isthmus of Panama). His rule was prosperous, and he remitted large surplus revenues to Spain, but an attempt to relax the commercial monopolies caused an outcry against him. He was ordered to turn over the government to the bishop of Lima, and was held in light captivity during nearly two years while the charges against him were tried. In the end he was exonerated, returned to Spain, and resumed his seat in the Council of the Indies until his death.

Cuffe (kuf), Lady **Sybil Marjorie.** b. Oct. 3, 1879; d. 1943. English novelist. She married (Dec. 8, 1926) Percy Lubbock. She was the author of *A Book of the Sea* (1918), *Four Tales by Zélide* (1925), and *Child in the Crystal* (1939) and editor of *A Page from the Past* (1936).

Cugerni (kụ.jėr′nī). See **Gugerni.**

Cui (kü.ē′), **César Antonovich.** [Russian, **Kyui.**] b. at Vilna, in Lithuania, Jan. 18, 1835; d. at Petrograd, in March, 1918. Russian composer, representative of the neo-Russian school of music. His works include operas, symphonies, songs, and piano pieces.

Cuiabá (kö.yą.bä'). [Former spelling, **Cuyabá.**] Capital of the state of Mato Grosso, in SW Brazil: distribution center for gold, diamonds, and ipecac. 24,119 (1950).

Cuiabá River. [Former spelling, **Cuyabá.**] River in W Brazil which flows SW to join the Paraguay River, through the São Lourenço. It is navigable to the town of Cuiabá.

Cuigh Uladh (kwē ö'lą). Irish name of **Ulster.**

Cuilcagh (kwil'ką). Mountain in Ulster province, Irish Republic, in County Cavan, situated on the Irish Republic-Northern Ireland border, ab. 24 mi. NW of Cavan. Elevation, ab. 2,188 ft.

Cuillin Hills (kö'lin). Small range of mountains in N Scotland, in Inverness-shire, situated on the Isle of Skye in the Inner Hebrides. The summit is Sgur Alasdair (3,309 ft.).

Cuilo (kwē'lö). Portuguese name of the **Kwilu.**

Cuitlahuatzin (kwēt.lä.wä'tsēn). [Also, **Citlahuatzin.**] b. c1470; d. at Mexico City, in September or October, 1520. Aztec Indian chief; brother of Montezuma. After Montezuma had been seized by the Spaniards (1520), Cuitlahuatzin was for a time in their power. He was elected war chief before the death of Montezuma, and immediately organized an attack on the Spanish quarters, in which Montezuma himself was killed. Cuitlahuatzin directed the Aztec forces during the Spanish retreat, and soon after was elected in Montezuma's place. He died of a pestilence a few weeks after.

Cuitzeo (kwēt.sā'ō), **Lake.** [Spanish, **Laguna de Cuitzeo.**] Lake in C Mexico, in Michoacán state. Length, ab. 31 mi.

Cujacius (kų.jā'shus). [Original name, **Jacques Cujas** (kü.zhäs).] b. at Toulouse, France, 1522; d. at Bourges, France, Oct. 4, 1590. French jurist. He studied under Arnaud Ferrier at the University of Toulouse, where in 1547 he began a course of instruction on the Institutes of Justinian. In 1555 he was called to the University of Bourges, whence he removed to Valence in 1557. After several changes he returned in 1577 to Bourges, where he passed the rest of his life. He wrote commentaries on the Institutes of Justinian, the Pandects and Decretals, including emendations of the text of legal and other manuscripts, under the title of *Observationes et emendationes.* An incomplete collection of his writings, edited by himself, was published in 1577. The first complete edition was published by Fabrot in 1658.

Cujavia (kū.jā'vi.ą). Division of the medieval kingdom of Poland, situated N and E of Great Poland and W of Masovia. It lay on both sides of the Vistula, S and W of Toruń. It was annexed to the kingdom of Poland early in the 14th century.

Culalok (kö.lä'lôk), **Brah Buddha Yot Fa.** See **Rama I.**

Culbertson (kul'bėrt.sǫn), **Ely.** b. in Rumania, in July, 1891—. American author, lecturer, and authority on contract bridge. He has been, at various times, editor of *The Bridge World Magazine,* captain of the American team in international bridge matches (1933–34, 1937), founder and president of World Federation, Inc. He is the author of *Contract Bridge Blue Book* (1930), *Red Book of Leads and Plays* (1934), *The World Federation Plan* (1942), *Total Peace* (1943), *Must We Fight Russia?* (1946), and other books.

Culbertson, William Smith. b. at Greensburg, Pa., Aug. 5, 1884—. American lawyer, diplomat, and author. A graduate of Yale (B.A., 1908; Ph.D., 1911), he practiced law (1912 *et seq.*) at Washington, was a member (1917–25) and vice-chairman (1922–25) of the U.S. Tariff Commission, and served as U.S. ambassador to Rumania (1925–28) and Chile (1928–33). He is the author of *Commercial Policy in War Time and After* (1919), *Political Economy of Total War* (1942), and other books.

Culdee (kul'dē). Member of a fraternity of priests, constituting an irregular monastic order, existing in Scotland, and in smaller numbers in Ireland and Wales, from the 9th or 10th century to the 14th or 15th century.

Culebra (kų.lā'brą; Spanish, kö.lā'ʙrä). Station in the Canal Zone, on the railroad ab. 10 mi. from Panama. The making of the Gaillard (formerly Culebra) Cut was one of the most difficult engineering operations in the construction of the Panama Canal, on account of landslides. The width of the cut at the bottom is 300 ft. for a distance of ab. 9 mi.

Culebra (kų.lā'brą). Name sometimes used for a region in N New Mexico, near the confines of Colorado, including a valley near the S part of the Sangre de Cristo Range and the surrounding mountains, which are sometimes called the Culebra Range.

Culiacán (kö.lyä.kän'). City in W Mexico, capital of Sinaloa state, at the site of the Aztec city Hucicolhuacán. 144,550 (1950).

Culin (kū'lin), **Robert Stewart.** b. at Philadelphia, July 13, 1858; d. April 8, 1929. American anthropologist, curator of ethnology in the Brooklyn Institute from 1903. He published *Korean Games* (1896), *Chess and Playing Cards* (1896), *American Indian Games* (1905), and others.

Culion (kö.lyōn'). Second in size of the Calamian Islands, NE of Palawan, in the Philippine Islands. Halsey Harbor and Culion are good harbors. Area, 150 sq. mi.; pop. 7,328 (1939).

Culion. [Also, **Port Culion.**] Bay and town on the E coast of Culion island, Palawan province, Philippine Islands: a large leper colony is located at the town. The harbor is safe for large craft in all weather.

Cullen (kul'ęn). Royal burgh and seaport in E Scotland, in Banffshire, situated on Cullen Bay (an inlet of Moray Firth), ab. 11 mi. W of Banff, ab. 590 mi. N of London by rail. The town is a fishing port. 1,656 (est. 1948).

Cullen, Countée. b. at New York, May 30, 1903; d. 1946. American Negro poet. He was graduated from New York University (B.A., 1925) and from Harvard (M.A., 1926), was assistant editor (1926–28) of *Opportunity: Journal of Negro Life,* and held a Guggenheim fellowship. He is the author of a novel, *One Way to Heaven* (1931), and of poetry including *Color* (1925), *Copper Sun* (1927), *The Ballad of the Brown Girl* (1927), *The Black Christ* (1929), and *The Medea and Some Other Poems* (1935).

Cullen, Paul. b. in County Kildare, Ireland, April 27, 1803; d. at Dublin, Oct. 24, 1878. Irish prelate. He was appointed archbishop of Armagh in 1849, of Dublin in 1852, and cardinal priest in 1866.

Cullen, Thomas Stephen. b. at Bridgewater, Ontario, Canada, Nov. 20, 1868—. American surgeon, gynecologist, and authority on cancer and tumors of the uterus. A graduate (M.B., 1890) of Toronto, he has been gynecologist (1892 *et seq.*) at the Johns Hopkins Hospital. He is the author of *Cancer of the Uterus* (1900), *Adenomyoma of the Uterus* (1908), *Early Medicine in Maryland* (1927), and other works.

Cullen, William. b. at Hamilton, Scotland, April 15, 1710; d. near Edinburgh, Feb. 5, 1790. Scottish physician and chemist.

Cullendale (kul'ęn.dāl). Unincorporated community in S Arkansas, in Ouachita County, near the Ouachita River ab. 5 mi. S of Camden. 3,225 (1950).

Cullera (kö.lyā'rä). Town in E Spain, in the province of Valencia, situated on the Júcar River, ab. 25 mi. SE of Valencia: center of a stock-raising district; fisheries. 15,005 (1940).

Cullinan Diamond (kul'i.nąn). Diamond discovered in the Premier Mine, near Pretoria, in the Transvaal, on Jan. 25, 1905. It was the largest ever found to that date, weighing 3,030½ carats (English carat) and measuring 4 by 2½ by 2 inches. It was given to the king of England by the Transvaal Colony. The largest two gems cut from it were a drop briolette, of 516½ carats, called the "Star of Africa" and set for the royal scepter, and a square English-cut brilliant, of $309\frac{3}{16}$ carats, set for the royal crown. Besides these the crystal furnished a drop diamond of 92 carats, a square brilliant of 62 carats, five other fine stones of from $18\frac{13}{32}$ to $4\frac{5}{16}$ carats, and 96 smaller brilliants with an aggregate weight of 7⅜ carats, not including nine unpolished ends.

Cullman (kul'mąn). City in N Alabama, county seat of Cullman County, ab. 43 mi. N of Birmingham: shipping point for strawberries. 7,523 (1950).

Culloden Moor (ku.lō'dęn). [Also, **Drummossie Moor.**] Moor ab. 5 mi. E of Inverness, Scotland. Here, on April 27, 1746, the forces of the English crown (ab. 10,000) under the Duke of Cumberland defeated the Highlanders (ab.

6,000) under Charles Edward Stuart, the Young Pretender.

Cullom (kul'om), **Shelby Moore.** b. in Wayne County, Ky., Nov. 22, 1829; d. Jan. 28, 1914. American lawyer and politician. He grew up in Illinois, where his father, an antislavery Southerner, settled in 1830. He began the practice of law and of politics in the same year, 1855, when he was admitted to the bar and elected as city attorney of Springfield. In 1858, influenced by his father's friend Abraham Lincoln, he joined the then new Republican Party. Meanwhile in 1856 he had been elected to the Illinois state legislature, and thereafter sat for several terms in that body. He was a member of the U.S. House of Representatives (1865–71), and governor of Illinois (1876–83) before entering on the long final phase of his career as a U.S. Senator (1883–1913). In 1896 he was among the contenders for the Republican Party nomination to the presidency of the U.S. He was defeated for renomination to the Senate in the Republican primary of 1912, and with his retirement in 1913, he ended what he himself called a political career of longer unbroken service than any other in American history. As governor of Illinois he had caused the enactment of a law regulating railroads, and his most memorable service in the U.S. Senate was the part he played in writing and securing passage of the legislation setting up the Interstate Commerce Commission. Staunchly loyal to his party, he nevertheless opposed its high tariff policy when he thought it was carried to extremes; he favored income and inheritance taxes when they were anathema to most Republican Party leaders, and as chairman of the Senate Committee on Foreign Relations, he opposed certain foreign policies which he considered to be of an imperialistic tendency.

Cullum (kul'um), **George Washington.** b. at New York, Feb. 25, 1809; d. there, Feb. 28, 1892. American soldier and military writer. He was graduated from the U.S. Military Academy in 1833, and entered the engineer corps. During the Civil War he was employed in a number of engineering operations, including the fortification of Nashville, Tenn., in 1864. He served as superintendent of the U.S. Military Academy from Sept. 8, 1864, to Aug. 28, 1866. He was brevetted major general on March 13, 1865. He published *Biographical Register of the Officers and Graduates of the United States Military Academy at West Point* (1868).

Cully (kul'i), **Sir Nicholas.** Foolish, gullible knight in Etherege's comedy *The Comical Revenge, or Love in a Tub.*

Culp (kulp; Dutch, kůlp), **Julia.** b. at Groningen, Netherlands, Oct. 1, 1881—. Dutch contralto. She studied at the Amsterdam Conservatory and first appeared (1901) at a concert at Magdeburg, Germany. She toured in Germany, France, and Austria, and made her first appearance in the U.S. in 1913. Notable as an interpreter of the lieder of the German composers, she has been considered particularly outstanding in her renditions of Schubert, Schumann, Hugo Wolf, and Brahms.

Culpeper (kul'pep"ėr). Town in N Virginia, county seat of Culpeper County, ab. 62 mi. SW of Washington: trading center for a farming area. It was both a Confederate and a Union base at different times during the Civil War. 2,527 (1950).

Culpeper, John. fl. 1678–80. American colonial politician. He headed the insurrection (1677–79) in North Carolina known as Culpeper's Rebellion, which deposed the president and deputies of the proprietaries, and established a new government.

Culpeper or **Colepeper** (kul'pep"ėr), Lord **Thomas.** b. 1635; d. at London, 1689. Colonial governor of Virginia. In conjunction with Lord Arlington he received in 1673 from Charles II a grant of the colony of Virginia, of which he acted as governor from 1680 to 1683.

Culpeper's Rebellion. In American colonial history, an uprising (1677–79) of North Carolina colonists against the proprietary regime, caused by the attempt to carry out the British trade laws. Under the leadership of John Culpeper, a party of colonists jailed the officials of the proprietary government and established their own regime, of which Culpeper served as governor.

Culross (kul'ros). Royal burgh and seaport in E Scotland, in Fifeshire, situated on the N bank of the Firth of Forth, ab. 6 mi. W of Dunfermline. The town has the ruins of a Cistercian abbey founded in 1217. Pop. 546 (est. 1948).

Culture. Prose work (1938) by Ezra Pound, in which the poet presents his "intellectual autobiography."

Culver City (kul'vėr). City in S California, in Los Angeles County, SW of Los Angeles: motion-picture studios. In the decade between the last two U.S. censuses its population more than doubled. 8,976 (1940), 19,720 (1950).

Cumae (kū'mē). In ancient geography, a city on the coast of Campania, Italy, ab. 10 mi. W of what is now Naples. It was founded (c1000 B.C.) by Greek colonists from Cyme in Euboea, was one of the chief Greek cities in Italy until the 5th century B.C., and became (338 B.C.) a Roman *municipium* (a town whose citizens enjoyed certain of the rights of Roman citizenship). It contained the cavern of the Cumaean sibyl, the most famous of these prophetesses of antiquity, and has some remnants of antiquity, including a Roman amphitheater, imperfectly excavated, but displaying 21 tiers of seats. The axes of the great ellipse are 315 and 255 ft., of the arena 240 and 180 ft. The inhabitants of Cumae founded Neapolis (now Naples) and Puteoli (now Pozzuoli).

Cumaná (kö.mä.nä'). [Also: **Santa Inés de Cumaná;** colonial name (1523), **Toledo la Nueva.**] City in NW Venezuela, capital of Sucre state, at the mouth of the Manzanares River: textile, coffee, tobacco, and fishing industries. Cumaná was founded by missionaries in 1512, abandoned and refounded in 1523, and is the oldest European city in South America. It has suffered greatly from earthquakes. 46,416 (1950).

Cumania (kų.mā'ni.ą). [Also: **Great Cumania, Kumania.**] Region in Hungary, E of the Tisza River.

Cumania, Little. [Also, **Little Kumania.**] Region in Hungary, W of the Tisza River.

Cumans (kū'mąnz, kö.mänz'). [Also: **Comans, Comanians.**] Tribe which spoke a Turkic tongue, and which invaded Hungary, probably in the 11th century. It was subdued and Christianized by the Hungarians in 1278 when Pope Nicholas IV proclaimed a crusade against the tribe.

Cumberland (kum'bėr.ląnd). See also **Cumberland River.**

Cumberland. Maritime county in NW England. It is bounded on the NW and N by Solway Firth, on the N by Scotland, on the E by Northumberland and Durham, on the SE and S by Westmorland and the detached portion of Lancashire, and on the W by the Irish Sea. Its surface is mountainous in the SW and E, and low in the N. The SW portion, which comprises part of the Lake District, is celebrated for its picturesque scenery, including the lakes Ullswater, Bassenthwaite, Derwentwater, Thirlmere, and others. It has virtually the only hematite iron-ore field of any importance in Britain. There is an iron and steel industry located along the coast in the west (at Workington) using some domestic ores combined with foreign ores. Cumberland also has coal mining, some coal going to London, but the mines are generally not very productive. Other industry includes low-priced boot and shoe manufactures, and flour milling. Oats are raised, and stock raised includes beef cattle and sheep. Carlisle is the county seat; area of administrative county, ab. 1,513 sq. mi.; pop. of administrative county, 285,347 (1951).

Cumberland. City in SE Kentucky, in Harlan County. Coal mining is the principal industry. 4,249 (1950).

Cumberland. City in NW Maryland, seat of Allegany County, on the Potomac River: industrial railroad center and second largest city in Maryland. The Cumberland coal region lies to the west. The city has manufactures of iron, steel, glass, tires, tin plate, and synthetic silk. Fort Cumberland, on whose site the city was built (1785) was Braddock's base and one of Washington's commands in the French and Indian Wars. In the early 19th century it was the eastern terminus of the Cumberland (or National) Road. 37,679 (1950).

Cumberland. Town in N Rhode Island, in Providence County: textiles and other manufactures. 12,842 (1950).

Cumberland. U.S. sloop of 30 guns in the Civil War. She was sunk by the Confederate ironclad ram *Merrimack* (*Virginia*) on March 8, 1862, off Newport News, Hampton Roads, Va. She went down with all on board and her colors flying, and most of her crew perished. Her commander was Lieutenant George U. Morris.

Cumberland, Duke of. Title of **Ernest Augustus,** son of George III (of England).

Cumberland, Duke of. A title of **Rupert,** Prince.

Cumberland, Duke of. Title of **William Augustus,** son of George II (of England).

Cumberland, Earl of. Title held by various members of the **Clifford** family.

Cumberland, Army of the. Division of the Union army in the American Civil War. It was organized in 1861 by Don Carlos Buell, commander of the department of the Ohio, and was originally known as the Army of the Ohio. Upon the establishment of the department of the Cumberland, on Oct. 24, 1862, under the command of W. S. Rosecrans, it was transferred to that department, and was renamed the Army of the Cumberland. Rosecrans relieved Buell of the command of the army at Louisville, Ky., on Oct. 30, 1862, and took up his headquarters in Nashville, Tenn., in November, 1862. He defeated Braxton Bragg at Stone River (Dec. 31, 1862–Jan. 3, 1863), which gave him possession of Murfreesboro, drove Bragg from middle Tennessee in a nine days' campaign around Tullahoma (June 24–July 3, 1863), and was defeated by Bragg at Chickamauga (Sept. 19–20, 1863). The department of the Cumberland was made part of the military division of the Mississippi, under command of General Grant, in October, 1863, when Rosecrans was relieved of command by George H. Thomas, and the Army of the Cumberland ceased to be an independent command.

Cumberland, Fort. See **Beauséjour, Fort,** and see also under **Cumberland,** Md.

Cumberland, Princess **Olive of.** Assumed title of **Serres, Olivia.**

Cumberland, Prince of. Title formerly bestowed on the successor to the crown of Scotland when succession was declared in the king's lifetime (the crown was originally not hereditary). In Shakespeare's *Macbeth* the title is given to Malcolm by his father Duncan.

Cumberland, Richard. b. at London, July 15, 1631; d. at Peterborough, England, Oct. 9, 1718. English divine and moral philosopher. His chief work is *De legibus naturae* (1672), a disquisition meant to refute the selfish philosophy of Thomas Hobbes. Cumberland maintains the moral good to be in that which benefits the mass of mankind, rather than the individual. He is regarded as the founder of the English utilitarian school.

Cumberland, Richard. b. at Cambridge, England, Feb. 19, 1732; d. at Tunbridge Wells, England, May 7, 1811. English dramatist and statesman; great-grandson of Richard Cumberland (1631–1718).

Cumberland Gap. Pass in the Cumberland Mountains, situated on the border between Kentucky and Tennessee, ab. 45 mi. NE of Knoxville, Tenn. It was an important strategic point in the Civil War. Elevation, 1,315 ft.

Cumberland House. Fur-trading post in E Saskatchewan, Canada, ab. 43 mi. W of The Pas, Manitoba. It was established in 1744 and has been one of the important posts of the Hudson's Bay Company, trading in the upper valleys of the Saskatchewan and Churchill rivers. It can now be reached by air, as well as by river. Pop. of township, 444 (1946).

Cumberland Peninsula. Eastern part of Baffin Island, in the Arctic Archipelago, bordering on Davis Strait.

Cumberland Plateau or **Mountains.** Range in the Appalachian system, separating Kentucky from Virginia, and extending generally SW through E Tennessee. The region is rich in minerals, especially coal. Width, ab. 50 mi.

Cumberland River. River in E central U.S., a southern tributary of the Ohio River. It rises in the Cumberland Plateau, in E Kentucky, flows through Kentucky and middle Tennessee, reënters Kentucky, and joins the Ohio at Smithland, Ky., ab. 43 mi. E of Cairo, Ill. Length, ab. 690 mi.; navigable to Nashville, Tenn. (nearly 200 mi.).

Cumberland Road. [Also: **U.S. Road, National Road.**] Road through Maryland, Virginia, Pennsylvania, Ohio, Indiana, and Illinois, with its E terminus at Cumberland, Md., and its W terminus at Vandalia, Ill., built (1811 *et seq.*) by the U.S. government. Much of the route was laid out over existing roads, such as Braddock's Road (in Pennsylvania) and Zane's Trace (in Ohio). That portion W of Wheeling, W.Va., was popularly called the National Road or the U.S. Road because of the government's building it. After 1822 tollgates were built when the road's maintenance was turned over to the several states. It was the country's first national road, and played an important role in the development of the area along the Ohio and the upper Mississippi. The present U.S. Route 40 follows the old road.

Cumbrae (kum.brā', kum'brā), **Great** and **Little.** [Also: **Cumbray;** collectively called "the **Cumbraes.**"] Two islands in W Scotland, in Buteshire, situated in the Firth of Clyde ab. 4 to 5 mi. SE of Bute. Little Cumbrae lies ab. 1 mi. S of Great Cumbrae. Length of Great Cumbrae, ab. 4 mi.; width, ab. 2 mi. Length of Little Cumbrae, ab. 2 mi.; width, ab. 1 mi.

Cumbre Pass (köm'brā). See **Uspallata Pass.**

Cumbri (kum'brī). See **Brython.**

Cumbria (kum'bri.ạ). In early British history, the Cymric lands between the Clyde and the Ribble (i.e., between what are now Lanarkshire, in S central Scotland, and Lancashire, in N central England), in the W of the island; or, the S portion of that region.

Cumbria. A former name of **Strathclyde.**

Cumbrian Mountains (kum'bri.ạn). Mountain region in NW England, chiefly in Cumberland. The mountains are rugged, with deep valleys, and are divided by cross-valleys into several blocks. The entire region is a resort center, and much visited by mountain climbers. The peak elevation is Sca Fell Pike (3,210 ft.), the highest summit in England.

Cumming (kum'ing), **John.** b. in Aberdeenshire, Scotland, Nov. 10, 1807; d. at London, July 5, 1881. Scottish clergyman and writer. His works include *Apocalyptic Sketches* (1849), *The Great Tribulation* (1859), and *Destiny of Nations* (1864).

Cumming, Roualeyn George Gordon-. b. March 15, 1820; d. at Fort Augustus, Inverness-shire, Scotland, March 24, 1866. Scottish traveler and sportsman, surnamed "the Lionhunter." He lived (1843–48) in South Africa as a hunter, and wrote *Five Years of a Hunter's Life in the Far Interior of South Africa* (1850).

Cummings (kum'ingz), **Bruce Frederick.** See **Barbellion, Wilhelm Nero Pilate.**

Cummings, Byron. b. at Westville, N.Y., 1861—. American archaeologist. He was graduated (B.A., 1889; M.A., 1892) from Rutgers, was professor and dean of the college of arts and sciences (1906–15) at the University of Utah, director (1915–38) of the Arizona state museum, and dean of the school of arts, letters, and sciences (1917–21) at the University of Arizona. He has conducted archaeological expeditions in Utah, Arizona, and Mexico. He wrote *Kinishba, a Prehistoric Pueblo of the Great Pueblo Period.*

Cummings, Edward Estlin. [As often written by him, **e e cummings.**] b. at Cambridge, Mass., Oct. 14, 1894—. American poet and painter. He received a B.A. (1915) from Harvard. During World War I he served (1917) with the Norton Harjes Ambulance service in France, before the U.S. entered the war. Through a misunderstanding, he was imprisoned as a spy by the French but released after six months. His experiences in the internment camp are recorded in his novel *The Enormous Room* (1922). He has exhibited his paintings at art shows at the American British Art Center (1944) and the Rochester Memorial Gallery (1945). He is the author of *Tulips and Chimneys* (1923), *XLI Poems* (1925), *&* (1925), *Is 5* (1926), *him* (1927, a play), an untitled volume of poems (1927), *Christmas Tree* (1928), *by E. E. Cummings* (1930), *CIOPW* (1931, art work in charcoal, ink, oil, pencil, watercolor), *ViVa* (1931), *No Thanks* (1935), *Tom* (1935, a burlesque of *Uncle Tom's Cabin*), *1/20* (1936), *Collected Poems* (1938), *50 Poems* (1940), *1 x 1* (1944), *Santa Claus* (1946), and other books. *Eimi* (1933) was published after his visit to Russia.

Cummings, Homer Stillé. b. at Chicago, April 30, 1870—. American lawyer and politician, U.S. attorney general (1933–39). He was graduated (1891) from Yale, where he also received (1893) his law degree. He was admitted to the Connecticut bar (1893), establishing his practice at Stamford, Conn., and later being admitted to practice before the U.S. Supreme Court. He was mayor of Stamford (1900–02, 1904–06) and served (1908–12) as its corporation counsel. Active in Democratic politics, he was a member (1900–25) of the Democratic national committee and served (February, 1919–July, 1920) as its chairman. He was (1914–24) state's attorney for Fairfield County, Conn., and on March 4, 1933, was sworn in as U.S. attorney general under President F. D. Roosevelt, after the sudden death of Thomas J. Walsh, who was to have had the post, on March 2. He resigned from that post on Jan 2, 1939. During his incumbency the federal penitentiary at Alcatraz was established, the federal prison system was improved, the powers of the FBI were extended, and the scope of federal power in regard to kidnaping and interstate crime was broadened. After leaving federal office he resumed his law practice at Stamford, Conn.

Cummings v. Missouri, 4 Wallace 277 (1867). U.S. Supreme Court decision declaring unconstitutional a provision in the Missouri constitution of 1865 requiring voters, candidates for public office, attorneys, and ministers to take a state test oath intended to keep ex-Confederates and their sympathizers from the enjoyment of the franchise, public office, or professional life. The invalidation was based on the ground that the clause in question was an ex post facto law and a bill of attainder.

Cummins (kum'inz), **Albert Baird.** b. at Carmichaels, Pa., Feb. 15, 1850; d. July 30, 1926. American politician. He served as governor (1902–08) of Iowa. As a U.S. senator (1908–26), he was coauthor (1920) with Representative John J. Esch of the Transportation Act, which aided the financial rehabilitation of the railroads.

Cummins, George David. b. near Smyrna, Del., Dec. 11, 1822; d. at Lutherville, Md., June 26, 1876. American clergyman. He left the Protestant Episcopal Church in 1873, and became the first bishop of the Reformed Episcopal Church.

Cummins, Maria Susanna. b. at Salem, Mass., April 9, 1827; d. at Dorchester (part of Boston), Oct. 1, 1866. American novelist. She wrote the successful *The Lamplighter* (1854), and *Mabel Vaughan* (1857), *El Fureidis* (1860), and *Haunted Hearts* (1864).

Cumnock and Holmhead (kum'nok; hōm'hed). Police burgh in S Scotland, in Ayrshire, situated on Lugar Water ab. 14 mi. E of Ayr, ab. 374 mi. N of London by rail. It includes the town of Old Cumnock. Alexander Peden (c1626–86) the Covenanter, who had a great following in S Scotland, is buried here. 4,586 (est. 1948).

Cumnor Hall (kum'nọr). Old manor house in the environs of Oxford, England, now destroyed. Scott made it famous as Cumnor Place, the house where Amy Robsart is kept and where she meets her death, in *Kenilworth.* W. J. Meickle wrote a ballad called *Cumnor Hall*, which was a lament for Amy Robsart.

Cumont (kü.môṅ), **Franz Valéry Marie.** b. at Aalst, East Flanders, Belgium, Jan. 3, 1868; d. 1947. Belgian Orientalist. He studied at Ghent, Bonn, Berlin, Vienna, and Paris, then resided at Athens (1890) and Rome (1891). He served as professor at Ghent (1892–1910), lecturer at Oxford (1902, 1906) on the history of religions, lecturer at the Collège de France (1905) and at Uppsala, Sweden (1911), and also lectured at various American universities. He was curator (1899–1912) of the Musée Royale du Cinquantenaire, Brussels, and associate of the French Academy of Inscriptions and Belles-Lettres (1913). His principal writings concern the Eastern cults in Rome at the beginning of the Christian era, such as *Les Religions orientales dans le paganisme romain* (1906) and his large work *Textes et monuments relatifs aux mystères de Mithra* (1894–1901; Eng. trans., *The Mysteries of Mithras*, 1903).

Cuna (kö'nạ). [Also: **Tule, San Blas Cuna;** called the **"White Indians."**] Indian tribe inhabiting a number of small islands (the San Blas archipelago) along the N coast of Panama and several river valleys in the mountainous area of the E part of that country. The Cuna language belongs to the Chibchan stock. The Cuna are famous for the unusual number of albinos among them; in recent decades the incidence of albinism in the villages of San Blas is about one albino in every 200 of the population, far exceeding the proportion, perhaps one in ten thousand, among other Indians or other peoples in the world. The albinos share all the physical characteristics of the rest of the population, except that they lack any pigmentation of the skin, eyes, and hair.

Cunard (kū.närd'), Sir **Samuel.** b. at Halifax, Nova Scotia, Nov. 21, 1787; d. at London, April 28, 1865. British civil engineer and merchant, founder of the Cunard (now the Cunard-White Star) Line of steamships. He was a merchant in the lumber, shipping, and banking businesses at Halifax when in 1839 he formed a company with the Burns brothers of Glasgow, David MacIver of Liverpool, and Robert Napier, among others, to carry the mail from Liverpool to America. This company, named the British and North American Royal Mail Steam Packet Company, but known as the Cunard Line, sent as its first vessel the *Britannia*, a wooden paddle-wheel ship, from Liverpool to Halifax and Boston, on July 4–19, 1840. Cunard was made a baronet in 1859.

Cunaxa (kū.nak'sạ). In ancient geography, a place in Babylonia near the Euphrates, probably ab. 75 mi. NW of Babylon. Here, in 401 B.C., a battle took place between Artaxerxes II, king of Persia (with 400,000–1,000,000 men), and his brother Cyrus the Younger (with 100,000 Asiatics aided by 13,000 Greeks). Cyrus was defeated and slain; the Greek contingent was successful in escaping to the Black Sea, as Xenophon, one of their leaders, relates in his *Anabasis.*

Cundell (kun'dẹl), **Henry.** See **Condell, Henry.**

Cundinamarca (kön″dē.nä.mär'kä). Department in C Colombia. It is in part an elevated plateau with a temperate climate. Capital, Bogotá; area, 9,108 sq. mi.; pop. 1,470,500 (est. 1950).

Cundwah (kund'wä). See **Khandwa.**

Cunego (kö.nä'gō), **Domenico.** b. at Verona, Italy, 1727; d. at Rome, 1794. Italian engraver. His most noted work is an engraving of Michelangelo's *Last Judgment.*

Cunegond (kū'nẹ.gond), Saint. [German, **Kunigunde.**] d. March 3, 1038. Wife of the emperor Henry II. According to legend she disproved a charge of conjugal infidelity by passing unhurt through an ordeal of fire. The same chastity test is credited to other women falsely accused, and is a popular theme of local legend and folklore. After the death of her husband in 1024 Cunegond retired to the cloister of Kaufungen, near Kassel.

Cunégonde (kü.nā.gôṅd). In Voltaire's novel *Candide*, the beloved of Candide.

Cunene (kö.nā'nẹ). [Also, **Kunene.**] River in SW Africa; it flows into the South Atlantic Ocean N of Cape Frio, and forms part of the boundary between South-West Africa and Angola. Length, ab. 725 mi.

Cuneo (kö'nā.ō). Province in NW Italy, in the *compartimento* (region) of Piedmont. Capital, Cuneo; area, ab. 2,900 sq. mi.; pop. 608,912 (1936), ab. 608,000 (est. 1946).

Cuneo. [Also, **Coni.**] City and commune in NW Italy, in the *compartimento* (region) of Piedmont, the capital of the province of Cuneo, situated at the junction of the Gesso and Stura rivers, SW of Turin. It has important chemical and metallurgical industries and silk manufactures and is a trade center for the products of the neighboring Alpine valleys; chestnuts are widely exported. It is also a communications center between Piedmont and the French Riviera. Cuneo is the seat of a bishopric, and has a technical institute and a library. The Church of San Francesco dates from the 15th century. The city became part of Savoy in 1382 and was frequently besieged in the wars of the 16th, 17th, and 18th centuries. Buildings of interest to tourists were undamaged in World War II. Pop. of commune, 35,321 (1936); of city, 18,852 (1936).

Cunha (kö'nyạ), **Euclides (Rodrigues Pimenta) da.** b. on a farm near Cantagalo, Brazil, Jan. 20, 1866; assassinated at Rio de Janeiro, Aug. 15, 1909. Brazilian writer, who became famous in his country after the publication of his first book, *Os sertões* (1902). This important sociological work was translated into English in 1943 as *Rebellion in the Backlands.* The book is the story of a backwoods revolt covered by Cunha as a newspaper reporter. His descriptions and comments on the state of the people are gloomy but penetrating. He was a military engineer, and had been appointed professor of logic at the Colégio Pedro II a few months before he was slain. Among his other works, the best known are *Perú versus Bolívia* (1907), *Contrastes e confrontos* (1907), and *Á margem da história* (1909).

Cunha, Tristão da. b. c1460; d. c1540. Portuguese navigator and diplomat. In the days during the early 16th century of Portugal's prominence in world exploration, he led expeditions to Africa and to India. Among his discoveries was a group of three islands in the south Atlantic Ocean, of which one is known by his name. He sat in the Portuguese royal council, and in 1514 was sent as a special legate of the king to the court of Pope Leo X.

Cunha Mattos (kö'nyą mä'tös), **Raymundo José da.** b. at Faro, Algarve, Portugal, Nov. 2, 1776; d. at Rio de Janeiro, March 2, 1839. Portuguese-Brazilian soldier and author. He joined an artillery regiment in 1790, was stationed on the island of São Tomé, near the African coast (1798–1816), and went to Brazil in 1817. He became field marshal in 1834. He published accounts of his travels in Brazil, historical works on São Tomé, Minas Gerais, and Goiás, a digest of military law, an account of the attack and defense (during the Napoleonic era) of the city of Oporto, and many papers and maps, all of great value. He was one of the founders of the Brazilian Instituto Historico e Geographico.

Cunliffe (kun'lif), **John William.** b. at Bolton, England, Jan. 20, 1865; d. at Ogunquit, Me., March 18, 1946. American educator and professor of English who served (1920–31) as director of the Columbia University School of Journalism. He received a B.A. (1884) from London University, and taught (1899–1905) at McGill, then was professor at Wisconsin (1906–12) and Columbia (1912–20). He wrote or edited *Century Readings in English Literature* (1910; 5th ed., 1940), *Shakespeare's Principal Plays* (1914; 3rd ed., 1935), and other books.

Cunliffe-Lister (kun'lif.lis'tėr), **Philip.** See **Swinton,** 1st Viscount.

Cunningham (kun'ing.ąm, -ham), Sir **Alan Gordon.** b. at Dublin, May 1, 1887—. British army officer; brother of Sir Andrew Browne Cunningham. He served (1914–18) in France during World War I, then as general staff officer (1919–21) in the Straits Settlements. He was commander (1937–38) of the first Division of Royal Artillery. During World War II he was general officer commanding the East Africa Forces (1940–41) and the eighth Imperial Army in the Middle East, Ethiopia, and Libya, and the Eastern Command (1944–45). After the war, he was high commissioner and commander in chief (1945 *et seq.*) in Palestine, being in charge of the British evacuation in 1948.

Cunningham, Alexander. [Title, 5th Earl of **Glencairn.**] d. Nov. 23, 1574. Scottish leader in the Reformation. He was a signer of a letter (1557) inviting John Knox to return from Geneva. He prevented the queen regent, Mary of Guise, from attacking the reformers at Perth (1559), and petitioned (1560) Elizabeth's aid against the French invasion which Mary called to strengthen her hand. Cunningham destroyed (1561) monasteries in western Scotland. In rebellion against Mary, Queen of Scots, he aided the earl of Moray in an attack (1565) on Edinburgh and was a leader in the army of James Douglas, 4th Earl of Morton, at the battle of Langside (1568). He was nominated for the regency in 1571, during the minority of James VI (later James I of England) but lost to Morton.

Cunningham, Alexander. b. at Cumnock, Scotland, c1655; d. at The Hague, Netherlands, in December, 1730. Scottish classical scholar. Educated in Holland and at Edinburgh, he became professor of civil law at Edinburgh (c1698), but was removed (1710) because his patron the duke of Queensberry was out of favor. He retired to The Hague on a pension granted by the duke. His classical scholarship is shown in his edition of Horace (1721) and of Vergil (1743). He attacked in the notes of his own 1721 edition Bentley's edition of Horace. Cunningham was known as a skilled chess player and is sometimes credited with the invention of the Cunningham gambit, still retaining some currency, but, as H. J. R. Murray has demonstrated in his *History of Chess,* this should be credited to another Alexander Cunningham (1654–1737), author of a Latin history of Great Britain of his times, who was in Europe immediately before the critic's Hague sojourn.

Cunningham, Sir **Alexander.** b. Jan. 23, 1814; d. Nov. 28, 1893. English military engineer and archaeologist; son of Allan Cunningham. He served in India from 1834 to 1885, first as a member of the engineers, and then, after his retirement from the army, as archaeological surveyor. His works include *An Essay on the Arian Order of Architecture* (1846), *Ladak, Physical, Statistical, and Historical* (1846), *Book of Indian Eras* (1883), and others.

Cunningham, Allan. b. at Keir, Dumfriesshire, Scotland, Dec. 7, 1784; d. at London, Oct. 30, 1842. Scottish poet and man of letters. He was apprenticed to a stone mason, but went to London in 1810, and became a reporter and writer on the *Literary Gazette.* He became (1814) secretary to the sculptor Francis Legatt Chantrey, a position which he retained until his death. He wrote *Traditional Tales of the Peasantry* (1822), *The Songs of Scotland, Ancient and Modern* (1825), *Lives of the Most Eminent British Painters, Sculptors, and Architects* (1829–33), and several romances.

Cunningham, Sir **Andrew Browne.** [Titles: 1st Viscount of **Hyndhope,** 1st Baron of **Kirkhope.**] b. at Dublin, Jan. 7, 1883—. British naval officer; brother of Sir Alan Gordon Cunningham. He joined the navy in 1898, served (1914–18) in World War I, and became a rear admiral serving (1933–36) in command of the Mediterranean fleet's destroyer flotillas. He was vice-admiral (1937–38) heading the battle-cruiser squadron and second in command in the Mediterranean, and deputy chief (1938–39) of the naval staff. As chief commander (1939–42) in the Mediterranean during World War II, with the rank of admiral, he successfully raided (November, 1940) the Italian fleet anchored in the Gulf of Taranto, was victorious (March, 1941) in the Ionian Sea, and had charge (November, 1942) of allied naval operations in the Northwest African theater. He was commissioned (1943) admiral of the fleet and commander in chief (1943) of the Allied naval forces in the Mediterranean under General Dwight Eisenhower. He served as first sea lord, and chief (October, 1943 to 1946) of the naval staff. Author of *A Sailor's Odyssey* (autobiography, 1951).

Cunningham, Sir **John Henry Dacres.** b. 1885—. British naval officer. He was in command (1928–29) of H.M.S. *Adventure,* was director (1930–32) of the plans division of the admiralty and assistant chief (1936–38) of the naval staff. As vice-admiral (1938–41) he headed the first cruiser squadron, and then became chief (1941–43) of supplies and transport as lord commissioner for the admiralty. In the field in World War II, he was commander in chief in the Mediterranean (1943–46), leading the Allied naval forces. He served as chief (1946 *et seq.*) of the naval staff.

Cunningham, Joseph Davey. b. at Lambeth (now part of London), June 9, 1812; d. near Ambala, India, Feb. 28, 1851. English soldier and author; son of Allan Cunningham. He entered the Bengal engineers (1831) and served (1837) as assistant to the political agent on the Sikh frontier, where he gathered information for his book on the Sikhs. He was present (1838 *et seq.*) at important conferences in the Sikh country and served during the Sikh wars in the 1840's. While political agent (1846) at Bhopal, he wrote the *History of the Sikhs* (published 1849). Its revelation of political secrets caused his removal (1850).

Cunningham, Peter. b. at London, April 1, 1816; d. at St. Albans, England, May 18, 1869. English antiquary and littérateur; son of Allan Cunningham. He wrote a *Handbook of London* (1849), and edited the works of Drummond, Goldsmith, and others.

Cunningham, William. b. at Hamilton, Scotland, Oct. 2, 1805; d. at Edinburgh, Dec. 14, 1861. Scottish clergyman and theologian, one of the founders of the Free Church. He became professor of theology in the Free Church College in 1843, professor of church history in 1845, and principal in 1847. He wrote *Historic Theology* (1862), and other works.

Cunningham, William. b. at Edinburgh, Dec. 29, 1849; d. at Cambridge, England, June 10, 1919. Scottish clergyman of the Anglican Church, pioneer in the study and writing of economic history in Britain, and theorist of Joseph Chamberlain's movement against free trade. He was professor of economics and statistics (1891–97) at King's College, London. Cunningham traveled widely in Europe, India, Palestine, South Africa, and America, and lectured (1899, 1914) on economic history at Harvard. He wrote *The Growth of English Industry and Commerce*

(1882; many editions), *Christian Opinion on Usury* (1884), *An Alternative to Socialism* (1885), *Modern Civilization in Some of Its Economic Aspects* (1896), *Alien Immigrants in England* (1897), *Western Civilization in Its Economic Aspect in Ancient Times* (1898), *Gospel of Work* (1902), *The Moral Witness of the Church on the Investment of Wealth* (1909), *Christianity and Social Questions* (1910), and *Increase of True Religion* (1917).

Cunninghame (kun'ing.ạm). [Also, **Cunningham.**] Northern division of Ayrshire, in S Scotland. It lies N of the river Irvine and is a dairying district.

Cunninghame Graham (kun'ing.ạm grā'ạm), **Robert.** See **Graham, Robert.**

Cunninghame Graham, Robert Bontine. b. at London, May 24, 1852; d. at Buenos Aires, March 20, 1936. Scottish essayist, short-story writer, biographer, socialist, politician, and traveler. In 1886 he won a seat as Liberal member of Parliament, but he lost the elections of 1892 and 1918. He was suspended from the House of Commons for using the word "damn" in the House, the first member, it is believed, to be so distinguished.

Cuno (kö'nō), **Wilhelm.** b. at Suhl, Germany, July 2, 1876; d. at Aumühle, near Hamburg, Germany, Jan. 3, 1933. German statesman. He was employed first in the treasury, and during World War I in the government food department. Later he became associated with the Hamburg shipping concern Hapag (Hamburg-American Steamship Line), eventually rising, after Albert Ballin's suicide (1918), to the position of head of the firm. In the critical period after the murders of Matthias Erzberger (1921) and Walter Rathenau (1922), Cuno was asked to form a nonparty cabinet. As chancellor (from November, 1922) he discontinued Karl Wirth's policy of treaty fulfillment, and organized passive resistance in the Ruhr against the French occupation. The monetary crisis following his policies forced him to resign in August, 1923. He then returned to the presidency of the shipping firm.

Cunobeline (kū'nọ.bẹ.līn″) or **Cunobelinus** (kū″nọ.bẹ-lī'nus). Semilegendary king of the Silures, the father of Caractacus. He is often confused with Cymbeline, whose adventures as related by Shakespeare are taken from the *Decameron*, but whose name was borrowed by Shakespeare from Holinshed. A historical king (d. c43 A.D.) of the name was an ally of Augustus.

Cuntisuyu (kön.tē.sö'yö). [Also, **Conde-suyu.**] Western quarter of the regions controlled by the Incas, extending from Cusco (in what is now Peru) W and SW to the coast. It derived its name from Cunti, a small region just W of Cusco, which was early conquered by the Incas.

Cunza (kün'zạ). See **Kunza.**

Cuore (kwô'rā). [Eng. trans., *"Heart."*] Book by Edmondo de Amicis, written in 1886. It is the daily records of the events of a school year as told by a boy pupil; to it are added letters from his parents and others. It was translated (1887) into English by Isabel F. Hapgood.

Cuorgnè (kwôr.nye'). Town and commune in NW Italy, in the *compartimento* (region) of Valle d'Aosta, in the province of Aosta, situated in the Locana Valley (Italian, Val di Locana), on the Orro River, N of Turin. The valley, rich in pasture land, is a cattle-raising district and has also numerous metallurgical establishments. Buildings of interest to tourists were undamaged in World War II. Pop. of commune, 10,983 (1936); of town, 3,278 (1936).

Cup, The. Poetical drama by Alfred Tennyson, produced at the Lyceum Theatre, London, in 1881.

Cupar (kö'pạr). [Also, **Cupar-Fife** (kö'pạr.fīf).] Royal burgh in E Scotland, county seat of Fifeshire, situated on the river Eden, ab. 9 mi. E of Falkland, ab. 438 mi. N of London by rail. It has a sugar-beet refining industry. The corporate existence of Cupar dates back more than 500 years. 5,211 (est. 1948).

Cupid (kū'pid). [Also: **Amor**; Greek, **Eros.**] In ancient Roman mythology, the god of love, the son of Mercury and Venus. The parallel Greek Eros is similarly son of Hermes and Aphrodite. He is generally represented as a beautiful boy with wings, carrying a bow and a quiver of arrows, and is often spoken of as blind or blindfolded. The bow is used to shoot the arrows, which are invisible and which cause the one shot to fall irrevocably in love. Cupid originally was depicted as a young man, as he is in the story of Cupid and Psyche, but with time developed into the cherubic little scamp of later myth. The name is often given in art to figures of children, with or without wings, introduced, sometimes in considerable number, as a motif of decoration and with little or no mythological allusion.

Cupid, Adam. See **Adam Cupid.**

Cupid, The Letter of. Poem by Thomas Hoccleve (Occleve) dated 1402, two years after Chaucer's death, attributed in the 1532 edition to Chaucer.

Cupid and Psyche (sī'kē). Episode in the *Golden Ass* of Apuleius. The beauty of Psyche, the youngest of three daughters of a certain king, and the homage paid to it, arouse the wrath of Venus, who commands Cupid to avenge her. In the attempt he falls in love with Psyche; she is borne to a lovely valley where every night Cupid, always invisible, visits her and commands her not to attempt to see him. Urged by her sisters and by her own curiosity, she violates this command, and is abandoned by the god. After toilsome wanderings in search of her lover, and many sufferings, she is endowed with immortality by Jupiter and united to Cupid forever. The tale, utilizing themes and motifs familiar in folk tales from all over the world, for example the taboo against looking at the supernatural husband and the search for the lost husband, is the clearest example of unadorned folk tale in classical literature. The story has served as a basis for many later accounts, such as the one by La Fontaine, and for paintings, one of the most familiar by Raphael.

Cupid and Psyche. Copy in marble, in the Capitol, Rome, of a Greek original of Hellenistic date, representing a boy and a girl embracing. Cupid is nude, Psyche draped from the hips down.

Cupid in Waiting. Comedy by William Blanchard Jerrold, produced on July 17, 1871.

Cupid's Revenge. Play by Francis Beaumont and John Fletcher. It was acted c1612, and published in 1615, and attributed, incorrectly, to Fletcher alone, though probably he wrote the major part of it. It is based on two of the stories in Sidney's *Arcadia.*

Cupis de Camargo (kü.pēs dẹ kà.màr.gō), **Marie Anne.** See **Camargo.**

Cuppy (kup'i), **Will.** [Full name, **William Jacob Cuppy.**] b. at Auburn, Ind., Aug. 23, 1884; d. at New York, Sept. 19, 1949. American critic and humorist. He received (1907) a Ph.B. from the University of Chicago, and served as a lieutenant in World War I. Cuppy was a member of the editorial staff of the New York *Herald Tribune.* His books include *How to be a Hermit* (1929), *How to Tell Your Friends from Apes* (1931), *How to Become Extinct* (1941), and *The Decline and Fall of Everybody* (1948).

Cura (kö'rä). See **Villa de Cura,** Venezuela.

Curaçao (kö.rä.sä'ō; Anglicized, kū'rạ.sō). [Also, **Netherlands Antilles.**] Former Dutch colony in the West Indies, comprising all the Netherlands Antilles, i.e., the Netherlands Windward Islands (Curaçao, Aruba, and Bonaire), off the N coast of Venezuela, and the Netherlands Leeward Islands (St. Eustatius, Saba, and the S part of St. Martin), E of Puerto Rico; now, in accordance with the 1922 constitution, an integral part (overseas territory) of the kingdom of the Netherlands. Capital, Willemstad (on Curaçao); area, 403 sq. mi.; pop. 164,073 (est. 1951).

Curaçao. [Also: **Curaçoa, Curazao.**] Island in the Caribbean Sea, N of Venezuela, part of the Dutch overseas territory (formerly a colony) of Curaçao. The chief industry is the refining of Venezuelan oil. It was settled by the Spaniards in 1527 and taken by the Dutch in 1634. Chief city (and capital of the territory), Willemstad; length, ab. 40 mi.; width, ab. 10 mi.; area, ab. 210 sq. mi.; pop. 102,206 (est. 1951).

Curan (kur'ạn). In Shakespeare's *King Lear,* a courtier.

Curci (kör'chē), **Carlo Maria.** b. at Naples, Italy, Sept. 4, 1809; d. at Villa Careggi, near Florence, June 8, 1891. Roman Catholic theologian and writer on church politics. He entered the order of the Jesuits in 1826, and was editor (1850–53) of the *Civiltà cattolica,* a Jesuit periodical. He was in 1877 expelled from his order on account of his opposition to the policy of the Pope toward the Italian government. He subsequently recanted, however, and was restored to membership in the order. He published *Lezioni esegetiche e morali sopra i quattro evangeli* (1874–

76), *Il Moderno dissidio tra la Chiesa e l'Italia* (1877), *La Nuova Italia ed i vecchi zelanti* (1881), and others.

Curé d'Ars (kü.rā dȧr). See **Vianney,** Saint **Jean Baptiste Marie.**

Cure for a Cuckold, A. Tragicomedy written by John Webster, assisted by William Rowley. It was published in 1661.

Curel (kü.rel), **François de.** b. at Metz, France, June 10, 1854; d. at Paris, 1928. French playwright belonging to the realist school. He was the author of *Les Fossiles* (1892), *La Nouvelle Idole* (1895), *Le Repas du Lion* (1897), *La Danse devant le miroir* (1913), and others. Son of a noble Lorraine family related to the De Wendel steel dynasty, he turned to literature as an avocation and lived the life of a gentleman of letters in the English tradition. His talent for combining realism with ideas early attracted such experts as André Antoine (who first staged his work at the Théâtre Libre), but his plays rarely pleased general audiences. He was elected to the French Academy in 1918.

Cure of Souls, A. Novel by May Sinclair, published in 1924.

Cures (kū'rēz). In ancient geography, a city of the Sabines, ab. 24 mi. NE of Rome: a legendary city of Numa Pompilius and Titus Tatius.

Curetes (kū̦.rē'tēz). In Greek mythology, attendants of Zeus, properly in Crete, who are often wrongly identified with the Corybantes, the Cabiri, and others. The Curetes were probably characters in a ceremony to Zeus the infant, and the myth explained their noisy dance. When Zeus was taken away and hidden from Cronus, who had swallowed his other children, the Curetes danced near him and, with the noise of spears and shields, drowned his infant cries so that his father might not hear them.

Cureton (kūr'to̦n), **William.** b. at Westbury, Shropshire, England, 1808; d. June 17, 1864. English Orientalist. He was appointed to a position in the Bodleian Library in 1834, undertook the cataloguing of Arabic books and manuscripts in the British Museum in 1837 (the first part of the catalogue appeared in 1846), and became chaplain to Queen Victoria in 1847 and canon of Westminster and pastor of Saint Margaret's in 1849. He is best known for his work in classifying and, in part, editing the important collection of Syriac manuscripts obtained (1841–43) by the British Museum from the monasteries of Nitria. His most important discovery was a manuscript of the *Epistles of Ignatius to Polycarp,* which he edited in 1845. He also discovered parts of a Syriac version of the gospels, differing from the Peshitta version, and now known in his honor as the *Curetonian Gospels.*

Curfew Must Not Ring Tonight. Ballad by Rose Hartwick Thorpe, published in a Detroit newspaper in 1867.

Curia Rhaetorum (kū'ri.a̦ rē.tō'rum). Latin name of **Chur.**

Curiatii (kū.ri.ā'shi.ī). In Roman legend, three brothers from Alba Longa, who fought against the three Horatii. They killed two of the Horatii, but the third slew the three Curiatii and then, when his sister Horatia grieved at the news, because she was betrothed to one of the Curiatii, he slew her.

Curicancha (kö.rē.kän'chä). Variant name of **Coricancha,** the great Inca temple at Cusco.

Curicó (kö.rē.kō'). Province in C Chile, S of Colchagua. It is mountainous in the E and W. Capital, Curicó; area, 2,215 sq. mi.; pop. 90,547 (est. 1950).

Curicó. Capital of Curicó province, in C Chile: cattle markets, flour mills, and distilleries. 21,153 (1940).

Curie, Ève Denise (kü.rē; Anglicized, kū̦.rē', kū'rē). b. at Paris, Dec. 6, 1904—. French pianist, writer, editor, and lecturer; daughter of Pierre Curie and Marie Curie. Her first love was music, and it might have remained her sole major interest had it not been for World War II. In 1925 she made her first bow as a concert pianist, at Paris, and thereafter played in many cities, chiefly in France and Belgium. She also engaged, under a pseudonym, in musical criticism. During World War II, living in the U.S., she gave her energies to the Free French movement, and as a correspondent visited some of the most active battlefronts, from which experience came her book *Journey Among Warriors* (1943). In 1945 she became one of the publishers of the newspaper *Paris Presse.* She had, however, turned to writing even before the war, and her absorbing story of her mother's life, *Madame Curie,* published in 1937, is regarded as one of the great biographies of recent times, and has been translated into many other languages. France made Ève Denise Curie a chevalier of the Legion of Honor and bestowed on her also the Croix de Guerre, and Poland conferred upon her the order of Polonia Restituta.

Curie or **Curie-Joliot** (kü.rē.jo̦.lyō), **Irène.** See **Joliot-Curie, Irène.**

Curie, Marie. [Maiden name, **Marja Skłodowska.**] b. at Warsaw, Poland, Nov. 7, 1867; d. in Haute-Savoie, France, July 4, 1934. Polish-French chemist and physicist; wife of Pierre Curie. She studied under her father, a physics teacher at Warsaw, and, after being involved in student troubles there, went to Paris in 1891 to study at the Sorbonne. She married (1895) Pierre Curie, with whom she worked in her investigations of radioactivity until his death in 1906. With him she discovered the elements radium and polonium (1898), reducing some eight tons of pitchblende to obtain less than a gram, not of pure radium but of radium salts. Together they discovered the radioactivity of thorium (1898) and the induction of radioactivity in other substances (1899). The two Curies and Antoine Henri Becquerel were awarded the Nobel prize in physics in 1903. When Pierre died in 1906, Mme. Curie became professor at the Sorbonne. In 1911 she was winner of the Nobel prize in chemistry. Her daughter Irène (b. 1897) won the Nobel prize for chemistry with her husband Frédéric Joliot (Joliot-Curie) in 1935; another daughter, Ève, is a musician and writer. The curie, a unit of radioactive measurement, and the element curium are named for Mme. Curie.

Curie, Pierre. b. at Paris, May 15, 1859; run over and killed by a dray, at Paris, April 19, 1906. French physicist; husband of Marie Curie. With his brother, he investigated (1880) piezoelectricity (the electricity produced from a crystal under pressure). He became director of laboratories (1882) and professor (1895) at the Paris School of Physics and Chemistry. In the latter year he married Marie Skłodowska, who became his collaborator in investigations of radioactivity. Also in 1895, he established Curie's law (the magnetic susceptibility of any substance is changed in inverse proportion to absolute temperature). With his wife he discovered the elements polonium and radium, thorium's radioactivity, and induced radioactivity (1898–99). He was awarded the Nobel prize in physics with his wife and Antoine Henri Becquerel (1903). From 1900 until his death he was professor at the Sorbonne.

Curières de Castelnau (kü.ryer de̦ kȧs.tel.nō), **Édouard,** Vicomte **de.** See **Castelnau, Édouard,** Vicomte **de Curières de.**

Curio (kū'ri.ō). Gentleman in attendance on the Duke of Illyria, in Shakespeare's *Twelfth Night.*

Curio, Gaius Scribonius. d. 53 B.C. Roman general and politician. He fought with Sulla against Mithridates II of Parthia, Tribune (90), consul (76), governor of Macedonia (75–73), he became pontifex maximus, the chief priest of the civic religion, in 57. He was the first Roman general to reach the Danube in Moesia, c73 B.C. He was an opponent of Caesar.

Curio, Gaius Scribonius. Killed at Utica, Africa, 49 B.C. Son of Gaius Scribonius Curio (d. 53 B.C.); a partisan of Caesar in the civil war. After struggling in Roman politics to prevent any action by the senate against Caesar, he took the field as leader of military forces, taking Sicily and besieging a Pompeian force in Utica.

Curiosities of Literature, The. Work by Isaac D'Israeli, containing anecdotes, criticism, and general information in all fields. It was issued anonymously, the first volume in 1791, a second in 1793, a third in 1817, a fourth and fifth in 1823, and a sixth and last in 1834.

Curious Impertinent, The. Episode in Cervantes's *Don Quixote.* John Crowne (c1640–1712) wrote a play, *The Married Beau, or The Curious Impertinent* (1694), the plot of which is taken from this. The story is that of two friends, one of whom induces the other, after much argument, to test the faithfulness of the former's wife. She proves to be not as virtuous as she should be and all ends tragically.

Curitiba (kö.rē.tē'ba̦). [Former spellings, **Coritiba, Corityba, Curityba, Curytiba.**] Capital of the state of

Paraná, in SE Brazil: railway shipping center for maté and coffee. 141,349 (1950).

Curium (kū'ri.um). Ancient city in Cyprus, W of the river Lycus, said to have been founded by the Argives. Its ruins contain a Phoenician temple, remarkable especially for its crypt of four rock-hewn chambers, ab. 23 ft. in diameter, connected by doors and a gallery. The objects in gold and silver constituting the "Treasure of Curium" in the Metropolitan Museum, New York, were found in these chambers.

Curle (kėrl), **Richard Henry Parnell.** b. at Melrose, Roxburghshire, Scotland, March 11, 1883—. English writer and traveler in South America, the West Indies, the Far East, and other regions. He is the author of books about Joseph Conrad, whom he knew as a friend. Among his works are *Wanderings, Oriental Trail, The Echo of Voices, Aspects of George Meredith, Caravansery and Conservation* (1937), and others.

Curley (kėr'li), **James Michael.** b. at Boston, Nov. 20, 1874—. American politician and public official. He served both in the municipal government of Boston and in the Massachusetts state legislature before his first election to the U.S. House of Representatives, where he served two terms before returning to the municipal arena in 1914, when he was elected mayor of Boston. His first term in the city hall ended in 1918, but subsequently he served two more terms as mayor (1922–26, 1930–34). His power was now state-wide, and he became (1937) governor of Massachusetts, serving until 1939. He went to Congress again (1943–46), and before the end of his term he was once more (1945) chosen mayor of his native city. In 1947 an action brought by the U.S. Department of Justice resulted in his conviction and imprisonment on a charge of using the mails to defraud. After he had served several months, his sentence was commuted by President Truman, who also in 1950 issued him a full pardon. Upon his release he resumed his functions as mayor of Boston, serving out his term until 1950, but his bid to succeed himself in that office failed, and he was defeated in the election of 1949.

Curley, Michael Joseph. b. at Golden Island, Athlone, Ireland, Oct. 12, 1879; d. May 16, 1947. Roman Catholic prelate. He was ordained a priest in 1904, served (1904–14) as a missionary in Florida, was consecrated (1914) bishop of St. Augustine, and in 1921 became archbishop of Baltimore.

Curll (kėrl), **Edmund.** b. 1675; d. at London, Dec. 11, 1747. English bookseller. He achieved a reputation for issuing obscene literature, which led to the use in his day of the word "Curlicism" as meaning indecency in literature. In 1716 he had a quarrel with Pope over his ascription of the anonymous *Court Poems* to Pope. The poet thereupon pilloried Curll in the *Dunciad.* He published a number of standard works; of his biographies Arbuthnot said they had added a new terror to death.

Curme (kėrm), **George Oliver.** b. at Richmond, Ind., 1860; d. 1948. American philologist and grammarian. He was graduated (M.A., 1885) from De Pauw University and received the Ph.D. (1926) from Heidelberg University. He lectured on German language and literature at the University of Washington, Cornell College, Iowa (1887–96), Northwestern (1896–1933), and the University of California. He was the author of works on English and German grammar, including *Parts of Speech and Accidence* (1935), and *A Grammar of the German Language* (1905; revised ed., 1922), a lavishly documented and comprehensive presentation of the facts of the language.

Curragh (kur'ạ). [Also, **Curragh of Kildare.**] Plain in Leinster province, Irish Republic, in County Kildare ab. 27 mi. SW of Dublin. The plain has a fine turf and is the site of the most famous racecourse in Ireland. The chief military training camp of the Irish Republic is also here. Formerly, the area was the property of the crown. Area, ab. 8 sq. mi.

Curran (kur'ạn), **Charles Courtney.** b. at Hartford, Ky., Feb. 13, 1861; d. 1942. American painter. He studied at the Cincinnati School of Design, the Art Students League and the National Academy of Design, both at New York, and at the Julian Academy, Paris, under Constant, Lefebvre, and Doucet. He became a member (1904) of the National Academy and instructor of life classes there. He received prizes from the National Academy (1888, 1893, 1895, 1919), from the Paris (1900), Pan-American (1901), and St. Louis (1904) expositions, and others. His *Cathedral Interior, Verona* is in the Metropolitan Museum at New York; *Perfume of the Roses* is in the National Gallery at Washington, D.C. He was the painter also of the Mark Twain portrait for the Mark Twain Memorial at Hartford, Conn.

Curran, John Philpot. b. at Newmarket, County Cork, Ireland, July 24, 1750; d. at Brompton, near London, Oct. 14, 1817. Irish orator. He studied at Trinity College, Dublin, and at the Middle Temple, London, and in 1775 was admitted to the Irish bar. In 1783 he entered the Irish Parliament, where he joined the opposition, of which Grattan was at that time the leader. When the government instituted its bloody series of prosecutions against the leaders of the Irish insurrection of 1798, he appeared for the prisoners, such as Wolf Tone, in nearly every case, and conducted the defense with extraordinary boldness and ability. Robert Emmett, who led an attempt to capture the viceroy in 1803, came out of hiding to visit Curran's daughter Sarah and was captured and hanged as a result. Curran was cleared of implication in the plot. He was (1806–14) master of the rolls in Ireland, and then retired to private life. See *Life of Curran*, by his son, W. H. Curran (1819); *Curran and his Contemporaries*, by Charles Phillips (1818); and *Curran's Speeches* (1806).

Currelly (ku.rel'i), **Charles Trick.** b. at Exeter, Ontario, Canada, Jan. 11, 1876—. Canadian archaeologist. A graduate of the University of Toronto, on the staff (1902–09) of the Egypt Exploration Fund he took part in the discoveries in the Sinai peninsula. He is responsible for such discoveries as the tombs of Ahmose and Menthuhotep III, and the Great Cow of Hathor and her shrine. He has served as director (1908 *et seq.*) of the Royal Ontario Museum of Archaeology and professor of archaeology at the University of Toronto. He is the author of *Abydos II* and the Stone Age volume of the *Cairo Catalogue*, and is coauthor with Sir William Matthew Flinders Petrie of *Researches in Sinai.*

Current (kur'ẹnt). River in SE Missouri which joins the Black River near Pocahontas, Randolph County, NE Arkansas. Length, over 225 mi.

Currie (kur'i), Sir **Arthur William.** b. at Napperton, Ontario, Canada, Dec. 5, 1875; d. at Montreal, Nov. 30, 1933. Canadian soldier and educator. He taught school at Sidney and Victoria, British Columbia. In World War I he commanded (1914–15) the 2nd Canadian infantry brigade, was appointed major general in command of the 1st Canadian division (1915), and then general in command of the Canadian corps in France (1917). He served as inspector general of Canadian militia and principal military councilor after his return to Canada. From 1920 to 1933 he was principal of McGill University.

Currie, James. b. at Kirkpatrick-Fleming, Dumfriesshire, Scotland, May 31, 1756; d. at Sidmouth, England, Aug. 31, 1805. Scottish physician who practiced at Liverpool. He wrote *Medical Reports on the Effects of Water, cold and warm,* as a *Remedy in Fevers and Febrile Diseases* (1797), and edited Burns's works (1800); his edition, prepared at the Burns family's request, remained the standard Burns for many years.

Currie, Lady **Mary Montgomerie.** [Pseudonym, **Violet Fane;** maiden name, **Lamb.**] b. at Beauport, Littlehampton, Sussex, England, Feb. 24, 1843; d. at Harrogate, Yorkshire, England, Oct. 13, 1905. English poet, essayist, short-story writer, novelist, and translator; wife (married 1894, as her second husband) of Sir Philip Henry Wodehouse Currie. She contributed many essays and poems to *Nineteenth Century, Blackwood's Magazine, Littel's Living Age*, and other periodicals. She took her pseudonym from a character in Disraeli's novel *Vivian Gray*, adopting it because her parents did not approve of a literary career. She appears as Mrs. Sinclair in William H. Mallock's satirical novel *The New Republic* (1876), which is dedicated to her. She was the author of *Laura Dibalzo* (1880), *Sophy* (1882), *Through Love and War* (1886), and *The Story of Helen Davenant* (1889), novels; *Edwin and Angelina Papers* (1878), *Two Moods of Man* (1901), *Collected Essays* (1902), *Are Remarkable People Remarkable Looking?, Enfants Trouvés of Literature, Feast of Kebobs,* and *Way of Dreams* (all 1904), essays; *From Dawn to Noon* (1872), *Great Peace-Maker* (1872), *Denzil*

Place: A Story in Verse (1875), *Queen of the Fairies* (1876), *Collected Verses* (1880), *Autumn Songs* (1889), *Under Cross and Crescent* (1895), *Betwixt Two Seas* (1900), and *In Winter* (1904), poetry.

Currie, Sir **Philip Henry Wodehouse.** [Title, 1st Baron **Currie of Hawley.**] b. at London, Oct. 13, 1834; d. at Hawley, England, May 12, 1906. English diplomat; husband of Lady Mary Montgomerie Currie. He joined (1854) the staff of the foreign office, where he became assistant undersecretary of state for foreign affairs (1882) and permanent undersecretary of state (1889). He served (1893–98) as British ambassador at Constantinople during a period of Turkish rioting and of war between Greece and Turkey. From 1898 to 1903 he was ambassador at Rome.

Currier (kur′i.ėr), **Nathaniel.** b. at Roxbury, Mass., March 27, 1813; d. at New York, Nov. 20, 1888. American publisher of prints and lithographs, and founder of the firm of Currier and Ives, which became "an American institution." He received the training that prepared him for his life work as an apprentice to John and William S. Pendelton, first at Boston and later, under John Pendelton, at Philadelphia and New York. Having served his apprenticeship, he went into business for himself and founded his firm at New York, in 1835. Fifteen years later he made James Merritt Ives (1824–95) a partner, and all the prints carried the name "Currier & Ives" after 1857. Currier retired in 1880, leaving his son to carry on with Ives. The firm was discontinued in 1907. The prints, the most famous of their kind, give a picture of American life, history, and character from 1835 until the end of the century. Sporting events, floods and fires, political campaigns, the Gold Rush in '49, the rise of railroads and of ships and the shipping industry, are presented vividly and strikingly, but not too artistically, the great value of the original prints as collectors' items being their comparative rarity. The volume *Currier & Ives, Printmakers to the American People* (1942), by Harry T. Peters, contains 192 plates, with 294 prints, 32 of them in full color.

Currier and Ives (īvz). American firm, publishers of lithographs. The firm dated from 1857, when Nathaniel Currier (1813–88), who had set up in business as a lithographer at New York in 1835, took into partnership the artist James Merritt Ives (1824–95), who had first found employment (c1850) with Currier as a bookkeeper but subsequently took charge of the art end of the business. Currier had already manifested great shrewdness in turning out relatively inexpensive lithographs dealing with current events and aspects of the American scene, which in those days before photography was much in use, and when newspapers carried few illustrations, were eagerly bought. Ives was equally alert in perceiving what subjects would find popular acceptance, and in addition to supplying drawings of his own for lithographic reproduction, he was a good judge of the work of other artists. After 1857 the name Currier & Ives appeared on all prints published by the firm. The increasing use of illustrations in newspapers and periodicals, which became even more widespread as photographic techniques improved, eventually dried up the market for such works as the Currier and Ives prints, the popularity of which during their time was, nevertheless, surpassed by their later fame. In the early decades of the 20th century the art of Currier and Ives was rediscovered, and their prints, showing scenes from American life, particularly rural life, hunting episodes, frontier battles and adventures, the clipper ships that carried the American flag around the world, early steamships, railroading as it developed with ever larger and more impressive locomotives, domestic scenes often inclining toward the sentimental, exciting views of horse races and trotting races, Biblical illustrations, and portraits of eminent 19th-century Americans, are justly considered to form an invaluable record of American life and progress in a great and crucial epoch. Original Currier and Ives prints, which originally sold for a few dollars, in later days have brought prices of hundreds or even thousands of dollars, and reproductions in book form, as separate prints, or as illustrations of calendars, have been circulated by the millions.

Curry (kur′i), **Arthur Mansfield.** b. at Chelsea, Mass., Jan. 27, 1866—. American musician. He studied violin with Franz Kneisel and composition with Edward MacDowell, became choral and orchestral conductor at Boston, and taught harmony at the New England Conservatory of Music. His compositions include the overtures *Blomidon* (1902) and *Elegie;* he has also composed songs and the symphonic poem *Atala* (1908).

Curry, Jabez Lamar Monroe. b. in Lincoln County, Ga., June 5, 1825; d. Feb. 12, 1903. American educator and statesman. A graduate of the University of Georgia, he won a law degree at Harvard in 1845. He was a member (1847, 1853, and 1855) of the Alabama legislature, and served (1857–61) in Congress. After service (1861–63, 1864) in the Confederate Congress, he was in the Confederate army (1864–65). He was minister (1885–88) and ambassador extraordinary (1902) of the U.S. to Spain. He was president (1865–68) of Howard College, Alabama, and professor (1868–81) of English at Richmond College (now the University of Richmond). As administrator (1888 *et seq.*) of the George Peabody Fund, agent (1890 *et seq.*) of the Slater Fund, and president (1899 *et seq.*) of the Southern Educational Board, he established, both for Negroes and whites, normal schools in 12 Southern states and graded public schools in many parts of the South.

Curry, John Steuart. b. at Dunavant, Kan., Nov. 14, 1897; d. at Madison, Wis., Aug. 29, 1946. American painter prominent in the tradition called "American Scene" painting, best known for pictures of the violent weather and rugged life in Kansas farming country. He studied at the Kansas City Art Institute and the Art Institute of Chicago, and became an illustrator for western-story magazines. After a year of study at Paris, with the help of Gertrude Vanderbilt Whitney he established a studio at Westport, Conn., where such paintings as *Baptism in Kansas* (1928), *Tornado Over Kansas* (1930; second prize, Carnegie International, 1933), and *Line Storm* (1934) were painted from memory. Appointed (1936) artist in residence at the University of Wisconsin College of Agriculture, he remained there until his death. He was the painter also of *Circus Elephants* (1932) and other circus pictures. His mural commissions include the Department of Justice and Department of Interior buildings at Washington, D.C., and the Kansas state capitol at Topeka, part of which is his panel *John Brown.* He is represented in the Metropolitan Museum of Art and the Whitney Museum of American Art, both at New York, the Addison Gallery of American Art, at Andover, Mass., the St. Louis Museum, and elsewhere. He became (1943) an academician of the National Academy of Design.

Cursa (kėr′sa̤). The third-magnitude star β Eridani. It is the star situated in the constellation at the beginning of the river (Eridanus), near Orion.

Curse of Kehama (kē.hä′ma̤), **The.** Poem by Robert Southey, first published in 1810. The theme is the curse of a charmed life, but without food or water, pronounced by Kehama on Ladurlad. Hindu mythology and folklore form the background.

Cursor (kėr′so̤r), **Lucius Papirius.** See **Papirius Cursor, Lucius.**

Cursor Mundi (kėr′so̤r mun′dī). Poem, in the northern Middle English dialect, written c1320, and founded on Caedmon's paraphrase of Genesis. It relates, in some 24,000 lines, the course of the world from the creation to doomsday. The whole poem was printed by the Early English Text Society (ed. by Richard Morris).

Curtain, The. London playhouse established in Shoreditch in 1576. It is thought that Shakespeare acted here in his own plays as a member of the Chamberlain's company. It remained open until the accession (1625) of Charles I, after which the drama gave way to exhibitions of athletic feats. It is said that it was called The Curtain because here the green curtain was first used; in 1678 Aubrey calls it "The Green Curtain."

Curtana (kėr.tā′na̤). [Also: **Courtain, Curtein** (kėr-tān′).] Name originally given to the sword of Roland (later Durandal), of which, according to the tradition, the point was broken off in testing it. The name is also given to the pointless sword (also called the sword of Edward the Confessor) carried before the kings of England at their coronation, and emblematically considered as the sword of mercy.

Curtatone (kōr.tä.tō′nā). Town and commune in N Italy, in the *compartimento* (region) of Lombardy, in the province of Mantua, situated on the Mincio River ab. 4 mi. W of Mantua. Here, in 1848, the Austrians under Radetzky defeated the Italians. Pop. of commune, 9,585 (1936); of town, 495 (1936).

Curtea-de-Argeş (kör′tyä.dā.är′jesh). Town in S central Rumania, ab. 96 mi. by rail NW of Bucharest. It is located on the E side of the Argeş River, in the S foothills of the Transylvanian Alps. The town was founded near the beginning of the 14th century as the capital of the Walachian princes. It has notable historical monuments, including a 14th-century church, a cathedral, and the old palace. In 1793 Curtea-de-Argeş was made the seat of a bishopric. 9,180 (1948).

Curtin (kėr′tin), **Andrew Gregg.** b. at Bellefonte, Pa., April 23, 1815; d. Oct. 7, 1894. American politician. He became a power in Pennsylvania politics, and in 1860 was nominated for the governorship in order to make sure that Pennsylvania would go to Lincoln, just as Henry S. Lane was to bring Indiana into the Lincoln camp. He was elected in 1860 and again in 1863, serving until 1867. After he lost the Republican vice-presidential nomination to Schuyler Colfax in 1868, he served (1869–72) in Russia as U.S. minister. On his return (1872) he threw his support in the presidential campaign to Horace Greeley, and against Grant, thus angering his political friends, and in the end he became a Democrat, being elected to Congress in 1880 and serving until 1887.

Curtin, Jeremiah. b. at Milwaukee, Wis., Sept. 6, c1840; d. Dec. 14, 1906. American ethnologist and writer, assistant ethnologist of the U.S. Bureau of Ethnology from 1883. From 1865 to 1870 he was secretary of the U.S. legation at St. Petersburg, and was (1865–66) acting consul general there. He published several translations of Polish and Russian fiction. One of the great linguists and folklorists of his time, Curtin published works on the American Indian, the Mongolians, the Celts, and the Slavs, and their several mythologies and folk tales. He is said to have known 70 languages.

Curtin, John. b. at Creswick, Victoria, Australia, Jan. 8, 1885; d. at Canberra, Australia, July 5, 1945. Australian journalist and political leader. He was prime minister (1941–45) of Australia during World War II. He was an astute parliamentarian who enjoyed the respect of opponents both in and out of the labor movement. At an early age he engaged in radical politics and journalism, influenced by the views of the English labor leader Tom Mann. He served as secretary (1911–15) of the Victoria Timber Workers' Union. He was an anticonscriptionist in World War I, then editor (1917–28) of the *Westralian Worker*, and later Labour member (1928–31 and 1934–45) of the federal house of representatives. He opposed the so-called conservative policies of the Scullin government, was leader (1935–41) of the opposition (Labour), and became (1941) prime minister and minister of defense.

Curtis (kėr′tis). Character in Shakespeare's comedy *The Taming of the Shrew*. This part was originally described in the dramatis personae as a serving-man, but it is now played as an old woman, the housekeeper of Petruchio.

Curtis, Benjamin Robbins. b. at Watertown, Mass., Nov. 4, 1809; d. at Newport, R.I., Sept. 15, 1874. American jurist, associate justice of the U.S. Supreme Court (1851–57); brother of George Ticknor Curtis. He wrote (1857) a dissenting opinion to Taney's Dred Scott decision, and served (1868) as Andrew Johnson's chief counsel at his impeachment trial, retiring thereafter from public life. He published *Reports of Cases in the Circuit Courts of the U.S.* (1854), *Decisions of the Supreme Court, Digest of the Decisions of the Supreme Court* (to 1854), and others.

Curtis, Charles. b. at North Topeka, Kan., Jan. 25, 1860; d. at Washington, D.C., Feb. 8, 1936. American statesman, 31st Vice-president (1929–33) of the United States, elected (1928) on the Republican ticket with Herbert Hoover. After admission (1881) to the bar he began law practice at Topeka, Kan., served as county attorney from 1884 to 1888, and was representative (1893–1909) to the U.S. Congress and senator (1907–13, 1915–29) from Kansas.

Curtis, Charles Gordon. b. at Boston, 1860; d. March 10, 1953. American inventor. He devised the Curtis steam turbine, selling the rights to the General Electric Company. He was graduated from Columbia (C.E., 1881) and from the New York Law School (1883), and for several years practiced as a patent lawyer. He founded the C. and C. Electric Motor Company, the first manufacturers of electric motors and electric fans.

Curtis, Cyrus Hermann Kotzschmar. b. at Portland, Me., June 18, 1850; d. at Wyncote, Pa., June 7, 1933. American publisher. Moving (1876) to Philadelphia from Boston, he founded the periodical *Tribune and Farmer*, predecessor of the *Ladies' Home Journal* (1883 *et seq.*), and established (1890) the Curtis Publishing Company, which purchased the *Saturday Evening Post* (1897) and the *Country Gentleman* (1911). When Curtis bought the *Post* its circulation was only about 2,000 copies; by 1933 it had a circulation, due to Curtis's happy choice of George Horace Lorimer as editor, of nearly two and three-quarters million copies. He remained head of the company until succeeded by Edward William Bok, his son-in-law. He acquired the Philadelphia *Public Ledger* (1913), the Philadelphia *Press* (1920), the New York *Evening Post* (1924), and the Philadelphia *Inquirer* (1930). He was noted for his philanthropies.

Curtis, George Carroll. b. at Abington, Mass., July 15, 1872; d. Feb. 2, 1926. American geographer and sculptor of topographical maps. He graduated (1896) from Harvard and did (1895–98) graduate study there in physiography and geographic modeling. His model of metropolitan Boston won (1900) the gold medal at Paris as the first example of applied aerial perspective to relief maps; his model (1902) of Washington, D.C., was the first city model based on a photographic survey. He made (1923–25) landscape paintings in relief of Yosemite, Niagara, and the Grand Canyon. As representative of the National Geographic Society on the Dixie expedition to the West Indies, he was first to reach the crater of La Soufrière, and discovered the new summit of Mount Pelée.

Curtis, George Ticknor. b. at Watertown, Mass., Nov. 28, 1812; d. at New York, March 28, 1894. American lawyer and legal writer; brother of Benjamin Robbins Curtis. He argued the case of Dred Scott, Negro slave, before the Supreme Court. His works include *The Law of Copyright* (1847), *The Law of Patents* (1849; 4th ed., 1873), *A History of the Origin, Formation, and Adoption of the Constitution of the United States* (1854–58), *Life of Daniel Webster* (1870), *Last Years of Daniel Webster* (1878), *Life of James Buchanan* (1883), and *Constitutional History of the United States from their Declaration of Independence to the Close of the Civil War* (2 vols., 1889, 1896, the latter ed. by J. C. Clayton).

Curtis, George William. b. at Providence, R.I., Feb. 24, 1824; d. on Staten Island, N.Y., Aug. 31, 1892. American journalist, orator, publicist, and author. He lived in the community at Brook Farm, remaining there 18 months, and traveled abroad (1846–50). On his return in the latter year he became connected with the New York *Tribune*, was subsequently associated (1852–57) with *Putnam's Monthly*, and became editor of the "Easy Chair" in *Harper's Magazine* in 1854, and in 1863 of *Harper's Weekly*. He was an influential advocate of civil-service reform. In 1871 he was appointed by Grant one of the commissioners to draw up rules for the regulation of the civil service, but resigned because of differences with the President. He was president of the New York State Civil Service League in 1880, and of the National Civil Service Reform League from its foundation until his death. Curtis was also an influential member of the woman's suffrage reform movement. He wrote *Nile Notes of a Howadji* (1851), *Howadji in Syria* (1852), *Lotus-Eating* (1852), *Potiphar Papers* (1853), *Prue and I* (1856), *Trumps* (186?), *From the Easy Chair* (1891), and *Washington Irving* (1891).

Curtis, Heber Doust. b. at Muskegon, Mich., June 27, 1872; d. Jan. 8, 1942. American scientist, astronomer of the Lick Observatory from 1909. He was a member of the U.S. Naval Observatory eclipse expedition to Sumatra in 1901, and was acting astronomer in charge of the Mills expedition (1906–09) to the Southern Hemisphere. He directed the Allegheny Observatory at the University of Pittsburgh (1920–30) and the observatories at the University of Michigan (1930 *et seq.*).

Curtis, Natalie. Maiden name of **Burlin, Natalie.**

Curtis Jadwin (jad′win). See **Jadwin, Curtis.**

Curtiss (kėr′tis), **Glenn Hammond.** b. at Hammondsport, N.Y., May 21, 1878; d. at Buffalo, N.Y., July 23,

1930. American aviator and aeronautical inventor. He was director of experiments of the Aërial Experiment Association founded by Alexander Graham Bell. On July 4, 1908, he won (in an airplane) the prize offered by the *Scientific American* for the first flight of one kilometer (record, 1¼ mi. in 1 min. 42 2/5 sec.). On July 17, 1909, he made a second record for the *Scientific American* trophy (24.7 mi. in 52 min. 30 sec.). At Reims, France, on Aug. 28, 1909, he won (in a biplane) the Gordon Bennett international aviation cup, flying 20 kilometers (12.42 mi.) in 15 min. 50 3/5 sec. On Sept. 12, 1909, at Brescia, Italy, he won the grand prize, making a flight of 31.05 mi. in 49 min. 24 sec. On May 29, 1910, he flew from Albany to New York (137 mi.) in 2 hrs. 32 min. He opened (1909) the first flying school in the U.S. He invented (1912) the flying boat and built two years later the first heavier-than-air craft intended for transatlantic flight. During World War I he produced over 5,000 of his planes (known as "Jennies") for military use, and later developed the "Wasp," in its day one of the world's speediest small planes. A Curtiss-built seaplane, the *NC-4*, was the first to fly (1919) the Atlantic.

Curtius (kůr'tsē̦.ůs), **Ernst.** b. at Lübeck, Germany, Sept. 2, 1814; d. at Berlin, July 11, 1896. German archaeologist and historian, professor (1844, 1863 *et seq.*) at the University of Berlin; brother of Georg Curtius. Curtius was responsible for the agreement whereby the important excavations at Olympia, Greece (1875–81), were to be done exclusively by the Germans. His works include *Peloponnesos, eine historisch-geographische Beschreibung der Halbinsel* (1851–52), *Die Ionier vor der ionischen Wanderung* (1855), *Griechische Geschichte* (1857–67; Eng. trans. by A. W. Ward, 1868–73), *Attische Studien* (1863–64), and others.

Curtius, Ernst Robert. b. at Thann, in Alsace, April 14, 1886—. German historian of literature and professor (1929 *et seq.*) of Romance philology at Bonn. He is a widely read interpreter of modern French literature and civilization through such books as *Die literarischen Wegbereiter des neuen Frankreichs* (1919), *Maurice Barrès und die geistigen Grundlagen des französischen Nationalismus* (1921), *Balzac* (1923), *Französischer Geist im neuen Europa* (1925), which contains a highly regarded study of Proust, and *Einführung in die französische Kultur* (1930). In his studies, *James Joyce* (1929) and especially *Deutscher Geist in Gefahr* (1932), Curtius took a stand on controversial matters which made it necessary for him to keep silent during the period of the Third Reich. In the course of these years he produced *Europäische Literatur und lateinisches Mittelalter* (1948), and encyclopedic work on the continued influence of medieval Latin rhetoric in European letters up to the 18th century. The work was included in the publications of the American Bollingen Foundation.

Curtius, Georg. b. at Lübeck, Germany, April 16, 1820; d. at Hermsdorf, Germany, Aug. 12, 1885. German philologist; brother of Ernst Curtius (1814–96). He was professor of classical philology (1862 *et seq.*) at Leipzig after occupying posts at Prague and Kiel. He wrote *Griechische Schulgrammatik* (1852), *Grundzüge der griechischen Etymologie* (1858–62), and others.

Curtius, Julius. b. at Duisburg, Germany, Feb. 7, 1877; d. at Heidelberg, Germany, Nov. 12, 1948. German politician of the Weimar republic. He was German People's Party member (1920 *et seq.*) of the Reichstag, minister of economics (1926), and minister of foreign affairs (1929–31). A follower of Gustav Stresemann's policies, he resigned in 1931 because French opposition brought about the failure of an economic agreement with Austria.

Curtius (kėr'shi.us, -shus), **Marcus.** fl. 4th century B.C. Roman legendary hero. In 362 B.C., a chasm having been formed in the Forum by an earthquake, the soothsayers announced that it could be closed only by the sacrifice of Rome's greatest treasure. The people were at a loss to interpret the oracle when Marcus Curtius, a noble youth, stepped forward and, declaring that the state possessed no greater treasure than a brave citizen in arms, leaped, mounted on his steed and in full armor, into the chasm, which closed after him. The Forum stood where a marsh, the Lacus Curtius, formerly existed, and this is simply one of three legends intended to explain the name, the others being that Mettius Curtius, a Sabine, fell here before Romulus's pursuit, and that Gaius Curtius was consul when lightning struck here to make the spot sacred.

Curtius (kůr'tsē.ůs), **Theodor.** b. at Duisberg, Germany, 1857; d. at Heidelberg, Germany, 1928. German organic chemist. He was professor at Kiel (1889), Bonn (1897), and Heidelberg (1898–1926). He did important work on compounds containing directly linked nitrogens. His work includes the discoveries of hydrazine, diazoacetic ester, hydrazoic acid, and the Curtius rearrangement of acid azides to isocyanates.

Curtius Rufus (kėr'shi.us, -shus, rö'fus), **Quintus.** fl. c50 A.D. Roman historian of the time of Claudius. He was the author of a history of Alexander the Great in ten books. Curtius was probably the first Roman historian to deal with an entirely foreign subject.

Curupira (kö.rö.pē'rä). Mythological being, originally pertaining to the cultures of the various Tupí tribes of Brazil, but now also to the rural populations of Indian or mixed Indian-Portuguese descent. Curupira is conceived as a dwarfish man with upturned feet, who protects game and aids humans who help him but punishes those who are rude to him.

Curuzú Cuatiá (kö.rö.sö' kwä.tyä'). City in E Argentina, in Corrientes province, ab. 335 mi. N of Buenos Aires. 15,440 (1947).

Curvetto (kėr.vet'ō). Old libertine, affecting youth, in Thomas Middleton's play *Blurt, Master Constable.* He is the butt of many practical jokes.

Curwen (kėr'wẹn), **John.** b. at Heckmondwike, Yorkshire, England, Nov. 14, 1816; d. at Manchester, England, May 26, 1880. English educator, founder of singing instruction according to Sarah Ann Glover's tonic sol-fa system. He established (1863) the music-publishing firm of Curwen and Sons, Limited, and founded the Tonic Sol-fa Association (1853) and the Tonic Sol-fa College (1879).

Curwen, John Spencer. b. at Plaistow, England, Sept. 30, 1847; d. at London, Aug. 6, 1916. English music teacher; son of John Curwen. He was head (1880 *et seq.*) of the Tonic Sol-fa College. He established (1882) the Stratford Festival to foster the existence of such competitive festival.

Curwensville (kėr'wẹnz.vil). Borough in W Pennsylvania, in Clearfield County, at the confluence of Anderson Creek and the West Branch River. Manufactures include fire brick and other clay products, leather, stone products, shirts, and hosiery. It was settled in 1812. Pop. 3,332 (1950).

Curwood (kėr'wůd), **James Oliver.** b. at Owosso, Mich., June 12, 1878; d. there, Aug. 13, 1927. American novelist, author of popular adventure stories set in the Northwest. Among his works are *The Courage of Captain Plum* (1908), *Kazan* (1914), *God's Country and the Woman* (1915), *The Grizzly King* (1916), *Nomads of the North* (1919), *The River's End* (1919), *The Valley of Silent Men* (1920), *A Gentleman of Courage* (1924), and *The Black Hunter* (1926).

Curytiba (kö.rē.tē'bạ). A former spelling of **Curitiba.**

Curzola (kör.tsō'lä). Italian name of **Korčula.**

Curzon (kėr'zọn), **George Nathaniel.** [Titles: 1st Baron **Curzon of Kedleston,** 1st Marquess **Curzon of Kedleston.**] b. at Kedleston, Derbyshire, England, Jan. 11, 1859; d. at London, March 20, 1925. English statesman and publicist. He was undersecretary of state for India (1891–92) and undersecretary for foreign affairs (1895–98). From 1898 to 1905 he was viceroy of India, pacifying the Northwest Frontier and reforming the administration, but he resigned as the result of a disagreement with the army commander, H. H. Kitchener. He was created Baron Curzon of Kedleston (1898), earl (1911), and marquess (1921). He was a member of the war cabinet and afterwards secretary of state (1919–24) in charge of foreign affairs. He was a proponent of the idea of easing the reparations burden on Germany. From 1916 to 1924 he headed the House of Lords. He wrote *Russia in Central Asia* (1889), *Persia and the Persian Question* (1892), *Problems of the Far East* (1894), *Lord Curzon in India* (1906), *Frontiers* (1908), and *Principles and Methods of University Reform* (1909). In 1908 he was elected a member of the British Academy.

Cusa (kū'zạ), **Alexander John.** See **Alexander John I** (of *Rumania*).

Cusa, Nicholas of. See **Nicholas of Cusa.**

Cuscatlán (kös.kä.tlän′). Department in C El Salvador: largely an agricultural mountain area. Formed in 1835, it later lost most of its area to the departments of Chalatenango (1855) and Cabañas (1875). Capital, Cojutepeque; area, 672 sq. mi.; pop. 106,079 (est. 1942).

Cusco or **Cuzco** (kös′kō). Department in S Peru. Capital, Cusco; area, 55,731 sq. mi.; pop. 672,383 (est. 1950).

Cusco or **Cuzco.** City in S Peru, capital of Cusco department, at an altitude ab. 11,380 ft. above sea level: seat of a cathedral and a university. It was founded, according to tradition, by Manco Capac in the 11th century, was the capital of the empire of the Incas, and was noted for its Temple of the Sun and the so-called fortress of the Incas. It had other temples, palaces, and schools for the youth of the nobility. Streets were paved and met at right angles. There were five or six squares where great public ceremonials were held. The inhabitants probably numbered ab. 200,000. The city was entered by Pizarro on Nov. 15, 1533, and was besieged and partly burned (1536) by Manco Capac Inca (often called Manco to distinguish him from the legendary founder of the Inca empire). 55,634 (est. 1950).

Cush (kush). [Also, **Kush.**] In the Old Testament, a geographical and ethnographical term usually rendered as Ethiopia in the Vulgate and Septuagint. Cush corresponded probably to Upper Egypt and N Nubia (now in the Anglo-Egyptian Sudan), including, perhaps, part of the modern Ethiopia and S Arabia. Some modern scholars believe that some of the references translated as Ethiopia refer to an area (Arabian Cush) in S and W Arabia.

Cush. [Also, **Kush.**] In the Old Testament, the eldest son of Ham.

Cushendun (kůsh′e̦n.de̦n), 1st Baron. [Title of **Ronald John McNeill.**] b. at Torquay, Devonshire, England, April 30, 1861; d. at Cushendun, County Antrim, Ireland, Oct. 12, 1934. Irish editor, politician, and author, known (he was taller than six feet six inches) as "Ulster's giant Irish peer." A graduate of Oxford, he was admitted (1888) to Lincoln's Inn. He edited (1900–04) the *St. James Gazette*, and was assistant editor (1906–11) of the eleventh edition of the *Encyclopaedia Britannica*. He served (1911–27) in the House of Commons, as parliamentary undersecretary for foreign affairs (1922–24 and 1925), financial secretary to the treasury (1925–27) chancellor of the duchy of Lancaster (1927–29), and acting secretary of state for foreign affairs (1928). Cushendun signed, in place of Austen Chamberlain, who was ill the Briand-Kellogg peace pact in August, 1928. His books include *Home Rule: its History and Danger* (1907) and *Ulster's Stand for Union* (1922).

Cushing (kůsh′ing). City in N Oklahoma, in Payne County, in an oil-producing, farming, and livestock-raising district: supply and market center. It has several oil refineries. 8,414 (1950).

Cushing, Caleb. b. at Salisbury, Mass., Jan. 17, 1800; d. at Newburyport, Mass., Jan. 2, 1879. American jurist, politician, and diplomat. He was a member of Congress (1835–43) from Massachusetts, and went to China to negotiate (1843–44) a treaty to open certain Chinese ports to American commerce. During the Mexican War he served (1847) as a colonel and a brigadier general, having organized a regiment at his own expense. He was attorney general (1853–57) under Pierce, who owed his nomination in great part to Cushing's activity at the Democratic national convention in 1852. In 1860 he supported Breckenridge rather than Douglas and, when the South seceded, he switched his political loyalties to the Republican Party. After the Civil War he was sent to Geneva, where he acted (1871–72) as U.S. counsel before the Alabama Claims Commission assembled to arbitrate the demand of the U.S. government for damages from Great Britain arising from the activities of the British-built Confederate raider *Alabama*. From 1874 to 1877 he was U.S. minister to Spain, after having been nominated as chief justice of the Supreme Court on the death of Salmon Chase. He withdrew his name from consideration when the nomination aroused a partisan political storm.

Cushing, Frank Hamilton. b. at Northeast, Pa., July 22, 1857; d. at Washington, D.C., April 10, 1900. American ethnologist, especially noted for his studies of the Zuñi Indians. He published *Zuñi Fetiches* (1883), *Adventures in Zuñi* (1883), *Zuñi Folk-tales* (1901), and others.

Cushing, Harvey (Williams). b. at Cleveland, Ohio, April 8, 1869; d. at New Haven, Conn., Oct. 7, 1939. American surgeon, known for his development of new techniques in brain surgery. He was graduated at Yale University in 1891 and took the degree of doctor of medicine at Harvard in 1895. He was associate professor of surgery at the Johns Hopkins University (1903–11) and professor of surgery at Harvard (1911 *et seq.*). He gave special attention to neurological and experimental surgery. He published *The Pituitary Body and its Disorders* (1912), *Life of Sir William Osler* (1925), which was awarded the Pulitzer prize, *From a Surgeon's Journal, 1915–1918* (1938), and others.

Cushing, Luther Stearns. b. at Lunenburg, Mass., June 22, 1803; d. at Boston, June 22, 1856. American lawyer and writer on legal subjects. His best-known works are *A Manual of Parliamentary Practice: Rules of Proceeding and Debate in Deliberative Assemblies* (1844; known as "Cushing's Manual") and *Elements of the Law and Practice of Legislative Assemblies in the United States* (1856).

Cushing, Thomas. b. at Boston, March 24, 1725; d. Feb. 28, 1788. American politician, speaker of the Massachusetts House of Representatives (1763) and lieutenant governor of Massachusetts (1779–88).

Cushing, William. b. at Scituate, Mass., March 1, 1732; d. there, Sept. 13, 1810. American jurist, appointed associate justice of the U.S. Supreme Court in 1789.

Cushing, William Barker. b. in Wisconsin, Nov. 4, 1842; d. at Washington, D.C., Dec. 17, 1874. American naval officer in the Civil War. He was noted for his exploit in blowing up the Confederate ironclad ram *Albemarle* at Plymouth, N.C., on the night of Oct. 27, 1864.

Cushites (kush′īts). Descendants of Cush, the first son of Ham, according to Genesis. They were made up of five principal peoples, the Seba, Havilah, Sabtah, Raamah, and Sabteca. The last four were located in south and central Arabia while the Seba, it is believed, inhabited the neighboring coast of Africa. Although names and places concerning these people are vague and confused, it seems probable that there was an Eastern and African group, in what is now Ethiopia, answering to this name. Modern inhabitants of Ethiopia, Eritrea, and Somaliland speak Cushitic languages.

Cushitic (kush.it′ik). Group of related languages of NE Africa, spoken by peoples inhabiting the "east horn" area, including Ethiopia, Eritrea, French Somaliland, Italian Somaliland, NE Kenya, NE Anglo-Egyptian Sudan, and SE Egypt. Cushitic and Berber are the two subgroups of Hamitic. Cushitic includes such languages as those of the Somali, Galla, Danakil, Amarar, Abadba, Bisharin, and Hadendowa.

Cushman (kůsh′ma̦n), **Allerton Seward.** b. at Rome, June 2, 1867; d. May 1, 1930. American chemist whose principal researches were concerned with the extraction of potash from feldspathic rocks, the use of ground rock as fertilizer, the properties of road materials, and the cause and prevention of rust on iron and steel. Graduated from Worcester Polytechnic Institute (1888) and from Harvard (Ph.D., 1897), he was chemist (1902–10) in charge of investigations for the U.S. Department of Agriculture and founder (1910) and director (1910–24) of the Institute of Industrial Research at Washington. He was the author of *The Corrosion and Preservation of Iron and Steel* (1910) and *Chemistry and Civilization* (1920).

Cushman, Charlotte Saunders. b. at Boston, July 23, 1816; d. there, Feb. 17, 1876. American actress. Originally trained for the opera, she abandoned it (c1835) for the legitimate stage, scoring her first dramatic success (1837) at New York, where she played the role of Nancy Sykes in *Oliver Twist*. She was stage manager (1842–44) of the Walnut Street Theatre at Philadelphia. She enjoyed English acclaim (c1845–49) and, returning with the repute won on the London stage, toured (1849–52) America before announcing her farewell to the theater. This was the first of several announced retirements. She later lived in England and at Rome. Returning to the U.S. in 1870, she engaged in stage appearances and in public readings of plays. Her last performance was given (June 2, 1875) at Easton, Pa. Among her best-known roles were Lady Macbeth and that of Meg Merrilies in *Guy Mannering.*

Cushman, Pauline. b. at New Orleans, June 10, 1835; d. at San Francisco, Dec. 2, 1893. American actress, and intelligence agent for the Union army during the Civil War. The daughter of a Spanish political refugee and of a Frenchwoman, she was brought up at Grand Rapids, Mich., but in her 18th year went to New York and quickly won a measure of success on the stage. A few years later she joined a troupe performing in her native city of New Orleans, and married a member of the company, Charles Dickinson, who during the Civil War enlisted in the Union forces as a musician, and died of illness while in service. Having been constrained, while playing at Nashville, to pretend a sympathy with the Southern cause which she did not feel, she determined to make patriotic use of the friendly regard in which, because of this incident, she was held by adherents of the Confederacy. Her offer to undertake intelligence work for the Union army was accepted, and to confirm belief in her Southern sympathies, she was ordered to leave Nashville, and had no difficulty in passing through the Confederate lines. Her secret instructions included a warning never to carry papers on her person, but the ease with which she could obtain military maps led her to disobey this order, and she was apprehended with such documents on her person, tried as a spy by a court-martial of General Bragg's army, and sentenced to be hanged. Pending the date set for her execution she was committed to a hospital, and when a few days later Bragg found it wise to leave Shelbyville, Tenn., in great haste, she was left behind. Rescued by the Union forces, she gave them useful information concerning Bragg's plans and his army's strength, but it was impossible for her any longer to operate in Confederate territory. Thereafter for some years she lectured in the North, billed as "The Spy of the Cumberland," and wearing a Union army uniform. Her later years were years of misfortune and unhappiness, and she died by her own hand. The Grand Army of the Republic gave her a funeral with military ceremonies.

Cushman, Robert. b. in England, c1580; d. there, 1625. English merchant, one of the founders of the Plymouth colony in America.

Cushny (kush'ni), **Arthur Robertson.** b. at Moray, Scotland, 1866; d. 1926. Scottish physician and pharmacologist. His career was international, in that he came to the U.S. and held a professorial chair at the University of Michigan (1893–1905), but returned to Great Britain, where he taught at the University of London (1905–18) and at the University of Aberdeen (1918–25). He was a specialist in urological, optical, and cardiac problems, and was especially known for his important studies of the effects of digitalis on the heart.

Cusins (kū'zinz), Sir **William George.** b. at London, Oct. 14, 1833; d. at Remonchamps, France, Aug. 31, 1893. English conductor and composer. He was conductor (1867–83) of the London Philharmonic Society. His works include the *Royal Wedding Serenata* (1863), the oratorio *Gideon* (1871), overtures, a piano concerto, and small pieces.

Cusio (kö'zyō), **Lago.** An Italian name of **Orta, Lake.**

Cusis (kū'sis). Fabulous country in Sir John Mandeville's *Voiage and Travaile.* The people of this country have but one foot, so large that it casts a shadow over the whole body, and with this one foot they make wonderful speed.

Cust (kust), Sir **Edward.** b. at London, March 17, 1794; d. there, Jan. 14, 1878. English soldier and military historian; grandson of Sir John Cust (1718–70). He served in the Peninsular War, and was appointed equerry (1816) to Prince Leopold of Saxe-Coburg, made master of ceremonies to Queen Victoria (1847), commissioned general (1866), and created baronet (1876) on retirement from the queen's service. He was the author of *Annals of the Wars of the Eighteenth Century* and *Lives of the Warriors of the Thirty Years' War.*

Cust, Henry John Cockayne. b. at London, Oct. 10, 1861; d. there, March 2, 1917. English editor, politician, and poet; nephew of Robert Needham Cust. Educated at Eton and at Trinity College, Cambridge, he was Conservative member of Parliament for Stamford (1890–95) and for Bermondsey (1900–06). He was also editor (1892–96) of the *Pall Mall Gazette*, and cofounder (August, 1914) with George W. Prothero of the Central Committee for National Patriotic Organizations, of which he was chairman; he is honored at Nottingham University by an annual Cust lectureship. His volume *Occasional Poems* was published at Jerusalem in 1918.

Cust, Sir **John.** b. at Westminster (now part of London), Aug. 29, 1718; d. at London, Jan. 24, 1770. British politician; grandfather of Sir Edward Cust (1794–1878). He was speaker of the House of Commons (1761, 1768–70) and privy councilor (1762).

Cust, Robert Needham. b. at Cockayne-Hatley, Bedfordshire, England, 1821; d. at London, Oct. 28, 1909. English Orientalist and Africanist; nephew of Sir Edward Cust. He entered the civil service of India in 1843 and retired in 1869. After that date he resided at London. His principal works are *Sketch of the Modern Languages of the East Indies* (1878), *Linguistic and Oriental Essays* (1880–91), *Sketch of the Modern Languages of Africa* (1883), *Notes on Missionary Subjects* (1887), and *Africa Rediviva* (1891).

Custance (kus'tạns), **Dame Christian.** See **Constance** (or **Custance**), **Dame Christian.**

Custer (kus'tėr), **Elizabeth Bacon.** b. at Monroe, Mich., 1843; d. April 4, 1933. American writer; wife of George Armstrong Custer, whom she accompanied on many campaigns. She was the author of *Boots and Saddles, or Life in Dakota with General Custer* (1885), *Tenting on the Plains* (1887), and *Following the Guidon* (1891).

Custer, George Armstrong. b. at New Rumley, Ohio, Dec. 5, 1839; d. near what is now Little Bighorn, Mont., June 25, 1876. American soldier, leader of frontier expeditions against the Indians, remembered for "Custer's Last Stand." Graduated (1861) from West Point, he achieved a distinguished record of service in the Union army during the Civil War. The Confederate flag of truce was delivered to him shortly before the surrender of the Southern forces. Brevetted (April 15, 1865) a major general of volunteers, he was returned to his regular rank of captain in 1866. Later in the same year, he was made a colonel and given the command (which he did not actively assume until 1876) of the 7th Cavalry. The interim years were spent chiefly in campaigns against the Indians. His death came in an action against a large force of Indians atop the slope of what is now known as Custer Hill after he had started (May 17, 1876) on an expedition to pacify the Sioux and Cheyennes. Everyone who was with him on the hill was killed. Critics have maintained that he was guilty of reckless behavior, while others have pointed out that he was only exercising his rightful command. He was the author of *My Life on the Plains* (1874), also known under its later title of *Wild Life on the Plains.*

Custer Battlefield National Monument. Site in SE Montana, ab. 65 mi. by road E of Billings, where George Armstrong Custer and 263 men were massacred in a battle with the Sioux and Cheyenne Indians on June 25, 1876. This was the last major Indian victory in the U.S. A national cemetery was established here in 1886, and in 1946 the area of the battle along the Little Bighorn River was made a national monument. Area, ab. 1.2 sq. mi.

Custine (küs.tēn), **Adam Philippe,** Comte **de.** b. at Metz, France, Feb. 4, 1740; guillotined at Paris, Aug. 28, 1793. French soldier. He fought under Soubise in the Seven Years' War, and was quartermaster general (1778–83) of the French forces in America, being present at the surrender of Yorktown (1781). He was deputed to the States-General in 1789 and in 1792 was appointed to the command of an army. He took Speyer (Sept. 29, 1792) and Mainz (Oct. 21, 1792), but failing in the campaign of 1793 to relieve Mainz, which had been recaptured by the forces of the alliance against France, he was executed on the charge of conspiring to effect a counter-revolution.

Custine, Astolphe, Marquis **de.** b. at Niederwiller, Meurthe-et-Moselle, France, March 18, 1790; d. near Pau, France, Sept. 29, 1857. French writer and traveler; grandson of Adam Philippe de Custine. He wrote *Mémoires et voyages* (1830) and *La Russie en 1839* (1843). The latter work, in an English translation, was published in 1950 as *Journey for Our Time.*

Custis (kus'tis), **George Washington Parke.** b. at Mount Airy, Md., April 30, 1781; d. at Arlington House,

Fairfax County, Virginia, Oct. 10, 1857. American playwright; grandson of George Washington's wife, Martha, through a son born of her first marriage. When the son, John Parke Custis, died in 1781, Washington adopted G. W. P. Custis and his sister Eleanor P. Custis as his own children.

Custom of the Country, The. Play by Fletcher and Massinger, produced before 1628 and printed in 1647. It is partly from a story of Cervantes and partly from a story in Cinthio's *Hecatommithi. Love makes a Man,* by Cibber, and *Country Lasses,* by Charles Johnson, were partly taken from it.

Custom of the Country, The. Play by Susannah Centlivre produced in 1715. It was originally a farce called *A Bickerstaff's Burial,* said, doubtfully, to be founded on one of Sinbad's voyages.

Custom of the Country, The. Novel by Edith Wharton, published in 1913.

Custozza (kös.tôd'dzä). [Also, **Custoza** (-tô'dzä).] Village in N Italy, in the *compartimento* (region) of Veneto, in the province of Verona, ab. 11 mi. SW of Verona. It was the scene of two battles: **1.** On July 25, 1848, the Austrians (ab. 33,000) under Radetzky defeated the Sardinians (ab. 25,000) under King Charles Albert. **2.** On June 24, 1866, the Austrians (ab. 75,000) under the archduke Albert defeated the Italians (ab. 130,000) under Victor Emmanuel.

Cüstrin (küs.trēn'). See **Kostrzyn.**

Cut Bank. Town in NW Montana, county seat of Glacier County, ab. 180 mi. N of Butte, in an oil and natural gas area. Part of the Blackfeet Indian Reservation adjoins the town. 3,721 (1950).

Cutch (kuch). See **Kutch.**

Cuthah (kū'thạ). [Also, **Cuth** (kuth).] In Biblical geography, a city in Babylonia from which Shalmaneser IV (727–722 B.C.) brought colonists into Samaria (2 Kings, xvii. 24). These Cutheans, mingling with other peoples, became the progenitors of the Samaritans. In the cuneiform inscriptions the city is often mentioned under the name of Kutu. It was situated a little to the E of Babylon, and is now represented by the ruins of Tel Ibrahim. The statement (2 Kings, xvii. 30) that the principal god of the Cutheans was Nergal (the god of war) is confirmed by the inscriptions. Nebuchadnezzar (604–561) records that he restored the temple of Nergal in the city of Cuthah.

Cuthbert (kuth'bėrt), Saint. d. at Farne, in Northumbria, March 20, 687. English monk. He was prior of Melrose from 661 to 664, and in 664 of Lindisfarne, and bishop of Lindisfarne from 685 to 687.

Cuthbert. City in SW Georgia, county seat of Randolph County: seat of Andrew College. Farm products, lumber, and cotton are produced in the area; the town has canneries and a plywood factory. 4,025 (1950).

Cuthbert Clutterbuck (klut'ėr.buk), **Captain.** See **Clutterbuck, Captain Cuthbert.**

Cuticle (kū'ti.kl), **Surgeon.** Character in *White-Jacket* (1850), novel by Herman Melville.

Cutler (kut'lėr), **Manasseh.** b. at Killingly, Conn., May 13, 1742; d. at Hamilton, Mass., July 28, 1823. American botanist and Congregational clergyman, one of the founders of Marietta, Ohio, in 1788.

Cutler, Timothy. b. at Charlestown (now part of Boston), Mass., May 31, 1684; d. at Boston, Aug. 17, 1765. American clergyman, president of Yale College from 1719 to 1722.

Cuttack (ku.tak'). [Also: **Cattack, Katak, Kuttack.**] District in Orissa, Union of India, bounded on the E and SE by the Bay of Bengal, and traversed by the Mahanadi River: forest products, wheat, and rice. Capital, Cuttack; area, 3,654 sq. mi.; pop. 2,431,427 (1941).

Cuttack. [Also: **Cattack, Katak, Kuttack.**] Capital of the district of Cuttack and of Orissa state, Union of India, on the Mahanadi River, ab. 250 mi. SW of Calcutta. It is on the main line of the railroad from Madras to Calcutta. Once a busy port, it is no longer important as such because the railroad has taken most of the coastal trade and the port is too shallow for the modern deep-drafted ships. Ravenshaw College, a government institution, is located here. The city was taken from the Mahrattas by the British in 1803. Pop. 74,291 (1941).

Cutten (kut'ẹn), **George Barton.** b. at Amherst, Nova Scotia, April 11, 1874—. American educator. Graduated from Yale (B.A., 1897; Ph.D., 1902; B.D., 1903), he was president of Acadia University, Nova Scotia (1910–22) and of Colgate University (1922–42) and acting president (1943–44) of Colgate-Rochester Divinity School. He is the author of *The Psychology of Alcoholism* (1906), *The Psychological Phenomena of Christianity* (1908), *Instincts of Religion* (1940), *Should Prohibition Return* (1944), and other books.

Cutter (kut'ėr), **Charles Ammi.** b. at Boston, March 14, 1837; d. at Walpole, N.H., Sept. 6, 1903. American librarian. He was librarian (1868–93) of the Boston Athenaeum, cofounder (1876) of the American Library Association and of the *Library Journal,* of which he was general editor (1881–93), and aided (1894) in the development of the Forbes Library at Northampton, Mass. His classification of books by author initial-marks and numbers is a basis for the system now in wide usage. He was the author of the *Catalogue of the Library of the Boston Athenaeum* (5 vols., 1874–82), *Rules for a Printed Dictionary Catalogue* (1875), and *Expansive Classification* (1891–94).

Cutter, George Washington. b. at Quebec, Canada, 1801; d. Dec. 25, 1865. American poet and lawyer. He was a member (1838–39) of the Indiana legislature and later a stump speaker for the Know-Nothing Party. A captain in the Mexican War, he was inspired by his experiences at Buena Vista to write his best-known work, published in *Buena Vista and Other Poems* (1848). He was the author also of *The Song of Steam and Other Poems* (1857) and *Poems, National and Patriotic* (1857).

Cutting of an Agate, The. Volume of essays by William Butler Yeats, published in 1912.

Cuttle (kut'l), **Captain Edward.** In Charles Dickens's *Dombey and Son,* "a kind-hearted, salt-looking" old retired sailor with a hook in place of his right hand. He is a friend of Sol Gills, the ships' instrument-maker. One of his favorite expressions is "When found, make a note on."

Cutts (kuts), **John.** [Title, Baron **Cutts of Gowran;** called **"Salamander."**] b. 1661; d. at Dublin, Ireland, Jan. 26, 1707. English soldier. Returned to England with William of Orange at the time of the revolution of 1688, soon becoming colonel of his regiment; distinguished himself at Boyne (1690) where Macaulay states he was at the head of his regiment, the 5th Fusiliers; wounded at the siege of Limerick; called "Salamander" for his bravery during the siege of Namur (1695); as brigadier general he accompanied (1701) Marlborough to Holland; third in command at the battle of Blenheim, where his division fought strenuously throughout the day; appointed commander in chief in Ireland under the Duke of Ormonde.

Cutwa (kut'wạ). See **Katwa.**

Cuverville Island (kū'vėr.vil). [Also, **Cavelier de Cuverville Island.**] Dark, rounded rock with precipitous cliffs in Antarctica, lying ab. 1 mi. NE of De Rongé Island along the Danco Coast, in ab. 64°40′ S., 62°33′ W.

Cuvier (kü.vyā), **Frédéric.** b. at Montbéliard, Doubs, France, June 27, 1773; d. at Strasbourg, France, July 25, 1838. French naturalist; brother of Georges Cuvier. He became director of the menagerie of the Jardin des Plantes, at Paris, in 1804, and in 1827 was appointed professor of comparative anatomy at the Jardin des Plantes. He wrote *Des dents des mammifères, considerées comme caractères zoologiques* (1825) and (in coöperation with Geoffroy Saint-Hilaire) *Histoire naturelle des mammifères* (1819–39).

Cuvier, Georges Léopold Chrétien Frédéric Dagobert, Baron. b. at Montbéliard, Doubs, France, Aug. 23, 1769; d. at Paris, May 13, 1832. French naturalist, the founder of the science of comparative anatomy; brother of Frédéric Cuvier. He was educated at the *Gymnasium* (advanced secondary school) at Montbéliard and the Academia Carolina at Stuttgart, was tutor (1788–94) in the family of the Comte d'Héricy, became assistant professor of comparative anatomy at the Musée d'Histoire Naturelle in 1795, and a member of the National Institute in 1795. He was named professor of natural history in the Collège de France in 1800, life secretary of the Academy of Sciences in 1803, and councilor of the Imperial University in 1808; was appointed councilor of state by Napoleon in 1814; was admitted to the French Academy in 1818; was president (1819–32) of the Committee of the Interior; received the title of baron in 1820; was appointed superintendent of the Faculty of Protestant Theology in 1822; was made grand officer of the Legion of Honor in 1826; and was created a peer of France in 1831. His chief works are *Anatomie comparée* (1800–05), *Recherches sur les ossements fossiles* (1812), *Le Règne animal* (1817), and *Histoire naturelle des poissons* (with Valenciennes; 1828–49). Cuvier was a persistent opponent of the evolutionary doctrines advanced by Lamarck and Geoffroy Saint-Hilaire.

Cuvilliès (kü.vē.yes), **François de.** [Also, **Cuvilles.**] b. at Soissons, France, 1698; d. 1767 or 1768. French architect and decorator. He went to Paris in his youth to study architecture, and as early as 1720 was commissioned to execute important works at Cologne for the elector James Clement. In 1738 he was appointed architect to the elector Charles Albert of Bavaria who, upon becoming emperor under the title of Charles VII, elevated him to the post of architect to the imperial court. He brought the German rococo style to its most lavish perfection, especially in some of his creations at Munich, best known of which is probably the Amalienburg pavilion.

Cuxhaven (kůks'hä.fẹn). [Also, **Kuxhaven.**] City in NW Germany, in the *Land* (state) of Lower Saxony, British Zone, formerly belonging to the free city of Hamburg, situated at the mouth of the Elbe River, ab. 57 mi. NW of Hamburg. It has large port facilities, shipyards, important fisheries (especially for herring and codfish), fish-smoking plants and fish markets, canneries, and metallurgical, electrical, leather, and other industries. It is also a seaside resort with a large bathing beach. The city was frequently bombed during World War II; the Döser Church was partly destroyed. The contents of the museum had been evacuated to safe storage and were thus saved. The increase in population between 1939 and 1946 amounted to 37.1 percent. 42,542 (1946), 46,861 (1950).

Cuyabá (kö.yạ.bä'). Former spelling of **Cuiabá.**

Cuyaguateje (kö.yä.gwä.te'ʜā). River in W Cuba, flowing S to the Caribbean Sea.

Cuyahoga (kī.hog'ạ, ku-, kī.ạ.hō'gạ). River in N Ohio which flows into Lake Erie at Cleveland. Length, ab. 90 to 100 mi.

Cuyahoga Falls. City in NE Ohio, in Summit County, on the Cuyahoga River near Akron. Manufactures include rubber goods, tools, and chemicals. 29,195 (1950).

Cuyler (kī'lėr), **Theodore Ledyard.** b. at Aurora, N.Y., Jan. 10, 1822; d. at Brooklyn, N.Y., Feb. 26, 1909. American clergyman and author. He was pastor of the Lafayette Avenue Presbyterian Church at Brooklyn (1860–90), and then retired to devote himself to temperance reform and other philanthropic work. He helped to organize the Republican Party in 1856. In addition to his *Recollections of a Long Life* (1902), he was the author of many religious works, contributions to periodicals, and others.

Cuyo (kö'yō). In the history of Spanish South America, a region E of the Andes. It was originally settled from Chile, and remained a province of that captain-generalcy until 1776, when it was united to the new viceroyalty of Buenos Aires. The limits were never definitely fixed, and the name is now obsolete.

Cuyo Islands. [Also, **Cuyos.**] Group of small islands in the Philippines, E of the N part of Palawan and belonging to that province.

Cuyp or **Kuyp** (koip), **Albert.** b. at Dordrecht, Netherlands, 1620; d. there, 1691. Dutch painter; son of Jacob Cuyp. He was a skillful painter of genre scenes, architectural views, and country landscapes and also of animals, all of which he especially liked to place against backgrounds of diffused golden light. Some of his best-known works are *Promenade, Dapple-grey Horses, View of Dordrecht,* and *Piper with Cows.*

Cuyp or Kuyp, Jacob Gerritsz. b. 1575; d. 1651. Dutch painter; father of Albert Cuyp. He was known for both portraits and landscapes.

Cuypers (koi'pėrs), **Petrus Josephus Hubertus.** b. at Roermond, Netherlands, May 16, 1827; d. there, March 3, 1921. Dutch architect. He is best known for his prize-winning design for the Rijksmuseum (built 1877–85) at Amsterdam. He studied at the Antwerp Academy and established (1852) a workshop for Christian art at Amsterdam and later at Roermond. He built many Catholic churches in Holland and the Central Railway Station (built 1881–89) at Amsterdam. He is remembered for his restoration (1872–75) of Mainz Cathedral, and he supervised with fine understanding the restoration (1874 *et seq.*) of many medieval buildings in the Netherlands.

Cuyuni (kö.yö'ni). River in NE British Guiana. It flows W and empties into the Essequibo. Length, ab. 500 mi.

Cuza (kö'zä), **Alexander John.** See **Alexander John I** (of *Rumania*).

Cuzco (kös'kō). See **Cusco.**

Cvijić (tsvē'yēch), **Jovan.** b. at Loznitsa, Serbia, 1865; d. 1927. Serbian geographer, who played an influential role at the Paris peace conference in support of South Slav claims. He was professor of geography (1893 *et seq.*) at the University of Belgrade and the author of *La Péninsule balkanique: Geógraphie humaine* (1918, and later editions).

CWA. See **Civil Works Administration.**

Cwmbran (kům'brän). Urban district and industrial center in W England, in Monmouthshire, ab. 4 mi. S of Pontypool, ab. 140 mi. W of London by rail. It has manufactures of iron and steel and is a coal-mining center. 13,162 (1951).

Cwmry (kům'ri). See **Cymry.**

Cyaxares (sī.ak'sạ.rēz). King of the Medes (625–584 B.C.). In the cuneiform inscriptions his name is Uvakshtra. He may be considered as the founder of Media's power and greatness. After repelling the hordes of the Scythian invasion, he captured Nineveh (608 B.C.), in alliance with Nabopolassar, viceroy of Babylonia, and destroyed the Assyrian empire. Toward the W Cyaxares conquered Armenia, and thus extended his dominion as far as the river Halys (the modern Kizil Irmak) in Asia Minor. He even attempted the conquest of Lydia on the other side of the Halys, but had to desist on account of an eclipse which took place (585) during the battle.

Cybele (sib'ẹ.lē). [Also, **Rhea.**] In Greek mythology, the wife of Cronos (Saturnus), and mother of the Olympian gods: hence called the "Great Mother of the Gods." The original home of her worship was Phrygia, in Asia Minor. Her priests were called Corybantes, and her festivals were celebrated with wild dances and orgiastic excesses amid the resounding music of drums and cymbals. She was conceived as traversing the mountains in a chariot drawn by lions. From Asia her worship came to Greece, and during the second Punic War in 264 B.C. it was introduced into Rome, where the Megalesia, later also the Taurobolia and Criobolia, were celebrated in her honor. The oak, pine, and lion were sacred to her. She is usually represented enthroned between lions, with a diadem on her head and a small drum or cymbal, the instrument used in her rites, in her hand.

Cyclades (sik'lạ.dēz). [Also: **Kikladhes, Kyklades, Kykladon Nesoi.**] Group of islands belonging to Greece, situated in the Aegean Sea. The name, from the Greek word for "circle," derived from the belief that they formed a ring about Delos. Among the major islands are Andros, Tenos, Keos, Syros, Naxos, Melos, and Paros. They now form, with neighboring islands, the *nomos* (department) of Cyclades, which includes the provinces of Andros, Thera, Kea, Milo, Naxos, Syra, and Tenos. Capital, Hermopolis; area, 1,023 sq. mi.; pop. 121,256 (1951).

Cyclic Poets (sī'klik). The authors of Greek epic poems, composed between 800 B.C. and 550 B.C., relating to the Trojan War and the war against Thebes. Among these poems are *Cypria* (The Cyprian Lays), *Aethiopis* (The Lay of Aethiopia), *The Sack of Troy, The Little Iliad, Nostoi* (The Homeward Voyages), *Telegonia* (The Lay of Telegonus), all belonging to the Trojan cycle, and the *Thebais* and the *Epigoni*, belonging to the Theban cycle. A few fragments of these poems are extant.

Cyclops (sī'klops) or **Cyclopes** (sī.klō'pēz). In Greek mythology, a race of one-eyed giants, represented in the Homeric cycle of legends as Sicilian cannibalistic shepherds, whose leader was Polyphemus. Hesiod names them as the three sons of Uranus and Gaea who helped Zeus in his struggle against Cronus, and who gave Zeus his thunderbolts. They were slain by Apollo. In later mythology they were assistant forgers to Hephaestus.

Cydamus (sī′dą.mus). Latin name of **Gadames.**

Cydippe (sī.dip′ę). See under **Acontius.**

Cydnus (sid′nus). In ancient geography, a river of Cilicia, Asia Minor, flowing into the Mediterranean Sea ab. 12 mi. S of Tarsus.

Cydonia (sī.dō′ni.ą). Ancient Greek name of **Canea,** city.

Cygnaeus or **Cygnäus** (süng.nā′ùs), **Fredrik.** b. 1807; d. 1881. Finnish poet, literary historian, and educator, writing in the Swedish language. His career as an educator began at his alma mater, the University of Abo (now Turku), but in 1854 he became professor of esthetics and literature at the University of Helsingfors (now Helsinki). His own creative work in poetry and the drama, and his historical and critical writings, were influential in the development of Finnish culture, especially as long as Swedish remained the literary language of that country.

Cygnus (sig′nus). Swan: an ancient northern constellation in the Milky Way.

Cymbeline (sim′bę.lēn). Drama by Shakespeare, produced probably c1610; so called from one of the chief characters, a legendary ruler (Cunobeline) of Britain. Part of the play was no doubt derived from Holinshed; the part relating to Iachimo is in Boccaccio's *Decameron.* It was first published in the folio of 1623. Garrick produced his alteration in 1762.

Cyme (sī′mē). Ancient Greek city in W Asia Minor, ab. 28 mi. N of what is now Izmir (Smyrna), Turkey, on a small coastal bay. It was founded in the early Greek colonization of Aeolis, and rose to prominence as the principal city of this region. In the 7th century B.C. Cyme was ruled by a king, but later it had oligarchic rule. It was involved in the intrigues between Athens and Sparta, and changed hands numerous times in the struggles between Greek and Persian empires. In 17 A.D. it was severely damaged by an earthquake. The site of Cyme is supposed to be at the small village of Namúrt Kjöi.

Cymric (kim′rik). See under **Welsh.**

Cymru (kim′rö). Welsh name of **Wales.**

Cymry (kim′ri). [Also: **Cymri, Cwmry, Kymry.**] Name given to themselves by the Welsh. In its wider application the term is often applied to that division of the Celtic peoples embracing the Welsh, and including also the Cornishmen and the Bretons or Armoricans.

Cynaegirus (sin.ę.jī′rus). Athenian soldier; brother of Aeschylus. He distinguished himself at the battle of Marathon in 490 B.C., in which, according to Herodotus, he pursued the Persians to the sea, and, having seized one of their triremes to prevent its putting off, fell with his right hand severed. Later writers add that, having lost both his hands, he seized the vessel with his teeth.

Cynewulf (kin′ę.wùlf) or **Cynwulf.** [Also, **Kynewulf.**] fl. in the latter part of the 8th century. Anglo-Saxon poet, probably Northumbrian; sometimes identified with a Cynewulf who was bishop of Lindisfarne from 737 to 780. The discovery of his putative identity was based upon runic inscriptions in the epilogues of four poems attributed to him, *The Ascension, The Legend of St. Juliana, Elene,* and *The Fates of the Apostles.* These poems are preserved in the collections of Old English poems known as the Vercelli Book and Exeter Book. Other works ascribed to Cynewulf include *The Dream of the Rood, Andreas,* and others in the so-called Cynewulfian cycle.

Cynics (sin′iks). School of Greek philosophers founded by Antisthenes of Athens (b. c444 B.C.), who sought to develop the ethical teachings of Socrates, whose pupil he was. The chief doctrines of the Cynics were that virtue is the only good, that the essence of virtue is self-control, and that pleasure is an evil if sought for its own sake. They were accordingly characterized by an ostentatious contempt of riches, art, science, and amusements. The most famous Cynic was Diogenes of Sinope, a pupil of Antisthenes, who carried the doctrines of the school to an extreme and ridiculous asceticism, and is improbably said to have slept in a tub which he carried about with him.

Cynosarges (sī.nǫ.sär′jēz). A gymnasium of very early foundation in ancient Athens, combined with a sanctuary of Hercules, and possessing a grove. The philosopher Antisthenes taught here, and his school was hence called the Cynic. The Cynosarges lay somewhat high up on the S slope of Lycabettus; its site is now occupied by the Monastery of the Asomatôn and the British and American schools of archaeology.

Cynoscephalae (sin.ǫ.sef′ą.lē). Heights in Thessaly, Greece, between ab. 10 and 20 mi. SE of Larissa. Here the Thebans under Pelopidas defeated (364 B.C.) Alexander of Pherae and the Romans under Flamininus defeated (197 B.C.) Philip V of Macedon.

Cynosura (sī.nǫ.shö′rą). In Greek mythology, a nymph of Ida, and nurse of Zeus, metamorphosed into the constellation Ursa Minor.

Cynosura. The constellation of Ursa Minor ("Little Bear") or Little Dipper, containing the polestar (which forms the tip of the tail), and thus often the object to which the eyes of mariners are directed.

Cynosuria (sī.nǫ.shö′ri.ą). See **Cynuria.**

Cynthia (sin′thi.ą). In Congreve's *Double Dealer,* a flippant fine lady, the daughter of Lord and Lady Pliant, in love with Mellefont.

Cynthiana (sin.thi.an′ą). City in C Kentucky, county seat of Harrison County, on the South Fork of the Licking River, ab. 48 mi. S of Cincinnati: residential community. Tobacco, horses, and farm products are raised in the area. Settled in 1793 and incorporated in 1806, it was the scene of John H. Morgan's raids in 1862 and 1864 during the Civil War. 4,847 (1950).

Cynthia's Revels, or The Fountain of Self-Love. "Comicall satyre" by Ben Jonson, acted by the Children of the Queen's Chapel in 1600. It was printed in quarto in 1601 and with large additions in a folio of 1616.

Cynthia, the Lady of the Sea. Elegy by Sir Walter Raleigh, in which he expresses his loyalty and devotion to Queen Elizabeth (who is called "Cynthia" in accordance with a custom common among Elizabethan poets) and his unhappiness at having lost her favor. The poem is mentioned in print for the first time by Spenser, in his *Colin Clout's Come Home Again* (1595), but Raleigh had already read it, or some part of it, to Spenser in or about 1589, when they were in Ireland. Exactly when it was composed is not known. It was long thought to be lost, but a portion of it was discovered, and printed for the first time in 1870, by John Hannah the younger, archdeacon of Lewes, in his volume *The Courtly Poets from Raleigh to Montrose* (later published as *Poems of Sir Walter Raleigh and Other Courtly Poets,* 1875 and 1892). Hannah thought that it was composed when Raleigh was a prisoner in the Tower of London under James I, but evidence indicates that the discovered fragment goes back to the earlier poem. It was Spenser's habit to call Raleigh "the Ocean" or "the Shepherd of the Ocean," a manner of address that Raleigh himself adopted, so that another name by which this poem is called, *The Ocean to Cynthia,* simply means Raleigh to Queen Elizabeth.

Cynthius (sin′thi.us). See also **Giraldi, Giovanni Battista.**

Cynthius. Epithet of Apollo, the sun god, as the moon goddess is called Cynthia.

Cynthus (sin′thus). In ancient geography, a mountain in Delos, from which are derived Cynthia and Cynthius, the surnames, respectively, of Artemis and Apollo.

Cynuria (sī.nū′ri.ą). [Also, **Cynosuria.**] In ancient geography, a district in Greece in the E part of the Peloponnesus, situated on the Gulf of Argolis.

Cynwulf (kin′wùlf). See **Cynewulf.**

Cyparissus (sip.ą.ris′us). In Greek mythology, a youth, a son of Telephus. He accidentally killed Apollo's favorite stag, and was so overcome with grief that Apollo metamorphosed him into a cypress.

Cypern (tsē′pėrn). German name of **Cyprus.**

Cypress Hills. Hilly region in SE Alberta and SW Saskatchewan, Canada, ab. 35 mi. SE of Medicine Hat, Alberta. The hills rise abruptly from the prairie and are quite rough and dissected. A scrubby growth of jack pine grows on the higher hills. The area is chiefly used for grazing. A provincial park now occupies part of the area in Saskatchewan. Peak elevation, ab. 4,810 ft. Length, ab. 80 mi.

Cypria (sip′ri.ą). [Also, **Cyprian Lays.**] One of the poems of the Trojan cycle, anciently attributed to Homer, and later to Stasinus, or Hegesias, or Hegesinus. It was so named either in reference to the home of the author (Cyprus), or because it celebrated the Cyprian Aphrodite.

It served as an introduction to the *Iliad*, relating the first nine years of the siege of Troy.

Cyprian (sip′ri.ạn), Saint. [Full Latin name, **Thascius Caecilius Cyprianus.**] b. c200; beheaded at Carthage, Sept. 14, 258. Christian church father, bishop, and martyr. Nothing is known of his early life, but he was a man of education and of considerable wealth when in middle age (according to tradition, in 246) he was converted to Christianity, became a priest, and in 248 was made bishop of Carthage. During the persecutions begun by Decius in 250, many Christians apostatized; subsequently some bishops took an unforgiving attitude toward the backsliders, but Cyprian, like Pope Calixtus I, urged a more compassionate course. He gave most of his income to the poor, worked ardently for church unity, and wrote much on theological matters in an elegant style (his works were edited at Rome in 1471, and several times since). He was greatly influenced by Tertullian, and in turn he influenced later theologians, including Saint Augustine. He suffered martyrdom, being beheaded during the persecution begun by Valerian.

Cyprus (sī′prus). [French, **Chypre**; German, **Cypern**; Greek, **Kypros**; Italian, **Cipro**; Turkish, **Kibris.**] British crown colony, one of the largest islands of the Mediterranean, situated in its E corner, ab. 40 mi. S of Turkey and ab. 240 mi. N of Egypt, with the mountain range of the Lebanon on the mainland to the E and that of Taurus to the N. Its name is supposed to be derived from its rich mines of copper (Greek, *kypros*). Cyprus has limestone mountains averaging ab. 2,000 ft. in elevation along its N coast, and a higher and more extensive range occupies the S and W parts of the island, culminating in Mount Olympus, or Troodos (6,000 ft.). Between these ranges lies a fertile plain where agriculture is well developed. Carobs (a kind of bean), potatoes, wines, spices, raisins, and tobacco are among the agricultural products exported. Besides copper, Cyprus produces gypsum, ochre, umber, asbestos, chromium, and other minerals. Agriculture and mining are the principal occupations, but there are factories processing tobacco and foodstuffs and making wines, soap, buttons, and artificial teeth, among other items. Livestock raising is also of some importance, and mules are among the exports. Cyprus has ab. 70 mi. of railroad. Famagusta is the chief seaport, and there is an airport at Nicosia. The principal religions of the inhabitants are Greek Orthodox and Mohammedan; the population contains elements of Greek, Turkish, and Armenian origin. Capital, Nicosia; area, 3,572 sq. mi.; pop. 450,114 (1946), 492,297 (est. 1951).

History. Cyprus was celebrated in antiquity as the birthplace and favorite abode of Aphrodite, and was famous for its beauty and wealth, but also for its licentiousness. It was early settled by Phoenicians, who were followed by Greeks. Its principal cities were Paphos (still known by that name) on the W coast (a center of the cult of Aphrodite), Salamis (near modern Famagusta) on the E, Kittim, or Citium (on the site of modern Larnaca) on the SE, and Amathus (near modern Limassol) on the S. In the center of the island were the Phoenician mining cities Tamassus and Idalium (modern Dali), with the celebrated grove of Aphrodite. For a time Cyprus was tributary to Assyria. Its name in the cuneiform inscriptions is Yatnan, and the Assyrian king Sargon relates that seven kings from this island (probably chiefs of the Phoenician colonies) brought him costly gifts and "kissed his feet," i.e., acknowledged his sovereignty. He in turn presented them with a marble stele containing a full-length sculptured portrait of himself, and an inscription commemorating his principal deeds. This monument was found in 1846, well preserved, near Larnaca (the ancient Kittim or Citium), and was acquired by the Royal Museum of Berlin. Cyprus was in succession subject to Persia, Macedon, and Egypt, and in 57 B.C. became a Roman province. In the Middle Ages it belonged alternately to the Byzantine Empire and the Saracens, and from 1192 formed a kingdom ruled by the house of Lusignan. In 1489 Caterina Cornaro transferred the sovereignty to Venice. In 1571 it was taken by the Turks. Cyprus began to be administered by Great Britain according to a convention between that country and Turkey in 1878. At the outbreak of World War I the British government annexed the island outright, and it was made a crown colony in 1925. A movement for union with Greece caused trouble in 1931 and again in 1948, when a split in the legislative assembly led to the dissolving of that body by the colonial administration.

Cypselus (sip′sẹ.lus). Tyrant of Corinth c655–625 B.C.

Cyrankiewicz (tsi.ran.kye′vēch), **Józef.** b. 1911—. Polish politician; premier of the post-World War II Polish government. Until World War II he was secretary of the Polish Socialist Party at Kraków. Sent by the Germans to the infamous concentration camp at Oswiecim (Auschwitz), he was liberated in 1944 and immediately joined the Soviet-controlled faction of the Socialist Party at Warsaw. As its general secretary he promoted the establishment of a united communist and socialist party (the United Workers' Party), as a member of which he became (1947) premier of the Polish government.

Cyrano de Bergerac (sē.rȧ.nō dẹ ber.zhẹ.räk; Anglicized, sir′ạ.nō dẹ bėr′zhẹ.räk). Play by Edmond Rostand, first produced in 1897. The character of the hero is modeled upon that of a historic original, but is sketched by the dramatist in superlative. He is depicted as extraordinarily brave, extravagantly lavish, superbly indifferent to patronage, extremely ugly (owing to his very large nose), and loyally self-sacrificing in his love for his cousin Roxane. The events of the play are, however, substantially those which are reported to have befallen the original Cyrano. The elder Coquelin (supported by Sarah Bernhardt as Roxane) originally played the part of Cyrano in French. Richard Mansfield, Walter Hampden, and (most recently) José Ferrer are among the well-known actors who have played it in English.

Cyrano de Bergerac. Opera in four acts by Walter Damrosch, first performed at the New York Metropolitan Opera House on Feb. 27, 1913. The libretto, by William J. Henderson, is based on the Rostand play.

Cyrano de Bergerac, Savinien. b. at the Château de Bergerac, in Périgord, France, c1620; d. at Paris, 1655. French writer and duelist. He was wounded at the siege of Arras in 1640, and devoted himself to study. Among his works are *Agrippine*, a tragedy (1653), *Le Pédant joué*, a comedy (1654), and two works published after his death, *Histoire comique des états et empires de la lune* (1656) and *Histoire comique des états et des empires du soleil* (1661). These two are said to have served to suggest at least *Micromégas* and *Gulliver's Travels*. Rostand's *Cyrano de Bergerac* takes his name, but only slightly parallels the actual course of his life.

Cyrenaica (sir.ẹ.nā′i.kạ). [Also, **Pentapolis.**] In ancient geography, a country in N Africa, lying between the Mediterranean on the N, Marmarica on the E, the desert on the S, and the Syrtis Major (modern Gulf of Sidra) on the W. It corresponded closely to the modern territory of the same name, in NE Libya, and was noted for its fertility. It was settled (c631 B.C.) by Therians, was subject to Egypt from 321 B.C., and formed (67 B.C.) with Crete a Roman province. Its cities were ruined by invasions of Persians and Saracens in the 7th century A.D.

Cyrenaica. [Also, **Cirenaica.**] Territory in NE Libya, N Africa, until 1951 a trust territory of the United Nations under British administration. Before World War II it formed the E portion of the Italian colony of Libya. It is bounded on the E by Egypt, on the S by the Libyan desert, on the W by Tripolitania, and on the N by the Mediterranean Sea. Under Turkish rule from the 16th to the 20th century, Cyrenaica was made part of the Turkish vilayet of Tripoli in 1835, and was occupied by Italy in 1911 and annexed in 1912. Libya became an autonomous kingdom in 1951. The chief towns are Bengasi and Tobruk. Area, ab. 330,000 sq. mi.; pop. 327,000 (est. 1938).

Cyrenaics (sī.rẹ.nā′iks). School of Greek hedonistic philosophers, founded by Aristippus of Cyrene, a disciple of Socrates.

Cyrene (sī.rē′nē). [Also, **Cirene.**] In ancient geography, the principal city in Cyrenaica, situated ab. 10 mi. from the Mediterranean coast. It was founded (c631 B.C.) by Therians, under Battus, and was a seat of Greek learning and culture. The modern town on its site contains many antiquities. It was the birthplace of Aristippus, Eratosthenes, and other famous men.

Cyrene. In Greek mythology, a nymph, mother of Aristaeus.

Cyril (sir'il), Saint. [Called Saint **Cyril of Jerusalem.**] b. at or near Jerusalem, c316; d. probably on March 18, 386. Christian theologian and bishop. Before becoming bishop of Jerusalem in 350, he seems to have hesitated for a time between Arianism and orthodoxy, but, at least after his elevation to the episcopacy, he was one of the foremost enemies of the Arian heresy, particularly crossing controversial swords with Acacius, the Arian bishop of Caesarea, who procured his deposition in 357. Cyril was in fact forced by his Arian enemies to go into exile three times, but he was finally securely restored to his see in 381. His writings, consisting chiefly of catechistical lectures (edited in 1720), throw much light on 4th-century theological thought, and it has been surmised that he, even more than Athanasius, may have been the father of the Nicene creed. His feast is celebrated on March 18.

Cyril, Saint. [Called Saint **Cyril of Alexandria.**] b. at Alexandria; d. there, in June, 444. Christian theologian and archbishop. Coming to the archiepiscopal see of Alexandria in 412, he is conceded by all students of early church history to have been intemperately zealous in his measures against pagans, Novatians, Nestorians, and Jews. He despoiled the Novatians of their church property, expelled the Jews from the city, and is supposed by some to have instigated the murder (422), by a lector of Alexandria, of the pagan philosopher Hypatia, although many historians consider the evidence of this to be questionable at best. Especially after 428 he led the struggle against Nestorianism, and presided at the Council of Ephesus (431) which condemned Nestorius as a heretic. The proceedings of the council were marked by extreme acrimony, leaving the Christians of Antioch so embittered that two years later Cyril had to come to a compromise with them, under a formula which maintained his orthodoxy but is said by some scholars to have opened the way to certain subsequent theological errors. Cyril was in the thick of the extremely intricate doctrinal debates of those times, and his writings (which were edited in 1638) are mainly controversial. He is commemorated in the Greek, Roman, and Anglican churches on January 28.

Cyril, Saint. [Called the **"Apostle of the Slavs"**; original name, **Constantine.**] b. at Thessalonica, 827; d. at Rome, Feb. 4, 869. Christian prelate and scholar. He engaged with his brother, Saint Methodius, in missionary labors among the Moravians, Bulgarians, and other Slavic nations. He translated the gospels and various liturgical works into Slavonic, and is said to have devised the Cyrillic alphabet.

Cyril, Mount. Mountain in Antarctica, in the Commonwealth Range, in ab. 83°57′ S., 172°55′ E. Elevation, ab. 6,100 ft.

Cyril Lucar (lö'kar). See **Lucaris, Cyrillus.**

Cyrnos (sir'nos, kür'nôs). Greek name of **Corsica.**

Cyropaedia (sī″rō.pē.dī'a), **The.** Work of Xenophon, in eight books, describing the education of Cyrus, the founder of the Persian Empire, his great deeds, and his dying advice to his sons and ministers.

Cyrrhestes (si.res'tēz), **Andronicus.** See **Andronicus of Cyrrhus.**

Cyrrhestica (si.res'ti.ka) or **Cyrrhus** (sir'us). In ancient geography, a region in N Syria, W of the Euphrates and S of Commagene.

Cyrus (sī'rus). [Called **Cyrus the Great**; name in the Old Testament, **Koresh**; in the cuneiform inscriptions, **Kurush, Kurshu**; Old Persian, **Kurush.**] d. 529 B.C. Founder of the Persian Empire. All accounts of his birth and early youth are heavily encrusted by various legends. However, much information of some historical repute has been obtained from the inscriptions, among them a cylinder belonging to Cyrus himself, discovered in the ruins of Babylon and Sepharvaim (Sippar), combined with the accounts of the Greek historians (Herodotus, Xenophon, and Ctesiphon). On his cylinder he calls himself the son of Cambyses, grandson of Cyrus and great-grandson of Shishpish (Theispes), who were all "Kings of Anshan." Anshan is evidently identical with Anzan, the plain of Susa, and stands for Elam, which was conquered by Theispes, the son of Achaemenes, founder of the dynasty. In 549 Cyrus, after conquering Ecbatana (modern Hamadan), dethroned Astyages, king of Media, and united Media with Persia. He then directed his arms against the Lydian kingdom of Croesus (who made an offensive and defensive alliance with Nabonidus, king of Babylonia, and the reigning pharaoh of Egypt), defeated him, and captured the capital Sardis. The ensuing years Cyrus used for consolidating his power in the conquered countries. In 538 he marched with a great army into Babylonia. Sepharvaim (Sippar) was captured without fighting, Nabonidus, who defended it, fled, and two days afterward Babylon itself, which was held by Nabonidus's son Belshazzar, fell into the hands of the conqueror, likewise "without battle and fight," as he records. According to Eusebius, Nabonidus after the fall of Babylon fortified himself in Borsippa; the city was besieged by Cyrus, and after it had capitulated he treated it and Nabonidus himself with mercy, allowing the latter to make his residence in Carmania (modern Kerman). It is certain that he showed great generosity and consideration to the conquered capital (Babylon), sparing its inhabitants and their religious feelings; he even represented himself as having been called by Merodach (Marduk), the god of the city, to avenge his neglect at the hands of the preceding kings. Cyrus's attitude toward the Jewish exiles in Babylonia is well known from the Old Testament (Ezra, i.). He permitted them to return to their own country (thus ending the Babylonian Exile), to rebuild Jerusalem, and to restore the temple, and even returned to them the vessels of the temple which had been carried away by Nebuchadnezzar. Cyrus's death, like his birth, is somewhat shrouded in legend. The most common view is that he fell in battle with the Messagetes on the river Jaxartes (modern Syr Darya).

Cyrus. [Called **Cyrus the Younger.**] d. 401 B.C. Persian satrap; son of Darius Nothus, king of Persia, and Parysatis. He sought to overthrow his brother Artaxerxes II, king of Persia, attacked him with the aid, among others, of the ten thousand Greeks (as described by Xenophon in the *Anabasis*), and perished on the battlefield of Cunaxa.

Cyrus. Ancient name of the **Kura.**

Cyrus Choke (chōk), **General.** See **Choke, General Cyrus.**

Cysarz (tsē'zärts), **Herbert.** b. 1896—. German historian of literature, professor at the University of Vienna. His *Literaturgeschichte als Geisteswissenschaft* (1926), as also his studies of less sweeping themes (*Von Schiller und Nietzsche*, 1928; *Deutsche Barockdichtung*, 1924; *Zur Geistesgeschichte des Weltkrieges*, 1930), illustrate his dissatisfaction with traditional methods, but are considered by some critics to raise more problems than they can cope with.

Cythera (si.thir'a). [Also: **Cerigo, Cerigotto**; Greek, **Kithira, Kythera, Kytherion.**] One of the Ionian Islands in S Greece, in the *nomos* (department) of Argolis and Corinthia, situated between 8 and 10 mi. S of Laconia. Grain, wine, and olives are produced. The village of Kythera (pop. 628, 1936) is the seat of a bishopric. There is an ancient shrine of Aphrodite on the island. Area, ab. 110 sq. mi.; pop. 9,022 (1936).

Cytherea (sith.e.rē'a) or **Cythera** (si.thir'a). In classical mythology, surnames of Aphrodite, from the island of Cythera, or from a place of the same name which once existed in Crete.

Cytherea. Novel by Joseph Hergesheimer, published in 1922.

Cythna (sith'na). Character in Shelley's poem *The Revolt of Islam.*

Cyveiliog (ku.vī'lyōg), **Hugh of.** See **Hugh of Cyveiliog** (or **Kevelioc**).

Cyveiliog, Owain. See **Owain Cyveiliog.**

Cyzicus (siz'i.kus). [Also, **Cyzicum** (-kum).] In ancient geography, the peninsula (modern Turkish, Kapidağı) projecting from Mysia, Asia Minor, into the Sea of Marmara; also, the Greek town on its isthmus. Among its ruins are a Roman amphitheater, a temple of Hadrian, and an ancient theater. The Roman amphitheater dates from the 2nd century A.D. The ruins still rise to a height of 65 ft., built of rubble faced with rusticated masonry in granite. There are 32 arched entrances in the lower story. The longer axis of the ellipse is 325 ft. The temple of Hadrian, dedicated in 167 A.D., was greatly admired in antiquity. It was a Corinthian *peripteros* (building surrounded by a row of columns) of six by 15 columns, of white marble. The cella, or main chamber, was small, without *pronaos* (vestibule) or *opisthodomos* (rear chamber); there were four interior rows of columns in front and two behind. The temple measured 112 by 301 ft.; the cella 70 by 140 ft. The columns were 7 ft. in base-diameter and 70 ft. high (the highest of any classical temple). The pediments and the cella were richly adorned. The ancient theater, apparently contemporaneous with the amphitheater, was in part built up of rough masonry and faced with marble. The diameter is 328 ft.

Czacki (chäts'kē), **Tadeusz,** Count. b. at Poryck, in Volhynia (a region, formerly Polish, now in the Ukraine), Aug. 28, 1765; d. at Dubno, in Volhynia, Feb. 8, 1813. Polish writer, and promoter of education in Poland. His chief work is one on the laws of Lithuania and Poland (1800).

Czajkowski (chī.kôf'skē), **Michał.** b. 1808; d. 1886. Polish novelist, and general in the Turkish service. His works include *Wernyhora* (1838) and other novels of Ukranian and Cossack life.

Czarniecki (chär.nyets'kē), **Stefan.** [Also, **Czarnecki** (-nets'kē).] b. in Poland, 1599; d. at Sokolowka, in Volhynia (a region, formerly Polish, now in the Ukraine), 1665. Polish general, who distinguished himself in the war against the Swedes (1655–58) and in that against the Russians and Cossacks (1660–65).

Czartoryski (chär.tô.ris'kē), **Adam Casimir,** Prince. b. c1734; d. at Sieniawa, in Galicia, March 19, 1823. Polish politician and general, a candidate for the Polish throne in 1763.

Czartoryski, Adam Jerzy, Prince. b. at Warsaw, Poland, Jan. 14, 1770; d. at Montfermeil, near Paris, July 15, 1861. Polish politician and general; son of Adam Casimir, Prince Czartoryski. He was in the Russian ministry of foreign affairs (1802–05) and was president of the Polish provisional government in 1830, and of the national government in 1831.

Czartoryski, Isabella, Princess. [Title, Countess of **Flemming.**] b. at Warsaw, Poland, c1746; d. at Wysock, in Galicia, June 17, 1835. Polish writer and patriot; wife of Adam Casimir, Prince Czartoryski.

Czartoryski, Michael (or **Fryderyk Michał**), Prince. b. 1697; d. 1773. Polish politician. When the elector of Saxony was also king of Poland with the title of Augustus II, this young scion of one of the first families of the Polish nobility won favor at the court of Dresden and was made vice-chancellor of Lithuania. He was among the nobles who endeavored to assure the succession of the Polish crown to Augustus II's son, who did in fact, after the second abdication of Stanislaus I, become Augustus III (1736). During his reign Czartoryski, who was elevated to the grand chancellorship of Lithuania in 1752, was the most influential of Polish leaders. He promoted an orientation of Polish foreign policy toward an alliance with Russia, Austria, and England to balk the meddling of France and Prussia in Polish affairs, and he endeavored to bring about internal reforms to curb the disastrous factionalism of the Polish nobility. In later years his policy was more vacillating, reflecting many frustrations, but within the frame of the troubled history of Poland in that period, he may be seen as a patriot and a statesman.

Czar und Zimmermann (tsär' ůnt tsim'ėr.män). [Eng. trans., "*Czar and Carpenter.*"] Comic opera in three acts by Albert Lortzing, first performed at Leipzig on Dec. 22, 1837. The libretto is by the composer. The story deals with the life of Peter the Great of Russia, and has been performed in English under the title *Peter the Shipwright.*

Czaslau (chäs'lou). A German name of **Čáslav.**

Czechoslovak Agrarian Party (chek.ọ.slō'väk, -vak). See **Agrarian Party.**

Czechoslovakia (chek"ọ.slō.vä'ki.ạ, **-vak'i.ạ**). [Czech, **Československo**; official Czech name, **Československá Republika.**] Country in E central Europe, bounded on the N and W by Germany, on the S by Austria and Hungary, on the E by the U.S.S.R., and on the NE by Poland. Capital, Prague; area, 49,355 sq. mi.; pop. 12,463,000 (est. 1949).

Terrain and Climate. The W, N, and NE frontiers are marked by densely forested mountain ranges which rise highest in the Tatra Mountains, on the NE, in the central Carpathians. There are two major breaks, however: one is the upper Odra (German, Oder) River basin around Ostrava, opening up toward W Poland; the other is the valley of the Ohře River W of Cheb which leads into Franconia, Germany. From the high Tatra Mountains the terrain ranges to the fertile plain of southern Slovakia, the rolling hills of the Moravian uplands, and the central Bohemian basin which is bounded by the Sudeten Mountains on the N and E, the Harz chain on the NW, and the Bohemian Forest on the S. The entire southern border is devoid of natural divisions. There is rolling hill country between Vienna and Brno and likewise along the Slovakian-Hungarian frontier between the Ipel River and the Ukrainian border; the Danube River, between the influx of the Morava and Ipel rivers, forms the only natural barrier in the otherwise open country, which is a continuation of the Hungarian plain. Within the country, two low mountain ranges divide Bohemia from Moravia-Silesia and the latter from Slovakia, respectively. In terms of river basins, the inner divisions of Czechoslovakia are distinct. Bohemia belongs in its entirety to the Labe (German, Elbe) River basin which points toward the North Sea and hence forms the connecting link with the West. Moravia-Silesia is divided in itself: Silesia lies in the Odra basin, which points toward the Baltic Sea and is now divided between Poland and Germany, with the Polish influence prevailing; Moravia, through the Morava River, and likewise all of Slovakia, are part of the Danube basin which points toward the Black Sea and the countries of the Middle East. The central Bohemian and Moravian plain and hill region and that part of Slovakia which adjoins the Hungarian plain are exceptionally fertile, with mild climate. Through southern Moravia and Slovakia runs the northern limit of wine cultivation in Europe. The mountains, particularly the Carpathians, have high precipitation and cold winters. On the whole the climate is more central European than east European in character.

Industry, Agriculture, and Trade. The country is well suited to a balanced economy, combining large areas of arable land with wooded regions, pasture, and a variety of natural resources ranging from coal and iron ore to uranium deposits in its western extremity. Its chief industries are glass, porcelain, and earthenware manufacture, brewing, machinery, textiles, and sugar refining, as well as the processing of a variety of other foodstuffs. Before World War II, its primary exports were in finished manufactured products. Its currency was the Czech *koruna* (crown), which was stable and commanded a good exchange rate on the world money market. Agriculture is highly developed and diversified. Rye, wheat, barley, and oats are grown. Hops are of excellent quality and form together with barley the basis for Czechoslovakia's well-known beer production. Other important products are sugar beets, potatoes, turnips, hemp, and flax. Cattle, pigs, goats, sheep, horses, and fowl are raised in considerable numbers. Czechoslovakia ranks among the most richly wooded countries in Europe. Agricultural, foodstuff, and timber industries are widely dispersed in the country. The mineral production includes both soft and hard coal: the chief hard-coal fields are near Ostrava, the chief soft-coal (lignite) fields near Most, Teplice-Šanov, Falknov, and Chomůtov. Kaolin, graphite, and silver are mined in Bohemia, some silver, iron, copper, and lead in Slovakia. Czechoslovakia is a country of mineral springs and spas. Of 19,695 factories which were counted in 1947, 2,827 were metal and machine factories, 2,286 textile mills, 2,558 glass, stoneware, and ceramics factories, 1,789 food-producing factories, and 1,164 wood and furniture factories. All these industries are highly diversified and comprise units producing raw materials, half-finished, and finished products. The textile industry produces cotton, woolen, linen, and silk yarns, and also cloth, hosiery, and knitwear. The leather industry comprises tanneries, Europe's most highly developed shoe industry, and the production of gloves and handbags. The metal and engineering industries produce numerous products, including aircraft engines. In the manufacture of glassware, porcelain, costume jewelry, and beer Czechoslovakia has long been of international importance. However, the East-West conflict into which Czechoslovakia has been drawn is detrimental to its sensitive commercial organism. A further element of uncertainty is introduced by the nationalization of industry and mines and by the land reform. On June 21, 1945, the decree on land reform was issued; on Aug. 25, 1945, the nationalization of mines and of many industries, as well as banks and insurance companies, was decreed. The nationalization of industry has been completed.

History and Government. The country has a long history. It was inhabited by Celtic tribes before the Christian Era and acquired its Slavic population during the great European migrations in about the 6th century. After a period of obscurity and after the rise in the 9th century of a short-lived Moravian empire, the kingdom of Bohemia and Moravia emerged as a prominent medieval state in the 11th century, its king later becoming one of the electors of the Holy Roman Empire as his lands and fortunes became more deeply involved in the politics of that empire. It rose to the pinnacle of its power in the 14th century when its king, Charles IV, became Holy Roman Emperor. In the 15th century, the country became the center of religious controversy and war and at the same time enjoyed a rapid development of national culture under the stimulus of the Hussite reform movement. After 1526 the land was governed by Hapsburg rulers, and it lost its political independence for 300 years when it tried to end the Hapsburg elective succession in 1620. Thereafter it was a crownland of the Austrian emperors until its restoration as an independent republic in 1918. The earlier history of Bohemia, Moravia, Silesia, and Slovakia is treated under the separate entries. The modern Czechoslovak state came into existence on Oct. 28, 1918, when the Czech national council took over the government of Bohemia, Moravia, and Silesia. Two days later, the Slovak national council expressed the desire to unite politically with the Czechs. On Nov. 14, 1918, the first national assembly formally declared the republic, with Thomas G. Masaryk as president. The treaty of St.-Germain in the following year added international recognition. Sub-Carpathian Ruthenia was joined to the state. The attempts of the Sudeten Germans to set up their own state were suppressed. The republic had a democratic constitution (1920), a president, a responsible cabinet, two legislative chambers, and a free judiciary. Personal and religious freedoms were guaranteed. As such it continued as the most stable and prosperous of the Austrian succession states, until it was compelled to cede territories to Germany and Hungary following the Munich pact. The decision of the Four-Power Conference (Great Britain, France, Germany, Italy) which was made at Munich on Sept. 29, 1938, broke up the territory of Czechoslovakia. The regions largely inhabited by Germans were formed into a Sudeten-German territory and incorporated into Germany. Southern Slovakia was returned to Hungary. Subsequently, Polish troops occupied the territory of Těšín. On March 14, 1939, the Slovakian diet declared Slovakia an independent state. On the next day, the Germans occupied Bohemia and Moravia, which were incorporated into the German Reich as the Protectorate of Bohemia and Moravia. This development was a large contributing factor to the outbreak of World War II. The German occupation became more and more oppressive and the Czech population restive as the war proceeded. A Czech government in exile was set up in London under the leadership of Dr. Eduard Beneš. In Czechoslovakia itself numerous executions and deportations took place. The number of victims is estimated at 250,000, more than half of these Jews. The military liberation by Russian and American armed forces took place between October, 1944 and May, 1945. The sovereignty of Czechoslovakia over Bohemia, Moravia, Silesia, and Slovakia was fully restored. However, sovereignty over the easternmost region, called Carpathian Ruthenia, was transferred to the U.S.S.R. The Sudeten-German problem was solved radically by the expulsion of the native German population to Germany. Only a few hundred thousand Germans, either declared anti-Nazis or indispensable technicians, remained in the country. At the same time, a population exchange with Hungary took place in Slovakia. The Czechoslovak republic, as it emerged from World War II, was again based on the constitution of 1920, as revised in conformity with the Košice program of 1945, insuring personal liberties and parliamentary government but seeking to eliminate those groups which had sympathized with the Fascist regime. Slovakia was granted self-government within the framework of the common state. Following a cabinet crisis in February, 1948, the second president, Eduard Beneš, resigned and the country came under Communist control following the general elections of 1948 and the elevation of Klement Gottwald to the presidency. The three provinces of Bohemia, Moravia-Silesia, and Slovakia were abolished by decree of Dec. 21, 1948, and replaced by 19 *kraj* (counties or regions), named for their chief cities.

Culture. Culture in Czechoslovakia is not uniform. The country is inhabited chiefly by two closely allied Slavic peoples, the Czechs and the Slovaks, and has had considerable German and Hungarian minorities. It is rich in monuments and institutions reflecting an ancient peasant tradition and recalling its prominence during the Gothic and Baroque periods. Bohemia, Moravia, and Silesia from the early Middle Ages formed part of the Holy Roman Empire, and from the middle of the 16th century they were united with Austria. They were within West-European civilization while Slovakia, a backward part of Hungary, merely formed an outlying bastion. The country suffered an intellectual and cultural eclipse during two centuries of Hapsburg and Jesuit rule which gave place to a national revival at the end of the 18th century. Emphasis was then placed on the study of Slavic antiquities (Dobrovský, Jungmann), history (Palacký, Havlíček), music (Smetana, Dvořák), and art (Mánes). Focal points around which this growth centered were the National Museum (1818), the revived Czech section of Charles University (1882), and the National Theater (1883). The achievement of political independence in 1918 greatly aided further cultural activities. Czech culture, on a peasant foundation, is urbanized while Slovak culture until recently has been entirely rural. However, both Czechs and Slovaks had to assert themselves against German and Hungarian dominance in commerce and industry, in literature, and in politics. The landed estates were in German and Hungarian hands. The strength of the native peasantry grew throughout the 19th century, but only the land reform of the 1920's decided their dominance. At the same time, the peasant-bred Czechoslovak intelligentsia took over the state. By that time, approximately one third of the population of Bohemia, Moravia, and Silesia was German and one fourth of the population of Slovakia Hungarian; the German settlement in Slovakia was sparse. The Germans and the Czechs had struggled for supremacy in Bohemia and Moravia since the dawn of history, when both found themselves inhabiting one country. The spirit of compromise was lacking and all attempts to arrive at a modus vivendi failed. In the end, the very oppressiveness of the German rule after 1938 resulted in their expulsion when the Nazi domination was overthrown. In its ethnic composition, the country is now more nearly homogeneous than before, but the losses in population are not yet replaced. In religion the majority of the population is Roman Catholic, but about one million former Roman Catholics adhere now to an independent Czechoslovak church. Hussite sentiments are strong and many nominal Catholics are actually freethinkers. About one million are Protestants, in part Lutherans, in part Czech Brethren. The former Greek-Orthodox minority was concentrated in Carpathian Ruthenia and most of its members now reside outside the state. The ancient Jewish minority has disappeared through deportation and extermination. The language of the Czechs belongs to the western Slavic group, and the language of the Slovaks is closely related to Czech. Education and youth movements are highly developed. The SOKOL youth organization was for decades the leader of the nationalist revival movement; these groups are now under government control. There are four universities, two technical universities, and a number of agricultural, commercial, mining, art, musical, and theological academies. There is a well-developed press and literature. The musical culture and the religious mysticism of Bohemia have been a continuing influence in European civilization.

Czechoslovak National Democratic Party. See **National Democratic Party.**

Czechoslovak Social Democratic Party. Oldest organized political group of its kind in Bohemia before World War I. It subscribed to the Erfurt program with other European Social Democratic parties. Its non-Marxist wing was founded in 1896 as the National Socialist Party, was renamed the Czechoslovak Socialist Party in 1918, but returned to its old name in 1925. It has no similarities or connections with the German party of that name, and had Eduard Beneš as one of its leading members. The party advocated evolutionary state socialism and the bettering of social and laboring conditions. The Czechoslovak Communist Party was created in 1920 after a split within the Social Democratic groups.

Czechs (cheks). Inhabitants of the western part of Czechoslovakia, especially Bohemia and Moravia, numbering about six million. Linguistically, they belong to the Western branch of the Slavic family, with the Poles. Throughout their history the Czechs have been largely dominated by the Austrians. The Catholic faith is predominant among them.

Czegléd (tseg'lād). See **Cegléd.**

Czeladź (che'lyäch). [German, **Tscheliads.**] Town in SW Poland, in the *województwo* (province) of Śląsk (Silesia), situated on the Brinitza River, ab. 4 mi. NW of Sosnowiec. A coal-mining town, it belonged until 1919 (plebiscite 1921) to Upper Silesia, Germany. 16,624 (1946).

Czelakowski (che.lä.kôf'skē). See **Čelakovský.**

Czenstochau (chen'stō.ċhou). German name of **Częstochowa.**

Czenstochowa (cheṅ.stô.ʜô'vä). See **Częstochowa.**

Czermak (cher'mäk), **Jaroslaw.** b. at Prague, in Bohemia, Aug. 1, 1831; d. at Paris, April 23, 1878. Bohemian historical painter; brother of Johann Nepomuk Czermak. His best-known works are paintings of life in Montenegro and Hercegovina.

Czermak, Johann Nepomuk. b. at Prague, in Bohemia, June 17, 1828; d. at Leipzig, Germany, Sept. 16, 1873. Bohemian physiologist; brother of Jaroslaw Czermak. He introduced the use of the laryngoscope and the rhinoscope.

Czernin (cher'nin), **Ottokar,** Count. b. at Dimokur, in Austria-Hungary, Sept. 26, 1872; d. at Vienna, April 4, 1932. Austro-Hungarian diplomat and statesman. During his service as minister to Rumania, he attempted to keep that nation neutral in World War I; as minister of foreign affairs he represented Austria at Brest (or Brest Litovsk) and at Bucharest (1918). He worked for an early peace and was forced to retire because of the "Sixtus letter" Emperor Charles had written during the negotiations for a separate peace. He wrote his memoirs, *Im Weltkriege* (1919).

Czernowitz (cher'nō.vits). German name of **Chernovtsy.**

Czerny (cher'nē), **Adalbert.** b. at Szcakowa, in Galicia, March 25, 1863; d. at Berlin, Oct. 3, 1941. German pediatrician. He became Privatdocent of pediatrics (1893) at the University of Prague, professor (1894) at the University of Breslau, professor at Strasbourg (1910), and in 1913 succeeded J. O. Heubner at Berlin. He made studies of the physiology and pathology of digestion and metabolism in children and of nutritional disorders. He is responsible for the concept of the "exudative diathesis" (1907) which is still important in concepts of the pathogenesis of children's diseases. Author of *Der Arzt als Erzieher des Kindes* (1908) and *Des Kindes Ernährung, Ernährungsstörungen und Ernährungstherapie* (1906–18).

Czerny, Karl. b. at Vienna, Feb. 20, 1791; d. there, July 15, 1857. Austrian pianist and composer, noted for his piano exercises. Among his pupils were Liszt, Kullak, Döhler, and Ninette von Belleville.

Czerny, Vincenz. b. at Trutnov in Bohemia, Nov. 19, 1842; d. at Heidelberg, Germany, Oct. 3, 1916. Bohemian surgeon. He was assistant to Theodor Billroth and served as professor at the universities of Freiburg (1871 *et seq.*) and Heidelberg (1877 *et seq.*), establishing (1906) at the latter the Institute for Experimental Cancer Research. He contributed successfully to experimental and clinical surgery, including the treatment of bone and joint tuberculosis, the operation of inguinal hernia, total hysterectomy by the vaginal route, the enucleation of subperitoneal uterine fibroids, and the resection of the intestines. He recommended intestinal suturing. In renal surgery he succeeded in pyelolithotomy (1880) and was very successful in plastic surgery. Author of *Beiträge zur operativen Chirurgie* (1887), *Über die Entwicklung der Chirurgie während des 19. Jahrhunderts und ihre Beziehung zum Unterricht* (1903), *Das Heidelberger Institut für experimentelle Krebsforschung* (1912), and *Über die neuen Bestrebungen, das Los der Krebskranken zu verbessern* (1913).

Czerny George (cher'ni jôrj). See **Karageorge.**

Częstochowa (cheṅ.stô.ʜô'vä). [Also: **Czenstochowa;** Russian, **Chenstokhov, Tschenstochow;** German, **Czenstochau.**] City in C Poland, in the *województwo* (province) of Kielce, situated on the Warta River, ab. 65 mi. W of Kielce. There are steel and iron, cotton and woolen textile, leather, and paper industries, and breweries; coal mines are in the vicinity. It is the seat of a bishopric and one of the most frequented places of pilgrimage in Poland because of the miraculous wooden image of the Holy Virgin contained in the Monastery of Jasnagora. The monastery was erected in 1382; the present church is in the baroque style. The city and monastery were defended successfully against the Swedes in 1665; the fortifications were razed by Czar Alexander I. Częstochowa was occupied by the Germans in November, 1914, and again in September, 1939. Pop. 101,255 (1946).

Człuchów (chlö'ʜöf). [German, **Schlochau.**] Town in NW Poland, in the *województwo* (province) of Szczecin, formerly in the *Grenzmark* (frontier district) of Posen-Westpreussen, Germany, situated near the former German-Polish border, ab. 120 mi. SW of Danzig: sawmills. The ruins of a 14th-century castle of the Teutonic Order are here. The town came under Polish administration in 1945. Pop. 6,029 (1939); 3,711 (1946).

Czolgosz (chôl'gôsh), **Leon F.** b. at Detroit, 1873; executed at Auburn, N.Y., Oct. 29, 1901. American assassin. Influenced by anarchistic teaching, he shot President McKinley in the Temple of Music of the Pan-American Exposition at Buffalo, N.Y., on Sept. 6, 1901.

Czuczor (tsö'tsōr), **Gergely.** b. at Andód, Neutra, Hungary, Dec. 17, 1800; d. at Pest (now part of Budapest), Sept. 9, 1866. Hungarian poet and lexicographer. His best-known poems are the *Battle of Augsburg* (1824) and *Diet of Arad* (1828).

D

Dā (däṅ). See **Dan.**

Dabaiba (dä.bī'bä) or **Dabaybe** (dä.bī'bā). [Also: **Davaive, Abibe.**] Name given in the early part of the 16th century to a region S of the Isthmus of Panama, somewhere in the vicinity of the Atrato River. It was probably the appellation of a chief, or his title, transferred by the Spaniards to the territory over which he ruled. According to reports Dabaiba contained a temple lined with gold, where human sacrifices were made. Balboa vainly searched for this temple in 1512 and 1515, and it was long an object of the Spanish expeditions.

D'Abernon (dab'ėr.non), 1st Viscount. [Title of **Edgar Vincent.**] b. 1857; d. at Hove, Sussex, England, Nov. 1, 1941. English financier and diplomat who was British ambassador (1920–26) to Germany. He served for five years in the Coldstream Guards. He became president (1883) of the council of the Ottoman public debt, was financial adviser (1883–89) to Egypt, and was governor (1889–97) of the Imperial Ottoman Bank at Constantinople. During his embassy in Germany, the Locarno agreements concerning maintenance of European peace and the admission of Germany to the League of Nations were negotiated. He was a Conservative member of Parliament (1899–1906) from Exeter. In 1929 he headed a British economic mission to Argentina and Brazil. He was the author of *Dawes to Locarno—1924–1926* and of a grammar of modern Greek adopted by the University of Athens.

Dabih (dä′bē). The third magnitude star β Capricorni. Originally the Arabs applied the name to the two stars α and β.

Dabit (då.bē), **Eugène.** b. at Paris, Sept. 21, 1898; d. of scarlet fever while en route to attend the funeral of Maxim Gorky, at Sevastopol, Russia, Aug. 21, 1936. French novelist. He was the author of *Hôtel du Nord* (1929; Eng. trans., 1931), *Petit-Louis* (1930), *Villa Oasis* (1932), *Faubourgs de Paris* (1933), *Un Mort tout neuf* (1934), *L'Ile* (1934), *La Zone verte* (1935), and *Trains de vie* (1936). Self-educated and very poor, he won the Populist prize with his first novel, was taken up by Gide, Roger Martin du Gard, and other influential patrons, and was, at the time of his death, considered one of the most promising of the young French novelists.

Dablon (då.blôn), **Claude.** b. at Dieppe, France, c1619; d. at Quebec, Sept. 20, 1697. French Jesuit missionary. He arrived in New France in 1655, was with Marquette on Lake Superior in 1668, and was appointed superior of the missions of the Upper Lakes in 1670, serving in that capacity during the period when the Jesuits accomplished their most notable explorations in the area. He edited the *Relation* of 1671–72, and compiled an account of Marquette's journey.

Dabney (dab′ni), **Charles William.** b. at Hampden-Sidney, Va., June 19, 1855; d. at Asheville, N.C., June 15, 1945. American chemist and educator, president of the University of Cincinnati from 1904 to 1920. He was graduated from Hampden-Sidney College in 1873 and the University of Virginia in 1877, and studied (1878–80) at Berlin and Göttingen. He was state chemist (1880–87) of North Carolina, professor of agricultural chemistry and director of the agricultural experiment station (1887–90) in the University of Tennessee, and president (1887–1904) of the university. He served (1894–97) as assistant secretary of agriculture. His publications include numerous papers on scientific and educational topics.

Dabo (dä′bō), **Leon.** b. at Detroit, July 9, 1868—. American muralist and landscape painter, whose works are collected by many large galleries in the U.S., France, Japan, and Canada. He studied at the École des Beaux-Arts and the Julian Academy, both at Paris; his works have been exhibited in the U.S., England, France, and elsewhere. He is an associate of the National Academy of Design, chevalier of the Legion of Honor, member of the Royal Society of Arts and Sciences at London, and of the National Arts Club. Among his works are *Moore Park, The Cloud, The Hudson, The Ocean, Gray Cloud, Lawn Party, Sun and Mist, Cooper's Lake,* and *The Storm;* also 20 religious panels in the Church of John the Baptist at Brooklyn, N.Y.

Dąbrowa Górnicza (dôm.brô′vä gör.nē′chä). [Also: **Dombrowa Gora;** German, **Dombrau.**] City in SW Poland, in the *województwo* (province) of Śląsk (Silesia), NE of Sosnowiec. It belonged formerly to the province of Kielce. It is the center of an important coal-mining district, and has zinc and iron foundries and timber, chemical, and food industries. 28,070 (1946).

Dąbrowska (dôm.brôf′skä), **Marja.** [English, **Maria Dabrowska.**] b. at Rusów, Kalisz province, in what was then Russian Poland, 1892—. Polish novelist, reformer, and playwright. She has written numerous studies of the peasant problem in Poland, including *The Landless* (1925), *Crossroads* (1937), and *Hand in Hand* (1939); also, two dramas on historical themes, *Orphan Genius* (1939) and *Bogumil and Bolesław* (1944), and especially the long novel *Nights and Days* (1932–34), which depicts the fortunes of a Kalisz family following the uprising of 1863. She is believed to be resident now in Poland.

Dąbrowski (dôm.brôf′skē), **Jan Henryk.** See **Dombrowski, Jan Henryk.**

Dacca (dak′ą). [Also, **Dhaka.**] Division in East Bengal, Pakistan. Jute is the most important crop in the area, followed by rice and tobacco. Capital, Dacca; area, 15,937 sq. mi.; pop. 16,683,714 (1941).

Dacca. [Also, **Dhaka.**] District in Dacca division, East Bengal, Pakistan. Capital, Dacca; area, 2,738 sq. mi.; pop. 4,222,143 (1941).

Dacca. [Also, **Dhaka.**] Capital of the division and district of Dacca, and of East Bengal province, Pakistan, on the Buriganga River, ab. 160 mi. NE of Calcutta. It was for many years the chief city of Bengal. It was noted for its muslin, and its jute industry is important. 273,159 (1951).

Dacca Jelalpur (je.läl′pör). See **Faridpur.**

Dach (däċh), **Simon.** b. at Memel, Lithuania, July 29, 1605; d. at Königsberg, in East Prussia, April 15, 1659. German poet, author of occasional lyrics that were not collected until after his death. The depressing period in which he lived and his own poor health (he died of tuberculosis) lent a somber cast to his writings. The poem for which he has been chiefly known, *Anke van Tharaw*, supposedly written by him for a friend's wedding and long accepted as a folk song, may actually have been written by some other poet.

Dachau (däċh′ou). Town in S Germany, in the *Land* (state) of Bavaria, American Zone, in the *Regierungsbezirk* (government district) of Upper Bavaria, situated on the Amper River, ab. 10 mi. NW of Munich: an agricultural market town, with lumber and paper mills, cement works, and a brewery. It is also a health resort, known for its mud baths. The castle, reconstructed in 1715, contains a local museum. In the vicinity was the huge concentration camp of Dachau, opened in 1933 and used for the imprisonment of victims of racial and political persecution during the entire period of the National Socialist regime. Many people were put to death here by various methods; others were shipped to death camps in eastern Europe after 1941. The camp was occupied by Allied troops on April 29, 1945, after a revolt of the surviving prisoners (of all European nations) had prevented further killings; 32,000 people were liberated. A monument to the dead has been erected on the site. 23,552 (1951).

Dachstein (däċh′shtīn). One of the chief peaks in the Salzkammergut region, in W central Austria, ab. 18 mi. S of Ischl. It is one of the highest peaks of this group. 9,829 ft.

Dacia (dā′shą). In ancient geography, a province of the Roman Empire, lying between the Carpathian Mountains on the N, the Tissus or Tisia (Tisza) on the W, the Ister (Danube) on the S, and the Tyras or Danastris (Dniester) on the E. It corresponded approximately to modern Rumania, including Transylvania. The inhabitants were the Getae or Daci. It was invaded by Alexander the Great in 335 B.C., by Lysimachus c292 B.C., and its people defeated the generals of Domitian in 86–90 A.D. It was conquered by Trajan in 101, and succeeding years, and made a Roman province. It was abandoned by the Romans in the reign of Aurelian (270–275), but not before the Romans, during some 200 years of occupation, had left their imprint on the region by establishing the language that has developed into modern Rumanian.

Dacia. Diocese in the N part of the later Roman prefecture of Illyricum (Serbia and W Bulgaria).

Dacicus (dā′si.kus). A surname of **Trajan.**

Dacier (då.syā), **André.** b. at Castres, France, April 6, 1651; d. at Paris, Sept. 18, 1722. French classical scholar and academician; husband of Anne Dacier. He translated into French (for the use of Monseigneur, the Dauphin, Louis de France) Valerius Flaccus, Horace, Epictetus, Aristotle's *Poetics*, and other ancient Greek and Latin works.

Dacier, Anne. [Maiden name, **Lefebvre** or **Lefèvre.**] b. at Saumur, France, in March, 1654; d. at Paris, Aug. 17, 1720. French classical scholar; wife of André Dacier. She translated the *Iliad* (1699), the *Odyssey* (1708), and other Greek and Latin classics into French.

Dacoit (dą.koit′). [Hindustani, **Dakait.**] A member of any of the groups of armed bandits who long fought British forces in Bengal, India. Dacoity was the term applied to the raids by guerrilla bands which harassed the British-Indian government in Burma after the defeat of King Thebaw in 1885, after the annexation of Burma, and at intervals until recent times. During the disturbances incident to World War II, the reoccupation, and the end of British rule in Burma, dacoity greatly increased and, in the form of armed gangsterism preying upon peaceful villages, has become a major problem for the new Burmese government. The term is occasionally applied also to outlawry in Thailand (Siam) where, likewise, it results from unsettled conditions.

Da Costa (dä kôs′tä), **Izaak.** b. at Amsterdam, Netherlands, Jan. 14, 1798; d. at Leiden, Netherlands, April, 28 1860. Dutch poet and Protestant theologian. His works include *Prometheus* (1820, a translation of Aeschylus's play), *Po zii* (1821–22), *Feestliederen* (1828), *Hagar* (1840), and various historical and theological treatises.

Dacre (dā'kėr), Baron. Title held by various members of the **Brand** family; see also **Fiennes, Thomas.**

Dacre of Gilsland (gilz'land), Baron. A title of **Howard, Charles** (1629–85).

Dacres (dā'kėrz), Sir **Richard James.** b. 1799; d. at Brighton, England, Dec. 6, 1886. British field marshal. He served in the Crimean War, commanding the royal horse-artillery at the battle of the Alma and the artillery at the battle of Balaklava.

Dacres, Sir Sidney Colpoys. b. at Totnes, Devonshire, England, Jan. 9, 1805; d. at Brighton, England, March 8, 1884. British admiral. He entered the Royal Navy in 1817, and became a captain in 1840. He commanded the *Sans Pareil* in the operations before Sevastopol, including the bombardment of Oct. 17, 1854, was placed in charge of the port of Balaklava, on Oct. 27, 1854, and was appointed captain of the fleet in the Mediterranean in 1859. He was commander in chief in the English Channel in 1863, first sea lord in 1868, and admiral in 1870.

Dactyls (dak'tilz) or **Dactyli** (dak'ti.lī) or **Daktyloi** (-loi). In Greek and Roman mythology, supernatural and magical beings living on Mount Ida in Phrygia, the discoverers of iron and copper and of the art of working them. They were transferred, in the legends, to Mount Ida in Crete, and were there identified with the Curetes, Corybantes, and other mountain-dwelling semidivine beings. Their number, originally three, was increased, in various accounts, to ten, and even to one hundred.

Dade City (dād). City in C Florida, county seat of Pasco County, NE of Tampa: center for a citrus and truck farming community. 3,806 (1950).

Daedalus (ded'a.lus, dē'da.lus). In Greek legend, an Athenian; son of Metion and grandson of Erechtheus. He was regarded as the personification of all handicrafts and of art, and as such was worshiped by artists' guilds in various places, especially in Attica, and was a central figure in various myths. He was said to have made various improvements in the fine arts, including architecture, and to have invented many mechanical appliances, as the ax, the awl, and the bevel. For the murder of his nephew Talus, of whose inventive skill he was jealous, he was driven to Crete, where he constructed, to contain the monster Minotaur, the famous labyrinth, in which he, with his son Icarus, was confined for furnishing the clue of it to Ariadne. (In another legend a different account of his imprisonment is given: he built a cow disguise for Pasiphaë in order that the bull sent by Poseidon might mount her.) Escaping, he and Icarus fled over the sea on wings of wax which they had made. Icarus soared too near the sun, his wings melted, and he fell into the sea (which has since been called, from him, the Icarian Sea). Many archaic wooden images were, in ancient times, believed to be the work of Daedalus (and figures of the type are still called Daedalian).

Daegsastan (dak'sä.stän), **Battle of.** Victory gained in 603 by the Northumbrian king Ethelfrith over the Scots under Aidan, supposedly near the river Tees.

Daendels (dän'dels), **Herman Willem.** b. at Hattem, Gelderland, Netherlands, Oct. 21, 1762; d. on the Gold Coast, Africa, May 2, 1818. Dutch general, and governor general of the Dutch East Indies (1808–11). He took part in the revolutionary agitation in the Netherlands in 1787, and was obliged to seek refuge in France. In 1793 he aided Dumouriez in the expedition against Holland, as colonel of a body of foreign volunteers; and in 1794 served with Pichegru as general of brigade. After this campaign he entered the service of the Batavian Republic as lieutenant general, and in 1799 commanded a division in the successful resistance to the Anglo-Russian invasion. In 1806 he entered the service of the king of Holland, and was made marshal in 1807. He became governor general of the Dutch East Indies under the Napoleonic regime. He inaugurated many of the reforms reintroduced by, and sometimes attributed to, Sir Thomas Stamford Raffles under an equally brief British regime in Java. Because of his uncompromising attitude and the disturbances which arose in Java from the disruption of the traditional economy under a wartime policy of enforced production for export, he was highly unpopular in spite of his humanitarian intentions. He served under Napoleon in the Russian campaign in 1812, and in 1814 was made governor of the Dutch colonies on the Gold Coast of Africa.

Daffodil Fields, The. Narrative poem (1913) by John Masefield.

Daffodil Murderer, The. Poem by Siegfried Sassoon, published in 1913 under the pseudonym Saul Kain. It was awarded the Chantrey prize.

Dafirah (dä.fē'ra). Rarely used name for the star β Leonis, usually known as Denebola.

Dafne (däf'nā) or **Daphne** (daf'nē). Musical work credited as being the first opera, as distinguished from a musical drama. It was produced (1596) by the Society of the Alterati at Florence, in the private house of Jacopo Corsi. The music was by Giulio Caccini and Jacopo Peri (who both invented recitative), the words by Ottavio Rinuccini. Opitz made a German translation of the text, and Heinrich Schütz wrote new music for it. This was the first German opera, and was produced (April 13, 1627) at Torgau, at the court of the elector John George I.

Dafoe (dā'fō), **Allan Roy.** b. May 29, 1883; d. at North Bay, Ontario, Canada, June 2, 1943. Canadian physician who successfully delivered (May 28, 1934) the Dionne quintuplets, at Callander, Ontario. He received (1907) a medical degree from the University of Toronto, and practiced (1909 *et seq.*) at Callander. He was the personal physician (1934–42) of the Dionne quintuplets. He wrote *Dr. Dafoe's Guide Book for Mothers* (1936).

Dafoe, John Wesley. b. in Ontario, March 8, 1866; d. Jan. 9, 1944. Canadian journalist. He was correspondent (1883 *et seq.*) at Ottawa, covering Parliamentary news for the Montreal *Star*. In 1901 he became editor in chief of the Manitoba (later Winnipeg) *Free Press*, expressing liberal views even when, as in the case of the government's trade policies, they were at variance with the publisher's. In 1919 he attended the Paris peace conference as press representative of the Canadian Department of Public Information. He was chancellor (1934 *et seq.*) of the University of Manitoba.

Dafydd ap Gwilym (dä'viᴛʜ äp gwi'lim). See **David.**

Dagami (dä.gä'mē). Town in the NE part of Leyte island in the Philippines. It is on the Binahaan River, at the head of navigation by *cascos* (native boats), ab. 15 mi. from the river's mouth. 3,460 (1948).

Dagari (dä.gä'rē). [Also: **Dagaba, Dagarti, Dagati, Dagatsi.**] Sudanic-speaking people of W Africa, inhabiting the NW part of the Northern Territories of the Gold Coast and E Ivory Coast. Their language is related to those of the Mossi and Dagomba. Their number is estimated at ab. 60,000 (by M. Delafosse, *Haut-Sénégal-Niger*, 1912). They practice hoe agriculture, and their principal food is millet. They are non-Mohammedan.

Dagda (däg'da). See under **Tuatha De Danann.**

Dagestan Autonomous Soviet Socialist Republic (dä.ge.stän'). [Also: **Dagestan, Daghestan.**] Republic in the U.S.S.R., in the Russian Soviet Federated Socialist Republic, located on the W shore of the Caspian Sea, N of the Azerbaijan Soviet Socialist Republic. The surface ranges from mountainous to very hilly. By far the most important product of the area is its oil, but there is also some production of sulfur. Crops include cotton, grapes, tobacco, citrus fruits, and flax. It was formerly a province in the Russian Empire, having submitted to Russia in 1859, and was the scene of an insurrection (1877–78). Capital, Makhachkala; area, 13,124 sq. mi.; pop. 930,527 (1939).

Daggett (dag'et), **David.** b. at Attleboro, Mass., Dec. 31, 1764; d. at New Haven, Conn., April 12, 1851. American jurist. He was a U.S. senator from Connecticut (1813–19).

Daggett, Naphtali. b. at Attleboro, Mass., Sept. 8, 1727; d. at New Haven, Conn., Nov. 25, 1780. American clergyman. He was acting president (1766–67) of Yale College.

Daghestan (dä.ge.stän'). See **Dagestan Autonomous Soviet Socialist Republic.**

Dagnan-Bouveret (dá.nyäṅ.böv.re), **Pascal Adolphe Jean.** b. at Paris, Jan. 7, 1852; d. 1929. French painter; a pupil of Gérôme. He obtained the second Prix de Rome in 1876. His pictures first appeared in the Paris Salon in 1877. He was awarded several medals, one of the first class in 1880.

Dagö (däg'ė''). See **Hiiumaa.**

Dagobert (dag'ǫ.bėrt). See also **Daimbert.**

Dagobert I (dag'ǫ.bėrt; French, dȧ.go.ber). b. c602; d. c639. Merovingian king of the Franks, son of Clotaire II, by whom he was appointed king of Austrasia in 622, and whom he succeeded as king of the Franks in 628. He founded the abbey of St.-Denis, and reduced to writing the customary laws of the barbarian tribes in his kingdom. During his reign the empire of the Franks attained a wide extent, namely, from the Weser River to the Pyrenees, and from the Western Ocean to the frontiers of Bohemia. Following his reign the Merovingian kings became figureheads while the mayors of the palace took over actual rule.

Dagobert (dȧ.go.ber), **Chanson du roi.** [Eng. trans., "*Song of King Dagobert.*"] Popular French song concerning King Dagobert I and his favorite counselor, Saint Eloi. It was in existence before the French Revolution. It is a satirical series of couplets sung to a hunting chorus, and has been modified to suit various political epochs. In 1814 it became immensely popular on account of the verses against Napoleon and the Russian campaign. It was forbidden by the police, but was revived on the return of the Bourbons. Every other stanza begins "Le bon roi Dagobert."

Dagomba (dä.gōm'bä). Sudanic-speaking people of W Africa, inhabiting the E part of the Northern Territories of the Gold Coast and N Togoland. Their language is known as Dagbane, and is related to that of the Mossi. Their population is estimated at ab. 190,000 (based on A. W. Cardinall, *The Gold Coast*, 1931). They are ruled by a hereditary king known as Na, and have exogamous patrilineal clans. They practice hoe agriculture, and their principal foods are yams, millet, sorghum, and maize. They are non-Mohammedan.

Dagon (dā'gon). In the Old Testament, a deity mentioned as the national god of the Philistines, and as worshiped especially in Gaza and Ashdod (Judges, xvi. 23, and 1 Sam. v.). The name is usually derived from Hebrew *dag* (fish), and it is assumed that Dagon was depicted as half man and half fish, and had his female counterpart in Derketo, who was worshiped in Ashkelon (Ascalon). 1 Sam. v. 4 would seem to favor this view. On the other hand, Assyro-Babylonian mythology also includes a divinity Dagan, but there he is, etymologically at least, not connected with the fish, as the Assyrian word for fish is not *dag* but *nun;* the meaning of the name Dagan has not as yet been determined, but may be connected with the word for grain. At the same time the Babylonian historian Berossus gives an account of such a being, half man and half fish, under the name Oannes, who in the beginning of history emerged at intervals from the sea and taught the Babylonians the arts of civilization. This Oannes of Berossus is identified by some scholars with Ea of the Assyro-Babylonian pantheon, the god of the ocean, and is conceived as a human figure with the skin of a fish on his shoulders as a garment, a representation of which is often met on the early monuments. In Phoenicia the name of the god was connected with *dagan* (corn) and is accordingly rendered into Greek in the fragments of Philo Byblius as *sitos* (grain). Dagon was then considered as the god of agriculture, a function which is also emphasized in the Oannes of Berossus.

Dagonet (dag'ǫ.net, -nẹt). Pseudonym of **Sims, George Robert.**

Dagonet, Sir. [Also, **Sir Daguenet** (dag'ẹ.net).] In Arthurian romances, the fool of King Arthur, who "loved him passing well and made him knight with his own hands." He was buffeted and knocked about a good deal, and is frequently alluded to by the dramatists of Shakespeare's time and later.

Daguerre (dȧ.ger), **Louis Jacques Mandé.** b. at Cormeilles, Seine-et-Oise, France, Nov. 18, 1789; d. at Petit-Brie-sur-Marne, France, July 12, 1851. French painter, and inventor (with Joseph Nicéphore Niepce) of the daguerreotype process of photography. He was at first in the internal revenue service, then devoted himself to scene painting, in which he attained celebrity, and in 1822, with Charles Marie Bouton, opened the Diorama (a theater containing painted scenes viewed through openings and so arranged that the light shone through them, giving the illusion of reality) at Paris (burned 1839). In the successful study of the problem of obtaining permanent pictures by the action of sunlight he was anticipated by Nicéphore Niepce, who began his investigations in 1814, and communicated some of his results to Daguerre, who was then occupied with the subject, in 1826; the two worked together from 1829 until Niepce's death in 1833. Daguerre's perfected process was communicated to the Academy of Sciences by Dominique François Arago, Jan. 9, 1839. The daguerreotype was made by exposure to light of a silver plate coated with silver iodide, development in mercury vapor, and fixation with sodium thiosulfate (hypo). In return for pensions granted to Daguerre and Niepce's heir, the process was detailed to the Academy and a description published by the French government.

Daguesseau (dȧ.ge.sō), **Henri François.** See **Aguesseau, Henri François d'.**

Dagupan (dä.gö'pän). Town in Pangasinan province, W Luzon, Philippine Islands: seaport on the SE shore of Lingayen Gulf. 11,254 (1948).

Dahalach or **Dahalak** (dä.ä.läk'). See **Dahlak Archipelago.**

Daheim (dä.hīm'). German illustrated weekly "for family and home," founded by Velhagen and Klasing in 1864 when the more radical *Gartenlaube* was banned in Prussia. Its first editor was Robert Koenig, well known as the author of a best-selling history of German literature.

Dahl (däl), **Hans.** b. at Hardanger, Norway, Feb. 19, 1849; d. 1919. Norwegian-born landscape and genre painter who worked in Germany. He studied under Riefstahl and Gude at Karlsruhe, then with Gebhart at Düsseldorf. In 1876 he first exhibited at Berlin, and finally settled there permanently in 1889. He injected much humor into his work, which was much appreciated in Norway.

Dahl, Johan Christian Clausen (or **Claussön**). b. at Bergen, Norway, Feb. 24, 1788; d. at Dresden, Germany, Oct. 14, 1857. Norwegian landscape painter.

Dahl, Michael. b. at Stockholm, 1656; d. at London, Oct. 20, 1743. Swedish portrait painter. He was a pupil of the Danish painter Ernst Klocke, and in 1688 settled at London, where he acquired an extensive patronage among the nobility and at court. He painted the portraits of the princess (afterward queen) Anne and Prince George, the portrait of Charles XI of Sweden at Windsor, and the series of portraits of admirals at Hampton Court.

Dahl, Vladimir Ivanovich. [Also: **Dal, Dale;** pseudonym, **Kossack Lugansky.**] b. at St. Petersburg, 1801; d. at Moscow, Nov. 3, 1872. Russian novelist, philologist, and littérateur. He published a *Dictionary of the Living Russian Tongue* (4 vols., 1861–66). He was a worker in the field and his investigations resulted in his amassing about 4,000 folk tales and some 30,000 proverbs. His tales of Russian life were popular.

Dahlak Archipelago (dä.läk'). [Also: **Dahalach, Dahalak; Dahlac.**] Group of islands in the Red Sea, NE Africa, off the seaport of Massawa, Eritrea.

Dahlberg (däl'bery'; Anglicized, -bėrg), Count **Erik Jönsson.** b. at Stockholm, Oct. 20, 1625; d. there, Jan. 26, 1703. Swedish military engineer and field marshal. He was one of those responsible for the famous forced march (1658) across the ice against Copenhagen by the army of Charles X (Charles Gustavus). From 1676 to 1702 he was his country's chief military engineer in both offensive and defensive operations, and came to be known as the "Vauban of Sweden." As governor of Livonia he twice successfully defended Riga. At his retirement in 1702 he held the rank of field marshal.

Dahlbom (däl'böm), **Anders Gustaf.** b. at Forssa, East Gotland, Sweden, March 3, 1806; d. at Lund, Sweden, May 3, 1859. Swedish entomologist. His chief work was *Hymenoptera europaea praecipue borealia* (1845).

Dahlgren (däl'grẹn), **Erik Wilhelm.** b. at Stockholm, June 7, 1848; d. 1934. Swedish geographer who served (1903 *et seq.*) as director of the royal library at Stockholm. He was the author of *Les Relations commerciales et maritimes entre la France et les côtes de l'Océan pacifique* (Commercial and Maritime Relations Between France and the Coasts of the Pacific Ocean, 1909), and *Les Débuts de la cartographie du Japan* (The Beginning of Japan's Cartography, 1911).

Dahlgren, John Adolphus Bernard. b. at Philadelphia, Nov. 13, 1809; d. at the Washington navy yard, July 12, 1870. American naval officer, noted as an inventor of ordnance and for his development of the ordnance department at the Washington navy yard. After several years of service at sea, he was appointed (1832) midshipman and served (1834–36) with the coast survey, helping to make in Long Island the first scientifically measured base line in the U.S. He was active in other triangulation work, but had to take a leave of absence when his eyesight became seriously impaired. He received treatment at Paris, retired to the country after his return to the U.S., and in 1843, his eyesight restored, rejoined the navy. In 1847 he went to the Washington navy yard, where he remained for 16 years, eventually becoming commandant of the yard and chief of the ordnance bureau. In his work at the yard, he was responsible for building up the ordnance establishment, for introducing the "Boat Howitzers" (adopted by the navy in 1850), and for designing the smoothbore 11-inch guns called "Dahlgrens," whose seaworthiness he personally supervised during an experimental cruise (1857–59) in the ship *Experiment.* His achievements did much to prepare the navy for its service in the Civil War, in which Dahlgren, as a rear admiral (promoted February, 1863), commanded the South Atlantic blockading squadron during part of the war. He was commander (1866–68) of the South Pacific squadron and again (1868–69) chief of the ordnance bureau, leaving that post to become commandant of the Washington navy yard. He was the author of *32 Pounder Practise for Ranges* (1850), *The System of Boat Armament in the United States Navy* (1852), *Naval Percussion Locks and Primers* (1853), and *Shells and Shell Guns* (1856), and served as professor of gunnery at Annapolis.

Dahlgren, Karl Fredrik. b. at Stensbruk, near Norrköping, Sweden, June 20, 1791; d. at Stockholm, May 2, 1844. Swedish poet, novelist, and humorist. He is best known for his lyric *Zephyr and the Maid,* but his satires and humorous works are first-class in their field. His complete works were published 1847–52.

Dahlmann (däl′män), **Friedrich Christoph.** b. at Wismar, Mecklenburg-Schwerin, Germany, May 13, 1785; d. at Bonn, Prussia, Germany, Dec. 5, 1860. German historian and statesman, appointed professor at Kiel in 1812, at Göttingen in 1829, and at Bonn in 1842. He was a member of the National Assembly at Frankfort on the Main (1848–49). His works include *Quellenkunde der deutschen Geschichte* (1830), *Geschichte von Dänemark* (1840–43), *Geschichte der englischen Revolution* (1844), *Geschichte der französischen Revolution* (1845), and others.

Dahlstjerna (däl′sher.nä), **Gunno.** [Original name, **Gunno Eurelius.**] b. at Öhr, Dalsland, Sweden, Sept. 7, 1661; d. in Pomerania, Sept. 7, 1709. Swedish poet. He wrote *Kungaskald* (1697), an elegy on the death of Charles XI, and a poem on Charles XII and Peter the Great.

Dahn (dän), **(Julius Sophus) Felix.** b. at Hamburg, Germany, Feb. 9, 1834; d. at Breslau, Jan. 3, 1912. German historian and poet. He studied history and jurisprudence at Munich and Berlin. In 1857 he became docent in the faculty of law at the University of Munich, and in 1862 was made professor. The succeeding year he went in the same capacity to Würzburg. In 1872 he became professor of law at the University of Königsberg, and in 1888 at Breslau. His most important works are, in history, *Die Könige der Germanen* (The Kings of the Germans, 1861–92), *Urgeschichte der germanischen und romanischen Völker* (Primitive History of the Germanic and Romance Peoples, 1881–90); in law, *Die Vernunft im Recht* (Reason in Law, 1879). A volume of poems, *Gedichte,* appeared in 1857, and a second collection in 1873; *Balladen und Lieder* (Ballads and Songs) in 1878. He was the author of several romances, the principal one, *Ein Kampf um Rom* (A Struggle for Rome), appeared in 1876, in four volumes; *Odhins Trost* (Odin's Consolation) in 1880. He wrote, also, a number of dramas, among them *Markgraf Rüdeger von Bechelaren* (1875).

Dahomey (dạ.hō′mi). Territory of French West Africa, extending from the Slave Coast inland to the Niger River and the Upper Volta territory. On the W it borders on Togo, on the E on Nigeria. The French occupied the coast in 1851, and in 1894 annexed the entire kingdom of Dahomey. Until 1900 the court at Abomey was allowed to exist, but in that year the king was seized and exiled to the Congo. The territory is administered by a governor, subject to the governor general of French West Africa, and assisted by a privy council and a secretary-general. The land is low and the climate unhealthful. The chief export is palm oil, and some progress is being made in growing cotton. The chief port is Cotonou, near Porto-Novo. Dahomey sends one deputy to the French National Assembly, and two each to the Council of the Republic and the Assembly of the French Union. The many human victims for which certain of their ceremonies are notorious resulted from tribal belief and custom rather than from cruelty; reports were exaggerated, but human sacrifice was based on belief in the king's need for attendants in the afterworld and other beliefs consonant with their philosophy of life and death. They are also called "Fon." Their language is closely allied to Ewe. Capital, Porto-Novo; area, 43,232 sq. mi.; pop. 1,478,020 (1948).

Dahomey. [Also: **Dahome, Dahomy.**] Former kingdom of a Sudanic-speaking people of W Africa, in the area of the present French colony of the same name, with its capital at Abomey. The Dahomeans speak a language related to that of the Ewe, known as Fon (also, Fo, Fou). They have exogamous patrilineal clans which control succession to political office. The king and his court were supported by taxes based on an annual census of livestock and granaries. Through human sacrifice and annual slave-raiding wars with the Yoruba, in which female warriors or "Amazons" took part, the Dahomey acquired an exaggerated reputation for bloodthirstiness, exceeding even that of the Edo. They practice hoe agriculture, and their principal crops are maize, yams, and manioc.

Dahra (dä′rä). [Also, **Ed Dahra.**] Mountainous region in NW Africa, in E French Morocco, close to the Algerian border. In its caverns, during one of the French colonial campaigns of the mid-19th century, ab. 500 to 600 members of the Kabyle tribe were suffocated (1845) by order of the French commander Colonel Aimable Jean Jacques Pélissier.

Dahshur (dä.shör′). [Also, **Dashur.**] Locality in NE Africa, in Egypt, W of the Nile River and directly S of the great Pyramids. It is noted for its pyramids, two of stone and two of unburned brick. The northernmost, of stone, is of remarkable size, measuring ab. 700 ft. square (originally ab. 720), and 326 ft. high (originally ab. 342½). There is a series of three chambers beneath it. The sides of the other stone pyramid are built in two angles, like a curb roof, from which it is sometimes called the Bent Pyramid. Most of the exterior casing of this pyramid remains; the interior chamber beneath it is ab. 80 ft. high.

Daigleville (dā′gl.vil). Unincorporated community in SE Louisiana, in Terrebonne Parish. 4,809 (1950).

Dai Hoku (dī hō.kö). Japanese name of **Taipei,** Formosa.

Daikoku (dī.kō.kö). Japanese Buddhist deity of good fortune, whose image is often found in farm houses and on plaques in shops, in association with Ebisu, god of honesty.

Dáil Éireann (dôl ā′ron). Popularly-elected representative chamber of the Oireachtas (National Parliament) of the Irish Republic. Every Irish citizen aged 21 years or more, not disqualified by any constitutional or legal provision, and without discrimination of sex, is eligible to vote for members of, and to stand for election to, this body, which is chosen in accordance with the principles of proportional representation, and to which the executive branch of the government, headed by the Taoiseach (Prime Minister), is responsible. The Sinn Fein organization, at its first convention after becoming a political party, in October, 1917, drew up a plan for a future revolutionary provisional government, in which the name Dáil Éireann was prescribed for the popular assembly-to-be. In a general election (covering Great Britain and Ireland) in December, 1918, the majority of Irish constituencies elected Sinn Fein candidates, who were pledged not to attend the Parliament of the United Kingdom, but to meet in and legislate for Ireland. Accordingly the first Dáil Éireann convened at the Mansion House in Dublin on January 21, 1919, with 27 members present (the full membership was 73, but as to most of this number, as their names were called, the clerk answered

"Imprisoned by the English"). During this first session of the Dáil, whose proceedings were wholly in Gaelic, Ireland was proclaimed a republic, a provisional constitution was adopted, an executive ministry was appointed, and delegates were named to the peace conference at Versailles. During the ensuing war with Britain the Dáil functioned with difficulty, but the recognition of the Irish Free State in December, 1921, enabled it to function freely, and it emerged from a period of civil war with its authority firmly established. During subsequent constitutional changes which transformed the Irish Free State into Éire and finally into the Irish Republic, the name Dáil Éireann continued to designate this house of the Oireachtas.

Daillé (då.yā), **Jean.** [Latinized, **Dallaeus.**] b. at Châtellerault, France, Jan. 6, 1594; d. at Charenton, near Paris, April 15, 1670. French Protestant divine and controversialist. A voluminous writer, his chief work is *Traité de l'emploi des saints pères pour le jugement des différends qui sont aujourd'hui en la religion* (1632; Latin trans., 1656).

Daily Courant (ku.rant'), **The.** The first successful British daily paper. It was begun on March 11, 1702, and ceased publication in 1735.

Daily Telegraph Affair. International incident precipitated by the publication in the London *Daily Telegraph* on Oct. 28, 1908, of a summary manuscript of a confidential talk between Kaiser Wilhelm II and an English friend in which the Kaiser criticized the Anglo-Japanese alliance. The tactlessness of Wilhelm's statements not only greatly increased friction between Germany and Great Britain, but also aroused German public opinion. The German chancellor, Prince Bernhard von Bülow, had the support of all parties when he advised Wilhelm II to act more cautiously and discreetly in the future. Wilhelm, though accepting von Bülow's demands, did not forgive his chancellor, whom he dismissed in the following year.

Daimbert (dañ.ber) or **Dagobert** (då.go.ber). fl. latter part of 11th century; d. in Sicily, 1107. First Latin patriarch of Jerusalem. He became archbishop of Pisa in 1092, and commanded the Pisan and Genoese army in the first Crusade. He was elected patriarch of Jerusalem in 1099.

Daimiel (dī.myel'). Town in C Spain, in the province of Ciudad Real, situated on the Azuer River, ab. 20 mi. NE of Ciudad Real. It has linen and woolen manufactures, distilleries, and wine and oil markets. The Gothic parish church is of interest. 19,759 (1940).

Daimler (dām'lėr; German, dīm'lėr), **Gottlieb.** b. at Schorndorf, Württemberg, Germany, March 17, 1834; d. at Cannstatt, near Stuttgart, Germany, March 6, 1900. German engineer and inventor, noted as a pioneer manufacturer of automobiles. He invented (1885) an internal-combustion engine for automotive vehicles and independently of Karl Benz, with whose company his later merged, constructed one of the first practical automobiles. A progenitor of the modern automotive industry, he founded (1890) the Daimler Motor Company at Cannstatt (later Daimler-Benz and Company), producing the Mercedes, one of the most famous of automobiles.

Daingerfield (dān'jėr.fēld), **Elliott.** b. at Harpers Ferry (then in Virginia, now in West Virginia), March 26, 1859; d. Oct. 22, 1932. American painter. He studied at the Art Students League of New York, and in Europe. His work consists of easel pictures and decorations, notably those of the Lady Chapel of the church of Saint Mary the Virgin, New York. In his figure work he formed himself mainly on Italian models, while in landscape he owed much to the friendship and influence of George Inness. In 1906 he was elected a member of the National Academy of Design.

Dai Nippon (dī nēp.pôn). A Japanese name of **Japan.**

Dainty (dān'ti), **Lady.** Fashionable, frivolous, fine lady in Colley Cibber's comedy *The Double Gallant:* "Dogs, doctors, and monkeys are her favorites." She is courted by Careless.

Daiquirí (dī.kē.rē'). Town on the E coast of Cuba, in Oriente province, ab. 15 mi. S of Santiago. In the Spanish-American War, on June 22, 1898, the American army of invasion (excepting Kent's division, which was disembarked at Siboney, June 23) made a successful landing at this place (which, in many of the reports from the front, was miscalled *Baiquirí*). Pop. under 5,000 (1943).

Dairen (dī'ren'). [Also: **Tairen, Tairend;** Chinese, **Talien, Talienwan;** Russian, **Dalny.**] Seaport in NE China, in the province of Liaoning, Manchuria, situated on the Liaotung Peninsula, ab. 20 mi. NE of Port Arthur. It is the chief port of Manchuria, exporting soybeans, iron and steel products, and wheat. It was founded by the Russians in 1899 and was designed to be the commercial terminus of the Trans-Siberian Railway. During the Russo-Japanese War (1904–05) it was captured by the Japanese. In September, 1906, it was made a free port. It was built up by the Japanese as a modern city and port, but was returned after World War II to China. It has a fine harbor, protected by a breakwater, and is connected by railway with Port Arthur, Mukden, Harbin, and the Eastern Chinese railway system. 722,950 (1946).

Dai Sen (dī sen). [Also, **Oyama.**] Mountain in S Japan. on the island of Honshu, ab. 130 mi. NW of Kyoto, Elevation, ab. 5,900 ft.

Daisy (dā'zi), **Solomon.** Bell ringer of Chigwell, near London, in Charles Dickens's *Barnaby Rudge*, a rusty little fellow who seems all eyes.

Daisy Miller (dā'zi mil'ėr). [Full title, **Daisy Miller: A Study.**] Novel by Henry James, published in 1879. Daisy Miller is a frank and innocent American girl who, by her unconventional conduct, alienates the American colony in Rome.

Daitya (dī'tya). In Hindu mythology, one of a race of demons and giants who warred with the gods and interferred with sacrifices: the Daityas are parallels of the Greek Titans.

Dajak (dī'äk). See **Dyak.**

Dajo (dä.hō'). Mountain on Jolo Island, Sulu Archipelago, in the Philippines. An engagement between U.S. troops and Moros took place here March 6–7, 1906. Fifteen Americans, three members of the native constabulary, and 600 Moros were reported killed. Elevation, ab. 2,100 ft.

Dakait (dä.kä'ēt). Hindustani form of **Dacoit.**

Dakar (dä.kär'). Seaport on the extreme point of Cape Verde, in Senegal territory, French West Africa: the administrative seat of the federation of French West Africa. Here the governor general resides and his privy council of officials meets with the general assembly of Europeans and natives elected by the various territories. In 1924 Dakar and the surrounding suburbs were constituted a *circonscription*, i.e., given a government of their own separate from that of Senegal, but in 1946 the city and port were reunited with the territory. Dakar is in a strategic position, being on the routes from Europe to S and W Africa, and also a port of call for many ships on the way to South America. A fortified naval station has been established there. Extensive additions and alterations to the port, begun in 1938, were interrupted by World War II but are now complete. Its growth has been phenomenal. With its excellently protected and developed harbor and strong defenses the city remained under the control of the Vichy government in 1940. It withstood an attempt (July 8, 1940) by the Free French to take the city, and was considered a nest for German submarines until the Allies gained command in Africa in 1943. Area of Dakar and the surrounding area (which formerly constituted the *circonscription* of Dakar and dependencies), 60 sq. mi.; pop. 151,000 (1945).

Dakers (dā'kėrz), **Jonathan.** Idealistic physician, the hero of Francis Brett Young's novel, *My Brother Jonathan* (1928).

Dakiki or **Daqiqi** (dä.kē'kē), **Abu Mansur.** fl. c1000 A.D. Persian poet, from Tus (in Khurasan) or Bukhara, author of many odes and sonnets. Dakiki had completed a thousand distichs of the *Shahnamah* (*Book of Kings*) when he was murdered. Firdausi represents him as appearing to him in a dream, and asking him to incorporate in his work the fragment. To Dakiki Firdausi ascribed the portion of the *Shahnamah* relating to Gushtasp and Zartusht (Zoroaster).

Dakin (dā'kin), **Henry Drysdale.** b. at London, 1880; d. Feb. 10, 1952. English biochemist, noted for study of the action of enzymes within the body. A researcher (1905–20) at the Herter Laboratory at New York, he compounded Dakin's solution, an antiseptic that liberates free chlorine, for the treatment of wounds during World War I. He won (1941) the Davy medal of the Royal Society. He is the coauthor of *Handbook of Chemical Antiseptics* (1917).

Dakka (dak'a). See **Loe Dakka.**

Dakota (dạ.kō'tạ). [Also, **Sioux.**] Group of North American Indian tribes, all speaking languages of the Siouan family, formerly inhabiting a large area of Minnesota, North and South Dakota, and Montana.

Dakota River. See **James River,** in North Dakota.

Dakota Territory. Former territory of the U.S., divided in 1889 into the states of North Dakota and South Dakota.

Daktyloi (dak'ti.loi). See **Dactyls.**

Dal (däl). [Swedish, **Dalälven** (*älven* = "the river").] River in S central Sweden, in the *län* (counties) of Kopparberg, Gävleborg, and Uppsala. It is formed by the union of the East Dal (Swedish, Österdalälven) and West Dal (Swedish, Västerdalälven) and flows SE, then NE into the Gulf of Bothnia, ab. 58 mi. N of Uppsala, ab. 10 mi. SE of Gävle. Length, ab. 250 mi.

Dal or **Dale** (däl), **Vladimir Ivanovich.** See **Dahl, Vladimir Ivanovich.**

Daladier (dà.là.dyā), **Édouard.** b. at Carpentras, Vaucluse, France, June 18, 1884—. French political leader, premier of France at the outbreak of World War II. A graduate of the École Normale Supérieure, he taught history at various schools before World War I; during the war he rose from private to captain. He served as a Radical Socialist deputy (1919–40) and held numerous cabinet posts, including minister of colonies (1924–25), public works (1930–32), foreign affairs (1934, 1940), and national defense (1936–40). He served as premier three times (January–October, 1933; January–February, 1934; April, 1938–March, 1940) and was twice vice-premier (June, 1936–June, 1937; January–April, 1938). He succeeded (January, 1934) Édouard Herriot as president of the Radical Socialist Party and was elected honorary president in 1945. Having resigned the premiership because of inability to cope with the fascist-monarchist riots of February, 1934, following the exposure of the Stavisky scandal, he joined the anti-fascist Popular Front formed the following year, but as premier (1938–40) turned increasingly against the Communists while seeking an agreement with Germany. He signed the Munich agreement (1938) and the declaration of war against Germany (1939). Though granted (August, 1939) temporary rights to rule by decree, he resigned (March 20, 1940) as premier on the eve of the invasion of France. After the armistice by which France surrendered to the Germans, he was arrested by the Vichy authorities, but strenuously denied at the Riom trial (February, 1942) that he had failed to give France the means of defense. He was imprisoned in France (1941–43) and in Germany and Austria (1943–45). He was elected (1946) to the National Assembly.

Dalaguete (dä.lä.gā'tā). Town in the SE part of Cebu, in the Philippine Islands. 2,576 (1948).

Dalai Lama (dä.lī' lä'mạ). Title of the temporal and spiritual ruler of Tibet, whose seat is at Lhasa. He is supposed to be a reincarnation of the Mahayana Buddhist deity Avalokiteshvara. The manner of his selection in each new physical incarnation is, by Western standards, extremely curious: he is born, in a manner of speaking (a Tibetan would say that he becomes incarnate), at the precise moment of the death of his predecessor. This means that after the death of a reigning Dalai Lama a considerable search is instituted to determine the whereabouts of a child who can be ascertained to have been born at exactly the moment the former ceased to live. The search is oftentimes lengthy, during which period Tibet is governed by a priestly junta (which also ordinarily serves as a regency during the minority of each new Dalai Lama). Moreover, from the standpoint of a Tibetan, the child thus found cannot properly be called a "new" Dalai Lama; this will be obvious when the reader recalls that the Dalai Lama is, by definition, a reincarnation of Avalokiteshvara, who may therefore be said to have had an uninterrupted existence in various incarnations (14, to date). From this point of view, there is never a "new" Dalai Lama, but only a new incarnation; as one incarnation "dies" the new one instantly begins to "live" (whence the importance of determining the exact moment of birth). From a Western point of view, of course, this concept of continuous reincarnation is difficult to understand, and hence (as in the entry immediately following) many Western scholars tend to think of the Dalai Lama as being, at any particular moment in time, a particular person with an ascertainable date of birth who must inevitably someday die.

Dalai Lama. b. at Gumbum, near Sining, Tsinghai, China, 1934—. Spiritual and (at least nominally) political leader of Tibet. The present holder of this title, a young boy, is the 14th reincarnation. The child was enthroned (1940) at Lhasa, but the actual power was for several years in the hands of a regency. After the Japanese surrender (1945), the regency through him backed the Kuomintang against the Communists in China, but with the collapse of the Kuomintang it ousted (1949) the Chinese Central Government mission from Tibet and sought outside aid to break the tie with China. However, in October, 1950, the determination of the Chinese Communist government to be the chief force in Tibetan political affairs was made bluntly evident by the Chinese invasion of Tibetan territory, and within a few months virtually all members of the Tibetan army (hardly a significant military force by Western standards) had been captured or dispersed. The Dalai Lama withdrew from Lhasa in December, 1950, and established himself with a considerable retinue in territory from which, if necessary, he could seek shelter in India; however, in the latter half of 1951, after negotiations with the Chinese Communists, he returned to Lhasa.

Dalälven (däl'el.vẹn). Swedish name of the **Dal.**

Dalarna (dä'lär.nä). Swedish name of **Dalecarlia.**

Dalayrac or **d'Alayrac** (dà.lā.ràk), **Nicolas.** b. at Muret, France, June 13, 1753; d. at Tontenay-aux-Roses, France, Nov. 27, 1809. French composer of comic operas. His works include *Le Petit Souper* (1781), *Le Corsaire* (1783), *Nina* (1786), *Le Poëte et le musicien* (1809), and others.

Dalbeattie (dal.bē'tẹ, dạl-). Police burgh in S Scotland, in Kirkcudbrightshire, situated on Dalbeattie Burn (a tributary stream of Urr Water), ab. 11 mi. NE of Kirkcudbright, ab. 347 mi. N of London by rail. 3,365 (est. 1948).

Dalberg (däl'berk), **Emmerich Joseph.** [Title, Duc de **Dalberg.**] b. at Mainz, Germany, May 30, 1773; d. at Herrensheim, near Worms, Germany, April 27, 1833. Peer of France; son of Wolfgang Heribert von Dalberg. He was created a duke by Napoleon in 1810, and peer by Louis XVIII in 1815. He went (1815) to the Congress of Vienna as one of Talleyrand's assistants and later served as ambassador at Turin and Vienna. His daughter married Sir R. E. Acton and was the mother of the historian Lord Acton (John Emerich Edward Dalberg-Acton, 1st Baron Acton).

Dalberg, Karl Theodor Anton Maria von. b. at Herrensheim, near Worms, Germany, Feb. 8, 1744; d. at Regensburg, Germany, Feb. 10, 1817. German nobleman, prelate, and littérateur, last archbishop-elector of Mainz; brother of Wolfgang Heribert von Dalberg. An adherent of Napoleon, he was prince-primate of the Confederation of the Rhine (1806–13), and was created (1810) grand duke of Frankfort. He was a patron of the arts and a friend of Goethe, Schiller, and Wieland.

Dalberg, Wolfgang Heribert von. b. at Herrensheim, near Worms, Germany, Nov. 18, 1750; d. at Mannheim, Germany, Sept. 27, 1806. German theater director and dramaturgist at Mannheim; descendant of the distinguished lords of Dalberg (or Dalburg) castle near Kreuznach; younger brother of Karl Theodor Anton Maria von Dalberg and father of Emmerich Joseph Dalberg. In his endeavor to establish a German national theater he succeeded in organizing what has been called "a model republic of the stage." In 1782 he staged Schiller's *Räuber*, and the following year he engaged Schiller as the Mannheim theater playwright. The poet's *Briefe an den Freiherrn von Dalberg* were published in 1819. Dalberg's own contributions to German stage literature include a number of adaptations of Shakespearian plays.

Dalberg-Acton (dôl'bėrg.ak'tọn), **John Emerich Edward.** See **Acton,** Lord.

D'Albert (dal'bėrt), **Eugène.** See **Albert, Eugène Francis Charles d'.**

D'Albiac (dal'bi.ak), **John Henry.** b. 1894—. British air officer who headed (June, 1943–1944) with rank of air vice-marshal the Royal Air Force tactical command during World War II. He served (1937–38) with the army coöperation group, which was later (June, 1943) merged with the Royal Air Force tactical command. He commanded (1940) the Royal Air Force units in Greece, and was appointed (1944) deputy commander of the Mediterranean Allied tactical air force. He was a staff member (1945–46) of the air ministry.

Dalbono (däl.bô'nō), **Edoardo** (or **Eduardo**). b. at Naples, Italy, 1843; d. 1915. Neapolitan painter of landscapes and historical and mythological scenes. He was schooled at Rome, and then returned to Naples to continue his studies. Later he went to Paris, and was awarded prizes there and elsewhere in Europe. His work was recognized in Italy, Austria, France, and the U.S. *Excommunication of King Manfred*, *Legend of the Sirens*, *Tarantella*, *Fishing Boats*, and *The Bay of Naples* are among his best-known works.

Dalby (dôl'bi), **Isaac.** b. in Gloucestershire, England, 1744; d. at Farnham, Surrey, England, Feb. 3, 1824. English mathematician, employed in the survey of England after 1791.

Dalcroze Institute (dal.krōz'). See **Jaques-Dalcroze Institute.**

Daldianus (dal.di.ā'nus), **Artemidorus.** See **Artemidorus Daldianus.**

Dale (dāl). Borough in SW Pennsylvania, in Cambria County, near Johnstown: coal mines. 3,310 (1950).

Dale, David. b. at Stewarton, Ayrshire, Scotland, Jan. 6, 1739; d. at Glasgow, March 17, 1806. Scottish philanthropist. He was the founder and first proprietor, with Richard Arkwright, of the Lanark mills, since made famous by their connection with his son-in-law, the socialist Robert Owen. About 1770 he retired from the established church of Scotland, and founded a new communion on congregational principles, known as the Old Independents, of which he was chief pastor. He was noted as a munificent benefactor of the poor.

Dale, Sir **Henry Hallett.** b. at London, 1875—. English physiologist. He studied at Cambridge, St. Bartholomew's Hospital, and University College at London. He directed the Wellcome Physiological Research Laboratories (1904–14), and the National Institute for Medical Research (1928–42) at Hampstead, England. He was professor (1942–46) and director of research at the Royal Institution of Great Britain. He served as secretary (1925–35) and president (1940–45) of the Royal Society, was a member (1927–37) of the General Medical Council, and shared (1936) the Nobel prize in physiology and medicine with Otto Loewi for investigations of the chemical transmission of nerve impulses.

Dale, J. S. of. See **Stimson, Frederic Jesup.**

Dale, Richard. b. near Norfolk, Va., Nov. 6, 1756; d. at Philadelphia, Feb. 26, 1826. American commodore. He served as first lieutenant under John Paul Jones on the *Bonhomme Richard* in the battle (Sept. 23, 1779) with the *Serapis*, and commanded (1801–02) a squadron in the Mediterranean during the hostilities with Tripoli.

Dale, Robert William. b. Dec. 1, 1829; d. March 13, 1895. English Congregational clergyman and author. He became associate pastor of the Congregational Church at Carr's Lane, Birmingham, in 1853, and sole pastor in 1859. He was for a number of years editor of the *Congregationalist*, and was chairman (1868–69) of the Congregational Union of England and Wales. In 1877 he delivered at Yale College a series of lectures on preaching (the first Englishman appointed to the Lyman Beecher Lectureship). He was the author of *The Jewish Temple and the Christian Church* (1863), *Sermons on the Ten Commandments* (1871), *The Atonement* (1874), and others.

Dale, Sir **Thomas.** d. at Masulipatam, India, Aug. 9, 1619. Colonial governor of Virginia. He became marshal of Virginia in 1609, and in 1611 succeeded Thomas West, Baron De la Warr, as governor, being relieved by Sir Thomas Gates in the same year. He was governor a second time (1614–16), and returned to England, taking with him Thomas Rolfe and Rolfe's wife Pocahontas. His administrations, which were characterized by great severity, were attended by order and prosperity. The first working code of laws in Virginia, noted for their severity, was called popularly Dale's Code.

Dalecarlia (dä.lẹ.kär'li.ä). [Swedish, **Dalarna.**] Region and former province of Sweden, corresponding to the *län* (county) of Kopparberg. Its surface is mountainous. Its people took (1519–23) the leading part in the independence movement under Gustavus I, Gustavus Vasa.

Dalén (dä.lān'), **(Nils) Gustaf.** b. at Stenstorp, Sweden, Nov. 30, 1869; d. at Stockholm, Dec. 9, 1937. Swedish industrialist and inventor, best known as the inventor of an automatic switch for controlling unattended beacons. He studied (1896–97) at the Zurich Polytechnikum, developed (1897–99) hot-air turbines, and served (1906–09) as chief engineer for the Gas Accumulator Company, making important improvements in the use of acetylene. He won (1912) the Nobel prize in physics. In 1913 he was blinded in an explosion. Among his other inventions are compressors, air pumps, an apparatus for pasteurization, and a milking machine.

Dalgarno (dal.gär'nō), **George.** b. at Aberdeen, Scotland, c1627; d. at Oxford, England, Aug. 28, 1687. British scholar and writer, inventor of a deaf-mute alphabet. He wrote *Ars Signorum* (1661), an essay on a language in which the letters would convey concepts, and *Didascalocophus* (1680), containing his two-hand symbols for deaf-mutes.

Dalgarno, Lord. Malevolent young man in Sir Walter Scott's *Fortunes of Nigel*. He is the secret enemy of Nigel and the favorite of Prince Charles. Having heartlessly betrayed the Lady Hermione, he is compelled by the king to do her justice. After leaving court in disguise, he is murdered.

Dalgetty (dal.get'i), **Captain Dugald.** Soldier of fortune in Sir Walter Scott's *Legend of Montrose*. He had been a divinity student in his youth, and became a mercenary. He was courageous, and not untrustworthy if well paid. The original is said to have been a man named Munro who belonged to a band of Scotch and English auxiliaries in Swinemünde (1630).

Dalhart (dal'härt). City in NW Texas, in the Panhandle, county seat of Dallam County and also partly in Hartley County, NW of Amarillo: distributing and shipping center for grain and cattle. 5,918 (1950).

Dalhousie (dal.hou'zi, -hö'zi). County seat of Restigouche County, New Brunswick, Canada, situated on the S shore of the Bay of Chaleur, near its head. It is connected by rail and road with central Canada, and is a paper-making center, with several mills. 4,939 (1951).

Dalhousie, Earl and Marquesses of. Titles held by various members of the **Ramsay** family.

Dalhousie University. Institution of higher learning, nonsectarian and coeducational, located at Halifax, Nova Scotia. The College of Halifax, founded in 1818, was renamed Dalhousie College in 1821, in honor of one of the earls of Dalhousie, who laid the cornerstone in 1820, but it did not actually function until 1838. Three years later it was granted university status, but in 1843 it closed down, not to reopen until 1863. In addition to faculties of arts and science, the university comprises schools of engineering, law, medicine and dentistry, and has mutual arrangements with the Halifax Conservatory of Music and with the Nova Scotia College of Pharmacy. It is also associated with the University of King's College, which, dating from 1789, became by royal charter in 1802 the first university in Canada.

Dali (dä'lē). Modern name of **Idalium.**

Dali, Salvador. b. at Figueras, in Catalonia, Spain, March 11, 1904—. Spanish surrealist painter and etcher of meticulously drawn pictures combining familiar objects in irrational situations, and called by him "paranoiac" in content. He attracted wide attention in America (1934; 1940 *et seq.*) with window designs, for Fifth Avenue, N.Y., stores, utilizing common household objects made of fur, with paintings employing recurrent symbols such as ants, telephones, crutches, drooping watches, and the like. A precocious and opinionated painter, he was expelled from the School of Fine Arts, Madrid; at Paris (1927 *et seq.*) he was associated with Picasso, Miró, and Tanguy, experimenting with various new techniques such as pointillism, futurism, constructivism, and scientific cubism, and studying Freudian psychology. He has lived, with some interruptions, in the U.S. since 1940. Characteristic titles among his paintings are *The Enigma of William Tell* (1934), *Nostalgic Echo* (1935), *Group of Women Imitating the Gestures of a Schooner* (1940), and *Soft Self-Portrait with Grilled Bacon* (1941); his portrait of his wife, *Portrait of Gala* (1935), is in the Museum of Modern Art, New York. Perhaps his best-known painting is *The Persistence of Memory*, a desolate landscape with limp watches sagging over cliffs, bare branches, and the like. He is the author of and designer of scenes and costumes for *Labyrinth* (ballet, 1941); with Luis Bunuel, the scenarist of the surrealist films *Le Chien andalou* and *L'Âge d'or;* the illustrator of Lautréamont's *Les Chants de maldoror*.

Dalías (dä.lē′äs). Town in E Spain, in the province of Almería, situated on the S slope of the Sierra de Gador, near the Mediterranean Sea, ab. 18 mi. W of Almería. It has lead mines and sulfur springs. 11,683 (1940).

Dalida (dal′i.dą). The Delilah of the Book of Judges is found as Dalila in the Vulgate, but is Dalida in Chaucer, and Dalida is the form used in Wycliffe's Bible. Chaucer uses the form Dalida in the *Monk's Tale* and in *The Book of the Duchess*.

Dalin (dä.lēn′), **Olof von.** b. at Vinberga, Halland, Sweden, Aug. 29, 1708; d. at Drottningholm, Sweden, Aug. 12, 1763. Swedish historian and poet. He was the son of a clergyman. He studied at Lund, and subsequently entered (1726) one of the public offices in Stockholm. He began his literary career by the publication of a weekly journal, *Den Svenska Argus* (The Swedish Argus), modeled after the *Spectator*, which he issued (1733–34) anonymously. This was followed by *Tankar om Kritiker* (Thoughts about Critics, 1736) in the style of Pope's *Essay on Criticism*, and, after his return from a tour through Germany and France, by the satiric prose allegory *Sagan om Hästen* (The Story of the Horse, 1738), which is modelled after Swift's *Tale of a Tub*, and the satiric poem *Aprilverk om vår herrliga tid* (April-work of Our Glorious Time, 1738). An epic poem in Alexandrines, *Svenska Friheten* (Swedish Liberty), appeared in 1742. He wrote a tragedy, *Brynhilda* (1738), and a comedy, *Den Afvundsjuke* (The Envious Man, 1738), deriving from French models. In 1751 he was made tutor to the crown prince (later Gustavus III), and ennobled. In 1753 he was made privy councilor. In 1756, suspected of being concerned in the revolution of that year, he was banished from the court, but returned in 1761. During this period he was engaged upon his principal work, *Svea Rikes historia* (History of the Kingdom of Sweden; 4 vols., 1746–62), which extends to 1611, the end of the reign of Charles IX. His collected literary works, *Samlade Vitterhetsarbeten*, appeared in 1767, in 6 volumes. Dalin was the leading Swedish writer of his day and with his polished style brought Swedish letters back to the level achieved elsewhere in 18th-century Europe.

Dalkeith (dal.kēth′, dąl-). Police burgh and market town in S Scotland, in Midlothian, situated on the river North Esk, ab. 7 mi. SE of Edinburgh, ab. 389 mi. N of London by rail. It has no direct rail connections for passengers, being reached by rail to Eskbank Station, ab. ½ mi. from the town. Dalkeith Palace (the residence of the dukes of Buccleuch) is in the vicinity. 8,354 (est. 1948).

Dalkey (dô′ki, dôl′ki). Former town in E Irish Republic, in County Dublin, on Dublin Bay ab. 9 mi. SE of Dublin, now a part of the city borough of Dun Laoghaire. Dalkey has a 15th-century castle, and was a port of some importance in the Middle Ages. It is now a seaside resort and suburban residential area.

Dall (dôl), **William Healey.** b. at Boston, Aug. 21, 1845; d. March 27, 1927. American naturalist. He took part in the international telegraph expedition to Alaska in 1865, was assistant to the U.S. Coast Survey (1871–84), and was paleontologist to the U.S. Geographical Survey (1884–1909). His works include *Alaska and Its Resources* (1870), *Scientific Results of the Exploration of Alaska by the Parties under the Charge of W. H. Dall* (1876), and others.

Dallaeus (da.lē′us). Latinized name of **Daillé, Jean.**

Dal Lake (däl). Lake in N India, in the Vale of Kashmir, in the W Himalaya highlands near Srinagar: one of the most popular and beautiful tourist centers in NW India.

Dallas (dal′ąs). Town in NW Georgia, county seat of Paulding County, ab. 30 mi. NW of Atlanta. Near here, at New Hope Church, Pickett's Mill, Pumpkin Vine Creek, and other points, there was continued fighting between the Union forces under Sherman and the Confederates under Johnston from May 25 to 29, 1864. Pop. 1,817 (1950).

Dallas. City in NW Oregon, county seat of Polk County, on La Creole Creek, in a lumbering area: milling of lumber, and drying and packing of prunes. It was settled in the 1840's and named for George Mifflin Dallas (1792–1864), U.S. vice-president. Early manufactures consisted of iron products and wool textiles. 4,793 (1950).

Dallas. City in C Texas, county seat of Dallas County, NE of Austin, on the Trinity River: second largest city in the state, and largest city in the cotton belt and in the "black prairie" of Texas. It is a distributing center for cotton and petroleum, a fashion center of the Southwest, and a manufacturing center for agricultural machinery, cotton-ginning machinery, oil-field equipment, textiles and clothing, cottonseed oil, flour, refined petroleum, cement, and airplanes. It was settled c1842 and incorporated in 1856. It is named for George Mifflin Dallas, vice-president of the U.S. from 1845 to 1849. It is the seat of Southern Methodist University and the Dallas Little Theater, and has a number of noteworthy museums, housing geology, natural history, fine arts, history, ethnology, and other collections. 294,734 (1940), 434,462 (1950).

Dallas, Alexander James. b. in Jamaica, British West Indies, June 21, 1759; d. at Trenton, N.J., Jan. 16, 1817. American statesman, secretary of the treasury from 1814 to 1816; father of George Mifflin Dallas. He was the son of a Scottish physician resident in Jamaica. Having studied law in England, he emigrated from Jamaica to Philadelphia in 1783, was admitted to the bar in 1785, and served for a number of years as secretary of the commonwealth of Pennsylvania. For a time he edited the reports, the first series prepared, of the U.S. Supreme Court. He was U.S. attorney (1801–14) for the eastern district of Pennsylvania, and secretary (1814–16) of the U.S. treasury under Madison, discharging (1815–16) also the functions of secretary of war. As secretary of the treasury (1814–16), he was instrumental in securing the passage of the bill establishing (April 3, 1816) the Second Bank of the United States and recommended the protective tariff system that prevailed for three decades thereafter. The treasury, which was bankrupt when he assumed his post, was in a strong position at his resignation. Among his works were *Features of Mr. Jay's Treaty* (1795), *Laws of the Commonwealth of Pa.* (4 vols., 1793–1801), *Reports of Cases Ruled and Adjudged in the Several Courts of the United States and Pennsylvania . . .* (4 vols., 1790–1807), and *Treasury Reports: An Exposition of the Causes and Character of the War* (1815).

Dallas, George Mifflin. b. at Philadelphia, July 10, 1792; d. there, Dec. 31, 1864. American lawyer, politician, and diplomat, Democratic Vice-president of the United States under Polk; son of Alexander James Dallas. He graduated (1810) from Princeton and was admitted (1813) to the bar. He was (1813 *et seq.*) secretary to Albert Gallatin on his mission to Russia to obtain Russian mediation to end the war of 1812 with Great Britain. He was chosen by the American peace commissioners to carry back from Ghent the British peace terms in 1814. After government service at Washington, he returned to Philadelphia, where he was active in Democratic politics, and served as deputy attorney general for the city and county of Philadelphia, mayor, and district attorney (1829–31). He filled a vacancy in the U.S. Senate (1831–33), was (1833–35) attorney general of Pennsylvania, and was minister to Russia (1837 *et seq.*). After serving as vice-president (1845–49), he became (1856) minister to Great Britain, where he conducted the negotiations that culminated in the Dallas-Clarendon convention (Oct. 17, 1856), relating to U.S.-British differences in Central America, and was successful in inducing Great Britain to yield her right of search *vis-à-vis* the U.S. He held the post of minister until 1861.

Dallas, Robert Charles. b. at Kingston, Jamaica, British West Indies, 1754; d. at Ste.-Adresse, in Normandy, France, Nov. 20, 1824. British author; brother of Alexander James Dallas. He was educated in England, returned, on coming of age, to Jamaica in the West Indies to take possession of the estates left him by his father, and eventually settled in England. He is noted chiefly for his intimacy with Byron, to whom he gave literary advice, and for whom he acted as agent in dealings with publishers. He wrote *Recollections of the Life of Lord Byron from the year 1808 to the end of 1814*, which was edited by his son, A. R. C. Dallas.

Dallastown (dal'as.toun). Borough in SE Pennsylvania, in York County, near York. 3,304 (1950).

Dalles (dalz). Succession of rapids in a narrow gorge in the Columbia River, near the city of The Dalles, Ore.; also the neighboring heights. The Cascade Locks, built here in 1896 by the U.S. government, made it possible for ships to bypass the rapids. There is a similar formation, also called the Dalles, in the St. Croix River near the village of St. Croix Falls, Wis. Dalles is also a name (now more often Dells) for cascades and curious rock formations in the Wisconsin River, in Wisconsin and in the St. Louis River in Minnesota.

Dalles, The. See **The Dalles.**

Dalliance of the Eagles, The. Short poem (1881) by Walt Whitman. It is in his *Leaves of Grass*, in the "By the Roadside" group.

Dallin (dal'in), **Cyrus Edwin.** b. at Springville, Utah, Nov. 22, 1861; d. at Arlington Heights, Mass., Nov. 14, 1944. American sculptor, particularly of American Indian subjects. As a student at Paris, he worked under Henri Chapu and others. He was made a member (1930) of the National Academy of Design, a fellow (1923) of the American Academy of Arts and Letters, and a member of the Royal Society of Arts, London. Prizes were awarded his work at the Paris Salon (1890, 1909), the Paris (1900), Pan-American (1901), and Panama-Pacific (1915) expositions, and others. He taught at the Massachusetts School of Art. Among his well-known sculptures are *Signal of Peace*, in Lincoln Park at Chicago, *Medicine Man*, in Fairmount Park at Philadelphia, the *Pioneer Monument* at Salt Lake City, *Appeal to the Great Spirit*, in the Boston Museum of Fine Arts, and *Massasoit* at Plymouth, Mass.

Dalling and Bulwer (dôl'ing; bůl'wėr), Baron. Title of **Bulwer, William Henry Lytton Earle.**

Dallmeyer (däl'mī.ėr), **John Henry.** b. at Loxten, near Versmold, in Westphalia, Germany, Sept. 6, 1830; d. on shipboard near New Zealand, Dec. 30, 1883. German optician. He went to England in 1851, became a manufacturer of telescopes at London in 1859, and patented a single wide-angle photographic lens in 1864. He was elected a fellow of the Royal Astronomical Society in 1861. His work on photographic and microscopic lenses, in both of which he made improvements, was complemented by a technical capability in celestial photography. He wrote *On the Choice and Use of Photographic Lenses*.

Dall'Ongaro (däl.lông'gä.rō), **Francesco.** b. at Mansue, Treviso, Italy, 1808; d. at Naples, Italy, Jan. 10, 1873. Italian poet, novelist, and political agitator. He was a member of Garibaldi's movement, held office under Mazzini in the republic, and fled when that fell. In 1860 he returned from France, to become professor of dramatic literature at Florence and Naples. His *Novelle vecchie e nuove* were published in 1869.

Dalloway (dal'ọ.wā), **Clarissa.** See under **Mrs. Dalloway.**

Dalman (däl'män), **Gustaf Hermann.** b. at Niesky, in Silesia, June 9, 1855; d. at Herrnhut, Germany, Aug. 19, 1941. German Protestant theologian, noted as a student of Aramaic. He was graduated from the Moravian theological school at Gnadenfeld, where he was professor (1881–87) of Old Testament and practical theology. He served (1887–1902) as professor and later director of the Institutum Delitzschianum at Leipzig, became (1890) associate professor of Old Testament exegesis at the University of Leipzig, was director (1902–17) of the German Evangelical Archaeological Institute at Jerusalem, and headed (1917 *et seq.*) the Dalman Institute for Palestine Research at Greifswald. He was the author of *Christus im Thalmud* (1891), *Grammatik des jüdisch-palästinischen Aramäisch* (1894), and *Worte Jesu* (1898).

Dalmatia (dal.mā'sha). [Serbo-Croatian, **Dalmacija** (däl.mä'tse.yä); German, **Dalmatien** (däl.mä'tē.en); French, **Dalmatie** (dål.må.sē); Italian, **Dalmazia** (dälmä'tsyä).] Southern and western part of the federative unit of Croatia in the federal people's republic of Yugoslavia; a narrow strip of rocky coastal country, bordering the Adriatic Sea and including many offshore islands. The surface is mountainous and in part eroded. In antiquity, under the name of Illyricum, Dalmatia formed part of the Roman Empire. It was overrun by Goths and Moors, and in the 7th century by Slavic tribes coming from the northeast. The coastal areas came under the sovereignty and influence of Venice. The Turks occupied the interior in the 16th century but conceded most of it to Venice in 1699 and 1718 (peace treaties of Karlowitz and Passarowitz). The peace of Campo Formio (1797) brought Dalmatia, with Venice, under Austrian rule to which it returned (1815) after a brief interlude of French influence in the Bonapartist Kingdom of Italy and in the Illyrian provinces of the French Empire. Dalmatia, exclusive of the city of Zadar (Zara) and the island of Lastovo (Lagosta), went to the kingdom of Yugoslavia in 1918, the larger northern part to the *banovina* (province) of Primorska, the smaller southern part to the banovina of Zetska. After Yugoslavia entered (1941) World War II, Dalmatia was occupied by Italy. In 1945 almost the entire coastal strip, inclusive of Zadar, became part of the federative unit of Croatia. Only the regions around Hercegnovi and Metovic, where the railroad line coming from Mostar ends, belong to the federative unit of Bosnia-Hercegovina; the region of Kotor (Cattaro) belongs to the federative unit of Montenegro.

Dalmatie (dål.må.sē), Duc de. Title of **Soult, Nicolas Jean de Dieu.**

Dalmia (däl'mi.a), **Seth Remakrishna.** b. 1893—. Indian industrialist, founder and head of the Dalmia-Jain group of industries embracing a wide range of financial companies, mills, and factories. His centers of industrial activities have developed into self-sufficient towns, named after his ancestors and relatives. He is also known as a benefactor of social institutions in India.

Dalmorès (dål.mo.res), **Charles.** b. at Nancy, France, Dec. 21, 1871; d. 1939. French tenor singer.

Dalny (däl'ni). Russian name of **Dairen.**

Dalou (då.lö), **Jules.** b. at Paris, Dec. 31, 1838; d. there, April 15, 1902. French sculptor. He studied under Duret at the École des Beaux-Arts, and assisted Carpeaux. He sent his first work to the Paris Salon in 1867. On account of complicity with the Commune in 1871 he was obliged to leave Paris, and went to London, where he was appointed professor of sculpture at South Kensington. He returned to Paris, and was associated with Aubé in competition for the monument to the Constitutional Assembly. Their scheme was unsuccessful, but Dalou's sketch for a relief upon the design attracted the attention of Gambetta and Turquet, and was developed into the great bas-relief of Mirabeau and De Dreux-Brezé in the National Assembly, which won the medal of honor in the Salon of 1883. It was accompanied by another bas-relief called *Le Triomphe de la république*, now in the Hôtel de Ville at Paris. His project of the monument to the republic in the Place de la République won the second prize, and was ordered by the state for La Place des Nations.

Dalriada (dal.ri.ā'da). In Irish history, an ancient Gaelic kingdom, situated in what is now Ulster province, in Northern Ireland, in the N part of County Antrim. From here, in c500 A.D., the Dalriad Scots migrated to Argyllshire, Scotland, and founded the Scottish kingdom of Dalriada. The Irish district, in present-day Ulster, is called "The Route."

Dalriada. Former name for that part of Argyllshire, in W Scotland, settled (c500) by the Dalriad Scots from Ireland. Originally it comprised only the Kintyre and Knapdale districts, but was gradually extended until it included the whole of Argyllshire. The Dalriad Scots and Picts were united in one kingdom by Kenneth MacAlpine, who removed his court from Dunstaffnage, Argyllshire, to Forteviot, Perthshire, c846.

Dalry (dal'ri). Civil parish in SW Scotland, in Ayrshire, situated on the river Garnock, ab. 6 mi. NE of Ardrossan, ab. 402 mi. N of London by rail. 6,827 (1931).

Dalrymple (dal'rim.pl, dal.rim'pl), **Alexander.** b. at New Hailes, near Edinburgh, July 24, 1737; d. June 19, 1808. Scottish hydrographer. He entered the East India Company's service in 1752, and in 1762 was appointed to the command of the *London*, with instructions to open the trade with Sulu, in the Philippine Islands. He returned to England in 1765, and was appointed hydrographer to the East India Company in 1779, and hydrographer to the admiralty in 1795. He was the author of *Account of Discoveries in the South Pacific Ocean before 1764* (1767), *Historical Collection of South Sea Voyages* (1770–71), and others.

Dalrymple of Hailes (hālz), Sir **David.** d. 1721. Scottish politician. He was made baronet in 1700, represented Culross in the Scottish parliament and served as solicitor-general to Queen Anne (1703), was a commissioner for the treaty of union (1706) with England and was elected (1707) to the English Parliament. He was Queen's advocate in Scotland (1709), and auditor to the Scottish exchequer (1720).

Dalrymple, Sir **David.** [Title, Lord **Hailes.**] b. at Edinburgh, Oct. 28, 1726; d. Nov. 29, 1792. Scottish judge and author. He was educated at Eton and at Utrecht, admitted to the Scottish bar in 1748, raised to the bench of the Court of Session with the title of Lord Hailes in 1766, and in 1776 became a judge of the justiciary or criminal court. His most notable works are *An Inquiry into the Secondary Causes which Mr. Gibbon has assigned to the Rapid Growth of Christianity* (1786), and *Annals of Scotland* (from Malcolm Canmore to Robert I, 1776; continued to the accession of the house of Stuart, 1779).

Dalrymple, Sir **Hew.** [Title, Lord **North Berwick.**] b. 1652; d. Feb. 1, 1737. Scottish statesman, advocate of the union of Scotland and England; third son of Sir James Dalrymple (1619–95) and brother of Sir James Dalrymple of Borthwick and Sir John Dalrymple (1648–1707). He represented New Galloway (1690) and North Berwick (1702), in the last Scottish parliament and served as lord president of session (1698–1737), a post to which he was originally named by William III and in which he succeeded his father. An enthusiastic advocate of union with England, he was in 1702 and 1706 one of the commissioners who drew up the articles. His *Decisions of the Court of Session from 1698 to 1718, Collected by the Right Honorable Sir Hew Dalrymple, President of that Court* (1758, 1792) was published at Edinburgh.

Dalrymple, Sir **James.** [Title, 1st Viscount **Stair.**] b. in Carrick, Scotland, in May, 1619; d. at Edinburgh, Nov. 25, 1695. Scottish lawyer and statesman. He was educated at Glasgow and Edinburgh, became professor of logic, morals, and politics in the University of Glasgow in 1641, and was admitted to the Scottish bar in 1648. Appointed a judge of the Court of Sessions by Cromwell in 1657, he was reappointed by Charles II in 1661 and became president of the court in 1670. He was admitted to the Scottish parliament in 1672, fled in 1682 to Holland to avoid the consequences of refusing to take the test oath, supported William III (William of Orange) in 1688, and was created Viscount Stair, Lord Glenluce and Stranraer, in 1690. His chief work is *Institutions of the Law of Scotland* (1681).

Dalrymple of Borthwick (bôrth′wik), Sir **James.** fl. 1714. Scottish antiquary; son of Sir James Dalrymple (1619–95) and brother of Sir Hew Dalrymple and Sir John Dalrymple (1648–1707). He was admitted to the Faculty of Advocates (1675), appointed one of the commissaries of Edinburgh and a principal clerk of the court of session, and created baronet in 1698. Author of *Collections concerning the Scottish History preceding the death of King David the First in 1153* (1705).

Dalrymple, Sir **John.** [Title, 1st Earl of **Stair.**] b. 1648; d. Jan. 8, 1707. Scottish lawyer and statesman; son of Sir James Dalrymple (1619–95). He was admitted to the Scottish bar in 1672, was appointed king's advocate by James II in 1685, supported in 1688 the cause of William III (William of Orange), whose chief adviser in Scottish affairs he became, and was sworn privy councilor under Queen Anne in 1702. He was created 1st Earl of Stair in 1703. He is noted chiefly for his connection with the massacre of the Macdonalds of Glencoe, which was undertaken (1692) by his advice.

Dalrymple, John. [Title, 2nd Earl of **Stair.**] b. at Edinburgh, July 20, 1673; d. there, May 9, 1747. Scottish general and diplomat; son of Sir John Dalrymple (1648–1707). He was educated at Leiden, Netherlands, is said to have served in various subordinate grades throughout the wars of William III (William of Orange) in Flanders, became aide-de-camp to the Duke of Marlborough in 1703, and commanded a brigade at the siege of Lille and at the battle of Malplaquet. He was commissioned general in 1712. In 1715 he was appointed minister plenipotentiary to Paris; he was raised to the rank of ambassador in 1719, and was recalled in 1720. He was created field marshal in 1742, and was made general of the marines in 1746. He is noted chiefly for the princely style in which he supported his mission at Paris, and for the comprehensive and invaluable information which he remitted in his dispatches concerning the secret intrigues of the French court and of the friends of the Stuart Pretender.

Dalrymple, John. [Title, 5th Earl of **Stair.**] b. 1720; d. Oct. 13, 1789. British politician and army captain; grandson of Sir John Dalrymple (1648–1707). He presented a petition to the House of Lords on behalf of Massachusetts (1774) and opposed measures which later contributed in part to the outbreak of the Revolutionary War.

Dalrymple, John. [Title, 6th Earl of **Stair.**] b. 1749; d. June 1, 1821. English soldier in America; eldest son of John Dalrymple (1720–89). He served (1781) as captain of an infantry regiment under Sir Henry Clinton during the Revolutionary War, and was present at the attack on New London and Fort Griswold (September, 1781). On Jan. 5, 1782, he was appointed minister plenipotentiary to the king and republic of Poland and later (Aug. 5, 1785) minister plenipotentiary to Berlin.

Dalton (dôl′tọn). City in NW Georgia, county seat of Whitfield County, ab. 28 mi. SE of Chattanooga: center of the candlewick-bedspread industry. Near here, on May 9, 1864, an engagement took place between part of Sherman's army and the Confederates. 15,968 (1950).

Dalton. Town (in Massachusetts the equivalent of township in many other states) and unincorporated village in W Massachusetts, in Berkshire County: manufactures of paper for use in currency. Pop. of town, 4,772 (1950); of village, 4,285 (1950).

Dalton, Hugh. b. at Neath, Glamorganshire, Wales, 1887—. English statesman and lawyer. He graduated from Cambridge, was a member (1924 *et seq.*) of Parliament, was appointed reader (1925–36) in economics at the University of London, and served as undersecretary (1929–31) in the Foreign Office. During World War II, he was minister (1940–42) of economic warfare, and president (1942–45) of the Board of Trade. He was chancellor (1945–47) of the exchequer and minister (1950) of town and country planning.

Dalton, John. b. probably at Dean, Cumberland, England, 1709; d. at Worcester, England, July 22, 1763. English poet and divine. He was graduated (B.A., 1730; M.A., 1734) from Oxford, appointed a canon of Worcester cathedral in 1748, and about the same time obtained the rectory of Saint Mary-at-Hill, London. His most notable work is an adaptation of Milton's *Comus* for the stage, published in 1738 under the title *Comus, a Mask, now adopted to the Stage, as altered from Milton's Mask.*

Dalton, John. b. at Eaglesfield, Cumberland, England, Sept. 6, 1766; d. at Manchester, England, July 27, 1844. English chemist and natural philosopher. He was the son of a poor weaver and acquired an education chiefly by private study. He began to teach in 1778, and was appointed (1793) teacher of mathematics and natural philosophy in New College, Manchester (which was removed to York in 1799). He became a member of the Literary and Philosophical Society of Manchester in 1794, was elected a fellow of the Royal Society in 1822, and was chosen corresponding member of the French Academy of Sciences in 1816 and foreign associate in 1830. He perfected c1804 the atomic theory, which he propounded in a work entitled *A New System of Chemical Philosophy* (1808–10 and 1827). Dalton made final the theory that there are classes of matter (elements) that combine in certain proportions as the result of their structure, and that each ultimate particle of such a substance is capable of combining by weight with similar particles of other elements. He suffered from color blindness, and on Oct. 31, 1794, read a paper before the Manchester Literary and Philosophical Society, in which he gives the earliest account of that peculiarity, which is known from him as Daltonism. Dalton was interested in almost everything and contributed papers to his several societies on matters from meteorology (he kept a meteorological diary from 1787 until the day before he died) to English grammar.

Dalton, John Call. b. at Chelmsford, Mass., Feb. 2, 1825; d. at New York, Feb. 12, 1889. American physiologist. He was professor of physiology in the College of Physicians and Surgeons at New York (1855–83) and was emeritus professor and president of the college from 1883 until his death. He wrote *Treatise on Human Physiology* (1859), *Treatise on Physiology and Hygiene* (1868), and others.

Dalton-in-Furness (fėr′nes). [Also, **Dalton.**] Urban district and market town in NW England, in Lancashire, ab. 4 mi. NE of Barrow-in-Furness, ab. 260 mi. NW of London by rail. It has communications with the sea by a canal ab. 4 mi. long. 10,394 (1951).

Daly (dā′li), **Arnold.** [Full name, **Peter Christopher Arnold Daly.**] b. at Brooklyn, N.Y., Oct. 22, 1875; d. at New York, Jan. 13, 1927. American actor, noted for introducing the plays of George Bernard Shaw to the New York stage. He produced and acted in *Candida* (1903) and introduced, among others, *You Can Never Tell* (1905), *John Bull's Other Island* (1905), and *Mrs. Warren's Profession* (1905). This last play, dealing with prostitution, was attacked by Anthony Comstock and banned in New York. Daly was arrested, but acquitted, in a widely publicized case.

Daly, Augustin. [Full name, **John Augustin Daly.**] b. at Plymouth, N.C., July 20, 1838; d. at Paris, June 7, 1899. American playwright and producer, noted as manager and director of Daly's Theatre at New York. His first theatrical success was *Leah the Forsaken* (first produced at the Howard Athenaeum at Boston, Dec. 8, 1862), adapted from the German play *Deborah*, by S. H. von Mosenthal. Following other adaptations of foreign plays, he produced his first known play, *Under the Gaslight* (New York Theatre, Aug. 12, 1867), followed by other melodramas like *A Flash of Lightning* (1868) and *The Red Scarf* (1869). His most outstanding play, *Horizon*, was produced at the Fifth Avenue Theatre in 1871. When this theater burned down in 1873, he leased the old New York Theatre and renamed it Daly's Fifth Avenue Theatre, managing it until 1877. Here, where Booth and Wallack, among others, acted under him, he produced such melodramas as *Pique* (1875) and *The Dark City* (1877). In 1879 he took over the Old Broadway Theatre, renaming it Daly's Theatre, and directed a company that included Ada Rehan, John Drew, and Otis Skinner. From this time onward he depended chiefly on foreign adaptations. He took his company to Europe in the 1880's and in the following decade gave notable productions of Shakespeare's plays. His achievements at Daly's Theatre rank him as one of the leading theatrical artists of his time. Among his other original plays were *Griffith Gaunt* (1868), *Frou Frou* (1870), *Seven-Twenty-Eight* (1897), and *A Night Off* (1897). He was also the author of a biography, *Woffington, A Tribute to the Actress and the Woman* (1888). See *The Life of Augustin Daly*, by Joseph F. Daly (1917).

Daly, Marcus. b. in Ireland, Dec. 5, 1841; d. Nov. 12, 1900. American mining financier, an organizer of the Anaconda Copper Mining Company and the Amalgamated Copper Company. He arrived in the U.S. at the age of 15 and became a California pick-and-shovel man. After discovering (c1876) copper in the Anaconda silver mine, he bought the mine and others within the area and organized supplementary enterprises. His business and political feud (1888–1900) with William A. Clark involved him in Western politics. Their struggle to control the mines and the political machinery made of Montana (admitted to the Union as a state in 1889) a battleground, figuratively in terms of money spent and actually in terms of bloodshed among the miners. Daly made large contributions to Democratic Party campaign funds, giving 50,000 dollars to Bryan's 1896 campaign.

Daly, Reginald Aldworth. b. at Napanee, Ontario, Canada, May 19, 1871—. American geologist and authority on the origin of glaciers. He was professor of physical geology (1907–12) at the Massachusetts Institute of Technology and professor of geology (1912–42) at Harvard. His works include *Our Mobile Earth* (1926), *Igneous Rocks and the Depths of the Earth* (1933), *The Changing World of the Ice Age* (1934), *Strength and Structure of the Earth* (1940), and *The Floor of the Ocean* (1942).

Daly, Thomas Augustine. b. at Philadelphia, May 28, 1871; d. there, Oct. 4, 1948. American journalist and poet, known for his Italian dialect verse. He was a staff member of the Philadelphia *Record* (1891–98, 1918–29) and Philadelphia *Evening Ledger* (1915–18) and a columnist (1929 *et seq.*) on the Philadelphia *Evening Bulletin.* His works include *Canzoni* (1906), *Carmina* (1909), *Madrigali* (1912), *McAroni Ballads* (1919), *McAroni Medleys* (1931), *Selected Poems of T. A. Daly* (1936), *Late Lark Singing* (1946), and other collections of verse.

Daly City. City in C California, in San Mateo County, S of San Francisco: residential suburb of San Francisco. 15,191 (1950).

Dalyell or **Dalzell** (both, dal′yel, dē.el′), **Thomas.** b. c1599; d. Aug. 23, 1685. British general. He participated in the Royalist rebellion in the Highlands of Scotland in 1654 and entered the Russian service c1655. Returning (1665) to England on the invitation of Charles II, he was appointed commander in chief in Scotland in 1666, was sworn a privy councilor in 1667, entered Parliament in 1678, and in 1681 was commissioned to enroll the celebrated regiment of the Scots Greys.

Dalzel (dal.zel′), **Andrew.** b. at Kirkliston, Linlithgowshire, Scotland, Oct. 6, 1742; d. Dec. 8, 1806. Scottish classical scholar. He studied at the University of Edinburgh, was for some years tutor in the Lauderdale family, was appointed professor of Greek in Edinburgh University in 1779, assisted in the founding of the Royal Society of Edinburgh in 1783, and became principal clerk to the General Assembly in 1789. He was the author of two collections of Greek miscellaneous pieces.

Dalziel (dal′zi.el), **Davison Alexander.** [Title, 1st Baron **Dalziel of Wooler.**] b. at London, Oct. 17, 1854; d. there, April 18, 1928. English newspaper proprietor and industrialist. Learning the newspaper business in the U.S., he returned (1893) to London and founded Dalziel's News Agency; in 1910 he purchased controlling shares in the *Standard* and the *Evening Standard*, London papers. He sold them in 1916 and then became active in the Pullman Car Company, International Sleeping Car Company, and similar enterprises. A Conservative member of Parliament (1910–27) for Brixton, he was made (1919) a baronet and became Baron Dalziel of Wooler in 1921.

Dalziel, James Henry. [Title, 1st Baron **Dalziel of Kirkcaldy.**] b. April 24, 1868; d. at Brighton, Sussex, England, July 15, 1935. English statesman and newspaper proprietor. Educated at Brogue Academy, Shrewsbury High School, and King's College, London, he began his newspaper career in the London office of the *Scottish Leader*, later joining the staff of *Reynolds' Newspaper*, a Sunday publication. He purchased (1917) the *Pall Mall Gazette*, a London evening paper, the *Era*, and the *Country World.* He also established the *Sunday Evening Telegram* and purchased (October, 1918), the entire business of United Newspapers, Ltd., which included the *Daily Chronicle, Lloyd's Sunday News,* and other papers. He served continuously as member of Parliament (1892–1921) for Kirkcaldy Burghs, and during World War I as chairman of a board in charge of German prisoners. Knighted in 1908, he was made privy councilor in 1912, a baronet in 1918, and a baron in 1921.

Dam (däm), **Henrik.** [Full name, **Carl Peter Henrik Dam.**] b. at Copenhagen, Feb. 21, 1895—. Danish biochemist. From 1920 to sometime in 1941 he was associated with his alma mater, the University of Copenhagen, as an instructor, assistant professor and associate professor in chemistry and biochemistry. Coming to America as a war refugee, he lectured in the U.S. and Canada, engaged in research at the University of Rochester, and in 1945 became an associate member of the Rockefeller Institute for Medical Research. His work has been largely in the fields of nutrition and vitamins, and his identification of vitamin K led to his receiving in 1943, jointly with Edward A. Doisy, the Nobel Prize in Physiology and Medicine.

Dama (dä′mä) or **Bergdama** (berg.dä′mä). [Also: **Bergdamara, Damra, Damara, Taldama.**] Khoisan-speaking people of S Africa, inhabiting the N part of South-West Africa. Their population is estimated at ab. 25,000 (by H. Bauman, R. Thurnwald, and D. Westerman, *Völkerkunde von Afrika*, 1940). They are true Negro in physical type, but they speak Nama, a Hottentot language. Dama servants are found among the Nama Hottentots, Dama herders among the Herero, and Dama hunters among the Bushmen. One group, the Bergdama, fled into the hills from the Nama and Herero and are nomadic hunters and gatherers whose culture resembles that of the Bushmen. Another group, the Taldama, have settled in the valleys, where they hunt and raise small numbers of goats and cattle. As among the Herero, every village has its sacred fire.

Damaged Souls. Biographical sketches by Gamaliel Bradford, published in 1923.

Daman (dạ.män'). See also **Damão.**

Daman (dä.män'). Region on the border of W Pakistan and Afghanistan, between the Indus River and the Suliman Mountains: sheep raising.

Damanhur (dä.män.hör'). [Ancient name, **Hermopolis Parva.**] City in NE Africa, in Lower Egypt, the capital of Beheira province, ab. 39 mi. SE of Alexandria on the Alexandria-Cairo railroad line. It occupies the site of ancient Egyptian and Roman cities. 84,983 (1947).

Damão (dạ.mouṅ'). [Also, **Daman.**] Seaport and settlement belonging to Portugal, on the W coast of India, ab. 100 mi. N of Bombay. It has a number of saltworks and much transit trade and shipping. It was acquired by Portugal in 1558. Pop. of settlement, 41,671 (1941).

Damar (dä.mär'). See **Dhamar.**

Damaraland (dam'ạ.rạ.land", dä.mä'rạ-). Region in the N central part of the mandated territory of South-West Africa. British officials withdrew from the territory in 1880 (except from Walvis Bay), and it was annexed by Germany in 1884. The former German colony was given to the Union of South Africa in 1920 as a mandate; it is now a trust territory of the United Nations.

Damascene (dam'ạ.sēn), Saint **John.** See Saint **John Damascene.**

Damascenus (dam.ạ.sē'nus), **Nicolaus.** Latin name of **Nicholas of Damascus.**

Damascius (dạ.mash'i.us). fl. 6th century A.D. Greek Neoplatonist philosopher. When the school of philosophy at Athens was closed by the emperor Justinian in 529, he, with other Neoplatonists, emigrated to Persia.

Damascus (dạ.mas'kus). [Arabic, **Dimisq, Esh Sham**; French, **Damas** (dȧ.mä); Hebrew, **Dameseq, Dammeseq**; Assyrian, **Dimasqu.**] Capital and most important city of Syria, situated in the fertile valley of Coele-Syria, E of the Anti-Lebanon Mountains, on the edge of the Syrian Desert: believed to be the oldest city in the world that has been in continuous existence; the seat of the national university and teachers' college. It is served by two railways, many highways, and several air lines. On account of its beautiful fertile surroundings, its lofty position, and its richness in fresh water, Damascus has been praised in antiquity and in modern times as the "paradise of the earth," "the eye of the desert," and "the pearl of the Orient." It is traversed, from the eastern gate to the western, by one of the most famous streets in the world, the Street Called Straight. A city even before the Hittite period (c2000 B.C. *et seq.*), it became the capital of Syria, and a great part of the country was called by its name. In modern times it became notorious in Western eyes when more than 3,000 Christians were massacred there in 1860. In the Old Testament the name of Damascus occurs as early as the history of Abraham (Gen. xiv. 15, xv. 2). After the time of David, Damascus often came into sharp collision with Israel. In the New Testament Damascus is known especially from the history of Paul (Acts, ix). 286,310 (1943).

Damaskinos (ᴛʜä"mä.skē.nôs'), Archbishop. [Original name, **Demetrios Papandreou.**] b. at Dorvitsa, in Nafpactia, Greece, 1890; d. 1949. Greek divine. Studied theology and law at University of Athens; served as private in Balkan War (1912). Took orders (1917); archimandrite (1917); reorganized monastery of Pendeli and drafted charter for Mount Athos monasteries in 1918. He was metropolitan (bishop) of Corinth from 1922 to 1938. Founded general union of clergy (1919) and was its president (1919–22). Led relief work after Corinth earthquake of 1928, visiting the U.S. to raise funds; again visited the U.S. in 1930 as representative of the Ecumenical Patriarch to reconcile factions in the U.S. Greek Church. Elected archbishop of Athens, primate of all Greece in 1938, but rejected in favor of Chrysanthus by Metaxas and exiled to a monastery on the island of Salamis; recalled by the Axis occupation forces in 1941, who deposed Chrysanthus. In spite of owing his position to the Axis powers, he was nevertheless an active leader of resistance, organizing the EOChA (National Organization of Christian Solidarity), which was of great help to the guerrillas. He was arrested by the Nazis in 1944. Regent of Greece (1945–46); prime minister (1945); delegate to Council of Foreign Ministers at London (1945).

Damasus I (dam'ạ.sus), Saint. b. c306; d. Dec. 11, 384. Pope from 366 to 384. He is now known to have been born of Spanish parents. His election was contested by the deacon Ursinus, who was subsequently banished by Pope Valentinian III. He opposed Apollinarists and Macedonians, whose errors were condemned in two synods at Rome, one in 368 and another in 369.

Damasus II. b. in Bavaria, Germany; d. Aug. 9, 1048. Pope from July 17 to August 9 in the year 1048; successor to Pope Benedict IX.

Damavand (dä'mä.vänd). See **Demavend.**

Damayanti (dä.mä.yän'tē). In Hindu legend, the wife of Nala, and the heroine of the tale of Nala and Damayanti, an episode of the *Mahabharata.*

Dambolo (däm.bō'lō). See **Dambulla.**

Dambrauskas (däm.brou'skäs), **Aleksandras.** [Pseudonym, **Adomas Jakštas.**] b. at Kuronys, Pagirys township, Lithuania, Sept. 8, 1860; d. at Kaunas, Lithuania, Feb. 19, 1938. Lithuanian poet, critic, journalist, and theologian. He was graduated (1884) from the Kaunas Roman Catholic Theological Seminary, and (1888) from the St. Petersburg Roman Catholic Theological Academy. As a chaplain of the Panevėžys high school he had forbidden the Catholic pupils to attend services at the Russian Orthodox Church and was deported into the interior of Russia (1889–95); professor (1902–06) at the St. Petersburg Theological Academy; president (1907–38) of the Saint Casimir book-publishing society at Kaunas; editor of the magazine *Draugija* (Society, 1907–14, 1920–22); pioneer of the Lithuanian Esperanto movement and editor (1922–26) of its magazine *Litova stello;* honorary professor of Kaunas University (Oct. 15, 1922); author of three books of poems, *Dainu skrynele* (Chest of Songs), *Rudens aidai* (Echoes of Autumn), and *Lyrika* (Lyrics), of a collection of essays on Lithuanian literature, and other works.

Dambulla (däm.bu̇l'ạ). [Also: **Dambolo, Dambul** (däm.böl').] Village in Ceylon, situated ab. 40 mi. N of Kandy: noted for its Buddhistic cave temples. It is a trading center served by two major highways.

Dame aux Camélias (dȧm ō kȧ.mā.lyȧ), **La.** [Eng. trans., "*The Lady of the Camellias.*"] Novel by the younger Alexandre Dumas, published in 1848 and dramatized by him in 1852. The English version of the play is called *Camille*, and that is the name of the heroine. The original French heroine is Marguerite Gautier.

Dame Blanche (dȧm bläṅsh), **La.** [English title, **The White Maid.**] Comic opera in three acts by Boieldieu, with libretto by Scribe, first produced at Paris on Dec. 10, 1825.

Dame Christian Constance (or **Custance**) (dām kris'chạn kon'stạns; kus'tạns). See **Constance** (or **Custance), Dame Christian.**

Dame du Lac (dȧm dü lȧk). French name of the **Lady of the Lake.**

Dame Durden (dām dėr'dẹn). See **Durden, Dame.**

Dame Pliant (plī'ạnt). See **Pliant, Dame.**

Damer (dā'mėr), **Anne Seymour.** b. 1749; d. May 28, 1828. English sculptor; daughter of Henry Seymour Conway. She executed in 1785 two allegorical heads, one representing the river Thames and the other the river Isis, for a bridge at Henly, near her father's house at Park Place, which have been much admired. She also produced a statue of George III and a bust of Nelson.

Dameron (dȧm.rôṅ), **Charles Émile.** b. at Paris, 1848; d. there, Jan. 22, 1908. French painter; a pupil of Pelousse. His works are chiefly landscapes.

Dame Sirith (dām sir'ith). The only true fabliau (c1250) in English before Chaucer. Dame Sirith, a hypocritical bawd, succeeds in terrifying a young wife named Margeri into accepting as a lover the clerk Wilekin. Although the plot is highly improbable, the tale is skilfully told with an abundance of natural dialogue.

Damian (dā′mi.ạn). Youth in Chaucer's "Merchant's Tale" in the *Canterbury Tales*. He languishes for and obtains the love of May, the young wife of old January.

Damian. Young squire in Sir Walter Scott's *Ivanhoe*, an aspirant for the holy Order of Templars.

Damian, Saint. See under **Cosmas** and **Damian,** Saints.

Damian, Saint **Peter.** [Italian, **Pietro Damiani** or **Damiano**; Latinized, **Petrus Damianus.**] b. at Ravenna, Italy, 1007; d. at Faenza, Italy, Feb. 22, 1072. Italian ecclesiastic. In 1035 he became a hermit at Fonte Avellano, near Gubbio in Umbria, and was soon head of all the surrounding hermits and monks. He was noted for his asceticism, and was influential as a reformer, condemning simony and marriage of the clergy. He was made bishop of Ostia and cardinal in 1058, and was the adviser and censor of a number of popes. His works include epistles, sermons, lives of saints, ascetic tracts, and poems. He was declared a Doctor of the Church in 1828.

Damien (då.myaṅ; Anglicized, dā′mi.ẹn), Father. [Original name, **Joseph de Veuster.**] b. at Tremeloo, Belgium, Jan. 3, 1840; d. on the island of Molokai, Hawaii, April 15, 1888. Roman Catholic missionary who devoted his life (from 1873) to the welfare of the lepers in the leper colony on the island of Molokai, Hawaii. He himself contracted leprosy in 1885. Certain allegations against Father Damien by a minister evoked Robert Louis Stevenson's *An Open Letter to the Rev. Dr. Hyde* (1890).

Damiens (då.myaṅ), **Robert François.** b. near Arras, France, 1715; executed at Paris, March 28, 1757. French assassin who made an unsuccessful attempt upon the life of Louis XV, on Jan. 5, 1757. Damiens approached the king at Versailles, as he was entering his carriage, and succeeded in stabbing him. In punishment for this deed, his right hand was burned in a slow fire; his flesh was torn with pincers and burned with melted lead; resin, wax, and oil were poured upon the wounds; and he was torn to pieces by four horses.

Damietta (dam.i.et′ạ). [Arabic, **Damiat, Dimyat, Dumiat.**] City in NE Africa, in Lower Egypt, between the Damietta Branch of the Nile River and Lake Manzala, ab. 7 mi. from the Mediterranean Sea. It was besieged and taken by the Crusaders in 1218–19 and in 1249. The modern city produces textiles. Its harbor fills up with silt very rapidly and therefore is of little use as a port. 53,620 (1947).

Damietta Branch. Chief eastern mouth of the Nile River, Egypt.

Damiotti (dam.i.ot′i; Italian, dä.myôt′tē), **Dr.** Italian charlatan who exhibits the magic mirror in Sir Walter Scott's *Aunt Margaret's Mirror*.

Damiri (dä.mē′rē), **al-.** [Also: **al-Demiri**; full name, **Kamal al-Din Mohammed ibn-Musa al-Damiri.**] b. at Cairo, Egypt, c1345; d. there, 1405. Arab jurist and naturalist, author of a *Life of Animals*.

Damiron (då.mē.rôṅ), **Jean Philibert.** b. at Belleville, Rhône, France, May 10, 1794; d. at Paris, Jan. 11, 1862. French writer on philosophy, professor of the history of philosophy in the Faculté des Lettres at Paris. He was the author of *Essai sur l'histoire de la philosophie en France au XIXe siècle* (1828), *Cours de philosophie* (1831), and *Essai sur l'histoire de la philosophie en France au XVIIe siècle* (1846).

Damis (då.mēs). Impetuous youth in Molière's play *Tartuffe;* the son of Orgon.

Damkina (dam.kī′nạ). In Assyro-Babylonian mythology, wife of Ea, the god of the ocean, whose center of worship was at Eridu.

Dammam (dam.mam′). See under **Saudi Arabia.**

Damnation de Faust (då.nå.syôṅ dẹ fōst), **La.** Opera or dramatic legend in four parts by Berlioz, first produced at the Paris Opéra-Comique on Dec. 6, 1846. The libretto, by the composer and Gandonnière, is based on Gérard de Nerval's treatment of Goethe's drama.

Damnation of Theron Ware (thir′ọn wãr), **The.** Novel (1896) by the American novelist Harold Frederic. The time is the latter part of the 19th century; the setting is a predominantly Catholic town, Octavius, in New York state. The chief characters are Theron Ware, a Methodist minister, who wants to write a great book; Father Forbes, a Catholic priest; Ledsmar, an agnostic physician; and Celia Madden, whose beauty arouses the man in the minister. Ware's "damnation" comes when he is made to realize his own shortcomings, and causes him to give up the ministry. Regarded as Frederic's best work, it is called *Illumination* in the English edition.

Damnonium (dam.nō′ni.um), **Promontorium.** Latin name of **Lizard, the.**

Damocles (dam′ọ.klēz). fl. in the first half of the 4th century B.C. Syracusan, a courtier of Dionysius the elder. Cicero relates that Damocles, having extolled the good fortune of Dionysius, was invited by the tyrant to taste this royal felicity, and that, in the midst of a splendid banquet and all the luxury of the court, on looking up he beheld above his head a sword suspended by a single horse-hair.

Damocles. King of Arcadia in Robert Greene's *Arcadia*.

Damodar (dä′mọ.där). [Also, **Damudar.**] River in NE Union of India. It rises in the Nazaribagh Mountains, in Bihar, flows E and SE, and joins the Hooghly River below Calcutta. Length, ab. 368 mi.

Damoetas (dạ.mē′tạs). Herdsman in Theocritus and Vergil; hence, in pastoral poetry, a rustic. Sir Philip Sidney introduces in his *Arcadia* a foolish country clown by that name, which afterward seems to have become proverbial for folly.

Damon (dā′mọn). Goatherd in Vergil's *Eclogues;* hence, in pastoral poetry, a rustic.

Damon, Samuel Foster. b. at Newton, Mass., Feb. 22, 1893—. American teacher and poet. He received B.A. and M.A. degrees from Harvard and taught at Brown University. His books of verse include *Astrolabe* (1927) and *Tilted Moon* (1929), and he is the author of such critical works as *William Blake; His Philosophy and Symbols* (1924) and *Amy Lowell* (1935).

Damon and Phillida (fil′i.dạ). Pastoral farce by Colley Cibber, produced in 1729 and published anonymously the same year.

Damon and Pithias (pith′i.ạs). Play by Richard Edwards, printed in 1571. Its main subject is tragic, but it was nominally a comedy.

Damon and Pythias (pith′i.ạs). fl. in the first half of the 4th century B.C. Pythagorean philosophers of Syracuse, celebrated for their friendship. Pythias (or Phintias) plotted against the life of Dionysius I of Syracuse, and was condemned to die. As Pythias wished to arrange his affairs, Damon offered to place himself in the tyrant's hands as his substitute, and to die in his stead should he not return on the appointed day. At the last moment Pythias came back, and Dionysius was so struck by the fidelity of the friends that he pardoned the offender, and begged to be admitted into their fellowship.

Damon and Pythias. Tragedy by John Banim and Richard Lalor Sheil, produced in 1821.

Damophon (dam′ọ.fon). b. at Messene, Greece; fl. 2nd century B.C. Greek sculptor. He was one of the masters of Hellenic art, and his work combines the decorative richness of his period with something of the monumental simplicity of the Phidian epoch. He is known to have executed statues of gods in combined wood and marble for Messene and other Peloponnesian cities, and to have done much work in ivory and gold (it was he who restored the *Zeus* of Phidias after the ivory cracked during an earthquake).

Damoreau (då.mo.rō), **Laure Cinthie.** [Stage name, Mademoiselle *Cinti;* maiden name, **Montalant.**] b. at Paris, Feb. 6, 1801; d. there, Feb. 25, 1863. French singer. In 1819 she made her first appearance as Cherubino in *Le Nozze di Figaro* at Paris. In 1822 she appeared at London, and in 1826 at the Grand Opéra, Paris. From this time she sang both in Europe and the U.S. with assured success until 1856, when she retired from the stage. In 1834 she was made professor of singing at the Paris Conservatory.

Dampier (dam′pir), **William.** b. at East Coker, Somersetshire, England, probably in June, 1652; d. at London, in March, 1715. English freebooter, explorer, and author. His seafaring life began in 1668, and until 1691 he led a life of the wildest adventure, as manager of a Jamaica plantation, as a logwood cutter in Mexico, but generally as a sailor on various piratical cruises, especially against the Spanish colonies on the western coast of America and elsewhere. During this time he circumnavigated the globe, having been marooned in the Far East and acting for a time as a semi-captive master gunner in a British fort. In 1697 he published his *New Voyage Round the World*, and this was supplemented by a second volume of travels in 1699. In 1699 as a member of the navy he was given command of a ship, the *Roebuck*, in which he again went round the world, exploring the coasts of Australia and New Guinea. He started again on a privateering cruise with two ships in 1703, but accomplished little, and his company was broken up; he reached England, after a third circumnavigation, in 1707. It was during this voyage that Alexander Selkirk, Robinson Crusoe's original, was marooned in the Juan Fernández islands. Subsequently he was pilot of the privateer *Duke*, and again went (1708–11) round the world, on this voyage rescuing Selkirk. He published a well-known *Discourse on the Winds*. The Dampier Archipelago near Australia, two sea passages near New Guinea, both called Dampier Strait, and Dampier Land in Australia were named for him.

Dampier Archipelago. Group of small rocky islands situated NW of Australia. They were discovered by William Dampier, the English explorer, and named for him.

Dampier Island. Former name of **Karkar Island.**

Dampier Land. Peninsular region in NW Australia, in Western Australia state, on the Timor Sea W of the mouth of the Fitzroy River. It was named for the English explorer William Dampier.

Dampierre (däṅ.pyer), **Auguste Henri Marie Picot,** Marquis **de.** b. at Paris, Aug. 19, 1756; d. near Vicogne, Nord, France, May 9, 1793. French revolutionary general. He distinguished himself in the campaigns of 1792–93, at Valmy, Jemappes, and Neerwinden, and died of wounds received in action.

Dampier Strait (dam'pir). Strait NW of New Guinea, in the SW Pacific, separating that island from Waigeo. It was named for the English explorer William Dampier. Length, ab. 100 mi.; width, ab. 35 mi.

Dampier Strait. Strait NE of the island of New Guinea, separating the trust territory of North-East New Guinea from New Britain. It was named for William Dampier, English explorer. Width, ab. 15 mi.

Damply (dam'pli), **Widow.** Character in David Garrick's play *The Male Coquette*.

Dampremy (däṅ.rẹ.mē). Town in S Belgium, in the province of Hainaut, situated on the Sambre River and th Brussels-Charleroi Canal, E of Mons. It has coal mines, iron foundries, and glassworks. 11,678 (1947).

Damra (däm'rä). See **Dama.**

Damrosch (dam'rosh; German, däm'rosh), **Clara.** [Married name, **Mannes.**] American musician; daughter of Leopold Damrosch (1832–85). She married David Mannes, with whom she conducted (1916 *et seq.*) the David Mannes Music School and with whom she gave sonata recitals at New York, Boston, and London (1913).

Damrosch, Frank Heino. b. at Breslau, June 22, 1859; d. at New York, 1937. Conductor of choral societies in and near New York, including the Oratorio Society, the Musical Art Society, and the People's Choral Union; son of Leopold Damrosch (1832–85). He was director (1905 *et seq.*) of the Institute of Musical Art at New York.

Damrosch, Leopold. b. at Posen (then in Germany, now Poznań, Poland), Oct. 22, 1832; d. at New York, Feb. 15, 1885. Conductor, solo violinist, and composer. He settled at New York in 1871, and was instrumental in the establishment of German opera at the Metropolitan Opera House, New York, where he conducted during the 1884–85 season. He was director of the Oratorio and Symphony societies and the Männergesangverein Arion, until his death.

Damrosch, Walter Johannes. b. at Breslau, Jan. 30, 1862; d. at New York, Dec. 22, 1950. Composer and conductor; son of Leopold Damrosch (1832–85). He was director (1885 *et seq.*) of the Oratorio Society, organizer (1894) of the Damrosch Opera Company, and conductor (1903–27) of the New York Symphony Society, with which he toured (1920) Europe; a founder of the Fontainebleau summer music school for American students; conducted (1925) first symphonic concert broadcast by radio; appointed (1927) musical counsel to the National Broadcasting Company. He composed the operas *The Scarlet Letter* (1894), *Cyrano de Bergerac* (1913), and *The Man without a Country* (1937); and choral works including *Manila Te Deum* (1899) and *Abraham Lincoln Song* (1936).

Damsel of Brittany. See **Eleanor of Brittany.**

Damsel of Darien (dãr'i.ẹn), **The.** Historical romance by William Gilmore Simms, published in 1839.

Damudar (dä'mu.där). See **Damodar.**

Damuras (dä.mö'räs). See **Tamyras.**

D'Amville (dam'vil). Atheist in Cyril Tourneur's play *The Atheist's Tragedy*.

Dan (dan). See also **Dan River.**

Dan. In the Bible, a son of Jacob by Bilhah, and founder of the tribe of Dan, one of the 12 tribes of Israel. Gen. xxx. 6.

Dan. Hebrew tribe. The portion allotted to the Danites, as described in Josh. xix., was the small but fertile hilly tract west of Benjamin and northwest of Judah to the sea, including the cities of Jaffa, Ekron, Gathrimmon, and others. But though the tribe of Dan was originally one of the strongest numerically, counting 62,000 to 64,000, it was not equal to the task of expelling the Ammonites, and later the Philistines, from that territory, and only for a time prevailed with the help of Ephraim and Judah. Consequently part of the tribe migrated to the extreme north of the country, and conquered the city of Laish, henceforth called Dan. That part which remained in the south, from which the hero Samson descended, disappeared from history, and seems to have been absorbed by the tribe of Judah.

Dan. [Older name, **Laish.**] In Biblical geography, a city situated on the slopes of Mount Hermon, not far from the modern Baniyas (still called Tel-el-Kadi, "hill of the Judge"), and often mentioned in the Old Testament as the most northern landmark of Palestine, in the formula "from Dan to Beersheba." It was named Dan after its capture by the Danites. It contained a sanctuary with an image the exact nature of which is not known. At the division of the kingdom Jeroboam put up there one of the golden calves worshiped at that time. It is first mentioned in Gen. xiv. 14 as the place at which Chedorlaomer, king of Elam, and his four allies were overthrown and defeated by Abraham. The occurrence in this account of the name which was given to the place many centuries later is variously explained. If the Dan of Gen. xiv. is identical with that of Judges, xviii., and if the account of Gen. xiv. is authentic, the name Dan may have been later inserted in the manuscripts for Laish, when the latter was superseded by the former.

Dan (dän). [Also: **Dã, Diabouba, Diafoba, Ge, Geme, Gio, Mebe, Ngere, Sa, Samia.**] Mande-speaking people of W Africa, inhabiting W Ivory Coast and C Liberia. Their population is estimated at ab. 100,000 (by C. Kjersmeier, *Afrikanske Negerskulpturer*). Culturally they resemble the Kpelle, but the boys' and girls' initiation schools are known as *Bo* and *Bwo*. Their carved wooden masks are highly regarded in the field of African art. They are not to be confused with the Dian of E Ivory Coast.

Dana (dā'nạ), **Charles Anderson.** b. at Hinsdale, N.H., Aug. 8, 1819; d. at West Island, near Glen Cove, Long Island, N.Y., Oct. 17, 1897. American newspaper editor, noted for his direction of the New York *Sun*. He attended Harvard and was a member (c1841–46) of the experimental Brook Farm colony. After working as the assistant editor of the Boston *Daily Chronotype*, he became a reporter, covering the 1848 European revolutions, and then was named city editor of the New York *Tribune*, later serving as its managing editor (1849–62). Resigning in 1862, he joined the staff of the war department and for a time was special commissioner at Grant's headquarters in the west, suggesting to Secretary of War Stanton that Grant be made supreme commander of the Union forces; as assistant secretary of war (1864–65), he performed valuable service as a field observer with the Union army. He resigned in 1865, subsequently edited the *Republican* at Chicago, and became part proprietor and editor (1868) of the New York *Sun*, which soon became known for its news style stressing "human interest." Dana fought against the corruption of the Tweed machine and, after supporting Grant in the 1868 campaign, against the Grant administration's corruption. In his insistence upon the vivid and the concise, Dana was a pioneer of modern news editing. Among the well-known writers who worked under him were Richard Harding Davis, David Graham Phillips, and Jacob Riis. He compiled *The Household Book of Poetry* (1857), was coeditor of the *American Cyclopaedia* (1858 *et seq.*) and wrote *The Art of Newspaper Making* (1895), *Recollections of the Civil War* (1898), and *Eastern Journeys* (1898).

Dana, Charles Loomis. b. at Woodstock, Vt., March 25, 1852; d. at Harmon, N.Y., Dec. 12, 1935. American pathologist, professor of nervous diseases in the Cornell Medical College from 1899. He published *A Text-book of Nervous Diseases and Psychiatry* (1892).

Dana, Edward Salisbury. b. at New Haven, Conn., Nov. 16, 1849; d. June 16, 1935. American mineralogist and physicist; son of James Dwight Dana. He was assistant professor of natural philosophy at Yale University until 1890, when he became professor of physics.

Dana, Francis. b. at Charlestown, Mass., June 13, 1743; d. April 25, 1811. American diplomat, jurist, and Revolutionary patriot; son of Richard Dana (1700–72). Graduated (1762) from Harvard, he received his M.A. (1765) there and in 1767 was admitted to the bar. Chosen (1774) as a Cambridge delegate to the first provincial congress of Massachusetts, he instead went to England to sound out sentiment there concerning reconciliation. He returned (1776) a convinced American patriot and served (1776–80) as a member of the Massachusetts Council, a delegate (selected in 1776) to the Continental Congress, and in 1779 went to France as secretary of the legation led by John Adams. He served (1780–83) as minister to Russia, although he was not recognized as such by the Russian government. He was appointed (1785) an associate justice of the Massachusetts supreme court, and was its chief justice from 1791 to 1806.

Dana, James Dwight. b. at Utica, N.Y., Feb. 12, 1813; d. at New Haven, Conn., April 14, 1895. American geologist and mineralogist, professor at Yale University from 1850. He was graduated from Yale in 1833, traveled in the Mediterranean as mathematical instructor of midshipmen in the U.S. navy (1833–35), was assistant to Silliman at Yale (1835–38), and took part in the Wilkes exploring expedition (1838–42). His important *Reports* of the expedition (on geology, corals, and crustaceans) were published between 1846 and 1854. His works include *System of Mineralogy* (1837), *Manual of Geology* (1862), *Text Book of Geology for Schools and Academies* (1864), *Corals and Coral Islands* (1872), and *Characteristics of Volcanoes* (1890).

Dana, John Cotton. b. at Woodstock, Vt., Aug. 19, 1856; d. at New York, July 21, 1929. American librarian, at various times head of the Denver Public Library (1889–98), the Springfield, Mass., City Library (1898–1902), and the Newark, N.J., Public Library (1902–29). He made the Newark library a popular institution, and helped to found (1909) the Newark Museum Association, becoming the museum's director. He was the author of *Library Primer* (1896) and *Libraries, Addresses and Essays* (1916).

Dana, Paul. b. at New York, Aug. 20, 1852; d. April 7, 1930. American editor; son of Charles Anderson Dana (1819–97). He was associated (1890 *et seq.*) with the New York *Sun*, of which his father was editor, and served (1897–1903) as editor of the *Sun*.

Dana, Richard. b. at Cambridge, Mass., June 26, 1700; d. May 17, 1772. American lawyer and patriot. He was a prominent member of the Boston bar, and, as a supporter of the popular cause, frequently presided over the Boston town meetings between 1763 and 1772, and otherwise took a prominent part in the movements which preceded the Revolutionary War.

Dana, Richard Henry. b. at Cambridge, Mass., Nov. 15, 1787; d. at Boston, Feb. 2, 1879. American poet and essayist; son of Francis Dana (1743–1811) and father of Richard Henry Dana (1815–82).

Dana, Richard Henry. b. at Cambridge, Mass., Aug. 1, 1815; d. at Rome, Jan. 6, 1882. American writer and lawyer, noted as the author of *Two Years Before the Mast* (1840); son of Richard Henry Dana (1787–1879). Compelled to leave Harvard because of impaired eyesight, he went to sea as a common sailor in 1834, and upon his return in 1836 resumed his studies at Harvard, graduating in 1837. He was an instructor in elocution (1839–40) at Harvard, was admitted to the bar in 1840, and began specializing in admiralty cases. His record of his sea adventures was an immediate success in the U.S. and became popular abroad. He also wrote a maritime law manual, *The Seaman's Friend* (1841), which became a standard work. He was one of the founders (1848) of the Free-Soil Party. He served as U.S. attorney (1861–66) for the district of Massachusetts, appeared as counsel (1867–68) for the U.S. in the treason proceedings against Jefferson Davis, and was senior counsel (1877) for the U.S. at the fisheries commission at Halifax. He was a lecturer (1866–68) in the Harvard Law School, wrote *To Cuba and Back* (1859), and brought out an edition of *Wheaton's Elements of International Law* (1866).

Dana, Richard Henry. b. at Cambridge, Mass., Jan. 3, 1851; d. Dec. 16, 1931. American lawyer; son of Richard Henry Dana (1815–82). He was the founder (1878–79) of the Associated Charities of Boston, originator (1884) of the Massachusetts Civil Service Reform Act, drafted (1888) the first Australian Ballot Act to be made law in the U.S., and was editor (1889–92) of the *Civil Service Record*. Author of *Double Taxation in Massachusetts* (1895) and *Hospitable England in the Seventies* (1921).

Dana, Samuel Luther. b. at Amherst, N.H., July 11, 1795; d. at Lowell, Mass., March 11, 1868. American chemist and writer on agricultural chemistry. He was employed as chemist to the Merrimac Print Works at Lowell upward of 30 years, and invented a new method of bleaching cotton, which was generally adopted.

Dana, William Parsons Winchester. b. at Boston, Feb. 18, 1833; d. April 8, 1927. American painter. In his youth he went to sea, but as early as 1854 he was enrolled at the École des Beaux-Arts, Paris, and he continued in that city, studying also with individual instructors, until 1862. In the latter year he opened a studio at New York, but in 1870 he went abroad, and eventually made his home in England. His paintings are mostly either marine or genre pieces, and he received the first prize for marine paintings at the Pennsylvania Academy of Fine Arts in 1881. He also won awards at international expositions at Paris in 1878 and 1889. From 1867 he was an academician of the National Academy of Design. Examples of his work are to be seen in various American galleries, including the Metropolitan Museum of Art in New York and the Pennsylvania Academy of Fine Arts in Philadelphia.

Dana Coman (kō′mạn), **Mount.** See **Coman, Mount.**

Danaë (dan′ạ.ē). In Greek mythology, the daughter of Acrisius of Argos and mother of Perseus by Zeus, who visited her, while she was shut up in a brazen tower by her father, in the form of a shower of gold. She was shut up with her child in a chest, thrown into the sea, and carried by the waves to the island of Seriphos. From various difficulties she was in the end rescued by Perseus and brought back to Greece.

Danaë. Subject of a number of famous paintings of the 16th and 17th centuries. Among them are: **1.** A painting by Rembrandt, in the Hermitage Museum at Leningrad. Danaë lies, undraped, on a bed covered with green silk; her unloosed girdle has fallen to the floor. An old woman is in attendance behind the curtains. **2.** A painting by Correggio, in the Borghese Gallery at Rome. She reclines smiling on her couch, while Cupid before her holds out a fold of the drapery over her knees to catch the golden shower. **3.** A painting by Titian in the Museo Nazionale at Naples, painted for the grandson of Pope Paul III. Danaë reclines on a couch while the golden shower falls upon her. **4.** A painting by Titian, in the Imperial Gallery at Vienna, one of a number which he made on this subject because of the popularity of the Naples *Danaë*. Danaë lies, nude, on a cushioned couch; the golden rain falls from a cloud over her, in which the face and hand of Jupiter appear. An old woman seeks to catch some of the shower in a dish.

Danai (dan′ạ.ī). [Also, **Danaoi.**] In ancient Greek history, the Argives; used by Homer to denote the Greeks generally.

Danaïdes (dạ.nā′i.dēz). In Greek legend, the 50 daughters of Danaus, by whose command they slew their husbands. According to later writers, they were condemned in Hades to pour water into sieves.

Danakil (dan′ạ.kil). [Also: **Afar Country, Country of the Danakil.**] Region in E Africa, in Ethiopia, lying behind (W of) southern Eritrea and French Somaliland; formerly it extended to the Red Sea coast.

Danakil. [Also: **Afar, Afara, Dankali.**] Cushitic-speaking people of NE Africa, inhabiting C and S Eritrea, N French Somaliland, and NE Ethiopia, in a triangular region NE of Addis Ababa and between Asmara and Djibouti. Their population is estimated at ab. 250,000 (by E. Cerulli, cited in M. A. Bryan, *The Distribution of the Semitic and Cushitic Languages of Africa*, 1947). They are Mohammedans, and are divided into numerous nomadic bands ruled by independent chiefs. They are pastoralists, herding cattle and camels, and their principal food is milk. They are predominantly Caucasoid in physical type, although their skin is dark.

Danao (dä.nä′ō). Town in the E part of Cebu, Philippine Islands: seaport. 3,100 (1948).

Danao River. River in Negros Occidental Province, Negros, Philippine Islands.

Danapris (da̤.nap′ris). An ancient name of the **Dnieper.**

Danastris (da̤.nas′tris). An ancient name of the **Dniester.**

Danaus (dan′a̤.us). In Greek legend, a son of Belus and grandson of Poseidon, the founder of Argos, and ancestor of the Danai. He was the brother of Aegyptus.

Danbury (dan′ber″i, -bėr.i). City in SW Connecticut, in Fairfield County, on the Still River, ab. 52 mi. NE of New York: one of the leading hat-manufacturing cities of the U.S., principally of felt hats. It is important for its contribution to labor history through the U.S. Supreme Court decision in the case of *Loewe v. Lawlor* (1908), popularly known as the Danbury Hatters' Case. Settled in 1684, it was burned by the British in 1777. It is the site of a popular annual county fair in September and October. 22,067 (1950).

Danbury Hatters' Case. See **Loewe v. Lawlor, 208 U.S. 274 (1908).**

"Danbury News Man." See **Bailey, James Montgomery.**

Danby (dan′bi), 1st Earl of. A title of **Osborne,** Sir **Thomas.**

Danby, Francis. b. at Wexford(?), Ireland, Nov. 16, 1793; d. at Exmouth, England, Feb., 1861. English historical and landscape painter.

Dance (dȧns), **George.** b. 1700; d. 1768. English architect, designer of the Mansion House at London, in 1739; father of George Dance (1741–1825) and Sir Nathaniel Dance-Holland (1734–1811).

Dance, George. b. 1741; d. at London, Jan. 14, 1825. English architect and artist; son of George Dance (1700–68) and brother of Sir Nathaniel Dance-Holland (1734–1811). He designed Newgate Prison at London, in 1770.

Dance-Holland (dȧns′hol′a̤nd), Sir **Nathaniel.** b. 1734; d. near Winchester, England, Oct. 15, 1811. English painter; son of George Dance (1700–68) and brother of George Dance (1741–1825).

Dance of Death. [Also, **Dance of Macaber;** French, **Danse Macabre;** Latin, **Chorea Machabaeorum.**] Originally, a kind of morality or allegorical representation intended to remind the living of the power of death. It originated in the 14th century in Germany, and consisted of dialogues between Death and a number of typical followers, which were acted in or near churches by the religious orders. Soon after, it was repeated in France. It became extraordinarily popular, and was treated in every possible way, in pictures, bas-reliefs, tapestry, and other forms. Death is made grotesque and a sort of "horrid Harlequin," a skeleton dancer or musician playing for dancing, leading all mankind. A dramatic poem which grew out of this was imitated in Spain in 1400 as *La Danza general de los muertos.* In 1425 the French, having illustrated each verse, had the whole series painted on the wall of the churchyard of the Monastery of the Innocents, where they acted the drama. In 1430 the poem and pictures were produced at London, and not long after at Salisbury (1460), Wortley Hall in Gloucestershire, and other places. In Germany it attained its greatest popularity. The drama was acted until about the middle of the 15th century, when the pictures became the main point of interest. A picture of this kind was painted in the Marienkirche at Lübeck, Germany, and one was on the cloister wall of Klingenthal, a convent at Basel, Switzerland, both of the 14th century; the latter disappeared in 1805. One in the Campo Santo at Pisa has been ascribed to Orcagna. In the reign of Henry VII a processional Dance of Death was painted around the cloisters of old Saint Paul's at London. The younger Hans Holbein left 53 sketches for engraving; these he called *Imagines Mortis;* they are, however, independent, and do not represent a dance. Lydgate wrote a metrical translation of the poem for the chapter of Saint Paul's, to be placed under the pictures in the cloister. Various explanations of the name Macaber or Macabre have been given.

Dance of Death, The. Satirical drama in verse (1933) by Wystan Hugh Auden. The theme of the play, as stated by an announcer at the opening, is the decline and the final death of the British middle class. The unusual nature of the work may be suggested by the fact that it closes with an announcement, made by Karl Marx, that the death has taken place. The title presumably derives from the German morality plays of the Middle Ages and from the famous 16th-century woodcuts designed by the younger Hans Holbein.

Dance of Life, The. Philosophical prose work (1923) by Havelock Ellis. The highly original theme of the work, regarded as his most popular one, is that life and art are identical, and that life, when it reaches its highest development, comes closest to resembling the art of dancing. Dancing, thinking, writing, religion, and morals, all parts of the "dance," are taken up in separate chapters. The idealistic conclusion is the author's belief, or hope, that the world will be saved when man, through his esthetic impulse, discovers the secret of finding pleasure and enjoyment in things without actually owning or possessing them.

Dance of Macabre. Short didactic poem by John Lydgate. It is in 24 quatrains and was written to accompany illustrations. It was printed in 1554, at the end of Tottell's edition of Lydgate's *Falls of Princes,* in 1658 in Dugdale's *St. Paul's,* and in 1794 in the Douce edition of the younger Hans Holbein's *Dance of Death* woodcuts. It was also published in 1840 in Holbein's *Alphabet of Death,* edited by the French scholar Montaiglon. One of his minor works, it has suffered the fate of all Lydgate's poetry, long or short: it is no longer read.

Dance to Death, The. Poetic tragedy (1882) by Emma Lazarus. It was published in her *Songs of a Semite.* Although the play deals with anti-Semitism in 12th-century Germany, it is also a passionate attack on Russian anti-Semitism in the 19th century, as practiced under the czars, and was inspired by the anti-Jewish outbreaks of 1881–82.

"Dancing Chancellor." Nickname of **Hatton,** Sir **Christopher.**

Dancla (däṅ.klȧ), **Jean Charles.** b. at Bagnères-de-Bigorre, France, Dec. 19, 1817; d. at Tunis, Tunisia, Nov. 8, 1907. French composer and violinist. He was professor (1857 *et seq.*) at the Paris Conservatory, and organized and played in a chamber music quartet. His compositions include violin concertos and études, symphonies, and quartets. He wrote *Les Compositeurs chefs d'orchestre* (1873), *Miscellanées musicales* (1876), and *Notes et souvenirs* (1893).

D'Ancona (däng.kō′nä), **Alessandro.** See **Ancona, Alessandro d'.**

Dancourt (däṅ.kör), **Florent Carton.** b. at Fontainebleau, France, Nov. 1, 1661; d. at Courcelles-le-Roi, in Berry, France, Dec. 7, 1725. French comedian and playwright. His plays deal almost exclusively with the middle class. Among them are *Le Chevalier à la mode* (1687), *Les Bourgeoises de qualité* (1700), and *Les Trois Cousins* (1700).

Dandelion Days. Autobiographical novel by Henry Williamson, published in 1922. It is the second volume of a tetralogy under the general title *The Flax of Dream.*

Dandhu Panth (dun′dö punt′). Original name of **Nana Sahib.**

Dandie Dinmont (dan′di din′mo̤nt). See **Dinmont, Dandie.**

Dandin (däṅ.daṅ), **Perrin.** Name given to an ignorant and preposterous judge in Jean Baptiste Racine's *Les Plaideurs* and in La Fontaine's *Fables.* He is taken from Rabelais's *Perrin Dendin.*

Dandolo (däṅ′dō.lō), **Andrea.** b. 1310; d. Oct. 7, 1354. Doge of Venice (1343–54). He joined (1343) the Crusade proclaimed by Clement VI against the Turks, which ended in a peace advantageous to Venice in 1346. He waged almost continuous war with Genoa (1348–54). He wrote *Chronicon Venetum*, a Latin chronicle of Venice, which terminates with the year 1339.

Dandolo, Enrico. b. at Venice, c1108; d. at Constantinople, June 14, 1205. Doge of Venice (1192–1205). He was the leader of the Venetians and Crusaders in the capture of Constantinople (1203 and 1204). He went as ambassador to the Byzantine court in 1173, and was blinded by order of the emperor Manuel.

Dandolo, Count **Vincenzo.** b. at Venice, Oct. 26, 1758; d. there, Dec. 13, 1819. Italian chemist and economist. He wrote *Fondamenti della fisico-chimica* (1796), *Discorsi sulla pastorizia . . .* (1806), and others.

Dandurand (dän.dü.rän), **Raoul.** b. at Montreal, Canada, 1861; d. at Ottawa, Canada, March 11, 1942. Canadian lawyer and politician and leader of the Canadian Liberal Party. Educated at Montreal College and Laval University, he was elected (1898) to the Canadian senate, served as speaker of the senate (1905–09) and member of the privy council (1909) and as minister without portfolio (1921–26, 1926–30) in the Dominion cabinet, was appointed Canadian representative (1924) to the League of Nations, president of the sixth League assembly (1925) and delegate to the League council (1927), and was appointed (1941) imperial privy councilor.

Dane (dān), **Clemence.** [Pseudonym of **Winifred Ashton.**] English novelist and playwright. Her novels include *Regiment of Women* (1917), *Legend* (1919), *Wandering Stars* (1924), *The Babyons* (1928), *Broome Stages* (1931), *The Moon Is Feminine* (1938), *The Arrogant History of White Ben* (1939), and *He Brings Great News* (1946); her plays, *A Bill of Divorcement* (1921), *Will Shakespeare* (1921), *The Way Things Happen* (1923), *Naboth's Vineyard* (1925), *Granite* (1926), *Mariners* (1926), *Moonlight Is Silver* (1934), *Cousin Muriel* (1940), and *Call Home the Heart* (1947); her essays, *The Women's Side* (1927) and *Tradition and Hugh Walpole* (1930). She edited the anthologies *The Shelter Book* (1939) and *The Nelson Touch* (1942).

Dane, Mrs. Wayward heroine of Henry Arthur Jones's problem play *Mrs. Dane's Defence* (1900). Mrs. Dane, a woman with a past, wishes to marry young Carteret, but under a merciless cross-examination by his foster father, Sir Daniel, she is forced to confess to an affair she had on the Continent. Like another unfortunate heroine of modern drama, Pinero's Paula Tanqueray, she finds out, too late, that a woman cannot live down her past.

Dane, Nathan. b. at Ipswich, Mass., Dec. 29, 1752; d. at Beverley, Mass., Feb. 15, 1835. American jurist. He drafted the ordinance relating to the government of the territory northwest of the Ohio River in 1786–87, and published *Abridgment and Digest of American Law* (1823–29).

Danegeld (dān′geld). English land tax during the late 10th and until the middle 12th century, originally levied to appease Danish raiders. Unable effectively to protect England against the plundering and ravaging Danes, Norwegians, and Swedes, King Ethelred II bought them off by paying tribute money, raised by taxation on land, in 991 and on four other occasions up to 1012. With the accession (1016) of the Danish King Canute to the English throne, the tax was no longer needed for its original purpose, but the name continued to be applied to taxes levied from time to time for purposes of defense. In the reign of Edward the Confessor the Danegeld fell into disuse, but William the Conqueror seized upon it as a means of raising revenue, and it was partly to facilitate this levy that the Domesday Book came into existence. Under the Norman regime taxes continued to be raised under the name of Danegeld until 1163, after which the designation disappears from the records. Even before the first English payment of Danegeld, similar means were sometimes used to buy off Danish raiders in France.

Danelaw (dān′lô). [Also: **Danelage, Danelagh;** Old English, **Dena Lagu.**] That part of England where the Danish influence was paramount during the 9th and 10th centuries. It corresponded to the modern counties of Yorkshire, Lincolnshire, Nottinghamshire, Derbyshire, Leicestershire, Rutlandshire, Norfolk, Suffolk, Essex, Cambridgeshire, Huntingdonshire, Northamptonshire, Buckinghamshire, Bedfordshire, and Hertfordshire.

Dänemark (dā′ne̜.märk). German name of **Denmark.**

Danemora (dä.ne̜.mö′rä). See **Dannemora,** Sweden.

Danenhower (dan′e̜n.hou.ėr), **John Wilson.** b. at Chicago, Sept. 30, 1849; committed suicide at Annapolis, Md., April 20, 1887. American naval officer and arctic explorer. A graduate (1870) of the U.S. Naval Academy, he was commissioned lieutenant in 1879 and joined Captain G. W. De Long's arctic expedition as executive officer on the *Jeannette*, which became wedged in an ice pack and was crushed two years later. Survivors made their way to the mouth of the Lena River where a few were rescued. *Lieutenant Danenhower's Narrative of the Jeannette* (1882) describes his experiences.

Danes (dānz). Natives of Denmark. They were first described early in the 6th century as on the W coast of the Chersonesus Cimbrica or Cimbrian peninsula (now called Jutland), in the territory formerly occupied by the Heruli, whither, according to Jordanes, they had come from Scandinavia. The Old Danish language is preserved in numerous runic inscriptions, the oldest of which date from the Viking age (700–1050), and in literature from the 13th century. Three principal dialectal groups are distinguished, which are typically represented by the dialects of Skåne (Scania) in southern Sweden, Zealand, and Jutland. The Zealand dialect became the literary form at about the time of the Reformation, and it is from this period that modern Danish dates.

Danev (dä′nef), **Stoyan.** b. at Shumen, Bulgaria, 1858; d. 1940. Bulgarian statesman and jurist. He served (1901–03, 1913) as prime minister and minister of foreign affairs during the critical years before World War I, and was professor of international law at the University of Sofia.

Danewerk (dän′e̜.verk). [Danish, **Dannevirke.**] Ancient intrenchment or wall erected by King Göttrik in the 9th century as a protection of Denmark against invasion from the S. It extended across what is now Schleswig-Holstein from the Schlei (or Sli) inlet to the Treene River, a tributary of the Eider. It was strengthened in the 10th century and later, and was captured from the Danes by the Prussians April 23, 1848.

Danforth (dan′fōrth, -fôrth), **Moseley Isaac.** b. at Hartford, Conn., Dec. 11, 1800; d. at New York City, Jan. 19, 1862. American painter and engraver. In 1818 he was apprenticed to a Hartford engraver. Quickly mastering the technique of the art, he set up in business for himself at New Haven in 1821, and shortly thereafter moved to New York, where he became a founding member of the National Academy of Design in 1826. In 1827 he went to England and remained there ten years, associating with people of eminence in the arts while he studied painting and continued to perfect his technique as an engraver. He also achieved a considerable mastery of water colors. His most notable and important achievement, however, was the execution of a series of excellent drawings of the Elgin Marbles. After his return to America, while he continued to paint and to do portrait engraving, he became engrossed chiefly in banknote engraving as a business. About 1850 he became a member of the firm of Danforth, Underwood and Company, which in 1858 was absorbed into the American Banknote Company, and of this concern he was vice-president until his death.

Dangeau (däṅ.zhō), Marquis **de.** [Title of **Philippe de Courcillon.**] French soldier, aide-de-camp to Louis XIV, whom he attended in all his campaigns. He wrote a voluminous journal, covering the period from 1684 to 1720, and giving in minute detail the events and manners of the court of Louis.

Danger (däṅ.zhā). See **Latude, Jean Henry.**

Dangla Range (däng′lä′). See **Tanglha Range.**

Dangle (dang′gl). Amateur critic, in Richard Brinsley Sheridan's farce *The Critic*, whose peculiarities are agreeably described by his wife in the first scene; supposed to be a satire on Thomas Vaughan, a playwright.

Dangs (dängz), **the.** Group of 14 native states in W central Union of India, now part of Bombay state.

Dania (dā′ni.a̜). City in Florida, in Broward County, N of Miami: center of a tomato-producing area. It is near the Seminole Indian Reservation. 4,540 (1950).

Danican (dȧ.nē.käṅ), **François André.** See **Philidor.**

Daniel (dan'yẹl). [Babylonian, **Belteshazzar.**] One of the prophets of the Old Testament. According to the book which bears his name, he (probably being of royal or noble descent) was carried off captive to Babylon in the third year of Jehoiakim (605 B.C.), and with three other Israelitish youths of noble blood, Hananiah, Mishael, and Azariah, was instructed in the language and learning of the Babylonians and educated for the king's service. They refrained from defiling themselves by partaking of the food of the king. Daniel was especially gifted with "understanding in all visions and dreams," and successfully exercised this gift by interpreting disquieting dreams of Nebuchadnezzar, and the mysterious writing on the wall which disturbed the revelry of Belshazzar (Dan. v. 5). At the accession of Darius he was made "one of the three presidents" of the empire. He was divinely delivered from the lion's den into which he was thrown for refusing to obey a decree of the king forbidding anyone except the king to ask a petition of God or man for 30 days. He was still prosperous under Cyrus. In the third year of Cyrus he saw the vision on the bank of the Tigris, and this is the last mention of him in the Old Testament. He is referred to by Ezekiel as a pattern of righteousness and wisdom. In addition to his Hebrew name a Babylonian one, Belteshazzar, was given him. Legends about him grew up, as in the apocryphal additions to the Biblical book which bears his name, *Bel and the Dragon*, the story of Susanna and Daniel. According to Mohammedan tradition, Daniel returned to Palestine, where he held the government of Syria, and finally died at Susa, where his supposed tomb is still shown and is visited by crowds of pilgrims.

Daniel. Last of a series of three poems attributed to the "school of Caedmon." The first two poems are *Genesis* and *Exodus*.

Daniel (då.nyel), Saint **Antoine.** [Also, Saint **Antony Daniel.**] b. at Dieppe, France, May 27, 1600 or 1601; d. at Teanaostae, Ontario, Canada, July 4, 1648. One of the Jesuit martyrs of North America. Joining the Society of Jesus in 1621, he accompanied Samuel de Champlain to Quebec in 1633, and served as a teacher in a school for Indian boys in that settlement for some two years before going to the mission at Ihonatiria, among the Hurons, where he was to spend the rest of his life. On July 4, 1648, an Iroquois war-party attacked the mission while the Huron warriors were away. Father Daniel, having shepherded the women and children into the chapel, where he pronounced general absolution and baptized a number of catechumens, faced the Iroquois alone, and died pierced by many arrows. He was beatified by the Roman Catholic Church in 1925 and canonized in 1930. His feast is celebrated in the Jesuit order on March 16, and in the Church at large on September 26.

Daniel, Arnaud (or **Arnault** or **Arnaut** or **Arnauto**). fl. 12th century. French troubadour, called *"gran maestro d'amore"* ("great master of love") by Petrarch. His poetic innovations were much admired and his original sestina stanzaic pattern served as a model to Dante.

Daniel (dan'yẹl), **Book of.** Book which in the English Bible, as in all other translations, follows Ezekiel as the fourth of the great prophets, while in the original Hebrew Bible it has its place in the third division of the Canon, the Hagiographa. It is generally divided into two parts. The first, chapters i.-vi., contains historical incidents; the second, chapters vii.-xii., visions. Chapters ii. 4-vii., inclusive, are written in Aramaic, the rest in Hebrew. The authenticity and historical character of the book were early called in question. Porphyry, in his discourses against the Christians, and most modern critics relegate the book in its present shape, on historical and linguistic grounds, to the period of the persecutions of Antiochus Epiphanes (c167 B.C.). The writer exhibits a familiarity with the history of that period, while his historical references to the time in which Daniel is supposed to have lived are vague and in many instances incorrect; as, for instance, that Nebuchadnezzar was the father of Belshazzar, that the latter was the last Babylonian king, and that Darius, and not Cyrus, was the successor of Nabonidus in the rule over Babylonia. The language of the book contains numerous Persian and Greek words which point to a time when these empires had long been established. The object of the author may have been to encourage his people to constancy and faithfulness in the desperate struggle for their country and faith, showing them how the constancy and fidelity of Daniel and his three companions were rewarded, and revealing to them the glorious future which is to follow their present sufferings. This, however, does not exclude a historical basis of the narratives contained in the book; and it is not impossible that a Daniel similar to the one described in the book not only existed during the exile, but that also some written materials were extant from him, which the author of the 2nd century cast, together with the traditions, into a literary form, with a special view to the circumstances of his own time.

Daniel (då.nyel), **Gabriel.** b. at Rouen, France, Feb. 8, 1649; d. at Paris, June 23, 1728. French Jesuit historian and theologian, author of *Histoire de France* (1713).

Daniel (dä'nē.el), **Hermann Adalbert.** b. at Köthen, Germany, Nov. 18, 1812; d. at Leipzig, Germany, Sept. 13, 1871. German geographer and theologian. He wrote *Thesaurus hymnologicus* (1841–56), *Lehrbuch der Geographie* (1845), and others.

Daniel (dan'yẹl), **John Moncure.** b. in Stafford County, Va., Oct. 24, 1825; d. at Richmond, Va., March 30, 1865. American journalist and diplomat. He edited the *Southern Planter* and was editor (1847–53, 1861–65) of the Richmond *Examiner*. He was appointed U.S. representative to Sardinia, where he remained until South Carolina seceded. He approved secession, advocated military conscription, and conducted a vigorous campaign against Jefferson Davis's administration. During the Civil War he served briefly in the Confederate army.

Daniel, Lewis C. b. at New York, Oct. 23, 1901—. American painter, etcher, and illustrator, best known for his illustrations of books and poems. He was a pupil at the National Academy of Design and the Art Students League of New York and worked (1935–37) at the MacDowell Colony on a fellowship. The Whitney Museum, New York Public Library, Pennsylvania Academy of the Fine Arts, Bibliothèque Nationale (Paris), Library of Congress, and Cooper Union Art School have collected his works, among which are *He That Is without Sin Among You* and *Song of the Open Road.* He has also illustrated Walt Whitman's *Leaves of Grass*, James Joyce's *Ulysses*, and *The Gospel of Saint John*, and has contributed illustrations to many magazines.

Daniel, Peter Vivian. b. in Stafford County, Va., April 24, 1784; d. at Richmond, Va., May 31, 1860. American jurist, associate justice (1841–60) of the U.S. Supreme Court. He was elected to the Virginia legislature (1809), and served as a member (1812–35) of the privy council of Virginia and during his latter years in office as lieutenant governor and ex-officio chairman of the council. He was appointed (1836) judge of the U.S. district court of Virginia and elevated (1841) by Van Buren to the high court.

Daniel, Samuel. b. near Taunton, Somersetshire, England, 1562; d. at Beckington, Wiltshire, England, Oct. 14, 1619. English poet and dramatist. He was educated at Oxford and was for a time tutor to William Herbert, a nephew of Sir Philip Sidney. In 1592 he issued a volume containing *Delia*, one of the first of the Elizabethan sonnet sequences and his best-known work, and *The Complaint of Rosamond*, a narrative poem. *Cleopatra* (1594) was an attempt at Senecan tragedy, as was *Philotas* (1605). His poem *Musophilis, or A General Defence of Learning* (1599) upholds poetry as part of the background of the courtier or the warrior. He wrote a *Defense of Rime* (1603) in answer to Thomas Campion's attack on English rhyme in *Observations on the Art of English Poesie* (1602). In 1595 he issued *The Civil Warres between the Two Houses of Lancaster and York* in four books, a verse history expanded in 1609 to eight books but left even then still incomplete. Between 1612 and 1617 he wrote a prose history of England. For a short period in 1599 he is said to have been poet laureate, but to have resigned the post in Ben Jonson's favor. He was appointed (1603) master of the revels and between 1604 and 1615, when he seems to have retired to his Wiltshire farm, he worked at turning out court masques. His complete works, edited by A. B. Grosart, were published in five volumes (1885–96).

Daniel Deronda (dan'yẹl dẹ.ron'dạ). Novel by George Eliot. It appeared in eight monthly parts, beginning in

February, 1876, and as a whole in 1877. The book unfolds the author's conceptions of social growth, the strength of tradition, and the impelling force of nationality.

Daniel Jazz, The. Volume of poetry (1920) by Vachel Lindsay. It is generally regarded as one of his poorer works and as marking the beginning of his artistic decline.

Daniell (dan'yel), **John Frederic.** b. at London, March 12, 1790; d. there, March 13, 1845. English physicist and chemist, inventor of a hygrometer (c1820). His works include *Meteorological Essays* (1823), *Introduction to Chemical Philosophy* (1839), and others.

Daniell, Samuel. b. at London, 1775 or 1777; d. in Ceylon, in December, 1811. English artist and traveler; nephew of Thomas Daniell.

Daniell, Thomas. b. 1749; d. at London, March 19, 1840. English landscape painter and engraver, best known for his illustrations of works on Eastern subjects.

Daniels (dan'yelz), **Frank (Albert).** b. at Dayton, Ohio, Aug. 15, 1856; d. at West Palm Beach, Fla., Jan. 12, 1935. American comedian. His first stage appearance (1879) was in *Chimes of Normandie* at Chelsea, Mass.; he made his English debut in 1883. Among the plays in which he appeared were *An Electric Doll*, *Little Puck*, *Miss Simplicity*, *The Idol's Eye*, *The Office Boy*, *The Tattooed Man*, *The Pink Lady*, *Wizard of the Nile*, *Sergeant Brue*, and *Girl in the Train.*

Daniels, Jonathan Worth. b. at Raleigh, N.C., April 26, 1902—. American journalist and author; son of Josephus Daniels. A graduate of the University of North Carolina, he joined (1925) the staff of the Raleigh *News and Observer*, his father's paper, acted as its editor from 1933 to 1942 while his father was U.S. ambassador to Mexico, and became its editor in 1948 when his father died. During World War II he held several administrative posts in Washington, acting as President F. D. Roosevelt's administrative assistant (1943–45) and as presidential press secretary (1945). He was appointed U.S. representative to the United Nations subcommittee on the prevention of discrimination and the protection of minorities, and was made (1948) a public member of the administrative board of the Economic Cooperation Administration. He has written a novel, *Clash of Angels* (1930), and *A Southerner Discovers the South* (1938), *A Southerner Discovers New England* (1940), *Tar Heels: A Portrait of North Carolina* (1941), *Frontier on the Potomac* (1946), and *The Man of Independence* (1950), a biography of Harry S. Truman.

Daniels, Josephus. b. at Washington, N.C., May 18, 1862; d. at Raleigh, N.C., Jan. 15, 1948. American journalist and statesman; father of Jonathan Worth Daniels. He was editor (1885 *et seq.*) of the Raleigh *State Chronicle*, and in 1894 consolidated that paper with the *North Carolinian* and the *News and Observer* as the Raleigh *News and Observer*, of which he was publisher and editor for 53 years. He was head of the Democratic national publicity bureau during Bryan's 1908 presidential campaign and Wilson's successful 1912 campaign. From 1913 to 1921, he was secretary of the navy. His assistant secretary was Franklin D. Roosevelt, who later, when he became president, appointed Daniels U.S. ambassador to Mexico (1933–42). He was the author of *The Navy and the Nation* (1919), *Our Navy at War* (1922), *Life of Worth Bagley* (1924), *Life of Woodrow Wilson* (1924), *Tar Heel Editor* (1939), *Editor: In Politics* (1941), *The Wilson Era* (1944–45), and *Shirt Sleeve Diplomat* (1947).

Daniels, Winthrop More. b. at Dayton, Ohio, Sept. 30, 1867; d. at Saybrook Point, Conn., Jan. 3, 1944. American transportation authority. A graduate (1888) of Princeton, he was professor of political economy (1892–11) at Princeton, a member (1911–14) of the Public Utilities Commission of New Jersey, member (1914–23) and chairman (1918–19) of the Interstate Commerce Commission, and professor of transportation (1923–40) at Yale. He was the author of *Elements of Public Finance*, *The Price of Transportation Service*, and other books.

Danielson (dan'il.son, dan'yel-). Borough in NE Connecticut, in Windham County, near the Quinebaug River: most important cotton-manufacturing center in the state. 4,554 (1950).

Danielson-Kalmari (dä'nyel.sôn.käl'mä.rē), **Richard.** [Full name, **Johan Richard Danielson-Kalmari.**] b. at Hauho, Finland, May 7, 1853; d. at Helsinki, Finland, May 23, 1933. Finnish political leader and historian, active in the government of Finland under Russian rule before World War I. He served in the Finnish legislature and executive branch until 1909. He was professor (1880–1913) of general history at Turku University, of which he was also vice-chancellor (1903–06) and chancellor (1921–26). He was the leader (1907–14) of the Old Finnish party. After early writings on English and French history, he specialized in the history of Finland.

Danilo I (dä.nē'lô). b. 1677; d. 1735 or 1737. Last elected, and first hereditary, prince-bishop (*vladika*) of Montenegro. In 1702, captured by the Turks, he barely escaped with his life, and in the following year he plotted an extensive massacre of Moslems which was carried out on Christmas Eve and has sometimes been called "the Montenegrin Vespers." Making his way to St. Petersburg in 1715, he won a pledge from Czar Peter I of Russian assistance to the Montenegrins in their resistance to Turkish encroachments. It became customary thereafter for the Montenegrin prince-bishops to visit St. Petersburg to renew the Russian alliance. Danilo I considerably enlarged the area of Montenegrin territory free from Turkish control. He succeeded in having the title of *vladika* or prince-bishop made hereditary in his family, and since the ecclesiastical half of the title called for celibacy, he designated his nephew to succeed him, a practice which long continued to be the rule.

Danilo II. b. 1826; d. 1860. Prince of Montenegro. He became prince-bishop in 1851, but being a modern-minded man (and, moreover, wishing to marry, which as bishop he could not do) in 1852 he devolved his churchly office upon an archbishop, and became a secular ruler. The victories of the Montenegrins under his leadership over the Turks in 1853 and again in 1858 assured the country's independence. Danilo's reforms, carried out with a strong hand, raised enemies, one of whom assassinated him.

Daniłowski (dä.nē.lôf'skē), **Gustaw.** b. 1871; d. 1927. Polish poet and novelist.

Danish (dā'nish). Language of Denmark. It is a Scandinavian language, very closely related to Swedish, Norwegian, and Icelandic.

Danish Academy of Sciences and Letters, Royal. See **Academy of Sciences and Letters, Royal Danish.**

Danish-American Treaty of 1916. See **American-Danish Treaty of 1916.**

Danites (dan'īts). Members of the Hebrew tribe of Dan.

Danites. Members of a secret organization in the original Mormon Church, sworn to support the heads of the church in all speech or action.

Danjon (däṅ.zhôṅ), **André.** b. at Caen, France, April 6, 1890—. French astronomer, director of the observatory at the University of Strasbourg. He determined the brightness of the sunlit earth as seen from outer space, and is also known for his work in optics.

Dankali (däng'kä.lē). See **Danakil.**

Dankl (däng'kl), Baron **Viktor von.** b. at Udine, Italy (in territory which was then part of Austria), Sept. 18, 1854—. Austro-Hungarian general. He held commands on the Eastern front in 1914 and on the Italian front in 1916. He retired in 1917, and after 1918 was active as a monarchist leader.

Danks (dangks), **Hart Pease.** b. at New Haven, Conn., 1834; d. at Philadelphia, 1903. American composer, remembered chiefly for his song *Silver Threads Among the Gold.* His other works include an operetta and many hymns.

Danmark (dän'märk). Danish name of **Denmark.**

Dan Michel of Northgate (dan mich'el; nôrth'gāt, -gat). See **Michel of Northgate, Dan.**

Dannat (dan'at), **William T.** b. at New York, 1853; d. March 17, 1929. American figure painter. He studied at Munich and Florence, and with Munkacsy at Paris, and received the third-class medal at Paris in 1883. He was made a commander of the Legion of Honor in 1900.

Dannecker (dän'ek.ėr), **Johann Heinrich von.** b. at Waldenbuch, near Stuttgart, Germany, Oct. 15, 1758; d. there, Dec. 8, 1841. German sculptor. In 1771 he entered the Karlsschule at Stuttgart, where he was associated with Schiller. He designed at an early age some statues of children and caryatids for the chateau of Stuttgart and Hohenheim. Appointed court sculptor (1780) to Duke Charles of Württemberg, he went to Paris, where he studied with Pajou. In 1785 he went to Rome, where he met Canova, Goethe, and Herder. His statue of *Ceres and Bacchus* procured him admission to the academies of Milan and Bologna. On his return to Stuttgart (1790) he was appointed professor at the academy. His most famous work is a statue of Ariadne on a panther. Among his other works are a statue of Sappho, a bust of Schiller, and a bust of Gluck (1809).

Dannemora (dan.ẹ.mō'rạ, -môr'ạ). Village in NE New York, in Clinton County, ab. 12 mi. W of Plattsburg. It is the seat of Clinton State Prison. Settled as an iron-mining center, it was named for Dannemora, Sweden. 4,122 (1950).

Dannemora (dän.nẹ.mö'rä). [Also, **Danemora.**] Small parish in the *län* (county) of Uppsala, Sweden, ab. 28 mi. NE of Uppsala. It is celebrated for its iron mines (among the best in Sweden). Pop. ab. 1,050.

Dannevirke (dä'nẹ.vir.kẹ). Danish name of the **Danewerk.**

Dannreuther (dan'roi.tėr; German, dän'-), **Edward George.** b. at Strasbourg, Nov. 4, 1844; d. at Hastings, England, Feb. 12, 1905. Pianist and musicologist. He made his debut at London in 1863 and afterward lived there. He founded (1872) the Wagner Society and was appointed (1895) professor at the Royal College of Music. His works include *Wagner and the Reform of the Opera* (1872), *Musical Ornamentation* (2 vols., 1893–95), and the sixth volume of the *Oxford History of Music.*

D'Annunzio (dän.nön'tsyō), **Gabriele.** [Pseudonym, **Duca Minimo**; title, Prince of **Monte Nevoso**; original surname (according to some sources), **Rapagnetta.**] b. at Francavilla al Mare, near Pescara, Italy, 1863; d. at Gardone Riviera, Italy, March 1, 1938. Italian poet and novelist. A rabid nationalist, he advocated Italy's entry into World War I on the side of the Allies, was an officer in the Italian air force, where he lost an eye in combat, and occupied (1919) Fiume at the head of a group of young Italian soldiers, until after the signing of the first treaty of Rapallo (1920) made it an independent city. D'Annunzio was an enthusiastic Fascist and was granted his title in 1924 for his efforts at Fiume. He wrote *Primo Vere* (1879), *Canto Nuovo* (1882), *Terra Vergine* (1882), *Intermezzo di rime* (1883), *Il Libro delle Vergini* (1884), *L'Isottèo: La Chimera* (1885–88), *San Pantaleone* (1886), *Elegie romane* (1887–91), *Il Piacere* (1889; Eng. trans., *The Child of Pleasure,* 1898), *Giovanni Episcopo* (1891; Eng. trans., *Episcopo and Company,* 1896), *Poema paradisiaco: Odi navali* (1891–93), *L'Innocente* (1891), *Trionfo della Morte* (1894; Eng. trans., *The Triumph of Death,* 1896), *Le Vergini delle Rocce* (1896), *La Città Morta* (1898), *La Gioconda* (1899), *Il Fuoco* (1900), *La Canzone di Garibaldi* (1900), *Francesca da Rimini* (1901), *Le Laudi* (1904), *La Fiaccola sotto il moggie* (1905), *Più che l'amore* (1906), *L'Orazione e la canzone in morte d'Giosuè Carducci* (1907), *La Nave* (1908), *Il Mistero di S. Sebastiano* (1911), *La Pisanelle* (1913), *Notturno* (1919), *Le Faville del maglio* (1924), *Juvenilia* (1925), *Canto novo* (1925). Among the actresses appearing in his plays were Sarah Bernhardt and Eleonora Duse, with whom the poet maintained a liaison for a number of years. D'Annunzio's style is rich and fluent in language, but neither deep in thought nor conscious of real social relationships.

Danny; The Story of a Dandie Dinmont (dan'i; dan'di din'mọnt). Dog novel by Alfred Ollivant, published in 1902.

Dan River (dan). River in S Virginia and N North Carolina, flowing generally E from the Blue Ridge to join the Staunton River just N of Clarksville, Va., forming the Roanoke River. In its upper course it flows through a great gorge, called the Pinnacles of Dan, where a series of power dams were completed in 1938. Length, ab. 180 mi.

Dan Russel (rus'ẹl). See **Russel, Dan.**

Danry (däṅ.rē), **Jean.** See **Latude, Jean Henry.**

Danse Macabre (däṅs mȧ.kábr). Orchestral poem (Opus 40) by Camille Saint-Saëns, composed in 1874, based upon a poem by Henri Cazalis.

Danse Macabre. French name of the **Dance of Death.**

Dansville (danz'vil). Village in W New York, in Livingston County, ab. 63 mi. SE of Buffalo in a farming and nursery region. Manufactures include heating equipment and shoes. The American Red Cross was founded here by Clara Barton in 1881. It is the seat of a sanitarium, reopened (1929) by Bernarr Macfadden. 5,253 (1950).

Dantan (däṅ.täṅ), **Antoine Laurent.** b. at St.-Cloud, France, Dec. 8, 1798; d. there, May 31, 1878. French sculptor, a pupil of Bosio, known for his portrait work; brother of Jean Pierre Dantan.

Dantan, Jean Pierre. b. at Paris, in December, 1800; d. at Baden-Baden, Germany, in September, 1869. French sculptor, noted especially for grotesque busts; brother of Antoine Laurent Dantan.

Dantan, Joseph Édouard. b. at Paris, Aug. 20, 1848; d. at Trouville, France, 1897. French painter; son of Jean Pierre Dantan. His works include religious, historical, and genre paintings, and book illustrations for, among others, works by Victor Hugo and Émile Zola. He made his bow at the Paris Salon in 1869 with *An Episode in the Destruction of Pompeii.* He is represented in the Luxembourg Museum at Paris and in other French collections. The Legion of Honor was conferred upon him in 1880.

Dantas (dun'tạsh), **Júlio.** b. at Lagos, Portugal, May 19, 1876—. Portuguese dramatist, poet, and prose writer. He is a doctor of medicine and has been a member of the Portuguese parliament and a cabinet minister several times. His first book was *Nada* (1897), a collection of poems. The works which gave him renown were chiefly *A Severa* (1901), *A ceia dos cardeais* (1907), and *Rosas de todo o ano* (1907). The last two have been translated into English and other languages.

Dantas, Manuel Pinto de Souza. b. in Bahia, Brazil, c1825; d. Jan. 15, 1894. Brazilian politician of the liberal party. He was senator from 1879, minister of justice in 1880 and of the interior in 1882, and prime minister from June 6, 1884, to May 7, 1885. He brought forward a bill for emancipation, which, though not passed at the time, led to complete abolition of slavery three years later.

Dante (dan'tē; Italian, dän'tā). [Full name, **Dante Alighieri**; original prename, **Durante.**] b. at Florence, in May, 1265; d. at Ravenna, Italy, Sept. 14, 1321. Italian poet, generally considered to be the supreme example of integral Christian humanism. In his Latin letters he gives his name variously as Dantes Alagherius and Dantes Alagherii. His family can be traced back to Adamo of Florence, the father of Cacciaguida who is mentioned in *Paradiso* (xv., 139–144) as having been killed during the second Crusade in 1147. Dante's first meeting with Beatrice Portinari, who was to become the object of his "courtly," artistic, ideal, moral, spiritual, and symbolic love and the source of his poetic inspiration, can be dated as May 1, 1274. His elementary education was entrusted to a professional teacher named Romano; but Dante attributes his higher intellectual inspiration to Brunetto Latini. Dante tells us in the *Convivio* that he spent three years in the "schools of the friars (*religiosi*) and the disputations of the philosophers." It was, however, to his lifelong habit of insatiable reading in the ancient classics, patristic writings, contemporary poets and chroniclers, and scholastic philosophers and theologians that he owed the extraordinarily wide knowledge that is revealed in his works. His first extant sonnet in honor of Beatrice was written in 1283, and published in his first work, the *Vita Nuova,* c1292. Shortly after the death of Beatrice in 1290, Dante married Gemma Donati, to whom he had been betrothed as a boy in 1277. Gemma was the mother of Dante's four children, Peter, James, John, and Antonia, the first two of whom wrote commentaries on the *Divina Commedia;* the last became a nun in Ravenna with the name Sister Beatrice. As a young man Dante was trained as a soldier and took part in the battle of Campaldino in 1289. In 1295 he began to play an active role in Florentine political life. The documents show that he took a firm stand against any outside, including papal, interference in the city government. His patriotism was rewarded in 1300 by his election to the highest political office in Florence. It was in this office, as *Priore,* that he was called upon to banish one of his dearest friends, Guido Cavalcanti, in an effort to curb the factious political rivalry of the Neri (the Blacks, the Guelph faction of the ancient nobility) and Bianchi (the Whites, the Guelph faction of the newly rich banking and commercial bourgeoisie). Shortly after his tenure of office he went to Rome to make the pilgrimage of the Holy Year of Jubilee proclaimed by Pope Boniface VIII. It seems to have been this experience of visiting the center of Christendom and the "capital of the world" that filled Dante with the vision of humanity in history and in eternal life which is the subject matter of the *Divina Commedia* (*The Divine Comedy*). During Dante's absence from Florence on an embassy to Pope Boniface VIII in 1301, the party of the Neri, aided by Charles de Valois, destroyed the property of the Bianchi, and Dante himself was condemned to exile in 1302. His resentment at this betrayal by his beloved but stony-hearted city is reflected in the passionate mood of the Pietra sonnets. Having failed, even with Ghibelline help, to change the situation in Florence, Dante decided to become a "party all by himself." His travels throughout Italy, where he found no less than 14 dialects, suggested to him a philosophico-philological work on "courtly" vernacular diction, *De vulgari eloquentia.* His philosophical reading and reflection prompted him to write the Banquet (*Convivio*) of ethical essays in which he hoped to discuss in detail the Aristotelian-Thomistic description of the 14 moral virtues. In 1307 he left both works unfinished, and appears to have gone for a period of study in the University of Paris. The crowning of Henry VII (Henry of Luxembourg) as emperor of the Romans in 1312 kindled once more Dante's hope of seeing realized a world society under the triple universal authority of law, truth, and grace, organized by the efforts of the emperor (*imperium*), the university (*studium*), and the Pope (*Sacerdotium*), and renewing the highest traditions of Rome, Athens, and Jerusalem in the spheres of civilization, culture, and religion. Dante hastily returned to Italy; but when Henry died in 1313, all Dante could do was to set forth a theory of proper Church-State relationships in his *Monarchia,* just as he had already given his theory of the relationship of imperial power to philosophical authority in Book IV of the *Convivio.* The years after 1314 were filled with the completion of the *Divina Commedia.* He interrupted the work in 1319 to conduct a correspondence in the form of *Eclogae* in Latin verses which are as classical in form as they are poetical in inspiration. On Jan. 20, 1320, in the presence of the lord of Verona Can Francesco della Scala (the Can Grande who patronized the arts and was, especially, Dante's protector) and of high ecclesiastical authorities, in the Chapel of Saint Helen, he formally defended, in Scholastic Latin, a *Quaestio de Aqua et Terra* in order to establish his position as an authorized teacher. An embassy to Venice undermined his health and he died on Sept. 14, 1321. The most authentic painting of Dante is that by his friend Giotto, still to be seen on a wall in the Bargello museum at Florence. However, the bust by Vincenzo Vela, based on the scientific examination of Dante's skull by Fabio Frassetto in 1921, is a trustworthy indication of the poet's appearance. The so-called "death-masks" have no authentic value. The bibliography on Dante's period, life, and works is immense.

Dante. Critical essay by James Russell Lowell in his *Among My Books* (1870; 2nd series, 1876). It is regarded highly by Dante students, and is considered one of the best examples of Lowell's literary criticism. In its way it did for Dante in America what Coleridge and Carlyle did for German literature in England.

Dante. Prose criticism (1929) by T. S. Eliot. It is an essay in appreciation and is intended to serve as an introduction to the work of the Italian poet. It was well received and did much to strengthen Eliot's already strong position as a critic. Eliot had discussed Dante, and other authors, in an earlier volume, *The Sacred Wood* (1921).

Dantès (däṅ.tes), **Edmond.** [Title, **Count of Monte Cristo.**] Principal character in *Le Comte de Monte Cristo,* novel by the elder Alexandre Dumas. He is originally an innocent youth, unjustly imprisoned. He escapes, becomes immensely wealthy, and carries out an elaborate system of revenge in the various disguises of the Count of Monte Cristo, Lord Wilmore, and the Abbé Busoni.

Dante Symphony (dan′tẹ, dän′tā). Orchestral and choral composition by Franz Liszt, composed in 1855, based upon *The Divine Comedy* and dedicated to Wagner.

Danti (dän′tē), **Vincenzo.** b. at Perugia, Italy, 1530; d. May 24, 1576. Italian goldsmith, sculptor, military architect, and poet. He made the *Decapitation of Saint John* over the door of the baptistery at Florence, and the statue of Pope Julius III at Perugia.

Danton (däṅ.tôṅ), **Georges Jacques.** b. at Arcis-sur-Aube, France, Oct. 28, 1759; guillotined at Paris, April 5, 1794. French politician, one of the foremost leaders of the French Revolution. He was a lawyer and president of the Cordeliers (a political club which called for drastic reform of the French government). He took part, perhaps as organizer, in the attack (Aug. 10, 1792) on the Tuileries, when the king and queen, Louis XVI and Marie Antoinette, were captured and imprisoned. Soon after, the monarchy was abolished and Danton became minister of justice in the republican government. He was implicated in the "September massacres" of prisoners of the Revolution at a time when it seemed that foreign enemies would march into Paris. In September, 1792, he became a member of the National Convention, where he sat on the "Mountain," the high seats where the Jacobins, the Cordeliers, and the Hébertists sat, near such men as Marat and Robespierre. He was one of those voting (January, 1793) for the death of the king. In March, he was made president of the Jacobins, and he moved the formation of the Revolutionary tribunal. He was one of the nine members, from April to September, 1793, of the Committee of Public Safety. Recognizing that the struggle between the Girondists (the moderates who were slowly swinging towards royalism) and the Jacobins might cause the Revolution to fail, and in view of military reverses, he joined in the purge (June 2, 1793) of the Girondists from the Convention. In March, 1794, he overthrew Jacques René Hébert and his extreme radical party of the Paris commune with the aid of Robespierre, and in turn was overthrown (March 30, 1794) by Robespierre, given a quick semblance of a trial, and executed. Danton was an orator of great power who recognized the need both of eliminating the oppressive monarchy and of preventing the Revolution from deteriorating into a formless anarchy of blood baths, but his lack of resolution in crises doomed him.

Dantzic (dän′tsik) or **Dantzig** (-tsiċh). See **Danzig.**

Dantzig (däṅ.tsēk), Duc **de.** Title of **Lefebvre, François Joseph.**

Danube (dan′ūb). [Czech, **Dunaj;** German, **Donau;** Hungarian, **Duna;** Rumanian, **Dunărea;** Russian, **Dunai, Dunay;** Serbo-Croatian and Bulgarian, **Dunav;** Latin, **Danubius** (dą.nū′bi.us), **Ister.**] Largest river of Europe next to the Volga, formed by the union of the Breg and Brigach near Donaueschingen in S Baden, Germany. It flows through Germany and Austria, separates the S central part of Czechoslovakia from Hungary, flows S through C Hungary into N Yugoslavia, separates NE Yugoslavia from Rumania, becomes the boundary between Bulgaria and Rumania, flows N through E Rumania to join the Prut on the border of the U.S.S.R., and empties into the Black Sea by three principal mouths. It is navigable to Ulm, in Germany. Its chief tributaries are, on the right bank, the Iller, Lech, and Isar in Germany, the Inn and Enns in Austria, the Rába (Raab) in Hungary, the Drava, Sava, Morava, and Timok in Yugoslavia, the Isker in Bulgaria; on the left bank, the Altmühl, Naab, and Regen in Germany, the Morava (March), Váh (Waag), and Hron (Gran) in Czechoslovakia, the Tisza (Theiss) in Yugoslavia, the Timiş (Temeš), Jiu (Schyl), Olt (Aluta), Argeş (Arjish), Ialomiţa (Yalomitza), Siret (Sereth), and Prut in Rumania. Area of basin, ab. 320,000 sq. mi. Length, ab. 1,770 mi.

Danubian Principalities (dan.ū′bi.ąn). The former principalities of Moldavia and Walachia, now included in Rumania.

Danum (dā′num). Latin name of **Doncaster.**

Danvers (dan′vėrz). Town in NE Massachusetts, in Essex County, ab. 17 mi. NE of Boston: manufactures of leather, chemicals, shoes, and crayons. Israel Putnam (1718–90) was born near here. 15,720 (1950).

Danville (dan′vil). City in E Illinois, county seat of Vermilion County: center of a farming and mining area. Its factories produce mining machinery, textiles, and bricks. 37,864 (1950).

Danville. Town in W central Indiana, county seat of Hendricks County, ab. 20 mi. W of Indianapolis in a farming area. It is the seat of Canterbury College. 2,802 (1950).

Danville. City in C Kentucky, county seat of Boyle County, ab. 39 mi. S of Frankfort. It is the seat of Centre College. It was founded in 1775. Pop. 8,686 (1950).

Danville. Borough in E Pennsylvania, county seat of Montour County: manufactures of iron, steel, and textiles. 6,994 (1950).

Danville. City in S Virginia, geographically in Pittsylvania County but independent of county administration, on the Dan River: trading and shipping center for tobacco; manufactures of cotton textiles. It was the capital of the Confederacy from April 3 to April 10, 1865. It is the seat of Averett College, the Danville Military Institute, and Stratford College. 35,066 (1950).

Danzi (dän'tsē), **Franz.** b. at Mannheim, Germany, May 15, 1763; d. at Karlsruhe, Germany, April 13, 1826. German composer. He was a member (1778 *et seq.*) of the elector palatine's band and *kapellmeister* (choir leader) at Karlsruhe; composer of operas and of orchestral, chamber, and church music.

Danzig (dan'sig; German, dän'tsich). [Also: **Dantzic, Dantzig**; Polish, **Gdańsk.**] City in N Poland, in the *wojewodztwa* (province) of Gdańsk, situated on a bay of the Baltic Sea called the Gulf of Danzig and on the Mottlau River, W of the mouth of the Vistula River: formerly a free city. It has a harbor and shipyards, trade in coal, grain, and lumber, chemical, metallurgical, fur, and textile industries, breweries, and distilleries. Danzig has a theater, a library, and a museum with art, archaeological, and natural science collections, which was reopened in 1948 as the National Museum; an institute of technology (rebuilt), the first Polish academy of medicine (1945), and other educational institutions. The city, a jewel of Renaissance architecture, was almost entirely destroyed by demolition and fighting toward the end of World War II. Among the destroyed or severely damaged monuments are the Church of Mary, an enormous building in the brick-Gothic style (erected in 1343 and later enlarged), the churches of Saint John, Saint Nicholas, and Saint Catherine (12th–15th centuries), the Church of Saint Peter (15th–16th centuries), the city hall and Artus Court (14th–16th centuries) in the Gothic and Renaissance styles, the armory, a brick building in the Renaissance style erected by a Flemish architect, and numerous gates, warehouses, and picturesque private buildings. However, reconstruction is under way; it is expected that most of the buildings of artistic and historical value will be reconstructed by 1955. In the vicinity are a number of seaside resorts and fishing villages. Nearby also is the concentration camp of Stutthof, where many Jewish and Polish civilian prisoners perished during World War II. 117,894 (1946), 175,043 (1950).

History. Danzig is first recorded as having been a missionary post among the Slavs in the 10th century; it was capital of the dukes of Pomerellia in the 12th century, was under the sovereignty of the Teutonic Order from 1309 to 1454, and became a member of the Hanseatic League in 1361. The city seceded from the Teutonic Order in 1454 and was under Polish protection from that year until 1793, during which period it attained a large degree of independence under the *privilegium Casimirianum.* Danzig flourished commercially, maintained its German ethnic character, and introduced the Lutheran Reformation (1523–57). It was besieged and sacked by the Russians in 1734, fell to Prussia in the third partition of Poland in 1793, was a free city from 1807 to 1814, belonged to Prussia (after 1871, Germany) from 1814 to 1919, and was capital of the province of Westpreussen (West Prussia) in the period 1816–23 and again from 1878 to 1919. The treaty of Versailles (1919) separated the city from Germany and it was declared a free state under the protectorate of the League of Nations in 1920; a customs union with Poland was concluded in 1922. Danzig suffered commercially through the competition of the new Polish port-city of Gdynia. It was annexed to Germany in 1939, immediately preceding the outbreak of World War II, was occupied by the Russians after heavy fighting on March 31, 1945, and was returned to Poland after the Four Power Conference at Potsdam in the same year.

Danzig. German name of **Gdańsk,** province.

Danzig Crisis. European crisis precipitated (1939) when, after the complete occupation of Czechoslovakia in March, 1939, Hitler began to press for the annexation of the free city of Danzig and a revision of the Polish Corridor. With Danzig in the hands of a Nazi regime that defied the League of Nations high commissioner, and with the threat of German force present, the British announced that they would come to the assistance of Poland if Hitler were to impose a solution by unilateral action. Backed by the Russo-German pact, Hitler demanded (Aug. 29, 1939) the cession of Danzig and other rights for Germany in the Corridor. Polish refusal to negotiate under threats led to the German invasion (Sept. 1) of Poland and the beginning of World War II.

Daphnae (daf'nē). [Also: **Daphne**; modern name, **Tel Defenneh**; in the Old Testament, **Tahapanes, Tahpanhes, Tahpenes.**] Town in ancient Egypt, ab. 25 mi. from Pelusium. Its site has been explored and has yielded archaeological finds of interest.

Daphnaida (daf.nạ.ē'dạ). Elegy (1590) by Edmund Spenser, on the death of Lady Douglas Gorges, whose husband, Sir Arthur Gorges, poet and translator, was Spenser's friend.

Daphne (daf'nē). See also **Dafne.**

Daphne. In ancient geography, a famous grove and sanctuary of Apollo, situated ab. 5 mi. SW of Antioch, in ancient Syria. It was established by Seleucus Nicator.

Daphne. In Greek mythology, a nymph, daughter of the river-god Peneius, or, in other accounts of Ladon, an Arcadian. Her lover Leucippus pursued her in woman's clothing, and was killed by the nymphs at the instigation of Apollo. When the god in turn pursued her, she entreated that she might be transformed into the bay tree, and he granted her petition.

Daphne. An asteroid (No. 41) discovered by H. Goldschmidt at Paris, May 22, 1856.

Daphnis (daf'nis). In Greek mythology, a shepherd, son of Hermes and a Sicilian nymph. Pan taught him to sing and play the flute, and the Muses endowed him with a love of poetry, and he is said to have originated bucolic poetry. He was turned into a stone according to one legend; according to another his eyes were torn out by a nymph for his infidelity to her, and he threw himself in despair into the sea. In ancient pastoral poetry his name was frequently given to shepherds.

Daphnis. Gentle shepherd in John Fletcher's play *The Faithful Shepherdess.*

Daphnis and Chloe (klō'ẹ). Greek pastoral romance attributed to Longus (4th or 5th century A.D.), a Greek sophist. It recounts the loves and pastoral life of Daphnis, foster son of Lamon, a goatherd, and Chloe, foster daughter of Dryas, a shepherd. The manuscript of Mont-Cassin, taken to Florence, does not name the author. It is known principally through the French version of Amyot (1559), revised by Courier. It has been translated and imitated in all European languages. Tasso's *Aminta,* Montemayor's *Diana,* d'Urfé's *Sireine,* Saint-Pierre's *Paul and Virginia,* and Allan Ramsay's *Gentle Shepherd* are founded on it.

Da Ponte (dä pōn'tā), **Lorenzo.** [Original name, **Emanuele Conegliano.**] b. at Ceneda, Italy, March 10, 1749; d. at New York, Aug. 17, 1838. Italian librettist and author. He wrote (1786–90) the librettos for Mozart's operas *Le Nozzedi Figaro, Don Giovanni,* and *Così fan tutte.* After spending some years in London as a writer, he moved (1805) to the U.S., where he became a teacher of Italian. In 1825 he was appointed professor of Italian language and literature at Columbia University. He is credited with being one of the first to arouse an interest in the U.S. in Italian culture, through his teaching, through his short-lived attempt to establish an Italian opera house in New York, and through his praises of Dante.

Dapper (dap'ėr). In Ben Jonson's comedy *The Alchemist,* a greedy and credulous lawyer's clerk who desires a "fly" (a spirit or familiar) of the Alchemist to enable him to cheat at horse races by giving him prior information.

Dapperwit (dap'ėr.wit). Vain, foolish, and boastful rake in Wycherley's *Love in a Wood.*

Dapple (dap'l). Name of Sancho Panza's donkey in Cervantes's romance *Don Quixote.*

Dapsang (dup.sung'). See **Godwin-Austen, Mount.**

Daqahliya (dä.kä.lē'yạ). Province of Lower Egypt, NE Africa, in the northern part of the Nile delta, E of the Damietta Branch of the river. Capital, Mansura; settled area, 1,023 sq. mi.; pop. 1,414,284 (1947).

Daquin or **d'Aquin** (då.kaṅ), **Louis Claude.** b. at Paris, July 4, 1694; d. there, June 15, 1772. French organist and composer. He was appointed to the Cordeliers convent (1732) and subsequently to the chapel royal (1739). His works include organ and harpsichord pieces as well as music for voice and chorus.

DAR. Abbreviation of **Daughters of the American Revolution.**

Darab (dä.räb'). [Also: **Darabgherd, Darabjird.**] Town in SW Iran, in the region of Fars, ab. 70 mi. N of Lar: a mountain trading center served by two important trails; oranges and lemons are produced in the surrounding area. Nearby are rock sculptures dating from the 3rd century A.D. It is sometimes identified with the ancient Pasargadae.

Darabani (dä.rä.bä'nē). Town in NE Rumania, in the province of Moldavia, ab. 43 mi. NE of Siret, near the Russian border. 11,379 (1948).

Daraga (dä.rä'gä). Town in Albay province, in the SE part of Luzon, Philippine Islands. The town is at the S base of Mayon volcano. 7,651 (1948).

Dar-al-Baida (där"äl.bī.dä'). An Arabic name of **Casablanca.**

Daram (dä räm'). Irregularly shaped island on the W coast of Samar, in the Philippines, E of Daram Channel. It is a part of Samar province. Area, 35 sq. mi.

Daram Channel. Channel N of Leyte Island, in the Philippines, It separates Biliran from Daram island, and is connected by Janabatas Channel with San Pedro Bay on the E coast of Leyte.

Darányi (dô'rä.nyē), **Koloman.** [Also, **Kálmán de Darányi.**] b. at Budapest, March 22, 1886—. Hungarian politician. He served (1928 *et seq.*) as political state secretary to minister presidents Bethlen, Karolyi, and Gömbös, became (1935) minister of agriculture, and succeeded Gömbös (October, 1936) as minister president.

Daras (dā'rạs). Ancient town of Mesopotamia, situated near Nisibis (Nusaybin), in what is now SE Turkey. It was a frontier post of the Byzantine Empire against Persia in the 6th century A.D.

Darbhanga (dạr.bung'gạ). [Also: **Darbhangah, Durbunga.**] District in Bihar state, Union of India, ab. 200 mi. NE of Benares: wheat, rice, and sugar. Capital, Darbhanga; area, 3,348 sq. mi.; pop. 3,457,070 (1941).

Darbhanga. [Also: **Darbhangah, Durbunga.**] Capital of Darbhanga district, Bihar, Union of India, ab. 200 mi. NE of Benares: important trading center and rail junction. It is the seat of a medical school. 69,203 (1941).

Darboux (dår.bö), **Jean Gaston.** b. at Nîmes, France, Aug. 13, 1842; d. at Paris, Feb. 25, 1917. French geometer, considered to have been one of his country's greatest. As professor at the Collège de France and the École Normale, member of the Academy of Sciences from 1884, and perpetual secretary of the Academy from 1900, he was active for almost half a century in organizations devoted to the teaching of mathematics. He studied at the École Normale and the École Polytechnique, receiving his doctorate in 1866 with a thesis on orthogonal surfaces. He was especially interested in the application of analysis and differential equations to geometry and mechanics. His most influential work was *Leçons sur la théorie générale des surfaces* (4 vols., 1887–96).

Darboy (dår.bwå), **Georges.** b. at Fayl-Billot, Haute-Marne, France, Jan. 16, 1813; shot at Paris, May 24, 1871. French prelate, archbishop of Paris (1863–71). He was arrested and assassinated by the Communards during the Paris uprising.

Darby (där'bi). Borough in SE Pennsylvania, in Delaware County, ab. 6 mi. SW of Philadelphia. It is a residential community, settled (1682) by Quakers. 13,154 (1950).

Darby, John. See under **Garretson, James Edmund.**

Darby, John Nelson. b. at London, Nov. 18, 1800; d. at Bournemouth, Hampshire, England, April 28, 1882. English theological writer, for a time minister of the Church of England. He was one of the founders of the Plymouth Brethren, also called Darbyites.

Darby, Mary. Maiden name of **Robinson, Mary.**

Darby and Joan (jōn). Married pair who are said to have lived in the 18th century in the West Riding of Yorkshire, noted traditionally for their long and happy married life. There is a ballad on the subject called *The Happy Old Couple*, supposed to have been written by Henry Woodfall, though it has been attributed to Mathew Prior. A poem *Dobson and Joan*, by "Mr. B.," is published with Prior's poems.

Darbyites (där'bi.īts). See **Plymouth Brethren.**

d'Arc or **Darc** (dårk), **Jeanne** (or **Jehanne**). See **Joan of Arc.**

Darcet (dår.se), **Jean.** b. Sept. 7, 1725; d. at Paris, Feb. 13, 1801. French chemist, noted for his achievements in industrial chemistry.

Darcet, Jean Pierre Joseph. b. at Paris, Aug. 31, 1777; d. Aug. 2, 1844. French chemist; son of Jean Darcet (1725–1801). He effected improvements in the manufacture of powder.

Darcy (där'si), **Mr.** Lover of Elizabeth Bennet, in Jane Austen's *Pride and Prejudice.*

Darcy, Thomas Darcy, Baron. b. 1467; d. 1537. English statesman and rebel.

Dardanelles (där.dạ.nelz'). [Turkish, **Çanakkale Boğazı**; Greek, **Dardanellia** (ᴛʜär"ᴛʜä.ne.lē'ä), **Ellespontos**; ancient name, **Hellespont.**] Strait connecting the Sea of Marmara with the Aegean Sea, and separating the peninsula of Gallipoli from Asia Minor, or European from Asiatic Turkey. As the Hellespont, it was celebrated in the legend of Hero and Leander. It was crossed by Xerxes in 480 B.C., and by Alexander the Great in 334 B.C. The passage was forced by the British fleet under Admiral Duckworth in 1807. It was closed against foreign men-of-war by stipulations of 1841, 1856, 1871, and 1878, but was passed by a British fleet in February, 1878, to protect Constantinople (now Istanbul) from the Russians. In 1891 an agreement between Russia and the Turkish government was reached, by which the ships of the so-called volunteer fleet of Russia, bearing the flag of the merchant marine, were allowed free passage of the Dardanelles. Length, ab. 45 mi.; average width, 3 to 4 mi.; narrowest point, ab. 1¼ mi.

Dardani (där'dạ.nī). Ancient Illyrian people of the southern highland of Moesia. The Dardani became subject to the Macedonians under the Antigoni, and later to the Romans. Their chief city was Dardanus, after which the strait of the Dardanelles was named.

Dardani. Inhabitants of Dardania, mentioned in the *Iliad.*

Dardania (där.dā'ni.ạ). [Also, **Dardanice** (där.dạ.nī'sẹ).] In ancient geography, a territory in Mysia, with uncertain boundaries. It is mentioned, indefinitely, in the *Iliad.*

Dardanius (där.dā'ni.us). Servant to Brutus in Shakespeare's tragedy *Julius Caesar.*

Dardanus (där'dạ.nus). [Also, **Dardanum** (-num).] In ancient geography, a city in Mysia, Asia Minor, situated on the Hellespont, ab. 9 mi. SW of Abydos.

Dardanus. In Greek legends, a son of Zeus and Electra, and mythical ancestor of the Trojans.

Darden (där'dẹn), **Miles.** b. in North Carolina, 1798; d. in Henderson County, Tenn., Jan. 23, 1857. American noted for his size. His height was said to be 7 feet 6 inches, and his weight (at death) about 1,000 pounds.

Dardistan (där.di.stän'). [Also, **Jahistan.**] Region in central Asia, chiefly on the NW borders of India (in what are now Kashmir and N Pakistan), referred to by ancient historians as the domain of certain Aryan peoples (the Dard or Dardu), who came there along the valley of the Indus River from the Punjab.

Dare (dãr), **Virginia.** b. on Roanoke Island, Virginia, in August, 1587; date of death not known. First child born of English parents in the New World. She was the daughter of William and Eleanor Dare, and the granddaughter of John White, governor of a colony which was sent out by Sir Walter Raleigh from Plymouth in April, 1587, and reached Roanoke Island in July. White soon went back to England for supplies, and when a relief expedition reached Roanoke in 1591, it found the island deserted (with the word CROATAN carved on a tree). The fate of the "lost colony" is unknown.

Daredevil (dãr'dev.il). Atheist in Thomas Otway's comedy of *The Atheist.* He is a cowardly, boasting fellow, who when in danger forgets his principles and says "two dozen paternosters within a half hour."

Dar-el-Beida (där"el.bā.dä'). An Arabic name of **Casablanca.**

Dares Phrygius (dãr′ēz frij′i.us, dā′rēz). [English, **Dares the Phrygian.**] Priest of Hephaestus in Troy mentioned in the *Iliad*. The authorship of a lost work on the fall of Troy, a pretended Latin translation of which was written about the 5th century A.D., was attributed to him in antiquity.

Dar-es-Salaam (där″es.sä.läm′). [Also, **Daressalam.**] City in E Africa, capital of Tanganyika territory: railway terminus and chief port of the area. In earlier days it was, with Bagamoyo, a chief meeting place of caravans from the lake region. It was ceded by the sultan of Zanzibar to the German East African Company in 1885. In 1920, with the mandated territory of Tanganyika, the port came into British hands. The railway from the port runs 775 mi. W to Kigoma on Lake Tanganyika. Because of the railway the port is able to serve most of Tanganyika and a small part of E Belgian Congo. 59,160 (1947).

Dareste de la Chavanne (då.rest dẹ lå shå.vån), **Antoine Élisabeth Cléophas.** b. at Paris, Oct. 28, 1820; d. at Lucenay-les-Aix, France, Aug. 6, 1882. French historian, author of *Histoire de France* (1865–73).

Dar Fertit (där′ fer.tēt′). Region in C Africa, on the border between Ubangi-Shari province, French Equatorial Africa, and SW Anglo-Egyptian Sudan, S of Darfur.

Darfield (där′fēld). Urban district in N central England, in the West Riding of Yorkshire, ab. 173 mi. N of London by rail. 6,238 (1951).

Darfur (där.för′). [Also, **Darfor.**] Province of the Anglo-Egyptian Sudan, in the E part, in NE Africa, bordering French Equatorial Africa. It is inhabited by Negroes and Arabs, and the religion is Mohammedanism. Darfur was conquered and annexed to Egypt in 1874, but revolted in 1882. It was finally subdued in 1916 by British forces. Capital, El Fasher; area, 138,150 sq. mi.; pop. 949,640 (est. 1949).

Dargan (där′gạn), **Edwin Preston.** b. at Barboursville, Va., Sept. 7, 1879; d. at Chicago, Dec. 13, 1940. American professor and writer on French literature. He was adjunct professor (1907–10) and assistant professor (1910–11) of French at the University of California, assistant professor (1911–15), associate professor (1915–18), and professor (1918 *et seq.*) of French literature at the University of Chicago. His works include *Aesthetic Doctrine of Montesquieu* (1907), *Hylas and Other Poems* (1910), *Honoré de Balzac—A Force of Nature* (1932), *Anatole France* (1937), and, with W. A. Nitze, *History of French Literature* (1922).

Dargan, Olive. [Pseudonym, **Fielding Burke;** maiden name, **Tilford.**] b. in Grayson County, Ky.— American poet and novelist. She attended the University of Nashville and Radcliffe College. She is the author of poetic dramas published in *Semiramis and Other Plays* (1904) and *Lords and Lovers and Other Dramas* (1912). Among her volumes of poetry are *Path Flowers and Other Poems* (1914), *The Cycle's Rim* (1916), and *Lute and Furrow* (1922). She is the author of a collection of Kentucky mountain stories, *Highland Annals* (1925), and of a novel concerning miners, *Sons of the Stranger* (1948). Under the pseudonym Fielding Burke, she has published two novels, *Call Home the Heart* (1932) and *A Stone Came Rolling* (1935).

Dargaud (dår.gō), **Jean Marie.** b. at Paray le-Monial, Saône-et-Loire, France, Feb. 22, 1800; d. Jan. 5, 1866. French historian and man of letters. His chief work is *Histoire de la liberté religieuse en France* (1859).

Dargomijsky (där.go.mish′ski), **Aleksandr Sergeyevich.** b. in the government of Tula, Russia, Feb. 14, 1813; d. at St. Petersburg, Jan. 17, 1869. Composer of the New Russian school. He was in the government service, but, forming a friendship with Glinka, adopted music as his profession. Of his earlier works the best known are the operas *Esmeralda* (1847, founded on Victor Hugo's *Notre Dame de Paris*) and *Russalka* (1856). He traveled in 1864, but met with little success except in Belgium. On his return he joined Balakiref, and became prominent in the New Russian school, his most notable composition being *The Stone Guest,* which, while it has not met with popular recognition, is regarded as a remarkable work, embodying the most advanced ideas of his school. Its text is Pushkin's poem *Don Juan*, and it was orchestrated by Rimsky-Korsakov after the composer's death and performed at St. Petersburg in 1872.

Dariel Pass (dar.i.el′). See **Daryal Pass.**

Darien (dãr.i.en′, dãr′i.ẹn). Town in SW Connecticut, in Fairfield County, on Long Island Sound: suburb of New York City. 11,767 (1950).

Darien (dãr′i.ẹn, dā′ri.ẹn). City in SE Georgia, in McIntosh County, near the mouth of the Altamaha River: fish canneries. It was formerly an important lumber-shipping point, settled early in the 18th century. 1,380 (1950).

Darien (dãr.i.en′, dãr′i.ẹn). [Spanish, **Darién,** in full, **Santa María de la Antigua del Darién;** also, **La Antigua.**] Colony founded on the Isthmus of Panama by the Spaniards early in the 16th century. After one or two failures it was taken over in 1510 by Balboa, who used it as a base for his explorations for a time. He was followed by Pedrarias (Pedro Árias de Ávila) who, as governor, moved the colony in 1519 to the site of the present city of Panama.

Darién (dãr.i.en′, dãr′i.ẹn; Spanish, dä.ryān′). Province in E Panama, for a time included in Panamá province. Capital, El Real; pop. 14,707 (1950).

Darien (dãr.i.en′, dãr′i.ẹn), **Colony of.** [Also, **Darien Scheme.**] Scottish colony on the Isthmus of Panama, founded by William Paterson. It was chartered by the Scottish Parliament in 1695; the enterprise was begun in 1698 and the settlement was abandoned in 1700.

Darien, Gulf of. [Spanish, **Golfo de Darién.**] Branch of the Caribbean Sea, lying N of the republic of Colombia and E of the Isthmus of Panama.

Darien, Isthmus of. See **Panama, Isthmus of.**

Darien Scheme. See **Darien, Colony of.**

Darinel (dar′i.nel). Comic shepherd, a character introduced into *Florisel de Niquea*, the tenth book of *Amadis of Gaul*.

Daring Young Man on the Flying Trapeze, The. Collection of short stories by William Saroyan, published in 1934.

Darío (dä.rē′ō), **Rubén.** [Pseudonym of **Félix Rubén García Sarmiento.**] b. at Metapa, Nicaragua, 1867; d. at León, Nicaragua, Feb. 7, 1916. Nicaraguan poet, the acknowledged master of the modernists and one of the most prominent figures in the field of Spanish-American verse. After the appearance of his prose-and-poetry *Azul* (1888), which virtually launched Spanish-American modernism, he was lionized wherever he went in Central and South America, Spain, France, and the U.S. Progressing from his near-worship of form to an awareness of the importance of content and simplicity of expression, he exhibited the peak of his art in *Cantos de vida y esperanza* (1905). He contributed to newspapers in South America and Europe, and held diplomatic posts for several Spanish-American countries. The 31 volumes of his complete works, published (1922) at Madrid, contain the famous *Prosas profanas* (1896), *El Canto errante* (1907), and others. He is buried in the cathedral of León, Nicaragua.

Dariorigum (dar.i.or′i.gum). Ancient name of **Vannes.**

Darius I (of *Persia*) (dạ.rī′us). [Called **Darius the Great;** also known as **Darius Hystaspis.**] b. c550 B.C.; d. c485 B.C. King of Persia; son of Hystaspes, and fifth in the descent from Achaemenes. He succeeded (521) Cambyses on the Persian throne, after defeating the Magian Gaumata, who claimed to be Bardiya (the Greek Smerdis), brother of Cambyses and son of Cyrus. A record of his reign is given by himself in the long trilingual (Old Persian, Elamite, and Babylonian) inscriptions of Behistun. Besides the revolt in Persia itself, caused by the impostor Gaumata, he had to suppress two uprisings in Babylonia, led by Nidintu-Bel and Arachu, who made claim to be Nebuchadnezzar, son of Nabonidus; in consequence of these uprisings he caused the fortifications of Babylon to be torn down. The other countries under Persian dominion also revolted in turn, but at last were brought to submission. After restoring order in the empire Darius turned his attention to reorganization and reforms of the administration. He divided the whole land into 20 satrapies, introduced regular taxation and uniformity of coinage, constructed roads, and founded a kind of postal system by placing stations and relays with saddled horses at regular intervals on the road between Susa and Sardis. To the capitals Susa in Elam, Ecbatana in Media, and Babylon, he added Persepolis in Persia proper, which was destroyed by Alexander the Great, but whose imposing ruins have survived. On account of his attention to trade and industry he was called "the Huckster." His expedition over the Bosporus and Danube into Scythia was unsuccessful (512). Toward the East he extended his supremacy to the Indus, and compelled north Africa to pay him tribute. Under him began also the great struggle between Persia and Greece, reaching a climax in the battle of Marathon in 490 at which the Greeks were victorious. His tomb is hewn in the rock at a place called Naksh-i-Rustam, near Persepolis, and is adorned with sculptures and inscriptions complementing those of Behistun. Darius I is referred to in the Old Testament in connection with the building of the temple of Zerubbabel. In the second year of his reign he allowed the resumption of the building, and in the sixth it was completed (Ezra, vi. 15).

Darius II (of *Persia*). [Original name, **Ochus;** Greek surname, **Nothus,** meaning "bastard."] Persian king from c423 to 404 B.C.; son of Artaxerxes I. Through his son Cyrus the Younger, and Tissaphernes and Artabazus, satraps in Asia Minor, he pushed the plan to conquer the Athenian power, allying himself with Sparta about 412.

Darius III (of *Persia*). [Surnamed **Codomannus.**] d. 330 B.C. Last king of Persia. He reigned from 336 to 330 B.C., when he was dethroned by Alexander the Great, after he had been defeated at Issus (333) and Arbela (the modern Erbil; the battle actually was fought at Gaugamela) in 331. Darius fled to the east, where he was slain by one of his satraps.

Darius the Mede (mēd). 6th cent. B.C. In the Bible, king of Chaldea or Babylonia after the overthrow and death of Belshazzar. He is said to have been a son of Ahasuerus (see Daniel, v. 31; vi. 28; ix. 1; xi. 1; and other passages). Some historians identify him with Cyaxares, son of Astyages, and uncle to Cyrus.

Darjeeling (där.jē'ling). [Also, **Darjiling.**] District in West Bengal, Union of India, at the foothills of the Himalayas, ab. 320 mi. N of Calcutta. Tea is the outstanding crop of the area. Capital, Darjeeling; area, 1,164 sq. mi.; pop. 376,369 (1941).

Darjeeling. [Also, **Darjiling.**] Town and sanatarium in Darjeeling district, West Bengal, Union of India. It is the chief health station in Bengal, and the city where Europeans from the valley areas near Calcutta spend the hottest and most humid months of the year. Elevation, ab. 7,000 ft.; pop. 21,000 (est. 1941).

Dark (därk), **Eleanor.** b. at Sydney, Australia, August 26, 1901—. Australian novelist whose works are distinguished by fine psychological insight. She is best known abroad for *The Timeless Land* (1941); also author of *Sun Across the Sky* (1937), *Waterway* (1938), *Storm of Time* (1950), and others.

"Dark Continent." See **Africa.**

Dark Fire, The. Volume of poetry by W. J. Turner, published in 1918.

Dark Flower, The. Novel by John Galsworthy, published in 1913. Divided into three parts, "Spring," "Summer," and "Autumn," it presents the amorous adventures of Mark Lennan.

Dark Forest, The. Novel by Hugh Walpole, published in 1916. It is based on the author's experiences (1914–16) with the Red Cross in Russia during World War I. *The Secret City* (1919) is a sequel.

Dark Island, The. Novel by V. M. Sackville-West, published in 1934.

Dark Lady, The. Woman mentioned in Shakespeare's later sonnets (numbers 127 *et seq.*), who has been thought by some scholars to have been Mary Fitton, a maid of honor to Queen Elizabeth in 1595. She was the mistress of William Herbert, Earl of Pembroke, who is celebrated in the earlier sonnets. Others have suggested Penelope Devereux, Lady Rich, or any of a number of other women of the court or of London. The speculation concerning her has produced a considerable body of carefully reasoned hypotheses, but as yet no absolute proof of her identity.

Dark Lady of the Sonnets, The. Comedy in one act (1910) by George Bernard Shaw, who calls it "this little pièce d'occasion" in his 28-page preface to the 14-page play. It was first produced at the London Haymarket, on Nov. 24, 1910, with Mona Limerick as the Dark Lady, Suzanne Sheldon as Queen Elizabeth, and Granville Barker as Shakespeare. The occasion for which the play was written and performed was to raise funds for a national theater to be erected as a tribute to Shakespeare.

Dark Laughter. Novel by Sherwood Anderson, published in 1925. John Stockton, dissatisfied with his life as a Chicago journalist, walks out on his wife and travels through the Midwest country. During the course of his journey Stockton hears the "dark laughter" of Negroes, symbolizing for him a free and happy acceptance of life. Using an assumed name he becomes a factory worker and elopes with his employer's wife, a woman who shares Stockton's alienation from the machine age.

Darkness. Three-act tragedy (1926) by Liam O'Flaherty.

Dark Night, The. Narrative poem by May Sinclair, published in 1924.

Dark of the Moon. Volume of poetry (1926) by Sara Teasdale. It is characterized, as the title suggests, by a serious and somber tone. *Wisdom* ("It was a night of early spring"), *The Solitary* ("My heart has grown rich with the passing of years"), and *The Flight* ("We are two eagles"), regarded by critics as three of her best poems in the volume, are to be found in various anthologies of American poetry.

Dark Wind, The. Volume of poems by W. J. Turner, published in 1920.

Darlan (dår.läṅ), **Jean Louis Xavier François.** b. at Nérac, Lot-et-Garonne, France, Aug. 7, 1881; assassinated at Algiers, French North Africa, Dec. 24, 1942. French naval officer and politician, a leading official of the Vichy regime during World War II, whose transfer of support to the Allied side caused wide controversy. He served as an aide (1926–28) to Georges Leygues, naval minister. After promotion (1929) to rear admiral he returned to duty in the naval ministry (1929–34), was a French delegate to the London conference (1930), and returned briefly to service in the naval ministry before being named (1936) chief of the French naval staff. Promoted to admiral, he took command (1939) of all French naval forces on the eve of World War II. After the defeat of France, he was named (June, 1940) naval minister in Pétain's cabinet, replaced Pierre Laval as vice-premier, and was named (February, 1941) as next in the line of succession to Pétain as chief of state. He quickly took over the ministries of foreign affairs and interior, as well as the Vichy propaganda system. He negotiated the surrender (July, 1941) of French Indochina to Japan. Though replaced (April, 1942) by Laval as vice-premier because of German pressure, he remained as naval minister and commander of all Vichy armed forces. He was in North Africa at the time of the U.S. invasion (November, 1942), was captured and then released by the Americans in order to authorize French units in North Africa to join the Allies, and was made chief of state (high commissioner) in North Africa, despite widespread criticism in Allied countries. He was shot to death by Fernand Eugène Bonnier de la Chapelle, a young French antifascist.

Darlaston (där'la̤s.to̤n). Urban district in C England, in Staffordshire, situated on the Bentley Canal, ab. 4 mi. SE of Wolverhampton, ab. 124 mi. NW of London by rail. It has an iron industry. 22,024 (1951).

Darley (där'li), **Felix Octavius Carr.** b. at Philadelphia, June 23, 1822; d. at Claymont, Del., March 27, 1888. American artist, noted as an illustrator. He illustrated Sylvester Judd's novel *Margaret* (1856), Irving's *Legend of Sleepy Hollow* and *Rip Van Winkle*, and the works of Dickens, Cooper, and others.

Darley, George. b. in Ireland, 1795; d. 1846. British poet, critic, and mathematician.

Darling (där'ling). [Also: **Barwan, Barwon, Calewatta, Macintyre.**] River in Australia which rises in SE Queensland, flows through New South Wales, and joins the Murray in the SW corner of New South Wales. It often dries up in places in the summer season. Length, ab. 1,100 mi.

Darling, Charles John. [Title, 1st Baron **Darling of Langham.**] b. Dec. 6, 1849; d. at Lymington, Hampshire, England, May 29, 1936. English judge, legal writer, and poet. Called to the bar in 1873, he was made queen's counsel in 1885, was Conservative member of Parliament (1888–97) for Deptford, and judge of the king's bench division from 1897 until his retirement in 1923. He was the author of *Scintillae Juris* (1877), *Medi-*

tations in the Tea Room (1879), *Seria Ludo* (1903), *On the Oxford Circuit and Other Verses* (1909), *Musings on Murder* (1925), *A Pensioner's Garden* (1926), *Reconsidered Rimes* (1930), and *Autumnal Leaves* (1933). Knighted in 1897, he was made a peer in 1924. He tried Sir Roger Casement, who was hanged by the British during World War I.

Darling, Grace Horsley. b. at Bamborough, Northumberland, England, Nov. 24, 1815; d. Oct. 20, 1842. English heroine who aided in rescuing (Sept. 7, 1838) five persons from the wreck of the steamer *Forfarshire* near Longstone lighthouse, Farne Islands, where her father was lighthouse keeper.

Darling, Jay Norwood. [Called (from his signature) **Ding.**] b. at Norwood, Mich., Oct. 21, 1876—. American cartoonist. The son of a Congregational clergyman, he was educated at Yankton College, in South Dakota, Beloit College, in Wisconsin, and Drake University, in Iowa. He originally intended to study medicine, an idea he gave up when he found that he could make more money as a newspaper cartoonist. He began his career as a reporter for the Sioux City (Iowa) *Journal*, and later became a cartoonist, doing a daily picture, for the Sioux City *Tribune*, his success in which led to his next position, on the staff of the Des Moines *Register*. During the period 1911–13 he was on the staff of the New York *Globe*, and from 1917 on he has been editorial cartoonist for the New York *Herald Tribune*, although continuing to live at Des Moines. In 1923 he won the Pulitzer prize for a four-strip cartoon, and in 1934 Henry A. Wallace, then secretary of agriculture, asked him to become the head of the U.S. Bureau of Biological Survey, a post he accepted and for which he was qualified by reason of his deep interest, going back to World War I, in game preservation and restoration. Darling is the author of *Ding Goes to Russia* (1932), a report, with illustrations, of his visit to and his impressions of the U.S.S.R., and *The Cruise of the Bouncing Betty* (1937), a record of a trailer trip he took from Iowa to Florida. He has frequently disagreed with the policies of the papers that employed him, as when he drew cartoons favoring the League of Nations, although the editorial page of the *Tribune* fought it bitterly. He is the creator of "Alonzo Applegate," a college character, and "the Iowa Farmer." Individual cartoons that have been praised, and that seem likely to be remembered for a long time, are those on the death of "Buffalo Bill" Cody and on the death of "T. R.," the latter showing the former president as a cowboy, riding a horse, and waving good-by as he disappears in the distance.

Darling, Mr. and Mrs. Parents of Wendy, Michael, and John, in Sir James M. Barrie's fairy play, *Peter Pan* (1904).

Darling, Samuel Taylor. b. at Harrison, N.J., April 6, 1872; d. in automobile crash at Beirut, Lebanon, May 20, 1925. American pathologist and authority on tropical medicine. A graduate (1903) of the Baltimore College of Physicians and Surgeons, he joined (1906) General W. C. Gorgas on the Isthmian Canal Commission and served as chief of laboratories (1906–15) in the Canal Zone. He was appointed (1915) to the International Health Board, became (1918) professor of hygiene and director of laboratories of hygiene at the São Paulo, Brazil, medical school, and was director (1922 *et seq.*) of the field laboratory for research in malaria under the International Health Board of the Rockefeller Foundation. He was the author of "The Spleen Index in Malaria," published (1924) in the *Southern Medical Journal*, and "Comparative Helminthology as an Aid in the Solution of Ethnological Problems," published (1925) in the *American Journal of Tropical Medicine*.

Darling, Wendy. Young girl in Sir J. M. Barrie's *Peter Pan* (1904). Wendy and her brothers, after Peter teaches them how to fly, accompany him to his home in the Never-Never Land to take care of him; Wendy's home calls her back but she makes Peter happy by her promise that she will return every spring.

Darling Downs. Region in E Australia, in SE Queensland, ab. 150 mi. W of Brisbane. It is an extensive flat to rolling plain in the upper drainage basin of the Darling River, noted for sheep farming and wheat growing.

Darling of the Gods, The. Tragedy by David Belasco and John Luther Long, produced in 1902.

Darling Range. Range of low mountains in W Australia, running parallel to the coast, behind and S of the city of Perth.

Darlington (där'ling.tọn). County borough, market town, and manufacturing center in NE England, in Durham, situated on the river Skerne, ab. 18 mi. S of Durham. It has manufactures of construction steel, locomotives, metal cables, worsteds, and clothing. It was the terminus of the Stockton and Darlington Railway, said to be the oldest railway in the world (opened in 1825). 84,861 (1951).

Darlington. Town in NE South Carolina, county seat of Darlington County: marketing center for tobacco and cotton; manufactures of textiles and chairs. 6,619 (1950).

Darlington, Henry (Vane Bearns). b. at Brooklyn, N.Y., June 9, 1889—. American Protestant Episcopal clergyman; son of James Henry Darlington. He has been rector (1922 *et seq.*) of the Protestant Episcopal Church of the Heavenly Rest at New York.

Darlington, James Henry. b. at Brooklyn, N.Y., June 9, 1856; d. Aug. 14, 1930. American Protestant Episcopal clergyman, consecrated (1905) first bishop of Harrisburg. He served as assistant (1882–83) and rector (1883–1905) of Christ Church at Brooklyn, N.Y., and archdeacon (1896–98) of Brooklyn. He was the author of *Pastor and the People* (1902), and *Verses by the Way* (1923).

Darlington, William. b. at Birmingham, Pa., April 28, 1782; d. at West Chester, Pa., April 23, 1863. American botanist and politician. He was elected to Congress as a Democrat in 1815, and again in 1819 and in 1821. He wrote *Flora Cestrica* (1837), and other works on botany and botanists.

Darmesteter (dȧr.mes.te.ter), **Arsène.** b. at Château Salins, in Alsace, France, Jan. 5, 1846; d. at Paris, Nov. 16, 1888. French lexicographer, an authority on medieval French. He studied the writings of French Jews in the Middle Ages, and from glosses on their manuscripts and the evidence of French words introduced into Hebrew, was able to throw much light on the development of Old French, the subject which he taught as a professor at the Sorbonne. He was coauthor of an extensive and basic work, *Dictionnaire général de la langue française*, published (1890–1900) after his death. His formulation of rules governing changes of Latin words into French is known as "Darmesteter's law."

Darmesteter, James. b. at Château Salins, in Alsace, March 28, 1849; d. Oct. 19, 1894. French Orientalist, professor of Iranian languages and literature (1885 *et seq.*) at the Collège de France; brother of Arsène Darmesteter and husband of Mary Darmesteter. He was the author of numerous works on Oriental subjects, including a complete translation into French of the *Avesta* (3 vols., 1892–93).

Darmesteter, Mary. [Full name, **Agnes Mary Frances Darmesteter**; maiden name, **Robinson.**] b. at Leamington, England, Feb. 27, 1857—. Poet and expert on English literature; wife (1888–94) of James Darmesteter and, after Darmesteter's death, of Pierre Émile Duclaux. She is the author of *Poésies* (1888), *Ernest Renan* (1898), *Grands Écrivains d'outre-Manche* (1901), and others. Her works in English include *A Handful of Honeysuckles* (1878), *The Crowned Hippolytus* (1880), a translation of Euripides (1881), and *The End of the Middle Ages* (1889; a historical work).

Darmstadt (därm'shtät; Anglicized, -stat). City in W Germany in the *Land* (state) of Hessen, American Zone, formerly the capital of the free state of Hesse, situated in the province of Starkenburg, ab. 16 mi. S of Frankfort on the Main. It has chemical and pharmaceutical industries (formerly Merck and Company), metallurgical, machine, paper, and leather-goods factories, and also manufactures orthopedic instruments, precision instruments, furniture, and tobacco. It is the seat of an institute of technology and other educational institutions. Valuable art and ethnographical collections, a notable collection of ceramics, various large libraries, a theater, and scholarly societies are among its cultural resources. Formerly it was known for its artists' colony and art exhibitions. The castle, in its oldest parts dating from the 14th century, was rebuilt in 1568, 1716, and 1786; the castle church dates from the 16th century. The oldest architectural monument, the town church, was built in the 14th century. Most of the official buildings date from the

18th century. Almost the entire city was laid in ruins in World War II; it was occupied by American troops on March 26, 1945. Darmstadt received town privileges in 1330, became part of Hesse in 1479, was declared capital in 1567, and developed largely in the reign of Grand Duke Louis I of Hesse-Darmstadt (1790–1830). The population declined 30.2 percent between 1939 and 1946. It is predominantly Protestant. 94,788 (1950).

Darnay (där.nā'), **Charles.** [Original surname, **St. Evrémonde.**] In Charles Dickens's *A Tale of Two Cities,* a young French nobleman who flees France in disgust with the excesses of the aristocracy, including his own family. He changes his name and marries Lucie Manette, but is condemned to death (partly on evidence obtained through a paper written in prison against his family by Doctor Manette, Lucie's father) and is saved only through the self-sacrifice of Sydney Carton.

Darnétal (dȧr.nā.tȧl). Town in NW France, in the department of Seine-Inférieure, situated on the Aubette River, ab. 2 mi. E of Rouen. It is a textile center, producing woolen and cotton materials. 7,765 (1946).

Darnley (därn'li), Lord. [Title of **Henry Stuart** or **Stewart.**] b. at Temple Newsam, Yorkshire, England, Dec. 7, 1545; killed near Edinburgh, Feb. 9 or 10, 1567. Second husband of Mary, Queen of Scots; father of James I of England. He was the son of Matthew Stuart, 4th Earl of Lennox, and Margaret Douglas, granddaughter of Henry VII of England, and was cousin-german to Mary, whom he married July 29, 1565. He was treated at first with much kindness by the queen, who promised to induce the Scottish Parliament to grant him a crown matrimonial, but eventually alienated her affections by his stupidity, insolence, and profligacy, and especially by his participation in the murder (March 9, 1566) of her favorite, the Italian secretary David Rizzio. He attempted to reëstablish himself with her by turning over to her his associates in the murder; but then he refused (December, 1566) to attend the baptism of his son James. While convalescent from an attack of illness, smallpox according to some, poisoning according to others, he was removed to a solitary house called the Kirk o' Field, near Edinburgh, which was blown up with gunpowder under the direction of the Earl of Bothwell, apparently with the queen's knowledge, if not her connivance, on the night of Feb. 9–10, 1567. Darnley's body was found in a garden some distance from the house, leading to the hypothesis that he was strangled and the house blown up to cover the crime.

Darrow (dar'ō), **Clarence Seward.** b. at Kinsman, Ohio, April 18, 1857; d. at Chicago, March 13, 1938. American lawyer. He acted professionally in many cases against monopolies or on the side of labor. He was counsel (1894) in the Debs strike case, and for the miners in the anthracite coal strike arbitration at Scranton and Philadelphia (1902–03); attorney for William (Big Bill) Haywood, Moyer, and Pettibone when they were tried for the murder of ex-Governor Steunenberg of Idaho in 1907; attorney for the McNamara brothers, defendants in the case of the destruction (Oct. 1, 1910) of the Los Angeles *Times* building in 1911. He defended Leopold and Loeb in their trial (1924) for the murder of young Bobby Franks and saved them from execution; lost his case when serving (1925), against William Jennings Bryan for the prosecution, as defense counsel to John Thomas Scopes, who had violated a Tennessee statute by teaching evolutionary theories in a public school; pleaded for the Negro defendants in the Scottsboro trial (1932). He was the author of the novel *Farmington* (1904), of *Crime, Its Causes and Treatment* (1907), and of *The Story of My Life* (1932), and other books, pamphlets, and articles. Darrow, president of the American League to Abolish Capital Punishment, often pointed out, with some pride, that none of his clients was ever executed.

Dar Runga (där rön'gä). [Also, **Dar Rounga.**] Former Negro kingdom and vassal state of Ouadai, in C Africa, on the borders of Chad and Ubangi-Shari territories, French Equatorial Africa, near the border of the Anglo-Egyptian Sudan.

Dart (därt). River in SW England, in Devonshire, rising in Dartmoor and flowing SE past Totnes to the English Channel at Dartmouth. Length (to Totnes), 36 mi.; the estuary (to Dartmouth) is additionally ab. 11 mi. long. The river is navigable to Totnes.

Dart, Raymond Arthur. b. at Toowong (now part of Brisbane, Australia, Feb. 4, 1893—. Australian neuroanatomist, palaeontologist, and anthropologist, professor of anatomy (1923 *et seq.*) at the University of Witwatersrand.

D'Artagnan (dȧr.tȧ.nyäṅ; Anglicized, där.tan'yạn). See **Artagnan, D'.**

D'Artagnon (dȧr.tȧ.nyôṅ). See **Artagnon.**

Dartford (därt'fọrd). Municipal borough and market town in SE England, in Kent, situated on the river Darent ab. 17 mi. SE of London by rail. Its industries are paper-making, drug and chemical manufacture, flour-milling, cement-making, and brewing. Dartford is a railway junction and has facilities for importing coal and raw materials. There are large chalk quarries nearby. It is a rapidly expanding town located beyond the Outer Ring of London. 37,905 (1951).

Dartiguenave (dȧr.tēg.nȧv), **Philippe Sudre.** President of Haiti (1915–22). He was chosen (Aug. 12, 1915) president by the Haitian congress during American intervention. He signed a treaty (1916) with the U.S. assuring aid for ten years in development of Haitian resources and in the establishment of a firm financial system. A revolt (July, 1918 *et seq.*) against U.S. authority was suppressed, and peace restored in May, 1920.

Dartle (där'tl), **Rosa.** In Charles Dickens's *David Copperfield,* Mrs. Steerforth's excitable companion, in love with Steerforth. She has a scar on her face, caused by Steerforth in his youth.

Dartmoor (därt'mör). Granitic moorland region in SW England, in Devonshire, situated N of Plymouth. It abounds in British antiquities, and is the seat of a prison (opened in 1809 as a military prison) where American seamen were detained in the War of 1812, and where French prisoners of war were confined during the wars with Napoleon; it was made into a convict prison in 1850. Elevation, ab. 1,500 ft.; length, ab. 25 mi.; breadth, ab. 15 mi.

Dartmouth (därt'muth). [Full official name, **Borough of Clifton Dartmouth Hardness.**] Municipal borough, seaport, and market town in SW England, in Devonshire, situated on the W side of the estuary of the river Dart, opposite Kingswear (the railway terminus), ab. 26 mi. S of Exeter, ab. 209 mi. SW of London by rail. Dartmouth is reached from Kingswear by steam ferries. The Royal Naval Cadet Training College is located here. Dartmouth was an important seaport in the Middle Ages, but is now only of minor importance. 5,842 (1951).

Dartmouth. Town in SE Massachusetts, in Bristol County, near Buzzards Bay: trading point for agricultural and dairy products. 11,115 (1950).

Dartmouth. Seaport in Halifax County, Nova Scotia, Canada, situated on the N side of Halifax Harbor across from the city of Halifax. It is served by motor road and rail line. 15,037 (1951).

Dartmouth, Barons and Earls of. Titles held by various members of the **Legge** family.

Dartmouth. A former name of **Anamosa.**

Dartmouth College. Nonsectarian, privately endowed institution of higher learning for men, founded by Eleazer Wheelock, chartered in 1769, opened in 1770, and situated at Hanover, N.H. For a time a state college was affiliated with Dartmouth, but in 1893 this was established separately and became the University of New Hampshire. Chiefly concerned with courses in the liberal arts, Dartmouth also comprises the Tuck School of Business Administration, the Thayer School of Civil Engineering, a school of medicine, and other divisions, as well as the Baker Memorial Library.

Dartmouth College Case. [Formally cited as **Trustees of Dartmouth College v. Woodward, 4 Wheaton 518 (1819).**] In the history of American jurisprudence, a case which derives great importance from its bearing on the law of corporations. It originated in a dispute between the president and trustees of Dartmouth College. The former, having been removed from office by the latter, appealed to the legislature of New Hampshire, which passed a bill amending the charter of the college, whereby a new corporation was created under the title of Dartmouth University, the property of the college being vested in the new corporation. The college trustees brought action in the Court of Common Pleas in 1817 to recover the property. The case came by appeal before the Supreme Court of the U.S., which in 1819 rendered a decision in favor of the trustees. The decision, by Chief Justice John Marshall, held that a charter is a contract between the state and the corporation created by the charter, and that, as the states are prohibited by the Constitution from passing any laws impairing the obligations of contracts, charters are unalterable except by consent of the corporations created by them. The plaintiffs were represented by Daniel Webster.

Darton (där'tọn). Urban district in N central England, in the West Riding of Yorkshire, situated on the river Dearne, ab. 4 mi. NW of Barnsley, ab. 194 mi. N of London by rail. 14,400 (1951).

Daru (dȧ.rü), **Napoléon,** Comte. b. at Paris, June 11, 1807; d. there, Feb. 19, 1890. French politician; son of Pierre Antoine Daru (1767–1829). He was vice-president (1850–51) of the Legislative Assembly, and minister of foreign affairs in 1870.

Daru, Pierre Antoine, Comte. [Full family name, **Pierre Antoine Noël Bruno.**] b. at Montpellier, France, Jan. 12, 1767; d. at Becheville, near Meulan, France, Sept. 5, 1829. French statesman and historian. Although an adherent of the principles of the French Revolution, he was imprisoned (1793–94). He became (c1795) intendant-general of the army of the Danube, and was named (c1805) councilor of state; became minister of state in 1811, and a member of the Chamber of Peers in 1819. His chief work is *Histoire de la république de Venise* (1819–21).

Darwar (där.wär'). See **Dharwar.**

Darwen (där'wẹn, dar'ẹn). [Also, **Over Darwen.**] Municipal borough, market town, and manufacturing center in NW England, in Lancashire, ab. 18 mi. NW of Manchester, ab. 203 mi. NW of London by rail. It has manufactures of coarse cotton cloth, primarily for the Oriental trade. Other industries include paper making, coal mining, and plastics and soap manufactures. Darwen formerly had an iron industry. 30,827 (1951).

Darwin (där'win). [Former name, **Palmerston.**] City in N Australia, a seaport and the principal urban settlement in Northern Territory. Situated on the Timor Sea, it is the administrative center for the Northern Territory. The city was almost completely destroyed by Japanese bombs during World War II. 5,543 (1937).

Darwin, Sir **Charles Galton.** b. at Cambridge, England, Dec. 19, 1887—. English physicist, son of Sir George Howard Darwin. He has been Tait professor (1923–35) of natural philosophy at the University of Edinburgh, and director (1939 *et seq.*) of the National Physical Laboratory. He is the author of *The New Conceptions of Matter* (1931) and other works.

Darwin, Charles Robert. b. at Shrewsbury, England, Feb. 12, 1809; d. at Down, Kent, England, April 19, 1882. English naturalist, original expounder of the theory of evolution by natural selection since known as Darwinism; grandson of Erasmus Darwin (1731–1802) and father of Sir Francis Darwin (1848–1925). Though he studied medicine at Edinburgh and began to prepare for the ministry at Cambridge, his absorbing interest in natural history brought him in touch with the botanist John Stevens Henslow, who secured Darwin's appointment as naturalist with the around-the-world expedition which sailed on H.M.S. *Beagle* in 1831. The *Beagle,* on a surveying cruise, stopped at various points along the South American coast and at such neighboring islands as the Galapagos; then it headed across the Pacific to Tahiti, New Zealand, Australia, Tasmania, the Maldives, St. Helena, Brazil, and the Cape Verde and Azores islands, returning to England in 1836. Darwin was much struck by the variations in species in adjacent areas at which the ship stopped, by the close resemblance of the island species to similar species on the mainland, by the differences between fossils and living species in the same area; and he began to attempt to formulate his ideas of the succession of the species. He became friendly with Sir Charles Lyell, the noted geologist, in the period 1838–41, when he was secretary of the Royal Geological Society. In 1842 he took up residence in the secluded village of Down, in Kent, where he devoted himself to a life of study and scientific research. Taking his inspiration from Thomas Malthus's *Essay on Population* (1798), which investigates the rigorous economic laws that limit the number of people capable of maintaining life in view of the available food supply, Darwin began to see illustrated in his materials a natural tendency towards selection of the individuals that survived. In 1857 he wrote to Asa Gray, the American botanist, outlining his theories. In 1858 he was the recipient of a manuscript from Alfred Russel Wallace that explained Darwin's own theory, independently arrived at by Wallace, then in the Molucca Islands. On the advice of Lyell and Sir Joseph Hooker, Darwin included Wallace's paper with a sketch of his own work in a communication to the Linnean Society (1858) and in 1859 he published his work, *On the Origin of Species by Means of Natural Selection, or the Preservation of Favoured Races in the Struggle for Life,* in which he propounded his theory of biological evolution, which came to be known as the Darwinian theory. This book, Darwin's most important and most noted work, discusses his theory of selection and variation of species and marshals the evidence from which the theory developed. The book is said to have sold its first edition in one day; factions sprang up for and against the theory, and within the year the book was beginning to bring to bear that influence that it still maintains as perhaps the leading work in natural philosophy in man's history. Darwin also wrote reports on the biological and geological findings of the *Beagle* expedition, and other books and monographs. The more important of his later works are *The Movements and Habits of Climbing Plants* (1865), *The Variation of Animals and Plants under Domestication* (1868), and *The Descent of Man, and Selection in Relation to Sex* (1871). Few men indeed have so greatly influenced human concepts of life and the universe as has Charles Robert Darwin.

Darwin, Erasmus. b. at Elston, Nottinghamshire, England, Dec. 12, 1731; d. of heart disease, at Derby, England, April 18, 1802. English physician, scientist, poet, and political and religious radical; grandfather, by his first wife, of Charles Robert Darwin, some of whose ideas on evolution he anticipated, and, by his second wife, of Francis Galton. He was educated at Chesterfield Grammar School, at Edinburgh University, where he studied medicine, and at St. John's College, Cambridge. As a prose author, he contributed to the *Philosophical Transactions,* and wrote *Zoonomia, or the Laws of Organic Life* (1794–96), *A Plan for the Conduct of Female Education in Boarding Schools* (1797), expressing views then considered liberal, if not radical, and *Phytologia, or the Philosophy of Agriculture and Gardening* (1799), which expresses many of his scientific speculations. His works in verse (they are hardly considered poetry today) are of the didactic type so popular in the 18th century. They are *The Botanic Garden* (1781), in two parts; the first part, *The Economy of Vegetation,* was published in 1792, the second part, *The Loves of the Plants,* having come out in 1789. Strangely enough, in view of its later, and present, reputation, it was successful at first, and was praised by Walpole, Cowper, and William Hayley. If the poem is not completely forgotten today it is because of Canning's parody of it, "The Loves of the Triangles," which appeared in his periodical, *The Anti-Jacobin.* Darwin had enough of a sense of humor (not apparent in his own verse) to laugh at the satire, and was honest enough to admit that it was a good one. His poetry also includes *On the Death of Frederick, Prince of Wales* (1795) and *The Temple of Nature, or the Origin of Society* (published 1803, a year after his death), a title that speaks for itself. Darwin knew Rousseau, Watt, Josiah Wedgwood, and Maria Edgeworth's father. Johnson he knew and disliked intensely, a feeling that Johnson fully returned, which was natural enough in view of the radicalism of the one and the conservatism of the other.

Darwin, Sir **Francis.** b. at Down, Kent, England, Aug. 16, 1848; d. at Cambridge, England, Sept. 19, 1925. English botanist; son of Charles Robert Darwin. He was long associated with Trinity Hall at Cambridge University, and conducted important botanical research. His intimate knowledge of his father's work and thought lend authority to his *Life and Letters of Charles Darwin* (1887) and *Foundations of the Origin of Species* (1909).

Darwin, Sir **George Howard.** b. at Down, Kent, England, July 9, 1845; d. at London, Dec. 7, 1912. English physicist and astronomer; son of Charles Robert Darwin. He was (1883–1912) Plumian professor of astronomy and experimental philosophy at Cambridge. The most notable of his works is *The Tides and Kindred Phenomena in the Solar System* (1898).

Darwin, Leonard. b. 1850; d. in Sussex, England, March 26, 1943. English engineer and economist, an advocate of world eugenic reforms; son of Charles Robert Darwin. He attended the Royal Military Academy at Woolwich, and served (1885–90) on the staff of the intelligence department of the war office. He was president (1908–11) of the Royal Geographical Society, headed (1911–28) the Eugenics Education Society, and was chairman (1913–20) of Bedford College for Women, University of London. His works include *Bimetallism* (1898), *Municipal Trade* (1903), and *The Need for Eugenic Reform* (1926). The Darwin Mountains in Antarctica were named for him.

Darwin, Mount. [Spanish, **Monte Darwin.**] One of the chief peaks in Tierra del Fuego, Chile. Elevation, ab. 6,900 ft.

Darwinism (där′win.iz.ẹm). Name given to the particular body of ideas concerning biological evolution set forth in the writings of Charles Robert Darwin. In the mid-19th century, the surmise of evolution, even in the biological realm, was widely accepted, but in the way of its further development stood the concept of the permanence of species. From his observations during a long cruise around the world, and from more than 20 years of study thereafter, Darwin adduced proofs of the mutability of species, and in his epoch-making book *On the Origin of Species by Means of Natural Selection, or the Preservation of Favored Races in the Struggle for Life* (1859), he undertook to show that variations are constantly occurring within species as the result of the struggle for survival, which compels individual members or components of a species to achieve better adaptation to environment, or perish. Proof of the origin of species as a result of such mutations made unnecessary the concept of special creation of each species, and this had profound effects upon late 19th- and early 20th-century philosophical and religious thinking. Popular fancy seized upon the notion that Darwinism meant among other things that men are descended from monkeys, an idea over which religious fundamentalists have waxed indignant. Long since, however, most theologians have conceded that the Scriptural account of the Creation is to be understood metaphorically, that its six "days" can be conceived of as vast periods of time, during which the process of evolution worked out, even to the emergence of man, at some unknown point, from lower forms of life. The theory of evolution, with additions to and modifications of Darwin's outline of it, is now universally accepted by scientists, and has become a background to the concepts of life and the universe held by most of literate mankind. Thus Darwinism may be said to have brought about one of the most profound and most far-reaching revolutions in human thought, in all of recorded history.

Darwin Mountains. Mountains in Antarctica, in the Britannia Range, rising NW of Barne Inlet, on the W side of the Ross Shelf Ice, in ab. 79°50′ S., 157°10′ E. They were discovered by the National Antarctic Expedition (1901–04), under the command of Captain Robert F. Scott, who named these mountains for Leonard Darwin, at that time honorary secretary, later president, of the Royal Geographical Society. Elevation, ab. 6,200 ft.

Darya-i-nur (där′yä.ē.nör′). [Eng. trans., "*Sea* (or *River*) *of Light.*"] Largest diamond belonging to the Shah of Iran. It weighs 186 carats and is rectangular in shape.

Daryal Pass (där.yäl′). [Also, **Dariel Pass.**] Chief pass in the Caucasus Mountains of the U.S.S.R., in the Georgian Soviet Socialist Republic, situated in the central part of the chain. It is traversed by a military road, the route between Tiflis (Tbilisi) and Dzaudzhikau (Vladikavkaz). It is probably the ancient Caucasian or Iberian Gates (Caucasiae Pylae). Elevation, ab. 6,000 ft.

Das (däs), **Chitta Ranjan.** b. at Calcutta, India, Nov. 5, 1870; d. at Darjeeling, India, June 16, 1925. Indian statesman. He gave up a lucrative law practice to become the foremost leader of the Indian nationalist movement after the early failure of the noncoöperation campaign (1918 *et seq.*). Breaking with Gandhi, he formed the Swaraj Party in 1923 in Bengal to capture legislative seats on behalf of the nationalist movement. Critical of the parliamentary practices and political organization imposed by contact with the West, he urged the establishment of institutions more consistent with Indian tradition, and stressed political freedom for the Indian masses as well as for the middle class. He was president (1922) of the Indian National Congress, and first mayor (1924) of Calcutta.

Dasara or **Dussera** (du′sạ.rạ). Hindu festival held in September-October which commemorates the victory of Durga, a form of Devi, consort of the god Shiva, over the buffalo-headed demon Mahisha. It also celebrates the victory of Rama, hero of the *Ramayana*, over Ravana, the demon king of Ceylon. Originally, it was a festival for the Ganges. Hindus worship household gods and sacred books on that day, and martial communities perform rites before their weapons. In general, ritual homage is paid to the means of livelihood. It is an auspicious day on which to begin the education of children. The nine preceding nights are known as Navaratri, "nine nights," during which hymns are read before the image of Durga, and flower offerings are placed there. On the tenth day the image is thrown into the water. The word Dasara is from the term for "ten days."

Dasent (dā′sẹnt), Sir **George Webbe.** b. on the island of St. Vincent, British West Indies, May 22, 1817; d. near Ascot, Berkshire, England, June 11, 1896. English lawyer and author, best known as a student of Scandinavian literature. While on diplomatic service at Stockholm in 1840, he was interested by Jakob Grimm in Scandinavian literature and began his investigations into Icelandic. He published a translation of *The Prose or Younger Edda* (1842), *Popular Tales from the Norse* (1859), *Saga of Burnt Njal* (1861), *The Vikings of the Baltic* (1875). From 1845–70 he was one of the assistant editors of the London *Times*. He was professor (1853) of English literature and modern history at King's College, London.

Dash (däsh), **Comtesse.** Pseudonym of **Saint-Mars, Gabrielle Anne de Cisternes de Courtiras,** Marquise **de Poilow de.**

Dashur (dä.shör′). See **Dahshur.**

Dashwood (dash′wůd), **Elinor** and **Marianne.** Two sisters in Jane Austen's novel *Sense and Sensibility.* Elinor represents "sense," as opposed to Marianne's "sensibility" or exaggerated sentiment.

Dashwood, Elizabeth Monica. [Pseudonym, **E. M. Delafield**; maiden name, **de la Pasture**; full name, **Edmée Elizabeth Monica Dashwood.**] b. in Sussex, England, 1890; d. at Cullompton, Devonshire, England, Dec. 2, 1943. English novelist, short-story writer, and dramatist; daughter of Lady Clifford, Mrs. Henry de la Pasture (a surname of which her pseudonym is an Anglicized version). She was author of the novels *Zella Sees Herself* (1917), *The Pelicans* and *The War-Workers* (both 1918), *Consequences* (1919), *Tension* (1920), *Heel of Achilles* and *Humbug* (both 1921), *The Optimist* (1922), *Mrs. Harter* (1924), *The Chip and the Block* (1925), *Jill* (1926), *The Way Things Are* (1927), *What is Love?* (1928; American title, *First Love*), *Diary of a Provincial Lady* (1931), *Challenge to Clarissa* (1931; American title, *House Party*), *The Provincial Lady Goes Further* (1932; American title, *The Provincial Lady in London*), *Thank Heaven Fasting* (1932; American title, *A Good Man's Love*), and *Gay Life* (1933). Her short stories were published in *Messalina of the Suburbs* (1924), *The Entertainment* (1927), and *Women Are Like That* (1929). She also wrote *To See Ourselves* (1932), *The Glass Wall* (1933), and *The Mulberry Bush* (1935), plays; *General Impressions* (1933), notebooks of sketches, *The Provincial Lady in America* (1934) and *The Provincial Lady in Wartime* (1940), travel books, and *Straw Without Bricks* (1937; American title, *I Visit the Soviet*).

Dashwood, Francis. [Title, 15th Baron **le Despencer.**] b. in December, 1708; d. at West Wycombe, England, Dec. 11, 1781. English nobleman notorious for his profligacy. He was expelled from Italy by the Roman Catholic Church, and obtained a minor post in the household of the Prince of Wales. He was also a member of Parliament

(1741, 1747, 1754, 1761). He organized (c1755) the "Hellfire Club" or "Monks of Medmenham Abbey," known after him also as the "Franciscans," whose orgies included obscene parodies of Franciscan rites. They borrowed their motto from Rabelais and carved it over a doorway in their ruined abbey: *"Fay ce que voudras"* ("do what you will"). Other leaders in the group were John Montagu, Earl of Sandwich (1718–92), John Wilkes (1727–97), and George Bubb Dodington (1691–1762).

Daskam (das′kạm), **Josephine Dodge.** See **Bacon, Josephine Dodge.**

Dass (däs), **Petter.** [Called the **"Father of Modern Norwegian Poetry."**] b. on the island of Nord Herø, Norway, 1647; d. 1707. Norwegian poet. He was the son of a Scot, Peter Dundas, who settled in Norway. From his remote northern birthplace he went to Copenhagen for his higher education, and became an ordained clergyman in 1672. In 1689 he was appointed to a living in northern Norway which assured him of opportunity to indulge his poetic talent. *Den norska Dale-Vise* (The Norwegian Song of the Valley) was published in 1696, but most of his writings, though widely circulated in manuscript, were never printed during his lifetime. Posthumously, his *Andelig Tidsfordriv* (Spiritual Pastime) was issued in 1711, but it was not until 1739 that his greatest poem, *Nordlands Trompet* (The Trumpet of Nordland), saw print. On this rests his enduring fame and his place in the hearts of his countrymen. By virtue of its lively verse, its humor, imagination, and echoes of ancient lore, this rhymed celebration of the province of Nordland, its beauties and its ways of life, remains vivid and vital, and Norwegians of all ranks and classes can quote long passages from it. Dass's collected works in three volumes were published in 1874.

D'Asumar (dȧ.zü.mȧr), **Count.** Character in Alain René Le Sage's *Gil Blas.*

Daszyński (dä.shin′skē), **Ignacy.** b. 1860; d. 1936. Polish politician and journalist, a leader of the Polish Socialist Party. He organized the Socialist Party in Galicia and Silesia (1892), was editor in chief of its daily newspaper, *Naprzód*, at Kraków, and a member of the Austrian parliament (1897–1918). With Pilsudski, whose political adherent he was, he founded a commission of parties which fought (1911–14) for Polish independence and sponsored the creation of secret military formations. During World War I, he was a member of the Polish National Committee at Kraków, which aimed at rebuilding a Polish state in coöperation with Austria. When Poland became independent (1918), he became premier of its first government. Afterwards he was a member of the parliament and its speaker (1928). He published a considerable number of political pamphlets and other works.

Data (dä′tä). Extinct volcano in the Caraballos Occidentales range, in the W central part of Mountain province, Luzon, in the Philippine Islands. 7,364 ft.

Datchery (dach′ėr.i), **Dick.** Mysterious person with white hair and a military air who appears inexplicably at Cloisterham, in Charles Dickens's *Mystery of Edwin Drood.*

Date 1601: Conversation, as it Was by the Social Fireside, in the Time of the Tudors. Humorous prose (1880) by Samuel Langhorne Clemens (Mark Twain). One of his minor works, it has been criticized for displaying a lack of good taste.

Dathan (dā′thạn). In Old Testament history, a Reubenite chieftain; son of Eliab, and brother of Abiram. He joined the conspiracy of Korah and was swallowed up by the earth.

Datia (du′ti.ä). [Also, **Datiya.**] Town in the Bundelkhand region, in Vindhya Pradesh (formerly Central India states), Union of India, ab. 120 mi. SW of Cawnpore: a trading center and major road and rail junction. 24,071 (1941).

Datis (dā′tis). Median general who, with Artaphernes, commanded the army of Darius I which was defeated (490 B.C.) at Marathon by the Athenians.

Dato Iradier (dä′tō ē.rä.ᴛʜyer′), **Eduardo.** b. at La Coruña, Spain, 1850; assassinated at Madrid, March 8, 1921. Spanish statesman and jurist. Elected deputy to the Cortes in 1883 he represented conservative interests and held the portfolio of the interior ministry under Maura (1899–1900). He served as minister of justice (1903–06) and was made alcalde of Madrid in 1907. As president of the Cortes and premier in the period 1913–15 and, after a short interval, again in 1915, it fell to his lot to declare Spain neutral in World War I. In 1918 he was minister of foreign affairs and was called back to the premiership in 1920. On March 8, 1921, he was assassinated by an anarchist bomb thrown during the uprisings at Barcelona which accompanied the general elections of that year. His contributions to social legislation were outstanding. In 1900 he proposed the first Spanish legislation for the benefit of labor, including accident insurance and a law protecting women and child workers. In 1920 he revived the Instituto de Reformas Sociales and created a ministry of labor.

Daub (doup), **Karl.** b. at Kassel, Germany, March 20, 1765; d. at Heidelberg, Germany, Nov. 22, 1836. German Protestant theologian, professor of theology (1795 *et seq.*) at Heidelberg. His works include *Lehrbuch der Katechetik* (1801), *Theologumena* (1806), *Die dogmatische Theologie jetziger Zeit* (1833), and others.

Daubenton (dō.bän.tôn), **Louis Jean Marie.** b. at Montbar, Côte-d'Or, France, May 29, 1716; d. at Paris, Jan. 1, 1800. French naturalist. He was the collaborator of Buffon, writing the physical descriptions of the animals, in the first part of his *Histoire naturelle* and author of numerous scientific treatises and monographs.

Daubeny (dô′bẹ.ni, dôb′ni), **Charles Giles Bridle.** b. at Stratton, Gloucestershire, England, Feb. 11, 1795; d. Dec. 13, 1867. English geologist and chemist. His chief work was *Description of Volcanoes* (1826).

Dauber (dôb′ėr). Narrative poem of the sea (1913) by John Masefield. The poem, named after its sailor hero, who is also an artist, is partly autobiographical in that it is based on the author's memories and experiences after he left his Shropshire home and ran away to sea. Dauber, who wants to paint the water he sails on, rather than clean the decks of the ship, is not understood by his rough comrades, and he finally dies in a storm.

Daubigny (dō.bē.nyē), **Charles François.** b. at Paris, Feb. 15, 1817; d. there, Feb. 19, 1878. French landscape painter, a pupil of Paul Delaroche and a member of the Barbizon School. In 1838 he made his debut at the Paris Salon with a view of Notre Dame and the Île St.-Louis, and was continuously represented in the Salons, except those of 1842–46. At the Salon of 1850–51 he exhibited *The Washerwomen of the River Oullins, The Vintage,* and other works, which created a sensation among artists and connoisseurs by their brilliant technique and emphasis on naturalism. He also painted *The Harvest* (1851–57), *The Lake of Glylieu* (1852–53), *The Lock of Optevoz* (1855), *The Graves of Villerville* (1859), *The Banks of the Oise* (1859), and others. He was made (July 15, 1859) chevalier of the Legion of Honor.

Daubigny, Karl Pierre. b. 1846; d. 1886. French painter; son of Charles François Daubigny.

Daudet (dō.de), **Alphonse.** b. at Nîmes, France, May 13, 1840; d. at Paris, Dec. 16, 1897. French humorist and novelist. He went to school at Lyons, and then worked as a tutor for two years. In 1857 he settled at Paris, and published shortly afterward a collection of poems, *Les Amoureuses.* The *Figaro* published his account of a tutor's hardships, *Les Gueux de province.* A series of papers contributed to the same journal came out in book form as *Le Chaperon rouge* (1861). A second collection of poems, *La Double Conversion,* was published in 1859. Daudet wrote his *Lettres sur Paris* to *Le Petit Moniteur* under the nom de plume of Jehan de l'Isle in 1865. His first real success, *Lettres de mon moulin,* signed with the name Gaston-Marie, were addressed to *L'Événement* in 1866. Daudet's early publications include *Le Petit Chose* (1868), *Lettres à un absent* (1871), *Les Aventures prodigieuses de Tartarin de Tarascon* (1872), *Les Petits Robinsons des caves* (1872), *Contes du lundi* (1873), *Contes et récits* (1873), *Robert Helmont* (1874), *Les Femmes d'artistes* (1874), and *Fromont jeune et Risler aîné* (1874), a great success. There followed *Jack* (1876), *Le Nabab* (1877), *Les Rois en exil* (1879), *Contes choisis, la fantaisie et l'histoire* (1879), *Numa Roumestan* (1881), *Les Cigognes* (1883), *L'Evangéliste* (1883), *Sapho* (1884), *Tartarin sur les Alpes* (1885), *La Belle Nivernaise* (1886), *Trente ans de Paris* (1887), *Souvenirs d'un homme de lettres* (1888), *L'Immortel* (1888), and *Port Tarascon* (1890). Either unassisted or in collaboration with others he dramatized a number of his works, leaving them with their original titles. In like manner he brought out *La Dernière Idole* (1862), *Les Absents* (1863), *L'Œillet blanc* (1864), *Le Frère aîné* (1868), *L'Arlésienne* (1872), *Lise Tavernier* (1872), and finally *La Lutte pour la vie*, based on his novel *L'Immortel*.

Daudet, Julie Rosalie Céleste. [Pseudonym, **Karl Steen;** maiden name, **Julie Rosalie Céleste Allard.**] b. at Paris, 1847; d. 1940. French poet and essayist; wife of Alphonse Daudet (1840–97). She was the author of *Enfance d'une Parisienne* (1883) and of collections of poems including *Reflets sur le sable et sur l'eau* (1903) and *Les Archipels lumineux* (1913). She is perhaps most valued today for her memoirs, *Souvenirs autour d'un groupe littéraire* (1909) and *Journal de famille et de guerre* (1920).

Daudet, Léon. b. at Paris, Nov. 16, 1867; d. at St.-Rémy-de-Provence, France, July 1, 1942. French journalist and writer; son of Alphonse Daudet (1840–97). He served as editorial writer (1908 *et seq.*) for the Royalist *Action Française.* Author of *Le Stupide 19 Siècle* (1922) and more than 80 other works, including novels, memoirs, and polemic essays, he is remembered less for his writing than as a public figure. Long a moving spirit among antirepublican Royalists, he amused two generations with his vigorous polemics against the government and with his escapades, which included his escape from political imprisonment, first word of which reached the public through a story in his own newspaper. He served as a deputy for Paris (1919–24), but failed to be elected when he ran for the senate in 1926.

Daudet, Louis Marie Ernest. b. at Nîmes, France, May 31, 1837; d. 1921. French journalist, historian, and novelist; brother of Alphonse Daudet. He was the author of *Histoire des conspirations royalistes du Midi* (1881), *Histoire de la restauration* (1882), *Histoire de l'émigration* (1886–89), and others. Among his numerous novels are *Thérèse* (1859), *Fleur de péché* (1872), *Daniel de Kerfons* (1878), *Dolorès* (1879), *Défroqué* (1882), and *Gisèle Rubens* (1887).

Daudin (dō.daṅ), **François Marie.** b. at Paris, March 25, 1774; d. there, 1804. French naturalist, author of numerous works on the various branches of zoölogy.

Dauferius (dô.fir'i.us) or **Daufar** (dô'fär). Original name of Pope **Victor III.**

Daugava (dou'gä.vä). Lettish name of the **Dvina,** in W U.S.S.R.

Daugavpils (dou'gäf.pēls). [German, **Dünaburg;** Lithuanian, **Daugpilis** (douk'pē.lēs); Russian, **Dvinsk.**] City and former fortress in NW U.S.S.R., in Latvia. It was founded by Livonian knights in the 13th century, and incorporated in Russia in 1772. It was strongly fortified. The modern city is a rail and market center for a farming and lumbering region. 45,000 (1939).

Daugherty (dô'ėr.ti), **Harry Micajah.** b. at Washington Court House, Ohio, Jan. 26, 1860; d. at Columbus, Ohio, Oct. 12, 1941. American lawyer, politician, and one-time (1921–24) U.S. attorney general, notable for his connection with the Teapot Dome scandal. Harding's close friend and a chief figure in securing his nomination, Daugherty resigned his cabinet post under pressure from Coolidge on March 28, 1924, after Harding's death. His exact connection with the bribes allegedly received by Secretary of the Interior A. B. Fall has never been established, but a Senate investigating committee charged Daugherty with dealings in Sinclair oil stock, and Sinclair was a chief beneficiary of Fall's mishandling of public lands. He was tried (1927) for conspiracy to defraud but the case died after jury disagreements. Daugherty's book, *The Inside Story of the Harding Tragedy* (1932), claims that the Harding administration has been misrepresented and that his own resignation from the cabinet was the result of animosities within Congress.

Daugherty, James Henry. b. at Asheville, N.C., June 1, 1889—. American mural painter, illustrator, lithographer, and writer. He was educated at the Corcoran School of Art at Washington, D.C., and the Pennsylvania Academy of the Fine Arts at Philadelphia, and he has exhibited widely in the U.S. He painted murals for the Stamford, Conn., High School, for Loew's Theater at Cleveland, Ohio, and for the Thomas Cook pavilion at the Philadelphia Sesqui-Centennial Exposition. Among the books he has illustrated are Carl Sandburg's *Abe Lincoln Grows Up*, Stephen Vincent Benét's *John Brown's Body*, and Washington Irving's *Knickerbocker's History of New York*. He was both author and illustrator of *Daniel Boone* and *Poor Richard*.

Daughter, The. Play in verse by J. Sheridan Knowles, produced in 1836.

"Daughter of the Confederacy." See **Davis, Varina Anne Jefferson.**

Daughter of the Forest. Opera in one act by Arthur Nevin, with a libretto by Randolph Hartley, first performed at the Chicago Auditorium on Jan. 5, 1918.

Daughter of the Middle Border, A. Autobiographical narrative by Hamlin Garland, published in 1921 as a sequel to *A Son of the Middle Border* (1917). It was awarded the Pulitzer prize in 1922.

Daughter of the Regiment, The. English title of **Fille du Régiment, La.**

Daughter of the Storage and Other Things in Prose and Verse, The. Volume of short narratives, sketches, and dialogues (1916) by William Dean Howells. The volume also includes *Self-Sacrifice: A Farce-Tragedy* and *The Night Before Christmas: A Morality.*

Daughter of the Tenements, A. Novel (1895) of Italian and Jewish life in New York City, by E. W. Townsend.

Daughters of the American Revolution. [Abbreviation, **DAR.**] Patriotic society organized at Washington, D.C., on Oct. 11, 1890. Any woman is eligible for membership who is descended from a man or woman, of recognized patriotism, who rendered material aid to the cause of independence. It maintains headquarters at Washington and has many local chapters.

Daughters of the Late Colonel, The. Psychological short story by Katherine Mansfield. It is included in her volume of 15 stories, *The Garden Party* (1922).

Daughters of the Revolution. Patriotic society organized at New York, on Aug. 20, 1891. Membership is restricted to women who are lineal descendants of an ancestor who was in actual military or naval service under any of the 13 colonies or states, or a member of the Continental Congress, or are descendants of one who signed the Declaration of Independence, or of an official who actually assisted in establishing American independence and became liable to conviction of treason against the government of Great Britain.

Daughter To Philip. Novel by Beatrice Kean Seymour, published in 1933.

Daukantas (dou.kän'täs), **Simanas.** b. at Kalviai, Skuodas township, Lithuania, Oct. 28, 1793; d. at Papilė, Lithuania, Dec. 6, 1864. Lithuanian patriot, author, and student of history.

Daulatabad (dou''lạt.ạ.bäd'). [Also, **Dowlatabad;** former names, **Deoghir, Deoghur.**] Ancient fortress in Hyderabad, Union of India, ab. 165 mi. NE of Bombay: noted for its strong position on an isolated rock.

Daulatshah (dou.lät.shä'). Persian writer of the 15th century, author of a biography of the celebrated poets of Persia.

Daule (dou'lā). City in W Ecuador, in Guayas province. 18,089 (est. 1944).

Daule River. River in W Ecuador. It flows S to the Gulf of Guayaquil.

Daulis (dô'lis). In ancient geography, a city in Phocis, Greece, situated ab. 12 mi. E of Delphi. It is the setting of the myth of Tereus, Philomela, and Procne.

D'Aulnoy or **D'Aunoy** (dō.nwȧ), Comtesse (or Madame). See **Aulnoy** or **Aunoy, Marie Catherine Jumel de Berneville,** Comtesse **d'.**

Daumas (dō.mȧ), **Melchior Joseph Eugène.** b. Sept. 4, 1803; d. near Bordeaux, France, May 6, 1871. French general and diplomat, and writer on Algeria. He was consul in Algeria (1837–39), and was occupied with important administrative duties during the struggle with Abd-el-Kadir. He wrote *Le Sahara algérien* (1845) and *Les Chevaux du Sahara et les mœurs du desert* (5th ed., 1858).

Daumat (dō.mȧ), **Jean.** See **Domat** or **Daumat, Jean.**

Daumer (dou'mėr), **Georg Friedrich.** b. at Nuremberg, Germany, March 5, 1800; d. at Würzburg, Germany, Dec. 13, 1875. German poet and philosophical writer.

Daumier (dō.myā), **Honoré.** b. at Marseilles, France, Feb. 20, 1808; d. at Valmondois, France, Feb. 11, 1879. French painter, lithographer, and caricaturist. His father was a glazier who published a small volume of verses in 1823, and who tried to keep his son from an artistic career. But Honoré learned lithography and joined the staff of the journal *La Caricature*, where he began his life-long series of satiric works on the bourgeoisie, the law, and government incompetence. In 1832 Honoré was condemned to six months' imprisonment for a lithograph depicting Louis Philippe as Gargantua. He subsequently joined the staff of *Charivari*, founded by Charles Philipon. He continued his work of bitingly sarcastic plates, picking on the inanities of the middle class and the counterfeit classicism of the times. His paintings, on the other hand, are sober and more traditional, but Daumier's realism, before realism in painting became popular, never received the recognition due it during his lifetime. He became completely blind sometime between 1850 and 1860, but not before he had turned out more than 3,950 lithographs and some 200 canvases.

Daun (doun), Count **Leopold (Joseph Maria) von.** [Also, **Dhaun.**] b. at Vienna, Sept. 24, 1705; d. there, Feb. 5, 1766. Austrian field marshal. He was distinguished in the Turkish war (1737–39) and in the Silesian wars (1741–45), defeated Frederick the Great at Kolín in 1757 and at Hochkirch in 1758, captured Finck's army at Maxen in 1759, and was defeated by Frederick at Torgau in 1760.

Daunou (dō.nö), **Pierre Claude François.** b. at Boulogne, France, Aug. 18, 1761; d. at Paris, June 20, 1840. French historian and politician. He was deputy (1792–95) to the Convention, first president of the Council of Five Hundred in 1795, and a member of the Tribunate (1800–02). His chief work is *Cours d'études historiques* (1842–49).

Dauphin (dô'fin). Town in the province of Manitoba, Canada, situated on the Vermilion River in the W part of the province. It is connected by rail and road with Portage la Prairie and Winnipeg, and is an agricultural market center specializing in wheat, cattle, and poultry. 6,007 (1951).

Dauphin (dō.fañ; Anglicized, dô'fin). Title borne (1364 *et seq.*) by any of several male heirs (there were no female claimants) to the French throne. It originated as the title of the rulers of the old county of Vienne, perhaps as a personal name, and was borne by the Dauphins of the Viennois on their coats of arms as a dolphin. In 1285 the name Dauphiné was first applied to the county ruled by Humbert, Dauphin of Vienne. When Philip VI of Valois, king of France, took possession of the lands, the title was given to his grandson, who was to become Charles V of France, the first to bear the title of Dauphin of France. The eldest sons of the French kings were inheritors of the title; most famous was Monseigneur, Louis de Bourbon, son of Louis XIV and grandfather of Louis XV; the last to bear the title was the eldest son of Charles X, Louis Antoine de Bourbon, Duke of Angoulême, who renounced the throne in 1830. The title was also used by the rulers of the dauphinate of Auvergne from 1155 to 1693.

Dauphiné (dō.fē.nā). [English, **Dauphiny** (dô'fi.ni); Medieval Latin, **Delphinatus.**] Region and medieval county of France, bounded by the Rhone River on the W and N, by Savoy on the N, Piedmont on the E, Provence on the S, and Comtat-Venaissin on the SW. Its territory formed the departments Isère, Drôme, and Hautes-Alpes. Its capital was at Grenoble. The surface is generally mountainous. In the early Middle Ages it belonged to the kingdom of Arles.

Dauphine (dô'fin), **Sir.** In Ben Jonson's comedy *Epicoene, or the Silent Woman*, the lively and ingenious nephew of Morose. He concocts the plot by which a portion of his uncle's money is given to him and his debts are paid.

Dauphins (dô'finz). See **Delphin Classics.**

Daurat (dō.rá), **Jean.** See **Dorat** or **Daurat, Jean.**

Dauria (dä.ö'ri.ạ) or **Daur** (dä.ör'). Name of a district in the former region of Trans-Baikal, Siberia, situated SE of Lake Baikal on the Chinese frontier; now part of the Buryat-Mongol Autonomous Soviet Socialist Republic.

Dauthendey (dou'tẹn.dī), **Max.** b. at Würzburg, Germany, July 25, 1867; d. at Malang, Java, in August, 1918. German lyric poet who wrote at first under the influence of Stefan George and the symbolists but found congenial themes and forms for his later works through contact with the Far East, especially Japan. His prose works include *Die acht Gesichter am Biwasee* (1911). His poetry is represented in *Ausgewählte Lieder* (1914). His play *Die Spielereien einer Kaiserin* (1910) treats of Catherine the Great and her lover Menshikov.

Dautry (dō.trē), **Raoul François.** b. in France, Sept. 16, 1880; d. Aug. 21, 1951. French railway executive and political leader, general administrator and government representative (1947 *et seq.*) of the French atomic energy board. He directed (1928–37) the state railway system, was administrative deputy (1937–39) of the Compagnie Générale d'Électricité, was minister of armaments (1939–40), headed (1944) the French charity organization L'Entr'aide Française, and was minister of reconstruction and town planning (1944–46).

Davaive (dä.bī'bā). See **Dabaiba.**

Davalos (dä.bä'lōs), **Gil Ramirez.** b. at Baeza, in Castile, Spain, c1505; d. at Riobamba, near Quito, Ecuador, after 1561. Spanish soldier. He went to Peru with the viceroy Mendoza in 1551, was corregidor of Cusco in 1553, and was expelled from the city by Giron and his followers. He took part in the campaign against Giron, and in 1556 was made justicia mayor of Quito, subdued the Cañaris Indians in 1557, and from 1558 to 1561 was governor of the so-called Land of Cinnamon, on the Napo River. He founded there Baeza, Archidona, and other towns.

Davao (dä.vou'). Province of the Philippine Islands, in the SE part of Mindanao island. It is bounded by Agusan on the N, the Pacific Ocean on the E and S, and Cotabato (separated by a mountain range) on the W. The S coast is indented by the Gulf of Davao, in which is situated Samal island, a part of the province. Among the bays on the E coast is Pujada Bay, a safe harbor in all weather. The district is very mountainous. The active volcano Apo (9,690 ft.) is in the range separating Davao from Cotabato. The Butulan Mountains extend from S to N parallel with the E coast. The largest river is the Agusan, which rises among the Butulan Mountains and flows N into Agusan province. Many other rivers water the district. Most of the staples, such as hemp and sugar cane, are produced. Forests of teak, ebony, and other valuable woods cover the mountains. Coal and iron are found near Mati, N of Pujada Bay. Capital, Davao; area, 7,450.5 sq. mi.; pop. 364,854 (1948).

Davao. City in the Philippine Islands, the capital of Davao province, situated on the Gulf of Davao, at the mouth of the Davao River on SE Mindanao island: airport. Hemp is grown in the surrounding area. 111,263 (1948).

Davao, Gulf of. Arm of the Pacific Ocean indenting the S coast of Davao province, Mindanao, Philippine Islands. It is partly occupied by Samal island.

Davao River. River in Mindanao, in the Philippine Islands. It rises in the E part of Cotabato province and flows SE through Davao province into the Gulf of Davao.

Daveiss (dā'vis), **Joseph Hamilton.** [Also, **Daviess.**] b. in Bedford County, Va., March 4, 1774; d. near Tippecanoe, Ind., Nov. 8, 1811. American lawyer, mortally wounded at the Battle of Tippecanoe, on Nov. 7, 1811.

Davenant (dav'ẹ.nạnt), **Charles.** [Original name, **D'Avenant.**] b. at London, 1656; d. Nov. 6, 1714. English writer on political economy; son of Sir William D'Avenant. His collected works were published in 1771.

D'Avenant or **Davenant** (dav'ẹ.nạnt), Sir **William.** b. at Oxford, England, in February, 1606; d. at London, April 7, 1668. English poet and dramatist. William Oldys is chiefly responsible for the story that D'Avenant was the son of Shakespeare, which seems to rest mainly on the fact that the latter used the inn of one John Davenant (the father of William), at Oxford on his journeys to and from Warwickshire. D'Avenant became (c1620) page to the Duchess of Richmond, and then to Fulke Greville, Lord Brooke. In 1628, after the murder of Greville, he began to write plays. In 1638 he was made poet laureate, and about this time had a severe illness which resulted in the loss of his nose, a fact frequently adverted to by the witty writers of the time. He was manager of Drury Lane Theatre for a time, but, becoming implicated in the various intrigues of the English Civil War, fled to France. Returning in 1643, he was knighted by the king, Charles I, at the siege of Gloucester. While on an expedition (1650) to colonize Virginia, he was captured in the English Channel by a Parliamentary ship. He was imprisoned for two years in the Tower of London for political offenses and expected to be hanged. According to one of John Milton's biographers, Milton was instrumental in saving D'Avenant's life, and after the Restoration (1660) he in turn saved Milton from punishment. Right after his release, he published *Gondibert* (1651), an epic poem consisting of 1,500 four-line stanzas. After the Restoration (1660) he was in favor at court, and continued to write till his death. Among his plays are *Albovine* (1629), *The Cruel Brother* (1630), *The Just Italian* (1630), *The Platonic Lovers* (1636), *The Wits* (1636), *The Unfortunate Lovers* (1643), *Love and Honor* (1649), *Law against Lovers* (played in 1662), and *The Rivals* (played in 1664). He produced alterations of *The Tempest* (with Dryden, 1667), of *Macbeth* (printed 1674), and of *Julius Caesar*. D'Avenant was the founder of English opera, his *Siege of Rhodes* (1656) being produced in the period when plays were banned. It was in this opera that a woman first appeared on the English stage.

Davenport (dav'ęn.pōrt, -pôrt). City in E Iowa, county seat of Scott County, on the Mississippi River. Manufactures include farm machinery, pearl buttons, lumber products, cement, cigars, beer, pumps, steel wheels, washing machines, men's clothing, wooden sole shoes, meat products, and wool textiles. Together with Rock Island, Moline, and East Moline (all in Illinois), it is informally part of a metropolitan area known as the "Quad Cities." It is the seat of St. Ambrose College and the Palmer School of Chiropractic. Davenport was founded in 1836 by George Davenport. It was the home of Dred Scott and of his master, John Emerson, and of Charles Edward Russell, Harry Hansen, Susan Glaspell, and Floyd Dell. 74,549 (1950).

Davenport, Charles Benedict. b. at Stamford, Conn., June 1, 1866; d. at Huntington, Long Island, N.Y., Feb. 18, 1944. American zoölogist, director of the Carnegie Institution Station for Experimental Evolution at Cold Spring Harbor, N.Y., from 1904. He wrote *Experimental Morphology* (1897–99), *Statistical Methods in Biological Variation* (1899), *Inheritance of Characteristics of Fowl* (1909), *Eugenics* (1910), *Elements of Zoölogy* (1911), *Race Improvement by Eugenics* (1911), and others.

Davenport, Edward Loomis. b. at Boston, Nov. 15, 1815; d. at Canton, Pa., Sept. 1, 1877. American actor. He had nine children, all of whom went on the stage (except two who died young), and of whom the most famous was Fanny Davenport.

Davenport, Fanny Lily Gypsy. b. at London, April 10, 1850; d. at South Duxbury, Mass., Sept. 26, 1898. American actress; daughter of Edward Loomis Davenport (1815–77). After appearing as a child actress with her father's company, she played in Mrs. Drew's and Augustin Daly's companies. She is remembered for her roles as Fédora and La Tosca in Sardou's plays and as Nancy Sykes in *Oliver Twist*.

Davenport, George. b. in Lincolnshire, England, 1783; murdered by robbers, July 4, 1845. American soldier and fur trader. He came (1804) to New York and joined the U.S. army. Settling (1816) at Rock Island, Ill., he traded independently with the Indians until 1826, when he became an agent for the American Fur Company. With associates he purchased (1835) land in Iowa which became the city of Davenport. Familiar with Indian frontier problems, he assisted in the negotiation of the second Black Hawk purchase (1837) and the 1842 Sac and Fox tribes treaty.

Davenport, Homer Calvin. b. at Silverton, Ore., 1867; d. 1912. American cartoonist. Growing up on a farm, he had no instruction in draftmanship, but, self-taught, was able in 1892 to secure employment as a cartoonist on the San Francisco *Examiner*, and displayed such ability that in 1895 William Randolph Hearst made him a member of the staff of the New York *Evening Journal*. Quickly acquiring national fame and political influence, he became one of the most highly paid cartoonists up to that time. He created a well-known caricature of Mark Hanna, dressed in a suit covered with dollar signs, and another representing the trusts, which he used persistently and with great popular effect. His version of Uncle Sam also caught popular fancy, and became part of the symbolism of cartoon art. In 1904, having left the Hearst papers to serve the New York *Evening Mail*, he drew a picture showing Uncle Sam with his hand affectionately on the shoulder of President Theodore Roosevelt, which, with the caption "He's Good Enough for Me," was circulated in millions of copies. Subsequently he returned to the Hearst papers. Equally notable with his cartoons dealing with the American scene were the drawings he made at Paris of persons concerned with the Dreyfus affair. Davenport was also a competent writer, and in addition to his book entitled *Cartoons* (1898), he published *The Bell of Silverton* (1899), *Other Stories of Oregon* (1900), *The Dollar or the Man?* (1900), *My Quest of the Arab Horse* (1909), and *The Country Boy* (1910).

Davenport, Ira Erastus. b. Sept. 17, 1839; d. at Mayville, N.Y., July 8, 1911. American entertainer and spiritualistic medium; brother and partner of William Henry Harrison Davenport (1841–77). Popular on both European and American stages, they developed a complex system of musical cabinets which were controversially described as sleight-of-hand by their detractors and as spiritual manifestations by their faithful followers.

Davenport, John. b. at Coventry, England, 1597; d. at Boston, in March, 1670. English Puritan clergyman who emigrated to Boston in 1637. He was one of the founders of the New Haven colony in 1638.

Davenport, Marcia. [Maiden name, **Gluck.**] b. at New York, June 9, 1903—. American music critic and novelist; daughter of Alma Gluck (1884–1938). She has been a staff member (1928–31) of *The New Yorker* and music critic (1934–39) of *The Stage Magazine*. Her works include the biography *Mozart* (1932) and the novels *Lena Geyer* (1936), *The Valley of Decision* (1942), and *East Side, West Side* (1947).

Davenport, Thomas. b. at Williamstown, Vt., July 9, 1802; d. July 6, 1851. American inventor, noted for devising a machine which operated on the principles of the modern electric motor. Beginning as a blacksmith's apprentice, he moved (1823) to Brandon, Vt., establishing a blacksmith shop there. His interest in an electric magnet led him to construct a crude but workable electric motor which he patented in 1837. His attempts to manufacture and market improved models of the machine did not succeed because of financial difficulties. His health broken, he retired to a farm at Salisbury, Vt., where just before his death he was engaged in experimental work on an electromagnetic player piano.

Davenport, William Henry Harrison. b. Feb. 1, 1841; d. in Australia, July 1, 1877. American entertainer and spiritualistic medium; brother and partner of Ira Erastus Davenport (1839–1911).

Daventry (dav'ęn.tri, dān'tri). Urban district and market town in C England, in Northamptonshire, situated between the rivers Leam and Nen and near the Grand Union Canal (which traverses the Northamptonshire Uplands by the water-gap at Daventry), ab. 12 mi. W of Northampton, ab. 74 mi. NW of London by rail. 4,078 (1951).

Davey (dā'vi), **John.** b. in Somersetshire, England, June 6, 1846; d. Nov. 8, 1923. American tree surgeon. In the greenhouse and landscape-gardening business at Kent, Ohio, he was an expert on ornamental and shade trees before the publication (1902) of his first book, *The Tree Doctor*, established him as a campaigner for tree care and culture. His other books are *A New Era in Tree Growing* (1905), *Davey's Primer on Trees and Birds* (1905), and *Instruction Books on Tree Surgery and Fruit Growing* (1914).

David (dā'vid). d. c960 B.C. Second king of Israel, c1000–c960 B.C. He was born at Bethlehem, the seventh and youngest son of Jesse of the tribe of Judah. At about the age of 18, while still shepherd of his father's flocks, he was secretly anointed king of Israel by the prophet Samuel. Later he came into a close personal relationship with Saul the king, perhaps through his friendship with the king's son Jonathan, but incurred his bitter enmity. David played music before the king and was his armor bearer. The Philistine giant Goliath was slain by David in single combat. His successes and the praises accorded to him by the people aroused the suspicion and jealousy of Saul (whose daughter Michal David married), which subsequently turned into deadly hatred, so that David was often in jeopardy of his life. He first sought refuge with Samuel, then with the priests in Nob, which resulted in their massacre by Saul, and was finally driven to seek safety with the enemies of his people, the Philistines. But the slayer of Goliath was recognized, and David fled to the wilderness of Judah, where he built a fort at Adullam. There rallied around him "men who were in distress, in debt, and discontented." At the head of these freebooters or outlaws he undertook many expeditions and fought many skirmishes, which made him increasingly popular with the people. All this time he was pursued by Saul, whose mind became more and more darkened; twice the king came into his power, but because of this awe of the "anointed of the Lord" David did not avail himself of these opportunities (1 Sam. xxiv. 4ff., xxvi. 7ff.). He was compelled to become the vassal of the Philistine king Achish of Gath, who gave him for his support Ziklag on the frontier of Philistia. From here he undertook expeditions against the nomadic tribes of the border, while Achish believed that they were directed against Israel (1 Sam. xxvii.). The Philistines gathered a large army against Israel. In the battle of Gilboa Saul and his host lost their lives. David, who was then about 30 years old, succeeded to the throne. For seven and a half years his reign was limited to Judah, the southern kingdom, with his seat at Hebron, while the other tribes were under the scepter of Ishbosheth, son of Saul, residing at Mahanaim, E of the Jordan. Ishbosheth, however, was murdered, and all the tribes recognized David as king; he reigned over the whole of Israel for 33 years. He removed his residence from Hebron to Jerusalem, which he took from the Jebusites, and there established himself in the "city of David," the oldest quarter of Jerusalem, on Mount Zion. Here also the temporary sanctuary was put up (2 Sam. vi.), which made the city the political and religious center of the nation, and gave to David's reign a genuinely royal character. Through a series of successful wars against the Philistines, Ammonites, Moabites, Edomites, Syrians, Amalekites, and others, and by the introduction of a regular administration and organization of court and army, he became the real founder of the monarchical government of Israel. The constitution of the tribes remained intact, but the military organization was a national one. Each tribe sent a contingent of men (over 20 years of age) to the national army, which stood under one commander in chief, Joab, David's nephew. The bodyguard was formed, it seems, of foreigners, the Cherethites and Pelethites (supposed to be Philistines). The nucleus of the army consisted of the band of heroes (*gibborim*) who rallied about David while he was still an exile. The king presided over judicial cases, and was surrounded by a regular staff of military and administrative counselors and officers. David was also the actual founder of a sanctifying, divine worship, refining and enriching it by the influence of music and psalmody. The last period of his reign was much darkened by national misfortunes and domestic rebellions, the rebellion of his son Absalom, the uprising of Sheba ben Bishri, a drought and famine lasting three years, and a pestilence induced by the counting of the people. Even in his last days when he was prostrated with the infirmities of age, his son Adonijah attempted to secure the succession to which David had appointed Solomon. Solomon was in the eyes of David's other sons, not the rightful heir; Bathsheba, David's wife, had been acquired sinfully and only her hold on the king pushed Solomon to the fore as David's successor. This rebellion, however, like all the others, was successfully repressed, and David died peacefully at the age of 70. He became in tradition the ideal king of Israel, the pattern and standard by which all succeeding rulers were measured, the prototype of the last perfect ruler, the Messiah, who would be descended from David and is sometimes simply called David. As regards the Psalms, modern criticism denies him the authorship of many psalms bearing in the Biblical Book of Psalms the superscription "of David," but there is no reason for entirely disconnecting David from this kind of Hebrew poetry. The probability is that not only did the psalm poetry develop and flourish under his favor, but also that he himself composed a number of the hymns.

David or **Dewi** (dā'wi), Saint. b. c495; d. c589. Patron saint of Wales. He was bishop of Menevia (afterward called St. David's), where he founded a monastery. According to an account which has no historical foundation, he was appointed metropolitan archbishop of Wales at a synod held at Brefi. The wearing of a leek by the Welsh on St. David's day (March 1) is said to stem back to a suggestion by this saint just before a battle with the Saxons that the Welsh should wear leeks and thus be able to distinguish friend from foe in the heat of battle.

David. [Welsh, **Dafydd ap Gwilym** or **Gwillum.**] b. probably at Bro Gynin, in Llanbadarn Vawr parish, Cardiganshire, Wales, c1340; d. c1400. Welsh 14th-century poet and anticlerical song-writer, contemporary with Edward III. His dates and the places of his birth and death are uncertain. According to some, his life span is the same as that of Chaucer; other sources indicate that he was born in 1300, near Llandaff, Glamorganshire, and that he died in 1368, at the Abbey of Talley, in Carmarthenshire. He knew Latin and Italian and is believed to have lived and studied in Italy. He wrote some 147 poems to Morvid (also variously Morvydd or Morfudd or Morfid) of Anglesey, who loved him and with whom he eloped after she had, against her will, married another; the husband, a wealthy old man, is satirized in David's poetry as "Little Hunchback." Fined and imprisoned for his romantic adventure, David was saved by the men of Glamorgan who paid the fine for him, a favor he returned by celebrating the county in his verse. His collected work, consisting of 262 poems, was published (1789) at London, and English translations were brought out in 1791 and 1834. Much of his poetry, in manuscript form, is in the British Museum.

David (dä.ʙᴇᴛʜ'). Town in SW Panama, capital of Chiriquí province, near the Pacific coast and the frontier of Costa Rica: leather, soap, and alcohol. 14,969 (1950).

David (dā'vid). Colossal statue by Michelangelo, in the Accademia at Florence. The youthful hero stands in a position of repose, holding his sling in his left hand and a pebble in the right. The form is still undeveloped and boyish, but full of power.

David. Statue by Donatello, in the Bargello at Florence. David stands resting, nude, with his shepherd's hat on his head, and his left foot resting on the helmeted head of Goliath, whose sword he still holds.

David. Novel in three parts by Naomi Royde-Smith, published in 1934.

David I (of *Scotland*). b. 1084; d. at Carlisle, England, May 24, 1153. King of Scotland; son of Malcolm III Canmore and Margaret, sister of Edgar Aetheling. He succeeded his brother Edgar as earl or prince of Cumbria, ruling southern Scotland, in 1107, and ascended the throne of all Scotland on the death of his brother Alexander I in 1124. His marriage (1113) to Matilda of Northumbria made him heir to the earldom of Huntingdon. He refused to recognize Stephen as king of England, and invaded that country in support of the claim of Matilda, who was his niece, to the throne but was defeated at the Battle of the Standard at Cutton Moor, near Northallerton, Aug. 22, 1138.

David II (of *Scotland*). [Also, **David Bruce.**] b. at Dunfermline, Scotland, March 5, 1324; d. at Edinburgh, Feb. 22, 1371. King of Scotland; son of Robert I (called Robert the Bruce) whom he succeeded in 1329 under the regency of the earl of Moray. The incompetent earl of Mar having succeeded to the regency on the death of Moray in 1332, the kingdom was invaded by Edward de Baliol, who seized the throne with the assistance of Edward III of England. David took refuge in France in the period 1334–41, until he was restored by the successes of his adherents Sir Alexander Murray of Bothwell, Robert the steward of Scotland, and Sir William the knight of Liddesdale. He invaded England in 1346, was defeated and captured at Neville's Cross, on Oct. 17 of that year, and was detained in captivity until 1357.

David (dä'fet), **Eduard.** b. at Ediger, Germany, June 11, 1863; d. at Berlin, Dec. 24, 1930. German politician. Originally a high-school teacher, he was a Social Democratic member (1896–1908) of the diet of Hesse, a member (1903–30) of the Reichstag, president (February,

1919) of the Weimar constitutional assembly, and minister of the interior (1919–20). He was the author of *Sozialdemokratie im Weltkriege* (1915) and *Sozialismus und Landwirtschaft* (1922).

David (da.vēd), **Félicien César.** b. at Cadenet, France, April 13, 1810; d. at St.-Germain-en-Laye, France, Aug. 29, 1876. French composer. He early became a disciple of St. Simon and of Enfantin. In 1833 he went to the Orient. He remained in obscurity till 1844, when he brought out his chief work, a choral symphony, *Le Désert*. Among his other compositions are the operas *La Perle du Brésil* (1851), *Herculanum* (1859), *Lalla-Roukh* (1862), and *Le Saphir* (1865).

David (dä′fēt), **Ferdinand.** b. at Hamburg, Germany, June 19, 1810; d. in Switzerland, July 18, 1873. German violinist, teacher, and composer, leader (1836–73) of the band at the Gewandhaus, Leipzig. Among his pupils were Joachim and Wilhelmj. He published the collection *Hohe Schule des Violinspiels*.

David (dä′vēt), **Gerard** (or **Gheerardt** or **Gheeraert**). [Also, **Davit.**] b. at Oudewater, in South Holland, c1460; d. at Bruges, in Flanders, Aug. 13, 1523. Flemish painter. He is mentioned by early writers, but was entirely lost sight of until 1860, when information about him was discovered in the archives of Bruges. He settled at Bruges in 1483 and lived there during the remainder of his life. Well-authenticated works by him are to be found in many European collections. He is one of the most important of the Flemish primitives.

David (dä.vēd), **Jacques Louis.** b. at Paris, Aug. 30, 1748; d. at Brussels, Dec. 29, 1825. French historical painter, pupil of François Boucher and Joseph Marie Vien, and founder of the French classical school. He was educated at the Collège des Quatre Nations. In 1775 he won the grand prix de Rome after three unsuccessful attempts, and remained at Rome until 1780, when he returned to Paris, and was elected associate member of the French Academy (full member in 1783). The first picture composed under the influence of his classical ideas was *Belisarius* (1780). He was made court painter to Louis XVI, and in 1784 painted for him the *Oath of the Horatii*, as well as a number of other paintings on subjects from ancient legend and myth. He entered heartily into the Revolution, was elected to the Convention in 1792, was associated with Robespierre, and voted for the death of the king. After Robespierre's downfall he was imprisoned for seven months. After his release he painted the *Rape of the Sabines* and *Leonidas at Thermopylae*. Napoleon made him court painter, and for Napoleon he painted the *Coronation* and *Napoleon on Horseback*. With the return of the Bourbons, he was exiled to Brussels, where he painted, again in the classical vein, until his death.

David, Pierre Jean. [Called **David d'Angers.**] b. at Angers, France, March 12, 1789; d. at Paris, Jan. 5, 1856. French sculptor. He executed works for the Pantheon at Paris.

David (dā′vid), Sir **Tannatt William Edgeworth.** b. near Cardiff, Wales, Jan. 28, 1858; d. at Sydney, Australia, Aug. 28, 1934. Australian geologist, university professor, and antarctic explorer. He was educated at Oxford (B.A., 1880; D.Sc., 1910). He was an assistant geological surveyor in New South Wales (1882–90) and held the chair of geology and physical geography at the University of Sydney (1890–1924). He accompanied (1907–08) the British explorer Sir Ernest Henry Shackleton to the Antarctic, and journeyed to the magnetic pole. As a geologist with the army in France in World War I, he held the rank of lieutenant colonel. He was working on the geology of Australia at the time of his death. His classic work, *New Geological Map of Australia with Explanatory Notes*, was published in 1932.

David (dä.vēd), **Toussaint Bernard.** See **Émeric-David, Toussaint Bernard.**

David and Bethsabe (dā′vid; beth.sä′bẹ). Tragedy by George Peele (1556–96) from the Old Testament, almost entirely in blank verse.

David Copperfield (dā′vid kop′ėr.fēld). Novel (1850) by Charles Dickens. It was originally published in serial form in monthly parts from May, 1849 to November, 1850. It does not have one plot, but, like Shakespeare's plays, many, and it has a staggering number of characters, both major and minor, which is typical of Dickens. In general it tells the story of the life, adventures, hardships, failures, and the final success and happiness of its hero. It shows us David as a child ("I Am Born" is the title of chapter one), growing up and going to school, struggling to make a living, as a young man trying to become an author, and, in the end, as a man, still young, who is a happy husband and a successful writer. Some of the characters in the huge portrait gallery are Clara Copperfield, a widow and David's mother; Edward Murdstone, his brutal stepfather; the members of the Peggotty family: Clara Peggotty (usually called by her last name), David's nurse, Dan'l Peggotty, a Yarmouth fisherman, Ham Peggotty, Dan'l's nephew, and Little Em'ly, Ham's cousin and engaged to him; Barkis (remembered for his message "Barkis is willin' "), Peggotty's husband; James Steerforth, David's schoolfellow, a handsome villain who seduces Em'ly and later dies in a shipwreck, although Ham tries to save him: Uriah Heep, an odious villain, a thief and a forger whose name has become a synonym for disgusting hypocrisy; Miss Betsy Trotwood, David's aunt and later his guardian; Mr. Dick, a harmless lunatic who is obsessed by the head of Charles I; Dora Spenlow, a silly creature, David's "child-wife," as he calls her; Agnes Wickfield, as lovely as Dora but more mature, his second wife; Mrs. Gummidge, a complaining widow; Miss Mowcher, a midget; Creakle, a tyrannical teacher; Tommy Traddles, David's friend, a good-natured plodder who finally becomes a barrister; and the immortal Wilkins Micawber, an incurable optimist who is always waiting for "something to turn up." The full title of the novel is *The Personal History, Experience and Observation of David Copperfield the Younger, of Blunderstone Rookery, Which He Never Meant to be Published On Any Account.* It is in 64 chapters, was illustrated by the famous "Phiz," and was Dickens's seventh novel. Of all his works, it was his favorite. "I like this the best," he tells us in his preface. "It will be easily believed that I am a fond parent to every child of my fancy, and that no one can ever love that family as dearly as I love them. But, like many fond parents, I have in my heart of hearts a favorite child. And his name is DAVID COPPERFIELD." An artist's estimate of his own work rarely coincides with general or popular opinion, but *David Copperfield* has long been considered one of his best works and one of the great triumphs of English fiction. Dickens's partiality may stem from the fact that the novel is largely autobiographical.

David Daw (dô), **Sir.** See **Daw, Sir David.**

Davideis (dạ.vid′ẹ.is). Epic poem by Abraham Cowley, on the subject of David, king of the Hebrews, published in 1656. The poem is incomplete.

David Elginbrod (dā′vid el′gin.brod). Novel by George Macdonald, published in 1863.

David Garrick (gar′ik). Play translated by T. W. Robertson from a French play, *Sullivan*, in 1864.

David Gellatley (gel′ạt.li). See **Gellatley, David.**

David Grieve (grēv). Novel by Mrs. Humphry Ward, published in 1892.

David Harum (hãr′um). Novel by Edward Noyes Westcott, published in 1898. The scene is laid in the central New York town of Homeville. The book won wide popularity through the shrewdness, humor, and homely philosophy displayed by its principal character, an old horse-trading country banker for whom it is named, and sold 400,000 copies in two years.

Davidov (dä.vē′dọf), **Charles** (or **Karl**). b. at Kuldiga, in Courland (now part of Latvia), March 17, 1838; d. at Moscow, Feb. 25, 1889. Russian cellist. He studied with Schmidt, Schuberth, and Grützmacher, and first appeared at the Gewandhaus, Leipzig, Dec. 15, 1859, where he became solo cellist of the orchestra. He also became a teacher in the Conservatory. After several concert tours he settled at St. Petersburg as solo cellist of the imperial orchestra, teacher in the Conservatory (1862), and later its director (1876–87). His compositions include a symphonic poem and an orchestral suite, chamber music, four concertos, and many solo pieces for his instrument. His method for the cello is widely known.

Davidović (dä.vē′dô.vēch), **Ljubomir.** b. at Vlaška, in Serbia, 1863; d. 1940. Serbian politician, leader of the Democratic Party. He was minister of education (1904–05, 1914–18) and prime minister (1919–20, 1924).

Davids (dā′vidz), **Thomas William Rhys.** b. at Colchester, England, May 12, 1843; d. Dec. 27, 1922. English lawyer and Orientalist. He studied at the University of Breslau, was appointed writer in the Ceylon civil service in 1866, was admitted to the bar in 1877, and became editor of the journal of the Pali Text Society in 1883, professor of Pali and Buddhist literature in University College, London, in 1882, and professor of comparative religion at Manchester in 1904. He was the author of *On the Ancient Coins and Measures of Ceylon* (1874), *Buddhism: being a Sketch of the Life and Teachings of Gautama the Buddha* (1877), and others.

Davidsbündler (dä′fēts.bün.dlėr). Imaginary group of anti-Philistines, invented by Robert Schumann and introduced into his articles for the *Neue Zeitschrift für Musik.* Mainly represented by the imaginary characters Eusebius and Florestan, the society also included figures from contemporary life such as Clara Schumann, Mendelssohn, Banck, and Wedel.

Davidson (dā′vid.sọn), **Donald** (**Grady**). b. at Campbellsville, Tenn., Aug. 18, 1893—. American writer. He has served as a member (1920 *et seq.*) of the English department, as professor from 1937, at Vanderbilt University, and was a founder (1922) of the periodical *The Fugitive.* He supported regionalism and agrarianism in contributions to *I'll Take My Stand, Who Owns America?,* and *Culture in the South,* and published the volume of verse *An Outland Piper* (1924), the blank-verse poem *The Tall Men* (1927), and *Lee in the Mountains* (1938). His other books include *The Attack on Leviathan* (1938) and *The Tennessee* (1946) in the Rivers of America series.

Davidson, George. b. at Nottingham, England, May 9, 1825; d. 1911. American geographer and astronomer. Brought to the U.S. in childhood, he was reared in Pennsylvania, and attended the Central High School at Philadelphia, where he attracted the notice of Alexander Dallas Bache, its principal. When Bache established the first magnetic observatory in this country, at Girard College, he appointed young Davidson an observer, and when in 1845 Bache became superintendent of the U.S. Coast Survey, he made Davidson his secretary. The association with that branch of the government, thus begun, ended only with his retirement in 1895. In 1850 he was sent to the Pacific coast to supervise the preparation of charts of the coastal waters, and the results of his work were published under the title of *The Pacific Coast Pilot.* In the period 1860–66 he was engaged in charting the Philadelphia area for military purposes; in 1867 he was employed in the tropics, making a preliminary survey of the Isthmus of Darien (Panama) in connection with plans for a canal in that region, and in the Arctic, investigating the resources of Alaska. He directed the work of the U.S. Coast Survey in the Pacific (1867–87), meanwhile heading expeditions to Japan in 1874 and to New Mexico in 1882 to observe the transit of Venus, building the first Pacific coast observatory in 1879, and conducting surveys of the California mountain ranges. His interest in astronomy continued throughout his life, and whenever a phenomenon such as a solar eclipse or a transit of Mercury occurred, he was among the observers. Among his publications were studies of stars and meteors. Another of his interests was irrigation, which he studied in the West and in the Orient. He served on many official bodies, and for some years was president of the California Academy of Sciences, and also headed the Geographical Society of the Pacific. He was the author of *The Tracks and Landfalls of Bering and Chirikof* (1901), *The Discovery of San Francisco Bay* (1907), and *Francis Drake on the Northwest Coast* (1908).

Davidson, Israel. [Original name, **Israel Movshovitz.**] b. at Yanova, Lithuania, May 27, 1870; d. at Great Neck, Long Island, N.Y., June 27, 1939. Hebrew scholar. He studied at the yeshivas at Grodno and Slobodka, came to the U.S. in 1888, graduated (1895) from the College of the City of New York, and received the Ph.D. (1902) from Columbia University. He was appointed (1905) instructor at the Jewish Theological Seminary of America, where he served (1916–39) as professor of medieval Hebrew literature. He was visiting professor (1926) at the Hebrew University, Jerusalem. He compiled the *Otzar Hashirah Vehapiyut* (4 vols., 1924–33), a thesaurus of medieval Hebrew poetry, and was the author of *The Parody in Jewish Literature* (1907).

Davidson, Jo. b. at New York, March 30, 1883; d. at Bercheron, France, Jan. 2, 1952. American sculptor, best known for his portrait busts of international celebrities. He studied at the Art Students League of New York and received his first commission in 1905. He went to Europe (1907) and there became interested in the effect of light on sculpture. He first exhibited at the Paris Salon of 1908, and his work was exhibited at New York in 1910. After that, his work was shown repeatedly at New York, Paris, and London. Many honors were accorded him, including designation as an associate of the National Academy of Design and a chevalier of the Legion of Honor. He was considered to be one of the world's foremost sculptors of his time, his work having unique poetic and rhythmic qualities. Some of his better-known works are *Earth, Russian Dancer, Eve, Dawn, Night, Beyond, A Study in Repose,* and busts of Anatole France, Gertrude Stein, Joseph Conrad, Marshal Foch, Woodrow Wilson, Franklin D. Roosevelt, Will Rogers, General Pershing, Lloyd George, Clemenceau, Paderewski, Masaryk, and many others. He wrote the autobiography *Between Sittings* (1951).

Davidson, John. b. at Barrhead, Scotland, April 11, 1857; d. by suicide at Penzance, Cornwall, England, March 23, 1909. English poet, dramatist, novelist, and essayist. He was educated at Greenock Academy, and attended (1876–77) Edinburgh University. He engaged in teaching (1877–89) before going (1890) to London, where he made a living as a ghost writer and by translating French novels. He enjoyed a brief period (1906 *et seq.*) of improved personal circumstances as a result of a government pension of 100 pounds a year. He was the author of books of verse, including *The North Wall* (1885), *In a Music Hall* (1891), *Fleet Street Eclogues* (1893; 2nd series, 1896), *Ballads and Songs* (1894), *St. George's Day* (1895), *New Ballads* (1897), *The Last Ballad* (1899), *Holiday* (1906), and *Fleet Street and Other Poems* (1909). He also wrote the plays *Bruce* (1886), *Smith* (1888), *An Unhistorical Pastoral, A Romantic Farce,* and *Scaramouch in Naxos* (all 1889), *Godfrida* (1898), and *The Knight of the Maypole* (1903); the novels *Perfervid* (1890), *Laura Ruthven's Widowhood* (1892), *Baptist Lake* (1894), *Wonderful Mission of Earl Lavender* (1895), and *Miss Armstrong's and Other Circumstances* (1896); *The Triumph of Mammon* (1907) and *Mammon and His Message* (1909), philosophical works; and a series of five *Testaments* in which he expounded his philosophy of life, *The Testament of a Vivisector* and *The Testament of a Man Forbid* (both 1901), *The Testament of an Empire-Builder* (1902), *The Testament of a Prime Minister* (1904), and *The Testament of John Davidson* (1908). He translated François Coppée's *For the Crown* (1890). Among his poems are *A Ballad of Hell, Ballad of a Nun, Imagination, The Outcast,* and *The Unknown.*

Davidson, Lucretia Maria. b. at Plattsburg, N.Y., Sept. 27, 1808; d. there, Aug. 27, 1825. American poet; sister of Margaret Miller Davidson. She was the author of *Amir Khan and other poems* (1829).

Davidson, Margaret Miller. b. at Plattsburg, N.Y., March 26, 1823; d. at Saratoga, N.Y., Nov. 25, 1838. American poet; sister of Lucretia Maria Davidson. The works of the two sisters were published in 1850.

Davidson, Mount. Highest summit of the Prince Albert Mountains in Antarctica, lying NW of Granite Harbor, Victoria Land, in ab. 76°46′ S., 162°08′ E. Elevation, ab. 8,100 ft.

Davidson, Randall Thomas. [Title, 1st Baron **Davidson.**] b. April 7, 1848; d. May 25, 1930. English prelate. He was educated at Harrow and at Trinity College, Oxford, and was chaplain and private secretary to archbishop Tait (1877–82) and to archbishop Benson (1882–83), dean of Windsor and domestic chaplain to Queen Victoria (1883–91), bishop of Rochester (1891–95) and of Winchester (1895–1903), and consecrated archbishop of Canterbury in 1903. Among his publications are *Life of Archbishop Tait* (1891; with W. Behman) and *The Christian Opportunity* (1904).

Davidson, Samuel. b. near Ballymena, Ireland, 1807; d. April 1, 1898. English Biblical scholar, author of *Introduction to the New Testament* (1848–51).

Davidson, Thomas. b. at Edinburgh, May 17, 1817; d. 1885. English paleontologist. He was educated in France, Italy, and Switzerland and also studied painting for use in illustrating his monograph on British fossil brachiopods (1850–70) and later supplements.

Davidson, Thomas. b. in Aberdeenshire, Scotland, Oct. 25, 1840; d. at New York, Sept. 14, 1900. Scottish-American philosopher, teacher, and historian of education. He was educated at King's College, Aberdeen, winning high honors in classics, and taught school at Aberdeen, Tunbridge Wells, Wimbledon, in Canada, at Boston, St. Louis (where he was editor of the *Western Educational Review*), and New York, where he finally settled and founded the Breadwinners' College for men and women. He traveled (1878–84) in Greece and Italy. During his stay in Canada he founded, after a series of conferences at London in 1883, the Fellowship of the New Life, which later gave rise to the Fabian Society. He was the author of *The Parthenon Frieze and Other Essays* (1882), *The Place of Art in Education* (1886), *Aristotle and the Ancient Educational Ideals* (1892), *The Education of the Greek People and Its Influence on Civilization* (1894), *Rousseau and Education According to Nature* (1898), *A History of Education* (1900), and *The Education of the Wage-Earner* (1905).

Davidson, William Lee. b. in Lancaster County, Pa., 1746; killed at Cowan's Ford, Mecklenburg County, N.C., Feb. 1, 1781. American brigadier general in the Revolutionary War. He was detached by General Greene to interrupt the passage of Cornwallis across the Catawba, on Jan. 31, 1781, and fell in the engagement on the following day.

Davie (dā′vi), **William Richardson.** b. at Egremont, Cumberland, England, June 20, 1756; d. Nov. 29, 1820. American Revolutionary soldier, lawyer, and governor (1798–99) of North Carolina. After service in the war, from which he emerged a colonel, he rode the circuits of North Carolina as a lawyer (1782 *et seq.*) and served (1786–98) in the state legislature, where he was influential in the revision and codification of the laws, the sending of representatives to the Annapolis and Philadelphia constitutional conventions, the cession of Tennessee to the Union, and the fixing of state boundaries. One of the chief founders of the University of North Carolina, he was also appointed brigadier general during hostilities with the French, peace commissioner (1799) to France, and negotiator of the Tuscarora treaty (1802).

Davies (dā′vēz), **Arthur Bowen.** b. at Utica, N.Y., Sept. 26, 1862; d. at Florence, Italy, Oct. 24, 1928. American painter, noted for his dreamlike landscapes with figures. He studied at the Art Institute of Chicago, the Gotham Art Students, and the Art Students League of New York, and was a contributor of illustrations (c1888–91) to *Saint Nicholas.* Aided by the art dealer William Macbeth, he established (c1894) a New York studio. With the help of the merchant and art collector Benjamin Altman he went to Europe, where he produced his first characteristic work. Later, in canvases drawing upon mythological themes, he produced such paintings as *The Girdle of Ares* and *Leda and the Dioscuri.* As president of the Society of Independent Artists, he participated in conducting the famous Armory Show (1913) at New York. He also executed murals, tapestry designs, and small sculpture. He is represented in many private collections.

Davies (dā′vēz, -vis), **Ben.** [Full name, **Benjamin Grey Davies.**] b. at Pontardawe, Glamorganshire, Wales, Jan. 6, 1858; d. at Bath, England, March 28, 1943. Welsh operatic and concert tenor. He attended (1878–80) the Royal Academy of Music, sang (1893) at the Chicago World's Fair on his first visit to the U.S., and participated (1926) in the Handel Festival in England.

Davies (dā′vēz), **Charles.** b. at Washington, Litchfield, County, Conn., Jan. 22, 1798; d. at Fishkill Landing (now part of Beacon), N.Y., Sept. 18, 1876. American mathematician, author of a series of mathematical textbooks. He was professor at Columbia College from 1857 to 1865.

Davies (dā′vēz, -vis), **David.** [Title, 1st Baron **Davies of Llandinam.**] b. at Llandinam, Wales, 1880; d. there, 1944. Welsh coal-mine operator, politician, and author. Educated at Cambridge, he was a member of Parliament (1906–29) from Montgomeryshire, an officer (1914–16) in the Royal Welsh Fusiliers during World War I, and private secretary (1916–29) to Lloyd George. He founded the New Commonwealth Society for the establishment of a world police force, was president of the National Library of Wales and of University College at Aberystwyth, and was active in the field of public health. He was the author of *The Problem of the Twentieth Century* (1932), *Suicide or Sanity* (1932), and *Nearing the Abyss* (1936).

Davies, Sir **Henry Walford.** b. at Oswestry, Shropshire, England, Sept. 6, 1869; d. near Bristol, England, March 11, 1941. English organist and composer. He was appointed (1917) musical director to the Royal Air Force, and served as chairman (1923 *et seq.*) of the National Council of Music; he was knighted in 1922. He was also organist (1927 *et seq.*) at Saint George's Chapel, Windsor, and succeeded (1934) Sir Edward Elgar as master of the king's music. His works include *The Temple* (1902), *Peter Pan Suite* (1909), *Festal Overture* (1910), *Heaven's Gate* (1916), and *Memorial Suite* (1923).

Davies, Hubert Henry. b. 1876; d. 1917. English dramatist.

Davies, Ivor Novello. Original name of **Novello, Ivor.**

Davies of Hereford (her′e̤.fo̤rd), **John.** b. at Hereford, England, c1565; d. at London, 1618. English writing-master and poet. He was said to be an accomplished penman, and some specimens of his work are preserved in *The Writing Schoolemaster or the Anatomy of Faire Writing* (published c1631 after his death). Among his works are *Mirum in Modum* (1602), *Microcosmos* (1603), *The Wittes Pilgrimage* (1605), *The Scourge of Folly* (1610 or 1611), and *Wit's Bedlam* (1617).

Davies, Sir **John.** b. at Tisbury, Wiltshire, England, in April, 1569; d. Dec. 8, 1626. English jurist and poet. He was called to the bar in 1595, disbarred in 1598, and readmitted in 1601. In that year he was returned to Parliament for Corfe Castle. In 1603 he was made solicitor general for Ireland, and in 1606 succeeded to the position of attorney general for Ireland. In 1614, and again in 1621, he was member of Parliament for Newcastle-under-Lyme. For the last ten years of his life he was a sergeant-at-law in England. He was made chief justice in 1626, but died before taking possession of the office. Among his works are *Orchestra* (on dancing, 1596), and *Hymns to Astraea* (1599), acrostics to Queen Elizabeth. A number of his epigrams, printed in the same volume as Christopher Marlowe's translation of Ovid's *Elegies,* were ordered burned in 1599 during the censorship campaign of John Whitgift, archbishop of Canterbury. *Nosce Teipsum* (1599), a series of rhyming decasyllabic quatrains, on the soul and its immortal nature, was a great success and remains one of the best didactic poetical works in English.

Davies (dā′vēz), **Joseph Edward.** b. at Watertown, Wis., Nov. 29, 1876—. American lawyer and diplomat. He was U.S. commissioner of corporations (1913–15), chairman (1915–16) and vice-chairman (1916–18) of the Federal Trade Commission. He served as U.S. ambassador to Russia (1936–38) and Belgium (1938–39), and as U.S. minister (1938–39) to Luxembourg. He acted as special adviser at the Berlin (Potsdam) Conference (1945). His book *Mission to Moscow* (1941) helped overcome some of the U.S. feeling of strangeness at being allied with the U.S.S.R. in World War II.

Davies (dā′vēz, -vis), **Julia Augusta.** See **Webster, Augusta.**

Davies, Sir **Louis Henry.** b. at Charlottetown, Prince Edward Island, Canada, May 4, 1845; d. at Ottawa, May 1, 1924. Canadian statesman and jurist. After holding office as prime minister and attorney general of Prince Edward Island (1876–79), he sat in the Dominion House of Commons (1882–1901) as a member of the Liberal Party, and under the premiership of Sir Wilfrid Laurier was minister of marine and fisheries (1896–1901). He was knighted in 1897. In 1901 he was named a justice of the Supreme Court of Canada, and in 1918 became chief justice of that tribunal.

Davies, Mary. b. at London, Feb. 17, 1855; d. at Hampstead, London, June 22, 1930. Welsh mezzo-soprano. She studied at the Royal Academy of Music and was president of the Welsh Folk Musical Society.

Leading soprano at London ballad concerts for many years, she received (1916) an honorary degree of doctor of music from the University of Wales.

Davies, Peter. Young clerk in a second-hand London bookshop, in Gilbert Cannan's autobiographical novel *Peter Homunculus* (1909).

Davies, Richard. b. at Plas y Person, Wales, c1505; d. in Wales, Nov. 7, 1581. Welsh clergyman, translator of the New Testament into Welsh. He was vicar of Burnham in 1550 and in 1555 fled to Frankfort to join the Protestants there. Returning when Elizabeth came to the throne, he was later (1561) made bishop of St. David's, was adviser to Archbishop Parker and to Cecil on Welsh affairs, and was a friend of the earl of Essex, with whom he founded Carmarthen grammar school (1576). With William Salisbury, or Salesbury, he translated the New Testament into Welsh (1567); he was responsible for Deuteronomy and 2 Samuel in the revision of the "Great Bible" known as the "Bishops' Bible" (1568).

Davies (dā'vēz), **Samuel.** b. in New Castle County, Del., Nov. 3, 1723; d. at Princeton, N.J., Feb. 4, 1761. American Presbyterian clergyman, president of the College of New Jersey (later Princeton University) from 1759 to 1761.

Davies (dā'vēz, -vis), **Sarah Emily.** b. at Southampton, England, April 22, 1830; d. at Hampstead, London, July 13, 1921. English feminist, educator, and author of works on education. She went in 1860 to London, where she founded (1866) the London Schoolmistresses' Association. She was also active in founding (1869) a college for women at Hitchin, which later became (1873) Girton College, Cambridge, of which she was mistress (1873–75) and secretary (1882–1904). She was instrumental in gaining the admission of Elizabeth Garrett Anderson to medical school, and in drawing up a petition for women's suffrage which John Stuart Mill presented to Parliament on June 7, 1866. Her works include *Application of Funds to the Education of Girls* (1865), *Higher Education of Women* (1866), and *Thoughts on Some Questions Relating to Women: 1860–1908* (1910).

Davies, Thomas. b. c1712; d. at London, May 5, 1785. English bookseller. He tried acting from time to time, but without success. In 1763 he introduced Boswell to Samuel Johnson. He republished a number of old authors, including William Browne, Sir John Davies, Lillo, and Massinger. In 1785 he published his *Dramatic Miscellanies*.

Davies, William Henry. b. at Newport, Monmouthshire, England, April 20, 1871; d. at Nailsworth, Gloucestershire, England, Sept. 26, 1940. English tramp, peddler, poet, novelist, dramatist, and anthologist. After losing his right leg while stealing a ride on a train in Canada, he decided to return to England and to take up literature as an occupation. He was the author of a considerable body of work in both prose and poetry; among his writings are *The Soul's Destroyer* (1907), *Nature Poems* (1908), *Songs of Joy* (1911), *Foliage* (1913), *Raptures* (1918), *Song of Life* (1920), *Hour of Magic* (1922), *Secrets* (1924), *Poet's Alphabet* (1925), *Song of Love* (1926), *Poet's Calendar* (1927), and *49 Poems* (1928), books of poetry; *A Weak Woman* (1911), *Adventures of Johnny Walker, Tramp* (1926), and *Dancing Mad* (1927), prose fiction; *Autobiography of a Supertramp* (1908), *Beggars* (1909), *Nature* (1913), *Later Days* (1925), *My Birds* and *My Garden* (both 1933), autobiography and essays; and *A Tramp's Opera in Three Acts* (1923). In 1922 and 1930 he edited two poetry anthologies, *Shorter Lyrics of the 20th Century* and *Jewels of Song*. Some of his best poems are *Days Too Short*, *The Moon*, *The Two Stars*, *Jenny Wren*, *The Hermit*, *When Yon Full Moon*, and *Sheep*.

Daviess (dā'vis), **Joseph Hamilton.** See **Daveiss, Joseph Hamilton.**

Dávila (dä'ʙē.lä), **Alonzo.** See **Ávila, Alonzo de.**

Dávila, Carlos Guillermo. [Full name, **Carlos Guillermo Dávila Espinoza.**] b. at Los Ángeles, Bío-Bío, Chile, Sept. 15, 1887—. Chilean newspaper editor and politician. Employed (1912–16) on the staff of *El Mercurio*, he was afterward editor (1917–27) of *La Nación* and editor (1931–32) of *Hoy*. He served from 1927 to 1931 as ambassador to the U.S. He was a member of the revolutionary junta which deposed (1932) President Montero and was provisional president (June-September, 1932) of Chile. He favored socialism, and was author of the "Dávila Plan" creating the Inter-American Development Commission.

Davila (dä'vē.lä), **Enrico Caterino.** b. near Padua, Italy, Oct. 30, 1576; killed near Verona, Italy, Aug. 8, 1631. Italian soldier and historian. His ancestors, from 1464, bore the title of Constable of Cyprus, and from this island his father was driven when it was captured by the Turks. Davila, when seven years of age, was taken to France, became a page of Catherine de Médicis, and later fought in the civil wars until the peace of 1598. He was appointed governor of Crema, in Lombardy, in 1598, and on his way to that place in 1631 was assassinated by a man with whom he had had a dispute about post horses. His chief work is *Storia delle guerre civili di Francia* (1630; Eng. trans., *History of the French Civil Wars*, 1647).

Dávila (dä'ʙē.lä), **Gil González.** See **González Dávila, Gil.**

Dávila, Pedrarias. See **Pedrarias.**

Dávila y Padilla (ē pä.ᴛʜē'lyä), **Agustín.** [Called **"Chronicler of the Indies."**] b. at Mexico City, 1562; d. at Santo Domingo (now Ciudad Trujillo), 1604. Mexican prelate and historian. He was prior of the Dominican convent at Puebla de los Angeles, Mexico, and a celebrated lecturer on theology. From 1599 until his death he was bishop of Santo Domingo. His principal work, *Historia de la fondación de la provincia de Santiago de Méjico de la Orden de Predicadores*, is a history of his order in Mexico and Florida, with much of general interest. First published at Madrid in 1596, it was republished at Valladolid in 1634 with the title *Varia historia de la Nueva España y Florida*.

Davin (dȧ.vaṅ), **Félix.** Pseudonym used by Balzac in the introduction to the *Études philosophiques*.

da Vinci (dä vēn'chē), **Leonardo** (or **Lionardo**). See **Vinci, Leonardo** (or **Lionardo**) **da.**

Davis (dā'vis). City in N central California, in Yolo County, near Sacramento: seat of a branch of the University of California College of Agriculture. In the decade between the last two U.S. censuses its population more than doubled. 1,672 (1940), 3,554 (1950).

Davis, Alexander Jackson. b. at New York, July 24, 1803; d. at Llewellyn Park, West Orange, N.J., Jan. 14, 1892. American architect. His drawings and lithographs of outstanding buildings in New York and in New England led to a partnership with Ithiel Town of New Haven, Conn., who at that time established an office at New York. Town and Davis designed many much-admired buildings, including the Customs House (later the Subtreasury) at New York, the Patent Office at Washington, and the state capitols of Ohio, Indiana, and Illinois. In collaboration with another architect, Davis also had a hand in designing the state capitol of North Carolina. After 1843 Davis practiced individually, and it is probably true that, as he asserted late in life, he was the designer of more structures (public edifices, commercial buildings, churches, and homes) than any other American architect up to that time. Although he was a great exponent of the classic style, and also skilled in Gothic design, he was forward-looking, an early experimenter with structural iron, and he left drawings of a planned structure, which was never built, calling for use of glass and metal in a manner that would have been considered modernistic 50 years later.

Davis, Benjamin Oliver. b. at Washington, D.C., July 1, 1877—. American cavalry officer who was the first Negro general officer in the U.S. army. He served (1898–99) as lieutenant of volunteers, enlisted (1899) in a regular army cavalry unit as a private, was commissioned (1901) a lieutenant in the cavalry, and was military attaché (1911–12) at Monrovia, Liberia. He also served (1905–09, 1915–17, 1929–30, 1937–38) as professor of military science at Wilberforce University and as professor of military science and tactics (1920–24, 1931–37) at Tuskegee Institute. He was appointed colonel (1930) and brigadier general (1940), assistant (1941) to the inspector general of the army, adviser (1942) to the commanding general of the European theater of operations on problems involving Negro military personnel, special assistant (1944) to the commanding general of the communications zone of the European theater, and special assistant to the secretary of the army. In 1945 he was awarded the Distinguished Service medal, and in 1948 he retired from active military service.

Davis, Bette. [Full name, **Ruth Elizabeth Davis.**] b. at Lowell, Mass., April 5, 1908—. American actress. After a career on the stage beginning in 1925, she went to Hollywood to make motion pictures. Her first great success was in the role of Mildred in *Of Human Bondage* (1934), playing opposite Leslie Howard. Winner of two "Oscars" presented by the Motion Picture Academy of Arts and Sciences (for *Dangerous*, 1935, and *Jezebel*, 1938), Miss Davis has starred in many pictures, among them *The Petrified Forest, The Sisters, Dark Victory, Juarez, The Old Maid, The Little Foxes, All This and Heaven Too, The Letter, Watch on the Rhine*, and *All About Eve*. She returned to Broadway in 1952 to star in the revue *Two's Company*.

Davis, Charles Harold. b. at Amesbury, Mass., Jan. 7, 1856; d. Aug. 5, 1933. American landscape painter. He began his art studies at Boston, and afterward lived and studied in France and exhibited at the Paris Salon annually from 1880 through 1890. After returning to the U.S. he became a celebrant in color of the rich beauties of American landscape, especially of the eastern mountains and the blue skies and white clouds over them. Examples of his work are to be seen in the Metropolitan Museum of Art and the Union League Club at New York, the Museum of Fine Arts at Boston, the Pennsylvania Academy of the Fine Arts at Philadelphia, the Corcoran Gallery and the National Gallery at Washington, and in galleries and museums at Pittsburgh, St. Louis, Minneapolis, Worcester, Providence, and other American cities.

Davis, Charles Henry. b. at Boston, Jan. 16, 1807; d. at Washington, D.C., Feb. 18, 1877. American naval officer. He entered the navy in 1823, obtained the rank of commander in 1854, and served as chief of staff and captain of the fleet in the expedition under Dupont which captured Port Royal, S.C., in 1861. Having in the meantime been placed in command of the Mississippi gunboat flotilla, he gained a victory over a Confederate fleet off Fort Pillow (May 10, 1862) and another (June 6, 1862) before Memphis, whose surrounder he received on the same day. He was promoted to the rank of rear admiral on Feb. 7, 1863. He wrote *The Coast Survey of the United States* (1849) and *Narrative of the North Polar Expedition of the U.S.S. Polaris* (1876).

Davis, Charles Henry. b. at Cambridge, Mass., Aug. 28, 1845; d. Dec. 27, 1921. American naval officer, appointed rear admiral in 1904; son of Charles Henry Davis (1807–77). He was graduated from the U.S. Naval Academy in 1864, attained the rank of captain in 1898, was superintendent of the naval observatory from 1897 to 1902 (except April–Sept., 1898), and commanded the auxiliary cruiser *Dixie* during the Spanish-American War (1898). He served as division commander of the battleship squadron in 1904, 1905, and 1906, and was a member of the international commission which investigated, at Paris (1904–05), the attack of the Russian squadron under Rozhestvensky upon the British fishing fleet in the North Sea. He retired in August, 1907.

Davis, Chester Charles. b. near Linden, Dallas County, Iowa, Nov. 17, 1887—. American agricultural and financial administrator. A graduate (B.A., 1911) of Grinnell, he began his career as a journalist (1911–17) in South Dakota and Montana, editor and manager (1917–21) of the Montana *Farmer*, and an executive (1925–33) in agricultural organizations. He served as administrator (December, 1933–June, 1936) in the Agricultural Adjustment Administration, president (April, 1941–March, 1943) of the St. Louis Federal Reserve Bank, and U.S. Department of Agriculture administrator of food production and distribution (March–June, 1943).

Davis, Clyde Brion. b. at Unadilla, Neb., May 22, 1894—. American journalist and novelist. He served in the U.S. army in World War I, and between 1919 and 1937 was a reporter for various U.S. newspapers, including the San Francisco *Examiner* (1921–22), the Denver *News* (1922–29), and the Buffalo *Times* (1930–37). His novels include *The Anointed* (1937), *"The Great American Novel—"* (1938), *Nebraska Coast* (1939), *Sullivan* (1940), *Follow the Leader* (1942), *The Stars Incline* (1946), *Jeremy Bell* (1947), *Temper the Wind* (1948), *Playtime Is Over* (1949), and *The Age of Indiscretion* (1950). He is also the author of *The Arkansas* (1940), in the Rivers of America series.

Davis, Cushman Kellogg. b. at Henderson, N.Y., June 16, 1838; d. at St. Paul, Minn., Nov. 27, 1900. American Republican politician. He was graduated from the University of Michigan in 1857, was admitted to the bar in 1859, and served in the Union army (1861–64) in the Civil War, rising to the rank of assistant adjutant general. He was elected to the Minnesota legislature in 1867, served as district attorney for Minnesota (1868–73) and as governor of Minnesota (1874–75), and was elected U.S. senator in 1887, in 1893, and in 1899. In August, 1898, he was appointed a member of the Spanish-American Peace Commission. He published *The Law in Shakespeare* (1884).

Davis, David. b. in Cecil County, Md., March 9, 1815; d. at Bloomington, Ill., June 26, 1886. American statesman and jurist. He was associate justice of the U.S. Supreme Court (1862–77), U.S. senator from Illinois (1877–83), and acting vice-president (1881–83).

Davis, Dwight Filley. b. at St. Louis, Mo., July 5, 1879; d. at Washington, D.C., Nov. 28, 1945. American public official who served (1925–29) as U.S. secretary of war. He was educated at Harvard and at Washington University and served in World War I, being appointed captain (May, 1917), major (November, 1917), and lieutenant colonel (October, 1918) and awarded (1923) the Distinguished Service Cross for bravery under fire. After the war he was director (1921–23) of the War Finance Corporation and governor general (1929–32) of the Philippines. In 1942 he was appointed director general of the U.S. Army Specialist Corps, and served in World War II in an advisory capacity with the Army Service Forces. He is also known as a national tennis doubles champion (1899, 1900, 1901), with Holcombe Ward, and as the donor (1900) of the Davis Cup, the international lawn tennis trophy which now denotes world match-play championship.

Davis, Edwin Hamilton. b. in Ross County, Ohio, Jan. 22, 1811; d. at New York, May 15, 1888. American physician and archaeologist. His works include *Monuments of the Mississippi Valley* (in *Smithsonian Contributions to Knowledge*, 1858), and others.

Davis, Elmer (Holmes). b. at Aurora, Ind., Jan. 13, 1890—. American journalist, writer, and radio commentator. He was a Rhodes scholar (1912–14) at Oxford, and has been a staff member (1914–24) of the New York *Times*, news analyst for the Columbia Broadcasting System (1939–42) and American Broadcasting Company (1945 *et seq.*), and director (1942–45) of the U.S. Office of War Information. He is the author of *History of the New York Times* (1921), *Times Have Changed* (1923), *Not to Mention the War* (1940), and other books.

Davis, Garret. b. at Mount Stirling, Ky., Sept. 10, 1801; d. at Paris, Ky., Sept. 22, 1872. American politician, U.S. senator from Kentucky from 1861 to 1872.

Davis, George Breckinridge. b. at Ware, Mass., Feb. 13, 1847; d. at Washington, D.C., Dec. 15, 1914. American soldier and jurist, judge advocate general of the U.S. army (1901–11). He published several works upon international and military law.

Davis, George Whitefield. b. at Thompson, Conn., July 26, 1839; d. July 12, 1918. American engineer, army officer, and administrator. After service in the Union army during the Civil War, he was commissioned captain (1867) in the regular army. He served in the Spanish-American War, was military governor (1899–1900) of Puerto Rico and commander (1902–03) of the Philippine division, and retired (1903) as a major general. Appointed (1904) a member of the Isthmian Canal Commission, he served as governor (1904–05) of the Canal Zone, organizing the new government. As chief of the planning board of engineers, he recommended the building of the sea-level canal.

Davis, Harold Lenoir. b. at Yoncalla, Ore., Oct. 18, 1896—. American writer. He worked as a typesetter, sheep and cattle rancher, deputy sheriff, deputy assessor, surveyor, newspaper editor, and radio singer, and served in World War I. In 1919, he received the Levison poetry prize from *Poetry Magazine*. He was (1932) recipient of a Guggenheim fellowship to write in Mexico. He was awarded a Pulitzer prize for his novel *Honey in the Horn* (1935), also a Harper prize winner. His other books include the collection of verse *Proud Riders* (1942), and the novels *Harp of a Thousand Strings* (1947) and *Winds of Morning* (1952).

Davis, Henry. b. at East Hampton, N.Y., Sept. 15, 1771; d. at Clinton, N.Y., March 8, 1852. American clergyman and educator, president of Middlebury College from 1809 to 1817 and of Hamilton College from 1817 to 1833.

Davis, Henry Gassaway. b. at Woodstock, Md., Nov. 16, 1823; d. at Washington, D.C., March 11, 1916. American businessman and politician. He amassed a fortune from railroads, lumbering, and coal fields in the upper Potomac region. Elected (1871, 1877) senator from West Virginia, he served as chairman of the Appropriations Committee for two years and as a member of a special committee on transportation routes to the seaboard. He was Democratic candidate (1904) for vice-president.

Davis, Henry Gassett. b. at Trenton, Me., Nov. 4, 1807; d. at Everett, Mass., Nov. 18, 1896. American pioneer in orthopedic surgery, founder of the so-called traction school. He was the author of *Conservative Surgery, as Exhibited in Remedying some of the Mechanical Causes that Operate Injuriously both in Health and Disease* (1867).

Davis, Henry William Banks. b. at Finchley, England, Aug. 26, 1833; d. at Glaslyn, England, 1914. English painter of landscapes and animals whose works were widely reproduced and distributed. He studied at the Royal Academy; between 1853 and 1893 he exhibited there regularly, and in 1877 he became a member. Other exhibitions of his work were held at Vienna and Paris. His paintings are in museums at Bristol, Hamburg, Manchester, Melbourne, and Sheffield. Among his representative works are *Spring Ploughing, Picardy Sheep,* and *Moonrise, Praetorium at Neufchatel.*

Davis, Henry William Carless. b. at Ebley, England, Jan. 13, 1874; d. at Edinburgh, June 28, 1928. English historian and editor of the *Dictionary of National Biography,* one of the most distinguished scholars specializing in the history of the Middle Ages. He acted as director of the *Dictionary of National Biography* (1902–28), was professor of modern history at the University of Manchester (1921–25), and regius professor of modern history at Oxford (1925–28). He was the author of *England Under the Normans and Angevins* (1905), *Medieval Europe* (1911), *The Political Thought of Treitschke* (1914), and *The Age of Grey and Peel* (1930). He also served in the World Trade Intelligence Department (1915), the War Trade Advisory Committee (1916), the British delegation to the Paris conference (1918–19), the Unemployment Insurance Committee (1925), and, as acting director, the Department of Overseas Trade (1925). He was curator of the Bodleian Library (1925).

Davis, Henry Winter. b. at Annapolis, Md., Aug. 16, 1817; d. at Baltimore, Md., Dec. 30, 1865. American lawyer and politician, noted for his forthright support of the Union cause in Maryland and for the authorship of the Wade-Davis manifesto (1864). He studied law at the University of Virginia, commenced his law practice at Alexandria, Va., and moved (1849) to Baltimore, where he became active in the Whig party. Going to Congress in 1855, he soon became known as a leading figure in the Know-Nothing Party; in 1860, when he cast the deciding vote for a Republican speaker of the House, he became associated with that party for a time, but shortly afterward took a prominent part in organizing the Bell and Everett (Union) party in Maryland. He later emerged as an ardent supporter of the Union government, in opposition to the Maryland state administration which recognized the right of secession for the Southern states. He failed to be reëlected in 1861, but was chosen for Congress in 1863, becoming chairman of the Committee on Foreign Relations. He became an opponent of many of Lincoln's policies and an ally of the Radical Republicans, virtually ruling the House together with Thaddeus Stevens. He sponsored a bill on reconstruction that passed both houses of Congress in 1864 but was vetoed by Lincoln. In the noted Wade-Davis manifesto (1864), he attacked Lincoln's plan of reconstruction, favoring a radical and thoroughgoing scheme. However, he supported Lincoln in the campaign of 1864, in which he himself was defeated.

Davis, Herbert John. b. at Long Buckby, Northamptonshire, England, May 24, 1893—. American educator and authority on Jonathan Swift. Appointed (1937) professor of English at Cornell, he served there as department head from 1938 and as Goldwin Smith professor of English literature (1939–40). In 1940 he was named president of Smith College. He is the editor of *Complete Prose Works of Jonathan Swift* (14 vols., in progress since 1938); his writings include *Swift's View of Poetry* (1931), *Stella, A Gentlewoman of the 18th Century* (1942), and *The Satire of Jonathan Swift* (1945).

Davis, James Cox. b. at Keokuk, Iowa, Sept. 2, 1857; d. Aug. 31, 1937. American lawyer, specialist in railroad litigation. Admitted (1877) to the bar; mayor (1885–87) of Keokuk, Iowa. Appointed general Iowa attorney (1903) and general solicitor (1918) for the Chicago and North Western Railway Company. He was general counsel (1920) for the U.S. Railroad Administration.

Davis, James John. b. at Tredegar, South Wales, Oct. 27, 1873; d. at Tokoma Park, Md., Nov. 22, 1947. American politician. He came to the U.S. in 1881. He served as director general (1906 *et seq.*) of the Loyal Order of Moose, increasing its membership from 247 to more than 600,000. He was (1921–30) U.S. secretary of labor under Harding, Coolidge, and Hoover. He was U.S. senator (1930–45) from Pennsylvania.

Davis, Jefferson. b. in SW Kentucky (in what is now Todd County), June 3, 1808; d. at New Orleans, Dec. 6, 1889. American soldier, plantation owner, legislator, and secretary of war; president of the Confederate States of America. When he was three years of age his family moved to Mississippi and settled near Woodville in Wilkinson County. He attended successively a Dominican school, Wilkinson Academy, and Transylvania University, and was graduated (1828) from West Point. He served in frontier garrisons until 1835, taking part in the Black Hawk War (1833) and, according to an apocryphal story, taking Abraham Lincoln's first oath of allegiance to the U.S. when Lincoln led a group of Illinois volunteers into the army. In 1835, he married Sarah Knox Taylor, against the will of her father, Colonel Zachary Taylor, who was later to be president of the U.S. He resigned his commission in the army and returned to Mississippi, where his wife died three months later of fever. From 1835 to 1845 he managed his Mississippi plantation, "Brierfield," was an unsuccessful candidate for the state legislature in 1843, married Varina Howell two years later, and in the same year won a seat in Congress. He commanded the volunteer "Mississippi Rifles" in the Mexican War, fighting under General Taylor his father-in-law, and won fame in battles at Monterey and Buena Vista. In the summer of 1847 he accepted an appointment to the U.S. Senate, and was later (1850) elected to that body, where he became a leader of the Southern nationalists, an exponent of state sovereignty and the legal rights of slaveowners. After reluctantly voting for the Compromise of 1850, he resigned (1851) his seat to run for the governorship of Mississippi, but was defeated by Henry S. Foote. Davis became secretary of war in Pierce's cabinet and for four years served with a distinction that made him the guiding force of the administration. From 1857 to 1861 he represented the Southern point of view in the Senate, urged free trade policies and the development of world markets, and opposed the territorial policies of Stephen Douglas. Davis was not an ardent secessionist after the election of Abraham Lincoln, for he feared a resulting war and desired to exhaust every means of peaceable settlement before using the final resort of state sovereignty. On Jan. 21, 1861, after Mississippi had seceded, he gave his farewell address in the Senate and resigned his seat. Against his will (his preference was for a military command), he was chosen as provisional president of the Confederacy and was inaugurated as such on Feb. 18, 1861, at Montgomery, Ala.; elected in October, 1861, under the Confederate constitution, he was inaugurated on Feb. 22, 1862, at Richmond, Va., as president of the Confederacy. As a war president he accomplished much in leading the South against the powerful North. Yet his sensitiveness, his ill health, and his failure to credit enemies with any patriotic motives handicapped him as a leader. As the chief executive he became embroiled with governors and legislators on the issue of the respective powers of state and Confederate governments. With every Southern defeat, his popularity waned. The vitriolic criticism of the Richmond *Examiner* and of congressmen stung him to the quick. As the Confederate congress became increasingly hostile, he was forced into many compromises, but his control was sufficient to prevent passage of any act over his veto. Until the collapse of the Confederacy, he worked always for Southern independence; his acts, wise or inept, were sincere efforts toward this goal. He fled south when the Confederate lines at Petersburg, Va., were breached, ostensibly attempting to reach the trans-Mississippi territory and establish a government in Texas. Actually his laggardly journey evidenced a preference for capture, which was accomplished by Union troops on May 10, 1865, at Irwinville, Ga. For two years he was imprisoned in Fortress Monroe, part of the time in shackles, which rewon for him the sympathy of the Southern people. He was released without trial, although he had been indicted for treason, and for more than 30 years engaged in a number of business ventures. As a speaker and writer he defended the Confederacy and his administration against the thrusts of enemies North and South. His *Rise and Fall of the Confederate Government* (2 vols., 1881) was a philosophic, factual, and somewhat disappointing account. Davis reached the apex of his statesmanship as secretary of war, and his many years and many controversies after 1867 added little to his stature. See *Jefferson Davis: The Unreal and the Real*, by Robert McElroy (2 vols., 1937).

Davis, Jefferson Columbus. b. in Clarke County, Ind., March 2, 1828; d. Nov. 30, 1879. Union general in the American Civil War. He served (1846–47) in the Mexican War. He was at Fort Sumter when it was bombarded by the Confederates (April 12–13, 1861). He commanded a division at Pea Ridge (March 7–8, 1862), at Stone River (Dec. 31, 1862–Jan. 3, 1863), and at Chickamauga (Sept. 19–20, 1863), and led a corps in Sherman's march to the sea in 1864.

Davis, John. See also **Davys, John.**

Davis, John. b. at Plymouth, Mass., Jan. 25, 1761; d. at Boston, Jan. 14, 1847. American jurist. He was appointed comptroller of the U.S. treasury in 1795, and in 1801 became judge of the U.S. district court in Massachusetts. He was the youngest member in the convention of 1789 which adopted the federal constitution, and survived all the other members.

Davis, John. [Called **"Honest John."**] b. at Northboro, Mass., Jan. 13, 1787; d. at Worcester, Mass., April 19, 1854. American lawyer and politician. He served as Congressman (1824–32), governor of Massachusetts (1833–35, 1840–41), and U.S. senator (1835–40, 1845–53).

Davis, John Chandler Bancroft. b. at Worcester, Mass., Dec. 29, 1822; d. at Washington, D.C., Dec. 27, 1907. American jurist and diplomat. He was agent of the U.S. at the Geneva tribunal (1871–72) and minister to Germany (1874–77).

Davis, Sir **John Francis.** b. at London, 1795; d. near Bristol, England, Nov. 13, 1890. English diplomat and writer on China. He was the author of *The Chinese* (1836), and others.

Davis, John William. b. at Clarksburg, W.Va., April 13, 1873—. American lawyer and politician. He received a B.A. (1892) and an LL.B. (1895) from Washington and Lee, and practiced law (1897 *et seq.*) at Clarksburg, W.Va. He served as congressman (1911–13) from West Virginia, and as U.S. solicitor general (1913–18). From 1918 to 1921 he was U.S. ambassador to Great Britain. After the dramatic deadlock at the 1924 Democratic national convention between the forces supporting Alfred E. Smith and William G. McAdoo failed to resolve itself, Davis was chosen as compromise candidate for president, but was defeated easily by Coolidge.

Davis, Kenneth S. b. at Salina, Kan., Sept. 29, 1912—. American journalist and author. He was graduated from Kansas State University and the University of Wisconsin, was a reporter on the Topeka (Kan.) *Daily Capital*, an information specialist with the U.S. Soil Conservation Service, and a World War II newspaper correspondent in the European theater. Among his novels are *In the Forests of the Night* (1942) and *The Years of the Pilgrimage* (1948). He is also the author of *Soldier of Democracy* (1945), a biography of General Dwight D. Eisenhower.

Davis, Mount. Summit in SW Pennsylvania, in Somerset County, on Negro Mountain ab. 8 mi. W of Meyersdale, Pa. It is the highest point in the state, and there is a state park here. Elevation, ab. 3,213 ft.

Davis, Nathan Smith. [Called the **"Father of the American Medical Association."**] b. at Greene, N.Y., Jan. 9, 1817; d. June 16, 1904. American physician and medical writer, one of the founders of the American Medical Association. He practiced at Binghamton, N.Y. (1838–47) and at New York City (1847–49), and was professor (1849–59) at Rush Medical College at Chicago, where he advocated a sewage system, an adequate water supply, and a public hospital. He was one of the founders (1859) of the medical department of Lind University (now the medical department of Northwestern University), in which he was professor of the principles and practice of medicine and dean of the faculty. His works include *A Text Book on Agriculture* (1848), *History of Medical Education and Institutions in the United States* (1851), *History of the American Medical Association* (1855), *Clinical Lectures on Various Important Diseases* (1873), *Lectures on the Principles and Practice of Medicine* (1884), and *History of Medicine, with the Code of Medical Ethics* (1903).

Davis, Norman H(ezekiah). b. in Tennessee, Aug. 9, 1878; d. at Hot Springs, Va., July 2, 1944. American financier and diplomat. He went (1902) to Cuba, where he organized (1905) and headed (1905–17) the Trust Company of Cuba. He served as finance adviser (1918) to the U.S. secretary of the treasury, and was appointed (1919) U.S. finance commissioner in Europe. He was assistant secretary of the treasury (1919–20) and undersecretary of state (1920–21). He was a member (1931–37) of the League of Nations financial committee. He was appointed (1932) U.S. delegate to the disarmament conference at Geneva, member (1933) of the International Economic Conference, head (1935) of the U.S. delegation at the five-power naval conference at London, and chairman (1937) of the U.S. delegation at the international sugar conference. He served as chairman (1938 *et seq.*) of the American Red Cross.

Davis, Owen. b. at Portland, Me., June 29, 1874—. American playwright. He attended the University of Tennessee and Harvard University. He is the author of comedies and melodramas including *Through the Breakers* and *Nellie: The Beautiful Cloak Model*, and also of *Icebound* (1923), which won the Pulitzer prize, *The Detour* (1923), *The Nervous Wreck* (1923), *Lazybones* (1924), *Easy Come, Easy Go* (1925), and *Beware of Widows* (1925). He also made stage adaptations of *The Great Gatsby*, by F. Scott Fitzgerald, and *Ethan Frome*, by Edith Wharton. His autobiography is entitled *Like To Do It Again* (1931).

Davis, Rebecca Blaine. [Maiden name, **Harding.**] b. at Washington, Pa., June 24, 1831; d. at Mt. Kisco, N.Y., Sept. 29, 1910. American novelist, short-story writer, and journalist; mother of Richard Harding Davis. She educated herself at home, chiefly by reading widely, and combined writing with raising a large family. Her works include *Dallas Galbraith* and *Waiting for the Verdict* (both 1868), *Berrytown* (1872), *John Andross* (1874), *A Law Unto Herself* (1878), *Natasqua* (1886), *Silhouettes of American Life* and *Kent Hampden* (both 1892), and *Dr. Warrick's Daughters* (1896).

Davis, Richard Harding. b. at Philadelphia, April 18, 1864; d. at Mount Kisco, N.Y., April 11, 1916. American journalist and author, noted as a war correspondent; son of Rebecca Blaine Harding Davis. He attended Lehigh University and the Johns Hopkins University and entered journalism in 1886, working for the *Record, Press,* and *Telegraph,* all at Philadelphia. He served (1889–90) on the staff of the New York *Sun*, and in 1890 became managing editor of *Harper's Weekly*, later going abroad for that magazine and writing a series of letters published in book form as *The Rulers of the Mediterranean* (1894). His other journeys at this time were described in *Our English Cousins* (1894) and *About Paris* (1895). Meanwhile, he had achieved success as a writer of popular fiction, publishing the favorably received *Gallegher, and Other Stories* (1891), and following it with *Van Bibber and Others* (1892), *The Exiles and Other Stories* (1892), and

The Lion and the Unicorn (1899). Investigating conditions in areas near the Canal Zone, he recorded his experiences in *Three Gringos in Venezuela and Central America* (1896). As a newspaper correspondent, he covered, in addition to minor wars in the Balkans and in Latin America, six wars: the Spanish War in Cuba, the Greco-Turkish, the Spanish-American, the Boer War, the Russo-Japanese, and World War I, producing, as the result of his experiences, *Cuba in War Time* (1897), *A Year from a Reporter's Note Book* (1898), *The Cuban and Porto Rican Campaigns* (1898), *With Both Armies in South Africa* (1900), *Notes of a War Correspondent* (1910), *With the Allies* (1914), and *With the French in France and Salonika* (1916). He also wrote *The Congo and the Coasts of Africa* (1907). As a foreign and war correspondent, he established a tradition of the venturesome, the daring and picturesque; his name still identifies a special type of sensational reporting. A prolific author, he wrote such popular novels as *Soldiers of Fortune* (1897), *The King's Jackal* (1898), *Captain Macklin* (1902), *The Bar Sinister* (1903), *Vera the Medium* (1908), and *The White Mice* (1909). His other collections of short stories include *Ranson's Folly* (1902), *The Scarlet Car* (1907), *Once Upon a Time* (1910), *The Man Who Could Not Lose* (1911), *The Red Cross Girl* (1912), *The Lost Road* (1913), and *The Boy Scout* (1917). He was also the author of 25 plays, among them *The Dictator* (produced 1904), *Miss Civilization* (1906), and *The Seventh Daughter* (1910).

Davis, Stuart. b. at Philadelphia, Dec. 7, 1894—. American painter and illustrator. A pupil of Robert Henri, he went along, from his student days, with the currents of modern art, and at the age of 19 saw his work hung in the renowned Armory Show in 1913. At that time he was a cartoonist for *Harper's Weekly*. His paintings include murals in the Radio City Music Hall, Rockefeller Center, New York, and in the studios of radio station WNYC in the same city. Other examples of his work are included in the permanent exhibitions of the Museum of Modern Art and the Whitney Museum at New York, the Phillips Memorial Gallery at Washington, the Museum of the Pennsylvania Academy, the Albright Art Gallery at Buffalo, and elsewhere. A comprehensive retrospective exhibition of his work was presented by the Museum of Modern Art in 1946.

Davis, Thomas Osborne. b. at Mallow, County Cork, Ireland, Oct. 14, 1814; d. at Dublin, Sept. 16, 1845. Irish poet and politician. He graduated at Trinity College in 1836, was admitted to the bar in 1838, became joint editor with John Blake Dillon of the *Dublin Morning Register* in 1841, and founded, with Charles Gavan Duffy and Dillon, the *Nation* in 1842. He joined in 1839 the Repeal Association, within which organization he founded the party of Young Ireland in opposition to O'Connell's leadership. His poems, collected after his death, form a volume of Duffy's *Library of Ireland* for 1846.

Davis, Varina. [Maiden name, **Howell.**] b. near Natchez, Miss., May 7, 1826; d. Oct. 16, 1906. First lady of the Confederacy; wife of Jefferson Davis (1808–89). She was her husband's amanuensis while he wrote *The Rise and Fall of the Confederacy* (1881), and after his death she wrote *Jefferson Davis, Ex-President of the Confederate States of America: A Memoir* (2 vols., 1890).

Davis, Varina Anne Jefferson. [Known as the **"Daughter of the Confederacy."**] b. at Richmond, Va., June 27, 1864; d. at Narragansett Pier, R.I., Sept. 18, 1898. American novelist; daughter of Jefferson Davis, president of the Southern Confederacy. She was the author of *An Irish Knight of the Nineteenth Century: Sketch of the Life of Robert Emmet* (1888), *The Veiled Doctor; A Novel* (1895), and *A Romance of Summer Seas; A Novel* (1899).

Davis, William Augustine. b. in Barren County, Ky., Sept. 21, 1809; d. at St. Joseph, Mo., Jan. 15, 1875. American postal employee, said to have been the inventor of the railroad-car mail-sorting system. He served in the Richmond, Va., post office (1830–55), as postmaster (1855–61) at St. Joseph, Mo., and thereafter as U.S. postmaster's assistant. In 1862 he suggested the plan of sorting mail in railroad cars to speed overland mail distribution at railroad-stagecoach junctions. Credit for the scheme is, however, given by some historians to George B. Armstrong, another post-office employee.

Davis, William Morris. b. at Philadelphia, Feb. 12, 1850; d. at Pasadena, Calif., Feb. 5, 1934. American geologist, professor of geology in Harvard University from 1899. He was graduated from the Lawrence Scientific School (Harvard) in 1869, was assistant in the Argentine National Observatory at Córdoba (1870–73), and was assistant professor (1885–90) and professor (1890–99) of physical geography at Harvard. In 1903 he acted as physiographer of the Pumpelly (Carnegie Institution) expedition to Turkestan, and in 1905 accompanied the British Association to South Africa. He was exchange professor at the University of Berlin in 1908–09, headed (1912) the American Geographical Society's transcontinental expedition, and served during World War I on the National Research Council as chairman of the geographic and geologic division. Among his works are *Elementary Meteorology* (1894), *Physical Geography* (1899), and *The Coral Reef Problem* (1928).

Davis, William Stearns. b. at Amherst, Mass., April 30, 1877; d. Feb. 15, 1930. American writer and teacher, professor (1909–27) of history at the University of Minnesota. He was the author of *A Friend of Caesar* (1900), *God Wills It* (1901), *Belshazzar* (1902), *The Friar of Wittenberg* (1912), *A Day in Old Athens* (1914), *The Roots of the War* (1918), *Life on a Mediaeval Barony* (1923), *The White Queen* (1925), *Europe Since Waterloo* (1926), and *Gilman of Redford* (1927).

Davis Mountains. Mountain area in W Texas, ab. 175 mi. SE of El Paso. The E part of the range is much dissected by canyons, and is very rough. There are many prominent peaks in the W Davis Mountains, of which Mount Livermore or Baldy Peak (8,382 ft.) is the highest. The McDonald Observatory, with its 82-inch reflecting telescope, is atop Mount Locke (6,791 ft.).

Davison (dā′vi.sọn), **Henry Pomeroy.** b. at Troy, Pa., June 13, 1867; d. May 6, 1922. American banker. He was chairman (1917–19) of the Red Cross War Council and for many years a partner in J. P. Morgan and Company. As president (1899 *et seq.*) of the Liberty National Bank, he conceived the plan for a national bank and insurance company depository which was realized as the Bankers' Trust Company. He also served as a member (1908) of the Monetary Commission to study the European system of national currency and as chairman (1910) of the Six-Power Chinese Loan Conference at Paris. His Red Cross activities included the raising and administration (1917–19) of 285 million dollars.

Davison, William. d. in December, 1608. British diplomat. As a secretary of state he procured Elizabeth's signature to the death warrant of Mary, Queen of Scots in 1587.

Davis Peninsula (dā′vis). Elongated, snow and ice covered peninsula in Antarctica, on the Queen Mary Coast, in ab. 66°35′ S., 98°45′ E. Elevation, ab. 600 ft.; width, ab. 5 mi.

Davisson (dā′vi.sọn), **Clinton Joseph.** b. at Bloomington, Ill., Oct. 22, 1881—. American physicist, known for research in electricity, magnetism, and radiant energy. Associated (1917–46) with Bell Telephone laboratories (later with the engineering department of Western Electric Company), he discovered (1927) with L. H. Germer the diffraction of electrons by crystals, and for this shared (1937) the Nobel prize in physics with the English physicist George Paget Thomson, who had independently discovered, by another method, the same phenomenon.

Davis Strait (dā′vis). Sea passage connecting the Atlantic Ocean and Baffin Bay, and separating Greenland from Baffin Island and the rest of the islands of the Arctic Archipelago. It was named for its discoverer, the English navigator John Davys. Width in the narrowest part, ab. 200 mi.

Davit (dä′vēt), **Gerard** (or **Gheerardt** or **Gheeraert**). See **David, Gerard** (or **Gheerardt** or **Gheeraert**).

Davitt (dav′it), **Michael.** b. at Straide, County Mayo, Ireland, March 25, 1846; d. at Dublin, May 31, 1906. Irish journalist and political leader. His parents were evicted and when he was ten years of age he was sent to work in a Lancashire cotton mill. He lost his right arm as the result of a factory accident in 1857, and became a newsboy. He joined the Fenian brotherhood in 1865, and in 1870 was arrested for attempting to send arms into Ireland, was sentenced to 15 years, and served seven years, being released on ticket of leave (paroled). He went to the U.S. to make contact with the Fenians and, returning to Ireland, founded, with C. S. Parnell and others, the Irish Land League in 1879 in an attempt to further the cause of Irish independence by enlisting the dissatisfied farm people. He was soon arrested for seditious speeches and imprisoned for two years; again, in 1883, he served three months on a new charge of seditious utterances. He was first elected to Parliament for County Meath, in 1882, but was disqualified by a special vote of the House of Commons for nonexpiration of the sentence in 1870 for treason-felony. He was elected Nationalist member for Meath, North, in 1892, but was unseated on petition, and sat for Cork, Northeast, in 1893 and as anti-Parnellite member for Kerry, East (1895–96) and Mayo, South (1895–99). He published *Leaves from a Prison Diary* (1884), *Defence of the Land League* (1891), *Life and Progress in Australasia* (1898), *The Boer Fight for Freedom* (1902), *Within the Pale* (1903), and *The Fall of Feudalism in Ireland: Story of the Land League Revolution* (1904).

D'Avolos (dav'ǫ.los). In John Ford's *Love's Sacrifice*, the duke's secretary (modeled on Shakespeare's Iago), a spy and "pander to the bad passions of others."

Davos (dä.vōs'). Health resort in SE Switzerland, comprising the adjoining villages of Davos-Platz and Davos-Dorf, situated in the highest part of the Alpine valley of Davos: famous as a resort for consumptives. The Swiss Research Institute for Alpine Physiology and Tuberculosis was founded here in 1923. Davos is the scene of Thomas Mann's novel *The Magic Mountain.* There are many hotels and fashionable shops. 9,259 (1941).

Davos Valley. Alpine valley in SE Switzerland, in the canton of Graubünden, SE of the city of Chur. Its chief place is Davos (the adjoining villages of Davos-Platz and Davos-Dorf), a noted health resort at an elevation of 5,115 ft. The Lake of Davos, now important for hydroelectric power, is in the valley.

Davout (dȧ.vö), **Louis Nicolas.** [Titles: Duc **d'Auerstädt,** Prince **d'Eckmühl.**] b. at Annoux, Yonne, France, May 10, 1770; d. at Paris, June 1, 1823. French marshal. He was a lieutenant in a cavalry regiment in 1788, served (1792–93) as chief of battalion under Dumouriez, was brigadier general in the army of the Moselle, fought under Pichegru and Moreau in the army of the Rhine, and went to Egypt on Napoleon's expedition there and fought with distinction, especially at Abukir. He was made general of division in 1800 and marshal in 1804, and fought at Austerlitz (1805), Auerstedt (1806), where with one corps he beat the Prussian army, Eggmühl (Eckmühl) and Wagram (1809), and in the Russian campaign (1812). He was minister of war during the Hundred Days in 1815. He became Duke of Auerstädt in 1808, and Prince of Eckmühl in 1809.

Davus (dā'vus). Conventional name for a slave in Latin comedies.

Davy (dā'vi), Sir **Humphry.** b. at Penzance, Cornwall, England, Dec. 17, 1778; d. at Geneva, Switzerland, May 29, 1829. English scientist. The son of a woodcarver, he grew up in Cornwall, receiving his elementary education at Truro, and becoming in 1795 an apprentice to an apothecary at Penzance. This was a fortunate beginning of his career, in that it confirmed his interest in chemistry, and as early as 1799 he discovered the effects of inhaling nitrous oxide (laughing gas) and experimented with inhalation of other gases. In 1801 he became a lecturer in, and from 1802 to 1813 was a professor of, chemistry at the Royal Institute, London. During this period he first isolated several of the elements by electrolysis. He is noted for his demonstration that the diamond is a carbon, and even more as the inventor of a safety lamp for use in mines, which was of importance in the extension of coal mining in Great Britain and other countries. He was also an early student of agricultural chemistry. He was knighted in 1812 and made a baronet in 1818. In 1820 he was elected president of the Royal Society. Among his important books were *On Some Chemical Agencies of Electricity* (1807) and *Elements of Agricultural Chemistry* (1813). His collected works were published (1839–40) in nine volumes.

Davy Jones. In nautical folklore, a personification of the sea, whence "Davy Jones's Locker" means the bottom of the sea, especially as the grave of the drowned. These terms, first current among sailors, are now parts of common speech, and universally understood among English-speaking peoples, but their origin is unknown. There is no legend of a real or mythical Davy Jones. A connection has been surmised between the name Jones and the prophet Jonah who is reported in the Bible to have been swallowed by a whale. The two names ("Davy" and "Jones") together strongly suggest that this modern mythological immortal may have been born in the imagination of Welsh mariners.

Davys (dā'vis), **John.** [Also, **Davis.**] b. at Sandridge, Devonshire, England, c1550; killed in the Strait of Malacca, Dec. 29, 1605. English navigator. He commanded expeditions in search of the Northwest Passage in 1585, 1586, and 1587, on the first of which he discovered Davis Strait. He discovered the Falkland Islands in 1592. He sailed with Raleigh on the raiding voyage to Cádiz and the Azores in 1596. He took service in 1604 as pilot in the *Tiger*, under Captain Sir Edward Michelborne, destined for a voyage to the East Indies, on which he was killed by Japanese pirates.

Daw (dô), **Marjorie.** See **Marjorie Daw.**

Daw, Sir David. Foolish baronet in Richard Cumberland's *Wheel of Fortune.*

Daw, Sir John. In Ben Jonson's comedy *Epicoene, or The Silent Woman,* a cowardly, foolish coxcomb.

Dawes (dôz), **Charles Gates.** b. at Marietta, Ohio, Aug. 27, 1865; d. at Chicago, April 23, 1951. American lawyer, financier, and politician who served (1925–29) as Vice-president of the United States. He graduated from Marietta College (1884) and from Cincinnati Law School (1886). After serving (1897–1902) as U.S. comptroller of currency, he organized (1902) and was president (1902–21) and chairman of the board of directors (1921–25) of the Central Trust Company at Chicago, and chairman of the board (1932 *et seq.*) of the City National Bank and Trust Company at Chicago. He served in World War I, being appointed brigadier general and chief of supply procurement for the American Expeditionary Forces in France. He was the first director (1921) of the U.S. Bureau of the Budget. In 1923 he was president of the International Commission on German reparations which produced a reparations payment scheme known as the Dawes Plan (in effect Sept. 1, 1924). He was U.S. ambassador (1929–32) to Great Britain, and president (1932) of the Reconstruction Finance Corporation. He shared (1925) the Nobel peace prize with Sir Austen Chamberlain of England. Among his books are *A Journal of the Great War* (1921), *Notes as Vice-President* (1935), and *A Journal of Reparations* (1939).

Dawes, Henry Laurens. b. at Cummington, Mass., Oct. 30, 1816; d. at Pittsfield, Mass., Feb. 5, 1903. American politician, member of Congress from Massachusetts (1857–75) and Republican U.S. senator (1875–93).

Dawes, Sophie. See **Feuchères,** Baronne **de.**

Dawes, William. b. at Boston, April 6, 1745; d. Feb. 25, 1799. American patriot who rode (April 18, 1775) with Paul Revere from Lexington toward Concord, rousing the countryside to prepare for the British advance. Though Revere was stopped by the British, either Dawes or Samuel Prescott, the third rider on the mission, alerted the patriots at Concord.

Dawes, William Rutter. b. at London, March 19, 1799; d. at Haddenham, Buckinghamshire, England, Feb. 15, 1868. English astronomer. He was educated at the Charter House school (1811–13), settled as a surgeon at Liverpool in 1826, and was for a time pastor of an independent congregation at Ormskirk, Lancashire. He had charge (1839–44) of the observatory at South Villa, Regent's Park, London, belonging to George Bishop, fitted up an observatory at Camden Lodge, near Cranbrook, Kent, in 1845, and discovered 15 new double stars in the period 1840–59.

Dawes Commission. [Also known as the **Commission to the Five Civilized Tribes.**] Commission appointed by President Cleveland in 1893 for the purpose of negotiating with the Indian tribes of the Seminole, Creek, Choctaw, Cherokee, and Chickasaw in order to bring them under the terms of the Dawes General Allotment Act of 1887. It succeeded in securing the tribal agreements and was dissolved in 1905.

Dawes General Allotment Act. [Called the **"Emancipation Act of the Indians."**] Law passed (1887) by the U.S. Congress providing for the reallotment of Indian reservation lands. Tribal ownership could, with presidential approval, be supplanted by individual ownership of 160-acre tracts for family heads and 80-acre tracts for unmarried Indians. Once ownership was established by patent, the occupants became U.S. citizens. Mortgage or sale of the land was forbidden for 25 years, after which time title was to be conferred. The government could purchase the land remaining in the reservation after allotment to resident Indians, and the acreage was opened to white ownership.

Dawes Plan. International scheme (announced April 9, 1924) which provided for changing the schedule of German reparations payments established after World War I. The plan took its name from Charles G. Dawes, who served as head of a commission of experts from the U.S., Great Britain, France, Italy, and Belgium, which devised the scheme. The Dawes Plan, superseded by the Young Plan on May 17, 1930, was based upon German capacity to pay. It called for a measure of foreign control over the German economy in return for a loan to Germany, which was intended to stabilize the German economy, dangerously near collapse as the result of the precipitous fall of the mark, and for evacuation of the Ruhr by the French, who had occupied that industrial area after Germany failed to observe the original reparations schedule. The commission reported the plan on April 9, 1924; it was accepted by the Germans on April 16, concurred in by a conference at London in August, and went into effect the following month.

Dawison (dä′vē.sôn), **Bogumił.** b. at Warsaw, Poland, May 15, 1818; d. near Dresden, Germany, Feb. 1, 1872. Polish actor. He first appeared in America in 1866. He at one time played Othello to Edwin Booth's Iago. He played both tragic and comic parts.

Dawkins (dô′kinz), **John.** Young pickpocket in the employ of Fagin, in Charles Dickens's *Oliver Twist;* called the "Artful Dodger" from his expertness at his trade.

Dawkins, Sir **William Boyd.** b. at Buttington, Welshpool, Montgomeryshire, Wales, Dec. 26, 1838; d. Jan. 15, 1929. English geologist and paleontologist, author of *Cave-Hunting* (1874), *Early Man in Britain* (1880), and others.

Dawley (dô′li). [Called locally **Little Dawley.**] Urban district in W England, in Shropshire, situated on the Shrewsbury Canal, ab. 4 mi. SE of Wellington, ab. 156 mi. NW of London by rail. 8,369 (1951).

Dawlish (dô′lish). Urban district and seaside resort in SW England, in Devonshire, situated on the English Channel ab. 10 mi. S of Exeter, ab. 186 mi. SW of London by rail. 7,512 (1951).

Dawn. Autobiographical work (1931) by Theodore Dreiser. Along with his other works of the same nature, *A Traveler at Forty* (1913), *A Hoosier Holiday* (1916), and *A Book About Myself* (1922; published in 1931 as *Newspaper Days*), it gives a frank picture of his thoughts and feelings as a man and of his development as a writer.

Dawn's Left Hand. Novel by Dorothy M. Richardson, published in 1931. It is the tenth section of *Pilgrimage* (1938), a novel sequence in 12 parts employing the stream-of-consciousness technique.

Daws (dôz), **Sophie.** See **Feuchères,** Baronne **de.**

Dawson (dô′sọn). City in SW Georgia, county seat of Terrell County, in a farming region. 4,411 (1950).

Dawson. Mining city and the capital of the Yukon Territory, Canada, situated on the Yukon River, near the Klondike gold fields and just W of the Alaska boundary. 783 (1951).

Dawson, A. J. [Full name, **Alec John Dawson.**] b. at London, Aug. 25, 1872—. English novelist. He served (1914–19) in World War I as a major. His books include *Middle Greyness, God's Foundling, Bismillah, Hidden Manna, The Message, Finn the Wolfhound, Jan: Son of Finn, A Temporary Gentleman in France, Peter of Monkslease: his Mortal Tenement* (1924), *The Emergence of Marie* (1926), and *The Case Books of X 37* (1930).

Dawson, Bertrand Edward. See **Dawson of Penn,** 1st Viscount.

Dawson, Bully. fl. in the 17th century. Notorious London sharper, a contemporary of Sir George Etherege.

Dawson, Coningsby William. b. at High Wycombe, Buckinghamshire, England, Feb. 26, 1883—. American writer. He came to the U.S. in 1905, and served (1916–18) with the Canadian 1st Division in World War I. He afterward lectured (1919–20) throughout the U.S. on postwar reconstruction problems and reported to Herbert Hoover on reconstruction problems of central and eastern Europe. His works include *The Worker and Other Poems* (1906), *The House of the Weeping Woman* (1908), *Murder Point* (1910), *The Garden Without Walls* (1913), *Living Bayonets* (1919), *Pilgrims of the Impossible* (1928), and *Inspirational Valley* (1935).

Dawson, Geoffrey. [Original surname, **Robinson;** full name, **George Geoffrey Dawson.**] b. at Skipton-in-Craven, Yorkshire, England, 1874; d. at London, Nov. 7, 1944. English journalist, editor, and civil servant. Educated at Eton and at Magdalen College, Oxford, he was a fellow of All Souls College, Oxford, held a post in the Colonial Office, and served (1901–05) as Lord Milner's private secretary in South Africa. There he became a correspondent for the London *Times* and editor (1905–10) of the Johannesburg *Star.* Returning to England in 1910, he served from August, 1912 to February, 1919 as editor of the *Times,* resigning (1919) because he did not agree with Lord Northcliffe's policies; he returned (1923) to the editorship after Northcliffe's death and retired in 1941. He changed his name to Dawson in 1917. He was estates bursar (1919–23) of All Souls and secretary (1921–22) of the Rhodes Trust. On Jan. 7, 1927, as editor of the London *Times,* he participated in the first transatlantic telephone conversation in history when he spoke to Adolph S. Ochs, publisher of the New York *Times.*

Dawson, George Mercer. b. at Pictou, Nova Scotia, Canada, Aug. 1, 1849; d. at Ottawa, March 2, 1901. Canadian geologist and explorer; son of Sir John William Dawson. He was appointed geologist and botanist to the Northwest Boundary Commission in 1873 and in 1875 joined the geological survey of Canada, of which he became assistant director in 1883 and director in 1895. In 1891 and 1892 he served on the Bering Sea Commission. His publications include *Report of the Geology and Resources of the Region in the Vicinity of the Forty-ninth Parallel* (1875), *Descriptive Sketch of the Physical Geography and Geology of Canada* (1884, with A. R. Selwyn), a preliminary report on the physical and geological features of a portion of the Rocky Mountains (1886), and many monographs.

Dawson, James. b. c1717; d. at Kensington Green, London, 1746. Young volunteer officer, of good family, in the service of Charles Edward Stuart, the Young Pretender. He was hanged, drawn, and quartered, and his heart burned, on July 30, 1746, for treason. His betrothed was present, and, when all was over, she died in the arms of a friend. William Shenstone made this the subject of a ballad, *Jemmy Dawson.*

Dawson, Sir **John William.** b. at Pictou, Nova Scotia, Canada, in October, 1820; d. at Montreal, Nov. 19, 1899. Canadian geologist and naturalist. He was principal of McGill College and University from 1855 to 1893. His works include *Acadian Geology* (1855), and others.

Dawson, Thomas Cleland. b. at Hudson, Wis., July 30, 1865; d. at Washington, D.C., May 1, 1912. American diplomat. He was assistant attorney general of Iowa (1891–94), took part in the work of the Republican national committee in 1900, was secretary of the U.S. legation to Brazil (1897–1904), minister resident and consul general in the Dominican Republic (1904–07), and minister to Colombia (1907–09), to Chile (1909), and to Panama (1910). In 1909 he was made chief of the division of Latin-American affairs in the department of state. He was the author of *South American Republics* (1903–04).

Dawson, William Harbutt. b. July 27, 1860—. English publicist, chiefly known as the author of numerous books and articles interpreting German culture to English readers.

Dawson, William James. b. at Towcester, Northamptonshire, England, Nov. 21, 1854; d. 1928. American Wesleyan clergyman, noted for his writings. He was ordained in 1875 and became (1892) pastor of the Highbury Quadrant Congregational Church at London. In 1905 he moved to the U.S., where he was pastor of the First Church at Newark, N.J. His writings include the novel

Robert Shenstone (1917), verse such as *A Vision of Souls* (1884), and the miscellaneous writings *The Threshold of Manhood* (1889), *Makers of English Poetry* (1890), *Makers of English Prose* (1899), *Makers of English Fiction* (1905), *The Empire of Love* (1907), *The Book of Courage* (1911), and *The Autobiography of a Mind* (1925).

Dawson Creek. Town in E central British Columbia, situated a few miles S of the Peace River near the Alberta boundary. It is the northern terminus of the railroad line from Edmonton to the Peace River country and is the actual starting point of the Alaska Highway. It has a number of grain elevators. Ab. 54 mi. N of Dawson Creek is Fort St. John, the site of a large strategically located airfield. 3,589 (1951).

Dawson of Penn, 1st Viscount. [Title of **Bertrand Edward Dawson.**] b. at Duppas Hill, Croydon, Surrey, England, March 9, 1864; d. at London, March 7, 1945. English physician who served as physician in ordinary (1907–45) to Edward VII, George V, Edward VIII, and George VI, kings of England. He saw service during World War I as major general in charge of medical service, and was president (1931–38) of the Royal College of Physicians.

Dax (dȧks). [Also: **Ax**; Latin, **Aquae Tarbellicae, Aquae Augustae.**] Town in SW France, in the department of Landes, situated on the Adour River, between Bordeaux and Bayonne. It is a winter resort, and has thermal baths patronized by many persons suffering from rheumatism. During the Middle Ages the town underwent many invasions by the Goths, Franks, Saracens, Normans, and English. 14,113 (1946).

Day (dā), **Benjamin.** b. 1838; d. 1916. American printer; son of Benjamin Harry Day. He invented a process for shading the plates used in printing illustrations and maps. This Ben Day, or Benday, process is a standard technique in printing and is very widely used. To this day printers speak of "Bendaying" an illustration, or "giving it a Benday."

Day, Benjamin Harry. b. at West Springfield, Mass., April 10, 1810; d. at New York, Dec. 21, 1889. American printer, journalist, and founder of the New York *Sun;* father of Benjamin Day (1838–1916) and grandfather of Clarence Day (1874–1935). His father was Henry Day, and his mother, Mary (Ely), traced her descent to William Brewster, who signed the Mayflower Compact in 1620. He began his newspaper career when he was 14, as an apprentice to Samuel Bowles, who had just founded the Springfield *Republican.* In 1830, a year before he married, he went to New York, where he worked for the *Evening Post,* the *Commercial Advertiser,* and the *Journal of Commerce.* In 1833, a year made memorable in the city by a depression, bank failures, and cholera, he founded the New York *Sun,* a penny newspaper. The first issue came out on Tuesday, Sept. 3, being printed in a small room at 222 William Street. It contained four pages, and its announced aim was "to lay before the public, at a price within the means of everyone, all the news of the day." Within four months the paper's circulation was 4,000 copies, and by April, 1834, it had reached 8,000 copies daily, both large figures for that time. In 1835 Day claimed that his 19,360 copies daily had passed the 17,000 figure of the London *Times.* Three years later, he sold the *Sun* to Moses Yale Beach, his brother-in-law, for the sum of 40,000 dollars. In 1883, in an interview published in the *Sun* on its 50th anniversary, he declared that "the silliest thing I ever did in my life was to sell that paper." In 1840 he founded another penny daily, the *True Sun,* but got rid of it in a few months. In 1842 he founded, with James Wilson, a monthly (it later became a weekly), *Brother Jonathan,* which made a feature of reprinting popular English novels. The Civil War, which caused a paper shortage, hurt his business, and he retired in 1862, to spend the rest of his life in ease and comfort. He was a man of strong character, was a hard worker, had his own opinions, could give and take in a battle, and had no objection to attacking, or being attacked by, his professional rivals.

Day, Clarence. [Original full name, **Clarence Shepard Day.**] b. at New York, Nov. 18, 1874; d. there, of pneumonia, Dec. 28, 1935. American humorist, essayist, Yale historian, and illustrator. He was the eldest son of Clarence Shepard Day, who was one of the governors of the New York Stock Exchange, and Lavinia ("Vinnie") Stockwell, and his grandfather was the founder of the New York *Sun,* Benjamin Harry Day. He was educated at St. Paul's School, at Concord, N.H., and at Yale University, graduating with the class of 1896. He is not famous for his first three books, but he is known and loved by Yale men for them: *The Decennial Record* (1907), *A Record of the Quindecennial Reunion of the Class of 1896* (1912), and *The '96 Half-Way Book* (1915). To a larger and more general public he is known for his humorous prose essays, sketches, and narratives. *This Simian World* (1920), unscientific reflections on evolution, *The Crow's Nest* (1921; later revised as *After All,* 1936), *In the Green Mountain Country* (1934), a tribute to Calvin Coolidge, and the books that have established his reputation, *God and My Father* (1932), *Life with Father* (1935), and *Life with Mother* (published 1937, and edited by his wife, Katharine Briggs Dodge, whom he married in 1928). His *Life with Father* is a humorous portrait of the senior Day, a most explosive character, thoroughly in love with, but exceedingly trying to, his wife and children. It was a huge success as a book, selling over 114,000 copies, was translated into German (1936) by Hans Fallada, and as a stage and screen play gave Howard Lindsay and William Powell, respectively, each one of his best roles. Apart from being a writer, Day was a clever artist with pen and pencil. He illustrated his own *Thoughts without Words* (1935) and *Scenes from the Mesozoic, and Other Drawings* (1936), as well as making 20 full-page drawings for Charles A. A. Bennett's *At a Venture* (1924) and illustrations for *The Delicatessen Husband* (1926) by Florence Seabury. He also wrote another work of limited interest, *The Story of the Yale University Press* (1920) and edited *The Colby Essays* (1926), a two-volume collection of essays by Frank Moore Colby. From 1898, when he was discharged from the U.S. navy (in which he had enlisted when the Spanish-American War broke out), until his death, he was a sufferer, but a brave and cheerful one, as his works show, from arthritis. He made the best of a bad condition, never lost his spirit, joked about himself, not only smiled but laughed, and made thousands laugh with him and at his humorous outlook. He dropped his middle name, always writing as Clarence Day.

Day, Clive. b. at Hartford, Conn., Feb. 11, 1871; d. at Greensboro, Vt., July 27, 1951. American political economist. He served at Yale as Knox professor of political economy from 1907 to 1936. He was the author of *Policy and Administration of the Dutch in Java* (1904), *History of Commerce* (1907), *History of Commerce of the U.S.* (1925), and *Economic Development in Modern Europe* (1933).

Day, Edmund Ezra. b. at Manchester, N.H., Dec. 7, 1883; d. March 23, 1951. American educator. He was professor of economics (1910–23) at Harvard, professor of economics (1923–27) and first dean (1924–27) of the business administration school (which he organized) at Michigan, director for social sciences (1928–37) with the Rockefeller Foundation, president (1937–49), chancellor (1949–50), and president emeritus (1950 *et seq.*) of Cornell. He was author of *Index of Physical Production* (1920), *Statistical Analysis* (1925), *The Defense of Freedom* (1941), and other books.

Day, Frank Miles. b. at Philadelphia, April 5, 1861; d. 1918. American architect. He was graduated from the University of Pennsylvania in 1883 and studied architecture at that university and in Europe. He was a fellow of the American Institute of Architects and was elected its president in 1906. He was also a trustee of the American Academy at Rome. He designed various college buildings, among others.

Day, Henry Noble. b. at Washington, Conn., Aug. 4, 1808; d. at New Haven, Conn., Jan. 12, 1890. American educator and philosophical writer; nephew of Jeremiah Day. He became professor of sacred rhetoric at Western Reserve College in 1840, and president of the Ohio Female College in 1854, and moved to New Haven in 1864. His works include *Logic* (1867), *Ethics* (1876), *Ontology* (1878), and others.

Day, Holman Francis. b. at Vassalboro, Me., Nov. 6, 1865; d. at Mill Valley, Calif., Feb. 19, 1935. American writer and editor. He was managing editor of the Union Publishing Company (1889–90) at Bangor, Me., and thereafter of the Lewiston (Me.) *Daily Sun*. His books include *Up in Maine* (1900), *Pine Tree Ballads* (1902), *Kin O'Ktaadn* (1904), *Squire Phin* (1905), *Along Came Ruth* (1914, a play), *When Egypt Went Broke* (1920), *The Loving are the Daring* (1923), *Leadbetter's Luck* (1923), *When the Fight Begins* (1926), *Starwagons* (1928), and *Ships of Joy* (1932).

Day, James Roscoe. b. at Whitneyville, Me., Oct. 17, 1845; d. at Atlantic City, N.J., March 13, 1923. American Methodist clergyman and educator. He served as a pastor from 1872 to 1894 and left the active ministry to become chancellor (1894) of Syracuse University. Between that time and his retirement (1922), the enrollment at Syracuse expanded from 750 students to more than 5,000. He was the author of *The Raid on Prosperity* (1907) and *My Neighbor the Workingman* (1920).

Day, Jeremiah. b. at New Preston, Conn., Aug. 3, 1773; d. at New Haven, Conn., Aug. 22, 1867. American mathematician, president of Yale College from 1817 to 1846. He published an *Algebra* (1814), *Navigation and Surveying* (1817), and other works.

Day, John. b. c1574; d. 1640. English dramatist and poet. He was educated at Cambridge, and collaborated (1598 *et seq.*) with William Haughton, Henry Chettle, Thomas Dekker, and others in numerous plays, all of which remained unprinted except *The Blind Beggar of Bednal Green*. He was the author of *The Blind Beggar of Bednal Green* (1600, with Chettle), *Isle of Gulls* (1606), *Law Tricks* (1608), and *Humour Out of Breath* (1608). His chief work is the poemlike masque or pageant *The Parliament of Bees* (c1607).

Day, John Godfrey Fitzmaurice. b. 1874; d. at Dublin, Sept. 26, 1938. Irish clergyman and Protestant primate of all Ireland. He was a member (1902–09) of the Cambridge mission to Delhi, India, vicar (1912–20) of Saint Ann's Church at Dublin, canon (1914–20) of Christ Church Cathedral at Dublin, professor (1917–20) of pastoral theology at the University of Dublin, and was appointed bishop of Ossory, Ferns, and Leighlin (1920) and archbishop of Armagh (1938).

Day, Mr. In Sir Robert Howard's play *The Committee*, the chairman of the committee, a kind of Tartuffe, under the thumb of his wife.

Day, Stephen. See **Daye, Stephen.**

Day, Thomas. b. at London, June 22, 1748; d. at Wargrave, Berkshire, England, Sept. 28, 1789. English follower of Rousseau's theories, educator, essayist, poet, and philanthropist. He was educated at the famous Charterhouse School (where Thackeray spent six years) and at Corpus Christi College, Oxford. He was a friend of Sir William Jones, of R. L. Edgeworth, Maria's father, and of Erasmus Darwin. As a child, he was in the habit of giving his pocket money to poor people, and was noted for his kindness to animals. In later life, he refused to obey Jones's request, "kill that spider," remarking that he had no more right to do so than he would have to kill Jones if some powerful person said "kill that lawyer." When he married a lady of means, in 1778, he made her take all necessary steps to make it impossible for him to touch her fortune. His theory that animals will always respond to kindness he carried to such an extreme that it caused his death. On a visit to his wife and mother he was thrown on his head by an unbroken colt, the animal becoming frightened and shying as they neared Wargrave. Day died within an hour, and his wife, who never recovered from the shock, died of a broken heart two years later. Day wrote *The Dying Negro* (1773), a poem, *The Desolation of America* (1777), *Reflections on the Present State of England and the Independence of America* (1782), *Letters of Marius, or Reflections upon the Peace, the East India Bill, and the Present Crisis*, and *Fragments of Original Letters on the Slavery of the Negroes* (both 1784), *Dialogue between a Justice of the Peace and a Farmer* (1785), and the *History of Little Jack* (which was published in the *Children's Miscellany*, and separately in 1788), some pamphlets and a few poems. He is remembered, however, as the author of a moral and didactic romance, *The History of Sanford and Merton* (3 vols., 1783, 1787, 1789), in which he sets forth his ideals of right character and conduct.

Day, William Rufus. b. at Ravenna, Ohio, April 17, 1849; d. July 9, 1923. American jurist. He was graduated from the University of Michigan in 1870 and was admitted to the Ohio bar in 1872. He succeeded John Sherman as U.S. secretary of state in April, 1898, but resigned in September to become chairman of the U.S. peace commission at Paris; judge of the federal circuit court, sixth circuit (1899–1903); appointed associate justice of the U.S. Supreme Court in 1903, serving until 1922.

Dayak (dī′ak). See **Dyak.**

Daye (dā), **Stephen.** [Also, **Day.**] b. at London, c1594; d. at Cambridge, Mass., Dec. 22, 1668. First printer in the Anglo-American colonies, in the English-American colonies, or in British America (as he is variously called). He was a locksmith at Cambridge, England (not a printer, and there is no evidence that he studied or knew anything about printing) when he married a baker's widow, Rebecca Bordman, in 1618. Twenty years later, he came to America with her, his two sons, and her son, sailing from London on the *John*. He was under a two-year contract to work for the Reverend Jesse (or Josse, or José) Glover, a dissenting clergyman, who was bringing with him paper, type, and a printing press, with which Daye was to set up a shop at Cambridge, Mass. Glover died before the ship reached America, but his wife, carrying out the intended plans of her husband, bought a dwelling for the Daye family at Cambridge (on what later became Holyoke Street), and Daye began his printing business. About six months later, in January, 1639, he issued a broadside, the *Oath of a Freeman*, the first piece of printed matter in what is now the U.S. Other works that he printed are *An Almanack, Calculated for New England, by Mr. William Pierce, Mariner* (1639), ten annual almanacs, a speller (1643), *The Book of General the Lawes and Libertyes* (1648), Norris's *Cathechism*, in the same year, and a series of Harvard College broadsides. The first book that he printed, and the first English book printed in the American colonies (not counting the almanacs and broadsides as such) was *The Bay Psalm Book* (1640). He also brought out Winthrop's *A Declaration of Former Passages and Proceedings betwixt the English and the Narrogansetts, with their Confederates, Wherein the Grounds and Justice of the Ensuing Warre are Opened and Cleared* (1645). On Dec. 10, 1641, the Cambridge General Court gave him 300 acres of land in recognition of the fact that he was "the first that sett upon printing." In or after 1643, Daye seems to have turned over the management of the press to his son Matthew, who, it is believed, had learned printing in England. The 1647 edition of the *Almanack* carries Matthew's name on the title page.

Day is Done, The. Poem by Henry Wadsworth Longfellow. It was written in 1844 and published in 1845 in a volume called *The Waif*. It is one of Longfellow's most popular pieces, and its opening lines,

> The day is done and the darkness
> Falls from the wings of Night,

are familiar to thousands, to children who read and hear it, and to adults who recall it as a part of their childhood.

Day-Lewis (-lö′is), **Cecil.** See **Lewis, Cecil Day.**

Day of Atonement. See **Atonement, Day of.**

Day of Doom, The. [Subtitle, **A Poetical Description of the Great and Last Judgment.**] Theological poem by Michael Wigglesworth, published in 1662. The popularity of the poem was attested by the fact that it sold one copy for every 20 persons in the New England colonies, and has gone through at least 18 editions, seven before 1701. The poem describes the condemnation and punishment on Judgment Day of such persons as sinners and infants who died without being baptized.

Day of Dupes. See **Dupes, Day of.**

Day of the Rabblement (rab′l.mẹnt), **The.** Essay in pamphlet form by James Joyce, published in 1901, bitterly attacking the Irish National Theatre movement.

Days. Poem in blank verse by Ralph Waldo Emerson, published in 1857.

Days of the Barricades. See **Barricades, Days of the.**

Days Without End. Play (1934) by Eugene O'Neill. It deals with the theme of Catholic belief.

Dayton (dā′tọn). City in N Kentucky, in Campbell County, on the Ohio River opposite Cincinnati and adjoining Newport. 8,977 (1950).

Dayton. City in SW Ohio, county seat of Montgomery County, on the Miami River, ab. 48 mi. NE of Cincinnati. Manufactures include refrigerators, computing machines, cash registers, lighting systems, and auto and airplane parts. It was settled in 1796 and incorporated in 1805. It is the seat of the University of Dayton and the Dayton Art Institute, and was the home of the Wright brothers and of the poet Paul Laurence Dunbar. One of the chief U.S. aviation centers, it has Wright, Patterson, Fairfield, and other airfields. 243,872 (1950).

Dayton. City in E Tennessee, county seat of Rhea County. Manufactures include hosiery, underwear, and canned foods. It achieved fame as the scene of the Scopes "Monkey Trial" in 1925, a test case of the Tennessee statute prohibiting the teaching of theories denying divine creation. William Jennings Bryan died here soon after the Scopes trial, in which he had served for the prosecution. It is the seat of a university named for him. 3,191 (1950).

Dayton. City in SE Washington, county seat of Columbia County: processing and shipping center for cattle, peas, apples, lumber, and boxes. It was made county seat in 1875. Pop. 2,979 (1950).

Dayton, Elias. b. at Elizabethtown, N.J., May 1, 1737; d. there, Oct. 22, 1807. American Revolutionary officer. He served throughout the Revolution, and participated in the battles of Springfield, Monmouth, Brandywine, and Yorktown. After the war he was made major general of militia in New Jersey, and was a member (1787–88) of the Continental Congress.

Dayton, Jonathan. b. at Elizabethtown, N.J., Oct. 16, 1760; d. there, Oct. 9, 1824. American politician; son of Elias Dayton. He was speaker of the national House of Representatives (1795–99) and U.S. senator from New Jersey (1799–1805).

Dayton, William Lewis. b. at Baskingridge, N.J., Feb. 17, 1807; d. at Paris, Dec. 1, 1864. American jurist and politician; nephew of Jonathan Dayton. He was associate judge of the supreme court of New Jersey (1838–42), U.S. senator from New Jersey (1842–51), Republican candidate for vice-president in 1856, and minister to France (1861–64).

Daytona Beach (dā.tō′na). City in E Florida, in Volusia County, SE of Jacksonville on the Atlantic Ocean: vacation resort. The 23-mi. ocean beach is frequently the scene of automobile speed trials. It is the seat of Bethune-Cookman College. 30,187 (1950).

Dayton-Goose Creek Railway Co. v. United States, 263 U.S. 456 (1924). Unanimous decision of the U.S. Supreme Court upholding the recapture provisions of the Transportation Act of 1920, by which a railroad having an income greater than what the Interstate Commerce Commission had established as a fair return had to maintain the excess in a special fund, half reverting to the government. The opinion delivered by Chief Justice William H. Taft stressed the principle of public interest and was notable for its articulation of broad national powers.

Daza (dä′sä), **Hilarión.** [Original name, **Hilarión Daza Grosolé** (or **Grossoli**).] b. at Sucre, Bolivia, 1840; killed by a mob, March 1, 1894. Bolivian general and politician. From 1858 he took part in various revolutionary disturbances until May, 1876, when he was proclaimed president of Bolivia. Following the seizure of Atacama he declared war on Chile, on March 1, 1879, and in April joined the Peruvian forces at Tacna; but his incompetence and cowardice led to a mutiny of the troops (Dec. 27, 1879), and this was quickly followed by a revolution at La Paz, by which he was overthrown.

Dazey (dā′zi), **Charles Turner.** b. at Lima, Ill., Aug. 13, 1855; d. Feb. 9, 1938. American writer of stage and screen plays, best known for *In Old Kentucky*, a popular melodrama. His other plays include *An American King, That Girl from Texas, The Suburban Home Folks, The Stranger*, and *When Fran Came Home;* for the screen he wrote the scenarios *Wolf Lowry, Redemption of Dave Parcey, Behind the Mask*, and *Shifting Sands.*

Dazzle (daz′l). Man who lives by his wits and cleverly contrives to be an invited guest at Oak Hall, the home of Squire Harkaway, in the comedy *London Assurance* by Dion Boucicault, produced in 1841.

D-Day. June 6, 1944: the day of the Allied invasion of western Europe in World War II. On that day the invasion armada, carrying American, British, and Canadian troops, and using landing craft, gliders, paratroops, and supporting air forces and naval vessels, made landings on four main points over ab. 60 mi. of beaches on the Normandy coast. Although the term D-Day is most often used in connection with this particular operation, its origin and meaning within the armed forces is more generic: "D" stands for "Day," i.e., the day of an invasion or the beginning of any major military operation. In this sense, there were, of course, many D-Days in World War II.

De (dā). [Also, **Dey.**] Sudanic-speaking people of W Africa, inhabiting W Liberia in the neighborhood of Monrovia. They are closely related to the Bassa in language and in culture. They practice hoe agriculture, and their principal crops are dry rice and cassava. Their houses are circular, with mud walls and with palm-leaf thatch.

De Aar (dę är′). Town in S Africa, an important rail junction in Cape of Good Hope province, Union of South Africa, situated in the middle of the province W of the Orange Free State border. It is the junction of the railroad lines from Port Elizabeth (339 mi.) and Capetown (500 mi.), and is the point at which the line to South-West Africa starts. It is also the site of large livestock fairs. 9,137 (1946).

Deacon (dē′kǫn), **Thomas.** b. in 1697; d. at Manchester, England, Feb. 10, 1753. English physician and nonjuring bishop. He became a priest in 1716, settled at Manchester as a physician in 1719 or 1720, and c1733 was consecrated a nonjuring bishop by Bishop Archibald Campbell. He published *The Doctrine of the Church of Rome concerning Purgatory proved to be contrary to Catholic Tradition* (1718), *A Full, True, and Comprehensive View of Christianity* (1747), and others.

Deacon's Masterpiece; or, The Wonderful "One-Hoss Shay," The. Poem by Oliver Wendell Holmes, published in *The Autocrat of the Breakfast-Table* (1858). It originally appeared in the *Atlantic Monthly* in 1858. A perfectionist deacon, desiring to build an unbreakable carriage, constructed the vehicle with all parts having the same strength as each other. A century after its creation, the carriage suddenly collapsed, going "to pieces all at once." The poem is an allegory on Calvinism.

Dead, The. Sonnet (1839) by Jones Very, an American mystic, friend of Emerson, and author of sonnets thought by Bryant to be "among the finest in the language." The thought of the sonnet, which is in the Shakespearian, or English, form is that the living, who have ceased to know the Living God, are the dead ones, not those in the ground for whom they shed tears.

Dead, The. Two sonnets, out of the *1914* group of five, by Rupert Brooke. The same title is given to the third sonnet ("Blow out, you bugles, over the rich Dead!") and to the fourth ("These hearts were woven of human joys and cares"). The fifth one in the group is the famous one with which the poet's name is perhaps chiefly associated, *The Soldier* ("If I should die, think only this of me").

Dead, The. Short story (1914) in a collection, *Dubliners*, by James Joyce. The main characters are a middle-aged Irish schoolteacher and book reviewer, Gabriel Conroy, his wife, Gretta, and Michael Furey, who is dead before the story opens, who loved her. Gretta, who has not been thinking of him, tells her husband that a song they have just heard at a party has brought Michael back to her mind. The confession makes Conroy unhappy as he feels that his wife has closed a door on him and that the dead lover has an advantage over him. The story has been praised for its descriptive as well as its narrative power, and was discussed, 20 years later, by T. S. Eliot in his book of criticism *After Strange Gods.* Dublin is the setting of all the stories, and *The Dead* is the fifteenth, and last, story.

Dead End. Play by Sidney Kingsley, produced in 1935 and published in 1936. Tommy, Dippy, T.B., Angel, and Spit are five embittered children from the slums who live at the dead end of a New York street on the periphery of a fashionable district. The plot involves the difficulties of the children and the contrast between their squalid existence and the lives of the neighboring rich.

Dea Dia (dē′a̧ dī′a̧). One of the most primitive deities of Italian mythology. Nothing is known of the rites associated with her cult until after the reorganization of religious ceremonies by Augustus; from these later ceremonies much may be inferred concerning the earlier rites. The worship of this goddess was entrusted to the Arval Brothers, from which it is thought that she may be in fact Acca Larentia, the mother of the original 12 Arval Brothers. There was a grove dedicated to her at Rome, and a temple in it, where professional priests assisted the 12 members of the brotherhood, who after Augustus always included the emperor, in rites which included the sacrifice of animals, prayer to wine jars, the wearing of wheat-ears as crowns, and ceremonious banquets. It is quite clear, especially as the chief ceremonies in her honor occurred in December and in May, that this was a goddess of the fields and the harvest; moreover, since Dea Dia is not a proper name but a descriptive term, it is certain that she was one of the very ancient deities whose names it was considered impious and dangerous to pronounce.

Deadlock. Novel by Dorothy M. Richardson, published in 1921. It is the sixth section of *Pilgrimage* (1938), a novel sequence in 12 parts employing the stream-of-consciousness technique.

Dead Sea. [Arabic, **Bahr Lut**; Latin, **Lacus Asphaltites, Mare Mortuum.**] Salt lake in Palestine, ab. 16 mi. SE of Jerusalem in the ancient "Vale of Siddim": the Sea of the Plain or of the Arabah, Salt Sea, or East Sea of the Bible. Its waters are intensely salt, and of very high specific gravity. Its principal tributary is the Jordan, but it has no outlet, and its surface is ab. 1,290 ft. below the level of the Mediterranean. Length, ab. 47 mi.; width, 6 to 9½ mi.; depth varies from 1,300 ft. to 3 or 4 ft. in the shallowest section.

Dead Souls. Novel by Nikolai V. Gogol, which appeared in 1842. He began to write it in 1837, and left it unfinished, destroying the concluding portions in a fit of religious mania. An English translation, entitled *Tchitchikoff's Journeys, or Dead Souls*, by Isabel F. Hapgood, was published (1886) at New York. At the time of serfdom a Russian proprietor's fortune was not valued according to the extent of his lands, but according to the number of male serfs who were held upon them. These serfs were called "souls." Chichikov, or Tchitchikoff, the hero of the book, an ambitious rascal, attempts to gain wealth by traveling about buying "dead souls" (serfs who had died but had not yet been listed as dead by the census), and using them to obtain possession of certain lands the government was offering to those who could prove they had the manpower to develop them. The importance of the book is in its realistic pictures of Russia before the liberation of the serfs, and in the stimulation it gave in the development of the Russian realistic novel of the 19th century. The book is a humorous satire based on a very serious attack on the principle of serfdom and on the idiocies of Russian officialdom.

Deadwood (ded'wu̇d). City in W South Dakota, county seat of Lawrence County, in the Black Hills: one of the principal mining and smelting centers in the state; notable for gold mining since 1876. In the Mt. Moriah (or "Boot Hill") Cemetery here are the graves of James Butler ("Wild Bill") Hickok and Martha Jane ("Calamity Jane") Burke. Black Hills National Forest is nearby. 3,288 (1950).

Deadwood Dick (ded'wu̇d dik'). [Original name, **Richard W. Clarke.**] b. at Hansborough, England, Dec. 15, 1845; d. at Deadwood, S.D., May 5, 1930. American frontiersman. Arrived in the U.S. at the age of 16, he traveled (c1874) to the Black Hills, S.D., probably as a scout for General Custer. He worked in the region thereafter as a Pony Express rider, Indian fighter, and guide to U.S. marshals.

Deae Matres (dē'ē mā'trēz). [Also, **Deae Matronae** (mā.trō'nē).] Fertility deities worshipped in ancient times in Belgic Gaul, and among the Teutons. Altars and inscriptions to these or similar deities have been found in those areas. Representations on altars and other monuments depict the Deae Matres as three seated women with baskets or bowls of fruit.

Deák (dā'äk), **Ferencz.** b. at Söjtör, Zala, Hungary, Oct. 17, 1803; d. at Budapest, Jan. 29, 1876. Hungarian statesman. He entered the Hungarian diet in 1832, and was minister of justice in 1848. When the Hungarians under Kossuth revolted against Austrian overlordship, Deák refused to join in what he considered an illegitimate procedure. After the suppression of Hungarian independence in 1849, he remained in retirement. When Lombardy was lost to Austria in 1859, attempts were begun to forestall comparable Hungarian moves. After Austria's defeat by Prussia in 1866 and Austria's ejection from the German union, Deák, Count Julius Andrássy, and Count Friedrich von Beust organized the *Ausgleich* (1867) in which Hungary became, alongside Austria, a separate kingdom, but jointly ruled by the Austrian emperor.

Deakin (dē'kin), **Alfred.** b. at Melbourne, Australia, Aug. 3, 1856; d. there, Oct. 7, 1919. Australian lawyer and political leader, three times prime minister of Australia. He was educated at Melbourne University, was admitted to the bar in 1877, added keen journalistic interests, and moved from there to politics, entering the lower house at Victoria in 1880. He won ministerial office first in 1883. He was identified with promoting irrigation in the state of Victoria. In 1887 he came to the notice of the Imperial authorities for outspokenness on colonial grievances; his reputation was enhanced at the Imperial Conference (1907). He was an early proponent of Australian federation, and played a large role in converting Victoria to the doctrine. He was sent to the federal house of representatives from 1901 to 1913, served as attorney general in Sir Edmund Barton's cabinet, and succeeded Barton as prime minister in 1902, serving until 1904. His second ministry lasted from 1905 to 1908, and his final term of office extended from 1909 to 1910. He retired in 1913 because of failing mental powers and did no public work after 1915. He left a vast legend concerning his powers as an orator, astute politician, and middle-class leader.

Deal (dēl). Municipal borough, market town, seaport; and seaside resort in SE England, in Kent, situated on the North Downs ab. 8 mi. NE of Dover, ab. 87 mi. SE of London by rail. It was formerly one of the Cinque Ports, and contains Deal Castle. The Justices of the Cinque Ports still sit here. Near here Julius Caesar is supposed to have made his first landing in Britain in 55 B.C. 24,276 (1951).

Dealey (dē'li), **James Quayle.** b. at Manchester, England, Aug. 13, 1861; d. Jan. 22, 1937. American political scientist. He came to America as a young man, and was instructor (1893–95) of Latin and professor (1895–1928) of political science at Brown University and editor (1929 *et seq.*) of the Dallas (Tex.) *News.* He was the author of *The Development of the State* (1909), *The Family in its Sociological Aspects* (1912), *Growth of State Constitutions* (1915), *Sociology—Its Development and Application* (1921), *State and Government* (1921), *Foreign Policies of the United States* (1927), and *Political Situations in Rhode Island* (1928), and coauthor with Lester F. Ward of *Textbook of Sociology* (1905).

Deal Island (dēl). [Former name, **Devil's Island.**] Island in SE Maryland, in Chesapeake Bay ab. 25 mi. SW of Salisbury, Md. The island is noted for its oyster and crab fisheries and for muskrat trapping. There are several packing plants and a large fleet of small vessels. Length, ab. 2½ mi.; pop. 957 (1950).

De Amicis (dā ä.mē'chēs), **Edmondo.** b. at Oneglia, Italy, Oct. 21, 1846; d. at Bordighera, Italy, March 11, 1908. Italian writer of travels. He was in the Italian army (1865–70), and fought at the battle of Custozza in 1866. His early works include *Ricordi di Londra* (1874), *L'Olanda* (1874), *Marocco* (1875), *Constantinople* (1877), *Pagine sparse* (1877), *Ricordi di Parigi*, and his most popular book, *Cuore* (1886), a series of essays and sketches ostensibly written by a schoolboy. Among his later works are *Poesie* (1880), *Ritratti letterarii* (1881), *Gli amici* (1882), *Alle porte d'Italia* (1886), *La Carrozza di tutti* (1898), *Speranze e gloria* (1900), *Memorie* (1900), *Ricordi d'infanzia e di scuola* (1901), *Capo d'anno* (1902), and *Giardino della follia* (1902).

De Amicitia (dē am.i.sish'i.ạ). [Eng. trans., *"On Friendship"*; also called **Laelius.**] Treatise by Cicero, in the form of a conversation between Laelius and his sons-in-law, C. Fannius and Q. Mucius Scaevola, devoted to the praise of friendship.

Dean (dēn), **Amos.** b. at Barnard, Vt., Jan. 16, 1803; d. at Albany, N.Y., Jan. 26, 1868. American jurist. He became chancellor and professor of history in the University of Iowa in 1855. He published *Medical Jurispru-*

dence (1854), *Bryant and Stratton's Commercial Law* (1861), and others.

Dean, Bashford. b. at New York, Oct. 28, 1867; d. at Battle Creek, Mich., Dec. 6, 1928. American zoölogist, professor of vertebrate zoölogy at Columbia University from 1904. He studied at the College of the City of New York and afterward at Columbia, Munich, Naples, and Misaki (Japan). In 1889–92 and 1900–01 he was engaged in biological work for the U.S. Fish Commission, and was curator of fishes at the American Museum of Natural History at New York from 1903 to 1910 and after 1911. He was the author of numerous works on the anatomy and embryology of fishes. He was also curator of arms and armor in the Metropolitan Museum of Art at New York, from 1903.

Dean, Forest of. Forest in Gloucestershire, England, situated between the lower Wye and the Severn, SW of Gloucester. It has been noted for its production of coal and iron. Its chief trees are oaks and beeches.

Dean, Jay Hanna. [Sometimes **Jerome Herman Dean**; called **Dizzy Dean.**] b. at Lucas, Ark., 1911—. American baseball pitcher, and radio and television broadcaster. He has at different times given different accounts of his age, his birthplace, and his given names (whether seriously or as a prank is not definitely known, although many suspect the latter). He was long known as Jerome Herman Dean, but later explained that he had called himself Jerome Herman to console the mother of a boyhood friend, of that name, who had died in his youth. His family were sharecroppers, and from childhood he picked cotton at 50 cents an hour until he joined the U.S. army at the age of 16. In the army it was discovered that he was a pitcher of considerable ability, and after his discharge he found employment in professional baseball, quickly becoming one of the most valued major league players, and one of the most popular by virtue of a personality which lent itself to exploitation by publicity men and sports writers, who, probably with reference both to the dazzling speed of his fast ball, and to his flamboyant and unpredictable ways, gave him the nickname "Dizzy." For several years (1932–38) the star pitcher of the St. Louis Cardinals of the National League, he was traded to the Chicago Cubs, but an injury to his pitching arm in 1937 had permanently impaired his efficiency, and in 1940 he was waived to a minor league team. But this, a common fate of major league players, did not suit "Dizzy," who in 1941 began to broadcast radio accounts of baseball games from a St. Louis station, with instant and spectacular success, due at least partly to his use of weird and amusing words and phrases, ostensibly derived from Arkansas hill-billy speech. On one occasion a delegation of high-school teachers of English protested to the radio station whose facilities he used that his broadcasts were corrupting the speech habits of their students. In 1950 he became a television commentator, broadcasting from a New York station.

Dean, Julia. b. July 22, 1830; d. at New York, March 6, 1868. American actress. She first appeared at the Bowery Theater as Julia in *The Hunchback*. She was the original Norma in Epes Sargent's *Priestess*, and also the original Leonor in Boker's tragedy *Leonor de Guzman*.

Dean, William F. b. at Carlyle, Ill., Aug. 1, 1899—. American soldier. In World War II, he served (1943–44) as chief of the requirements section at Army Ground Forces headquarters before taking command of the 44th infantry division, which he led in fighting in Germany and Austria. He was military governor (1947–48) of the U.S.-occupied areas in Korea, and, with the outbreak of the Korean War, assumed command (July 2, 1950) of all U.S. forces in Korea, serving until superseded (July 13, 1950) by Walton H. Walker. He led the 24th division in the action at Taejon, but in the retreat from the burning city disappeared and was reported missing in action July 22, 1950; he was later found to be a prisoner of the North Koreans, who released him in September, 1953.

Deane (dēn), **Charles.** b. at Biddeford, Me., Nov. 10, 1813; d. at Cambridge, Mass., Nov. 13, 1889. American historian. He was a merchant at Boston, for many years, and retired from business in 1864, settling at Cambridge, Mass. He collected a valuable library of books relating to early New England history, and edited *Bradford's History of Plymouth Plantation* (1856), *Wingfield's Discourse of Virginia* (1860), and other historical documents.

Deane, Henry. d. at Lambeth (now part of London), Feb. 15, 1503. Archbishop of Canterbury. He was chief of the English commissioners who concluded the treaty leading to the marriage between Margaret Tudor, daughter of Henry VII of England, and James IV of Scotland, in 1503.

Deane, Lucy. In George Eliot's novel *The Mill on the Floss*, a pretty, amiable girl, the cousin and rival of Maggie Tulliver.

Deane, Richard. b. at Guyting, Gloucestershire, England, 1610; d. in battle off North Foreland, June 3, 1653. English admiral, and one of the signers of Charles I's death warrant. He volunteered for the Parliamentary artillery and fought (1644) under Essex in Cornwall. At Naseby (1645) he was in command of the artillery and thereafter was one of Cromwell's principal aides. He had an important part, after 1649, in the establishment of the Parliamentary fleet, acting as one of the three commissioners, with the title of general-at-sea. He fought with the army at Worcester (1651) and in Scotland (1652).

Deane, Silas. b. at Groton, Conn., Dec. 24, 1737; d. aboard ship near Deal, England, Sept. 23, 1789. American Revolutionary patriot and diplomat, noted as the first foreign emissary of the American colonies. He was graduated (1758) from Yale, where he also took his M.A. (1763). Admitted to the bar (1761), he established his practice at Wethersfield, Conn., in 1762 and by a well-connected marriage received a mercantile business. In 1769 he was chairman of a Wethersfield committee to enforce a nonconsumption agreement, became a member of the General Assembly three years later, and was secretary (1773) of the legislative committee of correspondence. He was a member (1774–75) of the Continental Congress, serving on several committees responsible for naval preparations. He was chosen (March, 1776) to go to France as the first American representing the interests of the colonies overseas. He had a dual function: to handle commercial transactions, and to purchase arms and supplies for the American forces. He succeeded in his mission, and in September, 1776, was joined by Benjamin Franklin and Arthur Lee. Deane also commissioned and dispatched foreign officers, among them Lafayette, De Kalb, Pulaski, and Steuben, who aided the Revolutionary cause. He also sent over some poorly selected soldiers of fortune; this, combined with unfavorable reports submitted by Arthur Lee, resulted in his recall (1778). The advances he had made to the Revolutionary cause while abroad had not been covered by proper audits, and Deane later failed to secure an authorized statement. His faith in the Revolutionary government declined, and, while abroad attempting to obtain evidence that his accounts were legitimate, he wrote (1781) a number of letters to American friends counseling reconciliation with England. They were picked up by the British and published (1781) by the Loyalist press at New York; thereafter, Deane was regarded as a traitor to the government he had served. He died a bankrupt, on his way back to the U.S. Congress later (1842) made partial restitution to his heirs. See *Silas Deane*, by G. L. Clark (1913).

Deán Funes (dā.än' fö'nās). City in C Argentina, in Córdoba province: resort in the Sierras, frequented by hunters. 13,840 (1947).

Deán Funes, El. See **Funes, Gregorio.**

De Angelis (dē an'je.lis), **(Thomas) Jefferson.** b. at San Francisco, Nov. 30, 1859; d. March 20, 1933. American comedian and singer, said by some sources to have appeared for the first time on the professional stage at the age of 10. Whether this is true or not, he is known to have been in vaudeville by 1874, and later (1880–84) to have headed his own company on a tour of Australia, South Africa, and China. He was leading comedian (1890–93) at the Casino at New York, and starred in *Fantana*, *The Great White Way*, *Revelry*, *School for Scandal*, *The Royal Family*, and *Apron Strings*, besides appearing in more than a hundred operas. He took the part of Ko-Ko in 12 productions of Gilbert and Sullivan's *The Mikado*.

Deans (dēnz), **Douce Davie.** Cow-feeder in Sir Walter Scott's novel *The Heart of Midlothian*. He is the father of Jeanie and Effie, and is distracted between his religious principles as an ardent Cameronian and his desire to save his daughter Effie's life.

Deans, Effie or Euphemia. In Sir Walter Scott's *The Heart of Midlothian,* a beautiful and erring girl, the younger half sister of Jeanie Deans.

Deans, Jeanie. Heroine of Sir Walter Scott's novel *The Heart of Midlothian,* the half sister of Effie Deans. In her devotion to her sister she walks all the way to London to obtain pardon for Effie from the queen. Her good sense, calm heroism, and disinterestedness move the Duke of Argyle to procure her the desired interview, which is successful.

Dearborn (dir'bôrn, -bo̤rn). City in S Lower Michigan, in Wayne County, adjoining Detroit: home of the Ford Motor Company and allied Ford industries. The River Rouge plant of the Ford Company, one of the largest mass-production automobile factories in the world, is nearby. Dearborn was the birthplace of Henry Ford, founder of the Ford Company, who established Greenfield Village and the Edison Institute of Technology here. 94,994 (1950).

Dearborn, Fort. Fort established (1804) by the U.S. government, which became the nucleus of Chicago.

Dearborn, George Van Ness. b. at Nashua, N.H., Aug. 15, 1869; d. Dec. 12, 1938. American psychiatrist and physiologist. He was professor of physiology and director (1900–16) of the physiological laboratory at Tufts College, professor (1906–21) of psychology and education at the Sargent Normal School at Cambridge, Mass., surgeon (1921 *et seq.*) in the neuropsychiatric section of the U.S. Public Health Service, and medical officer expert (1924) of the U.S. Veterans' Bureau. His books include *The Emotion of Joy* (1899), *A Textbook of Human Physiology* (1908), *Moto-Sensory Development* (1910), *Relations of Mind and Body* (1914), *The Influence of Joy* (1916), *How to Learn Easily* (1916), *The Physiology of Exercise* (1918), and *The Psychology of Clothing* (1918).

Dearborn, Henry. b. at Hampton, N.H., Feb. 23, 1751; d. June 6, 1829. American soldier, legislator, and secretary of war (1801–09) under Jefferson. He studied medicine privately, establishing (1772) his practice at Nottingham Square, N.H. A captain of militia before the outbreak of the Revolution, he participated in the battle of Bunker Hill and in Arnold's expedition to Quebec, being taken prisoner during the American attack on the city. He was exchanged (1777) in time to take an active part in the campaign against Burgoyne. He was at Valley Forge (1777–78), participated in the battle of Monmouth (where his regiment's behavior earned a commendation from Washington), in General Sullivan's expedition against the Six Nations, and at Yorktown. The journal which he kept during almost the entire period of the war constitutes one of the very few eyewitness accounts of the American side of the Revolution. He left the army in 1783, became (1790) U.S. marshal for the District of Maine, and was its Republican representative (1793–97) in Congress. He was secretary of war in Jefferson's administration (1801–09). In 1803 he issued from Washington the order for the establishment of a fort at "Chikago." The important part which this post, Fort Dearborn, played in the early history of Chicago has given his name a lasting association with that city. He became collector for the port of Boston in 1809, and in 1812 was appointed by Madison as "Senior Major-General" in the U.S. army and assigned to the command of the area from the New England coast to the Niagara River. He prepared an extensive plan of campaign, calling for simultaneous attacks at strategic points along the border, but he lacked the vigor and ability to carry it out, thus contributing to the defeat of William Hull at Detroit through failure to provide a diversion. For his continued incompetence, he was relieved of his command in July, 1813, and assigned to that of New York City. He received his honorable discharge in 1815. He served as minister to Portugal from 1822 to 1824. His last years were spent in retirement.

Dearborn, Henry Alexander Scammell. b. at Exeter, N.H., March 3, 1783; d. at Roxbury, Mass., July 29, 1851. American politician; son of Henry Dearborn. He was collector of the port of Boston (1812–29), was elected to the Massachusetts legislature in 1829, became a state senator in 1830, was in 1831 elected to Congress, where he served one term, and was made adjutant general of Massachusetts in 1835, from which post he was removed in 1843 for having furnished arms to Rhode Island during Dorr's rebellion. He was mayor of Roxbury from 1847 until his death. He wrote *Internal Improvements and Commerce of the West* (1809).

Dear Judas (jö'da̤s). Narrative poem by Robinson Jeffers, title piece of a volume published in 1929.

Dearman (dir'ma̤n). Original name of **Irvington,** N.Y.

Dearmer (dir'mėr), **Percy.** b. at London, Feb. 27, 1867; d. at Westminster, London, May 29, 1936. English clergyman and authority on ecclesiastical art and music. He was chaplain (1915) to the British Red Cross in Serbia, professor (1919–36) of ecclesiastical art at King's College, London, and canon (1931–36) of Westminster. His books include *Highways and Byways in Normandy* (1900), *The English Liturgy* (1903), *False Gods* (1914), *Our National Church* (1934), and *Christianity as a New Religion* (1935).

Dearne (dėrn). Urban district in N central England, in the West Riding of Yorkshire, ab. 171 mi. N of London by rail. It comprises parts of the former urban districts of Bolton-upon-Dearne and Thurnscoe. It has manufactures of woolens, and was formerly a coal-mining center. 24,253 (1951).

Dearth (dėrth), **Henry Golden.** b. at Bristol, R.I., 1864; d. at New York, March 27, 1918. American landscape painter. He studied at the École des Beaux-Arts, Paris, later exhibiting at Paris as well as in the U.S. Several medals were awarded him, and he was made an associate of the National Academy of Design in 1902 and an academician in 1906. His works hang in the Metropolitan Museum and the Brooklyn Museum at New York, the National Gallery at Washington, D.C., the Detroit Museum, the Art Institute of Chicago, and the Carnegie Institute. His paintings include *Cornelia, Road and Canal, Gardenias, An Old Church at Montreuil, Dreamland, Virgin and Child,* and *The Three-Master.*

Déat (dā.ȧ), **Marcel.** b. at Guérigny, Nièvre, France, March 7, 1894—. French politician and newspaper editor. Quitting the Socialist Party in 1933, he served as a deputy (1926–29, 1932–36, 1939–40), as air minister (1936), and as labor minister (1944) under Pétain. Sentenced to death in absentia (June, 1945), he was subsequently reported in hiding in Italy and France. He wrote a famous editorial, *Why Die for Danzig?,* shortly before the outbreak of World War II.

Death and Transfiguration. English title of **Tod und Verklärung.**

Death Comes for the Archbishop. Historical novel (1927) by Willa Cather. It concerns the French bishop Jean Latour and his vicar Father Joseph Vaillant, who are aided by Kit Carson and Indian guides in winning the friendship of the Hopis and Navahos. The two missionaries overcome the hostility of the Spanish clergy and establish their religion in the inhospitable territories of Colorado and New Mexico. The scholarly bishop, whose character contrasts sharply with that of his good friend, the practical-minded and affable Father Vaillant, becomes archbishop of Santa Fe, and after his death is universally mourned.

Death in the Afternoon. Discursive narrative by Ernest Hemingway, published in 1932. It contains much specific and oftentimes fairly technical information about bullfighters and their techniques (Hemingway has long been interested in the subject, as evidenced by the importance of the bullfighter in the plot of his early novel *The Sun Also Rises,* and has a very respectable knowledge of it). However, the book is not simply an English-language guide to bullfighting; it might perhaps better be described as Hemingway's chief nonfictional attempt to express his attitude toward life and death. The bull may be viewed as the symbol of that which faces inevitable, but far from ignoble, destruction, and the bullfight itself becomes, in its final meaning, a highly formalized expression of several things in which Hemingway deeply believes: that death is not the supreme tragedy, that courage is very close to being the supreme virtue, and that, even though one of the two contestants may be foredoomed, a mortal struggle may lend dignity and nobility to those engaged in it (it is essential to this, of course, that the contestants should not lack respect for each other, and hence the bullfighter is in Hemingway's eyes no mere butcher, but a brave man fully cognizant of his role as a participant in a drama filled with symbolism).

Death in the School-Room. Short story (1841) by Walt Whitman. It was popular in its day and was published in several newspapers. It is the story of a brutal schoolmaster who flogs one of his students, a widow's son, until he dies. It seems to have been published at least once in the Brooklyn *Eagle* and belongs to what has been called Whitman's "newspaper period" (1838–44).

Death of a Hero. Satirical novel, a product of experiences in World War I, by Richard Aldington, published in 1929.

Death of a Salesman. Tragedy (1949) by Arthur Miller. The play, in two acts, tells the story of Willy Loman, a middle-aged salesman who is beginning to lose his grip on life and himself and who is afraid to face the truth. The action takes place in different rooms in Willy's house, inside and out, in various offices he visits at New York and Boston, and in his disordered mind, which is gradually breaking. By means of an interesting technique, which has aroused some discussion, although spectators sometimes found it confusing, the past and the present were blended, and past events, such as an old and long-forgotten affair with a woman in a cheap hotel, were presented as though they were taking place at the moment (as they were in Willy's mind). The play opened at the Morosco Theater at New York, on Feb. 10, 1949, and enjoyed a long run. Lee J. Cobb, Thomas Mitchell, Gene Lockhart (and others in road companies) all scored successes in their varied interpretations of the salesman. On the screen, Frederic March played the title role, and in both versions Mildred Dunnock won praise for her performance of Linda, Willy's faithful wife.

Death of Caesar (sē'zạr). Painting (1867) by Gérôme. Caesar's body lies at the foot of Pompey's statue; the conspirators, still holding their daggers, are grouped in the background, and all the senators but one have fled from their seats.

Death of Cuchulain (kö.ċhö'lin), **The.** Poem (1893) by William Butler Yeats. It tells the story of the great Irish hero, Cuchulain, who unknowingly kills his own son in battle (just as Rustum kills his son, Sohrab, in Arnold's poem). The story has been told in many forms by many Irish authors, and Yeats himself told it later (1904) in his play *On Baile's Strand.*

Death of Eve, The. Dramatic fragment (1912) by William Vaughn Moody. It is the third and last part of a trilogy of dramas in verse, the first being *The Fire Bringer* (1904), dealing with a Greek theme, Prometheus, and the second, *The Masque of Judgment* (1900), dealing with the medieval theme of man's relationship with God, and presenting the angel Raphael as the chief character. *The Death of Eve,* which was never finished, dealing with a Hebrew theme, shows how God and man are brought together through Eve's agency.

Death of General Montgomery (mọnt.gum'ėr.i), **The.** Tragedy in blank verse by Hugh Henry Brackenridge, written in 1777.

Death of General Wolfe (wůlf), **The.** Painting by Sir Benjamin West (1771), in the Grosvenor Gallery, London. The general lies on the ground supported and surrounded by soldiers, one of whom holds the Union Jack. In the distance a soldier runs toward the group, bearing a captured French flag.

Death of Little Boys. Poem by Allen Tate. It is included in his volume *Mr. Pope and Other Poems* (1928), and is to be found also in several anthologies. Short as the poem is (20 lines) it has been praised for its humanity, and its timeless and placeless quality.

Death of Marlowe (mär'lō), **The.** Tragedy by R. H. Horne, published in 1837.

Death of Slavery, The. Poem by William Cullen Bryant. It expresses his happiness at the abolition of Negro slavery, and was written in the same year (1865) as his *The Death of Lincoln.*

Death of Society, The. Novel by Romer Wilson (Mrs. Edward J. O'Brien), published in 1921. It was awarded the Hawthornden prize.

Death of the Flowers, The. Lamentation by William Cullen Bryant on the death of his sister, published in 1825.

Death of the Hired Man, The. Narrative in blank verse by Robert Frost, published in his *North of Boston* (1914). It describes the character and death of Silas, an old New England farmhand whose former pride and independence have given way to a pathetic need for a final "home."

Death of the Moth, and Other Essays, The. Volume of critical essays (1942) by Virginia Woolf. It expresses her views on various phases of the culture of her time, and was published a year after her death.

Death of Wallenstein (wol'ẹn.stīn; German, väl'ẹn.shtīn), **The.** Historical tragedy (1799) in three parts by Schiller, dealing with the Bohemian general and politician Albrecht Wenzel Eusebius von Wallenstein. It was translated into English (1798–99, published 1800) by Coleridge, who used manuscript versions, not a printed text, a fact which is used to explain or excuse what some German critics have pointed to as mistranslations. Schiller's trilogy consists of *Wallenstein's Lager, Die Piccolomini,* and *Wallenstein's Tod.*

Death's Head Corps. See **Black Brunswickers.**

Death's Jest Book, or The Fool's Tragedy. Tragedy by T. L. Beddoes, published in 1850. It is the true story of the stabbing of a duke in the 13th century by his court fool.

Death Song. Poem of five lines by Bede. It is the only poem by Bede that has survived, and that because it is quoted in a letter by Saint Cuthbert. Like *Beowulf,* it shows the great store that men set by an honorable name after death.

Death Valley. [Also, **Amargosa Desert.**] Desert region in Inyo county, E California, and in S Nevada, lying, at its lowest part, 280 ft. below sea level: made a U.S. National Monument in 1933. Area, 1,850,565 acres.

Deauville (dō.vēl). Town in NW France, in the department of Calvados, adjoining the town of Trouville-sur-Mer, situated on the English channel at the mouth of the Touques River, N of Lisieux. It is one of the chief resorts and bathing beaches on the Normandy coast; many fashionable sports events are held here. The resort was founded by the duke of Morny during the Second Empire. It suffered considerable damage (1944) during the Normandy invasion in World War II. 4,663 (1946).

Dea Vocontiorum (dē'ạ vọ.kon.ti.ō'rum). Ancient name of **Die.**

De Bardeleben (dẹ bär'dẹ.lā.bẹn), **Henry Fairchild.** [Called the **"King of the Southern Iron World."**] b. in Alabama, July 22, 1840; d. Dec. 6, 1910. American industrialist who developed the coal and pig-iron industries in Alabama. As ward (and later son-in-law) of Daniel Pratt, a wealthy industrialist, he inherited large mine holdings in Alabama. He was cofounder (1886) of the De Bardeleben Coal and Iron Company which, with the Pinckard and De Bardeleben Land Company, formed the town of Bessemer, near Birmingham, Ala. His interests were reorganized (1887) into one company and taken over (1891) by the Tennessee Coal, Iron and Railroad Company.

De Bary (dẹ bä.rē'), **Heinrich Anton.** b. at Frankfort on the Main, Germany, Jan. 26, 1831; d. at Strasbourg, Jan. 19, 1888. German physician and botanist, noted especially for his researches in cryptogamic botany. He became professor of botany at Freiburg in 1855, at Halle in 1867, and at Strasbourg in 1872.

Debatable Land. Region on the border of England and Scotland, between the Esk and Sark, formerly claimed by both kingdoms.

Debbitch (deb'ich), **Deborah.** In Sir Walter Scott's novel *Peveril of the Peak,* the governess of Alice Bridgenorth. She was coquettish and deceitful.

Debbora (deb'ọ.rạ). See **Deborah.**

Debeney (dẹ.bẹ.nā), **Marie Eugène.** b. at Bourg-en-Bresse, Ain, France, Jan. 5, 1864; d. there, Nov. 9, 1943, from injuries reportedly sustained in a bombing attack. French army officer, army commander during World War I. He commanded the 5th Army in the victory of Didier (1918), was named (1919) head of the École de Guerre and later (1924) chief of the general staff, and served as a member of the supreme war council until 1934. He supported the Pétain regime after the fall of France.

De Beringhen (dẹ ber'ing.ẹn). See **Beringhen, De.**

Debidour (dẹ.bē.dör), **Élie Louis Marc Marie Antoine.** [Called **Antonin Debidour.**] b. at Nontron, France, Jan. 31, 1847; d. at Paris, Feb. 21, 1917. French historian. He served as professor (1880 *et seq.*) at Nancy and

Paris. His works include *L'Église catholique et l'état sous la troisième république* (The Catholic Church and the State under the Third Republic, 1906–09), and *Vers la grande guerre* (Toward the Great War, 1917).

Debierne (dę.byern), **André Louis.** b. 1874—. French physicist. He discovered the element actinium (1899), and later assisted Marie Curie in the isolation of elemental radium (1910). He was professor of heat at the Municipal School of Chemistry and Physics, Paris.

Debije (dę.bī'). See **Debye, Peter Joseph Willem.**

De Bilt (dę bilt'). [Also: **De Bildt, de Bildt.**] Town in C Netherlands, in the province of Utrecht. It is an eastern suburb of the city of Utrecht and seat of a meteorological institute. 14,561 (1939).

Dęblin (dem'blēn). [Russian, **Ivangorod.**] Fortress town in S central Poland, at the confluence of the Vistula and the Wieprz rivers, ab. 72 mi. by rail SE of Warsaw. From the early 19th century there was a fortress here established by the Russians, which was later expanded to a fortified perimeter of ab. 14 mi., forming one of the key bastions for the defense of Russian Poland. In World War I the first battle in October, 1914 resulted in the withdrawal of German forces. A second attack in 1915 resulted in the capture of the fortress by the Germans on Aug. 4, 1915. The fortifications were destroyed in these battles.

Debonair. Novel by G. B. Stern, published in 1928 and dramatized in 1930.

Débonnaire (dā.bo.ner), **Louis le.** See **Louis I** (of the *Holy Roman Empire*).

De Bono (dā bô'nō), **Emilio.** b. at Cassano d'Adda, Italy, 1866; d. at Verona, Italy, Jan. 11, 1944. Italian general. An early Fascist, he was one of the quadrumvirate leading the March on Rome (October, 1922). He was named (1925) governor of Tripolitania and appointed (1925) senator, and served as minister (1929) of the colonies and high commissioner (1935) in Italian Africa. Having royalist leanings and being not in complete agreement with Mussolini, he voted (1943) against the Duce in the grand council; for this the Fascists condemned him to death as a traitor.

Deborah (deb'ǭ.rạ). [Also, **Debbora.**] In the Bible, a prophetess and judge of Israel. She lived on Mount Ephraim, between Ramah and Bethel. She summoned Barak to deliver the tribes under her jurisdiction from the tyranny of Jabin, prophesied success for him, and sang a famous song of triumph after his victory over the Canaanites (Judges, v.). This song is considered by critics to be one of the most ancient pieces in the Old Testament.

Deborah. German drama by S. H. Mosenthal, the original of *Leah.*

Deborah Debbitch (deb'ich). See **Debbitch, Deborah.**

De Bow (dē bō'), **James Dunwoody Brownson.** b. at Charleston, S.C., July 10, 1820; d. at Elizabeth, N.J., Feb. 27, 1867. American editor, journalist, and statistician.

Debra Markos (deb'rạ mär'kōs). Town in E Africa, in Ethiopia, in Salale province, midway between Addis Ababa and Lake Tana. It is on one of the main roads from the capital to Gondar, and is a local market and trade center. Pop. ab. 5,000.

Debrecen (de'bre.tsen). [Also: **Debreczen** (de'bre.tsen), **Debreczin** (-tsēn).] City in E Hungary, near the Rumanian border, ab. 120 mi. E of Budapest. It is one of the chief cities of Hungary, famous for the nearby Hortobágy Puszta, a wide area of dry, steppelike grazing land, and is a major commercial center, with annual fairs and horse markets. There are railroad repair shops, flour mills, and metallurgical and other industries. The city is the center of Magyar Calvinism, has a large Reformed Church and a Reformed college, founded in 1588, now succeeded by the Tisza István University. There is a museum and a large library; the first Hungarian printing establishment was founded in Debrecen in 1561. In this city, on April 14, 1849, the independence of Hungary from the Hapsburg crown and the existence of a republic were proclaimed under the leadership of Kossuth. 119,570 (1948).

Debrett (dę.bret'), **John.** b. c1752; d. at London, Nov. 15, 1822. English publisher. In 1781 he purchased the Piccadilly business of John Almon, bookseller and political journalist. He compiled and published *Peerage of England, Scotland, and Ireland, Containing an Account of all the Peers* (2 vols., May, 1802), which ran through 14 editions during his lifetime, and *Baronetage of England, Containing their Descent and Present State* (1808). Both works, bearing Debrett's name, are still published annually. He retired from business in 1814.

Debrosses (dę.bros), **Charles.** See **Brosses, Charles de.**

Debs (debz), **Eugene Victor.** b. at Terre Haute, Ind., Nov. 5, 1855; d. at Elmhurst, Ill., Oct. 20, 1926. American labor organizer and Socialist leader. At the age of 15 he went to work in a railroad shop, before long became a fireman, in 1875 helped organize, and became secretary of, a lodge of the Brotherhood of Locomotive Firemen, and in 1880 was made national secretary-treasurer of that Brotherhood and editor of its magazine. Meanwhile in 1879 he had been elected city clerk of Terre Haute, holding that office into 1883, after which by election in 1884 he served some years in the legislature of Indiana. In 1892 he tried to resign from his offices in the Brotherhood, but was unanimously reëlected. He had already concluded that craft unionism was an ineffective form of labor organization, and that it should be superseded by industrial unionism. In 1893 he was therefore the prime mover in the formation of the American Railway Union, which was open to all railroad workers. This pioneer industrial union, of which Debs was chosen president, won several strikes. In 1894, when the employees of the Pullman Palace Car Company struck, the American Railway Union directed its members to refuse to move Pullman cars. Debs, though he thought this decision unwise, in the prevailing circumstances, vigorously directed its implementation. President Grover Cleveland, on the ground that movement of the mails was being interrupted, sent federal troops into Chicago over the protest of John P. Altgeld, governor of Illinois, who pointed out that the labor struggle was accompanied by no disorders. A federal court issued an injunction against the American Railway Union's tactics, a federal grand jury indicted Debs and three others for conspiracy to obstruct the mails, and they were arrested; shortly afterward Debs and six others were arrested for violating the injunction. The conspiracy case ended in a mistrial, but on the contempt charge Debs and the others were sent to jail for six months. The most notable result of this sentence was perhaps that during his imprisonment Debs's reading and study led him to become a socialist, and in 1897 he organized the Social Democratic Party, which together with a faction of the Socialist Labor Party, nominated him for President of the United States in 1900, when he was credited with 96,000 votes. In 1901 the Social Democrats and seceding Socialist Laborites formed the Socialist Party; Debs was its presidential candidate in 1904, 1908, and 1912, rolling up votes of 402,000, 420,000, and 901,000. During these years he was an associate editor of the weekly newspaper *Appeal to Reason,* for which he went on lecture tours. In 1905 he helped establish the Industrial Workers of the World. Before long he withdrew from this group, but when some of its leaders were charged with murder he campaigned tirelessly in their defense. He approved the Socialist Party's stand against American participation in World War I, and his speech at the Ohio convention of the party in 1918 led to a sentence of ten years in prison for violation of the Espionage Act. While a prisoner in 1920 he received 919,000 votes for the presidency. On Christmas, 1921, he was freed by President Harding. He hailed the Russian Revolution, but protested to Lenin against the execution of dissident socialists. In 1924 he backed the Progressive Party candidate, Robert M. LaFollette. Failing health sent him twice to a sanitarium, where his death finally occurred.

Debs, In re, 158 U.S. 564 (1895). Case arising out of the Pullman railroad strike of 1894, in which the defendants, who had been found guilty of contempt and sentenced to jail for violating an injunction to abstain from interfering with trains in interstate commerce or those carrying mails, were denied a writ of habeas corpus by the U.S. Supreme Court. Justice David J. Brewer, speaking for a united court, declared: "The entire strength of the nation may be used to enforce in any part of the land the full and free exercise of all national powers and the security of all rights entrusted by the Constitution to its care. . . .

If the emergency arises, the army of the nation, and all its militia, are at the service of the nation to compel obedience to its laws."

Debt Funding Commission. Body created by an act of the U.S. Congress in February, 1922, for the purpose of making funding agreements with European debtor nations, including Great Britain, France, and Italy, which had received U.S. loans during World War I. The commission fixed sums, interest rates, and annuities. It was terminated in 1927.

Deburau or **Debureau** (dẹ.bü.rō), **Jean Gaspard.** [Original Czech name, **Jan Kaspar Dvořák.**] b. in Bohemia, 1796; d. 1846. French pantomimist. Reviving the figure of Pierrot, he gave it a character of wistful, pathetic charm, so that ever since his time all Pierrots, in pantomime and ballet, have reflected the Deburau Pierrot. His biography by Francis Kozik is entitled *The Great Debureau*, and he is the central figure of the play *Deburau*, by Sacha Guitry.

Debus (dā'bůs), **Heinrich.** b. at Wolfhagen, Germany, 1824; d. at Kassel, Germany, 1916. Early German organic chemist. He investigated the oxidation of alcohols, glycols, and glycerine, glyoxalic acid, madder-root chemistry, gunpowder chemistry, and other fields. He was professor at the Marine Academy, Greenwich, England, from 1873 to 1888.

Debussy (dẹ.bū'si; French, dẹ.bü.sē), **Claude Achille.** b. at St.-Germain-en-Laye, France, Aug. 22, 1862; d. at Paris, March 26, 1918. French composer, representative of the extreme left wing of the early 20th-century French school in finding new methods of expression and in harmonic combinations. He studied (1874–84) at the Paris Conservatory, made trips to Russia and Italy, and spent his life composing at Paris. His compositions include an opera, *Pelléas et Mélisande* (1902); cantatas, *Printemps* (1882), *L'Enfant prodigue* (1884), and *La Demoiselle élue* (1888); a string quartet; *Prélude à l'Après-midi d'une faune* (1894), *Nocturnes* (1893–99), *La Mer* (1903–05), *Rapsodie* 1905), *Images* (1906–12), and other pieces for) orchestra; (piano pieces, such as *Deux arabesques* (1888, *Rêverie* (c1890), *Children's Corner* suite (1908), preludes, and études; and such songs as *Clair de Lune* (1884) and *Pierrot* (1884).

Debye (dẹ.bī'), **Peter Joseph Willem.** [Dutch, **Debije.**] b. at Maastricht, Netherlands, March 24, 1884—. Dutch physicist. He studied at Aachen, Germany, where he received an engineering diploma with a silver medal, and taught at Munich (1910), Zürich (1911), Utrecht (1912 *et seq.*), Leipzig (1927 *et seq.*), and Berlin (1935 *et seq.*). He was recipient of the Rumford medal (1931), the Faraday medal (1933), and the Lorentz medal of the Royal Dutch Academy of Science (1935). He was appointed (1935) director of the Kaiser Wilhelm Institute for Physics at Berlin. In 1936 he was awarded the Nobel prize in chemistry for studies in molecular structure through investigations on dipole moments and on diffraction of x-rays and electrons in gases. He is largely responsible for the Debye equation, which connects dielectric constant, dipole moment, and temperature for gases. Other fundamental work includes a good theory of the dependence of ferromagnetic susceptibility upon temperature, and a recent important equation for light scattering by colloids. He came to the U.S. in 1940, and has been (1940 *et seq.*) head of the physics department of Cornell University. He is the author of *Quantentheorie und Chemie* (1928), *Polar Molecules* (1929), *Dipolmomente und chemische Struktur* (1929), and *Molekulstruktur* (1931).

Decadents. Literary term used to refer to a group of writers of the 19th century, chiefly French, although poets, novelists, dramatists, and artists of other countries may exhibit in their work or express sympathy with the tendencies associated with the French originators and leaders of the movement. In France, the outstanding names are Verlaine, Rimbaud, Baudelaire, Mallarmé, Francis Jammes, J. K. Huysmans, Villiers de l'Isle Adam, Régnier, and Pierre Louys, author of *Aphrodite*. The decadents rejected the ordinary and conventional modes of thought and conduct, and violated, both publicly and privately, the accepted rules of social, moral, and sexual behavior. They tend to show a preference for the morbid and the abnormal, as those terms are ordinarily used and understood, and they were either oversensitive to a degree, or they cultivated oversensitiveness. The pomp and pageantry of the medieval period appealed to many of them artistically and emotionally. The terms "vice," "virtue," "evil," "morality," and "immorality," which mean so much and play so large a part in ordinary life and work and play, either mean little to them, or carry a meaning that is radically different from the one generally accepted. With them, content, what the artist says, is inferior to form, which emphasizes how it is said. In England, those influenced by the movement are Arthur Symons, who translated Baudelaire and Louys, Ernest Dowson, who wrote the poem *Cynara*, Aubrey Beardsley, of the *Yellow Book*, and Frank Harris, biographer of Wilde and author of *My Life and Loves*, which no one has yet criticized for its reticence. A Spanish follower of decadence is Rubén Darío. In America, with some modifications, Poe, who was translated by Baudelaire and Mallarmé, and Whitman may be included as members of the group. Another American, of a later period, Edgar Saltus, wrote two works whose titles express decadent tendencies, *The Philosophy of Disenchantment* and *The Anatomy of Negation*. The term, which signifies decaying, dying, in Latin, probably refers to the disintegration of the old Roman Empire. It is used generally, if not always, in a derogatory sense, although, as frequently happens in such cases, the term is taken up by those against whom it is hurled as a mark or sign of distinction and honor. The French Decadents, certainly, did not object to the term or regard it as a handicap.

Decalogue (dek'ạ.lôg, -log). See **Ten Commandments.**

Decameron (dẹ.kam'ẹ.rọn). [Italian, **Il Decamerone; Principe Galeotto.**] Collection of 100 tales, by Giovanni Boccaccio, written probably not long after 1348. The tales are enclosed by a framework device giving a fictional account of how they came to be told: in the year 1348, in order to escape from the plague-ridden city of Florence, a gay company of seven young ladies and three young gentlemen retire to villas and pleasant gardens above the city where through the hot afternoon hours of ten summer days they pass the time by telling stories, one each on each day, under some general heading or subject matter proclaimed by the one who is elected king or queen for the day. The *Decameron* is a masterpiece of prose style and narrative art. It became a model for Italian prose for centuries after, and enjoyed great popularity throughout Europe. Not even the major part of the stories contained in it were invented by Boccaccio, but all are cast in a manner quite his own. Included are the tales of the day from the French *fabliaux*, from incidents of actual life, or from whatever source was open to the author. The collection has had, through the years, the reputation of being overly licentious, but the tales reflect the mid-14th century in its moral as well as its immoral aspects. They present a kind of "human comedy," rich in the variety of characters that people it, a "natural" world quite untouched by any sense of otherworldliness as might be expected in a work written less than half a century after Dante's *Divine Comedy*. Both the proem of the work with its dedication to the "idle ladies" (as its ideal public), and the framework where the author speaks out in his own person in defense of a serene and objective art free from allegory, moralism, and didacticism, give ample evidence that Boccaccio was aware that this "new" art might well be attacked by those who demand that literature should do more than entertain, a fear which history has shown to be not without some ground. The collection of tales is also entitled *Principe Galeotto*, an appellation which the deputies appointed for correction of the *Decameron* considered as derived from the 5th canto of Dante's *Inferno*, Galeotto being the name of the book which was read by Paolo and Francesca. Few works have had an equal influence on literature. From it Chaucer adopted the idea of the framework of his tales, and the general manner of his stories, while in some instances, he merely versified the novels of the Italian. In 1566, William Paynter printed many of Boccaccio's stories in English, in his work called *The Palace of Pleasure*. This first translation, containing 60 novels, was soon followed by another volume, comprising 34 additional tales. Shakespeare made considerable use of the tales as he found them in Paynter.

De Camp (dę kamp′), **Joseph Rodefer.** b. at Cincinnati, Ohio, Nov. 5, 1858; d. at Boca Grande, Fla., Feb. 11, 1923. American painter. He was a pupil of Frank Duveneck in this country and was one of a group who went to Europe with Duveneck for further study in France, Italy, and Germany. De Camp was for some time a student at the Royal Academy at Munich. Upon returning to the U.S., he settled at Boston, where he executed portraits and figure pictures, and was a teacher at the school of the Museum of Fine Arts. He was an Associate of the National Academy of Design, and a member of the National Institute of Arts and Letters. Examples of his very accomplished work are included in the collections of the Cincinnati Art Museum, the Corcoran Gallery at Washington, the Pennsylvania Academy of the Fine Arts, at Philadelphia, and other principal repositories of art in the U.S.

Decamps (dę.käṅ), **Alexandre Gabriel.** b. at Paris, March 3, 1803; d. (as the result of an accident) at Fontainebleau, France, Aug. 22, 1860. French painter, a pupil of Abel de Pujol. He visited Greece and the coast of Asia in 1827, and all his later work exhibits his preference for Oriental subjects.

Decapolis (dē.kap′ǫ.lis). [Eng. trans., *"Ten Cities."*] Name of an ancient confederation of cities W and E of the Jordan, inhabited for the most part by a non-Jewish population which probably enjoyed certain privileges and franchises. Pompey put them under the immediate jurisdiction of the governor of Syria. Among the cities belonging to this confederacy were Scythopolis (modern Beisan), on the W of the Jordan; on the E, Damascus, Hippos on the Sea of Galilee, Pella, Gadara, Philadelphia (modern Amman), Canatha (or Kanatha), and Gerasa (modern Jerash).

De Casseres (dę kas′ėr.ęs), **Benjamin.** b. at Philadelphia, 1873; d. at New York, Dec. 6, 1945. American journalist and author. He was a staff member (1903–06, 1907–19) of the New York *Herald*, drama critic (1922–33) of *Arts and Decoration*, and editor and writer of the columns "On the Nail" and "March of Events" for the New York *American* and other Hearst newspapers (1934 *et seq.*). He wrote *The Shadow-Eater* (1915), *Anathema* (1928), *Black Suns* (1936), and other books of poetry; his prose writings include *Mirrors of New York* (1925), *Broken Images* (1936), *Sir Galahad* (1938), and *Don Marquis* (1938).

Decatur (dē.kā′tėr). City in N Alabama, county seat of Morgan County, ab. 75 mi. N of Birmingham, on the Tennessee River: cotton mills, brickyards, and lumber mills. It is a river port and manufactures steel barges. 19,974 (1950).

Decatur. City in NW Georgia, county seat of DeKalb County: suburb of Atlanta. It is the seat of Agnes Scott College; the Columbia Theological Seminary is nearby. 21,635 (1950).

Decatur. City in C Illinois, county seat of Macon County, on the Sangamon River, ab. 38 mi. E of Springfield, in a farming area: important as a railroad center and for railroad repair shops. It is the seat of James Millikin University. 66,269 (1950).

Decatur. City in E Indiana, county seat of Adams County: processing center for soybeans and beet sugar. 7,271 (1950).

Decatur. City in C Texas, county seat of Wise County, NW of Dallas: shipping center for agricultural and dairy products. It is the seat of Decatur Baptist College. 2,922 (1950).

Decatur, Stephen. b. at Newport, R.I., 1752; d. at Frankford, near Philadelphia, Nov. 14, 1808. American naval officer; father of Stephen Decatur (1779–1820). He was placed in command of the *Delaware* in 1798, and afterward commanded a squadron on the Guadeloupe station. He was retired in 1801.

Decatur, Stephen. b. at Sinepuxent, Md., Jan. 5, 1779; d. at Bladensburg, Md., March 22, 1820. American naval officer, noted for his exploits in the Tripolitan War and in the War of 1812. He became (1798) a midshipman, went on sea duty in the West Indies during the naval war with France, and became a lieutenant in 1801. He achieved his first fame in the Tripolitan War, when he seized the ketch *Mastico* (renamed *Intrepid*) which, at his suggestion, was used in the daring and successful destruction (Feb. 16, 1804) of the frigate *Philadelphia*, which had been stranded and then taken by the enemy. He was promoted to captain and commanded a division in the successive bombardments of Tripoli. He became (1808) commander of the naval forces on the southeastern coast; in the War of 1812 he is best remembered for his command of the *President*, which captured (Oct. 25, 1812) the British *Macedonian* and, on Jan. 14, 1815, alone was pursued by four British blockaders. The *President* defeated the *Endymion*, but was forced to surrender by the three other ships. Decatur was wounded in the engagement and taken prisoner, but was paroled and returned to the U.S. in the following month to be acclaimed a hero. Later in 1815, he was instrumental in forcing the dey of Algiers to come to terms with the U.S. government; feted upon his return to America, he delivered his famous words at a dinner at Norfolk given in his honor: "Our country! In her intercourse with foreign nations may she always be in the right; but our country, right or wrong." He served (1815 *et seq.*) on the Board of Navy Commissioners, and was killed in a duel over service matters with the suspended Captain James Barron, former captain of the *Chesapeake*, at whose court-martial Decatur had been a judge.

Decauville (dę.kō.vēl), **Paul.** b. at Petit-Bourg, Seine-et-Oise, France, 1846; d. at Neuilly, Seine, France, 1922. French inventor and manufacturer, known for the development of a narrow-gauge railway system with portable trackage, adapted especially for use in agriculture. He served (1891 *et seq.*) as a member of the French senate.

Decazes (dę.kȧz), **Élie,** Duc. b. at St.-Martin-de-Laye, Gironde, France, Sept. 28, 1780; d. at Decazeville, France, Oct. 24, 1860. French jurist and statesman. He became minister of police on Sept. 24, 1815, and premier and minister of the interior in 1818. He resigned in 1820, and became ambassador at London. He was raised to a hereditary dukedom in the same year, and founded (c1827) Decazeville.

Decazes, Louis Charles Élie. [Title, **Duc de Glücksberg.**] b. at Paris, May 9, 1819; d. at his Château La Grave, Gironde, France, Sept. 16, 1886. French statesman; eldest son of Élie Decazes (1780–1860). He was minister of foreign affairs (1873–77).

Decazeville (dę.kȧz.vēl). Town in S France, in the department of Aveyron, NW of the town of Rodez. It is the center of the Aveyron coal fields and has blast furnaces, iron foundries, wood industries, and various manufactures. 12,138 (1946).

Deccan (dek′ạn). [Also: **Dekhan, Dekkan.**] Nonofficial designation for the peninsular portion of India lying S of the Narbada River, between the Bay of Bengal on the E and the Arabian Sea on the W; in a restricted sense, the country between the Narbada on the N and the Kistna on the S.

Decebalus (dē.seb′ạ.lus). Title of honor among the Dacians, meaning "chief" or "king," and borne by several of their kings; especially by a king, d. c106 A.D., who was at war with the Romans in the reigns of Domitian and Trajan. He committed suicide after his defeat by Trajan, and Dacia became a Roman province.

Deceleia (des.ę.lē′ạ). In ancient geography, a city and strategic point in Attica, Greece, situated ab. 14 mi. NE of Athens. It was occupied (413–404 B.C.) by the Spartans (Lacedaemonians) during the Peloponnesian War.

Deceleian War (des.ę.lē′ạn). Name frequently given to the third or final stage of the Peloponnesian War, on account of the occupation of Deceleia by the Spartans (Lacedaemonians).

December (dē.sem′bėr). Twelfth month of the year, containing 31 days. During this month the sun touches the tropic of Capricorn at the winter solstice. In the early Roman calendar it was counted as the tenth and last month.

Decembrist Conspiracy (dē.sem′brist). First revolutionary movement (1825) in modern Russia. When Czar Alexander I died, having failed to redeem his promises to institute a more modern and enlightened political and social order, it was expected that he would be succeeded by Constantine, the elder of his two brothers. But Constantine, upon marrying a Polish woman, had in 1823 secretly renounced his right of succession in favor of the youngest brother, Nicholas, who was especially unpopular with the members of certain secret societies which had parliamentary government as their aim. At the time of the coronation of Nicholas I, these secret societies, whose membership included grand dukes and high army officers, offered to support a dictatorship to be headed by Prince Trubetzkoy, but he rejected the role. Nevertheless on Dec. 14, 1825, the conspirators, supported by some groups of the army, refused the oath of allegiance to Nicholas and resorted to open rebellion. The movement was crushed, and several of the leaders were hanged. This first challenge to the autocratic rule of the czar on the one hand led to a heightened use of police terrorism, and on the other hand, to the dissemination of the concept of revolution among the intellectuals of Russia.

Decemvirate (dę.sem'vi.rąt). In Roman history, the commission of ten, presided over by Appius Claudius, sent c450 B.C. to Greece to study Greek law and codify the Roman law. It was renewed the next year, and drew up the Twelve Tables. During its existence it superseded provisionally the regular machinery of government, and was overthrown on account of its tyranny by a popular insurrection after Appius Claudius had attempted to make a slave of Virginia, daughter of Virginius, who became tribune after the decemvirs were deposed.

Deception Island. Volcanic island in the South Shetland group, S of Cape Horn. Its harbor is Port Foster.

De Cespedes (dā chās'pā.dās), **Alba.** b. at Rome, 1911—. Italian novelist. De Cespedes, whose father came from a famous Cuban family and whose mother was Italian, was educated in Italy and early tried her hand at writing, often contributing to the famous third page of Italian newspapers. She became an Italian citizen through her marriage to an Italian. Her first novel, *Nessuno torna indietro* (1938; Eng. trans., *There's No Turning Back*) met with great success. Her most recent (1949) novel, *Dalla parte di lei*, treats of the fundamental barrier that exists between men and women, a favorite theme of this author.

Decetia (dę.sē'shi.ą, -shą). Latin name of **Decize.**

Dechamps (dę.shäṅ), **Adolphe.** b. at Melle, Belgium, June 17, 1807; d. near Manage, near Brussels, July 19, 1875. Belgian Catholic statesman; brother of Victor Auguste Dechamps. He became a member of the second chamber in 1834, governor of the province of Luxembourg in 1841, and minister of public works in 1843, and was minister of foreign affairs from 1845 to 1846.

Dechamps, Victor Auguste. b. at Melle, Belgium, Dec. 6, 1810; d. at Mechelen (Malines), Belgium, Sept. 28, 1883. Belgian Redemptorist and Ultramontane leader; brother of Adolphe Dechamps. He became bishop of Namur in 1865, archbishop of Mechelen in 1867, and cardinal in 1875.

De Charms or **De Charmes** (dę shärmz'), **Richard.** b. at Philadelphia, Oct. 17, 1796; d. there, March 20, 1864. American Swedenborgian clergyman and author.

Déchelette (dāsh.let), **Joseph.** b. at Roanne, France, Jan. 8, 1862; killed in action during World War I at Aisne, France, Oct. 4, 1914. French archaeologist, one of the foremost scholars in the field of prehistoric archaeology. His main work was *Manuel d'archéologie préhistorique, celtique et gallo-romaine* (Textbook of Prehistoric Celtic and Gallo-Roman Archaeology, 1908–14).

Dechen (deċh'ęn), **Heinrich von.** b. at Berlin, March 25, 1800; d. at Bonn, Germany, Feb. 15, 1889. German geologist and mining engineer, for many years director of mines at Bonn. With Karsten he edited the *Archiv für Mineralogie, Geognosie, Bergbau, und Hüttenkunde* (1838–55).

Decimus Junius Juvenalis (des'i.mus jön'yus jö.vę-nā'lis). Full Latin name of **Juvenal.**

Decimus Tite Barnacle (des'i.mus tīt' bär'ną.kl), **Lord.** See **Barnacle, Lord Decimus Tite.**

Děčín (dye'chēn). See **Děčín-Podmokly.**

Décines-Charpieu (dā.sēn.shär.pyė). Town in SE France, in the department of Isère, situated at the NE corner of the department, between Villeurbane and Meyzieux, E of Lyons. It is an industrial town belonging to the metropolitan region of Lyons. 6,078 (1946).

Děčín-Podmokly (dye'chēn.pôd'mô.kli). [German, **Tetschen-Bodenbach.**] Twin cities in NW Czechoslovakia, in N Bohemia, situated on opposite banks of the Labe (Elbe) River, immediately S (ab. 6 mi.) of the East German border: a railroad station and junction point on the line from Prague to Dresden, with a customs administration. The cities are connected by a bridge. There are textile, metal, and chemical industries, flour mills, and breweries. Děčín is a river port and has a 17th century castle on a rock dominating the S entrance to the strategic Elbe valley route through the mountains. The area is a tourist center for the Saxon-Bohemian "Switzerland," a picturesque hilly and wooded region stretching on both sides of the river. The population declined with the Sudeten German exodus after 1945. Pop., including suburbs, 30,753 (1947).

Decius (dē'shus, desh'us). [Full name, **Gaius Messius Quintus Trajanus Decius.**] b. at Budalia, in Pannonia, 201 A.D.; killed in battle with the Goths, near the Danube, 251 A.D. Emperor of Rome (249–251). Having been sent by the emperor Philip the Arabian to restore subordination in the revolted army of Moesia, he was compelled by the army to assume the purple and march against Philip, who fell in battle near Verona in 249. He was defeated and slain in 251, near Abricium (in what is now Dobruja, Rumania), by the Goths, who had invaded his dominions. During his reign a bloody persecution of the Christians took place.

Decius Mus (mus), **Publius.** Killed at the battle of Vesuvius, 340 B.C. Roman plebeian consul, distinguished in the first Samnite and Latin wars.

Decius Mus, Publius. Killed at the battle of Sentinum (modern Sassoferrato, Italy), 295 B.C. Roman consul; son of Decius Mus (d. 340 B.C.).

Decius Mus, Publius. Killed in battle at Asculum Apulum (modern Ascoli Satriano, Italy), 279 B.C. Roman consul; son of Decius Mus (d. 295 B.C.).

De civitate Dei (dē siv.i.tā'tē dē'ī). [Eng. trans., *"Of the City of God."*] Celebrated treatise (c413–c426 A.D.) by Saint Augustine. Its theme is the permanence of the City of God, "which abideth forever," a thought made doubly impressive by the overthrow of Rome, the "eternal city," by Alaric.

Decize (dę.sēz). [Latin, **Decetia.**] Town in C France, in the department of Nièvre, situated on an island in the Loire River at the point where the river is joined by the Aron River and the Canal du Nivernais, ab. 18 mi. SE of Nevers. The ruined castle of the counts of Nevers and the coal mines of La Machine are nearby. 4,765 (1946).

Decken (dek'ęn), **Karl Klaus von der.** b. at Kotzen, Brandenburg, Germany, Aug. 8, 1833; d. 1865. German explorer of Africa. He was in the military service until 1860. In that year he sailed from Hamburg to East Africa, and gave the rest of his life and means to the exploration of what later became British East Africa. His first attempt at exploration was fruitless. On his second expedition (1861–62) he explored the region around Mount Kilimanjaro. In 1864 he led a great expedition to the exploration of the Sabaki, Tana, and Juba rivers, in what is now Kenya and Somaliland. He and almost all his companions were killed by the Somalis. His material was published in *K. K. v. der Decken's Reisen in Ost-Afrika* (1869–79). His collections were given to the National Museum at Berlin.

Deckendorf (dek'ęn.dôrf). See **Deggendorf.**

Decker (dek'ėr), **Frank.** Original name of **Duveneck, Frank.**

Decker, Jeremias de. See **Dekker, Jeremias de.**

Decker, Thomas. See **Dekker, Thomas.**

Declaration of Independence. Document, or public act, proclaimed and adopted by the 13 original states of the Union in which they declared that they were cutting off all their ties with the mother country, Great Britain. It was proclaimed by the Continental Congress on July 4, 1776, a significant date in American history, and the Declaration itself is certainly one of the most important statements of belief and action in world history. It opens with the famous sentence, "When in the course of human events, it becomes necessary for one people to dissolve the political bands which have connected them with another, and to assume among the powers of the earth, the separate and equal station to which the Laws of Nature and of Nature's God entitle them, a decent respect to the opinions of mankind requires that they should declare the causes which impel them to the separation." This introductory sentence is then followed by one of the most quoted statements ever made: "We hold these truths to be self-evident, that all men are created equal, that they are endowed by their Creator with certain unalienable Rights, that among these are Life, Liberty and the pursuit of Happiness." It closes with the assertion that "these United Colonies are, and of Right ought to be FREE AND INDEPENDENT STATES. . . . And for the support of this Declaration, with a firm reliance on the protection of Divine Providence, we mutually pledge to each other our Lives, our Fortunes, and our sacred Honor." The main body of the Declaration is devoted to a long recital of the tyranny and despotism of George III, who is called "the present King of Great Britain," and is then simply referred to, 18 times, in phrases beginning "He has" or "He is." The document was signed by 56 members, the first signer being John Hancock of Massachusetts, whose name has thereby become symbolic for a signature in general, and the last, Matthew Thornton of New Hampshire. The eighteenth signer was Jefferson, who is believed to be responsible, in lesser or greater degree, for the actual wording of the Declaration. The ideas in the document derive partly from the English philosopher John Locke, and partly from the doctrines of 18th-century French radical philosophers. The Declaration has had an exciting history since it was penned. It was almost destroyed by fire at least twice, and it was twice almost captured by the British, in the Revolutionary War and in the War of 1812. It is now in the Library of Congress, at Washington, where it has been since 1921, and where, one may presume, it will remain. Its formal, but never-used, name is "The Unanimous Declaration of the thirteen united States of America."

Declaration of Indulgence. See **Indulgence, Declaration of.**

Declaration of London. See **London, Declaration of.**

Declaration of Panama. See **Panama, Declaration of.**

Declaration of Right. Affirmation of the ancient constitutional rights of the English nation, prepared by the convention of the Commons, assented to by the Lords, and by William III and Mary II (who thereupon were declared king and queen, February 13), in February, 1689. It was confirmed by Parliament as the Bill of Rights in December, 1689.

Declaration of Rights. Resolution adopted (Oct. 14, 1774) at Philadelphia by the First Continental Congress (at which all of the colonies were represented, except Georgia). The declaration, consisting of 11 resolutions, invoked the colonists' rights as Englishmen in making a protest against the passage and enforcement of the Intolerable Acts, but also asserted colonial loyalty to the crown. The chief purpose of the declaration was to secure a fair hearing for a redress of colonial grievances.

Declaration of St.-Ouen (saṅ.twaṅ'). See **St.-Ouen, Declaration of.**

Declaration of the Rights of Man and of the Citizen. Formulation (1789) of the French Revolutionary principles of liberty, equality, and fraternity. Proposed by Lafayette and drafted by him and by Sieyès, this manifesto, drawn in part from the ideas of Jean Jacques Rousseau and in part from the American Declaration of Independence, and designed to be placed at the head of the contemplated new French constitution, was adopted by the Constituent Assembly on Aug. 26, 1789, accepted by Louis XVI on October 5, and incorporated as a preamble in the constitution of 1791. The Declaration sets forth the inherent rights of the individual to liberty, security, and property, and calls for freedom of religion, of speech, and of the press. It asserts the sovereignty of the people, and enumerates restrictions necessary to be imposed on the individual for social considerations. The Declaration of the Rights of Man was a dynamic influence in the French Revolution, and a source of inspiration for European liberals who during the earlier decades of the 19th century carried on the struggle against the reactionary regimes which were set up after the fall of Napoleon.

Declaratory Act. Act of the British Parliament (March 18, 1766) which accompanied the repeal of the Stamp Act and was intended as a formal assertion of the power of the crown and Parliament over the American colonies. Parliamentary legislation, it stated, was binding upon the colonies and people of America "in all cases whatsoever," and it denied all power on the part of the colonies to reject or disobey such authority. The colonists, in their joy over the repeal of the Stamp Act, did not take more than superficial notice of the Declaratory Act, but the subsequent assertion of parliamentary power over the colonies illuminated its significance.

Dècle (dekl), **Lionel.** b. in May, 1859; d. March 1, 1907. French traveler and ethnological collector. He started in July, 1891, from Mafeking, Bechuanaland, and visited Palapye, failed to enter the Barotse country (in what is now Northern Rhodesia), returned to Matebeleland and Mashonaland (Southern Rhodesia), where he explored the subterranean lakes of Sinoia, and again reached the Zambesi River on his way to Nyasaland, in 1892. Thence he proceeded up the Shire River to Lakes Nyasa and Tanganyika (1893), and came out by way of Zanzibar (1894).

Decline and Fall of the Roman Empire, The. Celebrated history by Edward Gibbon, published in six volumes (1776–88). It is regarded as one of the classical works of historical literature in the English language. Gibbon's panoramic sweep embraces three periods covering a total of some 13 centuries: from the rule of Trajan and the Antonines to the decay of the Western Empire; from the era of Justinian in the East to the founding of the German Empire of the West under Charlemagne; and from the restoration of the Western Empire to the capture (1453) of Constantinople by the Turks. Gibbon's point of view is suggested by his observation that history is a record of "little more than the crimes, follies, and misfortunes of mankind." He relies on fact and incident to carry his story, but he expresses a love for the classical and a dislike for Christianity despite his attempted "outside view."

Decline of the Roman People, The. Historical essay (1834) by George Bancroft, perhaps best known for his six-volume *History of the United States.* In this essay Bancroft explains how oligarchy leads to tyranny and despotism, and how the evils of irresponsible government are responsible for the latter.

De consolatione philosophiae (dē kon.sō.lā.shi.ō'nē fil-ǫ.sō'fi.ē). [Eng. trans., *"On the Consolation of Philosophy."*] Latin work in prose and verse, written by Boethius c525 A.D., while he was imprisoned and awaiting execution. It was translated into Old English by Alfred the Great. Chaucer translated it into English prose before 1382. Caxton published it in 1480.

de Coppet (dẹ kô.pā'), **Edward J.** b. May 28, 1855; d. April 30, 1916. American banker and music patron, founder of the stock-brokerage firm of De Coppet and Doremus. He was the organizer (1904) and chief supporter (although not himself a member) of the Flonzaley string quartet, considered for over 25 years one of the finest ensembles of its kind.

Decorah (dẹ.kō'rạ). City in NE Iowa, county seat of Winneshiek County, on the Upper Iowa River. Settled by Norwegians, it is the seat of Luther College, which includes a Norwegian-American historical museum; a Norwegian language newspaper is published here. 6,060 (1950).

Decoration Day. See **Memorial Day.**

De Corona (dē kọ.rō'nạ). See **Crown, Oration on the.**

De Coster (dẹ kos'tėr), **Charles Théodore Henri.** b. at Munich, 1827; d. 1879. Belgian author.

Decoto (dẹ.kō'tō). Unincorporated community in W California, in Alameda County S of Oakland. 2,830 (1950).

Decoud (dẹ.kö'), **Martin.** Latin American journalist and patriot in Joseph Conrad's novel *Nostromo* (1904).

Decoux (dẹ.kö), **Jean.** b. May 5, 1884—. French naval officer, governor general of French Indochina (1940–45). He continued as the French representative there after the Japanese occupation (July, 1941), was arrested by the Japanese in March, 1945, and in February, 1949, was cleared of charges of treason.

Decree of the Trianon (trē'ạ.non). See **Trianon, Decree of the.**

Decretals of the Pseudo-Isidore (sū'dō.iz'i.dôr). See **False Decretals.**

Decumates Agri (dek.ū.mā'tēz ag'rī). Name given by the Romans to the lands E of the Rhine and N of the Danube. About the beginning of the 2nd century A.D. they were incorporated in the Roman Empire as a part of Rhaetia. They paid the Romans a tithe of a tenth of their produce.

Dedalus (ded'a.lus, dē'da-), **May.** Wife of Simon, and mother of Stephen and Dilly, in James Joyce's autobiographical novel *Portrait of the Artist as a Young Man* (1916). A devout Roman Catholic who is stunned when her son leaves the Church, she is believed to be a portrait of the author's own mother. In *Ulysses*, part of Stephen's day-long thought complex is concerned with her death.

Dedalus, Simon. Stephen's father and May's husband in James Joyce's autobiographical novel *Portrait of the Artist as a Young Man* (1916). A careless, happy-go-lucky character, more interested in pleasure than responsibility, he is regarded as a partial portrait of the author's father. He appears in several scenes in *Ulysses*.

Dedalus, Stephen. Protagonist of *A Portrait of the Artist as a Young Man* (1916) and one of the chief characters in *Ulysses* (1922), two novels by James Joyce. Believed to be a portrait of the author, Stephen is a sensitive artist type whose rich imagination helps him rise above his drab background. In the *Portrait* he is shown in revolt against his Roman Catholic and national cultural heritage as he strives toward an articulated esthetic; in *Ulysses* he is employed as a counterpart of Telemachus in the *Odyssey* in his quest for a father symbol.

Dedan (dē'dan). In the Bible, a son of Raamah, son of Cush, son of Ham (Gen. x. 7); also, his descendants, the Dedanim.

Dedan. In the Bible, a son of Jokshan, grandson of Abraham and Keturah (Gen. xxv. 3). In the Prophets the Dedanites are referred to as being settled now in Edom (Idumea), now on the Persian Gulf. Some scholars (Gesenius, Winer) infer that the Cushite Dedanites and those from Keturah were in some way amalgamated by intermarriage, and formed a widely spread trading tribe. There are still ruins of a city in the N Hejaz, Arabia bearing the name of Dedan.

Dede Agach (de'de ä.gäch'). Turkish name of **Alexandroúpolis.**

Dedekind (dā'de.kint), **Friedrich.** b. at Neustadt an der Leine, Germany, c1525; d. 1598. German poet and pastor, remembered for his satirical Latin poem *Grobianus* (1549), directed at gluttony and drunkenness. The idea was derived from the chapter on "Grobe Narren" in Sebastian Brant's *Narrenschiff* (1494). Dedekind's mock epic, which fixed the word "Grobian" in the German language, was translated in 1551, with emendations by Kaspar Scheidt, into German. An English translation appeared in 1605.

Dedekind, Julius Wilhelm Richard. b. at Brunswick, Germany, Oct. 6, 1831; d. there, Feb. 12, 1916. German mathematician who contributed to analysis and the theory of functions, best known for the so-called Dedekind cut in the definition of real numbers. He is remembered also for his definition of infinite classes, on which he corresponded extensively with Georg F. L. P. Cantor. His chief works include *Stetigkeit und irrationale Zahlen* (1872), *Was sind und was sollen die Zahlen?* (1888), and *Über die Theorie der ganzen algebraischen Zahlen* (1894). The first two of these books appeared in numerous editions. His *Gesammelte mathematische Werke* appeared in three volumes in 1930–32.

Dedham (ded'am). Town in E Massachusetts, county seat of Norfolk County, ab. 10 mi. SW of Boston. Settled in 1635, it is now a residential suburb of Boston. It was the scene (1921) of the Sacco-Vanzetti trial. 18,487 (1950).

Dedlock (ded'lok), **Lady.** Wife of Sir Leicester Dedlock in Charles Dickens's novel *Bleak House:* a haughty woman of fashion, secretly consumed with terror, shame, and remorse. She has an illegitimate child, Esther Summerson, but marries Sir Leicester, who is ignorant of her history. Her secret becomes known to Mr. Tulkinghorn, her husband's legal adviser, who tells her of his design to reveal it to her husband. She leaves home and dies from exposure and remorse at the gate of the graveyard where Captain Hawdon, the father of her child, is buried.

Dedlock, Sir Leicester. Extremely ceremonious and stately old baronet in Charles Dickens's novel *Bleak House.* He is perfectly honorable, but prejudiced to the most unreasonable degree, with a genuine affection and admiration for Lady Dedlock.

Dee (dē). River in N central and E Scotland, in Kincardineshire and Aberdeenshire. It rises in the Cairngorm Mountains, near the Aberdeenshire-Banffshire-Inverness-shire boundary, and flows E across the S portion of Aberdeenshire, crossing ab. 9 mi. of the N part of Kincardineshire before continuing ab. 14 mi. along the Aberdeenshire-Kincardineshire boundary to the North Sea at Aberdeen. It is the chief water supply of the city of Aberdeen. Length, ab. 87 mi.

Dee. River in SW Scotland, in Kirkcudbrightshire. It rises in Loch Dee, ab. 10 mi. N of Kirkcudbright, and flows S to the Solway Firth at Kirkcudbright Bay. Above Loch Dee, the river (known as the Water of Ken), traverses Loch Ken, emptying immediately into Loch Dee. Total length of both rivers, ab. 50 mi.; length of river Dee proper, ab. 12 mi.

Dee. [Latin, **Deva.**] River in N Wales and W England, rising in Lake Bala, in Merionethshire, Wales, flowing through Denbighshire, Wales, and Cheshire, England, through Chester to its estuary on the Irish Sea. Length, ab. 70 mi. (including the estuary).

Dee, John. b. at London, July 13, 1527; d. at Mortlake-Surrey, England, in December, 1608. English mathema, tician and astrologer. He took the degree of B.A. at Cambridge in 1545, was appointed one of the foundation fellows of Trinity College, Cambridge, in 1546, and lectured (c1550) on the *Elements* of Euclid at Paris. He returned to England in 1551 and became astrologer to the queen, Mary Tudor, was prosecuted before the Star Chamber on the charge of magic but was released c1555, practiced the various arts of astrology and horoscopy at the court of Elizabeth, gave exhibitions of magic at the courts of various princes in Poland and Bohemia (1583–88), and was appointed warden of Christ's College, Manchester, in 1595. He was patronized by Queen Elizabeth, who received instruction from him in astrology in 1564. According to the *Athenae Cantabrigienses* he wrote 79 works, most of which have never been printed. His most notable work is *Monas Hieroglyphica* (1564). Dee's reputation was primarily that of a magician, and his experiments in crystal-gazing and the evocation of spirits show his interest in magic, but he was also a sober mathematician who advocated the adoption of the Gregorian calendar and who did geographical descriptions of the new lands in America.

Deeg (dēg). See **Dig.**

Deems (dēmz), **Charles Force.** b. at Baltimore, Dec. 4, 1820; d. at New York, Nov. 18, 1893. American clergyman and writer, pastor of the Church of the Strangers at New York. He founded the American Institute of Christian Philosophy in 1881.

Deep (dēp). River of North Carolina which unites with the Haw to form the Cape Fear River ab. 26 mi. SW of Raleigh. Length, over 120 mi.

Deep Are the Roots. Play in three acts (1945) by Arnaud d'Usseau and James Gow. It deals with race prejudice, its victim being a Negro soldier-hero in World War II, Brett Charles, who finds that he is just a Negro, not a hero, when he returns in May, 1945, to his home, "a small town in the Deep South," where the action takes place.

Deepening Stream, The. Novel by Dorothy Canfield Fisher, published in 1930.

Deephaven (dēp'hā.ven). Volume of local-color sketches by Sarah Orne Jewett, published in 1877. They are set against the background of Deephaven, a Maine seaport.

Deeping (dēp'ing), **Warwick.** [Full name, **George Warwick Deeping.**] b. at Southend, Essex, England, May 28, 1877; d. at Weybridge, England, April 20, 1950. English novelist. He studied medicine but abandoned it, after a year of practice, in favor of writing. During World War I he was on active service in Gallipoli, Egypt, and France. His books include *Uther and Igraine* (1903; rev. ed., 1927), *Bess of the Woods* (1906), *Bertrand of Brittany* (1908), *The Red Saint* (1909), *The Lame Englishman* (1910), *Joan of the Tower* (1911), *The House of Spies* (1913), *The King Behind the King* (1914), *Unrest* (1916),

Martin Valliant (1917), *Valour* (1918), *Lantern Lane* (1921), *Orchards* (1922), *Apples of Gold* (1923), *Sorrell and Son* (1925), *Doomsday* (1926), *Kitty* (1927), *Old Pybus* (1928), *Roper's Row* (1929), *Exile* (1930), *Old Wine and New* (1932), *Blind Man's Year* (1937), *The Man Who Went Back* (1940), *Mr. Gurney and Mr. Slade* (1944), *Repriere* (1945), and *The Impudence of Youth* (1946).

Deep Mrs. Sykes, The. Play (1945) by George Kelly, American actor and author of one-act sketches, who later turned his talents to full-length plays. It is a psychological portrait of a masterful woman, who must dominate everything and everybody, a theme that, 20 years earlier, won Kelly the Pulitzer prize for his *Craig's Wife*, still regarded as his best play.

Deep River. See **Deep,** and see under **Chalk River.**

Deep South. Name applied to the states of the U.S. South situated between, and including, South Carolina and Texas. The region is predominantly agricultural, and its chief crop is cotton. Before the Civil War it was characterized by slavery and the plantation economy; at present its agricultural system includes the use of many sharecroppers and tenant farmers.

Deer (dir), **Book of.** [Also, **Book of Deir.**] Ancient manuscript of the Gospels in Latin, with marginal notes and interlineations in Gaelic, found in the abbey of Deer or Deir, in the parish of Old Deer, Aberdeenshire, Scotland. These glosses, probably written in the 12th century or earlier, are in the oldest form of Gaelic found in any existing Scottish book, and are of interest to scholars as showing the uniformity of Gaelic in Ireland and in Scotland at that time. The manuscript is in the Cambridge University Library.

Deer, Old. Civil parish in E Scotland, in Aberdeenshire, ab. 10 mi. W of Peterhead. The ruins of Saint Mary's Abbey of Deer (or Deir), a Cistercian monastery established c1218, are here. Old Deer is the scene of the defeat of the Comyns by Edward Bruce. The town is noted for an ancient manuscript (*Book of Deer*) containing Saint John's gospel and parts of the other three, belonging formerly to the old abbey, and now in the Cambridge University library. 3,380 (1931).

Deere (dir), **John.** b. at Rutland, Vt., Feb. 7, 1804; d. May 17, 1886. American manufacturer of agricultural implements, noted for his improvements on the plow. He was apprenticed to a blacksmith at Middlebury, Vt., but in 1837 emigrated to the West, subsequently settling at Grand Detour, Ill., where he continued his trade and formed a partnership with Major Andrus. His experience in devising agricultural tool-parts for the farmers of the area aroused his interest in the need for a new plow suitable for working prairie land. Together with his partner, he constructed three improved plows with a steel moldboard; with continued experimentation, the business developed. To secure a better location, Deere sold (c1846) his share of the business to Andrus and founded a firm at Moline, Ill., where his need for the proper type of steel plate finally led to the manufacture of the first plow steel in the U.S., rolled (c1846) at the steel works of Jones and Quigg. By 1857, Deere's company was producing as many as 10,000 plows a year, later adding cultivators and other tools.

Deerfield (dir'fēld). Village in NE Illinois, in Lake County NW of Chicago. 3,288 (1950).

Deerfield. Town in N Massachusetts, in Franklin County, near the junction of the Deerfield River with the Connecticut River, ab. 32 mi. N of Springfield: seat of Deerfield Academy. Settled c1670, it was sacked and burned by French and Indians in 1704, and the village of South Deerfield (pop. 1,418, 1950) was the scene of the Bloody Brook massacre in 1675. Pop. 3,086 (1950).

Deerfield River. Small river in N Massachusetts, a western tributary of the Connecticut River, which it joins near Deerfield, in Franklin County. It rises in S Vermont.

Deering (dir'ing), **Charles.** b. at Paris, Me., 1852; d. Feb. 5, 1927. American manufacturer; son of William Deering (1826–1913). After serving in the U.S. navy, he became (1881) secretary of his father's company and was named (1902) chairman of the board of the International Harvester Company upon the merger of the two companies.

Deering, William. b. at South Paris, Me., April 25, 1826; d. at Cocoanut Grove, Fla., Dec. 9, 1913. American manufacturer of agricultural machinery, noted as the maker of a grain harvester with a device for automatic binding. Abandoning the study of medicine, he joined his father's woolen-manufacturing business and in 1856 established a dry-goods store at South Paris, which later became (1865) Deering, Milliken and Company, with central offices at Portland, Me., and a branch at New York. He left the wholesale dry-goods business to become the partner of Elijah H. Gammon (who had bought the rights to the Marsh harvester and established a plant at Plano, Ill.). Foreseeing the wide need for the harvester, Deering bought Gammon's interest in 1879 and moved to Chicago, where he was instrumental in adding improvements that eventually led to the harvester with automatic binding. His factory grew to become the largest agricultural machinery plant in the world. In 1883 it was incorporated as William Deering and Company; later called the Deering Manufacturing Company, it was absorbed (1902) by the International Harvester Company of Chicago. Deering retired in 1901. His gifts to institutions included those to Northwestern University, the Garrett Biblical Institute, and Wesley Hospital.

Deer Island. Island in S Maine, on the E side of the entrance to Penobscot Bay. It was once noted as the home of many old-time sea captains; today it is a resort and farming area. Length, ab. 9 mi.

Deer Lodge. City in W Montana, county seat of Powell County, ab. 28 mi. NW of Butte. It was a gold-mining town in the 1860's. 3,779 (1950).

Deer Park. Village in SW Ohio, in Hamilton County near Cincinnati. In the decade between the last two U.S. censuses its population more than doubled. 3,510 (1940), 7,241 (1950).

Deerslayer (dir'slā.ėr), **The.** Novel of frontier life (1841) by James Fenimore Cooper. It is one of the series of five stories known as "the Leather-Stocking Tales." The hero of the novel is Natty Bumpo, a young hunter living with the Delaware Indians and fighting the Hurons. The setting is the northern section of New York state, and the time is 1740–45. Other characters are a trapper, Henry March, known as "Hurry Harry," Tom Hutter, a settler, Judith Hutter, who loves Natty, her sister Hetty, who loves March, Chingachgook, a Delaware chief, Natty's friend, and Wahtawah, an Indian maid. Although it was published last, *The Deerslayer* should be read first. The other volumes in the series, in chronological reading order, are *The Last of the Mohicans, The Pathfinder, The Pioneers,* and *The Prairie.*

Dées (dā'āsh). See **Dej.**

Defarge (dẹ.färzh'), **Thérèse.** In Charles Dickens's *Tale of Two Cities,* the wife of the keeper of a wineshop. A type of the remorseless women of the St.-Antoine quarter of Paris during the French Revolution, she takes her seat daily in front of the guillotine and knits while the executions take place.

Defauw (dẹ.fō'), **Désiré.** b. at Ghent, Belgium, Sept. 5, 1885—. Belgian violinist and conductor. During World War I he formed, with Lionel Tertis, Woodhouse, and Doehard, the Allied Quartet. He was appointed professor at the Antwerp Conservatory. He founded and was conductor of the Defauw Concerts at Brussels, was musical director of Belgium's national radio institute, and became director of concerts of the Brussels Conservatory in 1925. He was guest conductor (1939) in the U.S., and conductor (1943) of the Chicago Symphony. He has conducted orchestras throughout Europe (especially Italy), and at Montreal.

Defence of Cony-Catching, The. Pamphlet (1592) written as an answer to two pamphlets by Robert Greene, one of which was entitled *A Notable Discovery of Cozenage Now Daily Practised by Sundry Lewd Persons, Called Cony-Catchers and Crossbiters* (1591). In Elizabethan English, a "cony-catcher" was a thief, a cheat, sharper, trickster, swindler, a criminal of any kind, male or female, and "cony-catching" was stealing, cheating, or swindling in the manner of a cony-catcher. The unknown author of the *Defence* signed himself "Cuthbert Cony-Catcher" and offered his work as "a confutation of those two injurious pamphlets published by R. G."

Defence of Cosmetics, A. Essay (1922) by Sir Max Beerbohm, English novelist, parodist, and humorist. It was written at Oxford, where he was a student at Merton College, and was later called *The Pervasion of Rouge.* It justifies, with a blending of humor and seriousness, the place of artificiality and some forms of trickery or craftiness in modern civilization.

Defence of Guinevere, and Other Poems, The. Volume (1858) by William Morris. As the title suggests, it gives a more favorable view and a more sympathetic and subtle portrait of Arthur's wife than is found in the older Arthurian romances. Several of the poems in this volume, which has been called "that extraordinary book of verse," were originally published in *The Oxford and Cambridge Magazine.* Critics have pointed out that it shows both the defects and the qualities of his age (Morris was 24 at the time) but they have praised the title poem and "King Arthur's Tomb" for their passion and fire and energy.

Defence of Poesie, The. Title given to Sir Philip Sidney's essay on poetry, written c1579 and printed by Ponsonby in 1595; another version of the essay, printed by Olney the same year, is called *An Apologie for Poetrie.* It is a reply to the *School of Abuse* (1579) by the Puritan Stephen Gosson, in which all secular literature is attacked.

Defence of Poetry. Volume in verse by Isaac D'Israeli (the father of Benjamin Disraeli), published in 1790. It was his first work.

Defence of Poetry, The. Literary essay (1821) by Percy Bysshe Shelley, probably his best-known prose work. Published the year before his death, it is an answer to *The Four Ages of Poetry,* by his friend Thomas Love Peacock, and a strong plea for imagination and love in poetry. Its thesis (that the poet is a social and moral force, and that the poet must be a teacher, as well as a singer) is expressed poetically in Shelley's *Ode to the West Wind* and *To a Skylark.* The essay naturally invites a comparison with Sidney's piece of literary criticism (written over 200 years earlier) *An Apologie for Poetrie,* or, as it was called in another edition, *The Defence of Poesie.*

Defence of Rime, A. Critical essay (1603) by Samuel Daniel, "the well-languaged" Daniel, in which he makes a plea for the use of English verse forms. It was written in reply to Campion's *Observations* (1602), advocating the use of Latin meters in English poetry.

Defender of the Faith. Title (in Latin, *Fidei Defensor*) conferred (Oct. 11, 1521) by Pope Leo X upon Henry VIII of England, in recognition of the latter's treatise *Assertio septem sacramentorum* (1521) against Luther. Pope Paul III retracted the title after Henry's break with the Roman Catholic Church, but in 1544 it was granted the king by Parliament and has been retained by succeeding English sovereigns.

Defense, Department of. Department (established 1949) of the executive branch of the U.S. government. Until 1947, responsibility for the national defense of the U.S. was divided between the War Department, the Navy Department, and, for a short time after World War II, the Air Force. The secretaries of war and of the navy sat in the president's cabinet, and the president was commander in chief, but there was no machinery for overall coördination of the defense establishments. New conditions and requirements of warfare revealed during and after World War II, especially the enhanced importance of the air arm, created a necessity for unified control of the army, navy, and air force; moreoever the vastly increased demand for weapons, munitions, planes, and all sorts of military materiel, led to competition between the different defense establishments in the market, causing sharp increases in prices and laying a heavy burden on the budget. These considerations led to the creation in 1947 of the Department of Defense (at that time called the National Military Establishment), headed by a secretary of defense, the first incumbent being James V. Forrestal, who as secretary of the navy had taken a leading part in urging unification of the services. Within this new framework it was hoped that it might be possible to coördinate the activities of the War and Navy departments, the Air Force, the joint chiefs of staff, the National Security Council, the National Security Resources Board, the Central Intelligence Agency, the Munitions Board, the Research and Development Board, and the War Council. By the terms of the National Security Act of 1949, the National Military Establishment was transformed into the Department of Defense, headed by a secretary of defense, who took his place in the cabinet, and to whom the secretaries of war, of the navy, and of the air force were made subordinate. The first secretary of defense was Louis Arthur Johnson.

Defense Plant Corporation. Federal corporation established under the U.S. government by the Reconstruction Finance Corporation (RFC) in 1940 for the purpose of acquiring and allocating strategic raw materials and critical industrial equipment in a move to further production for national defense.

Deffand (de.fäṅ), Marquise **du.** [Title of **Marie de Vichy-Chamrond.**] b. at the Château de Chamrond, France, 1697; d. at Paris, Sept. 24, 1780. French leader in Parisian literary and philosophical circles, noted for her wit and cynicism. She was married to the marquis du Deffand in 1718, but soon separated from him. In 1753, she became blind. She is noted for her correspondence with Voltaire, Hénault, Montesquieu, Horace Walpole, and other great men of her time.

Defiance (dẹ.fī′ạns). City in NW Ohio, county seat of Defiance County, on the Maumee River ab. 50 mi. SW of Toledo, in an agricultural area. Manufactures include machinery, radio and auto parts, steel, and dairy products. It is the seat of Defiance College. Fort Defiance, on the same site, was the scene of a battle between the Indians and the forces of "Mad" Anthony Wayne on Aug. 6, 1794. Pop. 11,265 (1950).

Defile of Stradella (strä.del′lä). See **Stradella, Defile of.**

De finibus (dē fin′i.bus). [Full title, **De finibus honorum et malorum,** meaning "*Of the Boundaries of Good and Evil.*"] Treatise in five books by Cicero, in the form of a dialogue, consisting in a presentation of the doctrines of the Greek schools concerning good and evil. It was written in 45 B.C.

De Flores (dẹ flō′rēz). In Thomas Middleton's play *The Changeling,* an ill-favored, broken gentleman in the service of Vermandero, the father of Beatrice-Joanna. He loves Beatrice, who loathes him. Trusting in his devotion and poverty, she induces him to murder Alonzo de Pivacquo, to whom her father has betrothed her though she loves Alsemero. In a powerful scene he declares to her that she shall never marry Alsemero unless she first yields to him. He never relents, and after killing Beatrice dies triumphant, by his own hand, when the double discovery of the liaison and murder is made.

Defoe (dẹ.fō′), **Daniel.** [Also, **De Foe.**] b. at London, 1660; d. there, April 26, 1731. English novelist and political journalist; son of a tallow-chandler and butcher who became a Dissenter after the Act of Uniformity (1662). Daniel's surname (originally Foe or De Foe, variously spelled) was usually written De Foe after 1703 (modern editors, however, universally spell it Defoe). He studied for the Presbyterian ministry at Morton's academy at Stoke Newington, and his first poems (in manuscript, 1681) were religious meditations; but he became a merchant. He traveled widely in Great Britain and on the Continent, and was once captured and held by Algerian pirates between Harwich and Holland. In 1684 he married Mary Tuffley, by whom he had seven children. After failing for 17,000 pounds through rashness and wartime difficulties (1692) he satisfied his creditors, but debts were often revived for political persecution and he died in hiding because of an old claim. He joined the rising under the Duke of Monmouth in 1685, entered London in triumph with William of Orange (William III) in 1688, and with few intervals from 1689 to 1731 served four sovereigns as a pamphleteer. He held minor offices under William III and became his trusted confidant, suggesting plans for peace and war. He defended the Dutch in *The True-Born Englishman* (1701), a poem ridiculing racial superiority. After William's death his ironical tract *The Shortest Way with the Dissenters* (1702) gave an excuse for his prosecution by Tories before alderman judges (partly Whigs) whom he had satirized. He was sentenced (July, 1703) to stand three times in the pillory, pay a heavy fine, give sureties for seven years, and remain in prison till all was performed. His business as a pantile manufacturer failed before Robert Harley procured his release (November, 1703) from Newgate Prison to serve the government. His *Review* (1704–13) was best known of many journalistic undertakings. He promoted the union with Scotland (1707), urged peace with France (1713), and supported the Hanoverian succession (1714). In 1713 he was imprisoned for a short time when Whigs professed that his ironical tracts against the Pretender were treasonable. Although a Whig and a Dissenter, he put national interests first, writing to make the government's policies intelligible and acceptable to the public, and his opponents usually welcomed his services when they got into office; but he never supported Jacobitism or intolerance. In 1719 he began the works of fiction for which he is best known: *The Life and Strange Surprizing Adventures of Robinson Crusoe, of York, Mariner* (1719), *The Memoirs of a Cavalier* (1720), *The Life, Adventures, and Piracies of the Famous Captain Singleton* (1720), *The Fortunes and Misfortunes of the Famous Moll Flanders* (1722), *A Journal of the Plague Year* (1722), *The History and Remarkable Life of Colonel Jacque, Commonly call'd Colonel Jack* (1722), and *Roxana*, or *The Fortunate Mistress* (1724). Among his later writings are *A Tour thro' the whole Island of Great Britain* (1724–27), *A General History of the Pirates* (1724–28), *The Compleat English Tradesman* (1725–27), *The Memoirs of Captain Carleton* (1728), and *Robert Drury's Journal* (1729). He wrote considerably more than 400 books and tracts, on most subjects of public interest, nearly all issued without his name. He developed a prose style remarkable for simplicity and directness. As a journalist and novelist he had an extraordinary ability to capture details of speech and incident, and in Robinson Crusoe and Moll Flanders he created two memorable characters. As a historical writer he was notable for visualizing and interpreting events; all historians who deal with his period stand (often unconsciously) in his debt. Benjamin Franklin acknowledged his obligation to *An Essay upon Projects* (1697). In his writings on public affairs Defoe expressed many of the best ideas of his age; his own proposals often anticipated the thought of today.

De Forest (dę for'ęst), **John William.** b. May 31, 1826; d. July 17, 1906. American novelist and soldier. He served through the Civil War from 1861 to 1865, in the Southwest and with Sheridan in the Shenandoah Valley. He received the brevet rank of major. From 1865 to 1868 he was adjutant general of the veteran reserve corps. Among his works are *History of the Indians of Connecticut* (1853), *Oriental Acquaintance* (1856), *Seacliff* (1859), *Miss Ravenel's Conversion from Secession to Loyalty* (1867), *The Oddest of Courtships* (1881), and *A Lover's Revolt* (1898). *A Volunteer's Adventures* (1946), a collection of his letters and articles, recounts some of his Civil War experiences.

De Forest, Lee. [Sometimes called **"the Father of Radio."**] b. at Council Bluffs, Iowa, Aug. 26, 1873—. American inventor. Throughout his career he has been concerned chiefly with devising and improving means for the transmission of sound. His early work in wireless telegraphy contributed greatly to the successful development of radio, and others of his inventions have been of the greatest importance in extending the range of telephony, both by wire and by air. For the U.S. government he designed and supervised construction of its first high-powered naval radio stations. The patents granted to Lee De Forest have numbered more than 300.

De Forest, Robert Weeks. b. at New York, April 25, 1848; d. May 6, 1931. American lawyer and social reformer. He was educated at Yale and Columbia universities, and was admitted to the bar in 1871. He was a director of many commercial enterprises, served as trustee (from 1889), secretary (from 1904), and vice-president (from 1910) of the Metropolitan Museum of Art, and was president (1888 *et seq.*) of the Charity Organization Society of the city of New York.

Deformed; or, Woman's Trial, The. Drama in verse by Richard Penn Smith, produced and published in 1830.

Deformed Transformed, The. Drama by Byron, published in 1824. It was partly founded on Goethe's *Faust*.

Defregger (dā'freg.ėr), **Franz von.** b. at Stronach, Tyrol, Austria, April 30, 1835; d. 1921. Austrian genre and portrait painter whose popular scenes met with great success. He studied in the Academy at Munich, after a trip to the U.S.; later he went to Paris. He established his reputation fairly early in life, obtained high prices for his work, and was awarded several prizes. Among his more important works are *Young Tyrolian Peasant*, *Council of War, 1809*, *The Last Levee, 1809*, *The Dance*, *Wandering Italian Singers*, and *Portrait of the Crown Prince and Princess*.

De Funiak Springs (dę fū'ni.ak). Town in NW Florida, county seat of Walton County, W of Jacksonville. The springs for which it is named feed a small lake, 80 ft. deep, which is a swimming resort. It is the site of the first Confederate monument in Florida (1871). 3,077 (1950).

De Garmo (dę gär'mō), **Charles.** b. at Mukwonago, Wis., Jan. 7, 1849; d. 1934. American educator, professor of the science and art of education at Cornell University from 1898. He was professor of psychology and education at the University of Illinois (1890–91), and president of Swarthmore College (1891–98). His publications relate chiefly to the principles and methods of secondary education.

Degas (dę.gä), **Hilaire Germain Edgar.** b. at Paris, July 19, 1834; d. 1917. French painter. He belonged to the group of Impressionists and was early associated with Manet, Monet, Renoir, and Fantin-Latour. His first successes were made with pictures representing race-courses, but his subjects were later usually taken from the theater, and he depicted life behind the scenes, especially of ballet dancers, with great appreciation; remarkable are also his studies of women in everyday poses. He visited America and painted a noted picture of Negroes loading cotton at New Orleans.

De Gasperi (dā gäs'pe.rē), **Alcide.** b. at Pieve Tesino, Italy, April 3, 1881—. Italian statesman. He was a supporter (1903) of the Irredentist movement in the Trentino region. He served before World War I in the Austrian chamber and was elected (1921) to the Italian chamber of deputies. In 1926 he was arrested by the Fascists for having led the Popularist Party; after the fall of Fascism he became minister of foreign affairs (1944), serving in the cabinets of Bonomi and Parri, and premier (1945).

de Gaulle (dę gōl), **Charles André Joseph Marie.** b. at Lille, France, Nov. 22, 1890—. French political leader and army officer, leader of the Free French movement during World War II. Graduated (1911) from the Saint-Cyr military academy with the rank of second lieutenant, he first saw World War I duty in the 33rd infantry regiment, commanded by (then) Colonel Philippe Pétain. Twice wounded (1914, 1915), he was again wounded while fighting at the defense of Verdun (1916). Captured by the Germans, he made five attempts to escape before the armistice (1918) brought release from captivity. During the Polish-Soviet war (1920–21), he served on the staff of General Maxime Weygand, the French military adviser to the Polish government. A tour of duty as professor of military history (1921–24) at Saint-Cyr was followed by studies at the École de Guerre and service as aide-de-camp (1924–27) to Marshal Pétain. He served (1927–29) in the army of occupation at Trier, Germany, as commander of the 19th Infantry Battalion, was sent on a mission (1929–32) to the Near East for the French government, and returned to France to serve as secretary-general (1932–36) of the supreme defense council, without effectively convincing that body of his doctrine of the role of tanks and motorized forces in modern warfare. He spent the following year (1936–37) at the center for high military studies, was in command (1937–39) of the 507th Tank Regiment, and was commander (1939–40) of the 5th Army Tank Brigade. Placed (May, 1940) at the head of the 4th Armored Division, he was given a field promotion to brigadier general on June 2, 1940. Four days later he was ordered to Paris, where he became undersecretary of state for national defense in the Reynaud cabinet. He was sent to London by Reynaud to coördinate British and French activity, and then returned to France. He went back to London after the formation of the Pétain government, and responded to Pétain's signature of the armistice with Germany by a broadcast over the London radio calling for continued resistance and the creation of Free French armed forces. The British recognized him as the Free French leader on June 27, 1940. He was condemned to death in absentia by a Vichy court, and established (Oct. 27, 1940) at Brazzaville, in French Equatorial Africa, a council for the defense of the empire which was subsequently recognized by the British as the authority in areas placing themselves under the council's control. A French national committee, with de Gaulle as president, was formed at London on Sept. 24, 1941, and received British recognition as representative of all Free French forces. He was accepted as Free French leader by certain Resistance groups in France in June, 1942, and later (November, 1942) by French trade-union forces in Great Britain. He took part in the Casablanca Conference (January, 1943) with Franklin D. Roosevelt and Winston Churchill. Following the Allied liberation of North Africa, he combined forces with General Henri Giraud, with whom he created a French committee of national liberation, of which he became president. Shortly after the Allied invasion of Normandy, he returned (June 14, 1944) to French soil, entered Paris (August, 1944), was named (November, 1945) head of the provisional government by the Constituent Assembly, and resigned this post on Jan. 21, 1946. He then withdrew from public political activity until the formation (April 1, 1947) of the Rassemblement du Peuple Français by his supporters. He thereafter urged strengthening of the French state and strongly criticized the constitution of the Fourth Republic. His published works are *La Discorde chez l'ennemi* (1924), *Au Fil de l'épée* (1932), *Vers l'armée de métier* (1933), and *La France et son armée* (1939).

Degée (dẹ.zhā), **Olivier.** Original name of **Tousseul, Jean.**

Degeer (dẹ.yār'), Baron **Karl.** See **Geer,** Baron **Karl de.**

Degener (dā'gẹ.nėr), **Frederik Schmidt-.** See **Schmidt-Degener, Frederik.**

Degeneration. Title of the English translation of *Entartung* (1893), by Max Nordau.

Deggendorf (deg'ẹn.dôrf). [Also, **Deckendorf.**] Town in S Germany, in the *Land* (state) of Bavaria, American Zone, in the *Regierungsbezirk* (government district) of Lower Bavaria-Upper Palatinate, situated on the Danube River ab. 30 mi. NW of Passau. It has cement works, sawmills, chemical and textile industries, and markets for cattle, grain, and lumber. It is a center for excursions in the region of the Bavarian Forest, and its Church of the Holy Sepulchre (begun in 1337) has long been known as a place of pilgrimage. After the conclusion of World War II it contained one of the largest camps for displaced persons in Bavaria. 16,328 (1950).

Degkwitz (dek'vits), **Rudolf.** b. at Ronneburg, Thuringia, Germany, Jan. 19, 1889—. German pediatrician. He became privatdocent of pediatrics (1925) and full professor (1935) at the University of Greifswald. He is known for his studies on the prophylaxis of measles and rickets and the physical chemistry of the fat cells. Author of *Die Masernprophylaxe und ihre Technik* (1923), *Milch* (1931), and *Lipoide und Ionen; eine biologische und ärztliche Studie über die physiologische Bedeutung der Zell-Lipoiden* (1933); coeditor of *Lehrbuch der Kinderheilkunde* (1933) and *Immunität, Allergie und Infektionskrankheiten* (1935).

Degoutte (dẹ.göt), **Jean Marie Joseph.** b. at Charnay, Rhône, France, April 18, 1866; d. there, Oct. 31, 1938. French army officer, commander (1923–25) of the French forces of occupation in the Ruhr district of Germany. In 1918 he commanded the French 4th Army, with which three American divisions served as reinforcements, and was placed on a mission with King Albert of the Belgians. He became (1920) a member of the superior war council, and was commander in chief (1920–25) of the Allied army of occupation in the Rhineland.

Degrelle (dẹ.grel), **Léon (Marie Joseph Ignace).** b. 1906—. Belgian politician. He was graduated (LL.D.) from the University of Louvain, practiced law, and founded (1932) the journal *Rex* (for Christus Rex) as the organ of a movement to reanimate and inspire Christian life. The movement later became political, and followers of Degrelle became known as Rexists; the political philosophy of the party was pro-fascist. Degrelle was defeated (1937) by Van Zeeland in a contest for a seat in parliament. He was arrested (1940) when the German armies invaded Belgium, but was released after the armistice of June, 1940, joined the German army, and served on the eastern front. In 1945 he fled to Spain. Request for his extradition was at first refused; later Spain announced he had disappeared; in October, 1946, the Belgian government on this account filed a complaint against Spain before the United Nations.

De Haas (dẹ häs'), **Maurice Frederick Hendrick.** b. at Rotterdam, Netherlands, Dec. 12, 1832; d. Nov. 23, 1895. American marine painter. He studied in his native city and at The Hague before coming to the U.S. in 1858. He established his studio at New York and was successful from the beginning. He was accepted into the National Academy of Design in 1867, and he helped organize the American Water Color Society. His painting of *Farragut Passing the Forts at New Orleans* is perhaps the best-known among his works, examples of which are found in many public and private collections.

Dehan (dē'han), **Richard.** Pseudonym of **Graves, Clotilde Inez Mary.**

De Haven (dẹ hā'vẹn), **Edwin Jesse.** b. at Philadelphia, May 7, 1816; d. May 1, 1865. American antarctic and arctic explorer. He became a midshipman in the U.S. navy in 1829, and ten years later, with the rank of acting master, sailed with the Wilkes expedition, which spent three years exploring the Pacific and Antarctica. He won a citation for bravery in the rescue of men imperiled when one of the ships of the expedition was wrecked, and in 1841 was given the rank of lieutenant. He saw service in the Mexican War. In 1850 he was chosen leader of an expedition, arranged and financed by Henry Grinnell with the support of the U.S. government, having for its object to find and rescue Sir John Franklin, the English explorer, and his party, which had disappeared in the arctic regions. De Haven's ships were caught in the ice and drifted a thousand miles. He did not find Franklin's party, but did discover a new arctic territory which became known as Grinnell Land. Later De Haven made deep-sea soundings for the Coast Survey (1853–57), but because of failing health spent his last years ashore.

de Havilland (dē hav'i.lạnd), Sir **Geoffrey.** b. 1885—. British aeronautical engineer and airplane designer (1908 *et seq.*); manufacturer of De Havilland aircraft. He was awarded (1946) honorary membership in the U.S. Institute of Aeronautical Sciences.

De Helder (dẹ hel'dėr). See **Den Helder.**

Dehli (de'lē). See **Delhi,** India.

Dehmel (dā'mẹl), **Richard.** b. at Wendisch-Helmsdorf, Germany, Nov. 11, 1863; d. at Berlin, Feb. 8, 1920. German poet; close friend of Detlev von Liliencron. He took a doctor's degree in economics, and served for years as secretary of an insurance association. At 51 years of age he entered World War I as a volunteer. His *Kriegsbuch* appeared in 1919. He wrote some dramatic works (*Der Mitmensch*, 1895; *Lucifer*, 1899; *Die Menschenfreunde*, 1917), but he was essentially a lyricist, whose poems are concerned largely with love (*Aber die Liebe*, 1893; *Weib und Welt*, 1896; *Die Verwandlungen der Venus*, 1907).

Dehn (dān), **Adolf Arthur.** b. at Waterville, Minn., Nov. 22, 1895—. American etcher, lithographer, painter, water-colorist, and writer, best known for his lithographs and black-and-white drawings. He studied at the Minneapolis Art School and the Art Students League of New York, then traveled (1918–29) in Europe, staying for the most part at Vienna. He did mostly lithographs, drawings, and etchings until 1937, when he began to produce water colors and oil paintings. His work is represented in the Metropolitan Museum, Whitney Museum, and Brooklyn Museum at New York, the Albertina at Vienna, the Library of Congress at Washington, D.C., the Boston Museum, Honolulu Museum, British Museum, and elsewhere. He has contributed articles to *The Arts*, *Time*, *Art News*, *Coronet*, and other periodicals, and illustrations to *Fortune*, *The New Yorker*, *Dial*, *Vogue*, *Masses*, and others.

Dehn, Siegfried Wilhelm. b. at Altona, Germany, Feb. 25, 1799; d. at Berlin, April 12, 1858. German musicologist, librarian (1842–48) of the musical works in the royal library at Berlin; author of *Theoretische-praktische Harmonielehre* (1840) and *Lehre vom Kontrapunkt* (1859).

De Hondt (dẹ hônt'), **Pieter.** Original name of **Canisius,** Saint **Petrus.**

Dehr (dār). See **El Dirr.**

Dehra Dun (dā'rạ dön). [Also, **Dehra.**] Town in the Meerut division of Uttar Pradesh (United Provinces), Union of India, NE of the city of Delhi. The surrounding region produces sugar, wheat, rice, and barley. The town is the seat of a forestry institute (founded 1914) and of a national defense academy (founded 1949). It is known for its Hindu temple, said to have been built in 1699 by Ram Rai.

Deianira (dē.yą.nī′rą) or **Dejaneira** (dej.ą.nī′rą). In Greek mythology, daughter of Oeneus and Althaea, sister of Meleager, and wife of Hercules. She inadvertently caused Hercules's death by giving him the blood-steeped shirt of the centaur Nessus to wear, after the latter, dying and seeking revenge on Hercules, who had shot him, had told her that she could compel the love of any one wearing it. It burned him mortally, and she killed herself for sorrow.

De imitatione Christi (dē im.i.tā.shi.ō′nē kris′tī). [Eng. trans., "*Imitation of Christ.*"] Religious treatise commonly ascribed to Thomas à Kempis, but about which there has been much controversy. It places the rule of life in seclusion and renunciation. Other candidates have been put forward as its author, among them John Gerson, the famous chancellor of the University of Paris, and an unidentified John Gersen, abbot of Vercelli (supported by the Benedictines), whose name appears as that of the author in one manuscript. For Gerson are brought forward a number of early manuscripts and editions in France and Italy. The name of Thomas à Kempis appears on many early editions, including one c1471 which appears to be the first. A general tradition from his own times, extending over most of Europe, has led a great majority (including the Sorbonne itself) to determine the cause in his favor. It is also said that a manuscript of the treatise *De imitatione* bears these words at the conclusion: "*Finitus et completus per manum Thomae de Kempis, 1441*" and that many erasures and alterations in this manuscript give it the appearance of his original autograph.

Deimling (dīm′ling), **Berthold von.** b. at Karlsruhe, Germany, March 21, 1853; d. 1944. German general and politician. He crushed the uprising of the natives in the German colony of South-West Africa (1906–07), and served in World War I until 1917. After the war he became active in the Democratic Party and in pacifist movements, and was expelled from the organization of German officers. In 1924 he was one of the cofounders of the political organization Reichsbanner Schwarz-Rot-Gold, established to protect the Weimar constitution against extremists on the left and on the right.

Deimos (dī′mos). A satellite of Mars, revolving about its primary in 30 hours and 18 minutes at a distance of 14,600 miles. Its estimated diameter of five miles makes it the smallest known satellite in the solar system. It, along with Phobos, Mars's other satellite, was discovered by Professor Asaph Hall, of the U.S. Naval Observatory at Washington, in August, 1877.

Deinocrates (dī.nok′rą.tēz). See **Dinocrates.**

Deïoces (dē′yǫ.sēz). According to Herodotus, the founder (reigned c709–656 B.C.) of the Median dynasty, and the builder of Ecbatana. In fact, he was probably a local chieftain named Dayukku whose grandson Cyaxares founded the Median empire in 625 B.C. and whose name was included in the list of Median kings as a matter of policy.

Deïotarus (dę.yot′ą.rus). d. c40 B.C. Tetrarch and king of Galatia, and an ally of the Romans. He was defended before Caesar by Cicero in 45 B.C. on a charge of plotting to assassinate Caesar. Throughout the Roman struggle for power he kept his throne, siding successively with Pompey, Caesar, Brutus, and the triumvirate of Augustus, Antony, and Lepidus.

Deïphobus (dę.if′ǫ.bus). In Greek legend, a Trojan warrior, son of Priam and Hecuba. He appears in Shakespeare's *Troilus and Cressida.*

Deipnosophists (dīp.nos′ǫ.fists). Set of imaginary dialogues by Athenaeus, in which 29 dinner guests spend several days recounting tales and anecdotes. In this way the author manages to present many stories and quotations from Greek literature. Among the imaginary guests are included some of the most eminent men of the day, for example Masurius Sabinus, Ulpian, and Galen.

Deir (dir), **Book of.** See **Deer, Book of.**

Deira (dē′i.rą). In the 6th century A.D., an Anglian kingdom in what is now Yorkshire, England, extending from the Humber to the Tees. It was united (c600) with Bernicia to form the kingdom of Northumbria, and was later created an earldom.

Deirdre (dir′drę, der′drā). Heroine of the greatest love story of old Irish legendry. She was the daughter of Felim, in some versions of the story called a harper, in others a story-teller to Conchobar, king of Ulster about the beginning of the Christian era. By some accounts it was while Conchobar was feasting at Felim's house that a girl-baby was born to Felim's wife, of whom the druid Cathbad prophesied that she would be the most beautiful of the women of Eire but would cause bloodshed and death. Conchobar said that he would avert that doom by marrying Deirdre when she should be of age for it, and she was entrusted to the nurse Lavarcham who brought her up in a house in a secluded woods, where she saw no one but a few servants. One day when she was in her fifteenth year she saw a raven drinking the blood of a calf that had been slain on the snow, and she told Lavarcham that the man she would love would not be an old man like Conchobar, but one who had skin like the snow, cheeks like the blood, and hair like the raven. The nurse said there was such a man, Naoise, son of Usnach, and she yielded to Deirdre's pleas to bring him to her. Others tell the story differently to this point, but all agree that in the end Naoise and his brothers Ainle and Ardan took Deirdre to Alba, or Scotland, where they lived for some years, until Conchobar persuaded the famous warrior Fergus to go to Alba and invite the fugitives to return, with a promise of the king's friendship. Deirdre foresaw tragedy, but the three brothers trusted Fergus and the king. When they came to Eire, Fergus was detained by a ruse of Conchobar's while the three sons of Usnach, with Deirdre, went to the Ulster capital. There Conchobar set his minions upon the three brothers, who after an epic battle were slain. Some say that Deirdre died at that time after lamenting the deaths of Naoise, Ainle, and Ardan; another story is that she had to live with Conchobar for a year but then killed herself. Fergus and many others deserted Conchobar because of his treachery, and by joining Queen Medb of Connacht in the war of the Tain Bo Cuailgne, ensured the fulfillment of the druid Cathbad's prophecy that because of this crime, Emain Macha (the capital of Ulster) would be destroyed and no son of Conchobar would ever rule in Ulster.

Deirdre. Adaptation by James Stephens of the tragic story of Deirdre, the lovely heroine of old Irish legends, published in 1923.

Deirdre of the Sorrows. Tragedy by John Millington Synge, published in 1910, a year after his death. It is one of the many retellings by other authors, both Irish and non-Irish, of the story of the beautiful but tragic maid of Irish legend. Although left in an unfinished state, the play is regarded as Synge's greatest work.

Deir-el-Bahri (dār.eı.bä′rē). [Also: **Deir-el-Bahari, Der-el-Bahri.**] Locality W of Thebes, Egypt, near the W bank of the Nile, famous for its ruins. Among the ruins is a temple built by Hatshepsut, sister of Thutmose II and III (c1500 B.C.). The enclosure is preceded by a passage 1,600 ft. long between lines of sphinxes, at the end of which rose two obelisks. The inner court is entered by a fine granite pylon, and behind it is the temple itself. The plan is peculiar, as the buildings extend up the slope of the mountain in stages connected by flights of steps. The masonry is of a beautiful fine limestone, and the sculptures are of great importance, representing especially sacrificial scenes, military triumphs and captives, and payment of tribute. A number of the inner chambers and passages are covered with pseudovaulting of stones corbeled out from the walls. Here, in 1881, Maspero made a remarkable archaeological discovery of a number of mummies of the Pharaohs, including those of some of the most famous of Egyptian kings, among them Thutmose II and Thutmose III, the conqueror of Assyria, Seti I, and the great Rameses II, the "Pharaoh of the Oppression." These mummies are in remarkable preservation, and supply a not inadequate picture of the features of the sovereigns in life. The discovery was made through a quarrel of some Arabs, who had found a pit near the Sheikh Abd-el-Gournah hill, and were surreptitiously removing the contents. The mummies had evidently been brought from the royal tombs, which lie at no great distance, and placed in this pit for safety during some threatened danger. They are now preserved in the Gizeh Museum, Cairo. A second important discovery of concealed mummies was made in 1891.

Deism, "Bible" of. See under **Tindal, Matthew.**

Deity, The. Short poem (1825) by John Greenleaf Whittier. His first work, it was published in the Newburyport (Mass.) *Free Press,* edited by William Lloyd Garrison. A religious poem, as the title indicates, it belongs in tone and spirit with his *Laus Deo!* and *The Eternal Goodness.* In editions of the *Complete Works,* it is grouped, usually at the end of the volume, with "Early and Uncollected Verses."

Deitzler (dēts'lėr), **George Washington.** b. at Pine Grove, Pa., Nov. 30, 1826; d. in Arizona, April 10, 1884. American antislavery leader. He emigrated (1855) to Lawrence, Kan., where he joined the free-state movement, being imprisoned for treason at Lecompton after the so-called Wakarusa war (1855). Freed in 1856, he was a member (1857–58) of the free-state territorial legislature, a member of the Kansas senate under the Topeka constitution, mayor (1860) of Lawrence, and treasurer (1866) of the University of Kansas. During the Civil War, he took part in the battle of Wilson's Creek (1861) as a colonel and in Price's Raid (1864) as a major general.

Dej (dāzh). [Also: **Dées, Dés.**] Town in NW Rumania, in the province of Transylvania, situated on the Someş River, ab. 32 mi. NE of Cluj: railroad junction. The salt mine of Ocna Dejului is in the vicinity. 14,681 (1948).

Dejaneira (dej.ạ.nī'rạ). See **Deianira.**

Déjazet (dā.zhà.ze), **Pauline Virginie.** b. at Paris, Aug. 30, 1798; d. there, Dec. 1, 1875. French actress. She went on the stage in early childhood, and was known as a comedienne. She appeared for the last time on Oct. 2, 1875.

Dejean (dẹ.zhäṅ), **Pierre François Aimé Auguste,** Comte. b. at Amiens, France, Aug. 10, 1780; d. at Paris, March 18, 1845. French soldier and entomologist. He served with distinction at Ligny and Waterloo, and was appointed general in 1810, aide-de-camp to Napoleon in 1813, and general of division in 1814. He was the author of a catalogue of his collection of insects (1821–33) and *Histoire générale des coléoptères* (1825–39).

Dejection: An Ode. Poem (1802) by Samuel Taylor Coleridge. It was published in *The Morning Post* on Wordsworth's wedding day (Oct. 4, 1802) and was, for some strange reason which is still unknown, written for and given to Wordsworth as a wedding present. In its original version, the poet is several times addressed by name, "William." Later, after the two poets had a misunderstanding, Coleridge changed "William" to "Edmund," to "Otway," and to "Lady" and "Dear Lady." Although the poem is regarded as one of his two "noble odes" (*France* being the other), critics also regard it as the beginning of the end of his supreme poetic mastery. Coleridge himself, at the end of the second stanza, expresses regret that now he can merely "see" beauty, but not "feel" it.

Déjerine (dāzh.rēn), **Augusta.** [Maiden name, **Klumpke.**] b. at San Francisco, Oct. 15, 1859; d. at Paris, Nov. 5, 1927. French specialist in nerve pathology; wife of Joseph Jules Déjerine. She studied at Lausanne and Paris as a pupil of E. F. A. Vulpian. She described lead palsies, paralysis of the brachial plexus (1885), named Klumpke's paralysis, and made studies of the pathological anatomy of the nervous system. She was a coworker of her husband for 30 years and after his death founded a neurological laboratory and a museum at the medical faculty of the University of Paris. Author of *Des polynévrites en général et des paralysies et atrophies saturnines en particulier* (1889), and, with her husband, of *Anatomie des centres nerveux* (1895–1901).

Déjerine, Joseph Jules. b. at Geneva, Switzerland, Aug. 3, 1849; d. at Paris, Feb. 26, 1917. French neurologist; husband of Augusta Déjerine. A pupil of E. F. A. Vulpian, he became (1879) chef de clinique at the Charité at Paris, and three years later was named médecin des hôpitaux. After heading the clinic at the Bicêtre, he became (1901) professor of clinical medicine at the University of Paris, and director (1911) of the clinic at the Salpêtrière. He made studies of tabes and hereditary muscular atrophy (1903), described (with Jules Sottas, 1893) progressive hypertrophic interstitial neuropathy, described (with G. Roussy, 1906) thalamic hyperesthetic anesthesia (called the Déjerine-Roussy syndrome), and described (with L. T. J. Landouzy, 1886) facioscapulohumeral atrophy (called Landouzy-Déjerine atrophy or type). He wrote on spinal radiculitis, interstitial neuritis (1890), lesions on the pons and medulla, on aphasia, encephalitis, poliomyelitis, and syringomyelia. Author of *Recherches sur les lésions du système nerveux dans la paralysie ascendante aiguë* (1879), *L'Héré dans les maladies du système nerveux* (1886), *Sur l'atrophie musculaire des ataxiques* (1889), *Anatomie des centres nerveux* (in collaboration with his wife, 1895–1901), *Cahier de feuilles d'autopsies pour l'étude des lésions du névraxe* (1895; Eng. trans., 1911), *L'Aphasie motrice et sa localisation corticale* (1907), *Clinique des maladies du système nerveux* (1911), *The Psychoneuroses and their Treatment by Psychotherapy* (1913), and *Sémiologie des affections du système nerveux* (1914).

De Jonge v. Oregon, 299 U.S. 353 (1937) (dẹ jong'; or'ẹ.gọn). Unanimous decision of the U.S. Supreme Court which declared unconstitutional a conviction under the Oregon criminal syndicalist law on the ground that it violated the due process clause of the 14th Amendment. The offense charged against the appellant was based upon his attendance at a Communist Party meeting. Speaking for the court, Chief Justice Charles Evans Hughes asserted that "mere participation in a peaceable assembly and a lawful public discussion" could not be made "the basis for a criminal charge."

De Kaap (dẹ käp'). See under **Barberton,** Union of South Africa.

De Kalb (dē kalb'). City in N Illinois, in De Kalb County, ab. 58 mi. W of Chicago: a center for the manufacture of barbed wire. It is the seat of the Northern Illinois State Teachers College. 11,708 (1950).

De Kay (dẹ kā'), **Charles.** b. at Washington, D.C., July 25, 1848; d. May 23, 1935. American author, poet, and critic. He was graduated from Yale in 1868, was literary and art critic of the New York *Times,* and was U.S. consul general at Berlin (1894–97). He was the originator and one of the founders of the National Sculpture Society (1892) and of the National Arts Club (1898). Among his publications in book form are *Hesperus, and other Poems* (1880), *The Vision of Nimrod* (1881), *The Vision of Esther* (1882), *The Love Poems of Louis Barnaval* (1883), and *Bird Gods* (1898).

Dekhan or **Dekkan** (dek'ạn). See **Deccan.**

Dekker (dek'ėr), **Eduard Douwes.** [Pseudonym, **Multatuli.**] b. at Amsterdam, March 2, 1820; d. at Nieder-Ingelheim, Netherlands, Feb. 19, 1887. Dutch writer and colonial reformer. His best-known work is his autobiographical novel *Max Havelaar* (1860), which dramatically recounted his unsuccessful efforts as assistant resident in West Java to protect the people under his care against the extortions of Javanese and European officials, and against the harsh exactions of the Culture System, a method applied to force the production of coffee and other export crops. This book, amplified by others, became a propaganda instrument of liberal reformers in the Netherlands and, in translation, still serves anti-imperialist agitation in different parts of the world.

Dekker, Jeremias de. [Also, **Decker.**] b. at Dordrecht, Netherlands, c1610; d. at Amsterdam, 1666. Dutch poet, author of the satire *Lof der Geldzucht* (Praise of Avarice). His collected works were published in 1726.

Dekker, Thomas. [Also, **Decker.**] b. at London, c1572; d. probably at London, after 1632. English dramatist, at various times a collaborator of Middleton, Webster, Massinger, Rowley, and others. Little is definitely known of his life. He is first noticed in Henslowe's diary in 1598; in February of that year he was imprisoned in the Counter. Between 1598 and 1602 he wrote eight plays alone and many others in collaboration. In 1601 he wrote *Satiromastix, or the Untrussing of the Humorous Poet* (published 1602), a satirical dramatic attack on Ben Jonson, with whom a quarrel had broken out before 1600 when Jonson reflected upon him in *Every Man out of his Humour* and *Cynthia's Revels.* In 1601 Jonson attacked Dekker and Marston vigorously in *The Poetaster. Satiromastix* was Dekker's retort, parodying and ridiculing Jonson's style. From 1613 to 1619 he seems to have been imprisoned in the King's Bench prison. He wrote many pamphlets ridiculing the follies of the times, and in the plays written with others he excelled in good shop scenes and those laid in inns, taverns, and suburban pleasure-houses. He also had a poetical and luxuriant fancy. He wrote alone *The Gentle Craft* (produced in 1599; published anonymously in 1600 as *The Shoemaker's Holiday, or the Gentle Craft*), *Bear a Brain* (1599), *Old Fortunatus* (1600); and, with Chettle, *Troilus and Cressida*, *Agamemnon*, and *The Stepmother's Tragedy* (1599); with Chettle and Haughton, *Patient Grissel* (1603); with Day and Haughton, *The Spanish Moor's Tragedy* (1600). With Webster and others he joined in 1602 in a play in two parts on Lady Jane Grey, which probably appeared as *The Famous History of Sir Thomas Wyat* in 1607. In 1603 he published an account of the plague at London, *The Wonderful Year*. The first part of *The Honest Whore* he wrote in 1604, perhaps with Middleton. The earliest edition known of the second part is dated 1630, and there is nothing to show that Middleton was concerned in it. *The Seven Deadly Sins of London*, a pamphlet, he published in 1606, and *News from Hell*, a moralizing tract, in the same year. He also wrote *Westward Ho!* (before 1605) and *Northward Ho!* (1607), both with Webster, *The Bellman of London* (1608, a pamphlet on crimes and criminals), *Lanthorne and Candlelight* (the second part of *The Bellman*, 1608), *The Gull's Hornbook* (1609, a pamphlet on how not to behave), *The Roaring Girl*, with Middleton (1611), *If it be not Good the Devil is in it* (1612), *The Virgin Martyr*, with Massinger (c1620), and *Match Me in London* (published 1631). *The Sun's Darling*, with John Ford, was published in 1656 (the lyrical portions are thought to be Dekker's); *The Witch of Edmonton*, with Ford and Rowley, probably written in c1621, published in 1658; and in 1637 Dekker republished *Lanthorne and Candlelight* as *English Villainies*, the last of his numerous works; it is thought that he died shortly after its publication.

De Koven (dẹ kō′vẹn), **(Henry Louis) Reginald.** b. at Middleton, Conn., April 3, 1859; d. at Chicago, Jan. 16, 1920. American composer of songs and of light and grand operas, music critic, and conductor. He was taken to England as a boy, and was educated at St. John's College, Oxford, receiving his degree in 1879. He received his musical education in Germany, Italy, Paris, and Vienna. His light operas are *The Begum* (1887), *Don Quixote* (1889), *Robin Hood* (1890), first produced at Chicago by the Bostonians, a company that sang it with success thousands of times for over 20 years, *The Fencing Master* (1892), *The Algerian* (1893), *The Tzigane* (1895), *The Mandarin* (1896), *The Paris Doll* and *The Highwayman* (both 1897), *The Three Dragoons* (1899), *Red Feather* (1903), *Happy Land* (1905), *The Student King* (1906), *The Golden Butterfly* (1907), *The Beauty Spot* (1909), *The Wedding Trip* (1911), and *Her Little Highness* (1913). For his two grand operas he went to English and American themes, writing *The Canterbury Tales* (1917) in Switzerland, during the first year of World War I, and *Rip Van Winkle* (1920), in both cases the book being written by Percy Mackaye. The great success of his last opera was marred, unfortunately, by its association with his sudden death. *Rip Van Winkle* was first performed at Chicago, at the Civic Opera House, on Jan. 2; on Jan. 16, for its third performance, the house was completely sold out, and a supper party was being given in De Koven's honor; at that party he was stricken with apoplexy and died in ten minutes. He wrote over 120 songs, of which "O Promise Me," from *Robin Hood*, and his setting for Kipling's *Recessional* are his best known, and several pieces for piano. In 1902 he founded, and for three seasons conducted, the Washington (D.C.) Philharmonic Orchestra. His critical standards are reflected by his contributions to the Chicago *Evening Post*, the New York *World* (from 1892–97, and 1907–12), and the New York *Journal*.

de Kruif (dẹ krīf′), **Paul.** b. at Zeeland, Mich., March 2, 1890—. American bacteriologist and writer. He has been bacteriologist at Michigan (1912–17) and at the Rockefeller Institute (1920–22), reporter (1925 *et seq.*) for the Curtis Publishing Company, and a contributing editor to the *Reader's Digest*. Among his books are *Our Medicine Men* (1922), *Microbe Hunters* (1926), *Hunger Fighters* (1928), *Seven Iron Men* (1929), *Men Against Death* (1932), *Why Keep Them Alive?* (1936), *The Fight for Life* (1939), *Health is Wealth* (1940), *Kaiser Wakes the Doctors* (1943), *The Male Hormone* (1945), and *Life Among the Doctors* (1949); he worked with Sinclair Lewis on *Arrowsmith* (1925).

De La Beche (del.ạ.besh′, del′ạ.besh), Sir **Henry Thomas.** See **Beche,** Sir **Henry Thomas de la.**

Delaborde (dẹ.lȧ.bôrd), **Henri** Vicomte. b. at Rennes, France, May 2, 1811; d. at Paris, May 18, 1899. French painter and writer on the history of art. He was a pupil of Paul Delaroche. His principal works in painting are *La Conversion de Saint-Augustine* and *La Mort de Sainte Monique* (1838). As a historian he published numerous and notable works, especially on the Renaissance. He was collaborator with Charles Blanc on the *Histoire des peintres de toutes les écoles*. He wrote also *La Gravure* (1882), *La Gravure en Italie* (1883), and *L'Académie des Beaux-Arts . . .* (1891).

Delacroix (dẹ.lȧ.krwä), **Ferdinand Victor Eugène.** b. at Charenton-St.-Maurice, near Paris, April 26, 1799; d. at Paris, Aug. 13, 1863. French painter, a leader of the romantic school, known for his brilliant draftsmanship and dramatic compositions, chiefly on historical subjects. Among his works are *Dante et Virgile* (1822), *Massacre de Chios* (1824), *Femmes d'Alger* (1834), and *Prise de Constantinople* (1841).

de Lacy (dẹ lā′si). See **Lacy.**

Delafield (del′ạ.fēld), **Edward.** b. May 7, 1794; d. Feb. 13, 1875. American ophthalmologist and surgeon. He received his M.D. (1816) from the College of Physicians and Surgeons at New York, did clinical work (1817) abroad, and returned to New York, where he worked in obstetrics and general surgery, also devoting himself to eye diseases. One of the first ophthamologists in the U.S., he established (1820) the New York Eye Infirmary, was cofounder and first president (1864) of the American Ophthamological Society, and served as professor of obstetrics and diseases of women and children (1825–38) and as president (1858–75) of the College of Physicians and Surgeons. He was the author of *An Inaugural Dissertation on Pulmonary Consumption* (1816) and editor of an American edition (1825) of Benjamin Travers's *Synopsis of the Diseases of the Eye and Their Treatment.*

Delafield, E. M. Pseudonym of **Dashwood, Elizabeth Monica.**

Delage (dẹ.lȧzh), **Yves.** b. at Avignon, France, May 13, 1854; d. at Paris, Oct. 8, 1920. French zoölogist. He was appointed (1866) professor of zoölogy at the Sorbonne and became (1901) director of the marine biology laboratory at Roscoff, Finistère. One of the pioneers in the scientific investigation of reproduction, hybridism, and heredity, he wrote studies of parthenogenesis, sponge culture, evolution, and the commercial utilization of seaweeds. His books include *L'Hérédité et les grands problèmes de la biologie générale* (1895) and *La Structure du protoplasme* (1895).

Delagoa Bay (del.ạ.gō′ạ). [Portuguese, **Bahia Delagoa.**] Inlet of the Indian Ocean, on the SE coast of Africa, in Mozambique. It was discovered by the Portuguese toward the end of the 15th century. In 1823 the natives ceded it to the English Captain W. F. W. Owen, who raised the British flag there; but by arbitration of President MacMahon of France it was awarded (1875) to Portugal. It is the terminus of a railway connecting the Transvaal, Union of South Africa, with the seaboard. The important port of Lourenço Marques is situated at the head of the inlet.

Delagoa Bay Railway. Railroad in S Africa, connecting Komatipoort on the Transvaal frontier with the port of Lourenço Marques, Mozambique. At Komatipoort the line connects with the South Africa railways system, and direct contact is made with Pretoria (347 mi.) and Johannesburg (365 mi.). It was built in the 1890's and has been the instrument in making Lourenço Marques the port that it is today. Length of line from sea to Transvaal frontier, 55 mi.

Delagrange (dẹ.lȧ.gräṅzh), **Léon.** b. at Orléans, France, March 13, 1872; d. at Pau, France, Jan. 4, 1910. French sculptor and aviator. He studied at the École des Beaux-Arts, Paris, and executed works of sculpture of recognized merit, including *The Florentine Page*, *A Templar*, *Love and Youth*, *Miserère*, and *A Huguenot*. Becoming interested in aviation, he made many notable flights (1907–09) in

France, Italy, and England, establishing a record of 124 miles at the rate of 49 miles per hour in a Blériot monoplane at Juvisy, France, on Dec. 30, 1909. He was killed as the result of an accident to his monoplane during experiments at Pau.

Delaharpe (dę.là.ärp), **Jean François.** Original name of **Laharpe** or **La Harpe, Jean François de.**

Delaherche (dę.là.ersh), **Félix Auguste.** b. 1857—. French ceramist. A creative artist-craftsman in the old tradition, he works without assistants or employees, firing his kiln in the village of La Chapelle-aux-Pots only once a year, and preserving only those pieces which completely satisfy him. Considered by many to be the greatest French potter of his time, he is an officer of the Legion of Honor.

De la Mare (dę là mãr′, del′ą.mãr), **Walter (John).** b. at Charlton, Kent, England, April 25, 1873—. English poet, novelist, short-story writer, and dramatist; son of James Edward Delamare, a Huguenot church warden. Through his mother, Lucy Sophia Browning, he is related to the Victorian poet. He was educated at Saint Paul's Cathedral Choir School, at London (founded by John Colet), but he did not go to college. From 1890 to 1908 he was a bookkeeper in the London office of an oil company, dealing with facts and figures, a strange occupation for one with his poetic fancy. In the latter year, at the suggestion of Sir Henry Newbolt, he was awarded a small grant and an annual pension by the Asquith ministry of a hundred pounds on the Civil List. He began his writing career with contributions to the *Sketch* and the *Cornhill Magazine.* In his early days he used "Walter Ramal," an inversion of his own name, as a pseudonym. His works are *Songs of Childhood* (1902), *The Return* (1910), *The Listeners* and *A Child's Day* (both 1912), *Peacock Pie* (1913), *Motley* (1918), *Flora* (1919), *The Veil* (1921), *Down-adown-Derry* (1922), *Ding Dong Bell* (1924), *Stuff and Nonsense* (1927), *The Fleeting* (1933), *A Forward Child* (1934), *Early One Morning* (1935), *The Wind Blows Over* (1936), *This Year, Next Year* (1937), all poetry, and various volumes called *Poems* (1906) and *Collected Poems* (1920, 1935, 1941). He has also edited two anthologies of English poetry, *Come Hither* (1923) and *Behold, This Dreamer!* (1939). His prose includes *Henry Brocken* (1904), a novel, *Memoirs of a Midget* (1921), also a novel, which won the highly-valued James Tait Black memorial prize, several collections of short stories, *The Riddle* (1923), *Broomsticks* (1925), *The Connoisseur* (1926), *On the Edge* (1930), and *The Lord Fish* (1933). For children, he has written *Told Again* (1927), new versions of old fairy tales, and *Stories from the Bible. Desert Islands and Robinson Crusoe* (1930) is an essay in symbolism, and *Crossings* (1921) is a play. His own poetry is represented in anthologies by *The Listeners, An Epitaph, The Truants, Old Susan, The Old Men, Some One* ("Some one came knocking"), *At the Keyhole, The Mocking Fairy, Sam, Berries, All But Blind, Summer Evening, There Blooms No Bud in May, The Scarecrow, The Ghost, Silver, Nod, Shadow, Unregarding, Remembrance, The Three Cherry Trees, Miss Loo, Sam's Three Wishes, or Life's Little Whirligig, The Song of Shadows, The Dreamer, The Scribe* ("What lovely things Thy hand hath made"), *The Veil, The Quiet Enemy, The Holly,* and *Lucy,* and by many other selections.

Delamater (dę.lam′ą.tėr), **Cornelius Henry.** b. at Rhinebeck, N.Y., Aug. 30, 1821; d. Feb. 7, 1889. American mechanical engineer. He was co-owner of the Phoenix Foundry (after 1856 known as the Delamater Iron Works), which built, from designs by John Ericsson, America's first iron boats and steam fire engines and the engines for the Union government's ironclad *Monitor* (1862). The foundry was also notable for its production of propeller steamers, air compressors, the 36-inch cast-iron pipe for the Croton Aqueduct, and 30 gunboats (1869) for the Spanish government, and for the construction (1881) of John P. Holland's first successful submarine torpedo-boat.

Delambre (dę.läṅbr), **Jean Baptiste Joseph.** b. at Amiens, France, Sept. 19, 1749; d. at Paris, Aug. 19, 1822. French astronomer, appointed permanent secretary of the French Institute in 1803, and professor at the Collège de France in 1807. His works include *Méthodes analytiques pour la détermination d'un arc du méridien* (1799), *Base du système métrique décimal, ou mesure de l'arc du méridien compris entre les parallèles de Dunkerque et Barcelone, executée en 1792 et années suivantes par MM. Méchain et Delambre* (1806–10), and *Histoire de l'astronomie* (1817–27).

Delamere (del′ą.mir) or **de la Mer** (del′ą.mãr), 1st Baron. Title of **Booth, George.**

Delamere or **de la Mer,** 2nd Baron. A title of **Booth, Henry.**

De Lancey (dę lan′si), **Étienne** (or **Stephen**). b. at Caen, France, 1663; d. 1741. Merchant at New York in colonial times. A Huguenot who fled from France following the revocation of the Edict of Nantes, he became a successful merchant at New York, and one of that rising city's wealthiest men. He married into the influential Van Cortlandt family, and served for many years in the colonial assembly. His wealth and standing in the community were evidenced by the town house he built, which later became, and still is, known as Fraunce's Tavern, and is one of the most noted of colonial structures still standing in the metropolis.

De Lancey, James. b. Nov. 27, 1703; d. July 30, 1760. English colonial politician in America, chief justice and lieutenant governor of New York; brother of Oliver De Lancey. He attended Corpus Christi College, read law at the Inner Temple, was admitted to the bar after his return to New York in 1725, and became (1729) a member of the Council. He was appointed (1731) second judge of the supreme court, was promoted (1733) to chief justice, and in that capacity sat at the trial of Peter Zenger. In 1753 he became lieutenant governor of the province of New York, continuing while in that position to maintain and build his already formidable political power. He presided over the Albany Convention (1754) and was present at the conference of governors (1755) with General Braddock at Alexandria, Va.

De Lancey, James. b. at New York, 1732; d. at Bath, England, 1800. Colonial politician, sportsman, and Loyalist; son of James De Lancey (1703–60). He attended Eton and Cambridge, served in the French and Indian Wars and, upon the death of his father in 1760, inherited the elder De Lancey's landowning and political responsibilities. In 1761 he lost his political influence to the Livingston party, but regained it in 1768 and 1769, emerging as a conservative opponent of British colonial policies. But he was opposed to a revolutionary program, casting his vote against the Assembly resolution which sought to approve the proceedings of the Continental Congress. As a member of the provincial aristocracy educated in England, he established soon after his return to the colonies one of the finest stables of running horses in America. His stud stable produced most of the leading American race horses up to the mid-19th century, and from it also came the horse from which the Morgan breed is descended. He sold out his stable holdings in 1775 and went to England. A Loyalist, he was named in the Confiscation Act of 1777 and in the Act of Attainder of 1779. After the Revolution he received somewhat more than half of the 284,000 dollars claimed by him as compensation, although the sale of his forfeited estates, on the site of the present-day lower East Side in New York, brought 234,000 dollars.

De Lancey, James. b. at New York, 1746; d. in Nova Scotia, May 2, 1804. Colonial politician at New York and Loyalist leader during the American Revolution; grandson of Étienne (or Stephen) De Lancey (1663–1746), and cousin of James De Lancey (1732–1800). He was a leader of the faction sometimes called "the De Lancey Party" in the politics of the colony of New York, and represented the borough of Westchester in the colonial Assembly from 1750 to 1768. During the Revolutionary War he commanded, under Governor Tryon's commission, a band of men whose depredations against patriots of the "Neutral Ground" north of Manhattan Island, being largely of the nature of cattle-stealing, won them the name of "cowboys," while De Lancey was sometimes called "the Outlaw of the Bronx." He was proscribed by an act of the New York state legislature in 1779, and fled to Nova Scotia in 1782. There he became a member of the Nova Scotia Assembly, and in 1794 was appointed to the Council.

De Lancey, Oliver. b. at New York, Sept. 16, 1718; d. at Beverley, England, Oct. 27, 1785. Politician in colonial New York, Loyalist leader during the American Revolution, and British army officer; son of Étienne (or Stephen) De Lancey (1663–1741), brother of James

De Lancey (1703–60), and uncle of James De Lancey (1746–1804). A successful merchant and a leader of the De Lancey faction in the politics of the colony, Oliver De Lancey often acted arbitrarily and spoke violently, and persons whom he affronted or imposed upon were at a disadvantage because, his brother being chief justice of the colony, lawyers were reluctant to take cases against him. He served as an alderman of the city and as a member of the colonial Assembly, and early in the Revolutionary War he organized a force of approximately 1,500 Loyalists, some of whom operated on Long Island while others joined the British army in the South. Popular feeling toward him was evidenced by the sacking of his mansion in one of the rural districts of Manhattan Island, in 1777, and in 1779 he was attainted by the state legislature, and his property was confiscated. He fled to England, where he passed the rest of his life.

De Land (dę land′). City in Florida, county seat of Volusia County, SE of Jacksonville in a citrus-producing region. It is the seat of John B. Stetson University. 8,652 (1950).

Deland (dę.land′), **Margaret.** [Full name, **Margaretta Wade Deland**; maiden name, **Campbell.**] b. at Allegheny, Pa., Feb. 23, 1857; d. Jan. 13, 1945. American writer. Among her works are *The Old Garden and other Verses* (1886), *John Ward, Preacher* (1888), *Mr. Tommy Dove* (1893), *Philip and his Wife* (1894), *Old Chester Tales* (1898), *Dr. Lavender's People* (1903), *The Common Way* (1904), *The Awakening of Helena Richie* (1906), *R. J.'s Mother and Some Other People* (1908), *The Iron Woman* (1911), *Around Old Chester* (1915), *The Rising Tide* (1916), *The Vehement Flame* (1922), *New Friends in Old Chester* (1924), *If This Be I* (1935), and *Golden Yesterdays* (1941).

Delane (dę.lān′), **John Thadeus.** b. at London, Oct. 11, 1817; d. Nov. 22, 1879. English journalist; son of William Frederick Augustus Delane (1793–1857). He was editor (1841–77) of the London *Times*.

Delane, William Frederick Augustus. b. c1793; d. July 29, 1857. English journalist; manager of the London *Times*.

Delano (del′ą.nō). City in S California, in Kern County, NW of Bakersfield, in a farm and orchard region. 8,717 (1950).

Delano, Columbus. b. at Shoreham, Vt., June 5, 1809; d. Oct. 23, 1896. American congressman (1845–47, 1865–69) from Ohio and U.S. secretary of the interior (1870–75); at various times lawyer, banker, and sheep raiser. He was appointed (1869) U.S. commissioner of internal revenue. During his service as secretary of the interior, charges of fraud were made against the Bureau of Indian Affairs; although an investigating committee found evidence of incompetence, no charges were made against the major officials, but Delano resigned (1875).

Delano, Jane Arminda. b. at Townsend, N.Y., March 12, 1862; d. April 15, 1919. American nurse. She was director (1902–06) of the Bellevue Hospital School of Nursing at New York (from which she had graduated in 1884), chairman (1909 *et seq.*) of the National Committee of Red Cross nurses, superintendent (1909–11) of the Army Nurse Corps, president (1909–12) of the American Nurses' Association, and director (1918–19) of the Department of Nursing, American Red Cross. Author, with Isabel McIsaacs, of *American Red Cross Textbook on Elementary Hygiene and Home Care of the Sick* (1913).

Delany (dę.lā′ni), **Martin Robinson.** b. at Charles Town, Va. (now in W.Va.), May 6, 1812; d. at Xenia, Ohio, Jan. 24, 1885. American Negro leader, physician, and army officer. He was the son of free Negroes, but persecution caused the family to move to Pennsylvania in 1822, and he received his education at a Negro school at Pittsburgh. In 1836 he charted his course to become a physician, but was unable to continue his medical studies at that time, and only in 1849 was admitted to Harvard as a medical student, after being rejected by educational institutions in Pennsylvania and in New York. Meanwhile he turned journalist, beginning in 1843 the publication of a paper called *Mystery*, which attracted favorable attention, and in 1847 becoming associated with Frederick Douglass in issuing the *North Star*. He was active in work for the betterment of the lot of the Negro people, and in 1852 published his thoughtful book, *Condition, Elevation, Emigration, and Destiny of the Colored People of the United States, Politically Considered.* In this he emphasized practical problems of employment and living, and he also became an advocate of a return of the Negroes to Africa. In the same year (1854) in which he displayed heroism serving the victims of a cholera outbreak at Pittsburgh, he was instrumental in bringing about the first National Emigration Convention, as a result of which he was appointed to lead an expedition to the Niger valley of Africa, to explore the possibilities of such a movement. During the Civil War he was a physician with the Union army, and was given the rank of major, being the first Negro to rise so high in the U.S. army. In the Reconstruction years he was attached to the Freedman's Bureau, served as a judge in Charleston, S.C., fought vigorously against political corruption, but was defeated when he stood for election as lieutenant governor of that state.

Delany, Mary. [Maiden name, **Granville.**] b. at Coulston, Wiltshire, England, May 14, 1700; d. at Windsor, England, April 15, 1788. English author, friend and correspondent of Swift and patron of Fanny Burney; wife of Patrick Delany. She was the friend of the duchess of Portland, and was called his "dearest Mrs. Delany" by George III. He gave her a house in Windsor, and a pension of 300 pounds a year. She presented to the queen some of the "paper mosaic" for which she was famous, and became a great favorite with the royal family. She left six volumes of autobiography and letters, which contain much interesting gossip of the society of the time.

Delany, Patrick. b. in Ireland, c1685; d. at Bath, England, May 6, 1768. Irish preacher, dean of Down, in Ireland; husband of Mary Delany. He is noted as having been the intimate friend of Swift. In 1757 he began to publish a paper called the *Humanist*, advocating the prevention of cruelty to animals. He wrote *Reflections on Polygamy* (1738), *The Life and Reign of David, King of Israel* (1740–42), *A Humble Apology for Christian Orthodoxy* (1761), and others.

de la Pasture (dę.lap′ą.tėr), Mrs. **Henry.** See Lady **Clifford.**

de la Pole (del.ą.pōl′), **William.** See **Pole, William de la.**

Delaporte (dę.lȧ.pôrt), **Louis Joseph.** b. at St.-Hilaire-du-Harcouet, France, 1874—. French Orientalist. He served as professor (1921 *et seq.*) at the Institut Catholique de Paris, and was the author of *La Mésopotamie, les civilisations Babylonienne et Assyrienne* (Mesopotamia, and the Babylonian and Assyrian Civilizations, 1923).

De La Rey (dę lä rī′), **Jacobus Hercules.** [Also: **Delarey;** called **Oom Koos.**] b. in the Orange Free State, South Africa, Oct. 22, 1847; d. Sept. 14, 1914. Boer general of French Huguenot descent. In 1893 he was elected member for the Lichtenburg district of the Transvaal in the Volksraad, and was a strong adherent of Joubert. He was one of the few members opposed to a rupture with England and favored a policy of conciliation, but at the outbreak of hostilities in 1899 advocated an aggressive military policy. He was elected to the command of the Lichtenburg burghers, who became part of Cronje's western column, and secured the first victory of the war at Kraaipan (Oct. 12–13, 1899). In 1902 he succeeded in capturing Lord Methuen, together with a number of British troops. He was a member of the Boer commission which arranged the terms of submission, and afterward one of a deputation which visited Europe and the U.S. to raise funds for the assistance of their countrymen.

de la Roche (dę lä rôsh′), **Mazo.** b. at Toronto, 1885—. Canadian novelist. She is the author of a series of books revolving around the mythical Whiteoak family, including *Jalna* (1927) which was awarded the 10,000-dollar Atlantic Monthly prize, *Whiteoaks of Jalna* (1929), which was dramatized in 1936, *The Master of Jalna* (1933), *Young Renny* (1935), and *Whiteoak Harvest* (1936), and the volumes of short stories *The Sacred Bullock* (1939), *Whiteoak Heritage* (1940), *The Building of Jalna* (1944), and *Renny's Daughter* (1951); and of *Explorers of the Dawn* (1922), *Possession* (1923), *Portrait of a Dog* (1930), *Growth of a Man* (1938), and *A History of the Port of Quebec* (1944).

Delaroche (dę.lȧ.rosh), **Paul.** [Full name, **Hippolyte, Paul Delaroche.**] b. at Paris, July 17, 1797; d. there, Nov. 4, 1856. French historical and portrait painter. He began by studying landscape under Watelet, which he gave up for history after entering the studio of Baron Gros. He first attracted attention by his picture *Joash Saved from Death by Jehoshabeth* (1822). He received the gold medal in 1824, became knight of the Legion of Honor in 1828, officer in 1834, member of the French Institute in 1832, and professor at the French Academy in 1833. The following year he went to Italy, and on his return painted the famous hemicycle of the École des Beaux-Arts. At the time of his second visit in July, 1844, he was made a member of the Academy of St. Luke.

Delarue (dẹ.lȧ.rü), **Gervais.** b. at Caen, France, **1751**; d. 1835. French historian and antiquary, professor at the University of Caen. He was the author of *Essais historiques sur les bardes, les jongleurs et les trouvères normands et anglo-normands* (1834).

De la Rue (del'ạ.rö, del.ạ.rö'), **Warren.** b. in Guernsey, Channel Islands, Jan. 18, 1815; d. at London, April 19, 1889. English astronomer and physicist, best known for the application of photography to astronomy. He was the collaborator of Balfour Stewart and Loewy in *Researches on Solar Physics.*

Delattre (dẹ.lȧtr), **Roland.** Original name of **Lassus, Orlandus.**

de Lattre de Tassigny (dẹ tȧ.sē.nyē), **Jean Joseph Marie Gabriel.** b. at Mouilleron-en-Pareds, Vendée, France, Feb. 2, 1889; d. near Paris, Jan. 11, 1952. French soldier. A graduate (1913) of St. Cyr, he fought in the dragoons and in the infantry in World War I, being wounded five times. He fought in Morocco against the Riffs in 1925, and by 1939 had risen to the rank of general. After the occupation of France by the Germans in World War II, he organized resistance against German occupation of the entire country, for which he was tried by the Vichy government and sentenced (1942) to ten years' imprisonment. He escaped in 1943 and fled to England. He took part in the invasion of southern France in 1944, fought through Alsace, across the Rhine, and into Austria. He was the signer for France of the official German capitulation (May 9, 1945). He became chief (1945) of the French general staff and was placed in charge of the ground troops of the Western Union after the war. In 1950 he was made high commissioner and put in direct command of the French troops in Indo-China and succeeded in reorganizing them to stop the rebel (Ho Chi Minh) troops' advance. He was made a marshal of France posthumously.

Delaunay (dẹ.lō.nā), **Charles Eugène.** b. at Lusigny, Aube, France, April 9, 1816; drowned near Cherbourg, France, Aug. 5, 1872. French astronomer, author of *Théorie de la lune* (1860–67).

de La Vallée Poussin (dẹ lȧ vȧ.lā pö.saṅ), Baron **Charles.** b. at Louvain, Belgium, Aug. 14, 1866—. Belgian mathematician and civil and mining engineer. He received (1891) his doctoral degree in physical and mathematical sciences, became (1893) professor of mathematical analysis at Louvain, and was a visiting professor or lecturer at Harvard, Paris, Geneva, Strasbourg, and Madrid. He has been president (1920) of the International Mathematical Union and has been made doctor (honoris causa) at the universities of Toronto, Strasbourg, Oslo, and Paris, member of the Pontifical Academy of Sciences (1936), and corresponding member of the French Academy of Sciences. His works include *Cours d'analyse infinitesimale* and numerous articles in mathematical and scientific journals.

Delavan (del'ạ.vạn). City in SE Wisconsin, in Walworth County: manufactures of bathing suits and knitted goods. 4,007 (1950).

Delavigne (dẹ.lȧ.vēny'), **(Jean François) Casimir.** b at Le Havre, France, April 4, 1793; d. at Lyons, France, Dec. 11, 1843. French dramatist and poet. He began his studies in his native city, and completed them at Paris. As early as 1811 he attracted the attention of Napoleon by his *Dithyrambe sur la naissance du roi de Rome.* The events connected with Napoleon's downfall led Delavigne to write three elegies, *Les Messéniennes.* Two of these, *Waterloo* and *La Dévastation du musée*, were subsequently published with an article *Sur le besoin de s'unir après le départ des étrangers*, and in this form they widely attracted attention and favor. *La Vie et la mort de Jeanne d'Arc, Tyrtée, Le Voyageur, À Napoléon*, and *Lord Byron* were well received in 1824. The following year was spent in Italy, where Delavigne wrote the *Nouvelles Messéniennes.* After the stormy days of the revolution of July, 1830, he composed *La Parisienne*, set to music by Auber; also the *Dies irae de Kosciusko* and *La Varsovienne.* In 1843, in collaboration with his brother, Germain, he wrote the libretto to Halévy's opera *Charles VI.* His contributions to the stage include the *Vêpres siciliennes* (1819), *Les Comédiens* (1820), *Le Paria* (1821), *L'École des vieillards* (1823), *La Princesse Aurélie* (1828), *Marino Faliero* (1829), *Louis XI* (1832), *Les Enfants d'Édouard* (1833), *Don Juan d'Autriche* (1835), *Une Famille au temps de Luther* (1836), *La Popularité* (1838), *La Fille du Cid* (1839), and *Le Conseiller rapporteur* (1840). He was elected to the French Academy on Feb. 24, 1825. His works were edited in full by his brother in 1845, 1855, and 1863. A separate reprint of his poems and plays was also made in 1863.

Delavignette (dẹ.lȧ.vē.nyet), **Robert.** b. at Ste.-Colombe-sur-Seine, Côte-d'Or, France, March 29, 1897—. French colonial administrator, director (1947 *et seq.*) of political affairs of the French colonial ministry. He was governor general (1946–47) of Cameroun.

Delaville (dẹ.lȧ.vēl), **Bernard Germain Étienne.** See **Lacépède, Bernard Germain Étienne de la Ville** (or **Delaville**), Comte **de.**

Delaware (del'ạ.wãr). [Also: **Lenape, Leni-Lenape.**] Confederation of North American Indian tribes, formerly inhabiting the Delaware River valley, Pennsylvania, and large parts of New Jersey and Delaware. Remnants of the group are now settled in Oklahoma. They spoke an Algonquian language.

Delaware. [Called the **"First State"**; also the **"Diamond State"** and the **"Blue Hen State."**] State of the E United States, bounded by Pennsylvania on the N and NW, Delaware River and Bay (separating it from New Jersey) and the Atlantic Ocean on the E, and Maryland on the S and W: a Middle Atlantic State and one of the 13 original states.

Population, Area, and Political Divisions. Delaware is divided for administrative purposes into three counties. The state sends one representative to Congress and has three electoral votes. Wilmington and Dover are the principal cities. Capital, Dover; area, 1,961.7 sq. mi. (2,399.2 sq. mi., including water); pop. 318,085 (1950), an increase of 19.4 percent over the figure for 1940. The state ranks 47th in area, and 47th (on the basis of the 1950 census) in population.

Terrain and Climate. Delaware consists mostly of low, flat land, but has moderately rolling, hilly land in the N, the highest point in the state being at Centerville (ab. 440 ft.). There is much marshland, particularly along Delaware Bay. Small streams, fresh-water lakes, Delaware Bay, and the Atlantic Ocean provide an abundance of fish. The climate is temperate.

Industry, Agriculture, and Trade. Fruit growing (especially apples and peaches) and poultry raising (broilers) are the principal agricultural pursuits. Milk, eggs, truck crops, wheat, and corn are produced. Fishing and canning of fruit are important. E. I. duPont deNemours Company, the nation's largest producer of chemicals, has its headquarters and research laboratories at Wilmington, although its factories are dotted throughout the country. Many other large American corporations have their headquarters at Wilmington also, attracted to the state by the liberality of its tax laws. The state itself is not highly industrial, and Wilmington is the leading manufacturing center, producing textiles, machinery, and hardware, among other items. The city is the site of important shipyards, the world's largest braided-rubber hose plant, and its largest cotton-dyeing plant; it is an international center for the manufacture of morocco leather, glazed kid, and vulcanized fiber. The state's chief port, it is served by the Delaware River. Clay, stone, sand, gravel, bog iron ore, and phosphate rock are found in the state. The annual income in Delaware from agriculture ranges as high as 87 million dollars; from manufacturing, as high as 339,126,434 dollars; from mineral output, as high as 131,000 dollars.

History. Delaware was first explored (1609) by Henry Hudson; and although a settlement, Swanendael, was made (1631) near the site of what is now Lewes by the Dutch West India Company, the first permanent settlement, Fort Christina (now Wilmington), was made (1638) by Swedes led by Peter Minuit, who designated as New Sweden the entire territory from the Delaware River to the mouth of the Schuylkill. The region was captured (1655) by the Dutch under Peter Stuyvesant and was under Dutch rule until 1664, when it went to the English. It became united (1682) with Pennsylvania as part of a grant made to William Penn and was granted (1703) a separate legislature but had a governor in common with Pennsylvania until the American Revolution (1776). The regiment furnished by Delaware in the Revolutionary War was, on account of its fighting qualities, known as the "Game Cock Regiment." One of its officers, Captain Caldwell, who was noted as a fancier of gamecocks, maintained that a true gamecock must of necessity be the progeny of a blue hen. Hence the origin of the name "Blue Hen State," sometimes applied to Delaware. The first state to ratify the Constitution of the United States, Delaware adopted its own first constitution in 1776 and its present constitution in 1897. Although a slave state, it sided with the Union cause in the Civil War. The whipping post is still maintained in Delaware under provision of a law dating from 1771.

Culture. Delaware's population is fairly evenly balanced between urban and rural, the urban being slightly greater (62.6 percent in 1950). The state motto is "Liberty and Independence." The state flower is the peach blossom.

Delaware. City in C Ohio, county seat of Delaware County, on the Olentangy River, ab. 23 mi. N of Columbus: trading center for an agricultural and livestock area. It was platted in 1804. It is the seat of Ohio Wesleyan University, and was the birthplace of President Rutherford B. Hayes. 11,804 (1950).

Delaware Bay. Arm of the Atlantic Ocean and estuary of the Delaware River, which separates Delaware from New Jersey. Its entrance to the Atlantic, between Capes May and Henlopen, is ab. 13 mi. wide. Length, ab. 55 mi.; greatest width, ab. 25 mi.

Delaware River. River in the E U.S. which rises in S New York, in Delaware County, and separates Pennsylvania and Delaware on the W from New York and New Jersey on the E. It expands into Delaware Bay ab. 40 mi. below Philadelphia. On its banks are Trenton, Easton, Philadelphia, Camden, Chester, and Wilmington. Its chief tributaries are the Lehigh and Schuylkill, on the W. Length, ab. 300 mi.; navigable for ocean steamships to Philadelphia; tidal as far as Trenton.

Delaware Water Gap. Gorge on the Delaware River, between Pennsylvania and New Jersey, ab. 65 mi. NW of New York, by which the river passes through the Kittatinny Mountains between walls ab. 1,400 ft. in height.

De La Warr (del'ạ.wạr), Baron. [Called **Lord Delaware;** title of **Thomas West.**] b. probably at Wherwell, Hampshire, England, July 9, 1577; d. at sea, June 7, 1618. First governor and captain-general of the colony of Virginia. He attended Queen's College, Oxford, and went to Parliament in 1597. He served with the army in the Low Countries and in 1599 was in Ireland with his cousin, Robert Devereux, 2d Earl of Essex, by whom he was knighted in the same year. He was imprisoned and fined for his part in the Essex rebellion (1600–01). Upon his father's death he was raised to the peerage and became a member of the Privy Council. Designated a grantee in the second charter to the Virginia Company of London, he was a member of its council in 1609, and in February, 1610, was appointed first governor and captain-general for life of the Colony of Virginia. He left England (April, 1610) with 150 colonists, arriving in Virginia just as the colony was about to be given up. After sending for supplies and aid, and ordering the construction of three forts, he appointed a deputy and departed for the West Indies to recover from the illness brought on by the Virginia heat. He returned (June, 1611) to England, and in the same year published *The Relation of the Right Honourable the Lord De-la-Warre, Lord Governour and Captaine Generall of the Colonie, planted in Virginea.* He devoted himself to securing support for the settlement and left England in March, 1618, at the head of 200 men bound for Virginia. He stopped at Terceira in the Azores where, it is thought, he was poisoned.

Delbœuf (del.bėf), **Joseph.** b. at Liége, Belgium, Sept. 30, 1831; d. at Bonn, Germany, Aug. 13, 1896. Belgian philosophical writer and psychologist, professor of classical philology at the University of Liége (1866–96). Among his works are *La Psychologie comme science naturelle* (1876), *Questions de philosophie et de science* (1883), *Examen critique de la loi psychophysique* (1883), and *La Matière brute et la matière vivante* (1887).

Delbos (del.bō), **Yvon.** b. at Thonac, Dordogne, France, May 7, 1885—. French political leader and journalist, foreign minister from 1936 to 1938 and a leader of the Radical-Socialist Party. Founder of the newspaper *L'Ere Nouvelle* (1919) and editor in chief of the newspaper *Dépêche de Toulouse,* he served (1924–36) in the Chamber of Deputies, of which he was vice-president (1932–36). He subsequently held the posts of minister of justice (1936), foreign affairs (1936–38), and national education (1939–40). Active in the Resistance after the fall of France, he was deported to Germany. He was liberated (1945), and became a deputy to the Constituent Assemblies and to the National Assembly. He became minister of state in 1947, minister for overseas France in 1948, and minister of education in 1949.

Delbridge Islands (del'brij). See **Dellbridge Islands.**

Delbrück (del'brük), **Clemens von.** b. at Halle, Germany, Jan. 19, 1856; d. at Jena, Germany, Dec. 18, 1921. German politician. He was mayor of Danzig (1896), became Prussian minister of commerce (1905), was named (1909) a state secretary in the Reich ministry of the interior, and in 1914 rose to the vice-presidency of the Prussian council of ministers. The principal aide of Reichschancellor von Bethmann-Hollweg, he became, under the chancellorship of Prince Max of Baden, chief of the privy council. He was a German National People's Party member of the Weimar constitutional assembly, and of the Reichstag (1920).

Delbrück, Hans. b. at Bergen, Germany, Nov. 11, 1848; d. at Berlin, July 14, 1929. German historian, notable in the field of military history, also as a politician. He served as professor (1885 *et seq.*) at the University of Berlin. His works include *Geschichte der Kriegskunst im Rahmen der politischen Geschichte* (History of the Art of Warfare in the Framework of Political History, 1900–01, 1920–27), *Bismarcks Erbe* (The Heritage of Bismarck, 1915), and *Weltgeschichte* (World History, 1924–28). For some time he edited (1883–1919), with Treitschke, the periodical *Preussische Jahrbücher* (Prussian Annals).

Delbrück, (Martin Friedrich) Rudolf von. b. at Berlin, April 16, 1817; d. there, Feb. 1, 1903. Prussian statesman. He entered the ministry of commerce (1848) and was president of the chancery of the North German Confederation (1867–70) and of the imperial chancery (1871–76).

del Campo (del käm'pō), **Estanislao.** [Pseudonym, **Anastasio el Pollo.**] b. at Buenos Aires, 1834; d. 1880. Argentine poet. His epic *Fausto* (1866) is, after Hernández's *Martín Fierro,* the most famous gaucho poem. In it, a gaucho describes to his friend a performance of Gounod's opera.

Delcassé (del.kȧ.sā), **Théophile.** b. at Pamiers, Ariège, France, March 1, 1852; d. at Nice, France, Feb. 22, 1923. French political leader and diplomat, best known for his contribution to the Entente Cordiale with Britain. Entering the Chamber of Deputies in 1889, he served (1893–95) as minister of colonies. During the crucial years (1898–1905) when France rebuilt her diplomatic system, he held the foreign ministry uninterruptedly. After having brought the English-French clash in the Sudan in the Fashoda incident (1898–99) to a peaceful conclusion, he achieved a reorientation in Anglo-French relations marked by the colonial agreement of July 7, 1904. His policy of sharp opposition to Germany brought claims of "encirclement" from Berlin; his intransigence during the Moroccan crisis caused him to lose support within the French cabinet and brought his resignation (June, 1905). In 1909, he forced Clémenceau's resignation on a naval question. He was naval minister (1911–13), served at St. Petersburg as ambassador (1913–14), and was foreign minister (1914–15) in the ministry of national defense during World War I, resigning when Bulgaria, a country he had courted for the Allies, entered the war on the side of the Central Powers.

Del City (del). Town in C Oklahoma, in Oklahoma County near Oklahoma City. 2,504 (1950).

Delectable History of Forbonius and Prisceria (fôr-bō′ni.us; pri.sē′ri.ạ). See **Forbonius and Prisceria, Delectable History of.**

Delectable Mountains. Range of mountains in Bunyan's *Pilgrim's Progress*, from which a view of the Celestial City is to be had. They are "Emmanuel's Land," and the sheep that feed on them are those for whom Christ died. Isa. xxxiii. 16, 17.

Deledda (dā.lād′dä), **Grazia.** b. at Nuoro, Sardinia, 1875; d. 1936. Italian novelist. She won the Nobel prize in 1926. Her best works are usually considered to be *Il Vecchio della montagna* (1900), *Elias Portoliu* (1903), *Cenere* (1904), *L'Edera* (1904), *Nostalgie* (1905), *L'Incendio nell'oliveto* (1918), and *La Madre* (1920; Eng. trans., *The Woman and the Priest*, 1922, and *The Mother*, 1923).

De l'éducation (dẹ lā.dü.kà.syôṅ). See **Émile.**

De Lee (dẹ lē′), **Joseph Bolivar.** b. at Cold Spring, N.Y., Oct. 28, 1869; d. April 2, 1942. American obstetrician and gynecologist. After studying at Vienna, Berlin, and Paris, he established his practice at Chicago, and was instrumental in the founding of the Lying-in Hospital and Dispensary there in 1895. He held professorial chairs at Northwestern University (1897–1929) and at the University of Chicago (1929–36). His published works include *Obstetrics for Nurses* (1904) and *Principles and Practice of Obstetrics* (1913).

Delehaye (de.lẹ.e), **Hippolyte.** b. at Antwerp, Belgium, 1859; d. 1941. Belgian Jesuit priest and mathematician. He was president of the Collège des Bollandistes at Brussels, edited sections of the Bollandist *Acta sanctorum*, was a contributor to *Analecta Bollandiana*, and wrote chiefly on ecclesiastical subjects. His best-known book is *Work of the Bollandists through the Centuries.*

Delémont (dẹ.lā.môṅ). [German, **Delsberg.**] Small town in W Switzerland, in the canton of Bern, situated on the Sorne River, S of the French (Alsatian) border, between Basel and Biel. It has watch and cement factories. 6,625 (1941).

De Leon (dē lē′ọn), **Daniel.** b. on the island of Curaçao, Dec. 14, 1852; d. at New York, May 11, 1914. American Socialist leader and writer. He was educated at Hildesheim, Germany, and at Amsterdam, arriving (c1874) in the U.S. and settling at New York, where he became active in journalism. He received (1878) the degree of LL.B. at Columbia, where he won (1883) a prize lectureship in Latin-American diplomacy which he held for two three-year terms. Interested in reform and labor movements, he joined (1890) the Socialist Labor Party, became (1891) its national lecturer, and in the same year was its gubernatorial candidate for New York. He was editor (c1892 *et seq.*) of the Socialist journal, *The People.* An advocate of Socialist industrial trade unions, he led (1895) a group out of the Knights of Labor, which he had joined in 1888, and organized the Socialist Trade and Labor Alliance. Dissatisfaction with his allegedly dictatorial methods caused the withdrawal (1899) from the Alliance of a wing which later became the Socialist Party of America. In 1905 he participated in the founding of the Industrial Workers of the World, merging the Alliance with it, and upon being excluded from the IWW convention in 1908 lent his support to the Workers' International Industrial Union. His ideas were later praised by Lenin, who said the Soviet structure was presaged by De Leon's writings. Among his works are *What Means This Strike?* (1898), *Two Pages from Roman History* (1903), *Socialist Reconstruction of Society* (1905), and translations of Karl Marx's *The Eighteenth Brumaire of Louis Napoleon* and the major part of Eugène Sue's *Mysteries of the People; or History of a Proletarian Family Across the Ages.*

Delescluze (dẹ.lā.klüz), **Louis Charles.** b. at Dreux, France, Oct. 20, 1809; killed on the barricades at Paris, May 28, 1871. French journalist and political agitator, leader of the Paris Commune (March–May, 1871).

de Lesseps (dẹ les′eps; French, dẹ le.seps), **Ferdinand Marie,** Vicomte. See **Lesseps, Ferdinand Marie, Vicomte de.**

Delessert (dẹ.le.ser), Baron (**Jules Paul**) **Benjamin.** b. at Lyons, France, Feb. 14, 1773; d. at Paris, March 1, 1847. French naturalist and philanthropist. He was a member (1817–38) of the Chamber of Deputies, and contributed much to the introduction of savings banks in France. He was a collaborator of De Candolle in the publication of *Icones selectae plantarum* (1820–46).

Delft (delft). City in W Netherlands, in the province of South Holland, situated on the Schie Canal, ab. 5 mi. SE of The Hague. It has important cattle, butter, cheese, and vegetable markets, and also construction works, metallurgical and instrument industries, and chemical, glass, and tobacco manufactures. The famous pottery and faience manufacture of Delft, which flourished in the 17th and 18th centuries, has been revived. The inner town, one of the most typical in the Netherlands, contains interesting buildings, such as the *Oude Kerk* (Old Church), which dates from the 13th–16th centuries; the *Nieuwe Kerk* (New Church), built in the 14th and 15th centuries, with the tomb of William I of Orange by Hendryk de Keyser, other tombs of the Nassau-Orange family, and the tomb of the jurist Hugo Grotius, who was born here; the *Stadhuis* (city hall); the Gemeenlandhuis. The Prinsenhof, where William I (William the Silent) of Orange was assassinated on July 10, 1584, contains municipal collections; art collections are in the house of Lambert van Meerten. There is an old arsenal and a warehouse of the East India Company. Delft was occupied by the Germans in May, 1940, in World War II. 66,067 (est. 1951).

Delhi (del′i). [Also: **Dehli, Dilli.**] State of the Union of India, between Uttar Pradesh (United Provinces) and the state of Punjab on the W bank of the Jumna River. It includes New Delhi, the former capital of British India and the capital of the Union of India. Area, 574 sq. mi.; pop. 1,743,992 (1951).

Delhi. [Also: **Dehli, Dilli.**] City in the state of Delhi, Union of India, on the Jumna River: officially separate from New Delhi, the capital of British India and of the Union of India. Pop., including New Delhi and suburbs, 521,849 (1941).

History. The city of Indraprastha is said (in the *Mahabharata*) to have been built near the site of Delhi, in the 15th century B.C. Delhi was captured by Mohammed of Ghor in 1193 A.D., and a few years later became the capital of a Mohammedan monarchy. It was sacked by Tamerlane in 1398, and captured by Baber in 1526. Delhi became the capital of the Mogul Empire, and was rebuilt by Shah Jehan in the period 1638–58. It was sacked by Nadir Shah in 1739, and occupied by the British under Lake in 1803, although it continued to be the residence of the titular Grand Mogul down to 1857. It was captured by the Sepoy mutineers on May 11, 1857, and was besieged in June by the British and retaken on Sept. 20, 1857.

Architecture. Among the notable structures in Delhi, are the tomb of Humayun Shah, and the palace and Great Mosque of Shah Jehan. The tomb of Humayun, Shah was completed by his successor Akbar in the second half of the 16th century. The plan is about square; the tomb chamber is octagonal, with great canopied portals on four of its sides and small octagonal chambers on the four others. The central space is covered by a graceful dome. The decoration is much simpler than that of the later Mogul architecture, consisting chiefly of keeled arcades of different sizes framed in rectangular panels. The palace was built by Shah Jehan in the middle of the 17th century. It has been called the most splendid of Oriental palaces. The massive towered wall encloses an area of ab. 1,600 by 3,200 ft. The main entrance opens on a noble vaulted hall 375 ft. long, from which are reached in succession two spacious courts. On the second of these faces the hall of public audience, an open arcaded structure with scalloped arches and coupled columns in the exterior range. On another court, toward the river, is the hall of private audience (*Dewan-i-Khas*), similar to the first, but with square piers to its arches and beautiful inlaying in colored stones. On the river side stands also the Rung Mehal, or Painted Hall, an admirable structure, which includes a bath. The Jami Musjid, or Great Mosque, was built by Shah Jehan in the middle of the 17th century. It is very large, and the grouping of the three lofty monumental gates and the kiosked angle towers of its court with the lofty minarets, the great entrance arch, and the three fine bulbous domes of the sanctuary produces an unusually impressive architectural effect. The court is raised on a high basement, and is surrounded by graceful open arcades. The minarets rise from the ends of the façade of the mosque proper, and between them and the central arch there are on each side five fine arcades surmounted by paneling in red sandstone and white marble. Above the cornice are placed a range of close-set, round-headed battlements.

Delhi (del'hī). Town (in New York the equivalent of township in many other states) and village in C New York, county seat of Delaware County. It is the seat of a state school of agriculture. Pop. of town, 3,311 (1950); of village, 2,233 (1950).

Delhi Sultanate (del'i). Former Moslem state in NW and N India, which extended S to include all of C India in the 14th century. In the period from 1173 to 1202 A.D. the vast extent of N India was conquered by the Afghanistanian Turks under Mohammed of Ghor. When he was assassinated in 1206, Kutbuddin Aibak assumed the title of sultan of Delhi and established a dynasty which lasted until 1414, with 26 rulers. It was organized as an autocratic kingdom, with a royal army, under which were provincial governors, each having a provincial army. During the 13th century the great threat of the Mongols on the NW kept the forces of the Delhi Sultanate concentrated in the N, but in the 14th century Malwa and Gujarat were annexed, incorporating most of India. This large and unwieldy state suffered numerous local revolts, and was in the process of breaking up when the Mongols under Tamerlane poured into the Indus valley and ravaged N India, capturing and sacking Delhi in December, 1398. The central power of the sultanate was thus finally destroyed, and the state disintegrated, although the last sultan ruled a small territory around Delhi until his death in 1414.

Delia (dē'li.ạ). Name given in ancient Greek myth and religion to Artemis, from the island of Delos, her birthplace. Similarly Apollo, the sun god, was called Delius.

Delia. Shepherdess in Vergil's *Eclogues*.

Delia. Sonnet sequence (1592) by "the well-languaged" Samuel Daniel. A collection of 50 sonnets, they are addressed to his patroness, the Countess of Pembroke, whose household he called "my best school." Twenty-eight of the sonnets had been published in 1591. Some of those that are considered the best and that appear most frequently in anthologies are numbers 11 ("Tears, vows, and prayers win the hardest heart"), 18 ("Restore thy tresses to the golden ore"), 25 ("False Hope prolongs my ever certain grief"), 30 ("My cares draw on mine everlasting night"), 31, or 39 in some editions ("Look, Delia, how we esteem the half-blown rose"), 41 ("When men shall find thy flower, thy glory pass"), 42 ("Beauty, sweet love, is like the morning dew"), 45, or sometimes 49 or 54 ("Care-charmer Sleep, son of the sable Night"), perhaps the best known, and 46, or 55 ("Let others sing of knights and paladins"). Daniel has been charged with not knowing when to stop, and the last line of his last sonnet, "I say no more; I fear I said too much," has been used against him, half-humorously, half-seriously, as a good piece of self-criticism that he should have accepted long before. His work, however, is usually regarded as being worthy to rank among the five outstanding Elizabethan amatory sequences, with Sidney's *Astrophel and Stella*, Drayton's *Idea*, Spenser's *Amoretti*, and Shakespeare's *Sonnets*.

Delian League (dē'li.ạn). [Also, **Confederacy of Delos.**] A Hellenic league, formed probably c477 B.C., with its political center at Athens and its treasury at Delos (removed later to Athens). The term is sometimes applied also to a similar league of 378–338 B.C. The great danger of conquest by the Persians compelled the Ionian Greek states, jealous of their independence, but mostly located on islands, and individually indefensible against Persian power, to find some means of collaboration. Beginning in 478 B.C. such maritime states as Aegina, Megara, Naxos, Thasos, Lesbos, Chios, Samos, and others accepted the plan of a league with a treasury and a council on the island of Delos, the assessments for the treasury to be set by Athens, and the council to be under Athenian presidency. The League accomplished its purpose of nullifying the Persian peril, but when, after the death of Xerxes, Naxos and Thasos attempted to withdraw from it, their secession was prevented by Athens. By diplomacy and by their greater power, the Athenians were able to hold the confederacy together and to increase its adherents, which eventually numbered well over 200 states. In 457 B.C. Sparta was deterred from a threatened attack, and Thebes was subdued. But in 454 B.C., when under the pretext of new danger from the Persian quarter, the treasury was removed to Athens, the League became in fact an Athenian empire, which lasted for a troubled half century but came to an end with the close of the Peloponnesian War, disastrously for Athens, in 404 B.C. Subsequent restoration of Athenian sea power led in 378 to the formation of a new league, Athenian-dominated, but its course was also a troubled one, and in 338 B.C. it was extinguished by the power of Macedon. The story of the Delian League is the story of the fatal unwillingness of the small Greek states to coalesce into a nation, and of the inability of Athens to enforce unity. It was the high point of the hope for such an eventuation, and its failure made inevitable first the Macedonian hegemony and eventually the conquest by Rome.

Delibes (dẹ.lēb), **Clément Philibert Léo.** b. at St.-Germain-du-Val, France, Feb. 21, 1836; d. at Paris, Jan. 16, 1891. French composer. He was a chorus conductor at the Paris Opéra, and in 1881 was appointed professor of composition at the Paris Conservatoire. His music consisted chiefly of ballets such as *Coppélia* (1870) and *Sylvia* (1876), and operas including *Le Roi l'a Dit* (1873), *Jean de Nivelle* (1880), and *Lakmé* (1883).

Delicate Situation, The. Novel by Naomi Royde-Smith, published in 1931.

Delijannis (ᴛʜe.lē.yän'ēs), **Théodore.** See **Delyannis** or **Delijannis, Théodore.**

Delilah (dẹ.lī'lạ). In the Bible, a Philistine woman of the valley of Sorek, mistress of Samson. She discovered that Samson's long hair represented the secret of his strength; she cut it off and betrayed him to the Philistines, who were then able to capture him. Judges, xvi.

Delille (dẹ.lēl), **Jacques.** [Also, **Delisle.**] b. at Aigueperse, Puy-de-Dôme, France, June 22, 1738; d. at Paris, May 1, 1813. French didactic poet and translator. His works include *Les Jardins* (1782), *La Pitié* (1803), and a translation of Vergil's *Georgics* (1769).

Delineator, The. Monthly magazine published at New York from 1873 to 1937. It featured fashions, fiction, and comment on the contemporary scene. Before merging (1937) with the *Pictorial Review*, the magazine attained a circulation of more than two million. Its editors included Theodore Dreiser and Honoré Morrow.

Deliniers-Brémont (dẹ.lē.nyā.brā.môṅ), **Jacques Antoine Marie.** Original French name of **Liniers y Bremont** (or **Liniers), Santiago Antonio María de.**

Deliro (de.lē'rō). Character in Ben Jonson's comedy *Every Man Out of His Humour:* a good, doting citizen, a fellow sincerely in love with his own wife, and so taken by an idealization of her perfections that he simply holds himself unworthy of her.

Delisle (dẹ.lēl; Anglicized, dẹ.līl'), **Guillaume.** b. at Paris, Feb. 28, 1675; d. there, Jan. 25, 1726. French scientist, one of the founders of modern geography; brother of Joseph Nicolas Delisle.

Delisle, Joseph Nicolas. b. at Paris, April 4, 1688; d. there, Sept. 11, 1768. French astronomer; brother of Guillaume Delisle. His works include *Mémoires pour servir à l'histoire et au progrès de l'astronomie* (1738) and *Mémoire sur les nouvelles découvertes au nord de la Mer du Sud* (1752).

Delisle, Léopold Victor. b. at Valognes, Manche, France, Oct. 24, 1826; d. at Paris, July 22, 1910. French historian, bibliographer, and paleographer. In 1852 he was appointed assistant in the manuscript department of the Bibliothèque Nationale at Paris, of which he later became conservator and was administrator general (1874–1905). He was made chevalier of the Legion of Honor in 1857, officer in 1877, and commander in 1883. He wrote many important papers on the history of France, particularly that of Normandy, and on paleography and bibliography.

Delitzsch (dā'lich). Town in C Germany, in the *Land* (state) of Saxony-Anhalt, Russian Zone, formerly in the province of Saxony, Prussia, situated on the Löbber River, ab. 12 mi. N of Leipzig. Before World War II it had shoe, cigar, and chocolate factories, flour mills, and a sugar refinery, as well as vocational schools and a local museum. Herman Schulze-Delitzsch, the founder of the producers' coöperative movement in Germany, was born here. The population, mostly Protestant, increased 39.6 percent between 1939 and 1946, largely because of the influx of East German refugees. 25,148 (1946).

Delitzsch, Franz. b. at Leipzig, Germany, Feb. 23, 1813; d. there, March 4, 1890. German exegete and Hebraist. He became professor of theology at Rostock in 1846, at Erlangen in 1850, and at Leipzig in 1867. He represented strict Lutheranism. His numerous works include commentaries on the Old Testament books of Habakkuk (1843), Genesis (1852), Hebrews (1857), Psalms (1859–60), and Job (1864); also *Sakrament des wahren Leibes und Blutes Jesu Christi* (1844) and *System der biblischen Psychologie* (1855).

Delitzsch, Friedrich. b. at Erlangen, Bavaria, Germany, Sept. 3, 1850; d. Dec. 19, 1922. German Assyriologist; son of Franz Delitzsch. He was appointed professor of Assyriology at Leipzig in 1877, at Breslau in 1893, and at Berlin in 1899. His works include *Wo lag das Paradies?* (1881), *Assyrisches Wörterbuch* (1887), *Assyrisches Handwörterbuch* (1894–96), and *Babel und Bibel* (1903).

Delium (dē'li.um). In ancient geography, a place in Boeotia, Greece, situated on the coast ab. 24 mi. N of Athens. Here during the Peloponnesian War the Boeotians defeated (424 B.C.) the Athenians.

Delius (dē'li.us). Surname of Apollo, from his birthplace in Delos.

Delius (dē'li.us, dēl'yus), **Frederick.** b. at Bradford, Yorkshire, England, Jan. 29, 1862; d. at Grez-sur-Loing, Seine-et-Marne, France, June 10, 1934. English composer. He lived as an orange planter in Florida, and at Leipzig and Paris. His works include an opera, *Koanga* (1895–97); the music dramas *A Village Romeo and Juliet* (1900–01) and *Margot la Rouge* (1902); several symphonic works, including *Florida* (1887), *Paris: The Song of a Great City* (1899), *Brigg Fair* (1907), *In a Summer Garden* (1908), *On Hearing the First Cuckoo in Spring* (1912), *North Country Sketches* (1913–14), and *Eventyr* (1917); choral works, such as *Appalachia* (1902), *Sea Drift* (1903), *A Mass of Life* (1904–05), and *Songs of Farewell* (1930); he also composed songs, concertos, and chamber music.

Delius (dā'lē.ůs), **Nikolaus.** b. at Bremen, Germany, Sept. 19, 1813; d. at Bonn, Germany, Nov. 18, 1888. German philologist and Shakespearian scholar, professor of Sanskrit, Provençal, and English literature at Bonn (1855–80). He was the author of a critical edition of Shakespeare (1854–61 and 1882), and other works.

Deliverance, The. Novel of Southern life and character (1904) by Ellen Glasgow. Its theme, and the theme of much of her work, is the conflict between the codes and ideals of the Virginia aristocracy and of the old South, before its defeat in the Civil War, and the political democracy that followed the freedom of the slaves.

Dell (del), **Ethel M.** [Full name, **Ethel May Dell**; married name, **Savage.**] d. at London, Sept. 17, 1939. English popular novelist and short-story writer. A prolific writer, she published at least one book a year between 1911 and 1939. She was the author of novels including *The Way of an Eagle* (1912), *Knave of Diamonds* (1913), *Keeper of the Door* (1915), *Bars of Iron* (1916), *Greatheart* (1918), *Lamp in the Desert* (1919), *Top of the World* and *The Hundredth Chance* (both 1920), *The Obstacle Race* (1921), *Charles Rex* (1922), *Unknown Quantity* (1924), *A Man Under Authority* (1926), *The Black Knight* (1927), *The Gate Marked "Private"* (1928), *The Prison Wall* and *The Silver Bride* (both 1932), *Dona Celestis* (1933), *The Electric Torch* (1934), *Desire of His Life* and *Where Three Roads Meet* (both 1935), *Juice of the Pomegranate* and *Serpent in the Garden* (both 1938), and *Sown Among Stars* (1939). Among her collections of stories are *The Swindler* (1914), *The Safety Curtain* (1917), *The Tidal Wave* (1920), *The Odds* (1922), and *The Passer-By* (1925).

Dell, Floyd. b. at Barry, Ill., June 28, 1887—. American novelist, dramatist, essayist, and editor. From 1905 to 1908 he was a reporter on Davenport (Iowa) and Chicago papers, after having worked as a factory hand and a laborer. His formal education ended at 16 when the poverty of the Dell family compelled him to leave high school before his graduation. From 1911 to 1913 he was literary editor of the Chicago *Evening Post*, and he was on the editorial staff of two radical papers, the *Masses* (1914–17), and the *Liberator* (1918–24), which succeeded it. When the former publication was accused of violating the Espionage Act, he was a defendant. His novels are *Moon-Calf* (1920), its sequel *The Briary-Bush* (1921), *Janet March* (1923), *Runaway* and *This Mad Ideal* (both 1925), *An Old Man's Folly* (1926), dealing with pacifists in World War I, *An Unmarried Father* (1927), *Souvenir* (1929), *Love Without Money* (1931), *Diana Stair* (1932), and *The Golden Spike* (1934). His nonfiction includes *Women as World-Builders* (1913), *Were You Ever a Child?* (1919), a study in child psychology, *Looking at Life* (1924), *Intellectual Vagabondage, an Apology for the Intelligentsia* (1926), *Upton Sinclair, a Study in Social Protest* and *The Outline of Marriage* (both 1927), and *Love in the Machine Age* (1930). As a dramatist he has written *The Angel Intrudes* (1918), *Sweet-and-Twenty* (1921), *King Arthur's Socks* (1922), one-act plays, and *Little Accident* (1928; a dramatization of his *Unmarried Father*) and *Cloudy with Showers* (1931), both in three acts and both with the actor Thomas Mitchell in a leading part. *Love in Greenwich Village* (1926), is a collection of short stories and verse, and *Homecoming* (1933) is his autobiography.

della Bella (del.lä bel'lä), **Stefano.** See **Bella, Stefano della.**

Della Crusca (del″ą krus'ką). Pseudonym of **Merry, Robert.**

Della Cruscans (del″ą krus'kąnz). Small clique of English poets of both sexes who originally met (c1785) at Florence. Their productions, which were affected and sentimental, were published in England in the *World* and the *Oracle*. They were attacked by William Gifford (1791–96) in *The Baviad* and *The Mæviad*. Robert Merry adopted the pseudonym "Della Crusca," Mrs. Hannah Cowley "Anna Matilda," and Edward Jerningham "The Bard." These, with Edward Topham, Charles Este, James Boswell, Mrs. Piozzi, and others, formed the group. They took their name from the Florentine Accademia della Crusca, of which Merry was a member.

della Paglia (del.lä päl'yä), **Antonio.** See **Paleario, Aonio.**

della Robbia (del.lä rōb'byä; Anglicized, del″ą rob'i.ą). See under **Robbia.**

Dellbridge Islands (del'brij). [Also, **Delbridge Islands.**] Group of four islets of volcanic origin in Antarctica, lying in McMurdo Sound S of Cape Evans on Ross Island, in ab. 77°40′ S., 166°25′ E.

Dellenbaugh (del'ęn.bô), **Frederick Samuel.** b. at McConnelsville, Ohio, Sept. 13, 1853; d. at New York, Jan. 29, 1935. American explorer and writer, librarian of the American Geographical Society (1909–11). He accompanied Major Powell on his second journey of exploration through the Grand Canyon of the Colorado (1871–73), and went with the Harriman expedition to Alaska in 1899. His works include *The North Americans of Yesterday* (1900), *The Romance of the Colorado River* (1903), *Breaking the Wilderness* (1905), and *A Canyon Voyage* (1908).

Dellinger (del'in.jėr), **John Howard.** b. at Cleveland, Ohio, July 3, 1886—. American radio engineer. He has been a physicist (1907 *et seq.*) with the U.S. Bureau of Standards, serving as chief of its radio section (1918–46) and also as chief of research in the radio section (1926–34) of the Department of Commerce aeronautics branch, chief engineer (1928–29) with the Federal Radio Commission, and chairman of the radio propagation section (1942–46) of the National Defense Research Committee. He is the author of the government publication *Radio Instruments and Measurements* (1918), as well as many articles on radio and electricity.

Dellinger (del'ing.ėr), **Rudolf.** b. 1857; d. 1910. German composer. His works include the operettas *Don Cesar* (1885), *Lorraine* (1889), *Saint Cyr* (1891), *Die Chansonette* (1895), *Jadwiga* (1901), and *Der letzte Jonas* (1910).

Dellys (de.lēs'). Small seaport in Algiers department, Algeria, in NW Africa, ab. 50 mi. E of Algiers, on the Mediterranean coast. The area about the town has been little colonized by Europeans and the port is of minor importance. 4,038 (1936).

Delmar (del'mär). Unincorporated community in E New York, in Albany County. Under the new urban definition established for use in the 1950 census it was counted with adjoining urban areas. The last official enumeration was 2,992 (1940).

Del Mar (del′mär), **Alexander.** b. at New York, Aug. 6, 1836; d. at Little Falls, N.J., July 1, 1926. American political economist, statistician, and mining engineer. He was the founder of the *Social Science Review* and its editor from 1864 to 1866. In 1867 he was director of the Bureau of Statistics, and in the same year president of the Washington Statistical Society. His works include *Gold Money and Paper Money* (1862), *Essays on Political Economy* (1865), *What is Free Trade?* (1868), *The Resources . . . of Egypt* (1874), *History of the Precious Metals* (1880), and *A History of Money . . .* (1885).

Delmar (del′mär), **Viña.** [Maiden name, **Croter.**] b. at New York, Jan. 20, 1905—. American writer. She is the author of somewhat sensational but realistic popular novels, including *Bad Girl* (1928), *Loose Ladies* (1929), *Kept Woman* (1929), *Women Live Too Long* (1932), *The Marriage Racket* (1933), and *The Marcaboth Women* (1951).

Delmenhorst (del′men.hôrst). Town in NW Germany, in the *Land* (state) of Lower Saxony, British Zone, formerly in the free state of Oldenburg, situated on the Delme River, ab. 9 mi. W of Bremen. Formerly the center of large linoleum works, it is now known for its woolen textile, garment, furniture, tool, and felt manufactures; there are also dairies and agricultural markets. The population, mostly Protestant, increased 35.9 percent between 1939 and 1946, largely because of the influx of East German refugees. 48,742 (1946), 57,273 (1950).

Delmonico (del.mon′i.kō), **Lorenzo.** b. at Marengo, Switzerland, March 13, 1813; d. Sept. 3, 1881. American restaurateur, noted for his part in introducing European gastronomy into the U.S. He left Switzerland at the age of 19 to join his two uncles in the catering and confectionery business at New York. At his suggestion the company, in which he became a partner, opened a restaurant on William Street, where Delmonico embarked on the skillful combination of European cuisine and American abundance and variety that subsequently drew the admiration of both natives and foreigners. Succeeding restaurants were opened on Broad Street, at Beaver and William streets, at Broadway and Chambers Street, at 14th Street and Fifth Avenue, and at Broadway and 26th Street. His restaurants became world-famous, and in New York, where he pioneered the eating establishment offering an elaborate menu, the restaurant became an accepted institution and was adopted in a similar fashion in other cities.

Delmonte y Tejada (del.mōn′tā ē tā.hä′ᴛʜä), **Antonio.** b. at Santiago de los Caballeros, Dominican Republic, Sept. 29, 1783; d. at Havana, Cuba, Nov. 19, 1861. Spanish-American historian. Driven from his country in 1804 by the revolutionists, he resided at Havana after 1806, practicing law and occupying several government positions. The first volume only of his *Historia de Santo Domingo* was published at Havana in 1853.

Delna (del.nȧ), **Marie.** [Original name, **Marie Ledan.**] b. at Paris, Aug. 3, 1875; d. 1932. French contralto singer. She sang at the Paris Opéra, the Opéra-Comique, and the Gaîté Lyrique. Her principal roles were Orphée, Dido in Berlioz's *Les Troyens*, Charlotte in *Werther*, Mistress Quickly in *Falstaff*, Marceline in *L'Attaque du Moulin*, Fides in *Le Prophète*, Delilah, and Carmen. She was a member of the Metropolitan Opera Company (1909–10), and was heard at New York in *Orphée* and *L'Attaque du Moulin*.

Delolme (dẹ.lolm), **Jean Louis.** b. at Geneva, Switzerland, 1740; d. in Switzerland, July 16, 1806. Swiss constitutional writer. Having offended the Genevan government by the publication of a pamphlet entitled *Examen des trois points des droits*, he emigrated to England, where he lived many years. He returned to Switzerland in 1775. His works include *Constitution de l'Angleterre* (1771), of which an English translation, prepared by himself, appeared (1775) as *The Constitution of England*.

De Lôme Letter (dẹ.lōm′), **The.** Letter written by Dupuy de Lôme, Spanish minister to the U.S., and published (Feb. 9, 1898) by the Hearst press. The letter, which was in the nature of private correspondence to a Cuban friend, had been stolen, and its contents revealed de Lôme's impression of President McKinley as a weak and wavering politician. The American public at that time was already hostile toward Spain because of the alleged atrocities committed by her military forces in Cuba. The indiscretion of the Spanish minister heightened the growing hysteria. De Lôme resigned immediately, and although the incident was officially closed, it is generally regarded as one of the series of events, culminating in the sinking of the *Maine*, which precipitated the Spanish-American War.

Deloncle (dẹ.lôṅkl), **Eugène.** b. c1892; d. at Paris, 1944. French engineer, and fascist leader best known as the organizer of the Cagoulards (1935–37). He supported the Pétain regime, but reportedly was imprisoned briefly (December, 1942) and thereafter left active political life.

Deloney or **Delone** (dẹ.lō′ni), **Thomas.** b. probably at London, c1543; d. c1607. English weaver, balladist, pamphleteer, and realistic prose fictionist. Author of more than 50 ballads, all written before 1596, he is best known for his contribution to English fiction in the form of three very popular narratives written after 1596 and before 1600, *Thomas of Reading, or The Six Worthy Yeomen of the West*, *Jack of Newbury*, and *The Gentle Craft*, glorifying, respectively, weavers, clothiers, and shoemakers. The importance of the last, apart from its own merits, is that Deloney's story of Simon Eyre, a shoemaker who became lord mayor of London, served as the basis of Thomas Dekker's *The Shoemaker's Holiday* (1599). The secondary title of Dekker's work is the same one used by Deloney.

De Long (dẹ lông′), **George Washington.** b. at New York, Aug. 22, 1844; d. in Siberia, Oct. 30, 1881. American arctic explorer. He was graduated from the U.S. Naval Academy in 1865, obtained the rank of lieutenant in 1869, and of lieutenant commander in 1879. He accompanied Captain D. L. Braine on his arctic expedition in 1873. Having been appointed to the command of the *Jeannette*, fitted out by James Gordon Bennett, Jr., for a three-year voyage of exploration in arctic waters, and placed under the authority of the U.S. government, he sailed from San Francisco on July 8, 1879, and proceeded to the coast of Siberia, whence he steamed northward until trapped by ice in about 71°35′ N., 175° W., on Sept. 5, 1879. The vessel drifted to the northwest, and was crushed in 77°15′ N., 155° E., on June 13, 1881. With 14 others he reached the mouth of the Lena River, Siberia, where the whole party perished of cold and starvation, except two men sent forward to obtain relief. His body and those of his companions were discovered on March 23, 1882, by Chief Engineer George W. Melville, who with nine companions had been detached and had succeeded in reaching a small village on the Lena.

Deloraine (del.ọ.rān′), **William of.** In Sir Walter Scott's poem *Lay of the Last Minstrel*, a borderer and trusty vassal of the Buccleuch family. He is sent by the Ladye of Branksome to fetch the magic book from the tomb of Michael Scott, the wizard.

Delord (dẹ.lôr), **Taxile.** b. at Avignon, France, Nov. 25, 1815; d. at Paris, May 16, 1877. French journalist, historian, and politician. His chief work is *Histoire du second empire* (1868–75).

Delorme (dẹ.lôrm), **Marion.** [Also, **de Lorme.**] b. near Châlons-sur-Marne, France, Oct. 3, 1613; said to have died at Paris, July 2, 1650. French courtesan, mistress of the marquis de Cinq-Mars. After his death (1642), she is supposed by some to have had several highly placed lovers, including George Villiers, 2nd Duke of Buckingham, Cardinal Richelieu, and Louis XIV. In 1650 she was ordered to be arrested by Mazarin for her complicity in the Fronde disorders, and was found dead by the officers. This, however, is thought to have been a ruse. She is even said to have lived to the age of 137, living a life crowded with incident. She was the friend of Ninon de l'Enclos. Victor Hugo wrote a novel with her name as title, and Bulwer-Lytton introduces her in his play *Richelieu;* she was also a principal character of the drama *Cinq-Mars* (1826), by Alfred de Vigny.

Delorme or **de l'Orme** (dẹ lôrm), **Philibert.** b. at Lyons, France, c1510; d. at Paris, Jan. 8, 1570. French architect. He was court architect under Francis I and Henry II of France. He and Jean Brillant were commissioned by Charles IX's mother, Catherine de Médicis, to erect the Tuileries. His best work is the Château d'Anet, which he built (1552–59) for Diane de Poitiers, Henry II's mistress; his tomb of Francis I and work at several famous chateaux is also of the first order.

Delos (dē′los). [Also: **Mikra Dilos**; ancient names, **Asteria, Ortygia.**] Smallest island of the Cyclades, in the *nomos* (department) of Cyclades, Greece, situated in the narrow passage between the islands of Mykonos and Rhenea. According to Greek myth it was originally a floating island, and was the birthplace of Apollo and Artemis. It was the seat of a great sanctuary in honor of Apollo, one of the most famous religious foundations of antiquity. From the time of Solon, Athens sent an annual embassy to the Delian festival. Delos was the center of the Delian League, formed to resist Persian aggression in 478 B.C. In 454 B.C. the sacred treasure of Delos was removed to the Athenian Acropolis. The island was an Athenian dependency down to the Macedonian period, when it became semi-independent, and in the 2nd century B.C. it again became subject to Athens. The city of Delos was made a free port by the Romans and developed into a great commercial mart. It was raided in 87 B.C. by the forces of Mithridates VI and soon fell to the status of an almost uninhabited place. The sanctuary of Apollo was excavated by the French School at Athens, beginning in 1873. The work ranks as one of the chief achievements of its kind. The buildings disclosed lie for the most part within the enclosure or temenos of Apollo, which is of trapeziform shape, and ab. 650 ft. to a side. In addition to the interesting finds of architecture and sculpture, epigraphical discoveries of the highest importance were made, bearing upon history and particularly upon the ceremonial and administration of the sanctuary. Area of the island, 2 sq. mi.

Delos, Confederacy of. See **Delian League.**

Delpech (del.pesh), **Jacques Mathieu.** b. at Toulouse, France, c1775; murdered at Montpellier, France, Oct. 29, 1832. French surgeon, author of *Traité de l'orthomorphie* (1828–29).

Delphi (del′fī). [Also, **Delphoi** (ᴛʜel.fē′).] In ancient geography, a town in Phocis, Greece, situated ab. 6 mi. from the Corinthian Gulf, at the foot of Mount Parnassus: the seat of the world-renowned oracle of Pythian Apollo, the most famous oracle of antiquity. The temple had been won by Apollo from an earth spirit, presumably a snake, who inhabited the spot. Within the sacred precinct was a stone, the Omphalos, believed to mark the center of the earth, and a chasm leading to the center of the earth from which vapors emerged (this chasm has not been found by excavators). The oracle, known as the Pythia or Pythoness, putting herself in a trancelike state, would answer the question asked and this answer, explained or interpreted by the priests of the temple, was returned as being given from Apollo. Myth and legend emphasize the importance of the oracle. In later times the cult of Dionysus obtained a foothold here and Dionysus was believed to be the oracular god at certain times of the year. The oracle dated from prehistoric times, and was still respected when silenced by the Christian emperor Theodosius at the end of the 4th century A.D. Through the gifts of states and individuals who sought or had obtained the aid of the oracle, the Delphic sanctuary became enormously rich, not only in architecture and works of art, but in the precious metals. Its treasures of metals were plundered in antiquity, and Nero and other emperors robbed it of an astonishing number of statues and other art works. French official excavators began work there in 1892. Little exploration had before been possible, because the village of Kastri covered the site of the sanctuary. The village was removed, preparatory to the French exploration. Besides the splendid temple of Apollo, the enclosure of the sanctuary contained a theater, the council house, the Lesche, the Portico of the Athenians, a number of treasuries belonging to different states, and countless statues and other votive offerings. Buildings only second in importance were ranged outside of the enclosure.

Delphi. Town in N central Indiana, county seat of Carroll County, on the Wabash River ab. 60 mi. NW of Indianapolis. 2,530 (1950).

Delphinatus (del.fi.nā′tus). Medieval Latin name of **Dauphiné.**

Delphin Classics (del′fin). Edition of the Latin classics prepared by order of Louis XIV for the use of the Dauphin, Louis de Bourbon ("*In usum Delphini,*" meaning "for the use of the Dauphin"). The first works were published in 1674 under the direction of Bossuet and Huet. They are sometimes called "dauphins."

Delphine (del.fēn′), **Madame.** See **Madame Delphine.**

Delphinus (del.fī′nus). One of the northern constellations, figured by the ancients as representing a dolphin. It is situated E of Aquila.

Delphos (del′fọs). City in W Ohio, in Allen and Van Wert counties, ab. 14 mi. NW of Lima: canneries, truck-assembly plant, and manufactures of paper. It was platted in 1845, and was an important center along the route of the Miami and Erie Canal. 6,220 (1950).

Delpit (del.pē), **Albert.** b. at New Orleans, Jan. 30, 1849; d. at Paris, Jan. 4, 1893. French dramatist, journalist, and poet. Among his plays are *Les Chevaliers de la patrie* (1873) and *Jean Nu-Pieds* (1875). He afterward published a novel, *Le Fils de Coralie* (which was successful and was dramatized in 1879).

Delray Beach (del′rā). City in E Florida, in Palm Beach County, on the Atlantic Ocean N of Miami: vacation resort. It is the center for a truck-gardening region. 6,312 (1950).

Del Rio (del rē′ō). City in W Texas, county seat of Val Verde County, SE of Lubbock on the Rio Grande: shipping center for wool, mohair, and wine grapes. The San Felipe Springs, used for irrigation, are nearby. 14,211 (1950).

Delsarte (del.sȧrt), **François Alexandre Nicolas Chéri.** b. Dec. 19, 1811; d. July 19, 1871. French musician and teacher, noted for his studies of the art of oratorical, musical, and dramatic expression. He had sung with the Opéra-Comique when he turned to teaching (1839 *et seq.*) his applied aesthetics, coördinating body movements with the spoken or sung word. The system he developed was used by several famous actors and actresses and, expanded to include more of the calisthenic exercise, was brought to the U.S. in 1872 by James Morrison Steele MacKaye.

Delsberg (dels′berk). German name of **Delémont.**

Delta (del′tạ). City in W Colorado, county seat of Delta County, on the Gunnison River: shipping center for apples, cherries, peaches, and other fruits. 4,097 (1950).

Delta. Pseudonym of **Moir, David Macbeth.**

Delta Amacuro (del′tä ä.mä.kö′rō). [Official name, **Territorio Federal** (or **T. F.**) **Delta Amacuro**; also, **Territorio Delta Amacuro.**] Territory in E Venezuela, bordering on British Guiana and the Atlantic Ocean. Oil is the principal product. Capital, Tucupita; area, 15,521 sq. mi.; pop. 30,957 (1950).

Delta Wedding. Novel (1946) by Eudora Welty. A regional novel, it exhibits her ability to handle descriptive and psychological details, as well as her narrative skill, and her personal knowledge (a result of her Southern birth, training, and education) of the psychology of the old South. Before appearing in book form, the novel was serialized in the *Atlantic Monthly.*

Delteil (del.tey′), **Joseph.** b. 1894—. French novelist and poet. He is the author of *Les Cinq Sens* (1925), *Les Poilus* (1926), *Le Vert galant* (1931), and other novels, as well as the fictionalized biography *Jeanne d'Arc* (1926), and of poems including *Le Cœur grec* (1918). Regarded at the beginning of his career as a novelist of importance, he has failed to hold public attention.

Deluc (dẹ.lük), **Guillaume Antoine.** b. at Geneva, Switzerland, 1729; d. there, Jan. 26, 1812. Swiss naturalist; brother of Jean André Deluc.

Deluc, Jean André. b. at Geneva, Switzerland, Feb. 8, 1727; d. at Windsor, England, Nov. 7, 1817. Swiss geologist and physicist. His works include *Recherches sur les modifications de l'atmosphère* (1772), *Lettres physiques et morales sur l'histoire de la terre* (1778–80), and *Traité élémentaire de géologie* (1809).

De Luca (dā lö′kä), **Giuseppe.** b. at Rome, Dec. 29, 1876; d. Aug. 26, 1950. Italian operatic baritone. He made his debut (1897) and sang for eight years at La Scala, Milan, creating the role of Sharpless in the first performance (1904) of *Madame Butterfly.* In 1915 he joined the Metropolitan Opera Company at New York, making his debut there as Figaro in *Il Barbiere di Siviglia.*

He has played leading roles in *Rigoletto, Don Giovanni, Otello, Damnation of Faust, Tannhäuser, Parsifal. Pagliacci*, and *Eugen Onegin*.

Deluge (del'ūj). See the **Flood.**

Delyannis or **Delijannis** (del.i.an'is: Greek, ᴛʜe.lē.än'ēs), **Théodore.** b. 1826; d. June 13, 1905. Greek statesman. From 1863 he was frequently in office as minister of foreign affairs, finance, or the interior. He represented Greece at the Congress of Berlin, and obtained an extension of Greek territory on the Thessalian frontier. He was five times premier (1885–86, 1890–92, 1895–April, 1897, 1902–03, and 1904–05). He was assassinated.

Dema (dā'mä). [Also: **Badema, Wadema.**] Bantu-speaking people of SE Africa, inhabiting W Mozambique, and closely related to the Nyanja in language and culture.

Demaratus (dem.a.rā'tus). fl. c510–480 B.C. Spartan king of the Eurypontid line, who reigned from c510 to 491 B.C. He shared with his colleague Cleomenes the command of the army sent in 510 to assist the Athenians in expelling Hippias. In 506 he prevented Cleomenes from restoring Hippias. He was deposed in 491 by Cleomenes, who elevated Leotychides to his place, after bribing the Delphic oracle to state that Leotychides and not Demaratus was the son of Ariston, the previous king. The last years of his life were spent at the court of Xerxes, whom he accompanied on the expedition against Greece in 481–480.

Demarçay (de.mȧr.sā), **Eugène Anatole.** b. at Paris, 1852; d. 1904. French chemist. He discovered (1901) the rare-earth element europium. He read "a . . . spectrum . . . like an open book. Everyone who thought he had found a new . . . element took it to Demarçay and was immediately enlightened." He worked in his own private laboratory.

Demas (dē'mas). See also **Dismas.**

Demas. In the Bible, a companion, for a time, of Saint Paul. 2 Tim. iv. 10, 11.

Demavend (dem'a.vend). [Also, **Damavand.**] Extinct volcano in N Iran, the highest mountain of the Elburz range, situated ab. 50 mi. NE of Tehran. 18,600 ft.

Dembea (dem'bē.a), **Lake.** See **Tana, Lake.**

Dembiński (dem.bēn'skē), **Bronisław.** b. at Mala Komora, Poland, Aug. 14, 1858; d. 1940. Polish historian who served as professor at Lemberg (Lvov), Warsaw, and Posen (Poznań). He was the author (in Polish) of *Russia and the French Revolution* (1896) and *Poland at the Critical Point* (1913).

Dembiński, Henryk. b. at or near Kraków, Poland, May 3, 1791; d. at Paris, June 13, 1864. Polish general. He served in the Polish revolution of 1830–31, conducted (1831) a celebrated retreat through Lithuania, was commander of the Hungarians in 1849, and lost (1849) the battles of Kápolna and Temesvár (Timişoara).

Demchukdonrob (dem.chök.dôn.rōb'). Mongol name of Prince **Te.**

Demelli (dā.mel'lē), **Francesco Ezechiele Ermenegildo Cavaliere Suppé.** See **Suppé, Franz von.**

Demerara (dem.e.rãr'a, -rä'ra). County in N British Guiana, formerly a separate colony. Capital, Georgetown; area, 4,420 sq. mi.; pop. 185,184 (1931).

Demerara River. [Also, **Demerary.**] River in N British Guiana which flows N into the Atlantic Ocean at Georgetown. Length, ab. 200 mi.; navigable ab. 70 mi.

Demerdjis (ᴛʜe.mer.jēs') or **Demerdzis** (ᴛʜe.mer.dzēs'), **Constantine.** b. at Athens, Greece, 1876; d. 1936. Greek lawyer and statesman. He studied law at the University of Athens (1892–96) and at Munich (1896–1900), practiced law at Athens, and acted as instructor of Roman law at Athens University (1901–02). He served in the government as deputy from Attica-Boeotia (1910–36), member of the constitutional convention of 1910, and minister of navy (1913–14, 1917), and helped found and was head of the Progressive (Union) Party (1924). As prime minister (1935–36), he was the last parliamentary premier of Greece until 1946. Author of *Necessary Succession in Roman and Modern Law, Liability of Government for Illegal Acts of Officials, Government Finances*, and others.

Demeter (de.mē'tėr). In ancient Greek mythology, daughter of Cronus and Rhea; the goddess of vegetation and of useful fruits, protectress of social order and of marriage; one of the great Olympian deities. She is usually associated, and even confounded, in legend and in cult, with her daughter Persephone (Proserpine) or Kore the Maiden, whose rape by Hades (Pluto) symbolizes some of the most profound phases of Hellenic mysticism. She was a principal character at the celebration of the Thesmophoria, a women's festival memorializing Demeter's establishment of the laws of civilization, and in the Eleusinian mysteries, where her withdrawal from the earth, the consequent failure of crops, the rebirth of the grain, and the whole cycle of the yearly change as symbolized in the Persephone myth, were enacted, presumably, since nothing definite is known of the Eleusinian ritual. The Romans of the end of the republic and of the empire assimilated to the Hellenic conception of Demeter the primitive Italic chthonian divinity Ceres.

Demeter. Poetic play (1905) by Robert Bridges. The nature of the work and its method are indicated by the subtitle, *A Masque*. Like his *Prometheus, Bacchus, Ulysses*, and *Achilles*, it illustrates the author's classical tastes and interests.

Demeter and Other Poems. Volume of 28 poems (1889) by Tennyson. It includes "On the Jubilee of Queen Victoria," "To Professor Jebb," "Vastness," "The Ring," dedicated to James Russell Lowell, "To Ulysses," "Merlin and the Gleam," "Romney's Remorse," a poem about the English painter, "By an Evolutionist," "The Snowdrop," "The Throstle," and "The Oak." The thin volume (of 175 pages) opens with "To the Marquis of Dufferin and Ava" and closes (in accordance with Tennyson's frequently expressed wish) with "Crossing the Bar." The title poem is the fourth one in the collection.

Demeter of Cnidus (nī'dus). Greek statue (c4th century B.C.) of the school of Scopas, now in the British Museum at London. The figure is seated, fully draped, and although damaged, gives a feeling of profound grief.

Demetrius (de.mē'tri.us). For Russian rulers, see **Dmitri.**

Demetrius. In Shakespeare's *Titus Andronicus*, a son of Tamora, queen of the Goths.

Demetrius. In Shakespeare's *A Midsummer Night's Dream*, a Grecian gentleman, in love with Hermia.

Demetrius. In Shakespeare's *Antony and Cleopatra*, a friend of Antony.

Demetrius. Son of the king in John Fletcher's *Humorous Lieutenant*, in love with Celia.

Demetrius I (of *Macedonia*). [Surnamed **Poliorcetes,** meaning "Taker of Cities" or "Besieger."] b. c336 B.C.; d. at Apamea, in ancient Syria, 283 B.C. King of Macedonia (294–288); son of Antigonus I, who was called Antigonus Cyclops. He liberated Athens and Megara in 307, defeated Ptolemy I in 306, unsuccessfully besieged Rhodes (305–304), and was defeated at Ipsus in 301. He was chosen king by the army in 294, gained control (293–289) of Greece, and invaded Asia, which Antigonus had held, with an inferior force in 287. He surrendered to Seleucus I in 285 and drank himself to death.

Demetrius II (of *Macedonia*). b. c276 B.C.; d. 229 B.C. King of Macedonia; son of Antigonus II Gonatas, whom he succeeded c239. During his reign the Macedonians fought to preserve their territory; the Demetrian War, so called, was fought against the Aetolian League and the Achaeans, but Demetrius was defeated in the north. Philip V of Macedon was his son by his second wife Phthia (or Chryseis).

Demetrius I (of *Syria*). [Surnamed **Soter,** meaning "Savior."] b. 187 B.C.; killed 150 B.C. King of Syria from 162 B.C.; grandson of Antiochus the Great. After living as a captive in Rome while his uncle, Antiochus IV, and his cousin, Antiochus V, sat on the throne, he escaped (162 B.C.), killed his cousin, and became king himself. He suppressed the revolt of Timarchus in Babylon and put down the Maccabee uprising in Palestine. But Alexander Balas, a pretender, claimed the throne, and, with the help of the Maccabees, Egyptians, and others, overthrew Demetrius.

Demetrius II (of *Syria*). [Surnamed **Nicator.**] b. c161 B.C.; d. near Tyre, c125 B.C. King of Syria (147–141 and 129–126 B.C.); son of Demetrius I. He overthrew Alexander Balas, the usurper, with the aid of Ptolemy VI (Ptolemy Philometor), obtaining both the throne and Ptolemy's daughter, Cleopatra Thea, wife of Alexander Balas. He defeated the attempt (145–142 B.C.) to place Antiochus VI, son of Alexander Balas, on the throne. In 141 he was captured by the Parthians and remained their prisoner for about ten years, his brother Antiochus VII occupying the throne in his absence and marrying Cleopatra, Demetrius's wife. Demetrius regained the throne in 129 but was soon after killed in a civil war. He was succeeded by his sons Seleucus V and Antiochus VIII.

Demetrius III (of *Syria*). [Surnamed **Euergetes** and **Philometor.**] King of Syria c94–88 B.C.; son of Antiochus VIII Grypus. He struggled for the throne with his cousin Antiochus X and his brother Philip; he was defeated, captured, and held prisoner until his death by the Parthians.

Demetrius Doboobie (dǫ.bö'bi), **Dr.** See **Alasco.**

Demetrius Fannius (fan'i.us). In Ben Jonson's play *The Poetaster,* a shifty "dresser of plays about the town here." The character was intended to humiliate Thomas Dekker, with whom Jonson had had a quarrel; Dekker answered with his burlesque of Jonson's style in *Satiromastix.*

Demetrius Phalereus (fą.lē'rös, fą.lir'ę.us). b. at Phalerus, in Attica, 345 B.C.; d. in Upper Egypt, 283 B.C. Athenian orator and politician. He entered public life c325 as a supporter of Phocion, and in 317 was placed by Phocion's successor, Cassander, at the head of the administration of Athens. Expelled from Athens in 307 by Demetrius I of Macedonia (Demetrius Poliorcetes), he retired to the court of Ptolemy Lagi at Alexandria, where he devoted himself wholly to literary pursuits. He was exiled by Ptolemy's successor to Upper Egypt, where he is said to have died of the bite of a snake.

Demidov (di.mē'dǫf), **Akinfi Nikitich.** d. c1740. Russian manufacturer; son of Nikita Demidov.

Demidov, Prince **Anatoli Nikolayevich.** b. at Moscow, 1812; d. at Paris, April 29, 1870. Russian noble and philanthropist; son of Nikolai Nikitich Demidov.

Demidov, Nikita. b. c1665; d. after 1720. Russian manufacturer, founder of the family of Demidov. The son of a serf, he rose into favor under Peter the Great by his skill in the manufacture of arms. He established the first iron foundry in Siberia in 1699, and received a patent of nobility in 1720.

Demidov, Count **Nikolai Nikitich.** b. at St. Petersburg, c1773; d. at Florence, 1828. Russian capitalist; nephew of Paul Grigoryevich Demidov.

Demidov, Paul Grigoryevich. b. at Reval, Russia, 1738; d. at Moscow, 1781. Russian scholar and patron of science; nephew of Akinfi Nikitich Demidov.

De Mille (dę mil', dē), **Agnes.** b. at New York, c1905—. American dancer and choreographer; daughter of William Churchill De Mille and granddaughter of Henry George. Having studied ballet dancing and choreography under skilled teachers, she won acclaim at her debut in 1928. In the following year she directed the dancing in a revival of *The Black Crook,* a famous 19th-century musical show; in 1933 she was choreographer for a production of the noted London impresario Thomas B. Cochran, and in 1936 for a motion-picture version of *Romeo and Juliet.* Her subsequent work with the Ballet Theatre, the Ballet Russe de Monte Carlo (for which she composed and danced in the ballet *Rodeo*), the Theatre Guild, and other groups, especially in connection with the choreography of successful musical comedies such as *Oklahoma!*, *Bloomer Girl, Allegro, Brigadoon,* and *Carousel,* doubtless spread appreciation of the ballet more widely than ever before in the U.S. Both as a dancer and as a choreographer she proved herself a master of humor and of pathos alike. Her autobiographical book *Dance to the Piper* was serialized in the *Atlantic Monthly* and published in 1952.

De Mille, Cecil Blount. b. at Ashfield, Mass., Aug. 12, 1881—. American motion-picture producer; son of Henry Churchill De Mille. He was the organizer and president (1918–23) of the Mercury Aviation Company at Hollywood, Calif., first commercial company to book passengers for regular flights, president (1921 *et seq.*) of Cecil B. De Mille Productions, Inc., and producer (1936–45) of the Lux Radio Theatre of the Air. His film productions, which began in 1915 (director since 1913), include *Carmen, Male and Female, Feet of Clay, Ten Commandments, The King of Kings, The Volga Boatman, The Sign of the Cross, Cleopatra, The Crusades, The Plainsman, The Buccaneer, Union Pacific,* and *Reap the Wild Wind.* De Mille popularized not only the spectacle motion picture but the type of the director, wearing open-collar shirt and puttees and speaking through a megaphone.

De Mille, Henry Churchill. b. at Washington, N.C., Sept. 17, 1853; d. at Pompton, N.J., Feb. 10, 1893. American playwright, sometime partner of David Belasco; father of William Churchill De Mille and Cecil Blount De Mille. A graduate (1875) of Columbia College, he soon became associated with the theater, as an actor for a short time and then as a producer. His first original play, *John Delmer's Daughters or Duty,* was produced in 1883. After *The Main Line or Rawson's Y,* written (1886) with Charles Barnard, followed his Belasco productions, *The Wife* (1887), *Lord Chumley* (1888), *The Charity Ball* (1889), and *Men and Women* (1890). His last play was *The Lost Paradise,* an English version of Ludwig Fulda's *Das Verlorene Paradies.*

De Mille, William Churchill. b. at Washington, N.C., July 25, 1878—. American playwright; son of Henry Churchill De Mille and brother of Cecil Blount De Mille. Author of *Strongheart, The Warrens of Virginia, The Land of the Free, The Woman,* and *Hollywood Saga;* coauthor of *The Royal Mounted, Classmates, The Genius,* and other plays.

Deming (dem'ing). Village in SW New Mexico, county seat of Luna County, in a fruit, livestock, and mineral producing area. 5,672 (1950).

Demiri (de.mē'rē), **al-.** See **Damiri, al-.**

Demme (dem'ę), **Hermann Christoph Gottfried.** [Pseudonym, **Karl Stille.**] b. at Mühlhausen, Thuringia, Germany, Sept. 7, 1760; d. at Altenburg, Germany, Dec. 26, 1822. German poet and novelist, author of *Pächter Martin und sein Vater* (1792–93) and others.

Demme, Wilhelm Ludwig. b. at Mühlhausen, Thuringia, Germany, March 20, 1801; d. at Würzburg, Bavaria, Germany, March 26, 1878. German jurist; son of H. C. G. Demme. He wrote *Buch der Verbrechen* (1851) and others.

Demmin (de.mēn'). Town in NE Germany, in the *Land* (state) of Mecklenburg, Russian Zone, formerly in the province of Pomerania, Prussia, situated on the Peene River, ab. 73 mi. NW of Stettin. Before World War II it was a port for coastwise shipping and had a sugar refinery, brewery, and agricultural markets. The medieval town walls are preserved. One of the oldest Slavic settlements in Pomerania, it was besieged (1148) in vain by German crusaders; taken (1164) by Henry the Lion, Duke of Saxony; became (1283) a member of the Hanseatic League; fell to Sweden in 1648 and to Prussia in 1720. Pop. 18,006 (1946).

Democedes (dem.ǫ.sē'dēz). b. at Crotona, Magna Graecia (now Crotone, Calabria, Italy); fl. in the second half of the 6th century B.C. Greek physician. He practiced at the courts of Polycrates of Samos and of Darius the Great (Darius I), but returned to practice in Greece.

Demochares (dę.mok'ą.rēz). fl. 322–280 B.C. Athenian orator; nephew of Demosthenes. He came forward in 322 B.C. as an orator of the anti-Macedonian party, and after the restoration of democracy by Demetrius I of Macedonia (Demetrius Poliorcetes) in 307 became the leader of the popular party. He was several times expelled by the antidemocratic party, returning the last time in 287 or 286. He was sent as ambassador to Lysimachus c282, and disappears from view in 280.

Democracy. Poem (1841) by John Greenleaf Whittier. In 18 four-line stanzas, it is included in the group called *Songs of Labor and Reform.* The poet hails democracy as "Bearer of Freedom's holy light," "Breaker of Slavery's chain and rod," and as "the foe of all which pains the sight Or wounds the generous ear of God."

Democracy. Address (1884) by James Russell Lowell. It was delivered as an inaugural address, on Oct. 6, 1884, when he became president of the Birmingham and Midland Institute, in England. It was published in 1887 in *Democracy and Other Addresses.* It opens with a striking sentence: "He must be a born leader or misleader of men, or must have been sent into the world unfurnished with that modulating and restraining balance-wheel which we call a sense of humor, who, in old age, has as strong a confidence in his opinions and in the necessity of bringing the universe into conformity with them as he had in youth."

Democracy: An American Novel. Novel by Henry Adams, published (anonymously) in 1880, a vehicle for discussion of intrigue for power in late 19th-century Washington, D.C. Madeleine Lee uses her admirer, John Carrington, to become acquainted with a political boss, Senator Ratcliffe, whose suit she rejects when his lack of scruples is ultimately brought to her attention. Disillusioned by his defection, Madeleine leaves Washington. Some critics feel that President Hayes is represented in the character of "Old Granite," an unsophisticated president from the Middle West who permits himself to be victimized by the astute and ambitious Ratcliffe.

Democracy and Education. Work on educational philosophy (1916) by John Dewey. It is the best known of his many works, was successful on its appearance, has been so ever since, and is now accepted as an educational classic. It is used as a standard text in many colleges, and in schools of education, and is studied along with the writings of Pestalozzi, Herbart, Froebel, Spencer, Huxley, and William James, as "an introduction to the philosophy of education," which is its subtitle. In its 26 chapters, Dewey discusses education as a necessity of life, as a social function, as direction and growth, as conservative and progressive, and such topics as aims and thinking in education, work and play, labor and leisure, geography, history, and science, practical studies, humanism, the individual and the world, and moral and educational values.

Democratic Group (of *Luxembourg*). [Former name, **Radical Liberal Party.**] Luxembourg political party which supports labor legislation and the progressive development of lay institutions.

Democratic League. Name adopted (1944) by the middle-of-the-road Chinese Federation of Democratic Parties, which was originally established (1941) jointly by the National Socialist Party, the China Youth Party, the Rural Reconstructionists, the Vocational Educational Association, the Third Party, and individual members of the National Salvation Association. After Japan's surrender (1945) the first two broke with the League and joined the Kuomintang-led government which (1947) outlawed the League. The League subsequently participated in the Communist-led government established (1949) at Peiping.

Democratic Party. In U.S. history, a political party which arose c1792. It was called first the Republican, later the Democratic-Republican, and afterward (c1828) simply the Democratic Party. Until the administration of Woodrow Wilson, it generally opposed a strong central government, and generally favored a strict construction of the Constitution. It has controlled the executive or the national government under the administrations of the following presidents: Jefferson, Madison, Monroe, Jackson, Van Buren, Polk, Pierce, Buchanan, Cleveland, Woodrow Wilson, Franklin D. Roosevelt, and Harry S. Truman. Its principal founder was Jefferson. It may be regarded as the successor of the Anti-Federalist (opponents of Hamilton's Federalists) and Democratic-Republican parties. Intraparty conflict has been frequent; the split between the Northern faction headed by Stephen Douglas and the Southern faction headed by J. C. Breckenridge helped establish the Republican Party as the strong power in politics both before and after the Civil War; the Southern states' rights wing has battled the Northern industrial labor group recurrently ever since the close of the Civil War. Unity within the party has been achieved most often under the rise of a reform president or candidate in time of crisis: Bryan in 1896, Wilson in 1912, Roosevelt in 1932. Traditionally the Democratic Party wins the electoral votes of the "Solid South," broken only seldom by Republican candidates.

Democratic People's Party (of *the Netherlands*). Dutch political party formed in October, 1947, as a result of a split in the Labor Party between those favoring the maintenance of private ownership in some fields and exponents of progressive state ownership of the means of production.

Democratic Union. Alliance of the Argentine Radical Party with other anti-Conservative groups to oppose Juan Domingo Perón, the government candidate for president. Its dissolution was announced on April 16, 1946, less than two months after Perón's victory at the polls.

Democratic Vistas. Prose work by Walt Whitman, published in 1871 and included in *Two Rivulets* (1876). It deals with the themes of democracy, individualism, and materialism.

Democritus (dḙ.mok′ri.tus). [Called **"the Abderite"** and **"the Laughing Philosopher."**] b. at Abdera, in Thrace, c460 B.C.; d. c357 B.C. Greek philosopher. He inherited an ample fortune, which enabled him to visit the chief countries of Asia and Africa in pursuit of knowledge. He adopted and expanded the atomistic theory of Leucippus, which he expounded in a number of works, fragments only of which are extant. He is said to have been of a cheerful disposition, which prompted him to laugh at the follies of men (hence the epithet "the Laughing Philosopher"). According to tradition he put out his eyes in order to be less disturbed by outward things in his philosophical speculations. He distinguished between the things belonging to a substance by convention (heat, hardness) and in reality (atoms). Even the soul was a manifestation of the real existence of the body and it perished with the body. His mechanistic philosophy extended to the gods, mortal to Democritus, though composed of finer atomic stuff than man was. His ethical system was based on pleasure as an end; pleasure was, however, to be tempered by avoidance of excess.

Democritus Junior. Pseudonym of **Burton, Robert.**

Demodocus (dḙ.mod′ǫ.kus). In the *Odyssey*, a famous blind bard who, during the stay of Ulysses at the court of Alcinous, delighted the guests by recounting the feats of the Greeks at Troy and singing the amours of Ares and Aphrodite.

Demogeot (dḙ.mo.zhō), **Jacques Claude.** b. at Paris, July 5, 1808; d. there, Jan. 9, 1894. French literary historian and writer, professor at the Sorbonne. He was the author of *Histoire de la littérature français* (1851).

De Moivre (dḙ mwä′vrḙ), **Abraham.** See **Moivre, Abraham de.**

Demolins (dḙ.mo.laṅ), **Edmond.** b. at Marseilles, France, 1852; d. at Roches, France, July 22, 1907. French historian and sociologist. In 1886 he founded, with others, *La Science Sociale*, a journal devoted to the study of social economics along then new lines following the methods of Le Play, of whom he was a pupil. Among the best known of his publications are *À quoi tient la supériorité des Anglo-Saxons* (1897), *Les Français d'aujourd'hui* (1898), *L'Éducation nouvelle* (1898), *Les Grandes Routes des peuples* (1904), and *Classification sociale* (1905).

Demon, The. [Italian title, **Il Demonio** (ēl dā.mō′nyō).] Opera in three acts by Anton Rubinstein. It was produced at St. Petersburg on Jan. 25, 1875, and at London on June 21, 1881.

De Montfort (dē mont′fǫrt). Tragedy by Joanna Baillie, produced in 1800.

Demopolis (dḙ.mop′ǫ.lis). City in W Alabama, in Marengo County, ab. 125 mi. N of Mobile at the confluence of the Tombigbee and Black Warrior rivers, in a cotton-producing region. The first white settlement here was made in 1818 by a group of refugees from France after the fall of Napoleon. 5,004 (1950).

De Morgan (dē môr′gạn), **Augustus.** b. at Madura, Madras, India, June 27, 1806; d. at London, March 18, 1871. English mathematician and logician. He was educated at Cambridge and at Lincoln's Inn, and was professor of mathematics at London University (1828–31) and at University College, London (1836–66). He was the author of *Elements of Arithmetic* (1831), *Elements of Algebra* (1835), *Elements of Trigonometry* (1837), *Essay on Probabilities* (1838), *Differential and Integral Calculus* (1842), *Formal Logic* (1847), and *Budget of Paradoxes* (1872).

De Morgan, William (Frend). b. at London, Nov. 16, 1839; d. at London, Jan. 13, 1917. English novelist, potter, stained-glass designer, and inventor. He was the son of the mathematician Augustus De Morgan, "the wisest and best man I have ever known," and he derived his middle name from his grandfather, William Frend, scientist and economic reformer. He was educated in London at the University College School and at the College, where his father had been a professor. At the Royal Academy school, which he entered in 1859, he met, and came to know as lifelong friends, Burne-Jones, D. G. Rossetti, and William Morris. Until 1905, when he retired, he was engaged in the manufacture of pottery and stained glass, both in his own factories and with partners. This phase of his life, of much longer duration than his writing activity, produced a paper on pottery which he read in 1892 before the Society of Arts (published in the 40th volume of its *Journal*), and a *Report on the Feasibility of a Manufacture of Glazed Pottery in Egypt* (1894), written in 1893 when he visited Egypt by special invitation. Always of a scientific turn of mind, an inheritance from his father and grandfather, he invented a mill for grinding clay, several tools and articles connected with pottery, and was working on various mechanisms associated with national defense, both air and submarine, at the time of his death. His first novel, generally considered his best, *Joseph Vance: An Ill-Written Autobiography* (1906), was published in his sixty-seventh year. It created a sensation and was enthusiastically praised by readers and critics. It is a story of low life in London, centering around the adventures of a gutter boy, and Lossie Thorpe, a lovable heroine, who finally marries him after both have had previous mates. His second novel was *Alice-for-Short* (1907), the story of Alicia Kavanagh, a London girl, and Charles Heath, an artist in whom, says De Morgan, "I put much of myself." It was followed in 1908 by *Somehow Good*, dealing with the problem of loss of memory as a result of shock. *It Never Can Happen Again* (1909) and *When Ghost Meets Ghost* (1914) are regarded as examples of Victorian fiction. *An Affair of Dishonor* (1910), a historical romance, and *A Likely Story* (1911), which is something less than a full-length novel, are considered inferior efforts. *The Old Madhouse* (1919) and *The Old Man's Youth* (1921), both left unfinished at his death, were completed by his wife, Evelyn Mary Pickering, 18 years his junior, whom he married in 1887. De Morgan has been compared to Dickens, whom he resembles in many respects, and he is regarded as a belated example of the Victorian type of novelist.

Demos and Dionysus (dē'mos; dī.ǫ.nī'sus). Dialogue in blank verse by Edwin Arlington Robinson, published in *Dionysus in Doubt* (1925). The forces of reason and equality exemplified in Demos are contrasted with those of passion and individualism symbolized by Dionysus.

Demosthenes (dẹ.mos'thẹ.nēz). d. at Syracuse, 413 B.C. Athenian general in the Peloponnesian War. In 425 he defended Pylos against the Spartans, and made the dispositions by which the enemy was forced to capitulate, although the glory of the exploit (the unheard-of capture of Spartan soldiery) was claimed by Cleon, who relieved him in the command. He commanded under Nicias in the unsuccessful expedition against Syracuse in 413. Having been captured in the retreat, he was put to death by order of the Syracusan assembly.

Demosthenes. b. at Paeania, in Attica, 384 or 383 B.C.; d. on the island of Calauria, in the Saronic Gulf, 322 B.C. Greatest of Greek orators. He is said to have been the pupil of the orator Isaeus, and entered public life as a speaker in the popular assembly in 355. In 351 he delivered the first of a splendid series of orations directed against the encroachment of Philip II of Macedon, three of which are specifically denominated *Philippics*. In 346 he served as a member of the embassy which concluded with Philip the so-called peace of Philocrates. As Philip immediately after broke this treaty, Demosthenes came forward as the leader of the patriotic party, in opposition to the Macedonian party which was headed by Aeschines. In 340 he caused a fleet to be sent to the relief of Byzantium, which was besieged by Philip. On the outbreak of the Amphictyonic War, he persuaded the Athenians to form an alliance with Thebes against Philip, who defeated the allies at Chaeronea in 338, and usurped the hegemony of Greece. He was one of the leaders of the unsuccessful rising which took place on the death of Philip in 336, was exiled by the Macedonian party in 324, was recalled by the patriotic party on the outbreak of a fresh rising at the death of Alexander in 323, and on the capture of Athens by Antipater and Craterus in 322 fled to Calauria, near Argolis, where he took poison in the temple of Poseidon to avoid capture. His chief orations are three *Philippics* (351, 344, 341), three *Olynthiacs* (349, 349, 348), *On the Peace* (346), *On the Embassy* (343), *On the Affairs of the Chersonese* (341), *On the Crown* (330). This last-named speech, the most famous of Demosthenes's orations, was in answer to Aeschines, who objected when Ctesiphon moved that a crown be given to Demosthenes for his services to the state. Demosthenes was the great opponent of the Macedonian conquest of Greece, holding that Athens, traditionally and actually, was the heart of any Greek nation, and that it was necessary that the spark be rekindled that had died during the Peloponnesian War. Many legendary stories are told of how he obtained his oratorical power: a stammerer, he taught himself to speak slowly by putting pebbles in his mouth; he went to the seashore and declaimed to the waves so that the noise of an audience would not disturb him; he would run uphill while orating in order to strengthen his weak voice; he shut himself in a cave and copied Thucydides's history eight times in order to attain to a fine style. He seems actually to have had a speech defect; his style in oratory is not complex, but simple and pithy, and effective. The first printed collective edition of his orations is that published by Aldus Manutius at Venice in 1504.

Demotika or **Demotica** (ᴛʜē.mô'tē.kä). See **Didymoteikhon.**

Demotike (ᴛʜē.mô.tē.kē'). [English, **Demotic.**] One of the two forms of written modern Greek (the other is Katharevousa). The word means "popular" and the ideal of the proponents of this movement was the formation of an acceptable standard literary language based on the common spoken dialects of Greece. It was first systematized by Jean Psichari in 1888, though a similar style had been used occasionally since 1800, and popular dialects had been used in verse for several centuries before that. Since Psichari it had gradually been modified in the direction of the Katharevousa, chiefly by dropping some dialect words and forms and some foreign loanwords, and by adopting some words from the Katharevousa. At various times, notably in 1902 and 1903, there have been riots directed against its use, particularly for translations from the Scriptures and from ancient Greek literature, but it is now the generally preferred form for fiction and poetry. Its use for other purposes is to some extent political: the further left politically, the more extreme the form of the Demotike used in journalism and serious writing. Its chief marks are (1) an inflection in basic agreement with that of educated speakers, the most obvious sign being the absence of final *-n* from many forms where it had been present in ancient Greek, and (2) a vocabulary of mixed origin, including a basis of spoken Greek with many borrowings from the Katharevousa and from other languages, but few new coinages.

Dempsey (demp'si, dem'si), **Jack.** [Original name, **William Harrison Dempsey**; called the **"Manassa Mauler."**] b. at Manassa, Colo., June 24, 1895—. American heavyweight fighter. He engaged in his first regulation fight in 1915. Dempsey knocked out Fred Fulton in 14 seconds (1918), and went on to knock out Jess Willard in the third round at Toledo, Ohio (July 4, 1919) to win the world's heavyweight championship. He defended his title against Georges Carpentier (1921), Tom Gibbons (1923), and Luis Firpo (1923), but lost it to James Joseph (Gene) Tunney at Philadelphia (Sept. 23, 1926). He failed to regain the title from Tunney at Chicago (Sept. 22, 1927), and retired from boxing after losing a decision to King Levinsky (Feb. 19, 1932). His fights were always colorful. He beat Willard (who was taller by a head) so badly that the champion was unable to leave his corner. The Firpo fight saw Dempsey come back to knock out the Argentine fighter after the latter had knocked Dempsey out of the ring. The second Tunney fight contained the "long count" incident: Dempsey knocked Tunney down and did not, as the rules required, go to a neutral corner, thus permitting Tunney to stay down for 14 seconds when he might have been counted out in ten. A controversial figure in World War I because he worked in a shipyard and was not in uniform, Dempsey was a physical training officer in the Coast Guard in World War II.

Dempster (demp'stėr), **Janet.** Woman in George Eliot's novel *Janet's Repentance* who is rescued from a passion for drink by her friend and pastor.

Dempster, John. b. at Florida, Fulton County, N.Y., Jan. 2, 1794; d. at Evanston, Ill., Nov. 28, 1863. American Methodist clergyman, founder of Biblical institutes at Concord, N.H., and Evanston, Ill.

Dempster, Thomas. b. at Cliftbog, Aberdeenshire, Scotland, Aug. 23, 1579; d. near Bologna, Italy, Sept. 6, 1625. Scottish scholar. He was educated at the Jesuit seminary at Douai and at the University of Paris, and c1619 was appointed professor of humanities at the University of Bologna. He was the author of *Historia ecclesiastica gentis Scotorum* (1627).

Demter (dem'tėr). See **Deventer.**

Demuth (dẹ.möth'), **Charles.** b. at Lancaster, Pa., 1883; d. there, Oct. 23, 1935. American painter, chiefly of water colors. His best-known works are precise studies of flowers and vegetables and of architectural subjects, combining a cubistic analysis of planes and shapes with an effect of delicacy and translucency. He studied at Drexel Institute, Philadelphia (1901), at the Pennsylvania Academy of the Fine Arts (1903) under Anschutz and Chase, and at Paris (1907–08, 1912–14). On his return from Paris he did a series of illustrations for works by Zola, Poe, Balzac, and Henry James. Among his paintings are *Acrobats, Corn* (c1925), *Poppies* (c1930), *In the Key of Blue, My Egypt* (1925; a picture of grain elevators), and others. He is represented in the Whitney Museum of American Art at New York, the Duncan Phillips Memorial Gallery at Washington, and elsewhere.

Demuth (dā'möt), **Fritz.** b. at Berlin, Jan. 11, 1876—. German industrialist. He served (1918–20) with the treasury department, and has been a member of the Reichstag and of the Berlin chamber of commerce.

Dena (dā'nạ). See **Elmina.**

Denain (dẹ.naṅ). Town in N France, in the department of Nord, situated at the junction of the Selle and Escaut rivers, ab. 7 mi. SW of Valenciennes. It is one of the most important steel centers in France. Coal is mined in the vicinity. Here Marshal Villars defeated (1712) the Imperial army under Prince Eugene of Savoy. 24,908 (1946).

Denali (dẹ.nä'lẹ). See **McKinley, Mount.**

De natura deorum (dē nạ.tū'rạ dē.ō'rum). [Eng. trans., "*On the Nature of the Gods.*"] Dialogues by Cicero, in three books, treating of the existence, nature, and providence of the gods.

Denbigh (den'bi). Municipal borough and market town in N Wales, in Denbighshire, situated on the river Clwyd, ab. 11 mi. W of Mold, ab. 209 mi. NW of London by rail. It is the county seat of Denbighshire. Denbigh has a ruined castle, which was taken by the Parliamentarians in 1645. Pop. 8,127 (1951).

Denbighshire (den'bi.shir) or **Denbigh.** Maritime county in N Wales. It is bounded on the N by the North Sea, on the NE by Flintshire, on the E by Cheshire (England), the detached portion of Flintshire, and Shropshire (England), on the S by Montgomeryshire and Merionethshire, and on the W by Caernarvonshire. The surface is mountainous in the S and W portions, hilly in the E part, and level to undulating in the N. The county is situated on the North Wales coal field and coal mining is an important activity. Iron, lead, and slate are also produced. County seat, Denbigh; area of administrative county, ab. 669 sq. mi.; pop. of administrative county, 170,699 (1951).

den Bosch (dẹn bôs'). See **'s Hertogenbosch.**

Denby (den'bi), **Charles.** b. in Botetourt County, Va., June 16, 1830; d. at Jamestown, N.Y., Jan. 13, 1904. American diplomat. He was educated at Georgetown University and at the Virginia Military Institute, and was admitted to the Indiana bar in 1855. He served in the Union army during the Civil War, rising to the rank of colonel, and was U.S. minister to China from 1885 to 1898. In 1898 he was appointed by the president a member of the commission for the investigation of the war with Spain, and in 1899 a member of the civil commission for the investigation of affairs in the Philippines.

Denby, Edwin. b. at Evansville, Ind., Feb. 18, 1870; d. at Detroit, Mich., Feb. 8, 1929. American politician, secretary of the navy under Harding, remembered for his association with the "Teapot Dome" scandal. He was graduated (LL.B., 1896) from the University of Michigan, served with the navy in the Spanish-American War, established his law practice at Detroit, was in the Michigan legislature (1903), and was a member of Congress (1905 *et seq.*). In World War I he enlisted as a private in the U.S. Marine Corps, was engaged in home duty, and was discharged as a major. His administration of the Navy Department was marred by a scandal concerning the transfer of naval oil reserves from public title to lease by private oil interests. Although there was no evidence that he was bribed, his signature appeared on the leases made out to the oil companies represented by Harry Sinclair and Edward L. Doheny. The lands were later restored to the government by legal proceedings following the revelation of the contracts. In February, 1924, a Senate resolution requested the dismissal of Denby, which Harding's successor, Coolidge, refused to carry out on the grounds that the leases had been authorized under law. Denby submitted his resignation on February 18, 1924, and it became effective on March 10. Later investigations of the scandal cleared Denby's name; he practiced law at Detroit until his death.

Denby Dale. Urban district in N central England, in the West Riding of Yorkshire, situated on the river Dearne, ab. 8 mi. SE of Huddersfield, ab. 214 mi. N of London by rail. 9,651 (1951).

Dendera (den'dėr.ạ). [Also: **Denderah**; ancient Greek, **Tentyra, Tentyris.**] Town in Upper Egypt, situated on the Nile. It is celebrated for its temple of the cow-goddess Hathor, which, notwithstanding its late date, begun by Ptolemy XI (Ptolemy Auletes), and the great *pronaos* (columned hall outside the temple proper) added as late as the time of Tiberius, is one of the most interesting buildings in Egypt, owing to its almost perfect preservation, even to the roof. The imposing hexastyle pronaos has four ranges of Hathoric columns; on its ceiling is a noted sculptured zodiac, combining Egyptian and classical elements. Next to the pronaos is a hypostyle hall (ceiling supported on columns) of six columns, from which three chambers open on each side, and beyond this is a vestibule before a large hall in which stands an isolated cella. This hall is surrounded by a series of chambers, one of which in the middle of the back wall contained the emblematic sistrum of the goddess. The whole interior surface is sculptured, the art, however, being inferior. On the roof there is a small six-chambered temple to the local divinity Osiris-An.

Dendermonde (den.dėr.mōn'dẹ). Flemish name of **Termonde.**

Dendi (dān'dē). Sudanic-speaking people of W Africa, inhabiting the Niger valley in N Dahomey and SW French Niger territory. Like their northwestern neighbors, the Djerma, they speak a dialect of Songhai. Their population is estimated at ab. 20,000 (by Y. Urvoy, *Petit atlas ethno-demographique du Soudan*, 1942). The Dendi are completely Mohammedanized.

Dendin (däṅ.daṅ), **Perrin.** Ignorant peasant, applied to as a judge, in François Rabelais's *Pantagruel.* His method was to let people fight till they were tired of it: a satire on lawyers who prefer the ruin of their client to the slightest concession. He loved eating and drinking, and settled the disputes of his neighbors while indulging these tastes.

Deneb (den'eb). Word meaning "tail," from Arabic, used as the name of several stars, in reference to their situation in the constellation to which they respectively belong. The principal are the following: **1.** Deneb Algedi (al'jẹ.dē), the third-magnitude star δ Capricorni. **2.** Deneb Algenubi (al.jẹ.nū'bē), the third-magnitude star η Ceti, at the root of the whale-monster's tail. **3.** Deneb-al-okab (al.ō.kôb'), the third-magnitude star ζ Aquilae. The name is also applied to ϵ Aquilae, close by. **4.** Deneb al-shemali (al-she.mä'lē), the fourth-magnitude star ι Ceti, at the tip of the northern fluke of the monster's tail. **5.** Deneb Cygni (sig'nī), the first-magnitude star α Cygni, otherwise known as Arided. **6.** Deneb Kaitos (kī'tos), the third-magnitude star β Ceti, at the tip of the southern fluke of the tail, otherwise called Diphda. When used alone, Deneb commonly refers to Deneb Cygni.

Denebola (dẹ.neb'ọ.lạ). The second-magnitude star β Leonis, also sometimes called Dafirah and Serpha.

Denfeld (den'feld), **Louis Emil.** b. at Westboro, Mass., April 13, 1891—. American naval officer. He was commissioned ensign in 1912 and served on the destroyers *Ammen* and *Lamberton* on escort duty during World War

I. In World War II he was assistant chief (1942–45) and chief (1945–47) of naval personnel. Promoted (1947) to admiral, he was commander in chief (1947) of the Pacific fleet, and served (1947–49) as chief of naval operations, retiring after a bitter quarrel with Defense Secretary Louis A. Johnson about the navy's place in the defense establishment.

Dengis (den.gēs'). See **Balkhash.**

Den Haag (dẹn häċh'). A Dutch name of **Hague, The.**

Denham (den'ạm), **Dixon.** b. at London, Jan. 1, 1786; d. in Sierra Leone, West Africa, May 8, 1828. African explorer. As a British officer he took part in the continental wars against Napoleon I. In 1821 he was sent to Africa with Oudney and Clapperton. From Tripoli they went over Murzuk and Fezzan to Lake Chad, and stayed some time at Kuka, the capital of the native kingdom of Bornu, in what is now Nigeria. In a war with the conquering Fulbe, Denham was taken prisoner, but contrived to escape. After exploring the south end of Lake Chad, he accompanied Clapperton to Sokoto, and returned in 1824. He died in 1828 as lieutenant governor of Sierra Leone.

Denham, Sir **John.** b. at Dublin, 1615; d. at London, in March, 1669. English poet. He took up arms for the king when the English Civil War began, and was made governor of Farnham Castle, from which he was driven and sent a prisoner to London. His fortunes varied, but revived at the Restoration. He was falsely accused in 1667 of murdering his wife by a poisoned cup of chocolate. He was the author of a tragedy, *The Sophy* (1642), a descriptive poem, *Cooper's Hill* (1642), and *Cato Major* (1648), adapted from Cicero.

Denhardt (den'härt), **Gustav.** b. at Zeitz, Germany, June 13, 1856; d. at Leipzig, Germany, July 19, 1917. German explorer; brother of Klemens Denhardt. An explorer of Africa and colonial pioneer, he acquired territory for Germany by friendly negotiations in East Africa; the territory was later ceded (1890) to England in exchange for Helgoland.

Denhardt, Klemens. b. at Zeitz, Germany, Aug. 3, 1852; d. at Sulza, Germany, June 7, 1929. German explorer of Africa; brother of Gustav Denhardt. He acquired territories in East Africa from the sultan of Witu, in what is now Kenya, and placed them under German sovereignty.

Den Helder (dẹn hel'dėr). [Also: **De Helder;** English, **The Helder.**] Town in W Netherlands, in the province of North Holland, situated on the Mars Diep, an outlet from the Wadden Sea into the North Sea, ab. 40 mi. N of Amsterdam. It occupies the northernmost tip of the mainland of North Holland. It is separated from the island of Texel by a narrow body of water, and is connected with the seaside resort of Huisduinen. Den Helder is the chief naval station of the Netherlands, with shipyards, docks, arsenal, marine school, meteorological institute, and a zoölogical and hydrographic station; it is also a port for fishing fleets. The Dutch under Ruyter and Tromp defeated the British here in 1673. New fortifications were erected by Napoleon I in 1811. Heavy damage was done to the harbor works and naval installations during World War II. 36,209 (est. 1951).

Denia (dā'nyä). [Ancient name, **Dianum.**] Town in E Spain, in the province of Alicante, situated on the Mediterranean Sea, ab. 45 mi. NE of Alicante. It is a seaport, exporting the excellent raisins which are grown in the vicinity. Notable buildings include a Moorish castle and remnants of Roman and other Moorish structures. 12,323 (1940).

De Nicola (dā nē.kô'lä), **Enrico.** b. at Naples, Italy, Nov. 9, 1877—. Italian statesman. He was elected (1909) to the chamber of deputies, of which he served (1920–23) as head, and was named (1929) to the senate. In 1946 he was elected as temporary head of the new Italian republic and in 1948 was named president of the republic; upon his retirement (May 11, 1948) life senatorship was conferred on him.

Denifle (den'ẹ.fle), **Heinrich Seuse.** [Original name, **Joseph Denifle.**] b. at Imst, in the Austrian Tyrol, Jan. 16, 1844; d. at Munich, June 10, 1905. Church historian. Educated at the seminary of Brixen (then part of Austria, now Bressanone, Italy), he became a Dominican in 1861. He subsequently studied at Graz, Marseilles, and Rome. He taught philosophy at Graz (1870–80) and became known in Austria as a preacher. In 1880 he was summoned to Rome and began collecting manuscripts for a critical edition of Thomas Aquinas. In 1883 he was made subarchivist of the Vatican. He is known for his editing of the *Chartularium,* or records of the University of Paris, which became a basis of research on medieval universities. He also wrote on medieval university life, the German mystics, the Hundred Years' War, clerical profligacy in the early 16th century, and on the genesis of Luther's theological ideas.

Denijn (dẹ.nīn'), **Jef.** See **Denyn, Jef.**

Deniker (dẹ.nē.ker), **Joseph.** b. at Astrakhan, Russia, March 6, 1852; d. at Paris, March 18, 1918. French anthropologist, who served (1888 *et seq.*) as librarian at the Museum of Natural History at Paris. He was the author of *Les Races de l'Europe* (The Races of Europe, 1908), and *Les Races et les peuples de la terre* (The Races and the Peoples of the Earth, 2nd ed. 1926).

Denikin (di.nyē'kin), **Anton Ivanovich.** b. Dec. 4, 1872; d. in the U.S., 1947. Russian general. The son of a former serf, he accomplished the unusual feat of rising from the ranks to high command in the czarist army. In the Russo-Japanese War he was a colonel, and in World War I a general in command of the southwestern theater of war. He opposed the Bolshevist revolution in 1917, was imprisoned, but escaped and joined with General Kornilov and others in setting up a counterrevolutionary regime and assembling an army in the Don country. Upon Kornilov's death in March, 1918, Denikin became commander of this army, and in September assumed the role of commander in chief of the White Russian forces in the south. He won a number of victories and by the end of the year was in control of Kharkov, Kiev, and Odessa, and had established liaison with the counterrevolutionary forces under Kolchak. In November, however, a Red army under Budenny inflicted decisive defeats on Denikin's force which, low in morale, thereafter became more and more demoralized and ineffective, until, early in 1920, Denikin retreated to the Crimea, resigned his command in favor of General Wrangel, and fled to England. Later he lived in France, but came to the U.S. in 1946.

Denina (dā.nē'nä), **Carlo Giovanni Maria.** b. at Revello, near Saluzzo, Italy, Feb. 28, 1731; d. at Paris, Dec. 5, 1813. Italian historian. He was professor at Turin and later at Berlin, became university librarian at Turin in 1800, and was imperial librarian at Paris after 1804. He wrote *Istoria delle rivoluzioni d'Italia* (1769–72), and others.

Denis or **Denys** (den'is; French, dẹ.nē), Saint. b. in Italy, date unknown. Apostle to the Gauls, and patron saint of France, beheaded, according to the legends, at Paris c250, under Decius. He was confounded, at an early date, with Dionysius the Areopagite.

Denis (dẹ.nē), **Jean Ferdinand.** b. at Paris, Aug. 13, 1798; d. there, Aug. 2, 1890. French author. He traveled in America from 1816 to 1821, and subsequently in Spain and Portugal, with the object of studying the literature of those countries. After 1838 he was prominently connected with the libraries of Paris, especially the Sainte Geneviève, of which he became conservator in 1841 and administrator in 1865. He wrote numerous works, historical and descriptive, on Brazil, the Platine States (Argentina, Uruguay, and Paraguay), Guiana, and Portugal, and on the literature of Portugal and Spain; also a great number of biographical and historical articles for various encyclopedic works, and a series of historical novels.

Denis, Louise. [Maiden name, **Mignot.**] b. c1710; d. 1790. Niece and companion of Voltaire. Her husband, whom she had married in 1738, died in 1744, and in 1754 she returned to Voltaire's house, which she kept for him until his death in 1778. In 1779, when in her 70th year, she married a Sieur du Vivier, who was about 60. She wrote several works and a play, *La Coquette punie.*

Denis, Maurice. b. at Granville, France, Nov. 25, 1870—. French neotraditionalist and symbolist painter and illustrator. He was the leader of the Nabis, a group which included P. Bonnard, E. Vuillard, and P. Sérusier, and was an important influence on G. Rouault. He studied at the Julian Academy and later at the École des Beaux-Arts, both at Paris. He traveled to Italy, where he found the religious painting of the Renaissance to be an inspiration. Poussin and Ingres were also important influences on him. In 1910 he was made a chevalier of the Legion of Honor and societaire of the Société Nationale des Beaux-Arts. His work hangs in most of the important galleries in Europe. Among the most noteworthy of his paintings are *Descent from the Cross, Homage to Cézanne, Virgin and Child, Promenade, Head of a Woman,* and illustrations for books by André Gide (*The Voyage of Urien*), Verlaine (*Wisdom*), P. Claudel, Alfred de Vigny, Dante, and others.

Denis Duval (den'is dụ̈.val'). Unfinished novel by Thackeray, published in 1864, after his death.

Denison (den'i.sọn). City in W Iowa, county seat of Crawford County, in an agricultural area. 4,554 (1950).

Denison. City in C Texas, in Grayson County, N of Dallas: railroad and shipping center for the Red River Valley. Denison Dam, the world's largest rolled earth-fill dam, is ab. 4 mi. NW of the city. 17,504 (1950).

Denison, Cape. Rocky cape in Antarctica, in the center of the S shore of Commonwealth Bay, on the George V Coast, in 67°00′ S. 142°40′ E.

Denison, Henry Willard. b. at Guildhall, Vt., May 11, 1846; d. July 3, 1914. American jurist. He was the legal adviser of the Japanese during the negotiation of the peace with Russia at Portsmouth, N.H., in 1905, and was a delegate to the second peace conference in 1907. In 1880 he was named legal adviser to the Japanese department of foreign affairs.

Denison Dam. Large dam on the Red River, in N Texas and S Oklahoma, ab. 4 mi. N of Denison, Tex. The immense earth-fill flood-control and power dam was built by the U.S. army, supervised by the Corps of Engineers, and was completed in 1944. The first 35,000-kilowatt power unit began operation in 1945, and a second was added in 1949. A third is projected. The large reservoir formed by the dam is ab. 40 mi. long, and is named Lake Texoma. Length of dam, ab. 15,200 ft.; height, ab. 165 ft.

Denizli (de.nēz.lē'). [Also, **Denisli.**] *Il* (province or vilayet) in SW Turkey, NW of Antalya: a rich farming area where cotton, cattle, wheat, sheep, and olives are the chief products. Capital, Denizli; area, 4,304 sq. mi.; pop. 340,010 (1950).

Denizli. [Also, **Denisli.**] Town in SW Turkey, near the Menderes River, ab. 110 mi. E of its mouth: cotton, opium, and grapes; several spinning mills. Pop. ab. 17,000.

Denkmäler Deutscher Tonkunst (dengk'mā.lėr doi'chėr tōn'kůnst). Series of publications (1892 *et seq.*) of notable music from the past. The original committee in charge of the project included Brahms, Spitta, Helmholtz, Joachim, and Chrysander. The German government financed the undertaking.

Denkyira (dān.kyē'rä). One of the Sudanic-speaking Akan peoples of W Africa, inhabiting S Gold Coast.

Denman (den'mạn), **Thomas.** [Title, 1st Baron **Denman.**] b. at London, Feb. 23, 1779; d. at Stoke Albany, Northamptonshire, England, Sept. 22, 1854. English jurist. He defended Queen Caroline in 1820, and was attorney general (1830–32) and lord chief justice of the King's Bench (1832–50).

Denman, Thomas. [Title, 3rd Baron **Denman.**] b. Nov. 16, 1874—. English official, appointed governor general of Australia in 1911; great-grandson of Thomas Denman, 1st Baron Denman (1779–1854). He was educated at the Royal Military College, Sandhurst, and in 1900 served in the South African war as captain of a squadron of the Imperial Yeomanry. He has been deputy speaker of the House of Lords.

Denmark (den'märk). [Danish, Norwegian, and Swedish, **Danmark;** German, **Dänemark;** official Danish name, **Kongeriget Danmark.**] Country in N Europe, bounded by West Germany on the S, by the North Sea and the Skagerrak on the W and NW, by the Kattegat and the Øresund (the Sound) on the NE and E, and by the Baltic Sea on the SE; the island of Bornholm lies in the Baltic Sea far to the east. Capital, Copenhagen; area, 16,576 sq. mi.; pop. 4,281,275 (1950).

Terrain and Climate. The country falls into two parts: the Jutland (Jylland) peninsula, geographically a part of North Germany, and a number of islands between Jutland and Sweden, the largest of which is Zealand (Sjælland), on which Copenhagen is situated. The fact that the capital city is located on the easternmost rim of the national territory points to the fact that formerly S Sweden was also part of the Danish domain; Denmark is then seen in its true role as a bridge between Germany and the Scandinavian North. Denmark has natural frontiers except toward Germany. It has no high elevations and no large rivers. Soils, except in the heath districts of central Jutland, are good. The climate is oceanic and mild.

Agriculture, Industry, Commerce. Denmark is one of the most highly developed agricultural countries in Europe. Grain culture was relegated to a minimum in the course of the 19th century and livestock raising was substituted, based in part on local food crops and pasture lands, in part on the import of grain, oilseeds, and various other fodder materials. Denmark had in 1948 (est.) 23,816,000 hens, 2,831,000 head of cattle, and 1,462,000 pigs. Dairying is Denmark's leading industry; dairy and farm products, particularly butter, eggs, and meats, are exported in large quantities to Great Britain, in somewhat smaller quantities to Germany and to other countries. There are also a number of sugar refineries, breweries, and distilleries. Fishery products, chiefly herring, are likewise exported. There are few woodlands. The amount of minerals found in Denmark and the available water power are inconsiderable; there are, however, shipyards, metallurgical industries, and manufactures of textiles, gloves, and porcelain. Denmark's commercial fleet, her highways and railroads are excellent; noteworthy are the railroad ferries connecting Denmark with Sweden and Germany and also the various Danish islands among themselves.

History. Some of the pagan Danish nobles were converted to Christianity in the 10th century, but the cult of Odin retained its power in the rural districts for a long time. In the 11th and 12th centuries, Danes were feared in northern Europe; their warriors conquered England and Norway, and the country itself was rent by civil unrest. Waldemar I established unity in 1157; under his successors the coastal rimlands of the Baltic Sea were made tributary; new internal strife ensued, aggravated by controversy with the Hanseatic League and by the continued struggle for the domination of Schleswig and Holstein, with their partly German, partly Danish inhabitants. In the 14th century, unity was reëstablished by Waldemar IV Atterdag; under Queen Margaret the Union of Kalmar was concluded (1397) by which Norway and Sweden were joined to Denmark. However, the jump from the precariously achieved unity of Denmark to the wider unity of the entire far-flung North was beyond the strength, technically and politically, which could be mustered at the time. Unity by domination failed; numerous armed conflicts with Sweden fill most of Denmark's subsequent history. The Union of Kalmar crumbled after 1471 when the Swedes under Sten Sture defeated the Danes. After a series of further unsuccessful campaigns Denmark ceded, in the peace of Brömsebro (1645), Jämtland and Herjedalen and the islands of Öel (Saaremaa) and Gotland to Sweden. King Christian III had introduced the Lutheran Reformation (1536); Christian IV, as a prince of the German Empire (for Holstein), entered the Thirty Years' War, but was attacked by Sweden at the same time. In the peace of Roskilde (1658) Denmark ceded Skåne, Halland, Blekinge, Trondheim, and Bohus to Sweden. From then on, Denmark's energies were turned to internal organization, in the 17th century in terms of the absolute power of the king, in the 18th century in terms of enlightened absolutism, leading to the curtailment of the privileges of the aristocracy, to the emancipation of the peasantry (1788), and to the establishment of a system of universal elementary instruction; commercial activities were furthered at the same time. The Napoleonic period saw Denmark's sea power attacked by England. The successful naval battle before Copenhagen of April 2, 1801, was followed by the bombardment of the city by an English naval squadron in 1807, after which the Danish navy was to be delivered into English hands. In the peace of Kiel (1814), Denmark ceded Helgoland to England, and Norway to Sweden. The 19th century saw, apart from continued internal development, the struggle between Denmark and the autonomist, later the German nationalist, movement in Schleswig-Holstein. Fighting occurred in the period 1848–50, confirming Danish sovereignty but hardening Danish rule; the two duchies were ceded to Austria and Prussia as the executors of the German Bund, after an unsuccessful war, in the peace of Vienna (1864). North Schleswig, that is, the part of the entire territory which was ethnically most clearly Danish in character, was returned to Denmark through a plebiscite after World War I. There remained some Danish propaganda in favor of the inclusion of the southern parts of the long embattled territory, some German propaganda aiming at regaining the northern districts; for the vast majority of both peoples the question of Schleswig-Holstein is settled. The Danish possessions in the West Indies (Virgin Islands) were ceded to the U.S. in 1917. A democratic constitution was introduced in Denmark in 1849; a new constitution was adopted in 1915. The leading party is the Social Democratic Party. During World War II, Denmark was invaded by the Germans in 1940 and served as springboard for the invasion of Norway. Iceland became an independent republic in 1944.

Government. Denmark is a constitutional monarchy; the ruling king is Frederick IX, who succeeded his father, Christian X, on April 20, 1947. The constitution is based on the charter of June 5, 1915, which supplanted the constitution of June 5, 1849, and was amended on Sept. 10, 1920. The legislative power is jointly exercised by the king and the diet (*Rigsdag*). The executive power is exercised by the cabinet ministers on behalf of the king; the cabinet is responsible to the diet, which consists of a lower and a higher house. All permanent residents of Danish nationality who are over 25 years of age have the vote. The king has the power to dissolve the lower house. The members of the cabinet can appear before both houses of the diet, but can vote only in the house of which they are members.

Culture. The Lutheran religion has been the established church of Denmark since 1536; there are nine bishops. There are equal rights for citizens of all faiths; the Roman Catholic, Jewish, and other minorities are small. Elementary education was made compulsory in 1814. For higher instruction there exist two universities (Aarhus and Copenhagen), veterinary, dental, pharmaceutical, and technical institutes, and a royal academy of arts. Denmark passed four Social Reform acts in 1933, dealing with public assistance, labor exchanges and employment insurance, accident insurance, and sickness, invalid, and old-age insurance. Denmark, like her sister countries in Scandinavia, is renowned for her progressive educational and social security institutions; they are based on the realized ideal of an educated peasantry. Accordingly, Denmark, along with Sweden and Norway, has contributed far more than her share to European literature. Andersen, Jacobsen, Nexø, Bang, Brandes, and others are writers of more than local significance.

Denmark. Town in S central South Carolina, in Bamberg County ab. 50 mi. S of Columbia, in a farming region. It is a railroad junction and manufacturing town. 2,814 (1950).

Denmark, Prince of. See under **Hamlet.**

Denner (den′ėr), **Johann Christoph.** b. at Leipzig, Germany, Aug. 13, 1655; d. at Nuremberg, Germany, April 20, 1707. German maker of woodwind instruments who invented (c1700) the clarinet.

Dennery (den.rē), **Adolphe Philippe.** Original name of **Ennery, Adolphe Philippe d′.**

Dennett (den′ẹt), **Richard Edward.** b. at Valparaíso, Chile, 1857; d. May 28, 1921. English trader and official in Africa, and author of books on African subjects. Educated (1869–74) at Marlborough College, he was employed (1875–79) by Thomas Wilson, Sons, and Company, an English firm trading in Africa. He edited the *Congo Mirror*, a manuscript newspaper in which he boldly attacked murders and atrocities committed by Congo officials, his protests leading to the organization of the Congo Reform Association; and called attention in numerous letters in the *African Mail* to the injustices of French rule. He served as a member (1902–18) of the Nigerian forest service, retiring on a pension. Among his books are *Seven Years Experience Among the Fjort, Being an English Trader's Experience in the Congo* (1887), *Notes on the Folk-Lore of the Fjort (French Congo)* (1898). *At the Back of the Black Man's Mind* (1906), *Nigerian Studies, or the Religious and Political System of the Yoruba* (1910), *Notes on West African Categories* (1911), and a language book, *My Yoruba Alphabet* (1916).

Dennett, Tyler. b. at Spencer, Wis., June 13, 1883; d. at Geneva, N.Y., Dec. 29, 1949. American historian and educator. He was chief (1924–29) of the publications division of the U.S. state department, professor of international relations (1931–34) at Princeton, and president (1934–37) of Williams College. His works include *The Democratic Movement in Asia* (1918), *Americans in Eastern Asia* (1923), *Roosevelt and the Russo-Japanese War* (1924), *Lincoln and the Civil War—Hay Diaries* (1939); his *Biography of John Hay* (1933) won a Pulitzer prize.

Dennewitz (den′ẹ.vits). Village in NE Germany, in the *Land* (state) of Brandenburg, Russian Zone, formerly in the province of Brandenburg, Prussia, ab. 40 mi. SW of Berlin. Here the Prussians under Bülow, with the aid of Russians and Swedes under Bernadotte, defeated the French army under Ney, on Sept. 6, 1813. Pop. 618 (1946).

Dennewitz, Count von. See under **Bülow,** Baron **Friedrich Wilhelm von.**

Dennie (den′i), **Joseph.** [Called the **"American Addison."**] b. at Boston, Aug. 30, 1768; d. at Philadelphia. Jan. 7, 1812. American editor and essayist. He was educated at Harvard, became associated with the literary supporters of Federalism, and was editor (1796–98) of the *Farmer's Weekly Museum*, in which his "Lay Preacher" essays appeared. He edited (1801–09) *The Port Folio* at Philadelphia. His essays were published in 1796 and 1816.

Dennis (den′is). Servant to Oliver in Shakespeare's *As You Like It.*

Dennis. Hangman in Charles Dickens's novel *Barnaby Rudge.*

Dennis, Geoffrey Pomeroy. b. at Barnstaple, Devonshire, England, Jan. 20, 1892—. English writer. He served (1920–37) on the League of Nations staff, becoming chief editor and head of the document services, and as chief of the Italian section of the European service of the British Broadcasting Corporation. He is the author of *Mary Lee* (1922), *Harvest in Poland* (1925), *The End of the World* (1930; awarded the Hawthornden prize), *Sale by Auction* (1932), *Bloody Mary's* (1934), and *Coronation Commentary* (1937).

Dennis, John. b. at London, 1657; d. Jan. 6, 1734. English critic. His writings annoyed Pope, who ridiculed him in the *Dunciad*. He also wrote indifferently successful plays.

Dennis Brulgruddery (brul.grud′ėr.i). See **Brulgruddery, Dennis.**

Dennison (den′i.sọn). Village in E Ohio, in Tuscarawas County, in a clay-producing area. It was established in 1864 and was formerly important for its railway division shops. Manufactures include sewer pipe and other clay products. 4,432 (1950).

Dennison, Aaron Lufkin. [Called the **"Father of American Watchmaking."**] b. at Freeport, Me., March 6, 1812; d. Jan. 9, 1895. American watch manufacturer, designer of the world's first factory-made watches. He was interested in the application of the interchangeable parts production method as a means of lowering the cost and increasing the accuracy of American watches. With associates he formed at Roxbury, Mass., the American Horologue Company. After being sold in bankruptcy the company was moved to Waltham, Mass., and finally became known as the American Waltham Watch Company.

Dennison, William. b. at Cincinnati, Ohio, Nov. 23, 1815; d. at Columbus, Ohio, June 15, 1882. American lawyer, elected (1859) governor of Ohio. He served (1848 *et seq.*) as a state senator in Ohio, and was an early member (1856) of the newly formed Republican Party. From 1864 to 1866 he was U.S. postmaster general.

Denny (den′i), **George Hutcheson.** b. in Hanover County, Va., Dec. 3, 1870—. American educator. He has been professor of Latin and German (1896–99) at Hampden-Sydney College, professor of Latin (1899–1911) and president (1902–11) of Washington and Lee University, and president (1912–37, 1942) and chancellor (1937–41, 1942 *et seq.*) of the University of Alabama. He is the author of *The Subjunctive Sequence after Adjective and Substantive Predicates and Phrases* (1896).

Denny and Dunipace (dun'i.pās). Police burgh in C Scotland, in Stirlingshire, ab. 7 mi. S of Stirling. 6,550 (est. 1948).

Denon (de.nôn), Baron **Dominique Vivant.** b. at Châlon-sur-Saône, France, Jan. 4, 1747; d. at Paris, April 27, 1825. French artist, archaeologist, diplomat, and administrator. He was the author of *Voyage dans la Basse et la Haute-Égypte* (1802) and *Monuments des arts du dessin* (1829).

Den Pasar (den' pä.sär'). Airfield on the island of Bali, Indonesia, occupation of which by Japanese forces in February, 1942, cut the communication between Java and Australia.

Denry the Audacious (den'ri). American title of a novel (1911) by Arnold Bennett, published in England as *The Card.* It is one of the so-called "Five Towns" novels and is concerned more with character than with plot. It is a humorous, but sympathetic, portrait of a young man whose chief quality is suggested by the title, a quality which, rather than real ability, enables him to achieve what he considers to be success in his career.

Dent (dent), **Hugh Railton.** b. 1874; d. at Elmstead, West Wittering, Sussex, England, Nov. 20, 1938. English publisher; son of J. M. Dent (1849–1926). He entered his father's bookbinding firm in 1888, when it became a publishing business, and remained with it until his death; author of additional chapters in *The House of Dent, 1888–1938* (1938).

Dent, J. M. [Full name, **Joseph Malaby Dent.**] b. at Darlington, Durham, England, Aug. 30, 1849; d. at Croydon, Surrey, England, May 9, 1926. English publisher and author, founder of the publishing house of J. M. Dent and Sons. After having served his apprenticeship, he began (1872) his own bookbinding business at Hoxton, a North London suburb. In 1888 he published Lamb's *Essays of Elia, Last Essays,* and Goldsmith's *Essays, Poems and Plays* as the first volumes in the Temple Library, so named because both authors had lived in the Temple; in 1890 he began the Medieval Towns series, following it with the Temple Shakespeare (40 vols., 1893–96) edited by Israel Gollancz, distinguished Shakespearian scholar; in 1896 he brought out the first volumes of the Temple Classics. He also published (1898) the Haddon Hall Library and, in 1899, the Waverley novels (40 vols.). In 1904 he began his most ambitious project, the Everyman's Library, securing as general editor Ernest Rhys, who had suggested the name. He also published a series of English novelists from Henry Fielding to Jane Austen, and translations of Balzac with introductions by George Saintsbury. He was the author of essays on various phases of making and printing books, introductions to several Everyman's Library volumes, and *Memoirs* (1928).

Dentatus (den.tā'tus), **Manius Curius.** fl. in the first part of the 3rd century B.C. Roman tribune, consul, praetor, and censor, celebrated as a model of the early Roman virtues of simplicity, frugality, and patriotism. He defeated Pyrrhus in 275, and the Samnites and Lucanians in 274.

Dent Blanche (dän bläṅsh). Mountain in the Alps of Valais, Switzerland, situated N of the Matterhorn. 14,318 ft.

Dent de Jaman (dän de zhȧ.män). Mountain in Vaud, Switzerland, situated E of the Lake of Geneva. 6,165 ft.

Dent de Vaulion (dän de vō.lyôn). Peak of the Jura Mountains, in Switzerland, ab. 18 mi. NW of Lausanne. 4,880 ft.

Dent du Midi (dän dü mē.dē). Mountain in the canton of Valais, Switzerland, situated NW of Martigny. Elevation, ab. 10,700 ft.

Denton (den'ton). Urban district in NW England, in Lancashire, ab. 7 mi. SE of Manchester, ab. 181 mi. NW of London by rail. It has manufactures of hats. 25,612 (1951).

Denton. City in C Texas, county seat of Denton County, NW of Dallas: seat of the North Texas State Teachers College and the Texas State College for Women. 21,372 (1950).

D'Entrecasteaux Channel (dän.tre.kȧs.tō'). Strait between Tasmania and Bruny Island to the S.

D'Entrecasteaux Islands. Group of small islands lying E of the island of New Guinea, belonging to Australia as part of the Territory of Papua. Area, ab. 1,200 sq. mi.

D'Entrecasteaux Point. Cape at the SW extremity of Australia.

Dentz (däṅts), **Henri.** b. at Roanne, Loire, France, 1881; d. at Paris, Dec. 13, 1945. French army officer who resisted the occupation (June, 1941) of Syria by British and Free French forces while Vichy high commissioner for Syria. As military governor of Paris, he surrendered (June, 1940) the French capital to the Germans. Condemned to death as a traitor (April, 1945) his sentence was commuted by General Charles de Gaulle.

Denver (den'vėr). City in C Colorado, capital of Colorado and county seat of Denver County, on the South Platte River in the foothills of the Rocky Mountains. It is an important railway center, a major center for finance, commerce, and meat packing in the West, and the leading Western market for livestock and agricultural produce; seat of the University of Denver, Regis College, and a U.S. mint. It was first settled in 1858–59, named for James William Denver, was both gold-mining and silver-mining boom town in the 19th century, and has become noted for its scenery and its dry climate. Elevation, 5,280 ft.; pop. 322,412 (1940), 415,786 (1950).

Denver, James William. b. at Winchester, Va., Oct. 23, 1817; d. at Washington, D.C., Aug. 9, 1892. American government official for whom Denver, Colo., was named. He was state senator (1852–53) of California, secretary of state (1853) in California, and U.S. congressman (1855–57) active in the promotion of the transcontinental railroad. He also served as federal commissioner of Indian affairs (1857, 1858–59). As secretary (1857–58) and governor (1858) of the Kansas Territory, he firmly established the territorial government during its critical period. In the Civil War, he served (1861–63) as a brigadier general in command of Kansas volunteers.

Denyn (de.nīn'), **Jef.** [Also, **Denijn.**] b. at Mechelen (Malines), Belgium, 1862; d. 1941. Belgian carilloneur. He enjoyed a universal reputation in the art form he had done so much to re-create, and was a composer and author of books on the artistry and technique of the carillon. He was honorary carilloneur of the town of Mechelen and director of the school for carilloneurs.

Denys (den'is; French, de.nē), Saint. See Saint **Denis** or **Denys.**

Denza (den'tsä), **Luigi.** b. at Castellammare di Stabia, Italy, Feb. 24, 1846; d. at London, Jan. 26, 1922. Italian musician. He lived at London after 1879, and was professor of singing (1898 *et seq.*) at the Royal Academy of Music. Among the most popular of his some 600 songs is *Funiculì Funiculà,* written for the opening (1880) of the funicular railway at Naples; he also composed the opera *Wallenstein* (1876).

Denzil (den'zil), **Guy.** In Sir Walter Scott's poem *Rokeby,* the chief of a marauding band made up from both Cavaliers and Roundheads.

Deoband (dē'ō.bund, dā'-). Town in the Saharanpur district, Uttar Pradesh (United Provinces), Union of India, ab. 75 mi. NE of Delhi: trading center. 22,126 (1941).

Déodat de Sévérac (dā.o.dȧ de sā.vā.rȧk), **Joseph Marie.** See **Sévérac, Joseph Marie Déodat de.**

De Officiis (dē ō.fish'i.is). [Eng. trans., *"Of Duties."*] Treatise in three books, by Cicero, on moral obligations, written c44 B.C.

Deoghir or **Deoghur** (dē'ō.gėr, dā'-). Former name of **Daulatabad.**

Deoprag (dā'ō.präg). See **Devaprayaga.**

De Oratore (dē or.a.tō'rē). [Eng. trans., *"Of the Orator."*] Rhetorical work by Cicero, in three books, written (55 B.C.) in the form of a dialogue, the principal characters being L. Crassus and M. Antoninus. Its style and varied contents make it one of Cicero's most polished works.

Deorham (de.ōr'häm). Place (identified with Dereham, Gloucestershire, England) where Ceawlin, king of the West Saxons, defeated (577) the Britons.

Deor's Lament (dā'ôrz). English poem (9th or 10th century) named after its reputed author, a gleeman who in the last section of the poem tells of his own misfortune. Most commentators believe that this gleeman is only a fiction, used by the true author for mouthpiece. The poem falls into seven sections of varying length. All but the sixth conform to one pattern: the gleeman cites a story, taken from Germanic legend, in which a victim or victims of misfortune outlive their trouble. Each of these sections ends with the same consolatory line: "That now is gone; this too will go." The sixth section deals with earthly misfortune in general, and adds words of consolation correspondingly generalized.

Departmental Ditties. Volume of poetry (1886) by Rudyard Kipling. The poems, which originally appeared singly in various issues of the Lahore *Gazette*, gave a picture of Anglo-Indian life, something new in literature at the time, and were welcomed accordingly. In *Plain Tales from the Hills* (1888) Kipling accomplished somewhat the same end in prose.

DePauw (dẹ.pô′), **Washington Charles.** b. at Salem, Ind., Jan. 4, 1822; d. May 5, 1887. American banker and manufacturer. He started (1853) a small bank, becoming a leading Indiana banker, and with earnings from Civil War securities invested profitably in manufacture. He was a trustee of Indiana Asbury University (founded 1837), which he endowed heavily. Its name was changed (1884) to DePauw University.

Depazzi (dä.pät′sē). Character in Shirley's play *The Humorous Courtier*.

Dependencias Federales (dā.pen.den′syäs fā.ᴛʜā.rä′lās). [English, **Federal Dependencies.**] Group of islands in the Caribbean Sea under the jurisdiction of Venezuela. Area, 46 sq. mi.; pop. 779 (1950).

De Pere (dẹ pir′). City in E Wisconsin, in Brown County: manufactures include boats, cattle feed, glassine paper, butcher paper, and medicines. It is the seat of St. Norbert College. The city occupies the site of the first permanent Jesuit mission established (1671) on the Fox River by Father Claude Allouez. 8,146 (1950).

Depew (dẹ.pū′). Village in W New York, in Erie County near Buffalo: railroad center; manufactures include storage batteries, food products, steel castings, and mattresses. 7,217 (1950).

Depew, Chauncey Mitchell. b. at Peekskill, N.Y., April 23, 1834; d. at New York, April 5, 1928. American lawyer, legislator, railway president, and orator. He was graduated (1856) from Yale and studied law at Peekskill, where he established his practice after being admitted to the bar in 1858. He entered politics as a Republican, served (1862–63) in the state legislature, and was (1863 *et seq.*) secretary of state for New York. He was appointed (1866) by President Johnson as the first U.S. minister to Japan, but resigned even before going to his post in favor of employment as counsel for Commodore Cornelius Vanderbilt's Hudson River and Harlem railroad lines. He became (1874) a director in the Vanderbilt railway system, and in 1875 became its general counsel. In 1882 he became second vice-president of the New York Central and Hudson River line, and in 1885 its president. Elected (1899) U.S. senator from New York, he left the presidency of the New York Central Railroad and became chairman of its board of directors. He was widely known as a wit and after-dinner speaker.

De Peyster (dẹ pīs′tėr), **Abraham.** b. at New Amsterdam (New York), July 8, 1658; d. at New York, Aug. 10, 1728. American merchant and official; son of Johannes De Peyster (1600–c1685). He was mayor of New York (1691–95) and later became chief justice of the province and president of the king's council. By virtue of the latter post he was acting governor in 1701.

De Peyster, Arent Schuyler. b. at New York, June 27, 1736; d. at Dumfries, Scotland, in November, 1832. Royalist officer; grandson of Abraham De Peyster. He commanded at Detroit, Mackinac, and various places in Upper Canada during the Revolutionary War, and by his tact and conciliatory measures succeeded in detaching the Indians of the Northwest from the colonists and allying them with the British.

De Peyster, Johannes. b. at Haarlem, Holland, 1600; d. at New York, c1685. Dutch colonist (1640 *et seq.*) at New Amsterdam (New York); father of Abraham De Peyster (1658–1728).

De Peyster, John Watts. b. at New York, March 9, 1821; d. there, May 4, 1907. American military and historical writer. His works include *History of the Life of Leonard Torstenson* (1855), *History of Carausius, the Dutch Augustus and Emperor of Britain* (1858), and *The Thirty-Years' War: With Special Reference to the Military Operations and Influence of the Swedes* (1884).

Dépit amoureux (dā.pē à.mö.rė), **Le.** [Eng. trans., "*The Loving Spite.*"] Comedy by Molière, produced at Montpellier in 1654, and at Paris in 1658. It was not printed until 1663. Many authors have adapted and rearranged it. The subject is partly borrowed from *L'Intéressé* of Nicolo Secchi.

Deposition from the Cross. See also under **Descent from the Cross, 4.**

Deposition from the Cross. Painting (with the Virgin, the Magdalen, Saint John, Joseph of Arimathea, and Nicodemus) by Perugino, in the Academy of Fine Arts at Florence. The expression and differentiation of character in the group of mourners is considered masterly, and the painting among Perugino's best.

Depot Island (dē′pō). Small, glaciated, granite island in Antarctica, lying ab. 2 mi. NW of Cape Ross, off the coast of Victoria Land, in ab. 76°43′ S., 163°00′ E.

Depping (dep′ing), **Georges Bernard.** b. at Münster, Germany, May 11, 1784; d. at Paris, Sept. 5, 1853. French historian, of German parentage. He wrote *Histoire générale de l'Espagne* (1811), *Histoire du commerce entre le Levant et l'Europe* (1832), and *Histoire de la Normandie* (1835).

Depretis (dā.prā′tēs), **Agostino.** b. at Mezzana-Corte-Bottaroni, near Stradella, Italy, Jan. 31, 1813; d. there, July 29, 1887. Italian statesman. He was four times premier (1876–77, 1877–78, 1878–79, 1881–87).

Deprez (dẹ.prā), **Marcel.** b. at Châtillon-sur-Loing, France, Dec. 19, 1843; d. 1918. French engineer and pioneer electrician. As early as 1872 he made experiments in the transmission of electrical power; he is credited with demonstrating (1882) the first successful long-distance transmission of electrical power by wires (over a distance of some 35 miles between Munich and Miesbach). He served (1890 *et seq.*) as professor of industrial electricity at the Conservatoire des Arts at Métiers. He also invented a self-compensating brake for testing motors.

De Prie (dẹ prē′), **Jaques.** Supposed beggar in Ben Jonson's comedy *The Case is Altered.* He is a miser, and is in reality Melun, steward to the old Chamont. He somewhat resembles Shylock, loving both his ducats and his daughter.

Deptford (det′fọrd). Metropolitan borough in SE London, in the County of London, situated on the S bank of the river Thames, ab. 5 mi. SE of Charing Cross station, London, and immediately W of Greenwich. Its industries include sawmills, soap works, sugar refineries, and chemical works. It was long noted for its dockyard, which was closed in 1869. Deptford was on the route of Watling Street, an old Roman road which ran from the Strait of Dover through London to Chester. 75,694 (1951).

Deptford (dep′fọrd). Burial Mound I culture (c700–900 A.D.) of Georgia and NW Florida, of which simple- and check-stamped pottery is characteristic.

Deputy Was King, A. Novel by G. B. Stern, published in 1926. It is the second panel in her trilogy of Jewish life, *The Rakonitz Chronicles* (1932).

De Queen (dẹ kwēn′). City in SW Arkansas, county seat of Sevier County: rail center. 3,015 (1950).

De Quincey (dẹ kwin′si, -zi), **Thomas.** b. at Manchester, England, Aug. 15, 1785; d. at Edinburgh, Dec. 8, 1859. English essayist and miscellaneous writer, famous for his *Confessions of an English Opium-Eater* (in book form, 1822). He was the son of Thomas Quincey, a wealthy wholesale merchant who died in 1793. His guardians entered him in the Manchester Grammar School in 1800, from which he ran away in 1802. After a tour on foot of Wales, Thomas lived for some months in direst poverty at London. Becoming reconciled with his guardians, he entered Oxford late in 1803. Here, a year later, he first began his use of opium, which he continued, in widely varying amounts, for the rest of his life. He left Oxford without taking a degree in 1808. Making the acquaintance of Lamb, Coleridge, and Wordsworth, he moved to Grasmere, where he married Margaret Simpson in 1817. By this time his use of opium had increased to the amount of 8,000 drops of laudanum (about seven wineglasses) a day. Financial difficulties forced him to go to London in 1821 in search of literary work. His *Confessions of an English Opium-Eater*, published anonymously that fall in *The London Magazine* and in book form the following year, established his reputation. His only other books were *Klosterheim* (1832), an unduly neglected Gothic novel, and *The Logic of Political Economy* (1844). He wrote for the *Westmoreland Gazette, Hogg's Weekly Instructor, Blackwood's, Tait's Edinburgh*, and other magazines nearly 200 articles on biographical, literary, philosophical, historical, classical, and miscellaneous subjects. Like Coleridge, De Quincey was extraordinarily well read, had an amazingly retentive memory, and was a brilliant conversationalist. At its worst, his work is prolix, wandering, pedantic, poorly organized, and often grossly inaccurate, even as to easily checked quotations and factual details. At its frequent best, for example in *The Revolt of the Tartars, On Murder Considered as One of the Fine Arts, The English Mail-Coach, On the Knocking at the Gate in Macbeth, The Spanish Military Nun*, and *Joan of Arc*, his style is highly polished, stately, musical, and imaginative, often humorous. His autobiographic writings rank with Rousseau's and Cellini's. His essays on his contemporaries, Lamb, Coleridge, Wordsworth, Hazlett, and others, are honest, charming, and intimate. He is placed by most critics among the great masters of English prose. His works were first collected and published by Ticknor and Fields (Boston, 1850–59, 24 vols.), with De Quincey's consent and remuneration, followed by Hogg's *Selections Grave and Gay* (Edinburgh, 1853–60, 14 vols.), and David Masson's definitive *Collected Writings* (Edinburgh, 1889–90, 14 vols.). The best biographical and critical works on De Quincey are by Horace Ainsworth Eaton (New York, 1936), and Edward Sackville West (New Haven, 1936).

De Quincy (dē kwin'si). Town in S Louisiana, in Calcasieu Parish. It has railroad shops and produces turpentine and other pine products and tung oil. In the surrounding region are truck farms, orchards, poultry farms, and livestock ranches. 3,837 (1950).

Dera Ghazi Khan (der'ạ gä'zē kän'). District in the Multan division, Punjab province. Pakistan, W of the Indus River: wheat and cotton growing and sheep raising. Chief town, Dera Ghazi Khan; area, 9,364 sq. mi.; pop. 581,350 (1941).

Dera Ghazi Khan. Chief town of Dera Ghazi Khan district, in Punjab, Pakistan, on the Indus River ab. 50 mi. W of Multan. It is an important trading center and is the terminus of two trails over the Sulaiman Mountains. 35,909 (1951).

Derain (dẹ.raṅ), **André.** b. at Chatou, France, June 10, 1880—. French painter and sculptor who was an original member of the Fauve group. He studied with Eugène Carrière, and worked with Maurice de Vlaminck at Chatou. At Paris, he and Vlaminck met Matisse, and the three men formed the nucleus of the Fauve movement; his work after 1913 was not purely Fauve, since many influences such as African sculpture and cubism helped him develop a distinctive style. The art of Gauguin, Van Gogh, and Seurat also influenced him. He exhibited in the first Fauve exhibition of 1905, at Paris, and has continued to be shown in almost every important exhibition of modern art since then. Among the many books he has illustrated are Guillaume Apollinaire's *L'Enchanteur Pourrissant*, V. Muselli's *La Cassette de plomb*, and G. Gabory's *Le Nez de Cleopatra*. He has also done settings for the Ballet Russe, and his more important paintings include *The Bridge at Chatou, Portrait of Chevalier X, Portrait of Kisling, Saturday, Nude in a Landscape, Banks of the Seine, Woman with Hat, Still Life*, and *Nude* (panel).

Dera Ismail Khan (der'ạ is.mä.ēl' kän'). District in the S part of the North-West Frontier Province, Pakistan. Chief town, Dera Ismail Khan; area, 4,216 sq. mi.; pop. 298,131 (1941).

Dera Ismail Khan. Chief town of Dera Ismail Khan district, Pakistan, near the Indus River ab. 200 mi. W of Lahore. It is an important trading center and the terminus of a caravan route across the mountains to Afghanistan. 41,613 (1951).

Derajat (der.ạ.jät'). Plain in NW Pakistan, between the Indus River and the Sulaiman Mountains, in the Punjab and the North-West Frontier provinces: a wheat, cotton, and jute growing area.

Derayeh (de.rä'ye) or **Deraiyeh** (de.rī'ye). Ruined town in Nejd, Arabia. It was the capital of the Wahabis until its destruction in 1818.

Derbe (dėr'bē). In ancient geography, a town in Lycaonia, Asia Minor, near the border of Cilicia, and on the highway from Cilicia to Iconium.

Derbent (der.bent'). [Also, **Derbend.**] Seaport in the U.S.S.R., in the Dagestan Autonomous Soviet Socialist Republic of the Russian Soviet Federated Socialist Republic, situated on the Caspian Sea at the foot of the Caucasus Mountains. It produces raw materials for the ceramic industry and is a food-processing center. The surrounding region was a country known to the ancients as Albania, and the narrow pass between sea and mountains at this point was called the Albanian, or Caucasian, Gates. Near here commences the Derbent Wall ("Caucasian Wall" or "Alexander's Wall"), an ancient fortification built by the Persians in the 6th century. The town was founded by the Persians, captured (728) and developed by the Arabs, taken by the Mongols c1220 and by the Russians in 1722 and 1796, and was formally incorporated with Russia in 1813. Pop. 11,535 (1939).

Derby (dėr'bi). Unincorporated community in N central Colorado, in Adams County: a northern suburb of Denver. 2,840 (1950).

Derby. City in SW Connecticut, in New Haven County, at the confluence of the Naugatuck and Housatonic rivers, ab. 9 mi. W of New Haven: important for the production of sponge rubber and metal products; formerly important for shipbuilding (1657–1868). It comprises the former towns of Derby and Birmingham. 10,259 (1950).

Derby (där'bi, dėr'bi). [Old Danish, **Deora-by.**] County borough and manufacturing town in N central England, in Derbyshire, situated on the river Derwent, ab. 42 mi. NE of Birmingham, ab. 129 mi. NW of London by rail. It is the county seat of Derbyshire. Its industries include aircraft-engine manufacture, a motorcar industry, locomotive building and repair shops, steelworks, electrical shops, and a cotton and silk textile industry. It anciently belonged to Peveril, an alleged son of William I, and was one of the Five Boroughs taken from the Danes by the West Saxons in the 10th century. It was the southernmost point reached by the Young Pretender in 1745, and was the birthplace of Samuel Richardson. 141,264 (1951).

Derby (där'bi; in the U.S. often dėr'bi). Annual English horse-racing event. It is named for one of the earls of Derby, who instituted it in 1780, and is run at Epsom Downs, a racecourse in the municipal borough of Epsom and Ewell, within the area of Greater London, on the Wednesday of the week after Trinity Sunday, which is variously the last Wednesday in May or the first Wednesday in June. The course measures 29 yards more than a mile-and-a-half, and the race is open only to three-year-old colts and fillies, colts being required to carry a minimum of 126 pounds, and fillies not less than 121 pounds. The prize money is not great by modern standards, but the race has acquired great prestige and horses, carefully trained for it, are entered not only by English breeders but by Eastern potentates and American politicians and industrial magnates. The British Parliament adjourns for Derby Day, and hundreds of thousands of people crowd Epsom Downs to see the race if possible, to gaze on royalty and the aristocracy, and to admire the latest women's fashions. The name Derby has come to be applied to other sporting events of real or asserted superior character or importance. Thus a race held annually since 1875 at Churchill Downs near Lexington, Ky., is known as the Kentucky Derby, and roller-skating "Derbies" are featured in various American cities.

Derby, Countess of. Title of **Farren, Elizabeth** (or **Eliza).**

Derby, Earl of. A title of **Henry of Lancaster** (c1299–1361).

Derby, Earl of. A title of **Thomas of Lancaster.**

Derby, Earl of. Title held by various members of the **Stanley** family, in Great Britain.

Derby (dėr'bi), **Elias Hasket.** b. at Salem, Mass., Aug. 16, 1739; d. there, Sept. 8, 1799. American merchant in the India and China trade, prominent in the equipment of privateers during the Revolutionary War.

Derby, Elias Hasket. b. at Salem, Mass., Jan. 10, 1766; d. at Londonderry, N.H., Sept. 16, 1826. American merchant; son of Elias Hasket Derby (1739–99). He is said to have introduced merino sheep into the U.S.

Derby, Elias Hasket. b. at Salem, Mass., Sept. 24, 1803; d. at Boston, March 31, 1880. American lawyer and writer; son of Elias Hasket Derby (1766–1826).

Derby, George Horatio. [Pseudonyms, **John Phoenix** and **"Squibob."**] b. at Dedham, Mass., April 3, 1823; d. at New York, May 15, 1861. American soldier and humorist. He was a graduate of West Point and served in the Mexican War. He later held various positions in the topographical bureau at Washington, finally becoming a captain of engineers, and was in charge of lighthouse construction on the Southern coast. He was the author of *Phœnixiana* (1855) and *The Squibob Papers* (1859).

Derby, Orville Adelbert. b. at Kelloggsville, N.Y., July 23, 1851; d. 1915. American geologist. He was graduated from Cornell University, and was instructor there from 1873 to 1875. He made short visits to Brazil in 1870 and 1871, and in 1875 took a place on the Brazilian geological commission. From that time he engaged in geological and geographical work in Brazil, acting on various commissions, and for some years as curator of the geological department of the national museum. He was chief of the geographical and geological survey of São Paulo (1886–1904) and from 1907 was chief of the geological survey of Brazil.

Derbyshire (där′bi.shir, dėr′-). [Also, **Derby.**] County in N central England, bounded on the N by Yorkshire, on the E by Nottinghamshire, on the SE by Leicestershire, on the S by Warwickshire, on the SW by Staffordshire, on the W by Staffordshire and Cheshire, and on the NW by Cheshire. South Derbyshire is generally flat or undulating; the Peak District, in the NW portion, is mountainous, and the remainder of the county is generally hilly. Derbyshire is an important coal-producing county, and it has important limestone and marble quarries. Many minerals are found, among them lead, zinc, manganese, fluorspar, feldspar, and gypsum. It was an important source of lead in Roman times, and was the chief lead-mining center in the 12th and 13th centuries. Lead mining continued up to a quite recent date, but has now been abandoned as no longer economical. There are lead smelters near Matlock, now using imported ores. Other industries include a quite extensive iron and steel industry, cotton textiles, lace and hosiery, silk, and clothing manufactures. The Vale of Trent, in the S part, is very fertile. The county has dairying, mostly in the south. County seat, Derby; area of administrative county, ab. 993 sq. mi.; pop. of administrative county, 685,072 (1951).

Dercetas (dėr′sę.tąs). Friend of Antony in Shakespeare's *Antony and Cleopatra.*

Derceto (dėr′sę.tō). [Also, **Derketo.**] Principal Philistine female deity, worshiped especially in Ashkelon (Ascalon). She was represented in the form of a woman terminating in a fish, and is considered the female counterpart of Dagon. She was a nature goddess, the principle of generation and fertility, and corresponds in her attributes and the mode of her worship to Ashtoreth (Astarte) of the Canaanites and Syrians (the Assyro-Babylonian Ishtar), and to Atargatis of the Hittites. She was the mother of Semiramis, who, though human, was the counterpart of the goddess.

Dercum (dėr′kum), **Francis Xavier.** b. at Philadelphia, Aug. 10, 1856; d. April 23, 1931. American neurologist from whose description (1892) of adiposis dolorosa the ailment became known as Dercum's disease. He started (1877) medical practice at Philadelphia, and was professor (1892–1925) of nervous and mental diseases at Jefferson Medical College. Among his books are *A Clinical Manual of Mental Diseases* (1913, 1917), *Hysteria and Accident Compensation* (1916), *The Biology of the Internal Secretions* (1924), and *The Physiology of Mind* (1925).

Dercyllis (dėr.sil′is). See **Dinias and Dercyllis.**

Dereham (dir′ąm). See under **Deorham** and under **East Dereham.**

Der-el-Bahri (der.el.bä′rē). See **Deir-el-Bahri.**

Derème (dę.rem), **Tristan.** [Pseudonym of **Philippe Huc.**] b. at Marmande, France, 1889; d. at Oloron, France, 1941. French poet. Author of *Petits poèmes* (1910), *La Flute fleurie* (1913), *Le poème de la pipe et de l'escargot* (1920), *Le Livre de Clymène* (1928), and others. Regarded as a superior technician but prone to write on inconsequential subjects, he is generally classified as a continuer of the "bohemian" tradition of Verlaine.

Derenbourg (dę.räṅ.bör), **Hartwig.** b. at Paris, June 17, 1844; d. there, 1908. French Orientalist; son of Joseph Derenbourg. He studied at Göttingen and Leipzig, Germany, assisted in editing the catalogue of Arabic manuscripts at the Bibliothèque Nationale at Paris, in 1875 became teacher and in 1879 professor of Arabic at the École Spéciale des Langues Orientales Vivantes, and in 1886 professor at the École Pratique des Hautes Études. Among his published works are *Le Dîwân de Nâbiqa Dhobyânî* (1869), *Chrestomathie élémentaire de l'arabe littéraire* (1885), and *Oumâra du Yémen* (1897).

Derenbourg, Joseph (Naftali). b. at Mayence, France (now Mainz, Germany), 1811; d. at Ems, Germany, July 29, 1895. French Orientalist. He supervised the government's printing of various Oriental works. After 1877 he was professor of Hebrew language and literature at the École Pratique des Hautes Études. In 1871 he became a chevalier of the Legion of Honor. Derenbourg was one of the leaders of the Jewish community in France, especially interesting himself in Jewish education. He was the author of *Essai sur l'histoire et la géographie de la Palestine d'après les Talmuds et les autres sources rabbiniques* (1867), *Deux versions hébraïques du livre de Kalilâh et Dimnâh*, editions of Lokman and Hariri, and other works, and with his son Hartwig edited a volume of the *Corpus Inscriptionem Semiticarum* (1889–92).

Derennes (dę.ren), **Charles.** b. at Villeneuve-sur-Lot, France, 1882; d. 1930. French poet and novelist. He was the author of numerous light novels, such as *Les Caprices de Nouché* (1909) and *Gaby mon amour* (1925), as well as several volumes of verse. His notoriety stems from his study of gambling, *La Fortune et le jeu* (1926), and his volume on famous cuckolds, *Les Cocus célèbres* (1927).

De Republica (dē rę.pub′li.ką). [Eng. trans., *"Of the Republic."*] Philosophical political treatise in six books, by Cicero, in the form of a dialogue between Africanus the younger (in whose gardens the scene is laid), C. Laelius, and others. The theme is the best form of government and the duty of the citizen. It was written c54–51 B.C. About one third of it has survived.

De rerum natura (dē rē′rum ną.tū′rą). [Eng. trans., *"Of the Nature of Things."*] Didactic poem by Lucretius. Written just before Lucretius's death in 55 B.C., the poem is one of the monuments of Roman literature, an exposition of things as they are in the world as viewed by an Epicurean. Lucretius discusses superstition, the nature of matter and of the universe, atoms, the mind, mortality, the senses, dreams, sex, the earth, man and society, and the phenomena of nature in the sky and on earth. It is in six books.

Derfflinger (der′fling.ėr), **Georg von.** b. at Neuhofen, Upper Austria, March 10, 1606; d. at Gusow, near Küstrin, Prussia, Feb. 4, 1695. Brandenburg general in the Thirty Years' War. He served at the battles of Warsaw (1656) and Fehrbellin (1675) and in the campaign against the Swedes (1678–79).

Derg (dėrg), **Lough.** Lake (formed by an expansion of the river Shannon) partially separating Connacht province from Munster province, in the Irish Republic. It forms part of the County Galway-County Tipperary and County Clare-County Tipperary boundaries. Length, ab. 24 mi.; greatest width, ab. 4 mi.

Derg, Lough. Lake in Ulster province, Irish Republic, in County Donegal ab. 8 mi. E of Donegal. It contains a shrine, Saint Patrick's Purgatory, situated at first on Saint's Island, but now on Station Island. Length, ab. 3 mi.; width, ab. 3 mi.

Derham (dėr′ąm), **William.** b. at Stoulton, near Worcester, England, Nov. 26, 1657; d. at Upminster, near London, April 5, 1735. English divine and natural philosopher. His chief works are *Physico-Theology* (1713), *Astro-Theology* (1715), and *Christo-Theology* (1730).

De Ridder (dę rid′ėr). City in S Louisiana, parish seat of Beauregard Parish: center of a grain and citrus-fruit farming region. Turpentine and resin are also produced. 5,799 (1950).

Derketo (dėr′kę.tō). See **Derceto.**

d'Erlanger (der.läṅ.zhā), **Frédéric.** See **Erlanger, Frédéric d'.**

Derleth (dėr′lęth), **August William.** b. at Sauk City, Wis., Feb. 24, 1909—. American writer and editor.

Among his books are *Murder Stalks the Wakely Family* (1934), *Place of Hawks* (1935), *Wind Over Wisconsin* (1938), *Atmosphere of Houses* (1940), *The Milwaukee Road* (1947), and others; editor of H. P. Lovecraft's *Beyond the Wall of Sleep* (1943), *20 Masterpieces of Horror for the Connoisseur* (1944), and other books.

Dermody (dėr'mọ.di), **Thomas.** b. at Ennis, County Clare, Ireland, in January, 1775; d. at Sydenham (now part of London), July 15, 1802. Irish poet. He published *Poems* (1792), *Poems, Moral and Descriptive* (1800), and *Poems on Various Subjects* (1802). His works were published as *The Harp of Erin* in 1807.

Dermot (dėr'mọt), **Jessie.** Original name of **Elliott, Maxine.**

Dermott (dėr'mọt). City in SE Arkansas, in Chicot County: rail shipping point; sawmills. 3,601 (1950).

Dern (dėrn), **George Henry.** b. at Hooper, Neb., Sept. 8, 1872; d. at Washington, D.C., Aug. 27, 1936. American politician and inventor, U.S. secretary of war from 1933 to 1936. He attended Nebraska State University, leaving school in 1895 to migrate to Utah, where he joined the Mercur Gold Mining and Milling Company, of which he later served as general manager (1901–13). Together with Theodore P. Holt, he invented the Holt-Dern ore roaster for the treatment of low-grade silver ores, and also took part in the development of a vacuum slime-filtration process evolved by George Moore. He helped place both of these on a commercial basis. He became (1915) a member of the Utah legislature, where he sponsored liberal labor legislation and an act for the regulation of public utilities. He was elected (1924) governor of Utah, thus becoming the second non-Mormon to hold that office. He was reëlected in 1928 and in 1933 was appointed secretary of war by President F. D. Roosevelt. He held the post until his death.

Derna (der'nạ). [Also, **Derne.**] Coastal town in Libya, N Africa, in the territory of Cyrenaica, formerly the capital of Derna province in the old Italian colony of Libya. It is situated on the Mediterranean shore W of Tobruk and E of Bengasi, and is connected with both of these points by the coast highway. It was the scene of bitter fighting between the Germans and the British in World War II. 21,547 (1938).

Dernburg (dern'bůrk), **Bernhard.** b. at Darmstadt, Germany, July 17, 1865; d. 1937. German economist and politician. He belonged to a distinguished German-Jewish family (the French branch changed the spelling of the name to Derenbourg). He began his career as banker, and served as director (1906–10) of the colonial department of the foreign office; a vigorous defender of the government's colonial policies. He was a leading member (1919 *et seq.*) of the Democratic Party, and was minister of finance from April to June, 1919.

Dernier Chouan (der.nyā shwäṅ), **Le.** Original title of **Chouans, Les.**

Deronda (dẹ.ron'dạ), **Daniel.** The hero of George Eliot's novel *Daniel Deronda*. He is Jewish, and when he discovers his parentage he resolves to devote his whole life to restoring the Jewish nation to its lost political position.

De Rongé Island (dẹ rôṅ.zhā'). [Also, **Rouge Island.**] High, rugged island in Antarctica, largest island of the group which forms the W side of Errera Channel along the Danco Coast, in ab. 64°42′ S., 62°36′ W. Length, ab. 5 mi.; width, ab. 2½ mi.

Déroulède (dā.rö.led), **Paul.** b. at Paris, Sept. 2, 1846; d. at Mont-Boron, near Nice, France, Jan. 30, 1914. French writer and politician, best known for his vigorous opposition to the third French republic. He was exiled (1900) for ten years for plotting against the safety of the state, but was granted amnesty in 1905. A founder of the League of Patriots, an ultra-nationalist group of which he was president (1886–1908), he campaigned (1887) for Boulanger, was a deputy (1889–92, 1898–1900), and unsuccessfully tried to organize a military putsch (1899). A playwright and poet, he defended the idea of revenge against Germany in his *Chants du soldat* (1872). His play *La Moabite* (1882) was banned. Among his other works are *Marches et sonneries* (1881), *Chants patriotiques* (1882), *Le Désarmament* (1891), *Chants du paysan* (1894), and the plays *Messire du Guesclin* (1895) and *La mort de Hoche* (1897).

Deroy (dẹ.rwȧ), **Henri.** b. at Paris, June 12, 1900—. French banker, governor of the Crédit Foncier de France, leading French land bank. He was a member of the general council of the Bank of France, president of the board of the Compagnie Internationale des Wagons-Lits et des Grands Express Européens, and director-general of the Caisse des Dépôts et Consignations. He served (1923–35) in the finance ministry.

Derpt (derpt). A former Russian name of **Tartu.**

Derr (der). See **El Dirr.**

Derry (der'i). See also **Londonderry.**

Derry. Town in SE New Hampshire, in Rockingham County, ab. 10 mi. SE of Manchester: manufactures of shoes, textiles, and clothing. 5,826 (1950).

Derry. Borough in SW Pennsylvania, in Westmoreland County near Johnstown. 3,752 (1950).

Dertona (dėr.tō'nạ). Latin name of **Tortona,** Italy.

Dertosa (dėr.tō'sạ). Latin name of **Tortosa,** Spain.

Derwent (dėr'wẹnt). Name of several rivers in England, as follows: **1.** River in NW England, in Cumberland, which flows into Solway Firth on the Irish Sea, ab. 7 mi. N of Whitehaven. Length, ab. 33 mi. **2.** River in N central England, in Derbyshire, which joins the Trent ab. 7 mi. SE of Derby. It is noted for its scenery. Length, ab. 60 mi. **3.** River in NE England, in Northumberland and Durham, which flows NE to the Tyne ab. 3 mi. W of Gateshead. Length, ab. 30 mi. **4.** River in NE England, in the North Riding of Yorkshire, rising ab. 6 mi. S of Whitby and flowing S to the Ouse, ab. 15 mi. SE of York. Length, ab. 57 mi.

Derwent. River in Tasmania at the mouth of which is situated the capital city of Hobart. The river empties into Storm Bay. Length, ab. 130 mi.

Derwentwater or **Derwent Water** (dėr'wẹnt.wô.tėr, -wot.ėr). One of the chief lakes in the Lake District in NW England, in Cumberland, lying directly S of Keswick. It is an expansion of the river Derwent. Length, 3 mi.; width, ab. 1 mi.; elevation, ab. 244 ft.

Derwentwater, 3rd Earl of. Title of **Radcliffe** or **Radclyffe, Sir James.**

Derzhavin (dir.zhä'vin), **Gavriil Romanovich.** b. at Kazan, Russia, July 14, 1743; d. at Svanka, near Novgorod, Russia, July 21, 1816. Russian lyric poet. His best-known poem outside Russia is *Ode to God* (1784), besides which he wrote *Felicia, Monody on Prince Mestcherski, The Nobleman, The Taking of Ismail, The Taking of Warsaw*, and others. His works were published 1810–15.

Dés (dāsh). See **Dej.**

Desaguadero (des"ä.gwä.ᴛʜä'rō). River in W Bolivia, the outlet of Lake Titicaca, which flows into Lake Poopó. Length, ab. 160 mi.

Desaguadero Basin. See **Titicaca Basin.**

Desaix de Veygoux (dẹ.ze dẹ vā.gö), **Louis Charles Antoine.** b. at St.-Hilaire-d'Ayat, near Riom, Puy-de-Dôme, France, Aug. 17, 1768; killed at Marengo, Italy, June 14, 1800. French general. He served in the battle of the Pyramids (1798), conquered Upper Egypt (1798–99), and decided the victory at Marengo.

De Sanctis (dā sängk'tēs), **Francesco.** b. at Morra Irpina, Avellino province, Italy, 1817; d. 1883. Italian literary historian, critic, educator, and patriot. From 1838 to 1848 he conducted a private school of literary studies, rejecting the aloof and romantic tendencies of those times, and insisting that students and teachers of literature must take account of contemporaneous life and its problems. He led his pupils in support of the 1848 revolution at Naples, and after its failure was imprisoned by the Bourbon regime for more than two years without trial, being finally released in the expectation that he would go into exile in America; but he made his way to Turin, where he became one of the circle of liberals who were planning national unification. Accepting a professorship of literature at Zurich, Switzerland, in 1856, he won a large following with his lectures. When the hour for action in Italy came, he resigned his professorial chair and proceeded to Naples, where Garibaldi appointed him governor of his native province of Avellino, in 1860. In the following year he entered Cavour's cabinet as minister of education, holding office at that time for one year only, but accepting the same post on two later occasions (1878 and 1879–81). During the years preceding complete unification of Italy, he called tirelessly for the extension of education and preached the responsibility of citizens to be worthy of the new nation. From 1871 to 1878 he was professor of comparative literature at the University of Naples. Apart from his political writings and career, De Sanctis is widely considered one of the greatest of Italian literary critics, and indeed one of the foremost critics of modern times regardless of country or nationality. He had the faculty of perceiving greatness in a work of literary art and of arousing others to share his perceptions. His most influential works are *Saggi critici* (Critical Essays, 1866), *Storia della letteratura italiana* (History of Italian Literature, 1871), and *Nuovi Saggi critici* (New Critical Essays, 1872).

Desargues (dę.zärg), **Gérard.** b. at Lyons, France, 1593; d. there, 1662. French army officer, engineer, and architect, one of the earliest mathematicians to develop the theory of conic sections from the point of view of projective geometry. His classic treatise, *Brouillon project d'une atteinte aux événements des rencontres d'un cône avec un plan,* appeared in 1639, but it was long overlooked. His *Œuvres* were published in two volumes in 1864.

Désaugiers (dā.zō.zhyā), **Marc Antoine.** b. at Fréjus, 1742; d. at Paris, Sept. 10, 1793. French composer of light operas. He also wrote the cantata *Hiérodrama* in celebration of the fall of the Bastille, and composed a requiem (1786).

Désaugiers, Marc Antoine Madeleine. b. at Fréjus, France, Nov. 17, 1772; d. at Paris, Aug. 9, 1827. French song writer and author of vaudevilles; son of Marc Antoine Désaugiers.

Desault (dę.zō), **Pierre Joseph.** b. at Magny-Vernois, Haute-Saône, France, Feb. 6, 1744; d. at Paris, June 1, 1795. French surgeon and anatomist.

Desbarres (dā.bär'), **Joseph Frederick Walsh** (or **Wallet**). [Also, **Des Barres.**] b. 1722; d. at Halifax, Nova Scotia, Oct. 24, 1824. English officer and hydrographer. He published *Atlantic Neptune* (1777), and others.

Desbordes-Valmore (dā.bôrd.vål.môr), **Marceline Félicité Josèphe.** [Maiden name, **Desbordes.**] b. at Douai, France, June 20, 1786; d. July 23, 1859. French poet and singer; wife (married 1817) of the actor François Prosper Lanchantin, who was called Valmore. Her poetry is distinguished for sweetness and pathos, without affectation. She was the author of *Élégies et romances* (1818) and *Élégies et poésies nouvelles* (1824).

Desborough (dez'bėr.ǫ), **Colonel.** "Brutally ignorant" brother-in-law of Cromwell in Sir Walter Scott's novel *Woodstock.*

Desborough or **Desborow** (dez'bėr.ǫ, -brǫ) or **Disbrowe** (diz'brǫ), **John.** b. 1608; d. at Hackney (now part of London), 1680. English military officer. He served as major during the battles of Langport (July 10, 1645), Hambleton Hill (Aug. 4, 1645), and the storming of Bristol (Sept. 10, 1645), where he commanded the regiment of horse. He was made colonel in 1648 and major general at Worcester (1651), and was chosen (1653) one of four generals of the fleet. In 1657 he was a member of Cromwell's privy council. He was imprisoned (1660) in the Tower of London on suspicion of having plotted to kill Charles II and Queen Henrietta Maria.

Desbruères (dā.brü.er), **Henri.** b. at St.-Hilaire-en-Morvan, Nièvre, France, April 15, 1907—. French airline executive, general manager of the Compagnie Nationale Air-France. He was graduated from the École Polytechnique and served (1932 *et seq.*) as a French air-force engineer.

Descabezado Grande (des.kä.ʙä.sä'ᴛʜō grän'dā). Inactive volcano in C Chile. Elevation, ab. 12,750 ft.

Descartes (dā.kärt'; French, dā.kårt), **René.** b. at La Haye, France, March 31, 1596; d. at Stockholm, Feb. 11, 1650. French philosopher and mathematician. He graduated at the age of 17 from the Jesuit college of La Flèche and later studied at the University of Poitiers, saw some brief military service, lived for a time at Paris, and spent several years in travel, visiting Germany, Italy, Holland, and Poland, studying and seeking knowledge. In 1628 he was at the siege of La Rochelle as a volunteer, but the following year he took up residence in Holland, where he lived a retired life, busily engaged, however, in elaborating and defending his philosophy and formulating his mathematical system, until 1649 when upon the invitation of Queen Christina of Sweden he went to Stockholm, only to die there of pneumonia five months later. He had been marked as a modern philosopher to be reckoned with since the publication in 1637 of his brief treatise entitled *Discours de la méthode.* The theories there set forth he supported in three essays, *La Dioptrique, Les Météores,* and *La Géométrie.* Others of his works published during his lifetime were *Meditationes de prima philosophia* (1641), *Principia philosophiae* (1644), *Traité des passions de l'âme* (1649), as well as a polemical pamphlet (1643) entitled *Epistola Renati Descartes ad Gisbertum Voëitium.* After his death his friends published his *De l'homme, Traité de la formation du fœtus, Le Monde ou traité de la lumière de Descartes* (all of the forgoing appearing in 1664), and a collection of his letters, issued between 1657 and 1667. In 1701 appeared, finally, *Opuscula posthuma, physica et mathematica.* Descartes was one of the great mathematicians of all times, adding much to the theories of algebra and geometry. His philosophical methodology was an attempt to extend the mathematical approach to all fields of human thought and investigation. His name still looms large in the history of philosophy, and his influence remains great. Rejecting scholasticism, he based his speculations upon pure reason, his point of basic approach being derived from his famous axiom, *Cogito, ergo sum* ("I think, therefore I am."). Willing to take nothing for granted (the point of the axiom cited above is, of course, that it enabled Descartes safely to assume his own existence), he proceeds to proof of the existence of God, and from that to a demonstration of the reality of the material world. Between the material world and the mind or soul he posits a complete gulf, which can be bridged only by the direct intervention of God. Writing at a time when speculation could take its stand upon pure reason (still within the framework of Roman Catholic theology) his system inevitably diminished in authority with the rise, beginning a century or so after his death, of the natural sciences as they have since come to be understood.

Descaves (dā.kåv), **Lucien.** b. at Paris, March 18, 1861; d. Sept. 6, 1949. French journalist, novelist, and dramatist of the naturalist school. He was the author of the novel *Sous-Offs* (1889) and other satires of military life, *Les Emmurés* (1894), *La Colonne* (1902), *Barabbas* (1914), and *L'Imagier d'Épinal* (1919). His dramas, almost invariably written in collaboration and less successful than his fiction, include *La Pelote* (1889), *Les Chapons* (1890), *Le Cœur ébloui* (1926), and *Les Fruits de l'amour* (1928). Originally a declared naturalist, he revolted against Zola with the other signers of *La Manifeste des Cinq;* his later writings evolve toward a much milder manner than that of his early work. He became literary editor of *Le Journal* in 1892; later served *L'Intransigeant* in the same capacity; was elected to the Goncourt Academy in 1900 and became its president in 1944.

Descent from the Cross. Subject of many religious paintings in the Renaissance and subsequent periods in the history of art. The traditional content of these pictures, with figures lifting down the dead body of Christ and mourners grouped at the foot of the Cross, gave painters scope for great variety and force in their compositions. Because paintings in these periods were most often designed for the walls or altarpieces of churches they were not marked with specific titles and the same work is sometimes known by several names. Most art historians agree, however, in designating a given picture of the actual removal of Christ's body as a *Descent,* or *Deposition, from the Cross,* while a portrayal of the mourners grouped on the ground around the dead Christ, while sometimes known by one of these titles, is more often called a *Pietà,* from the Italian word for "pity." Among the best-known *Descents* are: **1.** Painting (1504) by Sodoma (Giovanni Antonio Bazzi), in the Academy at Siena, Italy. The group of mourning women is especially admired for the beauty of its conception and execution. **2.** Painting by Paolo Cavazzola, in the Pinacoteca at Verona. It unites the naturalism of the 15th century with the freedom of the following period. With its companion pieces, the *Bearing of the Cross* and the *Agony in the Garden,* it has been called the painter's masterpiece. **3.** Painting by Correggio, in the Pinacoteca at Parma, Italy. **4.** [Also, **Deposition from the Cross.**] Painting by Rubens (1614), by some critics considered his masterpiece, in Antwerp cathedral, Belgium. The body has been detached and is being lowered by men on ladders; it is received below by Saint John, beside whom kneel Mary Salome and the Magdalen. The Virgin stands behind.

Descent into the Maelström, A. Story by Edgar Allan Poe, published (1841) in *Graham's Magazine* and included in the *Prose Tales of Edgar A. Poe* (1843).

Descent of Man, The. Scientific work (1871) by Charles Darwin. It is a further exposition of the theory of evolution, previously presented and explained by Darwin in his *Origin of Species* (1859), which caused a scientific and intellectual revolution when it appeared. The *Descent* is as important, as scientific, and as careful a work as the earlier one, but a dozen years makes a difference, and the work aroused nothing like the anger and excitement and resentment that greeted the *Origin of Species*.

Deschamps (dā.shäṅ), **Émile.** [Full name, **Émile Deschamps de Saint Amand.**] b. at Bourges, France, Feb. 20, 1791; d. at Versailles, France, in April, 1871. French poet.

Deschamps, Eustache. [Called **Morel Deschamps.**] b. at Vertus, in Champagne (now in Marne department), France, in the first part of the 14th century; d. early in the 15th century. French poet and author of ballades (1,175 in number), rondeaux (171), virelais (80), a long poem, the *Miroir de mariage*, and *L'Art de dictier et de fere chancons, balades, virelais et rondeaulx* (a treatise on French rhetoric and prosody).

Deschamps, Gaston. [Full name, **Charles Pierre Gaston Napoléon Deschamps.**] b. at Melle, France, Jan. 5, 1861; d. 1931. French journalist and literary critic of marked conservative tendencies. His best criticism is preserved in *La Vie et les livres* (6 vols., 1894–1904).

Deschanel (dā.shȧ.nel), **Émile Auguste Étienne Martin.** b. Nov. 14, 1819; d. Jan. 26, 1904. French writer and journalist. He was appointed (1842) professor of rhetoric at Bourges, and shortly after occupied the same chair at Paris. He entered journalism as a liberal, and was imprisoned and exiled in 1851. He returned to Paris in 1859, and became one of the editors of the *Journal des Débats*. In 1876 he was elected to the Chamber of Deputies as a republican, and in 1881 was elected a senator for life. He published a number of anthologies with comments, *Les Courtisanes grecques*, *Le Mal qu'on a dit des femmes*, *Le Bien qu'on a dit des femmes* (1855–58), *La Vie des comédiens* (1860), *Études sur Aristophane* (1867), *Le Peuple et la bourgeoisie* (1881), and *Benjamin Franklin* (1882). From 1882 to 1886 he published his lectures at the Collège de France, called *Le Romantisme des classiques*, much enlarged and revised.

Deschanel, Paul Eugène Louis. b. at Brussels, Belgium, Feb. 13, 1856; d. at Paris, April 28, 1922. French statesman and author, tenth president of the third French republic; son of Émile Auguste Étienne Martin Deschanel. He was secretary (1876–77) to two ministers of the interior, de Marcère and Simon, and after filling various minor offices was elected to the Chamber of Deputies in 1885, of which he was president (1898–1902, 1912 *et seq.*). He was elected to the presidency of the republic in 1920. He resigned because of ill health (September, 1920), was elected (1921) to the senate, and died from injuries caused in a fall from a railroad car. He was named a member of the French Academy in 1899 and of the Academy of Moral Sciences in 1918. His published work includes *La Question du Tonkin* (1883), *La Politique français en Océanie* (1884), *Les Intérêts française dans le Pacifique* (1885), *Orateurs et hommes d'état* (1888; crowned by the French Academy), *Figures de femmes* (1889; also crowned), *Figures littéraires* (1889), *Questions actuelles*, a collection of his principal speeches (1891), *La Décentralisation* (1895), *La Question sociale* (1898), *Quatre ans de présidence* (1902), *Politique intérieure et étrangère* (1906), and *À l'institut* (1907).

Deschapelles (dā.shȧ.pel), **Louis Honoré Lebreton.** b. 1780; d. 1847. French whist and chess player. He was considered the strongest chess master of his time, giving odds to all players and beating them. It is said that when one of his pupils grew strong enough to play him at an even game, Deschapelles retired (c1821) from chess and took up whist instead. The Deschapelles coup, the lead of a high card to lose it so that partner's cards may win tricks, is named for him. He published a treatise on whist in 1839.

Deschutes (dā.shöt'). River in C and N Oregon, rising in the Cascade Range and flowing generally N to join the Columbia River ab. 15 mi. E of The Dalles, Ore. The lower course of the Deschutes, descending from the lava plateau to the Columbia valley, flows in a deep gorge, and has many falls and rapids. Length, ab. 320 mi.

Desclée (dā.klā), **Aimée Olympe.** b. Nov. 18, 1836; d. at Paris, March 9, 1874. French actress. She excelled in the dramas *Frou-Frou, Diane de Lys,* and other plays popular in her day.

Description of New England, A. Narrative of colonial settlement and exploration by Captain John Smith (1580–1631), published in 1616.

Desdemona (dez.dẹ.mō'nạ). In Shakespeare's tragedy *Othello*, the wife of Othello the Moor, and the daughter of Brabantio, a Venetian senator. Othello smothers her in an outburst of rage produced by a belief in her unfaithfulness, carefully instilled by Iago.

Desdén con el desdén (dez.dān' kōn el dez.dān'), **El.** [Eng. trans., *"Disdain Met with Disdain."*] Play by Augustín Moreto y Cavaña (1618–69), adapted from episodes in the plays of Lope de Vega. It is not known when it was first produced, but it is still played, and is one of the four classical pieces of the older Spanish drama. Under the title of *Donna Diana* it is familiar in Germany, and in 1864 John Westland Marston produced it under the same name in England, his version being a translation of that of Schreyvogel. Molière's version, *La Princesse d'Élide*, was a failure. Count Carlo Gozzi produced it in Italian as *La Principessa Filosofa o il Contraveleno* (The Philosophical Princess or the Antidote).

Desdichado (des.di.chä'dō). In Sir Walter Scott's novel *Ivanhoe*, the device, meaning "The Disinherited," assumed by Ivanhoe in the tournament at Ashby.

Deseada (dā.sā.ä'dä). See **Désirade.**

De senectute (dē sen.ek.tū'tē). [Eng. trans., *"On Old Age"*; also, **Cato Major.**] Short treatise by Cicero, in the form of a conversation, devoted to the praise (in the person of Cato the censor) of old age. It was written in 45 or 44 B.C.

Desenzano del Garda (dā.sen.tsä'nō del gär'dä). [Also, **Desenzano.**] Town and commune in N Italy, in the *compartimento* (region) of Lombardy, in the province of Brescia, situated at the S end of Lake Garda, ab. 16 mi. SE of Brescia. It is a station on the railroad line from Verona to Milan. Buildings of interest to tourists, including the medieval castle, were undamaged in World War II. Pop. of commune, 10,360 (1936); of town, 5,058 (1936).

Deseret (dez.ėr.et'). See under **Utah.**

Desertas (dā.ser'täs). [Also, **Las Desertas.**] Group of small islands in the Atlantic, lying SE of Madeira.

Deserted Village, The. Poem by Oliver Goldsmith, begun in 1768 and published in 1770. It is a version in rhymed couplets of the popular declamation of the time against luxury and the depopulation of the countryside as the result of the siren call of industrial wages.

Desert of Zin (zin). See **Zin, Desert of.**

Desert Places. Short nature poem by Robert Frost. It appears in *A Further Range* (1936), in which volume it is the second poem in the grouping "Taken Singly." It is also to be found in his *Collected Poems* (1949), and in various anthologies. Its opening line is "Snow falling and night falling fast, oh, fast."

de Seversky (dẹ sẹ.ver'ski), **Alexander Procofieff.** b. at Tiflis, Russia, June 7, 1894—. American aviator and aeronautical engineer. He came to the U.S. in 1918 and became a naturalized citizen in 1927. He was founder (1931) and president (1931–39) of the Seversky Aircraft Corporation, pursuit plane manufacturers, and the inventor of various airplane devices, including a fully automatic bombsight which was bought by the U.S. His designs include the single-seater, low-winged fighter plane (1936) which was accepted as the U.S. army standard. In 1935 he broke the world's speed record for amphibious aircraft. He has served as personal representative of the U.S. secretary of war at the Bikini atom bomb tests (1946) and as a columnist (1943–44) on air power for the McNaught Syndicate, and is the author of *Victory*

Through Air Power (1942) and *Air Power; Key to Survival* (1950).

Desfontaines (dā.fôṅ.ten), **René Louiche.** b. at Tremblay, Ille-et-Vilaine, France, Feb. 14, 1750; d. at Paris, Nov. 16, 1833. French botanist. His chief work is *Flora Atlantica* (1798–1800).

Desful (des.föl′). See **Dizful.**

Desgraviers (dā.grȧ.vyā), **François Marceau-.** See **Marceau, François Séverin des Graviers.**

Deshayes (dā.ā), **Gérard Paul.** b. at Nancy, France, May 13, 1795; d. at Boiran, Oise, France, June 9, 1875. French naturalist, especially known as a paleontologist. Among his works are *Description des coquillages fossiles des environs de Paris* (1824–37), *Traité élémentaire de conchyliologie* (1839–58), and *Description des animaux sans vertèbres découverts dans le bassin de Paris* (1857–65).

De-shima (de.shē.mä). See under **Nagasaki.**

Deshoulières (dā.zö.lyer), **Antoinette du Ligier de la Garde.** b. at Paris, Jan. 1, 1638; d. there, Feb. 17, 1694. French poet. She was the author of verse, for the most part of the occasional order (idyls, odes, elegiacs, and songs) and of two unsuccessful tragedies.

Desiderio da Settignano (dā.sē.dā′ryō dä sät.tē.nyä′nō). b. at Settignano, near Florence, Italy, c1428; d. 1464. Florentine sculptor. He was accepted as a member of the stonecutters' guild of Florence in 1453, and in 1455 executed the tomb of Carlo Marsuppini in the Church of Santa Croce at that city. This is perhaps his greatest achievement, but his tabernacle in the Florentine Church of San Lorenzo is also accounted a masterpiece. In his brief career he mastered an unsurpassed delicacy, displayed in his busts and reliefs of women and children and in the decorative details of his monumental works, so that he is considered one of the great sculptors of the Renaissance. He was strongly influenced by Donatello. Examples of Desiderio's art are to be seen in the National Gallery of Art at Washington, and in the Institute of Art at Detroit.

Desiderius (des.i.dir′i.us). Last king of the Lombards; reigned 756–774. He was Duke of Tuscany when he was chosen to be king. Pepin the Short, his backer in the succession to the throne, married Desiderius's daughter to his son Charles, who came to the Frankish throne in 771. Charles, later to be known as Charlemagne, was appealed to by Pope Adrian I when Desiderius attempted to extend the Lombard domains to include papal lands. Charles sent his daughter back to Desiderius and, when Desiderius also refused to recognize Charles's dominion over the Franks, supporting his brother Carloman's children, Charles crossed (773) the Alps, captured Ticinum (now Pavia) after a siege in 774, and sent Desiderius off to spend the rest of his life in a French monastery.

Desiderius, Abbot. See Pope **Victor III.**

Desiderius, Father. Religious name of **Lenz, Peter.**

Desierto (dā.syer′tō). Spanish word for "desert": for places including this word in their names, see the specific elements of the names.

Design for Living. Comedy (1933) by Noel Coward. The main characters are three Bohemians (in spirit, not in nationality), and the three acts take place in Otto's Paris studio, in Leo's London flat, a year and a half later, and in Ernest's New York apartment, two years later. The feminine interest is supplied by Gilda, who finds that she cannot live without Otto and Leo, just as they in their turn find that they cannot live without her, or each other.

Desima (de.shē.mä). See under **Nagasaki.**

Desio (de′zyō). Town and commune in NW Italy, in the *compartimento* (region) of Lombardy, in the province of Milano, N of Milan. It is an important industrial center, with a number of silk and woolen textile establishments, shoe factories, and others. Pop. of commune, 13,499 (1936); of town, 11,788 (1936).

Désir (dā.zēr), **Le.** French title of **Trauerwalzer.**

Désirade (dā.zē.rȧd). [Also: **Deseada, La Désirade.**] Island in the Caribbean Sea, ab. 9 mi. E of Guadeloupe: a French colony. The production of cotton and henequen, and the raising of sheep are the major industries. It has an important leprosarium. Area, ab. 10 sq. mi.; pop. ab. 2,000.

Desire Under the Elms. Play by Eugene O'Neill, produced and published in 1924. The 75-year-old Ephraim Cabot, living complacently under an inflexible Puritanical code, marries a third wife, Abbie Putnam. In order to have an heir to Ephraim's money, Abbie seduces his stepson, Eben. Abbie develops a genuine attachment to her lover but, when Eben discovers her greedy purpose, he rejects her. The enraged and remorseful Abbie murders their child. Eben tells the police of Abbie's crime but, in the end, his love for her reawakened, he willingly surrenders himself with Abbie.

Desjardins (dā.zhȧr.daṅ), **Marie Catherine Hortense.** [Pseudonym, Madame **de Villedieu.**] b. near Fougères, France, 1631; d. there, in November, 1683. French writer and author of numerous works, among which are *Les Désordres de l'amour, Amours des grands hommes, Mémoires du serail,* and *Le Récit en prose et en vers des précieuses.*

Desjardins, Paul. b. at Paris, 1859; d. 1940. French essayist and critic, founder (1910) of the internationally famous intellectual conferences at Pontigny, France. He was the author of *Le Devoir présent* (1891; Eng. trans., *The Present Duty,* 1893) and other essays. His written work is less important than his initiation of what is now called "Moral Rearmament." He founded (1892) the Ligue pour l'Action Morale and influenced two generations in France by his constant affirmation of the necessity of spiritual values among men of good will.

Des Knaben Wunderhorn (dẹs knä′bẹn vůn′dėr.hôrn). See **Wunderhorn.**

Desmarets or **Desmaretz** (dā.mȧ.rā), **Jean.** [Title, Sieur **de Saint-Sorlin.**] b. at Paris, 1595; d. there, Oct. 28, 1676. French dramatist and poet. In the 1630's he became one of the coterie who gathered around Valentin Conrart, and with others of that circle he was a founder of the French Academy, and was its first chancellor. Richelieu became his patron, and it was at the great cardinal's request that he turned to the writing of plays. The comedy *Les Visionnaires* (1637) is considered his masterwork, but his tragedies *Érigone* and *Scipione* were admired in their time. In the controversies between the literary factions known as the Ancients and the Moderns, Desmarets energetically enlisted with the latter, for which he was censured by Boileau. In his later years he wrote religious poetry, and published a polemic against the Jansenists.

Desmarets, Nicolas. [Title, Marquis **de Maillebois**]. b. at Paris, Sept. 10, 1648; d. 1721. French statesman; nephew of Jean Baptiste Colbert (1619–83). He rose to high rank in the financial administration under Colbert's patronage, but was dismissed after the latter's death, only to be recalled to office in 1686. Time and again in memoranda prepared for various controllers-general he analyzed the rapidly degenerating economic position of the country, and when he became controller-general in 1708 he attempted to save the situation by a scheme of income taxes similar to proposals made by Vauban, but the privileged classes and the tax-farmers were able virtually to nullify this attempt. After the death of Louis XIV, Desmarets was removed from his post, and retired from public affairs.

Desmas (dez′mạs). See **Dismas.**

De Smet (dẹ smet′), **Pierre Jean.** [Called **"Blackrobe."**] b. at Termonde, Belgium, Jan. 30, 1801; d. May 23, 1873. Jesuit missionary in America. He arrived in the U.S. in 1821 and between 1821 and 1827 trained at Jesuit novitiates at Whitemarsh, Md., and Florissant, Mo. Ordained in 1827, he became a missionary to the Indians, serving (1838–40) at St. Joseph, Mo. He traveled widely in the U.S. and abroad to survey missionary possibilities and solicit support. Considered an effective mediator with the Indians, he attended (1851) the great council near Fort Laramie and mediated in the Mormon and Yakima Indian wars. He visited (1868) the hostile chief Sitting Bull, making peace eventually possible.

Des Moines (dẹ moin′). City in C Iowa, capital of Iowa and county seat of Polk County, on the Des Moines River: largest city in the state. Its industries produce meat products, cement, flour, tile, bricks, clothing, hosiery, wool textiles, cosmetics, leather, and grain and dairy products. Settled in 1843 as a military post and two years later as a town, it became the capital in 1858. It is the seat of Drake University. 177,965 (1950).

Des Moines River. River in Iowa which rises in SW Minnesota, and joins the Mississippi at the SE extremity of Iowa, ab. 4 mi. below Keokuk. Length, from the union of the east and west forks (in Humboldt County, Iowa), ab. 300 mi.; total length, ab. 500 mi.; navigable to the city of Des Moines.

Desmond (dez′mǫnd). Ancient kingdom in SW Ireland, comprising the region now included in County Cork and County Kerry, Irish Republic. It was created c200 A.D. by the division of Munster, but was merely a loose federation of local chiefs under a ruler. In the 12th century, the MacCarthys became kings of Desmond, and ruled until the 16th century. The earldom of Desmond was created in 1329, and went out of existence in 1583, as a political unit.

"Desmond." See **MacCarthy, Denis Florence.**

Desmond, Shaw. b. in County Waterford, Ireland, Jan. 19, 1877—. Irish novelist and poet, founder (1934) of the International Institute for Psychical Research. He is the author of *The Soul of Denmark* (1918), *Democracy* (1919), *Passion* (1920), *The Drama of Sinn Fein* (1923), *The Isle of Ghosts* (1925), *Ragnarok* (1926), *Windjammer: the Book of the Horn* (1932), *We Do Not Die* (1934), *World Birth* (1937), *Reincarnation for Everyman* (1939), *How you live when you Die* (1942), *The Story of Adam Verity* (1947), and *The Edwardian Story* (1950).

Desmoulins (dā.mö.laṅ), **Camille.** [Full name, **Lucie Simplice Camille Benoît Desmoulins;** called **Procureur de la lanterne.**] b. at Guise in Picardy (now in the department of Aisne), France, March 2, 1760; guillotined at Paris, April 5, 1794. French revolutionist, prominent as a pamphleteer and journalist. In July, 1789 his impassioned harangues contributed powerfully to the popular excitement which culminated in the storming of the Bastille. He was a deputy to the Convention in 1792. He earned his nickname by virtue of his pamphlet directed against the aristocracy, *Le Discours de la lanterne aux Parisiens.* He published the weekly *Les Révolutions de France et de Brabant* from 1789 to 1791, and other pamphlets and papers, attacking the moderate position of the Girondins, but in 1793, in the *Vieux Cordelier*, he supported Danton's softer policy. He was arrested with Danton, given a farcical trial, and was third of the group of 15 to be executed with Danton.

Desmukh (des.mök′), Sir **Chintaman Dwarkanath.** b. 1896—. Indian official, prominent in world economic conferences. Delegate to the world monetary conference (1944) and Indian governor (1946) of the International Monetary Fund and the International Bank, he also served as delegate (1931) to the Round Table Conference, was revenue and financial secretary (1932–39) of the Central Provinces and Berar, secretary (1939–41) to the central board of the Reserve Bank of India, and deputy governor (1941–43) of the bank.

Desna (dyis.nä′). River in W U.S.S.R., in W Russian Soviet Federated Socialist Republic and N Ukrainian Soviet Socialist Republic, rising in the Smolensk Hills and flowing generally S to join the Dnieper ab. 4 mi. above Kiev. The river is navigable for river steamers to Novgorod-Severskii, ab. 337 mi. from its mouth, and, in times of high water, to Bryansk, ab. 512 mi. from its mouth. It has a considerable traffic in timber and wood from the forest regions of the upper river S to the steppe region of the Ukraine. Length, ab. 733 mi.

Desnoyers (dā.nwȧ.yā), **Auguste Gaspard Louis Boucher,** Baron. [Called **Boucher-Desnoyers.**] b. at Paris, Dec. 20, 1779; d. there, in February, 1857. French engraver. His best-known works are copies after Raphael (*La Belle Jardinière* and the *Transfiguration*, and others).

Desolación (dā″sō.lä.syōn′). [English, **Desolation, Desolation Land.**] Island in the Pacific Ocean, off the coast of S Chile, E of Punta Arenas. It has belonged to Chile since 1881. Length, ab. 70 mi.

Desolation Island. See **Kerguelen.**

Desor (dā.zôr′), **Eduard.** b. at Friedrichsdorf, near Homburg, Prussia, Feb. 11, 1811; d. at Nice, France, Feb. 23, 1882. Swiss geologist, zoölogist, and archaeologist.

De Soto (dẹ sō′tō). City in E Missouri, in Jefferson County: shipping point for lead; railroad shops and hat and shoe factories. 5,357 (1950).

de Soto (dẹ sō′tō; Spanish, dā sō′tō), **Hernando.** b. at Barcarrota, Spain, c1500; d. somewhere along the Mississippi River, May 21, 1542. Spanish explorer, noted for his discovery of the Mississippi River. He made his first voyage to Central America at about the age of 19, and later participated (1532 *et seq.*) in the conquest of Peru under Francisco Pizarro and Diego de Almagro. His achievements as a conquistador drew the attention of Charles V of Spain, who gave him (1537) a contract to conquer Florida and made him governor of Cuba, which de Soto reached in 1538. Preparing his expedition of some 1,000 men there, he departed from Havana in 1539, reaching the Florida coast in the vicinity of Charlotte Bay on May 30. Fighting Indians almost all of the way, he led his expedition through what are now the states of Florida, Georgia, North and South Carolina, Tennessee, Alabama, Mississippi, Arkansas, Oklahoma, and Texas, seeking gold and other riches. In April, 1541, he discovered the Mississippi River, probably crossing it below what is now Memphis, Tenn. The expedition penetrated as far west as Oklahoma, and then gave up hope of finding treasure and turned back. De Soto died on the west bank of the Mississippi, to whose waters his followers delivered his remains. The survivors of the company reached Mexico on the Gulf Coast in 1543. See *Narratives of the Career of Hernando de Soto* by E. G. Bourne (2 vols., 1904).

Despair, Giant. Giant in Bunyan's *Pilgrim's Progress* who takes Christian and Hopeful while they are asleep and imprisons them in his dungeons in Doubting Castle. Christian, after three days without food or drink and after being cudgeled regularly, opens the dungeon lock with the key "Promise," and he and Hopeful escape.

Despard (des′pärd, -pạrd), **Edward Marcus.** b. in Queen's County (now County Laoighis), Ireland, 1751; d. Feb. 21, 1803. Irish conspirator. He entered the army in 1766, obtained the rank of captain c1780, and in 1784 was appointed superintendent of his majesty's affairs in the Spanish peninsula of Yucatán. Having been dismissed from this office on a frivolous charge, he organized a conspiracy against the government, in consequence of which he was arrested on Nov. 16, 1802, and hanged at London.

Despencer (dẹs.pen′sėr), 15th Baron **le.** Title of **Dashwood, Francis.**

Despenser (dẹs.pen′sėr), **Edward le.** d. 1375. British knight; grandson of Hugh le Despenser the younger (d. 1326). He fought at Poitiers and in other French campaigns of Edward III of England, and under Pope Urban V. He was a Knight of the Garter and a patron of Jean Froissart, the chronicler.

Despenser, Henry le. [Also, **Spencer.**] b. c1341; d. Aug. 23, 1406. British bishop and soldier, bishop of Norwich (1370). He defeated the Norfolk peasants at North Walsham during the Peasants' Revolt (1381). He led the campaign of Pope Urban VI in Flanders against the antipope Clement VII and won a victory at Dunkerque (1383) and raised the siege of Ypres (1383). He was denounced by Wycliffe for being a soldier and a bishop at the same time. He aided Richard II of England during the French invasion (1385). He suppressed the Lollards. Imprisoned (1399) by Henry IV, for his loyalty to Richard, he later was reconciled (1401) to the new king.

Despenser, Hugh le. d. Aug. 4, 1265. Justiciar of England. He first appears in 1256, when he was entrusted with Harestan Castle, in Derbyshire. The first mention of him as justiciar is found in the Fine Rolls in 1261. He joined the baronial party at the outbreak of the war with Henry III in 1263, and fell in the battle of Evesham.

Despenser, Hugh le. [Called **"the Elder"**; title, Earl of **Winchester.**] b. c1262; d. at Bristol, England, Oct. 27, 1326. English court favorite; son of the justiciar Hugh le Despenser, who fell (1265) in the baronial ranks at Evesham. He was with the king in Gascony in 1294, was present at the battle of Dunbar in 1296, accompanied the expedition to Flanders in 1297, was sent on a mission to Pope Clement V at Lyons in 1305, and was created Earl of Winchester in 1322. On the death of King Edward II's favorite Piers Gaveston in 1312, he became the leader of the court party in opposition to the baronial, and together with his son Hugh le Despenser obtained a complete ascendancy over the king. The unscrupulous manner in which the favorites used their power to further schemes of self-aggrandizement caused them to be banished (1321–22), and brought about a rising of the barons under Queen Isabella in 1326, which ended in the deposition of the king and the execution of the favorites. The elder Despenser was captured at the surrender of Bristol, where he was tried and executed on the charge of treason.

Despenser, Hugh le. [Called **"the Younger."**] d. at Hereford, England, Nov. 24, 1326. English court favorite; son of Hugh le Despenser, Earl of Winchester. He was appointed chamberlain to Edward II in 1313. Originally an adherent of the baronial party, he joined (c1317) his father in the support of the king, and obtained in an especial degree the royal favor. He was banished with his father in 1321, returning with him in 1322. On the rising of the barons under Queen Isabella in 1326, caused by his insolence and self-seeking to a greater degree than even his father's, he fled with Edward from London, on Oct. 2, 1326, but was captured at Llantrisant on Nov. 16, 1326, and was tried and executed at Hereford on the charge of treason.

Despenser, Thomas le. [Title, Earl of **Gloucester.**] b. 1373; beheaded at Bristol, England, 1400. British soldier; son of Edward le Despenser. He was created Earl of Gloucester (1397) for supporting Richard II against Thomas of Woodstock, Earl of Gloucester, Richard Fitzalan, 4th Earl of Arundel, and Thomas Beauchamp, Earl of Warwick. He led the rear guard in Richard's Irish expedition (1399), but lost the earldom (1399) for his part in the death of the duke of Gloucester. He was in conspiracy against Henry IV, but was betrayed (1400) and beheaded at the demand of the people of Bristol (1400).

Desperate Lovers, The. Three-act comedy (1926) by Alfred Sutro.

Despiau (des.pyō), **Charles.** b. at Mont-de-Marsan, Landes, France, Nov. 24, 1874; d. at Paris, Oct. 30, 1946. French sculptor, known for his portrait busts and allegorical groups. After Aristide Maillol, he was one of the most individual of modern French sculptors. Discovered by Rodin, whose assistant he became, he executed his most characteristic work in bronze. At the time of his death he left uncompleted the figure of Apollo destined for the Museum of Modern Art at Paris.

D'Espine (des.pēn), **Adolphe.** b. at Geneva, Switzerland, Feb. 20, 1846; d. at Cologny, Switzerland, July 5, 1930. Swiss pediatrician. He became professor of pathology (1876) and of pediatrics (1908) at the University of Geneva. He described a sign for tracheobronchial adenitis or mediastinal tumor (1907) in which whispered voice sounds are heard over the upper thoracic vertebrae (called the D'Espine sign). His works include *Manuel des maladies de l'enfance* (1877), *La Cure marine de la scrofule à l'asile Dollfus de Cannes* (1904), and *Le Diagnostic précoce de la tuberculose des ganglions bronchiques chez les enfants* (1907).

Des Plaines (dẹs plānz'). City in NE Illinois, in Cook County, near Chicago: residential and industrial community. 14,994 (1950).

Des Plaines River. [Also, **Aux Plaines River.**] River in SE Wisconsin and NE Illinois, which unites with the Kankakee to form the Illinois ab. 40 mi. SW of Chicago. It is part of the canal system serving Chicago. Length, ab. 150 mi.

Despoblado (des.pō.blä'ᴛʜō). [Also, **Puna.**] Name given in the Andean regions of South America to any barren plateau which is so high and cold as to be practically uninhabitable. Specifically it is applied in S Peru to the region between the central and western cordilleras, an undulating tract from 14,000 to 18,000 ft. high, with a general breadth of ab. 150 mi., narrowing N and extending S on the borders of Chile and Bolivia.

Desportes (dā.pôrt), **Alexandre François.** b. at Champigneul, France, 1661; d. at Paris, 1743. French painter. He received some instruction from a Flemish painter resident at Paris, but in the main was self-taught, achieving proficiency by natural talent. His work, running largely to hunting scenes and landscapes with animals, pleased Louis XIV, who employed him in decorating the palaces of Versailles and Fontainebleau, and made him royal painter. In 1699 he became a member of the Academy at Paris. He accompanied one of the French ambassadors to England and did some painting there. His work is very well represented in the Louvre at Paris.

Desportes, Philippe. b. at Chartres, France, 1546; d. Oct. 5, 1606. French poet, clergyman, and diplomat. A disciple of Ronsard, he was called by his contemporaries "the French Tibullus."

Despoto Dagh (des'pō.tō däg). See **Rhodope Mountains.**

Despoto Planina (des'pō.tō plä.nē.nä'). Bulgarian name of the **Rhodope Mountains.**

Després (dā.prā), **Suzanne.** b. 1875—. French actress. She distinguished herself first at the Théâtre Antoine (1897) and became a leading actress at the Comédie Française after 1902. She made tours to other European countries and left a particular impression on the Bulgarian theater.

Dessaix (dā.se), **Joseph Marie,** Comte. b. at Thonon, Haute-Savoie, France, Sept. 24, 1764; d. Oct. 26, 1834. French general in the Napoleonic wars. Napoleon called him "L'Intrépide" after the battle of Wagram (1809).

Dessalines (dā.sȧ.lēn), **Jean Jacques.** b. at Grande Rivière, Haiti, 1758; assassinated near Port-au-Prince, Haiti, Oct. 17, 1806. Negro revolutionist, emperor (1805–06) of Haiti. He was a slave, joined the insurrection of 1791, rose to be second in command under Toussaint L'Ouverture, and fought against the mulattoes. He was notorious for savage courage and cruelty. In 1802 he resisted Leclerc's army in the west, but finally submitted. After Toussaint had been carried to France he headed another revolt, and, aided by the English, drove out the French (1803). On Jan. 1, 1804, he was proclaimed governor general for life of Haiti, and on Oct. 8, 1804, emperor, as Jean Jacques I. His despotism incited hatred, and he was eventually waylaid and killed.

Dessau (des'ou). City in C Germany, in the *Land* (state) of Saxony-Anhalt, Russian Zone, formerly the capital of Anhalt, situated on the Mulde River near its junction with the Elbe River, ab. 71 mi. SW of Berlin: river port. Before World War II it had important machine industries, and manufactured railroad cars, gas apparatus, paper, textiles, and carpets (rugs); there were also distilleries, breweries, and sugar refineries. The large Junkers aircraft factories were frequently bombed during World War II. From 1925 to 1933 Dessau was the seat of the Bauhaus, a school of arts and crafts which pioneered in modern artistic expression; some of its outstanding members fled to the U.S. in 1933. The city has beautiful parks and a number of art galleries and museums. The Church of Mary (1506–12) contains paintings by Lucas Cranach. The former ducal castle and the Prince Frederic Palais date from the 18th century, the Prince George Palais from 1820, the *Rathaus* (city hall) from 1900. A Slavic settlement in the 7th century, Dessau is mentioned as a German town in the 13th century. The Austrian general Wallenstein defeated the Protestants under Count Peter Ernst von Mansfeld here in 1626. From 1603 the capital of Anhalt, Dessau was a cultural center in the reign of Duke Leopold III (1751–1817). The philosopher Moses Mendelssohn was born here. Allied troops occupied the city on April 21, 1945, in World War II. War damage was extensive. The population, almost entirely Protestant, declined 24.8 percent between 1939 and 1946, to 88,139 (1946).

Dessauer (des'ou.ėr), **Friedrich.** b. at Aschaffenburg, Germany, July 19, 1881—. German politician and scientist. He worked particularly on x-ray treatments as professor (1920 *et seq.*) at the University of Frankfort on the Main. He was a Centrist Party member of the Reichstag (1924–33), wrote political, scientific, and philosophical works, and developed an optimistic philosophy of technology. Dismissed by the Nazis, he emigrated to Switzerland and became a member of the faculty at the University of Fribourg. Among his numerous books are *Wissen und Bekenntnis* (1944) and *Philosophie der Technik* (3rd ed., 1945).

Dessauer, Joseph. b. at Prague, in May, 1798; d. at Mödling, Austria, July 8, 1876. Bohemian (Czech) composer of songs and operas, chamber music, piano works, and overtures.

Dessie (des'yā). [Also, **Dessye.**] Town in E Africa, in Ethiopia, in the highlands N of Addis Ababa and E of Lake Tana. It is a road junction on the roads from Gondar, Assab, and Asmara to Addis Ababa, and is also a local commercial center.

Dessolles or **Dessole** (de.sol), **Jean Joseph Paul Augustin,** Marquis. b. at Auch, Gers, France, Oct. 3, 1767; d.

at Paris, Nov. 4, 1828. French general and politician. He served with distinction under Moreau in Italy in 1799, in Germany in 1800, and was minister of foreign affairs (1818–19).

De Stefani (dā ste'fä.nē), **Alberto.** b. at Verona, Italy, Oct. 6, 1879—. Italian economist, who served as professor (1916 *et seq.*) at Padua, Venice, and Rome; also as Mussolini's minister of finance (1922 *et seq.*). He is the author of *La Restaurazione financiaria* (The Financial Reconstruction, 1926), and *La Legislazione economica della guerra* (The Economic Legislation of War, 1927).

Destêrro (dēsh.tār'rö). A former name of **Florianópolis.**

Destinn (des'tin), **Emmy.** [Original surname, **Kittl.**] b. at Prague, Feb. 26, 1878; d. 1930. Czech opera singer. She is said to have taken her stage name from that of Marie Loewe-Destinn, with whom she studied singing at Prague. She sang (1898–1908) at the New Royal Opera House, Berlin, and also performed at the Metropolitan Opera House, New York, at Covent Garden, London, and elsewhere. Among her principal roles were Mignon, Santuzza in *Cavalleria Rusticana*, Elizabeth in *Tannhäuser*, Salome, and Carmen. In 1910 she appeared in Puccini's *The Girl of the Golden West.*

Destiny. Novel by Susan E. Ferrier, dedicated to Sir Walter Scott, and published anonymously in 1831.

Destouches (dā.tösh), **André Cardinal.** b. at Paris, c1672; d. there, Feb. 8, 1749. French operatic composer. He was director (1728–31) of the Opéra; his operas include *Amadis de Grèce* (1699), *Omphale* (1701), *Sémiramis* (1718), and *Les Éléments* (1721).

Destouches, Franz Seraph von. b. 1772; d. 1844. German composer, notably of dramatic works. His other compositions include chamber music, orchestral pieces, and concertos.

Destouches, Louis Fuch. [Pseudonym, **Louis-Ferdinand Céline.**] b. at Paris, 1894—. French novelist and physician. He is the author of *Voyage au bout de la nuit* (1932; Eng. trans., *Journey to the End of Night*, 1934), *Mort à credit* (1936; Eng. trans., *Death on the Installment Plan*, 1938), and *Bagatelles pour un massacre* and *École des Cadavres* (both 1938). All his work is fiercely nihilistic in tone and has been frequently condemned for its relentless obscenity. Accused of collaboration with the Germans, he was *non grata* in France and lived in exile in Denmark until he was amnestied in 1951.

Destouches, Philippe. [Original surname, **Néricault.**] b.at Tours, France, in April, 1680; d. near Melun, France, July 4, 1754. French dramatist. Among his 17 comedies are *Le Curieux impertinent* (1710), *Le Philosophe marié* (1727), and *Le Glorieux* (1732).

Destrée (des.trā), **Jules.** b. at Marcinelle, Belgium, 1863—. Belgian lawyer, publicist, and politician. With his brother he took part in the lively controversies in the provocative *Jeune Belgique;* also collaborated with Emile Vandervelde in writing *Le Socialisme en Belgique.* His esthetic interest is reflected in a number of works on painters. He served as minister of sciences and arts.

"Destroyer Deal." Term sometimes applied to an exchange made through executive agreement by President Franklin D. Roosevelt with Great Britain on Sept. 3, 1940, by which the U.S. obtained on 99-year leases a chain of bases running from Newfoundland to Trinidad in return for 50 overage destroyers. Bases on Newfoundland and Bermuda were granted outright as gifts to the U.S.; those in the West Indies, Antigua, Jamaica, St. Lucia, Bahamas, Trinidad, and British Guiana, by lease.

Destructive Element, The. Critical work by Stephen Spender, published in 1935.

Destutt de Tracy (des.tüt dẹ trà.sē), **Alexandre César Victor Charles,** Comte. b. at Paris, Sept. 9, 1781; d. at Paray-le-Frésil, Allier, France, March 13, 1864. French officer, politician, and writer; son of Antoine Destutt de Tracy (1754–1836).

Destutt de Tracy, Antoine Louis Claude, Comte. b. at Paris, July 20, 1754; d. March 10, 1836. French philosopher, deputy to the Constituent Assembly in 1789. His chief works are *Éléments d'idéologie* (1801–15) and *Commentaire sur l'esprit des lois* (1811, 1819).

Desvalières (dā.vȧ.lyer), **Georges Olivier.** b. at Paris, March 14, 1861—. French landscape, religious, portrait, and genre painter, and pastel artist. His work, which approaches expressionism, can be considered the link between the religious art of Moreau and Rouault. He studied under Moreau and others, at Paris, in the École des Beaux-Arts, and first exhibited in the Paris Salon of 1883, and regularly thereafter. He was awarded many prizes, including the silver medal at the Exposition Universelle of 1900. He has done murals in churches and private homes, and illustrated *Rolla*, and other books. Among his best-known works are *The Kiss of Christ, Portrait of Mme. D., Ball Players*, and decorations for the chapel of Saint Privat, and the church at Pawtucket.

Desvres (devr). Town in N France, in the department of Pas-de-Calais, ab. 12 mi. E of Boulogne. It is an industrial town; the outstanding products are cement and pottery. 5,515 (1946).

Detaille (dẹ.tȧy'), **Jean Baptiste Édouard.** b. at Paris, Oct. 5, 1848; d. 1912. French painter of battle scenes. During the Franco-Prussian War he was the secretary of General Pajol, and later of General Appert. Many of his pictures show the result of his studies from life at this period. Among them are *En Retraite* (1873), *Charge du 9ème cuirassiers à Morsbronn* (1874), *Le Régiment qui passe* (1875), *Salut aux blessés* (1877), *Le Rêve* (1888), *Charge du 1er hussards* (bought for the Luxembourg in 1891). Besides some minor illustrations he furnished designs in the period 1885–88 for a book containing all the types and uniforms of the French army.

de Tassigny (dẹ tȧ. sē.nyē), **Jean Joseph Marie Gabriel de Lattre.** See **de Lattre de Tassigny, Jean Joseph Marie Gabriel.**

Deterding (dā'tėr.ding), **Sir Henri.** [Original name, **Hendrik Wilhelm August Deterding.**] b. at Amsterdam, April 19, 1866; d. Feb. 4, 1939. International oil magnate. The son of a poor seaman, he found employment in a bank at the age of 16, six years later went to the Dutch East Indies as an employee of the Netherlands Trading Society, before long transferred his services to the Royal Dutch Company for the Working of Petroleum Wells in the Dutch East Indies, and by 1900, at the age of 34, was managing director of this concern. Convinced of the vast future of the oil industry and of its profit-making possibilities, he set himself to curb waste and inefficiency in the industry by integrating production and sales and by promoting agreements among oil companies to keep prices up. In 1903 such an agreement was reached between Royal Dutch and certain companies under British and French control, the chief among which was the Shell Transport and Trading Company; Royal Dutch and Shell were later merged into one great corporation. These combined interests proved strong enough to hold their own against the largest American oil group. Properties were acquired in many parts of the world including the Far East, Russia, Venezuela, Mexico, and even in the U.S. After the Russian Revolution Deterding, who had a very large stake in the Baku oilfields, backed the White Russian General Denikin in the hope of preventing the extension of the revolution to that region, but in April, 1920, the Bolsheviks secured control of Baku and its oil wells and refineries. Thenceforth it became one of Deterding's chief aims, pursued ever more doggedly, to recover the Baku properties. As this was obviously impossible without the overthrow of the Soviet regime, he became one of the principal non-German subsidizers of Adolf Hitler, in the expectation that a Nazi Germany might probably attack and defeat the U.S.S.R. In his later days Sir Henri Deterding was considered by many to be the most powerful man in the world. Lord Fisher of the Royal Navy, who brought about the substitution of oil for coal in that navy, said that Deterding was "Napoleonic in his audacity and Cromwellian in his thoroughness."

Detmold (det'mōld; German, -molt). City in W Germany, in the *Land* (state) of North Rhine-Westphalia, British Zone, formerly the capital of Lippe, situated on the Werre River ab. 46 mi. SW of Hanover. It has metallurgical, electrical, textile, shoe, and leather factories, and also manufactures wooden articles and costume jewelry; marble and gypsum quarries are in the vicinity. Detmold has vocational schools, a school of painting, a music conservatory, a theater, library, museum of antiquities, and local museum. The former residential castle dates from the 16th century; the new Palais. in the midst of a large park, from the 17th century. The city is a center for excursions and a summer resort. Charlemagne defeated the pagan Saxons here in 783. Throughout the medieval and modern period (until 1918) it remained the capital of the principality of Lippe. Damage in World War II was light. The population is predominantly Protestant; the increase in population between 1939 and 1946 was 30.3 percent. 26,807 (1946), 30,178 (1950).

Detmold, Johann Hermann. b. at Hanover, Germany, July 24, 1807; d. there, March 17, 1856. German politician and satirical writer. He was elected to the national assembly in 1848, and in 1849 was for a short time minister of justice and of the interior. He wrote *Anleitung zur Kunstkennerschaft* (1833), *Randzeichnungen* (1843), and *Taten und Meinungen des Herrn Piepmeier* (1849).

Detour, The. Play by Owen Davis, produced in 1921 and published in 1922.

Detroit (dę.troit'). City in S Lower Michigan, county seat of Wayne County, on the Detroit River: fifth largest city in the U.S., noted as a great automobile-manufacturing center, with the General Motors, Fisher, Packard, Chrysler, and other company plants established here. Other large industries include manufactures of stoves, rubber, pharmaceutical and biological products, and adding machines. It is the seat of the Detroit Institute of Arts, Wayne University, Marygrove College, Detroit Institute of Technology, and the University of Detroit. A tunnel connects the city with Windsor, Canada. It was first settled by the French in 1701 and was taken by the British in 1760. Ceded to the U.S. in 1783, it was not occupied until 1796. It was surrendered by Hull to the British in 1812 and recovered by the U.S. in 1813. From 1837 to 1847 it was the state capital. 1,623,452 (1940), 1,849,568 (1950).

Detroit (dę.trwä'), **Karl.** Original name of **Mehemet Ali Pasha.**

Detroit Conservatory of Music (dę.troit'). Music school founded (1874) at Detroit, Mich., offering courses in all branches of the field.

Detroit Lakes. City in W Minnesota, county seat of Becker County, in a resort region of nearly 500 lakes. 5,787 (1950).

Detroit River. River which flows from Lake St. Clair into Lake Erie, and separates Michigan from the province of Ontario, Canada. Length, ab. 25 mi.

Detroit Symphony Orchestra. Ensemble established (1914) by Weston Gales, who conducted it from 1914 to 1918. Its next conductor (until 1935) was Ossip Gabrilovitch; among the conductors who followed were Victor Kolar and Karl Krueger.

Dett (det), **Robert Nathaniel.** b. at Drummondville, Quebec, Canada, Oct. 11, 1882; d. at Battle Creek, Mich., Oct. 2, 1943. American Negro conductor and composer, the first American to use Negro folk music for classical themes. He received the Mus.B. degree (1908) from Oberlin Conservatory, and was director (1913–35) of music at the Hampton Institute, where he was conductor of the choir which toured Canada, the U.S., and Europe. His compositions include *America the Beautiful, The Ordering of Moses,* an oratorio, and the symphony *An American Sampler.* He published *Religious Folksongs of the Negro* and the *Dett Collection of Negro Spirituals* (four books, 1937).

Dettifoss (det'ti.fôs). Waterfall in NE Iceland, in the Jökulsá River ab. 47 mi. E of Akureyri. It is the greatest falls in Iceland, formed where the river plunges into a narrow gorge eroded in the volcanic rock for a length of ab. 15 mi. Height of falls, ab. 352 ft.

Dettingen (det'ing.ęn). Village in Lower Franconia, Bavaria, situated on the Main River, ab. 16 mi. SE of Frankfort on the Main. Here, on June 27, 1743, the Anglo-German army under George II of England defeated the French under Marshal Adrien Maurice de Noailles.

Dettmann (det'män), **Ludwig.** b. at Adelbye, Germany, July 25, 1865—. German landscape, genre, and battle painter, who was director of the art academy at Königsberg. He studied at the Berlin Academy under E. F. P. Bracht and F. A. de Werner (1884–90) and then traveled throughout Germany, to France and England. He was awarded a silver medal at the Exposition Universelle of 1900 at Paris. Among his works are *Fisherman's Cemetery, The Last Supper,* and *View of a Village.*

Dettweiler (det'vī.lėr), **Peter.** b. at Winterstein, Rhenish Hesse, Germany, Aug. 4, 1837; d. at Cronberg, Germany, Jan. 12, 1904. German physician, founder of a sanatarium for tuberculous patients at Falkenstein (Taunus). He became (1876) director of this institute, introducing rest cures on deck-chairs on porches or in the open air, and recommended spitting vials for tuberculous patients. He was the author of *Die Behandlung der Lungenschwindsucht in geschlossenen Heilanstalten* (1880), "Ernährungstherapie bei Lungenkrankheiten" (in *Handbuch der Ernährungstherapie* by E. von Leiden, 1898), and *Die hygienisch-diätetische Anstaltsbehandlung der Lungentuberkulose* (1899).

Deucalion (dū̦.kā'li.on). In Greek legend, king of Phthia in Thessaly; son of Prometheus and Clymene, who with his wife Pyrrha was saved from a deluge sent by Zeus. On the advice either of his father or of Prometheus, he built a wooden chest in which he and his wife were saved. After floating for nine days he landed on Mount Parnassus and sacrificed to Zeus. To renew the human race, destroyed by the deluge, he and Pyrrha were directed to veil their faces and throw behind them the bones of their mother. Understanding this to mean their mother the earth they threw stones, and those thrown by Deucalion became men and those thrown by Pyrrha women; and with these Deucalion founded a kingdom in Locris.

Deucher (doi'ċhėr), **Adolf.** b. 1831; d. 1912. Swiss statesman. Trained as a physician, he became (1855) a member of the Thurgau canton council and took part in drafting (1868) a new constitution for that canton. He served (1869–73) on the Swiss National Council and was elected (1887, 1897, 1903) president of the Swiss Confederacy.

Deuil (dėy'). Town in N France, in the department of Seine-et-Oise, between the towns of St.-Denis and Pontoise. It belongs to the metropolitan region of Paris. It has chemical factories. The town suffered damage in World War II. 9,125 (1946).

Deurne (dėr'nę). Town in N Belgium, in the province of Antwerp, E of Antwerp, of which it is a suburb. It has carpet manufactures and canneries, and a large airport. 56,853 (1947).

Deurne. Town in S Netherlands, in the province of North Brabant, E of Eindhoven. It is an agricultural market center and has textile manufactures. 12,531 (1939).

Deus (dā'ösh), **Gaspar da Madre de.** See **Madre de Deus, Gaspar da.**

Deus, João de. [Full name, **João de Deus Ramos.**] b. at San Bartolomeu de Messines, Portugal, March 8, 1830; d. at Lisbon, Portugal, Jan. 11, 1896. Portuguese poet who has been praised by many as the purest lyric poet of Portugal since Camoens. His poems are to be found in *Flores do campo* (1868), *Fôlhas sôltas* (1876), and *Campo de flores,* a collection of his complete poetical production, compiled by Teófilo Braga (1893) and enlarged in the 1896 edition. As an educator, he wrote *Cartilha maternal* (1876), which was officially adopted in Portuguese schools in 1888. His prose writings were published posthumously with the title *Prosas* (1898).

Deusdedit (dē'us.ded.it), Saint. [Called **Adeodatus I.**] b. at Rome; d. Nov. 8, 618. Pope from 615 to 618. Remembered for his devotion to the people during a year of pestilence, he authorized celebration of more than one mass on Sunday in churches unable otherwise to accommodate their parishioners, and was supposedly the first Pope to use the leaden seal (*Bulla*), whence the name for papal bulls is derived.

Deussen (doi'sęn), **Paul.** b. at Oberdreis, Germany, Jan. 7, 1845; d. at Kiel, Germany, July 6, 1919. German philosopher and Sanskrit scholar, remembered for his work in the field of Indian philosophy, about which he wrote many books such as *Das System der Vedanta* (1883) and *Die Geheimlehre des Veda* (1907 *et seq.*). He served (1889 *et seq.*) as professor at the University of Kiel. He wrote also *Elemente der Metaphysik* (1877) and *Allgemeine Geschichte der Philosophie* (1894 *et seq.*).

Deutekom (dė'tę.kôm). See **Doetinchem.**

Deutero-Malay (dū'tėr.ō.mą.lā', -mā'lā) or **Deutero-Malaysian** (-mą.lā'zhąn, -shąn). [Also, **Malay, Malayan, Malay-Mongoloid.**] An individual belonging to a subdivision of the Southern Mongoloid race characterized, in contrast to the Proto-Malay subdivision, by greater stature, lighter skin, rounder head, narrower nose, straighter hair, and a greater incidence of the Mongoloid fold. The Deutero-Malay type is found among the Burmans, Siamese, Shan, Khmer, Malays, Japanese, and throughout the Malay Archipelago.

Deuteronomy (dū.tėr.on′ǫ.mi). Fifth and last book of the Pentateuch, containing the last discourses of Moses, delivered in the plain of Moab. It begins with a recapitulation of the events of the last month of the 40 years' wandering of the Israelites in the desert (i.-iv. 40); then follows the main body of the book, setting forth the laws which were to regulate the Israelites when they should become settled in the promised land; while chapters xxvi-xxxiii contain the farewell speeches of Moses. Deuteronomy is a manual of religion and social ethics. Compared with the other books of the Pentateuch it is distinguished by a warm, oratorical tone. The laws of the preceding books are modified, and their presentation is more spiritual and ethical. On account of these differences Deuteronomy is now assigned by many critics to a different author and date from the rest of the Pentateuch. Owing to the fact that the so-called reformation of King Josiah appears to carry out the principles of Deuteronomy, it is concluded that "the book of the law" discovered by the priest Hilkiah in the temple in 621 B.C., which began the reformation of Josiah, was Deuteronomy. But its composition must certainly have originated at an earlier date. This is put by many critics in the reign of Manasseh, c698–c643 B.C.

Deutsch (doich), **Babette.** b. at New York, Sept. 22, 1895—. American poet and novelist; wife of Avrahm Yarmolinsky (1890—). She is the author of *Banners* (1919), *Honey Out of the Rock* (1925), *Fire for the Night* (1930), *Epistle to Prometheus* (1930), *One Part Love* (1939), *Take Them, Stranger* (1944), and other collections of verse; her novels include *Mask of Silenus* (1933) and *Rogue's Legacy* (1942). She has also published a book of criticism, *This Modern Poetry* (1935).

Deutsch, Emanuel, Oscar Menahem. b. at Neisse, Prussia, Oct. 28, 1829; d. at Alexandria, Egypt, May 12, 1873. German Orientalist, for many years an assistant in the British Museum library.

Deutsch, Ernst. b. at Prague, Sept. 16, 1890—. Austrian actor. He first appeared as an actor of unusual vocal power at Vienna and Dresden, winning attention in the last-mentioned city with his terse and forceful style in the early expressionist drama, Reinhard Sorge's *Der Bettler* (1912). Subsequently he acted for Reinhardt in Berlin and became a leading actor of the Staatstheater. After 1924 he also appeared in German films.

Deutsch Brod (doich′ brōt′). German name of **Havlíčkův Brod.**

Deutsch de la Meurthe (dėch dę là mėrt), **Henri.** [Original name, **Henri Deutsch.**] b. at Paris, Sept. 25, 1846; d. at the Château Romainville-les-Mureaux, Seine-et-Oise, France, Nov. 24, 1919. French industrialist and philanthropist, organizer of the first petroleum refineries in France. He sponsored various prizes for development of the automobile and aviation, and was founder of the Cité Universitaire at Paris.

Deutsche Chronik (doi′chę krō′nik). [Later name, **Vaterländische Chronik.**] German semiweekly journal of radical views in politics and literature, founded in 1774 by Christian Friedrich Daniel Schubart (1739–91), and continued after 1777 (while Schubart was confined in the fortress prison of Hohenasperg) by Johann Martin Miller (1750–1814). It changed names repeatedly. After Schubart's release (1787) it became the *Vaterländische Chronik.*

Deutscher Bund (doi′chėr bůnt). German name of the **German Confederation.**

Deutsche Rundschau (doi′chę růnt′shou). German literary and critical magazine published at Berlin. It was founded in 1874 and edited for many years by Julius Rodenberg. It was never the organ of a special group, but sought general excellence and as wide an audience as possible.

Deutsches Meer (doi′chęs mār). A German name of the **North Sea.**

Deutsches Theater (doi′chęs tā.ä′tėr). Most important theater of Berlin, notable for its uninterrupted and progressive production of modern drama. It was founded in 1883 by Adolf L'Arronge, who carried on the classical-historical tradition of the Meinigen Company. From 1894 to 1905, Otto Brahm gave this theater a naturalistic style. In 1905, Max Reinhardt brought with him a baroque approach and produced all styles of drama, romantic and symbolist as well as realistic. The theater collapsed during World War I, but it was revitalized for a short time by Heinz Hilpert in 1933.

Deutsch-Eylau (doich′ī′lou). German name of **Iława.**

Deutsch-Krone (doich′krō′nę). German name of **Wałcz.**

Deutschland (doich′länt) or **Deutsches Reich** (doi′chęs rīch). German names of **Germany.**

Deutschland, Deutschland über alles (doich′länt, doich′länt ü′bėr äl′ęs). German patriotic hymn, at one time a German national anthem. It was written in 1841 by Hoffman von Fallersleben, then a political fugitive on Helgoland (at that time British territory). The inspiration and some of the phraseology came from a song by Walther von der Vogelweide. It was adapted to a melody by Haydn (1797) which had previously been used for the Austrian national anthem. It came into vogue in Germany during the last quarter of the 19th century.

Deutsch-Südwestafrika (doich′züt.vest.äf′rē.kä). German name of **German Southwest Africa.**

Deutsch-Wagram (doich′vä′gräm). See **Wagram,** Austria.

Deutz (doits). [Latin, **Divitia**; medieval name, **Tuitium.**] Town in W Germany, in the *Land* (state) of North Rhine-Westphalia, British Zone, formerly in the Rhine Province, Prussia, situated on the E bank of the Rhine River, opposite Cologne. It is incorporated into the city of Cologne.

Deux Amis (dė.zà.mē), **Les.** [Eng. trans., *"The Two Friends."*] Play by Beaumarchais, produced in 1770.

Deux Journées (dė zhör.nā), **Les.** [English title, **The Water Carrier.**] Opera in three acts by Cherubini, with a libretto by Bouilly, first performed at the Théâtre Feydeau on Jan. 16, 1800. Based on an actual incident, the work deals with Count Armand who, in order to escape Mazarin, is taken from Paris in a water barrel.

Deux-Ponts (dė.pôṅ). French name of **Zweibrücken.**

Deux-Sèvres (dė.sevr). Department of France, in the W part, bounded by the department of Maine-et-Loire on the N, the department of Vienne on the E, the departments of Charente and Charente-Maritime on the S, and the department of Vendée on the W. The department was formed chiefly from parts of the old provinces of Poitou, Aunis, and Saintonge. It suffered in the religious wars and again during the insurrection of the Vendée at the time of the French Revolution. The department is known for its green pastures, its flower gardens, its canals, and its historic monuments dating from the medieval and Renaissance periods. Its economy is essentially agricultural; grain, vegetables, fruits, and wines are produced. Horses, mules, cattle, goats, hogs, and poultry are raised. Eggs and dairy products are exported in considerable quantities. It has active trade in lumber and in agricultural products, and a number of small industries. Capital, Niort; area, 2,337 sq. mi.; pop. 312,756 (1946).

Deva (dā′vä). [Also: **Déva**; German, **Diemrich.**] Town in NW Rumania, in the province of Transylvania, situated on the Mureş River, ab. 80 mi. SE of Arad: manufactures include canned foods and candies. The town is known for its beautiful castle. Here, in 1849, was fought a battle between the Austrians and the Hungarian insurgents. 12,959 (1948).

Deva (dā′vą). In Hindu and Buddhist belief, a deity. The Hindu Devas are reckoned as 33; this number includes 12 Adityas, eight Vasus, 11 Rudras, and two Ashvins. In Zoroastrian belief, the Devas are evil spirits, created by Ahriman, lord of darkness.

Deva (dē′vą) or **Devana Castra** (dę.vā′ną kas′trą). A Latin name of **Chester,** England.

Deva. Latin name of the river **Dee,** in N Wales.

De Valera (dev.ą.lār′ą), **Eamon.** b. at New York, Oct. 14, 1882—. Irish political leader and statesman; son of an Irish mother and Spanish father. He studied at Blackrock College and the Royal University at Dublin. At the time of its organization he became (1913) a member of the Irish Volunteers. He was commandant (1916) in the Irish national insurrection, and was condemned to life imprisonment but was released (1917) by a general amnesty. Arrested again in 1918 in a general clean-up of revolutionary elements, he was imprisoned, but in an escape organized by Michael Collins, De Valera fled (1919) to the U.S. He traveled (1919–20) in America to raise funds for an Irish republican government to whose leadership he had been elected (1919). He was president of the Irish Volunteers (1917–21) and of the Sinn Fein (1917–26). As a member (1917 *et seq.*) of the legislature, he headed (December, 1921–January, 1922) in the Dáil Éireann the opposition to the Anglo-Irish treaty establishing the Irish Free State as a dominion, which had been signed by his colleagues Michael Collins and Arthur Griffith; this led to his resignation (January, 1922) of the presidency and his formation of a militant group to oppose the treaty. He was founder and president (1924) of the Fianna Fáil, a group of extreme republicans. In 1926 he resigned as head of Sinn Fein and, after swearing allegiance to the king, the very oath he and his followers had fought against so bitterly for ten years, he brought (August, 1927) the Fianna Fáil into the Free State parliament. He served as president of the executive council and minister (1932–37) of external affairs and prime minister (1937–48) of the Irish government under the new constitution, which ignored the whole matter of Irish allegiance to the British crown. During World War II he insisted on Ireland's neutrality, maintaining it even in the face of the obvious endangering of the Normandy invasion by the activities in Ireland of Axis official representations. Out of power from 1948 to 1951, when a coalition made J. A. Costello premier, he again became prime minister in 1951 when the Fianna Fáil carried the election.

Devambez (dẹ.väṅ.bā), **André Victor Édouard.** b. at Paris, 1867; d. 1944. French landscape, figure, historical, and genre painter and illustrator, especially noted for his small, realistic portrayals of genre scenes. He was schooled at Paris under Benjamin Constant and J. Lefèbvre, and obtained a Prix de Rome in 1900. In 1889 he was made a member of the Société des Artistes Français and exhibited in their Salons regularly, where he also won two prizes. A list of his works includes *The Manifestation, Gulliver Received by the Lilliputians*, and *A Première in a Montmarte Theater.*

Devaprayaga (dā″vạ.prä.yä′gạ). [Also, **Deoprag.**] Sacred city of the Hindus, in Tehri-Garhwal, Uttar Pradesh (United Provinces), Union of India, ab. 150 mi. NE of Delhi, where the Alaknanda and Bhagirath rivers unite to form the Ganges.

Devar Malai (dā′vär mä.lī′). See under **Cardamom Hills.**

Devarshis (dā.vär′shēz). In Hindu belief, *rishis*, or sages, who have attained perfection upon earth, and have been exalted as demigods to heaven.

Dévaványa (dā′vô.vä′nyô). Town in E Hungary, N of the Kőrös River and E of the city of Mezőtúr. The population is predominantly Protestant. 15,653 (1948).

De Vecchi di Val Cismon (dā vek′kē dē väl′ chēz.mōn′), Count **Cesare Maria.** b. at Casale Monferrato, Italy, Nov. 14, 1884—. Italian government official. An early Fascist, he founded the Piedmontese group, was elected (1921) to the chamber of deputies, and headed (1921–22) the Fascists in the senate. He took part in the March on Rome, subsequently serving as finance minister (1923), governor (1923–28) of Italian Somaliland, minister (1928) of state, ambassador (1929–34) to the Vatican, minister (1935–36) of education, and governor (1936–40) of the Italian possessions in the Aegean. He was named senator (1924) and given (1925) the title of count. He voted (July 24–25, 1943) against Mussolini in the Grand Fascist Council and for this was condemned (1944) to death by the Fascists; he was later condemned (1947) to five years' imprisonment by the Italian republicans for his previous activities. Both trials, however, took place in absentia, as he had moved to Argentina.

Devens (dev′ẹnz), **Charles.** b. at Charlestown, Mass., April 4, 1820; d. at Boston, Jan. 7, 1891. American jurist and Civil War general. He served with distinction in the Army of the Potomac (1861–65), and was attorney general of the U.S. from 1877 to 1881.

Deventer (dā′vẹn.tėr). [Also, **Demter.**] Town in E Netherlands, in the province of Overijssel, situated on the Ijssel River ab. 22 mi. NE of Arnhem, and connected by canals with Zwolle and Almelo. It has chemical, machine, and cigar factories, and canneries; biscuits, called Deventer Koek, are a specialty; there are also large meat markets. The town has preserved its medieval appearance, and contains numerous old churches, towers, municipal buildings, and patrician houses. It has a municipal museum and various educational institutions. The Stadhuis has a painting by Ter Borch; the Landhuis dates from 1632. An ancient commercial settlement, the town was plundered by the Saxons in 778 and by the Normans in 883. It came later under the bishopric of Utrecht, fell in 1528 to Charles V of Spain, and in 1571 to William I of Orange (William the Silent). The college or brotherhood of Deventer, known as the Brethren of the Life in Common or the Good Brethren and Sisters, planned by Gerard Groot, became known in the Low Countries and in Germany after 1400 and exerted considerable influence because of the strict community life, devotion to manual labor, and mystical tendencies of its members. 47,195 (est. 1951).

Deventer, Sir **Jacob Louis van.** b. in Orange Free State, South Africa, 1874; d. 1922. South African soldier.

de Vere (dẹ vir′). See also under **Vere, de.**

de Vere, Sir **Aubrey.** b. at Curragh Chase, County Limerick, Ireland, Aug. 28, 1788; d. there, July 5, 1846. Irish poet. He published *Julian the Apostate* (1822), *The Duke of Mercia, The Song of Faith* (1842), *Mary Tudor* (1847: posthumously published), and others.

de Vere, Aubrey Thomas. b. at Curragh Chase, County Limerick, Ireland, Jan. 10, 1814; d. there, Jan. 20, 1902. Irish poet, critic, and essayist; friend of Cardinal Newman, Wordsworth, Tennyson, and Carlyle; son of Sir Aubrey de Vere. He was educated by tutors and at Trinity College, Dublin, and traveled frequently in England and Italy. He entered (1851) the Roman Catholic Church. Among his works are volumes of verse including *Waldenses* (1842), *The Search After Proserpine* (1844), *A Year of Sorrow* (1847), *Poems: Sacred and Miscellaneous* (1854), *May Carols* (1857), *Legends of St. Patrick* (1872), *Alexander the Great* (1874), *St. Thomas of Canterbury* (1876), *Antar and Zara* and *The Fall of Rora* (both 1877), *Poetical Works* (3 vols., 1884–89), *Legends and Records of the Church and Empire* (1887), *St. Peter's Chains* (1888), and *Medieval Records and Sonnets* (1893). He also wrote *English Misrule and Irish Misdeeds* (1848), *Picturesque Sketches of Greece and Turkey* (1850), *The Church Settlement of Ireland* (1866), *Ireland's Church Property* and *Pleas for Secularization* (both 1867), *Legends of the Saxon Saints* (1879), *Constitutional and Unconstitutional Political Action* (1882), *Ireland and Representation* (1885), *Critical Essays* (3 vols., 1887–89), and *Recollections* (1897).

De Vere, Maximilian Schele. See **Schele De Vere, Maximilian.**

Devereux (dev′ėr.ö, -öks). Novel by Edward Bulwer-Lytton, published in 1829.

Devereux, Penelope. [Married name, **Rich**; called **Stella** by Sidney.] Lady loved by Sir Philip Sidney, and celebrated by him in his group of sonnets entitled *Astrophel and Stella.* She was the daughter of Walter Devereux (1541–76), whose plan it was for her to marry Sidney. However, she actually married Robert Rich, 3rd Baron Rich, but did not therefore repudiate Sidney's devoted attentions (literary and otherwise).

Devereux, Robert. [Title, 2nd Earl of **Essex.**] b. at Netherwood, Herefordshire, England, Nov. 19, 1566; beheaded at London, Feb. 25, 1601. English nobleman; son of Walter Devereux, 1st Earl of Essex of the Devereux line; a favorite of Queen Elizabeth. He was appointed in 1585 general of the horse to the expedition sent under Robert Dudley, 1st Earl of Leicester, his stepfather, to the aid of the States-General in the Netherlands. In 1587 he attended the court of Queen Elizabeth, who at this time began to show him unmistakable signs of attention, emphatically so after the death (1588) of Leicester. He secretly married (1590) the widow of Sir Philip Sidney, Frances Walsingham, daughter of Elizabeth's secretary of state. Despite Elizabeth's great anger when she heard of the marriage, he made his peace with her and became a privy councilor in 1593. He commanded the land forces in the successful raiding expedition against Cádiz in 1596 but failed to win a complete victory or to capture the Spanish treasure ships and was reprimanded by the queen. In 1597 he led an expedition against the Azores, again failing to accomplish a real victory, permitting the Argentine ships to escape and almost falling into a trap. But Elizabeth made peace with him and he was appointed earl marshal of England in 1597. He became chancellor of Cambridge University in 1598. In 1599 he was appointed lord lieutenant of Ireland, in which post he aroused the queen's anger by the failure of his operations against the Irish rebels, and by his inability to follow orders from the queen. He made a truce with Hugh O'Neill, the Earl of Tyrone, leader of the Ulster rebels, and, leaving his post without authorization, returned (September, 1599) to England to lay his defense before the queen in person. Failing to regain his standing at court, and after a trial as the result of which he was stripped of his offices, he formed a conspiracy with Charles Blount, Baron Mountjoy, and Henry Wriothesley, 3rd Earl of Southampton, to compel her by force of arms to dismiss his enemies in the council, who were and had been the Cecil faction. On Feb. 8, 1601, he led a group of his retainers through the streets of London, trying to arouse the citizenry to join him; but this half-formed uprising was met with apathy and he returned to his palace, Essex House, where he was captured. He was tried for treason; Francis Bacon, who had consistently attempted to mediate between Essex and Elizabeth, prosecuted the charge virulently; and Essex was found guilty and executed on the charge of treason.

Devereux, Robert. [Title, 3rd Earl of **Essex.**] b. at London, 1591; d. Sept. 14, 1646. English general; son of Robert Devereux, 2nd Earl of Essex of the Devereux line. He was appointed general of the Parliamentary army on the outbreak of the English Civil War in 1642, fought the Royalist forces in the drawn battle of Edgehill in 1642, captured Reading, relieved Gloucester, and gained the first battle of Newbury in 1643. He lost his army in the unsuccessful campaign in Cornwall in 1644, and resigned (1645) his command on the passage of the Self-Denying Ordinance, which denied public office to members of Parliament.

Devereux, Walter. [Titles: 1st Viscount of **Hereford,** 3rd Baron **Ferrers.**] b. before 1490; d. Sept. 27, 1558. English soldier and courtier; grandfather of Walter Devereux (c1541–1576). He succeeded (1501) his father as 3rd Baron Ferrers. He engaged (1512–13, 1523) in military campaigns under Admiral Thomas Howard, 3rd Duke of Norfolk, and Charles Brandon, 1st Duke of Suffolk, against France, was created (1523) Knight of the Garter, and became (1550) Viscount Hereford. He was appointed (1525) steward of the household of Princess Mary of Wales (later Queen Mary Tudor) and chief justice of South Wales. In 1526 he was named chamberlain.

Devereux, Walter. [Titles: 1st Earl of **Essex,** 2nd Viscount of **Hereford.**] b. in Carmarthenshire, Wales, probably in 1541; d. at Dublin, Sept. 22, 1576. English nobleman. He raised in 1569 a troop of soldiers to assist in suppressing the northern rebellion under the earls of Northumbria and Westmorland, for which service he was created Earl of Essex, the first of the Devereux line, in 1572. He made an unsuccessful attempt (1573–76) to subdue and colonize Ulster.

Deveron (dev'ėr.on). River in E Scotland, in Aberdeenshire and Banffshire. It rises in Banffshire, near the Aberdeenshire-Banffshire boundary, ab. 37 mi. W of Aberdeen, and flows NE across a portion of Aberdeenshire, reëntering Banffshire and flowing N to enter the North Sea ab. 1 mi. E of Banff. Length, ab. 61 mi.

Devers (dev'ėrz), **Jacob Loucks.** b. at York, Pa., Sept. 8, 1887—. American field-artillery officer. Graduate (1909) of U.S. Military Academy; executive officer of field artillery school in World War I; instructor of military tactics at West Point; specialist in mechanized warfare. Chief of staff (1939–40) of Panama department, supervised mechanization of Panama Canal defenses; placed in command (1940) of Fort Bragg; given command (1941) of armored forces; promoted to major general (1940) and lieutenant general (1942); appointed (1943) chief of U.S. forces in Europe; promoted (1945) to general; commanding general (1945–49) of army ground forces.

Devi (dā'vē). See **Mahadevi;** see also **Parvati.**

Devil, The. Tavern in Fleet street, London, near Temple Bar. The Apollo Club was held here. It was presided over by Ben Jonson, Shakespeare, Beaumont, and Fletcher, and other celebrities frequented it. The tavern was absorbed by Child's Bank, one of the oldest banks in London, which occupied the next house.

Devil and Daniel Webster, The. Short story (1937) by Stephen Vincent Benét. Now recognized as an American classic, it shows how the great American statesman defeated Satan and won a case for his client, Jabez Stone. It has enjoyed popularity in several forms, in its original one as a short story, as a one-act opera, as a play, and as a motion picture, in which Edward Arnold and Walter Huston scored great successes. It was originally published in the *Saturday Evening Post,* and in a volume of short stories, *Thirteen O'Clock* (1937).

Devil Is an Ass, The. Comedy by Ben Jonson, first acted in 1616. Jonson evidently had in mind the title of Dekker's play (published 1612) *If it be not Good the Devil is in it.* The devil in Jonson's play is an ass in comparison to the characters who buffet and completely overreach him.

Deville (dẹ.vēl), **Charles Sainte-Claire.** See **Sainte-Claire Deville, Charles.**

Déville-lès-Rouen (dā.vēl.le.rwäṅ). Town in NW France, in the department of Seine-Inférieure, ab. 4 mi. NW of Rouen. It has metallurgical and textile industries. 7,567 (1946).

Devil Postpile National Monument. National monument in E central California, in the Sierra Nevada mountains ab. 70 mi. NE of Fresno. It is a mass of hexagonal volcanic rocks (basaltic lava) standing in vertical columns, and was established as a national monument in 1911. Area, ab. 1¼ sq. mi.

Devil's Bridge. Stone bridge over the Reuss River, in the canton of Uri, Switzerland, on the St. Gotthard Pass near Andermatt. It was partly destroyed by the French in 1799. A new bridge (near the original one) was built 1828–30.

Devil's Bridge. [Also, **Pont-y-Mynach.**] Bridge over the gorge of the Mynach, near Aberystwith, in Wales.

Devil's Dictionary, The. Collection of newspaper squibs by Ambrose Bierce, published (1906) as *The Cynic's Word Book* and reissued under the present title in 1911. Its "definitions" reflect the biting wit and wry pessimism so characteristic of Bierce's work.

Devil's Disciple, The. Comedy (1897) of the American Revolution by George Bernard Shaw, who calls it a melodrama. It is one of his "Three Plays for Puritans," the others being *Caesar and Cleopatra,* a history, and *Captain Brassbound's Conversion,* an adventure. The time of the play is the winter of 1777, and the scene of action is New Hampshire, in the Dudgeon and Anderson homes, and in the town hall, council chamber, and market place. The main characters are Dick Dudgeon, the "disciple," a radical; his mother, a thoroughly disagreeable woman, whose husband has just died; his brother, Christie, Anthony Anderson, a Presbyterian minister; his lovely wife, Judith; Essie, a frightened 17-year-old girl who is never allowed to forget her irregular birth; other characters who are brought in for satirical and comic purposes; and the historical personages, General ("Gentleman Johnny") Burgoyne, and Brudenell, a chaplain. The play, with its satire on British slowness and stupidity, its sly digs at Puritanism, religion, respectability, and conventional morality, and its cynical treatment of love and romance, has always been popular on the stage and has had many revivals, in both England and America. In the attractive role of dashing Dick Dudgeon, Richard Mansfield and Maurice Evans scored great successes.

Devil's Dyke. Ancient earthwork, 18 ft. high, of prehistoric origin, in Cambridgeshire, England, extending from Reach to Wood-Ditton. There is another natural "Devil's Dyke" near Brighton, England.

Devil's Hole. See **Peak Cavern.**

Devil's Island. [French, **Île du Diable.**] Island in the Atlantic Ocean, off the coast of French Guiana, formerly used as a penal colony by France. Alfred Dreyfus was imprisoned (1895–99) here.

Devil's Island. Former name of **Deal Island.**

Devils Lake. Salt lake in the NE part of North Dakota. Length, ab. 30 mi.

Devils Lake. City in NE North Dakota, county seat of Ramsey County, near Devils Lake ab. 85 mi. NW of Grand Forks. It was founded in 1883 on the shore of the lake, which since that date has receded, the level of the water (salt) having dropped more than 25 ft. 6,427 (1950).

Devil's Law-Case, The. Tragicomedy by John Webster, printed in 1623.

Devil's Parliament. Nickname given to the English Parliament which met at Coventry, England, in 1459. It attainted the leading Yorkists.

Devil's Thoughts, The. Short poem by Coleridge and Southey, sometimes known as *The Devil's Walk.*

Devils Tower National Monument. National monument in NE Wyoming, ab. 70 mi. NW of the Black Hills, S.D. The Devils Tower is a straight-sided vertical mass of gray volcanic rock formed as an erosion remnant of igneous rock which once filled the neck of a volcanic cone. Its sheer walls have been climbed by a few persons, including at least one woman. It was the first U.S. national monument, established in 1906. Height of tower, ab. 720 ft.; elevation of top, ab. 5,117 ft.

Devil's Wall. Popular name for the S portion of the Roman fortification called the Pfahlgraben, near Regensburg, Germany.

Devil upon Two Sticks, The. Comedy by Samuel Foote, first played on May 30, 1768, and printed in 1778. Foote took it from Alain René Le Sage's *Le Diable boiteux,* and himself played the part of the devil.

Devine (dę.vīn'), **Edward Thomas.** b. at Union, Hardin County, Iowa, May 6, 1867; d. 1948. American sociologist, general secretary of the Charity Organization Society of the city of New York, and professor of social economy in Columbia University. He was graduated from Cornell College, Iowa, in 1887, studied in Germany (1890–91), took his Ph.D. (1893) at the University of Pennsylvania, and spent several years in teaching. His publications include *Economics* (1898), *The Practice of Charity* (1901), *The Principles of Relief* (1904), *Efficiency and Relief* (1906), *Misery and its Causes* (1909), and others. He was the editor (1897–1912) of *The Survey.*

De Vinne (dę vin'i), **Theodore Low.** b. at Stamford, Conn., Dec. 25, 1828; d. Feb. 16, 1914. American printer, noted for his excellent craftsmanship, notably in wood engravings and half-tone plates. He became (c1842) a printer's apprentice with the Newburgh *Gazette,* moved (1848) to New York, and in 1858 became a junior partner in the firm of Francis Hart, on whose death (1877) De Vinne became sole owner. An expert in the history and craft of printing, he performed outstanding work on the *Century Magazine, Scribner's Monthly,* and *St. Nicholas.* He was instrumental in securing the invention of coated paper for work with fine wood engravings and plates. Among his outstanding productions are the *Century Dictionary,* the Book of Common Prayer, the "Jade" book, and the early books of the Grolier Club, of which he was a founder and president. His firm, which became Theo. L. De Vinne and Company in 1877, was incorporated (1908) as The De Vinne Press. He was one of the founders of the Typothetae of the City of New York and of the United Typothetae of America. His wide learning in the craft, which enabled him to raise printing to a new eminence in the U.S., is apparent in his writings, which include *The Printers' Price List* (1869), *The Invention of Printing* (1876), *Historic Printing Types* (1886), *The Practice of Typography* (4 vols., 1900–02, 1904), *Title-Pages as Seen by a Printer* (1901), and *Notable Printers of Italy During the Fifteenth Century* (1910).

Devious Ways. Novel by Gilbert Cannan, published in 1910.

Devizes (dę.vī'zęz). Municipal borough and market town in S England, in Wiltshire, situated on the river Kennet and the Avon Canal ab. 27 mi. SE of Bristol, ab. 86 mi. W of London. It has a trade in grain and was formerly a textile center. There is a rather remarkable "staircase" of 29 locks on one canal at Devizes. 7,892 (1951).

Devlin (dev'lin), **Joseph.** b. at Belfast, Ireland, 1872; d. there, Jan. 18, 1934. Irish politician, an advocate of Irish home rule and of union with the Irish Free State. He served as a member of Parliament (1902–22, 1929–34) and as member of the parliament of Northern Ireland (1921–29), was owner of the *Irish News,* and headed six missions to the U.S. and one to Australia on behalf of the Nationalist Party.

Devolution (dev.ǫ.lö'shǫn), **War of.** War (1667–68) that derived its name from an ancient law of Brabant, the *droit de dévolution.* This provided that upon the death of one of a married couple, the survivor enjoyed only the use of a property, but title passed to children. When Marie Thérèse, daughter of Philip IV of Spain, became the wife of Louis XIV of France, he agreed to her relinquishment of her rights of inheritance in consideration of the promise of a rich dowry. After Philip's death, Louis, alleging that the dowry had not been paid, claimed the Spanish Netherlands, including Brabant, in his wife's right, since they were a personal estate of the Spanish royal family, and should devolve upon Marie Thérèse as the daughter of Philip's first wife, whereas Philip's successor to the Spanish throne, Charles II, was the child of a later marriage. French armies overran not only a large area of the Spanish Netherlands, but also Franche-Comté, then a Spanish possession, but when Holland, England, and Sweden formed an alliance against him in January, 1668, Louis came to terms which restored Franche-Comté to the Spanish crown, but left him in possession of 12 strategically important towns on the borders of the Spanish Netherlands.

Devon (dev'ǫn). See also **Devonshire.**

Devon. Unincorporated community in SW Connecticut, in New Haven County near the Housatonic River: residential suburb. Under the new urban definition established for use in the 1950 census it was counted along with adjoining urban areas. The last official enumeration was 6,726 (1940).

Devonian Period (dę.vō'ni.an). Period in the Paleozoic Era when fish were the dominant life form. See table at end of Vol. III.

Devon Island (dev'ǫn). [Former name, **North Devon.**] Island of the Arctic Archipelago, N of Baffin Island, S of Ellesmere Island, and W of Greenland. Area, 20,484 sq. mi.; pop. 11 (1941).

Devonport (dev'ǫn.pōrt). Former county borough, now a civil parish, in SW England, in Devonshire, situated on the Hamoaze (the estuary of the river Tamar), ab. 227 mi. SW of London by rail. It is now part of Plymouth, and was called Plymouth Dock until 1824, when it was renamed. It has an important naval arsenal, and is noted for its dockyards specializing in the building of warships. 84,690 (1931).

Devonshire (dev'ǫn.shir) or **Devon.** [Old English, **Defena scīr.**] Maritime county in SW England, lying between Bristol Channel on the W and N, Somersetshire and Dorsetshire on the NE and E, the English Channel on the SE and S, and Cornwall on the W. It is the largest administrative county in England. It has manufactures of coarse woolens, lace, linens, gloves, shoes, and paper. Devonshire also has important fisheries, especially of pilchard and mackerel. Many minerals and kinds of stone are found in the county, and it was formerly an important producer of copper and tin, but foreign competition has now largely eliminated this industry; china clay and pipe clay are mined, however. The county is noted for its Devonshire cattle, a breed with long, straight horns and a red coat, and for its dairy products and cider, largely exported. The Island of Lundy, in Bristol Channel, belongs to Devonshire. Dartmoor, the Vale of Exeter, and the western part of Exmoor are noted natural features. Exeter is the county seat; area, ab. 2,582 sq. mi.; pop. 798,283 (1951).

Devonshire, Duke of. Title held by various members of the **Cavendish** family, in Great Britain.

Devonshire, Earl of. A title of **Blount, Charles** (1563–1606); also of **Courtenay, Henry.**

Devonshire, 1st Earl of. Title of **Cavendish, William** (d. 1626).

Devonshire Club. Liberal club at London, established in 1875.

Devonshire House. House in Piccadilly, London, near Berkeley Street, the residence of the duke of Devonshire, and for more than a century one of the headquarters of the leaders of the Whig Party. It was built in the second half of the 17th century and at first called Berkeley House. In the period following World War I the original structure was dismantled.

De Voto (dę vō'tō), **Bernard Augustine.** b. at Ogden, Utah, Jan. 11, 1897—. American writer and editor. He has been a member (1929–36) of the English department at Harvard, editor (1935 *et seq.*) of "The Easy Chair" in *Harper's Magazine*, and editor (1936–38) of *The Saturday Review of Literature*. His works include *The Crooked Mile* (1924), *The Chariot of Fire* (1926), *The House of Sun-Goes-Down* (1928), *Mark Twain's America* (1932), *Forays and Rebuttals* (1936), *Minority Report* (1940), *Mark Twain at Work* (1942), *The Year of Decision: 1846* (1943), *Mountain Time* (1947), *Across the Wide Missouri* (1947), *The World of Fiction* (1950), and *The Course of Empire* (1952).

Devoy (dẹ.voi'), **John.** b. near Kill, County Kildare, Ireland, Sept. 3, 1842; d. at Atlantic City, N.J., Sept. 30, 1928. Irish Fenian and American journalist, long a leader of the revolutionary Irish nationalist movement in the U.S. In 1861 he joined the Irish Republican Brotherhood, known also as the Fenians, and also enlisted in the French Foreign Legion to acquire military experience. Returning to Ireland in 1862, he became active in spreading Fenianism, and in October, 1865, was put in charge of the task of winning Irish soldiers in the British army to the patriot cause. For this he was apprehended in 1866, convicted and sentenced to 15 years in prison, but in 1871 he was released upon condition that he go into exile and never again set foot in Ireland. On February 9 of that year Devoy and four other Irish exiles were welcomed to New York by a great military and civil parade. He found employment on the New York *Herald*, became its foreign editor, but was discharged because of his views of Irish matters. Devoy established and edited a newspaper, the *Irish Nation*, organized the rescue of Irish political prisoners in Australia by the American ship *Catalpa*, reorganized the Fenian movement in the U.S. under the secret name of the United Brotherhood and the public name Clan-na-Gael (which might be translated either as *Irish People* or *Irish Nation*), successfully opposed factionists who, employing violence, sought to use the organization for political purposes, supported the agrarian program of the Land League, and in 1878 inaugurated the New Departure policy of coöperation with the Irish party in the British House of Commons, under the leadership of Charles Stewart Parnell, on condition that Parnell should support the land agitation and leave the door open for future realization of Irish independence. In the 1890's and early 1900's the organized Irish nationalists in the U.S. under Devoy's leadership, with the aid of Senator Matthew Stanley Quay and others, were able on three occasions to cause the rejection by the U.S. Senate of treaties with Great Britain which they considered to be concealed alliances and inimical to American interests. In 1903 Devoy founded the *Gaelic American*, a weekly newspaper which he edited until his death. Anticipating from the early 1900's a war between Great Britain and Germany, he took steps to rebuild the Fenian organization (Irish Republican Brotherhood) in Ireland, and with the outbreak of World War I he established contact with the German government which led to the German mission of Roger Casement and to the unsuccessful effort to land arms and munitions from Germany in Ireland. Under his leadership the Clan-na-Gael supplied most of the funds which made the Easter Week Rebellion (1916) possible, and subsequently established the Friends of Irish Freedom, which grew to a membership of many hundreds of thousands. The Clan and the Friends were mainly instrumental in selling millions of dollars' worth of Irish Republic Bond Certificates after the arrival of Eamon De Valera in the United States, but De Valera in his enmity toward certain of Devoy's associates did not hesitate to attack "the Old Man" and to split the unprecedently united and powerful Irish forces in this country. Nevertheless Devoy and his associates were able to influence leaders of the Republican Party to prevent American adherence to the League of Nations, which they believed dangerous to America and to Ireland. In 1924 John Devoy, once exiled by the British government with orders never to return to Ireland, was officially welcomed at Cobh by the government of the Irish Free State, and by vast multitudes who agreed with Padraic Pearse that he was "the greatest of the Fenians."

Devrient (dẹ.vrēnt', dẹ.vrē.äṅ'), **Gustav Emil.** b. at Berlin, Sept. 4, 1803; d. at Dresden, Germany, Aug. 7, 1872. German actor; brother of Karl August Devrient and Philipp Eduard Devrient, and nephew of Ludwig Devrient. His playing of Hamlet at Dresden was his most notable role.

Devrient, Karl August. b. at Berlin, April 5, 1797; d. at Lauterberg, in the Harz, Germany, Aug. 3, 1872. German actor; brother of Gustav Emil Devrient and Philipp Eduard Devrient, and nephew of Ludwig Devrient. He was noted for his Shakespearian roles, especially King Lear.

Devrient, Ludwig. b. at Berlin, Dec. 15, 1784; d. there, Dec. 30, 1832. German actor notable in his day for Shakespearian roles, both tragic and comic. He was an intimate friend of Ernst Theodor Wilhelm Hoffman.

Devrient, Max. b. 1857; d. 1929. German actor, last of the Devrient family in the German theater; son of Gustav Emil Devrient.

Devrient, Otto. b. at Berlin, Oct. 3, 1838; d. June 23, 1894. German actor, theatrical manager, and dramatist; son of Philipp Eduard Devrient (1801–77). As an actor he made his first bow to the public at Karlsruhe in 1856. In 1873 he became manager of the theater at Weimar, and after serving in the same capacity at Mannheim, Frankfort on the Main, and other cities, he was appointed director of the court theater of Berlin in 1889, but resigned in the following year. In collaboration with his father he translated and edited some of the works of Shakespeare in German. His own dramatic works include *Zwei Könige* (1867), *Tiberius Gracchus* (1871), *Kaiser Rotbart* (1873), and *Luther* (1883).

Devrient, Philipp Eduard. b. at Berlin, Aug. 11, 1801; d. at Karlsruhe, Baden, Germany, Oct. 4, 1877. German actor, dramatic writer, and playwright; brother of Karl August Devrient and Gustav Emil Devrient, and nephew of Ludwig Devrient. He was director of the court theaters at Dresden and Karlsruhe. His chief work is a *Geschichte der deutschen Schauspielkunst* (5 vols., 1848–74; reprinted in 2 vols., 1905).

De Vries (dẹ vrēs'), **David Pietersen.** b. at La Rochelle, France, c1592; d. c1655. Dutch merchant skipper and colonist in America. He was a partner (c1631) in the Dutch West India Company colony founded in Delaware but soon destroyed by Indians. On his last voyage (1638–44) he founded a colony on Staten Island and one near Tappan, N.Y., both destroyed by the Indians in 1643. He recounts his travels in *Korte Historiael, ende Journaels aenteyckeninge Van verscheyden Voyagiens in de vrier deelen des Wereldts-Ronde, als Europa, Africa, Asia, ende Amerika gedaen* (1655).

De Vries, Hendrik de. b. 1896—. Dutch poet and painter. His magical and haunted poetry reflects the same nightmarish dream world as that portrayed in his paintings. His poetical works include *Lofzangen* (Songs of Praise, 1923), *Stormfakkels* (Storm Torches, 1932), *Nergal* (1937), *Atlantische Balladen* (1937), and *Robijnen* (Rubies, 1944). He also did translations of Spanish folksongs in *Copla's* (1935).

De Vries, Hugo de. b. at Haarlem, the Netherlands, Feb. 16, 1848; d. at Lunteren, The Netherlands, May 21, 1935. Dutch botanist, professor of plant anatomy and physiology at the University of Würzburg. He was noted for his contributions to the theory of evolution and especially for his researches on mutation in plants. He studied at the universities of Leiden, Heidelberg, and Würzburg, and became professor of botany at the University of Amsterdam in 1878, and at the University of Würzburg in 1897. He published various works on botanical subjects, among them *Eine Methode zur Analyse der Turgorkraft* (1884), *Plasmolytische Studien über die Wand der Vaculoen* (1885), *Leerboek der Plantenphysiologie* (1885), *Intracellulare Pangenesis* (1889), *Monographie der Zwangsdrehungen* (1892), *Die Mutationstheorie* (1900–03), *Plant Breeding* (1907), and *Die Mutationem in der Erblichkeitslehre* (1912).

De Walden (dẹ wôl'dẹn), **T. B.** fl. second half of the 19th century. American dramatist, whose plays were highly successful throughout the U.S. during the 1860's and 70's, and later. He wrote *Sam* (1865), *British Neutrality* (1869), an exciting war play, *Kit, the Arkansas Traveler* (1870, first produced in that year, on Feb. 14, at the Boston Theater), and *The Baroness* (1872), which was a hit at the New York Fifth Avenue Theater. His best-known drama, *Kit, the Arkansas Traveler*, was long popular, the character of Kit Redding being one of the most successful roles of Francis S. Chanfrau, American actor of French birth, who acted it for 12 successive seasons from 1872 until his death in 1884, and of his son, Henry Chanfrau, who played it as late as 1894.

Dewangiri (dā.wän.gē′rē). [Also, **Diwangiri.**] Place on the boundary of the Kamrup district, Assam, Union of India, ab. 360 mi. NE of Calcutta: scene of engagements between the Bhutias and English troops in 1865.

Dewar (dū′ạr), Sir **James.** b. at Kincardine-on-Forth, Perthshire, Scotland, Sept. 20, 1842; d. March 27, 1923. British physicist and chemist, professor of experimental philosophy at Cambridge and of chemistry at the Royal Institution, London. He was best known for his investigations of the properties of matter at the lowest temperatures and for the invention of the Dewar flask, a container designed to prevent heat radiation (a flask with a silvered outer surface is placed within another with a silvered inner surface so that a vacuum exists between the two), the prototype of the familiar thermos bottle. With Sir Frederick Abel he invented cordite. He was knighted in 1904.

Dewar, John. d. Jan. 22, 1880. British whiskey distiller and merchant. Established successful whiskey-distilling business at Perth, Scotland; founder of John Dewar and Sons; succeeded after death by two sons, Thomas and John Dewar.

Dewer Rides (dū′ėr). Novel by L. A. G. Strong, published in 1929.

D'Ewes (dūz), Sir **Simonds.** b. at Coxden, Dorsetshire, England, Dec. 18, 1602; d. at Stow Langtoft Hall, Suffolk, England, April 8, 1650. English antiquary and chronicler. He collected journals of all the Parliaments during the reign of Queen Elizabeth (published 1682). His manuscripts were sold, after his death, to Sir Robert Harley (afterward Earl of Oxford), and are now in the British Museum.

De Wet (dẹ vet′), **Christiaan Rudolf.** b. in the Orange Free State, South Africa, Oct. 7, 1854; d. at Bloemfontein, Orange Free State, Feb. 3, 1922. Boer general. He was a member (1889–97) of the Volksraad, at the outbreak of the South African war in 1899 was appointed vice-commandant in Natal, and in December of the same year was made general on the western frontier under the command of General Cronje. He was most successful in guerrilla warfare, and was distinguished as a leader and strategist. After the close of the war he was a member of the committee for raising funds for the distressed Boers. In 1902 he published *Three Years' War.* In 1907 he was made minister for agriculture of the Orange River Colony (now Orange Free State). He was imprisoned (1914–15) as a result of his rebellion against the South African state during World War I.

De Wette (dẹ vet′ẹ), **Wilhelm Martin Leberecht.** b. at Ulla, near Weimar, Germany, Jan. 12, 1780; d. at Basel, Switzerland, June 16, 1849. German Protestant theologian and Biblical critic, professor at Heidelberg (1807–10), at Berlin (1810–19), and at Basel (1822–49). His chief works are *Beiträge zur Einleitung in das Alte Testament* (1806–07), *Kommentar über die Psalmen* (1811), *Lehrbuch der hebraïsch-jüdischen Archäologie* (1814), *Über Religion und Theologie* (1815), *Lehrbuch der Christlichen Dogmatik* (1813–16), and others.

Dewey (dū′i). City in NE Oklahoma, in Washington County ab. 45 mi. N of Tulsa. Laid out in 1898, it was named for the Spanish-American War admiral George Dewey. Cement is manufactured and an annual rodeo is held here. 2,513 (1950).

Dewey, Charles Melville. b. at Lowville, N.Y., July 16, 1849; d. Jan. 17, 1937. American painter. He was a pupil of Carolus Duran at Paris (1876–77). His work is composed of landscapes which usually represent the subdued light of morning or evening, with masses of dark trees against the sky. He won silver medals at the Pan-American Exposition at Buffalo in 1901, and at the Louisiana Purchase Exposition at St. Louis in 1904, and was elected associate of the National Academy of Design in 1903 and member in 1907.

Dewey, Chester. b. at Sheffield, Mass., Oct. 25, 1784; d. at Rochester, N.Y., Dec. 15, 1867. American clergyman and botanist.

Dewey, Davis Rich. b. at Burlington, Vt., April 7, 1858; d. at Cambridge, Mass., Dec. 13, 1942. American economist; elder brother of John Dewey (1859–1952).

Dewey, George. b. at Montpelier, Vt., Dec. 26, 1837; d. at Washington, D.C., Jan. 16, 1917. American naval officer, noted for his defeat of the Spanish squadron in Manila Bay during the Spanish-American War. He graduated (1858) from Annapolis, was commissioned lieutenant (1861), and as executive officer of the *Mississippi* took part under Farragut in the naval operations against New Orleans and Port Hudson during the Civil War. He was again under Farragut as executive officer of the flagship *Monongahela* on the lower Mississippi River. The postwar years were filled with various tours of duty, leading up to his appointment (1889) as chief of the bureau of equipment in the Navy Department, his designation (1895) as president of the Board of Inspection and Survey, and his assignment (1897) to the command of the Asiatic squadron. He reinforced his already impressive knowledge of the Philippines, and upon his arrival in the Far East prepared a base at Mirs Bay, at Hong Kong, on the Chinese mainland, also taking other measures to bring his fleet up to battle fitness. When war with Spain broke out, Dewey faced in the Far East a Spanish squadron which many believed to be superior to the American. However, the epic battle of Manila Bay (May 1, 1898) demonstrated Dewey's superior seamanship. Within the space of less than seven hours, his U.S. squadron virtually destroyed the Spanish ships and shore batteries, and at noon the American battle vessels were anchored off Manila. The Spanish lost all of their ships and suffered 381 casualties; the American loss was damage to four ships and eight wounded. The battle restored America's confidence in her navy, made the U.S. a power in the Far East, and brought Dewey the laurels of a popular hero. Congress gave him the rank of admiral of the navy and the people made him a gift of a home at Washington. His last service with the navy was as president (1900–17) of the general board of the Navy Department. See *Autobiography of George Dewey* (1913).

Dewey, John. b. at Burlington, Vt., Oct. 20, 1859; d. at New York, June 1, 1952. American philosopher, teacher, and author. He was educated at local schools, at the University of Vermont, and at the Johns Hopkins University. In addition to the B.A. and Ph.D., he held honorary degrees from Wisconsin, Peking National University, Oslo, the University of Paris, and Vermont and Johns Hopkins. In 1886, on July 28, he married one of his Michigan students, Alice Chipman (who died in 1927). His daughter Evelyn collaborated with him on *Schools of To-Morrow* (1915), one of his best-known books. As a professor of philosophy, Dewey served successively at three large American universities: the University of Michigan (1884–88, and 1889–94, spending the year in between at the University of Minnesota), the University of Chicago (1894–1904), to which he was called by its first president, William Rainey Harper, and, as a direct result of the name he made for himself there, Columbia University, from 1904 until he retired in 1930. A prolific writer, some of his works are *Psychology* (1886), *Leibnitz* (1888), *Critical Theory of Ethics* and *Study of Ethics* (both 1894), *School and Society* (1899), *Studies in Logical Theory* (1903), *How We Think* (1909), *Influence of Darwin on Philosophy and Other Essays* (1910), *Interest and Effort in Education* (1913), *Democracy and Education* (1916), *Human Nature and Conduct* (1922), *Experience and Nature* (1925), *The Public and Its Problems* (1927), *The Quest for Certainty: A Study of the Relation of Knowledge and Action* and *Impressions of Soviet Russia and the Revolutionary World* (both 1929), *Philosophy and Civilization* (1931), *Art as Experience* (1934), *Liberalism and Social Action* (1935), *Logic* (1938), *Freedom and Culture* (1939), *Education Today* (1940), and *Problems of Man* (1946). Dewey traveled very widely, visiting China, Japan, Constantinople, Russia, and England, studying their educational systems and their ways of living and thinking. What he found out and what conclusions he reached he expressed in *Reconstruction in Philosophy* (1920), in his *Impressions*, and in the Gifford Lectures that he delivered in 1929 at Edinburgh. Although primarily a philosopher, and thought of as a man most at home in the field of the abstract, he was interested during his life in practical political, social, and economic problems. He believed in action as well as thought, and was not averse to serving on committees.

Dewey, Melvil. [Original name, **Melville Louis Kossuth Dewey.**] b. at Adams Center, N.Y., Dec. 10, 1851; d. in Florida, Dec. 26, 1931. American librarian, advocate of reformed spelling, and founder of the "Dewey Decimal System" of cataloguing books. He was educated at the local Hungerford Collegiate Institute and Oneida Seminary, both of which he attended for very short periods, and at Amherst College, from which he received his B.A. in 1874. In 1876 he published *A Classification and Subject Index for Cataloguing and Arranging the Books and Pamphlets of a Library* (13th ed., 1932), which later developed into the system which is his chief contribution to furthering knowledge. From 1883 to 1888 he was chief librarian at Columbia University and professor of library economy. He served as director (1889–1906) of the (Albany) New York State Library and for practically the same period was director of the New York State Library School, which he founded in 1887. He was editor of the *Library Journal* (1876–81) and *Library Notes* (1886–98), both of which he founded. He was also interested in English spelling and in 1876 he organized the Spelling Reform Association, of which he served as secretary for many years. At Columbia, in 1887, he opened a School of Library Economy for women students, but he was suspended by the board of trustees on Nov. 5, 1888 because of some of the items on a questionnaire he required the students to fill out. He resigned, on Dec. 20, after the suspension had been terminated, and his resignation was accepted on Jan. 7, 1889. The school transferred to Albany the next year, and Dewey went with it. His first wife, Annie Roberts Godfrey, whom he married on Oct. 19, 1878, was a librarian at Wellesley College; she died Aug. 3, 1922, at Lake Placid, N.Y., where Dewey was president of the Lake Placid Club, founded by him and his wife in 1893. Dewey's full given name was Melville Louis Kossuth, but he dropped his middle names in his early twenties, and the *le* from his first name.

Dewey, Orville. b. at Sheffield, Mass., March 28, 1794; d. there, March 21, 1882. American Unitarian clergyman and writer. His works include *Human Nature*, *Human Life*, *Unitarian Belief*, and others.

Dewey, Thomas Edmund. b. at Owosso, Mich., March 24, 1902—. American lawyer and politician. A graduate of Michigan (B.A., 1923) and of Columbia (LL.B., 1925), he served (1933) as U.S. attorney for the southern district of New York, and as special prosecutor (1935–37) to investigate organized crime in New York City. In this position and as district attorney (1937–38) for New York County Dewey rose to national recognition as an able prosecutor who smashed several of the rackets plaguing the city. Governor (1942 *et seq.*) of New York, he was the Republican candidate (1944, 1948) for president, losing a wartime election to F. D. Roosevelt and a surprising postwar contest to Harry S. Truman. He is the author of *The Case Against the New Deal* (1940).

Dewi (dā′wi), Saint. See Saint **David** or **Dewi.**

de Windsor (dę win′zǫr), **Alice.** See **Perrers, Alice.**

De Windt (dę wint′), **Harry.** b. at Paris, in April, 1850; d. Nov. 30, 1933. English traveler and explorer. He was educated at Cambridge, was aide-de-camp (1876–78) to Raja Brooke of Sarawak, his brother-in-law, traveled from Peiping to France by land in 1887, rode from Russia to India through Persia in 1889, and attempted to travel from New York to Paris by way of Alaska, but nearly lost his life in Bering Strait, where he was rescued by a whaler. In 1901–02 he made the trip by land from Paris to New York. He traveled through the Balkan states in 1905 and crossed Lapland in the winter of 1908. He published a number of books of travel, including *From Paris to New York by Land* (1903), *Through Savage Europe* (1905), *Moles and their Meaning* (1908), and *Notes of a Restless Life* (1908).

Dewing (dū′ing), **Francis.** fl. late 17th–early 18th centuries. American engraver. Born in England, his arrival at Boston was noted in a newspaper of that city late in July, 1716, with the information that he was prepared to engrave coats of arms and other designs on copper or on silver plates, and also to execute woodcuts for the printing of textiles. His best-known surviving work is a large map of Boston which he engraved and published in 1722.

Dewing, Maria Richards Oakey. b. at New York City, 1845; d. 1927. American painter; wife of Thomas Wilmer Dewing. She studied at the National Academy of Design in New York and under John LaFarge and others. She painted especially flowers, figure compositions, and portraits.

Dewing, Thomas Wilmer. b. at Boston, May 4, 1851; d. Nov. 6, 1938. American painter. He studied art (1876–79) under Jules Lefebvre at Paris, was elected associate of the National Academy of Design in 1887 and academician in 1888, and won the Clarke prize at the Academy in 1887. His work includes figure pictures and interiors admired for their delicacy and refinement.

De Wint (dę wint′), **Peter.** b. at Stone, Staffordshire, England, 1784; d. at London, 1849. English painter, especially in water colors. He rejected a career in medicine to study painting, first under private teachers and later in classes of the Royal Academy. He did not entirely neglect oil painting, but by far the greater part of his work was done in water colors. He became a member of the Royal Water-Colour Society in 1812, and exhibited chiefly at that Society's shows. His subjects were chiefly landscapes depicting the Staffordshire and Lincolnshire countryside. Some of his oils, and many of his water colors, are in the collections of the South Kensington Museum and the National Gallery, at London.

De Winter (dę win′tėr), **Jan Willem.** b. on the island of Texel, Netherlands, 1750; d. at Paris, June 2, 1812. Dutch admiral, commander at the battle of Camperdown (Oct. 11, 1797).

De Witt (dē wit′). City in SE Arkansas, county seat of Arkansas County, ab. 60 mi. SE of Little Rock. It has cotton gins and rice mills and ships livestock and lumber. 2,843 (1950).

De Witt. City in E Iowa, in Clinton County, ab. 60 mi. SE of Cedar Rapids. It was named for De Witt Clinton. 2,644 (1950).

De Witt (dę wit′), **Cornelius.** b. at Dordrecht, Netherlands, 1623; murdered at The Hague, Aug. 20, 1672. Dutch politician and naval officer; brother of Jan De Witt.

De Witt, Jan. b. at Dordrecht, Netherlands, Dec. 25, 1625; murdered at The Hague, Aug. 20, 1672. Dutch statesman. He became grand pensionary of Holland in 1653 and terminated the war with England (which had broken out in 1652) by a treaty with Cromwell in 1654. He carried on a war with England (1665–67) after the Restoration had put the Stuart James II on the throne of England. In 1668 he procured the passage of the Perpetual Edict (directed against the house of Orange) and in the same year negotiated with England and Sweden the Triple Alliance, which frustrated the design of Louis XIV to annex the Spanish Netherlands. He was overthrown by the Orange party in 1672 when Louis XIV invaded the Netherlands, and with his brother Cornelius was torn to pieces at The Hague by an infuriated mob.

Dewsbury (dūz′bėr.i). County borough, market town, and manufacturing center in N central England, in the West Riding of Yorkshire, situated on the river Calder, ab. 8 mi. SW of Leeds, ab. 182 mi. N of London by rail. It is a center of the shoddy manufacture, and also has some carpet manufactures. 53,476 (1951).

Dexileus (dek.sil′ę̄.us), **Monument of.** Monument on the Street of Tombs at Athens. It is a beautiful stele bearing in relief a youthful horseman who has ridden down an enemy. Dexileus fell before Corinth in 394 or 393 B.C.

Dexippus (dek.sip′us), **Publius Herennius.** b. c210 A.D.; d. c280 A.D. Greek historian. He commanded a band of patriots in 262 against the Goths or Scythians who invaded Greece and captured Athens. He wrote an account of this invasion, entitled *Skythika*, fragments of which are extant.

Dexter (deks′tėr). Town (in Maine the equivalent of township in many other states) and unincorporated village in C Maine, in Penobscot County: woolen textiles. Pop. of town, 4,126 (1950); of village, 2,809 (1950).

Dexter. City in SE Missouri, in Stoddard County: processing point for poultry products, cotton, and flour. 4,624 (1950).

Dexter, Henry Martyn. b. at Plympton, Mass., Aug. 13, 1821; d. at New Bedford, Mass., Nov. 13, 1890. American Congregational clergyman and historian, editor of the *Congregationalist* (at Boston) 1851–66 and from 1867. His works include *The Voice of the Bible* (1858), *Congregationalism* (1865), *Church Policy of the Puritans* (1870), *The Congregationalism of the last Three Hundred Years* (1880; including a bibliography of over 7,000 titles), and *Common Sense as to Woman Suffrage* (1885). *A Bibliography of the Church Struggle in England during the Sixteenth Century* and *A History of the Old Plymouth Colony* were in preparation at his death.

Dexter, Samuel. b. at Boston, May 14, 1761; d. at Athens, N.Y., May 4, 1816. American jurist and politician. He served as secretary of war in 1800 and secretary of the treasury in 1801.

Dexter, Timothy. [Called **"Lord Timothy Dexter."**] b. at Malden, Mass., Jan. 22, 1747; d. at Newburyport, Mass., Oct. 23, 1806. American merchant and eccentric. He settled (1769) at Newburyport, Mass., after serving his apprenticeship on a farm and at dressing skins, and entered business as a leather dresser. He made his fortune by buying up depreciated Continental currency whose value was stabilized in 1791. Thereafter he engaged in a variety of mercantile undertakings and speculations, amassing riches which enabled him to buy some stately homes at Newburyport. His eccentricity (he gratuitously added the title of "Lord" to his name) converted his High Street mansion into a bizarre showplace. A ship-carver was commissioned to make more than 40 life-sized and colored statues, among them representations of Saint Paul, Saint John, Saint Peter, Adam and Eve, Lord Nelson, Washington, Jefferson, and Louis XIV. A statue of himself, arranged like the others to public view, bore an inscription that read, in part: "I am first in the East." Later in his life he conducted a mock funeral before his own coffin, beating his wife when she did not cry. Having written a book, *Pickle for the Knowing Ones* (1802), which was criticized because it had no punctuation at all, he issued a second edition with a page-full of commas and periods, asking his readers to use them as they pleased. He bequeathed gifts to several church and charitable institutions. See *Lord Timothy Dexter*, by John P. Marquand (1925).

Dey (dā). See **De.**

Dey, Frederick Van Rensselaer. See **Carter, Nick.**

de Young (dẹ yung′), **Michel Harry.** b. at St. Louis, Mo., Sept. 30, 1849; d. Feb. 15, 1925. American newspaper editor, cofounder (1865) of the San Francisco *Daily Dramatic Chronicle* (now the San Francisco *Chronicle*). Brought to California in childhood, he and his brother, Charles de Young (1847–80), made the *Chronicle* the West's most influential paper, successfully attacking (1872) land monopoly and agitating (1879) for a new state constitution. Its sole owner and editor in chief (1880 *et seq.*), he was also director for 25 years of the Associated Press.

Deyssel (dī′sẹl), **Lodewijk van.** [Pseudonym of **Karel J. L. Alberdingk Thijm.**] b. 1864—. Dutch essayist and novelist, leading critic of the "Movement of 1880," credited with reviving the Dutch art of prose writing. At first he was a passionate partisan of naturalism and *l'art pour l'art* tendencies; later, he turned to symbolism in such works as *De Dood van het Naturalisme* (Death of Naturalism, 1891) and *Van Zola tot Maeterlinck* (1895). Author of *In de zwemschool* (In the Swimming School), *Menschen en Bergen* (Men and Mountains, 1891), *Jeugd* (Youth, 1892), *Kindleven* (Child Life, 1904), *Vebeeldingen* (Imaginations, 1908). His novels include *Een Liefde* (Love, 1887) and *De kleine republiek* (The Small Republic, 1888). His *Collected Works* (8 vols.) were published 1922–24. English translations of his works are found in *Harvest of the Lowlands*, by J. Greshoff.

Dezhnev (dyezh′nif) or **Dezhneva** (dyezh′ni.vạ), **Cape.** See **East Cape,** U.S.S.R.

Dezhneva (dyezh′ni.vạ), **Mys.** Russian name of **East Cape,** U.S.S.R.

Dhahran (dä.rän′). [Former name, **Qatif** or **El Qatif.**] City in Saudi Arabia, on the E coast, on the Persian Gulf near the island of Bahrein: site of one of the largest oil fields in Arabia, controlled by American companies. A large refinery has been located at nearby Ras Tannura. The largest American population in the Middle East is found in this completely modern city.

Dhaka (dä′kä). See **Dacca.**

Dhalim (ᴛʜä′lim). The third-magnitude star β Eridani. It is more often called Cursa.

Dhamar (dä.mär′). [Also, **Damar.**] Town in S central Yemen, Arabia, ab. 65 mi. S of San'a, on the caravan route between San'a and Aden. The town is the chief center of a mountain valley basin on the E slope of the Yemen highlands. The region is an important cereal-growing area. Elevation, ab. 7,650 ft.; pop. ab. 40,000 (1945).

Dhammapada (däm.ạ.pä′dạ). Portion of the Buddhist Scriptures, the second division of the *Khuddakanikaya* or *Collection of Short Treatises.* It contains 423 stanzas in 26 chapters, and is a manual of ethics.

Dhar (där). One of the former states of Central India, now (since 1948) merged with Madhya Bharat, Union of India, NE of Bombay: cotton, wheat, cattle, and millet. Capital, Dhar; pop. 253,210 (1941).

Dhar. Town in Madhya Bharat, Union of India, former capital of Dhar state, ab. 300 mi. NE of the city of Bombay: trading center. Pop. ab. 20,000.

Dhar Adrar (där′ ä.drär′). See **Adrar.**

Dharmashastra (där.mạ.shäs′trạ). Body of Hindu law; more especially, the laws ascribed to Manu, Yajnavalkya, and other sages believed to have been given divine inspiration. These works are generally in three parts: (1) *achara,* rules of conduct; (2) *vyavahara,* judicature; (3) *prayashchitta,* penance. The inspired lawgivers are spoken of as 18 but 42 are mentioned. Manu and Yajnavalkya stand at their head. A general collection of the *Dharmashastras* has been printed at Calcutta by Jivananda under the title of *Dharmashastrasangraha.*

Dharwar (där.wär′). [Also: **Darwar, Dharwad** (-wäd′).] District in Bombay state, Union of India, E of Goa. It produces cotton, wheat, tobacco, and spices. Chief town, Dharwar; pop. 1,201,016 (1941).

Dharwar. [Also: **Darwar, Dharwad.**] Chief town of Dharwar district, Bombay state, Union of India, ab. 80 mi. E of Goa: trading center, served by a railroad and three major roads. It was taken by Hyder Ali in 1778, and retaken by the Mahrattas in 1791. Pop. 41,671 (1941).

Dhaulagiri (dou.lạ.gir′i). [Also: **Dhawalagiri, Dhwalagiri.**] Peak in the Himalayas, in Nepal, ab. 80 mi. NW of Patan. It was once supposed to be the highest mountain in the world, but now takes fifth position. Elevation, ab. 26,492 ft.

Dhaun (doun), Count **Leopold Joseph Maria von.** See **Daun,** Count **Leopold (Joseph Maria) von.**

Dhawalagiri (dou.lạ.gir′i). See **Dhaulagiri.**

Dhegiha (dā′gē.hä). Division of the Siouan North American Indian language family, embracing the Ponca, Omaha, Kansa, Osage, and Quapaw tribes.

d'Hérelle (dā.rel), **Félix Hubert.** b. at Montreal, April 25, 1873—. Canadian bacteriologist, noted for the discovery (1917) of bacteriophage. Bacteriologist (1902–06) to the government of Guatemala; director (1907–08) of the government bacteriological laboratory at Mérida, Mexico; assistant (1908–14) and chief (1914–21) at the Pasteur Institute at Paris; head (1921–23) of the laboratory at the University of Leiden, Netherlands; professor (1928–33) of bacteriology at Yale; professor (1934 *et seq.*) at the University of Tiflis in Russia. Author of *Le Cocobacille des Sauterelles* (1914), *Le Bactériophage, son rôle dans l'immunité* (1921; Eng. trans., 1922), *Bacterial Mutations* (1934), *Le Phénomène de la Guérison* (1938), and *Étude d'une maladie, le Choléra* (1946).

Dhiban (ᴛʜē.bän′, dē-). [Ancient name, **Dibon.**] Town in Jordan, ab. 37 mi. S of Amman and ab. 14 mi. E of the Dead Sea. It is a trading center in the midst of some of the best agricultural land in Jordan. A Moabite stone found here in 1868 carried a lengthy Hebrew inscription from c850 B.C. The ancient city of Dibon was fortified by the Gadites (Num. xxxii. 3,34), but allotted to the tribe of Reuben (Josh. xiii. 9,17). The stone discovered there is thought to be the stele of the Moabite king Mesha (2 Kings, iii. 4).

Dhipotamo (ᴛʜē.pô′tä.mô). See **Pamisos.**

Dhoire (dur′ẹ). Irish name of **Londonderry** city.

Dhoire, Conndae. Irish name of County **Londonderry.**

Dholpur (dōl′pör). Former native state in the Rajputana region, N Union of India, since 1949 merged with Rajasthan Union, ab. 150 mi. S of Delhi: wheat, cotton, barley, and millet. Area, 1,197 sq. mi.; pop. 286,901 (1941).

Dhritarashtra (dri.tạ.räsh′trạ). In Hindu legend, the eldest son of Vichitravirya or Vyasa, and brother of Pandu. He had by Gandhari a hundred sons, of whom the eldest was Duryodhana. Dhritarashtra was blind, and Pandu was affected with a disease supposed from his name, "the pale," to have been leprosy. The two brothers renounced the throne, and the great war recorded in the *Mahabharata* was fought between their sons, one party being called Kauravas after an ancestor named Kuru, the other Pandavas after their father Pandu.

Dhu-l-Hijja (döl.hēj′jä). [Also, **Dulheggia.**] Moslem month, twelfth of the calendar, having 29 days in regular years and 30 days in intercalary years.

Dhu-l-Kada (döl.kä′dä). [Also, **Dulkaada.**] Moslem month, eleventh in the year, having 30 days.

Dhwalagiri (dwä.lạ.gir′i). See **Dhaulagiri.**

Dhyani Buddha (dyä′nē bůd′ạ, bö′dạ). In Buddhist theology, one of the Buddhas evolved from the Adi-Buddha, and producing, by wisdom and contemplation, the Bodhisattva. The earlier Buddhism teaches that above the worlds of the gods there are 16 *Brahmalokas* ("worlds of Brahma"), one above another. Those who attain on earth to the first, second, or third *dhyanas*, or states of "mystic meditation," are reborn in the lower of these worlds, three being assigned to each stage or dhyana. Those who attain the fourth enter the tenth and eleventh Brahmalokas. The remaining five are assigned to those who attain to the third path on earth, and who will reach Nirvana in the new existence, the third path being that of those who will never return to this world, in whose hearts, the last remnants of sensuality and malevolence being destroyed, not the least low desire for oneself, or wrong feeling toward others, can arise. To each of these five groups of worlds the Great Vehicle, the northern school of Buddhism, assigns a special Buddha, called Dhyani Buddha. These five Buddhas correspond to the last four Buddhas, including Gautama, and the future Buddha, Maitreya. Each of these human Buddhas has his corresponding Bodhisattva and Dhyani Buddha, the latter being his pure and glorious counterpart in the mystic world, free from the debasing conditions of the material life. The material Buddha is only the emanation of a Dhyani Buddha living in the ethereal mansions of mystic trance.

Diabe (dē.ä′bā). [Also: **Askikaso, Sikasso.**] One of the Sudanic-speaking Anyi peoples of W Africa, inhabiting SE Ivory Coast between the Bonda and Ndenie peoples.

Diabelli (dē.ä.bel′ē), **Antonio.** b. at Mattsee, Austria, in September, 1781; d. at Vienna, April 7, 1858. Austrian composer and founder (1824) of the music-publishing firm of Diabelli and Company. He composed an operetta, masses, songs, and piano works; one of his waltzes served as the theme for Beethoven's *33 Variations* (Opus 120).

Diable (dyȧbl), **Île du.** French name of **Devil's Island.**

Diable boiteux (dyȧbl bwȧ.tė), **Le.** [Eng. trans., "*The Lame Devil.*"] Satirical romance by Alain René Le Sage, published in 1707. It was an imitation of a Spanish work entitled *El Diablo cojuelo*, written by Luis Vélez de Guevara, and first printed in 1641, and of other satires (by Cervantes and others) long current. The whole work is in dialogue form. Samuel Foote took from it his play *The Devil on Two Sticks*. The title *Le Diable boiteux* has been given to a number of other publications.

Diablerets (dyȧ.blẹ.re). Group of mountains in Switzerland, on the borders of Vaud, Valais, and Bern cantons, NE of St. Maurice. Highest point, ab. 10,650 ft.

Diablintes (dī.ạ.blin′tēz) or **Diablindi** (-blin′dī). Tribe of NW Gaul, allies of the Veneti against Caesar in 56 B.C. The Diablintes are thought to have lived near Le Mans. They were one of four tribes forming a group known as the Aulerci. The other three members of this group were the Cenomani, the Eburovici, and the Brannovici.

Diablo Dam (dī.ab′lō). Power dam in NW Washington, in the Skagit River ab. 58 mi. E of Bellingham, Wash. It was built in 1927–30 by the city of Seattle as a municipal power plant. Length of dam, ab. 1,180 ft.; height, ab. 389 ft.; installed capacity of the two power stations, ab. 196,000 kw.

Diabouba (dē.ä.bö′bạ). See **Dan.**

Diaconus (dī.ak′ọ.nus), **Paulus.** See **Paulus Diaconus.**

Diadochi (dī.ad′ọ.kī). The Macedonian generals of Alexander the Great who, after his death in 323 B.C., divided his empire. Literally, the name means "successors." The several empires that were established were the Seleucid in Syria and Asia Minor, the Ptolemid in Egypt, the Attalid in Pergamum, and the Antigonid in Macedonia.

Diadumenos (dī.ạ.dū′mẹ.nos). Athlete binding his brow with a fillet, a good Roman reproduction of a famous statue by Polyclitus, found at Vaison, France, and acquired by the British Museum.

Diafoba (dē.ä.fō′bạ). See **Dan.**

Diafoirus (dē.ȧ.fwȧ.rüs). Name of the physician in Molière's *Malade imaginaire* to whose son Thomas Argan wishes to betroth his daughter Angélique. The father is very comical, and the son, full of folly and erudition, no less so.

Diaghilev (dyä′gẹ.lif), **Sergei Pavlovich.** b. at Perm, Novgorod, Russia, March 19, 1872; d. at Venice, Aug. 19, 1929. Russian ballet producer. He founded (1899) *Mir Ikusstra*, an art review at St. Petersburg which was widely influential in the Russian art of the period, began (1907) producing Russian ballets and operas, and organized (1909) the Ballet Russe, which performed at Paris, London, Berlin, and other cities in Europe and the U.S. He was associated with such artists as Nijinsky, Pavlova, Massine, Karsavina, Fokine, Lifar, Stravinsky, and Bakst.

Diagoras (dī.ag′ọ.rạs). [Surnamed **"the Atheist."**] b. on the island of Melos, in the Aegean Sea; fl. last half of the 5th century B.C. Greek philosopher, accused by the Athenians of impiety because of his attacks on the Eleusinian mysteries.

Diaguita (dyä.gē′tä). Loosely organized group of Indian peoples divided into subgroups, each made up of a variable number of tribes, who lived originally in NW Argentina. Sometime before the Spanish conquest they also expanded into parts of N Chile, where their culture was submerged by that of the Incas. One of the chief subgroups, the Calchaqui, became so famous for their fierce resistance to the Spanish that their name has sometimes been applied to the Diaguita group as a whole. Their culture was of a simplified Andean type with an agriculture based on maize. Stone architecture was used for the villages and fortresses. There was an emphasis on hunting, and the herding of llamas and alpacas was of importance. Many subgroups fiercely resisted the Spaniards, and the latter were finally forced to deport them piecemeal into various parts of Spanish territory.

Diaguitan (dyä.gē′tạn). Independent linguistic stock of the Diaguita, comprised of a number of languages and dialects.

Dial, The. American literary quarterly and organ of the Transcendentalists published at Boston and edited (1840–42) by Margaret Fuller, assisted by George Ripley, Ralph Waldo Emerson, and others. It was edited (1842–44) by Emerson.

Dial, The. Monthly journal of literary criticism, published from 1880 to 1929. Under the editorship (1916 *et seq.*) of Conrad Aiken, Randolph Bourne, and Van Wyck Brooks the publication lost its conservative tone, publishing contributions by writers including Dewey, Veblen, and Laski. After Scofield Thayer became its editor in 1920, *The Dial* served as a leading American organ for new developments in art and literature.

Dialogue of Death. Book by William Bullein, published 1564–65. The whole title is *A Dialogue bothe pleasaunte and pietifull, wherein is a goodly regimente against the fever Pestilence, with a consolacion and comfort against death.*

Dialogues in Limbo. Ten philosophical discourses by George Santayana, published in 1926. The shades of Democritus, Alcibiades, Aristippus the Cyrenaic, Dionysius the Younger, Socrates, Avicenna, and the spirit of an anonymous figure still living on earth discuss esthetics, ethics, politics, and the nature of the universe.

Dialonke (dyä.lōn′kā). [Also, **Yalunka.**] Mande-speaking people of W Africa, inhabiting W French Guinea and NW Sierra Leone. Their population is estimated at more than 100,000 (based on Y. Urvoy, *Petit Atlas ethno-*

demographique du Soudan, 1942, and T. N. Goddard, *The Handbook of Sierra Leone*, 1925). They are becoming Mohammedanized.

Diamand (dyä'mänt), **Herman.** b. 1860; d. 1931. Polish socialist, one of the founders (1891) of the Polish Social-Democratic Party under the Austrian regime. He was a member of the Second International, representing (1904 *et seq.*) Polish socialists from all parts of the then partitioned country, a member (1906–18) of the Austrian parliament, and a member (1918–35) of the Polish parliament. As an expert on economic matters, he conducted negotiations (1924–28) with Germany. His published works deal mostly with statistical matters.

Diamante (dyä.män'tā). Town in E Argentina, in Entre Ríos province. 13,600 (1947).

Diamante River. See **Neuquén River.**

Diamantina (dē''ą.mun.tē'ną). [Former name, **Tejuco.**] City in E Brazil, in the state of Minas Gerais: the center of the Brazilian diamond industry. It was settled c1728. Pop. 10,177 (1950).

Diamantino (dē''ą.mun.tē'nö). Town in the state of Mato Grosso, Brazil, near the headwaters of the Paraguay River: the center of an abandoned diamond district. Pop. under 5,000 (1940).

Diamants de la Couronne (dyȧ.mäṅ dę lȧ kö.ron), **Les.** [Eng. trans., *"The Crown Diamonds."*] Opera in three acts by Auber, with a libretto by Scribe and St. George, first performed at the Opéra-Comique at Paris on March 6, 1841. The work deals with the comic adventures of Don Enriquez, culminating in his happy marriage to the Queen of Portugal.

Diamond or **Dyamond** (dī'ą.mǫnd). One of three brothers, sons of the fairy Agape, in Spenser's *Faerie Queene.* When he is slain by Cambell, his strength passes into his surviving brothers.

Diamond Head. Volcanic crater on the coast of SE Oahu, Hawaii, ab. 5 mi. SE of Honolulu. It is a noted landmark on the eastern sea approach to Honolulu. The crater is about 7/10 of a mile in diameter. Peak elevation, 761 ft.

Diamond Lens, The. Story by Fitz-James O'Brien, originally published in the *Atlantic Monthly* (January, 1858), and included in his volume *Poems and Stories* (1881).

Diamond Mountains. [Korean, **Kumgang-San**; Japanese, **Kongo-San.**] Mountain group in SE North Korea, ab. 45 mi. SE of Wonsan (Genzan). The mountains are extremely rugged and picturesque, with thick forests of pines and maples, topped by jagged, bare rock peaks. There are numerous old Buddhist temples and monasteries here, some of them having great images. Peak elevation, ab. 5,373 ft.

Diamond Necklace Affair, The. In French history, a celebrated episode which discredited the court on the eve of the French Revolution. A necklace (valued at about 300,000 dollars), originally ordered for Madame du Barry, was negotiated for (1783–84) by Cardinal de Rohan through an intermediary, the adventuress Countess de Lamotte. The cardinal had probably been duped by forged notes into thinking that Marie Antoinette, with whom he was infatuated, wanted him to get the necklace for her. Despite the charges of her contemporaries, the queen was probably innocent of complicity.

"Diamond State." A nickname of **Delaware.**

Diamond Wedding, The. Poem (1859) by Edmund Clarence Stedman.

Dian (dē.än'). Sudanic-speaking people of W Africa, inhabiting E Ivory Coast, N of the Lobi people. Their number is estimated at ab. 10,000 (by H. Labouret, *Les Tribus du Rameau Lobi*, 1931). They have exogamous patrilineal clans, and chiefs were lacking before the establishment of French rule. They practice hoe agriculture, and their principal food is millet. About 80 percent have adopted Mohammedanism. They should not be (but sometimes are) confused with the Dan of the W Ivory Coast and C Liberia.

Diana (dī.an'ą). Ancient Italian divinity, goddess of the moon, protectress of the female sex, later identified with the Greek Artemis. Like Artemis she was goddess of the hunt and the woods, protectress of chastity, and patroness of childbirth. Her famous shrine in the grove at Aricia was the scene of the custom investigated by Sir J. G. Frazer in the *Golden Bough.* Her companion, Virbius or Hippolytus, was worshiped there with her. Her priest, who came to his office by killing his predecessor in single combat, likewise might be killed by one in similar straits (specifically, a runaway slave).

Diana. Sonnet sequence (1592) by Henty Constable. The first edition contained 23 poems, which was increased to 76 in the second edition of 1594. Eight of these are known to be by Sidney, but it has not been proved that Constable is not the author of the remaining sonnets. Some of those included in anthologies are those whose first lines are "Mine eye with all the deadly sins is fraught," "Dear to my soul, then leave me not forsaken!" "To live in hell and heaven to behold," "Fair grace of graces, muse of muses all," and one called *To Sir Philip Sidney's Soul* ("Give pardon, blessed soul, to my bold cries"). The full title of the sequence is *Certaine sweete sonnets in the praise of his mistress, Diana.*

Diana. In Shakespeare's *All's Well that Ends Well*, the daughter of the Florentine widow with whom Helena lodges. She reconciles Bertram and Helena by a stratagem.

Diana. Character in Honoré d'Urfé's *Astrée*, taken from the *Diana Enamorada* of Jorge de Montemayor.

Diana and Actaeon (ak.tē'ǫn). Painting by Titian (1559), in the Bridgewater collection, London. The hunter and his dogs come suddenly upon the startled goddess and her nymphs at the bath. Diana looks angrily at the intruder, but has not yet taken action. It was painted for Philip II of Spain.

Diana and Callisto (ką.lis'tō). Painting (1559) by Titian, in the Bridgewater collection, London. The goddess sits on a bank beside a stream, and at her command, several of her nymphs hold the offending Callisto, forcibly, while another tears away her drapery. It was painted for Philip II of Spain.

Diana Enamorada (dyä'nä e.nä.mō.rä'ᴛʜä). [Eng. trans., *"Diana Enamored."*] Chief work of Jorge de Montemayor. An important pastoral romance, it was the most popular one published in Spain after *Amadis of Gaul.* It was first printed at Valencia in 1542. It was left unfinished, but in 1564 Antonio Pérez of Salamanca wrote a second part. In the same year Gaspar Gil Polo of Valencia wrote another continuation. There were many other imitations. Sir Philip Sidney translated some of the short poems. The original work was modeled to a degree on Jacopo Sannazaro's *Arcadia* (1504).

Diana of the Crossways (dī.an'ą). Novel by George Meredith, published in 1885. It deals with the romantic complications in the life of Diana Merion. She leaves her husband, Warwick, has an affair with the young politician Percy Dacier, and finally marries Thomas Redworth after Warwick's death. The character of Diana was popularly connected with Caroline Norton, Richard Brinsley Sheridan's granddaughter.

Diana of Versailles (vėr.sālz', ver.sī'). [Also, **Diana the Huntress.**] Greek statue in the Louvre, Paris, commonly regarded as a companion piece to the Apollo Belvedere, though inferior in execution. The goddess is advancing, clad in the short Dorian tunic and himation girded at her waist; she looks toward the right, as with raised arm she takes an arrow from her quiver.

Diana (or **Di**) **Vernon** (dī vėr'nǫn). See **Vernon, Diana** (or **Di**).

Diana with her Nymphs. Painting by Domenichino, in the Palazzo Borghese, Rome.

Diane de France (dyȧn dę fräṅs). [English, **Diana of France**; title, Duchesse **de Montmorency et d'Angoulême.**] b. in Piedmont, Italy, 1538; d. Jan. 3, 1619. Illegitimate daughter of Henry II of France, who played an influential part in French politics during the reigns of Henry III and Henry IV. Her mother was a Piedmontese.

Diane de Poitiers (dę pwȧ.tyā). [English, **Diana of Poitiers**; titles, Comtesse **de Brézé,** Duchesse **de Valentinois.**] b. Sept. 3, 1499; d. at Anet, in Orléanais, France, April 22, 1566. Mistress of Henry II of France, noted for her influence at the French court. She was a member of a noble family of Dauphiné, and married (1512) Louis de Brézé, grand seneschal of Normandy, who died in 1533.

Dianora and Gilberto (dyä.nō′rä; jēl.ber′tō). One of Boccaccio's tales, the fifth novel of the tenth day of the *Decameron*. Chaucer took his *Franklyn's Tale* from this story.

Dianum (dī.ā′num) or **Dianium** (dī.ā′ni.um). Ancient name of **Denia.**

Diaphanous Silkworm, Sir. See **Silkworm, Sir Diaphanous.**

Diarbekir (dē.är.be.kēr′) or **Diarbekr** (-bek′ėr). See **Diyarbakir.**

Diary of an Ennuyée. Diary by Mrs. Anna Brownell Jameson (Anna Murphy), published in 1826.

Diary of C. Jeames de la Pluche. Short story by Thackeray. It was originally published in the humorous weekly *Punch* (November, 1845–February, 1846) and was reprinted in Thackeray's *Miscellanies* (1856). The story tells the adventures of James Plush, a footman who becomes wealthy through buying railway shares, changes his ordinary name to a more aristocratic form, and takes a bachelor apartment in the aristocratic London *Albany* (where Byron, Macaulay, "Monk" Lewis, and Bulwer-Lytton once lived). He becomes engaged to the daughter of Lord Bareacres, Lady Angelina (who runs away with another suitor), loses his fortune, as quickly as he made it, in a market crash, settles down as a public-house keeper, and marries Mary Ann Hoggins.

Dias (dē′ąs), **Antônio Gonçalves.** b. on a farm near Caxias, Maranhão, Brazil, Aug. 10, 1823; d. in the shipwreck of the *Ville de Boulogne*, off the coast of Maranhão, Nov. 3, 1864. Brazilian poet, ethnographer, and scholar. The creator of Indianism in Brazilian poetry, he is generally called Brazil's national poet. He was educated at Coimbra, Portugal, was a college professor at Rio de Janeiro, and traveled in the north of the country and in Europe on government missions. His books of poetry include *Primeiros cantos* (1846), *Segundos cantos* (1848), *Últimos cantos* (1851), and *Os timbiras* (1857). He also published historical and ethnological papers, some dramas, and a dictionary of the Tupí language (1858).

Dias (dē′ąsh), **Bartolomeu.** [Also, **Díaz.**] b. c1450; d. in May, 1500. Portuguese navigator. He was a gentleman of the royal household, and in 1487 was made commander of one of two small vessels (João Iffante commanding the other) meant to explore further the coast of Africa. They passed the farthest point attained by Diogo Cam, followed the coast to the present-day Diaz Point, and thence sailed south in the open sea for 13 days in wind and storm, suffering greatly from cold. They turned eastward in search of land, and, not finding it, bore to the north, striking the coast at Mossel Bay, east of the Cape of Good Hope, and following the coast to a point beyond Algoa Bay. The sailors refused to go farther; and, after taking possession of the land for Portugal, they returned (1488) around the cape, named by him or by King John II of Portugal Cabo da Boa Esperanza (Cape of Good Hope), and reached home in safety. Some accounts say that Dias was driven beyond the cape by a storm without observing it; in any case, he and his companions were the first to double the south end of Africa. In 1497 Dias sailed with the expedition of Vasco da Gama, but remained trading on the West African coast. In 1500 he commanded a ship in the fleet commanded by Pedro Álvares Cabral that discovered Brazil; Dias was lost in a storm after leaving the Brazilian coast probably off the Cape of Good Hope.

Dias (dē′ąs), **Henrique.** b. at Pernambuco (now Recife), Brazil, c1600; d. c1660. Brazilian Negro soldier, in whose honor Brazil still maintains a regiment under Negro command. A freed Negro, he fought against Dutch domination of Brazil and became (1639) supreme commander of Negro troops in the Brazilian army.

Díaz (dē′äs), **Alberto Cabero.** See **Cabero Díaz, Alberto.**

Díaz (dē′äts), **Armando.** [Title, Duca **della Vittoria.**] b. at Naples, Italy, Dec. 5, 1861; d. at Rome, Feb. 29, 1928. Italian general and statesman. After serving (1912) in the Libyan campaign he was secretary (1913) to the chief of staff and assisted (1914) Cadorna with the reorganization of the army. He was commanding officer of the 49th division (1916–17) and the XXI army corps (May, 1917); replaced (November, 1917) Cadorna as army chief and his defense (June, 1918) at the Grappa-Piave line saved the army; conducted (October–November, 1918) the successful Vittorio-Veneto campaign. Served (1922–24) as minister of war in Mussolini's cabinet and was named (1924) marshal of Italy; bad health forced him to retire in the same year.

Díaz (dē′ąsh), **Bartholomeu.** See **Dias, Bartolomeu.**

Díaz (dē′äth), **Carlos Jiménez.** See **Jiménez Díaz, Carlos.**

Díaz, Eduardo Acevedo. See **Acevedo Díaz, Eduardo.**

Díaz, Melchior. d. cJan. 1, 1541. Spanish captain in Mexico. From c1536 to 1539 he commanded Culiacán. In November, 1539, he was sent by the viceroy Mendoza to verify the tale of Fray Marcos as to wealthy cities in the north. Going as far as "Chichilticalli," he was forced back by cold. He rejoined Coronado at Chiametla, sending a report to the viceroy. This was not favorable to Marcos, but secrecy was preserved by his superiors and the expedition proceeded. Later he escorted the discredited friar back. Executing, then, orders to explore northwest from Corazones, he crossed with 25 men NW Mexico and SW Arizona (the first to do this) to the Colorado River, which he reached (1540) ab. 80 mi. above its mouth, soon after Alarçon, the first to ascend, had passed on his return. Crossing the river, which he called Río del Tizon, he went west four days. Throwing a spear at an unruly dog, Díaz was accidentally so injured that he died. He was one of the most judicious and trusted officers of the period.

Díaz (dē′äs), **Porfirio.** [Full name, **José de la Cruz Porfirio Díaz.**] b. in Oaxaca, Mexico, Sept. 15, 1830; d. at Paris, July 2, 1915. Mexican general and statesman, president (1877–80,1884–1911) of Mexico. He served as a soldier in the war with the U.S. in 1847, led a battalion against Santa Anna in 1854, and adhered (1858) to Juárez and the liberal party in the War of the Reform. In 1861 he was a deputy, but soon took the field. During the French invasion he was one of the leaders of the defense, was captured at Puebla, in May, 1863, but escaped and headed the army of resistance in Oaxaca. Forced to surrender (February, 1865), he again escaped and raised new forces. After the withdrawal of the French army he rapidly gained ground against Maximilian's generals, taking Puebla (April 2, 1867), and finally entering Mexico City (June 21, 1867). Soon after, he was a candidate (1867) for the presidency, but Juárez was elected. General Díaz kept up a continual opposition to Juárez and his successor, Sebastián Lerdo de Tejada, and headed several revolts. In 1876 he finally drove Lerdo out, served (1876–77) as provisional president, and in May, 1877, became president of Mexico. He quickly restored order and started an era of prosperity for the country. Not being by the constitution eligible to immediate reëlection, he was succeeded by his friend, General González, in December, 1880. He was again elected in 1884, and reëlected in 1888, 1892, 1896, 1900, 1904, and 1910, the constitution having been amended to permit this. His dictatorial regime brought foreign capital to Mexico but small benefit to the average Mexican. He resigned on May 25, 1911, faced with the revolt under Francisco Madero, Pancho Villa, and Emiliano Zapata, and died in exile.

Díaz de Armendaris (dē′äth dā är.men.dä′rēs), **Lope.** [Title, Marquis of **Cadereita.**] b. in Quito (now Ecuador), c1575; d. probably at Badajoz, Spain, after 1641. Spanish naval officer and administrator. He commanded various fleets from 1603 to 1623. He was ambassador to Germany and Spain, major-domo to Queen Isabel de Borbon, and viceroy of Mexico (1635–40). Subsequently he was bishop of Badajoz.

Díaz de Bivar (dā bē.ᴃär′), **Rodrigo** (or **Ruy**). Original name of **Cid, the.**

Díaz de Guzmán (dē′äs dā gös.män′), **Ruy.** See **Guzmán, Ruy Díaz de.**

Diaz de la Peña (dyáz dę lá pā.nyá), **Eugène Émile.** b. at Paris, Feb. 27, 1837; d. at Coleville, Sept. 12, 1901. French composer; son of Narcisse Virgile Diaz de la Peña (c1807–1876). Among his compositions are the operas *Le Roi Candaule* (1865), *La Coupe du Roi de Thulé* (1867), and *Benvenuto Cellini* (1890), as well as songs.

Diaz de la Peña, Narcisse Virgile. b. at Bordeaux, France, Aug. 20, 1807; d. at Menton, France, Nov. 19, 1876. French landscape and genre painter of the Fontainebleau school. He made his debut at the Paris Salon in 1831. In 1844 he obtained a medal of the third class, in 1846 one of the second class, and in 1848 one of the first class. He became a chevalier of the Legion of Honor in 1851.

Díaz del Castillo (dē'äth del käs.tē'lyō), **Bernal.** b. at Medina del Campo, Spain, c1492; d. in Guatemala, c1581. Spanish soldier and author. He went, as a common soldier, to Darien with Pedrarias (Pedro Arias de Ávila) in 1514, thence crossed to Cuba, was with Francisco Fernández de Córdoba in the discovery of Yucatán in 1517, and with Juan de Grijalva in Mexico in 1518. He subsequently joined Cortés, and served through the conquest of Mexico (1519–21). He settled at Coatzacoalcos, and in 1524 rejoined Cortés in the Honduras campaign. Díaz settled in Guatemala, at Santiago de los Caballeros de Guatemala, where he began writing (c1556) his three-volume *Historia verdadera de la conquista de Nueva España*, which covers the period 1514–68 and includes his first-hand report of the conquest of Mexico, contradicting in many ways that of Cortés's chaplain, Francisco López de Gómara. It was first published at Madrid in 1632 by Friar Alonzo Remón. The original was preserved in the archives of Guatemala and was published by Garcia in 1904.

Díaz de Mendoza (dā men.dō'thä), **Fernando.** See **Mendoza, Fernando Díaz de Mendoza.**

Díaz Mirón (dē'äs mē.rōn'), **Salvador.** b. 1853; d. 1928. Mexican poet, notable for his influence on Darío and Chocano as well as for his own strongly individual and flawlessly constructed verse. *Poesías* (1886) and *Lascas* (1901) are collections of his poems, of which *A Gloria* is perhaps best known.

Díaz Rodríguez (rō.ᴛʜrē'ges), **Manuel.** b. 1868; d. 1927. Venezuelan novelist, the most famous adherent in his country of the modernist movement. He was the author of *Cuentos de color* (c1898), *Idolos rotos* (1901), *Sangre patricia* (1902), the book-length essay *Camino de perfección* (1907), and others.

Dibang (dē.bäng') or **Dibong** (dē.bông'). One of the chief tributaries of the Brahmaputra River. It rises in the Kangri Karpo Pass in Assam, India, and flows S until it joins the Brahmaputra E of Sadiya in Assam. Length, ab. 120 mi.

Dibdin (dib'din), **Charles.** b. at Southampton, England, March 4, 1745; d. at London, July 25, 1814. English song writer and composer, especially noted for his songs of the sea. He went on the stage as a "singing actor" when about 15 years old, and soon began to write operas and other dramatic pieces, for which he sometimes wrote the words as well as the music, and in which he also played. In 1789 he began his series of "table entertainments," which he wrote, acted, sang, and accompanied. Nearly all his best songs (*The Flowing Can*, *Ben Backstay*, *Tom Bowling*, and others) were written by him for these entertainments, which were called *The Whim of the Moment*, *Oddities*, *The Wags*, and *The Quizzes*, among others. He wrote several novels and *The History of the Stage* (c1800), his own *Professional Life* (1803), poems, and about 70 operas and musical dramas.

Dibdin, Charles Isaac Mungo. b. 1768; d. 1833. English dramatist and song writer; son of Charles Dibdin. He managed and wrote plays and spectacles for the Sadler's Wells Theatre.

Dibdin, Thomas Frognall. b. at Calcutta, India, 1776; d. at Kensington, London, Nov. 18, 1847. English bibliographer; nephew of Charles Dibdin (1745–1814). He published *Bibliomania* (1809–11), *Typographical Antiquities of Great Britain* (1810–19), and others.

Dibdin, Thomas John. b. at London, March 21, 1771; d. there, Sept. 16, 1841. English song writer and dramatist; son of Charles Dibdin (1745–1814).

Dibelius (dē.bā'lē.ụs), **Martin.** b. at Dresden, Germany, Sept. 14, 1883—. German theologian. He was educated at the universities of Neuchâtel, Leipzig, Tübingen, and Berlin, lectured (1910–15) at the University of Berlin, and became (1915) professor of New Testament theology at the University of Heidelberg. He is an advocate of the so-called *Formgeschichte* school of church historians. His works include *Die Lade Jahwes* (1906), *Die Geisterwelt im Glauben des Paulus* (1909), *Die Formgeschichte des Evangeliums* (1919), *Jesus* (1939), and *The Sermon on the Mount* (1940).

Dibër (dē'bėr). [Italian, **Dibra.**] One of the ten prefectures of Albania, in the NE part. Capital, Peshkopijë; pop. 86,992 (1930).

Dibich-Zabalkanski (dē'bich.zä.bäl.kän'ski), Count **Ivan Ivanovich.** [Also: **Diebitsch Sabalkanski**; original name, **Hans Karl Friedrich Anton von Diebitsch und Narden.**] b. at Grossleippe, near Breslau, May 13, 1785; d. at Kleczewo, near Pułtusk, Poland, June 10, 1831. Russian general, of German parentage. He served with distinction at Leipzig in 1813, took Varna in 1828 and Silistria in 1829, crossed the Balkans in 1829 (hence surnamed Zabalkanski, meaning "Balkan-crosser"), and commanded against the Poles at Grochów and Ostrołęka in 1831.

Dibio (dib'i.ō). A Latin name of **Dijon.**

Dibon (dī'bon). Place in S Judea, toward Edom (Neh. xi. 25), probably identical with Dimonah of Josh. xv. 22.

Dibon. Ancient name of **Dhiban.**

Dibong (dē.bông'). See **Dibang.**

Dibra (dē'brä). Italian name of **Dibër.**

Dibse (dib'sẹ). See **Thapsacus.**

Dibutades (dī.bū'tạ.dēz). Greek sculptor of Sicyon, the reputed inventor of relief sculpture.

Dicaearchus (dī.sē.är'kus). fl. c320 B.C. Greek geographer, historian, and philosopher of the Peripatetic school; a disciple of Aristotle. Fragments of his *Life of Hellas* (an account of the geography and political and social life of Greece) have been preserved.

Dicaeopolis (dī.sē.op'ǫ.lis). See under **Segeste.**

Dice (dī'sē) or **Dike** (dī'kē). In Greek mythology, one of the Horae, the personification of justice; daughter of Zeus and Themis (law), and sister of Irene (peace) and Eunomia (order).

Dicenta (dē.then'tä), **Joaquín.** b. 1863; d. 1917. Leading Spanish proletarian dramatist. His play *Juan José* (1895) was one of the most successful of the late 19th century, and remains even today the most popular among the Spanish working class.

Dicey (dī'si), **Albert Venn.** b. 1835; d. April 7, 1922. English jurist; brother of Edward Dicey. He was graduated at Balliol College, Oxford, in 1858, was called to the bar in 1863, and was professor of English law at Oxford from 1882 to 1909. He published *Lectures Introductory to the Study of the Law of the Constitution* (1886).

Dicey, Edward. b. at Claybrook Hall, Leicestershire, England, in May, 1832; d. at London, July 7, 1911. English journalist and historian; brother of Albert Venn Dicey. He was graduated at Trinity College, Cambridge, in 1854, was called to the bar at Gray's Inn in 1875, and was editor (1870–89) of the London *Observer.* He wrote *Rome in 1860* (1861), *Cavour: a Memoir* (1861), *Six Months in the Federal States* (1863), *The Schleswig-Holstein War* (1864), *The Battle-Fields of 1866* (1866), *England and Egypt* (1881), and *The Egypt of the Future* (1907).

Dichterbund (diċh'tėr.bu̇nt), **Göttinger.** See **Hainbund.**

Dichtung und Wahrheit (diċh'tu̇ng u̇nt vär'hīt). [Eng. trans., "*Poetry and Truth.*"] Autobiographical history of Goethe's life, from his birth till his settlement at Weimar. The first five books appeared in 1811, the next five in 1812, and the third instalment in 1814; the conclusion appeared posthumously in 1833. The original title was *Aus meinem Leben Dichtung und Wahrheit.* Reimer wanted Goethe to change it to *Wahrheit und Dichtung* and this form was often used, but has now fallen into disuse.

Dick (dik), **George Frederick.** b. at Fort Wayne, Ind., July 21, 1881—. American physician; husband (married 1914) of Gladys Dick, with whom he isolated the germ of scarlet fever, originated a serum, and devised the Dick test to determine susceptibility. He was professor and head of the medical department at Rush Medical College (until 1933) and at Chicago (1933 *et seq.*).

Dick, Gladys. [Maiden name, **Henry.**] b. at Pawnee City, Neb., Dec. 18, 1881—. American physician; wife (married 1914) of George Frederick Dick. She received the B.S. from the University of Nebraska (1900) and an M.D. from the Johns Hopkins University (1907), and served on the staff (1914–c1936) of the McCormick Institute for Infectious Diseases. In 1933 she received with her husband the Cameron prize of the University of

Edinburgh in recognition of their work on the etiology and treatment of scarlet fever.

Dick, Mr. Mildly demented gentleman, whose real name is Richard Babley, in Charles Dickens's *David Copperfield.* Aunt Betsey Trotwood thinks he is a genius, but he has trouble constantly with an intrusive vision of King Charles's head.

Dick, Thomas. b. near Dundee, Scotland, Nov. 24, 1774; d. at Broughty Ferry, near Dundee, July, 1857. Scottish writer on astronomical and religious subjects. He published *The Christian Philosopher* (1823).

Dick Amlet (am'lẹt). See **Amlet, Dick** (or **Richard**).

Dickason (dik'ạ.sọn), **Mount.** Mountain in Antarctica, lying W by SW of Mount Melbourne, in ab. 74°35′ S., 163°52′ E. Elevation, ab. 7,000 ft.

Dick Datchery (dach'ėr.i). See **Datchery, Dick.**

Dick Distich (dis'tik). See **Distich, Dick.**

Dickens (dik'ẹnz), **Charles.** [Pseudonym, **Boz;** full name, **Charles John Huffam Dickens.**] b. at Landport, near Portsmouth, England, Feb. 7, 1812; d. at Gadshill, near Rochester, England, June 9, 1870. English novelist, after Scott undoubtedly the most influential of all British fiction writers. He was the son of John Dickens, who served as a clerk in the navy pay office and afterward became a newspaper reporter. Young Charles received an elementary education in private schools, served for a time as an attorney's clerk, and in 1835 through his shorthand skill became a reporter for the London *Morning Chronicle,* having already been employed as a reporter in the House of Commons by the *True Sun* and the *Mirror of Parliament.* In 1833 he published in the *Monthly Magazine* his first story, entitled "A Dinner at Poplar Walk," which proved to be the beginning of a series of papers printed collectively as *Sketches by Boz* in 1836. He married Catherine, daughter of George Hogarth, one of the leading figures on the *Morning Chronicle,* in 1836. They separated in 1858. In 1836 and 1837 he published the *Pickwick Papers,* by which his literary reputation was established. He was the first editor (January-February, 1846) of the London *Daily News,* but he did much more important editorial work upon his own family-magazines, *Household Words* (established 1850) and its successor *All the Year Round* (established 1859), in which he published not only his own work but that of Wilkie Collins, Mrs. Gaskell, and many lesser writers who shared his literary ideals. He visited America in 1842 and again in 1867–68, when he read from his own works with overwhelming success. His chief works are *Pickwick Papers* (1836–37), *Oliver Twist* (1837–39), *Nicholas Nickleby* (1836–39), *Master Humphrey's Clock* (including *The Old Curiosity Shop* and *Barnaby Rudge,* 1840–41), *American Notes* (1842), *A Christmas Carol* (1843), *Martin Chuzzlewit* (1843–44), *The Chimes* (1844), *The Cricket on the Hearth* (1845), *Dombey and Son* (1846–48), *David Copperfield* (1849–50), *Bleak House* (1852–53), *Hard Times* (1854), *Little Dorrit* (1855–57), *A Tale of Two Cities* (1859), *The Uncommercial Traveler* (1860), *Great Expectations* (1860–61), *Our Mutual Friend* (1864–65), and *Mystery of Edwin Drood* (1870, unfinished). His *Life of Our Lord,* which he had conceived of originally as a tale for his children, was published during the 1930's in Great Britain and the U.S. He is buried in Westminster Abbey. Most of his novels were first published in monthly parts. His writing was matched by a very able group of illustrators: George Cruikshank, Phiz (Hablot Knight Browne), Marcus Stone, John Leech, and Robert Seymour, illustrator of the first sections of *Pickwick Papers.* Dickens was importantly influenced by the picaresque novels of Tobias Smollett, with their eccentric character-types. His characteristic note is a romantic treatment of realistic materials. Though essentially a humorist, he was often led toward didacticism by his idealism and moral earnestness. As he grew older, he worked away from both the high spirits and the semi-fantastic method of *The Pickwick Papers;* and some of his later novels, such as *Hard Times* (which attacks political economy of the Manchester school) and *Little Dorrit* (which involves imprisonment for debt), are very sombre and sociological. His friend Wilkie Collins was simultaneously exercising an influence in the direction of a more highly organized plot: see *Bleak House,* where the Chancery suit is all-pervasive, *A Tale of Two Cities,* and *The Mystery of Edwin Drood.* Like Scott, Dickens had the power to create scores of characters who talk themselves alive. Many of these have been called "caricatures," but they were not created under the inspiration of modern naturalistic ideals, and there is no denying their tremendous vitality. Even the inanimate often comes alive in Dickens; there survives in his pages much of the folklore quality known to primitive man. At the same time, his technique is often astonishingly forward-looking: see, for example, the short story "George Silverman's Explanation," where he makes use of what would now be called "stream-of-consciousness." Though Dickens's death-bed scenes, and the like, often seem very sentimental to 20th-century readers, he was, judged by Victorian standards, a daring crusader against prudery and hypocrisy. He was always the most passionately loved of Victorian novelists, and his critical reputation now seems to have recovered completely from the attacks made upon him, as a part of the anti-Victorian reaction of about a generation ago. The authorized *Life* by John Forster (1872–74) was brought up to date by J. W. T. Ley (1928). Dickens's *Letters* (first collected, 1880–82) have now been greatly enlarged in volumes 21–23 of "The Nonesuch Dickens" (1937–38). Una Pope-Hennessy's *Charles Dickens* (1945) is an excellent modern biography, except for its uncritical acceptance of the unverified legend of Dickens's liaison with Ellen Ternan, for which see Edward Wagenknecht, "Dickens and the Scandal-Mongers," *College English,* April, 1950. The latter author's *The Man Charles Dickens* (1929) is an elaborate study of Dickens's personality. There is excellent criticism in George Gissing, *Charles Dickens* (1898); G. K. Chesterton, *Charles Dickens* (1906); Walter C. Phillips, *Dickens, Reade, and Collins, Sensation Novelists* (1919); George Santayana, *Soliloquies in England* (1922); J. B. Van Amerongen, *The Actor in Dickens* (1927); George Orwell, *Dickens, Dali, and Others* (1946).

Dickens, Charles. b. at Holborn, London, Jan. 6, 1837; d. at West Kensington, London, June 20, 1896. English compiler and publisher of a series of dictionary guides; eldest son of Charles Dickens (1812–70). He published *Dictionary to London* (1879), which was followed by similar works on the Thames (1880), Continental railways (1880), Paris (1882), and Oxford and Cambridge (both 1884), and edited (1892–93) a new edition of his father's works for Macmillan, by whom he was employed as a publisher's reader.

Dickens, Sir **Henry Fielding.** b. at London, Jan. 16, 1849; d. Dec. 21, 1933. English lawyer and author; sixth son of Charles Dickens (1812–70). Educated at the old Wimbledon school and at Trinity Hall, Cambridge, he studied law, and was called to the bar in 1873, engaging in practice at London. He was recorder for Deal, and recorder (1892–1918) for Maidstone; appointed king's counsel in 1892 and knighted in 1922. Author of *Memories of My Father* (1929), originally published (1928) in the London *Times,* and *Recollections* (1934).

Dickens, Monica Enid. b. at London, May 10, 1915—. English writer; great-granddaughter of Charles Dickens (1812–70). Her books *One Pair of Hands* (1939) and *One Pair of Feet* (1942) are both autobiographical; she is the author also of *Mariana* (1940), *The Fancy* (1943), *Thursday Afternoons* (1945), and *The Happy Prisoner* (1946).

Dickerson (dik'ėr.sọn), **Mahlon.** b. at Hanover Neck, N.J., April 17, 1770; d. Oct. 5, 1853. American lawyer, manufacturer, and senator (1817–33). He served as member (1811–12) of the New Jersey Assembly from Morris County, justice of the state supreme court, governor (1815–17) of New Jersey, U.S. senator (1817–33), and secretary of the navy (1834–38). Owner of the Succasunna (N.J.) ironworks, he was an ardent protectionist.

Dickins (dik'inz), **John.** b. at London, cAug. 24, 1747; d. Sept. 27, 1798. American Methodist Episcopal clergyman, prominent in establishing that church in America. He was associated in the founding of Cokesbury College and of the Methodist Book Concern, and was publisher of the *Arminian Magazine* (1789–90) and the *Methodist Magazine* (1797–98).

Dickinson (dik'in.sọn). [Former name, **Pleasant Valley Siding.**] City in SW North Dakota, county seat of Stark County, near Heart River: shipping point for grain and cattle; manufactures of bricks and pottery. It is the seat of a state teachers college. 7,469 (1950).

Dickinson. Unincorporated community in SE Texas, in Galveston County near Galveston. 2,704 (1950).

Dickinson, Anna Elizabeth. b. at Philadelphia, Oct. 28, 1842; d. Oct. 22, 1932. American lecturer and advocate of woman suffrage, labor reform, and stringent reconstruction measures for the South. She lectured during the Civil War on war issues, and afterward generally on political subjects. In 1876 she went on the stage, but did not meet with success. She wrote a play, *An American Girl* (1880), and *What Answer?* (a novel, 1868), *A Paying Investment* (1876), and *A Ragged Register of People, Places, and Opinions* (1879).

Dickinson, Charles Monroe. b. near Lowville, N.Y., Nov. 15, 1842; d. at Binghamton, N.Y., July 3, 1924. American newspaperman, diplomat, and writer, now chiefly remembered as one of the principal organizers of the Associated Press. Acquiring (1878) a controlling interest in the Binghamton *Republican*, he was its manager until 1911. He was appointed (1897) consul general to Turkey by President McKinley, and served as diplomatic agent (1901) to Bulgaria and consul general at large (1906) for the entire Middle East.

Dickinson, Clarence. b. at Lafayette, Ind., May 7, 1873—. American organist and composer, founder of the Music Art Society. He has served as organist (1909 *et seq.*) at the Brick Presbyterian Church and at Temple Beth-El, New York, and professor of music (1912 *et seq.*) at the Union Theological Seminary, New York. His works include vocal solos and choruses as well as anthems. He is the editor of *Sacred Choruses* and of the *Historical Recital Series for Organ;* author with his wife of *Excursions in Musical History.*

Dickinson, Donald McDonald. b. at Port Ontario, N.Y., Jan. 17, 1846; d. at Trenton, Mich., Oct. 15, 1917. American lawyer, politician, and cabinet member. A graduate (1867) of Michigan Law School, he served as a defender of the homesteaders before the U.S. Supreme Court, senior consul (1896) for the U.S. before the international high commission on the Bering Sea claims, and U.S. member (1902) of the arbitration court during the U.S.-El Salvador dispute. He was also secretary (1872 *et seq.*) and chairman (1876 *et seq.*) of the Democratic central committee of Michigan, and a member (1880–85) of the Democratic national committee. He was U.S. postmaster general from 1888 to 1889.

Dickinson, Emily (Elizabeth). b. at Amherst, Mass., Dec. 10, 1830; d. there, May 15, 1886. American poet. Her father, Edward Dickinson, a lawyer, a Congressman, and treasurer of Amherst College, has been compared in his character and personality, in his relation to his daughter, and in his attempt to dominate her, to Elizabeth Browning's father. Her mother, Emily Norcross, who seems to have had no influence on her daughter, and who appears to have been a colorless individual, is generally not even mentioned in accounts of her daughter's life. Emily Dickinson was educated at the local schools, at Amherst Academy, and at the South Hadley Female Seminary (which later became Mt. Holyoke College). At the Academy she met Leonard Humphrey, the principal, whose chief distinction (he died at 26) is perhaps that he encouraged her to write. At the Seminary she met Helen (Fiske) Hunt Jackson, author of *Ramona*, who became her closest friend. In 1854 she went, with her mother, and her younger sister, Lavinia, to Washington, where her father was (Congress being in session), and on the way back she paid a brief visit to a Philadelphia school friend. In 1864 she went to Boston to see an eye specialist, and once again, in 1865, for the same reason. The years before, in between, and after, until her death, she spent at Amherst. Her outward life was as uneventful as, or even more so than, that of Jane Austen. What she thought and felt in her own heart and mind she put on paper, and she did it secretly. She wrote upwards of 1,500 short, intense, passionate, ecstatic poems, which would have been destroyed if Lavinia had carried out her sister's request. Of these poems, only two were published during her lifetime, one in the Springfield *Republican* (Feb. 14, 1866), edited by Samuel Bowles, a family friend, and the other, without her name, in G. P. Lathrop's *A Masque of Poets* (1878), and these two without her consent or knowledge. The great body of the work by which she is known and which has brought her recognition as one of America's great and original poets was published after her death in a series of volumes: *Poems* (1890, 1891, 1896), *Further Poems* (1929), *Unpublished Poems* (1936), *Poems: Centenary Edition* (1930), *The Single Hound* (1914), and *Bolts of Melody* (1945). Like Jane Austen, she never married, but love is not absent from her poetry. She is supposed to have loved, and to have been loved by, a young minister, whom she gave up when she found that he was not free, legally or morally, to marry her, and it is also claimed, without evidence, that she was in love with Captain Edward Bissell Hunt, the first husband of her friend, who returned her feeling. In a letter to Thomas Wentworth Higginson, she has given a pleasing self-portrait: "I am small, like a wren, and my hair is bold, like the chestnut burr, and my eyes, like the sherry in the glass that the guest leaves." She is the heroine of Helen Hunt Jackson's novel *Mercy Philbrick's Choice* (1876) and of Susan Glaspell's play *Alison's House* (1930). A revised and enlarged edition of her *Letters* (1894) appeared in 1931.

Dickinson, Goldsworthy Lowes. b. Aug. 6, 1862; d. Aug. 3, 1932. English author. He was educated at the Charterhouse and at King's College, Cambridge, was a fellow and lecturer of King's College, Cambridge, and a lecturer at the London School of Economics and Political Science. He delivered the Ingersoll lecture at Harvard in 1909. He published *The Development of Parliament in the Nineteenth Century* (1895), *The Greek View of Life* (1896), *Letters from a Chinese Official* (1903), *Justice and Liberty* (1908), *Religion and Immortality* (1911), *The European Anarchy* (1916), *War: its Nature, Cause, and Cure* (1923), and *After Two Thousand Years* (1930).

Dickinson, John. b. at Crosia, Talbot County, Md., Nov. 8, 1732; d. at Wilmington, Del., Feb. 14, 1808. American statesman; brother of Philemon Dickinson. He was a member of the Colonial Congress of 1765, and founder of Dickinson College at Carlisle, Pa.

Dickinson, Jonathan. b. at Hatfield, Mass., April 22, 1688; d. Oct. 7, 1747. American Presbyterian clergyman, first president (May–October, 1747) of the College of New Jersey (later Princeton University). He championed Presbyterian revivalism in the 1730's and, recognizing the need of the Middle Colonies for an institution of higher learning, he obtained (1746), after an unsuccessful try, the charter for the College of New Jersey.

Dickinson, Philemon. b. April 5, 1739; d. Feb. 4, 1809. American Revolutionary soldier and congressman; brother of John Dickinson (1732–1808). As a major general and commander in chief of New Jersey state militia, he is remembered for his participation in the Staten Island landing (1777), for delaying the British retreat, under Clinton, from Philadelphia toward New York and thus contributing to Washington's victory at the battle of Monmouth (1778), and for his attack at the battle of Springfield (1780). Member (1776) of the New Jersey provincial congress; elected (1782) to the Continental Congress from Delaware; member (1785) of commission to select the federal capital site; U.S. senator (1790–93) from New Jersey.

Dickinson, Sidney Edward. b. at Wallingford, Conn., Nov. 28, 1890—. American portrait painter, teacher at the Art Students League of New York and the National Academy of Design art schools. He was a pupil of Charles Bridgman, Douglas Volk, and W. M. Chase, exhibited extensively in the U.S., and won several medals and prizes. In 1927 he was made an academician of the National Academy of Design. The Art Institute of Chicago, Corcoran Gallery at Washington, D.C., City Art Museum at St. Louis, and other large galleries have collected his works, among which are *Self-Portrait, Unrest, The Young Painter, The Black Cape,* and *Mary.*

Dickman (dik'man), **Joseph Theodore.** b. at Dayton, Ohio, Oct. 6, 1857; d. at Washington, D.C., Oct. 23, 1927. American army officer. Graduated (1881) from the U.S. Military Academy, West Point, he served in the West against the Indians, and in the Spanish-American War (in the Santiago and Panay campaigns). He was subsequently chief of staff of U.S. forces in China, and was appointed (1917) a brigadier general in the regular army. In France during World War I, as a major general, he commanded the 3rd division on the south bank of the Marne River during the last German offensive, the 4th corps (August–October, 1918), and the 1st corps (October–November, 1918), participating in the St.-Mihiel and Meuse-Argonne operations. Given command (1918–19) of the 3rd army, he organized it for the occupation of Germany. He retired (1921) and wrote *The Great Crusade* (1927).

Dick's Coffee House. Old coffee house, formerly No. 8 Fleet Street (on the south side, near Temple Bar), London, originally "Richard's." It was named for Richard Torner, or Turner, to whom the house was let in 1680. The coffee room long retained its old paneling, and the staircase its original balusters. Richard's, as it was then called, was frequented by William Cowper when he lived in the Temple.

Dicksee (dik'sē), Sir **Francis Bernard.** b. at London, Nov. 27, 1853; d. 1928. English painter of figure subjects, portraits, and landscapes who was one of the leaders of the conservative school. He was educated at the Royal Academy Schools, where he received gold and silver medals; from 1872 on, he exhibited regularly at the Academy; in 1891 he was elected a member. Besides his membership in numerous organizations of artists, he was also a trustee of the British Museum and of the National Portrait Gallery. His principal works include: *Harmony* (Tate Gallery), *Landscape of Surrey* (Cardiff), and *The Foolish Virgins* (Leicester).

Dickson (dik'sọn). Town in W Tennessee, in Dickson County: manufactures include cigars, raincoats, and shuttles. 3,348 (1950).

Dickson, Leonard Eugene. b. at Independence, Iowa, Jan. 22, 1874—. American mathematician, author of many papers and books, especially on aspects of algebra, including the theory of numbers, the theory of equations, and the theory of groups. He received his doctorate at the University of Chicago in 1896 and taught there from 1900 to 1941. He received numerous awards and honorary degrees. Besides many unusually successful elementary textbooks on the theory of equations and the theory of numbers, his books include *Linear Groups* (1901), *Linear Algebras* (1914), *Algebraic Invariants* (1914), *History of the Theory of Numbers* (3 vols., 1920–23), *Algebras and Their Arithmetics, Modern Algebraic Theories* (1926), and *Researches on Waring's Problem* (1935).

Dickson, Samuel Henry. b. at Charleston, S.C., Sept. 20, 1798; d. at Philadelphia, March 31, 1872. American physician. He received an M.D. (1819) from the University of Pennsylvania, was a founder (1833) and professor of institutes and practice of medicine (1833–47; 1850–58) of the Medical College of South Carolina, and a professor (1847–50) at the University of the City of New York and (1858–72) at the Jefferson Medical College, Philadelphia. He was the author of *Manual of Pathology and Practice* (1839), *Essays on Pathology and Therapeutics* (2 vols., 1845), *Essays on Life, Sleep, Pain, Intellection, and Hygiene* (1852), *Elements of Medicine* (1855), and *Studies in Pathology and Therapeutics* (1867).

Dickson City. Borough in NE Pennsylvania, in Lackawanna County, ab. 3 mi. NE of Scranton: coal mining. 8,948 (1950).

Dick Swiveller (swiv'ẹl.ėr). See **Swiveller, Dick.**

Dick Tinto (tin'tō). See **Tinto, Dick.**

Dick Turpin (tėr'pin). See **Turpin, Richard.**

Dicquemare (dēk.mår), Abbé **Jacques François.** b. at Le Havre, France, March 7, 1733; d. March 29, 1789. French naturalist and astronomer, professor of experimental physics at Le Havre. He invented several instruments used in astronomy and navigation.

Dictator, The. Play by Richard Harding Davis, produced in 1904.

Dictionary of American Biography. Reference work containing biographies of leading Americans published in 20 volumes (1928–36) and one supplement (1944). Sponsored by the American Council of Learned Societies, it was financed to a large extent by the New York *Times*. The first seven volumes were edited by Allen Johnson, the remainder by Dumas Malone, and the first supplement by Harris E. Starr. The total work includes individual biographical sketches of 14,285 persons.

Dictionary of American English, A. Reference work (1936–44) in four volumes compiled at the University of Chicago and edited by Sir William Craigie and James R. Hulbert.

Dictionary of American History. Reference work compiled under the direction of James Truslow Adams, published in 1940 in six volumes (including an index). A second and revised edition was issued in 1946.

Dictionary of Americanisms, A. Reference work in two volumes, edited by Mitford M. Mathews, published in 1951. It lists and defines, with quotations from original sources and with etymologies, those words and expressions which have come into the English language in the U.S., whether they be original coinages, borrowings from other languages such as Spanish, or new meanings of older English words. The work was in preparation 1944–50.

Dictionary of National Biography. Reference work in 63 volumes and three supplementary volumes, listing and giving brief to rather extensive memoirs of persons prominent in English life since the beginning of English history. The series was founded in 1882 by George Smith, London publisher, and the volumes, edited by Leslie Stephen and subsequently by Sidney Lee, appeared quarterly from 1885 to 1900. The supplementary volumes were published under Lee's editorship in 1901, covering mainly biographies of those who had died since publication had been begun in 1885. In 1912 appeared the first volume of a series supplementary to the main work and intended to include one volume for each decade of the century. Additional volumes have appeared at intervals since. The editors of this series have been Lee, H. W. C. Davis and J. R. H. Warren, and L. G. Wickham Legg.

Dictionnaire raisonné des sciences, des arts et des métiers (dēk.syo.ner re.zo.nā dā syäṅs, dā zår ā dā mā.tyā). Full title of the **Encyclopédie.**

Dicts and Sayings of the Philosophers, The. Prose work (1477) translated from the French of Guillaume de Tignonville by Anthony Wydeville. Printed in November, 1477, on Caxton's famous Westminster press, established the year before, it is historically important as the first book printed on English soil, and the first book printed in England with a date. A passage on women, by Socrates, which Rivers left out, was added by Caxton. The French title of the work is *Les Ditz moraulx des philosophes.*

Dictum of Kenilworth (ken'il.wėrth). Decision forced from Henry III of England by the Commons in 1266 during the siege of Kenilworth. It reëstablished Henry's authority, proclaimed amnesty, annulled the provisions of Oxford (forced on the king in 1258 and providing for a regulating council of barons), and provided that the king should keep the charter to which he had sworn.

Dictys Cretensis (dik'tis krẹ.ten'sis). Reputed author, a native of Cnossus, Crete, of a narrative of the Trojan War, entitled (in the pretended Latin translation of Q. Septimius) *Ephemeris Belli Trojani*, the introduction to which represents him as a follower of Idomeneus in the Trojan War. This narrative, with *De excido Trojae* of Dares Phrygius, was one of the chief sources from which the heroic legends of Greece passed into the literature of the Middle Ages. It was probably composed by Septimius c300 A.D.

Didapper (dī'dap.ėr), **Beau.** In Henry Fielding's *Joseph Andrews*, a rich, weak-minded fop.

Diderot (dē.drō), **Denis.** b. at Langres, Haute-Marne, France, Oct. 5, 1713; d. at Paris, July 31, 1784. French philosopher, encyclopedist, and man of letters. After his formal schooling at Paris he spurned the professions, pursued against his father's wishes the study of Latin, mathematics, science, Italian, and English, and married secretly in 1743. His first literary labors were as a publishers' aid. He translated into French Temple Stanyan's *Histoire de la Grèce* (1743), Shaftesbury's *Essai sur le mérite et la vertu* (1745), and, with three collaborators, Robert James's *Dictionnaire universel de médicine, de chimie, de botanique* (6 vols., 1746–48). The publishers of this work, impressed with his knowledge and skill, soon associated him with Jean le Rond d'Alembert and made him general editor of *L'Encyclopédie*, the greatest publishing venture of the 18th century. In the face of severe censorship and repeated suppressions, and with a final resort to secret printing, Diderot was responsible for the publication of the first 28 volumes (17 of text, 11 of plates) over a period of more than 20 years (1751–72). Five volumes of addenda and two of tables brought the total to 35 by 1780. Diderot's interest in medical and biological sciences led him to write *Lettre sur les aveugles*

(1749), *Lettre sur les sourds et muets* (1751), *Pensées sur l'interprétation de la nature* (1753), and *Le Rêve de d'Alembert* (1769, published in 1830). These works show a thorough understanding of the physiological arguments for evolutionary transformism and a naturalistic philosophy of science applied to problems of ethics and esthetics. His *Salons*, written for the foreign subscribers to the *Correspondance littéraire*, reveal Diderot's superior talents and prophetic insight as critic of literature and the fine arts. Two plays, *Le Fils naturel* (1757) and *Le Père de famille* (1758), were produced, without great success, and published during his lifetime, accompanied by interesting and revolutionary essays on dramatic art. The third and best, *Est-il bon, est-il méchant?*, and the justly praised *Paradoxe sur le comédien* (1830) were left in manuscript for posterity. The same destiny attended his narrative fiction, except for the only occasionally interesting *Bijoux indiscrets* (1748) and two short stories. Posthumously published were *La Religieuse* (1796), *Le Neveu de Rameau* (1823), believed by many to be his masterpiece, *Jacques le fataliste* (1796), and a number of short stories, among the best of which is *Ceci n'est pas un conte*. His *Supplément au voyage de Bougainville*, written in 1772, first printed in 1796, shows (even by 20th-century standards) ultramodern views concerning religion, sex, and politics. Diderot received financial support from Catherine II of Russia, who bought his valuable library, but left him the use of it during his lifetime. He went to St. Petersburg in 1773–74 to express his gratitude, wrote a *Projet d'une université pour la Russie*, and left in manuscript very frank and critical *Observations* on Catherine's *Instructions* to her legists for a code of laws based on the principles of Montesquieu and other writers of the French enlightenment. Diderot's *Lettres à Sophie Volland* reveal the extraordinary character of the writer and the man, and justify his growing reputation as the great seminal mind of his century. A noteworthy collection of Diderot manuscripts has recently been rescued from oblivion by Herbert Dieckmann, author of "Bibliographical Data on Diderot" (in *Studies in Honor of Frederick W. Shipley*, 1942). Available works on Diderot in English are scarce, but include *Diderot and the Encyclopaedists*, by John Morley (1878), *The Censoring of Diderot's Encyclopédie*, by Douglas H. Gordon and Norman L. Torrey (1947), and *Diderot, Interpreter of Nature* (with translations of *Le Rêve de d'Alembert*, *Le Neveu de Rameau*, and others), by Jonathan Kemp and Jean Stewart (1938). In French, see *L'Humanisme de Diderot*, by Jean Thomas (1936), and *Diderot*, by A. Billy (1932).

Didinga (di.ding'gä). [Also, **Dodinga.**] African people of SE Anglo-Egyptian Sudan and N Uganda, in E Africa, occupying a range called the Didinga Hills near the borders of these two countries and that of Kenya. Their language is related to the Nilotic and Nilo-Hamitic linguistic groups. Their population is estimated at more than 25,000 (by J. H. Driberg, 1922). Political authority is divided among the chiefs of eight independent districts, grouped in two large divisions. The Bokorora, Lakorechoke, and Lomongole form the eastern Didinga, and the Patalado, Thuguro, Kademakuch, Lokorechoke, and Lomongole form the western Didinga. Raiding occurred between the E and W divisions, but not within them. They have exogamous patrilineal clans and age grades. They practice agriculture with wooden hoes, and herding, with the cattle complex. Their principal crops are sorghum and millet.

Didius Julianus (did'i.us jö.li.ā'nus). [Full name, **Marcus Didius Salvius Julianus;** later called **Marcus Didius Commodus Severus Julianus.**] d. at Rome, June 1, 193 A.D. Emperor of Rome (March–June, 193). He served with distinction in the army, and twice held the consulship, the last time in 179. On the murder of the emperor Pertinax by the praetorian guards in 193, the guards sold the imperial dignity to Didius, who had as his competitor Sulpicianus, the father-in-law of Pertinax. His elevation was not recognized by Septimius Severus, who marched with an army against Rome, whereupon the praetorian guards hastened to purchase the favor of Severus by putting the emperor to death.

Dido (dī'dō). Surname of the Phoenician goddess of the moon (Astarte), who was worshiped as the protecting deity of the citadel of Carthage. Her name was in later time appropriated by the Tyrian Elissa, founder of Carthage, who was the mistress of Aeneas in Vergil's *Aeneid* and killed herself when he left her.

Dido and Aeneas (ē.nē'as). Opera in three acts by Henry Purcell, with a libretto by Nahum Tate, first performed (c1688) at Chelsea. Dealing with Aeneas's sojourn at Carthage, the opera contains the duet *Our plot has took, the queen's forsook* and the aria *When I am laid in Earth.*

Dido Building Carthage. Large painting by J. M. W. Turner, in the National Gallery, London. The scene is on a river bank, with classical buildings in course of erection. Dido and her attendants are seen on the left.

Didon (dē.dôṅ), **Henri Gabriel.** b. at Touvet, France, March 17, 1840; d. at Toulouse, France, March 13, 1900. French Dominican priest, preacher, writer, and educator. After entering the Dominican order at the age of 18, studying at Rome, and teaching for some years, he began his career as a preacher in 1868. It was in Paris that he first displayed that natural eloquence which, heightened by oratorical art, so well served his ardent purpose of spreading the faith. Certain of his sermons on the indissolubility of marriage caused such controversy in the secular press that he discontinued them at the request of the archbishop of Paris, but they were subsequently published. This was in 1879, and in 1880, as a result of criticism of the stand he took in conferences on problems of the relation of the church to modern society, his superior sent him to Corsica. There he spent seven years (broken by visits to Palestine and to Germany) writing a *Life of Christ* which was published in 1890 and was widely circulated, and translated into several other languages. In 1892 he resumed preaching in Paris, but his later years were devoted to the education of youth. He was a progressive in education, as he was in his social ideas and in his support of the French Republic. Among his books, which had a considerable following in his day, are *Les Allemands* (1884), *Lettres à Mlle. Th. V.* (1900), *Lettres à un ami* (1902), and *Lettres à Mère Samuel* (1907–08).

Didone Abbandonata (dē.dō'nā äb.bän.dō.nä'tä). [Eng. trans., "*Dido Forsaken.*"] Tragedy by Metastasio, produced at Naples in 1724; his first dramatic work. It had great success, and is probably the best play written on the subject in comparatively modern times. It has been set to music by more than 40 composers.

Dido, Queen of Carthage (dī'dō), **The Tragedy of.** Tragedy by Marlowe, published in 1594. Nashe is said to have finished it after Marlowe's death. Dido has been the subject of many plays in English and in French, notably by Jodelle in 1552, La Grange in 1576, Hardy in 1603, Scudéry in 1636, and Franc de Pompignan in 1734.

Didot (dē.dō), **Ambroise Firmin.** b. at Paris, Dec. 7, 1790; d. there, Feb. 22, 1876. French publisher; son of Firmin Didot (1764–1836). He published with his brother Hyacinthe many important works, including *Bibliothèque des auteurs grecs*, *L'Univers pittoresque*, and *Nouvelle biographie générale*.

Didot, Firmin. b. at Paris, April 14, 1764; d. April 24, 1836. French publisher, printer, type founder, and author; son of François Ambroise Didot and brother of Pierre Didot (1760–1853).

Didot, François. b. at Paris, 1689; d. Nov. 2, 1757. French printer and bookseller, founder of the firm of Didot at Paris in 1713.

Didot, François Ambroise. b. at Paris, Jan. 7, 1730; d. July 10, 1804. French printer and publisher; son of François Didot. He was noted for his improvements in type founding and printing.

Didot, Henri. b. 1765; d. 1852. French type founder; son of Pierre François Didot (1732–95). He published editions in microscopic types.

Didot, Hyacinthe Firmin. b. at Paris, March 11, 1794; d. at Dandon, Orne, France, Aug. 7, 1880. French publisher; son of Firmin Didot, brother of Ambroise Firmin-Didot, and the latter's business associate after 1827.

Didot, Pierre. b. Jan. 25, 1760; d. Dec. 31, 1853. French publisher and printer; eldest son of François Ambroise Didot (1730–1804). He published *Virgil* (1798), *Horace* (1799), *Racine* (1801–05), and other classics.

Didot, Pierre François. b. at Paris, July 9, 1732; d. Dec. 7, 1795. French printer, publisher, and paper manufacturer; son of François Didot and brother of François Ambroise Didot (1730–1804).

Didrikson (did'rik.sọn), **Babe.** [Full original name, **Mildred Babe Didrikson**; married name, **Zaharias.**] b. at Port Arthur, Tex., June 26, 1913—. American athlete, generally known as Babe (not a nickname, but one of her given names). She began playing basketball at high school at the age of 14, and at 16 was employed by an insurance company so that she might join its girl employees' basketball team. During the next two years she was twice named as All-American women's basketball forward; as captain of the company's women's track team she secured it second place in national ranking, winning most of its points herself; she set eight new Southern and three new national track and field records, won 92 medals, and helped win 17 cups. By 1932 she held the record for the Southern Amateur Athletic Union in every track and field sport in which she participated. In that year she became internationally famous when in the Olympic Games at Los Angeles she broke four women's world records, and there was wide agreement with a sports writer who called her "the athletic phenomenon of all time, man or woman." In 1932 also she turned professional, and toured with the Babe Didrikson All-American Basketball team, all members but herself being men. She also went on the vaudeville circuit, and signed a series of syndicated newspaper articles on sports. Having saved a considerable sum of money, she spent three years learning to play golf, winning her first championship, in the Texas Women's Golf Association tournament, in 1935. The U.S. Golf Association barred her from further amateur play, but after turning professional she won numerous titles and tournaments; and her amateur standing having been restored, she continued her triumphs, taking among others the U.S. national amateur title in 1946 and the British amateur title in 1947. She was married in 1938 to George Zaharias, a businessman and former wrestler.

Didron (dē.drôṅ), **Adolphe Napoléon.** b. at Hautviller, Marne, France, March 13, 1806; d. at Paris, Nov. 13, 1867. French archaeologist, author of *Manuel d'iconographie chrétienne* (1845).

Didyme (did'i.mē). Ancient name of **Salina.**

Didymoteikhon (ᴛʜē.ᴛʜē.mô'tē.ċhôn). [Also: **Demotika, Demotica, Dimotika.**] Town in NE Greece, on the Maritsa River ab. 23 mi. S of Edirne. Pop. ab. 9,500.

Didymus (did'i.mus). [Surnamed **Chalcenterus.**] fl. in the second half of the 1st century B.C. Alexandrian grammarian and critic. He was a follower of the school of Aristarchus, and a contemporary of Cicero and the emperor Augustus. His works, consisting chiefly of compilations, covered a great variety of subjects, and were estimated by Seneca at four thousand; none of them is extant.

Didymus. [Often called **Didymus of Alexandria**; surnamed **"the Blind."**] b. 308, 309, or 314 A.D.; d. 394, 395, or 399 A.D. Alexandrian scholar and theologian. He lost his sight in childhood, but nevertheless became one of the most learned men of his time. He was a teacher in the catechetical school of Alexandria upward of 50 years, and numbered among his pupils Jerome, Palladius, Ambrose of Alexandria, Evagrius, and Isidore of Pelusium. He opposed the Arians with great spirit, but supported Origen. His extant works include a treatise on the Trinity, translated into Latin by Jerome.

Didymus. Greek name of the apostle **Thomas.**

Die (dē). [Ancient name, **Dea Vocontiorum.**] Town in SE France, in the department of Drôme, situated on the Drôme River ab. 27 mi. SE of Valence. The Porte de St. Marcel is a relic of the ancient town.

Diebitsch Sabalkanski (dē'bich zä.bäl.kän'ski). See **Dibich-Zabalkanski,** Count **Ivan Ivanovich.**

Diebitsch und Narden (dē'bich ůnt när'dẹn), **Hans Karl Friedrich Anton von.** Original name of **Dibich-Zabalkanski,** Count **Ivan Ivanovich.**

Dieckhoff (dēk'hof), **Hans Heinrich.** b. at Strasbourg (then in Germany), Dec. 23, 1884—. German diplomat. He became a member of the foreign service in 1912, was appointed (1930) chief of the Anglo-American department of the German foreign office, became (1936) head of the political department and was subsequently state secretary for foreign affairs, and served (1937–41) as German ambassador to the U.S.

Diedenhofen (dē'dẹn.hō.fẹn). German name of **Thionville.**

Diederichs (dē'dẹ.riks), **Helene Voigt-.** See **Voigt-Diederichs, Helene.**

Die erste Walpurgisnacht (dē ers'tẹ väl.půr'gis.näċht). German title of **Walpurgis Night.**

Diefenbach (dē'fẹn.bäċh), **Lorenz.** b. at Ostheim, Hesse, Germany, July 29, 1806; d. at Darmstadt, Germany, March 28, 1883. German philologist, ethnologist, and novelist, librarian at Frankfort on the Main (1865–76). His works include *Celtica* (1839–42), *Vergleichendes Wörterbuch der gothischen Sprache* (1846–52), the novel *Ein Pilger und seine Genossen* (1851), *Origines Europaeae* (1861), *Vorschule der Völkerkunde* (1864), and others.

Dieffenbach (dē'fẹn.bäċh), **Johann Friedrich.** b. at Königsberg, in East Prussia, Feb. 1, 1795; d. at Berlin, Nov. 11, 1847. German surgeon, appointed (1832) professor at Berlin. He wrote *Die operative Chirurgie* (1844–48).

Diego (dẹ.ā'gō). Waggish sexton in Fletcher and Massinger's *Spanish Curate.* He longs for a less healthy parish and more funerals.

Diego Garcia (dẹ.ā'gō gär.sē'ä). Largest and most important island of the Chagos Archipelago (Oil Islands), in the Indian Ocean, ab. 1,100 mi. SW of Cape Comorin, India. Exports include coconut oil, coconuts, copra, guano, and salted fish. Length, ab. 12 mi.; width, ab. 6 mi.; area, 75 sq. mi.; pop. 501 (1944).

Diégo-Suarez (dẹ.ā'gō.swä'rās). [Also, **Antsirane.**] Port at the N end of the island of Madagascar, off SE Africa. From 1885, when it was surrendered to the French, until 1896 when it became a part of Madagascar colony, Diégo-Suarez was a separate colony. Its harbor is one of the finest in the world. The port was captured by British forces in World War II. 14,375 (1946).

Diegueños (dē.ā.gā'nyōs). Collective term for the North American Indian tribes which once inhabited the region near what is now San Diego, Calif. All spoke languages of the Yuman family.

Diehl (dēl), **Karl.** b. at Frankfort on the Main, Germany, March 27, 1864; d. at Freiburg im Breisgau, Germany, May 12, 1943. German economist. He was professor at the Universities of Halle, Rostock, and Freiburg (1908 *et seq.*). Author of *P. J. Proudhon, seine Lehre und sein Leben* (3 parts, 1886–96) and *Theoret. Nationalökonomie* (3 vols., 1916–27). With P. Mombert he edited *Lesestücke zum Studium der polit. Ökonomie* (16 vols., 1910 *et seq.*).

Diekirch (dē'kirċh). Town in Luxembourg, situated on the Sure (Sauer) River, N of the city of Luxembourg: agricultural trade center. The parish church dates back to the 10th century. Toward the end of World War II, on Dec. 16, 1944, the Germans launched their last offensive from here, striking in the direction of Bastogne; the Americans crossed the Sure River between Dec. 29 and Dec. 31, 1944; the final assault on the Siegfried Line was started on Feb. 13, 1945. About 90 percent of the town's buildings were damaged. 3,809 (1948).

Diel du Parquet (dyel dü pȧr.ke), **Jacques.** b. in France, c1600; d. at St.-Pierre, Martinique, Jan. 3, 1658. French soldier and administrator. He was governor of Martinique (1638 *et seq.*).

Dielman (dēl'mạn), **Frederick.** b. at Hanover, Germany, Dec. 25, 1847; d. Aug. 15, 1935. American figure painter. He was president of the National Academy of Design (1889–1909), and professor of descriptive geometry and drawing in the College of the City of New York (1903–18).

Diels (dēls), **Otto.** b. at Hamburg, Germany, Jan. 23, 1876—. German chemist, cowinner of the 1950 Nobel prize in chemistry. He taught (1904–16) at the University of Berlin, and was professor (1916 *et seq.*) of chemistry and chemical technology at the University of Kiel, acting also as director of the chemical institute there. He did important research on cholesterol, but it was for his work in diene synthesis, performed with his former student and fellow prize-winner Kurt Adler, that he won the Nobel prize; the synthesis is of major importance in the analysis and development of plastic compounds.

Diemen (dē'mẹn), **Anton van.** b. 1593; d. at Batavia, Dutch East Indies, April 19, 1645. Dutch admiral and colonial administrator. In 1636 he was made governor general of the Dutch East India Company's settlements. He ruled capably, seized the Portuguese colonies in Ceylon and Malacca, established trade with Tonkin, China, and Japan, and in general greatly extended Dutch commerce and influence in the East Indies. The navigator Abel Tasman, sailing under van Diemen's orders, gave to a large island he discovered in 1642 the name of Van Diemen's Land. Later, in honor of the discoverer, the name was changed to Tasmania.

Diemrich (dēm′rich). German name of **Deva,** Rumania.

Dieng Plateau (dēng). High plateau in the N part of Central Java, ab. 5,980 ft. long and 2,700 ft. wide, covered with ruins of Shivaistic stone temples. Once a great religious center, the plateau has been called "the Benares of Java." Only eight temples are standing today, but 40 groups of temples were described at the beginning of the 19th century. Among the buildings are the oldest monuments of Hindu-Indonesian art, dating possibly from the end of the 7th century A.D. (earliest dated Dieng inscription is 809 A.D.; the latest, 1210), yet it is a mature art, the product of centuries of esthetic evolution and artistic tradition.

Diepenbeeck (dē′pen.bāk), **Abraham van.** b. at Boisle-duc ('s Hertogenbosch), Netherlands, 1599; d. at Antwerp, Belgium, 1675. Flemish painter and designer. He went to Antwerp c1629, and studied with Rubens. His earlier achievements were in the field of stained glass, and his windows in the cathedral of Antwerp have long been admired, but after returning to Antwerp following a period of study in Italy, he devoted himself to oil painting and to executing designs for books. During a visit to England he made many designs for the duke of Newcastle. Some of his oils have been rated with the work of Van Dyck. He is represented in the Antwerp Museum, the Berlin Gallery, the Brussels Museum, the Bordeaux Museum, the Dresden Gallery, the Frankfort Städel, the Munich Gallery, the Vienna Gallery, and the Louvre at Paris.

Dieppe (di.ep′; French, dyep). Town in NW France, in the department of Seine-Inférieure, situated on the English Channel, at the mouth of the Arques River, NE of Le Havre, and surrounded by high chalk cliffs. It is a resort and has a beautiful bathing beach. It is the seat of various industries, particularly the lace, food, and machine industries, and naval construction works. It has an excellent port, which specializes in fisheries, the import of bananas, and passenger service between England and France. The Church of Saint Jacques, damaged in World War II, is in pure Gothic style; the castle dates mainly from the 15th century. The town contains also an art museum and a casino. Dieppe began to be of importance in the late Middle Ages. It was bombarded by an Anglo-Dutch fleet in 1694. The harbor, improved during World War I, suffered heavy damage during World War II. It was the scene of the Dieppe Raid of Aug. 19, 1942. Pop. 21,770 (1946).

Dieppe Raid. Amphibious raid on the French coastal town of Dieppe in World War II. It was spearheaded by Canadians, and included British Commandos, American Rangers, and Free French units. Carried out during the early morning hours of Aug. 19, 1942, it probed German defenses, destroyed some radio installations, and captured some prisoners for questioning. About one half of the force of 7,500 attackers was lost, and considerable criticism was made of the raid, which had been given air cover and destroyer escort.

Diersheim (dērs′hīm). Village in Baden, SW Germany, situated near the Rhine River, ab. 8 mi. NE of Strasbourg. Here, on April 20, 1797, the French under Jean Victor Moreau defeated the Austrians.

Dierx (dyerks), **Léon.** b. on the island of Réunion, in the Indian Ocean, 1838; d. at Paris, June 11, 1912. French poet of the Parnassian school. Author of *Aspirations* (1858), *Poèmes et poésies* (1864), *Les Lèvres closes* (1867), and others. His complete works were published in 1888–89.

Dies (dīz), **Martin.** b. at Colorado, Tex., Nov. 5, 1901—. American lawyer and politician. He attended the University of Texas, received the LL.B. from National University at Washington, D.C., and began (1920) his law practice at Marshall, Tex. He served (1931–45) in the U.S. House of Representatives, being designated (1938) chairman of a special House committee (popularly called the Dies Committee) for the investigation of un-American activities. In 1945 he resumed law practice at Lufkin, Tex.

Dies Committee. Special committee of the U.S. House of Representatives headed originally by Democratic Representative Martin Dies of Texas which was established in 1938 for the investigation of un-American activities. While it received ready financial support from Congress, the committee met with criticism of its methods, particularly in connection with charging public officials with Communism. After Dies's retirement from the House of Representatives in 1945, the committee was established as a permanent body and designated as the Committee on Un-American Activities.

Diesel (dē′zel), **Rudolf.** b. at Paris, March 18, 1858; d. Sept. 29 or 30, 1913. German mechanical engineer, noted as the inventor of a type of internal-combustion engine later called the Diesel engine. He was educated at the Munich Polytechnic School. In 1893 he published *The Theory and Construction of a Rational Heat Motor*, a work embodying his investigations of an engine which he patented in 1893; the engine, which he developed between 1893 and 1897, had its first public exhibition (1898) at Munich. He established (1899) a plant at Augsburg for the manufacture of the engine. He died by drowning after falling overboard from an English Channel steamer. The full development of the Diesel engine came only after his death; the main features of the engine are its operation on cheap crude oil, its water-cooling system, and auto-ignition.

Dies Irae (dē′äs ē′rä, dī′ēz ī′rē). [Eng. trans., "*Day of Wrath.*"] Sequence appointed in the Roman missal to be sung between the Epistle and the Gospel in masses for the dead; named from its first words. The text was written probably by Thomas de Celano, the friend of Saint Francis of Assisi, and is a hymn in triple-rhymed stanzas. Its subject is the day of judgment. The transition from the terror of the day of wrath (*dies irae*) to hope in salvation is used as a natural preparation to the concluding prayer for eternal rest. Sir Walter Scott's translation in *The Lay of the Last Minstrel,* beginning "O day of wrath, O dreadful day," is well known. There have been numerous versions and translations. The author of the old ecclesiastical melody to which it is sung is not known, but it was adapted to the words at the time they were written. It has been a popular subject with many modern composers, notably Colonna, Bassani, Cherubini, Berlioz, Verdi, and Gounod in *Mors et Vita.* It is also introduced with magnificent effect in Mozart's *Requiem.*

Dieskau (dēs′kou), Baron **Ludwig August.** b. in Saxony, 1701; d. near Paris, Sept. 8, 1767. German general in the French service. He became brigadier general of infantry and commander of Brest in 1748, and in 1755 was sent to Canada with the rank of major general to conduct the French campaign against the English. With 1,200 Indians and Canadians and 200 regulars he undertook an expedition against Fort Edward in 1755. He was opposed by William Johnson, with 2,200 men, encamped on Lake George. Having ambushed and routed a detachment of 1,000 men under Colonel Ephraim Williams, he was himself defeated and captured in the ensuing attack on the British camp.

Diest (dēst). Town in C Belgium, in the province of Brabant, situated on the Demer River, ab. 32 mi. NE of Brussels. It has textile manufactures, breweries, and cattle markets. The Church of Saint Sulpice is in the late Gothic style; there are other medieval buildings. 8,576 (1946).

Diesterweg (dē′stėr.vāk), **Friedrich Adolf Wilhelm.** b. at Siegen, Westphalia, Prussia, Oct. 29, 1790; d. at Berlin, July 7, 1866. German educator and writer on pedagogics. He was a teacher in various institutions at Worms, Frankfort on the Main, Elberfeld, Mörs, and Berlin.

Dieterici (dē.te.rē′tsē), **Friedrich Heinrich.** b. at Berlin, July 6, 1821; d. there, Aug. 18, 1903. German Orientalist and philosophical writer; son of K. F. W. Dieterici (1790–1859). He published *Chrestomathie ottomane* (1854), various works on Arabic philosophy and literature, and others.

Dieterici, Karl Friedrich Wilhelm. b. at Berlin, Aug. 23, 1790; d. there, July 29, 1859. German statistician and political economist, director (1844 *et seq.*) of the Prussian bureau of statistics. His works include *Statistische Übersicht der wichtigsten Gegenständ* (1838–57), *Der Volkswohlstand im preussischen Staate* (1846), and others.

Diethelm (dē.telm), **André.** b. July 3, 1896—. French political leader, an official in the World War II Free French regime of General Charles de Gaulle. After holding a high post in the finance ministry, he left France for London in August, 1941; became (September, 1941) commissioner for interior, labor, and information; assumed (August, 1942) the posts of finances, economy, and merchant navy, and those of production and trade in June, 1943; and became war commissioner in April, 1944.

Dietmar von Aist (dēt′mär fon īst). [Also: **Thietmar von Aist** (or **von Eist**).] d. c1171. One of the earliest Middle High German minnesingers. He seems to have been an Austrian. Some of his poems, which are strong in emotional expressiveness, show the beginning influence of troubadour conventions. However, there is in them less pining for the unattainable than delight with triumphs achieved.

Diet of Worms (wėrmz). See **Worms, Diet of.**

Dietrich (dē′trich), **Albert Hermann.** b. at Golk, Germany, Aug. 28, 1829; d. at Berlin, in November, 1908. German composer. He was conductor (1855 *et seq.*) and head (1859 *et seq.*) of municipal music at Bonn, and after 1861 was *Kapellmeister* (choir leader) to the court at Oldenburg. His works include the opera *Robin Hood* (1879), a symphony, an overture, concertos, piano works, and pieces for choir.

Dietrich or **Dietrici** or **Dietricy** (dē.trē′tsē), **Christian Wilhelm Ernst.** b. at Weimar, Germany, Oct. 30, 1712; d. at Dresden, Germany, April 24 (or 23), 1774. German painter and engraver, noted especially for landscapes.

Dietrich (dē′trik), **Marlene.** b. at Berlin, Dec. 27, 1904—. American actress. A student of Max Reinhardt, she was on the Berlin stage for several years before turning to motion pictures. In *The Blue Angel* (1930), a German picture in which she played opposite Emil Jannings, she scored a great success; in addition to considerable acting ability, she displayed a perfect pair of legs, which soon became her "trademark." She came to the U.S. in 1930 and was naturalized as an American citizen in 1937. Among her principal films are *Morocco, Shanghai Express, Song of Songs, The Devil Is a Woman, Desire, The Garden of Allah, Destry Rides Again,* and *Golden Earrings.* During World War II she made numerous appearances at army camps.

Dietrichson (dē′trik.sôn), **Lorentz Henrik Segelcke.** b. at Bergen, Norway, Jan. 1, 1834; d. 1917. Norwegian critic and poet, professor (1875 *et seq*) of the history of art at the University of Christiania (now Oslo). His works include *Omrids af den norske Poesies Historie* (Outline of the History of Norwegian Poetry, 1866–69).

Dietrichstein (dē′trich.shtīn), Count **Albert von Mensdorff-Pouilly-.** See **Mensdorff-Pouilly-Dietrichstein,** Count **Albert von.**

Dietrich von Bern (fon bern′). In medieval Germanic legend, a figure corresponding to Theodoric the Great, historical king (474–526) of the Ostrogoths (East Goths), whose residence was at Verona. His life and adventures are the subject of the Icelandic *Thidrekssaga* (*Saga Thidhreks konungs af Bern*), also called the *Wilkina Saga,* whose material is from German sources, and is an element in various Middle High German poems, among them the *Nibelungenlied, Biterolf,* the *Rosengarten,* and *Ermenrichs Tod.* The South German cycle of Dietrich songs includes *Dietrichs Flucht, Alpharts Tod,* and the *Rabenschlacht,* all from the latter part of the 13th century. The *Hildebrandslied* treats a related theme. The figure of Dietrich appears also in the otherwise unrelated *Nibelungenlied.* There is no unified German Dietrich epic. His birth and death are mysterious; he is descended from a spirit, and disappears, ultimately, on a black horse. His name is still preserved in popular legends. In the Lausitz, the Wild Huntsman, the being who rides in furious haste across the heavens in violent storms, is called Dietrich von Bern. The name is also given to Knecht Ruprecht, the bringer of gifts or punishment at Christmas. Many large buildings in different parts of Italy, among them the amphitheater at Verona and the Castle of Sant' Angelo at Rome, have been popularly ascribed to him.

Dietz (dēts). See **Diez.**

Dietz, Feodor. b. at Neunstetten, Baden, Germany, May 29, 1813; d. at Gray, Haute-Saône, France, Dec. 18, 1870. German historical and battle painter. His works include *Death of Gustavus Adolphus, Storming of Belgrade,* and others.

Dietz, Howard. b. at New York, Sept. 8, 1896—. American writer and librettist. He has been a director (1918–24) and vice-president (1940 *et seq.*) in charge of publicity and advertising for Goldwyn Pictures Corporation, which merged (1924) into Metro-Goldwyn-Mayer. He collaborated with Jerome Kern on *Dear Sir* (1924), Morris Ryskind on *Merry-Go-Round* (1927), George S. Kaufman on *Bandwagon* (1932), and Reuben Mamoulian on *Sadie Thompson* (1944).

Dietz, Johann Christian. b. at Darmstadt, Germany, 1788; d. in the Netherlands, c1845. German instrument manufacturer, inventor of the claviharpe, the trochleon, and of a type of small piano called by him the melodeon.

Dietzenschmidt (dēt′sẹn.shmit). [Pseudonym of **Anton Franz Schmidt.**] b. at Teplitz-Schönau (now Teplice-Šanov, Czechoslovakia), Dec. 21, 1893—. German playwright and story writer. His play about a streetwalker, *Kleine Sklavin* (1918), created a sensation and helped bring him the Kleist prize a year later. The tales in *König Tod* (1918) already show the preoccupation with the fantastic and legendary which was to mark his later work. Saints' legends became his chief interest, and he put Saint Christopher and the Christ Child into a play (*Christofer,* 1920). Other such treatments are *Die Sankt Jacobs Fahrt* (1920) and *Die Nächte des Bruders Vitalis.*

Dieudonné d'Artois (dyė.do.nā dȧr.twȧ), **Henri Charles Ferdinand Marie.** See **Chambord,** Comte **de.**

Dieulafoy (dyė.lȧ.fwȧ), **Georges.** b. at Toulouse, France, Nov. 18, 1839; d. at Paris, Aug. 16, 1911. French clinician; brother of Marcel Auguste Dieulafoy. He was a pupil of Armand Trousseau and became professor of pathology at the University of Paris. He was a specialist in the treatment of the diseases of the lungs and the nervous system. Among his great contributions to the progress of medicine are his invention (1869) of a pump troicar for the evacuation of pleural effusions and the discovery of the three symptoms of objective evidence of appendicitis (Dieulafoy's triad): excessive hypersensitiveness of the skin, reflex contraction of the muscles, and abnormal sensitiveness to the touch at a specific point. He described also a type of gastric erosion which complicates pneumonia (Dieulafoy's ulcer or erosion). Author of *Manuel de pathologie interne* (1880–84; Eng. trans., *A Textbook of Medicine,* 1910), *Clinique médicale de l'Hôtel Dieu de Paris* (1896–99), *De l'aspiration pneumatique souscutanée. Méthode de diagnostic et de traitement* (1870; Eng. trans., *On Subcutaneous Pneumatic Aspiration, as a Method of Diagnosis and of Treatment,* 1870), and *Traité de l'aspiration des liquides morbides* (1873; Eng. trans., *A Treatise on the Traumatic Aspiration of Morbid Fluids,* 1873).

Dieulafoy, Jeanne Paule Henriette Rachel. [Maiden name, **Magre.**] b. at Toulouse, France, July 29, 1851; d. at Paris, 1916. French archaeologist; wife of Marcel Auguste Dieulafoy. She was the author of fiction and of *La Perse* (Persia, 1886), a description of her stay in that country with her husband.

Dieulafoy, Marcel Auguste. b. at Toulouse, France, Aug. 3, 1844; d. at Paris, Feb. 24, 1920. French archaeologist and engineer of roads and bridges; brother of Georges Dieulafoy. He explored the remains of the palaces of Darius I and Artaxerxes at Susa, Persia. Author of *L'Art antique de la Perse* (Ancient Persian Art, 1884–89) and *L'Acropole de Suse* (The Acropolis of Susa, 1890–93).

Diez (dēts). [Also, **Dietz.**] Town in W Germany, in the *Land* (state) of Rhineland-Palatinate, French Zone, formerly in the province of Hesse-Nassau, Prussia, situated on the Lahn River, ab. 19 mi. E of Koblenz. It has livestock markets, stone quarries, and small industries, and a medieval castle. 7,019 (1946).

Diez, Friedrich Christian. b. at Giessen, Hesse, Germany, March 15, 1794; d. at Bonn, Prussia, Germany, May 29, 1876. German philologist, the founder of scientific Romance philology. He was named (1830) professor at Bonn. Among his works are *Grammatik der romanischen Sprachen* (1836–42) and *Etymologisches Wörterbuch der romanischen Sprachen* (1853).

Differdange (dē.fer.däṅzh). [German, **Differdingen** (dif′ėr.ding.ėn).] Town in Luxembourg, situated in the "Red Earth" district near the French border, ab. 12 mi. SW of the city of Luxembourg. It is located in the "Minette" iron-ore field, stretching from Lorraine (near Longwy) into Luxembourg, and has iron mines, blast furnaces, and metallurgical industries. 15,243 (1948).

Difficulty, The Hill. Hill, in Bunyan's *Pilgrim's Progress*, encountered by Christian in his journey to the Celestial Country.

Diff'rent. Play by Eugene O'Neill, produced in 1921.

Dig (dēg). [Also, **Deeg.**] Fortified place in Rajasthan state, in the Rajputana region, Union of India, ab. 90 mi. S of Delhi. It was captured by the British in 1804. It contains a palace, built by Suraj Mull toward the middle of the 18th century. The portion completed is ab. 700 ft. square, and is traversed by a garden with beautiful architectural adornment. The north pavilion contains a fine audience hall, 77 by 54½ ft., divided by a central range of arches. An adjoining side of the court is occupied by a great hall 108 by 87 ft., open on two sides and including four ranges of columns with arcades edged with sharply cut cusps. The cornices are particularly noteworthy: they are wide-spreading, often double, and supported by very richly sculptured brackets.

Digby (dig′bi). Small seaport in Nova Scotia, Canada, on Annapolis basin, ab. 17 mi. SW of Annapolis. It is the county seat of Digby county and is connected by ferry with St. John, New Brunswick, and by rail with Halifax: center of Nova Scotian herring fishery. 2,047 (1951).

Digby, Sir Everard. b. May 16, 1578; d. Jan. 30, 1606. English conspirator; father of Sir Kenelm Digby. He inherited large estates in Rutlandshire, Leicestershire, and Lincolnshire from his father, Everard Digby of Stoke Dry, Rutland; and in 1603 was knighted by James I. He was one of the leading conspirators in the Gunpowder Plot (1605), being entrusted with the task of preparing for a rising in the midland counties to take place simultaneously with the blowing up and destruction of the Houses of Parliament. He was apprehended after the plot failed, confessed his guilt at his trial, and was hanged, drawn, and quartered at London.

Digby, George. [Title, 2nd Earl of **Bristol.**] b. at Madrid, October, 1612; d. at London, March 20, 1677. English Royalist soldier and politician; son of John Digby, 1st Earl of Bristol. His career was limited by his conversion (c1657) to Roman Catholicism and by his erratic instability of character. After graduation from Oxford (M.A., 1636), he attacked Roman Catholicism in letters (1638) to his cousin, Sir Kenelm Digby (1603–65). His speech (1641) in the House of Commons against the third reading of the attainder bill (which he had at first supported) concerning the earl of Stratford was burned by the common hangman. He fled to Holland as a result of his raising troops for Charles I, and was impeached for treason by the House of Commons. He joined the Royalist troops in the English Civil War, but resigned his command after a quarrel with Prince Rupert. He was secretary of state and privy councilor (1643), and lieutenant general of Royalist forces north of the Trent (1645). After defeat at Carlisle Sands (1645), he fled to France and became (1651) a lieutenant general in the French army. He fought brilliantly in the Fronde disorders, but was expelled from France for plotting to take Mazarin's place as royal minister. He was secretary of state (1657) to Charles II but lost his position as a result of his conversion to Roman Catholicism. He attempted to impeach Edward Hyde, the Earl of Clarendon, for his opposition to Digby's aim of an Italian marriage for Charles II. He retired from political life until the fall of Clarendon (1667).

Digby, John. [Title, 1st Earl of **Bristol.**] b. in February, 1580; d. at Paris, Jan. 16, 1653. English diplomat. He conducted negotiations for marriages between Prince Henry (d. 1612), son of James I, and Anne, daughter of Philip III of Spain (1611) and between Prince Charles (later Charles I) and Philip's younger daughter Maria (1614, 1618). He was made privy councilor (1616). In 1621 he was sent to advise on the dispute between Frederick V, elector palatine, son-in-law of James I, and the Holy Roman emperor, Ferdinand II. He returned to Spain (1622) to renew marriage arrangements, but in his attempts to come to agreement with Spain he offended Prince Charles and George Villiers, 1st Duke of Buckingham, and he had difficulty in obtaining a trial to answer charges brought by Charles I (1626). He was restored to the House of Lords (1628) after a period of imprisonment in the Tower of London. He supported Charles in the English Civil War and was one of those ordered by Parliament to be removed from the court in the Oxford peace propositions (1643).

Digby, Sir Kenelm. b. at Gothurst, Buckinghamshire, England, June (or July) 11, 1603; d. at London, June 11, 1665. English philosopher, naval commander, diplomat, and Royalist; son of Sir Everard Digby, who was executed for his participation in the Gunpowder Plot. He was educated at Gloucester Hall (later Worcester College), Oxford. In 1641 he fought a duel at Paris in defense of his royal master, Charles I; in 1644 he was made chancellor to Charles's queen, Henrietta Maria, and in 1645 at Rome (he was a Roman Catholic) he pleaded for Charles with Pope Innocent X. He was twice banished from England, in 1643 and again in 1649. He was visited during his exile by Evelyn, and he came to know Descartes. Some of his many works are *A Conference with a Lady about Choice of Religion* (Paris, 1638; London, 1654), *Observations upon Religio Medici* (1643), a criticism of Sir Thomas Browne's work, and often reprinted with it, *Observations on the 22nd Stanza in the Ninth Canto of the Second Book of Spenser's "Faery Queene"* (1644), *A Treatise of the Nature of Bodies* (Paris, 1644; London, 1658, 1665, 1669), *A Treatise declaring the Operations and Nature of Man's Soul, out of which the Immortality of reasonable Souls is evinced* (Paris, 1644; London, 1645, 1657, 1669), *Letters Concerning Religion* (1651), *A Discourse Concerning Infallibility in Religion* (1652), *A Discourse concerning the Vegetation of Plants* (1661), a lecture delivered at Gresham College, Jan. 23, 1661, in which he announced his discovery of the necessity of oxygen for the life of plants. As a philosopher, Digby was a follower of Aristotle and the Schoolmen. As a scientist he is not thought of too highly today, despite the fact that he unquestionably had much genuine scientific curiosity. Evelyn called him "an errant mountebank," after seeing his Paris laboratory, and Lady Fanshawe described him as "a person of excellent parts and a very fine-bred gentleman," apart from his tendency to lie about his experiments. His "sympathetic powder" or "powder of sympathy," for curing wounds, has long since been dismissed as being a quack preparation of no medical value.

Digby, Kenelm Henry. b. at Clonfert, Ireland, 1800; d. at London, March 22, 1880. English antiquary. He graduated, with the degree of B.A., at Cambridge in 1819, and spent most of his subsequent life in literary pursuits at London. His chief works are *The Broadstone of Honour, or Rules for the Gentlemen of England* (1822, anonymous; enlarged edition, with second title omitted, 1826–27), and *Mores Catholici, or Ages of Faith* (1831–40).

Digby Grant. See **Grant, Digby.**

Digby Plays. Collection of four late 15th-century religious plays, which exist in manuscript form in the Oxford Bodleian Library. The first play deals with *The Massacre of the Innocents and the Flight into Egypt* (also known as *The Killing of the Children*); the second with the *Conversion of Saul* (or Saint Paul), in which the unknown author quotes the "byble" as his authority; the third, regarded as the most important, is a *Mary Magdalene* miracle, the manuscript of which appears to be of the early 16th century, with the Seven Deadly Sins, Tiberius Caesar, and the king of Marseilles as characters; and the fourth, dealing with the burial and resurrection of Christ, is a morality play, named, after its chief characters, *Mind, Will, and Understanding*, with, of course, Satan, and his familiar "Ho, ho, ho!" In spite of their subjects, these plays have scenes of rough and vulgar humor, degenerating into coarse burlesque, which seem strangely out of place and, according to later notions, in bad taste. The first play is also called *Parfre's Candelmas-Day*, after its transcriber, Jhon (not John) Parfre, and the last is known as one of the "Macro

Moralities," the manuscript once being the property of the 18th-century antiquary Cox Macro.

Digest, The. See **Pandects of Justinian.**

Digger Indians. See under **Paiute.**

Diggers. Collective name popularly given to a number of North American Indian tribes of diverse linguistic affiliation who inhabited portions of California, Oregon, Idaho, Utah, Nevada, and Arizona. It refers to the root-collecting activities of the desert tribes of the area.

Digges (digz), Sir **Dudley.** b. 1583; d. 1639. English diplomat and parliamentarian; son of Thomas Digges (d. 1595). He was a member of the English Parliament from 1604 to 1629. James I employed him in diplomatic missions to Russia and the Netherlands. After the accession of Charles I he hoped for advancement through the king's favorite, the Duke of Buckingham, but these expectations failing, he took a leading part in the impeachment proceedings against Buckingham, and in opposition to the king, supported the Petition of Right (1628). After 1630, however, he was a supporter of the king's policies. He was a member of the court of high commission, and in 1636 was appointed master of the rolls.

Digges, Leonard. d. c1571. English mathematician. He studied at Oxford (without, however, taking a degree), and inherited a competent fortune, which enabled him to devote himself to scientific pursuits. His chief work is *A Booke named Tectonicon, briefly showing the exact measuring and speedie reckoning all manner of land, squares, timber, stone* . . . (1556).

Digges, Thomas. d. Aug. 24, 1595. English mathematician; son of Leonard Digges. He graduated, with the degree of B.A., at Cambridge in 1551, became a member of Parliament in 1572; and was muster-master-general of her majesty's forces in the Low Countries (1586–94). His works include *A Geometrical Practice, named Pantometria* (1571), *A Prognostication . . . contayning . . . Rules to judge the Weather by the Sunne, Moone, Stars* . . . (1578), and *An Arithmeticall Militare Treatise, named Stratioticos* (1579).

Digges, Thomas Atwood. b. c1741; d. c1821. American novelist, patriot, traveler, and friend of Washington, Jefferson, Franklin, and Madison. He is the author, or the generally accepted author, of *The Adventures of Alonzo: Containing some Striking Anecdotes of the Present Prime Minister of Portugal* (1775). It is an imitation of the picaresque novel, and tells the story of a young Portuguese merchant. It was published as being by "a native of Maryland, some years resident in Lisbon," both details applying to Digges, who is referred to as "a Maryland gentleman," and who is known to have lived at Lisbon during the Revolutionary War. His novel, which has been regarded by some as the first one by an American, is American in that sense only; as the title clearly indicates it does not deal with an American character or background, and it was not written in America.

Diggon (dig'ọn). Shepherd in Spenser's *Shepherd's Calendar*. He has traveled far and lost all his flock to sharp strangers.

Diggory (dig'ọ.ri). Loutish servant in Oliver Goldsmith's comedy *She Stoops to Conquer*.

Dighton (dī'tọn). Town in SE Massachusetts, in Bristol County, near the Taunton River: marketing point for agricultural products; formerly important for shipbuilding and fishing. Near it is the Dighton Rock, with an inscription formerly attributed to the Northmen, but now generally believed to be American Indian. 2,950 (1950).

Di Giacomo (dē jä'kō.mō), **Salvatore.** b. at Naples, Italy, 1860; d. 1934. Italian dialectal poet, novelist, and playwright.

Digna (dig'nạ), **Osman.** See **Osman Digna.**

Digne (dēny'). [Ancient name, **Dinia.**] Town in SE France, the capital of the department of Basses-Alpes, situated in a mountainous region on the Bléone River, NW of Nice. It is a tourist center and health resort with thermal springs considered useful in the treatment of rheumatism, gout, and skin diseases. It produces dried fruits, marmalades, honey, and hides. It is the seat of annual fairs for the sale of perfumes and essences, particularly lavender and mint. The cathedral of Saint Jérôme dates from the 15th century, the church of Notre-Dame-du-Bourg, one of the most majestic Romanesque churches of Provence, from the 12th and 13th centuries. The town suffered damage in World War II. 9,342 (1946).

Dignity and Impudence. Painting by Sir Edwin Landseer, in the National Gallery, London. It is a group consisting of a large, solemn-looking bloodhound and a pert Scotch terrier.

Digo (dē'gō). [Also: **Wadigo, Wadigu.**] One of nine Bantu-speaking peoples of E Africa known collectively as Nyika. The Digo inhabit Digo district in SE Kenya and Tanga district in NE Tanganyika, and their population is estimated at ab. 30,000 (by I. Schapera, *Some Problems of Anthropological Research in Kenya Colony*, 1940).

Digoin (dē.gwaṅ). Town in E France, in the department of Saône-et-Loire, situated on the Loire River and the Canal du Centre ab. 16 mi. W of Charolles. It is an industrial town, producing faïence earthenware and pottery. 6,357 (1946).

Dihang (dē.häng') or **Dihong** (dē.hông'). Name of the **Brahmaputra** in Assam.

Dijon (dē.zhôṅ). [Latin, **Divio, Dibio.**] City in E France, the capital of the department of Côte-d'Or, situated at the junction of the Ouche and Suzon rivers. It is a center for the trade in Burgundy wines and has chemical, metallurgical, and wood industries. Specialties of the department are liqueurs, cookies (*pain d'épice*), and mustards. The city is architecturally interesting because of its churches, its old houses and hotels, and the remarkable town hall in the former palace of the dukes of Burgundy. The cathedral of Saint Bénigne was started as a Romanesque basilica in 1001, but has an entirely Gothic superstructure. The churches of Saint Philibert, Saint Michel and Saint Jean date from the 14th and 15th centuries; Notre Dame, with a famous façade, from the 12th century. Dijon has a university and is the seat of a bishopric. The city flourished as long as it was a chief city (and finally, the capital) of the powerful duchy of Burgundy (1015–1477). Afterward, it was for a long time contested for by the French crown and the Hapsburgs. It was occupied by the Germans in 1870 and in 1940, and suffered damage toward the end of World War II. 100,664 (1946).

Dikaearchia (dī''kē.är.kī'ạ). Greek name of **Pozzuoli.**

Dike (dī'kē). See **Dice.**

Dikranakerd (dē.krä.nä.kerd'). Armenian name of **Diyarbakir.**

Diksmuide (diks.moi'dẹ). [Also: **Dikmuide**; French, **Dixmude.**] Small town in NW Belgium, in the province of West Flanders, situated on the Yser River, ab. 20 mi. SW of Bruges. It was severely damaged in World War I. Pop. ab. 3,000.

Diktonius (dik.tō'ni.us), **Elmer Rafael.** b. at Helsingfors (now Helsinki), Finland, 1896—. Finnish poet and prose writer. The son of a printer, he studied music and literature in France, England, and Czechoslovakia, and was one of the founders of the literary magazines *Ultra* and *Quosego*. Although he was at first a violent radical in his views and poetic form, Diktonius has slowly come to adopt an attitude expressing greater reconciliation to life. His verse is often an explosion of expressionistic modernism, always tempered, however, by his fine musical sensibility. Nature and man as the child of nature are central themes of his work, which is written in Swedish. English translations of his work may be found in *Voices From Finland* (1947) and *Modern Swedish Poems* (1948). His poetical volumes include *Min dikt* (My Poetry, 1921), *Hårda sånger* (Hard Songs, 1922), *Taggiga lågor* (Jagged Flames, 1924), *Stark men mörk* (Strong But Dark, 1930), *Gräs och granit* (Grass and Granite, 1936), *Jordisk ömhet* (Earthly Tenderness, 1938), and *Varsel* (Omen, 1942).

Dilettanti Society. London society devoted to the encouragement of a taste for the fine arts, founded in 1734.

Dilke (dilk), **Charles Wentworth.** b. Dec. 8, 1789; d. Aug. 10, 1864. English journalist, editor (1830–46) of the London *Athenaeum* and (1846–49) of the *Daily News*. He was the author of essays on the *Letters of Junius*. He did valuable research on Alexander Pope's life and continued the series of *Old Plays* begun by Robert Dodsley.

Dilke, Sir **Charles Wentworth.** b. at London, Feb. 18, 1810; d. at St. Petersburg, May 10, 1869. English politician; son of Charles Wentworth Dilke (1789–1864). He was a promoter of the London exhibition of 1851, commissioner to the New York industrial exhibition of 1853, and one of the royal commissioners for the London exhibition of 1862. He was made a baronet in 1862 and entered Parliament in 1865.

Dilke, Sir **Charles Wentworth.** b. at Chelsea, London, Sept. 4, 1843; d. at London, Jan. 26, 1911. English Radical Liberal politician and author; son of Sir Charles Wentworth Dilke (1810–69). He graduated at Cambridge in 1866 and was called to the bar in 1866, elected member of Parliament for Chelsea in 1868, appointed undersecretary of state for foreign affairs in 1880, and became president of the Local Government Board with a seat in the cabinet in 1882. He lost his seat in Parliament in 1886 after he had been named correspondent in a divorce case, but again became a member in 1892. He published *Greater Britain* (1868), *Parliamentary Reform* (1879), *Present Condition of European Politics* (1887), *The British Army* (1888), *Problems of Greater Britain* (1890), *Imperial Defense* (with Spenser Wilkinson, 1892), *The British Empire* (1898), and others. He married twice, his second wife being Emilia Frances Strong, Lady Dilke, noted art critic.

Dilke, Lady **Emilia.** [Maiden name, **Emilia Frances Strong.**] b. at Ilfracombe, Devonshire, England, Sept. 2, 1840; d. at Woking, Surrey, England, Oct. 24, 1904. English critic and historian of French art; daughter of Major Henry Strong; wife (married 1861) of Mark Pattison (1813–84) and (married 1885) of Sir Charles Wentworth Dilke (1843–1911). Educated at the South Kensington Art School; interested in social questions, labor unions, and votes for women; one of the founders of the Women's Trades Union League, the annual congresses of which she attended from 1884 to 1904. Contributed writings on art to the *Academy*, *Magazine of Art*, and other periodicals. Author of *The Renaissance of Art in France* (1879), *Art in the Modern State* (1884), *French Painters* (1889), *French Architects and Sculptors* (1900), *French Engravers and Draughtsmen* (1902), the last three dealing with the 18th century; she also wrote two collections of mystical stories, *The Shrine of Death* (1886), and *The Shrine of Love* (1891), and *The Book of the Spiritual Life* (1905).

Dill (dil), Sir **John Greer.** b. at Belfast, Ireland, Dec. 25, 1881; d. at Washington, D.C., Nov. 4, 1944. British soldier who served (1941–44) as a member of the joint Anglo-American board of strategy. He entered the army in 1901 and served in the Boer War (1901–02), and in World War I. He was director (1934–36) of military operations and intelligence in the War Office, and commanded British forces in Palestine. He led (1939–40) the First Army Corps in France, was appointed general (1939) and later field marshal. He accompanied (December, 1941) Winston Churchill to Washington. He was chief (1940–41) of the imperial general staff. Dill was responsible for the rebuilding of the British army after the Dunkerque disaster of 1940, when it was all but completely disorganized.

Dill, Ludwig. b. at Gerbsbach, Germany, Feb. 2, 1848; d. 1940. German landscape and marine painter. He studied under K. von Piloty and Seitz in the academy at Munich, and then traveled to Italy, France, and Switzerland, finally returning to Munich. He was awarded a Grand Prix in France at the Exposition Universelle of 1900. His work is in collections in Germany, France, and Argentina. Some of his better-known works are *Dutch Canal*, *Near the River*, *Canal at Venice*, *Venetian Fishing Boats*, and *Seascape*.

Dill, Sir **Samuel.** b. at Hillsborough, Ireland, March 26, 1844; d. at Belfast, Ireland, May 26, 1924. Irish classical scholar, educational administrator, and historian of Roman society in its period of decay and transformation. He was professor of Greek at Queen's College, Belfast (1890–1918), high master of Manchester Grammar School (1877–88), and is best remembered as author of *Roman Society in the Last Century of the Western Empire* (1898), *Roman Society from Nero to Marcus Aurelius* (1904), and *Roman Society in Gaul in the Merovingian Age* (1926).

Dillard (dil'ạrd), **James Hardy.** b. in Nansemond County, Va., Oct. 24, 1856; d. Aug. 2, 1940. American educator. After teaching mathematics at Washington and Lee University, he served as principal of various schools in the South before becoming professor of Latin at Tulane University, a chair he filled from 1891 until he resigned in 1907 to become president of the Jeanes Foundation, which promoted the betterment of education for Negroes in the South. In addition to serving in this capacity until 1931, he was director of the John F. Slater Fund (1910–17) and vice-president of the Phelps-Stokes Fund (1925). In 1928 his work in behalf of Negro education and better race relations won him the gold medal of the Harmon Foundation. He wrote and edited a number of books in the fields of mathematics, classical studies, and poetry, including *Fifty Letters of Cicero* (1902) and *Favorite German Poems* (1903). Dillard University at New Orleans is named for him.

Dillard University. Accredited, interdenominational, coeducational, privately controlled college for Negroes, at New Orleans. The outcome of an amalgamation of New Orleans University (Methodist) and Straight College (Congregationalist), it was chartered in 1930, named for James Hardy Dillard in recognition of his services to Negro education in the South, and opened in 1935. It has schools of arts and sciences, nursing, and business, and is affiliated with the Flint-Goodrich Hospital.

Dillenburg (dil'ẹn.bu̇rk). Town in W Germany, in the *Land* (state) of Hessen, American Zone, formerly in the province of Hesse-Nassau, Prussia, ab. 41 mi. NE of Koblenz. It has tool and machine, chemical, and rubber factories and manufactures musical instruments and costume jewelry. Count William I of Nassau (William the Silent) was born here; the ruins of his ancestral castle are preserved. 10,116 (1950).

Dillenius (di.lē'ni.us; German, di.lā'nē.u̇s), **Johann Jakob.** [Also, **Dillen** (dil'ẹn).] b. at Darmstadt, Germany, 1687; d. at Oxford, England, April 2, 1747. German botanist, professor at Oxford from 1728. He wrote *Catalogus plantarum sponte circa gissam nascentium* (1719), *Hortus elthamensis* (1732), and *Historia muscorum* (1741).

Dilli (dil'ē). See **Delhi,** India.

Dillingen (dil'ing.ẹn). Town in S Germany, in the *Land* (state) of Bavaria, American Zone, in the *Regierungsbezirk* (government district) of Swabia, situated on the Danube River, ab. 23 mi. NW of Augsburg. It has cement works, breweries, and machine and textile manufactures. Noteworthy buildings include a number of convents and churches of the baroque period (Jesuit Church and Parish Church, 17th century; Convent Church, 1735), a castle dating from the 13th century, the library, and the college of the Benedictines of Saint Ottilien. The town was the residence of the bishops of Augsburg from 1286 to 1803, and the seat of a university from 1554 to 1804. It became part of Bavaria in 1803. In World War II, Dillingen was occupied by Allied troops on April 27, 1945; war damage was considerable. 8,566 (1946).

Dillinger (dil'in.jėr), **John.** b. at Indianapolis, 1902; d. at Chicago, 1934. American bank robber. His criminal career began early, and he was at liberty on parole after a term in prison for attempted robbery when in 1933 he undertook, at the head of a gang of criminals, a campaign of bank robberies which terrorized the Middle West until in 1934 he was shot in Chicago by operatives of the Federal Bureau of Investigation.

Dillingham (dil'ing.ham, -ạm), **Charles Bancroft.** b. at Hartford, Conn., May 30, 1868; d. Aug. 30, 1934. American theater manager and producer, mainly of musical plays. He was manager of the Globe Theatre at New York and was associated with A. L. Erlanger in 20 other theaters, producing (1900 *et seq.*) some 200 plays.

Dillingham, William Paul. b. at Waterbury, Vt., Dec. 12, 1843; d. at Montpelier, Vt., July 12, 1923. American politician. He was elected governor of Vermont (1888) and U.S. senator (1900), holding the latter post until his death. As chairman (1903–11) of the Committee on Immigration, he is best known for his advocacy of the quota principle of immigration restriction, which formed the basis for the Immigration Law of 1921.

Dillmann (dil'män), **(Christian Friedrich) August.** b. April 25, 1823; d. July 4, 1894. German Orientalist and Protestant theologian, an authority on the Ethiopian language and literature and Old Testament criticism. He became (1869) professor at Berlin. His works include a grammar (1857) and lexicon (1865) of the Ethiopian language, and commentaries on Job, Genesis, Exodus, and Leviticus.

Dillon (dil'on). City in SW Montana, county seat of Beaverhead County, ab. 53 mi. S of Butte: wool-trading center. It is the seat of a state teachers college. 3,268 (1950).

Dillon. Town in NE South Carolina, county seat of Dillon County: shipping point for tobacco, cotton, and wheat; manufactures of textiles. 5,171 (1950).

Dillon, Arthur. b. at Roscommon, Ireland, 1670; d. at St.-Germain, France, 1733. English soldier, a general in the French army. He served as colonel of a Jacobite regiment under Louis XIV in Spain (1693–97), in Germany (1701), and in Italy (1702). Commissioned maréchal-de-camp (1704) and lieutenant general (1707), he was in charge of entrenchments at the siege of Barcelona (1714).

Dillon, Arthur Richard. b. at Braywick, Berkshire, England, 1750; guillotined in France, April 14, 1794. English soldier, a general in the French army; grandson of Arthur Dillon (1670–1733). He became a colonel (1767) under Louis XV; during the American Revolution he served in the West Indies and became governor of St. Kitt's.

Dillon, Charles. b. in England in 1819; d. there, June 27, 1881. English actor. He excelled in romantic drama, in such parts as Belphegor.

Dillon, Emile Joseph. b. at Dublin, Ireland, 1854; d. at Barcelona, Spain, June 9, 1933. English scholar, journalist, traveler, and editor. He traveled widely on the Continent, studying at the universities of Louvain, St. Petersburg, and Kharkov; founded (1885) *Le Muséon*, a French review, and was foreign editor of the Odessa *Messenger;* under the pseudonym E. B. Lanin he wrote (1889) articles on "Russian Characteristics" for the *Fortnightly Review;* became prominent as an expert on foreign affairs writing on France, Spain, China, and other countries for the *Contemporary Review* and the London *Daily Telegraph,* for which he covered the Dreyfus case. Author of translations, works on philology, *Maxim Gorky* (1902), *A Scrap of Paper* (1914), *Why Italy Went to War* and *Ourselves and Germany* (both 1916), *The Eclipse of Russia* (1918), *President Obregón* (1923), *Russia Today and Yesterday* (1929), and *Leaves from Life* (1932).

Dillon, George. b. at Jacksonville, Fla., Nov. 12, 1906—. American poet. Awarded (1932, 1933) Guggenheim fellowship; editor of *Poetry—A Magazine of Verse;* awarded Pulitzer prize in poetry for *The Flowering Stone* (1931). Author of *Boy in the Wind* (1927); translated (1935), with Edna St. Vincent Millay, Baudelaire's *Les Fleurs du Mal.*

Dillon, Sir **James.** fl. 1667. Irish soldier, the first of his family to serve European governments. He left Ireland for the Continent as a result of activities in the Leinster revolt (1652). He saw service thereafter as a brigadier general in the armies of Spain and of the Fronde; granted (1662) pension by Charles II for his services to Charles. I.

Dillon, John. b. 1851; d. Aug. 4, 1927. Irish politician, one of the leaders of the Irish National party. He entered Parliament in 1880 and became one of Parnell's supporters. He was imprisoned (1881–82) and again in 1891 for advocating resistance to rent collection and for assisting in the formation of the plan to have tenants pay into a central fund which would support them in case of eviction. Despite his opposition to the British government's policies in Ireland, he supported the crown in World War I. He was chairman (1918) of the Irish National Federation but suffered in its general defeat (1918) by the Sinn Fein.

Dillon, Wentworth. See **Roscommon,** 4th Earl of.

Dilly (dil'i), **Charles.** b. at Southill, Bedfordshire, England, May 22, 1739; d. at Ramsgate, Kent, England, May 4, 1807. English bookseller, publisher of Boswell's *Life of Johnson.* In partnership with his older brother, Edward Dilly (1732–79), he published Boswell's *Corsica,* Lord Chesterfield's *Works,* and many other outstanding 18th-century works; alone, he published Boswell's *Journal of a Tour to the Hebrides* (1780) and the *Life of Samuel Johnson, LL.D.* (1791; 2nd ed., 1793; 3rd ed., 1799). Both brothers were known for the famous dinners they gave to literary lights, and Charles was noted for the liberal terms he extended to his authors. Boswell's *Life* is full of references to "my worthy booksellers and friends," with Boswell more than once paying tribute to their "hospitable and well-covered table."

Dilmun (dil.mön'). Ancient city situated on an island, or rather peninsula, in the Persian Gulf, now included in the lowlands of the coast. Sargon II, king of Assyria (722–705 B.C.) relates on his monolith, found in Cyprus, that he received gifts and homage from Uperi, king of Dilmun.

Dilthey (dil'tī), **Wilhelm.** b. at Biebrich, Germany, Nov. 19, 1833; d. at Seis, Austria (now in Italy, near Bolzano), Oct. 3, 1911. German philosopher who did pioneer work for the systematic foundation of mental sciences, as differentiated from the natural sciences. He served as professor at the universities of Basel (1866), Kiel (1868), Breslau (1871), and Berlin (1882). His *Systematische Philosophie* (1907) reflects a positive idealism resulting from strongly empirical and historical tendencies. Between his *Einleitung in die Geisteswissenschaften* (1883) and *Der Aufbau der geschichtlichen Methode in den Geisteswissenschaften* (1910) the transformation of literary historiography from a technique of fact-recording into a vital science of ideas and human values had taken place. In this change Dilthey was largely instrumental, particularly with his essays on Lessing, Goethe, Novalis, Hölderlin, written at various times but published in 1905 under the title of *Das Erlebnis und die Dichtung.* Dilthey's other works include *Das Leben Schleiermachers* (1870), *Jugendgeschichte Hegels* (1905), and *Weltanschauung und Analyse des Menschen seit Renaissance und Reformation* (2 vols., 1921).

Di Maggio (dẹ mä'ji.ō), **Joseph Paul.** b. at Martinez, Calif., 1914—. American baseball player. His competence at bat and in the field led to his purchase in 1935 by the New York Yankees of the American League, and he quickly became one of the most noted and popular professional practitioners of the American national pastime. In 1937 he had a batting average of .347, and in 1941 he was credited with safe hits in 56 consecutive games, a record. He served with the U.S. army in World War II, after which he returned (1946) to the Yankees. He retired from baseball after the 1951 season had been completed. His autobiography, *Lucky to be a Yankee,* was published in 1946.

Diman (dī'mạn), **Jeremiah Lewis.** b. at Bristol, R.I., May 1, 1831; d. at Providence, R.I., Feb. 3, 1881. American historical writer and Congregational clergyman, professor of history at Brown University. He wrote *Theistic Argument* (1879) and *Orations and Essays* (published 1882).

Dimanche (dē.mänsh), **Monsieur.** [Eng. trans., *"Mr. Sunday."*] In Molière's *Don Juan* or *Le Festin de Pierre,* a tradesman who tries to collect money due him, but is never allowed even to ask for it, being constantly interrupted.

Dimetian Code (dī.mē'shi.ạn). Custom by which the youngest child received the dwelling house when property was divided by inheritance. It was practiced in Wales before the 10th century, according to the laws of Hywel Dda (Howel the Good), the different editions of which are included in the Dimetian Code for S Wales, in the Venedotian Code for N Wales, and in the Gwentian Code for NE Wales.

Diminuendo. Prose sketch (1896) by Max Beerbohm. Something of its whimsical, facetious nature may be gathered from the fact that it appeared in his first book, *The Works of Max Beerbohm,* which the author pretends is to be his last, and in which it is the closing selection. "I feel myself a trifle outmoded. I belong to the Beardsley period," and "I stand aside with no regret," Beerbohm tells his reader, in apparent sincerity. The meaning of the title in music (diminishing in loudness) is appropriate to the title of the sketch.

Dimisq (dē.mēsk'). An Arabic name of **Damascus.**

Dimitriev (dē.mē'trē.ef), **Radko.** [Also, **Dmitriev.**] b. at Gradets, Bulgaria, 1859; executed in Russia, 1919. Bulgarian general, who played a prominent role in military and political affairs as a friend of Russia. He participated in the overthrow (1886) of Prince Alexander of Battenberg because of the latter's anti-Russian policy, served as military commander during the Balkan wars (1912–13), as ambassador at St. Petersburg (1913–14), and as general in the Russian army during World War I.

He was executed by the Bolsheviks as a Czarist sympathizer.

Dimitrijević (dē.mē′trē.ye.vich), **Dragutin.** [Known as **"Apis."**] b. at Belgrade, Serbia, 1877; executed at Salonika, Greece, 1917. Serbian military and political figure, noted as a participant in conspiracies leading to the assassination of King Alexander I of Serbia in 1903 and of Crown Prince Francis Ferdinand in 1914. He founded (1911) the terrorist organization Union or Death, also known as the Black Hand. He was tried at Salonika by a Serbian military court and executed for treason against the Karageorgević dynasty.

Dimitri Roudine (dē.mē.trē rö.dēn). Name used in the French translation of the novel *Rudin*, by Ivan Turgenev, for the chief character. Now generally spelled Dmitri Rudin in English translations, the character is nevertheless sometimes entered in older English reference works under this French spelling.

Dimitrov (dē.mē′trŭf), **Georgi Mihailov.** b. at Kovachevtsi, Bulgaria, 1882; d. at Moscow, 1949. Bulgarian Communist leader, noted as secretary general (1935–42) of the Comintern (Communist International), and as first prime minister (1946–49) of the Bulgarian People's Republic. Member of Social Democrat and, after 1919, Communist parties; led abortive uprising (1923) in Bulgaria and went into exile; accused by Nazis of complicity in Reichstag fire, and acquitted at Leipzig trial (1933).

Dimitrov, Georgi Mihov. b. in Thrace (then part of Turkey), 1903—. Bulgarian agrarian leader, secretary general (1947 *et seq.*) of the International Peasant Union. He began his political career as secretary (1921–23) of the Bulgarian Agrarian Youth League, obtained a degree in medicine (1931), and served as a member of parliament (1931–34), representing the Agrarian National Union. He went into exile in 1941, and returned in 1944 as leader of the Agrarian National Union, but resigned (1945) under Communist pressure and again went into exile.

Dimmesdale (dimz′dāl), **Arthur.** Puritan clergyman in *The Scarlet Letter* (1850) by Nathaniel Hawthorne. He has a delicately sensitive nature, unable to bear the strain of the concealment of his sin with Hester Prynne, which he finally confesses publicly.

Dimnet (dēm.ne), **Ernest.** [Often referred to as **Abbé Dimnet.**] b. at Trelon, France, 1869—. French abbé, lecturer, writer, and authority on the Brontës. He is the author of *La Pensée catholique dans l'Angleterre contemporaine* (1905), *Figures de moines* (1909), *Les Sœurs Brontë* (1910), *L'Art de penser* (1928; Eng. trans., *The Art of Thinking*, 1930), and *What We Live By* (1932; original publication in English). He achieved popularity as lecturer and writer on self-improvement for American audiences.

Dimonah (di.mō′nạ). See under **Dibon,** Judea.

Dimotika (dē.mô′ti.kä). See **Didymoteikhon.**

Dimple Hill. Novel by Dorothy M. Richardson, published in 1938. It is the twelfth section of *Pilgrimage* (1938), a novel sequence in 12 parts employing the stream-of-consciousness technique.

Dimsdale (dimz′dāl), **Thomas.** b. in Essex, England, May 6, 1712; d. in Hertfordshire, England, Dec. 30, 1800. English physician, known chiefly as an advocate of inoculation for smallpox. He took up the practice of medicine at Hertford, and in 1767 published *The Present Method of Inoculation for the Small Pox,* which obtained for him in 1768 an invitation to St. Petersburg to inoculate the empress Catherine and the grand duke Paul.

Dimyat (dim.yät′). Arabic name of **Damietta.**

Dinagat (dē.nä′gät). Long, narrow island of the Philippines, belonging to Surigao province and lying N of Mindanao and E of Leyte, from which it is separated by Surigao Strait. It is traversed from N to S by mountains, of which Redondo, a peak at the N extremity, is the highest. Cagdayanao, at the SE end of the island, is a good harbor in all weather for large vessels. Area, 309 sq. mi.; pop. 14,606 (1939).

Dinah (dī′nạ). [Also, **Dina.**] In the Bible, the daughter of Jacob by Leah. She was raped by Shechem; in return her brothers Simeon and Levi destroyed eight of the Amorite cities after causing the men of the land to be disabled. Shechem wanted to marry Dinah, but the brothers insisted that she could not marry one who was a member of an uncircumcised people. Therefore Shechem's father, the king, ordered his male subjects to be circumcised. Gen. xxx, xxxiv.

Dinah, Aunt. In Laurence Sterne's *Tristram Shandy*, the aunt of Walter Shandy, who occupies himself with schemes for spending the money she leaves him.

Dinah Morris (mor′is). See **Morris, Dinah.**

Dinajpur (dē.näj′pör). [Also, **Dinagepore.**] District in the Rajshahi division, East Bengal, divided in 1947 between Pakistan and the Union of India, NE of the Ganges River. Rice and sugar are the important crops in the area. Capital, Dinajpur; area, 3,946 sq. mi.; pop. 1,926,833 (1941).

Dinajpur. [Also, **Dinagepore.**] Capital of Dinajpur district, Pakistan, ab. 220 mi. N of the city of Calcutta. It is an important road junction, with roads leading to Bhutan, Nepal, the valley of the Brahmaputra River, and the valley of the Ganges River. 34,271 (1951).

Dinan (dē.näṅ). Town in NW France, in the department of Côtes-du-Nord, picturesquely situated on an escarpment above the Rance River, ab. 29 mi. NW of Rennes. It is a tourist center, particularly frequented by British travelers, because of its medieval castle and ramparts, old streets and houses, and interesting environs. The Church of Saint Sauveur shows Romanesque, Gothic, and Renaissance characteristics. The British besieged the town twice (1344 and 1364). It was the meeting place for the estates of Brittany from 1643 to 1717. Pop. 12,737 (1946).

Dinant (dē.näṅ, dē.nänt′). Town in S Belgium, in the province of Namur, situated on the Meuse River, ab. 14 mi. S of Namur. It is fortified, and was formerly noted for its copper and brass wares. It was sacked by the Burgundians in 1466, and captured by the French in 1554 and 1675 and by the Germans in 1914. Pop. 7,046 (1947).

Dinant (di.nänt′). In John Fletcher and Philip Massinger's *Little French Lawyer*, a gentleman who formerly loved and still pretends to love Lamira.

Dinapore (dē′nạ.pōr). [Also, **Dinapur** (-pör).] Town in the district of Patna, Bihar state, Union of India, on the Ganges River ab. 12 mi. W of Patna. It has been known as an important military station, and was the scene of the start of the mutiny of the Sepoy regiments in the district in July, 1857. Pop. 24,221 (1941).

Dinar (dē.när′). [Ancient name, **Celaenae.**] Town in W central Turkey, in the *il* (province or vilayet) of Afyon, ab. 90 mi. N of Antalya. It stands on the site of an ancient city of Phrygia, once of great size and importance. It became a royal residence in the time of Xerxes. Traditionally Apollo flayed Marsyas here after he had beaten the upstart in a musical contest. Celaenae was situated at the source of both the Marsyas and Maeander rivers. Pop. ab. 4,000.

Dinard (dē.nàr). Town in NW France, in the department of Ille-et-Vilaine, situated at the mouth of the Rance River and on the English Channel, facing St.-Malo and St.-Servan. It is a fashionable seaside resort, famous for its mild climate. The town hall and the church were seriously damaged during the World War II bombardment of August, 1944. Pop. 8,428 (1946).

Dinaric Alps (di.nar′ik alps′). [Serbo-Croatian, **Dinara Planina** (dē′nä.rä plä′nē.nä).] Name given to those mountain ranges in Yugoslavia which are a continuation of the main Alpine system. They run parallel to the Adriatic Sea coast through Slovenia, Croatia, and Bosnia-Hercegovina. Highest peak, Voljnac (ab. 7,800 ft.).

Dinarzade (dē.när.zä′dẹ). Sister of Scheherazade in *The Arabian Nights' Entertainments.* She passes the night in the bridal chamber, and daily asks her sister, who is condemned to die each morning unless she can win a stay by telling another story, to relate for the last time one of her "agreeable tales."

Dindigul (din.di.gul′). [Also, **Dindigal.**] Town in Madras state, Union of India, ab. 120 mi. N of Cape Comorin. It is a major rail and road junction and is a large trading center. 56,275 (1941).

Dindings (din′dingz). [Also, **Dinding Isles.**] Administrative division of the former British colony of Straits Settlements (now part of the Federation of Malaya), situated on the W side of the Malay Peninsula, ab. 320 mi. NW of Singapore. The division is well known to stamp collectors, as it issued many beautiful series.

Dindorf (din′dôrf), **Wilhelm.** b. at Leipzig, Germany, Jan. 2, 1802; d. there, Aug. 1, 1883. German classical philologist. He was one of the collaborators in the revision of Stephanus's *Thesaurus linguae Graecae* (1831–65), and edited *Demosthenes* (1846–51), *Poetae scaenici Graeci* (1830), and others.

d'Indy (dañ.dē), **Vincent**. See **Indy, (Paul Marie Théodore) Vincent d'.**

Dindymene (din.di.mē'nē). [Also, the **Dindymenian Mother.**] Cybele, the Phrygian mother-goddess: so called from Mount Dindymus in Galatia.

Dindymus (din'di.mus). [Also, **Dindymum** (-mum).] In ancient geography, a mountain in Galatia, sacred to Cybele.

Dinesen (dē'ne.sen), **Isak.** [Pen name of Baroness **Karen Blixen** (**Finecke**); maiden name, **Dinesen.**] b. at Rungsted, Denmark, April 17, 1885—. Danish writer, who won a world circle of readers with her *Seven Gothic Tales* (1934). These show strong literary influences from 18th-century romantic writers. Her next book, *African Farm* (1937), was based on 18 years of living in East Africa. She returned to the romantic strain in *Winter's Tales* (1943) and used the romantic atmosphere to disguise a political message in *The Angelic Avengers* (1947), which she wrote under the pen name Pierre Andrézel.

Ding (ding). Signature used professionally by the cartoonist **Darling, Jay Norwood.**

Dingelstedt (ding'el.shtet), Baron **Franz von.** b. at Halsdorf, Hesse, Germany, June 30, 1814; d. at Vienna, May 15, 1881. German poet and novelist, director of the court theater at Stuttgart (1846–51), Munich (1851–56), and Weimar (1857–67) and of the Vienna Burgtheater (1872–81). He is considered one of the better political poets of the 1840's (*Lieder eines kosmopolitischen Nachtwächters*, 1841), and his tragedy *Das Haus des Barneveldt* (1850) was a success. He was the author also of the novels *Unter der Erde* (1840) and *Die Amazone* (1868). One of his great achievements was the staging at Weimar of a cycle of Schiller plays, and of Shakespeare's historical dramas in chronological order.

Dingle (ding'gl), **Herbert.** b. at London, Aug. 2, 1890—. English astronomer and physicist. He was reader and professor (1918–46) of natural philosophy at the Imperial College of Science and Technology, professor (1946 *et seq.*) of the history and philosophy of science at University College at London, and a member of the British government eclipse expeditions of 1927, 1932, and 1940. His written works include *Relativity for All* (1922) and *Modern Astrophysics* (1924).

Dingley (ding'li), **Nelson.** b. at Durham, Me., Feb. 15, 1832; d. Jan. 13, 1899. American editor, governor and congressman, author of the Dingley Tariff (1897). As editor (1856 *et seq.*) of the Lewiston (Me.) *Evening Journal*, he endorsed the newly formed Republican Party. Entering actively into Republican politics, he served (1861 *et seq.*) in the state legislature, was governor (1874–75) of Maine, and U.S. congressman (1881–99). As chairman (1895 *et seq.*) of the House Ways and Means Committee, he drafted the Dingley Tariff (passed 1897), the highest to that date.

Dingley Tariff. Act of the U.S. Congress, passed in 1897, which was effective in raising protective duties on imported commodities to a higher level, despite President William McKinley's inaugural statement promising a tariff for revenue purposes. The chief increases in the schedules applied to silks, linens, and chinaware. The 1890 duties on metals were restored and higher duties were reimposed on hides and wool.

Dingras (dēng.gräs'). Town in Ilocos Norte province, in the NW part of Luzon, Philippine Islands. 5,479 (1948).

Dingwall (ding'wôl, -wal). Royal burgh in N Scotland, in the county of Ross and Cromarty, situated near the head of Cromarty Firth, ab. 8 mi. N of Beauly, ab. 577 mi. N of London by rail. It is the county seat of Ross and Cromarty. 3,363 (est. 1948).

Dinia (dī'ni.a). Ancient name of **Digne.**

Dinias and Dercyllis (din'i.as; dėr.sil'is). Chief characters (and usual title) of an old Greek romance. (The work is sometimes also entitled *Of the Incredible Things in Thule.*) Their love story furnishes the plot. According to Photius it was written soon after the death of Alexander the Great; others, however, believed it had been written by Antonius Diogenes, who was thought to have lived in Syria in the 2nd century B.C.

Diniz (dē.nēsh'). [Also: **Dinis**; English form, **Denis** or (sometimes) **Dionysius.**] b. at Lisbon, Portugal, Oct. 9, 1261; d. at Santarem, Portugal, Jan. 7, 1325. Sixth king (1279–1325) of Portugal. He was the son of Alfonso III of Portugal and Beatriz de Guzman, an illegitimate daughter of Alfonso X of León and Castile. From 1277 to 1279 he was in revolt against his father, and when he succeeded to the throne in 1279 was faced by the revolt of his brother Alfonso. He married (1281) Isabel (often known as Saint Elizabeth of Aragon), daughter of Peter III of Aragon. Diniz earned his epithet, *O Rei Lavrador* ("the farmer king"), by his agricultural reforms, introducing new methods of farming and establishing agricultural schools. He limited the authority of the feudal rulers of the kingdom and helped to establish centralized authority in the throne. Despite quarrels with the neighboring kingdoms, he stabilized the political situation of Portugal by judicious marriages of his children. He is generally considered the best Portuguese medieval poet. His lyric poems were preserved in the *Cancioneiro da Vaticana* (Codex Vaticanus 4803) and reproduced in a critical edition (1892) by H. R. Lang. A second edition, with introduction, appeared in 1894. He ordered the translation into Portuguese of two works by his grandfather, King Alfonso X (known as Alfonso the Learned) of León and Castile: *Crónica general* and *Libro de las siete partidas*. They became the first literary works in Portuguese prose. Diniz was the founder (1290) of the University of Coimbra.

Diniz, Júlio. [Pseudonym of **Joaquim Guilherme Gomes Coelho.**] b. at Oporto, Portugal, Nov. 14, 1839; d. there, in September, 1871. Portuguese writer who is credited with having introduced realism and rustic characters in the literature of his country with great success. His most popular rural novels were *As pupilas do Sr. Reitor* (1867), *A morgadinha do canaviais* (1868), and *Os fidalgos da Casa Mourisca* (1871). *Uma família inglesa* (1868), another well-known novel, deals, however, with city life.

Dinka (ding'kä). [Also, **Dyangeh.**] Nilotic-speaking people of S Anglo-Egyptian Sudan in NE Africa, occupying the basin of the Bahr-el-Ghazal, SW of Malakal, and a smaller area downstream on the right bank of the White Nile. They call themselves *Jieng* (singular, *Jiang*); Dinka is a corruption of their Arabic name, *Denkawi*. Their population is estimated at ab. 500,000 (by A. N. Tucker, 1935). They comprise a number of independent subgroups, including the Rek, Agar, Ngok, Twij, Malual, Dongjol, Palyoupiny, Twi, Ruweng, Gok, Bor, and Ciec. They are divided into numerous subgroups ruled by local headmen. They have military age grades and exogamous patrilineal clans. They practice hoe agriculture and herding, with the cattle complex, and their principal foods are generally milk and millet.

Dinkard (dēn.kärd'). Largest and most important Pahlavi work in existence, containing a vast amount of information regarding the legends, writings, doctrines, and customs of the Zoroastrian religion. In its present state much of the work consists of a descriptive catalogue of the contents of the original compilation, interspersed with extracts in detail. The date of its latest revision must have been subsequent to the Mohammedan conquest of Persia.

Dinkelsbühl (ding'kels.bül). Town in S Germany, in the *Land* (state) of Bavaria, American Zone, in the *Regierungsbezirk* (government district) of Middle and Upper Franconia, situated on the Wörnitz River, ab. 44 mi. SW of Nuremberg. It has agricultural markets, and small industries producing baskets, toys, and furniture. It is one of the best preserved medieval towns in S Germany, with walls and gates dating from the 15th century, the German House (1543), and the Church of Saint George, which is a notable example of the late Gothic style. Dinkelsbühl was a free imperial city from 1351 to 1802; it became part of Ansbach in 1804 and of Bavaria in 1806. The Swedes conquered the town in 1632. Pop. 6,928 (1946).

Dinmont (din'mont, -mont), **Dandie** (or **Andrew**). Border farmer in Sir Walter Scott's novel *Guy Mannering*. He is the grateful friend of Brown, who had saved his life. Sent by Meg Merrilies, he protects Brown in the Portanferry jail and, after their escape helps him, under the guidance of Meg, to capture Hatteraick. He is the owner of Mustard and Pepper, the progenitors of the Dandie Dinmont terriers.

Dinner at Eight. Play (1932) by George S. Kaufman and Edna Ferber.

Dinocrates or **Deinocrates** (dī.nok′rą.tēz). fl. 4th century B.C. Ablest of the architects of Alexander the Great. He planned the new city of Alexandria, and rebuilt the Artemisium of Ephesus after its destruction by fire. He had a plan, never executed, of making a huge statue of a seated figure of Mount Athos (the mountain, personified, was to have a city in one hand and a basin to catch the rivers in the other).

Dinorah (di.nō′rą). [French title, **Le Pardon de Ploërmel.**] Opera in three acts by Meyerbeer, with libretto by Carré and Barbier, first produced at Paris, April 4, 1859.

Dinosaur National Monument. Large tract in NE Utah and NW Colorado, extending along the Green River and its tributary, the Yampa River. It includes areas of fossil remains, and the great Lodore Canyon of the Green River, in Colorado, with waterfalls and wild scenery. It was established in 1915. Area, ab. 298 sq. mi.

Dinslaken (dins′lä.kęn). Town in W Germany, in the *Land* (state) of North Rhine-Westphalia, British Zone, formerly in the Rhine Province, Prussia, situated near the Rhine River ab. 10 mi. N of Duisburg. It has metallurgical, electrical, machine, shoe, garment, and foodstuff industries, large iron and steel works, sawmills, and brick factories; coal mines are in the vicinity. 31,949 (1950).

Dinsmoor (dinz′mōr, -mör), **Robert.** [Also, **Dinsmore.**] b. at Windham, N.H., Oct. 7, 1757; d. March 16, 1836. American poet, known for poems in Scottish dialect. An edition of his poetry (1828) was edited and arranged (1898) as *Poems of Robert Dinsmoor, the Rustic Bard.* He was encouraged by John Greenleaf Whittier, who wrote an essay about him, "Robert Dinsmore" in *Old Portraits and Modern Sketches* (1850).

Dinsmore (dinz′mōr), **Charles Allen.** b. at New York, Aug. 4, 1860; d. at New Haven, Conn., Aug. 14, 1941. American Congregational clergyman and Dante scholar. Ordained (1888); pastor (1905–20) of the First Church at Waterbury, Conn.; professor (1920 *et seq.*) of the spiritual content of literature at the Yale Divinity School. His studies on Dante were published in *The Teachings of Dante* (1901), *Aids to the Study of Dante* (1903), and *Life of Dante* (1919); author also of *Atonement in Literature and Life* (1906), *The New Light on the Old Truth* (1912), *Religious Certitude in an Age of Science* (1924), *The English Bible as Literature* (1931), and *The Great Poets and the Meaning of Life* (1937).

Dinsmore, Elsie. Heroine of the 26 "Elsie Books" (1868–1905) by Martha F. Finley. Elsie is assiduously dedicated to virtue and to the resistance of all temptations, however minor, even when proffered by her father and friends. In the series she progresses from childhood to grandmotherhood, maintaining her remarkable virtue and immunity to temptation throughout.

Dinsmore, Robert. See **Dinsmoor, Robert.**

Dinter (din′tėr), **Gustav Friedrich.** b. at Borna, in Saxony, Feb. 29, 1760; d. at Königsberg, in East Prussia, May 29, 1831. German writer on pedagogics, professor of theology at Königsberg from 1822. His chief work is the *Schullehrerbibel* (1825–28).

Dinuba (di.nū′bą). City in C California, in Tulare County, NW of Los Angeles in a fruit-raising region. 4,971 (1950).

Dinwiddie (din′wid.i), **Robert.** b. at Germiston, near Glasgow, Scotland, 1693; d. at Clifton, Bristol, England, July 27, 1770. British colonial official in America. He was important in at least three respects: for his role in the French and Indian Wars, for his promotion of the westward movement, and for his influence on young George Washington. Placed by the British government in positions of increasing responsibility, he was assigned (1721 *et seq.*) to the island of Bermuda in charge of admiralty affairs, served (1727 *et seq.*) as collector of customs for Bermuda, and was promoted (1738) to surveyor-general (and in 1743 to the additional office of inspector-general) of customs for the southern part of America. In 1741 he became a member of the governor's council in Virginia, where finally in 1751 he was elevated to the position of lieutenant governor. With the approval of the Board of Trade, he led the colonial governors in opposing French domination of North America, and thereby greatly affected the course of American history. He promoted, in part to checkmate the French, the interests of the land venture known as the Ohio Company. In 1753 he dispatched 21-year-old George Washington to the French in the Lake Erie region, warning them to withdraw from that area. When the French continued their penetration into the Ohio valley, Dinwiddie in 1754 sent Washington against them with a small contingent, which the French forced to capitulate at Fort Necessity. Throughout the French and Indian Wars, his interest in military affairs was unflagging. He urged coöperation on the part of the colonies, was the first to place Washington in a position of military responsibility, and, for the most part, supported him even in defeat. In spite of occasional misunderstandings with Washington and with the burgesses, there was mutual confidence and respect. Contrary to popular belief he was not recalled, but left Virginia voluntarily in 1758 because of ill health.

Dio (dē′ō). Portuguese name of **Diu.**

Diocaesarea (dī.ǫ.sē.zą.rē′ą). Latin name of **Sepphoris.**

Dio (or **Dion**) **Cassius** (dī′ō, dī′on; kash′us, kash′i.us, kas′i.us). [Surnamed **Cocceianus.**] b. at Nicaea, in Bithynia, c155 A.D.; d. there, after 230 A.D. Historian of Rome. He was consul c220 and 229, and wrote in Greek a history of Rome in 80 books, covering the period from Aeneas to his own. Books 36–60 are extant.

Diocles (dī′ǫ.klēz). fl. 5th century B.C. Syracusan popular leader, the reputed (chief) author of a code of laws named for him.

Diocles Carystius (ką.ris′ti.us). b. at Carystus, in Euboea; fl. 4th century B.C. Greek physician.

Diocletian (dī.ǫ.klē′shąn). [Full Latin name, **Gaius** (or **Caius**) **Aurelius Valerius Diocletianus**; surnamed **Jovius.**] b. at Dioclea (whence his name), near Salona, in Dalmatia, 245 A.D.; d. near Salona, in Dalmatia, 313 A.D. Emperor of Rome. He entered the army at an early age, and, although of obscure origin, rose to important commands under Probus, Aurelian, and Carus. On the death of Numerianus, joint emperor with Carinus, he was proclaimed emperor by the army at Chalcedon in 284, and advanced against Carinus who was killed by one of his own officers. In 286 he adopted Maximian as his colleague in the government, dividing the empire into eastern and western parts for greater efficiency in government. In 292 the joint emperors appointed Galerius and Constantius Chlorus as their associates, and intending them as their successors. Diocletian and Maximian retained the title of Augusti, while Galerius and Constantius were denominated Caesars. Each of the rulers was independent in the local administration of his province, but the three junior rulers acknowledged Diocletian as the head of the empire. The empire was divided among them as follows: Diocletian received Thrace, Egypt, Syria, and Asia, with Nicomedia (modern Izmit, Turkey) as his capital; Maximian, Italy, Africa, Sicily, and the islands of the Tyrrhenian Sea, with Mediolanum (modern Milan) as his capital; Galerius, Illyricum and the countries of the Danube with Sirmium (near modern Sremska Mitrovica, Yugoslavia) as his capital; and Constantius, Britain, Gaul, and Spain, with Augusta Trevirorum (modern Trier or Treves, Germany) as his capital. Diocletian subdued a revolt in Egypt in 296, Constantius restored the allegiance of Britain in the same year, and Galerius forced the Persians to sue for peace in 297. Under Diocletian, the Roman Empire became more tranquil and prospered greatly. Republican forms of government finally disappeared during his reign; the monarchy became absolute. His economic measures were generally sound, but his attempt in 301 to fix prices and wages, during an economic crisis caused by speculation and bad crops, was a disastrous failure, causing an upheaval in food distribution and ruining many commercial enterprises. In 303 Diocletian, persuaded, it is said, by the false accusations of Galerius, ordered a general persecution of the Christians throughout the empire. He abdicated in 305, compelling Maximian to do the same, and retired to Salona in Dalmatia (near modern Split, Yugoslavia), where he spent his remaining years in the cultivation of his gardens. Diocletian and Maximian were succeeded as Augusti by

Galerius and Constantius, who in turn appointed Severus and Maximinus Caesars.

Diodati (dē.ǫ.dä'tę), **Charles.** b. c1608; d. 1638. English physician and scholar of the classics, famous for being a close friend of Milton; son of Theodore Diodati. He became friend to Milton at St. Paul's School. He received an M.A. from Oxford (1628) and an M.A. from Cambridge (1629), and practiced medicine near Chester. To him Milton addressed his first and sixth Latin elegies and an Italian sonnet. His death while Milton was abroad was lamented in *Epitaphium Damonis* (1640), considered by many to be the greatest of Milton's Latin poems.

Diodati, Domenico. b. at Naples, Italy, 1736; d. there, 1801. Italian archaeologist. His works include *De Christo graece loquente exercitatio* (1767), and others.

Diodati, Giovanni. b. at Geneva, Switzerland, June 6, 1576; d. there, Oct. 3, 1649. Swiss Protestant theologian, professor of Hebrew and later of theology at Geneva. He translated (1607) the Bible into Italian, revised an earlier French translation of the Bible, and translated into French Paolo Sarpi's *History of the Council of Trent.*

Diodati, Theodore. b. at Geneva, Switzerland, c1574; d. at London, 1651. English physician; father of Charles Diodati. His family emigrated to England, where he was educated as a doctor; he had Prince Henry and Princess Elizabeth as patients; he took his M.D. (1615) at Leiden. Florio, in his dedication of his translation of Montaigne's *Essays,* acknowledged Diodati's aid.

Diodorus (dī.ǫ.dō'rus). [Surnamed **Siculus,** meaning "of Sicily."] b. at Agyrium, Sicily; fl. in the second half of the 1st century B.C. Greek historian, author of an unreliable history in 40 books entitled *Historical Library.* The first five (dealing with the legendary histories of Egypt, Assyria, Ethiopia, and Greece) and the 11th to 20th books (beginning with the Persian War and ending with the events following Alexander's death) are all that have survived.

Diogenes (dī.oj'ę.nēz). See also **Romanus IV Diogenes.**

Diogenes. b. at Sinope, in Asia Minor, c412 B.C.; d. at Corinth, 323 B.C. Greek Cynic philosopher, famous for his eccentricities. He emigrated to Athens in his youth, became the pupil of Antisthenes, and lived, according to Seneca, in a tub. While on a voyage from Athens to Aegina, he was captured by pirates who exposed him for sale on the slave market in Crete. When asked what business he understood, he replied, "How to command men," and requested to be sold to some one in need of a master. He was purchased by Xeniades, a wealthy citizen of Corinth, who restored him to liberty, and in whose house he passed his old age. At Corinth he was, according to tradition, visited by Alexander the Great. Alexander inquired whether he could oblige him in any way. "Yes," replied Diogenes, "stand from between me and the sun." Diogenes taught and believed in an extreme of asceticism as a means of attaining truth and good. As a result he was looked down upon and in turn rejected his contemporaries. The story of his search with a lighted lamp in broad daylight (as he said, "for an honest man"), true or not, vividly illustrates this.

Diogenes, Antonius. Author of the romance *Dinias and Dercyllis.*

Diogenes Laërtius (lą.ėr'shi.us). fl. probably in the early 3rd century A.D. Historian and biographer, author of lives of the Greek philosophers in 10 books, from the early schools to the Epicureans. His work is chiefly valued as containing information preserved nowhere else.

Diogenes of Apollonia (ap.ǫ.lō'ni.ą). b. at Apollonia, Crete; fl. in the 5th century B.C. Greek natural philosopher, a pupil of Anaximenes.

Diogo Cam (dyō'gö kouṅ). See **Cão, Diogo.**

Diola (dē.ō'lä). [Also, **Dyola.**] Sudanic-speaking people of W Africa, inhabiting W Gambia, and SW French Senegal, S of Bathurst. They are non-Mohammedan. They are not to be confused with the Diula of N Ivory Coast.

Dioliba (di.ol'i.bą). See **Niger River.**

Diomede Islands (dī'ǫ.mēd). Group of small islands in Bering Strait. The international date line and the international frontier between Alaska and the U.S.S.R. separate the two main islands.

Diomedes (dī.ǫ.mē'dēz). In Greek legend, a king of Argos, and a leader of the Greek warriors at the siege of Troy. He was the son of Tydeus, who fell in the expedition against Thebes. He went with Sthenelus and Euryalus to Troy as the commander of a fleet of 80 ships carrying warriors from Argos, Tiryns, Hermione, Asine, Troezen, Eionae, Epidaurus, Aegina, and Mases. He was, next to Achilles, the most valiant of the Greeks before Troy, and fought against the most distinguished among the Trojans, including Hector and Aeneas. He and Odysseus carried off the Palladium, without which Troy must fall, in a night expedition.

Diomedes. In Greek legend, a Thracian king, son of Ares, and owner of the horses captured by Hercules as one of his labors. The horses were flesh-eaters and Hercules killed Diomedes and fed him to his own horses.

Diomedes. In Shakespeare's *Troilus and Cressida,* a Grecian commander.

Diomedes. In Shakespeare's *Antony and Cleopatra,* an attendant of Cleopatra.

Diomedes or **Diomidis** (ᴛʜē.ô.mē'ᴛʜēs), **Alexander.** b. at Athens, 1875; d. there, Nov. 11, 1950. Greek statesman. He studied law at the University of Athens, economics and political science at Berlin and Paris, and was a lecturer in administrative law at Athens. He was later governor of Attica-Boeotia (1906), a delegate to the Hague Conference (1907), and prefect of Athens (1909). Elected (1910) deputy from Spetsai, he was minister of finance (1911–15; 1922) and of foreign affairs (1918–19). In the period after World War I he was a cogovernor of the national bank of Greece (1918–23), and its governor (1923–28); he was governor of the bank of Greece from its founding in 1928 till 1931. After World War II he was deputy prime minister (1949), and prime minister (1949–50). He was author of *The State Budget* (1905), *Towns and Villages* (1911), and others.

Dion (dī'on). b. at Syracuse, c408 B.C.; assassinated there, 354 or 353 B.C. Syracusan philosopher, a disciple of Plato. He was an uncle of Dionysius the Younger and when Dion was in Greece studying with Plato and Dionysius confiscated his property and married his wife to someone else, Dion returned and expelled (356) his nephew from Syracuse. Dion became ruler of the city in 355, was overthrown in a short time, regained his position, and was killed by one of his companions.

Dion. Father of Euphrasia in Beaumont and Fletcher's *Philaster.*

Dion. Sicilian noble in Shakespeare's *The Winter's Tale.*

Dion Cassius (dī'on kash'us, kash'i.us, kas'i.us). See **Dio** (or **Dion**) **Cassius.**

Dion Chrysostomus (kri.sos'tǫ.mus). [Also, **Chrysostom.**] b. at Prusa, in Bithynia, c50 A.D.; d. at Rome, c117 A.D. Greek rhetorician and philosopher. His 80 extant orations were edited in 1784.

Dione (dī.ō'nē). In very early Greek mythology, the consort of Zeus; his feminine counterpart as sky deity. In later mythological genealogy, she is a female Titan, daughter of Oceanus and Tethys, and mother by Zeus of Aphrodite.

Dione. The fourth satellite of Saturn, discovered by Jean Dominique Cassini in March, 1684.

Dione. Pastoral tragedy by John Gay, published in 1720.

Dionne (di.on', -ōn'), **Cécile, Yvonne, Annette, Émilie,** and **Marie.** b. at Callander, Ontario, Canada, May 28, 1934—. Canadian quintuplets, prematurely born to Elzire, wife of Oliva Dionne; delivered by Dr. Alan Roy Dafoe. They are said to be the first set of quintuplets in medical history to have survived infancy.

Dionysia (dī.ǫ.nis'i.ą). Ancient Greek festivals in honor of Dionysus, a fertility god. Those held at Athens were the chief ones, and are usually considered to have been four in number: the Lesser or Rural Dionysia, the Lenaea, the Anthesteria, and the Greater or City Dionysia. It now seems proved, however, that the Lenaea and the Anthesteria were, in historic times at least, identical, and merely interchangeable names for the festival which centered about the Lenaeum, or sanctuary of Dionysus in the marshes, whose shrine was opened on only one day in the year. The date of this festival was from the 11th to the 13th of Anthesterion (about March 2–4). The Lesser Dionysia were wine-feasts of very early origin, a solstice celebration held throughout the Attic demes between the 9th and 11th of Poseideon (about Dec. 19–22), accompanied by drinking, boisterous processions, and dramatic performances, of which those at the Piraeus had the chief reputation. The Greater Dionysia were celebrated at Athens, probably from the 9th to the 13th of Elaphebolion (about March 28–April 2), a spring equinox observance.

Dionysius (dī.ō.nish′i.us, -nish′us). [Surnamed **"the Elder."**] b. c430 B.C.; d. at Syracuse, 367 B.C. Tyrant of Syracuse. He contrived in 405 to have himself appointed sole general of the forces of the republic in the war against Carthage, whereupon he surrounded himself with a strong bodyguard of mercenaries and usurped the government. He strengthened his position by marrying the daughter of the deceased party leader Hermocrates, and concluded peace with Carthage in 404. He declared war against Carthage in 398, and was besieged in 396 at Syracuse by the Carthaginians, who were compelled by pestilence and a successful sally of the Syracusans to raise the siege after an investment of 11 months. He concluded an advantageous peace in 392. He captured Rhegium in 387 and Croton in 379 (Reggio di Calabria and Crotone, in Italy), which gave him a commanding influence among the Italian Greeks. He fought two further wars with Carthage. His power and influence are said to have exceeded those of any other Greek before Alexander the Great. He encouraged letters, invited Plato to his court, and himself gained the chief prize at the Lenaea with a play entitled *The Ransom of Hector*. His reputation was, despite his literary and scholarly pretensions, one of a despot and an arbitrary ruler.

Dionysius. [Surnamed **"the Younger."**] b. c395 B.C.; d. probably at Corinth, after 343 B.C. Tyrant of Syracuse; a relative of Dion, and son of Dionysius the Elder whom he succeeded in 367. He was under the influence of Dion for several years, but then drove Dion from Syracuse and, despite Plato's desire to set up under Dionysius an ideal state, ruled with a profligate hand. He was expelled by Dion in 356, became tyrant of Locri, where he exhibited such cruelty that his wife and daughters were slaughtered when he left to take possession again of Syracuse in 346. He was finally expelled from Syracuse in 343 by Timoleon.

Dionysius. b. in Calabria (or perhaps Greece); d. Dec. 26, 268. Pope from 259 to 268. He was a man of charity and learning, reputedly the first Pope not to die a martyr. He condemned the Sabellian heresy and Subordinationism, and upheld the decision of the synod of Antioch deposing Paul of Samosate.

Dionysius Exiguus (eks.ig′ū.us). b. in Scythia; fl. in the 6th century A.D. Monk and scholar of the Western Church who, in his *Cyclus paschalis*, introduced the annunciation of the birth of Christ as the starting point of modern chronology, thus establishing the Christian or Dionysian era. He placed the birth of Christ from three to six years too late. His surname means "the Little" in Latin.

Dionysius of Alexandria, Saint. [Called **Dionysius the Great.**] b. at Alexandria, c190 or earlier; d. there, c264 or 265. Roman Catholic theologian. Converted from paganism in his youth, he studied under Origen and Heraclas and himself succeeded the latter as head of the catechetical school of Alexandria and then as bishop (247–248). He was arrested under the persecution of Decius, but escaped. He sided with Pope Cornelius against the antipope Novatian. During the persecution of Valerian he was banished to Kephro in the Merotis (257) but returned under Gallienus in 260. He wrote against the Chiliasts, who misinterpreted the Apocalypse, and on doctrinal subjects. Much of his writing was in the form of letters.

Dionysius of Halicarnassus (hal″i.kär.nas′us). b. at Halicarnassus, in Caria; d. at Rome c7 B.C. Greek rhetorician and historian, author of a history of Rome (*Archaeologia*). In this work, as the Scottish classicist Richard Jebb has pointed out, Dionysius "aimed at writing an *Introduction* to Polybius. He maintains, on fanciful grounds, that the Romans, who deserve to rule the world, are no "barbarians," but of Greek descent. We have Books I.–X., going down to 450 B.C., and fragments of Book XI. He did a better work in his rhetorical writings, and above all in his excellent essays on the Greek orators."

Dionysius Periegetes (per″i.ę.jē′tēz). fl. about the 4th century A.D. Author of a geographical poem, *Periegesis*, a geographical description of the earth.

Dionysius the Areopagite (ar.ę.op′ą.jīt). fl. 1st century A.D. Athenian scholar, a member of the Areopagus, converted to Christianity by Saint Paul c50 A.D. He was long regarded as the author of several Greek treatises (*The Celestial Hierarchy, The Ecclesiastical Hierarchy, Concerning the Names of God, Of Mystical Theology, Epistles* and a Liturgy) which appeared in the 6th century and were probably written in the 5th. They have been (see the entry immediately following) the subject of much theological and critical discussion.

Dionysius the Pseudo-Areopagite. fl. c500 A.D. Author whose identity is unknown, long identified incorrectly with the convert of Saint Paul. The actual writer may have been a Syrian and lived not before the second half of the 5th century. He was well acquainted with neo-Platonist writings, with sacred Scripture and the writings of the Fathers up to Cyrial of Alexandria. He seems to have deliberately created the impression of living in apostolic times by referring as an eye-witness to events of that period. His works were esteemed in the Middle Ages and were not challenged till the 15th century, after which both Catholic and Protestant scholars stood for and against their authenticity. In the latter half of the 19th century the higher criticism threw more light on the origin of the writings of the Pseudo-Areopagite and disproved his identification with the convert of Saint Paul.

Dionysius Thrax (thraks). b. at Alexandria, Egypt; fl. c100 B.C. Greek grammarian. He studied at Alexandria, taught there and at Rhodes and Rome, and wrote *The Art of Grammar*, the first written study of that subject in Greek. This work, which has come down to us, probably with later alterations and additions, is not exhaustive, but Dionysius's approach and method greatly influenced later grammarians. He is known also to have written commentaries on the works of ancient writers.

Dionysus (dī.ō.nī′sus). See also **Bacchus.**

Dionysus. In Greek mythology, a fertility god; often limited to his specific gift of the vine and called the god of wine. He was, according to the common tradition, the son of Zeus and Semele, the daughter of Cadmus of Thebes. Hera, jealous of the attention which Zeus bestowed on Semele, came to her in the guise of a friendly old woman and persuaded her to request him to approach her in the same majesty in which he approached his wife. Zeus appeared in thunder and lightning, with the result that Semele was burned to ashes and in her agony gave birth to Dionysus, whom Zeus rescued from the flames and sewed up in his thigh until he came to maturity. He was brought up by Ino and Athamas at Orchomenus, spent many years in wandering about the earth, introducing the cultivation of the vine, and eventually rose to Olympus. He was also called, both by the Greeks and the Romans, Bacchus, i.e., the riotous god, originally a surname of Dionysus. Dionysus was one of the principal cult gods of Greece. He was the central figure of the Orphic mysteries and appeared in a minor role in the Eleusinian mysteries. He was identified with Zagreus, murdered by the Titans, whose heart Zeus swallowed to bring forth the god again: an explanation of his epithet Dithyrambus, said to mean "twice-born." Violence was attendant on the Dionysian myth, despite his role as culture-bringer. He was attended by Bacchantes, Maenads, Bassarides, and other groups of frenzied women; lustful satyrs and drunken sileni also form part of his train. The cult had its phallic aspects as well. Dionysus is pictured as a mild god, but terrible in anger. Pentheus, king of Thebes, refused to permit the introduction of the Dionysian cult. He was induced to watch the secret rites of the women in Dionysus's cult, was seen by them, and was torn to bits by the frenzied devotees, who included his mother.

Dionysus in Doubt. Collection of poems by Edwin Arlington Robinson, published in 1925. It includes the blank-verse dialogue "Demos and Dionysus."

Dionyza (dī.ō.nī′zą). In Shakespeare's *Pericles*, the wife of Cleon, governor of Tharsus. She attempts the murder of Marina, and with her husband is burned to death in revenge.

Diophantus (dī.ō.fan′tus). fl. at Alexandria, c250 A.D. Greek mathematician, sometimes referred to, with al-Khowarizmi, as the "father of algebra." His most important work was the *Arithmetica*, a treatise in 13 books of which only the first six have survived. The *Arithmetica* is devoted largely to the solution of equations in integers, a subject which consequently has become known as "Diophantine analysis." An English edition of the extant works of Diophantus, edited by T. L. Heath, was published in 1885, with a second edition in 1910.

Dioscorides (dī.os.kor′i.dēz). Ancient name of **Socotra.**

Dioscorides, Pedacius or **Pedanius.** b. probably in Cilicia; fl. in the 1st or 2nd century A.D. Greek physician, author of a treatise on materia medica.

Dioscorus (dī.os′kō.rus). b. at Alexandria; fl. 6th century. Antipope from Sept. 22 to Oct. 14, 530. He was chosen by a dissident faction on the death of Saint Felix IV, who had foreseen the dissension and had designated the archdeacon Boniface to succeed him.

Dioscuri (dī.os.kū′rī). Castor and Pollux (Polydeuces), according to Greek legend the sons of Leda and Zeus, or of Leda and Tyndareus (whence their patronymic *Tyndaridae*), and brothers of Helen.

Dioscurus (dī.os.kū′rus). d. at Gangra, in Paphlagonia, 454. Bishop of Alexandria from 444 to 451. Having sided with the heretic Eutyches against Flavian, bishop of Constantinople, he convoked a synod at Ephesus in 449, which sustained the former and condemned the latter. This synod, over which he presided, was conducted with so much violence that it was stigmatized as the "Robber Synod." He was condemned and deposed by the Ecumenical Council of Chalcedon in 451.

Diósgyőr (dē′ōsh.dyėr). Town in NE Hungary, in a mountainous region W of Miskolc. It has large steel mills and other industries. 26,535 (1941).

Diospolis Magna (dī.os′pō.lis mag′nạ). See **Thebes.**

Diotima (dī.ō.tī′mạ). Priestess of Mantinea, the reputed teacher of Socrates, mentioned in Plato's *Symposium.* She is probably fictitious.

Dipavali (dē.pä.vä′lē). See **Divali.**

Diphda (dif′dạ). A name often used for the star β Ceti. It is also called Deneb Kaitos.

Diphilus (dif′i.lus). b. at Sinope, in Asia Minor; fl. c300 B.C. One of the chief Athenian poets of the New Comedy, a contemporary of Menander. He is said to have written a hundred plays. Fragments of his works are extant.

Diplomacy. Play adapted by Bolton and Savile Rowe from Sardou's *Dora,* produced in 1878.

Dipoenus and **Scyllis** (dī.pē′nus; sil′is). fl. c580 B.C. Greek sculptors of the archaic period. They worked together and their names are always coupled. They executed sculptures in wood and ivory and also, it is thought, in marble. Little is really known about them, although Pliny the Elder mentions that they worked at Sicyon, and it is thought that the noted school of sculpture at that city owed its rise to them.

Dippel (dip′ẹl), **Johann Andreas.** b. at Kassel, Germany, Nov. 30, 1866; d. 1932. German operatic tenor. He sang (1898–1908) with the Metropolitan Opera at New York, where he was joint manager (1908–10) with Gatti-Casazza. Later he was manager (1910–13) of the Chicago Opera; and subsequently organized a light opera company under his own direction.

Dippel, Johann Konrad. b. at Frankenstein, near Darmstadt, Germany, Aug. 10, 1673; d. at Berleburg, Prussia, April 25, 1734. German mystic and alchemist. He invented Dippel's animal oil, and discovered the pigment known as Prussian blue.

Dipper, Big (or **Great**). See under **Ursa Major.**

Dipper, Little. See under **Ursa Minor.**

Dipsodes (dip′sōdz). People in François Rabelais's *Gargantua and Pantagruel.* They were ruled by King Anarche, and many of them were giants. Pantagruel subdued them.

Dipylon Gate (dip′i.lon). Chief gateway of ancient Athens, traversing the walls on the NW side. As its name indicates, it was in fact a double gate, consisting of a strongly fortified rectangular court between an outer and an inner portal. Each portal also was double, having two doors, each 11⅓ ft. wide, separated by a central pier. The foundations of this gate, alone among those of ancient Athens, survive in great part, and from it toward the SW extends a beautiful stretch of the original wall of Themistocles, built under Peloponnesian menace after the Greek victories over the Persians in 480 and 479 B.C. This wall, in its contrasted construction of admirably fitted blocks and rough stones, confirms literary witness to the haste of work spurred on by emergency. The Dipylon is identical with the Sacred Gate, and among the roads diverging from it is the Sacred Way to Eleusis. It was long held that an opening in the wall immediately SW of the Dipylon was the Sacred Gate, but Dörpfeld found that this was a passage for the stream which he identified as the Eridanus.

Diquis (dē′kēs). River in S Costa Rica. It flows W to the Pacific Ocean.

Dirac (di.rak′), **Paul Adrien Maurice.** b. at Bristol, England, Aug. 8, 1902—. English mathematician and scientist, author of a series of important papers on quantum mechanics. He studied at Bristol University and received his Ph.D. degree at Cambridge University in 1926. In 1930 he was elected to the Royal Society and in 1932 he became Lucasian Professor of Mathematics at Cambridge. In 1933 he shared with Schrödinger the Nobel prize for discoveries in atomic theory. He is the author of *The Principles of Quantum Mechanics* (1930).

Dirce (dėr′sē). In Greek mythology, the second wife of Lycus, put to death by Amphion and Zethus, sons of Antiope, in revenge for her ill treatment of their mother. She was bound to the horns of a bull and dragged to death. (Her execution is represented in the famous sculpture group *The Farnese Bull.*) Her body was thrown into a well on Mount Cithaeron thereafter known as the fountain of Dirce.

Dirceu (dēr.sā′ö), **Marília de.** See **Marília de Dirceu.**

Directory. Body of five who held the executive power in France from Oct. 27, 1795, to the coup d'état of 1799 (18th Brumaire, November 9). It succeeded the Convention according to the constitution of the year III (1795). One member retired every year and was succeeded by a new member elected by the Council of the Ancients on nominations submitted by the Council of Five Hundred. During the period of the Directory occurred the campaigns of Napoleon in Italy and Egypt, and other campaigns in Germany and elsewhere; French influence became powerful in Italy and Switzerland, the treaty of Campo Formio was concluded with Austria, and France was nearly embroiled in a war with the U.S. The personnel (originally Barras, Lazare Nicolas Carnot, La Révéillère-Lépeaux, Charles Louis Letourneur, and Rewbell) of the Directory was modified by a coup d'état, 18th Fructidor (Sept. 4), 1797, in which the republicans triumphed over the reactionaries, Carnot escaping, François de Barthélemy being sent off to America. Toward the close of the period the Directory became discredited by defeats in Italy, and was overthrown by Napoleon with the aid of Sieyès and Pierre Roger Ducos and succeeded by the Consulate.

Diredawa (dir.ẹ.dä′wạ, dē″re.dạ.wä′). [Also: **Dire Dawa, Dire Daua.**] City in E Africa, in Ethiopia, halfway on the railroad line between Addis Ababa and Djibouti. It is the second most important commercial city of the country and has cotton mills and railroad repair shops. It is also an important local distributing center for Harar province. It is ab. 35 mi. from Harar, another important commercial center. Pop. ab. 30,000.

Dirichlet (dē.rē.klā′), **Peter Gustav Lejeune.** b. at Düren, Prussia, Germany, Feb. 13, 1805; d. at Göttingen, Hanover, Germany, May 5, 1859. German mathematician, successor to Gauss as professor of mathematics at Göttingen in 1855. He is best known for his work in the theory of numbers.

Dirk Hatteraick (dėrk hat′ėr.ăk). See **Hatteraick, Dirk.**

Dirr (dir), **El.** See **El Dirr.**

Dirschau (dēr′shou). German name of **Tczew.**

Dis (dis). In Roman mythology, a name of Pluto, and hence of the lower world.

Disabled American Veterans. Organization composed of honorably discharged veterans who were incapacitated while serving in the armed forces of the U.S. during World Wars I and II. Incorporated in 1921, it has been active in securing benefits for disabled ex-servicemen.

Disbrowe (diz′brō), **John.** See **Desborough** or **Desborow** or **Disbrowe, John.**

Disciples of Christ. [Also popularly known as **Campbellites;** one branch now denominated **Churches of Christ.**] Protestant religious body of American origin, founded in 1809. Thomas Campbell (1763–1854), an Irishman and a minister of the Seceders' wing of the

Presbyterian Church, immigrated to western Pennsylvania in 1807, continuing his ministry. Finding that the division of Christians into many sects made the maintenance of religious spirit and the work of the church difficult on the frontier, he promoted common worship and coöperation across the lines of sectarian differences. For this he was reproved by his superiors, but with a strong conviction that he was right, Thomas Campbell, in association with his son Alexander Campbell (1788–1866), in 1809 founded the Christian Association of Washington, Pa., and issued a Declaration and Address, which remains a fundamental statement of the principles of this denomination. Thomas and Alexander Campbell had no purpose to set up still one more sectarian organization, but on the contrary took their stand on the thesis that the church of Christ inherently consists of all, throughout the world, who believe in Jesus Christ, obey His teachings as contained in the Holy Scriptures, and make their faith manifest in their lives. In 1811 an independent church was built at Brush Run, Pa., of which Alexander Campbell became minister. At that time other small groups had left the Presbyterian fold and called themselves simply Christians; there were also some congregations of dissident Methodists and Baptists. The Campbells and other independent Presbyterians adopted baptism by immersion, and became nominally Baptists, but in the 1830's differences of opinion and method became so marked that the Campbellites formed separate congregations and called themselves Disciples of Christ. Many of the Christians joined the Disciples; others organized the Christian Church, which in 1931 was merged with the Congregational Church. During the first decade of the 20th century some congregations withdrew from the Disciples and by 1906 had formed a new organization known as Churches of Christ. The Disciples of Christ have grown to be a numerous body in the U.S., and their missionaries have established congregations in many other lands.

Disco (dis'kō). See **Disko.**

Discobolus (dis.kob'ǫ.lus). Statue of a discus thrower by Myron, Greek sculptor of the 5th century B.C. The body is bent forward and turned toward the right as the heavy discus is swung back, wonderful art being shown in the choice and expression of the moment of repose when, the backward motion completed, the powerful cast forward is on the point of execution. It is known only through copies, one of which is in the Vatican at Rome.

Discordia (dis.kôr'di.ạ). Latin name of **Eris.**

Discourager of Hesitancy, The. Short story (1885) by Francis Richard (Frank) Stockton, who specialized in his day in the "surprise ending," anticipating its later use by O. Henry. It is a sequel to *The Lady or the Tiger?* (1882), but is not as well known and failed to duplicate its sensational success.

Discours du docteur O'Grady (dēs.kör dü dok.tėr ō.grā.dē), **Les.** Fictional sketches (1922) by the French writer André Maurois (1885—), based on his experiences as a liaison officer with British troops in World War I.

Discourse der Mahlern (dēs.kör'zẹ dėr mä'lėrn). German-Swiss magazine edited by J. J. Bodmer and J. J. Breitinger. It appeared at Zurich from 1721 to 1723. In spite of its short span of life, the publication, fashioned on the model of Addison's *Spectator*, was instrumental in changing Swiss literary tastes by drawing attention to English literature, thought, and customs.

Discourse of English Poetrie, A. Prose critical essay (1586) by William Webbe. The subtitle of the work is *Together with the Author's judgment touching the reformation of our English verse.*

Discoveries. Volume of essays by William Butler Yeats, published in 1907.

Discoveries Made Upon Men and Matters. Prose work (1641) by Ben Jonson. It is not a systematic, organized work, but a collection of miscellaneous material on a variety of subjects. It is a result of Jonson's reading, scholarship, observation, and experience. Some of the pieces are as long as a Bacon essay, and some no longer than a sentence.

Discovery. Small ship which, under command of Captain George Waymouth, was sent out by the East India Company to "find the passage best to lye towards the parts or kingdom of Cataya or China, or the backe side of America." She sailed with the *Godspeed* from the Thames on May 2, 1602, intending to make the coast of Greenland; but the voyage had no important result, though Waymouth probably paved the way for Hudson's discovery. In April, 1610, the latter sailed in the *Discovery*, and entered the strait which bears his name in June. Early in August he entered Hudson Bay. He spent three months in exploring it, and in November the vessel was frozen in. In June of the following year she was released, and shortly thereafter a mutiny occurred. Hudson and others were set adrift, and were never again seen. The *Discovery* was taken home by the mutineers, and two years after this she was again sent to the Northwest with the *Resolution* under the command of Sir Thomas Button. He discovered Nelson's River, which he called Port Nelson, and several points. In 1615 the *Discovery* set out with William Baffin and Robert Bylot, and again in 1616. In both these voyages many important discoveries and explorations were made.

Discovery. One of the steam vessels of the British polar expedition (under Captain Sir George Nares) of 1875–76; the other was the *Alert.*

Discovery. Ship in which Captain Robert F. Scott made the antarctic expedition of 1901–04. Under the sponsorship of the British Admiralty, the Royal Society, and the Royal Geographical Society, the expedition sailed south from New Zealand, reaching the ice pack near the Antarctic Circle on Jan. 1, 1902. It touched at Victoria Land and Ross Island and, following the Ross Shelf Ice eastward, discovered Edward VII Peninsula. Returning to Ross Island, the *Discovery* remained frozen in, in McMurdo Sound, until February, 1904, and exploration was carried on by sledge parties, one of which went 380 mi. to the south.

Discovery Bluff. [Former name, **Rendezvous Bluff.**] Conspicuous headland in Antarctica, forming the W entrance to Avalanche Bay in Granite Harbor, Victoria Land, in ab. 77°00′ S., 162°41′ E. It was discovered by the *Discovery* expedition (1901–04), commanded by Captain Robert F. Scott, who referred to this feature as Rendezvous Bluff. It was renamed for the *Discovery* by Scott's second expedition (1910–13). Elevation, ab. 1,600 ft.

Discovery of the Great West, The. See **LaSalle and the Discovery of the Great West.**

Disentis (dē'zẹn.tēs). [Also: **Dissentis;** Romansh, **Mustèr.**] Village in SE Switzerland, in the canton of Graubünden, situated on the Mittel Rhine River and the Lukmanier road. It is noted for its Benedictine abbey, founded in 720 by Saint Sigisbert of Ireland, and rebuilt in the 17th century, now a boys' school; hence the name Mustèr, from Latin *Monasterium.* 2,173 (1941).

Disgrazia (dēz.grä'tsyä), **Monte della.** Mountain peak in the Alps, on the border of Italy and the canton of Graubünden, Switzerland, NW of Sondrio. Elevation, ab. 12,050 ft.

Dishart (dish'ạrt), **Gavin.** Hero of *The Little Minister* (1891), a novel and play (1897) by James M. Barrie.

Disko (dis'kō). [Also, **Disco.**] Island belonging to Denmark, situated at the entrance of Davis Strait into Baffin Bay off the W coast of Greenland, in ab. lat. 69°30′ N. It contains the harbor and settlement of Godhavn. Area, ab. 3,200 sq. mi.

Disko Bay. [Also, **Disco Bay.**] Bay on the W coast of Greenland, SE of Disko island.

Dismal Swamp. Morass in SE Virginia and NE North Carolina. It extends from near Norfolk, Va., 20 to 30 mi. southward. It contains Drummond Lake, and is traversed by the Dismal Swamp canal, which connects Chesapeake Bay and Albemarle Sound. Part of the swamp has been reclaimed.

Dismas (diz'mạs). [Also: **Demas, Desmas, Dysmas.**] Legendary name of the penitent thief crucified with Christ.

Disney (diz'ni), **Walt.** [Full name, **Walter Elias Disney.**] b. at Chicago, Dec. 5, 1901—. American producer of animated pictures. He studied at the Chicago Academy of Fine Arts, became a commercial artist, and in 1923 went to Hollywood and began making motion pictures by means of animated drawings, in which each drawing in a long series differs almost imperceptibly from the one before it, so that when they are photographed seriatim and thrown on the motion-picture screen in rapid succession, the drawn figures appear to be moving and acting. His series of pictures featuring *Oswald, the Rabbit* first won wide favor, after which his characters *Mickey Mouse* and *Donald Duck* made millions laugh throughout the world, became household words in every continent, and were widely used in advertising a great variety of products. Other world-famous Disney pictures were *Three Little Pigs, Ferdinand the Bull, Snow White and the Seven Dwarfs, Pinocchio,* and *Fantasia.*

Disowned, The. Novel by Edward Bulwer-Lytton, published in 1829.

Displaced Persons. [Called **DPs.**] Term used after World War II to describe the large masses of people driven from their homes in the Baltic states, Hungary, the Balkan countries, Poland, and later Czechoslovakia during the war. These persons, numbering millions, came under the protection of the United Nations Rehabilitation and Relief Administration (UNRRA) and the International Refugee Organization (IRO), mostly in camps in Germany, Austria, and Italy. Strenuous efforts have been made to resettle these people throughout the world (especially in the U.S., Australia, and South America) but in part they now almost certainly constitute permanent additions to the population of Western Europe. In 1950 refugees from East Germany were declared eligible as Displaced Persons by the U.S.

Disquisition on Government. Treatise written (1843–48) by John C. Calhoun, setting forth his views on the nature of government. A development of the ideas expounded by him in the *South Carolina Exposition* (1828), it emphasizes the concept of the concurrent majority as a means of protecting minority interests against majority rule. Granting the validity of the major premise, the logic is forceful and impeccable. The treatise is important as an expression of the rationale of a large and influential segment of the Southern ruling circle apprehensive over the expanding power of the North, and illuminates the sectional differences prevailing in the U.S. in the critical decades before the Civil War. The *Disquisition* appears in the first volume of Calhoun's *Works* (1851–55), edited by R. K. Crallé.

Disraeli (diz.rā'li), **Benjamin.** [Title, 1st Earl of **Beaconsfield**; nicknamed **Dizzy**; pseudonym, **Runnymede.**] b. at London, Dec. 21, 1804; d. there, April 19, 1881. English statesman and novelist; son of Isaac D'Israeli. He was descended from an aristocratic Sephardic family, but joined the Anglican Church in 1817. He was educated at home, and did not go to Oxford or Cambridge. He entered politics in 1832, and for the next three years made several unsuccessful attempts to gain a seat in Parliament. Finally, in 1837, he was elected Conservative member of Parliament for Maidstone. In 1839 he married Mary Ann Evans (Mrs. Wyndham Lewis), a widow 15 years his senior. She was "a perfect wife" for him, and her death, on Dec. 15, 1872, was a tragedy which made him feel that he "no longer had a home." His first speech in Parliament, in 1837, was a complete failure, giving no indication of the great man that he was to become or the great career that was to be his. In 1841 he represented Shrewsbury, and from 1847 to 1876 he was a member of Parliament from Buckinghamshire. In 1847, also, he was made the leader of the opposition in the House of Commons, a post that he held for a quarter of a century. He was three times Chancellor of the Exchequer, in 1853, 1857–58, and again in 1867, and he was twice Queen Victoria's prime minister, an office which since his childhood days he had hoped to hold. He became the queen's first minister in February, 1868, but resigned after the general election at the end of the year; he headed the government again from 1874 to 1880, resigning again after the Tory defeat in April, 1880. He was made Earl of Beaconsfield in 1876, the year in which he had Victoria proclaimed Empress of India, and he entered the House of Lords. He attacked Peel for his repeal of the Corn Laws in 1846, Gladstone's financial policy in 1860 and 1862, and his Irish and foreign policies during the period 1868–73. At the Congress of Berlin, which he forced on Russia in 1878, he accomplished his last great act of political genius, his "Peace with Honor," which brought his popularity to its highest point and won him the honor of being made a Knight of the Garter, on July 22, 1878. When he died, three years later, he was honored as no Englishman had been since Wellington. Had he wished it, he could have been buried in Westminster Abbey, but he was buried at Hughenden, in accordance with his expressed wishes, beside his wife. Victoria expressed her own feeling and that of the nation when she called "the death of my dear Lord Beaconsfield a national calamity." April 19, the day of his death, was, and is, called Primrose Day in his honor, because the primrose was his favorite flower, and a Conservative political organization, the Primrose League, was founded to carry on his principles and to keep his memory alive. As a novelist, Disraeli wrote *Vivian Grey* (1826), of autobiographical interest, *The Young Duke* (1831), *Contarini Fleming* (1832) and *The Wondrous Tale of Alroy* (1833), both of Jewish interest, revealing his pride in the Jewish people, a pride that he always maintained despite the fact that he had departed from the faith of his fathers. He also wrote *Henrietta Temple,* remembered for its Roman Catholic priest, *Glastonbury,* and *Venetia* (both 1837), *Coningsby* (1844), dealing with the English peasantry, *Sybil* (1845), which was instrumental in factory reform, and *Tancred* (1847). Two of his political novels, *Lothair* (1870) and *Endymion* (1880), which he wrote as the leader of "Young England," are regarded as inferior. Most of these works are in three volumes, except *Contarini Fleming,* which is in four, and *Vivian Grey,* in five. His nonfictional works, which now have only historical interest, are *An Enquiry into Plans of American Mining Companies, Lawyers and Legislators,* and *The Present State of Mexico* (both 1825), *England and France* (1832), *Vindication of the English Constitution* (1835), *The Spirit of Whiggism* (1836), and *Lord George Bentinck* (1852), a biography. His *Home Letters,* written in 1830–31, *Correspondence,* written 1852–53, *Selected Speeches,* in 2 volumes, and his *Letters* to Lady Bradford and to Lady Chesterfield, all published after his death, reveal facets of both his personal and his political lives.

D'Israeli (diz.rā'li) or **Disraeli, Isaac.** b. at Enfield, England, May, 1766; d. at Bradenham House, Buckinghamshire, England, Jan. 19, 1848. English miscellaneous writer; father of Benjamin Disraeli, 1st Earl of Beaconsfield. His chief works are *Curiosities of Literature* (6 vols., 1791–1834), a miscellaneous collection of anecdotes, quotations, and odd information, *Essay on the Literary Character* (1795), *Miscellanies, or Literary Recreations* (1796), *Calamities of Authors* (1812), *Quarrels of Authors* (1814), *Commentary on the Life and Reign of King Charles I* (1828–31), and *Amenities of Literature* (1841).

Diss (dis). Urban district and market town in E England, in Norfolk, situated on the river Waveney ab. 22 mi. N of Ipswich, ab. 95 mi. NE of London by rail. It was formerly a textile center. 3,505 (1951).

Dissentis (dis'en.tēs). See **Disentis.**

Distaffina (dis.ta.fē'na). Beloved of Bombastes Furioso in Rhodes's burlesque opera of the latter name. She jilted Bombastes for the king.

Distaff's Day, Saint. January 7, so called because according to tradition on that day the women who have kept the Christmas festival till Twelfth Day (Jan. 6) return to their distaffs, or ordinary work. As a distaff is also called a rock, the day is sometimes called Rock Day.

Distant Lamp, The. Historical novel by Harold Begbie, published in 1912. It is a story of the Children's Crusade of 1212, and is laid in France, Egypt, and the Holy Land.

Distant Prospect of Eton College (ē'ton), **Ode on a.** Poem by Thomas Gray, written in 1742 and published anonymously by Robert Dodsley in 1747.

Distich (dis'tik), **Dick.** Poet and satirist met in a madhouse by Sir Launcelot Greaves, in Tobias Smollett's novel of the latter name. Alexander Pope used this signature in *The Guardian.*

Distinguished Service Order. [Abbreviation, **D.S.O.**] British naval and military order of distinction, instituted on Sept. 6, 1886. It consists of the sovereign and those officers who have been mentioned in dispatches for meritorious or distinguished service in the field, or before the enemy, and upon whom the sovereign wishes, therefore, to confer honor. The badge of the order is a gold cross, enameled white, bearing upon the obverse the imperial crown within a wreath of laurel, and on the reverse the imperial cipher within a wreath of laurel. It is suspended by a red ribbon edged with blue. Foreign officers are, under certain conditions, eligible to honorary membership.

Distressed Mother, The. Tragedy by Ambrose Philips, produced in 1712. It was adapted from Racine's *Andromaque.*

Distresses, The. Play by Sir William D'Avenant, thought to have been the same as *The Spanish Lovers,* licensed in 1639.

District of Columbia (kǫ.lum′bi.ạ). [Sometimes called **"the District."**] Federal district of the U.S., coextensive with the national capital, Washington. It lies on the E bank of the Potomac River, between Maryland and Virginia.

Population, Area, and Political Status. The district is under the control of the federal government through three commissioners appointed by the president and confirmed by the Senate. Residents of the district have no vote, although persons from other states residing in the district as government appointees do not relinquish their state voting privileges. Only city, Washington; area, 61 sq. mi. (69 sq. mi., including water); pop. 802,178 (1950), an increase of 21 percent over the figure for 1940 (the figure is estimated to have soared as high as 1,250,000 at the height of World War II). For census purposes the Bureau of the Census classes the district as a state, giving it 36th rank. Negroes make up ab. 27 percent of the population. There are few foreign-born residents.

History. The District of Columbia was formed of cessions made by Maryland in 1788 and Virginia in 1789, these lands comprising 100 sq. mi.; organized in 1790–91. The seat of the national government was removed there from Philadelphia on June 10, 1800, during the administration of John Adams. Washington was incorporated as a city in 1802. The Virginia portion (Alexandria, W of the Potomac) was retroceded in 1846. Territorial government was established in 1871, succeeded by a provisional government in 1874. The present form of government was established in 1878. Georgetown, a former town within the district, was annexed to Washington in 1878, thus making the district and Washington coextensive. The motto of the district is *Justitia Omnibus,* meaning "Justice to All." The official flower is the American Beauty rose. For further details see **Washington,** D.C.

Distrito Federal (dēs.trē′tō fä.dẹ.räl′). [English, **Federal District.**] District in E Brazil, administered by the national government. Capital, Rio de Janeiro; area, 452 sq. mi.; pop. 2,413,152 (1950).

Distrito Federal (dēs.trē′tō fā.ᴛʜā.räl′). [English, **Federal District.**] Civil division in S Mexico, consisting chiefly of Mexico City and its suburbs. Area, 573 sq. mi.; pop. 2,942,594 (1950).

Distrito Federal. [English, **Federal District.**] Civil division in N Venezuela, on the Caribbean coast: seat of the national government of Venezuela. Organized in 1936, it includes Caracas, La Guaira, and neighboring towns. Capital, Caracas; area, 745 sq. mi.; pop. 700,149 (1950).

Dithmarschen (dit′mär.shẹn). [Also: **Ditmarsh;** early medieval name, **Nordalbingia.**] Region and former independent territory in W Holstein, in the *Land* (state) of Schleswig-Holstein, N Germany, situated between the Elbe and Eider rivers. A peasant republic in the Middle Ages, it was incorporated in Holstein in 1559, and annexed to Prussia in 1866.

Diti (dē′tē). In Hindu mythology, the name of a goddess without any distinct character. The name is formed by popular etymology from *Aditi,* as if that were *A-diti* ("not Diti"). In epic poetry Diti is a daughter of Daksha and wife of Kashyapa. The race of Daityas, or implacable enemies of the gods, are described as her progeny or descendants.

Ditmars (dit′märz), **Raymond Lee.** b. at Newark, N.J., June 20, 1876; d. 1942. American naturalist and author. He was graduated (1891) from Barnard Military Academy, served as assistant curator of entomology at the American Museum of Natural History, was a court reporter (1898–99) for the New York *Times,* became (1899) curator of reptiles at the New York Zoölogical Park, and in 1910 was named head of the park's department of mammals. He was the author of *The Reptile Book* (1907), *Reptiles of the World* (1909), *Strange Animals I Have Known* (1931), *Thrills of a Naturalist's Quest* (1932), *Forest of Adventure* (1933), *Confessions of a Scientist* (1934), *The Book of Prehistoric Animals* (1935), *The Making of a Scientist* (1937), and *The Book of Insect Oddities* (1938).

Ditmarsh (dit′märsh). See **Dithmarschen.**

Dittenberger (di′tẹn.ber.gėr), **Wilhelm.** b. at Heidelberg, Germany, Aug. 31, 1840; d. at Halle, Germany, Dec. 29, 1906. German classical scholar. He served as professor (1874 *et seq.*) at the University of Halle, and was the author of *Sylloge inscriptionum Graecarum* (Collection of Greek Inscriptions, 1883), and *Orientis Graeci inscriptiones selectae* (Selected Inscriptions of the Greek East, 1903–05).

Dittersdorf (dit′ėrs.dôrf), **Karl Ditters von.** [Original name, **Karl Ditters.**] b. at Vienna, Nov. 2, 1739; d. in Bohemia, Oct. 24, 1799. Austrian violinist and composer. He was *Kapellmeister* (choir leader) (1764–69) to the bishop of Grosswardein at Pressburg (Bratislava), and served (1769–95) as director of music to the prince bishop of Breslau. The best of his many operas, *Hieronymus Knicker* (1787) and *Doktor und Apotheker* (1786), long retained a place on the stage. His symphonies on Ovid's *Metamorphoses* (published in 1785) are remarkable specimens of early program music, and his string quartets foreshadow some of the developments of Haydn and Mozart.

Dittmann (dit′män), **Wilhelm.** b. at Eutin, Germany, Nov. 13, 1874—. German politician. Originally a cabinetmaker, he became a Social Democratic journalist, and served (1912–18, 1920–33) as a member of the Reichstag, as cofounder (1916) of the Independent Social Democratic Party, and as a member (November, 1918) of the council of the people's deputies. He organized strikes (1918) in the munitions factories, and was sentenced to five years' hard labor, but was released in November, 1918. He rejoined the Social Democrats in 1922, eventually to become vice-chairman of the party.

Ditton (dit′ọn), **Humphrey.** b. at Salisbury, England, May 29, 1675; d. Oct. 15, 1715. English mathematician. He wrote *General Laws of Nature and Motion* (1705), *An Institution of Fluxions* (1706), and others.

Ditzen (dit′sẹn), **Rudolf.** Original name of **Fallada, Hans.**

Diu (dē′ö). [Portuguese, **Dio.**] Portuguese colony in NW India, ab. 170 mi. NW of Bombay. The colony consists of the island of Diu (area, ab. 13½ sq. mi.), the village of Gogolá, on the mainland opposite (area, ab. 1 sq. mi.), and the minute territory of Simbor, on the coast ab. 15 mi. E of Diu. The Portuguese built a fort on the island in 1535–36 to protect their trade along the coast. It successfully withstood assaults by Indian armies in 1538 and 1546. The chief port and town of Diu grew up around the fort. In 1670 it was raided by Arabs from Muscat. The decline of Diu dates from the 18th century, when the English trade with India increased greatly. The chief industries now are fishing and salt production. Pop. of colony, 19,731 (1940).

Diula (dē.ö′lä). [Also, **Dyoula.**] Mande-speaking people of W Africa, scattered in small groups through N Ivory Coast. Their population is estimated at ab. 55,000 (by Y. Urvoy, *Petit Atlas ethno-Demographique du Soudan,* 1942). Culturally they are related to the Bambara, but the great majority have adopted Mohammedanism. They are not to be confused with the Diola of W Gambia and SW French Senegal.

Divali (dē.vä′lē) or **Dipavali** (dē.pä.vä′lē). Hindu festival in October-November. The term means a row of lamps; homes and shops are lavishly decorated with illuminations on this day. It is dedicated to Lakshmi, goddess of prosperity. Accounts of the origin of the festival varyingly attribute it to the celebration of the coronation of Rama, hero of the epic *Ramayana,* or to the rejoicing on the victory of the god Krishna over a demon.

Dive Bouteille (dēv bö.tey′), **La.** [Eng. trans., *"The Divine Bottle."*] Oracle to which Panurge in François Rabelais's *Pantagruel* makes a long journey in order to determine whether he shall marry. The oracle responds with one word, "Trinq." The Order of the Dive Bouteille was instituted in France in the 16th century by the most "illustrious drinkers" in honor of Rabelais, and in order to put in practice their "pantagruelism."

Diverting History of John Bull and Brother Jonathan, The. American prose satire (1812) aimed at the English, by James Kirke Paulding. It expresses the strong nationalistic feeling of the time, and derives from (although it is not a copy of) another anti-British satire, *A Pretty Story* (1774), by Francis Hopkinson.

Diverting History of John Gilpin, The. Humorous poem (1782) of the ballad type, by William Cowper, better known for his poems of melancholy and intense religious devotion. It is frequently called *Gilpin's Ride, John Gilpin's Famous Ride*, and by other inaccurate names, but its full and correct title, which is a good summary of the action, is *The Diverting History of John Gilpin, Showing How He Went Further than He Intended and Came Safe Home Again.*

Dives (dēv). [Full name, **Dives-sur-Mer.**] Town in NW France, in the department of Calvados, situated on the English Channel, W of Deauville. It is a medieval town, with a church dating from the 14th and 15th centuries, and a small port. The town, as well as the nearby fashionable seaside resort of Caubourg, suffered considerable damage in World War II. 5,300 (1946).

Dives (dī'vēz), **Crassus.** See **Crassus, Marcus Licinius.**

Divide, Continental. See **Continental Divide.**

Divide, The Great. See **Great Divide, The.**

Divina Commedia (dē.vē'nä kôm.mā'dyä). [Eng. title, **The Divine Comedy**; original Italian title, **Commedia.**] Celebrated epic poem by Dante, in three parts: *Inferno* (Hell), *Purgatorio* (Purgatory), and *Paradiso* (Paradise). It seems probable that the *Inferno* was begun after Dante's return from a pilgrimage to Rome in the jubilee year 1300, that the *Purgatorio* was finished about 1314, and that the composition of the *Paradiso* occupied the next five or six years of his life. The poem consists of 14,233 eleven-syllable lines arranged in tercets with the rhyming scheme known as *terza rima*, a b a, b c b, c d c, and so forth. After an introductory canto, the remaining 99 cantos are equally divided between the three parts. Read simply as a myth for the imagination, the poem describes a journey to the abodes of the dead. Thus in canto IV of the *Inferno*, Dante guided by Vergil visits the spirits of the heroes, heroines, and philosophers of antiquity who are enjoying a high but purely human happiness in the Noble Castle of Limbo. In the next canto he meets the sinners suffering for illicit love (Semiramis, Cleopatra, Paris, Tristram, and the rest) and sings the immortal tragedy of Paolo and Francesca. In canto X he meets the Epicurean aristocrat, Farinata degli Uberti, suffering for denying the immortality of the soul. Following a carefully worked out system of sins based on Aristotelian and Ciceronian ethics, with subdivisions borrowed from patristic and scholastic ideas and with elements taken from the Roman law and the "code of chivalry," the pilgrim sees the torments of every type of sinner until, at the center of the earth, in the mouths of the three heads of Satan, he finds Judas, the traitor to the Founder of a universal faith, and Brutus and Cassius who betrayed Caesar's efforts to establish a rule of universal law. What, however, gives passion to the poetic vision is the meaning which is addressed to the reader's mind. The great inverted cone of Dante's Hell is, allegorically, the human heart, and the poet's pilgrimage is a vision of human nature in the utmost depths of its possible degradations. In the same way, the seven-story mountain of Dante's *Purgatorio* is a vision of the human will struggling upwards in humanity's historical efforts to reach, by culture and civilization, the highest happiness and peace that men can hope for in a reign of light and law. So, too, the *Paradiso* can be enjoyed as a myth in which Dante meets the lovely Piccarda, the emperor Justinian, Saint Thomas Aquinas, and many others, but what accounts for the passionate poetry and inimitable music in this part is the poet's all-but-mystical vision of the efficacy of supernatural religion in elevating humanity to consummation in the perfect peace and possession of ultimate goodness, truth, and beauty. Thus the poem is about redemption in the widest sense. The six guides who lead "Dante" (that is "fallen" humanity) from the "dark wood" of sin, through the "divine forest" of innocence and upwards to "the light which in itself is true" and "the love which binds in a single volume the scattered leaves of all the universe," are Vergil, Cato, Statius, Matelda, Beatrice, and Bernard. Vergil is a symbol of reason in the form of Hellenic philosophy and Roman law (*ordinatio rationis*); Cato (a combination of Cato the Censor and Cato the Stoic, who preferred liberty with death to tyranny) is a symbol of reason in the form of conscience (*dictamen rationis*). Beatrice represents the role of grace, that is, of divine revelation and redemption and, hence, the ministry of the Church (*Sacerdotium*) as Vergil represents the authority of the State (*Imperium*). Bernard stands to Beatrice somewhat as Cato stands to Vergil. He is a symbol of mystical intuition or the religious light and force of holiness that come from direct communion with God. Statius (a combination of the historical figures of the pagan poet, author of the *Thebaid* and *Achilleid*, and of Statius, the converted rhetorician and teacher of Toulouse) stands for the Christian school (*Studium*) as the *bella donna* Matelda stands for the Christian home, for the role of love in the "age of innocence," for parental guidance in the period of childhood. The root idea of the whole poem is, as Dante tells us in a Latin letter to Can Grande, Can Francesco della Scala, that of human responsibility in the face of divine justice, *homo justitiae obnoxius*. The individual is responsible for his personality, for his inner freedom from the tyranny of ignorance and passion; the parent is responsible for the ministry of love, the teacher for the ministry of truth, the ruler for the ministry of justice, the priest for the ministry of grace, the saint for that holiness which is the nearest image we can know in history of the very life of God. Dante's sinners and saints suffer or rejoice because of the failure or fulfilment of their commission to reach and reveal some image of the divine, whether this be freedom, truth, goodness, beauty, justice, love, or holiness. It is this profound sense of the meaning of man and of history set to incomparable music and illumined and lifted up by "anagogic" intimations of the mystery of man's immortal destiny that has put the *Commedia* in the very forefront of the world's supreme works of art. The poem has been translated into all the great languages of the world, including Japanese and Arabic. Of the many translations into English by Cary, Longfellow, Norton, Fletcher, Wheeler, Binyon, Cummins, Lawrence White, and others, not one conveys the subtle and varied music of the original. The Carlyle-Wicksteed prose version, with its excellent introductions and notes to each canto may, however, serve as a good introduction to the poem. The poem was illustrated (1826–27) by William Blake, and his engravings have been hailed for their "breath-taking grandeur."

Divina Commedia. Six sonnets by Henry Wadsworth Longfellow written (1864–67) to accompany his translation *Dante's work* (3 vols., 1865–67).

Divine (di.vīn'), Father. b. c1882—. American religious cult founder. There is little reliable information concerning his origins and early years, but it is supposed that his original name was George Baker, that he was born near Savannah, Ga., and that he had long practice as a preacher in the South before beginning his career under the name of Major M. J. Divine in Northern cities. As he won a large and devoted following, he began to call himself Father Divine, and eventually intimated, or at least allowed his followers to assert, that he is God. The headquarters of his Peace Mission movement were for some years in the Harlem area of New York City, but were moved to Philadelphia to avoid the execution of judgments against the leader obtained in various legal actions brought by former "angels," as his followers are called. The Peace Mission movement acquired many properties, urban and rural, where "heavens" were established, as gathering places, residences, and refectories, and opened a number of restaurants serving the general public good meals at low prices. The movement is nonsectarian and interracial, though by far the greater number of its adherents are Negroes, and it has spread not only to many parts of the U.S. but even to other countries. It inculcates temperance, frugality, industry, and happiness, and its watchword is "Peace, it's wonderful!"

Divine Fire, The. Novel by May Sinclair, published in 1904. It tells the story of the beautiful Lucia Harden; Keith Rickman, a Cockney poet who has the "divine fire" in him; and Horace Jewdwine, an Oxford man. Keith is believed to be a fictional portrait of Ernest Dowson.

Divine Lady, The. Historical novel by Lily Adams Beck under the pseudonym E. Barrington, published in 1924. It is set in Naples and London in the years 1782–1803. The "divine lady" is Emma Lyon-Hart, Lady Hamilton (c1761–1815), mistress of Sir Charles Greville, of his uncle, Sir William Hamilton (who later married her), and of Lord Nelson (to whom she bore a daughter, Horatia).

Divine Tragedy, The. Poem by Henry Wadsworth Longfellow, published in 1871. It was later included in *Christus, a Mystery* (3 vols., 1872).

Divine Vision, The. Book of poems by "Æ" (George William Russell), published in 1904.

Divinity School Address. Address delivered by Ralph Waldo Emerson at Harvard on July 15, 1838. The subject so upset clergymen that it was almost 30 years before Emerson was again invited to speak at Harvard.

Divino (dē.ʙē′nō), **El.** See **Herrera, Fernando de.**

Divino, El. See **Morales, Luis de.**

Divino (dē.vē′nō), **Il.** See **Titian.**

Divio (div′i.ō). A Latin name of **Dijon.**

Divion (dē.vyôṅ). Town in N France, in the department of Pas-de-Calais, situated ab. 8 mi. SW of Béthune. It is a lignite-coal-mining center. 10,200 (1946).

Divitia (di.vish′ı.ạ). Latin name of **Deutz.**

Divitiacus (div.i.ti′ạ.kus). Aeduan noble, brother of Dumnorix. He was an ally of Rome, and a warm personal friend of Caesar. He was the guest of Cicero during a political visit to Rome. He rendered services to Caesar against Ariovistus and against the Belgae. Through his intercession Dumnorix's treason in 58 B.C. was pardoned by Caesar.

Divodurum (dī.vọ.dūr′um) or **Divodurum Mediomatricum** (mē″di.ọ.mat′ri.kum). Ancient names of **Metz.**

Divoire (dē.vwȧr), **Fernand.** b. at Brussels, Belgium, March 10, 1883—. French critic and poet. He is the author of *L'Amoureux* (1912), *Âmes* (1918), and *Itinéraire* (1928). His works also include studies of occultism and modern dancing.

Divona (dī′vọ.nạ, div′ọ.nạ). A Latin name of **Cahors.**

Diwala (di.wä′lạ). See **Duala.**

Diwangiri (dē.wän.gē′rē). See **Dewangiri.**

Diwaniyah (dē.wä.nē′yạ). *Liwa* (province) in C Iraq, ab. 100 mi. S of Baghdad, lying in the plain of the Euphrates River: a fertile farming area producing cotton, wheat, tobacco, and a large assortment of fruits. Capital, Diwaniyah; area, 5,765 sq. mi.; pop. 383,787 (1947).

Dix (diks), **Beulah Marie.** Maiden name of **Flebbe, Beulah Marie.**

Dix, Dorothea Lynde. b. at Hampden, Me., April 4, 1802; d. at Trenton, N.J., July 18, 1887. American reformer, educator, and writer, noted for her labors in behalf of the mentally ill, of the blind, and of deaf mutes, and for improvement of prisons. At 14 she opened a school at Worcester, Mass., and subsequently a day and boarding school in her grandmother's home at Boston. Natural science was important in the curriculum. Her text, *Conversations on Common Things*, went through 60 editions (1824–28). When ill health forced her to close her school in 1836 she visited England, where she met leading humanitarians of the day. She returned to the U.S. in 1837, a semi-invalid. In 1841 a visit to the East Cambridge jail, where degenerates, criminals, and the mentally ill were indiscriminately confined, was the beginning of a new career. An 18-months survey of jails and almshouses in Massachusetts inspired a stirring memorial and shocked the legislature into passing (1843) appropriate legislation. Despite delicate health, Miss Dix investigated state after state, appealing to legislatures, and enlisting public opinion in behalf of tax-supported institutions for the mentally ill. Her pamphlet *Remarks on Prisons and Prison Discipline* was long regarded as an authoritative manual on prison administration. In 1848 she sought but failed to secure from Congress a grant of half a million acres of the public domain to be used by states in providing for the mentally ill. In 1854 President Pierce vetoed a bill setting aside ten million acres for care of the mentally ill, and two and a half million acres for the blind, and the deaf and dumb. In Europe (1854–57) she succeeded in having the Royal Scotch Lunacy Commission set up by Queen Victoria, and in the reform by Pope Pius IX of hospitals in the Papal States. Her labors of 40 years resulted in 32 new hospitals in the U.S., several in Europe, and two in Japan. During the Civil War she was the first U.S. superintendent of nurses. Her published writings include *Evening Hours* (1825), *Hymns for Children* (1825), *Meditations for Private Hours* (1828), *Garland of Flora* (1829), *American Tales for Young Persons* (1832), and *Letter to Convicts in the Western State Penitentiary of Pennsylvania* (1848). See *Dorothea Dix: Forgotten Samaritan*, by Helen E. Marshall (1937).

Dix, Dorothy. See **Gilmer, Elizabeth.**

Dix, Fort. U.S. Army post in C New Jersey, ab. 18 mi. SE of Trenton. It was first established in World War I, and is one of the principal infantry-training centers in the NE U.S. Area, ab. 15 sq. mi.

Dix, John Adams. b. at Boscawen, N.H., July 24, 1798; d. at New York, April 21, 1879. American soldier and politician. Commissioned an ensign at the age of 14, he took part in the War of 1812; he remained in the army, eventually attaining the rank of major, studied law, and was admitted (1824) to the bar. He later resigned from the army and settled (1828) at Cooperstown, N.Y., where he practiced law and became active in politics. He was appointed (1830) adjutant general of New York State and served (1833–39) as its secretary of state, returning to his law practice in 1840 and founding a literary and scientific journal, the *Northern Light* (1841–43). Elected (1845) to the U.S. Senate, he filled an unexpired term, served as president (1854–57) of the Chicago and Rock Island and the Mississippi and Missouri railroads, and transferred his law practice to New York. He was (January–March, 1861) the last secretary of the treasury under Buchanan, and during his brief service strengthened the position of the department. Commissioned (1861) a major general, he served as commander of the Department of Maryland and of the Department of the East. He was (1866–69) U.S. minister to France and in 1872 was elected governor of New York. His writings include *A Winter in Madeira; and a Summer in Spain and Florence* (1850), *Speeches and Occasional Addresses* (2 vols., 1864), and translations of *Dies Irae* (1863) and *Stabat Mater* (1868).

Dix, John Alden. b. at Glens Falls, N.Y., Dec. 25, 1860; d. April 9, 1928. American politician. He was educated at Cornell University, was interested in several manufacturing enterprises, and was a director of the First National Bank at Albany. He was nominated for lieutenant governor in 1908, was chairman of the New York Democratic state committee in 1910, and was Democratic governor of New York, 1911 and 1912.

Dix, Morgan. b. at New York, Nov. 1, 1827; d. April 29, 1908. American Protestant Episcopal clergyman; son of John Adams Dix (1798–1879). He was associated for many years with Trinity Church, at New York, serving (1862–1908) as rector. He was the author of the *Book of Hours* (1866), written for the Sisterhood of Saint Mary, *Harriet Starr Cannon* (1896), a life of the sisterhood's first Mother Superior, *Lectures on the Calling of a Christian Woman* (1883), and several scholarly works, including *An Exposition of the Epistle of St. Paul to the Romans, According to the Analogy of the Catholic Faith* (1862), *Memoirs of John Adams Dix* (2 vols., 1883), and *A History of the Parish of Trinity Church in the City of New York* (4 vols., 1898–1906).

Dix, Mount. See **Dix Mountain.**

Dix, Otto. b. at Gera, Germany, 1891—. German painter, lithographer, and water-colorist. He participated in the Exposition of Contemporary German Painters at Paris in 1929. His work shows some influence of Toulouse-Lautrec. *Portrait of a Woman* (lithograph), *Artists, Portrait of the Artist*, and *Portrait of a Man* (water color), are among his better-known works.

Dix Ans Plus Tard, ou le Vicomte de Bragelonne (dē.zäṅ plü tȧr ö lẹ vē.kôṅt dẹ brȧzh.lon). [Eng. trans., "*Ten Years After, or the Vicomte de Bragelonne*"; shortened title, **Le Vicomte de Bragelonne.**] Novel by Alexandre Dumas *père*, published (1848–50) in 26 parts. It is the third part of the trilogy of which *Les Trois Mousquetaires* (*The Three Musketeers*) was the first, and *Vingt ans après* (*Twenty Years After*) the second. *Ten Years After* is the longest of the series, and parts of it have been published as separate novels: *Louise de la Vallière* and *The Man in the Iron Mask.*

Dixie (dik′si) or **Dixie's Land.** Said to have been originally a Negro name for New York or Manhattan Island, later applied to the South. The phrase originated in New York early in the 19th century; it developed into a song, or rather into many songs, the refrain usually containing the word "Dixie" or "Dixie's Land." In the South, Dixie is regarded as meaning the Southern states, the word being supposed to be derived from "Mason and Dixon's line," which formerly divided the free and slave states. It is said to have first come into use there when Texas joined the Union, and the Negroes sang of it as "Dixie."

Dixie. Song written in 1859 by Daniel D. Emmett, a minstrel-show performer. It achieved great popularity as a minstrel number and became the martial air of the Confederate forces during the Civil War.

Dixiecrats (dik'si.krats). See **States Rights Democrats.**

Dix Mountain. [Also, **Mount Dix.**] One of the principal summits of the Adirondacks, in N New York. 4,842 ft.

Dixmude or **Dixmuide** (dēks.müd). See **Diksmuide.**

Dixon (dik'sọn). City in N Illinois, county seat of Lee County, ab. 98 mi. W of Chicago: cement-manufacturing center. 11,523 (1950).

Dixon, George. d. c1800. English navigator. He served as a petty officer on the *Resolution* during Cook's last voyage. In 1785 he was appointed to the command of the *Queen Charlotte* in Nathaniel Portlock's exploring expedition along the NW coast of America. He was detached for the purpose of independent exploration, on May 14, 1787, and shortly after discovered the Queen Charlotte Islands. He published *A Voyage round the World* (1789).

Dixon, Henry Hall. [Pseudonyms: **General Chassé, The Druid.**] b. at Warwick Bridge, Cumberland, England, May 16, 1822; d. at Kensington, London, March 16, 1870. English novelist and writer on sport, agriculture, and law. Educated at Rugby and at Trinity College, Cambridge, he wrote (1853 *et seq.*) articles on sport for the *Daily News, Illustrated London News, Sporting Magazine*, and others. He was the author of the novels *Post and Paddock* (1856), *Silk and Scarlet* (1859), and *Scott and Sebright* (1862), first published as serials in the *Sporting Magazine;* also wrote *The Law of the Farm* (1858; many editions), a legal treatise; *The Breeding of Shorthorns* (1865), and *Field and Fern* (1865) and *Saddle and Sirloin* (1870), dealing, respectively, with Scottish and English cattle.

Dixon, Richard Watson. b. at Islington, London, May 5, 1833; d. at Warkworth, Northumberland, Jan. 23, 1900. English poet, church historian, and friend of Burne-Jones and William Morris; son of James Dixon (1788–1871), a Wesleyan minister whose *Life* (1874) he wrote. He was educated at King Edward's School, Birmingham, and Pembroke College, Oxford. Ordained in 1859, he was master (1863–68) and canon (1868–75) of Carlisle Cathedral, vicar at Cumberland (1875–83), and at Warkworth from 1883 until he died. He was the author of the prize-winning works *The Close of the Tenth Century of the Christian Era* (1857), an historical essay, *St. John in Patmos* (1863), a religious poem, and *Christ's Company* (1861); also of *Historical Odes* (1864), *Mano* (1883), a long poem, *Odes and Eclogues* (1884), *Lyrical Poems* (1887), *The Story of Eudocia and Her Brothers* (1888), and *Last Poems* (pub. 1905, edited by Mary Elizabeth Coleridge). His prose works are *History of the Church of England From the Abolition of the Roman Jurisdiction* (5 vols., 1878–1902, the last being published after his death), *Seven Sermons* (1888), *A Sermon Preached on the Occasion of the Diamond Jubilee of Queen Victoria* (1897), and other religious works. *Fallen Rain, The Feathers of the Willow, On Conflicting Claims, On Advancing Age,* and *The Spirit Wooed* are among his best poems.

Dixon, Roland Burrage. b. at Worcester, Mass., Nov. 6, 1875; d. Dec. 19, 1934. American anthropologist. He was an assistant (1897–1901), instructor (1901–06), assistant professor (1906–15), and professor (1916 *et seq.*) of anthropology at Harvard University, and served (1918–19) on the American commission to negotiate peace at Paris. His written works include *Oceanic Mythology* (1916), *Racial History of Man* (1923), and *The Building of Cultures* (1928).

Dixon, Thomas. b. at Shelby, N.C., Jan. 11, 1864; d. at Raleigh, N.C., April 3, 1946. American Baptist clergyman (at New York, 1889–99) and novelist whose book *The Clansman* (1905) was adapted by D. W. Griffith into motion-picture form as *The Birth of a Nation* (1915). He was the author also of *The Leopard's Spots* (1902), *The Southerner* (1913), *A Man of the People* (1920), *Flaming Sword* (1939), and other novels; coauthor with Harry M. Daugherty of the *Inside Story of the Harding Tragedy* (1932).

Dixon, William Hepworth. b. at Newton-Heath, England, June 30, 1821; d. at London, Dec. 27, 1879. English author and journalist. He was editor (1853–69) of the *Athenaeum*, and author of *New America* (1867), *Spiritual Wives* (1868), *Free Russia* (1870), and *Her Majesty's Tower* (1869–71).

Dixon Entrance. Sea passage, W of British Columbia, which separates Prince of Wales Island, Alaska, from the Queen Charlotte Islands, British Columbia, Canada.

Dixonville (dik'sọn.vil). Former name of **Columbiana.**

Dixville Notch (diks'vil). Ravine in N New Hampshire, in Coos County, N of the White Mountains. It is traversed by a tributary of the Connecticut River.

Dixwell (diks'wel), **John.** b. 1608; d. at New Haven, Conn., March 18, 1689. English regicide, a refugee in America after the Restoration.

Diyala (dē.yä'lạ). *Liwa* (province) in E central Iraq, ab. 75 mi. NE of the city of Baghdad, bordering on Iran: a flat, dry area irrigated by the Tigris and its tributaries, producing wheat, tobacco, subsistence crops, sheep, and goats. Capital, Diyala; area, 6,154 sq. mi.; pop. 273,336 (1947).

Diyarbakir (dē.yär.bä.kēr'). [Also: **Diarbekir, Diarbekr, Diyarbekir** (-be.kēr'); Armenian, **Dikranakerd.**] *Il* (province or vilayet) in SE Turkey, in the valleys of the upper Tigris and upper Euphrates rivers. Important crops are cotton, wheat, barley, and tobacco; there are large chromium mines. Capital, Diyarbakir; area, 5,742 sq. mi.; pop. 294,618 (1950).

Diyarbakir. [Also: **Diarbekir, Diarbekr, Diyarbekir, Kara Amid**; Armenian, **Dikranakerd**; ancient name, **Amida.**] City in SE Turkey, the capital of the *il* (province or vilayet) of Diyarbakir, situated near the Tigris River, ab. 125 mi. W of Lake Van. An important trading center, served by three highways and one railway line, it has manufactures of red and yellow morocco and exports chromium. It was a Roman colony c230 A.D., was sacked by Tamerlane near the end of the 14th century, and in 1515 was captured by the Turks. 45,495 (1950).

Dizengoff (dē'zẹn.gôf), **Meier.** b. at Akimowzi, in Bessarabia, 1861; d. at Tel-Aviv, Palestine, 1936. Zionist leader and pioneer in Palestine. He studied at the University of Paris, and in 1905, on his second journey to Palestine, took part in pioneering a land settlement near Jaffa. A founder of the city of Tel-Aviv, whose foundation stone he laid in 1909, he was twice (1921–25, 1935–36) its mayor. He was a member (1926–27) of the Zionist Executive.

Dizful (dēz.föl'). [Also, **Desful.**] Town in W Iran, in Khuzistan, situated ab. 77 mi. N of Ahwaz. It was a collecting center for materials to Russia during World War II. The ancient city of Susa was near here. Pop. ab. 35,000.

Dizzy (diz'i). Character in David Garrick's play *The Male Coquette.*

Dizzy. Nickname of **Disraeli, Benjamin.**

Djagatai (jag.ạ.tī'). See **Jagatai.**

Djago (jä'gō), **Chandi.** Most important sepulchral temple of the earliest phase of the great period (mid-13th century A.D.) of art in eastern Java. It was decorated with stone figures and reliefs. The statues, predominantly Buddhistic, reveal a recent wave of influences from southern India; they are now dispersed among many museums. The continuous relief bands are executed in an entirely different, probably indigenous, non-Indian style (Wayang style); they illustrate fables and events from the Hindu-Javanese epics.

Djailolo (jī.lō'lō). See **Halmahera.**

Djailolo Passage. [Also: **Gilolo Passage, Jailolo Passage.**] Sea passage separating the island of Halmahera, in Indonesia, from several smaller islands on the E. Length, ab. 100 mi.

Djambi (jäm'bē). See **Jambi.**

Djamileh (jä.mē.le′). Opera in one act by Georges Bizet, with a libretto by Louis Gallet, first performed at the Paris Opéra-Comique on May 22, 1872.

Djanelidze (jä.ne.lē′dze), **Yustin Yulianovich.** b. at Samtredy, in the Caucasus, Russia, Aug. 2, 1883—. Russian surgeon. He became (1950) chief surgeon of the Red Fleet. He introduced a method of reduction of shoulder dislocations, made studies on fusion of ankle joints, on restoration of the flexor digitorum, on dislocation of the hip joint, on congenital false articulation of the tibia, and on suture technique in fractures of the patella. He was the first in Russia to suture a wound of the heart (1912), experimented with surgery of the heart and blood vessels, recommended a special treatment of burns (1938), worked on traumatic injuries in the lungs and pleura, on diaphragmatic hernias, and on bronchopleural fistulas.

Djarai (jä.rī′). See **Jarai.**

Djawa-Barat (jä′vä.bä.rät′). See **West Java.**

Djawa-Tengah (jä′vä.teng.gä′). See **Central Java.**

Djawa-Timur (jä′vä.tē.mör′). See **East Java.**

Djebeïl (jù.bīl′). See **Byblos.**

Djebel (je.bel). See under **Jebel.**

Djemal Pasha (je.mäl′ pä.shä′), **Ahmed.** b. at Constantinople, May 1, 1861; assassinated at Tiflis, Russia, July 22, 1922. Turkish general and politician. He was governor general (1911) of Baghdad, a divisional commander during the Balkan War (1912 *et seq.*), and served as minister of public works and minister of marine. During World War I he commanded a Turkish army against the British; fleeing Turkey in 1918, he lived in Germany, Switzerland, Russia, and Afghanistan. Author of *Memories of a Turkish Statesman, 1913–19* (1922).

Djenné (je.nā′). [Also: **Jenné, Jinne.**] Town in French Sudan, French West Africa, ab. 250 mi. SW of Tombouctou (Timbuktu), on the flood plain of the Niger River.

Djerba (jer′bą). [Also, **Jerba;** ancient name, **Meninx.**] Island off the N coast of Africa, in the Gulf of Gabès, belonging to Tunisia. It was the scene of a massacre of Christians by the Turks, on May 11, 1560; the bones were piled to form a pyramid 20 ft. high that was not pulled down until 1848.

Djerid (je.rēd′), **Beled el.** See **Beled el Jerid.**

Djerid Salt Lake. See under **Beled el Jerid.**

Djerma (jer′mä). [Also: **Dyerma, Zerma.**] Sudanic-speaking people of W Africa, inhabiting the Niger valley in SW French Niger territory, in the neighborhood of Niamey. Their language is a dialect of Songhai, the language of their NW neighbors further up the Niger. Their population is estimated at ab. 185,000 (by Y. Urvoy, *Petit Atlas ethno-demographique du Soudan*, 1942). All but ab. 10 percent have been Mohammedanized.

Djevriye (jev.rē.ye′), **Ismet.** Original name of **Inönü, Ismet.**

Djibouti (ji.bö′ti). [Also, **Jibuti.**] Main seaport and, since 1892, the seat of the government of French Somaliland, E Africa. It is situated on the S shore of the Gulf of Tadjoura, and is the terminus of the railway (496 mi.) to Addis Ababa, the capital of Ethiopia. The port was created in 1888 and has been under continuous development by the French ever since that time. 10,421 (1944).

Djinnestan or **Jinnestan** (jin.ę.stän′). Land of the Djinns or Jinn in Persian and Oriental fairy lore.

Djof (jōf). See **Jauf.**

Djokjakarta (jōk.yą.kär′tą). See **Jogjakarta.**

Djollof (jol′ǫf). See **Jolof.**

Djollof or **Djolof** or **Djoloff** (jol′ǫf). See also **Wolof.**

Djonga (djōng′gä). [Also, **Badjonga.**] Central subgroup of the Bantu-speaking Tonga people of S Mozambique, in SE Africa.

Djugashvili (jö.gą.shvē′li), **Joseph Vissarionovich.** See **Stalin, Joseph Vissarionovich.**

Długosz (dlö′gôsh), **Jan.** [Latin name, **Johannes Longinus.**] b. at Brzeznica, Poland, 1415; d. at Kraków, Poland, May 19, 1480. Polish churchman, diplomat, and historian. Ordained to the priesthood in 1440, he became thereafter tutor of the children of Casimir IV, king of Poland, and was subsequently that monarch's ambassador to the courts of Bohemia and of Hungary. He also represented the Polish hierarchy on a mission to Pope Eugenius II. In his late years he was archbishop of Lvov. He used his considerable wealth to build churches and monasteries and to help poor students. He wrote the lives of several saints, but his great literary monument is the *Historia Polonia* in 12 volumes. For the better carrying out of this work he learned several foreign languages, and went to original sources in the oldest available Polish, Ruthenian, Czech, Hungarian, and German records, so that it remains even today a valuable chronicle of eastern European history in general as well as a source of information concerning ancient Polish history.

Dmitri (dmē′trē, dę.mē′-). [Also, **Demetrius.**] d. 1591. Czarevich of Russia; son of Ivan the Terrible. At the death of Ivan in 1584, his son Feodor became czar, but the real power rested with his brother-in-law, the ambitious and unscrupulous Boris Godunov. Dmitri, another son of Ivan, obviously stood in the way of Godunov's plan to seize the throne, and accordingly in 1591 Dmitri disappeared. It is accepted that Godunov had him done to death, though by exactly what means is still not known. At the death of Feodor in 1598, Boris Godunov became czar, and was succeded in 1605 by his son Feodor. Meanwhile there appeared in Poland a man who claimed to be the supposedly assassinated Dmitri. It is generally accepted that he was an impostor, but he won a considerable following.

Dmitri. [Also, **Demetrius I** (of *Russia*).] Killed at Moscow, May 17, 1606. Usurper of the throne of Russia (1605–06), often called Pseudo-Demetrius. He seems to have been a Polish monk who claimed to be the czarevich Dmitri (killed by Boris Godunov c1591). He ruled for about one year.

Dmitri. [Also, **Demetrius II** (of *Russia*).] Murdered Dec. 11, 1610. Usurper of the throne of Russia (1607–10).

Dmitriev (dmē′trę.if, dę.mē′-), **Ivan Ivanovich.** b. in the government of Simbirsk, Russia, Sept. 20, 1760; d. at Moscow, Oct. 15, 1837. Russian poet and politician, minister of justice from 1810 to 1814. He was the author of a translation of La Fontaine's fables, and other works.

Dmitriev, Radko. See **Dimitriev, Radko.**

Dmitrievsk (dmē′trę.ifsk). Former name of **Makeyevka.**

Dmitri Rudin (dmē′trē rö′dyin). Chief character of the novel *Rudin*, by Ivan Turgenev. He represents one of the earliest appearances in Russian literature of the young idealist of "advanced" ideas who is at the same time utterly incapable of decisive action.

Dmitrov (dmē′trǫf, dę.mē′-). [Also, **Dmitrof.**] Town in the U.S.S.R., in the Moscow *oblast* (region) of the Russian Soviet Federated Socialist Republic, ab. 43 mi. N of Moscow. It is an important textile town. Pop. ab. 6,000.

Dmitrovsk-Orlovski (dmē′trǫfsk.or.lôf′ski, dę.mē′-). [Former name, **Dmitrovsk.**] Town in the U.S.S.R., in the Kursk *oblast* (region) of the Russian Soviet Federated Socialist Republic, ab. 130 mi. N of Kharkov. There is some metal working in the town, but it is mainly a food-processing center. Pop. ab. 5,500.

Dmowski (dmôf′skē), **Roman.** b. 1864; d. 1939. Polish statesman, founder and leader of the National Democratic Party. A member of the Russian Parliament and chairman of its Polish group, he traveled to Switzerland during World War I to contact diplomatic agents of France and Great Britain. At Lausanne, where he founded (1917) the Polish Agency, a unique embassy of a country that had not yet regained its independence, he formed, with the support of Paderewski, a Polish National Committee (1918) to combat Pilsudski's pro-Austrian policy and solve the Polish question in coöperation with the nations of western Europe and the U.S. He reconciled his differences with Pilsudski after Poland became independent, became first Polish delegate to the peace conference, and signed the Treaty of Versailles. A member of the Polish parliament and minister of foreign affairs in 1920, he sought after Pilsudski's coup d'état to organize groups which opposed Pilsudski. Soon afterwards he retired from political life.

Dnepr (dnye′pėr). Russian name of the **Dnieper.**

Dneprodzerzhinsk (dnye″prǫ.dzer.zhinsk′). [Also: **Dnieprodzerzhinsk;** former name, **Kamenskoye.**] City in the U.S.S.R., in the Ukrainian Soviet Socialist Republic, ab. 80 mi. SW of Dnepropetrovsk. Blast furnaces, iron and steel manufacturing, and engineering works are important here. The Dneproges dam at Zaporozhe produces much of the power used. 147,829 (1939).

Dneproges (dnye.prǫ.ges′). [Former name, **Dneprostroi** (dnye.prǫ.stroi′).] Hydroelectric power station in SW

U.S.S.R., in E central Ukrainian Soviet Socialist Republic, in the Dnieper River ab. 3 mi. NW of Zaporozhe. It is the largest existing hydroelectric plant (1951) in the U.S.S.R., with a capacity of ab. 558,000 kw., and was built in the period 1928–32 with the aid of American consulting engineers. In 1941 the dam was breached and the machinery destroyed in the Soviet retreat. Dneproges was reoccupied in 1943, and reconstruction began almost immediately. In 1947 power production began again. Power is supplied to numerous industries in the region, and the Dnieper is made navigable where there had been rapids before the dam was built. Length of dam, ab. 2,495 ft.; height, ab. 145 ft.

Dnepropetrovsk (dnye″prǫ.pi.trôfsk′). [Also, **Dniepropetrovsk.**] *Oblast* (region) in the U.S.S.R., in the Ukrainian Soviet Socialist Republic, centered ab. 100 mi. SW of Kharkov. The area is hilly and is a large manufacturing center. There are several iron and steel works in the oblast as well as chemical and food-processing plants; it is also a great cereal-producing region. The Dneproges dam produces hydroelectric power for the city. During World War II this land was greatly damaged by the German forces which overran it. Capital, Dnepropetovsk; area, 13,432 sq. mi.; pop. 2,495,000 (1933).

Dnepropetrovsk. [Also: **Dniepropetrovsk**; former name, **Ekaterinoslav** or **Yekaterinoslav,** also **Ekaterinoslaff,** and various other spellings.] City in the U.S.S.R., in the Ukrainian Soviet Socialist Republic, capital of the *oblast* (region) of Dnepropetrovsk, situated on the Dnieper River above the rapids. Iron ore and pig iron are made here. Machine construction and metal works, textiles, chemical works, and petroleum refining are also important. The Dneproges dam at Zaporozhe produces much of the power used here. 500,662 (1939).

Dnestr (dnyes′tėr). Russian name of the **Dniester.**

Dnieper (nē′pėr, dnye′pėr). [Russian, **Dnepr**; Ukrainian, **Dnipro**; Polish, **Dniepr** (dnye′pėr); ancient name, **Borysthenes,** later **Danapris**; Turkish, **Uzi.**] River of the U.S.S.R., after the Volga and Danube the largest in Europe. It rises in the Smolensk *oblast* (region) of the Russian Soviet Federated Socialist Republic, and flows into the Black Sea by the Dnieper estuary, E of Odessa. Its leading tributaries are the Desna, Soj, Pripet, and Berezina. Smolensk, Kiev, Cherkassy, Kremenchug, Dnepropetrovsk, Zaporozhe, Nikopol, and Kherson are on its banks. The Dneproges dam at Zaporozhe supplies power over a large area. Length, ab. 1,200 mi.; navigable from Dorogobuzh.

Dnieprodzerzhinsk (dnye″prǫ.dzer.zhinsk′). See **Dneprodzerzhinsk.**

Dniepropetrovsk (dnye″prǫ.pi.trôfsk′). See **Dnepropetrovsk.**

Dniester (nēs′tėr, dnyes′tėr). [Russian, **Dnestr**; Ukrainian, **Dnister**; Polish, **Dniestr** (dnye′stėr); Rumanian, **Nistrul, Nistru**; Turkish, **Turla**; ancient names, **Tyras, Danastris.**] River in the U.S.S.R., which forms the boundary between the Ukrainian Soviet Socialist Republic and the Moldavian Soviet Socialist Republic for ab. 150 mi. It rises in the Carpathian Mountains, and flows into the Black Sea ab. 30 mi. SW of Odessa. Formerly it was the boundary between Bessarabia (then in Rumania) and the U.S.S.R. Length, ab. 800 mi.

Dnipro (dnē′prō). Ukrainian name of the **Dnieper.**

Dnister (dnēs′ter). Ukrainian name of the **Dniester.**

Doab (dō.äb′). [Also, **Duab**; Eng. trans., *"Two Rivers."*] In India, a name given to a tract of country between two rivers. It is applied especially to the region between the Ganges and the Jumna, of great fertility, ab. 500 mi. in length.

Doak (dōk), **William Nuckles.** b. at Rural Retreat, Va., Dec. 12, 1882; d. Oct. 23, 1933. American labor leader and cabinet member. He was associated (1908 *et seq.*) with the Brotherhood of Railroad Trainmen as general chairman (1908–16) of its units within the Norfolk and Western system, as vice-president (1916–28) and as national legislative representative (1916 *et seq.*). He served during World War I on the railway board of adjustment of the U.S. Railroad Administration. During the latter part of the administration of President Hoover he was U.S. secretary of labor. He was also editor and manager (1928 *et seq.*) of *The Railroad Trainmen.*

Doane (dōn), **George Washington.** b. at Trenton, N.J., May 27, 1799; d. at Burlington, N.J., April 27, 1859. American bishop of the Protestant Episcopal Church. He published *Songs by the Way* (1824), and others.

Doane, William Croswell. b. at Boston, March 2, 1832; d. May 17, 1913. American Protestant Episcopal bishop; son of George Washington Doane. Ordained in 1856, he was consecrated bishop (1869) of the Albany diocese. He served as trustee and honorary chancellor of Hobart College and as regent and chancellor of the University of the State of New York. His works include a biography of his father, *The Life and Writings of George Washington Doane, with a Memoir* (4 vols., 1860–61), *Rhymes from Time to Time* (1901), and the hymn *Ancient of Days.*

Dobberan (dob′ę.rän). See **Doberan.**

Dobbie (dob′i), Sir **William George Shedden.** b. at Madras, India, July 12, 1879—. British army officer. General staff officer (1926–28) at the War Office; brigade commander (1928–32) in Egypt; general officer (1933–39) in command of Malaya; governor (1940–42) of Malta with the rank (1941 *et seq.*) of lieutenant general.

Dobbin (dob′in), **James Cochran.** b. at Fayetteville, N.C., Jan. 17, 1814; d. Aug. 4, 1857. American lawyer, secretary of the navy (1853–57). He reformed and enlarged the navy, inaugurating a new retirement system for officers, a merit system for promotion, a naval apprentice system, and provisions for better treatment and terms for seamen.

Dobbin, Major William. Modest young officer in Thackeray's novel *Vanity Fair.* He marries Amelia Sedley after the death of her first husband, George Osborne.

Dobbins (dob′inz), **Humphrey.** Rough but grateful servant in Colman's comedy *The Poor Gentleman.*

Dobbs (dobz), **Arthur.** b. at Castle Dobbs, County Antrim, Ireland, April 2, 1689; d. March 28, 1765. Irish colonial governor (1754–62) of North Carolina. Member (1727 *et seq.*) of the House of Commons of the Irish Parliament; engineer in chief and surveyor-general (1730 *et seq.*) of Ireland; co-purchaser (1745) of 400,000 acres of land in North Carolina; appointed (1754) governor of North Carolina.

Dobbs Ferry (dobz fer′i). Village in SE New York, in Westchester County, on the Hudson River ab. 20 mi. N of New York City. It is the site of "Children's Village," a school for problem children. Here in the old Livingston mansion in 1783, Washington, George Clinton, and Guy Carleton met to settle the precise terms under which England would remove her troops from American soil. 6,268 (1950).

Dobell (dō.bel′), **Sydney Thompson.** [Pseudonym, **Sydney Yendys.**] b. at Cranbrook, Kent, England, April 5, 1824; d. at Nailsworth, Gloucestershire, Aug. 22, 1874. English poet. He was a wine merchant at Cheltenham from 1848 until his death. His works (a complete edition of which appeared in 1875–76) include *The Roman* (1850), *Balder* (1854), and *England in Time of War* (1856).

Döbeln (dė′bęln). Town in E Germany, in the *Land* (state) of Saxony, Russian Zone, formerly in the free state of Saxony, situated on the Mulde River, ab. 28 mi. W of Dresden. Before World War II it had metallurgical, machine, chocolate, and cigar factories and a sugar refinery. There are commercial and agricultural schools. The Church of Saint Nicholas was erected between 1479 and 1485. The population is predominantly Protestant. 28,841 (1946).

Dobenek (dō′bę.nek), **Johann.** Original name of **Cochlaeus, Johannes.**

Doberan (dō′bę.rän). [Also, **Dobberan.**] Town in NE Germany, in the *Land* (state) of Mecklenburg, Russian Zone, formerly in the free state of Mecklenburg, situated near the Baltic Sea, ab. 9 mi. W of Rostock. A health resort, it has radioactive ferruginous thermal springs. Doberan was formerly known for its horse races. It has a former convent of Cistercian monks, containing tombs of the princes of Mecklenburg; the Gothic Church of Mary is a brick building dating from the 14th century. The population is predominantly Protestant. 10,957 (1946).

Döbereiner (dė′bę.rī.nėr), **Johann Wolfgang.** b. near Hof, Bavaria, Germany, Dec. 15, 1780; d. at Jena, Germany, March 24, 1849. German chemist. He was professor of chemistry, pharmacy, and technology at the University of Jena from 1810 until his death. He discovered that spongiform platinum has the property of igniting hydrogen. Author of *Zur pneumatischen Chemie* (1821–25), and others.

Dobie (dō'bi), **James Frank.** b. in Live Oak County, Texas, Sept. 26, 1888—. American writer and teacher, chiefly known as an authority on the folklore of the American Southwest. He has been head of the English department at Oklahoma Agricultural and Mechanical College, head of the English department (1925–47) at the University of Texas, and a visiting professor of American history (1943–44) at Cambridge, England. His books include *A Vaquero of the Brush Country* (1929), *Coronado's Children* (1931), *Apache Gold and Yaqui Silver* (1939), *The Longhorns* (1941), *A Texan in England* (1945), *The Voice of the Coyote* (1949), *The Ben Billy Legend* (1950), and *The Mustangs* (1952).

Döblin (dėb'lin), **Alfred.** b. at Stettin, Germany, Aug. 10, 1878—. German physician, novelist, and historian. He was on the staff of mental hospitals at Regensburg and Buch (near Berlin), and was a practicing physician at Berlin (1911 *et seq.*) until Hitler came into power. He became famous as a writer of novels and historical works attacking traditional ways of life and pointing to the need for social progress. He is the author of *Gedächtnisstörungen bei der Korsakoff'schen Psychose* (1905); among his best-known novels are *Die drei Sprünge des Wang-lun* (1915), *Wadzek's Kampf mit der Dampfturbine* (1918), *Berge, Meere und Giganten* (1924), *Alexanderplatz Berlin* (1930), and *Bürger und Soldaten* (1941). His most famous work on a historical subject is *Wallenstein* (1920). He also wrote an epic poem, *Manas* (1927), and the essays *Das Ich über der Natur* (1927) and *Wissen und Verändern* (1931).

Dobneck (dob'nek), **Johann.** Original name of **Cochlaeus, Johannes.**

Doboobie (dọ.bö'bi), **Dr. Demetrius.** See **Alasco.**

Dobrée (dō'brẹ), **Bonamy.** b. 1891—. English literary historian, an authority on Restoration drama; husband (married 1913) of Valentine Dobrée. He served with the Royal Air Force in France and Palestine (1914–18) and during World War II (1939–45). His professional career includes professorships of English at the Egyptian University (1926–29) at Cairo and at the University of Leeds (1936 *et seq.*). He is the author of *Restoration Comedy* (1924), *Restoration Tragedy* (1929), *Giacomo Casanova* (1933), and *Modern Prose Style* (1934); coauthor of *The Victorians and After* (1938).

Dobree (dō'brẹ), **Peter Paul.** b. on the island of Guernsey, Channel Islands, 1782; d. at Cambridge, England, Sept. 24, 1825. English Greek scholar. M.A. Cambridge (1807); aided in founding Valpy's *Classical Journal* (1810); served as professor of Greek at Cambridge (1823–25). Edited Porson's *Aristophanica* (1820) and his *Photius lexicon* (1822); his notes on Greek and Latin authors were published by Professor Scholefield in *Adversaria* (1831–33).

Dobrée (dō'brẹ), **Valentine.** [Full name, **Gladys May Mabel Dobrée**; maiden name, **Brooke-Pechell.**] b. 1894—. English author; daughter of Sir Augustus Alexander Brooke-Pechell (1857–1937), and wife (married 1913) of Bonamy Dobrée. Her works of fiction include *Your Cuckoo Sings by Kind* (1927), *Emperor's Tigers* (1929), and *To Blush Unseen* (1935).

Döbrentei (dė'bren.te.ē), **Gábor.** b. at Nagyszöllös, Hungary (now Vel'ký Sevluš, in the Ukraine), Dec. 1, 1786; d. near Budapest, March 28, 1851. Hungarian scholar and poet. He published *Ancient Monuments of the Magyar Language* (1838–46).

Dobrich or **Dobric** (dô'brich). See **Tolbukhin,** Bulgaria.

Dobrizhoffer (dō'brits.hof.ėr), **Martin.** b. at Graz, Styria, Austria, Sept. 7, 1717; d. at Vienna, July 17, 1791. Jesuit missionary and author. From 1749 until the expulsion of the Jesuits in 1767 he resided in Paraguay, and seven years of this period were passed among the savage Abipone Indians. After 1767 he resided at Vienna, where he published his Latin *Historia de Abiponibus* in 1784, a work of considerable ethnological value. A German edition appeared in the same year; there was also an English translation by Sara Coleridge, with the title *An Account of the Abipones* (3 vols., London, 1822).

Dobropolje (dô'brô.pô.lye), **Battles of.** [Also, **Battles of Monastir-Doiran.**] Offensive (September, 1918) of World War I, representing a combined effort by Italian, Serbian, British, French, and Greek troops. This offensive, while not of major proportions, forced Bulgaria to sue for an armistice. The British and Greek troops had little success in the mountain fortifications of Doiran, but the French and Serbian troops in the center were able to slash through and cause panic among the weary Bulgarian defenders. The height of battle occurred between Sept. 15 and Sept. 24, and the armistice came on Sept. 29.

Dobrovský (dô'brôf.skē), **Josef.** b. at Gyermet, near Győr (Raab), Hungary, Aug. 17, 1753; d. at Brno (Brünn), in Moravia, Jan. 6, 1829. Czech philologist, the founder of Slavic philology. He became a member of the order of Jesuits in 1772. His works include *Geschichte der böhmischen Sprache und ältern Literatur* (1792), *Institutiones linguae slavicae dialecti veteris* (1822), and *Scriptores rerum bohemicarum* (1783–84).

Dobruja (dō'brö.jạ). [Also: **Dobrudja**; Rumanian, **Dobrogea** (dō'brō.jä); Bulgarian, **Dobrudzha** (dô'brö.jä).] Province in SE Rumania, bounded by Bulgaria on the S, the Black Sea on the E, the Danube River on the N and the Rumanian province of Muntenia on the W. Area, 8,979 sq. mi. In 1940 the region of Cadrilater, in the S part, was ceded to Bulgaria. Therefore the population decreased from 811,000 in 1930 to 503,217 in 1948.

Dobšiná (dôp'shē.nä). [Hungarian, **Dobsina** (dōp'shē.nô); German, **Dobschau** (dop'shou).] Town in Czechoslovakia, in E Slovakia, situated in the Carpathian Mountains SW of Spišska Nová Ves. It is noted for its ice caverns, which cover an area of 7,000 sq. meters. There is iron-ore mining and iron and wood manufactures. 3,957 (1947).

Dobson (dob'sọn), **Austin.** [Full name, **Henry Austin Dobson.**] b. at Plymouth, England, Jan. 18, 1840; d. at Ealing, London, Sept. 2, 1921. English poet, critic, essayist, and biographer. Son of a civil engineer, he was educated in French and English schools. Returning to England in 1856, he was until his retirement in 1901 a clerk in the Board of Trade. Beginning in 1904 he received a government pension of 250 pounds a year and devoted himself entirely to research. He was the author of *The Civil Service Handbook of English Literature* (1874), *Four Frenchwomen* (1890), *Eighteenth Century Vignettes* (1892; 2nd series, 1894; 3rd series, 1896), *Miscellanies* (1898), *A Paladin of Philanthropy* (1899), *Side-Walk Studies* (1902), *Old Kensington Palace* (1910), *At Prior Park* (1912), *Rosalba's Journal* (1915), and other collections of essays and papers; also wrote *Hogarth* (1879; final revision, 1907), *Fielding* (1883), *Thomas Bewick and His Pupils* (1884), *Steele* (1886), *Goldsmith* (1888), *Horace Walpole* (1890), *Samuel Richardson* (1902), and *Fanny Burney* (1903); *Vignettes in Rhyme* (1873), *Proverbs in Porcelain* (1877), *Old-World Idylls* (1883), *At the Sign of the Lyre* (1885), *The Sun Dial* (1890), *The Ballad of Beau Brocade* (1892), *The Story of Rosina* (1895), and *Complete Poetical Works* (1923). Among his poems are *Farewell, Renown, Before Sedan, Rose-Leaves, Ballade of Prose and Rhyme, In After Days, The Sick Man and the Birds,* and *Prayer of the Swine to Circe.* Dobson was one of the group (c1875) who introduced into English poetry such forms as the ballade, the rondel, the triolet, and the villanelle from French.

Dobson, Frank. b. at London, Nov. 18, 1887—. English modernist sculptor. At first he studied painting, but from 1913 on devoted himself to sculpture, and became a leader among the modernists. He became professor of sculpture at the Royal College of Art, and was elected an Associate of the Royal Academy in 1942. His method consists essentially in eliminating naturalistic details to achieve massive form, with the use of distortion where it will serve his design. He has also, however, executed some much-admired (and more conventional) portrait busts. Examples of his work are to be seen at the Tate Gallery, London, and in public museums at Manchester, Leeds, and Glasgow.

Dobson, William. b. at London, 1610; d. at Oxford, 1646. English portrait and historical painter, a pupil and imitator of Van Dyck, whom he succeeded as painter to Charles I. He painted the portraits of Charles I, the Prince of Wales, Prince Rupert, and various courtiers.

Doce (dō′sẹ). River in E Brazil which flows into the Atlantic Ocean. Length, over 360 mi.; navigable for ab. 90 mi.

Docetism (dō.sē′tiz.ẹm). The earliest heresy to arise in the Christian church. Its propagators and participants were first called "Docetae" or "Illusionists" by Serapion, bishop of Antioch from 190 to 203, but it troubled the church from the earliest days. The gist of Docetism was that Jesus Christ only appeared to have taken human form, that his birth, life, sufferings, and death were illusory. It was an intrusion of Gnosticism into Christianity; Gnostics in considerable numbers joined the early Christian congregations, but with their fixation upon the concept of the complete emancipation of the spiritual from the material, they could not accept the doctrine that "the Word was made flesh." Docetism troubled the church greatly in its early centuries, and was only exorcised by the earnest efforts of numerous patristic writers and preachers.

Dochart (doȯh′ȧrt). See under **Tay.**

Dock Junction. Unincorporated community in SE Georgia, in Glynn County, near Brunswick. 4,160 (1950).

Dockwra (dok′rạ) or **Dockwray** (dok′rā), **William.** d. Sept. 25, 1716. English merchant who played a chief part in establishing the penny postal system at London. This system had already been partly put into practice by Robert Murray, an upholsterer. Dockwra's contribution was to improve on it by setting up six large offices and a receiving house in each of the principal streets. Mails were collected hourly, and delivery was made four times daily in the suburbs and six to eight times in the principal business streets.

Doctor, The. Romance (7 vols., 1834) by Robert Southey. It was at first published anonymously, and he explicitly denied his authorship. In it he exhibits his vast store of learning in a rambling manner. The children's tale of *The Three Bears* first appeared here, invented by Southey from incidents in German and Norwegian folk tales.

Doctor Angelicus (an.jel′i.kus). See **Aquinas,** Saint **Thomas.**

Doctor Dodipoll (dod′i.pōl). Comedy (1600) the author of which is unknown. Dr. Dodipoll is a foolish, doddering creature.

Doctor Faustus (fôs′tus, fous′-). [Original full title (on the quarto edition of 1604), **The Tragicall History of D. Faustus.**] Tragedy in blank verse and prose by Christopher Marlowe. It was written, and probably first produced, in 1588, and published in 1604, although it was listed for publication as early as 1601. It is one of the first, if not the first, treatments in English of the old German Faust legend, of a man who enters into a bargain with the devil and sells his soul to him. Marlowe, it is presumed, knew, either in the original German, or in an English translation that appeared in 1588, a *Faustbuch* (Frankfort, 1587), translated as *The History of the Damnable Life and Deserved Death of Dr. John Faustus,* dealing with the magic deeds of a 16th-century German quack, Dr. Johann Faust. The play opens with a short summary of the plot, delivered by the Chorus (regarded and listed as a character), and then shows us Faustus, a great scholar who has mastered law, medicine, theology, and philosophy, in his study, alone, not satisfied with his vast knowledge but thirsting for more. In response to his request, made, of course, in Latin (that being the language of the devil and of evil spirits, whence Marcellus's cry in *Hamlet,* "speak to it, Horatio"), Mephistophilis appears. An agreement is reached and Faustus sells himself to the devil, who swears to serve him in all things for a period of 24 years, at the end of which period Faustus is to give him his soul. The period, although it seems long, at the time, to the young and eager Renaissance scholar, passes all too quickly and Faustus is called upon to meet the terms of the contract that he signed with his own blood. The play ends with his being dragged down, in horror and agony, to hell. He appeals in vain to God and Christ but the life he has led makes his prayers worthless. The tragedy contains many examples of what is known as Marlowe's "mighty line," the most famous one being his apostrophe to Helen:

Was this the face that launched a thousand ships
And burnt the topless towers of Ilium? (Scene 13)

The play ends with Faustus's agonized cries, "See, see where Christ's blood streams in the firmament! One drop would save my soul—half a drop," "My God! my God! look not so fierce on me!" and his final terrible, beautiful, pathetic, terrifyingly human cry, "I'll burn my books!"

Doctor Invincibilis (in.vin.sib′i.lis). See **Ockham** or **Occam, William of.**

Doctor Marigold (mar′i.gōld). Story by Charles Dickens, published in 1865 in a collection called *Doctor Marigold's Prescriptions.* Its narrator and chief character is Doctor Marigold himself, a wandering auctioneer (called, in England, a "Cheap Jack"), with whose life the story is chiefly concerned.

Doctor North and His Friends (nôrth). Novel by S. Weir Mitchell, published in 1900 as a sequel to *Characteristics* (1892).

Doctor of Alcantara (al.kan′tạ.rạ), **The.** Opera by Julius Eichberg, produced in 1862.

Doctor's Christmas Eve, The. Novel by James Lane Allen, published in 1910.

Doctor's Dilemma, The. Play (1906) by George Bernard Shaw, in which he satirizes doctors and the medical profession.

Doctor Serocold (ser′ọ.kōld). Novel by Helen Ashton, published in 1930.

Doctor Solemnis (sọ.lem′nis). See **Henry of Ghent.**

Doctor's Tale, The. See **Physician's Tale, The.**

Doctor Subtilis (sub.tī′lis). See **Duns Scotus, John.**

Doctor Universalis (ū″ni.vėr.sā′lis). See **Alain de Lille;** see also **Albertus Magnus.**

Doctrine and Discipline of Divorce, The. Prose pamphlet (1643) by John Milton. It is the first of a series of four so-called divorce tracts. His first wife, Mary Powell, a Royalist, left him in 1642, a few weeks after their marriage, and did not return at the time agreed on, although she did so later. To what extent the pamphlets represent personal anger and to what extent abstract theory, are questions that have been widely discussed. The first edition was anonymous, but the second carried Milton's name. The pamphlet was dedicated to Parliament.

Dóczy or **Dóczi** (dō′tsē), Baron **Louis (or Ludwig) von.** b. at Odenburg, Hungary, 1845; d. 1919. Hungarian author and playwright. Beginning his career as a journalist, after 1867 he was for some years a government employee. During this period his comedy *The Kiss* (1871), which brought him the award of the Hungarian Academy, established his reputation as a playwright, which was sustained by later successful works. He published original work in prose and poetry, and translated into Hungarian the poetry of Schiller and Part I of Goethe's *Faust.*

Dod (dod), **Charles Roger Phipps.** b. in Ireland, May 8, 1793; d. Feb. 21, 1855. Compiler of the *Parliamentary Companion* (1832 *et seq.*).

Doda Betta (dō′dạ bet′ạ). See under **Nilgiri Hills.**

Dodd (dod), **Frank Howard.** b. at Bloomfield, N.J., April 12, 1844; d. Jan. 10, 1916. American publisher. He joined (1859) a publishing house which had been established by his father, and became its president in 1870. In that same year he became partner of Edward S. Mead and B. Van Wagenen in Dodd, Mead and Company, which included among its 19th-century successes such works as E. P. Roe's *Barriers Burned Away,* Ian Maclaren's *Beside the Bonnie Brier Bush* (1894), and Paul Leicester Ford's *Janice Meredith* (1899). He was a founder of *The Bookman,* planned and published (1902–04) the original *New International Encyclopaedia,* and began (1907) the *New International Yearbook* as a supplement to the *Encyclopaedia.*

Dodd, James William. b. in London, c1740; d. 1796. English actor. He was a member of Garrick's company, and was especially successful as Sir Andrew Aguecheek and Abel Drugger.

Dodd, Lee Wilson. b. at Franklin, Pa., July 11, 1879; d. May 16, 1933. American playwright, novelist, and poet. His plays are *The Return of Eve* (1909), *Speed* (1911), *His Majesty Bunker Bean* (1915), *Pals First* (1917), and *The Changelings* (1923); his novels include *The Book of Susan* (1920), *Lilia Chenoworth* (1922), and *The Girl Next Door* (1923); his poems are collected in *The Middle Miles* (1915), and *The Great Enlightenment* (1928).

Dodd, William. b. at Bourne, Lincolnshire, England, May 29, 1729; d. June 27, 1777. English clergyman and author. He studied at Cambridge, was ordained deacon in 1751, and was appointed chaplain to the king in 1763. In 1777 he forged the name of Lord Chesterfield, his former pupil, to a bond for 4,200 pounds, and in spite of the efforts of Dr. Johnson and other influential persons was executed at London. He wrote *Beauties of Shakespeare* (1752) and *Thoughts in Prison* (1777).

Dodd, William Edward. b. at Clayton, N.C., Oct. 21, 1869; d. at Round Hill, Va., Feb. 9, 1940. American historian and diplomat. He was a professor (1900–08) of history at Randolph-Macon College, and professor (1908–33) of American history at the University of Chicago. Observations made during his ambassadorship (1933–37) to Germany were published as *Ambassador Dodd's Diary* (1941). His other works include *Jefferson's Rückkehr zur Politik (1796)* (1900), *Life of Nathaniel Macon* (1903), *Life of Jefferson Davis* (1907), *Statesmen of the Old South* (1911), *Expansion and Conflict* (1915), *Woodrow Wilson and His Work* (1920), and *Lincoln or Lee* (1928); coeditor with Ray Stannard Baker of *The Public Papers of Woodrow Wilson* (1924–26).

Doddridge (dod′rij), **Philip.** b. at London, June 26, 1702; d. at Lisbon, Oct. 26, 1751. English dissenting clergyman. He was pastor of an Independent congregation at Northampton from 1729 until his death. He is known chiefly as the author of *Rise and Progress of Religion in the Soul* (1745), and *The Family Expositor* (6 vols., 1739–56), and for his hymns.

Dodds (dodz), **Alfred Amédée.** b. at St.-Louis, Senegal, Feb. 6, 1842; d. at Paris, July 18, 1922. French colonial officer, best known for the so-called model campaign (1892) in Dahomey. He escaped twice from captivity and internment during the Franco-Prussian War (1870–71), saw duty in Senegal (1871–83, 1887–91) and Indochina (1883–87), and was commander in chief (1903–07) of all French colonial troops.

Dodds, Harold Willis. b. at Utica, Pa., June 28, 1889—. American political scientist, president (1933 *et seq.*) of Princeton University. He has been editor (1920–33) of *National Municipal Review*, an electoral adviser to the governments of Nicaragua (1922–24, 1928) and Cuba (1935), and professor of political science (1927 *et seq.*) at Princeton. He was chairman (1943) of the American delegation at the Anglo-American refugee conference in Bermuda. In 1951 he became chairman of the Carnegie Foundation for the Advancement of Teaching. His written works include *Out of This Nettle . . . Danger* (1943).

Dodecanese (dō.dek.ą.nēz′, -nēs′). [Greek, **Dodekanesos** (ᴛʜō.ᴛʜe.kä′nē.sôs), meaning "Twelve Islands."] Group of Greek islands in the SE part of the Aegean Sea near the SW coast of Turkey, including the *nomoi* (departments) of Rhodes, Kalymnos, Karpathos, and Kos. There are 12 main islands (Astypalaia, Khalke, Kalymnos, Karpathos, Kasos, Kos, Leros, Nisyros, Patmos, Rhodes, Syme, and Telos) and many small ones. The seat of administration is at Rhodes. The islands were part of the Turkish Empire from the 16th century until 1912, when they were occupied by Italy in the war with Turkey. By the treaty of Sèvres (1922) they were awarded to Italy, which held them until the German occupation in World War II. The peace treaty of 1947 awarded the islands to Greece, their population being predominantly Greek. Area, 1,035 sq. mi.; pop. 121,074 (1951).

Döderlein (dė′dėr.līn), **Albert.** b. at Augsburg, Germany, July 5, 1860; d. at Erlangen, Germany, Dec. 10, 1941. German obstetrician. He was assistant (1884–93) to E. Zweifel at Erlangen and Leipzig, became (1887) Privatdocent of gynecology and obstetrics at the University of Leipzig, was named professor (1893) and full professor (1897) at Groningen, and became professor at Tübingen (1897) and at the University of Munich (1907). He conducted investigations in the pathogenesis of puerperal fever (1887), wrote a study of vaginal secretion in relation to puerperal fever (1892), described a bacillus that bears his name, wrote on asepsis during delivery, recommending gloves (Döderlein's gloves), and was an early advocate of the radiative treatment of uterine cancer.

Döderlein, Ludwig. b. at Jena, Germany, Dec. 19, 1791; d. at Erlangen, Germany, Nov. 9, 1863. German classical philologist, professor at Erlangen (1819 *et seq.*). His works include *Lateinische Synonymen und Etymologien* (1826–38), *Homerisches Glossarium* (1850–58), and editions of Tacitus, Horace, and the *Iliad*.

Dodge (doj), **Augustus Caesar.** b. at Ste. Genevieve, Mo., Jan. 2, 1812; d. Nov. 20, 1883. American diplomat and U.S. senator; son of Henry Dodge (1782–1867). Delegate (1840–46) for Iowa Territory in Congress; first U.S. senator (1848–55) from Iowa; supported the Compromise of 1850, the Kansas-Nebraska bill, and the Fugitive-Slave law, condemning abolitionism; U.S. minister (1855–59) to Spain.

Dodge, Bayard. b. at New York, Feb. 5, 1888—. American educator. He has been a faculty member (1913 *et seq.*) and president (1923 *et seq.*) of the American University at Beirut, Syria, and director (1920–21) of Near East Relief in Syria and Palestine.

Dodge, Charles Wright. b. at Cape Vincent, N.Y., Jan. 15, 1863; d. 1934. American naturalist, professor of biology at the University of Rochester from 1892. He was graduated from the University of Michigan in 1886. He published an *Introduction to Elementary Practical Biology* (1894), and others.

Dodge, David Low. b. at Brooklyn, Conn., June 14, 1774; d. April 23, 1852. American pacifist and merchant. Established (1802) stores at Hartford and Litchfield, Conn.; partner (1807) in jobbing business with his wife's cousins, the Higginsons of Boston; manager (1813) of a Norwich, Conn. cotton mill. A philanthropist and pacifist, he propagandized widely against war (he founded (1815) and became first president of the New York Peace Society, which merged (1828) with the American Peace Society).

Dodge, Grace Hoadley. b. at New York, May 21, 1856; d. there, Dec. 27, 1914. American social worker and philanthropist, founder (1907) of the New York Travelers Aid Society. Founder of a working girls' club (nucleus for the Associations of Working Girls' Societies); member of the New York City Board of Education (1886); vice-president of the Industrial Education Association (founded 1884), which developed into the New York College for the Training of Teachers (1889) and then into Teachers College, Columbia University, with Grace Dodge as acting treasurer. She founded the American Social Hygiene Association, and worked with Young Women's Christian Association, serving (1906) as president of its national board.

Dodge, Grenville Mellen. b. at Danvers, Mass., April 12, 1831; d. Jan. 3, 1916. American soldier and civil engineer. He served through the Civil War, rising to the rank of major general of volunteers in 1864, and resigned from the army in 1866. He was a member of Congress from Iowa (1867–69), and was chief engineer of the Union Pacific Railroad (1866–70) and of the Texas and Pacific Railway (1871–81). In 1898 he was appointed president of the commission for investigating the management of the war with Spain.

Dodge, Henry. b. at Vincennes, Ind., Oct. 12, 1782; d. June 19, 1867. American soldier, governor and U.S. senator (1848–57) from Wisconsin.

Dodge, Joseph Morrell. b. at Detroit, Mich., Nov. 8, 1890—. American banker and administrator. After holding several positions as banking and financial examiner for the state of Michigan, he became (1932) a bank executive and subsequently a director of a number of business organizations. During World War II he was head of the army's price adjustment board, and later directed the Army Service Forces renegotiation division. With the establishment of the military government in Europe, he became its financial adviser, represented the U.S., with the rank of minister, on the Austrian Treaty Commission (1947), was a member of the financial advisory committee of the Economic Coöperation Administration, and in 1949 went to Japan as special adviser to General Douglas MacArthur on Japanese budgetary problems, then in a rapidly deteriorating state. In 1953, after the election of Dwight Eisenhower as President of the United States, Dodge was appointed to confer with the outgoing Truman administration on financial matters. He became (1953) budget director for the new administration.

Dodge, Mary Abigail. [Pseudonym, **Gail Hamilton.**] b. at Hamilton, Mass., March 31, 1833; d. at Wenham, Mass., Aug. 17, 1896. American writer. Her works include *Country Living and Country Thinking* (1862), *Gala Days* (1863), *New Atmosphere* (1864), *Woman's Wrongs* (1868), *Twelve Miles from a Lemon* (1873), and *Our Common School System* (1880).

Dodge, Mary Elizabeth. [Maiden name, **Mapes.**] b. at New York, Jan. 26, 1831; d. at Onteora Park, in the Catskill Mountains, N.Y., Aug. 21, 1905. American juvenile author and editor. She was educated by private tutors and by her father, James Jay Mapes, a scientist. In 1851 she married William Dodge, a lawyer, who died seven years later, leaving her with two boys to support. She thereupon did the only thing she knew and liked: she took up writing. She began with a series of sketches, *Irvington Stories* (1864), and she wrote for the *Atlantic Monthly, Harper's Magazine*, and the *Century.* From 1870 to 1873 she was associate editor of *Home and Hearth.* In the latter year a magazine for young people was founded, *St. Nicholas;* she was made its first editor and she occupied that position with marked success until her death a generation later. Bryant, Longfellow, Whittier, and Kipling (who had been a reader when he was a boy) contributed to its pages. The juvenile classic, Mrs. Burnett's *Little Lord Fauntleroy,* was serialized in it before appearing in book form. In 1865 she published her most successful work, *Hans Brinker, or the Silver Skates,* which is still read with pleasure by many children and some grown-ups. Others of her works are *A Few Friends and How They Amused Themselves* (1869), *Theophilus and Others* (1876), *Donald and Dorothy* (1883), *Baby World* (1884), and *The Land of Pluck* (1894). *Rhymes and Jingles* (1874), *Along the Way* (1879), and *When Life Is Young* (1894) are volumes of verse. As girl and woman, she counted among her friends Bryant, Greeley, Mark Twain, Brander Matthews, John Burroughs, and Maude Adams.

Dodge, Raymond. b. at Woburn, Mass., Feb. 20, 1871; d. at Tryon, N.C., April 8, 1942. American psychologist, notable for his discovery of the fundamental law of visual perception in reading. He was a graduate (1893) of Williams and professor (1924–36) at Yale, and one of the original directors of the Yale Institute of Human Relations. He is known also for his researches on inhibition modification of reflex response.

Dodge, Steadfast. American newspaperman in *Homeward Bound* (1838) and *Home as Found* (1838) by James Fenimore Cooper. He typifies the vulgarity which Cooper resented in his countrymen.

Dodge, Theodore Ayrault. b. at Pittsfield, Mass., May 28, 1842; d. Oct. 25, 1909. American soldier and author. He served through the Civil War and in the war department, rising to the rank of brevet colonel. He retired in 1870. Among his works are *Chancellorsville* (1881), *Civil War* (1883), *A Chat in the Saddle* (1886), *Alexander* (1890), *Hannibal* (1891), *Caesar* (1892), *Riders of Many Lands* (1894), *Gustavus Adolphus* (1890–95), and *Napoleon* (1904–07).

Dodge, William De Leftwich. b. at Liberty, Va., March 9, 1867; d. March 25, 1935. American mural painter. He studied at the École des Beaux-Arts at Paris, and also for a time at Munich. After returning to the U.S. he taught for many years at Cooper Union and at the Art Students League, both at New York. His first notable work was the decoration (1893) of the dome of the Administration Building of the World's Columbian Exposition at Chicago. He is also known for his mural panels in the Library of Congress at Washington, the Hall of Records at New York, the Academy of Music at Brooklyn, the city hall of Buffalo, N.Y., and the state capitol at Albany, N.Y. He also executed murals for the Café de l'Opéra and for the Folies Bergère at Paris.

Dodge, William Earl. b. at Hartford, Conn., Sept. 4, 1805; d. at New York, Feb. 9, 1883. American merchant and philanthropist, an organizer of the Y.M.C.A. He was noted also for his efforts on behalf of the freedmen, temperance, and foreign missions.

Dodge City. City in SW Kansas, county seat of Ford County, on the Arkansas River: a trading center of the Kansas wheat belt. At one time, as the "Cowboy Capital of the Southwest," it was a shipping point for buffalo hides, and for cattle driven north from Texas (it was then the westernmost terminus of the U.S. railroad network). 11,262 (1950).

"Dodger, Artful." See under **Dawkins, John.**

Dodgeville (doj'vil). City in SW Wisconsin, county seat of Iowa County, ab. 40 mi. SW of Madison. Settled in 1827, it was named for Henry Dodge (1782–1867), who later was governor of the Wisconsin Territory. It was a lead-mining center until the mid-19th century, and is now marketing and shipping center for a dairying, farming, and stock-raising region. 2,532 (1950).

Dodgson (doj'sọn), **Charles Lutwidge.** [Pseudonym, **Lewis Carroll.**] b. at Daresbury, Cheshire, England, Jan. 27, 1832; d. at Guildford, Surrey, Jan. 14, 1898. English mathematician, now best remembered as the author of the two immortal Alice books. He was educated at home by his father, a clergyman, at Rugby, and at Christ Church College, Oxford, where he later taught mathematics. He became a "member of the College" (as English students are called), and he remained that for almost half a century until his death. From 1855 to 1881 he was at Christ Church as a lecturer, a position corresponding to a professor in an American college. He wrote *Euclid and His Modern Rivals* (1879), *Curiosa Mathematica* (1888), and other technical works in his field, but he lives by his authorship of *Alice's Adventures in Wonderland* (1865), which was first called *Alice's Adventures Underground* and *Alice's Hours in Elfland,* and its sequel, *Through the Looking-Glass and What Alice Found There* (1871). His other juvenile books are *The Hunting of the Snark* (1876), *A Tangled Tale* (1885), and *Sylvie and Bruno* (1889). He wrote the works that made him famous under the name of "Lewis Carroll" and he made the name famous. (Neither the works nor the name can be said at first to have claimed Dodgson's serious attention. He thought of *Alice's Adventures in Wonderland* as no more than a fanciful tale contrived for the entertainment of a little girl named Alice Liddell, the daughter of Henry George Liddell, a leading 19th-century classicist and one of Dodgson's friends. It almost certainly never entered Dodgson's head that his name would not be remembered primarily for his achievements as a mathematician.) In 1867 he broke the routine of his Oxford life by visiting Russia, and *A Russian Journal,* a diary, was the result.

Dodinga (dō.ding'gä). See **Didinga.**

Dodington (dod'ing.tọn), **George Bubb.** [Title, Baron **Melcombe.**] b. in Dorsetshire, England, 1691; d. at Hammersmith (now part of London), July 28, 1762. English politician. He was created Baron Melcombe of Melcombe Regis, Dorsetshire, in 1761. He patronized men of letters, and was complimented by Edward Young, Henry Fielding, and Richard Bentley. He left a diary covering the period from 1749 to 1761, which was published in 1784. He was one of the group calling itself the "mad monks of Medmenham Abbey," along with Francis Dashwood, John Wilkes, and others.

Dodoma (dō'dọ.mạ). Town in E Africa, in Tanganyika territory, situated on the Central Railway of Tanganyika, ab. 288 mi. W of Dar-es-Salaam. It is the administrative headquarters of the Central Province, seat of an Anglican bishopric, and the chief native produce and livestock market in the region. Important roads link it with Arusha in the N; it is linked by the Great North Road with the Rhodesias and Nyasaland in the S.

Dodona (dō.dō'nạ). In ancient geography, a city in Epirus, probably situated on or near Mount Tomarus, SW of Ioannina. It was the seat of the oldest Greek oracle, dedicated to Zeus, in an oak grove hung with vessels of brass, by which the god's voice was thought to be made audible.

Dods (dodz), **Meg.** Landlady of the inn, in Sir Walter Scott's *St. Ronan's Well.*

Dodsley (dodz'li), **Robert.** b. probably at Mansfield, on the border of Sherwood Forest, Nottinghamshire, England; d. at Durham, England, Sept. 23, 1764. English dramatist, poet, editor, anthologist, and bookseller, and founder of the *Annual Register.* He was a prolific author, as well as a publisher of the works of others, and he wrote in a variety of forms, including plays, poems, songs, and satires. As a publisher, with a shop in Pall Mall, Dodsley published Pope's *First Epistle of the Second Book of Horace,* poems by Young and Akenside, Goldsmith's *Polite Learning,* and Johnson's *Rasselas, The Vanity of Human Wishes,* and *Irene.* In 1758 he founded a work that is still published, the *Annual Register*, a record, as the title indicates, of the significant events of the past year. He paid Burke, whom he engaged as editor, a hundred pounds a year. Johnson thought well of him and said, "Doddy, you know, is my patron, and I would not desert him." Nichols, of the *Literary Anecdotes*, praises him as "that admirable patron and encourager of learning," and Walpole, in a letter to George Montagu, touches a vital point in his character: "You know how decent, humble, inoffensive a creature Dodsley is; how little apt to forget or disguise his having been a footman."

Dodson (dod′sọn). Family name of the three aunts in George Eliot's *The Mill on the Floss*, Aunt Pullet, Aunt Glegg, and Aunt Tulliver. Their inherited customs and peculiarities are amusing, and are always referred to with respect by the phrase "No Dodson ever did" so and so.

Dodson and Fogg (fog). In Charles Dickens's *Pickwick Papers*, the legal advisers of Mrs. Bardell in the celebrated breach-of-promise case.

Dodsworth (dodz′wėrth). Novel by Sinclair Lewis, published in 1929. With Sidney Howard, the author wrote a stage version produced in 1934. Samuel Dodsworth, a Zenith automobile manufacturer, goes to Europe with his spoiled and shallow wife, Fran, who amuses herself with a series of affairs. In his loneliness Dodsworth becomes involved with Edith Cortright, an American widow who orients him to an appreciation of European culture. Dodsworth eventually leaves his wife for Edith.

Dodwell (dod′wel, -wẹl), **Edward.** b. c1767; d. at Rome, May 13, 1832. English antiquary and artist. He published *Classical and Topographical Tour through Greece* (1819), *Cyclopean or Pelasgic Remains in Greece and Italy* (1834), and others.

Dodwell, Henry. b. at Dublin, Ireland, in October, 1641; d. at Shottesbrooke, Berkshire, England, June 7, 1711. British classical scholar and controversialist. He studied at Trinity College, Dublin, removed to London in 1674, and was Camden professor of history at Oxford (1688–91). His chief work is *De veteribus graecorum romanorumque cyclis* (1701).

Doe (dō), **John.** Originally, the name of the fictitious plaintiff in actions of ejectment; the use of the name is now extended to include other actions or proceedings to which a person whose name is not known must be a party.

Doeg (dō′eg). In the Bible, the chief of the herdsmen of Saul. He slew four score and five priests of Nob.

Doeg. In the second part of John Dryden and Nahum Tate's *Absalom and Achitophel*, a character intended to represent Elkanah Settle.

Doenitz or **Dönitz** (dė′nits), **Karl.** b. 1891—. German admiral. He is believed to have been one of the German military leaders active in the scheme put into effect during the 1930's to construct submarines and train their crews, both of which activities were in violation of the Versailles treaty. During World War II, in 1943, he succeeded Admiral Erich Raeder as chief of the German navy. In the document published (April, 1945) as Hitler's "Political Testament" he was appointed successor to Hitler; surrendered (May 7, 1945) to the Allies. The international war crimes tribunal sentenced him to ten years' imprisonment.

Doerr (dėr), **Robert.** b. at Técsö, Hungary, Nov. 1, 1871—. Bacteriologist. He took his medical degree at Vienna, was a surgeon in the Austro-Hungarian army, and became Privatdocent of general and experimental pathology in 1908 and professor in 1912. During World War I he was director of the bacteriological laboratory of the Austro-Hungarian Committee of Military Hygiene. He became (1919) full professor of hygiene and bacteriology at the University of Basel. He published important studies on dysenteric toxin (1903), anaphylaxis, and allergy, on pappataci fever (1908), and spotted fever. Author of *Das Dysenterietoxin* (1907), *Pappatacifieber* (1909), *Dysenterietoxin und Antitoxin* (1911), *Allergie und Anaphylaxie* (1913), *Allergische Phaenomene* (1929), *Herpes Zoster und Encephalitis* (1930), *Die Lehre von den Infektionskrankheiten in allgemeiner Darstellung* (1931), and *Filtrierbare Virusarten* (1933).

Does (dös), **Jacobus van der.** b. at Amsterdam, Netherlands, March 4, 1623; d. at Sloten, Netherlands, Nov. 17, 1673. Dutch landscape and animal painter.

Does, Jan Van der. See **Dousa, Janus.**

Doesburg (dös′bėrċh), **Theo van.** [Pseudonym of **C. E. M. Kupper,** who also called himself **I. K. Bonset.**] b. at Utrecht, Netherlands, 1883; d. at Davos, Switzerland, 1931. Dutch nonobjective (neo-plastic) painter, architect, editor, and theorist, who was the founder of the De Stijl group and magazine at Leiden (1917). He was a self-educated painter, and worked mostly in Holland, although he did spend the period 1920–28 at Berlin, Paris, and Strasbourg. He exhibited at the Independents in 1929. Gropius, Le Corbusier, and Mies van der Rohe were influenced by him in their architectural designs. A list of his work includes *Self-Portrait, Card Players, Composition IX; Card Players, Russian Dance, Three Graces, Arithmetical Composition, Simultaneous Counter-Composition, Counter Composition in Dissonances,* and *Aesthetic Transformation of the Object.*

Doesticks, P.B. (dō′stiks), **Q.K. Philander.** Pseudonym of **Thomson, Mortimer Neal.**

Doesticks, What He Says. Series of sketches by Mortimer Neal Thomson, published in 1855 under the pseudonym Philander Doesticks (in full, Q.K. Philander Doesticks, P.B.).

Doetinchem (dö′tin.ċhẹm). [Also: **Deutekom, Doetichem** (dö′ti.ċhẹm).] Town in E Netherlands, in the province of Gelderland, situated on the Ijssel River, E of Arnhem. Manufactures include electric motors, enamelware, and canned food. There is a church in the late Gothic style and a town hall dating from the 18th century. 21,858 (est. 1951).

Dogali (dō.gä′lē). Place near Massawa, E Africa. Here, on Jan. 26, 1887, the Italian force under Gené was defeated and nearly destroyed by the Ethiopians under Ras Alula.

Dogberry (dog′beri″). Absurd constable in Shakespeare's *Much Ado about Nothing.*

Doge's Palace (dō′jẹz). Palace of the doges of Venice. The present building was begun by Marino Faliero in 1354, but only the south and west façades retain their characteristic Gothic style of architecture. The basement is a noble and massive arcade with cylindrical columns; above this is another arcade, with twice the number of columns, and graceful, sharp-cusped arches with a range of quatrefoils above them. The upper part of the building is a square mass, with later enriched balconies in the middle of each façade, broad pointed windows irregularly placed, a line of small circles above, and flamed battlements. The superstructure is in itself heavy, but is rendered effective by the color of its diaperwork of pink and white marble. The allegorical and Biblical sculptures of the capitals of the lower arcade and of the three angles of the palace are famous. The great entrance, the Porta della Carta, the court, and the Giants' Staircase with its colossal figures of Mars and Neptune are excellent works of the Renaissance. The halls of the interior are adorned with the masterpieces of Tintoretto, Titian, Paolo Veronese, and other great Venetians.

Dogger Bank (dog′ėr). [Also, **Doggerbank.**] Sand bank in the central North Sea. It is noted for its extensive and valuable fisheries. It was the scene of an indecisive naval battle between the English under Sir Hyde Parker and the Dutch in 1781. In 1904 a Russian fleet on its way to the Far East during the Russo-Japanese War fired on some British fishing vessels off Dogger Bank. The incident caused ill feeling for a time, but the claims were settled by a commission. A naval engagement of World War I took place (Jan. 24, 1915) here. This engagement was a defeat for German naval strength and resulted in the loss of the cruiser *Blücher* and heavy damage to two battle cruisers. The British squadron of Admiral Beatty had its flagship *Lion* damaged.

Doggett (dog′ẹt), **Thomas.** b. at Dublin, Ireland; d. Oct. (or Sept.) 21 or 22, 1721. English actor. He was before the public from 1691 to 1713. He established in 1716 a prize in the Thames rowing match, given every year on the first of August. It was an orange-colored livery and a badge, and was given in honor of George I. The custom is still kept up under the supervision of the Fishmongers' Company.

Doggrell (dog′rẹl). Foolish poet in Abraham Cowley's play *The Guardian.* He was omitted in *The Cutter of Coleman Street,* a revision.

Dogon (dō′gōn). [Also: **Habbe, Kado, Tombo.**] Sudanic-speaking people of W Africa, inhabiting S French Sudan, S and E of the Niger River. Their population is estimated at ab. 180,000 (by Y. Urvoy, *Petit Atlas ethno-demographique du Soudan*, 1942). They live in villages on the rocky cliffs of the region. They practice agriculture with wooden hoes, and their principal food is millet. They are non-Mohammedans.

Do-Good Papers. Essays by Benjamin Franklin published in *The New England Courant* in 1772.

Dog River. Former name of **Hood River.**

Dogs, Isle of. Peninsula in SE England, in London, in Poplar metropolitan borough. It projects into the river Thames opposite Greenwich and is cut across from E to W by the canal of the West India Docks. It contains docks and shipbuilding yards.

Dog Star. See **Sirius.**

Doğubayazit (dō.gö″bä.yä.zēt′). [Turkish, **Doğubayazıt;** former names: **Ağri, Bayazit** (or **Bayazid** or **Bayezid**).] Town on the E border of Turkey, in the *il* (province or vilayet) of Ağri, S of Mount Ararat. It was taken by the Russians in the wars of 1828 and 1877. Pop. ab. 1,800.

Doheny (dō.hē′ni), **Edward Laurence.** b. at Fond du Lac, Wis., Aug. 10, 1856; d. at Beverly Hills, Calif., Sept. 8, 1935. American oil speculator and financier, involved in the Teapot Dome scandals (1921 *et seq.*). Discovered (1892) oil near Westlake Park, Calif., starting a Los Angeles oil boom; organized Mexican Petroleum Company of California when wide automobile usage created a great demand for products of his oil interests; received (1922) U.S. government contract to build a naval fueling station at Pearl Harbor, and obtained leased drilling rights on naval oil reserve land at Elk Hills, Calif. When it was learned that he had sent 100,000 dollars in cash to U.S. Secretary of the Interior Albert B. Fall in 1921, he was investigated, indicted (1925) with Fall for bribery and conspiracy, but acquitted on both counts. The leases, however, had been canceled, and restitution was demanded on his profits from them.

Doherty (dō′ėr.ti), **Charles Joseph.** b. at Montreal, May 11, 1855; d. 1931. Canadian jurist and statesman. He was a judge of the superior court of the province of Quebec (1891–1906), a member of the Dominion House of Commons for some years beginning in 1908, minister of justice (1911–21), and for many years professor of civil and international law at McGill University, Montreal. He was a member of the Canadian delegation to the Paris Peace Conference after World War I, a signatory for Canada of the Versailles Treaty, and Canadian representative in the Assembly of the League of Nations (1920–21).

Doherty, Henry Latham. b. at Columbus, Ohio, May 15, 1870; d. at Philadelphia, Dec. 26, 1939. American utilities executive. Engineer and manager (1890–1905) of various utilities companies, he founded (1905) Henry L. Doherty and Company. He was a chief organizer (1910) and first president (1910–39) of the Cities Service Company, a holding company for almost 200 public utilities and petroleum properties (in recent years, almost entirely the latter) with assets of over a billion dollars.

Doherty, Robert Ernest. b. at Clay City, Ill., 1885; d. 1950. American educator. Associated (1909–31) with the General Electric Company, he was dean of the school of engineering (1933–36) at Yale, and became president (1936) of the Carnegie Institute of Technology at Pittsburgh. He wrote *Mathematics of Modern Engineering* (with E. G. Keller, 1936).

Dohm (dōm), **Ernst.** b. at Breslau, May 24, 1819; d. at Berlin, Feb. 5, 1883. German journalist and humorist; husband of Hedwig Dohm. He was for most of his life editor of *Kladderadatsch.* This comic Berlin weekly, one of a host of papers started when the censorship was lifted in 1848, became under his guidance (1849 *et seq.*) one of the wittiest publications in Germany, known for its literary quality and for its trenchant political satire. Dohm's play *Der trojanische Krieg* (1864) was itself a political satire. He also wrote *Das erste Debüt* (1860), *Ihr Retter* (1862), *Komm her* (1864), and translated La Fontaine's fables (1876–77).

Dohm, Hedwig. b. at Berlin, Sept. 20, 1833; d. there, Jan. 6, 1919. German feminist, playwright, and novelist; wife of Ernst Dohm. She wrote vigorously in favor of the emancipation of women (*Der Jesuitismus im Hausstand,* 1873; *Die Frau in der Wissenschaft,* 1874; *Der Frauen Natur und Recht,* 1876). She is also the author of light dramas (*Vom Stamme der Asra,* 1876; *Ein Schuss ins Schwarze,* 1878) as well as stories (*Frau Tannhäuser,* 1889) and novels (*Plein air,* 1891). Sharing with her husband an interest in Spanish culture, she wrote a history of Spanish literature (1867).

Dohnanyi (dō′nä.nyē), **Ernst von.** [Hungarian, **Ernő Dohnányi.**] b. at Pressburg, Hungary (now Bratislava, Czechoslavakia), July 27, 1877—. Hungarian composer and conductor. Studied at the Royal Academy of Music at Budapest; toured (1897–1908) in Europe, England, and the U.S. as a pianist; appointed (1908) professor of piano at the Hochschule at Berlin; director (1919) of the Budapest Conservatory. His compositions include the operas *Tante Simona* (1912), *Ivas Turm* (1922), and *The Tenor* (1929); important among his other works are the *Suite in F-sharp Minor* (Opus 19) for orchestra, and his four *Rhapsodies* (Opus 11) for piano. He has also composed a pantomime, concertos, string quartets, and piano works.

Dohrn (dōrn), **Anton.** b. at Stettin, Germany, 1840; d. at Munich, Germany, Sept. 26, 1909. German naturalist. He founded and directed the zoölogical station at Naples.

Doihara (dô.ē.hä.rä), **Kenji.** b. in Okayama prefecture, Japan, 1883; d. 1948. Japanese soldier, sometimes called the "Japanese Colonel Lawrence" (after the Englishman T. E. Lawrence). Doihara is famous as the behind-the-scenes instigator of several international incidents, particularly in China, which resulted usually in some Japanese aggressive action on that country. He was, for example, mayor of Mukden at the time of the Manchuria incident of 1931. Indicted as a war criminal after World War II, he was tried and sentenced to death by hanging.

Doisy (doi′zi), **Edward Adelbert.** b. at Hume, Ill., Nov. 13, 1893—. American biochemist. He has been professor of biochemistry (1923 *et seq.*) at the St. Louis University Medical School and director (1924 *et seq.*) of the biochemistry department at St. Mary's Hospital, St. Louis. Notable for his work on blood buffers, he isolated (1929) the sex hormones theelol, theelin, and dihydrotheelin, isolated two forms of crystalline vitamin K, and synthesized vitamin K 1 antibiotic compounds. He shared the Nobel prize in physiology for 1943 with Henrik Dam.

Dokhosie (dō.kōs′yā). See **Dorhosye.**

Doktor Faust (dok′tôr foust). Opera by Ferruccio Busoni, with a libretto by the composer giving his own adaptation of the story, first performed at Dresden on May 21, 1925.

Dol (dol). [Full name, **Dol-de-Bretagne** (dol.dẹ.brẹ-tány′).] Town in W France, in the department of Ille-et-Vilaine, formerly situated on the Bay of Mont-St.-Michel (today separated from it by the swampland of Dol), ab. 14 mi. SE of St.-Malo. The cathedral, dating mainly from the 13th century, with later additions, is in the Norman Gothic style. The town witnessed many sieges in the Middle Ages, one (1075) by William the Conqueror. 4,861 (1946).

Dola (dō′lä). See **Zula.**

Dolabella (dol.ạ.bel′ạ), **Publius Cornelius.** b. c70 B.C.; d. at Laodicea, in Asia Minor, 43 B.C. Roman patrician, noted chiefly as the son-in-law of Cicero. Ruined by his profligate habits, he sought to restore his fortunes by joining the standard of Caesar in the civil war. He commanded Caesar's fleet in the Adriatic in 49, and in 48 participated in the battle of Pharsalus. He obtained the consulship after the death of Caesar in 44. At first he acted in support of the senate, but was subsequently influenced by bribery to join the party of Antony. He received from Antony the province of Syria as his proconsulate, but was defeated at Laodicea by Cassius. He was, at his own request, killed by one of his soldiers in order not to fall into the hands of the enemy.

Dola Sequanorum (dō′lạ sek.wạ.nōr′um). Latin name of **Dôle,** France.

Dolbear (dol′bär), **Amos Emerson.** b. at Norwich, Conn., Nov. 10, 1837; d. Feb. 23, 1910. American physicist and inventor, professor of physics at Tufts College from 1874, best known for his inventions in telephony and wireless telegraphy. He invented the static telephone in 1879 and the air-space cable in 1882.

Dolbeau (dol.bō'). Town in Quebec, Canada, on the Mistassini River ab. 20 mi. N of Lake St. John and ab. 96 mi. NW of Chicoutimi. It has small industries, which use the water power generated in the area. 4,307 (1951).

Dolce (dōl'chā), **Lodovico.** b. at Venice, c1508; d. there, c1568. Italian poet and prolific miscellaneous writer, by profession a proofreader. He died in great poverty.

Dolci (dōl'chē) or **Dolce** (dōl'chē), **Carlo** (or **Carlino**). b. at Florence, May 25, 1616; d. there, Jan. 17, 1686. Florentine painter of religious subjects, a pupil of Jacopo Vignali.

Dol Common (dol kom'on). See **Common, Dol.**

Dôle (dōl). [Latin, **Dola Sequanorum.**] Town in E France, in the department of Jura, situated on the Doubs River and the Rhine-Rhone Canal, ab. 27 mi. SE of Dijon. The former capital of the Franche-Comté, it was ceded to France in 1678. It preserves the architectural character of the 16th and 17th centuries and has various old churches and secular buildings. There are numerous medieval castles in the region. The town has stone quarries, potteries, and metallurgical and chemical industries. 18,250 (1946).

Dôle. [Also, **La Dôle.**] One of the highest mountains of the Jura range, situated in the canton of Vaud, Switzerland, near the French border, ab. 17 mi. N of Geneva. Elevation, ab. 5,505 ft.

Dole (dōl), **Nathan Haskell.** b. at Chelsea, Mass., Aug. 31, 1852; d. at Yonkers, N.Y., May 9, 1935. American author, journalist, and translator. He was the author of *A Young Folks' History of Russia* (1881), *A Score of Famous Composers* (1891), *The Hawthorn Tree, and Other Poems* (1895), *Omar, the Tent-maker* (1899), *Peace and Progress* (1904), reissued as *The Building of the Organ* (1906), *The Pilgrims* (1908), and *A Teacher of Dante* (1908), and translator of works from many languages, among them Spanish, Italian, French, and Russian (including the writings of Tolstoy).

Dole, Sanford Ballard. b. at Honolulu, April 23, 1844; d. June 9, 1926. American jurist; president of the republic of Hawaii and first governor of the Territory of Hawaii. The son of a New England missionary who brought Christianity to the Hawaiian Islands, he was educated in missionary schools there, attended Williams College, was admitted to the bar in Massachusetts, and established his practice at Honolulu. He was elected (1884, 1886) to the Hawaiian legislature and helped lead the so-called bayonet revolution of 1887 which established certain constitutional reforms limiting the power of the monarchy; at the end of the year he was appointed associate justice of the supreme court. He held his post until his resignation (1893) when he became head of the revolutionary provisional government which overthrew the monarchy of Queen Liliuokalani, after the queen had attempted to do away with the 1887 constitution. From 1894, when the republic of Hawaii was formally declared, he served as its president, attempting to have Hawaii annexed to the U.S., but without success because of the opposition of President Cleveland. When McKinley became president, annexation (1897) quickly took place, and Dole was appointed first governor (1900–03) of the Territory of Hawaii. Resigning that post, he served until 1915 as judge of the U.S. district court for Hawaii.

Dolega-Kamieński (dô.le'gä.kä.myen'skē). Pseudonym of **Kamieński, Lucian.**

Dolet (do.le), **Étienne.** b. at Orléans, France, 1509; hanged and then burned at Paris, Aug. 3, 1546. French scholar and printer. Educated at Paris and Padua, he was secretary to the French ambassador at Venice, returned to Toulouse to study law, and was expelled after joining in disputes there. He obtained the right from Francis I to publish certain works, but, because of his entering into religious controversy, was accused of publishing atheistic material. He was imprisoned twice but released; a third time he was held guilty and executed.

Dolgelley (dol.gel'i). [Also, **Dolgelly.**] Urban district and market town in N Wales, in Merionethshire, situated at the confluence of the rivers Aran and Wnion, ab. 9 mi. E of Barmouth, ab. 224 mi. NW of London by rail. Dolgelley is the county seat of Merionethshire. It is one of the few places in Wales where the curfew is still rung nightly. 2,246 (1951).

Dolgeville (dolj'vil). Village in E New York, in Fulton and Herkimer counties: manufactures of felt. 3,204 (1950).

Dolgoruki (dôl.go.rö'ki), **Ivan Alekseyevich.** Executed at Novgorod, Russia, Nov. 6, 1739. Russian noble, accused of conspiracy against the czarina Anna.

Dolgoruki, Ivan Mikhailovich. b. April 18, 1764; d. Dec. 16, 1823. Russian poet. He was governor of Vladimir from 1802 to 1812. The first edition of his poetical works appeared in 1806.

Dolgoruki, Katarina Mikhailovna. b. 1846; d. 1922. Second wife (July 31 1880) of Czar Alexander II of Russia. She published, under the pseudonym Victor Laferté, *Alexandre II: détails inédits sur sa vie intime et sa mort* (1882).

Dolgoruki, Peter Vladimirovich. b. at Moscow, 1807; d. at Bern, Switzerland, Aug. 17, 1868. Russian writer, exiled on account of his work *La Vérité sur la Russie* (1860).

d'Olier (dōl'yā), **Franklin.** b. at Burlington, N.J., April 28, 1877—. American insurance executive who was elected (Nov. 12, 1919) first national commander of the American Legion. He was a U.S. army officer (1917–19) in France during World War I and served as chairman (1944–46) of the U.S. Strategic Bombing Survey in Germany and Japan in World War II.

Dollallolla (dol.a.lol'a), **Queen.** Wife of King Arthur and mother of Huncamunca in Henry Fielding's burlesque *The Tragedy of Tragedies, or the Life and Death of Tom Thumb the Great.* She is entirely faultless, except that she is a little given to drink, is a little too much of a virago toward her husband, and is in love with Tom Thumb.

Dollar (dol'ar). Police burgh in C Scotland, in Clackmannanshire, situated near the river Devon, at the foot of the Ochil Hills, ab. 5 mi. NE of Clackmannan, ab. 424 mi. N of London by rail. It has an academy, founded in 1818. 1,583 (est. 1948).

Dollar, Robert. b. at Falkirk, Scotland, March 20, 1844; d. at San Rafael, Calif., May 16, 1932. American shipowner, engaged chiefly in Far East trade. In the lumbering business (1882 *et seq.*), he bought (1893) his first ship to expedite lumber transportation in California. He turned to building cargo ships and began (1901) his Orient trade.

"Dollar Diplomacy." Epithet applied originally to the foreign policy of the U.S. under William Howard Taft and his secretary of state, Philander C. Knox. The Taft administration (1909–13) announced its intention not only to protect existing American overseas investments but also to encourage American industry and finance to seek foreign outlets for capital. With such support large sums were invested in China, particularly in the construction of railroads. The epithet was soon expanded to describe that area of U.S. foreign policy which seemed to be influenced by American economic interests abroad, notably in Latin America.

Dollar Law (dol'ar lô''). Mountain in S Scotland, in Peeblesshire, situated ab. 9 mi. SW of Peebles. Elevation, ab. 2,680 ft.

Dollart (dol'art). [Dutch, **Dollard** (dôl'ärt).] Arm of the North Sea at the mouth of the Ems River, between the NW part of Germany (former province of Hanover, Prussia) and the province of Groningen, Netherlands. It was formed by inundations in 1277 and subsequently. Length, 10 mi.; breadth, 4 to 8 mi.

Dollfuss (dol'fus), **Engelbert.** b. at Texing, Austria, Oct. 4, 1892; assassinated at Vienna, July 25, 1934. Austrian statesman. A Christian Socialist, he was minister of agriculture (1931–34) and served (1932–34) as chancellor, and as minister of foreign affairs and of defense and security. He tried to establish an authoritarian regime with Italian, British, and French assistance, the three countries supporting him in an attempt to preserve Austria as an independent nation, not only as a counter to the German Nazi state, but as part of the historical policy of resisting an Anschluss, an economic union of the German-speaking countries of central Europe. Opposed to both Socialists and Nazis, Dollfuss forcibly suppressed the Socialists at Vienna (February, 1934) and promulgated an authoritarian constitution for a corporate state, aided principally by his minister of justice Kurt von

Schuschnigg, and supported by the rightist militia forces under Emil Fey and Prince Ernst Rüdiger von Starhemberg, thus turning towards Italy for help rather than towards Germany. In July, he was assassinated by the Austrian Nazis in their abortive attempt to overthrow the government of Austria.

Dollier de Casson (do.lyā dẹ kȧ.sôṅ), **François.** fl. second half of 17th century. French missionary in Canada. He spent (c1668) a winter among the Nipissings, and in 1669 accompanied La Salle on an exploring expedition to the Ohio River. He separated from the expedition in the same year, with the view of establishing a mission among the Pottawattamies who inhabited the region of the upper lakes; but, finding the field occupied by the Jesuits, returned to the Sulpician seminary at Montreal. He was the author of *Histoire de Montréal.*

Döllinger (dėl′ing.ėr), **Ignaz.** b. at Bamberg, Bavaria, May 24, 1770; d. at Munich, Jan. 14, 1841. German physiologist and comparative anatomist, professor successively at Bamberg, Würzburg, Landshut, and Munich. He wrote *Werth und Bedeutung der vergleichenden Anatomie* (1814), *Grundzüge der Physiologie* (1835), and others.

Döllinger, Johann Joseph Ignaz von. b. at Bamberg, Bavaria, Feb. 28, 1799; d. at Munich, Jan. 10, 1890. German theologian, a leader in the "Old Catholic" movement; son of Ignaz Döllinger. He published *Kirche und Kirchen, Papstthum und Kirchenstaat* (1861), *Papstfabeln des Mittelalters* (1863), and others, and opposed decrees of the Vatican council (1869–70). He was excommunicated (1871).

Dolliver Romance (dol′i.vėr), **The.** Fragment by Nathaniel Hawthorne, the beginning of which was published in the *Atlantic Monthly* in July, 1864. It was published in 1876.

Dollond (dol′ọnd), **John.** b. at London, June 10, 1706; d. there, Nov. 30, 1761. English optician, the inventor of the achromatic telescope (1757–58); father of Peter Dollond.

Dollond, Peter. b. Feb. 24, 1730; d. at Kensington, London, July 2, 1820. English optician and maker of instruments; son of John Dollond.

Doll's House, A. Play by Henrik Ibsen, brought out (1879) at Christiania (Oslo). The chief character is Nora Helmer. Nora, having been sheltered by her husband from the realities of life, commits forgery when faced with a real-life situation. Out of this experience come her realization that she can live her own life, and her decision to leave the husband who has been treating her like a pampered doll.

Doll Tearsheet (dol′ tär′shēt). See **Tearsheet, Doll.**

Dolly's (dol′iz). Tavern in Paternoster Row, London, dating from the time of Queen Anne.

Dolly Varden (dol′i vär′dẹn). See **Varden, Dolly.**

Dolly Winthrop (win′thrọp). See **Winthrop, Dolly.**

Dolomieu (do.lo.myė), **Déodat Guy Silvain Tancrède Gratet de.** b. at Dolomieu, Isère, France, June 24, 1750; d. at Châteauneuf, Saône-et-Loire, France, Nov. 26, 1801. French geologist and mineralogist, for whom dolomite was named. His works include *Voyage aux îles de Lipari* (1783), *Mémoires sur les îles Ponces* (1788), and *Philosophie minéralogique* (1802).

Dolomites (dol′ọ.mīts). [Also: **Dolomite Alps, Dolomite Mountains.**] Group of limestone mountains in the Alps, in N Italy (Italian Tyrol). Highest peak, Marmolada (ab. 11,000 ft.).

Dolon (dō′lon) or **Dolon Nor** (dō′lon nôr′). See **Tolun.**

Dolopathos (do.lo.pȧ.tos). French romance of adventure, the work of Herbers, a trouvère of the 13th century. He says that he translated it from an old Latin manuscript of Dom Jéhans (Jean), a monk of the Abbaye d'Hauteselve or Hauteseille. The subject and style both show Oriental influence. It is a form of the old Eastern romance *The Seven Wise Men* (known also as the *Book of Sindibad*).

Dolores (dō.lō′rās). City in SW Uruguay, in Soriano department, on the San Salvador River: shipping point for grain. Pop. ab. 11,500.

Dolores, Grito de. [Eng. trans., "*Cry of Dolores.*"] First signal of revolt against Spanish rule in Mexico, and hence the overt beginning of the war for independence. On Sept. 16, 1810, the parish priest of Dolores, in Guanajuato, Miguel Hidalgo y Costilla, headed a band which freed some political prisoners. Hidalgo, after celebrating mass in the church, proclaimed a revolt; the raising of a banner was greeted with loud shouts against the government, and the outbreak soon assumed formidable proportions. The town of Dolores was later renamed Dolores Hidalgo.

Dolores, Mission. [Original name, **Mission of San Francisco de Asís.**] Franciscan mission founded under Father Junípero Serra in October, 1776, on the lagoon of Nuestra Señora de los Dolores (Our Lady of Sorrows), within the limits of the present city of San Francisco.

Dolores Hidalgo (dō.lō′rās ē.ᴛʜäl′gō). [Former name, **Dolores.**] City in C Mexico, in Guanajuato state, near the Río de la Laja River. It was named for Miguel Hidalgo y Costilla, revolutionist, who began the revolt against Spain here (1810) with the *Grito de Dolores* ("Cry of Dolores"). 5,915 (1940).

Dolores River (dọ.lō′rẹs). River in Colorado and Utah, a tributary of the Colorado River. It flows through a canyon 3,000 ft. deep. Length, ab. 250 mi.

Dolorosa (dol.ọ.rō′sạ), **Via.** See **Via Dolorosa.**

Dolorous Valley. In the Arthurian romances, a name for Edinburgh.

Dolton (dôl′tọn). Village in NE Illinois, in Cook County, near Chicago: residential community. 5,558 (1950).

Dolunnor (dō.lůn.nôr′). See **Tolun.**

Dom (dōm). Peak in S Switzerland, in the Valais Alps ab. 17 mi. SW of Brigue. It is the highest peak entirely in Swiss territory. Elevation, ab. 14,942 ft.

Domagk (dō′mäk), **Gerhard.** b. 1888—. German chemist and physician. He discovered (1932) the antibacterial action of the dye and sulfa-drug forerunner Prontosil, but did not realize that its action was due to its sulfanilamide portion (the discovery was publicized in 1935). Further study in France (despite German refusal to furnish Prontosil), England, and the U.S. led to sulfa-drug development in these countries. Domagk directed I. G. Farben's research institute at Elberfeld (1927 *et seq.*). He was offered, but did not accept, the Nobel prize in medicine for 1939.

Domain of Arnheim (ärn′hīm), **The.** Story by Edgar Allan Poe, published in 1847.

Domas y Valle (dō′mäs ē ʙä′lyā), **José.** b. at Cartagena, Spain, c1717; d. at Guatemala City, Oct. 9, 1803. Spanish naval officer and administrator. He distinguished himself as chief of a squadron on the coasts of Spain and Italy, commanded fleets in the West Indies during the war with England (1778–80), and was at the taking of Pensacola (1781) and the siege of Gibraltar (1783). From 1786 to 1794 he was governor of Panama, and from 1794 to 1801 captain-general of Guatemala.

Domaszewski (dō.mä.shef′skē), **Alfred von.** b. at Temesvár, Hungary (now Timişoara, Rumania), Oct. 30, 1856; d. at Heidelberg, Germany, July 2, 1927. German historian of ancient Roman life. He was professor (1890 *et seq.*) at the University of Heidelberg, and the author of *Die Religion des römischen Heeres* (The Religion of the Roman Army, 1895) and *Geschichte der römischen Kaiser* (History of the Roman Emperors, 1909).

Domat (do.mȧ) or **Daumat** (dō.mȧ), **Jean.** b. at Clermont, in Auvergne (now Clermont-Ferrand, Puy-de-Dôme), France, Nov. 30, 1625; d. at Paris, March 14, 1696. French jurist, author of *Les Lois civiles dans leur ordre naturel* (1689–97).

Domažlice (dô′mäzh.lē.tse). [German, **Taus, Tauss.**] Town in Czechoslovakia, in W Bohemia, situated on the Rubřina River, ab. 29 mi. SW of Plzeň. It is a station on the railroad line from Plzeň to Regensburg, in Bavaria. It is in the district of the "Chodove," the ancient guardians of the Czech frontier. The Germans were defeated here in 1040, and in 1431 by the Hussites. Buildings of interest include the castle of the Chodove, the Gothic Church of All Saints, and a museum. 7,228 (1947).

Dombasle (dôṅ.bäl), **Christophe Joseph Alexandre Mathieu de.** b. 1777; d. 1843. French agriculturist and innovator. He studied agricultural methods in other countries, and applied to French farming certain techniques borrowed from foreign practice, introducing also new products, and teaching the importance of improved care for livestock. In 1822 he established an agricultural school and a model farm near Nancy, and throughout his career he urged his ideas in numerous writings. A form of plow which he invented was named for him.

Dombasle-sur-Meurthe (dôṅ.bäl.sür.mėrt). [Also, **Dombasle.**] Town in E France, in the department of Meurthe-et-Moselle, situated at the junction of the Sanon and Meurthe rivers and the Marne-Rhine Canal, ab. 13 mi. SE of Nancy. It has a large soda factory. 8,036 (1946).

Dombey and Son (dom′bi). Novel by Dickens, issued originally in numbers, the first of which appeared in October, 1846. It was brought out in one volume in 1848. The original title was *Dealings with the Firm of Dombey and Son, Wholesale, Retail, and for Exportation.* Mr. Dombey, the father of little Paul and Florence, is a cold, unbending, pompous merchant. His chief ambition is to perpetuate the firm-name. However, after the death of his only son, little Paul, and the loss of his money, his obstinacy and pride are softened. Little Paul, the "son" in the title of the firm, is a delicate child who dies young. Florence, his devoted sister, marries Walter Gay, a clerk in her father's bank. Edith Dombey, the beautiful and scornful second wife of Mr. Dombey, elopes with Carker, his manager.

Dombrau (dom′brou). German name of **Dąbrowa Górnicza.**

Dombrowa Gora (dôm.brô′vä gö′rä). See **Dąbrowa Górnicza.**

Dombrowski (dôm.brôf′skē), **Jan Henryk.** [Also, **Dąbrowski.**] b. near Kraków, Poland, Aug. 29, 1755; d. at Wina-Gora, Posen, Prussia, June 6, 1818. Polish general. He served in the campaign of 1792 and in 1794 fought at Warsaw with Kosciusko. For Napoleon he organized (1797) the Polish legion at Milan, fighting in the several Italian campaigns until 1801. He served (1807) with distinction at Friedland, against the Austrians in 1809, and in the Russian campaigns of 1812–13. After Napoleon's fall, he became a general (1815) and senator palatine of the Polish kingdom. He retired in 1816.

Dom Casmurro (dōng käz.mör′rö). One of Brazil's outstanding novels, by Machado de Assís (1839–1908). It was published in 1900 at Rio de Janeiro, where its action takes place.

Domdaniel (dom.dan′yẹl). In the continuation of the *Arabian Nights' Entertainments* of Chavis and Cazotte, a seminary for evil magicians founded by the great magician Hal-il-Maugraby. It was an immense cavern "under the roots of the ocean" off the coast of Tunis, the resort of evil spirits and enchanters. It was finally destroyed. Southey makes its destruction the theme of his *Thalaba.*

Dôme de Chasseforêt (dōm dẹ shäs.fo.re). Central point of the Vanoise range, in the Tarentaise Alps, in SE France. Elevation, ab. 11,800 ft.

Domenech (do.me.nek), **Emmanuel Henri Dieudonné.** b. at Lyons, France, Nov. 4, 1825; d. 1905. French traveler and writer. He was an honorary canon of Montpellier, with the title of abbé.

Domenichino (dō.mā.nē.kē′nō). [Also: **Il Domenichino;** original name, **Domenico Zampieri.**] b. at Bologna, Italy, Oct. 21, 1581; d. at Naples, Italy, April 15, 1641. Italian painter. He was a student of the Carracci. Among his works are *Communion of Saint Jerome* (in the Vatican), *Martyrdom of Saint Agnes* (at Bologna), *Diana and her Nymphs* (at Rome), *Adam and Eve,* and *Saint Cecilia* (in the Louvre, Paris).

Domesday Book (dömz′dā). [Also, **Doomsday Book.**] Book containing a digest, in Latin, of the results of a census or survey of England undertaken by order of William I (William the Conqueror), and completed in 1086. It consists of two volumes in vellum, a large folio containing 382 pages and a quarto containing 450. They form a valuable record of the ownership, extent, and value of the lands of England (1) at the time of the survey, (2) at the dates of their bestowal (that is, at the time when they had been granted by the king), and (3) at the time of Edward the Confessor. The numbers of tenants and dependents, amount of livestock, and the like, were also recorded. The book was long kept under three different locks in the exchequer, along with the king's seal, but is now kept in the Record Office at London. In 1783 an edition, printed from types made for the purpose, was issued by the British government. The counties of Northumberland, Cumberland, Westmorland, and Durham were not included in the survey. There existed also local domesday books.

Domestic Symphony. English title of **Sinfonia Domestica.**

Domett (dom′ẹt), **Alfred.** b. at Camberwell Grove, Surrey, England, May 20, 1811; d. in England, Nov. 2, 1887. English poet and colonial statesman. He was educated at Cambridge and was called to the bar in 1841. In 1842 he went to New Zealand, where he filled many of the chief offices of the colony; he returned to England in 1871. He was the intimate friend of Robert Browning, who writes of him in *Waring* and *The Guardian Angel.* Among his works are volumes of poems published in 1833 and 1839. His "Christmas Hymn" appeared in *Blackwood's Magazine* about that time. He published *Ranolf and Amohia* (1872) and *Flotsam and Jetsam* (1877). He also wrote several official publications relating to New Zealand.

Domeyko (dō.mā′kō), **Ignatius.** b. at Niedzviadka, Lithuania, July 31, 1802; d. at Santiago, Chile, Jan. 23, 1889. Polish scientist. He was involved in the Polish revolt of 1830 and was compelled to leave the country, taking refuge at Paris. For several years he was engaged in mining work in Alsace. On invitation of the government of Chile he went to that country in 1838, founded a school of chemistry and mineralogy at Coquimbo, and was professor at the University of Santiago from 1839, and rector from 1867. Through his influence improved methods of mining were introduced into Chile, and the resources of the country were greatly developed. Besides numerous scientific papers and textbooks, he wrote *La Araucania y sus habitantes* (Santiago, 1845), a book on Chile (in the Polish language), and others.

Domfront (dôṅ.frôṅ). Town in NE France, in the department of Orne, situated on the Varenne River ab. 20 mi. N of Mayenne. It has a ruined castle, and was long one of the chief Norman strongholds. It was captured by William the Conqueror in 1048, and was often besieged in the English and religious wars. Pop. ab. 3,000.

Domingue (do.maṅg), **Michel.** Haitian Negro general and politician. He became president of the republic in June, 1874, and after a period of almost unequaled anarchy and tyranny directed against the mulatto party was forced to resign in 1875.

Domínguez (dō.mēng′geth), **José López.** See **López Domínguez, José.**

Dominic (dom′i.nik), Saint. [Original Spanish name, **Domingo de Guzmán.**] b. at Calaruega, in Old Castile, Spain, 1170; d. at Bologna, Italy, Aug. 6, 1221. Founder of the order of the Dominicans. He studied at the University of Palencia, and in 1194 became a canon of the cathedral at Osma. In 1204 he removed to Languedoc, where he preached with much vehemence against the Albigenses, debating with them and attempting their conversion, and founded the order of the Dominicans, which received papal confirmation in 1216. He was subsequently appointed *magister sacri palatii* (the Pope's own theologian) at Rome.

Dominica (dom.i.nē′kạ). [French, **La Dominique.**] Island in the Caribbean Sea, NE of Venezuela, between Martinique and Guadeloupe: one of the Windward Islands, a British colony. The chief products are citrus, bananas, and vanilla. It is the site of the last Carib settlement in the West Indies. Capital, Roseau; area, 305 sq. mi.; pop. 52,858 (est. 1949).

Dominican Republic (dọ.min′i.kạn). [Official Spanish name, **República Dominicana;** former names, **Santo Domingo, San Domingo.**] Republic in the E and larger part of the island of Hispaniola, in the Caribbean Sea, contiguous with Haiti.

Area, Population, Political Divisions. The republic is divided into 19 provinces for administrative purposes. Capital, Ciudad Trujillo; area, 19,129 sq. mi.; length, 240 mi.; width, 170 mi.; pop. 2,121,083 (1950).

Terrain and Agriculture. It is traversed by four mountain ranges, the largest being the Cordillera Central. In the interior there are elevated plains, especially the Vega Real, of great fertility and beauty. Sugar, cacao, and coffee are the principal exports.

History. The republic was formed in 1844, after a revolution by which it was separated from Haiti. From 1861 to 1865 it was held by Spain. In 1869 the president (Buenaventura Báez) signed with President Grant a treaty of annexation with the U.S., which the Senate at

Washington refused to ratify. There have been various wars with Haiti, political revolutions, and changes of the constitution. The U.S. maintained (1916–24) a military government here for the purpose of collecting debt payments. Generalissimo Rafael Leonidas Trujillo Molina was elected president in 1930 and again in 1942. In 1951 he was requested by the chamber of deputies to serve for a third term, but he refused and was succeeded (1952) by his brother Hector Trujillo Molina.

Dominicans (dǫ.min'i.kąnz). [Also, **Order of Preachers.**] Roman Catholic religious order, founded by Saint Dominic (c1170–1221). It was his observation of the prevalence of the Albigensian heresy in Languedoc which fired him with a purpose to institute an order to defend and propagate the Catholic faith by active, evangelistic preaching of the Gospel in all lands. Sent to Languedoc with one companion by Pope Innocent III in 1204, he established his first house for religious women at Prouille near Toulouse in 1206, and gradually gathered a small company of followers, which numbered 16 when in 1215 the Bishop of Toulouse granted them a church and recognized them as a congregation of his diocese. An ecumenical council at Rome in that year having declared against the establishment of new religious orders, Dominic and his followers adopted the Augustinian rule; but in 1216 Pope Honorius III confirmed them as an order and authorized their mission. In 1217, though only 17 in number, they dispersed throughout much of Europe, winning recruits, rapidly growing in numbers, and establishing communities at Rome (where the Pope gave them the church of Saint Sixtus), Bologna, Toulouse, Lyons, Paris, Madrid, Segovia, and other cities, especially at centers of learning. In 1219 the first general chapter of the order came into being at Bologna, and by the year of Saint Dominic's death it numbered eight national provinces. Dominicans, who wore a white habit, to which they added a black mantle when preaching (from this acquiring the name of Black Friars), were dedicated to the propagation of Catholic doctrine, the promotion of good morals, and the uprooting of heresy, by means of learning and teaching (their particular method of teaching being by way of preaching). The authority they acquired by their diligent theological studies resulted among other things in their close association with the Inquisition. The glory of the Dominican order is Saint Thomas Aquinas, but their roster includes many other notable names, as diverse as Albertus Magnus and Savonarola. In modern times the Dominicans continue to be the great evangelistic order of the Roman Catholic Church; in the U.S. they commonly conduct the missions held periodically in Catholic parishes for the instruction of the faithful and the revival of religious zeal. The Dominicans are governed by the decisions of annual general chapters, composed chiefly of elected delegates, and the priors of houses and provinces are chosen by election for limited terms. Because of the tradition that the Blessed Virgin Mary gave the rosary to Saint Dominic in a vision, that form of prayer is especially used and inculcated by Dominicans. Associated with them are sub-orders of Dominican Sisters (contemplative nuns) and of Brothers of Penitence of Saint Dominic (third order, or tertiaries).

Dominie Sampson (dom'i.ni samp'sǫn). See **Sampson, Dominie.**

Dominion (dǫ.min'yǫn). Coal-mining town on Cape Breton Island, Nova Scotia, situated at the E end of the southern peninsula of the island, near the city of Sydney. It is connected by rail and road with the other nearby mining towns. 3,143 (1951).

Dominion Day. National holiday of Canada, observed on July 1, which is the anniversary of the establishment, in 1867, of the Dominion of Canada as a union of Upper Canada, Lower Canada, New Brunswick, and Nova Scotia.

Dominis (dô'mē.nēs), **Marco Antonio de.** b. on the island of Rab (Arbe), in Dalmatia, 1566; d. at Rome, in September, 1624. Italian theologian and natural philosopher. He wrote *De radiis visus et lucis in vitris perspectivis et iride* (1611), *De republica ecclesiastica* (1617), and others.

Domino Noir (do.mē.nō nwär), **Le.** [Eng. trans., *"The Black Domino."*] Comic opera by Auber, words by Scribe, first produced at Paris in 1837.

Domitian (dǫ.mish'ąn). [Full Latin name, **Titus Flavius Domitianus Augustus.**] b. at Rome, Oct. 24, 51 A.D.; d. there, Sept. 18, 96 A.D. Roman emperor (81–96); second son of Vespasian and Flavia Domitilla, and the brother of Titus, whom he succeeded. He undertook a campaign against the Chatti in 83, in the course of which he began the construction of a boundary wall between the Danube and the Rhine. This wall was guarded by soldiers settled upon public lands (*agri decumates*) along its course. He carried on (86–90) unsuccessful wars against the Dacians under Decebalus, finally purchasing peace by the promise of a yearly tribute. He recalled Agricola, whose victories (78–84) in Britain aroused his jealousy. Though the beginning of his reign had been marked by sincere attempts to govern well, to enforce the laws, to build temples, and to supervise the government closely, the last years of his reign were sullied by cruelty and tyranny, induced by fear of revolt and assassination. He was murdered by the freedman Stephanus, at the instance of the empress and several officers of the court, who were in fear of their lives.

Domitilla (dom.i.til'ą). In James Shirley's play *The Royal Master*, a girl of 15 years who, in an innocent delusion, fixes her love upon the king, mistaking his promise to provide her with a husband for a proof of personal affection.

Domitilla, Flavia. First wife of Vespasian. She was the mother of Titus and Domitian.

Domitilla, Flavia. Wife of the consul Flavius Clemens, said to have been banished to Pandataria by Domitian for atheism (probably she followed Christian rites). She is regarded as a saint in the Roman Catholic Church.

Domitius Ulpianus (dǫ.mish'us ul.pi.ā'nus). See **Ulpian.**

Dom Juan, ou le festin de pierre (dôṅ zhü.äṅ ö lę fes.taṅ dę pyer). Comedy by Molière, first played in 1665. In 1673 it was turned into verse by Thomas Corneille. The second title is a mistake of Dorimond who first introduced Don Juan to the French stage c1658 in a play called *Le Festin de Pierre* (The Feast of Pierre), which he translated from the Spanish phrase *el convidado de piedra* (in French *le convié de pierre*, "the stone guest," referring to the statue of the commandant whom he named Pierre to explain it). Molière, finding the title established, adopted it.

Domleschg (dōm'leshk). Valley along the lower part of the Hinter Rhein, in the canton of Graubünden, Switzerland, S of Chur.

Dom Miguel (dôṅ mē.gel'). See **Miguel.**

Domna (dom'nạ), **Julia.** See **Julia Domna.**

Domnarvet (dôm.när'vet). Industrial center in C Sweden, in the *län* (county) of Kopparberg, on the Dal River ab. 14 mi. by rail SW of Falun. The Stora Kopparberg works here is one of the chief iron and steel works in Sweden, with blast furnaces, Bessemer ovens and electric ovens, a rolling mill, and fabricating mill. High-quality steel products are produced. The plant was established in 1878, and the industrial city of Borlänge which has grown up around it had a population of 20,947 in 1950.

Domnei: a Comedy of Woman Worship (dom'ni). Novel by James Branch Cabell, published in 1920. It is a revised version of his earlier novel *The Soul of Melicent* (1913).

Domnus (dom'nus). See **Donus.**

Domodossola (dǫ.mō.dôs'sō.lä). [Also, **Domo d'Ossola.**] Town and commune in NW Italy, in the *compartimento* (region) of Piedmont, in the province of Novara, situated in the Val d'Ossola (Ossola Valley) on the Toce River, ab. 47 mi. N of Novara, near the Swiss border. Owing to its location at the S end of the Simplon tunnel, which connects N Italy via Switzerland with the Rhine valley and with France, it is one of the most important railroad stations of Italy. It has a museum of natural history, and wine and fruit markets. It belonged in the Middle Ages to the bishop of Novara, in the 15th and 16th centuries to Switzerland, in 1714 became part of Austria, and in 1735 of Savoy. Napoleon I improved the road over the Simplon pass; the railroad was opened in 1906. Buildings of interest to tourists were undamaged in World War II. Pop. of commune, 10,645 (1936); of town, 9,193 (1936).

Dom Pedrito (dōm pę.drē'tö). City in S Brazil, in the state of Rio Grande do Sul. 11,465 (1950).

Domremy-la-Pucelle (dôṅ.rę.mē.là.pü.sel). [Also, **Domremy.**] Village in E France, in the department of Vosges, situated on the Meuse River, ab. 29 mi. SW of Nancy. It was the birthplace of Joan of Arc; the house where she was born has been preserved. 283 (1946).

Don (don). River in C England, in the West Riding of Yorkshire, rising near the Cheshire-Yorkshire border and flowing SE to Sheffield, thence NE past Rotherham, Doncaster, and Thorne to the river Ouse at Goole. The artificial channel from Snaith to Goole is known as the Dutch River. Length, ab. 70 mi.; navigable to Sheffield (39 mi).

Don. River in E Scotland, in Aberdeenshire. It rises on the Aberdeenshire-Banffshire boundary, ab. 10 mi. N of Braemar. It flows E across the county, reaching the North Sea ab. 2 mi. N of Aberdeen. The river is noted for the good fishing it provides. Length, ab. 82 mi.

Don (don; Russian, dôn). [Tartar, **Duna**; ancient name, **Tanais.**] River in the U.S.S.R. rising near Tula, ab. 90 mi. S of Moscow, and flowing generally S to the Sea of Azov. Before reaching the Sea of Azov it makes a large bend to the east, flows S past Stalingrad, and W past Rostov. Its chief tributary is the Donets. Length ab. 1,100 mi.

Doña Emilia (dō'nyä ā.mē'lyä). Charles Gould's wife in Joseph Conrad's novel *Nostromo* (1904).

Donaghadee (don"ą.ċhą.dē'). Urban district and seaport in Ulster province, Northern Ireland, in County Down, situated on the North Channel ab. 17 mi. E of Belfast. 3,455 (1947).

Donalbain (don'ąl.bān). In Shakespeare's *Macbeth*, son of Duncan, king of Scotland.

Donald (don'ąld), **William Henry.** b. in New South Wales, Australia, 1874; d. Nov. 9, 1946. Australian journalist and adviser to Chinese government officials. Donald gained his early experience on newspapers at Sydney and Melbourne; he was with the *China Mail* at Hong Kong from 1902 to 1910, and subsequently he was editor of the *Far Eastern Review* (from 1911 to 1919). He was associated with Chinese officials as adviser from 1911 (when he was associated with Sun Yat-sen); later, he was associated with Chang Hsueh-liang. For many years he advised Chiang Kai-shek, playing a notable role in the Sian kidnaping affair of 1936, when Chiang was abducted by Chang Hsueh-liang. He was captured at Manila by the Japanese in 1940, and was interned until 1945.

Donaldson (don'ąld.sǫn), Sir **James.** b. at Aberdeen, Scotland, April 26, 1831; d. March 9, 1915. Scottish Hellenist. He became principal of the united colleges of St. Salvator and St. Leonard in the University of St. Andrews in 1886, and in 1890 principal of the university. He was knighted in 1907. He edited, in conjunction with Alexander Roberts, *The Ante-Nicene Christian Library* (1867–72), and was author of *Critical History of Christian Literature and Doctrine from the Death of the Apostles to the Nicene Council* (1864–66).

Donaldson, Jesse Monroe. b. in Shelby County, Ill., Aug. 17, 1885—. American public servant, U.S. postmaster general (1947–51). He first became a postal employee in 1908, being stationed in Illinois and later in Oklahoma until his promotion to the rank of post office inspector, in which capacity he served at Chattanooga, Tenn., and Kansas City, Mo., from 1915 to 1933. Thereafter he was successively deputy second assistant and deputy first assistant postmaster general, chief inspector of the department, and first assistant postmaster general, until Nov. 26, 1947, when by nomination of President Truman he became postmaster general, the first Post Office Department career man ever to hold that post.

Donaldson, John William. b. at London, June 7, 1811; d. there, Feb. 10, 1861. English classical philologist and Biblical critic. His works include *New Cratylus* (1839), *Varronianus* (1844), and *Jashar* (1854).

Donaldson, Thomas Leverton. b. at London, Oct. 19, 1795; d. there, Aug. 1, 1885. English architect and author. He was professor of architecture in University College, London (1841–65), and emeritus professor from 1865 until his death. His works include *Pompeii* (1827) and *A Collection of the Most Approved Examples of Doorways from Ancient Buildings in Greece and Italy* (1833).

Donaldsonville (don'ąld.sǫn.vil). City in SE Louisiana, parish seat of Ascension Parish. Rice, sugar, and cotton are produced in the area. 4,150 (1950).

Donalsonville (don'ąl.sǫn.vil). City in SW Georgia, county seat of Seminole County, ab. 50 mi. NW of Tallahassee, Fla. Farm products, naval stores, and lumber are produced in the region, and it is popular with hunters. The city has a number of peanut-shelling plants. 2,569 (1950).

Donar (dō'när). German form of **Thor.**

Donatello (don.ą.tel'ō; Italian, dō.nä.tel'lō). [Full original name, **Donato di Niccolò di Betto Bardi.**] b. at Florence, Italy, c1368; d. there, Dec. 13, 1466. Florentine sculptor, one of the great artists of the Renaissance. It has been said that the Renaissance began in Florence with Donatello, but in his first period (1410–24) his work was not so much influenced by the relics of antiquity as by his own insistence on realism. As much as any other artist of the Renaissance, he broke forever the grip of the static art of the early Middle Ages, but his earlier work is closer to the Gothic than to the Classic style, and he was a precursor not only of Michelangelo but of Rodin, especially in the creation that was his own favorite, the *Zuccone* ("Pumpkin-head") in the Campanile at Florence. After 1425, having had an opportunity to study, which he did avidly, the remains of ancient art then existing in Rome, he conformed his style ever more closely to classic models, first in such works as the mausoleums of Pope John XVIII at Florence, of Cardinal Brancacci at Naples, and of Bartolommeo Aragazzi at Montepulciano, and later in masterpieces such as the *David*, the *Cupid*, and the *Angel with Tambourine.* In this period he executed a number of notable works in Padua, including the powerful figure of the warrior *Gattemalata*, the first bronze equestrian statue of modern times, which is generally rated with the renowned figure of Colleone by Donatello's pupil Verocchio. It is related that Donatello turned his back on the praise and emoluments which rewarded his work in Padua because he felt that the critical fault-finding of his Florentine compatriots was necessary to his artistic growth. Not only Verocchio, but also the painters Masaccio, Pollaiuolo, Andrea del Castagno and Desiderio da Settignano were powerfully influenced by Donatello.

Donatello. Character in *The Marble Faun* (1860) by Nathaniel Hawthorne. He is an impulsive young Tuscan count whose likeness to the statue of the faun by Praxiteles gives the title to the book.

Donati (dō.nä'tē), **Giovanni Battista.** b. at Pisa, Italy, Dec. 16, 1826; d. at Florence, Sept. 20, 1873. Italian astronomer. He discovered (June 2, 1858) the comet named for him. He was director (1864) of the observatory at Florence, and that year, by subjecting the light of a comet to spectrographic analysis, demonstrated the gaseous nature of comets.

Donation of Constantine (kon'stąn.tīn, -tēn), **The.** Medieval forgery, of unknown date and origin, which pretends to be an imperial edict issued by Constantine I (Constantine the Great) in 324 conferring the temporal and spiritual sovereignty of Italy and the West on the papal see. It was probably composed about the middle of the 8th century; in 1444 Lorenzo Valla demonstrated that it was a forgery.

Donatists (don'ą.tists). Early Christian sect in Africa which originated in a dispute over the election (311 A.D.) of Caecilian to the see of Carthage, occasioned by his opposition to the extreme reverence paid to relics of martyrs and to the sufferers for the Christian faith called confessors.

Donatus (dǫ.nā'tus). fl. early 4th century. Bishop of Casae Nigrae during the Diocletian persecution, and leader of a party which courted martyrdom with fanatical enthusiasm, and regarded with horror the traditores, or those who to escape their persecutors delivered up to them the sacred books. This division was the starting point of the Donatist schism, though the party was probably named from Donatus the Great, rather than from Donatus of Casae Nigrae.

Donatus, Aelius. fl. in the middle of the 4th century A.D. Roman grammarian and rhetorician; teacher of

Saint Jerome. Of his works we possess a Latin grammar, *Ars grammatica*, a commentary on Terence, and the preface and introduction (with other fragments) of a commentary on Vergil. The grammatical work was extremely popular and was translated into Greek; its reputation was such that it became the common name for an elementary grammar (donet, donat) and was thus used in English as late as the 16th century.

Donatus the Great. fl. 4th century A.D. Bishop of Carthage (315 *et seq.*). He was elected by the rigorists or opponents of the moderate party or traditores to succeed Majorinus who had been elected by them in opposition to Caecilian, elected by the moderates and deposed by the rigorists in a council assembled at Carthage. It was for this Donatus that the Donatist party probably was named.

Donau (dō′nou). German name of the **Danube.**

Donaueschingen (dō.nou.esh′ing.ẹn). Town in S Germany, in the *Land* (state) of Baden, French Zone, formerly in the free state of Baden, situated at the union of the Brigach and Brege rivers, considered the source of the Danube River, ab. 30 mi. E of Freiburg im Breisgau. It has small industries including brewing and brush manufactures, and cattle and lumber markets, and is frequented as a health resort. The Church of Saint Sebastian dates from 1614. The castle of Count Fürstenberg, erected in 1722, contains art collections, with important old German paintings of the 15th and 16th centuries, and a large library and archives of over 150,000 volumes, incunabula, and manuscripts, among others Codex C of the *Nibelungenlied* and the *Schwabenspiegel* of 1286, an outstanding source of medieval law. In the early Middle Ages the town belonged to the convent of Reichenau; it became part of Baden in 1806. The population is predominantly Roman Catholic. 6,911 (1947).

Donau Moos (dō′nou mōs′). [Former name, **Schrobenheimer Moos.**] Marshy district in Bavaria, S Germany, lying S of the Danube near Ingolstadt.

Donauwörth (dō′nou.vėrt). Town in S Germany, in the *Land* (state) of Bavaria, American Zone, in the *Regierungsbezirk* (government district) of Swabia, situated at the junction of the Wörnitz and Danube rivers, ab. 25 mi. N of Augsburg. It has livestock and lumber markets, brewing, basket weaving, and tool manufactures. Architecturally the town has preserved its medieval character. Structures of interest include walls and gates, numerous old houses, the *Rathaus* (town hall), customs house, and dance hall (14th and 15th centuries), the Fugger House (16th century), and the church of the Holy Cross, in the Gothic style. There are a number of educational institutions, mostly under ecclesiastical guidance. In the 12th century part of the Hohenstaufen domain, Donauwörth became a free imperial city in 1348. When in 1606 the Protestant population intercepted a Catholic procession, the town was condemned by the emperor Rudolf II and occupied by Duke Maximilian I of Bavaria; this was one of the incidents leading to the outbreak of the Thirty Years' War. The town was occupied by Gustavus II (Gustavus Adolphus) of Sweden in 1632, and by Emperor Ferdinand II in 1634. It was again a free city for a short period (1705–14) and from then on definitely belonged to Bavaria. The population is predominantly Roman Catholic. 7,298 (1946).

Donawitz (dō′nä.vits). Town in E Austria, in the province of Styria, a station on the railroad line from Leoben to Hieflau, W of Leoben. It has iron foundries and steelworks of the Austrian Alpine Montan Company. Soft coal (lignite) is mined in the vicinity. The town has recently been incorporated into the city of Leoben.

Donbas or **Donbass** (don.bäs′). See **Donets Basin.**

Don Benito (dōm bā.nē′tō). Town in W Spain, in the province of Badajoz, situated near the Guadiana River, ab. 57 mi. E of Badajoz: marketing point for wine, olive oil, and melons. 20,931 (1940).

Don Carlos (don kär′lọs). See also **Carlos, Don.**

Don Carlos. [Full title, **Don Carlos, Prince of Spain.**] Tragedy in rhymed verse by Thomas Otway, produced in 1676. The story is taken from the Abbé de St. Real, and the plot is simpler than in Schiller's play on the same subject.

Don Carlos. Play in blank verse by Schiller, completed in 1787. The play contrasts despotism and intolerance, embodied in Philip II of Spain, with liberalism and religious freedom, whose protagonists are Don Carlos, the king's son, and the Marquis Posa, his friend.

Don Carlos. Opera by Michael Andrew Agnus Costa, words by Tarantini, produced at London on June 20, 1844.

Don Carlos. Opera by Verdi, words by Joseph Méry and Camille du Locle, first produced at Paris, on March 11, 1867.

Doncaster (dong′kạs.tėr). [Latin, **Danum**; Saxon, **Donecester, Doneceaster.**] County borough, market town, and industrial center in N central England, in the West Riding of Yorkshire, situated on the river Don ab. 32 mi. S of York, 156 mi. N of London by rail. Its industries include coal mining, iron and steel works, and locomotive building and repairing. Doncaster is the shopping and social center of a thickly populated district. It was a river port in the Middle Ages. 81,896 (1951).

Doncaster, 1st Viscount of. A title of **Hay, James.**

Don César de Bazan (dôn sā.zàr dẹ bà.zän). French comedy by Philippe François Pinel Dumanoir and Adolphe Philippe Dennery, from an episode in Victor Hugo's play *Ruy Blas*, produced in 1844. The comedy has also been played in English. Don César is the ruined Count of Garofa; he assumes the name of Zafari, and retains in his rags his frank, gay nonchalance.

Don César de Bazan. Comic opera by Jules Massenet, first produced at Paris, on Nov. 30, 1872.

Don Cossacks (don kos′aks), **Province** (or **Territory**) **of the.** Former district in S Russia, situated in the valley of the lower Don River. The area has now been divided between the Rostov and Stalingrad *oblasts* (regions) of the Russian Soviet Federated Socialist Republics.

Donder (dôn.der), **Théophile de.** b. at Brussels, Belgium, 1872—. Belgian professor. He was graduated from the University of Brussels, where he taught mathematical physics, and was a visiting lecturer (1926) at the Massachusetts Institute of Technology.

Donderberg (dun′dėr.bėrg). [Also, **Dunderberg.**] Chief mountain at the S entrance to the Highlands of the Hudson, in SE New York, opposite Peekskill. Elevation, ab. 865 ft.

Donders (dôn′dėrs), **Frans Cornelis.** b. at Tilburg, Netherlands, May 27, 1818; d. at Utrecht, Netherlands, March 24, 1889. Dutch oculist. His chief work is *Anomalies of Accommodation and Refraction of the Eye* (published by the Sydenham Society, 1865).

Dondo (don′dō). Town in Angola, in SW Africa, on the right bank of the Cuanza River and at the head of river navigation, ab. 100 mi. SE of Luanda. It is the terminus of several caravan roads, and the principal market for the coffee grown in the region. Pop. ab. 4,000.

Dondra Head (don′drạ). Southernmost cape of Ceylon, projecting into the Indian Ocean.

Donegal (don′ẹ.gôl, don.ẹ.gôl′). [Irish, **Dún na nGall.**] Maritime county in Ulster province, Irish Republic, the northwesternmost of the Irish counties. It is bounded on the N and W by the Atlantic Ocean, on the E by Counties Londonderry and Tyrone (Northern Ireland), on the SE by County Fermanagh (Northern Ireland), and on the S by County Leitrim (Irish Republic) and Donegal Bay. The coastline is rugged and deeply indented. The surface is generally barren and mountainous, with many bogs and lakes. Most of the settlement is confined to the coastal plain where fishing and subsistence agriculture can be carried on. Large numbers of sheep are pastured on the uplands, providing wool for Donegal tweeds. There is no factory production, the textile manufacture being of the home-industry type. Donegal is the county seat; area, ab. 1,865 sq. mi.; pop. 131,511 (1951).

Donegal. Town in NW Irish Republic, county seat of County Donegal, at the head of Donegal Bay ab. 40 mi. SW of Londonderry. It is a small seaport and market town exporting grain, eggs, and butter, and has a castle, and ruins of a Franciscan monastery. 1,315 (1936).

Donegal Bay. Inlet of the Atlantic Ocean, lying between Connacht and Ulster provinces, and between Counties Donegal, Leitrim, and Sligo, in the Irish Republic, on the W coast of Ireland. Width, ab. 30 mi.

Donelaitis (dō.ne.lī′tis), **Kristijonas.** [Latinized, **Donalitius.**] b. at Lazdynėliai, in East Prussia, Jan. 1, 1714; d. at Tolminkiemis, Feb. 18, 1780. Most prominent of earlier Lithuanian poets. He studied Protestant theology at the University of Königsberg, and was pastor at Tolminkiemis from 1743 on. He was a strong supporter of the Lithuanian traditions and folkways in East Prussia, which was being Germanized in his time. In classical form, using the hexameter, he realistically portrayed the life and poverty of the Lithuanian serfs in the idyls *Pavasario linksmybes* (The Joys of Spring), *Vasaros darbai* (Summer's Toil), *Rudens gerybes* (The Fruits of Autumn), and *Žiemos rūpesčiai* (Winter's Hardships); he also wrote some fables in hexameter. These idyls were published posthumously in 1818 by L. Rėza (Rhesa) and are known as *Metai* (The Seasons). Other editions of his works by A. Schleicher (1865), G. F. F. Nesselmann (1869), J. Šlapelis (1914), M. Biržiška (1921, 1927), J. Ambrazevičius (1940).

Donelson (don'ẹl.sọn), **Andrew Jackson.** b. near Nashville, Tenn., Aug. 25, 1800; d. at Memphis, Tenn., June 26, 1871. American diplomat and politician; son of the brother-in-law of Andrew Jackson. He graduated from West Point and served under Jackson in the Seminole War. He was secretary to Jackson during the latter's term as president. Donelson was in charge of the negotiations concerning the annexation of Texas to the U.S., a matter he successfully concluded. He was U.S. minister to Prussia (1846–49), and was the unsuccessful candidate of the American Party (the Know-Nothings) for vice-president in 1856, running on the ticket headed by Fillmore.

Donelson, Fort. Fortification in NW Tennessee, situated on the Cumberland River ab. 63 mi. W by NW of Nashville. In the Civil War it was invested (Feb. 12–14, 1862) by Union forces under General Grant. Having sustained a bombardment by the Union gunboats under Commodore Foote on February 14, the garrison (which numbered ab. 18,000 effectives) made an unsuccessful sortie on February 15. The fort was surrendered by General Buckner on February 16; his senior officers, Generals Floyd and Pillow, escaped by the river. The Union troops numbered 15,000 at the beginning of the investment, and ab. 27,000 at the surrender. It was on this occasion that Grant, in replying to Buckner's statement of conditions for capitulation, wrote the well-known words: "No terms except an unconditional and immediate surrender can be accepted." The Union loss (army and navy, February 14–16) was 510 killed, 2,152 wounded, and 224 missing; the Confederate loss was ab. 2,000 killed and wounded, and 13,000 captured. The area is now a national military park.

Donets (do.nyets'). [Also: **Donetz, Donez.**] River in the U.S.S.R., chiefly in the Ukrainian Soviet Socialist Republic and in the Rostov *oblast* (region) of the Russian Soviet Federated Socialist Republic, the chief tributary of the Don, which it joins ab. 75 mi. above its mouth. Flowing generally SE through the Ukraine, the river makes a wide swing to the S and SW before it joins the Don. In this bend is the Donets Basin (called the Donbas), one of the chief industrial regions of the U.S.S.R. Length, ab. 650 mi.

Donets Basin. [In Russia called the **Donbas** or **Donbass.**] Region in SW U.S.S.R., in the Donets River valley, in E Ukrainian Soviet Socialist Republic and NW Rostov *oblast* (region) of the Russian Soviet Federated Socialist Republic. It is the greatest coal-mining region in the Soviet Union, with a production of ab. 78 million metric tons in 1938 (ab. 59 percent of the national total). The coal reserves are estimated at ab. 55 billion tons, of which over two thirds is anthracite. Coal mining began in 1790, and expanded especially in the last half of the 19th century, but the great growth of industrial cities and coking plants, chemical industries, iron and steel plants, and machinery industries took place in the 20th century. The Donbas was occupied by Axis armies in October, 1941 and was liberated by Russian forces in early 1943. Great damage was suffered by the mines and industries. Area, ab. 12,000 sq. mi.; pop. ab. 5,000,000 (1948).

Donez (do.nyets'). See **Donets.**

Don Felix (don fē'liks). See **Felix, Don.**

Don Fernando de Taos (don fėr.nan'dō dẹ tä'ōs, tous). See under **Taos** village.

Don Ferolo Whiskerandos (don fẹ.rō'lō hwis.kėr.an'dōz). See **Whiskerandos, Don Ferolo.**

Dongan (dong'gạn), **Thomas.** [Title, **Earl of Limerick.**] b. at Castletown, County Kildare, Ireland, 1634; d. at London, Dec. 14, 1715. Colonial governor of New York (1683–88). He was lieutenant governor (c1678–80) of Tangier and in 1682 was appointed governor of New York by the duke of York (later James II of England), replacing Edmund Andros. His governorship was marked by a stiffening of defenses against the French, including the establishment of a protectorate over the Iroquois and diplomatic and military moves. When New York was added to the Dominion of New England in 1688 he was superseded by Andros. In 1698 he became the 2nd Earl of Limerick, succeeding an elder brother.

Dongan Charter. Charter for the city of New York, granted by Thomas Dongan, lieutenant governor and vice-admiral of New York and its dependencies under James II of England, dated April 27, 1686. It remained in force until 1730. An early charter of the city of Albany, by the same authority, is known by the same name.

Don Garcia (dōn gär.chē'ä). Tragedy by Count Vittorio Alfieri, produced in 1785. It is drawn from the history of the Medici family; Don Garcia was one of the sons of Cosimo I (1519–74).

Don Garcie de Navarre (dôṅ gär.sē dẹ nȧ.vȧr). Play (1661) by Molière.

Don Giovanni (don jọ.vän'i; Italian, dōn jō.vän'nē). [Full title, **Don Giovanni, ossia il dissoluto punito;** Eng. trans., "*Don Juan, or the Libertine Punished.*"] Opera in two acts by Wolfgang Amadeus Mozart, with libretto by Lorenzo Da Ponte, first produced at Prague on Oct. 29, 1787. The legendary Spanish libertine, accompanied by his faithful but timorous servant Leporello, flees from the scorned Donna Elvira and from Donna Anna, whose father, the commendatore, he has slain. Don Giovanni becomes involved in a country wedding, at which he attempts to seduce Zerlina, the bride. His pursuers find him there, but again he manages to evade them by various tricks; his downfall comes when the murdered commendatore's statue comes to him at dinner to summon him to hell. The opera contains the duet *La ci darem la mano* and arias by Leporello (the catalogue aria) and Zerlina (*Batti, batti, o bel Masetto*).

Dong Nai (dông' nī'). [Also, **Donnai.**] River in SE Indochina, flowing from the high plateau of S Annam (Central Viet-Nam) generally SW to join the Saigon River in Cochin China (South Viet-Nam) ab. 5 mi. E of Saigon. In its middle course it descends sharply from the plateau to the lowland, with numerous falls. Length, ab. 280 mi.

Dongola (dong'gọ.lạ). Former province of the Anglo-Egyptian Sudan, now part of Northern Province. Merowe was the former capital. Dongola was captured (1885) by the Mahdi but was regained by the Egyptian army under General Kitchener, March–September, 1896.

Dongola. [Also: **Ordeh, New Dongola.**] Town in Northern Province, Anglo-Egyptian Sudan, in NE Africa, on the Nile River above the third cataract. It was built c1820, and was the largest town in the old province of Dongola. It was abandoned by the Anglo-Egyptian forces to the Mahdists in 1885, and was recaptured by the Egyptian army under General Sir Herbert Kitchener, on Sept. 23, 1896. Pop. ab. 9,000.

Dongola, Old. Ruined town in Nubia, NE Africa, situated on the Nile ab. 76 mi. SE of the modern town of Dongola (or New Dongola).

Dongson (dông'sôn'). **1.** Archaeological site in N Annam (Central Viet-Nam), where excavation of a cemetery of the 1st century A.D. yielded bronze objects of a previously unknown culture. **2.** Tentative name given to the Bronze Age culture of further India which, c300 B.C. or earlier, reached Indonesia and introduced there bronze casting (tools, weapons, ornaments, ceremonial drums), probably weaving (*ikat*), and a style of art characterized by an exuberance of decorative detail with curvilinear design elements.

Donham (don'ạm), **Wallace Brett.** b. at Rockland, Mass., Oct. 26, 1877—. American educator. He has been dean (1919–42) of the Harvard graduate school of business administration, and professor of administration (1942 *et seq.*). He is the author of *Business Adrift*, *Business Looks at the Unforeseen*, *Education for Responsible Living*, and other books.

Doniol (do.nyol), **Jean Henri Antoine.** b. at Riom, France, April 20, 1818; d. at Paris, June 19, 1906. French historian. He served (1882 *et seq.*) as director of the state printing office. His main work was *Histoire de la participation de la France à l'établissement des États-Unis d'Amérique* (History of the Participation of France in the Foundation of the United States, 1886–99).

Doniphan (don'i.fan), **Alexander William.** b. in Mason County, Ky., July 9, 1808; d. at Richmond, Mo., Aug. 8, 1887. American officer in the Mexican War. He was an eminent lawyer in Missouri from 1830, successfully defending in criminal cases. He commanded a brigade against the Mormons and refused to carry out a court-martial sentence of death against Joseph Smith and other Mormon leaders, a sentence later revoked. During the Mexican War, he was commanding officer in New Mexico, but gave the command over and conducted a regiment of Missourians from Valverde, N.M., to Chihuahua (December, 1846–March, 1847), fighting two battles on the way and covering more than 5,500 miles by land and water. This expedition is said to be one of the most brilliant long marches ever made.

Dönitz (dė'nits), **Karl.** See **Doenitz** or **Dönitz, Karl.**

Donizetti (don.i.zet'i; Italian, dō.nē.dzāt'tē), **Gaetano.** b. at Bergamo, Italy, Nov. 29, 1797; d. there, April 8, 1848. Italian operatic composer. He composed some 65 operas, among which are *Anna Bolena* (1830), *L'Elisire d'Amore* (1832), *Lucia di Lammermoor* (1835), *Lucrezia Borgia* (1834), *La Favorita* (1840), *La Fille du Regiment*, afterward *La Figlia del Reggimento* (1840), *Linda di Chamounix* (1842), and *Don Pasquale* (1843).

Don John (don' jon'). See **John, Don.**

Don Juan (don' wän'; also, especially in Byron, don jö'an; Spanish dōn hwän'). Legendary character of European tradition whose name is of Spanish origin. In the principal form of the legend, Don Juan Tenorio, who lived in the 14th century, the son of an illustrious family of Seville, killed the commandant Ulloa after having seduced his daughter. The Franciscan monks, wishing to put an end to the debaucheries of Don Juan, enticed him to their monastery and killed him, giving out that the statue of his victim (which had been erected there), incensed at an insult offered him (in the plays the statue of Ulloa is jeeringly invited to supper, and does come to the meal), had come down and dragged him to hell. Spanish and Italian plays were written on the subject, and Nicholas Drovin Dorimond introduced him to the French stage. Don Juan is the symbol of skeptical libertinism, and as such has been made the subject of the 17th-century drama *El Burlador de Sevilla y Convidado de Piedra* (The Deceiver of Seville and the Guest of Stone), by Gabriel Téllez (Tirso de Molina); of Molière's comedy *Don Juan, ou le festin de Pierre* (1665); of Mozart's opera *Don Giovanni* to Lorenzo da Ponte's libretto; of Christian Dietrich Grabbe's German drama *Don Juan und Faust* (1828); and of works by Thomas Corneille, Thomas Shadwell, Antonio de Zamora, Carlo Goldoni, Christoph Willibald Gluck, Alexandre Dumas the elder, José Zorilla y Moral, G. B. Shaw, and others. His name has become a synonym for libertine or rake. Byron's Don Juan takes only his name from the legend, the youthful introspective Byronic hero having no other connection with the cynical gallant of legend.

Don Juan. Incomplete poem by Byron, written in 1818 and published 1819–24.

Don Juan de Mañara (don wän' dā män.yä'ra). Opera in four acts by Eugene Goossens, with a libretto by Arnold Bennett, first performed at Covent Garden, London, on June 24, 1937.

Donker (dông'kėr), **Anthonie.** [Pseudonym of **N. A. C. Donkersloot** (dông'kėr.slōt).] b. 1902—. Dutch poet and essayist. A professor of Dutch literature at Amsterdam, he was a leader of the artists' resistance during the German occupation in World War II. His mildly melancholy poetry includes *Acheron* (1926), *Grenzen* (Boundaries, 1928), *Kruistochten* (Crusades, 1929), *De draad van Ariadne* (Ariadne's Thread, 1930), *Gebroken Licht* (Broken Light, 1934), *Onvoltooide Symphonie* (Unfinished Symphony, 1938), and *Orpheus and Eurydice* (1942). Some of his penetrating and well-considered essays (mainly published in *Vrije Bladen*, *Niuuwe Stem*, and *Critisch Bulletin*) were collected in *Fausten en Faunen* (1930), *Ter Zake* (To the Matter, 1932), *De Schichtige Pegasus* (Skittish Pegasus, 1932), and *Hannibal over de Helicon?* (1940). He has also written some novels and plays.

Donna (don'a). City in S Texas, in Hidalgo County, SW of Corpus Christi: shipping point for citrus fruits, winter vegetables, and canned goods. 7,171 (1950).

Donna Anna (dôn'nä än'nä). See **Anna, Donna.**

Donnacona (don.a.kō'na). Town in Portneuf County, Quebec, Canada, situated on the N bank of the St. Lawrence River, ab. 31 mi. W of the city of Quebec. 3,663 (1951).

Donna del Lago (dôn'nä del lä'gō), **La.** [Eng. trans., "*The Lady of the Lake.*"] Opera, based on Sir Walter Scott's poem, by Rossini, with a libretto by Tottola, first produced at Naples on Oct. 4, 1819.

Donnai (dôn'nī'). See **Dong Nai.**

Donnay (do.nā), **Maurice.** [Full name, **Charles Maurice Donnay.**] b. at Paris, Oct. 12, 1859; d. March 31, 1945. French playwright. He was a versatile author of frivolous comedies like *Education de Prince* (1900) and *La Patronne* (1908); librettos for musical comedy, such as *Le Mariage de Télémaque* (1910, with Jules Lemaître) and *Le Roi Candaule* (1920); psychological dramas, including *La Douloureuse* (1897) and *L'Autre Danger* (1902); satires, such as *La Clairière* (1900, with Lucien Descaves); problem plays such as his study of the Jewish question *Le Retour de Jérusalem* (1903). A trained engineer and graduate of the Central School in 1885, he made his theatrical debut with a semiprofessional troupe at the Chat Noir cabaret (1890–92). His plays are marked by his active sense of humor and great common sense. His incidental writings include a biography of Musset (1926) and three volumes of memoirs.

Donn-Byrne (don'bėrn'), **Brian Oswald.** [Known as **Donn Byrne.**] b. at New York, Nov. 20, 1889; d. in County Cork, Ireland, June 18, 1928. Irish-American novelist and short-story writer. He was a staff member of the *New Catholic Encyclopedia*, the *New Standard Dictionary*, the *Century Dictionary*, the New York *Sun*, and the Brooklyn *Eagle*, and contributed stories to *The Smart Set* and *Harper's*. He was the author of *The Stranger's Banquet* (1919), *The Foolish Matrons* (1920), *Messer Marco Polo* (1921), his great success; *The Wind That Bloweth* (1922), *The Changeling* (1923), *Blind Raftery* (1924), *Hangman's House* (1926), *Brother Saul* (1927), *Crusade* (1928), *Destiny Bay* (1928), and *Field of Honor* (1929).

Donndorf (don'dôrf), **Karl Adolf.** b. at Weimar, Germany, Feb. 16, 1835; d. 1916. German sculptor, professor of sculpture at the art school at Stuttgart from 1877.

Donne (dun, don), **John.** b. at London, in 1571 or 1572 (1573 according to his friend and biographer Isaak Walton); d. there, March 31, 1631. English poet and divine, the first and greatest of the so-called metaphysical poets. On his mother's side he was connected with Sir Thomas More and John Heywood. He was brought up as a Roman Catholic, and was educated at Oxford (1584), Cambridge (1587), and Lincoln's Inn (1592). In 1596 and 1597 he took part in the expeditions led by the earl of Essex against Cádiz and the Azores. In 1597 he was appointed secretary to Sir Thomas Egerton, Lord Keeper of the Great Seal, but lost his post in 1601 by his clandestine marriage to Egerton's niece, and was imprisoned (1602) for a time, the marriage being a violation of both common and canon law. After several years spent in fruitless attempts to obtain a position through court favor, his *Pseudo-Martyr* (1610) won him the notice of King James I. James, however, refused to promote him except in the Anglican Church, and at last, in 1615, Donne received Anglican orders. He was appointed successively royal chaplain, reader in divinity at Lincoln's Inn, and finally, in 1621, dean of Saint Paul's. In his later years he was widely regarded as the foremost preacher of his day.

Writings. Most of Donne's poems circulated in manuscript during his lifetime, and his collected poems were not published until 1633, after his death. His prose works include over 150 sermons, *Ignatius his Conclave* (a satirical attack on the Jesuits), and a small book of *Devotions* (written during a serious illness in 1623), from which Ernest Hemingway took the title *For Whom the Bell Tolls*. Donne's reputation stood very high during the 17th century, but during the 18th and 19th centuries, though never completely forgotten, he was little read. His modern reputation owes much to the edition of the *Poems* by H. J. C. Grierson (1912) and to the influence of the criticism of T. S. Eliot. Donne is best known for his love poems, his sonnet to Death (*Death, be not Proud*), and his *Anniversaries*, two elegies in memory of the 16-year-old Elizabeth Drury. His poetry is contrary to the courtly Petrarchan tradition established in English by Wyatt and Surrey; his approach is more natural, his attitude towards woman cynical, his writing more abrupt and witty.

Donne, John. [Called **the Younger.**] b. in May, 1604; d. at London, 1662. English writer; son of John Donne (c1573–1631). He was educated at Westminster School and at Oxford, where he was known for his dissipations. After an acquittal on a charge of manslaughter for the death of a young boy, he left for Padua, where he became a doctor of laws; upon his return to England he took holy orders (c1638). Some of his father's papers he gave to Izaak Walton the younger. He was the author of *Donnes Satyr* (1661–62), an indecent volume.

Donnelly (don'ẹl.i), **Ignatius.** b. at Philadelphia, Nov. 3, 1831; d. at Minneapolis, Jan. 1, 1901. American author, politician, and reformer. He settled in Minnesota in the 1850's, going into farming after the failure of a land venture in the panic of 1857. He became a Republican in politics, and at 28 years of age became lieutenant governor of Minnesota, later serving (1863–69) as a member of Congress. Abandoning the Republican ranks, he became a crusader against vested interests, edited (1874–79) the weekly *Anti-Monopolist*, served (1874–78) as a member of the state senate, and was affiliated on separate occasions with the Liberal Republican, Granger, and Greenback parties. Retiring from politics for a time, he took to study and writing, producing *Atlantis: The Antediluvian World* (1882), whose thesis is that civilization began in the legendary land of Atlantis; *Ragnarok: The Age of Fire and Gravel* (1883), in which the author argues the earth's collision with a comet in prehistoric times; and *The Great Cryptogram* (1888), in which he undertook to prove that Bacon was the author of Shakespeare's plays. He also wrote the futuristic novel *Caesar's Column; a Story of the Twentieth Century* (1891). In the late 1880's he became president of the Minnesota Farmers' Alliance, and led it into the Populist Party, in which he took a leading role. In his later years he edited the Populist *Representative* and served again in the Minnesota state legislature. Donnelly's success as a writer (both *Atlantis* and *Ragnarok* were very well received) was matched by his fame as an orator.

Donner (don'ėr), **Georg Raphael.** b. at Essling, Austria, May 25, 1692; d. at Vienna, Feb. 15, 1741. Austrian sculptor. He entered the imperial service in 1724, and in 1729 that of Prince Esterházy. His greatest works are the fountain on the Mehlmarkt and the fountain of Perseus at the old town hall, Vienna.

Donner Lake (don'ėr). Small lake in Nevada County, E California, in the Sierra Nevada.

Donner Party. Group of emigrants (including the Donner family from Sangamon County, Ill.) who camped (1846–47) at Truckee Lake (now Donner Lake) in the Sierra Nevada mountains while en route to California. Because of a wrong turn they lost time after leaving Fort Bridger, in Wyoming, and were trapped when heavy October snows blocked the passes. Their winter stay was marked by extreme hardship caused by starvation and bitter cold; of the 87 who originally made camp, only 47 survived, and most or all of these lived only because of their recourse to cannibalism. The survivors were finally rescued by California settlers who broke through the snowdrifts.

Donner Pass. Pass in N central California, through the Sierra Nevada range ab. 96 mi. by road NE of Sacramento. In the winter of 1846–47 the Donner Party, traveling overland from Illinois to California, was trapped in the severe winter conditions of this region, and nearly half of the group of 87 persons perished. The main transcontinental railroad to San Francisco traverses the pass, and in January, 1952, the modern streamlined train *City of San Francisco* was marooned in snowdrifts for four days here. Elevation, ab. 7,135 ft.

Donnissan (do.nē.säṅ), **Marie Louise Victoire de.** See **La Rochejacquelein** or **La Rochejaquelein, Marie Louise Victoire de Donnissan,** Marquise **de.**

Donnithorne (don'i.thôrn), **Arthur.** In George Eliot's novel *Adam Bede*, a vain, weak, good-natured young man, whose remorse for Hetty Sorrel's ruin lies chiefly in his chagrin at being found out and losing the approbation of his acquaintances.

Donnybrook (don'i.brůk). Town and parish in Leinster province, Irish Republic, in County Dublin. Donnybrook is now a part of the city of Dublin, located ab. 3 mi. SE of the city center. The town was formerly famous for its fair (held in August), proverbial for its good-humored rioting, established under King John and suppressed in 1855. It is now the center of an expensive residential district. 278 (1936).

Dono (dô'nō), **Paolo di.** See **Uccello, Paolo.**

Donora (dọ.nôr'ạ). Borough in SW Pennsylvania, in Washington County, on the Monongahela River near Pittsburgh: zinc smelting; manufactures of iron, steel, and wire. Founded in 1900, it was incorporated in 1901. Donora became the center of a news sensation in 1948 when smoke-impregnated fog blanketed the town, causing 20 deaths and making over 5,000 persons ill. 12,186 (1950).

Donoso (dō.nō'sō), **Justo.** b. at Santiago, Chile, 1800; d. at La Serena, Chile, Feb. 22, 1868. Chilean bishop. He was rector of a theological seminary at Santiago, lecturer at the university, and judge of the ecclesiastical court. He was named bishop of Ancud, Chile, in 1844, and was translated to the see of La Serena in 1855. His works on canonical law are authoritative throughout South America. A founder of *Revista Católica*, he wrote *Instituciones de derecho canónico americano* (1849), and others.

Donoso Cortés (kôr.tās'), **Juan Francisco María de la Salud.** [Title, Marquis of **Valdegamas.**] b. at El-Valle, Estremadura, Spain, May 6, 1809; d. at Paris, May 3, 1853. Spanish politician, diplomat, and writer. His works include *Consideraciones sobre la diplomacia* (1834) and *La ley electoral* (1835).

Donovan (don'ọ.vạn), **Dick.** Pseudonym of **Muddock, Joyce Emerson Preston.**

Donovan, Edward. d. at London, Feb. 1, 1837. English naturalist concerning whose personal history little is known except that he was in early life possessed of a considerable fortune, which enabled him to travel and make collections of objects in natural history. His chief work is *General Illustrations of Entomology.*

Donovan, William Joseph. [Called **"Wild Bill" Donovan.**] b. at Buffalo, N.Y., Jan. 1, 1883—. American soldier and lawyer. Received A.B. (1905) and LL.B. (1907) from Columbia; served in World War I as colonel of 42d infantry division; received (1918) Congressional Medal of Honor for bravery in action near Landres and St.-Georges, France; assistant (1925–29) to U.S. attorney general; served (July, 1941–June, 1942) as U.S. coördinator of information; chief (1942–45) of office of strategic services; promoted to brigadier general (1943) and major general (1945); resumed (1945) law practice.

Don Pasquale (dōn päs.kwä'lā). Opera in three acts by Donizetti, with libretto by Cammerano, first produced at Paris on Jan. 4, 1843. The story deals with the machinations of Dr. Malatesta to secure Don Pasquale's consent to the marriage of Ernesto, the Don's nephew, to Norina.

Don Pedro (dōn pā'drō). See **Pedro, Don.**

Don Quichotte (dôṅ kē.shot). Opera in five acts by Jules Massenet, with a libretto by Henri Cain based on Cervantes's work, first produced at Monte Carlo in February, 1910.

Don Quixote (don kẹ.hō'tē, kwik'sọt; Spanish, dōn kē-hō'tā). [Full Spanish title, **Don Quijote de la Mancha.**] Spanish satirical romance by Cervantes, printed at Madrid in two parts, the first in 1605, the second in 1615. When the second part was nearly completed (1614), an impudent attempt to malign the character of Cervantes was made by Alonso Fernandes de Avellaneda of Tordesillas (thought to be a pseudonym of Luis de Aliaga), who produced a pretended continuation of the first part. Translations of *Don Quixote* have appeared in every European language, including Turkish. The principal English translations are those of Shelton (1612–20), Motteux

(1719), Jarvis (1742), Ormsby (1885), and Putnam (1949). The book is named after its hero, a Spanish country gentleman, who is so imbued with tales of chivalry that he saddles up his nag Rosinante and sets forth with his squire Sancho Panza in search of knightly adventure to honor his lady Dulcinea del Toboso, really an ordinary country girl. At the beginning of the work Cervantes announces it to be his sole purpose to break down the vogue and authority of books of chivalry, and at the end he declares anew that he had "had no other desire than to render abhorred of men the false and absurd stories contained in books of chivalry," exulting in his success as an achievement of no small moment. The work was considered at first to be no more than hilarious satire (the Spanish themselves were notoriously slow to value the book properly), but in time perceptive readers of all countries saw beyond the surface laughter to the thoughtful and skillfully handled treatment of the idealist in a materialistic world, so that its comedy becomes the comedy of irony, not too far removed from something akin to tragedy.

Don Quixote. Orchestral tone poem (Opus 35) by Richard Strauss, composed in 1897 and first performed at Cologne in 1898. The work, in the form of variations, takes Don Quixote (cello) and Sancho Panza (viola) through their adventures; the music is often imitative, for instance in the bleating of sheep as portrayed by woodwinds.

Don Quixote in England. Comedy by Henry Fielding, produced in 1734.

Don River (don; Russian, dôn). See **Don.**

Dons (dôns), **Aage Bergishagen.** b. at Svanholm, Denmark, Aug. 19, 1903—. Danish novelist, whose best novel is said to be *Her mødes alle Veje* (Where All Roads Meet, 1941). He is noted for sensuous background and exciting plots.

Don Saltero's Coffee House (don sôl.tãr'ōz). House formerly standing in Cheyne Walk, Chelsea, London. It contained not only an eating house but a museum of natural curiosities. It was founded by John Salter c1690. It was torn down in 1866.

Don Sanche d'Aragon (dôṅ säṅsh dȧ.rȧ.gôṅ). Comedy by Pierre Corneille, produced in 1650. It was partly taken from a Spanish play, *El Palacio confuso.*

Don Sebastiano (dōn sä.bäs.tyä'nō). Opera by Gaetano Donizetti, first produced at Paris in 1843.

Don Segundo Sombra (dōn sä.gōn'dō sōm'brä). Prose work in the gaucho tradition by the Argentine writer Ricardo Guiraldes (1886–1927). Published in 1926, it was Guiraldes's last extended work.

Dont (dont), **Jacob.** b. at Vienna, March 2, 1815; d. Nov. 17, 1888. Austrian virtuoso violinist. He taught (1873 *et seq.*) at Vienna and composed violin studies.

Donus (dō'nus). [Also, **Domnus.**] b. at Rome; d. April 11, 678. Pope from 676 to 678. Little is known of his brief reign. Under him Archbishop Reparatus submitted to the Holy See, thus ending the minor schism begun by Archbishop Maurus when he declared the church of Ravenna to be independent.

Donzel del Phebo (dôn.zel' del fā'bō). See **Phebo, Donzel del.**

Doo (dö), **George Thomas.** b. at Christchurch, Surrey, England, Jan. 6, 1800; d. at Sutton, Surrey, England, Nov. 13, 1886. English engraver and painter. He was historical engraver in ordinary to William IV (1836–37), and to Queen Victoria in 1842. His first published engraving, *The Duke of York*, appeared in 1824.

D'Ooge (dō'gi), **Benjamin Leonard.** b. at Grand Rapids, Mich., Jan. 10, 1860—. American classical scholar, professor of ancient languages at the Michigan State Normal College from 1886. He was graduated from the University of Michigan in 1881, and took his doctor's degree at the University of Bonn in 1901. His works include textbooks, editions of Latin texts, and others.

Dooley (dö'li), **Mr.** Humorous character created by Finley Peter Dunne. Mr. Dooley is an Irish-American saloon-keeper in "Archey Road," Chicago, whose comments on topics of the day are compounded of shrewd wit and common sense. The Mr. Dooley books appeared from 1898 (*Mr. Dooley in Peace and in War*) to 1919 (*Mr. Dooley on Making a Will*); the Dooley sketches appeared from 1893.

Doolin de Mayence (do.o.laṅ dẹ mȧ.yäṅs). [Also, **Doon de Mayence.**] French *chanson de geste* of the 14th century, adapted as a prose romance in the 15th century. It was first published in 1501. Alxinger, a German poet, made (1787) a translation in the form of an epic poem. Doolin, or Doon, was the son of Guy of Mayence, and the ancester of Ogier the Dane. His name is attached to a whole cycle of the Charlemagne *chansons de geste*, those dealing with the false knights, the family of Ganelon; included here are such chansons as *The Four Sons of Aymon.*

Doolittle (dö'lit.l), **Hilda.** [Pseudonym, **H.D.**] b. at Bethlehem, Pa., Sept. 10, 1886—. American imagist poet. She attended Bryn Mawr College, went (1911) to Europe, and in 1913 married the poet and novelist Richard Aldington. One of the first Imagist poets, and influenced by the work and encouragement of Ezra Pound, she is the author of *Sea Garden* (1916), *Hymen* (1921), *Heliodora and Other Poems* (1924), *Collected Poems* (1940). Her novels include *Palimpsest* (1926), *Hedylus* (1928), and *The Hedgehog* (1936). Among her later poetic writings are *The Walls Do Not Fall* (1944), *Tribute to Angels* (1945), and *Flowering of the Rod* (1946).

Doolittle, James Harold. b. at Alameda, Calif., Dec. 14, 1896—. American air-force officer, notable as leader of the first bombing raid over Japan in World War II. Trained at the University of California, he served as a flight and gunnery instructor during World War I; engaged after the war in stunt flying; served (1919–21) with the border patrol; was an army flier until 1930. He received an M.S. (1924) and a D.Sc. (1925) from Massachusetts Institute of Technology; worked (1924 *et seq.*) in aviation research and testing; winner of numerous speed records (1922; Bendix trophy 1931; world's landplane record 1932, and others); appointed (1934) member of U.S. air corps investigating commission. He was recalled (1940) to army duty as major; awarded Congressional Medal of Honor for B-25 raid on Tokyo (April, 1942), the raid marking the first attack by medium bombers from an aircraft carrier; major general in command (1942) of U.S. air forces in North African invasion; commanded (1944 *et seq.*) 8th air force in Europe; promoted (1944) to lieutenant general; retired (1946) from army.

Doolittle Raid. Earliest attempt by the U.S. in World War II to strike direct return blows at the Japanese. The raid was carried out by a bombing squadron of 16 B-25 planes led by Colonel James Doolittle. The planes took off from the aircraft carrier *Hornet* on April 18, 1942, and dropped their explosives over Tokyo. After the raid it was necessary to make landings on the Asiatic mainland; some men were lost in these landings, while others found safety with Chinese rescuers.

Doomsday (dömz'dā). Novel by Warwick Deeping, published in 1926. The title derives from a Sussex farm where the action of the story takes place.

Doomsday. See **Judgment Day.**

Doomsday Book. See **Domesday Book.**

Doon (dön). River in SW Scotland, in Ayrshire. It rises in Loch Doon, on the Ayrshire-Kirkcudbrightshire boundary, and flows NW to the Firth of Clyde ab. 2 mi. S of Ayr. It is celebrated in the poetry of Burns. Length, ab. 27 mi.

Doon de Mayence (do.ôṅ dẹ mȧ.yäṅs). See **Doolin de Mayence.**

Doorman (dōr'män), **Karel Willem Frederik Marie.** b. at Utrecht, Netherlands, April 23, 1889; d. Feb. 26, 1942. Dutch naval officer. He was trained at the Royal Naval Institute of Den Helder. He met his death in World War II as commander of the Dutch fleet in the battle of the Java Sea.

Doorn (dōrn). Commune and village in C Netherlands, in Utrecht province, ab. 10 mi. SE of the city of Utrecht. The *Huis te Doorn*, now a museum, was the exile residence of Kaiser Wilhelm II of Germany from 1919 until his death in 1941. Pop. of commune, 6,313 (1949); of village, ab. 4,000 (1949).

Doornik (dōr'nik). Flemish name of **Tournai.**

Door Peninsula (dōr, dôr). Peninsula in NE Wisconsin, between Green Bay and Lake Michigan. It is a well-developed farming and resort area. North of Sturgeon Bay there are extensive cherry orchards, and on the W side of the peninsula, very picturesque limestone rock formations along Green Bay. Area, ab. 700 sq. mi.; pop. 32,844 (1950).

Doppler (dop'lėr), **Christian Johann.** b. at Salzburg, Germany, Nov. 30, 1803; d. at Venice, March 17, 1853. German physicist and mathematician, professor of experimental physics (1851–53) at the University of Vienna. The important principle that when the source of waves of light or sound moves away from the observer the waves appear to become less frequent, and vice versa, was announced by him in his paper *Über das farbige Licht der Doppelsterne* (1842). Explained by Armand Fizeau in 1848, this principle has been used to build a picture of an expanding universe in the modern astronomical theories; the spectra of distant universes show a shift of lines towards the red end of the spectrum, indicating that the nebulae so photographed are moving away from the earth because the frequency of spectral lines is less than it would be if the observed star systems were relatively stationary with respect to the earth.

Dor (dôr). [Also: **Dora** (dō'rạ).] Site of an ancient city in W Israel, ab. 15 mi. S of Haifa. It was the southernmost of the early Phoenician cities, was conquered by Joshua (Josh. xi. 1, 2; xii. 23), and was incorporated in the kingdom of Solomon as a district capital. Later it was tributary to Assyria, and in the 5th century B.C. to Athens. Dor was destroyed in the wars of the Diadochi in the late 4th century B.C. Later rebuilt, it was annexed to the Roman Empire by Pompey in 63 B.C. Dor was a small city, but heavily fortified. Its heaps of formless ruins lie just N of Tantura or Nasholim, on the coast.

Dora (dō'rạ). Play by Victorien Sardou, produced in 1877, and played in English under the title *Diplomacy.*

Dora. Poem by Alfred Tennyson.

Dora, Sister. See **Pattison, Dorothy Wyndlow.**

Dora Baltea (dō'rä bäl'tā.ä). [Latin, **Duria Major.**] River in N Italy, a tributary of the Po, in Piedmont. It rises in the Mont Blanc group, and joins the Po E of Turin. Length, ab. 100 mi.

Dora d'Istria (dō'rä dēs'trē.ä). [Pseudonym of **Helene Ghica,** Princess **Koltzoff Massalsky.**] b. at Bucharest, Rumania, Feb. 3, 1828; d. at Florence, Nov. 17, 1888. Rumanian writer. Among her works are *La Vie monastique dans l'église orientale* (1855), *La Suisse allemande* (1856), *Les Femmes en Orient* (1860), *Des femmes par une femme* (1864), and others.

Dorak-el-Atik (dō.räk'el.ä.tēk'). Town in W Iran, in Khuzistan, ab. 50 mi. NE of Abadan: a minor trading center. Pop. ab. 12,000.

Doralice (dō.rä.lē'chä). Daughter of the king of Granada in Ariosto's *Orlando Furioso.* She becomes the wife of Mandricardo, but is also loved by Rodomonte, to whom she had been betrothed. After the death of Mandricardo she is willing to give herself to his victor, Ruggiero.

Doralice. Tale, form of the Cinderella story, in Straparola's *Nights.*

Doralice (dor'ạ.lis). Wife of Rhodophil in John Dryden's comedy *Marriage à la Mode,* remarkable for her brilliant philosophy of flirtation in the last act.

Doralice (dō.rä.lē'chä). Opera by Mercadante, first produced at Vienna in 1824.

Doran (dō'rạn), **John.** b. at London, March 11, 1807; d. there, Jan. 25, 1878. English journalist and miscellaneous writer. He was editor of *Notes and Queries* from 1869 until his death. His works include *Lives of the Queens of England of the House of Hanover* (1855), *Their Majesties' Servants* (1860), and many works on stage history.

Dorante (do.ränt). Liar in Pierre Corneille's comedy *Le Menteur.* He surpasses even the women of the play in dissimulation. He seems to lie in a spirited manner for the sake of lying, not from self-interest. In the sequel to this play (*La Suite du Menteur*) he has reformed.

Dorante. Name of three courtly and witty gallants, somewhat differing in characteristics, in Molière's comedies *Le Bourgeois Gentilhomme* (where he is a count enamored of the Marquise Dorimène), *L'École des femmes,* and *Les Fâcheux.*

Dora Riparia (dō'rä rē.pä'ryä). [Latin, **Duria Minor.**] River in N Italy, a headstream of the Po, which it joins near Turin.

Dora Spenlow (dō'rạ spen'lō). See **Spenlow, Dora.**

Dorat (do.rà) or **Daurat** (dō.rà), **Jean.** b. at Limoges, France, c1508; d. at Paris, Nov. 1, 1588. French poet and scholar. A member of the Pléiade (among which were his pupils Ronsard, du Bellay, Belleau, and Baïf) he was called by his contemporaries "the modern Pindar." His influence as mentor and president of the Pléiade was great; his own writing was minor poetry. He was appointed professor of Greek in the Royal College in 1560.

Dorax (dō'raks). Renegade in Dryden's tragedy *Don Sebastian:* a noble Portuguese, formerly Don Alonzo de Sylvera, governor of Alcazar. He has been thought to be the best of Dryden's tragic characters.

Dorcas (dôr'kạs). [Also, **Tabitha.**] In the New Testament (Acts, ix. 36), a woman who was full of good deeds, and made coats and garments for the poor; hence, a Dorcas society is a society of the women of a church who supply garments to the needy.

Dorcas. In Shakespeare's *The Winter's Tale,* a shepherdess.

Dorcas Zeal (zēl). See **Zeal, Arabella** and **Dorcas.**

Dorchester (dôr'ches"tėr, -chẹs.tėr). [Middle English, **Dorchestre, Dorcestre;** Old English, **Dorceaster, Dorce-ceaster, Dorces ceaster, Dorcaceaster;** Latin, **Durnovaria.**] Municipal borough, and the county seat of Dorsetshire, in SW England, situated on the river Frome ab. 6 mi. N of Weymouth, ab. 135 mi. SW of London by rail. It has a Roman amphitheater known as Maumbury Rings. 11,623 (1951).

Dorchester. Village in Oxfordshire, England, situated near Oxford, important in the early Middle Ages.

Dorchester. Formerly a town in E Massachusetts, in Norfolk County, situated on Massachusetts Bay ab. 4 mi. S of Boston. It was annexed to Boston in 1870.

Dorchester, 1st Baron. Title of **Carleton, Sir Guy.**

Dorchester, Countess of. Title of **Sedley, Catharine.**

Dordogne (dor.dony'). Department in W France, bounded by the departments of Haute-Vienne on the N, the departments of Corrèze and Lot on the E, the department of Lot-et-Garonne on the S, and the departments of Charente, Charente-Maritime, and Gironde on the W. It corresponds to the old province of Périgord and parts of Limousin, Angoumois, and Saintonge. It went to the crown of France in the reign of Henry IV. The department contains a number of churches and other monuments dating from the Middle Ages. The city of Bergerac, made famous by Rostand's play *Cyrano de Bergerac,* is within its borders. It is a predominantly agricultural department, producing grain, potatoes, wine, hogs, and poultry. Truffles are a specialty. There are a number of industries, mainly flour mills, dairies, canning factories, and metallurgical plants. The population is declining. Capital, Périgueux; area, 3,550 sq. mi.; pop. 387,643 (1946).

Dordogne River. [Latin, **Duranius.**] River in W France which joins the Garonne ab. 14 mi. N of Bordeaux. Length, ab. 300 mi.; navigable for steamships to Libourne.

Dordrecht (dôr'drecht). [Also, **Dort.**] Town in W Netherlands, in the province of South Holland, situated on an island in the Maas (Meuse) River, ab. 12 mi. SE of Rotterdam. It is a river port, with shipyards and considerable trade. Machinery, instruments, chemicals, and biscuits are produced. The older part of the town is traversed by canals; it has a Gothic cathedral with an unfinished tower, interesting houses and gates of the Renaissance period, and art collections. The town was founded in 1018, was one of the wealthiest commercial centers of the country in the Middle Ages, and was a member of the Hanseatic League. The first assembly of the Protestant provinces of the Netherlands after the successful revolt against Spain was held here on July 15, 1572. It was the scene of a religious convention, known as the Synod of Dort, in the period 1618–19. The harbor installations were heavily damaged in World War II. 71,808 (est. 1951).

Dore (dôr), **Monts** or **Mont.** [Also, **Mont-Dore.**] Mountain mass in S central France, in the department of Puy-de-Dôme. Highest peak, Puy-de-Sancy (6,185 ft.).

Doré (do.rā), **Paul Gustave.** b. at Strasbourg, Jan. 6, 1832; d. at Paris, Jan. 23, 1883. French artist. From 1848, when he made his first series of sketches for the *Journal pour Rire,* he executed a great number of designs, paintings, and statues, and by 1850 had made his reputation. In 1861 he was decorated with the cross of the Legion of Honor. His work, originally woodcuts and then engravings by others of his pen drawings, is highly imaginative and relies on his keen sense of humor and fantasy. He illustrated *Œuvres de Rabelais* (1854), *Légende du Juif errant* (1856), *Contes drôlatiques de Balzac* (1856), *Essais de Montaigne* (1857), *Voyage aux Pyrénées de M. Taine* (1859), *Divina Commedia de Dante* (1861), *Contes de Perrault* (1861), *Don Quichotte* (1863), The Bible (1865–66), *Fables de La Fontaine* (1867), Tennyson's poems *Elaine* and *Viven* (1866–68), and others. Among his oil paintings are *Paolo and Francesca da Rimini*, *Rebel Angels Cast Down* (1866), *Gambling-Hall at Baden-Baden*, *The Neophyte* (1868), *The Triumph of Christianity*, and *Christ leaving the Praetorium*.

Doremus (dọ.rē′mus), **Charles Avery.** b. at New York, Sept. 6, 1851; d. Dec. 2, 1925. American chemist; son of Robert Ogden Doremus. He was professor of chemistry and toxicology in the medical department of the University of Buffalo (1877–82) and in the American Veterinary College of New York (1882–92), adjunct professor in Bellevue Hospital Medical College (1879–97), assistant professor of chemistry in the College of the City of New York (1897–1903), and acting professor there (1903–04). He published *Report on Photography, Vienna Exposition* (1873), "Gaseous Poisons" in *Textbook of Legal Medicine and Toxicology* (1903), and others.

Doremus, Robert Ogden. b. at New York, Jan. 11, 1824; d. there, March 22, 1906. American chemist, professor of chemistry and toxicology and medical jurisprudence in the Bellevue Hospital Medical College, and of chemistry and physics in the College of the City of New York.

Doremus, Sarah Platt. [Maiden name, **Haines.**] b. at New York, Aug. 3, 1802; d. Jan. 29, 1877. American philanthropist and social worker. She organized a home (now Isaac T. Hopper House) for discharged women prisoners, and assisted in the founding of the House and School of Industry (1850), The Nursery and Child's Hospital (1854), the Woman's Hospital of the State of New York (1855), and the Woman's Union Missionary Society (1860).

Dörfler (dėrf′lėr), **Peter.** b. at Untergermaringen, Germany, 1878—. German novelist. As a South German Catholic priest he has been interested in the religious aspects of his characters' lives and in the social problems of the peasantry. The scene of his stories is the Algäu (or Allgäu), a mountainous district in S Bavaria. The most ambitious of these are the two trilogies *Appolonia* (1930–32) and *Allgäu* (1934–36).

Dorfman (dôrf′mạn), **Joseph.** b. at Ramanovska, Russia, March 27, 1909—. American teacher and economist. He was graduated from Reed College (B.A., 1924) and Columbia (Ph.D., 1935), and in 1948 became full professor at Columbia. His works include *Thorstein Veblen and His America* (1934) and *The Economic Mind in American Civilization* (Vols. I–II, 1946; Vol. III, 1949).

Dorgan (dôr′gạn), **Thomas Aloysius.** [Pseudonym, **"Tad."**] b. at San Francisco, April 29, 1877; d. at Great Neck, N.Y., May 2, 1929. American cartoonist and sports commentator. He was cartoonist (until 1902) on the San Francisco *Bulletin* and (1902 *et seq.*) on William Randolph Hearst's New York *Journal*, creator of the cartoon characters "Judge Rumhauser" and "Silk Hat Harry," and credited with originating the slang expressions "23 skidoo" and "Yes, we have no bananas."

Dorgelès (dôr.zhẹ.les), **Roland.** [Pseudonym of **R. Lécavelé**; full name, **Roland Lécavelé.**] b. at Amiens, France, June 15, 1886—. French novelist. He is the author of *Les Croix de bois* (1919; Eng. trans., *Wooden Crosses*, 1921), *Le Cabaret de la Belle Femme* (1919; Eng. trans., *The Cabaret up the Line*, 1930), and *Le Réveil des morts* (1923), as well as of travel books and two volumes on Bohemian life on Montmartre, *Le Château des brouillards* (1932) and *Quand j'étais montmartrois* (1936). Leaving the École des Arts Decoratifs (c1902), he lived the Bohemian life of Montmartre for a decade, served in the army in World War I, and emerged with the manuscript of what proved an immensely successful novel of soldier life; none of his later work has achieved the popularity of *Les Croix de bois*. He was elected to the Goncourt Academy in 1929.

Dorhosye (dōr.hōs′yä). [Also: **Dokhosie, Dorossie.**] Sudanic-speaking people of W Africa, inhabiting E Ivory Coast, to the W of the Lobi people. Their population is estimated at ab. 4,000 (by H. Labouret, *Les Tribus du Rameau Lobi*, 1931). They have exogamous matrilineal clans, and chiefs were lacking before the establishment of French rule. They practice hoe agriculture, and their principle food is millet. They have adopted Mohammedanism.

Doria (dō′ryä), **Andrea.** [Called **"Liberator of Genoa."**] b. at Oneglia, Italy, Nov. 30, 1468; d. at Genoa, Italy, Nov. 25, 1560. Genoese admiral and statesman. He was a captain-general under Francis I of France, but when the king refused to fulfill his contract with Doria, the latter left his service. He joined the forces of the emperor Charles V and in 1528 he freed Genoa from the French. Doria set up a republic, aristocratic and under the protection of the emperor, but independent. He served with distinction in the imperial forces against the Turks, and achieved the capture of Tunis (1535) in Charles V's expedition against the Turkish city. He retired (1544) to Genoa from the emperor's service, but was forced to flee the city when a conspiracy against him flared up in 1547. He returned and regained his old power, suppressing vigorously all further factional disputes. From 1553 to 1555, in his eighties, he led the Genoese forces against the French on Corsica after the French had seized the island. There is a celebrated portrait of him, by Sebastiano del Piombo, in the Palazzo Doria, Rome.

Dorian Hexapolis (dō′ri.ạn hek.sap′ō.lis). See **Hexapolis, Dorian.**

Dorians (dō′ri.ạnz). One of the traditional branches of the ancient Greek people.

Doricha (dō′ri.kạ). Real name of **Rhodopis.**

Doricourt (dor′i.kōrt). Brilliant man of the world in Hannah Cowley's comedy *The Belle's Stratagem.* His wit, humor, and courtliness make him the fashion, while his taste for French piquancy renders him impervious to the charm of English beauty.

Dorigen (dor′i.gẹn). In Chaucer's *Franklin's Tale*, the faithful wife of Arviragus. She was beloved by Aurelius, "a lusty squire," and to escape his importunity said she would never listen to him till all the rocks on the seashore were removed. He having by magic removed them, Arviragus sacrificed her to her promise. When Aurelius beheld her gentle obedience to her husband's overstrained sense of honor, he released her from the bargain. Chaucer took the story from Boccaccio's *Dianora and Gilberto.*

Dorigny (do.rē.nyē), **Michel.** b. at St. Quentin, France, 1617; d. 1666. French painter and engraver; father of Sir Nicolas Dorigny (c1657–1746). Examples of his work as a painter are preserved in the Louvre and in the Madrid Gallery, but he is better known for his powerful work as an engraver.

Dorigny, Sir **Nicolas.** b. at Paris, c1657; d. 1746. French engraver; son of Michel Dorigny (1617–66). Although he studied under his father, he turned to the law as a profession, and practised for several years until at the age of 30 deafness interfered with his career. Returning thereupon to art, he went to Italy for further study and remained there more than 20 years. Thereafter he went to England by invitation of Queen Anne to make engravings from works of Raphael at Hampton Court. These were completed by 1719, and in recognition of their excellence, Dorigny was made a knight by George I in 1720. In 1725 he returned to France, and became a member of the French Academy.

Dorimant (dor′i.mant). In Etherege's comedy *The Man of Mode, or Sir Fopling Flutter*, a witty and fashionable libertine, intended as a portrait of the Earl of Rochester.

Dorimène (do.rē.men). In Molière's *Le Cocu imaginaire*, the wife of Sganarelle. Dorimène is also introduced in a later play, *Le Mariage forcé*, where she consents to marry Sganarelle, who is much older than she, with the intention of deceiving him.

Dorimène. Lady of rank in Molière's comedy *Le Bourgeois Gentilhomme.* She is loved by Dorante.

Dorinda (dō.rēn′dä). [Also, **Dorine.**] In Guarini's *Pastor Fido*, an impulsive, passionate girl.

Dorinda (dọ.rin′dạ). Sister of Miranda in Dryden and D'Avenant's version of *The Tempest.* Like Miranda, she has seen no man but her father.

Dorinda. In Farquhar's comedy *The Beaux' Stratagem*, the daughter of Lady Bountiful. She falls in love with and marries Aimwell, whose stratagem to win a rich wife thus succeeds.

Dorine (do.rēn). In Molière's comedy *Tartufe*, the caustic but faithful waiting woman of Marianne. This name was given in the old French theatrical nomenclature to an intriguing soubrette.

Dorion (do.ryôṅ), Sir **Antoine Aimé.** b. at Sainte Anne de la Pérade, Quebec, Canada, Jan. 17, 1816; d. at Montreal, May 31, 1891. Canadian politician and jurist. He was admitted to the bar in 1842, achieved prominence as a lawyer, and entered politics in 1854, being elected to the legislative assembly of Canada, where he became the leader of the young liberals. He was to the fore in demanding representation according to population. At first he advocated federation of the provinces, later opposed it as inimical to French Canadian interests, but accepted it when the Dominion of Canada was established, and sat in the Dominion House of Commons from 1867 to 1874. He accepted the post of minister of justice in 1873, but resigned in 1874 upon his appointment as chief justice of the court of Queen's Bench of the Province of Quebec. He was made a knight in 1877.

Doriot (do.ryō), **Jacques.** b. at Bresles, Oise, France, 1898; d. in SW Germany, as a result of an airplane attack, in February, 1945. French fascist leader, one of the most active supporters (1937–45) of collaboration with Nazi Germany. A Communist leader (1920–34), he turned to fascism, founding the Parti Populaire Français in 1936; was forced to resign (1937) as mayor of the Paris suburb of St.-Denis for irregularities in office; after the fall of France organized an anti-Bolshevist legion; and fought (1942) in the German army on the Russian front. His efforts to enter the Vichy government failed. Documents found after the defeat of Germany showed that he had been an agent of the Gestapo since 1935.

Doris (dō'ris, dor'is). In ancient geography, a territory in C Greece, surrounded by Phocis, Locris, Aetolia, and Malis; a valley between Oeta and Parnassus.

Doris. In ancient geography, a part of the coast of Caria, Asia Minor.

Doris. In classical mythology, the daughter of Oceanus and Tethys. She married Nereus, and their 50 daughters were called the Nereides. The name Doris is sometimes given to the sea by the poets, as by Vergil.

Doris. Asteroid (No. 48) discovered by Goldschmidt at Paris, Sept. 19, 1857.

Dorking (dôr'king). Urban district and market town in SE England, in Surrey, situated at the water gap of the river Mole through the North Downs near the base of Box Hill, ab. 22 mi. SW of London by rail. It is famous for its breed of fowls, and is the scene of the fictitious Battle of Dorking. 20,252 (1951).

Dorking, Battle of. Occurrence in an imaginary narrative of an invasion and conquest of England by a foreign army, written by General Sir Geroge T. Chesney in 1871 and published under the title *The Battle of Dorking, or Reminiscences of a Volunteer*. It called attention to the need of an improved system of national defense, and attracted much notice.

d'Orléans (dôr.lā.äṅ), Duchesse. Title of **Henrietta Anne.**

Dorléans or **D'Orléans, Louis.** b. at Paris, 1542; d. there, 1629. French poet and satirist.

Dörmann (dėr'män), **Felix.** [Pseudonym of **Felix Biedermann.**] b. at Vienna, May 29, 1870; d. there, Oct. 26, 1928. Austrian writer who was especially successful in the dramatic field and as a librettist. His lyrics are characterized by the decadent themes typical of his period.

Dormitor (dôr'mi.tọr). See **Durmitor.**

Dormont (dôr'mont). Borough in SW Pennsylvania, in Allegheny County near Pittsburgh: residential community. It was incorporated in 1909. 13,405 (1950).

Dorn (dôrn), **Erik.** See **Erik Dorn.**

Dorn, Heinrich (Ludwig Egmont). b. at Königsberg, in East Prussia, Nov. 14, 1804; d. at Berlin, Jan. 10, 1892. German operatic composer, conductor (1847–68) of the Royal Opera at Berlin. His chief opera is *Die Nibelungen* (1854).

Dorn, Johann Albrecht Bernhard. b. at Scheuerfeld, Coburg, Germany, May 11, 1805; d. at St. Petersburg, May 31, 1881. German Orientalist, professor (1835), and later (1843) chief librarian of the imperial public library at St. Petersburg. His works include *History of the Afghans* (1829–36), *Über die Sprache der Afghanen* (1840), *Chrestomathy of the Pushtu or Afghan Language* (1847), *Caspia* (1875), and others.

Dornbirn (dôrn'birn). Town in W Austria, in Vorarlberg province, situated on the Dornbirner Ache, a tributary of the Rhine River, ab. 7 mi. S of Bregenz. It is a station on the Bregenz-Feldkirch railroad and has cotton mills, machine factories, and a school of embroidery. 22,508 (1951).

Dorner (dôr'nėr), **August.** b. at Schiltach, Baden, Germany, May 13, 1846; d. at Hanover, Germany, April 17, 1920. German Protestant theologian and philosopher; son of Isaak August Dorner. He attended the universities of Berlin, Göttingen, and Tübingen, served (1869 *et seq.*) as minister of the German congregations at Marseilles and Lyons, and held the posts of professor and director of the Wittenberg Theological Academy until 1890, when he became professor at the University of Königsberg, where he served (1908–09) as rector. He was known as an advocate of a critical and speculative philosophy of religion. His works include *Augustinus* (1873), *Grundriss der Religionsphilosophie* (1903), and *Die Metaphysik des Christentums* (1913).

Dorner, Isaak August. b. at Neuhausen, near Tuttlingen, Württemberg, Germany, June 20, 1809; d. at Wiesbaden, Prussia, Germany, July 8, 1884. German Protestant theologian. He became (1862) professor at Berlin. His chief works are *Entwickelungsgeschichte der Lehre von der Person Christi* (1839, 1845–56; Eng. trans., *History of the Development of the Doctrine of the Person of Christ*, 1859), *Geschichte der protestantischen Theologie* (1867), and *System der christlichen Glaubenslehre* (1880–81).

Dornier (dôr.nēr', dôr.nyā'), **Claude.** b. in Bavaria, Germany, 1884—. German aeronautical designer and industrialist. Educated at the Munich Technical University, he was employed (1910 *et seq.*) by Count Zeppelin; he was among the first to use duralumin in aircraft construction and pioneered in seaplane design. Together with his brother, Maurice Dornier, he organized (1929) the Dornier Werke at Friedrichshafen, which produced many types of all-metal aircraft, among them the *DO-X*, a giant seaplane which carried 169 passengers to New York on its first transatlantic flight in 1931. During World War II the Dornier factories manufactured combat aircraft for the German air forces.

Dornoch (dôr'noċh, -noċh). City and royal burgh in N Scotland, in Sutherland, situated on Dornoch Firth, ab. 5 mi. N of Tain, ab. 647 mi. N of London by rail. It contains a 13th-century cathedral, rebuilt in the period 1835–37, and now used as a parish church. Dornoch has what is said to be one of the finest golf courses in the United Kingdom. It is the county seat of Sutherland. 765 (est. 1948).

Dornoch Firth. Inlet of the North Sea in N Scotland, lying between the county of Ross and Cromarty and the county of Sutherland. Length, ab. 20 mi.; width at entrance, ab. 9 mi.

Dornröschen (dôrn'rės"ċhẹn). See **Sleeping Beauty.**

Dornton (dôrn'tọn), **Harry.** Son of Old Dornton in Holcroft's *Road to Ruin*. His exploits give the name to the play. He is saved from ruin by Sulky, his father's friend.

Dornton, Old. Fond, confiding, but justly offended father of Harry Dornton in Holcroft's *Road to Ruin*.

Dorobo (dō.rō'bō). [Also: **Ildorobo, Ogyiek, Okiek, Ndorobo, Wandorobo.**] Nilo-Hamitic-speaking people of E Africa, scattered among the Handi, whose language they have adopted, and the Masai, Kikuyu, and other peoples of W Kenya and N Tanganyika. The two subgroups in Tanganyika are known as Mosiro and Aramanik. The Dorobo differ from their neighbors in that they practice neither farming nor herding. They are nomadic hunters and gatherers, whose only domesticated animal is the dog.

Dorobornensis (dō"rọ.bôr.nen'sis), **Gervasius.** Latinized name of **Gervase** (or **Gervaise**) of **Canterbury.**

Dorobrevum (dō.rọ.brē′vum). A Latin name of **Rochester,** England.

Dorogobuzh (do″rọ.gọ.bösh′). [Also, **Dorogobush.**] Town in the U.S.S.R., in the Smolensk *oblast* (region) of the Russian Soviet Federated Socialist Republic, ab. 52 mi. NE of Smolensk, situated on the Dnieper River. Food processing is important here. Pop. ab. 7,000.

Dorohoi (dō.rō.hoi′). [Also: **Dorogoie** (dô.rô.gô′ye), **Dorohoïu** (dō.rō.hō′ē).] Town in NE Rumania, in the province of Moldavia, ab. 24 mi. E of Siret. 15,036 (1948).

Doron (dō′ron). Character in Robert Greene's *Menaphon*, which Simpson, in his *School of Shakespeare*, attempted to identify with Shakespeare.

Dorosma or **Dorózsma** (dō′rōzh.mô). See **Kiskundorozsma.**

Dorossie (dō.rōs′yä). See **Dorhosye.**

Dorotea (dō.rō.tā′ä). Dramatic prose romance by Lope de Vega, written in his youth but later carefully revised by him, and first printed in 1632. He calls it "the most beloved of his works." The career of the hero Fernando is to some degree autobiographical.

Dorothea (dor.ọ.thē′ạ), Saint. d. c311. Virgin martyr. She was tortured and decapitated in the persecution of Diocletian. Her festival is celebrated Feb. 6 in the Roman Church. She was said to have sent roses and apples miraculously from paradise to a doubting spectator of her martyrdom, Theophilus, who jestingly asked her to do so. He was converted by this miracle, and later tortured and then decapitated. Dorothea was introduced as a character of much grace and tenderness by Massinger and Dekker in *The Virgin Martyr*.

Dorothea. The "peerless Queen of Scots" in Greene's play *James the Fourth*.

Dorothea. Very beautiful and unfortunate woman in an episode of Cervantes's *Don Quixote*.

Dorothea. In Fletcher's comedy *Monsieur Thomas*, a bright, affectionate English girl, the sister of Monsieur Thomas.

Dorothea. Vessel which was sent under command of Captain Buchan, with the *Trent* under Franklin, in 1818, on an expedition to the arctic regions.

Dorothea (dō.rō.tā′ä), **Hermann und.** See **Hermann und Dorothea.**

Dorothea Brooke (dor.ọ.thē′ạ brůk). See **Brooke, Dorothea.**

Dorotheus (dọ.rō′thē.us). fl. in the 6th century. Jurist at Berytus (modern Beirut), Syria; one of the compilers of Justinian's *Digest*.

Dorothy's Wedding (dor′ọ.thiz). Novel by Ethel Sidgwick, published in 1931.

Dorothy Vernon of Haddon Hall (dor′ọ.thi vėr′nọn; had′ọn). Novel by Charles Major, published in 1902.

Dorp (dôrp). Former manufacturing town in W Germany, in the Rhine Province of Prussia, situated on the Wupper River, ab. 17 mi. NE of Cologne: united in 1889 with Solingen.

Dorpat (dôr′pät) or **Dörpt** (dėrpt). German names of **Tartu.**

Dörpfeld (dėrp′felt), **Wilhelm.** b. at Barmen, Germany, Dec. 26, 1853; d. on the island of Leukas, Greece, April 25, 1940. German archaeologist and architect. An authority on excavations and the ancient Greek theater, he served as director (1887 *et seq.*) of the German archaeological institute at Athens, also as professor (1919 *et seq.*) at the University of Jena. He supervised such excavations as Olympia (1875 *et seq.*) and Troy (1874 *et seq.*, with Heinrich Schliemann). Among his works are *Das griechische Theater* (The Greek Theater, 1896; with Reisch), *Troja und Ilion* (Troy and Ilion, 1902), *Die Heimkehr des Odysseus* (Odysseus' Return, 1924), *Alt-Ithaka* (Ancient Ithaca, 1927), and *Alt-Olympia* (Ancient Olympia, 1935).

Dorpmüller (dôrp′mül.ėr), **Julius.** b. at Elberfeld, Germany, July 24, 1869—. German railroad official. He served (1907–17) as a railroad specialist to the Chinese government. During World War I he was in charge of the trans-Caucasian railroads. Later he became (1925) director of German railroads and served (May, 1945) as a member of the short-lived cabinet under Admiral Doenitz. He was captured by the Allied forces.

Dorr (dôr), **Benjamin.** b. at Salisbury, Mass., March 22, 1796; d. at Germantown, Pa., Sept. 18, 1869. American clergyman of the Protestant Episcopal Church. He was rector of Christ Church, Philadelphia, from 1837 until his death. His works include *The History of a Pocket Prayer-Book, Written by Itself*, *A Memoir of John Fanning Watson*, and others.

Dorr, John Van Nostrand. b. at Newark, N.J., Jan. 6, 1872—. American metallurgical engineer, known for his inventions including the Dorr classifier, Dorr thickener, and Dorr agitator, used in ore dressing, hydrometallurgy, and chemical and industrial processes. He has been research assistant (1893–95) to Thomas A. Edison, and president (1916 *et seq.*) of Dorr Company; author of *The Cyanidation and Concentration of Gold and Silver Ores* (1936).

Dorr, Julia Caroline. [Maiden name, **Ripley.**] b. at Charleston, S.C., Feb. 13, 1825; d. Jan. 18, 1913. American poet and novelist. She was the author of *Poems* (1871), *Friar Anselmo and Other Poems* (1879), *Afternoon Songs* (1885), *Poems Complete* (1892), and *Afterglow* (1900). Among her prose writings are *Farmingdale* (1854), *Lanmere* (1856), *Sibyl Huntington* (1869), *Expiation* (1872), *Bermuda* (1884), *The Flower of England's Face* (1895), *A Cathedral Pilgrimage* (1896), and *In King's Houses* (1898).

Dorr, Rheta Childe. b. at Omaha, Nebr., c1866; d. Aug. 8, 1948. American journalist, feminist, and author. She first became well known in journalistic circles and to a wide public during her years (1902–06) as editor of the women's department of the New York *Evening Post*. In 1907 she became a staff writer for *Hampton's Magazine*, and during the next ten years contributed to that and other periodicals articles dealing with political, social, and feminist questions. Her book stating the case for woman suffrage, *What Eight Million Women Want*, appeared in 1910. In 1917–18 she was in Europe as a war correspondent for the New York *Evening Mail* and other newspapers, and she returned to Europe in 1921 as a foreign correspondent, remaining there until 1923. Other books by Mrs. Dorr are *Inside the Russian Revolution* (1917), *A Soldier's Mother in France* (1918), *A Woman of Fifty* (her autobiography, 1924), *Susan B. Anthony* (a biography, 1928), and *Drink—Coercion or Control?* (1929), a study of liquor legislation in the Scandinavian countries.

Dorr, Thomas Wilson. b. at Providence, R.I., Nov. 5, 1805; d. Dec. 27, 1854. American politician and reformer, leader of the popular suffrage movement and Dorr's Rebellion in Rhode Island. Graduated (1823) from Harvard, he studied law at New York, was admitted to the bar (1827), and took his seat as a representative in the Rhode Island Assembly in 1834. Taking a prominent part in agitation in behalf of the Rhode Island Suffrage Association (founded in 1840), he became the leader of a reform movement to extend the franchise in the state. Rhode Island was governed, not by a state constitution, but by the charter granted it as a colony. The restrictions set up by the ruling group had the result that only some 3,500 voters existed in a population of over 100,000. Property qualifications held not only at the polls but in the courts as well. When the charter legislature failed to satisfy the grievances of the unenfranchised, the People's Party adopted and submitted to popular vote a reform constitution, gaining what was supposedly a majority of the legal voters. Thereafter there were two state administrations, one under Governor Samuel King, the other under Dorr, who had been elected under the "rebel" constitution, each claiming legal authority; and when Dorr took steps in May, 1842, to set up a government, the existing state administration began imprisoning his followers. On May 17, 1842, Dorr led 234 men in an unsuccessful attack upon the Providence Arsenal; he fled the state to seek support elsewhere, but soon gave up his fight. On June 26, 1842, martial law was declared in Rhode Island and a reward of 5,000 dollars was offered for the capture of Dorr, despite the fact that he had earlier announced the disbanding of his movement. He surrendered voluntarily to the authorities at Providence, stood trial for treason, and was sentenced to solitary confinement at hard labor for life. He was released (1845) after an act of general amnesty was passed. In 1851 he was returned to full civil rights.

Dorrego (dôr.rā′gō), **Manuel.** b. at Buenos Aires, 1777; executed there, Dec. 13, 1828. Argentine politician, elected (August, 1827) governor of Buenos Aires. His efforts to establish a confederation of the provinces were at first successful, and the war with Brazil was brought to a close (1828), both countries recognizing the independence of Uruguay. The revolt of Lavalle drove Dorrego from Buenos Aires; he was defeated in an attempt to recover the city, captured, and shot without trial.

Dorriforth (dor'i.fôrth). In Mrs. Inchbald's *Simple Story,* a Roman Catholic priest. He is the guardian of Miss Milner, who falls in love with him. He becomes the Earl of Elmwood, is released from his vows, and marries her.

Dorrit (dor'it), **Amy.** [Called **"Little Dorrit."**] In Charles Dickens's *Little Dorrit,* the unselfish daughter of the debtor William Dorrit, born in prison.

Dorrit, William. Father of Amy Dorrit, in Charles Dickens's *Little Dorrit.* He is a weak, selfish, good-looking man confined in the Marshalsea prison for a long time for debt, and hence called "the Father of the Marshalsea."

Dorr's Rebellion (dôrz). In U.S. history, a revolutionary movement under the leadership of Thomas Wilson Dorr to introduce a new state constitution in Rhode Island. It was caused by dissatisfaction with the existing fundamental law (a charter granted by Charles II, in 1663), which placed a heavy property qualification on the suffrage. A People's Party was organized under the leadership of Dorr in 1840. It held a mass meeting at Providence on July 5, 1841, and authorized the calling of a constitutional convention, which met at Providence on Oct. 4, 1841. The constitution proposed by this convention was submitted to the people (Dec. 27–29, 1841) and received a majority of the popular vote, Dorr's followers claiming also a majority of the legally qualified voters of the state. A government with Dorr at its head was elected under this constitution on April 18, 1842, and the state was for a time under dual government. The Dorr wing made an unsuccessful attempt to seize the arsenal at Providence on May 18, 1842, and was dispersed on June 25, 1842.

Dorset (dôr'sẹt). See also **Dorsetshire.**

Dorset. Eskimo culture extending from Hudson Bay to N Greenland, Labrador, and Newfoundland during the period from c100 to 900 A.D. The Dorset Eskimos lived in semisubterranean houses and hunted sea mammals with harpoons. The harpoon heads were of a unique type, with rectangular sockets and gouged line holes instead of the drilled holes of the remaining Eskimos.

Dorset, Earl of. A title of **Beaufort, Edmund.**

Dorset, 1st Earl of. A title of **Sackville, Thomas.**

Dorset, Marquis of. A title of **Beaufort, John.**

Dorset, Marquis of. Title held by various members of the **Grey** family.

Dorset, Marion. b. at Columbia, Tenn., Dec. 14, 1872; d. at Washington, D.C., July 15, 1935. American chemist, noted for researches on the chemical and biological nature of the tubercle bacillus and the bacteriology and chemistry of meats. He is credited with codiscovery of the hog-cholera serum. He was assistant chemist (1894–1903) and head (1904 *et seq.*) of the biochemic division of the U.S. Department of Agriculture.

Dorsetshire (dôr'sẹt.shir) or **Dorset** (dôr'sẹt). Maritime county in SW England, lying between Somersetshire and Wiltshire on the N, Hampshire on the E, the English Channel on the S, and Devonshire and Somersetshire on the W. It has some manufactures of paper, silk, gloves, pottery, and tiles, and has important fisheries, especially of mackerel. Ball clay and fine pipe clay are mined in the vicinity of Poole, some of which is supplied to the Potteries. Portland stone and Purbeck marble also come from Dorsetshire. Much of the county is traversed by the North and South Downs and it is noted for its breed of sheep pastured there. Dairying is highly developed, and much dairy produce is supplied to the London markets. Dorsetshire contains many British and Roman antiquities. County seat, Dorchester; area, ab. 970 sq. mi.; pop. 291,157 (1951).

Dorsey (dôr'si), **George Amos.** b. at Hebron, Ohio, Feb. 6, 1868; d. at New York, March 29, 1931. American naturalist, assistant curator (1896–97) and curator (1897–1915) of anthropology in the Field Museum at Chicago; brother of Herbert Grove Dorsey. In 1900 he was appointed professor of comparative anatomy at Northwestern University; he became assistant professor of anthropology at the University of Chicago in 1905 and associate professor in 1909. He served with naval intelligence during World War I, as naval attaché (1919–21) at Lisbon, and was a lecturer (1925 *et seq.*) at the New York School for Social Research. He published numerous anthropological and anatomical papers, including *Why We Behave Like Human Beings* (1925).

Dorsey, Herbert Grove. b. at Kirkersville, Ohio, April 24, 1876—. American physicist and oceanographer; brother of George Amos Dorsey. He has been a staff member (1926 *et seq.*) of the U.S. Coast and Geodetic Survey, and is known for his inventions of acoustical devices such as the Dorsey Phonelescope, a dynamic loudspeaker, and a "fathometer."

Dorsey, James Owen. b. at Baltimore, Oct. 31, 1848; d. Feb. 4, 1895. American ethnologist and linguist. He was ordained (1871) a Protestant Episcopal deacon, and served as a missionary (to 1880) among the Pawnee Indians of the Dakota Territory; as an agent of the U.S. Bureau of American Ethnology, he made studies of the Omaha Indians. He was the author of technical papers published (1881–94) in the *Annual Reports* of the United States Bureau of American Ethnology: *The Cegiha Language* (vol. VI, 1890) and *Dakota Grammar, Texts and Ethnography* (vol. IX, 1893).

Dorsten (dôr'stẹn). Town in W Germany in the *Land* (state) of North Rhine-Westphalia, British Zone, formerly in the province of Westphalia, Prussia, situated on the Lippe River, ab. 25 mi. NW of Dortmund. It has metallurgical, construction, chemical, paper, and textile industries, and an agricultural school. The majority of the population is Roman Catholic, but there is a considerable Protestant minority. The increase in population between 1939 and 1946 was 139.1 percent. 25,952 (1946), 27,945 (1950).

Dort (dôrt). See **Dordrecht.**

Dort, Synod of. Assembly of the Reformed Church of the Netherlands, with delegates from England and other countries, convened by the States-General for the purpose of deciding the Arminian controversy, and held at Dordrecht (Dort) from 1618 to 1619. It condemned the doctrines of the Arminians or Remonstrants.

Dorten (dôr'tẹn), **Adam.** b. at Endenich, Germany, Feb. 10, 1880—. German separatist. He was active at Mainz in 1919 and 1923, and later fled to France.

Dortmund (dôrt'mụnt). City in W Germany, in the *Land* (state) of North Rhine-Westphalia, British Zone, formerly in the province of Westphalia, Prussia, situated near the Emscher River, on the Dortmund-Ems Canal, E of Essen: one of the largest industrial centers in the Ruhr. 507,349 (1950).

Industries. Located on the border between the southern and northern coal-bearing zones of the Ruhr district, Dortmund is the seat of important mining enterprises and of large iron and steel works including the Vereinigte Stahlwerke-Dortmunder Union, Hörder Verein, Hösch, and other units; there are rolling mills and pipe, cable, railroad equipment, machine, and machine-tool factories. Huge enterprises (Klönne, Jucho) specialize in the building of bridges and similar engineering features. There are large breweries, chemical and construction industries, and manufactures of rubber articles, leatherware, garments, musical instruments, and canned foods. Dortmund has excellent shipping, port, and warehouse facilities in connection with the Dortmund-Ems Canal, and is a busy commercial center. It has not been ascertained whether the grain and foodstuff exchange, the iron and metal, exchange, and the livestock markets that existed before World War II have been restored.

Culture and Architecture. Dortmund has a number of educational institutions and vocational schools, a museum of arts and crafts, a museum of natural history, and a theater. The city was badly battered in World War II; the museum buildings, the 13th-century *Rathaus* (city hall) and the 15th-century Gildenhaus were wrecked. Churches including the Reinoldikirche, one of the finest Gothic buildings of Westphalia (13th century), the Petrikirche (14th century), the Marienkirche, a Romanesque building of the 12th century (all these Protestant), and the Catholic Probsteikirche (15th century) were heavily damaged; most of their art treasures, however, had been stored away and are safe.

History. Dortmund, mentioned in the 9th century as Throtmannia, in the 12th century as Tremonia, was frequently used as a residence by the medieval German emperors. The city received privileges and prospered commercially, becoming a member of the Hanseatic League. After the Thirty Years' War, its decline was complete. It became part of Prussia in 1815, and grew steadily in the 19th century and even more in the 20th century, after the opening of the Dortmund-Ems Canal in 1899. It was occupied by French troops from Jan. 16, 1923, to Oct. 22, 1924. Frequently bombed between 1943 and 1945, it was occupied by Allied troops in April, 1945. The population decreased 19.5 percent in the period 1939–47.

Dortmund-Ems Canal (dôrt′mu̇nt.ems′). Canal in NW Germany, built in the period 1892–99 to connect the Ruhr industrial area with the North Sea by way of the Ems River. It is navigable by ships of light draft up to 600 tons. The canal has not been a serious competitor of the Rhine route, and has been used mainly for Scandinavian trade with the Ruhr, importing chiefly Swedish iron ore and lumber. Total length (including branch to Herne), ab. 175 mi.

Dorus (dō′rus). In Greek mythology, the ancestor and eponym of the Dorians, generally represented as the son of Hellen.

Dorus. In Sir Philip Sidney's romance *Arcadia*, the name under which Musidorus, in the disguise of a shepherd, pretends to love Mopsa.

Dorval (dôr.vȧl′). Town on Montreal Island, Quebec, Canada, situated on the S side of the island, ab. 8 mi. from Montreal: site of the main airport used by the city of Montreal. 5,293 (1951).

Dory (dō′ri). Vociferous and faithful servant of Sir George Thunder, in O'Keefe's *Wild Oats*.

Dory, John. See **John Dory.**

Dorylaeum (dor.i.lē′um). Latin name of **Eskişehir,** town.

Dos Hermanas (dōs er.mä′näs). Town in S Spain, in the province of Sevilla, ab. 10 mi. S of the city of Seville: agricultural trade center. 20,330 (1940).

Dositheans (dọ.sith′ẹ.ạnz). Samaritan sect, named after Dositheus, a false Messiah, who appeared about the time of Christ. The sect, though small in numbers, existed for several centuries.

Dospad Dagh (dōs.päd′ däg′). Turkish name of the **Rhodope Mountains.**

Dos Passos (dọs pas′ọs), **John (Roderigo).** b. at Chicago, Jan. 14, 1896—. American writer of novels, plays, and travel books. He received a B.A. (1916) from Harvard and served in World War I as a member of the ambulance corps connected with the French and with the Italian armies, and in the U.S. army medical corps. He is the author of *One Man's Initiation* (1920; republished as *First Encounter,* 1945), *Three Soldiers* (1921), *Streets of Night* (1923), *Manhattan Transfer* (1925), *Orient Express* (1927); the trilogy *U.S.A.* (1938) embracing the novels *The 42d Parallel* (1930), *1919* (1932), and *The Big Money* (1936); *Adventures of a Young Man* (1939), *The Ground We Stand On* (1941), *Number One* (1943), *State of the Nation* (1944), *Tour of Duty* (1946), *The Grand Design* (1949), *The Prospect Before Us* (1950), *Chosen Country* (1951), and other books. His plays include *The Garbage Man* (1926), *Airways Inc.* (1929), and *Fortune Heights* (1933). He published the volume of verse *A Pushcart at the Curb* (1922). Dos Passos's technique of interspersing headline material and atmospheric historical background with short narrative passages, worked out in *Manhattan Transfer* and culminating in *U.S.A.*, was calculated to develop a novel in which individual characterization was subordinated to the panoramic effect of history sweeping people along.

Dosso Dossi (dôs′sō dôs′sē). [Original name, **Giovanni de Luteri** or **Giovanni di Nicolò di Lutero;** also known as **Giovanni Dossi.**] b. probably near Ferrara, Italy, c1479; d. 1542. Italian painter. In his earlier years he worked at Modena, but in 1512 it is supposed that he studied with Lorenzo Costa in Mantua, and thereafter spent ten years or more at Rome and at Venice. It is clear from his paintings that he was strongly influenced by Raphael, Giorgione, Titian, and Costa. Subsequently he was employed by successive dukes of Ferrara, both in the execution of frescoes for the adornment of the ducal palace, and in the painting of portraits and landscapes. Examples of his work are to be seen in the palace, the Certosa and the church of San Agostino in Ferrara, in the Uffizi Gallery and the Pitti Palace in Florence, in the Borghese and the Doria Palaces in Rome, in the Brera and in the Ambrosiana, Milan, in several churches at Modena, in the Berlin Gallery and the Dresden Gallery, and in the National Gallery in London. The Metropolitan Museum of Art in New York exhibits his *Three Ages of Man,* and the National Gallery of Art in Washington possesses his *Standard Bearer* and his *Saint Lucretia.* Dosso Dossi was a friend of Ariosto, made designs for the *Orlando Furioso,* and is mentioned by the poet in that book.

Dost Mohammed Khan (dōst mọ.ham′ẹd). b. 1793; d. June 9, 1863. Amir of Kabul. He ascended the throne in 1826. In 1839 the Indian government, on account of his refusal to become an ally of the British, sent an army into Afghanistan, drove him from his throne, and placed Shah Shuja upon it. In 1841 an insurrection broke out in Kabul, and in 1842 the British army was massacred in its retreat. This was followed by a second invasion by the British, who decided to reinstate Dost Mohammed (1842). He made an alliance with the British in 1855, fought against the Persians with them in 1857, and maintained strict neutrality during the Indian Mutiny. He captured Herat from the Persians in 1863.

Dostoevski (dos.to.yef′ski), **Feodor** (also **Fëdor, Fiodor,** or **Fyodor**) **Mikhailovich.** b. at Moscow, Nov. 11 (or, by the old style calendar then still used in Russia, Oct. 30), 1821; d. at St. Petersburg, Feb. 9 (old style, Jan. 28), 1881. Russian novelist, short-story writer, and journalist. His father, of Ukrainian origin, was an army surgeon; his mother came from a well-to-do Moscow business family. He was educated at Moscow, and at the St. Petersburg School of Military Engineering, where he made a fine record. From 1841 to 1844 he served in the army, resigning in the latter year because he felt that he wanted to make literature his life work. In the late 1840's he was a member of the radical Petrashevski group, and, as one of them, he was arrested on April 23, 1849, and spent the next eight months in prison. He was tried as a conspirator, found guilty, sentenced to death by shooting, and then deported to Siberia. The death sentence was recalled, but Dostoevski and his comrades were not allowed to know it until they had been tortured by being made to believe that the original decree was to be carried out. He listened to the formal reading of the death sentence, 20 times witnessed the long and detailed preparations for the execution, and waited blindfolded for the fatal shot to be fired before being informed, when the "joke" could not be further prolonged, that he was not to be killed. This experience, which took place on Dec. 21, 1849, did nothing to help his epilepsy, of which he was a victim from early childhood, and which figures prominently in his novels, as does his passionate fondness for gambling. In 1854 he was released from the Omsk penal colony, and sent to another part of Siberia as a private in the army. He was restored to his former rank in 1855, pardoned in 1859, and allowed to return to St. Petersburg. With his brother, Michael (d. 1864), he edited a review, *Vremya* (the *Times*), which although attacked by both the left and the right and suppressed by the government in 1863, was a success, and its successor, *Epokha* (the *Epoch*), which failed and was discontinued. He began his literary career as a novelist, with a work that immediately brought him recognition as a major force in Russian literature and was praised by the influential critic Belinsky. *Poor Folk* (also *Poor People,* finished 1845, published 1846) is an epistolary novel, telling the story of Makar, a poor government clerk, and Varvara, a poor orphan seamstress, whom he loves but cannot afford to marry, although he goes without food in order to buy her luxuries. He sinks lower and lower in the social scale, falls into debt, sells his clothing, is evicted from his room because he cannot pay his rent, becomes a drunkard, and is forced to accept charity from his superior. Varvara, who blames Makar for his extravagance, without realizing that she is the cause of it, meets Bykov, a wealthy man, and accepts his offer of marriage, without loving him, because she knows that it will mean the end of drudgery and drabness. Makar is left alone with a bitter heart and memories and the prospect of a dull and lonely future. *The Double* (1846) shows that sympathy for the underdog and deep interest in abnormal psychology which are characteristic of Dostoevski. His *Netochka Nezvanova* (1849) is a study in feminine psychology dealing with a "proud woman" type suggestive of the women he married. *The Manor of Stephanchikovo* (1859, also called *The Family Friend*), written in Siberia, is famous for the character of the repulsive Foma Opiskin, regarded as one of the greatest portraits in Russian fiction. *The House of Death* (also *The House of the Dead,* 1861) is a record of his prison impressions and experiences, both of which he never forgot. The sadistic brutality and savagery of the guards, the beatings and floggings, the deadly prison routine (and the pathetic ways in which the convicts sought to break it), their quarrels (frequently brought on by a need for varying the monotony), the psychology of men in chains, all these details of the prison life he saw are realistically described. *The Insulted and the Injured* (1861–62, also known as *The Downtrodden and the Oppressed*) is Dickenslike in its sympathy with the poor, and in its sentimentality. His *Letters from the Underworld* (1864, also called *Memoirs from the Underground* and *Notes from Underground*) is a cross between philosophy and fiction. A short work, in two parts, it deals with a man who takes pleasure in torturing himself and others. The narrative part which deals with Lisa, a prostitute, a familiar Dostoevski type, is almost overshadowed by psychological analysis of and philosophical comments on the nature of evil, and the evil man. It is told in the first person by the hero, who represents spite or malice. In the opinion of most modern critics it may usefully serve the beginning reader of Russian literature as a general introduction to all of Dostoevski. Other short works, long short-stories or novelettes rather than novels, are *The Gentle Maiden* and *The Landlady. Crime and Punishment* (1866), one of his greatest works, is generally regarded also as one of the greatest psychological novels in world literature. The main characters (there are many, Dostoevski being not unlike Dickens in this respect) are Raskolnikov, a poor, sick student, his mother and sister, Pulcheria and Eudoxia, Sonia, a high-minded prostitute, whom he loves and who becomes the means of his regeneration, Luzhin, to whom Eudoxia is engaged, and Petrovitch, a shrewd lawyer and police inspector. The crime is Raskolnikov's hatchet-murder of an old, repulsive, selfish, woman money-lender, and her sister, an act that turns out to be senseless as he does not benefit from it in any way. The punishment is not the seven-year sentence he receives, but the torture of his conscience. Dramatized versions have been successful on English, American, and European stages. His Letters (c1867) deal with his frequent financial distress, his battle with poverty, his study of literature, his life in Siberia, his travels in France, Germany, Italy, and Switzerland, his passionate feeling for Russia (which was so great that he could not be happy or productive anywhere else), his gambling excesses at Baden-Baden, which led him to lose his wife's wedding ring, his quarrel with Turgenev, and his deep conviction, born during his prison days, that Christ belonged to Russia and the Russian people. *The Idiot* (1868–69) is autobiographical in the sense that its Christlike hero, Prince Myshkin, is an epileptic. He is loved by two women, Aglaia, whom he refuses to marry because he feels that he will not be able to make her happy, and Nastasia, whom he is willing to marry in a spirit of self-sacrifice because she has been thrown over by a former lover. His creator represents him as an "idiot" in a double sense, as a pure, gentle, childlike, honest, unambitious character, laughed at by St. Petersburg fashionable society, and as insane, a real idiot, at the end of the story, as a result of spending the night with the jealous Rogozhin, who has murdered Nastasia, and her dead body. Another short novel, *The Eternal Husband* (1871), tells the story of a wife who fools her husband and of what happens, to him, the wife, and the lover, when he finds out. It has been called "a Russian *Madame Bovary.*" *The Demons* (1871, also *The Possessed*) is an anti-Nihilistic novel. Its characters are Nikolay Stavrogin, son of a wealthy widow, Peter Verhovensky, a cold, ruthless Nihilist, Shatov, a peasant and servant, the only decent person in the story, Lebyadkin, army captain and blackmailer, his sister Marya, a half-wit, and Kirillov, an engineer. As in *Hamlet*, most of the characters kill themselves or are killed at the end. *A Raw Youth* (1875), generally considered an inferior work, is the story of a father and his illegitimate son, who is obsessed by a desire to become a millionaire. Both are in love with the same woman and both do not hesitate to use blackmail when it serves their ends. His third masterpiece is *The Brothers Karamazov* (1880). The brothers are Dmitri, a soldier, Ivan, an intellectual and atheist, and Aloysha, a religious mystic, the sons of a drunken, depraved sot. When he is murdered, suspicion falls on Dmitri, whose hatred for his father was well known, but the act was committed by an illegitimate son of the old man, Smerdyakov, an epileptic, whose mother was an imbecile. The cause of the crime is the conflict between Dmitri and his father over Grushenka, the son wanting her as his wife, the father as his mistress. Different shadings of guilt are finely illustrated: actual or technical guilt by Smerdyakov, who kills himself, moral guilt by Ivan, who planted the seed of the crime in Smerdyakov's mind, and subconscious guilt by Dmitri, who wanted the crime committed, and who pays the legal penalty for it. Dostoevski is recognized as one of the great figures in world literature, and his works have been translated into the chief European languages. To English readers he is known through the translations of Constance Garnett, C. J. Hogarth, S. S. Koteliansky, J. Middleton Murry, and Ethel C. Mayne. He was influenced by Gogol, Balzac, and Dickens, but much of his style and technique was uniquely his own, coming from his experience and observation rather than from reading.

"Dot" (dot). See under **Peerybingle, Mrs.**

Dothan (dō′thạn). City in SE Alabama, county seat of Houston County: trading center for peanuts, cotton, potatoes, corn, and fruits. 21,584 (1950).

Dothan. [Also, **Dothaim** (dō.thā′im).] In Biblical geography, a place in Samaria, Palestine, situated ab. 10 mi. N of Shechem.

Dotheboys Hall (dö′ᴛʜẹ.boiz). Yorkshire school in Charles Dickens's *Nicholas Nickleby*, kept by Mr. Squeers, in which Nicholas served a short time as an under-master.

Dotterel (dot′ėr.ẹl), **Mrs.** Character in David Garrick's play *The Male Coquette.*

Dotzauer (dots′ou.ėr), **Justus Johann Friedrich.** b. at Hildburghausen, Germany, June 20, 1783; d. March 6, 1860. German cellist and composer. His works include an opera, a symphony, chamber music, cello concertos, masses, and overtures.

Dou or **Douw** or **Dow** (dou), **Gerard.** b. at Leiden, Netherlands, April 7, 1613; d. there, in February, 1675. Dutch painter of genre scenes, a pupil of Rembrandt. Among his best-known works are portraits, and the *Woman Sick of the Dropsy,* in the Louvre at Paris.

Douai (dö.ā′; French, dwā). [Former spelling, **Douay;** Latin, **Duacum.**] Town in N France, in the department of Nord, situated on the Scarpe River, ab. 18 mi. S of Lille. The Old Testament of the Douay Bible was published here in 1609–10. The town has metallurgical and textile industries, and is particularly known for its lace and its candies. The Hôtel de Ville and the Church of Notre Dame, beautiful Gothic buildings, were built in the 13th, 14th, and 15th centuries. The Church of Saint Pierre dates from the 18th century. The museum contains paintings, sculpture, and archaeological materials. There are various vocational schools. The town belonged originally to Flanders, then to Spain and to France. It finally went to France through the Treaty of Utrecht (1713). Douai was severely damaged in World Wars I and II; a large part of the town, including the Church of Notre Dame, was destroyed. 37,258 (1946).

Douai, Merlin de. See **Merlin,** Comte **Philippe Antoine.**

Douala (dö.ä′lạ). See also **Duala.**

Douala. [Also, **Duala.**] Chief port of the French trust territory of Cameroun. It is situated on the S shore of the Cameroon River estuary and possesses fine docks and a good harbor. It is connected by rail with the capital, Yaoundé, ab. 100 mi. to the E. Pop. ab. 30,000.

Douanier (dwȧ.nyā), **Le.** See **Rousseau, Henri.**

Douarnenez (dwȧr.nẹ.nez). Town in NW France, in the department of Finistère, beautifully situated on a bay named for the town, ab. 21 mi. SE of Brest. It has old churches, a picturesque fishing port, and important sardine and tuna fisheries. It is also a tourist center. 20,564 (1946).

Douaumont (dwō.môṅ). Ruined fortress in NE France, on a high ridge ab. 5 mi. NE of Verdun. One of the key forts of Verdun in World War I, it changed hands several times during the savage battles in 1916, and was finally reoccupied by the French on Dec. 15, 1916. In 1927 a great monument was dedicated, towering over the ossuary containing the remains of some 300,000 unidentified French soldiers who perished on the Verdun battlefields.

Douay (dö.ā', dwā). Former spelling of **Douai.**

Douay, Charles Abel. b. at Besançon, France, in March, 1809; killed at the battle of Wissembourg, France, Aug. 4, 1870. French general, distinguished in the Crimean War at the storming of the Malakhov (at Sevastopol) in 1855, and at Solferino in 1859; brother of Félix Charles Douay.

Douay, Félix Charles. b. at Besançon, France, Aug. 24, 1816; d. at Paris, May 4, 1879. French general; brother of Charles Abel Douay. He distinguished himself at Sedan in 1870, in the Franco-Prussian War, and in the suppression (1871) of the Paris Commune.

Douban (dö.bän'). In the story of "The Greek King and Douban the Physician," in *The Arabian Nights' Entertainments,* a physician who cures the king of leprosy. Believing him to be a traitor, the king orders his execution. Douban gives the king a book, assuring him that his head, after it is cut off, will answer any questions if he will first read a certain line on the sixth page. The pages are poisoned, and the king, moistening his fingers to turn them, instantly dies. Scott introduces a royal slave and physician of this name in *Count Robert of Paris.*

Doubleday (dub'l.dā), **Abner.** b. at Ballston Spa, N.Y., June 26, 1819; d. at Mendham, N.J., Jan. 26, 1893. American soldier, the reputed inventor of the game of baseball. According to a high commission of baseball authorities which delivered a formal report in 1908, Doubleday originated the game of baseball in 1839 while attending school at Cooperstown, N.Y., where he combined the elements of existing bat-and-ball games to formulate an approximation of modern baseball. More recent research, however, indicates that baseball was played in the U.S. perhaps even before Doubleday was born. After studying at Cooperstown, he was graduated (1842) from West Point, served in the Mexican War, and at the opening of the Civil War aimed the initial shot fired from Fort Sumter against the Confederate attack. He was appointed (Feb. 3, 1862) a brigadier general of volunteers in the Union army, commanded a brigade in the Second Battle of Bull Run, and led a division at Antietam and Fredericksburg. Appointed (Nov. 29, 1862) a major general of volunteers, he commanded a corps during the first day of the battle of Gettysburg, and a division on the second and third days. He became (Sept. 15, 1867) a colonel in the regular army, and while on duty (1869–71) at San Francisco secured the charter for the first cable street-railway. He retired from active duty in 1873. He wrote *Reminiscences of Forts Sumter and Moultrie in 1860–'61* (1876) and *Chancellorsville and Gettysburg* (1882).

Doubleday, Edward. b. at Epping, Essex, England, 1811; d. at London, Dec. 14, 1849. English naturalist. He was appointed an assistant in the British Museum in 1839, with special charge of the collections of butterflies and moths. His chief work is *On the Genera of Diurnal Lepidoptera.*

Doubleday, Frank Nelson. b. at Brooklyn, N.Y., Jan. 8, 1862; d. at Coconut Grove, Fla., Jan. 30, 1934. American publisher; husband of Neltje Doubleday. While associated (1877–95) with Charles Scribner's Sons, he reëstablished (1884) and edited *The Book Buyer* and was named (1886) manager of the newly established *Scribner's Magazine.* He was later connected (1897–1900) with Doubleday and McClure Company, president (1900–27) of Doubleday, Page and Company, and chairman (1928 *et seq.*) of the board after the firm became Doubleday, Doran and Company.

Doubleday, Neltje. [Pseudonym, **Neltje Blanchan;** maiden name, **de Graff.**] b. at Chicago, Oct. 23, 1865; d. at Canton, China, Feb. 21, 1918. American naturalist and writer of books on nature; wife of Frank Nelson Doubleday. She was the author of *The Piegan Indians* (1894), *Bird Neighbors* (1896), *Birds that Hunt and Are Hunted* (1898), *Nature's Garden* (1900), *How to Attract the Birds* (1902), *Birds that Every Child Should Know* (1907), *The American Flower Garden* (1909), *Birds Worth Knowing* (1917), *Birds* (1926), and numerous magazine articles, some published in *Country Life.*

Double Dealer, The. Comedy by Congreve, produced in 1693.

Double Falsehood, The. Play published by Theobald in 1728 as by Shakespeare. It is based on the story of Cardenio in *Don Quixote,* and is thought to have been very probably written by Shirley.

Double Gallant, or The Sick Lady's Cure, The. Comedy produced in 1707, compiled by Colley Cibber from Susannah Centlivre's *Love at a Venture* (which owed something to Thomas Corneille's *Le Galant double*) and Burnaby's *The Lady's Visiting Day* and *The Reformed Wife.*

Double Heart, The. Biographical study by Naomi Royde-Smith, published in 1931. It deals with Julie de Lespinasse, who was in love with d'Alembert, the Marquis de Mora, and Count Jacques Antoine Guibert.

Double Marriage, The. Tragedy by John Fletcher, assisted by Philip Massinger, apparently produced after Burbage's death. It was printed in 1647.

Doublin (dub'lin). Former name of **Dublin,** Tex.

Doubris (dö'bris). See **Rochester,** England.

Doubs (dö). Department in E France, bounded by the departments of Haute-Saône and Belfort on the N, Switzerland on the E and S, and the departments of Jura and Haute-Saône on the W. The region was subject to the invasion of a number of Germanic tribes at the end of the Roman era. In the late Middle Ages it was part of the domain of Burgundy, and then of the Spanish Hapsburgs; it was only after the death of Charles V, in the reign of the French king Louis XIV, that Doubs went finally to the French crown. Its cities have preserved their medieval character. The mountainous regions are comparatively barren, but the plains are fertile, producing mainly grains. The department has some of the most important metallurgical and mechanical industries in France. Besançon, Montbéliard, and Pontarlier are centers of the watchmaking, precision instrument, automobile, tractor, and bicycle industries. Other places produce nails, bolts, and similar articles; there are also textile, leather, and paper industries. The department is traversed by the Rhine-Rhone Canal. Capital, Besançon; area, 2,018 sq. mi.; pop. 298,255 (1946).

Doubs, Falls of the. [French, **Saut du Doubs.**] Cataract in the Doubs River, on the border of France and Switzerland, ab. 13 mi. NW of Neuchâtel. Height, ab. 86 ft.

Doubs River. [Latin, **Dubis.**] River in E France which forms part of the French-Swiss border and joins the Saône at Verdun. Length, ab. 270 mi.

Doubtful Heir, The. Romantic comedy by James Shirley, originally produced at Dublin under the title of *Rosania, or Love's Victory,* and licensed in 1640 under that name.

Doubting Castle. Abode of the Giant Despair, in Bunyan's *Pilgrim's Progress,* in which he locked up Christian and Hopeful.

Douce (dous), **Francis.** b. at London, 1757; d. there, March 30, 1834. English antiquary. He was for a time keeper of the manuscripts in the British Museum, in which capacity he took part in cataloguing the Lansdowne manuscripts, and in revising the catalogue of Harleian manuscripts. Having been left one of the residuary legatees of the sculptor Nollekens in 1823, he came into possession of a competent fortune, which enabled him to make a fine collection of books, manuscripts, prints, and coins. This collection was bequeathed to the Bodleian Library. His chief work is *Illustrations of Shakspere* (1807).

Douce Davie Deans (dös' dā'vi dēnz'). See **Deans, Douce Davie.**

Doucet (dö.se), **Charles Camille.** b. at Paris, May 16, 1812; d. there, April 1, 1895. French dramatist and critic. He was the drama critic of the *Moniteur Parisien,* was appointed (1853) chief of the theater division in the state department, and became (1863) director of theaters in the imperial household. He was elected (1876) to the French Academy as successor to Alfred de Vigny and became its perpetual secretary in 1876. His works include *Léonce* (1838; with Bayard), *Un Jeune Homme* (1841), *L'Avocat de sa cause* (1842), *La Chasse aux fripons* (1846), *Velasquez* (1847), *La Barque d'Antonio* (1849), *Les Ennemis de la maison* (1851), *Le Fruit défendu* (1858), *La Considération* (1860), and *Concours littéraires* (1886).

Doudney (död'ni), **Sarah.** b. at Portsmouth, Hampshire, England, Jan. 15, 1843; d. Dec. 15, 1926. English novelist, poet, and author of books for juveniles. Her novels include *The Strength of Her Youth* (1880), *The Family Difficulty* and *A Woman's Glory* (both 1885), *The Missing Rubies* and *Where Two Ways Meet* (both 1886), *When We Two Parted* (1887), *Under False Colours* (1889), *Through Pain to Peace* (1892), *Violets for Faithfulness* (1893), *A Romance of Lincoln's Inn* (1894), *Katherine's Keys* (1895), *Pilgrims of the Night* (1896), *Silent Strings* (1900), *One of the Few* (1904), *Shadow and Shine* (1906), and *Lady Dye's Reparation* (1907); she also wrote *Miss Irving's Bible* (1875), and other works for children.

Dougal (dö'gạl). Wild, shock-headed follower of Rob Roy, in Sir Walter Scott's novel *Rob Roy*.

Dougga (dö'gạ). [Ancient name, **Thugga.**] Former city in N Tunisia, ab. 66 mi. by road SW of Tunis. It was a flourishing native center in the 4th century B.C., and was tributary to Carthage until the first half of the 2nd century B.C. when Massinissa, a Numidian king, ruled it. In 46 B.C. it was conquered by the Romans, who retained the native government, setting up Roman magistrates. Roman colonization dates from the period of Augustus, and during the following two centuries it became Romanized. Today it is one of the chief archaeological sites in North Africa, with a large collection of Roman ruins.

Dougherty (dō'ėr.ti), **Denis J.** b. at Girardville, Pa., Aug. 16, 1865; d. at Philadelphia, May 31, 1951. American Roman Catholic prelate. He was educated at the American College at Rome, ordained priest in 1890, and consecrated bishop of Nueva Segovia in the Philippines in 1903. Subsequently he was bishop of Jaro, in the Philippines (1908), and Buffalo, N.Y. (1915), and archbishop of Philadelphia (1918); created cardinal March 7, 1921. He was papal legate to the International Eucharistic Congress at Manila, P.I., in 1937 and became known for his promotion of diocesan secondary schools at Philadelphia.

Dougherty (dok'ėr.ti), **Paul.** b. at Brooklyn, N.Y., Sept. 6, 1877; d. Jan. 9, 1947. American landscape and marine painter, best known for his ocean scenes; brother of the actor Walter Hampden. He studied alone at Paris, London, Florence, Venice, and Munich, later exhibiting in the U.S. and Canada. He was made an academician of the National Academy of Design (1907), and was also a member of the National Institute of Arts and Letters and the National Arts Club. Many large museums have collected his works, which include *The Land and the Sea*, *Flood Tide*, *Moonlight Cove*, *Sun and Storm*, *Autumn Oaks*, *Storm Quiet*, *Lake Louise*, and *Heavy Sea*.

Doughet (dö.ge), **Gaspar.** See **Poussin, Gaspar.**

Doughfaces (dō'fās"ẹz). Term used by Northerners in the pre-Civil War era in the U.S. to describe contemptuously those Northern persons who aligned themselves with the South on basic policies, such as the institution of slavery and its status in the territories.

Doughton (dou'tọn), **Robert Lee.** b. at Laurel Springs, N.C., Nov. 7, 1863—. American legislator. He was active (1894–1911) as a merchant and farmer and served as a member (1909–11) of the North Carolina state board of agriculture, a member (1908–10) of the state senate, and as a Democratic member (1911 *et seq.*) of the U.S. House of Representatives. He was chairman (1933–47) of the House Ways and Means Committee.

Doughty (dou'ti), **Charles Montagu.** b. in Suffolk, England, Aug. 19, 1843; d. at Sissinghurst, Kent, England, Jan. 30, 1926. English poet, scientist, explorer, and traveler. He was educated at the universities of London, Cambridge, Oxford, Leiden, and Louvain, and traveled in Norway, France, Spain, Italy, Greece, Tunis, Algeria, Damascus, Palestine, and Egypt. He was the author of the classic *Travels in Arabia Deserta* (1888), a work notable for its style, of which *Wanderings in Arabia* (1908) is a condensation; he also wrote scientific essays and reports of his exploring trips. Among his other works are *Under Arms* (1890), *The Dawn in Britain* (1906), an epic poem in 30,000 lines, *Adam Cast Forth* (1908), a verse drama dealing with the expulsion, separation, and reunion of Adam and Eve, *The Cliffs* (1909), *The Clouds* (1912), *The Titans* (1916), and *Mansoul, or the Riddle of the World* (1920).

Doughty, Thomas. b. at Philadelphia, July 19, 1793; d. at New York, July 24, 1856. American landscape painter.

Douglas (dug'lạs). City in SE Arizona, in Cochise County, on the Mexico border: principally important for copper smelting. It was named for James Douglas (1837–1918). 9,442 (1950).

Douglas. City in S Georgia, county seat of Coffee County, in a farming region: seat of South Georgia College. 7,428 (1950).

Douglas. Municipal borough, seaport, and seaside resort on the Isle of Man, situated on the E coast at the confluence of the rivers Dhoo and Glas. It is the capital of the Isle of Man. The port is the first in the world to have been radar controlled. 20,288 (1951).

Douglas. Town in S Massachusetts, in Worcester County, near the borders of Connecticut and Rhode Island: textiles. 2,624 (1950).

Douglas. Civil parish in S Scotland, in Lanarkshire, situated on Douglas Water (a tributary of the river Clyde), ab. 9 mi. SW of Lanark. In the neighborhood are Saint Bride's Church and the ruins of old Douglas Castle. 2,948 (1931).

Douglas. Town in E Wyoming, county seat of Converse County, on the North Platte River ab. 45 mi. E of Casper. It has wool and cattle markets and seed-pea packing plants and is the seat of the annual state fair. 2,544 (1950).

Douglas. Tragedy by John Home, first produced at Edinburgh on Dec. 14, 1756. It is partly founded on a Scottish ballad, *Childe Maurice*.

Douglas, Amanda Minnie. b. at New York, July 14, 1831; d. July 18, 1916. American author of books for children. She was a contributor of short stories to the New York *Ledger*, the *Saturday Evening Post*, and the *Lady's Friend*. Her books include *In Trust* (1866), *Red House Children at Grafton* (1913), *Larry*, which won a *Youth's Companion* prize (1893), the Kathie Series, the Little Girl Series, and the Helen Grant Series.

Douglas, Sir Archibald. b. c1296; killed at the battle of Halidon Hill, near Berwick-upon-Tweed, Northumberland, England, July 19, 1333. Scottish soldier and regent of Scotland (1333); son of Sir William Douglas, "the Hardy" (d. 1298). As a supporter of David Bruce (David II of Scotland) he defeated the newly crowned Edward de Baliol at Annan (1332), was made regent (March, 1333), and was defeated and slain at Halidon Hill.

Douglas, Archibald. [Title: 3rd Earl of **Douglas;** called **"the Grim"** and **"the Black Douglas."**] b. c1328; d. c1400. Scottish soldier and lawmaker; natural son of Sir James Douglas, "the Good" (c1286–1330). His wife was Joanna Moray (or Murray), heiress of Bothwell. He was constable of Edinburgh (1361), and warden of the western marches (1364, 1368). He was the ambassador from David Bruce (David II of Scotland) to the French court in the matter of divorce against David's wife (1369), and again on an embassy announcing Robert II's succession and renewing the French alliance (1371). With Robert, Earl of Fife, he invaded England (1389). The inclusion of Scotland in the peace between England and France was partly due to his efforts (1389, 1391).

Douglas, Archibald [Titles: 4th Earl of **Douglas,** 1st Duke of **Touraine;** called **"Tyneman."**] b. c1369; d. in France, Aug. 17, 1424. Scottish nobleman; second son of Archibald Douglas, 3rd Earl of Douglas (c1328–c1400). He married (1390) Margaret Stewart, daughter of the earl of Carrick (later Robert III). He was captured by the English while he was on a border raid in 1402, fought at Shrewsbury (1403) and was captured by Henry IV of England, and was kept a prisoner until 1408. In 1423 he commanded a Scottish army sent to the support of the French against the English, and in the same year was created Duke of Touraine by Charles VII of France. He fell in the battle of Verneuil, in France.

Douglas, Archibald. [Titles: 5th Earl of **Douglas,** 2nd Duke of **Touraine.**] b. c1391; d. at Restalrig, near Edinburgh, Scotland, June 26, 1439. Scottish soldier and statesman; son of Archibald Douglas, called "Tyneman" (c1369–1424). He fought for Charles VI of France against the English in the battle of Beaugé in France (1421). He accompanied James I of Scotland home from his captivity in England, was shortly after arrested (1424) by the king, soon released, but was later (1431) imprisoned again for a brief period: the arrests were the result of James's attempts to divide the nobility. He served as lieutenant general of Scotland (1438–39).

Douglas, Archibald. [Title, 5th Earl of **Angus**; called **"the Great Earl"**; nicknamed **"Bell-the-Cat."**] b. c1449; d. 1514. Scottish nobleman; son of George Douglas, 4th Earl of Angus. He was one of the disaffected nobles who overthrew and murdered James III's favorite, the Earl of Mar, Robert Cochrane, in 1482. At a meeting of the nobles to concert a plan of attack on the favorite, Lord Gray compared the meeting to that of the mice in the fable who proposed to string a bell round the cat's neck, and asked, with reference to the favorite, "Who will bell the cat?" Douglas answered, "I will bell the cat" (whence his epithet). He plotted with Edward IV of England and Alexander Stuart, Duke of Albany, against James III, but got out of the conspiracy. In the reign of James IV he was chancellor (1493–98) of the kingdom. In Scott's poem *Marmion* he is represented as entertaining Marmion and Lady Clare at his castle by command of the king.

Douglas, Archibald. [Title, 6th Earl of **Angus.**] b. c1489; d. in January, 1557. Scottish nobleman; stepfather of James V of Scotland; grandson of Archibald Douglas, 5th Earl of Angus. He married in 1514 Margaret, widow of James IV of Scotland and sister of Henry VIII of England. Their daughter was Margaret, Countess of Lennox, the mother of Henry Stuart, Lord Darnley. He was thus the great-grandfather of James I of England. Douglas was one of those who declared (1515) the duke of Albany, John Stuart, regent of Scotland. Albany then demanded and obtained custody of the young king, James V, despite Margaret's resistance. When Albany went (1517) to France, Douglas was among those acting on the council of regents in his absence. He ousted James Hamilton, Earl of Arran, from the presidency of the council, but when Albany returned he was exiled to France. During the period of his exile James was declared king, and in 1524 Douglas returned to Scotland. Relying on the backing of Henry VIII, he refused to obey Margaret's orders to stay away from the court. He managed to maintain his influence over James V despite intrigues and the use of force and despite James's desire to rid himself of his stepfather. In 1526 he was chancellor of Scotland, but Margaret divorced him in 1528 and James fled to her. Douglas was forced to go into exile again until after James's death in 1542. He then returned to Scotland to serve the new queen, Mary, Queen of Scots, during the regencies of Arran and Mary of Guise, the queen-mother. He fought at the battle of Pinkie (1547) and was lieutenant of southern Scotland.

Douglas, Archibald. [Title, 8th Earl of **Angus.**] b. 1555; d. at Smeaton, near Dalkeith, Scotland, Aug. 4, 1588. Scottish soldier and supporter of the Presbyterian party; nephew of James Douglas, 4th Earl of Morton (d. 1581), whose policies he supported. A member of the privy council (1573), he became warden of the west marches (1577) and took his uncle's part when Morton was removed from the regency (1578). Lieutenant general on Morton's return, he conspired for an English invasion after Morton's fall (1580) and fled to England after Morton's execution. He was well received by Elizabeth and became a friend of Sir Philip Sidney. He was pardoned by James (1582) but attainted (1584) for rebellion against James; fled to England and became a leader in the invasion of Scotland which resulted in the restoration of the exiled lords (1585). He was appointed warden of the western marches and lieutenant general (1586). His death from consumption was attributed to sorcery.

Douglas, Archibald. [Titles: 3rd Marquis and 1st Duke of **Douglas.**] b. 1694; d. at Edinburgh, July 21, 1761. Scottish supporter of George I during the revolt of 1715. He had obtained his dukedom (1703) by patent from Queen Anne. He fought for the king at Sheriffmuir (1715). His estates were settled on Archibald Douglas (1748–1827), son of his sister, Lady Jane Douglas (1698–1753).

Douglas, Camp. Reception and training point (1861–65) for Illinois volunteers in the Union forces during the Civil War, situated near what was then the southern city line of Chicago. It also served as a prison camp for Confederates.

Douglas, Charles Winfred. b. at Oswego, N.Y., Feb. 15, 1867; d. 1944. American Protestant Episcopal clergyman and musician. He was organist (1892–93) at the Church of Saint Zion and Saint Timothy, New York, associate editor of the *New Hymnal*, and lecturer (1928–34) at the Union Theological Seminary, New York. He compiled and edited such publications as *The Canticles at Evensong* (1915), *The American Psalter* (1929), and *The Praise of God—Church Music in History and Practice* (1936).

Douglas, Clifford Hugh. b. Jan. 20, 1879; d. Sept. 29, 1952. English economist and engineer. As head reconstruction adviser (1935) to the government of Alberta, Canada, he sought to indoctrinate the province with his social credit plan. He was the author of *Economic Democracy* (1919), *Credit Power and Democracy* (1920), *Social Credit* (1923), *The Monopoly of Credit* (1931), and *The Alberta Experiment* (1937).

Douglas, David. b. at Scone, Scotland, 1798; killed in the Hawaiian Islands, July 12, 1834. Scottish botanist. He visited the U.S. as botanical collector for the Royal Horticultural Society in 1823, and subsequently made several scientific journeys in America, spending the years 1829–32 chiefly in California. He contributed a number of papers to scientific journals.

Douglas, Ellen. Daughter of the outlawed James Douglas, in Sir Walter Scott's poem *The Lady of the Lake*. Going to Stirling with the signet ring given her by the Knight of Snowdon (the king) she obtains the pardon of father and lover, though the generous king himself had loved her in disguise.

Douglas, Fort. U.S. military post, ab. 3 mi. E of Salt Lake City.

Douglas, Gawin (or **Gavin**). [Also, **Gawain Douglas.**] b. c1474; d. at London, in September, 1522. Scottish poet and bishop; younger son of Archibald (Bell-the-Cat) Douglas, 5th Earl of Angus. He prepared a translation of the *Aeneid* into Scottish verse (1513; printed 1553), the first translation, after Caxton's feeble rendering of the *Aeneid*, of a classical work into any form of the English language. He also wrote the allegory *The Palice of Honour; King Hart*, an allegory of the heart, the senses, and the like; and *Conscience*, a conceit.

Douglas, George. [Title, 1st Earl of **Angus.**] b. c1380; d. in England, 1403. Scottish soldier; natural son of William Douglas, 1st Earl of Douglas (c1327–84) and Margaret, Countess of Angus. He was granted the title of Earl of Angus by charter of Robert II (1389). Captured at the battle of Homildon (1402), he was taken to England, where he died of the plague.

Douglas, George. [Titles: 4th Earl of **Angus,** Lord of **Douglas.**] b. c1412; d. 1462. Scottish nobleman. He remained loyal to James II in a rising of his kinsmen against the king, and commanded the royal forces at the battle of Arkinholm on May 1, 1455, in which the insurgents were defeated. He received as a reward large grants of land from the confiscated estates, and may be regarded as the founder of the position of the earls of Angus as border chiefs.

Douglas, George. In Sir Walter Scott's novel *The Abbot*, the seneschal of Lochlevel Castle during his father's absence. Falling in love with his prisoner, Mary, Queen of Scots, he aids her escape and dies at the battle of Langside.

Douglas, George. Pseudonym of **Brown, George Douglas.**

Douglas, Sir **Howard.** b. at Gosport, England, July 1, 1776; d. at Tunbridge Wells, England, in November, 1861. English general and military writer. He was the author of *Treatise on Naval Gunnery* (1820) and other works.

Douglas, Sir **James.** [Title, Lord of **Douglas;** called **"the Good Sir James"** and **"the Black Douglas."**] b. c1286; killed in Spain, probably on Aug. 25, 1330. Scottish nobleman. He was the terror of the English in his border raids. His name of "the Black Douglas" is either from this reputation or from his dark skin. He had no hesitation, twice, in destroying his own castle when it was occupied by the British. His exploits on the border were many and romantic, being climaxed in 1327 by his almost capturing Edward III of England in a night raid on the English camp. He joined the standard of Robert Bruce (Robert I of Scotland) in 1306, and commanded the left wing of the Scottish army at the battle of Bannockburn, on June 24, 1314. In accordance with the dying request of Bruce, he set out on a journey to the Holy Land, carrying with him Bruce's heart incased in a casket of gold. Arrived in Spain, he offered his services to Alfonso, king of Castile and León, against the Saracens of Granada, and fell in battle.

Douglas, James. [Title, 2nd Earl of **Douglas and Mar.**] b. c1358; d. 1388. Scottish nobleman; son of William Douglas, 1st Earl of Douglas. He commanded a force of 300 horse and 2,000 foot which ravaged the eastern border in 1388, and probably on the 19th of August in that year (on the 9th according to the English chroniclers, on the 15th according to Froissart) defeated a superior force of the levy of the northern counties of England under Lord Henry Percy (Harry Hotspur) at Otterburn; Hotspur was captured, along with his brother, but Douglas fell at the moment of victory. His fame is celebrated in the Scottish ballad *The Battle of Otterburn* and the English ballad *Chevy Chase.*

Douglas, James. [Titles: 7th Earl of **Douglas,** Earl of **Avondale;** called **"the Gross"** or **"the Fat."**] b. c1371; d. at Abercorn, Scotland, March 24, 1443. Scottish noble; son of Archibald Douglas "the Grim" (c1328–c1400). The regent Albany kept his support by allowing him to profit from the customs. He was a member of the assizes at the trial of the duke of Albany (1425), was created Earl of Avondale (1437), and was suspected of being implicated in the murder of his grandnephew, William Douglas, 6th Earl of Douglas (c1423–1440).

Douglas, James. [Title, 9th Earl of **Douglas.**] b. 1426; d. at Lindores, Scotland, July 14, 1488. Last Earl of Douglas. He headed a rebellion against James II of Scotland in 1452 but James, supported by George Douglas, 4th Earl of Angus, defeated him. Again in 1455, he rebelled, and again was defeated, in consequence of which he was banished and deprived of his estates. He was captured (1484) while he was on a raid from England into Scotland and was imprisoned in the abbey at Lindores for the rest of his life.

Douglas, James. [Title, 4th Earl of **Morton.**] b. at Dalkeith, Scotland, 1530; beheaded at Edinburgh, June 2, 1581. Regent of Scotland; second son of Sir George Douglas of Pittendriech. In 1553 he succeeded to the earldom of Morton through marriage with Elizabeth, daughter of the third earl. On the return of Mary, Queen of Scots, in 1561 he was made privy councilor, and in 1563 lord high chancellor. He was a prime mover in the assassination of Rizzio, and in securing the abdication of Mary at Lochleven. In October, 1572, he became regent on the death of the earl of Mar. He resigned when James VI assumed the government, and was condemned on the accusation of James Stuart (afterward earl of Arran) for complicity in the death of Darnley, the king's father.

Douglas, James. [Title, 4th Duke of **Hamilton.**] b. April 11, 1658; killed in a duel at Hyde Park, London, Nov. 15, 1712. Scottish nationalist and politician; son of William Douglas, 3rd Duke of Hamilton (1635–94). He was known for his opposition to the treaty of union with England (1707); commanded regiment of horse against Monmouth's rebellion (1685); accompanied James II until he left England (1688); as Duke of Hamilton became leader of nationalists in Scottish parliament and spoke against union but foiled attempt at armed rising (1707); chosen one of 16 representative peers to sit in English Parliament (1708); member of privy council (1710), ambassador extraordinary to France to negotiate peace of Utrecht, but killed in duel by Lord Mohun before he sailed.

Douglas, James. [Titles: 2nd Duke of **Queensberry,** 1st Duke of **Dover.**] b. Dec. 18, 1662; d. July 6, 1711. Scottish politician, supporter of the house of Hanover; eldest son of William Douglas, 1st Duke of Queensberry (1637–95); educated at Glasgow University; privy councilor under James II (1684), went over to William of Orange and was made privy councilor, appointed lord high treasurer (1693), appointed king's commissioner to meeting of Scottish estates (1700) and made Knight of the Garter (1701) for his able handling of that meeting; under Queen Anne one of the secretaries of state for Scotland (1702). Unknowingly aided Jacobites through his ignorance of Fraser's true aims (1703) and resigned his offices; his innocence resulted in reinstatement as lord privy seal (1705); negotiated treaty of union (1706); created Duke of Dover (1708) as reward; third secretary of state (1709).

Douglas, Sir **James.** b. in Lanarkshire, Scotland, June 5, 1803; d. at Victoria, British Columbia, Aug. 1, 1877. Canadian fur trader and colonial administrator. He went to Canada in 1820 and was in the service of the North West Company until its merger in the following year with the Hudson's Bay Company, when his long association with the latter began. In 1824, with John McLoughlin, he made his first trip of exploration into the region around the Columbia River. In 1840 he was appointed chief factor, and in 1846, senior officer, of the Hudson's Bay Company's territories west of the Rocky Mountains. In 1843 he built Fort Victoria on a site on Vancouver Island which is now included in the city of Victoria. In 1851 he was made governor of Vancouver Island, which had been ceded to the British crown, and in 1858 he was appointed governor also of the new colony of British Columbia. In accepting these offices, he ended his long association with the Hudson's Bay Company. He administered the affairs of both colonies with marked ability, and his services were recognized when knighthood was conferred on him in 1863, on the eve of his retirement from office.

Douglas, James. b. at Quebec, Nov. 4, 1837; d. June 25, 1918. Canadian metallurgist and mining engineer.

Douglas, Lady **Jane.** b. March 17, 1698; d. at Edinburgh, Nov. 22, 1753. Sister of Archibald Douglas, 1st Duke of Douglas (1694–1761). Her secret marriage to Colonel John Stuart (1746) led to a great Douglas lawsuit (1769) in which her son, Archibald James Edward Douglas (1748–1827) was declared legitimate heir to the Douglas estates.

Douglas, John. b. at Pittenweem, Fifeshire, Scotland, July 14, 1721; d. at Salisbury, England, May 18, 1807. British prelate and writer. He was appointed bishop of Carlisle in 1787, transferred to Salisbury in 1791, and became dean of Windsor in 1788. Among his works are *Milton vindicated from the Charge of Plagiarism* (1751), and a book attacking Hume's argument on the miracles, entitled *The Criterion* (1752).

Douglas, John Sholto. See **Queensberry,** 8th Marquis of.

Douglas, Lewis Williams. b. at Bisbee, Ariz., July 2, 1894—. American politician and diplomat; grandson of James Douglas (1837–1918). Miner and rancher (1921 *et seq.*) in Arizona; served (1923–25) in Arizona legislature; U.S. congressman (1927–33) from Arizona; served (1933–34) as U.S. budget director; principal and vice-chancellor of McGill University, Montreal (1938–39); president (1940–47) of New York Mutual Life Insurance Company; deputy administrator (May, 1942–March, 1944) of war shipping board; U.S. ambassador to Great Britain (1947–50).

Douglas, Lloyd Cassel. b. at Columbia City, Ind., Aug. 27, 1877; d. at Los Angeles, Calif., Feb. 13, 1951. American Lutheran clergyman and novelist. He was educated at Wittenberg College and Hamma Divinity School at Springfield, Ohio, and ordained (1903) in the Lutheran ministry. His books include *Magnificent Obsession* (1929), *Forgive Us Our Trespasses* (1932), *Precious Jeopardy* (1933), *Green Light* (1935), *White Banners* (1936), *Home for Christmas* (1937), *Disputed Passage* (1939), *Dr. Hudson's Secret Journal* (1939), *Invitation to Live* (1940), *The Robe* (1942), *The Big Fisherman* (1948), and *A Time to Remember* (1951), his autobiography.

Douglas, Lady **Margaret.** [Title, Countess of **Lennox.**] b. at Harbottle Castle, Northumberland, England, 1515; d. March 7, 1578. English noblewoman; granddaughter of Henry VII and mother of Lord Darnley (1545–67). Placed (1531) by Henry VIII at Beaulieu in household of Princess Mary (later queen) whose friendship she held throughout Mary's life; her private betrothal to Lord Thomas Howard, uncle to Anne Boleyn, displeased Henry who imprisoned her in Syon Abbey; declared illegitimate and thus ineligible for crown by Henry and was restored to favor; married Matthew Stuart, Earl of Lennox (1516–71), who was appointed Henry's governor of Scotland;

Henry's will excluded her from succession because of her Catholic leanings (1546); planned marriage between Mary, Queen of Scots and her son Lord Darnley, but arrested by Elizabeth on suspicion of treason (1562); released but sent to Tower of London after Darnley's marriage to Mary (1565); accused Mary of Darnley's murder at Elizabeth's court, but reconciled to her (c1572).

Douglas, Norman. [Full name, **George Norman Douglas.**] b. 1868; d. on Capri (the scene of *South Wind*), Feb. 9, 1952. English novelist. He was the author of *Unprofessional Tales* (1901), *Siren Land* (1911), *South Wind* (1917), *They Went* (1921), *Old Calabria* (1928), *Three of Them* (1930), *Goodbye to Western Culture* (1930), *Paneros* (1931), *Looking Back* (2 vols., 1933), and *Late Harvest* (1946).

Douglas, Paul Howard. b. at Salem, Mass., March 26, 1892—. American economist, U.S. senator (1948 *et seq*). From 1916 to 1920, as instructor, assistant professor, and associate professor, he taught economics at the University of Illinois, at Reed College in Portland, Ore., and at the University of Washington. In 1920 he became assistant professor, in 1923 associate professor, and in 1925 professor of industrial relations at the University of Chicago. He has been a member of many commissions and committees concerned with economic and industrial problems, and especially has served the U.S. government as an adviser in matters of wage laws and in measures for social security. In 1942 he enlisted in the U.S. Marine Corps, was wounded at Okinawa and awarded the bronze star for heroic conduct in action, and rose to the rank of lieutenant-colonel. As a Democrat, he was elected to the U.S. Senate from Illinois in 1948. He is the author of *Real Wages in the United States, 1890–1926* (1930), *The Theory of Wages* (1934), *Controlling Depressions* (1935), *Social Security in the United States* (1936), *Economy in the National Government* (1952), and *Ethics in Government* (1952).

Douglas, Sir **Sholto.** [Full name, **William Sholto Douglas.**] b. 1893—. British air officer who served (1946–47) as commander in chief of British forces in Germany and governor of British zone. Served during World War I and World War II; instructor (1932–35) of Imperial Defence College; director (1936–37) of staff duties at air ministry. Assistant chief of air staff (1938–40); commander in chief (1940–42) of fighter command; headed (1942–44) Middle East British air force; commanded (1944–45) Royal Air Force coastal command with rank of air chief marshal.

Douglas, Sholto George Watson. [Title, 20th Earl of **Morton.**] b. Nov. 5, 1844; d. in Scotland, Oct. 8, 1935. Representative peer (1886 *et seq.*) of Scotland. Educated at Trinity College, Cambridge; served as head coast watcher in royal navy during World War I; known as yachtsman during Victorian era.

Douglas, Stephen Arnold. [Called **"the Little Giant."**] b. at Brandon, Vt., April 23, 1813; d. at Chicago, June 3, 1861. American politician and legislator, noted as the proponent of "popular sovereignty" in the slavery crisis preceding the Civil War. He studied law in Ontario County, N.Y., where he also attended Canandaigua Academy, and in 1833 migrated to the West, settling at Winchester, Ill., where he conducted a school. He was licensed (at Jacksonville, Ill.) to practice law, and shortly afterward was elected state's attorney for the first judicial district. He was a leading spirit in the building of the Democratic organization in Illinois, in which he became a power before reaching his 35th year, and was elected to the state legislature as a Democratic member from Morgan County. After the session ended, he became register of the land office at Springfield, and in 1840 was appointed secretary of state. He was subsequently appointed a judge in the state supreme court. After terms (1843–47) in the House of Representatives, he became (1847) a member of the U.S. Senate, where he was made chairman of the Committee on Territories. In this position he was at the very center of the problems concerned with the extension of slavery, and helped frame the compromise bills establishing territorial governments for Utah and New Mexico (1850). In the same year he secured the passage of the Illinois Central Railroad bill. In the debates on the Kansas-Nebraska bill (1854) he originated the phrase "popular sovereignty," crystallizing his views on the question of slavery in the territories. While he supported the Kansas-Nebraska bill, which divided the Nebraska territory into two states and permitted the inhabitants to decide whether or not they wanted slavery (a denial of the Missouri Compromise of 1820 which forbade slavery in the territory), in order to keep his party from being divided, his action created hostility among Northern Democrats, and there was a section of opinion which held that Douglas had surrendered to the Southern faction in order to better his presidential ambitions. However, his uncompromising stand (1857) against the Lecompton constitution, a proslavery constitution adopted in Kansas after antislavery adherents failed to vote on it, signalized his break with the proslavery element in the Democratic Party. In 1858 he conducted his famous debates with Lincoln which brought the latter to national attention for the first time, and, because of some of his statements, widened the breach between Douglas and the Southern Democrats. Running against Lincoln, he was reëlected to the Senate in 1859, and upon his return to Washington became progressively further removed from the Southern wing of his party. He was nominated as presidential candidate by the Democratic convention at Baltimore after the Southern delegations had withdrawn at Charleston. Even while conducting his campaign in 1860, he made attempts to keep the Democratic Party from falling apart. Alone among the four presidential candidates who ran that year, he received votes in every section of the country; and in the North he ran second to Lincoln. Upon the outbreak of the Civil War, he threw his full support to Lincoln. He died while on a speaking tour to rally the forces of the country behind the government. See *Stephen A. Douglas: a Study in American Politics*, by Allen Johnson (1908).

Douglas, Sir **William.** [Title, Knight of **Liddesdale.**] b. c1300; killed 1353. Scottish nobleman. He sided with David II against Edward Baliol, and obtained as a reward the lordship of Liddesdale, whence he was surnamed "the Knight of Liddesdale." He was killed during a hunt in Ettrick forest by his kinsman William, Lord (afterward Earl) of Douglas.

Douglas, William. [Title, 1st Earl of **Douglas and Mar.**] d. 1384. Scottish nobleman; nephew of James Douglas, "the good Sir James." He was trained in arms in France; returned to Scotland c1348; recovered his paternal estates from the English; conducted numerous raids on the English border; was appointed a warden of the east marches c1356; and was created Earl of Douglas by David II in 1358.

Douglas, William. [Titles: 6th Earl of **Douglas,** 3rd Duke of **Touraine.**] b. c1423; beheaded at Edinburgh, Nov. 24, 1440. Scottish noble and claimant to the Scottish throne; son of Archibald Douglas (c1391–1439). At a banquet given by James II at Edinburgh, he was seized and soon after beheaded.

Douglas, William. [Title, 8th Earl of **Douglas.**] b. c1425; d. 1452. Scottish nobleman; son of James Douglas, 7th Earl of Douglas. He conspired against James II, by whom he was decoyed by a safe-conduct to Stirling Castle and put to death.

Douglas, William. [Title, 7th (or 8th) Earl of **Morton.**] b. 1582; d. at Kirkwall, Scotland, 1650. Scottish politician; grandson of Sir William Douglas of Lochleven (d. 1606). Commanded (1627) Scots regiment in Rochelle expedition; lord high treasurer of Scotland (1630–35); member (1641) Scottish parliament; his nomination (1641) for the chancellorship was defeated by his son-in-law, the Earl of Argyll; rewarded (1643) by Charles I with a charter of Orkney and Shetland Islands for advancement of money.

Douglas, William. [Titles: 11th Earl of **Angus,** 1st Marquis of **Douglas.**] b. 1589; d. at Douglas, Scotland, Feb. 19, 1660. Scottish nobleman. Created (1633) Marquis of Douglas, fought (1645) on the side of Montrose at Philiphaugh; imprisoned (1646) and released on signing Solemn League and Covenant; fined (1654) by Cromwell.

Douglas, Sir **William.** [Titles: 1st Earl of **Queensberry,** Viscount of **Drumlanrig.**] d. March 8, 1640. Scottish politician; son of Sir James Douglas (d. 1616). Created (1617) Viscount of Drumlanrig by James I; created (1633) 1st Earl of Queensberry by Charles I.

Douglas, William. [Title, 3rd Duke of **Hamilton.**] b. Dec. 24, 1635; d. at Holyrood Castle, Edinburgh, April 18, 1694. Scottish nobleman. Fined (1654) 1,000 pounds by Cromwell; privy councilor (1660–76) in Scotland; opposed (1672) Lauderdale's land tax; ejected (1676) from the council; privy councilor of England in 1687; royal commissioner (1689 and 1693) under William III.

Douglas, William. [Titles: 3rd Earl and 1st Duke of **Queensberry.**] b. 1637; d. March 28, 1695. Scottish politician; grandson of Sir William Douglas (d. 1640). Privy councilor (1667); lord justice general of Scotland (1680–86); created Duke of Queensberry (1684); one of the lords of privy council in both kingdoms (1687).

Douglas, William. [Titles: 3rd Earl of **March,** 4th Duke of **Queensberry;** latterly known as **"Old Q."**] b. 1724; d. at London, Dec. 23, 1810. Scottish politician, notorious for his dissolute life and extravagances. He attempted to develop horse racing as a science; Knight of the Thistle, 1761; representative peer for Scotland in the same year; vice-admiral (1767–76) of Scotland; created (1786) Baron Douglas of Amesbury in British peerage; satirized by Burns, called "degenerate Douglas" by Wordsworth, and basis of a character in Thackeray's *Virginians.*

Douglas, Sir **William de.** [Called **"the Hardy";** also known as Sir **William of Douglas.**] d. in the Tower of London, 1298. Scottish crusader and fighter for national independence; believed to have joined Crusades; among barons refusing to recognize John de Baliol as king of Scotland, but later gave homage; captured when Edward I took Berwick after Baliol's forced abdication, but released upon oath of fealty to Edward; joined Wallace in fight for independence and, when the barons submitted to Edward at Irving Water, Ayrshire (1297) was imprisoned in the Tower of London until his death (1298).

Douglas, William Lewis. b. at Plymouth, Mass., Aug. 22, 1845; d. Sept. 17, 1924. American shoe manufacturer, governor (1905–06) of Masschusetts. Member (1884) of Massachusetts legislature; state senator (1886).

Douglas, William Orville. b. at Maine, Minn., Oct. 16, 1898—. American jurist. Associated (1929–32) with U.S. Department of Commerce in bankruptcy studies; Sterling professor of law (1932–39) at Yale; member (1934–36) and chairman (1936–39) of Securities and Exchange Commission; appointed (1939) associate justice of U.S. Supreme Court. Douglas's interest in mountain climbing and exploration is reflected in his books *Of Men and Mountains* (1950), *Strange Lands and Friendly People* (1951), and *Beyond the High Himalayas* (1952).

Douglas of Kirkcudbright (kėr.kö′bri), **William.** b. at Fingland, Kirkcudbrightshire, Scotland, c1672; d. 1748. Scottish poet, author of *Annie Laurie.* The daughter of Sir Robert Laurie, of Maxwellton House, Dumfriesshire, Annie Laurie (1682–1764) broke her engagement with Douglas in order to marry (1709) James Fergusson, of Craigdarroch. Douglas later eloped with Betty Clark, of Glenboig, Galloway, but he made his earlier love famous with his song which is known and sung all over the world. *Annie Laurie* was first published as a poem in 1824, and the music was composed (1835) by Lady John Douglas Scott.

Douglas of Lochleven (loċh.lē′vẹn), Sir **William.** [Title, 6th (or 7th) Earl of **Morton.**] d. Sept. 27, 1606. Scottish courtier and soldier. Took part (1566) in murder of Rizzio; custodian (1567) of Mary, Queen of Scots after her surrender at Carberry Hill; commander (1568) of rear guard at Langside; signed bond (1582) as supporter of James VI; banished (1583) in the counterrevolution at St. Andrews; organized in France (1585) overthrow of Arran; made (1588) Earl of Morton.

Douglass (dug′lạs), **Andrew Ellicott.** b. at Windsor, Vt., July 5, 1867—. American astronomer and dendrochronologist, notable for researches in determining date of prehistoric ruins by tree rings. He is the author of *Climatic Cycles and Tree Growth* (3 vols., 1919, 1928, 1936).

Douglass, Frederick. [Original name, **Frederick Augustus Washington Bailey.**] b. at Tuckahoe, Md., c1817; d. at Anacostia Heights, D.C., Feb. 20, 1895. American abolitionist, orator, and journalist. He was born into slavery; sent to Baltimore in 1825 as a houseboy, he there learned to read and write. Growing accustomed to the relative liberty of a town slave, and becoming engaged to a free woman, he escaped (1838) and settled at New Bedford, Mass., where he became an odd-jobs laborer. After making a spontaneous speech at the convention of the Massachusetts Anti-Slavery Society at Nantucket, he was hired as an agent of the society. Schooled by William Lloyd Garrison and Wendell Phillips, he soon became an effective speaker; to answer those who doubted that he had spent 20 years in slavery, he wrote his *Narrative of the Life of Frederick Douglass* (1845), which was also printed in England and translated into French and German. In order to escape reënslavement after rendering this frank account of his slave experiences, and to seek British support for the abolitionist cause, he went to Great Britain and Ireland, remaining for nearly two years. His success abroad was great; British admirers raised money to purchase his freedom from his former master, and to enable him to found (1847) an abolitionist weekly, the *North Star.* During the 1850's he was in constant demand as a lecturer, his imposing physique and rolling voice lending themselves well to an impassioned eloquence. He was prominent in the temperance crusade and the woman's rights movement. He fled from the U.S. within three days after John Brown's abortive raid at Harpers Ferry in 1859, thus forestalling any effort by the state government of Virginia to seize him. In the Civil War, after an audience with President Lincoln, he aided in the recruiting of Negro troops, his own sons being his first two recruits. During the Reconstruction period he was a leading exponent of suffrage and civil rights for the emancipated Negroes. A staunch Republican, he was rewarded for his loyal support by appointment as marshal (1877–81) and later recorder of deeds (1881–86) of the District of Columbia, and as U.S. minister (1889–91) to Haiti. He wrote *My Bondage and My Freedom* (1855) and *Life and Times of Frederick Douglass* (1884).

Douglasville (dug′lạs.vil). Town in NW Georgia, county seat of Douglas County: formerly the site of an Indian village. 3,400 (1950).

Douhet (dö.ā′), **Giulio.** b. at Caserta, Italy, May 30, 1869; d. at Rome, Feb. 15, 1930. Italian flyer and general. After studying electrical engineering at Turin, he joined the army and became a major. He commanded (1911–15) the first Italian air battalion and served (1915) as chief of staff of the 5th division. He left (1917) active service after publishing his opinions of war conduct, in which he criticized the high command. His *Il Dominio dell'aria* (Air Domination, 1921), which first proposed an independent air force and advanced the hypothesis of saturation bombing since sometimes called the "Douhet Theory," had a great influence on German and Italian tactics in the Spanish Civil War.

Doukato (dö.kä′tō), **Cape.** [Also: **Cape Ducato;** ancient name, **Leucadia.**] Cape at the S extremity of the island of Leukas, Ionian Islands, Greece. Sometimes called "Lover's Leap," it is the traditional scene of the death of Sappho.

Doukhobors (dö′kọ.bôrz). See **Dukhobors.**

Doullens (dö.läṅ). Town in N France, in the department of Somme, situated at the junction of the Authie and Grouches rivers, ab. 19 mi. N of Amiens. It is a center for the exploitation of phosphates and has chemical and textile factories. It has an old citadel and a museum. Here, in the spring of 1918, Clemenceau and Lloyd George met to discuss the unification of the Allied command. The town, including the Church of Saint Pierre, was severely damaged during World War II. 5,404 (1946).

Doulton (dōl′tọn), Sir **Henry.** b. at Lambeth, London, 1820; d. at London, Nov. 17, 1897. English potter, said to have been "the greatest potter of the 19th century." Born of a potter's family, Henry Doulton was graduated from University College school in 1835. He worked on his foot-wheel and soon became an expert "thrower," and made (1841) his first distinct success with glazed pipes for sanitary purposes. His work received (1851, 1862) medals. He began (1870) to develop his famous "sgraffite" ware, a revival in a modified form of the old "agate" or self-glazed stoneware of the late 17th century. At the exhibition (1871) at South Kensington, this display won wide acclaim. After further success at Vienna (1873) and Paris (1878), Doulton concentrated on its production, employing at one time 400 male and female designers.

His rule was to leave no copy of previous patterns and no duplicate for later imitation. His more famous products include the Lambeth Faïence, Doulton Impasto, Silicon, Chiné, Marquetrie, and Burslem wares. He was vice-president (1890–94) of the Society of Arts.

Doumer (dö.mer), **Paul.** b. at Aurillac, Cantal, France, March 22, 1857; d. at Paris, May 7, 1932, after an attack by an assassin. French political leader, 13th president of the French third republic. He interrupted a parliamentary career (1888–96) to serve as governor general of Indochina (1896–1902). He returned (1902) to the Chamber of Deputies, was an unsuccessful candidate (1906) for president of the republic against Armand Fallières, served as finance minister in the Briand cabinets of 1921 and 1926, and was chosen president of the senate in 1927. He was elected president of the republic on May 13, 1931, and was shot by a Russian émigré on May 6, 1932.

Doumergue (dö.merg), **Gaston.** b. at Aigues-Vives, Gard, France, Aug. 1, 1863; d. there, June 18, 1937. French statesman and lawyer, president (1924–31) of the French third republic. A deputy (1893–1910) and a senator (1910–24, 1931 *et seq.*), he was colonial minister (1902–05, 1914–16), minister of commerce (1906), minister of public instruction (1906–10), premier (December, 1913–June, 1914, February–November, 1934), foreign minister (August, 1914), and president of the senate (1923–24). After completing his term as president, he returned to political life to become (Feb. 9, 1934) premier after the riots provoked by the Stavisky scandal, retiring in November.

Doumic (dö.mēk), **René.** b. at Paris, 1860; d. 1937. French critic and editor. He was the author of *De Scribe à Ibsen* (1893), *Essai sur le théâtre contemporain* (1897), and *Études sur la littérature française* (6 vols., 1896–1908). From teaching rhetoric at the famous Collège Stanislas, he turned (1897) to writing criticism for the *Correspondant, Revue Bleue, Journal des Débats,* and *Revue des Deux Mondes.* He was elected to the French Academy in 1910, became editor of the *Revue des Deux Mondes* in 1916, and was perpetual secretary of the Academy from 1919 until his death.

Doune (dön). Police burgh in C Scotland, in Perthshire, situated near the river Teith, ab. 6 mi. NW of Stirling, ab. 426 mi. N of London by rail. It contains the ruined Doune Castle. 868 (est. 1948).

Dour (dör). Town in S Belgium, in the province of Hainault, ab. 9 mi. SW of Mons: coal-mining town. 11,642 (1947).

Dourdan (dör.däṅ). Village in N France, in the department of Seine-et-Oise, ab. 25 mi. SW of Paris. It contains a church and a ruined castle.

Douro (dō′rö). [Spanish, **Duero;** Latin, **Durius.**] River in Spain and N Portugal which rises in the province of Soria, Spain, forms part of the boundary between the two countries, and flows into the Atlantic Ocean 3 mi. W of Oporto. Length, ab. 500 mi.; navigable ab. 90 mi.

Douro Litoral (dō′rö lē.tö.räl′). Province of Portugal, bounded by Minho on the N, Tráz-os-Montes e Alto Douro on the E, Beira Alta on the SE, Beira Litoral on the S, and the Atlantic Ocean on the W. It contains the district of Pôrto. It comprises mountainous parts and fertile districts around the Douro River valley; commercial and industrial activities are concentrated in the city of Oporto. Capital, Oporto; area, 1,269 sq. mi.; pop. 1,104,925 (1940).

Dousa (dö′sạ), **Janus.** [Latinized name of **Jan Van der Does.**] b. at Noordwijk, near Leiden, Netherlands, Dec. 6, 1545; d. there, in October, 1604. Dutch scholar, poet, historian, and patriot. He defended Leiden (1574–75), and became first curator of the University of Leiden in 1575. He published *Annals of Holland* (1599), and others.

Dousabel (dö′sạ.bel). [Also, **Dowsabel.**] Common name for a rustic sweetheart in old pastoral poems.

Dousterswivel (dös′tėr.swiv.ẹl), **Herman.** In Sir Walter Scott's novel *The Antiquary,* a German adventurer who tricks Sir Arthur Wardour by a pretended magical discovery of treasure, and is himself similarly tricked by Ochiltree. The nickname Dousterswivel was given to the phrenologist Johann Kaspar Spurzheim.

Douville (dö.vēl), **Jean Baptiste.** b. at Hambie, Manche, France, Feb. 15, 1794; d. in Brazil, c1837. French adventurer. He published in 1832 a book entitled *Voyage au Congo et dans l'intérieur de l'Afrique équinoxiale,* which purported to be an account of explorations made by himself in central Africa between 1828 and 1830. The gold medal of the Geographical Society at Paris was awarded to him for the most important discovery in 1830, and he was made secretary of the society for 1832. It was later shown, however, that the *Voyage* was a mere fabrication based on early Portuguese expeditions.

Douvres (dövr). French name of **Dover,** England.

Douw (dou), **Gerard.** See **Dou** or **Douw** or **Dow, Gerard.**

Dove (duv). River in N central England, in Derbyshire and Staffordshire, forming part of the Derbyshire-Staffordshire boundary, rising 4 mi. SW of Buxton and flowing to its juncture with the Trent ab. 3 mi. NE of Burton-upon-Trent. It is celebrated in the writings of Izaak Walton. Length, ab. 45 mi.

Dove. Pinnace of about 50 tons, one of the vessels (the other being the *Ark*) in which Lord Baltimore sent out a colony of "gentlemen adventurers," including his brothers George and Leonard Calvert, to Maryland in 1633. They landed near the mouth of the Potomac in 1634.

Dove, Doctor. Chief character in Southey's *The Doctor.*

Dove (dō′fẹ), **Heinrich Wilhelm.** b. at Liegnitz, Prussia, Oct. 6, 1803; d. at Berlin, April 4, 1879. German physicist, professor at Berlin from 1829, noted for his researches in meteorology and electricity. His chief works are *Meteorologische Untersuchungen* (1837), *Über die nicht-periodischen Änderungen der Temperaturverteilung* (1840–59), and others.

Dove (duv), **Lady.** In Cumberland's play *The Brothers,* a termagant, the mother of the principal female character.

Dove, Patrick Edward. b. at Lasswade, near Edinburgh, July 31, 1815; d. April 28, 1873. British editor and philosophical writer. He published *The Theory of Human Progression, and Natural Probability of a Reign of Justice* (1850), in which, among other doctrines, he maintained that rent belongs to the nation, and thus, in a measure, anticipated the single-tax theory of Henry George.

Dove (dō′fẹ), **Richard Wilhelm.** b. at Berlin, Feb. 27, 1833; d. at Göttingen, Germany, Sept. 18, 1907. German canonist; son of the physicist Heinrich Wilhelm Dove. He was professor successively at Tübingen (1862), Kiel (1865), and Göttingen (1868). He was elected a deputy to the Reichstag in 1871.

Dovedale (duv′dāl). Picturesque valley of the river Dove, in N central England, on the Derbyshire-Staffordshire boundary, NW of Burton-upon-Trent.

Dover (dō′vėr). City in C Delaware, capital of Delaware and county seat of Kent County, on Jones Creek. It has important canning industries. Settled c1684, it has been state capital since 1777. Pop. 6,223 (1950).

Dover. [French, **Douvres;** Old English, **Dofre, Dofere;** Latin, **Dubrae, Dubris, Portus Dubris.**] Municipal borough, seaport, and seaside resort in SE England, in Kent, situated on the Strait of Dover, ab. 77 mi. SE of London by rail. It is the chief of the Cinque Ports, a favorite seaside resort, and the terminus of packet-lines to Calais, France (22 mi. away), and Ostend, Belgium (68 mi. away), and is on one of the main lines between London and the Continent. Dover has little freight traffic, being chiefly a passenger port, but it handles imports of wines, skins, and light manufactured articles. Exports are few: yarns, textiles, and clothing mostly. Dover is located on the East Kent coalfield. Its chief points of interest include Dover Castle, situated on a cliff nearly 350 ft. high, Shakespeare Cliff (mentioned in *King Lear*), the Pharos, or lighthouse, which guided Roman supply ships into Dover harbor (and is the oldest standing building in England), and the Admiralty Pier. The town was burned by the Normans in 1066, became an important naval station, resisted the French in 1216, and fell into the hands of the Parliamentarians in 1642. Pop. 35,217 (1951).

Dover. City in SE New Hampshire, county seat of Strafford County, on the Cocheco River, ab. 11 mi. NW of Portsmouth. Manufactures include printing presses, cotton and woolen goods, woodworking machinery, and shoes. Settled in 1623, it is the oldest town in the state. 15,874 (1950).

Dover. Town in N New Jersey, in Morris County, ab. 32 mi. NW of New York: shipping center for iron ore. Munitions plants and a government arsenal are in the vicinity. 11,174 (1950).

Dover. [Former name, **Canal Dover.**] City in E Ohio, in Tuscarawas County, ab. 70 mi. SE of Cleveland. Coal and clay are produced in the area. Manufactures include tanks, plates, bricks, tiles, chemicals, and machine-shop equipment. It was settled in 1807 by Germans and was formerly a canal port. 9,852 (1950).

Dover, 1st Duke of. A title of **Douglas, James.**

Dover or **Dover Center.** Former names of **Westlake,** Ohio.

Dover, Battle of. Naval victory (August 21, 1217) of an English fleet from the Cinque Ports over a French fleet led by Eustace the Monk. Hubert de Burgh, afterwards regent in the minority of Henry III, led the English against the French vessels, which were coming to the aid of the barons in revolt against King John and his son Henry.

Dover, Strait of. [French, **Pas de Calais;** Latin, **Fretum Gallicum, Fretum Oceani.**] Strait separating England from France, and connecting the English Channel with the North Sea. Steamers cross daily from Dover to Calais and to Ostend. Width at Dover, 21 mi.

Dover, Treaty of. Secret treaty concluded May 22, 1670, at Dover, England, between Charles II of England and Louis XIV of France. The former was to aid in the designs of France against Holland, and the latter was to furnish subsidies and troops. The province of Zealand and the adjacent islands were to be reserved for England. Charles was to receive 200,000 pounds a year if he declared himself a Roman Catholic. By this treaty Louis broke up the triple alliance of England, Holland, and Sweden against him.

Dover-Foxcroft (-foks'kroft). Town (in Maine the equivalent of township in many other states) and unincorporated village in C Maine, county seat of Piscataquis County, on the Piscataquis River: woolen manufactures. Pop. of town, 4,218 (1950); of village, 2,566 (1950).

Dovers (dō'vėrz), **Cape.** Prominent cape in Antarctica, lying ab. 4 mi. S by SW of Henderson Island, on Queen Mary Coast, in ab. 66°28′ S., 97°00′ E. It was discovered by the Australasian Antarctic Expedition (1911–14), under the leadership of Sir Douglas Mawson, and named for G. Dovers, cartographer at the expedition's West Base.

Dove's Nest, The. Title story of a collection of short stories by Katherine Mansfield, published in 1923.

Doves Press (duvz). English publishing venture (1900–1916) concerned with the making of beautiful books. The press was set up in the Hammersmith borough of London by T. J. Cobden-Sanderson and Emery Walker, both of whom had worked with William Morris at the Kelmscott Press. The Doves type, designed by Walker, was a variant of the famous 15th-century Jenson type. The books printed at the Doves Press, including the renowned Doves Bible, had a great influence on the arts of typography and printing in the early part of the 20th century. When the venture came to an end in 1916, all fonts of Doves type were put beyond possibility of further use by being thrown into the Thames River.

Dovrefjell (dô'vrę.fyel). [Also: **Dovre Fjeld, Dovrefjeld.**] Spur of the Scandinavian Mountains, situated in Norway. It separates N and S Norway. Highest peak, Snøhetta (7,500 ft.).

Dow (dou), **Gerard.** See **Dou** or **Douw** or **Dow, Gerard.**

Dow, Herbert Henry. b. at Belleville, Ontario, Canada, Feb. 26, 1866; d. at Rochester, Minn., Oct. 15, 1930. American chemist and manufacturer. Evolved numerous chemical processes, among them the electrolysis of brine for the production of bromine, chlorine, magnesium chloride, Epsom salts, and iodine; developed processes for the synthetic production of indigo, phenol, and aniline, and for the production of magnesium alloys.

Dow, Lorenzo. b. at Coventry, Conn., Oct. 16, 1777; d. at Washington, D.C., Feb. 2, 1834. American itinerant preacher, of the Methodist belief. He made two missionary tours in England and Ireland, one in 1799 and one in 1805. He was noted for his eccentricities of manner and dress. His *Journal and Miscellaneous Writings* were edited by John Dowling in 1836.

Dow, Neal. b. at Portland, Me., March 20, 1804; d. there, Oct. 2, 1897. American advocate of prohibition. He drafted the noted "Maine (prohibitory) Law" in 1851 and was the candidate of the Prohibition Party for president in 1880.

Dowagiac (dǫ.woj'ak). City in S Lower Michigan, in Cass County, ab. 35 mi. SW of Kalamazoo: manufactures of stoves and furnaces. 6,542 (1950).

Dowden (dou'dẹn), **Edward.** b. at Cork, Ireland, May 3, 1843; d. at Dublin, April 4, 1913. Irish Shakespearian editor, critic, biographer, poet, and teacher. Educated at Queen's College (Cork) and Trinity College (Dublin), he was graduated (1863) from Trinity, where he was professor of English literature from 1867 until his death, except for short periods as Taylorian lecturer (1889) at Oxford, Clark lecturer (1893–96) at Cambridge, and special lecturer (1896) at Princeton in celebration of the 150th anniversary of the university. He was (1896–1901) commissioner of national education of Ireland. He was the author of the biographies *Southey* (1880), *Life of Shelley* (1886), *Robert Browning* (1904), and *Montaigne* (1905); of the critical and historical works *Shakespeare: A Critical Study of His Mind and Art* (1875), *Shakespeare: Scenes and Characters* (1876), *A Shakespeare Primer* (1877), *Studies in Literature: 1789–1877* (1878), *Introduction to Shakespeare* (1893), *The French Revolution and English Literature* (1897), *History of French Literature* (1897), *Puritan and Anglican* (1900), *Milton in the 18th Century* (1908), and *Essays: Modern and Elizabethan* (1910); and also of *Poems* (1876, 1914) and *A Woman's Reliquary* (1913). He edited Southey's *Correspondence* (1881), Shakespeare's *Sonnets* (1881), *The Passionate Pilgrim* (1883), *Hamlet* (1899), *Romeo and Juliet* (1900). *Cymbeline* (1903), and Browning's *The Ring and the Book* (1912).

Dowdey (dou'di), **Clifford (Shirley), Jr.** b. at Richmond, Va., Jan. 23, 1904—. American novelist. He attended Columbia University, was a reporter and book reviewer (1925–26) for the Richmond *News-Leader,* and from 1926 to 1935 was on the editorial staffs of *Munsey's Argosy,* and the Dell Publishing Company. His novels include *Bugles Blow No More* (1937), *Gamble's Hundred* (1939), *Sing For a Penny* (1941), *Tidewater* (1943), and *Where My Love Sleeps* (1945). He is also the author of the historical study *Experiment in Rebellion* (1946), dealing with the Southern Confederacy.

Dowding (dou'ding), Sir **Hugh Caswell Tremenheere,** [Title, 1st Baron **Dowding.**] b. in Cornwall, England. 1882—. British soldier who commanded (1936–40), with the rank of air chief marshal, the Royal Air Force fighter command during World War II. He was educated at the Royal Military Academy at Woolwich and served with the British air forces in World War I, particularly in the Near and Middle East. He was director of training at the air ministry and member (1930–36) for research and supply of the air council, and retired (1942) from the Royal Air Force; created (1943) baron by King George VI.

Dowgate (dou'gāt). Original water gate of the City of London.

Dowie (dou'i), **John Alexander.** b. at Edinburgh, May 25, 1847; d. at Chicago, March 9, 1907. Scottish-American fanatic. He came to the U.S. in 1886, and in 1896 organized the "Christian Catholic Apostolic Church in Zion," of which he was "general overseer," establishing it in 1901 at Zion City, near Chicago. In 1906 his followers brought various charges against him, including that of financial mismanagement, and deposed him.

Dowland (dou'lạnd), **John.** b. 1563; d. 1626. English lutanist at various European courts, remembered chiefly as one of the earliest writers of the art song.

Dowland, Robert. b. c1585; d. c1641. English lutanist; son of John Dowland (1563–1626). He was musician (1626 *et seq.*) to Charles I.

Dowlatabad (dou'lạt.ä.bäd'). See **Daulatabad.**

Dowler (dou'lėr), **Captain.** Retired military man in Charles Dickens's *Pickwick Papers,* noted for his bluster and brag, and his extraordinarily fierce and disjointed manner of talking.

Down (doun). Maritime county in Ulster province, Northern Ireland. It is bounded on the N by County Antrim and Belfast Lough, on the E and SE by the Irish Sea, on the SW by Carlingford Lough, and on the W by County Armagh. The coastline is much indented by many large and small inlets. The surface consists of numerous lowlands interspersed with hills, rising in the south of the county to the Mourne Mountains, of which the highest summit is Slieve Donard (2,796 ft.). The Mourne Mountains reach to the coast on Carlingford Lough and at Newcastle. Most of the land of the county lies below 500 ft. elevation, and there are large areas of pleasant farming country, especially in the eastern portion. Large numbers of sheep are raised on the uplands; beef cattle are more common on the lowland pastures. Poultry-raising and egg production for the Belfast market and for export is important in the area about Ballynahinch, S of Belfast. The principal crops raised are oats and potatoes. Newry is the leading seaport of the county. There are seaside resorts at Bangor and at Newcastle. The valley of the river Lagan, along the N boundary, is an industrial area, principally devoted to linen manufactures, the leading industry of the county. There are also cotton and leather manufactures. Downpatrick is the county seat; area, ab. 951 sq. mi.; pop. 230,064 (1947).

Down-Easters (doun'ēs'tėrz), **The.** Novel by John Neal, published in 1833.

Downers Grove (dou'nėrz grōv'). Village in NE Illinois, in Du Page County, near Chicago: manufactures tools and other items. 11,886 (1950).

Downes (dounz), **Andrew.** b. in Shropshire, England, c1549; d. at Coton, England, Feb. 2, 1628. English Greek scholar and Biblical translator. He was one of the translators of the Apocrypha for the Authorized Version of the Bible.

Downes, John. b. at Canton, Mass., Dec. 23, 1784; d. at Charlestown, Mass., Aug. 11, 1854. American naval commander. He served as lieutenant in the *Essex* under Captain Porter in the War of 1812, and commanded the *Épervier* in the war against Algiers. In 1832 he obtained command of a squadron in the Pacific Ocean, and bombarded Kuala Batu, on the coast of Sumatra, in retaliation for an outrage committed on an American vessel. He commanded the navy yard at Boston (1837–42, 1850–52).

Downes, Olin. [Full name, **Edwin Olin Downes.**] b. at Evanston, Ill., Jan. 27, 1886—. American music critic. Reviewer for the Boston *Post* (1906–24) and the New York *Times* (1924 *et seq.*); author of *The Lure of Music* (1918), *Symphonic Broadcasts* (1932), and *Symphonic Masterpieces* (1935).

Downey (dou'ni). Unincorporated community in S California, in Los Angeles County. Under the new urban definition established for use in the 1950 census it was counted with adjoining urban areas; the last official enumeration was 9,364 (1940).

Downey, Fairfax Davis. b. at Salt Lake City, Utah, Nov. 28, 1893—. American writer. He was graduated (B.A., 1916) from Yale, served in the U.S. army in World Wars I and II, and was a member of newspaper staffs of the Kansas City *Star* and the New York *Herald-Tribune*. His works include *A Comic History of Yale* (1924), *When We Were Rather Older* (1926), *Burton, Arabian Nights Adventurer* (1931), *Richard Harding Davis—His Day* (1933), *Portrait of an Era, As Drawn by C. D. Gibson* (1936), *Dog of War* (1943), and *Our Lusty Forefathers* (1947).

Downing (dou'ning), **Andrew Jackson.** b. at Newburgh, N.Y., Oct., 1815; drowned near Yonkers, N.Y., July 28, 1852. American landscape gardener and pomologist; brother of Charles Downing. He published *Theory and Practice of Landscape Gardening* (1841), *Cottage Residences* (1842), *The Fruits and Fruit Trees of America* (1845, with Charles Downing), *Architecture for Country Houses* (1850), and others. His books on country architecture, illustrated by Alexander Jackson Davis, and containing plans and elevations, were widely read and consulted, doing much to spread the Gothic revival in domestic buildings.

Downing, Charles. b. at Newburgh, N.Y., July 9, 1802; d. Jan. 18, 1885. American pomologist and horticulturist; brother and partner (1834–39) of Andrew Jackson Downing in a commercial nursery. In a testing orchard, he developed and classified varieties of apples, pears, and other fruits. He was the author with his brother of *The Fruits and Fruit Trees of America* (1845).

Downing, Sir **George.** b. probably in August, 1623; d. 1684. English soldier and politician. He emigrated with his parents in 1638 to New England (where he was the second graduate of Harvard College), but subsequently returned to England, and in 1650 was scoutmaster-general of Cromwell's army in Scotland. He was appointed resident at The Hague in 1657, and there is said to have arranged a secret meeting with Charles II, warned him of Cromwell's intention to seize him in Holland, and thereby to have saved Charles's life. He was retained in office by Charles II on the Restoration in 1660, and was created a baronet in 1663. He was given a grant of land in what is now Downing Street, in Whitehall, London, which derives its name from him.

Downing, Sir **George.** b. c1684; d. in Cambridgeshire, England, June 10, 1749. English philanthropist, the founder of Downing College; grandson of Sir George Downing (d. 1684). He was a member of the Parliaments of 1710 and 1713, and kept his seat from 1722 until his death.

Downing, Major **Jack.** Pseudonym of **Smith, Seba.**

Downing College. One of the colleges of Cambridge University. It was founded in 1800 by a bequest of Sir George Downing, of Gamlingay Park in Cambridgeshire, who died in 1749, but did not open until 1807, when its first buildings were erected. It is the college of Sir Busick Harwood, famous physician and medical professor, William Frere, who later became its master, and of Thomas Starkie and Andrew Amos, both Downing professors of law. Its founder was the grandson of the 17th-century Sir George Downing who built the famous London street named after him.

Downing Street. Street in the West End of London, leading from Whitehall. It contains the building (No. 10) in which the prime minister generally resides, the treasury building, and the foreign office; hence the name Downing Street has come to be used to symbolize the prime minister and his cabinet. It was built by Sir George Downing (1623–84) on a grant of land from Charles II.

Downingtown (dou'ning.toun). [Former name, **Milltown.**] Borough in SE Pennsylvania, in Chester County, on the East Branch of Brandywine Creek: manufactures of paper, textiles, and metal products. It was incorporated in 1859. 4,948 (1950).

Downpatrick (doun.pat'rik). Urban district and market town in Ulster province, Northern Ireland, county seat of County Down, situated on the river Quoile near its influx to Strangford Lough, ab. 21 mi. SE of Belfast. It is reputed to be one of the oldest towns of Ireland. Its cathedral was sacked in 1538 and remained a ruin until it was restored in 1790. The burial-place of Saint Patrick, believed to have died in 463 A.D., is here. 3,471 (1947).

Downright (doun'rīt). Rude but manly and consistent squire in Ben Jonson's comedy *Every Man in His Humour*. He is courageous, of plain words and plain actions.

Downs (dounz), **Battle of the.** Indecisive battle between the English and Dutch fleets, in the first days of June, 1666, off the E coast of Kent, England. The English were commanded by Monk, and the Dutch by De Ruyter and Tromp. It is sometimes claimed as an English victory.

Downs, the. Chalk hills in SE England, S of London and extending E to Dover. The two most prominent ridges are the North Downs and the South Downs, separated by the vales of Kent and Sussex from the Weald, a central ridge. The upland "downs" have a thin soil, and were natural grasslands, favored as sites of prehistoric settlement. Today they are divided up into rather large farms, and used principally for grazing sheep, of which the Southdown breed is a notable type originating in this region.

Downs, the. Part of the North Sea immediately offshore from SE England, off the E coast of Kent, at Deal. It forms a roadstead protected by the Goodwin Sands. There are many shoals and sandbanks. Length, ab. 8 mi.; width, ab. 6 mi.

Downshire (doun'shir), 1st Marquis of. A title of **Hill, Wills.**

Dowsabel (dou'sa̤.bel). See **Dousabel.**

Dowse (dous), **Thomas.** b. at Charlestown, Mass., Dec. 28, 1772; d. at Cambridgeport, Mass., Nov. 4, 1856. American book-collector. He bequeathed his collection to the Massachusetts Historical Society.

Dowson (dou'so̤n), **Ernest.** [Full name, **Ernest Christopher Dowson.**] b. in Kent, England, Aug. 2, 1867; d. at London, Feb. 23, 1900. English poet, short-story writer, and translator, often grouped with the so-called

Decadents in late 19th-century English literature. His short life was sickly; he was tubercular and his latter years were spent in poverty. He was the author of *Dilemmas* (1895), *Verses* (1896), *The Pierrot of the Minute* (1897), a poetic drama, and *Poems* (1905); and he translated works by Voltaire, Balzac, Zola and other French authors. He is best remembered for his lyric *Non Sum Qualis Eram Bonae Sub Regno Cynarae,* with its repeated "I have been faithful to thee, Cynara! in my fashion" (the work is commonly referred to simply as *Cynara*). The actual Cynara was the daughter of a French café-keeper in London, who later married a waiter. Among other short poems by Dowson are *Extreme Unction, You Would Have Understood Me, A Last Word, Spleen,* and *To One in Bedlam.*

Dowton (dou'tọn), **William.** b. at Exeter, England, 1764; d. at Brixton, Surrey, England, 1851. English actor. He made his first appearance in 1781, and came to New York in 1836. He had two sons, William and Henry, both of whom became actors. The former afterward became a brother of the Charter House, and died there at the age of nearly 90.

Doyen (dwå.yañ), **Gabriel François.** b. at Paris, 1726; d. at St. Petersburg, June 5, 1806. French painter, a pupil of Van Loo.

Doyle (doil), Sir **Arthur Conan.** b. at Edinburgh, May 22, 1859; d. at Crowborough, England, July 7, 1930. English writer of fiction, creator of Sherlock Holmes. A medical doctor, he practiced from 1882 to 1890, but meanwhile began his career in literature with the publication of *A Study in Scarlet* (1887), a crime-and-mystery story in which he introduced the character destined to make his fame and fortune, the detective Sherlock Holmes. He did not immediately concentrate upon Holmes, but during the next four years, besides publishing the historical novels *Micah Clarke* (1889), and *The White Company* (1891), he contributed further stories of Holmes's exploits to the *Strand Magazine,* and when these appeared in book form as *The Adventures of Sherlock Holmes* (1891), their success was sensational. Doyle continued to work the rich vein he had opened, but in the last story of *The Memoirs of Sherlock Holmes* (1893), either tiring of the game or fearful of his invention flagging, he killed off the hero—or so he thought. But the Sherlock Holmes cult continued to recruit avid readers who demanded more adventures, and were glad to accept the implausible explanation that the great detective had disappeared but had not died, since this made possible *The Return of Sherlock Holmes* (1905), and *The Last Bow* (1917). A final collection of stories, *The Case Book of Sherlock Holmes* (1927), completed the portrait and the history of a fictitious character who, more than any other in modern literature, seemed to millions of readers almost more real even than his creator. The name Sherlock Holmes, or merely Sherlock, in English-speaking countries has come to be synonymous with "detective." Certain illustrations of the early stories depicted Holmes as a thin-faced man wearing a peculiar checked cap, smoking an underslung pipe and carrying a magnifying glass; this visualization of his appearance was brought to life by the American actor William Gillette in his play *Sherlock Holmes,* and has become a part of the conventional symbolism of American cartoonists. Doyle also wrote a number of plays, one of which, *The Story of Waterloo,* successfully provided a starring vehicle for Sir Henry Irving. During the Boer War he spiritedly defended the British cause in a book, *The War in South Africa; its Causes and Conduct,* which led to his being knighted, and during World War I his pamphlet, *Cause and Conduct of the World War,* was circulated in millions of copies in a dozen languages. The loss of a son in that war led to the interest in psychic phenomena which made Sir Arthur in his last years a firm believer in spiritualism.

Doyle, Sir **Francis Hastings Charles.** b. at Nunappleton, near Tadcaster, Yorkshire, England, Aug. 21, 1810; d. at Berkeley Square, London, June 8, 1888. English balladist, poet, and teacher. Educated at Eton and at Christ Church, Oxford, he studied at the Inner Temple, being called to the bar in 1837 and elevated (1839) to the baronetcy on the death of his father. He gave up law practice to accept positions in the customs office, holding (1846–69) the receiver-generalship of customs, and serving (1869–93) as commissioner. He was professor of poetry (1867–77) at Oxford. Among his works are *Miscellaneous Verses* (1834, 1840), *Oedipus, King of Thebes* (1849), a translation of Sophocles, *The Return of the Guards and Other Poems* (1866), *Lectures* (1869, 1877), and several ballads.

Doyle, John Andrew. b. at London, May 14, 1844; d. at Oxford, Aug. 4 or 5, 1907. English essayist, historian, and librarian. He was educated at Eton and at Balliol College, Oxford, graduating in 1867, was a fellow (1867–1907) of All Souls College, Oxford librarian (1881–88), and author of a prize essay (1869) on *The English Colonies in America Before 1776.* He also wrote *A Summary History of America* (1875), *A History of the American Colonies Down to the War of Independence* (5 vols., 1882–1907), *The Puritan Colonies* (1887), *The Middle Colonies* (1907), and *The Colonies Under the House of Hanover* (1907). Doyle also contributed articles to the *Dictionary of National Biography* and the *Cambridge Modern History.*

Doyle, Lynn. [Pseudonym of **Leslie Alexander Montgomery.**] b. at Downpatrick, County Down, Ireland, 1873—. Irish writer. He is the author of collections of short stories such as *Ballygullion* (1908), *Lobster Salad—Irish Short Stories* (1922), *Dear Ducks* (1925), and *Me and Mrs. Murphy* (1930). His plays include *Love and Land* (1913; produced 1925 as *Perseverance*), *The Lilac Ribbon* (1919), and *Turncoats* (1922). Among his novels are *Mr. Wildridge of the Bank—a novel* (1916) and *Fiddling Farmer* (1937). He has also published a book of verse entitled *Ballygullion Ballads* (1936).

Doyle, Richard. b. at London, 1824; d. there, Dec. 11, 1883. English artist. He was a member of the staff of *Punch* (1843–50). Among his best-known works are the illustrations to Thackeray's *Newcomes* (1853–55) and a series of elfin scenes entitled *In Fairy-Land* (1870).

Doylestown (doilz'toun). Borough in SE Pennsylvania, county seat of Bucks County: residential community; manufactures of pottery. It was settled in 1735 and is the seat of an agricultural college (founded 1848). 5,262 (1950).

D'Oyly Carte (doi'li kärt), **Richard.** See **Carte, Richard D'Oyly.**

Dozy (dō'zē), **Reinhart.** b. at Leiden, Netherlands, Feb. 21, 1820; d. May 3, 1883. Dutch Orientalist and historian, professor of history at Leiden from 1850. His works include *Recherches sur l'histoire et la littérature d'Espagne pendant le moyen âge* (1849), *Histoire des Musulmans d'Espagne* (1861), *Supplément aux dictionnaires arabes* (1877–81), and others.

DPs. See **Displaced Persons.**

Drač (dräch). Serbo-Croatian name of **Durrës,** city.

Drachenfels (drä'ċhẹn.fels). [Eng. trans., "*Dragon's Rock.*"] Steepest of the Siebengebirge range of mountains, in W Germany, situated on the E bank of the Rhine, near Königswinter. It is now ascended by a mountain railway. In its side is the Drachenhöhle (dragon's cave), where lived the legendary dragon slain by Siegfried. Elevation, ab. 1,053 ft.

Drachman (drak'mạn), **Bernard.** b. at New York, 1861; d. 1945. American rabbi. He was graduated (1885) from the Jewish Theological Seminary of Breslau, and was a founder (1886) of the Jewish Theological Seminary, where he served as professor of Biblical exegesis and Jewish philosophy (1887–1902), as dean (1889–1902), and as professor of Bible and rabbinical codes. He was rabbi of Congregation Beth Israel Bikkur Cholim, Congregation Zichron Ephraim, and Congregation Oheb Zedek, all at New York, and was known as an exponent of orthodox Judaism. Author of *From the Heart of Israel* (1905) and *Looking at America* (1934).

Drachmann (dräċh'män), **Holger Henrik Herholdt.** b. at Copenhagen, Oct. 9, 1846; d. at Hornbæk, Denmark, Jan. 14, 1908. Danish poet and author. From 1866 to 1870 he studied art at Copenhagen. In 1872 he published a volume of poems. This was followed by *Dæmpede Melodier* (Repressed Melodies, 1875), *Sange ved Havet* (Songs by the Sea, 1877), *Ranker og Roser* (Vines and Roses), and *Ungdom i Digt og Sang* (Youth in Poetry and Song, 1879). The romantic poems *Prindsessen og det halve Kongerige* (The Princess and Half the Kingdom) and *Oesten for Sol og Vesten for Maane* (East of the Sun and West of the Moon) appeared in 1878 and 1880 respectively. In prose he wrote, among other long stories, *En Overkomplet* (1876) and *Tannhäuser* (1877). The shorter tales *Ungt Blod* (Young Blood) and *Paa Sømands Tro og Love* (On a Sailor's Word) appeared in 1877 and 1878 respectively. The most popular of his prose works is the series of sketches *Derovar fra Grændsen* (From the *Frontier*, 1877). A translation of Byron's *Don Juan* appeared in 1881. His later poetical works include *Dybe Strenge* (1884), *Fjældsange og Æventyr* (1885), *Sangenes Bog* (1889), *Ungdomsidgte* (1898), and *Broget Løv* (1901). He wrote also an autobiographical romance, *Den hellige Ild* (1899), *Smaa Fortællinger* (1884), *Med den brede Pensel* (1887), *Forskrevet* (1890), *Dædalus* (1900), and a number of dramatic works.

Draco (drā'kō) or **Dracon** (drā'kon). fl. in the last half of the 7th century B.C. Athenian legislator. According to tradition, he formulated the first written code of laws for Athens in 624 or c621 B.C., at which, there having been no written code previously, the people were so overjoyed that they smothered Draco accidentally under a deluge of cloaks. On account of the number of offenses to which it affixed the penalty of death, his code was said to have been written in blood. His code was superseded for the most part by that of Solon (594).

Draco. Northern constellation. As pictured since ancient times, the figure is that of a serpent with several small coils. It appears at a very ancient date to have had wings in the space now occupied by the Little Bear.

Dracontius (dra.kon'shi.us, -shus), **Blossius Aemilius.** Christian poet of the 5th century, an advocate in Carthage. Among his works are the didactic *De laudibus Dei*, as well as short epics on legendary subjects, two epithalamia, and an apologetic elegy.

Dracut (drā'kut). Town in NE Massachusetts, in Middlesex County, near the border of New Hampshire: center of a farming community. 8,666 (1950).

Draeseke (drā'ze.ke), **Felix (August Bernhard).** b. at Coburg, Germany, Oct. 7, 1835; d. Feb. 26, 1913. German composer and writer on music. His works include operas, church music, choral and solo voice works, and symphonic and chamber pieces.

Draft Riot. Riot (July 13–16, 1863) at New York against the enforcement of the draft for the Union army. During its progress scores of Negroes were killed and many others were wounded. The riot, which cost a number of lives variously estimated between 300 and 500, was finally suppressed by the police and militia. Property damage caused by pillaging and fire was estimated at as high as two and a half million dollars.

Draga (drä'gä). b. 1867; d. in June, 1903. Wife of Alexander I, king of Serbia. The widow of an engineer, Draga Mashin was a member of the entourage of the queen-mother of King Alexander when he fell in love with her. Rightly or wrongly it was generally supposed that she was an adventuress whose past conduct had not measured up to conventional moral standards, so that the young king's insistence on marrying her caused widespread indignation. Alexander's political course at this time also raised enemies, especially in the army, and a conspiracy took form under the leadership of a brother of Draga's first husband. On June 10, 1903, soldiers directed by the conspirators invaded the royal palace, shot Alexander and Draga (and also repeatedly stabbed Draga), and assassinated the prime minister and other officials of the government. The long and implacable feud between the Obrenovich dynasty, represented by Alexander I, and the Karageorgevich line, unquestionably had something to do with these events, which forever extinguished the Obrenovich power, and restored the Karageorgeviches to the throne in the person of Peter I.

Dragerton (drā'gėr.ton). Unincorporated community in E central Utah, in Carbon County. 3,453 (1950).

Drago (drä'gō), **Luis María.** b. at Buenos Aires, May 6, 1859; d. there, June 9, 1921. Argentine jurist and diplomat whose proposed corollary to the Monroe Doctrine (viz., that public debts of American states cannot be collected through armed intervention by European powers) was stated (1902) in a note to the U.S. State Department in connection with such intervention against Venezuela by Great Britain, Italy, and Germany. Largely based on the earlier Calvo Doctrine, which left jurisdiction over such disputes to the local authorities and ruled out international interference altogether, the Drago Doctrine was brought before the Hague Conference of 1907, but was put aside in favor of the less restrictive Porter proposition, which looked towards arbitration of claims but did not rule out force.

Drago Doctrine. Doctrine of international law propounded (1902) by the Argentine foreign minister Luis María Drago, which bars the use of armed force by one nation against another to compel payment of public debts. Intended as a corollary to the Monroe Doctrine, the Drago Doctrine was motivated specifically by the Joint British, Italian, and German intervention against Venezuela in 1902. It applies, in a much narrower context, the broad principle of nonintervention enunciated (1868) in the Calvo Doctrine. Although placed before the Hague Conference in 1907 for consideration, the Drago Doctrine was set aside in favor of the less restrictive Porter proposition, which did not rule out force but maintained it as a last resort after arbitration.

Dragomirov (drä.go.mē'rof), **Mikhail Ivanovich.** b. 1830; d. at Konotop, Russia, Oct. 28, 1905. Russian general. He served in the Russo-Turkish war, was wounded at Shipka Pass, and was later appointed director of the Academy of the General Staff. In 1889 he was appointed governor general of Kiev, Podolia, and Volhynia. He published various important works on tactics and military administration. He retired in 1904.

"Dragon Boat Festival." See **Tuan Yang.**

Dragonetti (drä.gō.nāt'tē), **Domenico.** b. at Venice, April 7, 1763; d. at London, April 16, 1846. Italian double-bass player. Engaged at London for concerts and opera; met (1809) Beethoven at Vienna; friend of Haydn; composer of double-bass sonatas; led (1845) the double-bass section at the Bonn Beethoven festival.

Dragon in Shallow Waters, The. Novel by V. Sackville-West, published in 1921.

Dragonnades (drag.o.nādz'). Form of persecution inflicted by the government of Louis XIV upon the French Protestants in the period preceding the revocation of the edict of Nantes. It consisted in billeting troops upon the inhabitants as a means of converting them, license being given to the soldiery to commit all manner of misdeeds.

Dragon of Wantley (wont'li), **The.** Old ballad, preserved by Percy, which describes the victory over this dragon (who devoured damsels, houses, and trees) by More of More Hall, who provided himself with armor covered with spikes.

Dragon's Blood. Novel by Romer Wilson (Mrs. Edward J. O'Brien), published in 1926.

Dragon's Mouth (or **Mouths**). [Spanish, **Boca de Dragón, Bocas del Dragón.**] Sea passage of the Caribbean, between Trinidad and the South American mainland (Paria peninsula, Venezuela). It is said to have been so named by Columbus, who sailed through it in 1498. The channel contains several islands.

Dragontea (drä.gōn.tā'ä), **La.** Poem by Lope de Vega on the subject of Sir Francis Drake's last expedition and death. It consists of ten cantos of octave verse.

Draguignan (drá.gē.nyäṅ). [Latin, **Forum Julii.**] Town in SE France, the capital of the department of Var, situated in a hilly region, near the Nartuby River NW of Fréjus. There are a number of Roman remains, including an amphitheater and aqueduct, and the Gothic cathedral of Notre Dame. The town has textile and tanning industries, and is the center of an olive-growing region. There is some resort trade. 11,801 (1946).

Dragut (drä'göt). [Also, **Torghud.**] d. at Malta, July 23, 1565. Algerian corsair. He was a native of Asia Minor, and became a lieutenant of the Greek-born Algerian corsair Barbarossa II (called Khair ed-Din), on whose death in 1546 he became governor of Tripoli. He defeated (1560) the Spaniards at Gerbes and was killed at the siege of Malta.

Drake (drāk), **Alexander Wilson.** b. near Westfield, N.J., Sept. 4, 1843; d. Feb. 4, 1916. American wood engraver and draftsman on wood, art director of *The Century Magazine* from 1870 (*Scribner's Monthly 1870–81*). He studied art at the Cooper Institute and the National Academy of Design, New York, and was largely instrumental in founding and developing the American school of wood engraving. He was one of the founders of the Grolier Club at New York.

Drake, Benjamin. b. at Mays Lick, Ky., 1795; d. April 1, 1841. American lawyer and author; brother of Daniel Drake (1785–1852). He was a prolific contributor of articles, editorials, and stories to newspapers and journals, especially the *Literary Gazette, Western Monthly Magazine,* and *Southern Literary Messenger;* cofounder and editor (1826–34) of the *Cincinnati Chronicle:* publisher (1827) with E. D. Mansfield of *Cincinnati in 1826,* a statistical account; author of *Tales and Sketches from the Queen City* (1838), *The Life and Adventures of Black Hawk, with Sketches of Keokuk, the Sac and Fox Indians, and the Late Black Hawk War* (1838), *Sketches of the Civil and Military Services of William Henry Harrison* (1840, with C. S. Todd), and *Life of Tecumseh and his Brother, the Prophet, with an Historical Sketch of the Shawanoe Indians* (1841).

Drake, Charles Daniel. b. April 11, 1811; d. April 1, 1892. American lawyer and U.S. senator; son of Daniel Drake (1785–1852). A radical Republican leader in Missouri during the Civil War period, he agitated for immediate, uncompensated emancipation and was one of the principal drafters (1865) of the new Missouri constitution. As U.S. senator from Missouri (1867–70), he supported radical Reconstruction measures and participated in Andrew Johnson's trial. He was chief justice (1870–85) of the U.S. Court of Claims.

Drake, Daniel. b. at Plainfield, N.J., Oct. 20, 1785; d. at Cincinnati, Ohio, Nov. 6, 1852. American physician. He published *Treatise on the Principal Diseases of the Interior Valley of North America* (1850–54), and other works.

Drake, Edwin Laurentine. b. at Greenville, N.Y., March 29, 1819; d. at Bethlehem, Pa., Nov. 8, 1880. American oil industry pioneer. President (1858 *et seq.*) of the Seneca Oil Company, he was the first to tap an oil reservoir (at Titusville, Pa., 1859) beneath the earth's surface by drilling.

Drake, Sir **Francis.** b. probably at Tavistock, Devonshire, England, c1540; d. off Portobelo, Panama, Jan. 28, 1596. English naval hero. In 1567–68 he commanded a small vessel, the *Judith,* one of two which escaped from the destruction of Sir John Hawkins's fleet by the Spanish in the Gulf of Mexico. Under Elizabeth's commission as a privateer, he visited the West Indies and the Spanish Main in 1570 and 1571, and became convinced that the towns there would fall an easy prey to a small armed force. Accordingly, in 1572, he fitted out what was properly a freebooting expedition, England being then at peace with Spain. With only three vessels and 100 men he took the town of Nombre de Dios on the Isthmus of Panama and an immense treasure; but he was badly wounded in the attack, and his men abandoned both town and treasure. Soon after, he burned a Spanish vessel at Cartagena, in what is now Colombia, captured many ships, and intercepted a train loaded with silver on the isthmus. He also crossed to Panama, and was the first English commander to see the Pacific. From his return, in August, 1573, to September, 1576, Drake served under Walter Devereux, 1st Earl of Essex, in Ireland. In December, 1577, with the express purpose of penetrating to the Pacific through the Straits of Magellan, he started on another freebooting expedition with five ships and 166 men. Two ships were abandoned on the west coast of South America, and after the passage of the Straits of Magellan, which took 16 days, his ship became separated from the other two, which returned to England. Drake continued in the *Golden Hind,* obtained an immense booty on the Pacific coast of Spanish America, crossed the Pacific, and returned to England by way of the Cape of Good Hope, arriving in September, 1580, with a vast treasure. This was the first English circumnavigation of the globe. Queen Elizabeth knighted Drake on his own ship, and ordered that the *Golden Hind* be preserved as a monument. (It rotted and was broken up some hundred years later.) Drake was mayor (1581) of Plymouth. In 1584–85 he was a member of Parliament. From 1585 to 1586 he commanded a powerful expedition to the West Indies and the Spanish Main, in which he took and ransomed Santo Domingo and Cartagena, ravaged the coasts of Florida, and on his way back brought off the remnant of the English Virginia colony founded by Sir Walter Raleigh in 1585. In 1587 he made a descent on the coast of Spain, and in the Bay of Cádiz destroyed numerous unfinished vessels intended for the Spanish Armada, besides capturing a rich Portuguese East Indiaman. In July, 1588, as a vice-admiral, he commanded under Lord Charles Howard in the combat with the Spanish Armada, capturing a large Spanish galleon; and next year he was one of the commanders in a descent on the Spanish and Portuguese coasts, which proved unsuccessful. For several years thereafter he was engaged in peaceful pursuits, and in 1593 he was again elected to Parliament. In 1595 he commanded another West India expedition, which met with little success, and in which both he and Sir John Hawkins died.

Drake, Francis Marion. b. at Rushville, Ill., 1830; d. 1903. Union Army officer in the Civil War, railroad president, and governor of Iowa (1896–98).

Drake, Francis Samuel. b. at Northwood, N.H., Feb. 22, 1828; d. at Washington, D.C., Feb. 22, 1885. American historian; son of Samuel Gardner Drake (1798–1875) and brother of Samuel Adams Drake (1833–1905). He was the author of *Dictionary of American Biography Containing Nearly Ten Thousand Notices* (1872), *List of Members of the Massachusetts Society of the Cincinnati* (1872), *Memorials of the Society of the Cincinnati* (1873), *The Life and Correspondence of Henry Knox* (1873), *Indian History for Young Folks* (1885), *The Town of Roxbury* (1878), and *Tea Leaves, Being a Collection of Letters and Documents Relating to the Shipment of Tea to the American Colonies* (1884); contributor to Justin Winsor's *Memorial History of Boston;* and editor (1884) of Schoolcraft's *Indian Tribes of the United States.*

Drake (drä'kȩ), **Friedrich.** b. at Pyrmont, Waldeck, Germany, June 23, 1805; d. at Berlin, April 6, 1882. German sculptor, best known from his portrait statues of Frederick William III and others.

Drake (drāk), **Joseph Rodman.** b. at New York, Aug. 7, 1795; d. there, Sept. 21, 1820. American poet. He was a New York physician who, with Fitz-Greene Halleck, his friend, published a series of witty poems under the name "Croaker and Co." in the New York *Evening Post* (1819). Drake was the author of the poems *The Culprit Fay* (1816) and *The American Flag* (1819). Halleck's eulogy to Drake, "Green be the turf above thee," is a tender tribute to a friend who died young. His collected works were published in 1935.

Drake, Nathan. b. at York, England, 1766; d. at Hadleigh, Suffolk, England, June 7, 1836. English physician and author. He practiced medicine at Hadleigh, in Suffolk, from 1792 until his death. His most notable work is *Shakspere and his Times* (1817).

Drake, Samuel Adams. b. at Boston, Dec. 19, 1833; d. at Kennebunkport, Me., Dec. 4, 1905. American historian; son of Samuel Gardner Drake (1798–1875) and brother of Francis Samuel Drake (1828–85). He was the author of *Old Landmarks and Historic Personages of Boston* (1873), *Historic Fields and Mansions of Middlesex* (1874), *Nooks and Corners of the New England Coast* (1875), *The Heart of the White Mountains* (1882), *The Making of New England* (1886), *The Making of the Great West* (1887), *The Making of Virginia and the Middle Colonies* (1893), *The Making of the Ohio Valley States* (1894), *Our Colonial Homes* (1894), and a novel, *The Young Vigilantes, a Story of California Life in the Fifties* (1904).

Drake, Samuel Gardner. b. at Pittsfield, N.H., Oct. 11, 1798; d. at Boston, June 14, 1875. American antiquary. He published *Book of the Indians* (1833), *History and Antiquities of Boston* (1856), *Early History of New England* (1864), *Annals of Witchcraft in the United States* (1869), *History of the French and Indian War* (1870), and others.

Drakenborch (drä'kȩn.bôrċh), **Arnold.** b. at Utrecht, Netherlands, Jan. 1, 1684; d. there, Jan. 16, 1748. Dutch philologist. He edited *Silius Italicus* (1717), *Livy* (1738–46), and others.

Drakensberg (drä'kȩnz.bėrg). [Also: **Drakenberge, Kathlamba, Quathlamba.**] Range of mountains in SE Africa, in the Union of South Africa. It lies partly on the border between Cape of Good Hope province and Natal on one side and Basutoland and the Orange Free State on the other, and culminates in Champagne Castle (ab. 10,500 ft.) and Mont Aux Sources (10,761 ft.).

Drake's Bay (drāks). Indentation of the Pacific in W California, in Marin County NW of San Francisco.

Drama (drä'mạ). *Nomos* (department) in N Greece, situated in Macedonia. Capital, Drama; area, 1,349 sq. mi.; pop. 119,009 (1951).

Drama. Town in N Greece, the capital of the *nomos* (department) of Drama, situated between the Struma and Nestos rivers, ab. 78 mi. NE of Salonika: railroad station on the line from Salonika to Istanbul. The environs are very fertile and grow much tobacco. Drama is the seat of a bishopric. 32,895 (1951).

Drama of Exile, A. Poem by Elizabeth Barrett Browning, published in 1844.

Dramatic Poesy, An Essay of. Work by Dryden (1668), written in the form of a dialogue between four friends: Neander (Dryden), Lisideius (Charles Sedley), Crites (Sir Robert Howard), and Eugenius (Charles, Lord Buckhurst, afterward 6th Earl of Dorset).

Drammen (dräm'ẹn). City in S Norway, the capital of the *fylke* (county) of Buskerud, situated at the mouth of the Drammen River, at the N end of Drammen Fjord, a branch of the Oslo Fjord, SW of Oslo. It has a harbor and shipyards and is the center of the Norwegian lumber trade, with large lumberyards, sawmills, paper, pulp, and cellulose factories; there are also breweries. It is a modern town; the old town was destroyed by fire in 1866 and 1870. Drammen was occupied by the Germans in 1940 during World War II. 26,994 (1946).

Drammen River. [Also: **Drams** (dräms); Norwegian, **Drammenselv** (dräm'ẹns.elv) (*elv* = "river").] River in S Norway, the outlet of Lake Tyrifjord. It flows into the Drammen Fjord at Drammen. Length, ab. 163 mi.

Drancy (drän̆.sē). Town in N France, in the department of Seine, NE of Paris. During World War II, it was used by the Germans as one of the chief assembly points for political deportees and Jews, who were shipped from there to extermination camps in Germany and E Europe. 42,166 (1946).

Dranesville (drānz'vil). Village in Fairfax County, Va., ab. 21 mi. NW of Washington, D.C. Here, on Dec. 20, 1861, part of the Army of the Potomac under Ord defeated the Confederates under Stuart.

Drangiana (dran.ji.ā'nạ). [Also, **Drangiane** (-ān').] In ancient geography, a region in C Asia, in what is now SW Afghanistan and E Iran; the modern name is Seistan.

Drang nach Osten (dräng' näċh os'tẹn). German phrase, meaning in literal translation, the "push or impulse toward the East." The phrase has been used to describe the eastward movement of German migration and conquest from the 10th to the 18th centuries. The expression has also been used to characterize German desires for expansion into the Balkans and Turkey under William II. During World War I it was used to describe the policies culminating in the Treaty of Brest-Litovsk. Hitler considered the eastward trend of Germany the inevitable course for the achievement of the German domination of the Continent.

Draper (drā'pėr). Unincorporated community in N North Carolina, in Rockingham County: manufactures include bedding, curtains, rugs, and woolen goods. 3,629 (1950).

Draper, Andrew Sloan. b. at Westford, N.Y., June 21, 1848; d. April 27, 1913. American educator. He was New York state superintendent of public instruction (1886–92), superintendent of schools (1892–94) at Cleveland, Ohio, president (1894–1904) of the University of Illinois, commissioner of education (1904 *et seq.*) on the New York state board of regents; member (1902 *et seq.*), later chairman, U.S. board of Indian commissioners.

Draper, Henry. b. in Prince Edward County, Va., March 7, 1837; d. at New York, Nov. 20, 1882. American scientist, especially noted for his labors in celestial photography; son of John William Draper.

Draper, John. b. Oct. 29, 1702; d. Nov. 29, 1762. American printer and publisher. He succeeded (1733) his father-in-law, Bartholomew Green, as publisher of the Boston *News-Letter*, the oldest colonial newspaper, and was the printer of Jeremiah Gridley's *Weekly Rehearsal* and *Ames Almanac.*

Draper, John William. b. at St. Helen's, near Liverpool, England, May 5, 1811; d. at Hastings-on-Hudson, N.Y., Jan. 4, 1882. American chemist, physiologist, and historian, noted for researches in spectrum analysis and photography. He emigrated to America in 1832, graduated from the medical department of the University of Pennsylvania in 1836, was appointed professor of chemistry in the University of New York in 1837, and was president of its medical college (1850–73). He continued to lecture at the university until 1881. He wrote *Text Book on Chemistry* (1846), and on *Natural Philosophy* (1847), *Human Physiology* (1856), *History of the Intellectual Development of Europe* (1862), *History of the American Civil War* (1867–70), and *Scientific Memoirs* (1878).

Draper, Lyman Copeland. b. at Hamburg, Erie County, N.Y., Sept. 4, 1815; d. at Madison, Wis., Aug. 26, 1891. American antiquary. He was corresponding secretary of the state historical society of Wisconsin at Madison, Wis. (1853–87), with the exception of two years (1858–59) when he was state superintendent of instruction, and was the editor of *Collections of the State Historica-Society* (1853–87).

Draper, Margaret. [Maiden name, **Green.**] fl 1750–1807; d. at London. American publisher; wife of Richard Draper. She continued after her husband's death (1774) the publication of *The Massachusetts Gazette and Weekly News-Letter*, in partnership (until the Revolutionary War) with John Boyle and then with John Howe, until the evacuation of Boston by the British.

Draper, Richard. b. Feb. 24, 1726/7; d. June 5, 1774. American publisher and printer; son of John Draper (1702–62). He continued publication (after 1762) of his father's paper, the Boston *Weekly News-Letter*, changing its name (1763) to *The Massachusetts Gazette and Weekly News-Letter*, in partnership with John Boyle.

Draper, Ruth. b. at New York, Dec. 2, 1889—. American monologuist. Performed (1918) in U.S. army camps in France; toured U.S. (1924–28), South Africa (1935), Far East (1938), South America (1940), Canada and U.S. (1940–41); commands repertory of 36 original monologues and 57 characters. She translated (from the Italian of Lauro de Bosis) the poetic drama *Icaro.*

Draper, Sir William. b. at Bristol, England, 1721; d. at Bath, England, Jan. 8, 1787. English army officer. He took the degree of B.A. at King's College, Cambridge, in 1740, and was subsequently fellow of his college. In 1744 he entered the army, and in 1762 commanded, with the rank of brigadier general, a successful expedition against Manila. He published in 1769 a letter, dated Jan. 26 of that year, defending the Marquis of Granby against the aspersions of "Junius," which led to a spirited controversy. He was promoted to major general in 1772. The correspondence between Draper and "Junius" was published separately under the title of *The Political Contest* (1769).

Drapier's Letters (drā'pi.ėrz). Series of letters published in 1724 by Jonathan Swift, under the pseudonym M. B. Drapier. They were directed against the acceptance in Ireland of a copper coinage the patent for supplying which had been accorded to William Wood, who with the duchess of Kendal, the king's mistress (who obtained him the privilege), was to divide the profit arising from the difference between the real and the nominal value of the halfpenny (about 40 percent). Owing to the public excitement raised by these letters the patent was canceled. Wood was compensated with a pension, and Swift gained a popularity which he never lost till his death. A large reward was offered at the time for the discovery of the author.

Drau (drou). German name of the **Drava.**

Draupadi (drou'pä.dē). In Hindu legend, daughter of Drupada, king of Panchala, and wife of the five Pandu princes. She plays an important part in the story of the *Mahabharata.*

Drava (drä'vä). [German, **Drau** (drou); French, **Drave** (dräv); Hungarian, **Dráva** (drä'vô); Latin, **Dravus** (drā'vus).] River in Austria and Yugoslavia which rises in East Tyrol province, Austria, traverses the provinces of Carinthia and Styria and N Yugoslavia, forms the boundary between Hungary and Yugoslavia, and joins the Danube ab. 14 mi. E of Osijek. Its chief tributary is the Mur. Length, ab. 450 mi.; navigable for steamers ab. 95 mi.

Draveil (drȧ.vey'). Town in N France, in the department of Seine-et-Oise, situated on the Seine River, between Paris and Corbeil. It belongs to the metropolitan region of Paris. 10,510 (1946).

Dravida (drä'vi.dą). Region in which the Tamil language is spoken, extending from Madras to Cape Comorin, in S Union of India.

Dravidian (drą.vid'i.ąn). Pre-Aryan group of people in India, comprising the majority of the inhabitants. Their descendants, now of Negroid admixture, comprise a large percentage of the population of S India.

Dravidian. Group of languages spoken by some 60 million people, mainly in south India. They are known not to be related to the Indo-European languages spoken in northern India or to any other linguistic stock. The principal Dravidian languages are Tamil, Malayalam, Telugu, and Kanarese. One Dravidian language, Brahui, is geographically isolated from the others, being spoken by about 200,000 people in Baluchistan, in W Pakistan.

Dravosburg (drą.vōs'bėrg). Borough in SW Pennsylvania, in Allegheny County, on the Monongahela River near Pittsburgh. 3,786 (1950).

Dravus (drā'vus). Latin name of the **Drava.**

Drawcansir (drô'kan.sėr). In Buckingham's burlesque *The Rehearsal*, a boasting and vainglorious bully. Almanzor, Dryden's favorite hero, was parodied in this character. The name became a synonym for a braggart.

Drax (draks), **Reginald Aylmer Ranfurly Plunkett-Ernle-Erle-.** See **Plunkett-Ernle-Erle-Drax, Reginald Aylmer Ranfurly.**

Drayton (drā'tǫn), **John.** b. near Charleston, S.C., June 22, 1766; d. at Charleston, S.C., Nov. 27, 1822. American politician and jurist, twice governor of South Carolina; son of William Henry Drayton (1742–79). Lieutenant governor (1798–1800), of South Carolina; governor (1800–04, 1808–10); influential in establishment (1801) of South Carolina College (now University of South Carolina); judge (1812–22) of U.S. court for district of South Carolina. Author of *Letters written during a Tour through the Northern and Eastern States of America* (1794), *A View of South Carolina, as Respects her Natural and Civil Concerns* (1802), and editor of a collection of his father's manuscripts, *Memoirs of the American Revolution, from its Commencement to the Year 1776, Inclusive; as Relating to the State of South-Carolina and Occasionally Referring to the States of North-Carolina and Georgia* (2 vols., 1821).

Drayton, Michael. b. at Hartshill, Warwickshire, England, 1563; d. at London, Dec. 23, 1631. English poet. He was buried in Westminster Abbey, and his epitaph is said to be by Ben Jonson. His chief works are *Idea; the Shepherd's Garland* (1593), a pastoral sequence; *Idea's Mirror* (1594), a sonnet sequence; *Mortimeriados* (1596; this afterward appeared with many alterations as *The Barons' Wars*, 1603); *England's Heroical Epistles* (1597); *Poems, Lyric and Pastoral* (c1606, containing "The Ballad of Agincourt" and "To the Virginian Voyage"); *Poly-Olbion* (1613–22), a description of England both topographical and legendary; *Nimphidia, the Court of Faery* (1627), a light-touched fairy poem; and *The Muses' Elysium* (1630).

Drayton, Percival. b. in South Carolina, Aug. 25, 1812; d. at Washington, D.C., Aug. 4, 1865. American naval officer; son of William Drayton (1776–1846). Although a member of a South Carolina family, he sympathized with the Union cause, and participated (1861) in DuPont's expedition against Port Royal, S.C., which was defended by his brother, General Thomas F. Drayton (1808–91) and other Confederate relatives. Commanding the *Passaic*, he attacked Fort McAllister and participated in DuPont's attack on Fort Sumter; on the *Hartford*, he fought at Mobile Bay under Farragut.

Drayton, Thomas Fenwick. b. in South Carolina, Aug. 24, 1808; d. at Florence, S.C., Feb. 18, 1891. American planter, railroad president, and Confederate officer in the Civil War; son of William Drayton (1776–1846). President (1853–61) of the Charleston and Savannah Railroad; commissioned (1861) brigadier general in the Confederate provisional army; in command of Port Royal, S.C. (1861) when it was attacked by Union ships under DuPont, one of which was commanded by his brother, Percival Drayton (1812–65).

Drayton, William. b. in South Carolina, March 21, 1732; d. May 18, 1790. American jurist. Chief justice (1767–76) of the province of East Florida; suspended (1776) because he advocated extension of local self-government; reinstated (1776); suspended again (1777). Appointed (1789) first judge of the U.S. court for the district of South Carolina after service as associate justice of the state supreme court.

Drayton, William. b. at St. Augustine, Fla., Dec. 30, 1776; d. May 24, 1846. American lawyer and congressman (1825–33) from South Carolina. Judge and recorder (1819–23) of the city court of Charleston; elected as a Union Democrat to Congress, where he fought the tariff but opposed nullification; chief organizer of Union party in South Carolina; president (1841 *et seq.*), Bank of the United States.

Drayton, William Henry. b. at Drayton Hall, on the Ashley River, S.C., in September, 1742; d. at Philadelphia, Sept. 3, 1779. American patriot; cousin of William Drayton (1732–90). He became chief justice of South Carolina in 1776, and in the same year delivered to the grand jury a charge which gave great impetus to the cause of independence. He was a member of the Continental Congress from 1778 until his death.

Drdla (dėrd'lä), **Franz.** b. at Saar, Moravia (now part of Czechoslovakia), Nov. 28, 1868—. Czech violinist and composer. He studied at the Prague and Vienna conservatories and played in the Vienna court opera orchestra. His compositions include *Souvenir*, *Vision*, and *Serenade in A Major*, dedicated to Kubelik, by whom it was first played.

Dreadnought (dred'nôt). British battleship, launched in 1906. It was of 17,900 tons displacement; length, 490 ft.; beam, 82 ft.; draft, 26½ ft.; had belt armor 11 inches thick; ten 12-inch guns; 5 torpedo tubes; 27,500 indicated horsepower; and a maximum speed of 21.85 knots. It gave its name to the class of heavy battleships before, during, and after World War I.

Dream, Chaucer's. Poem, probably spurious, added by Speght in 1598 to his edition of Chaucer. The proper title is *The Isle of Ladies.* (It is not the same as *The Dream of Chaucer*, which is genuine.)

Dream, The. Short poem by Byron, composed in 1816.

Dreamers, The. Three-act play about Robert Emmet, by Lennox Robinson, published in 1915.

Dream Life. Collection of essays by Ik Marvel (Donald G. Mitchell), published in 1851. It is the sequel to *Reveries of a Bachelor* (1850).

Dream of Eugene Aram (ū.jēn' ā'rąm), **The.** Poem by Thomas Hood, published in 1829.

Dream of Fair Women, A. Poem by Alfred Tennyson.

Dream of Fair Women, The. Autobiographical novel by Henry Williamson, published in 1924. It is the third volume of a tetralogy under the general title *The Flax of Dream.*

Dream of Gerontius (ję.ron'ti.us), **The.** Oratorio (Opus 38) by Sir Edward Elgar, based upon Cardinal Newman's poem of that title, first performed at the Birmingham Festival on Oct. 3, 1900.

Dream within a Dream, A. Poem by Edgar Allan Poe.

Drebbel (dreb'ęl), **Cornelis van.** b. at Alkmaar, Netherlands, 1572; d. at London, 1634. Dutch natural philosopher. He published *De natura elementorum* (1621) and others.

Dred, A Tale of the Great Dismal Swamp (dred). Novel by Harriet Beecher Stowe, published in 1856, showing the state of alarm and misery in which the slaveowners as well as slaves lived. Dred is a runaway Negro living in the Dismal Swamp. A new edition, called *Nina Gordon*, was published in 1866.

Dred Scott Case. [Formally cited as **Dred Scott v. Sandford, 19 Howard 393 (1857).**] In American history, a celebrated decision by the U.S. Supreme Court, which derived its importance from its bearing on the constitutionality of the Missouri Compromise of 1820. Dred Scott, a Missouri slave who had been taken to Wisconsin in the territory covered by the Missouri Compromise, and had therefore sued (1848) for his freedom, was sold to a citizen of another state. He then transferred his suit from the state to the federal courts, under the power given to the latter to try suits between citizens of different states; and the case came by appeal to the

Supreme Court. The decision of the Supreme Court, rendered in 1857, put Scott out of court on the ground that under the Constitution a slave, or the descendant of a slave, could not be a citizen of the U.S. or have any standing in federal courts. The opinion of chief justice Roger B. Taney also attacked the validity of the Missouri Compromise, on the ground that one of the constitutional functions of Congress was the protection of property, that slaves were recognized by the Constitution as property, and that Congress was therefore bound to protect slavery in the territories.

Drees (drās), **Willem.** b. at Amsterdam, Netherlands, July 5, 1886—. Dutch statesman, prime minister (1948 *et seq.*) of the Netherlands. He attended a commercial school at Amsterdam, and entered the employ of the Twentsche Bank. Chairman (1911–31) of the Hague branch of the Social Democratic Labor party; stenographer (1917–19) of the states general; official in The Hague municipality and in the province of South Holland; member (1933–40) of the second chamber of the states general; imprisoned by the Germans at Buchenwald and St. Michielsgestel (1940–41). He was minister of social affairs in the Schermerhorn cabinet.

Dreiherrnspitze or **Dreiherrn Spitze** (drī'hern'shpit.sẹ). One of the chief peaks of the Hohe Tauern, in the Austrian Alps, SW of the Grosse-Venediger. Elevation, ab. 11,480 ft.

Drei Pintos (drī pin'tos), **Die.** Unfinished opera by Carl Maria von Weber, composed c1821 with a libretto by Hell; rearranged by Carl von Weber and completed by Gustav Mahler; the latter conducted its first performance, at Leipzig, on Jan. 20, 1888.

Dreiser (drī'sėr), **Theodore (Herman Albert).** b. at Terre Haute, Ind., Aug. 27, 1871; d. at Hollywood, Calif., Dec. 28, 1945. American novelist and editor, notable as a writer of naturalistic fiction. He was editor of *Smith's Magazine* (1905–06) and *Broadway Magazine* (1906–07); editor in chief (1907–10) of Butterick publications, including *The Delineator;* and editor until 1934 of *The American Spectator.* He was the author of *Sister Carrie* (1900), *Jennie Gerhardt* (1911), *The Financier* (1912; revised ed., 1927), *The Titan* (1914), *The Genius* (1915), *A Hoosier Holiday* (1916), *Free And Other Stories* (1918), *Twelve Men* (1919), *The Color of a Great City* (1923), *An American Tragedy* (1925), *Chains* (1927), *Dawn* (1931), *Tragic America* (1932), *The Bulwark* (1946), *The Stoic* (1947), and other works. He published the tragedy *The Hand of the Potter* (1919), and was author of *Moods* (1926), a book of verse, and *Dreiser Looks at Russia,* published (1928) after a visit to Russia in 1927. Dreiser was often attacked for his lack of style, but his novels, remarkably complete in wealth of detail and powerful because of the stories they told, were widely read. *Sister Carrie* was removed from sale by its publisher; *Jennie Gerhardt* was attacked for its supposed immorality. Frank Cowperwood, central figure of *The Financier* and *The Titan,* is an accurate picture of the grasping businessman and his environment. *An American Tragedy,* his greatest success, is the story of a youth whose weakness and inability to resist the forces surrounding him bring him to destruction. Dreiser is a naturalist rather than a realist, depicting human beings swept along by events stronger than mere humanity and broken or elevated by chance or by some natural law that the author cannot fathom.

Drelincourt (drẹ.laṅ.kör), **Charles.** b. at Sedan, France, July 10, 1595; d. at Paris, Nov. 3, 1669. French Protestant clergyman. He was the author of *Consolations de l'âme fidele contre les frayeurs de la mort* (1651).

Drente (dren'tẹ). [Also, **Drenthe.**] Province of the Netherlands, in the NE part, bounded by Groningen on the N and NE, Germany on the E, Overijssel on the S, and Friesland and Overijssel on the W. It is one of the poorer provinces of the Netherlands; much of the soil is either sandy or swampy and the population density is not high. Agriculture and livestock raising are the principal occupations. Capital, Assen; area, 1,030 sq. mi.; pop. 285,079 (est. 1950).

Drepanum (drep'ạ.num). Ancient name of **Trapani,** Italy.

Drescher (dresh'ėr), **Martin.** b. at Wittstock, Germany, 1863; d. in the U.S., 1920. American poet who wrote in German. After studying law at Göttingen he entered the Prussian civil service, but came to America in 1891 and from his early American experiences emerged an impassioned Marxist. He was editor of the Detroit weeklies *Der Herold* and *Der arme Teufel.* He published volumes of verse (*Gedichte,* 1909; *Stille und Sturm,* 1913; *New York und die Welt,* 1913; *Krieg, Gedichte der Zeit,* 1914) and an autobiography (*Vom Sturm gepeitscht. Skizzen und Geschichten aus einem Zigeunerleben,* 1913).

Dresden (drez'dẹn). City in E Germany, in the *Land* (state) of Saxony, Russian Zone, formerly the capital of the free state of Saxony, situated on both sides of the Elbe River, ab. 63 mi. SE of Leipzig. Before World War II, the most important industry was cigarette manufacture, with many large and small enterprises; next in importance were the chemical and pharmaceutical industry, the manufacture of photochemical and photographic articles (Zeiss-Ikon), and the manufacture of chocolates and candies; there were also glass, porcelain, and majolica factories, paper mills, and machine shops. Dresden is now the center of cigarette manufacture in Eastern Germany and an important railroad junction and river port. It is the seat of a Lutheran bishopric and has an institute of technology, a music conservatory and dramatic academy, and an art academy (all three institutions of excellent reputation), and a number of other educational institutions and vocational schools. Its art gallery possesses works by Italian, Dutch, and Flemish masters (including the famous *Sistine Madonna* by Raphael) and well-known collections of porcelain, arms, coins, and jewelry. Before World War II Dresden was one of the most beautiful cities of Germany, dominated by the high cupola of the Frauenkirche (1726–43), a masterpiece of German baroque by Georg Bähr. The Catholic *Hofkirche* (Court Church) was erected (1738–55) in the baroque style of Rome by Gaetano Chiaveri. The Zwinger, a collection of buildings around a central courtyard, started in 1711 in the purest rococo style by Daniel Pöppelmann, was completed (1847–56) in the same style by Gottfried Semper. Other baroque and rococo buildings were the old *Rathaus* (city hall), the Neustädter Rathaus, the Neustädter Hauptwache, the Japanese Palais (by Pöppelmann), the Palais on the Zinzendorf Street, the Prinzen Palais, and the Johanneum. The former royal *Schloss* (castle) is a 16th-century building, renovated at the end of the 19th century. Other structures, such as the opera house, the new city hall, and others, are good examples of 19th and 20th century architecture, fitted into the general picture. The Brühl'sche Terrasse lined the banks of the Elbe River. Almost all these buildings are gone. The Frauenkirche is completely destroyed; the Hofkirche, Schloss, and Zwinger are largely ruined. The same may be said of large parts of the city; it is doubtful whether the unique flavor of Dresden's architecture will ever be restored.

History. Originally a Slavic fishing village, the German town of Dresden grew around a castle of the margraves of Meissen, but remained small until it became the residence of the rulers of Saxony of the Albertine line of the house of Wettin at the end of the 15th century. Lutheranism was introduced in 1539. The period of architectural activity and court splendor started in the reign of Johann Georg II in the middle of the 17th century and continued on a larger scale in the 18th century in the reign of August II and III, who at the same time were kings of Poland; Dresden was then one of the most grandiose courts of Europe. In the Seven Years' War Dresden surrendered to Prussian troops in 1756, was reconquered in 1759, and was bombarded by the Prussian army under Frederick II in 1760. It became Napoleon's chief arsenal and headquarters after his retreat from Russia; one of his last victories was won in the battle of Dresden (Aug. 26–27, 1813). The fortifications were razed after 1817. Steamship traffic on the Elbe River was introduced in 1836 and one of the first German railroads reached the town in 1839. Dresden was at this time the seat of a school of painting and architecture. A bloody revolution took place here in the spring of 1849, gravely damaging some of the buildings; it was suppressed. In 1851, a conference of the German states was held here on the initiative of Austria and Prussia. In 1866 the city was occupied by Prussian troops without a fight; the transition from monarchy to republic in 1918 was also bloodless. The city experienced devastating air raids in World War II;

it was occupied by Russian forces on May 8, 1945. The population, mostly Protestant, declined between 1939 and 1946 by 27.7 percent. 467,966 (1946).

Dresden, Treaty of. Treaty concluded on Dec. 25, 1745, between Prussia, Austria, and Saxony, ending the second Silesian war. Frederick the Great was confirmed in the possession of Silesia.

Dresden Codex. See under **Codex.**

Dresden Diamond. [Also, **Dresden Green Diamond.**] Diamond which was at one time in the collection belonging to the Saxon crown. It weighs approximately 40 carats and has a greenish tinge.

Dresser (dres'ėr), **John Alexander.** b. at Richmond, Quebec, Canada, June 27, 1866—. Canadian geologist and petrographer, geologist of the Canadian Geological Survey from 1909. He has been lecturer on geology at McGill University since 1907.

Dresser, Paul. [Surname originally **Dreiser.**] b. 1857; d. 1911. American song writer; brother of Theodore Dreiser. With no pretensions to high literary or musical quality, some of his songs, sentimental and melodious, caught the popular fancy. Two which swept the country were *On the Banks of the Wabash, Far Away,* and *The Blue and the Gray.* The last-named work was exceedingly popular during the Spanish-American War (1898).

Dressler (dres'lėr), **Marie.** [Original name, **Leila Koerber.**] b. at Cobourg, Ontario, Canada, Nov. 9, 1871; d. July 28, 1934. American actress. She was leading comedienne (1906 *et seq.*) with the Weber company at New York, where she played the part of Tillie Bob in *Tillie's Nightmare,* which she repeated (1916) in the motion picture *Tillie's Punctured Romance,* co-starring with Charles Chaplin. Other films in which she appeared are *Anna Christie, Emma, Caught Short, Reducing, Min and Bill, Politics, Prosperity, Dinner at Eight, Tugboat Annie,* and *The Late Christopher Bean.*

Dreux (drė). Medieval county in N France, W of Paris, whose chief town was Dreux.

Dreux. [Ancient names, **Durocasses, Drocae.**] Town in W France, in the department of Eure-et-Loir, situated on the Blaise River near its junction with the Eure River, ab. 45 mi. W of Paris. It is a center for trade in grain, poultry, and other agricultural products and has tanning, metallurgical, hat, shoe, and food (beer, liquor, cider, biscuits) industries. The church of Saint Pierre has a beautiful Renaissance bell tower. The chapel of Saint Louis, the burial place of the house of Orléans, built in the beginning of the 19th century, was damaged during World War II. 14,184 (1946).

Dreux, Battle of. In French history, name given to the defeat (Dec. 19, 1562) by Montmorency, with ab. 15,000 men, of an equal number of Huguenots under Condé, who was taken prisoner.

Drew (drö), **Daniel.** b. at Carmel, N.Y., July 29, 1797; d. Sept. 18, 1879. American railroad capitalist and speculator, noted for his role in the so-called Erie War. Starting out as a cattle drover and horse trader in New York state, he soon rose to a prominent position as a cattle buyer. Moving to New York in 1829, he entered (1834) the steamboat business, running boats on the Hudson River in competition with Cornelius Vanderbilt. He also set up a steamboat line on Lake Champlain and for many years controlled the Stonington Line on Long Island Sound. With his earnings he formed (1844) the Wall Street house of Drew, Robinson and Company, later becoming an independent operator known for his shrewdness. He sustained his first serious defeat in 1864, when he lost out to Vanderbilt and John Tobin in the Harlem Railroad corner; the stock manipulations cost Drew a half-million dollars. In alliance with James Fisk and Jay Gould, he carried out the notorious "Erie War" (1866–68) against Vanderbilt and his group. The affair, marked by duplicity, violence, court proceedings, and corruption, startled the country with its demonstration of the power wielded by reckless men in defiance of public responsibility. He was later betrayed in a financial deal by his confederates, Gould and Fisk, and after the panic of 1873 saw his fortune disappear. His bankruptcy schedule filed in 1876 indicated that his liabilities exceeded one million dollars. See *The Book of Daniel Drew,* by Bouck White (1910).

Drew, Georgiana Emma. See **Barrymore, Georgiana Emma Drew.**

Drew, John. b. at Dublin, Sept. 3, 1827; d. at Philadelphia, May 21, 1862. American actor; husband of Louisa Drew. He made his first appearance in 1845 at New York, and in 1852 at Philadelphia, where he became a great favorite. In 1853 he became (with William Wheatley) manager of the Arch Street Theatre. He played in England in 1855, in California in 1858, in Australia in 1859, and made his last appearance in 1862.

Drew, John. b. at Philadelphia, Nov. 13, 1853; d. at San Francisco, July 9, 1927. American actor, noted for his creations of high comedy roles; son of John Drew (1827–62) and Louisa Drew (1820–97). His first appearance on the stage was in a farce, *Cool as a Cucumber,* produced in 1873 at the Arch Street Theatre at Philadelphia. He went (1875) to New York to act with Augustin Daly's company, making his first appearance with that group as Bob Ruggles in *The Big Bonanza,* produced at the Fifth Avenue Theatre. He later appeared in Shakespearian roles and then joined his brother-in-law, Maurice Barrymore, in a barnstorming tour that took him to Texas. Drew rejoined Daly's company in 1879, remaining with it for the next 14 years, during which time he established his reputation, particularly in Shakespearian parts played opposite Ada Rehan. His first appearance as a star was opposite Maude Adams in Charles Frohman's New York production (1892) of *The Masked Ball,* an adaptation by Clyde Fitch. For the next 23 years, until Frohman was lost with the *Lusitania,* Drew played under Frohman's management in plays like *The Bauble Shop* and *The Liars,* by Henry Arthur Jones, *Rosemary,* by Louis N. Parker and Murray Carson, *The Tyranny of Tears,* by C. Haddon Chambers, and *The Mummy and the Humming Bird,* by Captain Marshall, being supported in the latter by his nephew, Lionel Barrymore. He played (1921–23) in *The Circle,* by Somerset Maugham, and later appeared in several revivals, particularly Pinero's *Trelawney of the Wells,* which he played with an all-star company. He was the author of *My Years on the Stage* (1923). See *A Splendid Gypsy: John Drew,* by Peggy Wood (1927).

Drew, Louisa. [Maiden name, **Lane.**] b. at London, Jan. 10, 1820; d. at Larchmont, N.Y., Aug. 31, 1897. American actress; wife of John Drew (1825–62). She married Henry Hunt, a singer, in 1836, and after separating from him married George Mossop, an Irish actor, who died in 1849. In 1850 she married John Drew. She went on the stage very young, came to America in 1828, and acted in all the important cities in the country. In 1861 she became sole manager of the Arch Street Theatre at Philadelphia.

Drew, Samuel. b. at St. Austell, Cornwall, England, March 6, 1765; d. at Helston, Cornwall, England, March 29, 1833. English Methodist clergyman and theologian. He wrote *Essay on the Immateriality and Immortality of the Soul* (1802), *Essay on the Identity and General Resurrection of the Body* (1809), and others.

Drewrys Bluff (drö'riz). [Also, **Drury's Bluff.**] Point on the James River, near Fort Darling, ab. 8 mi. S of Richmond, Va. Here, on May 16, 1864, the Confederates under Beauregard repulsed the Union forces under Butler. Union loss (May 12–16), 3,012; that of the Confederates, 2,500.

Drews (dröz), **Arthur.** b. at Ütersen, Holstein, Germany, Nov. 1, 1865; d. at Achern, Germany, July 19, 1935. German philosopher, professor (1898 *et seq.*) at Karlsruhe, who, influenced by Eduard von Hartmann and G. W. F. Hegel, propagated the so-called *Konkreter Monismus* (concrete monism). He is remembered as author of *Die Christusmythe* (1909–11), denying the historical existence of Jesus. Among his other books are *Die deutsche Spekulation seit Kant* (1893), *Das Lebenswerk E. v. Hartmanns* (1907), *Der Monismus* (1909), and *Die Entstehung des Christentums aus dem Gnostizismus* (1924).

Drexel (drek'sel), **Anthony Joseph.** b. at Philadelphia, Sept. 13, 1826; d. at Carlsbad, Germany (now Karlovy Vary, Czechoslovakia), June 30, 1893. American banker and philanthropist; son of F. M. Drexel (1792–1863). He became (1847) a member of Drexel and Company which, upon his father's death, came under his direction and that of his older brother, Francis. The firm's expansion after the Civil War, and its emergence as an investment brokerage firm, were largely due to his judgment and foresight. He took over the sole direction of the firm in 1885, when his brother Francis died. He made many gifts to charitable and church institutions. A part owner of the Philadelphia *Public Ledger*, he participated in establishing the Childs-Drexel Home for Aged Printers at Colorado Springs, Colo. His outstanding contributions, totaling some three million dollars, were made to Drexel Institute at Philadelphia, which he founded.

Drexel, Francis Martin. b. at Dornbirn, in the Austrian Tyrol, April 7, 1792; d. June 5, 1863. American banker. He founded (1837) the banking house of Drexel and Company at Philadelphia.

Dreyer (drī′ėr), **John Louis Emil.** b. at Copenhagen, Feb. 13, 1852; d. 1926. Danish astronomer, who worked in Ireland. He went to Ireland in 1874 to become astronomer of the observatory of the earl of Rosse at Birr, served as assistant astronomer of the observatory of the University of Dublin from 1878 to 1882, and from the latter date to 1916 was director of the observatory at Armagh, studying particularly the formation of nebulae and the motions of stars. He edited the *Second Armagh Catalogue of 3,300 Stars* (1886), and prepared a *New General Catalogue of Nebulae and Clusters of Stars* (1888). As a historian of his chosen science he wrote a *History of the Planetary Systems from Thales to Kepler* (1906), and edited the works of Sir William Herschel and the earlier volumes of the collected writings of Tycho Brahe.

Dreyer, Max. b. at Rostock, Germany, Sept. 25, 1862—. German dramatist and novelist. His greatest success was *Der Probekandidat* (1899), a play in which a brave young teacher tries to tell the truth about evolution and loses his job and financée. His humor at the expense of ruling houses in *Das Tal des Lebens* (1902) brought the ban of the Prussian censor, an act which helped the popularity of the play elsewhere. He is the author also of the novels *Nachwuchs* (1917), *Das Gymnasium von St. Jürgen* (1925), and *Der Weg durchs Feuer* (1930). For several years he taught in a *Gymnasium* (advanced secondary school), and for a decade he edited the Berlin *Tägliche Rundschau*, and has done best when drawing on these experiences.

Dreyfus (drā′fus, drī′-; French, drā.füs), **Alfred.** b. at Mulhouse, in Alsace, Oct. 9, 1859; d. at Paris, July 12, 1935. French army officer of Jewish descent, central figure in the celebrated Dreyfus affair. He was convicted (1894) by a secret military tribunal of having divulged state secrets to a foreign power, and was sentenced to penal servitude for life. He was imprisoned on Devil's Island, French Guiana. The so-called *bordereau* (a list of papers supposedly to be turned over by Dreyfus to the Germans), the principal piece of evidence in Dreyfus's conviction, was sufficient evidence to sway the anti-Semitic military court. However, in 1896 Colonel Picquart, of army intelligence, discovered, and in 1897 Dreyfus's brother Mathieu made public, evidence indicating that not Dreyfus but Major Marie Charles Ferdinand Walsin Esterhazy was the writer of the bordereau. The case rapidly became a public scandal and liberals and republicans sided against militarists and royalists in an attempt to reopen the case and obtain justice for Dreyfus. Such men as Émile Zola (convicted in 1898 for printing his pro-Dreyfus series of articles *J'accuse*, which summed up the evidence against the army), Jaurès, Anatole France, and Clemenceau attacked the rightists, who included Déroulède and Barrès. To support their case, the anti-Dreyfus forces made use of manufactured evidence, building a house of cards that tumbled with the suicide in prison of Lieutenant Colonel Henry, of army intelligence, who with Esterhazy was actually responsible for the bordereau. Dreyfus was accorded a second trial at Rennes (Aug. 7–Sept. 9, 1899), and was recondemned and sentenced to ten years' imprisonment, but was pardoned by President Loubet for by this time it was obvious that the case was not being tried on its merits. The decision of the court of cassation, the supreme appeals court of France, announced on July 12, 1906, quashed the verdict of the Rennes tribunal and completely vindicated Dreyfus. Restored (1906) to military rank as a major, he was decorated with the Legion of Honor, served in the French army in World War I, and retired as a lieutenant colonel after holding the temporary rank of brigadier general. Subsequent revelations (1930) indicated the absolute guilt of Major Esterhazy in forging the documents originally ascribed to Dreyfus. The Dreyfus case was used by the anticlerical party in France to further their aim of complete separation of church and state; on the other hand, the antirepublicans made every attempt, including armed resistance to the government, to use the affair to discredit the republic.

Dreyschock (drī′shok), **Alexander.** b. at Zack, in Bohemia, Oct. 15, 1818; d. at Venice, April 1, 1869. Czech pianist and composer. Professor of the pianoforte (1862 *et seq.*) at the conservatory of St. Petersburg, director of the imperial school of theatrical music, and court pianist.

Dreyse (drī′zẹ), **Johann Nikolaus von.** b. at Sömmerda, Prussia, Nov. 20, 1787; d. Dec. 9, 1867. German mechanician, inventor of the muzzle-loading needle gun (1827) and of the breech-loader (1836).

Dr. Faustus (fôs′tus, fous′-). See **Doctor Faustus.**

Dr. Grimshawe's Secret (grim′shôz). Prose romance by Nathaniel Hawthorne. It was left in an unfinished state, not being published until 1882 when it was edited by his son, Julian. The setting is a town in New England, and the time is the early part of the 19th century. The plot centers around an English estate which, since the time of Charles I, has had a bloody footstep on its threshold, a mark left by the last heir when he suddenly disappeared.

Dr. Heidegger's Experiment (hī′dẹ.gėrz). Short story by Nathaniel Hawthorne, included in his *Twice-Told Tales* (1837). The theme of the story is the old legend of the famous Fountain of Youth, which Ponce de Leon searched for.

Dr. Heidenhoff's Process (hī′dẹn.hofs). Psychological novel (1880) by Edward Bellamy. It was highly praised by William Dean Howells, who regarded it as "one of the finest feats in the region of romance" that he knew. Like its author's later *Miss Ludington's Sister* (1884), it deals with psychic material.

D'ri and I (drī). Novel by Irving Bacheller, published in 1901. The story involves the experiences of a hired man, Darius Olin, and Ramon Bell, son of Olin's employer.

Driburg (drē′bu̇rk). Resort town in W Germany, in the *Land* (state) of North Rhine-Westphalia, formerly in the province of Westphalia, Prussia, ab. 11 mi. E of Paderborn: mineral springs. Pop. about 4,000.

Driebergen-Rijzenburg (drē′ber″ċhẹn.rī′zẹn.bėrċh). Town in C Netherlands, in the province of Utrecht, E of the city of Utrecht. The town has beautiful villas and parks; agriculture and the raising of meat cattle prevail in the district. 11,300 (1939).

Driesch (drēsh), **Hans Adolf Eduard.** b. at Kreuznach, Germany, Oct. 28, 1867; d. at Leipzig, Germany, April 17, 1941. German biologist and philosopher. From 1891 to 1900 he was engaged in research at Trieste and at the zoölogical station at Naples. Originally a disciple of Haeckel, he later became an opponent of philosophical mechanism and formulated his own system of dynamic vitalism and individuality. He served as professor of philosophy at Heidelberg (1911 *et seq.*), Cologne (1920 *et seq.*), and Leipzig (1921 *et seq.*). Author of *Analytische Theorie der organischen Entwicklung* (1894), *Geschichte des Vitalismus* (1905), *Leib und Seele* (1916; 3rd ed., 1923), *Das Problem der Freiheit* (1917), *Metaphysik* (1924), *Parapsychologie* (1932; 2nd ed., 1943), and *Die Maschine und der Organismus* (1935).

Driesche (drēs′ċhẹ), **Jan van den.** See **Drusius, Johannes.**

Drieu La Rochelle (drē.ė lȧ ro.shel), **Pierre.** b. at Paris, Jan. 3, 1893; committed suicide after the Allied liberation of France, 1945. French poet, novelist, and editor. He was the author of poems, including *Interrogation* (1917) and *Fond de Cantine* (1920); of novels, such as *L'Homme couvert de femmes* (1925) and *Une femme à sa fenêtre* (1930). Early a member of such diverse groups as the Communists, surrealists, and Action Française, he later joined the Parti Populaire Français of Jacques Doriot. He wrote a novel, *Gilles* (1939), about fighting for France, and accepted the editorship (1940) of the *Nouvelle Revue Française* directly after the French defeat by the Germans in World War II.

Driffield (drif′ēld). Urban district and market town in NE England, in the East Riding of Yorkshire, ab. 36 mi. E of York, ab. 216 mi. N of London by rail. 6,888 (1951).

Drift. Novel by James Hanley, published in 1930.

Driftless Area. Extensive area mostly in W central and SW Wisconsin, but extending also into NW Illinois, NE Iowa, and SE Minnesota, which was not covered by any of the recent continental glaciations. It is hillier than the surrounding glaciated areas, and is traversed by deep valleys, of which the largest are those of the lower Wisconsin and the Mississippi rivers. The highest elevations in the region are Rib Mountain, near Wausau, Wis. (1,940 ft.) and West Blue Mound, ab. 20 mi. W of Madison, Wis. (1,716 ft.). Area, ab. 15,000 sq. mi.

Drilo (drī'lō). Ancient name of the **Drin.**

Drin (drēn). [Also: **Drini** (drē'nē); ancient name, **Drilo.**] River which flows from Yugoslavia through N Albania and empties into the Adriatic near Lesh (Alessio). Length, ab. 175 mi.

Drina (drē'nä). [Latin, **Drinus.**] River in Yugoslavia which rises in Montenegro, flows generally N between Serbia and Bosnia-Hercegovina, and joins the Sava. Length, ab. 170 mi.

Drinkwater (dringk'wô.tėr, -wot.ėr), **John.** b. at Leytonstone, Essex, England, June 1, 1882; d. at London, March 25, 1937. English dramatist and poet. He worked in the insurance business at Manchester, Birmingham, and elsewhere, and before turning to full-time writing took part in founding (1907) the Pilgrim Players, an amateur dramatic group which later became the Birmingham Repertory Theatre. Among his historical plays are *Abraham Lincoln, a Play* (produced 1918), *Mary Stuart* (published 1921, produced 1922), *Oliver Cromwell, a Play* (published 1921, produced 1923), and *Robert E. Lee, a Play* (published and produced 1923). Among his other plays are *Rebellion: a Three Act Play in Verse* (1914), *Bird in Hand* (1927), and *Midsummer Eve* (1932). His biographical and critical works include *William Morris, a Study* (1912), *Swinburne, a Study* (1913), *The Pilgrim of Eternity—Byron* (1925), *Charles James Fox* (1928), *Pepys* (1930), and *Shakespeare* (1933). Among his works of poetry are *Poems* (1903), *Poems of Men and Hours* (1911), *Cromwell and Other Poems* (1913), *Poems* 1908–14 (1917), *Seeds of Time* (1921), *From an Unknown Isle* (1924), *Christmas Poems* (1931), and *Summer Harvest* (1933). He wrote two autobiographical volumes, *Inheritance, The First Volume of an Autobiography* (1931) and *Discovery, the Second Volume* (1932).

Drioton (drē.o.tôṅ), **Étienne Marie.** b. at Nancy France, 1889—. French ecclesiastic and Egyptologist He served as professor (1920 *et seq.*) at the Institut Catholique de Paris. Among his works is *Introduction à l'étude des hiéroglyphes* (Introduction to the Use of the Hieroglyphs; with Sottas, 1922).

Drisler (dris'lėr), **Henry.** b. on Staten Island, N.Y., Dec. 27, 1818; d. at New York, Nov. 30, 1897. American classical scholar, lexicographer, and educator. In 1843 he was appointed tutor in Columbia College (later Columbia University), and was continuously connected with that institution during the rest of his active life, becoming professor of Greek in 1867, and dean of the faculty of arts in 1889. In 1894 he resigned and was made professor emeritus. In 1867 and 1888–89 he was acting president of the university. He reëdited Liddell and Scott's edition of Passow's Greek lexicon (1851), and was associate editor of the seventh revised Oxford edition, published in 1883.

Drittes Reich (drit'ęs rīċh'). See **Third Reich.**

Driver (drī'vėr), **Samuel Rolles.** b. at Southampton, England, Oct. 2, 1846; d. Feb. 26, 1914. English scholar, regius professor of Hebrew and canon of Christ Church College in the University of Oxford from 1883. He was one of the revisers of the English translation of the Old Testament (1876–84). Among his works are *Isaiah* (1893), *An Introduction to the Literature of the Old Testament* (1897), and commentaries on Joel and Amos (1897), Daniel (1901), Deuteronomy (1902), *The Minor Prophets* (1905), Job (1905), Genesis (1909), and *Three Papers on the Higher Criticism*, with A. F. Kirkpatrick (1905).

Dr. Johns (jonz). Novel by Ik Marvel (Donald Grant Mitchell), published in 1866.

Dr. Lavendar's People (lav'ęn.dėrz). Collected short stories (1903) by Margaret Deland. They are studies of American character in American village life, and belong to the "local-color" school. They are written in the romantic and sentimental tradition which Edgar Lee Masters rebelled against in his *Spoon-River Anthology* (1915).

Drobisch (drō'bish), **Moritz Wilhelm.** b. 1802; d. 1896. German educator, mathematician, and philosopher. He shared and practiced the educational theories of Johann Friedrich Herbart. His principal works were *Neue Darstellung der Logik* (New Exposition of Logic, 1836), *Grundlehren der Religionsphilosophie* (Fundamentals of Religious Philosophy, 1840), and *Empirische Psychologie* (Empirical Psychology, 1842).

Drocae (drō'sē). An ancient name of **Dreux,** town.

Droch (drok). Pseudonym of **Bridges, Robert.**

Drogheda (drô'ę.dą). [Irish, **Droichead Átha.**] Urban district, seaport, and manufacturing center in Leinster province, Irish Republic, in County Louth, situated on the river Boyne ab. 4 mi. from its mouth, ab. 27 mi. N of Dublin. It has cotton textile manufactures. The port handles imports of coal and general cargo. During the 14th century, Drogheda was one of the four ports in Ireland from which export of staple goods was permitted. Until 1898 it formed with the surrounding district (9 sq. mi.) a county. "Poynings's Law" was passed here in 1494. The town was defended (1641–42) against O'Neill, was stormed by Cromwell and the garrison massacred (September, 1649), and surrendered to William III after the battle of the Boyne (1690). Pop. 16,773 (1951).

Drogheda, Statute of. See **Poynings's Law.**

Drogio (drō'ji.ō). Name given by the late 14th-century Venetian explorer Antonio Zeno to a country said to be S and W of Estotiland. It was of vast extent, and has been thought to include Nova Scotia and New England.

Drogobych (dro.gô'bich). [Polish, **Drohobycz** (drô.ʜô'bich).] Town in the U.S.S.R., in the Ukrainian Soviet Socialist Republic, ab. 40 mi. SW of Lvov. It has considerable trade, and salt-works. 32,000 (est. 1940).

Droichead Átha (drô'ęd ô'hą). Irish name of **Drogheda.**

Droichead Banndan (drô'ęd ban'dąn). Irish name of **Bandon,** Irish Republic.

Droitwich (droit'wich). [Also, **Droitwich Spa.**] Municipal borough, market town, and spa in W England, in Worcestershire, situated on the river Salwarpe, ab. 6 mi. NE of Worcester, ab. 126 mi. NW of London by rail. It is famous for its salt springs and saline baths, known since Roman times, and formerly had salt mines, now no longer worked. 6,453 (1951).

Drôme (drōm). Department in SE France, bounded by the department of Isère on the N, the departments of Isère and Hautes-Alpes on the E, the department of Basses-Alpes on the SE, and the department of Vaucluse on the S, and separated by the Rhone River from the department of Ardèche on the W. It contains the westernmost ranges of the Alps, sloping down to the fertile Rhone valley. There are pastures and forests in the mountains, and orchards, olive groves, and vineyards in the valley. Its wines are famous. There are various industries, among which the leather industry of Romans is notable. The important railroad line from Lyons to Marseilles runs through the department. The American Seventh Army and a French army advanced through Drôme in 1944. Capital, Valence; area, 2,532 sq. mi.; pop. 268,233 (1946).

Dromina (drom'i.ną). Novel (1909) by Monsignor Count Francis Browning Drew Bickerstaffe-Drew under the pseudonym John Ayscough. Based on a religious theme, it is set against the historical background of the 1820's. The Dauphin, son of Louis XVI, is a leading character.

Dromio of Ephesus (drom'i.ō; ef'ę.sus) and **Dromio of Syracuse** (sir'ą.kūs). In Shakespeare's *Comedy of Errors,* twin brothers, servants respectively of Antipholus of Ephesus and Antipholus of Syracuse. The Dromio of Ephesus is a stupid servant, the Dromio of Syracuse a witty one.

Dromore (drǫ.mōr', drō'môr). Urban district and market town in Ulster province, Northern Ireland, in County Down, situated on the river Lagan ab. 15 mi. SW of Belfast. The town has a cathedral. 2,176 (1937).

Drona (drō'ną). In Hindu legend, the teacher of the military art to the Kaurava and Pandava princes. In the great war of the *Mahabharata* he sided with the Kauravas, and after the death of Bhishma became their commander in chief.

Dronfield (dron'fēld). Urban district in N central England, in Derbyshire, ab. 6 mi. NW of Chesterfield, ab. 151 mi. NW of London by rail. 7,628 (1951).

Drontheim (drôn'hām). Former spelling of **Trondheim,** Norway.

Dropsie (drop'si), **Moses Aaron.** b. at Philadelphia, March 9, 1821; d. July 8, 1905. American lawyer, educator, and benefactor. After receiving training in the Jewish faith, and working as a watchmaker, he took up the study of law at the age of 27, and was admitted to the bar in 1851. He served as president (1862–82) of the Lombard and South Streets Railway, and became (1888) president of the Green and Coates Streets Passenger Railroad Company. He was secretary and president (1848–92) of the Hebrew Education Society of Philadelphia, served as president of the board of trustees of the Maimonides College of Philadelphia, the first Jewish college in America, and became president (1893) of Gratz College, the first Jewish teachers college in America. His entire estate was willed for the foundation of a college which others named the Dropsie College for Hebrew and Cognate Learning.

Droste-Hülshoff (dros'tę.hüls'hof), Baroness **Annette Elisabeth von.** b. at Hülshoff, near Münster, Prussia, Jan. 10, 1797; d. at Meersburg, on Lake Constance, Germany, May 24, 1848. German poetess. Her story *Die Judenbuche* (1842) tells with sternness and realism of the Westphalian country from which she derived much of her material. Her poetry (including *Gedichte,* 1838, and *Das geistliche Jahr,* 1852), is filled with the atmosphere of the same region.

Droste zu Vischering (tsö fish'ę.ring), Baron **Klemens August von.** b. at Münster, Prussia, Jan. 21, 1773; d. Oct. 19, 1845. German Roman Catholic prelate. He studied at the University of Münster and belonged to the learned circle of Baron von Fürstenberg. Ordained priest in 1798, he was elected coadjutor bishop in 1807, and six months later succeeded von Fürstenberg as administrator of the diocese. In 1813 Napoleon replaced him by Baron von Spiegel, without the Pope's knowledge, but he was restored in 1815. He clashed with the Prussian government and later withdrew to private life. Elected archbishop of Cologne in 1835, he again came into conflict with the government because he supported Pope Gregory XVI in the condemnation of Hermes's teachings, and in other matters. He was arrested on Nov. 20, 1837, but freed in April, 1839, after John Gorres's defense of him in *Athanasius.* The accusation made against him in the *Darlegung* (exposé) was retracted by Frederick William IV. In 1844 he refused the cardinalate offered him by the Pope. Among his writings is *Über den Frieden unter der Kirche und den Staaten* (Münster, 1843).

Drouais (drö.e), **François Hubert.** b. at Paris, 1727; d. there, 1775. French painter, portraitist of royalty; son of Hubert Drouais (1699–1767) and father of Jean Germain Drouais (1763–88). His father was his first instructor; even more important for his future career, however, he was a pupil of François Boucher. His early work in portraiture won him membership in the French Academy in 1758 and brought him to the favorable attention of Louis XV, with the result that he painted portraits of all members of the royal family, of Mme. du Barry and Mme. de Pompadour, and of other personages at the French court, especially its beautiful women. One of his portraits of Mme. de Pompadour is in the Museum at Lyons, and others of his works are in the Louvre at Paris.

Drouais, Hubert. b. at La Roque, Normandy, France, 1699; d. at Paris, 1767. French painter, especially of miniatures; father of François Hubert Drouais (1727–75). He studied in the studios of several fashionable painters and became one himself, being especially successful with his miniatures. He was received into the French Academy in 1730.

Drouais, Jean Germain. b. at Paris, Nov. 25, 1763; d. at Rome, Feb. 13, 1788. French historical painter, a pupil of Jacques Louis David; son of François Hubert Drouais.

Drouet (drö.e), **Jean Baptiste.** b. at Ste.-Menehould, Marne, France, Jan. 8, 1763; d. at Mâcon, France, April 11, 1824. French revolutionist. He caused the arrest of Louis XVI at Varennes (June 21, 1791), and was a member of the Convention in 1792 and of the Council of Five Hundred in 1795.

Drouet, Jean Baptiste, Comte **d'Erlon.** b. at Reims, France, July 29, 1765; d. at Paris, Jan. 25, 1844. Marshal of France. He distinguished himself in the Napoleonic wars, particularly at Jena in 1806 and at Friedland (Pravdinsk) in 1807. He served (1834–45) as governor general of Algeria.

Drouyn de Lhuys (drö.aṅ dę lü.ēs), **Édouard.** b. at Paris, Nov. 19, 1805; d. there, March 1, 1881. French diplomat and politician. He was minister of foreign affairs (Dec. 20, 1848–June 2, 1849; Jan. 10–24, 1851; July 28, 1852–May 3, 1855; October, 1862–Sept. 1, 1866).

Drown (droun), **Thomas Messinger.** b. at Philadelphia, March 19, 1842; d. Nov. 16, 1904. American chemist. He was professor of chemistry (1874–81) at Lafayette College, professor of analytical chemistry (1885 *et seq.*) and later, professor in charge of the chemistry and chemical engineering departments at M.I.T. As director (1887 *et seq.*) of the Massachusetts analytical laboratories, he took a chief part in studying the state water supplies. He was manager (1871–73), secretary (1873–83), and president (1897) of the American Institute of Mining Engineers; president (1895–1904) of Lehigh University.

Droylsden (droilz'dęn). Urban district in NW England, in Lancashire, situated on the Rochdale Canal ab. 5 mi. E of Manchester, ab. 188 mi. NW of London by rail. 26,365 (1951).

Droysen (droi'zęn), **Johann Gustav.** b. at Treptow (Trzebiatów), Pomerania, Prussia, July 6, 1808; d. at Berlin, June 19, 1884. German historian, professor at Berlin from 1859. His works include translations of *Aeschylus* (1832) and *Aristophanes* (1836), *Geschichte Alexanders des Grossen* (1833), *Geschichte des Hellenismus* (1836–43), *Geschichte der preussischen Politik* (1855–85), and others.

Droz (droz), **Antoine Gustave.** b. at Paris, June 9, 1832; d. Oct. 22, 1895. French novelist. His works include *Monsieur, madame, et bébé* (1866), *Entre nous* (1867), *Le Cahier bleu de Mlle. Cibot* (1868), *Une Femme gênante* (1875), *Tristesses et sourires* (1884), and *L'Enfant* (1885).

Droz, François Xavier Joseph. b. at Besançon, France, Oct. 31, 1773; d. at Paris, Nov. 5, 1850. French moralist and historian. He published *De la philosophie morale* (1823) and *Histoire du règne de Louis XVI* (1839–42).

Droz, Henri Louis Jacquet. b. at La Chaux-de-Fonds, Switzerland, Oct. 13, 1752; d. at Naples, Italy, Nov. 18, 1791. Swiss mechanician; son of Pierre Jacquet Droz.

Droz, Pierre Jacquet. b. at La Chaux-de-Fonds, Switzerland, July 28, 1721; d. at Biel, Switzerland, Nov. 28, 1790. Swiss mechanician, especially noted for the construction of a writing automaton.

Dr. Thorne (thôrn). Novel (1858) by Anthony Trollope. It is the third of the series known as the "Chronicles of Barsetshire."

Drude (drö'dę), **Oskar.** [Full name, **Karl Georg Oskar Drude.**] b. at Brunswick, Germany, June 5, 1852; d. at Dresden, Germany, Feb. 1, 1933. German botanist; stepbrother of P. K. L. Drude. He was professor of botany (1879–1921) in the Technische Hochschule at Dresden, and established a system of geographical subdivisions of the earth based upon climate zones and phytogeographical features.

Drude, Paul Karl Ludwig. b. at Brunswick, Germany, July 12, 1863; d. at Berlin, July 5, 1906. German physicist; stepbrother of Oskar Drude. He was educated at the universities of Göttingen, Freiburg, and Berlin; served as professor of physics at the University of Leipzig (1894–1900), the University of Giessen (1900–05), and the University of Berlin; edited (1900 *et seq.*) *Annalen der Physik.* He made investigations in electromagnetic oscillation and the theory of anomalous dispersion. Author of *Physik der Äthers* (1894) and *Lehrbuch der Optik* (1900).

Druentia (drö.en'shą). Latin name of the **Durance.**

Druid (drö'id), **Dr.** Welsh tutor of Lord Abberville, in Cumberland's play *The Fashionable Lover.*

Druid, The. A pseudonym of **Dixon, Henry Hall.**

Druid Circle, The. Play (1947) by John van Druten.

Druids (drö'idz). Ancient Celtic priests, ministers of religion, poets, teachers, and judges of Gaul, Britain, and Ireland. The chief seats of the Druids were in Wales, Brittany, and the regions around what are now the communities of Dreux and Chartres in France, although probably the Druids existed as a class among all the Celtic peoples of Europe and the British Isles. They are believed to have possessed some knowledge of geometry, the physical sciences, and the like. They superintended the affairs of religion and morality and performed the office of judges. They were not a hereditary class; their knowledge was transmitted orally; as a result, all direct knowledge of the Druids died out with them, and our principal sources of information are such writers as Caesar. They are said to have had a common superior, who was elected by a majority of votes from their own members, and who enjoyed his dignity for life. A yearly general meeting supposedly was held in Gaul, perhaps near the present Chartres. The oak and the mistletoe were held by them in the highest veneration; their places of worship were in oak groves; the cutting of the mistletoe, according to Pliny, was performed by a priest clad in white using a golden knife, and was signalized by the sacrifice of two white bulls at the spot. The Continental Druids, who opposed Roman conquest of Gaul, were wiped out as a result of Rome's victory, but they remained longer in the British Isles, succumbing eventually to Christianity's advance. As a result, they appear in the literature that has come down to us as sorcerers and magicians, surrounded by an aura of evil power. They probably performed human sacrifice, and one of their duties was divining the future, but the mystery of their belief and practice has attached to them strange rites at Stonehenge, England, and Carnac, Brittany, which, so far as is now known, are Stone Age relics with no connection to Druidism. The Druids were succeeded by the bards and *fili* (poets); some remnants of Druid powers are seen in the legendary attributes of the poets Merlin and Taliesin; much of the Druid glamour is attached to the Celtic saints. Cathbad, the Druid teacher of Cuchulain, is prominent in the Ulster cycle of Irish legend, in such tales as *The Cattle-Raid of Cooley*.

Druids. Members of a society called the United Ancient Order of Druids, founded at London in 1781 for the mutual benefit of the members, which later had numerous lodges, called groves, in America, Australia, Germany, and elsewhere.

Drum (drum), **Hugh Aloysius.** b. at Fort Brady, Mich., Sept. 19, 1879; d. at New York, Oct. 3, 1951. American infantry officer and business executive. Served in Philippines (1898–1901, 1908–10) and on Mexican border (1914); assistant chief of staff (1917) to General Pershing in France; chief of staff (1918–19) of U.S. First Army in Europe; promoted (1922) to brigadier general; served as assistant chief of staff (1923–26) of U.S. army, in charge of operations and training; appointed inspector general (1930) and deputy chief of staff (1933) of U.S. army; promoted (1931) to major general; commanded (1935–37) Hawaiian department; promoted (1939) to lieutenant general; chief (1940–43) of eastern defense command and First Army; appointed (1944) chairman of New York State Veteran's Commission; president (1944 *et seq.*) of Empire State, Inc.

Drumcairn (drum.kãrn'), Lord. A title of **Hamilton,** Sir **Thomas** (1563–1637).

Drumclog (drum.klog'). Place in Lanarkshire, Scotland, ab. 16 mi. SE of Glasgow. Here, on June 1 (by the old style calendar), 1679, the Scottish Covenanters defeated the Royalists.

Drumheller (drum'hel.er). City in Alberta, Canada, ab. 88 mi. NE of Calgary, in the SE central part of the province: the largest coal-producing city in the province. With the development of the coal resources several industries have sprung up in the city. It is connected by rail with Calgary and other points to the E and W. 2,601 (1951).

Drumlanrig (drum.lan'rig), Viscount of. A title of **Douglas,** Sir **William.**

Drummer, or the Haunted House, The. Play by Addison. It was first played in March, 1716, and not known to be Addison's till Steele published the fact, after the author's death.

Drummond (drum'ond), **Henry.** b. Dec. 5, 1786; d. at Albury, Surrey, England, Feb. 20, 1860. English politician and general writer. He was for many years partner in Drummond's Bank, London, was member of Parliament for Plympton Earle, Devonshire (1810–13) and for West Surrey from 1847 until his death, founded the professorship of political economy at Oxford in 1825, and was one of the founders of the Catholic Apostolic Church, in which he held the rank of apostle, evangelist, and prophet. Among his works are *Condition of Agricultural Classes* (1842) and *History of Noble British Families* (1846).

Drummond, Henry. b. at Stirling, Scotland, 1851; d. at Tunbridge Wells, England, March 11, 1897. Scottish clergyman and author. He was appointed lecturer on natural history and science at the Free Church College, Glasgow, in 1877. He was the author of *Natural Law in the Spiritual World* (1883), *Tropical Africa* (1888), and others.

Drummond, James. [Titles: 4th Earl and 1st titular Duke of **Perth.**] b. 1648; d. at St.-Germain, France, March 11, 1716. Scottish nobleman. He was appointed chancellor of Scotland by Charles II in 1684, and was retained in office on the accession of James II, whose chief agent he became in the Roman Catholic administration of Scotland. He was banished on the deposition of James.

Drummond, James. [Titles: 5th Earl and 2nd titular Duke of **Perth.**] b. 1675; d. at Paris, 1720. Scottish nobleman; son of James Drummond (1648–1716), 4th Earl of Perth. He participated in the Jacobite rising of 1715–16 in Scotland, during which he conducted an unsuccessful expedition against Edinburgh Castle and led the cavalry at the battle of Sheriffmuir. He escaped from Montrose with the Pretender in 1716.

Drummond, James. [Titles, 6th Earl and 3rd titular Duke of **Perth.**] b. in Scotland, May 11, 1713; d. aboard ship en route to France, May 13, 1746. Scottish Jacobite soldier under Prince Charles Stuart during the Jacobite rising (1745); son of James Drummond (1675–1720), 5th Earl of Perth. He assumed the title of duke although his father's attainder had made it void, joined the Young Pretender at Perth (1745) and led the left wing at the battle of Culloden (1746), and died on a French ship during the escape to France.

Drummond, Sir **James Eric.** [Title, Lord **Perth.**] b. Aug. 17, 1876; d. at Rogate, England, Dec. 15, 1951. English diplomat, second secretary general of the League of Nations. He was private secretary to Prime Minister Asquith (1912–15), private secretary to foreign secretaries Sir Edward Grey and Lord Balfour (1915–19), and secretary general of the League of Nations (1919–33). He was British ambassador to Italy in the period 1933–39; in House of Lords after 1941 and deputy leader of the Liberal Party after 1946.

Drummond, John. [Title, 4th Duke of **Perth.**] d. at the siege of Bergen-op-Zoom, Netherlands, 1747. Scottish Jacobite soldier under Prince Charles Stuart; son of James Drummond (1675–1720). As a member of the French army, he was sent with the Royal Scots regiment to join the Young Pretender in Scotland (1745); contributed greatly to victory at Falkirk (1746) and prevented retreat from Culloden (1746) from becoming rout.

Drummond, Lake. Lake in SE Virginia, in the middle of the Dismal Swamp.

Drummond, Thomas. b. at Edinburgh, Oct. 10, 1797; d. at Dublin, April 15, 1840. British engineer, inventor (1825) of the Drummond light (which was actually an early limelight). It was used in connection with a trigonometrical survey of Great Britain then being carried out by the Royal Engineers (of which Drummond was a member). From 1835 to the year of his death Drummond served as undersecretary of state for Ireland.

Drummond of Hawthornden, **William.** b. at Hawthornden, near Edinburgh, Dec. 13, 1585; d. there, Dec. 4, 1649. Scottish poet; son of John Drummond (1553–1610), 1st Laird of Hawthornden. He took the degree of M.A. at the University of Edinburgh in 1605, and studied law (1607–08) at Bourges and Paris. On succeeding his father, John Drummond, as laird of Hawthornden in 1610, he retired to his estate, and devoted himself to literature and mechanical experiments. He published *Tears on the Death of Meliades* (1613), *Poems* (1616), *Notes of Ben Jonson's Conversations, Flowers of Zion,* and *Cypress Grove* (1623).

Drummond, William. [Title, 1st Viscount of **Strathallan.**] b. c1617; d. at end of March, 1688. Scottish soldier. Royalist commander (1651) of a brigade at the battle of Worcester, where he was captured; served (1653) under the Earl of Glencairn in the Highlands; served (1655–65) in Russian service as lieutenant general and governor of Smolensk; appointed (January, 1666) major general of the forces in Scotland with a seat on the council; in collaboration with Dalyell, he was credited with introducing to Scotland a method of torture by the thumbscrew which he had seen used in Russia.

Drummond, Sir **William.** b. in Scotland, c1760; d. at Rome, March 29, 1828. British diplomat and writer. He was the author of *Origines, or Remarks on the Origin of several Empires, States, and Cities* (1824–29).

Drummond, William Henry. b. near Mohill, County Antrim, Ireland, April 13, 1854; d. at Cobalt, Ontario, Canada, April 6, 1907. Canadian physician and poet, known as "the poet of the habitant." He moved to Canada in his youth and was educated there. He began the practice of medicine in the province of Quebec, where he came in close contact with the French-Canadian voyageurs and habitants, about whom most of his poems were written. Later he removed to Montreal, and for some years was professor of medical jurisprudence at Bishop University. His works include *The Habitant, and Other French-Canadian Poems* (1897), *Phil-o-rum's Canoe and Madeleine Vercheres* (1898), *Johnnie Courteau* (1901), *The Voyageur, and Other Poems* (1905), and *The Great Fight* (1908).

Drummond Island. Westernmost island of the Manitoulin group in Lake Huron. It belongs to Chippewa County, in Michigan.

Drummondville (drum'ọnd.vil). Capital of Drummond County, Quebec, Canada, situated on the St. François River, ab. 60 mi. NE of Montreal: large paper mills and related industries. 14,341 (1951).

Drummossie Moor (dru.mos'i). See **Culloden Moor.**

Drumont (drü.môṅ), **Édouard Adolphe.** b. at Paris, May 3, 1844; d. there, Feb. 6, 1917. French politician and writer, noted as a bitter anti-Semite. He aroused public attention with a brochure, *La France juive* (1886), in which he violently attacked Jews and republican political leaders. His newspaper, *La Libre Parole*, founded in 1892, became the chief spokesman for anti-Semitism in France. He was a deputy (1898–1902) for one term.

Drumright (drum'rīt). [Former name, **Fulkerson.**] City in N Oklahoma, in Creek County, in a petroleum-producing area. 5,028 (1950).

Drums. Historical novel by James Boyd, published in 1925.

Drum-Taps. Collection of poems by Walt Whitman, published in 1865 and followed by the volume *Sequel to Drum-Taps* (1865–66). Both works were included in the 1867 edition of *Leaves of Grass.*

Drunken Parliament, The. Nickname of the Scottish Parliament which met in 1661.

Drury (drö'ri), **Robert.** Hero of Defoe's *Madagascar: or, Robert Drury's Journal, during Fifteen Years Captivity on that Island*, published in 1729. Most of the story is clearly fictitious, and the real Robert Drury could not have been the narrator, but Defoe, using every available oral or printed account of Madagascar, produced a book so accurate in many details that it is often cited as an authority on the island.

Drury Lane. Street in London, near the Strand, with which it communicates through Aldwych. It was one of the great arteries of the parish of Saint Clement Danes, an aristocratic part of London in the time of the Stuarts. It takes its name from Drury House, built by Sir William Drury in the time of Henry VIII, and is probably best known for the Drury Lane Theatre.

Drury Lane Theatre. One of the principal theatres of London, situated on Russell Street near Drury Lane. It was opened under Killigrew's patent in 1663, rebuilt by Sir Christopher Wren and reopened in 1674, and reopened in 1794 and 1812.

Drury's Bluff. See **Drewrys Bluff.**

Druses (drö'zẹz). [Also, **Druzes.**] People and religious sect of Syria and Lebanon, living chiefly in the mountain regions of Lebanon and the Anti-Liban and the district of Hauran, including the formerly autonomous region of Jebel ed Druz. The only name they themselves acknowledge is Unitarians (*Muahidin*); the name by which they are commonly known to others comes probably from Ismail Darazi, their first apostle in Syria. Their religion, a monotheistic and messianic form of Mohammedanism, is based on the belief that al-Hakim, sixth of the Fatimid caliphs of Egypt and North Africa, who reigned from 996 to 1021 and declared his own divine nature, was the last appearance to man of the Deity. In his next incarnation, Hakim or the Deity will lead the believers to the establishment of their faith over the world. Darazi, who accepted al-Hakim's divinity, fled from Egypt to Syria, where he converted the hillmen to this belief. The Druse religion is separate and different from the orthodox Mohammedan belief and their customs are separate from those of their neighbors, whether Moslem or Christian. They have been in conflict with these neighbors since the formation of the sect, most notably with the Maronites, a Christian group, whom the Druses several times in the 19th century raided and massacred. These disorders were the pretext for French intervention in Syria in the 19th century, which culminated in the French mandate over the area after World War I. The Druses, though their regional autonomy in the Jebel ed Druz was recognized in 1921, led an uprising against the French in 1925. The Druses supported the Free French in World War II and, in the republic proclaimed in 1944, the Druses gave up their autonomy in the Jebel ed Druz to stand on equality with other Syrian nationals.

Drusilla (drö.sil'ạ). d. 79 A.D. In the New Testament, a daughter of Herod Agrippa I, wife first of Azizus, king of Emesa, and then of Felix, procurator of Judea. She is mentioned in Acts, xxiv. 24.

Drusilla. Daughter of Germanicus and Agrippina, and sister and mistress of Caligula.

Drusilla. Daughter of Caligula by his wife Caesonia.

Drusilla Livia. See **Livia Drusilla.**

Drusius (drö'si.us), **Johannes.** [Dutch, **Jan van den Driesche.**] b. at Oudenarde, in Flanders, June 28, 1550; d. at Franeker, in Friesland, Feb. 12, 1616. Dutch Orientalist and exegete.

Drust (drůst). See under **Tristan.**

Drusus (drö'sus), **Marcus Livius.** d. probably 109 B.C. Roman politician. He was tribune of the plebs conjointly with Gaius Gracchus in 122, his election having been procured by the senate, whose members were alarmed at the democratic innovations of the latter. In collusion with the senate he opposed his veto to the bills brought forward by his colleague, and introduced instead bills of similar import, but making more extravagant concessions, which were passed by the senate. He was consul in 112, and while governor of Macedonia, which he obtained as his province, defeated the Thracian Scordisci and reached the Danube.

Drusus, Marcus Livius. d. at Rome, 91 B.C. Roman politician; son of Marcus Livius Drusus (d. 109 B.C.). He became in 91 tribune of the plebs, whose favor he won by largesses of grain and by the introduction of a bill providing for a new division of the public lands. This bill, together with another which restored to the senate the places on the juries of which it had been deprived by Gaius Gracchus, was passed by the comitiae, but declared null and void by the senate. He was assassinated as he was about to bring forward a proposal to bestow Roman citizenship on the Italians (that is to say, on the people of Italy as a whole and not simply those who lived in the city of Rome). His death gave the signal for the outbreak of the Social War.

Drusus, Nero Claudius. [Called **"Drusus Senior"**; surnamed **Germanicus.**] b. 38 B.C.; d. in Germany, 9 B.C. Roman general; brother of Tiberius. He was the son of Livia Drusilla by Tiberius Claudius Nero, and was born shortly after the marriage of his mother with the emperor Augustus. He was adopted, together with his brother Tiberius, by the emperor, and at an early age married Antonia, the daughter of Mark Antony. He subdued a revolt in Gaul in 13, and, starting in 12 from the left bank of the Rhine, undertook four campaigns in Germany proper, in the course of which he led the Roman armies to the Weser and the Elbe. He died on the way back, in consequence of a fall from his horse.

Drusus Caesar (drö'sus sē'zạr). [Called **"Drusus Junior."**] b. c13 B.C.; d. 23 A.D. Son of Tiberius and Vipsania. He quelled a mutiny of the legions in Pannonia in 14, was consul in 15, was appointed governor of

Illyricum in 16, was consul in 21, and in 22 was invested with the *tribunicia potestas*, whereby he was declared heir apparent to the throne. He was poisoned by Tiberius's favorite Sejanus, who aspired to the succession.

Druzes (drö'zęz). See **Druses.**

Dryander (drü.än'dėr), **Jonas.** b. in Sweden, 1748; d. at London, Oct. 19, 1810. Swedish botanist. He catalogued (1796–1800) the library of Sir Joseph Banks. He was also librarian to the Royal Society.

Dryasdust (drī'ąz.dust), **Rev. Dr.** Prosy parson who is supposed to write the introductory letters to several of Sir Walter Scott's novels. He also writes the conclusion to *Redgauntlet.* The name was used by Carlyle as a synonym for dreary platitude (especially in historical writing).

Drybob (drī'bob). In Thomas Shadwell's comedy *The Humorists,* a fantastic coxcomb and would-be wit.

Dryburgh Abbey (drī'bur.ǫ). Highly picturesque ruin ab. 4 mi. SE of Melrose, Scotland, whose fragments exhibit excellent Norman and Early English architectural details. It contains the tomb of Sir Walter Scott.

Dryden (drī'dęn), **John.** b. at the vicarage of Aldwinkle All Saints, Northamptonshire, England, probably on Aug. 9, 1631; d. at London, May 1, 1700. English poet, critic, and dramatist. He was graduated from Trinity College, Cambridge, in 1654. In 1663 he married Lady Elizabeth Howard, the sister of his friend Sir Robert Howard, and in 1664 he achieved his first independent stage success with *The Rival Ladies.* Originally a Parliamentarian (he mourned Cromwell's death in 1658 with his *Heroic Stanzas*), he went ever to the Royalist side, writing (1660) his *Panegyric on the Coronation* to celebrate the coronation of Charles II. He was poet laureate and historiographer royal from 1670 to 1688. In 1679 he had a quarrel with John Wilmot, 2nd Earl of Rochester, who is believed thereupon to have caused him to be cudgeled in the street by masked bravoes. The unsettled state of public feeling created by allegations of "popish plots" (which induced him to write the series of satires of which *Absalom and Achitophel* was the first) brought down upon him a storm of libels. He was converted to Roman Catholicism in 1685, but his sincerity has been impugned. His critical writings, among the most distinguished in English, were numerous and on various subjects. The most famous of these are *An Essay of Dramatic Poesy* (1668) and the prefaces to the *Virgil* (1697), and the *Fables* (1700). He was the first to recognize fully the greatness of Shakespeare and Chaucer. He wrote many prologues, epilogues, epistles, and dedications, and after his conversion to Roman Catholicism employed his pen in defense of his faith. His chief poems are *Heroic Stanzas* (1659), *Astraea Redux,* celebrating the Restoration (1660), *Annus Mirabilis* (1667), *Absalom and Achitophel,* considered by some the greatest satire in English verse (1681; the second part with Tate, 1682), *Mac Flecknoe, or a Satyr upon the True-Blew-Protestant Poet, T.S.* (1682), an attack on Thomas Shadwell, *Religio Laici,* in defense of Anglicanism (1682), *The Hind and the Panther,* in defense of Roman Catholicism (1687), *The Works of Virgil* (1697), *Alexander's Feast; or the Power of Music* (1697), *Fables Ancient and Modern* (1700); also translations of Juvenal, Ovid, and others. His chief plays include *The Indian Emperor, or, The Conquest of Mexico by the Spaniards* (1665), *Almanzor and Almahide, or the Conquest of Granada* (1670), *Aurengzebe* (1675), and *All for Love: or, the World well Lost* (1678). Other notable plays were *Marriage à la Mode* (1673), *Amboyna* (1673), and *The Spanish Friar* (1681). His complete works were edited by Scott in 18 volumes (1808), and revised (1882–93) by George Saintsbury. See his biography by George Saintsbury in the "English Men of Letters" series (1881).

Dryden, John Fairfield. b. at Temple Mills, Me., Aug. 7, 1839; d. Nov. 24, 1911. American industrial insurance pioneer, cofounder of the Prudential Insurance Company. After studying industrial insurance for wage earners, he formed (1875) at Newark, N.J., the Prudential Friendly Society, the name of which was changed (1878) to The Prudential Insurance Company. He served (1902–07) as U.S. senator from New Jersey, and was the author of *Addresses and Papers on Life Insurance and Other Subjects* (1909).

Dryfesdale (drīfs'dāl), **Jasper.** In Sir Walter Scott's novel *The Abbot,* the revengeful old steward at Lochleven Castle, who endeavors to poison Queen Mary and her attendants.

Drygalski (drē.gäl'skē), **Erich von.** b. at Königsberg, in East Prussia, Feb. 9, 1865—. German explorer. He conducted an expedition to Greenland (1891–93) and was the leader of an expedition to the Antarctic (1901–03). In the latter he reached the vicinity of Kaiser Wilhelm II Land (named by him), where his ship was frozen fast in the ice (Feb. 12, 1902); here he spent a year in scientific observation. He became professor extraordinary of geography at the University of Berlin in 1899.

Dryope (drī'ǫ.pē). In Greek mythology, a shepherdess. She was the playmate of the Hamadryads, and was changed by them into a poplar. By Apollo she was the mother of Amphissus.

Drystan (dris'tän). See under **Tristan.**

Dry Tortugas (drī tôr.tö'gaz). Group of coral keys in the Gulf of Mexico included in Monroe County, Florida. A penal station was established on one of them, at Fort Jefferson, during the Civil War.

Dschagga (jäg'ä). See **Chaga.**

Dschurdschewo (jör'je.vô). See **Giurgiu.**

D.S.O. See **Distinguished Service Order.**

Duab (dö.äb'). See **Doab.**

Duacum (dū.ā'kum). Latin name of **Douai.**

Duala (dö.ä'lä). See also **Douala.**

Duala. [Also: **Diwala, Douala, Dwala.**] Bantu-speaking people of C Africa, living at the mouth of the Cameroon River, in the vicinity of Douala in E (French) Cameroun. In Douala they have mixed with the Ewondo, Bamileke, Basa, and other peoples. Their population is estimated at ab. 23,000 (by I. Dugat, in *Inventaire ethnique du Sud-Cameroun,* 1949).

Duane (dū.ān'), **Alexander.** b. at Malone, N.Y., Sept. 1, 1858; d. June 10, 1926. American ophthalmologist; son of James Chatham Duane (1824–97). He was the author of "Some New Tests for Insufficiencies of the Ocular Muscles," in the New York *Medical Journal* (1889), "Paralysis of the Superior Rectus and its Bearing on the Theory of Muscular Insufficiency," in the *Archives of Ophthalmology* (1884), *A New Classification of Motor Anomalies of the Eye* (1897); contributor to G. E. de Schweinitz and B. A. Randall's *An American Text-Book of Diseases of the Eye, Ear, Nose and Throat* (1899), to W. C. Posey and W. G. Spiller's *Eye and Nervous System* (1906), and to J. E. Week's *A Treatise on Diseases of the Eye* (1910); translator (1892) of Ernst Fuch's *Textbook of Ophthalmology.*

Duane, James. b. at New York, Feb. 6, 1733; d. at Schenectady, N.Y., Feb. 1, 1797. American jurist. He was appointed (1774) to the committee of correspondence, one of the groups whose duty it was to inform and be informed about the activities of patriots in the other colonies. He served (1774–83) as member of the Continental Congress, assisting in the drafting of the Articles of Confederation. During the Revolutionary War he was one of those conservatives who opposed independence for the colonies, but his patriotism, though attacked, was real. He served as first mayor (1784–89) of New York City after the Revolution, and was first federal judge (1789–94) for the district of New York. He served in the Poughkeepsie Convention, where he advocated the ratification of the federal constitution by New York.

Duane, James Chatham. b. at Schenectady, N.Y., June 30, 1824; d. Nov. 8, 1897. American military and civil engineer; grandson of James Duane (1733–97). Graduate (1848) of U.S. Military Academy; in engineer corps, participated (1858) in Utah expedition under Johnston; during Civil War, with McClellan's Army of the Potomac, made notable contribution with his organization of engineer battalion and equipment; McClellan's chief engineer before Antietam and from 1863 to 1865; brigadier general and chief of engineers (1886–88) U.S. Army; member after 1888 of Croton Aqueduct Commission.

Duane, William. b. near Lake Champlain, N.Y., May 17, 1760; d. Nov. 24, 1835. American journalist, author, and politician, noted for his part in the early political controversies of the American Republic. He learned the printer's trade in Ireland, where he was taken in 1765, and went to India in 1787, founding the *Indian World* at Calcutta. His agitation against the East India Company contributed to his deportation and the confiscation of his property. After a stay in England, he settled at Philadelphia, where he joined Benjamin Franklin Bache in issuing the *Aurora*. Upon Bache's death (1798), Duane became editor, converting the *Aurora* into the leading Jeffersonian organ. His powerful and brilliant attacks led to his arrest in 1799, but he was acquitted of the charge of instigating a seditious riot by circulating petitions for the repeal of the Alien Law. Later in the same year he was indicted under the Sedition Law; however, after successive postponements, the charge was finally dismissed when Jefferson became president. His journalistic exposures sometimes brought him physical injury at the hands of his enemies. His outstanding contribution was his exposure of the Ross Election Bill, by which the Federalists hoped to prevent Jefferson's election. He edited the *Aurora* until 1822, and served as an adjutant general in the War of 1812. He became (c1824) prothonotary of the supreme court of Pennsylvania for the eastern district, holding the post until his death. His works include *Military Dictionary* (1810), *An Epitome of Arts and Science* (1811), *Handbook for Riflemen* (1813), *Handbook for Infantry* (1813), and *A Visit to Colombia in the Years 1822 & 1823* (1826).

Duane, William. b. at Philadelphia, Feb. 17, 1872; d. at Devon, Pa., March 7, 1935. American physicist. He was an assistant (1893–95) in physics, Tyndall fellow (1895–97), assistant professor (1913–17), and professor (1917 *et seq.*) of biophysics at Harvard University; professor (1898–1907) of physics at the University of Colorado. After engaging (1907–12) in research at the Curie Radium Laboratory of the University of Paris, he utilized his investigations into the composition of matter and the mechanics of radiation to develop techniques and machinery for the therapeutic use of x-rays and radium, especially in the attempted cure of cancer (for which he was awarded the John Scott medal (1922), the Comstock prize (1922), and in 1923 the first Leonard prize).

Duane, William John. b. at Clonmel, Ireland, May 9, 1780; d. at Philadelphia, Sept. 26, 1865. American lawyer and politician; son of William Duane (1760–1835). Duane was a prominent lawyer and a leading politician at Philadelphia; he also served in the Pennsylvania legislature. He was appointed secretary of the treasury by President Jackson in 1833, but was dismissed in the same year for refusing to remove the government deposits from the Bank of the United States without authority from Congress.

Duarte (dwär′tā). Province in E Dominican Republic. Capital, San Francisco de Macorís; area, 1,090 sq. mi.; pop. 165,433 (1950).

Duarte (dū.är′te). Brave but vainglorious man in John Fletcher and Philip Massinger's *Custom of the Country*. Colley Cibber introduces him in a somewhat modified form in his *Love Makes a Man*, taken from the former play.

Dubail (dü.bȧy′), **Auguste Yvon Edmond.** b. at Belfort, France, April 15, 1851; d. at Paris, Jan. 7, 1934. French general, whose mission (1911) to Russia resulted in the French-Russian staff plans put into effect at the outbreak of World War I. He was briefly chief of the general staff (1911), was (1914–16) a leading officer of the general staff during World War I until appointed (1916) military governor of Paris, and was named (1918) grand chancellor of the Legion of Honor.

Duban (dü.bäṅ), **Jacques Félix.** b. at Paris, Oct. 14, 1797; d. at Bordeaux, France, Dec. 20, 1870. French architect. In 1834 he took over the construction of the École des Beaux-Arts. He restored the chateaux of Blois and Dampierre, and carried forth improvements at Fontainebleau and Chantilly. From 1848 to 1854 he was architect of the Louvre, completing the restoration of several of the galleries. He became inspector general of public buildings.

du Barry (dū bar′i; French, dü bȧ.rē), Comtesse. [Original name, **Marie Jeanne Bécu**; sometimes (but incorrectly), **Marie Jeanne Gomard de Vaubernier.**] b. in Champagne, France, Aug. 19, 1746; guillotined at Paris, Dec. 7, 1793. Mistress of Louis XV after 1769. The illegitimate daughter of a seamstress, she went c1762 to Paris, worked in a milliner's shop, and under the name Mlle. Lange became a prostitute and mistress of Jean, Comte du Barry, a professional gambler. They soon schemed to have her placed at court and, through the king's valet de chambre, had her introduced to Louis. She became the king's mistress (her beauty and wit were remarked upon by the many famous persons who came to know her), was married to du Barry's brother Guillaume, and with this front of respectability was presented at court as the Comtesse du Barry. She exercised great influence over the king, slowly overcame his attachment to his family and advisers, and placed her own friends in power. She, through the triumvirate of the duc d'Aiguillon (reputedly her lover), René Nicolas de Maupeou, and the abbé Joseph Marie Terray, ruled the king and kingdom; the duke Étienne François de Choiseul, the leading French diplomat of the day, was dismissed through her influence; a mansion was built for her near Versailles. When the king died (1774) she was ordered to an abbey by Louis XVI, but instead she took up residence at her mansion with her lover, the count de Cossé-Brissac, after the queen interceded for her. In 1792 she made a trip to England to pawn some jewelry, and in 1793 was arrested as having conspired against the Republic, was tried before the Revolutionary Tribunal, and, still arguing her innocence of any crime, was carried off to the guillotine.

Dubawnt (dö.bônt′). River in N central Canada, in S Northwest Territories, rising NE of Lake Athabaska, and flowing generally NE through numerous large lakes to Baker Lake, at the head of Chesterfield Inlet, Hudson Bay. The lower course is in a barren tundra region. Length, ab. 580 mi.

Dubawnt Lake. Lake in Canada, in the Northwest Territories, on the border between the Mackenzie and the Keewatin districts. It is drained by the Dubawnt River and Chesterfield Inlet into Hudson Bay. Elevation, ab. 500 ft.; area, ab. 1,600 sq. mi.

Dubbhe or **Dubhe** (döb′e). The second-magnitude star α Ursae Majoris, the northern of the "two pointers" in the Dipper which indicate the direction of the polestar.

du Bellay (dü be.lā). See **Bellay.**

Dubhe (döb′e). See **Dubbhe.**

Dubh-linn (du̇v′lin). An Irish name of **Dublin,** Irish Republic.

Dubinsky (du.bin′ski), **David.** b. at Brest, in Byelorussia, Feb. 22, 1892—. As a boy he worked in his father's bakery shop, and as a member of the bakery workers' union was so active in agitation that while only 16 years of age he was banished to Siberia. Escaping, he made his way to the U.S. in 1911, became a cloak cutter, and promptly joined the International Ladies' Garment Workers Union. An able organizer, he rose through the grades of officialdom in this union to its presidency, which he has held since 1932. Leadership of the I.L.G.W.U., with its large membership and well-filled treasury, gave him importance in the American labor movement, so that he became vice-president and a member of the executive council of the American Federation of Labor in 1934; but being an advocate of industrial rather than craft unionism, in 1936 he led the I.L.G.W.U. into the Committee of Industrial Organizations (later the Congress of Industrial Organizations), and in that same year helped launch the American Labor Party in New York State. In 1942, believing that the A.L.P. was too much under Communist influence, to which he has always been vigorously opposed, he became a founder and vice-chairman of the Liberal Party, which like the A.L.P. exists only in New York. In 1945 he led his union back into the A.F.L. and was elected again to that organization's executive council. A supporter of the economic and social program which in the time of President Franklin D. Roosevelt was known as the New Deal, Dubinsky in 1947 was one of the principal founders of Americans for Democratic Action, a nation-wide body dedicated on the one hand to social progress and on the other hand to opposition to Communism. From the first he supported the foreign policies of the Truman administration, including the European Recovery Plan.

Dubious Battle, In. See **In Dubious Battle.**

Dubis (dū′bis). Latin name of the **Doubs River.**

Dublin (dub′lin). City in C Georgia, county seat of Laurens County, ab. 48 mi. SE of Macon: shipping point for hardwood lumber and agricultural products. 10,232 (1950).

Dublin. [Irish, **Dubh-linn,** meaning "Black Pool."] Maritime county in Leinster province, in the Irish Republic. It is bounded on the NW and N by County Meath, on the E by the Irish Sea, on the S by County Wicklow, and on the W by County Kildare. The coastline is generally irregular, Dublin Bay being the principal indentation. The surface of the county is mostly flat, except in the south, where the Wicklow Mountains rise to elevations of 2,000 ft. and more. Little of the land is under cultivation, livestock raising being the principal occupation. Potatoes are the chief crop where agriculture is carried on. The city of Dublin is the administrative center of the county as well as the capital of the Irish Republic. Area, ab. 356 sq. mi.; pop. 691,428 (1951).

Dublin. [Irish: **Bhaile** (or **Baile**) **Átha Cliath,** also **Dubh-linn,** meaning "Black Pool."] City and county borough, market town, seaport, and the commercial and industrial center of the Irish Republic, whose capital it is. Dublin is in Leinster province, in County Dublin, situated on Dublin Bay, at the mouth of the river Liffey, at the confluence with the river Dodder. It is the eastern terminus of the Grand and Royal canals, which connect the port with the river Shannon. It is also the terminus of an extensive road and rail network which converges on the city from all over Ireland, and is the leading seaport of all Ireland. During the 14th century, Dublin was one of the four ports in Ireland from which export of staple goods was permitted by Edward III. Its most important modern exports consist of livestock, sent mostly to England and Wales. Other exports are ales, stout, and porter, foodstuffs, and hides and skins. Dublin has the largest imports of coal in the Irish Republic. The city has a variety of industries, clothing manufacture employing the greatest number of the population, but brewing is the largest single industry. One of the largest breweries in the world is here. Other industries include distilleries, ironworks, shipyards, and mineral water bottling-works. A flourishing silk industry was developed here during the late 18th century by French Huguenot immigrants, and the manufacture of silk poplins has survived. The city contains Dublin Castle, the University of Dublin (Trinity College), the Roman Catholic University College, the Bank of Ireland (formerly the Parliament House), the Custom House, Phoenix Park, and the Four Courts. It was probably the ancient Eblana of Ptolemy. It was seized by the Danes in the 9th century, and was taken (1171) by Richard de Clare, Earl of Pembroke, known as Strongbow. Its castle was commenced in 1205. A massacre of the English residents by the native Irish occurred on Black Monday (Easter Monday) in 1209. The city was occupied by William III in 1689 after the battle of the Boyne. It was the scene of a conspiracy by the United Irishmen in 1798, of Robert Emmet's insurrection in 1803, of the Phoenix Park political assassinations, on May 6, 1882, and of the 1916 uprising known as the Easter Rebellion. 521,322 (1951).

Dublin. [Former name, **Doublin.**] City in C Texas, in Erath County, NW of Austin: trading center for agricultural products and livestock. 2,761 (1950).

Dublin, University of. [Also, **Trinity College.**] Leading educational institution in Ireland, said to have been founded by Queen Elizabeth in 1591. The chief front, toward College Green, is ornamented with Corinthian columns and pilasters and a pediment. The extensive buildings enclose several quadrangles or "squares." The chapel has a Corinthian portico; the decorations of the fine library are also Corinthian. The campanile, which stands alone, is a circular, domed, Corinthian belvedere, surmounted by a lantern, and resting on a rusticated basement pierced by arches. It has schools of law, medicine, divinity, science, economics, music, education, engineering, and arts. The library contains some 490,000 volumes.

Dublin Bay. Inlet of the Irish Sea, in Leinster province, Irish Republic, in County Dublin. The city of Dublin lies at its head. Length, ab. 7 mi.; width, ab. 6 mi.

Dublin Castle. Fortification of the 13th century, in the city of Dublin, Irish Republic. It has been restored and used as an official residence.

Dubliners (dub′lin.ėrz). Collection of sketches and short stories dealing with Dublin life and character, by James Joyce, published in 1914. Among the stories are "Counterparts," "The Dead," and "Ivy-Day in the Committee Room."

Dübner (düb′nėr), **Johann Friedrich.** b. at Hörselgau, near Gotha, Germany, Dec. 20, 1802; d. near Paris, Dec. 13, 1867. German classical philologist and critic. He was professor at the *Gymnasium* (advanced secondary school) at Gotha (1826–31), and in 1832 went to Paris to take part in the editing of Henri Estienne's (known as Stephanus's) *Thesaurus linguae Graecae.*

Dubno (döb′nô). Town in the U.S.S.R., in the Ukrainian Soviet Socialist Republic; an important rail and road junction in a wheat and corn growing area. Pop. ab. 15,000.

Duboc (dö′bok), **Julius.** b. at Hamburg, Germany, Oct. 10, 1829; d. at Dresden, Germany, June 11, 1903. German philosopher and publicist. He was the author of *Die Psychologie der Liebe* (1874), *Das Leben ohne Gott* (1875), *Der Optimismus als Weltanschauung* (1881), and *Die Lust als sozialethisches Entwicklungsprinzip* (1900).

Du Bois (dö′ bois, dö bois′). City in W Pennsylvania, in Clearfield County, ab. 48 mi. NW of Altoona, on Sandy Lick Creek, in a farming and coal-mining region: railroad repair shops; manufactures of metal products. It was settled in 1865. Pop. 11,497 (1950).

Dubois (dü.bwä), **Antoine,** Baron. b. at Gramat, Lot, France, 1756; d. at Paris, in March, 1837. French surgeon, noted as an obstetrician. He accompanied Napoleon in the Egyptian campaign. Dubois delivered Marie Louise in 1811 when she bore Napoleon II. He wrote very little but was famed for his clear explanations in his teaching.

Dubois (dö′bois, dö.bois′), **Augustus Jay.** b. at Newton Falls, Ohio, April 25, 1849; d. Oct. 19, 1915. American engineer. A graduate of the Sheffield Scientific School of Yale University, he became professor of mechanical engineering there in 1877, and professor of civil engineering in 1884, holding that chair until his death. He is credited with important contributions to engineering theory, and his books, *Elements of Graphical Statistics and Their Application to Framed Structures* (1875), *Stresses in Framed Structures* (1883), and *Elementary Principles of Mechanics* (3 vols., 1894–95), have been widely used. In a series of papers contributed to the *Century Magazine* in the years 1889 through 1894, Dubois drew analogies between basic principles of morals and of mechanics. His highly original thesis, supported by his customary logic, was again expounded in *The Yale Review* in 1913.

Dubois (dü.bwä), **Eugène.** [Full name, **Marie Eugène François Thomas Dubois.**] b. 1858; d. 1941. Dutch anatomist and physical anthropologist. He discovered the first skeletal remains of *Pithecanthropus erectus* (which he named) in Java in 1891–92. The genus, sometimes called Java man, is intermediate between man and the anthropoid apes, though possibly not in a direct line of descent.

Dubois, Guillaume. b. at Brives-la-Gaillarde, Corrèze, France, Sept. 6, 1656; d. at Versailles, France, Aug. 10, 1723. French cardinal and statesman. He was councilor of state in 1715 under the regency of Philippe, Duc d'Orléans, during the minority of Louis XV, negotiated the triple alliance between England, France, and Holland in 1717, and was prime minister in 1722.

duBois (dü.bwä′), **Guy Pène.** b. at Brooklyn, N.Y., Jan. 4, 1884—. American painter, writer, and illustrator; cousin of Raoul Henri Pène du Bois. He studied under Chase, DuMond, and Henri, later exhibiting widely in the U.S. and winning many prizes. His work is represented in the Metropolitan Museum and Whitney Museum at New York, the Phillips Memorial Gallery at Washington, the Detroit Institute of Art, the Pennsylvania Academy of Art, the Toledo Museum, and many other large institutions. Among his better-known works are *The Doll and the Monster, Carnival Interlude, Beach Scene, Soldier and Peasant, The Race Track, Yvonne in the Purple Coat, Waiter, People,* and *Along the River.* He also wrote for the New York *American,* was an art critic for the New York *Evening Post* and the *New Yorker,* edited *Arts and Decora-*

tion, and wrote an autobiographical volume, *Artists Say the Silliest Things*.

Dubois (dü.bwä), **Jean Antoine.** b. at St.-Ramèz, Ardèche, France, 1765; d. at Paris, Feb. 7, 1848. French missionary. He published *Description of the Character . . . of the People of India* (London, 1816), and *Pantchatantra, ou les cinq ruses, fables de Wichnou-Sarma* (1826).

Dubois (dü.bwä′, dọ.bois′), **John.** b. at Paris, Aug. 24, 1764; d. at New York, Dec. 20, 1842. French-American bishop of the Roman Catholic Church and missionary in Maryland. He founded Mount St. Mary's College, at Emmettsburg, Md., in 1809. He was consecrated third bishop of New York in 1826.

Dubois (dü.bwä), **Paul.** b. July 18, 1829; d. May 23, 1905. French sculptor and painter.

Dubois, Paul Antoine. b. at Paris, Dec. 7, 1795; d. there, in December, 1871. French obstetrician; son of Antoine Dubois.

Dubois, Paul Charles. b. at La Chaux-de-Fonds, Switzerland, Nov. 28, 1848; d. at Bern, Switzerland, Nov. 4, 1918. Swiss neurologist and pioneer psychotherapist. He was a pupil of B. Naunyn and H. I. Quincke, became Privatdocent of clinical medicine (1876) at Bern and professor of neuropathology in 1902. He worked on electrotherapy and designed a Volta-galvanometer. He dedicated his later work to psychotherapy, which he put upon a definite basis in his important work *Les Psychonévroses et leur traitement moral* (1904), involving explanation to the patient of his condition and coöperation by the patient in the treatment. He was cofounder of the Société Suisse de Neurologie and of the *Schweizer Archiv für Neurologie und Psychiatrie*. Author of *De l'influence de l'esprit sur le corps* (1901), *Die Einbildung als Krankheitsursache* (1907), *L'Éducation de soi-même* (1908), and *Pathogenese der neurasthenischen Zustände* (1909).

duBois (dü.bwä′), **Raoul Henri Pène.** b. Nov. 29, 1912—. American painter and stage designer, most noted for his stage settings and costumes for musical comedies and extravaganzas; cousin of Guy Pène duBois. He designed costumes and scenery for *Too Many Girls, DuBarry Was a Lady, Two for the Show*, Billy Rose's *Aquacade* at the New York World's Fair (1940), and the ballet *Ghost Town* for the Ballet Russe de Monte Carlo.

Dubois (dü.bwä), **Théodore.** [Full name, **Clément François Théodore Dubois.**] b. Aug. 24, 1837; d. at Paris, June 11, 1924. French composer and teacher. He became (1877) organist at the Madeleine, succeeding Camille Saint-Saëns, and was professor (1871 *et seq.*) of harmony at the Paris Conservatory, of which he was also director (1896–1905). His compositions include the operas *La Guzla de l'Emir* (1873) and *Aben Hamet* (1884); among his oratorios are *Le Paradis perdu* (1878), and *Les Sept Paroles de Christ* (1867).

Du Bois (dọ bois′), **William Edward Burghardt.** b. at Great Barrington, Mass., Feb. 23, 1868—. American educator, editor, and author. Of Negro ancestry, he received a B.A. (1890) and Ph.D. (1895) from Harvard. He was professor of economics and history at Atlanta University (1897–1910), editor of *Crisis* (1910–32) and *Phylon Quarterly Review* (1940–44), and professor of sociology (1932 *et seq.*) and department head (1933–44) at Atlanta. He is the author of *The Suppression of the Slave Trade* (1896), *The Philadelphia Negro* (1899), *The Souls of Black Folk* (1903), *John Brown* (1909), *The Negro* (1915), *Darkwater* (1920), *Black Reconstruction* (1935), *Color and Democracy* (1945), *The World and Africa* (1947), and other books; and editor of Atlanta University *Studies of the Negro Problem* (1897–1911) and *Encyclopedia of the Negro* (1933–45).

Du Bois-Reymond (dü bwä′rā.môṅ′), **Emil.** b. at Berlin, Nov. 7, 1818; d. there, Dec. 26, 1896. German physiologist; brother of P. D. G. Du Bois-Reymond. He became professor of physiology at the University of Berlin in 1855, and in 1867 was elected perpetual secretary of the Academy of Sciences at Berlin. He is best known for his researches and discoveries in animal electricity and the functions of the nerves. His works include *Untersuchungen über tierische Elektrizität* (1848–84), *Gesammelte Abhandlungen zur allgemeinen Muskel- und Nervenphysik* (1875–77), and others.

Du Bois-Reymond, Paul David Gustav. b. at Berlin, Dec. 2, 1831; d. at Tübingen, Germany, April 7, 1889. German mathematician and philosopher, known especially for his contributions to the theory of functions; brother of the physiologist Emil Du Bois-Reymond. He was educated at the University of Berlin and taught at the universities of Heidelberg, Tübingen, and Freiburg. His works include *Beiträge zur Interpretation der partiellen Differentialgleichungen mit drei Variabeln* (1864), *Abhandlungen über die Darstellung der Functionen durch trigonometrische Reihen* (1876), *Die allgemeine Functionentheorie* (1882), and *Über die Grundlagen der Erkenntnis in den exacten Wissenschaften* (1890).

du Bos (dü bos), **Charles.** b. at Paris, 1882; d. 1939. French literary critic. His work is largely collected in *Approximations* (7 vols., 1922–37) and his *Journal* (2 vols., 1932). He was especially successful as interpreter of English and American literature.

Dubos (dü.bos), **Jean Baptiste.** b. at Beauvais, France, in December, 1670; d. at Paris, March 23, 1742. French critic, historian, and diplomat. His works include *Réflexions critiques sur la poésie et la peinture* (1719) and *Histoire critique de l'établissement de la monarchie française dans les Gaules* (1734).

Dubos (dü.bos′, dü.bō′), **René Jules.** b. at St.-Brice, Seine-et-Oise, France, Feb. 20, 1901—. American bacteriologist, noted for his researches in internal medicine. He received a B.S. (1921) from the Institut National Agronomique, Paris, and a Ph.D. (1927) from Rutgers. He was naturalized (1938) as a U.S. citizen. He has been associated (1927 *et seq.*) with Rockefeller Institute for Medical Research, of which he is a member (1941 *et seq.*). He was professor of comparative pathology and tropical medicine (1942–44) at Harvard Medical School, and discovered a method of production of a substance from certain soil bacteria that is useful in treating bacterial infections. He is the author of *The Bacterial Cell* (1945).

Dubosc (dü.bosk′). In *The Lyons Mail* (formerly Stirling's *The Courier of Lyons*), a brutal highwayman who murders the courier and robs the mail. His extraordinary likeness to the mild and noble-minded Lesurques causes the latter to be arrested for the crime. Henry Irving was successful in the dual part, playing both characters.

Dubossary (dö.bo.sä′ri). [Also: **Dubosari, Dubossari.**] Town in the U.S.S.R., in the Ukrainian Soviet Socialist Republic, ab. 120 mi. NW of Odessa, situated on the Dniester River: long known for its wine. Pop. ab. 15,000.

Dubourg (dü.bör), **Antony.** A pseudonym of **Lacroix, Paul.**

Dubovka (dö.bôf′kạ). Town in the U.S.S.R., in the Stalingrad *oblast* (region) of the Russian Soviet Federated Socialist Republic, situated on the Volga River, ab. 35 mi. N of Stalingrad. Wood and paper industries are important. Pop. ab. 10,000.

Dubrae (dū′brē) or **Dubris** (dū′bris). Latin names of **Dover,** England.

Dubray (dü.brā), **Vital Gabriel.** b. at Paris, Feb. 27, 1818; d. there, Oct. 4, 1892. French sculptor, a pupil of Ramey. His best-known works are 16 reliefs in bronze for the memorial to Joan of Arc at Orléans, and portraits of Napoleon III, Josephine, and others.

Dubrovnik (dö′brôv.nik). [French, **Raguse;** Italian, **Ragusa.**] Seaport city in SW Yugoslavia, in the southernmost strip of the federative unit of Croatia, in the former *banovina* (province) of Zetska and the former Austrian crownland of Dalmatia, situated on the Adriatic Sea halfway between the Peljesac peninsula and the Gulf of Kotor, ab. 38 mi. NW of the city of Kotor. Famous for its beautiful location and sunny climate, Dubrovnik has a harbor which is deep enough for large vessels. It has railroad connection with the interior of the country. The city exports mineral products, olive oil, and agricultural commodities. Massive walls of medieval fortifications, imposing towers, a cathedral, mint, and palace of the rectors were all built under Venetian influence. The city was settled in the 7th century by Slavic fugitives from Epidaurum who fled before the Avars. It was a bishopric from the 11th century on, and was long under Venetian sovereignty, but was intermittently occupied by Byzantines, Normans, and Serbs; later it was under Hungarian and Turkish rule. In the 15th century it was a flourishing maritime state allied to Venice, then a republic under Turkish sovereignty. It was occupied by the French in 1806, incorporated into Austria in 1814, and into Yugoslavia in 1918. Because of its relative independence, Dubrovnik preserved the culture and literature of the Yugoslavs during the centuries of Turkish overlordship and became the seat of a literary renaissance movement in the 19th century. The city was occupied by the Italians during World War II. 16,060 (1948).

Dubs (dups), **Jakob.** b. at Affoltern, near Zurich, Switzerland, July 26, 1822; d. at Lausanne, Switzerland, Jan. 13, 1879. Swiss statesman and jurist, president of the Swiss Confederation in 1864.

Dubsky (dup'skē), **Marie,** Countess. See **Ebner-Eschenbach, Marie,** Baroness **von.**

Dubufe (dü.büf), **Claude Marie.** b. at Paris, c1790; d. there, April 21, 1864. French painter.

Dubufe, Édouard. b. at Paris, March 30, 1820; d. at Versailles, Aug. 11, 1883. French historical and portrait painter; son of Claude Marie Dubufe. He was a pupil of his father and of Delaroche.

Dubufe, Édouard Marie Guillaume. b. at Paris, May 16, 1853; d. May 27, 1909. French painter; son of Édouard Dubufe.

Dubuisson (dü.bwē.sôn), **Paul Ulrich.** b. at Laval, France, 1746; guillotined at Paris, March 23, 1794. French dramatist. He was a revolutionist, a follower of Hébert, whose fate he shared.

Dubuque (du.būk'). City in E Iowa, county seat of Dubuque County, on the Mississippi River: trading center for an agricultural area. Manufactures include lumber and metal products, tractors, and chemicals. Shipbuilding is also important. It is the seat of Wartburg Theological Seminary, the University of Dubuque, Loras College, Clarke College, and Saint Raphael's Cathedral. It was settled in the 1830's as a lead-mining center, and named for Julien Dubuque, who is buried nearby. 49,671 (1950).

Dubuque (du.būk'; French, dü.bük), **Julien.** b. at St. Pierre les Brecquets, Quebec, Jan. 10, 1762; d. March 24, 1810. First white settler of Iowa. He traveled on the western frontier, settling (1785) at Prairie du Chien, Wis. After securing (1788) from the Fox Indians the sole rights to lead mines on the Iowa side of the Mississippi River, he developed a large Indian trade north from St. Louis. Dubuque, Iowa, was named for him.

Duc (dük), **Joseph Louis.** b. at Paris, Oct. 25, 1802; d. Jan. 22, 1879. French architect. His chief work is the Palace of Justice at Paris.

Duca Minimo (dö'kä mē'nē.mō). Pseudonym of **D'Annunzio, Gabriele.**

Du Camp (dü kän), **Maxime.** b. at Paris, Feb. 8, 1822; d. there, Feb. 9, 1894. French author, journalist, traveler, and artist. He was one of the founders of the *Revue de Paris* (1851; suppressed in 1858), and contributed to the *Revue des Deux Mondes.* Among his works are *Souvenirs et paysages d'Orient* (1848), *Le Nil* (1854), and *Paris: ses organes, ses fonctions, sa vie* (1869–75).

Du Cange (dü känzh) or **Ducange,** Sieur. [Title of **Charles du Fresne** or **Dufresne.**] b. at Amiens, France, Dec. 18, 1610; d. at Paris, Oct. 23, 1688. French philologist and historian. He was the author of *Histoire de l'empire de Constantinople sous les empereurs français* (1657), *Glossarium ad scriptores mediae et infimae latinitatis* (1678), *Historia Byzantina* (1680), and *Glossarium ad scriptores mediae et infimae graecitatis* (1688).

Ducange, Victor Henri Joseph Brahain. b. at The Hague, Netherlands, Nov. 24, 1783; d. at Paris, Oct. 15, 1833. French novelist and dramatist. His works include *Agathe* (1819), *Valentine* (1821; an attack on the Royalists which brought a six months' imprisonment), *Léonide* (1823), and *Marc Loricot* (1832). He was several times imprisoned.

Ducarel (dü.kà.rel'), **André Coltée.** b. in Normandy, France, c1713; d. at London, May 29, 1785. English antiquary. His chief work is *Anglo-Norman Antiquities* (1754–67).

Ducas (dū'kas), **Constantine X.** See **Constantine X.**

Ducas, Joannes (or **John**) **III.** See **John III** (of the *Byzantine Empire*).

Ducas, Michael. fl. in the second half of the 15th century. Byzantine historian. He wrote a history of the Byzantine Empire for the period between 1341 and 1462 (first printed at Paris in 1649).

Ducas, Michael VII. See **Michael VII Ducas.**

Ducasse (dü.kàs), **Jean Baptiste.** b. at Bern, Switzerland, c1640; d. in France, in July, 1715. French naval commander. In 1691 he was made governor of the French colony in Santo Domingo. He attacked and laid waste the English settlements in Jamaica in 1694. His own colony was ravaged by the English in 1695, and in 1697 he commanded the land forces in the expedition which sailed from Santo Domingo and took Cartagena (in Colombia). In August, 1702, he fought against the English fleet of Benbow for four days, Benbow finally retiring. He served in Spain during the War of the Spanish Succession, and commanded the naval forces in the attack on Barcelona in 1714.

Ducasse, Jean Jules Amable Roger. [Also, **Jean Jules Amable Roger-Ducasse.**] b. at Bordeaux, France, April 18, 1873—. French composer. He was a pupil of Fauré at the Paris Conservatory, and received the second Prix de Rome in 1902. He has written a *Suite Française* for orchestra, a string quartet, a set of variations for harp and orchestra, a pastoral for organ, and a number of songs and piano pieces.

Du Casse, Pierre Emmanuel Albert, Baron. b. at Bourges, France, 1813; d. at Paris, March 15, 1893. French soldier and military writer. He was placed on the general staff in 1854, and for a time was adjutant to Prince Jérôme Napoléon. He published numerous works on military affairs and on French military history.

Ducato (dö.kä'tō), **Cape.** See **Doukato, Cape.**

Duccio di Buoninsegna (döt'chō dē bwô.nēn.sā'nyä). Sienese painter. He is first heard of in 1282, and was then a master at Siena. His famous altarpiece in the cathedral of Siena was begun in 1308, and on its completion was conveyed, like the Rucellai Madonna of Cimabue, from the workshop to the church in solemn procession to the sound of bell and drum.

Duce (dö'chā), **Il.** See **Mussolini, Benito.**

Du Chaillu (dü chà.yü), **Paul Belloni.** b. probably at Paris (although some sources claim New Orleans), July 31, 1835; d. at St. Petersburg, April 30, 1903. African explorer. The son of a French trader in the territory of Gabon, W central Africa, he made (1851) some exploratory tours in the vicinity of his father's trading establishment and became acquainted with the customs of the Mpongwe. In 1855 he came to America, which he made his home. Under the auspices of the Academy of Natural Sciences of Philadelphia, he undertook a four-year botanical and zoölogical exploration of the Ogowe River basin in what is now French Equatorial Africa. His accounts of the gorillas and Obongo dwarfs were contradicted by Gray and Barth, but later explorations confirmed them. In 1861 he published his *Explorations and Adventures in Equatorial Africa.* In 1863 he started on a second exploration; he visited the Ngunye Falls and Ashango Land, and returned in 1865. His principal works are *A Journey to Ashango Land* (1867), *My Apingi Kingdom* (1870), *The Country of the Dwarfs* (1872), and *The Land of the Midnight Sun* (1881). This last book was the result of a several years' stay in Sweden and Lapland.

Duchamp (dü.shän), **Gaston.** See **Villon, Jacques.**

Duchamp, Marcel. b. at Blainville, France, July 28, 1887—. French cubist, dadaist, and surrealist painter whose work *Nude Descending a Staircase* (1912) caused a sensation at the New York Armory Show of 1913; brother of Raymond Duchamp-Villon and Jacques Villon. He was one of the organizers of several groups of modern artists at both Paris and New York, including the Société Anonyme and the Society of Independent Artists. From 1916 to 1920, he was involved in the dada movement; in 1920 he gave up painting for chess, but later was associated with the surrealists. A list of his important works includes *Nude Descending a Staircase, The Bride Stripped Bare by Her Bachelors, Monte Carlo Share, Young Man in a Train, The King and Queen Surrounded by Quick Nudes,* and *The Candy Crusher.*

Duchamp-Villon (dü.shän.vē.yôn), **Raymond.** b. at Damville, France, Nov. 5, 1876; d. in France, Oct. 7, 1918. French cubist painter and sculptor; brother of Marcel Duchamp and Jacques Villon. He was first strongly influenced by Auguste Rodin. In 1912, he produced his first piece of cubist sculpture, *The Lovers,* in which the separation of the planes, which Jacques Lipschitz further developed in his work, is clearly seen. He died in 1918 as a result of gassing during World War I. His best works are usually considered to be *Song, Torso of a Man, Baudelaire, The Lovers, The Horse,* and *Woman Seated.*

du Châtelet (dü shä.tle), **Gabrielle Émilie le Tonnelier de Breteuil,** Marquise. b. at Paris, Dec. 17, 1706; d. at Lunéville, France, Aug. 10, 1749. French author and scholar; mistress of Voltaire.

Duchcov (döн'tsôf). [German, **Dux.**] Town in Czechoslovakia, in N Bohemia, situated at the foothills of the Krusnehory Mountains (Erzgebirge), between Teplice-Šanov and Most. It has lignite mines, glassworks, and other industries. There is a municipal museum and the former Waldstein Chateau, which contains Wallenstein souvenirs. The population, formerly predominantly German, is now entirely Czech but has declined from 13,040 (1930) to 8,229 (1947).

Duché (dö.shā'), **Jacob.** b. at Philadelphia, Jan. 31, 1738; d. Jan. 3, 1798. American clergyman of the Anglican Church. He was assistant rector (1759–75) of Christ Church and Saint Peter's at Philadelphia, of which he was later rector (1775–77). At first an enthusiastic supporter of the Revolutionary cause, he was made chaplain of the Continental Congress. However, he turned Loyalist (1776) and was forced to sail (1777) for England. He returned to America in 1792. He was the author of numerous published sermons, among them two patriotic sermons, *The Duty of Standing Fast in Our Spiritual and Temporal Liberties* (1775) and *The American Vine* (1777), and the letters of "Caspipina," originally in the *Pennsylvania Packet,* published (1774) as *Observations on a Variety of Subjects, Literary, Moral and Religious,* and *Discourses on Various Subjects* (2 vols., 1779).

Duchemin (dü.shmaṅ), **René.** b. 1875—. French banker and industrialist, chairman of the French employers' association before World War II. He was at various times regent of the Bank of France, a president of the Chemical Industries Group, and president of the Etablissements Kühlmann chemical concern. He held numerous directorships in railway, mining, and industrial concerns.

Duchenne (dü.shen), **Guillaume Benjamin Amand.** b. at Boulogne, France, Sept. 17, 1806; d. at Paris, Sept. 17, 1875. French physician, a pioneer in electro-therapy. In 1833 he began experimenting with the therapeutic use of electricity, in which thereafter he specialized. He is considered the pioneer in this field, and in the description and treatment by it of locomotor ataxia and other muscular diseases and nervous disorders.

Duchesne (dü.shen), **André.** b. at Île-Bouchard, in Touraine, France, 1584; d. May 30, 1640. French historian. He published numerous works, among them *Historiae Normannorum scriptores antiqui* (1619) and *Historiae Francorum scriptores* (1636–49).

Duchesne, Jean Baptiste Joseph. b. at Gisors, Eure, France, Dec. 8, 1770; d. there, March 25, 1856. French enamel and miniature painter.

Duchesne, Le Père. See **Hébert, Jacques René.**

Duchesne, Louis Marie Olivier. b. at St.-Servan, Brittany, France, Sept. 13, 1843; d. April 21, 1922. French Roman Catholic priest, historian, and educator. The history of the Christian church was his especial interest, and in connection with his investigations of that history in the early centuries he pursued his researches (1874–76) at Mount Athos and in Asia Minor. Following his publication in 1877 of his dissertations, *De Macario magnete* and *Étude sur le Liber pontificalis,* he was appointed to the professorship of church history at the Catholic Institute in Paris, a chair which he held for eight years, applying modern scientific critical methods to an extent previously unknown in that field, to the alarm of some of the more conservative theologians. In 1885 he became a lecturer at the École Pratique des Hautes Études, and subsequently for many years directed the French School of Archaeology at Rome, during this time also serving as president of a papal commission on the revision of the breviary. The *Bulletin Critique,* devoted to disseminating knowledge of historical criticism among French churchmen, was founded by Duchesne in 1880. In 1886–92 appeared his edition of the *Liber pontificalis.*

Duchesne, Rose Philippine. b. at Grenoble, France, Aug. 29, 1769; d. at St. Charles, Mo., Oct. 18, 1852. Roman Catholic religious, founder of the first house (in the U.S.) of the Society of the Sacred Heart. Educated by the Visitation nuns, she attempted reëstablishment, after the French Revolution, of a community near Grenoble, which she had entered. Received by Mother Barat into the Society of the Sacred Heart (1804), she came to America in 1818, settling her community first at New Orleans and then at St. Charles, Mo., whence other communities of the Society spread through the country. She was beatified in 1940.

Duchess, The. Pseudonym of **Hungerford, Margaret Wolfe.**

Duchess of Devonshire (dev'ọn.shir). Portrait by Sir Joshua Reynolds. The figure is shown in full length, wearing a plumed turban, and about to descend a flight of steps.

Duchess of Devonshire. Portrait by Thomas Gainsborough, stolen from Agnew's galleries, London, in 1876, and recovered in 1901. The duchess is represented standing in a garden walk, and wearing a broad-brimmed plumed hat.

Duchess of Malfi (mal'fi), **The.** Tragedy by John Webster, played c1613, and printed in 1623. There is a dramatic version of the story among Lope de Vega's works, and it forms the subject of one of Bandello's *Novelle;* Webster's direct source was the 23rd tale in William Painter's *Palace of Pleasure* (1566). It is Webster's most popular play, the one oftenest read, and the most original. The crime for which the duchess is reduced by her family to insanity and death is her secret marriage with her steward, whom she loved.

Duchess of Wrexe (reks), **The.** Novel by Hugh Walpole, published in 1914. The first volume of a trilogy, it is noted as an example of Walpole's skill in characterization; it was followed by *The Green Mirror* (1917) and *The Captives* (1920).

Duchies of Parma and Piacenza (pär'mạ; pyä.chen'tsä). See **Parma, Duchy of.**

Ducis (dü.sē), **Jean François.** b. at Versailles, France, Aug. 22, 1733; d. there, March 31, 1816. French dramatic poet, best known as an adapter of *Hamlet* and others of Shakespeare's plays to the French stage. One of his original works is *Abufar* (1795). He was elected to the French Academy in 1778, taking Voltaire's seat.

Duck (duk). River in C Tennessee, rising SE of Murfreesboro, and flowing generally W to join the Tennessee River ab. 65 mi. W of Nashville. The river is noted for fishing, and flows through a fertile agricultural valley. Length, ab. 220 mi.

Duckinfield (duk'in.fēld). See **Dukinfield.**

Duckworth (duk'wėrth), Sir **John Thomas.** b. at Leatherhead, Surrey, England, Feb. 28, 1748; d. at Devonport, England, Aug. 31, 1817. English admiral. He commanded a vessel under Lord Howe in the action with the French off Ushant, on June 1, 1794. He directed the operations which led to the surrender of the French under Rochambeau in Santo Domingo. He was promoted to vice admiral in 1804. Duckworth defeated a French squadron off Santo Domingo, on Feb. 6, 1806. In 1810 he was promoted admiral; was created a baronet in 1813; and was commander in chief at Newfoundland from 1810 to 1813.

Duclaux (dü.klō), **Mary.** See **Darmesteter, Mary.**

Duclaux, Pierre Émile. b. at Aurillac, France, June 24, 1840; d. 1904. French biochemist; second husband (married 1901) of Mary Darmesteter. He served as professor at Clermont-Ferrand, at Lyons, and at the Sorbonne, and was a member (1888 *et seq.*) of the French Academy of Sciences, and director (1895 *et seq.*) of the Pasteur Institute. Among his works are *Sur l'iodure d'amidon* (1872), *Etudes sur la nouvelle maladie de la vigne dans le sud-est de la France* (1873–75), and *Ferments et maladies* (1882).

Duclos (dü.klō), **Charles Pinot.** b. at Dinan, in Brittany, France, Feb. 12, 1704; d. at Paris, March 26, 1772. French historian and man of letters. His earliest works were romances. He also published *Considérations sur les mœurs de ce siècle* (1749) and *Mémoires secrets des règnes de Louis XIV et de Louis XV* (1791). As secretary of the French Academy he supervised the publication of the 4th edition (1762) of its celebrated dictionary.

Duclos, Jacques. b. at Louey, Hautes-Pyrénées, France, Oct. 2, 1896—. French political leader, a member of the central committee of the French Communist party since 1926. Named to the party's political bureau in 1931, he became its secretary in the same year, and was named (1936) to the Communist International and to the Communist Information Bureau in 1947. He was a deputy (1926–32, 1936–40) under the Third Republic and served under the Fourth Republic in the Constituent Assemblies (1945–46) and the National Assembly (1946). He resigned (January, 1948) the vice-presidency of the National Assembly.

Ducommun (dü.ko.mėn), **Élie.** b. 1833; d. 1906. Swiss journalist, pacifist, and Nobel prize winner. Long the editor of *Revue de Genève* and a contributor to many leading periodicals, in 1891 he organized the International Bureau of Peace, with its headquarters at Bern, and devoted his energies and talents to the pacifist cause. In 1902 he was awarded, jointly with Charles Albert Gobat, the Nobel prize for peace.

Ducornet (dü.kôr.ne), **Louis César Joseph.** b. at Lille, France, Jan. 10, 1806; d. at Paris, April 27, 1856. French historical and portrait painter, a pupil of Gérard. He was born without arms, and used his feet to paint.

Du Croisy (dü krwà.zē). Lover in Molière's *Les Précieuses Ridicules*. He and La Grange, his friend, send their valets, disguised as le Marquis de Mascarille and le Vicomte de Jodelet, to make love to *les précieuses*, Madelon and Cathos, and teach them that fine phrases do not make a gentleman.

Ducrot (dü.krō), **Auguste Alexandre.** b. at Nevers, France, Feb. 24, 1817; d. at Versailles, France, Aug. 16, 1882. French general. He received command of the 1st division of the 1st army corps under MacMahon at the beginning of the Franco-Prussian War (1870), served at the battle of Wörth, and was taken prisoner at Sedan. He went to Pont-à-Mousson on parole, but fled to Paris where he took command of the second army. He made unsuccessful sorties (Sept. 19, Oct. 21, and Nov. 30–Dec. 4, 1870, Jan. 19, 1871) against the German lines around Paris. He was given command of the 8th army corps by Thiers in September, 1872, and held the post until 1878.

Ducrotay de Blainville (dü.kro.tā dę blaṅ.vēl), **Henri Marie.** b. at Arques, near Dieppe, France, Sept. 12, 1778; d. near Paris, May 1, 1850. French naturalist. He published *Faune française* (1821–30), *De l'organisation des animaux* (1822), and *Ostéographie* (1839–49).

Duddell (du.del'), **William Du Bois.** b. 1872; d. Nov. 4, 1917. English electrical engineer and inventor. After years of apprenticeship and research, he opened an office in London as a consulting engineer. He made important discoveries in connection with electric arcs, invented the Duddell galvanometer or oscillograph, and was a pioneer contributor to the development of radio-telegraphy. He was a Fellow of the Royal Society.

Duddon (dud'ǫn). Small river in NW England, on the Cumberland-Lancashire border, flowing into the Irish Sea ab. 20 mi. NW of Lancaster. It is celebrated in the poetry of Wordsworth. Length, ab. 20 mi.

du Deffand (dü de.fäṅ), Marquise. See **Deffand, Marquise du.**

Dudelange (düd.läṅzh). [German, **Düdelingen** (dü'dę-ling.ęn).] Town in Luxembourg, situated in the "Red Earth" district, near the French border, ab. 10 mi. S of the city of Luxembourg. It is surrounded by the iron-ore mines of the "Minette," which are part of the Lorraine-Luxembourg field, and has metallurgical and other industries and blast furnaces. 12,680 (1945).

Duden (dö'dęn), **Konrad.** b. at Wesel, Germany, Jan. 3, 1829; d. at Sonnenberg, Germany, Jan. 8, 1911. German lexicographer. In accordance with a resolution adopted at a joint meeting of the major German, Austrian, and Swiss printers' associations at Konstanz in 1902, he compiled *Rechtschreibung der Buchdruckereien deutscher Sprache* (1903), designed to unify German orthography. It was followed by *Orthographisches Wörterbuch der deutschen Sprache,* whose eighth edition (1905) was combined with the second edition of the "Buchdrucker-Duden" (1907) as *Rechtschreibung der deutschen Sprache und der Fremdwörter* (1915; known as Duden's ninth edition). The tenth edition (1929) adopted the title *Der grosse Duden.* In the course of time Duden's orthography was adopted as standard (partly by legislation, partly through usage) in all German-speaking states and countries. Duden's name became a household word and has been used for other reference works (a grammar, also a picture dictionary with parallel French, English, and Spanish volumes), all published by the Bibliographisches Institut at Leipzig.

Dudeney (död'ni), Mrs. **Henry.** [Maiden name, **Alice Whiffin.**] b. Oct. 21, 1866; d. 1945. English popular novelist. Some of her many novels are *A Man with a Maid* (1897), *The Maternity of Harriott Wicken* and *Folly Corner* (both 1899), *Spindle and Plough* (1903), *The Story of Susan* (1903), *The Wise Woods* (1905), *The Orchard Thief* (1907), *Married When Suited* (1911), *Set to Partners* (1913), *The Secret Son* (1915), *Traveller's Samples* (1916), and *The Head of the Family* (1917).

Duderstadt (dö'dėr.shtät). Town in NW Germany, in the *Land* (state) of Lower Saxony, British Zone, formerly in the province of Hanover, Prussia, situated on the Hahle River, ab. 14 mi. E of Göttingen. Manufactures include electrical and precision instruments, machine tools, paper, toys, artificial wool, and cigars. It is the center of a fertile agricultural district. The Gothic Church of Saint Cyriacus, built in the 14th century, the monumental *Rathaus* (town hall), dating from the 15th and 16th centuries, remains of old fortifications, and numerous gabled houses contribute to preserve a medieval architectural character. The population is predominantly Roman Catholic. The town belonged to the ecclesiastical territories of Quedlinburg and Mainz until 1802, became part of Westphalia in 1808, of Hanover in 1816, and of Prussia in 1866. The town suffered no damage during World War II. 11,511 (1950).

Dudevant (düd.väṅ), Baroness **Amadine Aurore Lucie Dupin.** See **Sand, George.**

Dudevant, Maurice. See **Sand, Maurice.**

Dudley (dud'li). County borough, market town, and manufacturing center in W England, in Worcestershire, ab. 8 mi. NW of Birmingham, ab. 120 mi. NW of London by rail. It has manufactures of hardware. Dudley was formerly a mining center for a high grade of coal, but the reserves have been exhausted. The ruins of Dudley Castle are nearby. 62,536 (1951).

Dudley. Town in S Massachusetts, in Worcester County, near the border of Connecticut. 5,261 (1950).

Dudley, Ambrose. [Title, Earl of **Warwick.**] b. in England, c1528; d. at Bloomsbury, London, Feb. 20, 1590. English soldier; son of John Dudley (c1502–53). He was convicted of treason for support (1553) of Lady Jane Grey (his sister-in-law), but was pardoned (1554). Under Mary Tudor he led English troops in support of the Spaniards at the siege of St.-Quentin (1557). He was sent by Elizabeth to help the Protestants at Le Havre (1562), and forced to expel the French there because of a plot on his life (1563). When he was besieged by the French he was ordered by Elizabeth to capitulate. He was a privy councilor (1573), and participated in the trial of Mary, Queen of Scots (1586).

Dudley, Benjamin Winslow. b. in Spottsylvania County, Va., April 12, 1785; d. at Lexington, Ky., Jan. 20, 1870. American surgeon, especially noted as a lithotomist.

Dudley, Charles Benjamin. b. at Oxford, N.Y., July 14, 1842; d. Dec. 21, 1909. American chemist, employed (1875–1909) by the Pennsylvania Railroad Company. His researches were a contributory factor in persuading the officials of that railroad to buy materials by specifications, thus materially increasing both safety and efficiency of operation.

Dudley, Charles Edward. b. at Johnson Hall, Staffordshire, England, May 23, 1780; d. at Albany, N.Y., Jan. 23, 1841. American politician, U.S. senator from New York from 1829 to 1833. Dudley Observatory at Albany was founded by his widow.

Dudley, Edmund. b. c1462; executed at London, Aug. 18, 1510. English politician. He was educated at Oxford and at Gray's Inn, is said to have been made a privy councilor at 23, and was chosen speaker of the House of Commons in 1504. He was employed as a fiscal agent by Henry VII, and incurred popular odium by the rigor with which he enforced the extortionate claims of the crown. On the death of Henry VII in 1509, he was beheaded on the charge of treason, in company with Sir Richard Empson, another of Henry VII's fiscal agents.

Dudley, Lord **Guildford.** Executed at London, Feb. 12, 1554. English nobleman; son of John Dudley, Duke of Northumberland, and brother of Robert Dudley, Earl of Leicester. He married Lady Jane Grey on May 21, 1553. He was implicated in his father's ill-starred attempt to place Lady Jane on the throne on the death of Edward VI (July 6, 1553), and was executed on the charge of treason.

Dudley, Irving Bedell. b. Nov. 30, 1861; d. Nov. 27, 1911. American diplomat. He was ambassador to Brazil (1906–11) and minister to Peru (1897–1906).

Dudley, John. [Titles: Duke of **Northumberland,** Earl of **Warwick,** Viscount **Lisle.**] b. c1502; beheaded Aug. 22, 1553. English politician and soldier; son of Edmund Dudley, and father of Robert Dudley, 1st Earl of Leicester. He was made Viscount Lisle, warden of the Scottish marches, and great admiral by Henry VIII in 1542, and was created Earl of Warwick and high chamberlain of England on the accession of Edward VI in 1547. He was regent jointly with Edward Seymour, Duke of Somerset, but permitted Somerset, who had great influence with the new king, to be named protector without opposing him. He was instrumental in defeating the Scots at Pinkie (1547) but worked against Somerset until in 1549 he overthrew Somerset, and assumed the chief control of the government. His policies were much less popular than Somerset's and, when in 1551 a movement to bring Somerset back was begun in Parliament, he had Somerset arrested, tried, and executed (1552). He was created Duke of Northumberland in 1551. With the object in view of transferring the crown from the Tudors to his own family, he persuaded Edward VI to grant letters patent excluding Edward's sisters, Mary and Elizabeth, from the succession and appointing Edward's cousin, Lady Jane Grey, heir presumptive to the crown, whereupon he married (1553) Lady Jane to his son, Guildford Dudley. At the death (1553) of Edward, he found himself unable to prevent the accession of Mary, and was executed for treason.

Dudley, Joseph. b. at Roxbury, Mass., Sept. 23, 1647; d. there, April 2, 1720. American politician. He took part in the battle with the Narragansetts (King Philip's War) in 1675. He was one of the commissioners for the united colonies of New England (1677–81), and was appointed president of New England in 1686 until Sir Edmund Andros's arrival. He was appointed chief justice of the colonial supreme court in 1687, was chief justice of New York (1690–93), and governor of Massachusetts (1702–15).

Dudley, Paul. b. Sept. 3, 1675; d. at Roxbury, Mass., Jan. 25, 1751. American jurist; son of Joseph Dudley. He graduated at Harvard in 1690, and studied law at the Temple in London. He was made chief justice of Massachusetts in 1745. He is known chiefly as the founder of the Dudleian Lecture on religion at Harvard College, for which he bequeathed 100 pounds. He published several papers on New England natural history in the London Royal Society's *Transactions.*

Dudley, Plimmon Henry. b. at Freedom, Ohio, May 21, 1843; d. Feb. 25, 1924. American civil engineer, consulting engineer on rails, tires, and structural steel of the New York Central lines from 1880. He invented the dynagraph (telling of conditions in a railroad car in motion), the track-indicator, and the stremmatograph (giving stresses in the rails as a train passes), and designed the first 5-inch and 6-inch steel rails used in the U.S.

Dudley, Robert. [Title, Earl of **Leicester.**] b. June 24, 1532; d. at Cornbury, Oxfordshire, England, Sept. 4, 1588. English courtier, politician, and general; son of John Dudley, Duke of Northumberland, and brother of Guildford Dudley. He participated in the attempt of his father and brother to place Lady Jane Grey on the throne at the death of Edward VI in 1553, and was in consequence sentenced to death on the charge of treason in 1554, but was pardoned later in the same year. On the accession in 1558 of Elizabeth, whose affections he had gained during the ascendancy of his father at the court of Edward VI, he became her chief favorite, and intrigued, though unsuccessfully, to obtain the consent of the great nobles to a marriage, in the interest of which project he was said to have procured the murder of his wife Lady Amy (Amy Robsart) in 1560. He was created Earl of Leicester in 1564, presumably in order to facilitate his marriage to Mary, Queen of Scots, but she married Lord Darnley in 1565 and the projected scheme came to nothing. In 1575 he entertained Queen Elizabeth with great magnificence at Kenilworth, which had been given to him by Elizabeth some years earlier. In 1576 Walter Devereux, 1st Earl of Essex, died in Ireland, according to rumor poisoned at Leicester's instigation, and in 1578 Leicester married Lettice (born Lettice Knollys), Essex's widow. This marriage, unlike an earlier liaison with Lady Douglas Sheffield, came to Elizabeth's notice; her displeasure almost resulted in his going to the Tower. In 1585 he was appointed to the command of the English army sent to the aid of the States-General against the Spaniards. He was made governor of the provinces in revolt; this, however, exceeded the authority granted him by Elizabeth and he was forced to apologize to her. After a defeat at Sluys and as a result of disagreements with the States-General, he was recalled in 1587. He was, however, restored to favor on his return, and in 1588 was appointed lieutenant and captain general of the queen's armies and companies to resist the expected Spanish invasion. He died suddenly soon after the routing of the Spanish Armada. Leicester was a patron of the arts and especially of the drama; the Earl of Leicester's company of players were licensed by the queen to play at London in 1574; this was the company that later included the Burbages and Shakespeare and for which the first London theater, the Theatre, was built in 1576.

Dudley, Samuel William. b. at New Haven, Conn., Oct. 18, 1879—. American mechanical engineer. He received a Ph.B. (1900) and an M.E. (1903) from Yale. He was associated (1905–21) with the Westinghouse Air Brake Company. He has served as professor of mechanical engineering (1921 *et seq.*), department head (1923–46), and dean (1936 *et seq.*) at the Yale School of Engineering.

Dudley, Thomas. b. at Northampton, England, 1576; d. at Roxbury, Mass., July 31, 1653. Colonial politician; father of Joseph Dudley. He came to Massachusetts as deputy governor to John Winthrop in 1630. He was four times governor (1634–35, 1640–41, 1645–46, 1650–51), and deputy governor 13 times. He was a strict Puritan and clashed several times with Winthrop and often with other leaders of the colony who had, he felt, left the path of orthodoxy.

Dudley, William Russel. b. at Guilford, Conn., March 1, 1849; d. at Los Altos, Calif., June 4, 1911. American botanist, assistant professor at Cornell University (1876–92) and professor at Stanford University (1892–1908). He published works on local botany, *A Manual of Histology* (1894, with M. B. Thomas), and others.

Dudley Diamond. Diamond found in Africa in 1868, and bought from Nie Kirk, the master of the man who found it, by Hunt and Roskell for 12,000 pounds. The earl of Dudley bought it from them for 30,000 pounds. It is heart-shaped, extremely brilliant, and weighs 44½ carats cut; originally it weighed 88½ carats.

Dudone (dö.dō'nā). [English, **Dudon.**] Knight in Ariosto's *Orlando Furioso.*

Dudu (dö.dö'). In Byron's *Don Juan,* a pensive beauty of 17.

Dudweiler (döt'vī.lėr). Town in the Saar territory, formerly Saarland, Germany, situated on the Sulzbach, a tributary of the Saar River, ab. 4 mi. NE of Saarbrücken. It belongs to the metropolitan area of Saarbrücken, and has coal mines, iron foundries, and manufactures of mining cars and machinery. The population is predominantly Roman Catholic, with a large Protestant minority. Prior to 1919 Dudweiler belonged to the Rhine Province, Prussia. 24,601 (1939).

Duel after the Masquerade. Painting by Jean Léon Gérôme, in the Walters Art Gallery at Baltimore. The duelists and their seconds have come direct from a masked ball; one, dressed as a clown, has been severely wounded, and his adversary, an Indian, hurries away, attended by a harlequin, to his carriage.

Duellist, The. Comedy by William Kenrick, produced in 1773. Three editions were printed in the same year.

Duellists, The. Play by Douglas Jerrold, written in 1818. It was rechristened *More Frightened than Hurt,* was played at the Sadler's Wells Theatre (April 30, 1821), was afterward translated into French, played in Paris, retranslated by Kenney, and played at the Olympic as *Fighting by Proxy*. It contained much sparkling dialogue and a good plot of the low-comedy kind.

Duenna (dū.en′ạ), **The.** Comedy interspersed with songs, a musical mélange, though sometimes called an opera, by Richard Brinsley Sheridan, produced c1775. The plot was taken from Wycherley's comedy *The Country Wife*. Linley, Sheridan's father-in-law, wrote the music for the songs. It was acted 75 times in one season.

Duer (dū′ėr), **John.** b. at Albany, N.Y., Oct. 7, 1782; d. on Staten Island, N.Y., Aug. 8, 1858. American jurist; son of William Duer (1747–99). He published *Law of Representations in Marine Insurance* (1845), *Law and Practice of Marine Insurance* (1845–46), and *Duer's Reports*.

Duer, William. b. in Devonshire, England, March 18, 1747; d. May 7, 1799. American Revolutionary patriot, merchant, and financier. After service with the British army, he went to the West Indies to manage his portion of the plantations inherited from his father; while visiting New York in 1768, he made several investments, including the purchase of a large timber holding near Saratoga, N.Y., on which he set up sawmills. After returning to England in 1773, he settled in New York state. He was (1775) a delegate to the Provincial Congress, a delegate (1776) to the New York constitutional convention, and a member (1776) of the Committee of Public Safety. He served (1777–79) as a New York delegate to the Continental Congress, and was a member of the Board of War and a signer of the Articles of Confederation. His influence was instrumental in causing the failure of the Conway Cabal's plan to remove Washington from his command. He was (1777–86) the first judge of common pleas of Charlotte (now Washington) County, N.Y., played a large part in founding (1784) the Bank of New York, and was appointed (1786) secretary to the Board of the Treasury. He became (1786) a member of the New York Assembly and was (1789–90) assistant secretary of the U.S. Treasury. Involved in land and other speculations, he was imprisoned for debt in 1792 and died in prison.

Duer, William Alexander. b. at New York, Sept. 8, 1780; d. May 30, 1858. American jurist, president of Columbia College (1829–42); son of William Duer (1747–99) and brother of John Duer. He wrote *Constitutional Jurisprudence of the United States* (1856), and others.

Duero (dwā′rō), Marqués de. Title of **Concha, Manuel de la.**

Duero. Spanish name of the **Douro.**

Duesenberg (dö′zẹn.bėrg), **Frederick S.** b. at Lippe, Germany, c1877; d. at Johnstown, Pa., July 26, 1932. American racing driver and automobile manufacturer. He arrived in the U.S. at the age of eight. He won Indianapolis racing prizes with an automobile equipped with a patented (1913) rotary valve motor. He organized (c1917) Duesenberg Motors Corp.

Duessa (dū.es′ạ). Loathsome old woman, in Spenser's *Faerie Queene*, who under the guise of Fidessa, a young and beautiful woman, typifies the falsehood and treachery of the Church of Rome. She also represents Mary, Queen of Scots, as the type of Catholic hostility to Elizabeth. She deceives and nearly ruins the Red Cross Knight; but all her ignominy and loathsomeness are laid bare by Arthur, who is sent by Una to the rescue. She is taken from Ariosto's *Alcina*, and the scene where the "false Duessa" is stripped of her disguise is literally translated from the *Orlando Furioso*.

Dufaure (dü.fōr), **Jules Armand Stanislas.** b. at Saujon, Charente-Maritime, France, Dec. 4, 1798; d. at Paris, June 28, 1881. French statesman. He was minister of the interior (Oct. 13–Dec. 20, 1848; June 2–Oct. 31, 1849); minister of justice (Feb. 19, 1871–May 24, 1873; March 11, 1875–Aug. 12, 1876); and premier (March 9–Dec. 2, 1876; Sept. 14, 1877–Feb. 1, 1879).

Dufay (dü.fā), **Guillaume.** b. at Hainault, Belgium, c1400; d. at Cambrai, France, Nov. 27, 1474. Flemish composer and contrapuntist, originator of improvements in musical notation, such as the use of white notes.

Duff (duf), **Alexander.** b. at Moulin, Perthshire, Scotland, April 25, 1806; d. at Edinburgh, Feb. 12, 1878. Scottish missionary in India, belonging to the Church of Scotland, later to the Free Church. He wrote *India and India Missions* (1839), and other works.

Duff, Douglas Ainslie Grant. See **Ainslie, Douglas.**

Duff, Sir **Mountstuart Elphinstone Grant.** See **Grant Duff,** Sir **Mountstuart Elphinstone.**

Duff Cooper (kö′pėr, kůp′ėr), **Alfred.** See **Cooper, Alfred Duff.**

Duff Cooper, Lady **Diana.** See **Cooper,** Lady **Diana Duff.**

Duffel (duf′ẹl). Town in N Belgium, in the province of Antwerp, situated on the Nèthe River, ab. 10 mi. SE of Antwerp. It became known originally for its manufacture of coarse woolen cloth called "duffel," and now has distilleries and metallurgical and paper factories. 12,003 (1947).

Dufferin (duf′ėr.in), Countess of. A title of **Sheridan,** Lady **Helen Selina.**

Dufferin and Ava (ä′vạ), 1st Marquis of. See **Blackwood, Frederick Temple Hamilton-Temple.**

Duff-Gordon (duf′gôr′dọn), Lady **Lucie** (or **Lucy**). [Maiden name, **Austin.**] b. at Westminster, London, June 24, 1821; d. at Cairo, Egypt, July 14, 1869. English writer, best known as a translator from the German (Niebuhr, Von Ranke, and Sybel). She resided in Egypt from 1862. She married Sir Alexander Duff-Gordon in 1840.

Duffy (duf′i), Sir **Charles Gavan.** b. at Monaghan, Ireland, April 12, 1816; d. at Nice, France, Feb. 9, 1903. Irish journalist, historian, editor, and poet, political leader in Ireland and Australia. He began his career as a journalist at 17, writing for the *Northern Herald* and the *Vindicator*, Belfast papers, and for the Dublin *Morning Register*, and later was one of the founders (1842), with John Dillon and Thomas Davis, of the *Nation*, a Dublin weekly which became the organ of the Young Ireland party. He was one of the leaders of the movement to popularize Irish letters; he published the series "The Library of Ireland," shilling books of Irish poetry and the like; in 1891 he was chosen first president of the Irish Literary Society. He was associated politically with Daniel O'Connell but broke with O'Connell over the latter's moderation. After serving in Parliament (1852–55) for New Ross and failing in his aim to gain some unity on the land problem, he left Ireland for Australia, where he was elected to the Victoria parliament. He was minister of land and works (1857, 1862), prime minister of Victoria (1871–73), and speaker of the house (1877–80). He returned to Europe in 1880, spending the rest of his life in southern France. He was the author of *Young Ireland* (1880–83), *A Bird's-Eye View of Irish History* (1882), *The League of North and South: An Episode in Irish History* (1886), *Thomas Davis: An Irish Patriot* (1890), *A Fair Constitution for Ireland* and *Conversations With Carlyle* (both 1892), *Revival of Irish Literature* (1894), and *Short Life of Thomas Davis* (1895), *My Life in Two Hemispheres* (1898), autobiography, and *Lays of the Red Branch* (1901). He edited the anthology *The Ballad Poetry of Ireland* (1845).

Duffy, Francis Patrick. b. at Cobourg, Ontario, Canada, May 2, 1871; d. June 26, 1932. Roman Catholic priest. One of 11 children in a family where poverty made hard work the rule, his sickliness saved him from labor in a mill or factory and permitted him to study for the priesthood. He completed his studies after coming to the U.S., and was ordained in 1896. Two years later he was assigned as chaplain of the "Fighting 69th" regiment of the New York National Guard, then mobilizing for service in the Spanish-American War. In the pest-ridden camp at Montauk Point, Long Island, he contracted typhoid fever. After intervening years of parochial service, Duffy again accompanied the 69th when it was called into national service along the Mexican border in 1916. When the U.S. entered World War I, the 69th became the 165th regiment, a unit of the Rainbow Division, and Francis Patrick Duffy, accompanying it to the fronts, not only earned the Distinguished Service Cross, the cross of the Legion of Honor, the Croix de Guerre and other medals, but the affection of countless soldiers, the esteem of chaplains of other faiths, and nation-wide fame. In 1920 he was appointed pastor of Holy Cross Parish in the Times Square neighborhood of New York City, where he served until his death. In 1921, at the silver jubilee of his ordination, he was presented with a purse of $25,000 raised by a committee which included President Harding, Governor Miller of New York, General Pershing, Cardinal Hayes, and many leading citizens. A statue of Duffy, unveiled in 1937, on which occasion President Roosevelt wrote of him as "a great Samaritan, a great Catholic, a great soldier," stands in Times Square, New York.

Dufour (dü.för), **Guillaume Henri.** b. at Konstanz, Baden (now in Germany), Sept. 15, 1787; d. at Contamines, near Geneva, Switzerland, July 14, 1875. Swiss general, cartographer, and military writer. He suppressed (1847) the Sonderbund insurrection, and superintended preparation of a topographical map of Switzerland (published 1842–65). He wrote *Mémoires sur l'artillerie des anciens et sur celle du moyen âge* (1840), and others.

Dufour, Jean Marie Léon. b. at St.-Sever, Landes, France, 1782; d. there, April 18, 1865. French entomologist.

Dufour, Pierre. A pseudonym of **Lacroix, Paul.**

Dufourspitze (dü.för'shpit"se). Highest peak of Monte Rosa, in the Alps on the Swiss-Italian border.

Dufoy (dū.foi'). Impertinent French servant in Etherege's comedy *The Comical Revenge, or Love in a Tub.* He is the subject of the comical revenge, being fastened in a wooden tub with holes for the head and arms by some women, as a punishment for his boasting and railing against their sex.

Dufrénoy (dü.frā.nwȧ), **Ours Pierre Armand Petit.** b. at Sevran, Seine-et-Oise, France, Sept. 5, 1792; d. at Paris, March 20, 1857. French mineralogist and geologist. He was the collaborator of Élie de Beaumont in the preparation of a general geological map of France (published 1841), and author of various geological monographs.

du Fresne or **Dufresne** (dü fren), **Charles.** See **Du Cange** or **Ducange,** Sieur.

Dufresne, Charles George. b. at Millemont, France, Nov. 23, 1876—. French cubist painter, water-colorist, and engraver, who was also associated with Guillaume Appollinaire's movement, called orphism. He educated himself, and did not start to paint until he was 30; before then, he had been employed by an engraver and medallist. He has exhibited at the salons of the Société Nationale from 1910, and the Salon des Indépendants. He spent two years (1910–12) at Algiers, and since then his work has had an exotic flavor. He has designed stage settings and costumes also, including those for *Antar.* Other works are *The Card Party, Pastorale, The Temptation of Saint Anthony* (water colors), *The Dream, Still Life, Hunter and Odalisque, The Blue Corsage, The Repose, Scene of Colonial Life,* and *Hunting Scene.*

Dufresnoy (dü.fre.nwȧ), **Charles Alphonse.** b. at Paris, 1611; d. at Villiers-le-Bel, near Paris, 1665. French painter and poet, author of a Latin poem *De arte graphica* (1668).

Dufresny (dü.fre.nē), **Charles Rivière.** b. at Paris, 1654; d. there, Oct. 6, 1724. French dramatist; descendant of "La Belle Jardinière," a mistress of Henry IV. He wrote a number of comedies, some of them in collaboration with Regnard.

Dufy (dü.fē), **Jean.** b. at Le Havre, France, March 12, 1888—. French painter and water-colorist, whose works have been strongly influenced by those of his brother, Raoul. He studied at the École des Beaux-Arts at Le Havre. His work is very decorative and whimsical, and he has painted many circus scenes, jazz scenes, flowers, and seascapes. A list of his better-known paintings includes *At the Circus, At the Bal Tabarin, Clowns, Port of Le Havre, Landscape, Flowers and Fruits, House in the Flowers,* and *Boats at Le Havre.*

Dufy, Raoul. b. at Le Havre, France, June 3, 1877; d. near Avignon, France, March 23, 1953. French painter, lithographer, and decorator, considered by many to have been among the most original and fresh of contemporary artists. With a great economy of line and simplification of representation, he painted sweeping, motion-filled, decorative scenes. He studied at the École des Beaux-Arts, and first began to paint academic works. Soon he changed his style and painted many lively, brilliantly colored scenes of the races, views of Le Havre, and Trouville. His illustrations for Guillaume Apollinaire's *Bestiaire* (1911) were his first successes. Later he did illustrations for many other books, including Apollinaire's *Poet Assassinated* and Mallarmé's *Madrigals.* He also executed many lithographs in color, including a series entitled *The Sea.* Among his best-known works are *The Sea at Le Havre, Trouville, Races at Ascot, Boulevard at Nice, Regatta at Le Havre, The Park at St.-Cloud, Panorama of Paris, Antibes,* and *Nude with Raised Arms.*

Du Gard (dü gȧr), **Roger Martin.** See **Martin du Gard, Roger.**

Dugdale (dug'dāl), **Richard Louis.** b. at Paris, 1841; d. 1883. American sociologist. Brought to this country by his English parents in 1851, at an early age he developed an interest in social work, which at that time was far from well organized or well financed. In 1874 the New York Prison Association employed him to report on conditions in a number of county jails, and he came upon the data showing that in certain of these institutions a large percentage of the inmates, year by year, were members of a certain family, to which he gave the fictitious name of Juke. In one of the Prison Association reports (1875) his observations and deductions were published under the title, *The Jukes: a Study in Crime, Pauperism, Disease, and Heredity.* This was issued in book form together with *Further Studies of Criminals* (1877). The depressing facts revealed by Dugdale, together with his theory of inherited familial degeneracy, made worse and perpetuated by close inbreeding, aroused exceptionally wide interest, but his conclusions, in the main, are no longer accepted. The discovery in 1911 of his original manuscript, which revealed the real name of the "Juke" family, enabled a later sociologist to report on the family's record 40 years later, under the title, *The Jukes in 1915.* From 1868 Dugdale was a member of the executive committee of the New York Prison Association, and in 1880 he became the first secretary of the Society for Political Education. He was active in many sociological and civic groups and movements.

Dugdale, Sir **William.** b. at Shustoke, Warwickshire, England, Sept. 12, 1605; d. there, Feb. 10, 1686. English antiquary. He wrote *Monasticon Anglicanum* (1655–73), *Antiquities of Warwickshire* (1656), *History of St. Paul's Cathedral* (1658), *Baronage of England* (1675–76), and others.

Duggan (dug'ạn), **Eileen May.** b. at Tua Marina, Marlborough, New Zealand —. New Zealand poet. Her works include *New Zealand Bird Songs* (1929), *Poems* (1937), and *New Zealand Poems* (1940).

Duggar (dug'ạr), **Benjamin Minge.** b. at Gallion, Ala., 1872—. American botanist. He was graduated (Ph.D., 1898) from Cornell, studied in Italy, Germany, and France, was research professor of plant physiology (1912–27) at the Missouri Botanical Garden and Washington University, and served (1927–43) as professor of physiology and economic botany at the University of Wisconsin. As consultant (1944) in mycological research and production to the Lederle Laboratories, Inc., he developed aureomycin. Among his works are *Fungous Diseases of Plants* (1909), *Plant Physiology* (1911), and *Mushroom Growing* (1915).

Dugi Otok (dö'gē ô'tôk). [Also: **Dugi;** full name, **Ostrvo** (= island) **Dugi Otok;** Italian, **Isola Lunga** (or **Grossa**).] Island in W Yugoslavia, in the federative unit of Croatia, ab. 10 mi. W of Zadar: fisheries, vineyards, and olive culture. Pop. ab. 4,000.

Dugmore (dug'mōr), **Arthur Radclyffe.** b. 1870—. English naturalist and animal photographer and painter. He has exhibited his big-game paintings in England and the U.S. He is the author of such books as *Bird Homes* (1900), *Nature and the Camera* (1902), *Camera Adventures in the African Wilds* (1910), and *Through the Sudan* (1938).

Duguay-Trouin (dü.gā.trö.aṅ), **René.** b. at St.-Malo, France, June 10, 1673; d. at Paris, Sept. 27, 1736. French naval officer and general. From 1691 to 1697 he commanded a privateer, and in the latter year entered the French navy. Among his noted deeds were the capture of an English convoy in 1707, and the capture and sack of Rio de Janeiro (September, 1711). He subsequently served with the army, attaining the rank of lieutenant general.

Dugué (dü.gā), **Charles Oscar.** b. at New Orleans, May 1, 1821; d. at Paris, Aug. 29, 1872. American Creole poet. He was the author of *Philosophie morale* (1847),

Essais poétiques (1847), *Mila ou la mort de La Salle* (1852), and *Le Cygne ou Mingo* (1852). His best-known poem *Home*, appeared in 1872.

Du Guesclin or **Duguesclin** (dü.ge.klañ), **Bertrand.** b. near Rennes, in Brittany, France, c1320; d. at Châteauneuf-de-Randon, in Languedoc, France, July 13, 1380. French military commander, constable of France, distinguished in the campaigns against the English and Pedro el Cruel (Peter the Cruel of Castile and León). After having made a soldier's reputation for himself in tournaments and in fighting for Charles de Blois, he helped in the defense of Rennes, besieged (1356–57) by Henry of Lancaster. He was captured at Melun in 1359 by Sir Robert Knollys, but covered himself with glory. At Cocherel in 1364 he beat the forces of Navarre and captured Jean de Grailly, the Captal de Buch, Navarre's most famous soldier. At Auray the same year, Charles de Blois was killed and Du Guesclin was captured by Sir John Chandos. He was ransomed for 100,000 crowns, since his aid, as France's leading soldier, was necessary to preserve internal order. The Treaty of Bretigny (1360) had brought a temporary pause in the Hundred Years' War and bands of discharged soldiers, the so-called free companies, were pillaging the country. Du Guesclin organized them into an army and took them into Spain to fight for Henry of Trastamara (later Henry II of Castile) against Pedro el Cruel, but after success in 1366, he was defeated by Edward, the Black Prince of England, Pedro's ally, at Navarrete. He was again ransomed and in the battle of Montiel (1369) defeated Pedro and put Henry on the throne. Under Charles V of France he fought (1370–79) in the campaigns to clean the English out of southern and western France, winning for the French throne Poitou, Guienne, Auvergne, and Brittany. He died in a campaign to suppress disorders in Languedoc.

Duhalde (dö.äl′dā), **Alfredo.** b. at Río Bueno, Chile, 1898—. Chilean politician and agriculturist, leader of the Radical Party. He was national deputy (1924–30), ambassador (1939) to Peru, minister of national defense (1940, 1942), vice-president (1944–46) of Chile, acting president (Jan. 17–June 27, 1946), and president (June 27–Oct. 17, 1946).

Du Halde (dü åld), **Jean Baptiste.** b. at Paris, Feb. 1, 1674; d. there, Aug. 18, 1743. French Jesuit and geographer. He was the author of *Description géographique . . . de la Chine et de la Tartarie chinoise* (1735).

Duhamel (dü.å.mel), **Georges.** b. at Paris, June 30, 1844—. French poet, novelist, dramatist, and physician. Early a member (1906–07) of the Abbaye group of poets, he emerged as a dramatist with *La Lumière* (1911; Eng. trans., *The Light,* 1914) and *Dans l'ombre des statues* (1912; Eng. trans., *In the Shadow of Statues,* 1914); turned to fiction with *Vie des Martyrs* (1917; Eng. trans., *The New Book of Martyrs,* 1918) and *Civilisation* (1918; Eng. trans., 1919). Since World War I most of his effort has been expended on two cyclical novels, *Le Cycle de Salavin* (4 vols., 1920-32; Eng. trans., *Salavin,* 1936 *et seq.*) and *La Chronique des Pasquier* (10 vols., 1937–41; Eng. trans., *The Pasquier Chronicles,* 1937 *et seq.*). He has been a member of the French Academy since 1938.

Duhamel, Jean Marie Constant. b. at St.-Malo, France, Feb. 5, 1797; d. at Paris, April 29, 1872. French mathematician, author of *Cours d'analyse* (1840–41), *Cours de mécanique* (1845), and *Des méthodes dans les sciences du raisonnement* (1866–72).

Duhamel du Monceau (dü.å.mel dü môñ.sō), **Henri Louis.** b. at Paris, 1700; d. there, Aug. 12, 1781. French authority on botany and agriculture. He wrote *De la physique des arbres* (1758).

Duhm (döm), **Bernhard.** b. at Bingum, Germany, Oct. 10, 1847; d. at Basel, Switzerland, Aug. 31, 1928. German Protestant theologian. He was known for his Biblical criticism. He was the author of *Das Geheimnis in der Religion* (1896), *Das kommende Reich Gottes* (1910), *Israels Propheten* (1916), and *Die Psalmen* (1922).

Duhr (dör). The third-magnitude star δ Leonis, on the rump of the animal. It is sometimes also called Zosma and Zubra.

Dühring (dü′ring), **Eugen Karl.** b. at Berlin, Jan. 12, 1833; d. in Germany, Sept. 21, 1921. German political economist and philosophical writer, a disciple of Henry C. Carey. He published *Kritische Geschichte der Nationalökonomie und des Sozialismus* (1871), and others.

Duhring (dūr′ing), **Louis Adolphus.** b. at Philadelphia, Dec. 23, 1845; d. May 8, 1913. American dermatologist. Receiving his medical degree from the University of Pennsylvania in 1866, he went to Vienna and took up the special study of dermatology. Returning to Philadelphia, he established in 1870 the Dispensary for Skin Diseases, with which he remained connected until 1890. In 1871 he began lecturing on skin ailments at the University of Pennsylvania, and for many years he was consulting dermatologist at the Philadelphia Hospital. Before his time little attention had been paid to skin troubles by the American medical profession. The disease dermatitis herpetiform is sometimes called "Duhring's Disease," he having been the first to demonstrate its true character. He was the author of *Atlas of Skin Diseases* (1876), *Practical Treatise on Diseases of the Skin* (1877), and *Cutaneous Medicine* (1895–98).

Duhshasana (dö.shä′sa.na). In Hindu legend, one of the hundred sons of Dhritarashtra. When the Pandavas lost their wife Draupadi in gambling with Duryodhana, Duhshasana dragged her by the hair and otherwise ill-used her; for this Bhima vowed he would drink his blood, a vow performed on the 16th day of the great battle between the Pandavas and the Kauravas.

Duida (dwē′ᴛʜä). [Spanish, **Cerro Duida.**] **Precipitous** mountain in S Venezuela, near the Orinoco River. Elevation, ab. 8,500 ft.

Duilius (dū.il′i.us), **Gaius** (or **Caius**). fl. in the 3rd century B.C. Roman general, consul in 260 B.C. He defeated the Carthaginians near Mylae (modern Milazzo), on the N coast of Sicily, in 260. This was the first naval success gained by Rome. Duilius, a land officer placed in charge of the fleet by necessity, decided to fight the naval engagement as a land battle, and by using grappling hooks and boarding planks, won his battle.

Duinkerken (doin′ker.kẹn), **Anton Van.** [Pseudonym of **W. J. M. A. Asselbergs.**] b. 1903—. Dutch author, journalist, and professor, notable as a leader in the Roman Catholic literary movement and for his studies on Roman Catholic poetry in the Netherlands in former times. His works on modern problems of art and society include *Hedendaagsche ketterijen* (Present Heresies, 1929), *Katholiek Verzet* (Catholic Resistance, 1932), and *Verscheurde Christenheid* (Christianity, 1937). His poetry includes *Hart van Brabant* (Heart of Brabant, 1937).

Duisberg (düs′berk), **Carl.** b. at Barman, Germany, Sept. 29, 1861; d. at Leverkusen, Germany, March 19, 1935. German industrialist. He joined the Bayer chemical firm in 1884, and in 1900 became a member of its executive board; organized the I. G. Farben chemical trust, becoming its chairman in 1925; chairman of the National Association of German Industry.

Duisburg-Hamborn (düs′bůrk.häm′bôrn; Anglicized, döz′bėrg.ham′bôrn). [Also, **Duisburg.**] City in W Germany, in the *Land* (state of North Rhine-Westphalia, British Zone, formerly in the Rhine Province, Prussia, situated at the junction of the Rhine and Ruhr rivers, ab. 15 mi. N of Düsseldorf. It includes a number of formerly independent towns, such as Ruhrort, Meiderich, Neudorf, and Laar. Duisburg and Hamborn were combined in 1929. It is the largest river port of Europe, consisting of numerous separate harbor-basins, with repair and loading facilities, warehouses, and railroad connections. The Netherlands seaports, notably Rotterdam, are reached via the Rhine River, the German North Sea ports via the Rhine-Herne Canal, which connects with the Dortmund-Ems Canal. The chief export is the coal of the Ruhr basin; the chief imports are iron ore, lumber, grain, and petroleum. The city has large industrial enterprises including blast furnaces, iron foundries, rolling mills, zinc and copper mills, shipyards, construction works, machine, tool, and boiler factories, chemical, tar, soap, and oil industries, petroleum refineries, gasworks, cotton spinning and weaving mills, shoe, paper, and tobacco manufactures, sugar refineries, flour mills, breweries, and distilleries. There are a number of educational institutions, among which are nautical, commercial, industrial, and mining schools. The city was occupied by Belgian troops in the period 1921–25. During World War II it was frequently bombed (1943–45), with intense damage to town, port areas, and industries. The churches also suffered some damage. The population is predominantly Roman Catholic, with a large Protestant minority; the decline in the period 1939–46 was 21.4 percent. 356,408 (1946), 410,783 (1950).

Duitschland (doits'länt). Dutch name of **Germany.**

Duiveland (doi'vẹ.länt). Island, properly the E part of the island of Schouwen, in the province of Zealand, Netherlands.

Dujardin (dü.zhär.daṅ), **Édouard Émile Louis.** b. at St.-Gervais, France, Nov. 10, 1861—. French poet, dramatist, and critic. He is the author of various studies of Mallarmé, Laforgue, James Joyce, and others. His novel *Les Lauriers sont coupés* (1887) is sometimes regarded as an early example of the stream-of-consciousness technique in fiction.

Dujardin, Félix. b. at Tours, France, April 5, 1801; d. at Rennes, France, April 8, 1860. French naturalist, professor (1839 *et seq.*) at Rennes. He is best known for his investigations on the Infusoria.

Dujardin, Karel. b. at Amsterdam, Netherlands, c1625; d. at Venice, Nov. 20, 1678. Dutch painter and etcher, particularly known for his landscapes.

Dukas (dü.kȧ), **Paul.** b. at Paris, Oct. 1, 1865; d. 1935. French music critic and composer. He was a pupil at the Paris Conservatory, winning the second Prix de Rome. His works include the opera *Ariane et Barbe Bleue*, with text by Maeterlinck (1907), a symphony (1897), a piano sonata (1901), overtures, and the symphonic poem *The Sorcerer's Apprentice* (1897).

Duke (dūk), **Benjamin Newton.** b. near Durham, N.C., April 27, 1855; d. at New York, Jan. 8, 1929. American businessman and philanthropist, notable (with his brother James Buchanan Duke) as a pioneer in the manufacturing and marketing of cigarettes in the U.S. A director (1890 *et seq.*) of the American Tobacco Company, he engaged also in banking, railroading, real estate, cotton manufacturing, and development of hydroelectric power. His personal fortune is estimated to have reached 60 million dollars. Gifts totaling more than two million dollars were given (1898 *et seq.*) to Trinity College (now Duke University) following the college's decision (1892) to move to Durham, N.C., in accordance with Duke's wish.

Duke, James Buchanan. b. near Durham, N.C., Dec. 23, 1856; d. Oct. 10, 1925. American tobacco magnate and civic benefactor. Together with his brother, Benjamin Newton Duke, he began as an itinerant vendor of packaged tobacco in North Carolina; at the age of 18 he became a member of W. Duke and Sons, which in 1881 began making cigarettes, subsequently manufactured with vastly increased efficiency by the Bonsack machine which he helped improve. He made his start towards his fortune by halving the price of a package of cigarettes two months before a lowered government impost became effective. In 1884 he established a branch factory at New York, embarking on an advertising program and expanding his trade; by 1889 half the U.S. output of cigarettes came from his machines. In 1890, as the result of a merger, he became president of the American Tobacco Company, which soon consolidated with other companies turning out a variety of tobacco products. In the field of plug tobacco, he became (1898) president of the Continental Tobacco Company, helped form (1900) the American Snuff Company, the American Cigar Company in 1901, and went into retail operations with the United Cigar Stores Company. The Consolidated Tobacco Company, organized in 1901, was later dissolved and the chief properties reorganized as the American Tobacco Company, which in turn was ordered by a U.S. Supreme Court decree (1911) to be dissolved. At about this time his properties comprised 150 factories representing a capitalization of 502 million dollars. In 1905 the Southern Power Company was organized with his aid. In 1924 he set up a trust fund, of which the chief portion was used to aid Duke University.

Duke Humphrey's Walk (hum'friz). See **Paul's Walk.**

Duke Jones (jōnz). Novel by Ethel Sidgwick, published in 1914. It is a sequel to her novel *A Lady of Leisure* (1914).

Duke of Exeter's Daughter (ek'sẹ.tėrz). Name given to the rack which the Duke of Exeter introduced as an engine of torture in the Tower of London in 1447.

Duke of Guise (gēz), **The.** Tragedy by Dryden and Lee, published in 1682. It was an attack on Shaftesbury and Monmouth. In *The Vindication*, by Dryden alone, he did what he could to excuse himself.

Duke of Milan (mi.lan'), **The.** Tragedy by Philip Massinger, produced in 1623. It is a variation of the theme of Shakespeare's *Othello.* The duke is a passionate, weak man, without Othello's noble traits.

Duke of Stockbridge (stok'brij), **The.** Novel by Edward Bellamy, published as a serial in 1879 and completed after his death. It is based on the events of Shays's Rebellion.

Duke of York Island (yôrk). Mountainous island in Antarctica, lying in the S part of Robertson Bay and along the N coast of Victoria Land, in ab. 71°37′ S., 170°03′ E. It was first charted in 1899 by the British Antarctic Expedition (1898–1900), under the command of C. E. Borchgrevink.

Duke of York Islands. [Former German name, **Neu-Lauenburg.**] Group of islands in the Australian mandated territory of New Guinea, in St. Georges Channel ab. 20 mi. E of Rabaul, New Britain. There are eight inhabited islands, with numerous coastal villages, coconut plantations, and Methodist missions. Before World War I the islands were a German colony. Area, ab. 23 sq. mi.

Dukes (dūks), **Ashley.** b. at Bridgewater, Somersetshire, England, May 29, 1885—. English dramatist and theater manager. He has been drama critic (1900–14, 1919–25) on various publications, director (1933 *et seq.*) of the Mercury Theatre, and supervisor (1945 *et seq.*) of theatrical productions in the British zone of Germany. His plays include *One More River* (1927), *Matchmaker's Arms* (1930), and translations and adaptations of *Jew Süss* (1929), *The Dumb Wife of Cheapside* (1929) from Rabelais, and *Mandragola* (1939) from Macchiavelli; author also of *Modern Dramatists* (1911), *The Youngest Drama* (1923), and *Drama* (1926).

Dukesborough Tales (dūks'bur″ọ). Sketches of Georgia provincial life by Richard Malcolm Johnston, published in 1871 as a revision of his *Georgia Scenes* (1864). They were issued under the pseudonym Philemon Perch.

Duke Sebastian (sẹ.bas'chạn). Central character in *The Edwardians* (1930), a novel of English life and character in the period of Edward VII, by V. Sackville-West.

Duke's Mistress, The. Play by James Shirley, produced in 1636.

Duke's Motto, The. Adaptation of Paul Féval's play *Le Bossu*, by John Brougham, produced in 1863.

Duke's Theatre. London theater which was built in 1660. It was destroyed in 1666 in the great fire, and rebuilt in 1671 by Sir Christopher Wren. It stood until 1720, and was on the site of the Salisbury Court Theatre.

Duketown (dūk'toun). See under **Calabar.**

Dukhobors (dö'kọ.bôrz). [Also: **Doukhobors;** original Russian, **Dukhobortsy,** meaning "spirit wrestlers."] Religious sect originating among the Russian peasantry. The movement may have begun as early as the closing years of the 17th century, but attracted little attention until about the middle of the 18th, when it became widespread in the Dnieper region. The sect's rejection of both church and state brought persecution, but in 1801 its members were permitted to settle near the Sea of Azov, where they flourished until disorders in the colony and their resistance to military conscription led to their removal to a barren region of Transcaucasia. Here again they built up a flourishing agricultural settlement, but in 1895 their active opposition to war and militarism led to their forcible dispersal and to the exile of their leader Peter Veregin to Siberia. It seems to have been about this time that Orthodox Christians began to apply to them, contemptuously, the name they are now generally known by, though their own name for themselves, in English, means "Christians of the Universal Brotherhood." Count Tolstoy, whose pacifist principles agreed with theirs and may have been in part derived from them, took up their cause and aroused in other countries an agitation against their persecution, with the result that in 1898 the Russian government permitted them to emigrate. Most of them in the following year settled in the province of Manitoba, Canada. They acquired land not as individuals but as communities, and their agricultural industry and skill again made a wilderness to yield abundance. They developed, however, a tendency toward sudden fanaticisms. Thus a few years after settling in Canada they decided that all use of animals and animal products was sinful; they turned their cattle loose and took the place of their horses in drawing the plow and hauling their produce to market; they refused to pay taxes and resisted arrest by going nude. A rumor spreading among them that Jesus would appear at Winnipeg, 300 miles from their nearest village, thousands of them set out for that city in October, 1902, afoot in sub-zero weather, and had to be rounded up by the police and forcibly sent home. Peter Veregin, who had been detained in Siberia when his followers first migrated, was eventually allowed to go to Canada, but the Dukhobor settlements, while they continued to prosper, also continued to be frequently disturbed, and in 1924 Veregin was assassinated. His son, also Peter Veregin, came from Russia to assume leadership, and under his guidance more stable conditions were brought about. At his death in 1939 he left a document advising the Dukhobors to give up communal living, to obey the law, but to hold to their faith. Though probably more than one-third of their potential membership has drifted away, there are still upward of 10,000 of the sect in Canada. The essence of their creed is that God dwells within every man, and since, therefore, everyone's acts are guided by God, neither church nor rulers are needed; writing and reading are superfluous; the Bible has no authority; marriage is a matter which needs neither sanction nor ceremony; Christ was only a man without sin, and other men without sin who may follow Him are His equals in authority.

Dukinfield (duk′in.fēld). [Also, **Duckinfield.**] Municipal borough and manufacturing town in W England, in Cheshire, situated on the river Tame ab. 7 mi. E of Manchester, ab. 184 mi. NW of London by rail. It is a cotton-spinning center. 18,445 (1951).

Dulac (dü.lȧk′), **Edmund.** b. at Toulouse, France, Oct. 22, 1882—. English portraitist, designer, caricaturist, and decorator, who designed the coronation stamp (1937), and the cameo portrait stamp of King George VI, as well as other stamps and bank notes.

Dulaim (dö.līm′). *Liwa* (province) in W Iraq, bordered by Syria, Jordan, and Saudi Arabia: a very dry desert area. Most of the population live in trading towns or are migratory herders. The province is crossed by two oil pipe lines. Capital, Dulaim; area, 17,488 sq. mi.; pop. 193,294 (1947).

Dulany (dų.lā′ni), **Daniel.** b. in Queen's County (now County Laoighis), Ireland, 1685; d. at Annapolis, Md., Dec. 5, 1753. Lawyer and politician in colonial America. He was a representative (1722 *et seq.*) from Annapolis in the Maryland legislative assembly, judge of the admiralty (1734 *et seq.*), and a member (1742–53) of the governor's council. He championed codification in English statute of rights guaranteed in Maryland charter with his pamphlet *The Rights of the Inhabitants of Maryland to the Benefit of the English Laws* (1728).

Dulany, Daniel. b. at Annapolis, Md., June 28, 1722; d. at Baltimore, March 17, 1797. American lawyer and politician; son of Daniel Dulany (1685–1753). He was a member (1751 *et seq.*) of the Maryland legislative assembly, and secretary of the province (1761–74). An upholder of the "No Taxation without Representation" plea after the passage of the Stamp Act, he wrote a pamphlet entitled *Considerations on the Propriety of Imposing Taxes in the British Colonies, for the Purpose of raising a Revenue, by Act of Parliament* (1765). Always in opposition to radical factions, however, he soon lost popularity when he refused to support the American Revolution.

Dulaure (dü.lōr), **Jacques Antoine.** b. at Clermont-Ferrand, France, Sept. 3, 1755; d. at Paris, Aug. 19, 1835. French archaeologist and historical writer, a member of the National Convention. He was the author of *Histoire civile, physique et morale de Paris* (1821–22).

Dulcamara (döl.kä.mä′rä), **Doctor.** Charlatan (bass) in Donizetti's opera *L'Elisir d'Amore.*

Dulce (döl′sā). [Spanish, **Río Dulce.**] River in NW Argentina which rises in the province of Tucumán, becomes salty, and is finally lost in the salt marshes of Lake Porongos. In its lower course it is called the Saladillo.

Dulce, Gulf of. [Spanish, **Golfo Dulce.**] Arm of the Pacific Ocean, off the SW coast of Costa Rica.

Dulce Gulf. See **Izabal, Lake.**

Dulce y Garay (döl′thā ē gä.rī′), **Domingo.** [Title, Marquis of **Castell-Florit.**] b. at Sotés, Logroño, Spain, May 7, 1808; d. at Amélie-les-Bains, France, in December, 1869. Spanish general and administrator. He took part in the Carlist war, and aided the revolution of 1854, being then captain-general of Catalonia. From December, 1862, to May, 1866, he was captain-general of Cuba, and distinguished himself by his activity in suppressing the slave trade. He was again captain-general of Cuba in June, 1869, but the success of the insurrection and his ill health forced him to resign.

Dulcigno (döl.chē′nyō). Italian name of **Ulcinj.**

Dulcinea del Toboso (dul.sin′ē.ą del tō.bō′zō; Spanish, döl.thē.nā′ä del tō.ʙō′sō). Lady beloved by Don Quixote in Cervantes's romance. Her real name was Aldonza Lorenzo, but Don Quixote was of the opinion that Dulcinea was more uncommon and romantic (from the Spanish *dulce*, meaning "sweet"); and, as she was born at Toboso, he made her a great lady on the spot with the *del.*

Dulcy (dul′si). Play (1921) by Marc Connelly and George S. Kaufman. Dulcy, a stupid woman with good intentions, voluntarily lends her aid toward furthering one of her husband's business deals. Despite her mistakes, the negotiations end successfully, and Dulcy is credited with the acumen she totally lacks. The original for Dulcy, who is the central character of this satirical comedy, appeared originally in "The Conning Tower," when this newspaper column was still being written by Franklin Pierce Adams (F.P.A.).

Dulheggia (dul.hej′ą). See **Dhu-l-Hijja.**

Dulkaada (dul.kä′dą). See **Dhu-l-Kada.**

Dülken (dül′kẹn). Town in W Germany, in the *Land* (state) of North Rhine-Westphalia, British Zone, formerly in the Rhine Province, Prussia, situated near the Dutch border, ab. 20 mi. NW of Düsseldorf. It has linen, cotton, and silk textile industries (specializing in velvets, ribbons, and sewing thread), and also metallurgical industries and a sugar refinery. In World War II the town was occupied by Allied troops in March, 1945. The population is predominantly Roman Catholic. 18,842 (1950).

Dulles (dul′ẹs), **John Foster.** b. at Washington, D.C., Feb. 25, 1888—. American lawyer and U.S. secretary of state (1953 *et seq.*) under President Dwight D. Eisenhower. He practiced (1911 *et seq.*) law at New York. In 1918–19 he was American commission counsel at the peace negotiations following World War I, and served (1919) on the reparations commission and the supreme economic council. He was U.S. representative (1933) at the Berlin debt conferences, a member of the U.S. delegation at the San Francisco conference on world organization (1945), and a member of the Moscow meeting (1947) of the foreign ministers' council. After serving as U.S. senator from New York for a short period (1949), he was chosen (1950) delegate to the U.N. Assembly. He was adviser to the State Department (1950–52), resigning in the campaign year so that he might be free to criticize U.S. foreign policy. He is the author of *War, Peace and Change*, and *War or Peace* (1950).

Dullin (dü.lan̊), **Charles.** b. at Yonne, Savoie, France, May 12, 1885; d. at Paris, Dec. 11, 1949. French actor and director. He began his theatrical career as Smerdiakov in Jacques Copeau's production (1911) of *The Brothers Karamazov*, was associated with Copeau at the experimental Vieux Colombier theater (1913–19), opened his own Atelier theater in 1921 with great success, and afterward figured as one of the four foremost directors in France.

Dulong (dü.lôn̊), **Pierre Louis.** b. at Rouen, France, Feb. 12, 1785; d. at Paris, July 19, 1838. French physicist and chemist, professor of physics (1820 *et seq.*) at the École Polytechnique at Paris and permanent secretary (1832 *et seq.*) of the Academy of Sciences. With A. T. Petit he announced (1819) the law (Dulong and Petit's law) that the product of the specific heat of an element in the solid state multiplied by its atomic weight is approximately constant for all elements.

Duluth (du.löth'). City and lake port in E Minnesota, county seat of St. Louis County, on Lake Superior at the mouth of the St. Louis River: third largest city of Minnesota, and twin city of Superior, Wis. Duluth is the leading Great Lakes port, shipping iron ore, wheat, coal, lumber, and other products; it is also a railroad center and has manufactures of iron and steel. 104,511 (1950).

Duluth or **Du Lhut** (dü.lüt), **Daniel Greysolon,** Sieur. b. in France, 1636; d. near Lake Superior, 1709. French pioneer in America, for whom Duluth, Minn., is named. He came to Canada c1672, and became a trader and a leader of bushrangers. He established the sites of Detroit and Fort William, helped in the Canadian war against the Senecas (1687), and against the Iroquois (1689). He commanded Fort Frontenac in 1695.

Dulwich (dul'ij). District in SE London, in the County of London, in Camberwell metropolitan borough, ab. 4 mi. SE of London Bridge station, London. It is the seat of Dulwich College, founded by Edward Alleyn and opened in 1619. The college contains a noted picture gallery.

Duma (dö'mä). [Also: **Wadoma, Waduma.**] Subgroup of the Bantu-speaking Shona of SE Africa, inhabiting SE Southern Rhodesia.

Dumaguete (dö.mä.gā'tā). Town in the Philippine Islands, the capital of Negros Oriental province, on Negros island. It is situated on the E coast, near the S entrance to the Strait of Tañon. 9,366 (1948).

Dumain (dū.mān'). French lord in attendance on the King of Navarre, in Shakespeare's *Love's Labor's Lost.*

Dumanoir (dü.mȧ.nwȧr), **Philippe François Pinel.** b. in Guadeloupe, West Indies, July 31, 1806; d. at Pau, France, Nov. 16, 1865. French playwright, noted particularly as a writer of sketches for vaudeville.

Dumaran (dö.mä.rän'). Island in Palawan province, in the Philippine Islands. It is situated E of the N part of Palawan island, from which it is separated by Dumaran Channel. It is high and well wooded. Area, 125 sq. mi.; pop. 2,409 (1939).

Dumarchey (dü.mȧr.shā), **Pierre.** Original name of **Mac Orlan, Pierre.**

Dumarsais (dü.mȧr.se), **César Chesneau.** [Also, **Du Marsais.**] b. at Marseilles, France, July 17, 1676; d. at Paris, June 11, 1756. French grammarian and writer on philosophy, author of *Traité des tropes.*

Dumas (dö'mạs). Town in SE Arkansas, in Desha County, ab. 75 mi. SE of Little Rock, in a cotton-producing area. 2,512 (1950).

Dumas. City in NW Texas, county seat of Moore County, ab. 48 mi. by road N of Amarillo, on the high plains of NW Texas. It was first a cattle center, then developed wheat agriculture, and has recently become an industrial center with the discovery of large oil and gas fields. There are carbon black plants, a helium plant, a zinc smelter, and an oil refinery. In the decade between the last two U.S. censuses its population more than doubled. 2,117 (1940), 6,127 (1950).

Dumas (dü.mȧ), **Alexandre.** [Original name, **Alexandre Davy de la Pailleterie.**] b. at Jérémie, Haiti, March 25, 1762; d. at Villers-Cotterets, Aisne, France, Feb. 26, 1806. French general; son of Marquis Alexandre Davy de la Pailleterie and a Negress; father of Alexandre Dumas (1802–70). He was distinguished in the wars of the Revolution and of the Directory, and was called by Napoleon "the Horatius Cocles of the Tyrol." He commanded the French cavalry in the Egyptian expedition.

Dumas, Alexandre (dü.mȧ; Anglicized, dö'mä, dö.mä'). [Called **Dumas père** (per).] b. at Villers-Cotterets, Aisne, France, July 24, 1802; d. in his son's home, at Puys, near Dieppe, France, Dec. 5, 1870. French novelist and dramatist. His full name, now never used, is Alexandre Dumas-Davy de la Pailleterie. He is generally called Dumas père in order to distinguish him from his son, Dumas fils. Dumas was educated by a priest and became a clerk in the office of a local lawyer, later working as a law clerk at Crépy. In 1822 or 1823 he went to Paris, where he met the great French actor Talma, and where, through the aid of General Foy, he was taken into the service of the duke of Orléans. At about this time he began to write dramatic pieces with his Swedish friend Adolphe de Leuven. In 1823 he began an affair with Marie Catherine Labay, a French dressmaker, by whom he had a son, Alexandre, who was to become almost as famous as himself. In 1825 he wrote an *Elegy on the Death of General Foy.* He made his first success as a romantic dramatist with *Henry III and His Court,* which was produced at the Comédie Française on Feb. 11, 1829. It won him the friendship of Hugo, whose *Hernani* was hailed as a triumph of romanticism a year later, of de Vigny, and a promotion from the duke of Orléans, who made him librarian of the Palais Royal. At the Odéon in March, 1830, he duplicated the success of *Henry III* with *Christine,* a poetic play in five acts, with a prologue and an epilogue. The year 1831 saw the production of three more plays, *Napoleon Bonaparte* (at the Odéon on Jan. 10), *Antony* (at the Porte St.-Martin, May 3), a psychological drama whose Byronic hero is largely a self-portrait, and, at the same theater, *Richard Darlington* (Dec. 10), suggested by Scott's *Chronicles of the Canongate.* It is also the year in which Dumas admitted his paternity and acknowledged his son. In 1832 Dumas left Paris for political reasons. In 1840 he married Ida Ferrier, an actress; however, they did not live long together, the wife going to Italy shortly after the marriage. In February, 1847, he opened his own theater, the Historique, which he had founded for the production of his own plays, with a dramatization of his novel *Queen Margot.* In 1851 he was at Brussels, and in 1853, back at Paris, he was publishing *Le Mousquetaire,* a daily newspaper devoted to art and literature. Written almost entirely by Dumas, it contained his *Memoirs,* and lasted until 1857, when it became a weekly, the *Monte-Cristo,* that lived for three years. In 1858 he was in Russia, and in 1860 in Sicily with Garibaldi. He lived at Naples for four years and then returned to Paris. In 1868 his daughter, Madame Petel, came to live with and take care of him. Dumas was a terrific worker and he turned out a staggering amount of work, so much that it was not physically possible for all of it to be the product of one man working alone. He was aided by a group of authors, who gathered material for him under his direction, wrote it up according to his own plans, given to them in outline form, and he then supervised their work, revised it, and largely rewrote it in its final form. It is also believed that some novels bearing his name on the title page are the work of other hands. Dumas's novels are: *The Chevalier d'Harmenthal* and its sequel, *The Regent's Daughter* (1843, 1845), dealing with France in 1718–19, and Louis XV, Cardinal d'Alberoni, the duke of Orléans (the regent), and his daughter, Mademoiselle de Chartres, among the leading characters; *Ascanio* (1844), dealing with Paris and Fontainebleau in 1540, with Cellini and Francis I dominating the story. One of his best-known and most popular works is *The Count of Monte Cristo* (1844–45), the story of a brave sailor, Edmond Dantes, and of his friends and enemies. A period of 40 years (1625–65) is covered in the trilogy *The Three Musketeers, Twenty Years After,* and *The Vicomte de Bragelonne* (1844, 1845, 1848–50, the last in 26 vols.); 18th-century France, in the period 1770–93, is covered in a series of five romances, *Memoirs of a Physician* (1846–48), *The Queen's Necklace* dealing with one of the most famous affairs in French history, *The Taking of the Bastille* (1852, *Ange Pitou* in French), *The Countess of Charny* (1853–55, in 19 vols.), and *Le Chevalier de Maison Rouge* (1846). Some of the characters who walk through the pages of this quintet are Louis XV, du Barry, Swedenborg, John Paul Jones, Voltaire, Rousseau, Diderot, Louis XVI, Marie Antoinette, Lafayette, Mesmer, Robespierre, Marat, Madame de Staël, Rouget de Lisle, Thomas Paine, Guillotin (of the beheading machine), Napoleon, as a second lieutenant, Necker, Cagliostro, and Danton. *Marguerite de Valois* (1845) begins with the Saint Bartholomew Massacre and ends with the death of Charles IX and the crowning of Henry III. *Agénor de Mauleon* (1846) is a picture of Spain and France in the second half of the 14th century, with Don Pedro (called "the Cruel," king of Castile and León), Queen Blanche, Charles V of France, Edward, the Black Prince, and Pope Urban V as characters. *Chicot the Jester* (1846, *La Dame de Monsoreau*) and *The Forty Five Guardsmen* (1848, also *The Forty Five, Les Quarante-cinq* in French) are connected stories dealing with Henri III, Catherine de Médicis, Henry of Navarre, and Cardinal de Lorraine. *The Black Tulip* (1850), set in 17th-century Holland, tells the story of the horrible murder of the de Witt brothers, John and Cornelius. *Olympe* *de Clèves* (1852) is a picture of court life in the 18th century and the story of a beautiful actress. *The Companions of Jehu* (1857) shows us Napoleon as first consul, Josephine, his brothers Lucien and Joseph, Fouché, and the Chouan leader Georges Cadoudal. *The She-Wolves of Machecoul* (1859) has a 19th-century setting, the time being the period 1832–43, the theme the attempted Vendean rebellion of the duchess of Berry, and some of the characters Louis XVIII, Louis Philippe, and La Rochejacquelein. *The Neapolitan Lovers* and *Love and Liberty* (both 1864) deal with Naples and Sicily in 1798–99, and center around the career of Luisa San Felice, heroine of the Neapolitan Revolution. Nelson, King Ferdinand, Cardinal Ruffo, Sir William Hamilton, and his wife and Nelson's mistress Emma Hamilton are some of the historical characters. *The Whites and the Blues* (1868), with France at the end of the 18th century, shows us Napoleon,Madame de Staël, Madame Recamier, Constant, Talleyrand, Fouché, Murat, and Junot. *The Two Dianas* (1846–47) deals with France in the reigns of Henry II and Francis II, whose deathbed scene is described. Other characters are Diane de Poitiers, Catherine de Médicis, Mary Stuart (Mary, Queen of Scots), Marguerite de Valois, Queen Mary of England, Charles IX, and Philip II of Spain. Its sequel is *The Page of the Duke of Savoy* (1855), in which many of the same characters appear, as well as the duke of Guise, Coligny, Cardinal de Lorraine, and Cardinal Pole. Among those who are known to have helped Dumas, in lesser or greater degree, are Auguste Maquet, Paul Lacroix (who had many pseudonyms), Paul Bocage, J. P. Mallefille, and Pier Angelo Fiorentino, who, with Maquet, assisted him in writing *Monte Cristo*. All of *The Two Dianas* is believed to be the work of François Paul Meurice, although his name is not on the title page. In addition to his novelistic output, huge even with all allowances made for as much aid as he may have received, Dumas wrote *Louis XIV and his Century* (4 vols., 1845) and his interesting *Memoirs* (20 vols., 1852–54). His complete works were published at Paris (1860–64) in 277 volumes. Two English authors who knew how to tell a story, Thackeray and Stevenson, were Dumas enthusiasts and found reading his romances a pleasure that was not spoiled by repetition.

Dumas, Alexandre. [Called **Dumas fils** (fēs).] b. at Paris, July 27, 1824; d. there, Nov. 27, 1895. French dramatist, novelist, social reformer, and member of the French Academy, to which he was elected on Jan. 30, 1874; son of Alexandre Dumas (1802–70). He is usually referred to as Dumas fils to distinguish him from his father. The little formal schooling he had was made unhappy by the cruel insults and the callous jokes of his school fellows about his illegitimate birth, and, as his later writings show, it left wounds that never healed. As a poet he wrote *La Chronique* (1842) and *Péchés de jeunesse* (1847), and as an essayist, *Tue-la, Monsieur Alphonse* (1874), *La Question du divorce* (1880), and *La Recherche de la paternité* (1883), but it is not as a poet or a writer of essays on moral topics that he is remembered. Like his father, he wrote plays and novels, but, unlike his father, he is remembered chiefly for one play, *La Dame aux camélias*, whereas the name of the elder Dumas calls to mind half a dozen novels. His dramas include *Le Demi-Monde* (1855), a comedy of manners, *La Question d'argent* (1857), a "stock exchange" play, as its title suggests, *Le Fils naturel* (1858), and *Le Père prodigue* (1859), the very names of which are suggestive, one referring to his own condition, and the other to his father's mode of life. *L'Ami des femmes* (1864), *Une Visite de noces*, and *La Princesse Georges* (both 1871) are problem plays. He again uses the stage as a platform for the discussion of social and moral issues in *Les Idées de Madame Aubray* (1867), in which he develops the thesis that the seducer is morally bound to marry his victim, in *La Femme de Claude* (1873), which defends the right of the husband to slay a wife who has violated her marriage vows, and in *L'Étrangère* (1876), in which the husband is the wrongdoer. With six of the leading French actors (Coquelin, Got, and Mounet-Sully, Sarah Bernhardt, Sophie Croizette, and Madeleine Brohan) in the latter play, its success was assured. Other plays that came from his pen are *La Princesse de Bagdad* (1881), *Denise* (1885), and *Francillon* (1887). As a patriotic Frenchman, alive to the suffering and the weakness of his country, he wrote *Nouvelle lettre de Junius* (1870) and two *Lettres sur les choses du jour* (1872). His novels are *Césarine* (1848), *Le Docteur Servan*, *Antonine*, and *Tristan le Roux* (all 1849), *Henri de Navarre* and *Trois hommes forts* (both 1850), *L'Affaire Clémenceau, mémoire de l'accusé* (1866), in which he anticipates the thesis of *La Femme de Claude* and also that of a prose pamphlet, *L'Homme-Femme* (1872). His most famous work, *La Dame aux camélias*, is both a novel (1848) and a play (1849, but not produced, because of censorship regulations, until 1852). It is a sentimental but moving portrait of a Paris courtesan, Marguerite Gautier, who has had many love affairs but has never known love until she meets Armand Duval. At his father's request she gives him up, in order to "save" him and his career. When the father realizes his mistake, it is too late. Marguerite dies, happy in the knowledge that Armand is at her side and happy in his love. Camille, as the heroine is called from her extreme fondness for the flower (the play is usually called *Camille* in English translation), is one of a long line, if not the first, of long-suffering ladies who are victims of consumption, a condition that has romantic possibilities that the romantic writer has not neglected. Marguerite was based on a well-known Parisian woman, known to Dumas, and it is believed that she was his mistress. The Italian actress Eleonora Duse was the first to play the role, which has since been played by many English, American, and European artists, on the stage, the screen, and the air. The appeal of the play, of the heroine's story as Dumas tells it (in both forms), and of her character, has been discussed by critics and students of art and human nature in an attempt to discover the secret of the success of what is, after all, a rather conventional story. Dumas's interest in and extreme preoccupation with questions of morality and ethics has been considered strange in view of his own background and that of his father, but, from the psychological viewpoint, it is probably that very background, a personal matter with him, that accounts for and explains the interest.

Dumas, Jean Baptiste André. b. at Alais, Gard, France, July 14, 1800; d. at Cannes, France, April 11, 1884. French chemist and physiologist, professor of organic chemistry in the École de Médecine at Paris. He published *Traité de chimie appliqué aux arts* (1828–45), and various other works.

Dumas, Guillaume Mathieu, Comte. b. at Montpellier, France, Dec. 23, 1753; d. at Paris, Oct. 16, 1837. French general and historian, author of *Précis des événements militaires* (1816–26).

Du Maurier (dū̦ môr′i.ā), **Daphne.** [Title, Lady **Browning.**] b. at London, May 13, 1907—. English novelist and biographer; second daugher of Sir Gerald Du Maurier. She married (1932) lieutenant general Sir F. A. M. Browning of the Grenadier Guards. She is the author of a biography of her father, *Gerald, a Portrait* (1934), and of *The du Mauriers* (1937). Her novels include *The Loving Spirit* (1931), *Jamaica Inn* (1936), *Rebecca* (1938), *Frenchman's Creek* (1941), *Hungry Hill* (1943), *The King's General* (1946), *The Parasites* (1950), *My Cousin Rachel* (1952), and *Kiss Me Again, Stranger* (1953).

Du Maurier, George Louis Palmella Busson. b. at Paris, March 6, 1834; d. at London, Oct. 8, 1896. English artist and novelist. He was educated at Paris, and went to England at the age of 17, studying later at Paris with Gleyre. He was noted for his illustrations in *Punch* and other periodicals. He wrote and illustrated *Peter Ibbetsen* (1892), *Trilby* (1894), and *The Martian* (1897). The hypnotist Svengali in *Trilby* is his most famous character.

Du Maurier, Sir **Gerald.** b. March 26, 1873; d. at London, April 11, 1934. English actor-manager; son of George Louis Palmella Busson Du Maurier, and father of Daphne Du Maurier. He made his debut (1894) in *An Old Jew*, and toured with Forbes-Robertson and later with Beerbohm Tree. He was well known as a philanthropist. He performed in *Trilby*, *The Seats of the Mighty*, *Escape*, and other plays, including Shakespearian revivals.

Dumbarton (dum.bär′tǫn). Royal burgh, seaport, and market town in W central Scotland, county seat of Dumbartonshire, situated at the confluence of the rivers Leven and Clyde, ab. 13 mi. NW of Glasgow, ab. 416 mi. N of

London by rail. It has a shipbuilding industry and a linen trade. Dumbarton Castle is here. 24,563 (est. 1948).

Dumbarton Castle. Fortress overhanging the river Clyde, at Dumbarton, Scotland, on a rocky eminence 240 ft. high. It has been called the Gibraltar of Scotland.

Dumbarton Oaks Conference (dum′bär.tọn ōks′). Meeting (Aug. 21–Oct. 7, 1944) of representatives of Great Britain, the U.S., and the U.S.S.R. (China replaced the U.S.S.R. after Sept. 29) at a mansion ("Dumbarton Oaks") in the District of Columbia. The purpose of the meeting was to prepare a basic draft for a proposed world organization. Guided largely by draft proposals of the U.S. State Department, a text was written that afterwards (1945) formed the basis of the United Nations Charter at San Francisco. The main question on which agreement was not reached at Dumbarton Oaks was the veto problem; this was not settled until the Yalta and San Francisco conferences.

Dumbartonshire (dum.bär′tọn.shir) or **Dumbarton** (dum.bär′tọn). [Also: **Dunbartonshire, Dunbarton.**] Maritime and inland county in W central Scotland, consisting of a main portion and an exclave. The main portion is bounded on the N by Perthshire, on the NE and E by Stirlingshire, on the SE by Lanarkshire, on the S by Renfrewshire and the Firth of Clyde, and on the W by Loch Long and Argyllshire. The detached portion is contained between Stirlingshire on the N and Lanarkshire on the S. The surface in the northern portion, between Loch Long and Loch Lomond, is mountainous; southward, toward the Firth of Clyde, it is low-lying and level. There is much industry along the banks of the rivers Clyde and Leven; shipbuilding is particularly important along the Clyde. The county produces some coal, slate, and ironstone. Dumbarton is the county seat; area, ab. 241 sq. mi.; pop. 164,263 (1951).

Dumbiedikes (dum′bi.dīks). Awkward Scottish laird in Sir Walter Scott's novel *The Heart of Midlothian.* He wants to marry Jeanie Deans, but on being refused promptly marries another.

Dum-Dum (dum′dum). [Also, **Dumdum.**] Town and military station 4½ mi. NE of Calcutta, West Bengal, Union of India: site of a major airport. Pop. ab. 20,000.

Duméril (dü.mā.rēl), **André Marie Constant.** b. at Amiens, France, Jan. 1, 1774; d. at Paris, Aug. 2, 1860. French physician and zoölogist. He was the author of *Erpétologie générale* (1835–51).

Duméril, Auguste Henri André. b. at Paris, Nov. 30, 1812; d. there, Nov. 12, 1870. French naturalist; son of André Marie Constant Duméril. He wrote *Histoire naturelle des poissons* (1865–70).

Du Mez (dü.mā′), **Andrew Grover.** b. at Horicon, Wis., April 26, 1885—. American pharmaceutical chemist. Associated (1917–26) with U.S. Public Health Service hygienical laboratory; dean (1926 *et seq.)* of University of Maryland school of pharmacy; first to prepare emetine bismuthous iodide as remedy for amoebic dysentery. Editor of *The Yearbook of the American Pharmaceutical Association* (1921–34), *Pharmaceutical Abstracts* (1935–41), and other publications.

Dumfries (dum.frēs′). Royal burgh, river port, and manufacturing town in S Scotland, county seat of Dumfriesshire, situated on the river Nith, ab. 15 mi. NW of Annan, ab. 332 mi. N of London by rail. It has manufactures of tweeds, hosiery, and farm machinery. Dumfries was famous in early border warfare. The tomb of Robert Burns and the house where he died in 1796 are here. Dumfries is the principal town in S Scotland. Maxwelltown is a suburb. 27,128 (est. 1948).

Dumfriesshire (dum.frēsh′shir) or **Dumfries** (dum.frēs′). Maritime county in S Scotland. It is bounded on the N by Lanarkshire, Peebleshire, and Selkirkshire, on the NE by Roburghshire, on the SE by Cumberland (in England), on the S by Solway Firth, on the SW and W by Kirkcudbrightshire, and on the NW by Ayrshire. The coastline is low and sandy. Dumfriesshire contains the valleys of Eskdale in the eastern part, Annandale in the center, and Nithsdale in the west. The leading occupation is the rearing of livestock. Lead, coal, red sandstone, and limestone are worked. The county has manufactures of tweeds. County seat, Dumfries; area, ab. 1,075 sq. mi.; pop. 85,656 (1951).

Dumiat (dụm.yät′). Arabic name of **Damietta.**

Dümichen (dü′mē.ċhen). **Johannes.** b. at Weissholz, in Silesia, Oct. 15, 1833; d. at Strasbourg, Feb. 7, 1894. German Egyptologist. He was appointed professor of Egyptology at Strasbourg in 1872, and published *Bauurkunde der Tempelanlagen von Dendera* (1865), *Geographische Inschriften altägyptischer Denkmäler* (1865–85), *Altägyptische Kalenderinschriften* (1866), *Historische Inschriften altägyptischer Denkmäler* (1867–69), *Resultate einer auf Befehl Sr. Majestät des Königs Wilhelm von Preussen 1868 nach Ägypten gesendeten archäologisch-photographischen Expedition* (1871), and others.

Dummer (dum′ėr), **Jeremiah.** b. at Newbury, Mass., Sept. 14, 1645; d. May 25, 1718. American silversmith, engraver, and portrait painter. In his 14th year he began an eight-year apprenticeship under John Hull, after which he established his own workshop, prospered, and became a leading citizen of Boston, an officer in the militia and the incumbent successively of several public offices. He was a most accomplished craftsman, with excellent taste, and some of the most admirable silverware of that period came from his shop. Exhibitions of his work in recent times at the Boston Museum of Fine Arts and at the Metropolitan Museum of Art in New York revived appreciation of his accomplishments. Little is known of his work as an engraver except that he executed plates for the printing of money for Connecticut. That he also painted portraits seems to have been known to few in his own day and was forgotten until in modern times several such paintings, including a self-portrait and one of his wife, and bearing his name as painter, were discovered. It seems probable that he was the first native-born American portraitist.

Dummer, Jeremiah. b. at Boston, c1680; d. at Plaistow, England, May 19, 1739. American scholar; son of Jeremiah Dummer (1645–1718). He was agent for Massachusetts in England (1710–21) and wrote *Defence of the New England Charters* (1728).

Dümmler (düm′lėr), **Ernst.** b. at Berlin, Jan. 2, 1830; d. at Friedrichroda, Germany, Sept. 11, 1902. German historian. He served as professor (1858 *et seq.*) at the University of Halle, also as president of the central directorate of the *Monumenta Germaniae historica.* Author of *Geschichte des ostfränkischen Reiches* (History of the East-Frankish Empire, 1862–65).

Dumnorix (dum′nọ.riks). Killed in Gaul, 54 B.C. A chief of the Aedui; brother of Divitiacus. Pardoned once by Caesar for permitting hostile forces through his territory, he led his cavalry from the Roman camp as Caesar prepared the British invasion and was captured and killed.

Dumont (dū′mont). Borough in NE New Jersey, in Bergen County near Paterson. 13,013 (1950).

Du Mont, Allen Balcom. b. at Brooklyn, N.Y., Jan. 29, 1901—. American radio and television engineer. He graduated (1924) from Rensselaer Polytechnic Institute and, after a period with Westinghouse (1924–28) and De Forest Radio (1928–31), established (1931) his own company in Passaic, N.J., to manufacture cathode ray equipment. He invented the so-called magic eye tube for visual radio tuning. The commercial development of television is in large part due to his pioneering work in cathode ray tube improvements.

Dumont (dü.môn), **Henri.** b. near Liége, Belgium, c1610; d. at Paris, May 8, 1684. Belgian church composer. He was organist (1639–84) at St. Paul's, Paris, where he also directed (1665 *et seq.*) the court chapel.

Dumont, Jean. d. at Vienna, 1726. French publicist and historical writer. He was the author of *Nouveau voyage au Levant* (1694) and *Mémoires politiques pour servir à la parfaite intelligence de l'histoire de la paix de Ryswick* (1699).

Dumont, Pierre Étienne Louis. b. at Geneva, Switzerland, July 18, 1759; d. at Milan, Italy, Sept. 29, 1829. Swiss scholar, literary coadjutor of Mirabeau. He was a disciple of Bentham, whose system he expounded in *Traité de la législation* (1802), *Théorie des peines et des récompenses* (1811), *Tactique des assemblées legislatives* (1815), *Preuves judiciaires* (1823), and *De l'organisation judiciaire* (1828).

Dumont d'Urville (dür.vēl), **Jules Sébastien César.** b. at Condé-sur-Noireau, Calvados, France, May 23, 1790; killed near Paris, May 8, 1842. French navigator and rear admiral. He took part (1819–20) in an expedition to the Greek archipelago and the Black Sea, and circumnavigated the globe as commander of two expeditions (*Astrolabe*, 1826–29, and *Zelée*, 1837–40); on the second he discovered the Adélie Coast and other points in Antarctica. He wrote narratives of his voyages.

Dumoulin (dü.mö.laṅ), **Charles.** [Latinized surname, **Molinaeus.**] b. at Paris, 1500; d. 1566. French jurist. He became a Calvinist, and for a time had to live in exile in Germany, but eventually returned to France. He was involved in many controversies, being at times attacked by Calvinists as well as by Catholics. Denouncing feudal privileges, and exalting the monarch as the sole source of legal authority, he had an influence of considerable importance at that historical momnet of transition. Friends and opponents alike acknowledged his eminence as a jurisconsult. Perhaps his two most important works were *Sommaire du livre analytique des contrats, usures, rentes constituées intérêts et monnoyes* and *Extricatio labyrinthi dividui et individui.*

Dumoulin Islets (du.mö'lin, dü.mö.laṅ'). Group of about 10 small islets in Antarctica, paralleling the coast directly W of Point Géologie, along the Adélie Coast, in ab. 66°37′ S., 140°10′ E. The French expedition under J. S. C. Dumont d'Urville landed on one of these islets in 1840.

Dumouriez (dü.mö.ryā), **Charles François.** b. at Cambrai, France, Jan. 25, 1739; d. at Turville Park, near Henley-on-Thames, England, March 14, 1823. French general. He served in the Seven Years' War, obtained the rank of captain in 1763, served as quartermaster general in the expedition against Corsica in 1768, was sent by the duc de Choiseul to Poland on a secret mission in 1770, and was promoted to major general in 1788. At the beginning of the French Revolution he joined the Jacobins and pronounced in favor of political reform without abandoning his loyalty to the court, and in 1792, after Mirabeau's death, joined the Girondins and held separately for a short period the ministries of foreign affairs and of war. He was subsequently appointed to the command of the north as lieutenant general under Marshal Nicolas Luckner, and in conjunction with François Christophe Kellermann inflicted a decisive defeat (Sept. 20, 1792) on the Prussian troops at Valmy. He conducted an expedition (1792–93) against the Austrian Netherlands, in the course of which he gained a victory over the Austrians at Jemappes (Nov. 6, 1792) and occupied Brussels, but was defeated at Neerwinden (March 18, 1793). Estranged from the republican party by the execution of the king, he was recalled by the Convention, but instead of returning to France he fled to the Austrian camp, and passed the rest of his life in exile, intriguing with French royalists and advising in the military campaigns against Napoleon.

Dun (dun), **Robert Graham.** b. at Chillicothe, Ohio, Aug. 7, 1826; d. Nov. 10, 1900. American mercantile credit specialist. Joined (1850) the mercantile agency of Tappen and Douglass; became owner (1859), changing name first to Dun, Boyd and Company and later to R. G. Dun and Company (now Dun and Bradstreet, Inc.). The original firm supplied credit ratings of country merchants for New York wholesale houses and expanded widely as business and communication facilities improved. A weekly report of business conditions, *Dun's Review*, was started in 1893.

Duna (dö'nô). Hungarian name of the **Danube.**

Duna (dö'nä). Tartar name of the **Don,** U.S.S.R.

Düna (dü'nä). German name of the **Dvina,** in W U.S.S.R.

Dünaburg (dü'nä.bu̇rk). German name of **Daugavpils.**

Dunaföldvár (dö'nô.féld'vär). [Also, **Duna-Földvár.**] Town in C Hungary, on the W bank of the Danube River ab. 48 mi. S of Budapest. It has flour mills, potteries, and hemp and flax processing plants. 11,256 (1948).

Dunagiri (dö.na̤.gir'i). Peak in N Union of India, in N Uttar Pradesh state (United Provinces), in the main range of the Himalayas ab. 12 mi. NW of the great peak of Nanda Devi. Elevation, ab. 23,182 ft.

Dunai or **Dunay** (dö.nī'). Russian name of the **Danube.**

Dunaj (dö'nī). Czech name of the **Danube.**

Dunajec (dö.nä'yets). River in S Poland, rising on the N slopes of the High Tatra Mountains, and flowing generally NE to join the Vistula ab. 36 mi. E of Kraków. It twists through a scenic mountain valley and cuts through several chalk ridges before emerging onto the plain of the Vistula. Length, ab. 129 mi.

Dunant (dü.näṅ), **Jean Henri.** b. at Geneva, Switzerland, May 8, 1828; d. at Heiden, Switzerland, Oct. 30, 1910. Swiss philanthropist, founder of the Red Cross and winner (1901) with Frédéric Passy of the first Nobel peace prize. While visiting (1859) the battlefield of Solferino, in Italy, he observed the lack of an adequate ambulance corps, and thereafter applied himself to urging measures for the relief of the wounded in wartime. His efforts, sustained by his countrymen, resulted in the conference which adopted the Geneva Convention (an international agreement setting up a code for the treatment in wartime of prisoners of war and the sick and wounded) in 1864 and established the International Red Cross. Having devoted his whole fortune to the cause, he was forced to support himself by teaching, but received a pension from the empress of Russia. His *Souvenir de Solferino* (1862) made a deep impression on the public. He published also *Fraternité et charité internationale en temps de guerre* (1864), and other works.

Dunărea (dö'nu.ryä). Rumanian name of the **Danube.**

Dunav (Serbo-Croatian, dö'näv; Bulgarian, dö'näf). Serbo-Croatian and Bulgarian name of the **Danube.**

Dunbar (dun.bär'). Royal burgh, seaport, and holiday resort in SE Scotland, in East Lothian, situated on the North Sea near the mouth of the Firth of Forth, ab. 11 mi. NE of Haddington, ab. 364 mi. N of London by rail. The ruins of Dunbar Castle, celebrated in Scottish history, are here. It was besieged by the English in 1336. Dunbar was formerly an important herring fishery center, but the trade has now practically disappeared. The town is becoming a popular seaside resort. At the battle of Dunbar (1296) Edward I of England defeated John Baliol, a result of the victory being Edward's declaration of himself as king of Scotland. Dunbar is notable in history also as the place from which Edward II embarked in 1314 after his defeat at Bannockburn, and as the place from which Mary, Queen of Scots, eloped with Bothwell in 1567. Cromwell's forces inflicted a crushing defeat here on the Scots on Sept. 3, 1650. Pop. 3,888 (est. 1948).

Dunbar (dun'bär). City in W West Virginia, in Kanawha County, in an oil and gas producing area. The city manufactures glassware, farm machinery, and enamelware. 8,032 (1950).

Dunbar (dun.bär'), **Agnes.** [Title: Countess of **Dunbar and March;** called **"Black Agnes."**] b. c1312; d. 1369. Scottish heroine, noted for her successful defense of Dunbar Castle in 1337–38. She was given the epithet "Black Agnes" because of her dark skin.

Dunbar, Battle of. Battle (April 27, 1296) at Dunbar, Scotland, in which the Scots under John Baliol were defeated by the English under John de Warenne, Earl of Surrey and Sussex, with the result that Baliol resigned the crown of Scotland, and that the government was placed in the hands of an English regent. This name is also given to the battle between the Parliamentary army under Cromwell and the Scottish Royalists under Leslie, which was fought at Doon Hill near Dunbar, on Sept. 3, 1650, and in which the Scots were totally defeated.

Dunbar (dun'bär), **Charles Franklin.** b. at Abington, Mass., July 28, 1830; d. Jan. 29, 1900. American economist, first professor of political economy (1869–1900) at Harvard University.

Dunbar, Paul Laurence. b. at Dayton, Ohio, June 27, 1872; d. there, Feb. 9, 1906. American Negro author and poet. He was engaged in journalistic work at Dayton and New York, and was employed in the Congressional Library at Washington. Among the better known of his works are *Oak and Ivy* (1893), *Majors and Minors* (1895), *Lyrics of Lowly Life* (1896), *Lyrics of the Hearthside* (1899), *The Strength of Gideon* (1900), *The Fanatics* (1901), *The Sport of the Gods* (1902), a novel; *Lyrics of Love and Laughter* (1903), and *Lyrics of Sunshine and Shadow* (1905).

Dunbar (dun.bär'), **William.** b. probably in East Lothian, Scotland, c1460; d. c1525. Scottish poet. He was a Franciscan who did diplomatic service in France for James IV of Scotland and was afterward attached to the court as laureate. He is one of the Scottish Chaucerian school. His works include *The Thrissil and the Rois*

(The Thistle and the Rose, 1503), a prothalamium in honor of James IV and Margaret Tudor; *The Golden Targe*, a dream allegory on beauty and love; *Dance of the Seven Deadly Sins, Merle and Nightingale, The Two Mariit Wemen and the Wedo*, a lusty discourse that outdoes Chaucer's wife of Bath; and *Lament for the Makaris*, an elegy on the poets (makers) who preceded him.

Dunbarton (dun.bär′tọn) or **Dunbartonshire** (dun.bär′-tọn.shir). See **Dumbartonshire.**

Dunblane (dun.blān′). Police burgh and market town in C Scotland, in Perthshire, situated on Allan Water, ab. 5 mi. N of Stirling, ab. 422 mi. N of London by rail. It has a noted cathedral, restored in the period 1889–93, one of a very few Scottish specimens of Gothic architecture. The town was formerly the seat of a bishop. 2,895 (est. 1948).

Duncan (dung′kạn). City in S Oklahoma, county seat of Stephens County, in a petroleum, livestock, and farming area. It has a plant where oil-well equipment is manufactured and is a processing center for petroleum, cotton, and cottonseed and a marketing center for dairy products. 15,325 (1950).

Duncan. Unincorporated community in NW South Carolina, in Greenville County. 3,950 (1950).

Duncan I (of *Scotland*). King of Scotland. He succeeded to the throne c1034 on the death of his grandfather Malcolm II, and was assassinated by Macbeth, near Elgin, in 1040 or 1039. He appears in Shakespeare's *Macbeth.*

Duncan, Adam. [Title, 1st Viscount **Duncan of Camperdown.**] b. at Lundie, Scotland, July 1, 1731; d. in Scotland, Aug. 4, 1804. British admiral. He gained the victory of Camperdown over the Dutch fleet, on Oct. 11, 1797.

Duncan, Sir **Andrew Rae.** b. 1884; d. March 30, 1952. British statesman. Member (1940 *et seq.*) of Parliament; president (1940, 1941–42) of the Board of Trade; minister (1940–41, 1942–45) of supply.

Duncan, Donald Bradley. b. in Michigan, Sept. 1, 1896—. American naval officer. He served as deputy and chief of staff to the commander in chief of the U.S. Pacific fleet with the rank of vice-admiral. He was deputy chief (1947) for naval operations for air, and was appointed (March, 1947) to the National Advisory Committee for Aeronautics. He was assigned (1948) as commander of the U.S. navy second task fleet and became (1951) vice-chief of naval operations.

Duncan, Isadora. b. at San Francisco, May 27, 1878; d. at Nice, France, Sept. 14, 1927. American esthetic dancer, noted for her creative interpretations of music and poetry, danced in bare feet with the dancer clad in flowing scarves. Together with the other children in her family, she became interested in the dance at a very early age, and with her sister, Elizabeth, taught dancing at San Francisco. At New York, she was for two years a member of Augustin Daly's company. Leaving for England with members of her family, she studied Greek art at the British Museum, making great sacrifices, almost to the point of privation, but learning much that later influenced her dancing. Coming under the sponsorship of Mrs. Patrick Campbell, she soon became noted among a small but influential circle at London and Paris, and made a Continental tour as a member of Loie Fuller's company. She and her family spent a year at Athens, where they made an unsuccessful effort to establish a temple of dancing. On various occasions after 1906 she went on tour, rendering her unique interpretations of Chopin's *Marche Funèbre*, the *Marseillaise*, and Tschaikowsky's *Marche Slav*, among others. An advocate of free love, she bore two children out of wedlock, in 1905 and 1908; one was fathered by Edward Gordon Craig, the theatrical designer, and the other by a millionaire admirer who often gave her financial aid. The two children were drowned in an accident (1913) in France. A later child by an Italian sculptor was still-born. She toured South America in 1916 and the U.S. in 1917; when her attempt to set up her school at Athens was frustrated, she accepted the invitation of the Soviet authorities to establish it at Moscow. While in Russia, she married the revolutionary poet Sergei Yesenin, who committed suicide in 1925. She departed from Russia in 1924, and lived at Paris and Nice, experiencing difficult times. She died in an accident, when a long scarf she was wearing was caught in the moving wheels of an automobile. She wrote *My Life* (1927) and *The Art of the Dance* (1928).

Duncan, James. b. in Kincardinshire, Scotland, May 5, 1857; d. Sept. 14, 1928. American labor leader and first vice-president (1900–28) of the American Federation of Labor, for many years an associate of Samuel Gompers. Arrived (1880) in U.S.; delegate (1898) to the British Trade Union Conference; representative (1911) of the American Federation of Labor at an international conference at Budapest; U.S. envoy extraordinary (1917) with the Root mission to Russia; member (1919) of the American Labor mission to the Peace Conference at Paris.

Duncan, John. b. at Gilcomston, near Aberdeen, Scotland, 1796; d. at Edinburgh, Feb. 26, 1870. Scottish Hebraist and clergyman of the Presbyterian Church.

Duncan, Norman. b. at Brantford, Ontario, Canada, July 2, 1871; d. Oct. 18, 1916. Canadian educator and author. He was on the staff of the New York *Evening Post* (1897–1901), and was professor of rhetoric at Washington and Jefferson College (1902–06) and adjunct professor of English literature at the University of Kansas (1907–10). He published *The Soul of the Street* (1900), *Doctor Luke of Labrador* (1904), *Dr. Grenfell's Parish* (1905), *The Mother* (1905), *Every Man for Himself* (1908), *The Suitable Child* (1909), *The Measure of a Man* (1911), and others.

Duncan, Sir **Patrick.** b. Dec. 21, 1870; d. at Pretoria, South Africa, July 17, 1943. South African lawyer and politician, who served (1937–43) as governor general of the Union of South Africa. Entered (1894) British colonial service; treasurer (1901), colonial secretary (1903–06), and acting lieutenant governor (1906) of the Transvaal Colony; minister of interior, public health, and education (1921–24), and minister of mines (1933–36) of the Union of South Africa.

Duncan, Robert Kennedy. b. at Brantford, Ontario, Canada, 1869; d. 1914. American industrial chemist and educator. A graduate of the University of Toronto, he spent the years 1901–1906 in Europe, during some of that time studying radioactivity in the laboratory of the Curies. While professor of industrial chemistry (1906–10) at the University of Kansas, he originated the plan of industrial fellowships to promote research with the purpose of making chemistry more serviceable to industry. The results of this innovation led to an offer of the chair of industrial chemistry at the University of Pittsburgh, which he held from 1910 to 1914, and to the establishment at that university, in 1913, of the Mellon Institute of Industrial Research. Duncan was the author of *The New Knowledge* (1905), *The Chemistry of Commerce* (1907), and *Some Chemical Problems of Today* (1911).

Duncan, Thomas. b. at Kinclaven, Perthshire, Scotland, May 24, 1807; d. at Edinburgh, May 25, 1845. Scottish historical and portrait painter. Among his best-known works are *Charles Edward Asleep* and *Charles Edward and the Highlanders Entering Edinburgh.*

Duncansby Head (dung′kạnz.bi). [Also, **Duncansbay Head** (-bā).] The NE extremity of Scotland, near John o' Groat's House.

Duncan's Camp. See under **Birnam Hill.**

Dunce Boy, The. Play (1925) by Lula Vollmer.

Dunciad (dun′si.ad), **The.** Satirical poem (1728–42; published in four books, 1743) by Alexander Pope, directed against various contemporary writers. The goddess of dullness elects Lewis Theobald poet laureate of that realm. Owing to a quarrel between Colley Cibber and Pope, the latter substituted Cibber for Theobald in the fourth part, published in 1742. The bestowal of the laureateship on Cibber may have added to Pope's venom.

Duncker (dủng′kėr), **Karl.** b. at Berlin, March 25, 1781; d. there, July 15, 1869. German publisher at Berlin.

Duncker, Maximilian Wolfgang. b. at Berlin, Oct. 15, 1811; d. at Ansbach, Bavaria, Germany, July 21, 1886. German historian; son of Karl Duncker. He was professor at Halle (1842–57) and at Tübingen (1857–59). In the latter year he entered the service of the government. His works include *Origines Germanicae* (1840), *Geschichte des Altertums* (1852–57; 5th ed., 1878–83), and others.

Dundalk (dun.dôk'). [Irish, **Dún Dealgan.**] Urban district, market town and seaport in Leinster province, Irish Republic, county seat of County Louth, situated on the river Castletown near its influx to Dundalk Bay, ab. 46 mi. N of Dublin. Its port exports oats and livestock, and imports coal. Industries of the town include breweries and distilleries, flour mills, linen mills, and tobacco factories. The workshops of the Great Northern Railway are here. Dundalk is the county seat of County Louth, and a customs station. It was here that Sir John de Bermingham, at the head of 15,000 troops, met (1318) the Scots under Edward Bruce. After a short combat, the Scots were decisively defeated and Edward Bruce killed. 19,661(1951).

Dundalk Bay. Large bay in Leinster province, Irish Republic, in County Louth. Dundalk urban district and Dundalk harbor are at its head. Width at entrance, ab. 10 mi.

Dundas (dun'dạs). Town in Wentworth County, Ontario, Canada, situated ab. 6 mi. W of Hamilton, which is on Burlington Bay at the W extremity of Lake Ontario. 6,846 (1951).

Dundas (dun.das', dun'dạs), Sir **David.** b. at Edinburgh, 1735; d. Feb. 18, 1820. British army officer. He was appointed (1809) commander in chief of the army to succeed the duke of York, a position which he held until 1811, a period during which the victories of Talavera de la Reina and Bussaco were achieved in the Peninsular War. He devised a system for the British infantry and cavalry patterned after the Prussian code of tactics. Adopted by the duke of York, the system provided unity of action.

Dundas, Henry. [Titles: 1st Viscount **Melville,** Baron **Dunira.**] b. at Edinburgh, April 28, 1742; d. May 28, 1811. British statesman. He was lord advocate of Scotland from 1775 to 1783. He was an intimate friend and trusted lieutenant of Pitt, during whose first administration he was home secretary (1791–94) and secretary of war (1794–1801). In 1802 he was raised to the peerage as Viscount Melville by Addington, and in 1804, on the accession of Pitt's second ministry, was appointed first lord of the admiralty. He was impeached in 1806 on the charge of appropriating public money, but was acquitted by the House of Lords. During the impeachment he resigned his position in the cabinet.

Dundas, Henry. [Title, 3rd Viscount **Melville.**] b. 1801; d. near Edinburgh, Feb. 1, 1876. Scottish soldier; eldest son of Robert Saunders Dundas (1771–1851). Appointed (Nov. 28, 1841) colonel and aide-de-camp to the queen for his vigorous suppression of the Canadian rebellion (1837–38), during which he repulsed a group of American brigands near Prescott, in Ontario; second in command during the siege and capture of Multan, in India; commanded (1856–60) the forces in Scotland; general (Jan. 1, 1868).

Dundas, Robert. [Called Lord **Arniston the elder.**] b. 1685; d. 1753. Scottish jurist, noted for reintroducing "guilty" or "not guilty" as possible jury verdicts. He was solicitor general of Scotland (1717–20), lord advocate (1720), and dean of the Faculty of Advocates (1721); member of Parliament (1722); subsequently (1748–53) lord president of session.

Dundas, Robert. [Called Lord **Arniston the younger.**] b. July 18, 1713; d. at Edinburgh, Dec. 13, 1787. Scottish judge; son of Robert Dundas (1685–1753). Educated at Edinburgh University and studied Roman law at Utrecht and Paris; solicitor general for Scotland (1742–46); lord advocate (1754); member of Parliament for Midlothian (1754); lord president (1760 *et seq.*). His popularity declined in the celebrated Douglas peerage case when, on July 7, 1767, he cast his vote against Archibald (Stuart) Douglas, rendering a decision that was reversed by the House of Lords two years later.

Dundas, Robert Saunders. [Title, 2nd Viscount **Melville.**] b. in Scotland, 1771; d. near Edinburgh, June 10, 1851. English politician; son of Henry Dundas (1742–1811). Member of Parliament for Hastings (1794) and for Rye (1796); privy councilor and president of board of control in cabinet of duke of Portland (1807). He became Irish secretary (1809), but left it for former position in board of control (1809). Under Lord Liverpool he was first lord of the admiralty (1812–27); Melville Sound was named after him for his interest in arctic exploration.

Dundas Strait (dun'dạs). Strait which separates Melville Island from Cobourg Peninsula in the N part of Northern Territory, Australia.

Dundee (dun.dē'). City, royal burgh, seaport, market town, and manufacturing center in E Scotland, in Angus, situated on the N bank of the Firth of Tay at the foot of the Sidlaw Hills, ab. 18 mi. NE of Perth, ab. 452 mi. N of London by rail. Its industries include shipbuilding (especially of cargo craft), textile machinery manufactures (especially machinery for the jute, hemp, and linen trades), jute, hemp, and linen manufactures, fruit-preserving and confectionery trades (especially marmalade manufactures, for which it is noted), and linoleum and plastics manufactures. Dundee ranks second in Scottish commerce and is the most important center of jute manufactures in the British Isles. The jute trade began c1830. Imports consist chiefly of raw jute and flax, and linen yarns. Docks are extensive, occupying ab. 2 mi. of the riverside. Dundee is the seat of a university college, founded in 1882 and united with the University of St. Andrews in 1896. During the Reformation it was called the "Scottish Geneva." It was stormed by the marquis of Montrose in 1645, and by Monk in 1651. Dundee is the fourth largest city in Scotland. 177,333 (1951).

Dundee. Former name of **Aberdeen,** Miss.

Dunderberg (dun'dėr.bėrg). See **Donderberg.**

Dundonald (dun.don'ạld), 10th Earl of. Title of **Cochrane, Thomas.**

Dundreary (dun.drir'i), **Lord.** Indolent, foolish, and amusing Englishman in Tom Taylor's comedy *Our American Cousin.* To this part originally only 47 lines were given; but E. A. Sothern, to whom it was assigned, introduced various extravagances to suit himself. He became famous in it, and the whole play hinged on it. The side-whiskers called Dundrearies are named for the character.

Dundrennan Abbey (dun.dren'ạn). Ancient monastery near Kirkcudbright, Scotland. Now in ruins, it was built in 1140.

Dundrum Bay (dun'drum, dun.drum'). Inlet of the Irish Sea, in Ulster province, Northern Ireland, in County Down. Width, ab. 10 mi.

Dunedin (dun.ē'din). City in W Florida, in Pinellas County, on the Gulf of Mexico ab. 5 mi. N of Tampa. It is a tourist resort; vegetables and citrus fruits are produced in the area. 3,202 (1950).

Dunedin. Seaport on South Island, New Zealand, on Otago Harbor at the S end of the Canterbury Bight. It was founded in 1848. Gold was discovered in its neighborhood in 1861. Otago University, a branch of New Zealand University, is located here, and includes a school of mines. Pop., with suburbs, 95,457 (1951).

Dunellen (dun.el'ẹn). Borough in C New Jersey, in Middlesex County: printing establishments. 6,291 (1950).

Dunes, Battle of the. Victory gained by the allied French and English under Turenne, who were besieging Dunkerque, France, over the Spaniards under Don John of Austria, on the dunes near Dunkerque, on June 4, 1658.

Dunfermline (dun.fėrm'lin). City, royal burgh, and manufacturing town in E Scotland, in Fifeshire, ab. 13 mi. NW of Edinburgh, ab. 410 mi. N of London by rail. Dunfermline is situated on the Fifeshire coal field, and is an important industrial town whose manufactures include iron and brass, soaps and dyes, rayon and linen textiles, and tobacco. It has long been noted for its damasks. The town has a famous Benedictine Abbey dating from the 11th century. It was a burial place for many of the Scottish kings (11th to 14th centuries); among them, Robert I (Robert the Bruce), who is buried underneath the pulpit of the abbey church. Dunfermline was formerly a royal residence. Here Charles II signed the Covenant in 1650. Pop. 44,710 (1951).

Dunfermline, 1st Baron. Title of **Abercromby, James.**

Dungannon (dun.gan'ọn). Urban district and market town, in Ulster province, Northern Ireland, in County Tyrone ab. 34 mi. W of Belfast. It was the ancient seat of the O'Neils (or O'Neills). 4,345 (1947).

Dungannon, Baron of. See **O'Neill, Hugh.**

Dungarvan (dun.gär'vạn). Urban district, market town, and seaport in Munster province, Irish Republic, in County Waterford, situated on the river Colligan at its influx to Dungarvan Harbour, ab. 25 mi. SW of Waterford. 5,426 (1951).

Dungarvan Harbour. Inlet of St. George's Channel, in Munster province, Irish Republic, in County Waterford. Dungarvan urban district is at its head. Length, ab. 4 mi.; width at entrance, ab. 2 mi.

Dungeness (dunj'nes'). Low headland in SE England, at the S extremity of Kent, ab. 11 mi. SE of Rye.

Dungi (dün'gē). [Also, **Shulgi.**] fl. about the 21st century B.C. Mesopotamian king. His capital was in Ur. Many temples are extant undertaken by him and his father and predecessor in the third dynasty of Ur, Ur-Nammu (Urgur or Ur-Engur), who called themselves "Kings of Ur, Kings of Shumir (Shinar) and Akkad (Accad)."

Dunglison (dung'gli.sọn), **Robley.** b. at Keswick, England, Jan. 4, 1798; d. at Philadelphia, April 1, 1869. American physician and medical writer, author of *Dictionary of Medical Science and Literature* (1833).

Dunheved (dön'he''ved). Ancient name of **Launceston,** England.

Dunhill (dun'hil), **Thomas Frederick.** b. at London, Feb. 1, 1877; d. 1946. English composer. He studied at the Royal College of Music, London, and was assistant music master (1899–1908) at Eton College. His compositions include the comic operas *Happy Families* and *Tantivy Towers* (1931), the latter based upon an A. P. Herbert libretto. The opera *Enchanted Garden* was awarded publication (1925) by the Carnegie Trust. He also wrote a symphony in A minor.

Duni (dö'nē), **Egidio Romoaldo.** b. at Matera, Italy, Feb. 9, 1709; d. at Paris, June 11, 1775. Italian composer of operas, commonly considered a founder of the opéra bouffe. His most famous work is *Ninette à la cour.*

Dunira (dun.ir'ạ), Baron. See **Dundas, Henry.**

Dunk (dungk), **George Montagu.** [Title, 2nd Earl of **Halifax;** called **"Father of the Colonies."**] b. in England, Oct. 5, 1716; d. there, June 8, 1771. English politician, called "Father of the Colonies" for his work in extending American trade; son of George Montagu (d. 1739). He took the name of Dunk on marrying an heiress of that name. For his aid in founding the colony of Nova Scotia when president of the Board of Trade (1748–61), the city of Halifax was named after him (1749). He was nominated lord lieutenant of Ireland (1761) and created first lord of the admiralty and made secretary of state (1762), and was a member of the triumvirate with Sir Charles Wyndham, 2nd Earl of Egremont, and George Grenville (1763), but the ministry was dismissed (1765). Under his nephew Frederick North, Lord North, he became lord privy seal (1770).

Dunkards (dung'kạrdz). [Also: **Dunkers** or (sometimes) **Tunkers.**] Popular name, derived from the German word meaning "to dip," of a sect of German Baptists, which by various secessions has become divided into several denominations. Founded in 1708 by Alexander Mack, a miller, at Swartzenau on the Oder, they became the objects of persecution, and a group of them led by Peter Becker migrated to Pennsylvania and settled in Germantown (now part of Philadelphia) in 1719. Subsequently they established other communities in Pennsylvania, and in small numbers spread to the West and to Canada. Their first church was erected at Germantown in 1723, and there they set up a press which printed the first German Bible in America. Becker's followers organized as the Church of the Brethren, and this denomination, also known today as Conservative Dunkers, remains the largest, with more than 1,000 churches and upward of 180,000 members, governed by regional conferences and an annual general conference; it supports colleges, home and foreign missions, and a publishing house. The first schism occurred in 1728, when the German Seventh Day Baptists (not identical with the Seventh Day Baptist Church), established the famous Ephrata Cloisters, famous for music and artistic crafts, where communal living was practiced; but celibacy also being a rule of this group, it has almost disappeared, its decline not checked even by the abandonment of celibacy and of community of goods. Another secession led to the setting up, in 1848, of the Church of God, whose members, now thought to number less than 1,0[illegible], are known as New Dunkers. A third separation occurred in 1881, resulting in the denomination known as Old German Baptist Brethren, or Old Order Dunkers, who have several score of churches and a membership approaching 4,000; while the Brethren Church, or Progressive Dunkers, the outcome of a fourth schism, in 1882, claims upward of 17,000 members. The Dunkards try to live simply and strictly by the precepts and examples of the Holy Scriptures as they understand them, carried into all the affairs of life, and to reject all vanity and all worldly ways for which they can find no Biblical authority. Excepting the Progressives, they dress severely, shun dancing and other frivolities, permit no musical instruments in their homes, forbid their members to make, sell or use intoxicants, to seek higher education, or to engage in politics. They were also among the earliest opponents of slavery. They practice "trine immersion," each candidate for church membership being "dipped" three times as the names of the Holy Trinity are invoked. The divisions of the sect were occasioned by the revolt of some groups against too strict insistence upon, and by others against too much relaxation of, these austerities. The Progressives, while holding to the concept of conforming life to the Bible, have lifted many of the primitive restrictions, notably in matters of education and of dress.

Dunkeld (dun.keld'). Registration district and market town, in C Scotland, in Perthshire, situated on the river Tay ab. 13 mi. NW of Perth, ab. 456 mi. N of London by rail. It was a seat of the Culdees from the 8th to the 12th century. The cathedral, built in the 14th and 15th centuries, is roofless except the choir, which has been restored and serves as the parish church. There is a square western tower, with turrets. Pop. of registration district, 751 (1931).

Dunkerley (dung'kėr.li), **William Arthur.** See **Oxenham, John.**

Dunkerque (dun'kėrk; French, deṅ.kerk). [Former French spelling, **Dunquerque;** English, **Dunkirk;** German, **Dünkirchen;** Eng. trans., *"Church on the Dunes."*] Town in N France, in the department of Nord, situated on the Strait of Dover, at the junction of a number of canals, near the border of Belgium. It is the fourth largest port in France, exporting the industrial products of the department of Nord and importing the raw materials which these industries consume. It is also an important fishing port, particularly for herring, and has shipyards and naval construction works, and linen, jute, cotton, metallurgical, and chemical industries. The center of the town is surrounded by old ramparts. It has a museum and a number of historic churches and houses. The Hôtel de Ville was built (1896–1901) after plans by Louis Cordonnier. Dunkerque belonged originally to the counts of Flanders, and the population still retains a Flemish dialect along with French. The town was often besieged, belonging successively to England, Burgundy, Spain, and France. It fell again to England in 1658, but was sold to France by Charles II in 1662. It was fortified by Vauban. Among its naval heroes was Jean Bart. The British besieged it unsuccessfully in 1793. It suffered bombardment in World War I. At the beginning of World War II, it saw the spectacular evacuation (May 28–June 4, 1940) of more than 330,000 British, Belgian, and French soldiers. Later in World War II it was subjected to damaging air bombardments, in the course of which a large part of the town, including the Church of Saint Eloi, was destroyed. 10,575 (1946).

Dunkerque, Battle of. Military operation in World War II after the fall (May 28, 1940) of Belgium and the subsequent collapse of the Allied lines. The British expeditionary forces were cut off and pinned against the Channel coast. Their removal from the beaches near Dunkerque was one of the great military evacuations of history. Using virtually every ship which could make the Channel crossing, over 330,000 men were rescued (May 28–June 4) despite constant air and artillery attack. In addition to 30,000 men who were killed by strafing and in rear-guard defense, the British lost much valuable materiel, as well as several destroyers and small craft.

Dunkerque, Treaty of. A 50-year Anglo-French treaty of alliance, of largely military significance, signed on March 4, 1947. It provides for common consultation and action to forestall a German policy of aggression or "an initiative likely to make possible such a policy." It also pledged the signatories to consult on economic relations between the two countries.

Dunkers (dung'kėrz). See **Dunkards.**

Dunkery Beacon (dung'kėr.i). See under **Exmoor.**

Dünkirchen (dün'kir.ċhen). German name of **Dunkerque.**

Dunkirk (dun'kėrk). City in E Indiana, in Blackford and Jay counties. 3,048 (1950).

Dunkirk. City in SW New York, in Chautauqua County, on Lake Erie ab. 35 mi. SW of Buffalo. Manufactures include oil-refinery machinery, boilers, radiators, shovels, and silk. 18,007 (1950).

Dunkirk. English name of **Dunkerque.**

Dún Laoghaire (dön la'ri). [Former names, **Kingstown, Dunleary** (dun.lir'i).] Borough, seaport, and resort in Leinster province, Irish Republic, in County Dublin, situated on Dublin Bay ab. 7 mi. SE of Dublin. It is now included within the boundaries of the city of Dublin, and forms the lower port of that city. The port was built in 1817. It is the headquarters of several yacht clubs and is the terminus of the passenger and mail steamer line from Holyhead, Wales. 47,963 (1951).

Dunlap (dun'lap), **John.** b. at Strabane, County Tyrone, Ireland, 1747; d. Nov. 27, 1812. American printer and publisher. He came (c1757) to America, and was owner (after 1766) of a bookselling and printing shop in Philadelphia. He was publisher (1771 *et seq.*) of a weekly newspaper, *The Pennsylvania Packet, or the General Advertiser,* which became (1784) the first daily newspaper in the U.S. In his office were printed the Declaration of Independence and the Constitution.

Dunlap, William. b. at Perth Amboy, N.J., Feb. 19, 1766; d. at New York, Sept. 28, 1839. American playwright, theater manager, painter, and historian. He early displayed an aptitude for drawing and studied under the painter Benjamin West at London, where he developed an interest in the theater which he manifested upon his return to America. His first successful play (1789) was a comedy, *The Father; or American Shandyism* (reprinted as *The Father of an Only Child*). His other plays include *Leicester* (produced in 1794); the first Gothic-type plays written in America, *Fontainville Abbey* (produced in 1795) and *Ribbemont; or, the Feudal Baron* (produced in 1796); *André* (produced in 1798); and *The Italian Father* (produced in 1799). In 1796 he bought an interest in the Old American Company, at that time the only theatrical firm in New York, of which he became (1798) the sole director and manager. After producing many successful plays adapted from the French and German, he fell into difficulties and was forced into bankruptcy (1805). He devoted himself to painting for a time, and in 1806 became general assistant to T. A. Cooper, manager of the Park Theatre. He left this post in 1811 to resume painting and for a brief time in 1813 managed a magazine, the *Monthly Recorder.* Again in financial straits, he found relief after his appointment (1814) as assistant paymaster-general to the state militia, a post he held until 1816, when he again took up portrait painting. In 1826 he helped to found the National Academy of Design, of which he was vice-president (1831–38) and in which he held a professorship of historical painting for some years. His later years saw the writing of his most important works, the *History of the American Theatre* (1832) and the *History of the Rise and Progress of the Arts of Design in the United States* (2 vols., 1834). His other works include *Memoirs of George Fred. Cooke, Esq., Late of the Theatre Royal, Covent Garden* (1813), *Life of Charles Brockden Brown* (1815), *Thirty Years Ago; or, the Memoirs of a Water Drinker* (1836), *A History of New York, for Schools* (1837), and *History of the New Netherlands, Province of New York, and State of New York, to the Adoption of the Federal Constitution* (2 vols., 1839–40).

Dun-le-Roi (dėṅ.lę.rwȧ). See **Dun-sur-Auron.**

Dunloe (dun.lō'), **Gap of.** Mountain pass in Munster province, Irish Republic, in County Kerry, ab. 6 mi. SW of Killarney. It passes between Macgillicuddy's Reeks on the W and Purple Mountain on the E, at a maximum elevation of 795 ft. It is noted for its grand and rugged beauty. Length, ab. 4 mi.

Dunlop (dun'lop, dun.lop'), **Cape.** [Also: **Dunlop Point, Rocky Point.**] Rocky headland in Antarctica, lying ab. 13 mi. S by SE of Cape Roberts, along the Wilson Piedmont Glacier of Victoria Land, in ab. 77°12′ S., 163°25′ E. It was first charted by the British Antarctic Expedition (1908–09).

Dunlop, John Boyd. b. at Dreghorn, Scotland, Feb. 5, 1840; d. at Dublin, Ireland, Oct. 23, 1921. Scottish veterinary surgeon, remembered chiefly for his invention of the pneumatic tire (c1887), first used on tricycles, later on bicycles and automobiles. One of the biggest tire manufacturers of Britain was named after him the Dunlop Rubber Company, Ltd.

Dunlop, John Colin. b. in Scotland, 1785; d. there, 1842. Scottish author and critic. He published *History of Fiction* (1814), adversely criticized by Hazlitt in the *Edinburgh Review; History of Roman Literature, from the Earliest Period to the Augustan Age* (1823–28), *Memoirs of Spain during the Reigns of Philip IV and Charles II* (1834), and *Selections from the Latin Anthology, Translated into English Verse* (1838).

Dunlop Island. [Also, **Terrace Island.**] Island in Antarctica, triangular in shape, lying along the Wilson Piedmont Glacier of Victoria Land, and NE of Cape Dunlop, in ab. 77° 12′ S., 163°27′ E.

Dunmail Raise (dun.māl'). Pass in NW England, situated on the Cumberland-Westmorland border, in the Lake District. It is on the route between Ambleside and Keswick. Elevation, ab. 780 ft.

Dunmore (dun'mōr, dun.mōr'). [Former name, **Buckstown.**] Borough in NE Pennsylvania, in Lackawanna County: anthracite coal mining; manufactures of silk yarn. Settled in 1783, it was renamed in 1840. Pop. 20,305 (1950).

Dunmore, Earl of. Title of **Murray, John** (1737–1808).

Dunmow (dun'mō). Rural district in SE England, in Essex, situated on the river Chelmer ab. 40 mi. NE of London by rail. It includes the villages of Great Dunmow and Little Dunmow. 18,214 (1951).

Dunmow. Local name for **Great Dunmow.**

Dunmow Flitch. Flitch of bacon awarded to any married pair who could take oath at the end of the first year and a day of their married life that there had not only been no jar or quarrel, but that neither had ever wished the knot untied. The custom, it is said, was originated in the priory of Little Dunmow, England, by Robert Fitzwalter, in 1244. The first recorded presentation of the bacon is dated 1445 (Chartulary of Dunmow Priory). Similar customs exist elsewhere, in England, Brittany, and other parts of Europe.

Dunn (dun). Town in C North Carolina, in Harnett County: marketing center for an agricultural area. 6,316 (1950).

Dunn, Beverly Wyly. b. at Clinton Parish, La., 1860; d. at New York, May 10, 1936. American army officer and ordnance expert who invented the high explosive known as "explosive D" or "dunnite." A graduate (1883) of the U.S. Military Academy, he organized (1908) the Bureau of Explosives for the American Railway Association, and retired (1911) from the army to serve (until 1934) as a member of it. He was one of the official investigators of the Black Tom explosion of July 30, 1916, at Jersey City, N.J., and reëntered the U.S. army for the duration of World War I. He developed one of first time-fuses for high-explosive shells.

Dunn, Gano. b. at New York, Oct. 18, 1870; d. there, April 10, 1953. American electrical engineer, noted for dynamo designs, and work on hydroelectric development and power distribution in factories. He was a U.S. delegate and executive committee member at an international conference (1936) on the use and development of electric power. He was a member (1939–41) of the U.S. Patent Office advisory committee, and (during World War II) a special consultant on power and steel to the U.S. Office of Production Management.

Dunn, Joseph. b. at New Haven, Conn., 1872; d. there, April 9, 1951. American linguist. Graduated from Yale, he studied in France and Germany, and in 1904 was named professor of Celtic language and literature at the Catholic University of America. Author of *A Grammar of the Portuguese Language* (1927).

Dunn, Samuel Orace. b. at Bloomfield, Iowa, March 8, 1877—. American editor and transportation authority.

He was the editor of *Railway Age Gazette* and *Railway Age* (1908 *et seq.*). He is the author of such books as *American Transportation Question* (1912) and *Government Ownership of Railways* (1913).

Dún na nGall (dön′ nąng ôl′). Irish name of County **Donegal.**

Dunne (dun), **Finley Peter.** b. at Chicago, July 10, 1867; d. April 24, 1936. American journalist and humorist, best known for his creation of "Mr. Dooley." He was a reporter for various Chicago newspapers from 1885 to 1891, city editor (1891–92) of the *Times*, on the staffs of the *Evening Post* and *Times-Herald* (1892–97), and editor (1897–1900) of the *Journal* (all at Chicago). His Mr. Dooley essays, in the form of dialogues (or rather monologues), first appeared in the *Evening Post.* The witty dialect series took the public fancy with apt commentary on the national scene, the foibles of the day, and the like. His works include *Mr. Dooley in Peace and in War* (1898), *Mr. Dooley in the Hearts of his Countrymen* (1898), *Mr. Dooley's Philosophy* (1900), *Mr. Dooley's Opinions* (1901), *Observations by Mr. Dooley* (1902), *Dissertations by Mr. Dooley* (1906), *Mr. Dooley Says* (1910), and *Mr. Dooley: On Making a Will and Other Necessary Evils* (1919).

Dunne, John William. b. 1875; d. Aug. 24, 1949. British airplane designer and philosopher. He designed and constructed (1906–07) the first British military airplane, and propounded the philosophical theory of "Serialism" through such books as *An Experiment With Time* (1927), *The Serial Universe* (1934), and *The New Immortality* (1938). His theories of time have influenced a number of writers, including W. Somerset Maugham and J. B. Priestley.

Dunnet Head (dun′ęt). Promontory in N Scotland, in Caithness-shire, ab. 8 mi. NE of Thurso. It is the most northerly point on the Scottish mainland. (John O'Groat's House, ab. 11 mi. E of Dunnet Head, is commonly said to be the most northerly point, but Dunnet Head lies ab. 2 mi. farther north.) Elevation, 346 ft.

Dunning (dun′ing), **John.** See **Ashburton,** 1st Baron.

Dunning, William Archibald. b. at Plainfield, N.J., May 12, 1857; d. Aug. 25, 1922. American historian. Serving for most of his professional life as a teacher of history at Columbia University, he was that institution's first Lieber professor of history and political science (1904–22), and a pioneer specialist in the history of the Reconstruction era. He was a cofounder and president (1913) of the American Historical Association, and editor (1894–1903) of the *Political Science Quarterly.* His works include *Essays on the Civil War and Reconstruction* (1898), *A History of Political Theories; Ancient and Mediaeval* (1902), *From Luther to Montesquieu* (1905), *Reconstruction, Political and Economic, 1865–1877* (1907), *The British Empire and the United States* (1914), and *From Rousseau to Spencer* (1920).

Dunnottar Castle (du.not′ąr). Ruined castle in Kincardineshire, Scotland, situated near the North Sea 1½ mi. S of Stonehaven. The existing structure dates from 1392.

Dunnville (dun′vil). Town in Ontario, Canada, situated on the Grand River a few miles from where it enters Lake Erie. It is the trading center for a rich farming area. 4,478 (1951).

Dunois (dü.nwå), **Jean.** [Title, Comte **de Dunois;** called the **"Bastard of Orléans."**] b. at Paris, Nov. 23, 1402; d. at St.-Germain-en-Laye, near Paris, Nov. 24, 1468. Natural son of the brother of Charles VI, Louis, Duke of Orléans (1372–1407), and Mariette d'Enghien, celebrated for his military prowess and his gallantries. He first came into prominence at Montargis in 1427, when he raised the siege and defeated the English. At the "battle of the herrings" near Rouvray in 1429 (when the French attacked an English wagon train, and the English defended themselves from behind barrels of herring) he was wounded, but that same year succeeded in holding out at Orléans until Joan of Arc arrived to drive off the English and defeat them at Patay. He carried on the fight after she was killed and by 1436 had retaken Paris. In 1440 he was for a time in league with the nobles against Charles VII in the Praguerie, but after the truce of 1444 was broken campaigned vigorously against the English. He took (1449–51) Harfleur, Honfleur, Cherbourg, Blaye, Bordeaux, and Bayonne, driving the English out of northern France altogether and restricting them in the west. Charles made him a prince of the royal blood, but Louis XI, when he came to the throne in 1461, stripped him of his honors. Dunois joined the League of the Public Good, a group of nobles in revolt against Louis's attempt to consolidate an absolute monarchy, and negotiated the compromising peace of Conflans. He is introduced in Scott's *Quentin Durward* and in the first part of Shakespeare's *Henry VI.*

Dunoon (dun.ön′). Police burgh and seaside resort in W central Scotland, in Argyllshire, situated on the W bank of the Firth of Clyde ab. 27 mi. W of Glasgow. It has no direct rail connections for passengers, being reached by rail to Glasgow, ab. 401 mi. N of London; thence by steamer. 10,020 (est. 1948).

Dunoyer de Segonzac (dü.nwå.yā dę sę.gôṅ.zåk), **André Albert Marie.** b. at Boussy-St.-Antoine, France, July 6, 1884—. French painter, etcher, and water-colorist. He was educated at the École des Beaux-Arts and the Julian Academy, both at Paris, and elsewhere. From 1907 to 1920 he exhibited at the Salon des Indépendants and the Salon d'Automne; by 1910 his own personal style began to be formulated with such paintings as *The Drinkers.* Although familiar with all of the important art movements in France, he has remained independent of them. He has worked chiefly in the provinces of France, mainly in the South, painting, illustrating books, and making etchings. Among his most important works are *The Village, Nude, Bathers, The River, The Bridge at Joinville, The Bread of Fantasy,* and *The Tree* (oils); *Landscape at Morin, Gardens at St.-Cloud, Nude,* and *Eight Illustrations of War* (etchings); *Isadora Duncan, Notes Taken at The Front,* and *Scheherazade* are some of the books he has illustrated.

Dunquerque (dėṅ.kerk). Former French spelling of **Dunkerque.**

Dunraven and Mount-Earl (dun.rā′ven; mount.ėrl′), **3rd** Earl of. A title of **Quin, Sir Edwin Richard Windham Wyndham-.**

Dun Rig (dun rig′). Mountain in S Scotland, situated on the Peeblesshire-Selkirkshire boundary. Elevation, ab. 2,433 ft.

Dunrobin Castle (dun.rob′in). Seat of the duke of Sutherland, near Golspie, Scotland. The present building is comparatively modern, although it incorporates the remains of an 11th-century stronghold.

Duns (dunz, duns). [Also, **Dunse.**] Police burgh and market town in S Scotland, in Berwickshire, ab. 13 mi. W of Berwick-upon-Tweed, Northumberland (England), ab. 356 mi. N of London by rail. Duns is the county seat of Berwickshire and the largest town in the county. 1,958 (est. 1948).

Dunsany (dun.sā′ni), Lord. [Full name, **Edward John Moreton Drax Plunkett;** title, 18th Baron **Dunsany.**] b. July 24, 1878—. Irish poet and dramatist; nephew of Sir Horace Curzon Plunkett (1854–1932). As a member of the Coldstream Guards, he served in the Boer War and in World War I. He was Byron professor of English literature at Athens University, Greece. His many poems and tales include *The Gods of Pegana* (1905), *Evil Kettle* (1926), *Fifty Poems* (1929), *Travel Tales of Mr. Jorkens* (1931), *My Talks With Dean Spanley* (1936), *Patches of Sunlight* (1938), *Mirage Water* (1938), and *Rory and Bran.* He achieved early acclaim as a dramatist with *Glittering Gates* (produced 1909 by W. B. Yeats at the Abbey Theatre, Dublin); among his other plays are *The Gods of the Mountain* (1911), *A Night at an Inn* (1916), *If* (1921), *Cheezo, The Laughter of the Gods,* and *Lord Adrian* (1933). Dunsany's stories and plays are fantasies dealing with the supernatural and supernatural beings; his style is simple yet deals in the paradoxes of human existence.

Dunsinane (dun.si.nān′, dun′si.nān). [Also: **Dunsinane Hill, Dunsinnan.**] One of the Sidlaw Hills, in C Scotland, in Perthshire, ab. 8 mi. NE of Perth. Here, in 1054, Siward, Earl of Northumberland, defeated Macbeth. The ruins of an ancient fortress, locally known as Macbeth's Castle, are here. Elevation, ab. 1,012 ft.

Duns Scotus (dunz skō′tus), **John.** [Called **Doctor Subtilis.**] b. at Duns, Scotland, c1265; d. at Cologne, Germany, Nov. 8, 1308. Scholastic theologian, one of the most influential in the history of medieval Europe. He was the founder of the scholastic system called Scotism, which long contended for supremacy among the schoolmen with the system called Thomism, founded by Thomas Aquinas. Nothing is known with certainty concerning his personal history. According to the commonly accepted tradition, he was born c1265 at Duns (or Dunse), Berwickshire, Scotland (hence his surname Scotus, or Scot), was a fellow of Merton College, Oxford, became a Franciscan friar, was chosen professor of theology at Oxford in 1301, removed in 1304 to Paris, where, in a disputation on the Immaculate Conception of Jesus Christ by the Virgin Mary he displayed so much ingenuity and resource as to win the title of Doctor Subtilis, and where he rose to the position of regent of the university. He died at Cologne, Germany, on Nov. 8, 1308, while on a mission in the interest of his order. His name, Duns, Dunse, or Dunce, came to be used as a common appellative, meaning "a very learned man," and, being applied satirically to ignorant and stupid persons as being as sensible as the extreme scholastics, gave rise to "dunce" in its present sense. Scotism, the movement he founded, was an extreme form of realism and anti-intellectualism. Instead of the middle of the road between faith and reason sought by Saint Thomas Aquinas, Duns Scotus restricted the sphere of rational thought, thus eventually driving the wedge between philosophy and religion that emancipated the philosophers from strict adherence to religious subjects, an effect opposite to the one Scotus attempted to achieve. The argument concerning the Immaculate Conception found the Thomists on one side and the Scotist Dominicans on the other; the latter were joined by the Franciscans, the Jesuits, and the Sorbonne theologians; the feud was dissolved with the publication (in 1854, after five and one half centuries of argument) of the papal bull *Ineffabilis Deus* of Pope Pius IX. Scotus held that true knowledge could be reached only through revelation from God. As a corollary to this, he held that the existence of God was essentially unprovable (it must be presupposed) and that God's nature was incomprehensible to man.

Dunstable (dun'stą.bl). Municipal borough and market town in E central England, in Bedfordshire, ab. 35 mi. NW of London by rail. Its industries include printing, straw plaiting, and the manufacture of straw hats. A considerable development and growth of population has occurred in Dunstable since 1933. Dunstable Downs, a part of the Chiltern Hills, are nearby; they are a popular week-end resort, and have recently become noted as a gliding center. 17,108 (1951).

Dunstable or **Dunstaple** (dun'stą.pl), **John.** d. Dec. 24, 1453. English composer, chief of the early school of contrapuntists, said to have been the inventor of true counterpoint.

Dunstan (dun'stąn), Saint. b. near Glastonbury, England, 924 or 925 A.D.; d. at Canterbury, England, May 19, 988 A.D. Archbishop of Canterbury. He was the son of Heorstan, a West Saxon noble, and was brought up at the abbey of Glastonbury and at the court of Ethelstan. But the scorn of his friends and the influence of the bishop of Winchester, to whom he fled, combined with a grave illness, made him take monastic vows. He was appointed abbot of Glastonbury by Edmund not later than 945. He became the chief adviser of Edred (reigned 946–955), but was banished by Edred's successor, the young king Edwig (955–959), whose ill will he incurred by refusing to consent to a marriage upon which the young king had set his heart, and by rudely bringing him back to the banqueting hall when, at his coronation, he left it for the society of the lady of his choice. Dunstan went to Flanders. He was recalled by Edwig's successor, Edgar (reigned 959–975), by whom he was created archbishop of Canterbury in 959 and restored to political power. He retained his influence at court during the reign of Edward (975–978), but appears to have lost it on the accession of Ethelred II (Ethelred the Unready) in 978. Dunstan's civil policies were aimed at integrating the Danes and the English as a nation; in this civil area and ecclesiastically his basic tenet was the rule of law. He fostered the strict Benedictine rule and campaigned against simony. His feast day is May 19.

Dunstan, Guy Mainwaring. Original name of **Morton, Guy Mainwaring.**

Dunster (dun'stėr), **Henry.** b. in Lancashire, England, 1609; d. at Scituate, Mass., Feb. 27, 1658 or 1659. First president of Harvard College. He was inaugurated in 1640 and resigned in 1654.

Dun-sur-Auron (dėṅ.sür.ō.rôṅ). [Also, **Dun-le-Roi.**] Town in central France, in the department of Cher, situated on the Auron River and the Canal du Berry, ab. 17 mi. SE of Bourges. It has coal mines. It is a town of medieval character, with a beautiful Romanesque church and a number of industries. 3,676 (1946).

Dunton (dun'tǫn), **John.** b. at Graffham, Huntingdonshire, England, May 4, 1659; d. 1733. English bookseller and author. In 1694 Dunton printed *The Ladies Dictionary* described as "a *Compleat Directory* to the *Female-Sex* in all *Relations, Companies, Conditions,* and *States* of Life." He wrote *Life and Errors of John Dunton* (1705), and *Letters from New England* (published in 1867).

Düntzer (dün'tsėr), **Johann Heinrich Joseph.** b. at Cologne, Germany, July 12, 1813; d. there, Dec. 16, 1901. German literary historian and philologist. He became (1846) librarian of the Roman Catholic *Gymnasium* (advanced secondary school) at Cologne. He published numerous critical works on Goethe, *Homer und der epische Cyclus* (1839), and others.

Dunwich (dun'ich). Civil parish and village in E England, in East Suffolk, situated on the coast of the North Sea ab. 4 mi. SW of Southwold, ab. 90 mi. NE of London. It was the seat of the bishopric of East Anglia, said to have been founded c630, and was important in the early Middle Ages. Successive inroads of the sea have destroyed churches and other buildings, leaving only a small village. 174 (1931).

Dunwoody (dun'wůd.i), **Robert.** Central character in *The Wayward Man* (1927), a novel by St. John Ervine.

Dupanloup (dü.päṅ.lö), **Félix Antoine Philibert.** b. at St.-Félix, near Chambéry, France, Jan. 3, 1802; d. Oct. 11, 1878. French prelate. He was made bishop of Orléans in 1849, was elected deputy to the National Assembly in 1871, and became a life senator in 1875.

Duparc (dü.pårk), **Marie Eugène Henri Fouques.** b. at Paris, Jan. 21, 1848; d. 1933. French composer. He studied under César Franck and helped found the Société Nationale. His compositions include the symphonic poem *Lenore,* the nocturne *Aux Étoiles,* the three-voice motet *Benedicat vobis Dominus,* and *Feuilles Volantes,* for piano, as well as many songs for which he is chiefly remembered.

Dupaty (dü.på.tē), **Charles Marguerite Jean Baptiste Mercier.** b. at La Rochelle, France, May 9, 1746; d. at Paris, Sept. 17, 1788. French jurist. He was the author of *Réflexions historiques sur les lois criminelles* (1788).

Dupe (dūp), **Lady.** Old lady in Dryden's comedy *Sir Martin Mar-all.*

Duperrey (dü.pe.rā), **Louis Isidor.** b. at Paris, Oct. 21, 1786; d. Sept. 10, 1865. French naval officer and scientist. He served as hydrographer in the *Uranie,* under de Freycinet, who made explorations (1817–20) in the North Pacific, and commanded (1822–25) the *Coquille* in a scientific expedition to Oceania and South America. He determined the positions of the magnetic poles and the figure of the magnetic equator. He contributed the volumes on hydrography and physical science to *Voyage autour du monde, exécuté par ordre du roi sur la corvette La Coquille pendant les années 1822, 1823, 1824, et 1825* (1826–30).

Duperron (dü.pe.rôṅ), **Jacques Davy.** b. at St.-Lô, France, Nov. 15, 1556; d. at Paris, Sept. 5, 1618. French cardinal, instrumental in converting Henry IV to Catholicism.

Dupes, Day of. Name given to Nov. 11, 1630, when the enemies of Richelieu were foiled in their intrigues against him with Louis XIII. Richelieu, apparently ruined in the eyes of the king, had an interview with him and emerged completely in favor again.

Dupetit-Thouars (dü.ptē.twår), **Abel Aubert.** b. at Saumur, France, Aug. 3, 1793; d. at Paris, March 17, 1864. French rear admiral; nephew of L. M. A. Dupetit-Thouars. He circumnavigated the globe (1837–39), extended a French protectorate over Tahiti and the Marquesas islands in 1842, and over the entire Society group in 1843.

Dupetit-Thouars, Louis Marie Aubert. b. at Bournois, near Saumur, France, Nov. 5, 1758; d. at Paris, May 11, 1831. French botanist and traveler. He visited (1792–1802) Mauritius, Madagascar, and Réunion.

Dupin (dü.paṅ), **André Marie Jean Jacques.** [Called **"Dupin the Elder."**] b. at Varzy, Nièvre, France, Feb. 1, 1783; d. at Paris, Nov. 18, 1865. French lawyer and politician; brother of François Pierre Charles, Baron Dupin. He was president (1832–40) of the Chamber of Deputies, and in 1849 was elected to the assembly. Author of *Principia Juris Civilis* (5 vols., 1806).

Dupin, François Pierre Charles, Baron. b. at Varzy, Nièvre, France, Oct. 6, 1784; d. at Paris, Jan. 18, 1873. French mathematician and politician who published numerous books on geometry and military matters; brother of André Marie Jean Jacques Dupin. He was educated at the École Polytechnique and entered the maritime service, becoming minister of marine in 1834 and a senator in 1852. He was elected to the Academy of Sciences (1832) and served as councilor of state (1831). In mathematics he is remembered for the "Dupin indicatrix" of differential geometry. His books include *Développements de géométrie* (1813), *Voyages dans la Grande-Bretagne* (1820–24), *Applications de géométrie* (1825), and *Forces productives des nations* (1851).

Du Pin or **Dupin** (dü.paṅ), **Louis Ellies.** b. June 17, 1657; d. June 6, 1719. French Catholic clergyman and church historian. He studied at the Sorbonne, and taught at the Collège de France, becoming known for his notes on the works and teachings of the Church Fathers. Bossuet attacked him in 1692, condemning him for audacity as a critic and demanding his censure by ecclesiastical authority.

Dupleix (dü.pleks), **Joseph François,** Marquis. b. at Landrecies, Nord, France, Jan. 1, 1697; d. at Paris, Nov. 10, 1763. French general, governor general (1742–54) of the French East Indies. The son of a director of the French East India Company, he made his reputation as administrator of Chandernagor after 1730; in 1742 he was appointed governor general of the French establishments in India. His subsequent attempts to expand French influence in India brought him into conflict with Robert Clive, whose military abilities were greater than Dupleix's. Dupleix made treaties with various native princes and organized native troops on a European basis. He clashed with Bertrand François Mahé, Comte de la Bourdonnais. La Bourdonnais had captured (1746) Madras and when he wished to return it to the English was ordered not to by Dupleix, his nominal superior. Dupleix successfully defended Pondichéry against the English siege in 1748, a siege which ended with the news of the signing (in Europe) of the treaty of Aix-la-Chapelle between the British and the French. He then began diplomatic maneuvers to control large areas in India, the Coromandel Coast, the Carnatic, and the Deccan. But Clive resisted and the French government, not wishing to antagonize the English, superseded Dupleix rather than risk war, and he returned to France in 1754. There he discovered that neither the company nor the government would recompense him for the large personal fortune he had spent in trying to extend French interests; he died in poverty.

Duplessis (dü.ple.sē), **Georges Victor Antoine Gratet-.** b. at Chartres, France, March 19, 1834; d. March 26, 1899. French critic and historian of art, custodian of the department of prints in the Bibliothèque Nationale at Paris. He published numerous works.

Duplessis, Maurice Le Noblet. b. at Three Rivers (Trois Rivières), Quebec, Canada, April 20, 1890—. Canadian politician. He was elected (1927) to the Quebec legislature and by 1933 had risen to the leadership of the Quebec Conservative Party. In 1936, after forming a new political party, Union Nationale, Duplessis won a striking victory at the polls and overthrew a Liberal Party ascendancy in Quebec politics that had lasted for four decades; he became premier, attorney general, and president of council in the provincial government. A vigorous advocate of French-Canadian autonomy, Duplessis established a strict regime which, because of such stringent legislation as the "Padlock Law" of 1937 that attempted to prevent the dissemination of radical literature, was accused of incipient fascism. Such accusations, combined with Duplessis's determination to maintain local rule and customs in the face of a growing federal power in Canada, caused his defeat at the polls in 1939, when he campaigned on an antimilitary platform. From 1939 to 1944 he was leader of the opposition, but in 1944 scored a crushing victory over his opponents and again became premier. He was reëlected in 1948 and 1952.

Duplessis-Mornay (-môr.nā). See **Mornay, Philippe de.**

Duplex Printing Press Co. v. Deering, 254 U.S. 443 (1921) (dir'ing). U.S. Supreme Court decision holding that a secondary boycott by a labor union constituted unlawful interference with interstate commerce and hence did not come under the protection of the Clayton Antitrust Act. It applied the principle of equity to labor unions and effectively weakened the anti-injunction provisions of the Clayton Act. The majority opinion was written by Justice Pitney; Justice Brandeis wrote a dissenting opinion, concurred in by Justices Clark and Holmes.

Duplin Moor (dup'lin). See **Dupplin Moor.**

Duployé (dü.plwȧ.yā), **Émile.** b.1833; d. 1912. French inventor of a shorthand system. The Duployé stenographic method, which he developed and which is named for him, has been (and still is) widely used in France.

Dupnica or **Dupnitsa** (döp'nē.tsä). Former name of **Marek.**

Du Ponceau (dū pon'sō; French, dü pôṅ.sō), **Pierre Étienne.** [Also, **Peter Stephen Duponceau.**] b. at Île-de-Ré, France, June 3, 1760; d. at Philadelphia, April 1, 1844. French-American lawyer and philologist. He published *Memoir on the Indian Languages of North America* (1835), and others.

Dupong (dü.pôṅ), **Pierre.** b. Nov. 1, 1885—. Luxembourg statesman and lawyer. He studied at the universities of Berlin, Fribourg (Switzerland), and Paris; member of parliament; minister of finance and social welfare (1926–37); prime minister since 1937. During World War II he was in Canada with the government-in-exile until September, 1944, when he resumed his functions in Luxembourg.

du Pont (dụ.pont', dū'pont). Name of a family prominent since the latter part of the 18th century in American industrial, financial, and political life. It may be said to have been established, as an American family, by Éleuthère Irénée du Pont and Victor Marie du Pont, who were the sons of Pierre Samuel du Pont de Nemours, a figure of considerable importance in the history of France during the latter part of the 18th century. The spelling of the name now preferred, and generally used, by all members of the family is "du Pont"; the spellings "Du Pont" or "DuPont" are seldom, if ever, used by the du Ponts themselves (except at the beginning of a sentence or in other situations requiring a capital letter), although they have wide usage in American general reference books.

Dupont (dụ.pont'). Borough in E Pennsylvania, in Luzerne County, in an anthracite coal mining area. 4,107 (1950).

du Pont (dụ.pont', dū'pont), **Éleuthère Irénée.** b. at Paris, June 24, 1771; d. at Philadelphia, Oct. 31, 1834. American manufacturer, founder of the du Pont powder works in Delaware; son of Pierre Samuel du Pont de Nemours (1739–1817). In 1788 he was placed under Lavoisier in the laboratory of the royal powder works at Essonne, and after the French Revolution managed his father's printing-house at Paris. When the establishment was suppressed in 1797, he left (1799) with his father, some relatives, and his own family for America, where he conceived the idea of setting up an American gunpowder works. In 1801 he secured the necessary designs and machinery in France and, with the backing of funds supplied largely by his father's company, which had originally contemplated land exploitation, he established a powder works on a farm near Wilmington, Del. He settled there in 1802, supervised the erection of the mills, and by 1804 had powder ready for sale. Transactions with the U.S. government netted the company good profits, and its operations were further stimulated by the War of 1812. He became the chief maker of powder for the U.S. government, and also supplied South American countries. The name E. I. du Pont de Nemours and Company is borne by the vastly expanded modern successor to this original company.

du Pont, Henry. b. at Eleutherian Mills, Wilmington, Del., Aug. 8, 1812; d. Aug. 8, 1889. American soldier and manufacturer of explosives; son of Éleuthère Irénée du

Pont (1771–1834). Graduated (1833) from West Point, he was for a time on duty in the Creek Indian country of Alabama but resigned (1834) his commission to become active in his father's gunpowder works. In 1850, in partnership with his brother and their nephew Irénée du Pont, he became head of E. I. du Pont de Nemours and Company. He was responsible for expanding the operations of the firm, buying (1859) mills on Big Wapwallopen Creek, Luzerne County, Pa., for the manufacture of blasting powder, purchasing controlling interests in the Hazard Powder Company and in the California Powder Works in 1876, and working out, during the post-Civil War years, a method of making special cakes of large-grain powder for big guns. During the Civil War he served as major general of the Delaware armed forces and sold powder to the Union army and navy. He undertook the manufacture of Hercules powder in 1876.

du Pont, Henry Algernon. b. near Wilmington, Del., July 30, 1838; d. Dec. 31, 1926. American soldier, industrialist, and legislator; elder son of Henry du Pont. Graduated (1861) from West Point, he took part in many Civil War actions, chiefly as a commander of Union artillery. Promoted to the rank of lieutenant colonel in 1864, he received the Congressional Medal of Honor for distinguished services and extraordinary gallantry at Cedar Creek. Leaving the service in 1875, he became (1878) a member of E. I. du Pont de Nemours and Company and was instrumental in securing the charter for incorporation (1899), after which he became a vice-president. He became (1879) president of the Wilmington and Northern Railroad and as a member (1906–17) of the U.S. Senate was chairman of the military affairs committee from 1911 to 1913. His writings include *The Early Generations of the Du Pont and Allied Families* (1923), *Campaign of 1864 in the Valley of Virginia* (1925), and *Rear-Admiral Samuel Francis Du Pont, a Biography* (1926).

du Pont, Irénée. b. Dec. 21, 1876—. American industrialist; great-grandson of Éleuthère Irénée du Pont (1771–1834). Educated at Massachusetts Institute of Technology; associated (1903 *et seq.*) with E. I. du Pont de Nemours and Company as vice-president and chairman of executive committee (1914–19), president (1919–26), and vice-chairman of board and chairman of finance committee (1926–40).

Dupont (dü.pôṅ) or **Dupont de l'Eure** (dü.pôṅ dẹ lėr), **Jacques Charles.** b. at Neubourg, Eure, France, Feb. 27, 1767; d. on his estate, Rouge Pierre, in Normandy, France, March 3, 1855. French politician. He became president of the imperial court at Rouen in 1811, was a member (1817–48) of the Chamber of Deputies, was minister of justice for about six months in 1830, and was president of the provisional government formed in February, 1848.

du Pont (dų̈.pont′, dū′pont), **Lammot.** b. Oct. 12, 1880; d. July 24, 1952. American industrialist; great-grandson of Éleuthère Irénée du Pont (1771–1834). He joined (1902) E. I. du Pont de Nemours and Company, and has served as vice-president in charge of miscellaneous manufacturing (1917 *et seq.*), president (1926–40), and chairman (1940–48) of the company.

Dupont (dü.pôṅ), **Pierre.** b. at Lyons, France, April 23, 1821; d. there, July 24, 1870. French lyric poet. He was a collaborator (1842–47) on the dictionary of the French Academy. His works include *Les Deux Anges* (1842; crowned by the Academy), *Les Bœufs* (1846), *Le Chant des nations,* and *Le Chant des ouvriers.*

du Pont (dų̈.pont′, dū′pont), **Pierre Samuel.** b. at Wilmington, Del., Jan. 15, 1870—. American industrialist; great-grandson of Éleuthère Irénée du Pont (1771–1834). He joined (1890) E. I. du Pont de Nemours and Company as chemist, and became a director and member of the company's finance committee.

du Pont, Samuel Francis. b. at Bergen Point, N.J., Sept. 27, 1803; d. at Philadelphia, June 23, 1865. American naval officer; son of Victor Marie du Pont. Appointed a midshipman by President Madison in 1815, he did not see active sea duty until 1817, when he embarked on a series of cruises that took him to European and South American waters. Promoted (1826) to lieutenant, he became a commander in 1842, served (1849) on Secretary of the Navy George Bancroft's board on the organization of the Annapolis naval school, and during the Mexican War served chiefly in the vicinity of Lower California. In the years between the wars he served on various tours of duty, and was promoted to the rank of captain in 1855, in which year he commanded the frigate *Minnesota* on a cruise to China. He became (1860) commandant of the Philadelphia navy yard, later served as the senior member of the Commission of Conference, which prepared naval operations plans, and in September, 1861, became commander of the South Atlantic blockading squadron, leading the successful Union expedition against Port Royal. Promoted to the rank of rear admiral in 1862, he later led operations along the southern coast. Heading a fleet of ironclads in 1863, he directed the unsuccessful attack upon the defenses of Charleston; relieved at his own request, he left active duty and performed his final service for the navy as a member of a naval board (1865) passing upon promotions for officers.

du Pont, Thomas Coleman. b. at Louisville, Ky., Dec. 11, 1863; d. Nov. 11, 1930. American industrialist and senator; great-grandson of Éleuthère Irénée du Pont (1771–1834). He was associated (1883 *et seq.*) with Kentucky coal and iron mining interests, was president (1902–15) of E. I. du Pont de Nemours and Company, and served as U.S. senator (1921–28).

du Pont, Victor Marie. b. at Paris, Oct. 1, 1767; d. at Philadelphia, Jan. 30, 1827. American manufacturer and merchant; son of Pierre Samuel du Pont de Nemours (1739–1817). A member of the French diplomatic service, he served as attaché (1787 *et seq.*) to the first French legation in the U.S., as second secretary of legation (1791–92) and, in 1795, as first secretary of legation, later becoming consul for the Carolinas and Georgia and consul general in the U.S. However, he was not accredited by President John Adams as holder of this latter post because of existing differences between the U.S. and France. Returning to France, he joined his family and again embarked for America, where he settled at Alexandria, Va., and devoted his efforts to furthering the land company organized by his father and to an independent mercantile firm bearing his own name. Both this and a later land-development venture failed, and he subsequently removed to Wilmington, Del., where he became manager of woolen mills established by his brother, Éleuthère Irénée. He later became a director of the Bank of the United States and a member of the Delaware legislature.

Dupont de l'Étang (dü.pôṅ dẹ lā.täṅ), Comte **Pierre.** b. at Chabanais, Charente, France, July 14, 1765; d. at Paris, March 7, 1840. French general, distinguished at Marengo and other battles, and especially at Friedland (1807). He capitulated at Bailén in 1808.

du Pont de Nemours (dü pôṅ dẹ nẹ.mör; Anglicized, dų̈ pont′ dẹ nẹ.mör′), **Pierre Samuel.** b. at Paris, Dec. 14, 1739; d. near Wilmington, Del., Aug. 6, 1817. French political economist and politician. He assisted (1774–76) Turgot, was a deputy to the States-General in 1789, and became a member of the Council of the Ancients in 1795. He emigrated (1799) to the U.S., returned to France in 1802, and again went to the U.S. in 1815. He wrote *Physiocratie, ou constitution naturelle du gouvernement le plus advantageux au genre humain* (1768) and *Philosophie de l'univers* (1796).

Duport (dü.pôr), **Jean Pierre.** b. at Paris, Nov. 27, 1741; d. at Berlin, Dec. 31, 1818. French cellist. He was a member (1773–1811) of the orchestra and leader (1787–1806) of concerts at the Berlin court.

Düppel (düp′ẹl). German name of **Dybbøl.**

Düppel, Lines of. In European history, name given to a chain of Danish fortifications W of Sønderborg on the island of Als (German, Alsen). They were stormed by the Prussians on April 18, 1864. They took their name from the town of Dybbøl (German, Düppel).

Dupplin Moor (dup′lin). [Also, **Duplin Moor.**] Moor in Perthshire, Scotland, ab. 7 mi. SW of Perth. Here Edward Baliol defeated (1332) the Scottish Royalists under the earl of Mar.

Duprat (dü.prà), **Antoine.** b. at Issoire, Puy-de-Dôme, France, Jan. 17, 1463; d. at Rambouillet, France, July

9, 1535. French cardinal and politician. He became chancellor and prime minister in 1515.

Duprat, Pascal Pierre. b. at Hagetmau, Landes, France, March 24, 1815; d. Aug. 17, 1885. French politician and journalist. He took part in the February revolution in 1848, founded with Lamennais *Le Peuple Constituant*, opposed the coup d'état in 1851, and was arrested and obliged to leave France. He was a member of the National Assembly in 1871, and, later, of the Chamber of Deputies. Sent as ambassador to Chile in 1883, he died on the return journey.

Duprato (dü.prȧ.tō), **Jules Laurent.** b. at Nîmes, France, 1827; d. at Paris, in May, 1892. French composer. He won the prix de Rome in 1848, and became professor of harmony at the Paris Conservatory in 1866. Among his operas are *Les Trovatelles* (1854), *Pâquerettes* (1856), *Salvator Rosa* (1861), and *Le Cerisier* (1874).

Dupray (dü.prā), **Louis Henri.** b. at Sedan, France, Nov. 3, 1841; d. in April, 1909. French military painter.

Dupré (dü.prā'), **August.** b. at Mainz, Germany, Sept. 6, 1835; d. at Sutton, England, July 15, 1907. Analytical chemist. He studied at Darmstadt, Giessen, and Heidelberg, went to London in 1855, was lecturer on chemistry (1864–97) at Westminster Hospital, became chemical referee to the medical department of the Local Government Board in 1871, and was also chemical adviser to the explosives department of the Home Office. Besides publishing many papers on scientific subjects, he collaborated with others in writing *The Nature, Origin, and Use of Wine* and a *Manual of Inorganic Chemistry*.

Dupré, Ernest Pierre. b. at Marseilles, France, 1862; d. at Deauville, France, Sept. 2, 1921. French physician. He was an intern under L. Landouzy and A. M. E. Chauffard, and later a pupil of J. M. Charcot, J. J. Déjerine, and E. Brissaud. In 1918 he became professor of psychiatry at Paris. He wrote a monograph on paralysis and on the history of psychopathy. Author of *Le Méningisme* (1894), *La Mythomanie* (1905), *Le Langage musical* (1911), *Anthropologie psychique*, and *Pathologie de l'imagination et de l'émotivité* (1925).

Dupré, Giovanni. b. at Siena, Italy, March 1, 1817; d. at Florence, Jan. 10, 1882. Italian sculptor. Among his works are *Abel* and *Cain* (Pitti Palace, Florence), *Sappho, Giotto,* and the Cavour monument at Turin.

Dupré, Jules. b. at Nantes, France, April 5, 1812; d. at L'Isle-Adam, France, Oct. 6, 1889. French landscape painter. He was originally a porcelain painter in his father's factory. He received a second-class medal at the Exposition Universelle in 1867, a second-class medal in 1883, and a medal of honor at the Exposition Universelle in 1889. He spent his winters at Paris from 1876 to 1882. He was the first and last of the group of Fontainebleau artists of 1830, also called the Romantic or Natural School (including Rousseau, Delacroix, Corot, Diaz, Millet, Troyon, and others). His studio was for some years in the Abbey of Saint Pierre in the forest of Fontainebleau, and afterward at L'Isle-Adam. Several of his pictures are in the Luxembourg Museum, one at Lille, and a number are owned in the U.S.

Duprez (dü.prā), **Caroline.** [Married name, Madame **Van den Heuvel.**] b. at Florence, 1832; d. at Pau, France, April 17, 1875. French opera singer; daughter of G. L. Duprez.

Duprez, Gilbert Louis. b. at Paris, Dec. 6, 1806; d. Sept. 23, 1896. French tenor singer and composer. He published *L'Art du chant* (1845), *La Mélodie* (1873), and *Souvenirs d'un chanteur* (1888).

Dupuis (dü.pwē), **Adolphe.** b. at Paris, Aug. 16, 1824; d. at Nemours, France, Oct. 25, 1891. French actor.

Dupuis, Charles François. b. at Trie-le-Château, Oise, France, Oct. 16, 1742; d. at Issur-Tille, Côte-d'Or, France, Sept. 29, 1809. French scholar and man of letters. He was the author of *L'Origine de tous les cultes, ou la religion universelle* (1795).

Dupuy (dü.pwē), **Charles Alexandre.** b. at Le Puy, Haute-Loire, France, Nov. 5, 1851; d. at Ille-sur-Têt, Pyrénées-Orientales, France, July 23, 1923. French political leader, best known for his cool behavior during a bomb attack (Dec. 9, 1893) upon the French Chamber of Deputies, over which he was presiding. "Gentlemen, the session continues," he said, calming the meeting. He was professor of philosophy at the lycée (state-maintained secondary school) of Le Puy (1876) and of St.-Étienne (1880), and inspector of the academy at Ajaccio (1884). He entered politics in 1885, and was minister of public instruction under Ribot in 1892, president of the council and minister of the interior (1894, 1898–99), president of the Chamber of Deputies and minister of the interior (1893–94), and senator from Haute-Loire (1900–09). He was also premier (1893, 1894–95, 1898–99).

Dupuy, Jean. b. at St.-Palais, Gironde, France, Oct. 1, 1844; d. at Paris, Dec. 31, 1919. French political leader and journalist, during World War I member of the war committee of the French cabinet. He was editor of the newspapers *Le Siècle* and *Le Petit Parisien,* was a deputy and a senator, and held the posts of minister of agriculture, commerce, and public works. He built up *Le Petit Parisien* into a mass-circulation newspaper.

Dupuytren (dü.pwē.traṅ), **Guillaume,** Baron. b. at Pierre-Buffière, Haute-Vienne, France, Oct. 6, 1777; d. at Paris, Feb. 8, 1835. French surgeon and anatomist.

Duque Job (dö'kā ᴴōb), **El.** Pseudonym of **Gutiérrez Nájera, Manuel.**

Duquesne (dū̦.kān'). City in SW Pennsylvania, in Allegheny County, on the Monongahela River ab. 1 mi. NW of McKeesport: manufactures of steel. It was named for Fort Duquesne. 17,620 (1950).

Duquesne (dü.ken; Anglicized, dū̦.kān'), **Abraham,** Marquis. b. at Dieppe, France, 1610; d. at Paris, Feb. 2, 1688. French naval commander, distinguished in the wars against the Spanish and Dutch. He defeated the combined Spanish and Dutch fleets under De Ruyter off the Sicilian coast on April 21, 1676.

Duquesne (dū̦.kān'), **Fort.** Fort erected by the French in 1754 on the site of what is now Pittsburgh, Pa. It was the initial objective of General Edward Braddock's ill-fated expedition (1755) and was taken by the English in 1758 after being abandoned by the French, and renamed Fort Pitt.

Duquesne University. Accredited coeducational institution of higher learning, conducted by the Roman Catholic Order of the Holy Ghost, at Pittsburgh, Pa. Known at first as Pittsburgh Catholic College of the Holy Ghost, it began offering instruction in 1878, was incorporated in 1882, and raised to university status under its present title in 1911. With an enrollment of about 5,000, it comprises a college of liberal arts and sciences, schools of law, pharmacy, business administration, education, music, and nursing, and a graduate school.

Duquesnoy (dü.ke.nwȧ), **François.** [Called **François Flamand.**] b. at Brussels, Belgium, 1594; d. at Leghorn, Italy, July 12, 1646. Dutch sculptor, son of an excellent sculptor from whom he received his first lessons. At an early age he made the figure of Justice on the portal of the Chancellerie at Brussels, and two angels for the door of the Jesuit church. In 1619 he was sent by the archduke Albert to study at Rome. He is especially famous for the children which he executed in marble and bronze, but more frequently in ivory, for drinking cups and the like.

Du Quoin (dö koin'). City in S Illinois, in Perry County ab. 70 mi. N of Cairo: coal-mining community. It was named for Jean Baptiste Du Quoigne, an Indian chief of the Kaskaskia tribe. 7,147 (1950).

Dura (dū'ra̦). See **Dura-Europos.**

Durack Range (dū'rak). Range of mountains in the N part of Western Australia, running S from Joseph Bonaparte Gulf.

Dura Den (dū'ra̦ den'). Small glen in E Scotland, in Fifeshire, ab. 3 mi. E of Cupar. It is noted for the fossil fish found in its sandstone.

Dura-Europos (dū'ra̦.ū̦.rō'pos). [Also, **Dura.**] Ancient city on the Euphrates founded around a rock fortress by a satrap of the Seleucid empire about the end of the 4th century B.C. It developed into an important town as the river station for caravans on the route from Palmyra to the East, and its walls were ab. 70 ft. high and ab. 2 mi. long. It belonged to the Parthian empire, and was taken by the Romans in 165 A.D. It remained on the border of Roman conquests, and was abandoned by them about the middle of the 3rd century A.D. Emperor Gordian III was killed here in a soldiers' revolt in 244 A.D. The ancient city site was discovered (in SE Syria at Salahiya, ab. 27 mi. NE of the Iraq border) by British troops in March,

1921, and has since been excavated by many expeditions, yielding rich archaeological discoveries.

Durán (dö.rän′), **Agustín.** b. at Madrid, Oct. 14, 1789; d. there, Dec. 1, 1862. Spanish critic and littérateur. He wrote *Sobre la decadencia del teatro español* (1828), and edited old Spanish romances and comedies.

Duran (dü.räṅ), **Carolus-.** [Original name, **Charles Auguste Émile Durand.**] b. at Lille, France, July 4, 1837; d. 1917. French genre and portrait painter, a pupil of Souchon. He studied at Paris, and afterward in Italy and Spain. He painted portraits, especially of women, with great success, and was also a sculptor. He received medals in 1866, 1869, 1870, 1878, and 1879.

Durance (dü.räṅs). [Latin, **Druentia.**] River in SE France which joins the Rhône ab. 3 mi. SW of Avignon.

Durand (dụ.rand′). City in C Lower Michigan, in Shiawassee County near Flint: railroad and manufacturing center. 3,194 (1950).

Durand (dü.räṅ), **Alice Marie Céleste.** See **Gréville, Henry.**

Durand (dụ.rand′), **Asher Brown.** b. at Jefferson Village, near Newark, N.J., Aug. 21, 1796; d. there, Sept. 17, 1886. American engraver and painter, noted for his pastoral landscapes. In 1812 he was apprenticed to a steel engraver, Peter Maverick, becoming the latter's partner in 1817; his accomplishment in the field was so outstanding that he was selected to engrave John Trumbull's painting *"The Signing of the Declaration of Independence.* Durand, in the meantime, set up his own establishment, and completed the Trumbull engraving in 1823, later producing a series of engravings, notably that of John Vanderlyn's *Ariadne,* which added to his reputation. Much of his work, remarkable for its craftsmanship, was devoted to engraved portraits of leading contemporaries. He also did engravings after the work of popular painters for such gift-books as *The Talisman, The Atlantic Souvenir, The Token,* and *The Gift.* In 1836 he abandoned the burin for the brush, and spent the remainder of his career as a painter, doing his best work as a painter of nature scenes drawn from New York and the New England states. With Thomas Cole, he is accounted as having established the American school of landscape painting. He was a charter member of the National Academy of Design and was its president from 1845 to 1861.

Durand, Edward Dana. b. at Romeo, Mich., Oct. 18, 1871—. American economist and statistician. Secretary (1900–02) of U.S. industrial commission; director (1909–13) of U.S. census; professor of economics (1913–17) at University of Minnesota; staff member (1917–19) of U.S. food administration in Europe; adviser (1919–21) to Polish food minister; chief economist (1930–35) and member (1935 *et seq.*) of U.S. tariff commission. Author of *Finances of New York City* (1898), *The Trust Problem* (1915), *Industry and Commerce of the United States* (1930), and other works.

Durand (dü.räṅ), **Nicolas.** See **Villegaignon,** Chevalier **de.**

Durand (dụ.rand′), **William Frederick.** b. at Bethany, Conn., March 5, 1859—. American mechanical engineer, notable for work in hydrodynamic and aerodynamic science. Served (1880–87) in U.S. navy engineering corps; professor of mechanical engineering at Michigan State (1887–91) and Stanford (1904–24); professor of marine engineering (1891–1904) at Cornell. Author of *Fundamental Principles of Mechanics* (1889), *Resistance and Propulsion of Ships* (1898), *Practical Marine Engineering* (1901), *Motor Boats* (1907), *Hydraulics of Pipe Lines* (1921), and other works; general editor of *Aerodynamic Theory* (6 vols., 1934).

Durandana (dū.rạn.dä′nạ). [Also: **Durandal** (dū′rạn-däl), **Durenda, Durendal, Durindana.**] Sword of Orlando (Roland). It possessed magic qualities, was made by the supernatural smiths, and was once owned by Hector. In the French Roland poems, it is called Durendal or Durandal and was presented to Roland by Charlemagne.

Durandarte (dö.rän.där′tā). Legendary Spanish hero whose exploits are related in old Spanish ballads and in *Don Quixote.* He was the cousin of Montesinos, and was killed at the battle of Roncesvalles. One of the ballads, a fragment, can be traced to the *Cancionero* of 1511, and one, *Durandarte, Durandarte,* to the old *Cancioneros Generales.*

Durandus (dụ.ran′dus), **Guilelmus.** [Also: **Durantus;** French, **Guillaume Durand;** Italian, **Duranti** or **Durantis;** called **"the Speculator."**] b. at Puimisson, near Béziers, France, 1237; d. at Rome, Nov. 1, 1296. French prelate and jurist. He wrote *Speculum judiciale* (1271; revised 1287, 1291), a fundamental source on the history of western liturgy, and *Rationale divinorum officiorum* (c1286), the first non-Biblical book to be printed (1459).

Durango (dụ.rang′gō). City in SW Colorado, county seat of La Plata County, on the Animas River: marketing center for agricultural produce. 7,459 (1950).

Durango (dö.räng′gō). State in N Mexico, lying between Chihuahua on the N, Coahuila on the E, Zacatecas on the SE, Jalisco and Nayarit on the S, and Sinaloa on the W. Capital, Durango; area, 47,691 sq. mi.; pop. 629,502 (1950).

Durango. [Full name, **Victoria de Durango;** former name, **Guadiana.**] City in N Mexico, capital of Durango state, near the foot of the Sierra Madre Occidental. The center of a mining region, it has metal foundries, and textile, glass, tanning, sugar-refining, and flour-milling industries. Iron ore for the iron and steel industry of Monterrey is mined just N of the city. Elevation, ab. 6,200 ft.; pop. 33,412 (1940).

Duranius (dụ.rā′ni.us). Latin name of the **Dordogne River.**

Durant (dụ.rant′). City in S Oklahoma, county seat of Bryan County: marketing center for livestock, cotton, grain, potatoes, hay, and peanuts; processing center for wild pecans, cottonseed, and bois d'arc (Osage orange). It is the seat of Southeastern State College and the Oklahoma Presbyterian College for Girls. Denison Dam is nearby. 10,541 (1950).

Durant, Henry. b. at Acton, Mass., June 18, 1802; d. Jan. 22, 1875. American Congregational clergyman, first president (1870–72) of the University of California. Ordained (1833) pastor of Congregational Church, Byfield, Mass.; moved (1853) to California and immediately aided the founding of Contra Costa Academy in Oakland; obtained charter (1855) for College of California which the legislature incorporated (1868) into the newly established University of California.

Durant, Henry Fowle. [Original name, **Henry Welles Smith.**] b. at Hanover, N.H., Feb. 20, 1822; d. Oct. 3, 1881. American lawyer, founder (1870) of Wellesley College. Graduate (1842) of Harvard; admitted (1843) to the bar; practiced (1843–48) at Lowell, Mass., and (1848–63) at Boston, changing his name (1851) because of many lawyers named Smith in Boston. He abandoned the law (1863) upon the death of his son, and conducted revivalist meetings in Massachusetts. After serving as a trustee of Mount Holyoke College, he obtained a charter (1870) for Wellesley College, of which he was treasurer (1870–81).

Durant, Thomas Clark. b. at Lee, Mass., Feb. 6, 1820; d. at North Creek, N.Y., Oct. 5, 1885. American railroad promoter, vice-president (1863–69) of the Union Pacific Railroad Company. Constructor with Henry Farnam of the Michigan Southern Railroad and other roads in the Midwest. As vice-president of the Union Pacific Company, he subscribed or guaranteed three fourths of the original capital. When funds seemed insufficient, he obtained the charter of the Crédit Mobilier (which undertook to complete the road) and served as its president (1863 *et seq.*). A struggle for control of the enterprise developed with the Ames brothers of Boston, and he lost (1867) his Crédit Mobilier directorate. He remained a Union Pacific director, however, and drove through to completion of construction, which was achieved on May 10, 1869, when the Union Pacific tracks westward met the Central Pacific tracks coming eastward. He was ousted by the Ames group from his Union Pacific connections a little more than two weeks thereafter.

Durant, Will. [Full name, **William James Durant.**] b. at North Adams, Mass., Nov. 5, 1885—. American educator and writer. Professor of Latin and French (1907–11) at Seton Hall College; director (1914–27) New York's Labor Temple School; professor of philosophy (1935 *et seq.*) at the University of California at Los Angeles. He is the author of *Philosophy and the Social Problem* (1917), *The Story of Philosophy* (1929), *Adventures in Genius* (1931), *On the Meaning of Life* (1932), *The Story of Civilization* (1935), *The Life of Greece* (1939), *Caesar and Christ* (1944), *The Age of Faith* (1950), and other books.

Durant, William Crapo. b. at Boston, Dec. 8, 1861; d. at New York, March 17, 1947. American auto industrialist. He founded (1886) the Durant-Dort Carriage Company at Flint, Mich., and successively organized the Buick Motor Car Company (1905), the General Motors Company (1908), and the Chevrolet Motor Company (1915). He acquired (1915) the controlling interest in General Motors, holding it until 1920, and in 1921 organized Durant Motors, Inc. He subsequently became a director of the Industrial Rayon Corporation.

Durante (dö.rän'tā). Original prename of **Dante.**

Durante, Francesco. b. at Frattamaggiore, Italy, March 15, 1684; d. at Naples, Italy, Aug. 13, 1755. Italian composer of sacred music. In 1742 he succeeded Porpora at the Conservatory of Santa Maria di Loreto at Naples, where he died.

Durante (dụ.ran'ti), **James Francis.** [Known as **Jimmy Durante;** nicknamed **"Schnozzola."**] b. at New York, Feb. 10, 1893—. American actor. Noted for his large nose and for his mangling of polysyllabic words, Durante has been a successful comedian in several mediums: stage, motion pictures, vaudeville, phonograph records, radio, and television. He is possibly best remembered as a night-club entertainer in the team of Clayton, Jackson, and Durante, but his musical-comedy appearances (*Strike Me Pink, Red, Hot, and Blue, Jumbo,* and others) and his radio (especially as the partner of Garry Moore) and television programs have made him known to a much wider audience.

Duranty (dụ.ran'ti), **Walter.** b. at Liverpool, England, May 25, 1884—. American journalist and author. Staff member (1913–39), Moscow correspondent (1921–35), and roving correspondent (1934–39) of New York *Times;* awarded Pulitzer prize for reporting (1932) and O. Henry short-story prize (1929) for his tale of Russia *The Parrot.* Author of *I Write as I Please* (1935), *One Life, One Kopek* (1937), *The Gold Train* (1938), *The Kremlin and the People* (1942), *Search for a Key* (1943), *USSR* (1944), *Stalin and Co.* (1949), and other books.

Durão (dö.rouṅ'), **José de Santa Rita.** b. at Cata Preta (now Santa Rita Durão), Minas Gerais, Brazil, c1720; d. at Lisbon, Portugal, Jan. 24, 1784. Brazilian poet, chiefly remembered for his epic poem *Caramurú* (1781). He was an Augustinian monk, a graduate and a professor of the University of Coimbra, and is believed to have lived for nine years in Italy.

Duras (dü.ràs). See under **Bonhomme Richard.**

Durazno (dö.räz'nō). Department in C Uruguay. Cattle are raised here. Capital, Durazno; area, 5,527 sq. mi.; pop. 97,140 (est. 1947).

Durazno. [Also, **San Pedro del Durazno.**] City in S Uruguay, capital of Durazno department. Cattle and grain are raised in the surrounding area. Pop. ab. 27,000.

Durazzo (dö.rät'tsō). Italian name of **Durrës,** city.

Durazzo (dö.rät'sō). Facetious and lively old man in Philip Massinger's play *The Guardian.* He is the guardian of Caldoro.

Durban (dėr'bạn). [Also, **D'Urban.**] [Former name, **Port Natal.**] City in S Africa, in Natal province, Union of South Africa, situated near Natal Bay on the E coast of the Union, ab. 295 mi. from Capetown by sea and 812 mi. and 494 mi. by rail from Capetown and Johannesburg respectively. It ranks with Capetown as a chief port of the country; further expansion of the city is planned. It is the port nearest to the gold fields of the Witwatersrand and the coal fields of the Transvaal, and is the terminus of the railway to the interior. It was renamed for Sir Benjamin D'Urban. 369,579, including 128,382 Europeans (1948).

D'Urban (dėr'bạn), Sir **Benjamin.** b. 1777; d. at Montreal, Canada, May 25, 1849. English soldier and colonial administrator in Africa. He served (1808–13) against the French in the Peninsula War and became a major-general in the Portuguese army (holding at the same time the rank of colonel in the British army). He was subsequently lieutenant governor of and commander in chief in British Guiana (1821–25) and Barbados (1825–29). During his term (1842–47) as governor of and commander in chief in the Cape of Good Hope colony he occupied (1843) Natal as a measure to counter heavy Boer immigration. The city of Durban, formerly Port Natal, was renamed for him. He died while in command of British forces in Canada.

Durbin (dėr'bin), **John Price.** b. in Bourbon County, Ky., Oct. 10, 1800; d. at Philadelphia, Oct. 19, 1876. American clergyman of the Methodist Episcopal Church, president of Dickinson College (1834–45). He was secretary of the Missionary Society of the Methodist Episcopal Church (1850–72). He wrote *Observations in Europe* (1844), *Observations in Egypt* (1845), and others.

Durbunga (dur.bung'gạ). See **Darbhanga.**

Durden (dėr'dẹn), **Dame.** Notable housewife in a famous English song; hence the nickname given to the careful and conscientious Esther Summerson in Charles Dickens's *Bleak House.*

Durdles (dėr'dlz), **Stony.** "A stone-mason, chiefly in the gravestone, tomb, and monument way, and wholly of their color from head to foot," in Charles Dickens's *Mystery of Edwin Drood.* He is usually drunk, and has wonderful adventures in the crypt of the cathedral.

Düren (dü'rẹn). [Ancient name, **Marcodurum.**] City in W Germany, in the *Land* (state) of North Rhine-Westphalia, British Zone, formerly in the Rhine Province, Prussia, situated on the Roer River ab. 23 mi. SW of Cologne. It has large paper, machine, and cloth manufactures, a sugar refinery, and dairies. Buildings of interest include a library, theater, and museum of art and antiquities. There were before World War II various medieval buildings, most of which were damaged; the Church of Saint Anna (13th–16th centuries) and the *Rathaus* (city hall) were completely destroyed. Düren was an important city under the Frankish kings and under Charlemagne. It came in 1238 under the rule of the counts of Jülich, was burned down by the army of the emperor Charles V in 1543, fell to France in 1801, and to Prussia in 1814. Heavy fighting occurred around Düren between December, 1944, and March, 1945, in World War II. The population, chiefly Roman Catholic, declined in the period 1939–46 by 37.2 percent. 27,653 (1946), 35,234 (1950).

Durenda (dü.rẹn.dä) or **Durendal** (dū'rẹn.däl). See **Durandana.**

Dürer (dü'rėr), **Albrecht.** b. at Nuremberg, Germany, May 21, 1471; d. there, April 6, 1528. German painter, draftsman, and engraver, of Hungarian descent. The son of an able goldsmith, he learned that craft before entering the studio of the painter Michel Wohlgemut in 1486. Later he studied with Martin Schongauer at Colmar, and visited Venice, studying with most interest the works of Mantegna and Bellini, before setting up his own studio at Nuremberg in 1497. His principal achievements at this time were in the field of portraiture. In 1505 he went to Venice again, and stayed two years. Back at Nuremberg, his period (1505–20) of greatest activity ensued, during which especially he brought to superbly powerful perfection his drawings, copper engravings, and woodcuts. Nuremberg at that time was a center of intellectual activity; Humanism and Protestantism were in the air. Dürer, though he was patronized by, and painted the portraits of, the emperors Maximilian I and Charles V, was also a friend of Luther and Melancthon. It is believed, however, that he remained a Catholic, and the Christian tradition, certainly gave him by far the greater number of his subjects, as shown by his numerous paintings, engravings, and woodcuts deriving from the stories of the Fall, the Nativity, the Flight into Egypt, the Passion, and the lives of the early Christian saints and martyrs. Although it was said by some Italian painters that if he had been an Italian, Dürer would have been the greatest of Italian artists, his work in all media is almost wholly Gothic in derivation, markedly different from the pictures of the Italian High Renaissance. His portraits of this period are solid, shrewd, uncompromisingly realistic; his copperplates and woodcuts are full of energy, crowded with invention, often grim, sometimes grotesque. Contrasting with all this vehemence and exuberance are many painted landscapes and drawings of small animals or patches of grass and flowers, of a calm and touching beauty. In 1521 he visited the Netherlands;

he was received with enthusiasm and respect, and he improved the opportunity to learn from the works of the Van Eycks, whose influence is evident in some of the work of his own last years, especially in the *Four Evangelists*, which some consider his masterpiece. Others give that title to his *Adoration of the Magi* at Florence. But it is perhaps a futile critical exercise to try to name as a masterpiece any particular creation of one whose work was all masterly. Dürer was not, certainly, one of the great colorists, but as a draftsman, as a portraitist, and as a designer, he is among the very greatest in the history of art. That his accomplishments were the reflection of a keen intelligence is shown by his writings on perspective and other aspects of graphic technique, and by his autobiographical writings. The most notable Dürer paintings known today are *Virgin and Child with Saints Anthony and Sebastian* and a *Crucifixion*, at Dresden; *Martyrdom of the Ten Thousand* and a *Madonna*, at Venice; *Virgin Crowned by Two Angels* and a portrait of Hieronymous Holzschuber, at Berlin; *Adoration of the Magi*, in the Uffizi at Florence; *A Young Man*, and portraits of Oswald Krell and Michel Wohlgemut, at Munich; and self-portraits at Leipzig, Madrid, and Munich. There are extensive collections of his drawings and engravings at Vienna, Berlin, London, Florence, Milan, and the Louvre at Paris.

Durey (dü.rā), **Louis.** b. at Paris, May 27, 1888—. French impressionistic composer. He joined (1917) a group of composers including Honegger, Auric, Milhaud, Poulenc, and Taillefere, which became known (with Durey) as "The Six." Among his compositions are the orchestral work *Pastorale*, the choral work *Éloges*, the opera *Judith*, and *Neige*, for piano.

Durfee (dėr′fẹ), **Job.** b. at Tiverton, R.I., Sept. 20, 1790; d. there, July 26, 1847. American jurist and philosophical writer, chief justice of the Rhode Island supreme court (1835–47). He wrote *Panidea* (1846) and others.

Durfee, William Franklin. b. at New Bedford, Mass., Nov. 15, 1833; d. Nov. 14, 1899. American engineer, a pioneer in the modern steel industry. With a natural talent for mechanics, developed under his father's instruction and at the Lawrence Scientific School of Harvard University, at the age of 20 he set up at New Bedford as an engineer and architect. A few years later he had a brief political career, being elected in 1861 to the state legislature, where he proposed a resolution calling upon Congress to repeal "all laws which deprive any class of loyal subjects of the Government from bearing arms for the common defense." The purpose of this was to open the way for the employment of Negro troops in the Civil War, and it was probably the first definite step taken in a Northern legislature toward that end. In 1862 he went to the iron-bearing region along Lake Superior to investigate the qualities of its ores with a view to their refinement by the methods proposed by William Kelly, and in September, 1864, he supervised the construction of a mill at Wyandotte, Mich., where with apparatus of his design the first steel produced by this process in the U.S. (called Bessemer steel, after Sir Henry Bessemer, whose process resembled Kelly's) was turned out. At Wyandotte Durfee also established the first laboratory in America for the systematic study of the problems of steelmaking. He also built a steel mill at Milwaukee, Wis., and a copper refinery at Ansonia, Conn., which was the first such plant in the U.S. to make use of gaseous fuel. Durfee, who was exceptionally well read in the history of engineering, contributed papers to technical periodicals, and accumulated a valuable collection of books which is now in the library of the Engineering Societies at New York.

D'Urfey (dėr′fi), **Thomas.** [Called **Tom D'Urfey.**] b. in Devonshire, England, 1653; d. at London, Feb. 26, 1723. English dramatist and humorous poet. His songs, which appeared for the most part in his successul and (at the time) greatly admired plays, were published as *Wit and Mirth; or Pills to Purge Melancholy* (1719–20).

Durga (dör′gä). See also **Parvati.**

Durga. In Hindu mythology, one of the malignant forms of Devi, the wife of Shiva.

Durham (dur′ạm). Administrative and geographical county in NE England. It is bounded on the N by Northumberland, on the E by the North Sea, on the S by Yorkshire, on the SW by Westmorland, and on the W by Cumberland. The surface in the W portion (in the region of the Pennines) consists of fertile valleys enclosed by hill ranges; the E part is more level, except in the NE, where it is undulating. Wheat, barley, oats, and root crops are raised. Durham is famous for its shorthorn Durham cattle. It has important coal fields, mostly worked in the S portion of the county. Other minerals are salt, lead, zinc, and limonite (except for salt, all are little worked now). Industries include shipbuilding, iron and steel production, chemical manufactures, and woolen and worsted manufactures. Durham is the county seat; area of geographical county, ab. 1,016 sq. mi.; of administrative county, ab. 974 sq. mi.; pop. of administrative county, 902,821 (1951).

Durham. [Middle English, **Durem, Duresme;** old English, **Dūnholm, Dunholme.**] Municipal borough, market town, and episcopal city in NE England, county seat of Durham, situated on the river Wear ab. 15 mi. S of Newcastle, ab. 254 mi. N of London by rail. Durham stands on the historical routeway from England to Scotland. Its industries include iron and steel production, coal mining, shipbuilding, chemical manufactures, and machine shops. On a rocky peninsula, almost surrounded by the river Wear, the old city contains a castle founded in 1072 by William the Conqueror and rebuilt by Bishop Hugh of Puiset a hundred years later. The interior possesses many features of interest, as the beautiful Norman arcade, door, and gallery, the Norman chapel beneath the 14th-century keep, the 14th-century refectory, and a 17th-century carved staircase of oak. The castle is now occupied by the University of Durham (founded by Cromwell in 1646, later dissolved, and reëstablished in 1832). The cathedral of Durham is a monument of great intrinsic importance, which is enhanced by its imposing position on the brink of a steep hill above the river Wear. The west front is flanked by two massive square towers, and a tower of similar form rises high over the crossing. The present church was founded at the end of the 11th century, and was practically completed by the middle of the 12th. A 12th-century knocker on the door was a place of sanctuary for fugitives who clung to it. The Lady Chapel or Galilee is later, and the curious east transept called the Nine Altars, at the eastern extremity of the choir, is of the early 13th century. The cloister is in Perpendicular style. The Norman interior is exceedingly impressive. The piers of the nave are alternately cylindrical and square, with engaged shafts; the former are covered with zigzag and other line patterns. The altar screen and episcopal throne date from the 14th century, the stalls from the 17th. The eastern or Nine Altars transept is architecturally beautiful, and is very skilfully joined to the older work. The Galilee chapel, projecting in front of the western façade, has four interior walls resting on round chevron-molded arches which spring from slender clustered columns, the whole supporting the roof in a manner rather Saracenic than Northern. The dimensions of the cathedral are 510 by 80 ft., length of transepts 170 ft., height of vaulting 70 ft., of central tower 214 ft. The old monastic buildings are still almost complete, and are of high interest. Durham was possibly a Roman station. It became the seat of the old Bishopric of Lindisfarne in 995, and its bishops were, in the Middle Ages, nearly independent rulers over the palatinate of Durham. 19,283 (1951).

Durham. Town (in New Hampshire the equivalent of township in many other states) and unincorporated village in SE New Hampshire, in Strafford County, ab. 10 mi. NW of Portsmouth. It is the seat of the University of New Hampshire, founded (1866) as a branch of Dartmouth, from which it was separated in 1890. Settled in 1635, Durham suffered from Indian attacks during King Philip's War and later. It was the home of General John Sullivan, whose house still stands. Pop. of town, 4,770 (1950); of village, 4,172 (1950).

Durham. City in C North Carolina, county seat of Durham County, NW of Raleigh: a leading center for the manufacture of cigarettes. Among its other products are silk hosiery, bricks, cotton textiles, and tobacco-packing machinery. It is the seat of Duke University and the North Carolina College for Negroes. 71,311 (1950).

Durham, 1st Earl of. Title of **Lambton, John George.**

Durham, Battle of. See under **Neville's Cross.**

Durham, Simeon (or **Symeon**) **of.** See **Simeon** (or **Symeon) of Durham.**

Durham, University of. University at Durham, England, reëstablished in 1832 (the university traces its origin, with a considerable interruption, to an order issued by Cromwell in 1646). It comprises the Durham division of eight colleges situated at Durham, and the Newcastle division (King's College, including the medical school) at Newcastle. The combined libraries have a total of some 256,000 volumes.

Durham Book, The. [Also: **Durham Gospels, Saint Cuthbert's Book.**] Latin text of the gospels with an interlinear gloss in Northumbrian Saxon.

Durham Letter. Letter written in 1850 by Lord John Russell, British prime minister, to the bishop of Durham, denouncing the newly established Roman Catholic hierarchy in England and Wales, and the ritualistic tendencies in the Church of England.

Durham Station. In U.S. history, a place (now partly included in the city of Durham) in North Carolina, ab. 29 mi. NW of Raleigh. Here, on April 26, 1865, the Confederate general J. E. Johnston surrendered with 29,924 men to General W. T. Sherman.

Duria Major (dū′ri.ạ mā′jọr). Latin name of the **Dora Baltea.**

Duria Minor (mī′nọr). Latin name of the **Dora Riparia.**

Durindana (dū.rin.dä′nạ). See **Durandana.**

Düringsfeld (dü′rings.felt), **Ida von.** b. at Militsch, in Silesia, Nov. 12, 1815; d. at Stuttgart, Württemberg, Germany, Oct. 25, 1876. German poet and novelist. Her works include *Skizzenaus der vornehmen Welt* (1842–45) and *Antonio Foscarini* (1850).

Durius (dū′ri.us). Latin name of the **Douro.**

Dürkheim (dürk′hīm). [Also, **Bad Dürkheim.**] Town in W Germany, in the *Land* (state) of Rhineland-Palatinate, French Zone, formerly in the Bavarian Palatinate, on the Isenach River at the slopes of the Hardt Mountains, ab. 13 mi. W of Mannheim. Situated in the largest wine-growing community in Germany, it is a center of the Palatinate wine trade; besides wine cellars, it has canneries and small industries. It is a health resort, visited for its grape-cures and its saline thermal springs, by people with intestinal and liver diseases. The castle church dates from the 15th century, the *Stadthaus* (town hall) from the 18th century. The name of Dürkheim appears in records as early as 742. It belonged from the Middle Ages to the counts of Leiningen. During the 17th and 18th centuries it was occupied several times by the French. The population is predominantly Protestant. 10,615 (1950).

Durkheim (dür.kem), **Émile.** b. 1858; d. 1917. French sociologist and philosopher, a student of national economics, folk psychology, and cultural anthropology. Durkheim centered his attention on social or moral aspects of group life. He founded a school of sociology which emphasized a particular type of coercive and external social fact as the data of scientific sociological research. He served as editor of the French sociological journal *Année Sociologique* from 1896 to 1913. His important works were *De la division du travail social* (1893, translated as *The Division of Labor in Society*, 1933), *Les Règles de la méthode sociologique* (1895, translated as *The Rules of Sociological Method*, 1938), *Le Suicide* (1897), and *Les Formes élémentaires de la vie réligieuse* (1912, translated as *The Elementary Forms of Religious Life*, 1915).

Durkin (dėr′kin), **Martin P.** b. at Chicago, March 18, 1894—. American labor leader, U.S. secretary of labor (1953 *et seq.*) under Eisenhower. A steamfitter by trade, he became his union's business manager in 1921 and later president of the national union. He served (1933–41) as Illinois state director of labor. During World War II he was a member of the national war labor board.

Durlach (dör′läch). Town in S Germany, in the *Land* (state) of Württemberg-Baden, American Zone, situated on the Pfinz River ab. 3 mi. E of Karlsruhe. It was formerly the capital of Baden-Durlach. Industries include machine, bicycle, and leather manufactures and a factory for dental instruments. It is a marketing center for a fruit and vegetable growing suburban district. For administrative and census purposes it is part of Karlsruhe.

Durmitor (dör′mi.tôr). [Also: **Durmitar** (-tär), **Dormitor** (dôr′-).] Highest summit in the mountains of Montenegro, Yugoslavia. Elevation, ab. 8,294 ft.

Durnovaria (dėr.nọ.vãr′i.ạ). Latin name of **Dorchester,** Dorsetshire, England.

Dürnstein (dürn′shtīn). [Also: **Dürrenstein, Tirnstein.**] Village in E Austria, in the province of Lower Austria, beautifully situated on the N bank of the Danube River, at the entrance to the Wachau region, W of Krems. It is overlooked by the ruins of a medieval castle, destroyed by the Swedes in 1645. Here, in 1193, Richard I of England (Richard Coeur-de-Lion), on his way back from the Holy Land, was kept prisoner by Leopold VI of Austria, his opponent in the Crusade. The present parish church, founded in 1410, was rebuilt (1720–33) in Austrian baroque style. 605 (1946).

Durobrivae (dū.rọ.brī′vē). Latin name of **Rochester,** England.

Duroc (dü.rok), **Géraud Christophe Michel.** [Title, Duc **de Friuli.**] b. at Pont-à-Mousson, near Nancy, France, Oct. 25, 1772; d. near Markersdorf, Saxony, Germany, May 22, 1813. French general and diplomat. He became (1796) aide-de-camp to Napoleon, whom he accompanied to Egypt in 1798. He took a prominent part in the overthrow (1799) of the Directory, and was employed by the first consul in diplomatic missions to Berlin, St. Petersburg, Stockholm, and Copenhagen. He accompanied Napoleon in the campaigns of 1805–06 and 1807, and was mortally wounded by the emperor's side near Markersdorf. He was a favorite officer of Napoleon.

Durocasses (dū.rọ.kas′ēz). An ancient name of **Dreux,** town.

Durocher (dů̇r.ō′chėr), **Leo (Ernest).** b. 1906—. American baseball player and manager. A light-hitting member of the New York Yankees of the Babe Ruth-Lou Gehrig period, Durocher did not become notable as a player until he played with the St. Louis Cardinals, the Gas-House Gang, in the early 1930's, when his competitive spirit was given full rein. Durocher became noted for his will to win at almost any cost and, as manager of the Brooklyn Dodgers, whom he led to a National League championship in 1941, he was famous for his arguments with umpires. He became (1948) manager of the New York Giants, intracity rivals of the Brooklyn team. In 1951, leading his team from an almost hopeless position behind the league-leading Dodgers, Durocher, the game's leading exponent of "percentage" baseball, overcame a 13½ game disadvantage in winning 37 of the remaining 44 games, finished the regular season in a tie with the Dodgers, and in a three-game playoff series, climaxed by a game won in the ninth inning by a home run, won the league pennant.

Durocornovium (dū″rọ.kôr.nō′vi.um). A Latin name of **Cirencester.**

Durocortorum (dū″rọ.kôr.tō′rum). An ancient name of **Reims.**

Duronceray (dü.rôṅs.rā), **Marie Justine Benoîte.** See **Favart,** Madame.

Durovernum (dū.rọ.vėr′num). Latin name of **Canterbury,** England.

Dürrenberg (dür′ẹn.berk). [Also, **Bad Dürrenberg.**] Town in C Germany, in the *Land* (state) of Saxony-Anhalt, Russian Zone, formerly in the province of Saxony, Prussia, situated on the Saale River W of Leipzig. It is a health resort with strong saline springs, visited by people suffering from nervous and respiratory diseases. The population is predominantly Protestant. 13,823 (1946).

Dürrenstein (dür′ẹn.shtīn). See **Dürnstein.**

Durrës (dör′rẹs). One of the ten prefectures of Albania, in the W part. Capital, Durrës; pop. 77,890 (1930).

Durrës. [Italian, **Durazzo**; Serbo-Croatian, **Drač**; ancient Greek, **Epidamnos**; Latin, **Epidamnus, Dyrrhachium.**] Seaport in W Albania, capital of Durrës prefecture, situated on the Adriatic Sea. It was founded by Corcyreans c625 B.C., and became the terminus of a great Roman road. Caesar was repulsed here by Pompey in 48 B.C., and here Robert Guiscard defeated the emperor Alexius I Comnenus in 1081, and took the city in 1082. It was part of the Turkish Empire from the 16th century until 1912. Pop. 8,739 (1930).

Dürrheim (dür'hīm). [Also, **Bad Dürrheim.**] Town in S Germany, in the *Land* (state) of Baden, French Zone, situated in the Black Forest N of Donaueschingen. It is a health resort with saline thermal springs, visited by people suffering from rheumatism and respiratory and nervous diseases, and also has small industries. The population is predominantly Roman Catholic. 2,180 (1947).

Dur Sharrukin (dör shär.rö.kēn'). See under **Khorsabad.**

Durtain (dür.taṅ), **Luc.** b. at Paris, 1881—. French poet, novelist, and critic. He is the author of various "cosmopolitan" novels including *Quarantième étage* (1927).

Duruma (dö.rö'mä). [Also, **Waduruma.**] One of nine Bantu-speaking peoples of E Africa known collectively as Nyika. They inhabit a district in SE Kenya, and their population is estimated at ab. 33,000 (by I. Schapera, *Some Problems of Anthropological Research in Kenya Colony*, 1949).

Duruy (dü.rü.ē), **(Jean) Victor.** b. at Paris, Sept. 11, 1811; d. there, Nov. 25, 1894. French historian and statesman, minister of public instruction (1863–69). He became a senator in 1869. His works include *Histoire des Romains* (1843–44), *Histoire de France* (1852), *Histoire de la Grèce ancienne* (1862), *Histoire moderne* (1863), and *Histoire des Grecs* (1887–89). Several of his works form part of the *Histoire universelle* (1846 *et seq.*) published under his direction.

Durvasas (dör'vä.säs). In Hindu legend, a sage noted for irascibility. Many fell under his curse. In Kalidasa's drama *Shakuntala* he curses Shakuntala for keeping him waiting at the door, and so causes the separation between her and king Dushyanta.

D'Urville Wall (dėr'vil). Great glacier-cut wall of granite in Antarctica, several thousand feet high, in Victoria Land, in ab. 75°18′ S., 162°00′ E. It was discovered by the British Antarctica Expedition (1908–09), under the command of Sir Ernest Shackleton, who named this feature for J. S. C. Dumont D'Urville, French naval commander and explorer who made a voyage of discovery (1837–40) in the South Seas.

Durward (dėr'wạrd), **Quentin.** Young archer of the Scottish Guard in Sir Walter Scott's novel *Quentin Durward.* After many adventures he marries Isabelle de Croye.

Duryea (dur'yā, dur'i.ā). Borough in E Pennsylvania, in Luzerne County: anthracite coal mining; manufactures of silk textiles. 6,655 (1950).

Duryea (dur'yā), **Charles Edgar.** b. near Canton, Ill., Dec. 15, 1861; d. at Philadelphia, Sept. 28, 1938. American manufacturer who is credited with developing (1895) the first modern U.S. automobile and many automotive devices. Built (1892) gasoline motorcar; organized (1895) Duryea Motor Wagon Company, Springfield, Mass.; sold first car in 1896; founded (1900) Duryea Power Company for automobile manufacture. His other contributions include a spray carburetor (1892) and pneumatic tires for automobiles.

Duryée (dur'yā), **Abram.** b. at New York, April 29, 1815; d. Sept. 27, 1890. American officer, with the Union army in the Civil War. An officer (1833–59) of various regiments of the militia, he organized (1861) a voluntary regiment known as "Duryée's Zouaves" which served at Big Bethel, Federal Hill, and in other engagements during the Civil War; appointed (1861) brigadier general; brevet major general of volunteers after the war. He was later (1873) police commissioner of New York City.

Duryodhana (dör.yō'dạ.nạ). Eldest son of Dhritarashtra, and leader of the Kaurava princes in the great war related in the *Mahabharata.* Upon the death of his brother Pandu, Dhritarashtra took his five sons, the Pandava princes, to his own court, and had them educated with his hundred sons. Jealousies sprang up, and Duryodhana took a special dislike to Bhima from his skill in the use of the club. He poisoned Bhima, who was restored to life by the Nagas. He was the occasion of the exile of the Pandavas. After their return he won in gambling from Yudhishthira everything he had, including his own freedom and that of his brothers, and his wife Draupadi. The result of the gambling was a second exile of 13 years. In the great battle he fell by the hand of Bhima, who had vowed to break his thigh in consequence of the insult to Draupadi.

Duse (dö'zā), **Eleonora.** [Sometimes spelled **Eleanora.**] b. in a railway carriage between Venice and Vigevano, Italy, Oct. 3, 1859; d. at Pittsburgh, Pa., April 21, 1924. Italian tragic actress. Her early life was full of hardships and was saddened by the death of her mother when she was 14. The same year (1872) in Verona, she played Juliet with great success. In 1879, the important manager Cesare Rossi engaged her for his company. Her repertoire soon included *Divorçons*, *Fedora*, *La Locandiera*, and *Theodora.* She toured South America in 1885, and in 1892 she electrified Vienna with her performance in *La Dame aux Camélias.* She made her debut in the U.S. in 1893. In 1895, while playing at London, she engaged in a historic contest with Sarah Bernhardt; both played Sudermann's *Magda* and invited the critics to make their choice. (George Bernard Shaw declared Duse far superior.) In 1899, Duse began her romantic and artistic association with the Italian playwright Gabriele D'Annunzio, having acted in his plays *La Città morta* and *La Gioconda.* In 1902, she came to America with her D'Annunzio dramas, having added *Francesca di Rimini* to her repertoire. She retired prior to World War I, but in 1921 she returned to the stage after a 12-year absence; in 1923 she played a series of matinees at London, and then gave eight performances at New York at the Metropolitan Opera House. Duse is considered by many to have been the greatest tragic actress of the modern theater, and perhaps her most important contribution was her playing of Ibsen's heroines (Nora in *A Doll's House*, Rebecca West in *Rosmersholm*, and *Hedda Gabler*) throughout Europe and America; among her best roles were Juliet, Francesca da Rimini, Camille, and Fernande.

Dushenka (dö'shin.kạ). Romantic poem by the 18th-century Russian poet I. F. Bogdanovich, published in 1775.

Dushman (dösh'mạn), **Saul.** b. at Rostov, Russia, July 12, 1883—. American physical chemist. He arrived (1891) in the U.S. and was associated (1912 *et seq.*) with the General Electric Company's research laboratory at Schenectady, N.Y. He was later (1922–25) director of research at the Edison Lamp Works, Harrison, N.J., and returned (1928) to Schenectady as assistant director of the main research laboratory. He is the author of *High Vacuum* (1923), *Elements of Quantum Mechanics* (1937), and other works.

Dushrattu (dösh.rät'tö). [Also, **Tushrattu.**] King of Mitanni mentioned in the Tel-el-Amarna tablets. From his diplomatic correspondence with the Egyptian king Amenhotep III (of the XVIIIth dynasty, c1500 B.C.), it appears that there existed an old friendship between Egypt and Mitanni, and that Amenhotep had married Dushrattu's daughter.

Dushyanta (dösh.yän'tạ). In Hindu mythology, a king of the lunar race, and descendant of Puru and husband of Shakuntala, by whom he had a son Bharata. The loves of Dushyanta and Shakuntala, her separation from him, and her restoration through the discovery of his lost ring in the belly of a fish, form the plot of Kalidasa's drama *Shakuntala.*

Dussek (dö'sek), **Jan Ladislav.** b. at Czaslau, in Bohemia, Feb. 9, 1761; d. at St.-Germain, near Paris, March 12, 1812. Bohemian pianist and composer. After successfully touring the Continent as a virtuoso (1782 *et seq.*), he made his debut at London in 1790; subsequently he became court musician to the prince von Ysenburg. Among his patrons were Talleyrand and Prince Louis Ferdinand of Prussia. He composed many sonatas, concertos, waltzes, rondos, quartets, and variations.

Düsseldorf (düs'ẹl.dôrf). City in W Germany, the capital of the *Land* (state) of North Rhine-Westphalia, British Zone, formerly in the Rhine Province, Prussia, situated on the E bank of the Rhine River ab. 21 mi. NW of Cologne. It is a river port and an important industrial center, with large machine, metallurgical, electrical, and chemical industries (including Vereinigte Stahlwerke, Mannesmann Röhrenwerke, and Rheinische Metallwaren und Maschinenfabrik); there are also flour mills, sawmills, sugar refineries, paper and leather manufactures, and active trade in metals, scrap, machines, chemicals, lumber, grain, fodder, and livestock. Cultural institutions include a medical school, an art academy, libraries, archives, theaters, an art museum, an arts and crafts museum, a museum of natural history, and a museum of social science and economics. Düsseldorf is the seat of a number of artistic and scholarly societies and also of a number of central industrial administrations, particularly of the German iron and steel industry and of the trade-union movement. It is a modern city with beautiful parks and promenades. There are some old buildings, including the Church of Saint Lambert (12th and 13th centuries), the Church of Saint Andrew (1622–29), the Maximilian Church (1659–1737), the Reformed Church (1684), and the baroque monument to the prince-elector Johann Wilhelm. 420,909 (1946), 500,516 (1950).

History. Düsseldorf was given municipal privileges by Count Adolph of Berg in 1288, and from 1511 was a royal residence. It came in 1609 under the rule of the palatinates of Neuburg of the house of Wittelsbach. It prospered in the reign of the prince-elector Johann Wilhelm (1690–1716), who founded the art gallery which in 1805 was transferred to Munich, to become an integral part of the Bavarian art collections. The art academy was founded by the prince-elector Carl Theodor in 1767. The city was occupied by France in 1795 and was chiefly under French rule until it fell to Prussia in 1814. It was the seat of an influential school of painting and sculpture in the 19th century. The poet Heinrich Heine was born here. Düsseldorf was occupied by the French after World War I (March 8, 1921–Aug. 25, 1925). In World War II it was frequently bombed; grave damage was done in the city and to many public buildings, including the abovementioned churches. Fighting occurred here in March and April, 1945; the city was occupied on April 17, 1945.

Dussera (dus'ėr.ạ). See **Dasara.**

Dust Bowl. Name given (1933) to that part of the high plains of the U.S. between a line near the 100th meridian, on the E, and the Rocky Mountains, on the W. More particularly, it applies to the high plains of the Southwest. Intense dust storms and drought prevailing in the first half of the 1930's brought the term into popular use.

Duster, A Gentleman With a. Pseudonym of **Begbie, Harold.**

Dustin (dus'tin), **Hannah.** [Maiden name, probably, **Emerson.**] b. at Haverhill, Mass., Dec. 23, 1659; date of death not known. American pioneer, captured (1697) by Indians and taken to a river island (now called Dustin's Island) near Concord, Mass. She escaped by killing nine of the Indians, returning with the scalps of her victims as proof of the adventure.

Dutch (duch). **1.** Nationals of the kingdom of the Netherlands, the native speakers of the Dutch language; the Low Germans. **2.** By extension, the nationals of Germany, the native speakers of the German language; the High Germans.

Dutch. Language spoken in the Netherlands, a Germanic language, sometimes called the Hollandish language (which differs very slightly from Flemish, spoken in parts of the adjoining kingdom of Belgium). It is called distinctively Low Dutch. Also, popularly still and formerly, the term is applied sometimes to the language spoken by the Germans, German or High German. This language was formerly and is still occasionally called distinctively High Dutch.

Dutch Borneo (bôr'nē.ō). See under **Borneo.**

Dutch Courtezan, The. Comedy by John Marston, printed in 1605.

Dutch Guiana (gē.ä'nạ). See **Surinam.**

Dutch Harbor. Port in SW Alaska, ab. 1 mi. N of the village of Unalaska, in the E Aleutian Islands. Once an important trading center and center of the fur-sealing industry, Dutch Harbor is now a naval air base, and its trade functions have transferred to Unalaska. It was bombed by Japanese planes in 1942. The harbor is a natural bay ab. 2 mi. long.

Dutchman's Fireside (duch'mạnz), **The.** Novel by James Kirkel Paulding, published in 1831.

Dutch Republic, The Rise of the. See **Rise of the Dutch Republic, The.**

Dutch River. See under **Don,** England.

Dutch Wars. Name applied collectively to three distinct conflicts (1652–54, 1664–67, 1672–78) in the 17th century. The Dutch and the English had long been competitors as carriers of commerce in European waters and to the East and the West Indies. In more recent years, they had also become bitter rivals in the Spitsbergen fisheries. Under the doctrine of the freedom of the seas the Dutch claimed the right to carry goods to France, with which England was embroiled in an undeclared war; against this the English set up, and exercised, the right of search and seizure. The English Navigation Act of 1651, banning Dutch trade with English colonies, brought matters to a head. Cromwell's government had ample funds confiscated from the Royalists, and the English navy was under unified control; the Dutch were dependent for their naval power on the money earned by their commerce, and its effectiveness was hampered by the fact that five provincial admiralties had a say in its use. After many naval actions, in which victory lay variously with the Dutch under Admiral Maarten Tromp and with the English under Admiral Robert Blake, the Dutch were defeated in a major engagement on July 31, 1653, and when peace was concluded by the Treaty of Westminster in April, 1654, the Dutch were constrained to accept English terms. Ten years later English and Dutch rivalry for the privilege of seizing and selling Africans into slavery led to English operations against Dutch trading posts in Africa and to English occupation of New Amsterdam in America. In June, 1664, the Dutch were worsted off Lowestoft, England. But the ravages of the plague retarded English operations until 1666, when several naval engagements were fought with varying fortune. In June, 1667, a Dutch fleet under Admiral De Ruyter sailed up the Thames almost to London, inflicting great damage on English shipping, and in July the Peace of Breda was signed, by which the Dutch ceded New Netherlands, while the English gave them back Surinam and modified the Navigation Laws to Dutch advantage. The attempt of Louis XIV of France to seize the Spanish Netherlands in the War of Devolution (1667–68) led the Dutch and the English, so lately enemies, to become allies, along with Sweden, to balk Louis's plans. But by secret treaty in 1670, England and France became allies, with a view to another assault upon the Netherlands. Operations began in 1672 with English harassments of Dutch convoys, and presently the French attacked by land, being stopped before Amsterdam only by the opening of the dikes. Dutch resistance hardened under the leadership of William of Orange, and the emperor, Spain, Brandenburg, and Denmark entered the conflict as allies of the Netherlands. The war was very unpopular in England, and in 1674 Charles II and the Dutch came to terms of peace. Hostilities between the French and the allies continued with varying fortunes until 1678, when the Treaty of Nijmegen, substantially favorable to the Dutch, was signed.

Dutch West India Company. Commercial and colonizing association (1623–1791) originally chartered in the Netherlands in 1621. Among the important grants it received from the Dutch government were the exclusive right of trading with a large part of the coasts of America and Africa, the authority to plant colonies and build forts, the privilege of employing soldiers and fleets, the power to make treaties, and license to attack the commerce and colonies of Spain and Portugal. It absorbed the United New Netherland Company, which was already engaged in trading around the lower Hudson River. At first the company's efforts were chiefly concerned with settling colonies in Brazil, but in 1654 the Portuguese colonists drove the Dutch out of that region. Thereafter operations in New Netherlands were pressed more vigorously, only to come to nothing with the capture of that colony by the English in 1664. The company continued its operations in the West Indies, in Guiana, and along the Gold Coast of Africa, and its powerful fleets made many descents on the coasts of Spanish and Portuguese America, captured many ships of those nationalities, and obtained vast amounts of booty. But its wars were expensive, it lost some of its colonies, and as a losing venture it was dissolved in 1674. A new company under the same name was formed in 1675, and existed until 1791, but it never greatly prospered.

Dutens (dü.tän), **Louis.** b. at Tours, France, Jan. 15, 1730; d. at London, May 23, 1812. French antiquary, numismatist, and writer. He published *Recherches sur l'origine des découvertes attribuées aux modernes* (1766) and

Mémoires d'un voyageur qui se repose (1806), and edited Leibnitz's works (1769).

Dutertre (dü.tertr), **Jean Baptiste.** b. at Calais, France, 1610; d. at Paris, 1687. French Dominican missionary and author. He served in the army and navy before joining the Dominicans in 1635. From 1640 to 1657 most of his time was spent in the French West Indies, where he witnessed many events of the Carib wars. His *Histoire générale des îles Saint Christophe, de la Guadeloupe . . .* (1654) was enlarged and republished as *Histoire générale des Antilles habitées par les Français* (4 vols., 1667–71).

Dutra (dö'trạ), **Eurico Gaspar.** b. at Cuiabá, Brazil, May 18, 1885—. Brazilian soldier, politician, and president (1946–51) of Brazil. He was commissioned (1910) a second lieutenant of cavalry, was appointed (1935) general in command of the 1st military area, served (1936–45) as minister of war, and organized (1944) Brazilian forces which fought in Italy.

Dutrochet (dü.tro.she), **René Joachim Henri.** b. at Néon, in Poitou, France, Nov. 14, 1776; d. at Paris, Feb. 4, 1847. French physiologist and physicist. He wrote *Nouvelles recherches sur l'endosmose et l'exosmose* (1828).

Dutton (dut'ọn), **Clarence Edward.** b. at Wallingford, Conn., May 15, 1841; d. at Englewood, N.J., Jan. 4, 1912. American geologist. After service in the Civil War as a captain, he joined the U.S. Geological and Geographical Survey, studying (1875–85) the plateau region of Utah and Arizona. He was the author of *Report on the Geology of the High Plateau of Utah* (1879–80), *Tertiary History of the Grand Canyon District* (1882), *Mount Taylor and the Zuñi Plateau* (1886), and *Earthquakes in the Light of the New Seismology* (1904).

Dutton, Edward Payson. b. at Keene, N.H., Jan. 4, 1831; d. at Ridgefield, Conn., Sept. 6, 1923. American publisher, noted for the distribution in America of the "Everyman" series of reprints of English-language classics. He was a member (1852–58) of the firm of Ide and Dutton, Boston booksellers, until he bought out (1858) Ide's interests and reorganized the firm as E. P. Dutton and Company, of which he became president. In 1864 he acquired the retail business of Ticknor and Fields at Boston. He also took over the General Protestant Episcopal Sunday School Union and Church Book Society of New York, and in 1869 moved the headquarters of his firm to New York, where it still remains.

Dutton, Joseph Everett. b. 1874; d. 1905. English biologist. In 1901, in the course of work in Africa, he made the important discovery of the type of flagellate infusorians which, in the human blood, cause sleeping sickness.

Dutuit Collection (dü.twē'). Collection of works of art and historic interest in the possession of the city of Paris.

Duun (dön), **Olav.** b. at Namdalen, Norway, Nov. 21, 1876; d. Sept. 13, 1939. Norwegian novelist, noted for his series *Juvikfolke* (The People of Juvik, 1918–23), an epic of farmers and fisher folk in his native community, which reflects at the same time the culture conflict of old and new and the problems of individual conscience.

Duval (dö.val'), **Claude.** b. at Domfront, in Normandy, France, 1643; executed at Tyburn, London, Jan. 21, 1670. Highwayman in England. His adventures as a highwayman and as a gallant form the subject of a number of novels and ballads.

Duval (dü.vȧl), **Jean Jacques.** See **Esprémesnil** or **Éprémesnil, Jean Jacques Duval d'.**

Duval, Jules. b. at Rodez, Aveyron, France, 1813; killed in France, Sept. 20, 1870. French political economist. He was the author of *Histoire de l'émigration européene, asiatique et africaine au XIXème siècle* (1862).

Duval, Paul. See **Lorrain, Jean.**

Duval (dụ.val'), **William Pope.** b. near Richmond, Va., 1784; d. at Washington, D.C., March 19, 1854. American frontiersman, Congressman, and territorial governor. As a youth of 15 or 16 years he left home for the frontier country of Kentucky, studied law, set up in practice at Bardstown in 1804, entered politics, and was elected to the U.S. Congress for the term 1813–15. In 1821 by appointment of President James Monroe he became the first judge of the superior court of East Florida, and in the following year he was named the first civil governor of the territory. He effected the peaceable transfer of the Seminole Indians to the southern part of the peninsula. He governed ably until 1833, but as the population of the territory grew, and with it the desire for statehood, Duval came to be regarded as a symbol of rule from Washington, and so many conflicts arose that President Andrew Jackson removed him from his office. He helped write the constitution of the state of Florida in 1838, and failed by one vote only to be elected president of the constitutional convention. He was a state senator (1839–42), a member (1845) of the commission to define the northern boundary of Florida, and an unsuccessful candidate (1848) for Congress. William Pope Duval was the model of two characters in early American fiction, namely Ralph Ringwood in Washington Irving's *Wolfert's Roost*, and Nimrod Wildfire in the romance of that name, by James K. Paulding.

Duveen (dụ.vēn'), **Joseph.** [Title, 1st Baron **Duveen of Millbank.**] b. at Hull, England, Oct. 14, 1869; d. May 25, 1939. English art dealer. His father and other members of his family being dealers in pictures, objects of art, and antiques, he entered the business as a young man and eventually became sole proprietor of the firm of Duveen Brothers. A salesman of almost uncanny sagacity and persuasiveness, possessing remarkable self-confidence and audacity, he operated in the grand manner, making art-dealing a sensational, and highly lucrative, business. Employing Bernard Berenson to expertize his purchases, he acquired during his career many of the greatest works of Italian Renaissance painters and of 18th-century English artists, which he sold chiefly to wealthy American collectors, often at fabulous prices. The fact that a picture had been for a time in the Duveen collection, and was bought from Duveen, gave it such enhanced prestige that men like Henry Clay Frick, Andrew Mellon, Henry E. Huntington, Joseph E. Widener, Samuel H. Kress, and William Randolph Hearst cheerfully paid prices which netted him sometimes hundreds of thousands of dollars profit on a single work. He is credited with having inspired Andrew Mellon to provide the funds for the establishment of the National Gallery of Art at Washington and to leave his collection, housed in that gallery, to the nation. For his benefactions to the National Gallery and the Tate Gallery at London, and to British painters, particularly through the British Artists Exhibitions Organization, and in recognition of his endowment of a professorship of the history of art at the University of London, he was knighted in 1919, made a baronet in 1926, and created 1st Baron Duveen of Millbank in 1933. His book *Thirty Years of British Art* was published in 1930.

Duveke (dü'vẹ.kẹ). See **Dyveke.**

Duveneck (dū'vẹ.nek), **Frank.** [Original name, **Frank Decker.**] b. at Covington, Ky., Oct. 9, 1848; d. at Cincinnati, Ohio, Jan. 3, 1919. American painter, etcher, sculptor, and teacher. He began his career as an apprentice to ecclesiastical decorators at Covington and Cincinnati, and at the age of 22 left for Munich, Germany, where he became a student at the Royal Academy. His talents won him a promotion to Wilhelm Dietz's painting class; while at Munich, he painted his well-known *Whistling Boy.* He returned to America in 1873, established a reputation with the paintings he exhibited at the Boston Art Club in 1875, and returned to Munich, where he spent most of his time until 1878, when he established his own school of painting. Following the death of his wife (1888), he settled at Cincinnati, where he was dean of the faculty at the Cincinnati Art Academy. A signal honor was conferred upon him in 1915, when a special gallery at the San Francisco Panama-Pacific Exposition was devoted to an exhibition of his works and a special medal awarded to him by an international jury.

Duvergier de Hauranne (dü.ver.zhyā dẹ ō.rȧn), **Jean.** b. at Bayonne, France, 1581; d. at Paris, Oct. 11, 1643. French Jansenist theologian, abbé of Saint Cyran. He became director of Port Royal in 1636.

Duvergier de Hauranne, Prosper. b. at Rouen, France, Aug. 3, 1798; d. in the Château Herry, near Samerques, Cher, France, May 19, 1881. French royalist politician and publicist. He was imprisoned by Napoleon in 1851, and banished for a brief period. He published *Histoire de gouvernement parlementaire en France* (1857–72).

Duverney (dü.ver.nā), **Guichard Joseph.** b. Aug. 5, 1648; d. Sept. 10, 1730. French anatomist.

Duvernois (dü.ver.nwȧ), **Clément.** b. at Paris, April 6, 1836; d. there, July 8, 1879. French politician and publicist.

Duvernois, Henri. [Pseudonym of **Henri Simon Schwabacher.**] b. at Paris, March 4, 1875; d. there, Jan. 30, 1937. French playwright and novelist. He was the author of several hundred short stories, novels, skits, comedies for the stage, and radio scenarios, and is familiar to American readers because of the appearance of his short stories, in translation, in mass circulation weeklies in the U.S.

Duvernoy (dü.ver.nwȧ), **Georges Louis.** b. at Montbéliard, France, Aug. 6, 1777; d. at Paris, March 1, 1855. French naturalist, a collaborator of Cuvier.

Duveyrier (dü.vā.ryā), **Anne Honoré Joseph.** [Pseudonym, **Mélesville.**] b. at Paris, Nov. 13, 1787; d. there, in November, 1865. French dramatist, a collaborator of Scribe and others; brother of Charles Duveyrier.

Duveyrier, Charles. b. at Paris, April 12, 1803; d. there, Nov. 10, 1866. French dramatic author; brother of A.H. J. Duveyrier. He was a firm believer in the social theories of Saint-Simon.

Duveyrier, Henri. b. at Paris, Feb. 28, 1840; d. by suicide at Sèvres, France, April 25, 1892. French explorer and geographer; son of Charles Duveyrier. He made a preliminary tour to the Sahara (March-April, 1857) and published valuable contributions to Berber ethnology and linguistics (1859). In 1858 he undertook, in the service of the French government, his exploration of the Sahara, which lasted until 1861. He did much to extend French influence. In 1874 he made another expedition to the south of Tunis and in 1876 he was sent on a political mission to Morocco. Most of his works are found in German and French scientific journals. His principal book is *Exploration du Sahara* (1864).

Duvieusart (dü.vyė.zär), **Jean.** b. at Frasnes-lez-Gosselies, Hainaut, Belgium, April 10, 1900—. Belgian politician. He served as mayor (1927–42) of his native town, deputy for the province of Hainaut (1933–36), and member of the house of representatives (1940 *et seq.*). A leader of the Christian Social Party, he was minister of economic affairs (1947–50, 1952 *et seq.*) and served as premier from June to August, 1950, resigning after the abdication of Leopold III, whom he had supported.

du Vigneaud (dų vēn'yō), **Vincent.** b. at Chicago, May 18, 1901—. American biochemist, notable for his researches on hormones, insulin, amino acids, proteins, and vitamins, and on sulfur in bodily chemistry. He received his B.S. (1923) from the University of Illinois and his Ph.D. (1927) from the University of Rochester. He has been a professor of biochemistry and department head (1932–38) at George Washington University medical school, and professor of biochemistry (1938 *et seq.*) at Cornell University medical college.

Dux (dụks). German name of **Duchcov.**

Duxbury (duks'ber".i, -bėr.i). Town in SE Massachusetts, in Plymouth County, on the coast of Plymouth Bay ab. 31 mi. SE of Boston. It was founded early in the 17th century by members of the Plymouth Colony. In its Old Burying Ground is the grave of Miles Standish (1584–1656). 3,167 (1950).

Duyckinck (dī'kingk), **Evert Augustus.** b. at New York, Nov. 23, 1816; d. there, Aug. 13, 1878. American author. He edited (1840–42) *Arcturus*, a literary journal, and published (1848–53) the *Literary World.* He prepared, conjointly with his brother George, a *Cyclopedia of American Literature* (2 vols., 1855; supplement 1865).

Duyckinck, George Long. b. at New York, Oct. 17, 1823; d. there, March 30, 1863. American biographer and critic; brother of Evert Augustus Duyckinck.

Duyse (doi'zẹ), **Prudens van.** b. at Termonde, Belgium, Sept. 17, 1804; d. at Ghent, Belgium, Nov. 13, 1859. Flemish poet and essayist, curator of the archives at Ghent. His poems were collected in *Vaderlandsche Poezy* (1840), *Het Klaverblad* (1848), and others.

Dvina (dvē.nä'). [Also: **Northern Dvina;** Russian, **Severnaya Dvina.**] Large river in NW U.S.S.R., traversing the Arkhangelsk *oblast* (region) of the Russian Soviet Federated Socialist Republic. It is formed by the confluence of the Vichegda and Sukhona rivers and flows generally NW to the White Sea at Arkhangelsk. It is navigable for its entire length, and is important also for logging and fishing. Great quantities of timber are floated down to supply the lumbering industry of Arkhangelsk. The Dvina system is linked by canals to the Kama and to the upper Volga via the Sheksna. Area of drainage basin, ab. 139,700 sq. mi.; length, ab. 470 mi.

Dvina. [Also: **Southern Dvina, Western Dvina** (Russian, **Zapadnaya Dvina**); Lettish, **Daugava**; German, **Düna.**] River in W U.S.S.R., which rises in the Kalinin *oblast* (region) of the Russian Soviet Federated Socialist Republic and flows into the Gulf of Riga ab. 5 mi. N of Riga. Length, 500–600 mi.; navigable to Vitebsk.

Dvina Gulf. [Also: **Dvina Bay, Gulf of Dvinsk;** Russian, **Dvinskaya Gruba** (dvēn'skạ.yạ gö.bä'); former (English) names, **Archangel Bay, Gulf of Archangel.**] Arm of the White Sea near Arkhangelsk (Archangel), in N U.S.S.R.

Dvinsk (dvēnsk). Russian name of **Daugavpils.**

Dvořák (dvôr'zhäk), **Antonín.** [Also, **Anton Dvorak.**] b. at Nelahozeves, in Bohemia, Sept. 8, 1841; d. at Prague, May 1, 1904. Czech composer. In 1873 his hymn *Die Erben des Weissen Berges*, for chorus and orchestra, brought him before the public. He soon received a state stipend. He conducted his *Stabat Mater* at London in March, 1884, and in the autumn of the same year at the Worcester musical festival. He was director (1892–95) of the National Conservatory of Music at New York, and director (1901–04) of the Conservatorium at Prague. Among his works are the operas *King and Collier* (produced in 1874), *The Pigheaded Peasants* (1874), *Vanda* (1876), *The Peasant a Rogue* (1877), *Dimitrije* (1882), and *The Devil and Kate* (1888); he also composed *Slavonic Dances* (1878) for duo piano, vocal duets, *The Spectre's Bride*, a cantata (1885), *St. Ludmila*, an oratorio (1886), *Requiem Mass* (1891), symphonies including *From the New World* (produced at New York, 1893, and usually known as the *New World Symphony*), concertos, string quartets, songs, impromptus, intermezzos, chamber music, and others. He introduced two original Bohemian forms, the *dumka* (elegy) and the *furiant* (a scherzo), in his symphonies and chamber music.

Dvorsky (dvôr'ski), **Michael.** See **Hofmann, Josef.**

Dvůr Králové nad Labem (dvôr' krä'lô.ve näd lä'bem). [Also: **Dvůr Králové**; German, **Königinhof, Königinhof an der Elbe.**] Town in Czechoslovakia, in NW Bohemia, situated on the Labe (Elbe) River between Jaromer and Vrchlabí, ab. 64 mi. NE of Prague. There is a considerable textile industry, and also a machine factory and a brewery. Here, on June 29, 1866, the Prussians defeated the Austrians. In 1818, a document was found here, which has become known as Královédvorský Rukopis (German, Königinhofer Handschrift), supposedly dating from the 13th century and containing the origins of Czech literature. The document was soon recognized as a forgery but continued to play a great role in the Czech cultural revival during the 19th century. 13,675 (1947).

Dwala (dwä'lä). See **Duala.**

Dwarka (dwär'kä). [Also: **Dwaraka, Jigat.**] Town in Bombay state, Union of India, at the mouth of the Gulf of Kutch, celebrated as the residence of Krishna, and a sacred Hindu city. It is a famous place of pilgrimage and a port of call on the Bombay-Karachi route. Steamers lie at some distance from shore and the trade is chiefly local. Pop. ab. 9,000.

Dweller of the Threshold, The. In Edward Bulwer-Lytton's novel *Zanoni*, a powerful and malignant being:

Whose form of giant mould
No mortal eye can fixed behold.

Dwiggins (dwig'inz), **William Addison.** b. at Martinsville, Ohio, 1880—. American type designer, book designer, and calligrapher. As an advertising artist and layout man, he perceived the need of type faces expressly suggestive of the modern machine age, and he designed a number of types to meet that need. In *An Investigation into the Physical Properties of Books* (1919) he animadverted severely on the state of things in American book design at that time. This led to his employment by the publisher Alfred A. Knopf to design a number of books which had the effect of greatly improving book design in the U.S. He did much also to revive interest in calligraphy. Some of his writings on the graphic arts have been collected under the title of *Mss. by W A D* (1949). His *Layout in Advertising* has been since its publication in 1928 an immensely influential work.

Dwight (dwīt). Village in N central Illinois, in Livingston County, ab. 55 mi. SW of Chicago. 2,843 (1950).

Dwight, Harrison Gray Otis. b. at Conway, Mass., Nov. 22, 1803; killed in a railroad accident in Vermont, Jan. 25, 1862. American Congregational clergyman, missionary to the Armenians.

Dwight, Henry Otis. b. at Constantinople, June 3, 1843; d. at Roselle, N.J., June 20, 1917. American writer and editor; son of Harrison Gray Otis Dwight. Secular agent (1867–74) in Turkey for the American Board of Commissioners for Foreign Missions; correspondent (1875–92) in Turkey for the New York *Tribune.* Author of *Turkish Life in War Time* (1881), *Treaty Rights of American Missionaries in Turkey* (1893), *Constantinople and Its Problems* (1901), *The Blue Book of Missions* (1905, 1907); editor of *Sir James Redhouse's Turkish and English Lexicon* (1890) and the *Encyclopaedia of Missions* (1904).

Dwight, John. b. 1637 or c1640; d. 1703. English potter, remembered for his petition of 1671 for a patent in which he claimed the discovery of the mystery hitherto attached to the making of transparent earthenware, commonly known as porcelain or china, or Persian ware. Whether the porcelain Dwight referred to was porcelain as later made is not certain, but he did bring the manufacture of stoneware to perfection. It is certain that Dwight did make some ware similar to porcelain, and also statues or figures. His wares are now in the British Museum and the South Kensington Museum.

Dwight, John Sullivan. b. at Boston, May 13, 1813; d. there, Sept. 5, 1893. American music critic and editor. He was graduated (1832) from Harvard, was among the organizers (1837) of the group which later became the Harvard Musical Association, and was an active member of the Transcendental Club, becoming (1841) a teacher of music and Latin at Brook Farm. He contributed articles on music and other subjects to the *Harbinger*, the Boston *Daily Chronotype*, and *Sartain's Magazine*, and for a time in 1851 was music editor of the Boston *Commonwealth.* He edited (1852–81) *Dwight's Journal of Music*, took a leading role in founding (1865) the Boston Philharmonic Society, was president (1873–93) of the Harvard Musica Association, and aided in establishing (1876) a professorship of music at Harvard.

Dwight, Mabel. b. at Cincinnati, Ohio, Jan. 29, 1876—. American etcher, painter, and lithographer, perhaps best known for her lithographs, which have been collected by museums and institutions at Paris, Berlin, and London, as well as in the U.S. She was educated at the Hopkins School of Art, San Francisco, and has exhibited widely in the U.S. and Europe. She has also done many water colors of the American scene. The Metropolitan Museum, Whitney Museum, and Brooklyn Museum at New York, Boston Museum, Fogg Art Museum at Cambridge, Mass., Art Institute of Chicago, Detroit Museum, Berlin Museum, Victoria and Albert Museum at London, and the Bibliothèque Nationale at Paris have collected her works, among which are *The Ferry Boat, Life Class, Sacco and Vanzetti, Circus Act, Barnyard, Nova Scotia, The Ocean,* and *Scene from Green Pastures.*

Dwight, Sereno Edwards. b. at Greenfield Hill, Conn., May 18, 1786; d. at Philadelphia, Nov. 30, 1850. American Congregational clergyman and author; son of Timothy Dwight (1752–1817). He was president of Hamilton College (1833–35), and wrote *Life of Edwards* (1830) and *The Hebrew Wife* (1836), and edited Jonathan Edwards's works (1829).

Dwight, Theodore. b. at Northampton, Mass., Dec. 15, 1764; d. at New York, June 12, 1846. American journalist and politician; brother of Timothy Dwight (1752–1817). He served as a Federalist representative from Connecticut in the 9th Congress (Dec. 1, 1806–March 3, 1807), was secretary of the Hartford Convention in 1814, and founded (c1817) the New York *Daily Advertiser*, with which he was connected until 1835.

Dwight, Theodore. b. at Hartford, Conn., March 3, 1796; d. at Brooklyn, N.Y., Oct. 16, 1866. American author; son of Theodore Dwight (1764–1846). He wrote *History of Connecticut* (1841).

Dwight, Theodore William. b. at Catskill, N.Y., July 18, 1822; d. at Clinton, N.Y., June 29, 1892. American jurist; grandson of Timothy Dwight (1752–1817). He was graduated from Hamilton College, Clinton, N.Y., in 1840, and was professor of municipal law (1858–91) at Columbia College. He published *Argument in the Court of Appeals in the Rose Will Case* (1863) and *Cases extracted from the Report of the Commissioners of Charities in England, and the Disposition of Property for Charitable Uses* (1864).

Dwight, Thomas. b. at Boston, Oct. 13, 1843; d. Sept. 9, 1911. American surgeon and anatomist. He received his M.D. (1867) from the Harvard Medical School, and was thereafter an instructor in comparative anatomy (1872–77, 1880–83) at Harvard, succeeding (1883) Oliver Wendell Holmes as Parkman professor of anatomy. He was the author of *The Intracranial Circulation* (1867), which won the Boylston prize, *The Structure and Action of Striated Muscle Fibers* (1873), *The Anatomy of the Head, with . . . Plates Representing Frozen Sections* (1876), *Frozen Sections of a Child* (1881), *Notes on the Dissection and Brain of the Chimpanzee "Gumbo"* (1895), *Description of the Human Spine Showing Numerical Variations* (1901), and *Thoughts of a Catholic Anatomist* (1911).

Dwight, Timothy. b. at Northampton, Mass., May 14, 1752; d. Jan. 11, 1817. American Congregational minister, educator, and writer. A grandson of Jonathan Edwards, he was a child prodigy, able to read the Bible before the age of four. He graduated (1769) from Yale, served as principal of the Hopkins Grammar School at New Haven, and was a tutor (1771–77) at Yale, where he also received his master's degree (1772). Licensed to preach (1777) by a committee of the Northern Association of Massachusetts, he was appointed later in the same year as chaplain of a Connecticut brigade in the Continental Army, resigning from the post in 1779. Returning to Northampton, he became active in politics and sat (1781–82) in the state legislature. In 1783 he took a pastorate at the Greenfield Hill Congregational Church, where he was ordained later in the same year. The successor to Ezra Stiles, he was (1795–1817) president of Yale College, where he also served as professor of theology and taught several other subjects; he founded the medical department at Yale and liberalized campus life. In addition, he helped organize the Missionary Society of Connecticut, the Andover Theological Seminary, and the American Board of Commissioners for Foreign Missions. A stern Calvinist, he expounded his views in *Theology, Explained and Defended* (5 vols., 1818–19), originally delivered as sermons to Yale students. He also wrote *A Discourse on the Genuineness, and Authenticity of the New Testament* (1794) and *The Nature, and Danger, of Infidel Philosophy* (1798). A Federalist in politics, he wrote *The Duty of Americans, at the Present Crisis* (1798) and the *Discourse . . . on the Character of George Washington, Esq.* (1800). His first publication, *A Dissertation on the History, Eloquence, and Poetry of the Bible* (1772) is the acknowledged fountainhead of the literary school known as the Connecticut (or Hartford) Wits. *The Conquest of Canaan* (1785) was styled by Dwight as the first American epic poem. His other poetical works include *Greenfield Hill* (1794) and *The Triumph of Infidelity, a Poem* (1788). Important as a historical source is his *Travels in New England and New York* (4 vols., 1821–22).

Dwight, Timothy. b. at Norwich, Conn., Nov. 16, 1828; d. May 26, 1916. American scholar; grandson of Timothy Dwight (1752–1817). He was graduated at Yale College in 1849, studied divinity at Yale (1851–55) and at Bonn and Berlin (1856–58), became professor of sacred literature and New Testament Greek in the divinity school at Yale in 1858, was appointed president of Yale College in 1886 (resigned 1899), and was a member of the New Testament Revision Company. He published *The True Ideal of an American University* (1872), among others.

Dwinger (dving'ėr), **Edwin Erich.** b. at Kiel, Germany, April 23, 1898—. German novelist. He experienced World War I at its worst: he was captured by the Russians, held prisoner in Siberia, then fought under Kolchak against the Bolsheviks, and finally escaped to Germany five years after he had left it. In the trilogy *Die Armee hinter Stacheldraht* (1929; *Prisoner of War*, 1930), *Zwischen Weiss und Rot* (1930; *Between White and Red*, 1932), and

Wir rufen Deutschland (1932), written in diary form, he has set forth the unspeakable horrors he felt and saw. The first volume particularly is considered by many to be one of the most unforgettable of the books about World War I.

Dwyfor (dü.ē'vôr), 1st Earl of. Title of **Lloyd George, David.**

Dyak (dī'ak). [Also: **Dayak, Dajak.**] Collective term for the pagan natives of Borneo, including these distinct tribal groupings: Land Dyak (SW), Ngadju Dyak (SE), Iban or Sea Dyak (W), Bahau (E), and Klamatan (Sarawak and British North Borneo). They number between one and one-and-a-half million. Their languages all belong to the Malayo-Polynesian stock.

Dyar (dī'ạr), **Harrison Gray.** b. at New York, Feb. 14, 1866; d. at Washington, D.C., Jan. 21, 1929. American entomologist. He was custodian of Lepidoptera (1897–1929) at the U.S. National Museum, which now houses his large collection. His most important work was research on the mosquito, and he published *The Mosquitoes of North and Central America* (4 vols., 1912–17), with Frederick Knab and L. O. Howard, and *The Mosquitoes of the Americas* (1928). He was also publisher of a monthly journal, *Insecutor Inscitiae Menstruus*, and editor (1904–07) of the *Journal of the New York Entomological Society.*

Dyar, Mary. See **Dyer** or **Dyar, Mary.**

Dyardanes (dī.är.dā'nēz). An ancient name of the **Brahmaputra.**

Dyamond (dī'ạ.mọnd). See **Diamond.**

Dyangeh (dyäng'ge). See **Dinka.**

Dyarse (dyär'se). See **Yarse.**

Dybbøl (düb'ėl). [German, **Düppel.**] Village in S Jutland, Denmark, opposite Sønderborg, ab. 28 mi. NE of Schleswig. The allied German troops were defeated here by the Danes on May 28, 1848, and again on June 5. The redoubts were stormed by the Saxons and Bavarians on April 13, 1849, and by the Prussians on April 18, 1864. Pop. ab. 1,000.

Dyce (dīs), **Alexander.** b. at Edinburgh, June 30, 1798; d. at London, May 15, 1869. British literary critic and Shakespearian scholar; cousin of William Dyce. He received a B.A. at Oxford in 1819, entered the ministry c1822, abandoned the clerical profession in 1825, and devoted himself to literature. He edited a number of English classics, including the works of William Collins (1827), George Peele (1828–39), John Webster (1830), Robert Greene (1831), James Shirley (1833), Thomas Middleton (1840), Beaumont and Fletcher (1843–46), and Christopher Marlowe (1850), but is chiefly known for his edition of Shakespeare (1857; revised 1866). He was one of those exposing John Payne Collier's inventions in Elizabethan literature. Dyce was a founder of the Percy Society, dedicated to publishing old poetry in English.

Dyce, William. b. at Aberdeen, Scotland, Sept. 19, 1806; d. at Streatham, England, Feb. 14, 1864. British historical painter, founder of the Pre-Raphaelite movement in the English school of painting; cousin of Alexander Dyce. He graduated with the degree of M.A. at the University of Aberdeen in 1822, and exhibited his first picture, *Bacchus Nursed by the Nymphs of Nyssa*, at the Royal Academy, London, in 1827; he painted a *Madonna and Child* in the Pre-Raphaelite style in 1828. He lived as a portrait painter at Edinburgh (1830–37), was headmaster of the School of Design at Somerset House, London (1840–43), and was appointed professor of fine arts in King's College, London, in 1844. He designed the fresco *Baptism of Ethelbert* for the House of Lords in 1846. He published *Theory of the Fine Arts* (1844), *The National Gallery, its Formation and Management* (1853), and others.

Dyche (dīch), **Thomas.** d. c1735. English schoolmaster, compiler of grammars, vocabularies, and dictionaries. Master of Stratford Bow school (after 1710); convicted of libel (1719) for his exposure of the peculations of John Ward of Hackney. Compiler of *Vocabularium Latiale* (1708 or 1709), *A Guide to the English Tongue* (1709), *The Spelling Dictionary* (1725), and *A New General English Dictionary* (3rd ed., 1740).

Dyer (dī'ėr), Sir **Edward.** d. 1607. English poet and courtier. He was employed in several embassies by Queen Elizabeth, by whom he was knighted in 1596. He was a friend of Raleigh and Sidney, and wrote a number of pastoral odes and madrigals. He is known chiefly as the author of a poem descriptive of contentment, beginning "My mind to me a kingdom is" (set to music in William Byrd's *Psalmes, Sonets, and Songs*, 1588).

Dyer, Eliphalet. b. at Windham, Conn., Sept. 14, 1721; d. there, May 13, 1807. American lawyer. He was a member (1747–62) of the Connecticut general assembly, and subsequently (1762–84) of the governor's council. An associate justice (after 1766) of the superior court of Connecticut, he was also a delegate (1774 *et seq.*) to the Continental Congress. Earlier (1754) he was an organizer of the Susquehanna Company to lay out a Connecticut settlement in the Wyoming Valley, west of what was then New York province. After years of adjudication with Pennsylvania, the case was argued by Dyer before a congressional committee, and the title was awarded to Connecticut (although these and other western lands were ultimately lost by Connecticut).

Dyer, George. b. at London, March 15, 1755; d. there, March 2, 1841. English scholar. He graduated at Cambridge University in 1778, and subsequently became pastor of a dissenting congregation at Cambridge. Having abandoned the clerical profession, he settled in 1792 at London, where he devoted himself to literature. His chief works are *History of the University and Colleges of Cambridge* (1814) and *Privileges of the University of Cambridge* (1824).

Dyer, Isadore. b. at Galveston, Tex., Nov. 2, 1865; d. Oct. 12, 1920. American dermatologist and leprologist. He was an associate professor of dermatology (1905–08), and later full professor and dean (1908–20), at Tulane University, Louisiana. He was a founder and first president (1894) of the Louisiana Leper Home (later the National Leprosarium). He was the author of *The Art of Medicine and Other Addresses, Papers, etc.* (1913); editor (1896–1920) of the *New Orleans Medical and Surgical Journal* and coeditor (1914–16) of the *American Journal of Tropical Diseases and Preventative Medicine.*

Dyer, John. b. at Aberglasney, Carmarthenshire, Wales, c1700; d. July 24, 1758. English poet. He became vicar of Calthorp, Leicestershire, in 1741, and subsequently held several church posts in Lincolnshire. He published *Grongar Hill* (1726), which with James Thomson's *The Seasons* is generally recognized as the first of the romantic pastoral poems, *Ruins of Rome* (1740), and *The Fleece* (1757).

Dyer or **Dyar, Mary.** Hanged at Boston, June 1, 1660. Quaker martyr. A Quaker intent on visiting her fellow Quakers imprisoned at Boston, she was twice banished from the Massachusetts colony on pain of death, and, when she returned again, was hanged on Boston Common.

Dyer, Nehemiah Mayo. b. at Provincetown, Mass., Feb. 19, 1839; d. Jan. 27, 1910. American naval officer, with the Union navy in the Civil War. He served on the *Metacomet* at Mobile Bay, was commissioned lieutenant and lieutenant commander during 1868, and as captain (1897) in command of the *Baltimore* participated in Dewey's victory at Manila Bay. He retired (1901) as a rear admiral.

Dyer, Reginald Edward Harry. b. at Simla, India, Oct. 9, 1864; d. at Long Ashton, Bristol, England, July 23, 1927. British general now generally held to have been immediately responsible for the "Amritsar Massacre" of 1919 in India. He entered the British army in India in 1885, and thereafter participated in many operations against Indian and Burmese objectors to British rule, and rose to command of an infantry brigade at the time of World War I. On April 13, 1919, he ordered troops under his command to fire on an assemblage of about 5,000 men, women, and children who had gathered for a religious observance in the Jalianwala Bagh, a public garden in the Punjab city of Amritsar. The casualties were nearly 400 killed and about 1,200 wounded. By General Dyer's further order, no one was allowed throughout the day to give medical aid, water, or other help to the wounded. When it became evident that these procedures had awakened profound anger throughout India, and caused unfavorable comment around the world, a commission of inquiry was set up. It heard General Dyer, who had been promoted to a higher command, admit that the gathering in the Jalianwala Bagh had no political character and had been entirely unarmed and peaceful (he is said to have regretted, however, that he had not had still more shot, the better to further his primary purpose of quelling anti-British activity in the Punjab). The commission censured the general; the commander in chief in India permitted him to resign; his admirers gave him a handsome sword; and he passed his last years in scientific studies, particularly concerning military aircraft. "Remember Amritsar" became an Indian nationalist slogan, and most historians now believe that Dyer's exploit actually therefore did much to hasten the eventual withdrawal of the British from India.

Dyer, Samuel. b. at London, 1725; d. there, Sept. 15, 1772. English translator, a friend of Samuel Johnson. He matriculated (1743) at Leiden, and intended originally to enter the ministry, but took up literary work at London. Member of the club organized (1749) by Johnson which met at the King's Head in Ivy Lane; translated lives of Pericles and Demetrius for Tinson's edition of *Plutarch's Lives* (1758); joined Johnson's Literary Club (1764) and became a friend of Edmund Burke; credited by Sir Joshua Reynolds and Malone with the authorship of the *Letters of Junius*.

Dyer, Thomas Henry. b. at London, May 4, 1804; d. at Bath, England, Jan. 30, 1888. English historian. He was for some time employed as a clerk in the West India House, and eventually devoted himself wholly to literature. He wrote *History of Modern Europe* (1861–64), *A History of the City of Rome* (1865), and others.

Dyerma (dyer'mä). See **Djerma.**

Dyersburg (dī'ėrz.bėrg). City in W Tennessee, county seat of Dyer County, in a cotton area: manufactures of cotton textiles. 10,885 (1950).

Dying Alexander (al.eg.zan'dėr). Name given to a sculptured head, held to be a Greek original of Hellenistic date, very remarkable for the intensity of its expression of pain, and of admirable execution.

Dying Gaul (gôl), **The.** [Formerly called **The Dying Gladiator.**] Ancient statue of the Pergamene school, in the Capitoline Museum, Rome. The warrior, nude, sits on the ground with bowed head, supporting himself with his right arm. The statue is considered especially fine in the mastery of anatomy displayed, and in its characterization of the racial type. It is thought possibly to have been commissioned by Attalus as a monument to his victories over the Gauls.

Dyk (dik), **Viktor.** b. at Psovka, Czechoslovakia, 1877; d. at Dubrovnik, Yugoslavia, 1931. Czech poet, dramatist, and novelist. As a young journalist he edited and wrote for periodicals of the anti-Austrian Radical Progressive Party, and throughout his life, nationalist sentiment dominated his work. In 1917 he was imprisoned by the Austrian authorities, but after the attainment of Czechoslovak independence he became a member of parliament and eventually a senator. He is esteemed chiefly as a poet, one of his best-known works being *The Window*, which was inspired by his prison experiences. Some of his short stories, of a romantic turn, are much admired, but some critical opinion holds that his novels are weak in construction and too verbose. As a dramatist he was successful both with historical plays and with satirical comedies.

Dykes (dīks), **John Bacchus.** b. at Hull, England, March 10, 1823; d. at St. Leonards, England, Jan. 22, 1876. English composer of church music, notably hymns such as *Nearer, My God, to Thee, The Day is Past and Over*, and *Jesus, Lover of My Soul.* He was an editor of *Hymns, Ancient and Modern.*

Dykh-Tau (dich.tou'). Peak in SW U.S.S.R., in the C Caucasus Mountains, ab. 50 mi. SE of Mount Elbrus. It is a sharp peak with mountain glaciers. Elevation, ab. 17,053 ft.

Dykstra (dīk'strą), **Clarence Addison.** b. at Cleveland, Ohio, Feb. 25, 1883; d. at Laguna Beach, Calif., May 6, 1950. American educator. He was professor of political science (1909–18) at Kansas. He served as commissioner (1923–26) and director of personnel and efficiency (1926–30) in the Los Angeles department of water and power, and was chosen city manager (1930–37) of Cincinnati, Ohio. He was president (1937–44) of the University of Wisconsin, served (1940–41) as U.S. selective service director while on leave of absence from Wisconsin, and was provost (1944 *et seq.*) of the University of California.

Dymoke (dim'ǫk), **Robert.** d. April 13, 1546. English soldier; son of Sir Thomas Dymoke (c1428–1471). He acted (1484, 1502, and 1509) as sheriff of Lincolnshire, was champion at the coronations of Richard III, Henry VII, and Henry VIII, and distinguished himself at the siege of Tournai.

Dymoke, Sir Thomas. b. c1428; beheaded at London, 1471. English soldier, attached to the Lancastrian faction in the Wars of the Roses. He aided his brother-in-law Sir Robert Wells in raising a force (1471) in Lincolnshire in support of Henry VI. Captured by Edward IV at Edgecote, he was taken to London and beheaded.

Dymond (dī'mǫnd), **John.** b. in Canada, May 3, 1836; d. March 5, 1922. American sugar planter. Broker (1863 *et seq.*) with Dymond and Lally at New York; New Orleans office (opened 1866) to trade in sugar, molasses, and coffee led to purchase of two sugar plantations on the Mississippi River. As manager of the plantations, he innovated many devices for the improvement of sugarcane growing.

Dymond, Jonathan. b. at Exeter, England, Dec. 19, 1796; d. May 6, 1828. English author. He followed the occupation of a linen-draper at Essex, where in 1825 he founded an auxiliary society of the Peace Society. His chief work is *Essays on the Principles of Morality* (1829).

Dynamo. Play (1929) by Eugene O'Neill. An electrical dynamo displaces God in the hierarchy of the universe, assuming the role of a cruel, relentless potentate.

Dynasts, The. Poem by Thomas Hardy, published in three parts, in 1903, 1905, and 1908. This is a gigantic epic drama (130 scenes in 19 acts) dealing with the Napoleonic wars, with interspersed lyrics and philosophical comments by supernatural spirits and choruses. In spite of its formal and stylistic defects, *The Dynasts* has been acclaimed as the greatest work, at least in its conception, produced by any English poet since Milton's *Paradise Lost.*

Dyola (dyō'lä). See **Diola.**

Dyoor (dūr). See **Lwo.**

Dyoula (dū'lä). See **Diula.**

Dyrrhachium (di.rā'ki.um). A Latin name of **Durrës,** city.

Dysart (dī'zart). Seaport, incorporated (1930) in Kirkcaldy royal burgh, in E Scotland, in Fifeshire, situated on the N bank of the Firth of Forth, ab. 2 mi. NE of Kirkcaldy proper. The port exports coal from the Fifeshire coal field.

Dyscolus (dis'kǫ.lus), **Apollonius.** See **Apollonius Dyscolus.**

Dysmas (diz'mąs). See **Dismas.**

Dyson (dī'sǫn), Sir **Frank Watson.** b. in Ashby de la Zouch, England, 1868; d. at sea en route to South Africa from Australia, May 25, 1939. British astronomer, who served as astronomer royal of Scotland (1905–10) and of England (1910–33). Member of eclipse expeditions to Portugal (1900), Sumatra (1901), and Sfax, Tunisia (1905); verified (1919) Einstein theory of effect of gravitation on light; president of International Astronomical Union.

Dyson, William Henry. b. at Alfredton, Victoria, Australia, Sept. 23, 1880; d. at London, Jan. 21, 1938. Australian cartoonist and satirical etcher. He gained great fame in England after 1910, especially as staff cartoonist for the Labourite *Daily Herald* (1912–16), where his satirical work on British complacency took the public fancy. He reached the peak of his popularity during World War I. He was associated (1925–30) with the Melbourne *Herald*, but returned to London and the *Daily Herald*, to which he contributed until his death.

Dyushambe (dų.shäm'bę). Former name of **Stalinabad.**

Dyveke (dü'vę.kę). [Also: **Duveke, Duiveke;** Latin, **Columbula,** meaning "Little Dove."] b. at Amsterdam, Netherlands, 1491; d. probably by poison, 1517. Mistress of Christian II of Denmark. Christian met her (1507) at Bergen, Norway, where her mother kept a small inn. She accompanied him to Oslo as his mistress, a relationship which she maintained even after his elevation to the throne in 1513, and his marriage (1515) to Isabella, sister of the emperor Charles V. She has been made the subject of an 18th-century tragedy, and of various novels and poems.

Dza-chu (dzä'chö'). Tibetan name of the **Mekong.**

Dzaudzhikau (dzou.jē.kou'). [Former names, **Ordzhonikidze, Ordjonikidze, Vladikavkaz.**] City in the U.S.S.R., capital of the North Ossetian Autonomous Soviet Socialist Republic, in the Russian Soviet Federated Socialist Republic, situated on the Terek River at the base of the Caucasus Mountains. Zinc, lead, silver, and copper are mined here and a large sulfuric acid plant is located in the city. It is a railroad terminus, a fortress, and an important center of transit trade. 127,172 (1939).

Dzerzhinsk (dzer.zhinsk'). [Former name, **Rastyapino.**] City in the U.S.S.R., in the Gorki *oblast* (region) of the Russian Soviet Federated Socialist Republic, ab. 25 mi. W of Gorki. It has dye factories and cotton and linen mills. 103,415 (1939).

Dzerzhinsky (dzer.zhin'ski), **Felix Edmundovich.** b. at Vilna, Lithuania (then a part of the Russian empire), 1877; d. in July, 1926. Russian political agitator and politician. He joined the Social Democratic Party in 1895, was banished to Siberia in 1897, escaped in 1899, was arrested again in 1900, escaped again in 1902, took a hand in the unsuccessful revolution of 1905, was again banished, and returned in 1912 only to be arrested once more and sentenced to prison at hard labor. Released in the early days of the revolution of 1917, he became a member of the group which planned the successful Bolshevik coup in November of that year, and in December was assigned to organize the Cheka, or secret police. In 1919 he was named commissar of the home department, and subsequently became commissar of transport, and finally head of the supreme economic council.

Dzhambul (jäm.böl'). [Former name, **Aulie-Ata, Auliye-Ata.**] City in the U.S.S.R., in the Kazakh Soviet Socialist Republic: a fast-growing city producing foodstuffs and textiles. 62,723 (1939).

Dzhibkhalantu (jēp.нä.län.tö'). [Also: **Jibhalanta;** Mongolian, **Uliassutai, Ulasutai.**] City in the Mongolian People's Republic, ab. 400 mi. W of Ulan Bator, the capital. It is a trading center and caravan meeting-place on one of the important trade routes from the W part of the country to the U.S.S.R. Pop. ab. 6,000.

Dzhugashvili (jö.gą.shvē'li), **Joseph Vissarionovich.** See **Stalin, Joseph Vissarionovich.**

Dzierzon (je'zhôn), **Johann** (or **Jan**). b. Jan. 16, 1811; d. Oct. 26, 1906. Polish-German apiculturist, noted as the discoverer of parthenogenesis in the drones of the honeybee. He also devised the Dzierzon hive (with cupboard opening at one end). He was the author of *Theorie und Praxis des neuen Bienengreundes* (1848), *Rationelle Bienenzucht* (1861; Eng. trans., *Dzierzon's Rational Beekeeping*, 1882), and *Der Zwillingsstock* (1890).

Dzierżoniów (jer.zhô'nyöf). [German, **Reichenbach.**] Town in S Poland, in the *województwo* (province) of Wrocław, formerly in Silesia, Germany, situated on the slopes of the Eulengebirge and on the Peile River ab. 32 mi. SW of the city of Wrocław (Breslau). It has cotton textile mills, livestock markets, and grain trade. Jewish textile workers' coöperatives from Poland settled here after World War II. There are various educational institutions. Here, on Aug. 16, 1762, Frederick the Great defeated the Austrians under Laudon; and here a convention (called the Convention of Reichenbach) was signed, on July 27, 1790, by which the emperor Leopold agreed not to annex Turkish territory, while Prussia gave up plans for annexations in Poland. A treaty was concluded here, on June 15, 1813, by which Great Britain agreed to subsidies for Russia and Prussia in the war against Napoleon. The town became part of Poland as a result of the decisions made at the Potsdam Conference (or Berlin Conference) in 1945. Pop. 17,253 (1939), 16,646 (1946).

Dzugashvili (dzö.gą.shvē'li), **Joseph Vissarionovich.** See **Stalin, Joseph Vissarionovich.**

Dzungaria (zúng.gãr'i.ą). [Also: **Songaria, Soongaria, Sungaria, Zungaria;** sometimes called the **"Northern Circuit."**] Name given to a former province of Ili, in the Chinese empire, S of the Altai, W of Mongolia, and E and S of Asiatic Russia; also sometimes restricted to a part of this province. It was the nucleus of a Mongol kingdom, that of the Songares, in the 17th and 18th centuries. It is now a part of the Chinese province of Sinkiang.

Dzungarian Alatau (zúng.gãr'i.ąn ä.lä.tou'). Mountain range in the U.S.S.R., in the Kazakh Soviet Socialist Republic, Asiatic Russia, on the boundary between that government and the Chinese province of Sinkiang. Elevation (average), ab. 13,000 ft.; length, ab. 350 mi.

Dzungarian Basin. [Also, **Dzungaria.**] Basin in NW China, in the province of Sinkiang. Bordered on the S by the Tien Shan mountain range and on the N by the Altai range, it is a desert region similar to the more moist parts of the Gobi. Length, ab. 450 mi.; width, ab. 200 mi.

Dzyubin (dzyö'bin), **Eduard Georgiyevich.** See **Bagritski, Eduard.**

E

Ea (ā'ä). One of the supreme gods of the Sumerians and Babylonians, enumerated in the first triad (with Anu and Enlil) of the 12 great gods. He was the god of the ocean and the subterranean springs. As god of the people he was also "lord of profound wisdom" and counsel, patron of sciences and arts, creator, bringer of culture, healer, and god of fertility.

Eabani or **Ea-bani** (ā.ä.bä'nē). See **Enkidu.**

Each and All. Poem by Ralph Waldo Emerson, published in 1839.

Eachard (ēch'ąrd), **John.** b. in Suffolk, England, c1636; d. at Cambridge, England, July 7, 1697. English divine and satirical writer. He was chosen master of Catharine Hall, Cambridge University, in 1675, and vice-chancellor of the University in 1679 and 1695. He wrote *The Grounds and Occasions of the Contempt of the Clergy and Religion* (1670, published anonymously), and others.

Eadbert (ed'bėrt) or **Eadberht** (ad'berċht), Saint. d. 698. Bishop of Lindisfarne in 688, the successor of Saint Cuthbert.

Eadburga (ed'bėr.gä) or **Eadburgh** (ad'börċh). [Also, **Eadburh** (ad'börċh).] fl. c800. Daughter of Offa, king of Mercia, and wife of Brihtric (Beorhtric), king of the West Saxons. She attempted to poison a favorite of Brihtric, but the cup was accidentally drained by her husband. She fled to Charlemagne, who appointed her abbess of a nunnery, a post from which she was later dismissed for immorality. She is said to have died a beggar in the streets of Pavia.

Eadfrid (ed'frid) or **Eadfrith** (ad'frith). d. 721. Bishop of Lindisfarne from 698 to 721.

Eadgar (ed'gar, ad'gär). See **Edgar.**

Eadgar the Ætheling (ath'ę.ling). See **Edgar** (or **Eadgar**) **Ætheling.**

Eadgyth (ad'yüth). See **Edith.**

Eadie (ē'di), **John.** b. at Alva, Stirlingshire, Scotland, May 9, 1810; d. at Glasgow, June 3, 1876. Scottish theologian and Biblical critic, appointed professor of Biblical literature in the United Secession Divinity Hall in 1843. He wrote commentaries on Ephesians, Colossians, Philippians, and Galatians (1854–69), *Bible Cyclopaedia* (1848), *The English Bible: an external and critical History of various English Translations of Scripture* . . . (1876), and others.

Eadmer (ed'mėr). See **Edmer.**

Eadmund (ed'mund). See **Edmund.**

Eadred (ed'rẹd). See **Edred.**

Eadric Streona (ed'rik strā'ǫ.nä). See **Edric or Eadric Streona.**

Eads (ēdz), **Hervey Lauderdale.** b. near South Union, Ky., April 28, 1807; d. there, Feb. 13, 1892. American bishop and theologian, author of works on Shakerism, and an outstanding leader of that sect in Kentucky. He was a relative of James Buchanan Eads, American engineer and inventor.

Eads, James Buchanan. b. at Lawrenceburg, Ind., May 23, 1820; d. at Nassau, Bahama Islands, March 8, 1887. American engineer and inventor, noted for his work on the Eads Bridge across the Mississippi at St. Louis. After working as a clerk during his early years, he became (1838) a purser on a Mississippi River steamboat. Patenting his invention of a diving bell, he left his job as purser to enter steamboat salvaging, in which he used his diving bell to good effect. After an unsuccessful venture in glass manufacturing at St. Louis, he resumed salvaging and became an authority on river control. Called to Washington by President Lincoln in 1861, he recommended to the Union government means of employing the Western rivers for war operations, and undertook to construct, in what was virtually record time, the fleet of steam-powered, armor-plated gunboats which he had proposed. He built a total of 14 armored vessels featuring ordnance inventions patented by him. His best-known achievement was the construction (1867–74) of a steel and masonry bridge across the Mississippi at St. Louis, incorporating engineering features that conquered difficulties which had been pronounced insuperable by prominent authorities of the day. His reputation as a hydraulic engineer was established with his river control work (completed 1879) at South Pass in the Mississippi, whereby he was able to control the placement of the river's sediment so as to keep the channel clean. He also contributed his knowledge to the improvement of harbor facilities at Liverpool, Toronto, Tampico, and Veracruz. He was awarded (1884) the Albert Medal by the British Society for the Encouragement of Art, Manufacture, and Commerce. Shortly before his death he clashed with Ferdinand de Lesseps over the place for the proposed canal across Central America. Eads favored a route across the isthmus of Tehuantepec, which (in comparison with the Panama route) would have considerably shortened the New York-to-San Francisco voyage, and he was working on this plan when his final illness forced him to stop.

Eadward (ed'wạrd) or **Eadweard** (ad'werd). See **Edward.**

Eadwig (ad'wēy'). See **Edwy** or **Eadwig.**

Eadwine (ad'wi.ne) or **Eadwin** (ad'win). See **Edwin** or **Eadwine** or **Eadwin.**

Eagle (ē'gl), **Solomon.** Pseudonym of **Squire, J. C.**

Eagle Grove. City in N Iowa, in Wright County near Fort Dodge. 4,176 (1950).

Eaglehawk (ē'gl.hôk). Mining town in SE Australia, in Victoria state, ab. 100 mi. NW of Melbourne. For administrative and census purposes it is part of Bendigo.

Eagle Island. See **Achill.**

Eagle Lake. City in SE Texas, in Colorado County, near the Colorado River ab. 60 mi. SW of Houston. It is a railroad junction and rice-milling center. 2,787 (1950).

Eagle of the Doctors. Epithet of **Ailly** or **Ailli, Pierre d'.**

Eagle; or Dartmouth Centinel (därt'muth sen'ti.nẹl), **The.** Newspaper published (1793–99) at Dartmouth College, Hanover, N.H. Among its contributors were Royall Tyler and Joseph Dennie.

Eagle Pass. [Spanish, **El Paso del Aguila.**] City in SW Texas, county seat of Maverick County, on the Rio Grande and the Mexican border: tourist resort. It is the site of a former U.S. military camp (which was called Camp Eagle Pass). The town was established in 1850 and called El Paso del Aguila. The site of nearby Fort Duncan, abandoned since the close of the Indian wars, is of some historical importance from its association with the Confederate cavalry unit under Joseph Shelby which withdrew across the Rio Grande River into Mexico on July 4, 1865, rather than surrender. (Shelby threw the unit's battle flag into the river in order to keep it from falling into Union hands, and thus led some historians to make occasional reference to the site as "the grave of the Confederacy.") 7,276 (1950).

Eaglesham (ē'gl.shạm), 9th Lord of. Title of **Montgomerie, Sir John.**

Eagle's Nest. Rock, ab. 1,200 ft. in height, among the Killarney Lakes in County Kerry, Ireland.

Eagle That Is Forgotten, The. Poem by Vachel Lindsay, published in *General William Booth Enters into Heaven and Other Poems* (1913). It celebrates the memory of John Peter Altgeld, governor of Illinois.

Eahfrith (aċh'frith). See **Aldfrith.**

Eaker (ā'kėr), **Ira Clarence.** b. at Field Creek, Llano County, Tex., April 13, 1896—. American air-force officer who commanded the first heavy-bomber mission over Europe in World War II. He transferred (1917) from the U.S. ground forces to the air corps. In 1926 he flew on a good-will tour of South America. He was chief pilot of the army plane, *Question Mark*, which set the world endurance flight record (1929). He completed (1936) the first transcontinental flight on instruments. Advanced to brigadier general (January, 1942), he was appointed chief (July, 1942) of the U.S. bomber command in Europe, promoted (September, 1942) to major general, and appointed (February, 1943) head of the U.S. army air force in Europe. He was promoted (September, 1943) to lieutenant general, and commanded (1944–45) the Mediterranean allied air forces. He was chief (1945–47) of U.S. army air staff.

Eakins (ā'kinz), **Thomas.** b. at Philadelphia, July 25, 1844; d. June 25, 1916. American painter, sculptor, and teacher. He attended the Pennsylvania Academy of the Fine Arts and in 1866 went to Paris, where he studied at the École des Beaux-Arts for three years. During a stay in Spain beginning in 1869, he came under the influence of Velázquez, Goya, Ribera, and other Spanish masters, some of whose traits were later apparent in Eakins's canvases. Returning (1870) to Philadelphia, where he spent the remainder of his career, he took up the study of anatomy at Jefferson Medical College, developing a knowledge and interest which appear in his later studies, the *Clinic of Dr. Agnew* and the *Clinic of Dr. Gross.* The latter, completed in 1875, is by some critics accounted his finest work, and reflects, as do many of his other works, his profound realism and his mastery of the human structure. In 1873 he began teaching at the Pennsylvania Academy of the Fine Arts, where for many years he was chief instructor and of which he ultimately became dean. Among his other well-known paintings are: *The Writing Master, Between Rounds, Biglen Brothers Turning the Stakeboat, Pair-Oared Shell, Chess Players, The Thinker,* and a number of portraits. The chief collection of his paintings is at the Pennsylvania Museum at Philadelphia. His sculpture includes work on the soldiers and sailors monument at Brooklyn, N.Y., and on the battle monument at Trenton, N.J.

Ealdfrith (ald'frith). See **Aldfrith.**

Ealdred (ald'red). See **Aldred.**

Ealdred's Gate. See **Aldersgate.**

Ealhwine (alċh'wi.ne). Anglo-Saxon name of **Alcuin.**

Ealing (ē'ling). Municipal borough in SE England, in Middlesex, ab. 6 mi. W of Paddington station, London. It was the birthplace of Thomas Huxley. 187,306 (1951).

EAM. Initials of Greek words meaning "National Liberation Front." This was the largest political organization for resistance during the Axis occupation of Greece in World War II. Founded in 1941, it was replaced by the rebel "Free Greek Government" in 1947. At the outset it was an alliance of various left-wing parties, with Communists most numerous in the leadership and least so in the rank and file. A combination of maneuvering by the Communists and violent opposition from the British forced it constantly further to the left, until finally it was almost purely Communist. The ELAS was its fighting force.

Eames (āmz), **Emma.** b. at Shanghai, China, Aug. 13, 1865; d. at New York, June 13, 1952. American operatic soprano. She made her debut in Gounod's *Romeo and Juliet* at the Opéra, Paris, in 1889. She married Julian Story on Aug. 1, 1891, and divorced him in 1907; married (1911) Emilio de Gogorza, a baritone with whom she appeared in recitals until her retirement in 1914.

Eames (ēmz), **Henry Purmort.** b. at Chicago, Sept. 12, 1872—. American pianist and teacher. He studied under Clara Schumann and Paderewski in Europe, toured (1895–97) the U.S. and Europe as a concert pianist, founded the Omaha School of Music, was vice-president and director (1912–20) of the piano and orchestra department of the Cosmopolitan School of Music, Chicago, and was president (1916–17) of the Society of American Musicians.

Eames, Wilberforce. b. at Newark, N.J., Oct. 12, 1855; d. at New York, Dec. 6, 1937. American librarian and bibliographer. He was associated (1885–95) with the Lenox Library until its merger with the New York Public Library. He was the author of articles on bibliographies of the *Bay Psalm Book* (1885), of Ptolemy's *Geography* (1886), of *Sir Walter Raleigh* (1886), and of *Captain John Smith* (1927), and of the books *List of Editions of the Margarita Philosophica* (1886), *The First Year of Printing in New York* (1928), and *Bibliography of Amerigo Vespucci* (1935).

Eames, William S. b. at Clinton, Mich., Aug. 4, 1857; d. March 5, 1915. American architect. He studied at the École des Beaux-Arts, Paris, and at Rome, and practiced his profession at St. Louis from 1882. He was deputy commissioner of public buildings at St. Louis (1881–83), U.S. representative at the International Congress at Madrid in 1904, and president (1904–05) of the American Institute of Architects.

Eanfled (en′fled) or **Eanflæd** (an′flad). b. April 17, 626; date of death not known. Daughter of Edwin, king of Northumbria, and wife of Oswy, king of Northumbria. She was baptized in infancy by Bishop Paulinus, and was the first Northumbrian to receive the rite.

Earby (ir′bi). Urban district and manufacturing town in N central England, in the West Riding of Yorkshire, ab. 7 mi. SW of Skipton, ab. 230 mi. N of London by rail. It has cotton manufactures. 5,384 (1951).

Eardwulf (ard′wůlf) or **Eardulf** (ar′důlf). d. 810. King (796–810) of Northumbria. He was driven from the throne in 808, but was restored in 809.

Earhart (ãr′härt), **Amelia.** [Married name, **Putnam.**] b. at Atchison, Kan., July 24, 1898; d. probably in July, 1937. American aviator, notable for making the first unaccompanied flight by a woman across the Atlantic (1932) and over the Pacific (1935) from Hawaii to California. She gave up teaching (1927) in Massachusetts in order to take part as the first woman in a transatlantic flight (June, 1928) with Wilmer Stutz and Louis Gordon from Newfoundland to Burry Port, Wales. She was aviation editor (1928–30) of *Cosmopolitan Magazine*, and vice-president (1930–31) of Ludington Airlines, Inc. She was lost (1937) while flying over the Pacific on a round-the-world flight. She married (1931) George Palmer Putnam, who edited her book *Last Flight* (1938); she was the author also of *20 hrs. 40 min.* (1928).

Earine (ē.ar′i.nē). In Ben Jonson's *The Sad Shepherd*, a beautiful shepherdess.

Earle (ėrl), **Alice Morse.** [Mrs. **Henry Earle.**] b. at Worcester, Mass., April 27, 1853; d. at Hempstead, Long Island, N.Y., Feb. 16, 1911. American writer on colonial history. Among her works are *The Sabbath in Puritan New England* (1891), *Customs and Fashions in Old New England* (1893), *Colonial Dames and Goodwives* (1895), *Colonial Days in Old New York* (1896), *Home Life in Colonial Days* (1898), *Child Life in Colonial Days* (1899), *Stage Coach and Tavern Days* (1900), *Old-time Gardens* (1901), *Sun-dials and Roses of Yesterday* (1902), and *Two Centuries of Costume in America* (1903).

Earle, John. b. at York, England, c1601; d. at Oxford, England, Nov. 17, 1665. English divine, appointed bishop of Worcester in 1662, and translated to the see of Salisbury in 1663. He wrote various poems (*On the Death of Beaumont, 1616*, *Hortus Mertonensis*, written while a fellow of Merton College) and *Microcosmographie, or a Peece of the World Discovered in Essayes and Characters* (1628, published anonymously), a humorous work which enjoyed great popularity.

Earle, John. b. at Churchstow, Devonshire, England, Jan. 29, 1824; d. at Oxford, England, Jan. 31, 1903. English scholar. He graduated at Oxford in 1845, became a fellow of Oriel College in 1848, was appointed professor of Anglo-Saxon in 1849 for five years, and was college tutor in 1852. He was presented to the rectory of Swanswick, near Bath, in 1857, and was prebend of Wanstow in Wells Cathedral in 1871 and rural dean of Bath from 1873 to 1877. He was reëlected professor of Anglo-Saxon at Oxford in 1876, the professorship having been made permanent. Among his works are *Two of the Saxon Chronicles Parallel* (1865), *The Philology of the English Tongue* (1866), *Book for the Beginner in Anglo-Saxon* (1866), *English Plant Names . . .* (1880), *Anglo-Saxon Literature* (1884), *A Hand Book to the Land Charters . . .* (1888), *English Prose . . .* (1890), and others.

Earle, Pliny. b. at Leicester, Mass., Dec. 17, 1762; d. there, Nov. 29, 1832. American inventor. His chief invention was a machine for making cards for cotton and wool carding.

Earle, Pliny. b. at Leicester, Mass., Dec. 31, 1809; d. at Northampton, Mass., May 17, 1892. American physician and writer on the treatment of the insane; son of Pliny Earle (1762–1832). He was appointed professor of psychology in Berkshire Medical Institution at Pittsfield, Mass., in 1852, and was superintendent of the Massachusetts State Hospital for the Insane from 1864 to 1885, when he retired. Author of *A Visit to Thirteen Asylums for the Insane in Europe* (1839) and *The Curability of Insanity* (1887).

Earle, Ralph. b. at Worcester, Mass., May 3, 1874; d. Feb. 13, 1939. American naval officer and educator. As rear admiral he headed (1916–19) the Bureau of Ordnance of the Navy Department and originated several ordnance projects, such as the 14-inch naval railway batteries in France during World War I. Retiring (1925) from the navy, he assumed the presidency (1925–39) of Worcester Polytechnical Institute. He was the author of *Life at the U.S. Naval Academy* (1917) and *Practical Interior Ballistics* (1917).

Earle, Thomas. b. at Leicester, Mass., April 21, 1796; d. at Philadelphia, July 14, 1849. American lawyer and writer; son of Pliny Earle (1762–1832). He practiced his profession at Philadelphia many years, was an influential member of the state constitutional convention in 1837, and was the vice-presidential candidate of the Liberty Party in 1840.

Earlington (ėr′ling.tọn). City in W Kentucky, in Hopkins County, in a coal-mining area: railroad junction. 2,753 (1950).

Earlom (ėr′lọm), **Richard.** b. at London, 1743; d. there, Oct. 9, 1822. English mezzotint engraver.

Earlston (ėrl′stọn). [Former name, **Erceldoune** or **Ercildoune.**] Parish and market town in SE Scotland, in Berwickshire, ab. 38 mi. by road SE of Edinburgh. The ruin of the "Rhymer's Castle" of Thomas Learmont (c1220–1294), an early Scottish poet called Thomas of Erceldoune or Thomas the Rhymer, is here. Textiles are woven, and there is a market. 1,689 (1931).

Earlston, Thomas of. See **Thomas the Rhymer.**

Early (ėr′li), **Jubal Anderson.** b. in Franklin County, Va., Nov. 3, 1816; d. at Lynchburg, Va., March 2, 1894. American Confederate soldier. Graduated (1837) from West Point, he was on duty in Florida against the Seminoles and resigned his commission as lieutenant in 1838. He studied law, was admitted to the bar (1840), and, until the Civil War, based his practice at Rocky Mount, Va. He was a member (1841–42) of the state legislature and served in the Mexican War. Although opposed to secession, he joined the Confederate army, took part as a colonel in the first battle of Bull Run, was promoted to brigadier general and served with the Army of Northern Virginia, attaining the rank of major general in 1863 and that of lieutenant general in 1864, having served in the Chancellorsville, Gettysburg, and Wilderness campaigns. As the commander of a corps, he was ordered (1864) to the Shenandoah Valley, where he exercised an independent command. He defeated Lew Wallace at Monocacy, but his attempt to take Washington (July 11–12, 1864) was unsuccessful, and he devoted his later efforts to harrying the Maryland and Pennsylvania areas. In September and October, 1864, he was driven back by Sheridan at Winchester and Cedar Creek, and in March, 1865, his command was virtually wiped out at Waynesboro by Custer. Relieved of his command by Lee, he set out westward to carry on the fight with Confederate forces in Mississippi, but upon learning of the surrender of the latter contingents went to Mexico and then to Canada, where he published *A Memoir of the Last Year of the War for Independence in the Confederate States of America* (1866). He took up his law practice at Lynchburg, Va., in 1869 and later served as president of the Southern Historical Society.

Early, Stephen. [Full name, **Stephen Tyree Early.**] b. at Crozet, Va., Aug. 27, 1889; d. at Washington, D.C., Aug. 11, 1951. American journalist. He was a member of the United Press (1908–13) and Associated Press (1913–17, 1920–27) staffs at Washington. He served as assistant secretary (1933–37) and secretary (1937–45) to

President F. D. Roosevelt, and secretary and special assistant to President Harry Truman (1945–49). In 1949 he was appointed undersecretary of defense.

Early Autumn: A Story of a Lady. Novel by Louis Bromfield, published in 1926 and awarded the Pulitzer prize in 1927.

Early English Text Society. Society founded in 1864 by F. J. Furnivall (1825–1910) and directed by him. Its object was the promotion of the study of early English. It rendered valuable service to literature in the publication of specially prepared editions of early English works.

Early History of Jacob Stahl (jā′kọb stäl, yä′kop shtäl), **The.** See **History of Jacob Stahl, The Early.**

Early Hours, The. Novel by Marmaduke Pickthall, published in 1921.

Earn (ėrn). River in C Scotland, in Perthshire. It is the outlet of Loch Earn. The river flows E from Loch Earn to the river Tay ab. 6 mi. SE of Perth. Length, ab. 46 mi.

Earn, Loch. Lake in C Scotland, in Perthshire, situated ab. 26 mi. W of Perth. Length, ab. 7 mi.; width, less than 1 mi.

Earth. The planet inhabited by man, the fifth largest of the bodies revolving about, and third in order from, the star called the Sun. It has an equatorial diameter of 7926.68 mi. but its diurnal revolution imposes an ellipsoidal figure and there is a polar "flattening," or oblateness, amounting to 26.7 mi. Its mass may be computed as 6.6 times 10^{21} tons, and its mean density as 5.52 times that of water. Of the 196,950,000 sq. mi. of surface, 57,470,000 sq. mi. is land, and the remaining 70.8 percent of area is water. If all irregularities were smoothed Earth would be wholly covered by an ocean with a uniform depth of 10,200 ft. Life is possible on this globe because of the energy supplied by the Sun, at a rate equivalent to 1.71 times 10^{14} kilowatts per second, although the Sun may be said to be, for all ordinary purposes, some 93 million mi. distant from the Earth. One complete rotation is accomplished in a sidereal day, which is 3 minutes 55.91 seconds shorter than the mean solar day of common use. This rotation is about an axis inclined 23 degrees and 27 minutes to the pole of the ecliptic, or orbit, causing, with the revolution around the Sun in 365.2422 days, the seasonal changes. Its orbital velocity is 18.49 mi. per second. The Earth has one satellite, the Moon.

Earth Horizon. Autobiography by Mary Austin, published in 1932.

Earthly Paradise, The. Collection of narrative poems (1868–71) by William Morris.

Easdale (ēz′dāl). [Also, **Eisdale.**] Small island in W Scotland, in Argyllshire, situated in the Firth of Lorne, ab. 11 mi. SW of Oban. It is important for its slate quarries. The island measures less than 1 mi. in length and width.

Easley (ēz′li). City in NW South Carolina, in Pickens County: trading and manufacturing center for cotton. 6,316 (1950).

East (ēst), Sir **Alfred.** b. at Kettering, England, Dec. 15, 1849; d. at London, Sept. 29, 1913. English landscape painter and etcher, closely identified with the conservative tradition of the Royal Academy. He began to study art in 1872 at Glasgow; later he studied at the École des Beaux-Arts and the Julian Academy at Paris, under Bouguereau and others. Soon he exhibited regularly at the Royal Academy; in 1889 he received a gold medal at Paris; subsequently he exhibited at Brussels, Munich, Berlin, Vienna, Venice, Rome, and The Hague. His work is represented in museums at Birmingham, Budapest, Chicago, Leeds, Milan, Pittsburgh, Sydney, and Zurich, among others. His principal works include *Hayle, a View of Lelant* (Birmingham), *The Valley of Gold* (Leeds), and *The Valley of Cambounes, Berkshire* (Sydney).

East, Edward Murray. b. at Du Quoin, Ill., Oct. 4, 1879; d. Nov. 9, 1938. American biologist. He was associated (1900–05) with the University of Illinois Agricultural Experimental Station, assistant professor (1909–14) and professor (1914–26) of experimental plant morphology, and professor (1926 *et seq.*) of genetics at Harvard University, and an investigator (1908–18) of methods of breeding tobacco for the U.S. Department of Agriculture. He wrote *Heterozygosis in Evolution and Plant Breeding* (1912), *Inbreeding and Outbreeding* (1919), *Mankind at the Crossroads* (1923), and *Heredity and Human Affairs* (1927), and edited *Biology in Human Affairs* (1931).

East, Far. See **Far East.**

East, Middle. See **Middle East.**

East, Near. See **Near East.**

East, the. In Biblical geography, the countries SE, E, and NE of Palestine, such as Moab, Ammon, Arabia Deserta, Assyria, and others.

East, the. One of the four great prefectures into which the Roman Empire was divided in its later history. It comprised the dioceses of Asia, Pontus, the East, and Egypt, and the diocese of Thrace (from the Aegean Sea to the Danube River).

East, the. Diocese in the prefecture of the East, in the later Roman Empire. It was somewhat more comprehensive than Syria.

East, the. The countries comprised in the Byzantine (or Eastern) Empire.

East, the. In Church history, the church in the Byzantine (or Eastern) Empire and countries adjacent, especially those on the east, as "the West" designates the church in the Western Empire.

East, the. In modern use, Asia; the Orient.

East, the. Popular designation of the states of the U.S. lying along the Atlantic seaboard, especially those north of Maryland. The term was also commonly once (but is now infrequently) applied to the New England states: Maine, New Hampshire, Vermont, Massachusetts, Rhode Island, and Connecticut.

East Abington (ab′ing.tọn). Former name of **Rockland,** Mass.

East Africa (af′ri.kạ), **British.** See **British East Africa.**

East Africa, German. See **German East Africa.**

East Africa, Italian. See **Italian East Africa.**

East Africa, Portuguese. See **Mozambique.**

East African (af′ri.kạn) or **East Africa Protectorate.** Former name of **Kenya.**

East Ahmedpur (ä.med.pör′). See **Ahmedpur.**

East Alton (ôl′tọn). Village in SW Illinois, in Madison County: important ammunition-manufacturing center. 7,290 (1950).

East Anglia (ang′gli.ạ). Ancient English kingdom, corresponding to the modern counties of Norfolk and Suffolk. Redwald was its first historical king (c593–617); its last under-king was Edmund (killed 870). It formed later a part of the Danelaw, and was one of the four earldoms of Canute.

East Anglian (ang′gli.ạn). General term for the dialects of England spoken in the eastern districts (those NE of London).

East Angus (ang′gus). Town in SE Quebec, Canada, situated on the Coaticook River, ab. 14 mi. E of Sherbrooke. 3,714 (1951).

East Aurora (ô.rō′rạ). Village in W New York, in Erie County: manufactures of toys. It was the home of Elbert Hubbard and until 1939 the headquarters of the Roycrofters, a handcraft group founded by Hubbard. 5,962 (1950).

East Avon (ā′vọn, av′ọn). See **Avon River,** S and W England.

East Bakersfield (bā′kėrz.fēld). Unincorporated community in S central California, in Kern County near Bakersfield. 38,177 (1950).

East Barnet (bär′nẹt). [Also, **East Barnet Valley.**] Urban district in E central England, in Hertfordshire, ab. 2 mi. SE of Barnet, ab. 8 mi. NW of King's Cross station, London. It is included in the London "Green Belt Scheme." 40,414 (1951).

East Bengal (ben.gôl′, beng-). Province of Pakistan, comprising the E portion of this divided country, bounded on the N, E, and W by the Union of India, on the S by the Bay of Bengal, and on the SE by Burma; composed of the eastern territories of the former province of Bengal (divided between India and Pakistan in 1947) and the former Assam district of Sylhet. Most of the inhabitants are Moslem farmers whose chief crops are jute, rice, sugar, and tea. The province is short on cereals and is subject to many floods from the mouths of the Ganges and Brahmaputra rivers. The chief port is Chittagong. Capital, Dacca; area, 54,501 sq. mi.; pop. 41,932,329 (1951).

East Borneo (bôr′nẹ.ō). Region in the Republic of Indonesia, in the island and province of Borneo, formerly

(1946–50) a *daerah* (autonomous area) of the United States of Indonesia, located in the NE section of what was formerly Dutch Borneo.

Eastbourne (ēst′bôrn, -bọrn). County borough and seaside resort in SE England, in East Sussex, situated on the English Channel ab. 3 mi. E of Beachy Head, ab. 66 mi. SE of London by rail. It was formerly a fishing village, growing rapidly during the 19th century after the building of the railroad. It is now connected with London by fast train service. 57,801 (1951).

East Bridgewater (brij′wô.tėr, -wot.ėr). Town in SE Massachusetts, in Plymouth County: residential community. 4,412 (1950).

East Cape. [French, **Cap Est.**] Cape in the Indian Ocean, on the NE coast of Madagascar, at the easternmost point of the island.

East Cape. Cape at the E extremity of the North Island of New Zealand.

East Cape. [Also: **Cape Dezhnev** (or **Dezhneva**); Russian, **Mys Dezhneva,** formerly **Mys Vostochny.**] Cape in the U.S.S.R., in the Khabarovsk *krai* (territory) of the Russian Soviet Federated Socialist Republic, Siberia: the easternmost headland in Asia, projecting into Bering Strait. Although still widely known as East Cape or the Russian equivalent (Mys Vostochny), it was officially renamed in 1898 for the navigator who discovered it.

Eastcheap (ēst′chēp). Originally, the E market place of the City of London, located at the junction of Watling Street and Ermine Street. It was quite large, including the site of modern Billingsgate and Leadenhall markets. Eastcheap is now a small street running E and W near the N end of London Bridge.

Eastchester (ēst′ches″tėr). Town in SE New York, in Westchester County. It includes the villages of Bronxville and Tuckahoe, chiefly residential suburbs of New York with some small industries at Tuckahoe. Formerly larger in extent, it included what is now the city of Mount Vernon. 27,174 (1950).

East Chicago (shi.kô′gō, -kä′-). City in Indiana, in Lake County, on Lake Michigan ab. 17 mi. SE of Chicago: heavy concentration of industries, with manufactures of steel, cement, chemicals, coke, petroleum products, lead, zinc, gypsum, railway equipment, and tinplate. 54,263 (1950).

East China Sea (chī′nạ). [Also: **Eastern Sea;** Chinese, **Tung Hai;** Japanese, **To Kai.**] That part of the Pacific Ocean which is included between China, Formosa, the Ryukyu Islands, and the Yellow Sea. Area, ab. 482,000 sq. mi.; greatest depth, ab. 10,500 ft.

East Cleveland (klēv′lạnd). City in NE Ohio, in Cuyahoga County, ab. 3 mi. NE of Cleveland: suburb of Cleveland. It was incorporated as a city in 1911. Pop. 40,047 (1950).

East Columbus (kọ.lum′bus). Unincorporated community in C Indiana, in Bartholomew County. Under the new urban definition established for use in the 1950 census it was counted with adjoining urban areas. The last official enumeration was 2,723 (1940).

East Conemaugh (kon′ẹ.mô). Borough in SW Pennsylvania, in Cambria County, ab. 26 mi. SW of Altoona: coal mines. 4,101 (1950).

East Coolgardie Gold Field (köl.gär′di). Mining area in SW Australia, in S central Western Australia, ab. 380 mi. by rail E of Perth. Gold was discovered here in 1892, and rapid settlement and development followed. In 1903 a water main 351 mi. in length was completed from Mundaring Weir, near Perth, which supplies about 2 billion gallons of water annually to the gold fields. The East Coolgardie field, surrounding the town of Kalgoorlie, is the richest in Australia, and has produced over half the total output of Western Australia. Area, ab. 632 sq. mi.

East Cowes (kouz). Former urban district, now a part of Cowes urban district, in S England, in the Isle of Wight (an administrative county of the geographical county of Hampshire), situated on the river Medina, at its influx to the Solent, opposite West Cowes. Near it is the former royal residence of Osborne, now a convalescent home. 4,604 (1931).

East Dereham (dir′ạm). [Also, **Dereham.**] Urban district and market town in E England, in Norfolk, ab. 16 mi. W of Norwich, ab. 125 mi. NE of London by rail. It is an East Anglian market town producing fences and poultry runs, and was formerly a textile center producing worsteds. 6,441 (1951).

East Detroit (dẹ.troit′). City in S Lower Michigan, in Macomb County: residential suburb of Detroit. In the decade between the last two U.S. censuses its population more than doubled. 8,584 (1940), 21,461 (1950).

East End or **East-End.** Name popularly given to that part of London which lies east of the Bank of England (here taken to represent the center of the city). It coincides roughly with Stepney, Poplar, Shoreditch, and Bethnal Green metropolitan boroughs. Whitechapel district and the Limehouse district are also in the East End. The term East End began to appear at the end of the 17th century, with the development of the fashionable West End. Shipbuilding was important here in the 19th century. Stepney and Poplar metropolitan boroughs have some of the docks of the port of London, and Stepney has considerable manufactures of clothing. Shoreditch and Bethnal Green have manufactures of furniture. Fur dressing and furriery are also important in parts of the East End.

Easter (ēs′tėr). Christian festival, commemorating the resurrection of Jesus Christ: probably adapted from the Jewish Passover or Pesach (from which the common European name, Pascua or one of its variants, is derived) and taking its English name from a pagan Teutonic goddess of springtime who was celebrated in a spring festival. Easter falls on the first Sunday following the first full moon after the vernal equinox (about March 21), but many disputes about the date existed in the early days of the Church. The date of Easter affects the dates of all other movable feasts in the Christian calendar. Easter is preceded by the 40 days of Lent; the paschal season lasts 50 days, until Whitsunday. Popularly, the custom of distributing colored eggs is a feature of the festival.

Easter Anstruther (an′struᴛʜ.ėr). See **Anstruther.**

Easter Island. [Spanish, **Isla de Pascua.**] Island in the E Pacific, ab. 2,000 mi. W of Chile: noted for its gigantic prehistoric statues. It belongs to Chile, and is administered as part of Valparaíso province.

Eastern Aden Protectorate (ā′dẹn, ä′-). See under **Aden Protectorate.**

Eastern Alps (alps). See **Alps, Eastern.**

Eastern Bengal and Assam (ben.gôl′, beng-; as.sam′). Former province of British India, formed from Assam and the E part of Bengal in October, 1905. It consisted of the territories formerly governed by the chief commissioner of Assam, to which were added the Dacca and Chittagong divisions, with the districts of Rajshahi, Dinajpur, Jalpaiguri, Rangpur, Bogra, Pabna, and Malda. It was bounded on the N by the Himalayas, on the E by Burma, on the S by Burma and the Bay of Bengal, and on the W by Bengal. The capital of the province was Dacca city, and the seaport Chittagong. The imperial proclamation at Delhi, on Dec. 12, 1911, provided for the disappearance of the province as a separate lieutenant-governorship.

Eastern Colorado (kol.ọ.rad′ọ̄, -rä′dō). See **Colorado River,** Texas.

Eastern Cordillera (kôr.dil′ėr.ạ). English name of **Cordillera Oriental.**

Eastern Empire or **Eastern Roman Empire** (rō′mạn). See **Byzantine Empire.**

Eastern Front. See under **World War I** and **World War II.**

Eastern Ghats (gôts, gäts) or **Ghauts** (gôts). See under **Ghats.**

Eastern Karelia Dispute (kạ.rē′li.ạ, -rēl′yạ). Dispute, between Russia and Finland over the autonomous territory of Eastern Karelia (in the E part of what is now the Karelo-Finnish Soviet Socialist Republic, or Karelia), which broke out in November, 1921. Claiming mistreatment of inhabitants by the Russians, Finland appealed to the Council of the League of Nations, which in turn appealed to the Permanent Court for an advisory opinion. The court did not give a decision, because of Russia's refusal to appear before it, and the matter was dropped.

Eastern Manych (mä.nich′). See **Manych, Eastern.**

Eastern Polder. See **Oostelijke Polder.**

Eastern Province. [Former name, **Stanleyville**; French, **Province Orientale.**] Province in NE Belgian Congo, bounded on the N by French Equatorial Africa and the Anglo-Egyptian Sudan, on the E by Uganda, on the S by Kivu province, and on the W by Equator province. There are gold mines in the NE part. Capital, Stanleyville; area, ab. 204,160 sq. mi.; pop. ab. 2,300,000.

Eastern Province. Province in NE Ceylon, in a hilly and mountainous area. Mica and zircons are mined in the hills; fishing is important in the coastal villages. Capital, Trincomalee; area, 3,840 sq. mi.; pop. 279,112 (1946).

Eastern Province. Province of Uganda protectorate, British East Africa, occupying the area N of Lake Victoria and immediately W of Kenya. It is divided into the districts of Busoga, Mbale, and Teso. Capital, Jinja; area (exclusive of open water), 11,698 sq. mi.; pop. (adult males) 320,000 (est. 1947).

Eastern Province. English name of **Simat-i-Mashriqi.**

Eastern Question. Name given collectively to the several problems or complications in the international politics of Europe growing out of the presence of the Turkish power in the SE, particularly in the latter half of the 19th century.

Eastern Region. See **Oriente,** Ecuador.

Eastern Samoa (sa̧.mō'a̧). See **American Samoa.**

Eastern Sea. See **East China Sea.**

Eastern Shore. The part of Maryland which lies E of Chesapeake Bay.

Eastern Wei (wā). See under **Northern Dynasties.**

Eastern Zone. See **German Democratic Republic.**

Easter Rebellion. See under **Sinn Fein.**

East Flanders (flan'dėrz). [Flemish, **Oost Vlaanderen**; French, **Flandre Orientale.**] Province of Belgium, bounded by the Netherlands on the N, Antwerp and Brabant on the E, Hainaut on the S, and West Flanders on the W. Apart from some sandy stretches in the central part, it is almost entirely composed of a fertile, low-lying, intensely cultivated, and densely populated plain, yielding abundant harvests of agricultural and horticultural products and offering good pasturage. It also contains textile and other manufactures. It is watered by the Lys, Dender, and Schelde rivers, and is connected with the sea by a network of canals. The population is entirely Flemish. It was part of the independent countship of Flanders in the Middle Ages. Capital, Ghent; area, 1,147 sq. mi.; pop. 1,226,602 (est. 1949).

East Friesland (frēz'la̧nd). [German, **Ostfriesland.**] Region in NW Germany, in the W part of the *Land* (state) of Lower Saxony, British Zone; formerly part of the province of Hanover, Prussia. It is bounded on the W by the Netherlands, on the N by the North Sea, and includes the adjacent islands (E Frisian Islands) in the North Sea. Originally it included the Dutch province of Groningen and the N part of Oldenburg in Germany. It became part of Prussia in 1744, of the Netherlands in 1807, of Hanover in 1815, and again of Prussia in 1866. Most of the region consists of fertile lowlands, some of it reclaimed from swamps. Livestock raising is important.

East Frisian Islands (frizh'a̧n). See under **Frisian Islands.**

East Gaffney (gaf'ni). Unincorporated community in N South Carolina, in Cherokee County near Gaffney. 4,289 (1950).

East Gary (gãr'i). Town in NW Indiana, in Lake County. 5,635 (1950).

East Gastonia (gas.tō'ni.a̧, -tōn'ya̧). Unincorporated community in W North Carolina, in Gaston County near Gastonia. 3,733 (1950).

East Germany. See **German Democratic Republic.**

East Godavari (gō̧.dä'va̧.rē). See under **Godavari.**

East Goths (goths). See **Ostrogoths.**

East Grand Forks. City in NW Minnesota, in Polk County, on the Red River: sugar-beet refineries. 5,049 (1950).

East Grand Rapids. City in S Lower Michigan, in Kent County near Grand Rapids. 6,403 (1950).

East Greenwich (gren'ich). Town in C Rhode Island, county seat of Kent County: manufactures of textiles and textile machinery; shipping point for shellfish. It was incorporated in 1677. Pop. 4,923 (1950).

East Grinstead (grin'sted, -stȩd). Urban district and market town in SE England, in East Sussex, ab. 14 mi. NE of Horsham, ab. 30 mi. S of London by rail. 10,845 (1951).

East Griqualand (grē'kwa̧.land, grik'wa̧-). See **Griqualand East.**

East Ham (ham). County borough, seaport, manufacturing town, and residential center in SE England, in Essex, situated on the N bank of the river Thames, ab. 2 mi. SW of Barking, ab. 6 mi. E of Fenchurch Street station, London. East Ham is an eastern suburb of London. Its urban development is continuous with the County of London. The N portion of East Ham is mainly residential in character. The S part (fronting on the river Thames) has important industrial developments and contains major portions of the Royal Albert Dock and the King George V Dock (London's most modern). They are a part of the largest single enclosed dock system in the world. 120,873 (1951).

East Hampton (hamp'to̧n). Town in C Connecticut, in Middlesex County, on Pine Brook River: important for the manufacture of bells. 4,000 (1950).

Easthampton (ēst.hamp'to̧n). Town in C Massachusetts, in Hampshire County, ab. 12 mi. NW of Springfield: manufactures of yarn, thread, elastic, and buttons. It is the seat of Williston Academy. 10,694 (1950).

East Hampton (hamp'to̧n). Town (in New York the equivalent of township in many other states) and village in SE New York, in Suffolk County, on Long Island: resort and residential community. Settled c1648, it was the home (1799–1810) of Lyman Beecher, and the birthplace of John Howard Payne. Pop. of town, 6,325 (1950); of village, 1,737 (1950).

East Harbor. Former name of **Ambrose Channel.**

East Hartford (härt'fo̧rd). Town in N Connecticut, in Hartford County, on the bank of the Connecticut River, opposite Hartford: important for the manufacture of airplane engines and parts. 29,933 (1950).

East Haven (hā'vȩn). Town in S Connecticut, in New Haven County, on Farm River E of New Haven: truck-gardening and residential community. 12,212 (1950).

East Hempstead (hemp'stȩd, hem'-). Unincorporated community in SE New York, in Nassau County, on Long Island. Under the new urban definition established for use in the 1950 census it was counted with adjoining urban areas. The last official enumeration was 2,881 (1940).

East Hills. Residential village in SE New York, in Nassau County on Long Island: an eastern suburb of New York City. In the decade between the last two U.S. censuses its population grew from 343 (1940) to 2,547 (1950).

East India (in'di.a̧). See **India, Further.**

East India Company. Name of various mercantile associations formed in different countries in the 17th and 18th centuries for the purpose of conducting under the auspices of their governments a monopoly of the trade of their respective countries with the East Indies: **1.** The Danish East India Company was organized in 1618. It was dissolved in 1634, reorganized in 1670, and finally dissolved in 1729, when its possessions, the chief of which was Tranquebar on the Coromandel coast of India, were ceded to the government. **2.** The Dutch East India Company was formed by the union of several smaller trading companies on March 20, 1602. It received from the state a monopoly of the trade on the further side of the Strait of Magellan and of the Cape of Good Hope, including the right to make treaties and alliances in the name of the States General, to establish factories and forts, and to employ soldiers. It founded Batavia in Java on the site of a native city in 1619, and in the middle of the 17th century held the principal seats of commerce throughout the Indian archipelago, including Ceylon, Sumatra, Java, and Borneo, and had flourishing colonies in South Africa. It was dissolved and its territories transferred to the state on Sept. 12, 1795. **3.** The British (English) East India Company, composed originally of London merchants, was incorporated by Queen Elizabeth on Dec. 31, 1600, under the title of the "The Governor and Company of Merchants of London trading with the East Indies." It obtained from the court of Delhi, India, in 1612 the privilege of establishing a factory at Surat, which continued to be the chief British station in India until the organization of Bombay. In 1645 it received permission of the natives to erect Fort St. George at Madras. In 1661 it was invested by Charles II with authority to make peace and war with infidel powers, erect forts, acquire territory, and exercise civil and criminal jurisdiction in its settlements. In 1668 it obtained a grant of the island of Bombay, which formed part of the dower of Catharine of Portugal. In 1675 it established a factory on the Hooghly River in Bengal, which led to the foundation of Calcutta. In 1749 it inaugurated, by the expulsion of the rajah of Tanjore, a series of territorial conquests which resulted in the acquisition and organization of British India. As the result of Robert Clive's military exploits (1751 *et seq.*) the English company ousted the French almost completely in India. Clive's administration (1764–67) in Bengal helped establish British control in the peninsula on a solid basis. A government board of control was established by Parliament in 1784, the company's trade monopoly was ended in 1813, and in 1858 the company relinquished altogether its functions of government to the crown. **4.** The French East India Company was founded by Colbert in 1664. It established a factory at Surat, India, in August, 1675, and acquired Pondichéry, which became the capital of the French possessions on the Coromandel coast. It was dissolved on Aug. 13, 1769, when its territories were ceded to the crown. **5.** The Swedish East India Company was formed at Göteborg, Sweden, in 1741, and was reorganized in 1806.

East Indian Archipelago. See **Malay Archipelago.**

East India United Service Club. London club established in 1848.

East Indies (in′dēz). [Formerly sometimes **East Indias:** so called in distinction from the newly discovered countries in America, supposed at first to be remoter parts of India, and called the West Indies or West Indias.] Vague collective name applied in the past to India, Farther India, and the Malay Archipelago. It has come to be limited in general usage to the Malay Archipelago, including chiefly, as political units, the Republic of Indonesia, the British possessions in Borneo and New Guinea, and sometimes also the Philippine Islands.

East Indonesia (in.dọ.nē′zhạ). [Also, **Indonesia Timoer.**] Former *negara* (state) of the United States of Indonesia, formed in December, 1946, and comprised of the eastern group of the former Netherlands East Indies, i.e., the islands E of Borneo, including Bali, Flores, Lombok, Soembawa, Celebes, the Moluccas, Salajar, the Sangihe group, Ceram, Soemba, the W part of Timor, and other small islands. Its capital was Makassar. With the formation (1950) of the Republic of Indonesia this unit was replaced by the three provinces of Celebes, Moluccas, and Lesser Sunda Islands. The proposal to add Netherlands New Guinea remained unsettled in 1952.

East Islip (ī′slip). Unincorporated community in SE New York, in Suffolk County, on Long Island. 2,834 (1950).

East Java (jä′vạ, jav′ạ). [Also, **Djawa-Timur.**] Province of the Republic of Indonesia, formerly (1946–50) a *negara* (state) of the United States of Indonesia, located in approximately the E third of the island of Java; under Dutch rule it was a province of the Netherlands Indies. Capital, Surabaya; area, ab. 18,503 sq. mi.; pop. 18,622,960 (1951).

East Keansburg (kēnz′bėrg). Unincorporated community in E New Jersey, in Monmouth County, on Raritan Bay. 2,596 (1950).

East Khandesh (kan′desh). See under **Khandesh.**

Eastlake (ēst′lāk). Residential village in NE Ohio, in Lake County E of Cleveland. 7,486 (1950).

Eastlake, Sir **Charles Lock.** b. at Plymouth, England, Nov. 17, 1793; d. at Pisa, Italy, Dec. 24, 1865. English painter, critic, and designer. He lived at Rome (1817–30) and at London (1830–55), was keeper of the National Gallery (1843–47), was president of the Royal Academy from 1850 until his death, and was knighted in 1850. Though popular in his day for paintings of religious and historical subjects, such as *Pilgrims in Sight of Rome* (1828), and of "banditti" and other Mediterranean types sketched on his travels, he was more influential in his selection of works for the National Gallery, as a critic (with several works on art, including a translation of Goethe's *Theory of Colors*, 1840), and as a designer, especially of stained glass. His emphasis, in his books and designs, was on the intrinsic decorative possibilities of the materials themselves and on the spirit rather than the exact forms of former great periods of art, especially the Gothic, which in his time was being slavishly and sentimentally copied by many architects and designers. His style, often called Eastlake Gothic, is associated with that of William Morris as part of a wholesome trend away from earlier 19th-century eclecticism.

Eastland (ēst′lạnd). City in C Texas, county seat of Eastland County, NW of Austin, in a petroleum region. 3,626 (1950).

East Lansdowne (lanz′doun). Borough in SE Pennsylvania, in Delaware County near Philadelphia. 3,527 (1950).

East Lansing (lan′sing). City in S Lower Michigan, in Ingham County, twin city of Lansing: residential community and seat of the Michigan State College of Agriculture and Applied Science. In the decade between the last two U.S. censuses its population more than tripled. 5,839 (1940), 20,325 (1950).

Eastlawn (ēst′lôn). Unincorporated community in SE Lower Michigan, in Washtenaw County near Ann Arbor. 4,127 (1950).

Eastleigh (ēst′lē). Municipal borough and industrial town in S England, in Southampton (an administrative county of the geographical county of Hampshire), ab. 73 mi. SW of London by rail. It is a railway construction and repair center. 30,557 (1951).

East Liverpool (liv′ėr.pöl). [Former names: **Fawcett's Town, Liverpool.**] City in E Ohio, in Columbiana County, on the Ohio River ab. 35 mi. NW of Pittsburgh: a leading center for the manufacture of pottery. Among its other products are barrels and steel. It was settled in 1798. Pop. 24,217 (1950).

East Loch Tarbert (loċh tär′bėrt). See **Tarbert, West Loch** and **East Loch.**

East London (lun′dọn). [Former name, **Port Rex.**] Seaport in Cape of Good Hope province, Union of South Africa, situated at the mouth of the Buffalo River ab. 150 mi. E of Port Elizabeth. It is connected by rail with the interior and is ab. 888 mi. from Capetown and 664 mi. from Johannesburg. Its chief exports are wool, citrus fruits, and meat and dairy products, all produce of the area back of the port. 78,530, including 39,646 Europeans (1946).

East Longmeadow (lông′med′ō). Town in S Massachusetts, in Hampden County, near the Connecticut River: apple growing and poultry farming; formerly important for the quarrying of sandstone used in brownstone buildings. 4,881 (1950).

East Los Angeles (los an′jẹ.lẹs, -lēz; ang′gẹ.lẹs; lōs). Township in S California, in Los Angeles County near Los Angeles. 81,664 (1950).

East Lothian (lō′ᴛʜi.ạn). [Former names, **Haddington, Haddingtonshire.**] Maritime county in S Scotland. It is bounded on the N by the Firth of Forth, on the NE and E by the North Sea, on the S by Berwickshire, and on the W by Midlothian. The Lammermuir Hills are in the S portion, reaching an elevation of 1,750 ft. From here the surface slopes with little interruption to the coast. The principal industries are fishing, agriculture, and coal mining. The county also has dairy and pig farms. Crops raised are chiefly potatoes, wheat, turnips, and barley. About two thirds of the total area of the county is under cultivation or in pasture. County seat, Haddington; area, ab. 267 sq. mi.; pop. 52,240 (1951).

East Lyme (līm). Town in SE Connecticut, in New London County: residential community. 3,870 (1950).

Eastmain (ēst′mān). River in N Quebec, Canada, which flows into the E side of James Bay. Length, ab. 375 mi.

East Main (mān). Name given at one time to a portion of the Northwest Territories, Canada, lying E of Hudson Bay and W of Labrador proper. It is now part of the province of Quebec.

Eastman (ēst′mạn). City in C Georgia, county seat of Dodge County: center for a cotton and pecan producing area. 3,597 (1950).

Eastman, Charles Alexander. [Indian name, **Ohiyesa.**] b. at Redwood Falls, Minn., 1858; d. 1939. American physician and author, of Sioux Indian parentage. He was graduated from Dartmouth College in 1887 and from the Boston University School of Medicine in 1890. In 1891 he married the poet Elaine Goodale. He was government physician at the Pine Ridge Agency in South Dakota (1890–93), was in charge of the Indian work of the Young Men's Christian Association (1894–97), and served as attorney for the Santee Sioux at Washington, D.C. (1897–1900) and as government physician at Crow Creek, S.D. (1900–03). He published *Indian Boyhood* (1902), *Red Hunters and the Animal People* (1904), *Old Indian Days* (1907), *Wigwam Evenings* (1909), *The Soul of the Indian* (1911), and others.

Eastman, Charles Gamage. b. at Fryeburg, Me., June 1, 1816; d. at Burlington, Vt., Sept. 16, 1860. American poet and journalist. He was for many years proprietor and editor of the Vermont *Patriot*, published at Montpelier, Vt. In 1848 he published a volume of poetry.

Eastman, George. b. at Waterville, N.Y., July 12, 1854; committed suicide at Rochester, N.Y., March 14, 1932. American inventor, industrialist, and pioneer in the manufacture of photographic supplies. He secured (1879) patents for a photographic coating process on dry plates and opened a business with Henry A. Strong. After the perfection of flexible paper-backed film, he organized the Eastman Dry Plate and Film Company. Successive developments included the various models of Kodak cameras (from 1888), transparent and daylight-loading film, color film, and film for motion pictures. With the profits from his expanding firm, he contributed millions of dollars to such organizations as the Rochester Dental Dispensary, the Eastman School of Music, the University of Rochester, and others.

Eastman, John Robie. b. at Andover, N.H., July 29, 1836; d. Sept. 26, 1913. American astronomer. He was assistant astronomer (1862–65) and professor of mathematics (1865–98) at the Naval Observatory, editor (1872–82) of observatory publications, and author of *Second Washington Catalogue of Stars* (1898) and *History of the Town of Andover, N.H., 1851–1906* (1910).

Eastman, Joseph Bartlett. b. at Katonah, N.Y., June 26, 1882; d. March 15, 1944. American transportation official. Received B.A. (1904) from Amherst; engaged in community welfare work; secretary of Boston's Public Franchise League; served (1915–19) on Massachusetts Public Service Commission; member (1919 *et seq.*) of Interstate Commerce Commission; served (1933–36) as federal coördinator of transportation; director (December, 1941–44) of Office of Defense Transportation.

Eastman, Max. [Full name, **Max Forrester Eastman.**] b. at Canandaigua, N.Y., Jan. 4, 1883—. American editor, writer, and translator. He edited *The Masses* (1913–17) and *The Liberator* (1918–22), and has been a roving editor (1941 *et seq.*) of the *Reader's Digest*. He is the author of *Enjoyment of Poetry* (1913; revised ed., 1921), *Journalism Versus Art* (1916), *Understanding Germany* (1916), *Marx and Lenin, the Science of Revolution* (1926), *Enjoyment of Laughter* (1936), *The End of Socialism in Russia* (1937), *Marxism, Is It Science?* (1940), *Enjoyment of Living* (1947), and other books; his poetry includes *Colors of Life* (1918), *Kinds of Love* (1931), and *Lot's Wife* (1942). He has translated (from the Russian) Pushkin's *Gabriel* (1929) and works by Leon Trotsky including *The Real Situation in Russia* (1928), *The History of the Russian Revolution* (3 vols., 1932–33), and *The Revolution Betrayed* (1937); compiled and narrated a film history of the Russian Revolution entitled *From Czar to Lenin* (1937).

Eastman, Seth. b. at Brunswick, Me., Jan. 24, 1808; d. at Washington, D.C., Aug. 31, 1875. American brigadier general. He was employed (1850–55) in the bureau of the commissioner of Indian affairs to illustrate the work entitled *History, Condition and Future Prospects of the Indian Tribes of the United States*, published (1850–57) by order of Congress.

East Marion (mar'i.ọn, mãr'-). Unincorporated community in W North Carolina, in McDowell County near Marion and E of Asheville. 2,901 (1950).

East Mauch Chunk (môk' chungk'). Borough in E Pennsylvania, in Carbon County, on the Lehigh River. 3,132 (1950).

East McKeesport (mạ.kēz'pōrt). Borough in SW Pennsylvania, in Allegheny County: residential community near Pittsburgh. It was incorporated in 1895. Pop. 3,171 (1950).

East Meadows. Unincorporated community in SE New York, in Nassau County, on Long Island. Under the new urban definition established for use in the 1950 census it was counted with adjoining urban areas. The last official enumeration was 3,145 (1940).

East Moline (mọ.lēn'). City in NW Illinois, in Rock Island County: important center for the manufacture of farm implements. It is informally part of a larger metropolitan area called the "Quad Cities." 13,913 (1950).

East Northport (nôrth'pōrt). Unincorporated community in SE New York, in Suffolk County, on Long Island. 3,842 (1950).

Easton (ēs'tọn). Town in C Maryland, county seat of Talbot County, near the Tred Avon River: agricultural trading center; manufactures include clothing, lumber, and canned goods. Its Friends' Meeting House (c1682) is one of the oldest wooden churches in the U.S. 4,836 (1950).

Easton. Town in SE Massachusetts, in Bristol County, ab. 25 mi. SW of Boston. It has iron manufactures. 6,244 (1950).

Easton. City in E Pennsylvania, county seat of Northampton County, at the confluence of the Lehigh and Delaware rivers, ab. 52 mi. N of Philadelphia: railroad and industrial center. Manufactures include textiles, metal products, and hosiery. It is the seat of Lafayette College. Settled in the mid-18th century, it was incorporated as a city in 1887. Pop. 35,632 (1950).

Easton, Nicholas. b. in England, 1593; d. at Newport, R.I., Aug. 15, 1675. Colonial governor of Rhode Island. He came from Wales in 1634, and resided successively at Ipswich (Massachusetts), Newbury (Massachusetts), Hampton (New Hampshire), and Newport (Rhode Island). He was governor of the united colonies of Rhode Island and Providence (1650–52).

East Orange (or'ạnj). City in NE New Jersey, in Essex County: suburb of Newark. Manufactures include electric motors, generators, and machinery. It is the seat of Upsala College and a college of physical education and hygiene. 79,340 (1950).

East Palestine (pal'ẹs.tīn). City in NE Ohio, in Columbiana County: manufactures include pottery, automobile tires, electrical refractories, and high-pressure steel tanks. The town was established in 1828. Pop. 5,195 (1950).

East Patchogue (pạ.chôg'). Unincorporated community in SE New York, in Suffolk County, on Long Island. 4,124 (1950).

East Paterson (pat'ėr.sọn). Borough in NE New Jersey, in Bergen County: industrial suburb of Paterson; textile manufactures. In the decade between the last two U.S. censuses its population more than tripled. 4,937 (1940), 15,386 (1950).

East Peoria (pẹ̄.ō'ri.ạ). City in N Illinois, in Tazewell County, across the Illinois River from Peoria: important for the manufacture of tractors. 8,698 (1950).

East Pittsburgh (pits'bėrg). Borough in SW Pennsylvania, in Allegheny County, ab. 3½ mi. NE of McKeesport: manufactures of electrical equipment, iron, and dynamos. 5,259 (1950).

East Point. City in NW Georgia, in Fulton County: industrial suburb of Atlanta. 21,080 (1950).

Eastport (ēst'pōrt). City in E Maine, in Washington County, on Moose Island in Passamaquoddy Bay. It is the easternmost city of the U.S. Sardine canning and herring, haddock, and cod fishing are the most important industries. 3,123 (1950).

Eastport. Unincorporated community in C Maryland, in Anne Arundel County, on Chesapeake Bay. 4,594 (1950).

East Prairie (prãr'i). City in SE Missouri, in Mississippi County ab. 140 mi. SE of St. Louis, in a grain and cotton producing region. 3,033 (1950).

East Providence (prov'i.dẹns). Town in N Rhode Island, in Providence County: industrial suburb of Providence. Manufactures include baking powder, refined petroleum, and dairy products. It was settled by Roger Williams in 1636. Pop. 35,871 (1950).

East Prussia (prush'ạ). [German, **Ostpreussen.**] Former province of Germany, separated in 1919 from the main portion of Prussia by the Polish Corridor. It was bordered on the W by the free state of Danzig and by Poland, on the S and SE by Poland, on the NE by Lithuania, and on the NW by the Baltic Sea. The coastal region has two large lagoons, separated from the Baltic Sea by sand spits, which have dunes as high as 200 ft. Much of the interior is rolling, and in the S and SE is the Masurian Lake region with some 3,300 lakes in a hilly morainic region. The greatest elevation is in the SW, ab. 1,024 ft. The climate is continental, with warm summers and cold winters. Originally largely forested, East Prussia developed into a rich agricultural region, with many great landed estates; about half the total population was employed in agriculture and forestry, with farming specialized in dairying and stock raising. Fishing is carried on both in the sea and in the lakes. Amber is still an important product of the Samland district. East Prussia was established by the Teutonic Knights in the 13th century and was the original heart of the duchy of Prussia, founded in 1525. In the period 1708–11 it was devastated by the plague, and recolonized by Protestants from Salzburg, the Palatinate, and Switzerland. Ermeland belonged to Poland until 1772, when it was annexed to East Prussia. East Prussia was the stronghold of the Junkers, the old Prussian military aristocracy, whose great estates occupied much of the province. In World War I Russian armies invaded East Prussia, but were decisively defeated in the battle of Tannenberg in August, 1914. In 1919 a strip of territory N of the Memel River was made an independent territory similar to Danzig, and detached from East Prussia. In World War II, East Prussia was conquered and occupied by Soviet armies in early 1945, and the province was divided between Poland and the U.S.S.R., with the larger portion going to Poland. The population of East Prussia was predominantly German, with a considerable proportion of Polish population in the S border regions. The German population was expelled after World War II and the area has been resettled by Slavs. Area, 14,283 sq. mi. (before 1939); pop. 2,333,301 (1939).

East Punjab (pun.jäb′, pun′jäb, -jab). See **Punjab** state, Union of India.

East Retford (ret′fọrd). [Called, locally, **Retford.**] Municipal borough and market town in N central England, in Nottinghamshire, situated on the river Idle and the Chesterfield Canal, ab. 19 mi. NW of Newark, ab. 139 mi. N of London by rail. 16,312 (1951).

East Ridge. Town in SE Tennessee, in Hamilton County, near Chattanooga. In the decade between the last two U.S. censuses its population more than tripled. 2,939 (1940), 9,645 (1950).

East Riding of Yorkshire (rīd′ing; yôrk′shir). See **Yorkshire, East Riding of.**

East River. Strait between Manhattan and Long Island, connecting Long Island Sound with Upper New York Bay, and separating the boroughs of Manhattan and the Bronx on the W from Brooklyn and Queens on the E. Length to the entrance of the Harlem River, ab. 9 mi.; to Fort Schuyler (at Throg's Neck, on Long Island Sound), ab. 16 mi. Width between Manhattan and Brooklyn, ½ to ¾ mi.

East Rochester (roch′es″.tėr, -ẹs.tėr). Village in W New York, in Monroe County: piano factories. 7,022 (1950).

East Rockaway (rok′ạ.wā). Village in SE New York, in Nassau County, on Long Island. 7,970 (1950).

East Rockport (rok′pōrt). Former name of **Lakewood,** Ohio.

East Rutherford (ruᴛʜ′ėr.fọrd). [Former name, **Boiling Springs Township.**] Borough in NE New Jersey, in Bergen County: suburb of Rutherford. 7,438 (1950).

East Sea. See under **Dead Sea.**

East Side, Lower. See **Lower East Side.**

East St. Louis (sānt lö′is). City in SW Illinois, in St. Clair County, on the Mississippi River opposite St. Louis: the most important bauxite-processing center in the U.S. It is also a major meat-packing center. 82,295 (1950).

East Stroudsburg (stroudz′bėrg). Borough in E Pennsylvania, in Monroe County, in an agricultural and summer resort area. 7,274 (1950).

East Suffolk (suf′ọk). [Also, **Suffolk East.**] Administrative county of the geographical county of Suffolk, in E England. It is a highly developed agricultural region and has important fisheries, especially at Lowestoft. A high proportion of the land is under crops and relatively little under pasture. There has been much land reclaimed from the sea. Ipswich is the county seat; area, ab. 858 sq. mi.; pop. 321,849 (1951).

East Sussex (sus′iks). [Also, **Sussex East.**] Administrative county in SE England, part of the geographical county of Sussex. It has many seaside resorts; however, it is primarily an agricultural county. Lewes is the county seat; area, ab. 781 sq. mi.; pop. 618,083 (1951).

East Syracuse (sir′ạ.kūs). Village in C New York, in Onondaga County, near Syracuse. 4,766 (1950).

East Thomaston (tom′ạs.tọn). Village in W Georgia, in Upson County. Peaches are raised in the surrounding region. 3,082 (1950).

East Tirol (tir′ol). [German, **Ost-Tirol.**] Territorial exclave of the Austrian province of Tirol, bounded by the provinces of Salzburg and Carinthia on the N and E and by Italy on the S and W. It was created by the cession of the S part of Tirol to Italy in 1918. The principal place is Lienz.

East Tualaty Plains (tö.ä′lạ.ti). A former name of **Hillsboro,** Ore.

East Turkistan or **Turkestan** (tėr.ki.stan′, -stän′). See under **Sinkiang.**

Eastview (ēst′vū). Suburb of the city of Ottawa, Ontario, Canada, situated on the right bank of the Ottawa River, a few mi. E of the city. 13,799 (1951).

Eastward Ho! Comedy written chiefly by George Chapman and John Marston, with contributions by Ben Jonson. It was written and acted during the winter of 1604–05, and was entered upon the Stationers' Register on Sept. 4, 1605. The authors were imprisoned for satirizing the Scots in this play, and sentenced to have their ears and noses split, feeling at the time about the Scots being especially sensitive because the new king, James I, was a Scot. Jonson, though not responsible for the obnoxious passages, gave himself up with his friends. The play was revived in 1751 as *The Prentices,* and in 1775 as *Old City Manners.*

Eastwick (ēst′wik), **Edward Backhouse.** b. 1814; d. at Ventnor, England, July 16, 1883. English Orientalist, diplomat, and author. After taking a degree at Oxford, he served with the East India Company in Kathiawar and Sind, India, and as professor of Hindustani (1845) at the East India College at Haileybury. At the closing of this school he was employed (1859) in the India Office, and later was secretary of legation in Persia (1860) and a member of the commission for a Venezuelan loan (1864, 1867). He translated Saadi's *Gulistan* (*Rose Garden,* 1852) and other Oriental classics, and also wrote on his experiences as a diplomat.

East Windsor (win′zọr). Town in N Connecticut, in Hartford County: marketing and processing point for shade-grown tobacco. 4,859 (1950).

East Windsor. Former industrial suburb of Windsor, Ontario, Canada, annexed to Windsor in 1935. It was first incorporated in 1913, and had several large automobile factories. 16,200 (1931).

Eastwood (ēst′wůd). Urban district in N central England, in Nottinghamshire, ab. 9 mi. NW of Nottingham, ab. 136 mi. N of London by rail. It has coal mines, and is noted as the place where the old Midland railway (later absorbed into the London, Midland, and Scottish system) was begun. 9,896 (1951).

Easy (ē′zi), **Sir Charles.** The "careless husband" in Colley Cibber's comedy of that name.

Eaton (ē′tọn). Village in SW Ohio, county seat of Preble County: residential community. It was established in 1806, and named for William Eaton (1764–1811). 4,242 (1950).

Eaton, Amos. b. at Chatham, N.Y., May 17, 1776; d. May 10, 1842. American natural scientist. He was a public lecturer (1817 *et seq.*) on botany and geology in New England and New York, and was professor of natural history (1820 *et seq.*) at Castleton, Vt., Medical School; senior professor (1824–42) at Rensselaer College (now Rensselaer Polytechnic Institute). He was the author of *A Manual of Botany for the Northern States* (1817).

Eaton, Daniel Cady. b. at Fort Gratiot, Mich., Sept. 12, 1834; d. at New Haven, Conn., June 29, 1895. American botanist; grandson of Amos Eaton. He graduated in 1857 from Yale, in which institution he became professor of botany in 1864. He published "Ferns of the Southwest" (*United States Geological Survey,* Vol. VI, 1878) and *Ferns of North America* (1878–79).

Eaton, Dorman Bridgman. b. at Hardwick, Vt., June 27, 1823; d. Dec. 23, 1899. American lawyer, civil service official, and author. He practiced law at New York (until 1870) with William Kent. An ardent advocate of the merit system and the abolition of the spoils system, he was appointed (1873) by Grant chairman of the U.S. Civil Service Commission. When the funds for the commission were suspended (1875), Eaton traveled to England to study the civil service system as it was being applied in that country. He drafted the Pendleton Act of 1883 establishing a permanent civil service system, and was reappointed chairman (1883, 1885) of the Civil Service Commission. His study of city administration is embodied in *The Government of Municipalities* (1899). He bequeathed funds for the Eaton professorship of the science of government at Harvard and the Eaton professorship of municipal science at Columbia. He was the author of *The Civil Service in Great Britain: A History of Abuses and Reforms and their Bearing Upon American Politics* (1880).

Eaton, George W. b. at Henderson, Huntingdon County, Pa., July 3, 1804; d. at Hamilton, N.Y., Aug. 3, 1872. American educator and Baptist clergyman. He was president of Madison University (now Hamilton) from 1856–1868, and of Hamilton Theological Seminary from 1861 to 1871.

Eaton, John Henry. b. June 18, 1790; d. at Washington, D.C., Nov. 17, 1856. American politician and lawyer, remembered for his association with Andrew Jackson. He attended the University of North Carolina, studied law, and settled (c1808–09) at Franklin, Tenn. He served for a time in the War of 1812 and began his connection with Andrew Jackson by marrying Myra Lewis, a ward of Jackson. He helped write *The Life of Andrew Jackson, Major General in the Service of the United States* (1817 and in 1818 was appointed to the U.S. Senate, serving until his resignation in 1829, when he became Jackson's secretary of war. Eaton's second wife, Peggy O'Neill (or O'Neale), became the center of a battle, waged as a war in Washington society, between the Jackson forces and their opponents. The affair contributed to the reshuffling of the cabinet, from which Eaton resigned in 1831. He became (1834) governor of Florida and served (1836 *et seq.*) as minister to Spain.

Eaton, Nathaniel. b. c1609; d. at London, 1674. First headmaster of Harvard College; brother of Theophilus Eaton and Samuel Eaton. He was appointed in 1637. In 1639 he was fined 100 marks for gross brutality to one of his ushers, Nathaniel Briscoe, whereupon he fled to Virginia, leaving debts to the amount of 1,000 pounds.

Eaton, Peggy. See **O'Neill, Margaret.**

Eaton, Samuel. b. at Crowley, Great Budworth, Cheshire, England, c1596; d. Jan. 9, 1665. Anglican clergyman; brother of Theophilus Eaton and Nathaniel Eaton. He emigrated (1637) with his brothers to New Haven, becoming the colleague of John Davenport, whom he assisted in establishing a local church, and returned (1640) to England.

Eaton, Theophilus. b. 1590; d. at New Haven, Conn., Jan. 7, 1658. First governor of the colony of New Haven; brother of Nathaniel Eaton and Samuel Eaton. He came in 1637 from London to New England with John Davenport, whom he assisted in the purchase of Quinipiak from the Indians as a site for the colony of New Haven, which was planted in 1638. In 1639 he was elected governor of the colony, which post he retained until his death.

Eaton, Walter Prichard. b. at Malden, Mass., Aug. 24, 1878—. American author and drama critic who served (1933–47) as associate professor of playwriting at Yale. Graduated (1900) from Harvard, he joined (1902) the drama department of the New York *Herald-Tribune* and also was drama critic for the New York *Sun*. He has taught at Columbia, the Cambridge School of Drama, and the University of Miami, and has served as a member of the drama jury of the Pulitzer prize committee. His works include *The American Stage of Today* (1908), *The Man Who Found Christmas* (1913), *The Idyl of Twin Fires* (1915), *Plays and Players* (1916), *Green Trails and Upland Pastures* (1917), *Ten Years of the Theatre Guild* (1929), *The Drama in English* (1930), *Wild Gardens of New England* (1935), and *The Runaway Place*. He is also the author of a book of verse, *Echoes and Realities* (1918), and wrote in collaboration with David Carb the play *Queen Victoria* (1923).

Eaton, William. b. at Woodstock, Conn., Feb. 23, 1764; d. at Brimfield, Mass., June 1, 1811. American naval officer and state department official, consul at Tunis from 1799 to 1803. He was subsequently appointed U.S. naval agent to the Barbary States, and during the Tripolitan War organized a movement among the natives to restore the brother of the reigning bey to the Tripolitan throne. With the assistance of the American squadron he took Derna in 1805, and was about to march on Tripoli when peace was concluded between the U.S. and the reigning bey. Eaton, Ohio, was named for him.

Eaton, Wyatt. b. at Philipsburg, Quebec, Canada, May 6, 1849; d. at Newport, R.I., June 7, 1896. American figure and portrait painter. He studied at the National Academy of Design at New York, and with Gérôme at Paris.

Eaton Rapids. City in S Lower Michigan, in Eaton County on the Grand River: center of a sheep-raising area. 3,509 (1950).

Eatonton (ē'tọn.tọn). City in N central Georgia, county seat of Putnam County, ab. 65 mi. SE of Atlanta in a farming region. It was the birthplace of Joel Chandler Harris. 2,749 (1950).

Eatontown (ē'tọn.toun). Borough in E New Jersey, in Monmouth County ab. 38 mi. E of Trenton. Fort Monmouth, a large training post for the U.S. Army Signal Corps, is nearby. 3,044 (1950).

Eau Claire (ō klãr'). Town in C South Carolina, in Richland County: residential suburb of Columbia. It is the seat of Columbia College and a Lutheran seminary. In the decade between the last two U.S. censuses its population more than doubled. 3,508 (1940), 9,238 (1950).

Eau Claire. City in W Wisconsin, in Eau Claire and Chippewa counties, on the Eau Claire and Chippewa rivers ab. 83 mi. SE of St. Paul: county seat of Eau Claire County. Manufactures include furniture, sashes, doors, books, kitchen utensils, farm machinery, stationery, mill tools, refrigerators, automobile tires and accessories, and sewer pipe. It is the seat of a state teachers college. In the early 19th century it was a lumbering center. 36,058 (1950).

Eaux-Bonnes (ō.bon). [Also, **Les-Eaux-Bonnes.**] Village in SW France, in the department of Basses-Pryénées, situated in mountainous surroundings near the Sourde River, ab. 28 mi. S of Pau. It is a health resort, having thermal springs considered useful in the treatment of various ailments. It is also a tourist and winter-sport center. 462 (1946).

Éauze (ā.ōz). Town in SW France, in the department of Gers, ab. 29 mi. NW of Auch. It is on the site of the Roman Elusa. Pop. ab. 2,000.

Ebal (ē'bạl), **Mount.** [Arabic, **Jebel Eslamiyah.**] Mountain (3,084 ft.) in Palestine, forming the N side of the fertile valley in which lies Nablus, the ancient Shechem. From Ebal the curse for disobedience to the law was pronounced, the blessing for obedience being given from Mount Gerizim, which lies opposite on the S side of the valley. Upon Ebal Joshua erected the first altar to Jehovah after conquering Canaan. Deut. xvii. 13.

Ebb and Flood. Novel by James Hanley, published in 1932.

Ebbinghaus (eb'ing.hous), **Hermann.** b. 1850; d. 1909. German psychologist. He received his degree from Bonn in 1873 and during the next seven years, while still independent of a formal university connection, he began his experimental studies of memory; he became docent at Berlin in 1880, and in 1885 published the results of his original studies of memory in *Über das Gedächtnis* (Eng. trans., 1913). Since Ebbinghaus's pioneering work, the field of memory and learning has been one of the most active fields of psychology. He showed how repetitions could be used as a measure of learning, and how the difference between the number of repetitions required for original learning and the number required for relearning (the "saving" of repetitions) could be used as a measure of retention. He pointed out the relation between memory and (1) the number of items in the list, (2) the position of the items in the list, (3) the number of repetitions of the list, and (4) the time elapsed since the original learning of the list. The latter relationship is described in his famous "Forgetting Curve." He invented the nonsense syllable (two consonants separated by a vowel) for the study of memory. In 1894 he became professor at Breslau. He invented (1897) the now common completion test in an early attempt to measure the intelligence of children. He helped found, with Arthur König, the *Zeitschrift für Psychologie und Physiologie der Sinnesorgane* (1890). His other books are *Grundzüge der Psychologie* (1897, 1902) and *Abriss der Psychologie* (1908). In the latter is his famous opening sentence "Psychology has a long past, but only a short history."

Ebbsfleet or **Ebbs Fleet** (ebz'flēt"). Hamlet in SE England, in Kent, situated on Pegwell Bay, in the Isle of Thanet, ab. 4 mi. SW of Ramsgate. It was the landing place of Hengist and Horsa in 449, and of Saint Augustine in 597.

Ebbw Vale (eb'ö). Urban district and industrial center in W England, in Monmouthshire, situated on the river Ebbwfawr ab. 5 mi. NW of Abertillery, ab. 155 mi. W of London by rail. Its industries include steel and tinplate manufactures. 29,205 (1951).

Ebco von Repgow (ep'kō fon rep'gō) or **Repkow** (rep'kō). See **Eike von Repgow** or **Repkow.**

Ebe (ā'bẹ), **Gustav.** b. at Halberstadt, Germany, Nov. 1, 1834; d. cMay 15, 1916. German architect. His work was typical of the so-called "Grunder-Barock" (an architectural style) palace representative of the 1870's and 1880's, using the forms of the German late Renaissance style in designs for private residences. He was awarded the first prize for the Vienna *Rathaus* (city hall), but his design was not executed. He is best known for the Palais Rudolf Mosse (built 1882–84) at Berlin, the house of the well-known newspaper owner.

Ebel (ā'bẹl), **Hermann Wilhelm.** b. at Berlin, May 10, 1820; d. at Misdroi, Pomerania, Prussia, Aug. 19, 1875. German philologist, especially distinguished in Celtic philology. He became (1872) professor at Berlin. His chief work is a revision of Zeuss's *Grammatica celtica* (1871).

Ebeling (ā'bẹ.ling), **Adolf.** b. at Hamburg, Germany, Oct. 24, 1827; d. July 23, 1896. German writer. He traveled in Brazil, lived at Paris as a teacher and newspaper correspondent until 1870, and then lived successively at Düsseldorf, Cologne, Metz, Cairo, and again at Cologne. His works include *Lebende Bilder aus dem modernen Paris* (1866–76), *Bilder aus Cairo* (1878), and others.

Ebeling, Christoph Daniel. b. at Garmissen, near Hildesheim, Germany, Nov. 20, 1741; d. at Hamburg, Germany, June 30, 1817. German geographer. He contributed to Büsching's *Erdbeschreibung* the volumes on America (1794–1816).

Ebelsberg (ā'bẹls.berk). [Also, **Ebersberg.**] Village in C Austria, in the province of Upper Austria, situated on the Traun River SE of Linz. Here the French defeated the Austrians in 1809. After World War II, it was the site of a Displaced Persons camp. It is now incorporated in the city of Linz.

Ebenezer (eb.ẹ.nē'zėr). In Biblical history, a stone set up by Samuel, after a defeat of the Philistines, as a memorial to divine aid.

Ebenezer Scrooge (skröj). See **Scrooge, Ebenezer.**

Eben Holden, a Tale of the North Country (hōl'dẹn). Novel by Irving Bacheller, published in 1900.

Ebensburg (eb'ẹnz.bėrg). Borough in SW Pennsylvania, county seat of Cambria County, in a bituminous coal mining area. It was settled by Welsh immigrants c1800 and was made county seat in 1805. Pop. 4,086 (1950).

Ebensee (ā'bẹn.zā). Village in C Austria, in the province of Upper Austria, situated at the influx of the Traun River into the Traunsee, between Gmunden and Ischl. It has a factory for the production of soda. The saltworks, constructed in 1607, are supplied with brine from Ischl and Hallstadt. During the Nazi occupation of Austria a concentration camp was located here. 10,329 (1951).

Eber (ē'bėr). See **Heber.**

Eberbach (ā'bėr.bäċh). Town in S Germany, in the *Land* (state) of Württemberg-Baden, American Zone, formerly part of Baden, situated on the Neckar River SE of Mannheim: wine and lumber trade; metallurgical and textile industries. It is an old town; above it is the Stolzeneck castle which in the 12th century belonged to the Hohenstaufen domain. 11,038 (1950).

Eberhard (ā'bėr.härt). d. at the battle of Andernach on the Rhine, 939. Duke of the Franks (or Franconia) and brother of Conrad I of Germany.

Eberhard I. [Titles: 5th Count and 1st Duke of **Württemberg.**] b. Dec. 11, 1445; d. Feb. 24, 1496. First Duke of Württemberg, 1495. He consolidated the country, framed its constitution, and established (1477) the University of Tübingen.

Eberhard, Johann August. b. at Halberstadt, Prussia, Aug. 31, 1739; d. Jan. 6, 1809. German philosopher, professor at Halle (1778 *et seq.*). He published *Neue Apologie des Sokrates* (1772) and others.

Eberhard, Konrad. b. at Hindelang, Bavaria, Germany, Nov. 25, 1768; d. at Munich, March 13, 1859. German sculptor. His most notable works were collected at Munich.

Eberl (ā'bėrl), **Anton.** b. at Vienna, June 13, 1766; d. there, March 11, 1807. German pianist and composer, a friend of Mozart. He was *Kapellmeister* (choir leader) from 1796 to 1800 at St. Petersburg.

Eberle (eb'ėr.li), **Abastenia St. Leger.** b. at Webster City, Iowa, April 6, 1878; d. 1942. American sculptor. She was a student at the Art Students League of New York, and of George Grey Barnard, and won awards from the National Academy of Design (1910), the Panama-Pacific Exposition (1915), the National Sculpture Society (1931), and others. Among her works are *Mowgli* (in the Metropolitan Museum), *Little Mother* (Art Institute of Chicago), *Hurdy Gurdy* (Detroit Institute of Arts), *Girl on Roller Skates* (Whitney Museum of American Art), and others.

Eberle (ā'bėr.lẹ), **Adolph.** b. at Munich, Jan. 11, 1843; d. Jan. 24, 1914. German genre and animal painter. He was a student of Karl von Piloty in the Academy at Munich, and lived most of his life at that city. His work has been exhibited at Vienna, where he won a medal in 1873, at Dresden, Hamburg, Munich, New York, and elsewhere. Among his better-known works are *Provisions of the Hunt, Pastorale, Temptation,* and *Fish Story.*

Eberle (eb'ėr.li), **Edward Walter.** b. at Denton, Tex., Aug. 17, 1864; d. at Washington, D.C., July 6, 1929. American naval officer. A graduate (1885) of the U.S. Naval Academy, he was a lieutenant (j.g.) on the *Oregon* during that vessel's famous Spanish-American War cruise around Cape Horn and in the battle of Santiago. As a flag lieutenant (1903–05) in the Atlantic fleet, he drew up the first naval wireless procedures and codes; superintendent (1915–17) U.S. Naval Academy; chief of naval operations (1923–27); retired (1928) as rear admiral.

Eberle (ā'bėr.lẹ), **Johann Ernst.** See **Eberlin, Johann Ernst.**

Eberle (eb'ėr.li), **John.** b. at Hagerstown, Md., Dec. 10, 1787; d. at Lexington, Ky., Feb. 2, 1838. American physician and medical writer.

Eberlein (ā'bėr.līn), **Gustav.** b. at Spiekershausen, near Hann-Munden, Germany, July 14, 1847; d. at Berlin, Feb. 5, 1926. German sculptor. Beginning his career as a neoclassicist, as in his *Dornauszieher* (1880) at the Berlin National Gallery, he later turned toward neobaroque expression influenced by R. Begas. Among his best-known works are his monuments of the emperor Wilhelm I (1890) at Mannheim, Richard Wagner (1901) at Berlin, and Goethe (1902) at Rome. He is represented in America by his monument (1910) at Buenos Aires in honor of the 100th anniversary of Argentina's independence.

Eberlin (ā'bėr.lin) or **Eberle** (ā'bėr.lẹ), **Johann Ernst.** b. at Jettingen, Bavaria, Germany, March 27, 1702; d. at Salzburg, Austria, June 21, 1762. German church composer and court organist (1754 *et seq.*) at Salzburg. He composed oratorios, motets, and masses, and wrote toccatas and fugues for the organ.

Ebers (ā'bėrs), **Emil.** b. at Breslau, Dec. 14, 1807; d. at Beuthen (Bytom), in Silesia, 1884. German painter.

Ebers, Georg Moritz. b. at Berlin, March 1, 1837; d. at Tutzing, Bavaria, Germany, Aug. 7, 1898. German Egyptologist and novelist. He first studied jurisprudence at Göttingen, then Oriental languages and archaeology at Berlin. In 1865 he became docent in Egyptian language and antiquities at the University of Jena; in 1870 he was called to Leipzig as professor in the same field. His first work was *Ägypten und die Bücher Moses* (Egypt and the Books of Moses, 1867–68). In 1869–70 he made a journey to Egypt, which was repeated in 1872–73, when he discovered the so-called *Papyrus Ebers*, an ancient medical treatise which he found at Thebes and published in 1874 under the title *Papyrus E., ein hieratisches Handbuch der Ägyptischen Medizin. Durch Gosen zum Sinai* (Through Goshen to Sinai) appeared in 1872; *Ägypten in Wort und Bild* (Egypt in Word and Picture) in 1878. Among his romances, principally historical novels set in Egypt and meant to popularize knowledge about Egypt, are *Eine Ägyptische Königstochter* (An Egyptian Princess, 1864), *Uarda* (1877), *Homo Sum* (1878), *Die Schwestern* (The Sisters, 1880), *Der Kaiser* (The Emperor, 1881), *Serapis* (1885), *Die Nilbraut* (The Bride of the Nile, 1887), and *Joshua* (1889).

Ebers, Karl Friedrich. b. March 25, 1770; d. at Berlin, Sept. 9, 1836. German composer and arranger. Of his works, consisting of four operas, cantatas, dances, overtures, and symphonies, only the drinking song *Wir sind die Könige der Welt* has survived.

Ebersbach (ā′bėrs.bäċh). Town in E Germany, in the *Land* (state) of Saxony, Russian Zone, formerly in the free state of Saxony, situated near the source of the Spree River and the border of Czechoslovakia, E of Dresden: textile and lumber industries. Its Protestant church (built in 1738) has one of the finest organs in Saxony. 11,315 (1946).

Ebersberg (ā′bėrs.berk). See **Ebelsberg.**

Eberswalde (ā′bėrs.väl.dẹ). City in NE Germany, in the *Land* (state) of Brandenburg, Russian Zone, formerly in the province of Brandenburg, Prussia, situated near the Berlin-Stettin Canal, ab. 28 mi. NE of Berlin. Industries include iron foundries, railroad repair shops, lumber mills, and brick factories. It is the seat of an academy of forestry and has a museum of forestry as well as a local museum. Parts of the medieval town walls have been preserved. The Church of the Magdalen dates from the 14th century, the *Rathaus* (town hall) from the 18th century. Nearby, in 1914, important prehistoric finds were made, consisting of numerous golden utensils and artefacts. The pieces were placed in the Berlin Museum für Vorgeschichte. The population of Eberswalde decreased in the period 1939–46 by 21.1 percent. 30,186 (1946).

Ebert (ā′bėrt), **Adolf.** b. at Kassel, Prussia, June 1, 1820; d. July 1, 1890. German Romance philologist, professor at Leipzig from 1862.

Ebert, Friedrich. b. at Heidelberg, Germany, Feb. 4, 1871; d. at Berlin, Feb. 28, 1925. First president of the German Reich (Weimar Republic). Ebert was a saddlemaker but early in life became a Social Democratic journalist and functionary; as a union leader at Bremen he became a member of the party's executive board (1905). Elected to the Reichstag in 1912, he became party leader in 1913, and induced the party to vote for war credits at the outbreak of World War I. He opposed strikes as a means of bringing about peace. In September, 1918, he entered the cabinet of Maximilian, commonly called Prince Max of Baden, and was offered the chancellorship; he accepted (Nov. 9) and formed a cabinet of three Majority Socialists and three Independent Socialists. He insisted on early elections for a constitutional assembly and was appointed Reichspresident by this body, on Feb. 11, 1919. His tenure was extended by the Reichstag until June, 1925. He served with distinction and tact under extremely difficult conditions. Both the leftist Spartacist revolt and the rightist Kapp putsch were suppressed by him, but his attempts to tread a middle path came under attack from extremists, especially those of the right who resented a plebeian head of the government. His untimely death has been attributed by some to unfounded attacks on his patriotism.

Ebert, Friedrich Adolf. b. at Taucha, near Leipzig, Germany, July 9, 1791; d. at Dresden, Germany, Nov. 13, 1834. German bibliographer. He was librarian at Wolfenbüttel (1823), and later (1825) at Dresden. His principal work is *Allegemeines bibliographisches Lexikon* (1821–30).

Eberth (ā′bėrt), **Karl Joseph.** b. at Wurzburg, Bavaria, Germany, 1835; d. 1926. German bacteriologist, pathologist, anatomist, and professor at Zurich and Halle universities. He studied medicine at Wurzburg under Kolliker and Virchow, two of the greatest names in 19th-century anatomy and pathology. He went to Zurich in 1874, and to Halle in 1881. He is noted for his many contributions to pathology and bacteriology, and for identification of the typhoid fever bacillus in 1880. "Eberth's bacillus" is named in his honor.

Eberton (eb′ėr.tọn). Former name of **West York, Pa.**

Eberwein (ā′bėr.vīn), **Karl.** b. at Weimar, Germany, Nov. 10, 1786; d. 1868. German composer and violinist; brother of Traugott Maximilian Eberwein. He was a member and conductor of the court orchestra at Weimar. His works include operas, chamber music, and incidental music to some of Goethe's dramas

Eberwein, Traugott Maximilian. b. at Weimar, Germany, Oct. 27, 1775; d. at Rudolstadt, Germany, Dec. 2, 1831. German composer and violinist; brother of Karl Eberwein. He was a member (1797 *et seq.*) and *Kapellmeister* (choir leader) (1817 *et seq.*) of the Rudolstadt court orchestra. His works include operas, symphonies, chamber works, concertos, and cantatas.

Ebingen (ā′bing.ẹn). City in S Germany, in the *Land* (state) of Württemberg-Hohenzollern, French Zone, formerly in the Schwarzwald *Kreis* (district) of Württemberg, situated ab. 35 mi. S of Stuttgart. Manufactures include tools, precision instruments, musical instruments, leather, and shoes. 17,076 (1950).

Ebionites (ē′bi.ọn.īts). Party of Judaizing Christians which appeared in the Church as early as the 2nd century A.D., and disappeared about the 4th century. They agreed in the recognition of Jesus as the Messiah, the denial of his divinity, belief in the universal obligation of the Mosaic law, and rejection of Paul and his writings. The two great divisions of Ebionites were the Pharisaic Ebionites, who emphasized the obligation of the Mosaic law, and the Essenic Ebionites, who were more speculative and leaned toward Gnosticism.

Ebisu (e.bē.sö). [Also, **Yebisu.**] Japanese Shinto deity of good fortune, whose image is often found in farmhouses and on plaques in shops, in association with Daikoku; one of the Seven Gods of Happiness.

Eblana (eb′lạ.nạ). See under **Dublin** city, Irish Republic.

Eblis (eb′lis). [Also, **Iblis.**] In Arabian mythology, the chief of the evil spirits; the devil; a fallen prince of the angels. Beckford introduces him in *Vathek*.

Ebner (āb′nėr), **Anton Gilbert Victor.** [Title, Ritter **von Rosenstein.**] b. at Bregenz, Vorarlberg, Austria, Feb. 4, 1842; d. at Vienna, March 20, 1925. Austrian histologist. A pupil of E. W. von Brücke and A. Rollet, he was assistant (1868–70) at the physiological laboratory at Graz, privatdocent of histology and embryology (1870–73) at the University of Innsbruck, and full professor (1873 *et seq.*) at the University of Graz. He is remembered for his description (1890) of the fibrils in the dentin and cementum of the teeth (Ebner's fibrils), the serous glands of the tongue, called Ebner's glands (1873), and for a method for decalcifying bones (1875). Author of *Über den Bau der Aortenwand* (1870), *Untersuchungen über den Bau der Samencanälchen und die Entwicklung der Spermatozoiden* (1871), *Die acinösen Drüsen der Zunge und ihre Beziehungen zu den Geschmacksorganen* (1873), *Untersuchungen über das Verhalten des Knochengewebes im polarisierten Lichte* (1874), *Über den feineren Bau der Knochensubstanz* (1875), *Mikroskopische Studien über Wachsthum und Wechsel der Haare* (1876), *Strittige Fragen über den Bay des Zahnschmelzes* (1890), and, with A. von Kölliker, *Handbuch der Gewebelehre des Menschen* (1902).

Ebner-Eschenbach (āb′nėr.esh′ẹn.bäċh), **Marie,** Baroness **von.** [Maiden name, **Marie,** Countess **Dubsky.**] b. at the castle of Zdislavic, near Ungarisch-Hradisch (Uherské Hradiště), in Moravia, Sept. 13, 1830; d. at Vienna, March 12, 1916. Austrian author, the outstanding woman writer in Austrian literature. Her work describes with great skill and insight the life and mores of the Viennese nobility and of the Bohemian country folk, peasantry, and landed gentry. She is unquestionably one of the great masters of the 19th-century *novelle*. Perhaps her most important long work is the novel *Das Gemeindekind* (1887; Eng. trans., *The Child of the Parish*, 1893). Among her numerous short stories *Lotti die Uhrmacherin* (Lotti the Watchmaker, 1881), *Krambambuli* (1913–15), and *Der Kreisphysikus* (The District Doctor, 1913–15) could be singled out as particularly successful.

Eboe (ē'bō). See **Ibo.**

Eboli (e'bō.lē). [Ancient name, **Eburum.**] Town and commune in S Italy, in the *compartimento* (region) of Campania, in the province of Salerno, situated near the Sele River, ab. 45 mi. SE of Naples. The surrounding district produces principally livestock, and also excellent wines and olive oil; there are extensive fisheries .A huge medieval castle is among the tourist attractions; the ruins of ancient Paestum, including beautiful Greek temples, are nearby. In the Middle Ages, the town was favored by the emperor Frederick II because of its adherence to the Hohenstaufen cause. Considerable damage was suffered during World War II by some buildings of tourist interest, but repairs have been completed or are being carried out. Pop. of commune, 14,727 (1936); of town, 12,057 (1936).

Éboli (ā'bō.lē), Princesa **de.** [Title of **Ana de Mendoza.**] b. 1540; d. at Pastrana, Spain, Feb. 2, 1592. Daughter of Don Diego Hurtado de Mendoza, viceroy of Peru, and (according to some authorities) mistress of Philip II of Spain. She married in 1559 the favorite Rui Gómez de Silva, prince of Eboli. While mistress of the king she maintained similar relations with the minister Antonio Pérez (some sources dispute the probability of the liaison with Philip). She was, in consequence of a political intrigue, betrayed by Juan de Escobedo, the secret agent at the court of Don John of Austria. Escobedo being murdered soon after by Pérez, she was suspected of complicity in the crime, and was banished from court in 1579. She figures as one of the characters in Schiller's *Don Carlos.*

Ebon (eb'on). Island in the Ralik Chain, Marshall Islands, the most southerly of the group. It is an important commercial port and the site of an American mission station.

Ebora Cerealis (eb'ō.ra sir.i.ā'lis). Roman name of **Évora,** city.

Eboracum (eb.ō.rā'kum). Latin name of **York,** England.

Éboué (ā.bwā), **Félix Adolphe.** b. at Cayenne, French Guiana, Dec. 26, 1884; d. at Cairo, Egypt, May 17, 1944. French colonial official, best known for bringing (August, 1940) the support of the Chad region, of which he was governor, under the Free French regime of General Charles de Gaulle. He was later governor general (December, 1940–May, 1944) of French Equatorial Africa. A Negro, he was particularly interested in the cultural life of the Ubangi region, where he served for 23 years.

Ebrard (ā'brärt), **Johann Heinrich August.** b. at Erlangen, Bavaria, Germany, Jan. 18, 1818; d. there, July 23, 1888. German clergyman of the Reformed Church, and theological and miscellaneous writer.

Ebro (ā'brō). [French, **Èbre** (ebr); Latin, **Iberus.**] River in Spain which rises in the province of Santander and flows into the Mediterranean. It is a source of irrigation water and hydroelectric power. Saragossa is situated on it. Length, ab. 500 mi.

Ebrodunum (eb.rō.dū'num). Ancient name of **Embrun.**

Ebudae (ē.bū'dē). An ancient name of the **Hebrides.**

Ebura (eb'ū.ra). An ancient name of the **Eure River.**

Eburacum (eb.ū.rā'kum). An ancient name of **York,** England.

Eburodunensis (eb"ū.rō.dö.nen'sis), **Lacus.** Ancient name of **Neuchâtel, Lake of.**

Eburodunum (eb"ū.rō.dū'num). Ancient name of **Yverdon.**

Eburum (eb'ū.rum). Ancient name of **Eboli.**

Ebusus (eb'ū.sus). Ancient name of **Iviza,** island.

Eça (ā'sa), **Matias Aires Ramos da Silva de.** Full name of **Aires, Matias.**

Ecbasis captivi (ek'ba.sis kap.tī'vī). Title of the oldest known medieval beast epic, composed by a monk of Toul c940 in Latin hexameters. It tells of an erring calf that falls into the clutches of a wolf and is rescued by the coöperation of other animals. It is an allegory of temptation, sin, and salvation. The genre of which this is the precursor reached its peak in the satirical Reynard epic of the 12th and 13th centuries.

Ecbatana (ek.bat'a.na). Ancient name of **Hamadan.**

Eccard (ek'ärt), **Johann** (or **Johannes**). b. at Mühlhausen, in Thuringia, 1553; d. 1611. German musician, noted as a composer of church music. In 1589 he was made *Kapellmeister* (choir leader) to the margrave of Brandenburg at Königsberg, and in 1608 was given the same position under the elector at Berlin. He wrote both sacred music and songs.

Ecce Homo (ek'sē hō'mō, ek'e). Name given (from the words of Pilate) to representations of Christ with the crown of thorns. Among the best-known paintings of this subject is one by Titian (1543), in the art museum at Vienna. Christ, bleeding and crowned with thorns, is led out from the palace above a flight of steps by soldiers. Below are a mocking company of soldiers and people, in which a portrait of the sultan Suleiman is conspicuous.

Ecce Homo: A Survey of the Life and Work of Jesus Christ. Work by John Robert Seeley of Cambridge, England. It was first published anonymously in 1865. It created much excitement among various Protestant denominations, and elicited a number of replies.

Ecclefechan (ek.l.feċh'an, -fek'an). Village in S Scotland, in Dumfriesshire, ab. 13 mi. E of Dumfries, ab. 319 mi. N of London by rail. It is noted as the birthplace and burial-place of Thomas Carlyle. The population is variously given in the 1931 census as 614 to 988, depending upon the exact limits of the various types of districts listed.

Eccles (ek'lz). Municipal borough and manufacturing town in NW England, in Lancashire, situated on the river Irwell, ab. 4 mi. W of Manchester, ab. 187 mi. NW of London by rail. It is an outlying suburb of Manchester, and has manufactures of cotton. 43,927 (1951).

Eccles, Marriner Stoddard. b. at Logan, Utah, Sept. 9, 1890—. American banker and economist. Active as banker and business executive in Utah (1914–34); governor (1934–36) of Federal Reserve Board; chairman (1936–51) of governing board of Federal Reserve System; member (1942–46) of U.S. Economic Stabilization Board; member (1947 *et seq.*) of United Nations Investment Commission. Author of *Beckoning Frontiers* (1951), a survey of contemporary U.S. financial history.

Ecclesfield Urban (ek'lz.fēld ėr'ban) or **Ecclesfield.** Civil parish, containing parts or the whole of four wards of Sheffield, in N central England, in the West Riding of Yorkshire, ab. 168 mi. N of London by rail. It has iron and steel manufactures. 10,950 (1931).

Eccleshall (ek'l.shal, -shôl). Market town in C England, in Staffordshire, ab. 7 mi. by road NW of Stafford. It is noted for a fine early English church, and the ruins of a castle, built in 1315, which was the residence of the bishops of Lichfield until 1867. Pop. 3,532 (1931).

Ecclesiastes (ē.klē.zi.as'tēz). [Also, **The Preacher.**] Book of the Old Testament, traditionally ascribed to Solomon, but probably of later date (perhaps as late as 200 B.C.). It is one of the so-called wisdom books of the Bible, expanding on the themes "all is vanity" and the impermanence of man and man's works. The text seems to have been confused by an editor, but the general lightly cynical pessimism has led some modern critics to assume Greek influence. Ecclesiastes is included in both the Jewish and the Christian canon.

Ecclesiasticus (ē.klē.zi.as'ti.kus). Latin name of a book of the Greek Bible (Septuagint), apocryphal in the Authorized Version, but declared canonical by the Council of Trent (1545–64); it is entitled *Wisdom of Jesus the Son of Sirach,* and was probably written in the first third of the 2nd century. The Hebrew original, which had been lost, was rediscovered as separate fragments (published 1896–1900) but is in mutilated form. The book, part of the Biblical wisdom literature, is mainly proverbial and extols the value of wisdom.

Ecclesiazusae (ē.klē"zi.a.zö'sē). Comedy of Aristophanes, exhibited in 392 B.C. In it the women meet in parliament (whence the name), and decide to take control of the state, with community of goods and husbands.

Eccleston (ek'lz.ton), **Samuel.** b. in Kent County, Md., June 27, 1801; d. at Georgetown, D.C., April 21, 1851. American prelate of the Roman Catholic Church. He became archbishop of Baltimore in 1834.

Ecco von Repgow (ek'ō fon rep'gō) or **Repkow** (rep'kō). See **Eike von Repgow** or **Repkow.**

ECE. See **United Nations Economic Commission for Europe.**

Ecgberht (eg'berċht). See **Egbert** or **Ecgberht.**

Echegaray y Eizaguirre (ā"chā.gä.rī' ē ā.thā.gėr'rā), **José.** [Often called the **"Spanish Ibsen."**] b. at Madrid, 1832; d. 1916. Spanish professor of mathematics, engineer, statesman, and dramatist. Rooted in the Romantic school, he combined the thesis play with the honor drama of the 17th-century Spanish dramatist Calderón. His *El Gran Galeoto* (Eng. trans., *The World and his Wife*, 1881) was acclaimed in Europe and the U.S. as one of the greatest plays of the 19th century. He was made professor of mathematics in the Engineering College of Madrid in 1858, became a member of the Academy of Sciences in 1866, and was the author of a number of mathematical works of recognized value. He became a member of the Cortes in 1868, was minister of commerce, education, and finance (1868–74), withdrew from political life in 1874, and was again minister of finance in 1905. Among his best-known works are *La Esposa del vengador* (1874), *La Última Noche* (1875) *O locura o santidad* (1877), *En el seno de la muerte* (1879), *Mariana* (1892), *El Hijo de Don Juan* (1892), *Mancha que limpia* (1895), and *El Loco dios* (1900). Many of his plays have been translated into other languages. In 1904 he received, with Mistral, the Nobel prize for literature.

Echenique (ā.chā.nē'kā), **José Rufino.** b. at Puno, Peru, 1808; d. at Arequipa, Peru, Oct. 18, 1879. Peruvian general and statesman, president (1851–55) of Peru. He served under Santa Cruz, but after the defeat at Yungay (January, 1839) he gave his allegiance to Gamarra. In 1843 he was one of the leaders of the revolt against Vivanco. He was elected president of Peru (April 20, 1851). Revolts against him, beginning in 1853, resulted in his defeat by Castilla and exile (January, 1855). He returned in 1862, aided in the defense of Callao in 1866, and was again a presidential candidate in 1872.

Echeverría (ā"chā.ʙer.rē'ä), **Esteban.** b. at Buenos Aires, 1805; d. at Montevideo, Uruguay, 1851. Argentine poet who, despite his strong advocacy of cultural independence for America, is generally credited with the introduction of European romanticism into Spanish-American letters following a sojourn (1826–30) in France. His political activities forced him to spend the last 11 years of his life in exile. Author of *Elvira o la novia de la Plata* (1832), *Los Consuelos* (1834), *Rimas* (1837; containing "La Cautivo," his famous poem of the Pampas), *La Guitarra* (1842), and others. His complete works (1874) fill five volumes.

Echeverría, Francisco Javier. b. in Jalapa, Mexico, July 25, 1797; d. at Mexico City, Sept. 17, 1852. Mexican financier. He was secretary of the treasury (1834, 1838, 1839–41). In 1839 he succeeded in funding the Mexican debt. He was acting president for a short time in 1841.

Echidna (ẹ.kid'nạ). In Greek mythology, a monster half maiden, half serpent; daughter of Chrysaor and Callirrhoe (or of Phorcys and Ceto), and by Typhon mother of the Chimaera, the Hydra of Lernea, and Cerberus, and by Orthus, of the Sphinx and other monsters. She was slain while asleep by the many-eyed Argus.

Echinades (ẹ.kin'ạ.dēz). In ancient geography, a group of islands W of Acarnania in Greece, formed in and near the mouth of the Achelous River and now reunited, in part, to the mainland.

Echmiadzin (ech"mē.ä.dzēn'). Monastery in SW U.S.S.R., in W Armenian Soviet Socialist Republic, ab. 12 mi. by road W of Erivan. It was founded in the 4th century A.D., in the period of the establishment of Christianity as the state religion of Armenia. It was a great center of Armenian culture which flourished about the 7th century. The monastery has a collection of 8,000 ancient Armenian manuscripts, and a historical and ethnographic museum. Echmiadzin is the residence of the *katholikos*, or primate of Armenia.

Echo (ek'ō). In Greek mythology, a nymph who by her prattling prevented Hera from surprising her husband Zeus in the company of the nymphs. The goddess punished her by condemning her never to speak first and never to be silent when any one else spoke. She pined away to a bodiless voice (echo) for love of Narcissus. According to another explanation, she repulsed Pan's advances and he caused her to be torn to pieces by maddened shepherds. Ge (the earth mother) hid the pieces, which still respond to sounds.

Echo, The. Verse satire by the Connecticut Wits, published (1791–1805) in the *American Mercury* and printed as an independent work in 1807. It expressed the Federalist point of view in politics.

Echo Canyon. Deep and precipitous canyon in the Wasatch Mountains, in N Utah, now traversed by a railroad. In the first part of the 19th century a trail through the canyon was used by emigrants on their way to the West, notably by the Donner Party in 1846 and by the Mormons under Brigham Young on their way to Salt Lake City in 1847.

Echo Lake. Name of various small sheets of water: **1.** A lake in New Hampshire, in the Franconia Notch. **2.** A lake near North Conway, N.H.

Echt (eċht). Town in SE Netherlands, in the province of Limburg, ab. 20 mi. NE of Maastricht: agricultural community. 10,573 (1939).

Echtermeyer (eċh'tėr.mī.ėr), **Ernst Theodor.** b. at Liebenwerda, Germany, 1805; d. at Dresden, Germany, May 6, 1844. German literary critic, coeditor with Arnold Ruge (1802–80) of *Hallische Jahrbücher für deutsche Wissenschaft und Kunst* (1838–41) and editor of *Auswahl deutscher Gedichte* (1836), which the original publishers (Buchhandlung des Waisenhauses at Halle) have kept in print for more than a century. The 48th (centennial) edition brought the total of copies distributed to 360,000.

Echternach (eċh'tėr.näċh). Town in Luxembourg, on the Sauer River, ab. 18 mi. NE of the city of Luxembourg. It is an ancient town, with remnants of medieval fortifications. There are potteries and distilleries. The yearly religious dancing-procession, held at Whitsuntide, is celebrated. It is said to have originated in an effort to prevent a return of an epidemic which visited the place in the 8th century. The town formed the southern anchorage of the German offensive in the Battle of the Bulge (Battle of the Ardennes), Dec. 16–31, 1944; almost all of the buildings were damaged. 3,141 (1948).

Echuca (e.chö'kạ). Town in SE Australia, in Victoria state, at the junction of the Campaspe and Murray rivers ab. 110 mi. N of Melbourne. 4,491 (1947).

Écija (ā'thē.ʜä). [Ancient names: **Astigi** or **Astigis, Augusta Firma.**] City in S Spain, in the province of Sevilla, situated on the Genil River, ab. 47 mi. NE of the city of Seville. Long famous for its shoemakers, it also manufactures olive oil, soap, straw hats, and pottery. It is the seat of a bishopric. The medieval walls are in ruins, but the gateways, the church towers with their glazed tiles, and the balconied mansions still recall the Moorish period. It was a flourishing Roman colony in ancient times, and there are remains of Roman structures. 34,944 (1940).

Eck (ek), **Johann.** [Original surname, **Mayr** (or **Maier**), and hence sometimes written, in full, **Johann Maier von Eck.**] b. at Eck (now Egg), in Swabia, Nov. 15, 1486; d. at Ingolstadt, in Bavaria, Feb. 10, 1543. German Roman Catholic theologian, a notable opponent of Luther and the Reformation. He attended Heidelberg, Tübingen, Cologne, and Freiburg universities, mastering a wide variety of subjects and joining the Humanist movement. He taught theology at Freiburg (1506–10), was ordained priest in 1508, and became pro-chancellor of Ingolstadt in 1512, where he taught for 32 years. He wrote much and became an authority on disputed theological issues. He was named papal legate, and acted as ecclesiastical counselor to the Bavarian dukes. In 1539 he published a German version of the Bible.

Eck, Johann Friedrich. b. at Mannheim, Germany, 1766; d. at Bamberg, Germany, c1809. German violinist and composer of violin music. He was a member (1778–88) of the Munich court orchestra and subsequently operatic conductor there until 1801.

Eckardt (ek'ärt), **Julius von.** b. at Wolmar (Valmera), Russia, Aug. 1, 1836; d. at Weimar, Germany, Jan. 20, 1908. German journalist and consular official. Eckardt left his native Russia because of the government's Russification campaign. As a German journalist he became a vigorous defender of Chancellor Caprivi's policies. From 1900 to 1907 he was a member of the German consular service.

Eckart (ek'ärt), **Dietrich.** b. at Neumarkt, in the Palatinate, Germany, March 23, 1868; committed suicide at Berchtesgaden, Bavaria, Germany, Dec. 12, 1923. German journalist, poet, and playwright; intimate friend of Adolf Hitler and editor (1921–23) of the Nazi party paper, *Völkischer Beobachter*. A follower of Count Joseph

Arthur de Gobineau and of Houston Stewart Chamberlain, he deeply influenced Hitler's ideas. He died shortly after his prison sentence (imposed for his part in the Beer Hall Putsch) had been commuted, and the National Socialist party glorified him as a martyr and one of Germany's greatest men of letters. His plays include *Heinrich der Hohenstaufe* (1915) and *Lorenzaccio* (1918). Among his essays *Der Bolschewismus von Moses bis Lenin* (1925) may be mentioned. His song *Sturm, Sturm, Sturm* . . . has the refrain "Deutschland erwache!" which became a Nazi war cry.

Eckart or **Eckardt, Johannes.** See **Eckhart** or **Eckart** or **Eckardt, Johannes.**

Eckart, the Trusty. See **Eckhardt** or **Eckart, the Trusty.**

Eckener (ek'e.nẹr), **Hugo.** b. at Flensburg, Germany, Aug. 10, 1868—. German aeronautical engineer and airship pilot. He was educated at the universities of Graz and Berlin, and received the Ph.D. at the University of Freiburg. He became (1905) assistant to Count Zeppelin, was named (1909) manager of the Zeppelin factory, became (1912) director of the Deutsche Luftschiff A.G. (DELAG), served in the German navy during World War I, and subsequently became a partner and president of the Zeppelin company. He made the first transatlantic airship flight (1924), piloting the *ZR-3* (later known as the *Los Angeles*) from Friedrichshafen, Germany, to Lakehurst, N.J. He commanded the *Graf Zeppelin,* in which he made a global flight (1929) and crossed the Atlantic many times, and designed many airships, including the *Hindenburg* (destroyed in an explosion at Lakehurst in 1937).

Eckermann (ek'ėr.män), **Johann Peter.** b. at Winsen, Germany, Sept. 21, 1792; d. at Weimar, Germany, Dec. 3, 1854. German writer, a friend and literary executor of Goethe. He is known chiefly for his *Gespräche mit Goethe* (1836–48).

Eckernförde (ek'ėrn.fėr.dẹ). Town in NW Germany, in the *Land* (state) of Schleswig-Holstein, British Zone, formerly in the province of Schleswig-Holstein, Prussia, situated on a land tongue on Kiel Bay, NW of Kiel. It is a seaport, and has fisheries, fish-smoking establishments, canneries, and metallurgical, rubber, furniture, and paperware manufactures. A battle between a Danish naval unit and Schleswig-Holstein coastal batteries took place here in 1849. The population is predominantly Protestant; an increase in population of 95.7 percent, due to the large influx of East German refugees, occurred in the period 1939–46. Pop. 24,394 (1946), 23,356 (1950).

Eckersberg (ek'ėrs.berg), **Kristoffer Vilhelm.** b. at Varnæs, near Aabenraa, Denmark, Jan. 2, 1783; d. at Copenhagen, July 22, 1853. Danish historical and marine painter.

Eckersley (ek'ėrz.li), **Peter Pendleton.** b. at Puebla, Mexico, Jan. 6, 1892—. English communications engineer. Studied (1912–15) at Manchester University; wireless equipment officer (1915–19) in the Royal Flying Corps; headed (1919–23) the experimental section of the Marconi Wireless Telegraph Company's designs department. As head engineer (1923–29) of the British Broadcasting Corporation, he was the first regular broadcaster (1921–22) in Britain and the first to introduce (1925) a high-power long-wave sending station; planner of the British scheme of regional alternating broadcasting programs; author of *The Power Behind the Microphone* (1941).

Eckert (ek'ėrt), **Karl Anton Florian.** b. at Potsdam, Germany, Dec. 7, 1820; d. at Berlin, Oct. 14, 1879. German composer, instrumentalist, and conductor. He was *Kapellmeister* (choir leader) at Stuttgart (1860–67) and subsequently at Berlin. His works include three operas, such as *Das Fischermädchen,* church music including the oratorio *Ruth,* chamber music, and a symphony.

Eckert, Thomas Thompson. b. at St. Clairsville, Ohio, April 23, 1825; d. at Long Branch, N.J., Oct. 20, 1910. American telegrapher and business executive. He organized the Union military telegraph service in 1862; brevetted brigadier general in 1865; assistant secretary of war (1866–67); became president of the Atlantic and Pacific Telegraph Company in 1875, president of the American Union Telegraph Company in 1880, vice-president and general manager of the Western Union Telegraph Company in 1881, and president in 1893.

Eckford (ek'fọrd), **Henry.** b. at Irvine, Scotland, March 12, 1775; d. at Constantinople, Nov. 12, 1832. American shipbuilder. He came to New York in 1796, was employed by the U.S. government to construct ships of war on the Great Lakes during the War of 1812, was appointed naval constructor in the U.S. navy yard at Brooklyn in 1820, and in 1831 became chief naval constructor for the Ottoman Empire.

Eckhardt (ek'härt) or **Eckart** (ek'ärt), **the Trusty.** [Also: **Eckehart;** German, **der getreue Eckart.**] Old man in German traditional lore, in the legend of Frau Holle or Holda (Venus). He appears in the Mansfeld country on the evening of Maundy Thursday with a white staff to save the people from the Wild Hunt, the furious host which travels in Holle's train. His duties differ in different traditions. Sometimes he is the companion of Tannhäuser, and has even been considered to be the same person. He is also said to be in the service of Holle, and to sit outside the Venusberg to warn passing knights of the dangers therein, to which the enamored Tannhäuser has abandoned himself. He is also a knight captured by the Wild Hunt and doomed to abide at the Venusberg till the judgment. He appears as a knight in the *Harlungen Saga* and the *Nibelungenlied.*

Eckhart (ek'härt) or **Eckart** or **Eckardt** (ek'ärt), **Johannes.** [Called **Meister Eckhart.**] b. at Hochheim, near Gotha, in Thuringia, c1260; d. probably at Cologne, c1328. German Dominican, founder of German mysticism. He was prior (1314) at Strasbourg and then at Cologne. He was accused of heresy in 1326, but denied the charge and appealed to Pope John XXII, who declared in 1329 (in the bull *In Coena Domini,* March 27) that Eckhart's doctrines were partly heretical. His philosophy, very influential on later thinkers, holds that all existence is in God, that creation is eternal because God has neither past nor future, but only the present. This apparently pantheistic philosophy is related, though no direct linkage or borrowing is known, with Plotinus and Neoplatonism, with Mahayana Buddhism, and with Vedanta.

Eckhout (ek'hout), **Gerbrand van den.** See **Eeckhout** or **Eckhout, Gerbrand van den.**

Eckmühl (ek'mül). See **Eggmühl.**

Eckmühl (dek.mül), Prince **d'.** A title of **Davout, Louis Nicolas.**

Eckstein (ek'shtīn), **Ernst.** b. at Giessen, Germany, Feb. 6, 1845; d. at Dresden, Germany, Nov. 18, 1900. German journalist and author of humorous verse epics and prose stories. He was for a time on the *Neue Freie Presse* of Vienna, then was editor of *Deutsche Dichterhalle* and the comic weekly *Der Schalk.*

Eclectic Magazine, The. Literary journal published monthly (1819–1907) at New York, Philadelphia, and Boston. It was initially brought out under the title *The Philadelphia Register and National Recorder* and became known as *The Eclectic Magazine* in 1844.

Eclympasteyre (e.klim.päs.tā'rẹ). Name given by Chaucer in *The Book of the Duchess* to the heir of Morpheus, the god of sleep.

> Morpheus, and Eclympasteyre
> That was the god of slepes heyre.

Ecnomus (ek'nō.mus). Hill near the modern town of Licata, on the S coast of Sicily. Here the Carthaginians defeated (311 B.C.) the Syracusan tyrant Agathocles. Near here the Roman fleet defeated (256 B.C.) the Carthaginians.

Ecole d'Arcueil (ā.kol dár.kėy'). Group of contemporary French composers established (1923) at the home of its leader, Erik Satie. Among its members are Henri Sauguet, Maxime Jacob, Henri Cliqué-Pleyel, and Roger Désormière.

École des Beaux-Arts (ā.kol dā bō.zȧr). French national school of fine arts at Paris, located on the Quai Malaquais. It was founded in 1648 and represented a merging of three academies of painting, sculpture, and architecture, a department of engraving being added later. It is free, coeducational, and is not limited to French students (although these naturally form the largest part of its student body). Admission is secured through satisfactory completion of a rigorous examination. The age limits are from 15 to 30. A grand prize, the Prix de Rome, is competed for annually by the students, and is their main objective. It was created by Louis XIV in 1666. It entitles the winner to a four-year scholarship at the French Academy of Art, at Rome, an annual income of 4,000 francs, and exemption from military service. The faculty of the École consists of the most distinguished French artists, who are allowed to teach students privately at their own studios. The original name of the school, École Académique, was changed to its present one in 1793. The old Hôtel de Conti and the Hôtel Chamay were purchased, respectively, in 1860 and 1885 for use as studios.

École des Femmes (lā.kol dā fàm), **Critique de l'.** [Eng. trans., *"Critique of the School of Wives."*] Brilliant short play by Molière, as a satirical reply to the critics of his *L'École des femmes.* It was produced on June 1, 1663.

École des Femmes, L'. [Eng. trans., *"The School of Wives."*] Comedy by Molière, produced on Dec. 26, 1662.

École des Maris (lā.kol dā mà.rē), **L'.** [Eng. trans., *"The School of Husbands."*] Comedy by Molière, produced in 1661. Sganarelle, as the guardian of a young girl, is the hero of this play, the plot of which is partly taken from Terence, Boccaccio, and Lope de Vega.

École Polytechnique (ā.kol po.lē.tek.nēk). French school of technology, founded by decree of the Convention, on March 11, 1794. From its origin and object of its foundation it was devoted to instruction in purely scientific and technical branches, such as artillery, military and civil engineering, the building of roads and bridges, shipbuilding, and the like. There were at first 360 students, and the course was three years. The number was later decreased to 200, and the terms shortened to two years. After graduation the students choose between a military and a civil career. The military students go to the École d'Application at Fontainebleau for two years, after which they enter the army as lieutenants of artillery or engineers. The others enter various special schools at Paris, such as the École des Ponts et Chaussées, École Spéciale des Mines, École Centrale des Arts et Manufactures, and others.

Ecological Society of America. Organization founded in 1915 for the purpose of promoting the scientific study of organisms in relation to their environment. It publishes *Ecology* (quarterly), *Ecological Monographs* (quarterly), and a *Bulletin* (quarterly).

Econometric Society. Organization with U.S. and foreign membership, founded in 1930 for the purpose of advancing economic theory in relation to mathematics and statistics. It maintains headquarters at the University of Chicago and publishes *Econometrica* (quarterly).

Economic and Social Council, United Nations. See **United Nations Economic and Social Council.**

Economic Commission for Asia and the Far East, United Nations. See **United Nations Economic Commission for Asia and the Far East.**

Economic Commission for Europe, United Nations. See **United Nations Economic Commission for Europe.**

"Economic Royalists." Epithet applied by President Franklin D. Roosevelt to the businessmen and financiers who had opposed the economic legislation of his New Deal on the grounds that it constituted excessive government interference in private enterprise. In his Philadelphia speech accepting the Democratic nomination for a second term (1936), Roosevelt said: "The economic royalists complain that we seek to overthrow the institutions of America. What they really complain of is that we seek to take away their power. Our allegiance to American institutions requires the overthrow of this kind of power."

Economic Welfare, Board of. See **Board of Economic Welfare.**

Economites (ę.kon'ǫ.mīts). See **Harmonists.**

Economo (ā.kō'nō.mō), **Constantin.** [Title, Baron **von Sanderff.**] b. at Brăila, Rumania, Aug. 21, 1876; d. at Vienna, Oct. 21, 1931. Austrian psychiatrist. He worked with E. Kraepelin at Munich and with H. Nothnagel and J. Pal at Vienna. He was assistant (1906–19) to Wagner-Jauregg, and became privatdocent of psychiatry and neurology (1913) at the University of Vienna, where he was named professor in 1921. He founded a research institute and was the first to describe (1917) encephalitis lethargica epidemica. He described also the topography of the cerebral cortex (1925). Author of *Die Encephalitis lethargica* (1918; Eng. trans., *Encephalitis lethargica; Its Sequelae and Treatment,* 1931), *The Cytoarchitectonics of the Human Cerebral Cortex* (1929; original German ed., 1925), *Über den Schlaf* (1925), *Die Pathologie des Schlafes* (1926), and *Zellaufbau der Grosshirnrinde des Menschen* (1927).

Economy (ę.kon'ǫ.mi). Township in W Pennsylvania, in Beaver County, ab. 17 mi. NW of Pittsburgh. The borough of Ambridge, within the township, is the site of the third communal settlement, which was named Economy, founded (1825) by the Harmony Society. 2,905 (1950).

Écorcheurs (ā.kôr.shėr), **Les.** Bands of armed adventurers who, favored by the Hundred Years' War, ravaged France and Belgium in the 15th century, beginning c1435. Among their leaders were Villandras and Crabannes the Bastard. They were called Ecorcheurs, or flayers, probably because they "not only waylaid and plundered their victims, but stripped them of every vestige of clothing, leaving them nothing but their shirts."

Ecorse (ę.kôrs', ē'kôrs). City in S Lower Michigan, in Wayne County: manufactures of steel products. 17,948 (1950).

ECOSOC. See **United Nations Economic and Social Council.**

Écosse (ā.kos). French name of **Scotland.**

Écrins (ā.krañ), **Barre** (or **Pic**) **des.** See **Barre des Écrins.**

Ector (ek'tǫr), **Sir.** [Also, **Sir Hector.**] In the Arthurian romances, a faithful knight who with his wife was entrusted with the upbringing of the infant Arthur. He was the father of Sir Kay.

Ector de Maris (dę mar'is), **Sir.** [Also: **Sir Hector de Maris, Sir Ector de Mares, Sir Hector de Mares.**] In Arthurian romance, the brother of Sir Lancelot. He mourned Lancelot's death with a bitter lament, and afterward went with Sir Bois and seven other knights to the Holy Land, where they died on a Good Friday.

Ecuador (ek'wą.dôr; Spanish, ā.kwä.ᴛʜōr'). [Full name, **República del Ecuador,** meaning (originally) "Republic of the Equator."] Republic of South America, lying between Colombia on the N, Peru on the E and S, and the Pacific Ocean on the W. The country is traversed from N to S by the Andes, which form a continuous eastern range and a roughly parallel but much broken western range, containing some of the highest peaks in South America and numerous volcanoes. Between the mountains there are several high tablelands or basins. The coast regions and those E of the mountains are low, hot, and covered in great part with forest. The principal products and exports are cacao, rice, straw hats, coffee, bananas, nuts, and rubber. The inhabitants are whites (of Spanish descent), Indians, and mixed races. The executive is vested in a president elected for four years, and a unicameral congress or chamber of deputies. There are 17 provinces besides the Galapagos Islands (Archipiélago de Colón). The Roman Catholic was formerly the state religion, but now complete freedom of worship is granted. At the time of the Spanish conquest the greater part of Ecuador was subject to the Incas of Peru. It was conquered (1533–34) by the Spaniards, and under the name of Quito was a presidency attached to the viceroyalty of Peru. The Spanish rulers being expelled (1822–23) with the aid of Bolívar, the country was united to the Colombian Confederation until 1830, when it seceded and adopted its present name. Since then it has suffered from political revolutions and from border disputes with Peru, the latest of which was settled in 1942. The present constitution was adopted in 1945. Capital, Quito; area, ab. 104,000 sq. mi.; pop. 3,076,933 (1950).

Ed (āt), **Ida.** Maiden name of **Boy-Ed, Ida.**

Edam (ē'dąm; Dutch, ā.däm'). Town in W Netherlands, in the province of North Holland, situated near the Ijsselmeer (Zuider Zee) ab. 11 mi. NE of Amsterdam. It is the chief market for Edam cheese; the nearby village of Volendam has extensive fisheries. The Groote Kerk (church) has stained-glass windows and a chime of bells; other buildings of interest include an old town hall and a historical museum. 8,941 (1939).

Edcouch (ed'kouch). Town in S Texas, in Hidalgo County, in the Rio Grande valley near Brownsville: railroad junction. 2,925 (1950).

Edda (ed'ạ). Work written (in prose and verse) by Snorri Sturluson (1178–1241), containing the old mythology of Scandinavia and the old rules for verse-making; also, another work, a collection of ancient Icelandic poems. The name Edda (whether given by Snorri himself is not known) occurs in the inscription of one of the manuscripts of the work. Snorri's *Edda* as it was originally written consisted of three parts: the *Gylfaginning* (delusion of Gylfi), an epitome of the old mythology; *Skaldskaparmal* (art of poetry), an explanation of poetical expressions and periphrases; and *Hattatal* (list of meters), a laudatory poem on the Norwegian king Hakon Hakonsson, and Jarl Skuli, in which all forms of verse used in the old poetry are exemplified. To this was ultimately added a *Formali* (preface), and the *Bragaroedhur* (sayings of Bragi), describing the origin of poetry, and in some manuscripts *Thulur*, or a rhymed glossary of synonyms, list of poets, and similar material. The work was intended as a handbook of poets. In the year 1643 the Icelandic bishop Brynjulf Sveinsson discovered a collection of old mythological poems which was erroneously ascribed to Sæmund Sigfusson (1056–1133), and hence called from him *Sæmundar Edda hins Frodha* (The Edda of Sæmund the Learned). The poems that compose this *Edda* are of unknown origin and authorship. They are supposed to have been collected about the middle of the 13th century, but were composed at widely different periods down from the 9th century, to the first half of which the oldest is to be assigned; hence the name now given to this collection, the *Elder* or *Poetic Edda*, in distinction from the *Younger* or *Prose Edda* of Snorri, to which alone the name *Edda* legitimately belonged. The *Elder Edda* is usually considered to include 32 poems (some of them fragmentary).

Ed Dahra (ed dä'rạ). See **Dahra.**

Eddin (ed.dēn'), **Nasir.** See **Nasir ed-din al-Tusi, Mohammed ibn-Mohammed ibn al-Hasan.**

Eddington (ed'ing.tọn), Sir **Arthur Stanley.** b. at Kendal, England, Dec. 28, 1882; d. at Cambridge, England, Nov. 22, 1944. English mathematician, astronomer, and astrophysicist, noted for his association of mathematical concepts with the structure of the universe. He calculated the "Eddington number" which he supposed to represent the total number of particles in the universe. He studied at the universities of Manchester and Cambridge, did research at the Cavendish Laboratory, became chief assistant at the Royal Observatory, and in 1913 succeeded Sir George Darwin at Cambridge. He was elected to the Royal Society in 1914, and was president of the Royal Astronomical Society (1921–23), president of the Physical Society (1930–32), and president of the International Astronomical Union (1938 *et seq.*). He was knighted in 1930. His works include *Stellar Movements and the Structure of the Universe* (1914), *Space, Time and Gravitation* (1920), *The Mathematical Theory of Relativity* (1923), *Internal Constitution of the Stars* (1926), *Stars and Atoms* (1927), *The Nature of the Physical World* (1928), *New Pathways in Science* (1935), *Relativity Theory of Protons and Electrons* (1936), *The Philosophy of Physical Science* (1939), and *The Combination of Relativity Theory and Quantum Theory* (1943).

Ed Dirr (ed dir'). See **El Dirr.**

Eddy (ed'i), **Clarence.** b. at Greenfield, Mass., June 23, 1851; d. at Chicago, Jan. 10, 1937. American organist and composer. He studied at Berlin under Haupt, became (1874) organist of the First Congregational Church at Chicago, was named (1876) director of the Hershey School of Musical Art, and was chosen honorary member of the Accademia Santa Cecilia at Rome. His publications include *The Church and Concert Organist* (2 vols., 1882, 1885) and *The Organ in Church* (1887); he translated Haupt's *Theory of Composition and Fugue.*

Eddy, Manton Sprague. b. at Chicago, May 16, 1892—. American soldier. Commissioned a second lieutenant in 1916, he saw service in France in World War I, and afterward rose through the ranks to become a general officer. In World War II he commanded the 9th infantry division through the fighting in Tunis, Sicily, and France, and was appointed (1944) commander of the XII army corps, operating in France, Luxembourg, and Germany. He headed the Third Service Command in 1946, was chief of army information in 1947, and served as commanding general of the Leavenworth staff college in 1948. In 1950 he assumed command of the 7th army in Germany and in 1952 became commanding general of the U.S. army in Germany; later, when command of the North Atlantic Treaty Organization armies was divided, he headed the central army group of U.S. and French troops.

Eddy, Mary Baker. b. at Bow, near Concord, N.H., July 16, 1821; d. at Chestnut Hill, Boston, Mass., Dec. 3, 1910. Founder of Christian Science. Her full maiden name was Mary Morse Baker; she was of Scotch-English extraction and numbered among her ancestors members of the Continental Army in the Revolutionary War. She received her education at academies in Tilton and Plymouth, N.H., and also from private tutors. Her first church connection was with the Congregational Church. She married George Washington Glover, a building contractor, in December, 1843, and went with him to Charleston, S.C., and later to Wilmington, N.C., where she was left a widow in June, 1844. She returned to New Hampshire soon after, where her only child, George Washington Glover, was born in September. From early childhood she was not strong physically, and in her search for health she sought relief through various healing systems including allopathy, homeopathy, hydropathy, electricity, and various others, but without success. She regarded her discovery of Christian Science as resulting directly and immediately from an accident which occurred in Lynn, Mass., in 1866. While on her way to a meeting of Good Templars, she fell on an icy street and was severely injured. She was carried to a nearby residence where she was attended by a physician and cared for during the night. The next day she was removed to her home in the adjacent town of Swampscott in a critical condition. On the third day following the injury, when apparently near death, she asked for her Bible, opened it to Mat. ix. 2, and reading the account of the healing of the palsied man by Jesus, was herself healed and able to rise from her sickbed. She married Asa Gilbert Eddy on Jan. 1, 1877 (he died in 1882). She published the Christian Science textbook *Science and Health with Key to the Scriptures* in 1875, and organized the first Christian Science church in 1879. This church was dissolved, and in 1892 she organized The First Church of Christ, Scientist, at Boston (known also as The Mother Church). She established The Christian Science Journal in 1883, and in 1898 founded The Christian Science Publishing Society. Her writings, all published at Boston by the trustees under her will, include: *Science and Health with Key to the Scriptures* (1875; final revision, 1906), *Miscellaneous Writings* (1896), *Retrospection and Introspection* (1891), *Unity of Good* (1887), *Pulpit and Press* (1895), *Rudimental Divine Science* (1891), *No and Yes* (1891), *Christian Science Versus Pantheism* (1898), *Messages to the Mother Church* (for 1900, 1901, 1902), *Christian Healing* (1886), *The People's Idea of God* (1886), *The First Church of Christ, Scientist, and Miscellany* (1913), *Poems* (1910), *Christ and Christmas* (1897), *Church Manual* (1895; final revision, 1908). Besides *The Christian Science Journal* (founded 1883), her Church periodicals comprise: the *Christian Science Sentinel*, the *Christian Science Quarterly, The Herald of Christian Science* (published in German, French, Scandinavian, Dutch, Spanish, and Braille in English).

Eddy, Sherwood. b. at Leavenworth, Kan., Jan. 19, 1871—. American official of Y.M.C.A. and writer. Served as Y.M.C.A. secretary for India (1896–1911) and Asia (1911 *et seq.*); Y.M.C.A. secretary with British army (1915–17) and U.S. army (1917–18). Author of *India Awakening* (1911), *The New Era in Asia* (1913), *The Students of Asia* (1915), *With Our Soldiers in France* (1917), *Religion and Social Justice* (1928), *A Pilgrimage of Ideas* (1935), *Revolutionary Christianity* (1939), *Pathfinders of the World Missionary Crusade* (1945), *Is God in History?* (1947), and other books.

Eddy, Spencer (Fayette). b. at Chicago, June 18, 1874; d. Oct. 7, 1939. American diplomat. He was attached to the American embassy at London (1899) and to that at Paris (1899–1901), was first secretary of legation at Constantinople (1901–03), at St. Petersburg (1903–06), and at Berlin (1906–07), and was minister to Argentina (1908–09). He became minister to Rumania, Serbia, and

Bulgaria in 1909, but resigned from the diplomatic service in that year.

Eddy, William Abner. b. at New York, Jan. 28, 1850; d. at Bayonne, N.J., Dec. 26, 1909. American meteorologist. An accountant by profession, in 1890 he began experiments in kite-flying for scientific purposes. By means of kites with the necessary apparatus attached he secured records of temperature at varying heights (1891), photographs taken in mid air (1895), and facts concerning air currents, atmospheric electricity, and the like. In 1903 he experimented with model airplanes released from kites in mid air. He also devised instruments for recording tremors of the earth. Much of his work was done in connection with the U.S. Weather Bureau.

Eddystone (ed′i.stōn). Borough in SE Pennsylvania, in Delaware County near Philadelphia: locomotive works. A munitions center in World War I, it was the scene of a serious explosion (April 10, 1917) of unknown origin. 3,014 (1950).

Eddystone Rocks (ed′i.stōn, -stọn). Dangerous reef in the English Channel, S of Cornwall, ab. 14 mi. SW of Plymouth. On it a famous lighthouse was erected 1696–99, and has been rebuilt in 1706, 1756–59, and 1879–82. In the present structure the light (159,600 candle power) is 133 ft. above the sea, and can be seen for 17½ mi.

Ede (ā′dā). Large town in W Africa, in Western Provinces, Nigeria, connected by road with Lagos and other large centers in the SW corner of the country. 51,000 (est. 1950).

Ede (ā′dẹ). Commune and town, consisting of seven settlements, in E Netherlands, in the province of Gelderland, ab. 13 mi. NW of Arnhem: agricultural and stock-raising district. 45,896 (est. 1951).

Edelinck (ā′dẹ.lingk), **Gérard.** b. at Antwerp, Belgium, Oct. 20, 1640; d. at Paris, April 2, 1707. Flemish copperplate and portrait engraver. At Antwerp he studied under Cornelisz Galle and Gaspard Huybrecht, and at Paris, in 1665, under François de Poilly. Louis XIV thought highly of his work, gave him a pension, and appointed him instructor at the Gobelins academy for training tapestry workers on the advice of its director, Le Brun, whose enthusiastic opinion confirmed his own. Edelinck was the first to use the lozenge shape in making prints. He is credited with 341 works, of which some of the best known are *Combat of Four Knights*, after da Vinci, the *Holy Family*, after Raphael, *Penitent Magdalene, Christ Surrounded by Angels, Saint Louis Praying, Saint Charles Borromeo Before a Crucifix*, all after Le Brun, and *La Couseuse*, after Guido Reni. He made portraits, over 200 altogether, of contemporaries including Philippe de Champagne (which he regarded as his best work), Santeuil, La Fontaine, Colbert, Descartes, Dryden, Louis XIV, and Le Brun. With Nanteuil and Masson he belongs to the trinity of famous portrait engravers in France. His brothers, Jean and Gaspard François, and his son, Nicolas, followed his profession.

Eden (ē′dẹn). In Biblical history, the name of the first abode of man, in the midst of which a garden, the garden of Eden (the "paradise"), was planted. The position of Eden is described in Gen. ii. 8ff. by four rivers that go out from it, and by the countries they surround or pass in their course. Of these two, the Euphrates and Tigris (Hebrew, Perath and Hiddekel), are the well-known rivers of Mesopotamia; the other two, Pishon and Gihon, have been identified with various streams. The hypothesis of Friedrich Delitzsch assumed that the narrator in Genesis thought Eden located near the city of Babylon and meant by the rivers Pishon and Gihon two canals; Delitzsch also attempted to identify the countries mentioned in this passage with territories in that region. Adam and Eve were banished from Eden for eating of the forbidden fruit. An enclosed garden of paradise appears in Persian myth; a tree of life in a gardenlike park is mentioned in Babylonian myth.

Eden. River in NW England, in Westmorland and Cumberland, rising on the E border of Westmorland and flowing into Solway Firth, ab. 8 mi. NW of Carlisle. Length, ab. 65 mi.

Eden, Anthony. [Full name, **Robert Anthony Eden.**] b. at Ferry Hill, Durham, England, June 12, 1897—. English diplomat; second surviving son of the 7th baronet of Windlestone Hall, Durham, descendant of the father of the 1st Baron Auckland (William Eden). He graduated (1922) from Oxford with a first class in Oriental languages, after having served (1915–19) in World War I with the King's Royal Rifle Corps, of which he was captain, and as general staff officer and brigade major. He was awarded the military cross. A member (1923 *et seq.*) of Parliament, he was parliamentary private secretary (1926–29) to Sir Austen Chamberlain, the then secretary of state for foreign affairs, parliamentary undersecretary (1931–33) in the Foreign Office, lord privy seal (1934–35) and member of the privy council. He was minister (1935) without portfolio for League of Nations affairs, secretary of state for foreign affairs (1935–38, 1940–45), for dominion affairs (1939–40), and for war (1940). From 1942 to 1945 he was leader of the House of Commons. He was chancellor (1945 *et seq.*) of the University of Birmingham. During his first term as secretary for foreign affairs, he negotiated (1937) with Count Ciano the "gentlemen's agreement" in regard to the Mediterranean, and acted as British representative (1937) to the nine-power conference over the Sino-Japanese conflict. He resigned (1938) his office after the conclusion of the Munich pact in protest against the administration of Neville Chamberlain. With the victory of the Conservatives in 1951, he again became foreign secretary.

Eden, Sir **Ashley.** b. at Hertingfordbury, Hertfordshire, England, Nov. 13, 1831; d. in India, July 9, 1887. English colonial official in India; grandson of the 1st Baron Auckland (William Eden). Appointed magistrate at Murshidabad (1856) and did much to avert mutiny there (1857); secretary to governor of Bengal (1860–71). When envoy to Bhutan (1863) was forced to sign disadvantageous treaty. Appointed first civil governor of British Burma (1871), served as lieutenant of Bengal (1877–82), and as member of secretary of state's council (1882–87).

Eden, Emily. b. at Westminster, London, March 3, 1797; d. at Richmond, Surrey, England, Aug. 5, 1869. English novelist, traveler, and travel writer. She was the seventh daughter of the 1st Baron Auckland (William Eden), and the sister of the 1st Earl of Auckland (George Eden). When her brother went to India as governor general, she accompanied him and, with a sister, Frances, stayed with him during his entire term (1835–42). This period of residence resulted in two books, *Portraits of the People and Princes of India* (1844, when she was back in England) and *Up the Country: Letters Written to her Sister from the Upper Provinces of India by the Hon. Emily Eden* (1866; other eds., 1867, 1872). She translated Hugo's tragedy *Marion Delorme* into English blank verse, and she wrote two gently satirical novels, *The Semi-detached House* (1859) and *The Semi-attached Couple* (1860), which have been paid the high compliment of being compared to Jane Austen. Successful in their day, they were reprinted in 1928 after being long forgotten.

Eden, George. See **Auckland,** 1st Earl of.

Eden, Martin. See **Martin Eden.**

Edén (e.dān′), **Nils.** b. at Piteå, Sweden, Aug. 25, 1871; d. at Stockholm, June 16, 1945. Swedish political leader and historian, who as premier (October, 1917–March, 1920) during and just after World War I favored trade relations with Germany and the other Central Powers. At first extremely conservative in his political attitude, he shifted toward an advance liberal position at about the time his parliamentary career began (1909). He sponsored social reforms and followed a vacillating policy toward Finland on the Aaland Islands question. He remained in the *Riksdag* (parliament) until 1924, serving also (1920 *et seq.*) as governor of Stockholm province. His important writings include *Om centralregeringens organisation under den äldre Vasatiden (1523-94)* (1899), *Den svenska centralregeringens utveckling till collegial organisation . . .* (1902), *1809 års rewolution* (2 vols., 1911), *Peder Swarts Konung Gustaf I's krönika* (1912), and *Gustaf Wasas bref* (1917).

Eden (ē′dẹn), **Richard.** b. c1521; d. 1576. English translator. He studied at Cambridge, held a position in the treasury (1544–46), and was appointed to a place in the English treasury of Prince Philip of Spain in 1554, a position which he soon lost, owing to an accusation of heresy. In 1562 he entered the service of a French nobleman, with whom he traveled extensively. Eden's name as a translator is appended to many books on geography, travels, navigation, and the like. Among these are *A*

Treatyse of the Newe India (1553, a translation of part of Munster's *Cosmographia*), which is the first intelligible description in English of America, and *Decades of the Newe World* (1555, mainly a translation of Peter Martyr's work).

Eden, William. See **Auckland,** 1st Baron.

Edenhall (ē′dẹn.hôl). Seat of the Musgraves of Cumberland, England, near Penrith.

Edenkoben (ā′dẹn.kō.bẹn). Town in W Germany, in the *Land* (state) of Rhineland-Palatinate, French Zone, formerly in the Bavarian Palatinate, situated on the slopes of the Hardt Mountains, ab. 15 mi. SW of Speyer. It is a center of the Palatinate wine trade and has small industries. Above the town are the ruins of the Rietburg castle; in the vicinity is the villa Ludwigshöhe, built in 1846 for the Bavarian royal house. 5,433 (1946).

Edenton (ē′dẹn.tọn). Town in NE North Carolina, county seat of Chowan County, near Albemarle Sound. It is a port for shad and herring fisheries and a marketing, processing, and shipping point for peanuts. Other important crops traded here include cotton, corn, soybeans, tobacco, cantaloupes, and watermelons. It was a major 18th-century shipbuilding center. Settled by Jamestown colonists in 1658, it achieved fame as the site of the first Revolutionary feminine "tea party," held on Oct. 25, 1774. Pop. 4,468 (1950).

Eder (ā′dėr), **Joseph Maria.** b. at Krems, Austria, 1855; d. 1944. Austrian pioneer photochemist. His researches include the introduction, in 1884, of erythrosine for long wave-length sensitization of photographic plates, which for the next 50 years was used in orthochromatic films. He edited the *Jahrbuch für Photographie und Reproduktionstechnik* (1887–1911) and was research director (1888 *et seq.*) of the Teaching and Experimental Institute for Photography at Vienna (which became the Graphic Teaching and Experimental Institute in 1889).

EDES (e′ᴛʜes). Name, formed from the initials of Greek words meaning "Greek Democratic National Army," of the second most important (ELAS was first) of the guerrilla groups fighting in Greece during the Axis occupation in World War II. It was organized and led by Napoleon Zervas, and seems to have been at first liberal, though anticommunistic. It lasted from 1943 to 1946, and was always strongest in Epirus and Thessaly. Its internal warfare with ELAS was generally unsuccessful, and toward the end it was forced back to Corfu. Possibly as a result of this warfare, it became more and more rightist, eventually monarchist and strongly nationalistic.

Edessa (ẹ.des′ạ). Ancient name of **Urfa.**

Edessa. [Also: **Edhessa, Vodena;** ancient name also **Aegae.**] Town in N Greece, the capital of the *nomos* (department) of Pella, situated ab. 48 mi. NW of Salonika. It was formerly the capital of the Macedonian kings. The modern town is a railroad station on the Salonika-Monastir line, and manufactures textiles; tobacco is grown in the vicinity. It is the seat of a bishopric. Philip II of Macedonia was assassinated here in 336 B.C. 15,415 (1951).

Edfelt (ed′felt), **Johannes.** [Full name, **Bo Johannes Edfelt.**] b. at Kyrkefalla, Västergötland, Sweden, 1904—. Swedish poet and literary critic. Edfelt went to college in the ancient town of Skara. Later he studied at the University of Uppsala, and worked as a teacher (1931–34). He is the literary critic for the Stockholm newspaper *Dagens Nyheter.*

Edfu (ed′fö). [Also: **Idfu;** ancient name, **Apollinopolis Magna;** Coptic, **Atbo.**] Town in Upper Egypt, situated near the left bank of the Nile. The celebrated temple of Edfu is one of the most perfect existing examples of an ancient Egyptian religious edifice. It was begun by Ptolemy III Euergetes in 237 B.C. The entrance is a massive double pylon 250 ft. wide and 115 ft. high, from which the strong enclosing wall is carried around the temple. Within the pylon lies the great court with its peristyle of columns. Behind it lies the hypostyle hall, to the rear of which is a second hall with three ranges of four columns, from which opens the double vestibule of the isolated sanctuary, on the passage around which are placed, as was usual, a number of small chambers. The abundant sculptures, though in style mere imitations of the older Pharaonic work, are from their subjects both interesting and instructive. The length of the temple is 450 ft.

Edgar or **Eadgar** (ed′gạr). [Called **"the Peaceful."**] b. 944; d. July 8, 975. King of England; son of Edmund I (Eadmund) and Aelfgifu. In 957 he was made king of Mercia and Northumbria by nobles dissatisfied with Edwy's rule. He ascended the throne in 959 as successor to his brother Edwy (Eadwig); for some reason, his coronation did not occur until 973. He ruled the whole nation (West Saxons, Northumbrians, and Mercians), and his quiet reign, under his adviser Dunstan, whom he made archbishop of Canterbury, gained for him the surname "the Peaceful." He is said to have ceded Lothian (northern Bernicia) to Kenneth of Scotland. He married twice; Ethelflaed, his first wife, was the mother of Edward, known as the Martyr, who reigned from 975 to 978; Aelfthryth, whom he married in 964, was the mother of Ethelred II (Ethelred the Unready), who was on the throne from 978 to 1016. Edgar is said to have received the homage of eight kings soon after his coronation.

Edgar. In Shakespeare's *King Lear,* the son of the Earl of Gloucester.

Edgar, Sir John. Pseudonym of Sir Richard Steele, under which he conducted the theatrical journal *The Theatre* from January, 1720, until April, 1720.

Edgar (or **Eadgar**) **Ætheling** (ath′ẹ.ling). [Also, **Edgar** (or **Eadgar**) **the Ætheling.**] b. probably in Hungary, before 1057; d. in the first part of the 12th century. English prince; grandson of Edmund II (Edmund Ironside). In 1066, on the death of Harold, he was chosen by earl Morcar as successor to the English throne, but he relinquished his claim to William I (William the Conqueror) when the latter made it plain that he would fight for the crown. He nevertheless joined (1068, 1069) in two attempts to dethrone William. He went then to Scotland, where his sister, later known as Saint Margaret of Scotland, married Malcolm III, king of Scotland. After 1074 he lived in France, but in 1094 was allied with Malcolm in border warfare against the English in Northumbria. He helped place his nephew Edgar on the Scottish throne in 1097, unseating Donald III. In 1099 he went on the crusade with Robert II, Duke of Normandy; on his return he sided with Robert against Henry I of England but was captured (1106) at Tinchebrai, Normandy, when Henry defeated the barons. He was soon released and lived thereafter in obscurity, dying probably some quarter of a century later.

Edgar Huntly; or, Memoirs of a Sleep-Walker (hunt′li). Epistolary novel by Charles Brockden Brown, published in 1799.

Edgar, Master of Ravenswood (rā′vẹnz.wůd). See **Ravenswood, Edgar, Master of.**

Edgartown (ed′gạr.toun). Town in SE Massachusetts, in Dukes County, on Martha's Vineyard ab. 74 mi. SE of Boston. Formerly a whaling port, it is now a summer resort. 1,508 (1950).

Edge (ej), **Walter Evans.** b. at Philadelphia, Nov. 20, 1873—. American journalist, politician, and diplomat. He founded the Atlantic City *Daily Press* and Atlantic City *Evening Union,* and served as governor (1917–19, 1944–47) of New Jersey, U.S. senator (1919–29) from New Jersey, and U.S. ambassador (1929–33) to France. He coöperated with Secretary of the Treasury Mellon in negotiating the Franco-American accord of July 6, 1931.

Edgecote (edj′kōt). Place in Northamptonshire, England, ab. 17 mi. SW of Northampton. Here the Parliamentary forces under Robin of Redesdale defeated (July 26, 1469) the Royalists under the earl of Pembroke.

Edgefield (ej′fēld). Town in W South Carolina, county seat of Edgefield County, in a cotton-producing region ab. 55 mi. SW of Columbia: railroad junction. 2,518 (1950).

Edge Foreign Banking Act. Act of the U.S. Congress, drafted by Walter Evans Edge and passed in 1919, authorizing federally chartered foreign banking corporations under the control of the Federal Reserve Board to finance foreign trade. The directors must be American citizens and the majority of the stock under American control.

Edge Hill or **Edgehill** (ej′hil). Ridge in Warwickshire, C England, situated ab. 12 mi. S of Warwick. Here was fought (Oct. 23, 1642) the first battle of the English Civil War, between the Royalists under Charles I and the

Parliamentarians under Robert Devereux, 3rd Earl of Essex. The result of the battle was indecisive.

Edge Hill. Unincorporated community in SE Pennsylvania, in Montgomery County near Philadelphia. Under the new urban definition established for use in the 1950 census it was counted with adjoining urban areas. The last official enumeration was 2,681 (1940).

Edgemere (ej'mir). Unincorporated community in N Maryland, in Baltimore County. Under the new urban definition established for use in the 1950 census it was counted with adjoining urban areas. The last official enumeration was 5,698 (1940).

Edgerton (ej'ėr.tọn). City in S Wisconsin, in Rock County ab. 20 mi. SE of Madison: trading, processing, and distributing center for tobacco. 3,507 (1950).

Edgerton, Harold Eugene. b. at Fremont, Neb., April 6, 1903—. American electrical engineer, chiefly known for his pioneering work in the field of stroboscopic photography. He received his B.S. from the University of Nebraska (1925) and his Sc.D. from the Massachusetts Institute of Technology (1931), serving thereafter (1932 *et seq.*) as a professor of electrical engineering at the latter institution. In collaboration with James R. Killian, Jr., he is the author of *Flash!* (1933).

Edgewater (ej'wô.tėr, -wot.ėr). Town in N central Colorado, in Jefferson County: western suburb of Denver. 2,580 (1950).

Edgewater. Borough in NE New Jersey, in Bergen County, on the Hudson River: tapestry manufacturing and automobile assembling plants. 3,952 (1950).

Edgewood (ej'wu̇d). Borough in SW Pennsylvania, in Allegheny County: eastern suburb of Pittsburgh. 5,292 (1950).

Edgeworth (ej'wėrth), **Francis Ysidro.** [Original name, **Ysidro Francis Edgeworth.**] b. at Edgeworthstown, County Longford, Ireland, Feb. 8, 1845; d. at Oxford, England, Feb. 13, 1926. Irish economist; a half-nephew of Maria Edgeworth; noted as an early exponent of strictly formal and mathematical treatment of economic theory. He was professor of political economy at the University of Oxford from 1891 to 1922, and served as first editor from its foundation in 1891 of the *Economic Journal* and president of the Royal Statistical Society (1912–14). He was the author of *New and Old Methods of Ethics* (1877), *Mathematical Physics, an essay on the application of Mathematics to the Moral Sciences* (1881), *Metretike, or the Method of Measuring Probability and Utility* (1887); later contributions, of which there are many, appeared mostly in the learned journals.

Edgeworth, Maria. b. at Black Bourton, Oxfordshire, England, Jan. 1, 1767; d. at Edgeworthstown, County Longford, Ireland, May 22, 1849. English novelist, known especially for her Gothic tales; daughter of Richard Lovell Edgeworth, and aunt of Thomas Lovell Beddoes. She wrote, in conjunction with her father, *Essays on Practical Education* (1798) and *Essay on Irish Bulls* (1802). Her chief independent works are *Castle Rackrent* (1800), *Belinda* (1801), *Moral Tales for Young People* (1801), *Popular Tales* (1804), *Tales of Fashionable Life* (1809–12), *Leonora* (1806), *The Absentee* (1812), *Patronage* (1814), *Ormond* (1817), and *Helen* (1834). She was a friend of Sir Walter Scott, who acknowledged in the preface to *Waverly* his debt to Miss Edgeworth's novels of Irish life.

Edgeworth, Richard Lovell. b. at Bath, England, May 31, 1744; d. at Edgeworthstown, County Longford, Ireland, June 13, 1817. English author and inventor who made the first attempt at telegraphic communication father of Maria Edgeworth. His attempt at telegraphy is said to have stemmed from a desire to learn the results of horse races as quickly as possible. He also invented a velocipede, a land-measuring machine, sailing carriages, and was able to obtain government approval of a telegraph line between Dublin and Galway (1804). He became a friend of Thomas Day (1748–89) and Erasmus Darwin; visited Rousseau (1771) and presented his son to him (the son had been brought up according to child-raising precepts derived from Rousseau's *Émile*); enrolled (1798) a corps at Edgeworthstown against the Irish insurgents who attempted in that year (with French help) to achieve Irish independence. In addition to works on mechanical subjects and on education, he collaborated with his daughter Maria on *Essays on Practical Education* (1798), a modification of Rousseau's theories, and on *Essay on Irish Bulls* (1802).

Edhem Pasha (ed.hem' pä.shä'). b. 1851; d. 1909. Turkish army officer. He led (1877) a brigade at the siege of Pleven, and during the Greco-Turkish war (1897) was commanding general of the Turkish army. He was named minister of war in 1909.

Edhessa (e'THe.sä). See **Edessa.**

Edib (e.dib'), **Halidé.** [Married name, **Adnan-Adívar.**] b. at Constantinople (Istanbul), 1884—. Turkish author, teacher, and feminine emancipationist. Active in the Young Turk movement, she joined (1919) the Nationalist Party, supported Mustafa Kemal's cause, and was an army officer (1922) in the war against Greece. Fleeing Turkey when she came under suspicion of organizing opposition to Kemal, she lectured in American and Indian universities, and later returned to her native country, where she became professor of English literature at the University of Istanbul. She is the author of *Memoirs of Halidé Edib, The Turkish Ordeal, Turkey Faces West, Inside India* (1937), and *The History of English Literature* (3 vols., 1940, 1944, 1948).

Edict by the King of Prussia (prush'ạ). Satire by Benjamin Franklin, published in 1773.

Edict of Amboise (äṅ.bwȧz'). See **Amboise, Edict of.**

Edict of Milan (mi.lan'). See **Milan, Edict of.**

Edict of Nantes (nants, näṅt). See **Nantes, Edict of.**

Edict of Nemours (nẹ.mör'). See **Nemours, Edict of.**

Edict of Restitution. See **Restitution, Edict of.**

Edie Ochiltree (ē'di ō'ċhil.trē, ō'kil-, oċh'il-, ok'il-). See **Ochiltree, Edie.**

Edina (ẹ.dī'nạ). Village in SE Minnesota, in Hennepin County, near Minneapolis. 9,744 (1950).

Edinburg (ed'in.bėrg). Town in S central Indiana, in Bartholomew and Johnson counties, on the Blue River ab. 30 mi. S of Indianapolis. Manufactures include furniture and veneers. 3,283 (1950).

Edinburg. City in S Texas, county seat of Hidalgo County, SW of Corpus Christi: shipping center for fruits and vegetables, with a large car-icing plant. 12,383 (1950).

Edinburgh (ed'in.bur.ọ). [Older spellings: **Edinborow, Edinbro:** Middle English, **Edenborow;** earlier **Edwinesburch, Edwinesburg;** popularly called **"Auld Reekie."**] City, royal burgh, seaport, and commercial, industrial, administrative, and cultural center of Scotland, in S Scotland, in Midlothian, situated on the S bank of the Firth of Forth ab. 42 mi. E of Glasgow, ab. 393 mi. N of London by rail. It is the capital of Scotland and of various departments of government, the military headquarters of Scotland, and the county seat of Midlothian. Its port, the parliamentary burgh of Leith, is included now within the limits of Edinburgh, and is the second-ranking port in Scotland. Leith has a shipbuilding industry and extensive imports. Edinburgh is an important publishing and literary center, having many trades associated with the industry. Other industries include brassworks, rubber factories, breweries, distilleries, and machinery manufactures. The city is noted for its picturesque situation on ridges near Calton Hill and Arthur's Seat. It grew up around Edinburgh Castle, dating from the 7th century, built in the middle of the city on a rock which falls 270 ft. on three sides. Edinburgh Castle was captured by Edward I in 1296 and remained in English hands until it was recaptured (1314) in the name of Robert I of Scotland (Robert Bruce) by Thomas Randolph, 1st Earl of Moray, and 30 men who surprised the English garrison. The exterior of the castle has been greatly modified, but much of the interior remains as of old, including some of the royal apartments and the Romanesque chapel. James VI of Scotland (later James I of England) was born in the castle in 1566. Here, in the castle, are preserved the royal regalia of Scotland. Adjoining the castle is the Scottish National War Memorial, containing a shrine and a gallery of honor which has a barrel-vaulted roof supported by octagonal columns, forming 12 bays, one for each of the Scottish regiments. The Parliament House is now occupied by the Supreme Law Courts. It is a large Renaissance building, with porticoes of Ionic columns over an arcaded and rusticated basement. The Parliament House includes the Advocate's Library. The great hall has a handsome roof of oak, and contains interesting portraits and statues. Edinburgh is the seat of a university, founded in 1582 by James VI. Also of note are the ruins of Holyrood Abbey, founded in 1128 by David I, and the adjoining Holyroodhouse, or Holyrood Palace, still used as a royal residence. Holyroodhouse has many associations with Mary, Queen of Scots. It was here that David Rizzio was murdered by the Scottish lords at the instigation of Henry Stuart, Lord Darnley. Rizzio and Darnley are buried at Holyrood Abbey. The palace contains a picture gallery notable for its collection of 110 portraits of Scottish kings, painted in the 17th century by a Dutch artist. It was in this picture gallery that Prince Charlie (Charles Edward Stuart, the "Young Pretender" to the English throne) gave a ball, in 1745, while Edinburgh Castle held out against him. The National Gallery of Scotland, in Edinburgh, contains a valuable art collection, one of its best-known paintings being *Christ in the House of Mary and Martha* by Jan Vermeer. Saint Giles's Church (the cathedral) was founded in the 12th century, but the present structure is of the 15th. The interior has high nave-pillars and Gothic pointed arches. The transept is Norman, with massive piers supporting the tower. The fine recessed and sculptured west doorway is modern. Saint Mary's Episcopal Cathedral, the work of Sir George Gilbert Scott, was completed in 1879. It is a spacious structure in the Early English style, with an imposing central spire 295 ft. high. Other interesting structures in Edinburgh are the Scott monument, the Royal Institution, John Knox's house, Moray House (twice occupied by Cromwell) in the summer house of which the Treaty of Union between England and Scotland was signed, and various charitable and educational institutions. Edinburgh is famous for its colleges and schools. The city was fortified by the Northumbrian king Edwin (whence its name Edwinesburg) c617, succeeded Perth as the Scottish capital in 1437, was taken and sacked by the English in 1544 and again (by Cromwell) in 1650, and was occupied by the Young Pretender in 1745. Fragments of the old town wall still remain. Edinburgh is famous in the literary history of the last half of the 18th and first half of the 19th century, through its connection with Hume, Robertson, Dugald Stewart, Adam Smith, Burns, Scott, John Wilson (Christopher North), the *Edinburgh Review*, and others. It is often called the "modern Athens" or "Athens of the North," both from its topography and as a seat of learning, also "Queen of the North." 466,770 (1951).

Edinburgh, Duke of. [Title of **Philip Mountbatten;** additional titles, Earl of **Merioneth,** Baron **Greenwich.**] b. on the Greek island of Corfu, Ionian Islands, June 10, 1921—. Greek and Danish prince and English duke; husband of Queen Elizabeth II of England (who was Princess Elizabeth when he married her on Nov. 20, 1947). Queen Victoria was his great-great-grandmother, and Christian IX of Denmark his great-grandfather. His parents are the late Prince Andrew of Greece, and Princess Alice, sister of Viscount Mountbatten, former governor general of India. His grandfather, Prince Louis of Battenberg, became a British subject, an admiral in the Royal Navy, and changed the family name to its present one, Mountbatten, which is an English version of Battenberg. Philip's early education was obtained at Paris at the American Kindergarten, and at an American school at St.-Cloud, France. At the age of eight he was taken to England, continuing his education at the Cheam Preparatory School in Surrey, at the Salem School in Baden, Germany (where his failure to be properly impressed by the Nazi salute is said to have brought a sudden end to his stay), and in Scotland at the Gordonstoun School, near Moray Firth. In 1939 he began his naval studies at the Dartmouth (Devonshire) Naval College, the English equivalent of the U.S. naval academy at Annapolis. During World War II he saw sea service in the Mediterranean, first in 1940 as a midshipman on the *Ramillies*, in 1941 on the *Valiant*, which clashed with the Italian fleet at Cape Matapan, and in 1942 as sublieutenant and lieutenant on the *Wallace*. He was transferred to the Pacific in 1944 as first lieutenant on an English destroyer, and in September, 1945, he witnessed the signing of the Japanese surrender at Tokyo Bay. On Feb. 28, 1947, he became a British subject and also a commoner (giving up, as is required by British law, all his Greek and Danish titles). On July 9 of the same year, his engagement to Princess Elizabeth was officially announced. The day before the wedding, King George VI made him Duke of Edinburgh, the title by which he is now known, and also Earl of Merioneth and Baron Greenwich; on the same day he also made him a member of the Order of the Garter (founded by Edward III in 1348), and gave him the title of His Royal Highness (which makes him an equal of the dukes of Gloucester, Kent, and Windsor). He is also a field marshal, admiral of the fleet, and air chief marshal.

Edinburgh, Duke of. A title of **Alfred,** Prince.

Edinburgh, University of. Scottish seat of learning, founded in 1582 by James VI. It comprises the faculties of arts, science, divinity, law, and medicine. Its library contains over 400,000 volumes. Conjointly with the universities of St. Andrews, Glasgow, and Aberdeen, it formerly sent three members to Parliament.

Edinburgh Review. Literary and political review, founded at Edinburgh in 1802 by Francis Jeffrey, Sydney Smith, Henry Peter Brougham, and others.

Edinburghshire (ed'in.bur.o̧.shir). Former name of **Midlothian.**

Edinger (ā'ding.ėr), **Ludwig.** b. at Worms, Germany, April 13, 1855; d. at Frankfort on the Main, Germany, Jan. 26, 1918. German neurologist. He was assistant to A. Kussmaul (1877) and to F. Riegel (1880) at Giessen, where he became (1881) privatdocent. He lectured on neurology (1883–88) at Frankfort on the Main. He became the head of a special neurological department at the Senckenberg Institute at Frankfort, and full professor of neurology at the newly founded University of Frankfort. He described (1885) with C. F. O. Westphal, an accessory nucleus of the oculomotor nerve (the pupilloconstrictor center, known as the Edinger-Westphal nucleus).

Edington (ed'ing.to̧n). [Former name, **Ethandun.**] Village in SW England, in Wiltshire, ab. 30 mi. by road SE of Bristol. It is noted as the site of a victory of Alfred over the Danes c879 A.D.

Edirne (e.dėr'ne). [Also: **Edirneh, Edreneh;** former name, **Adrianople.**] *Il* (province or vilayet) in European Turkey, NW of the Sea of Marmara: tobacco, fruit, and barley. Capital, Edirne; area, 2,920 sq. mi.; pop. 221,125 (1950).

Edirne. [Also: **Edirneh, Edreneh;** former name, **Adrianople;** ancient name, **Uscudama;** Roman, **Adrianopolis, Hadrianopolis.**] City in NW European Turkey, the capital of the *il* (province or vilayet) of Edirne, on the Maritsa River, near the borders of Greece and Bulgaria. A place of great strategic and commercial importance, it was founded by the Roman emperor Hadrian c125 A.D., on the site of an older city; it was the residence of the sultans from 1361 to 1453. It was besieged by the Avars in 586, stormed by the Bulgarians in 922, entered by the Crusaders in 1189, taken by the Turks in 1361, taken by the Russians under Dibich-Zabalkanski in 1829, again occupied by the Russians in January, 1878, and besieged by the Bulgarians in 1912. Baldwin I (of Jerusalem) was taken prisoner at Adrianople by the Bulgars in 1205. Its most notable building is the 16th-century mosque of the sultan Suleiman II (Suleiman the Magnificent). It is preceded by a fine portico of monolithic columns, and flanked by four slender fluted minarets ab. 200 ft. high. The span of the dome (106 ft.) is greater than that of Santa Sophia at Istanbul; it rests on four colossal porphyry columns. Pop. ab. 30,000.

Edison (ed'i.so̧n), **Charles.** b. at Llewellyn Park, West Orange, N.J., Aug. 3, 1890—. American business executive and public official, U.S. secretary of the navy (1939–40); son of Thomas Alva Edison. He attended the Massachusetts Institute of Technology and later joined his father's ventures, becoming president and director of Thomas A. Edison, Inc., and a director of its various affiliates. After serving with the National Recovery Administration and the Federal Housing Administration, he served (1937–39) as assistant secretary of the navy and as secretary of the navy from 1939 to 1940. He was Democratic governor of New Jersey from 1941 to 1944.

Edison, Thomas Alva. b. at Milan, Ohio, Feb. 11, 1847; d. at Menlo Park, N.J., Oct. 18, 1931. American inventor. He was born of a Dutch father and a Scottish mother. He had no formal education worthy of the name, his schooling being limited to 12 weeks at a Port Huron (Mich.) public school, but during his life he took out over a thousand patents for different inventions. At the age of 12 he was selling newspapers on the Grand Trunk Railway, on its line into Detroit. In his early teens he was a telegraph operator in various parts of Canada and the U.S. He began his inventing career in 1868 with an electrical vote-recording machine. During 1877–78 he invented a carbon telephone transmitter, and in 1877, a phonograph or speaking machine, which is probably one of the most famous products of his inventive mind. He is said to have given light to the world by his invention in 1879 (Oct. 21) of an incandescent lamp. In 1883 he took out a patent for "the Edison effect," which allows electricity to pass from a filament to a metal plate inside an incandescent lamp. In 1885 he devised a telegraphic system for communicating with moving ships and trains. Among his other inventions are the automatic telegraph repeater, the quadruplex and printing telegraph, which he soon followed with the sextuplex transmission method, the kinetoscope, which, like his phonograph, led to new ways of living and making a living, and spreading thought and news, the cinematograph, the electric pen, the microphone, the "Ediphone" for office dictation, the alkaline storage (the Edison) battery, and the mimeograph. During World War I he devoted his energies to working on naval and chemical problems connected with the national military effort. By April, 1928, he had been granted 1,033 patents. The French government made him a chevalier, and later an officer and a commander, of the Legion of Honor. Union College, Princeton, and the University of the State of New York gave him honorary degrees. It has been pointed out by some authorities that Edison was not a great scientist (in fact, not a scientist at all, by ordinary standards), but rather a man who had an amazing practical genius for compelling science to serve immediate utilitarian ends. The popular American saying that genius is "99 percent perspiration and 1 percent inspiration" has been attributed to him (and whether or not he actually coined it, the fact remains that it does certainly state the manner of his own dogged approach to the problems he faced). His life has been the subject of many biographies and at least two films have been made about him.

Edison Electric Institute. Organization founded in 1933 for the purpose of scientific research and operating methods in the production, transmission, and distribution of electricity. Its membership is composed of operating and holding companies. The organization maintains headquarters at New York and issues a monthly *Bulletin* and *Electrical Research Statistics* (monthly).

Edissa (e.dis'ạ). See **Esther.**

Edisto (ed'is.tō). River in South Carolina, formed by the union of a north and a south branch, and flowing into the sea by two channels ab. 25 mi. SW of Charleston. Length, over 150 mi.

Edith (ē'dith). [Also, **Eadgyth.**] d. at Winchester, England, Dec. 19, 1075. Anglo-Saxon queen. She was the daughter of Godwine, Earl of Wessex, and married Edward the Confessor in 1045, receiving Winchester and Exeter as her morning gift, i.e., the gift to the bride on the morning following consummation of the marriage. She is said to have planned the murder of Gospatric, one of the king's thanes, in 1064, at the instigation of her brother Tostig, Earl of Northumberland. She founded a church at Wilton, which was consecrated in 1065; and on the death (1066) of her husband retired to Winchester, in the quiet possession of which she was allowed to remain by William the Conqueror.

Edith. One of the principal characters in Francis Beaumont and John Fletcher's *The Bloody Brother.*

Edith. Maid of Lorn in Sir Walter Scott's poem *The Lord of the Isles.*

Edith Bellenden (bel'ẹn.dẹn). See **Bellenden, Edith.**

Edith Ronne Land (ron'i). That portion of Antarctica extending from the base of the Palmer Peninsula SE to Coats Land. It was discovered by the Ronne Antarctic Research Expedition (1947–48), under the leadership of Commander Finn Ronne.

Edith Swan-neck (swon'nek). fl. 11th century. Mistress of Harold II, king of the English, and mother, probably, of some of his children. By her aid the mutilated body of Harold was identified after the battle of Hastings (1066). She appears as a greatly idealized character in romance and poetry.

Edman (ed'mạn), **Irwin.** b. at New York, Nov. 28, 1896—. American philosopher and writer. He was graduated (B.A., 1917; Ph.D., 1920) from Columbia, where he was a lecturer (1918–20), instructor (1920–24), assistant professor (1925–31), associate professor (1931–35), and professor (1935 *et seq.*) of philosophy. His works include *Human Traits and Their Social Significance* (1920), *Richard Kane Looks at Life* (1926), *Four Ways of Philosophy* (1937), *Philosopher's Holiday* (1938), *Arts and the Man* (1939), and *Philosopher's Quest* (1947).

Edmands (ed'mạndz), **John.** b. at Framingham, Mass., Feb. 1, 1820; d. Oct. 17, 1915. American librarian. He was assistant (1851–56) in the Yale College Library, librarian (1856–1915) of the Mercantile Library at Philadelphia, and originator of a book classification system. His works include *Subjects for Debates, with References to Authorities* (1847), *Explanation of the New System of Classification Devised for the Mercantile Library of Philadelphia* (1878), *Reading Notes on Luther* (1883), *Reading Notes on Wycliffe* (1884), and *The Evolution of Congregationalism* (1916).

Edmer or **Eadmer** (ed'mėr). b. c1060; d. c1124. English monk and historian, of Canterbury. He was elected (1120) archbishop of St. Andrews through recommendation of Alexander I, king of Scotland, but the king would not allow Edmer to be consecrated by English primates. Edmer wrote a chronicle of contemporary events, *Historia novorum,* covering the period c1066–1122, and a *Life of Saint Anselm,* Anselm being one of his close friends.

Edmond (ed'mọnd). City in C Oklahoma, in Oklahoma County: trading center for an agricultural and oil-producing area. It is the seat of Central State College. 6,086 (1950).

Edmond Dantès (ed.môṅ däṅ.tes). See **Dantès, Edmond.**

Edmonds (ed'mọndz), **Walter Dumaux.** b. at Boonville, N.Y., July 15, 1903—. American novelist and short-story writer. He is the author of *Rome Haul* (1929), *The Big Barn* (1930), *Erie Water* (1933), *Mostly Canallers* (1934), *Drums Along the Mohawk* (1936), *Chad Hanna* (1940), *The Matchlock Gun* (1941), *Wilderness Clearing* (1944), *In the Hands of the Senecas* (1947), *The Wedding Journey* (1947), and other books.

Edmonton (ed'mọn.tọn). Capital of Alberta, Canada, on the North Saskatchewan River. It is the largest city in the province and the ninth largest in Canada; its growth has been extremely rapid. The city is the entryway to the vast Canadian northland and is the S terminus of the Alaska Highway. It is the site of one of the largest airports in the country and of numerous industries. The University of Alberta is situated here. The main line of the Canadian National Railway passes through the city. Pop., including suburbs, 173,075 (1951).

Edmonton. Municipal borough in SE England, in Middlesex, ab. 8 mi. N of Liverpool Street station, London. 104,244 (1951).

Edmund (ed'mund) or **Eadmund,** Saint. [Called **Edmund the Martyr.**] b. c840; killed by the Danes, 870. King (855–870) of East Anglia. Details of his life are legendary. He is supposed to have been a Saxon, born at Nuremberg, son of King Alkmund, and to have been adopted by Offa, whom he succeeded as king. In 870 he met the Danes at Hoxne and was defeated by them, dying on the field or, according to one story, being bound to a tree and beheaded, or shot with arrows, when he refused to forswear Christianity or acknowledge Danish overlordship.

Edmund, Saint. [Called **Edmund Rich** (rich) and **Edmund of Pontigny** (pon.tēn'yē, pôṅ.tē.nyē).] b. at Abingdon, England, Nov. 20, probably between 1170 and 1175; d. at Soisy, France, Nov. 16, 1240. Archbishop of Canterbury. He was the son of one Edward or Reinald Rich, studied and later lectured at Oxford and Paris, and in 1233 was appointed archbishop of Canterbury. He came forward as a champion of the national church against papal encroachment; but, finding himself unable to resist the appointment of 300 Italians to as many English benefices, abandoned his archiepiscopal see in 1240 and took refuge in the monastery of Pontigny, in France.

He died at Soisy, whither he had gone for the benefit of his health, and was canonized in 1247. His feast day is observed November 16.

Edmund. In Shakespeare's *King Lear*, a bastard son of the Earl of Gloucester.

Edmund or **Eadmund I.** [Called **Edmund the Magnificent** and **the Deed-doer.**] b. c922; killed at Pucklechurch, Gloucestershire, England, May 26, 946. King of the West Saxons and Mercians. He was the son of Edward the Elder, and half-brother of Athelstan, whom he succeeded in 940. He had fought at Brunanbuth for Athelstan, but after he became king he lost a large part of his kingdom to invaders from Ireland, but won it back in 944 or 945. He subdued Cumbria (945), which he bestowed on Malcolm I of Scotland. He was killed by a robber named Liofa while keeping the feast of Saint Augustine of Canterbury at Pucklechurch, Gloucestershire. The robber having entered the hall unbidden, the king ordered a cup-bearer to remove him, and when the robber resisted came to the cup-bearer's relief. In the struggle that ensued he was stabbed to death with a dagger. Edmund was married twice, to Ælfgifu, the mother of Edwy and Edgar, and to Ethelflæd.

Edmund or **Eadmund II.** [Called **Edmund Ironside.**] b. probably c989; d. probably at London, Nov. 30, 1016. King of the West Saxons. He was the son of Ethelred II (Ethelred the Unready), whom he succeeded in April, 1016. After many victories over the Danes, he was defeated in a bloody battle at Assandun (Ashington) in Essex by Canute, with whom he was forced to divide his kingdom, provision being made, it is said, that the survivor should be sole king. He retained Wessex, Essex, East Anglia, and London, while Canute received Northumberland and Mercia. His death, which was probably due to natural causes, has been attributed by later tradition to poison administered by Edric Streona, his brother-in-law, at the instance of Canute. After his death Canute took possession of the whole kingdom.

Edmunds (ed'mundz), **Albert Joseph.** b. at Tottenham, near London, Nov. 21, 1857; d. Dec. 17, 1941. American librarian and Buddhist scholar. He came to the U.S. in 1885, and was cataloguer (1891–1936) for the Historical Society of Pennsylvania. His works include *Marvellous Birth of the Buddhas* (1899), *Hymns of the Faith* (1902), *Buddhist and Christian Gospels* (1902), *A Dialogue Between Two Saviors* (5th ed., 1931), *Lucy Edmunds (1859–1935) in the Two Worlds* (1935), and *Leaves from the Gospel of Mark* (1936).

Edmunds, George Franklin. b. near Richmond, Vt., Feb. 1, 1828; d. at Pasadena, Calif., Feb. 27, 1919. American lawyer and legislator, author of the act (1882) making polygamy illegal in U.S. territories and chief framer of the Sherman Anti-Trust Act of 1890. He studied law privately in Vermont and at Washington, D.C., was admitted to the bar in 1849 and established his practice at Richmond, later moving it to Burlington. He served (1854–59) in the state legislature, and was speaker from 1857 to 1859; he was (1861–62) a member of the state senate and was president pro tempore; and in 1864 was appointed special counsel by Secretary of State Seward for the purpose of securing the extradition of the Confederate raiders on St. Albans, Vt. A Republican, he went to the U.S. Senate in 1866 to fill an unexpired term, and on the day (April 6) after being sworn in cast the deciding vote for the Civil Rights Bill which carried it over Johnson's veto. He was affiliated with the Radical Republicans during the Reconstruction period; in 1867, he was named chairman of the committee which arranged the rules of procedure for Johnson's trial. He served in the Senate until his retirement (1891), and was chairman of the committee on the judiciary (1872–91, with the exception of 1879–81). He secured the act of Jan. 29, 1877, which set up an electoral commission to supervise the disputed Tilden-Hayes contest of 1876 and was responsible for the Electoral Count Act of 1887. During his career in the Senate, he achieved a reputation with the law cases he handled before U.S. circuit courts and the U.S. Supreme Court. One of his outstanding cases, in which he won his argument against the unconstitutionality of the income tax, was *Pollock v. The Farmers' Loan and Trust Company* (decided 1895).

Edmunds, John. Felon, the principal character of the tale "The Convict's Return," in Charles Dickens's *Pickwick Papers*.

Edmundston (ed'mun.stọn). County town of Madawaska County, New Brunswick, Canada, situated on the St. John River, ab. 190 mi. from the city of St. John: paper mills. The main line of the Canadian National Railways from Quebec passes through the town as does the main highway from C Canada. 10,753 (1951).

Edna (ed'nạ). Town in S Texas, county seat of Jackson County, NE of Corpus Christi, in a petroleum-producing region: residential community. 3,855 (1950).

Edo (ā'dō). [Also, **Bini.**] Sudanic-speaking people of W Africa, inhabiting an area in the vicinity of the town of Benin in S Nigeria. Their population is estimated at ab. 500,000 (based on P. A. Talbot, *The Peoples of Southern Nigeria*, 1926). They are divided into 19 subgroups including the Bini (also called Edo), Esa, Sobo, Isoko, and 15 other peoples known as Kukuruku. The Bini kingdom has its capital at Benin, which is also known as Edo. The Edo have exogamous patrilineal clans. They practice hoe agriculture, and, except in the case of the Sobo and the Isoko, their principal crop is yams.

Edo. A former name of **Tokyo.**

Edom (ē'dọm). [Also: **Idumea, Seir.**] In Biblical geography, the region in the lowland S of the Dead Sea, bounded on the W by the desert of Paran, and on the NE by the mountains of Moab: the modern Wadi el Araba and the surrounding mountainous country, extending S to the Gulf of Aqaba, and including the seaports Elath (Aqaba) and Eziongeber. The most important cities of this rugged barren territory were Bozrah, the capital, Maon, Phunon, and Sela, afterward called Petra, from which the whole district was named Arabia Petraea. The Edomites were descendants of Esau, the brother of Jacob, and were, therefore, designated as "brothers of Israel" (Num. xx. 14, Deut. ii. 4, 8), but became later the hereditary enemies of Israel; Saul attacked them (1 Sam. xiv. 47) and subdued them (2 Sam. vii. 13). After the division of the Israelitish kingdom they came under the supremacy of Judah, but made frequent and sometimes successful attempts to regain their independence. They were for the last time subjected by Uzziah about the middle of the 8th century B.C. Tiglath-Pileser III of Assyria made (c743) Kaus Malik, king of Edom, tributary. Esarhaddon (680–668) mentions Kaus Gabri of Edom among the tributary kings. In the time of Nebuchadnezzar II (605–562) Edom, still ruled by a king, was attacked by the Babylonians. During the captivity in Babylonia of the Judeans, the Edomites took possession of portions of Judea, while their own territory was occupied by Arabic tribes, the Nabathaeans, and was called, after the city of Petra, Arabia Petraea. The Hasmonean king John Hyrcanus took Dora and Morissa and forced the Edomites to accept Judaism c130 B.C. Afterward they became the rulers of the Jews in the person of Antipater and his descendants the Herodians. The last king of this race, Herod Agrippa II, died c100 A.D., but the name of Edom vanishes from history with the fall of Judea.

Édouard (ā.dwàr). One of the central characters in *Les Faux-monnayeurs* (1926; Eng. trans., *The Counterfeiters*) by the French writer André Gide. In some respects, for instance his being a novelist engaged in writing a novel about the theme of counterfeiting, he may be taken to represent Gide.

Edred or **Eadred** (ed'rẹd). d. at Frome, England, Nov. 23, 955. King of England; youngest son of Edward the Elder and Eadgifu, and brother of Edmund I, whom he succeeded in 946. His government was controlled by his mother and Saint Dunstan; his reign was marked by revolts in Northumbria.

Edrei (ed'rẹ.ī). In the Old Testament, the capital of Og, king of Bashan. Near it Og was defeated by the Israelites. The city was with the territory assigned to the tribe of Manasseh. Josh. xiii. 31.

Edremit (e.dre.mēt'). [Also: **Edremid;** Biblical name, **Adramyttium;** Greek, **Adramyti.**] Town in W Turkey near the head of the Gulf of Edremit, an arm of the Aegean Sea, ab. 135 mi. SW of Istanbul: a trading center served by a railway and two highways. Olive oil, produced in several pressing plants, is the chief export. Pop. ab. 12,000.

Edremit, Gulf of. [Former name, **Gulf of Adramyttium.**] Arm of the Aegean Sea, on the W coast of Turkey, N of Mytilene. It separates the mainland of Turkey from the island of Mytilene, which belongs to Greece. Length, ab. 50 mi.; width, ab. 15 mi.

Edreneh (e.dre.ne'). See **Edirne.**

Edric or **Eadric Streona** (ed'rik strā'ǫ.nä). Put to death by Canute, 1017. English nobleman, ealdorman of Mercia, chief adviser of Etheldred II (Ethelred the Unready). He married Ethelred's daughter, but his loyalties seem to have been with the Danes. He dissuaded both Ethelred and his son Edmund II from fighting against the Danes, and when Edmund did meet Canute at Assandun (Ashington) Edric's treachery caused the English to be defeated. It is also said that he poisoned Edmund. Canute made Edric earl of Mercia, but had him killed rather than risk his treachery.

Edrinus (ed'ri.nus), **Lacus.** Latin name of **Idro, Lake.**

Edrisi (e.drē'sē). See **Idrisi.**

Edschmid (āt'shmit), **Kasimir.** [Original name, **Eduard Schmid.**] b. at Darmstadt, Germany, Oct. 5, 1890—. German novelist, one of the most outspoken of the German expressionists. His *Über den Expressionismus in der Literatur* (1918) set forth his theories, which he has exemplified in numerous narratives including *Das rasende Leben* (1916), *Die achatnen Kugeln* (1920), *Lord Byron; Roman einer Leidenschaft* (1929; Eng. trans., *Lord Byron; the Story of a Passion,* 1930), and *Afrika nackt und angezogen* (1929).

Edstrom (ed'strǫm), **David.** b. at Hvetlanda, Sweden, March 21, 1873; d. Aug. 12, 1938. American sculptor, best known for his psychological sculptures and portraits. He studied at the Royal Academy of Fine arts, Stockholm, as well as in Italy, France, and the U.S., to which he had come in 1880. To save money enough to study, he worked in factories and at odd jobs, then earned his passage to Europe by stoking coal. His sculpture has been exhibited widely in Europe and the U.S. Among his better-known works are *Fear, Pride, Envy, Caliban, The Cry of Poverty,* the busts of *Crown Prince and Princess of Sweden, Princess Patricia of Connaught,* and the statue *H. M. Whittier.* He also wrote *The Testament of Caliban,* an autobiography, and articles on politics, art, and other topics for magazines and newspapers.

Edström (ed'strėm), **Sigfrid.** [Full name, **Johannes Sigfrid Edström.**] b. at Morlanda, Sweden, Nov. 21, 1870—. Swedish businessman, known for his leadership in international business and sports organizations. He was president of the International Amateur Athletic Federation, of the International Olympic Committee, and honorary president of the International Chamber of Commerce. He was employed (1893-97) by U.S. electrical manufacturing concerns, including the Westinghouse Electric Manufacturing Company and the General Electric Company, directed tramway companies at Zurich, Switzerland (1897–1900) and Göteborg, Sweden (1900–03), served (1903–33) as president of the Asea Electric Company, and was a director of numerous electrical and steel firms. He was a member of the American Institute of Electric Engineers and the Institute of Electrical Engineers (London), and was (1934) chairman of the Swedish Employers Association.

Education, United States Office of. Governmental agency established on March 2, 1867, by Congress, becoming in 1869 a bureau in the Department of the Interior. Its purpose is to collect, and to make available, statistics and various types of information dealing with schools and to make surveys of school systems, both state and national. These surveys, of which more than 200 have been made, include grade and high schools, colleges, universities, and Negro and land-grant colleges. Its chief publication is the *Biennial Survey of Education,* and its library, limited to educational works, is the largest of its kind in the country. Its head, appointed by the President, is called a commissioner, an office that has been held by Henry Barnard (the first one), John Eaton, William T. Harris, Elmer Ellsworth Brown (long associated with New York University), Philander P. Claxton, and George F. Zook.

Education of Henry Adams (hen'ri ad'ạmz), **The.** Autobiography of Henry Adams, privately printed in 1907 and posthumously published in 1918. It delineates the conflict which he felt between the individual and an impersonal, highly mechanized society. Adams interweaves portions of his personal history (told in the third person) with an analysis of lines of historical force drawn between the unity, as Adams conceived it, of the 13th century and the multiplicity of his own age. The work presents the author's theory of the law of acceleration in historical development. Some of the ideas are set forth in the earlier *Mont-Saint-Michel and Chartres* (1904).

Edward or **Eadward** or **Eadweard** (ed'wạrd). [Called **Edward the Elder.**] d. at what is now Farndon, Northamptonshire, England, 924. King of the West Saxons; son of Alfred the Great, whom he succeeded in 901. He defeated his cousin Ethelwold, who disputed his title to the throne. On the death of his sister Ethelfleda (Elfleda), the widow of Ethelred, ealdorman of Mercia, he incorporated Mercia (which had long acknowledged the overlordship of the West Saxon kings) with Wessex. He completed the conquest of the Danelaw, begun by him with Ethelfleda's aid earlier, conquered East Anglia and Essex, and received the submission of Strathclyde and all the Scots. On this Scottish submission (denied later by the Scots) was based the claim of later English kings to Scotland. At his death he ruled Wessex, Kent, and Sussex by inheritance; Mercia, Essex, and East Anglia by conquest; and Northumberland, Wales, Scotland, and Strathclyde as overlord. He was succeeded by Æthelstan, his son by Ecgwyn; two sons by Eadgifu, his third wife, Edmund I and Edred, later reigned.

Edward or **Eadward.** [Called **Edward the Martyr.**] b. probably in 963; murdered March 18, 978. King of the West Saxons; son of Edgar, whom he succeeded in 975, and Ethelflæd. He was elected by the witan through the influence of Saint Dunstan, primate of England, in spite of the measures taken by his stepmother, Elfrida, to secure the crown for her son Ethelred. He was murdered by her order, according to tradition, and was succeeded by his stepbrother, Ethelred II (Ethelred the Unready). His youth and popularity led to his recognition as a martyr as early as 1001.

Edward or **Eadward.** [Called **Edward the Confessor.**] b. at what is now Islip, Oxfordshire, England, c1004; d. Jan. 5, 1066. King of the West Saxons; son of Ethelred II (Ethelred the Unready) and Emma of Normandy. He lived chiefly in Normandy during the Danish supremacy, and was elected to the throne of his father through the influence of Godwin, Earl of Wessex, on the death of Harthacnut, in 1042. He married Edith (Edgitha), daughter of Godwin, in 1045. Edward chose as chief advisers a number of Frenchmen and thus came into conflict with Godwin's power. His appointment of Robert of Jumièges as Archbishop of Canterbury, after the regular election of Godwin's relative Ælfric, caused a break with Godwin, and when, soon after, Dover offered resistance to Edward's brother-in-law Eustace II of Boulogne, Edward ordered Godwin to punish the town. This Godwin refused to do and, Edward threatening to try him for an old alleged crime, Godwin and his sons fled to France and Ireland. The next year (1052) Godwin raised a force and invaded England; Edward lacked support and restored Godwin to favor. He and his son Harold after him became the king's ministers while Edward applied himself to religious study. When his favorite, Tostig, Godwin's son, was faced with revolt in Northumbria in 1065, Edward was forced to submit to Tostig's removal. This and the realization that a struggle over the succession to the English throne among Harold, Harold III (Harold Haardraade) of Norway, Edgar Ætheling, and William of Normandy was due to break probably hastened his death. He died without issue, and was succeeded by his wife's brother Harold, whose title was disputed by William, Duke of Normandy. The so-called Laws of Edward the Confessor, compiled in 1070, were made from sworn statements of 12 men of each shire. He was canonized in 1161.

Edward. [Titles: 1st Duke of **Cornwall** and Prince of **Wales,** Prince of **Aquitaine and Gascony;** called **the Black Prince;** occasionally known also as **Edward IV** and **Edward of Woodstock.**] b. at Woodstock, England, July 15, 1330; d. at Westminster (now part of London), June 8, 1376. Eldest son of Edward III and Philippa of Hainaut. He was made (1333) Earl of Chester and became

(1337) Duke of Cornwall, the first man in England to hold a dukedom. In 1346 he fought well in the victory at Crécy, and in 1347 at the siege of Calais. In 1355 and 1356 he led raiding expeditions out of Gascony, culminating in the brilliant victory (Sept. 19, 1356) at Poitiers, where King John II of France was captured; next year Edward led him in triumph through London. In 1361 he married Joan of Kent, a granddaughter of Edward I; their only son later ruled England as Richard II. Edward was given (July, 1363) all the English possessions in southern France and was made Prince of Aquitaine. He took up residence in France, but his preference for Englishmen in making appointments antagonized the French nobles despite Edward's many attempts to win them over. Pedro the Cruel of Castile and León, deposed by Henry of Trastamara, won Edward over to his plan of regaining his crown, and in 1367 Edward advanced into Spain at the head of an army. At Navarrete (Nájera) in April he defeated Bertrand du Guesclin and put Pedro back on the throne. During the summer he contracted a disease and returned with his army to France. His attempt to recoup by a special tax financial losses suffered in the Spanish adventure met with the resistance of the barons, who appealed to the French king at Paris. Edward refused to be ruled by the French, whereupon the king, Charles V, declared forfeit all the English lands in France. Fighting broke out and the Black Prince took Limoges (1369) and massacred the inhabitants, but, finding himself too ill to sit in the saddle, gave the defense of Gascony into the hands of his brother John of Gaunt, and returned to England. There he found it necessary to oppose the Lancastrian policies, John of Gaunt, Duke of Lancaster, having become in the old age of Edward III the great political power in England. Edward rallied to his side the clerical party, who were opposed by Lancaster, his aim principally being to insure the accession of his son Richard to the throne.

Edward I (of *England*). [Called **Edward Longshanks.**] b. at Westminster (now part of London), June 17 or 18, 1239; d. at Burgh-on-the-Sands, near Carlisle, England, July 7, 1307. King of England from 1272 to 1307. He was the son of Henry III and Eleanor of Provence. In 1254 he married Eleanor of Castile, half sister of Alfonso X of Castile. He took an active part in the struggle between his father and the barons, inflicting a decisive defeat on their leader, Simon de Montfort, at Evesham in 1265. He engaged (1270–72) in the seventh Crusade, and was returning from the Holy Land when he heard of his accession to the throne. He returned slowly, visiting his lands in Gascony, and reaching England in 1274, in which year he was crowned. In 1277 he began the conquest of Wales, which had become practically independent during the barons' wars, and in 1284, after defeating Llewelyn, annexed that country to England. He expelled the Jews from England in 1290. On the death (1290) of Margaret, the Maid of Norway, granddaughter and heiress of Alexander III of Scotland, the Scottish estates were unable to decide between the two chief claimants to the throne, John de Baliol and Robert Bruce, with the result that Edward was appointed arbitrator. He decided in favor of Baliol, whose homage he received. In 1294 he became involved in a war with France, Philip IV of France forming an alliance with Scotland. In 1296 he defeated the Scots at Dunbar, compelled Baliol to resign the crown, carried the Scotch coronation stone (the Stone of Scone) to London, and placed Scotland under an English regent, who was, however, defeated by the patriot Sir William Wallace at Stirling in 1297. Edward defeated the Scots under Wallace in the battle of Falkirk, on July 22, 1298. In 1303 he concluded the peace of Amiens with France, having married in 1299 Philip IV's sister, Margaret. Invading Scotland in 1303, he received the submission of Bruce, and in 1305 he ordered the execution of Wallace, who had been betrayed to the English. He died on the way to Scotland, where a new insurrection had placed Robert Bruce, grandson of the claimant against whom Edward had earlier decided, on the throne in 1306. Edward's reign is of great importance in the internal history of England. The statutes of Westminster (1275, 1285, 1290) revised the landholding system and limited the feudal political power; although the aim was to break altogether the barons' power, Edward was forced, through need of money to finance his foreign struggles, to grant exemptions from the rules and to confirm the charters granted by John and Henry III. The old King's Court was separated into three tribunals: the Court of Exchequer, the Court of King's Bench, and the Court of Common Pleas. The jurisdiction of the Royal Council (later the Star Chamber) was established. In 1279, the statute of mortmain was promulgated, forbidding the extension of clerical landholding without the king's consent. This was opposed by the clergy and they received backing from Pope Boniface VIII, whose bull *Clericos Laicos* (1296), though intended to stop Philip IV of France from taxing the clergy, was applied in 1297 in England when the English clergy refused to contribute to Edward's campaign against France. Edward then announced that he could no longer protect the church holdings against the possible inroads of the barons. But when the barons allied themselves with the clergy, Edward gave way, reaffirmed the charters, and signed further articles against arbitrary taxation without parliamentary consent. In 1295 Edward convened the so-called Model Parliament, with representation from all three estates (clergy, nobility, commons), the type after which later Parliaments were formed. Edward established the royal power over the clergy when Pope Clement V, an Englishman, permitted him to suspend (1306) Robert de Winchelsea, archbishop of Canterbury, one of the leading ecclesiastical opponents of the king. Edward's reign is marked by his victory over the barons and the clergy, his conquest of Wales, his victory over Philip IV of France, and his firm establishment of the royal power under law in England.

Edward II (of *England*). [Full name, **Edward II of Caernarvon** (or **Carnarvon**).] b. at Caernarvon, Wales, April 25, 1284; murdered at Berkeley Castle, near Gloucester, England, Sept. 21, 1327. King of England from 1307 to 1327. He was the fourth son of Edward I by his first wife, Eleanor of Castile. He was created (1301) the first Prince of Wales. On his accession to the throne he recalled his favorite, Piers Gaveston, who had been banished as being a bad influence on Edward by Edward I. He married Isabella of France in 1308. The insolence of Gaveston having aroused the anger of the barons, the favorite was banished through their influence in 1308, only to be shortly recalled by the king. In 1310, in consequence of the incompetence of Edward, who was completely under the ascendancy of Gaveston, the government was entrusted by the barons to 21 ordainers, who procured the passage of the ordinances of the Parliament of 1311, in accordance with which Gaveston was exiled, and provisions were made for annual Parliaments and for the reform of administrative abuses. In 1312 the barons brought about the execution of Gaveston, who had been again recalled by the king. In 1314 Edward was defeated by the Scots under Robert I (Robert the Bruce) at the battle of Bannockburn (June 24). The exile of his new favorites, the two Despensers, by Parliament in 1321 involved him in a war with the barons, who were defeated at the battle of Boroughbridge in 1322. In 1323, after an unsuccessful invasion of Scotland, he concluded a peace for 13 years with Bruce, whose assumption of the royal title of Scotland was passed over in silence. His queen, Isabella, having in 1325 been sent to France, accompanied by the prince Edward, heir to the throne, to negotiate with her brother Charles IV concerning the English fiefs in France, intrigued with Roger de Mortimer, her lover, and other disaffected barons, landed in England in 1326, captured Bristol, executed the Despensers, and imprisoned Edward. Edward, the prince, refused to become king as long as his father claimed the throne, so Edward II was deposed by Parliament, forced to resign his claim, and brutally murdered in Berkeley Castle.

Edward III (of *England*). [Called **Edward of Windsor.**] b. at Windsor, England, Nov. 13, 1312; d. at Shene (Richmond), England, June 21, 1377. King of England from 1327 to 1377. He was the son of Edward II and Isabella of France. On the deposition of his father, he was proclaimed king under a council of regency, the actual government being exercised by the queen and her favorite, Roger de Mortimer. He married (1328) Philippa of Hainaut, and in the same year concluded the treaty of Northampton with the Scots, in which Robert I (Robert Bruce) was recognized as king. In 1330 he took the government into his own hands, securing the execution of Mortimer and removing the queen-mother from any further influence. On the death of Robert I in 1329, Edward Baliol seized the Scottish crown, to the exclusion of Robert's young son David (1324–71), who, despite his years, was already Edward's brother-in-law. Baliol did homage to Edward, and a revolt of the nobles drove him across the border. Edward defeated the national party at Halidon Hill in 1333, and restored Baliol, who was soon driven out by the Scots. In 1337 he became involved in a war with France (the Hundred Years' War), whose throne he claimed in right of his mother. His claim brought him as allies the Flemings, who were subject to the French king; he made alliances with the emperor Louis IV and with other German princes. The naval victory at Sluys (1340) gave England control of the Channel. In 1346, at the battle of Neville's Cross, his army defeated the invading Scots under David II (Bruce), who had recovered the Scottish throne in 1342; the Scots, however, succeeded in maintaining their independence. He gained with his son, Edward the Black Prince, the victory of Crécy over the French in 1346, and reduced Calais in 1347, while the Black Prince gained the battle of Poitiers in 1356. In 1360 he concluded with the French the peace of Brétigny, by which he renounced the French crown and Normandy, Anjou, Maine, and Touraine, in return for the cession in full sovereignty to England of Aquitaine, Ponthieu, Guisnes, and Calais. He subsequently, in a war with Charles V, lost all his possessions in France, with the exception of Bordeaux, Calais, and Bayonne, due principally to the incompetence of John of Gaunt, who replaced the Black Prince, Edward, as steward of the English possessions in France. During his reign occurred several visitations of the Black Death (1348–49, 1361, and 1369). This plague, by halving the population of England, caused a social revolution that was stopped neither by an ordinance (1349) fixing wages and prices nor by the Statute of Laborers (1351) to force the unemployed to work at the fixed wages. This emancipation of labor from the feudal system was accompanied by a growth of class-consciousness reflected in such literary works as *Piers Plowman* and in the rapid spread of Lollardy. The reign of Edward III was also marked by a revolt against the papal authority and the establishment of national strictures on the power of the papacy, then resident at Avignon and under the influence of the French. This was only one aspect of the growth of national feeling: among other such manifestations was the establishment of the English language on an official basis in the courts, the schools, and Parliament, where until then French had held sway. The business class grew in importance and asserted its right to be heard. Parliament, obtaining the whip hand because of Edward's need of money for his wars, consolidated its position as a check on monarchal power. In his later years Edward turned over actual rule of the kingdom to Edward the Black Prince and then, in the latter's illness, to John of Gaunt. The latter, with the support of the king's mistress Alice Perrers, rallied to himself the forces of the court, and was opposed by the parliamentary and clerical factions. After the Black Prince's death, John of Gaunt was actual ruler of England until the accession of Richard II. Edward III had 12 children; of his seven sons, five grew to manhood and were of importance to history: Edward of Woodstock, the Black Prince; Lionel of Antwerp (the place names indicate where the princes were born), Duke of Clarence; John of Gaunt (i.e., Ghent), Duke of Lancaster, whose descendants formed the Lancastrian party in the later Wars of the Roses; Edmund of Langley, later 1st Duke of York, from whom the Yorkists took their name; and Thomas of Woodstock, later Duke of Gloucester.

Edward IV (of *England*). See also **Edward,** the Black Prince (1330–76).

Edward IV (of *England*). b. at Rouen, France, probably April 28, 1442; d. April 9, 1483. King of England from 1461 to 1483. He was the son of Richard Plantagenet, 3rd Duke of York, and Cecily Neville, daughter of the earl of Westmorland. He was known as the Earl of March previous to his accession, and played a prominent part in the struggle of his house (the house of York) with that of Lancaster for the possessions of the throne. In conjunction with the earls of Salisbury and Warwick, his uncle and his cousin, both named Richard Neville, he defeated the Lancastrians under Henry VI at Northampton in 1460, and took the king prisoner. His father, the duke of York, was defeated and killed at the battle of Wakefield later in the same year, whereupon Edward succeeded to the title, defeated the Lancastrians at the battle of Mortimer's Cross in 1461, and was proclaimed king at London on March 4, 1461. The early part of his reign was disturbed by constant attempts of the Lancastrians to regain the throne. In 1464 he secretly married Elizabeth Grey, daughter of Richard Woodville, Baron Rivers, and widow of Sir John Grey, a Lancastrian. This caused a revolution under the earl of Warwick, who joined forces with the Lancastrians and proclaimed the deposed and captive Henry VI king. Edward fled to France, but returned and suppressed the rising in the battles of Barnet (April 14, 1471) and Tewkesbury (May 4, 1471); in the former Warwick was slain and following the latter Henry VI died, probably murdered, in the Tower of London. Edward's reign thereafter was more or less peaceful, only the rivalry of his brothers, the dukes of Clarence and Gloucester, marring the domestic scene (this was ended with Clarence's murder in 1478) and a war with France in 1475 disturbing the peace. From the French war came a subsidy which enabled Edward to avoid going to Parliament for money. As a result Edward reverted to autocracy and attempted to live the life of a Renaissance despot. His profligacy was well known; Jane Shore is the most famous of his several mistresses.

Edward V (of *England*). b. in Westminster Abbey, London, Nov. 2 or 3, 1470; murdered in the Tower of London, 1483. King of England from April to June, 1483. He was the son of Edward IV by Elizabeth Woodville. He succeeded to the throne under the regency of his uncle Richard, Duke of Gloucester, who secretly put him and his brother to death and usurped the government as Richard III. The mystery surrounding the deaths of Edward and his younger brother Richard, Duke of York, has never successfully been solved, but there is little doubt that Richard III procured their deaths through Sir James Tyrell after the Tower's constable, Sir Robert Brackenbury, refused to kill them.

Edward VI (of *England*). b. at Hampton Court, England, Oct. 12, 1537; d. at Greenwich, near London, July 6, 1553. King of England from 1547 to 1553. He was the son of Henry VIII by his third queen, Jane Seymour, and succeeded to the throne under the regency of his uncle, Edward Seymour, Duke of Somerset, who was supplanted c1550 by John Dudley, Duke of Northumberland. During his reign occurred the publication of the 42 articles of religion (1553) and the introduction of the Book of Common Prayer (1549), compiled by Thomas Cranmer. Before his death he was induced by the duke of Northumberland to assign the crown to Northumberland's daughter-in-law, Lady Jane Grey, to the exclusion of Henry VIII's children Mary and Elizabeth.

Edward VII (of *England*). [Full name, **Albert Edward;** called **the Peacemaker.**] b. at London, Nov. 9, 1841; d. there, May 6, 1910. King of Great Britain and Ireland and emperor of India from 1901 to 1910; eldest son of Victoria. He married Princess Alexandria, daughter of Christian IX of Denmark, on March 10, 1863. In 1860 he made a tour of the U.S. and Canada, in 1862 of Egypt and Palestine, and in 1875–76 of British India, the latter visit laying the groundwork for Victoria's assumption (1877) of the title Empress of India. As king he fostered international agreements with France, Germany, Italy, Portugal, and Spain. He ascended the throne as Edward VII on Jan. 22, 1901. He died during the parliamentary crisis of 1910–11 over the veto power of the House of Lords, in which dispute he preserved a neutral stand. Edward was a popular king, and his genial taste for good food, wine, and other attributes of a gay life (including love affairs; he appeared as a witness not only in a divorce suit but in a libel suit in connection with an alleged instance of cheating in gambling) probably actually added to the affection in which he was held by most of his subjects (after the austerity of Victoria, his escapades had the effect of reminding the world that an English ruler could be, so to speak, more human without thereby becoming less royal). His horses won the Derby several times and his racing yacht was one of the best of the times. As Albert Edward, Prince of Wales, he was an ambassador of good will both internationally and domestically, making it evident that the king would participate in national life without necessarily attempting to direct political matters.

Edward VIII (of *England*). [Full name, **Edward Albert Christian George Andrew Patrick David**; known after his abdication as Duke of Windsor.] b. at White Lodge, Richmond, England, June 23, 1894—. King of England from Jan. 20 to Dec. 10, 1936 (324 days). The eldest son of King George V and Mary (Victoria Mary of Teck), he became Prince of Wales in 1911, making his investiture speech at Caernarvon Castle in Welsh. During World War I he served with the British Expeditionary Forces in France, Flanders, and Italy. Following the war, his travels in Canada, the U.S., Australia, the West Indies, South Africa, and Latin America made him a familiar figure in the British Empire and the world at large. On the death of George V in 1936 he succeeded to the throne, still unmarried. Later that year it became known that he was planning to marry Mrs. Wallis Warfield Simpson, an American divorcee who was about to divorce her second husband. The proposed marriage was met with opposition from the cabinet, led by the Conservative Stanley Baldwin. The king insisting on his right to choose a wife and the king's ministers insisting that the king must accede to his subjects' wishes, a constitutional crisis developed that was resolved only with Edward's abdication. In a speech that has since become famous he declared that he could not "carry on the heavy burden of responsibility and discharge the duties of King as I would wish to do without the help and support of the woman I love." The abdication speech, delivered over the air on Dec. 11, has been many times reprinted in full, or quoted in part. He was succeeded by his brother, the duke of York, as George VI. On June 3, 1937 Edward, now known as Duke of Windsor, married Mrs. Simpson in France. He served for a short time in France in World War II and then was appointed governor of the Bahama Islands, a post he held from 1940 to 1945. Students of his character have called attention to apparent contradictions in his acts and utterances. His sympathies with miners and with other workers, and with the unemployed, are well known, but one of his best friends is Charles Bedaux, associated with a "speed-up" system that is highly unpopular with labor groups in England and elsewhere. When he left England in 1937 he found a welcome in the home of his friend, Baron Rothschild, but when he went to Germany, "to study labor conditions," he called on, and posed with, Hitler, Goebbels, and Goering. His story, told by himself, has been serialized and published in book form in *A King's Story* (1951).

Edward I. Play by George Peele, printed in 1593.

Edward II. Tragedy by Christopher Marlowe, entered on the Stationers' Register on July 6, 1593. It was probably written c1590, but was not published till 1598, after Marlowe's death.

Edward III. Tragedy attributed to Christopher Marlowe, founded on Holinshed's *Chronicle,* acted in 1590. It was entered on the Stationers' Register in 1595, was printed anonymously in 1596, and at one time was attributed to Shakespeare.

Edward IV. Play by John Heywood, printed in 1600.

Edward, Lake. [Also: **Edward Nyanza**; former name, **Albert Edward Nyanza**; native name, **Muta Nzige.**] Lake in E central Africa on the border between Uganda and the Belgian Congo, S of Lake Albert, and connected with the latter by the Semliki River. It was discovered by Henry M. Stanley in 1877 and revisited by him in 1888–89. Until 1909 it was known as Albert Edward Nyanza (it was named for the Prince of Wales, Albert Edward, and became Lake Edward when he ascended the throne as Edward VII). Area, 830 sq. mi.

Edward, Mount. Highest point in the Sweeney Mountains, in Antarctica, lying in the center of the group, which rises above the Joerg Plateau, in ab. 75°48′ S., 67°40′ W.

Edward Augustus (ô.gus′tus), Prince. [Additional title, Duke of **Kent and Strathern.**] b. at Buckingham House, London, Nov. 2. 1767; d. at Sidmouth, Devonshire, England, Jan. 23, 1820. Fourth son of George III of England, and father of Queen Victoria. On May 28, 1818, he married Victoria Mary Louisa, widow of Emich Charles, prince of Leiningen-Dachsburg-Hardenburg. Their only child, Victoria, was born at Kensington Palace, on May 24, 1819.

Edward Casaubon (ką.sô′bǫn), **Rev.** See **Casaubon, Rev. Edward.**

Edward Cuttle (kut′l), **Captain.** See **Cuttle, Captain Edward.**

Edwardes (ed′wąrdz), Sir **Herbert Benjamin.** b. at Frodesley, Shropshire, England, Nov. 12, 1819; d. at London, Dec. 23, 1868. English general and author, distinguished in the Sikh wars in India (1845–49). He published *A Year on the Punjab Frontier* (1851) and other works.

Edward Fairfax Rochester (fãr′faks roch′es″tėr, -ęs.tėr). See **Rochester, Edward Fairfax.**

Edward Glendinning (glen.din′ing). See **Glendinning, Edward.**

Edwardians (ed.wär′di.ąnz), **The.** Novel of English life in the time of Edward VII, by V. Sackville-West, published in 1930.

Edward Longshanks (lông′shangks). See **Edward I** (of *England*).

Edward Murdstone (mėrd′stōn, -stǫn). See **Murdstone, Edward.**

Edward II of Caernarvon (or **Carnarvon**) (kär.när′vǫn). See **Edward II** (of *England*).

Edward of Windsor (win′zǫr). See **Edward III** (of *England*).

Edward of Woodstock (wůd′stok). See **Edward,** the Black Prince (1330–76).

Edward VII Peninsula. [Also, **King Edward VII Land.**] Peninsula of the mainland of Antarctica, extending NW from Marie Byrd Land, E of the Ross Shelf Ice, in ab. lat. 77°45′ S. and long. 156° W. Length, ab. 100 mi.

Edwards (ed′wąrdz), **Albert.** Pseudonym of **Bullard, Arthur.**

Edwards, Alfred George. b. at Llanymawddwy, Wales, Nov. 2, 1848; d. at St. Asaph, Wales, July 22, 1937. Welsh clergyman of the Anglican church and first primate (1920–34) of the Church of Wales. He received an M.A. from Oxford, entered the church in 1885, and was appointed (1889) Bishop of St. Asaph. He served as headmaster and headwarden of the College of Llandovery for 10 years, and retired in 1934.

Edwards, Amelia Ann Blandford. b. at London, 1831; d. at Weston-super-Mare, Somersetshire, England, April 15, 1892. English novelist and Egyptologist; cousin of Matilda Barbara Betham-Edwards (1836–1919). She showed talent for drawing and music, and in 1853 began to write for periodicals. After 1880 she devoted herself to archaeological studies. In 1883 she became the honorary secretary of the Egyptian exploration fund. *A Thousand Miles up the Nile* (1877) was illustrated from her own sketches. She also wrote *A Summary of English History* (1856), *An Abridgment of French History* (1858), and *Pharaohs, Fellahs, and Explorers* (1891).

Edwards, Bryan. b. at Westbury, Wiltshire, England, May 21, 1743; d. at Southampton, England, July 15, 1800. English West India merchant and historian. He lived in Jamaica, finally returning to England in 1792. He established a bank at Southampton, and in 1796 was elected to Parliament. He is best known for his *History of the British Colonies in the West Indies,* of which the first two volumes were published in 1793; later editions were greatly enlarged, the best being that of 1819. His *Historical Survey of St. Domingo,* first published in 1797, is generally appended to the later editions of the *History.*

Edwards, Clarence Ransom. b. at Cleveland, Ohio, Jan. 1, 1860; d. at Boston, Feb. 14, 1931. American army officer. Graduated (1883) from the U.S. Military Academy at West Point; served in War Department as chief (1902–12) of its bureau of insular affairs; promoted to brigadier general (1912) and major general (1921) in regular army; headed (1915–17) U.S. troops in the Panama Canal Zone; after organizing (1917) the 26th division he commanded (1917–18) that group in France; commander (1917, 1918–20) of the northeastern department; became (1921) major general and head of 1st corps area headquarters at the Boston army base and served there until his retirement (1922).

Edwards, Eli. Pseudonym of **McKay, Claude.**

Edwards, George. b. at Stratford, Essex, England, April 3, 1693; d. at Plaistow, near London, July 23, 1773. English naturalist. He published a *History of Birds* (1745–51), *Gleanings of Natural History* (1758–64; 3 vols. additional to the *History*), and others.

Edwards, George Wharton. b. at Fair Haven (now part of New Haven), Conn., 1859; d. at Greenwich, Conn., 1950. American portrait and mural painter, and author. He was educated at Antwerp and Paris, studying under Eugène Féyén. From 1898 to 1903 he was art director for *Collier's* Magazine, and later was manager (1904–12) of the art department of the American Bank Note Company. He won medals at Boston in 1884 and 1890, for drawings, and repeated his success with paintings at the 1901 Buffalo Exposition and the 1902 South Carolina Exposition, also winning, in the latter year, honors at the Barcelona Exposition in Spain. His mural decoration *Henrik Hudson* is at the U.S. Military Academy. He was made a chevalier of the French Legion of Honor (1925), of the Belgian Order of the Crown and the Spanish Order of Isabella the Catholic (both 1927), and of the Royal Order of the Crown of Italy (1929). In 1920 he was awarded a medal of the Order of the King of Belgium, the honor being conferred by the king, and he was made a member of the National Academy of Design in 1930. He wrote *Thumbnail Sketches* (1886), *P'tit Matinic Monotones* (1887), *Break o' Day and Other Stories* (1889), *Holland of Today* (1909), *Brittany and the Bretons* (1910), *Some Old Flemish Towns* (1911), *Marken and Its People* (1912), *The Forest of Arden* (1914), *Vanished Towers and Chimes of Flanders* (1916), *Vanished Halls and Cathedrals of France* (1917), *Alsace-Lorraine* (1918), and *Belgium, Old and New* (1920). He illustrated Oliver Wendell Holmes's *Last Leaf* (1885), Austin Dobson's *Sun Dial* (1892), Spenser's *Epithalamium* (1895), *Old English Love Songs* (1896), *Old English Ballads* (1897), and R. H. Barham's *Jackdaw of Rheims* (1919). Other travel books that he wrote are *London* (1921), *Paris* (1924), *Spain* (1925), *Rome* (1928), and *Constantinople* (1930).

Edwards, Harry Stillwell. b. at Macon, Ga., April 23, 1855; d. Oct. 22, 1938. American journalist and author. He was assistant editor and editor of the Macon *Telegraph* (1881–87) and of the *Evening News* and *Sunday Times* (1887–88). In 1900 he became postmaster of Macon. Among his publications are *Two Runaways, and Other Stories* (1889), *Sons and Fathers*, for which he was awarded the 10,000-dollar prize in a contest sponsored by the Chicago *Record* (1895), *The Marbeau Cousins* (1898), *His Defense, and Other Stories* (1899), *Fifth Dimension* (1912), and *Little Legends of the Land* (1930).

Edwards, Henry Waggaman. b. at New Haven, Conn., in October, 1779; d. July 22, 1847. American lawyer; son of Pierpont Edwards (1750–1826) and grandson of Jonathan Edwards (1703–58). He was a U.S. congressman (1819–23), U.S. senator (1823–27), governor of Connecticut (1833–34, 1835–38). He favored abolition of the property qualification for voting, the division of the state into districts for the choice of national representatives, and a measure of governmental control over business interests.

Edwards, John. b. in Stafford County, Va., 1748; d. in Bourbon County, Ky., 1837. American planter and politician in Kentucky. Although twice (1782–83, 1785–86) a member of the Virginia House of Delegates, he favored separation from Virginia and statehood for Kentucky. He was active in framing the Kentucky constitution (1792), was the first U.S. senator (1792–95) from Kentucky, and was thereafter (1796–1800) a member of the Kentucky state senate.

Edwards, Jonathan. b. at East Windsor, Conn., Oct. 5, 1703; d. of smallpox, at Princeton, N.J., March 22, 1758. American theologian, philosopher, metaphysician, and college president. He was the fifth child and the only son of his parents. He was educated at home before he entered Yale at the age of 13, graduating (at the age of 17) at the top of his class. He read Latin at 6, wrote a pamphlet (*The Nature of the Soul*) at 10, a scientific essay (*The Habits of Spiders*) at 12, and at 14 read Locke's *Essay Concerning Human Understanding*, which is ordinarily regarded as a difficult book. After his graduation he spent two additional years at Yale studying theology. In 1722–23, he was pastor of a Presbyterian church at New York. In 1726 he was assistant minister to his grandfather, whose death, two years later, enabled him to become minister of one of the largest and richest churches in all Massachusetts. In July, 1727, he married Sarah Pierrepont, a girl of 17, who became the mother of their 12 children. He had loved her since meeting her four years previously, and his description of her, in a beautiful prose-poem, is one of his best-known and most popular pieces of writing. Its opening lines have been many times quoted: "They say there is a young lady [in New Haven] who is beloved of that Great Being who made and rules the world, and that there are certain seasons in which this Great Being, in some way or other invisible, comes to her and fills her mind with exceeding sweet delight, and that she hardly cares for anything except to meditate on Him. . . . She has a strange sweetness in her mind, and singular purity in her affections; is most just and conscientious in all her conduct; and you could not persuade her to do anything wrong or sinful, if you would give her all the world, lest she should offend this Great Being. . . . She will sometimes go about from place to place, singing sweetly, and seems to be always full of joy and pleasure, and no one knows for what. She loves to be alone, walking in the fields and groves, and seems to have some one invisible always conversing with her." From 1750 until his death he was a missionary to the Indians at Stockbridge, Mass. In the last year of his life, he was elected president of the College of New Jersey (now Princeton University). Appointed on Sept. 26, 1757, he served for less than three months, coming to Princeton early in January, 1758. He wrote *Resolutions* (1722–23), outlining a drastic spiritual program, *A Narrative of Surprising Conversions* (1735), *A Personal Narrative* (1739), describing his own conversion in 1719, *A Treatise Concerning the Religious Affections* (1742–43, 1746), collected sermons, *Qualifications for Full Communion in the Visible Church* (1749), *Of Insects* (1751), *The Great Christian Doctrine of Original Sin Defended* (1758), which claims that man is naturally bad, *History of the Work of Redemption* (1765), an unfinished work, a philosophical discussion of life, heaven, hell, and earth, that its author intended to be a masterpiece, and *The Nature of True Virtue* (1772). *Sinners in the Hands of an Angry God* (1741), a sermon preached at Enfield during "the Great Awakening," is famous for its vivid picture of man hanging over hell. His great work, the one by which he is remembered, is *A Careful and Strict Enquiry into the Modern Prevailing Notions of that Freedom of the Will which is Supposed to be Essential to Moral Agency, Virtue and Vice, Reward and Punishment, Praise and Blame* (1754), regarded as one of the greatest philosophical works written in America, as a masterpiece of logical reasoning, as the product of a tremendous intellect, and as one of the first American works to attract European attention. Edwards has been called "the greatest single figure produced by Puritanism and Calvinism," "the greatest American mind of the Colonial Period," "the most saintly American that ever lived," "the intellectual flower of New England Puritanism," and "one of the finest minds ever developed on the American continent." He has been compared to Saint Francis of Assisi, and as a mystic he has been contrasted with the practical Franklin.

Edwards, Jonathan. [Called **the Younger.**] b. at Northampton, Mass., May 26, 1745; d. at Schenectady, N.Y., Aug. 1, 1801. American Congregational clergyman; son of Jonathan Edwards (1703–58). He was president of Union College at Schenectady from 1799 to 1801.

Edwards, Justin. b. at Westhampton, Mass., April 25, 1787; d. at Virginia Springs, Va., July 23, 1853. American clergyman, author of various tracts on temperance, and other works.

Edwards, Matilda Barbara Betham-. See **Betham-Edwards, Matilda Barbara.**

Edwards, Ninian. b. in Montgomery County, Md., March 17, 1775; d. at Belleville, Ill., July 20, 1833. American lawyer and politician; nephew of John Edwards (1748–1837). He practiced law (1795 *et seq.*) in Kentucky, and was appointed (1807) chief justice of the Kentucky court of appeals. He served as governor (1809–18) of the Illinois Territory until it became a state and thereafter as U.S. senator (1818–24) from Illinois and governor (1826–30) of Illinois.

Edwards, Ninian Wirt. b. at Frankfort, Ky., April 15, 1809; d. Sept. 2, 1889. American lawyer, first superintendent of public instruction (1854–57) of Illinois; son of Ninian Edwards (1775–1833). He was attorney-general (1834–35) of Illinois and served in the state legislature as a representative (1836–40, 1848–51) and as a state senator (1844–48). As superintendent of public instruction, he secured passage (1855) of a school law which laid the basis for the state's school system. He was a friend of Abraham Lincoln; his wife's sister, Mary Todd, met (1839) Lincoln at Edwards's house, where they were eventually married. Author of *History of Illinois from 1778 to 1883 and Life and Times of Ninian Edwards* (1870).

Edwards, Pierpont. b. at Northampton, Mass., April 8, 1750; d. April 5, 1826. American lawyer and judge; son of Jonathan Edwards (1703–58). He practiced law (1771 *et seq.*) at New Haven, Conn., served (1777, 1784–85, 1787–90) in the Connecticut state legislature, and was a delegate (1787–88) to the Constitutional Convention. An early Jeffersonian Republican, he was a leader of that party in his state, and a member (1818) of the Connecticut constitutional convention which drafted the new state constitution. As judge (1806–26) of the Connecticut district court, he presided over the trials of clergymen and editors accused of libeling President Jefferson and the administration (although his jurisdiction was finally declared invalid on constitutional grounds by the Supreme Court).

Edwards, Richard. b. in Somersetshire, England, c1523; d. Oct. 31, 1566. English dramatist. In 1561 he was appointed master of the Children of the Chapel. He wrote a drama, *Damon and Pythias* (1571; reprinted by Dodsley), and a number of poems, some of which appeared in *The Paradyse of Daynty Devises* (1576).

Edwards Bello (ād.wärdz′ bā′yō), **Joaquín.** b. at Valparaíso, Chile, May 10, 1887—. Chilean journalist, editor (1920 *et seq.*) of *La Nación* at Santiago. His sketches of his countrymen at home and abroad, especially of the common man, are noted for their realism. Author of *El Roto* (1920), *El Chileno en Madrid* (1928), and others.

Edwards v. California, 314 U.S. 160 (1941) (ed′wạrdz; kal.i.fôr′nyạ). Unanimous decision of the U.S. Supreme Court which invalidated a California law aimed at excluding paupers or indigent persons from the state. Justice James J. Byrnes, in delivering the court's opinion, declared that the California statute set up "an unconstitutional barrier" to interstate commerce. Two concurring opinions based the right of migration upon the privileges and immunities clause of the Constitution.

Edwardsville (ed′wạrdz.vil). City in SW Illinois, county seat of Madison County, ab. 17 mi. NE of East St. Louis: coal-mining community. It was platted in 1813 and named for Ninian Edwards, governor (1809–18) of Illinois Territory. 8,776 (1950).

Edwardsville. Borough in E Pennsylvania, in Luzerne County, ab. 3 mi. N of Wilkes-Barre, in an anthracite coal area. It was incorporated in 1884. Pop. 6,686 (1950).

Edward the Black Prince (ed′wạrd). See **Edward** (1330–76).

Edward the Confessor. See **Edward** or **Eadward** (c1004–1066).

Edward the Elder. See **Edward** or **Eadward** or **Eadweard** (d. 924).

Edward the Martyr. See **Edward** or **Eadward** (963–978).

Edward the Peacemaker. See **Edward VII** (of *England*).

Edwin or **Eadwine** or **Eadwin** (ed′win). b. probably in 585; d. 633. King of Northumbria (617–633); son of King Ælla of Deira. With the help of Redwald, king of East Anglia, he overcame Ethelfrith of Bernicia, who attempted to keep him from his throne, and when Redwald died inherited his lands too. He was the fifth Bretwalda (ruler of the British), and his overlordship extended over all seven kingdoms of Teutonic Britain except Kent. He was defeated and slain in the battle of Heathfield in 633 by the rebellious Mercians under Penda in alliance with Cadwallon of Wales. During his reign Christianity was introduced into Northumbria, Edwin being baptized in 627. He established Paulinus as bishop of York.

Edwin and Angelina (an.jẹ.lī′nạ). Ballad by Oliver Goldsmith, privately printed originally for the countess of Northumberland. The ballad was first published in *The Vicar of Wakefield*, and is also called "The Hermit."

Edwin and Angelina. Opera by Victor Pelissier, with a libretto by Elihu H. Smith, first performed at New York on Dec. 19, 1796. Although its production followed by eight months that of Benjamin Carr's *The Archers*, it was composed at an earlier date than the latter, and thus has a claim to being the first American opera.

Edwin and Emma (em′ạ). Ballad by David Mallet, written in 1760.

Edwin Clayhanger (klā′hang.ėr). See **Clayhanger.**

Edwy (ed′wi) or **Eadwig** (ad′wēy′). [Called **Edwy the Fair.**] b. c940; d. 959. Son of Edmund I and Ælfgifu. He became king of Wessex in 955, succeeding his uncle Edred. When at his coronation feast he retired to the company of his intended wife and her mother, his nobles grew angry and an open fight was prevented only when Saint Dunstan convinced Edwy that he must return to the table. In 957 he exiled Dunstan for his part in the affair. That year Mercia and Northumbria rebelled and chose Edgar as king, but Edwy died in 959 before fighting took place.

Eeckeren (āk′ẹ.rẹn). See **Ekeren.**

Eeckhout (āk′hout) or **Eckhout** (ek′hout), **Gerbrand van den.** b. at Amsterdam, Netherlands, Aug. 19, 1621; d. there, Sept. 29, 1674. Dutch painter, a pupil of Rembrandt.

Eecloo (āk′lō). See **Eekloo.**

Eeden (ā′dẹn), **Frederik van.** b. 1860; d. 1932. Dutch novelist, poet, playwright, and essayist. He attacked naturalism to promote idealistic conceptions of art. He tried to realize Tolstoyan and communistic theories in his colony "Walden" near Bussum (influenced by Thoreau), but the experiment was a failure; in connection with this colony he made a lecture tour of the U.S. in 1908. He was converted to Roman Catholicism in 1922. His first novel, *De Kleine Johannes* (Eng. trans., *Little Johannes*, 1885), a symbolic fairy tale, contrasted sharply with his psychoanalytic novels, such as *Van de koele meren des doods* (1900; Eng. trans., *The Deeps of Deliverance*) and *De Nachtbruid* (1909; Eng. trans., *The Bride of Dreams*). He wrote simple nostalgic verse (*Ellen*, 1891) as well as philosophic poetry typified by *Het Lied van schijn en wezen* (The Song of Appearance and Essence, 3 vols., 1895–1922). His dramatic poetry included *De Broeders, tragedie van 't Recht* (The Brothers, Tragedy of Justice, 1894), on a Faustian theme, and *Lioba* (1897). Other plays are *Don Torribio* (1887; Eng. trans., *The King's Dream*), *Ysbrand* (1908; trans. into English), *Het Beloofde Land* (The Promised Country, 1909), and *'t Paleis van Circe* (1910), all more or less satires on the failure of his reform experiment. In reaction to World War I he wrote a successful historical play on human and divine justice, *De Heks van Haarlem* (The Witch of Haarlem, 1915). English translations of his work can also be found in *Coming After*, by A. J. Barnouw, and *Flowers From a Foreign Garden*, by A. L. Snell.

Eekhoud (āk′hout), **Georges.** b. at Amsterdam, Netherlands, May 27, 1854; d. at Brussels, Belgium, May 28, 1927. Flemish novelist and poet. He wrote realistic portrayals of Flemish life. His books of poetry include *Myrtes et cyprès* (1876), *Zigzags poétiques* (1877), and *Les Pittoresques* (1879). Among his novels are *Kees Dvorik* (1883), *Les Milices de Saint-François* (1886), *La Nouvelle Carthage* (1888), *Le Cycle patibulaire* (1891), *La Faneuse d'amour* (1900), and *Les Libertins d'Anvers* (1913).

Eekloo (āk′lō). [Also, **Eecloo.**] Town in NW Belgium, in the province of East Flanders, ab. 12 mi. NW of Ghent, connected by canals with Ghent and with Zeebrugge. It has cotton, linen, and woolen textile manufactures. 16,903 (1947).

Eesti (ās′tē) or **Eestimaa** (ās′tē.mä). Estonian name of **Estonia.**

Efate (e.fä′te). [Also: **Sandwich Island, Vaté, Vati.**] One of the southern islands of the New Hebrides condominium, Pacific Ocean. It possesses the two finest harbors in the New Hebrides group. Length, 26 mi.; width, 14 mi.; pop. ab. 2,000.

Efe (ā′fā). [Also: **Efeh** (ā′fe), **Ifi.**] One of the eastern pygmy groups of C Africa, inhabiting the forests of NE Belgian Congo. They speak a Sudanic language.

Effen (ef′ẹn), **Justus van.** b. at Utrecht, Netherlands, 1684; d. at 's Hertogenbosch, Netherlands, 1735. Dutch journalist, translator, and diplomat. He was educated at the universities of Utrecht and Leiden, and taught the sons of Dutch noblemen. He obtained his knowledge of English life and manners in 1715–16 and again in 1727–28, when he was at London as secretary of the Dutch embassy. In 1711 he began to publish a weekly periodical in French, the language he usually wrote, called *Le Misanthrope*, which was an imitation of the *Spectator* papers of Addison and Steele, and from 1731 until his death he wrote another series of periodical essays, the *Hollandsche Spectator*, again imitating, with some degree of success, the style of the aforenamed famous English authors. From 1715 to 1718 he was the chief contributor to a review, the *Journal Littéraire*, published at The Hague. He translated *Robinson Crusoe* and Swift's *Tale of a Tub* into French, and was praised for his rendering. His second imitation of the *Spectator* is the only work he wrote in his native tongue, and it is considered his best.

Effie Deans (ef′i dēnz). See **Deans, Effie** (or **Euphemia**).

Effingham (ef′ing.ham). City in E Illinois, county seat of Effingham County, in a dairying and farming region. 6,892 (1950).

Effingham (ef′ing.ham, -ạm). Surname of characters in *Homeward Bound* (1838), *Home as Found* (1838), and other novels by James Fenimore Cooper.

Effingham (ef′ing.ạm), Earl of. Title held by various members of the **Howard** family.

Efik (ā′fēk). [Also, **Fi.**] Subgroup of the Semi-Bantu-speaking Ibibio peoples of W Africa, inhabiting SE Nigeria in the neighborhood of Calabar. Their population is estimated at ab. 30,000 (by P. A. Talbot, *The Peoples of Southern Nigeria*, 1926). With the Efik proper are included three related subgroups, the Effiatt, Odott, and Uwett.

Efros (ef′ros), **Israel Isaac.** b. in the Ukraine, Russia, 1891—. Jewish Semitic scholar, rabbi, and poet. He arrived in the U.S. in 1906, was graduated (Ph.D.) from Columbia, and was ordained (1915) to the rabbinate at the Jewish Theological Seminary. He was a founder (1918) of the Baltimore Hebrew College and Teachers Training School, on whose faculty he served until 1928, lecturer (1928 *et seq.*) and head (1934–40) of the Semitics department at the University of Buffalo. In 1940 he became associate professor at Hunter College, New York. He is the author of *Space in Medieval Jewish Philosophy* (1917), *Philosophical Terms in the More Nebukim* (1924), and others.

Efutu (e.fö′tö). [Also, **Fetou.**] One of the Sudanic-speaking Akan peoples of W Africa, inhabiting S Gold Coast, between Winneba and Accra.

Ega (ā′gạ). Former name of **Tefé,** Brazil.

Egadi Islands (eg′ạ.di). [Italian, **Isole Egadi;** ancient names, **Aegates, Aegadian Isles.**] Group of small islands W of Sicily, belonging to the province of Trapani. The chief islands are Favignana, Marèttimo, Levanzo, and Formica. Tuna fishing is an important occupation. The Romans defeated the Carthaginians in a naval battle near the islands in 241 B.C. Area, ab. 15 sq. mi.; pop. ab. 7,000.

Égalité (ā.gȧ.lē.tā), **Philippe.** Name given during the French Revolution to Louis Philippe Joseph, Duc d'Orléans.

Egan (ē′gạn). Unincorporated community in NW Georgia, in Fulton County near Atlanta. Under the new urban definition established for use in the 1950 census it was counted with adjoining urban areas. The last official enumeration was 3,032 (1940).

Egan, Maurice Francis. b. at Philadelphia, May 24, 1852; d. Jan. 15, 1924. American author and diplomat, envoy extraordinary and minister plenipotentiary to Denmark (1907 *et seq.*), important in the purchase (1916) of the Virgin Islands. He was editor of *The Freeman's Journal* (1881–88), professor of English literature at the University of Notre Dame (1889–95), and professor of the English language and literature in the Catholic University at Washington, D.C. (1895–1907). His works include *Preludes* (1880), *Songs and Sonnets* (1892), *The Flower of the Flock* (1894), *The Chatelaine of the Roses* (1897), *From the Land of St. Lawrence* (1898), *The Leopard of Lancianus* (1898), *The Dream of Gerontius* (1903), *St. Martin's Summer* (1905), *The Ghost in Hamlet, and Other Essays* (1906), *The Wiles of Sexton Maginnis* (1909), *Everybody's Saint Francis* (1912), and others.

Egan, Patrick. b. at Ballymahon, Ireland, Aug. 13, 1841; d. at New York, Sept. 30, 1919. American politician, diplomat, and one-time Irish nationalist. He helped organize (1869) the Home Rule League and was named (1879), with Charles Parnell and Thomas Brennan, to the Executive Council of the Irish National Land League, serving as treasurer and directing the entire anti-British movement until, threatened with arrest, he sailed (1883) to the U.S. A founder (1883) of the Irish National League of America and its president for two years (1884–86), he proved (1889) himself and Parnell innocent of complicity in the Phoenix Park murders. As an American, he is best remembered as minister (1889 *et seq.*) to Chile.

Egan, Pierce. b. at London, 1772; d. there, Aug. 3, 1849. English writer on sports; father of Pierce Egan (1814–80). He was the author of a monthly serial, *Boxiana; or Sketches of modern Pugilism* (1818–24), and of *Life in London* (1821), a serial illustrated by George and Isaac R. Cruikshank.

Egan, Pierce. b. at London, 1814; d. July 6, 1880. English novelist and artist; son of Pierce Egan (1772–1849). He wrote *Wat Tyler* (1851), *Paul Jones* (1842), *The Snake in the Grass* (1858), and other novels.

Egaña (ā.gä′nyä), **Juan.** b. at Lima, Peru, 1769; d. at Santiago, Chile, April 13, 1836. Chilean jurist, statesman, and author. A lawyer at Santiago, he took an active part in the revolution of 1810, and was a leading spirit in the first Chilean congress. He was imprisoned by the Spaniards in 1814 at Juan Fernández, Chile, was released in 1817, and shortly after was again a member of the Chilean congress and a planner of the constitution. Among his numerous published works, which have been collected in 10 volumes, are *Tratados jurídicos, Descripción geológica y mineralógica de Chile, Memorias políticas,* and *Tratado de educación.*

Egba (eg′bä). Subgroup of the Sudanic-speaking Yoruba of W Africa, inhabiting SW Nigeria, N of Lagos. Their population is estimated at ab. 190,000 (by P. A. Talbot, *The Peoples of Southern Nigeria,* 1926). Their king is the Alake of Abeokuta, which is their capital city.

Egbado (eg.bä′dō). Subgroup of the Sudanic-speaking Yoruba of W Africa, inhabiting SW Nigeria, W of Abeokuta. Their population is estimated at ab. 30,000 (by P. A. Talbot, *The Peoples of Southern Nigeria,* 1926).

Egbert (eg′bėrt) or **Ecgberht** (ej′berċht). b. c775; d. 839. King of Wessex (802–839). He received the submission of Mercia and Northumberland in 829, and became lord of all England. He was probably the son of a Kentish underking who was exiled from England to the court of Charlemagne by King Offa of Mercia and King Beorhtric of Kent. In 802 he returned and ascended the throne of Wessex. In 815 he attacked the West Welsh in Cornwall, and in 825 defeated Beornwulf of Mercia at Ellandum, thus obtaining the submission of Kent, Surrey, Sussex, and Essex. Soon after the East Anglians acknowledged him, and in 829 Mercia and Northumbria submitted, thus making him overlord of all the English. He engaged in battles with the Danes, and in 838 beat them and the West Welsh, their British allies, in Cornwall. He was succeeded by his son Ethelwulf.

Egede (ā′gẹ.dẹ), **Hans.** [Called the **Apostle of Greenland.**] b. at Senjen, Norway, Jan. 31, 1686; d. on the island of Falster, Denmark, Nov. 5, 1758. Norwegian missionary. He was stationed (1721–36) among the Eskimos of Greenland, where he founded (1721) the colony of Godthaab. He became (1740) superintendent of the Greenland mission, and resided many years at Copenhagen. He wrote several works on the history of Greenland.

Egede, Paul. b. at Vaagen, Norway, 1708; d. at Copenhagen, 1789. Norwegian missionary; son of Hans Egede. He was stationed (1734–40) in Greenland, succeeded his father as superintendent of the Greenland mission, and lived many years in Copenhagen. He completed a translation, begun by his father, of the New Testament into the Eskimo language. He also compiled a catechism and a ritual in that language.

Egedesminde (ā′gẹ.ᴛʜẹs.min″ẹ). [Native name, **Ausiait.**] Settlement in W Greenland, on a small low island ab.

42 mi. S of Godhavn. It was founded in 1759 as a Danish mission station. 712 (1945).

Eger (e′ger). [German, **Erlau.**] City in NE Hungary, situated between Budapest and Miskolc. It is the seat of an archbishopric, has a cathedral and a number of other noteworthy sacred and secular buildings, mainly from the 18th century. The Servitan Church was formerly a Turkish mosque; the minaret is preserved. There are theological and law academies, a library, and a museum of art. Eger is a commercial center, has sugar and cement factories, and is noted for its excellent red wines. The city was destroyed by the Mongols in 1242, defended against the Turks in 1552, but conquered by them in 1596. It fell to the Hapsburgs in 1687. Pop. 29,428 (1948).

Eger (ā′gėr). German name of **Cheb;** also of the **Ohře.**

Egerbrunnen (ā′gėr.brůn.e̩n). A German name of **Františkovy Lázně.**

Egerdir Lake (e.ger.dir′). See **Eğridir Lake.**

Egeri (ā′ge̩.rē). See **Ägeri.**

Egeria (ē̩.jir′i.a̩). [Also, **Aegeria.**] In Roman mythology, one of the Camenae, or nymphs of springs, by whom Numa was instructed with regard to the forms of worship he was to introduce.

Egeria. [Also, **Aegeria.**] An asteroid (No. 13) discovered at Naples by De Gasparis, Nov. 2, 1850.

Egerton (ej′ėr.to̩n), **Francis.** [Title: 3rd Duke of **Bridgewater;** called the **"Father of British Inland Navigation."**] b. 1736; d. at London, March 3, 1803. British nobleman; last Duke of Bridgewater, younger son of the first duke by his second wife. He is notable as the projector of a canal from Worsley to Manchester (the first in England throughout its course entirely independent of a natural stream), and of one from Manchester to Liverpool.

Egerton, Francis. [Titles: 1st Earl of **Ellesmere,** Viscount **Brackley;** original surname, **Leveson-Gower.**] b. at London, Jan. 1, 1800; d. there, Feb. 18, 1857. English politician and man of letters; son of George Granville Leveson-Gower, Marquis of Stafford and Duke of Sutherland. He was a member of Parliament (1822–46), a lord of the treasury in 1827, undersecretary of state for the colonies in 1828, chief secretary for Ireland (1828–30), and secretary for war in 1830. He was created Viscount Brackley of Brackley and Earl of Ellesmere of Ellesmere in 1846, and was president of the Royal Asiatic Society in 1849 and of the Royal Geographical Society in 1854–55. He wrote *Mediterranean Sketches* (1843) and others.

Egerton, Francis Henry. [Title, 8th Earl of **Bridgewater.**] b. Nov. 11, 1756; d. at Paris, Feb. 11, 1829. English nobleman and clergyman, founder, by his will, of the Bridgewater Treatises.

Egerton, Hugh Edward. b. at London, April 19, 1855; d. at Oxford, England, May 21, 1927. English historian, a pioneer in the field of colonial history, first occupant of the chair of colonial history at Oxford founded (1905) by Alfred Beit. He was the author of *Short History of British Colonial Policy* (1897), *Federation and Union within the British Empire* (1911), and *Causes and Character of the American Revolution* (1923).

Egerton, John. [Title, 1st Earl of **Bridgewater.**] b. 1579; d. at Ashridge, England, Dec. 4, 1649. English politician; son of Sir Thomas Egerton. Served in Essex's Irish expedition (1599); created (1603) a Knight of the Bath by James I; created Earl of Bridgewater (1617); privy councilor (1626). He became lord lieutenant of Wales in 1631 (it was his taking up of this appointment that occasioned the writing and performance (1634) of Milton's *Comus* at Ludlow Castle).

Egerton, John. [Title, 2nd Earl of **Bridgewater.**] b. 1622; d. in England, Oct. 26, 1686. English politician; son of John Egerton (1579–1649).

Egerton, John. [Title, 3rd Earl of **Bridgewater.**] b. in England, Nov. 9, 1646; d. there, March 19, 1701. English politician; son of John Egerton (1622–86). He was a knight of the shire (1685) and later lord lieutenant of Buckinghamshire, but was removed (1687) from the latter office by James II for his lack of loyalty. He was reinstated (1688) by William III.

Egerton, Mount. Mountain peak in Antarctica, rising ab. 10 mi. S of Mount Hamilton and ab. 25 mi. W by NW of Cape Douglas, on the W side of the Ross Shelf Ice, in ab. 80°50′ S., 158°25′ E. Elevation, ab. 7,660 ft.

Egerton, Sir **Thomas.** [Titles: Baron **Ellesmere,** Viscount **Brackley.**] b. in Cheshire, England, c1540; d. at London, March 15, 1617. English jurist, lord chancellor of England from 1603 to 1617.

Egestorff (ā′ge̩.shtôrf), **George.** Pseudonym of **Omteda,** Baron **Georg von.**

Egeus (ē̩.jē′us). Father of Hermia in Shakespeare's *Midsummer Night's Dream.*

Egg (eg). See also **Eigg.**

Egg, Augustus Leopold. b. at London, May 2, 1816; d. at Algiers, Algeria, March 26, 1863. English painter of historical and genre scenes.

Egga (eg′a̩). Town in W Africa, in Northern Provinces, Nigeria, on the lower Niger River.

Egge (eg′e̩), **Peter Andreas.** b. at Trondheim, Norway, April 1, 1869—. Norwegian novelist, known for his studies of repressed characters and the effects of small-town suspiciousness, especially in *Jægtvig og hans Gud* (Jaegtvig and his God, 1923), and in *Hansine Solstad* (1925).

Eggers (eg′ėrz), **George William.** b. at Dunkirk, N.Y., Jan. 31, 1883—. American art teacher, writer, lithographer, and water-colorist. He has served as director of several museums and as the head of the art department at the College of the City of New York. He was educated at Pratt Institute, Brooklyn, then traveled in Europe. He taught at Pratt (1905–06), was head of the art department of Chicago Normal College (1906–16), was art editor of the *Rocky Mountain News* and *Webster's New International Dictionary,* and was director of the Art Institute of Chicago (1917–21), the Denver Art Museum (1921–26), and the Worcester, Mass., Art Museum (1926–30). He organized many exhibitions of American art in Europe, exhibited his own water colors in 1932, and is represented in the Art Institute of Chicago, the New York Public Library, and elsewhere. He wrote *George Bellows* and was coauthor of *Teaching of Industrial Arts;* he has also written many articles for art magazines, museum bulletins, and educational journals.

Eggertsville (eg′ėrts.vil). Unincorporated community in W New York, in Erie County near Buffalo. Under the new urban definition established for use in the 1950 census it was counted with adjoining urban areas. The last official enumeration was 5,708 (1940).

Egg Harbor City (eg′ här′bo̩r). City in S New Jersey, in Atlantic County: notable as a center for making wine and grapejuice. It is the site of the Atlantic County Agricultural Society fair grounds. 3,838 (1950).

Eggischhorn (eg′ish.hôrn). Mountain in the Alps, near the head of the Rhone valley, in the canton of Valais, Switzerland. Elevation, ab. 9,625 ft.

Eggleston (eg′l.sto̩n), **Edward.** b. at Vevay, Ind., Dec. 10, 1837; d. at Joshua's Rock, Lake George, N.Y., Sept. 2, 1902. American author; brother of George Cary Eggleston. In 1856 he became a Methodist preacher, and was editor at different times of periodicals such as *The Little Corporal, The Sunday School Teacher,* the New York *Independent,* and *Hearth and Home.* In 1879 he retired from the pastorate of the Church of the Christian Endeavor at Brooklyn, N.Y., and devoted himself entirely to literature. His chief works of fiction are *The Hoosier Schoolmaster* (1871), *The End of the World* (1872), *The Mystery of Metropolisville* (1873), *The Circuit Rider* (1874), *Roxy* (1878), *The Hoosier Schoolboy* (1883), *The Graysons* (1887), *The Faith Doctor* (1891), and *Duffels* (1893). He also wrote *Household History of the United States* (1888), *History of the United States for Schools* (1888), *The Beginners of a Nation* (1896), and *The Transit of Civilization* (1901).

Eggleston, Sir **Frederic William.** b. at Melbourne, Australia, Oct. 17, 1875—. Australian lawyer, politician, publicist, and public servant; knighted in 1941. He was educated at Melbourne and Cambridge universities, and became a member of the bar of the state of Victoria in 1897. He served in the Australian Imperial Forces in World War I, on the staff of the Australian delegation to Versailles in 1919, and as a member of the Victoria legislative assembly from 1920 to 1927; minister of water supply, and railways (1924–26); attorney general and solicitor general (1924–27); chairman of the Australian delegations to the imperial preference conferences of 1927, 1929, and 1936; chairman commonwealth grants committee (1933–41); minister to China (1941–44); minister to the U.S. (1944–46). His chief publications are *Life of George Swinburne* (1931), *State Socialism in Victoria* (1932), and *Search for a Social Philosophy* (1941). He is the editor of and a contributor to several volumes of essays on public affairs.

Eggleston, George Cary. b. at Vevay, Ind., Nov. 26, 1839; d. at New York, April 14, 1911. American journalist and author; brother of Edward Eggleston (1837–1902). He studied at Richmond College, Virginia, and began the practice of law in that state, but abandoned it to enlist in the Confederate army, in which he served throughout the Civil War. Later, at New York, he held editorial positions on various newspapers, among others the *Evening Post* (1875–81), the *Commercial Advertiser* (1884–89), and the *World* (1889–1900). He published many novels and other books, including *A Rebel's Recollections* (1874), *Southern Soldier Stories* (1898), *A Carolina Cavalier* (1901), *Evelyn Byrd* (1904), *A Daughter of the South* (1905), *Two Gentlemen of Virginia* (1908), *Westover of Wanalah* (1910), and *The History of the Confederate War* (2 vols., 1910).

Eggmühl (ek′mül). [Also, **Eckmühl.**] Village in S Germany, in Lower Bavaria, situated on the Grosse Laber River, ab. 13 mi. SE of Regensburg. Here, on April 22, 1809, Napoleon defeated the Austrians under the archduke Charles. For his part in the battle the French marshal Louis Nicolas Davout was created Prince d'Eckmühl.

Egham (eg′ạm). Urban district in SE England, in Surrey, situated on the river Thames ab. 2 mi. W of Staines, ab. 21 mi. W of Waterloo station, London. The district contains Runnymede, where the Magna Charta was signed, on June 15, 1215. Pop. 24,515 (1951).

Egilsson (ā′gils.sôn), **Sveinbjørn.** b. at Innri-Njardrik, Iceland, 1791; d. at Reykjavík, Iceland, Aug. 17, 1852. Icelandic philologist. His chief work is a *Lexicon poëticum antiquae linguae septentrionalis* (1854–60).

Eginhard (ā′gin.härt). See **Einhard.**

Egirdir Lake (e.gir.dir′). See **Eğridir Lake.**

Eglamore (eg′lạ.mōr) or **Eglamour** (-mör), **Sir.** Valiant knight and heroic champion of the Round Table, in the Arthurian cycle of romances. There is a ballad which recounts how he "slew a terrible huge great monstrous dragon."

Eglamour (eg′lạ.mör). In Shakespeare's *Two Gentlemen of Verona*, the agent for Sylvia's escape.

Eglantine (eg′lạn.tīn). In the story of *Valentine and Orson*, a romance of the Charlemagne cycle, the bride of Valentine and daughter of King Pepin.

Eglantine, Madame. In Chaucer's *Prioress's Tale*, the prioress.

> Full well she sang the servicè divine,
> Entunèd in her nose full seemèly.
> And French she spoke full fair and fetisly,
> After the school of Stratford-atte-Bow;
> For French of Paris was to her unknow.

Églantine (dā.gläṅ.tēn), **Philippe François Nazaire Fabre d'.** See **Fabre d'Églantine, Philippe François Nazaire.**

Egleston (eg′l.stọn), **Thomas.** b. at New York, Dec. 9, 1832; d. Jan. 15, 1900. American mineralogist. He was a graduate (1854) of Yale. He submitted (1863) a *Proposed Plan for a School of Mines and Metallurgy in New York City* to the trustees of Columbia College, and the department was opened (1864) as the School of Mines, the first such specialized school in the U.S. Author of *The Metallurgy of Silver, Gold and Mercury in the United States* (2 vols., 1887, 1890).

Egli (eg′lē), **Johann Heinrich.** b. at Seegräben, Switzerland, March 4, 1742; d. at Zurich, Switzerland, Dec. 19, 1810. Swiss composer of church and secular music. He taught music at Zurich.

Eglinton (eg′lin.tọn), **Earl of.** Title held by various members of the **Montgomerie** family.

Eglinton, John. Pseudonym of **Magee, William Kirkpatrick.**

Egloff (eg′lof), **Gustav.** b. at New York, Nov. 10, 1886—. American chemist, notable for his achievements in petroleum chemistry. Research director (1917 *et seq.*) of Universal Oil Products Company, Chicago; influential in developing petroleum-refining industry in China; increased production of high-octane gasoline from crude oil by application of multiple-coil process; manufactured rubber from butane gas. Author of *Earth Oil* (1933), *Isomerization of Pure Hydrocarbons* (1942), *The Physical Constants of Hydrocarbons* (3 vols., 1939, 1940, 1946), and other works.

Eglon (eg′lon). In Old Testament history, a king of the Moabites who captured Jericho and occupied it for 18 years, during which he oppressed the Hebrews and obliged them to pay tribute.

Egmond (eg′mond, -mọnd; Dutch, eċh′mônt). See under **Alkmaar.**

Egmont (eg′mont). Tragedy by Goethe, published in 1788.

Egmont (eg′mont, -mọnt), **Earl of.** Title held by various members of the **Perceval** family.

Egmont (eg′mont; Flemish, eċh′mônt) or **Egmond** (eg′mond), **Lamoral.** [Titles: Count of **Egmont** and Prince of **Gâvre.**] b. at La Hamaide, Hainaut (now part of Belgium), Nov. 18, 1522; d. at Brussels, June 5, 1568. Flemish general and popular hero. He headed the embassy to England that arranged the marriage of Mary Tudor to Philip of Spain (later Philip II). He fought under the emperor Charles V in Algiers, Germany, and France, and led the cavalry for Philip II of Spain at St.-Quentin in 1557 in the victory over the French, and at Gravelines in 1558. The latter victory made an enemy of the duke of Alva, who advised against the battle. He was for a time governor of Flanders and Artois, and was a member of the council of state under the regent, Margaret of Parma. Although a Catholic and a courtier, he opposed the absolute government which Philip II attempted to introduce into the Netherlands under cover of religion. Although he abstained from any overt resistance to Philip, his sovereign, he was treacherously seized by the duke of Alva (Sept. 9, 1567), and executed in company with the Count of Horn after a mockery of a trial by the Council of Blood. The revolt of the Netherlands is usually considered as beginning with Egmont's death.

Egmont, Mount. Extinct volcano in New Zealand, situated in the SW corner of the North Island. It was discovered by Cook on Jan. 13, 1770, and named in honor of Count Egmont. 8,260 ft.

Egoist, The. [Full title: **The Egoist: a Comedy in Narrative.**] Novel by George Meredith, published in 1879. The central character is the vain and selfish Sir Willoughby Patterne, whose cunning exploitation of others to further his purposes finally leads to his own humiliation.

Egoryevsk (yi.gôr′yifsk). See **Yegoryevsk.**

Egremont (eg′rẹ.mont). Former urban district, now a parish and market town, in NW England, in Cumberland, situated on the river Ehen ab. 5 mi. SE of Whitehaven, ab. 208 mi. NW of London by rail. It is an iron-mining center. The ruins of Egremont Castle are W of the town. 6,017 (1931).

Eğridir Lake (eg.ri.dir′). [Also: **Egerdir** (or **Egirdir**) **Lake;** Turkish, **Eğridir Gölü** (gė.lü′).] Lake in the *il* (province or vilayet) of Konya, Turkey, ab. 80 mi. N of the city of Antalya. Length, ab. 30 mi.

Egripo (eg′rē.pô). See **Chalcis.**

Egripo. Turkish name of **Euboea.**

Egripos (eg′rē.pôs). See **Evripos.**

Eguiara y Eguren (ā.gyä′rä ē ā.gö′ren), **Juan José.** b. at Mexico City, c1695; d. there, Jan. 29, 1763. Mexican author. He took orders, and was professor of theology and rector of the University of Mexico. His most important work is the *Biblioteca mexicana*, a bibliographical dictionary, of which only a part was printed (Mexico City, 1755). He also wrote numerous philosophical and theological treatises.

Egypt (ē′jipt). [Arabic, **Misr;** Biblical name, **Mizraim;** Latin, **Aegyptus.**] Country in NE Africa, famous for the great antiquity and former splendor of its civilization. It is bounded by the Mediterranean Sea on the N, and extends S, including the delta and the valley of the Nile River, to the second cataract of the Nile and the border of the Anglo-Egyptian Sudan. On the E it is bounded by Israel, the Gulf of Aqaba, and the Red Sea, and on the W by Libya. It includes the Sinai Peninsula, between the gulfs of Suez and Aqaba. The usual geographical divisions are the Nile valley region from Cairo south, called Upper Egypt, and the delta region, called Lower Egypt. Alexandria is the seaport.

Population, Area, and Political Divisions. The country is administratively divided into five governorships (*muhafzas*) and 15 provinces (*mudirias*). The government is a hereditary monarchy ruled by a king with a parliament consisting of a chamber of deputies and a senate, and with a council of ministers appointed by the king but responsible to the parliament. Capital, Cairo; area, ab. 386,198 sq. mi.; pop. 19,087,304 (1947).

Terrain and Climate. Egypt proper (i.e., the settled area) consists practically of the delta and a narrow strip on each side of the Nile. The soil of this region has been celebrated for its productiveness, resulting from the inundations of the river, and it was long the granary of Rome. The rest of the country is mostly desert, inhabited by nomads. The highest elevations (ab. 8,000 ft.) are in the Sinai Peninsula; mountains near the Red Sea coast reach ab. 6,000 ft., and plateaus elsewhere in the desert regions average ab. 1,500 ft. The climate is semitropical, with moderate cold in the winter and temperatures up to 110° F. in the summer months, high humidity throughout the year but rain only during the winter, and occasional sand storms in the summer.

Industry, Agriculture, and Trade. Egypt's economy is primarily agricultural, although recent years have seen considerable industrial development. The productivity of the Nile valley has been increased by the construction of the great dam at Aswan, completed in 1902; its height was increased in the period 1907–12. Cotton is by far the most important crop, amounting to about half of the nation's agricultural output. Rice, barley, and other cereals, sugar, legumes, flax, peanuts, and citrus fruits are also grown. Fish is exported. Mineral products include phosphates, oil, asbestos, chromite, and limestone. From its large cotton crop, Egypt makes yarns and textiles, the latter on both hand and mechanical looms. Woolen, rayon, and silk yarns and cloth are also made. Other industries include food processing, cigars and cigarettes, chemicals, and leather.

History. The history of ancient Egypt was given by Manetho under 31 dynasties. The dynasties are thus grouped by Breasted: the Old Kingdom (c3400–c2475 B.C.), dynasties I–VI; the Middle Kingdom (c2445–1580), dynasties IX–XVII; the New Kingdom or Empire (1580–1090), dynasties XVIII–XX. The first dynasty was founded by Menes c3400 B.C. During the early dynasties Memphis was the leading city, and in the time of the IVth dynasty occurred the building of the Pyramids (c2900–2800 B.C.). The construction of Lake Moeris and the Labyrinth are assigned to the XIIth dynasty. Thebes now became the center, and later the invasion of the Hyksos occurred (in the XVth dynasty). After a period of confusion and obscurity Egypt was united under the great Theban XVIIIth dynasty, and under this and the XIXth dynasty reached its highest point in extent and in the grandeur of its monuments. Among the great sovereigns were Thutmose III, Seti I, and Rameses II. The "Pharaoh" of the Exodus has frequently been identified with Merneptah or Meneptah of the XIXth dynasty, and the date stated approximately at c1300 B.C., but he is now dated at 1225–1215 B.C. With the next dynasty began the decline of the country's power. There were some revivals of power, and in the 7th and 6th centuries Greek settlements began, but in 527 B.C. Egypt was conquered by Cambyses, and this Persian dynasty ranks as the XXVIIth. From 406 B.C. native rulers again held power, but in 340 B.C. a short-lived Persian dynasty (the XXXIst and last of Manetho) began; this was overthrown in 332 B.C. by Alexander the Great. After his death Egypt was ruled by his general Ptolemy and Ptolemy's successors down to the death of the famous Cleopatra (Cleopatra VII or VI) in 30 B.C., when Augustus annexed it to the Roman Empire. Egypt was an important center of Christianity. In c640 it was conquered by the Saracens, and formed in later times part of the Ommiad and Abbasside empires. The Fatimites ruled it from 909 to 1171, and thereafter the Ayubites until 1250; they were succeeded by the Mamelukes, who in turn were overthrown by the Turks under Selim I in 1517. Egypt was invaded by Napoleon in 1798, but the French were expelled in 1801. In 1806 Mehemet Ali became pasha, and the country developed greatly. A successful war with Turkey was cut short in 1840 by the intervention of the European powers. In 1869 the Suez Canal was opened. From 1879 France and England exercised a joint supervision over the khedive, but a native revolt, begun under Arabi Pasha in 1881 and suppressed by England in 1882, was followed in 1883 by the abolition of the joint control, and the appointment of an English financial adviser. The Mahdists in the Sudan revolted (1881–85), and in spite of the resistance of Gordon at Khartoum and the campaigns of Wolseley and others the provinces S of the second cataract were lost. By the campaigns of 1896–99 the authority of the government was reëstablished. The predominant position of Great Britain was formally recognized by France in the Anglo-French agreement of April, 1904, and various decrees gradually removed all of the restrictions governing the management of finance. In 1914 Egypt was proclaimed a British protectorate, and the late khedive was deposed, to be replaced by Hussein Kamil (of the family of Mehemet Ali) who became sultan of Egypt. The protectorate terminated in 1922 and the sultan became king. Since then Egypt has been an independent state but with treaties of alliance with Great Britain. In 1936 a 20-year treaty was signed between the two nations providing for the withdrawal of all British troops except those needed to protect British interests in the Suez Canal. In 1947, at the request of the Egyptian government, negotiations were undertaken to change the terms of the treaty, and in 1948 Great Britain gave up all her rights in Egypt and withdrew her troops. However, Britain maintained her hold on the Suez Canal, and in 1951–52 fighting broke out between the British army units and Egyptian guerrillas, the Egyptians demanding withdrawal of the foreigners. The crisis deepened to the point where, in 1952, King Farouk was forced to abdicate in favor of his infant son. The resulting regency was strongly nationalistic.

Culture. The population, besides Egyptians and Europeans, includes Armenians, Nubians, Sudanese, Turks, Syrians, and others. The leading religion is Mohammedanism, but there are many Copts, and also other Christians, and Jews. The prevailing language is Arabic. In the 1947 census some 50,000 of the inhabitants were estimated to be nomads. Education is compulsory up to the age of 12; higher education is available in secondary schools, in a number of technical colleges, and in the University of Fuad I (founded 1908) at Cairo and the University of Farouk I (founded 1943) at Alexandria. Both universities are state-supported and coeducational.

Egypt. Diocese of the prefecture of the East, in the later organization of the Roman Empire.

Egypt Conference. Series of informal meetings on the U.S. battleship *Augusta* in February, 1945, between President Roosevelt and various Near Eastern leaders including King Farouk of Egypt, Ibn Saud of Arabia, and Haile Selassie of Ethiopia. No concrete decisions were made, these conferences having been intended by Roosevelt primarily as a gesture and an indication of the feeling on the part of the U.S. that it had a commitment in the Near East.

Egyptian Expedition (ẹ.jip′shạn). Expedition undertaken by the French against Egypt in 1798–1801, with the ultimate object of attacking the British empire in India. It was commanded by Napoleon, sailed from Toulon with 35,000 men May 19, 1798; conquered Malta June 12, 1798; defeated the Mamelukes in the battle of the Pyramids July 21, 1798; captured Cairo July 22, 1798; suffered the loss of its fleet by the victory of Nelson at Abukir Aug. 1, 1798; and in 1799 invaded Syria, but was in the same year repulsed by the Turks and the English at Acre, and retreated to Cairo. In August, 1799, Nạpoleon returned to France, leaving in command Kléber, who was murdered in 1800, and was succeeded by Menou. Menou concluded a treaty with the English at Cairo in 1801, in accordance with which Egypt was restored to the Ottoman Empire, and the French army transported to France by the English fleet.

Egyptian Princess, An. [German, **Ägyptische Königstochter.**] Novel (1864) by Ebers. The scene is laid in Egypt and Persia about 522 B.C.

Egyptian Thief. Thyamis, the lover of Chariclea, referred to in Shakespeare's *Twelfth Night.*

Ehard (ā′härt), **Hans.** b. at Bamberg, Germany, Nov. 10, 1887—. German politician. He served (1919–21, 1923–24) as public prosecutor at Munich, where he helped prosecute Hitler after the Beer Hall Putsch of November, 1923. He was appointed state secretary of the ministry of justice in 1945. A member of the Christian Social Union, he was elected (1947) to the Bavarian diet and became Bavarian minister president in December, 1947. He was elected chairman of the Christian Social Union in May, 1949.

Eheberg (ā′e̜.berk), **Karl Theodor von.** b. at Munich, Germany, Jan. 31, 1855—. German political economist, notable in the field of the science of finance. He served as professor (1882 *et seq.*) at the University of Erlangen. Author of *Finanzwissenschaft* (Science of Public Finance, 1903) and *Die Kriegsfinanzen* (The War Finances, 1917).

Ehecatl (ā.ā.kä′tl). In Aztec religion, the wind god, one of the many forms of Quetzalcoatl.

Ehingen (ā′ing.e̜n). Small town in Württemberg, SW Germany, on the Danube River ab. 15 mi. SW of Ulm.

Ehoue (ā′wā). See **Ewe.**

Ehrenberg (ā′re̜n.berk), **Christian Gottfried.** b. at Delitzsch, Prussia, April 19, 1795; d. at Berlin, June 27, 1876. German naturalist, especially noted for his studies of Infusoria. He wrote *Die Infusionstierchen als vollkommene Organismen* (1838) and *Mikro-Geologie* (1854).

Ehrenberg, Richard. b. at Wolffenbüttel, Germany, Feb. 5, 1857; d. at Rostock, Germany, Dec. 19, 1921. German economist. Originally a banker, he became a professor of economics in 1897, teaching first at the University of Göttingen, and later at Rostock. He did considerable writing on the history of free enterprise, his best-known work being *Das Zeitalter der Fugger* (3rd ed., 1922). He founded (1909) an institute for economic research.

Ehrenberg-Böhlitz (-bė′lits). Town in E Germany, in the *Land* (state) of Saxony, Russian Zone, formerly in the free state of Saxony, situated on the border between Saxony and Saxony-Anhalt, NW of Leipzig: a suburb of Leipzig. It has manufactures of musical instruments (Hupfeld-Zimmermann), and metallurgical and woodenware industries. The population is predominantly Protestant. 10,453 (1946).

Ehrenbreitstein (ā.re̜n.brīt′shtīn). Former town in W Germany, in the *Land* (state) of Rhineland-Palatinate, French Zone, formerly in the Rhine Province, Prussia, situated on the Rhine River opposite Koblenz: noted for its fortress, located on a steep rock above the river. It was taken by the French in 1631, by the Imperialists in 1637, again by the French in 1799. It was modernized in the 19th and 20th centuries, but razed after World War I. In World War II the town was taken by the Allies on March 27, 1945. It is now incorporated into the city of Koblenz.

Ehrenburg (e′re̜n.börk), **Ilya Grigoryevich.** b. at Moscow, 1891—. Russian journalist, novelist, and poet who lived for many years in Western Europe. He began by writing imitative verse, later turning to facile tales which satirized communism and free enterprise alike. In the 1930's he began to picture Soviet life more sympathetically and soon his enthusiasm for it was complete. During World War II he became the most popular Soviet journalist and a semi-official spokesman for the regime. All of his writings, some of which were in verse, were directed to helping the war effort. In 1946 he visited the U.S. and subsequently recorded his unfavorable impressions of that country. Several of his novels, notably *The Fall of Paris* (1943) and *Storm* (1949), a panorama of the recent armed conflict, and some of his war and post-war sketches, are available in English.

Ehrencron-Kidde (ā′re̜n.krōn.kiᴛʜ′e̜), **Astrid.** b. at Copenhagen, Jan. 4, 1871—. Danish novelist; wife of Harald Kidde. Several of her novels are romantic, warmhearted studies of folk types in the Swedish district of Värmland; these include the trilogy *Brødrene Nystad* (1925), *Brødrehuset* (1926), and *Bjærgmandsgaarden* (1927).

Ehrenfeld (ā′re̜n.felt). Commune in W Germany, in the *Land* (state) of North Rhine-Westphalia, British Zone, formerly in the Rhine Province, Prussia: a suburb of Cologne.

Ehrenfels (ā′re̜n.fels), Baron **Christian von.** b. at Rodaun, Austria, June 20, 1859; d. at Lichtenau, Austria, Sept. 8, 1932. Austrian philosopher who served (1896 *et seq.*) as professor at the University of Prague. While at Vienna he published his most important paper, "Über Gestaltqualitäten," (*Vtljsch, f. wiss. Philos.*, 14 (1890) pp. 249–292). This concept of *Gestaltqualität* (form-quality), which anticipated the later school of Gestalt psychology, was a reaction against the then current elementism of W. Wundt. The concept held that form was not a combination of other qualities, but a new quality: a square was not simply a sum of the four lines (the *Fundamente*), but was a new quality that emerged from the foundation (the *Grundlage*) formed by the arrangement of the four lines. He was the author also of *System der Werttheorie* (1897, 1898), *Sexualethik* (1907), *Kosmogonie* (1916), and *Die Religion der Zukunft* (1929).

Ehrenstein (ā′re̜n.shtīn), **Albert.** b. at Vienna, Dec. 22, 1886—. Austrian writer, a typical representative of expressionism in the prose and lyric genres. He was also a translator and essayist.

Ehrhardt (ār′härt), **Heinrich.** b. at Zella-Mehlis, Germany, Nov. 17, 1840; d. there, Nov. 20, 1928. German industrialist. Originally a locksmith, he founded a metal products factory, and in 1901 became an arms manufacturer.

Ehrhardt, Hermann. b. at Diersburg, Germany, Nov. 29, 1881—. German naval officer. After World War I he organized a free corps which took part in the Kapp putsch of 1920; later founded a secret organization, Consul, which was involved in the assassination of both Erzberger and Rathenau. Arrested, he was allowed to escape; continued to plot against the Weimar Republic. In 1933 he joined the Nazi party.

Ehringsdorf Man (ā′ringz.dôrf). See under **Neanderthal Man.**

Ehrismann (ā′ris.män), **Gustav.** b. 1855—. German historian of literature, professor at Greifswald. He is especially known for his *Geschichte der deutschen Literatur bis zum Ausgang des Mittelalters* (1918 *et seq.*) and *Der Geist der deutschen Dichtung im Mittelalter* (1925).

Ehrlich (ār′lich), **Arnold Bogumił.** b. at Włodawa, in what was then Polish Russia, Jan. 15, 1848; d. Nov. 5, 1919. Bible scholar. Studied at Leipzig; came (1878) to U.S. Author of *Mikra ki-Pheschuto* (3 vols., 1899–1901), *Die Psalmen* (1905), and *Randglossen zur hebräischen Bibel* (7 vols., 1908–14), considered today to be outstanding contributions to scholarly Bible interpretations.

Ehrlich, Heinrich. [Full name, **Alfred Heinrich Ehrlich.**] b. at Vienna, Oct. 5, 1822; d. Dec. 29, 1899. Austrian pianist and writer on music. Court pianist at Hanover; professor (1864–72) at the Berlin Stern Conservatorium; composed many piano pieces, such as *Conzertstück in Ungarischer Weise.* Author of *Musikstudien beim Klavierspiel* (1891).

Ehrlich, Paul. b. at Strehlen (Strzelin), in Silesia, March 14, 1854; d. at Homburg, Germany, Aug. 20, 1915. German biochemist. In 1910, he discovered the salvarsan arsenicals, famous pioneer chemotherapeutic agents, formerly of greatest importance in the cure of syphilis. Arsphenamine, number 606 in the series of chemicals tested, was later superseded by the less toxic neosalvarsan. Moreover, he conceived the "lateral chain theory," announced in 1897, which played an important part in the explanation of the facts of immunization, and for which he received half of the 1908 Nobel prize in medicine. He did important work on the staining of microscopical specimens, on the tubercle bacillus, and the like. He was head of the Koch Institute for Infectious Diseases (1890), director of the Institute for Serum Research at Dahlem (1896), which in 1899 became the Institute for Experimental Therapy at Frankfort on the Main, and professor at Frankfort (1914).

Éibar (ā′ʙär). Town in N Spain, in the province of Guipúzcoa, situated in the center of the Basque country, ab. 27 mi. W of San Sebastián: known for its long-established manufacture of arms and steel products. 11,772 (1940).

Eibenstock (ī'bḙn.shtok). Town in E Germany, in the *Land* (state) of Saxony, Russian Zone, formerly in the free state of Saxony, situated in the Erzgebirge, near the Zwickauer Mulde River, ab. 16 mi. SW of Zwickau: summer resort. Before World War II it had manufactures of curtains, lace, and embroidery, which had been introduced in 1775 to aid the starving population, and was noted for its tambour embroidery. It has a school for the textile industry. 8,250 (1946).

Eibergen (ī'ber.ċhḙn). Town in E Netherlands, in the province of Gelderland, situated on the Berkel River near the German border, NE of Arnhem. It has agricultural markets, construction industries, and textile manufactures. 10,257 (1939).

Eibler (ī'blėr), **Joseph Edler von.** See **Eybler** or **Eibler, Joseph Edler von.**

Eichberg (īċh'berk), **Julius.** b. at Düsseldorf, Germany, June 13, 1824; d. at Boston, Jan. 18, 1893. Composer and conductor. He was for some time a professor in the Conservatory at Geneva, Switzerland. In 1857 he went to New York, and in 1859 to Boston, where he was director of the orchestra at the Boston Museum for seven years. In 1867 he established the Boston Conservatory of Music, of which he remained the head until his death. He composed, among other works, four operettas: *The Doctor of Alcantara, The Rose of Tyrol, The Two Cadis,* and *A Night in Rome.*

Eichelberger (ī'kḙl.bėr.gėr), **Robert Lawrence.** b. at Urbana, Ohio, March 9, 1886—. American infantry officer. Graduate (1909) of U.S. Military Academy; served on Mexican border (1911), in Panama (1911–15), in Siberia (1918), and in Far East (1920–21); superintendent (1940–42) of West Point; appointed major general (1941) and lieutenant general (October, 1942); commanded forces in capture (January, 1943) of Buna, New Guinea, and at New Britain; participated (1944–45) in reoccupation of Philippines; commander (1946–49) under MacArthur of Allied and U.S. occupation forces in Japan. Author of *Our Jungle Road to Tokyo* (1950).

Eichelberger, William Snyder. b. at Baltimore, Sept. 18, 1865; d. at Buffalo, Feb. 3, 1951. American astronomer and mathematician. He taught (1890–96) mathematics and astronomy at Wesleyan University, and in 1900 he was appointed professor of mathematics at the U.S. Naval Academy. In 1900, 1901, and 1905, he was a member of U.S. eclipse expeditions to Pinehurst, N.C., Sumatra, and Daroca in Spain. From 1898 to 1929 he was with the U.S. Naval Observatory, and in 1929 he joined the staff of the Eastman Kodak Company at Rochester, N.Y. He was elected to scientific societies in England, Germany, and America. His chief work is *Positions and Proper Motions of 1504 Standard Stars* (1925), and he was coauthor (with Arthur Newton) of *The Orbit of Neptune's Satellite and the Pole of Neptune's Equator* (1926). With F. B. Littell, he compiled a catalogue of 23,521 stars.

Eichendorff (ī'ċhḙn.dôrf), Baron **Joseph von.** b. at Lubowitz (his father's estate), near Ratibor (Racibórz), in Silesia, March 10, 1788; d. at Neisse (Nysa), in Silesia, Nov. 26, 1857. German poet and novelist, considered to have been one of the best lyricists of the Romantic Movement in Germany. While studying at Halle (1805–06) and Heidelberg (1807–08) he associated with one or another of the romanticists. He served in the Wars of Liberation (1813 and 1815) and later was in government service at Breslau, Danzig, and Königsberg. While at Königsberg he interested himself in the restoration of Marienburg, ancient seat of the Teutonic Order. His novel *Ahnung und Gegenwart* (1815) touches on the contemporary Napoleonic war. His story *Aus dem Leben eines Taugenichts* (1826) is considered by many to be the gem of all German romantic narratives. His lyrics have in many cases attained the popularity of folk songs (*In einem kühlen Grunde, O Täler weit und Höhen, Wem Gott will rechte Gunst erweisen, Wer hat dich, du schöner Wald,* and others).

Eichhorn (īċh'hôrn), **Emil.** b. at Röhrsdorf, Germany, Oct. 9, 1863; d. at Berlin, July 26, 1925. German politician. He served (1903–11) as a member of the Reichstag, joined (1918) the newly founded German Communist Party, and was chief (November, 1918–January, 1919) of the Berlin police; his removal by Ebert caused the street fighting in Berlin of January, 1919. He was a Communist member of the Weimar constitutional assembly (1919–20) and of the Reichstag (1920–25).

Eichhorn, Hermann von. b. at Breslau, Feb. 13, 1848; assassinated at Kiev, Russia, July 30, 1918. German general; a grandson, on the maternal side, of the German philosopher F. W. Schelling (1775–1854). He saw service during the campaigns of 1866 and 1870–71. During World War I he fought in the battle of the Masurian lakes (1915) and later that same year took Kovno and Grodno on the Russian front. From 1916 to 1918 he was in command of an army group; he became (1917) a general field marshal. While commanding at Kiev he was assassinated by Russian revolutionists.

Eichhorn, Johann Gottfried. b. at Dörrenzimmern, in Hohenlohe-Öhringen, Germany, Oct. 16, 1752; d. at Göttingen, Germany, June 27, 1827. German scholar, historian, and Biblical critic, professor at Göttingen (1788 *et seq.*). Among his critical works are *Einleitung in das Alte Testament* (1780–83) and *Einleitung in das Neue Testament* (1804–14).

Eichhorn, Karl Friedrich. b. at Jena, Germany, Nov. 20, 1781; d. at Cologne, Germany, July 4, 1854. German jurist; son of Johann Gottfried Eichhorn. His chief work is *Deutsche Staats- und Rechts-geschichte* (1808–23).

Eichler (īċh'lėr), **August Wilhelm.** b. at Neukirchen, in Hesse, Germany, April 22, 1839; d. 1887. German botanist, professor of botany at the universities of Graz, Kiel, and Berlin. He is remembered chiefly for his system of classifying plants and for his descriptive studies of Brazilian plant life. He was trained at the University of Marburg (which is noted for its botanical gardens).

Eichrodt (īċh'rōt), **Ludwig.** [Pseudonym, **Rudolf Rodt.**] b. at Durlach, Germany, Feb. 2, 1827; d. at Lahr, Germany, Feb. 2, 1892. German poet and jurist, best known for the characters Biedermaier and Treuherz, which he created in "Biedermaiers Liederlust," humorous poems published in *Fliegende Blätter*. Like his colleague and friend Viktor Scheffel, he cultivated the humor and sentimentality of academic life. There is a typical selection of his poetry in *Lyrischer Kehraus* (1869). He edited an anthology of light verse under the title *Hortus deliciarum* (1876–80).

Eichstädt (īċh'shtet), Prince of. See **Beauharnais, Eugène de.**

Eichstätt (īċh'shtet). [Also, **Eichstädt.**] Town in S Germany, in the *Land* (state) of Bavaria, American Zone, in the *Regierungsbezirk* (government district) of Middle and Upper Franconia, situated on the Altmühl River ab. 38 mi. S of Nuremberg. It has small metallurgical, knitwear, and paperware industries. It is the seat of a Roman Catholic bishopric; the cathedral is a Gothic building, started in the 11th century and several times altered (the last 1881–1903). Other buildings are mostly in the baroque style; these include the churches of Saint Peter, of the Guardian Angel, and of Notre Dame, and the Benedictine Convent of Saint Walburga. The former episcopal residence is also in the style of the 17th and 18th centuries; the library there has more than 80,000 volumes and manuscripts. Above the town is the Willibaldsburg, a castle in the Rennaissance style, erected in the 17th century according to designs by Elias Holl. Town and bishopric were founded (740) by Saint Boniface, who appointed an English monk, Saint Willibald, as the first bishop. The bishopric, during the Middle Ages one of the wealthiest in Germany, was secularized in 1802, became part of Bavaria in 1805, and was recreated in 1821. Pop. 10,883 (1950).

Eichwald (īċh'vält), **Karl Eduard.** b. at Jelgava, in Courland, July 4 (by the Old Style calendar then still used in Russia), 1795; d. at St. Petersburg, Nov. 10, 1876. Russian naturalist, author of *Zoölogia specialis* (1829–31), *Die Urwelt Russlands* (1840–47), and others.

Eickemeyer (ī'kḙ.mī.ėr), **Rudolf.** b. at Altenbamberg, Bavaria, Germany, Oct. 31, 1831; d. Jan. 23, 1895. American inventor and manufacturer. He came (1850) to America after the failure of the 1848 revolution, and opened (1854) a repair shop at Yonkers, N.Y., where he invented and patented a "whip-stitch" for leather hatbands, a hat-blocking machine (1865), a hat-stretching machine, a machine to pounce hats, and other machinery which revolutionized the hat industry. He also perfected

(1870) a differential gear for reaping and mowing machines. Experimentation in electricity and armatures resulted in his invention of the first symmetrical drum armature, the iron-clad dynamo, and the first direct-connected railway motor. His business was consolidated (1892) with the General Electric Company. He discovered the talents of, and was the first to employ, Charles P. Steinmetz.

Eider (ī'dėr). River in N Germany, in Schleswig-Holstein, which flows into the North Sea ab. 25 mi. N of the mouth of the Elbe. Length, ab. 115 mi.

Eidlitz (īd'lits), **Leopold.** b. at Prague, March 29, 1823; d. at New York, March 22, 1908. American architect. He was educated at the polytechnic school at Prague, and, after a course of study at Vienna, came to America and established himself at New York. He was associated with H. H. Richardson in the construction of the state capitol at Albany and designed a number of churches and other buildings in the Gothic style.

Eidsvoll (āts'vôl). [Also, **Eidsvold.**] Commune in SE Norway, in the *fylke* (county) of Akershus, ab. 40 mi. by road NE of Oslo. It is noted as the locality in which the earliest known Norse council, the Eidsivating, met. In 1814 an elected national assembly met here and drafted the Norwegian constitution of May 17, 1814, which is the basic law of Norway. The assembly building is preserved as a national monument on its original site at Eidsvolls Verk. Pop. ab. 11,000.

Eielsen (ā'ẹl.sẹn), **Elling.** b. at Voss, Norway, Sept. 19, 1804; d. at Chicago, Jan. 10, 1883. American religious leader and lay preacher. He preached widely throughout Norway, Sweden, and Denmark before emigrating (1839) to the U.S. Settling at the Fox River Settlement, La Salle County, Ill., he preached in the surrounding territory and in the "meeting-house" in his own home. He traveled (1859) to the Texas settlements, doing missionary work among the Missouri Potawatomi. He organized (1846) the Evangelical Lutheran Church of America.

Eifel (ī'fẹl). Volcanic mountainous and picturesque region in W Germany, between the valleys of the Rhine, Moselle, and Roer. It is divided into the Schnee-Eifel and the Vorder-Eifel. Elevation of the Hohe Acht, 2,490 ft.

Eiffel (ī'fẹl; French, e.fel), **Alexandre Gustave.** b. at Dijon, France, Dec. 15, 1832; d. at Paris, Dec. 28, 1923. French engineer. He took charge (1858) of constructing the iron bridge over the Garonne River at Bordeaux, and subsequently built the railroad bridge over the Douro at Oporto, Portugal, designed locks for the French Panama Canal Company, constructed the iron framework for Bartholdi's Statue of Liberty, and built the iron span over the Tardes near Montluçon. His most notable engineering feat was the Eiffel Tower, constructed (1887–89) on the Champ-de-Mars at Paris. He also built the Aerodynamics Laboratory (the first of its kind) at Auteuil, later presenting it to the French government, and made important researches in aerodynamics.

Eiffel Tower. Tower, 984 ft. high, built of iron framework, in the Champ-de-Mars at Paris, for the exhibition of 1889. The general form is that of a concave pyramid. The base consists of four inclined piers set at the angles of a square of 336 ft. The piers are connected on the sides of the square by huge arches. After rising ab. 600 ft., the four piers are merged into one. There are three platforms at different heights: the top one, over 900 ft. from the ground, is surrounded by a balcony and covered with a glass pavilion 54 ft. square. Above this rises the lantern, which is fitted for scientific observations.

Eigenbrakel (ī'ċhẹn.brä.kẹl). Flemish name of **Braine-l'Alleud.**

Eigenmann (ī'gẹn.män), **Carl H.** b. at Flehingen, Germany, March 9, 1863; d. in California, April 24, 1927. American ichthyologist. He was professor of zoölogy (1891 *et seq.*) and dean of the graduate school (1908–27) at Indiana University and curator of fishes (1909–18) at the Carnegie Museum, Pittsburgh. With his wife, Rosa Smith, whom he married in 1887, he studied South American catfishes, California fishes, and the blind fish of the Indiana and Kentucky caves. He was the author of *Cave Vertebrates of America, a Study in Degenerative Evolution* (1909), *The Fresh-water Fishes of British Guiana* (1912), *The Fresh-water Fishes of Northwestern South America* (1922), and *The Fresh-water Fishes of Chile* (1927).

Eiger (ī'gėr). One of the highest mountains of the Bernese Oberland, Switzerland, NE of the Jungfrau. Elevation, ab. 13,042 ft.

Eigg (eg). [Also, **Egg.**] Small island in the Inner Hebrides, in N Scotland, in Inverness-shire, lying between the Sound of Sleat on the E and the Sea of the Hebrides on the West, ab. 10 mi. N of Ardnamurchan Point. Length, ab. 5 mi.; greatest width, ab. 4 mi.

Eight, the. See under **Society of Independent Artists.**

Eighteen Hundred and Seven or **Friedland** (frēd'lạnd). Large painting by Meissonier (1876), now in the Metropolitan Museum of Art at New York. It represents a regiment of cuirassiers passing at a gallop in a grain field before Napoleon, who sits on a white horse at the left, attended by his marshals and staff.

Eighteenth Amendment. Amendment to the Constitution of the U.S. which, after failing to secure a two-thirds vote in the House of Representatives in 1914, was submitted to the states in 1917 and ratified in 1919. Its creation was the result of agitation for national prohibition led by temperance organizations. The amendment declared illegal the manufacture, transportation, sale, importation, or exportation of intoxicating beverages and sanctioned Congress and the states with concurrent powers for enforcement. The Volstead Act of 1919 defined the meaning of intoxicating beverages (more than 0.5 percent alcohol) and set up federal enforcement procedures. The act was vetoed by President Wilson but passed over the veto by Congress. The amendment was repealed by the Twenty-first Amendment in 1933.

Eighth of January, The. Play by Richard Penn Smith, produced and published in 1829.

Eight Immortals. [Chinese, **Pa-Hsien.**] Eight characters of Chinese legend, of very ancient origin, but interpreted as rebels against Sung-dynasty conventions. They are said to be immortal, and their nonsense is construed as great wisdom in that it defies man-made codes.

Eight Trigrams. [Chinese, **Pa-Kua.**] Eight combinations of lines, arranged in circular form. They consist of groups of three whole or divided lines. They are said to have been devised by the legendary emperor Fu Hsi, and figure prominently in the ancient Chinese *Classic of Changes* and are also used for purposes of divination. The above simple combinations were later increased to 64.

Eijkman (īk'män), **Christiaan.** b. at Nijkerk, Netherlands, Aug. 11, 1858; d. at Utrecht, Netherlands, Nov. 5, 1930. Dutch hygienist. He was director (1888–96) of the pathological institute at Weltevreden, in Java, and professor of hygiene (1898–1928) at the University of Utrecht. He was the first to produce a deficiency disease experimentally, in fowls (1893), discovering that a nutritional deficiency is responsible for beri-beri. He also discovered (1897–1900) that in removing the husks of the rice grain an important substance was lost in the polishing process; with this discovery he gave the first impulse to the theory of the avitaminoses (deprivation or deficiency diseases). In 1929 he was awarded (with Frederick G. Hopkins) the Nobel prize in medicine for the discovery of the antineuritic vitamin B_1 (thiamine). Author of *Over gezondheid en ziekte in heete gewesten* (1898) and *Specifieke antistoffen* (1901).

Eike von Repgow (ī'kẹ fon rep'gō) or **Repkow** (rep'kō). [Also spelled **Eyke, Eiko, Ecco,** or **Ebco.**] fl. first half 13th century. German nobleman and author of the *Sachsenspiegel* (c1223), the earliest effective codification of German (in contrast to Roman) law. It was written in Latin, but only the author's own translation into Low German prose is extant. It appeared in Dutch, Czech, and Polish adaptations, and served as the model for a later *Schwabenspiegel, Frankenspiegel, Laienspiegel, Ritterspiegel,* and many others. Luther called the Decalogue the *Sachsenspiegel* of the Jews. In his rhymed prologue, Eike explains that his book is called *Sachsenspiegel* ("mirror of the Saxons") because the Saxons can see in it their law as women see their faces in a looking glass.

Eikon Basilike (ī'kon ba.sil'i.kē). Book describing the sufferings of Charles I of England, published in 1649. It is usually attributed to Bishop Gauden.

Eikonoclastes (ī.kon.ọ.klas'tēz). Pamphlet written by John Milton in answer to Gauden's *Eikon Basilike.*

Eil (ēl), **Lower Loch.** See under **Linnhe, Loch.**

Eildon Hills (ēl'dǫn). Three peaks in S Scotland, in Roxburghshire, situated ab. 1 mi. S of Melrose. The remains of a Roman camp, and a barrow, supposedly of Druidical origin, are here. The hills are famous in Scottish legend. Elevation of highest summit, 1,385 ft.

Eilean Molach (ā'lin mǫ.läċh'). See **Ellen's Isle.**

Eileen Carmody (ī'lēn kär'mǫ.di). See **Carmody, Eileen.**

Eileithyia (ē.lę̄.thī'ą). An ancient name of **El Kab.**

Eilenburg (ī'lęn.bůrk). City in C Germany, in the *Land* (state) of Saxony-Anhalt, Russian Zone, formerly in the province of Saxony, Prussia, situated on the Mulde River ab. 14 mi. NE of Leipzig. Before World War II it had manufactures of cotton textiles, plastics, machinery, furniture, pianos, and candies. The *Nikolaikirche* (Church of Saint Nicholas) is a brick building dating from the 15th and 16th centuries; the *Rathaus* (town hall) dates from 1544. The town is named after the Ilburg, a frontier castle built for defense against the Slavs in the 10th century; it belonged to the house of Wettin from that time until 1815. The population is predominantly Protestant. 19,980 (1946).

Eilhart von Oberge (īl'härt fon ō'ber.gę). fl. c1180–1207. Medieval German poet from near Hildesheim, author of the first German version of the Tristan story. His *Tristrant und Isalde* (c1180), written in a Middle German dialect, had an unknown French source. Eilhart's epic exists in a fragment of 600 lines. However, there is a Czech translation, and also a German prose version printed in 1484. Eilhart is a forerunner of the so-called court poets.

Eilissos (ē.li.sôs'). Modern Greek name of the **Ilissus.**

Eilshemius (il.shē'mi.us), **Louis Michel.** b. at Arlington, N.J., Feb. 4, 1864; d. at New York, Dec. 29, 1941. American mystical painter, writer, and composer. He studied at Cornell University, then at New York and at the Julian Academy, Paris. He exhibited in France, Germany, and the U.S., having one-man shows at New York sponsored by the Société Anonyme, of which he was a member; he belonged also to the American Federation of Arts and the Modern Artists of America. He did not achieve recognition until he had become old and embittered. His work is represented in the Phillips Memorial Gallery at Washington, D.C., the Metropolitan Museum, Whitney Museum, and Museum of Modern Art at New York, Boston Museum of Fine Arts, Cleveland Museum, Luxembourg Museum at Paris, and Detroit Institute of Art. Among his better-known paintings are *Green Valley, Children in Central Park, Nymphs Teasing, Contentment, Roma, Low Tide, Storm Clouds, Morning, The Stream, Before the Promenade,* and *Rose Marie.*

Eily O'Connor (ī'li ǭ.kon'ǫr). See **O'Connor, Eily.**

Eimbeck (īm'bek). See **Einbeck.**

Eimeo (ī.mā'ō). See **Moorea.**

Einaudi (ā.nou'dē), **Luigi.** b. at Carru, Italy, March 24, 1874—. Italian statesman and journalist. On the staff (1900–25) of the daily *Corriere della Sera,* he was later (1930–36) editor of the *Riforma soziale,* a review. He was appointed (1945) a governor of the Bank of Italy. After being appointed (1947) vice-president of the council of ministers, he was elected (May 11, 1948) president of the Italian republic.

Einbeck (īn'bek). [Also, **Eimbeck.**] Town in NW Germany, in the *Land* (state) of Lower Saxony, British Zone, formerly in the province of Hanover, Prussia, situated on the Ilme River near its junction with the Leine River, ab. 37 mi. S of Hanover. It has textile manufactures, breweries, and a sugar refinery. It is a picturesque old town, with its medieval fortifications still standing, and containing a number of ecclesiastical and secular buildings of the Gothic and Renaissance periods. The Church of Saint James dates from the 13th century, the Church of Alexander from the 14th century, the Church of Mary from the 15th century; the *Rathaus* (town hall) was erected in the period 1550–56. The town came under the rule of the house of Welf in 1272. It prospered in the Middle Ages because of its well-known breweries; it is said that the term "Bock," indicating a strongly brewed brown beer, is derived from the name Einbeck. Except for the Stiftskirche, which suffered some minor roof damage, the town and the above mentioned buildings remained intact during World War II. The population is predominantly Protestant. 17,759 (1950).

Eindhoven (īnt'hō.vęn). City in S Netherlands, in the province of North Brabant, situated near the confluence of the Dommel and Tongel rivers ab. 55 mi. SE of Rotterdam. It is a manufacturing town containing the Philips factories (electrical and radio equipment) and also machine, glass and plate glass, tobacco, button, stone, and paper factories and breweries. There are a number of industrial and residential suburbs. In World War II, it was the southernmost point reached by Allied air-borne troops in September, 1944; a large part of the center of the city was damaged or destroyed. 143,965 (est. 1951).

Eindhoven Landing. Air-borne attack (Sept. 17, 1944) by U.S. paratroops of General Lewis Brereton's First Allied Airborne Army. This landing sought to seize advance positions on the Meuse and Waal rivers in the Netherlands. Unlike its unfortunate counterpart further N at Arnhem this landing was coördinated (Sept. 22) with other advances of the Allied armies.

Einem (ī'nęm), **Karl von.** [Also, **von Rothmaler.**] b. at Herzberg, Germany, Jan. 1, 1853; d. at Mülheim, Germany, April 7, 1934. Prussian general. He organized the military expedition to China (1900), commanded the seventh army corps (1909 *et seq.*), and led the German third army in World War I.

Ein Feste Burg (īn fes'tę bůrk'). [Eng. trans., "*A Mighty Fortress.*"] First words of a hymn by Martin Luther ("Ein feste Burg ist unser Gott"), a version of Psalm xlvi. The hymn was probably written in 1527. The tune seems to have appeared in Köphl's *Psalmen und geistliche Lieder,* probably in 1538. The form now used is by Johann Sebastian Bach (in his *Cantata* No. 80 and also in a choral prelude) and differs slightly from Luther's original. The words have also been modernized.

Einhard (īn'härt). [Sometimes called **Eginhard.**] b. in Austrasia, c770; d. at Seligenstadt on the Main, Germany, probably on March 14, 840. Frankish scholar and biographer of Charlemagne. He was of noble birth, and was educated at the monastery of Fulda. He removed not later than 796 to the court of Charlemagne, who appointed him minister of public works and sent him in 806 as imperial legate to Rome. He was retained in office by Louis le Débonnaire, to whose son Lothaire he became tutor in 817. He retired in 830 to Mulinheim (which he named Seligenstadt), where he erected a monastery. He was married to Imma, who was the sister of Bernhard, bishop of Worms, but who was supposed by later tradition to be a daughter of Charlemagne. He wrote a life of Charlemagne, *Vita Caroli Magni.* He may have been the architect of the cathedral at Aachen.

Einhorn (īn'hôrn), **David.** b. at Dispeck, Bavaria, Germany, Nov. 10, 1809; d. at New York, Nov. 2, 1879. American theologian, rabbi, reform leader, and abolitionist. He received a thoroughly orthodox training, which is interesting in view of the fact that he later became an outstanding liberal and radical. He was educated at the village school, at the Fürth Talmudic Academy, and at the universities of Erlangen, Würzburg, and Munich. For ten years, from 1832, when he was qualified to become a rabbi, he was given no appointment in Germany because his views were considered dangerous. In 1842 he was called to head a congregation, but immediately found that he had little in common with those he was supposed to guide and inspire. After nine long years of unspiritual strife and conflict he left Germany for Pest, in Hungary. Two months later, in 1851, his temple was closed by government orders. In 1855, after four years of enforced idleness, he came to the U.S. to become the leader of a congregation at Baltimore. With a courage that was a credit to his heart, although it may not have been diplomatic, he began (writing in German) to attack slavery, which did nothing to increase his popularity in a city where most of the population was certainly opposed to the Abolitionists. On April 19, 1861, the famous Baltimore Riot broke out, and two or three days later he was forced to flee at night, under police protection, in order to escape being attacked by an angry mob. His coreligionists, who had nothing against him on other grounds, made it clear that they were willing to have him if he would agree not to mention slavery or to attack it in his sermons, but Einhorn refused to compromise with his principles. He then went to Philadelphia, where he accepted the post of rabbi to the Keneseth Israel Congregation. In approval of his attitude on the question of slavery, the Union League of Philadelphia made him an honorary member. In 1866 he was at New York, as rabbi of the Congregation Adath Jeshurun, which became Congregation Beth El after merging with another group in 1874. It was the last position he held, and he kept it until July, 1879, four months before his death. His works were *Das Prinzip des Mosaismus und dessen Verhältnis zum Heidenthum und Rabbinischen Judenthum* (1854), a system of Jewish theology published at Leipzig before he left for America, and *Ner Tamid, Die Lehre des Judenthums dargestellt fur Schule und Haus* (1866). His sermons were published in book form in 1880. In 1856 he founded a German-language monthly, *Sinai*, which he developed into an organ for reform Judaism. It lasted until 1863, when (as he said) "it died in the battle against slavery." He also issued *Olath Tamid* (1856), a reform version of the orthodox Jewish prayer book, to which he added a German translation. In his day he was recognized as a leading spirit of reform Judaism in America.

Einhorn, Max. b. at Suchowol, near Grodno, Russia, Jan. 10, 1862—. American physician. He was graduated (1884) at Berlin, was a pupil of Paul Ehrlich, and went (1885) to New York, where he was professor (1896–1922) at the New York Post Graduate School. He invented many ingenious devices and instruments, such as gastrodiaphany, also called Einhorn's method (1889), stomach buckets (1890) and duodenal buckets (1908) facilitating studies on pancreatic secretion, and a form of fermentation saccharimeter. He introduced the concept of a functional disorder of secretion, achylia gastrica (1892), and described (1895) gastric ulcer. Author of *Diseases of the Stomach* (1895), *Diseases of Intestines* (1900), *Practical Problems of Diet and Nutrition* (1905), *Lectures on Dietetics* (1914), *Duodenal Tube and Its Possibilities* (1920), *Methoden der künstlichen Ernährung* (1922), and *Diseases of the Stomach* (1929).

Einigen (ī'ni.gen), **Hans Müller-.** See **Müller, Hans.**

Einsame Insel (īn'zä.me in'zel). See **Hebrides, The.**

Einsiedeln (īn'zē.deln). Town in C Switzerland, in the canton of Schwyz. It is one of the most celebrated places of pilgrimage in Switzerland. The monastery was founded in the 9th century, and in 1294 received the standing of a principality from the German emperor Rudolph. The buildings date from the early 18th century, a good example of S German baroque architecture. Furniture, stucco decoration, and paintings were produced by the artist-brothers Adam of Bavaria. The library comprises more than 100,000 volumes, many incunabla, and medieval manuscripts. 8,392 (1941).

Einstein (īn'stīn; German, īn'shtīn), **Albert.** b. at Ulm, Württemberg, Germany, March 14, 1879—. Theoretical physicist. He was naturalized (1894) as a Swiss citizen, worked as an engineer (1902–09) in the patent office at Bern, Switzerland, was professor of theoretical physics at the University of Zurich, Switzerland (1909–11), at the German University, Prague (1911–12), and at the Federal Institute of Technology, Zurich (1912–14). He was elected (1913) a member of the Prussian Academy of Sciences at Berlin, and in 1914 became a German citizen once more. He was professor of physics (1914–33) at the University of Berlin and director (1914–33) of the Kaiser Wilhelm Physical Institute, Berlin. At the age of 26, in 1905, he published three papers (all in *Annalen der Physik*), each of which became the source of a new branch of physics: (1) explanation of the law of the photoelectric effect on the basis of the light-quantum hypothesis; (2) theory of the "Brownian movement" of barely visible particles; and (3) the special theory of relativity, asserting the invariance of natural laws under Lorentz transformations, that is, that the transformation of coördinates in the equations discovered in 1895 by Hendrik Lorentz was relative to both bodies and did not require one fixed location and another moving relative to it. Among the results of this last theory is such a striking fact as the equivalence of mass and energy. For his theory of the photoelectric effect he was awarded (1922) the 1921 Nobel prize in physics. He announced his general theory of relativity (1913–16), aiming to express all laws of physics by "covariant" equations, i.e., by equations having the same mathematical form irrespective of system of reference or of space-time variables used. This theory predicted (1911) that light beams from stars must be bent in passing the edge of the sun, predicted (1907) the red-shift of light rays emitted by a source located in a strong gravitational field, and explained (1915) the exact value of the rotation of the perihelion of Mercury. The unified field theory (1929 *et seq.*) has as its newest development the combining of gravitational and electromagnetic effects (1950). Einstein contributed greatly to the development of the quantum theory with discoveries in the photoelectric effect in 1905, specific heat in 1907, the emission and absorption of radiation in 1917, and the Bose-Einstein statistics in 1924–25. He arrived (1933) in the U.S. and was naturalized (1940) as a U.S. citizen, all his German property being confiscated and his citizenship revoked (1934) by the Hitler government. He was appointed (1933) a life member of the Institute for Advanced Study at Princeton, N.J., and there served as professor of theoretical physics (1933–45, emeritus since 1945). He was awarded (1935) the Medal of the Franklin Institute. He signed a letter to President Roosevelt (October, 1939) explaining the potentialities of atomic energy as a possible military weapon, thus providing the impetus for government atomic research. After the bombing of Hiroshima (1945) he became a militant advocate of world government as the only method to achieve and maintain international peace. He is the author of *The Meaning of Relativity* (1921; revised ed., 1945), *Sidelights on Relativity* (1922), *Investigations on the Theory of the Brownian Movement* (1926), *Einheitliche Feldtheorie* (1929), *On the Method of Theoretical Physics* (1933), *The World As I See It* (1934), and other works. He published, with Sigmund Freud, *Why War?* (1933), and, with Leopold Infeld, *The Evolution of Physics* (1938).

Einstein, Alfred. b. at Munich, Dec. 30, 1880; d. at El Cerrito, Calif., Feb. 12, 1952. German musicologist, professor of music (1939–50) at Smith College; cousin of Albert Einstein. He was editor of the *Zeitschrift für Musikwissenschaft* (1918 *et seq.*) and music critic of the *Berliner Tageblatt* (1927–33), left Germany in 1933, and came to the U.S. in 1939. Author of *A Short History of Music* (1936), *Mozart: His Character and His Work* (1945), *The Italian Madrigal* (1949), and others; one of his most important works is a revised edition (1937) of the Köchel listing of Mozart's compositions.

Einthoven (īnt'hō.ven), **Willem.** b. at Samarang, Java, May 21, 1860; d. at Leiden, Netherlands, Sept. 28, 1927. Dutch physiologist. Educated at the University of Utrecht, he was professor of physiology (1886–1927) at the University of Leiden. His perfection of the string galvanometer, and associated researches, laid the groundwork for electrocardiography. He was awarded (1924) the Nobel prize for physiology and medicine.

Éire (âr'e; Irish, ā're). Irish name of **Ireland** and, formerly, of the **Irish Republic.**

Eisdale (ēz'dāl). See **Easdale.**

Eiselsberg (ī'zels.berk), Baron **Anton von.** b. at Steinhaus, Upper Austria, July 31, 1860; d. Oct. 26, 1939. Austrian surgeon. He was assistant to Th. Billroth (1887), became privatdocent of surgery (1890) at the University of Vienna, was appointed full professor (1893) at the universities of Utrecht (1896) and Königsberg, and served (1901–31) at the First Surgical Clinic of the University of Vienna. He introduced an operation of the hypophysis (1907), an operation of pyloric exclusion, followed by gastroenterostomy (1889), produced experimentally (1892) tetany by excision of the thyroid of a cat and its relief by parathyroid transplants. He first removed an intramedullary tumor of the spinal cord, thus becoming a leader in neurosurgery. Author of *Über Tetanie im Anschluss an Kropfoperationen* (1890), *Die Krankheiten der Schilddrüse* (1901), *Die Krankheiten und Verletzungen der Schilddrüse* (1903), *Die heutige Behandlung der Knochenbrüche* (1905), *Vorkommen und Behandlung der Tetania parathyreopriva* (1908), *Aus der Werkstatt des Chirurgen* (1912), *Die Chirurgie der Schilddrüse* (1913), and *Lehrbuch der Chirurgie A. V. Eiselsberg* (1930); coeditor of *Mitteilungen aus den Grenzgebieten der Medizin und Chirurgie.*

Eisenach (ī'ze.näch). City in C Germany, in the *Land* (state) of Thuringia, Russian Zone, formerly in the free state of Thuringia, situated at the junction of the Nesse and Hörsel rivers ab. 31 mi. W of Erfurt. Before World War II it produced automobiles, bicycles, agricultural machinery, electrical articles, textiles, and beer, and was known as a favorite residence of retired officials. It is a health resort, with sulfurous saline springs. There are a number of educational institutions and museums, a library, and a theater. Buildings of interest include several churches dating from the 12th and 13th centuries, the *Rathaus* (town hall) from the 16th and 17th centuries, and the former grand-ducal castle, from the 18th century, which contains an art gallery. Above the town is the Wartburg, a huge medieval castle and one of the best-preserved Romanesque buildings in Germany, former seat of the landgraves of Thuringia; Martin Luther lived there from May 4, 1521, to March 1, 1522. It contains collections of arms and murals by Moritz von Schwind. A famous student demonstration took place here in 1817. Erected in the 11th and 12th centuries, the castle was renovated in the 19th century. The city of Eisenach was after 1596 the residence of the princes of the Ernestine line of the house of Wettin; this line was united with the line of Weimar in 1741. The composer Johann Sebastian Bach was born at Eisenach. In World War II the city was occupied by American troops in April, 1945. Pop. 57,834 (1946).

Eisenberg (ī'zęn.berk). City in C Germany, in the *Land* (state) of Thuringia, Russian Zone, formerly in the free state of Thuringia, situated near the Weisse Elster River ab. 33 mi. SW of Leipzig. Before World War II it had manufactures of porcelain, pianos, and sausages. Buildings of interest include churches dating from the 15th and 17th centuries; the old *Rathaus* (city hall) was erected in 1559. The Christiansburg castle, a baroque building of the 17th century, serves as the new city hall. The city belonged at various times to the margraves of Meissen, the landgraves of Thuringia, and the house of Wettin. It passed in 1826 to Saxe-Altenburg and in 1919 to the free state of Thuringia. 15,299 (1946).

Eisenerz (ī'zęn.erts). Town in E Austria, in the province of Styria, ab. 20 mi. NW of Bruck an der Mur: a station on the railroad to Leoben (Erzberg Railway). It is an old mining town. In the vicinity is the Erzberg ("ore mountain") which is so productive of spathic iron ore that it is possible to quarry it without the aid of mining operations. The Erzberg belongs to the Österreich-Alpine Montan Gesellschaft, which is now under government control. 12,759 (1951).

Eisenhower (ī'zęn.hou.ėr), **Dwight David.** [Called **"Ike."**] b. at Denison, Tex., Oct. 14, 1890—. American statesman, soldier, and educator, 34th President of the United States, supreme commander of Allied forces in W Europe in World War II. A graduate of the U.S. Military Academy (1915), he served in the tank corps in World War I under George Patton. He was a member (1935–39) of the U.S. military mission to the Philippines under Douglas MacArthur. In 1941 he was appointed brigadier general and, after the U.S. entered World War II, chief of the operations division of the U.S. general staff. He was appointed (June, 1942) lieutenant general commanding the U.S. forces in the European theater, both these appointments resulting from his brilliant conduct of the Louisiana maneuvers of the army in 1941. During the North African invasion (November, 1942) he served as Allied commander in chief, and in February, 1943, he was appointed general in supreme command of the Allied forces in North Africa and the western Mediterranean. He directed the invasions (1943) of Sicily and Italy. As Allied commander in chief (December, 1943, *et seq.*) in the European theater, he directed the Normandy invasion (June, 1944) and the conquest of western Germany (by May, 1945). He was appointed (December, 1944; permanent 1946) general of the army. He was the U.S. member (1945) of the Allied Control Commission for Germany. In November, 1945, he was appointed U.S. army chief of staff. He was president (1948 *et seq.*) of Columbia University. In 1950 he was appointed supreme Allied commander in Europe, in command of the Atlantic Pact forces integrated command. Eisenhower, who had been widely mentioned as a possible candidate for the presidency in 1948, resigned his NATO post in 1952 to seek the Republican nomination. He easily won a first-ballot nomination at the Chicago convention in July, and in November, gaining the largest popular vote ever cast for a U.S. presidential candidate, defeated Adlai Stevenson for the presidency (442 electoral votes to 89); Eisenhower's splitting the "solid South," winning Florida, Virginia, Texas, and other traditionally Democratic states, helped bring to the White House the first Republican president since 1933. He is the author of *Crusade in Europe* (1948).

Eisenlohr (ī'zęn.lōr), **August.** b. at Mannheim, Germany, Oct. 6, 1832; d. at Heidelberg, Germany, Feb. 24, 1902. German Egyptologist, professor of Egyptology at Heidelberg. He published *Der grosse Papyrus Harris* (1872) and others.

Eisenlohr, Wilhelm. b. at Pforzheim, Baden, Germany, Jan. 1, 1799; d. at Karlsruhe, Baden, Germany, July 10, 1872. German physicist, professor of physics (1840–65) at the polytechnic institute at Karlsruhe. His chief work is *Lehrbuch der Physik* (1836).

Eisenstadt (ī'zęn.shtät). [Hungarian, **Kis-Marton.**] Town in E Austria, the capital of the province of Burgenland (in what was formerly the county of Ödenburg, Hungary), ab. 25 mi. S of Vienna. It contains a chief castle of the Esterhazy family, built (1663–72) by an Italian architect. The composer Haydn, who was court conductor to a member of the Esterhazy family, lived here from 1766 to 1778; he is buried in the crypt of the cemetery. Eisenstadt was the seat of a Talmudic academy (*Yeshiva*) in the 17th, 18th, and 19th centuries. The historical collection of Sandor Wolf is now at Tel Aviv, Israel. There are new government buildings. The city was transferred in 1921 from Hungary to Austria. 5,388 (1951).

Eisenstein (ī'zęn.shtīn), **Ferdinand Gotthold.** b. at Berlin, April 16, 1823; d. there, Oct. 11, 1852. German mathematician and professor at the University of Berlin, known for his work on the invariants of algebraic forms and on elliptic functions. His works include *Théorèmes sur les formes cubiques* (1841), *Allgemeine Auflösung der Gleichungen der ersten vier Grade* (1844), *Allgemeine Untersuchungen über die Formen dritten Grades* (1844), and *Genaue Untersuchung der unendlichen Doppelproducte* (1847).

Eisenstein (ī'zęn.stīn; Russian, ā.zin.shtān'), **Sergei Mikhailovich.** b. in Russia, 1898; d. at Moscow, Feb. 10, 1948. Russian motion-picture director and producer, notable for his development of new film techniques, and acclaimed as one of the greatest directors of his time. Trained as civil engineer and architect; served (1918–20) in Bolshevik army as volunteer; staged plays for impresario Meyerhold; directed first film (*The Strike*) in 1924; worked at Paris and at Hollywood (1931); developed techniques of montage and dynamic progression through cutting and mounting film; pioneer in use of untrained actors to achieve "documentary realism." His productions include *Potemkin* (1926), *Ten Days That Shook the World* (1928), *Old and New* (1929), *General Line*, *Alexander Nevsky* (1939), *Ivan the Terrible* (part I, 1941), and the unfinished *Thunder Over Mexico*. Author of *The Film Sense*.

Eisernes Tor (ī'zėr.nęs tōr'). German name of the **Iron Gate.**

Eisfeld (īs'felt). Town in C Germany, in the *Land* (state) of Thuringia, Russian Zone, formerly in the free state of Thuringia, situated on the Werra River ab. 23 mi. SE of Meiningen. Before World War II it had manufactures of toys, china, and knitwear. It has a castle and a Gothic town church. 5,586 (1946).

Eisk (yā'ęsk). See **Yeisk.**

Eisleben (īs'lā.bęn). City in C Germany, in the *Land* (state) of Saxony-Anhalt, Russian Zone, formerly in the province of Saxony, Prussia, ab. 39 mi. NW of Leipzig. Copper and silver mines are in the vicinity; the city has small industries and is the center of a horticultural and market-gardening district, with trade in flower and vegetable seeds. There are schools of mining, commerce, and agriculture. The reformer Martin Luther was born here and died here; the house where he was born (now a museum) and the house where he died have been preserved. There are various churches dating from the 15th and 16th centuries; the *Rathaus* (town hall) was built in the period 1519–30. Mining activities have been carried on here for centuries. The population is predominantly

Protestant. The period 1939–46 saw an increase in population amounting to 25.9 percent. 29,095 (1946).

Eisler (īs′lėr), **Rudolf.** b. at Vienna, Jan. 7, 1873; d. there, Dec. 14, 1926. Austrian writer on philosophy. He was the author of *Wörterbuch der philosophischen Begriffe* (1899), *Philosophenlexikon* (1912), *Handwörterbuch der Philosophie* (1913), and *Kantlexikon* (1930).

Eislingen (is′ling.ẹn). Town in S Germany, in the *Land* (state) of Württemberg-Baden, American Zone, formerly in the free state of Württemberg, situated on the Fils River SE of Stuttgart: paper and lumber mills; metallurgical, textile, and leatherware manufactures. The population is predominantly Protestant. 13,399 (1950).

Eisner (īs′nėr), **Kurt.** b. at Berlin, May 4, 1867; assassinated by a political fanatic at Munich, Feb. 21, 1919. German politician and journalist. His early writings were published in the *Frankfurter Zeitung,* at which time he was associated with the National Socialists. Later he became a Social Democrat and was editor of the party paper, *Vorwärts,* from 1899 to 1905, when he was dismissed as a revisionist. He then became an editor at Nuremberg. At the outbreak of World War I he favored granting war credits. In 1917 he joined the Independent Social Democrats, and encouraged armament strikes for the enforcement of peace. Early in 1918 he was convicted of treason but was released in the fall of that year, later organizing the mass meetings at Munich (November 7) which helped overthrow the monarchy. He became president of the revolutionary government and opposed early elections. His publications accepting German war guilt and his Jewish descent increased his unpopularity. On his way to the Bavarian diet to proclaim the resignation of his government he was assassinated. Eisner's collected works were published in 1919.

Eissner (īs′nėr), **Clara.** See **Zetkin, Clara.**

Eist (īst), **von.** See **Dietmar von Aist.**

Eisteddfod (ā.steᴛʜ′vōd). Annual musical and literary festival and competition which originated in the triennial assembly of Welsh bards; the latter dates back to an early period. An Eisteddfod is mentioned as having been held in the 7th century. They are now held every year at various places in Wales. Concerts and competitions for prizes are still held; but, except that they take place in Wales and retain some ancient forms, they are no longer particularly national in character.

Eitherside (ē′ᴛʜėr.sīd, ī′-), **Sergeant.** Character in Macklin's *Man of the World.*

Eitherside, Sir Paul. In Ben Jonson's comedy *The Devil is an Ass,* a hard, unfeeling justice and superstitious wiseacre.

Eitner (īt′nėr), **Robert.** b. at Breslau, Oct. 22, 1832; d. at Templin, Germany, 1905. German teacher and musicologist. He was the founder (1868) of the Gesellschaft für Musikforschung at Berlin and editor (1869 *et seq.*) of its monthly publication, and also published the ten-volume *Biographisch-bibliographisches Quellen-Lexikon der Musiker und Musikgelehrten* (1900–04). He composed an opera, piano works, songs, and a cantata.

Eitorf (ī′tôrf). Town in W Germany, in the *Land* (state) of North Rhine-Westphalia, British Zone, formerly in the Rhine Province, Prussia, situated on the Sieg River ab. 28 mi. SE of Cologne. It has woolen textile, metallurgical, and chemical industries, a cannery, and a sugar refinery. 11,611 (1950).

Ekaterinburg (yi.kä″tyi.rin.börk′). Former name of **Sverdlovsk.**

Ekaterinoslav or **Ekaterinoslaff** (yi.kä.tyi.rē.nọ.släf′). Former name of **Dnepropetrovsk;** see also **Yekaterinoslav.**

Ek Chuah (ek chü′ä). In Maya religion, the Black War captain. He had two aspects: as a war god he was malevolent, and as a god of the merchants he was friendly.

Ekekete (ā.kā.kā′tā). [Also, **Quiquete.**] One of the 13 independent kingdoms of the Mbundu, a Bantu-speaking people of SW Africa, living in C Angola.

Ekelöf (ā′kẹ.lėv), **Gunnar.** [Full name, **Bengt Gunnar Ekelöf.**] b. at Stockholm, 1907—. Swedish poet and critic.

Ekelund (ā′kẹ.lünd), **Vilhelm.** [Full name, **Otto Vilhelm Ekelund.**] b. at Stehag, in Skåne, Sweden, 1880—. Swedish poet and essayist. Ekelund's significance is threefold: he may be regarded as the founder of modernist verse in Sweden, he is the country's most important aphorist, and he is a leading aesthetic philosopher in the classical tradition. The son of a blacksmith in southernmost Sweden, Ekelund attended college at Lund, and later studied at the university there. He held the Fröding literary fellowship (1926–33) and traveled widely. His poetry includes *Vårbris* (Spring Breeze, 1900), *Syner* (Visions, 1901), *Melodier i skymning* (Tunes in the Twilight, 1902), *Elegier* (Elegies, 1903), and *Dithyramber i aftonglans* (Dithyrambs in the Evening Glow, 1906). Among his collections of philosophical aphorisms *Concordia Animi* (1942) and *Atticism-humanism* (1943) are outstanding.

Ekeren (ā′kẹ.rẹn). [Also, **Eeckeren.**] Town in N Belgium, in the province of Antwerp, N of Antwerp, of which it is a suburb. 15,962 (1947).

Ekhmim (eċh.mēm′). See **Akhmim.**

Ekhof (ek′hōf), **Konrad.** b. at Hamburg, Germany, Aug. 12, 1720; d. at Gotha, Germany, June 16, 1778. German actor, founder of a theatrical academy. He was the leading member of the company of the National Theater at Hamburg (1767 *et seq.*), which has become famous through Lessing's *Hamburgische Dramaturgie,* and codirector of the court theater at Gotha (1775 *et seq.*), which was the first permanent theater in Germany. In 1777 Ekhof acted with Goethe and Duke Karl August in a private performance at Weimar. As an exponent of realism and naturalness he has been compared with Garrick and may be called the founder of the modern German theater.

Ekiti (ā.kē′tē). Subgroup of the Sudanic-speaking Yoruba of W Africa, inhabiting SW Nigeria, NW of Benin. Their population is estimated at ab. 225,000 (by P. A. Talbot, *The Peoples of Southern Nigeria,* 1926). They are divided politically into several small, independent kingdoms.

Ekkehard (ek′ẹ.härt). Historical novel by Scheffel, published in 1855.

Ekkehard I of St. Gallen (sänt gal′ẹn). b. c910; d. at St. Gallen, Switzerland, 973. Swiss monk. He later became dean at the famous monastery of St. Gallen. He wrote an epic, *Waltharius manu fortis,* in Latin hexameters, which deals with the escape of Walter of Aquitaine and Hiltgunt of Burgundy from the court of Attila.

Ekket (e′ket). Subgroup of the semi-Bantu-speaking peoples of W Africa, inhabiting SE Nigeria. Their population is estimated at ab. 30,000 (by P. A. Talbot, *The Peoples of Southern Nigeria,* 1926), including the related Ubium.

Ekman (āk′män), **Frans Gösta Viktor.** b. at Stockholm, Dec. 28, 1890; d. there, Jan. 12, 1938. Swedish actor. He became the leading man of the Swedish theater, playing a great variety of roles in both comedy and tragedy and appearing in all the important private and subsidized theaters of Sweden. He was especially successful in the roles of Hamlet, Shylock, and Fedya (in Tolstoy's *Redemption*).

Ekoi (e′koi). Semi-Bantu-speaking people of W Africa, inhabiting SE Nigeria and S British Cameroons, NE of Calabar. Their population is estimated at ab. 90,000 (by P. A. Talbot, *The Peoples of Southern Nigeria,* 1926). They are divided into 25 subgroups: the Afitopp, Akaju, Akparabong, Ama, Ambele, Anyang, Assumbo, Atamm, Banyangi, Befang, Befun, Ejagham, Ekomm, Itung, Kwa, Manta, Nde, Ngom, Nkumm, Nnamm, Nsele, Obang, Olulumaw, Otutu, and Wetshu.

Ekron (ek′ron). [Modern name, **Akir.**] In Biblical geography, one of the five chief cities of the Philistines, situated ab. 12 mi. NE of Ashdod. It contained an oracle.

Ektag Altai (ek.täg′ äl.tī′). See under **Altai.**

El Acola (el ak′ọ̄.lạ). See under **Alula Borealis and Alula Australis.**

Elagabalus (ē.lạ.gab′ạ.lus). [Also: **Heliogabalus;** as emperor called **Marcus Aurelius Antoninus;** original name, **Varius Avitus Bassianus.**] b. at Emesa (modern Homs), Syria, 205 A.D.; d. 222. Emperor of Rome. He was the son of Sextus Varius Marcellus and Julia Soæmias, and first cousin of Caracalla. He became while very young a priest in the temple of the sun god Elagabalus at Emesa. Being put forward as the son of Caracalla, he was proclaimed emperor by the soldiers in 218, in opposition to Macrinus who was defeated on the borders of Syria and Phoenicia in the same year. He gave himself up to the most infamous debauchery, and abandoned the government to his mother and grandmother. He adopted his cousin, Bassianus Alexianus, who succeeded to the throne as Severus Alexander. He was put to death at Rome by the praetorians.

Elah (ē'la̤). In Biblical geography, the valley in which the Israelites were encamped when the duel between David and Goliath occurred; probably the modern Wadi Es-Sunt.

Elaine (ȩ.lān'). In the Arthurian legends: **1.** The half sister of King Arthur. She bore a son, Mordred, to Arthur. **2.** The daughter of King Pelles. She was the mother of Lancelot's son Sir Galahad. **3.** The "lily maid of Astolat" who pined and died for Lancelot. Tennyson makes her story the subject of his *Elaine*. **4.** The daughter of King Brandegoris, who bore a child to Sir Bors de Ganis. In Malory's *Arthur* the statement is so worded that Elaine may be the name of the child. **5.** The wife of Ban of Benoic (Brittany), mother of Sir Lancelot. She was also called Elein.

El Alamein (el al.a̤.mān'), **Battles of.** Name applied to several military operations in North Africa, in World War II. The term is often applied specifically to the great artillery and tank engagement in which the British Eighth Army, under General Montgomery, broke through the lines of the Italians and of the German Afrika Korps in the fall of 1942. In July, 1942, the Germans, under Rommel, had bypassed the defenses of El Alamein, and the British retained the position, although it was for a time cut off. On Oct. 19, 1942, the British counterattacked with planes, artillery, and infantry. On Nov. 1 armored units followed and in one of the greatest tank battles of the war the Germans were forced to retreat many miles into Libya, having lost almost 90,000 men killed or taken prisoner.

El Alígero Clavileño (el ä.lē'ʜä.rō klä.ʙē.lā'nyō). See **Clavileño, El Alígero.**

Elam (ē'la̤m). [Also, **Susiana;** ancient Greek, **Elymaïs.**] Ancient country and empire E of the lower Tigris, S of Media, and N of the Persian Gulf. It is a region of fertile and picturesque mountains, valleys, and ravines, the only flat tract being on the shores of the Persian Gulf; and was in very high antiquity the seat of a mighty empire of which Susa was the capital. The oldest historical information about Elam is that it subjugated Babylonia in the period c2300–2076 B.C. The Elamite dynasty is identical with the Median of Berosus, which ruled over Babylonia from c2300 to 2076 B.C. Among these Elamite kings is also very probably to be counted Chedorlaomer (Kudur-Lagamaru) of Gen. xiv. The next historical notice is that Elam was subdued by Nebuchadnezzar 1, king of Babylonia, c1130 B.C. From the 8th century B.C. on, Elam was connected with the rivalry between Assyria and Babylonia, supporting the latter against the former. Elam was defeated by Sargon in 721 and 710, and by Sennacherib in several campaigns, especially in a decisive battle on the Tigris c691. In 645 Assurbanipal destroyed Susa. Soon after this catastrophe Elam is met with under the dominion of Theispes. In union with Media and Persia it helped to bring about the fall of Assyria and Babylonia. It shared thenceforth the fate of the other Assyrian provinces, and had no history of its own. The ancient Elamites were not Semites. This is ascertained by the names of their kings, which are alien to all of the Semitic dialects, and by their representations on the monuments, which exhibit a type widely different from the Semitic. The enumeration of Elam among the sons of Shem in Gen. x. 22 may perhaps be accounted for by the fact that the Elamite valley was early settled by the Semites, who predominated over the non-Semitic element of the population, and also by the fact that the Elamites had for more than two centuries the upper hand in Semitic Babylonia. The name Elymaïs was used either as an equivalent of Elam or for a part of it.

El Arahal (el ä.rä.äl'). Town in S Spain, in the province of Sevilla, situated in the Andalusian plain SE of the city of Seville: agricultural trade center. 13,517 (1940).

El Araish or **El Arish** (el ä.rīsh'). Arabic name of **Larache.**

El 'Arish (el ä.rēsh'). [Ancient name, **Rhinocolura.**] Town in NE Africa, in Egypt, on the Mediterranean shore of the Sinai Peninsula, W of the Israel frontier. It is connected by railroad with Jerusalem and with points on the Suez Canal. It was taken by the French in 1799, and retaken in 1799. A convention was signed here (1800) between Kléber and the grand vizir. Pop. ab. 10,000.

ELAS. Initials of Greek words meaning "Greek Popular Liberation Army." This was the fighting branch of EAM, and the strongest and most effective of the various guerrilla groups operating during the Axis occupation of Greece in World War II. It achieved dominance by acquiring the largest share of captive Italian arms. Its political coloration led it into fights not only with occupation troops, but also with rival guerrilla forces, particularly the EDES, which was decisively defeated by it more than once. At the time of liberation ELAS resisted certain orders of the temporary government and of the British General Scobie, thus beginning the Greek civil war which was finally brought under control in 1949. Though theoretically disbanded in 1945, many of its members undoubtedly provided a nucleus for the rebel army led by Marcos Vafiadis and later by Yoannidis. From 1943 till the official disbanding of ELAS, the principal general was Sarafis, who was exiled, along with another important officer, Colonel Bakerdjis, in 1946.

El Ashmunein (el äsh.mö.nān'). Arabic name of **Hermopolis Magna.**

Elatea (el.a̤.tē'a̤). See **Cithaeron.**

Elath (ē'lath) or **Eloth** (-loth). [Arabic, **Aqaba;** ancient name also **Aelana.**] In Biblical geography, a town of Edom, situated at the head of the Gulf of Aqaba. It was taken by David, and was the headquarters of Solomon's fleet. It was fortified by Uzziah.

Elathasi (el.a̤.thä'si). The fifth-magnitude star ζ Draconis. The name is of rare occurrence.

Elaver (ȩ.lā'vėr). Ancient name of the **Allier River.**

El-Azariyeh (el.ä.zä'ri.ye). Modern name of **Bethany,** Palestine.

Elâziğ (e.lä.zē'). [Also, **Elâziz** (-zēz').] *Il* (province or vilayet) in E Turkey, at the E end of the Anatolian plateau, W of Lake Van: a very hilly area devoted to subsistence crops and herding. It is the terminal of railway lines from Antalya and Ankara. Capital, Elâziğ; area, 5,858 sq. mi.; pop. 211,400 (1950).

Elba (el'ba̤). City in SE Alabama, a county seat (with Enterprise) of Coffee County, on the Pea River ab. 65 mi. SE of Montgomery, in a farming region. 2,936 (1950).

Elba. [Ancient names: **Ilva, Aethalia.**] Island in the Tyrrhenian Sea between the NE coast of Corsica and the coast of Tuscany, belonging to the province of Livorno, Italy. The chief town is Portoferraio. The surface is mountainous; wine and fruit are produced. There are deposits of iron ore, which have been worked since ancient times. Napoleon I was granted the island after his first abdication and resided here from May 1, 1814, until Feb. 26, 1815, when he left secretly for France. In World War II, French forces took the island from the Germans, June 17–19, 1944. Pop. 27,000 (est. 1931).

Elbasan (el.bä.sän'). [Also, **Elbasani** (-sä'nē).] One of the ten prefectures of Albania, in the C part. Capital, Elbasan; pop. 111,480 (1930).

Elbasan. [Also, **Elbasani.**] Town in C Albania, the capital of Elbasan prefecture, on the Shkumbi River: agricultural markets. 13,796 (1930).

Elbe (el'bȩ; Anglicized, elb). [Czech, **Labe;** Latin, **Albis.**] River in N Europe. It rises in the Riesengebirge, in Czechoslovakia, flows through Bohemia and Germany, generally in a NW direction, and empties into the North Sea ab. 65 mi. below Hamburg. Its chief tributaries are the Vltava (Moldau), Ohře (Eger), Mulde, Saale, and Havel (with the Spree). On its banks are Dresden, Torgau, Wittenberg, Magdeburg, and Hamburg. Length, ab. 725 mi.; navigable for ocean vessels to Hamburg, and for others to Mělník in Bohemia (over 500 mi.).

Elbe and Trave Canal (trä'vȩ). Canal in Germany joining the Elbe River at Lauenburg with the Trave River at Lübeck, thus connecting the North Sea with the Baltic. It is 41 mi. long, is 72 ft. broad, and has seven locks. It was completed in 1900 at a cost of nearly six million dollars.

El Bega (el bē.gä'). See **Bika, El.**

El Beni (el bā'nē). Full name of **Beni.**

Elberfeld (el'bėr.felt). Former city in W Germany, in the *Land* (state) of North Rhine-Westphalia, British Zone, formerly in the Rhine Province, Prussia, on the Wupper River ab. 24 mi. NE of Cologne. It forms with Barmen (which adjoins it) one of the most important manufacturing centers in Europe. Among the manufactures of the two cities are ribbons, chemicals, lace, thread, silk, cotton, and others. Since 1929 both have been part of Wuppertal.

Elbert (el'bėrt), **Mount.** Peak in C Colorado, in the Rocky Mountains ab. 13 mi. SW of Leadville. It is the highest peak in Colorado and the second highest in the U.S. The lower slopes are used for summer grazing. Elevation, ab. 14,431 ft.

Elberton (el'bėr.tọn). City in N Georgia, county seat of Elbert County, ab. 69 mi. NW of Augusta: granite quarrying. 6,772 (1950).

Elbeuf (el.bėf). Town in NW France, in the department of Seine-Inférieure, situated on a bend of the Seine River, ab. 13 mi. SW of Rouen. It has important textile manufactures, particularly of cloth and printed cotton goods, which have been known since the 15th century. Elbeuf suffered severe damage in World War II, the entire center of the town being destroyed. 15,958 (1946).

El Bika (el bi.kä'). See **Bika, El.**

Elbing (el'bing). German name of **Elbląg.**

Elbingerode (el'bing.ẹ.rō"dẹ). Town in C Germany, in the *Land* (state) of Saxony-Anhalt, Russian Zone, formerly in the province of Hanover, Prussia, situated in the Harz Mountains ab. 15 mi. SW of Halberstadt. It has stone quarries and lumber trade, and is known for its ruined castle. 4,291 (1946).

Elbistan (el.bi.stän'). [Also, **Albistan.**] Town in S central Turkey, on the Jihun River ab. 40 mi. NE of Maraş. The sultan Bibars defeated the Turks and Mongols here in 1277. Pop. ab. 6,000.

Elbląg (el'blông k). [German, **Elbing.**] City in N Poland, in the *województwo* (province) of Gdańsk, formerly in East Prussia, Germany, situated near the Frisches Haff, ab. 34 mi. SE of Danzig. Before World War II it had shipyards, lumber mills, woodenware, foodstuff, machine, and cigar industries, and livestock markets. Since the war the manufacture of cloth and garments has been introduced and a new mechanical workshop has been put into operation. The city has several educational institutions, including a school of agricultural administration, a school of inland navigation, and schools for the local industries. The old town, with gabled houses of the 15th–18th centuries, was badly damaged in the fighting that took place here at the conclusion of World War II. The churches of Saint Nicholas, Mary, the Holy Ghost, and Saint George, all Gothic buildings, date from the 13th–14th centuries. The town was founded in 1237 by German settlers from Lübeck. It was a member of the Hanseatic League, left the Teutonic Order in 1454 to accept Polish rule, became part of Prussia in 1772, and was occupied in World War II by Russian forces after heavy fighting which took place from Jan. 26 to Feb. 7, 1945. It came under Polish administration as a result of the Potsdam Conference in 1945. The German inhabitants have emigrated. 85,952 (1939), 20,924 (1946).

Elbogen (el'bō.gẹn). German name of **Loket.**

Elbogen, Ismar. b. at Schildberg, Posen, Germany, 1874—. German Jewish scholar and educator. Graduated from the University of Breslau and the Jewish theological seminary at Breslau; lecturer (1902–19) and professor (1919–34) of Biblical exegesis and Jewish history at the Lehranstalt für die Wissenschaft des Judentums at Berlin; came (1938) to the U.S., where he became research professor at several Jewish institutions of higher learning. He served on the editorial board of the *Jüdisches Lexikon*, the *Encyclopaedia Judaica*, and the *Universal Jewish Encyclopedia.* Author of *Die Religionanschauungen der Pharisäer* (1904), *Der jüdische Gottesdienst in seiner geschichtlichen Entwicklung* (1913), and *Geschichte der Juden seit dem Untergang des jüdischen Staates* (1919).

Elborus (el.bọ.rös'). See **Elbrus.**

Elbow (el'bō). In Shakespeare's *Measure for Measure*, a constable, an inferior Dogberry.

Elbrus (el'brös). [Also: **Elbruz, Elborus.**] Highest mountain of the Caucasus, in the U.S.S.R., in the Georgian Soviet Socialist Republic. Elevation, ab. 18,468 ft.

Elbsandsteingebirge (elp'zänt'shtīn.gẹ.bir"gẹ). German name of the **Saxon Switzerland.**

El Bukaa (el bu̇.kä'). See **Bika, El.**

Elburz (el.börz'). Range of mountains in N Iran, connected with the Caucasus and mountains of Armenia on the W, and with the Paropamisan Mountains on the E. They arch around the S shore of the Caspian Sea for a distance of ab. 450 mi. Highest summit, Mount Demavend.

El Buseira (el bu̇.sī'rạ, -sā'rạ). See **Bozrah.**

El Cajon (el kä.hōn'). City in S California, in San Diego County ab. 16 mi. E of San Diego. It is a local trade center in a region of fruit, truck, and poultry farming, and packs citrus fruit and vegetables for shipment. The area was once a Spanish *rancho*, opened for settlement in 1869. In the decade between the last two U.S. censuses its population more than tripled. 1,471 (1940), 5,600 (1950).

El Campo (el kam'pō). City in C Texas, in Wharton County, SE of Austin, in a petroleum-producing region: milling, trading, and shipping center for rice and cattle. 6,237 (1950).

El Caney (el kä.nā'). Village in Cuba, situated ab. 3 mi. NE of Santiago.

El Caney, Attack on. Military engagement at the village of El Caney, Cuba, flanking the San Juan position, which involved troops of opposing forces during the Spanish-American War. American infantry and artillery under General H. W. Lawton seized the village on July 1, 1898, in a move, timed with the frontal assault upon San Juan Hill, to open the road to Santiago.

El Capitan (el kap.i.tan'). Monolithic granite peak in Yosemite National Park, E central California, one of the most noted heights surrounding the Yosemite Valley. It rises ab. 3,604 ft. above the valley, and is the largest formation of its kind in the world.

El Centro (el sen'trō). City in S California, county seat of Imperial County, SE of Los Angeles. It is the second largest city below sea level in the U.S. (–52 ft. in elevation), and the chief storage and shipping center of the desert-reclaimed Imperial Valley. 12,590 (1950).

El Cerrito (el sẹ.rē'tō). City in W central California, in Contra Costa County, on San Francisco Bay NE of San Francisco. In the decade between the last two U.S. census its population more than doubled. 6,137 (1940), 18,011 (1950).

Elcesaites (el.sē'sạ.īts). [Also, **Elkesaites.**] Party or sect among the Jewish Christians of the 2nd century. They derived their name from Elkasai or Elxai, either their founder or leader, or the title of the book containing their doctrines, which they regarded as a special revelation. Their belief and practices were a mixture of Gnosticism and Judaism. They were finally confounded with the Ebionites.

El Chaco (el chä'kō). See **Chaco.**

Elche (el'chā). [Ancient name, **Ilici.**] City in E Spain, in the province of Alicante, situated on the Vinalapó River ab. 13 mi. SW of Alicante. Manufactures include leather, shoes, sandals, and esparto fabrics. The city is famous for its grove of date palms, the northernmost stand of this tree; it trades in dates and palm fronds. Elche is an episcopal see, and the scene of an annual mystery play. Architecturally the town has an African atmosphere, with picturesque churches. A Roman colony in ancient times, it was held by the Moors from the 8th to the 13th century. The castle of Calandura is in the vicinity. 55,877 (1950).

Elchingen (el'ċhing.ẹn). Village in S Germany, in Bavaria, situated near the Danube River ab. 7 mi. NE of Ulm. Here, on Oct. 14, 1805, the Austrians were defeated by Michel Ney (created afterward Duc d'Elchingen). The battle was followed by the capitulation of Ulm.

Elchingen, Duc d'. A title of **Ney, Michel.**

El Cid Campeador (el thēᴛʜ' käm"pā.ä.ᴛʜōr'). See **Cid, the.**

El Cobre (kō'ʙʀā). See **Cobre.**

Elda (el'dä). Town in E Spain, in the province of Alicante, situated on the Vinalapó River ab. 18 mi. NW of Alicante. It is an agricultural market town, with manufactures of paper and esparto articles. The ruins of a Gothic castle are of interest. 20,050 (1940).

El Deán Funes (el dā.än' fö'nās). See **Funes, Gregorio.**

Elder (el'dėr), **Eliza.** Maiden name of **Brightwen, Eliza.**

Elder Brother Society. See **Brothers' Society.**

Elder Knowell (nō′el), **the.** See **Knowell, the Elder.**
Elder Loveless (luv′les). See **Loveless, Elder.**
Elder Sister, The. Novel by Frank Swinnerton, published in 1925. It is a study of jealousy and the eternal triangle.
El Desdén con el desdén (el dez.dän′ kōn el dez.dän′). See **Desdén con el desdén, El.**
El Dirr (el dir′). [Also: **Ed Dirr, Dehr, Derr.**] Village in NE Africa, in Upper Egypt, on the Nile River ab. 70 mi. N of Wadi Halfa: noted for a small rock temple of Rameses II.
El Divino (el dē.bē′nō). Epithet of **Herrera, Fernando de.**
Eldon (el′don). City in C Missouri, in Miller County near Jefferson City: marketing center for a farming region. Manufactures include cheese and men's clothing. 2,766 (1950).
Eldon, 1st Earl of. Title of **Scott, John.**
Eldora (el.dō′ra). City in C Iowa, county seat of Hardin County, on the Iowa River, in a resort and farming region. 3,107 (1950).
El Dorado (el dō.rā′dō). City in S Arkansas, county seat of Union County: chief petroleum drilling and refining center in Arkansas. 23,076 (1950).
Eldorado (el.dō.rā′dō). City in SE Illinois, in Saline County: mining center. 4,500 (1950).
El Dorado (el dō.rā′dō). City in SE Kansas, county seat of Butler County, ab. 27 mi. NE of Wichita. Originally a cattle town, it is now a refining center for the state's richest oil-producing region. 11,037 (1950).
El Dorado (el dō.rä′ᴛʜō). [Also, **Manoa.**] Legendary city of great wealth which, during the 16th and 17th centuries and part of the 18th, was supposed to exist somewhere in the N part of South America. Beginning c1532, a number of expeditions were made by the Spaniards in search of this phantom; the explorers suffered terrible hardships, and hundreds died. The conquest and settlement of New Granada resulted from the quest; the mountain regions of Venezuela, the Orinoco and Amazon rivers, and the great forests E of the Andes were made known to the world; and later in the 16th century the English, led or sent by Sir Walter Raleigh, penetrated into Guiana, obtaining a claim on that country which resulted in their modern colony. The story of El Dorado arose from a yearly ceremony of an Indian tribe near what is now Bogotá, Colombia. According to the story, the chief of the Guatavitá in the highlands of Bogotá (Colombia) was periodically smeared with oil or balsam, and then covered with gold dust until his whole body had a gilded appearance, after which he threw gold, emeralds, and other precious stones into a sacred lake and then bathed there. This ceremony ceased upon the conquest of the tribe of Guatavitá by the Chibchans, but the tradition of this extraordinary rite remained and gradually spread very far, though in a more or less distorted form. In common and poetical language the name El Dorado, originally applied to the ruler, has now been transferred to the city or country which was the object of the quest.
"El Dorado" (el dō.rä′dō). Occasional nickname of **California.**
Eldorado Mines. See **Port Radium.**
Eldorado Springs (el.dō.rā′dō). City in SW Missouri, in Cedar County, ab. 60 mi. NE of Joplin, in the Ozark Plateau: mineral springs. 2,618 (1950).
Eldoret (el.dō.ret′). Town in British East Africa, in Kenya, situated in the highlands of the W part of the colony. It is the chief commercial and administrative center for the Uasin Gishu Plateau, a fertile grassland region and one of the most healthful regions in the country. Nearby is a large forest which supports a mill industry. The plateau is occupied almost entirely by European farmers, some of them descendants of the original Boer settlers. The town is ab. 577 mi. NW of Mombasa on the Kenya-Uganda railway. European pop., 600 (1946).
Eldridge (el′drij), **Paul.** b. at Philadelphia, May 5, 1888—. American novelist, short-story writer, poet, and teacher. He was graduated (B.S., 1909) from Temple University and from the University of Pennsylvania (M.A., 1911), served (1913) as lecturer on American literature at the Sorbonne, and was a teacher of romance languages (1914 *et seq.*) in the New York City high-school system. Among his volumes of verse are *Vanitas* (1920), *Our Dead Selves* (1923), *Cobwebs and Cosmos* (1930), and *I Bring A Sword* (1945). His novels include *If After Every Tempest* (1941) and *Madonna With the Cat* (1942); with George Sylvester Viereck, he was the coauthor of *My First Two Thousand Years* (1928), *Salome* (1930), and *The Invincible Adam* (1932). He has also published collections of short stories, including *And the Sphinx Spoke* (1921), *Irony and Pity* (1926), *One Man Show* (1933), *Virgins and Other Stories* (1945), *The Truth About Phyllis Warren* (1945), and *Men and Women* (1946).
Eldsich (el.dzik′). A rarely used name for the third-magnitude star ι Draconis.
El Duque Job (el dō′kā ʜōʙ′). Pseudonym of **Gutiérrez Nájera, Manuel.**
Eleanor of Aquitaine (el′a.nor; ak.wi.tān′). [Also: **Eleanor of Guienne**; French, **Aliénor.**] b. c1122; d. at Fontevrault, Maine-et-Loire, France, April 1, 1204. Queen of France and England. She was the daughter of William X, Duke of Aquitaine, and came into her inheritance on his death in 1137. She married the same year Louis of France, who within a month of the marriage became Louis VII of France. She accompanied him on the second Crusade and there, it is said (but without foundation) was improperly intimate with her uncle, Raymond of Antioch. In 1152, despite the fact that she had borne him two daughters, Louis divorced her (or had the marriage annulled) on the grounds of consanguinity. That same year she was married to the English prince, Henry of Anjou, bringing to him the possessions in Aquitaine. When he became king as Henry II in 1154, the stage was set for the long series of wars between England and France over the French territories of the English crown. Eleanor soon discovered that her husband was unfaithful and, though his affair with Rosamond Clifford occurred later, she soon grew to dislike him. In 1173 she backed her sons in their revolt against Henry and was kept under surveillance until Henry's death in 1189. She became a chief adviser to both Richard I and John. When John attempted to usurp the throne during Richard's absence on the third Crusade, she broke up the conspiracy and later reconciled the brothers. She was instrumental in ransoming Richard from his captivity in France. She saw to it that the succession passed to John and supported him against the claims of her grandson Arthur of Brittany. She was a patron of literature and maintained a brilliant court at Poitiers.
Eleanor of Brittany (brit′a.ni). [Called the **Damsel of Brittany.**] Daughter of Geoffroy, third son of Henry II of England (and hence a niece of King John). Geoffroy was the duke of Brittany through his wife Constance, the daughter and heiress of Duke Conan IV, and was succeeded by Eleanor's brother Arthur. She was imprisoned by John, and died in 1241.
Eleanor of Castile (kas.tēl′). d. at Grantham, England, in November, 1290. Sister of Alfonso X of Castile, and wife of Edward I of England.
Eleanor of Provence (pro.väṅs′). d. at Amesbury, England, 1291. Daughter of the Count of Provence, and wife of Henry III of England.
Eleatics (el. ē.at′iks). School of Greek philosophy founded by Xenophanes of Colophon, who resided in Elea, or Velia, in Magna Graecia. The most distinguished philosophers of this school were Parmenides and Zeno. The main Eleatic doctrines are developments of the conception that the One, or Absolute, alone is real.
Eleazar (el.ē.ā′zar). In the Bible, the third son of Aaron, and his successor as high priest.
Eleazar. In *Lust's Dominion*, all or parts of which have been attributed to Christopher Marlowe, a lustful and revengeful Moor, passionately loved by the sensual Queen of Spain. In his villainies he resembles Barabas in Marlowe's *Jew of Malta.*
Eleazar. Famous magician in Alain René le Sage's *Gil Blas.*
Electoral Hesse (hes). See **Hesse-Cassel.**
Electra (ē.lek′tra). City in C Texas, in Wichita County, NW of Dallas: oil wells; manufactures of drilling tools and oil-well machinery. 4,970 (1950).
Electra. In Greek mythology, the daughter of Oceanus and Tethys, who was the daughter of heaven.
Electra. In Greek legend, the daughter of Agamemnon and Clytemnestra, and sister of Orestes. The events of her

life have been dramatized by Aeschylus, by Sophocles in his *Electra*, by Euripides in his *Electra*, and by various modern poets.

Electra. In Greek mythology, one of the seven Pleiades.

Electra. The fourth-magnitude star 17 Tauri.

Electre (ā.lektr). Highly ironic play (1937), based on the familiar Electra myth, by the French writer Jean Giraudoux (1882–1944). Beneath the Greek trappings are concealed the author's deep concern and discouragement over the state of Europe just before World War II.

Electrides (ę.lek′tri.dēz). In Greek legend, the Amber Islands (where the trees weep amber), situated at the mouth of the fabulous Eridanus (later identified with the Po River in Italy). See also **Amber Islands.**

Elegy Written in a Country Churchyard. Elegiac poem by Thomas Gray, published in 1751. It went through 11 editions in a short time, and has been many times pirated, imitated, and parodied. (In the course of the several generations since it was written it has also been so often misquoted, in print, that few scholars now have the temerity to insist that anyone can be sure of exactly what all the original words and spellings may have been.) It has also been translated into Hebrew, Greek, Latin, Italian, Portuguese, French, Russian, and German.

Eleia (ę.lī′ạ). See ancient **Elis.**

Elein (ę.lān′). See under **Elaine,** 5.

Elektra (ę.lek′trạ). Opera in one act by Richard Strauss, with a libretto by Hugo von Hoffmannsthal, first produced at Dresden on Jan. 5, 1909. Taken from the Greek drama, the work depicts Electra's grief at the death of her father, and her final rejoicing when his murder is avenged by her brother Orestes.

Elementary Forms of Religious Life, The. See **Formes élémentaires de la vie religieuse, Les.**

Elements (of **Euclid**) (ū′klid). Most popular mathematical work of all time, the earliest extant Greek treatise on mathematics, and the oldest scientific textbook still in actual use. It is a book on geometry, both plane and solid, and the theory of numbers, a compendium of mathematical knowledge of the time, arranged in logical order. It was composed by Euclid c300 B.C., was frequently copied in manuscript, and was first printed in 1482. Since that time over a thousand editions have appeared.

Eleonora (el″ę.ǫ.nō′rạ). Poem written by Dryden, in 1692, in memory of the Countess of Abingdon.

Eleonora. Story by Edgar Allan Poe (1842) in *The Gift.*

Eleonora of Este (es′tā). b. June 19, 1537; d. Feb. 10, 1581. Italian princess; a friend of Tasso.

Elephanta (el.ę.fan′tạ). [Hindustani, **Gharapuri.**] Small island in Bombay harbor, Union of India, ab. 6 mi. E of Bombay, famous for its caves with Hindu sculptures.

Elephantine (el″ę.fan.tī′nē). [Arabic, **Geziret Aswan.**] In ancient geography, an island in the Nile, opposite Syene (Aswan). From it came Egyptian kings of the Vth dynasty. It contains monuments of Thothmes III and Amenhotep III, and a Nilometer of Ptolemaic date.

El Escorial (el es.kō′ri.ạl; Spanish, el es.kō.ryäl′). [Also, **Escorial de Arriba** (dā är.rē′ʙä).] Town in C Spain, in the province of Madrid, situated in the Sierra de Guadarama, NW of Madrid. It is a summer resort, known for its hotels and parks, famous military and ecclesiastical schools, and palace of Don Carlos. The Augustinian monastery of San Lorenzo del Escorial is famous as the former summer and autumn residence of the kings of Spain. It forms a huge rectangle flanked by towers and containing gardens, terraces, church, monastery, library, and apartments for the king and the royal court. The building was erected in the period 1563–86, but many changes were effected afterward; the best architects of Spain and Italy participated in the work. The church contains murals by Luca Giordano and others and the tombs of many Spanish kings. The library contains over 140,000 volumes and manuscripts, among them valuable Latin and Arabic codices.

Elets (yi.lets′). See **Yelets.**

Eleusinian Mysteries (el.ū̦.sin′i.ạn). Religious ceremonies performed in ancient Greece in honor of Demeter, the Greek equivalent of the Roman Ceres, and her daughter, Persephone (the Roman Proserpine). They were held at Eleusis, in Attica, about 10 miles from Athens, and were the chief cause of its fame. At first initiation into the mysteries was limited to residents of Attica; later it was extended to all Greek citizens, and still later, Romans were admitted to the privileges of membership. Barbarians (which initially of course, included the Romans), murderers, and all who were guilty of serious crimes were barred. A candidate for initiation was proposed by an Athenian citizen who already belonged. The candidates were called *mystae* before full initiation, and *epoptae,* or seers, after. The mysteries were divided into two parts, the Lesser, held in Antestherion, corresponding more or less to February, and the Greater, in Boedromion, equivalent to part of the end of September and the beginning of October. The mysteries were regarded by the ancients themselves as having moral and ethical values in that they promised, or seemed to promise, life after death as a reward for goodness. Hadrian and Marcus Aurelius did not think it beneath them to accept initiation. Valentinian, the Christian emperor, allowed the Eleusinian mysteries after he had abolished all others, but Theodosius did away with them at the end of the 4th century.

Eleusis (ę.lö′sis). *Deme* (administrative division) of Attica, Greece, the seat of a very ancient cult of Demeter, and of the famous Eleusinian Mysteries. The most important monuments lay within the sacred enclosure, which consisted of a spacious terrace on the E slope of the acropolis, surrounded by a massive wall. The precinct was entered by two propylaea or monumental gateways in succession, and its chief building was the temple of the mysteries, whose unique architecture and successive transformations, as well as those of the entire precinct, have been revealed by the excavations of the Archaeological Society of Athens, carried out at intervals since 1882.

Eleusis, Bas-relief of. Ancient Greek work of high artistic importance in the National Museum, Athens. It represents Demeter, Kora, and Triptolemus, and is most delicate in execution and expression. It dates from the early 5th century B.C.

Eleuthera (ę.lö′thėr.ạ). Island in the Atlantic Ocean, E of Miami, Fla.: part of the Bahama Islands. It was settled in 1647 under a grant of Charles I of England. The major industries are fishing and vegetable farming. Length, ab. 80 mi.; pop. 6,430 (1943).

Eleutherius (el.ū̦.thir′i.us), Saint. [Also, **Eleutheros** (ę.lö′thėr.os).] b. at Nicopolis, in Epirus; fl. second half of 2nd century. Pope from 175 to 189. He was an opponent of the Montanists.

Eleutheropolis (ę.lö.thėr.op′ǫ.lis). [Modern name, **Beit-Jibrin.**] In ancient geography, a town in Palestine, ab. 22 mi. SW of Jerusalem.

Eleutherus (ę.lö′thėr.us). In ancient geography, a river of Phoenicia, the modern Nahr el-Kebir ("Great River"), N of Tripoli. On its banks Jonathan the Asmonean met and defeated Demetrius.

Elevation of the Cross. [Also, **Raising of the Cross.**] Subject of religious paintings, notably two of the 17th-century Flemish school: **1.** Painting by Rubens (1610), in Antwerp cathedral, Belgium. The cross is being raised to position by a number of men pushing in front and others hauling by a rope behind. On the side panels are seen the holy women, soldiers, and the execution of the two thieves. **2.** Painting by Van Dyck (1632), in the Church of Notre Dame at Courtrai, Belgium. Christ is already fixed on the cross, which is being put in position by four men, attended by soldiers.

El Faiyum (el fī.öm′). See **Fayum,** city.

El Fasher (el fä′shėr). Capital of Darfur province, Anglo-Egyptian Sudan, in NE Africa. It is situated toward the N central part of the province and is the center of several caravan routes and roads. 23,250 (est. 1949).

Elfeld (el′felt). See **Eltville.**

El Ferrol del Caudillo (el fer.rōl′ del kou.ᴛʜē′lyō). [Also, **El Ferrol.**] Town in NW Spain, in the province of La Coruña, situated on the Atlantic coast ab. 11 mi. NE of La Coruña. It has a good natural harbor and is an important naval base, with an arsenal, docks, large shipyards used for naval construction, and a marine academy and nautical school. There are fisheries, and linen and leather factories. Nearby is the submarine base of La Graña. The town was a mere fishing village prior to the construction of the arsenal in 1726, after the selection of the site by Charles IV. The British defeated the French fleet here in 1805, forcing the town to surrender; the French occupied it again in 1809. In the Spanish civil war it was occupied by Nationalist troops in 1936. It was the birthplace of Generalissimo Franco and was renamed after him. 77,030 (1950).

Elfrida (el.frē'dạ). [Also, **Ælfthryth.**] b. c945; d. c1000. Anglo-Saxon queen, daughter of Ordgar, ealdorman of Devon, wife first of Aethelwald, ealdorman of the East Anglians, and, after his death, of King Edgar, by whom she was the mother of Ethelred II (Ethelred the Unready). She is said to have caused the murder of her stepson Edward, at Corfe, in order to secure the election of Ethelred.

El Fuerte (el fwer'tā). [Also: **Fuerte, Villa del Fuerte.**] Town in W Mexico, in Sinaloa state, on the Fuerte River. Pop. under 5,000 (1940).

Elgar (el'gạr, -gär), Sir **Edward William.** b. at Broadheath, Worcestershire, England, June 2, 1857; d. at Worcester, England, Feb. 23, 1934. English composer, professor of music (1904 *et seq.*) at Birmingham University. He wrote the oratorios *The Dream of Gerontius* (1900), *The Apostles* (1903), and *The Kingdom* (1906). He also composed much for the orchestra, including *The Enigma Variations* (1899), the overtures *Cockaigne* and *In the South, Symphony in A Flat* (1908), *Symphony in E Flat* (1911), and *Introduction and Allegro* for solo quartet of strings and string orchestra; wrote several marches under the title *Pomp and Circumstance.* Of his earlier cantatas *Light and Life, King Olaf,* and *Caractacus* are the most notable. He was knighted in 1904, having composed the *Coronation Ode* (1902) for King Edward VII.

Elgar, Francis. b. at Portsmouth, England, April 24, 1845; d. Jan. 17, 1909. British naval architect. He was adviser in naval construction to the Japanese government (1879–81), director of dockyards at the British admiralty (1886–92), and connected with private shipbuilding firms from 1892. He wrote *Ships of the Royal Navy* (1873), and numerous technical papers.

Elgin (el'jin). City in NE Illinois, in Kane and Cook counties, on the Fox River ab. 35 mi. NW of Chicago: manufactures include watches, machinery, paper products, butter, and processed milk. It is the seat of the Elgin Academy, the Elgin Observatory, and the Elgin Watchmakers College, and also of a large religious publications house. 44,223 (1950).

Elgin (el'gin). City and royal burgh in N Scotland, county seat of Moray, situated on the river Lossie ab. 13 mi. W of Buckie, ab. 572 mi. N of London by rail. It contains a cathedral, founded in 1224 but greatly damaged by fire and partly rebuilt toward the end of the 14th century. The architecture is chiefly Early English style. The ornament is rich, and the tracery of special beauty. There are two western towers, and a good chapter house. 10,831 (est. 1948).

Elgin. City in S central Texas, in Bastrop County, ab. 20 mi. E of Austin, in a farming and oil-producing region: railroad junction. 3,168 (1950).

Elgin (el'gin). Former name of **Moray** or **Morayshire.**

Elgin, Earl of. Title held by various members of the **Bruce** family in Scotland.

Elgin Marbles. Collection of Greek sculptures comprising the bulk of the surviving plastic decoration of the Parthenon, and a caryatid and column from the Erechtheum, and recognized as containing the finest existing productions of Greek sculpture. The marbles, now in the British Museum, were brought from Athens between 1801 and 1803 by Thomas Bruce, the 7th Earl of Elgin. The Parthenon sculptures were executed under the direction of Phidias, c440 B.C. The collection includes remains of the pediment statues in the round, a great part of the frieze, in low relief, ab. 525 ft. long, which surrounded the exterior of the cella, and 15 of the metopes of the exterior frieze, carved in very high relief with episodes of the contest between the Centaurs and the Lapiths. Among the chief of the pediment figures are the reclining figure of Theseus, Iris with wind-blown drapery, and the group of one reclining and two seated female figures popularly called the "Three Fates."

Elginshire (el'gin.shir). Former name of **Moray** or **Morayshire.**

El Giza or **El Gizeh** (el gē'zẹ). See **Giza,** city.

El Goléa (el gō.lā'ạ). Town and caravan station in S Algeria, in NW Africa, ab. 225 mi. S of Laghouat and 170 mi. SW of Ghardaïa. In 1891 it became an important French military post for the pacification of the Sahara. The oasis is important for its date palms and other fruit trees. It is on the main road crossing the Sahara. 6,279 (1948).

Elgon (el'gon), **Mount.** Extinct volcano in E Africa, on the border between Kenya and Uganda. It is 25 mi. E of Mbale, Uganda, and is the watershed between Lake Kyoga and Lakes Victoria and Rudolf. The mountain can be climbed easily. Elevation, ab. 14,140 ft.

Elgoni (el.gō'nē) or **Elgonyi** (el.gō'nyē). See **Kony.**

El Gran Presidente (el grän' prā.sē.ᴛʜen'tā). Epithet of **Montes, Ismael.**

El Greco (grek'ō). See **Greco, El.**

El Guayas (el gwä'yäs). See **Guayas,** province.

Elhanan (el.hā'nạn). In the Bible, according to 2 Sam. xxi. 19, the slayer of the brother of Goliath.

El Hasa (el has'ạ, hä'sạ). See **Hasa, El.**

Eli (ē'lī). [Also, **Heli.**] In the Bible, a Hebrew judge and high priest. He failed to punish the sins of his two sons Hophni and Phinehas, and the destruction of his house ensued. At news of a defeat of the Israelites by the Philistines, in which his sons had been killed and the Ark of the Covenant taken, he fell backward from his seat and broke his neck. He was a judge of Israel for 40 years, and was 98 years old when he died. 1 Sam. 12, etc.

Eli. Oratorio by Sir Michael Costa, produced at the Birmingham Festival, Aug. 29, 1855.

Elia (ē'li.ạ). Pseudonym of Charles Lamb in his essays contributed (1820 *et seq.*) to the *London Magazine.* They were collected as *Essays of Elia* in 1823, and *Last Essays of Elia* in 1833. The name was that of a clerk in the South Sea House, which Lamb remembered having heard there as a boy, and was at first used as a jest at the end of *Recollections of South Sea House,* the first of his essays. The Briget and James Elia of the essays are Mary and John Lamb, the brother and sister of the author.

Eliab (ẹ.lī'ab). Name of several persons mentioned in the Old Testament, including David's eldest brother. 1 Sam. xvi. 6.

Eliab. In Dryden and Tate's *Absalom and Achitophel,* Henry Bennet, Earl of Arlington.

Éliacin (ā.lyȧ.saṅ). Pseudonym of **Hervieu, Paul Ernest.**

Eliakim (ẹ.lī'ạ.kim). In the Old Testament, the name of several persons, of whom the most notable is the son of Hilkiah and master of Hezekiah's household. 2 Kings, xviii. 18, etc.

Éliante (ā.lyäṅt). In Molière's comedy *The Misanthrope,* a reasonable, lovable girl; contrasted with Célimène, the coquette.

Elias (ẹ.lī'ạs). Greek name of **Elijah.**

Elidure (el'i.dör). Legendary king of Britain, mentioned in Geoffrey of Monmouth's *Historia regum Britanniae.*

Élie de Beaumont (ā.lē dẹ bō.môṅ), **Jean Baptiste Armand Louis Léonce.** b. at Canon, Calvados, France, Sept. 25, 1798; d. there, Sept. 22, 1874. French geologist. He became professor of geology at the École des Mines in 1829, and at the Collège de France in 1832, and life secretary of the Academy of Sciences in 1853. He published *Recherches sur quelques-unes des révolutions de la surface du globe* (1829–30), *Carte géologique de France* (1843), *Notices sur les systèmes de montagnes* (1852), and other works.

Eliezer (el.i.ē'zėr, ē.li-). In the Old Testament, the name of several persons. The most notable are: **1.** The chief servant of Abraham, called Eliezer of Damascus. Gen. xv. 2. **2.** The second son of Moses and Zipporah. Ex. xviii. 4.

Eligius (ẹ.lij'i.us) or **Éloi** or **Eloy** (ā.lwȧ), Saint. b. near Limoges, France, c588; d. Dec. 1, 660. Bishop of Noyon-Tournai. He went to Paris in 610, and gained the favor of Clotaire II and Dagobert I both by his skill as a goldsmith and by his piety, which he displayed in founding churches and monasteries and in distributing alms to the poor. On the death of Dagobert in 639, he entered the priesthood and was chosen bishop of Noyon-Tournai in 640.

Elihu (ẹ.lī'hū). Name of several persons in the Old Testament, of whom the most notable is one of the friends of

Job. He describes himself as the youngest of the interlocutors. Job, xxxii.–xxxvii.

Elijah (ẹ.lī'jạ). [Greek, **Elias.**] Hebrew prophet of the 9th century B.C. An account of him is given in 1 Kings, xvii.–xxi., 2 Kings, i.–xi., and 2 Chron. xxi. 12–15. He appears before Ahab, king of Israel (who had given himself up to the idolatry of his Phoenician wife Jezebel), and predicts a great drought. Compelled to seek refuge in flight and concealment, he is miraculously fed by ravens in the torrent bed of the stream Cherith, and by the widow of Zarephath, whose dead son he restores to life. In the extremity of the famine he reappears before Ahab, before whom he calls down fire from heaven to consume a sacrifice to Jehovah, with the result that the king orders the extermination of the prophets of Baal, who are unable to call down fire to consume the offerings to Baal. Elijah then puts an end to the drought by prayers to Jehovah. Later he denounces Ahab and Jezebel for having despoiled and murdered Naboth, and is eventually carried to heaven in a chariot of fire. In the New Testament he is called Elias.

Elijah. Oratorio by Felix Mendelssohn, with words from the Old Testament. It was first performed at Birmingham, England, on Aug. 26, 1846.

Elijah Pogram (pō'grạm). See **Pogram, Elijah.**

Elikon (e.lē.kôn'). See **Helicon.**

Elim (ē'lim). In Biblical geography, a station in the wanderings of the Israelites, noted for its fountains; not identified.

Elimberum (el.im.ber'um). Gallic name of **Auch.**

Elimelech (ẹ.lim'ẹ.lek). In the Old Testament, the husband of Naomi. Ruth, i. 1–3.

Elinor Barley (el'i.nọr bär'li). Novelette by Sylvia Townsend Warner, published in 1930.

Elinor Dashwood (dash'wu̇d). See **Dashwood, Elinor** and **Marianne.**

Elío (ā.lē'ō), **Francisco Javier.** b. at Pamplona, Spain, March 4, 1767; d. at Valencia, Spain, Sept. 4, 1822. Spanish general. In 1805, having attained the grade of colonel, he was sent to the Río de la Plata, and given command of the forces operating against the English. In April, 1810, he was recalled to Spain, but returned at the end of the year as viceroy of Buenos Aires, appointed by the Spanish junta of the regency. The junta of Buenos Aires refused to recognize his commission, war followed, and Elío was besieged at Montevideo, but eventually arranged a treaty with the revolutionists by which both parties recognized the authority of Ferdinand VII and the unity of the Spanish nation, and agreed to refer their differences to the Spanish Cortes (Oct. 20, 1811). Elío was recalled to Spain two months after, and in 1812 and 1813 commanded against the French in Catalonia and Valencia, winning a series of brilliant victories. In 1814 he was made governor and captain-general of Valencia and Murcia. The revolution of 1820 caused his deposition and imprisonment. Some of his friends made an armed attempt to liberate him; the plot failed, and Elío, accused of instigating it, was found guilty by a court-martial and executed.

Eliocroca (ē″li.ọ.krō'kạ). Latin name of **Lorca.**

Eliot (el'i.ọt, el'yọt), **Charles William.** b. at Boston, March 20, 1834; d. at Northeast Harbor, Me., Aug. 22, 1926. American educator, president of Harvard, noted for his introduction of many progressive changes in the university's organization, administration, and curricula, and as editor of the well-known "five-foot shelf" of *Harvard Classics.* Graduated (1853) from Harvard, he became (1854) tutor in mathematics at that institution and served (c1858–63) as assistant professor of mathematics and chemistry. He became (1865) professor of chemistry at the Massachusetts Institute of Technology and drew notice with his two articles on "The New Education: Its Organization," which were published (1869) in the *Atlantic Monthly.* As successor to Thomas Hill, he was inaugurated as president of Harvard on Oct. 19, 1869. During his notable administration, which continued until his resignation in 1909, Harvard added graduate schools of arts and sciences and the applied sciences and business administration, increased its revenue-bearing treasury some ten times over, made important reforms in the administrative structure, raised the standards of medical education, introduced the elective system for undergraduates, and liberalized the disciplinary regulations at Harvard College. He was a member (1910–16) of the Harvard board of overseers and a member of the general education board and trustee of the Rockefeller Foundation and Carnegie Foundation for the Advancement of Teaching. Among his writings are: *The Happy Life* (1896), *American Contributions to Civilization* (1897), *Educational Reform* (1898), *The Religion of the Future* (1909), and *A Late Harvest* (ed. by M. A. DeWolfe Howe, 1924).

Eliot, Edward Granville. [Title, 3rd Earl of **St. Germans.**] b. in England, Aug. 29, 1798; d. there, Oct. 7, 1877. English diplomat. Envoy extraordinary (1834) to Spain during Carlist war where he concluded "Eliot Convention" for civilized treatment of prisoners. Member of Parliament (1837–45); chief secretary for Ireland (1841); and lord lieutenant (1852); postmaster general under Peel; viceroy of Ireland under Palmerston (1855) but shortly retired. Confidential adviser to Queen Victoria on family affairs.

Eliot, George. [Pseudonym of **Mary Ann** (or **Marian**) **Evans.**] b. at Arbury Farm, near Nuneaton, Warwickshire, England, Nov. 22, 1819; d. at Chelsea, London, Dec. 22, 1880. English psychological novelist, poet, and essayist. She is considered by some authorities the greatest of English women novelists and the equal of Dickens and Thackeray. She began her literary career by translating (1844–46) into English a life of Jesus written by the German theologian David Friedrich Strauss and as a contributor to and assistant editor of the *Westminster Review* (1850–53). Her career as a novelist opened (1857) with *The Sad Fortunes of the Reverend Amos Barton,* the beginning of *Scenes from Clerical Life* (1858). Her other major works include *Adam Bede* (1859), the story of an idealistic carpenter, *The Mill on the Floss* (1860), in which Tom and Maggie Tulliver represent the author and her brother Isaac, *Silas Marner* (1861), a long short-story rather than a novel, *Romola* (1863), an historical novel dealing with Florence in the days of Savonarola, and *Middlemarch* (1871–72), a psychological study of provincial life. Her lesser works, in the opinion of most modern critics, are *Felix Holt, the Radical* (1866), a political novel which has Gerald Massey, the English poet and radical, as its hero, *Daniel Deronda* (1876), her last fiction, a study of spiritual conflict and development, her poems *How Lisa Loved the King* (1867), *The Spanish Gypsy* (1868), and *The Legend of Jubal* (1870), and her satirical essays, *Impressions of Theophrastus Such* (1879). In 1854 she entered into a union (that lasted until his death) with the philosopher George Henry Lewes, who was unable to marry her because of the refusal of his wife to grant him a divorce. On May 6, 1880, she married an old friend, John Walter Cross, who later (1885–86) published *George Eliot's Life as Related in Her Letters and Journals.*

Eliot, George Fielding. b. at Brooklyn, N.Y., June 22, 1894—. American soldier, military analyst, and author. Taken to Australia as a child, and educated there, he served (1914–18) with the Australian Imperial Force in World War I. Arrived in the U.S., he began his writing career in 1926 and held a commission (1922–30) in the U.S. military intelligence reserve. He has served as military and naval correspondent for the New York *Herald Tribune* (1939 *et seq.*) and military analyst (1939–46) for the Columbia Broadcasting System. Author of *The Ramparts We Watch* (1938), *Bombs Bursting in Air* (1939), *Hour of Triumph* (1944), *The Strength We Need* (1946), and other books.

Eliot, Sir **John.** b. at Port Eliot, on the Tamar, England, April 20, 1592; d. in the Tower of London, Nov. 27, 1632. English patriot. He was educated at Oxford, studied law at London, and in 1625, as a member of the first Parliament of Charles I, came into prominence by the vehemence and irresistible eloquence with which he supported the measures of the constitutional party. As the leader of the opposition in the second Parliament (1626) he was sent to prison, in company with Sir Dudley Digges, by the king; but was released, together with Sir Dudley, when Parliament refused to proceed to business without them. In the third Parliament (1628–29) he had a principal share in drawing up the Remonstrance and the Petition of Right. He was arrested on the dissolution of Parliament in 1629, and sentenced, on a charge of conspiracy against the king, to a fine of two thousand pounds, and to imprisonment until he should acknowledge his guilt.

Eliot, John. [Called the **"Apostle of the Indians."**] b. at Nasing, Essex, England, 1604; d. at Roxbury, Mass., May 21, 1690. Missionary to the Indians of Massachusetts. His principal work is a translation of the Bible into the Indian language (1661–63). He also wrote an Indian catechism (1653) and grammar (1666).

Eliot, John. b. at Boston, May 31, 1754; d. there, Feb. 14, 1813. American clergyman and biographer. He published the *New England Biographical Dictionary* (1809) and others.

Eliot, Sir **John.** b. at Lamesley, Durham, England, May 25, 1839; d. at Cavalaire, France, March 18, 1908. Anglo-Indian educator and meteorologist. He was educated at St. John's College, Cambridge, and was professor of mathematics at the Rurki Engineering College in India (1869–72) and at the Muir Central College at Allahabad (1872–74), professor of physics at the Presidency College, Calcutta, and also meteorological reporter to the government of Bengal (1874–86), meteorological reporter to the government of India and director-general of Indian observatories (1886–1903), and on his retirement in 1903 was made Knight Commander of the Indian Empire. Besides many papers on meteorological subjects, he published *Handbook of Cyclonic Storms in the Bay of Bengal* and *The Climatological Atlas of India.*

Eliot, T. S. [Full name, **Thomas Stearns Eliot.**] b. at St. Louis, Mo., 1888—. American-born poet and critic who became (1927) a naturalized British subject. His poetic commentaries on the civilization and spirit of his day (notably *The Waste Land,* 1922, which was awarded the Dial poetry prize), with their distinctive technique of ironic juxtaposition of ideal and reality, subtle allusions to direct or disguised quotations from a great variety of earlier literary works, and a poetic logic which eliminated the conventional transitions between images and episodes, profoundly influenced younger writers on both sides of the Atlantic. He was awarded the 1948 Nobel prize for literature. Educated at Harvard, the Sorbonne, and Oxford, he lived (1914 *et seq.*) in England, where he worked first as a bank clerk and then with the publishing firm of Faber and Gwyer (later Faber and Faber), and until 1939 edited *The Criterion,* a literary review. His earlier poetry, characterized by pessimism, includes *Prufrock and Other Observations* (1917), *Poems* (1919), which includes "Portrait of a Lady," "Sweeney Among the Nightingales," "Gerontion," and 21 other poems, *The Hollow Men* (1925), and *Journey of the Magi* (1927). He then developed a more limpid and meditative style, as in *A Song for Simeon* (1928), *Animula* (1929), and *Marina* (1930). After turning to Anglo-Catholicism he struck a note of quietist religious acceptance in *Ash Wednesday* (1930), *The Rock* (1934), and *Four Quartets* (1944), in all of which works he made use of the Anglican liturgy and such mystical writers as Saint John of the Cross in order to present a mood of restrained penitential hope and faith. He is the author also of the poetic dramas *Murder in the Cathedral* (1935), *Family Reunion* (1939), and *The Cocktail Party* (1949). His critical essays appeared in *The Sacred Wood* (1920), *An Essay of Poetic Drama* (1928), *Dante* (1929), *Selected Essays* (1932), *The Use of Poetry and the Use of Criticism* (1933), *After Strange Gods* (1934), *Elizabethan Essays* (1934), *Essays Ancient and Modern* (1936), *The Idea of a Christian Society* (1939), *What is a Classic?* (1945), and *Notes toward the Definition of Culture* (1949).

Eliott (el'i.ọt, el'yọt), **George Augustus.** [Title, 1st Baron **Heathfield of Gibraltar.**] b. at Stobs, Roxburghshire, Scotland, Dec. 25, 1717; d. at Aix-La-Chapelle (now Aachen, Germany), July 6, 1790. Scottish soldier. He was appointed (1775) governor of Gibraltar, which he defended (1779 *et seq.*) against the Spanish during a three-year siege, surviving a blockade and erecting defenses which withstood red-hot shot. He was made a Knight of the Bath and raised (1787) to the peerage as Baron Heathfield of Gibraltar.

Eliphalet (ẹ.lif'ạ.let). [Also, **Eliphelet.**] Name of several persons in the Old Testament, of whom the most notable are two sons of David.

Eliphaz (el'i.faz). In the Bible, the chief of the three friends of Job, surnamed the "Temanite." Job, ii. 11, etc.

Elis (ē'lis). [Also, **Eleia.**] In ancient geography, a country in the W part of the Peloponnesus, Greece, lying between Achaia on the N, Arcadia on the E, Messenia on the S, and the Ionian Sea on the W. It comprised three parts: Elis proper or Hollow Elis, Pisatis, and Triphylia. It contained the temple of the Olympian Zeus.

Elis. [Also, **Ilia.**] *Nomos* (department) in S Greece, situated on the Peloponnesus. It includes the provinces of Elis and Olympia. Capital, Pyrgos; pop. 187,867 (1951).

Élisa (ā.lē.zȧ). [Full title, **Élisa ou le voyage au mont Bernard**; Eng. trans., *"Elisa, or the Journey to Mount Bernard."*] Opera by Cherubini, words by Saint-Cyr, produced at Paris on Dec. 13, 1794.

Elisabeth (ẹ.liz'ạ.bẹth). See also **Elizabeth.**

Élisabeth de France (ā.lē.zȧ.bet dẹ fräṅs), Madame. [Full name, **Élisabeth Philippine Marie Hélène;** called Madame **Élisabeth.**] b. at Versailles, France, May 3, 1764; guillotined at Paris, May 10, 1794. French princess; sister of Louis XVI.

Élisabeth de France. French name of **Elizabeth of Valois.**

Élisabeth, ou Les Exilés en Sibérie (ā.lē.zȧ.bet ö lā.zeg-zē.lā äṅ sē.bā.rē). [Eng. trans., *"Elizabeth, or the Exiles in Siberia."*] Romance by Madame Cottin, published in 1806. The subject is the same as that of Xavier de Maistre's *Jeune Sibérienne,* a young girl going on foot from Siberia to St. Petersburg to beg for the pardon of her exiled father.

Elisabethville (ẹ.liz'ạ.bẹth.vil). Capital of Katanga province, Belgian Congo, in C Africa: the second largest city in the colony, and the center of its mining area. It is connected by rail with Capetown via the Rhodesias (2,305 mi.), to Lobito, Angola, via the Benguela Railway (1,309 mi.), and with Port Francqui via the Bas Congo-Katanga railroad (650 mi.). It is the headquarters of the Union Minière du Haut Katanga, the great mining and smelting company which runs most of the mines and associated enterprises in the Katanga region. The city is the main distribution center in the colony for heavy mining and industrial equipment. The town was founded in 1910 and named after Elizabeth, then queen of the Belgians. It is a modern city, with wide streets, high buildings, and most of the facilities for modern living. Pop. 103,352, including 7,793 Europeans (1950).

Elisabethville. Former name of **Katanga** province.

Elisabeth von Lothringen (ā.lā'zä.bet fon lōt'ring.ẹn). [Also, **Elisabeth von Nassau** (nä'sou).] b. in Lorraine, before 1400; d. at Saarbrücken, Germany, Jan. 17, 1456. German princess and author. After the death (1429) of her husband, Count Philip of Nassau-Saarbrücken, she undertook to adapt into German prose four French *chansons de geste: Herpin* (after *Lion de Bourges*), *Loher und Maller, Sibille* (both after lost French originals), and *Hugo Scheppel.* These are notable as marking the transition from medieval epics to the prose novel of modern times.

Elisabetta, Regina d'Inghilterra (ā.lē.zä.bet'tä rā.jē'-nä dēng.gēl.ter'rä). [Eng. trans., *"Elizabeth, Queen of England."*] Opera by Rossini, written in 1815 for the San Carlos at Naples, and produced at Paris on March 10, 1822.

Elisavetgrad (yi.lē.zạ.vet.grät'). A former name of **Kirovograd.**

Elisavetpol (yi.lē.zạ.vet'pọl). A former name of **Kirovabad.**

Élise (ā.lēz). In Molière's *L'Avare* (The Miser), the daughter of Harpagon, in love with Valère.

Elisena (el.i.sē'nạ). In the Spanish cycle of romances, a princess of Brittany; the mother of Amadis of Gaul.

Eliseus (el.i.sē'us). See **Elisha.**

Elisha (ẹ.lī'shạ). [Also, **Eliseus.**] fl. in the 9th century B.C. Hebrew prophet, the attendant and successor of Elijah. 1 Kings, xix. 15–21.

Elishah (ẹ.lī'shạ). In the Bible, in Gen. x. 4, the eldest son of Javan: identified with the Aeolians, with Sicily, and with the N coast of Africa.

Elisheba (ẹ.lish'ẹ.bạ). [Also, **Elizabeth.**] In the Bible, the wife of Aaron.

Elisío (ā.lē.zē'ö), **Américo.** Pseudonym of **Bonifácio, José.**

Elisir d'Amore (lä.lē.zēr' dä.mō'rä), **L'.** [Eng. trans., *"The Elixir of Love."*] Opera in two acts by Donizetti, with a libretto by Romani, first produced at Milan in 1832. The English version was called *The Love Spell* and was produced at the Drury Lane Theatre, London, in 1839. The comic work shows the effect of a supposed love philter (in reality a bottle of wine sold by the quack Dulcamara) on a group of simple villagers.

Elissa (ẹ.lis'ạ). [Also, **Elisa.**] Under the name Dido, the heroine of the fourth book of Vergil's *Aeneid*. According to the tradition she was the daughter of King Matgen (or Belus), grandson of Eth-Baal of Phoenicia. She was married to her uncle Sicharbaal or Sicharbas (the Greek Acerbas and the Sychaeus of Vergil). After her husband was murdered by her brother Pygmalion, she set out at the head of Tyrian colonists to Africa. In Africa she bought as much land as could be enclosed in the hide of a bull, but by cutting the hide into thin strips managed to obtain a fairly large area on which she built the citadel around which Carthage grew up. To escape wedding the barbarian king Iarbas (Hiarbas) she erected a funeral pyre and stabbed herself upon it. According to Vergil her death was due to her despair at her desertion by Aeneas. In the popular mind she became confounded with Dido, a surname of Astarte as goddess of the moon, who was also the goddess of the citadel of Carthage.

Elissa. In the second book of Spenser's *Faerie Queene*, the eldest of three sisters who were always at odds. She is the sister of Medina and Perissa, and mistress of the rash Hudibras.

Eliud (ẹ.lī'ud). In the Bible, a Jew mentioned in the genealogy of Christ. He lived after the Babylonian exile.

Elizabeth (ẹ.liz'ạ.bẹth). See also **Elisheba.**

Elizabeth, Saint. In the Bible, the wife of Zacharias, a priest, the mother of John the Baptist, and a cousin of the Virgin Mary. She was childless until late in life, when an angel appeared to her husband and told him that she would give birth to a son. With her husband, Elizabeth is a saint of the Roman Catholic church, Nov. 5 being the day on which they are honored. Elizabeth is Greek for the Hebrew Elisheba, meaning "worshiper of God." Luke, i. 5–25.

Elizabeth (of *Austria*). [Full name, **Elizabeth Amelie Eugenie.**] b. at Possenhofen Castle, on Lake Starnberg, Munich, Dec. 24, 1837; stabbed to death at Geneva, Switzerland, Sept. 10, 1898. Empress of Austria from 1854 to 1898, and queen of Hungary from 1867. She was a daughter of Maximilian Joseph, Duke of Bavaria, and Louisa Wilhelmina, whose father was Maximilian I. On April 24, 1854, she was married at Vienna to her cousin Francis Joseph, emperor of Austria, who met her and her family in August, 1853, at Ischl, a watering-place in Upper Austria, and fell in love with her at first sight. She visited Hungary for the first time in 1857 and became its queen ten years later.

Elizabeth (of *Belgium*). b. July 25, 1876—. Queen of the Belgians (1909–34); mother of Leopold III. The daughter of Duke Charles Theodore of Bavaria, she married Prince Albert (later Albert I of Belgium) on Oct. 2, 1900. During World War I she remained with her husband at La Panne, near Ostend, where she served as a nurse in the Ocean Hospital. She was also instrumental in establishing many canteens and aid posts, and shared with Albert the well-merited affection of the Belgian people during and after the war.

Elizabeth (of *Bohemia*). [Full name, **Elizabeth Stuart.**] b. at Falkland, Scotland, in August, 1596; d. at London, Feb. 13, 1662. Queen of Bohemia; daughter of James VI of Scotland (James I of England) and Anne of Denmark, and wife of Frederick, elector palatine (later Frederick V of Bohemia). She was grandmother of George I of England. Both before and after her marriage she was the center of admiration for her beauty, earning the appellation "Queen of Hearts." Her misfortunes (defeat and deposition of her husband in 1620, the death of her son by drowning in 1629, her husband's death in 1632, the refusal of her son Charles Louis to support her, her rejection on all sides while living in the Netherlands) added to her romantic appeal. In 1661 she entered England despite Charles II's opposition to the move, and he had to grant her a pension.

Elizabeth (of *England*). [Also, **Elizabeth I, Elizabeth Tudor**; sometimes called **the Virgin Queen.**] b. at Greenwich Palace, London, Sept. 7, 1533; d. at Richmond, Surrey, March 24, 1603. Queen of England (1558–1603). She was the daughter of Henry VIII and his second wife, Anne Boleyn. Henry's marriage to Catherine of Aragon had been declared invalid by a court headed by Thomas Cranmer in 1533, and Henry married Anne Boleyn, one of the court ladies and a sister of one of Henry's former mistresses, Mary Boleyn. This marriage, secretly performed in January, 1533, was followed by Anne's coronation on Whitsunday, 1533; but while recognition of the marriage was official in England, Catherine and her adherents, including Pope Clement VII, refused to sanction the annulment of the previous marriage or the legitimacy of the issue of the new marriage. Thus, the right of Elizabeth to the throne was a live question throughout her reign and the many conspirators based their plots on what they considered a usurpation. In 1534, after the birth of Elizabeth, a parliamentary act of succession recognized the rights of Anne's issue as heirs to the throne; Elizabeth, who was to be Anne's only surviving child, became heir presumptive of England, taking place ahead of Mary, Catherine's child. In 1536, when Anne was tried and executed on a charge of adultery, Henry's second marriage was invalidated too; since this annulment constituted more than a divorce in that the offspring of the marriage were disowned, Elizabeth's claim to the English throne was afterwards called by many illegitimate, for the invalid marriage (the excuse for the annulment was that Anne Boleyn had been betrothed by contract to Henry Percy, Earl of Northumberland) was regarded as never having taken place legally and no heirs from the marriage could legally be recognized. Soon after the execution of Anne and the immediately following marriage of Henry to Jane Seymour, a new act of succession established the issue of the Seymour marriage in line of title. Later, after Jane's death in 1537 as the result of the birth of a male heir (who became Edward VI), parliament passed an act (following Henry's will) that put the order of succession as it actually later occurred: Edward, son of Jane Seymour; Mary, daughter of Catherine of Aragon; and Elizabeth, daughter of Anne Boleyn. Since none of these rulers had children and since Henry had no further issue from his three remaining marriages, the line of succession of the Tudors was not complicated further, and after Elizabeth's death the crown passed to James VI of Scotland, who as great-great-grandson of Henry VII, had next claim to the throne of England through his mother, Mary Queen of Scots. The Tudor line died with Elizabeth and the Stuarts came to the English throne.

Early Years. Elizabeth's education as a child and young girl was by teachers who followed the new Humanism of Erasmus, Colet, and More. She and her half-brother Edward were taught together and both were brought up as Protestants, since Henry had broken with the Roman Catholic Church over the question of the divorce from Catherine of Aragon. But whereas Edward was a deeply religious youth, Elizabeth's religious persuasion was never very strong; during Mary's reign she did not antagonize the Roman Catholics; during her own reign she did not persecute them. Among her tutors were Roger Ascham (who later wrote *The Scholemaster* and who became Elizabeth's secretary) and William Grindal. She became expert in languages, learning not only Greek and Latin, but French, German, and Italian as well. She was an accomplished writer and an eloquent speaker; tradition is quite specific about her command both of the courtly and flowery language and of the vigorous and vulgar tongue of her times. Elizabeth seems to have been rather handsome and, after Edward's accession as Edward VI, she was courted by Thomas Seymour, brother of the Protector, Edward Seymour, Duke of Somerset. Seymour, plotting to take his brother's place as the king's guardian, had married Catherine Parr, widow of Henry VIII, with whom Elizabeth lived after Edward became king. After Catherine Parr's death in 1548, Seymour openly tried to marry Elizabeth, but though it is possible that certain intimacies occurred, nothing came of the match. Seymour, was implicated in the plot that attempted to supersede the order of succession and place Lady Jane Grey on the throne and Elizabeth was severely questioned about the matter, but she was cleared of complicity; Seymour was executed. Elizabeth supported Mary Tudor's claim to the throne and when Mary came to London as queen after the suppression of the plot Elizabeth was at her side. Although she was not tied to the insurrection (1554) of Sir Thomas Wyatt to unseat Mary, who was about to make her unpopular marriage with Philip II of Spain, Elizabeth was nevertheless, as a danger to Mary's continuance on the throne, imprisoned in the Tower and later at Woodstock. She was afterwards received at court but spent most of her time until the end of Mary's reign in seclusion at Hatfield.

Accession and Consolidation. Mary died on Nov. 17, 1558, and Elizabeth, though opposed by Roman Catholics on the grounds of illegitimacy, came to the throne of England. The persecutions of Mary were fresh in the minds of the English and thus Roman Catholic objections to Elizabeth probably served only to strengthen her popular position. After a brief struggle with the English bishops over her position in the English church, Elizabeth saw to it that a bill of uniformity was passed in 1559 making her "Supreme Governor" (a compromise title in place of "Supreme Head") of the kingdom in religious matters. This compromise bill both placated the group that did not want to see a woman as head of the church and forestalled immediate action by the Roman Catholics and the Calvinists against her. Her coronation in 1559, however, was performed by the bishop of Carlisle, since the majority of the bishops refused to act. In choosing her privy council Elizabeth retained a number of people who had served under Mary, but she also appointed seven of her own people as advisers, including William Cecil (who was created Baron Burghley in 1571) as her secretary of state and Nicholas Bacon as lord privy seal and later as lord chancellor. There were no clerics on her privy council. Her principal subsequent appointment was of Francis Walsingham as Burghley's successor as secretary of state.

Foreign Policy. Elizabeth's reign was marked by the avoidance of war openly while at the same time it followed a policy of aggressive resistance to the spread of Spanish power and necessarily encouraged an atmosphere of extreme nationalism. The policy of the Tudors led them towards absolutism and Elizabeth early recognized that wars would mean expenditures heavier than the normal budget would allow, and that these expenditures would require the convening of parliament with its limiting power on the monarchy. Therefore, while her privateers waged unofficial war on Spain, returning huge fortunes to the royal coffers, officially England remained at peace for almost 30 years. Her armies and navies were only partly royal levies; a large proportion of her troops and ships were supplied by the great noblemen. Not until 1588 did open warfare really break out, and then nature and chance came to her defense by virtually destroying the Spanish Armada after it met (and was crippled by) the English. The later years of her reign were marked, however, by increasing taxes to support the war against Spain. Elizabeth came to the throne in the year that Calais was lost (January, 1588) to the French; English spirit and fortunes were at a low ebb. Her appointment of Cecil to handle her foreign affairs was a wise one. By the treaty of Cateau-Cambrésis (1559), France was to return Calais to England in eight years. England and Spain temporarily sided with one another; negotiations were going on for a marriage between Elizabeth and Philip II of Spain. Trouble now began over Scotland. Mary Stuart had married Francis of Valois, who came to the French throne in 1559 as Francis II. Mary claimed to be queen of both Scotland and England and issued orders to obtain Scottish conformity with the Roman Catholic Church. Elizabeth made an alliance with the Scottish reformers and, by July, 1560 (Treaty of Edinburgh), forced the withdrawal of the French from Scotland. Francis died in 1560 and Mary, returning to Scotland, became embroiled with the followers of John Knox. She married Lord Darnley and then, after his death, the earl of Bothwell, but eventually fled (1568) to England before the fury of the Scots and appealed to Elizabeth for sanctuary. Elizabeth, recognizing that she had her hands on a strong claimant to the English throne, kept Mary in custody for almost 20 years. Eventually, because of the many plots to free the Scots queen and to revive her claims to both thrones, Elizabeth permitted her execution in 1587. Before this, however, English alliance had swung from Spain to France. The marriage with Philip of Spain had fallen through and the activities of the Roman Catholics in England, supported by Philip, grew stronger and culminated in the rebellion in 1569 of the earls of Westmoreland and Northumberland. The piratical activities of Drake and Hawkins on the Spanish Main were a constant cause of friction, but Spain, faced with revolt in the Netherlands, could not afford an open break. Instead, Philip entered into further intrigue: the Ridolfi plot of 1571 was aimed at deposing Elizabeth (a papal bull had already deposed and excommunicated her) and placing Mary Queen of Scots on the throne along with Thomas Howard, the duke of Norfolk. The plot was exposed, Norfolk was executed, and Mary fell further into the queen's displeasure. The new reorientation of policy toward France was accompanied by marriage negotiations with the duke of Anjou (later Henry III of France) and François d'Alençon, but yet again the attempts to get the queen married came to nothing. When the Dutch revolted against Spain, Elizabeth supported them (treaty of alliance, 1577) and, therefore (after Elizabeth had returned the Spanish ambassador in 1586 for organizing plots against her), and also to put a halt to the increasingly serious raids of English mariners on his shipping, Philip determined to attack England. To this end he began gathering a fleet to carry soldiers to Britain. Francis Drake's daring raid on Cadiz in 1587 sank a sufficient number of ships to put off the invasion for a year, but in July, 1588, the Spanish Armada (the Invincible Armada) sailed with 25,000 troops and 30,000 seamen against England. It was supposed to pick up 25,000 more troops in the Netherlands before the invasion actually took place, but the English fleet under Charles Howard caught up with the Armada in the English Channel and for a week the 130 ships of the Armada were harried until on July 29 they were caught off Calais and scattered. The Spanish admiral, the duke of Medina-Sidonia, abandoned the plan to invade England and tried to get his ships back to Spain. The Channel was blocked and he sailed north around the British Isles. But the gale that had aided the English off Calais increased and the Armada was torn to bits off the Hebrides; fewer than half the ships ever got back to Spain. Now, after 30 years, Elizabeth found herself at war. In 1585, the earl of Leicester, Robert Dudley, had been sent to the Netherlands to aid the Dutch in their rebellion. In 1589 Drake raided Portugal (at the time a part of the Spanish king's domain) and raids were carried out against Cadiz (1596) and the Azores (1597). The Spanish war continued until the end of Elizabeth's reign. In 1597, the Irish rebelled; Robert Devereux, the earl of Essex, was sent to put down the revolt but he failed; not until 1603, after Charles Blount was appointed to the command there, was the rebellion suppressed.

Religion. Elizabeth's accession in 1558 followed a period of active suppression of Protestantism under Mary Tudor. The new queen was welcomed by the English who, with the rising feeling of nationalism, were turning against the rule of Rome in spiritual affairs. In 1559 two bills passed Parliament establishing the Church of England: the act of uniformity called for the use of the second Prayer Book (1552, by Thomas Cranmer) that made of the Roman Catholic Mass the Anglican Communion; the act of supremacy established Elizabeth as supreme governor in spiritual matters. Matthew Parker, who had been Anne Boleyn's chaplain, was appointed (1559) archbishop of Canterbury. Parker rewrote the 42 articles of convocation of Edward VI into the 39 articles (proclaimed by Elizabeth, 1563) and supervised the edition of the Bible known as the Bishop's Bible (1572). Elizabeth's policy, once the church had been cleared of ecclesiastics who refused to accept the acts of uniformity and supremacy, was one of toleration. Only the extreme Puritans (Brownists) and the Roman Catholics were not included in the new Anglican Church. Elizabeth supported the Calvinists in Scotland against the claims of the Roman Catholic Mary Queen of Scots, and under Elizabeth Protestantism was carried into Ireland. In 1570 Pope Pius V excommunicated her; she was faced, both before and after that, with several Roman Catholic plots to depose her and to bring Mary to the throne. The English Roman Catholics had set up a college at Douai in 1561 (located at Reims after 1571) from which missionary priests were sent to England to convert the English to Roman Catholicism and, incidentally, to support the plots against the queen. Among the famous priests who so acted were Edmund Campion (executed for conspiracy in 1581) and Robert Parsons (who later headed the English College at Rome). The controversy within the Anglican Church over Puritanism was carried even into Parliament, where members (like Peter and Paul Wentworth) agitated for reform. John Whitgift (later archbishop of Canterbury) and Thomas Cartwright (Cambridge professor of divinity, removed for his part in the argument) carried on a heated debate over conformity. The Martin Marprelate pamphlets of 1588–89 began a controversy concerning Whitgift's authority that ended with vigorous suppression of the pamphleteering.

Internal Policy. Elizabeth avoided, as long as she could, excess taxation, in the well-founded belief that thus she would avoid domestic unrest and would foster financial soundness within the country. Her avoidance of war was a result of this policy; when it was necessary to raise money, she sold royal lands rather than raise the tax burden. Her popularity, in fact, began to wane only after the beginning of the Spanish war in the late 1580's. Her shares of such matters as Drake's raiding voyage (1577–80) on Spanish shipping off South America were far from negligible. In 1560 and 1561 the coinage was standardized on a silver basis and in 1563 the Statute of Artificers set up a labor code that attempted to establish employment standards on a national basis, whereby unemployment would cease and wages would be regulated. This domestic policy culminated in the Elizabethan Poor Laws of 1597 and 1601 which made the parishes responsible for the care of the needy and imposed very heavy penalties for vagabondage. Elizabeth, true to the Tudor tradition, called few parliaments; in her more than 44 years on the throne only 13 parliaments were assembled. But even then Parliament made advances in these years; it grew from 308 to 372 members; it established its right to debate and legislate on matters only barely approaching those for which it was specifically called. Monopolies were granted by the crown in everything from foreign trade to domestic commodities, and while this helped in England's commercial and industrial expansion, it resulted in rising costs (as much as 400 percent) and the tyranny of arbitrary search and seizure. Elizabeth's later parliaments (1592, 1597, 1601) attempted to deal with the problems raised by these monopolies. In 1600 the East India Company, which in later years was to bring its richest empire to England, was chartered. A recurrent and a constant problem was Elizabeth's spinsterhood. Diplomatic marriages with Philip II of Spain or the French dukes of Anjou and Alençon were projected, but Elizabeth would not risk her hold on the throne by a foreign marriage. Despite certain rumored physical incapabilities (the legend that Elizabeth was really a man still has some currency), her liaisons with court favorites resulted in extreme jealousy on her part; perhaps her one real love was Robert Dudley, Earl of Leicester, but rumor made of him a wife-killer (Amy Robsart, his wife, had been killed in 1560, probably accidentally, when Leicester's marriage to Elizabeth was a strong possibility) and Elizabeth could not risk the scandal. Her affair with Robert Devereux, earl of Essex, towards the end of her life, ended unhappily with his rebellion and execution (1601). Elizabeth died, in 1603, the only English ruler of adult years since the Norman Conquest in 1066 who had not married. She recognized clearly the problem that would face the kingdom at her death and part of her reluctance to order the execution of Mary Queen of Scots is traceable to the fact that Mary's son, James VI of Scotland, was the logical successor to the English throne. On Elizabeth's death, he became James I of England.

The Elizabethan Age. The four and a half decades of Elizabeth's reign mark probably the most brilliant period in English history, and one of the top half dozen in world history. The long period of official peace with other nations built up about Elizabeth a colorful court whose energies were turned to other matters than war, although freebooting and soldiering expeditions by her military captains gave glamour to their names. Literature reached a golden age in this time, a period marked with Elizabeth's name, although much of the so-called Elizabethan literature (for example much of the body of dramatic literature) dates from the period of the first Stuart kings (1603–1642). Such poets as Spenser, Drayton, and Gascoigne, playwrights like Marlowe, Greene, Lyly, and Shakespeare, essayists, romancers, and critics of the stamp of Raleigh, Bacon, and Sidney make the period incomparable in its brilliance. Elizabeth's captains and advisers, the Cecils, Dudley, the Walsinghams, Raleigh, Hawkins, Drake, the Bacons, while not uniformly successful, were nevertheless instrumental in carrying out her policies. England became in Elizabeth's time a world power, not yet as strong as Spain but soon to surpass her; the English navy grew to be second to none; commerce expanded and colonies were established where such explorers as Frobisher and Drake had gone.

Elizabeth (of *England*). [Maiden name, Lady **Elizabeth Angela Marguerite Bowes-Lyon.**] b. in Hertfordshire, England, Aug. 4, 1900—. Queen mother of England; widow of King George VI, and mother of Elizabeth II; youngest daughter, of three, of Claude George Bowes-Lyon, 14th Earl of Strathmore and Kinghorn. On April 26, 1923, in Westminster Abbey, she married George VI, who was then Albert Frederick Arthur George, Duke of York. She became queen consort on Dec. 11, 1936, when her husband mounted the throne following the abdication of Edward VIII (formerly Prince of Wales, and now Duke of Windsor). She was crowned queen of England on May 12, 1937. In May and June, 1939, when she and the king visited America they were the first reigning English monarchs to visit the U.S. (and Canada).

Elizabeth I (of *England*). See **Elizabeth** (of *England*) (1533–1603).

Elizabeth II (of *England*). [Full name, **Elizabeth Alexandra Mary.**] b. at Buckingham Palace, London, April 21, 1926—. Queen of England; daughter of George VI (1894–1952), who was the Duke of York when she was born, and Queen Elizabeth (now queen mother). As a princess and a future queen, she was educated privately by a governess, and by tutors. She speaks French and German fluently, and Spanish and Italian slightly less so. Following the custom of her father (who was born on Dec. 14), she will celebrate her official birthday, as distinct from her private one, on June 5.

Elizabeth (of *Rumania*). [Full name, **Pauline Elizabeth Ottilie Luise**; pseudonym, **Carmen Sylva.**] b. at Neuwied, Germany, Dec. 29, 1843; d. at Bucharest, March 2, 1916. Queen of Rumania (1881–1916); daughter of Prince Hermann of Wied, and wife of Carol I of Rumania, whom she married Nov. 15, 1869. Under her pseudonym she became a well-known writer, in Rumanian, German, French, and English. She published *Sappho* (1880), *Hammerstein* (1880), *Stürme* (Storms, 1881), *Leidens Erdengang* (Sorrow on Earth, 1882), and others. In 1882 she published in French *Les Pensées d'une reine*, revealing her name, and later *Pelesch Märchen* (1883), *Le Pic aux regrets* (Paris, 1884), *Es Klopft* (Some One Knocks, 1887; translated into French in 1889, with a preface by Pierre Loti), and *Lieder aus dem Dimbovitzthal* (The Bard of Dimbovitza, 1889), a collection of folk tales. She also collaborated with Madame Mite Kremnitz under the signatures "Ditto" and "Idem," in writing *Aus zwei Welten* (1882), *Astra* (1886), and other works.

Elizabeth (of *Spain*). [Spanish, **Isabel**; also, **Isabella.**] b. at Fontainebleau, France, Nov. 22, 1602; d. at Madrid, Oct. 6, 1644. Queen of Spain; daughter of Henry IV of France, and wife of Philip IV of Spain; mother of Maria Theresa, wife of Louis XIV of France.

Elizabeth. City in N New Jersey, county seat of Union County, near Newark Bay and Staten Island Sound, ab. 12 mi. SW of New York and adjoining Newark. It is a center for the refining of copper and oil; manufactures include soap, clothing, chemicals, iron and steel machinery, hardware, and sewing machines. 112,817 (1950).

Elizabeth. Borough in SW Pennsylvania, in Allegheny County, on the Monongahela River, near Pittsburgh. 2,615 (1950).

Elizabeth. Novel by Frank Swinnerton, published in 1934.

Elizabeth. Pseudonym of **Russell, Elizabeth Mary.**

Elizabeth, Cape. Headland in Maine, projecting into the Atlantic ab. 8 mi. S of Portland.

Elizabeth, Mount. [Also, **Mount Elisabeth.**] Mountain in Antarctica, in the Queen Alexandra Range, rising

SW of Mount Anne at the head of the Ross Shelf Ice, in ab. 83°58′ S., 168°10′ E. Elevation, ab. 10,760 ft.

Elizabeth and Essex (es′iks). Biographical study by Lytton Strachey, published in 1928.

Elizabeth Bennet (ben′ẹt). See **Bennet, Elizabeth.**

Elizabeth Charlotte (shär′lọt). b. at Heidelberg, Baden, Germany, May 27, 1652; d. at St.-Cloud, France, Dec. 8, 1722. Palatine princess; second wife of Philip, Duke of Orléans (brother of Louis XIV of France).

Elizabeth Christine (kris.tē′nẹ). [Also, **Elisabeth Christine.**] b. Nov. 8, 1715; d. Jan. 13, 1797. Princess of Brunswick; wife of Frederick II of Prussia (Frederick the Great), whom she married on June 12, 1733.

Elizabeth City. Town in NE North Carolina, county seat of Pasquotank County, on the Pasquotank River ab. 39 mi. S of Norfolk: trading and shipping center for potatoes, cotton, corn, peanuts, soybeans, and fish; manufactures of cotton textiles and hosiery. It is the seat of a U.S. Coast Guard shipyard and air and supply base. It maintained an important West Indian shipping trade throughout the 18th and early 19th centuries. A naval victory was gained here, on Feb. 10, 1862, by a Union fleet under Commodore Rowan. 12,685 (1950).

Elizabeth Farnese (fär.nā′zā). b. Oct. 25, 1692; d. 1766. Queen of Spain and princess of Parma; wife of Philip V of Spain.

Elizabeth Islands. Group of 16 small islands, in SE Massachusetts, forming the town of Gosnold, Dukes County, lying between Buzzards Bay and Vineyard Sound.

Elizabeth of Bavaria (bạ.vãr′i.ạ). See **Isabeau of Bavaria.**

Elizabeth of Hungary (hung′gạ.ri), Saint. [Also, Saint **Elizabeth of Thuringia** (thủ.rin′ji.ạ).] b. at Pressburg (now Bratislava, Czechoslovakia), 1207; d. at Marburg, Germany, Nov. 19, 1231. Daughter of Andrew II of Hungary, and wife of Louis IV, landgrave of Thuringia, celebrated for her sanctity and charity to the poor. The death of her husband in 1227 left her with three infants and no income, since her brother-in-law drove her from her place as regent. She was offered the regency later, but renounced it to follow a life of penance and of nursing the sick. She is credited with several miracles.

Elizabeth of Valois (vá.lwá′, val′wä). [Also: **Isabella of Valois**; French, **Élisabeth de France**; Spanish, **Isabel.**] b. at Fontainebleau, France, April 13, 1545; d. at Madrid, Oct. 3, 1568. Queen of Spain; daughter of Henry II of France and Catherine de Médicis, and wife of Philip II of Spain. She was betrothed to Philip's son, Don Carlos, but after the death of Mary Tudor, Philip's second wife, and the refusal of Elizabeth of England to marry Philip, she married the father in preference to the son.

Elizabeth Petrovna (pi.trôv′nạ). [Russian, **Elizaveta Petrovna** (yi.lē.zạ.ve′tạ).] b. Dec. 18, 1709; d. Jan. 5, 1762. Empress of Russia (1741–62); daughter of Peter I (Peter the Great) and Catherine I. She took part against Frederick the Great (Frederick II of Prussia) in the Seven Years' War, in the course of which her army entered Berlin (1760) and pressed him so hard that he would probably have been overcome by the Allies except for her timely (from Frederick's point of view) death. She founded the University of Moscow, and the Academy of Fine Arts at St. Petersburg.

Elizabeth Point. Headland on the SW coast of Africa, midway along the coast of South-West Africa. It forms the W side of the bay on which the port of Lüderitz is situated.

Elizabeth the Queen. Drama in blank verse by Maxwell Anderson, produced in 1930 and published in the same year. The plot involves the British queen's unwavering determination to place national interests before all personal considerations. When Lord Essex, the court favorite, lends his aid to intrigues against Elizabeth, she divests him of his military power and orders his execution.

Elizabethton (ẹ.liz′ạ.bẹth.tọn). City in NE Tennessee, county seat of Carter County, at the confluence of the Watauga and Dee rivers. Manufactures include rayon textiles, twine, lumber, boxes, overalls, and flour. 10,754 (1950).

Elizabethtown (ẹ.liz′ạ.bẹth.toun″). City in C Kentucky, county seat of Hardin County: trading center for livestock, tobacco, and grain. It was platted in 1793, and was the home of Thomas Lincoln, father of Abraham Lincoln. 5,807 (1950).

Elizabethtown. Borough in SE Pennsylvania, in Lancaster County: marketing center for an agricultural area. Settled in 1732, it is the seat of Elizabethtown College. 5,083 (1950).

Elizabeth Town. Former name of **Hagerstown,** Md.

Elizabethtown. Former name of **Moundsville,** W.Va.

Elizabeth Tudor (tū′dọr). See **Elizabeth** (of *England*) (1533–1603).

Elizabeth Woodville (wủd′vil). b. probably in 1437; d. at Bermondsey (now part of London), June 8, 1492. Queen of Edward IV of England; daughter of Sir Richard Woodville, 1st Earl Rivers. After the death of her first husband, Sir John Grey, she married in 1464 Edward IV, by whom she became the mother of Edward V, who with another son, Richard, Duke of York, was murdered in the Tower, and of Elizabeth, queen of Henry VII.

El Jedida (el je.dē′dạ). Arabic name of **Mazagan.**

El Jezira (el je.zē′rạ). Arabic name of **Blue Nile** province.

El Jezireh (je.zē′re). See **Jezireh, El.**

El Jib (el jēb′). Arabic name of **Gibeon.**

Ełk (elk). [German, **Lyck.**] Town in E Poland, in the *województwo* (province) of Białystok, formerly in East Prussia, Germany, situated ab. 60 mi. NW of Białystok. It has livestock markets and a lumber industry. The castle once belonged to the Teutonic Order. In World War I, the town was occupied by the Russians from August to September, 1914. It came under Polish administration in 1945. Pop. 16,482 (1939); 6,104 (1946).

El Kab (el käb′). [Ancient names, **Eileithyia, Hebent.**] Place in NE Africa, on the right bank of the Nile River, in Upper Egypt, opposite and a little N of Edfu, on the railroad line from Cairo to Aswan, ab. 510 mi. S of Cairo. It is of interest for the ancient rock tombs and temples and the old city with its wall, which is now very much in ruins, believed to have been one of the oldest of Egyptian towns.

El Kahirah (el kä′hi.rạ). Arabic name of **Cairo,** Egypt.

El Kantara (kan′tạ.rạ). [Also, **El Qantara.**] Village in NE Egypt, on the Suez Canal ab. 27 mi. S of Port Said. It is a rail-ferry point on the only railway link between Egypt and the Levant.

El-Karidab (el.kar′i.dab). A very rarely used name for the third-magnitude star δ Sagittarii, more commonly called Kaus Media.

Elk City (elk). [Former name, **Busch.**] City in W Oklahoma, in Beckham County, in a dairy-farming region: trading and shipping center. 7,962 (1950).

El Kef or **El Keff** (el kef′). See **Le Kef.**

El Kerak (el ke′räk). [Also: **Kerak**; ancient names, **Kir-Hareseth, Kir Moab, Kir of Moab**; medieval name (in the crusades), **Le Crac.**] Town in W Jordan, ab. 48 mi. SE of Jerusalem. An ancient city, it once belonged to the Moabites. In 1167 it was held by the Christians. The castle of the Crusaders, built here c1131 by Foulques V, Count of Anjou, and king of Jerusalem, is one of the most imposing of medieval monuments. The walls and towers are lofty and massive; the passages, colonnades, cisterns, and moats are of great extent and interest. A subterranean chapel with frescoes is of unusual interest. Mesha sacrificed his son here (2 Kings, iii. 25–27). Pop. ab. 8,000.

Elkesaites (el.kē′sạ.īts). See **Elcesaites.**

El Khalil (el kä.lēl′, ḉhä-). Arabic name of **Hebron.**

El Kharga (el kär′gạ, ḉhär′-). See **Kharga.**

Elkhart (elk′härt). City in N Indiana, at the confluence of the Elkhart and St. Joseph rivers: important for the manufacture of musical instruments. The C. G. Conn Band Instrument Company factory is the largest of its kind in the world. Elkhart was the early home of Ambrose Bierce. 35,646 (1950).

Elkhorn (elk′hôrn). City in SE Wisconsin, county seat of Walworth County, ab. 40 mi. SW of Milwaukee. It is situated in a resort and farming region, and manufactures musical instruments. 2,935 (1950).

Elkhorn River. River in N and NE Nebraska, flowing generally SE across the prairies to join the Platte River ab. 20 mi. SW of Omaha. Length, ab. 330 mi.

Elkin (el'kin). Town in NW North Carolina, in Surry County, in an apple-producing region: manufactures of woolen blankets and wool textiles. 2,842 (1950).

Elkin, William Lewis. b. at New Orleans, La., April 29, 1855; d. at New Haven, Conn., May 30, 1933. American astronomer, director of the Yale Observatory from 1896 to 1910. He took part in investigations (1881–83) of the parallaxes of southern stars at the Royal Observatory, Cape of Good Hope.

Elkins (el'kinz). [Former name, **Leadsville.**] City in C West Virginia, county seat of Randolph County, ab. 92 mi. SE of Wheeling: railroad shops. Incorporated in 1890 and renamed for U.S. Senator Stephen B. Elkins, it was made county seat in 1900. It is the seat of Davis and Elkins College. 9,121 (1950).

Elkins, Stephen Benton. b. near New Lexington, Ohio, Sept. 26, 1841; d. Jan. 4, 1911. American legislator and capitalist, secretary of war (1891–93), noted as the author of the anti-rebate Elkins Act of 1903 and as joint framer of the Mann-Elkins Act of 1910, which widened the powers of the Interstate Commerce Commission. He was graduated (B.A., 1860; M.A., 1868) from the University of Missouri and served in the Union army in the Civil War as a captain of militia in the 77th Missouri Infantry. Admitted to the bar in 1864, he moved to New Mexico, where he established his practice at Messilia. He served in the territorial legislature until 1866, when he was appointed territorial district attorney, holding that post until 1867. He was also attorney general of the territory in 1867, was U.S. district attorney (1867–70), and in 1872 was elected as Republican territorial delegate to the national Congress, serving in that post until 1877. He was vice-president and a promoter of the West Virginia Central and Pittsburgh Railroad (Western Maryland) and in 1890 moved to Elkins, W.Va., a town he had developed in connection with his railroad and financial interests. He was appointed (1891) secretary of war by Harrison and was (1895–1907) Republican U.S. senator from West Virginia.

Elkins Act. Act passed (1903) by the U.S. Congress prohibiting the giving or receiving of rebates in railroad shipping and providing penalties for nonobservance. Any deviation from published rates was considered a misdemeanor.

Elkins Park. Unincorporated community in SE Pennsylvania, in Montgomery County near Philadelphia. Under the new urban definition established for use in the 1950 census it was counted with adjoining urban areas. The last official enumeration was 3,286 (1940).

Elk Island National Park (elk). Park in C Alberta, Canada, ab. 27 mi. by road E of Edmonton. It is the second largest animal reserve in Canada, established in 1913, and has large herds of buffalo, elk, deer, and moose. Area, ab. 75 sq. mi.

Elk Mountains and **West Elk Mountains.** Ranges of mountains in W Colorado, W of the Saguache range. Elevation of Castle Peak, 14,259 ft.

Elko (el'kō). City in NE Nevada, county seat of Elko County: chief trading center for a large cattle-producing area. It is also a vacation resort. 5,393 (1950).

Elkoyni (el.koi'nē). See **Kony.**

El Ksar el Kebir (el kẹ.sär' el ke.bir'). Arabic name of **Alcazarquivir.**

Elkton (elk'tọn). Town in NE Maryland, county seat of Cecil County, near the Delaware-Maryland-Pennsylvania border. Manufactures include flour, fertilizer, pulp, paper, and shirts. Once known as the Gretna Green of the eastern U.S., it was formerly a haven for eloping couples. 5,245 (1950).

Ella (el'ạ). See **Alla** or **Ella.**

Elland (el'ạnd). Urban district and manufacturing town in N central England, in the West Riding of Yorkshire, situated on the river Calder ab. 9 mi. SW of Bradford, ab. 193 mi. N of London by rail. It has a cotton-textile industry and a worsted-spinning industry. 19,273 (1951).

Ellandun (el'ạn.dun). Place in Wiltshire, England, near Wilton, where Egbert, king of Wessex, defeated (825 or 823) the Mercians.

Ellasar (el'ạ.sär, el.lā'sär). Biblical name of **Larsa.**

Ellaury (ā.you'rē), **José.** b. in Montevideo, Uruguay, c1831; d. in December, 1894. Uruguayan statesman. He was a lawyer, took part in politics, and in March, 1874, was elected president. In February, 1875, he was deposed by a military revolution.

Ellenborough (el'ẹn.bur.ọ), 1st Baron and 1st Earl of. Titles of **Law, Edward.**

Ellen Douglas (el'ẹn dug'lạs). See **Douglas, Ellen.**

Ellensburg (el'ẹnz.bėrg). [Former spelling, **Ellen's Burgh.**] City in C Washington, county seat of Kittitas County: distribution point for gold, coal, and agricultural and dairy products. It is the seat of the Central Washington College of Education. 8,430 (1950).

Ellen's Isle (el'ẹnz). [Also, **Eilean Molach.**] Wooded island in Loch Katrine, in C Scotland, in Perthshire ab. 8 mi. W of Callander. It is famous in early romance, and Scott makes it the favorite haunt of the *Lady of the Lake.*

Ellenville (el'ẹn.vil). Village in SE New York, in Ulster County, in the Shawangunk Mountains: resort center. 4,225 (1950).

Ellero (el'le.rō), **Pietro.** b. at Pordenone, Italy, Oct. 8, 1833; d. at Rome, 1933. Italian penologist. He taught at Milan and at Bologna (until 1889) and became deputy (1866) and senator (1889). He was the author of various texts and founder of *L'Archivio giuridico.*

Ellery (el'ėr.i), **William.** b. at Newport, R.I., Dec. 22, 1727; d. there, Feb. 15, 1820. American politician, one of the signers of the Declaration of Independence.

Ellesmere (elz'mir), 1st Earl of. A title of **Egerton, Francis** (1800–57).

Ellesmere, Baron. A title of **Egerton,** Sir **Thomas.**

Ellesmere Canal. Canal in N Wales and W England. In Wales it extends from Newtown (Montgomeryshire) on the river Severn, northward, paralleling the upper course of the river. It crosses a portion of Shropshire (England) past Whitchurch, and enters Cheshire, passing Nantwich and Chester, reaching the estuary of the river Mersey at Ellesmere Port. Length, ab. 69 mi.

Ellesmere Island. Northernmost island of the Arctic Archipelago, W of Greenland in the Arctic Ocean. Area, ab. 76,000 sq. mi.; pop. ab. 10.

Ellesmere Port. Urban district, seaport, and manufacturing center in W England, in Cheshire, situated on the river Mersey and the Manchester Ship Canal at its junction with the Ellesmere Canal, ab. 7 mi. N of Chester, ab. 191 mi. NW of London by rail. It is the first port of call on the Manchester Ship Canal, and the largest oil port in the United Kingdom. Its industries include chemical works, flour mills, paper mills, and galvanized sheet steel manufactures. The town has extensive residential areas. 32,594 (1951).

Ellespontos (e.lēs.pôn'tôs). A Greek name of the **Dardanelles.**

Ellet (el'ẹt), **Charles.** b. at Penn's Manor, Bucks County, Pa., Jan. 1, 1810; d. at Cairo, Ill., June 21, 1862. American engineer. He introduced the use of wire suspension-bridges into America, erecting one at Fairmount, Pa., in 1842, and another across the Niagara below the falls in 1847. He became a colonel of engineers in the Union army during the Civil War, and converted a fleet of Mississippi steamers into rams with which he sank or disabled several Confederate vessels off Memphis on June 6, 1862.

Ellet, Elizabeth Fries Lummis. b. at Sodus Point, N.Y., in October, 1818; d. at New York, June 3, 1877. American author; wife of William Henry Ellet. She wrote *The Women of the American Revolution* (1848) and others.

Ellet, William Henry. b. at New York, 1806; d. at New York, Jan. 26, 1859. American chemist; husband of Elizabeth F. L. Ellet.

El Libnan (el lēb.nän'). Arabic name of the **Lebanon** range.

Ellice Islands (el'is). [Also, **Lagoon Islands.**] Group of nine small coral islands in the South Pacific, N of the Fiji Islands, and NW of Samoa. They form part of the British crown colony of Gilbert and Ellice Islands. They were discovered by Captain Peyster, an American, in 1819. In 1892, Great Britain proclaimed a protectorate over the islands and, at the request of the native rulers, annexed them in 1915. Area, 14 sq. mi.; pop. 3,555 (est. 1945).

Ellichpur (el.ich.pör'). Former district in Berar, Union of India: now incorporated in the Amraoti district of Madhya Pradesh (Central Provinces). Area, 2,605 sq. mi.; pop. 988,524 (1941).

Ellichpur. Town in the Amraoti district, Madhya Pradesh (Central Provinces), Union of India, ab. 100 mi. W of Nagpur: trading center and a minor road junction. 26,082 (1941).

Ellicott (el′i.kọt), **Andrew.** b. at Solebury, Pa., Jan. 24, 1754; d. Aug. 28, 1820. American surveyor and mathematician. Publisher (1782 *et seq.*) of *The United States Almanack;* Virginia member of commission (1784) to extend the Mason and Dixon Line; member of Pennsylvania commission to survey the western (1785) and northern (1786) state boundaries and the Ohio and Allegheny river islands (1788); member (1789) of commission to fix southwestern boundary of New York; surveyed (1791–93) Washington, D.C., site for the federal capital redrawing L'Enfant's plan for the city; surveyed town of Presqu'Isle (now Erie), Pa. (1794), and the U.S.-Florida Territory frontier (1796), and the Georgia-South Carolina boundary (1811). Professor of mathematics (1813–20), U.S. Military Academy, West Point.

Ellicott, Charles John. b. April 25, 1819; d. Oct. 15, 1905. English Biblical commentator, bishop of Gloucester and Bristol (1863–97) and of Gloucester (1897–1905). He was Hulsean lecturer at Cambridge University in 1859. His lectures appeared as *On the Life of Our Lord Jesus Christ,* and he also published, besides minor works, a series of *Critical and Grammatical Commentaries* on most of the Pauline epistles. He was for 11 years chairman of the scholars who produced the revised version of the New Testament.

Ellicott City. Unincorporated community in N Maryland, county seat of Howard County, on the Patapsco River, ab. 10 mi. W of Baltimore: manufactures doughnuts. Several fine 18th-century mansions are in the vicinity, including Doughoregan Manor, which was the home of Charles Carroll of Carrollton. 2,682 (1940); with the adjoining community of Oella, 3,364 (1950).

Ellinwood (el′in.wụd). City in C Kansas, in Barton County, on the Arkansas River ab. 40 mi. NW of Hutchinson, in an oil-producing region. 2,569 (1950).

Elliot (el′i.ọt, el′yọt), **Daniel Giraud.** b. at New York, March 7, 1835; d. Dec. 22, 1915. American naturalist, honorary curator of zoölogy in the Field Columbian Museum, Chicago. He made extensive explorations in Canada, Alaska, South America, East Africa, Arabia, and elsewhere, and published about 20 volumes and several hundred papers on zoölogical (especially mammalogical and ornithological) subjects.

Elliot, Sir **Gilbert.** [Title, Lord **Minto.**] b. 1651; d. May 1, 1718. English judge. He was condemned to death (1685) for his active part in the Earl of Argyll's rising, but obtained royal pardon. Knighted and made clerk of privy council (1692); became judge of court of session with title of Lord Minto (1705).

Elliot, Sir **Gilbert.** [Title, 3rd Baronet of **Minto.**] b. in Scotland, in September, 1722; d. at Marseilles, France, Jan. 11, 1777. English politician and poet, friend of Hume; son of Sir Gilbert Elliot (1693–1766). He studied at the University of Edinburgh and at Leiden, was a member of Parliament (1754–77), and a lord of the admiralty (1756). He supported George III's harsh policy toward America and brought the king's influence to bear against a motion to allow colonies to tax themselves so that the motion was defeated.

Elliot, Jane or **Jean.** b. at Minto, Teviotdale, Scotland, 1727; d. March 29, 1805. Author of a single poem, *The Flowers of the Forest* (1756), at first believed, because of its genuine flavor, to be a true popular ballad; sister of Sir Gilbert Elliot (1722–77). Apart from her one poem, Jane Elliot is remembered for her charming cleverness at the age of 18 in saving her father, Sir Gilbert Andrew Elliot (1693–1766), from capture by a band of Jacobites; she was also the last lady in Edinburgh to use a sedan chair.

Elliot Islands. Group of small islands in Korea Bay, off the SE coast of the Liaotung Peninsula, NE China. They were used by the Japanese during the Russo-Japanese War as a naval base.

Elliot-Murray-Kynynmond (-mur′i.kin.in′mọnd), Sir **Gilbert.** [Title, 1st Earl of **Minto.**] b. at Edinburgh, April 23, 1751; d. June 21, 1814. British politician and diplomat; son of Sir Gilbert Elliot (1722–77). He was governor general of British India from 1807 to 1813.

Elliot-Murray-Kynynmond, Gilbert. [Title, 2nd Earl of **Minto.**] b. at Lyons, France, Nov. 16, 1782; d. July 31, 1859. British politician; son of Sir Gilbert Elliot-Murray-Kynynmond (1751–1814). He was lord privy seal (1846–52).

Elliot-Murray-Kynynmond, Gilbert John. [Title, 4th Earl of **Minto.**] b. July 9, 1845; d. March 4, 1914. British soldier and administrator; grandson of Gilbert Elliot-Murray-Kynynmond (1782–1859). He served with the Turkish army in 1877, in the Afghan war in 1879, in the Egyptian campaign in 1882, and as chief of staff in the rebellion in NW Canada in 1885. He succeeded to the title in 1891, was governor general of Canada (1898–1904), and was viceroy and governor general of India (1905–10).

Elliot-Murray-Kynynmond, Hugh. b. April 6, 1752; d. Dec. 10, 1830. English diplomat; son of Sir Gilbert Elliot (1722–77).

Elliotson (el′i.ọt.sọn, el′yọt-), **John.** b. at London, Oct. 29, 1791; d. there, July 29, 1868. English physician and physiologist. He wrote *Principles and Practice of Medicine* (1839), *Human Physiology* (1840), and others.

Elliott (el′i.ọt, el′yọt), **Aaron Marshall.** b. at Wilmington, N.C., Jan. 24, 1844; d. Nov. 9, 1910. American philologist and educator. Associate in languages (1876 *et seq.*), Johns Hopkins; founder (1883) of Modern Language Association and editor of its publications; founder (1894) of *Modern Language Notes,* the first such specialized journal in the U.S.

Elliott, Charles. b. in Ireland, May 16, 1792; d. Jan. 8, 1869. American Methodist clergyman and writer. He emigrated to the U.S. in 1815, and during the periods 1857–60 and 1864–67 was professor of Biblical literature (and president) at Iowa Wesleyan University.

Elliott, Charles Loring. b. at Scipio, N.Y., in December, 1812; d. at Albany, N.Y., Aug. 25, 1868. American portrait painter. He was elected to the National Academy of Design in 1846.

Elliott, Charles Wyllys. b. at Guilford, Conn., May 27, 1817; d. Aug. 20, 1883. American miscellaneous writer. He published *Saint Domingo* (1855), a *New England History* (1857), *Book of American Interiors* (1876), and *Pottery and Porcelain* (1877).

Elliott, Charlotte. b. at Clapham, London, March 17, 1789; d. at Brighton, Sussex, England, Sept. 22, 1871. English hymnist, best known for her *Just as I Am.* For 50 years an invalid, she came under the influence of Caesar H. A. Malan (1787–1864), a Swiss Protestant divine, and devoted her life to writing religious songs and poems. She was the author of *Hymns for a Week,* which had a sale of 40,000 copies, *Hours of Sorrow* (1840; many editions), and the *Invalid's Hymn Book* (1834; published privately), containing "Just as I am, without one plea," the most popular of her 150 hymns.

Elliott, Ebenezer. [Called the **"Corn-Law Rhymer."**] b. at Masborough, Yorkshire, England, March 17, 1781; d. near Barnsley, England, Dec. 1, 1849. English poet. He was the author of *Corn-Law Rhymes* (1831), *The Village Patriarch* (1829), *The Ranter, The Splendid Village,* and many other poems opposing the English Corn Laws as a "bread tax."

Elliott, Sir **Henry Miers.** b. at Westminster, London, 1808; d. at Simonstown, Cape of Good Hope, South Africa, Dec. 20, 1853. English historian, long in the service of the East India Company. He wrote a supplement to Wilson's *Glossary of Indian Terms, Bibliographical Index to the Historians of Muhammedan India* (vol. I, 1849), *History of India* (8 vols., 1867–77), and others.

Elliott, Jesse Duncan. b. in Maryland, July 14, 1782; d. at Philadelphia, Dec. 10, 1845. American naval officer. He was second in command under Commodore Perry at the battle of Lake Erie (Sept. 10, 1813), and the following month succeeded Perry in the command on Lake Erie. He commanded the sloop of war *Ontario* in Decatur's squadron employed against Algiers in 1815.

Elliott, John. b. in Lincolnshire, England, April 22, 1858; d. at Charleston, S.C., May 26, 1925. Scottish portrait and mural painter who spent the greater part of his life in America; husband of Maud Elliott. He began his artistic training by drawing from marble sculptures at the London British Museum and by doing cast drawing at the Paris École des Beaux-Arts. He later studied under

Duran at Paris, at the Julian Academy, and under di Villegas at Rome. Some of his best-known works are *The Triumph of Time*, a mural (in the Boston Public Library), a series of 16 *War Portraits*, red-chalk drawings of young Americans who were killed in action in World War I, and *Diana of the Tides*, another mural (both in the National Museum at Washington, D.C.). *The Vintage*, which he made for the Chicago home of Mrs. Potter Palmer, is regarded as one of his most beautiful pieces. As a portrait painter he is best known for those of King Humbert of Italy, the Marquis of Winchester, the Duke of Cambridge, Victor Chapman, Rose Farwell, General Arthur Wauchope, Lady Katherine Thynne (later Lady Cromer), and Samuel Gridley Howe and Julia Ward Howe, whose daughter, Maud, he married on Feb. 7, 1887.

Elliott, Maud. [Maiden name, **Howe.**] b. at Boston, Nov. 9, 1854; d. at Newport, R.I., March 19, 1948. American writer who was awarded (1917) with her sister Laura E. Richards the Pulitzer prize for *The Life and Letters of Julia Ward Howe* (1916), a biography of their mother. She married (1887) John Elliott, the painter. Her list of books includes *Mammon, Roma Beata, The Story of an Artist, Atlanta in the South, Three Generations, My Cousin, F. Marion Crawford* (1934), *Uncle Sam Ward and his Circle* (1938), *Recollections of the Civil War* (1943), and *This Was My Newport* (1944).

Elliott, Maxine. [Original name, **Jessie Dermot.**] b. at Rockland, Me., Feb. 5, 1871; d. at Juan les Pins, France, March 5, 1940. American actress. Married (1898) and divorced (1908) Nathaniel C. Goodwin after a previous divorce (1896) from George A. McDermott. Made her debut (1890) with E. S. Willard; hired (1894) as leading lady with Rose Coghlan, appeared (1895–97) in Shakespearian parts with Augustin Daly's company; co-starred (1898–1903) with Nat Goodwin in America and England; owner and manager (1908 *et seq.*) of the Maxine Elliott Theater at New York; her successes included *Her Own Way* (1903–05), *Her Great Match* (1905–07), *Under the Greenwood Tree* (1907), and *Myself–Bettina* (1908).

Elliott, Sarah Barnwell. b. in Georgia, 1848; d. at Sewanee, Tenn., Aug. 30, 1928. American novelist, short-story writer, and suffragist; granddaughter of the botanist Stephen Elliott (1771–1830). She became widely known through "Jerry," a serial (1890–91) in *Scribner's Magazine* and one of the first American novels concerned with Southern mountaineers. She held office in the Tennessee State Equal Suffrage Association, the Southern Woman Suffrage Conference, and the Civic League of Sewanee. Author also of *The Felmeres* (1879), *The Durket Sperret* (1898), *The Making of Jane* (1901), and the biography *Sam Houston* (1900).

Elliott, Stephen. b. at Beaufort, S.C., Nov. 11, 1771; d. at Charleston, S.C., March 28, 1830. American botanist. He was cofounder (1828) of the *Southern Review* and author of *Botany of South Carolina and Georgia* (1821–24).

Elliott, Stephen. b. at Beaufort, S.C., Aug. 31, 1806; d. at Savannah, Ga., Dec. 21, 1866. American bishop of the Protestant Episcopal Church; son of Stephen Elliott (1771–1830).

Elliott, William. b. at Beaufort, S.C., April 27, 1788; d. there, Feb. 3, 1863. American politician and writer.

Ellis (el'is). City in W central Kansas, in Ellis County, ab. 110 mi. W of Salina: railroad repair shops. 2,649 (1950).

Ellis, Alexander John. [Original surname, **Sharpe.**] b. at Hoxton, near London, June 14, 1814; d. at London, Oct. 28, 1890. English phonetician and mathematician. He wrote *Alphabet of Nature* (1845), *The Essentials of Phonetics* (1848), *On Early English Pronunciation* (1869–71), with especial reference to Shakespeare and Chaucer, and others.

Ellis, Augustine ap. See **Ap Ellis, Augustine.**

Ellis, Edward Sylvester. b. at Geneva, Ohio, April 11, 1840; d. at Cliff Island, Me., June 20, 1916. American writer of juveniles, dime novels, and popular works on history, notable as the author of *Seth Jones, or the Captive of the Frontier* (1860). One of the first dime novels, this work sold upwards of 600,000 copies. He also wrote textbooks on grammar, physiology, mythology, and arithmetic; his interpretations of current events included *Great Leaders and National Issues of 1896* (1896), *The Story of South Africa* (1899), and *Voters' Guide for the Campaign of 1900*.

Ellis, George. b. at London, 1753; d. April 10, 1815. English author. He published *Specimens of the Early English Poets* (1790; 6th ed., 1851), *Specimens of Early English Romances in Metre* (1805; ed. by Halliwell, 1848), and others.

Ellis, George Edward. b. Aug. 8, 1814; d. Dec. 20, 1894. American Unitarian clergyman. He was pastor of the Harvard Unitarian Church at Charlestown, Mass. (1840–69) and was professor of systematic theology in the Harvard Divinity School (1857–63). He wrote *A Half-Century of the Unitarian Controversy* (1857), and contributed to the *Narrative and Critical History of America*, edited by Justin Winsor.

Ellis, George Washington. b. at Weston, Platte County, Mo., May 4, 1875; d. at Chicago, Nov. 26, 1919. American lawyer, novelist, and diplomat. From 1902 to 1910 he was secretary of the U.S. legation in Liberia. When he returned to the U.S., he practiced law at Chicago, becoming known through his cases in every court in Illinois, and in the U.S. Supreme Court. For a brief period, from 1917 until his death, he was assistant corporation counsel for the city of Chicago. He was on the editorial staff of the *Journal of Race Development* (under the auspices of Clark University), and he wrote *Negro Culture in West Africa* (1914), *The Leopard's Claw* (1917), a novel of jungle adventure, both results of his eight-year stay in Liberia, and *Negro Achievements in Social Progress* (1915).

Ellis, Havelock. [Full name, **Henry Havelock Ellis.**] b. at Croydon, Surrey, England, Feb. 2, 1859; d. at Hintlesham, England, July 8, 1939. English man of letters and anthropologist. For a short time he practiced medicine in England, but left the medical profession to write. He edited the works of John Ford and of Christopher Marlowe in, and was over-all editor of, the Mermaid Series of old English dramatists, and wrote *The New Spirit* (1890), *The Criminal* (1890), *Man and Woman* (1894), *Affirmations* (1897), *The Evolution of Modesty* (1899), *Analysis of Sexual Impulse* (1903), *Sexual Selection in Man* (1905), *The Soul of Spain* (1908), *The Task of Social Hygiene* (1912), and *The Dance of Life* (1923); his seven separate volumes on the manifestations of sex form *Studies in the Psychology of Sex* (1897–1928). The latter work was of the greatest importance in changing the general attitude towards sex and the problems caused by it. Ellis's anthropo-sociological approach to the psychology of sexual abnormality has influenced almost all writers since on the subject.

Ellis, Sir **Henry.** b. at London, Nov. 29, 1777; d. there, Jan. 15, 1869. English antiquary, chief librarian of the British Museum (1827–56). He edited Brand's *Popular Antiquities* (1813) and, with others, Dugdale's *Monasticon* (1817–33), wrote the introduction to *Domesday Book* (1816), and published *Original Letters Illustrative of English History* (1824–46).

Ellis, Job Bicknell. b. near Potsdam, N.Y., Jan. 21, 1829; d. Dec. 30, 1905. American mycologist. His large collection of fungi is now housed in the herbarium of the New York Botanical Garden. He was coauthor with B. M. Everhart of *The North American Pyrenomycetes* (1892).

Ellis, Robinson. b. at Barming, near Maidstone, Kent, England, Sept. 5, 1834; d. at Oxford, England, Oct. 9, 1913. English classical scholar, philologist, teacher, and translator. He was educated at Elizabeth College, Guernsey, at Rugby, and at Balliol College, Oxford, winning scholarships and prizes. Elected a fellow of Trinity in 1858, he became later (1883) Oxford reader in Latin, Corpus professor of Latin literature (1893), and vice-president (1879–93) of Trinity. He was professor of Latin (1870–76) at London University College, and contributed to the *New English Dictionary*, the English and American *Journal of Philology*, and other classical organs. He was the author of *Poems and Fragments of Catullus Translated* (1866), *Commentary on Catullus* (1876), and an edition of Ovid's *Ibis* (1881).

Ellis, Sarah Stickney. b. at London, 1812; d. at Hoddesdon, Hertfordshire, England, June 16, 1872. English authoress; wife of William Ellis (1794–1872). She wrote *Women of England* (1838), *Daughters of England* (1842), and others.

Ellis, William. b. at London, Aug. 29, 1794; d. at Hoddesdon, Hertfordshire, England, June 9, 1872. English missionary in Polynesia; husband of Sarah Stickney Ellis. He published *Missionary Narrative of a Tour through Hawaii* (1827), *Polynesian Researches* (1829), *History of Madagascar* (1838), *Three Visits to Madagascar* (1858), and other works on missions.

Ellis, William. b. Jan. 1, 1801; d. at London, Feb. 18, 1881. English writer on social science. He became an assistant underwriter of the Indemnity Marine Insurance Company in 1824, and chief manager in 1827. He founded (1848–52) five schools, which he named Birkbeck schools. Author of *Outlines of Social Economy* (1846), *Education as a Means of Preventing Destitution* (1851), and *Philo-Socrates* (1861).

Ellis-Fermor (-fėr′môr), **Una Mary.** b. Dec. 20, 1894—. English lecturer and literary critic. She was a lecturer (1918–30) and reader (1930–47) in English literature at Bedford College, University of London. Her books include *Christopher Marlowe* (1926), *Jacobean Drama* (1936), *Some Recent Research in Shakespeare's Imagery* (1937), *The Irish Dramatic Movement* (1939), and *Frontiers of Drama* (1945).

Ellis Island. [Former names, **Bucking Island, Gibbet Island, Oyster Island.**] Small island in Upper New York Bay, ab. 1 mi. SW of the Battery: a U.S. immigrant station from 1891 to 1943. It was purchased (1808) by the government from New York state. At the height of immigration to the U.S. more than a million individuals were processed here annually. The immigrant reception center having been moved to Manhattan, the buildings on Ellis Island are used to house immigrants who must be detained or deported.

Ellison (el′i.sọn), **Mrs.** Character in Henry Fielding's *Amelia.*

Elliston (el′is.tọn), **Robert William.** b. at Bloomsbury, London, April 7, 1774; d. at Blackfriars, London, July 8, 1831. English actor and manager. He made his first appearance on April 14, 1791, at the Bath Theatre as Tressel in *Richard III*, and after a career showing great versatility and power, together with many excesses and absurdities, he died the first comedian of his day. Some of his best characters in comedy were Doricourt, Charles Surface, Rover, and Ranger, and in tragedy Hamlet, Romeo, and Hotspur.

Ellisville (el′is.vil). City in SE Mississippi, a county seat (with Laurel) of Jones County, near the Tallahala Creek. It is the seat of Jones County Junior College. The city was an antisecessionist center during the Civil War. 3,579 (1950).

Ellora (e.lō′rạ). [Also: **Elora, Elura.**] Town in Hyderabad, Union of India, ab. 167 mi. NE of Bombay. It contains a Dravidian rock-cut temple, anterior in date to 1000 A.D., remarkable not only in itself, but because the rock is cut away outside as well as inside, leaving the monument isolated and complete throughout. It consists of a central sanctuary or *vimana*, with a pyramidal roof ab. 80 ft. high, preceded by an enclosed porch of 16 columns, before which are two isolated pylons in succession, reached by bridges. The court is surrounded by a peristyle within which there is a series of cells. The sculptured decoration is elaborate, combining geometrical and arabesque motifs witb figure sculpture.

Ellore (e.lōr′). [Also, **Elur.**] City in the Kistna district, Madras state, Union of India, W of the mouths of the Godavari River, ab. 250 mi. N of the city of Madras: oilseeds, tobacco, rice, and cotton. 64,911 (1941).

Ellsberg (elz′bėrg), **Edward.** b. at New Haven, Conn., Nov. 21, 1891—. American naval officer, engineer, and author, noted as a naval salvage expert. Graduated (1914) from U.S. Naval Academy; awarded M.S. (1920) at Massachusetts Institute of Technology; served in World War I and World War II. Awarded Distinguished Service Medal of U.S. for work in directing salvage operations (1926) to raise U.S. submarine *S-51* which had sunk (1925) off Block Island after collision; also directed (1927) initial salvage operations on sunken U.S. submarine *S-4;* promoted (1929) to commander. Chief engineer (1926–35) of Tide Water Oil Company; invented improved methods of dehydrating and dewaxing lubricating oils; developed techniques of cracking crude oil for antiknock gasoline; inventor of underwater torch for cutting steel. Advanced to captain (1942) and awarded Legion of Merit for salvaging (1942) scuttled drydocks at Massawa, Eritrea, and later in salvaging vessels in North African area. Took part in installation of artificial harbors for Normandy invasion. His writings include *Salvage Operations on S-51* (1927), *On The Bottom* (1929), *Thirty Fathoms Deep* (1930), *Pigboats* (1931), *Ocean Gold* (1935), *Spanish Ingots* (1936), *Hell on Ice* (1938), *Men Under the Sea* (1939), *Captain Paul* (1941), *I Have Just Begun to Fight* (1942), *Under the Red Sea Sun* (1945), and *No Banners, No Bugles* (1949).

Ellsworth (elz′wėrth). City in SE Maine, county seat of Hancock County, on the Union River ab. 20 mi. SE of Bangor. It is a resort center for the Mount Desert region. Forest fires which swept this part of New England in 1947 and spread to many settled communities did extensive damage in the city. 3,936 (1950).

Ellsworth, Elmer Ephraim. b. at Mechanicsville, N.Y., April 11, 1837; shot at Alexandria, Va., May 24, 1861. American officer of Zouaves at the beginning of the Civil War. He moved to Chicago at an early age, and became a solicitor of patents. He accompanied Lincoln to Washington in March, 1861. In April, 1861, he organized at New York a Zouave regiment of firemen (the 11th New York), of which he became colonel. He occupied Alexandria, Va., with his regiment on May 24, 1861. Seeing a Confederate flag flying from the Marshall House, he ascended to the roof to remove it, and on descending was shot by James T. Jackson, the keeper of the hotel.

Ellsworth, Henry Leavitt. [Called the **"Father of the Department of Agriculture."**] b. at Windsor, Conn., Nov. 10, 1791; d. at Fair Haven, Conn., Dec. 27, 1858. American agriculturist and lawyer; son of Oliver Ellsworth and twin brother of William Wolcott Ellsworth. Practiced law (1813 *et seq.*) at Windsor, Conn.; president (1819–21) of Aetna Insurance Company, Hartford, Conn.; appointed commissioner (1832) to superintend resettlement of Arkansas Indians; as commissioner of patents (1835–45), he was influential in gaining the first congressional appropriation (1839) for agricultural research. Resigned (1845) to become an agent at Lafayette, Ind., for the purchase and settlement of Western lands.

Ellsworth, Lincoln. b. at Chicago, May 12, 1880; d. at New York, May 26, 1951. American engineer and polar explorer. He worked as a railroad and mining engineer in Canada and Alaska, led an expedition (1924) through the Andes to the headwaters of the Amazon, made a polar flight with Roald Amundsen in 1925, and was one of the leaders of the Amundsen-Ellsworth-Nobile transpolar flight (1926) from Spitsbergen to Alaska in the airship *Norge*. He was director of scientific investigation for the Wilkins-Ellsworth trans-Arctic submarine expedition in 1931, and in 1935 made a 2,300-mile flight across the Antarctic, claiming 300,000 sq. mi. of new territory for the U.S., and receiving a gold medal from the U.S. Congress in recognition of his achievement. Another flight made by him in 1939 into the interior of Antarctica enabled him to claim an additional 81,000 sq. mi. of land for the U.S. He is the author of *The Last Wild Buffalo Hunt* (1915), *First Crossing of the Polar Sea* (1926), *Search* (1932), and *Beyond Horizons* (1938).

Ellsworth, Oliver. b. at Windsor, Conn., April 29, 1745; d. Nov. 26, 1807. American jurist, Revolutionary patriot, and chief justice of the U.S. Supreme Court. He attended Yale and Princeton, studied law, and was admitted to the bar in 1771. Having set up his practice at Hartford, he moved there in 1775 and soon became recognized as one of Connecticut's foremost lawyers. During the Revolution he served on the Connecticut Committee of the Pay Table, performing some important missions for it, served (1777 *et seq.*) as a delegate to the Continental Congress, and in 1779 became a member of the Connecticut council of safety. He was a delegate to the Constitutional Convention, where he took part in bringing about the compromise providing for equality of representation in the Senate, and may have been the originator of the term "United States." He was one of Connecticut's first two senators under the new government, establishing a reputation as a statesman whose counsel was sought and esteemed. Among his achievements were the framing of the first bill regulating the consular service, the creation of the measure admitting

North Carolina, the framing of the nonintercourse act which brought Rhode Island into the Union, the reporting of the first 12 amendments and the first set of Senate rules, and his chairmanship of the committee which brought in the bill organizing the federal judiciary. Made chief justice in 1796, he served until 1799, when ne became commissioner to France, holding the latter post until 1800.

Ellsworth, William Wolcott. b. at Windsor, Conn., Nov. 10, 1791; d. at Hartford, Conn., Jan. 15, 1868. American politician and jurist; son of Oliver Ellsworth and twin brother of Henry Leavitt Ellsworth. He was governor of Connecticut from 1838 to 1842.

Ellwangen (el'väng.ẹn). Town in S Germany, in the *Land* (state) of Württemberg-Baden, American Zone, formerly in the Jagst *Kreis* (district) of the free state of Württemberg, situated on the Jagst River ab. 46 mi. NE of Stuttgart. It has knitwear and furniture manufactures, dairies and agricultural trade. There are various beautiful churches, including the Romanesque Church of Saint Veit, with baroque interior (13th century), the Wolfgang Church (15th century), and the Protestant parish church (18th century). The town grew from a Benedictine abbey, and became part of Württemberg in 1802. The majority of the population is Roman Catholic; there is a considerable Protestant minority. 10,390 (1950).

Ellwood (el'wůd), **Charles Abram.** b. near Ogdensburg, N.Y., Jan. 20, 1873; d. at Durham, N.C., Sept. 25, 1946. American sociologist. He was a professor at Missouri for 30 years and at Duke from 1930 to 1944. Author of *Sociology and Modern Problems* (1910), *The World's Need of Christ* (1940), and other books.

Ellwood, Thomas. b. at Crowell, Oxfordshire, England, 1639; d. at Amersham, Buckinghamshire, England, March 1, 1714. English Quaker, friend of Milton. He wrote *Sacred History of the Old Testament and New Testament* (1705–09), his autobiography (1714), and others.

Ellwood City. Borough in W Pennsylvania, in Beaver and Lawrence counties, on Connoquenessing Creek: manufactures of steel, steel pipe, and steel tubing. 12,945 (1950).

Elm (elm). Village in C Switzerland, in the canton of Glarus, noted for the fatal landslip of the Tschingelberg, Sept. 11, 1881. Pop. 785 (1941).

El Maghreb el Aqsa (el mä'greb el äk'sạ). Arabic name of **Morocco.**

El Majdal (el mäj'däl). Arabic name of **Magdala.**

Elmali (el.mä.li'). [Also: **Almali, Elmalu**; Turkish, **Elmalı.**] Town in S Turkey, near Antalya: sheep raising, cotton, and wheat. Pop. ab. 5,000.

Elman (el'mạn), **Mischa.** b. at Talnoi, in the province of Kiev, Russia, Jan. 21, 1891—. American violinist. He began his studies at Odessa, displaying unusual ability while still very young. In 1901 he went to St. Petersburg and became a pupil of Leopold Auer. He made his debut at Berlin, on Oct. 14, 1904, and has since appeared in most of the important cities on the Continent, in England, the Orient, and America. He made his New York debut (Dec. 10, 1908) with the Russian Symphony Orchestra, and became a U.S. citizen in 1923.

El Mansura (el män.sö'rạ). See **Mansura.**

Elmblad (elm'bläd), **Magnus Henrik.** b. at Herrestad, in Småland, Sweden, 1848; d. in Sweden, 1888. Swedish-American poet. Elmblad is regarded by some as the greatest American poet to have written in the Swedish language. He emigrated to America (Chicago) in 1871, subsequently working as a journalist and newspaper editor for the Swedish-American press. His powerful poetic descriptions of American freedom and natural beauty received attention in Sweden, and he received a prize from the then very conservative Swedish Academy. Elmblad returned to Sweden in 1884. His best-known works many be found in *Amerika-svensk lyrik genom 100 år* (American-Swedish Poetry Through 100 Years, 1949).

"Elm City." Nickname of **New Haven.**

El Mekheir (el me.ċhār'). See **Berber,** town.

Elmer Gantry (el'mėr gan'tri). Novel by Sinclair Lewis, published in 1927. The book has as its central theme the travesties on Christian ethics committed in the name of organized religion. Gantry is a hypocritical minister with a professional interest in conversion and an absorption in the lucrative aspects of his calling.

Elmes (elmz), **James.** b. at London, Oct. 15, 1782; d. at Greenwich (now part of London), April 2, 1862. English architect and writer on art. He published *Sir Christopher Wren and his Times* (1823), *Dictionary of the Fine Arts* (1826), and others.

Elmet (el'met). Small British kingdom conquered (c625) by Edwin, king of Northumbria. It corresponded roughly to the modern administrative county of West Riding in Yorkshire.

El Metemmeh (el me.tem'me). See **Metemmeh.**

Elmhurst (elm'hėrst). City in NE Illinois, in Du Page County: seat of Elmhurst College. 21,273 (1950).

Elmina (el.mē'nạ). [Also: **Dena**; Portuguese, **São Jorge da Mina.**] Town in Gold Coast colony, W Africa, ab. 5 mi. W of Cape Coast on the shore of the Gulf of Guinea. It was founded by the Portuguese, was conquered by the Dutch in 1637, and was transferred to the British in 1872. It is noted for its ancient fort, and for its ancient gold-mine workings. Pop. ab. 5,000.

El Mina (el mē'nạ). Seaport of Tripoli in NW Lebanon, on the Mediterranean coast ab. 47 mi. N of Beirut. Pop. ab. 7,000.

El Minya (el min'yạ). See **Minya.**

Elmira (el.mī'rạ). City in S New York, county seat of Chemung County, on the Chemung River. Manufactures include precision tools, structural steel, fire engines, fire-fighting apparatus, chemicals, knit goods, and glass bottles. It is the seat of Elmira College and a state reformatory. Samuel L. Clemens (Mark Twain) is buried at Elmira, which was his summer home for many years. 49,716 (1950).

Elmira Heights. Village in S New York, in Chemung County: northern suburb of Elmira. 5,009 (1950).

Elmire (el.mēr). In Molière's *Tartuffe,* the young wife of Orgon and sister of Cléante.

El Misti (el mēs'tē). See **Misti.**

Elmo (el'mō), **Castle of Saint.** See also **Sant'Elmo Castle.**

Elmo, Castle of Saint. Fort at Malta, said to be so named from Ermo, an Italianized variant of Erasmus (a Syrian martyr of the 3rd century).

Elmont (el'mont). Unincorporated community in SE New York, in Nassau County, on Long Island. Under the new urban definition established for use in the 1950 census it was counted with adjoining urban areas. The last official enumeration was 8,957 (1940).

El Monte (el mon'tẹ). Unincorporated community in W central California, in Contra Costa County E of San Francisco. 2,502 (1950).

El Monte. City in S California, in Los Angeles County, S of Los Angeles. It has a lion farm. 8,101 (1950).

Elmoran (el.mọ.ran'). See **Masai.**

Elmore (el'mōr), **Margaret.** In Lovell's play *Love's Sacrifice,* Matthew Elmore's daughter, who gives the name to the play by sacrificing her lover, giving him up because of her father's guilt.

El Morro National Monument (el mor'ō). National monument in W New Mexico, ab. 58 mi. by road SE of Gallup. The chief feature is a sandstone monolithic rock, covering 12 acres, known as Inscription Rock from the hundreds of inscriptions carved on it. The rock was a watering-place on the old Acoma-Zuñi trail, and has the ruins of two old Zuñi pueblos on top. The earliest legible date is 1605, carved by Juan de Oñate, the first colonizer of New Mexico. Area, ab. 0.4 sq. mi.

Elmosiro (el.mō.sē'rō). See **Mosiro.**

Elmsford (elmz'fọrd). Village in SE New York, in Westchester County near White Plains. 3,147 (1950).

Elmshorn (elms'hôrn). City in NW Germany, in the *Land* (state) of Schleswig-Holstein, British Zone, formerly in the province of Schleswig-Holstein, Prussia, ab. 19 mi. NW of Hamburg. It is a manufacturing center, with cement works, lumber mills, metallurgical, furniture, shoe, and leatherware manufactures, canneries, flour mills, a sugar refinery, and various foodstuff industries. The surrounding region is a dairying, cattle and hog raising, and market-gardening district. 36,186 (1950).

Elmsley (elmz'li), **Peter.** b. 1773; d. at Oxford, England, March 8, 1825. English philologist, principal of St. Alban Hall, Oxford, and professor of ancient history in the university (1823–25). He is known chiefly for his critical studies of Sophocles and Euripides.

El Mudo (el mö′ᴛʜō). Epithet of **Navarrete** or **Navarete, Juan Fernández.**

El Muerto (el mwer′tō). Mountain in the Andes of Chile, on the border of Argentina. Elevation, ab. 21,222 ft.

Elmwood (elm′wůd). Unincorporated community in C Connecticut, in Hartford County, SW of Hartford. Under the new urban definition established for use in the 1950 census it was counted with adjoining urban areas. The last official enumeration was 2,890 (1940).

Elmwood Park. Village in NE Illinois, in Cook County: suburb of Chicago. 18,801 (1950).

Elmwood Place. Village in SW Ohio, in Hamilton County: suburb of Cincinnati. 4,113 (1950).

Elnasl (el.nas′l). The third-magnitude star γ Sagittarii, sometimes called Warida.

El Nath (el nath′). See **Nath.**

Elnathan (el′nạ.than, el.nā′thạn). In the Bible, the maternal grandfather of Jehoiachin.

Elne (eln). [Ancient names, **Illiberis, Helena.**] Town in S France, in the department of Pyrénées-Orientales, ab. 13 mi. SE of Perpignan. It has a cathedral. Pop. ab. 4,000.

El Obeid (el ọ.bād′). Capital of Kordofan province, Anglo-Egyptian Sudan, in NE Africa, in about the middle of the province. Before its occupation by the Mahdi (1883), El Obeid was the great market for the Egyptian trade in gums and ostrich feathers. Later these articles were sent to Tripoli by way of Ouadai. Near here, on Nov. 3 (and the following days), 1883, the Mahdists exterminated an Egyptian army under Hicks Pasha (William Hicks). The town came under Anglo-Egyptian control in 1899. It is the center of a road network radiating in all directions, and is the western terminus of the railway from Khartoum via Sennar. 72,300 (est. 1949).

Elobey (ā.lō.ʙā′), **Great.** See **Great Elobey.**

Elobey, Little. See **Little Elobey.**

Eloesser (e.lės′ėr), **Arthur.** b. 1870—. German journalist, critic, and historian of literature at Berlin. He is the author of *Das bürgerliche Drama* (1898), *Heinrich von Kleist* (1904), *Thomas Mann* (1925), and *Die deutsche Literatur vom Barock bis zur Gegenwart* (1930).

Éloi (ā.lwȧ), Saint. See Saint **Eligius** or **Éloi** or **Eloy.**

Eloikob (e.loi′kōb). See **Lumbwa.**

Élomire (ā.lo.mēr). Anagram under which Molière was attacked by Le Boulanger de Challussay, an unknown author, in a scurrilous play *Élomire hypocondre, ou les médecins vengés* (1670). In 1663, in a play *Zélinde*, by De Villiers, various persons of quality meet and attack the reputation of Élomire (Molière).

Elora (e.lō′rạ). See **Ellora.**

El Oro (el ō′rō). Province in SW Ecuador. Capital, Machala; area, 2,288 sq. mi.; pop. 83,712 (est. 1944).

Eloth (ē′loth). An ancient name of **Aqaba;** see also **Elath.**

Eloy (ā.lwȧ), Saint. See Saint **Eligius** or **Éloi** or **Eloy.**

Eloy (ē′loi). Town in S Arizona, in Pinal County, on the Santa Cruz River ab. 50 mi. NW of Tucson, in a farming region. It was incorporated as a town in 1949. Pop. 3,580 (1950).

El Paraíso (el pä.rä.ē′sō). Department in S Honduras, on the Nicaraguan border: rubber. Capital, Yuscarán; area, 2,858 sq. mi.; pop. 82,572 (1950).

El Paso (el pas′ō). [Former name, **Franklin.**] City in W Texas, county seat of El Paso County, on the Rio Grande at the Mexican-U.S. border, opposite Ciudad Juárez, Mexico: rail, highway, and airline center, noted for its copper smelters and refineries, cotton gins, and cotton textile mills. It is the site of Fort Bliss, and the seat of the Texas College of Mines and Metallurgy. The passage of the Rio Grande through the mountains here was named El Paso del Norte by Spanish explorers in the 16th century. Missions were established in the area soon afterward, but the first permanent settlement on the present site was not made until the early 19th century, and it became part of Texas only after the Mexican War. 96,810 (1940), 130,485 (1950).

El Paso del Águila (el pä′sō del ä′gē.lä). Spanish name of **Eagle Pass.**

El Paso del Norte (el pä′sō del nôr′tā). Former name of **Ciudad Juárez.**

El Paso de Robles (el pas′ō dẹ rō′blẹs). [Also, **Paso Robles.**] City in SW California, in San Luis Obispo County, on the Salinas River ab. 25 mi. N of San Luis Obispo. It is a resort, with hot sulfur springs. Almonds are raised in the region. 4,835 (1950).

Elphege (el′fẹj), Saint. See Saint **Ælfheah.**

Elphin (el′fin). Town in Connacht province, Irish Republic, in County Roscommon, ab. 15 mi. N of Roscommon. It is the seat of a bishopric. 548 (1936).

Elphinstone (el′fin.stōn, -stọn), **Arthur.** [Title, 6th Baron **Balmerino.**] b. 1688; executed 1746. Scottish warrior and Jacobite leader.

Elphinstone, George Keith. [Title, Viscount **Keith.**] b. at Elphinstone Tower, near Stirling, Scotland, Jan. 7, 1746; d. at Tullyallan, March 10, 1823. British admiral. He was in 1800 appointed commander in chief in the Mediterranean, where he took Malta and Genoa. He subsequently coöperated with Abercromby in the military operations in Egypt, obtained the rank of admiral in 1801, and in 1814 was created Viscount Keith of the United Kingdom.

Elphinstone, Hester Maria. [Title, Viscountess **Keith.**] b. 1762; d. at London, March 31, 1857. Englishwoman, famous for her friendship with Samuel Johnson; daughter of Henry Thrale and his wife Hester (later Mrs. Piozzi), and herself wife (married 1808) of George Keith Elphinstone. Her education (from 1765) was directed by Johnson.

Elphinstone, James. [Title, 1st Baron **Balmerino.**] b. c1553; d. at Balmerino, Scotland, in July, 1612. Scottish politician. One of commissioners of the treasury known as the Octavians (1595); secretary of state (1598); nominated one of the commissioners to discuss union with England (1604). He was condemned to death (1609) for having gained James I's signature to a letter (1607) to Pope Clement VIII, which James had not read, that committed James to Catholicism; he was imprisoned, but was released in the same year.

Elphinstone, John. [Title, 2nd Baron **Balmerino.**] d. at Edinburgh, Feb. 28, 1649. Scottish politician; son of James Elphinstone, 1st Baron Balmerino. Elphinstone was noted for his active opposition to the ecclesiastical measures of Charles I.

Elphinstone, Mountstuart. b. Oct. 6, 1779; d. at Limpsfield, Surrey, England, Nov. 20, 1859. English statesman and historian, one of the chief founders of the Anglo-Indian empire. He entered the civil service of the East India Company in 1796, was appointed ambassador to the court of Kabul in 1808, was resident at the court of Poona (1810–17), and was governor of Bombay (1819–27). Author of *Account of the Kingdom of Cabul* (1815) and *History of India* (1841).

Elphinstone, William. b. at Glasgow, 1431; d. at Edinburgh, Oct. 25, 1514. Scottish prelate and statesman. He graduated with the degree of M.A. at the University of Glasgow in 1452, and subsequently studied law at the University of Paris, where he lectured for a time on this subject. He returned to Glasgow in 1474, was appointed bishop of Aberdeen in 1483, became lord privy seal in 1492, and in 1494 obtained a papal bull for the founding of King's College at Aberdeen, which was completed in 1506.

Elpidon (el.pē′dôn). Pseudonym of **Bałucki, Michał.**

El Progreso (el prō.grā′sō). Department in C Guatemala. Capital, El Progreso; area, 742 sq. mi.; pop. 46,555 (1950).

El Puerto (el pwer′tō). See **Puerto de Santa María.**

El Qantara (el kan′tạ.rạ). See **El Kantara.**

El Qatar (el kä′tär). See **Qatar.**

El Qatif (el kä′tif). Former name of **Dhahran.**

El Qoseir (el kō.sār′). See **Kosseir.**

El Quiché (el kē.chā′). See **Quiché,** Guatemala.

El Quds esh Sherif (el köts esh she.rēf′). Arabic name of **Jerusalem.**

El Quseir (el kö.sār′). See **Kosseir.**

El Qusur (el kö′sör). An Arabic name of **Luxor.**

El Recreo (el rā.krā′ō). [Also, **Sabana Grande.**] City in N Venezuela, in the Distrito Federal. 57,466 (1950).

El Reno (el rē′nō). City in C Oklahoma, county seat of Canadian County, ab. 25 mi. NW of Oklahoma City, near the North Canadian River: railway center; flour milling and marketing and shipping of agricultural products. Nearby is the U.S. military station, Fort Reno, from which the city derives its name. 10,991 (1950).

El Riachuelo (el rē.ä.chwā′lo). River in E Argentina, flowing into the Río de la Plata.

El Rosario (el rō.sä′ryō). See **Rosario,** Mexico.

Elsa (el′sạ). Town in S Texas, in Hidalgo County, in the Rio Grande valley ab. 45 mi. NW of Brownsville. In the decade between the last two U.S. censuses its population more than tripled. 1,006 (1940), 3,179 (1950).

Elsaesser (el′zes.ẹr), **Martin.** b. at Tübingen, Germany, May 28, 1884—. German architect. His designs, representing a sharp departure from traditional styles, are incorporated in many schools and churches built by him. He served as professor at the Technische Hochschule at Stuttgart and as director of the Academy of Applied Arts at Cologne, and became (1925) director of architecture for the city of Frankfort on the Main.

El Said (el sä.ēd′). See **Upper Egypt.**

El Salvador (el sal′vạ.dôr; Spanish, el säl.ʙä.ᴛʜōr′). [Also: **Salvador;** official Spanish name, **República de El Salvador.**] Smallest and most densely populated republic of Central America, bounded on the NW by Guatemala, on the N by Honduras, on the E by the Gulf of Fonseca and Honduras, and on the S by the Pacific Ocean.

Population, Area, Political Divisions. The republic is divided into 14 departments for administrative purposes. Capital, San Salvador; area, 13,176 sq. mi.; pop. 1,187,136 (1950).

Terrain. The surface is traversed by several mountain ranges with intervening fertile valleys and plains; there are many active or quiescent volcanoes, and earthquakes are frequent.

Industry, Agriculture, and Trade. Coffee is the principal export crop, although sugar cane, henequen, and balsam wood are also important, chiefly in trade with the U.S. Maize, which occupies the largest acreage, is consumed domestically. Its industries produce henequen bags, cotton textiles, and consumer goods.

History. The territory of El Salvador was invaded by Pedro de Alvarado in 1524, and conquered by Jorge de Alvarado in 1528. Independence was proclaimed in 1821, and from 1823 to 1839 the country was a state of the Central American Union. Since then, there have been frequent revolutions and wars with other Central American republics. The constitution of 1886 was abrogated in 1939, two years after El Salvador withdrew from the League of Nations. The country has a republican form of government; the national assembly is the legislative body. The president is elected for a term of four years and is not permitted to succeed himself.

Elsass (el′zäs). German name of **Alsace.**

Elsass-Lothringen (el′zäs.lō′tring.ẹn). German name of **Alsace-Lorraine.**

Elsberg (elz′bėrg), **Louis.** b. at Iserlohn, Prussia, April 2, 1836; d. at New York, Feb. 19, 1885. American physician, specializing in laryngology. In 1861 he gave a course, the first of its kind, on diseases of the throat, and in the following year he conducted the first public throat clinic. He founded the *Archives of Laryngology,* a quarterly, in 1880, and he was working on a textbook in his field when he died. In addition to his knowledge of the throat, both in health and in disease, Elsberg was a student of music, a combination that brought speech and voice students and opera singers to him as patients.

El Segundo (el sẹ.gun′dō). City in S California, in Los Angeles County, SW of Los Angeles: oil refineries and oil storage tanks. In the decade between the last two U.S. censuses its population more than doubled. 3,738 (1940), 8,011 (1950).

Elsene (el′sẹ.nẹ). Flemish name of **Ixelles.**

Elser (el′sėr), **Frank Ball.** b. at Fort Worth, Tex., Jan. 9, 1885; d. Feb. 1, 1935. American journalist and playwright. City editor (1908–14) of the Associated Press at New York; special correspondent (1915–16) abroad for the Associated Press and the New York *Times.* Author of the novel *The Keen Desire* (1926) and the plays *Mr. Gilhooley* (1930), *Low Bridge* (1932), and, with Marc Connolly, *The Farmer Takes a Wife* (1934), which was subsequently filmed.

Elsevier (el′zẹ.vēr). See **Elzevir.**

Elsheimer (els′hī.mėr), **Adam.** [Called (in Italy) **Adamo Tedesco,** meaning "Adam the German," or **Il Tedesco,** meaning "the German."] b. at Frankfort on the Main, Germany, 1578; d. 1620. German mythological and Biblical painter and etcher, teacher of Pieter Lastman, who taught Rembrandt. Art critics regard him as one of the founders of modern landscape painting. He was especially successful in securing light effects and he was fond of moonlight and torchlight scenes. Some of his best paintings are *John the Baptist Preaching* and *The Fall of Troy* (at Munich), *Saint Paul at Lystra* (Frankfort), *Ceres* (at the Prado, Madrid), *Phileomon and Baucis* (Dresden), *The Good Samaritan* (the Louvre, Paris), and *The Flight into Egypt.*

Elshender (el′shẹn.dėr). [Also called **Canny Elshie** (el′shi).] In Sir Walter Scott's novel *The Black Dwarf,* the name used by Sir Edward Mauley, the Black Dwarf.

Elsie Dinsmore (el′si dinz′mōr). See **Dinsmore, Elsie.**

Elsie Venner (el′si ven′ėr). Novel by Oliver Wendell Holmes, published in 1861.

Elsinore (el′si.nōr). English name of **Helsingør.**

Elskamp (els′kämp), **Max.** b. at Antwerp, Belgium, May 5, 1862; d. there, Dec. 10, 1931. Belgian poet. He was one of the leading exponents of symbolism in Belgian literature, and drew his themes from the life of the common people. Interested in folklore, he founded the Folklore Museum at Antwerp, of which he was the first director. His collected poems were published under the title *Louange de la vie* (1898). During the 1920's he was regarded by French-language Belgian poets as their master. Among his works are *Dominicales* (1892), *Salutations dont d'angéliques* (1893), *Sous les tentes de l'exode* (1921), *La Chanson de la rue St. Paul* (1922), *Aegri somnia* (1924), *Les Fleurs vertes* (1934), and *Les Joies blondes* (1934).

Elskwatawa (el.skwä′tạ.wạ). See **Tenskwatawa.**

Elsmere (elz′mir). Town in N Delaware, in New Castle County: residential suburb of Wilmington. In the decade between the last two U.S. censuses its population more than tripled. 1,630 (1940), 5,314 (1950).

Elsmere. Town in N Kentucky, in Kenton County near Covington. 3,483 (1950).

Elson (el′sọn), **Arthur.** b. at Boston, Nov. 18, 1873; d. 1940. American musicologist; son of Louis Charles Elson. He was the author of *A Critical History of Opera* (1901), *The Musician's Guide* (1912), *The Book of Musical Knowledge* (1914), and *A History of Vocal Music* (1918).

Elson, Henry William. b. in Muskingum County, Ohio, March 29, 1857—. American historian, lecturer, and educator. Professor of history and economics (1905–16) at Ohio University; president (1916–21) of Thiel College, Greenville, Pa.; lecturer on history (1927–32) at New York University. Author of *History of the United States* (5 vols., 1906), *A Guide to American History* (1909), *Guide to English History* (1911), *Modern Times and the Living Past* (1921), *United States—Its Past and Present* (1925), *Through the Years with Our Constitution* (1937), and other books.

Elson, Louis Charles. b. at Boston, April 17, 1848; d. there, Feb. 14, 1920. American music critic and writer. Among his works are *National Music of America and its Sources* (1899), *Shakespeare in Music* (1900), and *History of American Music* (1904). He edited *Modern Music and Musicians* (20 vols.) and the *University Encyclopedia of Music* (10 vols., 1912).

Elspeth (el′spẹth). In Sir Walter Scott's *Antiquary,* the old mother of Saunders Mucklebackit. She is apathetic and deaf, and keeps secret the crime of her mistress, in which she had assisted, till just before her death.

Elsschot (el′sċhôt), **Willem.** [Pseudonym of **Alfons de Ridder.**] b. 1882—. Flemish novelist. His sharp criticism of society and bourgeois morality is, in the opinion of many critics of modern Flemish literature, shrewdly camouflaged by a pleasant and humorous tone in such novels as *Villa des Roses* (1913), *Lijmen* (The Inveiglers, 1927), *Kaas* (Cheese, 1933), *Tsjip* (1934), *Pensioen* (1937), *Het Been* (The Leg, 1938), *De Leeuwentemmer* (The Lion Tamer, 1940), and *Het panterschip* (The Ironclad, 1941).

Elssler (els′lėr), **Fanny.** b. at Vienna, June 23, 1810; d. there, Nov. 27, 1884. Austrian dancer. She abandoned the stage in 1851. Her sister Thérèse (1808–78), also a dancer, contracted a morganatic marriage with Prince Adalbert of Prussia.

Elster (el′stėr). [Also, **Bad-Elster.**] Town in E Germany, in the *Land* (state) of Saxony, Russian Zone, formerly in the free state of Saxony, situated in the valley of the Weisse Elster River, near the border of Czechoslovakia, S of Plauen. It is a popular health resort with radioactive mineral springs and mud baths, parks, and a theater. The springs are visited by people suffering from dietetic, intestinal, and skin diseases, and anemia. 3,657 (1946).

Elster, Black. See **Schwarze Elster.**

Elster, Ernst. b. 1860—. German historian of literature, professor at Marburg. He is the editor of a critical edition of Heine's works (1924 *et seq.*), but chiefly known as the author of *Prinzipien der Literaturwissenschaft* (2 vols., 1897 *et seq.*), which represents an early attempt to emancipate literary historiography from mere data-gathering.

Elster, Julius. b. at Blankenburg, Germany, Dec. 24, 1854; d. at Wolfenbüttel, Germany, April 8, 1920. German physicist. In collaboration with H. F. Geitel he devised the earliest practical photoelectric cell. He also constructed an electroscope (named for him) for measuring the emanations of radioactive substances.

Elster, Schwarze. See **Schwarze Elster.**

El Supremo (el sö.prā′mō). See **Francia, José Gaspar Rodriguez.**

Elswick (elz′wik, el′sik). Ward of Newcastle, in NE England, in Northumberland, ab. 270 mi. N of London by rail. It has shipyards and ordnance manufactures. 13,028 (1931).

El Teb (el teb′). Locality between Tokar and Trinkitat, in what is now NE Anglo-Egyptian Sudan, in the vicinity of Suakim. Here, on Feb. 29, 1884, the British under General Graham defeated the Mahdists under Osman Digma.

Eltekeh (el′tę.ke). [Modern name, **Beit Likia.**] In ancient geography, one of the cities on the border of Dan. Near here Sennacherib defeated an Egyptian army which was coming to the relief of Ekron.

Elten (el′tęn), **H. D. Kruseman van.** See **Kruseman van Elten, H. D.**

Eltham (el′thạm). Former town in SE England, in Kent (now in the County of London, in SE London, in Woolwich metropolitan borough), ab. 9 mi. SE of Charing Cross station, London. It contains the ruins of Eltham Palace, formerly a royal residence.

Elton (el′tọn) or **Eltonskoe** (el′tọn.skọ.yę). Salt lake in the U.S.S.R., in the Stalingrad *oblast* (region) of the Russian Soviet Federated Socialist Republic, ab. 80 mi. E of Stalingrad: noted for its production of salt. Length, ab. 10 mi.

Elton, Oliver. b. at Holt, Norfolk, England, June 3, 1861—. English literary historian. Lecturer (1890–1900) at Owens College at Manchester; professor (1900–25) of English literature at Liverpool University. Author of *The Augustan Ages* (1899), *Modern Studies* (1907), a series entitled *Survey of English Literature: 1780–1830* (1912), *1830–80* (1920), and *1730–1780* (1928); *The English Muse* (1930), and *Essays and Addresses* (1939).

El Trocadero (el trō.kä.ᴛʜā′rō). See under **Puerto Real, Spain.**

Eltville (elt′vil). [Also: **Elfeld;** Latin, **Altavilla.**] Town in W Germany, in the *Land* (state) of Hessen, American Zone, formerly in the province of Hesse-Nassau, Prussia, situated on the Rhine River between Bingen and Mainz. The center of a wine, fruit, and vegetable growing district, it has wine trade and produces sparkling wines. Gutenberg opened a printing shop here in 1465. Pop. 6,304 (1946).

Éluard (ā.lü.är, -lwär), **Paul.** b. near Paris, Dec. 14, 1895; d. Nov. 18, 1952. French poet, notably successful in treating themes of pain and solitude. He is the author of *Capitale de la douleur* (1926), *Les Dessous d'une vie* (1926), *La Vie immédiate* (1932), and others. At first a Dadaist, he has occasionally collaborated with the surrealists, as in *L'Immaculée conception* (1930; with André Breton).

Elul (e.löl′). Twelfth month of the Hebrew civil year and sixth in the Hebrew ecclesiastical calendar, falling roughly during August or September. In the Babylonian system the month was known as Ululu.

El Uqsor (el ůk′sôr). Arabic name of **Luxor.**

Elur (e.lör′). See **Ellore.**

Elura (e.lö′rạ). See **Ellora.**

Elusa (e.lö′sa). See under **Eauze.**

Elvas (el′vạsh). [Arabic, **Balesh;** Latin, **Alpesa.**] City and *concelho* (commune) in E central Portugal, in the province of Alto Alentejo, in the district of Portalegre, situated on a tributary of the Guadiana River near the Spanish border, ab. 137 mi. NE of Lisbon. It is a center for the local wine, olive oil, and livestock trade and has metallurgical industries; copper and iron ore are mined in the vicinity. The cathedral is in Gothic style, with additions in the so-called Emmanuel style and Renaissance modifications; the convent and church of the Dominicans date from the 13th and 16th centuries; there is a library, theater, and museum, and the ruins of a medieval castle in Moorish-Romanesque style. The aqueduct of Amoeira was erected between 1498 and 1622. Formerly of considerable strategic importance, Elvas has strong fortifications which date from the 18th century. The city was a Moorish stronghold in the early Middle Ages and was retaken by Portugal in 1230. It was the seat of a bishopric from 1570 to 1882. Conquered by the French in 1808, it was ceded to Portugal by the convention of Sintra in the same year. Pop. of concelho, 28,602 (1940); of city, 12,413 (1940).

Elvehjem (el.vā′ęm), **Conrad Arnold.** b. at McFarland, Wis., May 27, 1901—. American biochemist, professor, educator, and author. He was educated at the Stoughton (Wis.) high school, and the University of Wisconsin, where, since 1930, he has been an assistant professor, associate professor, and full professor (since 1936), chairman of the biochemistry department (since 1944), and dean of the graduate school (since 1946). All his degrees (B.S., 1923; M.S., 1924, thesis on *Studies on Calcium Metabolism;* and Ph.D., 1927, thesis on *The Relation of Iron and Copper to Nutritional Anemia*) are from Wisconsin. From 1924 to 1929, after receiving his second degree, he was an instructor in biochemistry. The author of over 500 articles, and of special chapters to various books, he has contributed to *Nature*, the *American Journal of Public Health*, the *Scientific Monthly, Science, Chemical and Engineering News*, and the *Journal of Home Economics*. In 1941 he wrote *The Vitamin Content of Meat*, with Harry A. Waisman. He was selected to deliver the Harvey Society lecture in 1940, the Herter lecture in 1942, and the Sigma Xi lecture (he is a member of the honorary scientific fraternity) in 1943. Among prizes that he has won are the Mead Johnson award, in 1939, for his work on the vitamin B complex, the Grocery Manufacturers of America award, in 1942, and the Willard Gibbs medal, in 1943. In 1937 he made one of his outstanding discoveries, that nicotinic acid (niacin), which is part of the vitamin B complex, was a cure for black tongue in dogs, a disease corresponding to human pellagra, and his results were later applied to treating human beings. He also discovered that chick dermatitis was due to pantothenic acid deficiency, and that copper is essential to the formation of hemoglobin.

Elvestad (el′vę.stä), **Sven.** [Pseudonym, **Stein Riverton.**] b. at Halden, Norway, Sept. 7, 1884; d. 1934. Norwegian writer, best known for numerous detective stories published under his pseudonym. He also published essays and novels with literary pretensions.

Elvey (el′vi), Sir **George Job.** b. at Canterbury, England, March 27, 1816; d. at Windlesham, Surrey, England, Dec. 9, 1893. English organist and composer of religious works, such as anthems, oratorios, and odes. He was organist (1835 *et seq.*) at Saint George's Chapel, Windsor.

El Viejo (el вyā′hō). Volcano in W Nicaragua, NW of Managua. Elevation, ab. 5,838 ft.

Elvira (el.vī′rạ). In Dryden's *Spanish Friar*, a young wife who by the aid of the Spanish friar attempts to intrigue with Lorenzo, who turns out to be her brother.

Elvira. Sister of Don Duarte in Colley Cibber's *Love Makes a Man.*

Elvira. Mistress of Pizarro in Richard Brinsley Sheridan's *Pizarro*, adapted from Kotzebue.

Elvira (el.vē′rä). Name of the principal female character in Bellini's opera *I Puritani*, Verdi's opera*Ernani*, and Auber's opera *Masaniello.* In Mozart's opera *Don Giovanni*, she is a former mistress of Don Giovanni who attempts to prevent his further seductions.

Elvire (el.vēr.) Name of the principal female character in Molière's *Dom Juan.*

Elwell (el′wel), **Frank Edwin.** b. at Concord, Mass., June 15, 1858; d. Jan. 23, 1922. American sculptor. He studied sculpture at the École des Beaux-Arts at Paris and under Falguière, and modeled the first statue by an American sculptor to be placed in Europe (at Edam,